The Form Book®

JUMP RACING ANNUAL 2005-2006

The BHB's Official Record

Complete record of all Jump racing
from 24 April 2005 to 29 April 2006

totesport

Published by Raceform Ltd
Compton, Newbury, Berkshire, RG20 6NL
Raceform Limited is a wholly owned subsidiary of MGN Limited

ISBN 1-905153-09-9

Printed and bound in Great Britain by William Clowes Ltd, Beccles, Suffolk

Cover photo:Tony McCoy and Impek (leading) jump the fence in front of he stand on the first circuit in the Peterborough Chase at Huntingdon.
(Photo: © Jon Winter/Racing Post)

CONTENTS

Editor: Graham Dench

Head of Analysis Team: Ashley Rumney

Race Analysts & Notebook Writers:
Dave Bellingham, Mark Brown, Steffan Edwards,
Walter Glynn, Keith Hewitt, Richard Lowther,
Lee McKenzie, David Orton, Neville Ring,
Ashley Rumney, David Toft, Ron Wood, Richard Young.

Production: Ashley Rumney & Richard Lowther

The Form Book

●Jump Racing **2005-2006**

Welcome to the 2005-2006 edition of The Form Book Annual for Jump Racing, now in A4 format, to accomodate the increased fixture list and featuring enhanced editorial.

Race details contain Racing Post Ratings assessing the merit of each individual performance and speed figures for every horse that clocks a worthwhile time, weight-for-age allowance and the starting price percentage, in addition to the traditional features.

A race Focus is included after the result and endeavours to combine the opinions of the notebook writer, the handicapper, speed figure expert and where appropriate the paddock observer, in order to provide a snapshot of the merit of each individual race. The extended Notebook comments are printed below each race and cover all horses which are considered worthy of inclusion by our expert race-readers and analysts. The comments provide an analysis of the winning performance and, where applicable, explain possible reasons for improvement or attempt to explain why any horse failed to run to its best. More importantly, our team will also indicate the conditions under which horses are likely to be seen to best advantage .

●The official record

THE FORM BOOK records comprehensive race details of every domestic race, every major Irish Graded race and every foreign event in which a British-trained runner participated. In the **NOTEBOOK** section, extended interpretation is provided for all runners worthy of a mention, including all placed horses and all favourites. Generally speaking, the higher the class of race, the greater the number of runners noted.

MEETING BACK REFERENCE NUMBER is the Raceform number of the last meeting run at the track and is shown to the left of the course name. Abandoned meetings are signified by a dagger.

THE OFFICIAL GOING, shown at the head of each meeting, is recorded as follows: Turf: Hard; Firm; Good to firm; Good; Good to soft; Soft; Heavy. There may be variations for non-British meetings.

Where appropriate, there is a section indicating track bias and any differences to the official going indicated by race times.

THE WEATHER is shown below to the date for selected meetings.

VISIBILITY is good unless otherwise stated.

RACE NUMBERS for foreign races carry the suffix 'a' in the race header and in the index.

RACE TITLE is the name of the race as shown in the Racing Calendar.

COMPETITIVE RACING CLASSIFICATIONS are shown on a scale from Class 1 to Class 6. All Graded races are Class 1.

THE RACE DISTANCE is given for all races, and is accompanied by the number of fences or hurdles and number of flights bypassed (if any).

OFFICIAL RACE TIME as published in the Racing Calendar is followed in parentheses by the time when the race actually started. This is followed by the race class, age restrictions, handicap restrictions and the official rating of the top weight.

PRIZE MONEY shows penalty values for each placing; winner's prizemoney in bold type, remainder in parentheses.

IN THE RACE RESULT, the figures to the far left of each horse (under Form) shows the most recent form figures. The figure in bold is the finishing position in this race as detailed below.

1...40 – finishing positions first to fortieth; **b** – brought down; **c** – carried out; **f** – fell; **p** – pulled up; **r** – refused; **ro** – ran out; **s** – slipped up; **u** – unseated rider; **v** – void race.

A figure to the left of the Raceform Notebook comment is the last race in which the horse warranted an extended comment.

THE OFFICIAL DISTANCES between the horses are shown on the left-hand side immediately after their position at the finish.

NUMBER OF DAYS SINCE PREVIOUS RUN is the superscript figure immediately following the horse name and suffix.

PREVIOUS RACEFORM RACE NUMBER is the boxed figure to the right of the horse's name.

THE HORSE'S AGE is shown immediately before the weight carried.

WEIGHTS shown are actual weights carried.

OFFICIAL RATING is the superior figure directly after the horse's weight in the race result.

In handicaps, this figure is displayed in bold, and indicates the official BHB rating, at entry, from which the horse raced, after the following adjustments had been made:
(i) Overweight carried by the rider.
(ii) The number of pounds out of the handicap (if applicable).
(iii) Penalties incurred after the publication of the weights.
In non-handicaps, the rating is provided for information only, and is the bare BHB rating, at entry, with no adjustments.

HEADGEAR is shown immediately before the jockey's name and in parentheses and expressed as: **b** (blinkers); **v** (visor); **h** (hood); **e** (eyeshield); **c** (eyecover); **p** (cheekpieces); **t** (tongue tie).

THE JOCKEY is shown for every runner followed, in superscript, by apprentice allowances in parentheses.

CONDITIONAL JOCKEYS' ALLOWANCES The holders of conditional jockeys' licences, aged under 26 years, under the provisions of Rule 109(ii) (a) are permitted to claim the following allowances in Jumps races:

7lb until they have won 15 races;
thereafter 5lb until they have won 35 such races;
thereafter 3lb until they have won 65 such Flat races.

These allowances can be claimed in the steeplechases, hurdle races and National Hunt flat races set out below, with the exception of races confined to conditional jockeys:
(a) All handicaps except the Grand National Steeplechase
(b) All selling races.
(c) All weight-for-age races classified 3, 4, 5, and 6.
(d) All National Hunt Flat races

RACING POST RATINGS, which record the level of performance attained in this race for each horse, appear in the column headed RPR. These are the work of handicapper Steve Mason, who heads a dedicated team dealing with Jumps races for Raceform and sister publication, the *Racing Post*.

THE TRAINER is shown for every runner.

COMMENT-IN-RUNNING is shown for each horse in an abbreviated form. Details of abbreviations appear later in this section.

STARTING PRICES appear below the jockey in the race result. The favourite indicator appears to the right of the Starting Price; 1 for the favourite, 2 for the second-favourite and 3 for third-favourite. Joint favourites share the same number.

RACE TIMES in Great Britain are shown to a 10th of a second. Figures in parentheses following the time show the number of seconds faster or slower than the Raceform Median Time for the course and distance.

RACEFORM MEDIAN TIMES are compiled from all races run over the course and distance in the preceding five years. Times equal to the median are shown as (0.00). Times under the median are preceded by minus, for instance, 1.8 seconds under the median would be shown (-1.8). Course record times are indicated in parentheses.

GOING CORRECTION appears against each race to allow for changing conditions of the ground. It is shown to a tenth of a second and indicates the adjustment per furlong against the median time. The going based on the going correction is shown in parentheses and is recorded in the following stages:

Turf: HD (Hard); F (Firm); GF (Good to firm); G (Good); GS (Good to soft); S (Soft); HVY (Heavy).

WEIGHT-FOR-AGE allowances are given where applicable for mixed-age races.

STARTING PRICE PERCENTAGE follows the going correction and weight-for-age details, and gives the total SP percentage of all runners that competed. It precedes the number of runners taking part in the race.

Bookmakers have historically tended to bet to a margin of around 2% per horse (ie 110% for a five-runner race and 120% if there are ten runners). If the over-round is any bigger than this the market can be considered unduly skewed in their favour. However, percentages are usually significantly smaller at the big meetings, especially in handicaps, and in recent years the influence of betting exchanges and the arrival of 'new blood' among on course bookmakers has contributed to a general narrowing of the 'over round'.

SELLING DETAILS (where applicable) and details of any claim are given. Friendly claims are not detailed.

SPEED RATINGS appear below the race time and going correction. They are the work of time expert Dave Bellingham and differ from conventional ratings systems in that they are an expression of a horse's ability in terms of lengths-per-mile, as opposed to pounds in weight. They are not directly comparable with BHB and Racing Post ratings.

The ratings take no account of the effect of weight, either historically or on the day, and this component is left completely to the user's discretion. What is shown is a speed rating represented in its purest form, rather than one that has been altered for weight using a mathematical formula that treats all types of horses as if they were the same.

A comparison of the rating achieved with the 'par' figure for the grade of race - the rating that should be achievable by an everage winner in that class of race - will both provide an at-a-glance indication of whether or not a race was truly run and also highlight the value of the form from a time perspective.

In theory, if a horse has a best speed figure five points superior to another and both run to their best form in a race over a mile, the first horse should beat the second by five lengths. In a race run over two miles, the margin should be ten lengths and so on.

Before the speed figures can be calculated, it is necessary to establish a set of standard or median times for every distance at every track, and this is done by averaging the times of all winners over a particular trip going back several years. No speed ratings are produced when insufficient races have been run over a distance for a reliable median time to be calculated.

Once a meeting has taken place, a raw unadjusted speed rating is calculated for each winner by calculating how many lengths per mile the winning time was faster or slower than the median for the trip. A difference of 0.2 of a second equals one length. The raw speed ratings of all winners on the card are then compared to the 'par' figure for the class of race. The difference between the 'raw' speed rating and the 'par' figure for each race is then noted, and both the fastest and slowest races are discarded before the rest are averaged to produce the going allowance or track variant. This figure gives an idea as to how much the elements, of which the going is one, have affected the final times of each race.

The figure representing the going allowance is then used to adjust sent how fast the winners would have run on a perfectly good surface with no external influences, including the weather. The ratings for beaten horses are worked out by taking the number of lengths they were behind the winner, adjusting that to take into account the distance of the race, and deducting that figure from the winner's rating. The reader is left with a rating which provides an instant impression of the value of a time performance.

The speed 'pars' below act as benchmark with which to compare the speed figures earned by each horse in each race. A horse that has already exceeded the 'par' for the class he is about to run in, is of special interest, especially if he has done it more than once, as are horses that have consistently earned higher figures than their rivals.

Class 1 Grade One	117
Class 1 Grade Two	115
Class 1 Grade Three	113
Class 1 Listed	111
Class 2	109
Class 3	107
Class 4	105
Class 5	103
Class 6	101

Allowances need to be made for younger horses and for fillies. These allowances are as follows.

3-y-o	
Jul / Aug	-3
Sep / Oct	-2
Nov / Dec	-1
Races contested by fillies only	-3

Allowances are cumulative.

TOTE returns include a £1 stake. Exacta dividends are shown in parentheses. The Computer Straight Forecast dividend is preceded by the letters CSF, Computer Tricast is preceded by CT and Tote Trio dividend is preceded by the word Trio. Jackpot, Placepot and Quadpot details appear at the end of the meeting to which they refer.

OWNER is followed by the breeder's name and the trainer's location.

STEWARDS' INQUIRIES are included with the result, and any suspensions and/or fines incurred. Objections by jockeys and officials are included, where relevant.

HISTORICAL FOCUS details occasional points of historical significance.

FOCUS The Focus section has been enhanced to help readers distinguish good races from bad races and reliable form from unreliable form, by drawing together the opinions of handicapper, time expert and paddock watcher and interpreting their views in a punter-friendly manner.

NOTEBOOK horses marked with the ◆ symbol are those deemed by our racereaders especially worthy of note in future races.

OFFICIAL EXPLANATIONS, where the horse is deemed to have run well above or below expectation, are included in the Notebook section.

Key to racereaders' initials

WG ....Walter Glynn
KH ....Keith Hewitt
RL ....Richard Lowther
IM ....Iain MacKenzie
LM ....Lee McKenzie
JN ....Jonathan Neesom
DO ....Darren Owen
CR ....Colin Roberts
JR......................Joe Rowntree
JS ....John Santer
ST ....Steve Taylor
RY ....Richard Young

Abbreviations and their meanings

Paddock comments

gd sort - well made, above average on looks
h.d.w - has done well, improved in looks
wl grwn - well grown, has filled to its frame
lengthy - longer than average for its height
tall - tall
big - much larger than the average
rangy - lengthy and tall but in proportion, covers a deal of ground
athletic - well proportioned and active, fluent mover
medium-sized - medium sized
chasing type - with the physique to make a chaser in time
scope - scope for physical development
str - strong, powerful looking
w'like - workmanlike, ordinary in looks
lt-f - light-framed, not much substance
cmpt - compact
neat - smallish, well put together
leggy - long legs compared with body
angular - unfurnished behind the saddle, not filled to frame
unf - unfurnished in the midriff, not filled to frame
narrow - not as wide as side appearance would suggest
small - lacks any physical scope
nt grwn - not grown
lw - looked fit and well
bkwd - backward in condition
t - tubed
swtg - sweating
b (off fore or nr fore) - bandaged in front
b.hind (off or nr) - bandaged behind

At the start

stdd s - jockey purposely reins back the horse
dwlt - missed the break and left for a short time
s.s - slow to start, left longer than a horse that dwelt
s.v.s - started very slowly
s.i.s - started on terms but took time to get going
ref to r -does not jump off, or travels a few yards then stops
rel to r - tries to pull itself up in mid-race
w.r.s - whipped round start

Position in the race

led - in lead on its own
disp ld - upsides the leader
w ldr - almost upsides the leader
w ldrs - in a line of three or more disputing the lead
prom - on the heels of the leaders, in front third of the field
trckd ldr(s) - just in behind the leaders giving impression that it could lead if asked
chsd ldr - horse in second place
chsd clr ldrs - horse heads main body of field behind two clear leaders
chsd ldrs - horse is in the first four or five but making more effort to stay close to the pace than if tracking leaders.
clsd - closed
in tch - close enough to have a chance
hdwy - making ground on the leader
gd hdwy - making ground quickly on the leader, could be a deliberate move
sme hdwy -making ground but no real impact on race
stdy hdwy - gradually making ground
ev ch - upsides the leaders when the race starts in earnest
rr - at the back of main group but not detached
bhd - detached from the main body of runners
hld up - restrained as a deliberate tactical move
nt rcvr - lost all chance after interference, mistake etc.
wknd - stride shortened as it began to tire
lost tch - had been in the main body but a gap appeared as it tired
lost pl - remains in main body of runners but lost several positions quickly

Riding

effrt - short-lived effort
pushed along - received urgings with hands only, jockey not using legs
rdn - received urgings from saddle, including use of whip
hrd rdn - received maximum assistance from the saddle including use of whip
drvn - received forceful urgings, jockey putting in a lot of effort and using whip
hrd drvn - jockey very animated, plenty of kicking, pushing and reminders

Finishing comments

jst failed - closing rapidly on the winner and probably would have led a stride after the line
r.o - jockey's efforts usually involved to produce an increase in pace without finding an appreciable turn of speed
r.o wl - jockey's efforts usually involved to produce an obvious increase in pace without finding an appreciable turn of speed
unable qckn - not visibly tiring but does not possess a sufficient change of pace
one pce - not tiring but does not find a turn of speed, from a position further out than unable qckn
nt r.o. - did not consent to respond to pressure
styd on - going on well towards the end, utilising stamina
nvr able to chal - unable to produce sufficient to reach a challenging position
nvr nr to chal - in the opinion of the racereader, the horse was never in a suitable position to challenge.
nrst fin - nearer to the winner in distance beaten than at any time since the race had begun in earnest
nvr nrr - nearer to the winner position-wise than at any time since the race had begun in earnest
rallied - responded to pressure to come back with a chance having lost its place
no ex - unable to sustain its run
bttr for r - likely to improve for the run and experience
rn green - inclined to wander and falter through inexperience
too much to do - left with too much leeway to make up

Winning comments

v.easily - a great deal in hand
easily - plenty in hand
comf - something in hand, always holding the others
pushed out - kept up to its work with hands and heels without jockey resorting to whip or kicking along and wins fairly comfortably
rdn out - pushed and kicked out to the line, with the whip employed
drvn out - pushed and kicked out to the line, with considerable effort and the whip employed
all out - nothing to spare, could not have found any more
jst hld on - holding on to a rapidly diminishing lead, could not have found any more if passed
unchal - must either make all or a majority of the running and not be challenged from an early stage

Complete list of abbreviations

a - always
abt - about
a.p - always prominent
appr - approaching
awrdd - awarded
b.b.v - broke blood-vessel
b.d - brought down
bdly - badly
bef - before
bhd - behind
bk - back
blkd - baulked
blnd - blundered
bmpd - bumped
bnd - bend
btn- beaten
bttr - better
c - came
ch - chance
chal - challenged
chse - chase
chsd - chased
chsng - chasing
circ - circuit
cl - close
clr - clear
clsd - closed
comf - comfortably
cpld - coupled
crse - course
ct - caught
def - definite
dismntd - dismounted
disp - disputed
dist - distance
div - division
drvn - driven
dwlt - dwelt
edgd - edged
effrt - effort

ent - entering
ev ch - every chance
ex - extra
f - furlong
fin - finished
fnd - found
fnl - final
fr - from
gd - good
gng - going
gp - group
grad - gradually
grnd - ground
hd - head
hdd - headed
hdwy - headway
hld - held
hmpd - hampered
imp - impression
ins - inside
j.b - jumped badly
j.w - jumped well
jnd - joined
jst - just
kpt - kept
l - length
ld - lead
ldr - leader
lft - left
mod - moderate
m - mile
m.n.s - made no show
mde - made
mid div - mid division
mstke - mistake
n.d - never dangerous
n.g.t - not go through
n.m.r - not much room
nk - neck
no ex - no extra
nr - near
nrr - nearer
nrst fin - nearest finish
nt - not
nvr - never
one pce - one pace
out - from finish
outpcd - outpaced
p.u - pulled up
pce - pace
pckd - pecked
pl - place
plcd - placed
plld - pulled
press - pressure
prog - progress
prom - prominent
qckly - quickly
qckn - quicken
r - race
racd - raced
rch - reach
rcvr - recover
rdn - ridden
rdr - rider
reard - reared
ref - refused
rn - ran
rnd - round
r.o - ran on
rr - rear
rspnse - response
rt - right
s - start
sddle - saddle
shkn - shaken
slt - slight
sme - some
sn - soo
spd- speed
st - straight
stmbld - stumbled
stdd - steadied
stdy - steady
strly - strongly
styd - stayed
styng - staying
s. u - slipped up
swtchd - switched
swvd - swerved
tk - took
t.k.h - took keen hold
t.o - tailed off
tch - touch
thrght - throughout
trbld - troubled
trckd - tracked
u.p - under pressure
u.str.p- under strong pressure
w - with
w.r.s - whipped round start
wd - wide
whn - when
wknd - weakened
wl - well
wnr - winner
wnt - went
1/2-wy - halfway

Racing Post Ratings

Racing Post Ratings for each horse are listed after the Starting Price and indicate the actual level of performance attained in that race. The figure in the back index represents the BEST public form that Racing Post's Handicappers still believe the horse capable of reproducing.

To use the ratings constructively in determining those horses best-in in future events, the following procedures should be followed:

(i) In races where all runners are set to carry the same weight, no calculations are necessary. The horse with the highest rating is best in.

(ii) In races where all runners are set to carry different weights, add one point to the rating for every pound less than 12 st to be carried; deduct one point for every pound more than 12 st.

For example,

Horse	Age & Weight	Adj. from 12st	RRbase rating	Adj. rating
Azertyuiop	8-12-00	0	172	172
Well Chief	6-11-12	+2	168	170
Kadarann	8-11-10	+4	168	172
Contraband	7-11-06	+8	166	174

Therefore Contraband is top-rated (best-in)

NB No adjustments are made for weight for age in Racing Post ratings. The official weight for age scale is displayed for information purposes while any live weight for age conditions are displayed underneath each individual result.

The following symbols are used in conjunction with the ratings:

++ almost certain to prove better

+ likely to prove better

d disappointing (has run well below best recently)

? form hard to evaluate, may prove unreliable

t tentative rating based on race-time

Weight adjusted ratings for every race are published daily in Raceform Private Handicap, and on our new service, Raceform Private Handicap ONLINE (www.raceform.co.uk). For subscription terms please contact the Subscription Department on (01635) 578080.

The Official Scale of Weight, Age & Distance (Jumps)

The following scale should only be used in conjunction with the Official ratings published in this book. Use of any other scale will introduce errors into calculations. The allowances are expressed as the number of pounds that is deemed the average horse in each group falls short of maturity at different dates and distances.

Scale of Weight for Age for Steeple Chases and Hurdle Races

HURDLE RACES

The allowances, assessed in lbs, which three-year-olds and four-year-olds will receive from five-year-olds and upwards

Distance		JAN		FEB		MAR		APR		MAY		JUNE		JULY		AUG		SEPT		OCT		NOV		DEC	
Miles	Age	1/15	16/31	1/14	15/29	1/15	16/31	1/15	16/30	1/15	16/31	1/15	16/30	1/15	16/31	1/15	16/31	1/15	16/30	1/15	16/31	1/15	16/30	1/15	16/31
2	3	-	-	-	-	-	-	-	-	-	-	-	-	20	20	19	19	18	18	17	17	16	15	14	13
	4	12	11	10	9	8	7	6	5	4	4	3	3	2	2	1	1	-	-	-	-	-	-	-	-
2½	3	-	-	-	-	-	-	-	-	-	-	-	-	21	21	20	20	19	19	18	18	17	16	15	14
	4	13	12	11	10	9	8	7	6	5	5	4	4	3	3	2	2	1	1	-	-	-	-	-	-
3	3	-	-	-	-	-	-	-	-	-	-	-	-	22	22	21	21	20	20	19	19	18	17	16	15
	4	14	13	12	11	10	9	8	7	6	6	5	5	4	4	3	3	2	2	1	1	-	-	-	-

STEEPLE CHASES

The allowances, assessed in lbs, which four-year-olds and five-year-olds will receive from five-year-olds and upwards

Distance		JAN		FEB		MAR		APR		MAY		JUNE		JULY		AUG		SEPT		OCT		NOV		DEC	
Miles	Age	1/15	16/31	1/14	15/29	1/15	16/31	1/15	16/30	1/15	16/31	1/15	16/30	1/15	16/31	1/15	16/31	1/15	16/30	1/15	16/31	1/15	16/30	1/15	16/31
2	4	-	-	-	-	-	-	-	-	-	-	-	-	-	-	15	15	14	14	13	13	12	12	11	10
	5	9	8	7	6	5	4	3	3	2	2	1	1	-	-	-	-	-	-	-	-	-	-	-	-
2½	4	-	-	-	-	-	-	-	-	-	-	-	-	-		16	16	15	15	14	14	13	13	12	11
	5	10	9	8	7	6	5	4	4	3	3	2	2	1	1	-	-	-	-	-	-	-	-	-	-
3	4	-	-	-	-	-	-	-	-	-	-	-	-	-	-	17	17	16	16	15	15	14	14	13	13
	5	12	12	11	11	10	10	9	8	7	7	6	6	5	5	4	4	3	3	2	2	1	1	-	-

Course Descriptions

COURSE	COMMENT
AINTREE	Two left-handed courses. Grand National circuit, 2m2f, is flat and has big fences with drop on landing side and a long run-in. Mildmay Course, 1m3f, flat with conventional fences, is sharper than the hurdles course.
ASCOT	Right-handed, galloping, last mile mainly uphill, with stiff fences. Circuit 1m5f. Not in use in 2005/6
AYR	Left-handed, mainly flat. Circuit 1m4f.
BANGOR	Left-handed, sharp and flat with a long run-in. Circuit 1m4f.
CARLISLE	Right-handed, undulating, stiff and galloping. Circuit 1m5f
CARTMEL	Left-handed, sharp and undulating, with stiff fences and a 4f run-in for chases. Circuit 1m.
CATTERICK	Left-handed, sharp and undulating, suiting handy types. Circuit 1m3f.
CHELTENHAM *(old course)*	Left-handed, galloping, undulating and testing track with stiff fences. Circuit 1m4f.
CHELTENHAM *(new course)*	Left-handed, galloping, undulating and testing track with stiff fences. Circuit 1m4½f.
CHEPSTOW	Left-handed and undulating. Going can be very testing. Circuit 1m7f.
DONCASTER	Left-handed, galloping, generally flat. Heavy ground rare. Circuit 2m.
EXETER	Right-handed and undulating. Stiff test of stamina. Circuit 2m.
FAKENHAM	Left-handed, sharp, undulating, suiting nippy types. Circuit 1m.
FOLKESTONE	Right-handed, undulating oval of 1m2f
FONTWELL	Left-handed hurdle course. Figure-of-eight chase course does not suit long-striding gallopers. Ground can be testing. Circuit 1m.
HAYDOCK	Left-handed, flat and galloping. Drop fences and long run-in on chase course. Old hurdle course suits gallopers; new course much sharper. Ciruit 1m5f.
HEREFORD	Right-handed, sharpish and generally flat. Suits nippy types. Circuit 1m4f.
HEXHAM	Left-handed, severe and undulating, placing emphasis on stamina. Circuit 1m4f.
HUNTINGDON	Right-handed and galloping. Circuit 1m4f.

KELSO	Left-handed and undulating. Hurdles course of 1m1f is sharp, more so than 1m 3f chase track, which has 2f run-in.
KEMPTON	Triangular circuit 1m5f, practically flat. Circuit 1m5f. Not used in 2005/6.
LEICESTER	Right-handed and undulating, placing emphasis on stamina. Circuit 1m6f.
LINGFIELD	Left-handed, undulating and sharp. Chase circuit 1m5f, hurdles run on flat course.
LUDLOW	Right-handed. Chase course flat with sharp bends, circuit 1m4f. Hurdles track, 150y longer, slightly undulating, with easier bends.
MARKET RASEN	Right-handed oval, sharp and somewhat undulating. Circuit 1m2f.
MUSSELBURGH	Right-handed virtually flat track with sharp turns. Circuit 1m3f.
NEWBURY	Left-handed, flat and galloping, with stiff fences. Circuit 1m7f.
NEWCASTLE	Left-handed, with uphill finish. Going can be very testing. Circuit 1m6f.
NEWTON ABBOT	Left-handed oval, sharp with short run-in. Circuit 1m2f.
PERTH	Right-handed and flat, with tight bends. Chase course has long run-in. Circuit 1m2f.
PLUMPTON	Left-handed, undulating, sharp. Circuit 1m1f.
SANDOWN	Right-handed with stiff uphill finish. Chase course tricky, especially for novices. Hurdles run on flat course. Circuit 1m5f.
SEDGEFIELD	Left-handed, undulating oval, sharp bends. Chase course has easy fences. Circuit 1m2f.
SOUTHWELL	Left-handed oval, approx 1m round, with six portable fences. Outside half of jumps course used in summer.
STRATFORD	Left-handed, flat and sharp, with short finishing straight. Circuit 1m2f.
TAUNTON	Right-handed oval, on the sharp side with short run-in. Circuit 1m2f.
TOWCESTER	Right-handed, with last mile uphill. Very testing. Circuit 1m6f.
UTTOXETER	Left-handed with some undulations. Hurdle course is inside chase course. Circuit 1m3f.
WARWICK	Left-handed, with tight turns and short run-in. Circuit 1m5f.
WETHERBY	Left-handed oval, with easy bends. Circuit 1m4f.
WINCANTON	Right-handed rectangular track, mainly flat. Circuit 1m3f.
WINDSOR	Figure-of-eight track with tight turns, mainly flat. Circuit 1m4f.
WORCESTER	Left-handed 1m5f oval, flat with long straights and easy turns.

LUDLOW (R-H)

Sunday, April 24

OFFICIAL GOING: Good (good to firm in places)

Race times are best compared to meetings from last autumn/spring rather than those in midwinter, due to slight alterations to positioning of rails and hurdles.

Wind: almost nil Weather: fine

1 LUDLOW GOLF CLUB CLAIMING HURDLE (9 hdls) 2m

2:00 (2:01) (Class 4) 4-Y-0+ **£3,045** (£870; £435)

Form RPR

015- **1** **Ziggy Zen**[15] [4777] 6-11-10 117 NFehily 105
(C J Mann) *prom: led 4 out: hdd 2 out: rallied to regain ld run-in: r.o* **9/4**[1]

504- **2** *1½* **Pilca (FR)**[7] [4890] 5-10-13 93 DCosgrave[(7)] 99
(R Flint) *in tch: mstke 3rd: wnt 2nd appr 3 out: led 2 out: hdd run- in: nt qckn* **12/1**

560- **3** *8* **Bernardon (GER)**[7] [4881] 9-11-0 114 (p) JMMaguire 85
(A J Deakin) *midfield: hdwy 5th: rdn appr 3 out: one pce whn hung rt 2 out* **7/2**[2]

646- **4** *5* **Desert Spa (USA)**[15] [4776] 10-10-7 83 (t) AGlassonbury[(7)] 85+
(G E Jones) *prom: rdn in 3rd whn blnd 3 out: sn wknd* **25/1**

266- **5** *½* **Monsal Dale (IRE)**[28] [4579] 6-11-2 78 (v[1]) MAFitzgerald 82
(Mrs L C Jewell) *led to 4 out: wknd appr next* **16/1**

602- **6** *¾* **Cybele Eria (FR)**[22] [4684] 8-10-4 97 MNicolls[(5)] 74
(John Allen) *midfield: rdn appr 3 out: no imp* **15/2**

040- **7** *1* **Saddler's Quest**[55] [3121] 8-11-4 74 (p) JMogford 82
(B P J Baugh) *hld up: effrt appr 3 out: nvr trbld ldrs* **66/1**

6/0- **8** *5* **Moving On Up**[7] [4881] 11-11-0 120 (b) DVerco 73
(C N Kellett) *chsd ldrs tl rdn and wknd appr 3 out* **25/1**

560- **9** *3* **Saxe-Coburg (IRE)**[15] [4776] 8-10-7 77 MrSRees[(7)] 70
(K G Wingrove) *a towards rr* **50/1**

20P- **10** *7* **Brother Ted**[64] [3950] 8-11-0 88 (t) DRDennis 64+
(J K Cresswell) *chsd ldrs tl rdn and wknd appr 3 out* **40/1**

655- **11** *2½* **Margarets Wish**[24] [4667] 5-10-6 82 ONelmes[(3)] 55
(T Wall) *towards rr: effrt appr 3 out: sn btn* **18/1**

12 *17* **Look No More**[480] 4-11-3 PJBrennan 46
(W G M Turner) *nt fluent: a bhd* **40/1**

502- **F** **Sir Walter (IRE)**[42] [4343] 12-11-0 93 ChristianWilliams —
(D Burchell) *hld up: fell 2nd* **13/2**[3]

000- **P** **Regal Act (IRE)**[27] [4609] 9-11-2 90 (vt) AO'Keeffe —
(Jennie Candlish) *a bhd: t.o whn p.u bef 3 out* **50/1**

30P- **P** **Cantemerle (IRE)**[114] [3121] 5-10-4 76 TGreenway[(5)] —
(W M Brisbourne) *a bhd: reminders after 3rd: t.o 4 out: p.u bef next* **40/1**

3m 42.7s (-4.90) **Going Correction** -0.375s/f (Good)
WFA 4 from 5yo+ 5lb **15** Ran SP% **117.4**
Speed ratings: **97,96,92,89,89 89,88,86,84,81 79,71,—,—,—** CSF £27.42 TOTE £2.60: £1.80, £3.20, £1.90; EX 103.20.Pilca was claimed by Robert Stronge for £8,000

Owner All For One & One For All Partnership 2 **Bred** C A And R M Cyzer **Trained** Upper Lambourn, Berks

FOCUS

An ordinary event, run at a decent pace. The winner did not need to run to his recent level of form to score, and the runner-up ran to his mark.

NOTEBOOK

Ziggy Zen, found wanting in a handicap last time, was back in a more suitable grade. He tried to kick away once in line for home but the game appeared up when he was collared at the second last. His stamina not in question, he rallied on the flat. *(op 10-3)*

Pilca(FR) cut down the favourite at the second last and looked sure to win, but he was probably in front too soon and his rival rallied past him after the last. He has run two decent races since joining this yard but was claimed after the race to join Robert Stronge. *(op 10-1)*

Bernardon(GER) had the cheekpieces back on for this drop in class. He made promising headway *on the turn out of the back straight but could not sustain the progress once in line for home. (tchd 4-1)*

Desert Spa(USA), who had his tongue tied down, was on the retreat when blundering three from home. He has been a consistent sort in recent months.

Monsal Dale(IRE) was equipped with a visor for the first time instead of the cheekpieces/tongue strap combination he has worn of late. Setting a decent pace, he was collared at the last in the back straight, and although no threat to the principals from that point he did stick on.

2 TOTEPOOL AWAYBET NOVICES' CHASE (13 fncs) 2m

2:35 (2:35) (Class 3) 5-Y-0+ **£6,721** (£2,068; £1,034; £517)

Form RPR

241- **1** **Saafend Rocket (IRE)**[24] [4668] 7-11-6 108 RJohnson 123+
(H D Daly) *hld up: hdwy 4th: 2nd 9th: led appr 2 out: r.o wl* **13/8**[2]

/1P- **2** *6* **Saintsaire (FR)**[15] [4769] 6-11-6 MAFitzgerald 121+
(N J Henderson) *led: blnd and hdd 4th: regained ld 9th: hdd appr 2 out: no ex fr last* **11/8**[1]

5PP- **3** *3½* **Nopekan (IRE)**[185] [1792] 5-10-4 RSpate[(7)] 105+
(Mrs K Waldron) *hld up in tch: hdwy 7th: mstke whn chsng ldrs 4 out: sn one pce* **16/1**

003- **4** *12* **In The Frame (IRE)**[17] [4755] 6-10-11 JPByrne[(3)] 98+
(Evan Williams) *hld up: pckd 1st: hdwy 9th: btn fr 4 out* **14/1**

020- **5** *11* **Pennys From Heaven**[15] [4769] 11-11-0 OMcPhail 88+
(Mrs Tracey Barfoot-Saunt) *hld up: hit 9th: effrt whn mstke 4 out: sn wknd* **40/1**

33F- **6** *11* **Dabus**[51] [4155] 10-10-11 101 ACCoyle[(3)] 77+
(M C Chapman) *midfield: nt fluent 8th: hdwy appr 4 out: sn wknd* **11/1**[3]

PP3- **7** *3½* **Let's Rock**[24] [4668] 7-10-7 67 MrRHodges[(7)] 69
(Mrs A Price) *prom: niggled along fr 7th: wknd after 9th* **100/1**

8 *10* **No Can Do (IRE)**[15] 7-10-4 LVickers[(3)] 52
(K J Burke) *nt jump wl: bhd fr 5th (water)* **100/1**

0/6- **9** *16* **Moon Shot**[57] [3054] 9-10-11 97 DCrosse[(3)] 43
(A G Juckes) *plld hrd: blnd 2nd: sn prom: lft in ld 4th: clr after next (water): hdd 9th: weakeend appr 4 out* **22/1**

40P- **10** *dist* **Circle Of Wolves**[7] [4879] 7-10-7 85 (v) JAJenkins[(7)] —
(H J Manners) *rdn and bhd fr 2nd: t.o* **50/1**

PF5- **P** **Proper Poser (IRE)**[46] [4260] 9-10-7 72 CMStudd[(7)] —
(M C Chapman) *prom: blnd 1st: lost pl 3rd: bhd fr 5th (water): t.o wehn p.u bef 4 out* **100/1**

3m 50.4s (-13.80) **Going Correction** -0.675s/f (Firm)
WFA 5 from 6yo+ 3lb **11** Ran SP% **112.8**
Speed ratings: **107,104,102,96,90 85,83,78,70,— —** CSF £4.05 TOTE £1.90: £1.10, £2.10, £6.30; EX 2.80.

Owner Ludlow Racing Partnership **Bred** Mrs Carole Douglas **Trained** Stanton Lacy, Shropshire

FOCUS

A decent novice chase which could be rated a few pounds higher through the winner.

NOTEBOOK

Saafend Rocket(IRE), off the mark over course and distance last time, followed up in the style of a progressive performer. He seemed to relish this better ground and can win again. *(op 15-8)*

Saintsaire(FR) survived a bad blunder at the last fence with a circuit to go but forfeited the lead. Given time to recover, he was back in front at the last down the far side, but was no match for his market rival in the end. He is better than this. *(tchd 13-8)*

Nopekan(IRE), having his first start since the autumn, made a promising chasing debut. He looked to be going as well as the big two on the long home turn, but got in too close to the first fence in the straight and was never able to counter. A former useful hurdler in Ireland, he can win a novice chase. *(op 14-1)*

In The Frame(IRE) ◆, having his second run over fences, left the distinct impression he is capable of considerably better with this experience behind him. *(op 16-1)*

Moon Shot, a fair performer on the All-Weather, showed more than on his chase debut over Christmas but will need to settle better. *(op 28-1 tchd 20-1)*

3 MOORE SCOTT JUVENILE NOVICES' HURDLE (9 hdls) 2m

3:10 (3:12) (Class 4) 4-Y-0 **£4,118** (£1,267; £633; £316)

Form RPR

011- **1** **Ma Yahab**[31] [4533] 4-11-4 111 AO'Keeffe 106+
(Miss Venetia Williams) *midfield: hdwy after 4 out: led 2 out: hit last: sn shkn up: comf* **2/1**[2]

04- **2** *2* **Text**[9] [4852] 4-10-9 RHobson[(3)] 96+
(C J Down) *hld up: hdwy appr 3 out: mstke 2 out: sn swtchd lft: wnt 2nd after last: kpt on: nt trble wnr* **7/1**[3]

5- **3** *5* **L'Eau Du Nil (FR)**[32] [4514] 4-10-12 RJohnson 92+
(P J Hobbs) *in tch: hdwy appr 3 out: ev ch 2 out: mstke last: no ex* **15/8**[1]

44- **4** *2* **Mr Lewin**[28] [4585] 4-10-12 JMMaguire 88
(D McCain) *trckd ldrs: pushed along appr 3 out: outpcd bef last* **15/2**

004- **5** *4* **Charlie Bear**[39] [4401] 4-10-5 93 (t) PCO'Neill[(7)] 86+
(W K Goldsworthy) *led: hdd 2 out: wkng whn mstke last* **9/1**

00P- **6** *¾* **South Sands (IRE)**[14] [4789] 4-10-5 TScudamore 76
(M Scudamore) *hld up: niggled along after 6th: hdwy 3 out: nvr trbld ldrs* **50/1**

F5F- **7** *¾* **Sovereign Girl**[78] [3697] 4-10-5 WHutchinson 76
(A W Carroll) *trckd ldrs tl rdn and wknd appr 3 out* **100/1**

00P- **8** *1* **Greencard Golf**[149] [2454] 4-10-9 JPByrne[(3)] 82
(Jennie Candlish) *hld up: effrt appr 3 out: sn btn* **100/1**

9 *19* **Oration**[284] 4-10-12 JAMcCarthy 63
(Mrs P Robeson) *midfield: hdwy appr 5th: wknd bef 3 out* **28/1**

10 *½* **Weet An Haul**[6] 4-10-9 (t) ONelmes[(3)] 62
(T Wall) *midfield tl wknd 4 out* **50/1**

P0- **11** *26* **Hum (IRE)**[27] [4611] 4-9-12 MrSRees[(7)] 29
(Miss D A McHale) *prom tl wknd after 4 out* **100/1**

6P- **12** *nk* **Cloud Catcher (IRE)**[5] [2868] 4-10-2 (t) LVickers[(3)] 29
(M Appleby) *midfield tl wknd 4 out* **100/1**

PP0- **F** **Jaolins**[9] [4852] 4-9-13 ow1 BenOrde-Powlett[(7)] —
(M Appleby) *t.k.h: hld up: fell 5th* **150/1**

P- **F** **Zuleta**[15] [4776] 4-10-5 JamesDavies —
(B D Leavy) *midfield: niggled along and hdwy appr 4 out: sn wknd: bhd whn fell 3 out* **66/1**

3m 44.0s (-3.60) **Going Correction** -0.375s/f (Good) **14** Ran SP% **115.9**
Speed ratings: **94,93,90,89,87 87,86,86,76,76 63,63,—,—** CSF £15.46 TOTE £3.30: £1.30, £1.90, £1.10; EX 12.50.

Owner M J Pilkington **Bred** John Warren **Trained** Kings Caple, H'fords

FOCUS

A modest time for the grade, 1.3 seconds slower than the claimer. The winner stepped up slightly on recent form with the runner-up performing to his mark.

NOTEBOOK

Ma Yahab, back against his own age group, completed the hat-trick with a bit up his sleeve. He should continue to run well on decent ground on sharp tracks such as this. *(op 11-4)*

Text, in fourth place when untidy at the second last, kept staying on but did not seriously threaten the winner. Going the right way, he went well on fast ground on the Flat and there could be a little race for him over hurdles. *(op 9-1)*

L'Eau Du Nil(FR) came under pressure at the first flight in the home straight and could not match *his market rival for pace from that point. This ground might have been a bit lively for him. (op 5-4 tchd 2-1)*

Mr Lewin ran a third reasonable race and is now eligible for handicaps. *(op 7-1 tchd 13-2)*

Charlie Bear, with his tongue tied, set a moderate pace and only relinquished the lead at the second last. A sharp track seems to suit him. *(op 12-1)*

South Sands(IRE), out of a mare who was a successful hurdler for the Scudamore yard before *winning over fences for Nigel Twiston-Davies, showed signs that she is slowly finding her feet. (op 33-1)*

Weet An Haul *Official explanation: trainer said gelding ran without declared tongue-strap, which had come adrift and could not be refitted (op 33-1)*

4 TOTESPORT.COM H'CAP CHASE (17 fncs) 2m 4f

3:45 (3:45) (Class 3) (0-120,120) 5-Y-0+ **£6,747** (£2,076; £1,038; £519)

Form RPR

5F4- **1** **Cosmocrat**[29] [4564] 7-10-12 **106** RJohnson 121+
(R Lee) *t.k.h: hld up: hdwy appr 4 out: led and mstke 3 out: drvn out* **6/1**[3]

443- **2** *1¾* **Sky Warrior (FR)**[17] [4757] 7-11-9 **120** JPByrne[(3)] 132
(Evan Williams) *a.p: rdn appr 10th: ev ch 3 out: styd on* **5/1**[1]

210- **3** *6* **Toulouse (IRE)**[10] [4836] 8-11-0 **111** RWalford[(3)] 119+
(R H Alner) *in tch: hdwy 7th: ev ch 3 out: wknd run-in* **20/1**

F36- **4** *5* **Master Papa (IRE)**[17] [4757] 6-11-0 **108** CLlewellyn 109
(N A Twiston-Davies) *hld up: hdwy after 9th (water): rdn whn hit 4 out: wknd next* **11/1**

2F4- **5** *hd* **Kind Sir**[43] [4335] 9-10-6 **100** WHutchinson 103+
(A W Carroll) *led: hdd 3 out: sn wknd* **11/2**[2]

PP0- **6** *8* **River Pirate (IRE)**[74] [3761] 8-11-3 **111** MFoley 104
(N J Henderson) *bhd: effrt approahcing 4 out: sn btn* **20/1**

400/ **7** *2½* **Wave Rock**[393] [4572] 10-10-12 **106** NFehily 99+
(A W Carroll) *hld up: hdwy 10th: outpcd appr 13th: no imp after 4 out: n.d whn j.rt last* **12/1**

352- **8** *12* **Fiery Peace**[123] [2938] 8-11-4 **112** MBradburne 102+
(H D Daly) *hld up: mstke 10th: hdwy appr 13th: mstke 4 out: wkng whn j.rt and mstke 3 out* **7/1**

P12- **9** *21* **Lincoln Place (IRE)**[210] [1518] 10-11-3 **111** PJBrennan 68
(P J Hobbs) *prom: rdn appr 12th: wknd next* **7/1**

F24- **10** *10* **Celtic Star (IRE)**[24] [4670] 7-10-9 **103** DRDennis 50
(Mrs L Williamson) *midfield tl rdn and wknd appr 12th* **25/1**

P10- **P** **Talbot Lad**[7] 4880 9-11-8 **116**............(t) APMcCoy —
(S A Brookshaw) *prom: wkng whn mstke 12th: bhd whn blnd next: t.o whn p.u bef 4 out* **6/1**[3]

4m 51.3s (-14.50) **Going Correction** -0.675s/f (Firm) course record
WFA 5 from 6yo+ 4lb **11** Ran SP% **115.0**
Speed ratings: **102,101,98,96,96 93,92,87,79,75** — CSF £34.96 CT £563.32 TOTE £7.60: £2.20, £2.90, £4.30; EX 53.30 TRIFECTA Not won..
Owner M L Shone **Bred** Arthur E Smith **Trained** Byton, H'fords

FOCUS
A competitive handicap run at a good pace, and this looks a very solid piece of form.

NOTEBOOK
Cosmocrat, stepping up in trip, jumped well bar an error when in the thick of the action three out. He landed this competitive handicap in decent style under a patient ride and looks to be on the upgrade. *(op 13-2)*
Sky Warrior(FR), winner of this event last year off only a 2lb lower mark, did nothing wrong and went down fighting. This is his trip. *(op 4-1)*
Toulouse(IRE), sharper for his recent return to action, looked a threat from the home turn until crying enough on the flat.
Master Papa(IRE), down in trip, ran a respectable race but is finding it hard to get his head in front over fences. *(tchd 12-1)*
Kind Sir made the running as usual, but after getting in too close at the fourth from home the game was up at the next. This was a more encouraging effort than of late and he is a pound lower than when last winning a year ago. *(op 6-1)*
River Pirate(IRE), the blinkers discarded after failing to work, was never in the hunt but did stay on past beaten horses. *(op 16-1)*
Wave Rock, previously with Philip Hobbs, made a satisfactory return to the fray on his first start since March last year. It is four years since he tasted success over fences but he is undoubtedly well handicapped these days. *(op 10-1)*
Fiery Peace, having his first run since Christmas, was breathing down the leaders' necks on the home turn, but errors at the first two fences in the straight halted his progress. This trip stretches his stamina. *(op 8-1 tchd 9-1)*
Talbot Lad dropped out of contention rather tamely and has now been beaten twice off this mark since a course-and-distance win last month. *(op 9-1)*

5 TOTEEXACTA H'CAP HURDLE (11 hdls) 2m 5f
4:20 (4:22) (Class 3) (0-115,109) 4-Y-0+ **£5,418** (£1,667; £833; £416)

Form RPR
222- **1** **Water King (USA)**[15] 4780 6-11-1 **98**............ APMcCoy 110+
(R M Stronge) *midfield: hdwy appr 4 out: led on bit 3 out: clr bef last: comf* **5/1**[2]
001- **2** *8* **Rift Valley (IRE)**[7] 4889 10-11-3 **100** 7ex............(v) RJohnson 106+
(P J Hobbs) *trckd ldrs: led 7th: hdd and j.rt 3 out: j.rt again whn u.p fnl 2: no ch w wnr* **4/5**[1]
044- **3** *6* **Musally**[31] 4533 8-11-3 **100**............ CLlewellyn 98
(W Jenks) *hld up: hdwy appr 7th: outpcd after 4 out: rallied bef 2 out: styd on* **15/2**
303- **4** *2* **Vicario**[23] 4683 4-11-1 **109**............ StephenJCraine[(5)] 99
(D McCain) *trckd ldrs: ev ch appr 3 out: wknd bef last* **20/1**
650- **5** *5* **Burundi (IRE)**[23] 4678 11-11-12 **109**............ NFehily 102+
(A W Carroll) *hld up: hdwy after 4 out: chsd ldrs bef next: wknd last* **33/1**
030- **6** *3 ½* **Fast King (FR)**[21] 4723 7-9-12 **86**............ DrPPritchard[(5)] 74
(Dr P Pritchard) *hld up: sme hdwy 3 out: nvr on terms* **33/1**
345- **7** *2 ½* **Astyanax (IRE)**[23] 4679 5-11-1 **98**............ MAFitzgerald 83
(N J Henderson) *led: j.rt 6th: hdd next: wknd appr 3 out* **7/1**[3]
02P/ **8** *1 ½* **Linus**[446] 3655 7-10-9 **95**............ RHobson[(3)] 79
(C J Down) *a bhd* **66/1**
546- **9** *19* **Rumbling Bridge**[28] 4585 4-10-6 **95**............ MBradburne 54
(H D Daly) *midfield: rdn appr 4 out: sn wknd* **20/1**
0PP- **10** *dist* **Bude**[123] 2935 6-10-1 **87**............ JPByrne[(3)] —
(S A Brookshaw) *prom: reminders after 5th: wknd 7th: virtually p.u run-in* **66/1**
UF0- **U** **Murphy's Nails (IRE)**[14] 4799 8-10-7 **90**............ JPMcNamara —
(K C Bailey) *prom tl blnd and uns rdr 1st* **50/1**
4PP- **P** **Alchemystic (IRE)**[36] 4450 5-11-5 **102**............(t) AO'Keeffe —
(M A Barnes) *in tch: j. slowly 2nd: lost pl 6th: bhd after: t.o whn p.u bef 3 out* **66/1**

5m 3.90s (-9.60) **Going Correction** -0.375s/f (Good)
WFA 4 from 5yo+ 6lb **12** Ran SP% **118.3**
Speed ratings: **103,99,97,96,95 93,92,92,84,— —,—** CSF £9.09 CT £29.36 TOTE £5.60: £1.60, £1.10, £1.80; EX 16.90.
Owner Hellyer, Clark, St Quinton **Bred** Skymarc Farm Inc & Castlemartin Stud **Trained** Beedon, Berks

FOCUS
Not the most competitive of events, but improved form from the winner. The runner-up was 6lb off his recent win but the next four home all ran close to their marks.

NOTEBOOK
Water King(USA), raised another 3lb for finishing second at Hereford, was suited by this longer trip and gained reward for some consistent efforts. He soon made the race his once easing to the front and should be capable of building on this. *(op 4-1)*
Rift Valley(IRE), under a penalty for his facile win at Wincanton, ran his race but found the winner much too good. On this evidence he will struggle off his new mark of 105. *(op Evens)*
Musally, winner of this event twelve months ago when 2lb lower, ran another solid race without posing a real threat to the first two. *(op 8-1)*
Vicario ran respectably, and although his win came in testing ground the better underfoot conditions here appeared to suit. *(op 16-1)*
Burundi(IRE), who had a comeback run last month after more than eight months off, should be spot on with this outing behind him.
Astyanax(IRE), back in handicap company, remains an underachiever. *(tchd 15-2)*

6 50 YEARS IN RACING HUNTERS' CHASE (FOR THE LUDLOW GOLD CUP) (22 fncs) 3m 1f 110y
4:55 (4:57) (Class 6) 6-Y-0+ **£2,926** (£836; £418)

Form RPR
/4U- **1** **Chasing The Bride**[14] 12-11-11............ MissAGoschen[(3)] 115+
(Miss A Goschen) *hld up and bhd: staedy hdwy fr 17th: led 2 out: pushed out* **7/2**[2]
25- **2** *1 ½* **An Capall Dubh (IRE)**[17] 4750 9-11-7............ MrPCowley[(3)] 108+
(Mrs Edward Crow) *j.lft: prom: mstke 2nd: led bef 14th (water): hit 17th: clr appr 4 out: hdd 2 out: styd on but a hld* **15/8**[1]
/1P- **3** *5* **Teeton Priceless**[14] 10-10-10............ MrNPearce[(7)] 93
(Mrs Joan Tice) *led to 4th: remained prom: led 9th tl appr 14th (water): rdn bef 4 out: kpt on same pce fr 2 out* **20/1**
4 *dist* **Greenwich**[8] 11-11-7 85............ MissCStucley[(7)] 74
(Mrs Marilyn Scudamore) *midfield: reminder after 8th: hdwy after 9th: wknd 11th: mstke 12th: no ch whn mstke 16th: t.o* **7/1**
6PP- **P** **Robert The Rascal**[7] 12-11-3............ MrJBuxton[(7)] —
(Mrs C M James) *a bhd: t.o whn p.u bef 18th* **66/1**
FPF/ **P** **Autcaesar Autnihil (IRE)**[7] 10-11-3............ MrMMunrowd[(7)] —
(Mrs J Jeynes) *a bhd: hit 3rd: t.o whn p.u bef 15th* **40/1**
PPP- **P** **Major Bit**[8] 4870 9-11-7 57............(t) MissSBeddoes[(3)] —
(S A Brookshaw) *a bhd: lost tch 10th: t.o whn p.u bef 17th* **50/1**
40P- **P** **Good Bone (FR)**[10] 4840 8-11-10 88............(t) MrRhysHughes[(7)] —
(S Flook) *midfield: hdwy after 9th: wknd 11th: t.o whn p.u bef 4 out* **8/1**
U **Thebigfellow (IRE)**[289] 911 8-11-3............ MrRQuinn[(7)] —
(Richard Mathias) *prom: led 4th to 9th: losing pl whn blnd bdly and uns rdr 10th* **50/1**
F/3- **P** **Judaic Ways**[31] 4532 11-11-7 93............ MrAWintle[(3)] —
(H D Daly) *hld up: hdwy appr 15th: 4th whn sddle slipped 16th: nt rcvr: p.u bef 18th* **6/1**[3]
314- **P** **Mydante (IRE)**[14] 10-10-10 79............(t) MrRHodges[(7)] —
(S Flook) *trckd ldrs: mstke 15th: wknd 17th: mstke 3 out: bhd whn p.u bef last: dismntd* **10/1**

6m 29.4s **11** Ran SP% **116.6**
CSF £10.48 TOTE £5.80: £2.50, £1.10, £4.20; EX 15.30.
Owner The Florian Racing Partnership **Bred** Mrs S Hooper **Trained** Henstridge, Somerset

FOCUS
The field was soon well strung out in this fair hunter chase.

NOTEBOOK
Chasing The Bride, held up off the pace as usual, looked to have been set too much to do at one stage, but his trainer/rider had timed it right and he was well in command from the second last. He idled with his race won and is better than the bare result. *(op 9-4)*
An Capall Dubh(IRE) did not jump as well as he can. Clear on the turn for home, he was steadily reeled in by the patiently ridden favourite, but to his credit he was coming back for more near the line. *(op 9-4 tchd 5-2)*
Teeton Priceless, an infrequent runner under Rules, ran a most creditable race and finished a mile clear of the only other finisher. *(op 12-1)*
Judaic Ways was staying on, and certainly not out of calculations, when the saddle appeared to slip on landing over the seventh from home. Wintle did very well not to be unseated and to get his mount over the next before pulling up. *(op 13-2)*

7 JENKINSONS CATERERS INTERMEDIATE OPEN NATIONAL HUNT FLAT RACE 2m
5:25 (5:26) (Class 6) 4-6-Y-0 **£2,702** (£772; £386)

Form RPR
0- **1** **Kate's Gift**[50] 4193 4-10-13............ JamesDavies 90
(P R Webber) *in tch: rdn 3f out: led ins fnl f: r.o* **8/1**
2 *shd* **Paradise Bay (IRE)** 4-10-13............ MAFitzgerald 90
(N J Henderson) *hld up: hdwy 7f out: led over 2f out: rdn over 1f out: hdd ins fnl f: r.o* **3/1**[1]
4- **3** *2 ½* **Wotashambles (IRE)**[57] 4069 4-10-8............ MNicolls[(5)] 88+
(P R Webber) *midfield: hdwy 10f out: ev ch over 2f out: rdn and hung lft over 1f out: nt qckn* **15/2**[3]
- **4** *2 ½* **Highland Chief (IRE)**[70] 5-11-4............ TJMurphy 90
(Miss H C Knight) *hld up: stdy hdwy over 4f out: one pce fnl 2f* **7/2**[2]
06- **5** *½* **It's My Party**[152] 2413 4-10-13............ PJBrennan 84
(W G M Turner) *hld up in tch: hdwy over 3f out: rdn over 2f out: one pce* **33/1**
2- **6** *4* **Campaign Charlie**[50] 4179 5-11-1............ JPByrne[(3)] 87+
(H D Daly) *trckd ldrs: led 6f out: hdd over 2f out: wknd over 1f out* **9/1**
26- **7** *shd* **A Few Kind Words (IRE)**[26] 4644 4-10-6............ RSpate[(7)] 80
(Mrs K Waldron) *hld up: hdwy on ins over 3f out: rdn over 2f out: wknd over 1f out* **25/1**
050- **8** *2* **Slight Hiccup**[14] 4801 5-10-6............ LTreadwell[(5)] 76
(C W Moore) *wl bhd: rdn over 5f out: hdwy on ins over 3f out: nvr trbld ldrs* **100/1**
0- **9** *7* **Star Fever (IRE)**[102] 3325 4-10-13............ SThomas 71
(Miss H C Knight) *in tch: rdn over 5f out: wknd 4f out* **14/1**
10 *½* **Tom Tug (NZ)** 5-11-4............ CLlewellyn 75
(W Jenks) *prom tl rdn and wknd over 4f out* **20/1**
3- **11** *1* **Clifford T Ward**[36] 4465 5-11-4............ JMMaguire 74
(D McCain) *hld up: hdwy 5f out: rdn over 3f out: wknd over 2f out* **8/1**
0- **12** *3* **Silly Miss Off (IRE)**[147] 2506 4-10-6............ TScudamore 59
(M Scudamore) *racd keenly: prom: led after 4f: hdd 6f out: wknd 3f out* **33/1**
6- **13** *27* **Darnay Boy (IRE)**[22] 4690 5-11-4............ ATinkler 44
(Mrs P Ford) *a bhd* **66/1**
0- **14** *16* **Staley's Queen**[4] 4935 4-9-13............ JAJenkins[(7)] 16
(K G Wingrove) *trckd ldrs for 7f: sn wknd* **100/1**
00- **15** *7* **Crown Trix (IRE)**[36] 4451 6-11-4............ AO'Keeffe 21
(C W Moore) *led for 4f: wknd 1/2-way* **100/1**
P- **16** *dist* **General Oliver (IRE)**[4] 4935 5-10-11............ MrSRees[(7)] —
(K G Wingrove) *prom tl wknd 7f out: t.o* **100/1**
0- **S** **Georgie Girl Dove**[52] 4138 5-10-11............ WHutchinson —
(C J Price) *hld up whn stmbld and uns rdr after 3f* **100/1**

3m 39.3s (-7.70) **Going Correction** -0.375s/f (Good)
WFA 4 from 5yo+ 5lb **17** Ran SP% **118.8**
Speed ratings: **104,103,102,101,101 99,99,98,94,94 93,92,78,70,67** —,— CSF £29.30 TOTE £8.60: £1.90, £3.20, £2.20; EX 58.70 Place 6 £4.00, Place 5 £2.91..
Owner Mr & Mrs M J Dowd **Bred** S Hadley **Trained** Mollington, Oxon

FOCUS
A fair time for a bumper when compared to the two hurdle races over the same trip, but only modest form.

NOTEBOOK
Kate's Gift is out of a bumper winner from the family of The Tsarevich. Suited by better ground than he was faced with on his debut, he stayed on to show ahead inside the final furlong but only just held off the favourite's challenge. *(tchd 9-1)*
Paradise Bay(IRE), a half-brother to a Flat winner in Belgium, looked set to make a successful debut when striking the front but was soon under pressure. Collared inside the last, he battled right to the line. *(op 5-2 tchd 9-4)*
Wotashambles(IRE), a stablemate of the winner, ran another promising race despite edging to his left briefly in the straight, probably through greenness. *(op 13-2)*
Highland Chief(IRE), out of a winning hurdler, had been fourth to Joaaci in February on his sole run in an Irish point. This was a promising debut under Rules. *(op 4-1)*
It's My Party showed more than he did in two runs in the autumn.
Campaign Charlie showed a similar level of form as when runner-up in a five-runner affair in soft ground on his debut.
T/Jkpt: £7,859.40 to a £1 stake. Pool: £271,206.50. 24.50 winning tickets. T/Plt: £4.80 to a £1 stake. Pool: £42,631.75. 6,430.55 winning tickets. T/Qpdt: £3.20 to a £1 stake. Pool: £2,088.00. 475.30 winning tickets. DO

WETHERBY (L-H)

Sunday, April 24

OFFICIAL GOING: Good

The ground had dried out and was generally described as 'just on the easy side of good' at the start but by the last 'on the quick side of good'.

Wind: moderate; half-against Weather: fine and sunny

8 YELL.COM MAIDEN HURDLE (12 hdls) 2m 7f

2:20 (2:22) (Class 4) 4-Y-0+ **£2,933** (£838; £419)

Form RPR

65P- **1** **Ryhall (IRE)**[54] 4105 5-10-9 95 ....(b[1]) RGarritty 97
(T D Easterby) *trckd ldrs: wnt 2nd after 9th: hrd rdn and styd on to ld nr fin* **15/2**[3]

263- **2** ½ **Present Glory (IRE)**[46] 4267 6-11-2 .... TDoyle 105+
(C Tinkler) *w ldrs: led 7th: hit last: hdd nr fin* **7/4**[1]

005- **3** dist **Happy Boy (IRE)**[21] 4709 4-10-9 80 ....(t) JimCrowley 62
(M A Barnes) *in tch: drvn along 7th: outpcd 9th: kpt on to take 3rd nr line: btn 36 l* **33/1**

034/ **4** ½ **Nod Ya Head**[404] 4388 9-10-2 .... PKinsella[(7)] 61
(R E Barr) *chsd ldrs: jnd ldr 8th: wknd fr 3 out* **25/1**

660- **5** ¾ **Relix (FR)**[14] 4783 5-10-11 95 .... DMcGann[(5)] 67
(A M Crow) *chsd ldrs: outpcd fr 9th* **16/1**

423- **6** 11 **Bywell Beau (IRE)**[14] 4785 6-11-2 100 .... PRobson 56
(J I A Charlton) *chsd ldrs: mstke 8th: wknd next* **9/2**[2]

P- **F** **Royal Friend**[75] 3747 6-11-2 .... BHarding —
(C R Wilson) *chsd ldrs: fell 4th* **50/1**

0P- **P** **Derainey (IRE)**[81] 3648 6-11-2 ....(bt[1]) KJohnson —
(R Johnson) *sn bhd: t.o whn p.u bef 9th* **40/1**

P **Parsons Leap (IRE)** 6-11-2 .... ADempsey —
(I McMath) *bhd whn hmpd 4th: t.o whn p.u bef 7th* **25/1**

P **Stately Progress (IRE)**[357] 7-10-13 .... MrTGreenall[(3)] —
(C Grant) *bhd fr 6th: t.o whn p.u bef 9th* **50/1**

P- **P** **Pharnoon**[88] 3540 9-10-9 .... MJMcAlister[(7)] —
(E M Caine) *j. poorly: sn bhd: t.o 9th: p.u bef next* **100/1**

00/ **P** **Double Emblem (IRE)**[49] 8-10-4 .... DCCostello[(5)] —
(B R Foster) *chsd ldrs: rdn 6th: sn lost pl: bhd whn p.u bef 7th* **50/1**

235- **P** **Ironside (IRE)**[58] 4048 6-11-2 100 .... RThornton —
(H D Daly) *mde most tl hdd and mstke 7th: wknd 9th: poor 7th whn p.u bef 3 out* **9/2**[2]

443- **P** **Matmata De Tendron (FR)**[19] 4735 5-11-2 94 .... NPMulholland —
(A Crook) *chsd ldrs: reminders 6th: lost pl 8th: bhd whn p.u bef 3 out* **10/1**

5m 44.3s (-15.30) **Going Correction** -0.05s/f (Good)
WFA 4 from 5yo+ 6lb **14** Ran SP% **119.4**
Speed ratings: **101,100**,—,—,— —,—,—,—,— —,—,—,— CSF £20.22 TOTE £2.60: £2.60, £1.70, £6.50; EX 35.00.
Owner Mr & Mrs W J Williams **Bred** W J And Mrs M Williams **Trained** Great Habton, N Yorks
■ Stewards' Enquiry : T Doyle two-day ban: used whip with excessive frequency and without allowing gelding time to respond (May 5-6)

FOCUS

A weak maiden hurdle with the first two, both potential chasers, a long way clear of the third, who was beaten 36l.

NOTEBOOK

Ryhall(IRE), in first-time blinkers, never flinched and showed ahead near the line. Hopefully she will make a better chaser. *(op 8-1 tchd 7-1)*

Present Glory(IRE), a big type, went on and stepped up the pace but, after flattening the last, he just missed out. A good opportunity to break his duck over hurdles lost. *(op 2-1)*

Happy Boy(IRE), unplaced in five previous starts, was struggling to keep up with a circuit to go and in the end the first two were just a speck on the horizon.

Nod Ya Head, who is not very big, mixed it with the first two but faded badly over the final three flights.

Relix(FR), who is only small, has yet to prove his stamina. *(op 20-1)*

Bywell Beau(IRE) was disappointing and was already feeling the strain when getting the fifth last wrong. *(op 11-2)*

Ironside(IRE) set the pace but steopped to nothing on the final turn before being pulled up, reportedly lame. *Official explanation: vet said gelding was lame (op 4-1)*

9 "GO RACING IN YORKSHIRE" RACECARD COMPETITION AMATEUR RIDERS' H'CAP HURDLE (9 hdls) 2m

2:55 (2:55) (Class 4) (0-100,100) 4-Y-0+ **£3,122** (£892; £446)

Form RPR

220- **1** **Mr Bigglesworth (NZ)**[13] 4810 7-11-1 **96** .... WPKavanagh[(7)] 104+
(R C Guest) *chsd ldrs: led 2 out: styd on wl* **6/1**[2]

00P- **2** 6 **Shakwaa**[86] 3566 6-10-4 **85** .... MrTJO'Brien[(7)] 87
(E A Elliott) *trckd ldrs: led 3 out: hdd next: kpt on same pce* **50/1**

513- **3** 1¾ **Corrib Lad (IRE)**[44] 4298 7-11-4 **92** .... MrTGreenall 92
(L Lungo) *chsd ldrs: drvn along 3 out: styd on same pce* **7/2**[1]

652- **4** ½ **Gospel Song**[4] 4926 13-11-0 **95** .... GWhillans[(7)] 96+
(A C Whillans) *led to 3 out: one pce fr next* **9/1**

230- **5** 1 **Classic Calvados (FR)**[107] 3256 6-10-13 **94** ....(t) MrSFMagee[(7)] 93
(P D Niven) *hdwy 4th: sn chsng ldrs: one pce fr 2 out* **14/1**

22P- **6** shd **Miss Pross**[77] 3724 5-11-1 **96** .... MrMWalford[(7)] 95
(T D Walford) *hld up and bhd: hdwy 5th: styd on same pce fr 3 out* **20/1**

506- **7** shd **Mamore Gap (IRE)**[11] 4208 7-10-11 **90** .... MrPCallaghan[(5)] 89
(M E Sowersby) *rr-div: hdwy 6th: hung lft and styd on run-in* **33/1**

105- **8** 2 **Time Marches On**[13] 4387 7-11-0 **95** .... JReveley[(7)] 94+
(K G Reveley) *mid-div: hdwy 3 out: blnd last: nvr rchd ldrs* **14/1**

241/ **9** 3½ **Dilsaa**[75] 1623 8-11-12 **100** .... MissNCarberry 93
(K A Ryan) *bhd: sme hdwy 5th: one pce fr 2 out* **8/1**[3]

000- **10** hd **Ton-Chee**[44] 4303 6-11-3 **94** ow6 .... MrDJewett[(3)] 90+
(K W Hogg) *w ldrs: blnd 3 out: fdd next* **33/1**

00P- **11** 1 **Bromley Abbey**[14] 4785 7-9-7 **76** .... MrNJTerry[(7)] 68
(Miss S E Forster) *bhd: sme hewady 3 out: nvr nr ldrs* **100/1**

12 1½ **Ballyboe Boy (IRE)**[219] 1434 6-10-8 **85** .... TJDreaper[(3)] 75
(R C Guest) *rr-div: sme hewady 3 out: nvr a threat* **20/1**

P63- **13** 1 **Off The Edge (AUS)**[44] 4303 6-10-2 **83** .... EWhillans[(7)] 72
(N G Richards) *bhd: hdwy 5th: w ldrs 3 out: sn fdd* **10/1**

5P0- **14** nk **Pucks Court**[117] 3039 8-9-13 **76** .... MrNickyTinkler[(3)] 65
(I A Brown) *in rr whn mstke 1st: sme hdwy 3 out: nvr a factor* **100/1**

440- **15** ¾ **Speed Venture**[48] 4235 8-11-1 **96** ....(tp) MrGTumelty[(7)] 84
(J Mackie) *w ldrs: wknd 3 out* **14/1**

P00- **16** 6 **Al Mabrook (IRE)**[14] 4787 10-10-12 **93** .... MrCJCallow[(7)] 75
(N G Richards) *chsd ldrs: lost pl appr 3 out* **40/1**

030- **17** 3 **My Sunshine (IRE)**[14] 4782 4-10-3 **85** ....(t) MJMcAlister[(3)] 59
(M E Sowersby) *mid-div: reminders 6th: nvr on terms* **50/1**

030- **18** 1 **Only Words (USA)**[19] 4739 8-10-9 **90** .... PKinsella[(7)] 68
(A J Lockwood) *chsd ldrs: lost pl appr 3 out* **16/1**

2P4- **19** 8 **Ressource (FR)**[33] 4501 6-10-9 **90** ....(b) MrWRussell[(7)] 60
(G L Moore) *bhd fr 5th* **66/1**

000- **20** 1¼ **Mount Pekan (IRE)**[144] 2565 5-9-12 **79** ow4 .... MrDTStratton[(7)] 48
(J S Goldie) *chsd ldrs: mstke 3rd: lost pl appr 3 out* **40/1**

506- **21** ½ **It's Harry**[76] 3739 7-11-1 **96** .... ARAdams[(7)] 65
(Mrs S J Smith) *a in rr* **16/1**

600- **22** 10 **Bertie Arms**[46] 4261 5-9-9 **76** .... MrLGibson[(7)] 35
(J M Jefferson) *mstkes: a bhd* **100/1**

0P0- **23** 2½ **Gebora (FR)**[31] 3312 6-10-11 **92** .... MrABrooke[(7)] 48
(B R Foster) *a bhd* **66/1**

3m 55.4s (-1.80) **Going Correction** -0.05s/f (Good)
WFA 4 from 5yo+ 5lb **23** Ran SP% **128.6**
Speed ratings: **102,99,98,97,97 97,97,96,94,94 93,93,92,92,92 89,87,87,83,82 82,77,76**
CSF £293.16 CT £1235.70 TOTE £7.80: £1.90, £18.50, £2.00, £1.70; EX 1797.70.
Owner Bache Silk **Bred** Mrs E Alexander And W Alexander **Trained** Brancepeth, Co Durham

FOCUS

No better than a seller but a clear-cut winner of some potential. The form is solid for the grade and should work out.

NOTEBOOK

Mr Bigglesworth(NZ) in the end won going right away and the plan is to go novice chasing now. *(op 7-1)*

Shakwaa, pulled up when last seen out at Doncaster in January, showed a return to form.

Corrib Lad(IRE), hard at work coming off the final turn, proved just too slow over this trip on drying ground. A big type, he should make a better chaser. *(op 9-2)*

Gospel Song, a tough veteran, ran his heart out but the sun and the wind had turned the ground against him. *(op 10-1)*

Classic Calvados(FR), a maiden after eleven previous starts, had been absent since January and seemed to appreciate the much better ground he encountered here. *(op 16-1 tchd 12-1)*

Miss Pross, absent since pulling up at Hereford in February, ran better but she is a keen type and at present her own worst enemy.

Mamore Gap(IRE), last seen in action on the level, stayed on but hung quite badly on the run-in and does not look straightforward. *Official explanation: trainer said gelding lost front shoe*

Only Words(USA) *Official explanation: jockey said gelding bled from nose*

10 118 247 BEGINNERS' CHASE (18 fncs) 2m 7f 110y

3:30 (3:31) (Class 4) 5-Y-0+ **£3,916** (£1,205; £602; £301)

Form RPR

6F2- **1** **Bob Ar Aghaidh (IRE)**[66] 3906 9-11-2 .... TDoyle 117+
(C Tinkler) *chsd ldr: lft in ld after 9th: clr 3 out: eased towards fin* **85/40**[1]

06/ **2** 15 **Frankie Dori (IRE)**[11] 4833 6-11-2 .... RPMcNally 97
(S Donohoe, Ire) *hdwy to chse ldrs 10th: styd on to take 2nd last: no ch w wnr* **7/1**

443- **3** 10 **Lubinas (IRE)**[21] 4716 6-11-2 99 .... GLee 91+
(F Jordan) *mstke 6th: jnd ldrs 10th: rdn 4 out: wknd last* **10/3**[2]

5U6- **4** 1¼ **Sailor A'Hoy**[8] 4869 9-10-13 96 ....(p) RYoung[(3)] 86
(M Mullineaux) *in rr fr 10th: kpt on fr 2 out* **10/1**

/PP- **5** hd **Lambrini Bianco (IRE)**[7] 4875 7-10-9 65 ....(p) DLaverty[(7)] 86
(Mrs L Williamson) *bhd and reminders 6th: outpcd fr 13th: kpt on fr 2 out* **50/1**

303- **6** dist **High Rank**[50] 4171 6-11-2 ....(t) PMoloney —
(J Mackie) *chsd ldrs: lost pl after 13th: bhd fr 3 out: t.o* **14/1**

260- **F** **Isellido (IRE)**[22] 4694 6-10-9 .... HOliver —
(R C Guest) *j. ight: in rr tl fell 10th* **5/1**[3]

/P0- **P** **Manor Star**[41] 4369 6-9-13 67 .... DRCook[(10)] —
(B D Leavy) *chsd ldrs tl p.u bef 11th* **100/1**

P/P- **P** **Bobalong (IRE)**[114] 3122 8-11-2 109 .... AThornton —
(C P Morlock) *nt fluent: in rr tl p.u bef 4th* **14/1**

0/5- **P** **Seemore Sunshine**[340] 423 8-11-2 .... SCurran —
(M J Gingell) *led and sn clr: wknd: hdd and p.u after 9th* **100/1**

PPP- **P** **Seaniethesmuggler (IRE)**[31] 4536 7-11-2 95 .... FKeniry —
(S Gollings) *prom eraly: lost pl 4th: in rr whn p.u bef 11th* **25/1**

5m 56.2s (1.20) **Going Correction** -0.05s/f (Good) **11** Ran SP% **114.5**
Speed ratings: **98,93,89,89,89** —,—,—,—,— — CSF £17.04 TOTE £3.30: £1.80, £2.20, £1.60; EX 27.50.
Owner George Ward **Bred** George Ward **Trained** Compton, Berks

FOCUS

A very modest chase but an improved performance over fences by the winner, value for 20l, who can go on to better things.

NOTEBOOK

Bob Ar Aghaidh(IRE), who has taken time to come to terms with jumping fences, was springheeled and had this won some way out. He should find another race this summer now he has got his act together. *(op 5-2 tchd 2-1)*

Frankie Dori(IRE), an Irish point winner, kept on in his own time to finish clear second best in the end. *(tchd 13-2)*

Lubinas(IRE), basically a disappointing sort, tired badly late on and this trip looks beyond him. *Official explanation: jockey said gelding failed to stay (op 7-2)*

Sailor A'Hoy, suited by the better ground, stayed on in his own time but basically was never at the races.

Lambrini Bianco(IRE), in the Amberleigh House colours, is a brother to the 1995 Grand National winner Royal Athlete but that seems to be his only claim to fame.

Bobalong(IRE) *Official explanation: jockey said gelding made mistakes at first 3 fences*

11 "BOLTON PERCY CHALLENGE" (S) H'CAP HURDLE (10 hdls) 2m 4f 110y

4:05 (4:05) (Class 5) (0-90,90) 4-Y-0+ **£2,422** (£692; £346)

Form RPR

412- **1** **Irish Blessing (USA)**[25] 4662 8-11-1 **79** ....(p) TDoyle 80+
(F Jordan) *a.p: styd on fr 3 out: led last: drvn clr* **9/2**[1]

044- **2** 4 **Idlewild (IRE)**[19] 4734 10-11-5 **90** .... APogson[(7)] 90+
(C T Pogson) *led 3rd: mstke 2 out: blnd and hdd last: no ex* **28/1**

526- **3** 5 **Star Trooper (IRE)**[13] 4810 9-10-8 **77** ....(p) DCCostello[(5)] 69
(Miss S E Forster) *chsd ldrs: rdn 3 out: kpt on same pce* **15/2**[2]

556- **4** 4 **Approaching Land (IRE)**[14] 4783 10-11-2 **83** .... MrTGreenall[(3)] 72+
(M W Easterby) *t.k.h in rr: hdwy 7th: styd on fr 2 out* **14/1**

066- **5** 6 **College Cracker**[21] 4714 7-9-7 **64** .... EDehdashti[(7)] 49+
(J F Coupland) *chsd ldrs: one pce fr 3 out: j.rt last* **12/1**

F5P- **6** hd **Solway Gale (IRE)**[67] 3886 8-11-3 **81** .... BGibson 63
(L Lungo) *led to 3rd: chsd ldrs: outpcd fr 3 out* **22/1**

660- **7** ½ **Northern Echo**[14] 4783 8-10-7 **78** ....(p) GThomas[(7)] 59
(K S Thomas) *rr-div: hdwy u.p 7th: nvr nr ldrs* **33/1**

350- **8** *2 ½* **Francken (ITY)**[19] [4738] 6-10-7 **78** ow3..........................(b) MrMWalford[(7)] 57
(Lady Susan Watson) *hld up: stdy hdwy 7th: sn chsng ldrs: wknd 2 out* **12/1**

245- **9** *3* **In Good Faith**[95] [3422] 13-10-9 **80**.. PKinsella[(7)] 56
(R E Barr) *nvr bttr than mid-div* **25/1**

/P0- **10** *7* **Snails Castle (IRE)**[21] [4714] 6-10-12 **76**................................ ADempsey 45
(E W Tuer) *t.k.h in rr: stdy hdwy 5th: rdn after 7th: sn btn* **40/1**

11 *5* **Madhahir (IRE)**[62] [2052] 5-11-3 **81**.. SCurran 45
(M J Gingell) *chsd ldrs: lost pl appr 3 out* **33/1**

P24- **12** *¾* **Frankincense (IRE)**[19] [4738] 9-11-7 **85**..................................(p) ADobbin 48
(A J Lockwood) *chsd ldrs: wknd 3 out* **15/2**[2]

643- **13** *hd* **Casas (IRE)**[36] [4452] 8-10-7 **78**......................................(vt[1]) MrSFMagee[(7)] 41
(J R Norton) *a in rr* **25/1**

0P0- **14** *¾* **Quay Walloper**[14] [4783] 4-9-7 **70** oh6..........................(v) CDSharkey[(7)] 26
(J R Norton) *bhd: sme hdwy 7th: sn rdn and wknd* **100/1**

04P- **15** *nk* **Imperative (USA)**[6] [4798] 5-10-11 **85**...................... CareyWilliamson[(10)] 47
(M J Gingell) *in rr whn blnd 5th* **50/1**

403- **16** *7* **Chivvy Charver (IRE)**[14] [4783] 8-10-9 **80**............................ EWhillans[(7)] 35
(A C Whillans) *in rr: effrt 6th: sn btn* **10/1**[3]

050- **17** *10* **Martha Reilly (IRE)**[8] [4868] 9-11-8 **86**................................... AThornton 31
(Mrs Barbara Waring) *hld up in rr: sme hdwy 6th: sn lost pl: virtually p.u run-in* **22/1**

510- **18** *5* **Dennis The Mennis (IRE)**[14] [4783] 6-11-6 **84**........................ KJohnson 24
(R Johnson) *a bhd* **10/1**[3]

/0P- **P** **Mer Bihan (FR)**[167] [2099] 5-10-1 **68**.. GBerridge[(3)] —
(L Lungo) *sn bhd: p.u bef 3 out* **40/1**

P40- **P** **Rincoola (IRE)**[39] [4400] 6-11-10 **88**.. DO'Meara —
(J S Wainwright) *wl bhd whn p.u bef 7th* **40/1**

0P3- **P** **Jack Flush (IRE)**[27] [4623] 11-10-2 **69**..............................(vt) PBuchanan[(3)] —
(M E Sowersby) *bhd whn p.u bef 4th* **18/1**

00P- **P** **Kyle Of Lochalsh**[43] [4319] 5-11-4 **82**...(v[1]) GLee —
(J S Goldie) *in tch: lost pl 6th: bhd whn p.u bef 3 out* **11/1**

5m 7.50s **Going Correction** -0.05s/f (Good)
WFA 4 from 5yo+ 6lb **22** Ran SP% **131.5**
Speed ratings: **98,96,94,93,90 90,90,89,88,85 83,83,83,83,83 80,76,74,—,— —,—** CSF £141.42 CT £971.55 TOTE £4.80: £1.40, £5.30, £2.40, £3.00; EX 88.30.There was no bid for the winner.

Owner The Bhiss Partnership **Bred** Kenneth L Ramsey And Sarah K Ramsey **Trained** Adstone, Northants

FOCUS
They went a fair pace but this was a weak race. The first two are unlikely to be well handicapped after this.

NOTEBOOK
Irish Blessing(USA), proven in this class, made no mistake. *(op 11-2)*
Idlewild(IRE), back over hurdles, was getting the worst of the argument when getting the last all wrong. *(op 25-1)*
Star Trooper(IRE) again gave a good account of himself but the ground had dried out too much for him and a fourth career win is proving elusive. *(op 8-1 tchd 17-2)*
Approaching Land(IRE), no spring chicken, has three point wins to his credit. Very keen, he seemed to find this an insufficient test.
College Cracker has yet to finish in a place in nine starts now. *(op 14-1)*
Solway Gale(IRE) mixes hurdles and fences but to no avail. *(op 20-1)*
Martha Reilly(IRE) *Official explanation: jockey said mare lost her action (op 20-1)*
Rincoola(IRE) *Official explanation: jockey said mare bled from nose*

12 YELLOW PAGES H'CAP CHASE (18 fncs) 3m 1f
4:40 (4:41) (Class 3) (0-130,127) 5-Y-0+ **£7,673** (£2,361; £1,180; £590)

Form RPR

3P6- **1** **Tom's Prize**[22] [4692] 10-10-12 **120**.. TJDreaper[(7)] 129+
(J L Spearing) *led: hdd between last 2: led last: hld on gamely* **11/1**

412- **2** *½* **Jaoka Du Gord (FR)**[6] [4869] 8-10-4 **105**.................................... TDoyle 113
(P R Webber) *stdd s: hld up: stdy hdwy 10th: jnd ldr 4 out: tk nk advantage between last 2: hdd last: no ex nr fin* **9/2**[1]

3U2- **3** *5* **Blunham Hill (IRE)**[42] [4346] 7-9-9 **103** oh7 ow2................... DLaverty[(7)] 107+
(John R Upson) *chsd ldrs: hit 1st: one pce fr 3 out* **20/1**

/4P- **4** *8* **Barryscourt Lad (IRE)**[50] [4183] 11-10-9 **110**........................ JimCrowley 106+
(R D E Woodhouse) *mid-div: hdwy to chse ldrs 11th: outpcd fr 4 out* **20/1**

0P3- **5** *23* **The Kew Tour (IRE)**[43] [4331] 9-11-2 **117**.............................. DElsworth 89
(Mrs S J Smith) *chsd ldrs: lost pl appr 4 out* **5/1**[2]

2P5- **6** *9* **Jungle Jinks (IRE)**[44] [4302] 10-11-5 **120**.................................. FKeniry 83
(G M Moore) *w wnr: lost pl after 14th* **9/1**

1/3- **7** *17* **Stormy Skye (IRE)**[25] [4663] 9-10-2 **103**................................(b) JEMoore 61+
(G L Moore) *in rr: hdwy and prom 11th: lost pl after 14th: bhd whn eased run-in* **11/2**[3]

046- **P** **Winchester**[19] [4739] 10-11-5 **120**..(p) GLee —
(K A Ryan) *j.lft. stdd s. bhd whn p.u bef 14th* **16/1**

361- **P** **Wildfield Rufo (IRE)**[33] [4512] 10-10-8 **109**.......................... RMcGrath —
(Mrs K Walton) *bhd fr 9th: t.o whn p.u bef 14th* **10/1**

44P- **P** **Iron Express**[38] [4416] 9-9-9 **101** oh6................................(p) DCCostello[(5)] —
(G M Moore) *chsd ldrs: lost pl 8th: bhd whn p.u bef 14th* **33/1**

261- **P** **Coursing Run (IRE)**[42] [4346] 9-11-8 **123**............................ RThornton —
(H D Daly) *outpcd and reminders 5th: bhd whn p.u bef 7th* **13/2**

1/0- **P** **Jacdor (IRE)**[36] [4449] 11-10-10 **111**.......................................(v) AThornton —
(R Dickin) *prom: drvn along 11th: sn lost pl: bhd whn p.u bef 4 out* **12/1**

6m 20.8s (-15.30) **Going Correction** -0.05s/f (Good) **12** Ran SP% **117.0**
Speed ratings: **107,106,105,102,95 92,87,—,—,— —,—** CSF £59.22 CT £991.41 TOTE £13.20: £3.90, £2.30, £5.90; EX 25.30.

Owner Mrs P Joynes **Bred** Mrs P M Joynes **Trained** Kinnersley, Worcs

FOCUS
A fair handicap, the first two running to their marks.

NOTEBOOK
Tom's Prize, Hobdayed before his previous outing, proved very determined and his amateur rider is excellent value for his claim. *(op 12-1)*
Jaoka Du Gord(FR), given a very patient ride, took a narrow advantage between the last two fences but in the end the winner proved just too tough. His rating will rise after this. *(tchd 5-1)*
Blunham Hill(IRE), running from out of the handicap, is basically just a one-paced stayer.
Barryscourt Lad(IRE), injured when he won the 2003 Great Yorkshire Chase, gave his trainer some hope but he still has an awful lot to prove and time is not on his side. *(op 22-1)*
The Kew Tour(IRE) had the ground to suit but was on the retreat spinning off the home turn. *(op 4-1)*
Jungle Jinks(IRE) likes it round here, but he continues out of form and his trainer could not buy a winner at present.
Jacdor(IRE) *Official explanation: jockey said gelding had a breathing problem (tchd 11-1)*
Winchester *Official explanation: jockey said gelding moved badly throughout (tchd 11-1)*
Coursing Run(IRE) *Official explanation: jockey said gelding was unsuited by good ground (tchd 11-1)*

13 "BIG SCREEN ACTION HERE TODAY" H'CAP HURDLE (10 hdls) 2m 4f 110y
5:15 (5:17) (Class 3) (0-125,119) 4-Y-0+ **£5,167** (£1,590; £795; £397)

Form RPR

120- **1** **Stan (NZ)**[40] [4381] 6-11-8 **115**.. HOliver 127+
(R C Guest) *t.k.h: hdwy to trck ldrs 6th: led appr 3 out: shkn up between last 2: drvn out* **5/2**[1]

111- **2** *3 ½* **Pebble Bay**[29] [4557] 10-10-12 **105**.. DElsworth 111
(Mrs S J Smith) *trckd ldrs: wnt 2nd 3 out: swtchd lft between last 2: no real imp* **5/2**[1]

P0P- **3** *13* **Mister Moussac**[4] [4932] 6-9-11 **97**................................(p) SCrawford[(7)] 90
(Miss Kariana Key) *trckd ldr: led 3rd tl appr 3 out: one pce* **25/1**

253- **4** *1 ½* **Mighty Fine**[4] [4926] 11-10-4 **107**.. SGagan[(10)] 100+
(Mrs E Slack) *led to 3rd: chsd ldrs: one pce fr 3 out* **10/1**

361- **5** *25* **Ramblees Holly**[14] [4787] 7-10-6 **104**................................ DMcGann[(5)] 71
(R S Wood) *hdwy to join ldrs 4th: lost pl after 6th: sn bhd* **8/1**[3]

566- **6** *1 ¾* **Ireland's Eye (IRE)**[14] [4787] 10-9-13 **99**.......................... MrSFMagee[(7)] 64
(J R Norton) *chsd ldrs: drvn along 5th: lost pl after 6th* **25/1**

120- **7** *7* **Corlande (IRE)**[29] [4554] 5-11-2 **119**.................................. THalliday[(10)] 77
(Mrs S J Smith) *a in rr: t.o 7th* **12/1**

241- **8** *¾* **Constantine**[25] [4666] 5-11-12 **119**.......................................(b) JEMoore 76
(G L Moore) *prom: rdn and outpcd 7th: 6th and bhd whn blnd 2 out* **7/1**[2]

200- **P** **Honest Endeavour**[77] [3728] 6-11-1 **108**.. GLee —
(J M Jefferson) *hdwy to chse ldrs 3rd: pushed along 7th: sn lost pl: blnd next: bhd whn p.u bef 2 out* **12/1**

5m 3.20s (-4.30) **Going Correction** -0.05s/f (Good) **9** Ran SP% **112.9**
Speed ratings: **106,104,99,99,89 88,86,86,—** CSF £9.22 CT £116.17 TOTE £3.70: £1.40, £2.00, £3.30; EX 8.20.

Owner Paul Beck **Bred** Mrs M A Davies **Trained** Brancepeth, Co Durham

FOCUS
A race lacking strength in depth, but improved performances from the first two with the winner value for further.

NOTEBOOK
Stan(NZ), full of himself after a six-week break, took a keen grip but in the end scored in decisive fashion. A grand, big type, he looks ideal summer jumping material. *(tchd 3-1)*
Pebble Bay, 10lb higher, did not go down without a fight but in the winner he met an unexposed, probably useful type. *(tchd 11-4)*
Mister Moussac, in first-time cheekpieces, ran his best race for some time on his second outing in five days.
Mighty Fine, making a quick return to action, continues in good heart. He is at his best round Sedgefield.
Ramblees Holly was well below the form he showed when successful at Hexham two weeks earlier. *(op 7-1)*

14 NATIONAL FESTIVAL CIRCUS NOVICES' HURDLE (10 hdls) 2m 4f 110y
5:45 (5:46) (Class 4) 4-Y-0+ **£3,892** (£1,112; £556)

Form RPR

122- **1** **Notaproblem (IRE)**[36] [4457] 6-11-0 .... NHannity 90+
(G A Harker) *trckd ldrs: led 2 out: hld on towards fin* **5/4**[1]

/05- **2** *¾* **Iron Warrior (IRE)**[45] [4270] 5-11-0 91.. FKeniry 89+
(G M Moore) *led to 2 out: styd on: no ex towards fin* **9/2**[3]

320- **3** *nk* **Nifty Roy**[2] [4969] 5-11-0 83.. ADempsey 88
(K W Hogg) *hld up in rr: hdwy 5th: jnd ldrs 3f out: edgd rt between last 2: styd on wl towards fin* **12/1**

3- **4** *9* **Snow's Ride**[26] [4511] 5-11-0 .... GLee 80+
(M D Hammond) *chsd ldrs: wknd 2 out* **5/2**[2]

0PP- **5** *11* **Minster Abbi**[21] [4707] 5-10-7 ....(p) NPMulholland 61
(W Storey) *prom: outpcd 7th: wl btn 5th whn blnd 2 out* **66/1**

0U6- **6** *15* **Over To Joe**[19] [4735] 5-10-11 .... MrTGreenall[(3)] 53
(C Grant) *chsd ldrs: lost pl appr 3 out* **33/1**

P00- **7** *½* **Clouds Of Gold (IRE)**[21] [4715] 4-10-1 .... ARoss 39
(J S Wainwright) *bhd: hdwy 7th: sn rdn: wknd next* **50/1**

0- **8** *25* **Canterbury Bell**[95] [3425] 5-10-7 .... JimCrowley 20
(P D Niven) *bhd fr 5th* **40/1**

3- **9** *dist* **Zahunda (IRE)**[7] [4878] 6-9-11 .... CareyWilliamson[(10)] —
(M J Gingell) *chsd ldrs: lost pl 7th: virtually p.u run-in: t.o: fin lame* **16/1**

0- **P** **Stoneriggs**[14] [4788] 4-10-5 .... PBuchanan[(3)] —
(Mrs E Slack) *t.k.h in rr: blnd 1st: t.o 6th: p.u bef 3 out* **80/1**

060- **P** **Alethea Gee**[197] [1659] 7-10-7 .... RMcGrath —
(K G Reveley) *in rr: bhd fr 7th: t.o whn p.u bef next* **40/1**

P **Antigone's Fire**[24] 6-10-4 .... GBerridge[(3)] —
(P D Niven) *chsd ldrs: wknd qckly 5th: t.o whn p.u bef 3 out* **66/1**

0P/ **P** **Primitive Jean**[482] [3034] 6-10-7 .... PRobson —
(C R Wilson) *prom to 4th: lost pl and mstke next: sn bhd: t.o whn p.u bef 3 out* **50/1**

5m 10.4s (2.90) **Going Correction** -0.05s/f (Good)
WFA 4 from 5yo+ 6lb **13** Ran SP% **120.7**
Speed ratings: **92,91,91,88,83 78,78,68,—,— —,—,—** CSF £7.23 TOTE £2.20: £1.10, £2.30, £2.70; EX 6.90 Place 6 £24.59, Place 5 £12.61..

Owner John J Maguire **Bred** James Barry **Trained** Wensley, N Yorks

FOCUS
A very modest event, run in a slow time. Suspect form, rated through the second.

NOTEBOOK
Notaproblem(IRE), who took a bumper here in January, looked to have been found an ideal opportunity to get off the mark over hurdles, but he made very hard work of it and at the line was scrambling to hang on. *(op 6-4)*
Iron Warrior(IRE), given his own way out in front, did not go down without a fight. *(op 5-1)*
Nifty Roy, a weak-looking type, did not go unbacked. He ducked and dived between the last two flights but was closing the first two down at the line. *(op 14-1)*
Snow's Ride, well beaten on the level since his hurdling debut, may have to revert to Southwell's Fibresand surface and staying handicaps on the Flat.
Minster Abbi had been pulled up on her two most recent outings.
Zahunda(IRE) *Official explanation: jockey said mare finished lame (op 12-1)*

T/Plt: £5.40 to a £1 stake. Pool: £38,299.70. 5,125.55 winning tickets. T/Qpdt: £3.40 to a £1 stake. Pool: £1,977.00. 425.05 winning tickets. WG

The Form Book, Raceform Ltd, Compton, RG20 6NL

15 - 20a (Foreign Racing) - See Raceform Interactive

TOWCESTER (R-H)

Monday, April 25

OFFICIAL GOING: Good to firm

The forecast rain failed to reach the course and there were 30 non-runners on the card.

Wind: almost nil Weather: overcast

21 GG.COM NOVICES' HURDLE (8 hdls) 2m

2:10 (2:10) (Class 4) 4-Y-0+ **£4,231** (£1,302; £651; £325)

Form RPR

23- **1** **Mr Mischief**[52] 3545 5-11-0 APMcCoy 104+
(P C Haslam) *hld up: hdwy 5th: chsd ldr appr 2 out: led: j.rt and hit last: drvn out* **13/8**[2]

PPP- **2** ½ **Thieves'Glen**[13] 4814 7-11-0 115 (b) TScudamore 104+
(H Morrison) *led: hit 3 out: hdd and hmpd last: styd on* **15/2**[3]

3 9 **Rajayoga**[83] 4-10-9 LAspell 91+
(M H Tompkins) *hld up: bhd whn hmpd 3rd: hdwy 3 out: nt fluent last: styd on same pce* **16/1**

000- **4** 12 **Potts Of Magic**[44] 4324 6-11-0 73 PFlynn 82
(R Lee) *mid-div: rn in snatches: drvn and dropped rr 4th: n.d after* **50/1**

013- **5** 5 **Reservoir (IRE)**[23] 4696 4-11-2 116 RJohnson 81+
(P J Hobbs) *hld up in tch: chsd ldr 3 out: wknd next* **11/8**[1]

PP0- **6** 5 **Dry Old Party (IRE)**[28] 4621 6-11-0 (b) PHide 73+
(P Winkworth) *plld hrd: trckd ldr: swvd lft 4th: rdn and wknd after 3 out* **50/1**

300- **7** 10 **Ace Coming**[33] 4201 4-10-9 (p) JamesDavies 57
(D B Feek) *chsd ldrs to 3 out* **33/1**

6- **F** **Skibereen (IRE)**[8] 4885 5-10-7 (t) DLaverty[(7)] —
(Mrs A M Thorpe) *mid-div: fell 3rd* **20/1**

00- **U** **Alfadora**[16] 4775 5-11-0 SDurack 37
(M F Harris) *hld up: bhd whn hmpd 3rd: mstke 5th: n.d* **33/1**

42- **P** **Preston Hall**[202] 1605 4-10-9 (t) JPMcNamara —
(M J McGrath) *chsd ldrs tl wknd appr 3 out* **16/1**

3m 48.6s (-14.20) **Going Correction** -0.95s/f (Hard) **10** Ran SP% **118.3**

Speed ratings: **97,96,92,86,83 81,76,—,—,63** CSF £13.76 TOTE £2.60: £1.10, £2.10, £5.00; EX 16.30.

Owner Middleham Park Racing I & Mrs C Barclay **Bred** Mrs Maureen Barbara Walsh **Trained** Middleham Moor, N Yorks

FOCUS

The ground was described as "rough and patchy" by the riders in this opening event, in which there were seven non-runners. It was a modest event, lacking any strength in depth, that saw the first two come clear. The form should work out.

NOTEBOOK

Mr Mischief, third on the Polytrack at Wolverhampton on his last outing, travelled nicely into contention yet needed all of McCoy's strength to prevail in his battle with the runner-up on the run-in. This was his first success over timber at the third attempt - he was placed on both his previous efforts - and the faster ground was clearly to his liking. He can strike again under a penalty during the summer. *(tchd 6-4 and 7-4)*

Thieves'Glen, pulled up on his previous three outings, had never previously encountered ground this fast, but handled it well and went down all guns blazing. He was not helped by the winner jumping into him over the last flight, so could be considered a little unlucky, but he has two ways of running and remains one to have reservations about. *(op 8-1 tchd 9-1)*

Rajayoga, still a maiden and best known for his exploits in banded races on the Flat, was not disgraced on this hurdling debut and would most likely have preferred easier ground. He may also want a little further in due course. *(op 14-1 tchd 20-1)*

Potts Of Magic looked unsuited by the fast ground and shorter trip. He is bred to be useful over jumps and could do better over fences in time. *(op 33-1)*

Reservoir(IRE), whose sole win over hurdles came on similarly fast ground, dropped out tamely when push came to shove and must rate as disappointing. He is capable of better, and may prefer a sharper track, but this effort leaves him plenty to prove. *(op 13-8)*

22 WEATHERBYS INSURANCE H'CAP CHASE (18 fncs) 3m 110y

2:40 (2:40) (Class 4) (0-105,102) 5-Y-0+ **£4,114** (£1,266; £633; £316)

Form RPR

PP3- **1** **Over Zealous (IRE)**[29] 4584 13-10-0 **76** oh3 (b) PFlynn 85+
(John R Upson) *led to 14th: led appr 2 out: styd on wl* **4/1**

0P4- **2** 6 **Tommy Carson**[65] 3944 10-11-12 **102** MBatchelor 105+
(Jamie Poulton) *chsd wnr to 14th: sn rdn: wnt 2nd again appr last: no ex flat* **11/4**[2]

32P- **3** 13 **Paxford Jack**[16] 4778 9-11-8 **98** (v) OMcPhail 97+
(M F Harris) *hld up: hdwy 8th: mstke 13th: led next: hdd appr 2 out: rdn and wknd last: eased flat: fin lame* **15/8**[1]

3U5- **4** 18 **Maybeseven**[29] 4584 11-9-8 **77** JPritchard[(7)] 48
(R Dickin) *chsd ldrs: rdn 6th: lost pl 8th: sn bhd* **3/1**[3]

6m 16.8s **4** Ran SP% **106.4**

CSF £14.09 TOTE £5.80; EX 12.00.

Owner Middleham Park Racing X **Bred** Patrick Cronin **Trained** Maidford, Northants

FOCUS

Another race notable for its absentees, and it took little winning. The field came home strung out and the form needs treating with caution.

NOTEBOOK

Over Zealous(IRE), 3lb out of the handicap, set a brisk pace from the start and outstayed his rivals to score a game success. He had looked in decline in the past year, but the ground suited and he clearly still posseses stamina in abundance. Although he is due to be retired this year, he is still potentially very well treated on his previous best efforts and, granted a true stamina test, he could nick another race this summer. *(op 3-1)*

Tommy Carson tried in vain to peg back the winner in the straight, but was found out by the stiff finish and his big weight. He looked to find this ground a touch too fast, but still finished well clear of the rest and has another race in him on a sharper track. *(op 7-2)*

Paxford Jack looked to be going best of all before two out, but he soon came under heavy pressure and was disappointingly left behind by the front pair. He was found to have finished lame and deserves another chance. *Official explanation: vet said gelding finished lame (op 5-4 tchd 2-1)*

Maybeseven proved disappointing and his fate was on the cards a long way from home. He needs a shaper track over this trip. *(tchd 10-3 in a place)*

23 COMPARE ODDS @ GG-ODDS.COM NOVICES' (S) HURDLE (11 hdls) 2m 5f

3:10 (3:10) (Class 5) 4-Y-0+ **£2,975** (£850; £425)

Form RPR

5/4- **1** **Little Brave**[49] 4230 10-10-9 LStephens[(5)] 90+
(C Roberts) *hld up: hdwy 5th: chsd ldr 8th: led after 3 out: clr whn hit next: styd on wl* **3/1**[2]

465- **2** 10 **Chickapeakray**[35] 4495 4-9-10 63 StephenJCraine[(5)] 66+
(D McCain) *trckd ldrs: plld hrd: led 7th: rdn and hdd after 3 out: styng on same pce whn mstke last* **10/1**

P4P- **3** 2 **Monbonami (IRE)**[27] 4642 8-10-7 (p) RSpate[(7)] 76
(Mrs K Waldron) *hld up: hdwy 7th: rdn and ev ch after 3 out: styd on same pce* **12/1**

020- **4** 1¼ **Fille Detente**[22] 4714 5-10-7 77 WMarston 70+
(Mrs P Sly) *hld up: hdwy 6th: mstke next: rdn appr 3 out: nt running on whn nt fluent last* **5/1**

4P0- **5** 18 **Eastwell Violet**[7] 4911 5-10-7 75 RJohnson 53+
(Mrs A M Thorpe) *hld up: hdwy 7th: wknd appr 3 out* **5/2**[1]

PPP- **P** **Blow Me Down**[109] 3232 6-10-7 58 LAspell —
(F Jordan) *prom to 7th: t.o whn p.u bef 2 out* **20/1**

P **Mr Bill**[649] 5-11-0 JamesDavies —
(D B Feek) *hld up: hdwy 6th: hung lft and wknd bef next: t.o whn p.u bef 3 out* **20/1**

0U0- **P** **Dish**[28] 4609 6-10-4 57 ACCoyle[(3)] —
(Miss C J E Caroe) *chsd ldr tl nt fluent 3rd: rdn 5th: sn wknd: t.o whn p.u bef 7th* **66/1**

353- **P** **Cedar**[27] 4642 8-10-7 86 (b[1]) JPritchard[(7)] —
(R Dickin) *plld hrd: led: clr 3rd: hdd 7th: wknd after next: t.o whn p.u bef last* **9/2**[3]

5m 21.7s (-10.60) **Going Correction** -0.95s/f (Hard)

WFA 4 from 5yo+ 6lb **9** Ran SP% **116.2**

Speed ratings: **82,78,77,76,70 —,—,—,—** CSF £31.52 TOTE £4.70: £1.50, £2.80, £3.10; EX 40.60.There was no bid for the winner.

Owner James Hearne **Bred** C H Bothway **Trained** Newport, Newport

FOCUS

A poor event, even by selling standards, and it produced a very slow time indeed.

NOTEBOOK

Little Brave took up the running three out and had the race in the bag prior to making an error over the second last. This drop in class worked the oracle, this was his first success over timber from three outings and he handled the faster ground without fuss. However, he is far from certain to follow up back at a higher level. *(tchd 7-2)*

Chickapeakray got home well enough over this longer trip, without being a serious threat. She is clearly very limited. *(op 11-1 tchd 12-1)*

Monbonami(IRE), reverting to hurdles with the visor replaced by first-time cheekpieces, found nothing for pressure approaching two out and again looked to throw in the towel. *(tchd 14-1)*

Fille Detente lost her chance with some sloppy jumps late on and finished very tired. She is probably better over shorter, but is generally disappointing. *(op 6-1)*

Eastwell Violet never looked like getting to the leaders from off the pace and was disappointing. *She may have just found this ground fast enough and may prefer to race handy in this grade. (op 3-1 tchd 9-4)*

Mr Bill *Official explanation: jockey said gelding hung left and pulled up lame (op 14-1)*

Cedar was lit up early on by the first-time blinkers and it came as no real surprise that he failed to get home. *(op 14-1)*

24 CEDAR OPENACCOUNTS BEGINNERS' CHASE (14 fncs) 2m 3f 110y

3:40 (3:41) (Class 4) 5-Y-0+ **£4,056** (£1,248; £624; £312)

Form RPR

U22- **1** **Oulton Broad**[13] 4816 9-10-11 105 (p) JDiment[(5)] 100+
(F Jordan) *hld up: hdwy 7th: pckd 10th: led appr 2 out: sn clr: j.rt last: hung lft flat: lashed out twice whn hit run-in* **13/8**[2]

134- **2** 19 **The Bar Maid**[97] 3408 7-10-9 LAspell 77+
(O Sherwood) *led to 2nd: chsd ldrs: blnd 6th: rdn and wknd 2 out* **10/11**[1]

PUP- **3** 1¾ **Welsh Gold**[33] 4525 6-11-2 59 PFlynn 77
(S T Lewis) *chsd ldr tl led 6th: hdd next: led 3 out: hdd & wknd bef next* **14/1**

0/ **4** 28 **Tubber Streams (IRE)**[15] 8-11-2 BHitchcott 49
(B R Johnson) *j.lft: led 2nd to 6th: led 7th to 3 out: wkng whn hit next* **8/1**[3]

00P- **P** **Redvic**[27] 4642 5-10-12 59 JMogford —
(G J Smith) *hld up: nt fluent 1st: bhd fr 7th: t.o whn p.u bef last* **33/1**

5m 10.9s

WFA 5 from 6yo+ 3lb **5** Ran SP% **111.2**

CSF £3.72 TOTE £2.60: £1.30, £1.20; EX 4.80.

Owner Marcus Reeder **Bred** Fares Stables Ltd **Trained** Adstone, Northants

FOCUS

A weak event which provided a slow-motion finish. The form is hard to assess.

NOTEBOOK

Oulton Broad, despite looking distinctly resentful under pressure when in front after the second last, lashing out with his near-hind when hit, came right away from his tiring rivals and opened his account over fences at the fourth attempt. He deserved this success, and is capable of winning again over fences during the summer, but he has become quirky and is not one to place any great faith in. *(tchd 6-4)*

The Bar Maid, who showed a liking for this tack last year in novice hurdles and was making her chase debut for new connections, proved unsuited by this fast surface and her fate was on the cards from three out. She still shaped with promise, however, and can get off the mark over fences when reverting to easier ground. *(op 5-6 tchd Evens)*

Welsh Gold, pulled up over course and distance last time, ran with promise until his stamina gave way from three out. On this evidence he needs a sharper track and his confidence will have been boosted for a return to handicaps. *(op 18-1)*

Tubber Streams(IRE), making his chasing debut under Rules, had his limitations well and truly exposed. *(op 11-1 tchd 14-1)*

25 LONDON PERSONAL LOANS H'CAP HURDLE (8 hdls) 2m

4:10 (4:10) (Class 4) (0-85,85) 4-Y-0+ **£3,718** (£1,144; £572; £286)

Form RPR

00P- **1** **Little Rort (IRE)**[46] 4277 6-11-6 84 LTreadwell[(5)] 87
(S T Lewis) *led: mstke 3 out: rdn and hdd next: led last: styd on wl* **20/1**

600- **2** ¾ **Dash For Cover (IRE)**[47] 4269 5-11-5 78 JTizzard 80
(J G Portman) *chsd ldr tl led 2 out: rdn and hdd last: styd on* **33/1**

F01- **3** 1 **Rose Of York (IRE)**[6] 4918 5-10-4 70 7ex (t) DLaverty[(7)] 72+
(Mrs A M Thorpe) *chsd ldrs: nt fluent 4th: rdn whn hit last: styd on* **11/2**[2]

000- **4** 2½ **Dan De Lion**[22] 4714 6-11-5 78 SFox 77
(R C Guest) *hld up: hdwy 3 out: styd on u.p: nt rch ldrs* **10/1**

510- **5** ½ **Reach The Clouds (IRE)**[7] 4913 13-11-12 85 PFlynn 83
(John R Upson) *hld up: hdwy appr 2 out: nt rch ldrs* **20/1**

41P- **6** 3 **Princess Aimee**[175] 1948 5-11-7 80 (p) APMcCoy 75
(P Bowen) *hld up in tch: rdn appr 3 out: no imp fr next* **11/4**[1]

051- **7** ½ **Think Quick (IRE)**[32] 4529 5-10-11 80 AHawkins[(10)] 75
(R Hollinshead) *hld up in tch: effrt and nt fluent 2 out: sn hung rt: wkng whn mstke last* **10/1**

0PP- **8** 8 **Dunkerron**[70] 3852 8-10-8 74 SWalsh[(7)] 61
(J Joseph) *hld up: rdn 3 out: n.d* **20/1**

/U2- **9** nk **Not To Be Missed**[342] 408 7-11-3 76 WHutchinson 62
(R Dickin) *hld up: hdwy 4th: rdn and wknd appr 2 out* **16/1**

545- **10** *nk* **Compton Star**[8] 4890 5-11-9 82 TScudamore 68
(R J Hodges) *chsd ldrs to 5th* **8/1**[3]

0P3- **11** *1 1/2* **Wyoming**[38] 4442 4-11-5 83 NFehily 62
(Jedd O'Keeffe) *hld up: ridden 3 out: a in rr* **8/1**[3]

U60- **12** *hd* **Avanti**[30] 4565 9-10-10 72 RWalford(3) 56
(Dr J R J Naylor) *hld up: sme hdwy 3rd: wknd next* **10/1**

3P0- **13** *7* **Little Villain (IRE)**[44] 4325 7-10-7 73 (p) PMerrigan(7) 50
(T Wall) *hld up: rdn 4th: a in rr* **25/1**

000- **P** **Goodbye Chemo**[8] 4890 7-11-1 77 JPByrne(3) —
(Evan Williams) *chsd ldrs tl wknd appr 3 out: t.o whn p.u bef next* **25/1**

3m 53.2s (-9.60) **Going Correction** -0.95s/f (Hard)
WFA 4 from 5yo+ 5lb **14** Ran SP% **122.3**
Speed ratings: **86,85,85,83,83 82,81,77,77,77 76,76,73,—** CSF £524.88 CT £4094.61 TOTE £24.70: £5.70, £11.90, £1.80; EX 425.80.
Owner Simon T Lewis **Bred** N Hartery **Trained** Upton upon Severn, Gloucs
■ Stewards' Enquiry : J Tizzard two-day ban: used whip with excessive force (May 6,7)

FOCUS
A very moderate time for the grade. Low-level form, but there is no reason why it should not work out.

NOTEBOOK
Little Rort(IRE) , who recently won one of the new schooling trials at Cheltenham, enjoyed the switch to front-running tactics and ran out a game winner. He has fallen 26lb in the weights since switching from Ireland, and now he has proved himself on this ground, it is entirely possible he will defy a rise in the weights during the summer months. *(op 16-1)*
Dash For Cover(IRE) turned in his best effort over hurdles and just got run out of it after the final flight. The faster ground made all the difference and he looks to have found his level now. *(op 40-1 tchd 50-1)*
Rose Of York(IRE) , off the mark over course and distance in a selling handicap six days previously, looked held prior to clouting the final flight, but stuck bravely to her task up the run-in and registered a sound effort. She is clearly going the right way. *(op 4-1)*
Dan De Lion looked to have it all to do turning for home, but he was staying on with effect up the straight and posted a much more encouraging display. On this evidence, he could finally get off the mark if dropped back to plating-class over a touch further.

Not To Be Missed *Official explanation: jockey said mare lost a shoe (op 14-1)*
Goodbye Chemo *Official explanation: vet said gelding bled from nose*

26 WAYSIDE NOVICES' H'CAP CHASE (12 fncs) 2m 110y
4:40 (4:40) (Class 4) (0-105,105) 5-Y-0+ **£4,017** (£1,236; £618; £309)

Form RPR

5U2- **1** **Terrible Tenant**[33] 4525 6-9-11 **79** oh6 RYoung(3) 94+
(J W Mullins) *racd keenly: w ldr tl led 3rd: clr 2 out: j.rt last: jst hld on* **15/8**[1]

5P0- **2** *3/4* **Tosawi (IRE)**[10] 4855 9-11-1 **94** (p) TScudamore 106
(R J Hodges) *chsd ldrs: outpcd 7th: rallied 2 out: chsd wnr and j.rt last: styd on u.p* **4/1**

0/ **3** *18* **Multeen Gunner**[138] 2714 8-10-0 **79** oh1 PMoloney 77+
(Evan Williams) *led to 3rd: remained w wnr: pckd 5th: ev ch whn mstke 3 out: wkng whn j.rt last* **11/4**[3]

533- **4** *7* **Hi Fi**[13] 4816 7-11-12 **105** DRDennis 94+
(Ian Williams) *chsd ldrs: reminders 7th: wknd 9th* **9/4**[2]

4m 2.30s (-14.00) **Going Correction** -0.725s/f (Firm) **4** Ran SP% **112.2**
Speed ratings: **103,102,94,90** CSF £9.26 TOTE £3.60; EX 11.80.
Owner D I Bare **Bred** D I Bare **Trained** Wilsford-Cum-Lake, Wilts

FOCUS
A weak event, run at a strong pace, and the first two came clear. The winner can be rated value for slightly further.

NOTEBOOK
Terrible Tenant looked set for a cosy success approaching two from home, but his stride shortened soon after and he was all out to win at the end. He deserves credit as he helped set the generous pace from the start, this was the fastest surface he had encountered to date and he was racing from 6lb out of the handicap. He can defy a rise in the weights this summer. *(op 5-2)*
Tosawi(IRE) got outpaced when the tempo increased and was staying on again all too late under his big weight. This was by far his best effort since his chasing bow last year, and while he is not easy to catch right, he is capable of getting off the mark during the summer. *(op 5-1)*
Multeen Gunner , making his British debut for new connections from 1lb out of the handicap, was still in with every chance until he blundered three out and lost his momentum. This will have served his confidence well, and he enjoyed this fast ground, so providing he consents to settle, he could finally land a race this summer. *(op 9-4)*
Hi Fi ran disappointingly and continues to frustrate. *(op 2-1 tchd 5-2)*

27 GET BEST ODDS @ GG-ODDS.COM MARES' ONLY STANDARD OPEN NATIONAL HUNT FLAT RACE 2m
5:10 (5:10) (Class 6) 4-6-Y-0 **£2,303** (£658; £329)

Form RPR

1 **Granny Shona (IRE)** 4-10-9 TDoyle 81+
(P R Webber) *trckd ldrs: plld hrd: rdn over 3f out: led over 1f out: hung rt ins fnl f: r.o* **11/4**[1]

60- **2** *3/4* **Martovic (IRE)**[18] 4753 6-11-0 JPMcNamara 86
(K C Bailey) *sn led: rdn and hdd over 1f out: edgd rt ins fnl f: r.o* **10/1**

2- **3** *1/2* **Miss Midnight**[18] 4760 4-10-2 JamesWhite(7) 80
(R J Hodges) *chsd ldrs: rdn over 2f out: styd on ins fnl f* **7/2**[2]

4 *1 1/4* **Allez Melina** 4-10-9 ATinkler 79
(Mrs A J Hamilton-Fairley) *hld up: hdwy over 3f out: rdn over 1f out: styd on* **20/1**

643- **5** *2 1/2* **Air Of Affection**[15] 4788 4-10-9 DO'Meara 76
(J R Turner) *hld up: hdwy 1/2-way: styd on same pce appr fnl f* **6/1**[3]

6 *3 1/2* **Stormy Madam (IRE)** 5-10-7 MrRWakeham(7) 78
(J R Turner) *hld up: rdn over 3f out: nt clr run over 1f out: r.o ins fnl f: nt rch ldrs* **25/1**

7 *2 1/2* **Pairtree** 5-11-0 MBatchelor 75
(Jamie Poulton) *hld up: hdwy over 4f out: rdn and wknd over 1f out* **7/1**

8 *3* **Radigan Lane** 5-11-0 TScudamore 72
(J R Payne) *hld up: hdwy 3f out: wknd over 1f out* **33/1**

0- **9** *2 1/2* **Miss Sirius**[101] 3346 5-10-7 MrJNewbold(7) 70
(John R Upson) *hld up in tch: plld hrd: wknd 2f out* **33/1**

10 *5* **Silver Seline** 4-10-2 TMessenger(7) 60
(B N Pollock) *plld hrd and prom: ev chnace 3f out: sn wknd* **40/1**

00- **11** *2 1/2* **Touch And Weld (IRE)**[28] 4608 4-10-2 CMStudd(7) 57
(B W Duke) *plld hrd and prom: wknd over 3f out* **33/1**

00- **12** *4* **Posh Crack**[91] 3520 5-11-0 LAspell 58
(F Jordan) *hld up in tch: rdn and wknd over 2f out* **25/1**

13 *6* **Bob's Finesse** 5-11-0 AThornton 52
(J W Mullins) *chsd ldrs: lost pl 10f out: wknd over 5f out* **8/1**

3m 57.4s (-13.80) **Going Correction** -0.95s/f (Hard)
WFA 4 from 5yo+ 5lb **13** Ran SP% **119.6**
Speed ratings: **96,95,95,94,93 91,90,89,87,85 84,82,79** CSF £28.48 TOTE £3.20: £1.70, £2.60, £2.30; EX 41.50 Place 6 £414.72, Place 5 £220.07.
Owner Lightbody Celebration Cakes Ltd **Bred** Gainsborough Stud Management Ltd **Trained** Mollington, Oxon

FOCUS
An ordinary mares' bumper run at a sedate gallop. The moderate form is rated through the third and fifth placed horses.

NOTEBOOK
Granny Shona(IRE) , a half-sister to the useful Flat/hurdles winner Manoubi, ran freely through the early stages yet still produced the necessary turn of foot from two out to make a winning debut. She enjoyed this fast ground, shaped as though she will improve plenty for this experience and looks to have a future. *(tchd 5-2 and 3-1)*
Martovic(IRE) , last in the new mares-only bumper at Aintree previously, improved on that effort and went down fighting. She was unsuited by the modest gallop and will not peak until racing over further in due course.
Miss Midnight was staying on at the same pace under pressure and ran very close to the form of her recent Exeter debut. This half-sister to her yard's useful Goldbrook should find her way over hurdles in due course. *(op 5-1)*
Allez Melina , whose dam was a two-mile winner on the Flat and over hurdles, made a satisfactory debut and stayed on despite running green from two out. *(op 14-1)*
Air Of Affection again tried to challenge from off the pace, but never looked like getting there and may have found this ground a touch too fast. She helps set the standard for this form. *(op 4-1)*
Stormy Madam(IRE) , whose dam was a winning two-mile hurdler, shaped with promise and would have been closer with a clearer run entering the final furlong. She ran green and should improve a deal for this experience.
Silver Seline , a half-sister to 14-furlong winners Aurelian and Catullus, ran way too keen on this debut and it came as no surprise when she weakened in the straight. However, she still showed ability.
T/Plt: £676.30 to a £1 stake. Pool: £45,263.20. 48.85 winning tickets. T/Qpdt: £42.70 to a £1 stake. Pool: £3,608.30. 62.50 winning tickets. CR

28 - 31a (Foreign Racing) - See Raceform Interactive

NEWTON ABBOT (L-H)
Tuesday, April 26
32 Meeting Abandoned - waterlogged

39 - (Foreign Racing) - See Raceform Interactive

PUNCHESTOWN (R-H)
Tuesday, April 26
OFFICIAL GOING: Soft (yielding to soft on cross-country course)

40a EVENING HERALD CHAMPION NOVICE HURDLE (GRADE 1) 2m
2:35 (2:35) 5-Y-0+ **£43,971** (£13,475; £6,382; £2,127; £1,418)

RPR

1 **Wild Passion (GER)**[42] 4381 5-11-11 PCarberry 142
(Noel Meade, Ire) *cl up in 2nd: pushed along briefly 1/2-way: led fr 3 out: strly pressed fr bef last: all out* **7/4**[1]

2 *shd* **Kill Devil Hill (IRE)**[30] 4597 5-11-11 JLCullen 142
(Paul Nolan, Ire) *hld up in rr: hdwy after 3 out: 2nd and chal after 2 out: ev ch after last: jst failed* **12/1**

3 *2* **In Compliance (IRE)**[29] 4633 5-11-11 TJMurphy 140
(M J P O'Brien, Ire) *trckd ldrs in 5th: impr into 2nd bef 2 out: 3rd and rdn st: kpt on u.p* **9/2**[3]

4 *4* **Arteea (IRE)**[29] 4632 6-11-12 BJGeraghty 137
(Michael Hourigan, Ire) *trckd ldrs in 6th: rdn 3 out: hdwy on outer after 2 out: 4th bef last: no ex run-in* **20/1**

5 *3* **The Railway Man (IRE)**[28] 4647 6-11-12 BMCash 134
(A L T Moore, Ire) *settled 3rd: cl 5th 3 out: 3rd bef next: 5th and no ex st* **6/1**

6 *2* **Publican (IRE)**[42] 4381 5-11-11 RWalsh 131
(P A Fahy, Ire) *hld up towards rr: impr into 5th 2 out: sn no ex* **4/1**[2]

7 *1 1/2* **Man About Town (IRE)**[29] 4632 6-11-12 127 APMcCoy 130
(T J Taaffe, Ire) *led: rdn and hdd 3 out: wknd bef next* **10/1**

8 *8* **Ray Boy (IRE)**[52] 4196 6-11-12 CO'Dwyer 122
(P C O'Connor, Ire) *prom on outer: 3rd 3 out: wknd next: eased bef last* **16/1**

3m 58.0s **Going Correction** +0.025s/f (Yiel) **8** Ran SP% **116.3**
Speed ratings: **112,111,110,108,107 106,105,101** CSF £24.78 TOTE £2.60: £1.30, £3.70, £2.00; DF 55.90.
Owner D P Sharkey **Bred** M Ommer **Trained** Castletown, Co Meath

FOCUS
A second Grade 1 win for Wild Passion, who reproduced his Tolworth and Supreme Novices' form with a game effort, having been in front a long way out. Kill Devil Hill improved a little again, and so did In Compliance, as they were entitled to.

NOTEBOOK
Wild Passion(GER) needed plenty of help from the saddle after just a slow early pace had been set, but he answered all calls to deny the runner-up after being in front from the third last. He still has plenty of scope and his Cheltenham effort was not devalued here. *(op 13/8)*
Kill Devil Hill(IRE) put up a career-best performance here, pushing the winner to the extreme. Whether he stays hurdling next season or goes chasing, he can build on this.
In Compliance(IRE) just found the first pair too good for him but was not disgraced in defeat. He has the makings of a smart novice chaser. *(op 4/1 tchd 5/1)*
Arteea(IRE) put up a solid end of season effort, his best run to date.
The Railway Man(IRE) was found wanting in the straight. *(op 5/1)*
Publican(IRE) was not far off his Cheltenham form and simply doesn't look quite as good as his Naas maiden win suggested.

41a KERRYGOLD CHAMPION CHASE (GRADE 1) 2m
3:10 (3:10) 5-Y-0+ **£79,148** (£24,255; £11,489; £3,829; £2,553)

RPR

1 **Rathgar Beau (IRE)**[24] 4704 9-11-12 157 JRBarry 158
(E Sheehy, Ire) *hld up in tch: 5th 5 out: 3rd 4 out: 2nd and rdn after 3 out: chal after 2 out: led bef last: strly pressed run-in: all out* **8/1**[2]

2 *shd* **Moscow Flyer (IRE)**[18] 4763 11-11-12 180 BJGeraghty 161+
(Mrs John Harrington, Ire) *trckd ldrs in 3rd: 2nd 5 out: led next: nt fluent 3 out: sn rdn: bad mstke next: hdd bef last: rallied u.p: jst failed* **1/4**[1]

The Form Book, Raceform Ltd, Compton, RG20 6NL

3 *1* **Native Upmanship (IRE)**[24] [4704] 12-11-12 148 .... CO'Dwyer 157
(A L T Moore, Ire) *5th early: dropped to rr u.p 5 out: sn outpcd: styd on fr 3 out: 3rd after last: nrest at fin* **14/1**[3]

4 *4* **Ground Ball (IRE)**[28] [4650] 8-11-12 140 .... APMcCoy 153?
(C F Swan, Ire) *hld up: impr into 4th 4 out: 3rd next: sn rdn: no ex fr last* **16/1**

5 *4* **Central House**[28] [4650] 8-11-12 153 ....(b) PCarberry 149
(D T Hughes, Ire) *mainly 4th: 3rd after 5 out: 5th and rdn 3 out: no imp fr next* **14/1**[3]

6 *9* **Mossy Green (IRE)**[29] [4632] 11-11-12 145 .... RWalsh 140
(W P Mullins, Ire) *settled 2nd: 3rd 5 out: wknd after next* **25/1**

7 *10* **Colca Canyon (IRE)**[18] [4764] 8-11-12 143 ....(p) RMPower 130
(Mrs John Harrington, Ire) *led: hdd 4 out: 4th u.p bef next: sn wknd* **33/1**

4m 13.6s **Going Correction** +0.025s/f (Yiel) 7 Ran SP% **117.1**
Speed ratings: **119,118,118,116,114 109,104** CSF £11.61 TOTE £6.80: £2.00, £1.30; DF 9.70.
Owner One-O-Eight Racing Club **Bred** Liam Skehan **Trained** Graiguenamanagh, Kilkenny

FOCUS
The first time the remarkable Moscow Flyer has ever been beaten when completing over fences. He has had an arduous campaign and was more than a stone below his Cheltenham and Aintree form, yet he still ran close to the level he has run to on recent visits to Punchestown, which isn't his ideal track. Rathgar Beau has been rated as having run to his recent level, and Native Upmanship to his best in two years. Ground Ball's proximity is the worry.

NOTEBOOK
Rathgar Beau(IRE) showed tremendous determination after the door opened for him when Moscow Flyer blundered at the second last. He was just in front when having a good look at the last, but battled courageously to hold on by a hair's breadth. He has enjoyed a superb campaign and this first Grade 1 win was not undeserved. *(op 7/1)*
Moscow Flyer(IRE) was beaten for the first time in 20 completed starts over fence, but lost by the narrowest of margins in dramatic circumstances, having blundered badly at the second last. That mistake undoubtedly cost him the race, but he was already under pressure and had not quickened away when leading four out. Despite eight previous Punchestown wins, the course does not bring out the best in him, and despite being an outstanding champion, he seldom demonstrates an ability to quicken significantly. *(op 2/7)*
Native Upmanship(IRE) made up a tremendous amount of ground on the first pair, staying on powerfully between the last two fences. This was his best effort in a long time and he might not be finished yet.
Ground Ball(IRE) finished too close for comfort and appeared to show much imporoved form, even allowing for the favourite running well below his best. *(op 12/1)*
Central House could only plug on from three out. *(op 12/1)*

42a ELLIER DEVELOPMENTS NOVICE CHASE (GRADE 2) 2m 5f
3:45 (3:45) 5-Y-0+ **£25,393** (£7,450; £3,549; £1,209)

RPR

1 **Forget The Past**[28] [4648] 7-11-10 145 .... TJMurphy 154+
(M J P O'Brien, Ire) *settled 3rd: 2nd fr 6 out: led 4 out: clr after 3 out: styd on wl: comf* **7/4**[1]

2 *5* **Quazar (IRE)**[13] [4822] 7-11-6 ....(t) APMcCoy 138
(Jonjo O'Neill) *hld up towards rr: prog into 4th 1/2-way: 3rd and rdn 3 out: mod 2nd next: kpt on wout troubling wnr* **11/4**[2]

3 *3/4* **Davenport Milenium (IRE)**[28] [4648] 9-11-3 .... RWalsh 134
(W P Mullins, Ire) *hld up towards rr: prog into 5th whn slt mstke 4 out: 4th and rdn next: 3rd and no imp fr 2 out* **14/1**

4 *2* **Duncliffe**[59] [4064] 8-11-6 138 .... AThornton 135
(R H Alner) *led: slt mstke 7 out: hdd 4 out: sn rdn: outpcd after next: kpt on u.p fr 2 out* **7/1**

5 *25* **Strong Project (IRE)**[28] [4648] 9-11-3 .... GLee 107
(C F Swan, Ire) *cl up in 2nd: 3rd and pushed along 6 out: 4th u.p whn slt mstke 4 out: 5th and wknd next* **12/1**

6 *dist* **Sir Oj (IRE)**[40] [4407] 8-11-8 130 ....(b) PCarberry —
(Noel Meade, Ire) *5th early: pushed along and outpcd 7 out: mod 6th 4 out: sn no ex: t.o* **11/2**[3]

P **Talking Cents (IRE)**[269] [1084] 8-11-3 134 .... MAFitzgerald —
(S Donohoe, Ire) *hld up in tch: wknd bef 5 out: p.u bef 4 out* **25/1**

P **Feathered Storm (IRE)**[13] [4832] 7-11-3 .... JLCullen —
(Michael J O'Connor, Ire) *4th early: dropped towards rr 1/2-way: wknd fr 6 out: p.u bef 4 out* **33/1**

5m 35.6s **Going Correction** +0.025s/f (Yiel) 8 Ran SP% **112.1**
Speed ratings: **113,111,110,110,100** —,—,— CSF £6.78 TOTE £2.60: £1.30, £1.30, £2.80; DF 4.70.
Owner S Mulryan **Bred** M H Dare **Trained** Naas, Co Kildare

NOTEBOOK
Forget The Past went on four out to make it four out of six over fences. He is a late maturing sort and will be of real interest next season. *(op 2/1)*
Quazar(IRE) chased the winner over the last two after a mistake at the previous fence, but he was never going to get in an effective blow. *(op 5/2)*
Davenport Milenium(IRE) is still a maiden over fences but this dual Grade One winner over hurdles can still make his mark. *(op 12/1)*
Duncliffe did not appreciate the ground and, after leading to four out, was soon struggling. *(op 6/1)*
Strong Project(IRE) found the company too warm after blundering four out. *(op 14/1)*
Feathered Storm(IRE) *Official explanation: trainer said gelding choked in running (op 25/1)*

43a TOTE IRELAND 75TH ANNIVERSARY H'CAP HURDLE (LISTED RACE) 2m 4f
4:20 (4:21) (0-140,134) 4-Y-0+ **£34,627** (£10,159; £4,840; £1,648)

RPR

1 **Mansony (FR)**[28] [4649] 6-11-4 131 .... MissNCarberry(5) 136
(A L T Moore, Ire) *a in tch: 7th 1/2-way: 6th and hdwy 3 out: led after 2 out: rdn clr ent st: kpt on u.p fr last* **10/1**[3]

2 *1* **Raikkonen (IRE)**[6] [4635] 5-10-9 119 ....(t) RWalsh 121
(W P Mullins, Ire) *mid-div: 9th 5 out: 7th appr 2 out: 3rd bef last: kpt on wl u.p* **13/2**[2]

3 *shd* **City Of Sails (IRE)**[30] [4592] 6-9-10 110 .... PWFlood(3) 111
(A J McNamara, Ire) *a.p: 3rd fr 1/2-way: 2nd and rdn after 2 out: slt mstke last: kpt on u.p* **20/1**

4 *4* **Oodachee**[6] [1085] 6-10-1 116 .... JFLevins(5) 114
(C F Swan, Ire) *rr of mid-div: prog 5 out: 6th travelling wl 2 out: sn short of room and checked: rdn and kpt on st* **10/1**[3]

5 *1* **Macs Gildoran**[29] [4633] 11-10-9 119 .... DJCondon 116
(W P Mullins, Ire) *towards rr: styd on wl fr 3 out* **16/1**

6 *nk* **Hard Shoulder (IRE)**[28] [4649] 5-9-11 108 .... PCarberry 104
(Noel Meade, Ire) *rr of mid-div: prog into 8th 2 out: kpt on same pce st* **11/1**

7 *2* **Kilbeggan Lad (IRE)**[30] [4590] 7-9-6 110 .... DFFlannery(7) 104
(Michael Hourigan, Ire) *hld up: rdn and kpt on fr 2 out* **11/1**

8 *2* **Piercing Sun (IRE)**[30] [4590] 6-10-6 116 ....(tp) MAFitzgerald 109
(Anthony Mullins, Ire) *hld up: rdn and kpt on fr bef 2 out* **16/1**

9 *3* **Escrea (IRE)**[28] [4649] 6-10-2 113 .... APCrowe 102
(Paul Nolan, Ire) *mid-div on outer: 7th 3 out: 5th appr 2 out: 3rd early st: sn no ex* **12/1**

10 *1 1/2* **Basilea Star (IRE)**[10] [4862] 8-11-7 134 ....(t) KJMercer(5) 124
(Ferdy Murphy) *rr of mid-div: kpt on one pce fr 3 out* **14/1**

11 *2* **Keepthedreamalive**[46] [4316] 7-11-0 123 .... BHitchcott 110
(R H Buckler) *led: clr early: strly pressed 3 out: hdd after 2 out: sn wknd* **16/1**

12 *1/2* **Leaders Way (IRE)**[13] [4830] 10-10-9 119 ....(p) RGeraghty 105
(T K Geraghty, Ire) *nvr bttr than mid-div* **16/1**

13 *1/2* **One More Minute (IRE)**[107] [3285] 5-10-1 112 .... GLee 96
(C F Swan, Ire) *trckd ldrs: impr into 3rd appr 1/2-way: 2nd fr 5 out: chal 3 out: wknd fr 2 out* **20/1**

14 *2* **Joint Agreement (IRE)**[23] [4353] 8-9-11 108 .... GCotter 90
(T M Walsh, Ire) *mid-div: 12th 1/2-way: effrt 4 out: no ex after next* **9/2**[1]

15 *11* **Derawar (IRE)**[52] [4195] 6-9-9 109 .... DJHoward(3) 80
(A L T Moore, Ire) *nvr a factor* **16/1**

16 *4 1/2* **Doctor Linton (IRE)**[29] [4632] 6-10-10 122 .... TGMRyan(3) 91
(M J P O'Brien, Ire) *prom: 4th 4 out: 5th and rdn next: sn no ex* **20/1**

17 *20* **Barrow Walk (IRE)**[38] [4466] 6-9-3 107 .... AFreeman(7) 54
(Thomas Mullins, Ire) *a towards rr* **25/1**

18 *1 1/2* **Hordago (IRE)**[30] [4590] 5-9-8 112 .... BCByrnes(7) 57
(E McNamara, Ire) *nvr a factor* **16/1**

19 *20* **Mocharamor (IRE)**[155] [2398] 7-10-4 114 .... DNRussell 40
(C F Swan, Ire) *chsd ldrs on inner: 6th 1/2-way: wknd bef 3 out* **33/1**

20 *20* **Giolla De (IRE)**[44] [4353] 6-9-9 111 .... KTColeman(5) 16
(F Flood, Ire) *a towards rr* **20/1**

21 *7* **Urban (IRE)**[13] [4830] 4-9-10 110 .... JMAllen(3) 8
(Joseph Crowley, Ire) *a bhd* **16/1**

22 *1/2* **Demesne**[24] [4698] 5-9-13 110 .... TPTreacy —
(Paul Nolan, Ire) *hld up: slt mstke 6th: wknd fr 4 out* **16/1**

P **Hickory Hill (IRE)**[30] [4592] 7-9-12 109 ow1 .... JRBarry 7
(J Motherway, Ire) *prom on outer: 5th after 1/2-way: wknd fr 4 out* **25/1**

F **Emotional Article (IRE)**[28] [4649] 5-10-2 113 .... TJMurphy —
(T J Taaffe, Ire) *mid-div: 8th and in tch whn fell 4 out* **12/1**

P **Imazulutoo (IRE)**[28] [4649] 5-10-11 121 .... BJGeraghty —
(Mrs John Harrington, Ire) *chsd ldrs: 6th after 1/2-way: 4th and rdn 3 out: wknd next: p.u bef last* **16/1**

5m 9.50s **Going Correction** +0.025s/f (Yiel)
WFA 4 from 5yo+ 6lb 25 Ran SP% **171.0**
Speed ratings: 118,117,117,115,115 115,114,113,112,112 111,111,110,110,105 103,95,95,87,79 76,—,—,—, CSF £90.42 CT £1410.88 TOTE £10.00: £3.10, £2.00, £13.10, £2.30; DF 86.20.
Owner Michael Mulholland **Bred** M Hubert Bruckmann **Trained** Naas, Co Kildare

NOTEBOOK
Mansony(FR) gained his just reward for consistency at this level. *(op 8/1)*
Raikkonen(IRE) came with a sustained effort but the winner was always too good. *(op 7/1)*
Basilea Star(IRE) was never in contention, just staying on at the one pace from before two out.
Keepthedreamalive faded after being headed two out.
Hickory Hill(IRE) *Official explanation: trainer said gelding had a respiratory tract infection*

44a GOFFS LAND ROVER BUMPER 2m
4:55 (4:55) 4-5-Y-0 **£27,907** (£8,049; £4,503; £1,666; £957; £248)

RPR

1 **Its A Dream (IRE)**[70] [3864] 5-11-11 .... MrAFitzgerald 115
(N J Henderson) *a.p: 6th 1/2-way: impr to dispute ld over 3f out: rdn clr early st: styd on strly fnl f* **13/2**[3]

2 *4* **Virginia Preuil (FR)**[30] [4593] 4-11-0 .... NPMadden 100
(P Hughes, Ire) *hld up: 9th after 1/2-way: 6th and hdwy 4f out: 3rd and rdn appr st: mod 2nd and no imp fnl f* **5/1**[2]

3 *nk* **Tudorvic (IRE)**[37] 4-10-9 .... MrRO'Sullivan(5) 100
(John Joseph Murphy, Ire) *rr of mid-div: 9th and hdwy 5f out: 6th on outer early st: 3rd and styd on fnl f* **20/1**

4 *3* **Sir Overbury**[16] [4802] 4-11-0 .... MrJTMcNamara 97
(Daniel O'Connell, Ire) *led: hdd after 4f: remained prom: 4th into st: kpt on u.p* **16/1**

5 *2* **Macs Mandalus**[28] [4653] 5-11-7 .... MrJJCodd 102
(W P Mullins, Ire) *prom: 4th 1/2-way: impr to dispute ld over 3f out: hdd ent st: no ex fr 1 1/2f out* **9/1**

6 *2* **Sher One Moor (IRE)**[26] [4677] 4-10-9 .... MrGJPower(5) 93
(Joseph Crowley, Ire) *rr of mid-div: prog over 3f out: 8th 1 1/2f out: kpt on fnl f* **9/1**

7 *1 1/2* **Schindlers Hunt (IRE)** 5-11-2 .... RLoughran(5) 98
(D T Hughes, Ire) *mid-div: prog over 4f out: 5th and rdn early st: no ex fr over 1f out* **9/2**[1]

8 *1 1/2* **Major Hayward (IRE)**[26] [4677] 4-10-11 .... MrKEPower(3) 90
(E J O'Grady, Ire) *mid-div: 10th 1/2-way: 8th 5f out: no ex appr st* **8/1**

9 *3* **The Sham**[103] [3339] 5-11-0 .... PTEnright(7) 94
(Michael Hourigan, Ire) *mid-div: effrt and no imp fr over 3f out* **20/1**

10 *13* **Artic Web (IRE)**[31] [4575] 5-11-4 .... MrDerekO'Connor(3) 81
(F Flood, Ire) *towards rr: kpt on one pce fr 4f out* **16/1**

11 *2* **Rossmore Castle (IRE)**[9] [4898] 5-11-0 .... MrTDCarberry(7) 79
(Noel Meade, Ire) *hld up: kpt on one pce fr 3f out* **25/1**

12 *1* **Johnnybarry** 5-11-2 .... MissNCarberry(5) 78
(Thomas Gerard O'Leary, Ire) *towards rr: kpt on one pce fr over 4f out* **12/1**

13 *3/4* **Pure Palatial** 4-10-7 ....(t) MrRMHennessy(7) 70
(D T Hughes, Ire) *towards rr: hdwy after 1/2-way: 4th 5f out: wknd appr st* **14/1**

14 *8* **Hey Bob (IRE)**[30] [4593] 4-10-7 .... MrWJMcLernon(7) 62
(Joseph G Murphy, Ire) *hdwy to ld after 4f: hdd over 3f out: sn wknd* **20/1**

15 *4* **Western Dasher (IRE)** 4-11-0 .... MrAKWyse 58
(Thomas Gerard O'Leary, Ire) *towards rr: sme late prog* **16/1**

16 *3* **Thenford Trout (IRE)** 4-10-7 .... MrRPQuinlan(7) 55
(E J O'Grady, Ire) *nvr a factor* **16/1**

17 *9* **Steel Duke (IRE)**[30] [4593] 4-11-0 .... MrPFahey 46
(D Broad, Ire) *chsd ldrs to 6f out: sn wknd* **25/1**

18 *1/2* **Anaczar (IRE)** 5-11-0 .... MrDGPorter(7) 52
(P J Rothwell, Ire) *nvr a factor* **20/1**

19 *1/2* **Dunlo Society (IRE)**[30] [4593] 4-10-7 .... RMMoran(7) 45
(S J Treacy, Ire) *nvr a factor* **20/1**

20 *10* **Erritt (IRE)** 5-11-2 .... MrCJSweeney(5) 42
(John C Shearman, Ire) *nvr a factor* **20/1**
21 *2 1/2* **Fabro (IRE)**[5] [4952] 4-10-2 .... MrJTCarroll(7) 27
(P A Fahy, Ire) *prom: 3rd 1/2-way: wknd over 4f out* **20/1**
22 *7* **Adair Mohr (IRE)** 5-11-0 .... MrCPHuxley(7) 32
(Michael Hourigan, Ire) *a bhd* **20/1**
23 *25* **All Is Bright (IRE)** 5-11-2 .... MrROHarding(5) 7
(S J Treacy, Ire) *mid-div: wknd fr 5f out* **20/1**
24 *3* **Thinking Of You (IRE)** 5-11-0 .... MrBOWalsh(7) —
(Moses McCabe, Ire) *chsd ldrs: 8th 1/2-way: wknd fr 6f out* **33/1**
S **Jameson Prince (IRE)** 5-11-0 .... MrATDuff(7) —
(B P Galvin, Ire) *prom: 4th 1/2-way: chsng ldrs whn slipped up 5f out* **16/1**

3m 58.7s **Going Correction** +0.275s/f (Yiel)
WFA 4 from 5yo 5lb **25** Ran SP% **176.6**
Speed ratings: 107,105,104,103,102 101,100,99,98,91 90,90,89,85,83 82,77,77,77,72 71,67,55,53,— CSF £45.28 TOTE £6.80: £2.20, £1.50, £10.20, £6.10; DF 27.70.
Owner Mrs R Murdoch & David Murdoch **Bred** Mrs Esther Power **Trained** Upper Lambourn, Berks

NOTEBOOK
Its A Dream(IRE) certainly built on his Folkestone win with an emphatic success here, going clear in the straight and winning with something in hand. *(op 6/1 tchd 7/1)*
Sher One Moor(IRE) *Official explanation: jockey said gelding received a check down the back straight and lost ground (op 8/1)*
Western Dasher(IRE) *Official explanation: jockey said, regarding the running and riding, he missed the break and was one of the last to leave the chute, adding that he tried to put the gelding into the race down the back straight; vet said gelding finished lame behind*

45a MOUNTBROOK HOMES H'CAP CHASE 2m
5:30 (5:30) (0-140,130) 4-Y-0+ **£16,159** (£4,741; £2,258; £769)

RPR
1 **The Boys In Green (IRE)**[24] [4702] 8-10-9 111 .... APMcCoy 121
(C Roche, Ire) *mid-div: 7th 5 out: 5th and hdwy appr 3 out: 2nd fr 2 out: chal last: styd on wl u.p to ld cl home* **4/1**[1]
2 *1/2* **Cluain Rua (IRE)**[235] [1354] 10-9-10 99 .... PACarberry 107
(Liam P Cusack, Ire) *mid-div: hdwy 4 out: led next: slt mstke 2 out: strly pressed fr last: hdd cl home* **25/1**
3 *7* **Incas (FR)**[24] [4702] 9-10-1 106 .... DJHoward(3) 108
(A L T Moore, Ire) *hld up: prog 4 out: 6th after 3 out: 4th next: 3rd and no ex fr last* **5/1**[2]
4 *7* **Alphazar (IRE)**[61] [4039] 10-10-1 106 .... (p) MPMadden(3) 101
(Anthony Mullins, Ire) *led: hdd 4 out: 2nd next: 4th and no ex fr 2 out* **14/1**
5 *7* **Old Opry**[44] [4354] 8-10-6 111 .... DFO'Regan(3) 99
(Noel Meade, Ire) *towards rr: 10th and hdwy whn bad mstke 4 out: kpt on u.p fr next* **25/1**
6 *1/2* **Old Flame (IRE)**[29] [4636] 6-11-3 119 .... MAFitzgerald 107
(C F Swan, Ire) *settled 2nd: led 4 out: hdd next: 5th and no ex appr 2 out* **14/1**
7 *3* **Anxious Moments (IRE)**[51] [4216] 10-11-11 127 .... RWalsh 112
(C F Swan, Ire) *towards rr: bad mstke 4th: prog 3 out: 7th bef 2 out: 6th and no ex last* **9/1**[3]
8 *2* **Green Belt Flyer (IRE)**[28] [4650] 7-11-10 126 .... (b[1]) RMPower 109
(Mrs John Harrington, Ire) *prom: 5th 4 out: 3rd next: 4th and no ex appr 2 out* **9/1**[3]
9 *2 1/2* **Swordplay**[30] [4590] 7-11-3 122 .... TGMRyan(3) 102
(M J P O'Brien, Ire) *towards rr: impr into 9th appr 3 out: no ex fr next* **14/1**
10 *1* **Saddlers' Mark**[31] [4574] 10-9-5 99 .... (t) RJMolloy(5) 77
(D M Christie, Ire) *nvr a factor: mstke 2 out: kpt on fr last* **25/1**
11 *1* **Fiery Ring (IRE)**[28] [4650] 10-11-7 123 .... RGeraghty 101
(J R H Fowler, Ire) *rr of mid-div: no imp fr 4 out* **20/1**
12 *1* **City Hall (IRE)**[12] [2520] 11-11-10 126 .... (b) JLCullen 103
(Paul Nolan, Ire) *prom: 4th 4 out: wknd fr next* **20/1**
13 *6* **Cregg House (IRE)**[18] [4764] 10-12-0 130 .... DNRussell 101
(S Donohoe, Ire) *nvr a factor* **16/1**
14 *3/4* **Mr Flowers (IRE)**[28] [4651] 13-10-7 109 .... GCotter 79
(Miss S Barkley, Ire) *mid-div on outer: 8th 1/2-way: wknd after 4 out* **16/1**
15 *10* **Private Ben (IRE)**[23] [4732] 7-10-7 109 .... TPTreacy 69
(Mrs John Harrington, Ire) *trckd ldrs in 4th: 3rd 4 out: wknd next* **14/1**
16 *13* **Golden Row (IRE)**[30] [4590] 11-11-9 125 .... KWhelan 72
(Miss Mary Louise Hallahan, Ire) *hld up: hdwy on outer 4 out: no ex and wknd next* **33/1**
17 *1 1/2* **Transit**[39] [4443] 6-11-5 121 .... (p) GLee 67
(B Ellison) *nvr a factor: towards rr whn bad mstke last* **14/1**
18 *5* **Adarma (IRE)**[24] [4701] 7-11-5 121 .... CO'Dwyer 62
(C Roche, Ire) *nvr a factor* **9/1**[3]
19 *7* **Annshoon (IRE)**[225] [1425] 10-10-6 108 .... MDGrant 42
(M G Holden, Ire) *settled 3rd: dropped to 7th 4 out: sn wknd* **25/1**
F **Always**[164] [2210] 6-11-1 117 .... PCarberry —
(Noel Meade, Ire) *rr of mid-div: fell 5th* **9/1**[3]
P **The Moyne Machine (IRE)**[24] [4702] 9-9-12 100 .... JRBarry —
(Timothy Doyle, Ire) *mid-div: dropped to rr 5th: p.u bef next* **14/1**

4m 21.5s **Going Correction** +0.025s/f (Yiel) **21** Ran SP% **156.3**
Speed ratings: **99,98,95,91,88 88,86,85,84,83 83,82,79,79,74 67,67,64,61,— —** CSF £122.10 CT £574.48 TOTE £3.50: £1.50, £11.60, £1.40, £4.50; DF 422.40.
Owner John P McManus **Bred** Mrs Noeleen Roche **Trained** the Curragh, Co Kildare
■ Stewards' Enquiry : P A Carberry two-day ban: excessive use of the whip (May 5,6)

NOTEBOOK
Transit never got into it and was not a contender when blundering at the last.

CHELTENHAM (New Course) (L-H)
Wednesday, April 27

OFFICIAL GOING: Good
Wind: virtually nil

47 CHELTENHAM.CO.UK HUNTERS' CHASE (17 fncs) 2m 5f
5:25 (5:25) (Class 6) 5-Y-0+ **£3,290** (£940; £470)

Form RPR
/43- 1 **Let's Fly (FR)**[20] [4758] 10-12-0 .... MissPGundry 111
(Ross Oliver) *led to 3rd: chsd ldrs: led 11th: edgd rt towards fin: rdn out* **10/1**
/23- 2 *1/2* **Minella Silver (IRE)**[26] [4682] 12-12-0 .... MrRBurton 110
(G L Landau) *hld up in tch: chsd wnr 4 out: swtchd lft appr last: r.o* **4/1**[2]
40P/ 3 *1* **Mighty Montefalco**[25] 9-11-7 .... MissAdeLisleWells(7) 109+
(Mrs Alison De Lisle Wells) *chsd ldrs: rdn appraoching 2 out: styd on wl nr fin* **11/2**[3]
311- 4 *1/2* **Red Brook Lad**[26] [4682] 10-12-4 107 .... MissCTizzard(3) 116
(C St V Fox) *hld up: hdwy 12th: rdn appr last: no ex nr fin* **10/3**[1]
0/5- 5 *1 3/4* **Gaiac (FR)**[17] 11-11-7 .... (b) MissSSharratt(7) 108+
(Ms N M Hugo) *hld up: hdwy 7th: chsd wnr 13th to next: styd on same pce flat* **25/1**
26- 6 *1 1/4* **Sikander A Azam**[69] [3903] 12-12-4 .... MrTGreenall 110
(David M Easterby) *hld up: hdwy 4 out: rdn appr last: no ex flat* **4/1**[2]
0/3- 7 *12* **Scotmail Lad (IRE)**[10] 11-11-11 103 .... (b) MrCMulhall(3) 95+
(Mrs C M Mulhall) *hld up: hdwy 8th: wknd 2 out* **12/1**
511/ 8 *14* **Salford**[10] 10-11-7 .... MissTNewman(7) 80
(Miss Chloe Newman) *hld up: blnd 3rd: sme hdwy appr 2 out: nvr trbld ldrs* **25/1**
400- 9 *12* **Epsilo De La Ronce (FR)**[20] [4750] 13-11-7 96 .... MrPaulMorris(7) 68
(Paul Morris) *hld up: rdn 6th: a in rr* **40/1**
P/5- 10 *1 1/4* **Chief Mouse**[32] 12-11-7 65 .... (p) MrRHodges(7) 66
(Steve Isaac) *chsd ldrs: lost pl 5th: rdn and hit 7th: wknd 10th: bhd whn hit 13th* **100/1**
13U- 11 *dist* **Sporting Chance**[20] [4758] 13-11-11 83 .... MrMMunrowd(7) —
(Mrs Jo Sleep) *chsd ldr 3rd: led 8th to 11th: blnd next: wknd 4 out* **40/1**
/06- 12 *7* **Merry Minstrel (IRE)**[10] 12-11-7 88 .... (p) MrJOldring(7) —
(Mrs Jackie Hunt) *hld up: a in rr: bhd whn hmpd 13th* **100/1**
6/0- P **Magical Fun (IRE)**[12] [4856] 13-11-7 .... MissTHayes(7) —
(Mrs J A Hayes) *hld up: a bhd: p.u bef 2 out* **100/1**
/00- F **Captain Ron (IRE)**[55] [4144] 9-11-7 .... (b[1]) MrDEngland(7) —
(S Lycett) *led 3rd: mstke 5th: hdd 8th: wknd 12th: fell next* **100/1**
0P1- P **Mister Club Royal**[12] [4856] 9-11-13 82 .... MrRWoollacott(5) —
(Miss Emma Oliver) *chsd ldrs tl wknd after 13th: bhd whn p.u bef 2 out* **25/1**

5m 31.5s (20.50) **Going Correction** +0.90s/f (Soft) **15** Ran SP% **115.6**
Speed ratings: **96,95,95,95,94 94,89,84,79,79 —,—,—,—,—** CSF £45.89 TOTE £10.90: £2.80, £1.90, £1.80; EX 75.20.
Owner Ross Oliver **Bred** Neustrian Associates **Trained** Newquay, Cornwall

FOCUS
A decent hunter chase that looks reasonable form-wise and should produce the odd winner.

NOTEBOOK
Let's Fly(FR) has a marvellous record when completing and stepped up on his previous efforts to take this prize. He had one of the better jockeys on board and put his assured stamina to good use *in racing prominently throughout. A highly consistent sort, he should continue to pay his way. (op 11-1 tchd 12-1 in places)*
Minella Silver(IRE) went down fighting and received every assistance from the saddle. Like the winner he rarely runs a bad race and it will not be long until he is back winning. *(op 5-1)*
Mighty Montefalco ◆, who has been in cracking form in points, ran well on this return to hunter *chasing and was staying on all the time at the death, suggesting a return to three miles will suit. (tchd 6-1)*
Red Brook Lad is a solid performer at this level and ran another sound race without being quite good enough on the night. *(op 7-2 tchd 3-1 and 4-1)*
Gaiac(FR) has not won since coming to this country, and although he has run some good races, he remains winless in around five years.
Sikander A Azam was a little disappointing and was unable to quicken under pressure. *(tchd 9-2 and 5-1)*

48 FAUCETS THE LEADING INDEPENDENT BRASSWARE DISTRIBUTOR CHAMPION HUNTERS' CHASE (22 fncs) 3m 2f 110y
5:55 (6:04) (Class 6) 5-Y-0+ **£4,868** (£1,498; £749; £374)

Form RPR
P11- 1 **Mister Friday (IRE)**[13] [4840] 8-12-3 109 .... (v) MrCMulhall(3) 129+
(Mrs C M Mulhall) *hld up rr:hdwy to trck ldrs 10th:wnt 3rd 16th:slt ld 18th: qcknd 4l clr appr 2 out:kpt on under hand driving:readily* **5/2**[1]
532- 2 *1 3/4* **Mullensgrove**[13] [4840] 11-11-7 103 .... MissSSharratt(7) 118
(D Lowe) *in tch: outpcd 12th: rallied fr 17th: styd on u.p to go 2nd last: clsd on wnr run-in but a hld* **25/1**
5U3- 3 *5* **Gatsby (IRE)**[11] [4870] 9-11-11 .... MrRHFowler(3) 113
(J Groucott) *pressed ldr: chal fr 8th: stl upsides and rdn 3 out: outpcd appr next: lost 2nd last* **13/2**[3]
1- 4 *12* **Vinnie Boy (IRE)**[76] [3776] 8-12-3 .... MissPGundry 104
(Mrs O Bush) *chsd ldrs to 4 out: btn next* **20/1**
1- F **Coolefind (IRE)**[17] 7-12-0 .... MrSMorris —
(W J Warner) *fell 3rd* **9/2**[2]
12- R **Silver Castle**[26] [4682] 9-12-0 .... MrAWintle(3) —
(R J Rowsell) *blnd 3rd: rdr lost reins: blnd next: rn out 5th* **20/1**
F22- P **Bengal Bullet**[28] [4658] 8-11-9 107 .... MissTCave(5) —
(C Blank) *chsd ldrs tl blnd 7th: wknd 16th: t.o whn p.u after 18th* **9/1**
143- P **Montifault (FR)**[20] [4750] 10-12-6 120 .... (t) MrNWilliams 97
(P F Nicholls) *mde most and kpt narrow advantage tl hdd 18th: sn wknd: t.o whn p.u bef last* **9/2**[2]
11U- P **Cobreces**[20] [4750] 7-12-3 116 .... MrJSnowden(3) —
(Mrs L Borradaile) *chsd ldrs: hit 6th: reminders 7th: rdn 13th: wknd 17th: t.o whn p.u bef 2 out* **7/1**

7m 12.9s (22.10) **Going Correction** +0.90s/f (Soft) **9** Ran SP% **114.1**
Speed ratings: **103,102,101,97,— —,—,—,—** CSF £64.50 TOTE £3.90: £1.80, £4.00, £2.30; EX 52.80.
Owner Joseph Aaron Rea **Bred** Marion And Paddy Stack **Trained** Scarcroft, W Yorks

FOCUS
An average race rated through the runner-up, but Mister Friday is a really smart hunter chaser and recorded a smart time in again winning impressively, being value for further.

NOTEBOOK
Mister Friday(IRE) is quickly making up into a smart hunter chaser and this was his third impressive win of the month. A horse with a good change of gear, he see's this trip out well and will always be a threat when the ground is on the quick side. He now goes for the Intrum Justitia Cup at Stratford and will take the beating. *(tchd 9-4 and 11-4 in places)*
Mullensgrove ran a solid race in second, but was never a threat to the winner. He continues to run well in defeat. *(tchd 33-1)*
Gatsby(IRE) ran out of stamina up the hill, but had performed really well to a point and deserves a certain amount of credit. *(op 10-1)*
Vinnie Boy(IRE) kept plugging away and was not disgraced. *(op 16-1 tchd 25-1)*
Montifault(FR) used to be a class act, but has lost his way these days. *(op 7-2 tchd 5-1)*
Silver Castle *(op 7-2 tchd 5-1)*

49 THE WINNING POST AT CHELTENHAM HUNTERS' CHASE (27 fncs) 4m 1f

6:30 (6:31) (Class 6) 5-Y-0+ **£3,332** (£3,332; £784; £392)

Form RPR

P/6- **1** **No Retreat (NZ)**[20] [4750] 12-11-7 MrWHill(7) 111
(J Groucott) *led to 2nd: led 7th to next: remained handy: chsd ldr after 3 out: led last: rdn flat: jnd post* **16/1**

112- **1** *dht* **Paddy For Paddy (IRE)**[31] [4588] 11-12-4 MrRBurton 115
(G L Landau) *hld up in tch: chsd ldr 17th: lft in ld 22nd: hdd last: rallied to join wnr post* **4/1**[2]

232- **3** *12* **Mrs Be (IRE)**[10] [4879] 9-11-7 114 MissPGundry 93+
(J G Cann) *chsd ldrs: lost pl 13th: styd on fr 2 out: nt rch wnrs* **13/8**[1]

124- **4** *4* **Involved (IRE)**[11] [4870] 9-11-7 MrJJarrett(7) 98+
(Mrs Edward Crow) *hld up: hdwy 14th: mstke 20th: wkng whn j. slowly last* **25/1**

34P- **5** *15* **Samuel Wilderspin**[13] [4840] 13-12-0 98 MrNWilliams 80
(R Lee) *hld up: hdwy 17th: wknd 5 out* **22/1**

/21- **6** *6* **Tribal Run (IRE)**[48] [4282] 10-12-0 98 (t) MrSMorris 74
(Miss S A Loggin) *hld up: hdwy 17th: wknd 22nd* **11/1**

3/P- **7** *9* **Dunston Bill**[17] 11-11-7 107 MrAPuddy(7) 65
(Mrs K Smyly) *chsd ldrs: lost pl and hit 10th: n.d after* **14/1**

1P4- **8** *1* **Tanager**[13] [4840] 10-11-9 (b) MrBKing(5) 69+
(Mrs K Lawther) *chsd ldrs: j.rt: w wnr whn blnd 22nd: wknd appr 2 out* **8/1**[3]

4P6- **P** **Alska (FR)**[12] [4856] 12-11-0 75 MrRBandey(7) —
(P L Southcombe) *hld up: bhd fr 10th: p.u bef 22nd* **50/1**

/06- **P** **Strong Tea (IRE)**[18] 14-11-11 MissAGoschen(3) —
(Miss S Waugh) *hld up: bhd fr 10th: p.u bef 2 out* **50/1**

/23- **P** **Victoria's Boy (IRE)**[24] 12-11-7 87 MrMWalford(7) —
(Mrs W Wild) *hld up: bhd fr 17th: p.u bef last* **40/1**

43P- **P** **Maggies Brother**[11] 12-11-11 MrDBarlow(3) —
(R Shail) *chsd ldrs to 7th: bhd whn p.u bef 2 out* **33/1**

U **Golden Jack (FR)**[11] 11-11-7 (b) MrCMorris(7) —
(Mrs A L Tory) *led 2nd to 7th: led 8th: slt ld whn blnd and uns rdr 22nd* **66/1**

13P- **P** **Freedom Fighter**[31] [4588] 14-11-9 MrAndrewMartin(5) —
(Mrs Rosemary Gasson) *hld up: bhd fr 10th: p.u bef 20th* **100/1**

4P0- **P** **General Claremont (IRE)**[40] [4436] 12-11-11 100 (t) LHeard(7) —
(P F Nicholls) *hld up: hdwy 13th: wknd 20th: bhd whn p.u bef last* **12/1**

5/3- **P** **Ashgar (USA)**[17] 9-11-7 (p) MrTJO'Brien(7) —
(Mrs Nicola Sheppard) *hld up: hdwy 15th: hit 18th: wkng whn mstke 20th: bhd whn p.u bef next* **80/1**

8m 55.8s (-1.40) **Going Correction** +0.90s/f (Soft) **16** Ran SP% **119.0**
Speed ratings: **97,97,94,93,89 88,85,85,**—,—,— —,—,—,—,— — TRIFECTA Win PFP £2.30, NR £12.40. Place PFP £2.00, NR £5.70, MB £1.40. Exacta: PFP/NR £45.00, NR/PFP £50.90, CSF: PFP/NR £28.45, NR/PFP £37.
Owner M W & A N Harris **Bred** B G Francis, J S Mee And J R Watts **Trained** Much Wenlock, Shropshire
Owner Mrs Jane Thornton **Bred** Mrs Louise Cooper-Joyce **Trained** Frome, Somerset

FOCUS
A moderate race but a cracking finish and the race could be rated higher.

NOTEBOOK
No Retreat(NZ), last seen finishing sixth in the Topham, appreciated this extreme distance and stayed on well up the hill right the way to the line, looking unlucky to be joined by Paddy For Paddy who forced a deat heat. He is at his best on a sound surface, but it was slightly worrying that he was distressed after the race. *(tchd 7-2 and 5-1)*
Paddy For Paddy(IRE) showed a great attitude and rallied bravely up the hill to force a dead heat. He is less exposed than No Retreat and probably has more of a future. *(tchd 7-2 and 5-1)*
Mrs Be(IRE) set a good standard, but her lack of pace told on this decent ground and she could only plug on for a disappointing third. She is at her best with plenty of cut in the ground. *(op 2-1)*
Involved(IRE) ran well to a point, but was a blatant non-stayer. *(op 20-1)*
Samuel Wilderspin is a shadow of his former self. *(op 16-1)*

50 TIM POWELL MAIDEN HUNTERS' CHASE (17 fncs) 2m 5f

7:05 (7:05) (Class 6) 5-Y-0+ **£2,320** (£714; £357; £178)

Form RPR

4/2- **1** **Mr Splodge**[32] 11-11-9 MrJETudor(5) 103+
(Mrs T J Hill) *chsd ldrs: led 7th: drvn and styd on strly appr 2 out* **7/2**[2]

542- **2** *8* **Beauchamp Oracle**[10] 8-11-7 MrMWalford(7) 95
(S Flook) *chsd ldrs: wnt 2nd 11th: rdn fr 3 out and no imp* **5/1**[3]

32/ **3** *6* **Kasilia (FR)**[17] 7-11-7 MrMMackley(7) 89
(Tim Brown) *chsd ldrs tl lost position 12th: rallied fr 3 out: styd on run-in but nvr a danger* **20/1**

00P/ **4** *6* **Father Jim**[10] 10-11-7 MrFelixDeGiles(7) 85+
(J A T De Giles) *chsd ldrs: blnd 8th: lost position and rr 12th: styd on fr 2 out but nvr a danger* **40/1**

P- **5** *15* **Nautical Lad**[17] 10-11-7 MrJDocker(7) 68
(J H Docker) *bhd fr 9th* **10/1**

2U0/ **F** **Dragon's Dream**[24] 7-12-0 MrNWilliams —
(R Barber) *fell 2nd* **9/4**[1]

F **Raregem**[46] 7-11-7 MrWBiddick(7) —
(M Biddick) *blnd 3rd: disputing 2nd whn fell 10th* **8/1**

P **Drom Island**[10] 11-11-0 MrJSole(7) —
(Graham Richards) *blnd 6th: bhd: t.o whn p.u bef 12th* **100/1**

/P6- **F** **Round The Bend**[31] 13-11-7 MissLAllan(7) —
(Miss Louise Allan) *led to 7th: wknd 10th: fell 12th* **50/1**

/32- **P** **The Vintage Dancer (IRE)**[25] 9-11-7 MrGKerr(7) —
(Mrs Nicola Pollock) *bhd fr 7th: t.o whn p.u bef 12th* **33/1**

0PP/ **P** **Manor Down (IRE)**[30] 7-12-0 MrJMPritchard —
(Mrs C Maude) *prom early: bhd fr 6th: t.o whn p.u bef 10th* **25/1**

P **Waterloo Leader (IRE)**[32] 10-11-9 MrCGordon(5) —
(Mrs S Kellard-Smith) *in tch: rdn 6th: wknd 10th: t.o whn blnd 3 out: p.u bef next* **66/1**

P/ **P** **Physical Force**[17] 7-11-7 PKinsella(7) —
(Mrs Marjorie Fife) *chsd ldrs fr 5th: wknd 4 out: no ch whn blnd 3 out: t.o whn p.u bef last* **50/1**

R **Heisamodel (IRE)**[30] 7-11-11 MrMGMiller(3) 79
(J J Boulter) *bhd: hdwy 10th: trckd ldrs 10th: wnt 3rd 4 out: rdn and no imp fr next: wknd 2 out: 4th and no ch whn ref last* **10/1**

5m 32.8s (21.80) **Going Correction** +0.90s/f (Soft) **14** Ran SP% **119.3**
Speed ratings: **94,90,88,86,80** —,—,—,—,— —,—,—,— CSF £20.20 TOTE £4.10: £1.40, £2.70, £6.10; EX 28.30.
Owner Alan Hill **Bred** Mrs P J Fairbarns **Trained** Chinnor, Oxon

FOCUS
A modest maiden hunter chase, made weaker by the early exit of the favourite. However, the placed horses were close to their marks and the winner could rate higher.

NOTEBOOK
Mr Splodge, who had been successful in a point-to-point since his Leicester second, had his job made easier by the early departure of the favourite, but he ran out a good winner of this maiden chase. He may be stepped up in grade to contest the John Corbet Cup at Stratford next, but the competition will be a lot tougher there. *(op 4-1)*
Beauchamp Oracle ran a fair race in second but he is fairly exposed now and has not progressed as had once looked likely. *(op 6-1)*
Kasilia(FR) is still seeking his first win and, although he stayed on up the hill, he could never land a blow. A return to three miles will suit.
Father Jim, who is at his best going right-handed, has not won a race for almost three years. *(op 33-1)*
Nautical Lad failed to run up to his best at this meeting for the second year in succession. *(op 9-1)*
Heisamodel(IRE) may need top of the ground to show his best. *(op 8-1)*

51 COLIN NASH MEMORIAL (FOR HUNT STAFF BENEFIT SOC. UNITED HUNTS' CHALL. CUP) (HUNTERS' CHASE) (21 fncs) 3m 1f 110y

7:40 (7:41) (Class 6) 6-Y-0+ **£3,526** (£1,085; £542; £271)

Form RPR

122- **1** **Caught At Dawn (IRE)**[11] 11-11-10 MrTWeston(7) 128+
(M H Weston) *hld up: hdwy 11th: led 3 out: comf* **10/11**[1]

P/4- **2** *6* **Sherwood Rose (IRE)**[11] 9-11-5 MrMHarris(5) 109+
(Mrs N Field) *led: hit 2nd: clr 7th: hdd 3 out: ev ch whn hit next: no ch w easy wnr fr last* **7/1**[3]

UU5- **3** *9* **Kyalami (FR)**[26] [4682] 7-12-3 MissPGundry 104+
(B Tulloch) *hld up: hdwy 8th: ev ch 3 out: styd on same pce fr next* **4/1**[2]

0/5- **4** *29* **Rohan**[15] [4818] 9-11-10 (p) MissTessaClark(7) 79+
(R F Johnson Houghton) *hld up: blnd 7th: hdwy next: hit 4 out: sn wknd* **14/1**

/P0- **5** *2* **Carbonado**[12] [4856] 11-12-3 MrGBarfoot-Saunt 77
(H R Tuck) *hld up: sme hdwy 15th: sn wknd* **25/1**

PF5- **6** *6* **Totland Bay (IRE)**[11] 9-11-10 78 MrNHOliver(7) 73+
(Dr R D P Newland) *hld up in tch: hit 17th: sn wknd: bhd whn pckd 3 out* **33/1**

F **Champagneism (IRE)**[10] 8-11-10 MrJJarrett(7) —
(R A Wernham) *hld up: bhd whn fell 9th* **150/1**

4/P- **P** **Macy (IRE)**[10] 12-12-0 (p) MrDMansell(3) —
(Martin Jones) *chsd ldrs to 12th: p.u bef 14th* **40/1**

P54/ **P** **Slip The Ring**[17] 11-12-0 MrGHanmer(3) —
(P Senter) *hld up: bhd and rdn 11th: t.o whn p.u bef 17th* **50/1**

3- **U** **Bankit**[18] 12-11-10 MrHWhittington(7) —
(M G Hazell) *chsd ldr: disputing 2nd whn blnd and uns rdr 14th* **25/1**

P/1- **P** **Mustang Molly**[10] [4882] 13-11-5 MrAndrewMartin(5) —
(Andrew J Martin) *chsd ldrs to 6th: t.o whn p.u bef 17th* **20/1**

/3P- **P** **Prince Dundee (FR)**[28] [4658] 10-11-10 MrsBKeighley(7) —
(M Keighley) *mstkes: hld up: bhd whn blnd 16th: t.o whn p.u bef 2 out* **33/1**

6m 58.1s (26.80) **Going Correction** +0.90s/f (Soft) **12** Ran SP% **114.9**
Speed ratings: **94,92,89,80,79 78,**—,—,—,— —,— CSF £6.60 TOTE £1.90: £1.10, £1.70, £2.00; EX 7.70.
Owner M H Weston **Bred** Mrs Maura McSweeney **Trained** Hindlip, Worcs

FOCUS
A race for pointers from the South and West, Midlands, West and Welsh Borders. The winner is value for twice the official margin and close to his Aintree mark.

NOTEBOOK
Caught At Dawn(IRE), runner-up at Aintree earlier in the month, was sent off a short price and won easily. Connections now plan to run him in the Intrum Justitia Cup at Stratford next month, a race which is run over a further two and a half furlongs. The longer trip ought not to inconvenience him. *(op 6-4)*
Sherwood Rose(IRE), who has enjoyed a good time of it in point-to-points this season, ran a solid race in defeat, but she is flattered by her proximity to the winner. *(tchd 6-1)*
Kyalami(FR), who ran well at Newbury earlier in the month, may have found the ground softer than ideal, but this was still a fair performance. *(op 10-3 tchd 3-1)*
Rohan, who was wearing cheekpieces, was let down by some indifferent jumping. *(op 12-1 tchd 16-1)*
Totland Bay(IRE) made a mistake at the fifth last which quickly took its toll. *(op 25-1)*

52 AMATEUR JOCKEYS ASSOCIATION INVESTING IN RACING HUNTERS' CHASE (14 fncs) 2m 110y

8:10 (8:13) (Class 6) 5-Y-0+ **£3,024** (£864; £432)

Form RPR

U0P/ **1** **Galway (IRE)**[11] 12-11-5 MissCStucley(7) 96+
(Mrs Marilyn Scudamore) *led 3rd to 5th: led 6th: blnd 9th: hdd 10th: styd pressing ldrs: led last: drvn out* **3/1**[2]

F3U- **2** *3* **Enitsag (FR)**[11] 6-11-9 94 MrMWalford(7) 93
(S Flook) *bhd: hdwy 7th: trckd ldrs 4 out: chal fr next and stl ev ch last: one pce run-in* **6/1**

P04- **3** *2 ½* **Viscount Bankes**[11] 7-11-7 MrAndrewMartin(5) 87
(Mrs Rosemary Gasson) *led to 3rd: hdd 6th: styd chsng ldrs: one pce after 3 out: kpt on again run-in* **9/1**

6P2- **4** *½* **Jazz Night**[37] [4500] 8-12-2 MrTGreenall 91+
(S Lycett) *chsd ldrs: chal and stmbld 3 out: led next: hdd last and sn outpcd* **11/2**[3]

B1F- **5** *4* **Hot Plunge**[20] [4750] 9-11-11 MrJOwen(5) 96+
(Mrs J P Lomax) *planted s and lost half a f: rcvrd 6th: chsng ldrs whn blnd 7th: led 10th: rdn 3 out: hdd 2 out: wknd last* **11/4**[1]

U26- **6** *15* **Win The Toss**[10] 13-11-9 MrPYork(3) 70+
(P York) *bhd: effrt 10th: wknd and mstke 4 out* **20/1**

0P/- **7** *dist* **Gold Quest (IRE)**[11] 8-11-5 (t) MrNKent(7) —
(Nick Kent) *bhd fr 6th: t.o* **33/1**

0P0/ **8** *15* **One Of The Natives (IRE)**[380] 11-11-5 (t) MissJJenner(7) —
(Miss J H Jenner) *pulleed hrd: chsd ldrs: blnd 5th: blnd 8th and bhd: t.o* **80/1**

0 **P** **No Can Do (IRE)**[3] [2] 7-11-2 MrRHFowler(3) —
(K J Burke) *bhd fr 8th: t.o whn p.u bef last* **100/1**

0/1- **P** **Gray Knight (IRE)**[11] 8-11-11 MrJETudor(5) —
(Mrs T J Hill) *blnd 1st: chsd ldrs: blnd 7th and 10th: wknd 4 out: t.o whn p.u bef last* **7/1**

4m 21.4s (21.00) **Going Correction** +0.90s/f (Soft) **10** Ran SP% **113.8**
Speed ratings: **86,84,83,83,81 74,**—,—,—,— CSF £20.44 TOTE £3.90: £1.70, £3.00, £3.10; EX 32.40 Place 6 £39.53, Place 5 £16.01.
Owner Mrs Marilyn Scudamore **Bred** John Purfield **Trained** Naunton, Gloucs

FOCUS
A modest winning time but the form appears solid enough through those in the frame.

NOTEBOOK

Galway(IRE) had done all his previous winning in hunter chases and point-to-points over three miles, but this drop back to the minimum trip brought about plenty of improvement. There is a race at the big Stratford meeting next month for him over a similar trip and that looks the likely target, although the sharper track would not be sure to suit. *(op 11-2)*

Enitsag(FR), successful in hurdle races over this sort of trip in 2003, has been racing over further in chases of late, but did not mind the drop back in trip one bit. *(op 11-2)*

Viscount Bankes ran a couple of fair races in hunter chases over this trip last month and put in another solid effort. He seems to cope with most ground. *(op 7-1)*

Jazz Night could have done with quicker ground. *(op 13-2 tchd 5-1)*

Hot Plunge, runner-up in this race last year, lost almost 30 lengths when refusing initially to jump off as the tapes went up. He made up the lost ground to contest the lead, but the effort necessary to achieve that resulted in him being a spent force from the turn in. He clearly has the ability to win a race of this nature but his attitude leaves something to be desired. *(op 9-4)*

T/Plt: £51.00 to a £1 stake. Pool £37,990.00. 543.20 winning units T/Qpdt: £11.90 to a £1 stake. Pool 3,468.50. 215.20 winning units ST

EXETER (R-H)

Wednesday, April 27

OFFICIAL GOING: Heavy (soft in places)

The meeting went ahead following two inspections. The first flight after the winning post and the first two fences after the winning post were omitted.

Wind: strong half-behind

53 BRISTOL STREET RENAULT AMATEUR RIDERS' NOVICES' HURDLE (10 hdls 1 omitted) 2m 6f 110y

2:30 (2:30) (Class 4) 4-Y-0+ **£3,094** (£884; £442)

Form				RPR
064-	1		**Malaga Boy (IRE)**[28] [4654] 8-11-7 102 .... MrNWilliams	100+
			(C L Tizzard) *hld up in tch: led appr 3 out: kpt up to work fr 2 out* **11/8**[1]	
64F-	2	12	**Seeador**[73] [3831] 6-11-0 92 .... WPKavanagh(7)	83
			(J W Mullins) *trckd ldr 2nd to 6th: soon lost pl: rallied fr 3 out: plugged on to go 2nd run-in* **6/4**[2]	
01-	3	¾	**Shower Of Hail (IRE)**[9] [4911] 5-11-6 .... AGlassonbury(7)	90+
			(M C Pipe) *j.lft: trckd ldr to 3rd: led 7th: hdd bef stumbled 3 out: rdn and tired whn lost 2nd run-in* **9/2**[3]	
/00-	4	3	**Killarney Prince (IRE)**[7] [4933] 6-11-2 .... MrJOwen(5)	80+
			(Mrs J M Mann) *led: sn clr: rdn and hdd 7th: lost tch: rallied 2 out but nvr bk on terms* **33/1**	
0-	P		**Love At Dawn**[17] 11-11-0 .... MrPMason(7)	—
			(J A T De Giles) *hld up: j. slowly 2nd: lost tch 4th: t.o whn p.u bef next* **12/1**	

6m 6.30s (32.80) **Going Correction** +1.00s/f (Soft) **5** Ran SP% **110.9**

Speed ratings: **82,77,77,76,**— CSF £3.97 TOTE £2.70: £1.60, £1.30; EX 3.70.

Owner Alvin Trowbridge **Bred** G Hooper **Trained** Milborne Port, Dorset

FOCUS

This opener proved a slog in the conditions, and the form is weak.

NOTEBOOK

Malaga Boy(IRE) got the better of a tussle with the eventual third three from home, but was soon running on empty and he was a tired horse over the last couple of flights. He is well suited by testing ground but on this evidence a trip of around two and a half miles might prove best. *(op 15-8)*

Seeador, who came down with the race at his mercy here last time, dropped back to fourth with five flights to jump. He struggled on up the straight to salvage second prize but this has to go down as disappointing. *(op 15-8)*

Shower Of Hail(IRE) was a market drifter. He generally jumped better than on his two previous attempts over hurdles, but made an error at the third last when under pressure and that did for his chance. He probably needs better ground. *(op 11-4 tchd 5-1)*

Killarney Prince(IRE), an excitable type, dropped back once headed but did plug on again to reduce the gap. *(op 25-1)*

Love At Dawn, a fair point-to-pointer making his debut over hurdles, has shown all his form on much better ground. *(op 11-1)*

54 KINGS OF TAUNTON RENAULT H'CAP HURDLE (10 hdls 1 omitted) 2m 6f 110y

3:00 (3:00) (Class 3) (0-115,111) 4-Y-0+ **£4,888** (£1,504; £752; £376)

Form				RPR
445-	1		**Monger Lane**[13] [4837] 9-11-8 107 .... WHutchinson	112+
			(K Bishop) *led to 2nd: led briefly 3 out bef def ld next: rdn clr bef last* **5/1**[2]	
312-	2	10	**Master D'Or (FR)**[5] [4956] 5-10-9 94 .... RJohnson	94+
			(P J Hobbs) *hld up in rr: gd hdwy appr 3 out to ld: hdd bef next: hld whn blnd last: rdr lost irons: no ch after* **11/8**[1]	
340-	3	20	**Versus (GER)**[11] [4868] 5-11-9 111 .... (b) DCrosse(3)	94+
			(C J Mann) *a.p: led 4th tl hdd & wknd appr 4 out* **8/1**[3]	
P06-	4	dist	**Rutland (IRE)**[27] [4669] 6-10-1 89 ow2 .... AHoneyball(3)	—
			(Miss K M George) *mid-div tl wknd after 7th: t.o* **25/1**	
050-	P		**Scarlet Fantasy**[15] [4817] 5-11-5 104 .... CLlewellyn	—
			(P A Pritchard) *in tch tl after 4th: t.o whn p.u bef 3 out* **20/1**	
40F-	P		**Haydens Field**[17] [4791] 11-11-4 110 .... MrJCook(7)	—
			(Miss H Lewis) *led 2nd to 4th: wknd after next: t.o whn p.u bef 3 out* **8/1**[3]	
P04-	P		**General Duroc (IRE)**[10] [4889] 9-11-6 105 .... (bt) WMarston	—
			(R T Phillips) *in tch: rdn 4 out: wknd next: t.o whn p.u bef 2 out* **5/1**[2]	
316-	F		**Hattington**[24] [4717] 7-11-7 106 .... OMcPhail	97+
			(M F Harris) *hld up in rr: hdwy 7th: weakeneing and wl hld in 3rd whn fell last* **12/1**	

5m 52.5s (19.00) **Going Correction** +1.00s/f (Soft) **8** Ran SP% **114.0**

Speed ratings: **106,102,95,**—,— —,—,— CSF £12.64 CT £53.02 TOTE £7.80: £1.30, £1.10, £2.50; EX 17.10.

Owner Slabs And Lucan **Bred** K Bishop **Trained** Spaxton, Somerset

FOCUS

The riders took things steadily, though the time was still 13.8 seconds faster than the opener. Only the winner really got home.

NOTEBOOK

Monger Lane was the only runner to really get home, asserting between the last two flights. A winner in heavy ground over fences, she has largely disappointed since landing a couple of listed hurdles in her younger days, but had shaped quite well at Cheltenham on her latest start and this is her time of year. *(op 8-1)*

Master D'Or(FR) cruised up to challenge at the first in the home straight, but was untidy at the next and immediately came off the bridle, finding next to nothing. All but down at the final flight, his rider making a good recovery, he has now been beaten twice from this mark and as he goes up 16lb at the weekend his immediate prospects do not look rosy. *(op 6-5 tchd 6-4)*

Versus(GER), who has been running over further, tried to kick away at the end of the back straight but was easily pegged back going to the third last. *(tchd 9-1)*

Hattington improved together with the favourite from the back of the field, but was in trouble three from home and took a tired fall at the final flight when in third. He looks high enough in the weights now but may be suited by a return to two miles. *(op 11-1 tchd 14-1)*

55 MUMFORDS RENAULT H'CAP CHASE (15 fncs 2 omitted) 2m 7f 110y

3:30 (3:30) (Class 3) (0-135,119) 5-Y-0+ **£8,606** (£2,648; £1,324; £662)

Form				RPR
F22-	1		**Curtins Hill (IRE)**[32] [4562] 11-11-6 113 .... JMMaguire	121+
			(T R George) *hld up: stdy hdwy fr 8th: wnt 2nd 3 out: led next: styd on wl* **4/1**[1]	
21P-	2	4	**Ile De Paris (FR)**[55] [4135] 6-11-7 114 .... (b[1]) RJohnson	117
			(P J Hobbs) *a in tch: led 9th: rdn and hdd 2 out: kpt on one pce* **5/1**[3]	
246-	3	6	**Gumley Gale**[34] [4528] 10-11-8 115 .... (t) WHutchinson	114+
			(K Bishop) *trckd ldr: led appr 8th: hdd next: kpt on one pce fr 4 out* **12/1**	
024-	4	6	**Dear Deal**[24] [4726] 12-11-5 112 .... (b) JTizzard	103
			(C L Tizzard) *hld up: hdwy 9th: rdn after 11th: nvr on terms fr 4 out* **4/1**[1]	
FP5-	5	4	**Another Raleagh (IRE)**[102] [3358] 11-11-12 119 .... LAspell	107+
			(A Ennis) *in rr tl hdwy 9th: wknd after 11th* **7/1**	
310-	6	9	**Follow The Flow (IRE)**[15] [4815] 9-10-12 108 .... ONelmes(3)	88+
			(P A Pritchard) *trckd ldrs: weakeneing whn j.lft fr 4 out* **9/2**[2]	
265-	7	dist	**Prominent Profile (IRE)**[39] [4449] 12-11-6 113 .... CLlewellyn	—
			(N A Twiston-Davies) *led tl hdd appr 8th: sn wknd: t.o* **6/1**	

6m 4.40s (5.10) **Going Correction** +0.40s/f (Soft) **7** Ran SP% **109.3**

Speed ratings: **107,105,103,101,100 97,**— CSF £22.07 TOTE £6.10: £3.00, £2.70; EX 14.60.

Owner Mrs Elizabeth Pitman **Bred** Thomas Davis **Trained** Slad, Gloucs

FOCUS

Conditions did not appear to be quite as testing on the chase track. This was an ordinary handicap for the money, in which the topweight was rated 16lb below the permitted ceiling.

NOTEBOOK

Curtins Hill(IRE) had jumped repeatedly out to his right when runner-up at Newton Abbot and was happier going the opposite way round. Under a patient ride, he struck the front at the second last and soon had the race in safe keeping. While the manner of this victory was pleasing, he could struggle when he goes back up the handicap. *(op 7-2 tchd 9-2)*

Ile De Paris(FR) travelled sweetly and jumped fluently in the first-time blinkers but he did not have any answers when tackled at the second last. He still has a bit to prove. *(op 10-3)*

Gumley Gale, sharper for his return to action last month, ran a sound race on ground not really thought to suit him. He should enjoy a good summer with underfoot conditions more to his liking. *(op 9-1)*

Dear Deal, another for whom the ground was no help, is on a lengthy losing run and is not getting any younger. *(op 9-2 tchd 5-1)*

Another Raleagh(IRE) has yet to recapture his form since coming back from injury. *(tchd 13-2)*

Follow The Flow(IRE)has paid with the handicapper for his purple patch last term. *(op 5-1 tchd 11-2)*

56 RENAULT VANS THAT RUN AND RUN BEGINNERS' CHASE (10 fncs 2 omitted) 2m 1f 110y

4:00 (4:00) (Class 4) 5-Y-0+ **£4,176** (£1,285; £642)

Form				RPR
614-	1		**Nyrche (FR)**[19] [4762] 5-10-11 .... RThornton	136+
			(A King) *j.w: made all: drew clr after 4 out: eased run-in: promising* **4/9**[1]	
1/P-	2	22	**Simoun (IRE)**[62] [4024] 7-11-0 .... (t) JEMoore	114
			(M C Pipe) *trckd wnr: rdn appr 4 out: wknd after next* **5/1**[3]	
156-	3	dist	**Flame Phoenix (USA)**[32] [4553] 6-11-0 .... JMMaguire	—
			(D McCain) *a last but in tch tl rdn and wknd appr 4 out: t.o* **7/2**[2]	

4m 32.9s (12.90) **Going Correction** +0.40s/f (Soft)

WFA 5 from 6yo+ 3lb **3** Ran SP% **108.1**

Speed ratings: **87,77,**— CSF £2.89 TOTE £1.50; EX 2.90.

Owner Tony Fisher & Mrs Jeni Fisher **Bred** M Dolic **Trained** Barbury Castle, Wilts

FOCUS

An interesting beginners' chase in which all three of the runners had been useful hurdlers. The winner looks a useful recruit.

NOTEBOOK

Nyrche(FR) ◆ was the best of these over hurdles and he could rate even more highly over fences judging by this impressive debut. An athletic individual, he barely put a foot wrong and scored with a good deal in hand, despite the ground being much softer than he would like. He could run again at Warwick a week on Saturday before being put away for the summer. *(op 4-7 tchd 8-13)*

Simoun(IRE), lightly raced in the last year or so, was no match for the favourite, but he jumped well enough and a similar event should come his way. *(op 10-3 tchd 3-1)*

Flame Phoenix(USA), last of the trio throughout, lost touch over the final four fences and his jumping deteriorated, having been satisfactory in the first part of the race. He will be happier on much better ground. *(op 4-1 tchd 10-3)*

57 AKS YEOVIL RENAULT H'CAP CHASE (13 fncs 2 omitted) 2m 3f 110y

4:30 (4:30) (Class 4) (0-95,82) 5-Y-0+ **£3,626** (£1,036; £518)

Form				RPR
0PP-	1		**Heartache**[70] [3884] 8-10-4 60 .... (b[1]) WHutchinson	78
			(R Mathew) *trckd ldr: led 5th: clr 9th: sed to jump rt 4 out: hrd rdn after next: drvn out* **10/3**[2]	
4B5-	2	2½	**Borehill Joker**[76] [3766] 9-11-5 82 .... WKennedy(7)	97
			(J L Spearing) *hld up: hdwy to trck wnr 9th: ev ch 3 out: no hdwy fr next* **6/5**[1]	
P66-	3	30	**My Bold Boyo**[17] [4798] 10-10-10 71 .... TJPhelan(5)	56
			(K Bishop) *chsd ldrs tl lost tch after 9th* **4/1**[3]	
430-	4	27	**Rattina (GER)**[12] [4855] 9-11-12 82 .... SDurack	40
			(M F Harris) *led to 5th: wekaned qckly after 9th: t.o* **8/1**	
P00-	P		**Heritage Castle**[9] [4915] 6-11-2 75 .... (p) AHoneyball(3)	—
			(A E Jones) *t.k.h: hld up in tch: rdn and wknd rapidly after 9th: t.o whn p.u bef 2 out* **16/1**	

5m 3.60s (11.30) **Going Correction** +0.40s/f (Soft) **5** Ran SP% **105.5**

Speed ratings: **93,92,80,69,**— CSF £7.47 TOTE £4.60: £1.90, £1.20; EX 9.50.

Owner Robin Mathew **Bred** Robin Mathew **Trained** Little Barrington, Gloucs

■ Stewards' Enquiry : W Hutchinson two-day ban: used whip with excessive frequency and without giving gelding time to respond (May 8,9)

FOCUS

A low-grade handicap in which the weights were raised 12lb at the overnight stage. It took little winning and the form does not amount to much.

NOTEBOOK

Heartache, in first-time blinkers, raced less keenly than he has done in the past and, jumping out to his right when the pressure was on, stayed on under maximum pressure to see off the favourite. He has been dropped no less than 40lb since the start of last season and ran here off a BHB mark *of a mere 60. Official explanation: trainer said, regarding the improved form shown, gelding settled well with the first-time blinkers, was able to be ridden more prominently and runs well when fresh (tchd 7-2 in a place)*

Borehill Joker loomed up to challenge at the fourth from home but could never get his head in front. *A better horse over hurdles, he might just have needed this first run since February. (op 11-8 tchd 11-10)*

My Bold Boyo has won four times at this track over hurdles, but each time on firm ground. A maiden over fences, he has yet to convince he stays this far. *(tchd 5-1)*

58 RENAULT TRAFIC VAN MARES' ONLY NOVICES' HURDLE (7 hdls 1 omitted) 2m 1f

5:00 (5:00) (Class 4) 4-Y-0+ **£3,584** (£1,024; £512)

Form					RPR
620-	1		**Fallout (IRE)**[46] [4333] 4-10-4 .... RYoung(3)		83+
			(J W Mullins) *hld up in rr: hdwy appr 3 out: led next: drvn out run-in* **11/2**		
3-	2	*nk*	**Blueland (IRE)**[45] [4349] 6-10-12 .... BJCrowley		86
			(Noel T Chance) *in tch: trckd ldr 4th: led 3 out: hdd next: rallied gamely run-in: pressed wnr to line* **5/2**[1]		
060-	3	*2*	**Seemma**[34] [4540] 5-10-12 .... SDurack		85+
			(N I M Rossiter) *in tch: kpt on same pce fr 2 out* **7/1**		
25-	4	*5*	**The Wife's Sister**[49] [4252] 4-10-7 .... JMMaguire		74
			(D McCain) *mde most tl hdd 3 out: rdn and wknd run-in* **11/4**[2]		
06-	5	*1*	**One Wild Night**[42] [4406] 5-10-7 .... LTreadwell(5)		78
			(J L Spearing) *rn in snatches: rdn appr 3 out: sn btn* **16/1**		
560/	P		**Dolly Mop**[764] [4366] 9-10-5 .... MissVStephens(7)		—
			(Miss V A Stephens) *hld up in rr: wknd rapidly appr 3 out: t.o whn p.u bef next* **33/1**		
05-	P		**In Good Faith (USA)**[32] [4560] 4-10-7 .... MFoley		—
			(N J Henderson) *trckd ldr to 2nd: rdn after 4th: wkng and 4th whn blnd 3 out: p.u bef last* **4/1**[3]		

4m 34.9s (28.20) **Going Correction** +1.00s/f (Soft)
WFA 4 from 5yo+ 5lb **7** Ran SP% **111.9**
Speed ratings: **73,72,71,69,69** —,— CSF £19.28 TOTE £6.20: £2.50, £2.00; EX 27.40 Place 6 £6.77, Place 5 £5.95.
Owner Mrs Hilary Pike **Bred** Brian Miller **Trained** Wilsford-Cum-Lake, Wilts

FOCUS
A weak event run at a steady pace in a pedestrian time that produced something of a bunch finish.

NOTEBOOK
Fallout(IRE), who showed ability in bumpers, idled once in front and lost her lead after landing flat-footed at the last, but rallied close home. She may find things a struggle over hurdles now she has incurred a penalty. *(op 8-1)*
Blueland(IRE), another making her hurdling debut, nosed ahead on the run-in but was just denied. A step up in trip will help her. *(op 7-2 tchd 9-4)*
Seemma, who like the first two was tackling hurdles for the first time following four runs in bumpers, was more inconvenienced than most by the lack of pace but was keeping on at the finish. *(op 10-1)*
The Wife's Sisterwill be seen in a better light when faced with a greater test of stamina. *(tchd 3-1)*
One Wild Night, a keen mare making her hurdles debut, is probably flattered to finish so close. *(op 20-1)*
Dolly Mop *Official explanation: jockey said mare was unsuited by heavy, soft in places ground (op 9-4)*
In Good Faith(USA) *Official explanation: jockey said filly had a breathing problem (op 9-4)*
T/Plt: £16.30 to a £1 stake. Pool: £31,808.40. 1,421.90 winning tickets. T/Qpdt: £7.70 to a £1 stake. Pool: £1,495.40. 142.90 winning tickets. JS

KELSO (L-H)

Wednesday, April 27

OFFICIAL GOING: Soft (good to soft in places)
Wind: fresh, against

59 PETER ALLAN WEDDINGS AT THE RACECOURSE MAIDEN HURDLE (10 hdls) 2m 2f

5:40 (5:43) (Class 4) 4-Y-0+ **£3,926** (£1,208; £604; £302)

Form				RPR
243-	1		**Tandava (IRE)**[7] [4923] 7-11-2 107 .... MBradburne	101
			(Mrs S C Bradburne) *led to 5th: led briefly 4 out: drvn next: rallied to ld run in: kpt on wl* **2/1**[1]	
5-	2	*1 1/4*	**Bergerac (NZ)**[83] [3660] 7-11-2 .... HOliver	100
			(R C Guest) *keen: chsd ldrs: rdn to ld bef last: hdd run in: kpt on* **20/1**	
640-	3	*6*	**King's Protector**[120] [3039] 5-11-2 99 .... ADobbin	98+
			(M D Hammond) *in tch: pushed along whn blnd 3 out: no imp tl hung rt and styd on run in: no ch w first two* **10/1**	
550-	4	*shd*	**Bishop's Bridge (IRE)**[10] [4883] 7-10-6 109 .... (b[1]) DHarold(10)	95+
			(Andrew Turnell) *keen: hld up: hdwy on outside to ld after 4 out: hdd bef last: no ex* **6/1**	
034-	5	*2 1/2*	**Bollin Thomas**[16] [4270] 7-11-2 101 .... RGarritty	91
			(T D Easterby) *prom tl rdn and outpcd fr 2 out* **5/1**[2]	
0-	6	*17*	**The Maystone (IRE)**[46] [4323] 5-10-13 .... PBuchanan(3)	74
			(B Mactaggart) *in tch: outpcd bef 4 out: n.d after* **66/1**	
332-	7	*2 1/2*	**Quarry Island (IRE)**[17] [4782] 4-10-4 96 .... JimCrowley	60
			(M Todhunter) *hld up: sme hdwy after 4 out: no imp fr next* **6/1**	
000-	8	*1 3/4*	**Simon's Heights**[16] [4807] 4-10-11 .... KRenwick	65
			(Miss P Robson) *towards rr: n.d* **50/1**	
PP4-	9	*2 1/2*	**Lord Rosskit (IRE)**[16] [4807] 5-11-2 .... FKeniry	68
			(G M Moore) *a bhd* **20/1**	
50-	10	*1/2*	**Minnigaff (IRE)**[47] [4299] 5-11-2 .... BHarding	67
			(N G Richards) *hld up: shkn up 4 out: sn btn* **40/1**	
600-	11	*6*	**What A Night**[24] [4713] 6-11-2 .... ADempsey	61
			(Mrs A C Hamilton) *w ldr: led 5th: hit and hdd 4 out: btn after next* **100/1**	
00-	12	*18*	**Thepubhorse**[149] [2549] 5-10-11 .... DCCostello(5)	43
			(Mrs H O Graham) *nt fluent: in tch to 1/2-way: sn btn* **100/1**	
500-	P		**Claymills (IRE)**[32] [4559] 5-11-2 .... RMcGrath	—
			(P Beaumont) *a bhd: t.o whn p.u bef 2 out* **66/1**	
PP0-	P		**Flashy Filly**[120] [3043] 5-10-2 .... MJMcAlister(7)	—
			(J C Haynes) *a bhd: t.o whn p.u bef 2 out* **100/1**	
5-	P		**No Hesitation**[142] [2677] 4-10-11 .... NPMulholland	—
			(Mrs S C Bradburne) *sddle slipped and p.u bef 2nd* **100/1**	
/32-	U		**Fencote (IRE)**[16] [4807] 8-11-2 102 .... ATinkler	91
			(P Beaumont) *in tch: hdwy and 2l down whn stmbld bdly and uns rdr 2 out* **11/2**[3]	

4m 42.9s (11.40) **Going Correction** +0.35s/f (Yiel)
WFA 4 from 5yo+ 5lb **16** Ran SP% **123.9**
Speed ratings: **88,87,84,84,83 76,74,74,73,72 70,62,—,—,— —** CSF £46.45 TOTE £3.10: £1.10, £4.30, £3.20; EX 102.20.
Owner Black & White Communication (Scotland) Ltd **Bred** Newberry Stud Company **Trained** Cunnoquhie, Fife
■ Stewards' Enquiry : D Harold ten-day ban: failed to ride out for third place (May 8-17)

FOCUS
A very ordinary event and an ordinary pace resulted in a moderate time, 8.7 seconds slower than the later handicap over the same trip. As a result the race has been rated negatively.

NOTEBOOK
Tandava(IRE) looks fully exposed but probably did not have to improve too much to win a very ordinary event. He showed the right attitude but will be vulnerable under a penalty in this type of event or to progressive sorts in handicaps. *(op 11-4 tchd 3-1 in places)*
Bergerac(NZ) ◆, like several from this stable, failed to settle in the early stages but turned in an improved effort and looks likely to win an ordinary event in the North in due course. *(op 14-1)*
King's Protector was not disgraced on this first run since December but, although the step up to two and a half miles will suit, he is likely to continue to look vulnerable in this grade. *(op 11-1 tchd 12-1)*
Bishop's Bridge(IRE), tried in blinkers, ran a bit better than the bare form as he failed to settle and was asked for his effort a fair way out. However he does look exposed and is likely to remain vulnerable in this grade. *(op 9-1)*
Bollin Thomas was not disgraced in terms of form but has had plenty of chances and does not look one to place maximum faith in.
The Maystone(IRE) hinted at ability on this hurdles debut but will have to fare a good deal better to win in this grade. *(op 100-1 tchd 50-1)*
Quarry Island(IRE) is essentially a disappointing type who was below her best this time and remains one to to tread carefully with. *(op 11-2)*
No Hesitation *Official explanation: jockey said saddle slipped*

60 UBS LAING & CRUICKSHANK LTD NOVICES' CHASE (12 fncs) 2m 1f

6:10 (6:13) (Class 3) 5-Y-0+ **£5,434** (£1,672; £836; £418)

Form				RPR
221-	1		**Tribal Dispute**[22] [4734] 8-11-6 109 .... RGarritty	106+
			(T D Easterby) *prom: rdn to ld run in: kpt on* **5/4**[1]	
403-	2	*1 1/2*	**Your Advantage (IRE)**[10] [4873] 5-10-8 110 .... (tp) PBuchanan(3)	92
			(Miss Lucinda V Russell) *cl up: led 3rd to run in: kpt on* **5/2**[2]	
304-	3	*9*	**Snooty Eskimo (IRE)**[54] [4155] 13-10-10 66 ow3 .... MrHNorton(7)	90+
			(W T Reed) *chsd ldrs: outpcd 2 out: mstke last: no imp* **22/1**	
000-	4	*2*	**The Names Bond**[26] [4683] 7-10-4 .... DHarold(10)	86+
			(Andrew Turnell) *nt fluent and sn detatched: kpt on fr last: nvr nrr* **11/2**[3]	
550-	5	*1 1/4*	**Spectrum Star**[79] [3741] 5-10-11 .... PRobson	80
			(F P Murtagh) *prom tl mstke and outpcd 3 out: n.d after* **25/1**	
604-	6	*11*	**Moscow Dancer (IRE)**[10] [4873] 8-11-0 104 .... NPMulholland	77+
			(P Monteith) *cl up: ev ch 2 out: rdn and wknd last* **7/1**	

4m 30.6s (10.10) **Going Correction** +0.30s/f (Yiel)
WFA 5 from 6yo+ 3lb **6** Ran SP% **109.1**
Speed ratings: **88,87,83,82,81 76** CSF £4.61 TOTE £1.90: £1.30, £1.60; EX 4.50.
Owner Mrs Jennifer E Pallister **Bred** G R Parkin And Sons **Trained** Great Habton, N Yorks
■ Stewards' Enquiry : D Harold ten-day ban: breach of Rule 156, rode an ill-judged race (May 18-22,24-28)

FOCUS
Another uncompetitive race run at only a fair pace at best and a modest winning time for the grade. The winner is value for further with the third setting the standard.

NOTEBOOK
Tribal Dispute did not have to improve to win an uncompetitive event but, given his jumping was sound and he again travelled well, should be able to hold his own in ordinary handicap company around this trip. *(op 11-10 tchd 11-8 in a place)*
Your Advantage(IRE) looks exposed but had the run of the race and performed creditably with the first-time cheekpieces fitted. He is capable of winning a modest race over fences but looks vulnerable to anything progressive. *(op 3-1 tchd 10-3)*
Snooty Eskimo(IRE) looked to have a very stiff task at the weights and his proximity casts a doubt as to the true worth of this form. This longstanding maiden under Rules looks one to continue to field against. *(op 20-1)*
The Names Bond's rider was banned for ten days for riding an ill-judged race on this chase debut (below the pick of his hurdles form) but given he failed to have any sort of cut at his fences early on this looked a fairly harsh decision. He may be capable of better but is also not the most consistent and would not be one to lump on to make amends next time. *(tchd 5-1)*
Spectrum Star was not totally disgraced in the face of a stiff task on this chase debut, but his proximity is further proof that this bare form may not be totally reliable. *(tchd 20-1)*
Moscow Dancer(IRE), who has yet to reproduce the pick of his hurdles form over fences, ran a bit better than the bare form suggests, but again folded tamely and looks one to tread carefully with at present. *(tchd 8-1)*

61 ROYAL BANK OF SCOTLAND H'CAP HURDLE (10 hdls) 2m 2f

6:45 (6:46) (Class 3) (0-125,113) 4-Y-0+ **£7,020** (£2,160; £1,080; £540)

Form				RPR
54-	1		**Donovan (NZ)**[36] [4510] 6-10-12 102 .... (p) LMcGrath(3)	111+
			(R C Guest) *hld up: reminder 6th: hdwy to ld 3 out: kpt on wl* **7/1**[3]	
014-	2	*3 1/2*	**Dark Ben (FR)**[24] [4711] 5-11-3 109 .... DCCostello(5)	114
			(Miss Kate Milligan) *hld up in tch: hdwy appr 3 out: effrt next: kpt on fr last: nt rch wnr* **15/2**	
/03-	3	*1/2*	**River Alder**[12] [4847] 7-11-7 108 .... MBradburne	113
			(J M Dun) *prom: rdn and outpcd after 3 out: kpt on wl run in* **8/1**	
11F-	4	*3/4*	**Thoutmosis (USA)**[46] [4321] 6-11-9 113 .... GBerridge(3)	117
			(L Lungo) *hld up: outpcd 4 out: kpt on run in: no imp* **9/2**[2]	
OPP-	5	*3/4*	**Merryvale Man**[12] [4510] 8-10-10 102 .... DMcGann(5)	106+
			(Miss Kariana Key) *chsd ldrs: hit 6th and 3 out: outpcd last* **20/1**	
13U-	6	*1 1/2*	**Brave Vision**[32] [4553] 9-11-4 112 .... EWhillans(7)	115+
			(A C Whillans) *led to 2nd: cl up: ev ch to 2 out: hit last: outpcd run in* **12/1**	
OP-3	7	*11*	**Mister Moussac**[3] [13] 6-10-3 97 .... (p) SCrawford(7)	94+
			(Miss Kariana Key) *cl up: led 5th to 4 out: outpcd fr next* **20/1**	
OPP-	8	*5*	**Word Gets Around (IRE)**[103] [3350] 7-10-12 99 .... BGibson	85
			(L Lungo) *hld up: rdn 4 out: n.d* **11/1**	
306-	9	*8*	**Day Du Roy (FR)**[32] [4557] 7-11-7 108 .... JimCrowley	86
			(Miss L C Siddall) *hld up: hdwy after 4 out: rdn and wknd after next* **16/1**	
2F1-	10	*17*	**Classic Event (IRE)**[21] [4166] 4-11-7 113 .... RGarritty	69
			(T D Easterby) *plld hrd: hld up: rdn bef 3 out: sn btn* **10/1**	
360-	11	*4*	**Prize Ring**[32] [4553] 6-11-7 108 .... FKeniry	65
			(G M Moore) *led 2nd to 5th: wknd qckly after next* **16/1**	
1P/	12	*6*	**Blue Venture (IRE)**[280] [1355] 5-10-8 95 .... ADempsey	46
			(B Mactaggart) *plld hrd: chsd ldrs: led 4 out to next: sn btn* **50/1**	
052-	P		**Mazzareme (IRE)**[30] [4625] 7-11-9 110 .... ADobbin	—
			(N G Richards) *mstkes: hld up: wknd 4 out: t.o whn p.u and dismntd 2 out* **7/2**[1]	

4m 34.2s (2.70) **Going Correction** +0.35s/f (Yiel)
WFA 4 from 5yo+ 5lb **13** Ran SP% **124.1**
Speed ratings: **108,106,106,105,105 104,100,97,94,86 84,82,—** CSF £60.18 CT £441.94 TOTE £9.70: £2.90, £2.60, £2.50; EX 47.20.
Owner Concertina Racing Too **Bred** B C Morton **Trained** Brancepeth, Co Durham

FOCUS
An ordinary handicap in which the pace was sound and this form should prove reliable.

NOTEBOOK
Donovan(NZ) is a fair sort when on his game, had the race run to suit and notched his fourth win from his last ten starts. His stable is in decent heart and he appeals as the type to win more races. *(op 9-1)*

Dark Ben(FR), a dual winner over two miles and one furlong at Sedgefield, ran right up to his best and given he has only had eight races over hurdles, may well be capable of better in this sphere. He looks worth a try over two and a half miles. *(op 8-1 tchd 9-1)*
River Alder ◆ ran well given this course places more of an emphasis on speed than stamina, and she will be of much more interest returned to two and a half miles at courses like Hexham or Carlisle.
Thoutmosis(USA), from a stable going well at present, may not be the easiest of rides but ran *close to his best and left the impression that he is well worth another try over two and a half miles. (tchd 4-1 and 5-1 in a place)*
Merryvale Man has not proved entirely reliable but has slipped to a fair mark and ran his best race for some time over hurdles. Although he tends to make the odd mistake, he is one to keep an eye on in similar company. *(tchd 25-1)*
Brave Vision, from a stable going well, ran creditably but again left the impression that he is a few pounds too high in the weights at present. *(op 10-1)*
Classic Event(IRE) *Official explanation: jockey said gelding was unsuited by soft, good to soft in places ground (op 7-1)*
Mazzareme(IRE) *Official explanation: jockey said gelding lost its action (op 5-1)*

62 SIS H'CAP CHASE (FOR THE HADDINGTON JUBILEE CUP) (19 fncs) 3m 1f
7:20 (7:20) (Class 3) (0-125,125) 5-Y-0+ **£6,714** (£2,066; £1,033; £516)

Form RPR
53F- **1** **Time To Reflect (IRE)**^{11} [4864] 6-10-3 **102**..........(p) HOliver 111+
(R C Guest) *hld up: smooth hdwy 4 out: shkn up to ld run in: kpt on wl* **7/1**
216- **2** *2* **King's Bounty**^{44} [4370] 9-10-7 **106**..........(b) JimCrowley 111
(T D Easterby) *keen: chsd ldrs: led 13th: rdn 3 out: hdd run in: kpt on* **5/1**^{3}
61-P **3** *1 1/4* **Wildfield Rufo (IRE)**^{3} [12] 10-10-10 **109**..........(p) RMcGrath 113
(Mrs K Walton) *prom: effrt bef 3 out: outpcd after next: kpt on fr last* **11/1**
P34- **4** *1 3/4* **Wise Man (IRE)**^{6} [4946] 10-11-9 **125**.......... PBuchanan$^{(3)}$ 127
(N W Alexander) *hld up in tch: nt fluent and outpcd 4 out: kpt on fr 2 out: no imp run in* **8/1**
23- **5** *27* **Tarbolton Moss**^{46} [4318] 10-10-1 **100**.......... PRobson 92+
(M Todhunter) *chsd ldrs: rdn 13th: outpcd fr 3 out* **7/2**^{1}
50P- **6** *6* **Hussard Collonges (FR)**^{11} [4861] 10-11-12 **125**.......... RGarritty 114+
(P Beaumont) *cl up: led 8th to 13th: wknd fr 2 out* **4/1**^{2}
132- **P** **Heidi Iii (FR)**^{36} [4512] 10-10-13 **112**..........(v^{1}) ADobbin —
(M D Hammond) *led to 8th: rdn along 11th: wknd after 13th: t.o whn p.u bef 3 out* **4/1**^{2}
6m 31.6s (3.20) **Going Correction** +0.30s/f (Yiel) 7 Ran SP% **110.8**
Speed ratings: **106,105,104,104,95 93,—** CSF £38.81 CT £364.42 TOTE £9.10: £3.20, £3.90; EX 28.50.
Owner Concertina Racing Three **Bred** Edward Ryan **Trained** Brancepeth, Co Durham

FOCUS
A fair handicap with no progressive sorts on view and the pace was just fair. The winner can be rated better than the bare form.

NOTEBOOK
Time To Reflect(IRE) showed himself none the worse for his Ayr experience with his best effort yet. He is capable of winning after reassessment but it is worth remembering that he disappointed several times after winning in a similar manner at Catterick in January. *(op 6-1)*
King's Bounty took a good hold in a race run at just a fair pace but ran his race and looks a good guide to the level of this form. There is no reason why he should not continue to give a good account. *(tchd 11-2)*
Wildfield Rufo(IRE) is inclined to run the odd poor race, as he did at Wetherby three days earlier, but returned to something like his best this time. However, he is likely to remain vulnerable in competitive handicaps from his current mark. *(op 10-1 tchd 12-1)*
Wise Man(IRE), turned out quickly after his Perth exertions the previous week, fared a good deal better but, although a stiffer test of stamina on arguably softer ground would have suited, he is likely to continue to struggle from this mark. *(op 10-1)*
Tarbolton Moss should have been suited by the overnight rain but again disappointed and looks one to have serious reservations about at present. *(op 5-1 tchd 6-1)*
Hussard Collonges(FR), who looked a picture, has tumbled down the weights but continues to disappoint. *Official explanation: jockey said gelding lost a shoe (tchd 9-2)*
Heidi Iii(FR), closely matched with Wildfield Rufo on Wetherby form, was most disappointing tried *in the visor and he remains one to tread carefully with. Official explanation: jockey said gelding ran flat (op 5-2)*

63 CHARLIE BROWN UNITED BORDER HUNTERS' CHASE (19 fncs) 3m 1f
7:55 (7:55) (Class 6) 5-Y-0+ **£3,041** (£869; £434)

Form RPR
U46- **1** **Geordies Express**^{16} [4811] 13-11-11.......... EWhillans$^{(7)}$ 112+
(G T Bewley) *chsd ldrs: effrt 3 out: led last: styd on strly* **8/1**^{3}
1U4- **2** *19* **Emperor Ross (IRE)**^{26} [4682] 10-11-11 118.......... MrCJCallow$^{(7)}$ 93
(N G Richards) *hld up: hdwy 1/2-way: disp ld 3 out to last: sn rdn and hung lft: no ex* **4/5**^{1}
P/2- **3** *3 1/2* **Lord O'All Seasons (IRE)**^{10} [4877] 12-11-7 100.......... MissRDavidson$^{(5)}$ 86+
(Miss M A Neill) *mstkes: hld up: outpcd whn mstke 4 out: rallied between last two: no imp* **9/1**
P53- **4** *10* **High Expectations (IRE)**^{16} [4809] 10-11-7 72.......... MrTDavidson$^{(5)}$ 74
(J S Haldane) *cl up: chal 14th: led 4 out to last: sn btn* **33/1**
/3P- **5** *1* **Blyth Brook**^{47} [4304] 13-11-11 95.......... MrJARichardson$^{(7)}$ 83+
(W T Reed) *prom tl rdn and outpcd after 2 out: btn whn blnd bdly last* **25/1**
P3P- **6** *3/4* **Nisbet**^{16} [4811] 11-11-11 85.......... MissJRiding$^{(7)}$ 79+
(Miss M Bremner) *cl up: led 10th to 4 out: rdn whn hit 2 out: sn btn* **16/1**
41P/ **P** **Backsheesh (IRE)**^{17} 10-11-9..........(t) MrGTuer$^{(3)}$ —
(G Tuer) *led to 10th: lost pl 12th: t.o whn p.u bef 2 out* **11/4**^{2}
6m 38.3s (9.90) **Going Correction** +0.30s/f (Yiel) 7 Ran SP% **116.0**
Speed ratings: **96,89,88,85,85 85,—** CSF £16.28 TOTE £9.80: £2.00, £1.90; EX 22.20.
Owner G T Bewley **Bred** G Revitt **Trained** Hawick, Borders

FOCUS
The usual mixed bag and a race that did not take as much winning as had looked likely. The pace was just fair.

NOTEBOOK
Geordies Express took advantage of a below-par run by Emperor Ross to notch his fourth win over course and distance and he is a fair sort for this grade. *(op 9-1 tchd 10-1)*
Emperor Ross(IRE) looked the one to beat on his previous runs in this sphere but, after travelling strongly and jumping soundly, found next to nothing on this rain-softened ground. He will need a sound surface over this trip. *(op 10-11 tchd evens)*
Lord O'All Seasons(IRE) was not disgraced but will have to jump better than he did this time if he is to win races in this sphere. *(op 8-1)*
High Expectations(IRE) was not disgraced in the face of a stiff task and looks the type to win again in ordinary point company. *(op 25-1)*
Blyth Brook was not disgraced given he needs better ground and he would have finished closer but *for making a hash of the final fence. He is one to keep an eye out for back on a sound surface. (op 16-1)*
Nisbet was not totally disgraced in the face of a stiff task but remains below the pick of last season's form in this sphere.
Backsheesh(IRE) was most disappointing after a recent point victory but would not be one to write off yet. *(op 7-2 tchd 4-1 in places)*

64 ANDERSONS FARM BUSINESS CONSULTANTS H'CAP HURDLE (11 hdls) 2m 6f 110y
8:25 (8:26) (Class 3) (0-125,123) 4-Y-0+ **£4,927** (£1,516; £758; £379)

Form RPR
5/3- **1** **Ever Present (IRE)**^{46} [4321] 7-10-13 **110**.......... ADobbin 112+
(N G Richards) *hld up: hdwy whn nt fluent 3 out: led bef last: drvn out* **13/8**^{1}
532- **2** *1 3/4* **Roobihoo (IRE)**^{16} [4812] 6-10-10 **107**.......... RMcGrath 106+
(C Grant) *chsd ldrs: ev ch 3 out: sn drvn: kpt on fr last: nt rch wnr* **5/2**^{2}
6PP- **3** *3/4* **Hunters Tweed**^{6} [4946] 9-11-12 **123**..........(b) RGarritty 122+
(P Beaumont) *cl up: led after 3 out to bef last: rdn and nt qckn run in* **16/1**
F10- **4** *5* **Sikasso (USA)**^{4} [4977] 9-9-8 **98**.......... CDSharkey$^{(7)}$ 91+
(Mrs K Walton) *hld up in tch: effrt whn nt fluent 3 out: nt qckn next* **7/1**^{3}
000- **5** *8* **Divet Hill**^{32} [4549] 11-10-10 **110**.......... PBuchanan$^{(3)}$ 97+
(Mrs A Hamilton) *led to after 3 out: sn outpcd* **25/1**
502- **6** *1 1/2* **Crystal Gift**^{6} [4948] 13-10-6 **110**.......... EWhillans$^{(7)}$ 93
(A C Whillans) *prom: lost pl 1/2-way: rallied 4 out: sn btn* **8/1**
000- **7** *5* **Political Sox**^{53} [4186] 11-10-2 **106**.......... GThomas$^{(7)}$ 84
(R Nixon) *hld up: struggling bef 4 out: sn btn* **40/1**
010- **8** *27* **Mr Midaz**^{24} [4711] 6-10-4 **101**.......... BHarding 52
(D W Whillans) *in tch tl wknd bef 4 out* **14/1**
223- **9** *20* **Helvetius**^{70} [3886] 9-10-0 **97** oh4.......... KJohnson 28
(W T Reed) *prom to 5 out: sn lost pl* **25/1**
1/P- **P** **Intensity**^{206} [1565] 9-10-5 **102**.......... MBradburne —
(S B Bell) *hld up: struggling 5 out: t.o whn p.u bef 2 out* **33/1**
5m 45.0s (7.20) **Going Correction** +0.35s/f (Yiel) 10 Ran SP% **115.9**
Speed ratings: **101,100,100,98,95 95,93,83,77,—** CSF £5.96 CT £44.53 TOTE £1.80: £1.10, £1.40, £5.20; EX 8.00 Place 6 £89.10, Place 5 £42.18.
Owner Ramsay Donald Brown **Bred** Martin Cullinane **Trained** Greystoke, Cumbria

FOCUS
An ordinary handicap but one run at a fair pace and, with the first three close to their marks, this form should prove reliable.

NOTEBOOK
Ever Present(IRE) ◆ fully confirmed recent promise over this longer trip and, given he is in very good hands and is only lightly raced, appeals strongly as the type to win more races. *(tchd 6-5)*
Roobihoo(IRE) appreciated the overnight rain and again ran his race. He has proved a reliable sort *who looks a good guide to the level of this form and should continue to give a good account. (op 10-3 tchd 7-2)*
Hunters Tweed showed more than enough to suggest he can win races in this sphere, but he is vulnerable from his current mark to progressive or well handicapped types and he has also flattered to deceive on occasions.
Sikasso(USA) fared much better than in a recent outing at Market Rasen and, on this evidence, looks well worth a try over three miles. *(op 8-1 tchd 9-1 in a place)*
Divet Hill ◆ was anything but disgraced on ground that would have been plenty soft enough for him, and is one to keep a close eye on over hurdles when the ground firms up. *(op 20-1)*
Crystal Gift, flattered by his proximity to a progressive sort at Perth, was below that level on this occasion and, given he is not the most consistent and has not won since 2002, looks one to tread carefully with. *(op 7-1)*
T/Plt: £139.60 to a £1 stake. Pool: £47,308.25. 247.30 winning tickets. T/Qpdt: £34.60 to a £1 stake. Pool: £3,484.00. 74.40 winning tickets. RY

39 PUNCHESTOWN (R-H)
Wednesday, April 27
OFFICIAL GOING: Yielding to soft

65a AON GROUP/SEAN BARRETT BLOODSTOCK INSURANCE HURDLE 2m
2:00 (2:01) 4-Y-0 **£13,851** (£4,063; £1,936; £659)

RPR
1 **Strides Of Fire (IRE)**^{13} [4842] 4-10-7 92.......... RMMoran$^{(7)}$ 114
(John A Codd, Ire) *trckd ldrs in 4th: 3rd 3 out: cl 2nd travelling wl next: led ent st: sn rdn clr: styd on strly* **20/1**
2 *7* **Afrad (FR)**^{11} [4858] 4-11-7.......... MAFitzgerald 114
(N J Henderson) *settled 2nd: nt fluent early: led after 2 out: rdn and hdd ent st: sn outpcd: kpt on fr last* **4/1**^{2}
3 *3* **Dabiroun (IRE)**^{20} [4749] 4-11-2 124.......... MissNCarberry$^{(5)}$ 111
(Paul Nolan, Ire) *mid-div: hdwy on outer bef 4 out: 4th 3 out: 3rd and no imp after 2 out* **11/2**^{3}
4 *2* **Skyhawk (IRE)**^{40} [4433] 4-11-7.......... RWalsh 109
(Henry De Bromhead, Ire) *chsd ldrs in 3rd: 5th 3 out: kpt on u.p fr next* **12/1**
5 *4 1/2* **Hurricane Alley (IRE)**^{13} [4842] 4-11-7.......... SPMcCann 105
(G M Lyons, Ire) *led: j.lft 4th: hdd after 2 out: 4th and no ex early st* **12/1**
6 *2* **Articulation**^{13} 4-10-11.......... AndrewJMcNamara$^{(3)}$ 96
(C Byrnes, Ire) *rr of mid-div: prog into 9th after 2 out: rdn and kpt on* **25/1**
7 *2* **Dujareva**^{120} [3066] 4-10-4.......... JFLevins$^{(5)}$ 89
(J P Broderick, Ire) *hld up: rdn and styd on fr 3 out* **50/1**
8 *1 1/2* **Impartial**^{29} [4647] 4-11-7.......... PCarberry 99
(S J Mahon, Ire) *rr of mid-div: 11th 4 out: no imp fr next* **20/1**
9 *1* **Under Oath**^{52} [4224] 4-11-0 100..........(p) ADLeigh$^{(7)}$ 98
(Mrs John Harrington, Ire) *chsd ldrs: 8th 4 out: rdn and no imp fr next* **20/1**
10 *2 1/2* **Dalton (FR)**^{43} [4386] 4-11-7.......... DNRussell 96
(E J O'Grady, Ire) *mid-div: 10th 4 out: no imp fr next* **14/1**
11 *7* **Double Dizzy**^{30} [4616] 4-11-0.......... AThornton 82
(R H Buckler) *chsd ldrs: 6th early: 9th 4 out: no ex fr next* **25/1**
12 *4* **Levitator**^{29} [4646] 4-11-4.......... TGMRyan$^{(3)}$ 85
(M J P O'Brien, Ire) *trckd ldrs on inner: 6th 1/2-way: no ex after 3 out* **11/8**^{1}
13 *1/2* **Slightly Shifty (IRE)**^{2} [4727] 4-10-11..........(b) PWFlood$^{(3)}$ 77
(J T Gorman, Ire) *chsd ldrs: 7th and rdn 4 out: wknd after next* **25/1**
14 *7* **Twofan (USA)**^{272} 4-10-7.......... MJFerris$^{(7)}$ 70
(C Byrnes, Ire) *towards rr: effrt 2 out: sn no ex* **20/1**
15 *7* **Connemara Rose (IRE)**^{25} [4698] 4-10-6..........(t) APLane$^{(3)}$ 58
(Francis Ennis, Ire) *mid-div: 10th appr 1/2-way: no ex after 3 out: bad mstke next* **50/1**
16 *13* **Kyno (IRE)**^{13} [4842] 4-11-0.......... KWhelan 50
(Michael David Murphy, Ire) *rr of mid-div: no ex after 4 out* **33/1**

17 *4* **Gun Tote (USA)**[7] 4-11-0 .... JPElliott 46
(P Hughes, Ire) *rr of mid-div: wknd fr 4 out* **20/1**

18 *14* **Bakhtyar**[196] 4-10-11 .... MFMooney(3) 32
(A J Martin, Ire) *nvr a factor: t.o* **33/1**

19 *2* **Broken River (IRE)** 4-11-0 .... JLCullen 30
(P J Rothwell, Ire) *a bhd: t.o* **50/1**

20 *7* **Fourpointone** 4-10-7 .... BCByrnes(7) 23
(E McNamara, Ire) *a bhd: t.o* **50/1**

21 *3 1/2* **Areba Rocky (IRE)**[10] [4893] 4-10-11 .... AJDonoghue(3) 20
(P J Rothwell, Ire) *a bhd: trailing thrght: t.o* **66/1**

22 *1 1/2* **Clearwaterdreamer (IRE)**[13] [4842] 4-11-0 .... DTEvans 18
(Martin Brassil, Ire) *a bhd: t.o* **66/1**

23 *1* **Longueville Manor (FR)**[25] [4698] 4-11-0 .... CO'Dwyer 17
(Niall Madden, Ire) *rr of mid-div: wknd fr 4 out: t.o* **50/1**

24 *11* **Tuckerman**[13] [4842] 4-11-0 .... BMCash 6
(A J Martin, Ire) *a bhd: t.o* **33/1**

25 *nk* **Victory Lap (GER)**[13] [4842] 4-10-2 .... MTMannion(7) 1
(G T Lynch, Ire) *rr of mid-div: wknd 4 out: t.o* **66/1**

4m 1.50s **Going Correction** +0.20s/f (Yiel) **25** Ran SP% **158.0**
Speed ratings: 116,112,111,110,107 106,105,105,104,103 99,97,97,94,90 84,82,75,74,70 68,68,67,62,61 CSF £106.47 TOTE £108.80: £10.40, £1.60, £1.10, £1.60; DF 307.90.
Owner Make Six Syndicate **Bred** Kip McCreery **Trained** Clearistown, Co. Wexford

NOTEBOOK
Afrad(FR) was readily outpaced by the winner in the straight after leading briefly after the second last. *(op 4/1 tchd 7/2)*
Double Dizzy dropped right out after the third-last flight.
Levitator *Official explanation: vet said colt had a respiratory tract infection (op 5/4)*

66a BEWLEYS HOTELS EUROPEAN BREEDERS FUND MARES HURDLE (LISTED RACE) 2m 2f
2:35 (2:35) 4-Y-0+ **£23,085** (£6,773; £3,226; £1,099)

RPR

1 **Blazing Liss (IRE)**[29] [4647] 6-11-7 128 .... DNRussell 125
(John E Kiely, Ire) *trckd ldrs: 6th 1/2-way: impr to ld travelling wl after 3 out: stmbld and hdd briefly after 2 out: rdn and styd on wl fr bef last* **15/8**[1]

2 *2 1/2* **Mags Benefit (IRE)**[12] [4847] 5-11-3 113 .... (t) KHadnett 119
(T Hogan, Ire) *mid-div: 10th 4 out: 7th and hdwy next: 3rd 2 out: 2nd bef last: kpt on u.p* **16/1**

3 *1* **Greenhall Rambler (IRE)**[13] [4590] 6-11-4 118 .... GLee 119
(P A Fahy, Ire) *rr of mid-div: 11th 4 out: hdwy next: 3rd bef last: kpt on u.p* **12/1**

4 *2 1/2* **Sunami Storm (IRE)**[31] [4595] 7-11-4 115 .... RWalsh 116
(W P Mullins, Ire) *prom: 4th 1/2-way: 2nd after 3 out: rdn to ld briefly after 2 out: 4th appr last: kpt on same pce* **10/1**

5 *1 1/2* **Queen Astrid (IRE)**[31] [4595] 5-11-3 .... PCarberry 114
(D K Weld, Ire) *cl up: 2nd 4 out: 4th 2 out: 6th early st: kpt on* **7/1**[3]

6 *1 1/2* **Court Leader (IRE)**[31] [4595] 7-11-1 115 .... MAFitzgerald 110
(Thomas Mullins, Ire) *trckd ldrs: 5th 4 out: 3rd appr next: 6th and rdn 2 out: kpt on same pce* **14/1**

7 *shd* **American Jennie (IRE)**[25] [4699] 7-11-1 106 .... BMCash 110
(Michael Cullen, Ire) *hld up: prog into 9th after 4 out: kpt on fr 2 out* **33/1**

8 *14* **Shiminnie (IRE)**[31] [4599] 6-10-11 104 .... RGeraghty 92
(J R H Fowler, Ire) *towards rr: kpt on fr bef 2 out* **50/1**

9 *3* **Maryannthedancer (IRE)**[13] [4729] 5-11-3 106 .... JMAllen 95
(Ms M Flynn, Ire) *towards rr: hdwy into 9th 3 out: rdn and no imp fr next* **33/1**

10 *4* **Ocras Mor (IRE)**[38] [4486] 7-11-4 117 .... DFO'Regan 92
(Miss S Cox, Ire) *trckd ldrs in 5th: impr to ld after 5 out: hdd after 3 out: sn no ex* **12/1**

11 *7* **Waterlily (IRE)**[31] [4590] 6-11-1 113 .... BJGeraghty 82
(Mrs John Harrington, Ire) *trckd ldrs: 8th 4 out: 6th next: wknd 2 out* **20/1**

12 *1 1/2* **Mrs Wallensky (IRE)**[31] [4595] 7-11-4 122 .... JLCullen 83
(Paul Nolan, Ire) *towards rr: sme prog after 3 out: no imp fr next* **9/2**[2]

13 *3 1/2* **An Culainn Beag (IRE)**[30] [4635] 9-11-4 100 .... MJFerris 80
(Denis P Murphy, Ire) *mid-div: 9th 1/2-way: no ex after 4 out* **40/1**

14 *4 1/2* **Barrack Buster**[29] [4649] 6-11-7 131 .... APMcCoy 78
(Martin Brassil, Ire) *3rd early: led fr 4th: hdd after 5 out: wknd fr next* **9/1**

15 *2 1/2* **Rhapsody Rose**[31] [4585] 4-10-10 .... TDoyle 65
(P R Webber) *led: hdd 4th: 4th 4 out: wknd bef next* **14/1**

16 *14* **The Wrens Nest (IRE)**[38] [4486] 6-10-11 .... CO'Dwyer 52
(J A Berry, Ire) *rr of mid-div: wknd after 3 out: t.o* **100/1**

17 *nk* **Carriacou**[13] [4842] 4-10-3 .... PACarberry 44
(Dermot Day, Ire) *a towards rr: t.o* **66/1**

18 *dist* **Red Square Lady (IRE)**[223] [1432] 7-11-4 113 .... AndrewJMcNamara —
(Michael John Phillips, Ire) *mid-div: 12th 1/2-way: wknd bef 3 out: completely t.o* **33/1**

19 *dist* **Lickadoon (IRE)**[32] [4426] 4-10-3 82 .... BSCarey —
(P F O'Donnell, Ire) *a bhd: lost tch bef 1/2-way: completely t.o* **100/1**

4m 30.9s
WFA 4 from 5yo+ 5lb **19** Ran SP% **140.6**
CSF £39.52 TOTE £3.30: £1.70, £4.80, £3.40, £1.70; DF 74.20.
Owner Mrs N Flynn **Bred** Mrs N Flynn **Trained** Dungarvan, Co Waterford

NOTEBOOK
Blazing Liss(IRE) was in front and going on when stumbling badly after the second last. Quickly gathered up, she had recovered before the turn-in and was always on top from the last. *(op 2/1)*
Mags Benefit(IRE) is an improved mare and backed up her Ayr handicap win with a career-best effort here. *(op 14/1)*
Greenhall Rambler(IRE) stayed on well and will relish further.
Sunami Storm(IRE) looked set to take advantage of the winner after two out but was done with early in the straight. *(op 12/1)*
Queen Astrid(IRE) needs further but does not really show an aptitude for hurdling. *(op 6/1)*
Rhapsody Rose ran in front to the fourth but dropped right out from three out. *(op 12/1)*

67a BLUE SQUARE 1800 905050 H'CAP HURDLE 2m
3:10 (3:10) (0-140,130) 4-Y-0+ **£15,005** (£4,402; £2,097; £714)

RPR

1 **Stutter**[10] [2644] 7-10-2 106 .... PACarberry 115
(John G Carr, Ire) *hld up: 7th and hdwy after 2 out: styng on wl whn lft cl 2nd last: sn led and drew clr* **8/1**[3]

2 *5* **Native Stag (IRE)**[13] [4649] 7-10-11 114 .... CO'Dwyer 119
(P A Fahy, Ire) *trckd ldrs: 5th 4 out: led next: rdn and strly pressed after 2 out: hdd early st: sn outpcd: lft in ld whn hmpd last: no ex* **14/1**

3 *1 1/2* **Callow Lake (IRE)**[17] [1073] 5-11-4 121 .... BJGeraghty 125
(Mrs John Harrington, Ire) *trckd ldrs: 9th 4 out: impr into 2nd appr 2 out: 4th and rdn st: no imp whn lft 3rd fr last* **7/1**[2]

4 *1* **All Star (GER)**[46] [4332] 5-11-0 117 .... MAFitzgerald 120
(N J Henderson) *chsd ldrs: 7th 4 out: 6th and rdn after 2 out: styng on whn hmpd last: no ex* **16/1**

5 *2* **Baron De Feypo (IRE)**[7] [4371] 7-11-0 120 .... MFMooney(3) 121
(Patrick O Brady, Ire) *rr of mid-div: rdn and kpt on fr 2 out* **12/1**

6 *2* **Silk Screen (IRE)**[29] [4649] 5-11-3 120 .... DJCondon 119
(W P Mullins, Ire) *hld up towards rr: hdwy appr 2 out: lft 5th whn hmpd last: no ex* **12/1**

7 *4 1/2* **Patriotism**[32] [4568] 5-9-9 103 .... PWFlood(3) 95
(P A Fahy, Ire) *rr of mid-div: 8th 4 out: 3rd appr 2 out: no ex early st* **25/1**

8 *shd* **Top Strategy (IRE)**[42] [4397] 5-11-6 122 .... (b) RWalsh 117
(T M Walsh, Ire) *mid-div: 8th 1/2-way: 6th 4 out: no ex fr 2 out* **12/1**

9 *1* **Lagudin (IRE)**[122] [2980] 7-9-5 101 .... RJMolloy(5) 92
(Paul John Gilligan, Ire) *towards rr: kpt on fr bef 2 out* **33/1**

10 *1/2* **Ansari (IRE)**[7] [4830] 8-9-8 105 .... KHClarke(7) 96
(Patrick O Brady, Ire) *towards rr: kpt on one pced fr 3 out* **33/1**

11 *1 1/2* **Allez Petit Luis (FR)**[45] [4353] 7-10-8 112 .... JLCullen 102
(C A Murphy, Ire) *sn led: hdd 4th: remained prom: cl up and rdn 3 out: wknd next* **9/1**

12 *6* **Kentucky Charm (FR)**[10] [2982] 4-10-6 110 .... DNRussell 94
(E J O'Grady, Ire) *mid-div: prog after 3 out: 8th and in tch whn mstke next: sn no ex* **20/1**

13 *12* **Beechcourt**[40] [4438] 8-11-7 126 .... TGMRyan(3) 100
(M J P O'Brien, Ire) *towards rr: no imp fr 3 out* **12/1**

14 *1* **Miss Lauren Dee (IRE)**[32] [2054] 9-9-10 105 .... SERyder(5) 76
(M Flannery, Ire) *cl up to 1/2-way: wknd after 4 out* **40/1**

15 *shd* **Sea Skate (USA)**[114] [3216] 5-9-11 104 .... MPWalsh(3) 75
(R Donohoe, Ire) *nvr a factor* **25/1**

16 *3 1/2* **Zaydar (IRE)**[80] [3735] 5-10-0 104 .... APCrowe 71
(Paul Nolan, Ire) *cl up: led after 4 out: hdd next: sn wknd* **33/1**

17 *2* **Zum See (IRE)**[137] [2779] 6-11-9 128 .... DFO'Regan(3) 95
(Noel Meade, Ire) *nvr a factor* **20/1**

18 *shd* **Definate Spectacle (IRE)**[18] [4768] 5-11-11 127 .... PCarberry 94
(Noel Meade, Ire) *rr of mid-div: prog 3 out: 4th next: sn wknd* **9/2**[1]

19 *1/2* **Rayshan (IRE)**[36] [4510] 5-11-11 127 .... GLee 94
(J Howard Johnson) *prom early: wknd fr 1/2-way* **12/1**

20 *7* **King Carew (IRE)**[3] [17] 7-11-3 126 .... SJHassett(7) 86
(Michael Hourigan, Ire) *a bhd: t.o* **33/1**

21 *4 1/2* **Un Intello (IRE)**[736] [4741] 7-9-10 101 .... MDGrant 53
(E J O'Grady, Ire) *prom: led bef 4th: hdd & wknd after 4 out: t.o* **33/1**

22 *dist* **Pacolet (IRE)**[117] [3134] 6-10-13 116 .... JRBarry —
(Patrick J Flynn, Ire) *nvr a factor: t.o* **33/1**

23 *dist* **Lafayette (IRE)**[275] [1239] 7-10-9 119 .... DPMaher(7) —
(R J Osborne, Ire) *nvr a factor: wknd fr 4 out: completely t.o* **25/1**

P **Fenix (GER)**[18] [4770] 6-11-7 130 .... (b) ADLeigh(7) —
(Mrs L Wadham) *chsd ldrs: 6th bef 1/2-way: no ex after 3 out: p.u after next* **16/1**

F **I'Ll Call You Back (IRE)**[29] [4649] 6-11-0 117 .... RMPower —
(Mrs John Harrington, Ire) *hld up towards rr: 8th and hdwy after 3 out: 2nd next: rdn to ld early st: clr whn fell last* **25/1**

4m 1.60s **Going Correction** +0.20s/f (Yiel)
WFA 4 from 5yo+ 5lb **25** Ran SP% **153.7**
Speed ratings: 116,113,112,112,111 110,108,107,107,107 106,103,97,96,96 95,94,94,93,90 88,—,—,—,— CSF £119.87 CT £881.20 TOTE £8.50: £2.00, £4.00, £1.50, £7.40; DF 248.60.
Owner J Stanley **Bred** Whitsbury Manor Stud **Trained** Maynooth, Co. Kildare

NOTEBOOK
All Star(GER) was getting into full flow when hampered by the faller at the last.
Definate Spectacle(IRE) *Official explanation: vet said gelding coughed after race (op 4/1 tchd 5/1)*
Rayshan(IRE) was not a contender from halfway.
Fenix(GER) was prominent until three out and pulled up after the next. *Official explanation: jockey said saddle slipped (op 14/1)*

68a PUNCHESTOWN GUINNESS GOLD CUP CHASE (GRADE 1) 3m 1f
3:45 (3:47) 5-Y-0+ **£98,936** (£30,319; £14,361; £4,787; £3,191)

RPR

1 **Kicking King (IRE)**[40] [4435] 7-11-12 175 .... BJGeraghty 177+
(T J Taaffe, Ire) *trckd ldrs in 4th: impr into cl 2nd 6 out: led 4 out: clr after next: nt extended* **8/11**[1]

2 *3* **Rule Supreme (IRE)**[20] [4747] 9-11-12 164 .... RWalsh 170
(W P Mullins, Ire) *hld up in 5th: slow 3rd: 4th fr 6 out: impr into 2nd after 3 out: sn rdn: hit next: no imp fr last* **4/1**[3]

3 *15* **Pizarro (IRE)**[40] [4435] 8-11-12 149 .... DNRussell 155
(E J O'Grady, Ire) *cl up in 2nd: hit 7th: chal 5 out: 3rd and no ex after 3 out* **20/1**

4 *dist* **Kingscliff (IRE)**[122] [2943] 8-11-12 .... AThornton —
(R H Alner) *cl up in 3rd: slt mstke 9th: led after next: rdn and hdd 4 out: bad mstke 3 out: sn wknd: t.o* **7/2**[2]

5 *25* **First Gold (FR)**[20] [4748] 12-11-12 .... (b) APMcCoy —
(F Doumen, France) *led: hdd after 10th: sn rdn and wknd: t.o* **20/1**

P **Arctic Copper (IRE)**[18] [4772] 11-11-12 130 .... (p) PCarberry —
(Noel Meade, Ire) *a in rr: pushed along and lost tch 7th: t.o whn p.u bef 7 out* **66/1**

6m 26.3s **Going Correction** +0.20s/f (Yiel) **6** Ran SP% **111.1**
Speed ratings: **118,117,112,—,— —** CSF £4.06 TOTE £1.80: £1.40, £1.50; DF 3.20.
Owner Conor Clarkson **Bred** Sunnyhill Stud **Trained** Straffan, Co Kildare

FOCUS
A straightforward task for the King George VI and Gold Cup winner Kicking King, who is admirably consistent and ran to a similar level. Rule Supreme returned to his best level of the campaign, and Pizarro also ran to form.

NOTEBOOK
Kicking King(IRE) was quite magnificent here, executing the task with precision. Clear after the third last, he won without having a hard race, completing in exemplary fashion a superb campaign that has now yielded four major prizes. Still only seven, he is admirably consistent and should win many more if avoiding injury. His return in the autumn is eagerly awaited. *(op 4/6 tchd 4/5)*
Rule Supreme(IRE) moved into second after the third-last but was under pressure when blundering two out. His stamina carried him through to the end as he returned to his best level of the season, but he never threatened the winner. *(op 4/1 tchd 9/2)*
Pizarro(IRE) ran close to form again but was just a one-paced third from three out.
Kingscliff(IRE), who missed the Gold Cup after failing to please in a crucial gallop, was racing for the first time since chasing Kicking King home in the King George. He has run well fresh in the past, but this time relinquished his advantage four out, blundered badly at the next and was soon trailing. A disappointing effort.

First Gold(FR) ran in front but only on sufferance. Headed after the tenth, he was soon struggling. *(op 20/1 tchd 16/1)*

69a S.M.MORRIS LTD H'CAP CHASE (GRADE B) 2m 4f
4:20 (4:25) (0-150,142) 5-Y-0+ £25,393 (£7,450; £3,549; £1,209)

RPR

1 **Jasmin D'Oudairies (FR)**[31] 4590 8-10-8 126 BJGeraghty 139
(W P Mullins, Ire) *hld up towards rr: 7th and hdwy appr 4 out: 2nd next: sn chal: led appr last: styd on strly run-in* **14/1**

2 5 **Kymandjen (IRE)**[30] 4634 8-10-11 129 JLCullen 137
(Paul Nolan, Ire) *a.p: cl 2nd 6 out: led 3 out: sn rdn and strly pressed: hdd appr last: slt mstke: no ex run-in* **15/2**[3]

3 4 **Joueur D'Estruval (FR)**[32] 4567 8-10-8 126 RWalsh 130
(W P Mullins, Ire) *towards rr: prog appr 4 out: 5th 3 out: 4th bef next: 3rd and kpt on fr last* **7/1**[2]

4 7 **Dantes Reef (IRE)**[76] 3779 9-10-7 125 PCarberry 122
(A J Martin, Ire) *towards rr: 10th after 3 out: kpt on wl fr next* **5/1**[1]

5 4 **Oh Be The Hokey (IRE)**[42] 4398 7-10-5 123 CO'Dwyer 116
(C F Swan, Ire) *rr of mid-div: impr to trckd ldrs appr 1/2-way: 3rd 4 out: 4th u.p next: 3rd 2 out: sn no ex* **8/1**

6 2 ½ **Pearly Jack**[17] 4803 7-9-13 120 TGMRyan(3) 111
(D E Fitzgerald, Ire) *hld up: 9th 4 out: kpt on one pced fr 2 out* **12/1**

7 2 ½ **Simply Gifted**[18] 4772 10-11-5 137 APMcCoy 125
(Jonjo O'Neill) *towards rr: prog 6 out: 5th bef 4 out: 6th 3 out: sn no ex* **8/1**

8 ¾ **John James (IRE)**[19] 4764 9-11-2 134 KWhelan 121
(J H Scott, Ire) *cl up: led fr 5th: hdd 3 out: sn rdn: 5th next: wknd bef last* **25/1**

9 2 **Junior Fontaine (FR)**[20] 4751 8-10-4 125 DJHoward(3) 110
(A L T Moore, Ire) *mid-div: prog into 7th appr 3 out: no imp whn j. bdly lft next* **20/1**

10 2 ½ **Golden Storm (IRE)**[30] 4634 8-10-4 125 (b) JMAllen(3) 108
(Joseph Crowley, Ire) *mid-div: 12th 1/2-way: rdn and no imp fr 4 out* **25/1**

11 nk **Solar System (IRE)**[25] 4702 8-10-2 120 JPElliott 102
(T J Taaffe, Ire) *trckd ldrs: 4th 5 out: 6th whn slt mstke 4 out: sn no ex* **20/1**

12 1 ½ **Prince Of Pleasure (IRE)**[45] 4354 11-10-1 119 APCrowe 100
(D Broad, Ire) *led and disp: hdd 5th: remained cl up: 2nd whn slt mstke 4 out: wknd bef next* **25/1**

13 20 **Rheindross (IRE)**[94] 3503 10-9-10 114 PACarberry 75
(A L T Moore, Ire) *mid-div: 8th appr 4 out: sn no ex* **16/1**

14 5 **Guilt**[29] 4651 5-9-7 114 PWFlood(3) 70
(D T Hughes, Ire) *a bhd* **25/1**

15 4 **Jim (FR)**[20] 4748 8-11-10 142 MDGrant 94
(J T R Dreaper, Ire) *trckd ldrs: impr into 4th at 6th: lost pl after 6 out: sn no ex* **12/1**

16 5 **Fable (USA)**[165] 2210 9-9-13 117 NPMadden 64
(Noel Meade, Ire) *mid-div: wknd fr 5 out* **33/1**

17 9 **Alcapone (IRE)**[19] 4764 11-11-5 137 MAFitzgerald 75
(M F Morris, Ire) *chsd ldrs: 6th appr 1/2-way: wknd fr 5 out* **25/1**

18 8 **Balapour (IRE)**[40] 4438 7-9-5 114 (t) RJMolloy(5) 44
(Patrick O Brady, Ire) *a bhd* **20/1**

P **Carneys Cross (IRE)**[31] 4590 7-10-5 123 JRBarry —
(S J Treacy, Ire) *5th early: wknd after 5 out: p.u appr 3 out* **20/1**

P **Over The First (IRE)**[19] 4764 10-10-9 127 GLee —
(C F Swan, Ire) *rr of mid-div: no ex after 4 out: p.u bef last* **25/1**

U **Colonel Monroe (IRE)**[32] 4567 8-10-4 122 DNRussell —
(E J O'Grady, Ire) *rr of mid-div: bad mstke and uns rdr 5 out* **20/1**

P **Baily Mist (IRE)**[25] 4704 8-10-1 119 RGeraghty —
(M F Morris, Ire) *sn bhd and trailing: mstke 4th: t.o whn p.u bef 6 out* **33/1**

P **Winning Dream (IRE)**[19] 4764 11-10-13 131 GCotter —
(Oliver McKiernan, Ire) *chsd ldrs: 6th and rdn 4 out: sn wknd: p.u bef 2 out* **25/1**

5m 8.40s
WFA 5 from 7yo+ 4lb **25 Ran SP% 147.7**
CSF £110.37 CT £845.05 TOTE £31.60: £7.10, £2.20, £1.50, £2.00; DF 340.30.
Owner Decies & Dubs Syndicate **Bred** Cte Michel De Gigar **Trained** Muine Beag, Co Carlow

NOTEBOOK
Jasmin D'Oudairies(FR) showed more toe than the runner-up over this intermediate distance. *(op 12/1)*
Kymandjen(IRE) needs further to bring his stamina into play. *(op 8/1)*
Joueur D'Estruval(FR) does not find a great deal when asked, and frustrated once again. *(op 8/1)*
Dantes Reef(IRE) came from off the pace but never promised. *(op 5/1 tchd 9/2)*
Simply Gifted crept into it from five out but was never able to challenge. *(op 7/1)*
Over The First(IRE) *Official explanation: jockey said gelding made a respiratory noise in running*

70a PADDY POWER CHAMPION INH FLAT RACE (GRADE 1) (MARES & GELDINGS) 2m
4:55 (4:55) 4-Y-0+ £46,170 (£13,546; £6,453; £2,198)

RPR

1 **Refinement (IRE)**[18] 4774 6-11-9 (b¹) MrAJBerry 130
(Jonjo O'Neill) *trckd ldrs: 4th 6f out: led over 3f out: sn qcknd clr: styd on strly st: impressive* **6/1**[2]

2 9 **The Cool Guy (IRE)**[18] 4774 5-11-13 MrRWidger 125
(N A Twiston-Davies) *mid-div: 5th and hdwy ent st: mod 2nd over 1f out: kpt on u.p* **9/1**[3]

3 6 **Nicanor (FR)**[10] 4898 4-11-6 NPMadden 112
(Noel Meade, Ire) *rr of mid-div: 8th and smooth hdwy over 4f out: 3rd and rdn appr st: kpt on same pce fr 2f out* **10/1**

4 4 **Missed That**[42] 4399 6-12-0 MrJJCodd 116
(W P Mullins, Ire) *mid-div: prog into 5th 5f out: 3rd 3f out: 2nd and rdn ent st: 4th and no ex fr 1 1/2f out* **5/4**[1]

5 4 **Eye On The Ball**[42] 4399 6-11-11 MrKEPower(3) 112
(M F Morris, Ire) *hld up towards rr: hdwy 5f out: 5th 4f out: 6th appr st: kpt on same pce* **10/1**

6 2 ½ **Wheresben (IRE)**[10] 4898 6-12-0 MrJAFahey 110
(Seamus Fahey, Ire) *mid-div: impr into 6th 5f out: 4th 4f out: 6th and no ex early st* **25/1**

7 3 **Clew Bay Cove (IRE)**[42] 4399 5-11-13 (t) MrDerekO'Connor 106
(C A Murphy, Ire) *towards rr early: hdwy appr 1/2-way: cl 2nd over 5f out: led 4f out: hdd over 3f out: no ex ent st* **10/1**

8 ¾ **Knight Legend (IRE)**[45] 4357 6-12-0 MrRO'Sullivan 106
(Mrs John Harrington, Ire) *rr of mid-div: prog into 7th over 4f out: no ex st* **16/1**

9 2 **The Dasher (IRE)**[234] 1384 6-12-0 MrPTobin 104
(Sean Aherne, Ire) *towards rr: prog into 8th over 3f out: rdn and no imp st* **25/1**

10 2 ½ **Avoca Mist (IRE)**[18] 4774 5-11-8 MsKWalsh 95
(W P Mullins, Ire) *prom: 3rd 1/2-way: rdn and wknd fr 4f out* **25/1**

11 20 **Dawadari (IRE)**[10] 4898 5-11-13 MrKBBowens 80
(S J Mahon, Ire) *led: jnd appr 1/2-way: rdn and hdd 4f out: sn wknd* **14/1**

12 4 **Dark Artist (IRE)**[81] 3717 6-12-0 MissNCarberry 77
(John E Kiely, Ire) *nvr a factor* **25/1**

13 3 ½ **Skeheenarinky (IRE)**[80] 3738 5-11-13 MrSOO'Brien 73
(Sean O O'Brien, Ire) *a bhd* **25/1**

14 2 **Ballintra Boy (IRE)**[29] 4653 6-12-0 MrGElliott 72
(Noel Meade, Ire) *rr of mid-div: no ex fr over 4f out* **14/1**

15 ½ **Lyical Assassin (IRE)** 5-11-13 MrDRoche 70
(Paul A Roche, Ire) *a bhd* **100/1**

16 dist **Bit Of A Gift**[10] 4898 7-12-0 MrPFahey —
(Thomas Mullins, Ire) *cl up: disp ld appr 1/2-way: hdd & wknd 6f out: t.o* **14/1**

17 ½ **She's Our Daisy (IRE)**[46] 4333 5-11-8 MrAFitzgerald —
(S C Burrough) *chsd ldrs to 1/2-way: wknd over 5f out: t.o* **66/1**

18 dist **Dontbebrushedaside (IRE)**[488] 2972 6-12-0 MrDWCullen —
(R M Moore, Ire) *prom early: wknd appr 1/2-way: completely t.o* **66/1**

P **Littlejimmybrown (IRE)**[24] 4731 7-12-0 MrJTMcNamara —
(Patrick J Flynn, Ire) *3rd early: p.u injured 1/2-way: dead* **50/1**

3m 55.3s **Going Correction** +0.20s/f (Yiel)
WFA 4 from 5yo 5lb 5 from 6yo+ 3lb **19 Ran SP% 147.1**
Speed ratings: **123,118,115,113,111 110,108,108,107,106 96,94,92,91,91 —,—,—,—** CSF £65.82 TOTE £7.90: £1.90, £1.80, £2.30, £1.50; DF 50.00.
Owner M Tabor **Bred** M Tabor **Trained** Cheltenham, Gloucs

FOCUS
The second bumper win of the week for the visitors, following the success of Its A Dream on the opening day. Refinement was a revelation in the blinkers, winning impressively and returning her best figure since her second in Cheltenham's 2004 Festival Bumper. However, Missed That and several others were clearly well below the form they showed in Cheltenham's 2005 renewal.

NOTEBOOK
Refinement(IRE), aided by first-time blinkers, made amends for Cheltenham and Aintree with an emphatic success. *(op 9/2)*
The Cool Guy(IRE) finished clear of the rest but could not cope with the winner this time. *(op 8/1)*
Nicanor(FR) was outpaced in the straight.
Missed That ran way below his Cheltenham form and was possibly feeling the effects of the season. He remains a fine prospect. *(op 6/4)*
She's Our Daisy(IRE) found herself outclassed.

71a MASTERCHEF'S HOSPITALITY NOVICE CHASE 2m 2f
5:30 (5:30) 5-Y-0+ £12,696 (£3,725; £1,774; £604)

RPR

1 **Livingstonebramble (IRE)**[30] 4636 9-11-12 121 RWalsh 132
(W P Mullins, Ire) *trckd ldrs: 5th 4 out: sn pushed along: 2nd and rdn bef 2 out: swtchd rt to chal appr last: led early run-in: kpt on wl u.p* **5/2**[1]

2 ½ **Bizet (IRE)**[41] 4407 9-11-12 124 JLCullen 132
(F Flood, Ire) *trckd ldrs: 6th 6 out: impr into 3rd 4 out: led travelling wl 3 out: rdn clr next: strly pressed last: hdd early run-in: ra* **11/2**[3]

3 12 **Sandy Owen (IRE)**[29] 4648 9-11-12 124 BJGeraghty 120
(P A Fahy, Ire) *settled 4th: 3rd and rdn after 3 out: no ex after next* **3/1**[2]

4 1 ½ **Quarry Boy (IRE)**[14] 4831 9-11-9 MDarcy(3) 118
(E Sheehy, Ire) *prom: 2nd fr 6th: 3rd and rdn 3 out: 4th and no ex after 2 out* **12/1**

5 ½ **Leinster (IRE)**[500] 2759 8-11-2 PWFlood(3) 111
(D T Hughes, Ire) *mid-div: 8th 4 out: rdn and kpt on one pce fr next* **16/1**

6 8 **Roofing Spirit (IRE)**[11] 4867 7-11-12 115 NFehily 110
(D P Keane) *trckd ldrs in 7th: 6th and in tch 4 out: no ex fr next* **12/1**

7 3 ½ **Poker Pal (IRE)**[14] 4831 8-11-5 (t) APCrowe 99
(D T Hughes, Ire) *towards rr: effrt and no imp fr 4 out* **20/1**

8 ½ **Keevers (IRE)**[14] 4831 11-11-2 TGMRyan(3) 99
(W J Burke, Ire) *mid-div: 7th bef 4 out: no ex bef 2 out* **25/1**

9 25 **John Oliver (IRE)**[45] 4351 7-11-12 113 PCarberry 81
(John Queally, Ire) *led: hdd 3 out: sn wknd: eased fr last: t.o* **12/1**

10 4 **The Real Solara (IRE)**[34] 4542 8-10-12 96 DFFlannery(7) 70
(Michael Hourigan, Ire) *a bhd: t.o* **33/1**

11 8 **Rapide Plaisir (IRE)**[45] 4351 7-11-5 BMCash 62
(A L T Moore, Ire) *nvr a factor: t.o* **16/1**

12 dist **Moscow Parade (IRE)**[346] 390 7-11-5 KHadnett —
(Michael Hourigan, Ire) *a bhd: completely t.o* **40/1**

F **Addiction (IRE)**[14] 4831 8-11-5 MDGrant —
(Michael Hourigan, Ire) *bhd: fell 6 out* **50/1**

F **Rathmore (IRE)**[38] 6-10-12 MJFerris(7) —
(Eugene M O'Sullivan, Ire) *towards rr: fell 6 out* **66/1**

P **Benefit Of Caution (IRE)**[240] 1332 6-11-5 GCotter —
(Paul John Gilligan, Ire) *rr of mid-div: no ex after 6 out: p.u bef 4 out* **100/1**

F **Mambo Des Mottes (FR)**[18] 4769 5-11-5 AO'Keeffe —
(Miss Venetia Williams) *cl up in 2nd: slt mstke 2nd: 3rd fr 1/2-way tl fell 5 out* **7/1**

4m 50.3s
WFA 5 from 6yo+ 3lb **16 Ran SP% 134.7**
CSF £18.05 TOTE £2.30: £1.10, £1.80, £1.30, £2.10; DF 16.70.
Owner Favourites Racing Syndicate **Bred** Mrs Noelle Walsh **Trained** Muine Beag, Co Carlow

NOTEBOOK
Roofing Spirit(IRE) faded out from the third last, appearing unsuited by the ground. *(op 10/1)*
Mambo Des Mottes(FR) ran second and was still contesting third place when falling five out. *(op 8/1)*
Benefit Of Caution(IRE) *Official explanation: jockey said gelding was labouring at halfway (op 8/1)*

72 - (Foreign Racing) - See Raceform Interactive

HEREFORD (R-H)

Thursday, April 28

OFFICIAL GOING: Good to firm (firm in places)

With the forecast rain failing to materialise, there were 15 non-runners because of the fast ground.

Wind: fresh across Weather: some light rain before racing, then fine

73 LETHEBY & CHRISTOPHER MAIDEN HURDLE (13 hdls) 3m 2f

2:10 (2:13) (Class 4) 4-Y-0+ **£3,789** (£1,166; £583; £291)

Form				RPR
002-	1		**Jackson (FR)**[16] [4814] 8-11-3 125 .... RThornton (A King) *mde all: pushed along fr 2 out: styd on wl* **2/9**[1]	95+
366-	2	2 ½	**Vallica**[8] [4929] 6-10-3 79 .... DLaverty[(7)] (Mrs A M Thorpe) *sn prom: chsd wnr appr 10th: rdn appr 2 out: styd on same pce* **14/1**[3]	85
055-	3	4	**Monsieur Georges (FR)**[18] [4799] 5-11-3 100 .... TDoyle (F Jordan) *hld up: hdwy 9th: hit 10th: rdn after 3 out: one pce* **10/1**[2]	89+
/04-	4	dist	**Jacarado (IRE)**[90] [3573] 7-11-3 65 .... WHutchinson (R Dickin) *nt fluent: hld up in tch: reminders after 5th: rdn after 7th: wknd appr 10th: t.o* **100/1**	—
UP0-	5	7	**Meandmrsjones**[18] [4795] 6-10-7 .... (v[1]) DCrosse[(3)] (J G M O'Shea) *prom to 10th: t.o* **100/1**	—
2/6-	6	4	**Emanate**[186] [1831] 7-10-12 .... MNicolls[(5)] (John Allen) *w wnr tl appr 10th: wkng whn nt fluent 3 out: t.o* **33/1**	—
0/0-	P		**Carpenters Boy**[108] [3306] 5-10-12 .... LStephens[(5)] (C Roberts) *bhd fr 6th: t.o whn p.u bef 8th* **66/1**	—
00-	P		**Logger Rhythm (USA)**[134] [2442] 5-11-3 .... SThomas (R Dickin) *hld up: lost tch appr 10th: t.o whn p.u bef 2 out* **66/1**	—

6m 22.8s (-6.30) **Going Correction** -0.45s/f (Good) **8** Ran SP% **105.5**

Speed ratings: **91,90,89,—,— —,—,—** CSF £2.97 TOTE £1.10: £1.02, £1.90, £1.10; EX 3.40.

Owner C B Brookes **Bred** Mme Yves Priouzeau **Trained** Barbury Castle, Wilts

FOCUS

A weak race and a moderate winning time, though the in-form Alan King saddled his sixth consecutive winner.

NOTEBOOK

Jackson(FR) had been found an easy opening and fully justified being a red-hot favourite. *(op 2-7 tchd 3-10 in a place)*

Vallica got the trip well enough on this sound surface but the winner always appeared to have the upper hand. *(tchd 16-1)*

Monsieur Georges(FR) was another who appeared to put any stamina doubts to rest on the fast ground but he could not cope with the runner-up let alone the winner. *(op 13-2)*

74 FRANCIS CATERING EQUIPMENT NOVICES' H'CAP CHASE (14 fncs) 2m 3f

2:40 (2:42) (Class 4) (0-105,105) 5-Y-0+ **£4,173** (£1,284; £642; £321)

Form				RPR
U2-1	1		**Terrible Tenant**[3] [26] 6-10-2 80 7ex .... RYoung[(3)] (J W Mullins) *a gng wl: wnt 2nd 6th: led appr 3 out: sn clr: easily* **11/8**[1]	98+
6P4-	2	11	**Alexander Musical (IRE)**[38] [4497] 7-10-0 75 oh11 .... (v) PFlynn (S T Lewis) *led: rdn and hdd appr 3 out: sn btn* **16/1**	69+
444-	3	5	**Pollensa Bay**[11] [4879] 6-10-5 83 .... (p) JPByrne[(3)] (S A Brookshaw) *chsd wnr to 6th: wknd 8th* **3/1**[3]	71
625-	4	18	**Moorland Monarch**[58] [4113] 7-10-3 78 .... JTizzard (J D Frost) *bhd fr 8th* **11/4**[2]	48
0PP-	P		**Keltic Blue (IRE)**[79] [3747] 6-10-0 75 oh11 .... WHutchinson (R Dickin) *a bhd: t.o whn p.u bef 9th* **25/1**	—
536-	P		**Bowd Lane Joe**[31] [4614] 6-10-0 75 oh2 .... JMogford (A W Carroll) *a bhd: lost tch 8th: t.o whn p.u bef 4 out* **11/1**	—

4m 43.5s (-5.20) **Going Correction** -0.45s/f (Good) **6** Ran SP% **111.8**

Speed ratings: **92,87,85,77,— —** CSF £19.69 CT £57.23 TOTE £2.10: £1.10, £6.30; EX 15.10.

Owner D I Bare **Bred** D I Bare **Trained** Wilsford-Cum-Lake, Wilts

FOCUS

A very poor race decimated by five withdrawals because of the firm ground and the time was slow. The winner is value for more than double the official margin

NOTEBOOK

Terrible Tenant settled much better than when winning over the stiff two miles at Towcester three days earlier, and barely knew he had been in a race. *(tchd 6-4)*

Alexander Musical(IRE) had no answer to the winner from 11lb out of the handicap. *(tchd 22-1)*

Pollensa Bay, with the cheekpieces refitted, is struggling to find a suitable trip. *(tchd 11-4 and 10-3)*

Moorland Monarch may have found the ground too lively. *(op 3-1 tchd 10-3, 7-2 in a place)*

Keltic Blue(IRE) *Official explanation: trainer said gelding had a breathing problem (op 20-1)*

75 LETHEBY & CHRISTOPHER (S) H'CAP HURDLE (8 hdls) 2m 1f

3:10 (3:10) (Class 5) (0-95,95) 4-Y-0+ **£2,331** (£666; £333)

Form				RPR
000-	1		**Storm Clear (IRE)**[46] [4343] 6-10-7 76 .... WMarston (D J Wintle) *hld up and bhd: hdwy appr 5th: led after 2 out: drvn out* **11/2**[2]	84+
043-	2	4	**Sarena Special**[107] [3309] 8-10-3 77 .... CHonour[(5)] (J D Frost) *hld up in tch: wnt 2nd 5th: rdn and ev ch after 2 out: no ex flat* **7/1**	79
000-	3	6	**Final Command**[37] [4502] 8-11-4 87 .... (b[1]) SDurack (J C Tuck) *led after 2nd: rdn and hdd after 2 out: sn wknd* **6/1**[3]	83
/P0-	4	1 ½	**Island Warrior (IRE)**[56] [4139] 10-10-0 69 .... (p) JMogford (B P J Baugh) *hld up in tch: rdn after 3 out: wknd appr last* **40/1**	64
/0P-	5	1 ½	**Let's Celebrate**[131] [2899] 5-11-0 83 .... TDoyle (F Jordan) *hld up and bhd: hdwy and hit 3 out: sn rdn: wknd appr last* **16/1**	76
P46-	6	4	**Relative Hero (IRE)**[51] [2753] 5-10-6 75 .... (p) NFehily (Miss S J Wilton) *hld up in tch: lost pl appr 5th: short-lived effrt 2 out* **14/1**	64
/00-	7	1	**Sylcan Express**[107] [3309] 12-9-9 69 oh2 .... TJPhelan[(5)] (O O'Neill) *nvr nr ldrs* **33/1**	57
424-	8	3 ½	**Grand Prairie (SWE)**[10] [4913] 9-11-7 90 .... (p) JEMoore (G L Moore) *bhd fr 5th* **11/2**[2]	75
003-	9	nk	**Mersey Mirage**[3] [4602] 8-10-6 75 oh4 ow6 .... (p) SFox (R C Guest) *hld up in mid-div: hdwy appr 5th: rdn and wknd after 2 out* **14/1**	59
4FP-	10	2 ½	**Rocket Bleu (FR)**[12] [4871] 5-11-4 92 .... LStephens[(5)] (D Burchell) *hld up in mid-div: wknd after 3 out* **9/2**[1]	74
00P/	11	17	**Capacoostic**[327] 8-9-9 69 oh2 .... RStephens[(5)] (Miss H E Roberts) *prom tl wknd 4th* **33/1**	34
3PP-	P		**Beyond Borders (USA)**[49] [4277] 7-10-10 79 .... (b) RThornton (S Gollings) *bhd fr 3rd: p.u bef 5th* **11/1**	—
/0P-	P		**Mr Rhubarb (IRE)**[8] [4931] 7-11-12 95 .... (bt[1]) RJohnson (R T Phillips) *led tl after 2nd: wknd appr 5th: mstke 2 out: bhd whn p.u bef last* **16/1**	—

3m 54.6s (-9.40) **Going Correction** -0.45s/f (Good) **13** Ran SP% **117.5**

Speed ratings: **104,102,99,98,97 96,95,93,93,92 84,—,—** CSF £42.85 CT £241.04 TOTE £6.40: £2.40, £1.90, £2.80; EX 51.30.There was no bid for the winner

Owner Derek Boocock and Mrs Joan Egan **Bred** Jack Dorrian And Hugo Merry **Trained** Naunton, Gloucs

FOCUS

A modest seller but the winner is value for further.

NOTEBOOK

Storm Clear(IRE), who had shown a liking for fast ground in his younger days on the Flat, has *been slipping down the ratings and appreciated the drop in grade.Official explanation: trainer said, regarding the improved form shown, gelding may have benefited from the good to firm ground (op 7-1)*

Sarena Special, who has presumably been waiting for the ground to dry up, was encountering this sort of going for the first time over hurdles. *(op 13-2)*

Final Command, blinkered for the first time, was down in both class and distance but the game was up once he got collared. *(op 8-1)*

Island Warrior(IRE) was not inconvenienced by the faster going but the trip would have been on the short side for him.

Let's Celebrate likes this sort of ground but was not helped by missing out at the third last when working his way into contention. *(op 12-1)*

Beyond Borders(USA) *Official explanation: jockey said was unsuited by good to firm, firm in places ground (tchd 12-1)*

76 EASIBED H'CAP CHASE (19 fncs) 3m 1f 110y

3:40 (3:40) (Class 4) (0-105,104) 5-Y-0+ **£4,793** (£1,475; £737; £368)

Form				RPR
P22-	1		**Silver Samuel (NZ)**[13] [4853] 8-9-11 78 oh6 .... (t) JPByrne[(3)] (S A Brookshaw) *prom: lost pl 13th: rallied 3 out: lft in ld after 2 out: sn clr: eased towards fin* **5/2**[1]	88+
323-	2	2 ½	**Macgeorge (IRE)**[19] [4778] 15-11-10 102 .... PFlynn (R Lee) *j.lft: led to 10th: rdn 12th: outpcd 14th: rallying whn lft 2nd after 2 out: one pce* **5/1**[3]	105
0PP-	3	11	**Prince Highlight (IRE)**[11] [4886] 10-11-2 94 .... JMMaguire (Mrs Jeremy Young) *hld up and bhd: hdwy 5th: wnt 2nd 4 out: wknd 2 out* **10/3**[2]	86
210-	4	1 ¾	**Jazz Du Forez (FR)**[99] [3415] 8-9-11 80 oh9 ow2 .... MNicolls[(5)] (John Allen) *hld up: hdwy 11th: rdn 13th: wknd 3 out* **12/1**	70
P42-	F		**Yvanovitch (FR)**[32] [4578] 7-11-12 104 .... MFoley (Mrs L C Taylor) *hld up: fell 4th (water)* **15/2**	—
04P-	P		**Ungaretti (GER)**[90] [3575] 8-10-0 78 oh4 .... (p) WHutchinson (Ian Williams) *chsd ldr to 5th: wknd 8th: bhd whn p.u bef 3 out* **6/1**	—
1PU-	P		**Pete The Painter (IRE)**[13] [4853] 8-10-5 90 .... (b) MrJETudor[(7)] (J W Tudor) *hld up in tch: led 10th: hung lft appr 3 out: sddle slipped whn rn wd and hdd bnd after 2 out: sn p.u* **10/1**	90+

6m 17.1s (-16.70) **Going Correction** -0.45s/f (Good) **7** Ran SP% **111.2**

Speed ratings: **107,106,102,102,— —,—** CSF £14.68 CT £39.18 TOTE £4.90: £2.40, £2.60; EX 9.00.

Owner Redcroft Racing **Bred** H L Perry **Trained** Wollerton, Shropshire

FOCUS

An eventful race, with the leader pulling up on the home turn because of a slipping saddle. The race is rated through the runner-up with the winner value for further.

NOTEBOOK

Silver Samuel(NZ), 6lb 'wrong', had found a second wind when presented the race on the home turn. Whether he was a lucky winner is a matter of pure conjecture. *(tchd 11-4, 3-1 in a place)*

Macgeorge(IRE) had even faster ground to contend with this time and looked fortunate to finish second. *(op 9-2)*

Prince Highlight(IRE), who had been let down by his jumping since winning at Folkestone last November, was running on this sort of ground for the first time. *(op 4-1 tchd 3-1)*

Jazz Du Forez(FR) was 9lb out of the handicap for this first outing in over three months. *(op 11-1)*

Pete The Painter(IRE) could well have been an unlucky loser but one could say that his saddle *only began to slip because he started to hang left. Official explanation: jockey said saddle slipped (op 8-1)*

77 K.W. BELL CONSTRUCTION MARES' ONLY NOVICES' HURDLE (10 hdls) 2m 3f 110y

4:10 (4:11) (Class 4) 4-Y-0+ **£4,241** (£1,305; £652; £326)

Form				RPR
500-	1		**Blueberry Ice (IRE)**[94] [3511] 7-10-5 92 .... CMStudd[(7)] (B G Powell) *a.p: rdn to ld appr last: r.o* **20/1**	107+
241-	2	1 ½	**Bonny Grey**[6] [4958] 7-11-5 110 .... SCurran (P D Evans) *t.k.h: a.p: led 7th: rdn 2 out: hdd appr last: nt qckn flat* **9/4**[1]	112
/03-	3	1 ¼	**Samandara (FR)**[49] [4284] 5-10-12 .... RThornton (A King) *hld up: hdwy appr 6th: mstke 7th: rdn and swtchd rt appr last: sn ev ch: one pce flat* **5/2**[2]	106+
42-	4	12	**Separated (USA)**[33] [4560] 4-10-6 .... RJohnson (P J Hobbs) *hld up: hdwy appr 6th: ev ch 2 out: sn rdn: 4th and wkng whn nt fluent last* **11/4**[3]	90+
040-	5	30	**Vivre Aimer Rire (FR)**[8] [4933] 4-10-6 .... BJCrowley (M Scudamore) *a bhd* **66/1**	56
-	6	5	**The Risen Lark (IRE)**[626] 5-10-12 .... SThomas (Miss Venetia Williams) *led tl after 1st: prom: led appr 6th to 7th: wknd after 3 out* **16/1**	57
300-	7	3 ½	**Cotswold Rose**[68] [3946] 5-10-12 .... PHide (N M Babbage) *bhd fr 7th* **40/1**	53
00-	8	11	**Dorans Lane**[18] [4795] 7-10-12 .... PFlynn (W M Brisbourne) *hld up towards rr: hdwy after 6th: wknd after 3 out* **100/1**	42
	9	16	**Green Ocean**[132] 5-10-9 .... RHobson[(3)] (J W Unett) *a bhd: blnd last: t.o* **40/1**	26
430-	P		**Antinomy (IRE)**[14] [4841] 5-10-12 .... OMcPhail (N J Henderson) *a bhd: nt fluent 1st: t.o whn p.u bef 2 out* **12/1**	—
000-	P		**Roseville (IRE)**[32] [4589] 5-10-7 .... LTreadwell[(5)] (S T Lewis) *prom tl wknd after 4th: bhd whn p.u bef 7th* **100/1**	—
	P		**Dreams Of Zena**[948] 6-10-5 .... AScholes[(7)] (D Burchell) *led after 1st: clr after 3rd: hdd appr 6th: sn wknd: p.u bef 7th* **66/1**	—
0P-	F		**Queen Excalibur**[30] [4639] 6-10-12 .... AThornton (C Roberts) *hld up and bhd: hdwy appr 3 out: rdn and wknd after 2 out: 5th and no ch whn fell last* **25/1**	—

4m 41.8s (-6.70) **Going Correction** -0.45s/f (Good)
WFA 4 from 5yo+ 5lb **13** Ran SP% **118.0**
Speed ratings: **95,94,93,89,77 75,73,69,62,— —,—,—** CSF £64.24 TOTE £20.60: £4.90, £1.10, £1.60; EX 97.40.
Owner Mrs B M Studd **Bred** Michael Tierney **Trained** Morestead, Hants

FOCUS
Plenty of no hopers in this mares-only event and a slow time to boot. However, the placed horses were close to their marks so the form makes sense on paper.

NOTEBOOK
Blueberry Ice(IRE), who apparently has been more relaxed at home recently, showed plenty of improvement and it seems that fast ground is the key to her. She has already been schooled over fences. *Official explanation: trainer said, regarding the improved form shown, mare was better suited by today's faster ground and the fact that she had strengthened up after a long lay-off* *(op 16-1)*
Bonny Grey was not disgraced under a penalty for her win last week and does seem to act on all types of ground. *(tchd 2-1, 5-2 in a place)*
Samandara(FR) was 7lb better off than when three lengths behind Bonny Grey at Wincanton last month. She did not help her cause by dragging her hind legs through the fourth last over this longer trip. *(tchd 11-4)*
Separated(USA) appeared to get found out by the longer distance. *Official explanation: vet said filly lost a right fore shoe (op 3-1 tchd 10-3 in a place)*
Dreams Of Zena *Official explanation: jockey said mare lost her action, but returned sound (op 33-1 tchd 100-1)*

78 K.W. BELL NOVICES' H'CAP HURDLE (8 hdls) 2m 1f
4:40 (4:42) (Class 4) (0-105,103) 4-Y-O+ **£4,663** (£1,435; £717; £358)

Form	Pos	Dist	Horse	RPR
324-	1		**Phar Out Phavorite (IRE)**[21] [4759] 6-11-9 **100**.....(v) NFehily (Miss E C Lavelle) *led 2nd: rdn appr 2 out: r.o* **11/2**[2]	106+
030-	2	1 ½	**Dargaville (NZ)**[40] [4448] 6-11-4 **95**.....SFox (R C Guest) *hld up in tch: rdn and ev ch 2 out: kpt on same pce flat* **8/1**	99
F65-	3	¾	**Tom Bell (IRE)**[16] [4813] 5-10-8 **92**.....(v) NCarter(7) (J G M O'Shea) *a.p: hit 3 out: ev ch whn hit 2 out: rdn and r.o one pce* **14/1**	97+
0F1-	4	3 ½	**Alva Glen (USA)**[25] [4723] 8-11-6 **97**.....RJohnson (B J Llewellyn) *hld up and bhd: hdwy appr 2 out: nt rch ldrs* **9/1**	97
P31-	5	4	**Capitana (GER)**[32] [4579] 4-10-9 **91**.....MFoley (N J Henderson) *hld up towards rr: hdwy after 4th: wknd appr last* **11/2**[2]	88+
246-	6	10	**Innocent Rebel (USA)**[61] [4067] 4-11-5 **101**.....RThornton (A King) *hld up and bhd: mstke 3rd: hdwy after 3 out: wknd after 2 out* **4/1**[1]	82
F06-	7	1 ½	**Rudetski**[11] [4888] 8-11-4 **95**.....(t) PFlynn (M Sheppard) *led to 2nd: wknd after 4th* **20/1**	80
462-	8	8	**Barranco (IRE)**[19] [4776] 4-10-5 **87**.....(b) PHide (G L Moore) *hld up in mid-div: hdwy appr 5th: wknd appr 2 out* **20/1**	59
1PU-	9	13	**Looks The Business (IRE)**[11] [4890] 4-10-10 **99**.....(t) RLucey-Butler(7) (W G M Turner) *a bhd* **25/1**	58
001-	P		**Adjawar (IRE)**[19] [4776] 7-11-9 **100**.....SDurack (J J Quinn) *bhd fr 4th: p.u bef 5th* **11/1**	—
/PP-	P		**Gingko**[24] [471] 8-11-4 **95**.....TDoyle (P R Webber) *bhd fr 5th: t.o whn p.u bef last* **9/1**	—
600-	P		**Norwegian**[45] [4367] 4-10-7 **89**.....WHutchinson (Ian Williams) *a bhd: t.o whn p.u bef last* **25/1**	—
003-	P		**Arimero (GER)**[16] [4813] 5-11-3 **94**.....(bt) JTizzard (J G Portman) *prom tl wknd after 3 out: mstke 2 out: bhd whn p.u lame bef last* **7/1**[3]	—
04P-	P		**Fight The Feeling**[35] [4531] 7-10-10 **90**.....RHobson(3) (J W Unett) *prom: reminders after 3rd: wknd 5th: bhd whn p.u after 2 out* **33/1**	—

3m 52.7s (-11.30) **Going Correction** -0.45s/f (Good)
WFA 4 from 5yo+ 5lb **14** Ran SP% **129.5**
Speed ratings: **108,107,106,105,103 98,98,94,88,— —,—,—,—** CSF £49.47 CT £613.30 TOTE £7.50: £1.60, £2.90, £3.70; EX 85.90.
Owner Favourites Racing V **Bred** Mrs J Wilkinson **Trained** Wildhern, Hants

FOCUS
A moderate contest but the decent pace led to the comparative fastest time of the day, and the form looks solid for the grade

NOTEBOOK
Phar Out Phavorite(IRE), again in headgear, finally got off the mark on this return to a shorter trip. He was subsequently described as a bit of a monkey by his trainer. *(op 5-1)*
Dargaville(NZ), pulled out because of the soft ground at Kelso the previous evening, ran his race and simply met one too good. *(op 9-1 tchd 10-1)*
Tom Bell(IRE), tried in a visor, was rather let down by his jumping once things began to hot up but he kept on willingly to the end. *(tchd 16-1)*
Alva Glen(USA), raised 10lb, could never get to grips with the principals. *(op 8-1 tchd 10-1)*
Capitana(GER) was not knocked about once her chance had gone in the short home straight. *(op 4-1)*
Innocent Rebel(USA) could only manage a short-lived effort on this much faster surface. *(op 9-2)*
Fight The Feeling *Official explanation: jockey said gelding was unsuited by good to firm, firm in places ground (op 14-1)*
Arimero(GER) *Official explanation: jockey said gelding suffered an overreach (op 14-1)*

79 LETHEBY & CHRISTOPHER HUNTERS' CHASE (14 fncs) 2m 3f
5:10 (5:11) (Class 6) 5-Y-O+ **£1,736** (£496; £248)

Form	Pos	Dist	Horse	RPR
0PP/	1		**Willy Willy**[109] 12-11-11.....MrJSnowden(3) (Mrs Caroline Keevil) *a.p: led 2 out: rdn out* **20/1**	90
P0P-	2	1 ½	**Wings Of Hope (IRE)**[25] 9-11-11 64.....MrDSJones(3) (James Richardson) *led to 4th: prom: led after 4 out to 2 out: kpt on u.p flat* **10/1**	89
4B5-	3	1 ¼	**Guignol Du Cochet (FR)**[13] [4856] 11-12-0 102.....MrMWalford(7) (S Flook) *hld up: hdwy 11th: outpcd appr last: styd on flat* **5/1**[3]	94
5UP-	4	6	**Ivanoph (FR)**[29] [4658] 9-12-4 117.....MrLJefford (J J Boulter) *s.s: hld up: hdwy 9th: one pce fr 3 out* **14/1**	86+
UFF-	5	19	**Gue Au Loup (FR)**[18] 11-11-7 87.....MrMWall(7) (G C Evans) *prom: led 4th to 5th: wknd appr 3 out* **33/1**	66+
P0/	6	1	**Chaucers Miller**[11] 9-11-7.....MrDavidTurner(7) (R Bryan) *rdn 7th: a bhd* **66/1**	61
P6P-	7	14	**Worthy Man**[5] 8-11-11 64.....MrDMansell(3) (Mrs E England) *prom: led briefly 5th: wknd appr 3 out* **66/1**	52+
02P/	F		**Morph**[26] 11-11-9.....MrMarcBarber(5) (E W Morris) *hld up: fell 7th* **50/1**	—
PP-	P		**Spreejinsky**[33] 7-11-7.....MissKWood(7) (Robert Staley) *sn t.o: p.u bef 4th* **66/1**	—
3F4/	F		**Popgoestheweasel**[19] 10-11-0.....(t) MrPMason(7) (B Tulloch) *mid-div: fell 7th* **25/1**	—
U6P-	P		**Classic Revival**[5] 7-11-7.....MrRHodges(7) (Mrs A Price) *chsd ldrs tl p.u bef 6th* **22/1**	—
00P/	P		**Brandeston Ron (IRE)**[31] 6-11-11.....(t) MrDAlers-Hankey(3) (Miss T Pitman) *s.s: blnd 4th: bhd tl p.u bef 7th* **50/1**	—
/PF-	P		**Honest Yer Honour (IRE)**[18] 9-12-0.....MrRBurton (Mrs C J Robinson) *hld up towards rr: hmpd 7th: p.u bef 8th* **9/4**[2]	—
5PP-	P		**Gipsy Cricketer**[12] 9-11-7 69.....MrNHOliver(7) (Mrs Marilyn Scudamore) *chsd ldrs to 9th: t.o whn p.u bef 3 out* **25/1**	—
PP6/	P		**Contemporary Art**[31] 7-11-7.....(t) AGlassonbury(7) (N J Dawe) *a towards rr: mstkes 1st and 4th: t.o whn p.u bef 3 out* **33/1**	—
412-	P		**Phoenix Phlyer**[11] [4882] 11-12-0 104.....(v) MissCStucley(7) (Mrs Marilyn Scudamore) *prom: led after 5th tl after 4 out: sn wknd: p.u bef 3 out* **85/40**[1]	—

4m 40.4s (-8.30) **Going Correction** -0.45s/f (Good) **16** Ran SP% **126.3**
Speed ratings: **99,98,97,95,87 86,81,—,—,— —,—,—,—,—,—** CSF £195.08 TOTE £27.40: £6.60, £2.10, £2.50; EX 375.70 Place 6 £41.58, Place 5 £41.49.
Owner Mrs George Tricks **Bred** Mrs V M Tricks **Trained** Blagdon, Somerset

FOCUS
A modest hunter chase and best rated through the third..

NOTEBOOK
Willy Willy must have fast ground and took advantage of the fact that the rain stayed away.
Wings Of Hope(IRE), whose two wins over hurdles came on a similar surface, may have found this trip a shade on the short side for him.
Guignol Du Cochet(FR) is another who really wants a bit further. *(op 8-1)*
Ivanoph(FR) had done all his winning on soft going. *(op 10-1)*
Phoenix Phlyer, in headgear for the first time this year, may have found the ground too lively. *(op 15-8 tchd 7-4)*
Honest Yer Honour(IRE) was reported by his rider to have been kicked at the start and never happy on the fast ground. *Official explanation: trainer said gelding was kicked at start (op 15-8 tchd 7-4)*

T/Plt: £41.10 to a £1 stake. Pool: £39,788.75. 705.55 winning tickets. T/Qpdt: £15.50 to a £1 stake. Pool: £2,006.70. 95.50 winning tickets. KH

59 KELSO (L-H)
Thursday, April 28

OFFICIAL GOING: Good to soft (good in places)
Wind: fresh against

80 MOET & CHANDON CONDITIONAL JOCKEYS' H'CAP HURDLE (13 hdls) 3m 3f
5:50 (5:50) (Class 4) (0-100,95) 4-Y-O+ **£3,393** (£1,044; £522; £261)

Form	Pos	Dist	Horse	RPR
42P-	1		**Glenmoss Rosy (IRE)**[39] [4473] 6-10-9 **86**.....SMarshall(8) (N G Richards) *hld up: outpcd 9th: rallied 3 out: led run in: styd on wl* **15/2**	91
122-	2	2	**Gimme Shelter (IRE)**[6] [4970] 11-10-5 **77**.....DCCostello(3) (S J Marshall) *led to 8th: led 3 out to run in: kpt on same pce* **5/1**[2]	80
042-	3	6	**Fearless Foursome**[6] [4965] 6-10-9 **78**.....ONelmes (N W Alexander) *hld up: smooth hdwy 9th: effrt after 3 out: disp ld last: no ex run in* **4/1**[1]	75+
10P-	4	10	**You'Re The Man (IRE)**[5] [4977] 8-10-7 **86**.....(p) SGagan(10) (Mrs E Slack) *cl up: led 8th to 3 out: wknd next* **14/1**	73
4P0-	5	7	**Contract Scotland (IRE)**[17] [4812] 10-11-9 **95**.....GBerridge(3) (L Lungo) *hld up in tch: effrt bef 3 out: wknd after next* **8/1**	75
1P1-	6	dist	**The Merry Mason (IRE)**[50] [4254] 9-10-11 **88**.....THalliday(8) (Mrs S J Smith) *prom: disp ld 8th to 3 out: sn rdn and btn* **4/1**[1]	—
U35-	7	3 ½	**Mr Christie**[23] [4736] 13-11-1 **84**.....NPMulholland (Miss L C Siddall) *bhd: niggled 3rd: struggling 9th: n.d after* **20/1**	—
026-	8	2 ½	**Old Nosey (IRE)**[17] [4812] 9-11-8 **91**.....PRobson (B Mactaggart) *chsd ldrs to 9th: sn btn* **12/1**	—
0P2-	P		**Minster Fair**[8] [4924] 7-11-5 **91**.....GThomas(3) (A C Whillans) *hld up: rdn 4 out: sn btn: p.u bef 2 out* **7/1**[3]	—
P00-	P		**Bromley Moss**[17] [4807] 6-9-11 **69** oh5.....CDSharkey(3) (Miss S E Forster) *chsd ldr early: lost pl 8th: t.o whn p.u bef 3 out* **66/1**	—

6m 48.2s (13.50) **Going Correction** +0.725s/f (Soft) **10** Ran SP% **112.7**
Speed ratings: **109,108,106,103,101 —,—,—,—,—** CSF £43.87 CT £170.64 TOTE £8.60: £1.70, £2.30, £1.50; EX 59.40.
Owner West Coast Fiddlers **Bred** James Larkin **Trained** Greystoke, Cumbria

FOCUS
A modest handicap run at an ordinary gallop over the marathon trip with the runner-up the best guide to the level.

NOTEBOOK
Glenmoss Rosy(IRE), pulled up after a mistake last time, bounced back to record her first win. She was off the bridle some way out and looked to be struggling, but her stamina eventually won her the day. She may be retired now. *(op 8-1)*
Gimme Shelter(IRE) was returning to hurdles from a 13lb lower mark. A thorough stayer, she was in front for a second time three from home but was collared on the long run-in. *(op 6-1)*
Fearless Foursome is due to race off no less than 19lb higher in future handicaps so this was an opportunity missed. Despite making one or two jumping errors, he travelled well until this marathon trip found him out. Three miles should be within his compass, though. *(op 5-1 tchd 7-2)*
You'Re The Man(IRE) ran respectably, but he looks held from his current career-high mark. *(tchd 12-1)*
Contract Scotland(IRE), without a hurdles win since scoring over course and distance nearly three years ago, probably needs better ground. *(op 10-1)*
The Merry Mason(IRE), having his first run over hurdles since October 2002 and rated 18lb higher over fences, was a disappointment and the softish ground might have been a reason. *(tchd 9-2)*
Minster Fair *Official explanation: jockey said mare was never travelling*

81 BELHAVEN BEST H'CAP CHASE (17 fncs) 2m 6f 110y
6:20 (6:20) (Class 4) (0-90,88) 5-Y-O+ **£4,706** (£1,448; £724; £362)

Form	Pos	Dist	Horse	RPR
24P-	1		**Go Nomadic**[42] [4416] 11-11-1 **77**.....(tp) MBradburne (P G Atkinson) *mde all: rdn 3 out: styd on wl* **5/1**[1]	93+
462-	2	7	**Lochiedubs**[18] [4786] 10-11-4 **85**.....(p) DFlavin(5) (Mrs L B Normile) *mstkes: cl up: effrt 3 out: mstke next: kpt on same pce run in* **6/1**[2]	95+
P30-	3	14	**Jansue Charlie**[11] [4875] 11-10-8 **70**.....ADobbin (R Nixon) *hld up midfield: hdwy to chse ldrs 11th: rdn and outpcd fr 3 out* **12/1**	70+
UPP-	4	13	**Pornic (FR)**[11] [4874] 11-11-3 **82**.....ONelmes(3) (A Crook) *midfield: outpcd 13th: n.d after* **20/1**	64
120-	5	3	**Lanmire Tower (IRE)**[35] [4539] 11-10-13 **82**.....(p) WKennedy(7) (S Gollings) *chsd ldrs: hit 10th and next: wknd fr 4 out* **9/1**[3]	61

/55- **6** *7* **Hombre**[31] 4626 10-11-2 **78** BHarding 50
(M D Hammond) *in tch: hdwy 1/2-way: rdn and wknd bef 2 out* **16/1**

50P- **7** *dist* **Agincourt (IRE)**[31] 4627 9-10-5 **74** MrGTumelty[(7)] —
(John R Upson) *chsd ldrs to 11th: sn rdn and wknd* **16/1**

005- **F** **Sagardian (FR)**[11] 4872 6-10-7 **69** DO'Meara —
(L Lungo) *nt fluent: a bhd: fell 12th* **5/1**[1]

544- **P** **Gofagold**[42] 4418 10-11-6 **82** KRenwick —
(A C Whillans) *a bhd: t.o whn p.u bef 13th* **20/1**

333- **F** **Red Perk (IRE)**[42] 4416 8-11-12 **88** (p) KJohnson —
(R C Guest) *racd wd in midfield: fell 6th* **5/1**[1]

3/0- **P** **Northern Rambler (IRE)**[11] 4872 8-10-11 **73** RMcGrath —
(K G Reveley) *mstkes: a bhd: t.o whn p.u bef 13th* **20/1**

0P0- **P** **Pharagon (IRE)**[6] 4965 7-9-9 **62** oh3 DMcGann[(5)] —
(Mrs C J Kerr) *nt jump wl: a bhd: no ch whn hmpd 12th: p.u after next* **100/1**

P04- **P** **Fairwood Nickle (IRE)**[40] 4452 6-10-0 **65** (t) PBuchanan[(3)] —
(Miss Lucinda V Russell) *prom to 1/2-way: sn btn: t.o whn p.u bef 3 out* **16/1**

5m 56.6s (1.60) **Going Correction** +0.25s/f (Yiel) **13** Ran SP% **114.9**
Speed ratings: **107,104,99,95,94 91,—,—,—,— —,—,—** CSF £32.56 CT £340.61 TOTE £5.70: £2.10, £1.60, £3.30; EX 32.70.
Owner D G Atkinson **Bred** D G Atkinson **Trained** Yafforth, N Yorks

FOCUS
A modest handicap in which the winner produced his best run since 2004, although he was 12lb off his best form of that year.

NOTEBOOK
Go Nomadic, adopting his usual front-running role, saw off his pursuers to notch his first win in handicap company. Considered not to have been right for a lot of the time in recent months, he has been dropped around a stone since Christmas and had cheekpieces back on here. *(op 7-1)*
Lochiedubs, runner-up in a seller last time, ran creditably again despite a sticky round of jumping, but the drop in trip was not ideal.
Jansue Charlie, who went well here in his hurdling days, had the cheekpieces left off. Left behind by the first two from the third last, he is due to race off 3lb lower in future handicaps. *(op 14-1)*
Pornic(FR), who has lost his way of late, at least completed this time. *(op 16-1)*
Red Perk(IRE), whose best form is over further, took quite a heavy fall. *(tchd 11-2)*
Sagardian(FR), having only his second run over fences, had made mistakes prior to coming down. *(tchd 11-2)*

82 RMC MATERIALS NOVICES' HURDLE (8 hdls) 2m 110y
6:50 (6:50) (Class 3) 4-Y-0+ **£7,221** (£2,222; £1,111; £555)

Form RPR

230- **1** **Romany Prince**[41] 4434 6-11-0 TScudamore 101+
(S Gollings) *mde all: mstke 3 out: hdd briefly run in: kpt on gamely u.p* **7/4**[1]

511- **2** *hd* **Andre Chenier (IRE)**[25] 4709 4-11-3 114 NPMulholland 103
(P Monteith) *trckd ldrs: wnt 2nd gng wl 4 out: led briefly run in: sn rdn: kpt on: jst hld* **5/2**[2]

353- **3** *3 1/2* **Double Gem (IRE)**[17] 4807 6-11-0 PRobson 97
(J I A Charlton) *trckd wnr to 4 out: rdn next: kpt on same pce fr last* **33/1**

531- **4** *7* **Mohawk Star (IRE)**[12] 4446 4-10-8 112 PCO'Neill[(7)] 91
(Miss Venetia Williams) *hld up: effrt bef 3 out: outpcd fr next* **10/1**

035- **5** *7* **Neidpath Castle**[8] 4923 6-11-0 103 KRenwick 83
(A C Whillans) *hld up: hdwy bef 3 out: rdn and wknd bef 2 out* **12/1**

U- **6** *1/2* **Nobel (FR)**[25] 4709 4-10-2 MissRDavidson[(7)] 78+
(N G Richards) *mstke 1st: wl bhd tl styd on fr 2 out: n.d* **6/1**[3]

23- **7** *1/2* **You Do The Math (IRE)**[49] 4276 5-10-11 GBerridge[(3)] 82
(L Lungo) *hld up: pushed along 4 out: kpt on fr 2 out: n.d* **25/1**

216- **8** *7* **Italiano**[17] 4807 6-11-6 108 RGarritty 81
(P Beaumont) *prom tl wknd fr 2 out* **20/1**

051- **9** *11* **Lofty Leader (IRE)**[6] 4965 6-11-3 92 ONelmes[(3)] 70
(Mrs H O Graham) *hld up: hdwy 3 out: wknd next* **33/1**

50- **10** *2 1/2* **Another Taipan (IRE)**[12] 4865 5-10-7 EWhillans[(7)] 61
(A C Whillans) *nt fluent: nvr on terms* **100/1**

030- **11** *1 1/2* **Neven**[217] 1483 6-10-11 85 (t) PBuchanan[(3)] 60
(Miss Lucinda V Russell) *keen: hld up midfield: hit 2nd: wknd fr 4 out* **100/1**

460- **12** *5* **Acceleration (IRE)**[6] 4969 5-11-0 89 ADobbin 55
(R Allan) *chsd ldrs tl hit and wknd fr 3 out* **40/1**

0- **13** *4* **Alphecca (USA)**[12] 4858 4-10-9 RMcGrath 46
(K G Reveley) *hld up and a bhd* **50/1**

020- **14** *6* **King's Envoy (USA)**[48] 4303 6-11-0 100 JimCrowley 45
(Mrs J C McGregor) *a bhd* **66/1**

00- **15** *3* **Differentgear**[9] 4922 4-10-9 (t) FKeniry 37
(P C Haslam) *chsd ldrs to 4 out: sn struggling* **100/1**

006- **16** *dist* **The Rooken (IRE)**[81] 3730 6-11-0 KJohnson —
(P Spottiswood) *a bhd* **100/1**

0/0- **17** *dist* **Crumbs**[350] 332 5-10-7 BGibson —
(B Mactaggart) *prom to 4th: sn lost pl* **100/1**

0/0- **F** **Lady Godson**[144] 2652 6-10-2 DCCostello[(5)] —
(B Mactaggart) *bhd whn fell 3rd* **100/1**

P0- **F** **Hollywood Critic (USA)**[18] 4782 4-9-13 DDaSilva[(10)] —
(P Monteith) *hld up: hdwy 1/2-way: wknd 3 out: btn whn fell next* **100/1**

4m 9.20s (9.20) **Going Correction** +0.725s/f (Soft)
WFA 4 from 5yo+ 5lb **19** Ran SP% **123.3**
Speed ratings: **107,106,105,101,98 98,98,94,89,88 87,85,83,80,79 —,—,—,—** CSF £5.48 TOTE £2.60: £1.40, £2.10, £4.50; EX 9.60.
Owner J B Webb **Bred** P And Mrs Venner **Trained** Scamblesby, Lincs
■ Stewards' Enquiry : T Scudamore one-day ban: used whip with excessive frequency (May 9)

FOCUS
Quite a competitive novices' hurdle, although the winner was a stone below what he has shown over further and the form is probably not all that strong.

NOTEBOOK
Romany Prince, who has faced some stiff tasks over hurdles, stepped down in grade to get off the mark. Obliged to make his own running, he battled back bravely when the runner-up edged past him on the flat. He could go for the Chester Cup now, in which he has top weight. *(op 2-1)*
Andre Chenier(IRE) came close to completing a Kelso hat-trick, but the favourite, to whom he was conceding 3lb, would not be denied. *(tchd 11-4 in places)*
Double Gem(IRE), third in a similar event last time, handled this easier ground. He is now qualified for handicaps.
Mohawk Star(IRE) was held under the penalty he picked up for his controversial win at Bangor, having finished last on the Flat since then. *(op 9-1 tchd 11-1)*
Neidpath Castle did not see out the extended two and a half miles in soft ground last time but appeared to find this too sharp. *(op 16-1)*
Nobel(FR) found himself some way adrift following a first-flight error and could never get into the action. He is capable of better. *Official explanation: jockey said, regarding the running and riding, orders were to drop gelding in, get it settled and to ride the race as it developed, adding that gelding jumped novicey early on, was outpaced from approaching the third-last hurdle, and stayed on up the straight (op 9-2)*
You Do The Math(IRE), placed in both his bumpers, made a satisfactory hurdles debut over a trip which is likely to prove too short for him.

83 Z. HINCHLIFFE & SONS NOVICES' H'CAP CHASE (19 fncs) 3m 1f
7:20 (7:20) (Class 4) (0-105,100) 5-Y-0+ **£4,732** (£1,456; £728; £364)

Form RPR

31P- **1** **Diamond Cottage (IRE)**[11] 4875 10-10-8 **82** MBradburne 90
(S B Bell) *cl up: led 4 out: styd on wl* **5/1**[3]

501- **2** *2 1/2* **Brandy Wine (IRE)**[74] 3827 7-11-7 **95** ADobbin 100
(L Lungo) *hld up in tch: nt fluent 6th and next: hdwy 12th: chsd wnr 3 out: kpt on same pce last* **13/8**[1]

P62- **3** *12* **Wild About Harry**[11] 4872 8-10-0 **74** oh18 HOliver 67
(A R Dicken) *prom: outpcd 4 out: kpt on fr last: no imp* **16/1**

654- **4** *dist* **Goodbadindiferent (IRE)**[6] 4966 9-10-11 **85** BHarding —
(Mrs J C McGregor) *led: blnd 13th: hdd 4 out: wknd 2 out* **10/1**

6P5- **P** **Ladies From Leeds**[97] 3460 6-10-8 **82** NPMulholland —
(A Crook) *bhd: struggling whn mstke 11th: p.u after next* **50/1**

205- **P** **Sea Ferry (IRE)**[11] 4876 9-10-8 **85** (p) PBuchanan[(3)] —
(Miss Lucinda V Russell) *prom: blnd 13th: sn btn: t.o whn p.u bef 2 out* **14/1**

133- **P** **Dumadic**[12] 4864 8-11-12 **100** PRobson 92+
(R E Barr) *hld up in tch: hdwy to chse ldrs bef 3 out: outpcd after next: 4th and btn whn lost action and p.u run in* **9/4**[2]

6m 39.7s (11.30) **Going Correction** +0.25s/f (Yiel) **7** Ran SP% **109.1**
Speed ratings: **91,90,86,—,— —,—** CSF £12.93 CT £104.53 TOTE £10.40: £2.20, £1.70; EX 14.10.
Owner C H P Bell **Bred** Mrs Daphne Tierney **Trained** Swinhoe, Northumberland

FOCUS
Not a strong race and a moderate time. The winner improved on his previous form by 4lb with the runner-up rated to the level of his hurdles win.

NOTEBOOK
Diamond Cottage(IRE) jumped soundly and stayed on strongly to defy a mark 8lb higher than when successful two starts back. That win came in heavy ground but he appreciated the less testing conditions here. *(op 8-1)*
Brandy Wine(IRE), successful over hurdles last time out in February, was 9lb higher for this chasing bow. His jumping improved as the race progressed, but he was unable to peg back the winner. A three-parts brother to the good staying chaser Seven Towers, he should have learned from the experience. *(op 11-8)*
Wild About Harry, runner-up from 13lb out of the handicap at Carlisle, ran another decent race from no less than 18lb 'wrong'.
Goodbadindiferent(IRE) faded after making the running to the second last. *(tchd 9-1)*
Dumadic was beaten when pulling up after losing his action after the final fence. *(tchd 5-2)*

84 GLENDALE ENGINEERING H'CAP CHASE (12 fncs) 2m 1f
7:50 (7:52) (Class 4) (0-110,107) 5-Y-0+ **£6,948** (£2,138; £1,069; £534)

Form RPR

/P2- **1** **Little Flora**[11] 4873 9-9-11 **85** MJMcAlister[(7)] 105+
(S J Marshall) *prom: led 4 out: clr between last 2: styd on wl* **20/1**

F44- **2** *12* **Xaipete (IRE)**[26] 4689 13-11-3 **101** LMcGrath[(3)] 109
(R C Guest) *bhd: hdwy 4 out: effrt 2 out: kpt on: no ch w wnr* **16/1**

F21- **3** *2* **L'Oiseau (FR)**[19] 4780 6-11-4 **99** BGibson 105
(L Lungo) *hld up: smooth hdwy 4 out: chsd wnr 2 out: rdn and no ex last* **8/1**

501- **4** *10* **Fiori**[9] 4919 9-11-11 **106** 7ex FKeniry 104+
(P C Haslam) *led to 3rd: rdn 7th: outpcd fr 2 out* **9/2**[3]

333- **5** *15* **Mexican (USA)**[3] 4689 6-10-6 **87** (b) KRenwick 68
(M D Hammond) *hld up: hdwy 4 out: rdn 2 out: btn last* **16/1**

13F- **6** *19* **Celtic Legend (FR)**[81] 3729 6-10-11 **92** RMcGrath 54
(K G Reveley) *bhd and sn outpcd: nvr on terms* **14/1**

521- **7** *23* **Polyphon (FR)**[18] 4784 7-11-9 **104** ADobbin 68+
(P Monteith) *cl up: led 3rd to 4 out: wkng whn blnd 2 out* **11/4**[1]

332- **8** *15* **Vulcan Lane (NZ)**[31] 4614 8-10-5 **86** (p) HOliver 10
(R C Guest) *sn bhd: no ch fr 1/2-way* **4/1**[2]

315- **P** **Midlem Melody**[17] 4808 9-10-12 **93** ADempsey —
(W S Coltherd) *a bhd: no ch fr 1/2-way: p.u bef 2 out* **20/1**

140- **P** **Hollows Mill**[17] 4808 9-11-10 **105** PRobson —
(F P Murtagh) *in tch: lost pl whn blnd 8th: p.u after next* **40/1**

3P4- **P** **Javelot D'Or (FR)**[17] 4808 8-9-13 **83** (t) PBuchanan[(3)] —
(Mrs B K Thomson) *in tch: hit 5th: wknd after next: t.o whn p.u bef 3 out* **10/1**

4m 23.2s (2.70) **Going Correction** +0.25s/f (Yiel) **11** Ran SP% **115.4**
Speed ratings: **103,97,96,91,84 75,64,57,—,— —** CSF £280.03 CT £2760.28 TOTE £22.30: £4.00, £4.10, £2.30; EX 117.70.
Owner S J Marshall **Bred** Mrs S Gilchrist **Trained** Alnwick, Northumberland

FOCUS
This was run at a strong pace and the race could be rated a bit higher.

NOTEBOOK
Little Flora, who made a satisfactory chasing debut in heavy conditions, appreciated this better ground and stayed on strongly to score. The fast pace suited her. *(op 25-1)*
Xaipete(IRE), who is gradually slipping down the handicap, is without a win since September 2003 but has made the frame 21 times since then. *(op 9-1)*
L'Oiseau(FR), successful over hurdles last time, was 5lb higher. He travelled well but did not really pick up when he needed to. *(tchd 9-1)*
Fiori, penalised for his win at Towcester, ran creditably given that he helped set the strong pace. *(op 4-1 tchd 5-1)*
Mexican(USA), who had a run on Fibresand three days earlier, again did not find much in the latter stages.
Polyphon(FR) was largely responsible for setting the strong pace and was on the retreat when blundering two from home. *(op 5-2)*

85 BACK AND LAY AT GGBET.COM INTERMEDIATE HURDLE (11 hdls) 2m 6f 110y
8:20 (8:20) (Class 4) 4-Y-0+ **£3,510** (£1,080; £540; £270)

Form RPR

115- **1** **Hernando's Boy**[16] 1914 4-11-5 115 RMcGrath 112+
(K G Reveley) *keen: prom: wnt 2nd 1/2-way: led 2 out: drvn out* **2/1**[2]

11P- **2** *3 1/2* **Iris's Prince**[37] 4508 6-11-6 NPMulholland 107
(A Crook) *chsd ldrs: effrt bef 2 out: chsd wnr last: kpt on* **16/1**

2/1- **3** *12* **Monte Rosa (IRE)**[169] 2122 6-10-13 106 ADobbin 92+
(N G Richards) *mstkes: hld up in tch: outpcd bef 7th: rallied and cl up 3 out: outpcd bef last* **5/4**[1]

P04- **4** *9* **Opal's Helmsman (USA)**[17] 4812 6-11-0 87 ....(p) ADempsey 80
(W S Coltherd) *prom: lost pl 7th: styd on fr 2 out: no imp* **10/1**
01P- **5** *hd* **Lord Rodney (IRE)**[18] 4785 6-11-6 112 .... RGarritty 86
(P Beaumont) *keen: led to 2 out: btn last* **7/1**[3]
6/F- **6** *14* **Jockie Wells**[17] 4809 7-10-11 .... PBuchanan(3) 66
(Miss Lucinda V Russell) *sn bhd: nvr on terms* **40/1**
P60- **7** *6* **Venture More**[7] 4943 9-10-11 77 .... GBerridge(3) 60
(Mrs A F Tullie) *plld hrd: hld up: hdwy to chse ldrs 4th: wknd 3 out* **100/1**
050- **8** *14* **Parisian Rose (IRE)**[18] 4788 6-10-7 ....(t) MBradburne 39
(Mrs H O Graham) *sn bhd: no ch fr 1/2-way* **66/1**

6m 2.30s (24.50) **Going Correction** +0.725s/f (Soft)
WFA 4 from 6yo+ 6lb **8** Ran SP% **110.2**
Speed ratings: **86,84,80,77,77 72,70,65** CSF £28.00 TOTE £3.20: £1.10, £4.60, £1.10; EX 21.30 Place 6 £67.31, Place 5 £41.77.
Owner Crack of Dawn Partnership **Bred** T E Pocock **Trained** Lingdale, N Yorks

FOCUS
This was run at just a moderate pace and the time was therefore slow. Not an easy race to assess, but the winner was value for a bit further and the runner-up ran to his mark.

NOTEBOOK
Hernando's Boy had not run over hurdles since contesting a Listed event at Wetherby in October but has run two good races on the Flat this spring. A little keen over this longer trip, he responded well on the run-in to assert. *(op 5-2)*
Iris's Prince, pulled up on his debut for this yard last month after a lengthy absence, gave the impression he will be suited by a step up to three miles. *(op 9-1)*
Monte Rosa(IRE), not seen since scoring over three-quarters of a mile shorter at this venue in November, did not jump well and ran in snatches. *(tchd 11-8)*
Opal's Helmsman(USA), with cheekpieces on for the first time, again shaped as if he will be suited by a step up to three miles. *(op 12-1)*
Lord Rodney(IRE) set a modest pace before fading rather tamely. *(op 13-2)*
T/Plt: £111.00 to a £1 stake. Pool: £40,942.20. 269.25 winning tickets. T/Qpdt: £17.80 to a £1 stake. Pool: £3,952.90. 163.50 winning tickets. RY

[65]PUNCHESTOWN (R-H)
Thursday, April 28

OFFICIAL GOING: Soft

87a BLUE SQUARE CHASE (FOR THE LA TOUCHE CUP) 4m 2f (Banks Crse)
2:35 (2:35) 5-Y-0+ **£11,542** (£3,386; £1,613; £549)

RPR

1 **Good Step (IRE)**[22] 4744 7-12-3 107 .... MrJTMcNamara 115
(E Bolger, Ire) *hld up in tch: impr into 5th 6 out: 2nd 4 out: rdn bef 2 out: chal last: led early run-in: all out* **11/2**[2]
2 *1/2* **Shady Lad (IRE)**[2] 39 8-11-7 88 .... MissNCarberry(5) 110
(E Bolger, Ire) *a cl up: led and disp fr 18th: rdn and strly pressed fr 2 out: hdd after last: kpt on wl u.p* **10/1**
3 *14* **I'm On The Line (IRE)**[2] 39 9-11-0 .... MrCMMurphy(7) 91
(Mrs D A Love, Ire) *hld up: 10th 1/2-way: prog into 5th 4 out: 3rd bef 2 out: no ex bef last* **33/1**
4 *25* **Harry In A Hurry**[15] 4833 8-11-12 93 .... KWhelan 71
(Andrew Lee, Ire) *led and disp: hdd 5th: remained prom: led again 6 out: hdd 4 out: dropped to 5th bef 2 out: sn no ex* **20/1**
5 *6* **Three Mill (IRE)**[11] 8-11-2 .... MrJDMoore(5) 60
(Thomas Cleary, Ire) *towards rr: kpt on one pced fr 3 out* **25/1**
6 *7* **Andrewjames (IRE)**[2] 39 11-12-0 91 .... MrJCash(7) 67
(Peter McCreery, Ire) *mid-div: prog into 5th bef 1/2-way: rdn 19th: out pced 5 out: no ex after 3 out* **10/1**
7 *11* **Star Performance (IRE)**[139] 2747 10-11-12 109 ....(t) GCotter 47
(Oliver McKiernan, Ire) *racd wd in mid-div: impr into 6th bef 6 out: wknd after 4 out* **7/1**
F **Timucua (IRE)**[39] 4488 6-11-2 78 .... RLoughran(5) —
(D T Hughes, Ire) *mid-div: fell 14th* **33/1**
F **Luzcadou (FR)**[44] 4385 12-11-9 ....(b) KJMercer(3) —
(Ferdy Murphy) *trckd ldrs in 5th tl fell 16th* **6/1**[3]
P **Davids Lad (IRE)**[2] 39 11-11-12 123 ....(t) PCarberry —
(A J Martin, Ire) *hld up in tch: p.u lame bef 16th* **9/4**[1]
R **Desperately Frisky (IRE)**[2] 39 12-11-7 .... BMCash —
(D Broad, Ire) *nvr a factor: trailing whn ref 4 out* **66/1**
P **Mose Harper (IRE)**[71] 3897 13-11-12 64 ....(b) JPElliott —
(Thomas O'Neill, Ire) *prom early: wknd fr 1/2-way: p.u bef 4 out* **66/1**
P **Panchovillas Gleam (IRE)**[32] 4596 11-12-7 86 ....(b) PACarberry —
(Dermot Day, Ire) *nvr a factor: trailing fr 4 out: p.u bef last* **33/1**
U **Clawick Connection (IRE)**[89] 3579 10-11-7 75 .... RGeraghty —
(J N R Billinge) *hld up: 8th after 1/2-way: no imp fr 6 out: uns rdr 4 out* **33/1**
P **Pre Ordained (IRE)**[46] 13-11-0 .... RMMoran(7) —
(Mark Anthony Stafford, Ire) *cl up and disp ld: hdd bef 10th: wknd fr 17th: p.u bef 4 out* **33/1**
U **Takagi (IRE)**[31] 4634 10-11-12 139 .... DNRussell —
(E J O'Grady, Ire) *prom: led fr 10th tl mstke 18th: mstke 20th: 4th and rdn after mstke 3 out: no imp whn uns rdr next* **11/2**[2]

10m 19.3s **Going Correction** +0.70s/f (Soft) **16** Ran SP% **132.8**
Speed ratings: **111,110,107,101,100 98,96,—,—,— —,—,—,—,—,—** — CSF £58.42 TOTE £4.50: £1.30, £1.50, £9.20, £5.20; DF 21.20.
Owner John P McManus **Bred** Niall Flynn **Trained** Bruree, Co Limerick

NOTEBOOK
Good Step(IRE), from the dominant stable in this sphere, had it put up to him by his stable companion. *(op 5/1)*
Shady Lad(IRE), second here on Tuesday, ran another brave race and could be a traveller for the Pardubiche.
Luzcadou(FR) showed more enthusiasm here for the unique obstacles than he did 12 months ago. He was still in touch when falling at the 16th. *(op 5/2 tchd 11/4)*
Davids Lad(IRE) fractured a pedal bone and may not run again. *Official explanation: vet said gelding finished lame on its right fore (op 5/2 tchd 11/4)*
Clawick Connection(IRE) was well held when unseating four out. *(op 5/2 tchd 11/4)*

88a COLM MCEVOY AUCTIONEERS CHAMPION FOUR YEAR OLD HURDLE (GRADE 1) 2m
3:10 (3:10) 4-Y-0 **£48,368** (£14,822; £7,021; £2,340; £1,560)

RPR

1 **United (GER)**[45] 4367 4-10-9 .... LAspell 141+
(Mrs L Wadham) *settled 4th: impr to ld after 2 out: sn drew clr: unchal* **6/1**[3]
2 *12* **Strangely Brown (IRE)**[21] 4749 4-11-0 .... RWalsh 127
(E McNamara, Ire) *prom: 3rd 4 out: 5th u.p after 2 out: kpt on fr last to go mod 2nd nr fin* **7/2**[2]
3 *1/2* **Akilak (IRE)**[41] 4433 4-11-0 .... GLee 127
(J Howard Johnson) *hld up in tch: cl 5th appr 2 out: sn rdn: mod and no imp bef last: kpt on same pce* **8/13**[1]
4 *1/2* **Eye Candy (IRE)**[25] 4727 4-11-0 .... DJCondon 126
(Mrs Sandra McCarthy, Ire) *sn trckd ldr in 2nd: cl 3rd 2 out: kpt on same pce u.p* **50/1**
5 *shd* **Don't Be Bitin (IRE)**[41] 4433 4-11-0 .... BJGeraghty 126
(Eoin Griffin, Ire) *led: rdn and strly pressed after 3 out: hdd after next: sn outpcd: no ex fr last* **14/1**
6 *4* **Openide**[15] 4826 4-11-0 .... APMcCoy 122
(B W Duke) *cl up early: dropped to 6th 5 out: outpcd 3 out: kpt on fr last* **14/1**
7 *dist* **Maxxium (IRE)**[68] 3963 4-11-0 ....(t) PCarberry —
(M Halford, Ire) *hld up in rr: lost tch after 3 out: eased fr last: t.o* **50/1**

4m 3.10s **Going Correction** +0.475s/f (Soft) **7** Ran SP% **115.7**
Speed ratings: **123,117,116,116,116 114,—** CSF £28.20 TOTE £8.80: £2.80, £1.40; DF 24.10.
Owner R B Holt **Bred** Gestut Norina **Trained** Newmarket, Suffolk

FOCUS
A weak renewal both in terms of quality and quantity, and confirmation that the Irish juveniles are a moderate crop. Nevertheless, United confirmed herself a really smart recruit by retaining her unbeaten record in tremendous style, showing much improved form. Strangely Brown was below recent form and has been rated to the level of his earlier course win.

NOTEBOOK
United(GER) has a rather unorthodox hurdling technique but ran right away from these after the second last to retain her unbeaten record. She had looked a useful recruit since arriving from Germany, but the ease with which she won was still surprising as she barely came off the bridle. She looks a serious talent and could head for a championship event at Auteuil now. *(op 7/1)*
Strangely Brown(IRE) turned Cheltenham form around with the favourite but proved totally unable to go with the winner once she set sail. *(op 3/1)*
Akilak(IRE) was not travelling like a winner from as far out as the third last. He was probably over the top at this stage of the season, but easily his best two runs have been at Cheltenham and he may not be as effective elsewhere. *(op 4/6)*
Eye Candy(IRE) looked relatively exposed and appeared to run well above himself. His proximity raises a question mark over the race as a whole, although connections reportedly fancied him to run a big race. *(op 33/1)*
Don't Be Bitin(IRE) was the other to show improved form *(op 12/1)*
Openide was done with a long way out.

89a SWORDLESTOWN CUP NOVICE CHASE (GRADE 1) 2m
3:45 (3:45) 5-Y-0+ **£43,971** (£13,475; £6,382; £2,127; £1,418)

RPR

1 **War Of Attrition (IRE)**[19] 4769 6-11-12 140 .... CO'Dwyer 156
(M F Morris, Ire) *settled 3rd: 2nd whn slt mstke 3 out: sn rdn and outpcd: hdwy after 2 out: chal after last: styd on wl to ld cl home* **3/1**[2]
2 *1* **Watson Lake (IRE)**[30] 4648 7-11-12 .... PCarberry 155
(Noel Meade, Ire) *trckd ldrs: 2nd after 6th: led 4 out: drew clr after next: rdn after mstke 2 out: nt fluent last: strly pressed run-in: hdd* **7/4**[1]
3 *20* **Strike Back (IRE)**[31] 4636 7-11-12 .... RMPower 137+
(Mrs John Harrington, Ire) *trckd ldrs: 3rd 5 out: 2nd next: rdn 3 out: sn no ex* **10/1**
4 *3* **Euro Leader (IRE)**[30] 4648 7-11-12 120 .... RWalsh 132
(W P Mullins, Ire) *led: hdd after 6th: dropped to rr 5 out: kpt on onepced fr 3 out* **33/1**
5 *dist* **Newmill (IRE)**[67] 3984 7-11-12 .... AndrewJMcNamara —
(John Joseph Murphy, Ire) *hld up in rr: impr into 4th whn slt mstke 4 out: wknd after next: virtually p.u fr last: t.o* **10/1**
U **Fota Island (IRE)**[21] 4751 9-11-12 150 .... APMcCoy —
(M F Morris, Ire) *hld up in tch: mstke and uns rdr 5th* **4/1**[3]
F **Mariah Rollins (IRE)**[44] 4382 7-11-7 .... BJGeraghty —
(P A Fahy, Ire) *cl up in 2nd: led after 6th: rdn and hdd appr 4 out: btn whn fell next* **13/2**

4m 23.3s **Going Correction** +0.475s/f (Soft) **8** Ran SP% **115.8**
Speed ratings: **105,104,94,93,— —,—** CSF £9.39 TOTE £3.60: £2.20, £2.00; DF 7.00.
Owner Gigginstown House Stud **Bred** Miss B A Murphy **Trained** Fethard, Co Tipperary

FOCUS
The complexion changed dramatically from the second last. Watson Lake looked to have the rece sewn up, but a mistake appeared to knock the stuffing out of him and he capitulated in worrying fashion, conceding to War Of Attrition close home. The pair were a long way clear.

NOTEBOOK
War Of Attrition(IRE) appeared to have little chance two out but stayed on much the better to clinch it close home. He needs further but this was compensation for his Cheltenham and Aintree disappointments and he should enjoy a successful second season over fences now he has turned the corner. *(op 100/30 tchd 7/2)*
Watson Lake(IRE) threw magnificent jumps four out and three out but blundered badly at the second last and was tying up when none too clever at the last. In trouble on the run-in, he was not abused, and something may well have been amiss. *(op 7/4 tchd 13/8)*
Strike Back(IRE) had his chance four out before weakening. His future may lie in handicaps.
Euro Leader(IRE) was flying a bit high on just his third run over fences. He showed improved form in fourth and is going the right way. *(op 25/1)*
Newmill(IRE) continues to disappoint

90a BALLYMORE PROPERTIES CHAMPION STAYERS HURDLE (GRADE 1) 3m
4:20 (4:20) 4-Y-0+ **£74,751** (£22,907; £10,851; £3,617; £2,411)

RPR

1 **Carlys Quest**[20] 4767 11-11-12 .... KJMercer 142
(Ferdy Murphy) *towards rr: slt mstke 8th: hdwy after 5 out: led after 3 out: clr after 2 out: styd on strly* **25/1**
2 *9* **Kadoun (IRE)**[31] 4634 8-11-12 142 .... APMcCoy 133
(M J P O'Brien, Ire) *mod 6th: impr into 4th 5 out: rdn next: styd on fr 2 out: mod 2nd fr last* **14/1**
3 *2* **Basilea Star (IRE)**[2] 43 8-11-12 134 ....(t) GLee 131
(Ferdy Murphy) *bhd: 6th 5 out: styd on fr 3 out to go mod 3rd bef last* **25/1**
4 *20* **Homer Wells (IRE)**[32] 4597 7-11-12 136 .... DJCondon 111
(W P Mullins, Ire) *prom: 3rd 1/2-way: 2nd after 3 out: no ex after next* **16/1**
5 *7* **Solerina (IRE)**[14] 3845 8-11-7 158 .... JRBarry 99
(James Bowe, Ire) *attempted to make all: hdd after 3 out: 3rd and rdn next: sn wknd* **5/2**[2]
6 *dist* **Rosaker (USA)**[31] 4635 8-11-12 143 .... PCarberry —
(Noel Meade, Ire) *cl up in 2nd: outpcd after 3 out: trailing whn virtually p.u after 2 out: t.o* **10/1**

7 *dist* **Emotional Moment (IRE)**[42] 4409 8-11-12 150 .... BJGeraghty —
(T J Taaffe, Ire) *trckd ldrs in 4th: slt mstke 2nd: lost pl 5 out: virtually p.u fr next: completely t.o* 9/4[1]
P **Our Ben**[32] 4597 6-11-12 142 .... RWalsh —
(W P Mullins, Ire) *trckd ldrs in 5th: blnd 6th: sn p.u* 10/3[3]
P **Yogi (IRE)**[14] 4631 9-11-12 136 .... MAFitzgerald —
(Thomas Foley, Ire) *a bhd: trailing fr 7th: completely t.o whn p.u bef 4 out* 25/1

6m 16.0s **Going Correction** +0.625s/f (Soft) **10** Ran SP% **115.6**
Speed ratings: **113,110,109,102,100** —,—,—,— CSF £309.23 TOTE £44.00: £6.20, £3.00, £5.60; DF 240.10.
Owner Ms L Neville **Bred** R E A Bott (wigmore Street) Ltd **Trained** West Witton, N Yorks

FOCUS
Poor form by Grade 1 standards. Carlys Quest is thoroughly exposed, but he is an out-and-out stayer and was best equipped to take advantage of the conditions in a race in which none of the market leaders ran their races.

NOTEBOOK
Carlys Quest sprang the surprise of the meeting, stretching on from the third last and utilising his *undoubted stamina in a race in which the principals were all below form for one reason or another. Official explanation: trainer said, regarding the improved form shown, gelding was unsuited by the slower pace and faster ground at Aintree ;ast time, whereas today's softer ground was to its advantage (op 20/1)*
Kadoun(IRE), reverting to the smaller obstacles, ran well but proved no match for the winner from two out.
Basilea Star(IRE), stable companion of the winner, had made little show in a handicap earlier in the week but stayed on well here to go third in the straight. *(op 20/1)*
Homer Wells(IRE) went second after three out but could not sustain the run and ran well below his best.
Solerina(IRE) was headed three out and dropped away tamely. She might not get three miles but this was a weak effort. *(op 2/1)*
Rosaker(USA) ran second but cried enough after three out and was tailed off after the next. *(op 8/1)*
Emotional Moment(IRE) was another to run below par, trailing from the fourth last. *(op 9/4 tchd 5/2)*
Yogi(IRE) could not handle these. *(op 20/1)*
Our Ben, the market springer, hit the sixth and was pulled up soon afterwards. *(op 20/1)*

91a TATTERSALLS (IRELAND) LTD PAT TAAFFE H'CAP CHASE (GRADE B) 3m 1f
4:55 (4:55) (0-145,135) 5-Y-0+ **£25,393** (£7,450; £3,549; £1,209)

RPR
1 **No Half Session (IRE)**[31] 4637 8-10-0 111 .... PCarberry 136+
(Noel Meade, Ire) *hld up towards rr: 10th and hdwy 5 out: 4th travelling wl 3 out: cl 2nd whn forced lft next: sn led and drew clr: easily* 9/2[1]
2 *6* **Coolnahilla (IRE)**[31] 4634 9-10-10 121 .... KHadnett 131
(W J Burke, Ire) *hld up: mstke 1st: 9th 4 out: 7th and hdwy after next: mod 3rd bef last: kpt on* 9/1
3 *3/4* **What Odds (IRE)**[31] 4634 9-11-0 125 .... BJGeraghty 134
(T K Geraghty, Ire) *trckd ldrs: 5th 1/2-way: 4th 4 out: outpcd after 3 out: 6th 2 out: kpt on fr last* 10/1
4 *nk* **Ransboro (IRE)**[54] 4197 6-9-13 110 .... JRBarry 119
(C F Swan, Ire) *led and disp: rdn and strly pressed whn j. bdly lft 2 out: sn hdd: mstke last: no ex* 14/1
5 *1/2* **Berkley (IRE)**[18] 4804 8-9-11 111 ....(b) TGMRyan(3) 119
(Patrick Michael Verling, Ire) *prom: 3rd appr 1/2-way: 7th 5 out: no imp after 4 out: kpt on fr 2 out* 14/1
6 *2* **Hard Winter (IRE)**[31] 4637 8-9-10 110 .... PWFlood(3) 116
(D T Hughes, Ire) *cl up early: lost pl 8th: hdwy into 3rd 4 out: rdn next: no ex bef last* 14/1
7 *1* **Ossmoses (IRE)**[54] 4183 8-10-7 118 .... DRDennis 123
(D M Forster) *cl up: 2nd 1/2-way: chal bef 3 out: 4th bef next: onepced* 12/1
8 *2 1/2* **Like A Bee (IRE)**[54] 4197 7-9-11 108 .... APCrowe 111
(C Roche, Ire) *in tch: 6th 5 out: 7th and rdn after 3 out: no imp* 10/1
9 *13* **Bob Justice (IRE)**[25] 4733 9-10-0 111 ....(b) GCotter 101
(T M Walsh, Ire) *a towards rr: trailing fr 2 out* 20/1
10 *2* **Star Clipper**[31] 4634 8-10-8 122 .... DFO'Regan(3) 110
(Noel Meade, Ire) *mid-div on inner: hmpd 10th: slt mstke next: no imp whn mstke 3 out: trailing fr next* 16/1
11 *3/4* **Garvivonnian (IRE)**[31] 4634 10-11-6 134 .... AndrewJMcNamara(3) 121
(Edward P Mitchell, Ire) *mid-div: wknd 6 out: trailing fr 3 out* 25/1
F **Beau Colina (IRE)**[32] 4596 8-10-2 113 ow1 .... RWalsh —
(A J Martin, Ire) *hld up: fell 6 out* 5/1[2]
B **Munster (IRE)**[20] 4764 8-10-7 118 ....(t) GLee —
(A L T Moore, Ire) *towards rr whn b.d 6 out* 12/1
F **The Culdee (IRE)**[25] 2080 9-10-5 116 .... JLCullen —
(F Flood, Ire) *prom: 6th whn fell 10th* 12/1
P **Heroic (IRE)**[31] 4634 9-10-7 118 .... CO'Dwyer —
(C F Swan, Ire) *bhd: trailing whn hmpd 6 out: sn p.u* 16/1
P **Dark'n Sharp (GER)**[20] 4766 10-11-10 135 .... MAFitzgerald —
(R T Phillips) *mid-div: no ex fr 5 out: p.u bef 2 out* 33/1
P **This Is Serious (IRE)**[42] 4422 11-10-7 123 .... JFLevins(5) —
(C F Swan, Ire) *hld up in tch: wknd bef 5 out: p.u bef 4 out* 33/1
P **Ross River**[30] 4648 9-11-3 128 .... MrRWidger —
(S Donohoe, Ire) *hld up: sltly hmpd 10th: 8th 5 out: no ex fr next: p.u bef 2 out* 25/1
P **Sraid Na Cathrach (IRE)**[122] 3029 9-10-7 118 .... DJCondon —
(C Byrnes, Ire) *hld up: reminders after 6 out: no imp fr 4 out: p.u bef 2 out* 7/1[3]
P **Hume Castle (IRE)**[31] 4634 9-10-12 123 ....(t) RMPower —
(Mrs John Harrington, Ire) *rr of mid-div: impr into 7th bef 6 out: no ex after 5 out: p.u bef 2 out* 16/1
P **Golden Storm (IRE)**[1] 69 8-10-11 125 ....(b) JMAllen(3) —
(Joseph Crowley, Ire) *prom on outer: cl 2nd 5 out: 3rd next: wknd bef 3 out: trailing whn p.u bef last* 20/1

6m 46.4s **Going Correction** +0.625s/f (Soft) **21** Ran SP% **159.4**
Speed ratings: **103,101,100,100,100 99,99,98,94,94 93**,—,—,—,— —,—,—,—,— — CSF £54.35 CT £437.20 TOTE £5.40: £2.00, £1.70, £2.60, £7.50; DF 49.00.
Owner R D Murphy **Bred** John Neilan **Trained** Castletown, Co Meath

NOTEBOOK
No Half Session(IRE) is certainly exploiting his handicap mark and, 23lb higher than when starting his sequence, made it three in a row with an easy win. *(op 9/2 tchd 5/1)*
Coolnahilla(IRE), fifth in the Irish National, found the improver much too good and it was just stamina that saw him finish second. *(op 10/1)*
What Odds(IRE) kept on well after getting left behind three out.
Ransboro(IRE) was up front throughout but has a tendency to run down his fences, and he took the winner with him at the second last. He recovered well from a last fence error and stayed on again.
Ossmoses(IRE) only weakened from the second last.
Dark'n Sharp(GER) was struggling some way out. *(op 25/1)*
Sraid Na Cathrach(IRE) *Official explanation: trainer said gelding pulled up lame (op 25/1)*

92a LEMONGRASS RESTAURANTS H'CAP HURDLE 3m
5:30 (5:30) (88-130,128) 4-Y-0+ **£12,465** (£3,657; £1,742; £593)

RPR
1 **Gortinard (IRE)**[109] 3290 7-10-6 111 .... AndrewJMcNamara(3) 122
(C Byrnes, Ire) *sn trckd ldrs: 5th appr 3 out: impr to ld appr 2 out: rdn and jnd ent st: regained slt advantage after last: styd on wl cl* 7/2[1]
2 *1* **Kings Advocate (IRE)**[35] 4543 5-10-11 113 .... BJGeraghty 123
(T J Taaffe, Ire) *hld up: impr to trck ldrs 1/2-way: led 3 out: hdd appr next: rallied to dispute ld ent st: hdd after last: no ex nr fin* 9/1[3]
3 *8* **Final Act (IRE)**[70] 3913 9-10-4 106 .... APCrowe 108
(John Joseph Murphy, Ire) *towards rr: hdwy 3 out: lft 3rd next: kpt on u.p* 25/1
4 *nk* **Rackard**[15] 4830 6-10-2 104 .... JPElliott 106
(P Hughes, Ire) *hld up: hdwy appr 3 out: lft 6th 2 out: kpt on u.p* 33/1
5 *20* **Supreme Peace (IRE)**[26] 4700 7-10-4 111 .... KTColeman(5) 93
(F Flood, Ire) *mid-div: prog 6 out: 3rd after 3 out: 5th next: sn no ex* 16/1
6 *1/2* **Jack The Hough (IRE)**[46] 4353 8-9-13 106 .... RJMolloy(5) 87
(Philip Walsh, Ire) *mid-div: 9th and rdn after 4 out: kpt on same pce fr 2 out* 16/1
7 *2* **Mr Babbage (IRE)**[31] 4631 7-11-7 122 .... RWalsh 102
(W P Mullins, Ire) *hld up: impr into mid-div 4 out: rdn and no imp bef 3 out* 4/1[2]
8 *2 1/2* **Derawar (IRE)**[2] 43 6-10-7 109 .... RMPower 86
(A L T Moore, Ire) *towards rr: kpt on fr 3 out* 25/1
9 *1 1/2* **Killeaney (IRE)**[31] 4631 8-10-12 113 .... PACarberry 89
(John G Carr, Ire) *mid-div: 9th 1/2-way: no imp fr bef 3 out* 14/1
10 *2* **Gayle Abated (IRE)**[26] 4700 6-10-8 110 .... DJCondon 83
(W P Mullins, Ire) *rr of mid-div: prog after 1/2-way: 7th 3 out: mod 5th after 2 out: sn wknd* 20/1
11 *8* **Lovely Present (IRE)**[11] 4891 6-10-8 110 .... RGeraghty 75
(T K Geraghty, Ire) *nvr a factor* 12/1
12 *8* **Brigadier Brown (IRE)**[72] 3875 8-9-11 106 .... WOCallaghan(7) 63
(John Joseph Murphy, Ire) *towards rr: effrt and no imp fr 3 out* 16/1
13 *10* **Santa's Son (IRE)**[75] 3822 5-10-2 104 .... MDGrant 51
(J F O'Shea, Ire) *led: clr early: hdd appr 3 out: sn no ex* 12/1
14 *8* **Sum Leader (IRE)**[137] 2798 9-11-4 119 .... CO'Dwyer 59
(Miss Jane Thomas, Ire) *nvr a factor* 20/1
15 *3 1/2* **Snob Wells (IRE)**[18] 4804 8-10-7 109 ....(t) PCarberry 45
(Noel Meade, Ire) *a bhd* 20/1
16 *hd* **Haggle Twins (IRE)**[26] 4700 5-10-4 109 .... TGMRyan(3) 45
(Ms F M Crowley, Ire) *cl up: 4th 4 out: rdn and wknd next* 20/1
17 *11* **Touch Closer**[20] 4767 8-11-13 127 .... MAFitzgerald 54
(Miss V Scott) *mid-div: 10th and rdn 3 out: sn wknd* 16/1
18 *7* **Whatareyouhaving**[32] 4591 9-11-6 123 .... DFO'Regan(3) 43
(Henry De Bromhead, Ire) *cl up early: 7th whn reminders 1/2-way: wknd bef 4 out* 20/1
19 *13* **Teknash (FR)**[144] 2666 10-10-3 105 .... NPMadden —
(Niall Madden, Ire) *nvr a factor* 25/1
P **Columbus (IRE)**[5] 4976 8-11-6 123 ....(b) KJMercer(3) —
(Jennie Candlish) *a bhd: trailing whn p.u after 2 out* 50/1
F **Oulart**[42] 4412 6-11-11 128 .... PWFlood(3) —
(D T Hughes, Ire) *cl up: led after 4 out: hdd next: 3rd whn fell 2 out* 10/1
B **Slyguff Rory (IRE)**[15] 4830 7-10-12 113 ....(b) TPTreacy —
(Michael McCullagh, Ire) *prom: 4th 6 out: 6th whn b.d 2 out* 14/1
P **Major Shark (FR)**[17] 4812 7-10-8 110 ....(p) GLee —
(Jennie Candlish) *chsd ldrs early: wknd 1/2-way: trailing whn p.u bef 3 out* 25/1
P **Lotomore Lad (IRE)**[4] 18 7-10-3 105 ....(t) JRBarry —
(Donal Hassett, Ire) *nvr a factor: trailing 5 out: t.o whn p.u after 2 out* 12/1
P **What Perk (IRE)**[32] 4590 6-9-13 104 .... DJHoward(3) —
(A L T Moore, Ire) *trckd ldrs: 5th 1/2-way: wknd fr 4 out: p.u after 2 out* 20/1

6m 16.2s **Going Correction** +0.625s/f (Soft) **25** Ran SP% **170.1**
Speed ratings: **113,112,110,109,103 103,102,101,101,100 97,95,91,89,87 87,84,81,77**,— —,—,—,—,— CSF £40.36 CT £819.96 TOTE £5.50: £2.00, £2.20, £16.00, £32.20; DF 65.80.
Owner Danpaddyandy Syndicate **Bred** Noel Fenton **Trained** Ballingarry, Co Limerick

NOTEBOOK
Santa's Son(IRE) *Official explanation: trainer said gelding scoped dirty after race*
Touch Closer was not a threat from the third last.
Columbus(IRE) was tailed off when pulled up before the straight.
Major Shark(FR) pulled up before three out when tailed off.

93a KILDARE TRADERS/CLAIREFONTAINE (PRO-AM) INH FLAT RACE (MARES & GELDINGS) 2m
6:05 (6:05) 4-Y-0+ **£8,821** (£2,055; £906; £523)

RPR
1 **Silent Oscar (IRE)**[158] 2390 6-11-3 ow1 .... MrCJSweeney(5) 111+
(C P Donoghue, Ire) *mid-div: 12th 1/2-way: smooth hdwy over 4f out: 3rd and rdn to chal over 3f out: led early st: styd on wl fr 2f out* 9/1
2 *2 1/2* **Ballyagran (IRE)**[7] 4952 5-11-13 .... NPMadden 110
(Noel Meade, Ire) *trckd ldrs: prog into 4th 5f out: 3rd bef st: 2nd and rdn 2f out: kpt on wl wout threatening wnr* 15/8[1]
3 *3 1/2* **Bonne Noel'S (IRE)** 5-10-13 .... MrPCGreeves(7) 99
(C Roche, Ire) *hld up: prog over 3f out: 9th into st: styd on wl form over 1 1/2f out: nvr nrr* 20/1
4 *3 1/2* **Pay To Production (IRE)** 5-11-0 ow1 .... MrPRoche(7) 96
(C Roche, Ire) *mid-div: 11th appr 1/2-way: 7th and rdn appr st: kpt on fr over 1f out* 14/1
5 *1* **Ashamdil (IRE)**[42] 4432 6-11-4 .... RLoughran(5) 98
(P Hughes, Ire) *2nd early: 3rd 1/2-way: 5th 5f out: 2nd and chal over 3f out: no ex early st* 16/1
6 *3 1/2* **Alpha Royale (IRE)**[4] 19 5-11-6 ....(b) MJFerris(7) 98
(C Byrnes, Ire) *mid-div: hdwy 4f out: 5th 3f out: no imp st* 9/1
7 *5* **Blayney James (IRE)**[40] 5-11-1 .... MissNCarberry(5) 86
(Gerard Keane, Ire) *hld up: prog on outer over 4f out: 6th and rdn 3f out: no ex st* 16/1
8 *3/4* **Limestream (IRE)**[30] 4653 5-10-8 .... MrWJMcLernon(7) 80
(John G Carr, Ire) *prom: 3rd over 6f out: led over 3f out: sn rdn and strly pressed: hdd & wknd early st* 7/1[3]

9 *8* **Man Of Repute**[15] 4834 4-10-13 .... MrKBBowens(7) 77
(S J Mahon, Ire) *hld up in tch: 8th 1/2-way: rdn and no imp fr over 3f out* **14/1**
10 *6* **The Spoonplayer (IRE)**[120] 3092 6-11-11 .... MrKEPower(3) 79
(Henry De Bromhead, Ire) *trckd ldrs: 6th 5f out: no imp fr over 3f out* **10/1**
11 *3* **Phantom Plumber (IRE)**[138] 2783 5-10-13 .... KHClarke(7) 68
(V Bowens, Ire) *rr of mid-div: no imp fr 4f out* **66/1**
12 *5* **Last Hope (IRE)**[35] 4544 6-10-9 ....(t) AELynch(7) 59
(Miss Jane Thomas, Ire) *hld up: sme late prog* **66/1**
13 *hd* **Lady Accord (IRE)**[21] 4753 5-11-1 .... MsKWalsh(7) 65
(W P Mullins, Ire) *chsd ldrs: 9th 1/2-way: no ex fr 4f out* **16/1**
14 *2 1/2* **Media Man (IRE)** 5-10-13 .... MrRPQuinlan(7) 61
(E J O'Grady, Ire) *rr of mid-div thrght* **14/1**
15 *nk* **Gay Gladys**[21] 4753 5-11-1 .... BWharfe(7) 62
(T H Caldwell) *towards rr: last 6f out: kpt on fr over 3f out* **14/1**
16 *4* **Of Course (IRE)**[14] 4844 7-12-0 .... MrJJCodd 64
(W P Mullins, Ire) *led: hdd 6f out: rdn and wknd fr 5f out* **6/1[2]**
17 *2* **Dolly Of Dublin (IRE)**[26] 4703 7-10-9 .... MissDDuggan(7) 50
(J R H Fowler, Ire) *mid-div: impr into 6th 7f out: wknd fr 4f out* **33/1**
18 *9* **What A Gift (IRE)** 5-10-8 .... MrJDO'Neill(7) 40
(C Roche, Ire) *nvr a factor* **14/1**
19 *7* **Nilang (FR)** 4-10-3 .... MrLPFlynn(5) 26
(C F Swan, Ire) *a bhd* **16/1**
20 *2 1/2* **George Custer (IRE)**[474] 3299 7-11-0 .... MrMACahill(7) 37
(M A Gunn, Ire) *prom: 2nd bef 1/2-way: led 6f out: hdd & wknd over 3f out* **33/1**
21 *dist* **Coola Boola (IRE)**[39] 6-11-0 .... MrCPMcNally(7) —
(Adrian Maguire, Ire) *prom: 5th 1/2-way: 4th over 6f out: sn wknd: t.o* **25/1**
22 *2* **Daraheen Noora (IRE)** 5-10-8 .... MrDWhelan(7) —
(Dermot Day, Ire) *settled in mid-div: wknd over 5f out: t.o* **50/1**
23 *1/2* **Ruthie's Star (IRE)**[33] 4575 5-10-8 .... EoinMichaelKelly(7) —
(V Bowens, Ire) *a bhd: t.o* **25/1**
24 *5* **Itsachopperbaby (IRE)** 5-11-3 .... MrPCashman(3) —
(James J Kelly, Ire) *a bhd: t.o* **25/1**
25 *25* **Carrickbrack (IRE)** 5-10-8 .... APFagan(7) —
(D Broad, Ire) *whipped arnd s and slowly away: a bhd: t.o* **50/1**

4m 1.30s **Going Correction** +0.625s/f (Soft) **25** Ran SP% **176.6**
WFA 4 from 5yo 5lb 5 from 6yo+ 3lb
Speed ratings: **109,107,106,104,103 102,99,99,95,92 90,88,88,86,86 84,83,79,75,74**
—,—,—,—,— CSF £33.18 TOTE £12.20: £2.90, £1.60, £8.00, £9.20; DF 35.90.
Owner Patrick Convery **Bred** Patrick Sheridan **Trained** Monasterevin, Co Kildare

NOTEBOOK

Gay Gladys made little impression for her new stable, just staying on in the mid-division in the straight. *(op 12/1)*

T/Jkpt: @3,750.00. Pool of @50,000.00 - 10 winning units. T/Plt: @1,992.90. Pool of @10,629.00 - 4 winning units. II

BANGOR-ON-DEE (L-H)

Friday, April 29

OFFICIAL GOING: Good to soft (good in places)

Wind: nil Weather: fine

94 BERT LOUD 25TH ANNIVERSARY NOVICES' HURDLE (12 hdls) 3m

5:45 (5:46) (Class 4) 4-Y-0+ **£4,124** (£1,269; £634; £317)

Form RPR

2- **1** **Make It A Double (IRE)**[28] 4680 7-11-0 .... BJCrowley 102+
(Noel T Chance) *j. bdly rt: led: mstke 6th: hdd after 7th: lft in ld 9th: rdn after 3 out: hdd last: rallied to ld nr fin: all out* **4/9[1]**
026- **2** *3/4* **Combat Drinker (IRE)**[97] 3479 7-11-0 88 ....(t) ADobbin 92
(D McCain) *hld up: hdwy 8th: led last: hrd rdn and hdd nr fin* **11/2[3]**
010- **3** *15* **Simple Glory (IRE)**[28] 4679 6-10-3 98 .... JStevenson(10) 76
(R Dickin) *hld up: hdwy 7th: rdn and wknd appr 2 out* **5/1[2]**
POP- **4** *dist* **Edgemoor Princess**[20] 4775 7-10-4 ow4 .... MrRArmson(7) —
(R J Armson) *set slow pce to 1st: chsd wnr to 5th: lost pl 6th: last whn hmpd 9th: sn t.o* **80/1**
0/P- **F** **Carluccios Quest**[13] 4866 7-10-7 .... PMerrigan(7) —
(Mrs H Dalton) *hld up: wnt 2nd 5th: led after 7th: fell 9th* **22/1**

6m 23.6s (29.30) **Going Correction** +0.05s/f (Yiel) **5** Ran SP% **106.9**
Speed ratings: **53,52,47,—,—** CSF £3.19 TOTE £1.30: £1.10, £2.70; EX 2.50.
Owner A D Weller **Bred** Dr J F Gillespie **Trained** Upper Lambourn, Berks

FOCUS

A very weak novice hurdle in which Make It A Double scraped home having jumped badly to his right at nearly every hurdle and he is rated value for more than the winning margin. They went no pace which resulted in a pedestrian time..

NOTEBOOK

Make It A Double(IRE) shaped most encouragingly when second in just an ordinary maiden hurdle at Newbury on his previous start, but he could not have made harder work of this. With the pace very steady, he jumped badly to his right, forfeiting lots of ground, and it was only at full speed over the last couple of flights that his hurdling improved. His class saw him through in the end, but things could have been even tougher had Carluccios Quest not fallen and huge improvement is needed if he is to go on from this. He may do better in a stronger-run race on a right-handed track and it may be he needs fences sooner rather than later. *(op 2-5)*

Combat Drinker(IRE), back up in trip with a tongue-tie on for the first time, nearly took advantage of the favourite's waywardness. This was a good effort and he clearly has a race in him but, given *he was beaten in a claimer two starts back, he helps show what the winner achieved.* *(op 13-2 tchd 7-1)*

Simple Glory(IRE) managed to win a novice hurdle at Chepstow just two starts previously, but her long-term future is over fences. *(op 9-2)*

Carluccios Quest was still in contention and possibly about to confirm the promise he showed in pointing company until falling at the ninth. *(op 16-1)*

95 1905 R H DICKIN MEMORIAL NOVICES' H'CAP CHASE (12 fncs) 2m 1f 110y

6:15 (6:15) (Class 4) (0-100,96) 5-Y-0+ **£4,826** (£1,485; £742; £371)

Form RPR

20-1 **1** **Mr Bigglesworth (NZ)**[5] 9 7-11-9 96 .... LMcGrath(3) 107+
(R C Guest) *hld up: mstke 3rd: led appr 3 out: r.o wl* **11/10[1]**
000- **2** *2* **Quibble**[12] 4872 8-10-8 85 .... WKennedy(7) 88
(A Bailey) *hld up: hdwy 4 out: rdn appr 2 out: r.o flat: nt trble wnr* **10/1**
562- **3** *2 1/2* **Percipient**[32] 4617 7-10-4 74 ....(b) JTizzard 75+
(D R Gandolfo) *prom: led 3rd tl appr 3 out: ev ch 2 out: wknd flat* **5/1[2]**
53-P **4** *4* **Cedar**[4] 23 8-9-9 72 ....(v) JPritchard(7) 68
(R Dickin) *hld up: hdwy 4th: ev ch 3 out: sn rdn: wknd appr last* **13/2**
24F- **5** *14* **Alpha Image (IRE)**[208] 1579 6-10-7 77 .... OMcPhail 59
(Mrs L Williamson) *prom: jnd ldr 3rd: rdn after 7th: wknd after 3 out* **11/1**
006- **6** *3 1/2* **Bentyheath Lane**[9] 4934 8-10-1 74 ow3 ....(b[1]) ACCoyle(3) 53
(M Mullineaux) *hld up: hdwy 4th: wknd appr 3 out* **40/1**
254- **P** **Look To The Future (IRE)**[37] 4517 11-10-9 79 .... PFlynn —
(M J M Evans) *led tl 3rd: bhd fr 4th: t.o whn p.u after 8th* **6/1[3]**

4m 22.9s (-3.30) **Going Correction** -0.175s/f (Good) **7** Ran SP% **111.8**
Speed ratings: **100,99,98,96,90 88,—** CSF £11.99 TOTE £1.80: £1.30, £4.30; EX 16.00.
Owner Bache Silk **Bred** Mrs E Alexander And W Alexander **Trained** Brancepeth, Co Durham

FOCUS

A very moderate novices' handicap chase, but with the placed horses running to their marks the form should work out..

NOTEBOOK

Mr Bigglesworth(NZ), making his chasing debut, was able to race off the same mark as when winning a handicap hurdle at Wetherby on his previous start just five days before and took to the larger obstacles well to follow up. This was a weak race, but he is open to improvement and should complete the hat-trick. *(op 11-8)*

Quibble, without the blinkers, ran his best race to date over fences and, although no match for the winner, showed enough to suggest he can find a small race. *(op 9-1)*

Percipient, just touched off in a seller on his previous start, did not find as much as had looked likely and was a little disappointing. *(op 9-2 tchd 11-2)*

Cedar, pulled up in first-time blinkers over hurdles on his previous start, fared better with the visor fitted on this return to chasing and drop in trip, but he was still well held. *(op 15-2 tchd 6-1)*

Alpha Image(IRE), without the headgear on his return from 208 days off, was well beaten but could improve for the run. *(op 10-1)*

Look To The Future(IRE)'s jumping was not great and he could not build on the promise of his recent fourth. *Official explanation: jockey said gelding was never travelling (op 5-1)*

96 RED CROSS WEEK (S) H'CAP HURDLE (11 hdls) 2m 4f

6:45 (6:45) (Class 5) (0-95,95) 4-Y-0+ **£2,464** (£704; £352)

Form RPR

415- **1** **Ask The Umpire (IRE)**[9] 4934 10-10-10 79 ....(p) OMcPhail 89+
(B J Llewellyn) *chsd ldrs: led appr 6th tl appr 3 out: led appr 2 out: clr whn shkn up appr last: comf* **9/2[1]**
305- **2** *6* **Mantles Prince**[22] 4754 11-11-7 90 .... ATinkler 89
(A G Juckes) *a.p: led appr 3 out: rdn and hdd appr 2 out: one pce* **10/1**
454- **3** *24* **Christmas Truce (IRE)**[20] 4776 6-11-0 83 ....(p) ADobbin 64+
(Ian Williams) *hld up towards rr: hdwy appr 6th: hrd rdn appr 8th: wknd after 3 out: lft 3rd and hmpd 2 out* **9/2[1]**
/PU- **4** *1 1/4* **Bustisu**[75] 3838 8-10-5 79 .... TGreenway(5) 53
(D J Wintle) *hld up: mstke 3rd: rdn appr 6th: hdwy appr 8th: wknd after 3 out* **8/1[3]**
34P- **5** *3/4* **Sconced (USA)**[43] 4418 10-11-2 88 ....(b) LMcGrath(3) 67+
(R C Guest) *a bhd: reminders after mstke 3rd: rdn 5th: hmpd 6th: no ch whn hmpd 2 out* **6/1[2]**
0P0- **6** *12* **Henry's Luck Penny (IRE)**[13] 4866 5-9-7 69 oh5 ....(p) PMerrigan(7) 36+
(Mrs H Dalton) *hld up in mid-div: hdwy 6th: wkng whn n.m.r after 3 out: no ch whn hmpd 2 out* **16/1**
003- **B** **Penny's Crown**[20] 4776 6-10-10 86 .... DCosgrave(7) —
(G A Ham) *hld up and bhd: b.d 6th* **9/2[1]**
6P0- **F** **Spring Bee**[98] 3459 5-10-0 74 ow5 .... JDiment(5) —
(T Wall) *chsd ldr to 2nd: cl 3rd whn fell 6th* **14/1**
0/P- **P** **Susy Wells (IRE)**[27] 4684 10-9-13 71 .... JPByrne(3) —
(C W Moore) *a bhd: hmpd 6th: t.o whn p.u bef 3 out* **66/1**
PP0- **P** **Bint St James**[26] 4714 10-9-7 69 oh5 .... WKennedy(7) —
(J T Stimpson) *led tl appr 6th: wknd appr 7th: t.o whn p.u bef 3 out* **66/1**
050- **P** **Red Nose Lady**[64] 4022 8-11-5 95 ....(p) MrRArmson(7) —
(G J Smith) *chsd ldr fr 2nd tl appr 7th: wknd 8th: t.o whn p.u bef 2 out* **12/1**
15P- **F** **Greenacres Boy**[9] 4932 10-10-1 73 ow2 ....(b) ACCoyle(3) 58
(M Mullineaux) *plld hrd in rr: hdwy on ins 7th: 12 l 3rd and btn whn fell 2 out* **16/1**

4m 54.0s (0.20) **Going Correction** +0.05s/f (Yiel) **12** Ran SP% **118.1**
Speed ratings: **101,98,89,88,88 83,—,—,—,— —,—** CSF £49.23 CT £215.05 TOTE £5.80: £1.50, £4.20, £1.70; EX 90.90.The winner was bought in for 3,500gns.
Owner Mrs B C Richards **Bred** Michael Conroy **Trained** Fochriw, Caerphilly

FOCUS

A moderate handicap hurdle, even by selling standards, although the winner could rate higher.

NOTEBOOK

Ask The Umpire(IRE), returned to hurdles with cheekpieces on instead of blinkers, avoided the *trouble and won well. He is capable in this grade, including over fences, when things fall right.* *(tchd 5-1)*

Mantles Prince, nowhere near as good as he once was, did at least show enough to suggest he could find a similar event. *(op 12-1 tchd 14-1)*

Christmas Truce(IRE) had the cheekpieces back on, but they made little difference and he remains winless over hurdles.

Bustisu at least managed to complete this time, but she was well beaten. *(op 7-1)*

Sconced(USA), back over hurdles having been pulled over fences last time, and with blinkers on instead of cheekpieces, was not helped when hampered at the sixth, but was well beaten when finding trouble on landing after the second last. *(op 9-2)*

Greenacres Boy was well beaten in third when taking a horrible fall two out. *(op 13-2 tchd 4-1)*

Penny's Crown was brought down too early to know how she would have fared. *(op 13-2 tchd 4-1)*

Spring Bee fell too early to say how she would have got on. *(op 13-2 tchd 4-1)*

97 WYNNSTAY HUNT SUPPORTERS CLUB H'CAP CHASE (15 fncs) 2m 4f 110y

7:15 (7:15) (Class 3) (0-130,134) 5-Y-0+ **£10,351** (£3,185; £1,592; £796)

Form RPR

024- **1** **Gatorade (NZ)**[27] 4686 13-10-5 112 ....(p) LMcGrath(3) 121+
(R C Guest) *hld up: pckd 2nd: hdwy 8th: led 3 out: drvn out* **12/1**
461- **2** *2 1/2* **Mixsterthetrixster (USA)**[7] 4961 9-12-2 134 7ex .... JTizzard 142+
(Mrs Tracey Barfoot-Saunt) *t.k.h in tch: mstke 11th: ev ch 2 out: rdn and r.o one pce flat* **13/2[3]**
/21- **3** *1 1/2* **Jaffa**[26] 4718 13-10-5 116 .... MrRArmson(7) 121+
(Miss J Wormall) *hld up and bhd: hdwy 4 out: kpt on same pce u.p flat* **14/1**
0U2- **4** *3 1/2* **Killultagh Storm (IRE)**[132] 2898 11-11-1 119 ....(p) BJCrowley 121+
(Noel T Chance) *hld up: hdwy 4 out: rdn after 3 out: btn whn mstke 2 out* **7/1**
112- **5** *3 1/2* **Spring Lover (FR)**[36] 4530 6-11-1 124 .... LStephens(5) 123+
(Miss Venetia Williams) *led: hit 6th: hdd 3 out: sn rdn: wknd 2 out* **9/2[1]**
600- **6** *16* **Rathbawn Prince (IRE)**[21] 4764 13-11-2 120 .... JPMcNamara 101
(Miss H C Knight) *hld up: hdwy after 9th: wknd 4 out* **12/1**
/11- **7** *13* **Hallyards Gael (IRE)**[359] 184 11-11-12 130 .... ADobbin 98
(L Lungo) *prom tl wknd 9th* **11/2[2]**

013- **F** **Key Phil (FR)**[9] 4927 7-11-1 **119** .... WMarston 118
(D J Wintle) *prom: 5th and wkng whn fell 2 out* **11/2**[2]
543- **F** **Macnance (IRE)**[20] 4779 9-10-3 **107** .... PFlynn 93
(R Lee) *bhd most of way: blnd 6th: no ch whn fell 2 out* **10/1**
433- **P** **The Manse Brae (IRE)**[14] 4850 9-10-4 **108** .... (b) ARoss —
(J M Jefferson) *prom tl j.lft and hmpd 11th: p.u bef 4 out* **8/1**

5m 6.00s (-9.60) **Going Correction** -0.175s/f (Good) **10** Ran SP% **117.0**
Speed ratings: **111,110,109,108,106 100,95,—,—,—** CSF £88.70 CT £1115.32 TOTE £16.80: £4.30, £2.40, £3.00; EX 71.40.
Owner Paul Beck **Bred** Miss J N Fernie **Trained** Brancepeth, Co Durham

FOCUS
Pretty ordinary form for the grade in this handicap chase, but the time was respectable and the form looks solid.

NOTEBOOK
Gatorade(NZ) once again defied his years, winning off a mark 6lb higher than when last successful - the highest rating he has ever won off over fences. A rise will make things tougher, but further success cannot be ruled out whilst he is in this sort of form. *(op 14-1 tchd 16-1)*
Mixsterthetrixster(USA), twice a winner in novice chase company, including most recently at Newton Abbot, was 2lb well-in under his penalty for that success on this first run in handicap company over the larger obstacles, but the winner was just too strong.
Jaffa, the same age as the winner, ran well off a mark 6lb higher than when winning at Market Rasen on his previous outing. *(op 10-1)*
Killultagh Storm(IRE), returning from 132 days off, did not seem that enthusiastic and has yet to add to his Irish wins despite continually being dropped in the handicap.
Spring Lover(FR) has been in great form lately, but was 32lb higher than when first winning in this country in January. *(op 5-1)*
Hallyards Gael(IRE) was progressing well and developing into a very useful performer when last seen 359 days previously, but he did not show much on this return and it can only be hoped this run improves him significantly. *(op 6-1)*
The Manse Brae(IRE) still seemed to be going well when his rider opted to pull him up before the fourth last and it may be another horse jumped into the back of him at the previous fence. *(tchd 6-1)*
Key Phil(FR), 7lb higher than when winning here two starts previously, looked beaten when falling. *(tchd 6-1)*

98 JAMES GRIFFITH MEMORIAL NOVICES' HUNTERS' CHASE (18 fncs) 3m 110y
7:45 (7:47) (Class 6) 5-Y-0+ **£1,432** (£440; £220; £110)

Form RPR
241- **1** **Johns Legacy**[19] 4794 10-11-11 104 .... MissSarahRobinson(7) 97+
(Miss Sarah Robinson) *t.k.h: w ldr: led appr 8th: styd on wl fr 2 out* **2/1**[1]
P52- **2** *3 ½* **Another Club Royal**[12] 6-12-0 70 .... MrRBurton 85
(D McCain) *hld up in tch: rdn and ev ch 2 out: one pce* **9/4**[2]
/F2- **3** *2 ½* **Petolinski**[14] 4856 7-11-7 74 .... (p) TMessenger(7) 83+
(Mrs Sue Popham) *hld up: hdwy appr 8th: wnt 2nd 12th: rdn and ev ch 2 out: no ex flat* **7/1**
UU- **4** *5* **El Lute (IRE)**[5] 9-11-7 .... MrREGCollinson(7) 77
(Mrs E M Collinson) *hld up in tch: rdn after 11th: no hdwy fr 4 out* **20/1**
05- **5** *22* **Crested Penguin**[13] 7-11-11 .... (p) MrAWintle(3) 55
(Brian Perry) *led tl appr 8th: wknd 14th* **20/1**
P **Top Weld**[12] 10-11-7 .... MrSRoss(7) —
(K R Owen) *a bhd: rdn 11th: t.o whn p.u after 3 out* **16/1**
U **Achancyman (IRE)**[48] 10-11-7 .... MrDGreenway(7) —
(Richard Mathias) *prom: wkng whn blnd and uns rdr 13th* **33/1**
0/P- **P** **Clodagh Valley (IRE)**[12] 10-11-7 .... MrWKinsey(7) —
(R J Hewitt) *prom: wknd 8th: t.o whn p.u bef 4 out* **50/1**
P **Sarah's Party**[12] 9-11-11 .... MrGHanmer(3) —
(G D Hanmer) *hld up and bhd: hdwy 13th: wknd 4 out: bhd whn p.u bef last* **4/1**[3]

6m 23.4s (-0.30) **Going Correction** -0.175s/f (Good) **9** Ran SP% **116.9**
Speed ratings: **93,91,91,89,82 —,—,—,—** CSF £6.90 TOTE £3.00: £1.10, £1.20, £2.40; EX 8.30.
Owner Brian Robinson **Bred** S C Horn **Trained** Bridgwater, Somerset

FOCUS
An ordinary hunter chase, but the winner is value for more than double the official margin with the third setting the level.

NOTEBOOK
Johns Legacy ◆ followed up his recent Newton Abbot success and was value for quite a bit more than the winning margin would suggest - he had his ears pricked a fair way out and was always just doing enough. A reasonable sort, he looks well up to completing the hat-trick. *(op 15-8 tchd 9-4 and 5-2 in places)*
Another Club Royal, a winner of a point-to-point earlier in the month, but a beaten favourite in that sphere on his most recent start, ran well returned to Rules, but was no match for the winner and just gallops. Only six, there could be better to come. *(op 10-3)*
Petolinski has never been the most consistent, but this was another reasonable effort following his recent Taunton second. *(op 11-2 tchd 15-2)*
El Lute(IRE), runner-up in a point on his most recent start, acquitted himself creditably returned to Rules. *(op 16-1)*
Achancyman(IRE) got rid of his rider just before the race got really serious. *(op 20-1)*
Sarah's Party, had been in great form in point-to-points recently, winning his last two starts but, *switched Rules for the first time, he did not give his running. Official explanation: trainer said gelding was unsuited by good to soft ground (op 20-1)*

99 ROSE HILL H'CAP HURDLE (9 hdls) 2m 1f
8:15 (8:15) (Class 3) (0-125,125) 4-Y-0+ **£5,681** (£1,748; £874; £437)

Form RPR
541- **1** **Bogus Dreams (IRE)**[49] 4303 8-10-8 **107** .... BGibson 112+
(L Lungo) *hld up: rdn and sltly outpcd 5th: hdwy 6th: led 2 out: rdn out* **15/8**[1]
616- **2** *1 ½* **Top Achiever (IRE)**[12] 4883 4-9-13 **106** .... JPByrne(3) 102+
(C W Moore) *a.p: led briefly appr 2 out: sn rdn: r.o one pce flat* **10/1**
054- **3** *shd* **My Last Bean (IRE)**[28] 4678 8-11-2 **115** .... SCurran 116+
(M R Bosley) *hld up: hdwy and mstke 5th: rdn appr 2 out: kpt on u.p flat* **25/1**
U30- **4** *5* **Castleshane (IRE)**[42] 4438 8-11-5 **125** .... WKennedy(7) 121+
(S Gollings) *led: rdn and hdd appr 2 out: wknd appr last* **6/1**
P6P- **5** *¾* **Sachsenwalzer (GER)**[173] 2070 7-10-6 **105** .... RMcGrath 99+
(C Grant) *bhd tl styd on fr 2 out: n.d* **20/1**
312- **6** *6* **Crackleando**[33] 4576 4-10-12 **116** .... RThornton 102+
(A King) *chsd ldr tl after 6th: rdn whn mstke 3 out: sn wknd* **7/2**[2]
501- **7** *4* **It's Blue Chip**[30] 4660 4-10-11 **115** .... WMarston 98+
(Miss H C Knight) *prom: rdn after 5th: wknd 6th* **9/2**[3]
110- **P** **Broke Road (IRE)**[46] 4371 9-10-11 **117** .... PMerrigan(7) —
(Mrs H Dalton) *t.k.h: bhd fr 4th: t.o whn p.u bef 2 out* **14/1**

4m 7.60s (-1.40) **Going Correction** +0.05s/f (Yiel)
WFA 4 from 7yo+ 5lb **8** Ran SP% **113.8**
Speed ratings: **105,104,104,101,101 98,96,—** CSF £20.63 CT £350.54 TOTE £3.20: £2.00, £3.50, £2.80; EX 30.50 Place 6 £50.20, Place 5 £40.66.
Owner Mrs Tracey O'Hare **Bred** Elsdon Farms **Trained** Carrutherstown, D'fries & G'way

FOCUS
Just an ordinary handicap hurdle for the grade with the winner better than the bare result and the placed horses running to form.

NOTEBOOK
Bogus Dreams(IRE) defied an 18lb rise in the weights for his easy win in a minor novices' handicap hurdle at Ayr 49 days previously, although he was made to work quite hard. Clearly progressing, this once-smart Flat performer could well complete the hat-trick. *(op 2-1 tchd 7-4)*
Top Achiever(IRE), 7lb higher than when winning over course and distance two starts previously, ran creditably, but does not have much in hand of the Handicapper.
My Last Bean(IRE) ◆, who shaped well on his debut for these connections at Newbury, again offered promise and could do even better if given a chance over further. *(op 20-1)*
Castleshane(IRE) has dropped to a reasonable mark and would have appreciated this drop in grade. Without the cheekpieces this time, he showed enough to suggest he can find a similar race when he gets his favoured decent ground. *(op 5-1)*
Sachsenwalzer(GER) offered some promise on his return from 173 days off the track. *Official explanation: jockey said, regarding the running and riding, his orders were to jump gelding out behind the leaders and get it to settle because it is inclined to get "buzzy", adding that gelding did indeed pull hard for the first half of the race but emptied down the back straight (where he felt it prudent to keep hold of gelding's head to get it to finish) before running on past beaten horses in the latter stages*
Crackleando had it to do off a mark of 116 at this stage of his career, and the drop in trip probably did not help. *(op 9-2)*
It's Blue Chip had no easy task off a mark of 115, and probably would have preferred further, but this was still disappointing. *(op 4-1)*
T/Plt: £71.50 to a £1 stake. Pool: £31,870.35. 324.95 winning tickets. T/Qpdt: £36.40 to a £1 stake. Pool: £2,894.10. 58.70 winning tickets. KH

FONTWELL (L-H)
Friday, April 29

OFFICIAL GOING: Good
The ground was on the dead side, with the uphill finish providing a stiff test of stamina and fast ground horses at a disadvantage.
Wind: almost nil Weather: cloudy

100 CANTORSPREADFAIR.COM FOUR YEARS OLD ONLY INTERMEDIATE HURDLE (9 hdls) 2m 2f 110y
5:30 (5:30) (Class 4) 4-Y-0 **£3,412** (£975; £487)

Form RPR
124- **1** **At Your Request**[16] 4826 4-11-4 123 .... DRDennis 119+
(Ian Williams) *chsd ldrs: wnt 7 l 2nd at 6th: led last: edgd rt and flashed tail run-in: drvn out* **9/4**[1]
030- **2** *3* **Woody Valentine (USA)**[45] 4386 4-11-4 115 .... SThomas 114+
(Miss Venetia Williams) *led: qcknd 7 l clr at 6th: hdd last: no ex* **4/1**[3]
0- **3** *11* **Soleil Fix (FR)**[27] 4697 4-10-9 .... MrDHDunsdon(3) 96
(N J Gifford) *prom: lost pl appr 6th: styd on again run-in* **33/1**
122- **4** *¾* **Cunning Pursuit**[39] 4496 4-11-4 113 .... MFoley 101
(N J Henderson) *hld up in tch: hit 1st: chasing ldng pair whn hit 3 out: sn rdn and btn* **9/1**
04- **5** *8* **Maharaat (USA)**[41] 4446 4-10-12 .... RJohnson 87
(P J Hobbs) *towards rr: mstke and rdn 6th: nvr rchd ldrs* **14/1**
203- **6** *1 ¼* **La Concha (IRE)**[11] 4910 4-10-12 90 .... SDurack 86
(M J McGrath) *t.k.h in rr: rdn and sme hdwy after 6th: wknd after 3 out* **100/1**
01- **7** *5* **Atlantic City**[32] 4616 4-11-4 .... MBatchelor 87
(Mrs L Richards) *hld up towards rr: hdwy 5th: wknd 3 out* **16/1**
42-P **8** *26* **Preston Hall**[4] 21 4-10-12 .... LAspell 55
(M J McGrath) *a bhd* **100/1**
10F- **9** *9* **Verasi**[11] 4910 4-11-4 115 .... JEMoore 52
(G L Moore) *mid-div: nt fluent 2nd: rdn 5th: sn wknd* **7/1**
00- **10** *dist* **Can Can Flyer (IRE)**[59] 4110 4-10-12 .... JMogford —
(J C Tuck) *wd: hdwy and mstke 4th: wknd 6th* **25/1**
12- **P** **Vinmix De Bessy (FR)**[11] 4910 4-11-4 .... PHide —
(D B Feek) *chsd ldr tl wknd qckly 6th: wl bhd whn p.u bef 2 out: lame* **7/2**[2]

4m 28.6s (-4.70) **Going Correction** 0.0s/f (Good) **11** Ran SP% **116.8**
Speed ratings: **109,107,103,102,99 98,96,85,82,—** — CSF £11.15 TOTE £3.30: £1.30, £1.90, £8.40; EX 13.60.
Owner Cockbury Court Partnership **Bred** Gainsborough Stud Management Ltd **Trained** Portway, Worcs

FOCUS
A decent race run in a good time and the form should work out. The first two have plenty of ability and the third, in particular, showed promise for the future.

NOTEBOOK
At Your Request was undoubtedly the best at the weights but seemed to confirm that he is quirky once he hits the front, as he had been when winning at Huntingdon. His challenge should be delayed as late as possible for maximum effect. *(tchd 11-4 and 3-1 in a place)*
Woody Valentine(USA) looked to have stolen it along the back straight but could not quite hang on. Nonetheless, the tactics seemed effective and produced a performance that showed he is capable of winning more races over timber. *(op 9-2)*
Soleil Fix(FR) ◆ had run with promise in his only previous race, a bumper, and this was confirmation that he is one to keep an eye on. Not knocked about, he stayed on eyecatchingly from a wide berth and can improve enough to win races. He should stay a bit farther, too. *(tchd 40-1)*
Cunning Pursuit was not at his best at the hurdles, and the trip seemed to stretch him. He has plenty of speed and will bounce back at a modest level. *(op 8-1)*
Maharaat(USA) should be capable of making his mark in ordinary handicaps now he is qualified. *(op 12-1)*
La Concha(IRE) continues to race too keenly, which gave him little chance of lasting home in this competitive race. However, he did at least as well as expected and will be at home in run-of-the-mill company.
Atlantic City *Official explanation: trainer said gelding lost a hind shoe*
Can Can Flyer(IRE) was beaten a street but might have more chance now he is qualified for handicaps.
Vinmix De Bessy(FR) *Official explanation: vet said colt was lame on right hind (tchd 11-4 and 4-1 in a place)*

101 CANTORSPREADFAIR.COM H'CAP CHASE (19 fncs) 3m 2f 110y
6:00 (6:01) (Class 4) (0-95,91) 5-Y-0+ **£4,677** (£1,439; £719; £359)

Form RPR
P51- **1** **Robber (IRE)**[11] 4912 8-12-1 **91** 7ex .... SDurack 100+
(P Bowen) *mid-div: mstke 10th: effrt 14th: hrd rdn 4 out: wnt 5 l 2nd next: styd on to ld fnl 50 yds* **9/4**[1]

6P2- **2** *nk* **Alfred The Grey**[8] 4940 8-10-9 71 ....(p) PHide 83+
(G L Moore) *prom: led 10th to 14th: led and rdn 5 l clr 3 out: nt fluent last: idled and tired run-in: ct fnl 50 yds* **10/3**[2]

0P0- **3** *1 ¼* **Felix Darby (IRE)**[48] 4327 10-11-5 88 ....(b[1]) MrJSnowden[(7)] 96+
(Miss G Browne) *hld up in tch: trckd ldng pair 1/2-way: outpcd and nt fluent 3 out: rallied to press ldng pair whn nt clr run fnl 50 yds* **9/1**

5U6- **4** *12* **Flinders**[11] 4912 10-11-11 87 .... LAspell 82+
(R Rowe) *disp 2nd pl tl lft in ld after 6th: hdd 10th: led 14th tl wknd appr 3 out* **10/1**

0P0- **5** *dist* **Robbie's Adventure**[7] 4953 11-9-11 62 oh5 .... DCrosse[(3)] —
(D L Williams) *bhd: hdwy 7th: rdn 12th: mstke and wknd 14th* **20/1**

4PU- **P** **Kroisos (IRE)**[30] 4665 7-10-4 66 ....(b) TDoyle —
(R Curtis) *led tl p.u after 6th: lame* **5/1**[3]

346- **P** **Pangeran (USA)**[159] 2368 13-9-13 68 .... SWalsh[(7)] —
(N B King) *hld up towards rr tl p.u appr 14th* **20/1**

32P- **P** **Mr Banker**[83] 3696 10-11-0 81 .... RStephens[(5)] —
(J C Tuck) *mid-div tl j. slowly and lost pl fr 1/2-way: sn bhd and rdn: p.u bef 14th: b.b.v* **6/1**

6m 58.5s (-6.00) **Going Correction** -0.075s/f (Good) **8** Ran SP% **113.4**
Speed ratings: **105,104,104,100,— —,—,—** CSF £10.47 CT £53.03 TOTE £3.00: £1.40, £1.10, £3.50; EX 6.70.

Owner The Hedonists **Bred** David Valentine **Trained** Little Newcastle, Pembrokes

FOCUS

A weak contest, but a creditable weight-carrying victory in a messy finish. However, the third was close to his best and the race might work out.

NOTEBOOK

Robber(IRE) put up a fine weight-carrying performance, helped by the runner-up tying up badly from the last. *(op 2-1 tchd 5-2)*

Alfred The Grey ruined his chance of winning for only the second time by folding badly in the last 200 yards after looking sure to score. The uphill finish seemed to take a bit of getting at this meeting. *(op 7-2 tchd 4-1 and 3-1)*

Felix Darby(IRE) might have won with better fortune - letting the principals get first run on him *turning for home, then running into a dead end as he rallied. He stays well and is back in form. (op 10-1 tchd 11-1)*

Flinders helped to set the pace as usual but the weight anchored her from the home turn. *(op 9-1)*

Robbie's Adventure was in trouble setting out with a circuit to go, so achieved little. *(op 25-1)*

Pangeran(USA) was reported to be a possible withdrawal had there been overnight rain, which failed to materialise. Nonetheless, he gave the impression that, with this first run for five months behind him, a bolder show can be expected on genuinely fast ground. *(op 9-2 tchd 4-1)*

Mr Banker went to pieces around halfway but had a valid excuse. *Official explanation: vet said gelding bled from nose (op 9-2 tchd 4-1)*

Kroisos(IRE) bowled along until going wrong and being dismounted after one circuit. *Official explanation: trainer said gelding was lame (op 9-2 tchd 4-1)*

102 CANTORSPREADFAIR.COM CLAIMING HURDLE (10 hdls) 2m 4f

6:30 (6:30) (Class 4) 4-Y-0+ **£2,611** (£746; £373)

Form RPR

0- **1** **Bayadere (GER)**[10] 4920 5-10-8 .... SWalsh[(7)] 82+
(K F Clutterbuck) *hld up in rr: smooth hdwy whn hit 3 out: led next: drvn 3 l ahd run-in: tired fnl 50 yds: all out* **100/1**

66-5 **2** *½* **Monsal Dale (IRE)**[5] 1 6-11-2 78 ....(tp) LAspell 82
(Mrs L C Jewell) *hld up in rr: hdwy to chse ldng pair 2 out: styd on u.p run-in: nt catch tiring wnr* **25/1**

231- **3** *¾* **Tensile (IRE)**[37] 4522 10-11-6 118 .... TScudamore 86+
(R J Hodges) *hld up in tch: hdwy to ld after 7th: hdd 2 out: hit last: rallied and kpt on fnl 50 yds* **5/2**[2]

333- **4** *2* **Madison Avenue (GER)**[11] 4913 8-10-9 86 ....(b) RLucey-Butler[(7)] 79
(T M Jones) *trckd ldrs: outpcd appr 2 out: styd on again run-in* **12/1**[3]

2/0- **5** *10* **Queens Brigade**[57] 4139 13-10-7 85 .... MissVStephens[(7)] 69+
(Miss V A Stephens) *t.k.h: led and restrained in front: hit 7th: sn hdd: wknd appr 2 out* **66/1**

000- **6** *dist* **Prince Valentine**[11] 4913 4-11-0 87 ....(t) PHide —
(D B Feek) *mid-div tl wknd appr 3 out* **40/1**

/P0- **7** *28* **Kinda Crazy**[156] 2416 5-10-9 .... JAJenkins[(7)] —
(H J Manners) *plld hrd: chsd ldrs to 4th: bhd fr 7th* **66/1**

036- **P** **Mr Fernet**[46] 4380 8-10-11 98 .... StephenJCraine[(5)] —
(C J Mann) *chsd ldr tl p.u after 6th: sddle slipped* **12/1**[3]

101- **P** **Rob Leach**[83] 3708 8-12-0 124 .... JEMoore —
(G L Moore) *t.k.h towards rr: hdwy 3 out: cl 3rd whn broke leg and p.u appr 2 out: dead* **8/13**[1]

5m 6.10s (6.30) **Going Correction** 0.0s/f (Good)
WFA 4 from 5yo+ 6lb **9** Ran SP% **116.1**
Speed ratings: **87,86,86,85,81 —,—,—,—** CSF £1361.84 TOTE £71.50: £9.50, £3.50, £1.10; EX 347.20.

Owner K F Clutterbuck **Bred** A Pereira **Trained** Exning, Suffolk

FOCUS

A good favourite, whose sad demise inevitably affected the quality of the contest. The winner deserved her success, but the below-par effort of Tensile, over a trip short of his best, makes this a ordinary race and the time was slow to boot.

NOTEBOOK

Bayadere(GER)'s shock win was no fluke, though she was helped by the departure of the favourite. Travelling with remarkable ease during the race, she only had to prove her stamina, and that was achieved, albeit by a diminishing margin as the hill took its toll. It was a surprise that she was not claimed. *(op 66-1)*

Monsal Dale(IRE) is well exposed but this was a fair effort at the weights. However, with Rob Leach breaking down and Tensile apparently running below his best, it would be wise not to overstate the performance. *(op 20-1)*

Tensile(IRE) needs a stiffer test nowadays - this trip on a tough track like Towcester, or at least 2m6f around places like this. *(tchd 11-4 in a place)*

Madison Avenue(GER) was not well in at the weights but he ran his race and should continue to be there or thereabouts back in selling company.

Queens Brigade was too fresh, having had only one race in the last year, but he did well for a long way. *(op 40-1)*

Prince Valentine stopped to nothing at the end of the back straight and struggled home, finishing tired. *(tchd 33-1)*

Rob Leach was about to deliver his challenge when suffering an awful injury on the flat nearing the second last, which sadly proved fatal. *(op 4-5)*

Mr Fernet's saddle began to slip up his neck after the first few flights and his rider took the *sensible option setting out onto the final circuit. Official explanation: jockey said saddle slipped (op 4-5)*

103 LAURENT PERRIER H'CAP CHASE (15 fncs) 2m 4f

7:00 (7:02) (Class 3) (0-115,115) 5-Y-0+ **£5,512** (£1,696; £848; £424)

Form RPR

/64- **1** **Tamango (FR)**[27] 4693 8-11-12 115 .... RJohnson 132+
(P J Hobbs) *hld up in midfield gng wl: hdwy to chse ldng pair 11th: led appr 2 out: drvn 3 l ahd: hld on gamely run-in: all out* **3/1**[1]

324- **2** *hd* **Romany Dream**[142] 2701 7-9-12 90 ....(b) DCrosse[(3)] 106+
(R Dickin) *chsd ldrs: led 4 out and qcknd 6 l clr: j. slowly next: hdd appr 2 out: rallied wl run-in: jst hld* **13/2**

/50- **3** *21* **Mount Kimble (IRE)**[15] 4836 9-11-4 107 .... PHide 102
(P Winkworth) *prom: outpcd 11th: n.d after: mod 3rd fr 2 out* **20/1**

56P- **4** *2 ½* **Klondike Charger (USA)**[22] 4757 11-10-6 95 .... JGoldstein 87
(Miss J S Davis) *mde most to 4 out: sn outpcd* **25/1**

221- **5** *2 ½* **The Staggery Boy (IRE)**[8] 4942 9-10-6 95 7ex .... TScudamore 85
(M R Hoad) *in tch: rdn 9th: sn outpcd* **4/1**[2]

314- **6** *nk* **Master T (USA)**[8] 4942 6-11-5 108 .... MBatchelor 101+
(G L Moore) *nt jump wl: blnd 11th: bhd tl passed btn horses fr 3 out* **16/1**

545- **7** *20* **The Newsman (IRE)**[12] 4880 13-11-11 114 .... LAspell 84
(G Wareham) *w ldrs tl wknd 11th* **9/1**

641- **8** *10* **Harik**[30] 4663 11-11-9 112 ....(bt) JEMoore 72
(G L Moore) *hld up towards rr: mod effrt into midfield 10th: hrd rdn next: n.d after* **8/1**

322- **9** *1 ¼* **Walcot Lad (IRE)**[30] 4663 9-9-10 92 ....(p) DLaverty[(7)] 50
(A Ennis) *prom: pushed along 8th: wknd 10th: btn whn mstke next* **6/1**[3]

1P5- **P** **Melford (IRE)**[70] 3927 7-11-8 111 ....(b[1]) SThomas —
(Miss H C Knight) *bhd: rdn 8th: mstke 10th: t.o whn p.u bef 3 out* **12/1**

UF4- **P** **Hi Rudolf**[10] 4921 10-9-13 95 oh5 ow6 .... JAJenkins[(7)] —
(H J Manners) *mid-div: losing pl whn blnd 7th: sn wl bhd: p.u bef 3 out* **25/1**

5m 2.50s (0.20) **Going Correction** -0.075s/f (Good) **11** Ran SP% **119.8**
Speed ratings: **96,95,87,86,85 85,77,73,72,— —** CSF £23.22 CT £330.31 TOTE £4.30: £1.70, £2.30, £6.00; EX 28.50.

Owner The Brushmakers **Bred** Mme Dominique Le Drans **Trained** Withycombe, Somerset

■ Stewards' Enquiry : R Johnson two-day ban: used whip with excessive frequency (May 10,11)

FOCUS

A modest event and a race dominated by just two horses, with the extra class of the winner proving vital. The winner could rate higher but the also-rans are just typical Fontwell types.

NOTEBOOK

Tamango(FR) showed two admirable qualities - the ability to travel well, and plenty of guts in the finish, though his trainer says he is inclined to idle in front. His extra class was decisive, as was *Johnson's strength from the final fence, but his use of the whip cost him in the Stewards' room. (op 7-2 tchd 4-1)*

Romany Dream has been dropping to a winning mark and is capable of going one better if the Handicapper treats her fairly. *(op 8-1)*

Mount Kimble(IRE), having only his second race since arriving from Ireland, ran a fair if unexceptional race and could do with dropping a few pounds. His form is over two miles but he was plodding on at the finish, albeit rather slowly and without threatening the first two. *(tchd 25-1)*

Klondike Charger(USA) has not been at his best in recent races, but this was a shade better. However, further improvement is required for him to become competitive again. *(op 20-1 tchd 28-1)*

The Staggery Boy(IRE) kept on slowly over a longer trip than usual but prefers faster ground. He *was beaten much too far from home for the distance to be the reason.Official explanation: trainer said gelding was unsuited by good going (op 11-2 tchd 6-1)*

Master T(USA) put in a sloppy round of jumping, never having a cut at his fences and failing to threaten at any stage. This was his second successive poor effort following a winning reappearance last month.

Harik is useful on his day but rarely runs two races alike. After winning stylishly last time, he travelled well enough but failed to pick up when asked a mile from home. *(op 5-1)*

Walcot Lad(IRE) has been running well lately but this was a weak effort. He was already beginning *to struggle with a circuit left. Official explanation: trainer said he had no explanation for poor form shown (op 15-2)*

104 VIC FROST MEMORIAL BEGINNERS' CHASE (13 fncs) 2m 2f

7:30 (7:31) (Class 4) 5-Y-0+ **£4,704** (£1,447; £723; £361)

Form RPR

12P- **1** **Space Star**[20] 4777 5-10-13 113 .... TDoyle 106+
(P R Webber) *hld up towards rr: hdwy 4 out: rdn to ld last: styd on wl* **9/2**[3]

U20- **2** *1 ¼* **Flying Spirit (IRE)**[13] 2480 6-11-2 .... JEMoore 108+
(G L Moore) *hld up in tch: led 4 out: rdn 3 l ahd next: mstke 2 out: hdd last: kpt on* **15/8**[1]

005- **3** *9* **Winsley**[34] 4553 7-11-2 .... LAspell 100+
(O Sherwood) *hld up in tch: chsd ldrs 11th: one pce fr 3 out* **9/4**[2]

005- **4** *7* **Kyper Disco (FR)**[28] 4683 7-11-2 .... MFoley 92+
(N J Henderson) *prom tl dropped to rr 3rd: rallied 8th: rdn and lost pl next: brief effrt 3 out: no imp* **15/2**

104- **5** *1 ¾* **Celebration Town (IRE)**[213] 1532 8-10-9 102 .... SWalsh[(7)] 90
(Miss E C Lavelle) *hld up in rr: shkn up 3 out: nvr in chalng position* **16/1**

/33- **6** *1 ½* **Stopwatch (IRE)**[30] 4661 10-11-2 65 ....(p) PHide 90+
(Mrs L C Jewell) *w ldrs tl mstke and wknd 4 out* **18/1**

06P- **7** *22* **Down The Stretch**[11] 4914 5-10-6 102 ....(p) DLaverty[(7)] 67+
(A Ennis) *t.k.h: hdwy to ld 3rd: mstke 6th: hdd & wknd 4 out: bhd whn mstke 2 out* **33/1**

F0- **U** **Kjimmy (IRE)**[28] 4680 8-10-9 .... WPKavanagh[(7)] —
(J W Mullins) *led tl hdd and mstke 3rd: lost pl: in tch towards rr whn mstke and uns rdr 6th* **33/1**

4m 35.9s (-2.70) **Going Correction** -0.075s/f (Good)
WFA 5 from 6yo+ 3lb **8** Ran SP% **112.5**
Speed ratings: **103,102,98,95,94 93,84,—** CSF £13.56 TOTE £5.80: £1.90, £1.50, £1.50; EX 19.10.

Owner Skeltools Ltd **Bred** A B Phipps **Trained** Mollington, Oxon

FOCUS

A reasonably good contest for the track at this time of year that could be rated higher, with the winner taking well to fences and the next four home all capable of finding races.

NOTEBOOK

Space Star made a winning debut over fences and seems to have taken to it well. Making no obvious jumping errors, he finished the race off tidily and more success looks on the cards at this level. *(op 4-1)*

Flying Spirit(IRE) had a recent pipe-opener on the Flat and looked for a while to be on course for victory. There will be other days for this fast ground specialist. *(op 7-4 tchd 2-1 and 9-4 in places)*

Winsley, without the blinkers this time, made a fair chasing debut and should progress. A decent hurdler on his day, he is making the switch at the right time. *(op 5-2 tchd 11-4 in a place)*

Kyper Disco(FR) ran in snatches and does not look the most reliable proposition. However, he deserves a few more chances over fences to show what he can do. *(op 9-1 tchd 7-1)*

Celebration Town(IRE) ran with some promise after a long absence. There could be more to come. *(op 14-1)*

Stopwatch(IRE) could not be fancied at these weights but ran well enough for a while and will be more at home in lower grade. *(op 16-1 tchd 14-1)*

Down The Stretch, restrained in last place jumping the second fence, pulled his way to the front at the next and had run himself into the ground half a mile form home.*Official explanation: trainer said he had no explanation for poor form shown*

105 HARDINGS BARS & CATERING SERVICES H'CAP HURDLE (11 hdls) 2m 6f 110y
8:00 (8:00) (Class 4) (0-95,95) 4-Y-O+ **£2,688** (£768; £384)

Form					RPR
P00-	1		**Esters Boy**[19] 4799 7-11-12 **95**	JEMoore	102
			(P G Murphy) *blnd 1st and sn towards rr: hdwy 7th: led appr 2 out: hdd briefly after last: rallied gamely: drvn out*	**25/1**	
530-	2	2	**Coustou (IRE)**[13] 4579 5-11-2 **85**	(p) RJohnson	91+
			(R M Stronge) *hld up towards rr: hdwy 8th: pressing wnr whn mstke 2 out: led briefly after last: nt qckn fnl 100 yds*	**7/1**[2]	
06P-	3	10	**Charlie's Double**[68] 3975 6-10-2 **74**	DCrosse[(3)]	69
			(J R Best) *mid-div: outpcd and lost pl after 7th: styd on wl fr 2 out*	**15/2**[3]	
630-	4	2	**Manque Neuf**[8] 4939 6-10-9 **78**	(p) MBatchelor	71
			(Mrs L Richards) *hld up in tch: led after 7th tl appr 2 out: sn outpcd*	**16/1**	
5P2-	5	4	**Lancier D'Estruval (FR)**[34] 4565 6-10-8 **77**	(t) JMogford	72+
			(J C Tuck) *prom: drvn to chal whn blnd bdly 3 out: nt rcvr*	**7/1**[2]	
/02-	6	3	**Supreme Rullah (IRE)**[32] 4605 8-11-2 **85**	(t) LAspell	72+
			(Mrs L Wadham) *hld up towards rr: hdwy appr 8th: no imp fr 3 out*	**10/1**	
P25/	7	16	**Carl's Boy**[32] 9-9-12 **74**	(t) MrPSheldrake[(7)]	44
			(D A Rees) *chsd ldrs tl wknd 8th*	**20/1**	
F10-	8	17	**Lady Lisa (IRE)**[6] 4977 6-11-6 **89** 7ex	TScudamore	42
			(M C Pipe) *chsd ldrs tl wknd 8th*	**5/1**[1]	
0/4-	9	4	**Heavenly King**[20] 4780 7-11-0 **83**	(b) SDurack	32
			(P Bowen) *prom: led briefly 7th: hrd rdn and wknd 3 out*	**8/1**	
012-	10	2 ½	**Eau Pure (FR)**[11] 4914 8-11-3 **93**	EDehdashti[(7)]	40
			(G L Moore) *chsd ldrs tl wknd qckly 8th*	**5/1**[1]	
/35-	11	dist	**Paula Lane**[30] 4660 5-10-13 **82**	TDoyle	—
			(R Curtis) *a towards rr: no ch fr 8th*	**33/1**	
060-	12	1 ¾	**Ashgan (IRE)**[40] 4484 12-10-1 **80**	ODayman[(10)]	—
			(Dr P Pritchard) *mid-div: wknd 7th: sn t.o*	**25/1**	
4R0-	P		**Isam Top (FR)**[26] 4723 9-10-9 **81**	TJMalone[(3)]	—
			(M J Hogan) *hld up in rr: wl bhd fr 6th: p.u bef 8th*	**50/1**	
P05-	P		**Pace Stalker (USA)**[32] 4617 9-9-10 **72**	RLucey-Butler[(7)]	—
			(M R Hoad) *a bhd: hrd rdn 5th: sn t.o: p.u after 7th*	**66/1**	
5PP-	P		**Banjo Hill**[15] 4840 11-11-9 **92**	MFoley	—
			(Miss E C Lavelle) *led: nt fluent 5th: hdd 7th: sn wknd: bhd whn p.u bef 3 out*	**20/1**	
554-	P		**Wee Danny (IRE)**[206] 1594 8-11-1 **91**	DLaverty[(7)]	—
			(L A Dace) *in tch on outside: mstke 3rd: blnd next: wknd after 7th: t.o whn p.u bef 2 out*	**14/1**	

5m 40.2s (1.40) **Going Correction** 0.0s/f (Good) **16** Ran SP% **126.5**
Speed ratings: **97,96,92,92,90 89,84,78,76,75** —,—,—,—,— — CSF £189.09 CT £1481.77 TOTE £39.80: £7.60, £2.00, £3.10, £3.80; EX 340.40 Place 6 £75.24, Place 5 £47.49.
Owner J Cooper **Bred** Bram Davis And Mrs Louise A Murphy **Trained** East Garston, Berks

FOCUS
A run-of-the-mill contest that took little winning, with both joint favorites fading early on the final circuit.

NOTEBOOK
Esters Boy finally showed that this kind of trip is what he needs. This was a good effort off a stiff weight. *(op 16-1)*
Coustou(IRE) bounced back to form, and for a moment looked like scoring at the 13th attempt, only to be run out of it by the battling winner. The trip seemed to suit him well but a less stiff finish would have been in his favour. *(tchd 8-1)*
Charlie's Double looks a staying type and would be worth another attempt at three miles. *(op 12-1)*
Manque Neuf may be best around two and a half miles, having run with credit until the home turn.
Lancier D'Estruval(FR) is in reasonable form at present, but the bungle which nearly lost him his rider at the third last effectively ended his chance. *(op 8-1 tchd 9-1)*
Supreme Rullah(IRE) travels well enough to suggest some ability, albeit at a low level. She could not sustain her run but this is her kind of trip in less competitive company. *(op 12-1)*
Lady Lisa(IRE) is struggling off this higher mark. *(op 6-1)*
Eau Pure(FR) faded with great haste when the tempo increased. She is at her best on quicker *ground, and was not helped by it being on the dead side of good.Official explanation: trainer said mare was unsuited by good going (op 4-1)*
T/Plt: £183.50 to a £1 stake. Pool: £42,751.55. 170.00 winning tickets. T/Qpdt: £43.80 to a £1 stake. Pool: £3,160.50. 53.30 winning tickets. LM

SOUTHWELL (L-H)
Friday, April 29

OFFICIAL GOING: Good (good to firm in places)
The ground was described as 'well watered, just about perfect summer jumping ground, even all over and a credit to the groundstaff'.
Wind: slight, half behind Weather: fine and sunny

106 BIRCH TREE HOMES LTD NOVICES' H'CAP CHASE (16 fncs) 2m 5f 110y
2:30 (2:30) (Class 4) (0-100,100) 5-Y-O+ **£4,202** (£1,293; £646; £323)

Form					RPR
0P0-	1		**Lantaur Lad (IRE)**[44] 4405 11-10-12 **86**	WHutchinson	98+
			(A King) *in tch: hdwy to chse ldrs 11th: led 2 out: clr last: rdn out*	**22/1**	
233-	2	11	**Muttley Maguire (IRE)**[95] 3510 6-11-10 **98**	JTizzard	100+
			(B G Powell) *chsd ldrs: led after 9th: hdd 11th: upsides whn lft in ld 3 out: hdd next: sn btn*	**4/1**[2]	
226-	3	1 ¾	**Hot Produxion (USA)**[26] 4716 6-11-12 **100**	ADempsey	99
			(J Mackie) *chsd ldrs: reminders 9th: one pce fr 3 out*	**20/1**	
131-	4	7	**Ravenscar**[19] 4798 7-11-1 **96**	APogson[(7)]	90+
			(C T Pogson) *bhd: hdwy 10th: sn chsng ldrs: effrt after 13th: sn fdd*	**3/1**[1]	
6F3-	5	9	**Grandee Line**[7] 4955 10-9-11 **74** oh2	RWalford[(3)]	58+
			(R H Alner) *bhd: sme hdwy 10th: lost pl appr 3 out*	**11/2**[3]	
10P-	F		**Pottsy's Joy**[13] 4866 8-11-7 **95**	DElsworth	—
			(Mrs S J Smith) *rr-div: fell 10th*	**25/1**	
3/0-	F		**Kavi (IRE)**[13] 672 5-11-8 **100**	AThornton	100+
			(Simon Earle) *led to 2nd: led 11th tl fell 3 out*	**10/1**	
41-	P		**Camdenation (IRE)**[10] 4917 9-11-3 **91** 7ex	MAFitzgerald	—
			(J R Jenkins) *bhd fr 10th: p.u bef 3 out*	**14/1**	
142/	P		**Bell Lane Lad (IRE)**[497] 2833 8-11-8 **96**	RThornton	—
			(A King) *prom: lost pl 12th: bhd whn p.u bef 3 out*	**4/1**[2]	
PPU-	P		**High Peak**[49] 4313 8-9-13 **76**	RYoung[(3)]	—
			(J W Mullins) *led 4th tl after 9th: lost pl 12th: bhd whn p.u after next*	**16/1**	
0P5-	U		**Lonesome Man (IRE)**[32] 4614 9-11-6 **94**	(t) WMarston	—
			(R T Phillips) *led 2nd to 4th: hit 7th: lost pl next: bhd whn blnd and uns rdr 10th*	**50/1**	

5m 24.7s (-3.70) **Going Correction** -0.175s/f (Good)
WFA 5 from 6yo+ 4lb **11** Ran SP% **116.9**
Speed ratings: **99,95,94,91,88** —,—,—,—,— — CSF £106.77 CT £1826.32 TOTE £24.00: £3.70, £1.80, £4.60; EX 337.30.
Owner Mrs A A Shutes **Bred** John J Slattery **Trained** Barbury Castle, Wilts

FOCUS
An ordinary race with plenty of casualties but in the end a wide-margin winner and the form has a solid look.

NOTEBOOK
Lantaur Lad(IRE), who fractured a pelvis in the past, showed a return to form and broke his duck over fences at the seventh attempt. Now he has finally come good this dual Irish point winner should start making up for lost time.
Muttley Maguire(IRE), on his handicap bow, was left for dead by the winner over the final two fences. *(op 5-1 tchd 11-2)*
Hot Produxion(USA), looking his best on his second outing after a break, was struggling with a full circuit to go and looks a very one-paced stayer. *(op 18-1)*
Ravenscar, 8lb higher, sat at the back and never got competitive.
Bell Lane Lad(IRE), absent since December 2003, was making his chase debut and may need much softer ground. *(op 10-3 tchd 3-1)*
Kavi(IRE), fit from the Flat, was making his chasing bow but would have finished second at best but for crashing out. *(op 10-3 tchd 3-1)*

107 FORD AND SLATER DAF LTD BEGINNERS' CHASE (19 fncs) 3m 2f
3:00 (3:02) (Class 4) 5-Y-O+ **£4,095** (£1,260; £630; £315)

Form					RPR
P20-	1		**Special Conquest**[34] 4554 7-11-2 106	AThornton	110+
			(J W Mullins) *w ldrs: led 12th: qcknd next: styd on wl between last 2: rdn out*	**10/11**[1]	
PP2-	2	1 ¾	**No Further Comment (IRE)**[42] 4440 5-10-8	JMMaguire	97
			(Mrs Jeremy Young) *hld up: jnd ldrs 14th: wnt 2nd appr 3 out: sn chalng: nt qckn run-in*	**5/1**[3]	
P22-	3	15	**Thyne Man (IRE)**[19] 4796 7-11-2 103	PMoloney	95+
			(J Mackie) *trckd ldrs: blnd 13th: rdn and weakaning whn hit last 3*	**9/4**[2]	
452-	4	dist	**I'm For Waiting**[27] 4688 9-10-11 82	MNicolls[(5)]	—
			(John Allen) *mde most to 12th: wknd 14th: t.o 3 out*	**18/1**	
PFP-	5	shd	**Silver Styx**[19] 4796 6-10-9	APogson[(7)]	—
			(J R Holt) *last whn blnd 10th: bhd fr 14th: t.o 3 out*	**40/1**	
P0P-	P		**Comte De Chambord**[38] 4508 9-11-0 ow5	MrGBrewer[(7)]	—
			(Mark Campion) *t.k.h: hdwy to trck ldrs 5th: wknd 4 out: 4th and bhd whn p.u bef next*	**66/1**	

6m 41.4s (2.60) **Going Correction** -0.175s/f (Good)
WFA 5 from 6yo+ 8lb **6** Ran SP% **109.0**
Speed ratings: **89,88,83**,—,— — CSF £5.79 TOTE £1.90: £1.10, £2.40; EX 6.30.
Owner F G Matthews **Bred** F G Matthews **Trained** Wilsford-Cum-Lake, Wilts

FOCUS
In the end just a two-horse race and the form has a dubious look with the time also slow, but the winner should continue to make progress.

NOTEBOOK
Special Conquest, back over fences, stepped up the gallop early on the final circuit and was always doing enough. He should progress further. *(op Evens tchd 5-6)*
No Further Comment(IRE) looked like giving the winner a real fight but in the end he seemed less determined.
Thyne Man(IRE) wanted to do nothing but hang left and his jumping went to pieces late on. *Official explanation: jockey said gelding hung left handed (op 2-1 tchd 5-2)*
I'm For Waiting, who had a lot to find, seemed to find this trip well beyond him. *(op 14-1)*
Comte De Chambord *Official explanation: jockey said gelding had a breathing problem (op 50-1)*

108 WEATHERBYS BANK H'CAP CHASE (13 fncs) 2m 1f
3:30 (3:33) (Class 3) (0-125,121) 5-Y-O+ **£7,072** (£2,176; £1,088; £544)

Form					RPR
43P-	1		**Feel The Pride (IRE)**[15] 4837 7-10-11 **106**	MAFitzgerald	122+
			(Jonjo O'Neill) *trckd ldrs gng wl: led on bit 2 out: v smoothly*	**11/2**[3]	
33P-	2	2 ½	**Odagh Odyssey (IRE)**[97] 3492 11-11-11 **120**	(v[1]) JMMaguire	128+
			(Miss E C Lavelle) *chsd ldrs: rdn and sltly hmpd 3 out: wnt 2nd last: no ch w wnr*	**33/1**	
543-	3	2	**Enzo De Baune (FR)**[7] 4972 8-11-4 **120**	(p) BenOrde-Powlett[(7)]	126+
			(G A Harker) *trckd ldrs: led after 3rd: hit 6th: hdd 2 out: kpt on same pce*	**11/4**[1]	
F00-	4	¾	**Noshinannikin**[69] 3948 11-11-12 **121**	DElsworth	126+
			(Mrs S J Smith) *chsd ldrs: wnt 2nd 6th: one pce fr 3 out*	**22/1**	
563-	5	3	**Edmo Heights**[41] 4464 9-11-4 **113**	RGarritty	114
			(T D Easterby) *towards rr: hdwy 10th: one pce fr next*	**20/1**	
422-	6	1	**Kids Inheritance (IRE)**[18] 4808 7-11-5 **114**	JimCrowley	118+
			(J M Jefferson) *sn trcking ldrs: blnd 9th and 3 out: wknd 2 out*	**3/1**[2]	
P/6-	7	4	**Nephite (NZ)**[46] 4363 11-9-9 **95**	LTreadwell[(5)]	91
			(Miss Venetia Williams) *mid-div: hrd drvn to chse ldrs 10th: wknd fr next*	**33/1**	
041-	8	8	**Aelred**[41] 4458 12-11-4 **113**	(p) KJohnson	101
			(R Johnson) *chsd ldrs: lost pl 9th: sn bhd*	**20/1**	
200-	F		**Lik Wood Power (NZ)**[217] 1499 8-11-7 **116**	HOliver	—
			(R C Guest) *t.k.h towards rr: fell 9th*	**15/2**	
5/2-	F		**Montpelier (IRE)**[41] 12-10-13 **108**	(b) AThornton	—
			(Ms A E Embiricos) *hld up in rr: fell 3rd*	**50/1**	
/10-	P		**Fantasmic**[15] 4838 9-10-8 **106**	ONelmes[(3)]	—
			(O Sherwood) *led tl after 3rd: eased and p.u bef next: b.b.v*	**16/1**	
P26-	P		**Jodante (IRE)**[34] 4555 8-10-8 **103**	GLee	—
			(P Beaumont) *nvr gng wl: sn last: detached 5th: wl bhd whn p.u after 10th*	**13/2**	

4m 7.70s (-4.00) **Going Correction** -0.175s/f (Good) **12** Ran SP% **119.7**
Speed ratings: **102,100,99,99,98 97,95,92**,—,— —,— CSF £172.29 CT £610.34 TOTE £6.10: £3.00, £14.00, £1.70; EX 257.80.
Owner Mrs M Liston **Bred** Thomas B Russell **Trained** Cheltenham, Gloucs

FOCUS
A strongly-run race and with most of those close up running to their marks, the form should work out well.

NOTEBOOK
Feel The Pride(IRE) ◆ travelled supremely well and was never out of third gear. Rated 106, her hurdle mark is 130 and she will be of real interest even from her revised mark. *(op 4-1)*
Odagh Odyssey(IRE), back over fences and with the visor on, tried hard but the winner was simply toying with him. Tending to go left-handed under pressure, he may be better going the other way round. *(op 22-1)*
Enzo De Baune(FR), better going right-handed, could not totally dominate and he was firmly put in his place by the very easy winner. *(op 3-1)*
Noshinannikin, who has been out of sorts, was having his first outing for over two months and this trip is on the sharp side for him nowadays. *(op 16-1)*
Edmo Heights could never get competitive. He needs his rating to drop and can hopefully encounter some much easier ground this summer. *(op 14-1)*

Kids Inheritance(IRE) spoilt his chance with two bad jumping errors. *(op 6-1)*
Fantasmic *Official explanation: trainer said gelding was distressed (op 14-1)*

109 RBS HIGH FLYERS H'CAP HURDLE (13 hdls) 3m 2f

4:00 (4:01) (Class 3) (0-120,117) 4-Y-0+ **£5,736** (£1,765; £882; £441)

Form RPR

51F- **1** **Tomina**[16] 4820 5-11-12 **117**........ AThornton 128+
(Miss E C Lavelle) *hld up: stdy hdwy 7th: wnt 2nd 10th: led appr last: drvn clr* **15/2**[3]

212- **2** *5* **Harrycone Lewis**[55] 4189 7-10-13 **104**........(b) WMarston 111+
(Mrs P Sly) *trckd ldrs: led after 8th: hdd appr last: no ex* **5/2**[1]

433- **3** *3* **The Flyer (IRE)**[13] 4868 8-11-5 **110**........(t) JAMcCarthy 112
(Miss S J Wilton) *hld up in rr: gd hdwy 9th: sn chsng ldrs: one pce fr 2 out* **22/1**

F43- **4** *16* **Peddars Way**[19] 4799 6-10-9 **100**........(v) WHutchinson 86
(A King) *chsd ldrs: drvn along 6th: lost pl 3 out* **5/1**[2]

201- **5** *20* **Thyne For Intersky (IRE)**[19] 4797 6-11-6 **111**........(b) MAFitzgerald 77
(Jonjo O'Neill) *in tch: hdwy and prom 4th: rdn and wkng whn blnd 3 out* **5/1**[2]

R15- **6** *2 ½* **Magical Liaison (IRE)**[36] 4531 7-10-4 **95**........(b) CLlewellyn 59
(W Jenks) *sn bhd: rdn 8th: sn t.o* **28/1**

P34- **7** *nk* **Monte Cristo (FR)**[9] 4932 7-11-4 **109**........ MBradburne 72
(Mrs L C Taylor) *chsd ldrs: drvn along 6th: sn lost pl and bhd: t.o 3 out* **9/1**

POP- **8** *3* **Brush A King**[13] 4868 10-10-11 **109**........(p) APogson[(7)] 69
(C T Pogson) *chsd ldrs: lost pl 9th: sn bhd: t.o 2 out* **20/1**

010- **P** **Darab (POL)**[84] 3679 5-11-1 **106**........ DElsworth —
(Mrs S J Smith) *t.o 6th: p.u after 8th* **25/1**

5P0- **P** **Tee-Jay (IRE)**[151] 2547 9-11-8 **113**........ GLee —
(M D Hammond) *reminders and lost pl 6th: t.o whn p.u bef next* **33/1**

2PP- **P** **Reasonable Reserve (IRE)**[19] 4791 8-11-9 **114**........ JamesDavies —
(B G Powell) *rel to r: sn drvn along: t.o 8th: sn p.u* **33/1**

P35/ **P** **Hawthorn Prince (IRE)**[511] 2581 10-10-13 **104**........ PMoloney —
(Mrs P Sly) *led tl after 8th: sn lost pl: t.o whn p.u bef 2 out* **33/1**

1P4- **P** **Joris De Vonnas (FR)**[19] 4799 8-9-11 **93**........(t) TJPhelan[(5)] —
(Ian Williams) *chsd ldrs: lost pl after 7th: sn bhd: t.o whn p.u bef 2 out* **25/1**

6m 19.1s (-10.30) **Going Correction** -0.175s/f (Good) **13** Ran SP% **112.7**
Speed ratings: **108,106,105,100,94 93,93,92,—,— —,—,—** CSF £22.59 CT £391.32 TOTE £9.70: £3.60, £1.50, £5.10; EX 30.70.
Owner Paul G Jacobs **Bred** P G Jacobs **Trained** Wildhern, Hants

FOCUS
A fair contest for the time of year and a soundly-run race that should work out well.

NOTEBOOK
Tomina, none the worse for his tumble, was in no hurry to join issue over this extended trip. He came right away on the run-in and is sure to make a useful staying chaser in time. *(op 5-1)*
Harrycone Lewis, a stone lower, looked to have excellent prospects over these mini fences, but after going on he was firmly put in his place by an unexposed type. *(op 11-4)*
The Flyer(IRE), on a long losing run, just seems to stay these days. *(op 20-1 tchd 25-1)*
Peddars Way was soon making hard work of it and his enthusiasm seems strictly limited. *(op 11-2)*
Thyne For Intersky(IRE) was already feeling the strain when clattering through the third last obstacle. *(op 4-1 tchd 7-2)*
Reasonable Reserve(IRE) *Official explanation: jockey said gelding was never travelling (op 25-1)*

110 SOUTHWELL-RACECOURSE.CO.UK (S) HURDLE (11 hdls) 2m 5f 110y

4:30 (4:30) (Class 5) 4-Y-0+ **£2,681** (£766; £383)

Form RPR

223- **1** **Kings Castle (IRE)**[19] 4791 10-11-0 110........ AThornton 105+
(R J Hodges) *hld up: stdy hdwy 6th: sn trcking ldrs: led 2 out: clr last: heavily eased* **13/8**[1]

5RP- **2** *11* **Homeleigh Mooncoin**[15] 4835 10-11-0 112........ JamesDavies 88+
(B G Powell) *chsd ldrs: led appr 2 out: sn hdd: no ch w wnr whn eased run-in* **7/2**[2]

4P4- **3** *7* **Howaboys Quest (USA)**[152] 2508 8-10-4 89........(p) PJMcDonald[(10)] 80
(Ferdy Murphy) *bhd and reminders 6th: kpt on fr 3 out: tk remote 3rd last: greatly flattered* **12/1**

4 *2* **Phase Three (IRE)**[19] 8-11-0........ JMMaguire 78
(T R George) *jumpd lft: led tl hdd & wknd appr 2 out* **13/2**[3]

/PP- **5** *1 ¼* **Fullopep**[19] 4799 11-10-7 95........ APogson[(7)] 77
(J R Holt) *outpcd and bhd 6th: kpt on fr 3 out: nvr on terms* **25/1**

04P- **6** *16* **The Masareti Kid (IRE)**[94] 3528 8-11-0 84........(b[1]) GLee 61
(G A Harker) *chsd ldrs: rdn and wknd 8th: sn bhd* **14/1**

00P- **7** *17* **Calcar (IRE)**[67] 3208 5-10-7........(tp) CDSharkey[(7)] 44
(Mrs S Lamyman) *chsd ldrs to 6th: sn lost pl: wl bhd fr 2 out* **66/1**

/26- **P** **Step In Line (IRE)**[24] 4738 13-10-11 64........ ONelmes[(3)] —
(D W Thompson) *bhd: last whn blnd 7th: p.u bef next* **33/1**

100- **P** **Vitelucy**[188] 1719 6-11-0 93........(v) MAFitzgerald —
(Miss S J Wilton) *chsd ldrs: hit 5th: wknd 7th: t.o 3 out: p.u bef next* **13/2**[3]

/54- **P** **Special Constable**[317] 762 7-11-0 64........(b) JAMcCarthy —
(B I Case) *hld up: hdwy 5th: lost pl after 7th: t.o whn p.u bef 2 out* **33/1**

5m 17.2s (-5.50) **Going Correction** -0.175s/f (Good) **10** Ran SP% **112.6**
Speed ratings: **103,99,96,95,95 89,83,—,—,—** CSF £6.72 TOTE £3.30: £1.10, £2.30, £3.40; EX 9.00.There was no bid for the winner
Owner R J Hodges **Bred** Miss Katie Thorner And Joseph Kent **Trained** Charlton Adam, Somerset

FOCUS
A poor seller in which the winner outclassed the opposition and the third is greatly flattered, as both the first two were eased.

NOTEBOOK
Kings Castle(IRE), a big type, found this a very straightfoward task and was able to ease right off on the run-in. This looks his level at this advanced stage of his career. *(op 11-8)*
Homeleigh Mooncoin had 2lb in hand of the winner on official figures but it did not turn out anything like that. His best days look a long way behind him now. *(op 5-1)*
Howaboys Quest(USA), absent since November, kept on to take a remote third spot but, with the first two both eased, he is greatly flattered. *(op 11-1)*
Phase Three(IRE), out of sorts in points, continually lost ground jumping left-handed and after setting the pace he stopped in a matter of strides when headed. *(op 7-1 tchd 8-1 and 6-1)*
Step In Line(IRE) *Official explanation: jockey said gelding had breathing problem (op 25-1)*

111 NSPCC FULL STOP "NATIONAL HUNT" NOVICES' H'CAP HURDLE (11 hdls) 2m 5f 110y

5:00 (5:01) (Class 4) (0-105,110) 4-Y-0+ **£3,562** (£1,096; £548; £274)

Form RPR

032- **1** **Brigadier Benson (IRE)**[17] 4813 5-11-3 **96**........ AThornton 98
(R H Alner) *trckd ldrs: wnt 2nd 7th: slt ld last: hrd rdn and edgd lft: jst hld on* **7/2**[1]

/40- **2** *shd* **Random Precision (IRE)**[124] 2975 6-9-10 **82**........ CMStudd[(7)] 85+
(B G Powell) *mid-div: hdwy to ld 6th: hdd last: carried lft: jst failed* **7/1**

050- **3** *2 ½* **Waydale Hill**[156] 2428 6-9-11 **79** oh2........(p) RWalford[(3)] 78
(T D Walford) *in tch: jnd ldrs 7th: kpt on same pce fr 2 out* **66/1**

326- **4** *13* **Brooklyn Brownie (IRE)**[274] 1064 6-11-2 **95**........ GLee 81
(J M Jefferson) *rr-div: hdwy 7th: sn chsng ldrs: wknd 2 out* **11/1**

005- **5** *½* **Earls Rock**[38] 4507 7-10-4 **83**........ WHutchinson 69
(J K Cresswell) *mid-div: hdwy to chse ldrs 7th: wknd appr 2 out* **33/1**

21U- **6** *3* **Mac Hine (IRE)**[160] 2336 8-11-5 **98**........ BHarding 81
(Jonjo O'Neill) *hld up: hdwy 6th: sn chsng ldrs: lost pl appr 2 out* **4/1**[2]

005- **7** *19* **Amber Dawn**[19] 4795 6-9-11 **79** oh1........ ONelmes[(3)] 43
(J Gallagher) *bhd and drvn along 5th: nvr on terms* **33/1**

045- **8** *14* **Presenting Alf (IRE)**[64] 4026 5-10-10 **89**........ DElsworth 39
(Mrs S J Smith) *lost pl 3rd: sn bhd: blnd 2 out* **11/1**

030- **9** *3* **Star Prize (IRE)**[57] 4134 8-11-12 **105**........ MAFitzgerald 52
(N J Henderson) *chsd ldrs: rdn and lost pl after 3 out* **8/1**

500- **10** *10* **Idealko (FR)**[34] 4557 9-11-2 **95**........(p) PMoloney 32
(Ian Williams) *chsd ldrs: lost pl 7th: sn bhd* **28/1**

0P0- **P** **Jack White**[59] 4110 8-9-12 **87**........ THalliday[(10)] —
(Mrs S J Smith) *bhd fr 6th: blnd 3 out: t.o whn p.u bef next* **33/1**

000- **P** **Fenney Spring**[44] 4403 5-10-0 **79** oh10........(t) CLlewellyn —
(W Jenks) *in tch: lost pl 7th: bhd fr 3 out: t.o whn p.u bef last* **25/1**

0P2- **P** **Swifts Hill (IRE)**[20] 4775 7-10-11 **100**........ WMcCarthy[(10)] —
(T R George) *chsd ldrs: lost pl 6th: sn bhd: t.o whn p.u bef 2 out* **16/1**

561- **P** **Doof (IRE)**[7] 4960 5-11-10 **110** 7ex........ AGlassonbury[(7)] —
(M C Pipe) *led to 6th: hit 7th: lost pl and mstke next: sn bhd: t.o whn p.u bef 2 out* **13/2**[3]

5m 15.2s (-7.50) **Going Correction** -0.175s/f (Good) **14** Ran SP% **119.3**
Speed ratings: **106,105,105,100,100 99,92,87,85,82 —,—,—,—** CSF £26.18 CT £1383.66 TOTE £4.70: £2.50, £2.90, £12.00; EX 38.60 Place 6 £55.71, Place 5 £10.28.
Owner A Hordle **Bred** Mrs Mary Doyle **Trained** Droop, Dorset
■ A 191/1 four-timer for Andrew Thornton.
■ Stewards' Enquiry : A Thornton caution: careless riding

FOCUS
A poor contest but the first three finished well clear and the form looks solid.

NOTEBOOK
Brigadier Benson(IRE) seemed to appreciate this stiffer test but, going left-handed under a forceful right-hand drive on the run-in, he prevailed by a whisker. *(tchd 4-1)*
Random Precision(IRE), well supported on his first outing since Boxing Day, went down battling and was perhaps a shade unfortunate not to prevail. *(op 8-1 tchd 9-1)*
Waydale Hill, suited by this much better ground, ran her best race over hurdles on her seventh try. *(op 33-1)*
Brooklyn Brownie(IRE), on his handicap debut, was having his first outing since July and ran as if it was needed. *(op 10-1)*
Mac Hine(IRE) as usual moved up travelling smoothly, but on his first outing since November was unable to capitalize on a mark much lower than his chase mark. *(op 5-1)*
T/Plt: @150.30 to a £1 stake. Pool: £37,428.80 - 181.75 winning units T/Qpdt: @8.00 to a £1 stake. Pool: £3,592.20 - 330.50 winning units WG

[86]PUNCHESTOWN (R-H)

Friday, April 29

OFFICIAL GOING: Soft (yielding to soft in places)

112a FLOGAS IRELAND H'CAP CHASE 3m 1f

2:00 (2:00) (0-116,114) 4-Y-0+ **£9,234** (£2,709; £1,290; £439)

RPR

1 **Monterey Bay (IRE)**[43] 4431 9-10-9 96........ RWalsh 105
(Ms F M Crowley, Ire) *trckd ldrs: 7th 1/2-way: impr into 4th bef 4 out: 2nd and chal after next: led 2 out: styd on wl u.p* **9/1**[3]

2 *1 ½* **Osiris (IRE)**[49] 4312 10-11-6 106........(t) JRBarry 115
(Evan Williams) *chsd ldrs: 7th whn mstke 4 out: 4th after next: 2nd bef last: kpt on wl u.p* **12/1**

3 *3 ½* **Carndale (IRE)**[16] 4833 8-10-11 98........(b[1]) PCarberry 102
(Noel Meade, Ire) *hld up: prog 6 out: 5th next: 7th 3 out: rdn and kpt on fr 2 out* **16/1**

4 *2 ½* **Tristernagh (IRE)**[16] 4833 9-10-5 99........ AELynch[(7)] 101
(J A O'Connell, Ire) *a.p: 3rd 1/2-way: led after 4 out: hdd 2 out: 4th and no ex fr last* **25/1**

5 *3* **World Vision (IRE)**[72] 3888 8-11-9 112........ KJMercer[(3)] 112
(Ferdy Murphy) *settled 2nd: 3rd 6 out: 5th 3 out: kpt on u.p* **16/1**

6 *6* **Tribal Dancer (IRE)**[17] 4815 11-10-6 98........ PCO'Neill[(5)] 91
(Miss Venetia Williams) *led: clr early: hdd after 4 out: 6th next: kpt on same pce fr 2 out* **16/1**

7 *nk* **Wise Counsel (IRE)**[16] 4833 7-9-13 90........ TGMRyan[(3)] 81
(T J Taaffe, Ire) *trckd ldrs: 9th and rdn bef 4 out: no ex fr 2 out* **8/1**[2]

8 *nk* **Glabejet (IRE)**[43] 4431 7-10-3 91........ DJCondon 82
(John Brassil, Ire) *trckd ldrs: 6th 4 out: sn rdn: no imp fr 2 out* **14/1**

9 *1 ½* **Toto Caelo**[54] 4220 9-10-5 92........(p) APCrowe 82
(C Roche, Ire) *rr of mid-div: 10th 4 out: rdn and no imp next* **8/1**[2]

10 *15* **Rare Ouzel (IRE)**[16] 4833 9-10-10 97........ KWhelan 72
(A J Martin, Ire) *towards rr: kpt on one pced fr 4 out* **14/1**

11 *10* **Green River (IRE)**[32] 4634 11-11-5 112........ TJDreaper[(7)] 78
(J T R Dreaper, Ire) *rr of mid-div: no imp fr 3 out* **16/1**

12 *9* **Brownie Returns (IRE)**[40] 4488 12-11-1 101........(b) CO'Dwyer 58
(M F Morris, Ire) *chsd ldrs: 7th bef 1/2-way: no ex fr 5 out* **25/1**

13 *hd* **Rosses Folly (IRE)**[19] 4804 8-9-9 86........(b) JMAllen[(3)] 41
(Joseph Crowley, Ire) *a bhd: reminders bef 1/2-way: trailing fr 6 out* **25/1**

14 *3 ½* **Frankie Dori (IRE)**[5] 10 6-10-2 90........ RGeraghty 42
(S Donohoe, Ire) *prom: 4th 6 out: wknd fr next* **20/1**

15 *nk* **Old Pike Girl (IRE)**[40] 4487 8-10-6 98........ JFLevins[(5)] 50
(G M O'Neill, Ire) *a bhd: trailing fr 3 out* **25/1**

16 *8* **Ichi Cavalo (IRE)**[16] 4833 8-9-6 85........ RJMolloy[(5)] 28
(Niall Madden, Ire) *mid-div: bad mstke 8 out: wknd fr 6 out* **16/1**

17 *20* **Flaxen Town (IRE)**[33] 4596 10-9-13 87........ JPElliott 10
(Timothy Doyle, Ire) *nvr a factor: t.o* **33/1**

18 *4 ½* **Alberoni (IRE)**[19] 4804 9-11-2 105........ MPWalsh[(3)] 26
(Peter McCreery, Ire) *mid-div: wknd fr 6 out: t.o* **20/1**

P **Balto Rambler (IRE)**[99] 3452 8-10-9 96........(t) GCotter —
(D M Leigh, Ire) *chsd ldrs to 1/2-way: sn wknd: p.u bef 4 out* **40/1**

P **Nolans Pride (IRE)**[34] 4567 8-11-9 114........(b[1]) MrCJSweeney[(5)] —
(W J Burke, Ire) *nvr a factor: trailing whn p.u bef 2 out* **20/1**

P **Andiamo (IRE)**[34] 4569 10-9-3 84........ WOCallaghan[(7)] —
(John Joseph Murphy, Ire) *a bhd: trailing fr 5 out: p.u bef 4 out* **33/1**

P **Star Storm (IRE)**[26] [4733] 11-10-10 97 DNRussell —
(F Flood, Ire) *rr of mid-div: mstke 10th: no ex fr 5 out: p.u bef 3 out* **14/1**

P **Darrens Lass (IRE)**[19] [4804] 9-10-13 100 JLCullen —
(Robert Murphy, Ire) *mid-div whn bad mstke 2nd: trailing fr 5th: p.u bef 9th* **33/1**

F **Celtic Ross (IRE)**[16] [4833] 9-9-13 90 (p) PWFlood(3) —
(Robert Tyner, Ire) *trckd ldrs on outer: 6th 6 out: 7th and in tch whn fell 3 out* **8/1**[2]

P **Lord Alphieross (IRE)**[16] [4833] 7-11-10 110 BJGeraghty —
(W J Burke, Ire) *mid-div on outer: 10th 6 out: no ex fr 4 out: p.u bef 2 out* **5/1**[1]

6m 36.4s **Going Correction** +0.35s/f (Yiel) **25** Ran SP% **158.0**
Speed ratings: 108,107,106,105,104 102,102,102,102,97 94,91,91,89,89 87,80,79,—,— —,—,—,—, CSF £122.11 CT £1815.96 TOTE £7.50: £1.90, £3.10, £6.60, £17.70; DF 140.00.
Owner J J Power **Bred** Kilnamoragh Stud **Trained** Curragh, Co Kildare

NOTEBOOK
Osiris(IRE), a course winner over hurdles two years ago, held every chance once he recovered from a mistake four out, but the weight concession was too much from the last. *(op 10/1)*
World Vision(IRE) was struggling under the weight from the third last. *(op 14/1 tchd 20/1)*
Tribal Dancer(IRE) was done with once headed. *(op 12/1)*
Lord Alphieross(IRE) *Official explanation: trainer said gelding was never travelling and needs heavier ground (op 12/1)*

114a EMO OIL CHAMPION HURDLE (GRADE 1) 2m
3:10 (3:10) 5-Y-0+ **£70,354** (£21,560; £10,212; £3,404; £2,269)

RPR

1 **Brave Inca (IRE)**[20] [4771] 7-11-12 165 APMcCoy 167
(C A Murphy, Ire) *led: reminders after 4 out: rdn after 3 out: hdd bef last: rallied u.p to regain ld cl home* **2/1**[2]

2 *hd* **Harchibald (FR)**[45] [4383] 6-11-12 166 PCarberry 167
(Noel Meade, Ire) *hld up in tch: impr into 3rd 4 out: cl up travelling best fr 2 out: led last: sn rdn: hdd cl home* **4/6**[1]

3 *1* **Macs Joy (IRE)**[20] [4771] 6-11-12 160 BJGeraghty 166
(Mrs John Harrington, Ire) *trckd ldrs in 3rd: impr into 2nd 1/2-way: rdn to chal after 2 out: led briefly appr last: 3rd and no ex cl home* **11/2**[3]

4 *dist* **Bob What (IRE)**[12] [2006] 11-11-12 125 (t) RMPower —
(Thomas Mullins, Ire) *cl up in 2nd: slt mstke 4th: wknd bef 3 out* **125/1**

5 *25* **Publican (IRE)**[3] [40] 5-11-11 RWalsh —
(P A Fahy, Ire) *hld up in tch: cl 4th 2 out: sn rdn and no imp: blnd last and virtually p.u* **33/1**

4m 4.60s **Going Correction** -0.20s/f (Good) **5** Ran SP% **112.4**
Speed ratings: **93,92,92,—,—** CSF £3.97 TOTE £3.20: £1.70, £1.20; DF 4.10.
Owner Novices Syndicate **Bred** D W Macauley **Trained** Gorey, Co Wexford

FOCUS
Another thrilling finish was fought out by three of the principal members of a truly vintage crop of Irish hurdlers. Brave Inca benefited from the assistance of Tony McCoy for the first time, and that may well have been decisive. Harchibald confirmed himself a bridle horse.

NOTEBOOK
Brave Inca(IRE) responded well to the persistent pressure of new partner Tony McCoy and his gutsy attitude just won the day in another tight finish. He deserved this after a series of splendid efforts in defeat and his unlucky fall at Aintree. *(op 2/1 tchd 9/4)*
Harchibald(FR) travelled well and the race again looked there for the taking, but having committed earlier than at Cheltenham and gone a neck up at the last he refused to follow through with the effort and was denied by the braver winner. He is a bridle horse, but an extremely talented one, arguably inferior only to Hardy Eustace among a vintage crop. *(op 8/11 tchd 4/5)*
Macs Joy(IRE) had every chance between the other pair, only fading late on the run-in. Another rock solid effort. *(op 5/1)*
Bob What(IRE) was out of his depth and was trailing before the straight. *(op 100/1)*
Publican(IRE) stayed in touch until weakening after two out. He blundered badly at the last and walked home.

115a BETFAIR.COM NOVICE H'CAP CHASE (GRADE A) 3m 1f
3:45 (3:45) 5-Y-0+ **£43,971** (£13,475; £6,382; £2,127; £1,418)

RPR

1 **Pay It Forward**[48] [4339] 7-10-5 121 RMPower 128
(Mrs John Harrington, Ire) *trckd ldrs in 4th: 3rd whn slt mstke 6 out: 2nd and chal 3 out: sn led: rdn clr after 2 out: styd on wl fr last* **7/1**[3]

2 *2* **Joes Edge (IRE)**[13] [4861] 8-11-7 140 7ex KJMercer(3) 145
(Ferdy Murphy) *hld up towards rr: smooth hdwy 4 out: 4th after 3 out: 3rd travelling wl appr next: sn rdn: 2nd and kpt on wl fr last* **7/1**[3]

3 *4* **Mullacash (IRE)**[19] [4803] 7-10-3 119 (b) PCarberry 120
(Noel Meade, Ire) *mid-div: racd wd: hdwy into 4th 4 out: 3rd next: 2nd and rdn bef 2 out: 3rd and no imp fr last* **16/1**

4 *1 1/2* **Lincam (IRE)**[19] [4803] 9-10-4 120 CO'Dwyer 120
(C F Swan, Ire) *led: rdn and hdd after 3 out: 5th bef 2 out: kpt on* **7/1**[3]

5 *nk* **Numbersixvalverde (IRE)**[32] [4634] 9-11-4 134 RWalsh 133
(Martin Brassil, Ire) *hld up in tch: 6th whn mstke 4 out: sn rdn: kpt on one pced fr 2 out* **10/3**[1]

6 *2* **Well Presented (IRE)**[21] [4761] 7-11-4 134 (t) BJGeraghty 131
(Mrs John Harrington, Ire) *prom: 2nd fr 6th: 4th 3 out: sn rdn and one pced* **9/1**

7 *1 1/2* **Pearly Jack**[2] [69] 7-10-1 120 TGMRyan(3) 116
(D E Fitzgerald, Ire) *mid-div: rdn and wknd fr 4 out* **14/1**

8 *4* **Scarthy Lad (IRE)**[19] [4803] 7-11-10 140 APMcCoy 132
(Thomas Gerard O'Leary, Ire) *hld up in rr: prog after 4 out: 5th next: 4th and rdn bef 2 out: sn no ex: eased fr last* **5/1**[2]

9 *25* **G V A Ireland (IRE)**[19] [4803] 7-10-10 126 DNRussell 93
(F Flood, Ire) *prom: 3rd 1/2-way: 4th 5 out: rdn and wknd next: eased fr 2 out: t.o* **8/1**

10 *15* **Ballynattin Buck (IRE)**[34] [4567] 9-10-4 120 (t) TPTreacy 72
(A L T Moore, Ire) *mid-div: slt mstkes 3rd and 10th: wknd 5 out: eased fr 3 out: t.o* **25/1**

U **Aimees Mark (IRE)**[123] [3029] 9-9-12 119 KTColeman(5) —
(F Flood, Ire) *hld up in tch: impr into 6th after 1/2-way: cl up whn uns rdr 5 out* **20/1**

6m 34.7s **Going Correction** +0.35s/f (Yiel) **11** Ran SP% **119.5**
Speed ratings: **110,109,108,107,107 106,106,105,97,92** — CSF £56.86 CT £767.79 TOTE £8.90: £2.30, £2.80, £5.00; DF 48.10.
Owner Paid Thru The Nose Syndicate **Bred** J G Charlton **Trained** Stud Moone, Co Kildare

NOTEBOOK
Pay It Forward was running in his first handicap and his only previous success over fences was at Downpatrick. The faster ground saw him take control after three out and he was always holding the runner-up. He looks an interesting future prospect when conditions are right.
Joes Edge(IRE) had his chance but is very much in the Handicapper's grip.
Mullacash(IRE) has not won since gaining his only chase success in a handicap at Roscommon last October. He stayed on alright but does not quicken. *(op 14/1)*
Lincam(IRE) does not have to go out in front and his tendency to jump left did not help. His sole success from 27 outings was on heavy ground here.
Numbersixvalverde(IRE) has had a busy season and this Irish Grand National winner is now 29lb higher than when winning the Thyestes back in January. *(op 3/1 tchd 7/2)*
Well Presented(IRE), a stable companion of the winner, might have been feeling the effect of his Aintree exertions and was well beaten when blundering at the last. *(op 8/1)*
Scarthy Lad(IRE) began to feel the pinch after three out and was not persevered with from the next.
G V A Ireland(IRE) does not number consistency amongst his attributes these days.

116a MENOLLY HOMES CHAMPION NOVICE HURDLE (GRADE 1) 2m 4f
4:20 (4:20) 4-Y-0+ **£43,971** (£13,475; £6,382; £2,127; £1,418)

RPR

1 **Asian Maze (IRE)**[21] [4765] 6-11-7 144 PCarberry 142+
(Thomas Mullins, Ire) *mde all: rdn clr bef 2 out: eased fr last: impressive* **6/4**[1]

2 *5* **Kerryhead Windfarm (IRE)**[32] [4631] 7-11-12 AndrewJMcNamara 132
(Michael Hourigan, Ire) *trckd ldrs in 5th: impr into 3rd 3 out: 4th and rdn next: kpt on to go mod 2nd fr last* **25/1**

3 *3 1/2* **Washington Lad (IRE)**[42] [4434] 5-11-11 APMcCoy 128
(P A Fahy, Ire) *prom: 3rd 1/2-way: 2nd 4 out: 3rd and outpcd 2 out: kpt on same pce st* **7/1**

4 *3* **Petertheknot (IRE)**[31] [4647] 7-11-12 133 CO'Dwyer 126
(Patrick Sinnott, Ire) *trckd ldrs on outer: 5th and rdn 4 out: 4th next: mod 2nd 2 out: no ex st* **14/1**

5 *1/2* **Bagan (FR)**[14] [4849] 6-11-12 NFehily 125
(C J Mann) *towards rr: prog into 5th appr 2 out: mod 4th bef last: sn no ex* **14/1**

6 *13* **Major Vernon (IRE)**[32] [4633] 6-11-12 RWalsh 112
(W P Mullins, Ire) *trckd ldrs on inner: 6th 4 out: rdn and outpcd after next: no ex fr 2 out* **6/1**[3]

7 *nk* **Sher Beau (IRE)**[33] [4597] 6-11-12 133 DNRussell 112
(Philip Fenton, Ire) *mid-div: 8th after slt mstke 6 out: rdn and no imp fr 3 out* **7/2**[2]

8 *hd* **Keepthedreamalive**[3] [43] 7-11-12 123 BHitchcott 112
(R H Buckler) *chsd ldr in 2nd: 3rd and rdn 4 out: wknd bef next* **50/1**

9 *3 1/2* **Letterman (IRE)**[124] [2981] 5-11-11 TGMRyan 107
(E J O'Grady, Ire) *a towards rr: no ex fr 3 out* **40/1**

10 *9* **Macs Flamingo (IRE)**[54] [4224] 5-11-11 125 BJGeraghty 98
(P A Fahy, Ire) *towards rr: prog into 6th 4 out: wknd bef 2 out: eased* **12/1**

P **Django (IRE)**[48] [4336] 6-11-12 RMPower —
(Mrs John Harrington, Ire) *hld up in tch: rdn and wknd 5 out: p.u bef 2 out* **40/1**

4m 56.1s **Going Correction** -0.20s/f (Good) **12** Ran SP% **120.7**
Speed ratings: **119,117,115,114,114 109,108,108,107,103** — CSF £47.35 TOTE £2.40: £1.50, £7.40, £1.80; DF 104.20.
Owner Mrs C A Moore **Bred** Mrs C A Moore **Trained** Goresbridge, Co Kilkenny

FOCUS
Asian Maze has been one of the success stories of the campaign and proved different class in a race in which several of her main rivals were well below their best.

NOTEBOOK
Asian Maze(IRE) continued her amazing rate of improvement with an all-the-way success that saw her win virtually unchallenged, looking value for more like 20 lengths. Although she took nine races to get off the mark, this was her seventh win from her last eight starts and Racing Post Ratings have her improving more than 40lb since her first success. What's more, there is no sign of that improvement levelling off yet. She is versatile too, and connections may try her back at 2m one day. *(op 7/4)*
Kerryhead Windfarm(IRE), twice a winner around here, again showed his liking for the track with a career-best effort. *(op 20/1)*
Washington Lad(IRE) inflicted Asian Maze's only defeat this season when beating her at Leopardstown's Christmas meeting but, with less than fluent jumping, was no threat here after the third last. *(op 8/1)*
Petertheknot(IRE) went second two out but could not get on challenging terms. *(op 12/1)*
Bagan(FR) ran as well as could be expected but was toiling after two out. Underfoot conditions would not have suited him. *(op 12/1)*
Major Vernon(IRE) found this too quick and was struggling three out. *(op 5/1)*
Sher Beau(IRE) belied his strength in the market and lost his unbeaten record over flights with a *moderate effort. He was discovered to have a slight upper respiratory tract infection.Official explanation: vet said gelding was found to have a slight upper respiratory tract infection (op 3/1)*
Keepthedreamalive was done with before the third last.

117a OPEL NOVICE HURDLE 2m
4:55 (4:55) 5-Y-0+ **£13,851** (£4,063; £1,936; £659)

RPR

1 **Snoopy Loopy (IRE)**[44] [4394] 7-11-9 127 PWFlood(3) 130
(Miss V Scott) *trckd ldrs: 2nd fr 4 out: rdn to ld after 2 out: styd on wl u.p* **16/1**

2 *2 1/2* **The Railway Man (IRE)**[3] [40] 6-11-12 BMCash 128
(A L T Moore, Ire) *sn 2nd: led after 4th: rdn and hdd after 2 out: kpt on u.p* **7/2**[2]

3 *2 1/2* **Ray Boy (IRE)**[3] [40] 6-11-12 DJCondon 125
(P C O'Connor, Ire) *prom: 4th whn bad mstke 4th: impr into 5th 3 out: 4th and rdn next: kpt on same pce* **16/1**

4 *2 1/2* **Akshar (IRE)**[45] [4381] 6-11-12 128 BJGeraghty 123
(D K Weld, Ire) *trckd ldrs: impr into 3rd 4 out: rdn and no imp fr 2 out* **7/1**[3]

5 *5* **Sirius Storm (IRE)**[12] [4893] 5-11-11 JLCullen 117
(Paul Nolan, Ire) *towards rr: impr into 5th bef 3 out: kpt on* **11/1**

6 *10* **Proud To Be Irish (IRE)**[15] [4598] 6-11-5 108 MrJPO'Farrell(7) 108
(Seamus O'Farrell, Ire) *hld up: styd on fr 3 out* **33/1**

7 *4* **Augherskea (IRE)**[68] [3985] 6-11-12 PCarberry 104
(Noel Meade, Ire) *towards rr: prog 3 out: 12th next: kpt on* **11/4**[1]

8 *nk* **Davenport Democrat (IRE)**[15] [2738] 7-10-12 100 RJKiely(7) 96
(W P Mullins, Ire) *hld up: hmpd 1st: kpt on fr 3 out* **20/1**

9 *1 1/2* **Master Ofthe Chase (IRE)**[47] [4352] 7-11-7 125 JFLevins(5) 102
(C F Swan, Ire) *trckd ldrs: 5th 4 out: 4th appr next: wknd 2 out* **14/1**

10 *1/2* **Underwriter (USA)**[20] [4775] 5-11-8 KJMercer(3) 100
(Ferdy Murphy) *nvr bttr than mid-div* **16/1**

11 *2 1/2* **New Field (IRE)**[82] [3733] 7-11-12 116 CO'Dwyer 99
(Thomas Mullins, Ire) *rr of mid-div: hmpd 4 out: no imp fr next* **9/1**

12 *4* **Cash And Carry (IRE)**[16] [4827] 7-11-5 111 DNRussell 88
(E J O'Grady, Ire) *nvr a factor* **20/1**

13 *1 1/2* **Pom Flyer (FR)**[31] [4647] 5-11-11 122 FJFlood 93
(F Flood, Ire) *nvr a factor* **20/1**

14 3/4 **Daly Said It (IRE)**^{33} [4599] 5-11-4 .... JRBarry 86
(A J Martin, Ire) *nvr a factor* **14/1**
15 7 **Golden Exchange (IRE)**^{31} [4647] 5-11-11 116 .... MDGrant 86
(David Wachman, Ire) *mid-div thrght* **16/1**
16 1 1/2 **Wiscalitus (GER)**^{20} [4768] 6-11-7 .... PCO'Neill$^{(5)}$ 85
(Miss Venetia Williams) *mid-div: prog into 6th bef 3 out: wknd next* **25/1**
17 1 1/2 **Sky To Sea (FR)**^{26} [4225] 7-11-2 104 .... AO'Shea$^{(3)}$ 77
(Mrs A M O'Shea, Ire) *a bhd* **66/1**
18 11 **Mystical Memories (IRE)**^{186} [1840] 6-11-0 .... RWalsh 61
(W P Mullins, Ire) *a bhd* **20/1**
19 15 **Tycoon Hall (IRE)**^{73} [3872] 5-11-4 .... RMPower 50
(Mrs John Harrington, Ire) *chsd ldrs: 4th appr 1/2-way: 6th 4 out: sn wknd* **20/1**
20 **Laoch Dubh (IRE)**^{26} [4732] 6-11-5 97 .... MrJEBurns$^{(7)}$ 58
(Henry De Bromhead, Ire) *led: hdd after 4th: wknd after next: completely t.o* **50/1**
U **Boher Storm (IRE)**^{12} [4892] 5-11-8 .... TGMRyan$^{(3)}$ —
(P A Fahy, Ire) *uns rdr 1st* **20/1**
U **Monanore Melody (IRE)**^{138} [2797] 7-10-12 .... MJFerris$^{(7)}$ —
(W Harney, Ire) *uns rdr 1st* **100/1**
P **Barney McAll (IRE)**^{22} [4756] 5-11-11 .... (t) NFehily —
(R T Phillips) *prom early: wknd fr 1/2-way: p.u bef 2 out* **20/1**
U **Reine Des Reines (IRE)**^{16} [4827] 7-11-4 111 .... DFO'Regan$^{(3)}$ —
(John E Kiely, Ire) *towards rr: hmpd and uns rdr 4 out* **12/1**
P **Johnston's Swallow (IRE)**^{43} [4419] 7-11-12 .... APMcCoy —
(M J P O'Brien, Ire) *mid-div: prog into 5th 1/2-way: 4th 4 out: sn no ex: p.u bef 2 out* **16/1**

3m 54.4s **Going Correction** -0.20s/f (Good) 25 Ran SP% **174.7**
Speed ratings: 118,116,115,114,111 106,104,104,103,103 102,100,99,99,95 94,94,88,81,81 —,—,—,—,E CSF £85.51 TOTE £31.20: £4.90, £1.40, £5.90, £2.40; DF 171.40.
Owner Miss Victoria Scott Jnr **Bred** Mrs M Doran **Trained** Elsdon, Northumberland

NOTEBOOK
Snoopy Loopy(IRE) took over before the straight and, with the last flight bypassed, it was stamina that kept him in front. *(op 12/1)*
The Railway Man(IRE), turning out for a second time during the week, demonstrated the gap between the Grade One novices' hurdles and this class. He went on a long way out but was easily swept aside by the winner before they turned for home. *(op 4/1 tchd 9/2)*
Ray Boy(IRE) was a trailer in the same Grade One that The Railway Man contested on Tuesday but stayed on much better here despite a blunder at halfway.
Akshar(IRE) needs better ground than this. *(op 6/1)*
Augherskea(IRE) rather had the waiting tactics overdone. *(op 9/4)*
Underwriter(USA) never got into serious contention.
Wiscalitus(GER) flattered with a move before three out but soon dropped away.
Johnston's Swallow(IRE) *Official explanation: jockey said gelding was badly interfered with by a loose horse (op 12/1)*
Barney McAll(IRE) dropped away from halfway and was pulled up before the straight. *(op 12/1)*

113 - 118a (Foreign Racing) - See Raceform Interactive

HEXHAM (L-H)
Saturday, April 30

OFFICIAL GOING: Good (good to soft in places)
Wind: Light. Half behind.

119 RAMSIDE EVENT CATERING INTERMEDIATE CHASE (19 fncs) 3m 1f
5:25 (5:25) (Class 4) 5-Y-0+ **£3,711** (£1,142; £571; £285)

Form RPR
60-F 1 **Isellido (IRE)**^{6} [10] 6-10-9 .... HOliver 109+
(R C Guest) *hld up: hdwy 1/2-way: led 2 out: rdn and r.o wl* **3/1**^{1}
1P3- 2 4 **Jolika (FR)**^{10} [4928] 8-11-1 101 .... (p) JimCrowley 108
(L Lungo) *hld up: hdwy to chse ldrs whn blnd 4 out: rdn next: chsd wnr appr last: kpt on: no imp* **3/1**^{1}
204- 3 16 **Shannon's Pride (IRE)**^{27} [4708] 9-11-8 115 .... ADobbin 105+
(N G Richards) *cl up: led 10th: hdd 2 out: sn rdn and outpcd* **3/1**^{1}
12F- 4 5 **Kidithou (FR)**^{15} [4850] 7-11-8 112 .... KJohnson 99+
(W T Reed) *led to 10th: mstke 13th: lost pl whn blnd 4 out: n.d after* **7/2**^{2}
405- 5 18 **Now Then Sid**^{7} [4976] 6-10-13 86 .... KJMercer$^{(3)}$ 70
(Mrs S A Watt) *in tch: struggling 15th: sn btn* **7/1**^{3}
/PP- P **Blue Jar**^{20} [4798] 7-11-2 54 .... FKeniry —
(M Mullineaux) *chsd ldr to 8th: struggling 15th: t.o whn p.u bef 2 out* **100/1**

6m 27.2s (-5.60) **Going Correction** -0.125s/f (Good) 6 Ran SP% **110.7**
Speed ratings: **103,101,96,95,89** — CSF £12.31 TOTE £3.90: £3.30, £2.20; EX 24.70.
Owner C J Cookson **Bred** Hugh J Holohan **Trained** Brancepeth, Co Durham

FOCUS
An ordinary event in which the gallop was fair but the winner, who is value for nearly double the official margin, appeals as the type to win again over fences.

NOTEBOOK
Isellido(IRE) ◆ showed herself none the worse for a fall on her chasing debut six days earlier with a performance that matched the pick of her hurdles runs. She travelled strongly, jumped soundly and may be capable of better. *(op 10-3 tchd 7-2 and 11-4)*
Jolika(FR) is still not the finished article over fences but again showed enough to suggest she should be able to win in ordinary handicap company at up to this trip in the North. *(op 11-4)*
Shannon's Pride(IRE) looked to have solid claims at these weights but again found disappointingly *little off the bridle. He has had breathing problems and looks one to tread carefully with at present. (op 11-4)*
Kidithou(FR) looks to have lost his confidence at his fences after his Ayr fall and he will have to jump better than this before he is a betting proposition again. *(op 10-3 tchd 3-1)*
Now Then Sid had a stiff task at these weights but, although well beaten, may be happier on faster ground in ordinary handicap company. *(op 12-1 tchd 14-1)*
Blue Jar again achieved nothing.

120 NORTHUMBERLAND ASSOCIATION OF CLUBS FOR YOUNG PEOPLE (S) HURDLE (8 hdls) 2m 110y
5:55 (5:55) (Class 5) 4-Y-0+ **£2,513** (£718; £359)

Form RPR
000- 1 **Royal Glen (IRE)**^{25} [4738] 7-10-7 73 .... RMcGrath 91+
(W S Coltherd) *keen: hld up midfield: smooth hdwy bef 2 out: led run in: shkn up and kpt on strly* **66/1**
130- 2 3 **Talarive (USA)**^{10} [4926] 9-11-7 100 .... (tp) JimCrowley 102
(P D Niven) *cl up: led 3rd to run in: kpt on same pce* **6/1**^{3}
244- 3 7 **Polished**^{42} [4454] 6-11-7 84 .... (b^{1}) HOliver 95
(R C Guest) *keen: in tch: rdn and outpcd bef 2 out: kpt on fr last: no imp* **4/1**^{2}
1UP- 4 13 **Ball Games**^{19} [4810] 7-10-11 82 .... MMcAvoy$^{(10)}$ 92+
(James Moffatt) *hld up: hdwy to chal whn blnd and rdr lost irons 2 out: wknd bef last* **25/1**
660- 5 1 3/4 **Just Sal**^{10} [4928] 9-10-0 77 .... MrPCallaghan$^{(7)}$ 66
(R Nixon) *hld up midfield: outpcd after 5th: n.d after* **9/1**
PP0- 6 21 **Ghost Buster**^{87} [3648] 6-10-9 .... (p) DFlavin$^{(5)}$ 52
(Mrs L B Normile) *bhd: drvn along 5th: nvr on terms* **100/1**
U40- 7 6 **Jimmy Byrne (IRE)**^{7} [2293] 5-11-0 99 .... (p) ADobbin 46
(B Ellison) *chsd ldrs: chal after 3 out: wknd qckly bef next* **4/1**^{2}
304- 8 3 1/2 **Noras Legacy (IRE)**^{304} [843] 7-10-4 77 .... PBuchanan$^{(3)}$ 36
(Miss Lucinda V Russell) *hld up: rdn 5th: sn wknd* **33/1**
PPP- 9 nk **Eastern Tribute (USA)**^{21} [4711] 9-10-7 109 .... (b^{1}) EWhillans$^{(7)}$ 42
(A C Whillans) *led to 3rd: lost tch fr 3 out* **12/1**
030- 10 2 1/2 **Diagon Alley (IRE)**^{7} [4975] 5-11-0 .... PRobson 40
(K W Hogg) *hld up: struggling fr 1/2-way* **33/1**
050- 11 28 **Scamp**^{113} [3256] 6-10-7 73 .... KRenwick —
(R Shiels) *a bhd* **33/1**
P60- P **Sayoun (IRE)**^{27} [4714] 6-11-0 67 .... (b^{1}) BHarding —
(Mrs L B Normile) *hld up: struggling 4th: t.o whn p.u bef 3 out* **100/1**
P43- P **Top Style (IRE)**^{25} [4738] 7-11-7 95 .... GLee —
(J Howard Johnson) *cl up: chal 3rd: wknd qckly bef 2 out: p.u bef last* **5/2**^{1}

4m 12.4s (-1.60) **Going Correction** +0.075s/f (Yiel) 13 Ran SP% **116.7**
Speed ratings: **106,104,101,95,94 84,81,80,79,78 65,—,—** CSF £413.64 TOTE £47.90: £5.00, £1.90, £1.80; EX 289.00.The winner was bought in for 7,000gns.
Owner S Coltherd **Bred** R Goodwin **Trained** Selkirk, Borders

FOCUS
A poor race in which the pace seemed sound and the third sets the level.

NOTEBOOK
Royal Glen(IRE), an inconsistent sort who finished over 30 lengths behind Talarive on her previous start, turned in a much-improved display and there seemed no fluke about the manner of this win. However her record suggests she is not certain to put this in next time and she may be one to take on at short odds after reassessment. *(op 50-1)*
Talarive(USA) is not very consistent but had a good chance at the weights and ran better back in this grade than he had done in a Perth handicap. His stable is among the winners but he is not one to place maximum faith in. *(op 11-4)*
Polished, from a stable among the winners at present, was not disgraced back over hurdles in the *firs- time blinkers and he shaped as though a stiffer test of stamina would have been in his favour. (op 6-1)*
Ball Games, dropped in grade, ran better than the bare form as his rider lost his irons after a penultimate flight blunder but, while capable of winning a similar contest, is not one to place too much faith in. *Official explanation: jockey said he lost his irons*
Just Sal's two win have been over this course and distance but she again showed why she is not the best betting proposition around. *(op 16-1)*
Ghost Buster, dropped in grade and again in cheekpieces, offered no immediate promise. *(op 66-1)*
Top Style(IRE), who was not far behind Talarive at Sedgefield on his previous start, dropped out as *though something was amiss and remains one to tread carefully with at present.Official explanation: jockey said gelding moved poorly and ran flat (op 4-1)*

121 IBETX.COM BETTING EXCHANGE H'CAP HURDLE (10 hdls) 2m 4f 110y
6:25 (6:25) (Class 3) (0-125,122) 4-Y-0+ **£4,901** (£1,508; £754; £377)

Form RPR
/3P- 1 **River Mist (IRE)**^{351} [345] 6-10-0 **96** oh1 .... KRenwick 100+
(Karen McLintock) *hld up in tch: hdwy to ld 4 out: rdn and kpt on strly fr last* **20/1**
530- 2 2 1/2 **Wet Lips (AUS)**^{217} [1504] 7-11-7 **117** .... (t) HOliver 118
(R C Guest) *hld up: hdwy to chse ldrs 1/2-way: effrt and ev ch 2 out: kpt on same pce run in* **7/1**
50P- 3 3 **Hugo De Perro (FR)**^{19} [4812] 10-10-11 **110** .... (p) PBuchanan$^{(3)}$ 108
(Miss Lucinda V Russell) *chsd ldrs: led 6th to next: outpcd bef 2 out: kpt on fr last: no imp* **40/1**
5P6- 4 11 **Carapuce (FR)**^{27} [4711] 6-11-12 **122** .... BGibson 112+
(L Lungo) *prom: hdwy and cl up 4 out: rdn and wknd fr 2 out* **12/1**
/4P- 5 15 **Haystacks (IRE)**^{14} [4868] 9-11-0 **110** .... JimCrowley 82
(James Moffatt) *bhd: struggling 5th: rallied bef 2 out: no imp* **33/1**
P-30 6 12 **Mister Moussac**^{3} [61] 6-9-11 **96** oh1 .... (p) PAspell$^{(3)}$ 56
(Miss Kariana Key) *prom: led bef 5th to next: wknd after 3 out* **8/1**
443- 7 6 **Megapac (IRE)**^{21} [4775] 7-9-10 **99** .... WKennedy$^{(7)}$ 53
(Noel T Chance) *hld up: drvn and outpcd 6th: n.d after* **7/2**^{1}
142- 8 6 **Fishki's Lad**^{25} [4739] 10-11-0 **110** .... (p) BHarding 58
(E W Tuer) *mde most to bef 5th: lost pl after next: n.d after* **8/1**
/56- P **Didifon**^{155} [2465] 10-10-3 **102** .... (p) KJMercer$^{(3)}$ —
(N P McCormack) *sn bhd: t.o whn p.u bef 2 out* **33/1**
/PP- P **Eriskay (IRE)**^{133} [2887] 9-10-11 **107** .... ADobbin —
(L Lungo) *hld up: hit 2nd: struggling and p.u bef 7th* **14/1**
P34- P **Deja Vu (IRE)**^{25} [4736] 6-10-9 **105** .... GLee —
(J Howard Johnson) *w ldrs to 5th: lost pl qckly next: sn p.u* **4/1**^{2}
065- P **Notanotherdonkey (IRE)**^{141} [2744] 5-10-2 **98** .... TScudamore —
(M Scudamore) *cl up: outpcd whn hit 4 out: t.o whn p.u bef last* **13/2**^{3}

5m 5.40s (-1.50) **Going Correction** +0.075s/f (Yiel) 12 Ran SP% **117.7**
Speed ratings: **105,104,102,98,93 88,86,83,—,— —,—** CSF £149.39 CT £5488.49 TOTE £25.50: £7.60, £1.60, £9.10; EX 153.20.
Owner Mrs H Scotto **Bred** Mrs Hilary Scotto **Trained** Ingoe, Northumberland
■ Stewards' Enquiry : K Renwick two-day ban: used whip with excessive force and in the incorrect place (May 11,12)

FOCUS
A race in which the three market leaders disappointed but still a fair effort from the winner, who was having her first run for nearly a year. The form could be more solid.

NOTEBOOK
River Mist(IRE), off the course for nearly a year, turned in her best effort yet over hurdles and the way she travelled and jumped suggests she may well be able to hold her own after reassessment if all remains well. *(op 14-1)*
Wet Lips(AUS) has not won for over a year but ran up to his best with the blinkers left off for his in-form stable on this first run since September. He is capable of winning again over hurdles but is vulnerable to progressive sorts from his mark. *(op 8-1 tchd 13-2)*
Hugo De Perro(FR), who is back on a favourable mark, ran easily his best race for his current stable and is capable of winning a handicap from this mark but, given his antics at the start, is rarely one to go in head down for. *(op 33-1)*
Carapuce(FR) travelled well and ran as though coming to hand but may need to drop a few more pounds in the weights before he is able to pick up the winning thread. *(op 10-1)*
Haystacks(IRE) is not the most reliable around but left the impression that the return to three miles would be in his favour.
Mister Moussac is on a fair mark but has not won for some time and is anything but consistent. *He was below his best this time and remains one to tread carefully with.Official explanation: jockey said gelding hung right handed (op 12-1)*
Megapac(IRE), a rare runner at this course for his trainer, was soundly beaten on this handicap debut. However, given he is only lightly raced, he has to be worth another chance. *(op 5-1)*

Deja Vu(IRE) *Official explanation: trainers representative said gelding was over the top* (op 6-1 tchd 9-2)
Notanotherdonkey(IRE) *Official explanation: trainer had no explanation for poor form shown* (op 6-1 tchd 9-2)

122 IAN STRAKER MEMORIAL TROPHY (A H'CAP CHASE) (12 fncs) 2m 110y
6:55 (6:55) (Class 4) (0-100,97) 5-Y-O+ **£4,004** (£1,232; £616; £308)

Form RPR
05P- **1** **Risky Way**[19] [4810] 9-10-3 **74**… DO'Meara 88
(W S Coltherd) *mde all: rdn and styd on wl fr 2 out* **10/1**
35- **2** *3* **College City (IRE)**[33] [4628] 6-10-11 **82**…(p) HOliver 93
(R C Guest) *in tch: effrt and chsd wnr 3 out: kpt on same pce after last* **4/1**[1]
432- **3** *6* **Ameras (IRE)**[20] [4784] 7-10-0 **74**… MrCStorey(3) 79
(Miss S E Forster) *prom: outpcd after 4 out: kpt on fr last: no imp* **7/1**[3]
P5- **4** *6* **Jupiter Jo**[25] [4734] 9-10-0 **74**… PBuchanan(3) 73
(J B Walton) *in tch: outpcd 4 out: hit next: no imp fnl 2* **11/2**[2]
3U4- **5** *2* **Northern Flash**[13] [4874] 11-10-0 **71**…(p) FKeniry 68
(J C Haynes) *hld up: outpcd 4 out: nvr rchd ldrs* **33/1**
10P- **6** *6* **Cusp**[11] [4784] 5-10-13 **92**… DCCostello(5) 80
(C W Thornton) *midfield: outpcd 7th: nvr on terms* **12/1**
P03- **7** *3 ½* **Earl Sigurd (IRE)**[20] [4784] 7-11-12 **97**… BGibson 85
(L Lungo) *hld up: a bhd* **20/1**
0 **8** *6* **Ballyboe Boy (IRE)**[6] [9] 6-11-0 **85**… RMcGrath 67
(R C Guest) *sn bhd: nvr on terms* **16/1**
0U5- **9** *1 ¼* **Jamorin Dancer**[51] [4275] 10-9-7 **71** oh7…(p) TMessenger(7) 52+
(S G Chadwick) *cl up tl rdn and wknd fr 2 out* **80/1**
263- **10** *2* **Stormy Beech**[82] [3743] 9-11-0 **85**… KJohnson 63
(R Johnson) *hld up: sme hdwy after 4 out: wknd fr next* **9/1**
/34- **11** *dist* **Mister Magnum (IRE)**[8] [4968] 7-11-0 **95**… DDaSilva(10) —
(P Monteith) *a bhd: no ch fr 1/2-way* **16/1**
P63- **P** **Cool Carroll (IRE)**[33] [4624] 7-11-6 **91**… GLee —
(J Howard Johnson) *prom to 7th: t.o whn plld bef 3 out* **7/1**[3]
15-P **P** **Midlem Melody**[2] [84] 9-11-8 **93**… BHarding —
(W S Coltherd) *hld up: blnd bdly 6th: nt rcvr and p.u after next* **10/1**

4m 6.30s (-3.80) **Going Correction** -0.125s/f (Good)
WFA 5 from 6yo+ 3lb **13** Ran SP% **117.0**
Speed ratings: **103,101,98,95,95 92,90,87,87,86** —,—,— CSF £49.41 CT £304.52 TOTE £13.30: £6.40, £2.30, £2.00; EX 165.20.
Owner Mrs L J McLeod **Bred** Mrs N A Ward And W J Musson **Trained** Selkirk, Borders

FOCUS
A modest event in which the pace seemed sound and the form should stand up at a similar level.

NOTEBOOK
Risky Way, from a stable on the mark earlier this evening, jumped soundly and turned in his best effort for some time over fences. Two miles on a soundish surface seems to suit him well and he can win again on this evidence. *(tchd 9-1)*
College City(IRE), has not won for over two years and has yet to win over fences but is from an in-form stable and showed enough to suggest he can rectify matters, especially when returned to two and a half miles. *(op 5-1)*
Ameras(IRE) is a fairly reliable yardstick and was not disgraced in this modest handicap but her career record of no wins from 38 career starts means she has to be one to tread carefully with. *(op 9-1)*
Jupiter Jo was not disgraced on this handicap debut but left the impression that the step up to two and a half miles may be in his favour. *(op 6-1)*
Northern Flash is an inconsistent performer who was not totally disgraced given the way this race unfolded, but his inconsistency means he is of little interest for the future. *(op 25-1)*
Cusp, returned to fences after a spin on the Flat, did not show enough to suggest she will be one to be on in this type of event in the near future.
Cool Carroll(IRE) *Official explanation: jockey said mare ran flat (op 8-1)*

123 GEORGE F. WHITE HEART OF ALL ENGLAND MAIDEN HUNTERS' CHASE (19 fncs) 3m 1f
7:25 (7:25) (Class 6) 5-Y-O+ **£2,522** (£776; £388; £194)

Form RPR
P23- **1** **Imps Way**[46] [4392] 10-11-4… MrCMulhall(3) 86+
(Mrs T Corrigan-Clark) *midfield: hdwy 1/2-way: led bef last: readily* **11/2**[2]
2 *7 ¾* **Benbeoch**[34] 6-12-0…MissPRobson 87
(Dave Parker) *hld up and bhd: hdwy and in tch 13th: outpcd 3 out: kpt on fr last: fin 3rd, 6l & 1 3/4l: plcd 2nd* **6/4**[1]
5PP/ **3** *5* **Scenic Storm (IRE)**[20] 10-11-7… PKinsella(7) 82
(M E Broad) *bhd: rdn and no imp tl gd hdwy between last two: nvr rchd ldrs: fin 4th: promoted to 3rd* **50/1**
4 *16* **Mays Delight (IRE)**[6] 8-11-0… MrAWaugh(7) 59
(S G Waugh) *in tch tl rdn and wknd fr 3 out: fin 5th: promoted to 4th* **14/1**
P/ **5** *3 ½* **Natiain**[20] 6-11-7… MrJARichardson(7) 63
(Alistair M Brown) *keen: led 3rd to 3 out: wknd fr next* **9/1**
/24- **6** *2* **Buddy Girie**[20] 12-11-7… MrPCornforth(7) 61
(P Cornforth) *cl up tl rdn and wknd qckly fr 2 out* **6/1**[3]
0/P- **7** *dist* **Kelly Pride**[56] [4185] 8-11-7… MrNSSaville(7) —
(Niall Saville) *nt fluent: a bhd* **50/1**
404- **D** **Jupiter's Fancy**[43] [4445] 10-11-0… TMessenger(7) 80
(M V Coglan) *towards rr: hdwy to ld 3 out: lost weight cloth between last two: hdd bef last: no ch w wnr: fin 2nd, 6l: disqualified* **28/1**
F **Bobby Buttons**[20] 8-11-9… MissTJackson(5) —
(Mrs J Jones) *hld up: hdwy whn fell 6th* **14/1**
P **Rip Kirby**[6] 10-11-9… MrWLMorgan(5) —
(Mrs J Warwick) *mstkes: a bhd: t.o whn p.u bef 2 out* **25/1**
P0/ **U** **Wilfie Wild**[20] 9-11-7… MrsLWard(7) —
(Mrs Lynne Ward) *hld up: sme hdwy whn uns rdr 15th* **16/1**
05P- **P** **Mill Tower**[7] 8-11-9… MrPCallaghan(5) —
(R Nixon) *in tch to 1/2-way: t.o whn p.u bef last* **50/1**
FP2/ **P** **Mrs Sherman**[28] 10-11-0… MrCGillon(7) —
(Miss C Pennycook) *mstkes: sn bhd: t.o whn p.u after 13th* **25/1**
/24- **P** **Highland Brig**[19] [4809] 9-11-9…(p) MrRMorgan(5) —
(T Butt) *led to 3rd: cl up tl wknd bef 3 out: t.o whn p.u bef last* **16/1**
603/ **P** **Sea Knight (IRE)**[20] 8-11-7… MrAJFindlay(7) —
(Ms J M Findlay) *chsd ldrs tl wknd bef 3 out: t.o whn p.u bef last* **40/1**

6m 31.1s (-1.70) **Going Correction** -0.125s/f (Good) **15** Ran SP% **124.2**
Speed ratings: **97,94,92,87,86 86,—,95,—,— —,—,—,—,—** CSF £14.25 TOTE £7.00: £3.50, £1.90, £8.50; EX 22.60.
Owner Mrs T Corrigan-Clark **Bred** R Robinson **Trained** Scarborough, N Yorks

FOCUS
An ordinary renewal of this prestigious event but a sound pace and this form, rated through the runner-up, should prove reliable in similar events.

NOTEBOOK
Imps Way, who was in the process of running well until making a bad mistake in this race last year, jumped with fluency this year and turned in an improved effort. He is capable of winning again on this evidence. *(op 7-1)*
Benbeoch, a progressive sort in points, looked the one to beat after three straight wins but, although not beaten far proved a bit of a disappointment. However, he is only six and looks the sort to do much better in time. *(op 7-4)*
Scenic Storm(IRE) looked to have a stiff task on these terms but ran creditably and left the impression that a thorough test of stamina would have been in his favour.
Mays Delight(IRE) finished a similar distance behind Benbeoch in a point earlier this year and looked to give his running on this occasion. *(tchd 16-1)*
Natiain, unbeaten in three points last term, looks a bit better than the bare form as he failed to settle in a race run at a decent gallop and, given he is only six, is the type to make further progress in due course.
Jupiter's Fancy was in the process of reproducing that last year's career-best run (in this race) until finding things conspiring against her again and the fact her weight cloth came loose meant inevitable disqualification. *(op 25-1)*

124 ARUP NOVICES' HURDLE (12 hdls) 3m
7:55 (7:56) (Class 4) 4-Y-O+ **£3,402** (£972; £486)

Form RPR
61- **1** **Bellaney Jewel (IRE)**[20] [4785] 6-10-13… ADobbin 97+
(J J Quinn) *prom: hdwy and ev ch 2 out: sn drvn along: rallied to ld run in: styd on wl* **6/4**[2]
221- **2** *1 ½* **Rogues Gallery (IRE)**[39] [4508] 5-11-6… GLee 102
(J Howard Johnson) *keen: hld up in tch: hdwy to ld 4th: rdn appr last: hdd run in: kpt on* **6/5**[1]
045- **3** *3* **Uneven Line**[51] [4272] 9-10-4 67… MrCStorey(3) 86
(Miss S E Forster) *cl up tl lost pl 5th: rallied 2 out: kpt on fr last: nt rch first two* **20/1**
6- **4** *1 ¼* **Rhuna Red**[20] [4788] 6-10-7… KRenwick 85
(J R Bewley) *hld up in tch: outpcd 9th: rallied between last two: no imp run in* **33/1**
500- **5** *7* **Lothian Falcon**[10] [4935] 6-10-11… GCarenza(3) 85
(P Maddison) *keen: in tch: mstke 3rd: rdn and wknd between last two* **33/1**
350- **6** *2* **Primitive Poppy**[19] [4807] 6-10-4… PBuchanan(3) 76
(Mrs A Hamilton) *chsd ldrs tl wknd appr 2 out* **12/1**[3]
6- **7** *shd* **Beau Peak**[35] [4552] 6-10-0… EWhillans(7) 76
(D W Whillans) *prom: hdwy to press ldr 4th: ev ch tl wknd between last two* **20/1**
060- **P** **Tim's Moll**[35] [4552] 5-10-7… KJohnson —
(J B Walton) *nt fluent: a bhd: lost tch and p.u after 5th* **100/1**
0P/P **P** **Primitive Jean**[6] [14] 6-10-4…(t) PAspell(3) —
(C R Wilson) *hdwy and prom 5th: wknd 8th: t.o whn p.u bef 2 out* **100/1**
5P- **P** **Jealous Mead (IRE)**[52] [4259] 4-10-2…(p) DMcGann(5) —
(J Howard Johnson) *nt jump wl: keen: led to 4th: lost pl next: t.o whn p.u bef 3 out* **40/1**
000- **P** **Killwillie (IRE)**[14] [4865] 6-11-0…(t) PRobson —
(J I A Charlton) *hld up: stmbld after 8th: hdwy and cl up 3 out: wknd next: btn whn tried to refuse last: p.u flat* **33/1**

6m 17.1s (5.90) **Going Correction** +0.075s/f (Yiel)
WFA 4 from 5yo+ 7lb **11** Ran SP% **115.9**
Speed ratings: **93,92,91,91,88 88,88,—,—,— —** CSF £3.33 TOTE £2.10: £1.10, £1.10, £4.30; EX 3.20.
Owner J W Rosbotham **Bred** J W Rosbotham **Trained** Settrington, N Yorks
■ Stewards' Enquiry : A Dobbin one-day ban: used whip with excessive frequency (May 11)

FOCUS
A very modest contest run at a slow pace to this race and the proximity of the 67-rated third means it is not form to take at face value.

NOTEBOOK
Bellaney Jewel(IRE) ◆, whose forte is stamina, showed the right attitude in the closing stages of this messy contest to maintain her unbeaten record over hurdles. An end-to-end gallop would have suited much better and she looks very likely to progress again. *(op 11-8)*
Rogues Gallery(IRE) would have been suited by a much better gallop but, after looking sure to win for much of the way, was just outstayed in the closing stages. He looks sure to win again over hurdles in due course. *(op 11-8 tchd 11-10)*
Uneven Line's proximity in this slowly-run race gives this form a very dubious look and she is likely to continue to look vulnerable in this type of event. *(tchd 22-1)*
Rhuna Red was not disgraced on this hurdles debut but left the strong impression that a good test of stamina and modest handicaps will see her in her best light. *(op 25-1)*
Lothian Falcon did not get home on this hurdles debut having travelled strongly for much of the way and will be of more interest over shorter when handicapped. *(op 25-1)*
Primitive Poppy looks flattered by her proximity in this slowly-run race and is likely to continue to look vulnerable in this type of event. *(op 25-1 tchd 33-1)*

125 FLYING ACE HUNTERS' CHASE (19 fncs) 3m 1f
8:25 (8:26) (Class 6) 5-Y-O+ **£1,248** (£356; £178)

Form RPR
4F6- **1** **Red Rampage**[8] [4970] 10-12-0 101…(bt) PKinsella(7) 108
(H P Hogarth) *chsd ldrs: wnt 2nd 13th: effrt 2 out: led run in: styd on wl* **9/4**[1]
/F2- **2** *¾* **Silver Streak (IRE)**[13] 11-11-11 103… MrRArmson(3) 101+
(Milson Robinson) *led to 5th: led 8th to run in: kpt on* **9/4**[1]
/UP- **3** *17* **Kilcaskin Gold (IRE)**[6] 10-11-7… MrAJFindlay(7) 83
(R A Ross) *cl up: pushed along 1/2-way: outpcd fr 3 out* **12/1**
3/6- **4** *shd* **Lucky Master (IRE)**[13] 13-11-7… MissGSwan(7) 83
(Miss G Swan) *sn wl bhd: styd on fr 3 out: nvr rchd ldrs* **12/1**
6/1- **5** *9* **Dun Rose**[19] [4809] 11-11-7… MrRMorgan(5) 72
(Mrs P Claxton) *prom tl wknd fr 4 out* **13/2**[2]
10P- **6** *9* **Who Dares Wins**[13] 12-11-12 95… MissRachelClark(7) 70
(Ms S Duell) *sn wl bhd: nvr on terms* **12/1**
P3P- **7** *28* **Toad Hall**[203] [1662] 11-12-0 77… MissRCowie(7) 44
(Mrs L B Normile) *cl up tl wknd fr 15th* **25/1**
P/F- **8** *15* **Pilot's Harbour**[28] 9-11-7… MrCDawson(7) 22
(Mark Hughes) *mstkes: in tch to 13th: lost tch fr next* **66/1**
6P0/ **P** **Slaney Native (IRE)**[13] 12-11-7… MissMMullineaux(7) —
(Miss M Mullineaux) *j. slowly: sn t.o: p.u bef 12th* **10/1**[3]

6m 37.8s (5.00) **Going Correction** -0.125s/f (Good) **9** Ran SP% **112.4**
Speed ratings: **87,86,81,81,78 75,66,61,—** CSF £7.14 TOTE £3.90: £2.10, £1.40, £1.80; EX 6.10 Place 6 £143.86, Place 5 £80.61.
Owner H P Hogarth **Bred** N B Mason **Trained** Stillington, N Yorks
■ Stewards' Enquiry : Mr R Armson one-day ban: used whip in the incorrect place (May 11)

FOCUS
An ordinary event and a slow time compared with the other hunter chase, although the third and fourth ran pretty much to their marks.

NOTEBOOK

Red Rampage, turned out quickly after a solid effort at Perth, jumped soundly and ran up to his best to win his second race in this sphere. He is likely to win more races in this sphere. *(op 3-1)*

Silver Streak(IRE) jumped soundly in front and showed more than enough to suggest he can win again in this grade. *(op 7-4)*

Kilcaskin Gold(IRE), who won over this course and distance two year ago, came here on the back of a point win but, although not disgraced, continues to look vulnerable over the regulation fences.

Lucky Master(IRE) looked to face a stiff task on these terms but fared the best of those to come from off the pace and looks as though a thorough test of stamina would suit. *(op 25-1)*

Dun Rose, whose Kelso win represents only modest form, was found out in this stronger grade. *(op 5-1)*

Who Dares Wins won this race last year but had not been in much form since and was again a long way below that level. *(op 14-1)*

T/Plt: £172.80 to a £1 stake. Pool: £27,763.70. 117.25 winning tickets. T/Qpdt: £33.00 to a £1 stake. Pool: £3,156.30. 70.70 winning tickets. RY

UTTOXETER (L-H)

Saturday, April 30

OFFICIAL GOING: Soft

After overnight and morning rain the ground was described by the riders as 'genuine soft ground'. Third fence in back straight omitted in all chases.

Wind: moderate 1/2 against Weather: becoming fine, warm and sunny

126 TOTEPLACEPOT NOVICES' H'CAP CHASE (11 fncs 1 omitted) 2m

1:45 (1:45) (Class 4) (0-105,104) 5-Y-0+ **£3,770** (£1,160; £580; £290)

Form RPR

P5P- **1** **Itsuptoharry (IRE)**[65] 4022 6-11-12 **104** JMMaguire 120+
(D McCain) *hld up in tch: hdwy after 7th: hung lft fr next: led appr 2 out: styd on wl: bit slipped* **14/1**

642- **2** *11* **Vigoureux (FR)**[39] 4510 6-11-0 **99** (p) WKennedy[(7)] 103+
(S Gollings) *chsd ldrs: ev ch whn hit 8th: lft 2nd 2 out: no ch w wnr* **7/2**[2]

4P4- **3** *11* **The Mighty Sparrow (IRE)**[23] 4755 12-10-7 **85** MFoley 77
(A E Jones) *led: hdd and mstke 7th: sn wl outpcd* **20/1**

011- **4** *5* **Barneys Reflection**[27] 4714 5-11-5 **100** (v) NPMulholland 89+
(A Crook) *t.k.h: trckd ldrs: blnd 1st: led 7th: hit next: hdd 3 out: wknd next* **11/2**[3]

00-4 **5** *16* **Dan De Lion**[5] 25 6-10-3 **84** ow6 LMcGrath[(3)] 55
(R C Guest) *in rr: lost pl after 7th: bhd whn bdly hmpd 2 out* **7/2**[2]

224- **6** *3 ½* **Brigadier Du Bois (FR)**[60] 4116 6-10-3 **81** (t) LAspell —
(Mrs L Wadham) *trckd ldrs: lost pl 8th: sn bhd* **5/2**[1]

006- **F** **Lascar De Ferbet (FR)**[92] 3569 6-10-11 **89** ADempsey 93
(R Ford) *w ldrs: led 3 out: hdd and 2 l down whn fell next* **9/1**

4m 16.5s (14.30) **Going Correction** +0.975s/f (Soft)
WFA 5 from 6yo+ 3lb **7** Ran SP% **109.8**
Speed ratings: **103,97,92,89,81 79,—** CSF £58.45 CT £921.96 TOTE £18.20: £4.90, £2.80; EX 72.00.

Owner D M Proos **Bred** Mrs R Ardiff **Trained** Cholmondeley, Cheshire

FOCUS

A weak novices' handicap chase and difficult to rate, with the first two making their chasing bow, but a clear-cut winner who should progress.

NOTEBOOK

Itsuptoharry(IRE), who looks every inch a chaser, jumped soundly on his first try over fences but he persisted in hanging left and in the end the bit slipped through his mouth. He would not want the ground any softer than this. *(op 12-1)*

Vigoureux(FR), another making his chase debut, in the end finished clear second best but the winner was much too good. *(op 4-1)*

The Mighty Sparrow(IRE) made the running but over this trip, even on this ground, he was left toiling. *(op 16-1)*

Barneys Reflection, who has changed stables, was running from a mark 7lb higher than Market Rasen. He would not settle and did not respect his fences. *(op 5-1)*

Dan De Lion, making a quick return to action, was well in arrears when his rider was almost knocked out of the saddle two out on his first try over fences. *(op 10-3)*

Brigadier Du Bois(FR) did not improve for the drop back in distance and he is running out of excuses.

Lascar De Ferbet(FR), making his chasing bow, was clinging on to second spot when taking a crashing fall two out. *(op 8-1)*

127 TOTESPORT H'CAP HURDLE (12 hdls) 2m 4f 110y

2:20 (2:20) (Class 2) (0-140,141) 4-Y-0+

£15,399 (£5,841; £2,920; £1,327; £663; £398)

Form RPR

P44- **1** **Nonantais (FR)**[70] 3945 8-10-3 **117** MBatchelor 122
(M Bradstock) *led: hdd 3 out: styd on wl run-in: led nr fin* **20/1**

44B- **2** *½* **Turtle Soup (IRE)**[22] 4767 9-11-2 **140** WMcCarthy[(10)] 146+
(T R George) *jnd ldrs 6th: led 3 out: tired run-in: hdd nr fin* **16/1**

011- **3** *2* **Yes Sir (IRE)**[7] 4982 6-11-13 **141** LAspell 146+
(P Bowen) *chsd ldrs: hit 9th: sn outpcd: styd on gamely fr 2 out* **11/2**[2]

612- **4** *10* **Alikat (IRE)**[9] 4938 4-10-2 **125** TJMalone[(3)] 112
(M C Pipe) *chsd ldrs: lost pl after 3 out: kpt on run-in* **12/1**

001- **5** *hd* **Mcbain (USA)**[15] 4854 6-10-9 **123** RJohnson 115
(P J Hobbs) *hdwy 7th: chsng ldrs 9th: one pce fr next* **15/2**[3]

20-1 **6** *½* **Stan (NZ)**[6] 13 6-10-4 **121** 6ex LMcGrath[(3)] 114+
(R C Guest) *hdwy 6th: sn chsng ldrs: rdn 3 out: wknd run-in* **5/1**[1]

042- **7** *8* **Will Of The People (IRE)**[28] 4687 10-10-10 **124** (v[1]) JEMoore 108
(M C Pipe) *chsd ldrs: wknd after 3 out* **12/1**

115- **8** *2 ½* **Handy Money**[21] 4768 8-11-2 **130** RThornton 112+
(A King) *hdwy 7th: sn trcking ldrs: 4th and rdn whn mstke 3 out: wkng whn hit next* **9/1**

/06- **9** *dist* **First Love**[71] 3929 9-10-6 **120** MAFitzgerald —
(N J Henderson) *chsd ldrs: stmbld 3rd: reminders and lost pl 5th: lost pl 7th: sn bhd: t.o: btn 34 l* **40/1**

100- **10** *2 ½* **Mythical King (IRE)**[45] 4397 8-11-0 **128** JamesDavies —
(R Lee) *bhd and drvn along 7th: t.o* **25/1**

351- **11** *1 ¼* **Queen Soraya**[7] 4978 7-10-6 **120** WMarston —
(Miss H C Knight) *chsd ldrs: wknd after 3 out: heavily eased: t.o* **14/1**

36-4 **12** *3* **Master Papa (IRE)**[6] 4 6-10-5 **119** CLlewellyn —
(N A Twiston-Davies) *bhd fr 7th: t.o* **33/1**

20-0 **13** *12* **Corlande (IRE)**[6] 13 5-10-5 **119** DElsworth —
(Mrs S J Smith) *sn bhd and rdn alon: t.o* **50/1**

132- **14** *13* **Monolith**[125] 2972 7-11-4 **135** GBerridge[(3)] —
(L Lungo) *bhd fr 7th: t.o* **12/1**

020- **15** *15* **Very Optimistic (IRE)**[70] 3934 7-11-6 **134** (t) APMcCoy —
(Jonjo O'Neill) *reluctant to leave paddock: a in rr: bhd fr 7th: t.o* **11/2**[2]

410- **F** **Golano**[33] 2719 5-10-4 **118** (p) TDoyle —
(P R Webber) *w ldrs: wkng whn fell 7th* **20/1**

P31/ **P** **Mio Caro (FR)**[398] 4602 5-10-5 **119** BJCrowley —
(Noel T Chance) *sn bhd: p.u bef 8th* **40/1**

11P- **P** **Almnadia (IRE)**[16] 4837 6-10-5 **119** ATinkler —
(S Gollings) *chsd ldrs: lost pl 5th: p.u after next* **50/1**

5m 3.50s (0.90) **Going Correction** +0.45s/f (Soft)
WFA 4 from 5yo+ 6lb **18** Ran SP% **129.9**
Speed ratings: **116,115,115,111,111 110,107,106,—,— —,—,—,—,— —,—,—** CSF £301.18 CT £2027.17 TOTE £27.40: £7.20, £4.00, £1.90, £3.60; EX 424.80 Trifecta £398.20 Part won. Pool: £560.92 - 0.10 winning units..

Owner The Frankly Intolerable **Bred** Mle Isabelle Lelievre And Jean-Pierre Garcon **Trained** Letcombe Bassett, Oxon

FOCUS

A competitive and quite valuable handicap hurdle run at a strong pace in a fast time and in the end the first three clear. The form looks solid.

NOTEBOOK

Nonantais(FR), carrying a summer bloom, took them along at a strong pace and, sticking to his guns in valiant fashion, claimed the spoils near the line.

Turtle Soup(IRE), out of luck at Aintree, looked nailed on when going ahead but he rather hung fire on the run-in and had the prize whisked from under his nose near the line. *(op 18-1 tchd 20-1)*

Yes Sir(IRE), 6lb higher, was tapped for toe after hitting four out but, sticking to his guns in valiant fashion, was closing the first two down at the line.

Alikat(IRE), on the retreat after three out, was staying on again in her own time from the last and will be suited by three miles.

Mcbain(USA), with his confidence restored, tried to enter the argument on the run round to three out but this trip in this ground seems to stretch his stamina to the very limit. *(op 13-2)*

Stan(NZ) floundered in the ground and at the line was leg-weary. He does not want conditions as testing as he encountered here. *(op 9-2)*

Very Optimistic(IRE), in a first-time tongue strap, was most reluctant to leave the walkway exiting from the paddock and he was clearly in the wrong frame of mind. *(op 5-1 tchd 6-1)*

Almnadia(IRE) *Official explanation: jockey said mare hung right-handed (op 40-1)*

Mio Caro(FR) *Official explanation: jockey said gelding was never travelling (op 40-1)*

128 TOTEQUADPOT NOVICES' HURDLE (12 hdls) 2m 6f 110y

2:50 (2:51) (Class 4) 4-Y-0+ **£3,374** (£964; £482)

Form RPR

11- **1** **Standin Obligation (IRE)**[11] 4920 6-12-0 APMcCoy 125+
(M C Pipe) *w ldr: led 3rd: styd on wl fr 3 out* **1/1**[1]

/12- **2** *2* **Martha's Kinsman (IRE)**[38] 4526 6-11-7 RJohnson 116
(H D Daly) *hdwy to trck ldrs 7th: wnt clr 2nd next: effrt 3 out: styd on: no real imp* **9/4**[2]

003- **3** *29* **Classical Love**[20] 4789 5-10-0 (v[1]) SWalsh[(7)] 73
(C J Down) *chsd ldrs: outpcd 8th: kpt on to take remote 3rd last* **33/1**

03- **4** *¾* **Knocktemple Lass (IRE)**[20] 4793 6-10-7 NFehily 72
(D P Keane) *a in rr: bhd fr 7th: t.o 9th: kpt on fr 2 out* **25/1**

05- **5** *13* **Royal Cliche**[34] 4589 6-11-0 WMarston 66
(R T Phillips) *hdwy 7th: remote 3rd 2 out: wknd last* **33/1**

253/ **6** *19* **Captain Flinders (IRE)**[453] 3646 8-11-0 SThomas 47
(Miss H C Knight) *bhd fr 7th* **11/2**[3]

430- **7** *9* **Alfasonic**[42] 4463 5-11-0 WHutchinson 38
(A King) *chsd ldrs: hit 6th: wknd next: t.o 2 out* **12/1**

0/ **P** **Heathy Gore**[498] 2844 6-10-7 DRDennis —
(J K Cresswell) *bhd: t.o 9th: p.u bef next* **100/1**

0/ **P** **Lancastrian Island**[33] 7-10-4 ow4 MrRArmson[(7)] —
(John A Harris) *led to 3rd: j.rt and lost pl 8th: t.o whn p.u bef next* **100/1**

5m 44.7s (8.20) **Going Correction** +0.45s/f (Soft) **9** Ran SP% **115.6**
Speed ratings: **103,102,92,91,87 80,77,—,—** CSF £3.40 TOTE £2.00: £1.10, £1.20, £3.30; EX 2.40.

Owner D A Johnson **Bred** Mrs S Flood **Trained** Nicholashayne, Devon

FOCUS

An umcompetitive contest and a match over the final mile with the winner always looking to be holding the upper hand. however, the form looks solid enough for the grade.

NOTEBOOK

Standin Obligation(IRE), suited by going left-handed, made this a searching test and was firmly in command at the line. He looks an out-and-out stayer and his action suggests he will always prefer give underfoot. *(op 5-6 tchd 11-10)*

Martha's Kinsman(IRE) kept tabs on the winner but, tending to hang in behind him, was never going to get in a telling blow. He is sure to make a useful novice chaser after a summer break. *(op 5-2)*

Classical Love, in a visor this time, like the rest was hopelessly outclassed by the first two but to her credit kept on to snatch a remote third spot.

Knocktemple Lass(IRE), a poor pointer, shaped as if she will stay all day - in her own time. *(op 20-1)*

Royal Cliche, on his hurdling bow, showed a remote third at the penultimate flight but he tired noticeably on the run-in.

Captain Flinders(IRE), absent for over a year, clearly has had his problems and he never figured here. *(tchd 6-1)*

129 PETER J DOUGLAS (S) H'CAP HURDLE (12 hdls) 2m 4f 110y

3:25 (3:25) (Class 5) (0-100,100) 4-Y-0+ **£2,401** (£686; £343)

Form RPR

1 **Clearly Now (IRE)**[295] 910 7-10-4 **78** PMoloney 100+
(Bernard Jones, Ire) *mstke 3rd: hdwy to chse ldrs 6th: chalng whn blnd 3 out: sn led: clr last: eased last 100yds* **3/1**[1]

060- **2** *16* **Knockdoo (IRE)**[10] 4928 12-11-0 **95** MrGGoldie[(7)] 92
(J S Goldie) *hld up: hdwy 7th: chsd wnr after 3 out: wknd appr last* **14/1**

54P- **3** *hd* **Mead (IRE)**[14] 4871 8-10-12 **86** WMarston 83
(D J Wintle) *rr-div: drvn along 6th: hdwy 9th: wnt mod 3rd 2 out: blnd last: kpt on* **11/2**[3]

250- **4** *1* **Robbie On Tour (IRE)**[23] 4754 6-10-3 **80** (t) TJMalone[(3)] 76
(M C Pipe) *bhd: drvn along 7th: styd on fr 2 out* **7/1**

44-2 **5** *17* **Idlewild (IRE)**[6] 11 10-10-9 **90** APogson[(7)] 69
(C T Pogson) *chsd ldrs: led 9th: hdd after next: wknd qckly: eased run-in* **4/1**[2]

P20- **6** *dist* **Serious Position (IRE)**[11] 4918 10-11-4 **92** TDoyle —
(D R Stoddart) *w ldr: blnd 4th: led after 7th: hdd 9th: wknd qckly: sn bhd: t.o* **16/1**

040- **7** *3* **Damien's Choice (IRE)**[21] 4768 13-9-7 **77** oh3 ow3 ODayman[(10)] —
(Dr P Pritchard) *bhd: hdwy 7th: sn chsng ldrs: wknd after 9th: sn bhd: t.o* **25/1**

560- **8** *2* **Bobbi Rose Red**[11] 4918 8-10-2 **79** (p) RWalford[(3)] —
(P T Dalton) *bhd: hdwy to chse ldrs 7th: wknd next: sn bhd: t.o* **16/1**

1/3- **9** *22* **Better Moment (IRE)**[8] 4962 8-11-12 **100**...(v) JEMoore —
(M C Pipe) *led tl after 7th: wkng whn mstke 9th: sn bhd: t.o* **8/1**
00P- **P** **Javelin**[38] 4522 9-11-7 **95**... DRDennis —
(N J Hawke) *chsd ldrs: wknd qckly 7th: t.o whn plld after 8th* **12/1**
5m 14.1s (11.50) **Going Correction** +0.45s/f (Soft) **43** Ran SP% **114.0**
Speed ratings: **96,89,89,89,82** —,—,—,—,— CSF £42.69 CT £219.69 TOTE £3.90: £1.40, £4.20, £2.80; EX 90.70.The winner was bought in for 14,000gns.
Owner Mrs B Jones **Bred** J And Mrs Power **Trained** Saintfield, Co Down
■ The first winner in Britain for Northern Ireland trainer Bernard Jones.

FOCUS
A poor contest run in a slow time and a one-sided contest with the Irish-trained winner very much expected. The winner is value for 25 lengths with the third the best guide to the form.

NOTEBOOK
Clearly Now(IRE), absent since July, had bags of market confidence behind him and, surviving a bad mistake three out, he had it in the bag at the last, value for fully 25 lengths. Connections had to dig deep at the auction to retain him. *(op 9-2 tchd 11-4)*
Knockdoo(IRE), who has been bang out of form, looked a real threat when sent in pursuit of the winner after the third-last flight but he was soon comprehensively outstayed.
Mead(IRE), down in class, was struggling with a full circuit to go yet in the end just failed to collar the flagging second. *(op 4-1)*
Robbie On Tour(IRE), with the visor left off, was detached and taking no interest but in the end was hard on the heels of the placed horses, suggesting this was a very weak event apart from the winner.
Idlewild(IRE), making a quick return, tired badly after showing ahead and in the end struggled to reach the finishing line. *(op 7-2)*
Javelin *Official explanation: trainer said gelding lost his action (op 15-2 tchd 7-1)*

130 SEVERN TRENT/WATERAID H'CAP CHASE (16 fncs 2 omitted) 3m
4:00 (4:00) (Class 2) 5-Y-0+
£12,045 (£4,568; £2,284; £1,038; £519; £311)

Form RPR
PP3- **1** **Trust Fund (IRE)**[42] 4462 7-10-1 **115**... RWalford(3) 128+
(R H Alner) *wnt prom 9th: led 2 out: clr last: styd on wl* **16/1**
/6P- **2** *17* **A Piece Of Cake (IRE)**[14] 4861 12-11-0 **125**... ADempsey 123+
(J S Goldie) *chsd ldr: lft in ld appr 10th: hdd 2 out: wknd last* **16/1**
051- **3** *6* **Kock De La Vesvre (FR)**[9] 4946 7-11-10 **135**... SThomas 126+
(Miss Venetia Williams) *hld up: hdwy and prom 10th: wknd 3 out* **7/2[2]**
4F1- **4** *14* **Grey Report (IRE)**[47] 4368 8-10-12 **123**... RJohnson 112+
(P J Hobbs) *led: clr 7th: rel to r and hdd appr 10th: sn bhd and j.lft: t.o 2 out* **4/1[3]**
P52- **5** *shd* **Bee An Bee (IRE)**[28] 4692 8-10-9 **120**...(b) JMMaguire 96+
(T R George) *wnt prom 9th: upsides 4 out: sn rdn: wknd next: fin tired* **10/3[1]**
5P0- **6** *dist* **Black Frost (IRE)**[56] 4167 9-11-0 **125**... DElsworth —
(Mrs S J Smith) *chsd ldrs: rdn 10th: wknd appr 4 out: t.o 2 out* **33/1**
0U0- **P** **Avalanche (FR)**[8] 4972 8-11-9 **137**... DCrosse(3) —
(J R Best) *in rr: drvn along 9th: sn bhd: p.u bef 11th* **25/1**
403- **P** **Spring Grove (IRE)**[17] 4821 10-11-7 **132**... AThornton —
(R H Alner) *hld up: blnd 5th: wnt prom 10th: wknd 11th: bhd whn p.u bef 4 out* **8/1**
1/F- **P** **The Bushkeeper (IRE)**[45] 4398 11-11-0 **125**... MAFitzgerald —
(N J Henderson) *lost pl 3rd: reminders 5th: in rr whn blnd 7th: p.u bef next* **9/2**
6m 37.4s (7.00) **Going Correction** +0.975s/f (Soft) **9** Ran SP% **113.1**
Speed ratings: **111,105,103,98,98** —,—,—,— CSF £218.64 CT £1099.88 TOTE £18.40: £3.30, £2.80, £1.70; EX 137.80.
Owner Tim Collins **Bred** Mrs Violet Pollard **Trained** Droop, Dorset

FOCUS
A fair handicap run at a sound gallop and a true test in the conditions. The form is assessed using the runner-up and could be rated higher.

NOTEBOOK
Trust Fund(IRE), receiving weight all round, jumped a lot better and his stamina carried him well clear in the end.
A Piece Of Cake(IRE), pulled up in the Scottish National, kicked on with a circuit to go but in the end he was a tired horse on the run-in. *(op 18-1)*
Kock De La Vesvre(FR), 5lb higher, was attempting to repeat last year's success from a 3lb higher mark but this time his chance had gone three out. *(op 3-1)*
Grey Report(IRE) raced as sweet as a nut but passing the stands for a second time he reckoned that was enough and put the brakes on. Jumping left afterwards, he is obviously one to have severe reservations about.
Bee An Bee(IRE), 4lb higher, was bang in contentuion four out but on this ground emptied quickly and looked very tired in the end. *(op 5-2)*
The Bushkeeper(IRE)was soon struggling and after a bad mistake was wisely pulled up. *Official explanation: jockey said gelding made a bad mistake and lost his action (op 11-2)*

131 TOTESPORT 0800 221 221 STANDARD OPEN NATIONAL HUNT FLAT RACE 2m
4:35 (4:36) (Class 6) 4-6-Y-0 **£2,058** (£588; £294)

Form RPR
1 **Off Spin** 5-11-4... TDoyle 107+
(P R Webber) *str: cmpt: trckd ldrs: led over 5f out tl over 1f out: led ins fnl f: styd on wl* **9/2[2]**
2 *1* **Cloudy Lane** 5-11-4... JMMaguire 106
(D McCain) *rangy: in tch: outpcd 6f out: hdwy over 3f out: slt advantage over 1f out: hdd ins last: no ex* **22/1**
3 *5* **Kobai (IRE)** 6-11-4... RThornton 101
(A King) *medium-sized: lengthy: mid-div: hdwy 8f out: sn chsng ldrs: one pce fnl 2f* **8/1**
64- **4** *11* **Negus De Beaumont (FR)**[11] 4922 4-10-13... LAspell 85
(F Jordan) *led tl over 5f out: wknd fnl 2f* **12/1**
41- **5** *10* **Call Oscar (IRE)**[47] 4373 6-11-11... MAFitzgerald 90+
(C Tinkler) *trckd ldrs: wknd over 2f out* **3/1[1]**
6 *21* **Toothill Gunner** 4-10-13... DElsworth 54
(J K Cresswell) *neat: mid-div: sme hdwy 6f out: wknd 4f out* **66/1**
7 *nk* **The Laying Hen (IRE)** 5-10-11... NFehily 52
(D P Keane) *lengthy: unf: chsd ldrs: wknd over 3f out* **14/1**
4- **8** *16* **Haunted House**[76] 3837 5-11-4... AThornton 43
(H D Daly) *hld up in rr: hdwy after 6f: lost pl 5f out: sn bhd* **22/1**
3- **9** *7* **Kayceecee (IRE)**[56] 4179 4-10-13... RJohnson 31
(H D Daly) *hld up and bhd: hdwy 6f out: sn lost pl* **9/1**
10 *4* **Shinjiru (USA)** 5-11-1... RHobson(3) 32
(P A Blockley) *rangy: bkwd: hld up: bhd fnl 6f* **25/1**
11 *3* **Deuteronomy (IRE)** 4-10-13... SDurack 24
(E A Elliott) *rangy: scope: bhd: sme hdwy 7f out: sn lost pl* **40/1**
36- **12** *3* **Ice Bucket (IRE)**[47] 4373 5-11-4... SThomas 26
(Miss H C Knight) *chsd ldrs: lost pl 6f out: sn bhd* **12/1**
13 *dist* **Holme Lane (IRE)** 4-10-13... ARoss —
(J Hetherton) *lengthy: unf: t.k.h in mid-div: lost pl 6f out: t.o 3f out* **50/1**
2- **14** *1 1/4* **Thievery**[65] 4027 4-10-10... JPByrne(3) —
(H D Daly) *mid-div: lost pl 5f out: sn bhd: t.o 3f out* **8/1**
P **Bluemantle Maggie** 4-10-6... ADempsey —
(R Ford) *rangy: unf: sn in rr: t.o 7f out: p.u over 5f out* **66/1**
P **Accumulus** 5-11-4... BJCrowley —
(Noel T Chance) *lengthy: unf: hld up in rr: hdwy 6f out: hung rt and lost pl 4f out: sn eased and p.u* **7/1[3]**
3m 58.9s (8.70) **Going Correction** +0.45s/f (Soft)
WFA 4 from 5yo 5lb 5 from 6yo 3lb **16** Ran SP% **129.9**
Speed ratings: **96,95,93,87,82 72,71,63,60,58 56,55**,—,—,— — CSF £111.71 TOTE £5.40: £2.80, £6.20, £3.60; EX 109.10.
Owner D R Stoddart **Bred** D R Stoddart **Trained** Mollington, Oxon

FOCUS
A fair bumper with the first two likely to improve. The fourth sets the standard and the race could rate higher.

NOTEBOOK
Off Spin, from the same family as the Grand National winner Party Politics, is not that big but is well put together. He knew his job and, finding plenty, regained the upper hand inside the last. He clearly has a lot more stamina than speed. *(op 7-1 tchd 15-2)*
Cloudy Lane, a well-made, jumping-bred gelding, worked hard to go a neck up but in the end the winner proved simply too determined. He will want a trip over hurdles. *(op 33-1)*
Kobai(IRE), fitted with a cross noseband, is out of a mare that won over three miles over hurdles and he already looks a stayer in the making. *(op 7-1 tchd 13-2)*
Negus De Beaumont(FR), having his third run, made the running winding up the gallop in the process but he was out on his feet in the final quarter mile. *(op 10-1)*
Call Oscar(IRE), a nice type, kept tabs on the leaders but in the end the penalty proved too much on this rain-soaked ground.
Thievery *Official explanation: trainer had no explanation for the poor form shown*
Accumulus *Official explanation: jockey said gelding was unsuited by soft ground (op 9-2 tchd 8-1)*

132 TOTESPORT.COM H'CAP CHASE (13 fncs 2 omitted) 2m 4f
5:10 (5:10) (Class 4) (0-105,103) 5-Y-0+ **£4,803** (£1,478; £739; £369)

Form RPR
P32- **1** **Mandica (IRE)**[55] 4203 7-11-4 **95**... JMMaguire 110+
(T R George) *trckd ldrs: j.lft 10th: led last: rdn out* **9/4[1]**
/12- **2** *8* **Miss Wizadora**[31] 4665 10-10-5 **82**... WMarston 91+
(Simon Earle) *w ldrs: blnd 9th: led next: hdd last: one pce* **11/2[3]**
P/P- **3** *6* **Armageddon**[28] 4688 8-10-12 **89**... LAspell 88
(O Sherwood) *led to 4th: outpcd 9th: kpt on fr 2 out* **12/1**
0/4- **4** *3 1/2* **Chaos Theory**[19] 4811 10-11-1 **92**... SFox 90+
(R C Guest) *blnd 1st: chsd ldrs: led 4th to 10th: wknd appr 2 out* **11/2[3]**
P/4- **P** **Stone Cold**[27] 4718 8-11-2 **93**...(b) RGarritty —
(T D Easterby) *chsd ldrs: wknd 9th: bhd whn p.u befeore next* **4/1[2]**
PPP- **P** **Coastguard (IRE)**[74] 3871 11-9-9 **77** oh13...(b) TGreenway(5) —
(David Pearson) *lost pl after 6th: sn bhd: t.o whn p.u bef 9th* **33/1**
652- **P** **River Mere**[181] 1935 11-10-10 **87**... OMcPhail —
(Mrs L Williamson) *w ldrs: lost pl 5th: sn bhd: t.o whn p.u bef 9th* **6/1**
65/- **P** **Magic Of Sydney (IRE)**[488] 3041 9-11-12 **103**... MAFitzgerald —
(R Rowe) *in rr: pushed along 6th: sn bhd: t.o whn p.u bef 3 out* **14/1**
5m 32.8s (18.10) **Going Correction** +0.975s/f (Soft) **8** Ran SP% **113.1**
Speed ratings: **102,98,96,95**,— —,—,— CSF £15.08 CT £118.32 TOTE £3.70: £1.60, £1.70, £4.20; EX 11.10 Place 6 £270.16, Place 5 £83.04.
Owner R A Dalton **Bred** Harold Byrne **Trained** Slad, Gloucs
■ Stewards' Enquiry : J M Maguire two-day ban: used whip with excessive frequency (May 11,12)

FOCUS
A weak handicap with the winner's proven stamina carrying the day in the end. The winner comes from a rock-solid Kempton race and the runner-up ran to her mark.

NOTEBOOK
Mandica(IRE), 2lb lower, came clear on the run-in, his rider leaving nothing to chance but at a cost paying a compliment to his Kempton conqueror Change Agent. *(op 10-3)*
Miss Wizadora a lucky winner at Fontwell, is now 8lb higher and she was well and truly outstayed by the winner in the end. *(op 9-2)*
Armageddon, pulled up on his chasing debut four weeks earlier, looked a useful prospect when taking a bumper four years ago but he clearly has had his problems since. *(op 7-1)*
Chaos Theory, a dual point winner who returned under Rules in a hunter chase, soon took them along but in this ground he tired badly over the last two. *(op 6-1 tchd 5-1)*
Stone Cold stopped to nothing on ground a lot more testing than he prefers. *Official explanation: trainer's representative said gelding was unsuited by the soft ground (tchd 7-2 and 9-2)*
T/Plt: £1,217.90 to a £1 stake. Pool: £51,720.20. 31.00 winning tickets. T/Qpdt: £75.60 to a £1 stake. Pool: £3,004.70. 29.40 winning tickets. WG

WORCESTER (L-H)
Saturday, April 30

OFFICIAL GOING: Good to firm (good in places)
Wind: Nil Weather: Raining for last two races

133 IAN & TINA VALENTINE MAIDEN HURDLE (8 hdls) 2m
5:40 (5:41) (Class 4) 4-Y-0+ **£3,770** (£1,160; £580; £290)

Form RPR
246- **1** **Fairly High (IRE)**[18] 4813 5-10-9 82...(p) ATinkler 75+
(N G Ayliffe) *chsd clr ldr: led appr 2 out: rdn clr bef last: comf* **20/1**
34- **2** *12* **Lunar Exit (IRE)**[148] 2611 4-10-8... MrTGreenall(3) 66+
(Lady Herries) *in tch: hdwy 5th: rdn 3 out: styd on same pce: tk 2nd cl home* **6/4[1]**
606- **3** *nk* **Parsifal**[32] 4640 6-11-2 83...(v) SCurran 70
(P Wegmann) *taken to post early: t.k.h: led: clr after 2nd: drvn 3 out: sn hdd: nt fluent last: lost 2nd nr fin* **66/1**
4 *3/4* **Double Aspect (IRE)**[258] 4-10-11... APMcCoy 65+
(Jonjo O'Neill) *in tch: clsd after 5th: rdn next: hung lft u.p flat: styd on one pce* **15/8[2]**
00- **5** *3* **Seal Of Office**[33] 4621 6-11-2... JAMcCarthy 66
(A M Hales) *towards rr: hdwy after 5th: rdn 3 out: styd on same pce* **50/1**
6 *1/2* **Hillcrest (NZ)**[352] 6-11-2... DRDennis 66
(Ian Williams) *in rr: hdwy 5th: nt fluent last: kpt on flat* **40/1**
7 *3 1/2* **West End Wonder (IRE)**[48] 6-10-9... AScholes(7) 62
(D Burchell) *in tch: no imp on ldrs fr 3 out* **66/1**
0/0- **8** *8* **Simon The Poacher**[16] 4839 6-10-11... TJPhelan(5) 54
(L P Grassick) *towards rr: hdwy 5th: one pce fr next: fin lame* **100/1**
514- **9** *1 1/4* **Stagecoach Diamond**[56] 4172 6-11-2... PFlynn 55+
(Mrs S J Smith) *hld up towards rr: sme hdwy after 5th: hmpd 3 out: no ch after* **12/1**

0/0- **10** *3 ½* **Rush'N'Run**[155] [2466] 6-10-6 THalliday(10) 49
(Mrs S J Smith) *in rr: mstke 2nd: sme hdwy after 5th: wknd next* **80/1**
000- **11** *2 ½* **Kingcombe Lane**[10] [4933] 5-11-2 JPMcNamara 47
(P W Hiatt) *prom in chsng gp: rdn after 5th: sn wknd* **100/1**
60- **12** *8* **On Top (IRE)**[93] [3558] 5-10-9 MrPCowley(7) 39
(Mrs S E Busby) *prom in chsng gp tl wknd bef 3 out: mstke next* **100/1**
20- **13** *shd* **Waziya**[182] [1903] 6-10-2 DLaverty(7) 32
(Mrs L Williamson) *mid-div: hdwy 5th: drvn to chse ldrs next: wknd after 3 out* **50/1**
/00- **14** *11* **Huxley (IRE)**[172] [2102] 6-11-2 (t) BHitchcott 28
(M G Quinlan) *t.k.h: a in rr* **25/1**
/0P- **15** *2* **Luristan (IRE)**[113] [3261] 5-10-11 LTreadwell(5) 26
(S T Lewis) *in tch: rdn after 4th: sn wknd* **100/1**
16 *15* **Thiseldo Us**[776] 10-10-9 CMStudd(7) 11
(M B Shears) *prom in chsng gp: rdn 5th: sn wknd: t.o* **100/1**
00- **P** **Muffler**[123] [3052] 7-10-13 ONelmes(3) —
(J G M O'Shea) *a in rr: t.o fr 5th: p.u bef 3 out* **125/1**
00P- **B** **Kingscourt Lad (IRE)**[20] [4793] 7-10-6 WJones(10) —
(Jonjo O'Neill) *towards rr: no ch whn b.d 3 out* **40/1**
2/6- **F** **Supreme Hope (USA)**[45] [4401] 6-11-2 MBradburne —
(H D Daly) *mid-div: clsd after 5th: trcking ldrs whn fell 3 out* **11/1**[3]
P **Call Of The Seas (IRE)**[342] 6-10-9 NCarter(7) —
(J G M O'Shea) *in tch: nt fluent 3rd: wknd bef 5th: t.o whn p.u bef 3 out* **100/1**

3m 56.1s (5.90) **Going Correction** +0.275s/f (Yiel)
WFA 4 from 5yo+ 5lb **20 Ran SP% 119.2**
Speed ratings: **96,90,89,89,87 87,85,81,81,79 78,74,74,68,67 60,—,—,—,—** CSF £47.89 TOTE £26.00: £4.90, £1.10, £9.10; EX 66.60.
Owner D T Hooper **Bred** John Foley **Trained** Winsford, Somerset

FOCUS
A moderate contest and despite the large field few got into this. With the winner having been beaten in selling company this form is limited.

NOTEBOOK
Fairly High(IRE) chased the clear leader, herself some way ahead of the pack. Getting to the front before the second last, she kept up the gallop for a clear-cut victory. The faster ground obviously suited her. *(op 16-1)*
Lunar Exit(IRE), having his first run since December, lacked the pace to mount a serious challenge but stayed on to take second spot near the line. He needs further. *(op 7-4 tchd 15-8 and 11-8)*
Parsifal was taken to post very steadily and a long time before the others. Soon in a clear lead, he was cut down by the eventual winner in the straight, but stuck on and just missed out on second. *(op 50-1)*
Double Aspect(IRE), a useful handicapper at up to 12 furlongs on the Flat for Sir Michael Stoute, could never land a blow on this hurdling debut, and while he kept on for pressure he looked a bit of an awkward ride. *(op 7-4 tchd 2-1)*
Seal Of Office, a regressive sort on the Flat, ran his best race so far over hurdles on his third attempt. *(op 33-1)*
Hillcrest(NZ), who had one run on the Flat in New Zealand nearly a year ago, did not shape without promise on this hurdles debut. *Official explanation: jockey said gelding had breathing problem from 2 out (op 33-1)*
Simon The Poacher *Official explanation: jockey said gelding was lame (op 66-1)*
Huxley(IRE), a keen sort, was ridden differently to Huntingdon and was always at the back of the field. He is now qualified for handicaps and could do a bit better in that sphere. *(op 16-1)*
Supreme Hope(USA) was on the heels of the leaders when coming down at the third from home. He would have made the frame at least and obviously has the ability, although his jumping still needs improvement. *(op 9-1 tchd 12-1)*

134 CANNONS HEALTH CLUB MARES' ONLY (S) H'CAP HURDLE (8 hdls) 2m
6:10 (6:12) (Class 5) (0-95,85) 4-Y-0+ **£3,052** (£872; £436)

Form RPR
060/ **1** **Reverse Swing**[729] [82] 8-10-13 **72** APMcCoy 77+
(Mrs H Dalton) *hld up in mid-div: hdwy 4th: rdn appr 3 out: led flat: r.o* **13/2**[3]
53P- **2** *1 ¾* **Lyricist's Dream**[105] [3361] 6-10-7 **71** RStephens(5) 75+
(R L Brown) *a.p: led 2nd to 3rd: rdn appr 3 out: led 2 out: hit last: edgd rt and hdd flat: nt qckn* **14/1**
51-0 **3** *1 ½* **Think Quick (IRE)**[5] [25] 5-10-11 **80** AHawkins(10) 82
(R Hollinshead) *hld up in mid-div: hdwy appr 3 out: kpt on flat* **10/1**
602- **4** *½* **Macreater**[11] [4918] 7-10-4 **70** (p) SWalsh(7) 71
(K A Morgan) *led to 2nd: prom: led 5th: rdn appr 3 out: hdd 2 out: ev ch flat: no ex towards fin* **8/1**
054- **5** *6* **Twist N Turn**[7] [4975] 5-9-13 **63** StephenJCraine(5) 59+
(D McCain) *hld up in tch: rdn after 5th: wknd flat* **14/1**
036- **6** *8* **Somewin (IRE)**[134] [2866] 5-9-9 **61** (p) RSpate(7) 48
(Mrs K Waldron) *hld up and bhd: hdwy after 5th: wkng whn nt fluent 2 out* **14/1**
00P- **7** *2* **Princess Stephanie**[123] [3041] 7-9-12 **62** CHonour(5) 47
(M J Gingell) *t.k.h in rr: nt fluent 2nd: hdwy appr 3 out: no further prog fr 2 out* **40/1**
6PP- **8** *2* **Avenches (GER)**[12] [4913] 5-10-9 **68** CLlewellyn 51
(M J McGrath) *mid-div: rdn and lost pl 4th: styd on fr 2 out: n.d* **66/1**
335- **9** *4* **Private Jessica**[7] [4975] 4-11-2 **83** (b[1]) LMcGrath(3) 57
(R C Guest) *t.k.h: hdwy appr 4th: wknd after 3 out* **10/1**
00P- **10** *2* **Another Windfall**[48] [4344] 6-10-6 **65** (t) DRDennis 42
(C P Morlock) *nvr nr ldrs* **20/1**
0/P- **11** *13* **Hidden Smile (USA)**[11] [4918] 8-11-4 **77** JPMcNamara 41
(F Jordan) *a bhd* **16/1**
P/0- **12** *6* **Wearerich**[10] [4930] 8-10-10 **69** WHutchinson 27
(D J Wintle) *prom tl wknd 3 out* **11/2**[1]
502- **13** *shd* **Lovely Lulu**[12] [4913] 7-10-8 **67** JMogford 25
(J C Tuck) *hld up: short-lived effrt after 5th* **12/1**
625- **14** *1 ½* **Frambo (IRE)**[165] [2261] 4-11-7 **85** (tp) JTizzard 36
(J G Portman) *prom to 4th: no ch whn mstke last* **6/1**[2]
104- **15** *2 ½* **Spectacular Hope**[195] [1743] 5-11-5 **85** WPKavanagh(7) 39
(J W Mullins) *mid-div: rdn after 4th: sn bhd* **10/1**
P0P- **16** *1* **Threepenny Bit**[8] [4958] 7-10-5 **64** JAMcCarthy 17
(Mrs S M Johnson) *a bhd: hrd rdn 4th: no ch whn j.rt last* **100/1**
PP0- **17** *7* **Major Belle (FR)**[7] [4975] 6-11-8 **81** (p) SCurran 27
(M J Gingell) *prom: led and nt fluent 3rd: hdd 5th: sn wknd* **50/1**
/PP- **P** **Gordy's Joy**[8] [4958] 5-11-11 **70** (b) PFlynn —
(G A Ham) *bhd tl p.u bef 3 out* **80/1**
00-0 **P** **Bertie Arms**[6] [9] 5-11-3 **76** ATinkler —
(J M Jefferson) *mid-div: rdn after 4th: sn bhd: p.u bef 2 out* **40/1**
535- **P** **Soleil D'Hiver**[21] [4776] 4-10-11 **80** (p) LStephens(5) —
(M Sheppard) *hld up in tch: wkng whn nt fluent 5th: bhd whn p.u bef 3 out* **16/1**

3m 57.0s (6.80) **Going Correction** +0.275s/f (Yiel)
WFA 4 from 5yo+ 5lb **20 Ran SP% 136.2**
Speed ratings: **94,93,92,92,89 85,84,83,81,80 73,70,70,69,68 68,64,—,—,—** CSF £99.93 CT £947.52 TOTE £8.20: £2.10, £3.90, £4.00, £2.20; EX 144.10.There was no bid for the winner.
Owner The Herons Partnership **Bred** Mrs P Sly **Trained** Norton, Shropshire

FOCUS
A very modest mares-only seller although the placed horses ran to their marks.

NOTEBOOK
Reverse Swing, with an interesting jockey booking, made a successful return after an absence of exactly two years. *(op 9-2)*
Lyricist's Dream, back in the right sort of grade, appreciated the sounder surface and did nothing wrong despite coming off a true line on the run-in. *(tchd 16-1)*
Think Quick(IRE), making a quick reappearance, goes well for her young rider and showed no tendency to hang this time. *(tchd 11-1)*
Macreater, again in the cheekpieces, was slightly impeded by the runner-up on the run-in. She was beaten fair and square in the end. *(op 9-1)*
Twist N Turn was under pressure leaving the back straight and finally gave best in the closing stages.

135 CHELTENHAM & THREE COUNTIES CLUB CLASSIFIED CHASE (12 fncs) 2m
6:40 (6:41) (Class 4) 5-Y-0+ **£3,770** (£1,160; £580; £290)

Form RPR
24U- **1** **Apadi (USA)**[19] [4808] 9-10-13 85 LMcGrath(3) 98+
(R C Guest) *hld up towards rr: hdwy 6th: chsd ldr after 8th: led 4 out: rdn appr last: comf* **9/2**[3]
520- **2** *7* **Amptina (IRE)**[223] [1449] 10-10-6 71 THalliday(10) 83+
(Mrs S J Smith) *mid-div: hdwy 7th: rdn after next: chsd wnr 3 out: one pce bef last* **20/1**
325- **3** *4* **Vandante (IRE)**[144] [2695] 9-11-2 81 RJohnson 77
(R Lee) *nt fluent: prom tl hit 8th and lost pl: styd on again fr 2 out: nt trble ldrs* **11/4**[1]
615- **4** *nk* **Prince Of Aragon**[237] [1372] 9-11-2 79 (t) BHitchcott 77
(Miss Suzy Smith) *in tch: reminder 5th: rdn and lost pl 7th: styd on u.p flat* **16/1**
5UF- **5** *1 ¼* **Johnny Grand**[174] [2074] 8-11-2 73 NFehily 75
(D W Lewis) *in tch: rdn after 8th: one pce fr 3 out* **40/1**
30-4 **6** *11* **Rattina (GER)**[3] [57] 9-10-13 82 (v[1]) SDurack 61
(M F Harris) *lft in ld 1st: hdd 8th: sn rdn and wknd* **16/1**
B0- **7** *21* **Padamul**[15] [4853] 9-10-13 62 RYoung(3) 43
(J W Mullins) *a in rr: t.o fr 8th* **40/1**
5P0- **P** **Saragann (IRE)**[11] [4919] 10-11-2 85 PFlynn —
(M J M Evans) *a in rr: lost tch 8th: t.o whn p.u bef 4 out* **16/1**
UF0- **F** **Little Chartridge**[20] [4795] 7-10-13 85 (vt) TDoyle —
(P R Webber) *trckd ldrs tl led 8th: hdd and fell next* **22/1**
/5-P **R** **Seemore Sunshine**[6] [10] 8-11-2 90 SCurran —
(M J Gingell) *led tl blnd 1st: chsd ldr tl wnt rt, ref and uns rdr 4th* **100/1**
000- **F** **Silent Voice (IRE)**[56] [4166] 8-11-2 72 (t) RPMcNally —
(Sir John Barlow Bt) *in rr: mstkes: rdn 6th: lost tch 8th: wl bhd whn fell last* **25/1**
U04- **P** **Kercabellec (FR)**[27] [4716] 7-10-9 90 APogson(7) —
(J R Cornwall) *in tch: carried rt and j. slowly 4th: bhd fr 8th: no ch whn hmpd 4 out: p.u bef last* **7/1**
313- **P** **Cool Chilli**[33] [4614] 7-11-2 86 (t) APMcCoy 77
(N J Pomfret) *in tch: mstke 5th: clsd 7th: chsng ldrs whn hmpd 4 out: 3rd and one pce whn p.u bef last: dismntd* **3/1**[2]

3m 59.7s (1.10) **Going Correction** +0.20s/f (Yiel) **13 Ran SP% 118.8**
Speed ratings: **105,101,99,99,98 93,82,—,—,— —,—,—** CSF £92.24 TOTE £3.50: £1.60, £3.60, £2.00; EX 106.20.
Owner Mrs Anna Kenny **Bred** Juddmonte Farms Inc **Trained** Brancepeth, Co Durham

FOCUS
Not a strong event, although the winner is value for more than double the official margin with the fifth setting the level.

NOTEBOOK
Apadi(USA) customarily blazes a trail but a change to more patient tactics did the trick. In front at the first in the home straight, he went on to score with something to spare. *(op 5-2)*
Amptina(IRE), having his first run since September, went after the winner with three to jump but had nothing more to offer between the last two fences. He had plenty to find based on official figures and this was a creditable effort.
Vandante(IRE), down in trip for this first start since December, was less than convincing with his jumping and dropped back to a moderate sixth after belting the last fence on the far side. Rather held together in the home straight, he did stay on quite nicely and there could be a little race for him if he jumps better. *(op 9-2)*
Prince Of Aragon, a winner of a selling hurdle at this venue, had his ground for this first outing since September. Having only his second run over fences, he was staying on at the end and could need further. *(op 14-1)*
Johnny Grand, on his first start since November, put in a clear round which should have boosted his confidence.
Rattina(GER), making a quick reappearance and tried in a visor, had no more to give on the long turn out of the back straight. *(op 14-1)*
Cool Chilli was in third place, and appeared held, when losing his action after the second last. *Official explanation: jockey said gelding lost its action (op 7-2)*
Little Chartridge, a daughter of that fine mare Auntie Dot, has only a fraction of her dam's ability but she did show a bit more before coming down. *(op 7-2)*

136 ARENA LEISURE H'CAP HURDLE (8 hdls) 2m
7:10 (7:10) (Class 4) (0-110,110) 4-Y-0+ **£4,446** (£1,368; £684; £342)

Form RPR
516- **1** **O'Toole (IRE)**[18] [4817] 6-11-12 **108** RJohnson 115+
(P J Hobbs) *a.p: rdn to ld 3 out: drvn out* **7/1**[3]
104- **2** *3* **Salute (IRE)**[35] [4561] 6-11-6 **107** RStephens(5) 111
(P J Hobbs) *hld up in tch: rdn to chse wnr 2 out: one pce* **12/1**
2P6- **3** *1 ¾* **Lord Lington (FR)**[27] [4723] 6-11-9 **105** WMarston 107
(D J Wintle) *hld up and bhd: hdwy 3 out: r.o flat* **33/1**
042- **4** *½* **State Of Play**[33] [4622] 5-11-9 **105** (v[1]) TDoyle 107
(P R Webber) *hld up in tch: chsd wnr 3 out to 2 out: one pce* **12/1**
356- **5** *8* **Kalambari (IRE)**[185] [1856] 6-11-12 **108** (b) CLlewellyn 103+
(J Joseph) *hld up and bhd: styd on fr 2 out: nvr nrr* **20/1**
203- **6** *hd* **Wild Is The Wind (FR)**[57] [4159] 4-11-9 **110** APMcCoy 99
(Jonjo O'Neill) *hld up: racd wd bk st: hdwy 4th: wknd appr 2 out* **5/2**[1]
/P0- **7** *nk* **Lupin (FR)**[13] [4881] 6-11-11 **107** NFehily 100
(A W Carroll) *bhd tl r.o fr 2 out: nrst fin* **100/1**
02-F **8** *nk* **Sir Walter (IRE)**[6] [1] 12-10-6 **93** LStephens(5) 86
(D Burchell) *hld up in rr: late hdwy: nrst fin* **25/1**
033- **9** *nk* **Meadow Hawk (USA)**[13] [4883] 5-11-0 **96** (b) DRDennis 89
(Ian Williams) *hld up: rdn and hdwy appr 3 out: wknd appr 2 out* **14/1**

62P- **10** *nk* **Saorsie**[13] 4890 7-11-3 **99** ... SFox 91
(J C Fox) *mid-div: short-lived effrt after 5th* **33/1**

000- **11** *7* **Inducement**[14] 4030 9-10-5 **87** ... JEMoore 73+
(R M Stronge) *hld up in mid-div: hdwy 4th: rdn after 5th: no imp: hrd rdn and hung rt after 2 out: hit last* **100/1**

623- **12** *hd* **Soviet Joy (IRE)**[27] 4715 4-11-5 **106** ... ADempsey 86
(D Carroll) *chsd ldr: led after 2nd to 3 out: wknd 2 out* **14/1**

/PP- **13** *14* **Forzacurity**[13] 4881 6-11-2 **98** ... SDurack 69
(M Sheppard) *led tl after 2nd: prom: rdn after 5th: wknd 3 out* **40/1**

2/5- **14** *2 ½* **Shamsan (IRE)**[75] 3854 8-11-4 **107** ... (t) SWalsh(7) 76
(J Joseph) *prom tl wknd 3 out* **100/1**

503- **15** *¾* **Turn Of Phrase (IRE)**[20] 4787 6-11-8 **107** ... (v) PWhelan(3) 75
(R A Fahey) *mid-div: rdn 4th: sn bhd* **13/2**[2]

312- **16** *1 ½* **Golden Chalice (IRE)**[13] 4883 6-11-4 **107** ... PCO'Neill(7) 73
(Miss E C Lavelle) *a bhd* **13/2**[2]

040- **17** *5* **Salt Cellar (IRE)**[32] 4639 6-11-4 **100** ... (v) JamesDavies 61
(P R Webber) *hld up in mid-div: rdn whn mstke 4th: sn struggling* **18/1**

3m 53.7s (3.50) **Going Correction** +0.275s/f (Yiel)
WFA 4 from 5yo+ 5lb **17** Ran SP% **121.6**
Speed ratings: **102,100,99,99,95 95,95,94,94,94 91,91,84,82,82 81,79** CSF £81.44 CT £2599.10 TOTE £9.00: £2.00, £4.50, £16.30, £5.00; EX 62.30.
Owner Mrs L R Lovell **Bred** John Moclair **Trained** Withycombe, Somerset

FOCUS
A wide-open low-grade handicap and the form looks reasonably solid.

NOTEBOOK
O'Toole(IRE), again on a sound surface, was back down in distance and responded well to pressure. *(tchd 15-2)*
Salute(IRE) did not mind the faster ground. He stuck to his task but could make little impression on the winner. *(tchd 14-1)*
Lord Lington(FR) settled much better this time and did all his best work in the home straight. *(op 25-1)*
State Of Play ran a solid enough race on his handicap debut in the first-time visor but lacked the required turn of foot.
Kalambari(IRE) made a promising comeback after six months off and is worth bearing in mind over further.
Wild Is The Wind(FR) was rather disappointing on this switch to handicaps after his encouraging run at Newbury. *(op 11-4 tchd 9-4)*
Lupin(FR), whose hurdle win in France came on very soft ground, showed his first signs of ability over obstacles in this country. He may be capable of better things.

137 JON & MARGARET HEYS HAPPY DAYS NOVICES' H'CAP CHASE (18 fncs) 2m 7f 110y

7:40 (7:40) (Class 4) (0-105,105) 5-Y-0+ **£4,290** (£1,320; £660; £330)

Form RPR

201- **1** **He's The Biz (FR)**[20] 4790 6-10-10 **89** ... SDurack 102+
(Nick Williams) *hld up in rr: stdy hdwy fr 11th: rdn 2 out: chal last: sn led: styd on strly* **11/4**[2]

241- **2** *7* **Jack Of Spades (IRE)**[20] 4800 9-10-13 **92** ... WHutchinson 99+
(R Dickin) *in tch: clsd 10th: trckd ldr 12th: mstke next: rdn to chal 4 out: led appr 2 out tl sn after last: no ex* **6/4**[1]

2PP- **3** *dist* **Inland Run (IRE)**[78] 3796 9-10-12 **91** ... RJohnson 79
(R T Phillips) *led: j.rt at times: reminder 7th: rdn bef 4 out: hdd appr 2 out: wknd qckly* **8/1**[3]

320- **4** *15* **Monster Mick (FR)**[20] 4799 7-10-7 **86** ... JamesDavies —
(B G Powell) *trckd ldr tl after 9th: sn pushed along: wknd 12th: mstke 14th: t.o* **9/1**

5PU- **5** *dist* **Blazing Fire**[38] 4523 8-9-7 **79** oh11 ... CPoste(7) —
(M Wellings) *in tch: hdwy 8th: chsd ldr after 9th tl 12th: sn wknd: t.o fr 14th* **100/1**

/0P- **6** *dist* **Stormy Row (IRE)**[13] 4890 11-9-7 **79** oh4 ... (t) CMStudd(7) —
(M B Shears) *bhd tl clsd 4th: chsd ldrs 6th: rdn 11th: wknd next: t.o whn j. bdly rt last 2: virtually p.u* **100/1**

P40- **F** **Bodfari Creek**[221] 1467 8-11-12 **105** ... (t) AThornton —
(J G Portman) *trckd ldrs tl fell 6th* **11/1**

/0P- **F** **Caucasian (IRE)**[135] 2858 7-10-1 **80** ... DRDennis —
(Ian Williams) *hld up in rr: hdwy 10th: hit 12th: cl 3rd whn fell 14th* **33/1**

646- **P** **Point**[14] 4868 8-11-7 **100** ... CLlewellyn —
(W Jenks) *trckd ldrs: mstke 9th: dropped rr next: sn lost tch: t.o whn p.u after 14th* **8/1**[3]

6m 6.50s (5.40) **Going Correction** +0.20s/f (Yiel) **9** Ran SP% **112.1**
Speed ratings: **99,96,—,—,— —,—,—,—** CSF £7.32 CT £26.02 TOTE £3.70: £2.00, £1.10, £2.10; EX 6.30.
Owner Mrs Jane Williams **Bred** Mme Mariette Barth **Trained** George Nympton, Devon

FOCUS
A modest event won by an improving performer. The runner-up sets the standard but the form is not the strongest.

NOTEBOOK
He's The Biz(FR) ◆ was raised 5lb after Newton Abbot but that was nowhere near enough to stop him. He scored in a manner of a progressive chaser at a lowly level and there should be more to come. *(op 2-1 tchd 3-1)*
Jack Of Spades(IRE), who is reportedly not easy to train, like his brother Monsignor, ran a solid race from an 8lb higher mark but was put in his place by the winner on the run-in. *(op 7-4 tchd 2-1)*
Inland Run(IRE) made the running, but was eventually collared before the second last and finished a tired horse. Ridden this way, he did not appear to stay. *(op 9-1)*
Monster Mick(FR) has the size to jump fences, but he did not show any great aptitude on this chasing debut. *(op 10-1 tchd 8-1)*
Point, making his chasing debut, dropped to the back of the field early on the final circuit and did not look too keen from then on. *(op 10-1)*
Caucasian(IRE) did not show a great deal in bumpers or over hurdles, but he was right in the firing line when coming down at the fifth last on this chasing debut. *(op 10-1)*

138 FAMILY FUN DAY, SUNDAY MAY 8TH MAIDEN OPEN NATIONAL HUNT FLAT RACE 2m

8:10 (8:12) (Class 6) 4-6-Y-0 **£2,097** (£599; £299)

Form RPR

060- **1** **Ballymena**[20] 4801 4-10-1 ... LStephens(5) 89
(C Roberts) *hld up in tch: led over 5f out: rdn over 2f out: edgd rt 1f out: r.o* **14/1**

50- **2** *1* **Celtic Jem (IRE)**[51] 4290 5-11-4 ... RJohnson 100
(P Bowen) *hld up and bhd: stdy hdwy on ins over 5f out: chsd wnr wl over 2f out: ev ch whn rdn and edgd rt 1f out: nt* **4/1**[2]

0- **3** *22* **Il Capriccio (IRE)**[51] 4290 5-11-4 ... JTizzard 78
(B J M Ryall) *prom tl rdn and wknd 3f out* **16/1**

4 *1 ½* **Northern Endeavour** 6-10-11 ... DCosgrave(7) 77
(B De Haan) *hld up in mid-div: rdn and hdwy 4f out: wknd 3f out* **9/1**

5 *7* **Play It Again** 5-11-4 ... APMcCoy 70
(Simon Earle) *led: hdd over 5f out: wknd over 3f out* **11/4**[1]

0- **6** *2 ½* **Loada Baloney**[32] 4644 4-10-13 ... JPMcNamara 62
(Lucinda Featherstone) *hld up and bhd: sme hdwy over 3f out: nvr nr ldrs* **50/1**

7 *shd* **Berkeley Court** 4-10-13 ... JEMoore 62
(C A Cyzer) *hld up towards rr: hdwy and n.m.r over 6f out: rdn and rn green bnd 4f out: wknd 3f out* **5/1**[3]

6- **8** *4* **Willies Way**[85] 3689 5-11-1 ... AHoneyball(3) 63
(C J Down) *hld up and bhd: rdn and hdwy over 5f out: wknd 4f out* **50/1**

0- **9** *¾* **Bitta Dash**[70] 3960 5-11-1 ... RWalford(3) 62
(A J Wilson) *nvr nr ldrs* **50/1**

00- **10** *1* **Another Jameson (IRE)**[79] 3771 5-10-11 ... ATinkler 54
(J M Jefferson) *hld up in mid-div: hmpd over 6f out: bhd fnl 4f* **25/1**

0- **11** *2 ½* **Surfboard (IRE)**[40] 4499 4-10-13 ... VSlattery 54
(P A Blockley) *hld up in mid-div: rdn and hdwy 5f out: wknd over 3f out* **14/1**

0/0- **12** *¾* **Flurry**[20] 4801 6-10-11 ... PHide 51
(C J Down) *hld up in tch: wknd over 3f out* **8/1**

006- **13** *12* **Len Ross**[20] 4801 6-11-4 ... SDurack 46
(R Lee) *prom: rdn over 5f out: sn wknd* **11/1**

0-S **14** *½* **Georgie Girl Dove**[6] 7 5-10-11 ... WHutchinson 39
(C J Price) *prom tl rn wd bnd over 5f out: sn eased* **66/1**

15 *8* **River Iris** 4-9-13 ... CPoste(7) 26
(Lucinda Featherstone) *hld up and plld hrd: hdwy after 5f: wknd over 5f out* **66/1**

0- **16** *15* **The Langer (IRE)**[151] 2556 5-10-13 ... LTreadwell(5) 23
(S T Lewis) *prom: rdn over 6f out: wknd over 5f out* **100/1**

17 *23* **Frosty Moon (IRE)** 5-10-4 ... MrGTumelty(7) —
(B L Lay) *hdwy after 4f: wknd 10f out: t.o* **66/1**

18 *dist* **Meiklecantly Charm** 6-10-11 ... JGoldstein —
(G F Bridgwater) *a bhd: t.o fnl 7f: virtually p.u fnl 2f* **66/1**

006- **P** **Old Golden Bay**[33] 4615 5-11-1 ... JPByrne(3) —
(M Wellings) *hld up in mid-div: rdn after 6f: sn bhd: t.o whn p.u over 1f out* **100/1**

3m 47.2s (-0.60) **Going Correction** +0.275s/f (Yiel)
WFA 4 from 5yo+ 5lb **19** Ran SP% **129.7**
Speed ratings: **112,111,100,99,96 95,94,92,92,92 90,90,84,84,80 72,61,—,—** CSF £70.28 TOTE £13.20: £5.30, £2.20, £3.40; EX 135.00 Place 6 £188.45, Place 5 £87.43.
Owner Gallagher Enterprises Ltd **Bred** Gallagher Enterprises Ltd **Trained** Newport, Newport
■ Stewards' Enquiry : R Johnson caution: used whip without giving gelding time to respond

FOCUS
The first two drew right away in what was probably a very ordinary bumper and the form is somewhat muddling, though the winning time compared very favourably with the three hurdle races run over the same trip.

NOTEBOOK
Ballymena was able to hold her position this time and built on an improved effort over course and distance earlier in the month. *(op 10-1)*
Celtic Jem(IRE) looked a different horse on this faster ground and just lost out in what developed into a protracted duel in the home straight. *(tchd 7-2)*
Il Capriccio(IRE) stepped up on his debut but could not live with the two main protagonists. *(tchd 14-1)*
Northern Endeavour is out of a mare who won at up to two miles five furlongs over both hurdles and fences. *(op 14-1)*
Play It Again dropped out tamely after making the running. *(op 10-3 tchd 7-2)*
Another Jameson(IRE) *Official explanation: jockey said mare was hampered in back straight*
Meiklecantly Charm *Official explanation: jockey said he virtualy pulled up mare when he felt her go lame (op 50-1)*
T/Plt: £133.60 to a £1 stake. Pool: £32,576.45. 177.90 winning tickets. T/Qpdt: £23.40 to a £1 stake. Pool: £2,939.00. 92.90 winning tickets. KH/RL

139 - 146a (Foreign Racing) - See Raceform Interactive

SEDGEFIELD (L-H)

Monday, May 2

OFFICIAL GOING: Good (good to firm in places)

After 28mm of rain and water over the previous week the ground was described as 'near perfect, a credit to the ground staff'.
Wind: moderate half-behind Weather: fine and sunny but blustery shower race 6

147 BET365 CALL 08000 322 365 MAIDEN HURDLE (10 hdls) 2m 5f 110y

2:15 (2:15) (Class 4) 4-Y-0+ **£3,360** (£960; £480)

Form RPR

P0P- **1** **Miss Jessica (IRE)**[12] 4929 5-10-9 80 ... JMogford 81
(Miss M E Rowland) *chsd ldrs: led 3 out: rdn rt out: all out* **12/1**

562/ **2** *2* **Noble House**[535] 2139 8-11-2 ... ADobbin 86
(Mrs A Duffield) *led to 3rd: chsd wnr after 3 out: kpt on run-in* **3/1**[1]

P00- **3** *5* **Parisienne Gale (IRE)**[37] 6-9-13 ... MissCarolineHurley(10) 74+
(R Ford) *chsd ldrs: outpcd 7th: styd on fr 2 out: snatched 3rd on line* **18/1**

/06- **4** *shd* **French Tune (FR)**[37] 4550 7-11-2 85 ... AThornton 81
(Miss S E Hall) *a in tch: outpcd 7th: kpt on fr 2 out* **9/1**

P/0- **5** *6* **Wiseguy (IRE)**[341] 500 6-11-2 95 ... GLee 78+
(J Howard Johnson) *chsd ldrs: led 3rd to 3 out: 3rd and wkng whn mstke last* **3/1**[1]

F **Saddleback Prince** 6-10-9 ... MJMcAlister(7) —
(B Storey) *fell 1st* **66/1**

P **Max 'n Limbo (IRE)** 5-11-2 ... JMMaguire —
(R Ford) *bhd fr 5th: t.o whn p.u bef 2 out* **18/1**

P **Alderclad Lad (IRE)** 5-11-2 ... ADempsey —
(J Howard Johnson) *sn bhd: t.o 6th: p.u bef 3 out* **7/1**[3]

0/0- **P** **Whatdo You Want (IRE)**[22] 4788 5-10-9 ... (t) FKeniry —
(G M Moore) *sn bhd: t.o whn p.u bef 2 out* **50/1**

6P4- **P** **Yankee Crossing (IRE)**[121] 3146 7-10-13 94 ... KJMercer(3) —
(Ferdy Murphy) *in rr: p.u after 5th: dead* **9/2**[2]

00- **P** **The Yellow Earl (IRE)**[166] 2271 5-11-2 ... JimCrowley —
(J M Jefferson) *sn bhd: t.o whn p.u bef 7th* **33/1**

0-P **P** **Stoneriggs**[8] 14 4-10-11 ... BHarding —
(Mrs E Slack) *sn bhd: tried run out 5th: t.o whn p.u bef 2 out* **66/1**

4P6- **P** **Muller (IRE)**[305] 857 5-11-2 64 ... JPMcNamara —
(R W Thomson) *chsd ldrs: lost pl 6th: bhd whn p.u bef 3 out* **100/1**

5m 18.1s (7.40) **Going Correction** +0.10s/f (Yiel)
WFA 4 from 5yo+ 5lb **13** Ran SP% **117.8**
Speed ratings: **90,89,87,87,85 —,—,—,—,— —,—,—** CSF £47.81 TOTE £14.80: £2.40, £2.10, £6.40; EX 48.20.
Owner K Hopkin, S Deeman **Bred** Mrs Sheila O'Ryan **Trained** Lower Blidworth, Notts
■ Stewards' Enquiry : Miss Caroline HurleyW seven-day ban: failed to take all reasonable and permissible measures to obtain best possible placing (May 13-19)

FOCUS
A very poor event won by a mare with an official rating of just 80 and a slow time. the first two ran to their marks but the form is weak.

NOTEBOOK
Miss Jessica(IRE), already beaten in sellers and miles behind on her last two starts in handicaps, held a decisive advantage between the last two flights but at the line there was not an ounce to spare.
Noble House, absent since chasing home Patriarch Express at Newcastle in November 2003, is a big horse who should make a better chaser. *(tchd 10-3)*
Parisienne Gale(IRE), well beaten in selling company when last seen over hurdles, has since won a maiden point since. Left behind four out she stayed on in her own time under her inexperienced rider, setting the alarm bell off in the Stewards room! *(op 16-1)*
French Tune(FR), well beaten in two starts after a lengthy absence, ran as if the extended trip was in his favour. *(op 11-1 tchd 12-1)*
Wiseguy(IRE), keen in the past, ambled round in front but found nothing at all when challenged and dropped away in the tamest possible fashion. *(op 10-3 tchd 7-2)*
Alderclad Lad(IRE), a springer in the market, showed nothing at all before calling it a day. *(op 10-1 tchd 6-1)*

148 WARES TEESSIDE 01642 358040 NOVICES' CHASE (16 fncs) 2m 5f
2:45 (2:45) (Class 3) 5-Y-0+ **£5,473** (£1,684; £842; £421)

Form RPR
112- **1** **Mckelvey (IRE)**[19] [4825] 6-11-0 .... APMcCoy 113+
(P Bowen) *chsd ldrs: led 9th: pin broke and rdr lost nrside iron sn after last: hung bdly rt: hld on nr fin* **8/11**[1]
315- **2** *hd* **Page Point (AUS)**[15] [4881] 7-11-0 .... HOliver 111+
(R C Guest) *chsd ldrs: drvn along 8th: jnd wnr 2 out: carried rt run-in: jst hld* **4/1**[2]
023- **3** *dist* **Cumbrian Knight (IRE)**[44] [4447] 7-11-0 105.......... GLee 75
(J M Jefferson) *in tch: hdwy to chse ldrs 11th: wknd fr 3 out: btn 35 l* **9/2**[3]
446- **4** *1* **Kippour (FR)**[27] [4734] 7-10-11 87.......... (b) KJMercer(3) 75
(Ferdy Murphy) *nt fluent: w ldr: led 8th: hdd next: wknd 12th* **20/1**
52U- **5** *5* **Nomadic Blaze**[21] [4806] 8-10-11 .... LMcGrath(3) 74
(P G Atkinson) *chsd ldrs: blnd and lost pl 11th: bhd fr next* **20/1**
60U/ **U** **Percy Beck**[792] [3913] 9-11-0 .... FKeniry —
(P Needham) *in last and outpcd whn blnd and uns rdr 7th* **100/1**
/00- **P** **Riyadh**[141] [2785] 7-11-0 .... (b) JMMaguire —
(T P Tate) *mde most to 8th: hit 10th: sn lost pl: bhd whn p.u bef 12th* **20/1**

5m 18.6s (-0.70) **Going Correction** +0.10s/f (Yiel) **7** Ran SP% **111.4**
Speed ratings: **105,104,—,—,—** —,— CSF £3.75 TOTE £1.70: £1.10, £2.00; EX 2.80.
Owner N Elliott **Bred** John Quane **Trained** Little Newcastle, Pembrokes

FOCUS
A decent race of its type for the track and the 123-rated hurdler McKelvey looked to have been found a simple task on his chasing bow. However, circumstances counted against him and it could be argued that he had luck on his side in the Stewards' room.

NOTEBOOK
Mckelvey(IRE) looked to have been found an ideal opportunity on his chasing bow but his rider was in trouble landing after the last and it took all the champion's strength to get his head in front on the line. *(op 4-5)*
Page Point(AUS), making hard work of it with a circuit to go on this chasing bow, warmed to his task and if anything looked to be getting the better of the argument when knocked repeatedly out of his stride on the run-in. The winner's misfortune was clearly not of his own making but connections must be wondering just what must happen before the placings are reversed under the present guidelines. *(tchd 9-2)*
Cumbrian Knight(IRE) was left trailing by the first two over the final three fences and did not make *the expected improvement encountering much better ground. Two miles looks more his cup of* tea. *(op 11-2 tchd 6-1)*
Kippour(FR), with the blinkers on again, would not have a cut at his fences and after showing ahead seemed to give up very tamely. *(op 16-1)*
Nomadic Blaze was stopped in his tracks by a blunder six out.

149 MIKE BLOCKI 60TH BIRTHDAY H'CAP HURDLE (7 hdls 1 omitted) 2m 1f
3:20 (3:20) (Class 4) (0-100,100) 4-Y-0+ **£3,031** (£866; £433)

Form RPR
003- **1** **He's Hot Right Now (NZ)**[47] [4403] 6-10-12 86.......... (p) HOliver 100+
(R C Guest) *chsd ldrs: led 3 out: hrd rdn and kpt on: hld on wl towards fin* **6/1**[3]
00-0 **2** *1 ½* **Ton-Chee**[8] [9] 6-11-0 88.......... PRobson 98
(K W Hogg) *mid-div: hdwy to chse ldrs 5th: j.lft 2 out: edgd lft fnl f: hld towards fin* **16/1**
000- **3** *7* **Errol**[15] [4883] 6-10-12 93.......... EDehdashti(7) 96
(J F Coupland) *chsd ldrs: kpt on same pce fr 3 out* **40/1**
000- **4** *2* **Prince Adjal (IRE)**[72] [3950] 5-10-10 84.......... FKeniry 87+
(G M Moore) *w ldr: hit 3rd: outpcd fr 3 out* **20/1**
402- **5** *3 ½* **Donna's Double**[21] [4810] 10-11-7 95.......... ADobbin 94+
(Karen McLintock) *towards rr: hdwy whn hit 5th: kpt on fr next: nvr nr ldrs* **9/2**[2]
344- **6** *11* **Five Gold (IRE)**[21] [4810] 4-10-4 89.......... EWhillans(7) 72
(A C Whillans) *led: hit 3rd: hdd 3 out: sn wknd* **8/1**
046- **7** *4* **Lord Of The Land**[37] [4551] 12-10-9 93.......... SGagan(10) 76
(Mrs E Slack) *in tch: outpcd 5th: n.d after* **25/1**
530- **8** *1 ¼* **Siena Star (IRE)**[116] [3235] 7-11-3 91.......... APMcCoy 72
(P Bowen) *sn bhd: sme hdwy 2 out: nvr a factor* **11/4**[1]
036- **9** *6* **Young Tot (IRE)**[84] [3743] 7-10-11 88.......... (v) KJMercer(3) 63
(Mrs A Duffield) *bhd fr 3rd* **33/1**
503- **10** *12* **Petrolero (ARG)**[115] [3254] 6-11-1 89.......... JimCrowley 52
(James Moffatt) *staedied s: a bhd* **14/1**
430- **11** *8* **Dubonai (IRE)**[16] [2545] 5-11-6 99.......... DCCostello(5) 54
(Andrew Turnell) *bhd fr 5th* **16/1**
0P-2 **F** **Shakwaa**[8] [9] 6-10-11 85.......... PJBrennan —
(E A Elliott) *mid-div: fell 3rd* **9/1**
60U- **P** **Young Scotton**[64] [4085] 5-11-12 100.......... GLee —
(J Howard Johnson) *sn bhd: p.u after 3rd* **9/1**
P/5- **P** **Le Mino (FR)**[187] [1861] 6-10-12 89.......... GBerridge(3) —
(C W Thornton) *sn bhd: p.u bef 2 out* **40/1**

4m 2.10s (-0.60) **Going Correction** +0.10s/f (Yiel)
WFA 4 from 5yo+ 4lb **14** Ran SP% **125.1**
Speed ratings: **105,104,101,100,98 93,91,90,87,82 78,—,—,—** CSF £93.40 CT £3538.26 TOTE £7.40: £2.60, £7.60, £15.20; EX 211.20.
Owner Paul Beck **Bred** T W Jarvis **Trained** Brancepeth, Co Durham

FOCUS
A very moderate handicap in which the time was quite decent for the grade and the first two should continue to give a good account of themselves at this sort of level. The final flight was omitted resulting in a run-in of about three furlongs.

NOTEBOOK
He's Hot Right Now(NZ), placed just once in eight previous starts, has been improved by cheekpieces and his name certainly sums up his trainer's fortunes at present. *(op 5-1)*
Ton-Chee, still 1lb higher than for his sole success, appreciated the better ground and, despite a tendency to go to his left, he made the winner pull out all the stops.
Errol, still 6lb higher than his sole success at Doncaster in January, will continue to struggle until he is shown some leniency. *(tchd 50-1)*
Prince Adjal(IRE) has slipped down the weights and had the ground more in his favour this time. *(op 14-1)*
Donna's Double, 7lb higher, could never take a hand and prefers a much stiffer track. *(op 7-1)*
Five Gold(IRE) set a strong gallop, him and Prince Adjal raced clear, but they simply succeeded in cutting their own throats. *(op 11-1 tchd 12-1)*
Siena Star(IRE), absent since January, never figured and not even the champion could get him competitive. *Official explanation: jockey said gelding was never travelling (op 3-1 tchd 10-3)*

150 JOHN SMITH'S DURHAM NATIONAL (A H'CAP CHASE) (22 fncs) 3m 4f
3:50 (3:50) (Class 3) (0-125,120) 5-Y-0+
£12,180 (£4,620; £2,310; £1,050; £525; £315)

Form RPR
2F2- **1** **Prince Of Slane**[54] [4258] 6-9-9 94 oh4.......... DCCostello(5) 112+
(G A Swinbank) *bhd: gd hdwy 16th: sn chsng ldrs: blnd 4 out: wnt 2nd next: led 2 out: styd on u.p* **16/1**
512- **2** *5* **Lodestar (IRE)**[35] [4612] 8-10-11 105.......... (b) APMcCoy 116
(Ian Williams) *w ldrs: led 13th tl 2 out: no ex* **4/1**[1]
3F-1 **3** *18* **Time To Reflect (IRE)**[5] [62] 6-10-12 109 7ex.......... (p) LMcGrath(3) 102
(R C Guest) *in rr: hdwy to chse ldrs 15th: wknd 3 out* **7/1**
633- **4** *2* **Jacquemart Colombe (FR)**[20] [4815] 8-11-6 114.......... (p) SDurack 105
(P Bowen) *chsd ldrs: wnt 2nd 14th: wknd 3 out* **5/1**[3]
004- **5** *19* **Bright Approach (IRE)**[19] [4821] 12-11-5 116.......... TJMalone(3) 88
(J G Cann) *prom: outpcd 14th: sn lost pl: t.o 2 out* **9/2**[2]
110- **6** *½* **Caribbean Cove (IRE)**[23] [4773] 7-10-7 101.......... (b) HOliver 83+
(R C Guest) *rr-div: mstke 6th: hdwy to chse ldrs 17th: weakened next* **11/1**
135- **P** **Lord Capitaine (IRE)**[29] [4710] 11-11-3 111.......... GLee —
(J Howard Johnson) *mid-div: blnd 11th: sn bhd: p.u bef 13th* **17/2**
114- **P** **Dante Citizen (IRE)**[23] [4778] 7-11-1 109.......... JMMaguire —
(T R George) *chsd ldrs: lost pl 14th: sn bhd: t.o whn p.u bef 3 out* **14/1**
4R4- **P** **Ballinclay King (IRE)**[100] [3484] 11-11-5 120.......... TJDreaper(7) —
(Ferdy Murphy) *sn bhd: detached in last 12th: p.u after 14th* **16/1**
5P2- **P** **Cassia Heights**[19] [4821] 10-11-6 114.......... (t) ADobbin —
(S A Brookshaw) *led to 7th: lost pl after 13th: bhd whn p.u after 15th* **11/1**
405- **P** **Majed (FR)**[17] [4850] 9-10-13 112.......... (b) DFlavin(5) —
(Mrs L B Normile) *w ldrs: led 7th to 13th: weakaned 15th: sn bhd: t.o whn p.u bef 3 out* **33/1**

7m 6.60s (-4.70) **Going Correction** +0.10s/f (Yiel) **11** Ran SP% **115.9**
Speed ratings: **110,108,103,102,97 97,—,—,—,—** — CSF £80.24 CT £500.39 TOTE £18.10: £3.50, £1.90, £2.90; EX 113.00.
Owner J H Richardson **Bred** J Richardson **Trained** Melsonby, N Yorks
■ A downgraded but historic race won by the susequent Grand National winners Red Alligator in 1967 and Rubstic three times.

FOCUS
A fair handicap run at a decent gallop, although the form looks nothing special.

NOTEBOOK
Prince Of Slane, 4lb out of the handicap, made a sharp forward move with a full circuit to go. Surviving a blunder four out, in the end he scored in decisive fashion in this quite valuable prize, his first success on his 16th career start. A late developer and clearly an out-and-out stayer, there may be even better to come.
Lodestar(IRE), improved by blinkers, is still 12lb below his hurdle-race mark. Suited by the decent ground, he went on with just over a circuit to go but in the end was very much second best. There was no disgrace in this at all. *(op 3-1)*
Time To Reflect(IRE), making a quick retrurn, moved up looking a real threat but he stopped in a matter of strides three out.
Jacquemart Colombe(FR), tried in cheekpieces, went in pursuit of the leader but ultimately pulled out very little. *(tchd 11-2)*
Bright Approach(IRE), getting long in the tooth, was in trouble early on the final circuit. *(op 5-1 tchd 11-2)*
Caribbean Cove(IRE) would not get this trip in a horse box. *(op 12-1 tchd 10-1)*
Lord Capitaine(IRE) *Official explanation: jockey said gelding lost its action (op 8-1 tchd 15-2 and 9-1)*

151 P&C MORRIS EXPRESS CATERING UNITS HUNTERS' CHASE (16 fncs) 2m 5f
4:25 (4:29) (Class 6) 5-Y-0+ **£1,526** (£436; £218)

Form RPR
1U5- **1** **Swiftway**[21] [4811] 11-11-11 .... MrWLMorgan(5) 96
(Miss J Fisher) *chsd ldrs: mstke 1st: led 9th tl after 2 out: rallied run-in: led nr fin* **4/1**[2]
UP3- **2** *hd* **Bohemian Spirit (IRE)**[8] 7-12-0 107.......... MissRDavidson(5) 99
(Miss M A Neill) *uns rdr at false s: hld up: hdwy 7th: sn trcking ldrs: led after 2 out: rdn after last: hdd nr fin* **15/8**[1]
/04- **3** *3 ½* **Adolphus (IRE)**[22] 8-11-12 .... (p) MrCStorey 88
(C Storey) *chsd ldrs: mstke 3rd: outpcd 3 out: styd on wl appr last* **7/1**
P/-0 **4** *7* **Gold Quest (IRE)**[5] [52] 8-11-5 .... (p) MrNKent(7) 82+
(Nick Kent) *chsd ldrs: outpcd 3 out: wknd last* **33/1**
P01- **5** *15* **Natural (IRE)**[15] [4877] 8-11-11 77.......... (t) MrTDavidson(5) 70
(Mrs J Williamson) *chsd ldrs: outpcd fr 13th* **9/1**
630- **6** *21* **Donnybrook (IRE)**[25] [4750] 12-11-7 95.......... MrBWoodhouse(5) 45
(R D E Woodhouse) *chsd ldrs: drvn along 8th: sn lost pl* **9/2**[3]
PPP- **7** *13* **Oscar Pepper (USA)**[16] [4870] 8-11-5 .... MrSCharlton(7) 32
(M J Brown) *chsd ldrs: lost pl 12th: sn bhd* **40/1**
30P/ **P** **Jimmy Blues**[8] 10-11-9 .... (t) TJDreaper(3) —
(Ferdy Murphy) *sn bhd: t.o 8th: p.u bef 11th* **16/1**
630/ **P** **Whitley Grange Boy**[15] 12-11-5 .... PKinsella(7) —
(A J Lockwood) *in rr: bhd fr 10th: p.u bef 13th* **25/1**
/35- **U** **Orleans (IRE)**[8] 10-11-7 ow2.......... (p) MrSimonRobinson(7) —
(S J Robinson) *rel to r: whipped rnd and uns rdr sn after s* **20/1**
P- **P** **Dinan (IRE)**[8] 13-11-5 .... MrsJoanneBrown(7) —
(Mrs Joanne Brown) *chsd ldrs: lost pl 9th: sn bhd: t.o whn p.u bef 2 out* **33/1**
064/ **P** **Sparkey Smith (IRE)**[22] 13-11-5 .... MrWBRamsay(7) —
(Major General C A Ramsay) *j.rt: led to 9th: lost pl and blnd 11th: sn bhd: t.o whn p.u bef 2 out* **16/1**

5m 24.6s (5.30) **Going Correction** +0.10s/f (Yiel) **12** Ran SP% **124.2**
Speed ratings: **93,92,91,88,83 75,70,—,—,—** —,— CSF £12.38 TOTE £6.00: £2.30, £1.20, £2.10; EX 15.40.
Owner Miss J Fisher **Bred** Auldyn Stud Ltd **Trained** Kirknewton, Lothian

FOCUS
A modest hunter chase with the first two rated below their best and the third the best guide to the level.

NOTEBOOK
Swiftway put a poor run last time behind him and really battled up the final hill to pinch it in the last few strides. *(op 7-2)*
Bohemian Spirit(IRE) bloodied his rider's face when unseating her at the false start. Patiently ridden, he looked nailed on when jumping the last two lengths to the good but in the end he just missed out. *(op 9-4 tchd 5-2 and 7-4)*
Adolphus(IRE), winner of two of his four starts in points, finished with a real flourish and is the type to relish a severe test of stamina. *(op 13-2)*
Gold Quest(IRE), tried in cheekpieces this time, ran his best race for some time but his stamina looks limited. *(op 28-1)*
Natural(IRE) was readily left behind on this much better ground. *(op 8-1 tchd 10-1)*
Donnybrook(IRE), who jumped round Aintree last time, was the first in trouble. *(op 5-1 tchd 11-2)*

152 RACECOURSE VIDEO SERVICES H'CAP HURDLE (10 hdls) 2m 5f 110y
4:55 (4:56) (Class 4) (0-90,88) 4-Y-0+ £3,031 (£866; £433)

Form RPR
20-3 **1** **Nifty Roy**[8] [14] 5-11-4 **80** PRobson 88+
(K W Hogg) *chsd ldrs: led after 3 out: j.lft next: rdn clr* **4/1**[2]
60-0 **2** *10* **Northern Echo**[8] [11] 8-10-9 **78** (p) GThomas[(7)] 76
(K S Thomas) *bhd: hdwy 7th: styd on fr next: tk 2nd run-in: no ch w wnr* **40/1**
/PP- **3** *1* **Classic Lash (IRE)**[97] [3528] 9-10-10 **79** CDSharkey[(7)] 77+
(P Needham) *hdwy to chse ldrs 6th: wnt 2nd appr 2 out: kpt on same pce* **25/1**
064- **4** *3 1/2* **Book's Way**[35] [4604] 9-11-1 **80** KJMercer[(3)] 74
(D W Thompson) *chsd ldrs: one pce fr 3 out* **11/1**
605- **5** *6* **Cody**[16] [4871] 6-10-9 **81** (v) MMcAvoy[(10)] 69
(James Moffatt) *mid-div: hdwy to chse ldrs 7th: outpcd fr next* **22/1**
40-P **6** *3 1/2* **Rincoola (IRE)**[8] [11] 6-11-12 **88** DO'Meara 72
(J S Wainwright) *mid-div: effrt 7th: nvr nr ldrs* **66/1**
45-0 **7** *4* **In Good Faith**[8] [11] 13-10-11 **80** PKinsella[(7)] 60
(R E Barr) *bhd: sme hdwy 7th: nvr a factor* **16/1**
601- **8** *6* **Hello Baby**[22] [4783] 5-11-9 **85** KRenwick 59
(A C Whillans) *chsd ldrs: lost pl after 3 out* **6/1**[3]
050- **9** *10* **Lampos (USA)**[47] [2970] 5-11-9 **85** RGarritty 53+
(Miss J A Camacho) *bhd: sme hdwy 5th: lost pl 3 out: eased* **14/1**
051- **10** *6* **Kings Square**[64] [4089] 5-11-7 **83** ADempsey 47+
(M W Easterby) *trckd ldrs: lost pl after 3 out: sn bhd and eased* **5/2**[1]
606- **11** *2 1/2* **Swallow Magic (IRE)**[64] [4089] 7-11-9 **85** (b) BHarding 41
(Ferdy Murphy) *led tl after 3 out: sn lost pl: heavily eased run-in* **14/1**
00P- **12** *dist* **Sir Lamb**[48] [4387] 9-11-4 **85** (p) DCCostello[(5)] —
(Miss S E Hall) *bhd fr 7th: t.o after next* **20/1**
205- **13** *1 1/2* **Lagosta (SAF)**[211] [1568] 5-11-10 **86** FKeniry —
(G M Moore) *chsd ldrs: lost pl 7th: t.o 2 out: fin lame* **20/1**
004- **P** **Abbey Princess**[35] [4625] 5-11-3 **79** GLee —
(J Howard Johnson) *lost pl 6th: sn bhd and p.u: lame* **10/1**
000/ **P** **Jack Weighell**[379] [4879] 6-11-9 **85** JimCrowley —
(J M Jefferson) *bhd: blnd 4th: t.o whn p.u after 6th* **25/1**
5/0- **P** **Humming**[10] [4954] 8-11-2 **78** (t) JMogford —
(Miss M E Rowland) *chsd ldrs: lost pl 6th: bhd whn p.u bef 3 out* **66/1**

5m 13.6s (2.90) **Going Correction** +0.10s/f (Yiel) **16** Ran SP% **126.5**
Speed ratings: **98,94,94,92,90 89,87,85,82,79 78,—,—,—,— —** CSF £167.72 CT £3607.99 TOTE £5.30: £1.40, £11.80, £11.10, £3.50; EX 272.60 Place 6 £214.80, Place 5 £73.16.
Owner K W Hogg **Bred** Mrs Norma Peebles **Trained** Isle Of Man

FOCUS
A seller in all but name but a wide-margin, improving winner. The form looks solid enough for the grade.

NOTEBOOK
Nifty Roy again did not come home in a straight line but that did not prevent him coming right away up the final hill. *(op 7-2 tchd 9-2 in a place)*
Northern Echo sat away off a strong pace and staying on to chase the winner up the final hill may well have been flattered. *(op 33-1)*
Classic Lash(IRE), pulled up on his last two starts, emerged from the doldrums.
Book's Way continues to wage war with the official assessors. *(op 12-1)*
Cody, with the visor on again, has failed to hit the target in 26 starts now. *(op 25-1)*
Hello Baby *Official explanation: jockey said gelding was never travelling (op 7-1)*
Kings Square, well backed, kept tabs on the leaders in a race run at a strong pace. However, he stopped to nothing in a few strides after three out and in the end his rider was content just to nurse *him over the finishing line. Official explanation: trainer was unable to offer any explanation for poor form shown (op 5-1)*
Humming *Official explanation: jockey said gelding lost its action (op 50-1)*
T/Plt: £166.90 to a £1 stake. Pool: £38,542.20. 168.50 winning tickets. T/Qpdt: £80.90 to a £1 stake. Pool: £2,188.40. 20.00 winning tickets. WG

153 - 166a (Foreign Racing) - See Raceform Interactive

[53]EXETER (R-H)
Tuesday, May 3

OFFICIAL GOING: Heavy (soft in places)
Bottomless ground throughout the evening and runners finished tired.
Wind: slight across Weather: light showers

167 GG.COM CONDITIONAL JOCKEYS' NOVICES' H'CAP HURDLE (9 hdls 1 omitted) 2m 3f
5:45 (5:46) (Class 4) (0-95,93) 4-Y-0+ £3,234 (£924; £462)

Form RPR
022- **1** **Alessandro Severo**[17] [4871] 6-11-4 **85** (v) RStephens 89+
(Mrs D A Hamer) *a.p: pckd 4th: led after 6th: rdn appr last: r.o* **3/1**[1]
30F- **2** *2 1/2* **My Lady Link (FR)**[11] [4955] 6-11-3 **87** LTreadwell[(3)] 87
(Miss Venetia Williams) *hld up: hdwy 5th: disp ld after 6th to 2 out: r.o one pce* **8/1**
4- **3** *4* **Denarius Secundus**[34] [4662] 8-10-7 **74** DCrosse 70
(N R Mitchell) *hld up in tch: hdwy 5th: reminder after 6th: rdn appr 2 out: kpt on same pce* **16/1**
4P-5 **4** *18* **Sconced (USA)**[4] [96] 10-11-4 **88** (p) PCO'Neill[(3)] 66
(R C Guest) *prom: nt fluent 2nd: led appr 4th to 5th: sn wknd* **6/1**[3]
646- **5** *1* **Great Compton**[42] [4506] 5-10-13 **80** (p) JPByrne 57
(B J Llewellyn) *hld up mid-div: lost pl 4th: n.d after* **12/1**
024- **6** *5* **Algymo**[26] [4754] 5-11-1 **82** (b) AHoneyball 54
(S C Burrough) *led: rdn and hdd appr 4th: wknd 5th* **9/1**
PPP- **7** *1* **Earn Out**[15] [4913] 4-10-7 **87** CBonhoff[(8)] 53
(M C Pipe) *nvr nr ldrs* **14/1**
323- **8** *7* **Spiders Web**[14] [4579] 5-11-3 **90** (b) EDehdashti[(6)] 54
(G L Moore) *t.k.h in tch: 4th and wkng whn hit 3 out* **5/1**[2]
050- **9** *6* **Villago (GER)**[24] [4775] 5-11-5 **92** (b) StephenJCraine[(6)] 50
(C J Mann) *hld up in tch: rdn 4th: wknd appr 6th* **10/1**
00P- **10** *20* **Phairy Storm (IRE)**[18] [4853] 6-10-4 **76** (b[1]) SWalsh[(5)] 14
(J D Frost) *prom tl rdn and wknd appr 3 out* **25/1**
P00- **11** *23* **John Jorrocks (FR)**[54] [4289] 6-10-6 **73** RWalford —
(J C Tuck) *prom: led and hit 5th: hdd after 6th: sn wknd: t.o* **33/1**
P05- **P** **My Retreat (USA)**[37] [4579] 8-11-7 **88** TJPhelan —
(R Fielder) *a bhd: t.o whn p.u bef 2 out* **16/1**
3S2/ **P** **Proverbial Gray**[732] [82] 8-10-2 **69** ATinkler —
(D R Gandolfo) *a bhd: t.o whn p.u bef 3 out* **16/1**
P/P- **P** **Loramore**[250] [1297] 8-10-7 **74** JamesDavies —
(J C Tuck) *hld up: rdn 4th: sn bhd: t.o whn p.u bef 3 out* **50/1**

4m 54.2s (21.20) **Going Correction** +1.15s/f (Heav)
WFA 4 from 5yo+ 4lb **14** Ran SP% **126.9**
Speed ratings: **101,99,98,90,90 88,87,84,82,73 64,—,—,—** CSF £28.94 CT £351.08 TOTE £5.50: £1.20, £3.00, £5.20; EX 36.60.
Owner Mike Thomas **Bred** Peter Deal **Trained** Nant-y-caws, Carmarthens

FOCUS
A weak race with the runner-up the best guide to the form.

NOTEBOOK
Alessandro Severo has been running consistently well, finishing second the last twice, and deserved to get his head in front. He appeared to relish the bottomless ground and ploughed through it without too much fuss. He is still only six and has further improvement in him. *(op 5-1)*
My Lady Link(FR) showed no ill-effects of her fall over fences last time and ran a solid race in second. She has won over fences in France and is capable of doing so here if getting her jumping together. *(op 10-1)*
Denarius Secundus was nibbled at in the market and rewarded each-way backers. He was clear of the fourth and may have a similar race in him. *(op 25-1)*
Sconced(USA) claimed a moderate fourth and is not up to much these days. *(op 11-2)*
Great Compton would not have wanted the ground this soft and ran as expected. *(op 14-1)*
Spiders Web was the disappointment of the race, seeming to get bogged down in the ground. He may be worth another chance. *(op 4-1 tchd 7-2)*

168 BEARNES DIAMOND JUBILEE H'CAP HURDLE (12 hdls 1 omitted) 3m 110y
6:15 (6:15) (Class 3) (0-125,120) 4-Y-0+ £4,875 (£1,500; £750; £375)

Form RPR
/22- **1** **Admiral Peary (IRE)**[123] [3120] 9-11-2 **110** RThornton 117+
(C R Egerton) *a.p: jnd ldr and nt fluent 7th: led appr 3 out: rdn appr 2 out: edgd lft flat: styd on* **12/1**
221- **2** *3* **Global Challenge (IRE)**[306] [857] 6-11-12 **120** (b) APMcCoy 124
(Jonjo O'Neill) *a.p: w wnr appr 3 out: rdn appr 2 out: edgd lft and no ex flat* **9/2**[3]
1P1- **3** *13* **General Gossip (IRE)**[17] [4868] 9-11-1 **109** WMarston 100
(R T Phillips) *hld up: hdwy 9th: rdn and wknd appr 2 out* **5/2**[1]
020- **4** *1 3/4* **Lorgnette**[17] [4868] 11-11-2 **113** RWalford[(3)] 102
(R H Alner) *hld up: rdn appr 9th: sn struggling* **11/1**
45P- **5** *2 1/2* **Keepers Mead (IRE)**[34] [4655] 7-11-3 **111** AThornton 98
(R H Alner) *led: rdn and hdd appr 3 out: sn wknd* **15/2**
45-1 **6** *dist* **Monger Lane**[6] [54] 9-11-6 **114** 7ex PJBrennan —
(K Bishop) *w ldr to 7th: rdn 8th: sn wknd: t.o* **11/4**[2]
P61- **P** **Sungates (IRE)**[66] [4059] 9-11-9 **117** ATinkler —
(C Tinkler) *hld up: last whn hit 8th: sn rdn and lost tch: t.o whn p.u bef 3 out* **7/1**

6m 35.3s (35.30) **Going Correction** +1.40s/f (Heav) **7** Ran SP% **113.7**
Speed ratings: **99,98,93,93,92 —,—** CSF £63.80 CT £180.13 TOTE £14.20: £5.10, £2.50; EX 86.00.
Owner M Haynes **Bred** John Walsh **Trained** Chaddleworth, Berks

FOCUS
A hugely depleted field, with more than half the original declarations not taking part on account of the ground. The form is best not taken at face value.

NOTEBOOK
Admiral Peary(IRE) has shown many a time that he can go well fresh and he stayed on dourly under pressure to deny the top weight. He is a fairly consistent sort and, although he would be an obvious sort to 'bounce', it would not surprise to see him win again. *(op 10-1 tchd 14-1)*
Global Challenge(IRE), not for the first time, looked far from helpful once push came to shove and he was forced to settle for second even under the force of McCoy. *(op 7-2)*
General Gossip(IRE) comes from a stable who have been struggling for winners all season, albeit he won himself last time, and he was simply not good enough on the day. *(tchd 9-4)*
Lorgnette was never going particularly well and soon faded having momentarily posed a threat. *(op 12-1)*
Keepers Mead(IRE) travelled well to a point, but ended up fading out of things rather disappointingly. The sooner he is switched to fences the better. *(op 12-1)*

169 PERCY BROWNE MEMORIAL TROPHY NOVICES' H'CAP CHASE (15 fncs 2 omitted) 2m 7f 110y
6:45 (6:45) (Class 4) (0-95,93) 5-Y-0+ £3,720 (£1,209; £651)

Form RPR
0/6- **1** **Billy Ballbreaker (IRE)**[12] [4937] 9-10-7 **74** (t) ChristianWilliams 90+
(C L Tizzard) *hld up: hdwy appr 7th: led 4 out: rdn out* **14/1**
060- **2** *8* **Nurzyk (POL)**[13] [4928] 8-10-7 **74** JMMaguire 83+
(T R George) *led tl after 2nd: w ldr: j.rt 6th: led 9th: rdn and hdd 4 out: one pce fr 2 out* **14/1**
462- **3** *dist* **Gola Supreme (IRE)**[37] [4584] 10-11-12 **93** WMarston 62
(R Lee) *hld up: hdwy after 7th: rdn and wknd appr 4 out* **4/1**[2]
P43- **P** **Peejay Hobbs**[23] [4796] 7-11-2 **86** RHobson[(3)] —
(C J Gray) *a bhd: t.o whn p.u after 8th* **12/1**
PPP- **P** **The Pecker Dunn (IRE)**[35] [4641] 11-11-7 **88** JMogford —
(Mrs N S Evans) *a bhd: rdn 7th: t.o whn p.u bef 4 out* **40/1**
PPP- **U** **Curragh Gold (IRE)**[61] [4140] 5-10-3 **77** AProcter —
(Mrs P N Dutfield) *a bhd: rdn 7th: t.o whn blnd and uns rdr 11th* **40/1**
U42- **P** **General O'Keeffe**[23] [4790] 8-11-7 **88** AThornton —
(R H Alner) *hld up: rdn after 7th: sn bhd: t.o whn p.u bef 10th* **4/1**[2]
422- **P** **Sure Future**[15] [4912] 9-11-11 **92** RThornton —
(R M Stronge) *hld up: rdn appr 8th: sn struggling: t.o whn p.u bef 4 out* **3/1**[1]
00P- **P** **Always In Debt (IRE)**[13] [4932] 6-11-9 **90** PJBrennan —
(P J Hobbs) *prom: mstke 1st: rdn appr 8th: wknd appr 4 out: bhd whn p.u bef 3 out* **7/1**[3]
504- **P** **Ebony Jack (IRE)**[37] [4580] 8-10-1 **71** RYoung[(3)] —
(Mrs Tracey Barfoot-Saunt) *led after 2nd: bmpd 6th: hdd 9th: wknd after 11th: t.o whn p.u bef last* **20/1**
0P5- **F** **In The Park (IRE)**[23] [4790] 8-10-7 **74** (b) APMcCoy —
(Jonjo O'Neill) *prom: reminders after 3rd and 5th: rdn 9th: wknd appr 4 out: poor 4th whn fell 3 out* **8/1**

6m 15.1s (15.80) **Going Correction** +0.70s/f (Soft)
WFA 5 from 6yo+ 3lb **11** Ran SP% **119.3**
Speed ratings: **101,98,—,—,— —,—,—,—,— —** CSF £183.46 CT £936.08 TOTE £16.00: £3.20, £4.90, £1.80; EX 204.90.
Owner Blackmore Vale Syndicate **Bred** John And Philip Hore **Trained** Milborne Port, Dorset

FOCUS
A poor contest and a real slog in the mud with only three of the 11 runners managing to complete. Although there is not much to go on, the first two ran close to their marks.

NOTEBOOK
Billy Ballbreaker(IRE) was well supported when running well for a long way last time and connections clearly new he was nearing a win. Being by Good Thyne the prevailing conditions were only going to suit and he ploughed on stoutly under pressure to end up winning comfortably. He is a lowly-rated individual and, if staying sound, is capable of adding to this. *(op 16-1)*
Nurzyk(POL) was completely unexposed coming into this, with it being his first start over fences and he ran a huge race, just being outbattled by the winner. His trainer should get the best out of him and it will be disappointing if he cannot pick up a similar race in the short term.
Gola Supreme(IRE) was the only other to complete, albeit a distance back, and deserves a mention for being able to do so. He is handicapped up to the hilt and will struggle to win until dropping a few pounds, unless he reverts to hurdles. *(op 9-2 tchd 7-2)*
Sure Future set a reasonable standard and should have taken the beating, being so consistent and all, but he never at any point looked a likely winner and dropped out of it disappointingly. He is better than this, but now has a bit to prove. *(tchd 15-2)*
The Pecker Dunn(IRE) *Official explanation: trainer said gelding had breathing problem (tchd 15-2)*
Peejay Hobbs *Official explanation: jockey said gelding was never travelling (tchd 15-2)*
In The Park(IRE) is a moderate performer to say the least and will not be in his top owners colours for much longer unless getting his act together. *(tchd 15-2)*
Always In Debt(IRE) ran below expectations and was never really jumping with any fluency. *(tchd 15-2)*

170 DIAMOND EDGE H'CAP CHASE (10 fncs 2 omitted) 2m 1f 110y
7:15 (7:16) (Class 4) (0-110,107) 5-Y-0+ **£4,212** (£1,296; £648; £324)

Form RPR
4F- **1** **Dangerousdanmagru (IRE)**[24] [4773] 9-11-6 **101** .... MFoley 115+
(A E Jones) *a.p: led appr 4 out: rdn appr 2 out: drvn out* **9/2**[3]
P05- **2** *2* **Barren Lands**[13] [4932] 10-11-8 **103** .... PJBrennan 114
(K Bishop) *hld up: hdwy 5th: rdn appr 4 out: chsd wnr fr 3 out: kpt on towards fin* **6/1**
13- **3** *6* **Pequenita**[33] [4667] 5-11-8 **105** .... (p) HOliver 108
(R C Guest) *hld up: hdwy after 6th: hrd rdn appr 4 out: sn lost pl: styd on flat* **7/1**
5PP- **4** *1 ½* **Eggmount (IRE)**[74] [3931] 7-11-2 **97** .... JMMaguire 101
(T R George) *w ldr: led 6th tl appr 4 out: wknd 2 out* **5/2**[1]
321- **5** *2 ½* **Brooklands Lad**[30] [4724] 8-10-1 **85** .... RYoung(3) 87+
(J W Mullins) *hld up: hdwy appr 4 out: rdn appr 3 out: wknd last* **7/2**[2]
4PL- **6** *13* **Athnowen (IRE)**[91] [3638] 13-11-4 **99** .... AThornton 95+
(J R Payne) *unruly and w.r.s: wl bhd tl sme hdwy and j.rt 3rd: n.d after* **14/1**
425- **7** *11* **Loriko D'Airy (FR)**[31] [4689] 6-11-12 **107** .... NFehily 84
(C J Mann) *led to 6th: wknd appr 4 out* **10/1**
14P- **8** *1 ½* **Get The Point**[11] [4955] 11-10-10 **91** .... JamesDavies 67
(Dr P Pritchard) *hld up in tch: wknd appr 4 out* **14/1**

4m 36.5s (16.50) **Going Correction** +0.925s/f (Soft)
WFA 5 from 6yo+ 2lb **8** Ran SP% **118.2**
Speed ratings: **100,99,96,95,94 88,84,83** CSF £32.66 CT £188.89 TOTE £4.10: £1.80, £1.80, £2.10; EX 44.60.
Owner N F Glynn **Bred** Kashmir Breeding **Trained** Cove, Devon

FOCUS
Ordinary form but the winner could rate higher, with the third setting the level.

NOTEBOOK
Dangerousdanmagru(IRE), out of his depth at Aintree last time, was much more at home back in this grade and he stayed on strongly after the last, always holding Barren Lands. He is still relatively unexposed at this sort of level and is entitled to respect in a follow-up bid. *(op 7-2 tchd 3-1)*
Barren Lands finds it difficult to win and ran another solid race in defeat. He is on a fair enough mark, but could never be backed with confidence. *(op 7-1 tchd 8-1)*
Pequenita ran a reasonable race on ground she would most probably have found a little too testing. She will be more at home once the ground dries up a bit. *(op 5-1)*
Eggmount(IRE) had the potential to prove much better than these, but the ground was wrong for him and he appeared to find it all a bit too much. He has not gone on from his smart Cheltenham effort early last season and, at the moment, has become disappointing. *(op 3-1 tchd 7-2)*
Brooklands Lad travelled well, but was running on fresh air when his jockey asked him to pick up. He was another for whom this ground would have been too soft. *(op 5-1 tchd 6-1)*

171 LADIES CLUB & HOLNE CHASE HOTEL NOVICES' HUNTERS' CHASE (13 fncs 2 omitted) 2m 3f 110y
7:45 (7:46) (Class 6) 5-Y-0+ **£2,804** (£863; £431; £215)

Form RPR
1 **Virgos Bambino (IRE)**[23] 8-11-0 .... MissSGaisford(5) 90
(Miss V J Nicholls) *a.p: led after 9th to 4 out: led last: drvn out* **12/1**
F **2** *nk* **Raregem**[6] [50] 7-11-5 .... MrWBiddick(7) 97
(M Biddick) *hld up in tch: led briefly 9th: led 4 out to last: r.o* **5/1**[3]
3 *25* **Smart Cavalier**[17] 6-11-12 .... (t) MrNWilliams 77+
(R Barber) *hld up and plld hrd: hdwy 6th: ev ch 4 out: rdn and wknd appr 2 out* **6/5**[1]
/4P- **4** *2 ½* **Nickit (IRE)**[11] [4963] 9-11-12 .... MissPGundry 69
(Mrs Susan Smith) *chsd ldr to 7th: wknd appr 4 out* **7/2**[2]
0P/ **5** *6* **Itworked**[23] 10-11-5 .... AGlassonbury(7) 63
(E M Treneer) *hld up and bhd: nt fluent 4th: hdwy appr 8th: wknd appr 4 out* **50/1**
40/- **6** *3* **Teninarow (IRE)**[16] 11-11-5 .... MissVShaw(7) 60
(M Weir) *hld up in tch: wknd appr 7th* **14/1**
0/0- **7** *13* **River Bailiff (IRE)**[36] 9-11-9 **74** .... (p) MrPYork(3) 47
(R Gurney) *hld up and bhd: hdwy appr 9th: wknd appr 4 out* **7/1**
0/ **P** **Whats Up Maid**[36] 8-10-12 .... MrMMunrowd(7) —
(Mrs Jo Sleep) *a bhd: t.o whn p.u bef 3 out* **33/1**
PP4/ **P** **Emali**[45] 8-11-5 .... MrWWhite(7) —
(G Chambers) *hld up in tch: blnd 7th: sn rdn and wknd: t.o whn p.u bef 4 out* **50/1**
P6P- **P** **By My Side (IRE)**[11] [4963] 11-11-5 .... (b) LHeard(7) —
(M J Lethbridge) *led: sn clr: j.lft 4th: hdd 9th: sn wknd: t.o whn p.u bef 3 out* **25/1**

5m 10.6s (18.30) **Going Correction** +0.925s/f (Soft) **10** Ran SP% **121.9**
Speed ratings: **100,99,89,88,86 85,80,—,—,—** CSF £72.68 TOTE £11.60: £1.70, £2.10, £1.70; EX 114.10.
Owner Mrs Maureen Nicholls **Bred** J Shanahan **Trained** Yelverton, Devon

FOCUS
A modest hunter chase but a fair time for the grade.

NOTEBOOK
Virgos Bambino(IRE) showed an admirable attitude in battling on bravely to deny Raregem and causing a small surprise in the process. She was the trip out extremely well having been on the pace throughout and will continue to be a threat under similar conditions. *(op 16-1)*
Raregem, a faller at Cheltenham last week, is a three-time winner in points and bounced back to form. On this evidence he can pick up a small race. *(op 7-2)*
Smart Cavalier was well adrift of the front two in third and on the face of it disappointing. He is worth another chance on better ground and will hopefully settle better next time. *(op 11-8 tchd 11-10)*
Nickit(IRE) was another fancied runner to disappoint and he found very little for pressure. *(op 4-1 tchd 5-1)*

172 FARMERS FRIEND OF EXETER MAIDEN HURDLE (7 hdls 1 omitted) 2m 1f
8:15 (8:16) (Class 4) 4-Y-0+ **£3,360** (£960; £480)

Form RPR
/00- **1** **Itsmyboy (IRE)**[24] [4774] 5-10-13 .... TJMalone(3) 120+
(M C Pipe) *hld up: hdwy appr 2nd: led after 3 out: r.o wl* **7/4**[1]
2 *4* **Gironde**[263] 4-10-12 .... APMcCoy 108+
(Jonjo O'Neill) *hld up in tch: rdn to chse wnr appr last: no imp* **7/2**[3]
345- **3** *12* **Vingis Park (IRE)**[86] [3723] 7-11-2 105 .... (tp) ATinkler 100
(V R A Dartnall) *led: hdd after 4th: rdn appr 2 out: wknd last* **5/1**
FP2- **4** *3 ½* **Sargasso Sea**[11] [4958] 8-11-2 110 .... WHutchinson 97
(J A B Old) *a.p: led after 4th tl after 3 out: wknd after 2 out* **3/1**[2]
00- **5** *15* **Bottom Drawer**[13] [4930] 5-10-11 .... RStephens(5) 82
(Mrs D A Hamer) *hld up: hdwy 3rd: wknd appr 3 out* **66/1**
6 *10* **Almutasader**[599] 5-11-2 .... PJBrennan 72
(J A B Old) *hld up in tch: rdn and wknd appr 3 out* **13/2**
0/6- **F** **El Hamra (IRE)**[38] [4563] 7-11-2 .... JMMaguire —
(T R George) *w ldr to 2nd: prom whn fell 4th* **40/1**
P **Ly's West**[637] 5-11-2 .... AThornton —
(C L Tizzard) *hung lft thrght: a in rr: eased and p.u bef 3 out* **33/1**

4m 27.9s (21.20) **Going Correction** +1.40s/f (Heav)
WFA 4 from 5yo+ 4lb **8** Ran SP% **120.5**
Speed ratings: **106,104,98,96,89 85,—,—** CSF £8.95 TOTE £3.30: £1.40, £1.10, £2.30; EX 11.00 Place 6 £229.11, Place 5 £99.53.
Owner D A Johnson **Bred** Padraig Moroney **Trained** Nicholashayne, Devon

FOCUS
An uncompetitive race, but winner Itsmyboy can follow up if kept to a modest level. It was a fair winning time for the class.

NOTEBOOK
Itsmyboy(IRE) is not the biggest, but handled the conditions better than most and won with a bit in hand. He had shown some promise in the championship bumpers at Cheltenham and Aintree and is evidently going to make a better hurdler. If kept on the go he should have little trouble following up. *(op 2-1 tchd 5-2)*
Gironde was a fair performer on the level and made a pleasing start to his hurdling career. He is equally effective on a sound surface and should not be too troubled in winning. *(op 3-1)*
Vingis Park(IRE) is very slow and does not always see his races out as strongly as may be expected. He is not one to rely on. *(op 4-1 tchd 11-2)*
Sargasso Sea was a bit disappointing and failed to see his race out. He is better than this, but now has a bit to prove. *(op 5-2)*
Almutasader, a smart stayer on the Flat with John Dunlop a couple of seasons back, has clearly had his problems and was having his first start for nearly two years. Someone thought he may run a big race however, as he virtually halved in price, but once the race began to heat up he dropped away disappointing to finish last. He has some ability but is one to tread carefully with. *(op 12-1 tchd 6-1)*
Ly's West *Official explanation: jockey said gelding hung left*
T/Plt: £155.20 to a £1 stake. Pool £47,382.70. 222.75 winning units T/Qpdt: £19.00 to a £1 stake. Pool £3,924.20. 152.70 winning units KH

[1]LUDLOW (R-H)
Tuesday, May 3

OFFICIAL GOING: Good
Wind: almost nil Weather: fine, showers after race 5

173 J.P. SEAFOODS (S) HURDLE (9 hdls) 2m
2:10 (2:11) (Class 5) 4-6-Y-0 **£2,555** (£730; £365)

Form RPR
60- **1** **Trickstep**[46] [4444] 4-10-8 .... JMMaguire 84+
(D McCain) *led to 4th: remained prom: hmpd 5th: chsd clr ldr after 4 out: led appr last: rdn out* **8/1**[3]
200- **2** *4* **Honan (IRE)**[11] [4969] 6-10-12 95 .... (v) TScudamore 82
(M C Pipe) *prom: led appr 5th: sn clr: rdn bef 3 out: hdd bef last: no ex run-in* **5/6**[1]
F46- **3** *9* **Go Green**[7] [3433] 4-10-1 79 .... (t) SCurran 64+
(P D Evans) *hld up: hdwy 5th: rdn after 4 out: btn fr next* **7/2**[2]
00P- **4** *7* **Makandy**[36] [4625] 6-10-5 .... MrRArmson(7) 68+
(R J Armson) *chsd ldrs: hmpd 5th: sn lost pl and struggling: n.d whn blnd 3 out* **40/1**
0/5- **5** *dist* **Vrubel (IRE)**[71] [2581] 6-10-5 72 .... (tp) APogson(7) —
(J R Holt) *in tch: wknd bef 4 out: t.o* **14/1**
/40- **6** *4* **Giust In Temp (IRE)**[226] [1446] 6-10-7 80 .... StephenJCraine(5) —
(M J M Evans) *racd keenly: hld up: effrt appr 4 out: no imp: sn wknd: t.o* **12/1**
P **Key Of Gold (IRE)**[45] 4-10-8 .... JMogford —
(A G Juckes) *nt fluent: a bhd: t.o whn p.u bef 2 out* **25/1**
P- **F** **Nutley Queen (IRE)**[14] [2493] 6-9-13 ow1 .... (t) BenOrde-Powlett(7) —
(M Appleby) *racd keenly: prom after 3rd: led next: hdd appr 5th and fell* **33/1**

3m 51.1s (3.50) **Going Correction** +0.125s/f (Yiel)
WFA 4 from 6yo 4lb **8** Ran SP% **111.5**
Speed ratings: **96,94,89,86,— —,—,—** CSF £14.97 TOTE £10.10: £2.30, £1.02, £1.60; EX 22.10.The winner was bought in for 6,400gns
Owner Market Avenue Racing Club Ltd **Bred** P Onslow **Trained** Cholmondeley, Cheshire

FOCUS
A weak seller, with the favourite well below par. It has been rated through the third and is unlikely to rate higher.

NOTEBOOK
Trickstep, who had the cheekpieces left off, was previously with Gay Kelleway. Surviving being hampered in the back straight, he cut down the favourite between the last two flights to land this weak event.

Honan(IRE) was taking a big drop in class but failed to make it count. He held a sizeable lead at one stage but was caught between the last two flights and did not put up much of a fight. The visor had failed to have too much effect on two previous occasions. *(op 4-5 tchd 8-11 and 10-11 in places)*
Go Green, third on the Flat a week earlier, was without the visor. Her stamina remains in serious question. *(op 4-1)*
Makandy, formerly with Jill Wormall, is a very limited performer and a poor jumper of hurdles. *(op 33-1 tchd 50-1)*
Nutley Queen(IRE) became very keyed up when mounted in the paddock. Keen in the race, she soon pulled her way into the lead but had been headed before coming down. *(op 20-1)*
Key Of Gold(IRE) *Official explanation: jockey said gelding had breathing problem (op 20-1)*

174 EDDIE MAPP MEMORIAL NOVICES' CHASE (17 fncs) 2m 4f
2:40 (2:40) (Class 3) 5-Y-O+ **£5,323** (£1,638; £819; £409)

Form RPR
234- **1** **Tigers Lair (IRE)**[166] 2296 6-11-0 .... APMcCoy 117+
(Jonjo O'Neill) *j.lft several times: prom: led 4th: rdn out* **11/4**[2]
41-1 **2** *7* **Saafend Rocket (IRE)**[9] 2 7-11-12 108.......... RJohnson 120+
(H D Daly) *j.lft: hld up: stdy hdwy fr 11th: chsd wnr appr 4 out: no ex run-in* **7/2**[3]
256- **3** *5* **Angel Delight**[18] 4855 9-10-6 98.......... WKennedy(7) 101
(J L Spearing) *hld up: hdwy appr 10th: rdn to take 2nd briefly after 13th: wknd bef last* **7/1**
212- **4** *27* **On The Outside (IRE)**[237] 1394 6-10-7 ....(t) TDoyle 68
(S E H Sherwood) *led to 4th: remained prom: hung lft after 12th: sn rdn: wknd after 13th* **12/1**
040- **5** *14* **Magnificent Seven (IRE)**[42] 4502 6-11-0 95.......... SDurack 66+
(Miss H C Knight) *in tch: blnd bdly 6th: wknd appr 10th: mstke next* **25/1**
P3-0 **6** *hd* **Let's Rock**[9] 2 7-10-7 67.......... MrRHodges(7) 61
(Mrs A Price) *prom: rdn and wknd appr 10th: mstke next* **50/1**
263- **F** **Lord Dundaniel (IRE)**[128] 2944 8-11-0 111.......... NFehily —
(B De Haan) *hld up: mstke 3rd: fell 5th* **5/2**[1]
300- **U** **Gone Far (USA)**[16] 4881 8-11-0 115..........(b) TScudamore —
(M C Pipe) *trckd ldrs tl blnd bdly and uns rdr 5th* **12/1**

4m 58.5s (-7.30) **Going Correction** -0.25s/f (Good)
WFA 5 from 6yo+ 3lb **8** Ran SP% **111.2**
Speed ratings: **104,101,99,88,82 82,—,—** CSF £12.52 TOTE £3.70: £1.60, £1.20, £2.10; EX 10.40.
Owner Mrs Gay Smith **Bred** James F Whitehead **Trained** Cheltenham, Gloucs

FOCUS
Solid novice chase form, with Tigers Lair, who was value for a bit further, running up to his hurdles mark.

NOTEBOOK
Tigers Lair(IRE) was minus the blinkers for this first run since November. He jumped well on this chasing debut, if out to his left at times, and scored in pleasing fashion. He is capable of a bit better. *(op 5-2 tchd 3-1)*
Saafend Rocket(IRE) carried a double penalty for two wins at this track, his home from home, but both those victories came over two miles and he does not really see out this longer trip. He should not be written off. *(op 3-1)*
Angel Delight had conditions to suit, but she was taking on a couple of decent novices and she ran as well as could be expected in the circumstances. *(op 15-2 tchd 8-1)*
On The Outside(IRE), making his chase debut on his first start since September, was beaten on the long home turn and held together from that point.
Magnificent Seven(IRE), who did not show a great deal in bumpers or over hurdles, got away with a serious blunder on this chasing debut but was beaten in the back straight. *(op 20-1)*
Lord Dundaniel(IRE), appearing for the first time since Boxing Day, was a victim of the tricky first fence in the home straight. *(op 11-4)*

175 JANICE STEVENS BIG "O" INTERMEDIATE HURDLE (9 hdls) 2m
3:10 (3:10) (Class 4) 4-Y-O+ **£4,010** (£1,234; £617; £308)

Form RPR
24-1 **1** **At Your Request**[4] 100 4-11-8 123.......... DRDennis 121+
(Ian Williams) *plld hrd: prom: led last: pushed out* **6/4**[1]
P15- **2** *1 1/2* **Pak Jack (FR)**[94] 3593 5-11-0 .... RJohnson 109+
(P J Hobbs) *plld hrd: led after 3rd: rdn 3 out: hdd last: nt qckn* **5/2**[2]
602- **3** *4* **Nuit Sombre (IRE)**[34] 4660 5-11-6 112.......... MAFitzgerald 112+
(N J Henderson) *in tch: rdn whn hit 3 out: styd on same pce* **11/2**[3]
014- **4** *3 1/2* **Jack's Lad (IRE)**[19] 4839 6-11-1 120.......... LStephens(5) 107
(Mrs S M Johnson) *j.rt: racd keenly: led 1st: hdd after 3rd: remained prom: rdn whn ch 3 out: wknd run-in* **7/1**
306- **5** *13* **Charlie Chapel**[14] 4920 6-11-0 100.......... PFlynn 89+
(W M Brisbourne) *hld up: effrt appr 3 out: wkng whn hit 2 out* **20/1**
6 *9* **Boytjie (IRE)** 5-11-0 .... SThomas 79
(Miss H C Knight) *trckd ldrs: j. slowly 5th and 4 out: sn rdn whn hung lft: wknd appr 3 out* **18/1**
00P- **P** **Lewsher**[40] 4527 5-10-4 .... ACCoyle(3) —
(M Mullineaux) *nt fluent: led to 1st: sn bhd: t.o whn p.u bef 3 out* **50/1**

3m 52.3s (4.70) **Going Correction** +0.125s/f (Yiel) **7** Ran SP% **108.4**
Speed ratings: **93,92,90,88,82 77,—** CSF £4.92 TOTE £2.00: £1.50, £2.20; EX 5.40.
Owner Cockbury Court Partnership **Bred** Gainsborough Stud Management Ltd **Trained** Portway, Worcs

FOCUS
This was slowly-run and produced a moderate winning time for the grade. The form is obviously suspect, but that said most of the principals ran to within 4lb of their pre-race marks.

NOTEBOOK
At Your Request, quickly supplementing his Fontwell win, cruised to the front at the final flight and won comfortably. He flashed his tail again but that is just him. *(op 11-8 tchd 13-8 in places)*
Pak Jack(FR) had not run over hurdles in this country before, but on his hurdling debut at Auteuil he divided a couple of useful sorts in Exotic Dancer and Meryl. He was readily picked off by the favourite after setting a slow pace but a true gallop should show him in a better light.
Nuit Sombre(IRE) lacked a change of gear off what had been a decidedly steady pace.
Jack's Lad(IRE), as at Cheltenham last month, was done no favours by the lack of a real gallop. *(op 11-2)*
Charlie Chapel is normally keen in front but this time he was held up in what was a slowly-run affair. *(tchd 25-1)*
Boytjie(IRE), a half-brother to Be My Destiny, should improve for this debut experience. *(op 20-1)*

176 WOOD BREWERY SILVER JUBILEE H'CAP CHASE (19 fncs) 3m
3:40 (3:40) (Class 4) (0-105,102) 5-Y-O+ **£6,662** (£2,050; £1,025; £512)

Form RPR
23P- **1** **Maxie McDonald (IRE)**[61] 4135 12-11-9 99.......... CLlewellyn 110+
(N A Twiston-Davies) *prom: lost pl 7th: mstke 14th: rallied appr 4 out: led jst after last: r.o: collapsed after r: dead* **10/1**
P0R- **2** *1/2* **Bramblehill Duke (IRE)**[23] 4792 13-10-12 88..........(b[1]) SThomas 98
(Miss Venetia Williams) *trckd ldrs: led appr 12th: rdn and hung rt fr 4 out: hit next: hdd jst after last: styd on* **16/1**
324- **3** *8* **Tudor King (IRE)**[173] 2156 11-10-7 83.......... JEMoore 86+
(J S King) *led to 4th: remained handy: mstke 14th: rdn whn chsng ldrs 4 out: styd on same pce* **12/1**
/3-P **4** *1/2* **Judaic Ways**[9] 6 11-11-3 93.......... RJohnson 97+
(H D Daly) *held up: hdwy 12th: hit 15th: 2nd whn blnd bdly 4 out: hit 3 out: one pce fr next* **11/2**[1]
354- **5** *3 1/2* **Channahrlie (IRE)**[11] 4955 11-11-1 91..........(p) DRDennis 89
(R Dickin) *in tch: hdwy 15th: rdn 4 out: wknd run-in* **11/2**[1]
055- **6** *3/4* **Jupon Vert (FR)**[18] 4855 8-11-12 102.......... TScudamore 99
(R J Hodges) *hld up: hdwy 12th: rdn appr 4 out: wknd run-in* **16/1**
531- **7** *11* **Kimoe Warrior**[18] 4853 7-10-2 81..........(b) ACCoyle(3) 71+
(M Mullineaux) *bhd: effrt appr 4 out: no imp* **6/1**[2]
33P- **P** **Midnight Gunner**[24] 4778 11-11-9 99.......... TDoyle —
(A E Price) *a towards rr: p.u bef 14th* **9/1**[3]
403- **P** **Khaladjistan (IRE)**[60] 4157 7-10-0 76 oh3..........(tp) MBatchelor —
(Miss S J Wilton) *bhd fr 3rd: t.o whn p.u bef 4 out* **12/1**
135- **P** **Doe Nal Rua (IRE)**[84] 3749 8-11-12 102.......... RGarritty —
(T D Easterby) *j.rt: midfield: wknd 15th: t.o whn p.u bef 4 out* **12/1**
0FF- **P** **Fearless Mel (IRE)**[10] 4976 11-10-13 96.......... PMerrigan(7) —
(Mrs H Dalton) *j. slowly 3rd: towards rr: t.o whn p.u bef 4 out* **14/1**
1FP- **P** **Themanfromcarlisle**[13] 4928 9-11-10 100.......... GLee —
(S H Shirley-Beavan) *midfield: lost pl 7th: sn bhd: p.u bef 14th* **11/1**
P3P- **P** **Auditor**[19] 4836 6-10-11 87..........(v[1]) PFlynn —
(S T Lewis) *prom: led 4th: clr whn mstke 6th: nt fluent 11th (water): hdd appr 12th and mstke: sn wknd: p.u bef next* **50/1**

6m 0.60s (-8.50) **Going Correction** -0.25s/f (Good) **13** Ran SP% **115.9**
Speed ratings: **104,103,101,101,99 99,95,—,—,— —,—,—** CSF £151.20 CT £1933.48 TOTE £9.70: £2.40, £7.60, £2.60; EX 153.20.
Owner Mrs J E Meek **Bred** Miss M R Crozier **Trained** Naunton, Gloucs

FOCUS
A strongly-run handicap which had a tragic conclusion.

NOTEBOOK
Maxie McDonald(IRE) put up probably the best performance of his career but sadly died a few minutes after the race.
Bramblehill Duke(IRE), blinkered for the first time having refused at Newton Abbot, hung markedly to his right when the pressure was on up the home straight and was caught soon after touching down over the last. Not the horse he was, he has plummeted down the weights and this was a better effort than he has been putting up of late.
Tudor King(IRE) was unable to dominate, but this was an encouraging return to the track after nearly six months' absence. Although he is currently 10lb higher than when last winning, he has won off this mark before.
Judaic Ways, 7lb lower than when last in handicap company, ran another decent race at his favourite track but was stopped in his tracks by a blunder at the fourth from home.
Channahrlie(IRE), 9lb lower than when last successful, was back over a more suitable trip but could only plug on at the same pace when coming under pressure in the straight.
Jupon Vert(FR) is edging down to a winning mark, but has yet to prove that he really stays three miles. *(op 12-1)*
Fearless Mel(IRE) *Official explanation: jockey said gelding hung right (op 12-1)*

177 MOORE SCOTT H'CAP HURDLE (9 hdls) 2m
4:10 (4:10) (Class 4) (0-105,105) 4-Y-O+ **£4,738** (£1,458; £729; £364)

Form RPR
030- **1** **Kentmere (IRE)**[175] 2105 4-11-0 97.......... TDoyle 99
(P R Webber) *midifeld: niggled along appr 5th: lost pl bef 4 out: rallied next: led run-in: r.o* **7/2**[1]
235- **2** *1/2* **Absolut Power (GER)**[66] 4060 4-11-8 105.......... SDurack 107
(J A Geake) *a.p: led appr 3 out: hdd run-in: r.o* **5/1**[2]
0P0- **3** *1 1/2* **Nesnaas (USA)**[163] 2367 4-10-0 83 oh1.......... GLee 83
(M G Rimell) *hld up: hdwy after 4 out: rdn whn chsng ldrs 2 out: nt qckn run-in* **15/2**[3]
400- **4** *7* **New Currency (USA)**[117] 3235 5-11-9 102.......... TScudamore 101+
(M C Pipe) *midfield: rdn and hdwy appr 3 out: blnd 2 out: eased whn btn run-in* **15/2**[3]
006- **5** *nk* **Stage Friendly (IRE)**[42] 4502 6-10-11 90.......... CLlewellyn 87
(N A Twiston-Davies) *prom: rdn and outpcd approaching 3 out: kpt on run-in* **16/1**
0P-1 **6** *2* **Little Rort (IRE)**[8] 25 6-10-12 91 7ex.......... PFlynn 90+
(S T Lewis) *led: rdn and hdd appr 3 out: blnd 2 out: sn wknd* **11/1**
00P- **7** *3* **Contas (GER)**[30] 4723 5-10-8 87..........(t) OMcPhail 79
(M F Harris) *hld up: hdwy after 4 out: wknd 2 out* **16/1**
5/0- **8** *1 1/4* **Gentle Beau**[16] 4890 7-11-12 105.......... RJohnson 99+
(P J Hobbs) *hld up: hdwy appr 3 out: blnd last: sn wknd* **15/2**[3]
303- **9** *16* **Wages**[50] 4378 5-10-8 94..........(p) WKennedy(7) 68
(A M Hales) *hld up: hdwy appr 4 out: wknd bef next* **9/1**
643- **10** *1 3/4* **Salinas (GER)**[6] 4890 6-11-5 98.......... BHitchcott 71
(M F Harris) *hld up in tch: hdwy appr 5th: wknd after 4 out* **12/1**
200- **11** *29* **Suspicious Minds**[21] 4813 4-10-2 85.......... SCurran 25
(J W Mullins) *midfield: rdn and wknd 4 out* **33/1**

3m 46.5s (-1.10) **Going Correction** +0.125s/f (Yiel)
WFA 4 from 5yo+ 4lb **11** Ran SP% **114.9**
Speed ratings: **107,106,106,102,102 101,99,99,91,90 75** CSF £21.13 CT £122.42 TOTE £3.40: £2.10, £1.70, £2.00; EX 21.40.
Owner D Allen **Bred** G And Mrs Middlebrook **Trained** Mollington, Oxon

FOCUS
This was run at a good pace and it should produce winners. Kentmere was stepping up slightly on his form in the autumn and the second and third were both showing big improvement.

NOTEBOOK
Kentmere(IRE), absent since November, was driven to assert near the line. He is going the right way and faster ground will suit him. *(tchd 4-1 in places)*
Absolut Power(GER) was back at two miles for his handicap debut. He did nothing wrong, but was just outgunned by an opponent to whom he was conceding 8lb. There should be a race for him. *(op 9-2 tchd 11-2)*
Nesnaas(USA), having his first run for over five months, was ridden to get the trip and this was a considerable improvement on his previous form. *(op 8-1 tchd 9-1)*
New Currency(USA), returning after four months off the course, looks to be coming back to the level of form he showed for Jim Bolger in Ireland. *(op 8-1 tchd 7-1)*
Stage Friendly(IRE), dropped back in trip after a run over an extended 2m 6f, found this too sharp.
Little Rort(IRE), still well handicapped on his old form despite the Towcester penalty, was collared going to the first flight in the home straight and a blunder at the next ended any chance he had. *(op 10-1)*

178 WELSH GUARDS ASSOCIATION NOVICES' HURDLE (11 hdls) 2m 5f
4:40 (4:41) (Class 4) 4-Y-0+ **£4,049** (£1,246; £623; £311)

Form RPR

5/5- **1** **Amicelli (GER)**[373] 4 6-11-0 109.. RJohnson 114+
(P J Hobbs) *trckd ldrs: led appr 4 out: clr 2 out: eased run-in* **7/4**[1]

23S- **2** *16* **Reasonably Sure (IRE)**[74] 3921 5-10-11 110...................... ONelmes(3) 90
(O Sherwood) *bhd: niggled along after 4 out: styd on fr 3 out: tk 2nd run-in: no ch w wnr* **11/2**[3]

06-5 **3** *1* **One Wild Night**[6] 58 5-10-0 .... WKennedy(7) 83+
(J L Spearing) *in tch: hdwy appr 4 out: ev ch bef next: sn rdn: btn whn mstke 2 out* **33/1**

444- **4** *10* **The Gangerman (IRE)**[24] 4775 5-11-0 .... CLlewellyn 79
(N A Twiston-Davies) *hld up: outpcd after 4 out: kpt on fr 3 out: nvr on terms* **11/1**

5- **5** *5* **Beet De Bob (IRE)**[23] 4797 7-10-7 .... MrPCowley(7) 75+
(Mrs S E Busby) *midfield: blnd 3rd: nt fluent 4th: mstke 4 out: n.d after* **20/1**

051- **6** *6* **Cantgeton (IRE)**[13] 4933 5-11-4 .... TJMalone(3) 82+
(M C Pipe) *hld up: hdwy whn nt fluent 6th: cl up appr 3 out: sn wknd* **7/2**[2]

00-P **7** *13* **Fenney Spring**[4] 111 5-10-7 69..(bt[1]) PMoloney 48
(W Jenks) *trckd ldrs tl rdn and wknd after 4 out* **100/1**

04- **8** *30* **Corton (IRE)**[13] 4933 6-11-0 .... MAFitzgerald 25
(Jonjo O'Neill) *prom: blnd 1st: wknd after 4 out: t.o* **10/1**

/3P- **9** *22* **Nick The Jewel**[332] 646 10-11-0 86.. JEMoore 3
(J S King) *led: hdd appr 4 out: wknd bef next: t.o* **25/1**

0- **P** **Middleton Kate**[19] 4841 5-10-7 .... PFlynn —
(John R Upson) *a bhd: t.o whn p.u bef 3 out* **66/1**

2/6- **P** **Maljimar (IRE)**[144] 2744 5-11-0 .... SThomas —
(Miss H C Knight) *a bhd: t.o whn p.u bef 3 out* **8/1**

5m 11.6s (-1.90) **Going Correction** +0.125s/f (Yiel) **11 Ran SP% 116.5**
Speed ratings: **108,101,101,97,95 93,88,77,68,—** — CSF £11.05 TOTE £2.60: £1.40, £2.30, £7.30; EX 17.00.
Owner Jack Joseph **Bred** Gestut Brummerhof **Trained** Withycombe, Somerset

FOCUS
An ordinary novice event in which the winner, the clear form pick, was value for 24l.

NOTEBOOK
Amicelli(GER), last seen in action just over a year back when with Charlie Mann, had little to beat but did it very comfortably. He looks capable of winning again. *(op 9-4 tchd 5-2)*
Reasonably Sure(IRE) stayed on over the last three flights but was never anywhere near the winner. He is a quirky sort but capable of better than this. *(op 4-1)*
One Wild Night, run out of second spot on the flat, showed more than on her recent hurdling debut and needs one more run for a handicap mark.
The Gangerman(IRE) was tackling his longest trip to date but could need three miles on this evidence. He now qualifies for handicaps. *(op 14-1)*
Beet De Bob(IRE) confirmed that he has ability but did not jump fluently. *(op 16-1)*
Cantgeton(IRE) was one of three to pull clear of the remainder on the long home turn but was *soon back-pedalling in the straight. It turned out that there was a valid excuse.Official explanation: jockey said gelding injured its knee (op 10-3 tchd 4-1)*
Corton(IRE) appeared not to stay. *(op 8-1)*

179 WOOD'S SHROPSHIRE LAD STANDARD OPEN NATIONAL HUNT FLAT RACE 2m
5:10 (5:10) (Class 6) 4-6-Y-0 **£2,604** (£744; £372)

Form RPR

1 **Unjust Law (IRE)** 4-10-9 .... MrTGreenall(3) 89+
(N J Henderson) *midfield: hdwy over 3f out: led ins fnl f: r.o* **11/2**[2]

2 *2* **Bally's Bro (IRE)** 6-10-9 .... SCrawford(7) 88
(N A Twiston-Davies) *led: rdn and hung lft over 1f out: hdd ins fnl f: nt qckn* **5/1**[1]

3 *3 ½* **Oscar's Delight** 4-10-5 .... CLlewellyn 73
(J L Spearing) *racd keenly: hld up: hdwy over 4f out: ev ch over 2f out: one pce fnl f* **5/1**[1]

00- **4** *5* **Show Of Hands (IRE)**[126] 3052 5-10-9 .... NCarter(7) 80+
(J G M O'Shea) *midfield: hdwy over 6f out: rdn over 2f out: wknd fnl f* **20/1**

0- **5** *2 ½* **Keen Royal**[74] 3925 4-10-5 .... BHitchcott 66
(Miss Suzy Smith) *chsd ldrs: ev ch over 2f out: wknd over 1f out* **33/1**

6 *1 ¾* **Glendara (IRE)** 4-10-12 .... SDurack 71
(Miss H C Knight) *midfield: hdwy over 3f out: ev ch over 2f out: wknd over 1f out* **13/2**[3]

7 *½* **Bynack Mhor (IRE)** 4-10-12 .... SThomas 70
(Miss H C Knight) *in tch tl rdn and wknd 3f out* **7/1**

0-0 **8** *shd* **The Langer (IRE)**[3] 138 5-11-2 .... PFlynn 74
(S T Lewis) *midfield: lost pl bef 1/2-way: kpt on u.p fr 3f out: n.d* **66/1**

00- **9** *6* **Cadtauri (FR)**[74] 3932 4-10-12 .... PMoloney 64
(Miss H C Knight) *hld up: effrt over 4f out: wknd 3f out* **25/1**

10 *9* **Mister Tibus (FR)** 4-10-12 .... MAFitzgerald 55
(J A Geake) *midfield: lost pl over 6f out: bhd after* **7/1**

11 *2* **Commanche Gun** 5-11-2 .... TDoyle 57
(A E Price) *racd keenly: prom tl rdn and wknd 4f out* **25/1**

- **12** *2 ½* **Woolfall Princess** 6-10-9 .... TScudamore 48
(G G Margarson) *in tch tl rdn and wknd over 4f out* **7/1**

13 *dist* **No Girls Allowed** 5-10-13 .... KJMercer(3) —
(D Shaw) *plld hrd: hld up: hdwy after 6f: hung lft and wknd over 5f out: t.o* **14/1**

3m 51.4s (4.40) **Going Correction** +0.125s/f (Yiel)
WFA 4 from 5yo+ 4lb **13 Ran SP% 123.1**
Speed ratings: **94,93,91,88,87 86,86,86,83,78 77,76,—** CSF £32.22 TOTE £7.70: £2.40, £2.90, £3.90; EX 40.50 Place 6 £38.09, Place 5 £34.60 .
Owner The Dover Street Boys **Bred** Simon And Helen Plumbly **Trained** Upper Lambourn, Berks

FOCUS
A poor bumper, rated through the modest fourth.

NOTEBOOK
Unjust Law(IRE), whose dam was a winning two-year-old over five furlongs and also won a juvenile hurdle, is not very big, but he has ability and ran out a comfortable winner. This was a pretty modest event, though. *(op 5-1)*
Bally's Bro(IRE) is a brother to Ballynabragget, a decent chaser for the Twiston-Davies yard. Somewhat green for this debut, he held off all but one of his rivals and he should improve for the experience.
Oscar's Delight is out of a mare who was a fair hurdler at around two and a half miles for the Spearing yard. She evidently has ability and should make her mark in due course. *(tchd 11-2)*
Show Of Hands(IRE) showed much more than on his two previous attempts.
Keen Royal was well beaten on her debut at Fakenham in February but was a good deal sharper here. *(tchd 40-1)*
Glendara(IRE), a half-brother to an Irish Flat winner, did the best of the three Knight runners. *Slightly short of room inside the final two furlongs, he is entitled to come on for the outing. (op 10-1)*
Commanche Gun, out of a half-sister to 1982 Grand National winner Grittar, is quite a rangy individual who is going to need time.
T/Plt: £69.50 to a £1 stake. Pool: £29,301.05. 307.60 winning tickets. T/Qpdt: £51.40 to a £1 stake. Pool: £1,792.60. 25.80 winning tickets. DO

FAKENHAM (L-H)
Wednesday, May 4

OFFICIAL GOING: Good (good to soft in places)
Wind: blustery, various Weather: overcast, rain at times

180 FAKENHAM RACECOURSE FOR EQUESTRIAN HOLIDAYS (S) HURDLE (9 hdls) 2m
2:20 (2:20) (Class 5) 4-Y-0+ **£2,660** (£760; £380)

Form RPR

04- **1** **Lawaaheb (IRE)**[23] 2443 4-10-8 ....(v) MAFitzgerald 89+
(B R Johnson) *led bef 3rd: mstke 2 out: 4l clr bef last: drvn out* **11/4**[1]

56-4 **2** *3 ½* **Approaching Land (IRE)**[10] 11 10-10-9 83.................. MrTGreenall(3) 86
(M W Easterby) *handy: chsd wnr fr 3 out: rdn and nt fluenmt next: no imp after* **10/3**[3]

066- **3** *11* **Lazy Lena (IRE)**[11] 4975 6-10-5 83.. NPMulholland 71+
(Miss L C Siddall) *chsd ldrs: 5th and rdn 3 out: wnt 3rd and mstke next: no imp after* **10/1**

50-P **4** *3* **Red Nose Lady**[5] 96 8-11-5 95..(b) JMogford 80+
(G J Smith) *t.k.h: prom: chsd wnr 5th tl drvn 3 out: sn fnd little* **12/1**

00-6 **5** *16* **Prince Valentine**[5] 102 4-10-8 85..(bt) PHide 52
(D B Feek) *cl up: rdn whn mstke 6th: 3rd briefly 3 out: sn fdd tamely* **22/1**

050- **6** *2* **Domart (POL)**[37] 4613 5-10-12 84.. SDurack 54
(M Pitman) *led tl bef 3rd: pressed ldrs tl 3 out: drvn and sn fdd* **3/1**[2]

0- **7** *3* **Parisi Princess**[19] 4852 4-9-8 .... CMStudd(7) 40
(D L Williams) *j. poorly in last: no ch fr 6th* **25/1**

P40- **8** *½* **Royal Exposure (IRE)**[56] 4257 8-10-12 74.. JPByrne 51
(H Alexander) *towards rr: lost tch after 6th* **16/1**

5-PR **9** *6* **Seemore Sunshine**[4] 135 8-10-12 .... SCurran 45
(M J Gingell) *a bhd: lost tch bdly after 6th* **66/1**

P0-0 **10** *13* **Major Belle (FR)**[4] 134 6-10-9 81.. CareyWilliamson(10) 39
(M J Gingell) *sn towards rr: struggling 6th: t.o* **40/1**

0- **P** **Komena**[15] 2103 7-10-5 .... ATinkler —
(J W Payne) *plld hrd: chsd ldrs tl 5th: t.o and p.u last* **40/1**

00- **P** **Marylou Day (IRE)**[60] 4172 6-10-5 .... JEMoore —
(O Brennan) *bhd: rdn and labouring after 5th: t.o and p.u 3 out* **33/1**

03-0 **P** **Mersey Mirage**[6] 75 8-10-9 65..(b) LMcGrath(3) —
(R C Guest) *midfield whn blnd bdly 4th: stugging 6th: t.o and p.u 3 out* **14/1**

P- **P** **Belisco (USA)**[11] 4978 4-10-3 ow2..(t) MrMatthewSmith(7) —
(C A Dwyer) *dropped bk last and rdn after 5th: tailed moff and p.u 3 out* **40/1**

3m 58.9s (-4.10) **Going Correction** -0.15s/f (Good)
WFA 4 from 5yo+ 4lb **14 Ran SP% 124.0**
Speed ratings: **104,102,96,95,87 86,84,84,81,75 —,—,—,—** CSF £11.88 TOTE £3.80: £2.00, £1.20, £3.10; EX 13.60.The winner was bought in for 8,400gns.
Owner C Lefevre **Bred** Shadwell Estate Company Limited **Trained** Ashtead, Surrey

FOCUS
A very moderate race but a creditable winning time for a seller and the second sets the level for the form.

NOTEBOOK
Lawaaheb(IRE), who was a fourth to La Lambertine in a seller at Taunton back in November, scooted up despite ploughing through the second last. This was a poor race but he should remain equally effective in similar company and connections were forced to go to 8,400 gns to retain him. *He will now have a break and come back after the summer to continue as a dual-purpose horse. (tchd 5-2, 3-1 in places)*
Approaching Land(IRE) had appeared to find two miles on the sharp side when tried over it before. Travelling nicely throughout, he crept into contention approaching three out, but could never reel in the leader. A step-up in trip will suit him better. *(op 5-1)*
Lazy Lena(IRE), who had shown only a modicum of promise in her previous races, kept on very slowly to get a place and being under pressure from a long way out. She will struggle to find a race but a step-up in trip might help. *(op 15-2)*
Red Nose Lady had the blinkers refitted after trying cheekpieces last time. They had little effect and she only plodded on at one pace. *(op 8-1)*
Prince Valentine travelled kindly for a long way but was a spent force approaching the second last. He does not seem to get home over hurdles. *(op 20-1 tchd 25-1)*
Domart(POL) has been really disappointing since coming over from Poland. After racing up with the pace early, he dropped out of contention very quickly and looks as though he will be very hard to place. *(tchd 11-4 and 10-3)*
Belisco(USA) *Official explanation: jockey said gelding was unsuited by good, good to soft ground (op 33-1)*
Marylou Day(IRE) *Official explanation: trainer said mare bled (op 33-1)*

181 REMEMBER TO VOTE-OK H'CAP CHASE (16 fncs) 2m 5f 110y
2:50 (2:50) (Class 4) (0-90,89) 5-Y-0+ **£5,213** (£1,604; £802; £401)

Form RPR

30P- **1** **Make It Easy (IRE)**[18] 9-9-7 **63** oh2.. MissLHorner(7) 73+
(D L Williams) *hld up towards rr: stdy prog 10th: j. slowly 12th: sustained run after 2 out: chal last: pushed ahd fnl stride* **9/2**[1]

304- **2** *hd* **Tirley Storm**[38] 4581 10-10-11 **74**.. WMarston 85+
(J S Smith) *midfield whn j.v.slowly 5th: hdwy 11th: led bef 13th: bad blunder 2 out: hrd pressed last: drvn and jst ct* **10/1**

563- **3** *½* **New Perk (IRE)**[37] 4606 7-10-3 **66**.. SCurran 74+
(M J Gingell) *j.rt 1st: hdwy 8th: wnt 2nd bef 12th: lft w ldr 2 out: rdn and ev ch last: no ex cl home* **11/2**[3]

665- **4** *1* **Nosam**[263] 1176 15-11-9 **89**..(t) LMcGrath(3) 97+
(R C Guest) *hld up and bhd: stdy prog 12th: rdn in cl 4th whn nt fluent last: no imp after* **33/1**

0P2- **5** *10* **Backscratcher**[24] 4798 11-9-13 **67**..(b) MNicolls(5) 66+
(John R Upson) *pressed ldrs: blnd 7th: u.p 3 out: wknd bef next* **10/1**

12-2 **6** *12* **Miss Wizadora**[4] 132 10-11-5 **82**.. MAFitzgerald 66
(Simon Earle) *hit 3rd: trckd ldrs: wnt prom 9th: led bef 12th tl bef next: wknd qckly after 3 out* **5/1**[2]

/0P- **7** *shd* **Cromwell (IRE)**[11] 4980 10-10-3 **73**..(b) CMStudd(7) 57
(M C Chapman) *pressed ldrs: rdn 11th: struggling 13th* **40/1**

6P4- **8** *1 ½* **West Coaster (IRE)**[11] 4976 7-11-3 **83**.. MrTGreenall(3) 66
(M W Easterby) *chsd ldr after 2nd: mstke 8th: drvn and demoted after 9th: n.d fr 11th* **8/1**

315- **9** *1 ¼* **Tiger Talk**[29] 4737 9-11-5 **82**..(b) HOliver 64
(R C Guest) *nt a fluent: nvr bttr than midfield: no ch fr 11th* **6/1**

P00- **P** **Win Alot**[31] 4716 7-10-12 **78** ACCoyle(3) —
(M C Chapman) *mstke 2nd: last and rdn 8th: t.o and p.u 12th* **40/1**

326- **P** **Hatsnall**[77] 3880 7-11-3 **80** ARoss —
(Miss C J E Caroe) *hehind: reminders 7th: lost tch 11th: t.o and p.u 13th* **10/1**

1P0- **P** **Hisar (IRE)**[15] 4919 12-10-5 **68** (t) AThornton —
(P C Ritchens) *led after 2nd tl bef 12th: dropped out rapidly: p.u 3 out* **25/1**

545- **P** **Coral Island**[51] 4365 11-11-5 **82** RJohnson —
(R M Stronge) *led tl after 2nd: prom tl lost pl 9th: t.o and p.u 11th* **20/1**

5m 36.2s (2.23) **Going Correction** +0.10s/f (Yiel) **13** Ran SP% **119.3**
Speed ratings: **99,98,98,98,94 90,90,90,89,— —,—,—** CSF £45.49 CT £254.36 TOTE £5.30: £2.00, £2.70, £3.20; EX 62.10.
Owner Miss L Horner **Bred** E Mortell **Trained** Shefford, Berks

FOCUS
A poor race but a good debut by multiple winning pointer Make It Easy, who will be even more effective over slightly further. The form is not strong.

NOTEBOOK
Make It Easy(IRE) won five from five in Welsh points and was sold to current connections after winning his last race by a wide margin. There is definitely room for improvement in the jumping department but is obviously well handicapped after his spell between the flags and looks sure to win more races off his current mark. *(op 11-2 tchd 4-1)*
Tirley Storm has run his best races on a sound surface and was handicapped to go fairly close. He had a good record over the course prior to the race - two wins and a second from three runs - and the win column could have been improved had he not made two really bad jumping errors. That said, he ran a fine race and should find compensation soon.
New Perk(IRE) momentarily looked like breaking his maiden when he was virtually given the lead two out. He may need producing very late as when he hit the front he looks to idle. *(op 6-1)*
Nosam belied his years by running a fair race on his return to the track. A mistake at the last ended his chances but it was a good effort all the same. *(op 25-1)*
Backscratcher was to the fore before clouting a fence hard, and dropped away quickly when the pressure was applied. This was slightly disappointing given his improved effort at Worcester last time. *(op 15-2)*
Miss Wizadora raced close to the pace but dropped out quickly when headed. The rise in weights since her fortunate win keeps anchoring her. *(op 4-1)*
Tiger Talk looks to have lost his way recently. *(op 7-1)*

182 SIS NOVICES' HURDLE (13 hdls) 2m 7f 110y
3:25 (3:25) (Class 3) 4-Y-0+ **£5,382** (£1,656; £828; £414)

Form RPR

343- **1** **Common Girl (IRE)**[21] 4820 7-10-7 105 JEMoore 106+
(O Brennan) *settled last tl effrt after 8th: led 3 out: sn rdn clr: in n.d fr next: eased flat* **8/11**[1]

416- **2** *24* **Middleham Park (IRE)**[18] 4866 5-11-3 106 RYoung(3) 103+
(J W Mullins) *mostly 2nd tl led bef 3 out where jnd and blnd: btn whn mstke next* **9/4**[2]

600- **3** *20* **King's Mountain (USA)**[19] 5-10-7 67 SWalsh(7) 61
(R M Stronge) *set slow pce: niggled along fr 6th: drvn and hdd bef 3 out: sn lost interest and continued wl bhd ldng pair* **50/1**

06/ **4** *14* **Simon's Seat (USA)**[26] 4051 6-11-0 SDurack 47
(P Howling) *in tch tl rdn 9th: labouring bdly bef 3 out: drvn out to hold remote 4th* **8/1**[3]

0 **5** *1 1/4* **Madhahir (IRE)**[10] 11 5-11-0 81 SCurran 46
(M J Gingell) *wnt 2nd after 5th tl rdn 8th: nvr gng wl after: t.o bef 3 out: drvn out in vain attempt to seize 4th* **50/1**

20-4 **R** **Fille Detente**[9] 23 5-10-7 77 (b1) WMarston —
(Mrs P Sly) *ref to r* **12/1**

6m 8.90s (21.10) **Going Correction** -0.15s/f (Good) **6** Ran SP% **111.4**
Speed ratings: **58,50,43,38,38** — CSF £2.65 TOTE £1.60: £1.10, £1.50; EX 2.70.
Owner J W Hardy **Bred** Nicholas Keogh **Trained** Worksop, Notts

FOCUS
A moderate contest run in a painfully slow time, even for a race like this.

NOTEBOOK
Common Girl(IRE) has run well in the past without ever getting her head in front. Her effort last time at Cheltenham under professional handling was probably her best, and she made little fuss of winning after her only serious rival made a bad blunder three flights from home. She does not look to be anything special and might go chasing in the near future. *(op 10-11)*
Middleham Park(IRE) was going better than the eventual winner when crashing through the third last. That ended his challenge and he came home in his own time. He was dismounted after the line, but was reportedly merely winded after his blunder and in need of oxygen. Though probably still in reasonable form, this was a very poor race. *(op 2-1 tchd 5-2)*
King's Mountain(USA) was the early pace setter - at a very slow pace - but was readily passed and dropped as the principals started the last circuit. *(op 33-1)*
Simon's Seat(USA) never got into the race and was very disappointing. He had been in a bit of form on the All-Weather over the winter so it does not bode well for his future over timber. *(op 15-2 tchd 9-1)*
Madhahir(IRE) has a fantastic pedigree but no ability. *(op 25-1)*
Fille Detente stood still as the tapes rose and decided to take no part. *(tchd 10-1)*

183 GG.COM NOVICES' CHASE (18 fncs) 3m 110y
4:00 (4:00) (Class 3) 5-Y-0+ **£5,980** (£1,840; £920; £460)

Form RPR

01F- **1** **Kelly (SAF)**[20] 4836 8-11-6 107 SThomas 115
(Miss Venetia Williams) *led tl 2nd: trckd ldrs: drew clr chsng rival after 15th: looked hld bef last where lft w ch and sn drvn ahd: kpt on* **7/2**[3]

F1F- **2** *3/4* **Harry Collins**[20] 4836 7-11-1 103 CHonour(5) 115+
(B I Case) *racd enthusiastically: settled trcking ldrs: led 13th: 2l clr bef last where pckd and lost momentum and hdd: nt rcvr* **2/1**[1]

P13- **3** *dist* **Tipp Top (IRE)**[15] 4919 8-11-6 89 (t) JPMcNamara 80
(O Brennan) *prom: jnd ldr briefly 13th: rdn 15th: lost tch qckly next: btn 41l* **13/2**

110- **4** *14* **Jesper (FR)**[21] 4825 8-11-0 101 (t) RJohnson 67
(R T Phillips) *hld up: mstke 6th: hdwy to 2nd 10th tl 12th and briefly 15th: wknd and mstke 3 out: btn 55l* **6/1**

P5P- **P** **Tails I Win**[276] 1089 6-11-0 SFox —
(Miss C J E Caroe) *bhd: hit 10th and 11th: lost tch and mstke 14th: t.o and p.u 2 out* **50/1**

F5-P **P** **Proper Poser (IRE)**[10] 2 9-10-11 72 ACCoyle(3) —
(M C Chapman) *towards rr: last and u.p 11th: sn lost tch: t.o whn nrly fell 15th and p.u* **100/1**

/P4- **P** **Go White Lightning (IRE)**[48] 4411 10-11-0 110 MBatchelor —
(M Bradstock) *led 2nd: mstke 9th and hdd briefly: hdd again 13th: blnd next and fdd rapidly: t.o and p.u last* **11/4**[2]

6m 26.8s (-1.20) **Going Correction** +0.10s/f (Yiel) **7** Ran SP% **112.8**
Speed ratings: **105,104,—,—,— —,—** CSF £11.13 TOTE £3.60: £2.40, £1.20; EX 15.30.
Owner P A Deal **Bred** Litchfield Stud **Trained** Kings Caple, H'fords

FOCUS
A fair novices' chase for the track producing a close finish, with the first two close to their marks.

NOTEBOOK
Kelly(SAF) landed the spoils after a last-fence mishap by his closest rival. He has the scope to make a better chaser than a hurdler and may well take in more races during the summer. *(op 3-1)*
Harry Collins continues to have a few problems with jumping, and can be counted unlucky not to have taken the prize. He has plenty of ability and is sure to win more races when the jumping becomes more consistent. *(op 5-2 tchd 11-4)*
Tipp Top(IRE) has plenty of chasing experience but was rated well below the principals on official ratings. He ran as well as could have been expected but will need to come up against rivals of his own ability to be fully effective. *(op 8-1 tchd 17-2)*
Jesper(FR) made a few mistakes on his chasing debut and could never get into contention. He was well beaten but should be wiser for the outing. *(tchd 13-2)*
Go White Lightning(IRE) was probably feeling the effects of his good run at the Cheltenham Festival as he was beaten very early in the race. Even though his early wins were over sharp courses, a more galloping track might suit him much better now. *(op 9-4 tchd 3-1)*

184 ELDRED WILSON MEMORIAL FOX HUNTERS' CHASE (FOR THE ESSANDEM TROPHY) (18 fncs) 3m 110y
4:35 (4:36) (Class 6) 5-Y-0+ **£2,226** (£636; £318)

Form RPR

6-6 **1** **Sikander A Azam**[7] 47 12-12-4 MrTGreenall 116+
(David M Easterby) *hld up on ins: clsd 12th: lft 2nd at 15th: led after 2 out: sn rdn clr* **11/4**[1]

F/4- **2** *6* **Derrintogher Yank (IRE)**[18] 11-11-9 MrDMansell(3) 105+
(Miss R S Reynolds) *chsd ldr and clr of rest: led 6th: clr again w two rivals after 15th: hdd after two out: kpt on same pce u.p* **5/1**[3]

234- **3** *19* **Upham Lord (IRE)**[11] 4980 12-11-13 99 MrGBrewer(5) 91
(P Beaumont) *j. indifferently: led tl 6th: pressed ldr tl after 14th: wknd qckly after 3 out* **7/2**[2]

5/3- **4** *3 1/2* **Bush Hill Bandit (IRE)**[10] 10-11-5 MissLAllan(7) 82
(Mrs Anne-Marie Hays) *sn chsng pair who were 15l clr: clsd 12th: drvn and wknd after 14th* **5/1**[3]

P4P/ **5** *28* **Ain Tecbalet (FR)**[10] 7-11-5 MrGGreenock(7) 54
(N M Bloom) *stdd in rr: clsd briefly 12th: pushed along and lost tch 14th: t.o* **13/2**

0P-P **6** *3* **Good Bone (FR)**[10] 6 8-12-1 88 MrRhysHughes(7) 61
(S Flook) *bhd: effrt to midfield 13th: rdn and j. slowly next: lost tch qckly: t.o* **33/1**

/30- **U** **Tirley Gale**[24] 13-11-5 64 MrGTumelty(7) —
(Mrs N D Smith) *w.r.s and uns rdr* **50/1**

PP3/ **P** **Militaire (FR)**[18] 7-11-7 (t) MrJOwen(5) —
(J M Turner) *towards rr: drvn 11th: nt keen after: sn lost tch: t.o and p.u 3 out* **33/1**

P3P- **F** **Montys Tag (IRE)**[10] 12-11-5 MrMMackley(7) —
(S R Andrews) *hld up off pce in midfield: clsd 12th: wnt 1l 2nd and fell 15th* **14/1**

P24/ **P** **Straight On (IRE)**[10] 14-11-5 MrsSHodge(7) —
(A H B Hodge) *towards rr: nt fluent 5th: pckd 6th and lost tch: t.o and p.u 10th* **66/1**

P/P- **P** **Tubber Roads (IRE)**[11] 12-11-5 105 MrJJarrett(7) —
(M G Hazell) *chsd clr ldng pair early: rdn fr 5th: lost tch u.p 11th: t.o and p.u 3 out* **12/1**

6m 28.7s (0.70) **Going Correction** +0.10s/f (Yiel) **11** Ran SP% **119.3**
Speed ratings: **102,100,94,92,83 82,—,—,—,— —** CSF £17.16 TOTE £3.00: £1.30, £1.60, £1.10; EX 25.70.
Owner The Grand National Racing Club Limited **Bred** Miss H Day **Trained** Sheriff Hutton, N Yorks

FOCUS
A fair hunter chase run at a sound pace. The winner is classy on his day and returned to his best form to win with plenty in hand and could be rated higher.

NOTEBOOK
Sikander A Azam returned to the track at Cheltenham last week, after a short break, which put him right for this race. The extra distance suited him well and it would be no surprise to see him out again at Stratford for the Champion Hunters' Chase on May 21st given his light campaign to date and the prize money on offer. *(tchd 3-1)*
Derrintogher Yank(IRE) made all of the running at a good pace until being passed by the classy winner. He has had his problems with jumping in the past but he showed no signs. There is a hunters' chase at Market Rasen on May 15th which would suit him very well. *(tchd 9-2 and 11-2)*
Upham Lord(IRE) managed to lay up with the early pace, but found those exertions taking their toll as the race took shape. It is fair to say he is slightly on the downgrade now after his illustrious past, but he can still hold his own and will no doubt win another race before retiring. *(op 4-1)*
Bush Hill Bandit(IRE) had won a couple of ladies races under the experienced Alex Embiricos recently but never got into contention back in the hunter chase sphere. *(op 7-1)*
Ain Tecbalet(FR), who was once under the care of Nicky Henderson, was held-up in rear and never closed down the leaders. In all probability, he was found out in this class. *(op 7-1)*
Tirley Gale gave his rider the ignominy of coming off even before they jumped the first fence. *(op 11-1 tchd 14-1)*
Tubber Roads(IRE) usually has it all his own way in the lead in points, but was never quick enough to establish himself in front and may have sulked as a result as he was beaten a long way from home. *(op 11-1 tchd 14-1)*
Montys Tag(IRE) was still going well when coming to grief. It was too far out to know exactly how he would have fared had he stayed on his feet. He won the Champion Novices' Hunters' Chase at Stratford in the past so it would be no surprise to see him back at that meeting for the big one if he is alright after his fall. *(op 11-1 tchd 14-1)*

185 REMEMBER TO VOTE-OK MARES' ONLY H'CAP HURDLE (11 hdls) 2m 4f
5:05 (5:06) (Class 4) (0-95,94) 4-Y-0+ **£3,753** (£1,155; £577; £288)

Form RPR

505- **1** **Red Dahlia**[37] 4618 8-10-10 **75** ATinkler 82+
(M Pitman) *hld up: hdwy bef 3 out: drvn next: jnd ldng pair last: edgd clr flat* **8/1**

000- **2** *1 1/4* **Marathea (FR)**[69] 4029 4-9-9 **70** LTreadwell(5) 70
(Miss Venetia Williams) *trckd ldrs: chal 3 out: led bef next: drvn and jnd last: fin weakly* **11/2**[3]

553- **3** *6* **Nod's Star**[15] 4660 4-10-13 **83** (t) LAspell 79+
(Mrs L C Jewell) *settled in last trio: clsd 3 out: wnt 4th and tried to chal bef last: hung lft and sn btn* **7/1**

244- **4** *10* **Upright Ima**[24] 4797 6-10-13 **78** PMoloney 67
(Mrs P Sly) *t.k.h and prom: ev ch 3 out: drvn bef next: no rspnse and sn btn* **5/2**[1]

01-3 **5** *21* **Rose Of York (IRE)**[9] 25 5-10-2 **74** (t) DLaverty(7) 48+
(Mrs A M Thorpe) *cl up: mstke 6th: ev ch whn blnd 3 out: nt rcvr* **4/1**[2]

F10- **6** *2 1/2* **What's A Filly**[98] 3539 5-11-9 **91** LMcGrath(3) 56
(R C Guest) *cl up: led 3 out: rdn and hdd bef next: sn wknd* **8/1**

0/0- **7** *10* **Cash Return**[15] [4920] 6-10-4 **69** JEMoore 24
(Mrs S Lamyman) *led: drvn bef 8th: headed bef next where hmpd whn fading rapidly: t.o* **66/1**

060- **8** *9* **Hilarious (IRE)**[22] [4813] 5-11-4 **86** RWalford(3) 32
(Dr J R J Naylor) *cl up: lost pl and pckd 7th: struggling next: t.o* **20/1**

000- **P** **Land Of Nod (IRE)**[19] [4852] 4-9-7 **70** oh1 RLucey-Butler(7) —
(G Brown) *last trio: rdn 6th: wknd next: t.o and p.u last* **40/1**

000- **P** **Three Times A Lady**[218] [1540] 5-10-2 **70** ONelmes(3) —
(D W Thompson) *last trio: rdn 5th and nvr gng wl after: t.o and p.u 2 out* **50/1**

264- **F** **Festive Chimes (IRE)**[13] [4936] 4-11-3 **94** SWalsh(7) 94
(N B King) *hld up: effrt whn mstke 8th: rallied after next: jnd ldng pair and fell last* **9/1**

5m 7.00s (6.30) **Going Correction** -0.15s/f (Good)
WFA 4 from 5yo+ 5lb **11** Ran SP% **119.3**
Speed ratings: **81,80,78,74,65 64,60,57,—,—** — CSF £51.41 CT £329.75 TOTE £10.70: £3.30, £1.90, £1.80; EX 55.70 Place 6 £16.23, Place 5 £10.27.
Owner John Goodman **Bred** T G And Mrs Bish **Trained** Upper Lambourn, Berks
■ Stewards' Enquiry : P Moloney one-day ban: careless riding (May 15)

FOCUS
A poor fillies' event and a very slow time indeed for the grade.

NOTEBOOK
Red Dahlia was only slightly higher than her only winning mark, in a seller, and did enough after the last to gain her second success. She clearly is of limited ability and will probably be hard to place. *(op 9-1 tchd 10-1)*
Marathea(FR) ◆ had a very attractive handicap mark coming into the race and looked the most likely winner in the latter stages of the race. However, she did not get home quite as well as the winner when joined, and may have just needed it after a short break. Twice a winner on the Flat in France, it would be surprising if current connections could not find a suitable opening for her off her lowly rating. *(op 6-1 tchd 5-1)*
Nod's Star made a dash for glory after the second last that never quite took her into the lead. This was a fair effort but it will need to be a weak race for her to get her head in front. *(op 13-2)*
Upright Ima took a strong hold early and found very little when asked for an effort. She would probably be slightly better on a quicker surface. *(op 3-1)*
Rose Of York(IRE) moved into the race nicely before clattering into the third-last and ending her chance. This was the second race in a row she has made a serious jumping error. *(op 9-2)*
Cash Return *Official explanation: trainer said mare lost a front shoe (op 50-1)*
Hilarious(IRE) *Official explanation: trainer said mare suffered interference in running (op 12-1)*
Festive Chimes(IRE) had every chance when falling at the last fence. She has enough ability to win a race although she remains a maiden under both codes. *(tchd 12-1)*
T/Plt: £32.50 to a £1 stake. Pool: £35,225.65. 790.85 winning tickets. T/Qpdt: £6.90 to a 31 stake. Pool: £2,313.90. 246.10 winning tickets. IM

NEWTON ABBOT (L-H)
Thursday, May 5
186 Meeting Abandoned - Waterlogged

[8]WETHERBY (L-H)
Thursday, May 5

OFFICIAL GOING: Good
The ground was reckoned to be a bit quicker than the official version.
Wind: Blustery, half behind. Weather: Fine and sunny bit windy.

192 NIDD VALE WETHERBY CONDITIONAL JOCKEYS' NOVICES' HURDLE (9 hdls) 2m
5:50 (5:52) (Class 4) 4-Y-O+ **£3,766** (£1,076; £538)

Form RPR

23-1 **1** **Mr Mischief**[10] [21] 5-11-2 PMerrigan(5) 104+
(P C Haslam) *hld up in midfield: gd hdwy on outer appr 3 out: effrt next: rdn and qcknd to ld flat: styd on wl* **7/2**[2]

230- **2** *2 ½* **Magico (NZ)**[99] [3542] 7-10-11 102 PCO'Neill(3) 94
(R C Guest) *a trcking ldrs: hdwy 3 out: led next: rdn appr last: hdd flat and nt qckn* **2/1**[1]

0U5- **3** *4* **Sterling Guarantee (USA)**[32] [4714] 7-10-11 91 CDSharkey(3) 91+
(N Wilson) *hld up towards rr: hdwy 3 out: rdn along next: styng on whn hmpd last: kpt on flat* **50/1**

3-4 **4** *hd* **Snow's Ride**[11] [14] 5-11-0 NPMulholland 92+
(M D Hammond) *a promient: effrt and lft in ld 3 out: rdn and hdd next: drvn and hld whn hmpd last: drvn and one pce flat* **16/1**

5 *½* **Sarin**[598] 7-10-11 SThomas(3) 89
(Miss Venetia Williams) *in tch on outer: hdwy 3 out: rdn along next and kpt on same pce last* **6/1**

364- **6** *nk* **Humid Climate**[18] [4883] 5-11-0 104 KJMercer 89
(R A Fahey) *in tch: hdwy appr 3 out: rdn along next and sn btn* **4/1**[3]

PP0- **7** *5* **Diamond Vein**[5] [4261] 6-10-9 83 MrJEClare(5) 84
(S P Griffiths) *bhd: sme hdwy 3 out: sn rdn along and nvr a factor* **100/1**

8 *1* **Staff Nurse (IRE)**[14] 5-10-7 JamesDavies 76
(R Johnson) *bhd: mstke 4th: styd on fr 3 out: nvr a factor* **33/1**

000- **9** *3* **Dumfries**[22] [4826] 4-10-5 91 BWharfe(5) 76
(T H Caldwell) *in tch: hdwy on outer and cl up 3rd: rdn along appr 3 out: wknd appr next* **50/1**

4PP- **10** *5* **Martin House (IRE)**[38] [4611] 6-11-0 85 ONelmes 75
(D W Thompson) *in tch: pushed along and outpcd 4 out: bhd after* **50/1**

540- **11** *3* **Agnese**[118] [3256] 5-10-7 87 (p) TJPhelan 69+
(G M Moore) *cl up: rdn along fter 4 out: sn wknd* **33/1**

12 *3* **Penteli**[126] 5-10-7 PJBrennan 62
(C Grant) *a rr* **100/1**

040- **13** *8* **My Good Lord (IRE)**[16] [4922] 6-11-0 ATinkler 61
(B D Leavy) *bhd fr 1/2-way* **50/1**

14 *2 ½* **Messager (FR)**[367] 5-10-9 SWalsh(5) 59
(J A Supple) *a rr* **80/1**

000- **15** *hd* **Teeswater**[61] [4191] 5-10-11 StephenJCraine(3) 58
(Mrs P Sly) *in tch on inner: pushed along appr 4 out: sn wknd* **50/1**

00P- **16** *dist* **Spes Bona (USA)**[65] [4110] 4-10-7 DCCostello(3) —
(G M Moore) *chsd ldrs: mstke 3rd: rdn along appr 4 out: sn wknd* **66/1**

P **F** **Antigone's Fire**[11] [14] 6-10-7 GBerridge —
(P D Niven) *a rr: wl bhd whn fell 3 out* **100/1**

000- **R** **Ballinruane (IRE)**[79] [3865] 6-10-11 64 PAspell(3) —
(B S Rothwell) *led: rdn along 4 out: rn out next* **100/1**

243- **F** **Best Flight**[8] [4085] 5-11-0 105 PRobson 91
(N Wilson) *midfield: stdy hdwy 3 out: rdn to chal after next and ev ch whn fell last* **14/1**

600- **P** **High Window (IRE)**[112] [3332] 5-10-11 WKennedy(3) —
(S Gollings) *chsd ldrs on inner: rdn along and wknd 4 out: bhd whn hmpd next and p.u after* **80/1**

3m 56.5s (-0.70) **Going Correction** -0.025s/f (Good)
WFA 4 from 5yo+ 4lb **20** Ran SP% **125.5**
Speed ratings: **100,98,96,96,96 96,93,93,91,89 87,86,82,81,80** —,—,—,—,— CSF £10.63 TOTE £4.50: £1.80, £1.70, £13.90; EX 9.20.
Owner Middleham Park Racing I & Mrs C Barclay **Bred** Mrs Maureen Barbara Walsh **Trained** Middleham Moor, N Yorks

FOCUS
A moderate event run at just a steady gallop, but in the end the first two came clear and the race could be rated higher.

NOTEBOOK
Mr Mischief, given a very confident ride by his up-and-coming young rider, tended to hang left when called on for an effort but in the end he ran out a most decisive winner. He can turn out without a penalty at Ludlow next week. *(op 3-1)*
Magico(NZ), rested since January, travelled strongly but in the end could not match the winner for pace. *(op 9-4 tchd 15-8, 5-2 in a place)*
Sterling Guarantee(USA), beaten in a seller last time, deserves credit for the way he stuck on after being hampered when his stablemate came to grief at the final flight. He was almost certainly flattered by the way the race was run.
Snow's Ride, dropping back in trip, stayed on in his own time over the final three flights and was making no impression whatsoever when becoming entangled at the last. *(op 12-1)*
Sarin, rated 78 on the Flat, was last seen out in September 2003. A positive on the exchanges, he took a keen grip and was kept wide. Forced to check when the leader ran out three out, he then tended to hang left but then stayed on all the way to the line. This will have blown away the cobwebs and he would not need to improve much to find a race. *(op 5-1)*
Humid Climate did well to keep going all the way to the finish considering he took a fierce hold in mid-field. *(op 7-1)*
Best Flight travelled strongly on his return to this game but looked held when crashing out at the last. He rose to his feet only to be knocked clean over again. He may take time to get over this unhappy experience.
Ballinruane(IRE) was one one rein throughout and eventually ran out to the right at the third last flight.

193 CAR-BOOT SALE HERE EVERY SUNDAY NOVICES' H'CAP CHASE (15 fncs) 2m 4f 110y
6:25 (6:26) (Class 3) (0-115,113) 5-Y-O+ **£5,414** (£1,666; £833; £416)

Form RPR

422- **1** **Ashnaya (FR)**[12] [4979] 7-10-2 **94** (p) DCCostello(5) 115+
(G M Moore) *chsd ldr: hdwy to ld 3 out: rdn next: styd on strly and clr last: rdn out* **9/2**[3]

P21- **2** *17* **Encore Cadoudal (FR)**[14] [4944] 7-11-12 **113** DO'Meara 120+
(H P Hogarth) *hld up in tch: mstke 5th: hdwy 4 out: rdn and hdwy whn hit 2 out: sn drvn and kpt on: no ch w wnr* **9/4**[2]

123- **3** *2 ½* **Silvergino (IRE)**[18] [4888] 5-11-1 **105** PJBrennan 104
(Mrs Jeremy Young) *led: rdn along 4 out: hdd next: drvn and one pce fr 2 out* **2/1**[1]

604- **4** *12* **Tates Avenue (IRE)**[17] [4911] 7-10-9 **96** CLlewellyn 88+
(N A Twiston-Davies) *hld up: hdwy 4 out: rdn next and sn btn* **6/1**

/61- **U** **Stanway**[23] [4816] 6-11-9 **110** MAFitzgerald —
(Mrs Mary Hambro) *trckd ldng pair: hdwy 5 out: cl up whn blnd and uns rdr next* **6/1**

5m 14.4s (-5.00) **Going Correction** -0.025s/f (Good)
WFA 5 from 6yo+ 3lb **5** Ran SP% **110.9**
Speed ratings: **108,101,100,96,—** CSF £15.36 TOTE £6.10: £2.60, £1.60; EX 22.90.
Owner B P Bradshaw **Bred** P Dane Player **Trained** Middleham Moor, N Yorks

FOCUS
An improved performance from the winner from a stable back on the rails after a lengthy blank spell. The winner appeared to improve with the second below his best over this trip.

NOTEBOOK
Ashnaya(FR) jumped soundly and skipping clear was full value for the winning margin. This looked a much improved performance and three miles will not be a problem in time. *(op 5-1)*
Encore Cadoudal(FR), 5lb higher, survived one bad mistake and went in pursuit of the winner but he did not see out the extended trip anywhere near as well as that rival. *(tchd 2-1 and 5-2)*
Silvergino(IRE), determined to lead, jumped well in front but he carried his head very high and his response to pressure was limited to say the very least. *(tchd 9-4)*
Tates Avenue(IRE), a big, staying type, was keen in last place on his chasing bow. He tried to close starting the final turn but was much too slow to enter the argument and in the end simply completed in his own time. He will need three miles plus. *(op 7-1)*
Stanway, who looked really well, stuck to the inner on his handicap debut and was looking a real threat when he landed awkwardly and put his rider out through the side door four out. He would have finished second at worst. *(op 11-2)*

194 JEWSON NOVICES' HURDLE (SERIES QUALIFIER) (10 hdls) 2m 4f 110y
6:55 (6:55) (Class 3) 4-Y-O+ **£4,940** (£1,520; £760; £380)

Form RPR

0- **1** **Ponderon**[60] [4201] 5-11-0 MFoley 109+
(Mrs P Robeson) *trckd ldrs: hdwy to ld approachiong 3 out: rdn next: styd on strly last* **4/1**[2]

201- **2** *1 ¾* **Enhancer**[21] [4839] 7-11-10 117 CLlewellyn 117
(M J McGrath) *hld up: gd hdwy appr 3 out: rdn to chse wnr next: drvn appr last: kpt on* **6/1**[3]

F24- **3** *2* **Ungaro (FR)**[15] [4923] 6-11-0 103 JimCrowley 106+
(K G Reveley) *hld up: stdy hdwy appr 3 out: rdn to chse ldrs next: one pce whn hit last* **9/1**

5P-1 **4** *9* **Ryhall (IRE)**[11] [8] 5-10-13 95 (b) RGarritty 97+
(T D Easterby) *hld up and bhd: stdy hdwy appr 3 out: rdn to chse ldrs next: drvn and one pce whn hit last* **14/1**

450- **5** *9* **Coralbrook**[62] [4160] 5-11-0 95 MBradburne 87
(Mrs P Robeson) *chsd ldrs: rdn along 3 out: wknd and j. bdly rt next* **40/1**

22-1 **6** *¾* **Notaproblem (IRE)**[11] [14] 6-11-6 NHannity 92
(G A Harker) *trckd ldrs: pushed along appr 3 out: sn rdn and wknd appr next* **9/1**

05-3 **7** *8* **Happy Boy (IRE)**[11] [8] 4-10-9 80 (t) GLee 73
(M A Barnes) *led: rdn along 4 out: hdd & wknd bef next* **50/1**

0-0 **8** *27* **Alphecca (USA)**[7] [82] 4-10-9 RMcGrath 46
(K G Reveley) *trckd ldrs: pushed along 4 out: sn wknd and bhd fr next* **50/1**

400- **9** *5* **Spitfire Bob (USA)**[97] [3569] 6-10-11 92 PBuchanan(3) 46
(M E Sowersby) *cl up: rdn along and lost pl 1/2-way: sn bhd* **100/1**

112- **F** **Mister Mustard (IRE)**[21] [4839] 8-11-10 120 .... APMcCoy 108
(Ian Williams) *hld up and bhd: stdy hdwy 5th: chsd ldrs 3 out: rdn and hld in 5th whn fell next* **11/10**[1]

5m 6.80s (-0.70) **Going Correction** -0.025s/f (Good)
WFA 4 from 5yo+ 5lb **10** Ran SP% **115.9**
Speed ratings: **100,99,98,95,91 91,88,78,76,—** CSF £27.75 TOTE £6.30: £2.10, £2.40, £2.50; EX 34.60.
Owner Mrs P Robeson **Bred** Southcourt Stud **Trained** Tyringham, Bucks

FOCUS
No gallop at all for the first three quarters of a mile but the first three eventually came clear and will be of interest. The form looks sound and should work out.

NOTEBOOK
Ponderon, an 88-rated stayer on the Flat, came in for plenty of support to step up on his hurdling bow. He went on before three out and always looked in total command. His immediate future in uncertain, he could switch back to the level. *(op 9-2 tchd 7-2)*
Enhancer, conceding the winner 10lb, went in pursuit of him but was never going to get in a telling blow. *Time may show that this was a sound effort from this one-time useful bumper winner. (op 7-1 tchd 8-1 in a place)*
Ungaro(FR) travelled strongly. Switched left for no apparent reason two out, he was booked for third spot when clouting the last. His rider could certainly not be accused of knocking him about and he can do better and make his mark.
Ryhall(IRE), dropping back in trip, was dropped in at the start. Showing second three out, she soon struggled under her penalty and, after hitting the final flight, was eased right off. Chasing will be her game. *(op 12-1)*
Mister Mustard(IRE), dropped in at the start, went third three out but found little and was well held when departing at the next. *(tchd 5-4)*

195 WETHERBY RACECOURSE - "YOUR CONFERENCE VENUE FOR LEEDS" H'CAP CHASE (12 fncs) 2m

7:25 (7:31) (Class 3) (0-120,120) 5-Y-0+ **£5,707** (£1,756; £878; £439)

Form RPR

3P-1 **1** **Feel The Pride (IRE)**[6] [108] 7-11-5 **113** 7ex .... APMcCoy 128+
(Jonjo O'Neill) *hld up: smooth hdwy 7th: cl up 4 out: led after next: clr last: easily* **5/6**[1]

000- **2** *3* **Galway Breeze (IRE)**[24] [4808] 10-10-6 **107** .... CDSharkey(7) 114
(Mrs K Walton) *in toucjh: pushed along and outpcd 5 out: rdn 3 out: styd on wl fr next: no ch w wnr* **50/1**

66P- **3** *1 1/4* **The Nomad**[54] [4335] 9-11-4 **115** .... MrTGreenall(3) 122+
(M W Easterby) *a cl up: led 4 out: sn rdn: hdd after next: sn drvn and one pce* **20/1**

/10- **4** *1/2* **Star Jack (FR)**[28] [4750] 10-11-1 **109** ....(t) GLee 115
(Miss P Robson) *mde most tl rdn along and hdd 4 out: drvn next and kpt on same pce* **10/3**[2]

26-P **5** *9* **Jodante (IRE)**[6] [108] 8-10-9 **103** ....(b[1]) RGarritty 100+
(P Beaumont) *keen: chsd ldrs: rdn along appr 3 out: hit next and sn wknd* **20/1**

055- **6** *1 1/4* **Sir Storm (IRE)**[110] [3362] 9-11-12 **120** ....(p) ARoss 115
(G M Moore) *prom: rdn along appr 4 out: wknd bef next* **33/1**

POP- **7** *3/4* **Tacolino (FR)**[18] [4880] 11-11-8 **116** .... JPMcNamara 111
(O Brennan) *hld up towards rr: hdwy after 5 out: rdn to chse ldrs next: drvn 3 out and sn wknd* **33/1**

11P- **8** *shd* **Billie John (IRE)**[201] [1728] 10-11-9 **117** .... RMcGrath 111
(Mrs K Walton) *prom: rdn along 6th: sn outpcd and bhd fr 5 out* **25/1**

412- **9** *13* **Six Pack (IRE)**[140] [2847] 7-10-8 **102** .... ADempsey 88+
(Andrew Turnell) *hld up: a bhd* **9/1**[3]

121- **P** **Mumaris (USA)**[196] [1784] 11-11-2 **113** ....(p) PBuchanan(3) —
(Miss Lucinda V Russell) *mstke 1st: chsd ldrs: hit 5th and lost pl: nt fluent next and sn p.u* **14/1**

3m 58.5s (-5.00) **Going Correction** -0.025s/f (Good) **10** Ran SP% **115.5**
Speed ratings: **111,109,108,108,104 103,103,103,96,—** CSF £49.50 CT £429.35 TOTE £1.70: £1.30, £11.00, £3.30; EX 71.00.
Owner Mrs M Liston **Bred** Thomas B Russell **Trained** Cheltenham, Gloucs

FOCUS
A fair race of its type for the time of year and a decent winning time for the grade. After three jumped the last upsides, a very easy well-handicapped winner in the end. The form looks rock solid.

NOTEBOOK
Feel The Pride(IRE), banged up 12lb after Southwell, travelled strongly and skipped clear for a very easy win. She will not be resting on her laurels. *(op 4-5 tchd Evens)*
Galway Breeze(IRE), who looked in tip-top condition, was only fifth jumping two out. Fourth at the last, he finished with quite a flourish but the winner was already easing down. This marked a serious return to form over a trip short of his best.
The Nomad, back after a seven-week break, showed a return to form.
Star Jack(FR), heavily backed to upset the favourite, jumped soundly in front but in the end this hunter/pointer was simply not quick enough over this shorter trip. *(op 6-1)*
Jodante(IRE), tried in blinkers, was too keen for his own good and was already on the retreat when not going high enough three out. *(tchd 28-1)*
Sir Storm(IRE), who likes it here, was having his first outing since January and it is over a year now since he last tasted success.
Mumaris(USA) *Official explanation: jockey said gelding jumped poorly and felt wrong (tchd 12-1)*

196 PEOPLECO YORKSHIRE POINT-TO-POINT ASSOCIATION HUNTERS' CHASE (18 fncs) 2m 7f 110y

7:55 (7:58) (Class 6) 5-Y-0+ **£1,533** (£438; £219)

Form RPR

203- **1** **The Butterwick Kid**[18] [4877] 12-11-11 96 ....(b) MrRTATate(7) 94
(T P Tate) *mde all: j.w: rdn along 4 out: styd on strly* **11/4**[1]

23-1 **2** *1* **Imps Way**[5] [123] 10-11-8 .... MrCMulhall(3) 86
(Mrs T Corrigan-Clark) *hld up: hdwy to chse wnr fr 11th: pushed along 3 out: rdn next kpt on* **3/1**[2]

4- **3** *2* **Sams Way**[25] 8-11-7 .... PKinsella(7) 87
(Mrs S M Barker) *hld up: outpcd and pushed along appr 5 out: rdn next: styd on fr 3 out* **10/1**

03- **4** *5* **Ikdam Melody (IRE)**[11] 9-12-0 .... MissJFoster(7) 89
(Miss J E Foster) *chsd ldrs: rdn along appr 4 out: one pce fr next* **5/1**

503/ **5** *1 1/2* **San Francisco**[11] 11-11-7 .... MissFreyaHartley(7) 81
(Miss Freya Hartley) *prom: rdn along appr 4 out: sn wknd* **14/1**

42P- **6** *2* **Strongtrooper (IRE)**[11] 10-11-7 100 .... MissJCoward(7) 82+
(Mrs C A Coward) *chsd ldrs: rdn along after 5 out: mstke next and sn outpcd: hit 3 out and bhd whn mstke next* **10/3**[3]

0/4- **P** **The Graduate**[18] 11-12-0 .... MrSWalker —
(A J Walker) *hld up in rr: hdwy on outer 13th: chsd ldrs after 5 out: rdn next: sn wknd and bhd whn p.u bef last* **20/1**

6m 0.70s (5.70) **Going Correction** -0.025s/f (Good) **7** Ran SP% **111.9**
Speed ratings: **89,88,88,86,85 85,—** CSF £11.26 TOTE £4.40: £2.80, £2.40; EX 8.30.
Owner R T A Tate **Bred** Scorrier Stud **Trained** Tadcaster, N Yorks

FOCUS
In effect a confined hunter chase. They were all in contention five out but the winner soon put his stamp on the race, his second success in it in three years. the placed horses set the level although it could rate slightly higher

NOTEBOOK
The Butterwick Kid likes it round here and, given a most positive ride, had it in the bag jumping the last. *(tchd 3-1)*
Imps Way, given a most patient ride, looked poised to challenge four out but she let the winner get *first run. Closing the gap all the way up the run-in, she was never going to seriously threaten him. (tchd 5-2)*
Sams Way, twice a winner in points, was the first to come under serious pressure. He stayed on in determined fashion up the final straight and would not need to improve much to find a novices' hunters' chase. *(op 7-1)*
Ikdam Melody(IRE) jumped better but he faced a stiff task conceding weight all round. *(op 9-2)*
San Francisco, runner-up in his last four starts in points, is a grand schoolmaster.
Strongtrooper(IRE), in good form of late in points, was feeling the strain under his young rider when he got the big ditch, four out, all wrong. After that his jumping deteriorated. *(op 9-2)*

197 26TH MAY IS OUR "LADIES EVENING" H'CAP HURDLE (9 hdls) 2m

8:30 (8:32) (Class 4) (0-110,108) 4-Y-0+ **£3,654** (£1,044; £522)

Form RPR

0-11 **1** **Mr Bigglesworth (NZ)**[6] [95] 7-11-7 **103** 7ex .... HOliver 109+
(R C Guest) *in tch: hdwy on outer 4 out: cl up next: chal 2 out: rdn last: hrd drvn and hung lft flat: led last 100 yds* **11/8**[1]

621- **2** *1 1/4* **Lawgiver (IRE)**[24] [4810] 4-10-13 **99** .... ARoss 102+
(T J Fitzgerald) *in tch: hdwy 4 out: effrt appr 2 out: rdn and ev ch whn blnd bdly last: styd on strly flat* **10/1**

060- **3** *nk* **Beseiged (USA)**[52] [4371] 8-11-9 **108** .... PWhelan(3) 114+
(R A Fahey) *a.p: effrt 3 out: led next: sn rdn: drvn last: bdly hmpd and hdd 100 yds out: no ex* **8/1**[3]

PP-5 **4** *1 1/2* **Merryvale Man**[8] [61] 8-10-13 **102** .... SCrawford(7) 105+
(Miss Kariana Key) *led: rdn along 3 out: hdd and hit 2 out: sn drvn and one pce appr last* **12/1**

200- **5** *10* **Feanor**[40] [4557] 7-11-6 **105** ....(t) KJMercer(3) 97
(Mrs S A Watt) *hld up and bhd: hdwy 3 out: rdn along next: kpt on appr last: nt rch ldrs* **33/1**

656- **6** *1/2* **Dance Party (IRE)**[49] [4413] 5-11-6 **105** .... MrTGreenall(3) 97
(M W Easterby) *chsd ldrs: rdn along 3 out: sn wknd* **16/1**

06-0 **7** *shd* **Day Du Roy (FR)**[8] [61] 7-11-12 **108** .... JimCrowley 99
(Miss L C Siddall) *hld up and bhd: hdwy 3 out: styd on u.p fr next: nvr a factor* **20/1**

0P0- **8** *4* **Very Tasty (IRE)**[235] [1411] 8-10-0 **82** ....(p) GLee 69
(M Todhunter) *midfield:m hdwy on outer 4 out: chsd ldrs next: sn rdn and wknd next: hit last* **20/1**

60-0 **9** *3/4* **Prize Ring**[8] [61] 6-11-12 **108** .... FKeniry 95
(G M Moore) *in tch: poushed along 4 out: rdn and wknd bef next* **20/1**

412- **10** *13* **Noblefir (IRE)**[127] [3074] 7-11-2 **98** .... BGibson 72
(L Lungo) *hld up in rr: hdwy appr 4 out: rdn along bef next and sn wknd* **5/1**[2]

050- **11** *7* **Minstrel's Double**[55] [4303] 4-9-9 **86** oh6 .... DCCostello(5) 49
(F P Murtagh) *nt fluent in midfield: rdn along 4 out and sn outpcd* **40/1**

52P/ **12** *1 1/4* **Coulthard (IRE)**[388] [4786] 12-10-10 **97** .... StephenJCraine(5) 62
(Mrs P Sly) *trckd ldrs on inner: rdn along appr 3 out and sn wknd* **16/1**

005- **13** *4* **Rainbow River (IRE)**[44] [4510] 7-9-12 **90** .... DSwan(10) 51
(M C Chapman) *chsd ldr: rdn along 4 out: sn wknd* **33/1**

11-4 **14** *5* **Barneys Reflection**[5] [126] 5-11-1 **100** ....(v) ONelmes(3) 56
(A Crook) *midfield: hit 4th: sn lost pl and b ehind* **14/1**

3m 53.7s (-3.50) **Going Correction** -0.025s/f (Good)
WFA 4 from 5yo+ 4lb **14** Ran SP% **127.7**
Speed ratings: **107,106,106,105,100 100,100,98,97,91 87,87,85,82** CSF £15.56 CT £94.39 TOTE £2.20: £1.60, £2.80, £2.50; EX 19.40 Place 6 £30.36, Place 5 £18.59.
Owner Bache Silk **Bred** Mrs E Alexander And W Alexander **Trained** Brancepeth, Co Durham
■ Stewards' Enquiry : H Oliver three-day ban: careless riding (May 16-18)

FOCUS
A moderate event run at a strong gallop and the winner can rate higher.

NOTEBOOK
Mr Bigglesworth(NZ), hoisted 11lb after his win here, has since won over fences. His rider's use of the whip in his right hand on the run-in was careless to say the very least but he stayed on to account for the strong finishing runner-up. It was the second time in four days when it was underlined that for a winner to get thrown out under the present guidelines something exceptional has to occur. *(op 2-1 tchd 5-4)*
Lawgiver(IRE), a close third when he blundered at the last, finished with quite a flourish but just too late. He is much improved. *(op 9-1)*
Beseiged(USA), 8lb higher than his last success, travelled strongly on ground that suits him. After going on, he was booked for second spot when the winner went right across his bows on the run-in. The result was clearly affected, but the Stewards allowed the winner to keep the prize because the runner-up was not involved.
Merryvale Man, who gets no respite, ran one of his better races taking them along at a sound gallop and keeping on all the way to the line. *(op 10-1)*
Feanor, after two poor efforts, had her tongue tied down and ran better though never in the argument. *(op 25-1)*
Noblefir(IRE), absent since December, was back over hurdles but was under pressure and going nowhere four out. *(op 6-1 tchd 13-2)*
T/Jkpt: £79.30 to a £1 stake. Pool: £43,250.10 - 397.95 winning units T/Plt: £25.80 to a £1 stake. Pool: £3,069.50 - 87.90 winning units JR

198 - 200a (Foreign Racing) - See Raceform Interactive

WINCANTON (R-H)

Friday, May 6

OFFICIAL GOING: Good

Jockeys reported the ground to be on the fast side of good to firm.
Wind: virtually nil

201 ROYAL OAK AT SOMERTON "NATIONAL HUNT" NOVICES' HURDLE (11 hdls) 2m 6f

5:55 (5:56) (Class 4) 4-Y-0+ **£3,570** (£1,020; £510)

Form RPR

31P- **1** **Bowleaze (IRE)**[22] [4835] 6-11-7 122 .... AThornton 110+
(R H Alner) *hld up towards rr: hdwy fr 7th: rdn to chse ldr after 3 out: led appraoching last: sn in command: readily* **13/8**[1]

64-1 **2** *2 1/2* **Malaga Boy (IRE)**[9] [53] 8-11-2 102 .... MrNWilliams(5) 106+
(C L Tizzard) *in tch: hdwy after 6th: lft in ld 3 out: nt fluent 2 out: rdn and hdd appr last: no ex* **12/1**

/0P- **3** *12* **Glacial Delight (IRE)**[141] [2853] 6-11-0 .... MFoley 86
(Miss E C Lavelle) *mid div: tk clsr order 8th: rdn to chse ldrs after 3 out: kpt on same pce* **25/1**

F50- **4** *1* **Reelinga**[106] [3440] 6-10-7 81........ WMarston 78
(G A Ham) *hld up rr: sltly hmpd 6th: stdy hdwy whn nt fluent and rdr lost irons 3 out: styd on fr next* **66/1**

FP5- **5** *7* **Kellys Fable**[19] [4887] 5-10-11 .... RYoung(3) 78
(J W Mullins) *mid div tl lost pl and bhd 7th: styd on fr 2 out: nvr a danger* **100/1**

0PP- **6** *14* **Delphine**[43] [4534] 6-10-7 .... JMMaguire 57
(T R George) *hld up towards rr: n.d* **50/1**

600- **7** *11* **The Bag Man**[13] [4978] 6-11-0 ....(t) ChristianWilliams 53
(P F Nicholls) *hld up towards rr: sme hdwy after 7th: wknd after 3 out* **20/1**

1RR- **8** *1 3/4* **Tino (IRE)**[215] [1576] 9-11-0 .... PJBrennan 51
(J S King) *led tl 7th: wknd appr 3 out* **25/1**

004- **9** *1/2* **He's The Gaffer (IRE)**[19] [4887] 5-11-0 .... BHitchcott 51
(R H Buckler) *chsd ldrs tl 6th: sn wknd* **33/1**

06- **10** *12* **Classic Clover**[15] [4941] 5-11-0 .... TScudamore 39
(C L Tizzard) *in tch tl 8th* **50/1**

60- **11** *1 1/4* **Court Award (IRE)**[144] [2807] 8-11-0 .... JamesDavies 38
(B G Powell) *mid div: hmpd 6th: sn bhd* **66/1**

30U- **F** **Bee Hawk**[16] [4929] 6-11-0 105........(t) RWalsh —
(P F Nicholls) *in tch whn fell 6th* **7/2**[3]

0- **P** **Bhaydalko (FR)**[34] [4697] 5-11-0 .... RThornton —
(Mrs Jeremy Young) *a towards rr: t.o and p.u bef 2 out* **66/1**

62U- **P** **Lescer's Lad**[21] [4853] 8-10-11 76........ RWalford(3) —
(C L Popham) *chsd ldrs: hit 8th: sn wknd: p.u bef 2 out* **100/1**

00/ **P** **Winter Brook**[781] [4222] 7-10-7 .... BJCrowley —
(J A Geake) *dwlt: nvr fluent and a bhd: t.o and p.u bef 7th* **66/1**

P **Sportsfield Coogee (IRE)**[159] 6-11-0 .... NFehily —
(D P Keane) *chsd ldrs tl after 8th: sn wknd: p.u bef 2 out* **100/1**

2- **U** **Lease Back (FR)**[20] [4866] 6-11-0 .... JEMoore —
(L Wells) *trckd ldrs: led approachng 7th: travelling wl whn stmbld bdly and uns rdr 3 out* **9/4**[2]

5m 21.5s (-1.90) **Going Correction** -0.25s/f (Good) **17** Ran SP% **127.0**
Speed ratings: **93,92,87,87,84 79,75,75,74,70 70,—,—,—,— —,—** CSF £22.42 TOTE £3.00: £1.50, £2.30, £9.70; EX 29.70.
Owner Martin Short **Bred** Mrs E Tector **Trained** Droop, Dorset

FOCUS
A modest winning time for this fair novice event. Bowleaze has been rated 12lb off his Newbury win.

NOTEBOOK
Bowleaze(IRE) bounced back from his Cheltenham flop but did not need to be at his best to do so. He did not look to be going as well as the leader on the home turn, but got to the front between the last two flights and won comfortably. He really needs three miles and remains a nice chasing prospect. *(op 15-8 tchd 2-1 and 5-2 in a place)*
Malaga Boy(IRE), a winner in bad ground last time, had no problem with these faster conditions. Left in front at the third from home, he tried to get clear facing up to the last two flights but was worn down after the second last. *(op 8-1)*
Glacial Delight(IRE), an Irish point winner last year, ran his best race so far under Rules but could make no impression on the first two in the home straight. He is now eligible for handicaps.
Reelinga, taking a considerable step up in trip, stayed on from the rear of the field after things had not gone her way. She settled better and this was an encouraging performance. *(op 50-1)*
Kellys Fable, an exposed performer, was never in the hunt. *(op 66-1)*
Bee Hawk was not far behind the leaders when coming down. *(op 5-2 tchd 11-4)*
Lease Back(FR), ridden more prominently, was in front and travelling within himself when he stepped into the third last and gave Moore no chance. *(op 5-2 tchd 11-4)*
Bhaydalko(FR), making his hurdles debut, showed a hint of promise before weakening quickly on the home turn and being pulled up. *(op 5-2 tchd 11-4)*

202 DANEBURY VINEYARDS NOVICES' H'CAP CHASE (17 fncs) 2m 5f
6:25 (6:27) (Class 4) (0-100,100) 5-Y-0+ **£4,147** (£1,276; £638; £319)

Form RPR

413- **1** **Party Games (IRE)**[78] [3904] 8-11-12 **100**........ PHide 116+
(G L Moore) *a.p: led 11th tl next: slt advantage whn lft clr 2 out: comf* **4/1**[2]

UF3- **2** *2 1/2* **Ho Ho Hill (IRE)**[13] [4980] 7-11-3 **91**........ RWalsh 99
(P F Nicholls) *hld up: hdwy 12th: chsd ldrs after 4 out: lft 2nd 2 out: sn rdn: no imp* **3/1**[1]

U50- **3** *7* **Ideal Jack (FR)**[21] [4855] 9-10-8 **82**........ WMarston 85+
(G A Ham) *hld up: hdwy appr 9th: mstke 12th: rdn to chse ldrs after 13th: wkng whn blnd and lft 3rd 2 out* **11/1**

P0-2 **4** *2 1/2* **Tosawi (IRE)**[11] [26] 9-11-6 **94**........ TScudamore 94+
(R J Hodges) *chsd ldrs: rdn appr 10th: one pced fr 3 out* **11/2**[3]

0F0- **5** *1/2* **Ultimate Limit**[58] [4264] 5-10-0 **77** oh13........ PJBrennan 73+
(A Ennis) *mid div: n.m.r amd lost pl on bnd after 9th: hdwy whn j.lft 12th: sn rdn: wkng whn mstke 3 out* **66/1**

666- **6** *1 1/2* **Hill Forts Henry**[33] [4725] 7-10-1 **78**........ RYoung(3) 77+
(J W Mullins) *hld up: hdwy appr 4 out: rdn appr 3 out: lft 4th and mstke 2 out: wknd* **4/1**[2]

00- **P** **Ri Na Realta (IRE)**[20] [4866] 10-11-7 **95**........ AThornton —
(J W Mullins) **20/1**

P00- **P** **China Chase (IRE)**[54] [4343] 6-9-10 **77**........(p) WKennedy(7) —
(J L Spearing) *in tch tl 12th: sn bhd: p.u after 4 out* **33/1**

456- **P** **Land Rover Lad**[98] [3575] 7-9-7 **74** oh3........(b) SWalsh(7) —
(C P Morlock) *a bhd: lost tch fr 11th: t.o and p.u bef 4 out* **12/1**

4FP- **P** **Cloudy Blues (IRE)**[19] [4886] 7-10-2 **76**........ BHitchcott —
(R H Buckler) *chsd ldrs tl 10th: sn wknd: bhd and p.u after 4 out* **25/1**

054- **P** **Rings Of Power (IRE)**[24] [4816] 8-9-10 **77**........ TMessenger(7) —
(N R Mitchell) *chsd ldrs: mstke 8th and 11th: sn wknd: p.u bef 3 out* **12/1**

P- **U** **Supreme Tadgh (IRE)**[19] [4889] 8-11-7 **95**........ SDurack 103
(J A Geake) *led: hdd 11th tl next: rdn appr 3 out: jst hdd whn stmbld bdly and uns rdr 2 out* **25/1**

5m 17.0s (-5.60) **Going Correction** -0.525s/f (Firm)
WFA 5 from 6yo+ 3lb **12** Ran SP% **121.0**
Speed ratings: **89,88,85,84,84 83,—,—,—,— —,—** CSF £16.40 CT £125.77 TOTE £4.70: £2.00, £1.40, £2.30; EX 15.30.
Owner Goldfingers **Bred** G N Cannon **Trained** Woodingdean, E Sussex

FOCUS
A modest winning time for the grade. Party Games has been rated as value for seven lengths.

NOTEBOOK
Party Games(IRE) made a successful chasing debut. Jumping soundly, he had just moved to the front when he was left clear at the second last, and he was eased down with his race won on the run-in. There should be more to come. *(op 11-4)*
Ho Ho Hill(IRE) jumped well, if extravagantly at times, and looked a real danger facing up to the last three fences, but he came off the bridle going to the second last and the response was already a limited one when he was slightly hampered at that fence. *(op 7-2 tchd 4-1)*
Ideal Jack(FR) is creeping down the weights again and there still could be a small chase for him. *(op 10-1)*
Tosawi(IRE) was without the cheekpieces. He is due to go up 4lb now and may struggle from his revised mark. *(op 9-2 tchd 4-1)*
Ultimate Limit, placed in a maiden point in Ireland, had not shown much since but ran a decent race on this chase debut from nearly a stone out of the handicap. *(op 50-1)*
Hill Forts Henry made a satisfactory chasing debut and would have finished a bit closer but for an error at the second last, where he also gave a fallen rider a kick. *(op 10-1 tchd 11-1)*
Ri Na Realta(IRE) *Official explanation: jockey said gelding made a bad mistake in back straight (tchd 33-1)*
Supreme Tadgh(IRE), a dual pointing winner in Ireland, was fifth in a Clonmel hunter chase on his only previous run over regulation fences. After making much of the running, he had just been headed when he parted company at the second last. *(tchd 33-1)*
Cloudy Blues(IRE) *Official explanation: jockey said gelding had breathing problem (tchd 33-1)*
China Chase(IRE) *Official explanation: jockey said gelding made a bad mistake in back straight (tchd 33-1)*

203 JEWSON NOVICES' HURDLE (SERIES QUALIFIER) (8 hdls) 2m
6:55 (6:56) (Class 4) 4-Y-0+ **£3,475** (£993; £496)

Form RPR

2- **1** **Fandani (GER)**[76] [3959] 5-10-12 .... NFehily 123+
(C J Mann) *t.k.h in tch: hdwy after 3 out: led appr last: shkn up run-in: r.o wl* **11/8**[1]

031- **2** *3 1/2* **Earth Man (IRE)**[19] [4885] 6-11-4 .... RWalsh 123
(P F Nicholls) *chsd clr ldr fr 2nd: hdwy appr 2 out: ev ch approacing last: nt qckn* **7/4**[2]

PP-2 **3** *9* **Thieves'Glen**[11] [21] 7-10-12 115........(b) APMcCoy 109+
(H Morrison) *led at gd pce and sn clr: hit 2nd: rdn and mstke 2 out: sn hdd: no ex* **5/1**[3]

/00- **4** *4* **Shining Strand**[34] [4696] 6-10-12 .... MFoley 105+
(N J Henderson) *hld up rr: hdwy 5th: rdn to chse ldrs after 3 out: wknd next* **11/1**

5 *26* **Convent Girl (IRE)**[167] 5-10-5 .... PHolley 71
(Mrs P N Dutfield) *hld up: mstke 5th: sme hdwy next: wkng whn mstke 2 out* **33/1**

60- **6** *5* **Uncle Al (IRE)**[16] [4930] 6-10-12 .... WHutchinson 73
(K Bishop) *chsd ldrs: hit 4th: wknd appr 3 out* **150/1**

246- **7** *3* **Twentytwosilver (IRE)**[190] [1878] 5-10-12 94........ PJBrennan 70
(N J Hawke) *hld up: hdwy appr 3 out: sn wknd* **33/1**

P0P- **8** *20* **Debatable**[19] [4884] 6-10-9 .... AHoneyball(3) 50
(N J Hawke) *a bhd* **150/1**

4/6- **9** *4* **Bravura**[16] [4362] 7-10-12 .... PHide 46
(G L Moore) *a towards rr* **125/1**

6P0- **10** *18* **Jo's Sale (IRE)**[19] [4885] 6-10-12 .... ChristianWilliams 28
(Evan Williams) *mid div tl 3 out: sn wknd* **125/1**

P0P- **P** **Mansion Special (FR)**[69] [4062] 5-10-12 ....(b[1]) RThornton —
(A King) *in tch: wknd 3 out: p.u bef next* **40/1**

3m 39.0s (-9.00) **Going Correction** -0.25s/f (Good)
WFA 4 from 5yo+ 4lb **11** Ran SP% **114.7**
Speed ratings: **112,110,105,103,90 88,86,76,74,65** — CSF £3.91 TOTE £2.60: £1.40, £1.40, £1.30; EX 5.10.
Owner N Kempner & W J Smith **Bred** Dr W Spangler **Trained** Upper Lambourn, Berks

FOCUS
A strongly-run race and a decent winning time. This is good novice form, with the winner is rated value for further.

NOTEBOOK
Fandani(GER) split a useful pair in Cerium and McBain on his debut over course and distance in February. Given time since, he ran out a comfortable winner and he should be able to defy a penalty. *(op 11-10 tchd 13-8)*
Earth Man(IRE), suited by this faster pace, showed big improvement on his recent course win and *there was no disgrace in his defeat by a promising opponent to whom he was conceding 6lb. (op 2-1 tchd 13-8)*
Thieves'Glen, again somewhat keen in the blinkers, soon opened up a clear lead. Not jumping all that fluently, he was collared after the second last but stuck on for third. *(op 7-1)*
Shining Strand went out to his left as the tapes went up but soon recovered. Never close enough to get in a blow at the leaders, he needs one more run for a mark. *(op 10-1 tchd 12-1)*
Convent Girl(IRE), a useful mare at around a mile on the Flat, showed a bit of promise on this hurdling debut but is going to have to jump a lot better. *(op 25-1)*

204 R K HARRISON HUNTERS' CHASE (21 fncs) 3m 1f 110y
7:25 (7:26) (Class 6) 5-Y-0+ **£3,445** (£1,060; £530; £265)

Form RPR

0/3- **1** **Be My Dream (IRE)**[19] 10-11-5 .... MrMWilesmith(7) 100+
(Mrs C Wilesmith) *led tl 5th: w ldr: led 9th tl 16th: prom: rallying in cl 2nd whn lft wl clr 2 out* **3/1**[1]

2 *11* **Which Pocket (IRE)**[13] 7-11-5 ....(v[1]) MrMWall(7) 89+
(A D Peachey) *prom: led 5th tl 9th: w wnr: nt fluent 13th (water): j.lft fr next: rdn after 15th: wknd after 17th: lft 2nd 2 out* **14/1**

4P1- **3** *6* **Don Royal**[34] 11-12-2 100........ MrNHarris 84+
(J R Scott) *in tch: trckd ldrs: rdn appr 15th: one pced fr 4 out: lft 3rd 2 out* **9/1**

14-P **4** *dist* **Mydante (IRE)**[12] [6] 10-11-2 79........(t) MrMWalford(7) 62
(S Flook) *hld up: blnd 10th: hdwy appr 4 out: chalng for 3rd whn mstke 3 out: wkng whn lft 4th next* **20/1**

32-2 **U** **Mullensgrove**[9] [48] 11-11-12 103........ MissSSharratt(7) —
(D Lowe) *in tch whn mstke and uns rdr 12th* **7/2**[2]

1U5- **P** **Moor Lane**[20] [4870] 13-11-12 114........ MrABraithwaite(7) —
(A M Balding) *trckd ldrs tl p.u after 7th: lame* **4/1**[3]

P1-P **P** **Mister Club Royal**[9] [47] 9-12-0 82........ MrRWoollacott(5) —
(Miss Emma Oliver) *in tch: hdwy 14th: rdn after next: sn wknd: p.u bef 3 out* **25/1**

F- **F** **Caspers Case**[24] [4818] 12-11-12 .... MrNWilliams 100
(R Barber) *in tch: hit 12th: hdwy 14th: led 16th: rdn appr 3 out: 1 l clr whn fell 2 out* **10/1**

F42- **P** **Mollycarrs Gambul**[14] [4963] 6-10-12 .... MrTJO'Brien(7) —
(Miss Sarah Robinson) *hld up: nt fluent 6th and 13th: sme hdwy next: wknd 16th: bhd and p.u bef 4 out* **6/1**

6m 36.8s (-7.60) **Going Correction** -0.525s/f (Firm) **9** Ran SP% **115.9**
Speed ratings: **90,86,84,—,— —,—,—,—** CSF £43.29 TOTE £3.80: £1.60, £4.20, £3.10; EX 69.70.
Owner C W Booth **Bred** John Quane **Trained** Upton-on-Severn, Gloucs

FOCUS
An ordinary hunter chase in which the winner was rated 5lb below his best with the faller rated as having dead-heated.

NOTEBOOK

Be My Dream(IRE), in and out of the lead, was renewing his effort and might have won in any case when he was handed the prize on a plate at the second last. A thorough stayer, he is enjoying a good year *(tchd 4-1)*

Which Pocket(IRE) won an intermediate at Brampton Bryan on his latest start. A keen sort, he shaped with promise on his debut under Rules although he was fortunate to finish second in the end. *(op 16-1)*

Don Royal, who won a weak event at Stratford in March, was a beaten favourite in an open last time. *(op 10-1)*

Mydante(IRE) did not jump very well and that might have cost her third place in the end. *(tchd 22-1)*

Moor Lane appeared to go wrong going into the seventh fence and was pulled up straight after the obstacle. *(op 7-2 tchd 10-3)*

Caspers Case is remarkably lightly raced for his age and this was only the eighth run of his career and his second under Rules. He had jumped well enough, bar getting in to close to the 12th, but undid his good work by coming down at the last when he was still in a narrow lead. None the worse, although he lay winded for a time, he can win a hunter chase if his jumping holds up. *(op 7-2 tchd 10-3)*

205 BUSINESS MONEY PANTO PRINCE H'CAP CHASE (21 fncs) 3m 1f 110y

7:55 (7:56) (Class 3) (0-120,118) 5-Y-0+ **£7,114** (£2,189; £1,094; £547)

Form	Pos	Dist	Horse	RPR
134-	1		**Were In Touch (IRE)**[29] 4757 7-11-10 **116** ....(t) RWalsh (P F Nicholls) *hld up in tch: hit 15th: hdwy to go 2nd after 17th: chalng whn lft clr 3 out: idled and hdd sn after last: led cl home* **2/1**[2]	132+
P42-	2	shd	**Phar City (IRE)**[14] 4955 8-10-4 **96** .... BHitchcott (R H Buckler) *trckd ldrs: led 10th tl 13th: w ldrs tl sltly outpcd appr 3 out: rallied to ld run-in: ct cl home* **14/1**	106
010-	3	5	**Even More (IRE)**[29] 4757 10-11-8 **114** .... AThornton (R H Alner) *led tl 10th: outpcd after 14th: styd on again fr 3 out* **20/1**	119
24-4	4	7	**Dear Deal**[9] 55 12-11-6 **112** ....(b) ChristianWilliams (C L Tizzard) *chsd ldrs tl blnd 11th: sn rdn along in tch: one pced fr 4 out* **7/1**[3]	113+
/05-	5	4	**Lord 'N' Master (IRE)**[14] 4955 9-11-1 **107** .... MBatchelor (R Rowe) *hld up rr: mstke 17th: hdwy next: sn rdn: mstke 3 out: wknd* **14/1**	103+
6P5-	6	9	**Multi Talented (IRE)**[20] 4869 9-10-12 **104** ....(b) LAspell (L Wells) *bhd fr 13th* **33/1**	89
12P/	7	17	**Waterberg (IRE)**[573] 1617 10-11-6 **112** .... MBradburne (H D Daly) *hld up: hdwy 16th: cl 4th appr 4 out: rdn whn hmpd 3 out: wknd* **11/1**	80
111-	F		**Tom Sayers (IRE)**[19] 4886 7-11-5 **116** .... RStephens(5) (P J Hobbs) *in tch: led after 12th: jnd whn fell 3 out* **13/8**[1]	132

6m 26.6s (-17.80) **Going Correction** -0.525s/f (Firm) **8** Ran SP% **113.3**

Speed ratings: **106,105,104,102,101 98,93,—** CSF £27.73 CT £430.86 TOTE £3.00: £1.40, £3.20, £1.60; EX 47.90.

Owner Paul Barber,Malcolm Calvert,Colin Lewis **Bred** J J Fisher **Trained** Ditcheat, Somerset

FOCUS

A fair handicap chase for the time of year. The winner has been rated as value for 6l, while the faller has been rated as having dead-heated. The second and third ran to their marks.

NOTEBOOK

Were In Touch(IRE) was left in command at the third last when his market rival came down, but he wanted to down tools in front. Collared just after the last, he rallied well to salvage the situation. He is capable of a good deal better but may need holding up for as long as possible. *(op 5-2)*

Phar City(IRE), who ran his best race for a while at Chepstow last time, almost embarrassed the idling leader but, after nosing ahead on the run-in, he was just touched off. *(op 12-1 tchd 20-1)*

Even More(IRE), the early leader, struggled to stay in touch as the pace lifted but to his credit was staying on at the end. He does look high enough in the weights. *(op 16-1)*

Dear Deal was always up against it after a blunder at the eleventh.

Lord 'N' Master(IRE) has yet to recapture his form since returning from a lengthy absence. *(op 9-1)*

Waterberg(IRE), off the track since October 2003, was resuming off his last winning mark. He made an encouraging return to action before lack of race fitness told. *(op 10-1 tchd 9-1 and 12-1)*

Tom Sayers(IRE), bidding for the four-timer off a 12lb higher mark, had just been joined when he became a victim of the tricky first fence in the home straight. He had jumped well up to then. *(op 11-8 tchd 5-4 and 7-4)*

206 MIRAGE SIGNS H'CAP HURDLE (11 hdls) 2m 6f

8:25 (8:26) (Class 4) (0-100,98) 4-Y-0+ **£3,115** (£890; £445)

Form	Pos	Dist	Horse	RPR
6F2-	1		**The Kirk (NZ)**[26] 4797 7-11-3 **96** .... RLucey-Butler(7) (M Madgwick) *hld up bhd: hit 6th: stmbld 8th: gd hdwy after 3 out: nt clr run appr next: led appr last: kpt on wl: rdn out* **7/1**	100+
306-	2	1 3/4	**Kimono Royal (FR)**[143] 2824 7-11-11 **97** .... RThornton (A King) *in tch: hdwy whn nt clr run on inner and hmpd appr 2 out: sn rdn: kpt on to go 2nd sn after last* **5/2**[1]	100+
405-	3	3/4	**Knight Of Silver**[19] 4889 8-10-5 **82** .... RStephens(5) (S C Burrough) *chsd ldrs: sltly outpcd after 8th: rallied and ev ch appr 2 out: kpt on* **9/1**	83
POP-	4	1 1/4	**Supreme Return**[45] 4502 6-11-4 **90** .... WHutchinson (A King) *chsd ldrs: rdn to ld 2 out: hdd appr last: kpt on same pce* **12/1**	89
064-	5	2	**Vivante (IRE)**[19] 4884 7-10-2 **74** .... WMarston (A J Wilson) *mid div: pushed along fr 7th: hdwy 3 out: pressed ldrs appr 2 out: one pced after* **6/1**	71
125-	6	5	**Breaking Breeze (IRE)**[178] 2104 10-11-8 **94** .... PJBrennan (J S King) *keen: led: rdn and hdd appr 2 out: one pced* **11/2**[3]	86
244-	7	10	**Elheba (IRE)**[21] 4857 6-11-9 **98** .... RYoung(3) (C J Down) *mid div tl wknd after 3 out* **14/1**	80
PF0-	8	dist	**Honneur Fontenail (FR)**[303] 901 6-10-0 **72** oh8 .... BHitchcott (N J Hawke) *chsd ldrs: rdn and effrt after 3 out: wknd qckly next* **40/1**	—
000-	9	1	**Gondolin (IRE)**[14] 4956 5-10-13 **85** .... PFlynn (G Brown) *in tch tl 6th: sn bhd* **40/1**	—
10P-	P		**Sarasota (IRE)**[58] 4269 10-11-7 **93** .... APMcCoy (P Bowen) *keen in rr: hdwy 8th: sn rdn: wknd qckly and p.u bef 2 out* **5/1**[2]	—
5U0-	P		**Castleboy (IRE)**[56] 4316 7-11-7 **93** .... RJohnson (P J Hobbs) *hld up towards rr: mstke 3 out: wknd qckly and p.u bef next* **16/1**	—

5m 22.6s (-0.80) **Going Correction** -0.25s/f (Good) **11** Ran SP% **122.5**

Speed ratings: **91,90,90,89,88 87,83,—,—,— —** CSF £26.56 CT £164.97 TOTE £11.80: £2.70, £1.70, £2.80; EX 41.70 Place 6 £36.40, Place 5 £15.90..

Owner DDB Racing **Bred** J D Corcoran **Trained** Denmead, Hants

FOCUS

An ordinary hurdle run in a modest winning time for the grade. The winner improved on previous form and this was probably not a bad little handicap.

NOTEBOOK

The Kirk(NZ) confirmed the promise of his run at Worcester. Making steady headway from the rear to strike the front between the last two flights, he found sufficient to hold on despite edging left. *(op 6-1)*

Kimono Royal(FR), making his handicap debut on his first run since December, was short of room early in the home straight and then had to be switched between the last two flights. He stayed on when clear but could not get to the winner. *(op 4-1 tchd 9-2)*

Knight Of Silver, who is slipping down the handicap, ran his best race since joining this yard. He could be worth another try at three miles. *(op 14-1 tchd 16-1)*

Supreme Return was well beaten in four previous tries over hurdles but he improved for this faster ground. He looks a chasing type. *(op 9-1)*

Vivante(IRE) is a limited perfomer, but she is not running badly at present.

Breaking Breeze(IRE), having his first run over hurdles for three years, was only collared on the run to the second last. This should have sharpened him up for a summer campaign. *(op 13-2 tchd 7-1)*

Sarasota(IRE) *Official explanation: jockey said gelding lost its action (op 9-2)*

T/Plt: £58.30 to a £1 stake. Pool: £40,579.00. 507.85 winning tickets. T/Qpdt: £17.50 to a £1 stake. Pool: £3,136.40. 132.40 winning tickets. TM

HAYDOCK (L-H)

Saturday, May 7

OFFICIAL GOING: Flat course - soft; hurdle course - good to soft

Other races under Rules of Flat racing

Wind: moderate to fresh, against Weather: mainly fine

207 STANLEYBET LONG DISTANCE H'CAP HURDLE (12 hdls) 2m 7f 110y

1:20 (1:20) (Class 2) 4-Y-0+

£16,576 (£6,287; £3,143; £1,429; £714; £428)

Form	Pos	Dist	Horse	RPR
0/0-	1		**Mr Cool**[14] 4982 11-10-4 **135** .... JEMoore (M C Pipe) *chsd ldrs: wnt 2nd 7th: led appr 4 out: clr bef 2 out: drvn out* **33/1**	144+
302-	2	6	**Mr Ed (IRE)**[30] 4747 7-11-3 **148** ....(p) APMcCoy (P Bowen) *in rr: pushed along briefly after 6th: hdwy appr 3 out: j.rt next: wnt 2nd last: no real imp on wnr* **7/2**[1]	152+
20-0	3	3/4	**Very Optimistic (IRE)**[7] 127 7-10-1 **132** .... GLee (Jonjo O'Neill) *midfield: hdwy 7th: wnt 2nd appr 3 out and mstke: mstke next: lost 2nd last: kpt on same pce* **10/1**	135+
34R-	4	7	**Westender (FR)**[30] 4747 9-11-12 **157** ....(b) TScudamore (M C Pipe) *midfield: hdwy appr 7th: rdn bef 2 out: wknd bef last* **16/1**	152+
F11-	5	7	**Broken Knights (IRE)**[35] 4687 8-10-0 **131** oh1 .... ADobbin (N G Richards) *hld up: hdwy appr 7th: mstke 4 out: rdn and wknd appr 2 out* **4/1**[2]	118
00-0	6	2	**Mythical King (IRE)**[7] 127 8-10-0 **131** oh6 .... TDoyle (R Lee) *hld up: effrt 3 out: nvr on terms* **66/1**	116
0P0-	7	2 1/2	**Champagne Harry**[29] 4767 7-10-0 **131** .... CLlewellyn (N A Twiston-Davies) *chsd clr ldr to 7th: wknd appr 4 out* **25/1**	114
F00-	8	8	**Ardashir (FR)**[23] 4835 6-10-0 **131** oh6 .... WMarston (N A Twiston-Davies) *midfield: hmpd 7th: sn bhd* **100/1**	109+
011-	9	6	**Holland Park (IRE)**[29] 4767 8-10-9 **140** .... RJohnson (Mrs S D Williams) *in tch: rdn appr 3 out: wknd bef next* **4/1**[2]	115+
304-	10	4	**Quick**[23] 4835 5-10-8 **142** ....(v) TJMalone(3) (M C Pipe) *led: sn clr: rdn after 7th: hdd appr 4 out: wknd qckly bef next* **20/1**	107
141-	11	1	**The Persuader (IRE)**[20] 4881 5-9-9 **131** oh10 ....(t) RStephens(5) (P F Nicholls) *midfield: niggled along after 4th: wknd appr 4 out* **14/1**	101+
4B-2	F		**Turtle Soup (IRE)**[7] 127 9-10-4 **145** .... WMcCarthy(10) (T R George) *in tch: fell 7th* **8/1**[3]	—
560-	P		**Back To Ben Alder (IRE)**[29] 4767 8-10-0 **131** oh11 .... MFoley (N J Henderson) *chsd ldrs tl rdn and wknd qckly appr 7th: t.o whn p.u bef next* **33/1**	—

5m 46.3s (-23.10) **Going Correction** -0.575s/f (Firm) **13** Ran SP% **111.9**

Speed ratings: **115,113,112,110,108 107,106,103,101,100 100,—,—** CSF £134.58 CT £1262.37 TOTE £40.10: £7.80, £1.80, £3.30; EX 133.40 TRIFECTA Not won..

Owner N G Mills **Bred** Mrs N G Mills **Trained** Nicholashayne, Devon

FOCUS

A good, staying handicap hurdle run in a smart time that looks solid form-wise and should produce winners.

NOTEBOOK

Mr Cool, rated 14lb higher in his pomp, has had revolutionary treatment for tendon trouble and came into this having made a reasonable reappearance over an inadequate two miles. He got into a nice rhythm and kicked clear early in the straight, wrapping the event up and causing something of a shock in the process. He has always had a touch of class and it will be interesting to see what connections do with him now.

Mr Ed(IRE), able to race off the same mark as when second in a Grade Two at Aintree, stayed on from a long way back, but the winner had flown and he had to settle for the runner-up spot. He is a tough, progressive hurdler and will continue to fare well in similar events. *(op 3-1)*

Very Optimistic(IRE) ran his best race for some time and is creeping back to form. He was a useful novice and will be one for all the big staying handicap hurdles next season, with the Pertemps Final being an obvious target, assuming he stays over the smaller obstacles. *(op 12-1)*

Westender(FR) ran a smashing race under his big weight in ground that would have been too soft. He refused to race at Aintree last time, but was on his best behaviour here and will appreciate a return to faster ground.

Broken Knights(IRE) has a good wins-to-runs ratio, but was unable to cope with this rise in grade. He is still unexposed and the type to make a decent chaser. *(op 9-2)*

Mythical King(IRE) ran a lot better than his price entitled him to and plugged on through beaten horses down the straight.

Holland Park(IRE), winner of the big staying handicap hurdle at Aintree, failed to run his race and struggled badly off this 10lb higher mark. *(op 7-2)*

208 STANLEYBET H'CAP HURDLE (FORMERLY THE SWINTON HURDLE) (8 hdls) 2m

1:50 (1:55) (Class 1) 4-Y-0+

£40,600 (£15,400; £7,700; £3,500; £1,750; £1,050)

Form	Pos	Dist	Horse	RPR
112-	1		**Coat Of Honour (USA)**[22] 4845 5-10-0 **134** .... GLee (J Howard Johnson) *a.p: rdn to ld appr 2 out: clr after last: styd on wl* **6/1**[3]	143+
01-0	2	5	**Definate Spectacle (IRE)**[10] 67 5-10-0 **134** oh4 .... PCarberry (Noel Meade, Ire) *midfield: hdwy gng wl 3 out: wnt 2nd appr last and j.rt: sn one pce* **8/1**	138+
453-	3	1	**Crossbow Creek**[28] 4768 7-10-1 **135** .... JimCrowley (M G Rimell) *midfield: rdn and hdwy appr 2 out: styd on same pce* **9/1**	137

051- **4** 2 ½ **Rooster Booster**[15] 4973 11-11-12 **160**.................................. RJohnson 160
(P J Hobbs) *hekld up in rr: hdwy whn hung lft appr 2 out: no ex run-in* **8/1**
203- **5** 3 **Perouse**[15] 4973 7-11-2 **150**..(t) RWalsh 147
(P F Nicholls) *in tch: lost pl and outpcd 4 out: no imp after* **20/1**
111- **6** ¾ **Genghis (IRE)**[21] 4860 6-10-13 **147**... APMcCoy 144+
(P Bowen) *led: mstke 3 out: hdd appr next: wknd last* **3/1**[1]
032- **7** 1 ¼ **Cherub (GER)**[17] 4930 5-10-0 **134** oh4..(t) ADobbin 129
(Jonjo O'Neill) *in tch: hdwy 3 out: wknd next* **14/1**
002- **8** 1 ¼ **Penny Pictures (IRE)**[14] 4982 6-10-1 **135**......................... TScudamore 128
(M C Pipe) *midfield: effrt appr 3 out: wknd bef next* **20/1**
540- **9** 7 **Torrid Kentavr (USA)**[14] 4438 8-9-11 **134**..................... KJMercer(3) 120
(B Ellison) *a bhd* **20/1**
063- **F** **Fontanesi (IRE)**[14] 4982 5-9-13 **136**.................................... TJMalone(3) —
(M C Pipe) *hld up: fell 4 out* **20/1**
02F- **P** **Royal Shakespeare (FR)**[15] 4973 6-11-2 **150**...................... RThornton —
(S Gollings) *mstkes: trckd ldrs: rdn and wknd after 4 out: t.o whn p.u bef last* **5/1**[2]

3m 47.4s (-11.80) **Going Correction** -0.575s/f (Firm) **11** Ran SP% **113.9**
Speed ratings: **106,103,103,101,100 99,99,98,95,**— — CSF £47.66 CT £424.32 TOTE £6.70: £2.30, £2.50, £3.00; EX 78.10 TRIFECTA Not won..
Owner Andrea & Graham Wylie **Bred** Makio Shimoyashiki **Trained** Billy Row, Co Durham

FOCUS
A top two-mile handicap, run at just a fair gallop but the form looks strong, with two highly progressive horses finishing ahead of two solid performers in Crossbow Creek and former Champion Hurdle winner Rooster Booster. Genghis was disappointing and struggled off this 10lb higher mark for winning the Scottish Champion Hurdle.

NOTEBOOK
Coat Of Honour(USA), unsuited by a slow pace in a small field when turned over for the first time at Ayr latest, was given a positive ride by Lee and stayed on strongly having disposed of favourite Genghis, getting the season off to a flyer for racing's new 'dream team'. He is totally unexposed and could develop into a high-class hurdler later in the season, with races like the Totesport Trophy being obvious targets. In the meantime he reportedly has the Ebor as a target on the Flat. *(op 5-1)*
Definate Spectacle(IRE) bounced back from a poor showing at Punchestown and returned to something like his Aintree form. He again travelled well, but the winner was relentless and he was *never getting to him. A race at the Galway Festival is now the plan for him after a short break. (tchd 9-1)*
Crossbow Creek was on the premises in most of the big two-mile handicap hurdles last season, winning the Lanzarote, and ran another sound race. He was doing his best work late, but needs to improve over the summer if he is to defy the Handicapper later in the season. *(op 12-1)*
Rooster Booster bounced back to form when winning at Sandown last time, travelling like he used to in his pomp, but on this softer surface under his big weight he was not as effective, but ran well nonetheless. He will reportedly race on next season. *(op 15-2 tchd 7-1 and 9-1 in places)*
Perouse ran well on ground softer than ideal for him, but remains firmly in the grip of the Handicapper and is worth trying over fences now he has hit a brick wall in terms of progression as a hurdler. *(tchd 25-1)*
Genghis(IRE), who has been on a roll of late, scooping valuable prizes at Aintree and the Scottish Champion Hurdle at Ayr, struggled off a 10lb higher mark and was unable to match Coat Of Honour when he kicked again. He is probably ready for a break now and it will be interesting to see how he copes off this mark when returning. *(op 5-2)*
Cherub(GER) ran well to a point, but has had a disappointing season, partly down to the form of the stable, and could not go with the principals from the turn into the straight. He may bounce back next season, only being a five-year-old, and could prove well handicapped in time. *(op 12-1)*
Penny Pictures(IRE) ran his best race for some time when second at Sandown last month, but lacked the basic speed to cope at this trip and is best kept to two and a half miles, as he does not have the stamina for three plus. *(op 25-1)*
Royal Shakespeare(FR) has basically had a disappointing season and once again would have prefered quicker ground. He was in the process of going close against Rooster Booster at Sandown, in front when falling at the last, but he has had a 'nearly' season and it will be interesting *to see whether he is sent chasing later in the year.Official explanation: jockey said gelding was unsuited by good to soft ground (op 11-2)*

[119]HEXHAM (L-H)
Saturday, May 7

OFFICIAL GOING: Good (good to soft in places)
Wind: strong against

209 JOHN SMITH'S EXTRA SMOOTH "NATIONAL HUNT" NOVICES' HURDLE (DIV I) (8 hdls) 2m 110y
2:00 (2:00) (Class 4) 4-Y-0+ **£3,052** (£872; £436)

Form RPR
411- **1** **Portavadie**[26] 4807 6-11-7 .... AThornton 103+
(J M Jefferson) *prom: lft in ld 5th: drew clr bef last: easily* **2/7**[1]
406- **2** 10 **Mooramana**[17] 4923 6-11-0 **94**.. RGarritty 81+
(P Beaumont) *led to 3rd: cl up tl outpcd bef last* **8/1**[2]
0-PP **3** 11 **Stoneriggs**[5] 147 4-10-7 .... PBuchanan(3) 64+
(Mrs E Slack) *bhdd: hdwy after 3 out: styng on whn mstke last: no imp* **150/1**
/0-0 **4** 1 ¾ **Rush'N'Run**[7] 133 6-10-4 .... THalliday(10) 65
(Mrs S J Smith) *prom: effrt after 2 out: wknd bef next* **40/1**
0/0- **5** 23 **Loch Red**[46] 4513 6-11-0 .... NPMulholland 42
(C W Thornton) *nt fluent in rr: struggling 1/2-way: nvr on terms* **50/1**
/53- **6** shd **Loch Torridon**[218] 1548 6-11-0 .... RMcGrath 42
(James Moffatt) *prom to 5th: sn rdn and wknd* **20/1**[3]
00- **7** 1 ½ **Scarlet Memory**[26] 4807 6-10-7 .... PRobson 34
(G A Harker) *chsd ldrs tl wknd bef 2 out* **80/1**
000- **8** 21 **Solemn Vow**[46] 4513 4-9-10 .... SCrawford(7) 9
(P Maddison) *a bhd: no ch fr 1/2-way* **150/1**
0FP- **9** 3 ½ **Top Pack (IRE)**[32] 4735 6-11-0 .... BHarding 16
(N G Richards) *hld up: rdn 5th: sn btn* **50/1**
5-P **10** ½ **No Hesitation**[10] 59 4-10-7 .... ONelmes(3) 12
(Mrs S C Bradburne) *in tch to 1/2-way: sn struggling* **100/1**
R **Tin Healy's Pass**[55] 4357 5-10-7 .... MissLKendall(7) —
(I McMath) *cl up: led 3rd: rn out 5th* **33/1**
0- **U** **Solway Bob**[48] 4477 6-10-11 .... GBerridge(3) —
(L Lungo) *towards rr: outpcd 1/2-way: btn whn hit and uns rdr 2 out* **25/1**

4m 18.6s (4.60) **Going Correction** -0.05s/f (Good)
WFA 4 from 5yo+ 4lb **12** Ran SP% **110.3**
Speed ratings: **87,82,77,76,65 65,64,54,53,52** —,— CSF £1.96 TOTE £1.10: £1.02, £1.90, £23.70; EX 2.70.
Owner Ashleybank Investments Limited **Bred** Mrs J M F Dibben **Trained** Norton, N Yorks

FOCUS
An uncompetitive event in which the winner did not have to improve to win with plenty in hand and is value for half as much again as the official margin. A slow pace means this bare form is likely to prove unreliable.

NOTEBOOK
Portavadie did not have to improve to maintain his unbeaten record over hurdles in this most uncompetitive race. A stronger gallop will suit and he will be interesting in ordinary handicaps in due course. *(op 3-10 tchd 1-3)*
Mooramana fared better than of late dropped to this trip but looks flattered by his proximity to the easy winner and he is going to continue to look vulnerable to progressive sorts in this type of event. *(op 7-1)*
Stoneriggs ran easily his best race to date but, although flattered by his proximity, may be the type to fare better in low-grade handicaps when upped in distance. *(op 100-1)*
Rush'N'Run ran his best race over hurdles but this bare form looks decidedly ropey. However, he is in good hands and may be capable of better in modest handicaps. *(op 50-1)*
Loch Red achieved very little on this hurdles debut and is going to continue to look vulnerable in this grade. *(op 66-1)*
Loch Torridon was again well beaten and will have to show a good deal more before he is worth a bet. *Official explanation: jockey said gelding did not travel down the hill (op 25-1)*
Top Pack(IRE) *Official explanation: jockey said gelding had a breathing problem (op 40-1)*

210 JOHN SMITH'S EXTRA SMOOTH "NATIONAL HUNT" NOVICES' HURDLE (DIV II) (8 hdls) 2m 110y
2:30 (2:30) (Class 4) 4-Y-0+ **£3,052** (£872; £436)

Form RPR
0- **1** **Bannister Lane**[72] 4027 5-11-0 .... JMMaguire 100
(D McCain) *prom: rdn bef 2 out: chsd ldr and 6l down last: styd on to ld towards fin* **25/1**
535- **2** ½ **Dewasentah (IRE)**[27] 4783 6-10-7 **98**................................... AThornton 92
(J M Jefferson) *cl up: led 2nd: clr after 3 out: 6l up last: edgd lft u.p: no ex and ct nr fin* **5/4**[1]
03- **3** 9 **Duke Orsino (IRE)**[57] 4299 5-10-11 .... PBuchanan(3) 90
(Miss Lucinda V Russell) *midfield: outpcd 5th: styd on fr 2 out: nt rch first two* **6/1**[3]
0- **4** 7 **Longdale**[58] 4270 7-11-0 .... ADempsey 86+
(M Todhunter) *in tch: effrt bef 2 out: wknd appr last* **20/1**
221- **5** 6 **Pavey Ark (IRE)**[221] 1537 7-11-0 **66**...................................... RMcGrath 77
(James Moffatt) *cl up: outpcd after 3 out: no imp fr next* **4/1**[2]
- **6** 12 **Tullyhappy Lad (IRE)**[12] 31 4-10-10 .... ARoss 61
(I A Duncan, Ire) *hld up: sme hdwy after 3 out: rdn and no imp fr next* **7/1**
06-0 **7** 3 ½ **The Rooken (IRE)**[9] 82 6-11-0 .... KJohnson 62
(P Spottiswood) *hld up: rdn after 5th: sn btn* **100/1**
PP- **8** shd **Crofton Arch**[179] 2109 5-11-0 .... DO'Meara 61
(M A Barnes) *prom: lost pl whn mstke 3 out: wknd* **100/1**
POP- **8** dht **Casterflo**[53] 4393 6-10-7 **73**...(t) BHarding 54
(W S Coltherd) *a bhd* **18/1**
0PP- **10** 6 **Lucken Howe**[26] 4807 6-10-11 ....(t) GBerridge(3) 55
(Mrs J K M Oliver) *hld up: rdn bef 3 out: nvr on terms* **100/1**
P00- **11** 1 ¾ **Seafire Lad (IRE)**[34] 4709 4-10-5 **69**.................................. DMcGann(5) 50
(R Johnson) *a bhd* **25/1**
/0P- **12** 9 **Hot Air (IRE)**[94] 3648 7-11-0 ....(t) PRobson 45
(J I A Charlton) *led to 2nd: cl up tl wknd qckly bef 2 out* **20/1**

4m 17.6s (3.60) **Going Correction** -0.05s/f (Good)
WFA 4 from 5yo+ 4lb **12** Ran SP% **116.7**
Speed ratings: **89,88,84,81,78 72,71,71,71,68 67,63** CSF £55.69 TOTE £30.30: £3.40, £1.10, £2.30; EX 99.80.
Owner Shaw Hill Golf Club(Sage Cott Props Ltd) **Bred** Halewood International Ltd **Trained** Cholmondeley, Cheshire

FOCUS
Another very ordinary event and another steady gallop in the early stages means this bare form, rated through the third, may be less than reliable.

NOTEBOOK
Bannister Lane, who hinted at ability in a bumper on his debut, showed improved form on this hurdles debut and, although this was not much of a race, left the impression that he would be suited by a much stiffer test of stamina in due course.
Dewasentah(IRE), down in trip, looked the one to beat in this company but seemed to throw the race away after going clear and remains one to tread carefully with. *(op 6-4 tchd 13-8 in a place)*
Duke Orsino(IRE), who is now qualified for a handicap mark, left the strong impression that the step up to two and a half miles on a galloping course would be in his favour. *(op 13-2 tchd 5-1)*
Longdale hinted at ability in this very ordinary event and is likely to be suited by the step into modest handicap company in due course.
Pavey Ark(IRE), back over hurdles and down in trip on this first start since September, has still to come near the pick of his chase form in this sphere but left the impression that the return to further would suit. He may fare better in modest handicaps. *(tchd 7-2)*

211 FOSTERS SUPER CHILLED NOVICES' H'CAP CHASE (19 fncs) 3m 1f
3:05 (3:05) (Class 4) (0-100,95) 5-Y-0+ **£3,867** (£1,190; £595; £297)

Form RPR
4PU- **1** **Tina's Scallywag**[27] 4786 8-10-0 **69** oh9................................ DO'Meara 79+
(H P Hogarth) *cl up: led 14th: mde rest: styd on wl* **16/1**
52-2 **2** 1 **Another Club Royal**[8] 98 6-10-7 **76**...................................... JMMaguire 85+
(D McCain) *in tch: hdwy after 4 out: chsd wnr bef last: kpt on run in* **9/2**[3]
P0-P **3** 5 **Tee-Jay (IRE)**[8] 109 9-11-3 **86**... FKeniry 90+
(M D Hammond) *in tch: hdwy and reminder 13th: rdn bef 3 out: one pce fr next* **16/1**
1P-1 **4** 1 **Diamond Cottage (IRE)**[9] 83 10-11-0 **86**......................... PWhelan(3) 90+
(S B Bell) *chsd ldrs: ev ch whn hit 4 out: effrt bef next: one pce between last two* **3/1**[1]
3FP- **5** 13 **Just For Fun (IRE)**[80] 3886 7-10-8 **84**...........................(p) TJDreaper(7) 76+
(Ferdy Murphy) *bhd: struggling 15th: styd on fr 2 out: n.d* **10/1**
134- **6** 12 **Walking Sunday (IRE)**[16] 4940 7-11-1 **84**.....................(p) JPMcNamara 61
(K C Bailey) *in tch tl drvn and outpcd fr 3 out* **7/2**[2]
/0F- **7** 10 **Inglewood**[26] 4812 5-10-12 **88**.. PRobson 48
(Miss Kate Milligan) *bhd: rdn and wknd fr 14th* **33/1**
445- **8** 18 **Leopard Spot (IRE)**[17] 4925 7-11-5 **91**.........................(t) PBuchanan(3) 40
(Miss Lucinda V Russell) *prom: lost pl whn blnd 12th: sn btn* **6/1**
0P-F **9** dist **Pottsy's Joy**[8] 106 8-11-12 **95**.. DElsworth —
(Mrs S J Smith) *hld up: hdwy 1/2-way: wknd after 13th* **10/1**
500- **P** **Sea Maize**[59] 4258 7-10-0 **69** oh3...(p) BHarding —
(C R Wilson) *led to 14th: wknd 4 out: t.o whn p.u bef last* **25/1**

6m 30.2s (-2.60) **Going Correction** -0.175s/f (Good)
WFA 5 from 6yo+ 7lb **10** Ran SP% **116.4**
Speed ratings: **97,96,95,94,90 86,83,77,**—,— CSF £88.47 CT £1191.08 TOTE £20.20: £3.90, £2.00, £5.60; EX 92.40.
Owner Hogarth Racing **Bred** N B Mason **Trained** Stillington, N Yorks

FOCUS
A low-grade handicap in which the pace was fair, with those in the frame behind the winner close to their marks.

NOTEBOOK

Tina's Scallywag, from a stable among the winners, turned in her best effort to win from 9lb out of the handicap. Stamina is her strong suit but, given her record is one of inconsistency, may not be one to lump on at shortish odds next time.

Another Club Royal is progressing steadily over fences and showed enough to suggest a similar race can be found. He looks likely to be suited by an even stiffer test of stamina. *(op 11-4)*

Tee-Jay(IRE) seems to like it at this course and ran his best race over fences, but his record suggests he would be no certainty to reproduce this next time. *(op 20-1)*

Diamond Cottage(IRE), who won a modest event at Kelso on his previous start, was not disgraced from this 4lb higher mark. A good test of stamina seems to suit best and he should continue to give a good account. *(op 7-2)*

Just For Fun(IRE), who has a modest completion record over fences, was not totally disgraced but did not really show enough to suggest he is one to be on next time. *(op 11-1 tchd 9-1)*

Walking Sunday(IRE) had conditions to suit but was disappointing and a series of relatively quick races may have taken its toll. *(op 4-1 tchd 9-2)*

212 IBETX.COM BETTING EXCHANGE MAIDEN HURDLE (12 hdls) 3m
3:40 (3:42) (Class 4) 4-Y-0+ **£2,611** (£746; £373)

Form | | | | RPR
2F4- **1** **Arctic Lagoon (IRE)**^{17} [4928] 6-10-13 88............................(t) ONelmes$^{(3)}$ 90+
(Mrs S C Bradburne) *prom: drvn 4 out: rallied bef 2 out: led bef last: styd on wl* **5/1**^{3}
2 *5* **Royal Artisan (IRE)**^{5} [158] 7-11-2 .... ARoss 86+
(I A Duncan, Ire) *keen early: cl up: led 2 out to bef last: no ch w wnr* **9/2**^{2}
23-0 **3** *4* **You Do The Math (IRE)**^{9} [82] 5-10-13 .... GBerridge$^{(3)}$ 83+
(L Lungo) *hld up: hdwy and chsng ldrs whn hit 2 out: one pce last* **3/1**^{1}
50-6 **4** *14* **Primitive Poppy**^{7} [124] 6-10-9 80... RMcGrath 60
(Mrs A Hamilton) *prom tl rdn and outpcd bef 2 out* **8/1**
0P-P **5** *½* **Derainey (IRE)**^{13} [8] 6-11-2 .... KJohnson 69+
(R Johnson) *mde most to 2 out: wknd bef last* **66/1**
04-4 **6** *dist* **Opal's Helmsman (USA)**^{9} [85] 6-11-2 87.......................(p) ADempsey —
(W S Coltherd) *bhd: struggling 4 out: nvr on terms* **17/2**
00-0 **7** *18* **Thepubhorse**^{10} [59] 5-10-11 .... DCCostello$^{(5)}$ —
(Mrs H O Graham) *chsd ldrs tl wknd bef 2 out* **100/1**
556- **P** **Missoudun (FR)**^{17} [4925] 5-10-9 .... TJDreaper$^{(7)}$ —
(Ferdy Murphy) *nvr on terms: p.u bef 4 out* **40/1**
F **P** **Saddleback Prince**^{5} [147] 6-10-9 .... MJMcAlister$^{(7)}$ —
(B Storey) *nt fluent in rr: t.o whn p.u 1/2-way* **100/1**
360/ **P** **Loi De Martiale (IRE)**^{392} [4732] 7-11-2 .... ATinkler —
(J M Jefferson) *a bhd: t.o whn p.u bef 4 out* **20/1**
04U- **P** **Calamitycharacter**^{15} [4965] 6-10-9 85....................................... BHarding —
(I McMath) *a bhd: t.o whn p.u bef 2 out: lame* **33/1**
05- **P** **Gaelic Jig**^{14} [4981] 6-11-2 ....(t) PRobson —
(J I A Charlton) *prom to 1/2-way: t.o whn p.u bef 3 out* **50/1**
P0P- **P** **Killer (FR)**^{83} [3825] 7-10-13 ....(t) PBuchanan$^{(3)}$ —
(Miss Lucinda V Russell) *a towards rr: t.o whn p.u bef 4 out* **80/1**
05-2 **P** **Iron Warrior (IRE)**^{13} [14] 5-11-2 95.. FKeniry —
(G M Moore) *chsd ldrs: hit 8th: sn lost pl: t.o whn p.u bef last* **9/2**^{2}

6m 7.50s (-3.70) **Going Correction** -0.05s/f (Good) **14** Ran SP% **116.5**
Speed ratings: **104,102,101,96,96** —,—,—,—,— —,—,—,— CSF £25.97 TOTE £5.90: £2.00, £2.30, £1.90; EX 43.90.
Owner William A Powrie **Bred** Lord Vestey **Trained** Cunnoquhie, Fife

FOCUS

An ordinary maiden hurdle in which the gallop was only fair and rated through the winner and third, although could be assessed a lot higher.

NOTEBOOK

Arctic Lagoon(IRE), who is essentially a consistent sort, finally got off the mark over obstacles at the 27th attempt and he should continue to give a good account. *(tchd 11-2 in a place)*

Royal Artisan(IRE), who had shown ability in bumpers, ran right up to the pick of that form over this much longer trip on his hurdles debut. He looks capable of winning a similar event. *(tchd 11-2)*

You Do The Math(IRE) ◆, up markedly in trip, showed more than enough to suggest he can win in ordinary handicap company around this trip in due course. *(op 11-4 tchd 10-3, 7-2 in a place)*

Primitive Poppy has shown ability over hurdles but is likely to continue to look vulnerable in this type of event. *(op 16-1)*

Derainey(IRE) had the run of the race but nevertheless showed much improved form and is the type to win a small handicap for current connections. *(op 50-1)*

Opal's Helmsman(USA), again fitted with cheekpieces, disappointed back over a trip that should have been very much to his liking and he remains one to have reservations about. *(op 8-1 tchd 9-1)*

Iron Warrior(IRE) dropped out very tamely before stamina became any sort of issue over this *longer trip. He has yet to win a race and looks one to tread carefully with. Official explanation: jockey said gelding failed to pick up on final circuit (tchd 25-1)*

Loi De Martiale(IRE) *Official explanation: jockey said gelding was never travelling (tchd 25-1)*

213 TANT PIS H'CAP CHASE (12 fncs) 2m 110y
4:10 (4:12) (Class 4) (0-95,89) 5-Y-0+ **£3,507** (£1,002; £501)

Form | | | | RPR
41-1 **1** **Bogus Dreams (IRE)**^{8} [99] 8-11-12 89.................................... BGibson 116+
(L Lungo) *hld up in tch: smooth hdwy to ld 2 out: jst in front whn blnd last: rdn and kpt on strly* **8/11**^{1}
35-2 **2** *6* **College City (IRE)**^{7} [122] 6-11-5 85.................................(p) LMcGrath$^{(3)}$ 96
(R C Guest) *cl up: led 3 out to next: ev ch last: no ch w wnr run in* **8/1**^{2}
335- **3** *4* **Compadre**^{15} [4968] 7-11-6 83.. NPMulholland 90
(P Monteith) *chsd ldrs: drvn bef 3 out: rallied after next: kpt on run in* **14/1**^{3}
50-5 **4** *¾* **Spectrum Star**^{10} [60] 5-10-0 65 oh6...................................... RMcGrath 69
(F P Murtagh) *bhd tl styd on fr 2 out: n.d* **25/1**
U4-5 **5** *½* **Northern Flash**^{7} [122] 11-10-6 69...(p) FKeniry 75
(J C Haynes) *hld up: hdwy and prom 7th: rdn and outpcd fr 2 out* **33/1**
F6F- **6** *14* **Raise A McGregor**^{183} [2018] 9-11-3 80.................................... DElsworth 72
(Mrs S J Smith) *chsd ldrs tl wknd fr 3 out* **20/1**
5P-1 **7** *5* **Risky Way**^{7} [122] 9-11-4 81... DO'Meara 71+
(W S Coltherd) *led tl hit and hdd 3 out: rdn and btn next* **8/1**^{2}
0-45 **8** *nk* **Dan De Lion**^{7} [126] 6-11-1 78... HOliver 64
(R C Guest) *hld up: hdwy 1/2-way: wknd fr 3 out* **14/1**^{3}
55-6 **9** *10* **Hombre**^{9} [81] 10-10-9 72...(v^{1}) BHarding 48
(M D Hammond) *chsd ldrs tl wknd fr 2 out* **25/1**
04-P **10** *11* **Fairwood Nickle (IRE)**^{9} [81] 6-9-11 63 oh3................(t) PBuchanan$^{(3)}$ 28
(Miss Lucinda V Russell) *sn towards rr: rdn and struggling fr 1/2-way* **40/1**
/23- **11** *1½* **Corbie Abbey (IRE)**^{311} [844] 10-10-7 70.............................. ADempsey 34
(B Mactaggart) *prom to 1/2-way: sn lost pl* **25/1**
/P0- **P** **Hills Of View**^{63} [4166] 7-10-8 71.. ARoss —
(J M Jefferson) *a bhd: t.o whn p.u bef 3 out* **50/1**
0P0- **P** **Karyon (IRE)**^{32} [4738] 5-9-10 66...............................(p) DCCostello$^{(5)}$ —
(Miss Kate Milligan) *a bhd: t.o whn p.u bef 3 out* **100/1**
5P5- **P** **No Kidding**^{90} [3729] 11-11-11 88.. PRobson —
(J I A Charlton) *sn lost prom position: tailing off whn p.u after 6th* **40/1**

4m 3.90s (-6.20) **Going Correction** -0.175s/f (Good)
WFA 5 from 6yo+ 2lb **14** Ran SP% **120.5**
Speed ratings: **107,104,102,101,101 95,92,92,87,82 82**,—,—,— CSF £6.30 CT £51.79 TOTE £1.50: £1.20, £2.20, £3.00; EX 6.90.
Owner Mrs Tracey O'Hare **Bred** Elsdon Farms **Trained** Carrutherstown, D'fries & G'way

FOCUS

A moderate contest but the winner is value for more than double the official margin with the placed horses close to their marks.

NOTEBOOK

Bogus Dreams(IRE) ◆, over fences for only the second time and racing from a 25lb lower chasing mark, looks well ahead of the assessor over fences at present and was value for a fair bit more than the winning margin. He is in tremendous heart and is one to keep on the right side. *(op Evens)*

College City(IRE), from an in-form stable, almost certainly ran to the pick of his recent form but was unlucky to bump into a rival who had a good deal in hand of his mark. He has not won for some time but should continue to go well. *(op 9-1 tchd 10-1)*

Compadre is an honest sort who ran his race but is likely to continue to look vulnerable to anything progressive in this type of event. He looks worth another try over a bit further. *(op 10-1)*

Spectrum Star, having only his second start over fences, has yet to win a race but is going to need a much stiffer test than the one he got here if he is to do so in this sphere. *(op 20-1)*

Northern Flash was not disgraced but is vulnerable to progressive sorts and did not really leave the impression that he is a winner waiting to happen. *(op 25-1)*

Raise A McGregor, down in trip, got round this time but was below his best on this first start for six months. He is in good hands but will have to show more before he is worth a bet. *(op 14-1)*

Risky Way was closely matched with College City on a recent course and distance run, but *consistency is not his strongest suit and he capitulated quickly after a mistake at the third last. (op 7-1 tchd 13-2)*

214 KRONENBOURG 1664 (S) H'CAP HURDLE (8 hdls) 2m 110y
4:45 (4:46) (Class 5) (0-95,93) 4-Y-0+ **£2,471** (£706; £353)

Form | | | | RPR
44-3 **1** **Polished**^{7} [120] 6-11-0 84..(b) LMcGrath$^{(3)}$ 99+
(R C Guest) *hld up in tch: hdwy to ld 3 out: drew clr fr next: easily* **11/10**^{1}
50-0 **2** *15* **Scamp**^{7} [120] 6-10-4 71..(p) KRenwick 66
(R Shiels) *prom: effrt bef 2 out: kpt on: no ch w wnr* **25/1**
UP-4 **3** *½* **Ball Games**^{7} [120] 7-10-5 82.. MMcAvoy$^{(10)}$ 77
(James Moffatt) *hld up in tch: outpcd 3 out: rallied bef last: no imp* **11/2**^{3}
6U5- **4** *5* **Roadworthy (IRE)**^{32} [4738] 8-10-4 78.............................. MrSFMagee$^{(7)}$ 68
(J K Magee, Ire) *cl up: lost pl 1/2-way: rallied bef last: no imp* **20/1**
04-0 **5** *½* **Noras Legacy (IRE)**^{7} [120] 7-10-4 74.............................. PBuchanan$^{(3)}$ 63
(Miss Lucinda V Russell) *cl up: led 4th to 3 out: outpcd fr next* **14/1**
425- **6** *11* **Power And Demand**^{59} [4261] 8-10-3 75............................ DCCostello$^{(5)}$ 53
(C W Thornton) *hld up: hdwy after 3 out: rdn and outpcd after next* **9/2**^{2}
P0-0 **P** **Pucks Court**^{13} [9] 8-10-7 74... ATinkler —
(I A Brown) *sn bhd: p.u after 2nd* **10/1**
46-0 **P** **Lord Of The Land**^{5} [149] 12-11-2 93............................... SGagan$^{(10)}$ —
(Mrs E Slack) *led to 4th: lost pl next: t.o whn p.u bef 2 out* **12/1**
00P- **U** **Torkin Wind**^{58} [4270] 4-10-0 71 oh7......................................(p) DO'Meara —
(M A Barnes) *hld up: struggling 1/2-way: no ch whn swvd rt bef last: wnt rt and uns rdr run in* **66/1**

4m 12.3s (-1.70) **Going Correction** -0.05s/f (Good)
WFA 4 from 6yo+ 4lb **9** Ran SP% **114.7**
Speed ratings: **102,94,94,92,92 86**,—,—,— CSF £30.71 CT £114.45 TOTE £1.90: £1.10, £4.80, £1.80; EX 33.50.There was no bid for the winner.
Owner The Cherry Blossom Partnership **Bred** Ewar Stud Farms **Trained** Brancepeth, Co Durham

FOCUS

A poor event in which the pace was only fair. The winner is value for more than the official margin, but this race is unlikely to be throwing up many winners.

NOTEBOOK

Polished, with the blinkers on again, won a very poor race with a vast amount in hand. His stable are in tremendous form but he may find life much tougher after reassessment. *(op 13-8 tchd 7-4)*

Scamp has been soundly beaten over hurdles and, although fitted with first-time cheekpieces, did not achieve much in this weak event. A step up in trip may help but she will be one to field against at shortish odds next time. *(op 33-1)*

Ball Games is an inconistent performer but finished a similar distance behind the winner as he had done over this course and distance last month. He remains one to tread carefully with. *(op 4-1)*

Roadworthy(IRE), a modest and exposed maiden over hurdles, shaped as though a stiffer test would have suited but is of little immediate interest. *(op 12-1)*

Noras Legacy(IRE) may be suited by a stiffer test of stamina but will have to show more before she is a betting proposition. *(op 16-1)*

Power And Demand, down in trip, was below his recent best and, given he has yet to win in 42 Flat and jumping starts, remains one to place very little faith in. *(op 4-1 tchd 7-2)*

Pucks Court *Official explanation: jockey said gelding lost its action (op 7-1)*

215 JOHN SMITH'S NO NONSENSE H'CAP HURDLE (12 hdls) 3m
5:15 (5:17) (Class 4) (0-100,100) 4-Y-0+ **£2,709** (£774; £387)

Form | | | | RPR
FC3- **1** **Lanzlo (FR)**^{22} [4851] 8-11-10 98... RMcGrath 101
(James Moffatt) *hld up: hdwy bef 2 out: led run in: styd on wl* **8/1**
33-F **2** *¾* **Red Perk (IRE)**^{9} [81] 8-10-8 82..(p) KJohnson 84
(R C Guest) *hld up: hdwy and prom 5th: ev ch bef 2 out: sn rdn: kpt on run in* **5/1**^{1}
2F-4 **3** *1½* **Kidithou (FR)**^{7} [119] 7-11-9 100.................................... PBuchanan$^{(3)}$ 101
(W T Reed) *led or disp ld to run in: kpt on same pce* **8/1**
03-0 **4** *8* **Chivvy Charver (IRE)**^{13} [11] 8-9-11 78............................ EWhillans$^{(7)}$ 71
(A C Whillans) *bhd tl styd on fr 2 out: n.d* **33/1**
325- **5** *nk* **Tobesure (IRE)**^{26} [4812] 11-11-11 99.. PRobson 92+
(J I A Charlton) *in tch: effrt 3 out: wknd after next* **7/1**^{2}
000- **6** *3* **End Of An Error**^{32} [4739] 6-10-9 86...................................... ONelmes$^{(3)}$ 77+
(Mrs E Slack) *bhd: rdn 4 out: no imp tl hdwy 2 out: mstke last: kpt on* **12/1**
600- **7** *3* **Pikestaff (USA)**^{26} [4812] 7-10-11 85.......................................(t) DO'Meara 71
(M A Barnes) *hld up: outpcd 4 out: sme late hdwy: n.d* **25/1**
0P-4 **8** *1¾* **You'Re The Man (IRE)**^{9} [80] 8-10-1 85.........................(p) SGagan$^{(10)}$ 69
(Mrs E Slack) *prom to 4 out: sn lost pl: n.d after* **10/1**
064- **9** *11* **Terramarique (IRE)**^{48} [4473] 6-10-7 81.................................. BGibson 54
(L Lungo) *hld up: hdwy to chse ldrs 8th: wknd bef 2 out* **7/1**^{2}
26-0 **10** *1½* **Old Nosey (IRE)**^{9} [80] 9-11-2 90.. ADempsey 62
(B Mactaggart) *hld up: hdwy and cl up 5th: wknd bef 2 out* **25/1**
330- **11** *18* **Dark Thunder (IRE)**^{17} [4928] 8-10-6 87........................(v^{1}) TJDreaper$^{(7)}$ 41
(Ferdy Murphy) *a bhd: struggling fr 1/2-way* **25/1**
32/- **12** **Brackney Boy (IRE)**^{5} [153] 11-10-11 85... ARoss 39
(I A Duncan, Ire) *chsd ldrs tl wknd bef 2 out* **15/2**^{3}

50F- **13** **Premier Drive (IRE)**[26] [4812] 12-11-5 **98** .... DCCostello(5) 52
(G M Moore) *led or disp ld to bef 2 out: wknd qckly: virtually p.u run in* **33/1**

01-0 **P** **Hello Baby**[5] [152] 5-10-11 **85** .... KRenwick —
(A C Whillans) *prom tl lost pl bef 4 out: t.o whn p.u bef 2 out* **14/1**

440- **P** **Oscar The Boxer (IRE)**[99] [3566] 6-10-12 **86** .... ATinkler —
(J M Jefferson) *midfield: struggling bef 4 out: t.o whn p.u bef last* **12/1**

PP4- **P** **Putup Or Shutup (IRE)**[21] [4868] 9-11-7 **100** .... CHonour(5) —
(K C Bailey) *hld up midfield: hdwy and prom 4 out: wknd 2 out: t.o whn p.u bef last* **9/1**

6m 4.10s (-7.10) **Going Correction** -0.05s/f (Good) **16** Ran SP% **134.2**
Speed ratings: **109,108,108,105,105 104,103,102,99,98 92,92,92,—,— —** CSF £50.58 CT £350.16 TOTE £10.50: £4.00, £2.50, £3.00, £6.60; EX 65.30 Place 6 £11.49, Place 5 £10.88.
Owner The Sheroot Partnership **Bred** Alain Fabre And Mme Ursula Wittmer **Trained** Cartmel, Cumbria
■ Stewards' Enquiry : K Johnson two-day ban: used whip with excessive frequency (May 18,19)

FOCUS
Mainly exposed performers in this ordinary event and, given the pace seemed sound, this form could rate higher and should stand up at a similar level.

NOTEBOOK
Lanzlo(FR), down in grade, had no progressive sorts to cope with this time and ran right up to his best under ideal conditions. He should continue to give a good account at this sort of level. *(tchd 9-1)*
Red Perk(IRE), back over hurdles, ran right up to his best for a stable that is in tremendous form. He is not really one for maximum faith but is capable of winning a similar event from this sort of mark. *(op 6-1 tchd 13-2)*
Kidithou(FR), reverting to hurdles after seeming to lose his confidence over fences, ran creditably but still tends to make the odd mistake and is likely to continue to look vulnerable to progressive or well handicapped sorts. *(op 9-1 tchd 10-1)*
Chivvy Charver(IRE) ran creditably upped to this trip for the first time and did not fail through lack of stamina. However his lack of consistency means this is not sure to be reproduced next time. *(op 25-1)*
Tobesure(IRE) is mainly a consistent sort and was not disgraced, but the fact he is without a win since September 2003 is beginning to be a bit of a concern. *(tchd 8-1)*
End Of An Error was not totally disgraced but is another on a long losing run and his inconsistency means he is not one to place much faith in. *(op 11-1)*
Terramarique(IRE) ran a bit better than the bare form as he again did not seem to get home over this trip. However, he is in good hands and will be of interest around two and a half miles in modest company. *(op 6-1)*
T/Plt: £12.20 to a £1 stake. Pool: £24,857.45. 1,475.45 winning tickets. T/Qpdt: £5.10 to a £1 stake. Pool: £1,484.80. 215.30 winning tickets. RY

WARWICK (L-H)
Saturday, May 7

OFFICIAL GOING: Good to firm (firm in places)
There were 14 non-runners due to the ground having dried out during the day.
Wind: moderate across Weather: fine

216 RACING UK "NATIONAL HUNT" NOVICES' HURDLE (11 hdls) 2m 5f
5:50 (5:50) (Class 4) 4-Y-0+ **£3,549** (£1,014; £507)

Form RPR

202- **1** **Azzemour (FR)**[14] [4977] 6-11-0 94 .... (t) RWalsh 100+
(P F Nicholls) *hld up: stdy hdwy on ins after 6th: led appr 2 out: drvn out* **7/4**[1]

PPP- **2** *3* **Sylvan Shack (IRE)**[85] [3795] 7-11-0 .... MFoley 95
(S J Gilmore) *chsd ldr: rdn and ev ch appr 2 out: kpt on same pce flat* **66/1**

3 *3* **Kilty Storm (IRE)**[40] [4638] 6-11-0 .... JEMoore 92
(M C Pipe) *t.k.h: hdwy appr 5th: led 7th: rdn and hdd appr 2 out: no ex flat* **2/1**[2]

F60- **4** *½* **Thisisyourlife (IRE)**[42] [4554] 7-11-0 104 .... RJohnson 92+
(H D Daly) *hld up and bhd: hdwy after 8th: one pce fr 2 out* **7/2**[3]

/63- **5** *6* **Lyon**[18] [4920] 5-11-0 .... LAspell 85
(O Sherwood) *hld up: hdwy appr 7th: wknd appr 2 out* **10/1**

0P- **6** *29* **Teen House**[140] [2900] 6-10-7 .... BHitchcott 49
(Miss Suzy Smith) *nt jump wl: set slow pce: hdd 7th: mstke 8th: wknd after 3 out: t.o* **100/1**

000- **7** *dist* **Griffin's Legacy**[27] [4793] 6-11-0 .... GSupple —
(N G Ayliffe) *hld up in tch: nt fluent 7th: bhd whn mstke 8th: t.o* **66/1**

000- **8** *nk* **Ilongue (FR)**[15] [4958] 4-9-13 .... DCrosse(3) —
(R Dickin) *a bhd: hit 2nd: lost tch 7th: t.o* **100/1**

P **Lisaroon (IRE)** 7-11-0 .... BJCrowley —
(Miss E C Lavelle) *prom: reminders 5th: rdn and wknd appr 6th: t.o whn p.u bef 3 out* **25/1**

4m 55.2s (-17.90) **Going Correction** -1.025s/f (Hard)
WFA 4 from 5yo+ 5lb **9** Ran SP% **109.8**
Speed ratings: **93,91,90,90,88 77,—,—,—** CSF £97.26 TOTE £2.60: £1.02, £8.90, £2.00; EX 100.10.
Owner Tony Hayward And Barry Fulton **Bred** Hubert Carion **Trained** Ditcheat, Somerset

FOCUS
A slowly-run, modest affair and the form is somewhat suspect, although the winner is rated value for more than the official margin.

NOTEBOOK
Azzemour(FR), a brother to Montifault and Le Sauvigon, seems to have learnt to settle and probably had less to do back in novice company. His trainer thought the quick ground helped and he will be kept on the go over the summer. *(op 15-8 tchd 2-1)*
Sylvan Shack(IRE), the winner of all three of his points in 2003, had been pulled up in each of his starts under Rules. He would not have minded further, especially given the way things panned out, and it could be that fast ground is the key to him. *(op 50-1)*
Kilty Storm(IRE), a winner between the flags in Ireland, had finished fourth in a soft-ground bumper restricted to pointers at Fairyhouse in March. He was not disgraced on his hurdling debut on this totally different ground. *(tchd 7-4 and 9-4)*
Thisisyourlife(IRE) could not sustain a promising-looking effort. *(op 9-2)*
Lyon, trying a longer trip, may well have found the ground too lively. *(op 13-2)*
Griffin's Legacy *Official explanation: jockey said gelding was unsuited by good to firm, firm in places ground (op 50-1)*

217 RACING UK NOVICES' CHASE (12 fncs) 2m 110y
6:20 (6:20) (Class 3) 5-Y-0+ **£5,541** (£1,705; £852; £426)

Form RPR

P-11 **1** **Feel The Pride (IRE)**[2] [195] 7-11-5 118 .... APMcCoy 123+
(Jonjo O'Neill) *hld up: hdwy 7th: led 2 out: v easily* **8/15**[1]

0F4- **2** *2* **Emanic (FR)**[86] [3777] 5-10-12 120 .... (t) RWalsh 107+
(P F Nicholls) *hld up: nt fluent 1st: hdwy 8th: slipped bnd appr 2 out: kpt on flat: no ch w wnr* **7/2**[2]

PP-3 **3** *hd* **Nopekan (IRE)**[13] [2] 5-10-5 .... RSpate(7) 104
(Mrs K Waldron) *hld up in tch: rdn and sltly outpcd after 3 out: styd on flat* **25/1**

P1P- **4** *shd* **Major Euro (IRE)**[14] [4979] 8-11-6 104 .... JamesDavies 113+
(S J Gilmore) *led: rdn and hdd 2 out: one pce* **40/1**

00-4 **5** *7* **The Names Bond**[10] [60] 7-11-0 100 .... GLee 103+
(Andrew Turnell) *chsd ldr tl blnd 7th: wknd 4 out* **33/1**

151- **6** *8* **Sardagna (FR)**[15] [4968] 5-11-0 118 .... TJMalone(3) 94
(M C Pipe) *hld up and bhd: j.lft 2 out: nvr nr ldrs* **15/2**[3]

633- **7** *5* **Bolshoi Ballet**[92] [3144] 7-11-0 .... (b) PMoloney 86
(J Mackie) *prom tl wknd 7th* **50/1**

50P- **P** **Distant Romance**[125] [3176] 8-10-0 .... RLucey-Butler(7) —
(Miss Z C Davison) *bhd fr 6th: mstke 3 out: t.o whn p.u bef last* **150/1**

3m 55.8s (-4.50) **Going Correction** -0.70s/f (Firm)
WFA 5 from 7yo+ 2lb **8** Ran SP% **111.1**
Speed ratings: **82,81,80,80,77 73,71,—** CSF £2.55 TOTE £1.50: £1.10, £1.60, £2.60; EX 4.00.
Owner Mrs M Liston **Bred** Thomas B Russell **Trained** Cheltenham, Gloucs

FOCUS
A fair race of its type for the time of year although the time was slow, but the winning margin gave no reflection of the winner's superiority.

NOTEBOOK
Feel The Pride(IRE) loves fast ground and completed a quick hat-trick without knowing she had been in a race. She was merely toying with the opposition in the closing stages and will now be given a little break prior to a possible trip to the Galway Festival. *(op 4-7 after 8-13 and 4-6 in places)*
Emanic(FR), wearing a tongue tie for the first time, stuck to his task in the three-way battle for second but is greatly flattered by his proximity to the winner. *Official explanation: jockey said gelding slipped on final bend (op 10-3)*
Nopekan(IRE) appeared to find a second wind after the final fence but the winner was in a different league. *(op 20-1)*
Major Euro(IRE) showed that all was well after he had lost his action last time. However, he had no answer when brushed aside by the winner. *(op 25-1)*
The Names Bond was stopped in his tracks by a bad error at the second ditch. *Official explanation: jockey said gelding made bad mistake at open ditch*
Sardagna(FR) has won over hurdles on a sound surface but it was not as quick as this. *(op 7-1 tchd 8-1)*

218 HBG CONSTRUCTION H'CAP HURDLE (11 hdls) 2m 5f
6:50 (6:50) (Class 4) (0-105,105) 4-Y-0+ **£3,580** (£1,023; £511)

Form RPR

353- **1** **Vicentio**[14] [4977] 6-10-0 **79** oh3 .... GLee 84+
(T J Fitzgerald) *hld up: hdwy 3 out: led and j.rt last: drvn out* **7/4**[1]

PP-0 **2** *5* **Dunkerron**[12] [25] 8-9-7 **79** oh7 .... SWalsh(7) 79
(J Joseph) *led: rdn appr 2 out: hdd last: one pce* **16/1**

03P- **3** *1 ¼* **Welsh Dane**[44] [4531] 5-10-3 **82** .... (p) PJBrennan 82+
(M Sheppard) *hld up: hdwy appr 6th: rdn appr 2 out: one pce* **20/1**

50-3 **4** *1 ¾* **Waydale Hill**[8] [111] 6-9-13 **81** .... (p) RWalford(3) 78
(T D Walford) *hld up in tch: outpcd 7th: styd on flat* **4/1**[2]

163- **5** *¾* **At The Double**[18] [4918] 9-10-11 **90** .... (b) PHide 86
(P Winkworth) *prom: hit 3 out: one pce* **11/1**

F05- **6** *nk* **Georgian Harry (IRE)**[40] [4613] 8-11-3 **96** .... (t) RJohnson 93+
(R T Phillips) *hld up: hit 4th and 5th: hdwy 7th: rdn appr 2 out: wknd flat* **6/1**[3]

600- **7** *7* **Domenico (IRE)**[29] [4403] 7-10-11 **90** .... TScudamore 79
(J R Jenkins) *hld up: hdwy 7th: rdn and wknd appr 2 out* **16/1**

630- **8** *dist* **Stolen Song**[21] [3792] 5-11-2 **95** .... SDurack —
(M J Ryan) *prom tl wknd 7th: t.o* **10/1**

OPP- **U** **Nick The Silver**[19] [4914] 4-11-2 **100** .... JEMoore —
(M C Pipe) *hung rt thrght: racd wd: a bhd: t.o whn uns rdr after 7th* **8/1**

4m 50.8s (-22.30) **Going Correction** -1.025s/f (Hard)
WFA 4 from 5yo+ 5lb **9** Ran SP% **115.7**
Speed ratings: **101,99,98,97,97 97,94,—,—** CSF £29.34 CT £426.80 TOTE £2.30: £1.40, £6.30, £6.70; EX 29.00.
Owner Shaw Thing Partnership **Bred** Biddestone Stud **Trained** Malton, N Yorks

FOCUS
A very moderate race and the first two came from out of the handicap proper.

NOTEBOOK
Vicentio had the form of his third at Market Rasen boosted by the success of Azzemour in the opener. He drew away under pressure after jumping across the runner-up at the last despite being 3lb out of the handicap. *(op 5-2 tchd 11-4, 3-1 in a place)*
Dunkerron, 7lb 'wrong', bounced back to form with ground conditions in his favour. *(op 10-1)*
Welsh Dane was encountering this sort of ground for the first time and this was certainly a much better performance. *(op 12-1)*
Waydale Hill appears to need the combination of the top of the ground and a return to a longer trip. *(op 7-2)*
At The Double has shown his best form on soft ground but did keep plugging on after looking held when missing out at the third last. *(op 9-1)*
Georgian Harry(IRE) again ran as if this distance is beyond him. *(op 5-1 tchd 13-2)*

219 CENKOS CHASE (12 fncs) 2m 110y
7:20 (7:20) (Class 2) 5-Y-0+ **£10,114** (£3,112; £1,556; £778)

Form RPR

F23- **1** **Bambi De L'Orme (FR)**[30] [4751] 6-11-0 134 .... APMcCoy 143+
(Ian Williams) *hld up in rr: hdwy to ld 2 out: drvn out* **85/40**[1]

136- **2** *nk* **River City (IRE)**[28] [4769] 8-11-10 147 .... TDoyle 152
(Noel T Chance) *hld up: hdwy 3 out: ev ch fr 2 out: sn rdn: r.o flat* **3/1**[2]

546- **3** *8* **Kadarann (IRE)**[21] [4863] 8-11-10 150 .... (t) RWalsh 145+
(P F Nicholls) *w ldr: led after 5th to 4 out: rdn to ld briefly appr 2 out: wknd last* **10/3**[3]

102- **4** *½* **Almaydan**[23] [4838] 7-11-4 133 .... RThornton 138
(R Lee) *prom tl wknd 2 out* **7/2**

04F- **5** *16* **Bonus Bridge (IRE)**[21] [4863] 10-11-4 137 .... MBradburne 134+
(H D Daly) *led tl after 5th: rdn 7th: led 4 out tl appr 2 out: wkng whn mstke 2 out: stmbld last* **11/1**

3m 46.3s (-14.00) **Going Correction** -0.70s/f (Firm) course record **5** Ran SP% **110.6**
Speed ratings: **104,103,100,99,92** CSF £9.03 TOTE £2.60: £1.50, £1.40; EX 10.50.
Owner Mr & Mrs John Poynton **Bred** A F Peter And Classic Breeding Sarl **Trained** Portway, Worcs

FOCUS
A decent race run at a good pace and fast ground led to the course record held by the horse this race was named after being broken by 1.5 seconds. The form looks solid.

NOTEBOOK
Bambi De L'Orme(FR) gained due reward for some cracking efforts behind Fota Island. He handles this sort of ground but will be put away until the autumn to contest the top two-mile handicap chases. *(op 2-1 tchd 9-4)*

The Form Book, Raceform Ltd, Compton, RG20 6NL

River City(IRE) who may have found Aintree coming too soon after his third in the Arkle at Cheltenham, bounced back to form with a grand effort and lost nothing in defeat at these weights. *(op 9-4)*
Kadarann(IRE) was fitted with a tongue tie having been tried in blinkers when disappointing at Ayr. The ground may have been a bit lively for him. *(op 7-2 tchd 4-1)*
Almaydan was a pound worse off than when over 30 lengths behind the winner in the Grand Annual at the Cheltenham Festival. *(op 4-1 tchd 9-2)*
Bonus Bridge(IRE) would not have been beaten so far had his jumping not deteriorated in the home straight. *(op 10-1)*

220 WARWICK RACECOURSE FOR CONFERENCES H'CAP HURDLE (8 hdls) 2m

7:50 (7:50) (Class 4) (0-110,108) 4-Y-0+ **£3,444** (£984; £492)

Form RPR
214- **1** **Tiger Frog (USA)**[17] 3054 6-11-7 **101** (b) WMarston 103
(J Mackie) *a.p: led appr last: drvn out* **4/1**[3]
550- **2** ½ **Robyn Alexander (IRE)**[20] 4889 7-11-6 **100** RWalsh 101
(P F Nicholls) *prom: lost pl 5th: hdwy 2 out: ev ch last: hrd rdn: r.o* **11/4**[1]
034- **3** ¾ **Cream Cracker**[22] 4854 7-11-1 **95** JMMaguire 95
(Mrs Jeremy Young) *hld up and bhd: hdwy on ins appr 2 out: rdn and ev ch last: nt qckn* **11/1**
000- **4** 2 **Blue Hawk (IRE)**[34] 4714 8-10-7 **94** JPritchard(7) 92
(R Dickin) *tk keen hold: led: rdn and hdd appr last: no ex flat* **25/1**
000- **5** 2½ **Noble Pasao (IRE)**[39] 4279 8-11-6 **100** GLee 96
(Andrew Turnell) *hld up and bhd: hdwy appr 2 out: rdn and wknd last* **11/1**
225- **6** hd **A Bit Of Fun**[20] 4883 4-11-5 **108** LTreadwell(5) 100
(J T Stimpson) *hld up in mid-div: sltly outpcd 3 out: no real prog fr 2 out* **12/1**
530- **7** 3 **Avesomeofthat (IRE)**[35] 4691 4-10-13 **97** (t) PHolley 89+
(Mrs P N Duffield) *hld up and bhd: hdwy after 3 out: ev ch whn blnd 2 out: nt rcvr* **12/1**
020- **8** 1¼ **Blue Leader (IRE)**[44] 4533 6-11-8 **102** (t) ChristianWilliams 93
(W K Goldsworthy) *prom: rdn and wkng whn sltly hmpd 2 out* **8/1**
512- **F** **Wenger (FR)**[41] 4579 5-11-3 **97** (b) PHide 91
(P Winkworth) *hld up in tch: rdn and ev ch whn fell 2 out* **7/2**[2]

3m 37.0s (-17.10) **Going Correction** -1.025s/f (Hard)
WFA 4 from 5yo+ 4lb **9** Ran SP% **115.9**
Speed ratings: **101,100,100,99,98 98,96,95,—** CSF £15.92 CT £111.17 TOTE £4.50: £2.00, £1.10, £2.70; EX 20.40.
Owner Fools Who Dream **Bred** Camberwell Investments **Trained** Church Broughton, Derbys

FOCUS
A moderate contest that turned out to be very competitive with the runner-up setting the standard.

NOTEBOOK
Tiger Frog(USA), sharpened up by a run on soft ground on the Flat, does not mind hearing his feet rattle. He seems equally effective over both hurdles and fences. *(op 5-2)*
Robyn Alexander(IRE) delivered her challenge in the home straight after Walsh was content to let her lose her place. It was simply a case of meeting one too good on the day. *(op 4-1 tchd 5-2)*
Cream Cracker, 8lb lower than when previously in a handicap put a disappointing run last time behind her. *(op 8-1)*
Blue Hawk(IRE), who had done little since winning a fast-ground seller in September 2003, again showed a liking for these conditions. *(op 14-1)*
Noble Pasao(IRE) has slipped to a mark only a pound higher than when he scored at Haydock last November. The fast ground should not have bothered him. Official explanation: jockey said gelding was unsuited by good to firm, firm in places ground *(op 11-2 tchd 12-1)*
A Bit Of Fun has gone up 10lb without winning since he landed a Doncaster seller last December. *(op 10-1 tchd 14-1)*
Avesomeofthat(IRE) would have finished closer had he not made a nonsense of the penultimate hurdle. *(op 10-1 tchd 14-1)*
Wenger(FR) was still in contention but not going like a winner when crashing out at the penultimate hurdle. *(tchd 4-1)*

221 FINALE HUNTERS' CHASE (17 fncs) 2m 4f 110y

8:20 (8:20) (Class 6) 5-Y-0+ **£1,631** (£466; £233)

Form RPR
P23- **1** **Silence Reigns**[38] 4658 11-12-0 115 (bt) LHeard(7) 114+
(P F Nicholls) *hld up: hit 12th: hdwy appr 4 out: swtchd rt appr 2 out: rdn to ld flat: r.o wl* **5/2**[2]
/2P- **2** 2½ **Red Guard**[30] 4750 11-12-0 102 TMessenger(7) 108
(George Hosier) *hld up and bhd: hdwy 8th: chal on bit appr 2 out: ev ch flat: rdn and nt qckn* **33/1**
25-2 **3** ¾ **An Capall Dubh (IRE)**[13] 6 9-12-5 MrRBurton 105
(Mrs Edward Crow) *a.p: rdn to ld appr 2 out: hdd and no ex flat* **11/10**[1]
0P-2 **4** 14 **Wings Of Hope (IRE)**[9] 79 9-11-11 64 MrDSJones(3) 91+
(James Richardson) *w ldr: led 11th tl appr 2 out: 4th and wkng whn blnd last* **6/1**[3]
/40- **5** 1 **Cassia Green**[30] 4750 11-11-12 MrDGreenway(7) 90
(P H Morris) *prom: stdd and lost pl 3rd: mstke 5th: hdwy 10th: wknd after 3 out* **14/1**
3U-0 **6** 9 **Sporting Chance**[10] 47 13-11-12 83 MrMMunrowd(7) 81
(Mrs Jo Sleep) *prom: led after 4th to 11th: wknd after 3 out* **50/1**
00-0 **7** 6 **Epsilo De La Ronce (FR)**[10] 47 13-12-0 88 MrPaulMorris(7) 77
(Paul Morris) *bhd: mstke 5th: nvr nr ldrs* **40/1**
06-0 **8** 3 **Merry Minstrel (IRE)**[10] 47 12-12-0 79 (p) MrJOldring(7) 74
(Mrs Jackie Hunt) *chsd ldrs: rdn 13th: wknd 3 out: no ch whn hit last* **100/1**
55/ **9** 16 **Hip Pocket (IRE)**[577] 1580 9-11-12 (p) MrRMcCarthy(7) 56
(Robert Bowling) *a bhd* **20/1**
043- **P** **Imago Ii (FR)**[47] 4500 9-12-2 89 MrAWintle(3) —
(B R Summers) *a bhd: j.rt 12th: p.u bef 13th* **20/1**
03P/ **P** **Bengal Boy**[6] 9-11-12 MrNPearce(7) —
(Mrs Jane Knight) *led: mstke 4th: sn hdd: wknd appr 11th: t.o whn p.u bef 4 out* **66/1**
PPP- **P** **Pharbeitfrome (IRE)**[21] 11-12-4 87 (t) MrNMoore(3) —
(W B Stone) *mid-div: nt fluent 1st: bhd fr 11th: t.o whn p.u bef 4 out* **100/1**
00-F **P** **Captain Ron (IRE)**[10] 47 9-11-7 (b) MrRhysHughes(7) —
(S Lycett) *towards rr: mstke 3rd: blnd bdly and rdr lost iron 9th: t.o whn p.u bef 11th* **100/1**

5m 3.00s (-13.50) **Going Correction** -0.70s/f (Firm) **13** Ran SP% **118.5**
Speed ratings: **97,96,95,90,90 86,84,83,77,— —,—,—** CSF £79.14 TOTE £3.10: £1.80, £3.70, £1.20; EX 35.80 Place 6 £5.26, Place 5 £3.83.
Owner R P Blackburn **Bred** Cheveley Park Stud Ltd **Trained** Ditcheat, Somerset

FOCUS
A modest hunter chase in which the first three came clear.

NOTEBOOK
Silence Reigns had never previously run on ground this fast but came through to win going away. *(op 13-8)*
Red Guard does not mind this sort of ground but the winner proved far too strong when the chips were really down. *(op 16-1)*
An Capall Dubh(IRE) was worn down over a trip on the short side for him, especially on such a fast surface. *(op 7-4)*
Wings Of Hope(IRE) would have finished closer had he not made a real mess of the final fence. *(op 10-1 tchd 5-1)*
Cassia Green had been beaten over 30 lengths by the winner on soft ground at Bangor in February. *(tchd 18-1)*
T/Plt: £3.60 to a £1 stake. Pool £33,022.40, 6661.25 winning tickets T/Qpdt: £3.70 to a £1 stake. Pool £2,533.30. 2533.40 winning tickets KH

222 - 228a (Foreign Racing) - See Raceform Interactive

PLUMPTON (L-H)

Sunday, May 8

OFFICIAL GOING: Good to firm
Wind: Almost nil Weather: Mostly fine, heavy shower during race five (4.10)

229 SOUTHERN FM NOVICES' H'CAP HURDLE (14 hdls) 3m 1f 110y

2:10 (2:11) (Class 4) (0-95,95) 4-Y-0+ **£2,744** (£784; £392)

Form RPR
02P- **1** **Brisbane Road (IRE)**[18] 4929 8-11-4 **88** (bt[1]) MrRMcCarthy(7) 88+
(B J Llewellyn) *cl up: reminder after 9th: pressed ldr 3 out: led next: in command last: rdr nrly uns flat: styd on* **12/1**
66-2 **2** 4 **Vallica**[10] 73 6-11-1 **85** DLaverty(7) 80
(Mrs A M Thorpe) *pressed ldr: led 6th: rdn and hdd 2 out: one pce* **3/1**[1]
2U3- **3** 2 **Mistified (IRE)**[45] 4531 4-11-9 **95** RYoung(3) 82
(J W Mullins) *hld up in last: prog after 10th: outpcd bef 3 out: kpt on u.p fr next* **4/1**[2]
PP6- **4** hd **Salix Bay**[17] 4939 9-10-0 **70** (v) RLucey-Butler(7) 63
(P Butler) *prominent: trckd ldr 9th to 3 out: one pce after* **33/1**
P5P- **5** dist **Celtic Ruffian (IRE)**[42] 4582 7-10-6 **69** ow1 BJCrowley —
(R Rowe) *led: mstke 6th and hdd: mstke next: struggling fr 11th: t.o : btn 40 l* **6/1**[3]
3FR- **6** 5 **Lord Attica (IRE)**[41] 4620 6-10-5 **68** NFehily —
(M F Harris) *in tch: rdn 10th: sn struggling: t.o 3 out: btn 45 l* **7/1**
334/ **7** nk **Spider Boy**[552] 1929 8-10-1 **64** (p) BHitchcott —
(Miss Z C Davison) *chsd ldrs tl wknd 10th: t.o after next: btn 45 l* **40/1**
P06- **8** 14 **Charleston**[36] 4691 4-11-1 **84** LAspell —
(R Rowe) *j.rt: hld up: prog to trck ldrs 11th: wknd bef next : t.o: btn 59 l* **14/1**
530- **F** **Cannon Fire (FR)**[133] 2975 4-11-10 **93** AThornton —
(Evan Williams) *crumpled on landing and fell 1st* **4/1**[2]

6m 12.3s (-44.80) **Going Correction** -0.30s/f (Good) **9** Ran SP% **111.5**
Speed ratings: **101,99,99,99,— —,—,—,—** CSF £46.85 CT £168.85 TOTE £13.20: £4.20, £1.40, £1.90; EX 60.60.
Owner Chris Howell **Bred** John McEnery **Trained** Fochriw, Caerphilly

FOCUS
A poor race, run at a modest early gallop and the pace only lifted over the final mile. The form is weak.

NOTEBOOK
Brisbane Road(IRE), blinkered for the first time, appreciated being stepped up in trip again though the signs did not look great with over a circuit left as he was being given a couple of serious reminders. Getting stronger as the race progressed, he was in control when starting to hang coming to the last flight and nearly lost his rider when almost colliding with the stands' rail on the run-in. He will be fortunate to find another race like this, but remains unexposed over the trip. *(op 14-1)*
Vallica did her best under a positive ride, but she does lack a decisive turn of foot and that was again her downfall even over this trip. She is yet to win a race over hurdles after 22 attempts. *(op 11-4 and 10-3 in places)*
Mistified(IRE), like the winner, stepping up in trip, stayed on over the last half-mile but could never land an effective blow. He may be better with cut. *(op 7-2 tchd 9-2)*
Salix Bay, unplaced in all seven of his previous outings, was always thereabouts and managed to stay in the thick of the action for longer than might have been anticipated. His proximity drags the form right down. *(op 28-1 tchd 25-1)*
Lord Attica(IRE) never looked that happy on this return to hurdles and he may have found the ground too quick. *(op 12-1)*

230 JOE THE CAP FROM CARSHALTON MEMORIAL MAIDEN HURDLE (9 hdls) 2m

2:40 (2:42) (Class 4) 4-Y-0+ **£3,220** (£920; £460)

Form RPR
33- **1** **Kilindini**[23] 4852 4-10-12 BJCrowley 106+
(Miss E C Lavelle) *mde all: 4 l clr and rdn after 3 out: styd on wl* **3/1**[2]
2 1¼ **Settlement Craic (IRE)**[40] 4-10-12 JimCrowley 106+
(T G Mills) *hld up midfield: mstke 3rd: prog 6th: mstke 3 out: sn chsd wnr: rdn and no imp 2 out: styd on again flat* **11/4**[1]
100- **3** 14 **Sonic Sound**[36] 4696 6-11-2 (t) TDoyle 95+
(P R Webber) *settled in midfield: effrt and outpcd bef 3 out: pushed along and styd on bef next: tk modest 3rd last* **15/2**
023- **4** 3½ **Hatteras (FR)**[20] 4911 6-10-9 109 RLucey-Butler(7) 92
(Miss M P Bryant) *mstke 1st: towards rr: sme prog 3 out: chsd clr ldng pair 2 out: no imp: lost 3rd last* **6/1**[3]
220- **5** 10 **Whistling Fred**[151] 2705 6-11-2 NFehily 83+
(B De Haan) *hld up towards rr: outpcd fr 6th: mstke 3 out: shuffled along and kpt on steadily: nvr nr ldrs* **14/1**
034- **6** 1¾ **Cappanrush (IRE)**[31] 4760 5-11-2 LAspell 81+
(A Ennis) *hld up towards rr: prog 5th: chsd ldng trio bef 3 out: wknd bef next* **14/1**
P- **7** nk **The King Of Rock**[28] 4793 4-10-12 VSlattery 77+
(A G Newcombe) *hld up wl in rr: bhd fr 6th: shuffled along 3 out: sltly hmpd 2 out: styd on steadily: nvr nr ldrs* **100/1**
0P- **8** shd **Sean (IRE)**[326] 765 6-11-2 BHitchcott 79
(Mrs L C Jewell) *chsd ldrs: outpcd after 6th: wknd after 3 out* **100/1**
5/4- **9** 6 **Gemini Dancer**[21] 4885 6-11-2 JTizzard 73
(C L Tizzard) *hld up in rr: mstke 2nd: effrt 6th: sn outpcd: no ch fr 3 out* **10/1**
6- **10** 9 **Cicatrice**[50] 4446 4-10-12 MFoley 60
(D R Gandolfo) *chsd wnr to 2nd: wknd after 5th: wl bhd 2 out* **50/1**
0- **11** 28 **Balloch**[168] 2367 4-10-0 StephenJCraine(5) 25
(Mary Meek) *chsd ldrs to 4th: wknd: wl bhd fr 6th: t.o* **100/1**
0U0- **F** **The Last Over**[23] 4852 4-10-2 AHoneyball(3) —
(N J Hawke) *wl in rr: 13th whn fell 5th* **100/1**
L **Among Thieves (IRE)**[57] 5-10-2 LNewnes(7) —
(M D I Usher) *reluctant to go to post: ref to r: tk no part* **100/1**

0/ **F** **My Maite (IRE)**[83] 2778 6-11-2 ....(vt) MBatchelor 83
(R Ingram) *prom: chsd wnr 6th tl after 3 out: 4th and wkng whn fell 2 out: dead* **20/1**

P/0- **P** **Orthodox**[19] 4696 6-11-2 ....(p) PHide —
(G L Moore) *chsd wnr 2nd to 6th: wkng rapidly and wl bhd whn blnd 3 out: p.u bef next* **16/1**

3m 44.25s (-6.05) **Going Correction** -0.30s/f (Good)
WFA 4 from 5yo+ 4lb **15** Ran SP% **117.7**
Speed ratings: **103,102,95,93,88 87,87,87,84,80 66,—,—,—,—** CSF £11.28 TOTE £3.90: £2.20, £2.00, £2.30; EX 14.90.
Owner Nigel Foster **Bred** C N H Foster **Trained** Wildhern, Hants

FOCUS
A moderate maiden hurdle and, despite the big field, not that competitive. Nevertheless the form looks solid enough and should produce winners.

NOTEBOOK
Kilindini built on the promise he showed when third on his two previous runs over hurdles, keeping on well when challenged having been ridden positively throughout. Things will be harder in novice company under a penalty, but that division can be quite weak at this stage of the season and further success cannot be ruled out. He also has the option of going handicapping. *(op 9-4)*
Settlement Craic(IRE), an 87-rated dual middle-distance winner on the Flat, made a respectable hurdling debut, but was just found out by his inexperience in the hurdling department. This form falls some way short of the level he is at on the Flat, but he is open to improvement, ought to stay further, and should have little bother in winning races. *(op 5-2 tchd 7-2)*
Sonic Sound managed to win a bumper last season, but he has yet to go on from that over hurdles. Fitted with a tongue-tie for the first time, this was a little better, but he just lacked the pace of the front two and may want further. *(op 8-1 tchd 9-1)*
Hatteras(FR) once again found a few too good and, on the evidence of his recent form, his current rating flatters him. *(op 7-1)*
Whistling Fred showed little on his hurdling debut in a much better race than this at Newbury, but this seemed a little better and he only needs one more run for a handicap mark. *(op 16-1)*
My Maite(IRE) just seemed to be dropping out of contention when he fell fatally two out. *(op 16-1)*

231 JO EARL BIRTHDAY CELEBRATION BEGINNERS' CHASE (18 fncs) 3m 2f
3:10 (3:12) (Class 4) 5-Y-0+ **£4,745** (£1,460; £730; £365)

Form RPR
32-3 **1** **Mrs Be (IRE)**[11] 49 9-10-4 108.......... MissPGundry(3) 92+
(J G Cann) *mde virtually all: pushed along fr 13th: drew 4 l clr after 3 out: styd on wl* **1/2**[1]

050- **2** 3 ½ **Indian Squaw (IRE)**[43] 4560 6-10-7 ....(t) NFehily 85
(B De Haan) *t.k.h early: hld up: prog to chse wnr after 14th: rdn 2 out: tried to cl last: no imp flat* **8/1**[3]

PPP- **3** 21 **Hardy Russian (IRE)**[97] 3625 8-10-4 .... KBurke(10) 71
(P R Rodford) *trckd ldng pair: mstke 10th: lost pl and reminder 12th: outpcd fr 14th: tk modest 3rd again flat* **20/1**

F0-U **4** 3 ½ **Kjjimmy (IRE)**[9] 104 8-10-11 .... RYoung(3) 71+
(J W Mullins) *often plld hrd: hld up: nt fluent 10th: mstke 13th: outpcd after next: btn whn mstke 3 out: wknd* **40/1**

P **Taffy**[41] 8-10-7 .... JAJenkins(7) —
(H J Manners) *p.u bef 3rd: lame* **14/1**

/U4- **P** **Monsieur Rose (IRE)**[19] 4917 9-11-0 90.......... LAspell 66
(N J Gifford) *pressed wnr: upsides whn nt fluent 14th: wknd fr next: last whn p.u bef last* **11/2**[2]

6m 36.3s (-29.10) **Going Correction** -0.30s/f (Good) **6** Ran SP% **107.0**
Speed ratings: **103,101,95,94,—** — CSF £4.68 TOTE £1.30: £1.30, £2.80; EX 5.30.
Owner J H Burbidge **Bred** Edmond Cogan **Trained** Cullompton, Devon.

FOCUS
A very weak beginners' chase that is difficult to rate with confidence.

NOTEBOOK
Mrs Be(IRE) had by far the best form to her name - she was third in the Cross Country at the Cheltenham Festival - and did enough to gain her first win under Rules. The runner-up ensured she had to work for this, but she never really looked like being caught and could find a weak novice chase if connections opt to take that route. *(op 2-5 tchd 8-15 in a place)*
Indian Squaw(IRE) had shown some ability both in bumpers and over hurdles, and made an encouraging debut over fences. Having looked likely to pose a threat, she ultimately found the winner too strong, but was clear of the remainder and has the ability to find a similar race. *(op 9-2)*
Hardy Russian(IRE), pulled up on all three of his previous runs over fences, managed to complete this time and may have appreciated the decent ground. *(op 33-1)*
Kjjimmy(IRE)'s jumping was not always up to scratch, raced keenly and finished well beaten. *(op 50-1)*
Monsieur Rose(IRE) is unlikely to have appreciated ground this fast. *(op 8-1)*
Taffy *Official explanation: vet said gelding was lame on left fore (op 8-1)*

232 HENRY CARR CELEBRATES HIS 11TH BIRTHDAY CLAIMING HURDLE (9 hdls) 2m
3:40 (3:40) (Class 4) 4-Y-0+ **£2,723** (£778; £389)

Form RPR
36-P **1** **Mr Fernet**[9] 102 8-11-0 98.......... NFehily 96
(C J Mann) *trckd ldng gp: prog 6th: chal and bmpd 3 out: drvn to ld 2 out: edgd lft and lft clr last: tired bdly: jst hld on* **4/1**[3]

400- **2** shd **Caliban (IRE)**[21] 4881 7-11-3 106..........(b) AHoneyball(3) 102
(Ian Williams) *led: drvn 6th: hdd and bmpd 3 out: looked wl btn and mstke 2 out: lft disputing 2nd last: styd on wl: jst failed* **2/1**[1]

UPP- **3** 1 ¼ **Wild Tempo (FR)**[30] 4764 10-10-8 116.......... JKington(10) 99
(M Scudamore) *trckd ldrs: rdn and lost pl 6th: looked reluctant after: 15 l 5th 2 out: styd on strly flat: gaining at fin* **9/1**

10-5 **4** ¾ **Reach The Clouds (IRE)**[13] 25 13-10-7 85.......... MNicolls(5) 93+
(John R Upson) *trckd ldrs: chsd ldng trio 3 out: sn nt qckn: lft disputing 2nd at last: plugged on same pce* **8/1**

60F- **5** 11 **Outside Investor (IRE)**[141] 2899 5-10-9 82.......... MrRMcCarthy(7) 85
(P R Rodford) *hld up in rr: outpcd fr 6th: mstke 3 out: shuffled along and kpt on fr next: nvr nr ldrs* **16/1**

P/ **6** 8 **Raheel (IRE)**[30] 2205 5-10-12 .... LAspell 75+
(M R Hoad) *t.k.h: hld up wl in rr: mstke 4th: sme prog 6th: sn outpcd: nudged along and kpt on fr 2 out: nvr nr ldrs* **25/1**

0/ **7** 1 ¼ **Philosophic**[452] 3843 11-10-12 ....(p) BHitchcott 72
(Mrs L C Jewell) *chsd ldrs to 5th: sn lost pl: bhd and struggling fr next* **50/1**

R0-P **8** 18 **Isam Top (FR)**[9] 105 9-10-9 77..........(t) MrJMorgan(7) 58
(M J Hogan) *a towards rr: outpcd and bhd fr 6th: no ch after* **33/1**

0-0 **9** 1 ¾ **Parisi Princess**[4] 180 4-9-12 .... ONelmes(3) 41
(D L Williams) *t.k.h: hld up in last: mstke 2nd: nvr a factor: wl bhd fr 6th* **33/1**

6P-0 **P** **Cloud Catcher (IRE)**[14] 3 4-9-8 ....(t) LNewnes(7) —
(M Appleby) *plld hrd: prog to trck ldr and blnd 3rd: wknd 6th: t.o whn p.u bef 2 out* **50/1**

303- **R** **Shaman**[51] 4443 8-11-4 101.......... PHide 100+
(G L Moore) *trckd ldr to 3rd and again fr 6th: led 3 out: rdn and hdd next : upsides whn sltly intimidated and rn out last* **7/2**[2]

3m 46.1s (-4.20) **Going Correction** -0.30s/f (Good)
WFA 4 from 5yo+ 4lb **11** Ran SP% **116.2**
Speed ratings: **98,97,97,96,91 87,86,77,76,—** — CSF £12.08 TOTE £4.30: £1.70, £1.10, £3.60; EX 13.40.Mr Fernet was claimed by Milton Harris for £6,000.
Owner L Bolingbroke S Cannon N Gravett B Walsh **Bred** Cliveden Stud Ltd **Trained** Upper Lambourn, Berks

FOCUS
A modest race, but a very dramatic contest with several of these looking quirky to say the least.

NOTEBOOK
Mr Fernet, whose saddle slipped in his most recent outing, looking likely to win easily after his nearest rival ran out at the last, but he stopped to nothing on the run-in and would have been caught in another stride. He does give the impression that he is suited by a sound surface over hurdles, but that may be misleading given his form on soft ground on the level. *(op 11-2)*
Caliban(IRE) adopted his usual front-running role, but seemed to have run his race rounding the home turn. However, with one of the leaders running out and the other falling in a hole after the last, he very nearly took full advantage of the unexpected chance he was given. *(op 9-4 tchd 5-2 in places and 11-4 in a place)*
Wild Tempo(FR), very well in at the weights, was making his hurdling debut in this country after failing to complete against smart opposition in three outings over fences here. After showing up for over a circuit, he seemed to drop himself out but then consented to run on again as the shape of the race changed dramatically after the final flight. He is probably flattered by this and does not look one to rely on in any case. *(op 8-1 tchd 10-1)*
Reach The Clouds(IRE), who has not shown a great deal since returning to fences, was still in with a chance coming to the last, but although he had to swerve to avoid Shaman as he was being pulled up on the run-in, it made no difference to the result. He is unlikely to find too many more opportunities at his age.
Shaman, not the most straightforward of characters, was battling for the lead when the eventual winner hung in slightly towards him approaching the last and that was the only excuse he needed to dive the wrong side of the wing. He has talent, but simply cannot be trusted. *(op 11-4 tchd 4-1 in places)*

233 PLUMPTON RACECOURSE AMATEUR RIDERS' H'CAP HURDLE (12 hdls) 2m 5f
4:10 (4:11) (Class 4) (0-110,108) 4-Y-0+ **£3,503** (£1,078; £539; £269)

Form RPR
05-0 **1** **Time Marches On**[14] 9 7-10-5 94.......... JReveley(7) 101+
(K G Reveley) *cl up: mstke 4th: nt fluent 8th: led next: drew clr fr last: pushed out* **7/2**[2]

13- **2** 5 **Polar Scout (IRE)**[21] 4880 8-11-10 106..........(t) MrDHDunsdon 111+
(C J Mann) *mstkes: cl up: w wnr fr 9th: mstke and stmbld 3 out: stl upsides after 2 out: wknd flat* **2/1**[1]

0P6- **3** ½ **Joshua's Bay**[25] 4823 7-11-7 108.......... LNewnes(5) 109
(J R Jenkins) *hld up in detached last: mstke 1st: stdy prog fr 9th: chsd ldng trio after 3 out: styd on same pce fr next* **6/1**

020- **4** nk **Correct And Right (IRE)**[23] 4855 6-10-9 96..........(p) WPKavanagh(5) 97
(J W Mullins) *trckd ldrs: prog 9th: chsd ldng pair bef 3 out: rdn and no imp fr 2 out* **12/1**

1P2- **5** 8 **Unusual Suspect**[17] 4939 6-10-12 101..........(b) MrLHamilton(7) 94+
(G L Moore) *hld up in last trio: gng easily but steadily lost grnd fr 9th: no ch after 3 out: brief reminder flat: styd on: hopeless ta* **4/1**[3]

3P6- **6** ½ **L'Etang Bleu (FR)**[20] 4915 7-9-9 84 oh4 ow2(tp) MissGDGracey-Davison(7) 77
(P Butler) *t.k.h: prom: mstke 9th: sn pushed along and btn* **66/1**

500- **7** 5 **Cyindien (FR)**[28] 4799 8-10-1 90.......... MissPBuckley(7) 78
(D E Cantillon) *a towards rr: outpcd fr 9th: last and no ch 3 out: nudged along and one pce fr next* **12/1**

000- **8** shd **Boring Going (IRE)**[291] 1023 11-10-13 100 ow10.......... MrCGordon(5) 87
(Miss A M Newton-Smith) *led to 2nd: wknd after 9th* **50/1**

235- **9** 7 **Running Times (USA)**[16] 4956 8-9-10 85..........(b) MrSStockley(7) 65
(H J Manners) *t.k.h: led 2nd to 9th: wknd beofre 3 out* **16/1**

5m 6.20s (-24.10) **Going Correction** -0.30s/f (Good) **9** Ran SP% **114.6**
Speed ratings: **103,101,100,100,97 97,95,95,92** CSF £11.15 CT £39.23 TOTE £4.70: £1.70, £1.40, £2.20; EX 12.10.
Owner Mrs M B Thwaites **Bred** Mrs M B Thwaites **Trained** Lingdale, N Yorks
■ A first winner for sixteen-year-old rider James Reveley, son of trainer Keith.

FOCUS
A modest contest, run at a very slow early pace with the fourth the best guide to the level of the form.

NOTEBOOK
Time Marches On, just 1lb higher than for his last win, was always up with the pace and though his jumping was not foot-perfect, he jumped the last three flights much better than the runner-up and that proved crucial. This ground would have been plenty quick enough so he deserves extra credit. *(op 11-2)*
Polar Scout(IRE), running over hurdles for the first time in over a year, was given a positive ride but he did not give the obstacles enough respect and a bad blunder three out, followed by an couple of minor errors at the last two flights, did him no favours at all. *(op 7-4 tchd 9-4 in places)*
Joshua's Bay, racing off his correct mark this time, is now 2lb lower than for his last win. He did not get going until it was too late and may need a stiffer track or longer trip these days. *(op 5-1)*
Correct And Right(IRE) had every chance, but was found wanting for a turn of foot where it mattered. She stayed the trip well enough and might still have just needed it after her winter break.
Unusual Suspect, with the ground in his favour, may need further than this now but even so he was given a very strange ride. Held up out the back, his pilot did very little on him and the combination were never in the race with a chance. To be fair, his rider has little experience under Rules, but this did not look very appealing. *(tchd 7-2 and 9-2 in places)*

234 VI NICHOL HAPPY BIRTHDAY H'CAP CHASE (14 fncs) 2m 4f
4:40 (4:40) (Class 4) (0-110,110) 5-Y-0+ **£4,901** (£1,508; £754; £377)

Form RPR
4P3- **1** **Blakeney Coast (IRE)**[42] 4581 8-9-11 84 oh11..........(t) RYoung(3) 99+
(C L Tizzard) *led 2nd: mde rest and set str pce: in command 2 out: drvn out* **8/1**

2P0- **2** 1 ½ **Giorgio (IRE)**[31] 4757 7-11-9 107..........(b) NFehily 118
(Mrs Jeremy Young) *led to 2nd: chsd wnr after: rdn and hld bef 2 out: kpt on wl flat* **6/1**[3]

14-6 **3** 10 **Master T (USA)**[9] 103 6-11-9 107.......... PHide 111+
(G L Moore) *settled midfield: prog to chse ldng pair 4 out: rdn and nt qckn after next: no imp after* **15/2**

26P- **4** 9 **Joint Authority (IRE)**[15] 4984 10-10-13 104.......... MissLHorner(7) 96
(D L Williams) *chsd ldng trio: outpcd fr 10th: n.d after* **7/2**[1]

Form	Pos	Dist	Horse	RPR
U61-	5	15	**Lucky Pete**[20] 4915 8-10-13 **97** .... LAspell (P J Jones) *hld up midfield: outpcd and wl bhd fr 10th: no ch after* **4/1**[2]	74
P1F-	6	1	**Just Muckin Around (IRE)**[17] 4942 9-10-12 **96** .... BHitchcott (R H Buckler) *nvr gng wl: sn detached in last: brief effrt 9th: sn wl bhd* **7/1**	72
06P-	7	30	**Soeur Fontenail (FR)**[15] 4980 8-11-3 **101** .... AThornton (N J Hawke) *chsd ldng pair: wkng whn blnd 4 out: no ch after: virtually p.u flat* **8/1**	47
2P6-	F		**Quiet Millfit (USA)**[10] 2735 9-10-0 **84** oh2 .... MBatchelor (R Ingram) *s.s: hld up in last pair: reminders after 8th: last and wl bhd whn fell heavily 10th* **9/1**	—

4m 48.2s (-35.00) **Going Correction** -0.30s/f (Good) course record **8** Ran SP% **113.0**
Speed ratings: **103,102,98,94,88 88,76,**— CSF £53.51 CT £373.79 TOTE £9.50: £2.60, £2.50, £1.80; EX 54.80.

Owner The Jam Boys **Bred** Major F B And J G B Boyd **Trained** Milborne Port, Dorset

FOCUS

Just a modest handicap chase, but eventual winner Blakeney Coast ensured this was a decent test and can win again.

NOTEBOOK

Blakeney Coast(IRE) ◆ built on the promise he showed when fitted with a tongue-tie for the first time over course and distance on his previous outing, keeping on well right the way to the line having made this a good test almost from the start. This ended a losing run stretching back to 2003 and, a horse with rediscovered confidence, he is at the right end of the handicap and could follow up. *(tchd 10-1)*

Giorgio(IRE) has dropped 7lb since first running in a handicap and returned to form with a creditable effort, keeping the winner up to his work right the way to the line. Clear of the remainder, he could find a similar race whilst in this sort of form. *(op 8-1)*

Master T(USA) does not have a very good wins-to-run record but, although ultimately well held, this was an improvement on is last couple of efforts. *(op 7-1 tchd 8-1)*

Joint Authority(IRE), pulled up when well out of his depth in the Betfred Gold Cup on his previous outing, would have found this much less competitive and seemed to have conditions to suit, but he proved a little disappointing and may find this trip on the short side these days. *(op 10-3 tchd 4-1)*

Lucky Pete, 12lb higher than when successful over course and distance on his previous outing, *ran nowhere near that level of form but can be forgiven this as he finished lame.Official explanation: vet said gelding finished lame (op 10-3)*

Just Muckin Around(IRE) *Official explanation: jockey said gelding was unsuited by good to firm ground (op 11-2 tchd 5-1)*

Soeur Fontenail(FR) *Official explanation: jockey said mare was unsuited by good to firm ground (tchd 9-1)*

Quiet Millfit(USA) was well out the back when taking a horrible fall. *(op 12-1 tchd 8-1)*

235 HBLB INTERMEDIATE OPEN NATIONAL HUNT FLAT RACE 2m 2f

5:10 (5:12) (Class 6) 4-6-Y-O **£1,890** (£540; £270)

Form	Pos	Dist	Horse	RPR
06-5	1		**It's My Party**[14] 7 4-10-4 .... SHaddon(10) (W G M Turner) *trckd ldr after 4f to 9f out: bdly outpcd over 6f out: gd prog fr 3f out to ld 2f out: sn clr* **12/1**	101+
443-	2	11	**Maarees**[20] 4916 4-10-0 .... (p) RLucey-Butler(7) (G P Enright) *settled midfield: bdly outpcd over 6f out: kpt on fr over 2f out to take 2nd 1f out: no ch w wnr* **7/2**[2]	83
20-	3	1	**Benny**[28] 4801 4-10-7 .... MrNKinnon(7) (R H York) *t.k.h: led at stdy pce: qcknd clr 7f out: hdd and one pce 2f out* **12/1**	89
0-	4	1 ¼	**Victree (IRE)**[71] 4069 6-10-11 .... MrJMorgan(7) (L Wells) *prom: chsd ldr 9f out to over 6f out: outpcd and sn rdn: tried to cl fr 3f out: kpt on one pce* **5/1**[3]	92
	5	1	**Hill Forts Timmy** 5-11-4 .... SCurran (J W Mullins) *hld up in last: bdly outpcd over 6f out: effrt over 4f out: clsng in 6th pl whn hung bdly rt bnd 2f out: kpt on fnl f* **33/1**	91
	6	11	**Molly's Spirit (IRE)** 4-10-7 .... TDoyle (P R Webber) *prom but rn green: chsd clr ldr over 6f out: sn rdn: tried to cl 3f out: wknd over 2f out: eased* **5/4**[1]	74+
	7	9	**Rose Amber** 4-10-7 .... LAspell (J J Bridger) *in tch to 1/2-way: wl bhd over 6f out* **33/1**	60
0-	8	16	**Megalala (IRE)**[17] 4941 4-11-0 .... PHide (J J Bridger) *chsd ldrs: outpcd over 6f out: sn wknd: t.o* **33/1**	51
	9	dist	**Mad Louie** 5-11-4 .... MBatchelor (Miss Z C Davison) *chsd ldrs tl wknd 1/2-way: sn wl t.o* **33/1**	—
10-	P		**Dreams Jewel**[175] 2217 5-11-6 .... LTreadwell(5) (A G Newcombe) *in tch tl wknd and p.u 6f out: dismntd* **16/1**	—

4m 14.6s (-6.10) **Going Correction** -0.30s/f (Good)
WFA 4 from 5yo+ 4lb **10** Ran SP% **116.4**
Speed ratings: **97,92,91,91,90 85,81,74,**—,— CSF £52.23 TOTE £10.00: £2.20, £1.60, £3.10; EX 50.40 Place 6 £13.86, Place 5 £7.76.

Owner Mascalls Stud **Bred** Mascalls Stud **Trained** Sigwells, Somerset

■ Stuart Haddon's first winner.

FOCUS

A pretty moderate bumper but reasonably solid with the placed horses running to their marks.

NOTEBOOK

It's My Party built on the promise he showed on his return from a break at Ludlow, readily getting off the mark at the 12th attempt. His future could now lie over hurdles and, having proven his *effectiveness on fast ground, he could pick up a novice event or two in the summer months. (op 10-1 tchd 14-1)*

Maarees, in cheekpieces for the time, was no match for the winner late on, but seemed to run her race and gives a guide to the strength of the form. *(op 4-1 tchd 9-2)*

Benny was well beaten at Worcester on his previous outing, but this was more like the form he showed on his debut and he has ability. *(op 14-1)*

Victree(IRE) would have found this easier than the Kempton maiden he landed on his debut and seems to be progressing. *(op 4-1)*

Hill Forts Timmy, the first foal of a very moderate maiden jumper, stayed on well, but hung wide into the straight and may have found the ground fast enough. *(op 20-1)*

Molly's Spirit(IRE), a 29,000gns purchase, out of a half-sister to Irish National winner Son Of War, hails from a stable that has been doing well in this type of race and was very popular in the market, but she ran below expectations and was disappointing. She can, however, be given another chance. *(op 11-8 tchd 11-10 and 6-4 in places)*

Dreams Jewel *Official explanation: jockey said saddle slipped*

T/Plt: £27.00 to a £1 stake. Pool: £40,428.55. 1,092.55 winning tickets. T/Qpdt: £13.50 to a £1 stake. Pool: £1,984.70. 108.40 winning tickets. JN

126 UTTOXETER (L-H)

Sunday, May 8

OFFICIAL GOING: Good

One fence and one hurdle omitted in back straight on all circuits of all races

Wind: Fresh, against Weather: Cloudy with showers

236 COORS BREWERS MAIDEN HURDLE (12 hdls 2 omitted) 3m

2:30 (2:30) (Class 4) 4-Y-0+ **£3,290** (£940; £470)

Form	Pos	Dist	Horse	RPR
02P-	1		**Nite Fox (IRE)**[42] 4582 6-10-3 93 .... (p) PMerrigan(7) (Mrs H Dalton) *hld up: hdwy 7th: jnd ldr 4 out: swtchd rt flat: r.o to ld nr fin* **12/1**	94
33P-	2	½	**Rifleman (IRE)**[78] 3958 5-11-3 110 .... SDurack (P Bowen) *chsd ldr tl led 5th: rdn and hung lft flat: hdd nr fin* **2/1**[1]	102+
/2P-	3	18	**Having A Party**[113] 3370 7-10-10 .... PMoloney (J Mackie) *hld up: hdwy 7th: wknd appr 2 out* **11/2**[3]	79+
P5-P	4	21	**Ladies From Leeds**[10] 83 6-10-10 82 .... NPMulholland (A Crook) *led: mstke 4th: hdd next: wknd after 4 out* **50/1**	55
533-	5	1 ¼	**Superrollercoaster**[37] 4680 5-11-3 105 .... (p) GLee (O Sherwood) *chsd ldrs: rdn 4 out: wknd bef next* **9/4**[2]	60
	6	15	**Come To The Bar (IRE)**[41] 6-11-3 .... DRDennis (W W Dennis) *chsd ldrs tl wknd appr 3 out* **6/1**	45
U-	P		**Mister Julius**[26] 4814 8-11-3 .... ADobbin (P Bowen) *bhd and rdn 2nd: t.o whn p.u bef 5th* **28/1**	—
UP-	P		**Holly Park**[15] 4978 7-10-10 .... JPByrne (C N Kellett) *chsd ldrs to 7th: t.o whn p.u bef next* **100/1**	—
0P-4	P		**Edgemoor Princess**[9] 94 7-10-3 64 .... MrRArmson(7) (R J Armson) *hld up: lost tch 7th: t.o whn p.u bef 9th* **80/1**	—
4P-	P		**Merry Storm (IRE)**[40] 4641 6-10-10 .... RSpate(7) (Mrs K Waldron) *hld up in tch: mstke 4th: rdn 6th: wknd 8th: t.o whn p.u bef 3 out* **25/1**	—

6m 27.6s **10** Ran SP% **112.9**
CSF £35.47 TOTE £13.20: £3.20, £1.40, £1.50; EX 44.70.

Owner Mrs A Beard Miss M Knapper & J Dalton **Bred** John Smiddy **Trained** Norton, Shropshire

FOCUS

A modest maiden rated through the winner.

NOTEBOOK

Nite Fox(IRE) has generally been running better since the cheekpieces have been applied and finished strongly to win her first race. She is still only six and probably has a little improvement left in her. *(op 10-1)*

Rifleman(IRE) was basically disappointing and remains winless. He has had plenty of chances and become expensive to follow. *(tchd 15-8)*

Having A Party was well adrift of the front two and probably needs softer ground. *(op 6-1 tchd 13-2)*

Ladies From Leeds is a lowly performer and needs dropping into selling company before she wins. *(op 40-1)*

Superrollercoaster is very modest and the application of cheekpieces failed to make a difference. *(op 2-1)*

237 PETER J DOUGLAS ENGINEERING (S) H'CAP HURDLE (10 hdls 2 omitted) 2m 4f 110y

3:00 (3:00) (Class 5) (0-90,90) 4-Y-0+ **£2,457** (£702; £351)

Form	Pos	Dist	Horse	RPR
005-	1		**Angie's Double**[19] 4918 5-9-12 **65** .... TJMalone(3) (M Scudamore) *chsd ldrs: lost pl after 2nd: hdwy 6th: chsd ldr after next: led 3 out: clr next: comf* **9/1**[3]	84+
303-	2	10	**Coxwell Cossack**[214] 1615 12-11-6 **84** .... MBradburne (Mark Campion) *led to 2nd: led after 7th: hdd next: styd on same pce fr 2 out* **12/1**	86
PP6-	3	18	**Antony Ebeneezer**[55] 4369 6-11-9 **87** .... CLlewellyn (C R Dore) *hld up: hdwy 7th: wknd 3 out* **15/2**[2]	74+
00P-	4	3 ½	**Extremist (USA)**[22] 4871 6-11-1 **79** .... (b1) JPMcNamara (K C Bailey) *hld up: hit 3rd: hdwy 7th: wknd 3 out: mstke next* **20/1**	60
560-	5	8	**Fairmorning (IRE)**[76] 3041 6-10-12 **76** .... (b) JPByrne (C N Kellett) *hit 1st: sn prom: wknd 3 out: poor 4th whn blnd last* **40/1**	55+
010-	6	14	**Ascari**[16] 4714 9-10-9 **80** .... TBurrows(7) (A L Forbes) *chsd ldrs: led 3rd to 5th: wknd after 7th* **33/1**	39
300-	7	20	**Super Boston**[35] 4714 5-10-7 **71** .... NPMulholland (Miss L C Siddall) *prom: rdn 4th: hit 6th: wknd bef next* **20/1**	10
006-	P		**Waterline Blue (IRE)**[60] 4267 4-10-9 **78** .... ADobbin (P Bowen) *bhd fr 4th: t.o whn p.u bef 6th* **9/1**[3]	—
335-	P		**Oro Street (IRE)**[350] 475 9-11-5 **90** .... MrSPeltell(7) (G F Bridgwater) *sn bhd: t.o whn p.u bef 6th* **25/1**	—
040-	P		**River Of Fire**[13] 2717 7-10-2 **71** .... TGreenway(5) (C N Kellett) *bhd fr 5th: t.o whn p.u bef 3 out* **14/1**	—
/0P-	P		**Kadlass (FR)**[21] 4890 10-11-2 **83** .... RWalford(3) (Mrs D Thomas) *hld up in tch: wknd 7th: t.o whn p.u bef 3 out* **50/1**	—
1-	P		**Crazy Mazie**[372] 127 8-10-11 **82** .... SWalsh(7) (K A Morgan) *hld up: hdwy 7th: wknd bef next: bhd whn p.u bef 2 out* **10/1**	—
4P-3	P		**Monbonami (IRE)**[13] 23 8-10-10 **81** .... (p) RSpate(7) (Mrs K Waldron) *mid-div: hdwy 3rd: wknd 7th: t.o whn p.u bef 2 out* **18/1**	—
P4P/	P		**Sungio**[16] 2307 7-11-5 **90** .... TMessenger(7) (B P J Baugh) *hld up in tch: wkng whn hit 6th: t.o whn p.u bef 2 out* **20/1**	—
P0-4	P		**Island Warrior (IRE)**[10] 75 10-10-4 **68** .... (p) JMogford (B P J Baugh) *prom: mstke and wknd 7th: t.o whn p.u bef 2 out* **14/1**	—
510-	P		**Wally Wonder (IRE)**[28] 4783 7-11-5 **86** .... (b) HBastiman(3) (R Bastiman) *led 2nd to next: led 5th: mstke 7th: sn hdd & wknd: t.o whn p.u bef 2 out* **14/1**	—
12-1	P		**Irish Blessing (USA)**[14] 11 8-11-7 **85** .... (tp) MAFitzgerald (F Jordan) *prom: lost pl after 1st: hit 3rd: hdwy u.p after 6th: wknd after next: t.o whn p.u bef 2 out* **9/4**[1]	—

5m 29.1s (26.50) **Going Correction** +1.20s/f (Heav)
WFA 4 from 5yo+ 5lb **17** Ran SP% **130.1**
Speed ratings: **97,93,86,85,81 76,69,**—,—,— —,—,—,—,— —,— CSF £109.10 CT £877.38 TOTE £9.60: £1.70, £2.80, £2.40, £7.40; EX 156.90.The winner was sold to Nick Shutt for 6,500gns.

Owner P H Wafford **Bred** P And Mrs Wafford **Trained** Bromsash, Herefordshire

FOCUS

A bad race, as one would expect for the grade, although the winner is value for more than the official margin.

NOTEBOOK

Angie's Double has been running only moderately, but has been edging down the handicap as a result and was racing here off a mark of just 65. She cleared right away having taken it up around three out and it will be rather disappointing if she cannot add to this under a penalty.

Coxwell Cossack ran his race and was simply not good enough to match the winner, who was in receipt of much weight. He is not getting any better at the age of 12, but is clearly still capable of paying his way. *(tchd 14-1)*
Antony Ebeneezer was a further 18 lengths back in third and is only moderately handicapped. *(op 9-1)*
Extremist(USA) ran better than he has been in the first-time blinkers, but did not see his race out.
Fairmorning(IRE) ran a bit better than his price entitled him to. *(tchd 50-1)*
Irish Blessing(USA) was never really going and appeared to run flat. *Official explanation: jockey said gelding was never travelling (tchd 5-2 and 11-4 in places)*

238 DAVID AND BETTINE FERRAND 50TH ANNIVERSARY H'CAP HURDLE (9 hdls 1 omitted) 2m
3:30 (3:32) (Class 4) (0-100,98) 4-Y-0+ **£3,017** (£862; £431)

Form RPR
060- **1** **Tinstre (IRE)**[10] 2933 7-10-8 **80** SFox 92+
(P W Hiatt) *hld up in tch: hmpd and lost pl after 4 out: rallied and pckd next: sn led: styd on wl* **50/1**
003- **2** *5* **Arjay**[35] 4714 7-9-8 **73** (b) CDSharkey(7) 78+
(S B Clark) *hld up in tch: ev ch and mstke 3 out: sn rdn styd on same pce last* **11/1**
4PP- **3** *2* **Penric**[18] 4923 5-10-13 **85** ADobbin 87
(Miss V Scott) *led to 4th: w ldr whn mstke 6th: rdn appr 2 out: styd on same pce* **14/1**
403- **4** *1* **Pure Brief (IRE)**[131] 3041 8-10-3 **75** (b) PMoloney 76
(J Mackie) *w ldr tl led 4th: hdd after 3 out: wknd flat* **8/1**[3]
00-3 **5** *½* **Errol**[6] 149 6-11-7 **93** MAFitzgerald 94
(J F Coupland) *chsd ldrs: rdn 3 out: styd on same pce fr next* **9/2**[1]
P60- **6** *12* **Lone Soldier (FR)**[35] 4714 9-10-5 **84** MissRachelClark(7) 73
(S B Clark) *hmpd 1st: hdwy 4th: wknd 3 out* **20/1**
41/0 **7** *1¼* **Dilsaa**[14] 9 8-11-12 **98** GLee 85
(K A Ryan) *hld up: mstke 5th: hdwy u.p after next: blnd 3 out: sn wknd* **6/1**[2]
003- **8** *16* **West Hill (IRE)**[64] 4173 4-9-11 **76** oh5 KJMercer(3) 43
(D McCain) *hld up: rdn 6th: n.d* **12/1**
0P4- **9** *nk* **Celtic Romance**[56] 4343 6-10-8 **80** SDurack 51
(Ms Sue Smith) *mid-div: rdn 6th: sn wknd* **8/1**[3]
050- **10** *11* **Baker Of Oz**[12] 4714 4-9-7 **76** oh5 (p) AScholes(7) 32
(D Burchell) *plld hrd and prom: ev ch 3 out: wkng whn blnd next* **11/1**
150- **11** *5* **Viva Forever (FR)**[88] 3762 6-11-4 **90** (v[1]) MBradburne 45
(A M Hales) *hld up: hdwy 5th: wknd appr 3 out* **10/1**
336- **P** **Colophony (USA)**[53] 4403 5-10-10 **89** (t) SWalsh(7) —
(K A Morgan) *hld up: bhd fr 4th: t.o whn p.u bef 3 out* **9/1**
00-0 **P** **Dumfries**[3] 192 4-10-8 **91** BWharfe(7) —
(T H Caldwell) *hld up: hdwy 5th: wknd next: t.o whn p.u bef 3 out* **20/1**
P3P- **P** **Comete Du Lac (FR)**[78] 3950 8-10-6 **78** (p) LFletcher —
(Mrs N Macauley) *prom to 5th: t.o whn p.u bef 3 out* **33/1**
5P-F **P** **Greenacres Boy**[9] 96 10-10-0 **72** oh1 (b) OMcPhail —
(M Mullineaux) *hld up: plld hrd: hdwy 5th: wknd appr 3 out: p.u bef next* **16/1**
054/ **P** **Niciara (IRE)**[5] 4605 8-11-1 **90** ACCoyle(3) —
(M C Chapman) *chsd ldrs: lost pl 3rd: bhd fr next: j.rt 4th: t.o whn p.u bef 3 out* **20/1**

4m 13.6s (21.20) **Going Correction** +1.20s/f (Heavy)
WFA 4 from 5yo+ 4lb **16** Ran SP% **129.9**
Speed ratings: **95,92,91,91,90 84,84,76,75,70 67,—,—,—,— —** CSF £537.40 CT £7951.08 TOTE £88.60: £11.70, £3.00, £3.60, £1.70; EX 951.00.
Owner M Wennington **Bred** Hugo Merry **Trained** Hook Norton, Oxon

FOCUS
A moderate event with a shock winner and the form looks suspect, but the runner-up sets the standard.

NOTEBOOK
Tinstre(IRE) caused a huge surprise in landing this handicap, managing to overcome being hampered and coming with a determined challenge to win going away. This was an improved *effort, but he needs to show it was no fluke and will be hit by the Handicapper. Official explanation: trainer's representative said, regarding the improved form shown, gelding may have benefited from the good ground (op 66-1)*
Arjay kept plugging away for second and will be capable of winning a small race if able to hold this level of form.
Penric remains winless and needs dropping into selling level. *(tchd 16-1)*
Pure Brief(IRE) had nothing left to offer once headed and held on for fifth. *(op 9-1)*
Errol travelled well throughout, but failed to find anywhere near as much as expected off the bridle and could not quicken. *(op 11-2 tchd 6-1)*
Greenacres Boy *Official explanation: jockey said saddle slipped (op 14-1)*

239 CALL BET365 08000 322 365 NOVICES' CHASE (FOR THE HARRY BROWN TROPHY) (14 fncs 2 omitted) 2m 5f
4:00 (4:02) (Class 3) 5-Y-0+ **£5,700** (£1,852; £997)

Form RPR
60P- **1** **You Owe Me (IRE)**[30] 4767 8-11-0 CLlewellyn 125+
(N A Twiston-Davies) *chsd ldr: hit 9th: led appr next: chal whn lft clr 2 out* **3/1**[2]
04-P **2** *dist* **Kercabellec (FR)**[8] 135 7-10-7 90 APogson(7) 75
(J R Cornwall) *led: racd keenly: hit 7th: hdd appr 10th: wknd bef next: lft remote 2nd 2 out* **25/1**
03-6 **3** *1¾* **High Rank**[14] 10 6-11-0 (tp) PMoloney 73
(J Mackie) *chsd ldrs tl wknd appr 4 out: t.o whn j.lft next: lft remote 3rd 2 out* **16/1**
6P- **U** **Padre (IRE)**[82] 3859 6-11-0 SDurack —
(M Pitman) *hld up: blnd and uns rdr 5th* **28/1**
46P- **P** **Box On (IRE)**[99] 3582 8-11-0 GLee —
(Miss V Scott) *prom to 4th: t.o whn p.u bef 5 out* **11/1**
3F-6 **P** **Dabus**[14] 2 10-10-11 99 ACCoyle(3) —
(M C Chapman) *hld up: a bhd: t.o whn p.u bef 5 out* **14/1**
0-F1 **P** **Isellido (IRE)**[8] 119 6-10-13 HOliver —
(R C Guest) *hld up: mstke 7th: a in rr: t.o whn p.u bef 5 out* **11/4**[1]
100- **P** **Doce Vida (IRE)**[99] 3592 7-10-7 111 RThornton —
(A King) *hld up in tch: wknd appr 4 out: lft remote 3rd whn p.u bef 2 out* **4/1**[3]
353- **U** **Celtic Boy (IRE)**[111] 3390 7-11-0 96 ADobbin 120
(P Bowen) *hld up in tch: mstke 9th: chsd wnr appr 4 out: ev ch whn blnd and uns rdr 2 out* **11/2**

5m 36.1s (16.80) **Going Correction** +0.725s/f (Soft) **9** Ran SP% **115.2**
Speed ratings: **97,—,—,—,— —,—,—,—** CSF £64.15 TOTE £3.80: £1.40, £6.70, £3.00; EX 112.50.
Owner C Cornes **Bred** J F C Maxwell **Trained** Naunton, Gloucs

FOCUS
A moderate novice and hard to fathom what You Owe Me achieved in coming home alone, his three main rivals all failing to complete.

NOTEBOOK
You Owe Me(IRE), a useful hurdler, had the luxury of seeing all three of his serious challengers depart in one way or another and he was left clear two out, merely having to jump the last to collect. He may well have won anyway and looks an obvious type to score again for his chase orientated stable. *(op 7-2)*
Kercabellec(FR) is a moderate performer and was no match for the useful winner. He is hard to win with, but will stand more chance back down in grade. *(op 22-1)*
High Rank was the only other to complete, but achieved very little.
Celtic Boy(IRE) was still bang there when coming down two out and would have finished second *at worst. He is the type to do well in handicap chases during the summer and should pay his way. (op 13-2 tchd 5-1)*
Doce Vida(IRE) failed to run up to her hurdle form on this first crack at fences and has something to prove now. She is undoubtedly better than this and worth another chance. *(op 13-2 tchd 5-1)*
Isellido(IRE) has now failed to complete on two of her three starts over fences and is clearly not that reliable. The one she did manage to finish however did result in a win and she clearly has ability. *Official explanation: vet said mare finished distressed (op 13-2 tchd 5-1)*

240 SIR STANLEY CLARKE STAFFORDSHIRE CHASE (A H'CAP) (18 fncs 2 omitted) 3m 2f
4:30 (4:41) (Class 4) (0-110,108) 5-Y-0+ **£5,369** (£1,652; £826; £413)

Form RPR
PB2- **1** **Gallik Dawn**[29] 4778 7-10-6 **88** MAFitzgerald 111+
(A Hollingsworth) *hld up: hdwy 10th: led 3 out: clr next* **11/1**
1U/- **2** *19* **Romantic Hero (IRE)**[528] 2420 9-10-5 **87** (b) PMoloney 90+
(C R Egerton) *chsd ldr: pckd 12th: led 5 out: hdd 3 out: wknd next* **5/1**[1]
2P1- **3** *5* **Calcot Flyer**[18] 4931 7-11-5 **101** RThornton 99+
(A King) *hld up: hdwy 7th: wknd 3 out* **5/1**[1]
U41- **4** *1¼* **Stand Easy (IRE)**[59] 4278 12-10-4 **93** APogson(7) 88
(J R Cornwall) *hld up: j.rt: hit 12th: n.d* **25/1**
F6-1 **5** *dist* **Red Rampage**[8] 125 10-11-2 **98** (bt) DO'Meara —
(H P Hogarth) *hld up in tch: wknd 13th* **9/1**
0P-0 **6** *13* **Cromwell (IRE)**[4] 181 10-9-7 **82** oh9 (b) CMStudd(7) —
(M C Chapman) *bhd fr 6th* **66/1**
031- **P** **Benefit**[15] 4976 11-10-2 **84** GLee —
(Miss L C Siddall) *a bhd: t.o whn p.u bef 5 out* **6/1**[3]
0/2- **P** **Madam's Man**[61] 4239 9-11-12 **108** CLlewellyn —
(N A Twiston-Davies) *hld up: bhd fr 6th: t.o whn p.u bef 4 out* **8/1**
P35- **P** **Courage Under Fire**[41] 4605 10-11-8 **104** (b) JPMcNamara —
(C C Bealby) *prom: mstke 6th: rdn and wknd 11th: sn p.u* **33/1**
P54- **P** **Father Abraham (IRE)**[45] 4537 7-10-3 **85** SDurack —
(J Akehurst) *led: rdn and hdd 5 out: sn wknd: t.o whn p.u bef 3 out* **33/1**
PP1- **P** **Ankles Back (IRE)**[41] 4612 8-11-11 **107** MBradburne —
(H D Daly) *got loose bef s: chsd ldrs: rdn and wknd after 7th: bhd whn p.u bef 11th* **8/1**
524- **P** **Be Upstanding**[16] 4970 10-10-0 **89** TJDreaper(7) —
(Ferdy Murphy) *hld up: drvn along 8th: sme hdwy appr 12th: sn wknd: t.o whn p.u bef 2 out* **11/2**[2]

7m 6.10s (11.10) **Going Correction** +0.725s/f (Soft) **12** Ran SP% **114.8**
Speed ratings: **111,105,103,103,— —,—,—,—,— —,—** CSF £62.66 CT £313.02 TOTE £12.60: £4.60, £2.10, £2.20; EX 96.10.
Owner Perry Adams **Bred** Mrs D Jenks **Trained** Feckenham, Worcs

FOCUS
Modest stuff, but Gallik Dawn ran out an authoritative winner. The form does not look entirely reliable.

NOTEBOOK
Gallik Dawn is not the most consistent, but was on a going day and fairly romped home. As a result of his inconsistency he cannot be relied upon to repeat the form, but is still only a seven-year-old and may have some improvement in him. *(op 10-1 tchd 12-1)*
Romantic Hero(IRE) fared best of the rest, but was of no match to the winner. He is a consistent sort who should continue to pay his way. *(op 10-3)*
Calcot Flyer followed up his recent win with a fair third and looks to be building some consistency. *(op 11-2 tchd 9-2)*
Stand Easy(IRE) ran only reasonably and in firmly in the grip of the Handicapper.
Benefit *Official explanation: trainer said gelding was unsuited by slow ground (op 11-2)*
Be Upstanding finds winning hard and ran a below-par race in pulling up. *(op 11-2)*
Ankles Back(IRE) *Official explanation: trainer said gelding was never travelling (op 11-2)*

241 DERBY EVENING TELEGRAPH STANDARD OPEN NATIONAL HUNT FLAT RACE (DIV I) 2m
5:00 (5:12) (Class 6) 4-6-Y-0 **£1,603** (£458; £229)

Form RPR
03- **1** **Master Marmalade**[19] 4922 4-10-12 MAFitzgerald 89
(D Morris) *hld up: hdwy 1/2-way: led over 3f out: hdd over 2f out: rallied to ld over 1f out: drvn out* **3/1**[2]
2- **2** *2½* **Dan's Man**[19] 4922 4-10-12 CLlewellyn 87
(N A Twiston-Davies) *plld hrd and prom: outpcd over 2f out: styd on ins fnl f* **10/11**[1]
0- **3** *1¼* **Itsdowntoben**[43] 4559 4-10-12 JMMaguire 85
(D McCain) *hld up: hdwy 7f out: rdn and ev ch over 1f out: no ex ins fnl f* **20/1**
00- **4** *1¼* **Jontys'Lass**[35] 4720 4-9-12 CDSharkey(7) 77
(A Crook) *led 5f: remained handy: rdn over 2f out: styd on same pce appr fnl f* **50/1**
06- **5** *1¼* **Tickers Way**[19] 4922 4-10-5 APogson(7) 83
(C Drew) *plld hrd and prom: led 11f out: rdn and hdd over 3f out: led over 2f out: to over 1f out: sn hung lft and no ex* **16/1**
00- **6** *8* **Keen Warrior**[47] 4513 5-10-13 LVickers(3) 79
(Mrs S Lamyman) *hld up: hdwy 6f out: rdn and ev ch over 2f out: sn hung lft and wknd* **33/1**
7 *3½* **Ammunition (IRE)** 5-11-2 SDurack 75
(M Pitman) *hld up: sme hdwy over 4f out: wknd over 1f out* **13/2**[3]
0- **8** *27* **Hapthor**[22] 4865 6-10-9 DVerco 41
(F Jestin) *plld hrd and prom: wknd 5f out* **66/1**
0/0- **9** *1¼* **Pixley**[113] 3374 5-11-2 KJohnson 47
(T J Fitzgerald) *plld hrd and prom: rdn 7f out: sn wknd* **33/1**
10 *½* **Callingwood (IRE)** 5-10-13 KJMercer(3) 47
(Ferdy Murphy) *hld up: bhd fr 1/2-way* **12/1**

4m 9.60s (19.40) **Going Correction** +1.20s/f (Heavy)
WFA 4 from 5yo+ 4lb **10** Ran SP% **118.4**
Speed ratings: **99,97,97,96,95 91,90,76,76,75** CSF £5.89 TOTE £4.90: £1.10, £1.40, £4.20; EX 9.70.

The Form Book, Raceform Ltd, Compton, RG20 6NL

Owner Bloomsbury Stud **Bred** Bloomsbury Stud **Trained** Newmarket, Suffolk

FOCUS

Not a bad bumper although more slowly run than the second division. The front two, who ran to their previous marks, look a couple of fair performers.

NOTEBOOK

Master Marmalade had shown more than enough in two previous bumpers to suggest he could win one and he appreciated the sound surface, reversing Towcester form with the favourite in the process. He looks a fair prospect and it will be interesting to see how he takes to hurdles. *(op 7-2)*

Dan's Man did himself no favours in pulling hard and that appeared to take its toll late on. He is better than this and worthy of another chance. *(op Evens)*

Itsdowntoben improved on his initial effort and was simply outstayed by the front pair. He is evidently progressing and will appreciate further over hurdles. *(op 16-1)*

Jontys'Lass has improved with each run and ran better than her price entitled her to. She should improve for a switch to hurdles. *(tchd 40-1)*

Tickers Way did not look an easy ride, pulling and hanging, but he evidently has ability and should be capable of winning a small race once sent hurdling. *(op 12-1)*

Ammunition(IRE) is evidently one of his stable's lesser lights. *(op 7-1)*

242 DERBY EVENING TELEGRAPH STANDARD OPEN NATIONAL HUNT FLAT RACE (DIV II) — 2m

5:30 (5:39) (Class 6) 4-6-Y-O — **£1,603** (£458; £229)

Form					RPR
	1		**Ben's Turn (IRE)** 4-10-5 (A King) *hld up: hdwy 1/2-way: chsd ldr 7f out: led over 2f out: rdn clr over 1f out* **6/1**^{3}	RThornton	101+
	2	*10*	**Treacysdream (IRE)**^{35} 5-10-9 (Mrs K Waldron) *mid-div: hdwy to chse clr ldr 10f out: lft in ld 7f out: rdn and hdd over 2f out: sn wknd* **20/1**	RSpate(7)	100
2-	3	*9*	**Nevada Red**^{38} [4673] 4-10-12 (D McCain) *hld up: hdwy over 6f out: riden and wknd over 2f out* **3/1**^{2}	JMMaguire	87
05-	4	*15*	**Shakerattleandroll (IRE)**^{78} [3946] 4-10-12 (J Nicol) *hld up: hdwy over 6f out: rdn and wknd over 2f out* **8/1**	MAFitzgerald	72
	5	*5*	**Double Spread** 6-11-2 (M Mullineaux) *chsd ldrs: rdn over 6f out: wknd over 4f out* **18/1**	MBradburne	71
	6	*3*	**Tooka** 4-10-12 (J Gallagher) *bhd fr 1/2-way: t.o whn hung rt over 4f out* **33/1**	OMcPhail	64
034-	7	*dist*	**Code (IRE)**^{97} [3626] 4-10-12 (Miss Z C Davison) *a bhd* **6/1**^{3}	GLee	—
00-	8	*dist*	**Burnside Place**^{67} [3771] 5-10-9 (C C Bealby) *chsd ldrs to 1/2-way* **66/1**	JPMcNamara	—
-	P		**Beam Me Up** 5-11-2 (C N Kellett) *chsd clr ldr 6f: sn wknd: bhd whn hung rt over 4f out: sn p.u* **22/1**	SDurack	—
00-	P		**Youknowtheanswer**^{48} [4499] 5-10-9 (Miss L C Siddall) *sn bhd: t.o fr 1/2-way: p.u over 6f out* **66/1**	NPMulholland	—
	P		**Felix The Fox (NZ)** 5-11-2 (N A Twiston-Davies) *led and sn wl clr: wknd and hdd 7f out: sn t.o: p.u fnl 5f* **85/40**^{1}	CLlewellyn	—

4m 7.20s (17.00) **Going Correction** +1.20s/f (Heav)
WFA 4 from 5yo+ 4lb — **11** Ran SP% **117.0**
Speed ratings: **105,100,95,88,85 84,—,—,—,—** — CSF £121.56 TOTE £6.40: £2.10, £5.60, £1.20; EX 65.90 Place 6 £215.46, Place 5 £133.41.

Owner C B Brookes **Bred** Miss E Violet Sweeney **Trained** Barbury Castle, Wilts

FOCUS

Not an easy race to rate, but the time was faster than the first division.

NOTEBOOK

Ben's Turn(IRE) would no doubt have delighted connections with this winning debut, clearing away having come through to lead around quarter of a mile out. It will be interesting to see if she is asked to defy a penalty or goes hurdling. *(op 8-1)*

Treacysdream(IRE), an Irish point winner, ran above market expectations and should pick up a modest bumper during the summer.

Nevada Red needs more time and experience and will improve for jumping obstacles. *(op 9-4 tchd 2-1)*

Shakerattleandroll(IRE) failed to improve on his most recent effort and was a little disappointing. *(op 12-1)*

Double Spread made only a modest debut and is another who may need more time. *(op 25-1)*

Tooka *Official explanation: jockey said gelding hung right-handed*

Code(IRE) ran below expectations and something was clearly amiss. *(tchd 11-2)*

Burnside Place *Official explanation: trainer said mare "tied up" post race (op 50-1)*

Beam Me Up *Official explanation: jockey said gelding hung right-handed (op 2-1 tchd 5-2)*

Felix The Fox(NZ) *Official explanation: trainer was unable to offer any explanation for poor form shown (op 2-1 tchd 5-2)*

T/Plt: £693.40 to a £1 stake. Pool: £47,259.10. 49.75 winning tickets. T/Qpdt: £98.10 to a £1 stake. Pool: £2,573.30. 19.40 winning tickets. CR

133 WORCESTER (L-H)

Sunday, May 8

OFFICIAL GOING: Good to firm

243 CANNONS HEALTH CLUB FOUR YEARS OLD NOVICES' HURDLE (8 hdls) — 2m

2:20 (2:20) (Class 4) 4-Y-O — **£3,438** (£1,058; £529; £264)

Form					RPR
	1		**Natal (FR)**^{197} 4-10-12 (P F Nicholls) *hld up: hdwy appr 3rd: led appr 2 out: rdn clr flat: r.o wl* **10/1**^{3}	(t) ChristianWilliams	116+
453-	2	*10*	**Adjami (IRE)**^{41} [3441] 4-10-12 110 (A King) *hld up in tch: ev ch 3 out: one pce fr 2 out* **2/1**^{1}	RThornton	104+
046-	3	*7*	**Grouville**^{113} [3354] 4-10-9 93 (C J Mann) *hld up and bhd: hdwy 5th: nt fluent 2 out: sn wknd* **14/1**	DCrosse(3)	97+
540-	4	*shd*	**Antigiotto (IRE)**^{104} [3508] 4-10-12 102 (P Bowen) *hld up: hdwy 4th: wknd 2 out: nt fluent last* **12/1**	TScudamore	97+
13-5	5	*19*	**Reservoir (IRE)**^{13} [21] 4-11-5 114 (P J Hobbs) *hld up: short-lived effrt appr 2 out* **2/1**^{1}	RJohnson	91+
	6	*1½*	**Glide**^{331} 4-10-12 (J A B Old) *prom: mstke 5th: wknd 3 out* **33/1**	PJBrennan	75
P52-	7	*1¼*	**Moorlaw (IRE)**^{60} [4250] 4-10-12 110 (D McCain) *chsd ldr tl appr 3 out: wknd 2 out* **7/1**^{2}	JMMaguire	74
04-5	8	*1¼*	**Charlie Bear**^{14} [3] 4-10-12 98 (W K Goldsworthy) *led: rdn and hdd appr 2 out: sn wknd* **12/1**	(t) JamesDavies	73
0P0-	9	*dist*	**Heriot**^{23} [4852] 4-10-12 85 (S C Burrough) *a bhd: t.o* **100/1**	(t) WMarston	—
00F-	P		**Thespian Lady**^{17} [4936] 4-10-5 (Mrs A J Hamilton-Fairley) *hld up in tch: wknd after 5th: bhd whn p.u bef 2 out* **125/1**	ATinkler	—

3m 49.3s (-0.90) **Going Correction** +0.075s/f (Yiel) — **10** Ran SP% **115.0**
Speed ratings: **105,100,96,96,86 86,85,84,—,—** CSF £30.80 TOTE £11.70: £2.70, £1.40, £3.80; EX 30.20.

Owner Mrs Monica Hackett **Bred** Yves D'Armaille **Trained** Ditcheat, Somerset

FOCUS

Pretty solid form, and the winner has been rated as value for 12l.

NOTEBOOK

Natal(FR) had two runs in France, the second of them over hurdles. Tongue tied for this British debut, he ran out an impressive winner, surprising connections. He looks a nice prospect and his real future lies over fences. *(op 9-1 tchd 11-1)*

Adjami(IRE), third in a warm event at Taunton on his latest run over hurdles, has had an outing on the Flat since then. He ran a sound race but was put in his place by the winner from the second last. *(tchd 13-8)*

Grouville, taking a slight drop in grade, ran respectably but is the sort who is likely to do better in handicaps.

Antigiotto(IRE) was returning after a break. He ran with credit but does not seem to be getting home. *(op 16-1)*

Reservoir(IRE), who jumped slowly at the first flight in the back straight and dropped towards the rear, tried to get back into the action on the home turn but was soon beaten. He is going the wrong way. *(op 9-4 tchd 3-1)*

Glide, a fair maiden on the Flat for Roger Charlton, made an error at the last flight in the back straight and was soon in trouble. *(op 16-1)*

244 HAVE YOU THOUGHT OF SPONSORING A RACE BEGINNERS' CHASE (18 fncs) — 2m 7f 110y

2:50 (2:50) (Class 4) 5-Y-O+ — **£4,182** (£1,287; £643; £321)

Form					RPR
P2-	1		**Hold On Harry**^{28} [4794] 9-10-11 (Miss C J Williams) *j.rt: prom: led 5th: hit 2 out: sn rdn: r.o* **14/1**	RStephens(5)	96+
502-	2	*2½*	**Jivaty (FR)**^{17} [4937] 8-11-2 103 (Mrs A J Hamilton-Fairley) *a.p: lft 2nd 4 out: rdn and ch whn hung rt appr last: nt qckn flat* **8/1**^{3}	ATinkler	93
14P/	3	*13*	**Toon Trooper (IRE)**^{92} 8-11-2 (R Lee) *t.k.h: j.rt 2nd: nt fluent 5th: hdwy appr 4 out: sn no imp* **12/1**	WMarston	83+
P05/	4	*23*	**Saucynorwich (IRE)**^{453} [3756] 7-11-2 (J G Portman) *led to 3rd: mstkes 8th and 14th: sn wknd: hmpd 4 out* **25/1**	PJBrennan	57
P6P-	5	*dist*	**Uncle Ada (IRE)**^{66} [4142] 10-10-11 (D J Minty) *bhd: mstke and hmpd 1st: reminders 7th: lost tch 11th: t.o* **100/1**	TJPhelan(5)	—
U12-	6	*¾*	**Castlemore (IRE)**^{50} [4450] 7-11-2 (P J Hobbs) *led tl blnd 1st: led 3rd to 5th: nt fluent 6th: mstke 14th: sn wknd* **13/8**^{2}	RJohnson	—
000-	U		**Rigmarole**^{16} [4973] 7-11-2 (P F Nicholls) *hld up: unsighted and blnd bdly 2nd: hdwy 13th: 3 l 2nd and clsng whn blnd and uns rdr 4 out* **11/8**^{1}	(t) APMcCoy	—

6m 3.30s (2.20) **Going Correction** -0.20s/f (Good) — **7** Ran SP% **110.5**
Speed ratings: **88,87,82,75,— —,—** CSF £104.75 TOTE £9.50: £2.60, £2.20; EX 29.60.

Owner S J Williams **Bred** Miss B Palfrey **Trained** Bridgwater, Somerset

■ The first winner under Rules for Claire Williams.

FOCUS

A modest winning time for the class and with Rigmarole a casualty this took little winning. The winner's Newton Abbot second could arguably have been rated this high.

NOTEBOOK

Hold On Harry, runner-up in a hunter chase last time, ran out a surprise winner, helped by the market leaders' errors. He jumped out to his right almost throughout, and was less than fluent at times, but kept galloping to the line. *(tchd 16-1)*

Jivaty(FR), who has changed stables again, had his chance but not for the first time did not look the most enthusiastic. *(op 6-1)*

Toon Trooper(IRE), pulled up in a point-to-point in Scotland in February, took a keen grip in rear and merely plugged on for a fairly remote third place. *(op 11-1 tchd 10-1)*

Castlemore(IRE), a winning hurdler, made more than one serious error on this chase debut and *dropped right away up the home straight. Official explanation: vet said gelding suffered injury to left fore leg (op 7-4 tchd 15-8)*

Rigmarole, a high-class recruit to chasing, very nearly dislodged McCoy at the second and eventually did so at the fourth from home. He put in a mixed round apart from those two blunders, both at open ditches, and while he was going well enough in second place when coming down he was about to enter unknown territory stamina-wise. *(op 13-8 tchd 7-4 in a place)*

245 BBC HEREFORD AND WORCESTER HBLB MARES' ONLY H'CAP HURDLE (12 hdls) — 3m

3:20 (3:22) (Class 4) (0-105,102) 4-Y-O+ — **£3,445** (£1,060; £530; £265)

Form					RPR
303-	1		**Wayward Melody**^{16} [4956] 5-10-9 85 (G L Moore) *bhd: hrd rdn 7th: hdwy after 9th: hung lft fr 3 out: led flat: all out* **9/2**^{2}	JEMoore	91
52P-	2	*1*	**Shady Grey**^{45} [4531] 7-10-8 87 (C J Mann) *chsd ldr: led 7th: rdn appr 2 out: hdd flat: nt qckn* **10/1**	DCrosse(3)	92
510-	3	*7*	**Tirikumba**^{24} [4837] 9-11-3 98 (S G Griffiths) *a.p: rdn appr 3 out: wknd flat* **9/1**	RStephens(5)	96
023-	4	*1*	**Hylia**^{21} [4889] 6-11-2 92 (Mrs P Robeson) *led to 7th: prom: rdn 3 out: wknd flat* **2/1**^{1}	APMcCoy	89
540-	5	*2*	**Silver Gift**^{28} [4799] 8-10-5 88 (G Fierro) *hld up and bhd: hdwy 9th: sn rdn: wknd appr last* **12/1**	PCStringer(7)	83
P66-	6	*½*	**Earcomesannie (IRE)**^{28} [4795] 5-10-0 76 oh5 (P A Pritchard) *prom: led 4th to 7th: wknd flat* **25/1**	JGoldstein	72+
246-	7	*9*	**Bally's Bak**^{150} [2718] 7-11-2 102 (Mrs S J Smith) *hld up: hdwy 9th: wknd after 3 out* **11/1**	THalliday(10)	88
U50/	8	*dist*	**Erins Lass (IRE)**^{400} [4651] 8-10-4 90 (R Dickin) *mstke 2nd: a bhd: t.o* **33/1**	JStevenson(10)	—
500-	P		**Sovereign's Gift**^{107} [3459] 9-11-2 92 (Mrs S D Williams) *bhd tl p.u after 6th* **25/1**	RJohnson	—
200-	P		**Miniballist (IRE)**^{86} [3793] 7-11-7 100 (R T Phillips) *a bhd: t.o whn p.u bef 2 out* **16/1**	GCarenza(3)	—
2F0-	P		**L'Orage Lady (IRE)**^{121} [3258] 7-11-7 97 (Mrs H Dalton) *bhd fr 8th: t.o whn p.u bef 3 out* **16/1**	SThomas	—
40-5	P		**Vivre Aimer Rire (FR)**^{10} [77] 4-10-0 82 oh3 (M Scudamore) *prom tl wknd 7th: t.o whn p.u bef 3 out* **10/1**	TScudamore	—
3P4-	P		**Eagle's Landing**^{16} [4964] 7-10-1 77 (W K Goldsworthy) *mstke 1st: sn t.o: p.u bef 7th* **33/1**	(tp) JamesDavies	—
1P-6	P		**Princess Aimee**^{13} [25] 5-10-3 79 (P Bowen) *prom tl rdn and wknd after 9th: bhd whn p.u bef last* **8/1**^{3}	(p) ChristianWilliams	—

5m 52.6s (0.70) **Going Correction** +0.075s/f (Yiel)
WFA 4 from 5yo+ 6lb **14** Ran SP% **132.2**
Speed ratings: **101,100,98,98,97 97,94,—,—,— —,—,—,—** CSF £52.47 CT £409.40 TOTE £6.60: £2.60, £3.70, £3.00; EX 92.70.
Owner BHW Partnership **Bred** W D Hodge **Trained** Woodingdean, E Sussex
■ Stewards' Enquiry : J E Moore three-day ban: used whip with excessive frequency (May 19-21)

FOCUS
An ordinary handicap saw an unlikely winner in Wayward Melody, who looked set to finish out the back for much of the way. The third and fourth pretty much ran to their marks.

NOTEBOOK
Wayward Melody, a moody sort, was being ridden along before halfway and looked set to finish at the back of the field, but Moore's sterling efforts were rewarded as she came through to lead on the flat. She was well in on her old form and this was her first win away from Fontwell. *(op 5-1 tchd 11-2)*
Shady Grey, having her second run since leaving Karen Marks's yard, improved for this return to three miles. She is still a maiden over hurdles but is capable of putting that right. *(op 12-1)*
Tirikumba, 8lb higher than when successful at Wincanton in March, came under pressure leaving the back straight and eventually stayed on into third on the run-in. *(op 8-1 tchd 10-1)*
Hylia took an early lead, but was unable to dominate as she likes. She remained prominent until her stamina gave out in the latter stages over this longer trip. *(op 10-3 tchd 7-2)*
Silver Gift is on a long losing run, but she could put that right soon as she has become well handicapped. *(tchd 11-1)*
Earcomesannie(IRE), upped in trip and ridden more prominently, ran her best race to date over hurdles. *(tchd 33-1)*
Sovereign's Gift *Official explanation: jockey said mare lost her action (op 20-1)*
Princess Aimee *Official explanation: vet said mare was lame (op 20-1)*

246 CANCER RESEARCH UK'S RACE FOR LIFE H'CAP CHASE (12 fncs) 2m
3:50 (3:51) (Class 4) (0-110,108) 5-Y-O+ **£4,192** (£1,290; £645; £322)

Form RPR
13- **1** **Manoram (GER)**[178] 2147 6-11-4 **100**.....(v) APMcCoy 111+
(Ian Williams) *chsd ldr: mstke 3 out: nt fluent last: hrd rdn to ld nr fin: all out* **2/1**[1]
P05- **2** *nk* **Lord Of The Hill (IRE)**[21] 4888 10-11-5 **101**..... JEMoore 110
(G Brown) *led: hrd rdn appr last: hdd nr fin* **12/1**
40P- **3** *19* **Blazing Batman**[30] 4765 12-10-10 **97**..... TJPhelan[(5)] 87
(Dr P Pritchard) *hld up: hdwy appr 4th: lost pl after 6th: styd on flat: n.d* **25/1**
4U-1 **4** *hd* **Apadi (USA)**[8] 135 9-10-7 **92**..... LMcGrath[(3)] 85+
(R C Guest) *hld up and bhd: hdwy 6th: wknd 4 out* **3/1**[2]
312- **5** *5* **Green Gamble**[20] 4915 5-10-11 **95**..... JamesDavies 78
(D B Feek) *hld up: hdwy appr 4th: wknd appr 4 out* **7/2**[3]
060- **6** *2 ½* **Saby (FR)**[24] 4838 7-11-9 **105**..... RJohnson 87
(P J Hobbs) *a bhd* **12/1**
3P-P **7** *2 ½* **Auditor**[5] 176 6-10-2 **87**.....(v) DCrosse[(3)] 67
(S T Lewis) *hld up: hdwy 6th: rdn and wknd appr 4 out* **50/1**
533- **8** *3* **Flahive's First**[246] 1360 11-10-13 **100**..... LStephens[(5)] 77
(D Burchell) *a bhd* **14/1**
60-3 **P** **Bernardon (GER)**[14] 1 9-11-12 **108**.....(tp) PJBrennan —
(A J Deakin) *hld up: mstke 4th: blnd 5th: t.o whn p.u bef 8th* **16/1**

3m 54.0s (-4.60) **Going Correction** -0.20s/f (Good)
WFA 5 from 6yo+ 2lb **9** Ran SP% **114.3**
Speed ratings: **103,102,93,93,90 89,88,86,—** CSF £25.60 CT £459.72 TOTE £3.20: £1.40, £2.80, £6.30; EX 28.40.
Owner Willsford Racing Incorporated **Bred** Gestut Graditz **Trained** Portway, Worcs
■ Stewards' Enquiry : J E Moore one-day ban: used whip with excessive frequency (May 22)

FOCUS
A strongly-run race which few got into. It could be rated higher, but the winner probably ran to a similar level to his Cheltenham win.

NOTEBOOK
Manoram(GER), reappearing after a six-month break, wore a visor instead of the blinkers. Chasing the leader throughout, he looked held after an untidy jump at the final fence but responded bravely to McCoy's driving to put his head in front. He likes quick ground and will be kept going through the summer. *(op 11-4)*
Lord Of The Hill(IRE), having his fourth run for this yard, was still without the tongue tie. Adopting his favoured tactics, he seemed set to make all but, after holding the favourite at bay all the way up the home straight, was touched off near the line. *(op 14-1 tchd 16-1)*
Blazing Batman, back in realistic company, stayed on again in the latter stages having looked set to finish out the back.
Apadi(USA), 7lb higher, moved into third place on the home turn but could make no further inroads. This was disappointing. *(op 11-4 tchd 5-2)*
Green Gamble, back at two miles, was on the retreat on the run round to the home straight. *(tchd 10-3)*

247 ARENA LEISURE H'CAP HURDLE (8 hdls) 2m
4:20 (4:20) (Class 3) (0-130,123) 4-Y-O+ **£7,052** (£2,170; £1,085; £542)

Form RPR
134- **1** **Swift Swallow**[46] 4526 7-11-3 **114**..... JEMoore 115
(O Brennan) *hld up in mid-div: hdwy after 5th: rdn 3 out: r.o to ld post* **20/1**
PP-0 **2** *shd* **Forzacurity**[8] 136 6-10-0 **102** oh1 ow5..... LStephens[(5)] 104+
(M Sheppard) *led tl appr 2nd: chsd ldr: led 3 out: rdn after 2 out: hdd post* **80/1**
P6-3 **3** *5* **Lord Lington (FR)**[8] 136 6-10-9 **106**..... WMarston 103+
(D J Wintle) *hld up and bhd: hdwy appr 3 out: kpt on same pce flat* **14/1**
310- **4** *¾* **Half Inch**[21] 4883 5-10-1 **103**..... CHonour[(5)] 98
(B I Case) *bhd tl hdwy appr last: r.o flat: nrst fin* **25/1**
02/ **5** *½* **Heemanela (IRE)**[559] 1613 10-11-1 **112**..... RMcGrath 107
(Miss P Robson) *a.p: rdn appr 2 out: no ex flat* **20/1**
020- **6** *½* **Brooklyn's Gold (USA)**[113] 3359 10-11-2 **113**..... DRDennis 107
(Ian Williams) *hld up in tch: no hdwy fr 3 out* **14/1**
061- **7** *1 ¼* **Schapiro (USA)**[36] 4691 4-11-8 **123**..... APMcCoy 112
(Jonjo O'Neill) *hld up in tch: rdn appr 3 out: no imp* **2/1**[1]
124- **8** *5* **Cossack Dancer (IRE)**[142] 2878 7-10-9 **116**.....(p) JBunsell[(10)] 109+
(M Bradstock) *led appr 2nd: hdd 3 out: hit 2 out: wkng whn mstke last* **7/1**
000- **9** *hd* **Border Tale**[32] 4557 5-10-8 **105**..... JamesDavies 93
(James Moffatt) *hld up in tch: wknd 3 out* **20/1**
34B- **10** *7* **Monticelli (GER)**[157] 2593 5-11-4 **115**..... RJohnson 99+
(P J Hobbs) *a bhd* **4/1**[2]
30-2 **11** *25* **Magico (NZ)**[3] 192 7-10-2 **102**..... LMcGrath[(3)] 58
(R C Guest) *a bhd: t.o* **6/1**[3]
105- **P** **Davoski**[30] 4763 11-10-12 **114**..... TJPhelan[(5)] —
(Dr P Pritchard) *wl bhd fr 3rd: t.o whn p.u bef 2 out* **66/1**
52F/ **P** **Dileer (IRE)**[452] 3767 6-10-12 **112**..... GCarenza[(3)] —
(D J Wintle) *a bhd: rdn after 5th: t.o whn p.u bef 2 out* **33/1**
016- **P** **Debbie**[70] 3595 6-11-2 **123**..... DRCook[(10)] —
(B D Leavy) *hld up in tch: wknd appr 3 out: bhd whn p.u bef 2 out* **16/1**
600- **P** **Lord Joshua (IRE)**[37] 4678 7-11-3 **114**..... ATinkler —
(N J Henderson) *hld up in mid-div: lost pl appr 3 out: bhd whn p.u bef last* **20/1**

3m 47.7s (-2.50) **Going Correction** +0.075s/f (Yiel) **15** Ran SP% **127.9**
Speed ratings: **109,108,106,106,105 105,104,102,102,98 86,—,—,—,—** CSF £1066.13 CT £20630.24 TOTE £22.70: £5.10, £14.70, £5.50; EX 1656.20.
Owner Richard J Marshall **Bred** Ronald Wilkie **Trained** Worksop, Notts

FOCUS
Quite a competitive handicap run at a sound pace. The winner was stepping up on his previous form to the tune of 6lb.

NOTEBOOK
Swift Swallow put in a strong challenge on the run-in and got up right on the line. On the upgrade, he appreciated this faster ground and will not mind a return to further. *(op 25-1)*
Forzacurity, having his fourth run for this yard, jumped to the front at the first in the home straight. Not fluent at the next, he seemed sure to hold on under some firm driving but was pipped in the last stride. *(tchd 100-1)*
Lord Lington(FR), having his third outing since leaving Paul Nicholls, ran respectably again, but he is not getting much help from the handicapper. *(op 12-1)*
Half Inch, having her second run back from a winter break, was only getting going when the race was as good as over.
Heemanela(IRE) was successful in a similar event at Gowran Park in October 2003, but had not run since an outing on the Flat later that month. This was an encouraging return. *(op 25-1)*
Brooklyn's Gold(USA) ran creditably on this first start since January and remains on a decent mark.
Schapiro(USA), put up 12lb for winning at Newbury, was somewhat disappointing and the faster ground would not seem a valid excuse. *(op 9-4 tchd 5-2 in a place)*
Cossack Dancer(IRE), having his first run since December, set a sound pace until collared at the third last. He is potentially well in and is capable of winning a handicap. *(tchd 15-2)*
Debbie *Official explanation: jockey said mare lost her action (op 14-1)*

248 WORCESTER RACECOURSE FAMILY FUN DAY H'CAP CHASE (15 fncs) 2m 4f 110y
4:50 (4:50) (Class 3) (0-125,123) 5-Y-O+ **£5,921** (£1,822; £911; £455)

Form RPR
43-2 **1** **Sky Warrior (FR)**[14] 4 7-11-12 **123**..... ChristianWilliams 134+
(Evan Williams) *hld up in tch: blnd and lost pl 3rd: wl bhd 9th: hdwy appr 2 out: led last: drvn out* **6/1**[3]
34F- **2** *1 ¾* **Ball O Malt (IRE)**[52] 4407 9-11-6 **120**..... PWhelan[(3)] 127
(R A Fahey) *hld up: hdwy 10th: led 4 out to last: nt qckn* **7/1**
243- **3** *2* **Little Big Horse (IRE)**[64] 4167 9-11-7 **118**..... DElsworth 123
(Mrs S J Smith) *hld up in tch: lost pl 8th: rallied appr 2 out: styd on u.p flat* **4/1**[2]
253- **4** *2 ½* **Nagano (FR)**[35] 4724 7-10-8 **105**..... DRDennis 109+
(Ian Williams) *hld up and bhd: hdwy 10th: rdn and ev ch last: wknd* **9/1**
06U- **5** *shd* **Why The Long Face (NZ)**[15] 4979 8-10-4 **104**..... LMcGrath[(3)] 106
(R C Guest) *bhd: reminders after 3rd and 4th: styd on flat: nvr nrr* **16/1**
PP2- **6** *9* **Burning Truth (USA)**[203] 1746 11-11-1 **112**..... PJBrennan 108+
(M Sheppard) *led to 4 out: wknd last* **33/1**
525- **7** *20* **Bobosh**[15] 4979 9-10-0 **107**.....(p) JStevenson[(10)] 80
(R Dickin) *prom: bmpd 6th: sn lost pl: wl bhd fr 9th* **18/1**
311- **8** *5* **Renvyle (IRE)**[203] 1748 7-10-13 **110**.....(b) APMcCoy 86+
(Jonjo O'Neill) *hld up: hdwy whn bdly bmpd 6th: led briefly appr 4 out: wknd 3 out* **11/4**[1]
362- **9** *3 ½* **Duchamp (USA)**[21] 4880 8-11-9 **120**.....(b) JEMoore 85
(A M Balding) *w ldr: reminders after 3rd: lost 2nd 11th: sn wknd* **7/1**
51P- **P** **Up The Glen (IRE)**[24] 4836 11-10-10 **107**..... RMcGrath —
(A W Carroll) *hld up in tch: p.u lame bef 7th* **14/1**

5m 6.70s (-8.80) **Going Correction** -0.20s/f (Good) **10** Ran SP% **116.7**
Speed ratings: **108,107,106,105,105 102,94,92,91,—** CSF £47.96 CT £189.20 TOTE £6.50: £2.10, £2.20, £1.60; EX 47.20.
Owner Mr and Mrs Glynne Clay **Bred** Suc I B S Lewin **Trained** Cowbridge, Vale Of Glamorgan

FOCUS
The early pace was strong and fortunes changed several times up the home straight. The form looks suspect, but the second and third ran to their marks and it will be interesting to see if it works out.

NOTEBOOK
Sky Warrior(FR) dropped to the back of the field after a blunder at the third and was still a fairly remote eighth jumping the fourth from home, but he began to stay on down the outside and swept into the lead at the final fence. He won a shade comfortably in the end and there could be more to come. *(op 8-1)*
Ball O Malt(IRE) came from off the pace to show ahead at the fourth from home but was no match for the winner on the run-in. He stayed farther than this over hurdles and could benefit from a step up in trip. *(op 13-2 tchd 6-1)*
Little Big Horse(IRE) was renewing his effort at the end and continues in good heart. He will be suited by a return to three miles. *(op 5-1 tchd 11-2)*
Nagano(FR) ran a decent race but this longer trip eventually found him out. The drop back to two miles will suit him.
Why The Long Face(NZ), without the usual cheekpieces, never looked particularly happy but passed beaten rivals at the end. *(op 11-1)*
Burning Truth(USA), racing off his last winning mark, set a good pace until caught at the fourth from home and should strip fitter for this first start since the autumn. *(op 25-1)*
Renvyle(IRE), back over fences for this first run since October, survived a mishap at the sixth. He moved to the front on the turn out of the back straight but no sooner had he got there than he was collared and on the retreat. *(op 4-1)*
Up The Glen(IRE) *Official explanation: jockey said mare lost her action (op 12-1 tchd 16-1)*

249 COME EVENING RACING NEXT SATURDAY 14TH MAY INTERMEDIATE NATIONAL HUNT FLAT RACE 2m
5:20 (5:20) (Class 6) 4-6-Y-O **£2,030** (£580; £290)

Form RPR
6- **1** **Slick (FR)**[63] 4207 4-11-0..... ATinkler 84+
(N J Henderson) *hld up in tch: rdn to ld over 2f out: edgd rt ins fnl f: r.o* **6/4**[1]
2 *1 ½* **Even Flo** 4-10-4..... TJMalone[(3)] 75
(R Curtis) *hld up and bhd: hdwy on outside bnd 4f out: ev ch over 2f out: sn rdn: swtchd lft ins fnl f: kpt on* **16/1**
5- **3** *nk* **Sabreur**[43] 4559 4-11-0..... PJBrennan 82+
(Ian Williams) *hld up and bhd: hdwy over 3f out: sn rdn: kpt on ins fnl f* **9/4**[2]
00- **4** *1 ½* **Jimmy Bedney (IRE)**[64] 4193 4-10-9..... RStephens[(5)] 81
(Mrs D A Hamer) *led: rdn and hdd over 2f out: no ex towards fin* **9/2**[3]

0- **5** *5* **Lord Hopeful (IRE)**[40] [4644] 4-10-7 PCStringer(7) 76
(C P Morlock) *hld up: hdwy on ins 4f out: wknd over 2f out* **28/1**

0- **6** *½* **Batties Den (IRE)**[68] [4111] 5-11-1 GBerridge(3) 79
(P D Niven) *chsd ldr 7f: wnt 2nd again over 4f out: wknd 3f out* **8/1**

7 *17* **Escape Wall** 4-10-7 MrGTumelty(7) 58
(K Bishop) *hld up in tch: wknd 3f out* **16/1**

8 *22* **Country Rally** 6-10-13 TJPhelan(5) 40
(Mrs S Gardner) *a bhd: t.o* **33/1**

F **Charm Indeed** 5-10-11 SWalsh(7) —
(N B King) *hld up in tch: chsd ldr 9f out tl rdn over 4f out: wkng whn hung rt and rn wd ent st: collapsed over 2f out* **25/1**

3m 58.4s (10.60) **Going Correction** +0.075s/f (Yiel)
WFA 4 from 5yo+ 4lb **9** Ran SP% **122.1**
Speed ratings: **76,75,75,74,71 71,63,52,—** CSF £29.85 TOTE £2.60: £1.30, £3.80, £1.40; EX 36.90 Place 6 £7621.40, Place 5 £3281.21.
Owner Riverwood Racing II **Bred** Petra Bloodstock Agency Ltd **Trained** Upper Lambourn, Berks

FOCUS
A very slow time when compared with the earlier hurdle races over the same trip. The race has been rated through the winner and the sixth.

NOTEBOOK
Slick(FR) is a half-brother to a pair of middle-distance winners in France. Held in what has turned out to be a fairly ordinary Kempton bumper on his debut, he did not have to improve on that running to get off the mark. *(op 7-4 tchd 15-8)*
Even Flo, out of an unraced half-sister to Grand National winner Party Politics, is a half-sister to a winning hurdler and a bumper winner. A cheap purchase from a yard not noted for its bumper successes, she ran a good race on this debut, albeit in a weak event. *(tchd 20-1)*
Sabreur, who is a half-brother to the smart but injury-prone chaser Rockforce, did not show any improvement on this second outing. *(op 7-4 tchd 5-2)*
Jimmy Bedney(IRE), backed down on course from 20/1, set a modest pace and could not find a change of gear when tackled. *(op 20-1 tchd 25-1)*
Lord Hopeful(IRE) had been tailed off on his debut in heavy ground. *(op 33-1)*
T/Jkpt: Not won. T/Plt: £1,935.10 to a £1 stake. Pool: £47,848.80. 18.05 winning tickets. T/Qpdt: £208.10 to a £1 stake. Pool: £3,263.30. 11.60 winning tickets. KH

250 - 260a (Foreign Racing) - See Raceform Interactive

[21]TOWCESTER (R-H)
Monday, May 9

OFFICIAL GOING: Good (good to soft in places)
Wind: nil Weather: heavy rain for 2 hours before racing, then fine

261 CANTORSPREADFAIR.COM MAIDEN HURDLE (11 hdls) 2m 5f
6:00 (6:01) (Class 4) 4-Y-0+ **£4,212** (£1,296; £648; £324)

Form RPR

010- **1** **Flintoff (USA)**[30] [4774] 4-10-11 HOliver 95+
(R C Guest) *hld up midfield: prog and mstke 8th: trckd ldr next: led after 2 out: sn clr* **5/1**[3]

2 *10* **Auntie Kathleen**[64] 6-10-9 JEMoore 84+
(M C Pipe) *t.k.h: trckd ldr: led 6th: mstke 3 out: blnd 2 out: sn hdd and btn* **6/4**[1]

00-4 **3** *6* **Potts Of Magic**[14] [21] 6-11-2 87 PFlynn 82
(R Lee) *chsd ldrs: pushed along fr 6th: outpcd 3 out: plugged on one pce: mstke last* **14/1**

00-0 **4** *hd* **Cotswold Rose**[11] [77] 5-10-4 TJPhelan(5) 75
(N M Babbage) *last trio: outpcd and rdn 7th: sn struggling: prog u.p after 3 out: kpt on* **40/1**

46- **5** *17* **Touch Of Fate**[21] [4911] 6-11-2 MAFitzgerald 65
(R Rowe) *trckd ldrs tl wknd 3 out: sn bhd* **3/1**[2]

00-0 **P** **Posh Crack**[14] [27] 5-10-9 LAspell —
(F Jordan) *a in last trio: wknd 7th: sn t.o: p.u after 3 out* **100/1**

00-P **P** **The Yellow Earl (IRE)**[7] [147] 5-11-2 ARoss —
(J M Jefferson) *a in last trio: wknd 7th: t.o whn blnd 3 out and p.u* **50/1**

00P- **P** **Firstflor**[43] [4583] 6-10-4 70 JDiment(5) —
(F Jordan) *t.k.h: led to 6th: mstke 8th: wknd 3 out: wl bhd whn p.u bef last* **50/1**

/3F- **P** **Peppershot**[21] [4911] 5-11-2 100 RThornton —
(R Gurney) *trckd ldng pair: mstke 2nd: wknd 3 out: wl bhd whn p.u bef 2 out* **6/1**

5m 41.2s (8.90) **Going Correction** +0.075s/f (Yiel)
WFA 4 from 5yo+ 5lb **9** Ran SP% **110.0**
Speed ratings: **103,99,96,96,90 —,—,—,—** CSF £12.32 TOTE £4.60: £1.90, £1.10, £2.70; EX 15.80.
Owner Andrew Flintoff & Paul Beck **Bred** Mill Ridge Farm Ltd & Jamm Ltd **Trained** Brancepeth, Co Durham

FOCUS
Only a fair race, but the winner did it nicely and could make a useful handicapper. The third sets the standard.

NOTEBOOK
Flintoff(USA), making his hurdling debut, had too much class for rules debutant Auntie Kathleen and cleared away from two out to win tidily. Still only a four-year-old, he acts well on a sound surface and looks more than capable of defying a penalty. *(op 9-2 tchd 6-1)*
Auntie Kathleen, unbeaten in three points, was a little disappointing on this Rules debut, but may have bumped into a useful sort and is probably worthy of another chance. She should have little trouble winning races. *(op 5-4 tchd 6-5)*
Potts Of Magic lacked the pace of the principals and third was the best he could have hoped for. This was a fair effort and three miles in handicaps will be more his bag. *(tchd 18-1)*
Cotswold Rose is a lowly performer and will do better once handicapped.
Touch Of Fate is not really progressing over hurdles and was disappointing. *Official explanation: vet said gelding sustained cuts to its legs (op 9-2)*
Peppershot ran a rare bad race and may have been affected by his fall last time. *Official explanation: jockey said gelding had breathing problem (op 7-1 tchd 15-2)*

262 CANTORSPREADFAIR.COM H'CAP CHASE (18 fncs) 3m 110y
6:30 (6:30) (Class 4) (0-100,99) 5-Y-0+ **£4,153** (£1,278; £639; £319)

Form RPR

636- **1** **Uncle Mick (IRE)**[161] [2541] 10-11-12 99 (b) JTizzard 114+
(C L Tizzard) *wl in tch: trckd ldr 13th: led gng easily after 3 out: drvn and styd on after 2 out* **15/2**

414- **2** *5* **Sissinghurst Storm (IRE)**[19] [4929] 7-9-11 73 oh3 DCrosse(3) 83
(R Dickin) *in tch: rdn whn blnd 14th: effrt u.p to chse wnr 2 out: no imp* **9/4**[1]

P3-1 **3** *19* **Over Zealous (IRE)**[14] [22] 13-10-9 82 (b) PFlynn 73
(John R Upson) *mde most: pushed along after 9th: bmpd next: drvn and hdd after 3 out: wknd next* **8/1**

4P5- **4** *6* **Isou (FR)**[47] [4516] 9-10-4 77 (b[1]) ATinkler 64+
(V R A Dartnall) *mstkes: pressed ldr: chal and bmpd 10th: blnd 3 out and wknd* **9/2**[2]

/PP- **5** *dist* **Chancers Dante (IRE)**[145] [2837] 9-10-1 77 (b) KJMercer(3) —
(Ferdy Murphy) *a in rr: rdn and struggling after 6th: t.o 12th: j. last as 4th horse fin* **9/1**

PU-P **F** **Pete The Painter (IRE)**[11] [76] 8-10-10 90 (b) MrJETudor(7) —
(J W Tudor) *in tch: reminder 7th: fell next* **5/1**[3]

15-0 **U** **Tiger Talk**[5] [181] 9-10-9 82 (b) HOliver —
(R C Guest) *hld up: in tch whn mstke and uns rdr 11th* **8/1**

6m 31.5s **Going Correction** -0.575s/f (Firm) **7** Ran SP% **109.6**
Speed ratings: **101,99,93,91,— —,—** CSF £23.61 CT £127.24 TOTE £7.90: £3.90, £1.50; EX 18.00.
Owner D J Hinks **Bred** J L Rothwell **Trained** Milborne Port, Dorset

FOCUS
Poor form although the time was reasonable.

NOTEBOOK
Uncle Mick(IRE), giving upwards of 16lb to his field, put up a good weight-carrying performance and stayed on strongly under pressure to record his first victory since September 2003. He will do well to find a weak-enough race to follow up in . *(op 7-1)*
Sissinghurst Storm(IRE) gave chase to the winner best she could, but was never getting to him and had to settle for a clear second. She is still on a reasonable mark. *(op 11-4)*
Over Zealous(IRE), up 6lb from last time, struggled off this higher mark and was unable to make much of an impression on the front pair. *(op 5-1)*
Isou(FR) has not progressed as expected and was again disappointing. *(op 13-2)*

263 CANTORSPREADFAIR.COM (S) HURDLE (8 hdls) 2m
7:00 (7:00) (Class 5) 4-6-Y-0 **£2,884** (£824; £412)

Form RPR

4-31 **1** **Polished**[2] [214] 6-11-11 84 (b) PCO'Neill(7) 98+
(R C Guest) *t.k.h: hld up in tch: smooth prog to ld after 3 out: rdn next: kpt on* **5/6**[1]

04-0 **2** *1 ½* **Spectacular Hope**[9] [134] 5-11-1 85 RYoung(3) 80+
(J W Mullins) *trckd ldrs: bmpd by loose horse 4th: rdn after 3 out: chsd wnr 2 out: kpt on flat: nt quite able to chal* **15/2**

54-5 **3** *15* **Twist N Turn**[9] [134] 5-10-11 63 JMMaguire 60+
(D McCain) *led briefly 2nd: styd prom: led 5th: drvn and hdd after 3 out: blnd 2 out: wknd* **11/2**[2]

P-F **4** *9* **Nutley Queen (IRE)**[6] [173] 6-10-11 PFlynn 53+
(M Appleby) *plld hrd: hld up in last: rdn after 3 out: no ch w ldrs fr next: tired whn blnd last* **40/1**

P0-6 **5** *10* **Dry Old Party (IRE)**[14] [21] 6-11-4 83 (b) PHide 45
(P Winkworth) *trckd ldrs: rdn 3 out: sn wknd: blnd last* **12/1**

25-0 **6** *4* **Frambo (IRE)**[9] [134] 4-11-0 83 (tp) PJBrennan 37
(J G Portman) *led to 2nd: lft in ld 3rd: mstke 5th and hdd: wknd rapidly after 3 out* **6/1**[3]

U00- **R** **Reedsman (IRE)**[16] [4975] 4-10-11 72 (b) LMcGrath(3) —
(R C Guest) *plld hrd: led after 2nd tl rn out next* **25/1**

4m 14.8s (12.00) **Going Correction** -0.125s/f (Good)
WFA 4 from 5yo+ 4lb **7** Ran SP% **110.0**
Speed ratings: **86,85,77,73,68 66,—** CSF £7.18 TOTE £1.80: £1.20, £2.10; EX 4.60.The winner was sold to V Dartnall for 4,200gns
Owner The Cherry Blossom Partnership **Bred** Ewar Stud Farms **Trained** Brancepeth, Co Durham

FOCUS
A bad race and the front two pulled clear. The form is weak but solid enough for the grade.

NOTEBOOK
Polished, a winner only two days ago, was able to race off the same mark and won in workmanlike fashion. He is beginning to find his feet now and it will be interesting to see what the Handicapper does. *(op 8-11 tchd 10-11)*
Spectacular Hope pulled clear of the third, staying on well, but was always being held by the winner. *(op 8-1)*
Twist N Turn was well adrift of the front two and it will be a bad race he wins. *(op 15-2)*

264 CANTORSPREADFAIR.COM NOVICES' CHASE (14 fncs) 2m 3f 110y
7:30 (7:30) (Class 4) 5-Y-0+ **£4,140** (£1,345; £724)

Form RPR

13-3 **1** **Pequenita**[6] [170] 5-10-4 105 (p) HOliver 110+
(R C Guest) *j. slowly 1st: trckd ldr: led after 7th: drew clr fr 3 out: easily* **11/10**[1]

22-1 **2** *11* **Oulton Broad**[14] [24] 9-10-9 105 (p) JDiment(5) 105
(F Jordan) *nvr gng particularly wl: hld up: urged along to chse wnr sn after 3 out: no imp* **11/8**[2]

B0-0 **3** *dist* **Padamul**[9] [135] 9-10-11 62 RYoung(3) —
(J W Mullins) *prom: chsd wnr after 7th tl after 3 out: wknd: t.o* **15/2**[3]

PPP- **R** **Just Bryan**[85] [3838] 6-10-9 64 (bt[1]) TGreenway(5) —
(P A Pritchard) *racd v freely: led and sn clr: mstke 6th: hdd after next: 3rd whn rn out 8th* **20/1**

5m 17.6s **Going Correction** +0.05s/f (Yiel)
WFA 5 from 6yo+ 2lb **4** Ran SP% **106.3**
Speed ratings: **103,98,—,—** CSF £2.99 TOTE £2.30; EX 3.30.
Owner Paul Beck **Bred** Rodney Meredith **Trained** Brancepeth, Co Durham

FOCUS
A modest contest, but a straightforward victory for Pequenita who is rated value for more than the official distance.

NOTEBOOK
Pequenita is a consistent mare who has taken well to fences. She pulled right away from Oulton Broad and it will be interesting to see how she gets on once pitched into handicaps. *(tchd Evens)*
Oulton Broad has taken well to chasing, yet to finish out of the first two in four starts, but lacks scope and will always be vulnerable. *(tchd 5-4)*
Just Bryan ran well to a point, but was beaten when running out at the eighth. *Official explanation: jockey said gelding cocked jaw and ran out (op 12-1)*

265 CANTORSPREADFAIR.COM H'CAP HURDLE (8 hdls) 2m
8:00 (8:00) (Class 4) (0-105,99) 4-Y-0+ **£3,425** (£1,054; £527; £263)

Form RPR

605- **1** **Sunnyarjun**[46] [4533] 7-10-10 83 JMogford 95+
(J C Tuck) *hld up: prog 5th: trckd ldr bef 2 out and stl gng easily: delayed effrt tl after last: rdn to ld flat* **4/1**[3]

F0-U **2** *1* **Murphy's Nails (IRE)**[15] [5] 8-10-12 90 MNicolls(5) 97
(K C Bailey) *w ldr and clr of rest: led 3 out and drvn 4 l clr: hdd and outpcd flat* **11/1**

660- **3** *1 ¼* **Signature Tune (IRE)**[27] [4813] 6-11-9 96 PHide 102
(P Winkworth) *trckd ldrs: mstke 5th: rdn and outpcd next: styd on again u.p fr 2 out* **10/1**

P-16 **4** *13* **Little Rort (IRE)**[6] 177 6-10-12 **90** LTreadwell(5) 88+
(S T Lewis) *mde most to 3 out: wknd u.p bef next: no ch whn blnd bdly last* **3/1**[1]
32-0 **5** *16* **Vulcan Lane (NZ)**[11] 84 8-10-8 **84** (b) LMcGrath(3) 61
(R C Guest) *chsd ldng pair tl after 5th: sn wknd u.p: wl bhd 2 out* **7/2**[2]
35-0 **6** *25* **Paula Lane**[10] 105 5-10-8 **81** TDoyle 33
(R Curtis) *hld up in last: struggling fr 5th: t.o 2 out* **10/1**
2P-0 **U** **Saorsie**[9] 136 7-11-12 **99** (b) SFox —
(J C Fox) *hld up midfield: disputing 4th pl whn stmbld and uns rdr bnd bef 4th* **8/1**
00/P **U** **Jack Weighell**[7] 152 6-10-12 **85** ARoss —
(J M Jefferson) *hld up: rdn and wl btn in 5th whn stmbld bdly on landing 3 out and uns rdr* **14/1**

4m 7.90s (5.10) **Going Correction** -0.125s/f (Good) 8 Ran SP% **111.5**
Speed ratings: **103,102,101,95,87 74**,—,— CSF £42.81 CT £398.20 TOTE £4.60: £2.30, £3.30, £2.90; EX 73.90.
Owner The Sunny Five **Bred** J C Tuck **Trained** Oldbury on the Hill, Gloucs

FOCUS
Another bad contest but the time was reasonable and the winner is value for further.

NOTEBOOK
Sunnyarjun was given a good, confident ride by Mogford and was produced with impeccable timing to take this low-grade event. He is a fairly consistent sort and this seemed an improved effort. *(op 9-2 tchd 5-1)*
Murphy's Nails(IRE) is not up to much and has still to find ideal conditions. He ran well, but was always a sitting duck for the winner. *(op 8-1)*
Signature Tune(IRE) continues to shape as though a rise in distance will help. *(tchd 11-1)*
Little Rort(IRE) was already well held when whacking the last and probably needs to drop a few pounds before he is winning again as he is not really progressing. *(op 7-2 tchd 4-1)*
Vulcan Lane(NZ) ran a below par race and is probably worth giving another chance to. *(tchd 3-1)*
Saorsie was in the process of running a good race under his big weight and it will be interesting to see if he is turned out again quickly. *(op 11-2)*

266 CANTORSPREADFAIR.COM MAIDEN OPEN NATIONAL HUNT FLAT RACE 2m
8:30 (8:30) (Class 6) 4-6-Y-O **£2,324** (£664; £332)

Form RPR
0- **1** **Castlemainevillage (IRE)**[20] 4922 5-11-4 SCurran 84+
(M R Bosley) *chsd ldng pair: rdn over 3f out: clsd to ld over 2f out: tired and drvn over 1f out: hld on* **6/1**[3]
2 *1 1/2* **Musical Chord (IRE)** 6-11-4 TDoyle 81+
(C Tinkler) *trckd ldrs: rdn over 3f out: effrt u.p to chse wnr over 1f out: kpt on but a jst hld* **13/8**[1]
0-00 **3** *8* **The Langer (IRE)**[6] 179 5-11-4 PFlynn 74+
(S T Lewis) *settled in rr: pushed along 1/2-way: struggling 5f out: prog u.p over 2f out: one pce fnl f* **12/1**
4 **4** *8* **Allez Melina**[14] 27 4-10-7 ATinkler 56+
(Mrs A J Hamilton-Fairley) *trckd clr ldr: clsd to ld wl over 2f out: sn rdn and hdd: wknd over 1f out* **3/1**[2]
5 *6* **April Showers** 5-10-11 JMogford 52
(J C Tuck) *t.k.h: hld up in last: lost tch 7f out: no ch fnl 3f* **12/1**
6 *5* **Clintos** 4-11-0 WMarston 50
(G R I Smyly) *in tch tl wknd 3f out* **14/1**
0- **7** *3/4* **Essennbee**[16] 4981 5-10-13 TJPhelan(5) 53
(Mrs J R Buckley) *led and sn clr: stl 15 l ahd over 3f out: wknd and hdd wl over 2f out* **33/1**
6- **U** **Boysterous (IRE)**[32] 4760 5-10-11 PMerrigan(7) —
(Mrs H Dalton) *swvd and uns rdr s* **6/1**[3]

4m 10.8s (-0.40) **Going Correction** -0.125s/f (Good)
WFA 4 from 5yo 4lb 5 from 6yo 2lb 8 Ran SP% **116.7**
Speed ratings: **97,96,92,88,85 82,82**,— CSF £16.55 TOTE £7.30: £2.10, £1.40, £2.50; EX 50.30 Place 6 £32.02, Place 5 £20.38.
Owner Mrs Jean M O'Connor **Bred** James Dullea **Trained** Kingston Lisle, Oxon
■ Stewards' Enquiry : P Flynn three-day ban: used whip with excessive force and not giving gelding time to respond (May 20-22)

FOCUS
An ordinary bumper with the winner setting the level.

NOTEBOOK
Castlemainevillage(IRE) was running on fresh air in the final 100 yards, but the favourite never looked like he was quite getting past and he held on for victory. This was a step up on his debut effort and he should make a hurdler, as he has plenty of size and scope. *(op 15-2)*
Musical Chord(IRE) comes from a stable that had a good time of it with their bumper horses last season and on this evidence he should soon be getting his head in front. This was a promising debut. *(op 11-8 tchd 7-4, 15-8 in a place)*
The Langer(IRE) shaped as though a greater distance is going to suit once sent hurdling. *(op 20-1)*
Allez Melina did not show a great deal of improvement on her initial effort and failed to see out the race as well could have been expected. *(op 7-2)*
T/Plt: £149.50 to a £1 stake. Pool: £40,520.80. 197.75 winning tickets. T/Qpdt: £27.10 to a £1 stake. Pool: £2,942.50. 80.20 winning tickets. JN

267 - 270a (Foreign Racing) - See Raceform Interactive

73 HEREFORD (R-H)
Tuesday, May 10

OFFICIAL GOING: Good to firm
Wind: Almost nil Weather: Fine

271 BET365, CALL 08000 322365 MAIDEN CHASE (14 fncs) 2m 3f
2:10 (2:11) (Class 4) 5-Y-0+ **£4,143** (£1,275; £637; £318)

Form RPR
F3-2 **1** **Ho Ho Hill (IRE)**[4] 202 7-11-3 **91** RWalsh 110+
(P F Nicholls) *a.p: wnt 2nd 7th: led appr 2 out: drew clr bef last: easily* **13/8**[1]
2 *11* **Jolejoker**[114] 7-11-3 TDoyle 95+
(R Lee) *in tch: hdwy 4 out: rdn to chse ldrs appr 3 out: wnt 2nd 2 out: no ch w wnr* **16/1**
P53- **3** *13* **Montys Island (IRE)**[19] 4942 8-11-3 **99** NFehily 79
(C J Mann) *hld up: mstke 5th: rdn and outpcd 4 out: kpt on u.p fr 2 out* **11/2**[2]
444- **4** *shd* **Lightin' Jack (IRE)**[39] 4681 7-11-3 **104** BJCrowley 82+
(Miss E C Lavelle) *j.lft: led: hdd appr 2 out: sn wknd* **13/8**[1]
4F-2 **5** *30* **Seeador**[13] 53 6-11-3 AThornton 49
(J W Mullins) *nt jump wl: in tch: rdn and wknd 4 out* **12/1**[3]
P4-2 **6** *6* **Alexander Musical (IRE)**[12] 74 7-11-3 **64** (v) PFlynn 43
(S T Lewis) *chsd ldr to 7th: rdn appr 9th: wknd 4 out* **25/1**
P0-0 **7** *dist* **Kinda Crazy**[11] 102 5-10-7 JAJenkins(7) —
(H J Manners) *midfield: lost pl appr 7th: sn bhd: t.o* **100/1**
P **Anaclone (IRE)**[9] 7-11-3 (t) TScudamore —
(M Scudamore) *a bhd: t.o whn p.u bef 10th* **40/1**
0PP- **U** **Chita's Flight**[37] 4725 5-10-7 (t) MBradburne —
(S C Burrough) *hld up: 7th whn blnd and uns rdr 4 out* **66/1**

4m 42.2s (-4.40) **Going Correction** -0.10s/f (Good)
WFA 5 from 6yo+ 2lb 9 Ran SP% **113.9**
Speed ratings: **105,100,94,94,82 79**,—,—,— CSF £26.63 TOTE £2.60: £1.10, £5.00, £2.20; EX 35.00.
Owner Mrs Mary Coburn & Paul K Barber **Bred** James Meagher **Trained** Ditcheat, Somerset

FOCUS
A moderate contest but easy for Ho Ho Hill, who was value for 15 lengths. The third and fourth were below par.

NOTEBOOK
Ho Ho Hill(IRE), who jumped pretty well, moved smoothly to the front and scored with a bit in hand. Not winning out of turn, he now goes to Doncaster sales. *(op 15-8 tchd 2-1 and 9-4 in a place)*
Jolejoker, third in both his point-to-points, the latest in January, ran a promising race on this debut under Rules and should improve for the experience. *(tchd 20-1)*
Montys Island(IRE) stayed on from the second last to take third prize on the line. He is worth stepping up in trip. *(op 6-1 tchd 7-1)*
Lightin' Jack(IRE), who slipped going into the first open ditch, showed a tendency to jump out to his left. Not for the first time he found little when headed and, weakening, he was pipped for third place right on the line. *(tchd 5-4)*
Seeador found the ground too fast for him on this chase debut and made more than one mistake. *(op 9-1)*

272 GERRARD LADIES CHAMPIONSHIP HUNTERS' CHASE (FINAL OF THE 2005 CHAMPIONSHIP) (19 fncs) 3m 1f 110y
2:40 (2:40) (Class 6) 5-Y-0+ **£3,380** (£1,040; £520; £260)

Form RPR
11-4 **1** **Red Brook Lad**[13] 47 10-11-4 **107** MissCTizzard(3) 113+
(C St V Fox) *in tch: hdwy after 13th (water): led after 3 out: clr appr last: styd on wl* **2/1**[1]
4U-1 **2** *7* **Chasing The Bride**[16] 6 12-11-4 MissAGoschen(3) 105
(Miss A Goschen) *hld up: hdwy appr 2 out: styd on to take 2nd run-in: nt trble wnr* **11/4**[2]
0P/1 **3** *1 1/2* **Galway (IRE)**[13] 52 12-11-2 MissCStucley(5) 103
(Mrs Marilyn Scudamore) *trckd ldrs: wnt 2nd 10th: led next: hdd after 3 out: outpcd by wnr appr last: lost 2nd and no ex run-in* **14/1**
P/U- **4** *11* **Golfagent**[9] 7-10-10 (t) MissRachelReynolds(7) 88
(Nick Shutts) *in rr: mstke 2nd: struggling 4 out: nvr on terms* **11/1**[3]
0P/3 **5** *1 1/4* **Mighty Montefalco**[13] 47 9-11-3 MissAdeLisleWells(7) 94
(Mrs Alison De Lisle Wells) *racd keenly: mde most to 11th: remained prom: rdn appr 2 out: sn wknd* **2/1**[1]
PP- **6** *3/4* **Twilight Dancer (IRE)**[18] 4957 7-10-5 MrsLucyRowsell(5) 79
(Miss H E Roberts) *w ldr to 10th: remained handy: rdn and wknd appr 3 out* **50/1**

6m 31.8s (-2.40) **Going Correction** -0.325s/f (Good) 6 Ran SP% **110.3**
Speed ratings: **90,87,87,84,83 83** CSF £7.88 TOTE £3.00: £1.10, £2.00; EX 5.60.
Owner C St V Fox **Bred** T H Jagger **Trained** Gillingham, Dorset

FOCUS
An interesting event, but a slightly disappointing turnout for the final of this point-to-point series. Neither of the first two were at their best but the third and fourth ran to their pre-race marks.

NOTEBOOK
Red Brook Lad does much of his racing under Rules over shorter but he stays this trip well enough. Pulling clear on the home turn, he was never seriously challenged. *(op 15-8 tchd 85-40 in a place)*
Chasing The Bride stayed on from the rear as usual but the winner was clear by the time he got going. He needs a stronger pace. *(op 5-2)*
Galway(IRE) ran his race but seems happier over shorter, under Rules in any case. *(op 12-1)*
Golfagent has had a good season between the flags, but he was always at the back of the field prior to passing a couple of opponents on the run-in. *(op 8-1)*
Mighty Montefalco, in front of today's winner over a shorter trip at Cheltenham last time, did not jump particularly well. *(op 3-1)*
Twilight Dancer(IRE) landed a ladies' point first time out but has been found wanting three times in hunter chases since then. *(op 33-1)*

273 DEVINE WINES - YOUR MESSAGE ON A BOTTLE (S) HURDLE (10 hdls) 2m 3f 110y
3:10 (3:10) (Class 5) 4-7-Y-0 **£2,191** (£626; £313)

Form RPR
046- **1** **Morson Boy (USA)**[23] 4890 5-10-12 **99** RWalsh 91+
(P F Nicholls) *hld up: hdwy 3 out: wnt 2nd 2 out: led on bit appr last: clr run-in: easily* **4/7**[1]
46-6 **2** *7* **Relative Hero (IRE)**[12] 75 5-10-12 **73** (p) NFehily 76+
(Miss S J Wilton) *led to 2nd: led again 3rd: rdn appr 2 out: hdd bef last: no ch w wnr run-in* **10/1**[3]
06-5 **3** *18* **Charlie Chapel**[7] 175 6-10-12 **100** PFlynn 57
(W M Brisbourne) *hld up: hdwy 4 out: rdn after 3 out: wknd after next* **7/2**[2]
600- **4** *13* **Starmix**[34] 4110 4-10-7 **81** NHannity 39
(G A Harker) *hld up: hdwy 5th: wknd 2 out* **16/1**
0FP- **5** *17* **Iris's Queen**[62] 4252 5-10-5 JMMaguire 20
(D McCain) *led 2nd to 3rd: remained prom: j. slowly 6th: wknd after 3 out* **14/1**
000- **6** *3/4* **Sparkes**[18] 4958 7-10-5 JAJenkins(7) 26
(H J Manners) *racd keenly: chsd ldrs to 5th: wknd appr 4 out* **40/1**
0P-0 **7** *dist* **Threepenny Bit**[10] 134 7-10-0 **59** (t) LStephens(5) —
(Mrs S M Johnson) *hld up: rdn after 6th: wknd appr 4 out: t.o* **50/1**

4m 45.5s (-2.40) **Going Correction** -0.325s/f (Good)
WFA 4 from 5yo+ 4lb 7 Ran SP% **111.9**
Speed ratings: **91,88,81,75,69 68**,— CSF £7.26 TOTE £1.40: £1.10, £2.60; EX 5.00.The winner was bought by N Shutts for 14,500gns.
Owner Ged Mason **Bred** G A Seelbinder **Trained** Ditcheat, Somerset

FOCUS
A slow time, even for a seller, 8.3 seconds slower than the later handicap. The winner was value for around double the actual margin in this desperate affair.

NOTEBOOK
Morson Boy(USA), without the blinkers this time, cruised into the lead on the home turn and won without turning a hair. He changed hands for a big sum at the auction. *(op 4-6 tchd 8-11)*
Relative Hero(IRE), adopting different tactics on this step up in trip, tried to get clear going to the second last but the favourite had him covered. *(op 8-1)*
Charlie Chapel requires a stronger pace. *(tchd 3-1 and 4-1)*
Starmix, who had a run on the Flat last month, did not settle. He is on the downgrade. *(op 12-1)*

274 BET365.COM NOVICES' HURDLE (8 hdls) 2m 1f
3:40 (3:40) (Class 4) 4-Y-0+ **£4,498** (£1,384; £692; £346)

Form RPR
561- **1** **Darrias (GER)**[25] [4852] 4-11-3 RWalsh 115+
(P F Nicholls) *hld up in tch: hdwy 3 out: led after 2 out: sn clr* **7/4[2]**
1- **2** *13* **Argent Ou Or (FR)**[22] [4916] 4-10-10 APMcCoy 90
(M C Pipe) *w ldr: led 4th: hdd after 2 out: sn btn* **9/2[3]**
020- **3** *3/4* **Devil's Teardrop**[215] [1635] 5-11-0 98 NFehily 95+
(C J Mann) *hld up: outpcd appr 2 out: 4th whn hmpd last: n.d* **15/2**
03-3 **4** *16* **Samandara (FR)**[12] [77] 5-10-7 107 RThornton 88+
(A King) *racd keenly: chsd ldrs: wnt 2nd 4th to 2 out: 2nd again and wl hld whn blnd bdly last: nt rcvr* **11/8[1]**
0- **P** **Top Son**[364] [287] 6-11-0 CLlewellyn —
(D W Lewis) *plld hrd: led to 4th: rdn and wknd appr 4 out: t.o next: p.u bef 2 out* **80/1**
6-0 **R** **Cicatrice**[2] [230] 4-10-10 TDoyle —
(D R Gandolfo) *in rr: struggling after 4th: no ch whn jinked bdly lft and fell appr 2 out* **33/1**

3m 54.5s (-8.60) **Going Correction** -0.325s/f (Good) **6** Ran SP% **112.6**
Speed ratings: **107,100,100,93,—** — CSF £10.24 TOTE £2.80: £2.60, £2.40; EX 7.20.
Owner Formpave Ltd **Bred** Gestut Rottgen **Trained** Ditcheat, Somerset

FOCUS
The easy winner has been rated value for 18l, with the second running to the value of his bumper win.

NOTEBOOK
Darrias(GER), who was taken to post early, settled better this time but was still keen. Quckening clear after the second last to complete a facile hat-trick for the Nicholls-Walsh team, he will surely win more of these over the summer. *(tchd 13-8)*
Argent Ou Or(FR), winner of an ordinary bumper on his debut, tried to get away three from home but the winner was much too good. *(op 4-1 tchd 7-2)*
Devil's Teardrop ran a fair race on his first run since September and was in fourth, close behind the two in front of him, when he was hampered at the final flight. *(op 9-1 tchd 10-1)*
Samandara(FR) was stepping down in trip. She was well held by the winner, but would probably have been second, when she nearly came down at the final flight, Thornton doing well to retain his seat. *(op 13-8 after 7-4 in a place)*
Cicatrice, brought out quickly, was well beaten when he appeared to try to duck out on the approach to the second last and came down. *(op 20-1)*

275 2005 CHAMBER BUSINESS FESTIVAL H'CAP HURDLE (10 hdls) 2m 3f 110y
4:10 (4:10) (Class 4) (0-110,108) 4-Y-0+ **£5,642** (£1,736; £868; £434)

Form RPR
F1-4 **1** **Alva Glen (USA)**[12] [78] 8-11-1 97 PJBrennan 101
(B J Llewellyn) *hld up: rdn appr 6th: hdwy bef 4 out: led after next: clr bef last: styd on* **4/1[2]**
B5-2 **2** *6* **Borehill Joker**[13] [57] 9-10-11 100 WKennedy[(7)] 98
(J L Spearing) *midfield: hdwy 5th: rdn to chse wnr 2 out: one pce after* **9/1**
121- **3** *2 1/2* **Kadam (IRE)**[18] [4956] 5-11-10 106 (b) RWalsh 103+
(P F Nicholls) *in tch: rdn to chse ldrs appr 2 out: one pce* **11/8[1]**
000- **4** *1* **Courant D'Air (IRE)**[23] [4883] 4-11-3 104 CLlewellyn 94
(Lucinda Featherstone) *bhd: mstke 2nd: effrt whn n.m.r on bnd appr 2 out: kpt on u.p after* **22/1**
P3P- **5** *5* **Boing Boing (IRE)**[14] [2939] 5-11-0 96 NFehily 87+
(Miss S J Wilton) *mstke 2nd: mde most tl after 3 out: sn wknd* **18/1**
2P0- **6** *2 1/2* **Diamond Merchant**[102] [3571] 6-11-12 108 RThornton 95
(A King) *trckd ldrs: rdn appr 3 out: wknd after next* **5/1[3]**
06-0 **7** *2* **Rudetski**[12] [78] 8-10-11 93 PFlynn 78
(M Sheppard) *midfield: hdwy appr 5th: hung rt bef 3 out: sn wknd* **33/1**
F50- **8** *hd* **Three Lions**[43] [4613] 8-11-1 97 ChristianWilliams 82
(R S Brookhouse) *prom tl hmpd whn wkng on bnd appr 2 out* **11/1**
015- **9** *13* **Fard Du Moulin Mas (FR)**[28] [4817] 12-11-6 102 BJCrowley 74
(M E D Francis) *prom tl rdn and wkng whn hmpd on bnd appr 2 out* **20/1**
66-3 **10** *22* **My Bold Boyo**[13] [57] 10-10-6 93 TJPhelan[(5)] 43
(K Bishop) *a bhd* **20/1**

4m 37.2s (-10.70) **Going Correction** -0.325s/f (Good)
WFA 4 from 5yo+ 4lb **10** Ran SP% **119.2**
Speed ratings: **108,105,104,104,102 101,100,100,95,86** CSF £37.46 CT £73.93 TOTE £6.60: £1.90, £2.30, £1.10; EX 40.90.
Owner A M Prettyjohn **Bred** Mrs Yolande Seydoux **Trained** Fochriw, Caerphilly

FOCUS
Solid handicap form, with the winner improving around 10lb for this longer trip.

NOTEBOOK
Alva Glen(USA) was being shoved along by halfway, but found himself in front at the end of the back straight and was not going to be caught. The step up in trip was a big help. *(op 5-1)*
Borehill Joker, 16lb higher over hurdles than fences, was back over the smaller obstacles for the first time since January. He ran to his mark but could not catch the winner. *(op 8-1)*
Kadam(IRE), 6lb higher than at Chepstow, was not at his best but did stay on past beaten rivals. *(op 6-4)*
Courant D'Air(IRE), pinched for room on the flight leaving the back straight, did stay on after that. *(op 20-1)*
Boing Boing(IRE), who had a pipe-opener on the Flat last month, made much of the running until headed by the winner leaving the back straight. *(op 20-1)*
Diamond Merchant, tackling fast ground for the first time, was unable to raise his game when the race began in earnest. *(op 6-1 tchd 13-2)*
Rudetski *Official explanation: jockey said gelding hung badly right-handed (op 25-1)*

276 COURTYARD ARTS CENTRE, EDUCATING RITA H'CAP CHASE (19 fncs) 3m 1f 110y
4:40 (4:40) (Class 4) (0-95,94) 5-Y-0+ **£4,576** (£1,408; £704; £352)

Form RPR
25P- **1** **Team Captain**[159] [2591] 11-11-9 91 PHide 101+
(C J Down) *a.p: led 4 out: clr 2 out: hld on wl cl home* **9/1**
22-1 **2** *1/2* **Silver Samuel (NZ)**[12] [76] 8-11-1 83 (t) JPByrne 93+
(S A Brookshaw) *hld up in tch: hdwy 14th: outpcd 4 out: rallied to chse wnr appr last: carried hd awkwardly but r.o after last* **11/4[1]**
U5-4 **3** *7* **Maybeseven**[15] [22] 11-10-3 71 (p) CLlewellyn 74+
(R Dickin) *prom: led 5th: hdd 4 out: rdn after 3 out: wknd after next* **16/1**
P0-3 **4** *19* **Felix Darby (IRE)**[11] [101] 10-10-13 88 (b) PCO'Neill[(7)] 71
(Miss G Browne) *mstkes: nvr gng wl: wl outpcd 4 out* **9/2[3]**
446- **5** *1 1/2* **Brady Boys (USA)**[25] [4853] 8-9-11 68 oh12 (p) ONelmes[(3)] 50
(J G M O'Shea) *hld up: hit 2nd: hdwy 8th: wknd 14th* **12/1**
1/P- **6** *nk* **Boardroom Dancer (IRE)**[22] [4912] 8-11-10 92 PMoloney 73
(Miss I E Craig) *hld up: stdy hdwy whn blnd 15th: sn btn* **25/1**
346- **7** *dist* **Dragon King**[17] [4980] 13-11-7 94 (b) TGreenway[(5)] —
(P Bowen) *in tch: rdn after 10th: wknd 14th: t.o* **10/1**
UP-3 **P** **Welsh Gold**[15] [24] 6-10-0 68 oh9 (v[1]) PFlynn —
(S T Lewis) *led to 5th: rdn after 9th: sn wknd: t.o whn p.u bef 12th* **14/1**
PP5- **P** **Mr Jake**[57] [4377] 12-9-7 68 oh8 MrGTumelty[(7)] —
(H E Haynes) *hld up: rdn along appr 8th: wknd 11th: mstke next: t.o whn p.u bef 4 out* **25/1**
U54- **P** **Usk Valley (IRE)**[25] [4853] 10-11-2 84 JamesDavies —
(P R Chamings) *in tch: rdn and hdwy 12th: cl 3rd whn mstke 4 out: sn wknd: t.o whn p.u bef last* **3/1[2]**

6m 31.8s (-2.40) **Going Correction** -0.10s/f (Good) **10** Ran SP% **116.9**
Speed ratings: **99,98,96,90,90 90,—,—,—,—** CSF £35.41 CT £392.04 TOTE £8.90: £3.30, £1.30, £2.80; EX 23.80.
Owner P J Hickman **Bred** P J Hickman **Trained** Mutterton, Devon

FOCUS
A weak handicap that did not take much winning with the winner slightly below his best.

NOTEBOOK
Team Captain has been largely out of form since winning over course and distance 13 months ago, but he goes well fresh and had been dropped 4lb since his latest run in December. *(op 15-2)*
Silver Samuel(NZ) was 5lb higher than when landing a similar race here last month. The leaders got away from him down the back straight, and although he was staying on quite well at the end the line was always going to beat him. *(op 9-4 tchd 3-1 in places)*
Maybeseven showed a bit more spark in the first-time cheekpieces. *(op 12-1)*
Felix Darby(IRE), an inconsistent sort, finished a remote fourth. *(op 6-1)*
Boardroom Dancer(IRE), having his second run back after a lengthy absence, lost what chance he *had with a blunder at the fifth from home. Official explanation: jockey said gelding suffered interference*
Usk Valley(IRE) looked likely to be involved at the business end when one of three to pull clear in the back straight, but weakened quite tamely from the third last. *(op 4-1)*

277 FUTURE STARS STANDARD OPEN NATIONAL HUNT FLAT RACE 2m 1f
5:10 (5:10) (Class 6) 4-6-Y-O **£1,953** (£558; £279)

Form RPR
4- **1** **None-So-Pretty**[19] [4941] 4-10-7 BJCrowley 78+
(Miss E C Lavelle) *trckd ldrs: led over 3f out: drvn out* **5/1[3]**
00- **2** *nk* **Ice Cream (FR)**[87] [3810] 4-10-7 MAFitzgerald 78
(M E D Francis) *midfield: hdwy over 4f out: wnt cl 2nd over 3f out: r.o u.p towards fin* **7/2[2]**
30- **3** *19* **Xcentra**[118] [3325] 4-11-0 JamesDavies 66
(B G Powell) *led: rdn and hung lft whn hdd over 3f out: wknd over 2f out* **7/1**
4 *1 3/4* **Cutting Edge** 6-10-4 JAJenkins[(7)] 61
(A J Chamberlain) *hld up: rdn and outpcd 5f out: kpt on u.p fnl 2f: nvr on terms* **33/1**
5 *2* **South Shore One** 4-10-7 NHannity 55
(G A Harker) *hld up: rdn and outpcd 5f out: kpt on fnl 2f: nvr on terms* **5/4[1]**
5- **6** *1* **Pat Malone**[40] [4673] 5-11-4 JPMcNamara 65
(Lucinda Featherstone) *racd keenly: in rr: nvr able to chal* **33/1**
7 *18* **Simplyirresistible (IRE)** 5-10-11 PFlynn 40
(S T Lewis) *prom: rdn and lost pl 10f out: n.d after* **25/1**
13/ **8** *2* **Bula's Quest**[604] [1378] 6-11-8 MrLJefford[(3)] 52
(L G Cottrell) *racd keenly: in tch: hdwy after 4f: rdn and wknd 4f out* **9/1**
0- **9** *18* **Oui Exit (FR)**[99] [3626] 4-11-0 SThomas 23
(M Scudamore) *prom tl rdn and wknd 4f out* **16/1**

3m 57.6s (-3.50) **Going Correction** -0.325s/f (Good)
WFA 4 from 5yo 4lb 5 from 6yo 2lb **9** Ran SP% **121.4**
Speed ratings: **95,94,85,85,84 83,75,74,65** CSF £23.77 TOTE £7.60: £1.90, £2.60, £1.20; EX 18.00 Place 6 £17.27, Place 5 £9.82.
Owner Mrs P Thorne **Bred** Mrs P Thorne And Miss K Thorne **Trained** Wildhern, Hants

FOCUS
A poor bumper in which the first two finished clear and set the standard.

NOTEBOOK
None-So-Pretty had the benefit of a previous run but was still green, pricking her ears in front. This did not take much winning. *(op 9-2 tchd 11-2)*
Ice Cream(FR), not disgraced in a Grade Two event last time, went down fighting and finished a long way clear of the third. *(op 5-1)*
Xcentratried to steal the race but was swept aside with over three furlongs to run and hung when beaten on the bend. *(op 4-1)*
Cutting Edge is out of a half-sister to the useful two and a half-mile chaser St Alezan. *(tchd 40-1)*
South Shore One is a sister to useful bumper performer Jay Be Junior who won at this track last summer. She was a little disappointing, but was keeping on at the end and may improve with the experience behind her. *(op 6-4 tchd 13-8, 7-4 in a place)*
T/Plt: £6.30 to a £1 stake. Pool: £33,459.80. 3,857.00 winning tickets. T/Qpdt: £3.80 to a £1 stake. Pool: £1,884.00. 359.20 winning tickets. DO

HUNTINGDON (R-H)
Tuesday, May 10

OFFICIAL GOING: Good to firm
Wind: Virtually nil Weather: Bright

278 SHARP NUTRITION NOVICES' HUNTERS' CHASE (16 fncs) 2m 4f 110y
5:45 (5:48) (Class 6) 5-Y-0+ **£1,436** (£442; £221; £110)

Form RPR
04-3 **1** **Viscount Bankes**[13] [52] 7-11-9 MrAndrewMartin[(5)] 92+
(Mrs Rosemary Gasson) *a in tch: led 2 out: styd on wl run-in* **8/1**
62- **2** *3 1/2* **Coole Glen (IRE)**[24] 9-12-0 MrSMorris 87
(W J Warner) *led tl hdd 2f out: kpt on but nt qckn run-in* **6/1[3]**
P05/ **3** *nk* **Little Worsall (IRE)**[30] 12-11-7 MissHGrissell[(7)] 88+
(Mrs F Marshall) *mid-div: hdwy fr 3 out: styd on wl fr next* **10/1**
1F-5 **4** *shd* **Hot Plunge**[13] [52] 9-12-2 MrJOwen[(5)] 96+
(Mrs J P Lomax) *mid-div: mstke 10th: hdwy whn hit 4 out: styng on whn sltly hmpd last: nvr nrr* **6/1[3]**
04-3 **5** *1 1/4* **Snooty Eskimo (IRE)**[13] [60] 13-11-7 66 MrHNorton[(7)] 86
(W T Reed) *towards rr tl hdwy 9th: rdn 3 out: one pce fr next* **10/1**
P6-F **6** *dist* **Round The Bend**[13] [50] 13-11-7 MissLAllan[(7)] —
(Miss Louise Allan) *prom tl wknd 12th: t.o* **33/1**
0/ **P** **Rival (IRE)**[8] 6-11-7 MrMWalford[(7)] —
(S Flook) *a bhd: t.o whn p.u bef 12th* **66/1**
/-04 **F** **Gold Quest (IRE)**[8] [151] 8-11-7 (p) MrNKent[(7)] —
(Nick Kent) *in rr whn fell 10th* **16/1**
500/ **P** **Bede (IRE)**[38] 9-11-7 MrABraithwaite[(7)] —
(S H Marriage) *a bhd: t.o whn p.u bef 2 out* **33/1**
POP- **P** **Colombe D'Or**[10] 8-11-7 MissHannahWatson[(7)] —
(C J Leech) *a bhd: t.o whn p.u bef 2 out* **66/1**

65P/ **P** **Saxon Victory (USA)**[43] 10-11-11 ....(v) MrRArmson(3) —
(Tim Tarratt) *virually ref to r: p.u bef 4th* **33/1**

044/ **S** **Diamond Alpha (IRE)**[8] 11-11-7 ....(t) MrJMahot(7) —
(Ms Jane Evans) *in rr whn slipped up on bnd appr 7th* **25/1**

F26- **P** **Supercharmer**[9] 11-11-7 .... MrCDawson(7) —
(M A Humphreys) *trckd ldrs to 13th: sn wknd: t.o whn p.u bef last* **20/1**

6P-0 **P** **Worthy Man**[12] [79] 8-11-11 64 .... MrDMansell(3) —
(Mrs E England) *hld up: hdwy 12th: blnd 3 out: wknd qckly: p.u bef next* **100/1**

R **R** **Heisamodel (IRE)**[13] [50] 7-11-11 .... MrMGMiller(3) —
(J J Boulter) *in tch: mstke 10th: trcking ldrs whn blnd 12th: wl btn whn ref last* **4/1**[1]

F/ **F** **Cloudy Bay Boy**[16] 7-11-11 .... MrRCope(3) 90
(Mrs Caroline Bailey) *trckd ldr: chal 3f out and ev ch to next: rdn and hld whn fell last* **11/2**[2]

4m 56.7s (-9.40) **Going Correction** -0.625s/f (Firm) **16** Ran SP% **120.5**
Speed ratings: **92,90,90,90,90** —,—,—,—,— —,—,—,—,— — CSF £51.93 TOTE £10.10: £2.70, £2.40, £4.10; EX 53.40.
Owner Mrs Rosemary Gasson **Bred** Mrs Frank Campbell **Trained** Banbury, Oxon

FOCUS
They went a fair early pace in this novices' hunter chase and the form looks solid enough for the grade.

NOTEBOOK
Viscount Bankes ran well over two miles at Cheltenham recently and confirmed form with Hot Plunge despite being worse off at the weights. His last and only success in a point came over this intermediate distance back in January 2004 and the return to this longer trip proved to be in his favour. *(op 11-2)*
Coole Glen(IRE), who likes to be out in front, made all in a three-mile point last month. He adopted his usual pacemaking role again and ran a solid race in second. *(op 11-2 tchd 5-1)*
Little Worsall(IRE), successful in a couple of Ladies' Open point-to-points lately, had not run under Rules for over two years but translated her current good form to this novices' event. *(op 12-1)*
Hot Plunge, who ran well at Cheltenham last time despite giving the rest a big start, was a bit disappointing, and although the trip did not seem to be a problem, the quicker ground might have been. *(op 5-1)*
Snooty Eskimo(IRE) is an exposed performer in this sort of grade. *(tchd 12-1)*
Cloudy Bay Boy looked likely to be placed when departing at the last. He clearly has the ability to win a race of this nature and, being a relatively lightly-raced sort, is capable of doing better next season. *(op 11-2)*
Heisamodel(IRE) had no excuse on account of the ground this time. *(op 11-2)*

279 HUNTS ELECTRICAL SUPPLIES AMATEUR RIDERS' "HANDS AND HEELS" NOVICES' HURDLE (8 hdls) 2m 110y
6:15 (6:21) (Class 4) 4-Y-0+ **£3,311** (£946; £473)

Form RPR

44- **1** **Three Ships**[43] [4621] 4-10-7 .... MrMatthewSmith(7) 86
(Miss J Feilden) *t.k.h: sn prom: led appr 3 out: drvn out run-in: all out* **11/1**

40- **2** *nk* **Moldavia (GER)**[19] [3554] 4-10-7 .... MrTGreenall 80+
(M C Chapman) *t.k.h: hld up: hdwy 5th: 3rd whn hit 2 out: styd on wl u.p run-in* **33/1**

033- **3** *shd* **Classic Croco (GER)**[33] [4756] 4-11-0 99 .... MrNWilliams 86
(Mrs Jeremy Young) *bhd: slipped bnd after 3rd: rdn and hdwy fr next: chal 2 out: kpt on run-in* **7/2**[2]

4 *12* **Sort It Out (IRE)**[45] 8-11-1 110 .... TJDreaper(3) 78
(Ferdy Murphy) *mid-div: rdn to chal 5th: sn btn and one pce after* **7/1**[3]

3F-6 **5** *shd* **Celtic Legend (FR)**[12] [84] 6-10-11 83 .... JReveley(7) 78
(K G Reveley) *hld up: mde sme late hdwy but nvr on terms* **9/1**

31-4 **6** *3 1/2* **Mohawk Star (IRE)**[12] [82] 4-11-0 111 .... MrRMcCarthy(7) 77
(Miss Venetia Williams) *nvr travelling wl in rr: mstke 2nd and nvr on terms after 5th* **6/4**[1]

060- **7** *1/2* **Silistra**[35] [3344] 6-11-1 86 ....(p) MrJMorgan(3) 74
(Mrs L C Jewell) *w.w: hdwy appr 3 out: wknd qckly bef next* **25/1**

0- **8** *1/2* **Adalar (IRE)**[15] [1623] 5-10-11 .... MrMD'Arcy(7) 73
(P W D'Arcy) *in tch to 4th: wkng whn hit last* **50/1**

300/ **9** *7* **Prince Minata (IRE)**[376] [1231] 10-10-11 73 .... MissAHockley(7) 66
(M Appleby) *plld hrd: led 2nd and sn clr: hdd appr 3 out: wknd qckly* **80/1**

402- **10** *6* **Miss Merenda**[47] [4534] 4-10-0 94 ....(p) MissPBuckley(7) 49
(D E Cantillon) *led to to 2nd: prom tl wknd after 4th* **7/1**[3]

/PP- **11** *28* **Love Diamonds (IRE)**[277] [1137] 9-10-11 .... MissCDyson(7) 32
(Miss C Dyson) *in tch tl wknd 5th* **125/1**

0P-P **R** **Mr Rhubarb (IRE)**[12] [75] 7-10-11 90 .... MrNABChapman(7) —
(R T Phillips) *ref to r* **80/1**

04P- **U** **Government (IRE)**[20] [4930] 4-10-7 69 .... MrRQuinn(7) —
(M C Chapman) *trckd ldrs to 4th: bhd whn j.lft and uns rdr last* **100/1**

566/ **U** **Caroline's Rose**[497] [2691] 7-10-4 64 .... MrElmelov(7) —
(A P Jones) *bhd tl hdwy 4th: wknd 3 out: t.o whn uns rdr 2 out* **125/1**

3m 44.4s (-11.30) **Going Correction** -0.625s/f (Firm) **14** Ran SP% **119.4**
WFA 4 from 5yo+ 4lb
Speed ratings: **101,100,100,95,95 93,93,93,89,86 73**,—,—,— CSF £296.76 TOTE £12.40: £4.00, £4.90, £2.00; EX 223.30.
Owner Ocean Trailers Ltd **Bred** Juddmonte Farms **Trained** Exning, Suffolk

FOCUS
Not a strong race, andt they went a steady early pace in this modest novice hurdle for amateur riders, but the winner and third ran to their marks.

NOTEBOOK
Three Ships raced keenly but not as badly as he has in the past and on this quicker ground his stamina was preserved. He looked the more determined when tackled by Classic Croco on the run-in and held on well when Moldavia joined issue close home. *(op 10-1)*
Moldavia(GER), who had not got home in his previous two starts over hurdles due to soft ground, appreciated these quicker conditions and ran his best race to date over hurdles. *(op 28-1)*
Classic Croco(GER) had his chance to take the winner on the run-in but appeared the less hearty in the battle. *(op 5-1)*
Sort It Out(IRE), whose recent outings have been in three-mile point-to-points, was having his first start for his new stable. He kept on well enough without being able to keep tabs on the principal trio. *(op 10-1)*
Celtic Legend(FR), who last ran over hurdles in December 2003, has a rating of 83 and did not shape too badly in the circumstances. *(tchd 8-1)*
Mohawk Star(IRE) set a fair standard but all his form is on easier ground and he was never travelling on this quicker surface. *(tchd 7-4)*

280 J R DIMSDALE MEMORIAL HUNTERS' CHASE (19 fncs) 3m
6:45 (6:49) (Class 6) 5-Y-0+ **£1,617** (£462; £231)

Form RPR

1-F **1** **Coolefind (IRE)**[13] [48] 7-12-4 .... MrSMorris 110+
(W J Warner) *t.k.h: hld up: hdwy 14th: chal after 3 out: hit next: hung rt after: rdn to ld nr fin* **5/2**[2]

/21- **2** *1/2* **Find Me Another (IRE)**[17] 9-11-11 .... MissALStennett(7) 107
(Mrs Caroline Bailey) *a.p: led 15th: rdn and kpt on: hdd nr fin* **7/1**[3]

460- **3** *7* **Cape Stormer (IRE)**[33] [4750] 10-11-11 103 ....(b) MrMGorman(7) 101+
(Mrs C M Gorman) *led to 15th: rdn after 3f out: 3rd whn hit last: wknd run-in* **16/1**

46P/ **4** *13* **Torn Silk**[10] 11-11-11 .... MrCMulhall(3) 83
(P England) *a bhd: mde sme late hdwy: nvr on terms* **50/1**

22-1 **5** *4* **Caught At Dawn (IRE)**[13] [51] 11-12-0 .... MrTWeston(7) 101+
(M H Weston) *hld up: hdwy 12th: outpcd 3 out: 4th whn mstke last: eased run-in* **5/6**[1]

B5-3 **6** *20* **Guignol Du Cochet (FR)**[12] [79] 11-12-0 102 .... MrMWalford(7) 66
(S Flook) *in tch tl lost pl 12th: lost tch 15th* **22/1**

052/ **7** *1 1/4* **Highland Rose (IRE)**[24] 9-11-4 .... MrNMoore(3) 51
(Ms A E Embiricos) *nt fluent but prom: wkng and wl bhd whn hit 2 out* **25/1**

16F- **R** **Althrey Dandy (IRE)**[9] 10-12-0 .... MrJJarrett(7) —
(Miss C J Goodall) *ref to r* **33/1**

6m 4.70s (-7.60) **Going Correction** -0.625s/f (Firm) **8** Ran SP% **114.6**
Speed ratings: **87,86,84,80,78 72,71**,— CSF £18.57 TOTE £4.10: £1.60, £1.80, £3.40; EX 23.40.
Owner Mrs Judy Wilson **Bred** Michael Gowen **Trained** Northampton, Northants

FOCUS
Run in a time seven seconds slower than the following race, a slow early pace resulted in something of a sprint over the final few fences. The first two ran to previous course form with the third the best guide to the level.

NOTEBOOK
Coolefind(IRE), one of the least experienced runners in the line-up, had not run on ground as quick as this before, but he coped well with conditions, responding well to pressure from the turn into the straight to assume command close home. He looks open to further improvement in this sphere. *(op 3-1)*
Find Me Another(IRE) only gave best close home having fought the eventual winner from the turn into the straight. Successful three times in Ladies' Open point-to-points this spring, he clearly remains at the top of his game. *(op 15-2 tchd 8-1)*
Cape Stormer(IRE), whose successes under Rules have come over shorter, was still a player until blundering at the final fence. *(op 14-1)*
Torn Silk was never a threat to the principals but stayed on past beaten horses.
Caught At Dawn(IRE) was the disappointment of the race. He stays well and the slow early pace, *coupled with the quick ground, played against his strengths. Official explanation: vet said gelding had a high respiratory rate (tchd 10-11)*

281 HISCOX INTERMEDIATE POINT-TO-POINT CHAMPIONSHIP FINAL HUNTERS' CHASE (19 fncs) 3m
7:15 (7:18) (Class 6) 5-Y-0+ **£3,367** (£1,036; £518; £259)

Form RPR

600/ **1** **Martin Ossie**[17] 8-12-0 .... MrJMPritchard 102+
(R T Baimbridge) *mde all: j.w: lft clr 3 out: tired run-in but hld on wl* **9/4**[2]

2 *2* **Coomakista**[16] 8-11-2 .... MrRMorgan(5) 92
(Mrs E J Reed) *prom tl outpcd 12th: styd on after 3 out to chse and cl on wnr run-in* **7/1**[3]

42-2 **3** *6* **Beauchamp Oracle**[13] [50] 8-11-7 .... MrMWalford(7) 95+
(S Flook) *hld up: hdwy fr 12th: wnt 2nd 2 out: fdd fr last* **7/4**[1]

4 *8* **Catch The Bus (IRE)**[8] 8-11-9 .... MrJOwen(5) 86+
(Mrs K Smyly) *in front rnk: hit 8th: blnd 11th: lft 2nd 3 out: wknd next* **20/1**

235- **5** *9* **Raging Torrent**[23] 10-11-11 .... MrPYork(3) 76
(Mrs H J Cobb) *prom to 6th: lost pl 8th: bhd after* **22/1**

342/ **6** *3/4* **Misty Ramble (IRE)**[10] 10-11-7 .... MrLRPayter(7) 75
(Ms Jill Carenza) *mid-div: lost tch fr 15th* **40/1**

0/F- **7** *6* **Franco (IRE)**[38] 7-12-0 .... JDiment 69
(Mrs A E Brooks) *a struggling in rr* **7/1**[3]

P **Hi Tech Man (IRE)**[16] 7-11-11 .... MrNMoore(3) —
(E J Cantillon) *t.o 11th: p.u bef 13th* **18/1**

U **Skew Whip**[10] 7-11-7 .... MrRWakeham(7) —
(C Brader) *prom whn hit 11th: 4th but rdn whn blnd and uns rdr 4 out* **12/1**

F **U** **Bobby Buttons**[9] 8-11-9 .... MissTJackson(5) —
(Mrs J Jones) *prom: mstke 7th: 2nd whn hit and uns rdr 3 out* **20/1**

5m 57.7s (-14.60) **Going Correction** -0.625s/f (Firm) **10** Ran SP% **121.4**
Speed ratings: **99,98,96,93,90 90,88**,—,—,— CSF £18.42 TOTE £3.00: £1.40, £1.80, £1.80; EX 18.90.
Owner D Smith (saul) **Bred** D Smith **Trained** Herringswell, Suff
■ Stewards' Enquiry : Mr P York four-day ban: used whip causing injury, in the wrong place and when out of contention (May 21,25,26,28)

FOCUS
The time of this race compared favourably with the previous race over the same distance, being seven seconds quicker and the race is rated through the third.

NOTEBOOK
Martin Ossie, a winner of each of his seven starts in point-to-points this season, put up a splendid front-running performance on his Rules debut, jumping well throughout. He is clearly progressing well and, although the John Corbet Cup at Stratford on 20th May will be a tougher race, it is the logical target. *(op 7-4)*
Coomakista struggled to keep up with the pace set by the winner, but her stamina came into play late on and she cut Martin Ossie's advantage right down on the run-in. The ground may have been plenty quick enough for her and this lightly-raced mare has improvement in her.
Beauchamp Oracle is a consistent sort but looked more exposed than some of his rivals. He has yet to get his head in front this term and it was something of a surprise to see him sent off favourite. *(op 5-2)*
Catch The Bus(IRE) was left the nearest challenger to Martin Ossie when Bobby Buttons departed, but he just could not keep tabs with him and lost out on a place in the straight. *(tchd 22-1)*
Franco(IRE) is normally a front-runner and he completely failed to run his race under more patient tactics. *Official explanation: vet said gelding bled from nose (op 17-2)*
Bobby Buttons was running well until the moment he clouted the third last, giving his rider no chance. He fell on his only previous start under Rules so his jumping clearly needs working on, but he has the ability to score in this sphere. *(op 11-1)*
Skew Whip, for whom conditions might have been quicker than ideal, was under some pressure but staying on when depositing his rider on the ground. *(op 11-1)*

282 HONEYBELL HUNTERS' CHASE (19 fncs 6 omitted) 3m 6f 110y

7:45 (7:53) (Class 6) 5-Y-0+ **£1,596** (£456; £228)

Form				RPR
1-4	**1**		**Vinnie Boy (IRE)**[13] [48] 8-12-4 .... MissPGundry (Mrs O Bush) *hld up: stdy hdwy fr 10th: led last: styd on strly* **2/1**[1]	104+
654/	**2**	*7*	**Marrasit (IRE)**[10] 9-11-1 ow1 .... MrSCharlton(7) (H E Thorpe) *bhd tl hdwy 15th: wnt 2nd run-in: styd on but no ch w wnr* **33/1**	87
3P-P	**3**	*3/4*	**Maggies Brother**[13] [49] 12-11-11 .... MrDBarlow(3) (R Shail) *sn prom: led after 14th: rdn and hdd last: wknd run-in* **12/1**	92
	4	*2 1/2*	**My Best Buddy**[17] 9-11-11 .... MrRCope(3) (Mrs Caroline Bailey) *in tch: rdn and ev ch 2 out: wknd run-in* **9/1**	91+
P4-0	**5**	*9*	**Tanager**[13] [49] 10-11-13 ....(b) MrBKing(5) (Mrs K Lawther) *mid-div: hdwy 14t: wknd appr 3 out* **7/2**[2]	86+
P-5	**6**	*8*	**Nautical Lad**[13] [50] 10-11-7 .... MrJDocker(7) (J H Docker) *in tch tl hit 14th: sn wknd* **8/1**	73
0P/4	**7**	*13*	**Father Jim**[13] [50] 10-11-7 .... MrFelixDeGiles(7) (J A T De Giles) *prom to 15th: sn wknd* **14/1**	60
/P3-	**8**	*24*	**Castleford (IRE)**[30] 7-11-7 85........ MrWKinsey(7) (Mrs T R Kinsey) *a bhd* **7/1**[3]	36
	P		**Abrakadalpha (IRE)**[17] 11-11-7 .... MrJMahot(7) (Ms Jane Evans) *mstkes and a bhd: p.u after 14th* **100/1**	—
555/	**P**		**Redouble**[24] 9-11-7 ....(p) MrABraithwaite(7) (W B Stone) *mstkes and a bhd: t.o whn p.u after 14th* **66/1**	—
F/P-	**P**		**Lord Valnic (IRE)**[21] [4917] 9-11-11 .... MrNMoore(3) (Ms A E Embiricos) *mstke and lost pl 9th: t.o whn p.u bef 15th* **33/1**	—
005/	**P**		**Laras Grey (IRE)**[9] 12-11-7 ....(b[1]) MrMatthewSmith(7) (Martin Ward) *sn led: hdd after 14th: wknd qckly and p.u bef next* **66/1**	—
PPP/	**F**		**Dunmanus Bay (IRE)**[38] 8-11-7 .... MrMMackley(7) (Mrs Julie Read) *prom ttl blnd 13th: qckly lost palce and bhd whn fell 15th* **40/1**	—
P/1-	**P**		**Pennyahei**[8] 14-11-8 .... MissSBeddoes(3) (Miss H Brookshaw) *bhd and continually j.lft: hmpd 11th: t.o whn p.u bef last* **10/1**	—

7m 52.4s (-21.40) **Going Correction** -0.625s/f (Firm) **14** Ran SP% **124.9**
Speed ratings: **102,100,100,99,97 94,91,85,—,— —,—,—,—** CSF £79.61 TOTE £3.10: £1.50, £7.50, £4.50; EX 89.30.
Owner J H Burbidge **Bred** John J Duffy **Trained** Cullompton, Devon

FOCUS
A proper test of stamina with the winner the best guide to the level.

NOTEBOOK
Vinnie Boy(IRE), who won over an extended three miles one in bad ground at Wincanton in February and ran well in a better contest than this at Cheltenham last time, clearly relishes a test of stamina, and this trip brought out the best in him. *(op 11-4)*
Marrasit(IRE), a daughter of Zaffaran, was racing on fast ground for the first time and put up her best effort to date. *(op 28-1)*
Maggies Brother, whose last win came almost two years ago over four and a quarter miles at Uttoxeter, tried to make it a serious test by stretching the field going out onto the final circuit. He made a good fist of it and was only beaten on the run-in. *(op 14-1 tchd 16-1)*
My Best Buddy had never previously raced over as far as this, but it appeared to suit him as he reversed form with Nautical Lad, who beat him at Guilsborough in April. *(op 13-2)*
Tanager won a four-mile point-to-point earlier in the year so his stamina was not in doubt. The ground may have been quicker than ideal, though. *(tchd 3-1)*
Nautical Lad has failed to translate his point-to-point form to races under Rules. *(op 9-1)*

283 HUNTINGDON-RACECOURSE.CO.UK AMATEUR RIDERS' H'CAP HURDLE (10 hdls) 2m 5f 110y

8:15 (8:22) (Class 4) (0-100,98) 4-Y-0+ **£2,702** (£772; £386)

Form				RPR
100-	**1**		**Garnett (IRE)**[42] [3344] 4-10-13 **97**........(p) MissPBuckley(7) (D E Cantillon) *hld up: racd wd: hdwy appr 3 out: rdn to ld fnl 100yds* **9/4**[1]	95+
44-4	**2**	*1 1/4*	**Upright Ima**[6] [185] 6-9-13 **78**........ MissLAllan(7) (Mrs P Sly) *hld up: hdwy fr 5th: led appr 3 out: rdn and hdd fnl 100yds* **9/2**[2]	77
4P0-	**3**	*1 1/4*	**Killonemoonlight (IRE)**[43] [4611] 6-10-6 **78**........ JDiment (D R Stoddart) *led to 1st: outpcd and lost pl 6th: hdwy 3 out: styd on and swtchd rt run-in: kpt on* **18/1**	76
152-	**4**	*1 1/4*	**Another Promise (IRE)**[61] [4277] 6-11-5 **98**........ MrMatthewSmith(7) (J A Supple) *hld up: hdwy 5th: rdn and styd on fr 2 out* **13/2**[3]	95
350-	**5**	*3/4*	**Lord Lamb**[20] [4928] 13-11-2 **95**........ JReveley(7) (K G Reveley) *hld up: hdwy fr 4th: hung rt and no imp fr 2 out* **16/1**	91
23-0	**6**	*1 1/2*	**Helvetius**[13] [64] 9-11-2 **93**........ MrRMorgan(5) (W T Reed) *prom tl rdn and one pce appr 2 out* **16/1**	87
33-6	**7**	*nk*	**Stopwatch (IRE)**[11] [104] 10-10-4 **76**........ MissPGundry (Mrs L C Jewell) *bhd: mde sme late hdwy but nvr on terms* **14/1**	70
3/6-	**8**	*1 1/2*	**Count Oski**[379] [23] 9-10-13 **90**........ WPKavanagh(5) (M J Ryan) *a towards rr* **14/1**	82
P4-0	**9**	*nk*	**Ressource (FR)**[16] [9] 6-10-9 **88**........(b) MrWRussell(7) (G L Moore) *mid-div: hdwy 6th: wknd 2 out* **25/1**	80
P4-3	**10**	*2 1/2*	**Howaboys Quest (USA)**[11] [110] 8-11-0 **89**........(p) TJDreaper(3) (Ferdy Murphy) *prom: led 6th tl hdd appr 3 out: sn wknd* **8/1**	79
6P0-	**11**	*24*	**Regal Vision (IRE)**[55] [4404] 8-10-7 **86**........ MissCDyson(7) (Miss C Dyson) *led 2nd: hdd 6th: wknd appr 2 out* **25/1**	52
00P-	**12**	*18*	**Harry Bridges**[18] [4954] 6-9-7 **72** oh8........ MrTCollier(7) (R Lee) *a bhd* **33/1**	20
11/-	**P**		**Canny Scot**[536] [2288] 8-10-10 **85**........ MissSBeddoes(3) (R Curtis) *prom to 3 out: wknd qckly next: p.u bef last* **10/1**	—
560-	**U**		**Over Bridge**[17] [4977] 7-10-1 **80**........ MrRhysHughes(7) (Mrs S M Johnson) *in tch tl n.m.r and uns rdr on bnd after 5th* **20/1**	—

5m 2.40s (-8.40) **Going Correction** -0.625s/f (Firm)
WFA 4 from 6yo+ 5lb **14** Ran SP% **128.2**
Speed ratings: **90,89,89,88,88 87,87,87,87,86 77,70,—,—** CSF £13.09 CT £159.51 TOTE £3.60: £1.70, £1.90, £5.50; EX 24.20 Place 6 £132.24, Place 5 £40.20.
Owner Mrs Sue Catt **Bred** James Reardon **Trained** Newmarket, Suffolk
■ The first winner for Phoebe Buckley.

FOCUS
A moderate handicap run at a steady early gallop, resulting in a modest winning time for the grade, and won by the least exposed runner in the field. He is rated value for further and can rate higher.

NOTEBOOK
Garnett(IRE), in form on the Flat of late, appreciated the underfoot conditions and, racing wide for most of the way, was brought with a perfectly-timed run to take the race on the flat. This was a cosy success and he looks capable of better. *(op 7-2)*
Upright Ima looked to have made the race-winning move when kicking on rounding the bend into the straight as she soon had most of her pursuers in trouble, but the winner proved too strong after the last. *(op 5-1 tchd 4-1)*
Killonemoonlight(IRE) ran well on only her third start over hurdles, and she would have finished marginally closer still had she not been forced to switch on the run-in. *(op 16-1)*
Another Promise(IRE), who may have found the ground faster than ideal, is more exposed than one or two who finished in front of him, and the Handicapper looks to have his measure for the time being. *(op 15-2)*
Lord Lamb has dropped a fair way in the ratings but he is at the veteran stage now and is likely to continue to be vulnerable against younger, less-exposed rivals in handicap company. *(op 14-1)*
Helvetius put up a better effort with the ground more to his liking. *(op 10-1)*
Howaboys Quest(USA) failed to find the expected improvement for his recent comeback outing at Southwell. *(op 10-1)*
Canny Scot broke down. *(op 15-2)*
T/Plt: £295.70 to a £1 stake. Pool: £30,180.45. 74.50 winning tickets. T/Qpdt: £42.00 to a £1 stake. Pool: £2,449.30. 43.10 winning tickets. JS

NEWTON ABBOT (L-H)

Tuesday, May 10

OFFICIAL GOING: Good to firm (good in places)
The ground had dried out dramatically after the last two meetings had been off due to waterlogging but it was still rather tacky on the bends.
Wind: Almost nil. Weather: Fine.

284 PARTYFARECATERERS.CO.UK CONDITIONAL JOCKEYS' CLAIMING HURDLE (8 hdls) 2m 1f

6:00 (6:00) (Class 4) 4-Y-0+ **£2,562** (£732; £366)

Form				RPR
600-	**1**		**Brochrua (IRE)**[5] [4369] 5-10-0 90........ SWalsh(5) (J D Frost) *hld up: pckd 1st: chsd ldr appr 5th: led appr 2 out: clr last: r.o wl* **3/1**[3]	93+
00-2	**2**	*7*	**Caliban (IRE)**[2] [232] 7-11-6 106........(b) WHutchinson (Ian Williams) *j.rt: led: clr after 4th: rdn and hdd appr 2 out: one pce* **11/10**[1]	101
FF0-	**3**	*28*	**Lucky Do (IRE)**[93] [3720] 8-10-11 95........ DLaverty(3) (A E Jones) *nt fluent: hld up: wnt 3rd 3 out: sn struggling* **16/1**	67
0P0-	**S**		**Blues Story (FR)**[45] [4563] 7-11-0 77........(t) DCrosse (N G Ayliffe) *hld up: disputing 4th and in tch whn slipped up bnd appr 5th* **33/1**	—
523-	**P**		**Iambe De La See (FR)**[44] [4578] 9-10-12 .... ATinkler(3) (N J Henderson) *t.k.h: chsd ldr tl appr 5th: wknd qckly 3 out: t.o whn p.u bef 2 out* **11/4**[2]	—

4m 2.60s (-2.50) **Going Correction** +0.025s/f (Yiel) **5** Ran SP% **108.1**
Speed ratings: **106,102,89,—,—** CSF £6.73 TOTE £3.60: £2.50, £1.10; EX 9.50.
Owner Ms H Vernon-Jones **Bred** Nicholas Teehan **Trained** Buckfastleigh, Devon

FOCUS
A weak event rated through the winner with the second below par.

NOTEBOOK
Brochrua(IRE), sharpened up by an outing on the Flat last week, likes this sort of ground and proved far too good for the favourite. *(op 4-1 tchd 11-4)*
Caliban(IRE) may have had the edge taken off him by his hard race at Plumpton two days earlier. He proved no match for the winner at these weights. *(op 5-6)*
Lucky Do(IRE) hardly jumped a hurdle properly. *(op 12-1 tchd 20-1)*
Iambe De La See(FR) *Official explanation: trainer had no explanation for the poor form shown (op 9-4 tchd 10-3)*

285 SHERILEE AND NICKY, THE LOCOMOTIVE INN LANDLADIES MARES' ONLY NOVICES' HURDLE (8 hdls 1 omitted) 2m 3f

6:30 (6:30) (Class 4) 4-Y-0+ **£3,328** (£1,024; £512; £256)

Form				RPR
221-	**1**		**Latin Queen (IRE)**[6] [4376] 5-11-0 109........ CHonour(5) (J D Frost) *a.p: wnt 2nd 3rd: led sn after 3 out: clr 2 out: easily* **4/7**[1]	106+
060-	**2**	*10*	**Kentford Lady**[59] [4333] 4-10-7 .... AThornton (J W Mullins) *hld up: hdwy 3 out: chsd wnr appr 2 out: sn rdn and btn* **7/1**[3]	79
6-53	**3**	*1 1/2*	**One Wild Night**[7] [178] 5-10-7 .... LTreadwell(5) (J L Spearing) *hld up in tch: pushed along 5th: wknd appr 2 out: hit last* **9/1**	83+
0	**4**	*dist*	**Bob's Finesse**[15] [27] 5-10-9 .... RYoung(3) (J W Mullins) *chsd ldr to 3rd: lost pl 4th: t.o fr 5th* **33/1**	—
60-3	**F**		**Seemma**[13] [58] 5-10-12 .... JTizzard (N I M Rossiter) *led: hit 3 out: sn hdd and rdn: 12 l 4th and wkng whn fell 2 out* **4/1**[2]	78

4m 37.2s (4.20) **Going Correction** +0.025s/f (Yiel)
WFA 4 from 5yo+ 4lb **5** Ran SP% **109.1**
Speed ratings: **92,87,87,—,—** CSF £5.12 TOTE £1.40: £1.10, £3.00; EX 6.90.
Owner B S Williams **Bred** Cooliney Stud **Trained** Buckfastleigh, Devon

FOCUS
A slow winning time for the grade in this uncompetitive event. The winner is value for half as much again but the overall form is distinctly moderate. The first flight was omitted.

NOTEBOOK
Latin Queen(IRE) had less to do than when landing a similar event on this sort of ground at Taunton in May. She is likely to go novice chasing in the autumn. *(op 8-13 tchd 4-6 and 8-11 in places)*
Kentford Lady, who failed to progress in bumpers, found the winner too hot to handle. *(op 5-1)*
One Wild Night may have made the separate race for the runner-up spot more interesting had she not rapped the final flight. *(op 13-2)*

286 SWAN INN, STEPH'S 25TH ANNIVERSARY NOVICES' CHASE (13 fncs) 2m 110y

7:00 (7:01) (Class 3) 5-Y-0+ **£6,104** (£1,878; £939; £469)

Form				RPR
11F-	**1**		**Andreas (FR)**[18] [4968] 5-11-10 135........(t) RWalsh (P F Nicholls) *mde all: clr appr 2 out: blnd last: easily* **30/100**[1]	138+
20-2	**2**	*13*	**Flying Spirit (IRE)**[11] [104] 6-11-0 ....(p) JEMoore (G L Moore) *prom: nt fluent 1st: chsd wnr fr 5th: ev ch 4 out: sn rdn: one pce fr 3 out* **9/2**[2]	108
/6-0	**3**	*29*	**Moon Shot**[16] [2] 9-11-0 92........ ATinkler (A G Juckes) *plld hrd: prom: wnt 2nd briefly 4th: bhd fr 6th* **50/1**	79
/P-2	**4**	*15*	**Simoun (IRE)**[13] [56] 7-11-0 ....(t) TScudamore (M C Pipe) *chsd wnr to 4th: wknd 8th* **11/1**[3]	64
00-P	**P**		**Heritage Castle**[13] [57] 6-11-0 67........(b[1]) MFoley (A E Jones) *hit 1st: wl bhd fr 3rd: t.o whn p.u after 6th* **100/1**	—

4m 2.40s (-3.10) **Going Correction** +0.025s/f (Yiel) **5** Ran SP% **106.4**
Speed ratings: **108,101,88,81,—** CSF £2.01 TOTE £1.20: £1.10, £1.50; EX 2.30.

Owner Mark Tincknell **Bred** M Gosse And Mlle Noelle Bataille **Trained** Ditcheat, Somerset

FOCUS

An uncompetitive event but any easy winner, value for 20l.

NOTEBOOK

Andreas(FR) was rather unlucky to tip up with the race at his mercy at Perth last time. He made a far worse error at the final fence here but fortune was on his side. He will be put away with a view to coming back for a novice chase at Cheltenham in October. *(op 1-3 tchd 4-11 and 2-5 in places)*

Flying Spirit(IRE), with the cheekpieces refitted, found himself up against a useful novice for this time of the year. *(op 7-2)*

287 TLH LEISURE RESORT NOVICES' H'CAP HURDLE (10 hdls) 2m 6f

7:30 (7:30) (Class 4) (0-105,99) 4-Y-O+ **£3,427** (£1,054; £527; £263)

Form RPR

135- **1** **Altitude Dancer (IRE)**[22] 4914 5-10-13 **93** DLaverty(7) 100+
(Mrs A M Thorpe) *a.p: reminders after 4th: w ldrs 6th: led 7th: clr after 3 out: r.o wl* **7/2**[2]

003- **2** *11* **Dancinginthestreet**[42] 4640 5-11-7 **99** RStephens(5) 96+
(J L Flint) *chsd ldrs: hmpd and lost pl 6th: rallied and chsd wnr appr 2 out: sn no imp* **5/2**[1]

10-0 **3** *13* **Lady Lisa (IRE)**[11] 105 6-11-5 **92** TScudamore 78+
(M C Pipe) *led to 2nd: chsd ldr: led 6th to 7th: wknd after 3 out* **7/1**

4-3 **4** *6* **Denarius Secundus**[7] 167 8-9-12 **74** DCrosse(3) 51
(N R Mitchell) *hld up: rdn after 6th: sn wl bhd* **11/2**

46-5 **U** **Great Compton**[7] 167 5-10-7 **80** PJBrennan —
(B J Llewellyn) *hld up: last tl jinked and uns rdr 3rd* **13/2**

5- **U** **Nimvara (IRE)**[49] 4502 9-10-4 **77** ChristianWilliams —
(Evan Williams) *plld hrd: led 2nd: clr 3rd: hdd whn blnd and uns rdr 6th* **4/1**[3]

5m 19.2s (-1.10) **Going Correction** +0.025s/f (Yiel) **6** Ran SP% **112.0**

Speed ratings: **103,99,94,92,**— — CSF £12.90 TOTE £3.90: £1.80, £1.90; EX 7.20.

Owner Mrs A M Thorpe **Bred** M L Page And Orpendale **Trained** Bronwydd Arms, Carmarthens

FOCUS

This did not prove to be as competitive as the betting suggested and the runner-up provides the best line to the form.

NOTEBOOK

Altitude Dancer(IRE), 4lb higher than when winning at Plumpton in March, put a very disappointing display at the same venue last time behind her. *(op 11-4)*

Dancinginthestreet, a two-mile winner on the Flat, was stepping up in distance for this switch to handicaps with ground conditions in his favour. *(op 3-1 tchd 7-2)*

Lady Lisa(IRE), 15lb higher than when scoring over a shorter trip on soft ground here last month, has yet to show she can be effective on a fast surface. *(op 6-1)*

Denarius Secundus *Official explanation: jockey said gelding was unsuited by the fast ground (op 5-1 tchd 9-2)*

288 NEWTON ABBOT RACECOURSE FOR CORPORATE EVENTS H'CAP CHASE (16 fncs) 2m 5f 110y

8:00 (8:00) (Class 4) (0-100,98) 5-Y-O+ **£3,793** (£1,167; £583; £291)

Form RPR

PP0- **1** **Our Jolly Swagman**[22] 4912 10-11-0 **86** (p) AThornton 93
(J W Mullins) *hld up in tch: chal 3 out: rdn to ld flat: r.o* **9/1**

2P-3 **2** *hd* **Paxford Jack**[15] 22 9-11-12 **98** (v) OMcPhail 105
(M F Harris) *a.p: wnt 2nd 4th: led 3 out: hdd flat: r.o* **10/1**

25-3 **3** *1* **Vandante (IRE)**[10] 135 9-10-9 **81** TDoyle 91+
(R Lee) *chsd ldr to 4th: prom: chalng whn blnd 3 out (water): rallied and hung lft after 2 out: ev ch last: nt qckn* **11/4**[1]

13P- **4** *10* **Bill Owen**[23] 4888 9-11-7 **93** (b) NFehily 91+
(D P Keane) *led to 3 out: wknd last* **8/1**

543- **U** **Wun Chai (IRE)**[25] 4855 6-10-9 **81** (b) MFoley —
(A E Jones) *bhd tl blnd and uns rdr 6th* **10/3**[2]

/3-0 **P** **Stormy Skye (IRE)**[16] 12 9-11-10 **96** (b) JEMoore —
(G L Moore) *hld up: mstke 6th: bhd whn p.u bef 10th* **6/1**[3]

0P-F **P** **Caucasian (IRE)**[10] 137 7-10-8 **80** DRDennis —
(Ian Williams) *hld up: mstke 2nd: rdn 11th: sn lost tch: t.o whn p.u bef 2 out* **7/1**

0/P- **P** **Insurrection (IRE)**[131] 3107 8-9-13 **76** ow1 CHonour(5) —
(J D Frost) *hld up in tch: reminders after 6th: nt fluent 9th: wknd 10th: t.o whn p.u bef 4 out* **25/1**

5m 21.4s (-1.30) **Going Correction** +0.025s/f (Yiel) **8** Ran SP% **110.6**

Speed ratings: **103,102,102,98,**— —,—,— CSF £83.67 CT £298.45 TOTE £9.00: £3.20, £2.50, £1.30; EX 68.90.

Owner F G Matthews **Bred** Dennis Badham **Trained** Wilsford-Cum-Lake, Wilts

FOCUS

All four who completed were still in with a shout at the penultimate fence and the placed horses set the standard.

NOTEBOOK

Our Jolly Swagman handles all sorts of ground and bounced back to form off a mark no less than 30lb lower than when he last won at the end of 2003. *(op 10-1)*

Paxford Jack, again a stone lower than when successful at Towcester in November, lost nothing in defeat after finishing lame at the same venue last time. *(op 5-1)*

Vandante(IRE) ◆, back up in distance, deserves another chance for he lost more ground by leaving his hind legs in the water than the margin of this defeat. *(op 7-2)*

Bill Owen gives the impression that this trip is just beyond him. *(op 13-2)*

Stormy Skye(IRE) *Official explanation: jockey said gelding lost its action (op 9-2)*

289 DIAGEO H'CAP HURDLE (12 hdls) 3m 3f

8:30 (8:30) (Class 4) (0-110,107) 4-Y-O+ **£3,386** (£1,042; £521; £260)

Form RPR

121- **1** **Graffiti Tongue (IRE)**[19] 4939 12-11-12 **107** (p) APMcCoy 105
(Evan Williams) *rn in snatches in rr: hrd rdn and gd hdwy whn sltly hmpd 2 out: led last: styd on* **5/4**[1]

4P-P **2** *1 3/4* **Ungaretti (GER)**[12] 76 8-10-13 **94** DRDennis 91+
(Ian Williams) *chsd ldr: rdn whn lft in ld and hmpd 2 out: hdd last: nt qckn* **11/1**

034- **3** *1 3/4* **Wimbledonian**[48] 4524 6-10-9 **90** WMarston 87+
(R T Phillips) *hld up: rdn 9th: hdwy whn hmpd 2 out: no ex flat* **7/1**

166- **4** *28* **El Hombre Del Rio (IRE)**[73] 4057 8-11-9 **104** AThornton 70
(R H Alner) *chsd ldrs tl wknd 3 out* **11/2**[3]

/25- **F** **Witness Time (IRE)**[24] 4868 9-11-3 **103** MNicolls(5) 101
(B J Eckley) *led: rdn and 2 l ahd whn fell 2 out* **5/2**[2]

6m 45.5s (3.50) **Going Correction** +0.025s/f (Yiel) **5** Ran SP% **109.2**

Speed ratings: **95,94,93,85,**— CSF £13.07 TOTE £1.90: £1.10, £4.30; EX 18.80 Place 6 £6.30, Place 5 £4.46.

Owner Patrick Heffernan **Bred** Mrs M Farrell **Trained** Cowbridge, Vale Of Glamorgan

FOCUS

A modest winning time for the class but the form looks reasonably solid for the grade.

NOTEBOOK

Graffiti Tongue(IRE), up 4lb, is the ideal type for McCoy's never-say-die approach and the combination came through for an unlikely win after being available at 50/1 in running on the exchanges. *(op 5-6)*

Ungaretti(GER), reverting back to hurdles, seemed to be getting the worst of the argument when Witness Time fell and he then got swamped by the winner. *(op 16-1)*

Wimbledonian, who has dropped over a stone in the handicap, could not sustain her effort but it would be hard to say she did not get this marathon trip. *(op 5-1 tchd 9-2)*

Witness Time(IRE) had just come under pressure when coming to grief and whether he would have held on will have to remain a mystery. *(op 4-1)*

T/Plt: @4.50 to a £1 stake. Pool: £41,083.35 - 6,550.90 winning units T/Qpdt: @3.10 to a £1 stake. Pool: £2,388.40 - 552.60 winning units KH

290 - 293a (Foreign Racing) - See Raceform Interactive

[167]EXETER (R-H)

Wednesday, May 11

OFFICIAL GOING: Good to firm (firm in places)

Racing was delayed after a racegoer collapsed.

Wind: Slight, accross Weather: Sunny

294 SIMPKINS EDWARDS NOVICES' HURDLE (8 hdls) 2m 1f

1:50 (2:23) (Class 4) 4-Y-O+ **£3,562** (£1,096; £548; £274)

Form RPR

2 **1** **Gironde**[8] 172 4-10-10 APMcCoy 101+
(Jonjo O'Neill) *w ldr: led on bit appr 3 out: j.lft 2 out and last: dismntd after fin* **1/5**[1]

2 *1 1/4* **Fox 'N' Goose (IRE)** 5-11-0 AThornton 95
(P C Ritchens) *a.p: chsd wnr appr 2 out: kpt on same pce flat* **28/1**

3 *19* **Mr Dip**[8] 5-10-7 DLaverty(7) 76
(L A Dace) *hld up and plld hrd: rdn and no real prog fr 2 out* **25/1**

P/0- **4** *1 1/2* **Simiola**[27] 4839 6-10-2 63 LTreadwell(5) 67
(S T Lewis) *led: hdd appr 3 out: sn rdn: wknd appr 2 out* **40/1**

4- **5** *dist* **Lovers Lane (FR)**[39] 4690 5-11-0 JEMoore —
(M C Pipe) *hld up: nt fluent 1st and 2nd: rdn after 5th: sn struggling: t.o* **12/1**[2]

6 *4* **Sooty From Mitcham** 5-10-11 RWalford(3) —
(R H Alner) *hld up: nt fluent 4th: sn bhd: t.o* **20/1**[3]

P **P** **Ly's West**[8] 172 5-11-0 JTizzard —
(C L Tizzard) *plld hrd: hung and j.lft 3rd: t.o whn p.u bef 5th* **33/1**

4m 1.90s (-7.30) **Going Correction** -0.65s/f (Firm) **7** Ran SP% **108.5**

Speed ratings: **91,90,81,80,**— —,— CSF £9.09 TOTE £1.10: £1.10, £8.00; EX 11.90.

Owner Mrs Gay Smith **Bred** Ridgecourt Stud **Trained** Cheltenham, Glouc s

FOCUS

A bad race run in a modest time and rated through the fourth with the winner value for further.

NOTEBOOK

Gironde, who showed enough promise to win a novice on his debut here behind a decent sort, won with a bit in hand, not being given an overly hard time by McCoy, but it was worrying that he was dismounted after the finish and it may have been that he pulled up sore on account of the ground. If none the worse for this, he can follow up granted easier conditions. *(tchd 2-11)*

Fox 'N' Goose(IRE) made a highly pleasing start to his career and will no doubt have delighted connections. Further will suit in time and he looks a ready-made winner of a similar event. *(op 20-1 tchd 33-1)*

Mr Dip was no match for the front two and will do better once qualified for handicaps. *(tchd 28-1)*

Sooty From Mitcham did not show a great deal of promise and is likely to fare better once jumping fences. *(op 16-1 tchd 25-1)*

Ly's West *Official explanation: jockey said gelding hung left throughout (op 50-1 tchd 66-1)*

295 SOUTH-WEST RACING CLUB NOVICES' H'CAP HURDLE (10 hdls) 2m 3f

2:20 (2:48) (Class 4) (0-100,100) 4-Y-O+ **£3,549** (£1,092; £546; £273)

Form RPR

00-2 **1** **Dash For Cover (IRE)**[16] 25 5-10-13 **82** JTizzard 89+
(J G Portman) *prom: led after 3rd: hit 2 out and last: rdn out* **4/1**[3]

006- **2** *2 1/2* **Fu Fighter**[125] 3235 4-10-12 **86** ChristianWilliams 83
(Evan Williams) *hld up and bhd: hdwy after 7th: ev ch 3 out: sn rdn: nt qckn flat* **3/1**[2]

46-6 **3** *hd* **Innocent Rebel (USA)**[13] 78 4-11-12 **100** RThornton 97
(A King) *hld up in mid-div: hdwy after 4th: ev ch 3 out: sn rdn: nt qckn flat* **11/4**[1]

40- **4** *7* **City Affair**[19] 4962 4-10-6 **83** (p) AHoneyball(3) 73
(C J Down) *hld up and bhd: rdn and hdwy 3 out: no further progess fr 2 out* **7/1**

005/ **5** *3* **Notwhatshewanted (IRE)**[393] 4819 8-11-0 **86** RYoung(3) 78
(J W Mullins) *j.lft: led tl after 3rd: prom tl wknd after 3 out* **20/1**

05F- **6** *8* **Quel Fontenailles (FR)**[40] 3534 7-11-5 **95** DLaverty(7) 79
(L A Dace) *hld up in mid-div: hdwy after 7th: wknd 3 out* **10/1**

060- **7** *6* **Farceur (FR)**[19] 4962 6-11-0 **90** (v[1]) AGlassonbury(7) 68
(M C Pipe) *hld up in tch: rdn and wknd appr 3 out* **20/1**

042- **8** *12* **Tyup Pompey (IRE)**[26] 4854 4-10-13 **87** JGoldstein 48
(Miss J S Davis) *prom tl wknd appr 3 out* **14/1**

9 *2 1/2* **Rosemont (IRE)**[46] 10-9-8 **70** DJacob(7) 34
(N R Mitchell) *prom to 3rd: wl bhd fr 6th* **66/1**

4m 26.8s (-14.10) **Going Correction** -0.65s/f (Firm) **9** Ran SP% **110.9**

Speed ratings: **103,101,101,98,97 94,91,86,85** CSF £15.69 CT £35.51 TOTE £3.60: £1.50, £1.80, £1.10; EX 16.60.

Owner Eddis, Buchanan And Kottler **Bred** Oyster Farm **Trained** Compton, Berks

FOCUS

Fast ground clearly suits the winner who hung on despite hitting the final two flights. The race could be a few pounds out either way, but the time was reasonable and the form could work out.

NOTEBOOK

Dash For Cover(IRE) is a much better type when the ground rides on the fast side. Leading for almost all the race, he stretched out nicely when challenged and held some dangerous-looking rivals, even after hitting the final two hurdles. Further success over the summer looks assured. *(tchd 7-2)*

Fu Fighter ran one of his best races after a short break. Current connections are adept at getting improvement from this type of horse and he is capable of picking up a race at a weak level. *(tchd 7-2)*

Innocent Rebel(USA) moved nicely into the race but found much less than expected when produced with his effort. He is giving the impression he does not get home that well over hurdles. *(op 9-4 tchd 3-1)*

City Affair is consistent at his level - although already beaten in sellers- and never threatened in this grade. *(op 8-1)*

Notwhatshewanted(IRE) showed some promise on his first run in just over a year. However, he was decisively beaten at the end of the race and cannot be relied upon to reproduce this effort. *(tchd 22-1)*

Quel Fontenailles(FR) won a ladies race on the All-Weather recently, but continues to struggle over timber. *(op 14-1 tchd 9-1)*

296 HEAVITREE BREWERY NOVICES' CHASE (17 fncs) 2m 7f 110y
2:50 (3:15) (Class 3) 5-Y-0+ **£5,486** (£1,688; £844; £422)

Form				RPR
52F-	**1**		**Moscow Whisper (IRE)**[22] 4917 8-11-2 .... PJBrennan (P J Hobbs) *a.p: wnt 2nd 4th: led 13th: hit 3 out: sn rdn: drvn out* **5/4**[1]	94+
20-1	**2**	*1 ¼*	**Special Conquest**[12] 107 7-11-8 109 .... AThornton (J W Mullins) *racd wd: chsd ldr to 4th: outpcd 12th: rallied 3 out: styd on flat* **13/8**[2]	97+
54-P	**3**	*shd*	**Rings Of Power (IRE)**[5] 202 8-10-13 77 .... RYoung(3) (N R Mitchell) *hld up in tch: chsd wnr appr 4 out: sn rdn: no ex flat* **50/1**	90
1-	**4**	*dist*	**Pams Oak**[31] 4796 7-11-8 105 .... OMcPhail (P S Payne) *led: j.rt 1st: mstke 7th (water): wkng whn mstke 4 out: t.o* **9/1**[3]	76
06-4	**5**	*dist*	**Rutland (IRE)**[14] 54 6-10-13 .... (p) AHoneyball(3) (Miss K M George) *hld up: last whn hit 10th: hrd rdn after 13th: sn lost tch: t.o* **20/1**	—
40-F	**P**		**Bodfari Creek**[11] 137 8-11-2 105 .... (t) JTizzard (J G Portman) *hld up: p.u lame bef 5th* **11/1**	—

5m 52.1s (-6.50) **Going Correction** -0.25s/f (Good) **6** Ran SP% **107.6**
Speed ratings: **100,99,99,—,—** — CSF £3.43 TOTE £2.30: £1.50, £1.70; EX 4.50.
Owner Ms F Nasir **Bred** Frank Barry **Trained** Withycombe, Somerset

FOCUS
A modest chase run in only an average time. The form does look slightly suspect, particularly in view of the proximity of the third.

NOTEBOOK
Moscow Whisper(IRE), who got no further than the second last time out, showed dour staying qualities up the straight to hold off some persistent challenges. Idling after jumping the last, he made much harder work of it than looked necessary and is not one to be plunging on at a short price next time. *(op 11-8 tchd 6-4)*
Special Conquest stays further than this trip and struggled to get into contention on the quick ground. His jumping was far from fluent and he only managed to snatch second after the last. On quick ground, he will need a stiffer test. *(op 5-4)*
Rings Of Power(IRE) ran a blinder for a horse rated so lowly and was unlucky not to hold on for second after giving the winner a fair battle over the last couple of fences. If this effort can be believed, he looks sure to pick up a chase in the coming months.
Pams Oak did not get away with the errors that nearly cost him victory last time. He will remain a risky proposition over fences until he jumps more fluently. *(op 8-1 tchd 10-1)*
Rutland(IRE) showed nothing on his chasing debut to kindle any immediate enthusiasm. *(op 40-1)*
Bodfari Creek *Official explanation: jockey said gelding was lame (op 14-1)*

297 SIMPKINS EDWARDS H'CAP CHASE (19 fncs) 3m 1f 110y
3:25 (3:42) (Class 3) (0-115,115) 5-Y-0+ **£5,687** (£1,750; £875; £437)

Form				RPR
F1P-	**1**		**Presence Of Mind (IRE)**[38] 4726 7-10-6 **95** .... BJCrowley (Miss E C Lavelle) *prom: j. slowly and lost pl 4th: hdwy 9th: led 15th: clr whn j.rt fr 4 out: eased considerably flat* **4/1**[2]	121+
0R-2	**2**	*13*	**Bramblehill Duke (IRE)**[8] 176 13-10-0 **89** oh1 .... (b) JamesDavies (Miss Venetia Williams) *led: hdd and hit 14th: rdn and outpcd after 15th: styd on to take 2nd flat: no ch w wnr* **4/1**[2]	93
0P5-	**3**	*2*	**Dunster Castle**[46] 4562 10-11-12 **115** .... PJBrennan (P J Hobbs) *chsd ldr: led 14th to 15th: rdn and one pce fr 4 out* **8/1**	117
210-	**4**	*13*	**Tell Tale (IRE)**[34] 4757 13-10-12 **104** .... TJMalone(3) (J G Cann) *sn wl bhd* **9/2**[3]	93
210-	**5**	*11*	**Diletia**[27] 4837 8-10-8 **97** .... AThornton (R H Alner) *wl bhd fr 11th* **5/1**	75
46-3	**P**		**Gumley Gale**[14] 55 10-11-11 **114** .... (t) WHutchinson (K Bishop) *hld up: hdwy 9th: wkng whn blnd 15th: t.o whn p.u bef 4 out* **7/2**[1]	—

6m 15.5s (-12.50) **Going Correction** -0.25s/f (Good) **6** Ran SP% **108.2**
Speed ratings: **109,105,104,100,97** — CSF £18.73 TOTE £5.00: £3.20, £2.30; EX 34.50.
Owner Michael Coghlan **Bred** M Ryan **Trained** Wildhern, Hants

FOCUS
A very decent time for the grade and a winner is value for more and on an upward curve.

NOTEBOOK
Presence Of Mind(IRE) ◆ put the disappointment of his last effort behind him without the visor. Eased into the race from well off the strong pace, he took it up five out and won as he pleased. The one minus point was his tendency to jump badly out to the right over the final three fences. *(op 7-2)*
Bramblehill Duke(IRE) set a really good pace in front and unsurprisingly had very little left when the eventual winner sauntered past him after the fifth last. However, to his credit, he stuck on well and regained runners-up spot after rallying up the straight. The worrying statistic that he is winless since 2002 remains.
Dunster Castle probably stood little chance trying to give nearly a stone and a half to an improving youngster. The weight anchored him from the time of being passed by the winner and can be given another chance when he does not have to give so much weight away. *(op 7-1 tchd 13-2)*
Tell Tale(IRE) handles conditions well but could never get involved off the strong pace. He is a shade high in the handicap which will not help this 13-year-old. *(op 11-2)*
Diletia was held-up behind the strong pace but never got into contention at any stage. *(tchd 9-2)*
Gumley Gale was just starting to weaken when clouting the fifth last. *Official explanation: jockey said gelding was unsuited by good to firm, firm in places (tchd 9-2)*

298 MARLBOROUGH BOOKSHOP AND SPORTING GALLERY H'CAP HURDLE (13 hdls) 3m 110y
4:00 (4:10) (Class 4) (0-100,100) 4-Y-0+ **£3,136** (£896; £448)

Form				RPR
35-1	**1**		**Altitude Dancer (IRE)**[1] 287 5-11-6 **100** 7ex .... SWalsh(7) (Mrs A M Thorpe) *led to 2nd: prom: led after 10th: hrd rdn appr last: all out* **11/2**[3]	103
25/0	**2**	*2*	**Carl's Boy**[12] 105 9-9-8 **74** .... (t) MrPSheldrake(7) (D A Rees) *hld up in tch: nt clr run on ins and swtchd lft appr 3 out: sn rdn to chse wnr: styd on same pce flat* **10/1**	75
532-	**3**	*8*	**Good Man Again (IRE)**[65] 4233 7-11-12 **99** .... ChristianWilliams (Evan Williams) *hld up: hdwy 8th: rdn and wknd appr 3 out: wknd appr 2 out* **9/4**[1]	92
624-	**4**	*2 ½*	**Delaware (FR)**[19] 4962 9-11-0 **87** .... JMogford (H S Howe) *led 2nd to 4th: prom tl rdn and wknd after 10th* **14/1**	78
/4-1	**5**	*11*	**Little Brave**[16] 23 10-11-0 **92** .... LStephens(5) (C Roberts) *hld up: hdwy 9th: rdn appr 3 out: wknd appr 2 out* **8/1**	72
54-P	**6**	*dist*	**Wee Danny (IRE)**[12] 105 8-10-11 **91** .... DLaverty(7) (L A Dace) *prom: led 4th tl after 10th: sn wknd: t.o* **11/2**[3]	—
605-	**F**		**Rose Of The Hill (IRE)**[18] 4977 6-11-8 **95** .... JEMoore (M C Pipe) *hld up: fell 6th* **7/2**[2]	—
/0-5	**P**		**Queens Brigade**[12] 102 13-10-2 **82** .... MissVStephens(7) (Miss V A Stephens) *a bhd: lost tch 8th: t.o whn p.u lame 2 out* **20/1**	—

6m 1.20s (-12.10) **Going Correction** -0.65s/f (Firm) **8** Ran SP% **115.4**
Speed ratings: **93,92,89,89,85** —,—,— CSF £57.03 CT £158.60 TOTE £8.10: £2.70, £5.10, £1.10; EX 63.40.
Owner Mrs A M Thorpe **Bred** M L Page And Orpendale **Trained** Bronwydd Arms, Carmarthens
■ Stewards' Enquiry : S Walsh caution: used whip in an incorrect place

FOCUS
Not a strong race but a second victory within 24 hours for the winner. The form is highly debatable.

NOTEBOOK
Altitude Dancer(IRE) picked up his second race within twenty-four hours with a fluent display. Always travelling well close to the pace, he took it up on the far side and won with a bit to spare. In his current vein of form, the hat-trick must be highly possible if turned out quickly. *(op 4-1)*
Carl's Boy came from well off the pace to give chase to the winner. Receiving almost two stone in weight, he could never get to the winner but improved on his most recent efforts. Connections may want to exploit his lowly mark in a handicap chase during the summer given his background between the flags. *(op 16-1)*
Good Man Again(IRE)was slightly disappointing on ground thought to be advantageous for him. However, all his best recent form has been on ground with cut and that assumption may not be correct. *(tchd 5-2)*
Delaware(FR) has still to convince he stays this sort of trip and is without a win since 2002. *(op 12-1)*
Little Brave only won a weak seller at Towcester last time and never got to grips with these slightly better rivals. His handicap mark almost certainly flatters him. *(op 5-1)*
Wee Danny(IRE) led for most of the way before weakening badly up the straight. He is nicely handicapped but has done all his winning in late summer. *(op 8-1)*
Rose Of The Hill(IRE) departed very early in the race and gave his jockey no chance of staying on board. *(op 6-1 tchd 13-2)*

299 EXETER RACECOURSE INTERMEDIATE HUNTERS' CHASE (SERIES FINAL) (15 fncs 2 omitted) 2m 7f 110y
4:30 (4:41) (Class 6) 5-Y-0+ **£3,415** (£1,051; £525; £262)

Form				RPR
60/	**1**		**Teddy Boy**[25] 9-11-7 .... MrRWoollacott(5) (Miss E Thompson) *hld up and bhd: hdwy on outside appr 9th: hit 10th: led appr 4 out: rdn and hdd 2 out: led last: styd on wl* **3/1**[1]	88+
	2	*2*	**Dante's Promise (IRE)**[24] 9-11-5 .... MrJBarnes(7) (Richard J Smith) *reluctant and led to post: hld up in tch: led 2 out to last: no ex* **11/2**[3]	86
6-	**3**	*2 ½*	**Horizon Hill (USA)**[9] 5-11-5 .... MrNWilliams (T W Boon) *hld up in tch: lost pl after 11th: smooth hdwy 4 out: ev ch 2 out: sn rdn: wknd flat* **3/1**[1]	78+
	4	*13*	**O'Ech**[9] 11-10-12 .... AGlassonbury(7) (Mrs C Lawrence) *hld up: hdwy 9th: rdn 11th: wknd appr last* **14/1**	65+
33P-	**5**	*8*	**Bob's Lad**[39] 8-11-9 79 .... MissAGoschen(3) (D J Richards) *sn prom: hmpd 5th: sn lost pl: sme hdwy 4 out: n.d* **9/2**[2]	65+
3FP-	**6**	*7*	**Pinmoor Hill**[11] 9-11-5 .... (b[1]) MrMMunrowd(7) (Mrs Diane Wilson) *chsd ldr: lft in ld 9th: hdd appr 4 out: sn wknd* **33/1**	56
	7	*2 ½*	**Joli Christmas**[9] 8-11-5 .... MrWWhite(7) (G Chambers) *hld up: mstke 7th: hdwy appr 9th: ev ch appr 4 out: sn wknd* **25/1**	53
P-	**8**	*shd*	**Chapners Cross**[9] 9-11-5 .... (v[1]) MissJCongdon(7) (A W Congdon) *a bhd* **20/1**	53
6F-	**U**		**Frontenac (IRE)**[11] 9-11-5 .... MissRAGreen(7) (Mrs Mandy Hand) *led tl blnd and uns rdr 9th* **8/1**	—
	P		**Ryders Hill**[9] 6-10-12 .... MissVShaw(7) (M Weir) *hld up: hdwy after 8th: blnd 10th: sn wknd: t.o whn p.u bef 3 out* **33/1**	—

5m 57.0s (-1.60) **Going Correction** -0.25s/f (Good)
WFA 5 from 6yo+ 3lb **10** Ran SP% **115.8**
Speed ratings: **92,91,90,86,83 81,80,80,—,—** CSF £19.03 TOTE £3.60: £1.30, £2.60, £1.30; EX 18.50.
Owner R Mitford-Slade **Bred** P Trant **Trained** South Molton, Devon

FOCUS
An ordinary hunter chase and unlikely to have much bearing on future events. The open ditch in the back straight was omitted on both circuits.

NOTEBOOK
Teddy Boy, who won a mens open between the flags last month, was made to work very hard for victory but saw out the trip much better than his closest rivals. *(op 9-4)*
Dante's Promise(IRE) gave a little trouble going to post but showed plenty of willing in the final stages of the race. He handles conditions really well and almost certainly ran up to his best form between the flags. *(op 5-1 tchd 6-1)*
Horizon Hill(USA) moved stylishly into the race and looked the most likely winner as his jockey continually took a pull. However, when he was fully let down the response was minimal and never got his head in front. *(op 13-2)*
O'Ech never got competitive and only ran on when the leaders had flown. *(op 9-1)*
Bob's Lad has been in poor recent form and never threatened to break that cycle. *(op 8-1)*
Frontenac(IRE) was still in contention when giving his jockey no chance of staying in the saddle at the ninth.

300 DARREN HAMMETT 30TH BIRTHDAY MAIDEN OPEN NATIONAL HUNT FLAT RACE 2m 1f
5:05 (5:07) (Class 6) 4-6-Y-0 **£2,499** (£714; £357)

Form				RPR
	1		**Pan The Man (IRE)** 4-11-0 .... AThornton (J W Mullins) *hld up in tch: rdn to ld ins fnl f: drvn out* **11/1**	87
2-3	**2**	*hd*	**Miss Midnight**[16] 27 4-10-0 .... JamesWhite(7) (R J Hodges) *a.p: rdn to ld over 2f out: hdd ins fnl f: r.o* **13/8**[1]	80
	3	*6*	**Neodyme (FR)** 4-11-0 .... GSupple (M C Pipe) *hld up and bhd: hdwy on ins over 3f out: sn swtchd lft: rdn and rn green over 2f out: wknd fnl f* **8/1**	81
	4	*1*	**The Cliffe (IRE)**[52] 6-11-4 .... OMcPhail (J Rudge) *hld up: hdwy 8f out: led over 3f out tl over 2f out: wknd fnl f* **25/1**	84
06-	**5**	*5*	**Be Positive**[21] 4935 5-11-4 .... JamesDavies (C J Down) *plld hrd in mid-div: hdwy over 3f out: rdn whn swtchd rt over 2f out: wknd over 1f out* **13/2**[3]	79
6-U	**6**	*3 ½*	**Boysterous (IRE)**[2] 266 5-10-11 .... PMerrigan(7) (Mrs H Dalton) *prom tl wknd 3f out* **14/1**	75
02-	**7**	*2*	**Karawa**[27] 4841 6-10-11 .... JTizzard (C L Tizzard) *led: hdd 9f out: led 7f out: rdn and hdd over 3f out: wknd 2f out* **10/3**[2]	66
0	**8**	*6*	**Shinjiru (USA)**[11] 131 5-11-1 .... RHobson(3) (P A Blockley) *hld up: hdwy over 4f out: wknd 3f out* **33/1**	67
	9	*6*	**Hey You M'Lady** 5-10-8 .... MissEJJones(3) (J Rudge) *bhd fnl 4f* **33/1**	54
0/0-	**10**	*10*	**Bob's Temptation**[157] 2662 6-11-1 .... RWalford(3) (A J Wilson) *w ldr: ev ch over 3f out: sn wknd* **66/1**	51

11 1 ¾ **Knapp Bridge Boy** 5-11-4 .... TScudamore 49
(J R Payne) *hld up and bhd: hdwy to ld 9f out: hdd 7f out: wknd 4f out* **50/1**

12 9 **Legal Warning** 4-10-7 .... MissLGardner[7] 36
(Mrs S Gardner) *a bhd* **40/1**

13 1 **Mr Parson (IRE)** 5-11-4 .... PFlynn 39
(S T Lewis) *hld up in tch: rdn and wknd 8f out* **14/1**

3m 59.5s (-7.30) **Going Correction** -0.65s/f (Firm)
WFA 4 from 5yo+ 4lb **13** Ran SP% **122.9**
Speed ratings: **91,90,88,87,85 83,82,79,77,72 71,67,66** CSF £28.79 TOTE £14.40: £5.10, £1.10, £2.80; EX 48.50 Place 6 £5.00, Place 5 £4.47.
Owner Mark Adams **Bred** Miss Yvonne McClintock And Mrs Jean O'Brien **Trained** Wilsford-Cum-Lake, Wilts

FOCUS
An ordinary bumper in which the second gives the form a secure but moderate look.

NOTEBOOK
Pan The Man(IRE) was always travelling well on his debut and showed plenty of determination when challenged by the more experienced runner-up. He has the size to make a chaser and could be capable of carrying a penalty if the race is fairly weak.
Miss Midnight was well supported on the back of some fairly solid bumper form. Travelling well for most of the race, she did not find as much off the bridle as looked likely and failed to make use of the weight she received from the winner. Experience will continue to improve her as she was still a bit green in the latter stages. *(op 3-1 tchd 10-3 in places)*
Neodyme(FR) looked very green in the final stages of the race and is sure to improve from this effort. *(op 7-1)*
The Cliffe(IRE), already pulled up in a maiden point-to-point, showed enough on his debut under Rules to suggest he can pick up a small race somewhere.
Be Positive ran a similar race to Worcester last time out, again suggesting he has some talent. He has plenty of scope and gives the impression experience is doing him a lot of good. *(op 7-1)*
Boysterous(IRE) was on his best behaviour after dumping his jockey at the start at Towcester last time. He did not get home after showing up prominently early. *(op 11-1)*
Karawa travelled nicely until challenged early in the straight. The jockey did not overly persevere with her when she became unbalanced inside the final furlong and she is better than this showing. *(op 5-2)*
T/Plt: £7.00 to a £1 stake. Pool: £27,979.80. 2,883.85 winning tickets. T/Qpdt: £4.80 to a £1 stake. Pool: £1,342.20. 206.10 winning tickets. KH

PERTH (R-H)

Wednesday, May 11

OFFICIAL GOING: Good (good to firm in places)
Wind: breezy, behind

301 GUINNESS FROM DARKNESS COMES LIGHT MAIDEN HURDLE (10 hdls) 2m 4f 110y
6:30 (6:30) (Class 4) 4-Y-0+ **£3,747** (£1,153; £576; £288)

Form RPR

555- **1** **Downing Street (IRE)**[34] 4756 4-10-11 .... (b) JPMcNamara 94+
(Jennie Candlish) *hld up and bhd: stdy hdwy fr 4 out: shkn up to ld towards fin* **10/1**[3]

532- **2** 1 ¼ **Dawn Devoy (IRE)**[21] 4923 6-11-2 105 .... GLee 98+
(Miss V Scott) *cl up: effrt and ev ch 2 out: hit last: kpt on towards fin* **9/4**[1]

POP- **3** 1 ½ **Supply And Fix (IRE)**[32] 7-11-2 78 .... KWhelan 96
(J J Lambe, Ire) *mde most tl hdd and no ex towards fin* **16/1**

60-5 **4** ½ **Relix (FR)**[17] 8 5-10-11 93 .... (t) DMcGann[(5)] 95
(A M Crow) *cl up: drvn after 3 out: kpt on fr last* **16/1**

U-6 **5** 1 ½ **Nobel (FR)**[13] 82 4-10-4 .... MissRDavidson[(7)] 89
(N G Richards) *hld up: hdwy and prom 1/2-way: effrt bef 2 out: kpt on fr last* **10/3**[2]

423/ **6** 10 **Mounthooley**[531] 2402 9-11-2 .... ADempsey 84
(B Mactaggart) *hld up: hdwy 4 out: wknd after next* **20/1**

653- **7** ½ **Mr Tim (IRE)**[46] 4550 7-11-2 .... BGibson 83
(L Lungo) *chsd ldrs: mstke 3 out: sn rdn: wknd bef next* **9/4**[1]

P/P- **8** 10 **Lethem Air**[31] 7-10-13 .... ONelmes[(3)] 73
(Mrs H O Graham) *prom to 3 out: sn rdn and btn* **66/1**

0P-0 **9** *dist* **Bromley Abbey**[17] 9 7-10-9 73 .... KJohnson —
(Miss S E Forster) *in tch to 4 out: sn btn* **50/1**

00-P **P** **Killwillie (IRE)**[11] 124 6-11-2 .... (t) PRobson —
(J I A Charlton) *a bhd: t.o whn p.u bef 2 out* **50/1**

00- **P** **Up In The Sky (IRE)**[46] 4552 5-10-9 .... BHarding —
(Mrs R L Elliot) *sn bhd: t.o whn p.u after 6th* **100/1**

00- **P** **Dock Copper's Girl**[146] 2852 5-10-4 .... DCCostello[(5)] —
(J N R Billinge) *a bhd: t.o whn p.u bef 2 out* **100/1**

60-0 **P** **Venture More**[13] 85 9-10-13 77 .... GBerridge[(3)] —
(Mrs A F Tullie) *s.i.s: a bhd: t.o whn p.u bef 2 out* **100/1**

405- **P** **Starbright**[60] 4317 4-10-4 68 .... (p) MrJARichardson[(7)] —
(W G Young) *nt jump wl: sn bhd: t.o whn p.u bef 2 out* **100/1**

5-P0 **P** **No Hesitation**[4] 209 4-10-11 .... MBradburne —
(Mrs S C Bradburne) *midfield to 1/2-way: sn lost pl and p.u bef 7th* **100/1**

4m 59.8s (-8.40) **Going Correction** -0.30s/f (Good)
WFA 4 from 5yo+ 5lb **15** Ran SP% **120.6**
Speed ratings: **104,103,102,102,102 98,98,94,—,— —,—,—,—,—** CSF £32.82 TOTE £12.70: £2.30, £1.50, £3.30; EX 30.70.
Owner Reuben Fielding **Bred** M Stewkesbury And The Luna Wells Syndicate **Trained** Basford Green, Staffs

FOCUS
A race lacking strength but a decent gallop throughout. The fourth sets the standard and the form looks fairly solid.

NOTEBOOK
Downing Street(IRE) may not be entirely straightforward but had the race teed up for him and only had to be kidded along to win with a bit in hand over this longer trip. Things went his way this time but may not be one for short odds for a follow up. *(op 8-1)*
Dawn Devoy(IRE) ran creditably but left the impression that he would be much better suited by softer ground over this trip. He will stay three miles and looks sure to win an ordinary event. *(op 3-1)*
Supply And Fix(IRE) looked to have a stiff task at the weights but seemed to show much improved form. He looks capable of winning a small event but will find life tougher in handicaps after reassessment.
Relix(FR) ran creditably and should stay three miles but his record suggests he is no certainty to reproduce this next time. *(tchd 20-1)*
Nobel(FR) is now qualified for a handicap mark and has shown enough to suggest he can win a small event in due course. *(op 11-4)*
Mounthooley shaped as though retaining ability on this first start since November 2003 but is likely to continue to look vulnerable in this type of event.
Mr Tim(IRE) looked to have fair claims after an encouraging display at Carlisle but was disappointing after travelling strongly for a long way and he may be better with more cut in the ground. *(op 2-1 tchd 5-2 in places)*

302 TAITTINGER CHAMPAGNE MARES' ONLY INTERMEDIATE HURDLE (8 hdls) 2m 110y
7:00 (7:01) (Class 4) 4-Y-0+ **£3,445** (£1,060; £530; £265)

Form RPR

214- **1** **Millagros (IRE)**[5] 4845 5-11-5 .... JimCrowley 105+
(I Semple) *hld up in tch: smooth hdwy to ld appr 2 out: hit last: drvn out* **2/1**[2]

P44- **2** 2 **Farne Isle**[57] 4388 6-11-5 103 .... (p) NHannity 101
(G A Harker) *prom: effrt and pressed wnr 2 out: rdn and kpt on wl fr last* **13/2**[3]

313- **3** 5 **Zaffaran Express (IRE)**[39] 4694 6-11-5 104 .... BHarding 96
(N G Richards) *nt fluent 1st: mde most to appr 2 out: sn outpcd* **10/11**[1]

FPP/ **4** 1 ¼ **Blue Bar**[385] 4913 7-10-12 64 .... RMcGrath 88
(G A Harker) *in tch: effrt bef 2 out: kpt on same pce last* **50/1**

00-P **5** 17 **Three Times A Lady**[7] 185 5-10-9 70 .... ONelmes[(3)] 71
(D W Thompson) *chsd ldrs: hit 5th: outpcd after next* **100/1**

0UP- **6** 1 ¼ **High Class Pet**[71] 4108 5-10-12 83 .... PRobson 70
(F P Murtagh) *w ldr to after 3 out: btn next* **33/1**

0R- **7** 5 **August Rose (IRE)**[30] 4807 5-10-9 .... PBuchanan[(3)] 65
(Miss Lucinda V Russell) *nt fluent: a bhd* **66/1**

U44- **8** 2 ½ **Katie Kai**[31] 4782 4-10-1 83 .... CDSharkey[(7)] 58
(Miss S E Forster) *a bhd* **25/1**

5P0- **9** *hd* **Cashema (IRE)**[29] 4180 4-10-8 69 .... (t) KJohnson 58
(D R MacLeod) *keen: hld up: shortlived effrt bef 3 out: sn btn* **100/1**

00- **10** 2 ½ **Globe Pearl (IRE)**[118] 3332 5-10-7 .... DCCostello[(5)] 60
(F P Murtagh) *in tch to 4th: struggling fr next* **200/1**

0- **P** **Aba Gold (IRE)**[73] 4090 5-10-7 .... DFlavin[(5)] —
(Mrs L B Normile) *a bhd: t.o whn p.u bef 2 out* **50/1**

P **Stylistic (IRE)**[24] 4646 4-10-8 .... (p) KWhelan —
(J J Lambe, Ire) *hld up: sme hdwy 4 out: wknd next: t.o whn p.u after 2 out* **20/1**

3m 55.7s (-4.90) **Going Correction** -0.30s/f (Good)
WFA 4 from 5yo+ 4lb **12** Ran SP% **118.5**
Speed ratings: **99,98,95,95,87 86,84,83,82,81** —,— CSF £14.12 TOTE £3.30: £1.30, £2.10, £1.10; EX 14.00.
Owner James A Cringan **Bred** Elsdon Farms **Trained** Bowridge, S Lanarks

FOCUS
Just an ordinary gallop and, with Zaffaran Express proving a bit disappointing, this race did not take as much winning as seemed likely and the proximity of the fourth means this bare form may not be that solid and reliable.

NOTEBOOK
Millagros(IRE), back over hurdles, took advantage of a below-par display from the favourite to win with a bit in hand. She looks the type to progress further over obstacles. *(op 9-4)*
Farne Isle, tried in cheekpieces, returned to form dropped in trip but, although running creditably, left the impression that the return to further would suit. *(op 6-1)*
Zaffaran Express(IRE), back in trip, jumped a good deal better than at Newbury last time but left the impression that the return to two and a half miles would suit. *(op 11-10)*
Blue Bar's proximity holds this race down as this was the first time she had shown any worthwhile form on this first start for her new yard. She may be capable of better but will find things much tougher after reassessment in handicaps. *(op 40-1 tchd 66-1)*
Three Times A Lady is a poor performer who looks flattered by her proximity in this ordinarily run race. *(op 66-1)*
High Class Pet is likely to continue to look vulnerable in this type of event.
Stylistic(IRE) *Official explanation: vet said filly was slightly lame (tchd 66-1)*
Aba Gold(IRE) *Official explanation: jockey said mare was unsuited by good, good to firm in places ground (tchd 66-1)*

303 CARLSBERG NOVICES' CHASE (18 fncs) 3m
7:30 (7:30) (Class 3) 5-Y-0+ **£5,546** (£1,802; £970)

Form RPR

1P- **1** **Native Coral (IRE)**[62] 4272 7-11-0 .... BHarding 127+
(N G Richards) *trckd ldrs: rdn to ld bef last: r.o strly* **6/4**[1]

032- **2** 7 **Snowy (IRE)**[30] 4806 7-11-0 102 .... PRobson 117
(J I A Charlton) *cl up: led 13th: hdd bef last: no ch w wnr* **13/8**[2]

501- **3** *dist* **Winter Garden**[30] 4806 11-11-3 103 .... PBuchanan[(3)] 103
(Miss Lucinda V Russell) *led to 13th: outpcd 3 out: btn whn ref last: continued* **11/4**[3]

3PP- **P** **Mackenzie (IRE)**[20] 4947 9-10-9 64 .... DMcGann[(5)] —
(Mrs C J Kerr) *keen: prom tl wknd 8th: t.o whn p.u bef 13th* **33/1**

6m 7.30s (-5.30) **Going Correction** -0.30s/f (Good) **4** Ran SP% **107.7**
Speed ratings: **96,93,—,—** CSF £4.42 TOTE £2.00; EX 5.40.
Owner City Rovers Partnership **Bred** P Fitzgerald **Trained** Greystoke, Cumbria

FOCUS
A reasonable early gallop but a modest winning time for the class. The winner is value for nearly double the official margin with the second to mark.

NOTEBOOK
Native Coral(IRE) ◆ disappointed at Carlisle last time but showed what he was capable of on this debut over regulation fences and, although this was not much of a contest, looks the sort to progress again and win more races over fences. *(op 11-8)*
Snowy(IRE) is a reliable sort who ran creditably and looks a reasonable guide to the level of this form. He remains vulnerable to progressive sorts in this type of event, though. *(op 7-4)*
Winter Garden was closely matched with Snowy on recent Kelso but ran poorly for no apparent reason. *(op 3-1)*
Mackenzie(IRE) was again well beaten and has to show that he possesses ability. *(op 25-1)*

304 SCOTTISH FIELD H'CAP HURDLE (12 hdls) 3m 110y
8:00 (8:00) (Class 3) (0-115,113) 4-Y-0+ **£5,577** (£1,716; £858; £429)

Form RPR

1F-4 **1** **Thoutmosis (USA)**[14] 61 6-11-9 **113** .... GBerridge[(3)] 119+
(L Lungo) *hld up: smooth hdwy after 4 out: effrt and ev ch last: sn led: drvn out* **3/1**[1]

00-0 **2** 1 ½ **Political Sox**[14] 64 11-10-11 **105** .... GThomas[(7)] 109
(R Nixon) *hld up: hdwy to ld after 3 out: hdd after last: kpt on* **16/1**

523- **3** 3 ½ **Speed Kris (FR)**[20] 4948 6-11-6 **107** .... (p) MBradburne 107
(Mrs S C Bradburne) *hld up: effrt after 3 out: kpt on u.p fr last* **4/1**[2]

00-6 **4** 13 **End Of An Error**[4] 215 6-9-11 **87** oh1 .... ONelmes[(3)] 74
(Mrs E Slack) *bhd: drvn 4 out: styd on fr 2 out: n.d* **6/1**

-306 **5** *shd* **Mister Moussac**[11] 121 6-10-1 **95** .... (p) SCrawford[(7)] 82
(Miss Kariana Key) *chsd ldrs tl wknd bef 2 out* **10/1**

6 ½ **No Time At All (IRE)**[16] 30 5-9-7 **87** oh8 .... MrNMcKnight[(7)] 73
(Mayne Kidd, Ire) *chsd ldrs to 3 out: rdn and wknd bef next* **25/1**

4P-5 **7** *3 ½* **Haystacks (IRE)**[11] 121 9-11-7 **108** .... JimCrowley 91
(James Moffatt) *hld up: hdwy and prom bef 2 out: sn rdn and btn* **12/1**
444- **8** *4* **Caesar's Palace (GER)**[26] 4851 8-10-10 **100** ....(p) PBuchanan(3) 79
(Miss Lucinda V Russell) *cl up: outpcd after 7th: btn 3 out* **5/1**[3]
41-0 **9** *17* **Aelred**[12] 108 12-10-3 **90** ....(p) KJohnson 52
(R Johnson) *set decent pce to after 3 out: sn wknd* **16/1**
115/ **10** *dist* **Kilbride Lad (IRE)**[11] 142 11-10-9 **96** .... KWhelan —
(J J Lambe, Ire) *hld up in tch: drvn 4 out: wknd bef next* **12/1**

5m 58.5s (-12.40) **Going Correction** -0.30s/f (Good) **10** Ran SP% **116.0**
Speed ratings: **107,106,105,101,101 101,99,98,93,**— CSF £48.61 CT £195.63 TOTE £3.80: £1.80, £4.80, £1.50; EX 36.10.
Owner The Border Reivers **Bred** Cormal Investments **Trained** Carrutherstown, D'fries & G'way

FOCUS
An ordinary event but a strong gallop meant those held up had the edge. The first two are rated as having run to their marks.

NOTEBOOK
Thoutmosis(USA), tried again over this trip, benefited from the decent gallop and ran right up to his best. He has a good win record and should continue to progress. *(op 9-4 tchd 10-3)*
Political Sox is a law unto himself but elected to put it all in for a race that was run to suit. Whether this will be reproduced next time remains to be seen, though.
Speed Kris(FR) extended his run of creditable efforts and looks a good guide to the form but the fact that he has yet to win in 17 starts is becoming a bit of a worry. *(op 5-1)*
End Of An Error had the race run to suit but did not show enough given she had the race run to suit to suggest she is about to break her losing run. *(op 7-1)*
Mister Moussac fared the best of those that raced up with the decent gallop but, although on a fair mark, his inconsistency means he is not one to place much faith in. *Official explanation: jockey said gelding hung right-handed throughout (op 9-1 tchd 11-1)*
No Time At All(IRE) may be a bit better than the bare form and ran arguably her best race over hurdles. She should not mind the drop back to two and a half miles.

305 FAMOUS GROUSE H'CAP CHASE (12 fncs) 2m
8:30 (8:30) (Class 3) (0-125,115) 5-Y-0+ **£6,825** (£2,100; £1,050; £525)

Form RPR
124- **1** **Nowator (POL)**[164] 2502 8-11-12 **115** .... DRDennis 128+
(T R George) *cl up: led 3rd: set decent gallop: clr 4 out: rdn next: rdn and edgd rt fr 2 out: tired run in: all out* **4/1**[2]
263- **2** *½* **Kalou (GER)**[18] 4979 7-10-9 **101** .... MrTGreenall(3) 110
(C Grant) *hld up: hdwy 8th: drvn after next: styd on wl fr last: jst hld* **7/1**
01-4 **3** *1 ¼* **Fiori**[13] 84 9-11-0 **110** .... PCO'Neill(7) 118
(P C Haslam) *in tch tl lost pl 1/2-way: rallied 2 out: styd on wl fr last* **6/1**
522- **4** *nk* **Glenfarclas Boy (IRE)**[24] 4874 9-10-3 **95** ....(p) PBuchanan(3) 103
(Miss Lucinda V Russell) *towards rr: struggling 1/2-way: hdwy 2 out: kpt on wl fr last* **12/1**
P3P- **5** *nk* **Black Bullet (NZ)**[20] 4944 12-11-7 **110** ....(t) JPMcNamara 118+
(Jennie Candlish) *led to 3rd: pressed wnr: drvn bef 3 out: rallied: no ex run in* **25/1**
63-5 **6** *16* **Edmo Heights**[12] 108 9-11-8 **111** .... RGarritty 102
(T D Easterby) *prom: drvn and outpcd 8th: no imp fr next* **10/1**
P2-1 **7** *1* **Little Flora**[13] 84 9-10-0 **96** .... MJMcAlister(7) 86
(S J Marshall) *chsd ldrs tl outpcd after 4 out: btn next* **5/1**[3]
422- **U** **Brown Teddy**[53] 4447 8-11-5 **108** .... GLee —
(R Ford) *in tch whn blnd and uns rdr 7th* **7/2**[1]
U31- **P** **Runner Bean**[24] 4888 11-11-5 **108** .... SDurack —
(R Lee) *mstke 1st: a bhd: t.o whn p.u after 3 out* **8/1**

3m 56.6s (-6.20) **Going Correction** -0.30s/f (Good) **9** Ran SP% **117.4**
Speed ratings: **103,102,102,101,101 93,93,**—,— CSF £32.79 CT £167.91 TOTE £5.60: £2.20, £3.40, £2.80; EX 45.60.
Owner Mrs Sharon C Nelson **Bred** Sk Moszna **Trained** Slad, Gloucs

FOCUS
An ordinary event but a strong gallop throughout and the winner may be a bit better than the bare form. The third and fourth set the level and the race should work out.

NOTEBOOK
Nowator(POL) ◆ notched his second course and distance win with a gutsy display and may be better than the bare form as he ensured a strong gallop throughout. A test of speed suits and he appeals as the type to win again. *(op 11-2)*
Kalou(GER) ran creditably in this strongly-run race and, although yet to win over hurdles, will be suited by the step up to two and a half miles. *(op 10-1)*
Fiori ran creditably given this course was plenty sharp enough for him. The return to somewhere like Hexham or Towcester will suit and he appeals as the type to win again.
Glenfarclas Boy(IRE) ran creditably in terms of form but has not won for some time and did not look the easiest of rides. He remains one to tread carefully with. *(tchd 14-1)*
Black Bullet(NZ) was not disgraced given he was not allowed his own way in front, but his record suggests he is not the best betting proposition around. *(op 20-1)*
Edmo Heights was again below his best and he has not been very consistent since his last success in March of last year. *(op 8-1)*
Little Flora, up 11lb in the weights, handles a sound surface but was below the form he showed to win at Kelso last time. *(op 7-2)*

306 STEADFAST SCOTLAND H'CAP HURDLE (8 hdls) 2m 110y
9:00 (9:00) (Class 4) (0-85,85) 4-Y-0+ **£4,394** (£1,352; £676; £338)

Form RPR
0- **1** **Poor Tactic's (IRE)**[9] 154 9-11-7 **80** .... KWhelan 87
(J J Lambe, Ire) *in tch: drvn after 4 out: rallied after next: led run in: kpt on wl* **5/1**[2]
0P-P **2** *2 ½* **Kyle Of Lochalsh**[17] 11 5-11-6 **79** .... ADempsey 84
(J S Goldie) *in tch: drvn along fr 3 out: kpt on run in: nt rch wnr* **20/1**
005/ **3** *½* **Dream Castle (IRE)**[434] 4133 11-11-1 **81** .... PCO'Neill(7) 85
(Barry Potts, Ire) *led to run in: kpt on same pce* **25/1**
000- **4** *hd* **We'll Meet Again**[33] 3741 5-11-8 **84** .... MrTGreenall(3) 88
(M W Easterby) *hld up: drvn and no imp bef 3 out: hdwy next: kpt on wl run in* **12/1**
250- **5** *3* **Bridge Pal**[5] 4810 5-11-2 **85** ....(p) DDaSilva(10) 86
(P Monteith) *wl bhd tl gd hdwy appr 2 out: kpt on run in: no imp* **20/1**
00-4 **6** *½* **Prince Adjal (IRE)**[9] 149 5-11-6 **84** .... DCCostello(5) 85+
(G M Moore) *mstkes: cl up tl rdn and nt qckn between last two* **8/1**
6P0- **7** *4* **Sunnyside Royale (IRE)**[30] 4810 6-11-9 **85** ....(t) HBastiman(3) 81
(R Bastiman) *bhd: rdn bef 3 out: sme hdwy next: n.d* **12/1**
4P2- **8** *10* **Signed And Dated (USA)**[18] 4975 6-10-13 **82** ....(p) SGagan(10) 68
(Mrs E Slack) *bhd tl sme late hdwy: nvr on terms* **20/1**
PP-0 **9** *5* **Martin House (IRE)**[6] 192 6-11-9 **85** ....(v) ONelmes(3) 66
(D W Thompson) *cl up tl rdn and wknd fr 2 out* **33/1**
054- **10** *9* **The Rip**[165] 2483 4-11-8 **85** .... RGarritty 53
(T D Easterby) *midfield: hdwy and chsd ldrs 3 out: wknd after next* **11/2**[3]
14P/ **11** *8* **Lion Guest (IRE)**[634] 1143 8-11-12 **85** .... MBradburne 49
(Mrs S C Bradburne) *prom to 3 out: btn and eased next* **33/1**

PPP- **12** *3* **Sandy Bay (IRE)**[18] 4738 6-11-8 **81** ....(p) JPMcNamara 42
(W G Harrison) *a bhd* **100/1**
305- **13** *1* **Kalic D'Alm (FR)**[30] 4810 7-11-5 **78** .... DO'Meara 38
(W S Coltherd) *hld up: shortlived effrt 1/2-way: sn btn* **12/1**
30-0 **14** *18* **Neven**[13] 82 6-11-8 **84** ....(t) PBuchanan(3) 26
(Miss Lucinda V Russell) *a bhd: no ch fr 3 out* **14/1**
P20- **15** *2 ½* **Miss Ellie**[231] 1477 9-11-2 **80** .... DMcGann(5) 20
(Mrs C J Kerr) *in tch to 1/2-way: sn lost pl* **100/1**
050- **P** **Pacific Highway (IRE)**[50] 4511 6-11-7 **85** .... DFlavin(5) —
(Mrs L B Normile) *a bhd: t.o whn p.u bef 2 out* **50/1**
21-0 **U** **Polyphon (FR)**[13] 84 7-11-11 **84** .... GLee —
(P Monteith) *hld up: outpcd 4 out: no ch whn uns rdr bnd ent st* **5/2**[1]
P **Jungle Gingoes (IRE)**[85] 3872 5-11-10 **83** ....(b1) PACarberry —
(John G Carr, Ire) *a bhd: no ch whn blnd bdly and p.u 2 out* **16/1**

3m 54.6s (-6.00) **Going Correction** -0.30s/f (Good)
WFA 4 from 5yo+ 4lb **18** Ran SP% **135.3**
Speed ratings: **102,100,100,100,99 98,96,92,89,85 81,80,80,71,70** —,—,— CSF £111.67 CT £2380.45 TOTE £8.40: £2.50, £5.30, £7.40, £3.60; EX 444.50 Place 6 £79.75, Place 5 £36.94.
Owner R L Donn **Bred** James O'Connor **Trained** Dungannon, Co. Tyrone
■ Stewards' Enquiry : P C O'Neill two-day ban: careless riding (May 22,24)
S Gagan two-day ban: careless riding (May 22,24)

FOCUS
A low-grade event in which those that raced prominently held the edge. However, those in the frame ran to their marks and the race looks solid for the level.

NOTEBOOK
Poor Tactic's(IRE) has not been very consistent but elected to put his best foot forward to win an ordinary event. However, he left the impression that the return to further would be in his favour. *(op 9-1 tchd 10-1 in places)*
Kyle Of Lochalsh, with the headgear he wore for the first time last time, ran his best race for some time for a stable that is among the winners. This was not much of a race but he may be capable of a bit better.
Dream Castle(IRE) had not been in much form but had the run of the race and returned to something like his best. Whether this will be reproduced next time remains to be seen, though.
We'll Meet Again ran his best race over hurdles for some time but his record suggests he is no good thing to reproduce this next time. *(op 9-1)*
Bridge Pal was not disgraced in a truly-run race, but her record of no wins from 24 starts suggests she remains one to tread carefully with.
Prince Adjal(IRE) has not really progressed after his debut win and will have to brush up his jumping to do so on this evidence.
Polyphon(FR), reverting to hurdles and with patient tactics re-employed, was well below his chase form and is the type that needs things to fall perfectly. *(op 11-4 tchd 3-1 and 9-4 in places)*
T/Plt: £165.30 to a £1 stake. Pool: £41,569.35. 183.55 winning tickets. T/Qpdt: £98.80 to a £1 stake. Pool: £2,684.00. 20.10 winning tickets. RY

307 - 309a (Foreign Racing) - See Raceform Interactive

[173]LUDLOW (R-H)
Thursday, May 12

OFFICIAL GOING: Good to firm
Wind: slight, across Weather: fine

310 RED CROSS CONDITIONAL JOCKEYS' (S) H'CAP HURDLE (11 hdls) 2m 5f
5:40 (5:41) (Class 5) (0-95,94) 4-6-Y-0 **£2,541** (£726; £363)

Form RPR
36-6 **1** **Somewin (IRE)**[12] 134 5-9-6 **68** oh9........(p) RSpate(8) 73+
(Mrs K Waldron) *hld up: hdwy after 4 out: led 3 out: rdn out* **9/1**
P0-6 **2** *3* **Henry's Luck Penny (IRE)**[13] 96 5-9-6 **68** oh4........(p) PMerrigan(8) 70
(Mrs H Dalton) *hld up: hdwy appr 3 out: rdn to chse wnr 2 out: edgd lft and kpt on u.p run-in* **10/1**
FR-6 **3** *11* **Lord Attica (IRE)**[4] 229 6-9-11 **68** ....(b1) CPoste(3) 61+
(M F Harris) *trckd ldrs: led after 4 out: hdd next: wknd last* **12/1**
20P- **4** *12* **Royal Prodigy (USA)**[11] 4889 6-11-4 **94** .... JamesWhite(8) 73
(R J Hodges) *disp ld: def advantage 7th: hdd after 4 out: wknd appr 3 out* **5/2**[1]
5-06 **5** *¾* **Frambo (IRE)**[3] 263 4-10-10 **83** ....(b) PJBrennan 56
(J G Portman) *in tch: rdn and wknd appr 3 out* **10/1**
65-2 **6** *1 ¾* **Chickapeakray**[17] 23 4-10-0 **76** .... StephenJCraine(3) 48
(D McCain) *t.k.h: trckd ldrs: rdn and hung lft whn wkng after 4 out* **11/4**[2]
P0-5 **7** *dist* **Eastwell Violet**[17] 23 5-10-1 **72** .... DLaverty(3) —
(Mrs A M Thorpe) *disp ld: mstke and hdd 7th: wkng whn blnd 4 out: t.o* **4/1**[3]

5m 6.80s (-11.50) **Going Correction** -0.825s/f (Firm)
WFA 4 from 5yo+ 5lb **7** Ran SP% **111.1**
Speed ratings: **88,86,82,78,77 77,**— CSF £82.18 CT £1047.61 TOTE £13.80: £4.40, £4.50; EX 65.70.The winner was bought in for 9,000gns
Owner Nick Shutts **Bred** Bryan Ryan **Trained** Stoke Bliss, Worcs

FOCUS
A desperate seller run in a slow time with the third setting the level.

NOTEBOOK
Somewin(IRE) ran out a comfortable winner despite racing from 9lb out of the handicap. The longer trip appeared the answer. *(op 10-1)*
Henry's Luck Penny(IRE) had shown next to nothing previously, including in this grade. *(op 8-1)*
Lord Attica(IRE) wore blinkers for the first time, having been tried in cheekpieces and a visor before, and was rather keen. *(tchd 16-1)*
Royal Prodigy(USA), without the usual cheekpieces, was taken very steadily to post. He did not get home over this shorter trip. *Official explanation: jockey said gelding finished lame (op 2-1)*
Frambo(IRE) did not stay, which was surprising as she got two miles on the Flat. *(tchd 9-1)*
Eastwell Violet *Official explanation: jockey said mare finished lame (tchd 7-2 and 9-2)*

311 TANNERS WINES H'CAP CHASE (22 fncs) 3m 1f 110y
6:10 (6:10) (Class 3) (0-130,124) 5-Y-0+ **£8,096** (£2,491; £1,245; £622)

Form RPR
656- **1** **Moving Earth (IRE)**[25] 4880 12-11-4 **116** .... CLlewellyn 124
(A W Carroll) *hld up: hdwy appr 15th: chsd ldr 2 out: r.o to ld post* **10/1**
22-1 **2** *shd* **Curtins Hill (IRE)**[15] 55 11-11-7 **119** .... APMcCoy 127
(T R George) *midfield: hdwy 9th: led 15th: rdn appr last: hung lft run-in: ct post* **11/4**[1]
14P- **3** *1 ¾* **Parisian Storm (IRE)**[25] 4886 9-11-0 **112** .... AThornton 118
(Evan Williams) *hld up: hdwy 12th: lost pl bef 15th: rallied appr 4 out: styd on wl after last* **14/1**
P6-1 **4** *5* **Tom's Prize**[18] 12 10-11-5 **124** .... TJDreaper(7) 126+
(J L Spearing) *j.lft: led 2nd: hdd 15th: rdn appr 4 out: wknd last* **6/1**[3]
46-6 **5** *30* **Tribal Dancer (IRE)**[13] 112 11-10-0 **98** oh2........ AO'Keeffe 74+
(Miss Venetia Williams) *led to 2nd: remained prom: j.rt fr 13th: wknd 17th* **10/3**[2]

04-5 **6** *7* **Bright Approach (IRE)**[10] [150] 12-11-1 **116**........................ TJMalone(3) 80
(J G Cann) *trckd ldrs: blnd 2nd: sn lost pl: brief effrt appr 15th: sn btn* **10/1**

430- **7** *18* **Ballyvaddy (IRE)**[45] [4612] 9-11-6 **118**........................(v) SDurack 64
(J A Geake) *trckd ldrs: hit 10th and lost pl: sn bhd* **8/1**

10-P **8** *12* **Talbot Lad**[18] [4] 9-11-2 **114**........................(t) LAspell 48
(S A Brookshaw) *in tch tl rdn and wknd 17th* **20/1**

PP0- **9** *8* **Heart Midoltian (FR)**[20] [4972] 8-11-4 **116**........................(vt) JEMoore 42
(M C Pipe) *midfield: pckd 10th: hdwy 16th: wknd after 18th: n.d whn mstke 3 out* **20/1**

300- **U** **Make Haste Slowly**[141] [2937] 8-10-13 **111**........................ RJohnson —
(H D Daly) *hld up: mstke and uns rdr 15th* **16/1**

6m 17.3s (-17.90) **Going Correction** -0.70s/f (Firm) **10** Ran SP% **115.4**
Speed ratings: **99,98,98,96,87 85,79,76,73,**— CSF £38.76 CT £386.50 TOTE £9.80: £3.10, £1.40, £3.30; EX 36.00.
Owner Pursuit Media **Bred** Daniel C And Patrick Keating **Trained** Cropthorne, Worcs

FOCUS
Quite a competitive handicap with the third rated as having run to his best.

NOTEBOOK
Moving Earth(IRE), back over a more suitable trip, kept straight after the last and caught the hanging leader right on the line. *(op 8-1)*
Curtins Hill(IRE), successful in heavy ground at Exeter, for which he was raised 6lb, coped with these very different conditions. He looked in command all the way up the home straight, but after going a little to his right over the last he then hung left on the run-in and was touched off. *(op 3-1)*
Parisian Storm(IRE) ◆ lost his pitch towards the end of the back straight, but he rallied once in line for home and was closing the gap after the last. He looks one to keep an eye on.
Tom's Prize, raised 4lb, ran another honest race from the front but gave the impression he would be happier back on a left-handed track. *(op 9-2)*
Tribal Dancer(IRE), 10lb lower than when landing this event a year ago, did not last long in front. *(op 7-2 tchd 4-1 and 3-1)*
Ballyvaddy(IRE), equipped with a visor instead of cheekpieces, dropped to the back of the field with more than a circuit to run. He looks one to avoid for the time being. *(op 7-1)*
Heart Midoltian(FR), who has fallen steadily through the handicap during a lengthy spell in the doldrums, did not stay this trip. *(op 16-1)*

312 MOORE SCOTT NOVICES' H'CAP HURDLE (9 hdls) 2m
6:40 (6:41) (Class 3) (0-120,110) 4-Y-0+ **£4,667** (£1,436; £718; £359)

Form RPR

24-1 **1** **Phar Out Phavorite (IRE)**[14] [78] 6-11-8 **106**........................(v) NFehily 117+
(Miss E C Lavelle) *chsd ldr: led after 4 out: rdn and hung rt whn mstke 3 out: j.rt and mstke last: styd on wl* **7/2**[3]

35-2 **2** *4* **Absolut Power (GER)**[9] [177] 4-11-3 **105**........................(p) SDurack 107
(J A Geake) *led: hdd after 4 out: rdn appr next: j.rt last: no ex run-in* **9/4**[2]

3-11 **3** *4* **Mr Mischief**[7] [192] 5-11-12 **110**........................ APMcCoy 113+
(P C Haslam) *chsd ldrs: rdn appr 3 out: btn whn j.rt and hit last* **6/5**[1]

0P-0 **4** *dist* **Contas (GER)**[9] [177] 5-10-3 **87**........................(t) PJBrennan —
(M F Harris) *hld up: hdwy 5th: rdn after 4 out: sn wknd: n.d whn blnd 2 out: t.o* **40/1**

620- **P** **Amnesty**[9] [4482] 6-10-11 **95**........................(b) JEMoore —
(G L Moore) *t.k.h: a bhd: blnd 3rd: t.o whn p.u after 4 out* **8/1**

3m 38.4s (-13.90) **Going Correction** -0.825s/f (Firm)
WFA 4 from 5yo+ 4lb **5** Ran SP% **112.0**
Speed ratings: **101,99,97,**—,— CSF £12.17 TOTE £4.40: £1.30, £2.30; EX 15.10.
Owner Favourites Racing V **Bred** Mrs J Wilkinson **Trained** Wildhern, Hants

FOCUS
A fair little contest with the third to mark and the form should work out.

NOTEBOOK
Phar Out Phavorite(IRE) supplemented his Hereford win off a 6lb higher mark. He was in control up the home straight despite a couple of untidy jumps. *(op 3-1)*
Absolut Power(GER) raced keenly in the first-time cheekpieces but was held by the winner over the final three flights. He is due to race off 5lb higher now. *(tchd 2-1 and 5-2)*
Mr Mischief, on a hat-trick mission, was unpenalised for his win in a conditionals' race last time but the Handicapper left him on the same mark anyway. Unable to get to the first two when the pressure was on, he might have found conditions too fast. *(op 5-4, tchd 11-10 and 11-8 in places)*
Amnesty has been running creditably in blinkers on the Flat of late, but he looked less than *enthusiastic wearing the aids for the first time over hurdles.Official explanation: jockey said gelding was never travelling (op 9-1 tchd 10-1)*

313 LUDLOW FINAL HUNTERS' CHASE (17 fncs) 2m 4f
7:10 (7:14) (Class 6) 5-Y-0+ **£2,712** (£775; £387)

Form RPR

3/2- **1** **Longstone Boy (IRE)**[11] 13-11-11 87........................ DJacob(5) 107+
(E R Clough) *trckd ldrs: mstke 6th: sltly outpcd after 13th: rallied to ld 3 out: clr last: comf* **14/1**

43-P **2** *4* **Montifault (FR)**[15] [48] 10-12-2 120........................(t) MrNWilliams 104+
(P F Nicholls) *prom: mstke 6th: blnd 12th: led after 13th: hdd 3 out: no ex run-in* **11/10**[1]

3U-2 **3** *17* **Enitsag (FR)**[15] [52] 6-11-9 94........................ MrMWalford(7) 93+
(S Flook) *mstke and rdr lost iron 1st: bhd: hdwy 8th: n.m.r on bnd after 13th: kpt on fr 3 out: nt trble ldrs* **5/1**[2]

PP/1 **4** *¾* **Willy Willy**[14] [79] 12-11-13........................ MrJSnowden(3) 86+
(Mrs Caroline Keevil) *in tch: blnd 6th: rdn to chse ldrs appr 4 out: wknd bef last* **9/1**

5 *5* **The Unamed Man**[11] 9-11-5........................ MrAWadlow(7) 76
(J Groucott) *midfield: kpt on fr after 13th: nvr on terms* **66/1**

0F/ **6** *15* **Holding The Fort (IRE)**[74] 11-11-9........................ MrDBarlow(3) 61
(I Anderson) *chsd ldrs to 11th: btn whn mstke 4 out and blnd next* **50/1**

0-00 **7** *6* **Epsilo De La Ronce (FR)**[5] [221] 13-11-6 88 ow1....(p) MrPaulMorris(7) 56
(Paul Morris) *a bhd* **25/1**

030- **8** *12* **Fairtoto**[19] 9-11-5 71........................ MissAdeLisleWells(7) 43
(M D Jones) *midfield: bhd fr 6th* **33/1**

U **P** **Thebigfellow (IRE)**[18] [6] 8-11-5........................ MrRQuinn(7) —
(Richard Mathias) *a bhd: hit 5th: t.o whn p.u bef 10th* **66/1**

100/ **P** **Leaburn (IRE)**[25] 12-11-5........................ MissJHouldey(7) —
(Miss J Houldey) *a bhd: mstke 6th: t.o whn p.u bef 3 out* **25/1**

6U3- **P** **Wahiba Sands**[5] 12-11-7 107........................(p) MissLucyBridges(5) —
(Miss Lucy Bridges) *a bhd: t.o whn p.u bef 4 out* **14/1**

P5P/ **P** **The Welder**[10] 11-11-5........................(v[1]) MrMWall(7) —
(Miss S Jackson) *in tch: wkng whn blnd 12th: t.o whn p.u bef 4 out* **66/1**

2- **P** **Cider Man**[59] [4372] 10-11-12........................ MrJMPritchard —
(Mrs J Hughes) *midfield: mstke 6th: sn bhd: t.o whn p.u bef 4 out: dismntd* **13/2**[3]

F16- **U** **Step Quick (IRE)**[25] 11-11-9 92........................ MrGPWright(7) 90
(Mrs S E Busby) *midfield: pckd 5th: hdwy 12th: 4th and 5 l down whn mstke and uns rdr 3 out* **16/1**

11P/ **F** **Waterlaw (IRE)**[32] 11-11-9........................(t) MrTPFaulkner(7) —
(Mrs D C Faulkner) *led: blnd 3rd and 12th: hdd after 13th: niggled along in 2nd whn fell 4 out* **25/1**

4m 54.2s (-16.50) **Going Correction** -0.70s/f (Firm) **15** Ran SP% **127.8**
Speed ratings: **105,103,96,96,94 88,85,81,**—,— —,—,—,—,— CSF £31.32 TOTE £19.70: £4.10, £1.60, £2.80; EX 45.50.
Owner E R Clough **Bred** Mrs Diane C Watts **Trained** Narberth, Pembrokes

FOCUS
A reasonable hunter chase rated around the third and fourth.

NOTEBOOK
Longstone Boy(IRE) won two ladies' point-to-points in Wales during March. He was a little outpaced by the two in front of him on the long home turn, but steadily closed the gap and scored readily in the end. *(op 12-1)*
Montifault(FR) eased to the front on the long home turn but had no answers when headed three from home. He is more effective over further. *(op 5-4 tchd 11-8 in places)*
Enitsag(FR) stayed on from a good way back to snatch third near the line. *(op 6-1)*
Willy Willy, who won a weak race at Hereford, ran as well as could be expected and was only caught for third close home. *(op 10-1)*
The Unamed Man won a brace of points two years ago but had failed to get round in eight attempts between the flags since. *(op 100-1)*
Waterlaw(IRE), a winning handicapper when trained by Martin Pipe, had been pulled up in both his point-to-points this year. After setting a decent pace, he was in second when taking a crashing fall at the first fence in the home straight. *(op 33-1)*
Step Quick(IRE), a winner of three point-to-points this year under his inexperienced rider, might have finished third had he not departed three from home. *(op 33-1)*

314 WHITE COMPANY "NATIONAL HUNT" INTERMEDIATE HURDLE (9 hdls) 2m
7:40 (7:46) (Class 4) 4-Y-0+ **£3,970** (£1,221; £610; £305)

Form RPR

F0F- **1** **Reseda (GER)**[27] [4847] 6-10-12 105........................ APMcCoy 88+
(Ian Williams) *a.p: hit 2nd: led 4th: clr 3 out: comf* **4/7**[1]

3P-2 **2** *6* **Lyricist's Dream**[12] [134] 6-10-5 74........................ JPByrne 71
(R L Brown) *led: hdd 4th: rdn and outpcd after 4 out: chsd wnr 3 out: no ex run-in* **7/2**[2]

0P- **3** *4* **Master Fox**[25] [4885] 7-10-12........................ RJohnson 74
(T R George) *t.k.h: hld up: hdwy appr 3 out: wknd after last* **9/1**[3]

F50- **4** *8* **Pink Harbour**[95] [3724] 7-10-7 76........................ StephenJCraine(5) 66
(D McCain) *prom: rdn and wkng whn hit 3 out* **10/1**

0P-P **5** *15* **Distant Romance**[5] [217] 8-9-12 84........................ RLucey-Butler(7) 44
(Miss Z C Davison) *hld up: stmbld 5th: effrt after 4 out: sn wknd* **28/1**

0-P **6** *dist* **Middleton Kate**[9] [178] 5-10-5........................ PFlynn —
(John R Upson) *in tch: lost pl 4th: sn bhd: t.o* **40/1**

3m 41.8s (-10.50) **Going Correction** -0.825s/f (Firm)
WFA 4 from 5yo+ 4lb **6** Ran SP% **110.9**
Speed ratings: **93,90,88,84,76** — CSF £2.89 TOTE £1.50: £1.10, £1.80; EX 2.90.
Owner R J Turton **Bred** Gestut Gorlsdorf **Trained** Portway, Worcs

FOCUS
An uncompetitive and uneventful affair run in a moderate time. The winner is value for more than the official margin but the form looks weak.

NOTEBOOK
Reseda(GER), who had fallen on two of her last three runs, had a stone in hand on official figures and won with the minimum of fuss. *(tchd 4-6)*
Lyricist's Dream is an honest mare and her turn should come. *(op 4-1)*
Master Fox, having only his second run over hurdles, may have trouble staying the trip. *(op 14-1)*
Pink Harbour, returning after a three-month break, needs easier ground. *(op 8-1)*
Distant Romance, a huge mare, showed little on this return to hurdling. *(op 16-1)*

315 WEATHERBYS INSURANCE H'CAP HURDLE (12 hdls) 3m
8:10 (8:10) (Class 3) (0-125,120) 4-Y-0+ **£5,768** (£1,774; £887; £443)

Form RPR

01-2 **1** **Rift Valley (IRE)**[18] [5] 10-10-11 **105**........................(v) RJohnson 111+
(P J Hobbs) *a.p: led appr 8th: rdn and hung lft bef 3 out: j.rt fnl 3: hung lft again run-in: drvn out* **1/1**[1]

42P- **2** *3* **Idaho D'Ox (FR)**[19] [4982] 9-11-12 **120**........................ TScudamore 121
(M C Pipe) *hld up: hdwy appr 4 out: chsd wnr bef next: one pce run-in* **9/2**[2]

22P- **3** *2½* **Lord Nellsson**[154] [2734] 9-10-6 **100**........................ PJBrennan 98
(J S King) *led: hdd appr 8th: rdn bef 3 out: no ex run-in* **16/1**

50-5 **4** *5* **Burundi (IRE)**[18] [5] 11-10-12 **106**........................ NFehily 100+
(A W Carroll) *hld up: hit 6th: rdn and hdwy appr 3 out: wknd run-in* **7/1**[3]

000- **5** *dist* **Count Tony**[30] [4817] 11-11-2 **115**........................(p) LStephens(5) —
(Mrs D A Hamer) *prom: nt fluent 7th: sn niggled along: wknd after 4 out: n.d whn mstke next: t.o* **16/1**

110- **F** **It's Definite (IRE)**[190] [1982] 6-11-9 **117**........................(p) SDurack —
(P Bowen) *prom tl fell 5th* **9/2**[2]

5m 36.6s (-18.00) **Going Correction** -0.825s/f (Firm) course record **6** Ran SP% **110.6**
Speed ratings: **97,96,95,93,**— — CSF £5.97 CT £37.89 TOTE £1.60: £1.30, £2.20; EX 8.60.
Owner Mrs Kathy Stuart **Bred** Mrs Anne Macdermott **Trained** Withycombe, Somerset

FOCUS
This was not the most competitive of handicaps but the placed horses ran to their marks giving the form a fairly sound appearance.

NOTEBOOK
Rift Valley(IRE) enhanced his excellent win record when visored, despite racing from a 5lb higher mark than when beaten at odds on here last time. The longer trip helped, and he stayed on well despite jumping to his right at each of the last three flights and hanging the opposite way on the flat. *(op 11-10 tchd 5-4 and 11-8 in places)*
Idaho D'Ox(FR), down in grade, ran a respectable race but could not give away 15lb to the winner. He remains hard to win with.
Lord Nellsson ran his race on this first start since December but he is still to get his head in front. *(op 14-1)*
Burundi(IRE), who is dropping down the weights, was eventually found out by this longer trip. *(op 5-1 tchd 8-1)*
It's Definite(IRE) took a heavy fall on this first run since November. *(tchd 7-2)*

316 ST JOHN AMBULANCE STANDARD OPEN NATIONAL HUNT FLAT RACE 2m
8:40 (8:40) (Class 6) 4-6-Y-O **£2,534** (£724; £362)

Form RPR

1 **Keralam (FR)** 5-11-2........................ JTizzard 102+
(B G Powell) *trckd ldrs: wnt 2nd 3f out: led 2f out: pushed out* **4/1**[3]

2 *1½* **Princess Yum Yum** 5-10-9........................ LFletcher 92
(J L Spearing) *hld up in rr: hdwy 3f out: rdn and ev ch 2f out: nt qckn fnl f* **14/1**

2- **3** *2* **Crafty Lady (IRE)**[21] 4941 6-10-9 .... MBatchelor 90
(Miss Suzy Smith) *t.k.h: a.p: led over 3f out: hdd 2f out: kpt on same pce* **6/4**[1]

0- **4** *10* **Danbury (FR)**[24] 4916 5-11-2 .... LAspell 87
(O Sherwood) *hld up: rdn 5f out: wknd over 3f out* **2/1**[2]

5 *16* **Saddlers Lady (IRE)** 5-10-9 .... TDoyle 70+
(R Curtis) *led: hdd over 3f out: rdn and hung lft whn sn wknd* **6/1**

3m 41.0s (-11.20) **Going Correction** -0.825s/f (Firm)
WFA 4 from 5yo+ 4lb **5** Ran SP% **114.3**
Speed ratings: **95,94,93,88,80** CSF £47.19 TOTE £5.80: £1.80, £5.50; EX 52.30 Place 6 £125.94, Place 5 £6.73.
Owner Jim McCarthy **Bred** S A Aga Khan **Trained** Moretead, Hants

FOCUS
A weak bumper rated through the placed horses to their marks, but could be too high.

NOTEBOOK
Keralam(FR), out of a mare who won the Group Three Anglesey Stakes at two but failed to train on, changed hands for 6,500 gns as a three-year-old. Clearly travelling best turning for home, she was a comfortable winner of this weak race. *(tchd 5-1)*
Princess Yum Yum, whose dam never ran, showed the right attitude on this debut but the winner was too good. *(op 10-1)*
Crafty Lady(IRE), two places in front of subsequent winner None-So-Pretty at Fontwell, was found wanting in the final quarter-mile. She may need a stiffer test. *(op 11-10)*
Danbury(FR) looks a limited perfomer although he is entitled to improve when tackling a longer trip. *(op 11-4)*
Saddlers Lady(IRE) is bred to stay, being out of a mare who won two hurdles and a staying handicap on the Flat for the Curtis yard as well as finishing second in the Ascot Stakes. *(op 9-2 tchd 13-2)*
T/Plt: £213.60 to a £1 stake. Pool: £27,077.90. 92.50 winning tickets. T/Qpdt: £3.50 to a £1 stake. Pool: £3,449.90. 726.70 winning tickets. DO

301 PERTH (R-H)
Thursday, May 12

OFFICIAL GOING: Good to firm (good in places)
Wind: light, half across

317 PRICEWATERHOUSECOOPERS INTERMEDIATE HURDLE (12 hdls) 3m 110y
2:20 (2:20) (Class 4) 4-Y-0+ **£3,474** (£1,069; £534; £267)

Form RPR
2P5- **1** **Hot Weld**[20] 4967 6-11-9 117 .... KJMercer(3) 105+
(Ferdy Murphy) *mde all: rdn and styd on strly fr 2 out* **6/4**[1]

1P-2 **2** *7* **Iris's Prince**[14] 85 6-11-6 110 .... NPMulholland 89
(A Crook) *cl up: effrt bef 2 out: kpt on same pce last* **10/3**[2]

/0F- **3** *1 1/4* **High Bird Humphrey**[150] 2807 6-11-0 .... GLee 82
(Miss V Scott) *hld up: hdwy 4 out: effrt bef 2 out: one pce last* **16/1**

45-3 **4** *18* **Uneven Line**[12] 124 9-10-4 81 .... MrCStorey(3) 57
(Miss S E Forster) *chsd ldrs: outpcd 4 out: n.d after* **12/1**

5 *1/2* **Greenfort Brave (IRE)**[87] 3990 7-11-0 79 .... JLCullen 64
(J J Lambe, Ire) *chsd ldrs tl rdn and wknd bef 2 out* **25/1**

2FP- **6** *dist* **Mr Auchterlonie (IRE)**[47] 4551 8-11-0 95 .... ADobbin —
(L Lungo) *hld up in tch: stdy hdwy 8th: wknd after next* **4/1**[3]

250- **7** *dist* **Allez Scotia**[56] 4413 6-10-2 93 .... DCCostello(5) —
(R Nixon) *hld up: struggling 8th: sn btn* **11/1**

0-6 **8** *1/2* **The Maystone (IRE)**[15] 59 5-10-11 .... PBuchanan(3) —
(B Mactaggart) *nt fluent in rr: lost tch fr 4 out* **50/1**

6m 4.00s (-6.90) **Going Correction** -0.30s/f (Good) **8** Ran SP% **110.8**
Speed ratings: **99,96,96,90,90** —,—,— CSF £6.23 TOTE £2.60: £1.30, £1.20, £5.10; EX 4.50.
Owner S Hubbard Rodwell **Bred** Cartmel Bloodstock **Trained** West Witton, N Yorks

FOCUS
No strength in depth to this modest event, which was run at a steady early pace, and the first three came well clear. The winner did not have to be at his best to score.

NOTEBOOK
Hot Weld dictated the gallop from the off, and when asked to win his race from two out, quickened readily and ran out a clear-cut winner. He enjoyed this decent ground, does look best when able to dominate and he has the potential to keep improving when sent over fences in the autumn. *(tchd 7-4)*
Iris's Prince had his chance yet failed to see out this longer trip. He can win again at this level during the summer when reverting in trip, yet is another who appeals as the type to only peak when going chasing in due course. *(op 4-1 tchd 3-1)*
High Bird Humphrey, stepping up to three miles for the first time on this debut for new connections, turned in his best effort to date over hurdles and his confidence should have been boosted in the process. However, he was no match for the first two. *(op 14-1)*
Uneven Line failed to muster a change of pace when the tempo increased before four out and was well held. She remains a maiden under Rules.
Mr Auchterlonie(IRE), reverting to hurdles, again disappointed and he continues to frustrate. *(op 7-2)*

318 CORNELIAN ASSET MANAGERS INTERMEDIATE CHASE (12 fncs) 2m
2:50 (2:52) (Class 3) 5-Y-0+ **£5,395** (£1,660; £830; £415)

Form RPR
04-6 **1** **Moscow Dancer (IRE)**[15] 60 8-11-0 90 .... NPMulholland 113+
(P Monteith) *hld up: hdwy 8th: effrt 3 out: led last: edgd rt: kpt on wl* **20/1**

12-0 **2** *1 1/2* **Noblefir (IRE)**[7] 197 7-11-6 109 .... BGibson 117+
(L Lungo) *led and clr to 4 out: jnd next: hdd and hit last: edgd rt: kpt on* **11/2**[3]

405- **3** *3* **Gone Too Far**[167] 2465 7-11-6 112 .... (v) GLee 113
(P Monteith) *hld up: hdwy bef 3 out: kpt on fr next: no imp run in* **11/2**[3]

/22- **4** *1/2* **Kombinacja (POL)**[341] 642 7-10-7 .... RThornton 102+
(T R George) *blnd 1st: hit next: chsd clr ldr: effrt and ev ch 3 out: one pce after next* **11/10**[1]

4PP- **5** *13* **Simply Da Best (IRE)**[47] 4573 7-11-0 .... (b) JLCullen 97+
(J J Lambe, Ire) *hld up in tch: outpcd 8th: 6l down whn blnd bdly 3 out: no imp* **33/1**

P03- **6** *5* **The Miner**[20] 4968 7-11-3 92 .... MrCStorey(3) 100+
(Miss S E Forster) *in tch: outpcd whn hit 4 out: sn btn* **25/1**

3P5- **7** *11* **Vandas Choice (IRE)**[26] 4859 7-12-1 135 .... PBuchanan(3) 96
(Miss Lucinda V Russell) *prom tl lost pl bef 4 out: sn btn* **10/3**[2]

(-2.80) **Going Correction** -0.225s/f (Good) **7** Ran SP% **113.0**
Speed ratings: **98,97,95,95,89 86,81** CSF £119.06 TOTE £14.60: £5.50, £3.00; EX 138.80.
Owner J Stephenson **Bred** Gerald Mitchell **Trained** Rosewell, Midlothian
■ Stewards' Enquiry : B Gibson one-day ban: used whip without giving gelding time to respond (May 24)

FOCUS
A modest chase, run at a sound gallop, which produced a shock winner and the form may be suspect, although the runner-up fifth and six were close to their marks.

NOTEBOOK
Moscow Dancer(IRE) improved vastly on his previous chasing form and opened his account over fences at the fourth time of asking with a gritty success. He has proved hard to catch right since resuming in March this year after a long layoff, and this success will see him go up plenty in the ratings now, but he was progressive over hurdles in 2003 and could be on the up.*Official explanation: trainer said, regarding the improved form shown, gelding was suited by today's faster ground (tchd 25-1)*
Noblefir(IRE) set off at a brisk pace, and may have been a touch closer but for an error at the final fence, yet he was a sitting duck for the winner at that point. This was another fair effort, and he was nicely clear of the third horse, so should pick up another race over fences during the summer months. *(op 4-1)*
Gone Too Far, having his first outing since November 2004, ran a satisfactory race and should improve plenty for this experience. He has slipped to fair mark and should be placed to get closer during the summer. *(op 6-1)*
Kombinacja(POL), rated 120 over hurdles and well backed for this chasing bow, was none too fluent throughout and failed to quicken when it mattered. She is entitled to improve for the experience, but must do so in order to progress in this sphere. *(op 6-4)*
Vandas Choice(IRE) looked uneasy on the faster ground and his fate was apparent from some way out. *(op 5-2)*

319 BILL AND BUNNY CADOGAN MEMORIAL H'CAP HURDLE (9 hdls 1 omitted) 2m 4f 110y
3:25 (3:26) (Class 4) (0-110,109) 4-Y-0+ **£5,109** (£1,572; £786; £393)

Form RPR
3F6- **1** **Bodfari Signet**[74] 4088 9-11-12 109 .... MBradburne 112+
(Mrs S C Bradburne) *hld up: hdwy bef 2 out: kpt on run in: no ch w wnr: fin 2nd, 10l: awrdd r* **4/1**[1]

326- **2** *10 3/4* **Litron (IRE)**[188] 2029 8-11-3 100 .... JLCullen 101
(J J Lambe, Ire) *chsd ldr: effrt bef 2 out: kpt on same pce: fin 3rd, 10l & 3/4l plcd 2nd* **11/2**[2]

156- **3** *nk* **I Got Rhythm**[21] 4948 7-10-12 95 .... JimCrowley 96
(K G Reveley) *in tch: drvn bef 2 out: sn one pce: fin 4th: plcd 3rd* **11/2**[2]

004- **4** *8* **Lutin Du Moulin (FR)**[45] 4626 6-10-7 90 .... BGibson 83
(L Lungo) *hld up: drvn 7th: no imp fr 2 out: fin 5th: plcd 4th* **6/1**[3]

1P/0 **5** *19* **Blue Venture (IRE)**[15] 61 5-10-12 95 .... ADempsey 69
(B Mactaggart) *hld up: hdwy 1/2-way: wknd bef 2 out: fin 6th: plcd 5th* **20/1**

160- **6** *16* **Welsh Dream**[31] 4812 8-10-9 95 .... MrCStorey(3) 53
(Miss S E Forster) *in tch tl rdn and outpcd fr 7th: fin 7th: plcd 6th* **11/2**[2]

000- **7** *9* **Test Of Faith**[31] 4812 6-9-9 83 oh1 .... DCCostello(5) 32
(J N R Billinge) *bhd: rdn and no ch fr 7th: fin 8th: plcd 7th* **33/1**

OP-3 **D** **Supply And Fix (IRE)**[1] 301 7-9-7 83 oh5 .... MissJAKidd(7) 96+
(J J Lambe, Ire) *led and sn clr: tk wrong crse bef omitted 3 out: kpt on wl: fin 1st, 10l: disqualified* **11/2**[2]

53/- **P** **Golden Hawk (USA)**[1093] 251 10-10-0 83 oh10 .... KJohnson —
(R M Clark) *s.s: a bhd: t.o whn p.u bef 2 out* **33/1**

005- **P** **Tullimoss (IRE)**[20] 4969 10-9-11 83 oh1 .... KJMercer(3) —
(J N R Billinge) *keen: hld up: outpcd 7th: tk wrong crse at omitted 3 out: p.u next* **7/1**

5m 0.90s (-7.30) **Going Correction** -0.30s/f (Good) **10** Ran SP% **119.0**
Speed ratings: **97,96,96,93,86 80,76,101**,—,— CSF £26.61 CT £121.47 TOTE £3.80: £2.10, £1.60, £1.80; EX 36.40.
Owner Strath Pack Partnership **Bred** C J Hill **Trained** Cunnoquhie, Fife
■ Stewards' Enquiry : J L Cullen two-day ban: used whip with excessive force (May 24,25)
Miss J A Kidd 14-day ban: went wrong side of the dolls on the home bend (May 24-31, Jun 2, 4-9)

FOCUS
An unsatisfactory result to this moderate handicap, which saw the clear-cut winner disqualified for taking the wrong course at the bypassed third-last flight. The form still looks solid enough for the class, however.

NOTEBOOK
Bodfari Signet was firmly put in his place by the winner and was doing all of his best work late in that day. He has to rate a very fortunate winner to get the race in the Stewards' room. *(op 9-2)*
Litron(IRE), who refused at the final fence when last seen in action in 2004, showed the benefit of a break and turned in a much more encouraging effort on this return to hurdling. *(op 10-1)*
I Got Rhythm ran close to her mark and was not disgraced. She remains in the Handicapper's grip, however, and probably needs to drop back in class. *(op 6-1)*
Lutin Du Moulin(FR) *(op 5-1 tchd 7-1 in a place)*
Supply And Fix(IRE), who improved greatly to finish third over course and distance just 24 hours previously, confirmed that form with a comfortable success from the front. However, his rider took the wrong course at the omitted hurdle three out and he was subsequently disqualified from first place. He will now find life much tougher off a higher mark and has to rate as most unlucky. *(op 5-1)*

320 GRANT THORNTON INTERMEDIATE H'CAP HURDLE (8 hdls) 2m 110y
4:00 (4:00) (Class 4) (0-105,105) 4-Y-0+ **£4,778** (£1,470; £735; £367)

Form RPR
440- **1** **Travel (POL)**[197] 1854 5-11-12 105 .... RThornton 112
(T R George) *trckd ldrs: led and hung lft fr 2 out: drvn and hld on wl run in* **7/2**[1]

/6F- **2** *nk* **Heraclitean Fire (IRE)**[85] 3894 8-11-2 95 .... JLCullen 102
(J J Lambe, Ire) *in tch: smooth hdwy to chal 2 out: sn rdn: n.m.r run in: kpt on towards fin* **9/1**

51-0 **3** *5* **Lofty Leader (IRE)**[14] 82 6-11-3 99 .... ONelmes(3) 101
(Mrs H O Graham) *bhd tl styd on fr 2 out: mstke last: no ch w first two* **14/1**

00-1 **4** *shd* **Royal Glen (IRE)**[12] 120 7-10-3 82 .... RMcGrath 84
(W S Coltherd) *in tch: effrt bef 2 out: one pce appr last* **6/1**[3]

PP-0 **5** *4* **Word Gets Around (IRE)**[15] 61 7-11-4 97 .... ADobbin 96+
(L Lungo) *cl up: led 3 out to next: sn outpcd* **9/2**[2]

300- **6** *16* **Olympic Storm (IRE)**[20] 4969 7-10-9 88 .... PRobson 70
(N W Alexander) *hld up in tch: rdn and wknd bef 2 out* **25/1**

OP-0 **7** *4* **Casterflo**[5] 210 6-10-0 79 oh6 .... DO'Meara 57
(W S Coltherd) *bhd: drvn along 1/2-way: nvr on terms* **66/1**

63-0 **8** *11* **Off The Edge (AUS)**[18] 9 6-10-2 81 .... BHarding 48
(N G Richards) *hld up: rdn 3 out: btn next* **8/1**

223- **9** *13* **Named At Dinner**[39] 4709 4-10-6 92 .... (p) PBuchanan(3) 42
(Miss Lucinda V Russell) *led to 5th: wknd next* **8/1**

10 *3* **Luxi River (USA)**[145] 2909 5-11-2 95 .... (p) BMCash 46
(Michael McElhone, Ire) *cl up: led 5th to 3 out: rdn and wknd bef next* **10/1**

44-6 **U** **Five Gold (IRE)**[10] 149 4-9-13 89 .... EWhillans(7) —
(A C Whillans) *uns rdr 1st* **8/1**

20-0 **P** **King's Envoy (USA)**[14] 82 6-11-2 95 .... JimCrowley —
(Mrs J C McGregor) *bhd: t.o and p.u bef 5th* **16/1**

3m 57.2s (-3.40) **Going Correction** -0.30s/f (Good)
WFA 4 from 5yo+ 4lb 12 Ran SP% **125.0**
Speed ratings: **96,95,93,93,91 84,82,76,70,69** —,— CSF £37.74 CT £411.21 TOTE £3.90: £1.90, £3.70, £4.60; EX 80.10.
Owner Mrs Sharon C Nelson **Bred** Adam Milewski **Trained** Slad, Gloucs
■ Stewards' Enquiry : J L Cullen three-day ban: used whip with excessive force (May 26-28)
R Thornton two-day ban: careless riding (May 24-25)

FOCUS
A modest time for the grade, but the form appears fairly solid for the class.

NOTEBOOK
Travel(POL) , returning from more than three months off the track, hung left when in front two out, but still had enough guts to repel the runner-up late on and score a second course and distance success. This was his best effort to date, and while he remains open to further progression on this ground, he may just be at his best when fresh.
Heraclitean Fire(IRE) looked the most likely winner before two out but, despite being tight for room on the run-in, found less than expected under pressure and was just held at the finish. He may just be at his best over a touch further, but handled this faster ground well and a reproduction of this effort should see him gain compensation soon. *(op 8-1)*
Lofty Leader(IRE) , making his handicap debut, was staying on all too late yet still posted an improved display. He can progress again when reverting to an easier surface.
Royal Glen(IRE) , winner of a seller last time over this trip at Hexham, had her chance and was not at all disgraced in this better event.
Word Gets Around(IRE) had his chance, but failed to quicken when it mattered. Although he has become disappointing, this has to rate as a more enocuraging effort, and he could find a race from this lowly mark if able to build on this. *(tchd 5-1)*

321 ALLIED IRISH BANK (GB) H'CAP CHASE (18 fncs) 3m
4:35 (4:36) (Class 3) (0-115,114) 5-Y-0+ **£6,955** (£2,140; £1,070; £535)

Form RPR
UU6- **1** **Stack The Pack (IRE)**[20] 4969 8-10-2 **90**.............. RThornton 102+
(T R George) *cl up: hit 6th: mstke 10th: kpt on wl fr 3 out* **11/4**[2]
63-5 **2** *3 1/2* **World Vision (IRE)**[13] 112 8-11-7 **112**.............. KJMercer(3) 117+
(Ferdy Murphy) *hld up: hdwy to chse wnr 13th: effrt 3 out: kpt on same pce last* **5/1**
122- **3** *25* **Catch The Perk (IRE)**[27] 4850 8-11-9 **114**.............. PBuchanan(3) 93
(Miss Lucinda V Russell) *chsd ldrs: outpcd 1/2-way: rallied 13th: outpcd bef 3 out* **4/1**[3]
031- **4** *19* **Panmure (IRE)**[19] 4980 9-10-6 **94**.............. JimCrowley 54
(P D Niven) *hld up: drvn bef 4 out: nvr able to chal* **10/1**
12-2 **5** *8* **Lodestar (IRE)**[10] 150 8-11-3 **105**..............(b) GLee 57
(Ian Williams) *prom: blnd and lost pl 11th: n.d after* **9/4**[1]
4PF/ **6** *12* **False Tail (IRE)**[10] 157 13-9-8 **89**.............. AELynch(7) 29
(J J Lambe, Ire) *led to 11th: wknd fr 14th* **20/1**
0F5- **F** **Ornella Speed (FR)**[85] 3888 5-10-0 **95** oh12..............(t) BHarding —
(Ferdy Murphy) *nt fluent: hld up: fell 12th* **25/1**

6m 5.10s (-7.50) **Going Correction** -0.225s/f (Good)
WFA 5 from 8yo+ 7lb 7 Ran SP% **111.8**
Speed ratings: **103,101,93,87,84 80,**— CSF £16.25 CT £52.18 TOTE £5.10: £2.80, £2.20; EX 25.10.
Owner Mrs Christine Davies **Bred** Dr J M McKelvey **Trained** Slad, Gloucs

FOCUS
A modest handicap, run at a decent gallop, and the first two came clear. The winner can be rated value for further.

NOTEBOOK
Stack The Pack(IRE) , yet to complete in three previous outings over fences, was again none too fluent in his jumping, but still ran out a ready winner and can be rated value for further. This one-time bumper winner should be capable of further success while at this end of the handicap, and would be hard to stop under a penalty, yet his jumping remains cause for concern. *(op 3-1)*
World Vision(IRE) never looked like getting to the winner, but still ran another creditable race and had no trouble with this much faster ground. *(tchd 11-2)*
Catch The Perk(IRE) was unable to get to the front as he prefers and, as a result, ran well below his best. He can do better. *(op 7-2)*
Panmure(IRE) turned in a moody effort on this step up in distance and never looked like following up his recent Market Rasen success. *(op 9-1)*
Lodestar(IRE) lost his chance with a bad error at the water jump. He should be given another chance. *Official explanation: jockey said gelding was unsuited by the watered ground (op 2-1)*

322 ROYAL HIGHLAND SHOW LADIES DAY NOVICES' HUNTERS' CHASE (LINLITHGOW/STIRLINGSHIRE HUNT TRPHY) (15 fncs) 2m 4f 110y
5:05 (5:05) (Class 6) 5-Y-0+ **£2,743** (£844; £422; £211)

Form RPR
04-2 **1** **Jupiter's Fancy**[12] 123 10-10-10.............. TMessenger(7) 83
(M V Coglan) *chsd ldrs: led 3 out: styd on strly* **10/1**
/4P- **2** *1 1/4* **Good Heart (IRE)**[32] 10-11-3..............(t) MrNHOliver(7) 89
(R Ford) *hld up: hdwy 4 out: chsd wnr last: kpt on run in* **10/1**
3 *7* **Prioritisation (IRE)**[11] 6-11-5.............. MrBWoodhouse(5) 86+
(B R Woodhouse) *cl up: led 6th: blnd and hdd 3 out: one pce last* **7/2**[2]
U5-1 **4** *10* **Swiftway**[10] 151 11-11-13.............. MrWLMorgan(5) 82+
(Miss J Fisher) *chsd ldrs tl rdn and outpcd 3 out: btn whn hung rt after next* **7/4**[1]
5 *16* **Soldati (IRE)**[10] 157 7-11-7.............. AELynch(3) 56
(I R Ferguson, Ire) *towards rr: effrt u.p bef 4 out: nvr able to chal* **7/1**[3]
53-4 **6** *12* **High Expectations (IRE)**[15] 63 10-11-5 72.............. MrTDavidson(5) 44
(J S Haldane) *prom to 4 out: wknd bef next* **20/1**
P/P- **7** *2* **Mr Cooney (IRE)**[13] 113 11-11-3.............. MrSClements(7) 42
(J Clements, Ire) *a bhd: no ch fr 1/2-way* **66/1**
F- **8** *1/2* **Jupsala (FR)**[19] 8-11-3.............. MrCGillon(7) 42
(J Burke) *in tch tl wknd bef 4 out* **33/1**
32P- **9** *7* **Alittlebitopower**[18] 8-11-10.............. MrCStorey 35
(C Storey) *hld up: hdwy and prom whn blnd 4 out: nt rcvr* **10/1**
10 *18* **Kilifi Creek (IRE)**[19] 8-11-10..............(b[1]) MrBRHamilton 17
(J J Lambe, Ire) *led to 6th: cl up tl wknd fr 4 out* **33/1**
5P-P **U** **Mill Tower**[12] 123 8-11-5.............. MrPCallaghan(5) —
(R Nixon) *a bhd: t.o whn blnd and uns rdr 10th* **50/1**
P **Incroyable Mais Vrai (FR)**[18] 9-11-3..............(tp) MrJARichardson(7) —
(G F White) *a bhd: t.o whn p.u bef 2 out* **25/1**
/5P- **P** **Gunson Hight**[18] 8-11-3 74..............(tp) MrJThompson(7) —
(J L Gledson) *chsd ldrs: lost pl 9th: t.o whn p.u bef 11th* **40/1**
/0P- **P** **Red Marsala**[5] 7-11-7 59.............. MJMcAlister(3) —
(Miss J M Furness) *bhd: blnd 6th: nvr on terms: t.o whn p.u bef 12th* **50/1**
24-P **P** **Highland Brig**[12] 123 9-11-7.............. MrDJewett(3) —
(T Butt) *chsd ldrs: lost pl 9th: n.d after: t.o whn p.u bef 3 out* **20/1**

5m 9.90s (-5.40) **Going Correction** -0.225s/f (Good) 15 Ran SP% **125.5**
Speed ratings: **101,100,97,94,87 83,82,82,79,72** —,—,—,—,— CSF £96.35 TOTE £13.50: £2.60, £3.70, £2.10; EX 150.50.
Owner M V Coglan **Bred** Miss Julie Liddle **Trained** Crook, Co Durham
■ Victor Coglan's first winner under Rules.

FOCUS
A weak novices' hunter chase that saw the first two come well clear. The runner-up is rate to his mark and the race could rate a little higher.

NOTEBOOK
Jupiter's Fancy took up the running readly three out and never looked in danger thereafter. This first success under Rules must rate a personal best, she had no problems with this drop in trip, but may not have beaten a great deal this time and is not certain to follow-up.
Good Heart(IRE) stuck to his task gamely under pressure and finished a clear second best. He is a fair benchmark for the form.
Prioritisation(IRE) had his chance, and while it made no difference to the result, he would have been closer but for an error three from home. *(op 4-1 tchd 9-2 in a place)*
Swiftway got left behind from three out and was disappointing. He is capable of much better, but has a fair bit to prove now. *(tchd 2-1 and 6-4 in places)*

323 HERALD & POST INTERMEDIATE NATIONAL HUNT FLAT RACE 2m 110y
5:35 (5:36) (Class 6) 4-6-Y-0 **£2,324** (£664; £332)

Form RPR
5- **1** **Etched In Stone (IRE)**[129] 3217 6-11-4.............. MissRDavidson(7) 104+
(N G Richards) *mde virtually all: rdn and r.o wl fr 2f out* **5/4**[1]
2 *2 1/2* **Rossclare (IRE)**[251] 1355 5-10-11.............. PCO'Neill(7) 91
(J J Lambe, Ire) *in tch: effrt 3f out: pressed wnr over 1f out: nt qckn ins last* **5/1**[2]
0- **3** *2 1/2* **Chief Dan George (IRE)**[20] 4971 5-10-13.............. DMcGann(5) 89
(D R MacLeod) *bhd tl styd on fr 3f out: nrst fin* **100/1**
4 *4* **Nycos Des Ormeaux (FR)** 4-10-4.............. PJMcDonald(10) 81
(Ferdy Murphy) *in tch: effrt over 2f out: kpt on same pce* **14/1**
5 *3 1/2* **Talisker Rock (IRE)** 5-10-11.............. MJMcAlister(7) 82+
(B Storey) *cl up: ev ch 5f out: outpcd over 2f out* **40/1**
/06- **6** *5* **Our Men**[63] 4290 6-10-13.............. TGreenway(5) 76
(N W Alexander) *bhd tl styd on fr 2f out: nvr on terms* **33/1**
7 *3/4* **Lethem Present (IRE)**[40] 5-10-8.............. ONelmes(3) 69
(Mrs H O Graham) *chsd ldrs: disp ld over 5f out: wknd over 2f out* **20/1**
/62- **8** *29* **Rathowen (IRE)**[32] 4788 6-11-4.............. PRobson 47
(J I A Charlton) *hld up: pushed along over 4f out: n.d* **7/1**
045- **9** *7* **Alfie's Connection**[74] 4090 4-10-7.............. MrDTStratton(7) 36
(K G Reveley) *hld up: n.d* **13/2**[3]
000- **10** *1 1/2* **Crystal Runner**[85] 3891 5-10-4.............. SCrawford(7) 31
(E J Jamieson) *midfield: rdn over 5f out: sn btn* **100/1**
0- **11** *5* **Romanov Rambler (IRE)**[20] 4971 5-10-11.............. TMessenger(7) 33
(Mrs S C Bradburne) *hld up: rdn 1/2-way: n.d* **100/1**
0- **12** *4* **Theatre Rights (IRE)**[72] 4111 5-11-4.............. NPMulholland 29
(J S Haldane) *nvr on terms* **100/1**
0- **13** *3* **Brosie**[20] 4971 4-10-4.............. GBerridge(3) 15
(L Lungo) *hld up and a bhd* **25/1**
00- **14** *19* **Regal Leader**[94] 3744 6-11-1.............. MrCStorey(3) 7
(M A Barnes) *midfield: rdn over 5f out: sn btn* **100/1**
0- **15** *10* **What's Ahead**[61] 4323 5-10-4.............. GThomas(7) —
(Mrs J C McGregor) *a bhd: no ch fr 1/2-way* **66/1**
16 *3 1/2* **Chantilly Passion (FR)** 4-10-11.............. KJMercer(3) —
(B Storey) *bhd: lost tch 1/2-way: virtually p.u* **11/1**
0- **U** **Cloudmor (IRE)**[20] 4971 4-10-11.............. MrTGreenall(3) —
(Miss S E Forster) *in tch: drvn and outpcd whn swvd lft and uns rdr 4f out* **33/1**

3m 51.9s (-8.90) **Going Correction** -0.30s/f (Good)
WFA 4 from 5yo+ 4lb 17 Ran SP% **125.3**
Speed ratings: **108,106,105,103,102 99,99,85,82,81 79,77,76,67,62 60,**— CSF £6.80 TOTE £2.40: £1.10, £2.90, £111.50; EX 12.60 Place 6 £282.69, Place 5 £194.33.
Owner Mr & Mrs Duncan Davidson **Bred** Vincent Finn **Trained** Greystoke, Cumbria

FOCUS
A decent time for a bumper, 5.3 seconds quicker than the earlier handicap hurdle over the same trip. The form is hard to rate, with the first two making their British debuts, but both could rate higher.

NOTEBOOK
Etched In Stone(IRE) , making his British debut for new connections, made it two out of two in this sphere with a gutsy success under his penalty. He had no problems with the faster ground, should stay further in time and is an interesting prospect for novice hurdling. *(tchd 6-4)*
Rossclare(IRE) , another making his Brisish debut for new connections, had his chance yet was put in his place by the winner inside the final furlong. He did more than enough to suggest he should be winning in this division before too long. *(op 9-2)*
Chief Dan George(IRE) improved dramatically on his debut form and was staying with effect at the finish. He needs time to mature, but has a future. *(op 66-1)*
Nycos Des Ormeaux(FR) , a half-brother to a winning French chaser, showed with a fair bit of promise on this debut. He should improve when upped in trip over hurdles in due course. *(op 9-1)*
Talisker Rock(IRE) , half-brother to a winning French hurdler/chaser, had every chance and shaped as though he already needs a stiffer test. He should improve for the experience and looks to have a future. *(op 33-1)*
T/Plt: £713.30 to a £1 stake. Pool: £33,811.95. 34.60 winning tickets. T/Qpdt: £63.30 to a £1 stake. Pool: £2,875.40. 33.60 winning tickets. RY

324 - 328a (Foreign Racing) - See Raceform Interactive

AINTREE (L-H)
Friday, May 13

OFFICIAL GOING: Good changing to good (good to firm in places) after race 3 (7.00)
A keen breeze meant the ground was drying out all the time.
Wind: fresh across Weather: sunny

329 EMLYN HUGHES MEMORIAL MARES' ONLY H'CAP HURDLE (11 hdls) 2m 4f
6:00 (6:00) (Class 4) (0-110,106) 4-Y-0+ **£3,896** (£1,199; £599; £299)

Form RPR
0F-2 **1** **My Lady Link (FR)**[10] 167 6-10-8 **87**.............. SThomas 93+
(Miss Venetia Williams) *chsd ldr to 2nd: hld up in tch: j. slowly 5th: wnt 2nd after 8th: rdn to chal 3 out: led after 2 out: r.o wl* **5/1**[2]
104- **2** *3 1/2* **Tell The Trees**[21] 4960 4-11-8 **106**.............. APMcCoy 103
(M C Pipe) *hld up and bhd: rdn and hdwy appr 2 out: styd on u.p flat: nt trble wnr* **5/1**[2]
533- **3** *1/2* **Topanberry (IRE)**[23] 4924 6-11-2 **95**.............. ADobbin 96
(N G Richards) *hld up: rdn and hdwy 3 out: r.o one pce flat* **4/1**[1]
1F6- **4** *2* **She's My Girl (IRE)**[175] 2331 10-11-0 **93**..............(p) PACarberry 93+
(John G Carr, Ire) *led: sn clr: rdn and hdd after 2 out: no ex flat* **8/1**[3]
12-0 **5** *2* **Eau Pure (FR)**[14] 105 8-11-0 **93**..............(t) JEMoore 90
(G L Moore) *hld up: hmpd bnd after 2nd: hdwy appr 7th: hrd rdn appr 2 out: one pce* **10/1**

000- **6** *15* **Moon Catcher**[29] 4837 4-11-7 **105** .... RJohnson 85+
(D Brace) *prom: chsd ldr after 5th tl hrd rdn after 8th: wknd appr 2 out* **25/1**

001- **7** *19* **Hopbine**[40] 4717 9-11-12 **105** .... (p) GLee 68
(J L Spearing) *chsd ldr fr 2nd tl after 5th: rdn and wknd after 8th* **5/1**[2]

126- **8** *dist* **Cashel Dancer**[26] 4881 6-11-9 **102** .... JPByrne —
(S A Brookshaw) *hld up towards rr: sltly hmpd bnd after 2nd: rdn 8th: sn struggling: virtually p.u flat* **10/1**

P00- **P** **Journal Princess (IRE)**[65] 4252 6-10-0 **79** oh5 .... TScudamore —
(M Scudamore) *bhd tl p.u bef 6th* **20/1**

46-0 **S** **Bally's Bak**[5] 245 7-10-13 **102** .... THalliday(10) —
(Mrs S J Smith) *prom: 3rd whn slipped up bnd after 2nd* **16/1**

4m 57.1s (-6.60) **Going Correction** -0.10s/f (Good)
WFA 4 from 6yo+ 5lb **10** Ran SP% **113.8**
Speed ratings: **109,107,107,106,105 99,92,—,—,—** CSF £29.90 CT £108.59 TOTE £6.30: £1.70, £1.90, £2.00; EX 39.80.
Owner Six Diamonds Partnership **Bred** P Joubert **Trained** Kings Caple, H'fords

FOCUS
A typically modest mares-only event, but the time was reasonable and the form looks fairly solid for the grade.

NOTEBOOK
My Lady Link(FR), set to go up 6lb in future handicaps after finishing second last time, did not mind this much faster going and ran out a clear-cut winner. *(op 6-1)*
Tell The Trees, dropping back in distance, seems to need further these days especially on this sort of ground.
Topanberry(IRE), switching to handicaps, is another who ideally wants a longer trip on this type of surface. *(op 7-2)*
She's My Girl(IRE) ran her race but appears somewhat harshly treated compared with her Irish handicap mark.
Eau Pure(FR) had ground conditions to suit but this distance could be on the short side for her on a course as easy as this.
Journal Princess(IRE) *Official explanation: jockey said mare pulled up lame*

330 G.W. HELI-4-LEATHER H'CAP CHASE (19 fncs) 3m 1f (Mildmay)

6:30 (6:32) (Class 3) (0-120,120) 5-Y-0+ **£5,928** (£1,824; £912; £456)

Form RPR

552- **1** **Iverain (FR)**[126] 3259 9-10-8 **102** .... RMcGrath 108+
(Sir John Barlow Bt) *prom: lost pl 15th: hrd rdn and rallied appr last: led flat: all out* **12/1**

420- **2** *1 1/4* **Koquelicot (FR)**[58] 4398 7-11-12 **120** .... PJBrennan 124+
(P J Hobbs) *led: mstke 14th: hrd rdn and hdd flat: no ex* **7/2**[2]

P2-P **3** *3 1/2* **Cassia Heights**[11] 150 10-11-6 **114** .... (t) LAspell 117+
(S A Brookshaw) *hld up: hdwy 4th: chsd ldr appr 12th: rdn appr 2 out: ev ch whn jinked rt last: one pce* **8/1**[3]

FPP- **4** *15* **Cruise The Fairway (IRE)**[33] 4800 9-10-7 **101** .... PHide 88+
(B G Powell) *hld up: hdwy 9th: wknd appr 2 out* **16/1**

P3P- **P** **Ardent Scout**[99] 3659 13-11-0 **108** .... DElsworth —
(Mrs S J Smith) *chsd ldrs: lost pl 5th: lost tch fr 11th: t.o whn p.u bef 15th* **10/1**

3P0- **P** **Blazing Hills**[182] 2165 9-10-5 **99** .... TDoyle —
(P T Dalton) *j.rt: w ldr to 7th: wknd 10th: mstke 11th: sn bhd: t.o whn p.u bef 3 out* **14/1**

U63- **P** **Jones's Road (IRE)**[42] 4681 7-11-5 **113** .... APMcCoy —
(Jonjo O'Neill) *j.rt and bdly bmpd 2nd: j. slowly 3rd: sn bhd: t.o whn p.u bef 3 out* **3/1**[1]

1P-2 **P** **Ile De Paris (FR)**[16] 55 6-11-6 **114** .... (b) RJohnson —
(P J Hobbs) *hld up and bhd: mstke 13th: hdwy 14th: mstke 15th: j.rt and wknd 4 out: bhd whn p.u bef 2 out* **3/1**[1]

6m 26.7s (-3.70) **Going Correction** -0.10s/f (Good) **8** Ran SP% **112.7**
Speed ratings: **101,100,99,94,— —,—,—** CSF £53.51 CT £359.84 TOTE £22.20: £4.20, £1.80, £2.10; EX 120.00.
Owner Sir John & Lady Barlow **Bred** Suc Roger De Soultrait **Trained** Brindley, Cheshire

FOCUS
A fair handicap and a good finish despite the fact only four completed, and the form might work out.

NOTEBOOK
Iverain(FR), raised 5lb, had not been seen since finishing second at Musselburgh at the start of the year. Caught rather flat-footed at the end of the back straight, he deserves full marks for the way he battled back to pull the race out of the fire.
Koquelicot(FR) made a valiant attempt to make all under top weight but he had to give best towards the finish. *(op 4-1 tchd 9-2)*
Cassia Heights, set to go up 2lb in future handicaps, is a bit of an in-and-out performer. He lost valuable impetus when appearing to think twice about ducking out at the final fence. *(tchd 9-1)*
Cruise The Fairway(IRE), lightly-raced since winning at Newbury in December 2001, has tumbled down the ratings and at least managed to get round this time.
Jones's Road(IRE) seemed to get unsettled by the incident at the second fence and was never travelling thereafter. *Official explanation: jockey said gelding was never travelling (tchd 11-4)*
Ile De Paris(FR), again in blinkers, was let down by his jumping on this faster surface once things began to hot up. *(tchd 11-4)*

331 JEWSON NOVICES' HURDLE (SERIES QUALIFIER) (9 hdls) 2m 110y

7:00 (7:04) (Class 3) 4-Y-0+ **£5,122** (£1,576; £788; £394)

Form RPR

00-1 **1** **Itsmyboy (IRE)**[10] 172 5-11-6 .... APMcCoy 113+
(M C Pipe) *led: hdd after 6th: lft in ld 3 out: sn hrd rdn and edgd rt: hdd last: rallied to ld towards fin: all out* **8/11**[1]

2- **2** *1* **Forthright**[13] 4696 4-10-10 .... PHide 102
(G L Moore) *hld up in tch: nt clr run and switch lft 3 out: led last: hrd rdn and hdd towards fin* **2/1**[2]

200- **3** *10* **Buttress**[75] 4085 6-10-11 .... MrTGreenall(3) 97+
(M W Easterby) *hld up: smooth hdwy after 6th: sltly hmpd 2 out: sn rdn: wknd flat* **50/1**

4 *21* **Grey Clouds**[14] 5-10-7 .... RGarritty 72+
(T D Easterby) *hld up: hit 2nd: hdwy 5th: wknd appr 3 out* **14/1**

5 *dist* **Ocotillo**[21] 5-11-0 .... JimCrowley —
(James Moffatt) *a bhd: t.o fr 5th* **100/1**

20-0 **6** *3* **Waziya**[13] 133 6-10-0 82 .... DLaverty(7) —
(Mrs L Williamson) *a bhd: nt fluent 4th: t.o fr 6th* **100/1**

600- **P** **Majestic Class (USA)**[58] 4401 5-11-0 .... ADempsey —
(M W Easterby) *hld up: rdn 5th: sn struggling: t.o whn p.u bef 2 out* **100/1**

033- **U** **Reem Two**[55] 4446 4-10-3 100 .... GLee 86
(D McCain) *w wnr: led after 6th: blnd bdly and hdd 3 out: cl 3rd whn stmbld and uns rdr 2 out* **9/1**[3]

4m 3.50s (-1.10) **Going Correction** -0.10s/f (Good)
WFA 4 from 5yo+ 4lb **8** Ran SP% **112.8**
Speed ratings: **98,97,92,82,— —,—,—** CSF £2.40 TOTE £1.70: £1.10, £1.20, £3.90; EX 2.80.
Owner D A Johnson **Bred** Padraig Moroney **Trained** Nicholashayne, Devon

FOCUS
This eventually developed into the anticipated match and is rated through the runner-up to his mark.

NOTEBOOK
Itsmyboy(IRE) made heavy weather of winning on ground that was probably on the fast side for him and McCoy had to be at his strongest. *(op 4-5 tchd 10-11, evens in places)*
Forthright had run creditably at Goodwood since his promising hurdling debut. He looked set to gain the upper hand on the run-in but could not hold the winner's renewed effort. He should have little difficulty going one better. *(op 15-8 tchd 7-4)*
Buttress, who shaped with promise on this sort of ground in bumpers, ran by far is best race to date over hurdles. He did not find a lot when push came to shove but it is possible that he blew up on this first start for two months.
Reem Two was undoubtedly going better than the winner going to the third last but things quickly began to go wrong. *(op 10-1)*

332 G.W. 2 OVER PAR H'CAP HURDLE (9 hdls) 2m 110y

7:35 (7:36) (Class 3) (0-135,130) 4-Y-0+ **£7,491** (£2,305; £1,152; £576)

Form RPR

00-0 **1** **Border Tale**[5] 247 5-10-1 **105** .... JimCrowley 110+
(James Moffatt) *hld up in mid-div: pushed along and outpcd 6th: rallied and hit 3 out: rdn to ld flat: r.o* **20/1**

04-2 **2** *3/4* **Salute (IRE)**[13] 136 6-10-6 **110** .... RJohnson 114
(P J Hobbs) *hld up in mid-div: hdwy after 6th: led appr 2 out: hrd rdn and hdd flat: nt qckn* **10/3**[1]

033- **3** *9* **Borora**[42] 4678 6-11-12 **130** .... TDoyle 126+
(R Lee) *hld up and bhd: hdwy 6th: ev ch 2 out: wknd flat* **13/2**

4-1 **4** *1 1/2* **Donovan (NZ)**[16] 61 6-10-2 **109** .... (p) LMcGrath(3) 103
(R C Guest) *hld up and bhd: hdwy after 3rd: rdn 5th: ev ch 3 out: wknd appr last* **11/2**[3]

102- **5** *14* **Low Cloud**[160] 2112 5-10-6 **110** .... GLee 94+
(J J Quinn) *chsd ldr: led appr 3 out: hdd appr 2 out: sn wknd* **13/2**

000- **6** *15* **Rising Generation (FR)**[86] 3889 8-11-5 **123** .... ADobbin 88
(N G Richards) *prom tl wknd appr 3 out* **16/1**

41-0 **7** *1 1/2* **Constantine**[19] 13 5-11-0 **118** .... JEMoore 81
(G L Moore) *bhd: reminders after 1st: rdn appr 5th: sn struggling* **14/1**

15-1 **8** *4* **Ziggy Zen**[19] 1 6-10-13 **117** .... (b1) NFehily 76
(C J Mann) *led: hit 2nd: hdd appr 3 out: wknd qckly* **8/1**

3U-6 **9** *13* **Brave Vision**[16] 61 9-10-8 **112** .... KRenwick 58
(A C Whillans) *hld up and bhd: hdwy after 3rd: rdn 5th: wknd after 6th* **18/1**

344- **P** **Misty Dancer**[34] 4777 6-10-5 **109** .... SThomas —
(Miss Venetia Williams) *hld up: mstke 4th: sn bhd: t.o whn p.u bef 3 out* **4/1**[2]

3m 58.8s (-5.80) **Going Correction** -0.10s/f (Good) **10** Ran SP% **118.8**
Speed ratings: **109,108,104,103,97 90,89,87,81,—** CSF £89.31 CT £500.67 TOTE £34.20: £7.80, £2.10, £2.90; EX 159.40.
Owner Chadwick, Dyer & Flynn **Bred** M L Page **Trained** Cartmel, Cumbria

FOCUS
Wide-open betting in this fair handicap and five were still in contention at the third last. The fifth was close to his mark and the form looks solid.

NOTEBOOK
Border Tale was found to have had a vertebrae out since joining his present stable. All the better for his recent run at Worcester, he fought back after looking in trouble at the end of the back straight. There may be more improvement to come. *(op 16-1)*
Salute(IRE) is knocking on the door but could not quite overcome a 3lb hike in the weights. *(op 9-2)*
Borora, reverting to more patient tactics, found his big weight anchoring him from the final flight. *(op 9-2)*
Donovan(NZ), raised 7lb for his victory in much softer ground in Kelso, had previously scored on this sort of surface. *(op 9-2)*
Low Cloud had not been seen since running on the All-Weather last December. *(op 7-1)*
Misty Dancer *Official explanation: jockey said, regarding the running and riding, the key to gelding is to get it to relax early and, although it jumped the first two hurdles well, it then started to guess at its hurdles and may well have fallen if allowed to continue (op 5-1)*

333 NORTHERN BUILDING DESIGN ASSOCIATES NOVICES' HUNTERS' CHASE (17 fncs 2 omitted) 3m 1f (Mildmay)

8:10 (8:11) (Class 6) 5-Y-0+ **£2,470** (£760; £380; £190)

Form RPR

PF-P **1** **Honest Yer Honour (IRE)**[15] 79 9-12-0 .... MrRBurton 122+
(Mrs C J Robinson) *hld up: hdwy 7th: led appr last: styd on wl* **7/1**[3]

1/F- **2** *2* **Chabrimal Minster**[41] 4688 8-11-7 107 .... MrNHOliver(7) 118
(R Ford) *chsd ldr: led 6th tl appr last: nt qckn* **11/4**[2]

F/3- **3** *17* **Dawn's Cognac (IRE)**[13] 12-11-7 .... MissFWilson(7) 103+
(D Brace) *led to 6th: disp ld 12th: mstke 3 out: wknd 2 out* **9/1**

233- **4** *13* **Cloth Of Gold**[34] 8-12-0 .... MissEJJones 91+
(Miss T Spearing) *hld up in tch: rdn after 14th: wknd 2 out* **11/8**[1]

32/3 **5** *17* **Kasilia (FR)**[16] 50 7-11-7 .... MrMMackley(7) 71
(Tim Brown) *wl bhd 10th: sme hdwy appr 3 out: nvr nr ldrs* **12/1**

/5P- **P** **Head For The Hills**[78] 4028 12-11-7 .... MrNSSaville(7) —
(Niall Saville) *a bhd: blnd 8th: t.o whn p.u bef 10th* **14/1**

PU3/ **P** **Valman (IRE)**[6] 9-11-11 .... (v) MrPJMillington(3) —
(P J Millington) *bhd: mstke 5th: lost tch 9th: t.o whn p.u bef 13th* **66/1**

0/F- **P** **Edgar Gink (IRE)**[48] 11-11-9 .... MrDEdwards(5) —
(L Corcoran) *prom: hit 6th and 11th: wknd 13th: t.o whn p.u bef 2 out* **25/1**

6m 26.1s (-4.30) **Going Correction** -0.10s/f (Good) **8** Ran SP% **111.0**
Speed ratings: **102,101,95,91,86 —,—,—** CSF £25.94 TOTE £6.90: £1.70, £1.70, £1.90; EX 30.10.
Owner Sean P Burke **Bred** Mrs James Hannon **Trained** Shifnal, Shropshire

FOCUS
A modest novice event and a fair time, although the race could turn out better than rated. The cross fence was omitted on both circuits because of a low sun.

NOTEBOOK
Honest Yer Honour(IRE), who did not live up to failing by four lengths to give 8lb to Brave Inca over hurdles at Fairyhouse in November 2003, is a dual winner between the flags. Leaving behind his previous form in hunter chases on ground considered perfect for him, he could be on the upgrade. *(tchd 6-1)*
Chabrimal Minster lost little in defeat and this lightly-raced sort seems perfectly capable of taking a similar event. *(tchd 3-1)*
Dawn's Cognac(IRE) again put the value of his victories in Welsh points into context. *(op 14-1)*
Cloth Of Gold, the winner of two ladies' opens this year, folded tamely at the penultimate fence after coming under pressure towards the end of the back straight. *(op 5-4 tchd 6-5 and 11-10 in places)*

334 G.W. OVER THE HILL NOVICES' H'CAP HURDLE (13 hdls) 3m 110y
8:45 (8:48) (Class 4) (0-105,102) 4-Y-0+ £3,896 (£1,199; £599; £299)

Form RPR

501- 1 **Muckle Flugga (IRE)**[21] 4969 6-11-4 94 ADobbin 102+
(N G Richards) *hld up: hdwy 9th: rdn to ld appr 2 out: drvn out* **6/1**[3]

2 4 **Mary Macs Lad (IRE)**[76] 4080 6-10-5 81 (b[1]) RJohnson 86+
(John G Carr, Ire) *hld up: hdwy 7th: hrd rdn and one pce flat* **12/1**

26-2 3 2 **Combat Drinker (IRE)**[14] 94 7-11-0 90 (t) JMMaguire 92
(D McCain) *hld up and bhd: hdwy after 10th: styd on same pce flat* **11/1**

3P-1 4 1 **River Mist (IRE)**[13] 121 6-11-12 102 KRenwick 103
(Karen McLintock) *hld up towards rr: hdwy 6th: led appr 3 out tl appr 2 out: wknd flat* **10/1**

30-F 5 8 **Cannon Fire (FR)**[5] 229 4-10-11 93 ChristianWilliams 80
(Evan Williams) *hld up and bhd: hdwy 7th: hit 10th: wknd appr 2 out: mstke last* **16/1**

6 7 **Fakima (IRE)**[11] 154 7-11-5 95 PACarberry 84+
(John G Carr, Ire) *prom: lost pl 7th: bhd whn mstke 9th: sme hdwy appr 2 out: eased whn no ch flat* **7/2**[1]

45-0 7 1 3/4 **Presenting Alf (IRE)**[14] 111 5-10-11 87 DElsworth 71
(Mrs S J Smith) *prom tl wknd appr 3 out* **25/1**

P4-P 8 nk **Joris De Vonnas (FR)**[14] 109 8-11-0 90 DRDennis 74
(Ian Williams) *led tl appr 3rd: chsd ldr: led after 7th tl appr 3 out: wknd appr 2 out* **22/1**

P/5- 9 8 **Waynesworld (IRE)**[27] 7-11-0 90 TScudamore 66
(M Scudamore) *prom tl wknd appr 8th* **20/1**

3U4- 10 17 **Faraway Echo**[7] 2066 4-10-0 82 oh2 JimCrowley 35
(James Moffatt) *j.lft 1st: a bhd* **25/1**

00-F P **Silent Voice (IRE)**[13] 135 8-10-0 76 oh4 (t) RMcGrath —
(Sir John Barlow Bt) *a bhd: t.o whn p.u bef 3 out* **33/1**

02U- P **The Weaver (FR)**[75] 4089 6-11-6 99 GBerridge(3) —
(L Lungo) *mid-div: mstke 9th: sn bhd: t.o whn p.u bef 3 out* **9/2**[2]

06-5 U **Stage Friendly (IRE)**[10] 177 6-11-0 90 CLlewellyn —
(N A Twiston-Davies) *chsd ldr: led appr 3rd tl after 7th: cl 2nd whn blnd and uns rdr 8th* **12/1**

551- P **Dragut Torghoud (IRE)**[23] 4929 9-10-4 85 TJPhelan(5) —
(N M Babbage) *hld up and bhd: hdwy 10th: hung lft bnd appr 3 out: sn wknd: bhd whn p.u bef 2 out* **7/1**

6m 15.3s (-1.10) **Going Correction** -0.10s/f (Good)
WFA 4 from 5yo+ 6lb 14 Ran SP% 125.6
Speed ratings: **97,95,95,94,92 89,89,89,86,81** —,—,—,— CSF £72.76 CT £795.47 TOTE £5.60: £2.10, £3.10, £2.20; EX 64.10 Place 6 £87.67, Place 5 £54.00..
Owner Dr Kenneth S Fraser **Bred** Paul Murphy **Trained** Greystoke, Cumbria

FOCUS
Several of these were in decent form coming into this open-looking handicap and the placed horses set a reasonable standard.

NOTEBOOK
Muckle Flugga(IRE), defying a 6lb rise in the weights for her soft-ground win at Perth, had previously shown she could handle this type of surface. She is considered a chaser in the making. *(tchd 11-2)*
Mary Macs Lad(IRE), a stable companion of the well-backed favourite, was blinkered for the first time having been struggling on soft ground in Ireland. *(tchd 14-1)*
Combat Drinker(IRE), on the fastest ground he has encountered so far, does seem to have benefited from having his tongue tied. *(op 14-1)*
River Mist(IRE) had gone up 6lb for winning on her only start since being pulled up when favourite for this race last year. It could be that this trip proved just beyond her. *(tchd 9-1)*
Cannon Fire(FR) appeared not to stay and looked leg-weary when fluffing the last. *(op 9-1)*
Fakima(IRE), a well-backed favourite, could never really get back into it after losing his pitch at halfway. This ground could have been a bit lively for him. *(op 5-1)*
Dragut Torghoud(IRE) *Official explanation: jockey said gelding hung badly left-handed (tchd 15-2, 13-2 in places)*
T/Plt: £196.20 to a £1 stake. Pool: £48,461.85. 180.25 winning tickets. T/Qpdt: £22.40 to a £1 stake. Pool: £3,337.30. 110.20 winning tickets. KH

335 - 342a (Foreign Racing) - See Raceform Interactive

94

BANGOR-ON-DEE (L-H)
Saturday, May 14

OFFICIAL GOING: Good (good to firm in places)
The ground was patchy after watering in the wind and the times suggested it was slower than the official description.
Wind: mod across Weather: sunny

343 COURSES 4 HORSES NOVICES' HURDLE (9 hdls) 2m 1f
2:15 (2:15) (Class 4) 4-Y-0+ £3,569 (£1,098; £549; £274)

Form RPR

53-2 1 **Adjami (IRE)**[6] 243 4-10-8 110 RThornton 104+
(A King) *chsd ldr: led sn after 3 out: clr whn hit last: easily* **7/2**[3]

F1P- 2 9 **Terre De Java (FR)**[98] 3693 7-10-12 TDoyle 94
(Mrs H Dalton) *t.k.h in mid-div: hdwy 5th: lft 2nd 2 out: no ch w wnr* **10/3**[2]

00- 3 3 1/2 **Pearson Glen (IRE)**[5] 2432 6-10-12 GLee 93+
(James Moffatt) *a.p: mstke 3rd: rdn whn hmpd 2 out: btn whn mstke last* **50/1**

32-U 4 7 **Fencote (IRE)**[17] 59 8-10-12 102 RGarritty 85+
(P Beaumont) *hld up and bhd: hdwy 5th: wknd 2 out* **10/1**

P/P- 5 25 **Bodfari Rose**[28] 4871 6-9-12 85 (p) WKennedy(7) 52
(A Bailey) *hld up in mid-div: rdn appr 6th: no rspnse* **22/1**

P 6 11 **Sportsfield Coogee (IRE)**[8] 201 6-10-12 NFehily 48
(D P Keane) *nvr nr ldrs* **100/1**

0/0- 7 2 **Joe Malone (IRE)**[49] 4547 6-10-12 ADobbin 46
(N G Richards) *hld up in tch: wknd appr 5th* **14/1**

50-0 8 1 3/4 **Slight Hiccup**[20] 7 5-10-0 LTreadwell(5) 37
(C W Moore) *a bhd* **100/1**

P6- 9 dist **Bebe Factual (GER)**[29] 4852 4-10-3 CHonour(5) —
(J D Frost) *prom: rdn and wkng whn mstke 6th: t.o* **66/1**

00- 10 2 **Waterloo Son (IRE)**[61] 4373 5-10-12 RJohnson —
(H D Daly) *t.k.h in mid-div: bhd fr 5th: t.o* **10/1**

POP- 11 shd **Muraqeb**[49] 4565 5-10-12 75 (t) BHitchcott —
(Mrs Barbara Waring) *a bhd: t.o* **50/1**

F- P **Lord Tiddlypush (IRE)**[24] 4930 7-10-12 RMcGrath —
(Sir John Barlow Bt) *bhd: mstkes 1st and 2nd: t.o whn p.u bef 6th* **66/1**

30-1 F **Romany Prince**[10] 82 6-11-5 118 TScudamore 101
(S Gollings) *led: rdn and hdd sn after 3 out: 2nd and hld whn fell 2 out* **13/8**[1]

4m 12.6s (1.70) **Going Correction** +0.10s/f (Yiel)
WFA 4 from 5yo+ 4lb 13 Ran SP% 121.5
Speed ratings: **100,95,94,90,79 73,72,72**,—,— —,—,— CSF £15.89 TOTE £4.30: £1.60, £1.70, £7.30; EX 18.30.
Owner Let's Live Racing **Bred** His Highness The Aga Khan's Studs S C **Trained** Barbury Castle, Wilts

FOCUS
A modwerate novices' event in which few could be fancied on form and they went 10/1 bar three. The winner is value for more than the official margin and the form behind looks reasonable.

NOTEBOOK
Adjami(IRE) probably came up against a decent sort in Natal when fancied at Worcester last weekend. He had gained the upper hand when Romany Prince fell and was left to come home at his leisure. He can defy a penalty. *(op 4-1)*
Terre De Java(FR) was reported to have been unsuited by the soft ground when pulled up over fences back in February. He has some decent placed form to his name in novice hurdles but proved no match for the winner. *(op 7-2 tchd 3-1)*
Pearson Glen(IRE), reported by his rider to have had a breathing problem, was probably only fourth best on merit. *Official explanation: jockey said gelding had a breathing problem (op 66-1)*
Fencote(IRE) could not sustain a promising-looking effort and may need softer ground. *(op 8-1)*
Romany Prince, who made the running until inside the last half-mile in last week's Chester Cup, was in the process of having his measure taken when falling two out. He probably really wants further over hurdles. *(op 15-8 tchd 2-1 in places)*

344 NORTH WEST RACING CLUB NOVICES' CHASE (15 fncs) 2m 4f 110y
2:50 (2:50) (Class 3) 5-Y-0+ £5,760 (£1,872; £1,008)

Form RPR

34-1 1 **Tigers Lair (IRE)**[11] 174 6-11-6 APMcCoy 132+
(Jonjo O'Neill) *w ldr: led 4th: clr 3 out: eased flat* **4/5**[1]

3P1- 2 11 **Croix De Guerre (IRE)**[37] 4755 5-11-3 122 (b) RJohnson 114+
(P J Hobbs) *a.p: chsd wnr fr 5th: rdn whn mstke 4 out: sn no imp: mstke last* **2/1**[2]

64-6 3 11 **Humid Climate**[9] 192 5-10-8 PWhelan(3) 94+
(R A Fahey) *hld up: 3rd whn mstke 9th: n.d after* **25/1**

5P-1 P **Itsuptoharry (IRE)**[14] 126 6-11-6 114 JMMaguire —
(D McCain) *a bhd: t.o whn p.u bef 10th* **9/1**[3]

/02- U **Welsh Main**[35] 4777 8-11-0 CLlewellyn —
(Miss G Browne) *led to 4th: lost pl after 6th: poor 4th fr 9th: blnd and uns rdr last* **14/1**

5m 14.6s (2.10) **Going Correction** +0.10s/f (Yiel)
WFA 5 from 6yo+ 3lb 5 Ran SP% 109.4
Speed ratings: **100,95,91**,—,— CSF £2.85 TOTE £1.70: £1.20, £1.70; EX 2.70.
Owner Mrs Gay Smith **Bred** James F Whitehead **Trained** Cheltenham, Gloucs

FOCUS
This fair novices' chase for the time of year developed into the expected match some way out. The winner is value for more than the official margin and the race could be rated higher, but is held down by the time.

NOTEBOOK
Tigers Lair(IRE) ◆, who jumped left-handed at Ludlow last time, never put a foot wrong going this way round. A hat-trick looks on the cards. *(op Evens)*
Croix De Guerre(IRE) was not going as well as the winner when an error at the final ditch really put him on the back foot. *(op 13-8 tchd 9-4 in places)*
Humid Climate never posed a threat after missing out at the second ditch on his chasing debut. *(op 20-1)*

345 RED DRAGON NOVICES' H'CAP HURDLE (11 hdls) 2m 4f
3:20 (3:20) (Class 3) (0-110,102) 4-Y-0+ £4,903 (£1,508; £754; £377)

Form RPR

26-4 1 **Brooklyn Brownie (IRE)**[15] 111 6-11-5 95 GLee 110+
(J M Jefferson) *a gng wl: led and lft clr 2 out: easily* **3/1**[2]

P55- 2 24 **Lord Jay Jay (IRE)**[41] 4721 5-11-7 97 SThomas 82
(Miss H C Knight) *hld up: hdwy 8th: rdn and wkng whn lft 2nd 2 out* **5/1**[3]

21-3 3 3 1/2 **L'Oiseau (FR)**[16] 84 6-11-6 99 GBerridge(3) 81
(L Lungo) *hld up and bhd: hdwy 8th: rdn and wknd appr 2 out* **9/4**[1]

4P-P 4 18 **Fight The Feeling**[16] 78 7-11-0 90 (v) CLlewellyn 54
(J W Unett) *led to 3rd: w ldr: rdn appr 7th: hit 8th: sn wknd* **20/1**

600- 5 7 **Smileafact**[102] 3637 5-10-9 85 BHitchcott 42
(Mrs Barbara Waring) *prom: rdn appr 7th: wknd after 8th* **33/1**

35F- 6 1/2 **Beaugency (NZ)**[93] 3769 7-11-2 95 LMcGrath(3) 51
(R C Guest) *hld up and bhd: short-lived effrt whn hit 6th* **5/1**[3]

66-3 7 nk **Lazy Lena (IRE)**[10] 180 6-10-6 82 NPMulholland 38
(Miss L C Siddall) *hld up: rdn 8th: 4th and no ch whn hmpd 2 out* **14/1**

300- 8 4 **It's Ej**[21] 4978 7-11-12 102 DElsworth 54
(Mrs S J Smith) *bhd fr 7th* **14/1**

04P- F **Barton Sun (IRE)**[24] 4929 6-10-1 77 WHutchinson 84
(R N Bevis) *w ldr: led 3rd: hdd and fell 2 out* **20/1**

4m 59.4s (1.80) **Going Correction** +0.10s/f (Yiel) 9 Ran SP% 114.9
Speed ratings: **100,90,89,81,79 78,78,77**,— CSF £18.02 CT £38.89 TOTE £3.90: £1.70, £1.50, £1.40; EX 22.20.
Owner P Gaffney & J N Stevenson **Bred** John P A Kenny **Trained** Norton, N Yorks

FOCUS
An ordinary novice handicap with the winner rated value for a ten-length win over the faller.

NOTEBOOK
Brooklyn Brownie(IRE) ◆, sharpened up by his run at Southwell, was gaining command when Barton Sun departed two out. He likes the top of the ground and this lightly-raced sort does seem to have got his act together. He can score again. *(op 11-4)*
Lord Jay Jay(IRE), back up in distance, may well have been fortunate to finish second on this handicap debut. *(op 11-2)*
L'Oiseau(FR) was back on a sound surface for this return to hurdling. *(op 5-2)*
Beaugency(NZ) *Official explanation: jockey said gelding had a breathing problem*
Barton Sun(IRE), coming back from three miles, found the winner galloping all over him when coming to grief at the penultimate flight. However, this was still a big improvement and it seems he needs some decent ground. *(tchd 25-1)*

346 GALLAGHERS MITSUBISHI H'CAP CHASE (15 fncs) 2m 4f 110y
3:50 (3:50) (Class 3) (0-115,110) 5-Y-0+ £6,307 (£1,940; £970; £485)

Form RPR

00-0 1 **Idealko (FR)**[15] 111 9-10-9 93 (b) DRDennis 109+
(Ian Williams) *a.p: led 10th: clr appr 2 out: eased towards fin* **14/1**

44-2 2 12 **Xaipete (IRE)**[16] 84 13-11-0 101 LMcGrath(3) 109+
(R C Guest) *hld up and bhd: hdwy 8th: hit 9th: mstke 4 out: chsd wnr after 2 out: no imp* **5/1**[3]

123- 3 6 **Oso Magic**[99] 3677 7-11-4 102 DElsworth 103+
(Mrs S J Smith) *hld up: hdwy after 9th: chsd wnr appr 3 out tl after 2 out: 3rd and wkng whn blnd last* **5/2**[1]

52-P 4 11 **River Mere**[14] 132 11-10-2 86 OMcPhail 73
(Mrs L Williamson) *prom: rdn after 7th: wknd 11th* **12/1**

The Form Book, Raceform Ltd, Compton, RG20 6NL

P0-P **P** **Saragann (IRE)**[14] 135 10-9-9 **84** oh4 StephenJCraine(5) —
(M J M Evans) *bhd fr 9th: t.o whn p.u bef 4 out* **25/1**

531- **P** **The Extra Man (IRE)**[22] 4955 11-11-12 **110** (b) RThornton —
(A King) *prom tl wknd 8th: t.o whn plld bef 10th* **10/3**[2]

021- **P** **Ojays Alibi (IRE)**[34] 4792 9-11-6 **109** CHonour(5) —
(J D Frost) *a bhd: rdn after 6th: t.o 10th: p.u bef 3 out* **8/1**

/4-P **P** **Stone Cold**[14] 132 8-10-4 **88** (b) DO'Meara —
(T D Easterby) *prom tl wknd 8th: no ch whn blnd 4 out: t.o whn p.u after 3 out* **8/1**

FF-P **P** **Fearless Mel (IRE)**[11] 176 11-10-12 **96** (p) JPMcNamara —
(Mrs H Dalton) *chsd ldr: led 8th to 9th: wknd appr 11th: t.o whn p.u after 3 out* **14/1**

PP-1 **P** **Heartache**[17] 57 8-10-0 **84** oh17 (b) WHutchinson —
(R Mathew) *led: clr 4th: hdd 8th: led 9th: hung rt and hdd 10th: wknd 4 out: j.rt 3 out: sn p.u* **18/1**

5m 12.2s (-0.30) **Going Correction** +0.10s/f (Yiel) **10** Ran SP% **120.7**
Speed ratings: **104,99,97,92,**— —,—,—,—,— CSF £86.90 CT £239.86 TOTE £24.50: £3.50, £2.00, £1.40; EX 59.00.
Owner Mrs Maggie Bull **Bred** Scea Terres Noires **Trained** Portway, Worcs

FOCUS
This run-of-the-mill handicap may not have taken much winning, but the time was reasonable and the runner-up sets the level.

NOTEBOOK
Idealko(FR) bounced back to form in some style on this return to fences, but what he actually achieved remains to be seen.
Xaipete(IRE) proved no match for the winner on this return to a longer distance. *(tchd 11-2)*
Oso Magic, another back up in trip, did not get home on what the jockeys considered was not genuine fast ground after watering. *(op 7-2)*
River Mere would have been unsuited by the soft ground when pulled up last time. *(op 11-1)*
The Extra Man(IRE) *Official explanation: vet said gelding sustained an injury to a hind leg (tchd 3-1)*
Heartache *Official explanation: jockey said gelding hung badly right-handed (tchd 3-1)*

347 BANGOR RACES SUPPORT BROOKE HOSPITAL H'CAP HURDLE (9 hdls) 2m 1f
4:25 (4:25) (Class 3) (0-120,113) 4-Y-0+ **£6,479** (£1,993; £996; £498)

Form RPR

P-02 **1** **Forzacurity**[6] 247 6-10-4 **96** LStephens(5) 104+
(M Sheppard) *mde all: clr whn mstke last: r.o wl* **7/2**[2]

20-0 **2** *5* **Blue Leader (IRE)**[7] 220 6-10-13 **100** (vt[1]) ChristianWilliams 100
(W K Goldsworthy) *a chsng wnr: rdn appr 2 out: no imp* **16/1**

101- **3** *1 3/4* **Conroy**[27] 4883 6-11-12 **113** LAspell 111
(F Jordan) *t.k.h: sme hdwy 6th: kpt on same pce fr 2 out* **9/1**

6U-5 **4** *1* **Why The Long Face (NZ)**[6] 248 8-11-5 **109** (v[1]) LMcGrath(3) 109+
(R C Guest) *plld hrd early: in tch: mstke 3 out: sn rdn: one pce* **16/1**

6-00 **5** *17* **Day Du Roy (FR)**[9] 197 7-11-4 **105** AThornton 90+
(Miss L C Siddall) *nvr nr ldrs* **10/1**

14-1 **6** *12* **Tiger Frog (USA)**[7] 220 6-11-4 **105** (b) WMarston 73
(J Mackie) *prom tl rdn and wknd 5th* **9/2**[3]

2/P- **7** *29* **Cristoforo (IRE)**[106] 3574 8-10-8 **95** PMoloney 34
(B J Curley) *hld up in rr: struggling fr 6th: mstke 3 out: sn eased* **5/4**[1]

4m 14.6s (3.70) **Going Correction** +0.10s/f (Yiel)
WFA 4 from 6yo+ 4lb **7** Ran SP% **115.7**
Speed ratings: **95,92,91,91,83 77,64** CSF £50.95 CT £467.10 TOTE £5.00: £2.40, £7.20; EX 37.10.
Owner Don Gould, Mervyn Phillips & Jeff Smith **Bred** L A C Ashby **Trained** Eastnor, H'fords

FOCUS
A fair event for the time of year but a modest winning time for the grade, two seconds slower than the earlier novice event.

NOTEBOOK
Forzacurity was effectively 6lb lower than when touched off from just out of the handicap at Worcester when Stephens was unable to utilise his allowance. He had things his own way out in front this time. *(op 11-4)*
Blue Leader(IRE), tried in a visor following a couple of below-par efforts, had to be content to play second fiddle.
Conroy, raised 7lb, could have settled better on ground that may not have been quite quick enough to be ideal for him. *(op 7-1 tchd 10-1)*
Why The Long Face(NZ) was lit up early on in the first-time visor and could not raise his game after an error at the third last. *(op 11-1)*
Tiger Frog(USA), up 4lb, did not get the genuinely fast ground he needs. *(op 3-1)*
Cristoforo(IRE) has won on soft ground on the Flat, but there were apparently complaints from connections beforehand about the state of the watered ground.*Official explanation: jockey said gelding was never travelling (op 11-4 tchd 11-10)*

348 NORTH WESTERN AREA POINT TO POINT CHAMPIONSHIP (A HUNTERS' CHASE) (18 fncs) 3m 110y
5:00 (5:01) (Class 6) 5-Y-0+ **£4,048** (£1,245; £622; £311)

Form RPR

/6-1 **1** **No Retreat (NZ)**[17] 49 12-12-0 MrWHill(7) 117+
(J Groucott) *hld up in tch: led appr 2 out: clr last: styd on wl* **5/2**[2]

P/1- **2** *9* **Cornish Gale (IRE)**[12] 11-12-4 MrRBurton 106+
(D McCain Jnr) *hld up: hdwy 8th: led 3 out: sn hdd: one pce* **15/8**[1]

P/P- **3** *29* **Home Made**[12] 7-11-11 86 (p) MissSBeddoes(3) 72
(Miss H Brookshaw) *prom: jnd ldr 4th: wknd 14th* **20/1**

P40/ **4** *1/2* **Pristeen Spy**[12] 8-12-0 MrNWilliams 72
(Mrs Edward Crow) *led to 3 out: sn wknd* **9/2**[3]

652- **5** *1/2* **Returned Un Paid (IRE)**[14] 8-11-7 MrWKinsey(7) 71
(Mrs V Park) *bhd fr 9th* **33/1**

445- **P** **Quality First (IRE)**[21] 12-11-7 119 (p) MrGTumelty(7) —
(A N Dalton) *v rel to r: a t.o: p.u bef 2 out* **6/1**

40-5 **P** **Cassia Green**[7] 221 11-11-7 MrDGreenway(7) —
(P H Morris) *prom: lost pl 8th: mstke 9th: bhd whn p.u bef 14th* **20/1**

P/P- **U** **Be My Friend (IRE)**[47] 9-11-11 MrPCowley(3) —
(G D Hanmer) *hld up: hdwy 12th: ev ch whn blnd bdly and uns rdr 4 out* **10/1**

6m 18.4s (-4.80) **Going Correction** +0.10s/f (Yiel) **8** Ran SP% **117.4**
Speed ratings: **111,108,98,98,98** —,—,— CSF £8.04 TOTE £4.30: £1.40, £1.40, £4.60; EX 9.30.
Owner M W Harris **Bred** B G Francis, J S Mee And J R Watts **Trained** Much Wenlock, Shropshire

FOCUS
A decent race of its type and a smart winning time for a hunter chase.

NOTEBOOK
No Retreat(NZ) showed his wellbeing after finishing distressed when dead-heating over four miles at Cheltenham last time. He does seem to have had a new lease of life since returning after a long lay off this spring. *(op 3-1 tchd 7-2)*
Cornish Gale(IRE) has yet to win over three miles under Rules but did come up against a rival in top form. *(op 2-1 tchd 11-8)*
Home Made was left well behind, as he was entitled to be, by the front two.
Pristeen Spy, a multiple winner in points, set the pace on this debut over fences under Rules, but was left well behind in the straight. *(op 6-1 tchd 13-2)*

349 PATRICK BURLING DEVELOPMENTS MARES' ONLY STANDARD OPEN NATIONAL HUNT FLAT RACE 2m 1f
5:30 (5:31) (Class 6) 4-6-Y-O **£2,640** (£754; £377)

Form RPR

6- **1** **Camden Bella**[41] 4720 5-11-0 ADobbin 89+
(N G Richards) *mid-div: hdwy over 6f out: led over 2f out: rdn clr ins fnl f* **4/1**[2]

0- **2** *7* **Lunar Eclipse**[22] 4971 5-11-0 PRobson 82
(J I A Charlton) *mid-div: hdwy 6f out: styd on ins fnl f to take 2nd cl home: no ch w wnr* **25/1**

0- **3** *nk* **Eurydice (IRE)**[22] 4971 5-10-4 PJMcDonald(10) 82
(Ferdy Murphy) *hld up: hdwy 6f out: rdn 3f out: styd on u.p ins fnl f* **16/1**

054- **4** *1/2* **Lady Speaker**[34] 4788 4-10-10 RGarritty 77
(T D Easterby) *prom: led over 6f out: rdn and hdd over 2f out: wknd towards fin* **10/1**

5 *1 1/2* **Classy Chick (IRE)** 4-10-10 MBradburne 76
(H D Daly) *mid-div: pushed along 7f out: hdwy over 2f out: kpt on: nt rch ldrs* **8/1**[3]

40- **6** *3 1/2* **Call Me Bobbi**[61] 4373 6-10-9 RStephens(5) 76
(Mrs S M Johnson) *in tch: tk clsr order after 5f: rdn over 2f out: wknd over 1f out* **25/1**

24- **7** *6* **Autograph**[21] 4981 4-10-10 DElsworth 66
(Mrs S J Smith) *mid-div: hdwy 5f out: wknd 2f out* **4/1**[2]

8 *13* **Sister Bury** 6-11-0 ChristianWilliams 57
(W K Goldsworthy) *mid-div: outpcd 1/2-way: n.d after* **25/1**

60-2 **9** *1 1/2* **Martovic (IRE)**[19] 27 6-11-0 JPMcNamara 56
(K C Bailey) *led: hdd over 6f out: rdn and wknd over 4f out* **11/4**[1]

0- **10** *3 1/2* **Bint Sesaro (IRE)**[76] 4090 4-10-5 DFlavin(5) 48
(Mrs L B Normile) *bhd: hdwy 6f out: nvr rchd ldrs* **33/1**

11 *12* **So Cloudy** 4-10-10 JMMaguire 36
(D McCain) *t.k.h: mid-div: hdwy 1/2-way: wknd over 4f out: sn eased* **10/1**

12 *11* **She's Little Don**[35] 5-10-9 LStephens(5) 29
(V J Hughes) *prom tl rdn and wknd over 4f out* **14/1**

0- **13** *11* **Just Ruby**[34] 4801 4-10-5 JDiment(5) 14
(F Jordan) *mid-div: lost pl 1/2-way: sn bhd* **22/1**

040- **14** *3/4* **Olympian Time**[30] 4841 5-10-9 MNicolls(5) 17
(B J Eckley) *trckd ldrs tl rdn and wknd over 6f out* **33/1**

15 *dist* **She's A Terror**[49] 6-10-9 CHonour(5) —
(N B King) *mid-div: rdn and wknd 1/2-way* **16/1**

60- **16** *12* **Only Millie**[94] 3757 4-10-0 MMcAvoy(10) —
(James Moffatt) *in tch tl rdn and wknd 1/2-way* **33/1**

17 *dist* **Bustling Bay** 4-10-3 WKennedy(7) —
(S Gollings) *a bhd: t.o* **33/1**

0- **18** *dist* **Rosina Copper**[74] 4111 5-10-7 CEddery(7) —
(P Beaumont) *a bhd: t.o* **40/1**

4m 8.70s (-2.40) **Going Correction** +0.10s/f (Yiel)
WFA 4 from 5yo 4lb 5 from 6yo 2lb **18** Ran SP% **144.5**
Speed ratings: **109,105,105,105,104 102,100,94,93,91 86,80,75,75,**— —,—,— CSF £119.81 TOTE £6.10: £2.20, £9.50, £10.90; EX 117.30 Place 6 £27.68, Place 5 £8.78.
Owner Mrs Carole Stephenson **Bred** Mrs C Stephenson **Trained** Greystoke, Cumbria

FOCUS
This may have been a modest mares-only bumper but it was run at a good even pace. the fourth and sixth set the standard.

NOTEBOOK
Camden Bella ran out a convincing winner and certainly appears to be going the right way. *(tchd 9-2)*
Lunar Eclipse is another who stepped up on her debut, but by the time she really got going the winner was home and dry.
Eurydice(IRE) had finished 13 lengths behind Lunar Eclipse at Perth so connections are entitled to be pleased with this effort. *(op 14-1)*
Lady Speaker had the advantage of being more experienced than those who finished in front of her. *(op 9-1)*
Classy Chick(IRE) is out of a mare who won at up to two miles three furlongs over hurdles. *(tchd 15-2)*
Martovic(IRE) folded up tamely with over half a mile to go. *(op 9-2)*
So Cloudy *Official explanation: jockey said filly had run too keenly*
Rosina Copper *Official explanation: jockey said mare had a breathing problem (op 50-1)*
T/Plt: £26.40 to a £1 stake. Pool: £36,309.25. 1,003.85 winning tickets. T/Qpdt: £12.40 to a £1 stake. Pool: £2,072.20. 123.20 winning tickets. KH

236 UTTOXETER (L-H)
Saturday, May 14

OFFICIAL GOING: Good (good to soft in places)
Wind: Fresh, behind Weather: Cloudy with sunny spells

350 MOUNT ARGUS OPEN HUNTERS' CHASE (18 fncs 2 omitted) 3m 2f
6:10 (6:10) (Class 6) 5-Y-0+ **£2,324** (£664; £332)

Form RPR

452- **1** **Raiseapearl**[6] 10-11-5 MissTessaClark(7) 100+
(Patrick Thompson) *hld up: hdwy 8th: led 13th: clr 4 out: hit next: nt fluent last: eased flat* **5/1**[3]

3P-F **2** *12* **Montys Tag (IRE)**[10] 184 12-11-5 MrMMackley(7) 82
(S R Andrews) *hld up: hdwy 12th: chsd wnr 4 out: no imp* **7/2**[2]

PPP/ **3** *6* **The Eens**[12] 13-11-12 MrTGreenall 76
(D McCain Jnr) *chsd ldrs: rdn appr 14th: wknd next* **5/2**[1]

11P/ **P** **Game Gunner**[422] 4425 13-11-9 MissAGoschen(3) —
(Miss B Lewis) *plld hrd and prom: wknd 8th: t.o whn p.u bef 4 out* **5/2**[1]

/P6- **P** **Young Tomo (IRE)**[6] 13-11-7 64 (p) MrPCallaghan(5) —
(Miss C J Goodall) *led to 13th: wknd appr 4 out: bhd whn p.u bef next* **10/1**

/P-P **P** **Macy (IRE)**[13] 12-11-5 MrsBKeighley(7) —
(Martin Jones) *chsd ldrs: lost pl 10th: bhd whn hit 12th: t.o whn p.u bef 3 out* **25/1**

7m 13.3s (8.10) **Going Correction** +0.35s/f (Yiel) **6** Ran SP% **109.0**
Speed ratings: **101,97,95,**—,— — CSF £21.51 TOTE £8.70: £3.70, £2.00; EX 34.60.
Owner Mrs Anne Greenwood **Bred** Mrs Christine T Forber **Trained** Nantwich, Cheshire

FOCUS
A weak race devalued further by the poor performances of the two joint-favourites.

NOTEBOOK
Raiseapearl achieved little in winning a race with little or no depth, but he appreciates a stiff test nowadays. This was his first win under Rules, and his form between the flags is modest. *(op 6-1 tchd 13-2)*

Montys Tag(IRE) is still a shade better than his recent form figures suggest, but this comfortable defeat was a reminder that he is nowhere near as good as he was. *(tchd 10-3)*
The Eens had been in good form in point-to-points during the spring, so this was a disappointing effort. He is best on easier ground. *(op 3-1 tchd 9-4)*
Game Gunner was too headstrong on this first outing for 14 months. He is getting to the veteran stage but may still have something to offer if he returns to anything like his best. *(op 2-1)*

351 KENDRICK CONSTRUCTION NOVICES' HURDLE (10 hdls 2 omitted) 2m 4f 110y
6:40 (6:40) (Class 4) 4-Y-0+ **£3,458** (£988; £494)

Form RPR
OP-0 **1** **Greencard Golf**[20] [3] 4-10-8 95 .... AO'Keeffe 87+
(Jennie Candlish) *hld up: mstke 6th: hdwy appr 3 out: led 2 out: hung lft flat: drvn out* **11/2**
25-4 **2** *2½* **The Wife's Sister**[17] [58] 4-10-1 .... GLee 74
(D McCain) *chsd ldr: led appr 3 out: hdd 2 out: sn rdn: styd on same pce flat* **11/4**[2]
0/P- **3** *11* **The Muratti**[48] [4576] 7-10-13 .... PMoloney 78+
(Miss I E Craig) *hld up: hdwy whn hmpd 3 out: sn lost pl: n.d after* **10/1**
/P-F **4** *1¾* **Carluccios Quest**[15] [94] 7-10-6 .... PMerrigan[(7)] 73
(Mrs H Dalton) *hld up: mstke 3rd: hdwy 6th: rdn and wknd after 2 out* **8/1**
03/ **5** *17* **Optimism (FR)**[782] [4364] 7-10-13 .... AThornton 61+
(R H Alner) *chsd ldrs tl wknd appr 2 out* **5/1**[3]
0P-P **6** *26* **Lewsher**[11] [175] 5-10-3 .... (b[1]) ACCoyle[(3)] 23
(M Mullineaux) *led and sn clr: nt fluent: hit 5th: rdn after next: hung rt and hdd appr 3 out: wknd* **40/1**
7 *dist* **Si Anthony (FR)**[381] 5-10-6 .... TJDreaper[(7)] —
(Ferdy Murphy) *hld up: plld hrd: rdn and wknd after 7th* **9/4**[1]

5m 23.0s (10.90) **Going Correction** +0.35s/f (Yiel)
WFA 4 from 5yo+ 5lb **7** Ran SP% **112.1**
Speed ratings: **93,92,87,87,80 70,**— CSF £20.61 TOTE £7.50: £3.50, £1.70; EX 25.20.
Owner racingforyou.co.uk **Bred** David Jamison Bloodstock And J Dohle **Trained** Basford Green, Staffs

FOCUS
A poor race won by a horse with weak previous form and the time was very modest.

NOTEBOOK
Greencard Golf had started at 100-1 in all his previous races over hurdles - four of them - but he was good enough in a poor race. His previous race suggested he is improving a little, and this confirmed it over a longer trip which suited him.. *(op 5-1 tchd 9-2)*
The Wife's Sister will need to be aimed very low to have a chance of success, but this run showed she is not entirely without hope during the summer. *(op 6-4)*
The Muratti hinted at ability in bumpers two seasons ago and showed a glimmer of form, albeit at a very low level. *Official explanation: jockey said gelding lost a shoe (op 12-1)*
Carluccios Quest has only minor ability, but at least he completed this time. *(op 10-1 tchd 11-1)*
Optimism(FR) showed promise when last on the track two years ago. If he comes on for the run, he should improve. *(op 11-2 tchd 6-1)*
Lewsher needs to show more to enter future calculations. *Official explanation: vet said mare finished lame (op 33-1)*
Si Anthony(FR) was too headstrong, and his rider reported that he kept changing his legs. *Official explanation: jockey said gelding was changing legs on the ground (op 7-2)*

352 PETER J DOUGLAS ENGINEERING SUPER SELLER (A (S) H'CAP HURDLE) (10 hdls 2 omitted) 2m 4f 110y
7:10 (7:10) (Class 5) (0-100,100) 4-7-Y-O **£10,374** (£3,192; £1,596; £798)

Form RPR
U0F/ **1** **Kristoffersen**[425] [4378] 5-11-12 100 .... DRDennis 107
(Ian Williams) *hld up: hit 4th: hdwy appr 6th: chsd ldr 3 out: hrd rdn to ld nr fin* **25/1**
2P/0 **2** *1* **Linus**[20] [5] 7-11-4 95 .... RHobson[(3)] 101
(C J Down) *led to 2nd: led after 5th: rdn flat: hdd nr fin* **14/1**
50-4 **3** *18* **Robbie On Tour (IRE)**[14] [129] 6-10-6 80 .... (t) RGreene 68
(M C Pipe) *prom: chsd ldr 6th: sn rdn: wknd appr 2 out* **8/1**[3]
016- **4** *19* **Caper**[35] [4781] 5-10-2 86 .... (p) AHawkins[(10)] 55
(R Hollinshead) *hld up: n.d* **12/1**
406- **5** *5* **Sninfia (IRE)**[29] [4857] 5-11-5 100 .... DCosgrave[(7)] 64
(G A Ham) *hld up: plld hrd: hdwy and mstke 7th: wknd next* **16/1**
PP-0 **6** *5* **Earn Out**[11] [167] 4-10-6 85 .... TScudamore 39
(M C Pipe) *hld up: rdn 7th: a in rr* **16/1**
50-0 **7** *21* **Lampos (USA)**[12] [152] 5-10-8 82 .... SThomas 20
(Miss J A Camacho) *hld up: rdn 7th: a in rr* **8/1**[3]
506- **8** *2* **Bonnyjo (FR)**[108] [3539] 6-10-9 83 .... TDoyle 19
(P R Webber) *hld up: hit 2nd: a in rr* **11/2**[1]
005- **9** *dist* **Nice Baby (FR)**[22] [4962] 4-10-9 88 .... (v[1]) GSupple —
(M C Pipe) *hld up: bhd fr 6th* **16/1**
50R- **R** **Downtherefordancin (IRE)**[21] [4977] 5-11-1 96 .... (p) AGlassonbury[(7)] —
(M C Pipe) *ref to r* **25/1**
00-3 **S** **Parisienne Gale (IRE)**[12] [147] 6-10-8 82 .... GLee —
(R Ford) *chsd ldrs tl wknd and fell bnd after 7th* **10/1**
001/ **P** **Bravo**[783] [4338] 7-10-11 85 .... (v) PMoloney —
(J Mackie) *prom: hit 6th: sn wknd: t.o whn p.u bef 3 out* **15/2**[2]
410- **P** **Grand Manner (IRE)**[22] [4969] 5-10-11 85 .... RMcGrath —
(K G Reveley) *hld up: in rr whn hit 3rd: t.o fr 6th: p.u bef 3 out* **12/1**
456- **P** **Longstone Lass**[74] [4108] 5-11-3 91 .... ADempsey —
(D Carroll) *led 2nd tl after 5th: rdn and wknd 7th: t.o whn p.u bef next* **14/1**
005- **P** **Comfortable Call**[47] [4623] 7-11-7 95 .... (t) JPByrne —
(H Alexander) *hld up: rdn 5th: bhd fr next: t.o whn p.u bef 7th* **14/1**
05 **P** **Madhahir (IRE)**[10] [182] 5-10-1 75 .... JMogford —
(M J Gingell) *chsd ldrs: rdn and lost pl appr 3rd: sn bhd: t.o whn p.u bef 3 out* **66/1**
B14- **P** **Diamond Joshua (IRE)**[199] [1863] 7-11-7 95 .... (v) OMcPhail —
(J Gallagher) *hld up: rdn whn hit 3rd: bhd fr 5th: t.o whn p.u bef 3 out* **10/1**
00-P **P** **Vitelucy**[15] [110] 6-11-5 93 .... (v) MAFitzgerald —
(Miss S J Wilton) *chsd ldrs: rdn and lost pl after 4th: sn bhd: t.o whn p.u bef 7th* **22/1**

5m 14.9s (2.80) **Going Correction** +0.35s/f (Yiel)
WFA 4 from 5yo+ 5lb **18** Ran SP% **134.1**
Speed ratings: **108,107,100,93,91 89,81,80,**—,— —,—,—,—,— —,—,— CSF £357.27 CT £3087.53 TOTE £32.20: £6.60, £6.30, £1.60, £3.70; EX 1076.00.The winner was bought in for 8,200gns.
Owner Ian Williams **Bred** Five Horses Ltd **Trained** Portway, Worcs
■ Stewards' Enquiry : D R Dennis three-day ban: used whip with excessive force and frequency (May 25-27)

FOCUS
A valuable and well-contested seller, run at a strong pace, with the first two finishing clear and recording creditable figures. The form looks solid.

NOTEBOOK
Kristoffersen, racing for the first time since falling and injuring himself 14 months ago, did well to concede the weight. With he and the runner-up finishing clear off a strong pace, there is nothing wrong with the form. *(tchd 33-1)*
Linus has a good record in selling company and this good effort showed he can win again in that grade or in a modest handicap. *(op 12-1)*
Robbie On Tour(IRE) is one of his stable's more modest inmates and put up only a fair effort at the weights. His trainer will be hunting for a weak opening during the summer. *(op 11-1)*
Caper was never competitively placed but is capable of a bit better in fast-ground sellers.
Sninfia(IRE) was not at her best, but she will be at home in sellers on fast ground during the summer.
Earn Out needs to be competing in weaker sellers than this one. *(tchd 20-1)*
Bonnyjo(FR), dropped to selling company for the first time, did not run well but may be more competitive with this first run for three months behind him. *(op 6-1 tchd 13-2)*

353 WEATHERBYS INSURANCE H'CAP HURDLE (12 hdls 2 omitted) 3m
7:40 (7:40) (Class 3) (0-120,119) 4-Y-0+ **£5,206** (£1,602; £801; £400)

Form RPR
35/P **1** **Hawthorn Prince (IRE)**[15] [109] 10-10-11 104 .... WMarston 114+
(Mrs P Sly) *led to 2nd: chsd ldr 4th: led appr and hit 9th: drvn out* **33/1**
344- **2** *6* **Just Beth**[30] [4837] 9-11-2 114 .... DLaverty[(5)] 118+
(G Fierro) *a.p: chsd wnr after 4 out: rdn and hung lft appr last: no ex flat* **8/1**
202- **3** *3* **Bohemian Boy (IRE)**[28] [4868] 7-11-9 116 .... ATinkler 117+
(M Pitman) *hld up: hdwy 8th: rdn after 3 out: wknd last* **6/1**
22-1 **4** *17* **Water King (USA)**[20] [5] 6-11-1 108 .... MFoley 93+
(R M Stronge) *hld up: hdwy 7th: wknd after 3 out* **11/2**[3]
32-1 **5** *dist* **Brigadier Benson (IRE)**[15] [111] 5-10-8 101 .... AThornton —
(R H Alner) *hld up: hdwy and hit 6th: blnd 8th: wknd appr 3 out* **4/1**[2]
202- **6** *dist* **Called To The Bar**[37] [4754] 12-10-0 93 oh2 .... (v[1]) PMoloney —
(Evan Williams) *plld hrd: trckd ldrs: rdn appr 8th: sn wknd: t.o whn j.rt last* **16/1**
155- **7** *9* **Whispered Secret (GER)**[23] [4948] 6-11-9 119 .... TJMalone[(3)] —
(M C Pipe) *led 2nd: sn clr: hdd & wknd appr 9th* **16/1**
050- **P** **Bunkum**[30] [4836] 7-11-6 113 .... (b[1]) RThornton —
(R Lee) *hld up: bhd and rdn 7th: p.u bef next* **25/1**
324- **P** **Stamparland Hill**[60] [4387] 10-11-1 108 .... ARoss —
(J M Jefferson) *hld up: plld hrd: wknd 8th: t.o whn p.u bef 3 out* **16/1**
052- **P** **Mylo**[24] [4932] 7-11-8 115 .... (b) APMcCoy —
(Jonjo O'Neill) *hld up: bhd fr 4th: rdn and wknd after 7th: t.o whn p.u bef 4 out* **5/2**[1]
P22- **P** **Fabrezan (FR)**[34] [4791] 6-10-1 104 ow2 .... (p) DRCook[(10)] —
(B D Leavy) *prom: lost pl and mstke 5th: bhd fr 8th: t.o whn p.u bef 3 out* **20/1**

6m 8.40s (3.40) **Going Correction** +0.35s/f (Yiel) **11** Ran SP% **118.5**
Speed ratings: **108,106,105,99,**— —,—,—,—,— — CSF £274.69 CT £1826.09 TOTE £32.10: £4.80, £1.90, £2.70; EX 270.60.
Owner Messrs G A Libson,D L Bayliss & G Taylor **Bred** Miss Mary Rita Cahalan **Trained** Thorney, Cambs

FOCUS
A reasonable race of its type for the time of year, run at a strong pace. The winner is handicapped to win again as long as he is not raised more than a couple of pounds for this first success since May 2003.

NOTEBOOK
Hawthorn Prince(IRE) seemed to have benefited from his recent run and was suited by the strong tempo. *He will still be fairly handicapped next time if the Handicapper does not over-react.Official explanation: trainer said, regarding the improved form shown, gelding benefited from its previous run which came after a very long lay-off (op 25-1)*
Just Beth maintains a good level of form. It will not help her handicap mark, but her consistency is admirable. *(tchd 15-2)*
Bohemian Boy(IRE) is in decent form at present, simply finding a couple too good at the weights. *(tchd 7-1)*
Water King(USA)'s stamina was unproven and the way he faded in the straight suggests he may be best at shorter trips. *(op 10-3)*
Brigadier Benson(IRE) ran as if failing to stay, though he weakened so quickly there may have been more to it than that. *(op 5-1)*
Called To The Bar found this company too tough, and failing to settle made his task impossible. A drop back in class is required.
Mylo had plenty in his favour, so this was an abysmal effort. *Official explanation: trainer had no explanation for the poor form shown (op 3-1 tchd 10-3 in a place)*

354 FRANK COCKER'S 50TH, GO GENTLY BENTLEY H'CAP CHASE (11 fncs 1 omitted) 2m
8:10 (8:15) (Class 4) (0-110,102) 5-Y-0+ **£3,789** (£1,166; £583; £291)

Form RPR
F12- **1** **Danish Decorum (IRE)**[226] [1544] 6-11-10 100 .... ChristianWilliams 120+
(Evan Williams) *mde all: sn clr: blnd 5 out: nt fluent next: rdn appr last: styd on u.p* **10/3**[2]
064- **2** *5* **Papua**[29] [4855] 11-11-12 102 .... (b) DRDennis 117+
(N J Hawke) *prom: chsd wnr 6th: mstke 5 out: rdn next: no imp fr 2 out* **6/1**[3]
43-3 **3** *26* **Lubinas (IRE)**[20] [10] 6-11-6 96 .... MAFitzgerald 84
(F Jordan) *mid-div: hdwy 5th: rdn whn j.lft 3 out: sn wknd* **11/4**[1]
540- **4** *20* **Barnards Green (IRE)**[29] [4855] 7-10-7 83 .... AThornton 51
(R H Alner) *hld up: effrt after 5 out: wknd bef next* **10/1**
12-0 **P** **Six Pack (IRE)**[9] [195] 7-11-12 102 .... ADempsey —
(Andrew Turnell) *prom to 4th: t.o whn p.u bef 5 out* **10/1**
P4-P **U** **Javelot D'Or (FR)**[16] [84] 8-10-6 82 .... (t) MFoley —
(Mrs B K Thomson) *hld up: stmbld and uns rdr after 1st* **20/1**
0/P- **P** **Rash Decision (IRE)**[60] [4391] 10-10-12 91 .... LVickers[(3)] —
(I W McInnes) *hld up: bhd fr 5th: t.o whn p.u bef 3 out* **25/1**
6-P5 **P** **Jodante (IRE)**[9] [195] 8-11-10 100 .... (p) RGarritty —
(P Beaumont) *hld up: hdwy appr 7th: sn wknd: t.o whn p.u bef 3 out* **9/1**
03P- **P** **Cool Dante (IRE)**[191] [2002] 10-11-5 95 .... JMMaguire —
(T R George) *chsd ldrs to 4th: wkng whn hit 6th: t.o whn p.u bef 5 out* **12/1**
04-4 **P** **Tates Avenue (IRE)**[9] [193] 7-11-2 92 .... (t) CLlewellyn —
(N A Twiston-Davies) *chsd ldr 3rd to 6th: wknd appr 4 out: t.o whn p.u bef 2 out* **8/1**

4m 8.10s (3.10) **Going Correction** +0.35s/f (Yiel) **10** Ran SP% **119.6**
Speed ratings: **106,103,90,80,**— —,—,—,—,— CSF £24.97 CT £63.12 TOTE £5.00: £2.00, £2.60, £1.60; EX 17.10.
Owner W Ralph Thomas **Bred** Michael Doyle And Christy Ryan **Trained** Cowbridge, Vale Of Glamorgan

FOCUS
A fair race of its type for May, dominated by the winner.

NOTEBOOK
Danish Decorum(IRE) bounced back from a rest spell and dominated throughout. He is a decent sort at this level and there should be more to come. *(op 7-2 tchd 4-1)*
Papua goes well at this track and this was another good effort. A return trip should be noted. *(op 4-1)*
Lubinas(IRE) is better suited by an extra half mile. *(op 5-1 tchd 5-2)*
Barnards Green(IRE) has been below his best of late. *(op 9-1 tchd 12-1)*
Jodante(IRE) was wearing cheekpieces instead of blinkers this time, but they did not have the desired effect. *(op 8-1)*

355 LAURENT PERRIER MAIDEN OPEN NATIONAL HUNT FLAT RACE 2m
8:40 (8:44) (Class 6) 4-6-Y-O **£2,065** (£590; £295)

Form RPR
3- **1** **Scotts Court**[149] [2852] 5-11-4 RGarritty 98+
(N Tinkler) *led 2f: chsd ldr tl led over 4f out: rdn out* **7/1**
0- **2** *4* **Thenameescapesme**[65] [4290] 5-11-4 JMMaguire 93
(T R George) *hld up: plld hrd: hdwy over 3f out: chsd wnr over 2f out: sn rdn: edgd lft ins fnl f: no ex* **16/1**
3 *nk* **Hurricane Francis** 5-11-1 RWalford(3) 93
(T D Walford) *hld up: hdwy 1/2-way: rdn over 2f out: styd on same pce fnl f* **25/1**
2- **4** *3 1/2* **Delightful Cliche**[34] [4801] 4-11-0 WMarston 85
(Mrs P Sly) *prom: chsd wnr over 3f out to over 2f out: wkng whn swtchd rt ins fnl f* **13/2**[3]
5 *2 1/2* **Didn't You Know (FR)** 4-10-0 AGlassonbury(7) 76
(M C Pipe) *hld up: effrt over 2f out: n.d* **10/11**[1]
0- **6** *5* **Flyingwithoutwings**[51] [4540] 6-11-4 RThornton 82
(A King) *hld up: racd keenly: rdn over 3f out: sn btn* **7/2**[2]
0- **7** *22* **Edenderry (IRE)**[34] [4788] 6-11-4 ARoss 60
(A D Brown) *w ldr tl led 14f out: rdn and hdd over 4f out: sn wknd* **66/1**
0- **8** *27* **Tony's Pride**[84] [3953] 5-11-4 AThornton 33
(P T Dalton) *chsd ldrs: rdn over 6f out: wknd over 4f out* **28/1**

4m 25.7s (25.90) **Going Correction** +0.35s/f (Yiel)
WFA 4 from 5yo 4lb 5 from 6yo 2lb **8** Ran SP% **115.1**
Speed ratings: **49,47,46,45,43 41,30,16** CSF £102.46 TOTE £9.30: £1.70, £3.20, £3.90; EX 44.30 Place 6 £1,859.28, Place 5 £549.85.
Owner The Green Syndicate & W Hardie **Bred** A C M Spalding **Trained** Langton, N Yorks

FOCUS
A pedestrian time for a bumper run at a modest pace and rated through the winner.

NOTEBOOK
Scotts Court got the run of the race, but he is going the right way and further improvement can be expected. *(op 5-1 tchd 9-2 and 8-1)*
Thenameescapesme improved on his first effort and is capable of winning a little bumper, especially if he stops pulling so hard. *(op 12-1)*
Hurricane Francis, a 3,500gns yearling, has winners in the family and acquitted himself well on this first attempt. *(tchd 33-1)*
Delightful Cliche has now shown promise in two bumpers and should continue to be there or thereabouts at this level. *(op 6-1)*
Didn't You Know(FR), a half-sister to the useful hurdler and chaser Bounce Back, needs to improve but there was enough promise in this first effort to give connections optimism. *(op Evens tchd 11-10 in places)*
Flyingwithoutwings was disappointing, given the promise of his previous run. *(op 9-2 tchd 10-3)*
T/Plt: £1,107.70 to a £1 stake. Pool: £40,593.70. 26.75 winning tickets. T/Qpdt: £130.80 to a £1 stake. Pool: £3,218.40. 18.20 winning tickets. CR

[243]WORCESTER (L-H)
Saturday, May 14

OFFICIAL GOING: Good to firm (good in places)
Wind: Fresh, across

356 WORCESTERSHIRE NOW MAGAZINE NOVICES' HURDLE (8 hdls) 2m
6:00 (6:05) (Class 4) 4-Y-0+ **£3,458** (£1,064; £532; £266)

Form RPR
0/6- **1** **Beechwood**[34] [4793] 7-10-2 86 KBurke(10) 100+
(P R Rodford) *a in tch: hdwy to ld 3 out: clr fr next: v easily* **25/1**
0- **2** *17* **General Smith**[22] [4958] 6-10-12 VSlattery 83
(H J Evans) *hld up in rr: rdn and hdwy after 5th: styd on to go 2nd run-in* **66/1**
0 **3** *1 3/4* **West End Wonder (IRE)**[14] [133] 6-10-5 AScholes(7) 81
(D Burchell) *in rr tl styd on fr 3 out: nvr nr to chal* **20/1**
46-1 **4** *3/4* **Fairly High (IRE)**[14] [133] 5-10-12 99 (p) ATinkler 81
(N G Ayliffe) *trckd ldr: mstke 3 out: sn rdn: hmpd and lft 2nd last: wknd run-in* **4/5**[1]
050- **5** *18* **Sitting Duck**[108] [3539] 6-10-12 90 JTizzard 63
(B G Powell) *led tl hdd 3 out: sn wknd* **5/1**[2]
6 *nk* **Tog Go Boge (IRE)** 7-10-12 RJohnson 62
(R T Phillips) *a struggling in rr* **13/2**[3]
60-0 **7** *3* **On Top (IRE)**[14] [133] 5-10-12 PJBrennan 59
(Mrs S E Busby) *hld up in mid-div: rdn appr 3 out: sn wknd* **80/1**
F06- **8** *3/4* **Impero**[62] [4343] 7-10-12 74 (b) JGoldstein 58
(G F Bridgwater) *prom tl rdn 4th: wknd next* **40/1**
PP6- **P** **Gentle Warning**[24] [4930] 5-9-12 BenOrde-Powlett(7) —
(M Appleby) *a bhd: t.o whn p.u bef 3 out* **66/1**
PP- **P** **Golden Fitz (ARG)**[16] [1744] 6-10-5 SWalsh(7) —
(R M Stronge) *prom tl wknd 5th: t.o whn p.u bef 3 out* **80/1**
5- **F** **Pure Pleasure (NZ)**[24] [4930] 6-10-12 BJCrowley 83
(N M Babbage) *mid-div: hdwy appr 5th: 2nd but no ch w wnr whn fell last* **5/1**[2]

3m 50.3s (1.90) **Going Correction** +0.275s/f (Yiel) **11** Ran SP% **118.7**
Speed ratings: **106,97,96,96,87 87,85,85,—,—** — CSF £944.34 TOTE £24.20: £4.80, £21.40, £3.40; EX 376.50.
Owner Les Trott **Bred** Peter Taplin **Trained** Ash, Somerset

FOCUS
A very moderate event but an easy winner in Beechwood, who could rate higher.

NOTEBOOK
Beechwood, sharper for his recent return to action following more than a year off, was clearly going best turning for home and cleared right away from the second last. The fast ground was a big plus and he could have more improvement in him based on his old bumper form.
General Smith settled better than he had on his recent hurdles debut. Staying on up the run-in to finish a fairly remote second after being carried to his left at the final flight, he will be suited by a step up in trip.
West End Wonder(IRE) closed on the long home turn and looked a threat at the first flight in the straight, but the effort soon flattened out and he was held when hampered at the last. This was a step up on his recent debut over course and distance, when 20l behind today's fourth, and he needs one more run for a handicap mark. *Official explanation: jockey said gelding hung left (op 33-1 tchd 40-1)*
Fairly High(IRE) had her chance but was found wanting. She ran to a similar level as when an easy winner of a maiden over course and distance last time and will struggle in handicap company off her current mark. *(op 8-11 tchd 5-6 and 10-11 in places)*
Sitting Duck, back in trip for this first start since January, set a moderate pace before fading. *(op 6-1)*
Pure Pleasure(NZ), who ran once on the Flat and once over hurdles in his native New Zealand, showed more than on his recent British debut and would have been second but for falling at the last. *(op 8-1)*

357 DAVID LEES H'CAP HURDLE (10 hdls) 2m 4f
6:30 (6:31) (Class 4) (0-100,99) 4-Y-0+ **£3,185** (£910; £455)

Form RPR
60-1 **1** **Tinstre (IRE)**[6] [238] 7-11-0 **87** 7ex SCurran 98+
(P W Hiatt) *mid-div: stdy hdwy fr 3 out: hmpd by faller 2 out: led last: rdn clr* **6/1**[2]
556- **2** *6* **Roman Candle (IRE)**[257] [1331] 9-10-3 **76** JEMoore 79
(Lucinda Featherstone) *t.k.h in rr: rdn and hdwy appr 3 out: styd on to chse wnr run-in* **7/1**[3]
RRP- **3** *3/4* **Popsi's Cloggs**[181] [2224] 13-9-11 **73** oh9 DCrosse(3) 75
(D W Lewis) *led after 1st: hdd bef 2 out where lft in ld: hdd last: one pce run-in* **33/1**
2-F0 **4** *5* **Sir Walter (IRE)**[14] [136] 12-10-13 **93** MrRMcCarthy(7) 91+
(D Burchell) *bhd tl hdwy appr 3 out: styd on: nvr nr to chal* **11/1**
060- **5** *8* **Sandywell George**[34] [4799] 10-10-12 **90** (t) TJPhelan(5) 79
(L P Grassick) *led tl after 1st: trckd ldr tl rdn and wknd after 4 out* **25/1**
500- **6** *15* **Infidel (IRE)**[163] [2593] 5-11-7 **94** NFehily 68
(C J Mann) *hld up: hdwy on outside 4th: rdn and one pce fr 3 out* **10/1**
15-4 **7** *8* **Prince Of Aragon**[14] [135] 9-10-11 **84** (t) BHitchcott 50
(Miss Suzy Smith) *in tch: rdn after 5th: wknd appr 3 out* **6/1**[2]
P-0U **8** *4* **Saorsie**[5] [265] 7-11-12 **99** (v[1]) SFox 61
(J C Fox) *trckd ldrs tl wknd appr 3 out* **12/1**
000- **9** *8* **Fair Touch (IRE)**[72] [4132] 6-10-11 **84** (t) JAMcCarthy 38
(C P Morlock) *trckd ldrs tl rdn and wknd qckly appr 3 out* **11/1**
P0-0 **10** *17* **Heriot**[6] [243] 4-10-7 **85** (tp) PJBrennan 17
(S C Burrough) *in tch: rdn 5th: sn bhd* **33/1**
00-0 **11** *12* **Inducement**[14] [136] 9-10-12 **85** RJohnson 10
(R M Stronge) *mid-div: rdn and wknd appr 4 out* **10/1**
656- **12** *14* **Taranai (IRE)**[47] [4604] 4-10-3 **88** (t) CMStudd(7) —
(B W Duke) *a bhd: lost tch 4 out* **14/1**
/00- **P** **Neptune**[16] [3433] 9-10-9 **82** MBatchelor —
(J C Fox) *stmbld 1st: reminders 4th: bhd whn p.u bef 4 out* **25/1**
PU0- **P** **Monty Be Quick**[86] [3906] 9-10-4 **80** AHoneyball(3) —
(J M Castle) *mid-div: wknd 6th: t.o whn p.u bef 3 out* **33/1**
000- **P** **Miss Muscat**[98] [3690] 5-9-7 **73** oh5 SWalsh(7) —
(Evan Williams) *trckd ldrs: lost pl after 4th: t.o whn p.u bef 4 out* **25/1**
5-22 **F** **College City (IRE)**[7] [213] 6-11-0 **87** (b) HOliver 91+
(R C Guest) *hld up in mid-div: hdwy fr 4 out: led bef fell 2 out* **5/2**[1]

4m 55.8s (7.80) **Going Correction** +0.275s/f (Yiel)
WFA 4 from 5yo+ 5lb **16** Ran SP% **139.2**
Speed ratings: **95,92,92,90,87 81,77,76,73,66 61,55,—,—,—** — CSF £51.58 CT £1348.98 TOTE £9.20: £2.90, £2.40, £18.90, £2.40; EX 81.90.
Owner M Wennington **Bred** Hugo Merry **Trained** Hook Norton, Oxon

FOCUS
A very moderate handicap but Tinstre has been rated as value for eight lengths, although College City would have given him something to think about. The fourth is the best guide to the level.

NOTEBOOK
Tinstre(IRE) defied the penalty for his Uttoxeter victory. He had a bit to do entering the straight and was forced to sidestep the faller two out, but was well on top once striking the front at the final flight. *(op 9-2)*
Roman Candle(IRE), having his first run since August, ran up to the level of his course and distance effort the month before. *(op 8-1)*
Popsi's Cloggs was having his first run since November following a string of non-completions over fences. He showed plenty of spark out in front and was only seen off at the final flight.
Sir Walter(IRE) likes it here and was runner-up in this event a year ago. *(op 10-1)*
Sandywell George adopted more positive tactics and this was his best run since his last win in December 2003.
Infidel(IRE) ran an encouraging race on his first start since December. *(op 12-1)*
Saorsie, in a first-time visor, was well placed turning out of the back straight but his stamina then appeared to give way. *(op 11-1)*
College City(IRE), back over hurdles, got away with a mistake at the fourth from home but was not so lucky two flights later. He had just taken the lead when coming down and would have been second at worst. *(op 4-1)*
Monty Be Quick *Official explanation: trainer said gelding had a breathing problem (op 4-1)*

358 RACING BY THE RIVER BEGINNERS' CHASE (18 fncs) 2m 7f 110y
7:00 (7:00) (Class 4) 5-Y-0+ **£4,173** (£1,284; £642; £321)

Form RPR
33-2 **1** **Muttley Maguire (IRE)**[15] [106] 6-11-2 98 JTizzard 105+
(B G Powell) *trckd ldr: led 6th: clr 5 out: comf* **9/2**[2]
00-U **2** *11* **Rigmarole**[6] [244] 7-11-2 (bt) RWalsh 91
(P F Nicholls) *hld up: hmpd 5th: hdwy to trck wnr 5 out: rdn and no ex after 3 out* **8/13**[1]
PU-P **3** *5* **High Peak**[15] [106] 8-10-13 71 RYoung(3) 86
(J W Mullins) *hld up in rr: styd on appr 4 out: wknd appr 2 out* **25/1**
2/F- **4** *13* **Pharly Star**[27] [4879] 11-11-2 RJohnson 76+
(H D Daly) *led to 6th: mstke 13th: wknd next* **5/1**[3]
44-3 **5** *22* **Pollensa Bay**[16] [74] 6-11-2 81 LAspell 51
(S A Brookshaw) *j.rt thrght: a in rr: lost tch 13th* **16/1**
506/ **6** *21* **Matrix (AUS)**[412] 8-11-2 NFehily 30
(K McAuliffe) *in tch: hdwy 9th: rdn and wknd appr 4 out* **80/1**
020- **7** *dist* **Charm Offensive**[37] [4754] 7-10-2 68 (t) RLucey-Butler(7) —
(C J Gray) *a bhd: t.o fr 6th* **50/1**
030/ **P** **Ruby Dante (IRE)**[42] 7-10-2 SWalsh(7) —
(Mrs A M Thorpe) *trckd ldrs: wknd 8th: p.u after mstke next* **25/1**
600- **P** **Ballyaahbutt (IRE)**[43] [4680] 6-11-2 JamesDavies —
(B G Powell) *trckd ldrs: rdn 12th: wknd rapidly and t.o whn p.u bef 4 out* **66/1**

5m 59.4s (4.50) **Going Correction** +0.275s/f (Yiel) **9** Ran SP% **115.0**
Speed ratings: **103,99,97,93,86 79,—,—,—** CSF £7.92 TOTE £5.80: £1.40, £1.10, £7.00; EX 15.90.

Owner Mrs Jean R Bishop **Bred** A W Buller **Trained** Morestead, Hants

FOCUS
An ordinary novice chase, but Muttley Maguire jumped well out in front and turned over the odds-on Rigmarole, who failed to stay. The winner could be rated higher.

NOTEBOOK
Muttley Maguire(IRE) is apparently hard to get fit and needed his run at Southwell. Jumping soundly, if out to his right a lot of the time, he kept up the gallop to draw the sting out of the favourite. He is on the upgrade and there should be more to come. *(op 4-1 tchd 5-1)*
Rigmarole had the blinkers back on. A casualty on his recent chase debut here, he jumped better on this occasion but, after looking to be going well on the long home turn, he ran out of stamina *from the third last. He does not stay three miles but should get two and a half.Official explanation: jockey said gelding had a breathing problem (op 4-6)*
High Peak had ground conditions in his favour and this was his best run over regulation fences, although that is not saying a great deal. *(op 40-1 tchd 66-1)*
Pharly Star was unable to get his own way out in front and his jumping again lacked polish. *(tchd 9-2)*

359 CANNONS HEALTH CLUB NOVICES' HURDLE (12 hdls) 3m
7:30 (7:30) (Class 4) 4-Y-0+ **£3,445** (£1,060; £530; £265)

Form | | | | RPR
0U-F **1** **Bee Hawk**[8] [201] 6-11-0 105 ....(t) RWalsh 106+
(P F Nicholls) *hld up in rr: hdwy 4 out: smooth hdwy to ld last: sn clr* **1/2**[1]
00-1 **2** *9* **Esters Boy**[15] [105] 7-11-6 102 .... JEMoore 102+
(P G Murphy) *hld up: hdwy 8th: wnt 2nd 4 out: led next: rdn and hdd last: one pce run-in* **3/1**[2]
6PP- **3** *11* **Safe To Blush**[24] [4929] 7-10-7 87 .... MBradburne 80+
(P A Pritchard) *led tl hdd 3 out: sn btn and j. bdly rt last 2* **18/1**
5-5 **4** *½* **Beet De Bob (IRE)**[11] [178] 7-10-7 .... MrPCowley(7) 83
(Mrs S E Busby) *in tch tl rdn and one pce after 3 out* **8/1**[3]
P65- **5** *14* **Coyote Lakes**[23] [4938] 6-11-0 80 .... SDurack 69
(M J McGrath) *racd wd: a.p: chsd ldr 1/2-way tl mstke 4 out: wknd bef next* **66/1**
P0P- **6** *2 ½* **Pendil's Princess**[114] [3438] 6-10-7 .... JTizzard 60
(S E H Sherwood) *trckd ldrs to half way: wknd bef 4 out* **33/1**
U52/ **P** **Protection Money**[423] [4401] 5-10-9 85 .... TJPhelan(5) —
(L P Grassick) *t.k.h: hld up: lost tch 8th: t.o whn p.u bef last* **20/1**

6m 0.30s (11.10) **Going Correction** +0.275s/f (Yiel) **7** Ran SP% **117.2**
Speed ratings: **92,89,85,85,80 79,—** CSF £2.51 TOTE £1.60: £1.10, £2.20; EX 2.10.
Owner R D Cox **Bred** R D Cox **Trained** Ditcheat, Somerset

FOCUS
A slowly-run affair and a modest time for the type of race. The first two ran close to their marks.

NOTEBOOK
Bee Hawk was found a straightforward opportunity to get off the mark and accomplished it easily *enough. He jumped well and, a brother to Irbee, should make a chaser. (op 4-7 tchd 8-13 and 4-6 in places)*
Esters Boy did not seem all that happy on the fast ground but ran to his mark in defeat *(op 5-2 tchd 10-3)*
Safe To Blush was encountering fast ground for the first time. Headed at the third from home and quickly beaten, she veered badly out to her right at both the remaining obstacles. *(op 16-1 tchd 20-1)*
Beet De Bob(IRE) jumped these brush obstacles better and is now qualified for handicaps. *(op 16-1)*
Coyote Lakes has beaten just two rivals home in four attempts over hurdles.
Pendil's Princess *(op 20-1)*

360 BARBARA BRETHERTON BIRTHDAY H'CAP CHASE (15 fncs) 2m 4f 110y
8:00 (8:00) (Class 3) (0-125,123) 5-Y-0+ **£6,987** (£2,150; £1,075; £537)

Form | | | | RPR
P26- **1** **Luneray (FR)**[22] [4955] 6-10-8 **105** ....(t) RWalsh 122+
(P F Nicholls) *hld up: hdwy to go 2nd 9th: led 3 out: rdn clr appr last: idled and strly rdn run-in: jst hld on* **5/1**[3]
F4-5 **2** *shd* **Kind Sir**[20] [4] 9-10-1 **98** .... WHutchinson 112
(A W Carroll) *trckd ldr: ld appr 9th: rdn and hdd 3 out: clsd rapidly on wnr run-in: jst failed* **7/1**
323- **3** *8* **Deep King (IRE)**[212] [1720] 10-10-8 **108** .... RYoung(3) 116+
(J W Mullins) *in tch: hit 3 out: wkng whn blnd next* **5/1**[3]
0-F **4** *hd* **Lik Wood Power (NZ)**[15] [108] 8-11-5 **116** .... HOliver 124+
(R C Guest) *bhd whn hmpd 5th: nvr on terms* **4/1**[2]
U2-4 **5** *18* **Killultagh Storm (IRE)**[15] [97] 11-11-7 **118** ....(p) BJCrowley 106
(Noel T Chance) *trckd ldrs: mstke 10th: sn wknd* **7/1**
F1-4 **6** *1 ¾* **Grey Report (IRE)**[14] [130] 8-11-12 **123** .... RJohnson 109
(P J Hobbs) *led: hit 5th: stopped rapidly and hdd bef j. slowly 9th: sn wl bhd* **3/1**[1]
24-0 **7** *14* **Celtic Star (IRE)**[20] [4] 7-9-12 **98** ....(p) DCrosse(3) 70
(Mrs L Williamson) *bhd: mstke 8th: sn lost tch* **33/1**
0P-0 **P** **Tacolino (FR)**[9] [195] 11-11-2 **113** .... JPMcNamara —
(O Brennan) *mid-div: bhd whn p.u after 11th* **16/1**
25P- **P** **El Bandito (IRE)**[28] [4869] 11-11-4 **115** .... SDurack —
(R Lee) *hld up in tch: mstke 5th: rdn 6th: lost tch after next: t.o whn p.u bef 4 out* **14/1**

5m 9.90s (2.40) **Going Correction** +0.275s/f (Yiel) **9** Ran SP% **118.8**
Speed ratings: **106,105,102,102,95 95,89,—,—** CSF £40.98 CT £186.70 TOTE £9.00: £2.40, £4.00, £1.30; EX 50.30.
Owner Sandicroft Stud **Bred** Mrs Emile Ouvry **Trained** Ditcheat, Somerset
■ Stewards' Enquiry : R Johnson one-day ban: used whip with excessive force (May 25)

FOCUS
A fair handicap run at a decent pace. The winner has been rated as value for further.

NOTEBOOK
Luneray(FR), who had the tongue-strap refitted, went about five lengths up between the last two fences, but tied up badly on the run-in and the line arrived just in time. Although she has form over further this trip did appear to stretch her stamina. *(op 11-2)*
Kind Sir was unable to dominate with Grey Report in opposition but was left with the advantage after that rival pulled himself up. Headed at the third last, to his credit he did not drop away and, staying on willingly after the last, he nearly snatched the race. *(op 13-2)*
Deep King(IRE) paid his way last summer with a string of consistent performances and this was an encouraging return to action. *(op 6-1)*
Lik Wood Power(NZ), a faller on his return last month, was ridden with restraint this time. After improving leaving the back straight, he could make no further inroads once in line for home. He is well handicapped at present and there should be a race for him over the summer. *(op 9-2 tchd 5-1)*
Grey Report(IRE) was in front when suddenly deciding to draw stumps going to the middle fence down the back. He is an extremely risky proposition. *(op 4-1)*
Tacolino(FR) was pulled up after blundering at the 11th where his rider lost an iron. He was held at the time. *(op 12-1)*

361 HOME OF SUMMER JUMPING STANDARD OPEN NATIONAL HUNT FLAT RACE 2m
8:30 (8:30) (Class 6) 4-6-Y-0 **£1,951** (£557; £278)

Form | | | | RPR
1 **Tokala** 4-10-9 .... MrSWalker(5) 91
(B G Powell) *trckd ldrs: wnt 2nd 4f out: outpcd 3f out: rallied gamely u.p to ld wl ins fnl f* **12/1**[3]
2- **2** *¾* **Earl Of Forestry (GER)**[26] [4916] 4-11-0 .... RWalsh 90
(P F Nicholls) *hld up in tch: hdwy to go 2nd over 3f out: led over 2f out: strly rdn and hdd wl ins fnl f* **1/3**[1]
3 *3* **Ar Nos Na Gaoithe (IRE)**[49] 6-10-4 .... SWalsh(7) 85+
(Mrs A M Thorpe) *hld up in rr: rdn and hdwy fr 4f out: hung lft ins fnl 3f but kpt on wl fnl f* **50/1**
/0-0 **4** *5* **Flurry**[14] [138] 6-10-11 .... PHide 79
(C J Down) *hld up in rr: rdn 4f out: hdwy 3f out: one pce ins fnl 2f* **12/1**[3]
003- **5** *1 ¾* **Men Of Destiny (IRE)**[83] [3973] 4-10-7 .... WPKavanagh(7) 80
(B G Powell) *led for 2f: rdn 5f out: sn btn but kpt on one pce fnl 3f* **8/1**[2]
0-0 **6** *1* **Surfboard (IRE)**[14] [138] 4-11-0 .... VSlattery 79
(P A Blockley) *t.k.h: led after 2f: rdn and hdd over 2f out: sn wknd* **40/1**
7 *18* **Logies Lass** 6-10-11 .... PJBrennan 58
(J S Smith) *in rr whn rdn 4f out: sn wl bhd* **28/1**
8 *3* **Lens Boy** 6-10-11 .... MrRMcCarthy(7) 62
(D Burchell) *trckd ldr after 6f: wknd over 3f out* **33/1**

3m 49.3s (1.50) **Going Correction** +0.275s/f (Yiel) **8** Ran SP% **112.3**
Speed ratings: **107,106,105,102,101 101,92,90** CSF £16.17 TOTE £13.60: £2.50, £1.02, £8.20; EX 27.50 Place 6 £348.62, Place 5 £11.98.
Owner W Smith **Bred** Greenfield Stud S A **Trained** Morestead, Hants

FOCUS
A modest bumper, rated through the fourth and the sixth.

NOTEBOOK
Tokala is out of an unraced half-sister to Prix de Diane winner Lypharita who has produced four minor Flat winners and one over hurdles. Seeing a racecourse for the second time, having taken part in a schooling event at Cheltenham where he reportedly hated the testing ground, he showed a good attitude to see off the favourite. *(op 10-1 tchd 14-1)*
Earl Of Forestry(GER), runner-up in a weak event on his debut, struck the front in the straight but was worried out of it. A greater test of stamina will suit him. *(op 4-9 tchd 40-85 in a place)*
Ar Nos Na Gaoithe(IRE) failed to complete in a couple of point-to-points in March, the second of them in a tongue tie. She would have finished a bit closer to the first two had her rider not temporarily lost an iron in the final furlong. *(op 25-1)*
Flurry ran a reasonable race at this venue two outings ago but was well beaten here last time. *(op 10-1)*
Men Of Destiny(IRE) has not progressed since running out when looking likely to score on his debut in January. *(op 6-1 tchd 11-2)*
T/Plt: £621.10 to a £1 stake. Pool: £37,692.30. 44.30 winning tickets. T/Qpdt: £2.80 to a £1 stake. Pool: £3,593.70. 925.00 winning tickets. JS

LE LION-D'ANGERS (R-H)
Saturday, May 14

OFFICIAL GOING: Soft

362a PRIX ALAIN DU BREIL GRAND STEEPLE-CHASE DE PRINTEMPS 2m 7f
3:10 (3:11) 5-Y-0+ **£14,298** (£7,149; £4,170; £2,830; £1,340)

| | | | RPR
1 **Caprice Du Hasard (FR)**[1309] 7-9-13 .... AThierry —
(E Leray, France)
2 *15* **Satin Turk (FR)**[595] [1461] 9-10-7 .... RDelozier —
(G Chaignon, France)
3 *nk* **Le Grand Jeu (FR)**[226] 6-9-13 .... GOlivier —
(P Journiac, France)
4 *5* **Itador (FR)**[340] 9-10-3 .... —
(E Leray, France)
5 *3* **Muscat Du Turf (FR)**[683] 9-10-5 .... —
(E Leenders, France)
6 *2* **Luzcadou (FR)**[16] [87] 12-10-1 ....(b) KJMercer —
(Ferdy Murphy) *towards rr & making minor mstks early, closed up to 6th starting final circuit, ridden 3 out, gradually weakened*
7 *10* **Gosse D'Alleuds (FR)** 11-9-10 .... —
(G Lecomte, France)
P **Jurrassique (FR)**[45] 8-10-1 .... —
(F Doumen, France)
F **Hamcon Bleu (FR)**[391] 10-10-5 ....(b) —
(T Poche, France)
F **Tresor Clementais (FR)**[903] 7-10-9 .... —
(S Foucher, France)
F **Izmir Du Cosquet (FR)**[333] 9-11-0 .... —
(E Leenders, France)
P **Dauphin Des Carres (FR)**[125] [3292] 7-11-2 .... —
(T Civel, France)
P **Esprit Du Chene (FR)**[11] 8-10-9 .... —
(Mme D Guibourne, France)
U **Espoir Du Printemp (FR)**[125] [3292] 9-10-4 .... —
(P Peltier, France)

6m 17.63s **14** Ran
PARI-MUTUEL: WIN 5.00 (coupled with Itador); PL 3.10, 4.10, 3.40; DF 60.10.
Owner J Duchesne **Bred** J Juif **Trained** France

NOTEBOOK
Luzcadou(FR) did not jump fluently and, although he made his move from the rear beginning the final circuit, it was a short-lived effort.

180 FAKENHAM (L-H)

Sunday, May 15

OFFICIAL GOING: Good to firm (firm in places)

Wind: virtually nil Weather: bright and sunny

363 100 YEARS OF RACING AT FAKENHAM (S) H'CAP HURDLE (9 hdls) 2m

2:20 (2:22) (Class 5) (0-90,90) 4-Y-0+ **£2,597** (£742; £371)

Form RPR

4U0- **1** **Clydeoneeyed**[26] 4918 6-9-8 **65** ... SWalsh(7) 67+
(K F Clutterbuck) *bhd: rdn 5th: sn outpcd: 7th and drvn whn three ldrs departed 3 out: plugged into ld after next: kpt on gamely: unimpressiv* **5/1**[2]

00-0 **2** *2* **Reedsman (IRE)**[6] 263 4-10-4 **72** ...(b) HOliver 65
(R C Guest) *plld hrd in rr: mstke 2nd: jnd ldrs 5th: lft 2nd briefly 3 out: drvn to regain 2nd bef last: fnd nthing* **25/1**

0P-5 **3** *5* **Let's Celebrate**[17] 75 5-11-4 **82** ... LAspell 76+
(F Jordan) *t.k.h: towards rr early: rdn 6th: effrt and lft in ld next: drvn and hdd after next: fnd nil: btn 3rd whn mstke last* **11/2**[3]

PP-P **4** *5* **Beyond Borders (USA)**[17] 75 7-11-1 **79** ...(b) TDoyle 71+
(S Gollings) *rr and drvn 3rd: last after 5th and nt keen: wl bhd whn hmpd 3 out: plugged on in farcical event* **11/1**

/6P- **5** *11* **Glory Of Love**[182] 2219 10-10-11 **75** ... GSupple 51
(J A Supple) *nvr bttr than midfield: lost tch and hmpd 3 out* **80/1**

6-42 **F** **Approaching Land (IRE)**[11] 180 10-11-12 **90** ... APMcCoy —
(M W Easterby) *led tl fell 3 out* **10/11**[1]

4P-0 **B** **Imperative (USA)**[12] 11 5-10-9 **80** ...(v) MrMMackley(7) —
(M J Gingell) *chsd ldr tl 6th: jst losing 3rd whn b.d 3 out* **50/1**

0P-0 **B** **Princess Stephanie**[15] 134 7-9-12 **64** oh4 ow3 ... CHonour(5) —
(M J Gingell) *pressed ldrs: wnt cl 2nd bef 3 out where b.d* **16/1**

-PR0 **U** **Seemore Sunshine**[11] 180 8-11-5 **83** ... SCurran —
(M J Gingell) *bhd: struggling 5th: t.o whn hmpd by refusing rival and rdr flew off at last* **66/1**

323/ **R** **Estuary (USA)**[29] 10-11-7 **85** ... SDurack —
(Ms A E Embiricos) *chsd ldrs: wkng whn hmpd 3 out: remote 6th whn ref at hurdle lying flat on grnd at last* **10/1**

3m 54.8s (-14.10) **Going Correction** -1.00s/f (Hard)
WFA 4 from 5yo+ 4lb **10** Ran SP% **116.3**
Speed ratings: **95,94,91,89,83** —,—,—,—,— CSF £105.77 CT £713.35 TOTE £7.70: £1.90, £5.30, £1.70; EX 151.50.There was no bid for the winner.

Owner The T Class Partnership **Bred** Mrs Elizabeth Wilkinson **Trained** Exning, Suffolk

FOCUS
Awful stuff - as bad as it gets - and a dramatic conclusion with Approaching Land falling at the third last and bringing down his two closest pursuers. This left the way clear for Clydeoneeyed to get off the mark.

NOTEBOOK
Clydeoneeyed was a very fortunate winner. A poor horse, he was plugging on at his own pace when the three ahead of him departed, kindly leaving the path clear for him to score his first success. He was winning here off a mark of 65 and will need to improve if he is to defy a rise as he would only have finished third had they all stood up. *(op 9-1 tchd 10-1)*

Reedsman(IRE) is still only four and ran his best race to date. He was in the process of running well when running out last time and looks to be finding some form. He would have given the winner more to do had he not pulled so hard in the early stages. *(op 33-1 tchd 22-1)*

Let's Celebrate would only have finished sixth but for the incident at the third last and was lucky to collect some place money. *(op 9-2)*

Approaching Land(IRE) still looked the likeliest winner when coming down at the third last. He jumped the fence well enough, but came down on the landing side and can consider himself unlucky. He has yet to win under rules, but should not be too long in doing so. *(op Evens tchd 5-6, 11-10 in a place)*

Imperative(USA) was in the process of running a fair race, but was beginning to back track when brought down at the third last. *(op Evens tchd 5-6, 11-10 in a place)*

Princess Stephanie looked booked for at least second when brought down by the fall of the favourite. *(op Evens tchd 5-6, 11-10 in a place)*

364 GG.COM BEGINNERS' CHASE (12 fncs) 2m 110y

2:50 (2:51) (Class 4) 5-Y-0+ **£4,104** (£1,263; £631; £315)

Form RPR

03-4 **1** **In The Frame (IRE)**[21] 2 6-11-0 ... ChristianWilliams 110+
(Evan Williams) *chsd ldr: nt fluent 7th: demoted whn mstke pckd bdly 8th: lft 2nd 3 out: led nring 2 out: clr bef last: rdn out* **4/1**[2]

4-P2 **2** *5* **Kercabellec (FR)**[7] 239 7-10-7 90 ... APogson(7) 100
(J R Cornwall) *sent to post early: str hold in clr ld: pressed fr 9th: drvn and hdd bef 2 out: one pce after* **11/1**[3]

F4-2 **3** *5* **Emanic (FR)**[8] 217 5-10-12 120 ...(t) APMcCoy 98+
(P F Nicholls) *hld up: nt fluent 4th: wnt 2nd at 8th tl mstke 3 out and drvn: btn bef last: mstke and wknd* **4/11**[1]

25P- **4** *25* **Squeeze (IRE)**[42] 4716 7-11-0 112 ... TScudamore 75+
(B N Pollock) *last pair: lost tch 9th: sn wl bhd: eased flat* **16/1**

4m 3.70s (-16.90) **Going Correction** -1.00s/f (Hard)
WFA 5 from 6yo+ 2lb **4** Ran SP% **107.5**
Speed ratings: **99,96,94,82** CSF £28.71 TOTE £5.60; EX 33.80.

Owner The Gascoigne Brookes Partnership **Bred** Mull Enterprises Ltd **Trained** Cowbridge, Vale Of Glamorgan

FOCUS
A modest beginners' chase. The winner has been rated value for ten lengths but was still 7lb off his hurdles form.

NOTEBOOK
In The Frame(IRE) has made a good start to his chasing career and was getting off the mark over the larger obstacles at the third attempt. In truth it was a modest race, but now he has the win under his belt, should be able to progress. *(op 7-2 tchd 9-2)*

Kercabellec(FR) has long been a frustrating character and seems to have been around for ages, yet is remarkably only a seven-year-old. He ran his best race so far over fences but was still below his hurdles form and can never be backed with any confidence. *(op 14-1)*

Emanic(FR) has basically been disappointing and does not look to have taken as well to fences as was once hoped. This was around a stone off his best form over either hurdles or fences. *(op 2-5 tchd 4-9 in a place)*

Squeeze(IRE) offered little hope for the future.

365 EAST WINCH NOVICES' H'CAP HURDLE (13 hdls) 2m 7f 110y

3:20 (3:20) (Class 4) (0-100,95) 4-Y-0+ **£3,740** (£1,151; £575; £287)

Form RPR

6P-3 **1** **Charlie's Double**[16] 105 6-10-2 **74** ... DCrosse(3) 75+
(J R Best) *hld up in tch: wnt 2nd after 3 out: led next: edgd lft fnl turn: hld on wl flat: readily* **5/1**[2]

03-6 **2** *1* **La Concha (IRE)**[16] 100 4-11-3 **92** ... SDurack 85
(M J McGrath) *hld up in rr: drvn and prog in 4th after 3 out: wnt 2nd and tried to chal last: a hld flat* **25/1**

44-4 **3** *9* **The Gangerman (IRE)**[12] 178 5-11-4 **94** ... MGoldstein(7) 84
(N A Twiston-Davies) *cl up: lost pl 9th: drvn next: mod 6th bef 3 out: styd on after next to snatch 3rd* **13/2**

P-54 **4** *½* **Sconced (USA)**[12] 167 10-11-3 **86** ...(p) HOliver 76
(R C Guest) *rn in snatches and urged at several stages: last and drvn and nt looking keen after 9th: mod late prog to snatch 4th* **11/2**[3]

P3P- **5** *¾* **Walsingham (IRE)**[28] 4889 7-11-1 **84** ... SThomas 77+
(Mrs Jeremy Young) *led at modest pce: drvn and hdd 2 out: n.m.r bef last and plld outside: clr 3rd last but fdd bdly and hung lft nr fin* **16/1**

63-3 **6** *6* **New Perk (IRE)**[11] 181 7-11-2 **85** ... SCurran 69+
(M J Gingell) *prom tl rdn bef 3 out: lost tch bef next* **8/1**

12P- **7** *11* **Light Des Mulottes (FR)**[60] 4395 6-11-12 **95** ...(b) APMcCoy 72+
(C R Egerton) *nt a fluent: rr tl quick move to 2nd bef 9th: drvn 3 out: fnd nil: wl btn next* **13/8**[1]

566- **8** *16* **Seattle Prince (USA)**[22] 4977 7-10-12 **81** ... TScudamore 37
(S Gollings) *nt fluent 3rd: mstke 7th: handy tl dropped rr and drvn 9th: nvr gng wl after* **12/1**

5m 48.3s (-18.10) **Going Correction** -1.00s/f (Hard)
WFA 4 from 5yo+ 5lb **8** Ran SP% **112.0**
Speed ratings: **90,89,86,86,86 84,80,75** CSF £96.70 CT £810.95 TOTE £6.40: £1.60, £4.40, £2.00; EX 179.00.

Owner The Highly Hopeful Club **Bred** J R Heatley **Trained** Hucking, Kent

FOCUS
An ordinary event that did not take a lot of winning, but one that may produce the odd winner at a similar level.

NOTEBOOK
Charlie's Double, having his first start on a fast surface, improved on all previous form and responded gamely to his jockey's urgings to record his first success. The ground is clearly the key and he can now go about exploiting his lowly rating.

La Concha(IRE) is slowly getting the hang of racing and ran by far his best race to date here. It was the weight that made the difference in the end and he should soon be getting his head in front. *(op 20-1)*

The Gangerman(IRE) ran another reasonable race in defeat and his consistency will see him rewarded sooner rather than later. *(tchd 6-1)*

Sconced(USA) is a quirky old character and had to be coaxed along for much of the way. It is debatable whether he has the heart to win races these days. *(op 13-2 tchd 5-1)*

Walsingham(IRE) ran better than his finishing position suggests, being a clear third at the last before hanging and fading badly to end up fifth. He has a similar race in him, but the manner he finished the race was rather worrying. *(op 14-1)*

Light Des Mulottes(FR) has never been the heartiest of characters and found nothing when asked. He has plenty of ability, but is evidently not one to trust. *(tchd 7-4)*

366 FAKENHAM RACECOURSE CENTENARY CELEBRATION H'CAP CHASE (18 fncs) 3m 110y

3:55 (3:58) (Class 3) (0-115,114) 5-Y-0+ **£6,776** (£2,085; £1,042; £521)

Form RPR

P-32 **1** **Paxford Jack**[5] 288 9-10-10 **98** ...(v) APMcCoy 108
(M F Harris) *mde all: drew clr w one rival fr 15th: urged along and kpt finding ex fr next* **5/4**[1]

PP-3 **2** *10* **Prince Highlight (IRE)**[17] 76 10-10-4 **92** ... JMMaguire 98+
(Mrs Jeremy Young) *hdwy 5th: wnt 2nd at 12th: ev ch whn bmpd w wnr 3 out: sn drvn: 5l 2nd and btn whn blnd bdly last* **11/4**[2]

240- **3** *29* **Strong Magic (IRE)**[32] 4820 13-10-0 **95** ... APogson(7) 66
(J R Cornwall) *sn in last pair: rdn and lost tch 11th: lft v poor 3rd 3 out: pckd last* **5/1**[3]

46-P **4** *12* **Pangeran (USA)**[16] 101 13-9-7 **88** oh25 ... SWalsh(7) 47
(N B King) *s.i.s: bhd: mstke 7th: 15l adrift 13th: t.o 3 out* **33/1**

6P-4 **P** **Klondike Charger (USA)**[16] 103 11-10-3 **91** ... JGoldstein —
(Miss J S Davis) *chsd ldr tl rdn and lost pl 11th: poor last whn p.u after 14th* **7/1**

0/ **P** **Uncle Arthur (IRE)**[335] 744 11-11-3 **105** ... SDurack —
(Mrs D Haine) *chsd ldrs: mstke 10th: nt fluent 14th and rdn: sn outpcd: mod 3rd whn p.u 3 out: dismntd* **14/1**

6m 8.30s (-29.30) **Going Correction** -1.00s/f (Hard) **6** Ran SP% **109.9**
Speed ratings: **106,102,93,89**,— — CSF £5.12 CT £10.05 TOTE £1.90: £1.60, £1.60; EX 5.80.

Owner Mrs Ruth Nelmes **Bred** Shade Oak Stud **Trained** Edgecote, Oxon

FOCUS
Not much of a race, but Paxford Jack put up a strong galloping performance under a good ride from McCoy.

NOTEBOOK
Paxford Jack was given an aggressive ride by McCoy and galloped on far too strongly for anything else. He did it with quite a bit to spare in the end and is entitled to go close in a follow up bid. *(op 13-8 tchd 7-4 in a place)*

Prince Highlight(IRE) is on a winning mark and has fared much better the last twice. He still has his jumping problems though, as was evident with his blunder at the last, and he is never one to place total faith in. *(op 7-2)*

Strong Magic(IRE) was well adrift of the front two and achieved little back in third. *(op 7-2)*

Uncle Arthur(IRE) had run a fair race, but was well held when pulled up and dismounted three out. *(op 8-1)*

367 FAKENHAM & WELLS TIMES NOVICES' HURDLE (9 hdls 2 omitted) 2m 4f

4:25 (4:28) (Class 4) 4-Y-0+ **£4,134** (£1,272; £636; £318)

Form RPR

43-1 **1** **Common Girl (IRE)**[11] 182 7-10-12 110 ... JEMoore 106+
(O Brennan) *led at slow pce: rdn and jst hdd whn lft 4l clr at original 4 out: styd on: comf* **2/1**[2]

64-F **2** *2 ½* **Festive Chimes (IRE)**[11] 185 4-9-8 98 ow1 ... SWalsh(7) 90+
(N B King) *plld hrd in midfield: j. slowly 5th: rdn 3 out: wnt 2nd passing omitted next: drvn bef last: wl hld flat* **5/1**[3]

601- **3** *5* **Zaffre (IRE)**[24] 4936 6-10-5 100 ... RLucey-Butler(7) 95
(Miss Z C Davison) *last whn mstke and rdr lost iron 4th: stl 5th and rdn passing 2 out: styd on to snatch 3rd but n.d* **10/1**

00-5 **4** *shd* **Lothian Falcon**[15] 124 6-10-9 ... GCarenza(3) 95
(P Maddison) *pressed ldrs: 3rd and rdn passing 2 out: wknd bef last and nt fluent: demoted on line* **16/1**

0 **5** *6* **Messager (FR)**[10] 192 5-10-12 .... GSupple 89
(J A Supple) *prom early: rr 7th: wl bhd bef 3 out* **100/1**

0-1 **6** *7* **Bayadere (GER)**[16] 102 5-10-12 .... SCurran 82
(K F Clutterbuck) *bhd: hmpd 2nd: effrt to midfield whn hmpd again original 4 out: wnt 2nd briefly next but drvn: sn fdd tamely* **12/1**

0- **U** **Grey Prince**[27] 4916 4-10-1 ow1.............................. MrMatthewSmith(7) —
(G Prodromou) *j.rt and uns rdr 2nd* **100/1**

042- **F** **Emkanat (IRE)**[88] 3891 4-10-0 .... PJBrennan —
(K A Morgan) *cl 2nd tl led and fell heavily 4 out: dead* **33/1**

463- **B** **Nippy Des Mottes (FR)**[23] 4958 4-10-7 106.............................. (t) APMcCoy —
(P F Nicholls) *settled trcking ldrs: cl 3rd whn b.d 4 out* **13/8**[1]

4m 57.1s (-15.10) **Going Correction** -1.00s/f (Hard)
WFA 4 from 5yo+ 5lb **9** Ran SP% **115.7**
Speed ratings: **90,89,87,86,84 81,—,—,—** CSF £12.78 TOTE £2.80: £1.40, £1.30, £2.10; EX 14.70.
Owner J W Hardy **Bred** Nicholas Keogh **Trained** Worksop, Notts

FOCUS
The shape of the race changed in the final half mile with Emkanat bringing down Nippy Des Mottes. The proximity of the fifth is a concern, but the form looks solid and the first two have been rated to their marks. The second-last flight was omitted on both circuits.

NOTEBOOK
Common Girl(IRE) is a most consistent mare and although possibly a little lucky to win here, could not be begrudged victory. She will jump fences in time and may improve further for the larger obstacles. *(op 7-4 tchd 9-4)*
Festive Chimes(IRE) ran well on ground probably a bit quicker than ideal and, although fortunate to finish second, undoubtedly has a race of this nature in her. *(op 6-1)*
Zaffre(IRE) plugged on without ever posing a serious threat and stepped up on her maiden win. She should get further and is still open to further improvement. *(op 17-2)*
Lothian Falcon was robbed of third on the line, but has shown enough in two starts over hurdles to take a similar race. *(op 33-1 tchd 40-1)*
Emkanat(IRE) was in the process of running a huge race and still had every chance of winning when taking a crashing fall at the fourth last. Sadly she did not get up. *(op 7-4 tchd 6-4)*
Nippy Des Mottes(FR) was a little unfortunate to be brought down by the fall of Emkanat. He held *every chance at the time and should not be long in getting off the mark for top connections. (op 7-4 tchd 6-4)*

368 LIGHT DRAGOONS H'CAP CHASE (FOR THE PRINCE OF WALES CUP) (15 fncs 1 omitted) 2m 5f 110y
4:55 (4:56) (Class 4) (0-100,100) 5-Y-0+ **£4,202** (£1,293; £646; £323)

Form RPR

6/P- **1** **Gale Star (IRE)**[175] 2368 12-10-4 **78**.............................. (t) JEMoore 91+
(O Brennan) *keen in last: hdwy 12th: led sn after 2 out: clr flat: comf* **17/2**[3]

3P2- **2** *5* **Balla D'Aire (IRE)**[205] 1801 10-10-0 **74** oh2.............................. SCurran 82
(K F Clutterbuck) *led: drvn and hdd sn after 2 out: kpt on same pce* **12/1**

13-3 **3** *3* **Tipp Top (IRE)**[11] 183 8-11-0 **88**.............................. (t) JPMcNamara 93
(O Brennan) *hld up in tch: effrt in 3l 4th bef 13th: rdn and one pce fr next* **3/1**[2]

P02- **4** *3* **Guilsborough Gorse**[22] 4980 10-11-5 **100**.............................. MrMWalford(7) 103+
(T D Walford) *keen in 3rd: wnt 2nd at 11th: w ldr whn hit 3 out: rdn next: wknd bef omitted last* **3/1**[2]

034- **P** **Poly Amanshaa (IRE)**[48] 4606 13-11-6 **94**.............................. TDoyle —
(M C Banks) *nt fluent 9th: chsd ldr tl 11th: lost tch qckly 3 out: p.u next* **10/1**

04-2 **P** **Tirley Storm**[11] 181 10-10-2 **76**.............................. PJBrennan —
(J S Smith) *settled 4th: blnd 8th: b.b.v and collapsed nearing 10th: bk on feet within 5 minutes* **2/1**[1]

5m 25.7s (-18.80) **Going Correction** -1.00s/f (Hard) **6** Ran SP% **110.6**
Speed ratings: **94,92,91,90,—** — CSF £81.87 CT £359.55 TOTE £7.90: £4.20, £5.00; EX 46.00 Place 6 £1,900.71, Place 5 £632.53.
Owner O Brennan **Bred** Louis Vambeck **Trained** Worksop, Notts

FOCUS
The last fence was bypassed, leaving a three-furlong run-in. A minor surprise with what looked Owen Brennan's second string taking the spoils. Not a strong race, but the winner has been rated to the best of his Irish form and the next three were close to their marks.

NOTEBOOK
Gale Star(IRE) pulled up on the course on his first start since arriving from Ireland back in November and was having his first start since. He has clearly improved quite a bit on that initial effort and ran out a ready winner. He should be more than capable of winning again under a penalty. *(op 8-1 tchd 7-1)*
Balla D'Aire(IRE) was a bit unfortunate to bump into the unexposed winner and will find easier opportunities. *(op 11-2)*
Tipp Top(IRE) the seemingly better-fancied of the Brennan runners, has his chance and was not good enough on the day. *(op 4-1)*
Guilsborough Gorse was the only other to complete, but was comfortably held. *(op 11-4 tchd 7-2)*
Tirley Storm received sympathy from many after he burst in front of the stands with a circuit to run *and collapsed. He just needed some time to recover and was back up after the race had finished. (op 11-4)*
T/Plt: £1,847.00 to a £1 stake. Pool: £38,333.65. 15.15 winning tickets. T/Qpdt: £117.40 to a £1 stake. Pool: £3,095.40. 19.50 winning tickets. IM

MARKET RASEN (R-H)
Sunday, May 15

OFFICIAL GOING: Good (good to firm in places)
The well watered ground was descibed as 'just on the fast side of good'. Due to re-seeding work the third-last fence was omitted on each circuit.
Wind: almost nil Weather: fine and sunny

369 MERCEDES-BENZ OF HULL MAIDEN HURDLE (8 hdls) 2m 1f 110y
2:00 (2:00) (Class 4) 4-Y-0+ **£3,479** (£994; £497)

Form RPR

50-4 **1** **Bishop's Bridge (IRE)**[18] 59 7-11-2 105.............................. (b) RJohnson 102+
(Andrew Turnell) *wnt prom 5th: led appr 2 out: clr whn hit last: eased towards fin* **5/2**[1]

P62- **2** *10* **Leopold (SLO)**[28] 4890 4-10-5 98.............................. CPoste(7) 86+
(M F Harris) *hld up: hdwy after 5th: wnt 2nd appr 2 out: kpt on: no ch w wnr* **11/2**[3]

P55- **3** *10* **Given A Chance**[12] 4715 4-10-9 104.............................. LVickers(3) 76+
(Mrs S Lamyman) *chsd ldrs: led and hit 6th: hdd appr 2 out: fdd* **8/1**

05- **4** *11* **Encounter**[77] 4084 9-11-2 .... ARoss 68+
(A D Brown) *hld up and bhd: gd hdwy to chse ldrs 6th: wknd appr next* **100/1**

00- **5** *2 1/2* **Imperial Royale (IRE)**[42] 4715 4-10-2 .... TBurrows(10) 61
(P L Clinton) *sn bhd: kpt on fr 6th: nvr nr ldrs* **100/1**

0 **6** *1/2* **Tin Healy's Pass**[8] 209 5-11-2 .... BHarding 64
(I McMath) *mid-div: sme hdwy 5th: nvr nr ldrs* **28/1**

030- **7** *1* **Rocket Force (USA)**[43] 4166 5-11-2 102.............................. ATinkler 63
(S Gollings) *mid-div: hit 4th: nvr a threat* **16/1**

400- **8** *10* **All Marque (IRE)**[117] 3407 5-10-2 .... WKennedy(7) 46
(S Gollings) *in rr: nvr on terms* **66/1**

06-3 **9** *nk* **Parsifal**[15] 133 6-10-13 93.............................. (v) TJMalone(3) 53
(P Wegmann) *stdd s: hld up in rr: nvr on terms* **16/1**

P- **10** *2* **Desert Image (IRE)**[109] 3534 4-10-12 .... WHutchinson 47
(C Tinkler) *hdwy and prom 5th: lost pl appr 2 out* **9/1**

326- **11** *14* **Always Flying (USA)**[43] 3887 4-10-12 96.............................. PRobson 33
(N Wilson) *led and sn clr: jnd 5th: hdd next: sn lost pl* **10/1**

/00- **12** *18* **Blunham**[19] 3326 5-10-6 70.............................. DSwan(10) 19
(M C Chapman) *t.k.h: sn chsng ldr: lost pl 5th: sn bhd* **100/1**

13 *dist* **Scary Night (IRE)**[6] 5-11-2 .... SFox —
(M J Gingell) *bhd fr 5th: t.o* **100/1**

P **Raybers Magic**[20] 4-10-0 .... DCCostello(5) —
(J R Weymes) *sluggish s: bhd tl p.u bef 5th* **150/1**

4/ **P** **Joe Cooley (IRE)**[393] 4866 5-11-2 .... GLee —
(K A Ryan) *mid-div: hdwy 5th: sn chsng ldrs: 4th whn p.u bef 2 out* **7/2**[2]

40-0 **P** **Royal Exposure (IRE)**[11] 180 8-11-2 74.............................. JPByrne —
(H Alexander) *hdwy 4th: sn in tch: wknd 6th: bhd whn p.u bef next* **66/1**

4m 6.50s (-9.90) **Going Correction** -0.60s/f (Firm)
WFA 4 from 5yo+ 4lb **16** Ran SP% **119.2**
Speed ratings: **98,93,89,84,83 82,82,78,77,76 70,62,—,—,—** — CSF £15.84 TOTE £3.40: £1.60, £2.50, £3.10; EX 19.80.
Owner S Kimber **Bred** F Fennelly **Trained** Broad Hinton, Wilts

FOCUS
A weak maiden hurdle and the winner value for a bit further. the form could be rated higher but is limited by the time.

NOTEBOOK
Bishop's Bridge(IRE), who looked in peak trim, bounced off the ground and was value 15 lengths in a very weak maiden hurdle. *(tchd 11-4)*
Leopold(SLO), who had 7lb to find with the winner on official ratings, proved no match whatsoever. *(op 5-1)*
Given A Chance, a winner in rock-bottom grade on the level since his apparently much improved effort behind Admiral here six week ago, had the ground to suit but he was always tending to do too much and he faded badly over the last two flights. *(op 7-1)*
Encounter, a keen type, was having his first run for his new stable and he was ridden as if his stamina is suspect.
Imperial Royale(IRE), a winner at the the lowest level on the Flat, is struggling to make any impact over hurdles.
Joe Cooley(IRE) *Official explanation: jockey said gelding pulled up lame (tchd 4-1)*

370 GRIMSBY INSTITUTE H'CAP HURDLE (8 hdls) 2m 1f 110y
2:30 (2:30) (Class 4) (0-110,110) 4-Y-0+ **£4,927** (£1,516; £758; £379)

Form RPR

/30- **1** **Hilltime (IRE)**[169] 2481 5-11-0 **103**.............................. DCCostello(5) 108+
(J J Quinn) *chsd ldrs: led 3rd: rdn out* **10/1**

60-6 **2** *2 1/2* **Lone Soldier (FR)**[7] 238 9-10-0 **84**.............................. GLee 85
(S B Clark) *wnt prom 4th: styd on fr 2 out: tk 2nd run-in* **20/1**

60-3 **3** *2* **Beseiged (USA)**[10] 197 8-11-9 **110**.............................. PWhelan(3) 109
(R A Fahey) *trckd ldrs: t.k.h: chal appr 2 out: sn rdn: fdd run-in* **9/4**[1]

444- **4** *nk* **Ipledgeallegiance (USA)**[35] 4784 9-10-11 **95**.............................. DO'Meara 94
(N Waggott) *hdwy 5th: sn chsng ldrs: one pce fr 2 out* **16/1**

00- **5** *8* **Northern Friend**[100] 3676 5-10-2 **89** oh1 ow5.............................. (p) LMcGrath(3) 80
(R C Guest) *in rr: hdwy 6th: kpt on: nvr nr ldrs* **14/1**

5-22 **6** *1/2* **Borehill Joker**[5] 275 9-10-9 **100**.............................. WKennedy(7) 91
(J L Spearing) *chsd ldrs: wknd 2 out* **4/1**[2]

0-3P **7** *5* **Bernardon (GER)**[7] 246 9-11-2 **107**.............................. AHawkins(7) 93
(A J Deakin) *hld up in mid-div: effrt 5th: wknd next* **20/1**

0-35 **8** *3* **Errol**[7] 238 6-10-2 **93**.............................. EDehdashti(7) 76
(J F Coupland) *hdwy to chse ldrs 4th: wknd appr 2 out* **7/1**[3]

61-5 **9** *2* **Ramblees Holly**[21] 13 7-11-1 **104**.............................. DMcGann(5) 85
(R S Wood) *chsd ldrs: lost pl after 5th* **16/1**

124/ **10** *5* **Tory Boy**[980] 1182 10-10-7 **91**.............................. WMarston 67
(D T Turner) *a in rr* **20/1**

F-6P **11** *7* **Dabus**[7] 239 10-11-3 **104**.............................. ACCoyle(3) 73
(M C Chapman) *s.i.s: a in rr* **14/1**

F26- **12** *6* **All Bleevable**[27] 4443 8-11-1 **102**.............................. LVickers(3) 65
(Mrs S Lamyman) *chsd ldrs: lost pl after 6th* **12/1**

000- **13** *12* **Valuable (IRE)**[40] 4738 8-10-3 **87**.............................. (t) KJohnson 38
(R Johnson) *a bhd* **33/1**

00-P **14** *3/4* **Win Alot**[11] 181 7-9-7 **84** oh6.............................. CMStudd(7) 34
(M C Chapman) *led to 3rd: lost pl 5th: sn bhd* **50/1**

05-0 **P** **Rainbow River (IRE)**[10] 197 7-9-9 **89** ow4.............................. DSwan(10) —
(M C Chapman) *t.k.h: trckd ldrs: lost pl 4th: sn bhd: p.u bef 2 out* **33/1**

4m 4.30s (-12.10) **Going Correction** -0.60s/f (Firm) **15** Ran SP% **127.3**
Speed ratings: **102,100,100,99,96 96,93,92,91,89 86,83,78,77,—** CSF £203.01 CT £619.66 TOTE £13.80: £3.60, £7.60, £1.40; EX 466.60.
Owner Mrs S Quinn **Bred** Rossenarra Stud **Trained** Settrington, N Yorks

FOCUS
A moderate contest but rock solid form for the grade with the first four clear in the end.

NOTEBOOK
Hilltime(IRE), absent since November, had the ground to suit. His stamina is strictly limited and after looking in total command late on he had to be kept right up to his work. *(op 9-1)*
Lone Soldier(FR), who has won over fences and over further in the past, had Lee aboard and, with the ground to suit, he ran his best race for some time.
Beseiged(USA) as usual travelled strongly but it was two years to the day since he last won, from a 10lb lower mark, and his constant battle with the Handicappers seems to have dulled his will to win. *(op 5-2 tchd 11-4)*
Ipledgeallegiance(USA), back over hurdles, stuck on in willing fashion on ground plenty quick enough for him. *(tchd 20-1)*
Northern Friend, absent since February, was in effect 6lb out of the handicap and a selling hurdle may prove a more reachable target. *(op 12-1)*
Rainbow River(IRE) *Official explanation: jockey said gelding pulled up lame*

371 GEOFFREY & MOLLIE BOOTH MEMORIAL BEGINNERS' CHASE (12 fncs 2 omitted) 2m 6f 110y
3:00 (3:00) (Class 3) 5-Y-0+ **£5,586** (£1,815; £977)

Form RPR

PP-P **1** **Seaniethesmuggler (IRE)**[21] 10 7-10-9 95.............................. WKennedy(7) 109+
(S Gollings) *trckd ldrs: wnt 2nd 3 out: led appr next: sn drew clr* **13/2**[3]

U6-4 **2** *9* **Sailor A'Hoy**[9] 10 9-10-13 92.............................. ACCoyle(3) 100
(M Mullineaux) *chsd ldrs: wnt 2nd 8th: j.rt 2 out: sn btn* **4/1**[2]

30-2 **3** *dist* **Wet Lips (AUS)**[15] 121 7-10-13 ....(p) LMcGrath(3) 94
(R C Guest) *led to 2nd: lft in ld 4th: hdd appr 2 out: fnd nthing: 6l 3rd whn fell last: eventually rmntd* **4/7**[1]

00-P **F** **China Chase (IRE)**[9] 202 6-11-2 77....................(b[1]) WHutchinson —
(J L Spearing) *led 2nd: j. rt and fell 4th* **14/1**

004- **P** **Crosby Don**[89] 3869 10-11-2 57.................... BHarding —
(J R Weymes) *t.k.h: wnt 2nd 4th: wknd 8th: poor 4th whn p.u bef 2 out* **16/1**

5m 48.0s (1.60) **Going Correction** -0.45s/f (Good)
WFA 5 from 6yo+ 3lb **5** Ran SP% **109.5**
Speed ratings: **79,75,—,—,—** CSF £30.30 TOTE £6.60: £2.50, £1.60; EX 33.20.
Owner J B Webb **Bred** Mrs Grace Bracken **Trained** Scamblesby, Lincs

FOCUS
A dire beginners' chase run at a very steady pace and the form, rated through the winner's hurdle rating, looks distinctly moderate.

NOTEBOOK
Seaniethesmuggler(IRE), pulled up on all four starts since he took a weak novices' hurdle here in November, did not go without support and in the end came right away. A winning Irish pointer, he will be lucky to find another contest as poor. *(op 12-1 after early 16-1 in places)*
Sailor A'Hoy, rated 4lb behind the winner on official figures, was getting much the worst of the argument when diving right at the second last obstacle. *(op 5-2)*
Wet Lips(AUS), different class to these over hurdles, jumped soundly on his chasing bow but he emptied badly and was booked for a well-beaten third when he crashed out at the last. Even though this trip is beyond his best it was a disappointing start to this phase of his career. *(op 4-6)*
Crosby Don *Official explanation: jockey said gelding pulled up lame (op 14-1)*

372 HARRIS CONSTRUCTION (LEEDS) H'CAP HURDLE (10 hdls) 2m 6f
3:30 (3:30) (Class 3) (0-125,125) 4-Y-0+ **£4,901** (£1,508; £754; £377)

Form RPR

1P-P **1** **Almnadia (IRE)**[15] 127 6-11-6 **119**.................... RThornton 119
(S Gollings) *led tl hdd appr 4th: led appr 2 out: j.lft last: edgd lft run-in: all out* **11/1**

421- **2** *½* **Cottam Grange**[22] 4977 5-10-7 **109**.................... MrTGreenall(3) 108
(M W Easterby) *trckd ldrs: wnt 2nd 2 out: upsides whn bmpd last: hung rt and carried lft run-in: no ex nr fin* **3/1**[1]

212- **3** *14* **Nick's Choice**[23] 4960 9-10-12 **116**.................... LStephens(5) 103+
(D Burchell) *trckd ldrs: one pce fr 2 out* **11/2**[2]

244- **4** *2½* **Siegfrieds Night (IRE)**[25] 4930 4-10-10 **117**.................... ACCoyle(3) 97+
(M C Chapman) *mstkes: bhd: hdwy 3 out: kpt on fr next* **16/1**

51-0 **5** *18* **Queen Soraya**[15] 127 7-11-7 **120**.................... WMarston 85
(Miss H C Knight) *chsd ldr: led appr 4th: hdd appr 2 out: sn wknd* **3/1**[1]

000- **6** *3* **Migration**[19] 3592 9-11-6 **122**.................... LVickers(3) 84
(Mrs S Lamyman) *hld up in rr: hdwy 7th: rdn after next: wknd bef 2 out* **10/1**

42-0 **7** *dist* **Fishki's Lad**[15] 121 10-10-11 **110**....................(p) GLee —
(E W Tuer) *chsd ldrs: pushed along 5th: lost pl after next: bhd 3 out: sn t.o* **7/1**[3]

12P- **8** *¾* **Sister Cinnamon**[91] 3839 7-10-6 **105**.................... RJohnson —
(S Gollings) *chsd ldrs: lost pl 3 out: sn bhd: t.o* **11/1**

0UP- **P** **Plutocrat**[16] 4300 9-11-9 **125**....................(p) GBerridge(3) —
(L Lungo) *nt fluent in rr: t.o 7th: p.u bef 2 out* **14/1**

5m 17.9s (-10.40) **Going Correction** -0.60s/f (Firm)
WFA 4 from 5yo+ 5lb **9** Ran SP% **116.2**
Speed ratings: **94,93,88,87,81 80,—,—,—** CSF £45.40 CT £206.39 TOTE £12.90: £3.60, £1.30, £1.70; EX 73.00.
Owner J Hennessy **Bred** Barouche Stud Ltd **Trained** Scamblesby, Lincs

FOCUS
A modest handicap run at just a steady gallop and the first two who came clear, having had a coming together on the run-in. Both could struggle when reassessed.

NOTEBOOK
Almnadia(IRE), much happier going right-handed, came off best in a barging match from the final flight, postponing her retirement to the paddocks. *(op 14-1)*
Cottam Grange, 11lb higher, hung in behind the winner when called on for an effort between the last two. After collecting a bump at the last, they got into each others' way on the run-in and the suspicion was at the line he was just outbattled. *(op 7-2)*
Nick's Choice, on ground plenty quick enough for him, was left behind by the first two from two out. *(op 9-2)*
Siegfrieds Night(IRE) clattered his way round in the rear. Staying on when it was all over, this will put him right for Cartmel later in the month.
Queen Soraya, unable to dominate this time, eventually showed ahead but she dropped right out when headed. This looked a jaded effort. *(op 7-2)*
Migration, as usual walked to post, had a run on the Flat two weeks ago but he looks bang out of form over hurdles at present. *(op 9-1 tchd 11-1)*
Sister Cinnamon *Official explanation: jockey said mare finished distressed (op 10-1)*
Plutocrat *Official explanation: jockey said gelding bled from the nose (op 10-1)*

373 NAPOLEONS CASINO HULL H'CAP CHASE (12 fncs 2 omitted) 2m 6f 110y
4:05 (4:05) (Class 4) (0-100,88) 5-Y-0+ **£3,465** (£990; £495)

Form RPR

20-5 **1** **Lanmire Tower (IRE)**[17] 81 11-10-8 **77**....................(p) WKennedy(7) 89
(S Gollings) *a chsng ldrs: led 2 out: hld on wl towards fin* **5/1**[3]

P32- **2** *1* **Were Not Stoppin**[22] 4976 10-11-5 **88**.................... MissJFoster(7) 98
(R Bastiman) *led to 2 out: upsides last: nt qckn last 75yds* **10/3**[1]

31-0 **3** *1* **Kimoe Warrior**[12] 176 7-11-2 **81**....................(b) ACCoyle(3) 90
(M Mullineaux) *hdwy to chse ldrs 8th: upsides last: no ex* **4/1**[2]

PB0- **4** *1¾* **Master Jackson**[42] 4718 6-10-12 **77**.................... RWalford(3) 85+
(T D Walford) *j. slowly: chsd ldrs: styd on fr 3 out: kpt on wl run-in* **6/1**

PP-4 **5** *17* **Pornic (FR)**[17] 81 11-10-13 **78**....................(t) ONelmes(3) 68
(A Crook) *lost pl 7th: hdwy 3 out: chsng ldrs appr 2 out: sn wknd* **11/2**

P-06 **6** *nk* **Cromwell (IRE)**[7] 240 10-10-0 **69**....................(b) CMStudd(7) 59
(M C Chapman) *w ldrs: drvn along 5th: lost pl 3 out: sn bhd* **8/1**

PU0- **P** **Middleway**[159] 2695 9-10-2 **69**.................... DCCostello(5) —
(Miss Kate Milligan) *chsd ldrs: lost pl 9th: bhd whn p.u bef 2 out* **10/1**

45P- **P** **Atomic Breeze (IRE)**[138] 3044 11-11-0 **76**.................... RMcGrath —
(D M Forster) *wnt prom 5th: lost pl 8th: t.o whn p.u after 3 out* **20/1**

5m 35.3s (-11.10) **Going Correction** -0.45s/f (Good) **8** Ran SP% **114.4**
Speed ratings: **101,100,100,99,93 93,—,—** CSF £22.75 CT £72.45 TOTE £5.40: £1.60, £1.50, £2.00; EX 15.20.
Owner Mrs D Dukes **Bred** Miss Emer Carty **Trained** Scamblesby, Lincs
■ A 539/1 treble at his local track for trainer Steve Gollings.

FOCUS
A very moderate handicap chase, a seller in all but name, with the runner-up setting the standard.

NOTEBOOK
Lanmire Tower(IRE)dropped in the weights and back on his favoured good ground, took advantage of a weak handicap but nothing was left to chance. *(op 9-2 tchd 11-2)*
Were Not Stoppin, happy in front, battled all the way to the line and gets on well with this rider. *(op 3-1 tchd 7-2)*
Kimoe Warrior likes the track and the ground and this was one of his better efforts. *(tchd 7-2)*
Master Jackson, absent for six weeks, was hesitant at his fences but he stayed on all the way to the line giving connections some hope. *(op 5-1 tchd 7-1)*
Pornic(FR), in a first-time tongue tie, has run some of his best races in the past here but he looks very much on the downgrade now. *(op 5-1)*

374 GEOSTAR HUNTERS' CHASE (12 fncs 2 omitted) 2m 6f 110y
4:35 (4:35) (Class 6) 5-Y-0+ **£1,282** (£366; £183)

Form RPR

454- **1** **Royal Snoopy (IRE)**[14] 12-11-7 100....................(b) MrRAbrahams(7) 106+
(Mrs Sarah L Dent) *chsd ldrs: led and qcknd 8th: styd on fr 2 out* **6/5**[1]

1P-3 **2** *4* **Teeton Priceless**[21] 6 10-11-4 .... MrNPearce(7) 98
(Mrs Joan Tice) *chsd ldrs: wnt 2nd after 8th: nt qckn fr 2 out* **2/1**[2]

PP-0 **3** *dist* **Oscar Pepper (USA)**[13] 151 8-11-7 .... MrSCharlton(7) —
(M J Brown) *outpcd and bhd fr 6th: t.o 5th whn hit 3 out: lft distant 3rd last: btn 60 l* **14/1**

26-P **P** **Supercharmer**[5] 278 11-11-7 .... MissJRiding(7) —
(M A Humphreys) *led to 8th: sn wknd: distant 4th whn p.u bef 2 out* **9/2**[3]

P5P/ **U** **Rigadoon (IRE)**[63] 9-11-7 ....(p) MrJHaley(7) —
(Mrs J L Haley) *outpcd and bhd 6th: wnt mod 3rd appr 2 out: blnd and uns rdr last* **12/1**

5m 34.1s (-12.30) **Going Correction** -0.45s/f (Good) **5** Ran SP% **111.3**
Speed ratings: **103,101,—,—,—** CSF £4.23 TOTE £2.20: £1.50, £1.50; EX 4.90.
Owner Michael D Abrahams **Bred** Mrs M Doran **Trained** Billingham, Co Durham
■ A first winner under Rules for rider Rupert Abrahams.

FOCUS
A moderate hunter chase, but run marginally faster time than the preceding handicap.

NOTEBOOK
Royal Snoopy(IRE), bang out of luck in this last year, came here on the back of a point win and, kept right up to his work, always looked in command. *(op 11-10 tchd 5-4)*
Teeton Priceless, a winner of six points, is not as effective under Rules but to her credit she pushed the winner hard all the way to the line. *(op 6-4 tchd 85-40 in a place)*
Oscar Pepper(USA), a hesitant jumper, was struggling with a full circuit to go but in the end picked *up £183 prizemoney, a modest sum compared with what he earned in his prime on the level. (op 16-1 tchd 20-1)*

375 NAPOLEONS CASINO HULL STANDARD OPEN NATIONAL HUNT FLAT RACE 2m 1f 110y
5:05 (5:07) (Class 6) 4-6-Y-0 **£1,995** (£570; £285)

Form RPR

3- **1** **Alaskan Fizz**[104] 3626 4-10-5 .... WMarston 80+
(R T Phillips) *trckd ldrs: wnt 2nd over 4f out: led over 2f out: drvn rt out* **11/4**[2]

23/- **2** *3* **Lago D'Oro**[406] 4663 5-10-9 .... RGarritty 81+
(Miss J A Camacho) *trckd ldrs: led over 4f out tl over 2f out: kpt on wl* **5/2**[1]

0- **3** *5* **Cash On Friday**[60] 4406 4-10-9 .... LMcGrath(3) 78
(R C Guest) *rr-div: hdwy 4f out: hrd rdn and styd on fnl 2f* **14/1**

4 *hd* **Valhuec (FR)** 5-10-11 ow2.................... MrKGreen(7) 84
(Mrs J R Buckley) *rangy: unf: unruly s: hdwy 4f out: styd on fnl 2f* **40/1**

5 *7* **Talpour (IRE)** 5-10-13 .... ACCoyle(3) 75
(M C Chapman) *rangy: unf: chsd ldrs: wnt 3rd over 2f out: wknd 1f out* **14/1**

6 *nk* **Silent Age (IRE)** 4-10-12 .... RThornton 71
(S Gollings) *rangy: mid-div: hdwy 3f out: edgd lft and kpt on fnl f* **7/1**

7 *1¼* **Double Measure** 5-10-13 .... RWalford(3) 73
(T D Walford) *rangy: unf: rr-div: hdwy 6f out: nvr nr ldrs* **20/1**

8 *3* **Burgau (IRE)** 6-10-13 .... LVickers(3) 70
(A D Brown) *rangy: unf: sn bhd: hdwy u.p on outside 6f out: nvr on terms* **66/1**

9 *nk* **Jallopy (IRE)** 4-10-12 .... NHannity 66
(G A Harker) *rangy: bkwd: chsd ldrs: wknd over 3f out* **9/2**[3]

0/ **10** *2½* **Terimons Daughter**[583] 1605 6-10-9 .... GLee 60
(E W Tuer) *led tl 6f out: wknd 4f out* **18/1**

0/ **11** *2* **Mapilut Du Moulin (FR)**[430] 4277 5-11-2 .... AThornton 65
(C R Dore) *mid-div: sme hdwy 6f out: nvr on terms* **20/1**

5- **12** *4* **Penney Lane**[35] 4788 4-10-0 .... DCCostello(5) 50
(Miss Kate Milligan) *trckd ldrs: led 6f out tl over 4f out: wknd 3f out* **12/1**

13 *nk* **Ma Burls** 5-10-9 .... SFox 54
(M J Gingell) *leggy: lt-f: unf: rr-div: sme hdwy on outer 6f out: wknd over 4f out* **100/1**

0- **14** *12* **Birtley Boy**[245] 1415 6-11-2 .... KJohnson 49
(R Johnson) *stdd s: a bhd: t.o 6f out* **50/1**

0 **15** *dist* **Holme Lane (IRE)**[15] 131 4-10-12 .... ARoss —
(A D Brown) *trckd ldrs: lost pl 7f out: sn bhd: t.o 3f out* **66/1**

4m 10.9s (-5.60) **Going Correction** -0.60s/f (Firm)
WFA 4 from 5yo 4lb 5 from 6yo 2lb **15** Ran SP% **130.1**
Speed ratings: **88,86,84,84,81 81,80,79,79,77 77,75,75,69,—** CSF £10.36 TOTE £3.90: £2.00, £1.70, £6.00; EX 10.60 Place 6 £25.64, Place 5 £15.61.
Owner Mrs Claire Smith **Bred** Crandon Park Stud **Trained** Adlestrop, Gloucs
■ Stewards' Enquiry : L McGrath one-day ban: used whip with excessive frequency (May 26)

FOCUS
A steadily-run low-grade bumper rated through the winner.

NOTEBOOK
Alaskan Fizz, weak in the market, had finished third on her only previous start at Exeter in January. Long in the back, she looked in total command when taking charge but in the end had to be kept right up to her work. *(op 15-8)*
Lago D'Oro, having her fourth start, was having her first outing for over a year. She went on and stepped up the pace and to her credit fought back all the way to the line. *(op 3-1 tchd 7-2)*
Cash On Friday, who finished last but one on his debut two months earlier, stayed on under a hard ride to snatch third spot. *(op 20-1)*
Valhuec(FR), a handful at the start, stayed on in his own time and will hopefully settle down with racing.
Talpour(IRE), who continually wished his tail on his debut, tired badly late on. *(op 12-1)*
Silent Age(IRE), who swished his tail in the paddock, showed definite signs of inexperience on his racecourse debut. *(tchd 8-1)*
Jallopy(IRE), a cheap buy, looked fat and he was back-pedalling before the final turn. *Official explanation: jockey said gelding hung left-handed throughout (op 8-1 tchd 9-1)*
T/Plt: £37.60 to a £1 stake. Pool: £31,740.85. 614.75 winning tickets. T/Qpdt: £11.80 to a £1 stake. Pool: £1,590.70. 99.30 winning tickets. WG

376 - 383a (Foreign Racing) - See Raceform Interactive

[284]NEWTON ABBOT (L-H)

Monday, May 16

OFFICIAL GOING: Good (good to soft in places)

The ground had eased dramatically since the meeting last week after nearly an inch of rain had fallen on Saturday.

Wind: Almost nil Weather: Fine

384 PARTYFARECATERERS.CO.UK MAIDEN HURDLE (10 hdls) 2m 6f

2:20 (2:21) (Class 4) 4-Y-0+ **£3,445** (£1,060; £530; £265)

Form RPR

1 **Boulevardofdreams (IRE)**[50] 4-10-9 .... APMcCoy 96+
(M C Pipe) *mde all: hit 5th and 6th: rdn appr 2 out: clr appr last: styd on wl* **10/3**[2]

002- 2 7 **Thomo (IRE)**[36] [4793] 7-11-0 .... JamesDavies 93
(N E Berry) *hld up in mid-div: hdwy after 6th: hrd rdn after 3 out: kpt on flat: no ch w wnr* **16/1**

53/6 3 ½ **Captain Flinders (IRE)**[16] [128] 8-11-0 111 .... SThomas 92
(Miss H C Knight) *hld up towards rr: hdwy after 6th: rdn and edgd rt appr 2 out: one pce* **5/1**

00-0 4 10 **Griffin's Legacy**[9] [216] 6-10-11 83 .... DCrosse(3) 83+
(N G Ayliffe) *a.p: hit 3 out: rdn and c wd appr 2 out: wkng whn mstke last* **100/1**

43- 5 4 **Hunter Pudding**[128] [3279] 5-10-4 .... RWalford(3) 71
(C L Popham) *hld up in mid-div: hdwy appr 3rd: chsd wnr appr 7th: rdn and wknd appr 2 out* **50/1**

000- 6 20 **Long Night**[96] [3760] 6-11-0 88 .... RJohnson 58
(P J Hobbs) *chsd ldrs: rdn 5th: wknd appr 7th* **16/1**

PP0- 7 dist **Exclusive Air (USA)**[7] [4913] 6-10-7 62 .... TMessenger(7) —
(H H G Owen) *a bhd: t.o fr 3 out* **100/1**

P6 P **Sportsfield Coogee (IRE)**[2] [343] 6-10-7 .... DJacob(7) —
(D P Keane) *a bhd: t.o whn p.u bef 7th* **66/1**

P2- P **Cash Converter (IRE)**[24] [4964] 7-11-0 .... WMarston —
(R T Phillips) *a bhd: t.o whn p.u bef 7th: b.b.v* **11/1**

402- F **Edgar Wilde (IRE)**[28] [4911] 7-11-0 109 .... LAspell —
(R Rowe) *t.k.h: chsd wnr after 2nd: cl 3rd whn fell 5th* **7/2**[3]

6PP/ P **Besuto (IRE)**[393] [4895] 8-11-0 .... TScudamore —
(D D Scott) *mid-div: rdn after 3rd: sn bhd: t.o whn p.u bef 7th* **66/1**

60- P **Blazing The Trail (IRE)**[59] [4444] 5-11-0 .... (bt) NFehily —
(C J Mann) *hld up and bhd: hdwy appr 5th: wknd 7th: hit 3 out: t.o whn p.u after 3 out* **11/1**

03-2 P **Dancinginthestreet**[6] [287] 5-11-0 99 .... (b[1]) ChristianWilliams —
(J L Flint) *t.k.h: chsd wnr tl after 2nd: wnt 2nd again 5th: prom whn p.u bef 7th* **11/4**[1]

5m 26.1s (5.80) **Going Correction** +0.20s/f (Yiel)
WFA 4 from 5yo+ 5lb **13 Ran SP% 124.0**
Speed ratings: **97,94,94,90,89 81,—,—,—,— —,—,—** CSF £55.63 TOTE £4.20: £1.60, £3.90, £2.00; EX 75.40.
Owner D A Johnson **Bred** Nicholas O'Neill **Trained** Nicholashayne, Devon

FOCUS
A very modest maiden hurdle rated through the fourth and fifth.

NOTEBOOK
Boulevardofdreams(IRE), the winner of his only Irish point in March, was a bit novicey at some of his hurdles. However, the further he went the better he looked and he can defy a penalty. *(op 9-4 tchd 4-1, 9-2 in places)*
Thomo(IRE) shaped as though he might appreciate this much longer trip when second here last time and that certainly proved to be the case. *(op 14-1)*
Captain Flinders(IRE), all the better for his outing at Uttoxeter, just lost out in the separate battle for the runner-up spot. *(op 8-1)*
Griffin's Legacy, who may have been carried wide by the third nearing the second last, ran by far his best race to date over hurdles. It could be that this trip was just beyond him. *(op 66-1)*
Hunter Pudding, on better ground for this first run for a new stable, did not get home on this big step up in distance.
Dancinginthestreet was reported by his rider to have lost his action. *Official explanation: jockey said gelding lost its action (op 9-1)*
Cash Converter(IRE) *Official explanation: jockey said gelding bled from the nose (op 9-1)*

385 ANTIQUES FAIR HERE ON JUNE 11TH (S) HURDLE (8 hdls 1 omitted) 2m 3f

2:50 (2:50) (Class 5) 4-Y-0+ **£2,625** (£750; £375)

Form RPR

23-1 1 **Kings Castle (IRE)**[17] [110] 10-11-4 110 .... AThornton 102+
(R J Hodges) *hld up towards rr: hdwy appr 5th: led after 3 out: hit last: r.o wl* **1/1**[1]

50P- 2 1¾ **Fire Ranger**[24] [4962] 9-10-5 88 .... JAMcCarthy 88+
(J D Frost) *hld up and bhd: hdwy 5th: chsd wnr appr 2 out: sn rdn: mstke last: nt qckn* **14/1**

2PP- 3 14 **Alvaro (IRE)**[24] [4953] 8-11-3 105 .... (b) MrRMcCarthy(7) 92
(B J Llewellyn) *j.rt: sn led: pushed along after 4th: hdd 3 out: wknd appr 2 out* **12/1**

15-1 4 nk **Ask The Umpire (IRE)**[17] [96] 10-11-10 85 .... (p) OMcPhail 92
(B J Llewellyn) *hld up in mid-div: hdwy appr 5th: wknd 3 out* **7/1**[3]

260- 5 5 **Cracow (IRE)**[24] [4962] 8-10-12 70 .... ChristianWilliams 75
(W K Goldsworthy) *hld up in mid-div: wknd 5th* **12/1**

P0-S 6 nk **Blues Story (FR)**[6] [284] 7-10-12 77 .... (t) GSupple 75
(N G Ayliffe) *hld up and bhd: short-lived effrt appr 2 out* **40/1**

PP-3 7 12 **Wild Tempo (FR)**[8] [232] 10-10-12 116 .... TScudamore 66+
(M Scudamore) *led early: chsd ldr: led briefly 3 out: rdn and wknd appr 2 out* **9/4**[2]

00P- 8 dist **Katz Pyjamas (IRE)**[92] [3833] 4-9-7 69 .... EDehdashti(7) —
(G F H Charles-Jones) *prom tl wknd 5th: t.o* **50/1**

0P0/ P **Foreman**[1780] [721] 12-10-9 .... AHoneyball(3) —
(C J Down) *hld up in tch: nt fluent 1st: rdn and wkng whn n.m.r on ins bnd appr 5th: t.o whn p.u bef 2 out* **14/1**

0P-P P **Kadlass (FR)**[8] [237] 10-10-5 83 .... SWalsh(7) —
(Mrs D Thomas) *hld up: pushed along whn hdwy on ins and nt clr run after 4th: nt fluent 5th: sn wknd: t.o whn p.u bef 2 out* **50/1**

4m 36.8s (3.80) **Going Correction** +0.20s/f (Yiel)
WFA 4 from 7yo+ 4lb **10 Ran SP% 128.3**
Speed ratings: **100,99,93,93,91 91,85,—,—,—** CSF £20.50 TOTE £2.20: £1.10, £4.50, £4.00; EX 21.30.The winner was bought in for 4,500gns. Wild Tempo was claimed by Mrs Judith E. Wilson for £6,000.
Owner R J Hodges **Bred** Miss Katie Thorner And Joseph Kent **Trained** Charlton Adam, Somerset

FOCUS
A modest seller with the hurdle in the starting chute omitted. The form looks solid enough for the grade.

NOTEBOOK
Kings Castle(IRE) was written off by the vets after breaking down badly at Ascot just over a year ago. Following up his win at Southwell, he is still useful in this sort of grade. *(op 11-8)*
Fire Ranger appreciated this much better ground but did seem to be getting the worst of the argument when missing out at the final flight.
Alvaro(IRE) was inclined to jump right on this return to hurdles having twice won in this grade last season.
Ask The Umpire(IRE) may have been unsuited by the fact the ground was a shade quicker than when he scored at Bangor last month. *(tchd 13-2)*
Cracow(IRE) did not find a drop into a seller the answer. *(tchd 14-1)*

386 CAR BOOT SALE HERE ON MAY 22ND H'CAP CHASE (16 fncs) 2m 5f 110y

3:20 (3:20) (Class 3) (0-120,118) 5-Y-0+ **£6,163** (£1,896; £948; £474)

Form RPR

/31- 1 **Good Lord Louis (IRE)**[228] [1544] 7-11-5 **111** .... PJBrennan 132+
(P J Hobbs) *a.p: led 12th: rdn clr after 3 out: hit last: comf* **11/4**[1]

63-F 2 11 **Lord Dundaniel (IRE)**[13] [174] 8-11-5 **111** .... NFehily 117
(B De Haan) *led 1st to 12th: rdn 4 out: one pce fr 3 out* **5/1**[3]

226- 3 2½ **Mark Equal**[32] [4838] 9-11-10 **116** .... (t) TScudamore 121+
(M C Pipe) *hld up: hdwy appr 10th: rdn 4 out: one pce fr 3 out* **9/1**

11P- 4 1¾ **Bronzesmith**[345] [646] 9-11-9 **115** .... JTizzard 118+
(B J M Ryall) *j.rt 1st: mstke 2nd: sn bhd: styd on fr 2 out: mstke last: nvr nrr* **12/1**

55-6 5 5 **Jupon Vert (FR)**[13] [176] 8-10-9 **101** .... RJohnson 98
(R J Hodges) *hld up and bhd: hdwy after 10th: outpcd 11th: rallied after 4 out: sn no imp* **8/1**

050- 6 3½ **Search And Destroy (USA)**[139] [3056] 7-11-10 **116** .... (b) JMMaguire 110+
(T R George) *w ldr to 10th: wknd 11th: no ch whn mstke last* **9/2**[2]

1F3- 7 3 **Lord Strickland**[214] [1713] 12-11-9 **118** .... AHoneyball(3) 108
(P J Hobbs) *hld up in mid-div: bhd fr 11th* **12/1**

6P4- 8 5 **Fear Siuil (IRE)**[36] [4792] 12-11-3 **109** .... (t) DRDennis 94
(Nick Williams) *a bhd* **16/1**

225- 9 5 **Dun An Doras (IRE)**[104] [3638] 9-11-7 **113** .... JAMcCarthy 93
(J D Frost) *prom tl rdn and wknd 11th* **7/1**

2-F P **Yvanovitch (FR)**[18] [76] 7-10-12 **104** .... MFoley —
(Mrs L C Taylor) *hld up: hdwy appr 10th: wknd 10th: t.o whn p.u bef 3 out* **10/1**

P36- P **Francolino (FR)**[50] [4584] 12-10-0 **92** oh29 .... JMogford —
(Dr P Pritchard) *lost pl 3rd: j. slowly 5th: sn bhd: t.o whn j.rt 9th: sn p.u* **50/1**

5m 26.8s (4.10) **Going Correction** +0.425s/f (Soft) **11 Ran SP% 127.4**
Speed ratings: **109,105,104,103,101 100,99,97,95,— —** CSF £19.37 CT £117.37 TOTE £4.60: £2.40, £2.80, £3.10; EX 26.20.
Owner The Country Side **Bred** James Griffin **Trained** Withycombe, Somerset

FOCUS
A fair contest for the time of year but apart from the winner, who is value for more than the official margin, most of these were fully exposed.

NOTEBOOK
Good Lord Louis(IRE) ◆ has been difficult to train having suffered from a variety of niggling problems. He made this look pretty straightforward despite being 11lb higher than when winning at Hereford last September on his previous outing. He can make up for lost time providing the Handicapper is not too hard on him. *(op 4-1)*
Lord Dundaniel(IRE) could not go with the progressive winner from the water jump. *(op 4-1)*
Mark Equal, down 3lb, was still 5lb higher than when winning at Newbury in November.
Bronzesmith, who has gone well when fresh in the past, was doing all his best work late on after almost a year on the sidelines.

387 TOTESPORT SUMMER FESTIVAL 20TH & 21ST AUGUST H'CAP HURDLE (8 hdls 1 omitted) 2m 3f

3:50 (3:51) (Class 3) (0-130,123) 4-Y-0+ **£7,377** (£2,798; £1,399; £636; £318; £190)

Form RPR

/P0- 1 **Cool Spice**[32] [4837] 8-11-6 **117** .... RJohnson 124+
(P J Hobbs) *hld up and bhd: hdwy appr 5th: led appr 2 out: rdn and hit 2 out: r.o* **7/1**

032- 2 2 **Jockser (IRE)**[29] [4881] 4-10-8 **110** .... AThornton 111+
(J W Mullins) *hld up in mid-div: hdwy on ins 3rd: rdn whn mstke 2 out: wnt 2nd last: r.o one pce* **4/1**[3]

032- 3 1½ **Achilles Wings (USA)**[34] [4817] 9-10-10 **107** .... (p) SDurack 109
(Miss K M George) *hld up in mid-div: hdwy 3rd: wnt 2nd 4th: rdn and ev ch appr 2 out: no ex flat* **16/1**

01-5 4 5 **Mcbain (USA)**[16] [127] 6-11-7 **123** .... RStephens(5) 120
(P J Hobbs) *prom: rdn 5th: wknd appr 2 out* **7/2**[2]

253- 5 6 **Kildee Lass**[48] [4643] 6-10-4 **101** .... JTizzard 93+
(J D Frost) *hld up and bhd: hdwy appr 5th: wknd appr 2 out* **12/1**

2P1- 6 7 **Prince Of Persia**[26] [4932] 5-11-3 **114** .... (p) TScudamore 98
(R S Brookhouse) *hld up towards rr: hdwy appr 5th: wknd after 3 out* **12/1**

302- 7 4 **Latitude (FR)**[24] [4959] 6-11-11 **122** .... APMcCoy 102
(M C Pipe) *hld up and bhd: short-lived effrt appr 5th* **5/2**[1]

F42- 8 1½ **Imperial Rocket (USA)**[158] [2732] 8-10-0 **97** oh3 .... ChristianWilliams 76
(W K Goldsworthy) *led 1st: rdn and hdd appr 2 out: sn wknd* **33/1**

54-3 9 7 **My Last Bean (IRE)**[17] [99] 8-11-6 **117** .... SCurran 89
(M R Bosley) *a bhd* **14/1**

060- 10 19 **Polish Cloud (FR)**[71] [4204] 8-10-12 **109** .... JMMaguire 62
(T R George) *prom tl rdn and wknd 5th* **16/1**

F30- P **Fireball Macnamara (IRE)**[37] [4768] 9-11-2 **113** .... NFehily —
(M Pitman) *a bhd: t.o whn p.u bef 2 out* **12/1**

13P/ P **Citius (IRE)**[880] [2573] 9-10-3 **100** .... LAspell —
(R Rowe) *prom tl wknd after 4th: t.o whn p.u after 3 out* **20/1**

01P- P **Rydon Lane (IRE)**[39] [4759] 9-10-6 **103** .... (p) RThornton —
(Mrs S D Williams) *bhd fr 5th: t.o whn p.u bef 2 out* **20/1**

05-P P **Davoski**[8] [247] 11-11-3 **114** .... JAMcCarthy —
(Dr P Pritchard) *led to 1st: wknd 3rd: t.o whn p.u bef 5th* **33/1**

000/ P **The Grey Butler (IRE)**[397] [4836] 8-11-2 **120** .... DCosgrave(7) —
(B De Haan) *prom tl wknd appr 5th: t.o whn p.u bef 2 out* **16/1**

4m 30.2s (-2.80) **Going Correction** +0.20s/f (Yiel)
WFA 4 from 5yo+ 4lb **15 Ran SP% 146.1**
Speed ratings: **113,112,111,109,106 103,102,101,98,90 —,—,—,—,—** CSF £41.83 CT £478.52 TOTE £8.70: £3.20, £1.40, £4.30; EX 48.70.
Owner Celtic Racing **Bred** Mrs M S Thomas **Trained** Withycombe, Somerset

FOCUS
A fair contest in which the hurdle in the starting chute was omitted. A decent winning time for the grade and the form could be rated higher.

The Form Book, Raceform Ltd, Compton, RG20 6NL

NOTEBOOK

Cool Spice, dropped 3lb, was all the better for her outing at Cheltenham a month ago. She may also have benefited from this being a shorter trip. *(tchd 15-2)*

Jockser(IRE) ran another sound race off a mark 16lb higher than when he won at Huntingdon in February. The trouble is he is already set to go up another pound. *(op 9-2)*

Achilles Wings(USA), raised 2lb, has certainly been faring better since the ground has dried up and gave another good account of himself.

Mcbain(USA) had no excuses on account of the ground this time. *(op 9-2)*

Kildee Lass was another who would have appreciated the fact that the ground was much drier than she encountered last time.

Prince Of Persia was only 4lb higher than when successful at Worcester. *(op 11-1)*

Latitude(FR) was found to be lame on post race inspection by the Veterinary Officer. *Official explanation: vet said mare finished lame (op 4-1 after 6-1 in a place, tchd 9-2)*

My Last Bean(IRE) *Official explanation: trainer said gelding was unsuited by the ground - good, good to soft in places (op 12-1)*

388 NEWTONABBOTRACING.COM NOVICES' H'CAP CHASE (13 fncs) 2m 110y

4:20 (4:22) (Class 4) (0-100,98) 5-Y-0+ **£4,819** (£1,482; £741; £370)

Form				RPR
00-2	**1**		**Honan (IRE)**[13] 173 6-11-9 **95** (v) APMcCoy *(M C Pipe) a.p: led 3 out: sn rdn: clr appr last: r.o* **5/2**[1]	104+
0-24	**2**	1 ½	**Tosawi (IRE)**[10] 202 9-11-12 **98** (p) TScudamore *(R J Hodges) chsd ldrs: nt fluent 3rd: lost pl appr 7th: rallied appr 2 out: kpt on u.p flat* **5/1**[2]	104+
040-	**3**	¾	**Gin 'N' Fonic (IRE)**[167] 2550 5-10-9 **90** SWalsh[(7)] *(J D Frost) hld up towards rr: rdn 8th: hdwy appr 2 out: kpt on flat* **12/1**	92
0-46	**4**	5	**Rattina (GER)**[16] 135 9-10-1 **73** (v) PJBrennan *(M F Harris) chsd ldr: led sn after 4 out: hdd 3 out: sn rdn: wknd flat* **11/1**	74+
0FP-	**5**	25	**Mendip Manor**[31] 4855 7-11-4 **90** RPMcNally *(S C Burrough) led: hdd sn after 4 out: sn wknd* **22/1**	64
6P6-	**F**		**Bold Momento**[26] 4933 6-11-1 **87** (p) NFehily *(B De Haan) prom tl wknd 7th: fell 9th* **14/1**	—
024-	**F**		**Riccarton**[223] 1600 12-10-0 **72** WMarston *(D C Turner) hld up in mid-div: fell 8th* **11/1**	—
20-5	**U**		**Pennys From Heaven**[22] 2 11-9-9 **74** JStevenson[(7)] *(Mrs Tracey Barfoot-Saunt) bhd tl blnd and uns rdr 7th* **10/1**	—
652-	**P**		**Nazimabad (IRE)**[56] 4497 6-10-3 **75** (t) ChristianWilliams *(Evan Williams) hld up: hdwy 7th: wknd 2 out: p.u bef last* **5/2**[1]	70
U6-	**P**		**Take The Oath (IRE)**[73] 4157 8-10-0 **72** TDoyle *(D R Gandolfo) hld up and bhd: stdy hdwy 9th: wknd appr 2 out: p.u bef last* **9/1**[3]	—

4m 13.4s (7.90) **Going Correction** +0.425s/f (Soft)
WFA 5 from 6yo+ 2lb 10 Ran SP% **128.3**
Speed ratings: **98,97,96,94,82** —,—,—,—,— CSF £18.02 CT £137.29 TOTE £4.60: £1.40, £2.70, £3.50; EX 16.40.
Owner Eminence Grise Partnership **Bred** Miss Ashling O'Connell **Trained** Nicholashayne, Devon

FOCUS

This very moderate novices' handicap did not take much winning, although the winner is value for a little further.

NOTEBOOK

Honan(IRE), who became frustrating over hurdles, registered his first victory since landing a bumper under McCoy on this first outing over fences. *(op 3-1)*

Tosawi(IRE), with the cheekpieces refitted, could not overcome a 4lb higher mark and probably wants a bit further on a course as easy as this. *(op 6-1)*

Gin 'N' Fonic(IRE), without his regular cheekpieces, was not disgraced on his chasing debut. He would be entitled to come on for this first start for nearly six months. *(op 14-1)*

Rattina(GER), again in a visor, has tumbled down the ratings.

Nazimabad(IRE) was pulled up before the final fence as if something was amiss. *(op 11-4 tchd 3-1)*

389 RACECOURSE FOR ALL EVENTS H'CAP HURDLE (8 hdls) 2m 1f

4:50 (4:51) (Class 4) (0-100,100) 4-Y-0+ **£2,667** (£762; £381)

Form				RPR
0P4-	**1**		**Miss Lehman**[96] 3758 7-10-3 **84** ow8 MissSGaisford[(7)] *(J D Frost) hld up and wl bhd: gd hdwy after 3 out: led 2 out: qcknd clr flat: r.o strly* **20/1**	93+
P24-	**2**	5	**Amadeus (AUS)**[26] 4934 8-10-2 **76** TScudamore *(M Scudamore) hld up towards rr: hrd rdn and hdwy appr 2 out: kpt on same pce flat* **3/1**[2]	80
P50-	**3**	2	**Water Quirl (GER)**[37] 4777 6-11-12 **100** (bt[1]) SDurack *(M F Harris) chsd ldr: rdn to ld appr 2 out: sn hdd: no ex flat* **33/1**	102
650-	**4**	3 ½	**Club Royal**[90] 3858 8-10-7 **81** JamesDavies *(N E Berry) hld up towards rr: hdwy 5th: rdn appr 2 out: wknd appr last* **20/1**	80
0-02	**5**	1	**Blue Leader (IRE)**[2] 347 6-11-12 **100** (vt) ChristianWilliams *(W K Goldsworthy) a.p: led briefly after 3 out: sn rdn: wknd appr last* **10/1**	98
000-	**6**	5	**Thai Town**[43] 4721 6-10-0 **79** DLaverty[(5)] *(A E Jones) hld up towards rr: hdwy appr 5th: wknd 2 out* **20/1**	72
005-	**7**	10	**Real Cracker (IRE)**[46] 4671 6-11-1 **89** (b[1]) SThomas *(Miss Venetia Williams) led tl appr 5th: wknd appr 2 out* **10/1**	72
00-0	**8**	5	**John Jorrocks (FR)**[13] 167 6-10-0 **74** oh5 JMogford *(J C Tuck) hld up in mid-div: hdwy appr 5th: wknd appr 2 out* **20/1**	52
112-	**9**	23	**Damarisco (FR)**[24] 4962 5-11-9 **97** RJohnson *(P J Hobbs) hld up in tch: led appr 5th: blnd bdly 3 out: sn hdd & wknd* **5/2**[1]	77+
66P-	**10**	1 ¼	**Mevagissey (BEL)**[110] 3539 8-10-12 **86** PJBrennan *(J D Frost) a bhd* **16/1**	39
04P-	**11**	1 ¾	**Champagne Sundae (IRE)**[29] 4890 7-10-2 **76** LAspell *(P Winkworth) mid-div: bhd fr 3 out* **50/1**	28
060-	**12**	23	**Blue Nun**[88] 3905 4-9-7 **78** oh1 EDehdashti[(7)] *(G F H Charles-Jones) mid-div: rdn after 4th: sn lost pl: t.o* **33/1**	—
610-	**13**	13	**Tizi Ouzou (IRE)**[29] 4890 4-10-13 **98** (v) AGlassonbury[(7)] *(M C Pipe) chsd ldrs: rdn after 3rd: sn lost pl: t.o fr 5th* **12/1**	—
006-	**P**		**Chakra**[214] 1709 11-11-8 **99** RHobson[(3)] *(C J Gray) a bhd: t.o whn p.u bef 2 out* **25/1**	—
43-U	**P**		**Wun Chai (IRE)**[6] 288 6-11-3 **98** (b) SWalsh[(7)] *(A E Jones) mid-div: rdn 4th: bhd whn p.u bef 2 out* **12/1**	—
S2/P	**P**		**Proverbial Gray**[13] 167 8-10-0 **74** oh7 TDoyle *(D R Gandolfo) a bhd: t.o whn p.u bef 2 out* **20/1**	—
/6-F	**P**		**El Hamra (IRE)**[13] 172 7-10-5 **79** (b) JMMaguire *(T R George) prom tl mstke 5th: t.o whn p.u bef 2 out* **20/1**	—
321-	**P**		**Jayed (IRE)**[87] 3920 7-10-8 **92** JBunsell[(10)] *(M Bradstock) hld up in tch: rdn 5th: eased whn btn after 3 out: p.u bef 2 out* **9/1**[3]	—

4m 8.80s (3.70) **Going Correction** +0.20s/f (Yiel)
WFA 4 from 5yo+ 4lb 18 Ran SP% **143.3**
Speed ratings: **99,96,95,94,93 91,86,84,73,72 71,61,55**,—,— —,—,— CSF £83.67 CT £2161.42 TOTE £26.70: £4.70, £1.80, £5.60, £6.10; EX 235.90 Place 6 £207.73, Place 5 £70.07.

Owner P A Tylor **Bred** Mrs M C Reveley **Trained** Buckfastleigh, Devon

FOCUS

The moderate handicap in which field was soon well strung out and the winner came from the next parish, making the form look suspect.

NOTEBOOK

Miss Lehman, dropped out at the start, was soon some 30 lengths off the pace. Carrying a pound more than her handicap mark, with her rider unable to utilise her allowance, she may be flattered by this performance with the leaders having gone off too fast.

Amadeus(AUS) was coming back in distance for this return to hurdling. Like the winner, he came from a fair way back but had to be hard driven to make ground. *(op 4-1 tchd 11-4)*

Water Quirl(GER), tried in blinkers instead of a visor, was always near the pace in contrast to the first two. That makes this effort all the more praiseworthy.

Club Royal was another to come from a fair way back but could not sustain his effort.

Blue Leader(IRE) eventually found his exertions when second at Bangor on Saturday catching up with him. *(tchd 11-1)*

Damarisco(FR) effectively put himself out of the contest when Johnson did well to stay aboard at the third last. *(op 11-4 tchd 3-1)*

Jayed(IRE) *Official explanation: jockey said gelding was unsuited by the ground - good, good to soft in places (op 8-1 tchd 10-1)*

Wun Chai(IRE) *Official explanation: jockey said gelding had a breathing problem (op 8-1 tchd 10-1)*

T/Plt: £161.50 to a £1 stake. Pool: £38,943.30. 175.95 winning tickets. T/Qpdt: £49.10 to a £1 stake. Pool: £2,936. 90. 44.20 winning tickets. KH

390 - 393a (Foreign Racing) - See Raceform Interactive

[261]TOWCESTER (R-H)

Tuesday, May 17

OFFICIAL GOING: Good to firm changing to good (good to firm in places) after race 2 (6.30)

Wind: Nil Weather: Fine and sunny

394 WAYSIDE MAIDEN HURDLE (10 hdls) 2m 3f 110y

6:00 (6:01) (Class 4) 4-Y-0+ **£4,251** (£1,308; £654; £327)

Form				RPR
042-	**1**		**My Pal Val (IRE)**[159] 2731 5-11-2 (t) SThomas *(Miss H C Knight) settled trcking ldrs in slowly run r: wnt 2nd at 7th: rdn to ld 2 out: drvn clr bef last* **10/3**[2]	95+
03-3	**2**	6	**Classical Love**[17] 128 5-10-2 81 (v) SWalsh[(7)] *(C J Down) prom: wnt 2nd bef 5th: led and mstke next: rdn and hdd 2 out: outpcd bef last* **16/1**	82
	3	12	**Sound Skin (IRE)**[309] 939 7-11-2 LAspell *(A Ennis) hld up in tch: effrt in 3rd 3 out: sn drvn and lost tch w ldng pair: mstkes 2 out and last* **7/1**[3]	80+
00-0	**4**	21	**Kingcombe Lane**[17] 133 5-11-2 JPMcNamara *(P W Hiatt) led tl bef 2nd: chsd ldr tl lost pl bef 5th: wd bef next: remote fr 3 out* **100/1**	56
60-	**5**	10	**Wednesday Club**[80] 4069 4-10-6 TJPhelan[(5)] *(N M Babbage) j. v erratically in last pair: lost tch 5th: t.o 3 out* **50/1**	41
3	**6**	3 ½	**Mr Dip**[6] 294 5-10-11 DLaverty[(5)] *(L A Dace) last whn blnd 2nd: bhd tl sme prog bef 3 out where plenty to do and bdly hmpd: continued remote* **20/1**	58+
S40-	**F**		**Redspin (IRE)**[10] 2278 5-11-2 104 SDurack *(J S Moore) hld up: rdn to make prog in 5l 4th whn fell 3 out* **11/4**[1]	—
05-0	**B**		**Amber Dawn**[18] 111 6-10-9 78 OMcPhail *(J Gallagher) t.k.h: led bef 2nd: hdd 6th: 5th and wkng whn b.d 3 out* **50/1**	—
/0-4	**P**		**Simiola**[6] 294 6-10-9 63 PFlynn *(S T Lewis) keen: j. poorly: cl up tl lost pl and mstke 6th: wl bhd whn impeded 3 out: t.o whn crashed over next and p.u* **50/1**	—

5m 3.80s (-14.30) **Going Correction** -0.85s/f (Firm)
WFA 4 from 5yo+ 4lb 9 Ran SP% **79.8**
Speed ratings: **94,91,86,78,74 73**,—,—,— CSF £21.06 TOTE £2.30: £1.10, £2.60, £2.50; EX 17.50.
Owner Harold Winton **Bred** V I McCalla And Winton Bloodstock **Trained** West Lockinge, Oxon
■ Dubai Ace (2/1) was withdrawn on vet's advice. R4 applies, deduct 30p in the £.

FOCUS

Seamus Durack suffered a badly broken leg in this fall. A weak maiden, run at a sedate early gallop, and the form looks suspect. However, the winner can be rated value for further.

NOTEBOOK

My Pal Val(IRE), off for 159 days previously, got off the mark at the third attempt over hurdles under a decent ride from Thomas. He had no trouble with the underfoot conditions, appreciated the longer trip and could be rated value for further. While he did not have to be at his best to win this *weak affair, and should strike again during the summer, his future lies with the Handicapper. (op 3-1 tchd 4-1)*

Classical Love was firmly put in her place by the winner, but ran an improved race and was well clear of the rest. She looked happier over this shorter trip and should be placed to go one better this summer. *(tchd 18-1)*

Sound Skin(IRE) , last seen 309 days previously, got left behind when the tempo increased and ran very much as though the outing was needed. *(op 6-1)*

Kingcombe Lane *(op 66-1)*

Mr Dip would have been closer but for meeting trouble when Redspin fell three out and can be *rated better then his finishing position suggests.Official explanation: vet said gelding lost a front shoe (op 22-1 tchd 16-1)*

Redspin(IRE) had yet to be asked for maximum effort prior to departing three from home. *(tchd 5-2 and 3-1)*

395 JENKINSONS CATERERS H'CAP CHASE (12 fncs) 2m 110y

6:30 (6:31) (Class 4) (0-100,95) 5-Y-0+ **£3,513** (£1,081; £540; £270)

Form				RPR
21-5	**1**		**The Staggery Boy (IRE)**[18] 103 9-11-11 **94** TScudamore *(M R Hoad) trckd ldrs: chal to ld after 3 out: rdn and kpt on gamely fr last* **11/2**[2]	106
/6-0	**2**	1 ¼	**Nephite (NZ)**[18] 108 11-11-10 **93** SThomas *(Miss Venetia Williams) trckd ldrs: rdn and sltly outpcd 3 out: rallied to 2nd bef next: ev ch whn mstke last: kpt on at one pce after* **16/1**	104
30P-	**3**	3 ½	**Newick Park**[51] 4581 10-11-8 **91** WHutchinson *(R Dickin) hld up midfield: effrt and rdn 3 out: wnt 3rd after next: no imp on ldng pair after* **14/1**	98
2-11	**4**	6	**Terrible Tenant**[19] 74 6-11-3 **89** RYoung[(3)] *(J W Mullins) mostly 2nd fr 5th: j. slowly and landed v awkwardly 9th: demoted bef 2 out: wknd appr last* **7/4**[1]	94+

20-2 **5** *11* **Amptina (IRE)**[17] [135] 10-10-5 **74**.. DElsworth 70+
(Mrs S J Smith) *rr whn bdly hmpd 4th: sme prog bef 3 out: rdn and nvr nr ldrs after* **11/2**[2]

P-P0 **6** *1 3/4* **Auditor**[9] [246] 6-11-4 **87**..(b) JPMcNamara 78+
(S T Lewis) *led: clr 4th: hit 8th: taken to extreme outside bef 3 out: hdd on long run to next: sn btn* **33/1**

UF-5 **7** *shd* **Johnny Grand**[17] [135] 8-10-1 **73**.. DCrosse(3) 63+
(D W Lewis) *mstke 3rd: lost tch and mstke 8th: wl bhd whn mstke 2 out: styng on after last* **14/1**

36P- **8** *2 1/2* **Macgyver (NZ)**[67] [4311] 9-11-5 **95**.. MissLHorner(7) 81
(D L Williams) *pressed ldrs tl rdn and wknd after 3 out* **25/1**

P- **9** *2 1/2* **Major Reno (IRE)**[23] 8-10-3 **77**.. MNicolls(5) 60
(R C Harper) *mstke 4th: chsd ldr tl next: rdn 7th: wknd 9th* **80/1**

2-05 **10** *23* **Vulcan Lane (NZ)**[8] [265] 8-10-13 **85**..(b) LMcGrath(3) 45
(R C Guest) *bhd whn tried to refuse 5th and str reminders: lost tch and slow next: nt keen: t.o 9th* **17/2**[3]

0-54 **F** **Spectrum Star**[10] [213] 5-9-9 **71** oh8.. DCCostello(5) —
(F P Murtagh) *bhd whn fell 4th* **9/1**

4m 6.50s (-12.80) **Going Correction** -0.825s/f (Firm) **11** Ran SP% **114.9**
WFA 5 from 6yo+ 2lb
Speed ratings: **97,96,94,91,86 85,85,84,83,72** — CSF £81.25 CT £1163.92 TOTE £4.20: £1.70, £3.10, £4.50; EX 55.60.
Owner Foray Racing **Bred** Miss Terry Horgan **Trained** Lewes, E Sussex

FOCUS
A moderate handicap that saw the field finish strung out. The form, rated through the first two, looks sound for the class.

NOTEBOOK
The Staggery Boy(IRE) jumped smoothly throughout and got back to winning with a typically brave performance. He had never previously won off a mark this high, but he is in good heart at present and is undoubtedly better over a longer trip, so he could add to this during the summer months. *(op 7-1)*

Nephite(NZ) made the winner pull out all the stops and would have been closer but for getting the last fence all wrong. However, although he is undoubtedly on a decent mark at present, he never quite looked like getting on top this time and is not easy to win with. *(op 12-1)*

Newick Park kept on at his own pace under pressure from three out and ran close to his mark. This was a more encouraging effort. *(tchd 16-1)*

Terrible Tenant , bidding for the hat-trick, ran below his recent level and has to rate as *disappointing. However, he is better than this and is not one to write off just yet. (op 15-8 tchd 2-1 in places)*

Amptina(IRE) ran well below his best and advertised his stable's recent poor form.

Johnny Grand *Official explanation: jockey said gelding was unsuited by good ground (op 11-1)*

396 SEVERN VALLEY CATERING NOVICES' (S) HURDLE (8 hdls) 2m
7:00 (7:00) (Class 5) 4-Y-0+ **£3,003** (£858; £429)

Form RPR

43-2 **1** **Sarena Special**[19] [75] 8-10-12 82.. RJohnson 81+
(J D Frost) *sn cl up in chsng gp: chal after 3 out: ev ch fr next: sn drvn ahd but carried lft by hanging rival after* **2/1**[2]

01-P **2** *1/2* **Adjawar (IRE)**[19] [78] 7-11-5 100.. RGarritty 89+
(J J Quinn) *chsd long ldr: clsd fr 5th: led wl bef 2 out: hanging lft after: sn hdd flat: nt qckn* **7/4**[1]

0P-0 **3** *15* **Luristan (IRE)**[17] [133] 5-10-7 74.. LTreadwell(5) 66
(S T Lewis) *midfield: j. slowly 4th and rdn: drvn into 3rd bef 2 out: continued wl adrift of ldrs* **40/1**

00-1 **4** *5* **Storm Clear (IRE)**[19] [75] 6-11-5 86.. WMarston 69+
(D J Wintle) *bhd: rdn and mod prog 3 out: poor 4th bef next* **4/1**[3]

0/P **5** *16* **Lancastrian Island**[17] [128] 7-10-4 ow6..(p) MrRArmson(7) 38
(John A Harris) *prom in chsng gp: j. slowly 3rd: wknd qckly 5th* **50/1**

PP-0 **6** *9* **Just Bryan**[8] [264] 6-10-7 64..(bt) TGreenway(5) 36
(P A Pritchard) *led and sn 20l clr at hdstr pce: hdd on long run to 2 out: immediately fdd* **22/1**

0-00 **7** *11* **Parisi Princess**[9] [232] 4-9-8 .... CMStudd(7) 14
(D L Williams) *bhd: lost tch 5th: t.o bef 2 out* **40/1**

00-P **8** *4* **Muffler**[17] [133] 7-10-5 .... NCarter(7) 21
(J G M O'Shea) *rdn and struggling 5th: t.o after next: mstke last* **66/1**

F **City General (IRE)**[5] 4-10-5 .... DCrosse(3) —
(J S Moore) *fell 1st* **12/1**

P **Maid The Cut**[95] 4-10-1 .... VSlattery —
(A D Smith) *plld hrd in last: lost tch and mstke 3rd: sn hopelessly t.o: p.u 3 out* **33/1**

4m 3.80s (-7.60) **Going Correction** -0.85s/f (Firm)
WFA 4 from 5yo+ 4lb **10** Ran SP% **113.0**
Speed ratings: **85,84,77,74,66 62,56,54,—,—** CSF £5.51 TOTE £3.00: £1.30, £1.50, £7.10; EX 6.40.The winner was sold to Mrs Alison Thorpe for 3,400gns.
Owner Sarena Mfg Ltd **Bred** Bealy Court Stud **Trained** Buckfastleigh, Devon
■ Stewards' Enquiry : R Garritty caution: careless riding

FOCUS
A slow time, even for a seller, and the form is weak. The first two came well clear.

NOTEBOOK
Sarena Special gained a deserved success under a fine ride from Johnson. He has been in fair form at this level of late, and could strike again, but is far from certain to put his best foot forward next time. *(op 5-2)*

Adjawar(IRE) had every chance, but not for the first time looked reluctant to put it all in late on and again disappointed. He has a bad habit of ducking the issue if challenged late on and, although he *has the ability to win races at this sort of level, he is one to avoid in the main. (tchd 6-4 and 15-8 in places)*

Luristan(IRE) , making his handicap debut and competing in plating-class for the first time, was never a serious factor. However, this still rates as his best effort to date over timber. *(op 50-1)*

Storm Clear(IRE) , who beat the winner last time at Hereford, proved very easy to back and turned in a moody effort. *(op 11-4)*

397 GET A FREE £50 WITH GG-CASINO.COM H'CAP HURDLE (11 hdls) 2m 5f
7:30 (7:30) (Class 3) (0-120,115) 4-Y-0+ **£4,914** (£1,512; £756; £378)

Form RPR

032- **1** **Earlsfield Raider**[29] [4618] 5-11-2 **105**..(b) JEMoore 119+
(G L Moore) *hld up: effrt bef 3 out: led on bit bef next: in command whn j.rt and mstke last: eased 50 yds out* **5/2**[1]

23R- **2** *2 1/2* **Pardon What**[30] [4877] 9-9-12 **90**.. KJMercer(3) 97+
(Ferdy Murphy) *hld up trcking ldrs: j. slowly 6th: impeded next: 4l 7th 3 out: wnt 2nd next: sn rdn: nt looking keen whn slow and awkward* **16/1**

6U4- **3** *6* **Celtic Blaze (IRE)**[14] [4508] 6-10-12 **101**..(tp) ARoss 100
(B S Rothwell) *hld up in rr: effrt 8th: chal next: 3rd bef 2 out: rdn and wknd bef last* **20/1**

-164 **4** *10* **Little Rort (IRE)**[8] [265] 6-9-6 **89**.. LTreadwell(5) 78
(S T Lewis) *mde most: rdn and hdd bef 2 out: sn fdd* **11/1**

00-P **5** *3/4* **Miniballist (IRE)**[9] [245] 7-10-11 **100**..(t) RJohnson 88
(R T Phillips) *hld up last: effrt and hit 8th: ev ch next: rdn and wknd bef 2 out* **14/1**

P-P2 **6** *15* **Ungaretti (GER)**[7] [289] 8-10-5 **94**.. DRDennis 67
(Ian Williams) *prom: ev ch 3 out: rdn fnd nthing bef next* **4/1**[3]

RP-2 **7** *6* **Homeleigh Mooncoin**[18] [110] 10-11-2 **105**.. JamesDavies 72
(B G Powell) *prom: 2nd and ev ch whn pckd 3 out: fdd qckly bef next* **22/1**

35P- **P** **Majestic Bay (IRE)**[34] [4823] 9-11-12 **115**.. WHutchinson —
(J A B Old) *prom or disp ld tl broke leg on flat bef 7th* **8/1**

/5-0 **P** **Shamsan (IRE)**[17] [136] 8-10-9 **105**..(t) SWalsh(7) —
(J Joseph) *last whn mstke 4th: nt keen after: big jump 5th: t.o next: p.u 7th* **66/1**

4/2- **P** **Mumbling (IRE)**[15] [1611] 7-11-8 **111**.. JTizzard —
(B G Powell) *j. slowly 1st: handy tl c u.p 7th: lost tch bef 3 out: t.o and p.u next* **3/1**[2]

5m 26.5s (-14.70) **Going Correction** -0.85s/f (Firm) **10** Ran SP% **116.2**
Speed ratings: **94,93,90,86,86 80,78,—,—,—** CSF £39.33 CT £661.06 TOTE £3.20: £1.30, £5.20, £2.80; EX 25.10.
Owner Mrs R J Doorgachurn **Bred** Mrs R J Doorgachurn And C Stedman **Trained** Woodingdean, E Sussex

FOCUS
Not a strong race and could be rated too high, but the winner did the job impressively and is value for further.

NOTEBOOK
Earlsfield Raider was well backed to score, and did so with a stylish display, being value for at least six lengths. He seems to go on most ground, this looks to be his optimum trip and this effort rates as a personal best over hurdles. Further success looks assured. *(op 3-1)*

Pardon What , who had refused on his previous two outings, is flattered by his proximity to the winner, yet turned in a much-improved display on this return to hurdling. He will go up in the weights for this, however. *(op 20-1)*

Celtic Blaze(IRE) found less than looked likely when push came to shove and shaped as though she may prefer a longer trip on this ground. *(op 16-1)*

Little Rort(IRE) was found out by this step up in class. *(op 10-1)*

Ungaretti(GER) had his chance, but faded disappointingly from two out. He has it to prove now. *(op 5-1)*

Mumbling(IRE) , fit from a recent couple of spins on the level, proved most disappointing and may *need even faster ground. Official explanation: trainer said gelding was unsuited by good ground; vet said gelding lost two front shoes (op 5-2 tchd 10-3)*

398 CHRISTIE & CO. H'CAP CHASE (18 fncs) 3m 110y
8:00 (8:00) (Class 4) (0-95,93) 5-Y-0+ **£4,368** (£1,344; £672; £336)

Form RPR

F2-3 **1** **Petolinski**[18] [98] 7-10-0 **74**..(p) TMessenger(7) 83
(C L Popham) *hld up: stdy hdwy 8th: led 14th: drew clr w rival fr 3 out: hdd after next: drvn to regain advantage fnl stride* **7/1**

524- **2** *hd* **Sir Cumference**[30] [4875] 9-11-10 **91**..(b) SThomas 100
(Miss Venetia Williams) *led 6th tl 8th: led after 11th tl 15th: hit 14th and 15th: cl 2nd tl drvn into slt ld after 2 out: ct fnl stride* **9/4**[1]

PP-5 **3** *17* **Chancers Dante (IRE)**[8] [262] 9-10-7 **77**..(b) KJMercer(3) 69
(Ferdy Murphy) *midfield: effrt 14th: sn rdn w little rspnse: btn after 3 out: drvn to snatch poor 3rd* **25/1**

/6-1 **4** *shd* **Billy Ballbreaker (IRE)**[14] [169] 9-11-2 **83**..(t) JTizzard 75
(C L Tizzard) *towards rr whn blnd 4th and 5th: prog after 11th: rdn 13th: nt rch ldrs fr 3 out: 14l 3rd whn mstke next: demoted on line* **9/2**[3]

P-3P **5** *4* **Welsh Gold**[7] [276] 6-9-9 **67** oh8.. LTreadwell(5) 55
(S T Lewis) *plld hrd: prom: drvn bef 12th: stl mod 3rd 3 out: plodded on* **33/1**

5-0U **6** *3/4* **Tiger Talk**[8] [262] 9-10-6 **76**..(b) LMcGrath(3) 63
(R C Guest) *nt jump wl: racd on outside: bhd tl prog and j. slowly 12th: sn u.p: nt gng wl after: btn bef 3 out* **10/1**

0P-1 **7** *1 3/4* **Make It Easy (IRE)**[13] [181] 9-9-7 **67**.. MissLHorner(7) 59+
(D L Williams) *hld up towards rr: j. slowly 2nd and 5th: bdly hmpd 10th: effrt 14th: one pce and n.d fr next* **4/1**[2]

0P4- **8** *3* **Luckycharm (FR)**[27] [4931] 6-10-10 **77**.. PMoloney 59
(R Dickin) *nt jump wl in rr: bhd: hdwy 14th: 4th and rdn and outpcd 3 out: sn wknd* **20/1**

050- **F** **Mvezo**[49] [4640] 7-10-0 **67** oh3.. TScudamore —
(Evan Williams) *midfield tl fell 10th* **12/1**

20-4 **P** **Monster Mick (FR)**[17] [137] 7-11-0 **81**.. JamesDavies —
(B G Powell) *dropped rr and hrd drvn 7th: fnd nil: t.o after 10th: p.u 14th* **14/1**

05/4 **P** **Saucynorwich (IRE)**[9] [244] 7-11-12 **93**.. PJBrennan —
(J G Portman) *j. slowly 5th: midfield tl slow 11th: wknd and slow 13th: t.o 3 out: p.u next* **25/1**

PP-P **P** **Major Bit**[23] [6] 9-10-0 **67** oh10..(tp) JPByrne —
(S A Brookshaw) *set slow pce: mstke 2nd: hdd 6th: led again 8th tl after 11th: sn u.p: fdd after 15th: t.o and p.u 2 out* **66/1**

6m 23.4s (-23.20) **Going Correction** -0.825s/f (Firm) **12** Ran SP% **121.8**
Speed ratings: **104,103,98,98,97 96,96,95,—,— —,—** CSF £23.45 CT £390.53 TOTE £9.70: £2.00, £1.30, £5.90; EX 27.30.
Owner Friends Of Eddy Hall **Bred** Ford Farm Bloodstock **Trained** West Bagborough, Somerset
■ This broke a very long losing run for Chris Popham.

FOCUS
A poor handicap, but the first two came well clear, and the form looks fair for the class.

NOTEBOOK
Petolinski , placed in hunter chases on his last two outings, bravely put his best foot forward on the run-in to get back up at the line and score a narrow first success over fences. Considering he is rated 19lb higher over hurdles, he could still be well in despite an inevitable rise in the weights, and is clearly in good heart at present. *(op 15-2)*

Sir Cumference ◆ gave his all in defeat, and can be condisered a little unlucky, as he was miles clear of the rest. This better ground was much more to his liking and it is surely only a matter of time before he gains compensation this summer. *(op 7-2)*

Chancers Dante(IRE) improved on his latest effort over course and distance, but was never a threat to the front pair.

Billy Ballbreaker(IRE) was beaten by the faster ground, rather than the 9lb rise for winning at *Exeter last time, and can be given another chance when reverting to an easier surface. (tchd 4-1 and 5-1)*

Make It Easy(IRE) , 4lb higher than when getting off the mark under Rules last time, proved disappointing over this longer trip. It would be a surprise if he were not capable of getting closer once again when reverting to shorter, but he has it to prove now nonetheless. *(op 10-3 tchd 9-2)*

399 GG.COM CONDITIONAL JOCKEYS' MARES' ONLY H'CAP HURDLE (8 hdls) 2m
8:30 (8:30) (Class 4) (0-100,96) 4-Y-0+ **£3,393** (£1,044; £522; £261)

Form RPR

02-4 **1** **Macreater**[17] [134] 7-9-11 **72** ow1 ....(p) SWalsh[(5)] 73+
(K A Morgan) *cl up in chsng gp: chal 3 out: led next: wnt rt after 2 out: hung lft bef last: edgd rt flat: r.o under heavy press* **10/1**

00-2 **2** *1* **Marathea (FR)**[13] [185] 4-9-11 **74** .... AO'Keeffe[(3)] 71+
(Miss Venetia Williams) *hld up: midfield whn mstke 5th: chal 2 out: hmpd by wnr nring last and nt fluent: wnt 2nd flat: nt qckn* **7/2**[1]

05-1 **3** *nk* **Red Dahlia**[13] [185] 8-10-11 **81** .... ATinkler 80
(M Pitman) *prom bhd clr ldr: effrt in 4th and rdn bef 2 out: lft w ch briefly last: sn no ex* **5/1**[3]

20-4 **4** *1 1/4* **Correct And Right (IRE)**[9] [233] 6-11-12 **96** ....(p) RWalford 94
(J W Mullins) *hld up: hdwy 5th: 6th and hrd drvn bef 2 out: plugged on but unable to chal* **9/2**[2]

1-35 **5** *1* **Rose Of York (IRE)**[13] [185] 5-10-1 **74** ....(t) DLaverty[(3)] 72+
(Mrs A M Thorpe) *led tl after 1st: nt fluent 3rd: wnt 2nd at 5th untoil lost pl after next: styd on again after last* **5/1**[3]

P00- **6** *nk* **Grace Dieu**[28] [4920] 4-9-7 **75** oh3 ow1 .... JKington[(8)] 68+
(M Scudamore) *tk fierce hold and led after 1st: sn 8l clr: rdn and hdd whn mstke 2 out: wknd flat* **100/1**

100- **7** *2* **Fiddles Music**[14] [4269] 4-10-13 **92** .... MGoldstein[(5)] 82
(Miss Sheena West) *hit 2nd: nvr bttr than midfield: rdn and hdd bef 3 out: hit next: plodded on* **12/1**

P20- **8** *16* **Sylphide**[37] [4797] 10-10-7 **83** .... JAJenkins[(6)] 61
(H J Manners) *handy early: wknd after 5th* **20/1**

5/0- **9** *16* **It's Just Sally**[139] [3080] 8-10-2 **75** .... JamesDavies[(3)] 37
(B G Powell) *plld hrd: stdd in rr: lost tch 5th* **14/1**

35-0 **10** *3* **Private Jessica**[17] [134] 4-10-6 **83** ....(b) PCO'Neill[(3)] 38
(R C Guest) *effrt to chse ldrs whn hit 5th: sn rdn and wknd* **14/1**

F30- **U** **Breema Donna**[82] [4035] 7-10-10 **88** .... JStevenson[(8)] —
(R Dickin) *4th whn hit 4th and uns rdr* **50/1**

5-U **P** **Nimvara (IRE)**[7] [287] 9-10-7 **77** .... JPByrne —
(Evan Williams) *plld v hrd: last whn mstke 2nd: a bhd: mstke 3 out and drvn: p.u next* **11/1**

4m 0.40s (-11.00) **Going Correction** -0.85s/f (Firm)
WFA 4 from 5yo+ 4lb **12** Ran SP% **119.9**
Speed ratings: **93,92,92,91,91 91,90,82,74,72** —,— CSF £45.91 CT £202.65 TOTE £14.60: £3.30, £2.60, £1.80; EX 48.80 Place 6 £108.17, Place 5 £46.40.
Owner Nigel Stokes **Bred** J N Stokes **Trained** Waltham-On-The-Wolds, Leics
■ Stewards' Enquiry : S Walsh four-day ban: used whip with excessive frequency (May 28-31)

FOCUS
A weak conditional riders' mares-only handicap, run at a modest gallop, and lacking any strength in depth. Both the first two can be rated better than the bare form.

NOTEBOOK
Macreater made very heavy weather of things, but still had enough in reserve on the run-in to finally get off the mark at the 20th attempt. She still looks some way short of the level he achieved in bumpers in 2002/03, but has improved of late for the application of cheekpieces, and is clearly suited by this stiff two miles. *(op 8-1)*
Marathea(FR) lost momentum at the final flight and that ultimately cost her. She still managed to reverse her recent form with the third horse, however, and can be rated better than the bare form. Success against her own success during the summer months look assured. *(op 10-3 tchd 4-1)*
Red Dahlia failed to confirm her recent Fakenham form with the runner-up off this 6lb higher mark. She was not disgraced, however, and may need genuinely fast ground to be seen at best. *(op 8-1)*
Correct And Right(IRE) , who took this race last year off a 1lb lower mark, failed to quicken when it mattered under her big weight and ran a little below par. *(tchd 5-1)*
Rose Of York(IRE) , who beat the winner in a course and distance selling handicap in April, was never a serious threat yet improved for the return to this venue nontheless. *(op 7-1)*
T/Plt: £149.80 to a £1 stake. Pool: £44,152.90. 215.15 winning tickets. T/Qpdt: £8.50 to a £1 stake. Pool: £3,637.50. 313.70 winning tickets. IM

FOLKESTONE (R-H)
Wednesday, May 18
OFFICIAL GOING: Good to firm (firm in places)
Wind: almost nil Weather: fine

400 TIGER INN NOVICES' HUNTERS' CHASE (FOR THE GUY PEATE MEMORIAL CHALLENGE TROPHY) (19 fncs) 3m 2f
6:00 (6:00) (Class 6) 5-Y-0+ **£1,735** (£534; £267; £133)

Form RPR

/2P- **1** **Millenium Way (IRE)**[16] 11-11-10 .... MrPGHall[(7)] 98
(Mrs C L Taylor) *in tch: stdy prog to trck ldr 16th: led bef 2 out: sn clr: comf* **7/2**[2]

150- **2** *11* **Exodous (ARG)**[11] 9-11-12 .... MrCGordon[(5)] 87
(Mrs A Blaker) *nt fluent: hld up: prog to trck ldr 12th to 16th: rdn and btn after 3 out: kpt on to take 2nd flat: no ch w wnr* **5/1**[3]

3 *3 1/2* **Run Monty (IRE)**[11] 10-11-10 ....(p) MrMMackley[(7)] 83
(D J Lay) *settled in last trio: effrt 12th: outpcd fr 14th: kpt on u.p to snatch 3rd last stride* **25/1**

05/3 **4** *shd* **Little Worsall (IRE)**[8] [278] 12-11-10 .... MissHGrissell[(7)] 88+
(Mrs F Marshall) *led: clr fr 5th: mstke 11th: blnd 3 out: hdd bef 2 out: btn whn blnd 2 out: wknd and lost 2 pls flat* **7/2**[2]

P/4- **5** *20* **Runningwiththemoon**[11] 9-11-12 **68** .... MrJOwen[(5)] 63
(M S Burman) *chsd ldr to 12th: rdn 16th: wknd next: no ch whn mstkes 2 cut and last* **15/2**

F/3- **6** *1 3/4* **Tricky Trevor (IRE)**[16] 12-12-0 .... MrPYork[(3)] 61
(Mrs H J Cobb) *tended to jump lft: nvr gng particularly wl: in tch to 15th: struggling and wl btn 3 out* **3/1**[1]

3- **7** *6* **Just Lark**[18] 11-11-10 .... MrRBliss[(7)] 55
(Mrs V K Rickcord) *hld up in rr: nvr on terms w ldrs: no ch fr 3 out* **10/1**

4P2/ **P** **Castle Arrow (IRE)**[31] 12-11-10 .... MissRosemaryWilliams[(7)] —
(Miss R Williams) *prom to 6th: sn wknd: t.o 12th: p.u bef 14th* **50/1**

6m 26.5s (-16.60) **Going Correction** -0.75s/f (Firm) **8** Ran SP% **112.8**
Speed ratings: **95,91,90,90,84 83,81,**— CSF £21.09 TOTE £4.60: £1.70, £2.90, £5.40; EX 25.10.
Owner Mrs C L Taylor **Bred** J A Weld **Trained** Ashford, Kent

FOCUS
A very quick time for the race, only 4 seconds outside the course record. The race has been rated through the fourth.

NOTEBOOK
Millenium Way(IRE), who had to be ridden by another jockey due to the Jockey Club not allowing the usual pilot a licence because of an old injury, won very easily after making steady headway throughout the last furlong. The way the race was set up for him clearly helped and the quick ground held no fears either. *(op 9-2)*
Exodous(ARG), who once competed in Graded races in his native Argentina, kept on plugging away for pressure and ran on to take a distant runner's-up spot. *(op 9-2)*
Run Monty(IRE) kept on after being badly outpaced. The jockey deserves credit for getting him placed. *(op 20-1 tchd 28-1)*
Little Worsall(IRE), who had beaten the winner in a Ladies' Open race in March, set a really good pace, but was clearly tired jumping the last and lost places on the flat.
Runningwiththemoon was a very poor performer when last seen under Rules, but came into the race on the back of two wins in the point-to-point sphere. His chance was gone even before he hit the last two fences. *(op 12-1)*
Tricky Trevor(IRE) ran a moody race and never got into contention. *(op 11-4 tchd 10-3, 7-2 in places)*
Castle Arrow(IRE) *Official explanation: jockey said gelding lost a shoe (op 33-1)*

401 GRANT'S CHERRY BRANDY SOUTH EAST NOVICES' HUNTERS' CHASE (15 fncs) 2m 5f
6:30 (6:30) (Class 6) 5-Y-0+ **£2,736** (£842; £421; £210)

Form RPR

2/P- **1** **Trade Off (IRE)**[32] 7-12-0 **91** .... DJacob[(3)] 93+
(R H Alner) *chsd clr ldr to 9th: sn pushed along: styd prom: gd jump to ld 3 out: rdn bef next: styd on wl* **5/6**[1]

26U- **2** *3* **Blaze On**[18] 6-12-0 .... MrPYork[(3)] 89
(R H York) *hld up: nt fluent 3rd: prog 9th: cl up whn mstke 3 out: effrt to chse wnr bef next: kpt on but no imp* **3/1**[2]

3U5- **3** *10* **Badgers Glory**[32] 9-11-10 **58** .... MrPGHall[(7)] 79
(Miss Z Anthony) *fractious bef s: chsd clr ldng pair: chsd ldr 9th to 12th: fdd bef 2 out* **16/1**

4 *nk* **Knighton Combe**[10] 5-11-11 .... MrJSnowden[(3)] 76
(J W Dufosee) *hld up: effrt after 9th: rdn and in tch after 3 out: sn one pce and btn* **12/1**

5 *9* **Ballykilthy (IRE)**[32] 8-12-0 .... MrNMoore[(3)] 73+
(Ms A E Embiricos) *in tch: outpcd fr 11th: rdn and no prog after 3 out* **15/2**[3]

PPP- **6** *16* **Cheeky Lad**[39] 5-11-11 .... MrFHutsby[(3)] 51
(R C Harper) *plld hrd: led and sn clr: 25 l ahd 8th: hdd 3 out: wknd rapidly next* **25/1**

P- **P** **Sir Henrik (IRE)**[11] 7-12-3 .... MrSWalker —
(Mrs D H McCarthy) *in tch in rr: rdn and wknd bef 9th: t.o whn p.u bef 3 out* **33/1**

5m 11.1s (-13.30) **Going Correction** -0.75s/f (Firm)
WFA 5 from 6yo+ 3lb **15** Ran SP% **111.7**
Speed ratings: **95,93,90,89,86 80,**— CSF £3.63 TOTE £1.60: £1.60, £1.60; EX 4.30.
Owner C W W Dupont & Mrs P A Tory **Bred** Joseph O'Dwyer **Trained** Droop, Dorset

FOCUS
An ordinary hunter chase in which the first two pulled clear of the rest of the field. Not much Rules form to go on, and the time compared unfavourably to the other two races over the trip.

NOTEBOOK
Trade Off(IRE), switched to Robert Alner's yard after racing under his wife's name until recently, never managed to pick a race up when trained by Martin Pipe under Rules, but has found his feet in the pointing field and won in the style of an improving type. It would be no suprise to see the horse continue under Rules next season. *(tchd 4-5 and Evens)*
Blaze On was slightly disappointing last time when trying to complete a four-timer, but recaptured his best form to chase up the winner. He has time on his side and should win more races in the point-to-point field. *(op 7-2)*
Badgers Glory stays three miles really well and probably found the drop in trip against him. *(op 14-1)*
Knighton Combe was making only his fifth appearance and ran with credit against some much more experienced rivals. *(op 16-1)*
Ballykilthy(IRE) was readily left behind when the pace was increased. *(op 5-1)*
Cheeky Lad raced much too keenly in the early stages and never got home.

402 GUILLAINE OVENDEN'S 90TH BIRTHDAY OPEN HUNTERS' CHASE (STUART ADAMSON MEMORIAL) (18 fncs) 3m 1f
7:00 (7:00) (Class 6) 5-Y-0+ **£2,019** (£673)

Form RPR

3UF- **1** **Hot Toddy (IRE)**[26] [4963] 10-12-3 .... MrRBurton 86+
(G L Landau) *nt a fluent: settled in last tl trckd ldr 13th: chal bef 2 out: rdn to ld last: kpt on* **6/5**[1]

/45- **2** *1 1/4* **Little Farmer**[16] 11-11-13 ....(p) MrPGHall[(7)] 85
(Mrs D M Grissell) *led: rdn after 3 out: hdd last: no ex flat* **9/4**[2]

4F-4 **R** **Greenwich**[24] [6] 11-12-1 **84** .... MissCStucley[(5)] —
(Mrs Marilyn Scudamore) *trckd ldr to 13th: wknd 3 out: 30 l bhd whn ref last : dismntd* **5/2**[3]

6m 14.1s (-19.30) **Going Correction** -0.75s/f (Firm) **3** Ran SP% **104.8**
Speed ratings: **100,99,**— CSF £3.89 TOTE £2.10; EX 3.50.
Owner Gilbert C Hinckley **Bred** Hugh Harley **Trained** Frome, Somerset

FOCUS
A competitive little race but won comfortably by Hot Toddy who has been rated as value for a little further.

NOTEBOOK
Hot Toddy(IRE) has a superb winning record in the pointing field but came into the race on the back of two failures to finish. He sometimes did not jump all that fluently but his jockey produced him between the last two to win nicely. However, the race did not take a lot of winning. *(op Evens)*
Little Farmer, wearing first-time cheekpieces, has run at this meeting for the last three seasons now. Taking his rivals along for most of the race, he became a sitting target for the eventual winner and could not hold his challenge after the last. *(op 2-1 tchd 5-2 in a place)*
Greenwich is probably at his best when making the running but could never get to the lead. He was well behind and looked a bit sore when refusing to jump the last. *(op 7-2)*

403 SHEPHERD NEAME UNITED HUNTS OPEN CHAMPION HUNTERS' CHASE (22 fncs) 3m 7f
7:30 (7:30) (Class 6) 6-Y-0+ **£3,458** (£1,064; £532; £266)

Form RPR

P-P3 **1** **Maggies Brother**[8] [282] 12-11-11 .... MrDBarlow[(3)] 98+
(R Shail) *cl up: led 16th and kicked on: jnd 2 out: drvn and hld on gamely flat* **5/2**[2]

10-4 **2** *1 1/4* **Tell Tale (IRE)**[7] [297] 13-12-0 **104** .... MrRMorgan[(5)] 101
(J G Cann) *racd wd: cl up: lost pl 16th: prog to trck wnr next: chal 2 out: upsides last: rdn and nt qckn flat* **7/4**[1]

0PR/ **3** *2 1/2* **Good Vintage (IRE)**[16] 10-11-11 .... MrNBloom[(3)] 93
(S R Andrews) *sn in rr: prog to trck wnr 16th to next: outpcd and rdn 3 out: 8 l down 2 out: kpt on steadily bef last* **4/1**[3]

4/3- **4** *23* **Prime Course (IRE)**[18] 16-11-9 .... MrCGordon(5) 70
(Mrs A Farrant) *pressed ldr to 16th: sn rdn: outpcd fr 18th: no ch 3 out* **25/1**

64F/ **5** *17* **Glory Trail (IRE)**[16] 11-11-7 .... MissHGrissell(7) 53
(Mrs D M Grissell) *cl up: outpcd fr 17th: wl bhd 3 out: j. bdly lft 2 out and last* **8/1**

PPP- **P** **Silver Lake (IRE)**[11] 11-11-7 ....(p) MrMMackley(7) —
(C J Lawson) *in tch tl wknd rapidly 16th: p.u bef next* **14/1**

P0-5 **P** **Robbie's Adventure**[19] [101] 11-11-9 49..........(p) MissLHorner(5) —
(D L Williams) *mde most to 16th: sn wknd: t.o 3 out: p.u bef last* **25/1**

7m 49.9s **7** Ran SP% **110.4**
CSF £7.11 TOTE £3.50: £1.20, £1.90; EX 10.40.
Owner Mrs G M Shail **Bred** R J Shail **Trained** Hollybush, H'fords

FOCUS
A competitive hunter chaser where stamina was at a premium. The winner improved 6lb on his recent Huntingdon run.

NOTEBOOK
Maggies Brother, back to form over this sort of distance when third at Huntingdon last time, found plenty under pressure and was always holding favourite Tell Tale, running on gamely under pressure. This was a slightly improved effort and it will be interesting to see if he is turned out in the near future. *(tchd 11-4 in a place)*
Tell Tale(IRE) was given a fine ride and had every chance to pass the winner, but was simply unable to do so. He is a consistent sort, who will continue to pay his way. *(op 11-8)*
Good Vintage(IRE), who has developed into a useful pointer, found himself tapped for toe at a vital stage and was finishing well having got a bit behind. He may benefit from a more positive ride from the outset next time as speed is clearly not one of his main assets. *(op 6-1)*
Prime Course(IRE) was well adrift of the front three and ran as well as could have been expected for a 16-year-old. He was reportedly retired after the race. *(op 20-1)*

404 DEBORAH BUTTERWORTH IS 40 TOMORROW MAIDEN HUNTERS' CHASE (FOR CUCKOO MAIDEN CHALLENGE CUP (15 fncs) 2m 5f

8:00 (8:00) (Class 6) 5-Y-0+ **£1,722** (£530; £265; £132)

Form RPR

40/ **1** **Bell Rock**[4] 7-11-12 .... MrJETudor(5) 92+
(Mrs T J Hill) *settled midfield: prog to trck ldrs 9th: pushed along 3 out: prog to ld 2 out: clr last: rdn out* **7/1**[3]

0/P- **2** *5* **Machrihanish**[18] 5-11-7 ....(b[1]) MrRBliss(7) 82
(Miss S Brine) *sn t.o and jumping lft: sme prog and jst in tch 9th: outpcd 11th: r.o reluctantly fr 3 out: tk 2nd flat* **8/1**

/0-0 **3** *2 1/2* **River Bailiff (IRE)**[15] [171] 9-12-0 74.......... MrPYork(3) 82
(S Garrott) *cl up: blnd 6th: trckd ldr 11th: led 3 out: rdn and hdd 2 out: wknd last* **14/1**

3- **4** *2* **Lord Euro (IRE)**[24] 8-11-10 .... MrAMerriam(7) 80
(Mrs D M Grissell) *led 3rd and set str pce: hdd 3 out: wknd next* **5/1**[2]

/35- **5** *8* **Mister Pearly**[32] 8-11-10 .... MrJSole(7) 73+
(T D B Underwood) *wl in tch: trckd ldrs 9th: effrt to chal and nt fluent 3 out: rdn and wknd bef next* **5/1**[2]

6 *2* **Tellem Noting (IRE)**[16] 8-11-10 ....(t) MrDPhelan(7) 70
(David Phelan) *hld up in rr: prog 8th: chsd ldng gp 10th: no imp whn mstke 12th: no hdwy after* **33/1**

P/ **7** *dist* **Asabache (IRE)**[16] 10-11-10 ....(v[1]) MrMatthewSmith(7) —
(Sean Regan) *sn t.o in last trio: r.o to snatch remote 7th nr fin: btn 75 l* **33/1**

0P- **8** *3/4* **Carvilla (IRE)**[11] 10-11-10 .... MrNKinnon(7) —
(Mrs B Ansell) *plld hrd: prom: w ldr after 7th to 11th: wknd rapidly: t.o: btn 76 l* **50/1**

6/6- **9** *18* **Jack Of Kilcash (IRE)**[11] 11-11-10 .... MrNBenstead(7) —
(Nigel Benstead) *racd v wd: in tch to 4th: sn u.p and struggling: t.o 9th: btn 94 l* **25/1**

6/5- **P** **Blakes Road (IRE)**[16] 8-11-10 .... MsLisaStock(7) —
(Ms Lisa Stock) *sn t.o in last trio: p.u bef 3 out* **12/1**

P **Cosmic Sky**[11] 8-11-10 .... MrRStearn(7) —
(Robert Abrey) *chsd ldrs: mstke 8th: wknd after next: sn bhd: t.o in 9th whn p.u bef last* **7/1**[3]

4- **U** **No Reward (IRE)**[38] 9-11-10 ....(t) MrPGHall(7) 70
(Mrs D M Grissell) *settled at rr of main gp: outpcd after 9th: n.d after: 6th and wl btn whn uns rdr last* **4/1**[1]

P0/0 **P** **One Of The Natives (IRE)**[21] [52] 11-11-10 ....(p) MissJJenner(7) —
(Miss J H Jenner) *led to 3rd: chsd ldr tl after 7th: wknd rapidly: t.o whn p.u bef 3 out* **66/1**

5m 9.60s (-14.80) **Going Correction** -0.75s/f (Firm)
WFA 5 from 7yo+ 3lb **15** Ran SP% **117.0**
Speed ratings: **98,96,95,94,91 90,—,—,—,— —,—,—** CSF £58.16 TOTE £9.60: £3.00, £2.00, £4.30; EX 67.80.
Owner Alan Hill **Bred** A J Struthers **Trained** Chinnor, Oxon

FOCUS
A modest hunter chase, but two unexposed types fought out the finish. It has been rated through the fourth.

NOTEBOOK
Bell Rock, who has often looked a non-stayer over three miles, is more at home over this sort of distance and he pulled away after the last to win comfortably. He likes top of the ground and will continue to be an obvious type under similar conditions. *(op 8-1)*
Machrihanish, off the mark in a maiden point last month, looked awkward under pressure in the first-time blinkers and many would say unwilling. He is still only five and open to further improvement so not one to discount just yet. *(op 10-1)*
River Bailiff(IRE) had his chance and was not good enough to hold off a couple of unexposed sorts. *(op 16-1)*
Lord Euro(IRE) may have done a bit too much too soon and had nothing left to offer from the second last. *(tchd 9-2)*
Mister Pearlywas basically disappointing and a slight mistake three out ended all chance. *(op 7-2)*
No Reward(IRE) has been running well in points, but was comfortably held here when unseating at the last. *(op 7-2 tchd 9-2)*

405 KELLY'S BOY CELEBRATION OPEN HUNTERS' CHASE (FOR THE UNITED HUNTS CUP) (15 fncs) 2m 5f

8:30 (8:30) (Class 6) 5-Y-0+ **£1,876** (£536; £268)

Form RPR

32U- **1** **Satchmo (IRE)**[41] [4750] 13-11-10 101.......... MrPGHall(7) 105+
(Mrs D M Grissell) *trckd ldrs: led 6th: drew steadily away fr next: wl clr 3 out: unchal* **8/13**[1]

060/ **2** *26* **Lord Of The Flies (IRE)**[18] 12-11-10 .... MrJSole(7) 79
(Ms Lisa Stock) *hld up in detached last: stdy prog fr 9th: wnt 2nd after 3 out: no ch w wnr* **14/1**

0/3- **3** *3* **Royal Czarina**[16] 8-11-7 .... MrJSnowden(3) 69
(J W Dufosee) *trckd ldrs: chsd wnr 7th to 10th: sn struggling: kpt on to take modest 3rd flat* **3/1**[2]

6-00 **4** *1 3/4* **Merry Minstrel (IRE)**[11] [221] 12-11-10 79..........(p) MrJOldring(7) 74
(Mrs Jackie Hunt) *prom: chsd wnr 11th tl after 3 out: wknd* **33/1**

/P0- **5** *11* **Gratomi (IRE)**[10] 15-11-10 .... MrMMackley(7) 63
(Mrs A E Lee) *led at fast pce to 6th: chsd wnr to next and fr 10th to 11th: wknd 3 out* **40/1**

6P6/ **6** *dist* **Chief Chippie**[11] 12-11-10 .... MissRosemaryWilliams(7) —
(A C Simpson) *prom to 5th: sn wknd: wl t.o 9th: stl appr last as 5th horse fin* **50/1**

U3-P **P** **Wahiba Sands**[6] [313] 12-11-12 107..........(b[1]) MissLucyBridges(5) —
(Miss Lucy Bridges) *a in rr: pushed along and struggling 9th: t.o in 6th whn p.u bef 3 out* **7/1**[3]

5m 8.60s (-15.80) **Going Correction** -0.75s/f (Firm) **7** Ran SP% **113.4**
Speed ratings: **100,90,88,88,84 —,—** CSF £9.93 TOTE £1.60: £1.50, £3.20; EX 8.00 Place 6 £52.49, Place 5 £12.98.
Owner G J D Wragg **Bred** Patricia Mollahan **Trained** Brightling, E Sussex

FOCUS
Satchmo turned this into a procession. The race has been rated through the the third and fourth, both of whom ran to their marks.

NOTEBOOK
Satchmo(IRE) has always been a useful sort and he destroyed this modest field by an easy 26 lengths. This represented a big drop in grade and he would be a good thing were connections to find him a similar race in the near future. *(op 4-7)*
Lord Of The Flies(IRE) did best of the rest, but was no match for the winner and did not appear to achieve a great deal on this hunter chase debut. *(op 12-1)*
Royal Czarina was made to look pedestrian back in third and could only plod on. *(tchd 10-3)*
Wahiba Sands is a shadow of his former self and deserves to be retired. *(op 10-1)*
T/Plt: £68.60 to a £1 stake. Pool: £31,114.55. 330.65 winning tickets. T/Qpdt: £31.40 to a £1 stake. Pool: £2,277.05. 53.50 winning tickets. JN

[80]KELSO (L-H)

Wednesday, May 18

OFFICIAL GOING: Good to firm (good in places in home straight)
Wind: Light, half against

406 NICHOLSON BROS NOVICES' H'CAP HURDLE (8 hdls) 2m 110y

2:30 (2:33) (Class 4) (0-105,101) 4-Y-0+ **£4,927** (£1,516; £758; £379)

Form RPR

60-0 **1** **Acceleration (IRE)**[20] [82] 5-10-10 83..........(t) ADobbin 86
(R Allan) *in tch: hdwy 2 out: led last 100yds: styd on wl* **12/1**

00-4 **2** *3/4* **We'll Meet Again**[7] [306] 5-10-8 84.......... MrTGreenall(3) 87
(M W Easterby) *hld up: drvn and effrt bef 2 out: kpt on fr last: nt rch wnr* **4/1**[2]

21-2 **3** *shd* **Lawgiver (IRE)**[13] [197] 4-11-10 101.......... WMarston 100
(T J Fitzgerald) *cl up: led bef 2 out to run in: rallied: hld towards fin* **2/1**[1]

6- **4** *shd* **Miss Kilkeel (IRE)**[62] [4420] 7-10-7 83.......... SMcGovern(3) 86
(R T J Wilson, Ire) *midfield: effrt bef 2 out: ev ch run in: hld towards fin* **16/1**

0-14 **5** *1/2* **Royal Glen (IRE)**[6] [320] 7-10-9 82.......... GLee 84
(W S Coltherd) *keen: hld up in tch: hdwy to ld run in: hdd and no ex last 100yds* **8/1**

600- **6** *1 1/2* **Ready To Rumble (NZ)**[142] [2994] 8-11-0 90..........(p) LMcGrath(3) 91
(R C Guest) *keen early: led: drvn and hdd bef 2 out: nt qckn last* **7/1**[3]

4P6- **7** *7* **The Count (FR)**[200] [1474] 6-10-3 76.......... BHarding 70
(F P Murtagh) *bhd: effrt u.p 2 out: no imp run in* **66/1**

P-00 **8** *1* **Bromley Abbey**[7] [301] 7-9-13 75 ow2..........(p) MrCStorey(3) 68
(Miss S E Forster) *chsd ldrs tl wknd bef 2 out* **66/1**

0-00 **9** *3 1/2* **Alphecca (USA)**[13] [194] 4-10-0 77.......... RMcGrath 62
(K G Reveley) *prom tl wknd qckly fr 3 out* **7/1**[3]

00-0 **10** *1/2* **Simon's Heights**[21] [59] 4-10-13 90.......... KRenwick 75
(Miss P Robson) *hld up: shortlived effrt 3 out: sn btn* **16/1**

05-P **11** *4* **Tullimoss (IRE)**[6] [319] 10-10-4 82.......... DCCostello(5) 67
(J N R Billinge) *chsd ldrs tl wknd bef 3 out* **20/1**

664- **12** *27* **I'm Your Man**[38] [4785] 6-11-9 99.......... PBuchanan(3) 57
(Mrs Dianne Sayer) *a bhd* **33/1**

PP-P **13** *1 3/4* **Mackenzie (IRE)**[7] [303] 9-9-12 76.......... DMcGann(5) 32
(Mrs C J Kerr) *prom tl lost pl after 3rd: struggling fr next* **100/1**

000/ **P** **Weldman**[424] [4461] 6-10-3 76.......... JimCrowley —
(K G Reveley) *a bhd: t.o whn p.u bef 2 out* **28/1**

3m 48.5s (-15.20) **Going Correction** -0.725s/f (Firm) **14** Ran SP% **124.0**
Speed ratings: **106,105,105,105,105 104,101,100,99,98 97,84,83,—** CSF £59.93 CT £142.00 TOTE £12.90: £3.00, £1.60, £1.20; EX 64.30.
Owner Kim Marshall, Sue Rigby, Susan Warren **Bred** Cliveden Stud Ltd **Trained** Cornhill-on-Tweed, Northumberland

FOCUS
A race run at a fair pace, but still several had a major chance jumping the last and less than a length and a half covered the first five. The form should work out well enough.

NOTEBOOK
Acceleration(IRE), who has not been getting home in his recent races, battled on really well to finally get off the mark over timber at the 19th attempt in a driving finish. The combination of a 6lb lower mark, a return to faster ground and, probably most significantly, the fitting of a tongue tie *brought about the improvement. Whether he will repeat this is anyone's guess.Official explanation: trainer said, regarding the improved form shown, gelding benefited from the fitting for the first time of a tongue-strap and was also suited by the faster ground*
We'll Meet Again is sliding down the handicap and came as close to winning over hurdles as he has ever done. His only win on the Flat came over seven furlongs on very fast ground which demonstrates that he needs a sharp track to see out this trip. A repeat of this could net him a small *race, but considering how many chances he has had you would not want to bet on it. (op 9-2 tchd 7-2)*
Lawgiver(IRE), now 11lb higher than when getting off the mark over course and distance last month, had every chance but lacked a decisive turn of foot on the long run-in. He may prefer a slightly stiffer test now. *(tchd 5-2)*
Miss Kilkeel(IRE), an Irish-trained hurdler making her second appearance in Scotland, ran her race but is probably better suited by further.
Royal Glen(IRE) was in front starting up the run-in, but was just found wanting for a turn of foot. This was her second decent effort since her shock win in a Hexham seller. *(op 6-1)*
Ready To Rumble(NZ), given a positive ride in the cheekpieces, was just done for foot on the *climb from the second last. This was still his best effort since arriving from New Zealand. (op 8-1 tchd 10-1 in a place)*
Simon's Heights *Official explanation: jockey said gelding was never travelling (op 20-1)*

407 CHARLES CHURCH INTERMEDIATE CHASE (19 fncs) 3m 1f
3:05 (3:05) (Class 2) 5-Y-0+ **£14,882** (£5,645; £2,822; £1,283; £641)

Form			Horse	Jockey	RPR
23F-	1		**Smiths Landing**[158] [2768] 8-11-8 127	DElsworth	127
			(Mrs S J Smith) *mde all: drvn 2 out: hld on gamely*	**7/2**[2]	
12-1	2	*shd*	**Mckelvey (IRE)**[16] [148] 6-11-5	RJohnson	128+
			(P Bowen) *cl up: hit 10th: effrt and ev ch whn blnd last: rallied gamely run in: jst hld*	**6/4**[1]	
133-	3	*shd*	**Isard III (FR)**[26] [4974] 9-11-8 127	APMcCoy	127
			(M C Pipe) *chsd ldrs: hdwy 3 out: effrt and chal last: hrd rdn run in: hld cl home*	**6/4**[1]	
03-6	4	*25*	**The Miner**[6] [318] 7-11-5 92	MrCStorey	99
			(Miss S E Forster) *in tch tl wknd fr 14th*	**25/1**[3]	
6-00	5	*1*	**Old Nosey (IRE)**[11] [215] 9-11-0	ADempsey	93
			(B Mactaggart) *in tch to 13th: wknd next*	**33/1**	

6m 13.2s (-16.40) **Going Correction** -0.925s/f (Hard)
WFA 5 from 6yo+ 7lb **5** Ran SP% **109.0**
Speed ratings: **89,88,88,80,80** CSF £9.39 TOTE £4.10: £2.30, £1.90; EX 7.80.
Owner Billy McCullough **Bred** R H Smith **Trained** High Eldwick, W Yorks

FOCUS
A three-horse race to all intents and purposes and a contest run at a very modest pace, which developed into something of a sprint over the last half-mile. The winning time was moderate for a race of its type as a result, but nonetheless it produced a cracking finish. The form should work out.

NOTEBOOK
Smiths Landing, returning from a five-month break, has shown he can go well fresh in the past. Allowed the luxury of an uncontested lead, that was to prove vital as he kept on pulling out more when he was challenged on both flanks up the run-in. He is very well suited by going this way round. *(tchd 4-1)*
Mckelvey(IRE), encountering his fastest surface to date on only his second outing over fences, was always sat in the slipstream of the winner. He looked the first of the big three beaten on the turn to the last fence and did not jump the obstacle anything like as well as the other two. Rallying well up the inside rail on the run-in, given how narrowly he failed that last-fence blunder was probably very costly. *(tchd 11-8, 7-4 in a place)*
Isard III(FR), whose four previous wins under Rules have been over shorter, though he has won a point over this sort of trip, was held behind the front pair for most of the way. Brought with his effort at the last, he gave his all on the run-in, but could never quite get up. The modest pace meant that his stamina was not truly tested. *(tchd 7-4)*
The Miner had a mountain to climb at the weights and was always taking part in a separate match for fourth place, which he just about won. *(tchd 28-1)*

408 NEWTON INVESTMENT MANAGEMENT INTERMEDIATE HURDLE (11 hdls) 2m 6f 110y
3:35 (3:36) (Class 2) 4-Y-0+ **£12,087** (£4,584; £2,292)

Form			Horse	Jockey	RPR
11-3	1		**Yes Sir (IRE)**[18] [127] 6-11-8 144	APMcCoy	150+
			(P Bowen) *keen: mde all: drew clr fr 4 out: canter*	**1/3**[1]	
12-4	2	*dist*	**Alikat (IRE)**[18] [127] 4-10-9 125	RJohnson	103
			(M C Pipe) *chsd wnr tl outpcd fr 4 out: eased whn no ch run in*	**5/2**[2]	
0-	3	*dist*	**Comeonourfella (IRE)**[5] [335] 6-11-0 79	SMMcGovern	—
			(R T J Wilson, Ire) *chsd ldrs: struggling 4th: tailing off whn fell 7th: continued*	**33/1**[3]	

5m 16.8s (-20.90) **Going Correction** -0.725s/f (Firm)
WFA 4 from 6yo+ 5lb **3** Ran SP% **106.5**
Speed ratings: **107,—,—** CSF £1.54 TOTE £1.20; EX 1.10.
Owner Ms Y M Hill **Bred** Louis Hill **Trained** Little Newcastle, Pembrokes

FOCUS
Effectively a match and a straightforward victory for the long odds-on favourite, who has been rated as value for 35l. Despite the small field and the winner being heavily eased, the time was still 6.8 seconds faster than the later handicap.

NOTEBOOK
Yes Sir(IRE), 11lb well in with his main rival compared to a handicap, was positive from the start and never really looked in any danger. He would have worked harder on the gallops. *(op 1-4)*
Alikat(IRE), who would have been 11lb better off with the favourite in a handicap, was always in about the same place but was easily left behind over the last half-mile. He will find much easier opportunities. *(op 3-1 tchd 10-3)*
Comeonourfella(IRE), already a long way behind the front pair when coming down at the seventh, was remounted in order to collect the £2,292.40 for finishing third. *(tchd 40-1)*

409 BACK AND LAY AT GGBET.COM H'CAP CHASE (12 fncs) 2m 1f
4:10 (4:10) (Class 3) (0-125,124) 5-Y-0+
£12,203 (£4,628; £2,314; £1,052; £526; £315)

Form			Horse	Jockey	RPR
4-61	1		**Moscow Dancer (IRE)**[6] [318] 8-10-1 97 7ex	NPMulholland	116+
			(P Monteith) *j.rt: hld up in tch: stdy hdwy whn hit 8th: led last: rdn and r.o strly*	**5/2**[1]	
03P-	2	*10*	**Figaro Du Rocher (FR)**[26] [4974] 5-11-12 124	(t) APMcCoy	132+
			(M C Pipe) *w ldr: led bef 3 out: hit and hdd last: no ch w wnr*	**7/2**[2]	
05-3	3	*9*	**Gone Too Far**[6] [318] 7-11-2 112	(v) RThornton	114+
			(P Monteith) *prom: blnd and lost pl 4th: no imp fr 3 out*	**7/1**	
43-3	4	*8*	**Enzo De Baune (FR)**[19] [108] 8-11-5 122	(p) BenOrde-Powlett(7)	115+
			(G A Harker) *led: hdd whn mstke 3 out: rdn and wknd bef last*	**4/1**[3]	
1P-0	5	*9*	**Billie John (IRE)**[13] [195] 10-11-5 115	RMcGrath	96
			(Mrs K Walton) *chsd ldrs to 4 out: sn rdn and wknd*	**25/1**	
22-6	6	*18*	**Kids Inheritance (IRE)**[19] [108] 7-11-3 113	GLee	76
			(J M Jefferson) *hld up: lost tch 1/2-way: t.o*	**7/2**[2]	

4m 2.60s (-20.60) **Going Correction** -0.925s/f (Hard) **6** Ran SP% **109.4**
Speed ratings: **111,106,102,98,94 85** CSF £11.24 CT £46.40 TOTE £3.10: £2.10, £4.00; EX 13.40.
Owner J Stephenson **Bred** Gerald Mitchell **Trained** Rosewell, Midlothian

FOCUS
A decent time for the grade, just 0.2 seconds outside the 21-year-old course record, and the form looks fairly sound. The winner is progressive.

NOTEBOOK
Moscow Dancer(IRE) followed up his recent Perth success with a commanding performance under his 7lb penalty. He has clearly come right of late, but was techincally 8lb well in for this under the penalty, and if allowing for further improvement, he is going to find life difficult off his revised mark in the future. *(tchd 9-4)*
Figaro Du Rocher(FR) was a sitting duck for the winner even before he blundered at the final fence. Even though he looks held by the Handicapper at present, this was a much more encouraging effort and he looks best over this trip. *(op 3-1)*
Gone Too Far was always struggling after an early blunder and ran below his recent form with the progressive winner. He is capable of better, but is never one to place too much faith in. *(op 9-1)*
Enzo De Baune(FR) got his favoured lead, but made a bad error three out and went backwards thereafter. He is best over slightly further and is happier on an easier surface. *(tchd 5-1)*
Kids Inheritance(IRE) ran a moody race and looks held by the Handicapper now. *Official explanation: jockey said gelding slipped on stand bend and lost interest (tchd 4-1)*

410 SAVILLS H'CAP HURDLE (11 hdls) 2m 6f 110y
4:45 (4:45) (Class 3) (0-115,107) 4-Y-0+ **£5,603** (£1,724; £862; £431)

Form			Horse	Jockey	RPR
000-	1		**Bob's Gone (IRE)**[128] [3297] 7-11-5 100	ADobbin	106+
			(N G Richards) *set stdy pce: mde all: rdn and r.o wl fr last*	**11/2**	
30-0	2	*3*	**Siena Star (IRE)**[16] [149] 7-10-10 91	RThornton	93
			(P Bowen) *hld up in tch: effrt bef 2 out: chsd wnr run in: kpt on same pce*	**9/2**[3]	
23-3	3	*shd*	**Speed Kris (FR)**[7] [304] 6-11-12 107	(p) MBradburne	109
			(Mrs S C Bradburne) *chsd ldrs: effrt after 2 out: kpt on same pce fr last*	**5/2**[1]	
4-46	4	*9*	**Opal's Helmsman (USA)**[11] [212] 6-10-5 86	ADempsey	80+
			(W S Coltherd) *chsd ldrs: drvn fr 3 out: outpcd fr next*	**8/1**	
25-5	5	*3*	**Tobesure (IRE)**[11] [215] 11-11-3 98	PRobson	88
			(J I A Charlton) *cl up: ev ch 3 out: wknd last*	**7/2**[2]	
0-02	6	*6*	**Political Sox**[7] [304] 11-11-3 105	GThomas(7)	89
			(R Nixon) *hld up: mstke 4 out: sn rdn: outpcd fr next*	**15/2**	
/P-P	7	*dist*	**Intensity**[21] [64] 9-11-4 102	PWhelan(3)	—
			(S B Bell) *hld up: outpcd 4 out: btn next*	**25/1**	

5m 23.6s (-14.10) **Going Correction** -0.725s/f (Firm) **7** Ran SP% **111.1**
Speed ratings: **95,93,93,90,89 87,—** CSF £28.59 CT £73.37 TOTE £6.70: £3.10, £2.10; EX 33.90.
Owner Team Cobra Racing Syndicate **Bred** Denis Dunne And Thomas Phelan **Trained** Greystoke, Cumbria
■ Stewards' Enquiry : G Thomas caution: used whip when out of contention

FOCUS
A modest time for the grade, due to the stop-start gallop, and the first three came clear. The form is suspect.

NOTEBOOK
Bob's Gone(IRE) got back to winning ways under a shrewd front-running ride from Dobbin. This is his ground, he has clearly fallen to a decent mark and it should be noted that all of his wins over timber to date have come when he is allowed to dominate. He can strike again while the ground is quick. *(op 10-3 tchd 3-1)*
Siena Star(IRE) turned in one of his best efforts to date over hurdles, and deserves credit, as he was totally unsuited by the uneven gallop. This advertised the good recent form of his yard, but whether he can repeat this has to be questionable given his recent inconsistency. *(op 6-1)*
Speed Kris(FR) had his chance, but again proved one-paced at the business end of the race. This was a fair effort under top weight and he really does deserve to find a race in this country. *(op 7-2 tchd 4-1)*
Opal's Helmsman(USA) proved unsuited by the lack of pace on this drop back in trip and was never a serious factor. He remains a maiden. *(op 9-1)*
Tobesure(IRE), runner-up in this last year off a 6lb higher mark, was well backed to go one better and had every chance, but dropped out disappointingly from three out. He is regressing badly. *(op 9-2)*
Political Sox looked to have an obvious chance on the form of his latest effort at Perth, but he was unsuited by the lack of real pace, and failed to recover after a bad error four from home. He evidently has two ways of running and is one to avoid. *(op 5-1)*
Intensity *Official explanation: jockey said gelding had breathing problem (op 20-1)*

411 PERSIMMON HOMES HUNTERS' CHASE (19 fncs) 3m 1f
5:20 (5:20) (Class 6) 5-Y-0+ **£2,383** (£681; £340)

Form			Horse	Jockey	RPR
U4-2	1		**Emperor Ross (IRE)**[21] [63] 10-11-11 111	MrCJCallow(7)	120+
			(N G Richards) *hld and bhd: hdwy to chse ldr 14th: led bef last: sn clr*	**13/8**[2]	
3UP/	2	*12*	**Pharmistice (IRE)**[3] 14-11-7	MrsNNeill(7)	102
			(Mrs N C Neill) *in tch: rdn fr 15th: chsd wnr run in: no imp*	**12/1**[3]	
224-	3	*20*	**Coole Abbey (IRE)**[41] [4750] 13-11-11	TJDreaper(3)	87+
			(W Amos) *cl up: mde most fr 5th to bef last: outpcd run in*	**5/4**[1]	
24P-	4	*6*	**Primitive Way**[38] 13-11-7 95	(v) MrPMaitland-Carew(7)	76
			(C Storey) *towards rr: outpcd 1/2-way: n.d after*	**14/1**	
S/F-	5	*6*	**Wild Edgar (IRE)**[24] 8-11-7	MrRTrotter(7)	70
			(A R Trotter) *led to 5th: wknd fr 14th*	**40/1**	
3P-0	6	*8*	**Toad Hall**[18] [125] 11-12-3 69	MissRCowie(7)	72
			(Mrs L B Normile) *sn wl bhd: nvr on terms*	**66/1**	
351/	P		**Derryrose**[11] 12-12-0	MrTGreenall	—
			(T Butt) *towards rr: struggling and p.u bef 15th*	**20/1**	
P-PU	P		**Mill Tower**[6] [322] 8-11-9	MrPCallaghan(5)	—
			(R Nixon) *cl up tl wknd bef 14th: t.o whn p.u bef 3 out*	**100/1**	
/F-0	P		**Pilot's Harbour**[11] 9-11-9	(p) MrTDavidson(5)	—
			(Mark Hughes) *cl up to 13th: wknd bef next: t.o whn p.u bef 3 out*	**33/1**	

6m 18.9s (-10.70) **Going Correction** -0.925s/f (Hard) **9** Ran SP% **109.5**
Speed ratings: **80,76,69,67,65 63,—,—,—** CSF £17.06 TOTE £2.20: £1.10, £2.20, £1.10; EX 13.70 Place 6 £16.10, Place 5 £9.53.
Owner James Callow **Bred** Denis O'Gorman **Trained** Greystoke, Cumbria
■ Stewards' Enquiry : T J Dreaper seven-day ban: continued when gelding appeared to be lame (May 30-31, Jun 14, Jul 17, Aug 5, Sep 11, Oct 18)

FOCUS
A very slow winning time, even for a hunter chase, and the field came home well strung out behind the easy winner.

NOTEBOOK
Emperor Ross(IRE) relished the return to this faster ground and got back to winning ways with a comfortable success. He can be rated value for even further and is hard to beat in this sphere on his day. *(op 7-4 tchd 11-8)*
Pharmistice(IRE), fourth in a point three days previously, came home well clear of the rest, but was firmly put in his place by the winner. He has won three times at this venue in the past, and while he remains vulnerable to anything with a turn of foot, he may be able to find a weak race over course and distance. *(op 10-1)*
Coole Abbey(IRE), fourth in the Fox Hunters' at Aintree last time, stopped quickly before the final fence as though something may well have been amiss. The fast ground may well have been the contributing factor. *(op Evens tchd 6-4, 7-4 and 13-8 in a place)*
Primitive Way, with the visor back on, was never a factor and looks totally fed up with racing. *(op 16-1)*
Pilot's Harbour *Official explanation: vet said gelding bled from nose (op 50-1)*

T/Plt: £18.90 to a £1 stake. Pool: £32,785.55. 1,261 winning tickets. T/Qpdt: £10.00 to a £1 stake. Pool: £1,780.10. 131.30 winning tickets. RY

[147] SEDGEFIELD (L-H)

Wednesday, May 18

OFFICIAL GOING: Good to firm

Wind: nil

412 MISS DURHAM - 24TH MAY CONDITIONAL JOCKEYS' H'CAP HURDLE (8 hdls) 2m 1f

6:20 (6:20) (Class 4) (0-105,98) 4-Y-O+ **£3,419** (£1,052; £526; £263)

Form RPR

03-1 **1** **He's Hot Right Now (NZ)**[16] [149] 6-11-3 **95**....................(p) MrJEClare[8] 101+
(R C Guest) *hld up: hdwy to trck ldrs 1/2-way: led appr and hit 2 out: rdn last: styd on wl flat* **4/1**[2]

03-2 **2** *2* **Arjay**[10] [238] 7-10-3 **73**....................(b) DCCostello 74+
(S B Clark) *hld up: hdwy in in tch 1/2-way: effrt to chse wnr appr 2 out: rdn and hit last: kpt on same pce flat* **5/1**[3]

500- **3** *5* **Not Amused (UAE)**[9] [3676] 5-10-9 **79**....................(b[1]) WHutchinson 74
(Ian Williams) *led to 2nd: cl up tl led after 4th: rdn along and hdd bef 2 out: drvn appr last: wknd flat* **3/1**[1]

36-0 **4** *hd* **Young Tot (IRE)**[16] [149] 7-11-1 **85**.................... KJMercer 80
(Mrs A Duffield) *hld up and bhd: hdwy appr 3 out: rdn to chse ldrs next kpt on u.p appr last: nrst fin* **16/1**

00-0 **5** *11* **Al Mabrook (IRE)**[24] [9] 10-11-1 **90**.................... WMcCarthy[5] 74
(N G Richards) *chsd ldrs: rdn along appr 3 out and sn btn* **9/1**

0-62 **6** *2½* **Lone Soldier (FR)**[3] [370] 9-11-0 **84**.................... PAspell 65
(S B Clark) *cl up: led and hit 2nd: hdd after 4th: rdn along appr 3 out and sn wknd* **9/1**

03-4 **7** *½* **Pure Brief (IRE)**[10] [238] 8-10-5 **75**....................(b) TGreenway 56
(J Mackie) *prom: rdn along and mstke 5th: sn drvn and wknd* **6/1**

60-1 **8** *1¼* **Trickstep**[15] [173] 4-11-7 **98**.................... StephenJCraine[3] 74
(D McCain) *prom: rdn along 3 out and sn wknd* **16/1**

P-FP **9** *3½* **Greenacres Boy**[10] [238] 10-10-1 **71**....................(p) ONelmes 47
(M Mullineaux) *s.i.s: a bhd* **20/1**

0/0- **P** **Conor's Pride (IRE)**[346] [656] 8-11-12 **96**.................... GBerridge —
(B Mactaggart) *a rr: t.o whn p.u bef 2 out* **50/1**

(-6.50) **Going Correction** -0.30s/f (Good)
WFA 4 from 5yo+ 4lb **10** Ran SP% **114.4**
Speed ratings: **103,102,99,99,94 93,93,92,90,—** CSF £24.27 CT £67.29 TOTE £3.40: £2.20, £1.80, £1.80; EX 20.90.
Owner Paul Beck **Bred** T W Jarvis **Trained** Brancepeth, Co Durham

FOCUS
This was run at a good pace. The winner is rated value for further and the runner-up ran to his mark.

NOTEBOOK
He's Hot Right Now(NZ) defied a rise of 9lb for his course and distance win earlier in the month. Coming from just off the strong pace, he was in command when his rider dropped his stick between the last two flights. *(op 10-3 tchd 9-2 in places)*
Arjay remains in good form but continues to prove hard to win with. *(op 7-1)*
Not Amused(UAE), who showed improved form on the Flat when fitted with a visor, ran a decent race in headgear over jumps for the first time. *(op 4-1)*
Young Tot(IRE) stayed on from the back of the field and seems better without the headgear.
Lone Soldier(FR), a stablemate of the runner-up, might have found this coming too soon.

413 STANLEY THOMPSON MEMORIAL BEGINNERS' CHASE (16 fncs) 2m 5f

6:50 (6:51) (Class 4) 5-Y-O+ **£4,143** (£1,275; £637; £318)

Form RPR

560- **1** **Beat The Heat (IRE)**[25] [4711] 7-11-0 112....................(b) BHarding 102+
(Jedd O'Keeffe) *in tch: hdwy 8th: cl up next: led 2 out: sn rdn and styd on wl* **5/1**[3]

11-2 **2** *3* **Pebble Bay**[24] [13] 10-11-0 .... DElsworth 99+
(Mrs S J Smith) *cl up: led 3rd: pushed along 4 out: rdn and hdd 2 out: kpt on u.p* **7/2**[2]

U25- **3** *4* **Daguyda (FR)**[110] [3567] 6-10-11 91.................... KJMercer[3] 94
(Ferdy Murphy) *bhd tl styd on fr 4 out: nrst fin* **25/1**

33-4 **4** *7* **Hi Fi**[23] [26] 7-11-0 104....................(b[1]) DRDennis 89+
(Ian Williams) *mstke 1st: chsd ldrs on inner: rdn along 4 out: drvn next: wknd 2 out* **6/1**

2U-5 **5** *1¼* **Nomadic Blaze**[16] [148] 8-10-11 .... LMcGrath[3] 87+
(P G Atkinson) *led to 3rd: cl up: mstke 9th: rdn along next: grad wknd fr 4 out* **50/1**

0F-0 **6** *4* **Inglewood**[11] [211] 5-10-4 83.................... MJMcAlister[7] 79
(Miss Kate Milligan) *chsd ldrs: rdn along 9th: mstke next: sn lost pl and bhd* **100/1**

0U/U **P** **Percy Beck**[16] [148] 9-11-0 .... FKeniry —
(P Needham) *a bhd: p.u bef 3 out* **100/1**

0- **U** **The Hill (IRE)**[5] [335] 6-10-11 .... PBuchanan[3] 75
(D M Christie, Ire) *midfield: pshed along and bhd fr 5 out: blnd and uns rdr 2 out* **33/1**

0-45 **P** **The Names Bond**[11] [217] 7-11-0 100.................... GLee —
(Andrew Turnell) *in tch: mstke 11th and sddle slipped: sn lost pl and p.u after 4 out* **15/2**

1/ **P** **Windy Spirit (IRE)**[18] 10-11-0 99.................... ChristianWilliams —
(Evan Williams) *midfield: hdwy to chse ldrs 9th: rdn along and outpcd bef 4 out: bhd whn p.u bef 2 out* **9/1**

112/ **P** **Phar From Frosty (IRE)**[522] [2722] 8-11-0 .... JAMcCarthy —
(C R Egerton) *nt fluent: in tch: hdwy and cl up 1/2-way: rdn along and lost pl qckly 11th: p.u after 4 out* **5/2**[1]

5m 16.5s (-6.90) **Going Correction** -0.30s/f (Good)
WFA 5 from 6yo+ 3lb **11** Ran SP% **114.2**
Speed ratings: **101,99,98,95,95 93,—,—,—,— —** CSF £22.24 TOTE £6.80: £2.30, £1.80, £4.70; EX 28.80.
Owner Richard Berry **Bred** Moyglare Stud Farm Ltd **Trained** Middleham Moor, N Yorks

FOCUS
An ordinary event which could be rated higher, but the average time holds down the form.

NOTEBOOK
Beat The Heat(IRE) was having his first run over fences since January but has been in action over hurdles and on the Flat since. With blinkers on for the first time in more than two years, he jumped soundly and stayed on willingly to score. *(op 11-2 tchd 6-1 and 9-2)*
Pebble Bay ◆ made a promising chasing debut at the age of ten, jumping well out in front and trying all the way to the line once headed. He can go one better in ordinary company. *(op 5-2)*
Daguyda(FR), who was reluctant to line up, jumped better than he did last time but merely stayed on from the rear of the field. *(op 33-1)*
Hi Fi ran his race again, but is proving hard to win with and the blinkers did not bring about any discernible improvement. *(op 11-2 tchd 5-1)*
Nomadic Blaze ran his best race over this course and distance but that came in heavy ground.
Windy Spirit(IRE) showed little over fences in Ireland when trained by Jessica Harrington, for whom he acted as Moscow Flyer's lead horse. He has landed a couple of weak Welsh point-to-points in recent weeks but was well beaten on this return to regulation fences. *(tchd 10-3)*
The Names Bond was disputing fourth place, and not out of calculations, when he had to be pulled up with a slipping saddle before the third last. *Official explanation: jockey said saddle slipped (tchd 10-3)*
Phar From Frosty(IRE), a formerly decent hurdler absent since December 2003, was making his chasing debut. He did not jump particularly well and was well beaten when pulling up with three to jump. *(tchd 10-3)*

414 SALTWELL SIGNS NOVICES' H'CAP HURDLE (10 hdls) 2m 5f 110y

7:20 (7:21) (Class 4) (0-95,95) 4-Y-O+ **£2,702** (£772; £386)

Form RPR

04-5 **1** **Lutin Du Moulin (FR)**[6] [319] 6-11-7 **90**....................(v[1]) ADobbin 98+
(L Lungo) *hld up in midfield: hdwy and hit 3 out: led appr next: sn rdn and styd on wl* **7/2**[2]

06-2 **2** *7* **Fu Fighter**[7] [295] 4-10-12 **86**.................... ChristianWilliams 82+
(Evan Williams) *hld up: hdwy 7th: chsd ldr and mstke next: sn led: rdn and hdd bef 2 out: drvn and kpt on same pce* **5/2**[1]

5F-6 **3** *3½* **Beaugency (NZ)**[4] [345] 7-11-5 **95**.................... PCO'Neill[7] 92+
(R C Guest) *trckd ldrs: hdwy 4 out: rdn along after next: kpt on same pce fr 2 out* **10/1**

050- **4** *4* **That's Racing**[124] [3348] 5-10-7 **76**.................... GLee 69+
(J Hetherton) *hld up and bhd: stready hdwy fr 1/2-way: chsd ldrs after 3 out: sn rdn and kpt on same pce fr 2 out* **12/1**

/00- **5** *3* **Daily Run (IRE)**[151] [2888] 7-9-11 **71**....................(t) DCCostello[5] 60
(G M Moore) *in rr and rdn along 1/2-way: hdwy after 3 out: sn drvn and no imp fr next* **33/1**

06-6 **6** *20* **Bentyheath Lane**[19] [95] 8-10-1 **73**....................(b) ACCoyle[3] 42
(M Mullineaux) *a bhd* **66/1**

40P- **7** *½* **Clichy**[64] [4388] 5-10-8 **87**.................... THalliday[10] 60+
(Mrs S J Smith) *cl up whn hit 1st and rn v wd bnd after: led 3rd: mstke 7th: rdn along and hit next: sn hdd & wknd* **20/1**

P0-0 **8** *1½* **Quay Walloper**[24] [11] 4-9-11 **74** oh10....................(v) PAspell[3] 36
(J R Norton) *chsd ldrs: rdn along and hit 7th: sn wknd* **100/1**

0P-1 **9** *2* **Miss Jessica (IRE)**[16] [147] 5-11-1 **84**.................... JMogford 54+
(Miss M E Rowland) *chsd ldrs whn carried wd after 1st: hdwy to chse ldrs bef 3 out: sn rdn and wknd bef next* **10/1**

26-P **F** **Step In Line (IRE)**[19] [110] 13-9-11 **69** oh5....................(t) ONelmes[3] —
(D W Thompson) *led tl fell 2nd* **66/1**

0P-P **U** **Mer Bihan (FR)**[24] [11] 5-10-0 **69** oh1.................... DO'Meara —
(L Lungo) *midfield whn hmpd and uns rdr 2nd* **66/1**

0/PU **P** **Jack Weighell**[9] [265] 6-11-2 **85**.................... ARoss —
(J M Jefferson) *a rr: bhd whn p.u bef 2 out* **40/1**

21-5 **P** **Pavey Ark (IRE)**[11] [210] 7-10-11 **80**.................... RMcGrath —
(James Moffatt) *cl up: rdn along and wknd 8th: bhd whn p.u bef last* **4/1**[3]

00-6 **P** **Olympic Storm (IRE)**[6] [320] 7-11-5 **88**.................... PRobson —
(N W Alexander) *rel to r and wnt rt s: in tch whn hmpd 2nd: chsd ldrs lost pl and bhd fr 8th: p.u after 3 out* **14/1**

5m 8.60s (-7.10) **Going Correction** -0.30s/f (Good)
WFA 4 from 5yo+ 5lb **14** Ran SP% **118.9**
Speed ratings: **100,97,96,94,93 86,86,85,84,— —,—,—,—** CSF £12.26 CT £80.70 TOTE £4.40: £1.90, £1.60, £2.50; EX 17.30.
Owner K Foster **Bred** S C E A Moulin **Trained** Carrutherstown, D'fries & G'way

FOCUS
An average handicap in which the first four all ran to within a few pounds of their mark.

NOTEBOOK
Lutin Du Moulin(FR), who ran in snatches last time, gained his French chase win when wearing blinkers and the aids did the trick here. He could be capable of a bit more improvement over hurdles. *(tchd 3-1 and 4-1)*
Fu Fighter ran respectably, but while he did stay this longer trip the run might have come a little too quick for him. *(op 3-1 tchd 7-2)*
Beaugency(NZ), who reportedly had a breathing problem at Bangor four days earlier, travelled well but did not find a great deal when coming off the bridle. *(op 9-1)*
That's Racing, upped in trip for this handicap debut, was distracted by the antics of a rival at the start and got away very slowly. He made up the ground to get into contention but could make no further progress from the second last. *(op 14-1 tchd 11-1)*
Daily Run(IRE), without the visor on this first run since December, is clearly a very limited performer but did show a bit more promise over this longer trip.

415 GOSFORTH DECORATING AND BUILDING SERVICES NOVICES' HURDLE (8 hdls) 2m 1f

7:50 (8:00) (Class 4) 4-Y-O+ **£3,373** (£1,038; £519; £259)

Form RPR

3-44 **1** **Snow's Ride**[13] [192] 5-10-12 95.................... GLee 93
(M D Hammond) *trckd ldrs: hit 5th: pushed along next: hdwy to ld 2 out and sn rdn: drvn flat and styd on wl* **10/3**[1]

U5-3 **2** *1* **Sterling Guarantee (USA)**[13] [192] 7-10-12 93.................... PRobson 92+
(N Wilson) *in tch: hdwy after 3out: rdn appr last: drvn and ev ch flat tl hung bdly lft and no ex last 100 yds* **5/1**[2]

4 **3** *9* **Sort It Out (IRE)**[8] [279] 8-10-9 110.................... KJMercer[3] 85+
(Ferdy Murphy) *led: rdn along 3 out: hdd next: sn drvn: blnd last and sn wknd* **5/1**[2]

4 *1¼* **Lizarazu (GER)**[148] 6-10-12 .... APMcCoy 82
(C R Egerton) *hld up towards rr: smooth hdwy on inner 3 out: chsd ldrs and and rdn bef next: one pce* **10/3**[1]

5 *1¼* **Constable Burton**[27] 4-10-8 .... TScudamore 77
(Mrs A Duffield) *prom: mstke and lost pl 3rd: hdwy to join ldrs 5th: ev ch 3 out: sn rdn and wknd appr next* **22/1**

P00- **6** *6* **Qualitair Pleasure**[141] [3039] 5-10-5 .... ARoss 68
(J Hetherton) *chsd ldrs: effrt and ev ch 3 out: sn rdn and wknd: j. bdly lft 2 out* **20/1**

P00- **7** *½* **Fortune's Fool**[25] [4975] 6-10-12 71.................... ATinkler 74
(I A Brown) *hld up and bhd: hdwy 3 out: rdn along bef next and sn no imp* **100/1**

40-0 **8** *2½* **Agnese**[13] [192] 5-10-5 84....................(p) FKeniry 65
(G M Moore) *in tch: rdn along bef 3 out and sn outpcd* **25/1**

06 **9** *1* **Tin Healy's Pass**[3] [369] 5-10-12 .... BHarding 71
(I McMath) *bhd: hdwy into midfield 1/2-way: sn rdn along and wknd bef 3 out* **50/1**

00- **10** *24* **Master Nimbus**[190] [2109] 5-10-12 .... RGarritty 47
(J J Quinn) *a bhd* **66/1**

0-PP **11** *10* **The Yellow Earl (IRE)**[9] [261] 5-10-12 .... DO'Meara 37
(J M Jefferson) *in rr whn mstke 3rd: a bhd* **100/1**

00P- **12** *5* **Zeydnaa (IRE)**[69] 4270 5-10-9 ......(t) PAspell[(3)] 32
(C R Wilson) *chsd ldrs on inner: rdn along 1/2-way: sn lost pl and bhd* **200/1**

52-0 **13** *1 1/2* **Moorlaw (IRE)**[10] 243 4-10-8 110 ......(b[1]) JMMaguire 26
(D McCain) *keen: cl up: rdn along 6th: drvn 3 out and sn wknd* **6/1**[3]

14 *12* **Daring Games**[13] 4-10-1 ...... JimCrowley —
(B Ellison) *rr whn blnd 4th: sn bhd* **50/1**

4m 1.40s (-5.10) **Going Correction** -0.30s/f (Good)
WFA 4 from 5yo+ 4lb **14** Ran SP% **114.6**
Speed ratings: **100,99,95,94,94 91,91,89,89,78 73,71,70,64** CSF £17.85 TOTE £4.60: £1.40, £1.70, £1.80; EX 10.30.
Owner Oakwood Racing Partnership **Bred** Biddestone Stud And Partner **Trained** Middleham, N Yorks

FOCUS
Not a great deal of pace on in this modest novice event in which the first two both ran to their marks. The start was delayed for ten minutes after Phar Quicker (40/1, withdrawn) got loose.

NOTEBOOK
Snow's Ride, just behind today's runner-up at Wetherby, got off the mark over hurdles at the fourth attempt. He clearly likes fast ground and may get a bit farther. *(op 7-2 tchd 4-1)*
Sterling Guarantee(USA), a head in front of today's winner last time, stayed on to challenge at the last, but did not go forward in a straight line on the run-in and was just held. *(op 7-1)*
Sort It Out(IRE), who failed to stay three miles in points, made the running to the penultimate flight and was held in second spot when blundering at the last. *(tchd 9-2)*
Lizarazu(GER), a dual winner on the Flat in Germany, has left Frank Jordan's yard since his last run before Christmas. He showed ability on this hurdles debut, but did not appear to get home. *(op 7-2)*
Constable Burton only stayed a mile on the Flat and stamina could be a problem over hurdles. *(op 20-1 tchd 25-1)*

416 CALVERTS CARPETS H'CAP CHASE (16 fncs) 2m 5f
8:20 (8:25) (Class 4) (0-105,101) 5-Y-0+ **£4,754** (£1,463; £731; £365)

Form RPR

0/3 **1** **Multeen Gunner**[23] 26 8-10-2 77 ......(p) PMoloney 88+
(Evan Williams) *mde all: rdn along 4 out: 3 l clr last: drvn flat and jst hld on* **9/1**

6P0- **2** *shd* **Maidstone Monument (IRE)**[30] 4912 10-9-9 75 oh4 ...... DLaverty[(5)] 86+
(Mrs A M Thorpe) *a chsng wnr: hit 10th and next: sn pushed along: rdn 3 out: drvn next: styd on strly fr last: jst failed* **8/1**

6F-6 **3** *7* **Raise A McGregor**[11] 213 9-10-4 79 ...... DElsworth 83+
(Mrs S J Smith) *in tch: smooth hdwy to trckd ldrs 5 out: shkn up and outpcd after next: rdn and styd on bef 2 out: drvn and one pce last* **10/1**

65-4 **4** *8* **Nosam**[14] 181 15-10-11 89 ......(tp) LMcGrath[(3)] 86+
(R C Guest) *hld up: hdwy and in tch 1/2-way: effrt to chse ldrs 5 out: rdn along bef 3 out: drvn and one pce appr last* **7/1**[3]

006- **5** *14* **Mr Laggan**[157] 2784 10-9-7 75 oh5 ......(p) MJMcAlister[(7)] 56
(Miss Kate Milligan) *bhd: hdwy 1th: rdn along next and nvr nr ldrs* **66/1**

455- **6** *4* **Karo De Vindecy (FR)**[25] 4980 7-10-11 86 ......(t) GLee 63
(M D Hammond) *chsd ldng pair: pushed along 11th: rdn next and wknd 4 out* **8/1**

10-4 **P** **Jesper (FR)**[14] 183 8-11-12 101 ......(t) RJohnson —
(R T Phillips) *nt fluent: a bhd: p.u bef 2 out* **5/1**[2]

03-0 **P** **Earl Sigurd (IRE)**[18] 122 7-11-3 92 ...... BGibson —
(L Lungo) *in rr whn blnd 7th: wl bhd whn p.u after 9th* **20/1**

26-3 **P** **Hot Produxion (USA)**[19] 106 6-11-10 99 ...... ADempsey —
(J Mackie) *chsd ldrs: reminders 3rd: rdn along and lost pl 8th: bhd fr 4 out: p.u bef 2 out* **8/1**

45-0 **P** **Leopard Spot (IRE)**[11] 211 7-10-8 86 ......(tp) PBuchanan[(3)] —
(Miss Lucinda V Russell) *midfield: pushed along and mstke 9th: sn lost pl and bhd whn p.u bef 3 out* **9/1**

/0-0 **P** **Saddlers' Mark**[22] 45 10-11-4 93 ......(t) ADobbin —
(D M Christie, Ire) *hld up: hdwy 9th: in tch whn mstke 10th: sn rdn along and outpcd: bhd whn p.u bef 2 out* **7/2**[1]

5m 18.7s (-4.70) **Going Correction** -0.30s/f (Good) **11** Ran SP% **120.1**
Speed ratings: **96,95,93,90,84 83,—,—,—,— —** CSF £80.88 CT £745.47 TOTE £11.60: £3.90, £2.40, £3.10; EX 98.70 Place 6 £201.66, Place 5 £156.94.
Owner R E R Williams **Bred** Edward Roscoe Associates Ltd **Trained** Cowbridge, Vale Of Glamorgan

FOCUS
A poor handicap, rated through the winner to the best of his Irish form.

NOTEBOOK
Multeen Gunner, with the cheekpieces back in place for his second run in this country, enjoyed himself out in front and jumped soundly. Even halfway up the run-in he looked well in control, but he suddenly began to tie up and the line just saved him. *(op 10-1 tchd 11-1)*
Maidstone Monument(IRE) was in second place throughout. Outpaced on the home turn and three lengths down at the final fence, he kept staying on and very nearly caught the flagging winner. *(op 12-1)*
Raise A McGregor was tackling a more suitable trip on this second run after a break and kept plugging away. *(op 12-1)*
Nosam gained his last victory over this course and distance in September 2003 and it will take a very weak race if he is to add to his tally at his age. *(op 5-1 tchd 15-2)*
Saddlers' Mark does most of his racing in Ireland on easier ground. *(op 16-1)*
Earl Sigurd(IRE) *Official explanation: jockey said gelding finished distressed (op 16-1)*
Jesper(FR) *Official explanation: jockey said gelding was never travelling (op 16-1)*

417 GREAT NORTH AIR AMBULANCE H'CAP HURDLE (13 hdls) 3m 3f 110y
8:50 (8:53) (Class 4) (0-90,90) 4-Y-0+ **£2,968** (£848; £424)

Form RPR

544- **1** **Tickateal**[25] 4977 5-11-12 90 ...... JimCrowley 97+
(R D E Woodhouse) *hld up: smooth hdwy to join ldrs 8th: led 3 out: rdn next: styd on wl* **9/1**

05-5 **2** *5* **Cody**[16] 152 6-11-0 78 ......(v) ADobbin 79
(James Moffatt) *in tch: smooth hdwy 9th: chsd wnr 3 out: rdn along next: drvn and one pce last* **15/2**

30-0 **3** *3 1/2* **Dark Thunder (IRE)**[11] 215 8-10-11 85 ......(b) PJMcDonald[(10)] 83
(Ferdy Murphy) *prom: led 8th tl after next: rdn along 3 out and kpt on same pce fr 2 out* **8/1**

05-F **4** *30* **Sagardian (FR)**[20] 81 6-10-5 69 ...... BGibson 37
(L Lungo) *hld up and a bhd* **11/2**[3]

0P5- **5** *25* **Western Bluebird (IRE)**[260] 1340 7-10-1 70 ......(b) DCCostello[(5)] 13
(Miss Kate Milligan) *prom: led after 9th: rdn along and hdd 3 out: sn drvn and wknd* **33/1**

00-P **6** *5* **Sea Maize**[11] 211 7-10-4 71 ......(b[1]) PAspell[(3)] 9
(C R Wilson) *a bhd* **25/1**

240/ **7** *dist* **Mr Cavallo (IRE)**[11] 13-10-11 78 ...... PBuchanan[(3)] —
(Miss Lucinda V Russell) *led to 2nd: prom tl lost pl 7th: sn bhd and t.o fr 10th* **16/1**

000- **P** **Southbound (IRE)**[164] 2655 6-10-8 72 ...... BHarding —
(I McMath) *a bhd: p.u bef 9th* **40/1**

0-P6 **P** **Rincoola (IRE)**[16] 152 6-11-7 85 ...... DO'Meara —
(J S Wainwright) *a rr: bhd fr 10th: t.o whn p.u bef 2 out* **33/1**

00-0 **F** **Pikestaff (USA)**[11] 215 7-11-5 83 ......(t) GLee —
(M A Barnes) *trckd ldrs on inner: hdwy and cl up whn fell 9th* **9/2**[2]

6-22 **P** **Vallica**[10] 229 6-11-7 85 ...... APMcCoy —
(Mrs A M Thorpe) *hld up in tch: hdwy to join ldrs 9th: rdn along appr 3 out: sn wknd and p.u bef 2 out* **15/8**[1]

PP-P **P** **Blue Jar**[18] 119 7-10-0 67 ow3 ...... ACCoyle[(3)] —
(M Mullineaux) *cl up: led 2nd tl mstke and hdd 8th: lost pl after next and bhd whn hit 10th and sn p.u* **66/1**

6m 41.0s (-22.90) **Going Correction** -0.30s/f (Good) **12** Ran SP% **120.8**
Speed ratings: **101,99,98,90,82 81,—,—,—,— —,—** CSF £72.67 CT £573.75 TOTE £10.80: £2.50, £2.10, £2.40; EX 77.10.
Owner R D E Woodhouse **Bred** R D E Woodhouse And Mrs C Woodhouse **Trained** Malton, N Yorks
■ Trainer Bob Woodhouse's first winner since moving yards to Malton.

FOCUS
A weak race, but the first two look to be improving.

NOTEBOOK
Tickateal has found his feet since being upped in trip and this real test of stamina suited him. This was a good effort under topweight and he is on the upgrade. *(op 10-1)*
Cody, tackling his longest trip to date, ran a sound race but the winner proved too strong. *(op 7-1)*
Dark Thunder(IRE), who is slipping back down the weights, ran respectably back at his favourite venue and finished miles clear of the rest.
Sagardian(FR) was always at the back of field and merely passed a couple of flagging rivals in the home straight. *(op 8-1)*
Western Bluebird(IRE), having his first run since August, did not see out this marathon trip.
Pikestaff(USA) was travelling within himself when parting company. *(op 5-1)*
Vallica suddenly came under pressure going to the third last and, with no response forthcoming, was soon pulled up. She did not stay. *Official explanation: jockey said mare lost her action (op 5-1)*
Southbound(IRE) *Official explanation: jockey said gelding pulled up feelingly (op 5-1)*
T/Plt: £356.00 to a £1 stake. Pool: £46,257.20. 94.85 winning tickets. T/Qpdt: £90.70 to a £1 stake. Pool: £2,968.00. 24.20 winning tickets. JR

[406]KELSO (L-H)
Thursday, May 19

OFFICIAL GOING: Good to firm (good in places)
Wind: Breezy; half against.

418 QUEENS HEAD "NEW BEDROOMS" MAIDEN HURDLE (8 hdls) 2m 110y
6:05 (6:05) (Class 3) 4-Y-0+ **£7,033** (£2,164; £1,082; £541)

Form RPR

643- **1** **Chef De Cour (FR)**[75] 4180 4-10-12 ...... ADobbin 104+
(L Lungo) *hld up: hdwy 1/2-way: led run in: drifted lft: drvn out* **5/1**[3]

223- **2** *9½* **Summer Special**[28] 4943 5-11-2 107 ...... MBradburne 98
(Mrs S C Bradburne) *prom: ev ch 2 out: kpt on same pce fr last: fin 3rd: 3½l & 6l: plcd 2nd* **9/1**

53-3 **3** *6* **Double Gem (IRE)**[21] 82 6-11-2 104 ...... PRobson 93
(J I A Charlton) *trckd ldr: ev ch 3 out: outpcd after next: fin 4th: plcd 3rd* **3/1**[1]

304- **4** *8* **Lutea (IRE)**[27] 4958 5-11-2 ...... APMcCoy 87+
(M C Pipe) *led tl hdd 2 out: wknd last: fin 5th: plcd 4th* **5/1**[3]

06-6 **5** *4* **Our Men**[7] 323 6-10-11 ...... TGreenway[(5)] 81
(N W Alexander) *in tch: outpcd after 4 out: no imp fr next: fin 6th: plcd 5th* **40/1**

0 **6** *6* **Penteli**[14] 192 5-10-9 ...... DO'Meara 68
(C Grant) *in tch tl outpcd 1/2-way: n.d after: fin 7th: plcd 6th* **66/1**

F- **7** *1 1/4* **Skiddaw Jones**[164] 2674 5-10-13 ......(t) PWhelan[(3)] 73
(M A Barnes) *bhd: rdn 1/2-way: nvr on terms: fin 8th: plcd 7th* **50/1**

0- **8** *3* **Stravonian**[18] 4085 5-10-13 ...... GBerridge[(3)] 70
(D A Nolan) *a bhd: fin 9th: plcd 8th* **100/1**

50-0 **9** *5* **Parisian Rose (IRE)**[21] 85 6-10-2 ......(t) BenOrde-Powlett[(7)] 58
(Mrs H O Graham) *chsd ldrs: hit 4th: wknd after next: fin 10th: plcd 9th* **100/1**

5 **10** *1 3/4* **Ocotillo**[6] 331 5-10-13 ...... PAspell[(3)] 63
(James Moffatt) *a bhd: fin 11th: plcd 10th* **100/1**

11 *15* **Air Of Supremacy (IRE)**[127] 4-10-12 ...... WMarston 43
(Mrs K Walton) *bhd: no ch fr 1/2-way: fin 12th: plcd 11th* **25/1**

12 *1/2* **Galahad (FR)** 4-10-12 ...... ADempsey 42
(B Storey) *midfield: rdn and wknd fr 1/2-way: fin 13th: plcd 12th* **40/1**

0P0/ **13** *29* **Minster Meadow**[396] 4881 6-10-9 ......(t) SGagan[(7)] —
(S G Chadwick) *plld hrd: cl up to 4 out: sn btn: no ch whn blnd last: fin 14th: plcd 13th* **100/1**

40-3 **D** **King's Protector**[22] 59 5-11-2 101 ...... GLee 104
(M D Hammond) *cl up: led 2 out to run in: kpt on same pce: hld whn lost weight cloth cl home: fin 2nd, 3.5l: disqualified* **13/2**

3- **P** **Beaver (AUS)**[115] 3517 6-10-13 ...... LMcGrath[(3)] —
(R C Guest) *a bhd: t.o whn p.u bef 3 out* **10/3**[2]

P **Bluefield (IRE)**[34] 4-10-12 ...... NHannity —
(Mrs K Walton) *nt fluent in rr: t.o whn p.u bef 3 out* **100/1**

/0-0 **P** **Crumbs**[21] 82 5-10-9 ...... BGibson —
(B Mactaggart) *j. slowly 1st: midfield: wknd 4th: t.o whn p.u bef 2 out* **100/1**

3m 55.8s (-7.90) **Going Correction** -0.35s/f (Good)
WFA 4 from 5yo+ 4lb **17** Ran SP% **122.9**
Speed ratings: **103,98,95,91,90 87,86,85,82,82 75,74,61,101,— —,—** CSF £47.69 TOTE £6.00: £1.60, £2.40, £1.60; EX 41.50.
Owner Ashleybank Investments Limited **Bred** Andre Blee **Trained** Carrutherstown, D'fries & G'way

FOCUS
A race lacking strength but a fair pace and the winner appeals as the type to improve further.
Average form, with a big step up from the winner and the second and third running to their marks.

NOTEBOOK
Chef De Cour(FR) ◆ bettered the form of his hurdling debut and, although he had to be driven out, the way he travelled and the fact he is in good hands means there is a good prospect of further improvement. *(op 13-2)*
Summer Special, a long-standing Flat maiden who has yet to win over jumps, ran creditably and looks a good guide to the level of this form, but is not going to be easy to place in this grade or from his current mark in handicaps.
Double Gem(IRE), another who is vulnerable to progressive sorts in this grade, seemed to run his race but looks worth a try over two and a half miles. *(op 7-2 tchd 11-4)*
Lutea(IRE), back on a sound surface, was disappointing and will have to settle better if he is to progress in this sphere. *(op 7-2 tchd 11-2)*

Our Men was making his hurdling debut and his proximity confirms this bare form is nothing special. He shaped as though a stiffer test of stamina would be in his favour. *(op 33-1)*
King's Protector is exposed as ordinary and is vulnerable to an improver in this grade, but ran his race. The fact that his rider weighed in light after the weight cloth worked loose meant inevitable disqualification. *(op 7-1)*
Beaver(AUS) *Official explanation: jockey said gelding had a breathing problem and lost its action (op 4-1)*

419 ROYAL HIGHLAND SHOW LADIES' DAY NOVICES' CHASE (12 fncs) 2m 1f
6:35 (6:35) (Class 3) 5-Y-0+ **£6,773** (£2,084; £1,042; £521)

Form RPR
21-1 **1** **Tribal Dispute**[22] 60 8-11-10 114 DO'Meara 133
(T D Easterby) *chsd ldrs: wnt 2nd 2 out: sn rdn: led and edgd lft run in: r.o wl* **7/2**[2]
012- **2** 2 ½ **Escompteur (FR)**[28] 4943 5-10-10 APMcCoy 118+
(M C Pipe) *keen: led: j.w tl mstke last: hdd run in: no ex* **4/6**[1]
0-23 **3** 2 **Wet Lips (AUS)**[4] 371 7-10-9 (p) LMcGrath(3) 117
(R C Guest) *hld up: hdwy 8th: kpt on fr 2 out: nrst fin* **6/1**[3]
5/2- **4** 21 **What If (IRE)**[69] 4300 8-10-12 100 ADobbin 99+
(I Buchanan, Ire) *cl up: blnd 6th: wknd fr 2 out* **16/1**
32-3 **5** 13 **Ameras (IRE)**[19] 122 7-10-2 73 MrCStorey(3) 79+
(Miss S E Forster) *in tch: outpcd whn blnd 4 out: sn btn* **20/1**
P00/ **6** dist **Mccrinkle (IRE)**[26] 8-10-12 MBradburne —
(Mrs C J Kerr) *a bhd: t.o fr 1/2-way* **100/1**
P0-P **7** 21 **Pharagon (IRE)**[21] 81 7-10-7 54 DMcGann(5) —
(Mrs C J Kerr) *sn bhd: no ch fr 1/2-way* **150/1**
PP-P **P** **Alchemystic (IRE)**[25] 5 5-10-7 (tp) PWhelan(3) —
(M A Barnes) *towards rr: struggling 1/2-way: t.o whn p.u bef last* **40/1**

4m 12.7s (-10.50) **Going Correction** -0.475s/f (Good)
WFA 5 from 7yo+ 2lb **8** Ran SP% **111.2**
Speed ratings: **105,103,102,93,86** —,—,— CSF £6.22 TOTE £6.00: £1.40, £1.10, £1.90; EX 14.20.
Owner Mrs Jennifer E Pallister **Bred** G R Parkin And Sons **Trained** Great Habton, N Yorks

FOCUS
Another race lacking strength but a good gallop and an improved effort from hat-trick winner Tribal Dispute. The race could be rated a fair bit higher.

NOTEBOOK
Tribal Dispute is progressing well over fences and turned in his best effort yet to beat a useful hurdler that jumped well on its chase debut. He jumps soundly and may be able to hold his own in handicap company.
Escompteur(FR), a 126-rated hurdler, failed to match the pick of that form on this first run over fences for his current stable (has run over fences in France) and, given his jumping was really good, his finishing effort has to go down as disappointing. However he is sure to win races in this sphere. *(op 5-6)*
Wet Lips(AUS), from a bang-in-form stable, showed more than enough on only this second outing over fences to suggest that he can win races in this sphere, especially granted a stiffer test of stamina. *(op 9-2)*
What If(IRE), who faced no easy task at the weights, ran a bit better than the bare form suggests and will be suited by the return to further and the return to ordinary handicap company.
Ameras(IRE), a long-standing maiden, is not very consistent and will be seen to much better effect in low-grade handicaps. *(op 25-1)*
Mccrinkle(IRE) faced an impossible task on these terms. *(tchd 80-1)*

420 FHM DUNN CLASSIC INTERMEDIATE HURDLE (10 hdls) 2m 2f
7:05 (7:05) (Class 3) 4-Y-0+ **£7,464** (£2,831; £1,415; £643; £321)

Form RPR
1-31 **1** **Yes Sir (IRE)**[1] 408 6-11-8 144 APMcCoy 148+
(P Bowen) *early mstkes: mde all: drew clr bef 2 out: eased run in* **4/9**[1]
46-4 **2** 3 **All Star (GER)**[22] 67 5-11-5 118 ATinkler 125
(N J Henderson) *chsd wnr: effrt bef 2 out: sn outpcd: no imp run in: flattered by proximity to eased wnr* **10/1**
532- **3** dist **Aleron (IRE)**[13] 4978 7-11-8 133 ADobbin 93
(J J Quinn) *chsd ldrs tl wknd bef 4 out* **7/1**[3]
216- **4** 26 **Karelian**[42] 4749 4-11-4 125 GLee —
(K A Ryan) *chsd ldrs: rdn and rdr dropped whip after 5th: wknd after next* **9/2**[2]
06F- **5** dist **Spree Vision**[125] 3353 9-10-9 97 DDaSilva(10) —
(P Monteith) *sn detached: nvr on terms* **100/1**

4m 17.0s (-22.90) **Going Correction** -0.35s/f (Good)
WFA 4 from 5yo+ 4lb **5** Ran SP% **110.0**
Speed ratings: **110,108**,—,—,— CSF £5.79 TOTE £1.30: £1.20, £3.00; EX 5.70.
Owner Ms Y M Hill **Bred** Louis Hill **Trained** Little Newcastle, Pembrokes

FOCUS
With two of the three market leaders disappointing this did not take as much winning as seemed likely. Yes Sir has been rated as value for 20l, with the runner-up to form.

NOTEBOOK
Yes Sir(IRE), who has made up into a smart hurdler this year, gained another bloodless win at this two-day fixture in a race where his two market rivals disappointed. He was value for much more than the winning margin and, although this told us little new about him, he will be an interesting runner if going down the novice chase route next term. *(op 1-2 tchd 4-7 in a place and 8-15 in places)*
All Star(GER) was extremely flattered to get as close as he did to the eased-down winner but, given the manner in which he went through the race, will be interesting back in ordinary handicap company later this term. *(op 16-1)*
Aleron(IRE) was easy to back and ran disappointingly but, although this was nowhere near his true form, he may be difficult to place successfully from his current mark this term. *(op 11-2 tchd 5-1)*
Karelian may not be an easy ride and dropped himself out soon after his rider lost his whip, but this still has to go down as most disappointing and he looks one to tread carefully with. *(tchd 11-2)*
Spree Vision faced an uphill struggle on these terms. *(op 66-1)*

421 M & J BALLANTYNE H'CAP CHASE (19 fncs) 3m 1f
7:35 (7:35) (Class 4) (0-105,103) 5-Y-0+ **£6,825** (£2,100; £1,050; £525)

Form RPR
205- **1** **Ta Ta For Now**[27] 4970 8-10-7 84 MBradburne 95
(Mrs S C Bradburne) *prom: effrt after 4 out: led bef last: kpt on strly* **3/1**[2]
336/ **2** 5 **Carnacrack**[47] 11-10-4 84 MrCStorey(3) 92+
(Miss S E Forster) *w ldr: led 14th: nt fluent 4 out: hit next: hdd bef last: kpt on run in* **8/1**
F2-1 **3** 13 **Prince Of Slane**[17] 150 6-11-7 103 DCCostello(5) 97+
(G A Swinbank) *nt fluent: hld up in tch: hdwy 1/2-way: effrt 2 out: sn no ex* **2/1**[1]
01-3 **4** 11 **Winter Garden**[8] 303 11-11-9 103 (p) PBuchanan(3) 85
(Miss Lucinda V Russell) *mde most to 14th: rdn and wknd after 3 out* **10/1**
0/ **P** **Drumbo (IRE)**[103] 3716 9-10-12 89 GLee —
(I Buchanan, Ire) *in tch to 1/2-way: lost tch and p.u bef 13th* **9/1**
3U0- **P** **Wild Spice (IRE)**[27] 4970 10-11-1 92 (b) SThomas —
(Miss Venetia Williams) *hld up in tch: blnd bdly 2nd: hit 6th: struggling 1/2-way: t.o whn p.u bef 14th* **7/2**[3]

6m 20.7s (-8.90) **Going Correction** -0.475s/f (Good) **6** Ran SP% **110.8**
Speed ratings: **95,93,89,85**,— — CSF £24.09 CT £54.50 TOTE £4.00: £1.80, £4.80; EX 28.20.
Owner Mrs V M Stewart **Bred** Lawers Stud **Trained** Cunnoquhie, Fife

FOCUS
Mainly exposed horses, a fair gallop and modest winning time for the grade. The first two ran pretty much to their marks.

NOTEBOOK
Ta Ta For Now seems to come to hand around this time of year and, on his favoured fast ground, ran right up to his best. He is not the most consistent but should continue to go well in this company granted a sufficient test of stamina. *(op 7-2 tchd 11-4)*
Carnacrack, a pointing winner in February, had conditions to suit for this first run for nearly 500 days over regulation fences and showed enough to suggest a small race can be found this summer on his favoured fast ground. *(op 7-1)*
Prince Of Slane, up 9lb after his Sedgefield win, was anything but disgraced on ground that suited, but his jumping lacked fluency at times and he was a shade disappointing after travelling strongly for much of the way. *(op 9-4 tchd 5-2)*
Winter Garden, normally a fairly reliable yardstick, was again well beaten and his stable seems to have gone off the boil at present. *(op 6-1)*
Wild Spice(IRE) continues to be let down by his jumping and he is not a reliable betting proposition at present. *(op 4-1 tchd 9-2)*
Drumbo(IRE) again achieved nothing over fences. *Official explanation: jockey said gelding was never travelling (op 4-1 tchd 9-2)*

422 ALCAZAR LTD DEVELOPING OUTSTANDING BRANDS H'CAP HURDLE (11 hdls) 2m 6f 110y
8:05 (8:05) (Class 2) (0-140,138) 4-Y-0+
£12,354 (£4,686; £2,343; £1,065; £532; £319)

Form RPR
03-3 **1** **River Alder**[22] 61 7-9-11 112 oh3 PBuchanan(3) 117
(J M Dun) *chsd ldrs: rdn to ld last: styd on gamely* **7/1**[2]
02-0 **2** 1 ½ **Penny Pictures (IRE)**[12] 208 6-11-9 135 RThornton 138
(M C Pipe) *hld up: smooth hdwy and ev ch last: rdn and kpt on run in* **7/1**[2]
PP0- **3** 1 ¾ **Mondial Jack (FR)**[27] 4972 6-10-7 119 APMcCoy 120
(M C Pipe) *hld up: effrt u.p 3 out: kpt on fr last: nt rch first two* **7/1**[2]
P00- **4** nk **Model Son (IRE)**[130] 3290 7-9-11 116 PMerrigan(7) 117
(Mrs H Dalton) *hld up: smooth hdwy and ev ch 3 out: rdn next: one pce run in* **7/1**[2]
10-F **5** ¾ **It's Definite (IRE)**[7] 315 6-10-5 117 (p) RJohnson 117
(P Bowen) *led to last: kpt on same pce run in* **8/1**[3]
123- **6** 1 ¾ **Paddy The Piper (IRE)**[33] 4862 8-11-12 138 ADobbin 137
(L Lungo) *hld up: hdwy bef 3 out: effrt and ev ch 2 out: one pce run in* **9/2**[1]
0-01 **7** 29 **Border Tale**[6] 332 5-10-0 111 6ex JimCrowley 86+
(James Moffatt) *hld up: effrt 3 out: no imp fr next* **12/1**
055- **8** 16 **Scots Grey**[28] 4946 10-10-12 124 ATinkler 78
(N J Henderson) *chsd ldrs to 4 out: wknd next* **9/1**
142- **9** 2 ½ **Sully Shuffles (IRE)**[34] 4851 10-10-12 124 GLee 75
(M Todhunter) *in tch: hit and lost pl 7th: n.d after* **8/1**[3]
12P/ **10** dist **Jollyolly**[452] 3958 6-11-5 131 (p) WMarston —
(P Bowen) *cl up: mstke 3rd: blnd 4 out: sn btn* **20/1**
F6-2 **U** **Bodfari Signet**[7] 319 9-10-3 115 6ex MBradburne —
(Mrs S C Bradburne) *hld up in tch: hit and uns rdr 2nd* **25/1**

5m 23.0s (-14.70) **Going Correction** -0.35s/f (Good) **11** Ran SP% **116.7**
Speed ratings: **110,109,108,108,108 107,97,92,91**,— — CSF £55.31 CT £358.72 TOTE £9.10: £2.70, £3.30, £2.70; EX 75.90.
Owner J M Dun **Bred** Mrs A G Martin And R F And S D Knipe **Trained** Heriot, Borders
■ A first winner in seven years for one-horse permit holder Michael Dun.
■ Stewards' Enquiry : P Merrigan five-day ban: used whip with excessive force (May 30-31, Jun 2,4,5)

FOCUS
A decent field and a good gallop means the bare form of this contest should prove reliable.

NOTEBOOK
River Alder ◆, upped to a more suitable trip, travelled strongly and showed the right attitude in the closing stages. She will be equally at home on a more galloping course with cut in the ground and appeals as the type to win again either over hurdles or if sent over the larger obstacles. *(op 8-1 tchd 9-1)*
Penny Pictures(IRE), returned to this more suitable trip and in an easier race than at Haydock, ran right up to his best after travelling like the best horse for much of the way and he looks sure to make his mark in similar company. *(tchd 13-2)*
Mondial Jack(FR), returned to timber from this much lower hurdles mark, showed enough to suggest he can win races in this sphere, especially when back over three miles at a more galloping course. *(op 6-1 tchd 8-1)*
Model Son(IRE) ◆, having his first run for his new stable, travelled strongly for much of the way after this break of over four months and showed more than enough to suggest he can win races for his capable handler. *(op 10-1 tchd 11-1)*
It's Definite(IRE), given an attacking ride at a course that suits this style of racing, ran creditably with no excuses and just looks a few pounds too high in the weights at present. *(tchd 15-2 and 17-2)*
Paddy The Piper(IRE), another to travel strongly for much of the way, may be suited by the step up to three miles but does look vulnerable to progressive or well handicapped types from his current mark. *(op 4-1)*
Scots Grey *Official explanation: jockey said gelding was never travelling*

423 GGBET.COM BETTING EXCHANGE H'CAP CHASE (19 fncs) 3m 1f
8:35 (8:35) (Class 2) (0-150,140) 5-Y-0+
£17,935 (£6,803; £3,401; £1,546; £773; £463)

Form RPR
0U5- **1** **Ballycassidy (IRE)**[26] 4984 9-11-10 138 RJohnson 152+
(P Bowen) *mde virtually all: drew clr fr 3 out: eased run in* **3/1**[1]
2U4- **2** 22 **Double Honour (FR)**[33] 4861 7-11-12 140 (b) PJBrennan 127+
(P J Hobbs) *mainly chsd wnr thrght: drvn fr 14th: kpt on fr 3 out: no ch w wnr* **3/1**[1]
51-3 **3** 5 **Kock De La Vesvre (FR)**[19] 130 7-11-7 135 SThomas 121+
(Miss Venetia Williams) *hld up in tch: hdwy 1/2-way: rdn in 3rd whn blnd 2 out: no imp* **10/1**
6P-2 **4** 6 **A Piece Of Cake (IRE)**[19] 130 12-10-11 125 ADempsey 98
(J S Goldie) *prom: outpcd whn mstke 4 out: sme late hdwy: n.d* **16/1**
401- **5** 1 ¾ **Jordan's Ridge (IRE)**[38] 4812 9-10-0 114 oh4 NPMulholland 89+
(P Monteith) *hld up: rdn 13th: hdwy after 4 out: outpcd whn blnd 2 out* **9/1**[3]

045- **6** *4* **Montreal (FR)**[27] 4972 8-10-7 **121** .... APMcCoy 88
(M C Pipe) *hld up in tch: hmpd 11th: rdn whn nt fluent 15th: wknd fr 3 out* **7/2**[2]

P4F- **F** **Lord Noelie (IRE)**[36] 4821 12-11-10 **138** .... GLee —
(Mrs Jeremy Young) *prom whn fell heavily 11th* **10/1**

00-5 **P** **Divet Hill**[22] 64 11-10-11 **128** .... PBuchanan(3) —
(Mrs A Hamilton) *cl up tl lost pl 1/2-way: t.o whn p.u bef 15th* **12/1**

6m 14.1s (-15.50) **Going Correction** -0.475s/f (Good) **8** Ran SP% **114.0**
Speed ratings: **105,97,96,94,93 92**,—,— CSF £12.88 CT £77.11 TOTE £3.50: £2.00, £1.60, £2.50; EX 7.70.
Owner R Owen & P Fullagar **Bred** Michael Griffin **Trained** Little Newcastle, Pembrokes

FOCUS
A disappointing turnout for the money. The pace was sound. The impressive winner has been rated as value for further but the placed horses were below their best.

NOTEBOOK
Ballycassidy(IRE) has faced some very stiff tasks this year but routed this relatively uncompetitive field to win with even more in hand than the winning margin suggests. A sound surface suits but he is going to find life much tougher over fences after reassessment and he would be of more interest from his lower hurdles mark. *(op 10-3)*

Double Honour(FR) was not disgraced, but was not at his best at a course and on ground that placed more of an emphasis on speed than stamina. He is a useful stayer but may not find life easy from this mark this term. *(op 4-1)*

Kock De La Vesvre(FR) has now been below his best on both occasions since his Perth win but he does go particularly well at the last-named venue and will be of interest if returning there early next month.

A Piece Of Cake(IRE), who hasn't had much racing in recent times, was not totally disgraced in a race that did not play to his strengths stamina-wise, but has a bit to prove from his current mark against younger and more progressive sorts.

Jordan's Ridge(IRE) had conditions to suit but was below his best returned to fences from out of the handicap in a stronger race than he usually competes in. A drop in grade could ensure further success this summer. *(op 10-1)*

Montreal(FR) has been disappointing since his Perth success in June of last year and this run again showed that he is one to tread carefully with for the time being. *(op 9-2)*

424 DRYBURGH ABBEY HOTEL STANDARD NATIONAL HUNT FLAT RACE 2m 110y
9:05 (9:07) (Class 6) 4-6-Y-O **£3,705** (£1,140; £570; £285)

Form RPR

61- **1** **Malt De Vergy (FR)**[104] 3682 5-11-8 .... GBerridge(3) 108+
(L Lungo) *plld hrd: hld up: hdwy over 3f out: led over 1f out: drvn out* **9/4**[2]

2 *nk* **First Cry (IRE)** 5-11-4 .... WHutchinson 100+
(N G Richards) *prom: hung rt and led over 2f out: hdd over 1f out: rallied: hld cl home* **7/4**[1]

0-3 **3** *11* **Chief Dan George (IRE)**[7] 323 5-10-13 .... DMcGann(5) 89
(D R MacLeod) *trckd ldrs: effrt and ev ch over 2f out: sn rdn and one pce* **12/1**

4 *8* **Mulligan's Pride (IRE)** 4-10-9 .... DCCostello(5) 77
(G A Swinbank) *hld up: drvn and outpcd over 4f out: hdwy 2f out: kpt on: no imp* **7/2**[3]

003- **5** *1 3/4* **The Connor Fella**[81] 4090 4-10-9 .... StephenJCraine(5) 75
(F P Murtagh) *hld up: effrt u.p over 3f out: nvr rchd ldrs* **100/1**

6 *1* **Tongariro Crossing (IRE)**[25] 5-10-13 .... TGreenway(5) 78
(W T Reed) *chsd ldrs: ev ch whn rdr dropped whip over 2f out: sn rdn and btn* **100/1**

7 *5* **Exit To Saumur (FR)** 4-10-11 .... KJMercer(3) 69
(B Storey) *cl up tl wknd over 2f out* **20/1**

5 **8** *12* **Talisker Rock (IRE)**[7] 323 5-10-11 .... (t) MJMcAlister(7) 61
(B Storey) *led to over 2f out: sn btn* **25/1**

9 *9* **Commanche Girl**[40] 5-10-8 .... MrCStorey(3) 45
(Miss S E Forster) *in tch on outside tl wknd over 4f out* **66/1**

04- **10** *1 1/2* **Meda's Song**[92] 3891 6-10-11 .... PRobson 44
(D W Whillans) *chsd ldrs to over 4f out: sn lost pl* **12/1**

0- **11** *1 3/4* **Torgiano (IRE)**[33] 4865 4-11-0 .... NPMulholland 45
(P Monteith) *chsd ldrs tl wknd fr 3f out* **20/1**

12 *2* **My Countess** 4-10-0 .... TMessenger(7) 36
(A C Whillans) *bhd: rdn and no ch fr 1/2-way* **40/1**

13 *hd* **Over'n Out** 4-10-4 .... PAspell(3) 36
(A R Dicken) *a bhd: no ch fnl 4f* **50/1**

14 *22* **High Delight** 5-10-11 .... (t) TJDreaper(7) 25
(W Amos) *midfield: rdn and wknd 1/2-way* **66/1**

3m 53.0s
WFA 4 from 5yo+ 4lb **14** Ran SP% **127.5**
CSF £6.49 TOTE £2.40: £1.70, £1.60, £2.20; EX 5.40 Place 6 £23.63, Place 5 £11.53.
Owner Ashleybank Investments Limited **Bred** P Besson **Trained** Carruthertown, D'fries & G'way

FOCUS
A race lacking strength in depth but the first two pulled clear in this steadily-run race and could be fair prospects. It has been rated through the third.

NOTEBOOK
Malt De Vergy(FR) ◆, a progressive type, turned in his best effort yet and did well given that he had failed to settle for much of the way. He is likely to make his mark over hurdles, especially if learning to race with restraint. *(op 2-1 tchd 5-2)*

First Cry(IRE) ◆, out of an Irish bumper winner, attracted support and although hanging, perhaps due to greenness or the ground, he showed more than enough to suggest he should win a similar event at the very least before going over obstacles. *(tchd 15-8, 2-1 in places)*

Chief Dan George(IRE), who turned in an improved effort at Perth last time, again left the impression that a stiffer test of stamina would have been in his favour. *(op 9-1)*

Mulligan's Pride(IRE), whose dam is from the same family as Gold Cup winner Mr Mulligan, was the subject of favourable reports but, although not disgraced on this debut, left the impression that a stiffer test of stamina would have suited. *(op 9-1 tchd 10-1)*

The Connor Fella was not totally disgraced given this race was not really run to suit and he may do better in ordinary handicaps over obstacles with the emphasis on stamina.

Tongariro Crossing(IRE) had the rub of this slowly-run race on this bumper debut so may be flattered by his proximity and, in any case, is likely to continue to look vulnerable in this grade.

T/Plt: £201.90 to a £1 stake. Pool: £47,892.75. 173.15 winning tickets. T/Qpdt: £85.20 to a £1 stake. Pool: £3,306.10. 28.70 winning tickets. RY

[192]WETHERBY (L-H)
Thursday, May 19

OFFICIAL GOING: Good to firm (good in places)
Wind: Virtually nil

425 "WETHERBY RACECOURSE - YOUR CONFERENCE VENUE FOR LEEDS" CLAIMING HURDLE (10 hdls) 2m 4f 110y
2:00 (2:00) (Class 4) 4-Y-O+ **£2,691** (£769; £384)

Form RPR

30-2 **1** **Talarive (USA)**[19] 120 9-10-12 99 .... (tp) JimCrowley 102+
(P D Niven) *hld up: hdwy 4 out: rdn to chal after 2 out: led last and styd on wl* **5/1**[3]

31-3 **2** *5* **Tensile (IRE)**[20] 102 10-11-0 116 .... TScudamore 99
(R J Hodges) *hld up: hdwy 4 out: mstke next: rdn to ld after 2 out: drvn and hdd last: kpt on same pce* **2/1**[1]

0P-3 **3** *3* **Hugo De Perro (FR)**[19] 121 10-10-9 110 .... (p) PBuchanan(3) 94
(Miss Lucinda V Russell) *chsd ldrs: hdwy to ld appr 3 out: rdn next: sn hdd & wknd* **5/2**[2]

0-P4 **4** *2 1/2* **Red Nose Lady**[15] 180 8-10-4 94 .... (b) LTreadwell(5) 89
(G J Smith) *led: hit 5th: rdn along and hdd appr 3 out: grad wknd* **33/1**

P0P- **5** *11* **Dark Shadows**[38] 4812 10-11-1 92 .... KJMercer(3) 88+
(W Storey) *in tch: effrt appr 3 out: sn rdn along: hld whn hit 2 out* **33/1**

00-0 **6** *11* **Ballinruane (IRE)**[14] 192 6-11-12 64 .... ARoss 85+
(B S Rothwell) *chsd ldrs: rdn along bef 3 out and sn wknd* **150/1**

50-5 **7** *12* **Lord Lamb**[9] 283 13-10-12 95 .... (p) RMcGrath 58
(K G Reveley) *trckd ldrs: hdwy on outer to dispute ld whn mstke 6th: sn poushed along: rdn after 4 out and sn wknd* **8/1**

/51- **8** *18* **Court Of Justice (USA)**[16] 4667 9-11-2 108 .... PJBrennan 44
(K A Morgan) *chsd ldrs: nt fluent 3rd and sn rdn along: lost pl after next and bhd fr 1/2-way* **11/1**

10-P **P** **Darab (POL)**[20] 109 5-10-8 102 .... THalliday(10) —
(Mrs S J Smith) *prom: pushed along and lost pl bef 5th: bhd whn p.u b efore 3 out* **16/1**

4m 58.5s (-10.40) **Going Correction** -0.65s/f (Firm) **9** Ran SP% **110.4**
Speed ratings: **94,92,90,90,85 81,77,70**,— CSF £14.76 TOTE £8.00: £1.90, £1.30, £1.30; EX 17.50.The winner was the subject of a friendly claim of £5,000.
Owner Ian G M Dalgleish **Bred** Juddmonte Farms **Trained** Barton-le-Street, N Yorks

FOCUS
A pretty uncompetitive race on paper with only three of the nine runners looking to have a serious chance. It has been rated through the winner and the fifth.

NOTEBOOK
Talarive(USA), 7lb higher than when winning at Sedgefield last month, appreciated the step back up in distance on this faster surface and in the end stayed on too strongly for the favourite. He has really improved this year for the fitting of cheekpieces and should continue to pay his way. *(op 11-2)*
Tensile(IRE) is a smart sort at this sort of level but was put in his place by the winner from the final flight. He ideally requires a stiffer test. *(op 9-4 tchd 5-2)*
Hugo De Perro(FR) would have found this an insufficient test of stamina and he had no answer when the front pair went by. *(tchd 9-4)*
Red Nose Lady ran better than she was entitled to at the weights, but was always a sitting duck. *(op 28-1)*

426 BAKER TILLY NOVICES' HURDLE (12 hdls) 2m 7f
2:30 (2:31) (Class 3) 4-Y-O+ **£4,956** (£1,525; £762; £381)

Form RPR

0-54 **1** **Relix (FR)**[8] 301 5-10-9 93 .... (t) DMcGann(5) 93+
(A M Crow) *a.p: cl up fr 6th: led 3 out: hit next: sn rdn and kpt on gamely flat* **7/2**[2]

0-54 **2** *1 1/4* **Lothian Falcon**[4] 367 6-10-11 .... GCarenza(3) 91
(P Maddison) *hld up: hdwy to trck ldrs after 4 out: effrt 2 out: rdn and ev ch last: kpt on u.p flat* **13/2**[3]

P-14 **3** *1 1/4* **Ryhall (IRE)**[14] 194 5-10-13 103 .... (b) RGarritty 90+
(T D Easterby) *hld up in rr: hdwy to trck ldrs 1/2-way: effrt on inner and sn ev ch 3 out: rdn next: hit last: drvn and no ex flat* **10/11**[1]

00P- **4** *24* **Caipiroska**[139] 3114 6-10-11 .... KJMercer(3) 66
(Ferdy Murphy) *keen: trckd ldrs tl pushed along and sltly outpcd bef 3 out: styng on whn hit 2 out: sn wknd* **9/1**

5 *7* **Missy Moscow (IRE)**[39] 7-10-7 .... JMMaguire 56+
(T P Tate) *cl up: led 3rd tl rdn along and hdd 3 out: sn wknd* **14/1**

-PP3 **6** *3 1/2* **Stoneriggs**[12] 209 4-10-8 .... BHarding 49
(Mrs E Slack) *hld up in tch: hdwy to trck ldrs after 4 out: rdn next and sn wknd* **25/1**

P0P- **7** *dist* **Red Autumn**[177] 2404 8-11-0 .... RMcGrath —
(K G Reveley) *chsd ldrs: rdn along and lost pl after 6th: bhd fr next* **33/1**

0-P6 **P** **Middleton Kate**[7] 314 5-10-2 .... MNicolls(5) —
(John R Upson) *led to 3rd: cl up tl lost pl 6th and bhd whn p.u bef 3 out* **100/1**

P-F **P** **Royal Friend**[25] 8 6-10-11 .... (p) PAspell(3) —
(C R Wilson) *prom and j. slowly 1st: pushed along 3rd: rdn and bhd fr next: p.u bef 7th* **80/1**

5m 46.1s (-10.60) **Going Correction** -0.65s/f (Firm)
WFA 4 from 5yo+ 5lb **9** Ran SP% **113.6**
Speed ratings: **93,92,92,83,81 80**,—,—,— CSF £25.03 TOTE £4.90: £1.40, £2.40, £1.02; EX 30.00.
Owner Stuart Taylor, David Hardy, Lee Seaton **Bred** S N C Lagardere Elevage **Trained** Bonjedward, Borders

FOCUS
A modest race and a modest winning time to boot. The race has been rated through the winner.

NOTEBOOK
Relix(FR) was getting off the mark at the 15th attempt and saw his race out well in the second-time tongue tie. This is undoubtedly his sort of trip and he may be open to further improvement. *(op 10-3 tchd 4-1)*
Lothian Falcon is improving with racing and will have little trouble with a full three miles. He should be capable of winning a handicap or two. *(op 7-1 tchd 8-1)*
Ryhall(IRE) has definitely been helped by the blinkers and ran a reasonable race in defeat. She is worth a try in handicaps. *(op 11-10)*
Caipiroska was well adrift of the front three and did not get home having raced far too keenly early on. He still looks in need of more time and will eventually jump a fence. *(tchd 10-1)*

427 ROCOM PANASONIC H'CAP CHASE (13 fncs 2 omitted) 2m 4f 110y
3:00 (3:01) (Class 3) (0-135,128) 5-Y-O+ **£7,480** (£2,431; £1,309)

Form RPR

P0-2 **1** **Giorgio (IRE)**[11] 234 7-10-5 **107** .... (b) NFehily 118+
(Mrs Jeremy Young) *j.w: mde all: rdn appr 2 out and styd on wl* **9/4**[2]

00-2 **2** *6* **Galway Breeze (IRE)**[14] [195] 10-10-7 **109**.......... JimCrowley 114
(Mrs K Walton) *hld up: hdwy to to chazse wnr appr 4 out: rdn to chal next: drvn and one pce appr last* **11/2**

00-4 **3** *2 1/2* **Noshinannikin**[20] [108] 11-11-5 **121**.......... DElsworth 125+
(Mrs S J Smith) *chsd wnr: mstke 8th: pushed along bef 4 out: rdn and styd on fr 2 out* **4/1**[3]

212- **P** **Powder Creek (IRE)**[29] [4927] 8-11-0 **116**.......... RMcGrath —
(K G Reveley) *trckd ldng pair: hdwy 5 out: rdn after next: sn wknd and p.u after 2 out* **6/4**[1]

5m 6.30s (-14.40) **Going Correction** -0.525s/f (Firm) **4** Ran SP% **106.2**
Speed ratings: **106,103,102,**— CSF £12.15 TOTE £3.40; EX 11.90.
Owner Sir Robert Ogden **Bred** William Mangan **Trained** Charlton Mackrell, Somerset

FOCUS
A competitive race on paper despite a depleted field due to the ground. The well handicapped winner ran to his mark.

NOTEBOOK
Giorgio(IRE), who ran well in defeat last time, was soon in a good jumping rhythm and edged further and further away from his field before getting a little tired over the final couple of fences, albeit still keeping on well. The fitting of blinkers has improved him and he should be up to defying a penalty. *(op 2-1)*
Galway Breeze(IRE) kept battling away and got the beter of Noshinannikin for the runner-up spot. He was no match for the winner, but is on a winning mark. *(op 5-1)*
Noshinannikin does not find winning easy and is probably a fraction too high in the weights at present. *(op 7-2 tchd 10-3)*
Powder Creek(IRE) has developed into a consistently fair performer, but this was some way adrift *of his true form. He deserves another chance. Official explanation: jockey said gelding was unsuited by good to firm, good in places ground (op 2-1)*

428 RIPON MITSUBISHI H'CAP HURDLE (9 hdls) 2m
3:35 (3:36) (Class 4) (0-110,107) 4-Y-O+ **£3,486** (£996; £498)

Form RPR

/P-0 **1** **Cristoforo (IRE)**[5] [347] 8-11-0 **95**.......... PMoloney 111+
(B J Curley) *mde all: clr 3 out: rdn and hit last: styd on wl* **11/4**[2]

444- **2** *5* **Kingkohler (IRE)**[115] [3519] 6-11-10 **105**.......... PJBrennan 114+
(K A Morgan) *hld up: hdwy 1/2-way: chsd wnr 2 out: sn rdn and no imp* **5/2**[1]

340- **3** *8* **Once Seen**[72] [4242] 5-11-11 **106**.......... JAMcCarthy 107+
(O Sherwood) *hld up towards rr: hdwy after 6th: rdn 2 out: styd on u.p appr last: nrst fin* **13/2**

-005 **4** *6* **Day Du Roy (FR)**[5] [347] 7-11-10 **105**.......... AThornton 99
(Miss L C Siddall) *hld up: hdwy 1/2-way: chsd ldrs after 4 out: rdn along and one pce after next* **14/1**

P-54 **5** *1 1/2* **Merryvale Man**[14] [197] 8-11-0 **102**.......... SCrawford(7) 95
(Miss Kariana Key) *chsd ldrs: rdn along and outpcd appr 4 out: no ch after* **11/2**[3]

/00- **6** *1* **Sunridge Fairy (IRE)**[1] [4156] 6-10-10 **91**.......... WHutchinson 83
(L R James) *chsd wnr: rdn along 4 out: wknd next* **33/1**

P0-0 **7** *27* **Diamond Vein**[14] [192] 6-10-6 **87**.......... ARoss 52
(S P Griffiths) *a bhd* **16/1**

10P- **8** *6* **Seeyaaj**[75] [4184] 5-11-9 **107**..........(t) PBuchanan(3) 66
(Miss Lucinda V Russell) *chsd ldrs: rdn along 5th: wknd after next* **14/1**

4P-U **9** *dist* **Government (IRE)**[9] [279] 4-10-0 **88** oh16 ow3.......... ACCoyle(3) —
(M C Chapman) *a bhd: t.o fr 5th* **100/1**

F/0- **U** **Late Arrival**[24] [3655] 8-10-5 **86**.......... FKeniry —
(M D Hammond) *blnd and uns rdr 1st* **66/1**

00-5 **P** **Noble Pasao (IRE)**[12] [220] 8-11-5 **100**.......... TScudamore —
(Andrew Turnell) *a rr: mstke 2nd: t.o fr 6th: p.u bef last* **11/1**

3m 46.6s (-12.80) **Going Correction** -0.65s/f (Firm)
WFA 4 from 5yo+ 4lb **11** Ran SP% **116.9**
Speed ratings: **107,104,100,97,96 96,82,79,—,—** — CSF £10.22 CT £40.09 TOTE £3.50: £1.60, £1.50, £2.30; EX 12.90.
Owner P Byrne **Bred** Bill Dwan & Tom Lynch **Trained** Newmarket, Suffolk

FOCUS
Cristoforo, who was well in on his Kempton hurdles second in November 2003 let alone his Flat form, made every yard of the running at a decent pace and won well. This looks a decent piece of form.

NOTEBOOK
Cristoforo(IRE), coming into this on the back of two no-shows over hurdles since the start of the year, was in cracking form on the level last season and it was only a matter of time until he transferred the form over to obstacles. He went off at a decent gallop that did not relent and he powered home, despite hitting the last, for a comfortable win. *(op 3-1 tchd 13-8)*
Kingkohler(IRE), attempting to give the winner 10lb, proved no match, but was clear of the third and time will probably show he faced a very tough task. *(op 9-2)*
Once Seen does not find winning easy and is not one to make a habit of backing. On the plus side, he is still only a five-year-old and may yet improve. *(op 7-1 tchd 15-2)*
Day Du Roy(FR) ran a reasonable race under his big weight, but will always be vulnerable. *(tchd 16-1)*
Merryvale Man ideally wants a stiffer test than this and he never posed a threat. *(op 5-1 tchd 13-2)*
Government(IRE) *Official explanation: jockey said gelding finished distressed (op 80-1)*
Noble Pasao(IRE) *Official explanation: jockey said gelding was never travelling (op 10-1 tchd 12-1)*

429 "WETHERBY RACECOURSE FOR WEDDING RECEPTIONS" AMATEUR RIDERS' H'CAP HURDLE (12 hdls) 2m 7f
4:05 (4:06) (Class 4) (0-100,104) 4-Y-O+ **£2,859** (£817; £204; £204)

Form RPR

325- **1** **Getinbybutonlyjust**[29] [4928] 6-11-1 **93**.......... MissJSayer(7) 94
(Mrs Dianne Sayer) *a.p: led 7th to 4 out: rdn along next: styd on flat to ld nr fin* **15/2**

00-1 **2** *nk* **Garnett (IRE)**[9] [283] 4-11-6 **104** 7ex..........(p) MissPBuckley(7) 101+
(D E Cantillon) *racd wd: hld up and bhd: hdwy 4 out: cl up whn pckd next: rdn appr last: kpt on flat* **5/2**[1]

60-2 **3** *1/2* **Knockdoo (IRE)**[19] [129] 12-11-3 **95**.......... MrGGoldie(7) 95
(J S Goldie) *towards rr: hdwy after 4 out: rdn along 2 out: styd on wl fr last* **20/1**

020- **3** *dht* **Own Line**[118] [3463] 6-11-5 **97**.......... CLidster(7) 97
(J Hetherton) *trckd ldrs: hdwy 4 out: led after next: rdn appr last: hdd and no ex towards fin* **25/1**

5-00 **5** *1 1/2* **In Good Faith**[17] [152] 13-9-13 **77**.......... PKinsella(7) 76
(R E Barr) *hld up and bhd: hdwy 3 out: rdn next: styd on appr last: nrst fin* **33/1**

F-65 **6** *8* **Celtic Legend (FR)**[9] [279] 6-10-5 **83**.......... JReveley(7) 77+
(K G Reveley) *trckd ldrs: pushed along 3 out: rdn next and sn wknd* **7/2**[2]

063- **7** *8* **Betterware Boy**[161] [2729] 5-10-3 **81**.......... MrElmelov(7) 66+
(A P Jones) *hld up and bhd: gd hdwy appr 4 out: chsd ldrs next: sn rdn: hit 2 out and sn wknd* **20/1**

0F-0 **8** *12* **Premier Drive (IRE)**[12] [215] 12-11-9 **97**.......... TJDreaper(3) 68
(G M Moore) *prom: led 5th to 7th: led again 4 out: rdn along and hdd after next: grad wknd* **20/1**

P00- **9** *3 1/2* **Petite Salou**[53] [4583] 8-9-7 **71** oh7.......... MissKWood(7) 38
(C N Kellett) *a rr* **100/1**

64-4 **10** *nk* **Book's Way**[17] [152] 9-10-6 **77**.......... MrTGreenall 44
(D W Thompson) *prom: rdn along 4 out and sn wknd* **8/1**

54/P **11** *2* **Niciara (IRE)**[11] [238] 8-10-12 **90**.......... MrRQuinn(7) 55
(M C Chapman) *in tch: mstke 6th: rdn along and outpcd appr 4 out: sn bhd* **66/1**

65P- **P** **Modulor (FR)**[65] [4390] 13-9-11 **75**..........(t) TMessenger(7) —
(L R James) *led to 5th: sn lost pl and bhd whn p.u bef 7th* **40/1**

4-42 **U** **Upright Ima**[9] [283] 6-9-12 **76**.......... MissLAllan(7) —
(Mrs P Sly) *hld up in rr: gd hdwy on inner 1/2-way: chsd ldrs whn blnd and uns rdr 8th* **9/2**[3]

5m 47.1s (-9.60) **Going Correction** -0.65s/f (Firm)
WFA 4 from 5yo+ 5lb **13** Ran SP% **117.8**
Speed ratings: **91,90,90,90,90 87,84,80,79,79 78,—,—** CSF £24.40 TOTE £10.50: £3.10, £1.30; EX 39.00 TRIFECTA Pl: O.Line £3.10, Knockdoo £2.20. Tri: Getinbybutonlyjust, Garnett, O.Line £228.59; Gettinbybutonlyjust, Garnett, Knockdoo £184.70..
Owner Andrew Sayer **Bred** Mrs Hugh Maitland-Jones **Trained** Hackthorpe, Cumbria
■ A first winner for 16-year-old Jo Sayer, daughter of trainer Dianne.
■ Stewards' Enquiry : Mr G Goldie two-day ban: used whip with excessive frequency and out of stride pattern (May 30-31)

FOCUS
A low-grade handicap and a modest winning time for the class. The winner and Own Line ran to their marks, while Garnett may have been unlucky.

NOTEBOOK
Getinbybutonlyjust is a strong stayer and he rallied gamely under pressure to reclaim the lead from favourite Garnett. He should make up into a better chaser than hurdler and is open to further improvement. *(op 8-1)*
Garnett(IRE), up 7lb from when successful at Huntingdon, has proved a real money-spinner on the sand and over hurdles and he very nearly made it five wins from his last six starts. Still only a four-year-old, he will need to keep improving to defy his ever increasing mark. *(op 11-4 tchd 9-4)*
Knockdoo(IRE) plugged on to force a tie for third, but has not won for around four and a half years. Enough said. *(tchd 18-1)*
Own Line was tiring toward the end of the race and did well to cling on for a share of third. He is undoubtedly better at shorter. *(tchd 18-1)*
In Good Faith was doing his best work late having been given a patient ride, but his old legs could not carry him there in time. He is obviously not getting any beter, but still seems to enjoy his racing. *(op 25-1)*
Celtic Legend(FR) is better handicapped over hurdles compared to fences, but he was unable to justify his odds and was disappointing. *(op 4-1)*
Upright Ima was still in with as good a chance as any when unseating at the eighth. *(op 11-2 tchd 6-1)*

430 "DON'T MISS LADIES' EVENING - 26TH MAY" H'CAP CHASE (15 fncs 3 omitted) 3m 1f
4:40 (4:41) (Class 3) (0-115,106) 5-Y-O+ **£5,434** (£1,672; £836; £418)

Form RPR

214- **1** **Cool Cossack (IRE)**[54] [4558] 8-11-12 **106**.......... DElsworth 118+
(Mrs S J Smith) *a.p: mstke 10th: rdn along 3 out: styd on to ld next: rdn and j. slowly last: drvn flat and jst hld on* **13/2**

22-1 **2** *hd* **Ashnaya (FR)**[14] [193] 7-11-8 **102**..........(p) FKeniry 112+
(G M Moore) *trckd ldrs: hdwy 11th: led appr 3 out: rdr dropped whip and hdd next: rdn and kpt on flat: jst hld* **7/1**

31-P **3** *1 3/4* **Benefit**[11] [240] 11-10-4 **84**.......... AThornton 91
(Miss L C Siddall) *led: rdn along 11th: hdd appr 3 out: drvn and kpt on same pce fr next* **10/1**

16-2 **4** *3* **King's Bounty**[22] [62] 9-11-12 **106**..........(b) RGarritty 111+
(T D Easterby) *hld up in tch: hdwy 11th: rdn along 4 out: drvn and one pce bef 2 out* **5/1**[2]

54-5 **5** *15* **Channahrlie (IRE)**[16] [176] 11-10-9 **89**..........(p) WHutchinson 78
(R Dickin) *in tch: rdn along 4 out: drvn and wknd next* **7/1**

12-2 **F** **Jaoka Du Gord (FR)**[25] [12] 8-11-12 **106**.......... TDoyle —
(P R Webber) *hld up in rr: fell 5th* **9/4**[1]

4P-4 **U** **Barryscourt Lad (IRE)**[25] [12] 11-11-9 **103**.......... BHarding —
(R D E Woodhouse) *promtl blnd and uns rdr 5th* **6/1**[3]

6m 23.0s (-17.00) **Going Correction** -0.525s/f (Firm) **7** Ran SP% **109.1**
Speed ratings: **106,105,105,104,99** —,— CSF £44.57 CT £408.65 TOTE £5.50: £2.90, £3.10; EX 30.10.
Owner Trevor Hemmings **Bred** Michael Griffin **Trained** High Eldwick, W Yorks
■ Stewards' Enquiry : D Elsworth caution: used whip with excessive frequency

FOCUS
A good performance by co-top weight Cool Cossack, who battled on well to score his second win over fences. This is not strong form.

NOTEBOOK
Cool Cossack(IRE) has done little wrong since starting out on his chase career and, although he is capable of throwing in the odd blunder, jumped soundly in the main here. He looked to have it sewn up before two out, but got tired in front before picking up again once joined by Ashnaya. This was a good effort under co-top weight and he remains open to further improvement. *(op 7-1 tchd 6-1)*
Ashnaya(FR) looked set to reclaim the lead after the last, but Cool Cossack picked up again once she ranged alongside and she was forced to settle for second. She is consistent and remains open to a little further improvement. *(op 9-2)*
Benefit kept grinding away in third having been headed early in the straight. *(op 11-1 tchd 12-1)*
King's Bounty never reached a challenging position and looked rather paceless. *(op 6-1)*
Jaoka Du Gord(FR) would have gone close on the best of his form, but he got no further than the fifth fence. It remains to be seen how this affects his confidence. *(tchd 2-1 and 5-2)*

431 "CAR-BOOT SALE HERE EVERY SUNDAY" STANDARD OPEN NATIONAL HUNT FLAT RACE 2m
5:15 (5:15) (Class 6) 4-6-Y-O **£2,016** (£576; £288)

Form RPR

00-4 **1** **Jontys'Lass**[11] [241] 4-10-4.......... MrTGreenall(3) 77
(A Crook) *mde all: rdn 3f out: drvn wl over 1f out: kpt on gamely ins last* **10/1**

2 *hd* **Our Tees Component (IRE)** 4-10-7.......... RMcGrath 77
(K G Reveley) *hld up and bhd: hdwy over 4f out: pushed along over 2f out: rdn over 1f out: styd on strly ins last: jst failed* **6/4**[1]

5- **3** *5* **Trafalgar Man (IRE)**[58] [4513] 4-11-0.......... FKeniry 79
(M D Hammond) *hld up: hdwy 6f out: rdn along to chse wnr wl over 2f out: drvn and ch over 1f out: kpt on same pce fnl f* **5/2**[2]

0-6 **4** *4* **Batties Den (IRE)**[11] [249] 5-11-4.......... PMoloney 79
(P D Niven) *hld up: hdwy 6f out: rdn to chse ldng pair wl over 2f out: drvn and wknd wl over 1f out* **16/1**

5 11 **Nonotreally** 4-11-0 .... JMMaguire 64
(T P Tate) *hld up: hdwy over 6f out: pushed along and rn green home turn: rdn and hung lft over 3f out: sn no imp* **4/1**[3]

00- **6** 11 **Daniel's Dream**[71] 4263 5-10-11 .... MrTDavidson[(7)] 57
(J E Dixon) *chsd ldrs: hdwy to chse wnr 6f out: rdn along 4f out and sn wknd* **66/1**

U- **7** 29 **Stoneriggs Silver**[26] 4981 4-11-0 .... BHarding 24
(Mrs E Slack) *keen chsd ldrs: rdn along 6f out: sn wknd* **14/1**

0- **8** 2 **Just Scooby**[54] 4552 4-11-0 .... RGarritty 22
(M D Hammond) *chsd ldrs on inner: rdn along 6f out and sn wknd* **40/1**

3m 47.0s (-17.40) **Going Correction** -0.65s/f (Firm)
WFA 4 from 5yo 4lb **8** Ran SP% **114.1**
Speed ratings: **97,96,94,92,86 81,66,65** CSF £25.41 TOTE £8.90: £2.00, £1.20, £1.70; EX 39.40 Place 6 £77.85, Place 5 £66.34.
Owner A Crook - T Oglesby - S Hollingsworth **Bred** Mrs E M Charlton **Trained** Harmby, N Yorks

FOCUS
A poor bumper dominated by the two fillies. It has been rated through the winner and the fourth.

NOTEBOOK
Jontys'Lass was sent straight into the lead by Greenall and enjoyed the run of the race. She responded well to pressure and deserved to hang on. This was an improved effort and she should stay two and a half miles over hurdles. *(tchd 12-1)*
Our Tees Component(IRE) ◆ was clearly fancied to make a winning debut and would have done so had she been ridden closer to the pace. She looks nailed on to win a similar race in the coming weeks. *(op 15-8 tchd 2-1)*
Trafalgar Man(IRE) improved on his initial effort and will appreciate a greater test over hurdles. *(op 9-4 tchd 15-8)*
Batties Den(IRE) ran his best race to date, but does not have the speed to win a bumper. *(op 7-1)*
Nonotreally showed enough on this debut to suggest he can win a bumper, and judging by the way he ran around under pressure, the experience should do him good. *(op 11-2 tchd 7-1)*
T/Plt: £83.10 to a £1 stake. Pool: £34,332.35. 301.30 winning tickets. T/Qpdt: £43.30 to a £1 stake. Pool: £2,406.90. 41.10 winning tickets. JR

432 - 435a (Foreign Racing) - See Raceform Interactive

STRATFORD (L-H)
Friday, May 20

OFFICIAL GOING: Good
Wind: slight against Weather: overcast

436 GTH CONSTRUCTION NOVICES' H'CAP CHASE (16 fncs) 2m 5f 110y
6:10 (6:10) (Class 3) (0-110,108) 5-Y-0+ **£6,877** (£2,116; £1,058; £529)

Form RPR

P5-U **1** **Lonesome Man (IRE)**[21] 106 9-10-10 **92** .... RJohnson 100+
(R T Phillips) *led: hit 10th: hdd 13th: jnd ldr and lft in command 2 out: drvn out* **33/1**

241- **2** 3 ½ **Solve It Sober (IRE)**[28] 4953 11-9-9 **82** oh11 .... RStephens[(5)] 86
(S G Griffiths) *trckd ldrs: rdn and outpcd 13th: plugging on whn lft 3rd 2 out: wnt 2nd last: nt rch wnr* **16/1**

13-1 **3** 1 ½ **Party Games (IRE)**[14] 202 8-11-12 **108** .... PHide 116+
(G L Moore) *mstkes: pressed ldrs: rdn and ev ch 3 out: 2l 3rd whn lft 2nd and bdly hmpd 2 out: nt rcvr: demoted at last* **11/4**[1]

P61- **4** 9 **Reviewer (IRE)**[21] 4535 7-11-9 **105** .... RThornton 98
(M Meade) *bhd: drvn after 9th: a struggling after* **11/1**

02-2 **5** 2 ½ **Jivaty (FR)**[12] 244 8-11-7 **103** .... ATinkler 94
(Mrs A J Hamilton-Fairley) *cumbersme jumping in rr: detached fr rest by 4th: u.p 8th: sn lost tch* **12/1**

004- **U** **Murat (FR)**[70] 4311 5-11-0 **99** .... APMcCoy —
(M C Pipe) *mstke and uns rdr 1st* **5/1**[3]

220- **F** **Lough Rynn (IRE)**[145] 2944 7-11-10 **106** .... SThomas —
(Miss H C Knight) *j. slowly 6th: towards rr tl fell 7th* **10/3**[2]

40P- **F** **Anshabil (IRE)**[33] 4889 6-10-13 **95** .... WHutchinson 103
(A King) *pressed ldr: j. ahd 13th: drvn and jnd and fell 2 out* **11/1**

624- **P** **Mantilla**[269] 1269 8-10-10 **92** ....(v) DRDennis —
(Ian Williams) *ldr lost iron 4th: rr whn hmpd 7th: rdn and struggling next: t.o and p.u 11th* **7/1**

5m 19.8s (5.40) **Going Correction** +0.35s/f (Yiel)
WFA 5 from 6yo+ 3lb **9** Ran SP% **112.1**
Speed ratings: **104,102,102,98,98** —,—,—,— CSF £422.56 CT £1930.11 TOTE £40.30: £6.00, £4.20, £1.30; EX 148.50.
Owner P Docherty **Bred** James Wilson **Trained** Adlestrop, Gloucs

FOCUS
Reasonable form, the winner putting in his best run for ages. Anshabil was arguably unlucky.

NOTEBOOK
Lonesome Man(IRE) was once a promising hurdler in Ireland but he had shown very little since joining his current yard, reportedly suffering from a back problem last season. Setting a good pace and jumping soundly, he was headed with four to jump but was back upsides when left in command at the second last. He is still relatively unexposed and provided his problems do not resurface there could be more to come.
Solve It Sober(IRE), successful in a selling handicap on his latest start, ran a sound race from 11lb out of the handicap. He really needs a greater test of stamina.
Party Games(IRE), 8lb higher, did not jump with the fluency he showed at Wincanton, perhaps *finding the track too sharp, and was held when badly hampered by the faller at the second last. (op 9-4 tchd 3-1 in places)*
Reviewer(IRE), upped in trip, was being driven along early on the final circuit and could make no impression on those in front of him. *(op 10-1)*
Lough Rynn(IRE), having his first run since a disappointing effort on Boxing Day, was on the floor with just over a circuit to run. *(tchd 11-4 and 7-2)*
Anshabil(IRE), who went the wrong way over hurdles, showed a lot more on his chasing bow and was in there fighting when coming down two from home. Stratford's second last is a tricky obstacle and he had jumped soundly up to then. *(tchd 11-4 and 7-2)*

437 NEEDHAM & JAMES HUNTERS' CHASE (12 fncs 1 omitted) 2m 1f 110y
6:40 (6:41) (Class 6) 5-Y-0+ **£3,571** (£1,099; £549; £274)

Form RPR

23-1 **1** **Silence Reigns**[13] 221 11-12-4 115 ....(bt) MrCJSweeney[(3)] 115+
(P F Nicholls) *bdly hmpd 1st: bhd tl stdy prog 8th: effrt on bit fr 3 out: led last: sn rdn clr* **9/4**[1]

62-2 **2** 6 **Coole Glen (IRE)**[10] 278 9-12-0 .... MrSMorris 93
(W J Warner) *midfield whn bmpd rival 6th: clsd to ld after 8th: drvn 3 out: hdd last: immediately outpcd but wl in command of rest* **20/1**

/P-U **3** 3 ½ **Be My Friend (IRE)**[6] 348 9-12-0 .... MrRBurton 90
(G D Hanmer) *stdd in last: wl bhd tl 6th: prog after 8th: mstke 10th and rdn: wknd bef 2 out* **10/1**

P/13 **4** nk **Galway (IRE)**[10] 272 12-12-2 .... MissCStucley[(5)] 96
(Mrs Marilyn Scudamore) *outpcd in rr: kpt on past btn horses fr 3 out: hit next: styd on but unable to chal* **14/1**

F-54 **5** 1 ¼ **Hot Plunge**[10] 278 9-12-2 ....(p) MrJOwen[(5)] 96+
(Mrs J P Lomax) *hit 3rd: prom: 2nd and drvn whn hit 3 out: wknd next* **25/1**

4PP- **6** 2 ½ **Phildari (IRE)**[33] 4882 9-11-7 84 .... MrDEngland[(7)] 86
(Mrs Jelly O'Brien) *multiple errors: prom: 3rd and ev ch whn hit 3 out: fdd bef next* **33/1**

U-23 **7** 7 **Enitsag (FR)**[8] 313 6-12-0 94 .... MrMWalford[(7)] 88+
(S Flook) *pckd 3rd: nvr bttr than midfield: rdn 7th: hmpd next: struggling after* **14/1**

P2-4 **8** 1 ¾ **Jazz Night**[23] 52 8-12-4 .... TJDreaper[(3)] 84
(S Lycett) *pressed ldrs tl 8th: rdn and btn after 10th* **33/1**

43-1 **9** 1 **Let's Fly (FR)**[5] 10-12-0 .... MrWBiddick[(7)] 83
(Ross Oliver) *cl up tl put u.p 7th: blnd next and sn wknd* **9/1**[3]

P- **10** 11 **Lance Toi (FR)**[34] 6-11-11 ....(b[1]) MrPCowley[(3)] 65
(G D Hanmer) *midfield: effrt to chse ldrs and rdn bef 9th: sn struggling* **66/1**

P/14 **F** **Willy Willy**[8] 313 12-12-4 ....(p) MrJSnowden[(3)] —
(Mrs Caroline Keevil) *fell 1st: dead* **33/1**

P **Marton Mere**[6] 9-11-7 .... MissJFoster[(7)] —
(P Grindrod) *blnd 2nd: sn last: t.o and p.u 7th* **100/1**

0/P- **U** **Rhetoric (IRE)**[18] 6-11-7 .... MissSarah-JayneDavies[(7)] —
(Miss Sarah-Jayne Davies) *uns rdr 1st* **100/1**

/5-5 **B** **Gaiac (FR)**[12] 11-11-7 ....(b) MissSSharratt[(7)] —
(Ms N M Hugo) *mstke 4th: towards rr next: b.d 8th* **14/1**

532- **F** **Call Me Jack (IRE)**[13] 9-11-7 77 .... MissJCoward[(7)] —
(Mrs C A Coward) *blnd 2nd: towards rr tl fell 5th* **66/1**

/3-0 **P** **Scotmail Lad (IRE)**[23] 47 11-11-11 94 ....(b) MrCMulhall[(3)] —
(Mrs C M Mulhall) *bdly hmpd 1st: nvr rcvrd: wl bhd whn p.u 8th* **20/1**

10-4 **F** **Star Jack (FR)**[15] 195 10-12-2 109 ....(t) MrBWoodhouse[(5)] —
(Miss P Robson) *trckd ldrs: 5th and wl in tch whn fell 8th: dead* **3/1**[2]

FF-5 **P** **Gue Au Loup (FR)**[22] 79 11-11-7 78 .... MrMWall[(7)] —
(G C Evans) *chsd ldrs: hmpd 6th and rdn: outpcd after: t.o and p.u last* **100/1**

P/0- **F** **Workaway**[12] 9-11-11 .... MrAWintle[(3)] —
(M Keighley) *led and set furious gallop: j.rt: hit 7th: hdd after next: 7th and fading rapidly whn fell 3 out* **50/1**

4-31 **P** **Viscount Bankes**[10] 278 7-12-2 .... MrAndrewMartin[(5)] —
(Mrs Rosemary Gasson) *prom tl 5th: losing pl whn j.rt next and clashed w rival: no ch after 8th: wl bhd whn p.u 10th* **16/1**

4m 19.9s (7.40) **Going Correction** +0.35s/f (Yiel) **20** Ran SP% **130.9**
Speed ratings: **97,94,92,92,92 90,87,87,86,81** —,—,—,— —,—,—,—,— CSF £54.65 TOTE £3.00: £2.10, £5.40, £3.00; EX 69.40.
Owner Mrs M Findlay **Bred** Cheveley Park Stud Ltd **Trained** Ditcheat, Somerset
■ Stewards' Enquiry : Mr Andrew Martin one-day ban: careless riding (May 31)

FOCUS
A well-contested event run at a furious pace. There was plenty of grief and a safety factor of twenty does seem too high for a race of this nature. The first fence in the back straight was bypassed on the second circuit. The race has been rated around the fifth and sixth, the easy winner value for further.

NOTEBOOK
Silence Reigns, given a patient ride after surviving a scare at the first, quickened away on the run-in for a very easy victory. He has not needed to run to the form of his Bangor win at February in landing two victories this month. *(op 5-2)*
Coole Glen(IRE), tackling his shortest trip so far, ran another good race but came up against a smart performer for this grade. *(tchd 18-1)*
Be My Friend(IRE), in good form in points and bang there when unseating at Bangor, found the early pace too hot. He closed to chase the leaders but his progress was slowed by an error at the last ditch.
Galway(IRE) won over a furlong shorter at Cheltenham last month but he found himself taken off his feet. He stayed on in the last half mile and would have been third but for a mistake at the second last. *(tchd 16-1)*
Hot Plunge ran a solid race in the first-time cheekpieces.
Phildari(IRE), without the tongue tie this time, got away with a number of mistakes and only faded from the second last.
Star Jack(FR) appeared to be unsighted at the eighth and sadly took a fatal fall. *(op 9-2)*

438 JEWSON NOVICES' HURDLE (SERIES QUALIFIER) (9 hdls) 2m 110y
7:10 (7:12) (Class 3) 4-Y-0+
£6,066 (£2,301; £1,150; £523; £261; £156)

Form RPR

1 **1** **Natal (FR)**[12] 243 4-11-0 ....(t) RWalsh 106+
(P F Nicholls) *hld up in tch: wnt 2nd at 6th: led bef 2 out where nt fluent: drvn clr last* **6/4**[2]

11-1 **2** 4 **Portavadie**[13] 209 6-11-8 .... GLee 110+
(J M Jefferson) *wnt 2nd at 3rd: led 6th: qcknd after next: drvn and hdd bef 2 out: ev ch nring last: outpcd flat* **15/2**[3]

2-1 **3** 1 ½ **Fandani (GER)**[14] 203 5-11-4 .... NFehily 105+
(C J Mann) *hld up towards rr: trckd ldrs fr 5th: chal 2 out and ev ch bef last: outpcd whn nt fluent: no ex* **1/1**[1]

5/ **4** 25 **Willows Gate**[531] 2602 7-10-12 .... TDoyle 73
(P R Webber) *set slow pce: hdd 6th: wknd rapidly after 3 out* **40/1**

5 8 **Street Life (IRE)**[15] 7-10-12 .... LAspell 65
(W J Musson) *hld up last pair: lost tch 6th: far fr disgracd* **16/1**

P-0P **6** 4 **Cloud Catcher (IRE)**[12] 224 4-9-11 ow1 ....(bt[1]) MNicolls[(5)] 51
(M Appleby) *chsd ldr tl 3rd: lost tch 6th: sn wl bhd* **300/1**

0-14 **U** **Storm Clear (IRE)**[3] 396 6-10-11 86 .... RCummings[(7)] —
(D J Wintle) *pitched 1st and uns rdr* **100/1**

4m 3.90s (5.50) **Going Correction** +0.275s/f (Yiel)
WFA 4 from 5yo+ 4lb **7** Ran SP% **111.4**
Speed ratings: **98,96,95,83,79 78**,— CSF £12.14 TOTE £2.80: £1.40, £2.80; EX 9.20.
Owner Mrs Monica Hackett **Bred** Yves D'Armaille **Trained** Ditcheat, Somerset

FOCUS
This turned into something of a sprint off a slow pace and the form is suspect. Both the winner and third were below the form they showed when scoring last time.

NOTEBOOK
Natal(FR) took over at the second last where he was awkward, but a better leap at the final flight when being hotly pursued sealed the race for him. He was 10lb below the form he showed at *Worcester in winning this slowly-run affair and remains a promising youngster. (tchd 11-8 and 13-8 in places)*
Portavadie quickened the pace approaching the fourth last, and although outspeeded by the winner in the end he went down fighting. He could have done with a truer test throughout and this was a sound effort. *(op 7-1)*
Fandani(GER) was a little outpaced by the first two when the pace lifted and had to work to get *into contention. He will be seen to much better effect in a truly-run race. (op 6-5 tchd 5-4 and 11-8 in places)*
Willows Gate ran a satisfactory race on this hurdles debut and first run since December 2003. *(op 33-1)*

Street Life(IRE), four times a winner over ten furlongs on the Flat, was given a fairly kind introduction to hurdling and can do better in time. *(op 14-1)*

439 INTRUM JUSTITIA H'CAP CHASE (21 fncs) 3m 4f
7:40 (7:42) (Class 3) (0-120,120) 5-Y-0+ **£8,209** (£2,526; £1,263; £631)

Form RPR

B2-1 **1** **Gallik Dawn**[12] [240] 7-10-2 **96** 7ex ow1 RWalsh 115+
(A Hollingsworth) *hld up gng wl in rr: smooth prog in 4th at 15th: chal 3 out: led next: easily drew clr* **2/1**[1]

4-56 **2** *10* **Bright Approach (IRE)**[8] [311] 12-11-3 **114** MissPGundry[(3)] 120+
(J G Cann) *prom: rdn 7th: rn in snatches after: rallied after 16th: drvn ahd 3 out: hdd next: no ch w wnr after but kpt on* **20/1**

1P-1 **3** *5* **Presence Of Mind (IRE)**[9] [297] 7-10-8 **102** 7ex BJCrowley 99
(Miss E C Lavelle) *cl up: mstke 3rd: rdn 12th: disp 2nd fr next tl led 18th: hdd 3 out: ev ch bef next: drvn and wknd* **7/2**[2]

630- **4** *3* **Tipsy Mouse (IRE)**[55] [4548] 9-11-3 **111** (b[1]) DElsworth 105
(Mrs S J Smith) *led: drvn after 16th: hdd 18th: wknd u.p after 3 out* **8/1**

F05- **5** *5* **Alpine Slave**[32] [4912] 8-10-4 **98** LAspell 89+
(N J Gifford) *mostly 2nd tl after 16th: 4l 5th and drvn 3 out: sn wknd* **25/1**

061- **6** *dist* **Twisted Logic (IRE)**[38] [4815] 12-11-7 **118** RWalford[(3)] —
(R H Alner) *pushed along in rr 8th: t.o 15th: btn 88l* **14/1**

0P-3 **7** *1 ¾* **Blazing Batman**[12] [246] 12-10-3 **97** JMogford —
(Dr P Pritchard) *prom: lost pl 10th: t.o 15th: btn 90l* **33/1**

40P- **F** **Lucky Bay (IRE)**[27] [4984] 9-11-12 **120** GLee —
(Mrs Jeremy Young) *midfield and rdn 9th: fell 12th* **12/1**

01-1 **F** **He's The Biz (FR)**[20] [137] 6-10-7 **101** PJBrennan —
(Nick Williams) *hld up in rr: last trio passing 9th: fell 14th* **7/1**[3]

41-2 **P** **Jack Of Spades (IRE)**[20] [137] 9-10-0 **94** oh2 WHutchinson —
(R Dickin) *midfield: lost tch after 16th: t.o and p.u last* **10/1**

520- **P** **Count Campioni (IRE)**[143] [3049] 11-11-1 **109** NFehily —
(M Pitman) *hit 2nd: last and struggling 7th: stl labouring whn bdly hmpd 14th: continued t.o tl p.u 18th* **17/2**

7m 4.80s (-6.50) **Going Correction** +0.35s/f (Yiel) **11** Ran SP% **124.7**
Speed ratings: **109,106,104,103,102** —,—,—,—,— — CSF £45.14 CT £144.19 TOTE £3.40: £1.60, £5.00, £1.30; EX 46.70.

Owner Perry Adams **Bred** Mrs D Jenks **Trained** Feckenham, Worcs

FOCUS
A decent handicap run at a good pace, and the easy winner has been rated as value for 13 lengths.

NOTEBOOK
Gallik Dawn, under a confident ride, shrugged off the penalty for his win at Uttoxeter and ran out an easy winner. There should be more to come from this progressive young stayer. *(op 3-1)*
Bright Approach(IRE), due to drop 3lb in future handicaps, ran a solid race but ran into a progressive opponent. He has yet to win outside hunter chases/points.
Presence Of Mind(IRE), under a penalty for his Exeter win, was found out over this longer trip against slightly better opposition. He is probably better going right-handed. *(op 4-1)*
Tipsy Mouse(IRE), showing more zest than of late, made a lot of the running in the first-time blinkers but was beaten with three to jump. *(op 7-1)*
Alpine Slave, whose only chase win to date came at this track, ran a better race than of late but the step up in trip eventually told.
He's The Biz(FR), who was raised 12lb after Worcester, was in about seventh place and not out of contention when coming down. *(op 11-2)*

440 WEATHERBYS CHASE CHAMPION NOVICES' HUNTERS' CHASE (FOR THE JOHN CORBET CUP) (19 fncs 2 omitted) 3m 4f
8:10 (8:12) (Class 6) 5-Y-0+ **£12,478** (£4,864; £2,538; £1,269)

Form RPR

21- **1** **Lord Beau (IRE)**[28] [4963] 9-11-7 MrTJO'Brien[(7)] 113
(A J Bateman) *settled abt 4th and cl up: mstke 10th: led bef 2 out: hrd pressed passing omitted last: drvn and fnd ex: r.o gamely* **13/2**[3]

54/2 **2** *1 ¾* **Marrasit (IRE)**[10] [282] 9-11-0 MrSCharlton[(7)] 104
(H E Thorpe) *pressed ldr: mstke 9th: led 15th: hdd bef 2 out: rallied u.p passing last: no ex fnl 100 yds* **50/1**

3-12 **3** *10* **Imps Way**[15] [196] 10-11-4 MrCMulhall[(3)] 97+
(Mrs T Corrigan-Clark) *hld up in rr: prog after 16th: hmpd 18th: rdn and rallied after 3 out: sn no imp* **20/1**

4U- **4** *17* **Jimmy Cricket**[19] 8-11-7 MrNHOliver[(7)] 84
(Ms Caroline Walker) *sn settled in midfield: effrt bef 18th: sn outpcd: 10l 4th 3 out: wknd* **11/1**

5/P- **F** **Classify**[18] 6-11-11 MrJSnowden[(3)] —
(R Barber) *towards rr whn fell heavily 5th* **11/1**

PP/ **P** **The Grey Baron**[20] 8-11-9 MrPBull[(5)] —
(A Coveney) *sn bhd: struggling 11th: t.o and p.u 17th* **33/1**

1-41 **F** **Vinnie Boy (IRE)**[10] [282] 8-12-0 MissPGundry —
(Mrs O Bush) *handy early: mstke 10th: wkng whn fell 12th* **5/1**[2]

4-21 **P** **Jupiter's Fancy**[8] [322] 10-11-0 TMessenger[(7)] —
(M V Coglan) *travelled bdly in last pair: t.o and p.u 15th* **50/1**

F2 **F** **Raregem**[17] [171] 7-11-7 MrWBiddick[(7)] —
(M Biddick) *hld up towards rr: nt fluent 8th: prog 15th: 3l 5th whn fell 18th* **33/1**

P **Uncle Neil (IRE)**[20] 8-12-0 (b[1]) MrRBurton —
(Mrs Edward Crow) *led: hit 13th: hdd 15th: wkng whn blnd bdly 18th: p.u next* **14/1**

P1-3 **P** **Don Royal**[14] [204] 11-12-0 92 MrNHarris —
(J R Scott) *prom: 4th after 13th: drvn and wknd 16th: t.o and p.u 3 out* **100/1**

P-56 **P** **Nautical Lad**[10] [282] 10-11-7 (p) MrJDocker[(7)] —
(J H Docker) *urged along in rr but nvr looking keen: struggling 12th: t.o and p.u 15th* **33/1**

2-23 **P** **Beauchamp Oracle**[10] [281] 8-11-7 MrMWalford[(7)] —
(S Flook) *midfield: lost pl 14th: tring to cl but rdn and hld whn blnd 18th: p.u next* **28/1**

215- **P** **Denvale (IRE)**[36] [4840] 7-11-11 MrRCope[(3)] —
(Mrs Caroline Bailey) *nvr jumping fluently: midfield tl brief effrt to press ldrs 12th: rdn and wknd next: t.o and p.u 17th* **5/1**[2]

1- **P** **Lord Anner (IRE)**[38] [4818] 6-12-0 MrNWilliams —
(P F Nicholls) *nt fluent: hld up midfield: hdwy and mstke 9th: ev ch whn blnd 16th: 9l 3rd and fading whn slow 3 out: p.u next* **5/2**[1]

12-0 **P** **Silver Castle**[23] [48] 9-11-9 MrsLucyRowsell[(5)] —
(R J Rowsell) *tended to jump rt: prom fr 5th tl lost pl 9th: j. violently 13th and again whn struggling 18th: p.u after 3 out* **10/1**

7m 15.9s (4.60) **Going Correction** +0.35s/f (Yiel) **16** Ran SP% **129.6**
Speed ratings: **93,92,89,84**,— —,—,—,— —,—,—,— —,—,—,— — CSF £304.48 TOTE £7.60: £1.80, £11.80, £9.30; EX 697.60.

Owner P R Bateman **Bred** Michael Maye **Trained** Minehead, Somerset

FOCUS
The leading novice hunter chase of the season although this renewal was probably not that strong. It has been rated through the third. They went a good pace, putting the emphasis on stamina, and only four completed. The last fence was bypassed on the final two circuits.

NOTEBOOK
Lord Beau(IRE) ◆, who appreciated the faster ground, got the better of a drawn-out tussle with the eventual runner-up. He stays really well and, as this was only the fifth race of his life, has plenty of miles left on the clock. *(op 7-1)*

Marrasit(IRE), suited by a thorough stamina test, ran her best race yet and was brave in defeat. Surprisingly, she has yet to break her duck, although she has only run in two point-to-points to date.

Imps Way, patiently ridden again, made steady progress from the rear. She was still a threat after being hampered at the final ditch but faded on the home turn.

Jimmy Cricket won a four-miler between the flags last time and did not fail through lack of stamina.

Denvale(IRE) looked a bright prospect at Towcester but has twice failed to confirm that impression. *(op 4-1 tchd 11-2)*

Raregem had closed into contention when falling foul of the final open ditch. He is a promising youngster but still has something to learn about jumping racecourse fences. *(op 4-1 tchd 11-2)*

Uncle Neil(IRE), successful in his last five points, set a decent pace but had shot his bolt by the time he blundered at the fourth last. *(op 4-1 tchd 11-2)*

Lord Anner(IRE), a huge individual, made a number of jumping errors but remained in contention until weakening quickly at the third last. Although he was still in with a chance of some place money, his rider wisely called it a day. *(op 4-1 tchd 11-2)*

441 IRISH THOROUGHBRED MARKETING H'CAP HURDLE (14 hdls) 3m 3f
8:40 (8:41) (Class 3) (0-125,125) 4-Y-0+
£6,374 (£2,417; £1,208; £549; £274; £164)

Form RPR

5-11 **1** **Altitude Dancer (IRE)**[9] [298] 5-9-8 **100** 7ex SWalsh[(7)] 103+
(Mrs A M Thorpe) *keen: hmpd 5th: mostly 2nd: pckd 9th: led after 3 out: rdn and styd on tenaciously flat* **11/2**[2]

10-3 **2** *½* **Tirikumba**[12] [245] 9-9-9 **99** oh1 RStephens[(5)] 99
(S G Griffiths) *trckd ldrs: wnt cl up after 10th: chsd wnr after 3 out: rdn and no imp fr next* **9/1**

04-2 **3** *2* **Tell The Trees**[7] [329] 4-9-12 **106** TJMalone[(3)] 99+
(M C Pipe) *nt fluent: last tl after 7th: rdn 11th and plenty to do: no real prog tl 2 out: consented to run on stoutly after last* **8/1**

1P4- **4** *nk* **Kjetil (USA)**[27] [4979] 5-10-9 **108** (t) ChristianWilliams 106
(P F Nicholls) *bhd: rdn after 7th: prog after 10th: drvn and little imp fr bef 2 out: 3rd at last tl nr fin* **16/1**

02-1 **5** *2 ½* **Azzemour (FR)**[13] [216] 6-10-2 **101** ow1 (t) RWalsh 97
(P F Nicholls) *hld up in rr: smooth prog after 3 out: wnt 3rd bef next: sn rdn and fnd nil* **7/2**[1]

P2-5 **6** *½* **Unusual Suspect**[12] [233] 6-10-2 **101** (b) RJohnson 96
(G L Moore) *towards rr: drvn to improve after 10th: 4th and u.p after 3 out: fnd nthing bef next* **11/2**[2]

44-2 **7** *¾* **Just Beth**[6] [353] 9-10-10 **114** DLaverty[(5)] 108
(G Fierro) *bhd: prog 7th: hrd drvn 11th: one pce after next* **7/1**[3]

240- **8** *7* **Ice Crystal**[40] [4796] 8-10-13 **117** LStephens[(5)] 104
(W K Goldsworthy) *bef 2 out in rr: rdn and prog 11th: flattered briefly: fdd* **20/1**

10-3 **9** *1 ½* **Simple Glory (IRE)**[21] [94] 6-10-0 **99** oh1 WHutchinson 85
(R Dickin) *led 4th: j.rt after: hdd after 3 out: drvn and wknd on long run to next* **25/1**

206- **10** *dist* **No Picnic (IRE)**[28] [4967] 7-10-12 **114** ONelmes[(3)] —
(Mrs S C Bradburne) *set slow pce tl 4th: prom tl 10th: wkng whn blnd next: btn 58l* **10/1**

420- **11** *9* **Cosi Celeste (FR)**[65] [4404] 8-9-10 **100** oh6 ow1 MNicolls[(5)] —
(John Allen) *bhd: last at 10th: t.o 3 out: btn 67l* **40/1**

33P- **P** **Pougatcheva (FR)**[33] [4876] 6-10-7 **106** AO'Keeffe —
(Miss Venetia Williams) *sn midfield: wknd after 10th: t.o and p.u 2 out* **33/1**

61-P **P** **Sungates (IRE)**[17] [168] 9-11-2 **115** ATinkler —
(C Tinkler) *cl up whn stmbld 6th: rdn after 9th: sn dropped out: t.o and p.u after 3 out* **12/1**

6m 38.2s (4.40) **Going Correction** +0.275s/f (Yiel)
WFA 4 from 5yo+ 6lb **13** Ran SP% **123.3**
Speed ratings: **104,103,103,103,102 102,102,99,99**,— —,—,— CSF £53.86 CT £405.82 TOTE £7.70: £2.50, £3.20, £3.00; EX 117.00 Place 6 £514.20, Place 5 £166.78..

Owner Mrs A M Thorpe **Bred** M L Page And Orpendale **Trained** Bronwydd Arms, Carmarthens

FOCUS
A fair handicap in which Altitude Dancer has been rated as value for a bit further.

NOTEBOOK
Altitude Dancer(IRE), able to race off the same mark as when scoring at Exeter despite his penalty, was officially 5lb well in. Completing the hat-trick in game style, he has abundant stamina. *(op 5-1 tchd 9-2)*

Tirikumba, tackling her longest trip to date, went down fighting. This was just about her best run yet over hurdles. *(op 11-1)*

Tell The Trees, tackling this marathon trip for the first time, was held up a good way off the pace. She only really began to close from the second last and never reached the leading pair. *(op 7-1)*

Kjetil(USA), back over hurdles, was without the blinkers. Another upped in trip, he was found wanting from the second last.

Azzemour(FR) looked a threat on the turn for home but was then found out by the 6lb rise for his Warwick victory coupled with the extra demands of this trip. *(tchd 4-1 in places)*

Unusual Suspect did not fail through lack of stamina. *(op 15-2)*

T/Plt: £181.60 to a £1 stake. Pool: £50,340.65. 202.30 winning tickets. T/Qpdt: £70.60 to a £1 stake. Pool: £3,773.60. 39.50 winning tickets. IM

442 - 449a (Foreign Racing) - See Raceform Interactive

436 STRATFORD (L-H)

Saturday, May 21

OFFICIAL GOING: Soft

There were 24 non-runners due to the fact the going changed to soft after 6mm of rain before racing on already watered ground.

Wind: almost nil Weather: Fine after heavy rain before racing

450 PERTEMPS H'CAP HURDLE (9 hdls) 2m 110y

5:45 (5:46) (Class 3) (0-135,135) 4-Y-0+

£12,644 (£4,796; £2,398; £1,090; £545; £327)

Form			Horse	Jockey	SP	RPR
61-1	1		**Darrias (GER)**[11] 274 4-10-10 **123**	ChristianWilliams		126+
			(P F Nicholls) *hld up and bhd: hdwy 6th: led and nt fluent last: drvn out*		9/1	
110-	2	2 ½	**Genuine Article (IRE)**[203] 1907 9-10-1 **110**	GLee		114
			(M Pitman) *led: hit and hdd 6th: led 2 out to last: nt qckn*		8/1	
522-	3	2 ½	**Alrafid (IRE)**[68] 4362 6-10-6 **115**	PHide		116
			(G L Moore) *t.k.h: sn mid-div: hdwy appr 6th: rdn and one pce fr 2 out*		16/1	
12-2	4	1 ½	**Afrad (FR)**[24] 65 4-11-0 **127**	MAFitzgerald		124+
			(N J Henderson) *hld up in tch: hit 6th: rdn appr 2 out: one pce*		7/1³	
223-	5	½	**Dominican Monk (IRE)**[170] 2593 6-10-11 **120**	TDoyle		119
			(C Tinkler) *hld up in tch: ev ch whn nt fluent 2 out: wknd last*		16/1	
356-	6	6	**Xellance (IRE)**[28] 4982 8-10-12 **121**	RJohnson		114
			(P J Hobbs) *prom: rdn appr 3 out: wknd appr 2 out*		11/1	
1-00	7	5	**Constantine**[8] 332 5-10-1 **117**	EDehdashti(7)		105
			(G L Moore) *mid-div: rdn after 5th: no hdwy fr 3 out*		33/1	
241-	8	2	**Norma Hill**[42] 4777 4-11-1 **128**	DRDennis		110
			(R Hollinshead) *prom: led 6th: hit 3 out: hdd 2 out: sn wknd*		25/1	
/20-	9	3 ½	**Society Buck (IRE)**[188] 2213 8-10-5 **119**	MNicolls(5)		102
			(John Allen) *hld up towards rr: rdn after 5th: nvr nr ldrs*		66/1	
-021	10	1	**Forzacurity**[7] 347 6-9-11 **111** oh1 ow2	LStephens(5)		93
			(M Sheppard) *prom tl wknd after 3 out*		12/1	
01-3	11	½	**Conroy**[7] 347 6-10-4 **113**	LAspell		94
			(F Jordan) *hld up and bhd: hdwy appr 6th: wknd appr 2 out*		20/1	
641-	12	2 ½	**Full Irish (IRE)**[35] 4863 9-11-2 **125**	ADobbin		104
			(L Lungo) *nvr gng wl: nt fluent 3rd: j.rt 5th and 6th: a bhd*		9/2²	
P3P-	13	shd	**Caracciola (GER)**[44] 4751 8-11-5 **135**	VConte(7)		113
			(N J Henderson) *j.rt 5th: a bhd*		20/1	
111-	14	10	**Zonergem**[17] 1792 7-11-3 **129**	MrTGreenall(3)		97
			(Lady Herries) *a bhd*		4/1¹	
44-4	F		**Siegfrieds Night (IRE)**[6] 372 4-10-1 **117**	ACCoyle(3)		92
			(M C Chapman) *prom: wknd after 6th: hit 3 out: no ch whn fell last*		33/1	

4m 1.40s (3.00) **Going Correction** +0.375s/f (Yiel)

WFA 4 from 5yo+ 4lb **38** Ran SP% **120.3**

Speed ratings: **107,105,104,103,103 100,98,97,95,95 95,94,94,89,**— CSF £72.40 CT £1150.51 TOTE £11.20: £4.30, £2.40, £4.90; EX 108.20.

Owner Formpave Ltd **Bred** Gestut Rottgen **Trained** Ditcheat, Somerset

FOCUS

A very competitive handicap won by an improving type. The form is rated through the third and fifth.

NOTEBOOK

Darrias(GER), a progressive novice, completed a hat-trick on this transition to handicaps despite connections having reservations about the soft ground. *(op 8-1 tchd 10-1)*

Genuine Article(IRE), a winner on all five of his previous visits here, lost little in defeat on his first outing for nearly seven months. He won his bumper on this sort of ground but he seems at his best on a sound surface. *(op 9-1)*

Alrafid(IRE), who not for the first time proved difficult to settle, gave a good account of himself and does seem to handle all types of ground. *(op 12-1)*

Afrad(FR) developed into a decent novice hurdler last season and the Handicapper had given him his fair share of weight. *(op 13-2 tchd 8-1)*

Dominican Monk(IRE) was not disgraced on his first start for nearly six months on ground that would have been plenty soft enough for him. Improvement can be expected. *(tchd 18-1)*

Xellance(IRE) ran well for a long way over a trip well short of his best. *(op 10-1)*

Zonergem was always out with the washing on this rain-softened ground. *Official explanation: trainer said the gelding was unsuited by soft ground (op 9-2)*

451 JENKINSONS CATERERS AMATEUR RIDERS' H'CAP HURDLE (10 hdls) 2m 3f

6:15 (6:18) (Class 4) (0-110,109) 4-Y-0+ **£4,221** (£1,299; £649; £324)

Form			Horse	Jockey	SP	RPR
4-00	1		**Ressource (FR)**[11] 283 6-9-9 **85**	(b) MrWRussell(7)		89+
			(G L Moore) *hld up and bhd: hdwy on ins whn nt clr run bnd after 3 out: sn swtchd rt: swtchd lft and led last: r.o wl*		25/1	
16-F	2	4	**Hattington**[24] 54 7-11-8 **105**	MrTGreenall		103
			(M F Harris) *led: hdd appr 2 out: sn rdn: led briefly appr last: nt qckn*		8/1³	
	3	2	**Mantras (FR)**[624] 6-11-5 **109**	MrRQuinn(7)		105
			(M C Pipe) *a.p: rdn to ld appr 2 out: hdd appr last: one pce*		10/1	
43-0	4	½	**Megapac (IRE)**[21] 121 7-11-0 **97** ow1	(v¹) MrNHarris		93
			(Noel T Chance) *hld up towards rr: hdwy after 5th: sltly outpcd 3 out: kpt on same pce fr 2 out*		16/1	
10-4	5	¾	**Half Inch**[13] 247 5-10-13 **103**	TMessenger(7)		98
			(B I Case) *a.p: one pce fr 3 out*		10/1	
0F-P	6	3 ½	**Haydens Field**[24] 54 11-11-3 **105**	MrJCook(5)		97
			(Miss H Lewis) *hld up and bhd: hdwy after 2 out: nt rch ldrs*		16/1	
40-4	7	½	**Antigiotto (IRE)**[13] 243 4-10-7 **102**	MrTJO'Brien(7)		88
			(P Bowen) *hld up: hdwy after 5th: wknd appr last*		10/1	
050-	8	4	**Killer Cat (FR)**[61] 4496 4-10-3 **98**	AGlassonbury(7)		82+
			(M C Pipe) *hld up towards rr: rdn appr 6th: nvr trbld ldrs*		14/1	
U3-3	9	6	**Mistified (IRE)**[13] 229 4-10-2 **95**	WPKavanagh(5)		72+
			(J W Mullins) *nvr nr ldrs*		11/1	
5-01	10	1	**Time Marches On**[13] 233 7-10-10 **100**	JReveley(7)		80
			(K G Reveley) *n.d*		7/2¹	
526-	11	1	**Hamadeenah**[31] 4932 7-11-5 **107**	MrDEdwards(5)		86
			(C J Down) *chsd ldrs: pushed along 4th: wknd after 5th*		25/1	
400-	12	2 ½	**Euro Bleu (FR)**[31] 4932 7-10-7 **97**	MissALStennett(7)		74
			(Mrs L Wadham) *prom tl wknd after 3 out*		16/1	
033-	13	¾	**Knightsbridge King**[92] 3923 9-10-10 **98**	MrPCallaghan(5)		74
			(John Allen) *a bhd*		16/1	
22-1	14	4	**Alessandro Severo**[18] 167 6-10-6 **94**	(v) MrsLucyRowsell(5)		66
			(Mrs D A Hamer) *prom tl rdn and wknd appr 2 out*		7/1²	
35-P	15	24	**Oro Street (IRE)**[13] 237 9-10-0 **90**	MrDanielChinn(7)		38
			(G F Bridgwater) *a bhd: t.o fr 5th*		66/1	
23/R	16	1	**Estuary (USA)**[6] 363 10-9-10 **86** ow1	MissLisaMarriott(7)		33
			(Ms A E Embiricos) *hld up in tch: wknd 6th: t.o*		80/1	
PP0-	P		**Yer Father's Yacht (IRE)**[268] 1294 5-10-13 **103**	MrJNewbold(7)		—
			(Lady Connell) *mid-div: bhd whn p.u bef 7th*		100/1	

4m 48.2s (12.90) **Going Correction** +0.625s/f (Soft)

WFA 4 from 5yo+ 4lb **17** Ran SP% **123.0**

Speed ratings: **97,95,94,94,93 92,92,90,88,87 87,86,85,84,74 73,**— CSF £212.27 CT £2166.93 TOTE £41.40: £8.20, £2.10, £2.60, £2.90; EX 382.60.

Owner Miss S M Eastes **Bred** W Wolf **Trained** Woodingdean, E Sussex

FOCUS

A modest handicap but the winner was well-in on old form and was value for a bit further than the official margin of victory.

NOTEBOOK

Ressource(FR), who had previously shown he could handle soft ground albeit at a low level, finally lost his maiden tag and also gave his rider his first winner.

Hattington, who stays further, adopted a change of tactics with the big change in the going putting more of an emphasis on stamina.

Mantras(FR), three times a winner on good ground over hurdles and fences in the French Provinces in 2003, had not been seen since September of that year. The soft going should not have bothered him and Martin Pipe will have had him pretty straight. *(op 7-1 tchd 13-2)*

Megapac(IRE) may have been helped by the fact that the emphasis had switched to stamina in the soft ground and kept plugging away in the first-time visor. *(op 20-1)*

Half Inch appeared to get the longer trip well enough especially considering the ground had changed quite dramatically. *(op 9-1)*

Haydens Field has always done best when able to dominate and got going too late over a trip short of his best. *(op 10-1)*

Time Marches On, raised 6lb for winning a similar event over further at Plumpton last time, was *never in contention and this softer ground would not have been an excuse.Official explanation: trainer said the gelding was never travelling (op 5-1)*

452 IRISH THOROUGHBRED MARKETING H'CAP CHASE (13 fncs) 2m 1f 110y

6:45 (6:47) (Class 3) (0-135,135) 5-Y-£9,234 (£3,532; £1,789; £839; £443)

Form			Horse	Jockey	SP	RPR
030-	1		**Ghadames (FR)**[43] 4764 11-10-12 **121**	(p) HOliver		136+
			(R C Guest) *hld up: hdwy 7th: led 2 out: rdn clr last: eased towards fin*		8/1	
316-	2	9	**Old Marsh (IRE)**[44] 4751 9-11-5 **128**	JCulloty		136+
			(A W Carroll) *hld up: hdwy 7th: ev ch whn pckd 2 out: 4 l 2nd and btn whn blnd last*		4/1²	
3P-2	3	14	**Odagh Odyssey (IRE)**[22] 108 11-10-13 **122**	(v) BJCrowley		111+
			(Miss E C Lavelle) *mstkes: bhd fr 3rd: no ch whn blnd bdly last*		6/1³	
300-	4	1	**Power Unit**[68] 4371 10-10-0 **109** oh2	BHitchcott		95
			(Mrs D A Hamer) *wl bhd fr 6th*		25/1	
610-	5	18	**Palua**[64] 4437 8-11-5 **135**	(v¹) PCO'Neill(7)		103
			(Miss E C Lavelle) *chsd ldr tl appr 9th: sn wknd*		15/2	
/32-	F		**Lewis Island (IRE)**[15] 4369 6-10-6 **115**	(t) GLee		—
			(B Ellison) *hld up: bdly hmpd and fell 7th*		7/1	
230-	F		**Golden Crusader**[49] 4693 8-9-13 **111**	RYoung(3)		114
			(J W Mullins) *led: clr 8th: mstke 4 out: hdd and fell 2 out*		16/1	
056-	P		**Made In France (FR)**[29] 4974 5-10-10 **121**	APMcCoy		—
			(M C Pipe) *prom: j. bdly lft 7th: sn wknd: t.o whn p.u after 3 out*		11/4¹	
15P-	P		**Emperors Guest**[37] 4838 7-10-13 **122**	(b) NFehily		—
			(C J Mann) *hld up in tch: bdly hmpd and lost pl 7th: t.o whn p.u bef 4 out*		11/1	

4m 20.6s (8.10) **Going Correction** +0.625s/f (Soft)

WFA 5 from 6yo+ 2lb **21** Ran SP% **114.4**

Speed ratings: **107,103,96,96,88** —,—,—,— CSF £40.67 CT £206.90 TOTE £10.50: £2.40, £2.20, £1.40; EX 49.70.

Owner Paul Beck **Bred** Mrs A Daubin And Mrs Jean-Francois Daubin **Trained** Brancepeth, Co Durham

FOCUS

A race decimated by five withdrawals because of the soft ground. The impressive winner is rated value for seven lengths and, with the second and faller pretty much to marks, the form should work out.

NOTEBOOK

Ghadames(FR) had the cheekpieces back on after never featuring in the Topham at Aintree. With the rain-softened ground holding no terrors for him, he jumped the last two fences much better than the runner-up. *(op 10-1)*

Old Marsh(IRE) found that nodding on landing at the tricky penultimate fence put him on the back foot and he was fighting a losing battle when getting the last all wrong. He prefers a sounder surface. *(tchd 11-2)*

Odagh Odyssey(IRE) was let down by his jumping. *(op 5-1)*

Golden Crusader appeared to be about to have his measure taken when coming to grief at the second last. *(op 7-2)*

Made In France(FR) could never get to his favourite front-running position. *(op 7-2)*

453 47TH RUNNING OF THE INTRUM JUSTITIA CUP CHAMPION HUNTERS' CHASE (21 fncs) 3m 4f

7:20 (7:23) (Class 2) 5-Y-0+ **£18,656** (£7,136; £3,616; £1,696; £896)

Form			Horse	Jockey	SP	RPR
2-31	1		**Mrs Be (IRE)**[13] 231 9-11-7 108	MissPGundry		118+
			(J G Cann) *trckd ldrs on outside: effrt 14th: wnt 2nd appr 17th: drvn to ld bef 2 out: readily drew clr*		4/1¹	
/12-	2	6	**Yeoman Sailor (IRE)**[35] 4870 11-12-0	MrNHarris		119
			(Ms Grace Muir) *led after 5th: 7l clr 18th: rdn and hdd bef 2 out: kpt on gamely: no ch w wnr*		5/1²	
6-11	3	8	**No Retreat (NZ)**[7] 348 12-12-0 111	MrWHill		111
			(J Groucott) *sn prom: nt fluent 8th: rdn and wknd appr 18th*		5/1²	
2-2U	4	9	**Mullensgrove**[15] 204 11-12-0 103	MissSSharratt		103+
			(D Lowe) *handy early: sn mid field: wnt 3rd briefly bef 15th: rdn bef 17th: wknd 3 out*		20/1	
/3-1	5	28	**Be My Dream (IRE)**[15] 204 10-12-0	MrMWilesmith		77+
			(Mrs C Wilesmith) *nt a fluent: chsd ldrs: rdn after 15th: wknd bef 18th: t.o*		16/1	
121-	P		**Mr Mahdlo**[30] 4947 11-12-0 97	MrMWalford		—
			(R D E Woodhouse) *cl up tl 12th: rdn and lost pl 13th: t.o whn p.u 2 out*		12/1	
5-36	P		**Guignol Du Cochet (FR)**[11] 280 11-12-0 95	MrAWintle		—
			(S Flook) *hld up in rr: drvn 15th: sn struggling: t.o and p.u 18th*		100/1	
F2-2	P		**Silver Streak (IRE)**[7] 11-12-0 90	MrRArmson		—
			(Milson Robinson) *mid field: reminders 11th: wknd u.p 14th: t.o and p.u 17th*		40/1	

/31- **R** **Sir D'Orton (FR)**[21] 9-12-0 113................................ MissCTizzard —
(A J Tizzard) *towards rr: mstke 5th: nt fluent next: struggling fr 14th: t.o whn ref last* **20/1**

3P-5 **P** **Blyth Brook**[24] [63] 13-12-0 87.................................. MrRMorgan —
(W T Reed) *led tl after 5th: pressed ldr tl 13th: wkng whn mstke 17th: t.o and p.u 3 out* **100/1**

U-12 **P** **Chasing The Bride**[11] [272] 12-12-0 .... MissAGoschen —
(Miss A Goschen) *j. slowly in last: hit 13th: struggling whn mstke 15th: t.o and p.u 2 out* **20/1**

6-61 **F** **Sikander A Azam**[17] [184] 12-12-0 .... MrTGreenall 91
(David M Easterby) *hld up and bhd: nt fluent 11th: effrt bef 17th: no ch w ldrs tl bef 3 out: mod 6th whn fell next* **16/1**

/11- **F** **Ask The Natives (IRE)**[35] [4870] 11-12-0 .... MissCRoddick 96
(Miss C Roddick) *bhd: mstke 7th and reminder: hit 10th: hdwy 16th: 6l 3rd whn mstke 3 out: sn wknd: 5th whn fell next* **11/2**[3]

2-15 **P** **Caught At Dawn (IRE)**[11] [280] 11-12-0 .... MrTWeston —
(M H Weston) *mid-field: nt fluent 2nd: mstke 13th: effrt 15th: chsng ldrs whn blnd 17th and rdr lost iron: nt rcvr: bhd whn p.u 3 ou* **7/1**

7m 29.7s (18.40) **Going Correction** +0.775s/f (Soft) **14** Ran SP% **119.4**
Speed ratings: **104,102,100,97,89** —,—,—,—,— —,—,—,— CSF £22.12 TOTE £5.80: £1.50, £2.60, £2.90; EX 41.20.
Owner J H Burbidge **Bred** Edmond Cogan **Trained** Cullompton, Devon.

FOCUS
This was not a great renewal of the race formerly known as The Horse and Hound Cup.

NOTEBOOK
Mrs Be(IRE) is an out-and-out stayer who loved the fact that the heavy rain had made this into a real stamina test. *(op 13-2 tchd 7-1)*
Yeoman Sailor(IRE) ran another fine race on ground that would have been slower than ideal for him. *(op 3-1)*
No Retreat(NZ) had finished 12 lengths in front of the winner when dead-heating over the extended four miles on good ground at Cheltenham last month. *(op 13-2)*
Mullensgrove has yet to show he can be effective over this sort of distance, especially on soft ground. *(op 14-1)*
Ask The Natives(IRE) was fighting a losing battle after an error three out and came down at the next. *(op 4-1)*

454 GEORGE JONES MEMORIAL H'CAP CHASE (FOR THE GAMBLING PRINCE TROPHY) (16 fncs) 2m 5f 110y
7:50 (7:50) (Class 2) (0-140,137) 5-Y-0+**£12,378** (£4,825; £2,517; £1,258)

Form RPR

2F4- **1** **Spring Margot (FR)**[29] [4972] 9-10-12 **123**.............................. APMcCoy 139+
(P F Nicholls) *a.p: led 10th to 11th: led 12th: clr 3 out: j.lft 2 out: easily* **3/1**[1]

64-1 **2** *13* **Tamango (FR)**[22] [103] 8-10-9 **120**.. RJohnson 125+
(P J Hobbs) *a.p: pckd 7th: chsd wnr appr 12th: no imp fr 4 out* **7/2**[2]

3-21 **3** *8* **Sky Warrior (FR)**[13] [248] 7-11-3 **128**........................ ChristianWilliams 122
(Evan Williams) *prom: lost pl 7th: struggling 9th: wnt mod 3rd 2 out* **9/1**

2F4- **4** *9* **Marked Man (IRE)**[38] [4822] 9-11-3 **128**.................................. TDoyle 119+
(R Lee) *hld up and bhd: blnd 7th: mstke 8th: wknd after 3 out: disputing 3rd whn blnd bdly 2 out* **15/2**

23P- **P** **The Bandit (IRE)**[66] [4398] 8-11-5 **130**................................. JAMcCarthy —
(Miss E C Lavelle) *chsd ldr: led 11th to 12th: sn wknd: t.o whn p.u bef 2 out* **4/1**[3]

1P3- **P** **Harapour (FR)**[36] [4848] 7-11-7 **132**... PJBrennan —
(P F Nicholls) *hld up: mstkes 5th and 8th: hdwy 9th: wknd 11th: t.o whn p.u bef 4 out* **12/1**

024- **P** **Jimmy Tennis (FR)**[35] [4869] 8-10-3 **114**.............................(b) SThomas —
(Miss Venetia Williams) *led: mstke 4th: hdd 10th: wknd 12th: blnd 4 out: t.o whn p.u bef 2 out* **6/1**

5m 26.9s (12.50) **Going Correction** +0.775s/f (Soft) **7** Ran SP% **111.0**
Speed ratings: **108,103,100,97**,— —,— CSF £13.44 CT £77.89 TOTE £3.90: £1.70, £2.20; EX 9.00.
Owner Sir Robert Ogden **Bred** Yves Bourdin And Jean-Pierre Rouillay **Trained** Ditcheat, Somerset

FOCUS
Several of these were let down by their jumping in the soft ground, and with the second and third below their best it is not form to be confident about rating.

NOTEBOOK
Spring Margot(FR) had previously shown he could handle testing conditions and made short work of the remaining opposition. *(tchd 10-3)*
Tamango(FR), raised 5lb, has scored on good to soft over hurdles but proved no match for the winner on this ground. *(op 3-1)*
Sky Warrior(FR) was in trouble with a circuit to go. *(op 10-1 tchd 11-1)*
Marked Man(IRE) was one of those whose jumping was found wanting on ground softer than he prefers. *(op 7-1 tchd 8-1)*

455 STRATFORD MILLENNIUM ROSE BOWL LADIES' HUNTERS' CHASE (17 fncs 1 omitted) 3m
8:20 (8:20) (Class 6) 5-Y-0+ **£3,581** (£1,102; £551; £275)

Form RPR

/53- **1** **Tales Of Bounty (IRE)**[13] 10-10-10 106...................(b) MissRAGreen(7) 96+
(R Barber) *nearly uns rdr 1st: nt a fluent in rr: mstke 13th: stdy prog 15th: 6l 5th 3 out: cajoled along to ld last: rdn out* **9/2**[3]

3- **2** *1 ½* **Double Ange (FR)**[20] 7-10-7 .... MissFWilson(7) 89
(Mrs Katie Baimbridge) *hld up: hdwy 11th: wnt 2nd at 13th: led next: rdn and hdd last: nt qckn* **4/1**[2]

3 *3* **Sing High**[7] 9-10-0 .... MissHannahWatson(7) 79
(Mrs Rosemary Gasson) *keen in rr: hdwy 8th: wnt 2nd at 11th: demoted 14th: rdn and ev ch passing 2 out: btn whn hit last* **50/1**

FPP/ **4** *6* **Keltic Lord**[21] 9-10-11 ....(t) MissAGoschen(3) 82+
(Miss S Waugh) *mid field: nt fluent 3rd: mstke 10th: outpcd after 14th: unable to chal after* **14/1**

4-P4 **5** *¾* **Mydante (IRE)**[15] [204] 10-10-3 79...............................(t) MissSSharratt(7) 78+
(S Flook) *j. slowly and sn last: hmpd 9th: effrt after mstke 13th: one pce fr 3 out: mstke last* **13/2**

6- **6** *14* **Skip 'N' Tune (IRE)**[13] 8-10-2 .... MissCStucley(5) 58
(R N Miller) *nt fluent 6th: lost 2nd next: lft in ld and hmpd 9th: hdd and mstke 15th: sn wknd* **14/1**

03-4 **U** **Ikdam Melody (IRE)**[16] [196] 9-10-10 93...................(p) MissJFoster(7) —
(Miss J E Foster) *chsd ldr: blnd and uns rdr 7th* **9/2**[3]

/4-2 **F** **Derrintogher Yank (IRE)**[17] [184] 11-10-7 ...... MissRachelReynolds(7) —
(Miss R S Reynolds) *keen in ld tl fell 9th* **7/2**[1]

30-0 **P** **Fairtoto**[9] [313] 9-10-7 64.. MissAdeLisleWells(7) —
(M D Jones) *tubed: mid field: rdn 12th: wkng whn hit next: t.o and p.u last* **25/1**

6m 24.4s (22.20) **Going Correction** +0.85s/f (Soft) **9** Ran SP% **111.1**
Speed ratings: **97,96,95,93,93 88**,—,—,— CSF £22.18 TOTE £4.00: £2.00, £1.80, £5.20; EX 25.70.
Owner H B Geddes **Bred** John O'Connor And Jeremiah Aherne **Trained** Beaminster, Dorset

FOCUS
A race greatly weakened by the fact that the anticipated three market leaders were all scratched.

NOTEBOOK
Tales Of Bounty(IRE) should have won his last two points but ran out when looking the likely winner at Staffords Cross. *Already proven in soft ground, he overcame some indifferent jumping. (op 4-1 tchd 7-2)*
Double Ange(FR) had been troublesome at the start when all out to land a ladies open at Cold Harbour last time. This soft ground winner over fences in France did nothing wrong here and it was simply a case of meeting one too good. *(tchd 9-2)*
Sing High, mounted on the course and taken down early, had only been successful once in 23 points. *(op 20-1)*

456 GGBET.COM NOVICES' H'CAP HURDLE (9 hdls) 2m 110y
8:50 (8:50) (Class 4) (0-105,102) 4-Y-0+ **£4,340** (£1,410; £759)

Form RPR

000- **1** **Front Rank (IRE)**[22] [4554] 5-11-8 **98**................................(b) JPMcNamara 106+
(K C Bailey) *a.p: led on bit after 3 out: clr 2 out: easily* **4/1**[2]

000- **2** *12* **Virtus**[164] [2705] 5-10-7 **83**... RJohnson 79
(P J Hobbs) *hld up and bhd: hdwy whn blnd 6th: rdn 3 out: lft 2nd 2 out: no ch w wnr* **9/2**[3]

45-0 **3** *5* **Compton Star**[26] [25] 5-9-11 **80**.. JamesWhite(7) 73+
(R J Hodges) *hld up in mid-div: rdn and hdwy whn nt fluent 3 out: wkng whn hmpd 2 out: lft 3rd last* **11/2**

/6-0 **P** **Bravura**[15] [203] 7-10-13 **89**..(b) PHide —
(G L Moore) *a bhd: t.o whn p.u bef 2 out* **20/1**

00-5 **P** **Seal Of Office**[21] [133] 6-10-13 **89**..................................... JAMcCarthy —
(A M Hales) *a bhd: hit 5th: mstke 6th: t.o whn p.u bef 3 out* **16/1**

230- **U** **Bestam**[16] [4166] 6-11-3 **93**.. SThomas 86
(G C Bravery) *prom: ev ch after 3 out: 2nd and wkng whn blnd and uns rdr 2 out* **8/1**

00-5 **F** **Bottom Drawer**[18] [172] 5-10-8 **89**...................................... RStephens(5) 82
(Mrs D A Hamer) *prom: ev ch after 3 out: sn wknd: 3rd and btn whn fell last* **16/1**

04-1 **P** **Lawaaheb (IRE)**[17] [180] 4-11-1 **95**.................................(v) MAFitzgerald —
(B R Johnson) *led after 2nd to 4th: wknd after 3 out: t.o whn p.u bef 2 out* **3/1**[1]

060- **P** **Claim To Fame**[114] [3554] 4-10-2 **82**.. ATinkler —
(M Pitman) *hld up and bhd: mstke 2nd: hit 3rd: rdn after 5th: t.o whn p.u bef 3 out* **16/1**

530- **P** **Blazeaway (USA)**[235] [1529] 5-10-6 **82**..............................(b) TScudamore —
(R S Brookhouse) *led tl after 2nd: led 4th tl after 3 out: sn wknd: t.o whn p.u bef 2 out* **20/1**

4m 11.7s (13.30) **Going Correction** +0.85s/f (Soft)
WFA 4 from 5yo+ 4lb **10** Ran SP% **116.8**
Speed ratings: **102,96,94**,—,— —,—,—,—,— CSF £22.89 CT £96.80 TOTE £6.20: £2.00, £2.40, £1.80; EX 28.30 Place 6 £91.73, Place 5 £57.74.
Owner Off The Bridle Partnership **Bred** Ballymacoll Stud Farm Ltd **Trained** Preston Capes, Northants

FOCUS
With six withdrawals because of the soft ground this was little better than a seller. The winner was very well in on the best of his winter form.

NOTEBOOK
Front Rank(IRE), fit from the Flat, had not worn blinkers since being highly tried on his first two outings over timber last year. They certainly appeared to do the trick here, although the value of the form remains to be seen.
Virtus, who had shown little in his previous outings, was just working his way into the picture when making a hash of the fourth last. *(op 4-1)*
Compton Star would have preferred better ground but has already been beaten in sellers. *(op 6-1)*
Seal Of Office *Official explanation: jockey said the gelding was never travelling (op 7-2)*
Lawaaheb(IRE), a winner on the Polytrack, was left floundering in the soft ground. *(op 7-2)*
Claim To Fame *Official explanation: jockey said the gelding was never travelling (op 7-2)*
T/Plt: £1,419.60 to a £1 stake. Pool: £44,534.45. 22.90 winning tickets. T/Qpdt: £48.10 to a £1 stake. Pool: £4,995.60. 76.70 winning tickets. KH

[271]HEREFORD (R-H)
Sunday, May 22

OFFICIAL GOING: Good to firm changing to good to soft after race 2 (2.40)
Wind: Moderate, across Weather: Heavy rain before race 2 until after race 3; fine otherwise

457 BURCOTT NOVICES' HURDLE (8 hdls) 2m 1f
2:10 (2:11) (Class 4) 4-Y-0+ **£3,935** (£1,211; £605; £302)

Form RPR

416- **1** **Buena Vista (IRE)**[67] [4399] 4-10-10 .... APMcCoy 121+
(M C Pipe) *chsd ldr: led 5th: clr after 3 out: easily* **8/11**[1]

04-2 **2** *12* **Text**[28] [3] 4-10-7 109... RHobson(3) 101+
(C J Down) *a.p: chsd wnr fr 5th: hit 2 out: no imp* **6/1**[3]

33-1 **3** *13* **Kilindini**[14] [230] 4-11-3 .... BJCrowley 95+
(Miss E C Lavelle) *led to 5th: rdn and wknd appr 2 out* **7/2**[2]

0P- **4** *8* **Tuesday's Child**[170] [2604] 6-11-0 .... JCulloty 83
(Miss H C Knight) *hld up in mid-div: sme hdwy appr 5th: no further prog* **14/1**

0P-F **5** *4* **Queen Excalibur**[24] [77] 6-10-2 .... LStephens(5) 72
(C Roberts) *hld up and bhd: hdwy whn nt fluent 3 out: no further prog* **50/1**

PP3/ **6** *3* **Harry B**[13] [3841] 6-10-11 ow4.. MrSGray(7) 80
(R J Price) *hld up in mid-div: short-lived effrt 5th* **28/1**

7 *1* **Heisse**[75] 5-11-0 .... DRDennis 75
(Ian Williams) *j.big 1st: nvr nr ldrs* **12/1**

8 *7* **Irish Playwright (IRE)**[33] 5-11-0 .... OMcPhail 68
(D G Bridgwater) *a bhd* **100/1**

9 *10* **Bobering**[24] 5-11-0 .... JMogford 58
(B P J Baugh) *mstke 3rd: a bhd* **125/1**

P/P- **10** *5* **Frazers Fortune**[56] [4583] 5-11-0 .... SCurran 53
(H J Manners) *chsd ldrs tl wknd appr 3 out: nt fluent 3 out: sn bhd* **125/1**

/00- **11** *10* **Plantagenet Prince**[60] [4526] 6-11-0 .... JTizzard 43
(M Scudamore) *bhd fr 4th* **80/1**

0 **12** *6* **Weet An Haul**[28] [3] 4-10-7 ....(t) ONelmes(3) 33
(T Wall) *bhd fr 4th* **150/1**

0/P- **P** **Palmac's Pride**[220] [1714] 5-11-0 .... LAspell —
(P G Murphy) *a bhd: t.o whn p.u bef last* **100/1**

0-0 **P** **Oui Exit (FR)**[12] [277] 4-10-10 .... JamesDavies —
(M Scudamore) *plld hrd: a bhd: j. slowly 5th: t.o whn p.u bef 3 out* **100/1**

3m 50.4s (-12.70) **Going Correction** -0.65s/f (Firm) **14** Ran SP% **120.6**
Speed ratings: **103,97,91,87,85 84,83,80,75,73 68,65,—,—** CSF £5.85 TOTE £1.70: £1.10, £1.80, £1.30; EX 5.90.
Owner M Archer & The Late Jean Broadhurst **Bred** Lodge Park Stud **Trained** Nicholashayne, Devon

FOCUS
Not many got into this. The winner was value for 20 lengths and ran close to the level of his Cheltenham bumper effort.

NOTEBOOK
Buena Vista(IRE) ◆, sixth in the Champion Bumper at Cheltenham, ran out a very easy winner on this hurdling debut. Jumping well, bar rapping the last, he coasted home and looks a smart novice for the time of year. *(tchd 4-5 and 5-6 in places)*
Text was no match for the promising winner but continues to progress and his turn will come. *(op 13-2 tchd 7-1)*
Kilindini, adopting the tactics he showed when off the mark at Plumpton, was a little keen and had nothing to offer when passed by the favourite.
Tuesday's Child, off the track since his hurdling debut in December, showed his first sign of ability but was beaten a long way. *(op 18-1)*
Queen Excalibur, who took a heavy fall here on her previous start, was never a factor. *(op 33-1 tchd 66-1)*
Heisse, formerly useful on the Flat, did not jump fluently on this hurdling debut but gave the *impression he can do better given experience.Official explanation: jockey said the gelding had a breathing problem (op 14-1 tchd 16-1)*

458 HATTERALL HALL (S) HURDLE (10 hdls) 2m 3f 110y
2:40 (2:46) (Class 5) 4-Y-0+ **£2,394** (£684; £342)

Form RPR

P2-6 **1** **Burning Truth (USA)**[14] [248] 11-10-12 113 .... DRDennis 92+
(M Sheppard) *mde all: clr 7th: rdn appr last: unchal* **3/1**[1]

4P-3 **2** *7* **Mead (IRE)**[22] [129] 8-10-12 86 .... (t) CLlewellyn 86+
(D J Wintle) *hld up: hdwy appr 7th: stmbld 2 out: chsd wnr appr last: kpt on: nt trble wnr* **3/1**[1]

4-02 **3** *13* **Spectacular Hope**[13] [263] 5-10-7 84 .... RYoung(3) 69+
(J W Mullins) *hld up in mid-div: hdwy 5th: chsd wnr appr 7th tl appr last: sn wknd* **10/1**

0/ **4** *1 ¼* **Kilrossanty (IRE)**[22] 6-10-12 .... JPMcNamara 69
(R Flint) *hld up in mid-div: taken wd and hdwy appr 7th: wknd after 2 out* **33/1**

60-0 **5** *5* **Saxe-Coburg (IRE)**[28] [1] 8-10-5 77 .... MrSRees(7) 64
(K G Wingrove) *hld up in tch: rdn appr 5th: wknd 6th* **66/1**

0F-5 **6** *1 ¼* **Outside Investor (IRE)**[14] [232] 5-10-10 82 .... MrRMcCarthy(7) 68
(P R Rodford) *hld up in mid-div: rdn and styd on fr 3 out: n.d* **22/1**

221- **7** *16* **Luminoso**[160] [2813] 13-10-12 95 .... DLaverty(5) 52
(J D J Davies) *bhd fr 6th* **9/1**

00-0 **8** *6* **Sylcan Express**[24] [75] 12-10-7 67 .... RStephens(5) 41
(O O'Neill) *a bhd* **33/1**

/FP- **9** *3* **Selassie**[29] 6-10-2 .... JKington(10) 38
(M Scudamore) *hld up in tch: wknd after 3 out* **20/1**

0P- **10** *2 ½* **Ewar Bold**[168] [2657] 12-10-5 78 .... (t) WPKavanagh(7) 35
(K G Wingrove) *a bhd* **66/1**

/0-0 **11** *3 ½* **Moving On Up**[28] [1] 11-10-9 112 .... (b) RHobson(3) 32
(P R Johnson) *hld up and bhd: reminders after 3rd: hdwy after 4th: wknd 6th: mstke 3 out* **16/1**

0 **12** *2* **Thiseldo Us**[22] [133] 10-10-5 .... CMStudd(7) 30
(M B Shears) *rdn after 4th: a bhd* **66/1**

P03- **13** *dist* **Dunston Durgam (IRE)**[296] [1080] 11-10-12 64 .... JPByrne —
(Ms Sue Smith) *prom to 6th: t.o whn p.u bef 2 out* **50/1**

44-0 **P** **Elheba (IRE)**[16] [206] 6-11-3 95 .... MBradburne —
(C J Down) *rel to r: p.u after 1st* **8/1**[3]

1P0/ **P** **Wrangel (FR)**[510] [3050] 11-10-7 .... (p) LStephens(5) —
(Mrs S M Johnson) *prom tl wknd appr 7th: t.o whn p.u bef 2 out* **50/1**

06-5 **R** **Sninfia (IRE)**[8] [352] 5-10-3 98 .... EDehdashti(7) —
(G A Ham) *v rel to r: gd hdwy 2nd: rdn appr 6th: sn wknd: bhd whn ref and uns rdr 2 out* **4/1**[2]

0-4P **P** **Island Warrior (IRE)**[14] [237] 10-10-12 67 .... (p) JMogford —
(B P J Baugh) *prom: rdn after 6th: wkng whn mstke 3 out: bhd whn p.u bef 2 out* **33/1**

4m 48.0s (0.10) **Going Correction** +0.025s/f (Yiel) **17** Ran SP% **132.4**
Speed ratings: **100,97,92,91,89 89,82,80,79,78 76,75,—,—,— —,—** CSF £11.81 TOTE £3.20: £1.60, £1.50, £2.40; EX 21.00.There was no bid for the winner.
Owner G Jones **Bred** Juddmonte Farms **Trained** Eastnor, H'fords

FOCUS
A weak seller won comfortably by Burning Truth, who is better known as a chaser.

NOTEBOOK
Burning Truth(USA), reverting to hurdles, soon had his field stretched and was never seriously threatened. He is not as good over the smaller obstacles, but did not have to be to take care of this field and he does like this track. *(op 2-1)*
Mead(IRE), set plenty to do, already had too much on to get to the winner when he stumbled at the second last. This trip is on the sharp side for him. *(op 6-1)*
Spectacular Hope ran another decent race but it could be that she is best at around two miles.
Kilrossanty(IRE) won a Cork bumper on his racecourse debut two years ago, but had shown next to nothing snce, including in point-to-points this spring.
Selassie won a maiden point-to-point last month.
Island Warrior(IRE) *Official explanation: jockey said the gelding had a breathing problem*

459 SIR JOHN COTTERELL NOVICES' CHASE (14 fncs) 2m 3f
3:10 (3:15) (Class 3) 5-Y-0+ **£5,590** (£1,720; £860; £430)

Form RPR

0P0- **1** **Chivite (IRE)**[29] [4982] 6-10-12 .... PJBrennan 109+
(P J Hobbs) *led 2nd to 3rd: led 8th to 3 out: rdn to ld 2 out: clr last: eased cl home* **4/1**

062- **2** *2 ½* **Dad's Elect (GER)**[49] [4716] 6-10-12 .... DRDennis 102+
(Ian Williams) *hld up: hdwy 8th: rdn and outpcd 10th: styd on wl flat: nt trble wnr* **10/3**[2]

306- **3** *5* **Papillon De Iena (FR)**[30] [4960] 5-10-9 .... APMcCoy 93
(M C Pipe) *hld up: hmpd 2nd: hdwy 8th: led 3 out: hrd rdn and hdd 2 out: wknd flat* **3/1**[1]

PP-U **4** *12* **Chita's Flight**[12] [271] 5-10-2 .... (t) MBradburne 74
(S C Burrough) *hld up: j.rt 1st: hdwy 9th: no imp fr 4 out* **66/1**

0-5U **5** *dist* **Pennys From Heaven**[6] [388] 11-10-8 74 ow1 ...... MrGBarfoot-Saunt(5) —
(Mrs Tracey Barfoot-Saunt) *hld up: hdwy 5th: mstke 7th: no ch whn mstke 4 out: pckd last: t.o* **50/1**

230- **6** *29* **Chase The Sunset (IRE)**[175] [2514] 7-10-12 105 .... (b[1]) JCulloty —
(Miss H C Knight) *prom tl wknd appr 4 out: t.o* **8/1**

PP-P **P** **Gordy's Joy**[22] [134] 5-9-13 .... RYoung(3) —
(G A Ham) *a bhd: t.o whn p.u bef 3 out* **66/1**

660- **U** **Mister Flint**[39] [4825] 7-10-12 .... RJohnson —
(P J Hobbs) *j. sltly lft and uns rdr 1st* **7/2**[3]

/5P- **P** **Ham Stone**[315] [919] 7-10-12 .... JTizzard —
(B J M Ryall) *a bhd: mstke 4th: sn lost tch: t.o whn p.u bef 7th* **66/1**

3-06 **P** **Let's Rock**[19] [174] 7-10-6 67 ow1 .... MrRHodges(7) —
(Mrs A Price) *hld up in tch: rdn and wknd 6th: t.o whn p.u bef 4 out* **66/1**

1-4 **P** **Pams Oak**[11] [296] 7-11-4 100 .... OMcPhail —
(P S Payne) *led to 2nd: led 3rd: hit 6th: hdd 8th: sn wknd: p.u bef 10th* **16/1**

4m 48.8s (2.20) **Going Correction** +0.025s/f (Yiel)
WFA 5 from 6yo+ 2lb **11** Ran SP% **115.2**
Speed ratings: **96,94,92,87,— —,—,—,—,— —** CSF £17.78 TOTE £6.70: £2.30, £1.30, £1.60; EX 24.50.
Owner I Russell **Bred** B Kennedy **Trained** Withycombe, Somerset

FOCUS
A fair novice chase, which could be rated higher. Chivite won more comfortably than the margin suggests.

NOTEBOOK
Chivite(IRE) appeared the Hobbs second string, but was the best of these over hurdles. Always in the front rank, he was going worse than the favourite leaving the back straight, but responded to pressure to draw clear before the final fence. He jumped soundly and will be suited by genuine good ground. *(op 7-2 tchd 9-2)*
Dad's Elect(GER) was outpaced half a mile out, and although he stayed on again to claim second on the run-in he was never remotely a threat to the winner. *(op 5-1)*
Papillon De Iena(FR), making his chasing debut, moved up smoothly to challenge the eventual winner leaving the back straight. After taking a slight lead, he soon came under pressure and had nothing more to offer from the second last. On this evidence he did not stay, but he does look one to tread carefully with. *(op 5-2)*
Chita's Flight, a casualty on her recent chase debut at this track, gave the impression that she needs a greater test of stamina.
Chase The Sunset(IRE), off the track for six months, wore blinkers for the first time. After challenging in the back straight, he weakened rather tamely with four to jump and remains disappointing. *(tchd 6-1)*
Mister Flint, a stablemate of the winner, was in last place when dislodging Johnson at the first on this chasing debut. *(op 10-3 tchd 9-2)*
Let's Rock *Official explanation: jockey said gelding was unsuited by good to soft ground (op 10-3 tchd 9-2)*
Pams Oak *Official explanation: jockey said the gelding was unsuited by the good to soft ground (op 10-3 tchd 9-2)*

460 K W BELL CONSTRUCTION H'CAP HURDLE (8 hdls) 2m 1f
3:40 (3:44) (Class 3) (0-115,115) 4-Y-0+ **£10,588** (£3,258; £1,629; £814)

Form RPR

65-3 **1** **Tom Bell (IRE)**[24] [78] 5-10-2 98 ow4 .... (v) NCarter(7) 110
(J G M O'Shea) *hld up: hdwy after 4th: led appr 2 out: clr appr last: r.o wl* **4/1**[1]

4-11 **2** *18* **Phar Out Phavorite (IRE)**[10] [312] 6-11-12 115 .... (v) NFehily 109
(Miss E C Lavelle) *a.p: led sn after 5th: hdd appr 2 out: one pce* **4/1**[1]

26-0 **3** *2 ½* **Cashel Dancer**[9] [329] 6-10-11 100 .... JPByrne 92
(S A Brookshaw) *a.p: one pce fr 3 out* **16/1**

20F- **4** *2 ½* **La Lambertine (FR)**[38] [4837] 4-11-8 115 .... (v) APMcCoy 103+
(M C Pipe) *nvr gng wl: prom: lost pl appr 3rd: sn wl bhd: styng on whn hmpd last* **5/1**[2]

02-3 **5** *1* **Nuit Sombre (IRE)**[19] [175] 5-11-2 112 .... VConte(7) 102+
(N J Henderson) *led tl sn after 5th: one pce fr 3 out* **7/1**[3]

1-41 **6** *1 ¼* **Alva Glen (USA)**[12] [275] 8-11-2 105 .... PJBrennan 92
(B J Llewellyn) *hld up: lost pl 4th: n.d after* **7/1**[3]

3P5- **7** *7* **Don Valentino (POL)**[348] [686] 6-11-2 105 .... JMMaguire 85
(T R George) *prom tl wknd appr 5th* **20/1**

450- **8** *dist* **Pirandello (IRE)**[116] [3536] 7-11-12 115 .... JPMcNamara —
(K C Bailey) *bhd fr 4th: blnd 2 out: t.o* **12/1**

/6-1 **9** *30* **Beechwood**[8] [356] 7-10-6 105 .... KBurke(10) 92
(P R Rodford) *hld up in tch: hdwy 4th: 5th and wkng whn blnd bdly and miraculous rcvry last: virtually p.u: t.o* **10/1**

3-55 **10** *12* **Reservoir (IRE)**[14] [243] 4-11-7 114 .... (b[1]) RJohnson —
(P J Hobbs) *wl bhd fr 3rd: t.o whn j. slowly 3 out* **12/1**

46-0 **11** *2* **Twentytwosilver (IRE)**[16] [203] 5-10-2 94 .... ONelmes(3) —
(N J Hawke) *hld up: hdwy 3rd: wkng whn hit 5th: t.o* **25/1**

3m 59.5s (-3.60) **Going Correction** +0.025s/f (Yiel)
WFA 4 from 5yo+ 4lb **11** Ran SP% **120.6**
Speed ratings: **109,100,99,98,97 97,93,—,—,— —** CSF £21.34 CT £236.77 TOTE £4.60: £1.50, £2.60, £3.50; EX 25.60.
Owner K W Bell **Bred** John O'Connor **Trained** Elton, Gloucs

FOCUS
A step up of around 13lb from the winner, in line with the level of his best Flat form.

NOTEBOOK
Tom Bell(IRE) broke his duck over hurdles in a race sponsored by his owner, coming clear from the second last to turn around recent course form with Phar Out Favourite on considerably better terms. He is likely to go up a lot for this and could struggle off his new mark. *(tchd 7-2 and 9-2)*
Phar Out Phavorite(IRE), bidding for a hat-trick off a 9lb higher mark, ran his race but was no match for the well-handicapped winner from the second last. The ease in the ground did not help his cause. *(op 7-2 tchd 9-2)*
Cashel Dancer, down in trip again, was never far off the pace but had no answers when the winner went on. She looks high enough in the weights at present. *(op 20-1)*
La Lambertine(FR) was swishing her tail in the paddock and she did not look keen in the race. Dropping herself out before halfway, it was only due to McCoy's persistence that she finished as close as she did. She looks one to avoid. *(op 8-1)*
Nuit Sombre(IRE) set a strong pace on this handicap debut but was beaten with three to jump. *(tchd 15-2)*
Alva Glen(USA), 8lb higher, was always at the back of the field and found this too sharp.
Beechwood, with whom the Handicapper has taken no chances, was on the retreat before the second last. He would have had an 'F' next to his name but for a gravity-defying recovery by both horse and rider at the final flight. *(op 11-1)*
Reservoir(IRE) showed no enthusiasm in the first-time blinkers and has become one to be wary of. *(op 14-1)*

461 CHARLES DAWSON MEMORIAL H'CAP CHASE (18 fncs 1 omitted) 3m 1f 110y
4:10 (4:12) (Class 4) (0-105,101) 5-Y-0+ **£4,842** (£1,490; £745; £372)

Form RPR

15U- **1** **Dead-Eyed Dick (IRE)**[181] [2396] 9-11-11 100 .... PJBrennan 125+
(Nick Williams) *hld up and bhd: stdy hdwy 10th: led approachng 3 out: clr appr 2 out: eased considerably flat* **9/1**

R-22 **2** *16* **Bramblehill Duke (IRE)**[11] [297] 13-11-3 92 .... (b) AO'Keeffe 94+
(Miss Venetia Williams) *led tl appr 3 out: sn btn* **5/1**[3]

311- **3** *1 ¼* **Paddy The Optimist (IRE)**[43] 4778 9-11-2 **96**.................. LStephens(5) 96
(D Burchell) *hld up: hdwy 12th: wknd appr 4 out: lft 3rd 2 out* **7/2**[1]
R2S- **4** *25* **Filscot**[29] 13-10-7 **82**.. JPMcNamara 57
(P W Hiatt) *a bhd: lost tch 10th* **20/1**
U-PF **5** *11* **Pete The Painter (IRE)**[13] 262 8-11-1 **90**......................(b) MBradburne 54
(J W Tudor) *hld up in mid-div: struggling fr 14th* **12/1**
4-P3 **F** **Rings Of Power (IRE)**[11] 296 8-9-13 **77**............................. RYoung(3) —
(N R Mitchell) *fell 3rd* **5/1**[3]
46-5 **P** **Brady Boys (USA)**[12] 276 8-9-11 **75** oh19......................(v) ONelmes(3) —
(J G M O'Shea) *a bhd: t.o fr 13th: p.u bef last* **25/1**
U6-4 **P** **Flinders**[23] 101 10-10-8 **83**.. LAspell —
(R Rowe) *chsd ldr to 4th: lost pl 6th: t.o whn p.u bef 12th* **9/1**
PP-3 **P** **Hardy Russian (IRE)**[14] 231 8-9-8 **79** oh5 ow4.................. KBurke(10) —
(P R Rodford) *a bhd: lost tch 10th: t.o whn p.u bef 3 out* **33/1**
6-00 **F** **Rudetski**[12] 275 8-11-12 **101**...(t) DRDennis 91
(M Sheppard) *prom: chsd ldr 9th to 4 out: wknd 3 out: 3rd and btn whn fell 2 out* **28/1**
2-12 **P** **Silver Samuel (NZ)**[12] 276 8-11-0 **89**...............................(t) JPByrne —
(S A Brookshaw) *prom: chsd ldr 4th to 9th: blnd and rdr lost iron briefly 11th: rdn 13th: sn wknd: t.o whn p.u bef 3 out* **9/2**[2]

6m 35.0s (0.80) **Going Correction** +0.125s/f (Yiel) **11** Ran SP% **116.4**
Speed ratings: **103,98,97,90,86** —,—,—,—,— — CSF £51.51 CT £190.16 TOTE £11.20: £3.50, £2.10, £1.10; EX 43.00.
Owner Mrs Jane Williams **Bred** Edward And Teresa Forde **Trained** George Nympton, Devon

FOCUS
A personal best from Dead-Eyed Dick who has been rated as value for 20 lengths. The open ditch past the stands was bypassed on the second circuit.

NOTEBOOK
Dead-Eyed Dick(IRE) had not run since November but has overcome a similar absence before. Well at home in the rain-softened ground, he struck the front turning out of the back straight and soon had it sewn up. *(op 7-1)*
Bramblehill Duke(IRE) set a decent pace, but had no answers when the winner went past him and had to settle for second again. *(op 8-1)*
Paddy The Optimist(IRE), attempting a course-and-distance hat-trick, was found out by an 8lb hike plus this easier ground. *(op 10-3 tchd 4-1)*
Filscot has been well beaten between the flags this spring, usually in cheekpieces. He requires plenty of winding up and was only getting going when the race was over.
Pete The Painter(IRE) needs faster conditions underfoot.
Rudetski, reverting to fences and taking a big step up in trip, ran respectably but was a tired third when falling heavily at the second last. *(op 11-2)*
Silver Samuel(NZ) has been in good form at this venue of late, but the ground had gone against him. He lost his pitch after a blunder early on the final circuit and could never get back into contention. *(op 11-2)*

462 ADAM JONES AND JOSEPH JAMES MARES' ONLY H'CAP HURDLE (10 hdls) 2m 3f 110y
4:40 (4:43) (Class 4) (0-105,103) 4-Y-O+ **£4,143** (£1,275; £637; £318)

Form RPR
510- **1** **Kims Pearl (IRE)**[76] 4230 7-10-5 **87**.............................. LStephens(5) 105+
(D Burchell) *mde virtually all: clr after 2 out: r.o wl* **7/1**[3]
550/ **2** *9* **Sunnyland**[409] 4712 6-10-3 **80**.. RJohnson 89
(P J Hobbs) *hld up: wnt 2nd 6th: led briefly 3 out: rdn after 2 out: 8 l 2nd and btn whn mstke last* **3/1**[1]
6-61 **3** *24* **Somewin (IRE)**[10] 310 5-9-7 **77** oh5.................................(p) RSpate(7) 62
(Mrs K Waldron) *hld up: hdwy appr 7th: wknd appr 2 out* **10/1**
553- **4** *17* **Combe Florey**[42] 4795 6-10-11 **88**....................................... RThornton 56
(H D Daly) *prom: j.rt 1st: wknd appr 3 out* **10/3**[2]
331- **5** *10* **White Dove (FR)**[137] 3231 7-11-2 **93**..................................(b) DRDennis 51
(Ian Williams) *prom: hit 7th: sn wknd* **3/1**[1]
20-1 **P** **Fallout (IRE)**[25] 58 4-11-3 **99**.. AO'Keeffe —
(J W Mullins) *bhd fr 7th: t.o whn p.u bef 2 out* **9/1**
006- **P** **Lady Loveday**[106] 3690 4-10-0 **82** oh13.................................. PJBrennan —
(Nick Williams) *prom tl wknd 5th: t.o whn p.u bef 2 out* **28/1**
P0-F **P** **Spring Bee**[23] 96 5-9-11 **77** oh8.. ONelmes(3) —
(T Wall) *rn in snatches: a last: lost tch 5th: t.o whn p.u bef 2 out* **28/1**

4m 49.8s (1.90) **Going Correction** +0.125s/f (Yiel)
WFA 4 from 5yo+ 4lb **8** Ran SP% **111.6**
Speed ratings: **101,97,87,81,77** —,—,— CSF £27.52 CT £204.95 TOTE £6.80: £2.10, £2.50, £3.10; EX 43.40.
Owner John Richards **Bred** Mrs D McDonogh **Trained** Briery Hill, Blaenau Gwent

FOCUS
A weak race, devalued by five non-runners.

NOTEBOOK
Kims Pearl(IRE) was headed for a few strides at the third last but was quickly back in front again and steadily drew clear. Well treated on the form of her Chepstow win, she was not inconvenienced by the rain-affected ground. *(tchd 13-2 and 8-1)*
Sunnyland, having her first run for over a year, went past the eventual winner three from home but was soon headed and had no more to offer. She remains qualified for novice events and better ground should help. *(op 11-4)*
Somewin(IRE) was on her toes and attended by two handlers in the paddock. Raised 9lb for winning a poor Ludlow seller, she was well beaten but stuck on to suggest a geater test of stamina will suit her. *(op 9-1)*
Combe Florey had been seen off with three to jump on this handicap debut. *Official explanation: jockey said the mare had a breathing problem (op 7-2 tchd 4-1 in a place)*
White Dove(FR), successful without the headgear on her latest run here in in January, had run her race before the third last. *(tchd 10-3)*
Lady Loveday looked an excitable sort in the preliminaries. *(op 25-1)*

463 RACING ADVERTISER MAIDEN OPEN NATIONAL HUNT FLAT RACE 2m 1f
5:10 (5:10) (Class 6) 4-6-Y-0 **£2,016** (£576; £288)

Form RPR
5 **1** **Hill Forts Timmy**[14] 235 5-11-4 .... SCurran 96+
(J W Mullins) *hld up and bhd: stdy hdwy over 6f out: led over 3f out: rdn and hung lft over 1f out: r.o* **8/1**
2 **2** *1 ¼* **Treacysdream (IRE)**[14] 242 5-10-11 .... RSpate(7) 93
(Mrs K Waldron) *hld up in mid-div: hdwy 9f out: hrd rdn and ev ch 1f out: nt qckn* **11/4**[2]
3 *8* **Twist The Facts (IRE)** 5-10-11 .... APMcCoy 78
(M C Pipe) *hld up in mid-div: hdwy 9f out: rdn and hdd over 3f out: wknd fnl f* **9/4**[1]
4 *nk* **Judy The Drinker** 6-10-1 .... ENolan(10) 78
(J G M O'Shea) *hld up in mid-div: rdn 8f out: outpcd 5f out: styd on fnl 2f* **25/1**
60- **5** *11* **Mialyssa**[92] 3946 5-10-4 .... JAJenkins(7) 67
(M R Bosley) *led: hdd 5f out: wknd 4f out* **33/1**
6 *6* **Ravens Flight (IRE)** 4-11-0 .... JPByrne 64
(S A Brookshaw) *hld up in mid-div: hdwy 9f out: rdn over 4f out: wknd over 1f out* **8/1**
7 *1* **Pumpkin Pickle** 4-9-11 .... KBurke(10) 56
(P R Rodford) *prom tl wknd over 5f out* **16/1**
8 *1 ¼* **Alotdone (IRE)**[168] 6-11-4 .... JMogford 66
(Mrs N S Evans) *chsd ldr: rdn over 7f out: wknd 4f out* **50/1**
9 *2 ½* **Schindler's List** 5-10-13 .... LStephens(5) 63
(C Roberts) *a bhd* **11/2**[3]
00- **10** *dist* **Itsukate**[55] 4608 5-10-11 ....(t) OMcPhail —
(J Rudge) *a bhd: t.o* **40/1**
11 *dist* **April Rose** 5-10-4 .... MrSRees(7) —
(K G Wingrove) *a bhd: t.o* **25/1**
12 *9* **Georgie's Lass (IRE)**[22] 6-10-8 .... RHobson(3) —
(C Roberts) *prom 7f: virtually p.u over 4f out: t.o* **50/1**
13 *1* **Kinallen**[42] 5-10-11 .... MrRMcCarthy(7) —
(B J Llewellyn) *prom: rdn over 5f out: wknd over 4f out: sn eased: t.o* **50/1**

4m 1.40s (0.30) **Going Correction** +0.125s/f (Yiel)
WFA 4 from 5yo+ 4lb **13** Ran SP% **119.9**
Speed ratings: **104,103,99,99,94 91,91,90,89,**— —,—,— CSF £28.76 TOTE £6.90: £3.30, £1.80, £1.10; EX 21.00 Place 6 £10.92, Place 5 £10.02.
Owner Mrs J C Scorgie **Bred** R L And Mrs Scorgie **Trained** Wilsford-Cum-Lake, Wilts

FOCUS
A modest bumper but the winner could be the type to do better.

NOTEBOOK
Hill Forts Timmy, who hung in the other direction on his debut, still showed signs of greenness but found enough to hold off the strong challenge of the runner-up. This was an ordinary race but he could be the type to do a bit better. *(op 15-2 tchd 9-1)*
Treacysdream(IRE), a non-runner in a maiden hurdle earlier in the week, stayed on to have his chance after being carried towards the stands' rail in the straight. He has won a point-to-point over three miles and stamina looks his strong suit. *(op 4-1)*
Twist The Facts(IRE), out of an unraced half-sister to fair chaser Pennybridge, was mounted on the course and taken steadily to post. After travelling well, she came off the bridle before the home turn and did not find much. *(op 5-4)*
Judy The Drinker, whose dam was a middle-distance winner, did not shape badly under a jockey having his first ever ride. *(tchd 33-1)*
Mialyssa, whose dam was a winning hurdler, was well beaten on Polytrack last time but showed a bit more back on turf. *(op 25-1)*
T/Plt: £66.00 to a £1 stake. Pool: £40,595.65. 448.40 winning tickets. T/Qpdt: £68.40 to a £1 stake. Pool: £2,211.40. 23.90 winning tickets. KH

106 SOUTHWELL (L-H)
Sunday, May 22

OFFICIAL GOING: Good
Wind: Virtually nil

464 EXPERIENCE NOTTINGHAMSHIRE H'CAP CHASE (19 fncs) 3m 2f
2:00 (2:01) (Class 4) (0-90,88) 5-Y-0+ **£3,965** (£1,220; £610; £305)

Form RPR
PP-5 **1** **Lambrini Bianco (IRE)**[28] 10 7-9-7 **62**.....................(p) TMessenger(7) 74+
(Mrs L Williamson) *cl up: led 11th: rdn along 4 out: j.rt next: sn drvn and kpt on wl flat* **11/2**[2]
P00- **2** *1 ¼* **Cyanara**[30] 4953 9-9-9 **62** oh8... TJPhelan(5) 70
(Dr P Pritchard) *midfield: hdwy to chse ldrs 15th: effrt 3 out: rdn next: ev ch last: drvn flat and no ex nr fin* **40/1**
0-51 **3** *hd* **Lanmire Tower (IRE)**[7] 373 11-11-1 **84** 7ex...................(p) WKennedy(7) 92
(S Gollings) *trckd ldrs: hdwy to join wnr 13th: rdn along after 4 out: ev ch tl drvn and one pce last* **10/1**
302- **4** *hd* **Southerndown (IRE)**[30] 4953 12-11-2 **78**................................. TDoyle 87+
(R Lee) *hld up: rdn along and bhd 12th: styd on fr 4 out: chsd ldrs after next: sn rdn and one pce last* **8/1**
PU-1 **5** *3* **Tina's Scallywag**[15] 211 8-10-10 **72**.. DO'Meara 77
(H P Hogarth) *hld up in tch: hdwy to chse ldrs 1oth: rdn along 4 out: drvn and one pce fr next* **9/1**
B0-4 **6** *3 ½* **Master Jackson**[7] 373 6-10-12 **77**....................................... RWalford(3) 79
(T D Walford) *towards rr: hdwy appr 4 out: sn rdn along and no imp fr next* **13/2**[3]
00-0 **7** *10* **Cyindien (FR)**[14] 233 8-11-8 **87**... DCrosse(3) 82+
(D E Cantillon) *in tch: hdwy to chse ldrs 12th: rdn along to chse ldng pair after 4 out: drvn next and sn wknd* **25/1**
PP5- **8** *¾* **Spilaw (FR)**[30] 4953 9-9-11 **64** oh14 ow2................................ MNicolls(5) 55
(John Allen) *a towards rr* **80/1**
-066 **9** *shd* **Cromwell (IRE)**[7] 373 10-10-4 **69**......................................(b) ACCoyle(3) 60
(M C Chapman) *led to 11th: rdn along whn hit 14th: wknd fr 4 out* **22/1**
0-43 **10** *dist* **Robbie On Tour (IRE)**[8] 352 6-11-1 **80**............................(t) TJMalone(3) —
(M C Pipe) *midfield: blnd bdly 3rd and rdr lost irons: t.o fr 6th* **8/1**
P-PP **P** **Major Bit**[5] 398 9-9-7 **62** oh5...(bt¹) SWalsh(7) —
(S A Brookshaw) *a rr: bhd whn p.u bef 12th* **66/1**
000- **P** **Zaffisfaction**[33] 4920 5-10-0 **69** oh5.. TScudamore —
(K C Bailey) *a rr: bhd whn p.u bef 12th* **20/1**
524- **P** **Our Man Dennis**[286] 1158 11-10-11 **73**.. GLee —
(Mrs P Ford) *a rr: blnd 11th: bhd and p.u after next* **14/1**
36-P **P** **Francolino (FR)**[6] 386 12-9-12 **63**....................................... LVickers(3) —
(Dr P Pritchard) *racd wd: chsd ldrs tl lost pl after 12th: bhd whn p.u bef 4 out* **25/1**
1PP- **P** **Little Herman (IRE)**[106] 3696 9-10-11 **73**................................ WHutchinson —
(J A B Old) *chsd ldrs: rdn along 1/2-way: sn loost pl and bhd whn p.u bef 4 out* **7/1**
P0-1 **P** **Our Jolly Swagman**[12] 288 10-11-12 **88**..............................(p) AThornton —
(J W Mullins) *in tch: hdwy to chse ldrs 8th: rdn along 13th: mstke 15th and p.u after* **5/1**[1]

6m 34.6s (-4.70) **Going Correction** -0.275s/f (Good)
WFA 5 from 6yo+ 7lb **16** Ran SP% **127.8**
Speed ratings: **96,95,95,95,94 93,90,90,90,**— —,—,—,—,— — CSF £216.93 CT £2194.57 TOTE £8.50: £2.00, £24.20, £2.50, £2.20; EX 349.10.
Owner Halewood International Ltd **Bred** John Brophy **Trained** Saighton, Cheshire

FOCUS
A moderate staying event, but Lambrini Bianco is still only seven and may be capable of leaving the form behind, being a half-brother to Royal Athlete.

NOTEBOOK
Lambrini Bianco(IRE), a half-brother to Royal Athlete, obviously had little trouble seeing this trip out and kept on too strongly for Cyanara. He is quite a lazy individual and needed plenty of driving, but he did respond and should be capable of further progress off his lowly mark. *(op 7-1 tchd 15-2)*

Cyanara bounced back to form in second and it will be interesting to see if she can repeat the performance next time.
Lanmire Tower(IRE) ran well under a 7lb penalty and just got the better of another dour stayer in Southerndown for third. *(op 6-1)*
Southerndown(IRE) would gallop all day long if he could and he was just denied a placing close home.
Tina's Scallywag, finally off the mark at Hexham, ran well in this follow-up bid and could not stay on strongly enough to make a big impression. *(op 10-1)*
Our Man Dennis *Official explanation: jockey said the gelding pulled up lame (op 11-2 tchd 9-2)*
Our Jolly Swagman has never been the most consistent and gave one of his lesser efforts. *Official explanation: jockey said the gelding lost his action (op 11-2 tchd 9-2)*
Major Bit *Official explanation: jockey said the gelding lost its tongue strap (op 11-2 tchd 9-2)*

465 DINE IN THE QUEEN MOTHER RESTAURANT BEGINNERS' CHASE (16 fncs) 2m 5f 110y

2:30 (2:41) (Class 4) 5-Y-O+ **£4,309** (£1,326; £663; £331)

Form				RPR
/40-	**1**		**Nawow**[8] 2343 5-10-13 ATinkler (P D Cundell) *hld up: hdwy appr 12th: rdn 3 out: styd on to ld next: drvn and kpt on wl flat* **7/1**	99+
505-	**2**	*1*	**Milord Lescribaa (FR)**[30] 4960 5-10-10 TJMalone(3) (M C Pipe) *hld up: hdwy to trck ldrs 6th: jnd ldr 4 out: pushed along whn lft in ld next: sn hdd: drvn and rallied last: no ex flat* **7/2**[2]	96
003-	**3**	*4*	**Hey Boy (IRE)**[55] 4621 6-10-13 107 DCrosse(3) (C J Mann) *a.p: rdn along 4 out: drvn after next and one pce after 2 out* **16/1**	95
00-P	**4**	*dist*	**Ri Na Realta (IRE)**[16] 202 10-11-2 95 AThornton (J W Mullins) *a rr* **22/1**	—
/34-	**5**	*9*	**Balinahinch Castle (IRE)**[79] 4153 8-10-11 100 DFlavin(5) (Mrs L B Normile) *led to after 1st: chsd ldrs tl lost pl 7th: bhd fr 1/2-way* **10/1**	—
0PP/	**P**		**Bellefleur**[20] 8-10-6 LVickers(3) (N J Pomfret) *cl up: led 3rd to 7th: sn lost pl and bhd whn p.u bef 11th* **66/1**	—
F06-	**B**		**The Glen**[35] 4889 7-11-2 TDoyle (R Lee) *hld up in tch: hdwy whn hit 11th: styng on and cl 4th whn b.d 3 out* **13/2**	102+
0P0-	**P**		**Broughton Boy**[32] 4933 5-10-6 TMessenger(7) (G J Smith) *in tch: rdn along 5 out: sn wknd and bhd whn p.u bef 2 out* **100/1**	—
114-	**F**		**Bushido (IRE)**[230] 1275 6-11-2 DElsworth (Mrs S J Smith) *cl up: led 7th: pushed along 4 out: one l clr whn fell 3 out* **11/4**[1]	102+
0P-0	**P**		**Brother Ted**[28] 1 8-11-2 (t) WHutchinson (J K Cresswell) *hld up: hdwy 11th: rdn along and wknd next: b ehind whn p.u after 4 out* **50/1**	—
120/	**P**		**Gigs Bounty**[526] 2717 7-11-2 MAFitzgerald (C C Bealby) *cl up: led after 1st to 3rd: cl up tl rdn along and mstke 11th: sn lost pl and p.u after 4 out* **9/2**[3]	—

5m 22.5s (-4.70) **Going Correction** -0.275s/f (Good)
WFA 5 from 6yo+ 3lb **11** Ran SP% **116.7**
Speed ratings: **97,96,95**,—,— —,—,—,—,— — CSF £31.94 TOTE £11.20: £4.80, £1.10, £4.90; EX 60.50.
Owner Ian M Brown **Bred** Kirtlington Stud Ltd **Trained** Compton, Berks

FOCUS
A modest race in which the outcome changed significantly over the final few fences, with Bushido, leading at the time, falling and bringing down close fourth The Glen at the third last.

NOTEBOOK
Nawow, making his chase debut, ran out quite a tidy winner of what was admittedly a modest heat. He may have been a tad fortunate with Bushido falling when going well in front, but he jumped soundly and won with a little bit to spare. He has an obvious chance of following up if placed well by connections. *(op 6-1)*
Milord Lescribaa(FR), another debuting over fences, made the winner work hard enough for his win and did not go down without a fight. He was four lengths ahead of the third and should have little trouble winning a similar race. *(op 4-1)*
Hey Boy(IRE) improved on his hurdles form and is entitled to improve for this first outing over the 'big ones'. *(op 14-1)*
The Glen was still in with a chance when being brought down and he was probably denied a place. *(op 5-2 tchd 3-1)*
Bushido(IRE) was still going well in front when coming down at the third last and looked unfortunate. His chase-orientated stable are sure to win races with him, but it remains to be seen how this affects his confidence. *(op 5-2 tchd 3-1)*
Brother Ted *Official explanation: jockey said gelding had breathing problem (op 5-2 tchd 3-1)*
Gigs Bounty was never going after a mistake at the 11th and is better than he was able to show. *Official explanation: jockey said the gelding lost its action (op 5-2 tchd 3-1)*

466 PANTRY H'CAP CHASE (13 fncs) 2m 1f

3:00 (3:05) (Class 4) (0-110,110) 5-Y-O+ **£4,163** (£1,281; £640; £320)

Form				RPR
10-3	**1**		**Toulouse (IRE)**[28] 4 8-11-9 **110** RWalford(3) (R H Alner) *a.p: led 3 out: rdn next: styd on wl flat* **3/1**[1]	122+
-45P	**2**	*2*	**The Names Bond**[4] 413 7-11-2 **100** GLee (Andrew Turnell) *trckd ldrs: hdwy and cl up 7th: ev ch whn hit 3 out: sn rdn and kpt on same pce last* **5/1**[2]	108+
-P22	**3**	*1 ½*	**Kercabellec (FR)**[7] 364 7-10-1 **92** ow2 APogson(7) (J R Cornwall) *cl up: led appr 3rd: rdn along 4 out: hdd next: sn drvn and kpt on same pce fr 2 out* **11/2**[3]	100+
0-54	**4**	*1 ¼*	**Reach The Clouds (IRE)**[14] 232 13-10-2 **91** MNicolls(5) (John R Upson) *hld up: hdwy 8th: rdn along 4 out: styd on to chse ldrs next: sn drvn and one pce* **10/1**	95
42-2	**5**	*3*	**Vigoureux (FR)**[22] 126 6-10-8 **99** (p) WKennedy(7) (S Gollings) *trckd ldrs: rdn along 8th: drvn after 4 out and kpt on same pce* **11/2**[3]	100
4-PU	**6**	*15*	**Javelot D'Or (FR)**[8] 354 8-9-11 **84** oh2 (t) KJMercer(3) (Mrs B K Thomson) *in tch: rdn along 9th: outpcd fr 4 out* **16/1**	70
60-0	**7**	*23*	**Farceur (FR)**[11] 295 6-10-3 **87** (v) GSupple (M C Pipe) *led: j. bdly rt 2nd and sn hdd: pushed along and lost pl 5th: sn bhd* **11/1**	50
-6P0	**R**		**Dabus**[7] 370 10-10-12 **99** ACCoyle(3) (M C Chapman) *ref to r: tk no part* **20/1**	—
31	**P**		**Pequenita**[13] 264 5-11-7 **110** (p) LMcGrath(3) (R C Guest) *hld up in rr: j. slowly 4th and next: sn bhd and p.u bef 7th* **5/1**[2]	—

4m 5.90s (-5.70) **Going Correction** -0.275s/f (Good)
WFA 5 from 6yo+ 2lb **9** Ran SP% **117.2**
Speed ratings: **102,101,100,99,98 91,80**,—,— CSF £19.27 CT £79.06 TOTE £4.60: £2.00, £2.20, £2.00; EX 19.40.
Owner Pell-Mell Partners **Bred** D J Fitzpatrick **Trained** Droop, Dorset

FOCUS
A moderate event, but the winner, rated as value for further, still has the potential to do better. Pretty solid form.

NOTEBOOK
Toulouse(IRE), still 5lb higher than when last winning at Hereford back in November, is going the right way again and saw his race out well to record the third win of his career. He has yet to fulfil early promise, but is still only eight and probably has more to offer. *(op 10-3)*
The Names Bond lost momentum with a mistake at the third last and that prevented him running the winner closer. He has yet to win over fences, but showed enough here to suggest he should have little trouble doing so. *(op 13-2)*
Kercabellec(FR) undoubtedly has a small race in him over fences, but continues to frustrate and he was unable to hold the front two off despite being in receipt of plenty of weight. *(op 13-2)*
Reach The Clouds(IRE) plugged on for fourth, but was never in with a chance of getting to the front three.
Vigoureux(FR) has displayed enough ability in two starts over fences to suggest he can pick up a small race. *(op 5-1)*
Pequenita was never going and there may well have been something amiss. *Official explanation: jockey said the mare was never travelling (op 7-2)*

467 SOUTHWELL-RACECOURSE.CO.UK INTERMEDIATE HURDLE (9 hdls) 2m 1f

3:30 (3:33) (Class 4) 4-Y-O+ **£3,484** (£1,072; £536; £268)

Form				RPR
30-2	**1**		**Woody Valentine (USA)**[23] 100 4-11-1 117 SThomas (Miss Venetia Williams) *trckd ldng pair: smooth hdwy to ld appr 3 out: clr next: styd on wl* **1/1**[1]	121+
0-1F	**2**	*1 ¼*	**Romany Prince**[8] 343 6-11-5 118 TScudamore (S Gollings) *trckd ldrs: hdwy to chse wnr approacing 2 out: sn drvn and kpt on* **5/2**[2]	118
2UB-	**3**	*24*	**Dalriath**[74] 4259 6-10-9 90 ACCoyle(3) (M C Chapman) *led: rdn along and hdd bef 3 out: drvn and wknd bef next* **20/1**	87
4P5-	**4**	*hd*	**Medici (FR)**[37] 4857 7-11-5 112 GLee (Mrs Jeremy Young) *keen: prom:nt fluent 3rd: pushed along 4 out and wknd next* **11/2**[3]	94
030-	**5**	*6*	**Young Patriarch**[49] 4715 4-10-12 104 (p) DCrosse(3) (C J Mann) *in tch: effrt and pushed along whn hit 4 out: sn rdn and btn* **12/1**	84
4-25	**6**	*7*	**Idlewild (IRE)**[22] 129 10-10-12 92 APogson(7) (C T Pogson) *bhd fr 1/2-way* **25/1**	81
P-F4	**7**	*12*	**Nutley Queen (IRE)**[13] 263 6-10-0 StephenJCraine(5) (M Appleby) *a bhd* **66/1**	55
0	**8**	*24*	**Scary Night (IRE)**[7] 369 5-10-12 (t) SFox (M J Gingell) *a bhd* **100/1**	38
P-	**P**		**La Gitana**[52] 3943 5-10-5 WHutchinson (A Sadik) *a rr: drvn along 4th: bhd whn p.u bef next* **66/1**	—

3m 54.2s (-10.70) **Going Correction** -0.675s/f (Firm)
WFA 4 from 5yo+ 4lb **9** Ran SP% **114.2**
Speed ratings: **98,97,86,86,83 79,74,62**,— CSF £3.53 TOTE £1.70: £1.10, £1.10, £4.50; EX 4.30.
Owner Favourites Racing IX **Bred** J I Amos And Barbara F Amos **Trained** Kings Caple, H'fords

FOCUS
A two-horse race on paper and they finished well clear. The easy winner has been rated as value for seven lengths.

NOTEBOOK
Woody Valentine(USA) was winning his second race since turning his hand to hurdles, possessing too much speed for runner-up Romany Prince. Good ground is a must and he should continue to pay his way through the summer. *(tchd 10-11 and 11-10 in places)*
Romany Prince is ideally suited by further and he lacked the pace to get to the winner. This was a decent effort conceding weight and he was clear of the third. *(op 10-3)*
Dalriath was well adrift of the front two and simply outclassed. *(tchd 22-1)*
Medici(FR) found this an inadequate test and he struggled under his penalty. *(op 4-1)*
Young Patriarch has not really progressed from his Folkestone win last season and was beaten a long way. *(op 10-1 tchd 14-1)*
Nutley Queen(IRE) *Official explanation: jockey said the mare had a breathing problem*
Scary Night(IRE) *Official explanation: jockey said the gelding had a breathing problem (op 66-1)*
La Gitana *Official explanation: jockey said the mare was unsuited by the ground*

468 ARENA LEISURE H'CAP HURDLE (13 hdls) 3m 2f

4:00 (4:02) (Class 3) (0-115,113) 4-Y-O+ **£5,564** (£1,712; £856; £428)

Form				RPR
0F1-	**1**		**Cherry Gold**[30] 4957 11-10-13 **100** (p) ChristianWilliams (Evan Williams) *led: rdn along 4 out: hdd 2 out: swtchd rt and drvn: one l down whn lft clr last* **6/1**[2]	107
0P-0	**2**	*10*	**Brush A King**[23] 109 10-10-13 **107** APogson(7) (C T Pogson) *hld up: stdy hdwy 1/2-way: chsd ldrs 4 out: rdn next and sn outpcd: lft 2nd at last* **33/1**	104
33-3	**3**	*11*	**The Flyer (IRE)**[23] 109 8-11-9 **110** (t) JAMcCarthy (Miss S J Wilton) *bhd: rdn along 3 out styd on fr next: lft poor 3rd last* **9/1**[3]	96
PP-P	**4**	*2 ½*	**Reasonable Reserve (IRE)**[23] 109 8-11-6 **112** (b) JFLevins(5) (B G Powell) *chsd ldrs: hit 4th: rdn along bef 4 out and sn wknd* **14/1**	96
P1-6	**5**	*1*	**The Merry Mason (IRE)**[24] 80 9-10-0 **87** oh2 JimCrowley (Mrs S J Smith) *prom: rdn along 7th: drvn appr 4 out and sn wknd* **11/4**[1]	70
105-	**6**	*20*	**Simlet**[37] 4851 10-11-9 **113** (t) GBerridge(3) (E W Tuer) *hld up: hdwy 8th: rdn along next and sn btn* **14/1**	76
01-3	**U**		**Shower Of Hail (IRE)**[25] 53 5-11-6 **110** TJMalone(3) (M C Pipe) *uns rdr 1st* **9/1**[3]	—
245-	**P**		**Phase Eight Girl**[274] 1235 9-10-0 **87** oh4 WHutchinson (J Hetherton) *a rr: wl bhd whn p.u 9th* **25/1**	—
33P-	**P**		**Mrs Ritchie**[49] 4717 8-10-8 **98** LVickers(3) (Mrs S Lamyman) *prom: rdn along 4 out: hit next: sn wknd and puleld up bef 2 out* **16/1**	—
12-2	**F**		**Harrycone Lewis**[23] 109 7-11-8 **109** (b) WMarston (Mrs P Sly) *hld up: stdy hdwy to join ldrs 4th: cl up fr 6th: rdn along 4 out: drvn to ld 2 out: one l up and all out whn fell last* **11/4**[1]	118+

6m 14.9s (-14.50) **Going Correction** -0.675s/f (Firm) course record **10** Ran SP% **113.6**
Speed ratings: **95,91,88,87,87 81**,—,—,—,— CSF £156.96 CT £1751.93 TOTE £4.80: £1.60, £6.20, £2.50; EX 113.10.
Owner R Mason **Bred** R Burton **Trained** Cowbridge, Vale Of Glamorgan

FOCUS
A dramatic conclusion to the race with Harrycone Lewis falling at the last when still a length ahead. Cherry Gold was certainly not beaten and may have won anyway, but had his task simplified.

NOTEBOOK

Cherry Gold, better known as a hunter chaser, was in the process of making a good return to hurdles when Harrycone Lewis fell at the last, leaving him clear. He may have won anyway, but one could not say for certain. He would have finished clear of the third even if beaten and it will be interesting to see how the handicapper reacts. *(op 5-1)*

Brush A King ran his best race since August of last year and may be finding some form. He was a fortunate second, but finished clear of the third.

The Flyer(IRE) was well beaten back in third, but continues to pay his way. *(tchd 10-1)*

Reasonable Reserve(IRE) is back on a winning mark, but will need to show more than he did here. *(op 16-1)*

The Merry Mason(IRE) has not really cut the mustard since dropping back to hurdles and was disappointing. *(op 4-1)*

Harrycone Lewis was set to continue his consistent run of finishing first or second, and was still a length ahead, when taking a crashing fall at the last. It remains to be seen how this affects his confidence. *(op 5-2 tchd 3-1 in places)*

469 ENJOY HOSPITALITY AT SOUTHWELL CONDITIONAL JOCKEYS' H'CAP HURDLE (11 hdls) 2m 5f 110y

4:30 (4:30) (Class 4) (0-90,90) 4-Y-O+ **£4,023** (£1,238; £619; £309)

Form RPR

3P-5 **1** **Walsingham (IRE)**[7] [365] 7-11-6 **84**.....(b[1]) SThomas 90+
(Mrs Jeremy Young) *mde all: rdn clr after 3 out: styd on wl* **8/1**[3]

5- **2** 2 ½ **Squantum (IRE)**[93] [3923] 8-10-12 **84**..... PMerrigan(8) 86
(Mrs H Dalton) *midfield: hdwy toi trck ldrs 1/2-way: pushed along 3 out: rdn to chse wnr appr last: kpt on same pce flat* **8/1**[3]

4-40 **3** 3 **Book's Way**[3] [429] 9-10-13 **77**..... KJMercer 76
(D W Thompson) *a.p: chsd wnr fr 6th: rdn along 3 out: drvn and one pce fr next* **9/1**

P-02 **4** 1 ¾ **Dunkerron**[15] [218] 8-11-1 **82**..... SWalsh(3) 80+
(J Joseph) *hld up and bhd: hdwy after 3 out: effrt on outer next: sn rdn and kpt on: nrst fin* **8/1**[3]

PP-5 **5** 6 **Fullopep**[23] [110] 11-11-9 **90**..... APogson(3) 81
(J R Holt) *a chsng ldrs: rdn along and hit 4 out:d riven next and sn one pce* **14/1**

504- **6** ¾ **Mystic Glen**[161] [2786] 6-10-12 **76**..... DCCostello 66
(P D Niven) *midfield: hdwy on inner to chse ldrs 4 out: rdn along next: wknd appr 2 out* **9/1**

P0-0 **7** shd **Snails Castle (IRE)**[28] [11] 6-10-10 **74**..... GBerridge 64
(E W Tuer) *hld up and b ehind: hdwy appr 3 out: sn rdn and hit next: nvr a factor* **25/1**

0-34 **8** 10 **Waydale Hill**[15] [218] 6-11-3 **81**.....(p) RWalford 61
(T D Walford) *midfield: hdwy and in tch 6th: rdn along next and sn outpcd* **9/2**[1]

PR0U **9** ½ **Seemore Sunshine**[7] [363] 8-11-0 **83**..... PCStringer(5) 63
(M J Gingell) *hld up: effrt and somke hdwy 4 out: sn rdn along and wknd* **33/1**

P5-5 **10** 30 **Kellys Fable**[16] [201] 5-11-5 **83**..... TJMalone 33
(J W Mullins) *chsd ldrs on inner: rdn along 4 out and sn wknd* **5/1**[2]

0PP- **P** **Soroka (IRE)**[29] [4977] 6-11-12 **90**.....(p) LTreadwell —
(Jennie Candlish) *a rr: bhd whn p.u bef 2 out* **16/1**

50-P **P** **Pacific Highway (IRE)**[11] [306] 6-11-1 **82**..... DFlavin(3) —
(Mrs L B Normile) *a rr: bhd whn p.u bef 7th* **25/1**

/0-P **P** **Humming**[20] [152] 8-10-11 **78**.....(t) RLucey-Butler(3) —
(Miss M E Rowland) *bhd fr 1/2-way: p.u bef 2 out* **33/1**

600- **P** **Green Master (POL)**[162] [2370] 5-10-7 **76**..... WMcCarthy(5) —
(A Sadik) *in tch: rdn along whn hit 7th: sn bhd and p.u bef 2 out* **33/1**

05-5 **P** **Earls Rock**[23] [111] 7-11-3 **81**..... WHutchinson —
(J K Cresswell) *chsd ldrs: rdn along 3 out: drvn next: wknd qckly and p.u bef next* **8/1**[3]

5m 16.2s (-6.10) **Going Correction** -0.675s/f (Firm) **15** Ran SP% **128.4**
Speed ratings: **84,83,82,81,79 78,78,75,75,64** —,—,—,—,— CSF £71.37 CT £601.25 TOTE £7.00: £1.70, £5.10, £5.40; EX 144.10.
Owner Sir Robert Ogden **Bred** William McCarthy **Trained** Charlton Mackrell, Somerset

FOCUS

A weak race, but an improved performance by Walsingham in the first-time blinkers and over this shorter trip.

NOTEBOOK

Walsingham(IRE) has never been the most consistent, but the first-time blinkers worked the oracle and he stayed on strongly for an all-the-way success. It remains to be seen if the headgear has the same effect in future, but if it does he would have obvious claims for following up. *(op 16-1)*

Squantum(IRE) improved on his first start since arriving from Ireland and kept on well into second. He will be winning sooner rather than later. *(op 13-2)*

Book's Way is creeping down the weights and should be placed to find a race off his current mark. *(tchd 10-1)*

Dunkerron was doing his best work late and could have done with a more positive ride. He may still be a little high in the handicap. *(op 7-1)*

Fullopep failed to pick up under pressure and ended up well beaten.

Waydale Hill has been running reasonably well of late, but this was disappointing and she ran a rare bad race. *(op 11-2)*

Kellys Fable *Official explanation: jockey said the gelding had a breathing problem (op 9-2)*

Pacific Highway(IRE) *Official explanation: jockey said the gelding pulled up lame (op 10-1)*

Earls Rock *Official explanation: jockey said the gelding lost its action (op 10-1)*

470 SEE YOU IN JULY INTERMEDIATE OPEN NATIONAL HUNT FLAT RACE 2m 1f

5:00 (5:00) (Class 6) 4-6-Y-O **£2,037** (£582; £291)

Form RPR

2 **1** **Cloudy Lane**[22] [131] 5-11-4..... GLee 106+
(D McCain) *trckd ldrs: smooth hdwy 6f out: led 2f out: shkn up and clr over 1f out* **9/4**[1]

3-1 **2** 11 **Scotts Court**[8] [355] 5-11-11..... RGarritty 98+
(N Tinkler) *a.p: led 6f out: rdn along over 2f: sn hdd: drvn and nt pce of wnr appr last* **7/2**[2]

3 1 ½ **Snargate** 5-11-1..... RWalford(3) 87
(T D Walford) *hld up: hdwy and in tch 5f out: rdn along 3f out: kpt on appr last: nrst fin* **33/1**

4 **4** 1 ¼ **Valhuec (FR)**[7] [375] 5-10-11..... MrKGreen(7) 85
(Mrs J R Buckley) *hld up: hdwy on outer over 6f: rdn along 4f out: kpt on u.p fnl 2f: nrst fin* **8/1**

- **5** 1 ½ **Colline De Fleurs** 5-10-11..... WHutchinson 79+
(J A B Old) *racd wd: in tch: hdwy to chse ldrs over 4f out: rdn along whn hmpd 3f out: soo drvn and wknd fnl 2f* **6/1**

6 dist **Thunder Child** 5-10-13..... MNicolls(5) —
(John Allen) *cl up: rdn along over 4f out: drvn and wknd over 2f out* **25/1**

0-0 **7** 4 **Hapthor**[14] [241] 6-10-11..... DVerco —
(F Jestin) *led: rdn along and hdd 6f out: sn wknd* **50/1**

0-0 **8** 11 **Essenbee**[13] [266] 5-10-13..... TJPhelan(5) —
(Mrs J R Buckley) *chsd ldr: rdn along 1/2-way: sn wknd* **40/1**

00- **9** 12 **Silver Jade**[113] [3598] 4-10-4..... PAspell(3) —
(C J Teague) *chsd ldrs: pushed along and lost pl 1/2-way: sn bhd* **50/1**

0- **10** 14 **Tees Mill**[98] [3830] 6-11-1..... KJMercer(3) —
(D W Thompson) *a rr: bhd fr 1/2-way* **33/1**

B **Desperate Dex (IRE)** 5-10-13..... LTreadwell(5) —
(G J Smith) *hld up: stdy hdwy 6f out: rdn along to chse ldrs whn b.d home turn 3f out* **16/1**

S **Oscar's Lady (IRE)** 4-10-2..... DCCostello(5) —
(G A Swinbank) *in tch: hdwy on inner 1/2-way: rdn along and cl 3rd whn slipped up home turn 3f out* **5/1**[3]

3m 54.7s
WFA 4 from 5yo+ 4lb **12** Ran SP% **117.0**
CSF £9.09 TOTE £3.10: £1.60, £1.70, £5.80; EX 8.60 Place 6 £209.03, Place 5 £70.62.
Owner Trevor Hemmings **Bred** Gleadhill House Stud Ltd **Trained** Cholmondeley, Cheshire

FOCUS

The winner was rated value for 15l. The first five pulled clear of a bad, bad bunch.

NOTEBOOK

Cloudy Lane did not have to build much on his debut effort when second at Uttoxeter and he was found an ideal opportunity to get off the mark. He did it nicely and looks more than capable of winning more races once sent hurdling. *(tchd 5-2)*

Scotts Court fared with credit attempting to defy his penalty, but the winner was simply too strong and he now needs a switch to hurdles. *(op 11-4)*

Snargate made a pleasing debut and ran above market expectations. He will appreciate two and a half miles over hurdles.

Valhuec(FR), as on his debut, found two miles an inadequate test and is another for whom a stiffer test over hurdles will suit. *(op 10-1 tchd 15-2)*

Colline De Fleurs, whose stable had a good time of it last year with their bumper horses, made only a moderate debut and did not see her race out as well as one may have hoped. *(op 7-1)*

T/Plt: £394.60 to a £1 stake. Pool: £38,062.00. 70.40 winning tickets. T/Qpdt: £34.30 to a £1 stake. Pool: £2,510.10. 54.10 winning tickets. JR

BADEN-BADEN (L-H)

Sunday, May 22

OFFICIAL GOING: Soft

471a SCHMIDT-PAULI-JAGDRENNEN (CHASE) 2m 2f

5:15 (5:24) 5-Y-O+ **£2,837** (£1,135; £851; £567; £284)

RPR

1 **Hanseat (GER)**[336] 8-10-7..... J-GGueracague —
(Frau E Mader, Germany) **6/5**[1]

2 3 **Lutin Des Bordes (FR)**[559] 6-10-3..... DFuhrmann —
(J Vana Jr, Czech Republic) **6/4**[2]

3 dist **Water Quirl (GER)**[6] [389] 6-9-13..... CRafter —
(M F Harris) *led 3rd til headed 4 out, weakened* **102/10**

4 3 ½ **Joung Man (POL)** 8-9-13 ow7..... LSloup(7) —
(V Luka) **113/10**

5 ½ **Sunshine Story (IRE)**[392] 5-9-13..... MrTSteeger —
(C Von Der Recke, Germany) **76/10**[3]

6 shd **Art Aurel (GER)**[632] 6-10-6..... RMackowiak(4) —
(U Stoltefuss, Germany) **117/10**

P **Klimt (GER)**[975] 7-9-11..... PAJohnson —
(H Blume, Germany) **10/1**

4m 32.85s
WFA 5 from 6yo+ 2lb **8** Ran SP% **131.1**
WIN 22; PL 12, 12, 15; SF 38.
Owner Stall Africa **Bred** *unknown **Trained** Germany

NOTEBOOK

Water Quirl(GER) jumped well and made most of the running until the two favourites quickened away four out. He was beaten a total of 43 lengths.

472 - 478a (Foreign Racing) - See Raceform Interactive

412 SEDGEFIELD (L-H)

Tuesday, May 24

OFFICIAL GOING: Good to soft (soft in places)

Wind: Light, half behind

479 JOE RUTHERFORD MEMORIAL NOVICES' CHASE (13 fncs) 2m 110y

6:15 (6:15) (Class 4) 5-Y-O+ **£4,371** (£1,345; £672; £336)

Form RPR

1-P2 **1** **Adjawar (IRE)**[7] [396] 7-11-0 100..... RGarritty 117+
(J J Quinn) *mde all: drvn whn hit last: hld on gamely* **14/1**

-111 **2** ¾ **Mr Bigglesworth (NZ)**[19] [197] 7-11-0 105..... HOliver 117+
(R C Guest) *chsd ldrs: chal 9th: rdn and hung lft 2 out: blnd bdly last: r.o nr fin* **6/5**[1]

0-00 **3** 16 **Prize Ring**[19] [197] 6-11-0 104..... FKeniry 101+
(G M Moore) *in tch: outpcd 8th: rallied to chse clr ldrs bef last: no imp* **8/1**

1-40 **4** 11 **Barneys Reflection**[19] [197] 5-10-12 99.....(v) NPMulholland 89+
(A Crook) *cl up tl ouptaced fr 3 out* **16/1**

03-0 **5** 5 **Turn Of Phrase (IRE)**[24] [136] 6-10-11 105..... PWhelan(3) 83
(R A Fahey) *hld up in tch: drvn 7th: wknd next* **7/1**[3]

63-2 **6** 22 **Kalou (GER)**[13] [305] 7-11-0 103..... RMcGrath 61
(C Grant) *chsd ldrs: drvn 6th: lost tch after next: t.o* **3/1**[2]

4m 10.0s (-4.20) **Going Correction** -0.175s/f (Good)
WFA 5 from 6yo+ 2lb **6** Ran SP% **106.6**
Speed ratings: **102,101,94,88,86 76** CSF £29.94 TOTE £9.00: £2.70, £1.40; EX 43.50.
Owner Mrs Marie Taylor **Bred** His Highness The Aga Khan's Studs S C **Trained** Settrington, N Yorks

FOCUS

An ordinary event in which the pace was fair and the form should work out.

NOTEBOOK

Adjawar(IRE) jumped soundly in the main apart from a final fence error and showed the right attitude to win on this chasing debut and on ground that may have been softer than ideal. Consistency is not his strong suit though, so it remains to be seen whether this will be reproduced next time. *(op 12-1)*

Mr Bigglesworth(NZ) ◆ has been in tremendous form and, although hanging to his left again, may well have completed the four timer had he not ploughed through the final obstacle on this return to fences. He looks the type to win again in modest company. *(op 6-4)*

Prize Ring, making his chase debut, has mainly been disappointing since winning twice over hurdles in May last year and, although a similar distance behind the runner-up over hurdles last time, did not leave the impression he is about to be winning in this grade. *(op 14-1)*
Barneys Reflection, a dual hurdle winner on a sound surface earlier this year, is not the most consistent and was again well below the pick of his hurdle form back over the larger obstacles.
Turn Of Phrase(IRE), who has not won over hurdles for two years, was soundly beaten on this chase debut and looks one to tread carefully with at present. *(op 6-1 tchd 11-2)*
Kalou(GER) has won on easy ground over hurdles and ran creditably over fences last time but ran *poorly for no apparent reason. His very modest strike-rate means he is one to tread carefully with. Official explanation: jockey said gelding was unsuited by good to soft, soft in places, ground* *(op 9-4)*

480 JOHN WADE SKIP HIRE PREMIER (S) H'CAP HURDLE (FINAL) (10 hdls) 2m 5f 110y

6:45 (6:45) (Class 5) 4-Y-0+ **£6,721** (£2,068; £1,034; £517)

Form				RPR
-005	1		**In Good Faith**^{5} [429] 13-9-11 **77** .... PKinsella(7) (R E Barr) *hld up: hdwy bef 3 out: led after next: drvn out* **9/1**	85+
26-3	2	½	**Star Trooper (IRE)**^{30} [11] 9-10-1 **77** .... (p) MrCStorey(3) (Miss S E Forster) *cl up: led 4 out to after 2 out: kpt on fr last* **9/2**^{2}	85
05-P	3	22	**Comfortable Call**^{10} [352] 7-11-4 **91** .... (t) JPByrne (H Alexander) *cl up: rdn whn hit 3 out: outpcd next: btn whn mstke last* **12/1**	79+
24-0	4	5	**Frankincense (IRE)**^{30} [11] 9-10-8 **84** .... (p) PBuchanan(3) (A J Lockwood) *cl up tl rdn and wknd fr 3 out* **14/1**	65
0-05	5	1 ¾	**Al Mabrook (IRE)**^{6} [412] 10-10-10 **90** .... GThomas(7) (N G Richards) *bhd: drvn 1/2-way: sme late hdwy past btn horses: nvr on terms* **5/1**^{3}	69
-0U6	6	10	**Tiger Talk**^{7} [398] 9-11-3 **90** .... (b) HOliver (R C Guest) *hld up midfield: stdy hdwy 1/2-way: rdn and wknd bef 3 out* **8/1**	59
6-0P	7	6	**Lord Of The Land**^{17} [214] 12-10-12 **90** .... DCCostello(5) (Mrs E Slack) *hld up: struggling 4 out: nvr on terms* **33/1**	53
0-21	8	3 ½	**Talarive (USA)**^{5} [425] 9-11-12 **106** 7ex .... (tp) TJDreaper(7) (P D Niven) *hld up: hdwy and in tch 1/2-way: rdn and wknd bef 3 out* **7/2**^{1}	65
6-PF	9	26	**Step In Line (IRE)**^{6} [414] 13-9-11 **73** oh9 .... ONelmes(3) (D W Thompson) *towards rr: drvn 1/2-way: nvr on terms* **50/1**	6
P66-	P		**Amjad**^{200} [2021] 8-9-7 **73** oh9 .... MJMcAlister(7) (Miss Kate Milligan) *a bhd: struggling whn p.u bef 6th* **50/1**	—
530-	P		**Lord Pat (IRE)**^{119} [3528] 14-10-3 **76** .... PRobson (Miss Kate Milligan) *in tch to 1/2-way: t.o whn p.u bef 4 out* **33/1**	—
00-0	P		**Valuable (IRE)**^{9} [370] 8-11-0 **87** .... (p) KJohnson (R Johnson) *racd wd: cl up to 4 out: sn btn: t.o whn p.u bef 2 out* **33/1**	—
PP0-	P		**Christy Jnr (IRE)**^{133} [3314] 11-9-11 **73** oh12 .... (tp) PAspell(3) (C J Teague) *chsd ldrs: lost pl after 3rd: t.o whn p.u bef 2 out* **66/1**	—
06U-	P		**Barrow (SWI)**^{36} [4738] 8-10-12 **95** .... PJMcDonald(10) (Ferdy Murphy) *bhd: shortlived effrt 1/2-way: btn bef 3 out: p.u bef next* **16/1**	—
56-P	P		**Longstone Lass**^{10} [352] 5-11-3 **90** .... (v) ADempsey (D Carroll) *led and set decent gallop to 4 out: sn wknd: t.o whn p.u bef 2 out* **16/1**	—

5m 14.9s (-0.80) **Going Correction** +0.125s/f (Yiel) **15** Ran SP% **118.5**
Speed ratings: **106,105,97,96,95 91,89,88,78,**— —,—,—,—,— CSF £46.84 CT £498.02 TOTE £9.10: £3.70, £1.90, £7.20; EX 40.00.There was no bid for the winner.
Owner P Cartmell **Bred** C W Rogers **Trained** Seamer, N Yorks

FOCUS
A decent gallop resulted in a fair time for this valuable seller, 2.1 seconds faster than the later novices' handicap over the same trip. The form looks reasoanble for the grade.

NOTEBOOK
In Good Faith has not proved consistent since his last win in 2003 but was well suited by the decent gallop and found enough for pressure in the closing stages. He has been a grand servant for his stable and may well be capable of further success. *(tchd 8-1)*
Star Trooper(IRE) has not won for some time but shaped as though about to rectify that, He looks better than the bare form as he was up with the strong pace throughout and, although not 100% reliable, is capable of winning a similar event. *(op 7-1)*
Comfortable Call was not totally disgraced but is still operating a long way below the level of his three wins over hurdles in the first half of last year and remains one to tread carefully with. *(op 14-1)*
Frankincense(IRE) is an inconsistent performer who has not won for over two years and was again below his best with the cheekpieces on for the third time. *(op 12-1)*
Al Mabrook(IRE), back up in distance, had the race run to suit but was a long way below his best and remains best watched for now. *(tchd 7-2 and 11-2)*
Tiger Talk, from a stable in tremendous form, was a long way below his best returned to hurdles and is another who is not the most reliable around. *(op 6-1)*
Talarive(USA) had been running creditably but was found out back on this easier surface. He is not really one for short odds. *Official explanation: jockey said gelding struck into itself (tchd 4-1)*

481 GOSFORTH DECORATING & BUILDING SERVICES H'CAP CHASE (21 fncs) 3m 3f

7:15 (7:15) (Class 4) (0-105,91) 5-Y-0+ **£4,696** (£1,445; £722; £361)

Form				RPR
0-03	1		**Dark Thunder (IRE)**^{6} [417] 8-9-4 **65** .... (b) PJMcDonald(10) (Ferdy Murphy) *chsd ldrs: led 4 out: drew clr fr 2 out* **7/4**^{1}	87+
4P-1	2	13	**Go Nomadic**^{26} [81] 11-11-7 **86** .... (tp) MBradburne (P G Atkinson) *mde most to 4 out: no ex fr 2 out* **11/4**^{2}	96+
F5-F	3	13	**Ornella Speed (FR)**^{12} [321] 5-10-8 **83** .... (t) KJMercer(3) (Ferdy Murphy) *bhd tl hdwy 4 out: rdn and no imp fr next* **9/1**	75+
1-P3	4	16	**Benefit**^{5} [430] 11-11-5 **84** .... AThornton (Miss L C Siddall) *disp ld to 16th: wknd fr next* **11/2**^{3}	69+
41-P	5	18	**Camdenation (IRE)**^{25} [106] 9-11-5 **91** .... BenOrde-Powlett(7) (J R Jenkins) *in tch tl wknd fr 15th* **16/1**	53
P-45	P		**Pornic (FR)**^{9} [373] 11-10-13 **78** .... BHarding (A Crook) *hld up in tch: mstke 8th: wknd and p.u bef 15th* **12/1**	—
024-	P		**Cill Uird (IRE)**^{86} [4095] 7-11-11 **90** .... GLee (J J Lambe, Ire) *chsd ldrs: rdn 14th: wknd next: p.u bef 16th* **14/1**	—

6m 58.8s (-8.00) **Going Correction** -0.175s/f (Good) **7** Ran SP% **108.7**
WFA 5 from 7yo+ 7lb
Speed ratings: **104,100,96,91,86** —,— CSF £6.54 CT £26.31 TOTE £3.00: £2.20, £1.90; EX 7.60.
Owner Anthony O'Gorman **Bred** Miss Josephine McClements **Trained** West Witton, N Yorks
■ The first winner in Britain for rider P. J. McDonald.

FOCUS
An uncompetitive handicap in which the pace was fair and the placed horses were close to their marks.

NOTEBOOK
Dark Thunder(IRE), a soft-ground hurdle winner at this course, had run creditably over hurdles last time, attracted support and ran his best race over the larger obstacles. Stamina is his strong suit and he may be able to pick up a similarly uncompetitive race after reassessment. *(op 7-2)*
Go Nomadic, up 9lb for his Kelso victory, ran his race and looks a reasonable guide to the worth of this form. He is an honest type who should continue to give it his best shot but is vulnerable to progressive types. *(op 5-2 tchd 9-4 and 3-1)*
Ornella Speed(FR) ran arguably her best race over fences and has a little ability. She was not knocked about and may be capable of picking up a small race when there is more of an emphasis on stamina. *(op 11-1)*
Benefit ran creditably at Wetherby last time but all his best efforts and wins have been on a sound surface and he was well beaten on this rain-softened ground. *(op 4-1)*
Camdenation(IRE) is an inconsistent performer who was again well below the level of his Towcester win last month. *(op 12-1)*
Pornic(FR) was not sure to stay this far but was beaten before stamina became an issue and remains one to tread carefully with. *(op 9-1)*

482 V.P.T.A. H'CAP HURDLE (8 hdls) 2m 1f

7:45 (7:45) (Class 4) (0-110,105) 4-Y-0+ **£3,354** (£1,032; £516; £258)

Form				RPR
0-02	1		**Ton-Chee**^{22} [149] 6-11-1 **94** .... PRobson (K W Hogg) *chsd ldrs: led after 3 out: clr whn j.lft last: hung lft: all out* **8/1**	103+
3-11	2	1	**He's Hot Right Now (NZ)**^{6} [412] 6-11-2 **95** .... (p) HOliver (R C Guest) *in tch: outpcd 4 out: rallied and chsd wnr after next: rdn and no imp 2 out: kpt on fr last: jst hld* **6/4**^{1}	101
545	3	6	**Merryvale Man**^{5} [428] 8-11-2 **102** .... SCrawford(7) (Miss Kariana Key) *led to after 3 out: outpcd whn mstke next* **4/1**^{2}	104+
62-2	4	½	**Leopold (SLO)**^{9} [369] 4-10-8 **98** .... CPoste(7) (M F Harris) *hld up in tch: hdwy 4 out: outpcd next: n.d after* **7/1**	93
0P6-	5	4	**Hope Sound (IRE)**^{13} [4213] 5-11-12 **105** .... (v) ADobbin (B Ellison) *cl up tl wknd fr 3 out* **11/1**	100
6F-2	6	2 ½	**Heraclitean Fire (IRE)**^{12} [320] 8-11-8 **101** .... GLee (J J Lambe, Ire) *hld up in tch: drvn and wknd bef 3 out* **5/1**^{3}	94

4m 8.60s (2.10) **Going Correction** +0.125s/f (Yiel)
WFA 4 from 5yo+ 4lb **6** Ran SP% **108.6**
Speed ratings: **100,99,96,96,94 93** CSF £19.84 TOTE £9.90: £3.50, £1.40; EX 28.50.
Owner Anthony White **Bred** Auldyn Stud Ltd **Trained** Isle Of Man

FOCUS
Another run-of-the-mill handicap in which the pace was only fair but the form looks sound enough.

NOTEBOOK
Ton-Chee confirmed previous course and distance promise to win with little to spare but, given that he has looked more effective on a sound surface, may be a bit better than the bare form. His tendency to hang is a worry, though. *(op 7-1 tchd 9-1)*
He's Hot Right Now(NZ) has been in good heart since the cheekpieces have been fitted and, unpenalised for last week's course and distance win, ran right up to his best. He left the impression that he would be suited by a try over further. *(op 7-4 tchd 15-8 and 11-8)*
Merryvale Man had the run of the race but folded tamely and, although well treated on the pick of last year's form, he looks one to tread carefully with at present. *(op 9-2)*
Leopold(SLO) had been running creditably on a sound surface but, although not disgraced on easy ground, is likely to continue to look vulnerable from his current mark. *(op 11-2 tchd 15-2)*
Hope Sound(IRE), whose form has been patchy since his chase win here in December, was below his best returned to hurdles and is another who does not inspire confidence. *(op 10-1 tchd 16-1)*
Heraclitean Fire(IRE), who ran well on fast ground at Perth last time, has form on soft ground but was well below that level for no apparent reason. *(op 4-1)*

483 HARRY COATES MEMORIAL NOVICES' H'CAP HURDLE (10 hdls) 2m 5f 110y

8:15 (8:15) (Class 4) (0-105,102) 4-Y-0+ **£3,380** (£1,040; £520; £260)

Form				RPR
4-51	1		**Lutin Du Moulin (FR)**^{6} [414] 6-11-4 **94** 7ex .... (v) ADobbin (L Lungo) *prom: rdn after 4 out: rallied next: led between last 2: styd on wl* **6/5**^{1}	104+
P-14	2	7	**River Mist (IRE)**^{11} [334] 6-11-12 **102** .... KRenwick (Karen McLintock) *cl up: led whn nt fluent 6th: hdd between last 2: one pce* **7/2**^{2}	104+
10-4	3	hd	**Sikasso (USA)**^{27} [64] 9-11-0 **97** .... (p) CDSharkey(7) (Mrs K Walton) *led to 1/2-way: cl up: rdn 3 out: one pce next* **9/2**^{3}	98
0-00	4	10	**Lampos (USA)**^{10} [352] 5-10-4 **80** .... (v) GLee (Miss J A Camacho) *hld up in tch: rdn and wknd after 3 out* **20/1**	71
06-4	5	6	**French Tune (FR)**^{22} [147] 7-10-8 **84** .... AThornton (Miss S E Hall) *chsd ldrs to 3 out: sn rdn and wknd* **6/1**	69
00P-	6	2 ½	**Charnwood Street (IRE)**^{89} [4035] 6-10-1 **80** .... (v) ONelmes(3) (D Shaw) *hld up: struggling 1/2-way: sn btn* **33/1**	62

5m 17.0s (1.30) **Going Correction** +0.125s/f (Yiel) **6** Ran SP% **107.8**
Speed ratings: **102,99,99,95,93 92** CSF £5.48 TOTE £2.00: £1.30, £2.10; EX 2.70.
Owner K Foster **Bred** S C E A Moulin **Trained** Carruthertown, D'fries & G'way

FOCUS
An ordinary event in which the gallop increased markedly at the fourth last. the placed horses were to their marks and the form looks reasonable.

NOTEBOOK
Lutin Du Moulin(FR) ◆ followed up his recent course and distance win on these softer conditions and, although showed a tendency to go in snatches, is the type to improve further upped to three miles. He looks sure to win more races. *(op 10-11 tchd 5-6, 5-4 in a place)*
River Mist(IRE) has been running creditably and may be a bit better than the bare form as he increased the pace a long way from home. She should continue to give a good account around this trip. *(op 4-1 tchd 9-2)*
Sikasso(USA) was not disgraced but left the impression that a stiffer test of stamina would be in her favour. *(op 6-1)*
Lampos(USA) continues below his best and did not really leave the impression that a return to *winning ways was on the cards. Official explanation: jockey said gelding had breathing problem (op 12-1 tchd 22-1)*
French Tune(FR), an inconsistent maiden, left the impression that he would have been suited by less of a test of stamina. *(op 12-1 tchd 14-1)*
Charnwood Street(IRE), whose sole win from 49 starts was on the Flat in 2002, looks one to leave alone. *(op 10-1)*

484 HAPPY 50TH BIRTHDAY, JIM TONES STANDARD OPEN NATIONAL HUNT FLAT RACE 2m 1f

8:45 (8:45) (Class 6) 4-6-Y-0 **£1,897** (£542; £271)

Form				RPR
0-	1		**Lindbergh Law (USA)**^{163} [2790] 5-11-4 .... ADobbin (G A Swinbank) *hld up in tch: smooth hdwy 4f out: led over 1f out: pushed out* **11/4**^{1}	94+
025-	2	6	**Arctic Minster**^{59} [4552] 6-11-4 .... NHannity (G A Harker) *led to over 1f out: kpt on same pce* **3/1**^{2}	88

3 6 **Phantom Major (FR)** 4-10-7 .... MissRDavidson(7) 78+
(Mrs R L Elliot) *hld up: hdwy fr over 2f out: kpt on strly fnl f: no ch w first two* **11/1**3

0-3 4 3 **Itsdowntoben**16 [241] 4-11-0 .... GLee 75
(D McCain) *hld up midfield: effrt over 3f out: no imp fr 2f out* **11/4**1

5 1 **Stoneriggs Merc (IRE)** 4-11-0 .... BHarding 74
(Mrs E Slack) *bhd tl hdwy over 2f out: kpt on fnl f: no imp* **20/1**

6 23 **Paddy George (IRE)** 4-11-0 .... DO'Meara 51
(A J Lockwood) *chsd ldrs tl outpcd over 3f out: n.d after* **25/1**

0 7 1 **Burgau (IRE)**9 [375] 6-11-1 .... LVickers(3) 54
(A D Brown) *cl up to 4f out: sn btn* **12/1**

0-U 8 3/4 **Cloudmor (IRE)**12 [323] 4-11-0 .... KJohnson 49
(Miss S E Forster) *prom tl wknd fr 4f out* **20/1**

0/0 9 5 **Terimons Daughter**9 [375] 6-10-8 .... KJMercer(3) 41
(E W Tuer) *a bhd* **25/1**

0 10 dist **Chantilly Passion (FR)**12 [323] 4-11-0 .... RMcGrath —
(B Storey) *keen in midfield: rdn and wknd 4f out* **33/1**

000- 11 14 **Crackington (FR)**65 [4477] 5-11-4 .... JPByrne —
(H Alexander) *plld hrd: in tch tl wknd over 4f out* **100/1**

0- 12 21 **Maddy The Hatter**63 [4513] 6-10-4 .... MissTJackson(7) —
(Miss T Jackson) *racd wd: hld up: shortlived effrt 1/2-way: sn btn* **100/1**

13 13 **Callitwhatyoulike** 4-11-0 .... PRobson —
(Miss Kate Milligan) *bhd: rdn 1/2-way: sn btn* **25/1**

4m 10.1s (3.20) **Going Correction** +0.125s/f (Yiel)
WFA 4 from 5yo 4lb 5 from 6yo 2lb **13** Ran SP% **120.3**
Speed ratings: **97,94,91,89,89 78,78,77,75,— —,—,—** CSF £9.99 TOTE £4.10: £1.60, £1.40, £5.30; EX 12.00 Place 6 £13.57, Place 5 £7.73.
Owner Mrs F H Crone & Mrs J A Lawson **Bred** Caboodee Stud **Trained** Melsonby, N Yorks

FOCUS
A fair gallop but almost certainly ordinary form. The third sets the standard and the performance of the third caught the eye.

NOTEBOOK
Lindbergh Law(USA) left his debut form some way behind on this easier ground and, although this bare form is nothing special, he appeals as the type to win races over obstacles. *(op 7-2 tchd 4-1)*
Arctic Minster is a reliable sort who seemed to run his race and he looks a good guide to the level of this form. He should pick up a small race over hurdles in due course. *(op 4-1 tchd 9-2)*
Phantom Major(FR) ◆, a half-brother to a winning hurdler/chaser in France, very much caught the eye on this racecourse debut without being at all knocked about and looks likely to leave this bare *form behind granted a stiffer test over hurdles.Official explanation: jockey said, regarding the running and riding, orders were to put the colt in the race and to see how the race unfolded, adding that colt ran in snatches and after having a breather at the top of the hill it ran on in the straight (tchd 14-1)*
Itsdowntoben had his limitations exposed and left the impression that he would be suited by a decent test of stamina when sent over obstacles. *(op 9-4 tchd 15-8)*
Stoneriggs Merc(IRE), out of a winning Irish chaser, ran creditably on this debut but looks more of a long-term prospect. *(tchd 16-1 and 25-1)*
Paddy George(IRE), out of an unraced half-sister to a winning Irish pointer, was well beaten on this debut but is entitled to come on for the experience. *(op 14-1)*
T/Plt: £35.10 to a £1 stake. Pool: £44,387.50. 921.65 winning tickets. T/Qpdt: £5.40 to a £1 stake. Pool: £3,392.10. 460.70 winning tickets. RY

356 WORCESTER (L-H)
Tuesday, May 24

OFFICIAL GOING: Good (good to firm in places)
Wind: Slight, across Weather: fine

485 LADIES DAY IS JUNE 4TH FOUR YEAR OLD NOVICES' HURDLE (8 hdls) 2m
6:25 (6:25) (Class 4) 4-Y-O **£3,406** (£1,048; £524; £262)

Form RPR

3 1 **Rajayoga**29 [21] 4-10-12 .... LAspell 99+
(M H Tompkins) *t.k.h: hdwy 2 out: hit last: sn led: rdn out* **10/1**

1-2 2 5 **Argent Ou Or (FR)**14 [274] 4-10-12 .... APMcCoy 94
(M C Pipe) *hld up in tch: wnt 2nd 3rd: led 2 out: sn rdn: hdd sn after last: one pce* **3/1**3

30-1 3 1 3/4 **Kentmere (IRE)**21 [177] 4-11-5 104 .... TDoyle 99
(P R Webber) *led: reminder after 4th: rdn appr 3 out: hdd 2 out: one pce flat* **2/1**2

4 29 **Alekhine (IRE)**214 4-10-12 .... RJohnson 63
(P J Hobbs) *chsd ldr: j.big and pckd 2nd: j. slowly and lost 2nd 3rd: rdn after 5th: wknd appr 2 out* **7/4**1

5 2 1/2 **Magic Amigo**24 4-10-12 .... TScudamore 61
(J R Jenkins) *hld up: struggling appr 3 out* **22/1**

6 dist **Kilminchy Lady (IRE)**293 4-10-5 .... ChristianWilliams —
(B Llewellyn) *a bhd: t.o fr 5th* **100/1**

4m 2.00s (13.60) **Going Correction** +0.15s/f (Yiel) **6** Ran SP% **109.1**
Speed ratings: **72,69,68,54,52** — CSF £38.00 TOTE £11.50: £1.30, £2.30; EX 33.00.
Owner Mystic Meg Limited **Bred** Mystic Meg Limited **Trained** Newmarket, Suffolk

FOCUS
A decent pace but the time was poor as the runners had stood still for 16 seconds after the starting tape went back. The form appears reasonable for the grade.

NOTEBOOK
Rajayoga was suited by the fact they eventually went a good clip and won going away. *(op 8-1 tchd 13-2)*
Argent Ou Or(FR) looked set to score when leading at the penultimate hurdle. However, he was well outpointed by the winner in the end. *(op 9-4 tchd 10-3)*
Kentmere(IRE) could not overcome a penalty for his win in a Ludlow handicap. *(tchd 5-2)*
Alekhine(IRE), a seven-furlong winner on his debut as a juvenile, stayed a mile and a quarter on the Flat. Very novicey early on, he did jump better as the race progressed and it remains to be seen if stamina is going to be a problem. *(op 5-2)*

486 HOSPITALITY BESIDE PARADE RING NOVICES' H'CAP CHASE (15 fncs) 2m 4f 110y
6:55 (6:55) (Class 4) (0-105,105) 5-Y-O+ **£4,121** (£1,268; £634; £317)

Form RPR

53-U 1 **Celtic Boy (IRE)**16 [239] 7-11-10 **103** .... RJohnson 125+
(P Bowen) *hld up: hdwy 6th: mstke 8th: led 9th: j.rt fr 10th: clr 3 out: unchal* **7/4**1

-242 2 23 **Tosawi (IRE)**8 [388] 9-11-5 **98** .... (p) TScudamore 90+
(R J Hodges) *chsd ldr: led 4th: mstke 5th: hdd 6th: led 7th: j.rt thereafter: hdd 9th: no ch w wnr fr 3 out* **4/1**3

00-P 3 7 **Ballyaahbutt (IRE)**10 [358] 6-10-2 **81** .... JamesDavies 63
(B G Powell) *hld up: mstke 8th: rdn 9th: struggling fr 11th: tk 3rd flat* **8/1**

40-0 4 4 **Saddler's Quest**30 [1] 8-10-5 **84** .... JMogford 63+
(B P J Baugh) *hld up and bhd: rdn and hdwy after 11th: wkng whn lft 3rd 3 out* **20/1**

4F0/ P **Lovers Tale**488 [3447] 7-10-6 **85** .... PFlynn —
(G A Ham) *prom: wkng whn mstke 7th: t.o whn mstke 10th: p.u after 11th* **50/1**

60-0 U **Court Award (IRE)**18 [201] 8-9-7 **79** oh3 .... CMStudd(7) —
(B G Powell) *j.rt: hld up in tch: rdn appr 7th: wkng whn mstke and uns rdr 8th* **14/1**

44-4 P **Lightin' Jack (IRE)**14 [271] 7-11-11 **104** .... BJCrowley —
(Miss E C Lavelle) *led to 4th: led 6th to 7th: wknd 11th: bhd whn p.u bef 4 out* **3/1**2

142- F **Dramatic Quest**35 [4917] 8-11-9 **105** .... (p) DCrosse(3) —
(A G Juckes) *hld up: mstke 4th: reminders after 6th: rdn 9th: hdwy 11th: 8 l 3rd and btn whn fell 3 out* **14/1**

5m 12.5s (5.00) **Going Correction** +0.225s/f (Yiel) **8** Ran SP% **112.5**
Speed ratings: **99,90,87,86,— —,—,—** CSF £9.31 CT £41.80 TOTE £2.40: £1.30, £1.10, £2.60; EX 6.60.
Owner Walters Plant Hire Ltd **Bred** William G Corrigan **Trained** Little Newcastle, Pembrokes

FOCUS
An uncompetitive event which took little winning although the winner is value for further.

NOTEBOOK
Celtic Boy(IRE) made amends for his untimely exit at Uttoxeter and drew right away despite jumping right-handed. This form does not amount to much. *(op 6-4 tchd 15-8)*
Tosawi(IRE) began to jump right even earlier than the winner and was fighting a losing battle when particularly bad at the third last. *Official explanation: jockey said gelding bled from nose (op 3-1)*
Ballyaahbutt(IRE) just plodded on to secure the minor berth. *(op 14-1)*
Saddler's Quest was making his chasing debut over a distance he never seemed to get over timber.
Dramatic Quest, possibly slightly distracted when coming to grief, would have finished at least third. *(op 9-2)*
Lightin' Jack(IRE) *Official explanation: jockey said gelding was never travelling (op 9-2)*

487 CANNONS HEALTH CLUB MARES' ONLY MAIDEN HURDLE (10 hdls) 2m 4f
7:25 (7:27) (Class 4) 4-Y-O+ **£3,507** (£1,002; £501)

Form RPR

2P-2 1 **Shady Grey**16 [245] 7-11-0 92 .... NFehily 100+
(C J Mann) *prom: led 3rd: rdn clr last: r.o* **5/2**1

P0-3 2 4 **Killonemoonlight (IRE)**14 [283] 6-11-0 78 .... TDoyle 95
(D R Stoddart) *hld up and bhd: hdwy 6th: outpcd appr 3 out: styd on flat: nt trble wnr* **20/1**

3 1/2 **Keep On Movin' (IRE)**18 4-10-9 .... APMcCoy 90
(T G Mills) *t.k.h: a.p: wnt 2nd appr 5th: rdn and ev ch 2 out: one pce* **8/1**3

PP-6 4 13 **Delphine**18 [201] 6-11-0 .... JMMaguire 82
(T R George) *hld up and bhd: rdn and hdwy 7th: wknd after 3 out* **40/1**

6- 5 nk **Lets Get Busy (IRE)**176 [2542] 5-10-11 .... RYoung(3) 86+
(J W Mullins) *hld up towards rr: hdwy after 4th: rdn after 7th: wkng whn mstke 3 out: no ch whn mstke last* **66/1**

42-4 6 dist **Separated (USA)**26 [77] 4-10-9 .... RJohnson —
(P J Hobbs) *hld up towards rr: hdwy appr 7th: rdn and wknd appr 3 out: t.o* **7/2**2

PP-6 7 4 **Twilight Dancer (IRE)**14 [272] 7-10-9 .... RStephens(5) —
(Miss H E Roberts) *led to 3rd: hit 6th: wknd after 7th: t.o* **40/1**

04 8 nk **Bob's Finesse**14 [285] 5-10-11 .... RWalford(3) —
(J W Mullins) *a bhd: t.o fr 5th* **100/1**

30-U 9 29 **Breema Donna**7 [399] 7-11-0 88 .... DRDennis —
(R Dickin) *a bhd: t.o fr 7th* **25/1**

0PP- 10 11 **Hayley's Pearl**100 [3841] 6-11-0 65 .... JamesDavies —
(Mrs P Ford) *a bhd: t.o fr 7th* **100/1**

000- P **Miss Trooper**104 [3760] 5-10-9 .... JDiment(5) —
(F Jordan) *j.rt: prom to 5th: t.o whn p.u bef 3 out* **100/1**

320- P **Floranz**187 [2290] 9-11-0 86 .... JMogford —
(Mrs M Evans) *prom to 4th: wknd qckly: bhd whn p.u bef 6th* **40/1**

05- P **Colorado Pearl (IRE)**34 [4933] 4-10-9 .... (t) ChristianWilliams —
(Miss G Browne) *a towards rr: t.o whn p.u bef last* **25/1**

0-3F P **Seemma**14 [285] 5-11-0 .... MAFitzgerald —
(N I M Rossiter) *mid-div: j.rt 4th: wknd and p.u bef 6th: dismntd* **28/1**

P **Ballydoyle Counsel (IRE)**23 7-10-7 .... PMerrigan(7) —
(T Wall) *prom: rdn appr 4th: wknd appr 5th: t.o whn p.u bef 3 out* **20/1**

3-34 F **Samandara (FR)**14 [274] 5-11-0 103 .... WHutchinson 95
(A King) *hld up in mid-div: hdwy 6th: 2 l 3rd and rdn whn stmbld and fell 2 out* **5/2**1

4m 48.7s (0.70) **Going Correction** +0.15s/f (Yiel)
WFA 4 from 5yo+ 5lb **16** Ran SP% **122.9**
Speed ratings: **104,102,102,97,96 —,—,—,—,— —,—,—,—,— —** CSF £55.51 TOTE £3.80: £1.40, £4.50, £3.80; EX 91.50.
Owner P A Sweeney **Bred** A Dawson **Trained** Upper Lambourn, Berks

FOCUS
A poor contest, and although the form looks messy the time was reasonable.

NOTEBOOK
Shady Grey sensibly had plenty of use made of her having run so well over three miles here last time. *(op 3-1 tchd 7-2)*
Killonemoonlight(IRE) eventually found her second wind and this Irish point winner needs a return to a longer trip.
Keep On Movin'(IRE), a ten-furlong Polytrack winner, stayed a mile and a half. This was a satisfactory start to her hurdling career, albeit at a low level. *(op 9-1)*
Delphine could only manage a short-lived effort. *(tchd 33-1)*
Lets Get Busy(IRE) did not appear to get the trip on her hurdling debut. *(op 50-1)*
Floranz *Official explanation: trainer said mare lost a shoe and returned sore (op 2-1 tchd 11-4, 3-1 in a place)*
Samandara(FR) did not appear to be going as well as the winner when she was unlucky to come to grief two out. *(op 2-1 tchd 11-4, 3-1 in a place)*
Seemma *Official explanation: jockey said mare was lame (op 2-1 tchd 11-4, 3-1 in a place)*
Colorado Pearl(IRE) *Official explanation: jockey said filly had breathing problem (op 2-1 tchd 11-4, 3-1 in a place)*

488 SUE AND BOB DANIEL SILVER WEDDING ANNIVERSARY H'CAP HURDLE (10 hdls) 2m 4f
7:55 (7:57) (Class 3) (0-115,114) 4-Y-O+ **£5,083** (£1,564; £782; £391)

Form RPR

04P- 1 **Lady Racquet (IRE)**40 [4837] 6-11-6 **108** .... ATinkler 111+
(Mrs A J Bowlby) *hld up: hdwy appr 7th: led 2 out: sn rdn and hung rt: hung lft flat: drvn out* **20/1**

P0-0 **2** *1* **Lupin (FR)**[24] [136] 6-11-3 **105** NFehily 106
(A W Carroll) *hld up and bhd: hdwy 7th: rdn and ev ch last: nt qckn towards fin* **20/1**
15-6 **3** *3 ½* **Magical Liaison (IRE)**[25] [109] 7-10-4 **92** (b) WMarston 90
(W Jenks) *hld up: hdwy after 4th: led 7th to 2 out: sn hrd rdn: no ex flat* **50/1**
22F- **4** *9* **Mini Dare**[38] [4868] 8-11-3 **105** (p) LAspell 94
(O Sherwood) *hld up and bhd: hdwy appr 3 out: nvr trbld ldrs* **14/1**
25-6 **5** *2 ½* **A Bit Of Fun**[17] [220] 4-10-9 **107** LTreadwell[(5)] 89+
(J T Stimpson) *hld up in mid-div: hdwy appr 6th: rdn appr 3 out: wknd appr 2 out* **16/1**
3P-2 **6** *7* **Rifleman (IRE)**[16] [236] 5-11-7 **109** (v) RJohnson 91+
(P Bowen) *led appr 2nd: mstke 6th: hdd 7th: wknd appr 3 out* **10/3**[1]
15-0 **7** *8* **Fard Du Moulin Mas (FR)**[14] [275] 12-10-12 **100** BJCrowley 71
(M E D Francis) *prom to 6th* **20/1**
P1-6 **8** *14* **Prince Of Persia**[8] [387] 5-11-12 **114** (p) TScudamore 71
(R S Brookhouse) *hld up in mid-div: hdwy 5th: rdn and wknd after 7th* **14/1**
165- **9** *4* **Bill Brown**[72] [4343] 7-10-6 **94** BHitchcott 47
(R Dickin) *hld up: rdn 6th: sn bhd* **20/1**
112- **10** *4* **Wilfred (IRE)**[210] [1849] 4-11-3 **110** (b) APMcCoy 54
(Jonjo O'Neill) *w ldr: mstke 5th: wknd appr 7th* **4/1**[2]
F-P6 **11** *19* **Haydens Field**[3] [451] 11-11-3 **105** (p) ChristianWilliams 35
(Miss H Lewis) *prom: rdn appr 4th: wknd appr 5th* **14/1**
P6-3 **R** **Joshua's Bay**[16] [233] 7-11-6 **108** JCulloty —
(J R Jenkins) *in rr whn rn out 2nd* **9/1**
3P3- **P** **Mystery (GER)**[34] [4932] 7-10-10 **98** (t) JMMaguire —
(T R George) *hld up: bhd whn p.u bef 6th* **5/1**[3]
23P/ **P** **Beaver Lodge (IRE)**[31] [1359] 8-11-8 **110** JMogford —
(B P J Baugh) *led tl appr 2nd: hit 5th: sn wknd: bhd whn p.u bef 3 out* **66/1**

4m 46.4s (-1.60) **Going Correction** +0.15s/f (Yiel)
WFA 4 from 5yo+ 5lb **14** Ran SP% **118.1**
Speed ratings: **109,108,107,103,102 99,96,91,89,87 80,—,—,—** CSF £332.81 CT £17945.32 TOTE £23.20: £5.20, £19.70, £8.20; EX 471.40.
Owner The Norman Partnership **Bred** Martin Molony **Trained** Kingston Lisle, Oxon

FOCUS
A modest handicap but the first and third ran to their marks and the time was decent enough.

NOTEBOOK
Lady Racquet(IRE) took advantage of a drop in grade but hung both ways under pressure on ground that could have been on the fast side for her.
Lupin(FR) appreciated the return to a longer trip but could not quite take advantage of the winner's foibles. *(tchd 25-1)*
Magical Liaison(IRE) stepped up on his two previous outings this spring but really needs extreme distances.
Mini Dare, another who stays well, requires softer ground to be really affective over this sort of trip.
A Bit Of Fun got found out by the extra half-mile. *(op 14-1)*
Rifleman(IRE), narrowly beaten over three miles last time, may have done too much in the lead in the first-time visor. *(op 9-2)*
Wilfred(IRE) was stepping up in distance on this first run for seven months. *(op 3-1)*
Mystery(GER) *Official explanation: jockey said gelding was never travelling (op 6-1 tchd 9-2)*

489 ARENA LEISURE H'CAP CHASE (18 fncs) 2m 7f 110y
8:25 (8:25) (Class 3) (0-120,118) 5-Y-0+ **£5,551** (£1,708; £854; £427)

Form RPR
UPP- **1** **Personal Assurance**[44] [4792] 8-11-3 **109** (b[1]) APMcCoy 117+
(Jonjo O'Neill) *hld up: hdwy 8th: hit 3 out: led appr last: hdd flat: rallied to ld cl home: all out* **7/1**
6-3P **2** *shd* **Gumley Gale**[13] [297] 10-11-8 **114** (t) PJBrennan 122+
(K Bishop) *a.p: wnt 2nd 12th: rdn to ld appr 2 out: hdd and swtchd rt appr last: led flat: hdd cl home: r.o* **10/1**
4P- **3** *10* **Navarone**[52] [4692] 11-11-2 **108** PMoloney 105
(Ian Williams) *led: rdn and hdd appr 2 out: wknd appr last* **12/1**
26-3 **4** *1 ¼* **Mark Equal**[8] [386] 9-11-10 **116** (t) TScudamore 112
(M C Pipe) *hld up and bhd: hdwy 11th: rdn and wknd 2 out* **12/1**
33-4 **5** *15* **Jacquemart Colombe (FR)**[22] [150] 8-11-8 **114** ChristianWilliams 95
(P Bowen) *chsd ldrs tl wknd 12th* **10/3**[1]
353- **6** *10* **Farnaheezview (IRE)**[138] [3240] 7-11-9 **115** LAspell 86
(O Sherwood) *hld up: mstke 7th: bhd fr 10th: j.rt thereafter* **12/1**
/0-P **7** *16* **Jacdor (IRE)**[30] [12] 11-10-11 **103** JEMoore 58
(R Dickin) *rdn 12th: a bhd* **22/1**
061- **8** *28* **Mounsey Castle**[47] [4757] 8-11-5 **111** RJohnson 38
(P J Hobbs) *chsd ldr: mstke 3rd: lost 2nd 12th: wknd after 14th* **9/2**[2]
53P- **P** **Mercato (FR)**[79] [4205] 9-10-9 **104** DCrosse[(3)] —
(J R Best) *nt jump wl: a bhd: t.o whn p.u bef 12th* **13/2**[3]
P1-P **P** **Ankles Back (IRE)**[16] [240] 8-11-1 **107** MAFitzgerald —
(H D Daly) *hld up in tch: hit 8th: wknd 12th: bhd whn p.u bef 4 out* **8/1**

5m 54.9s **Going Correction** +0.225s/f (Yiel) **10** Ran SP% **114.7**
Speed ratings: **109,108,105,105,100 96,91,82,—,—** CSF £72.32 CT £824.58 TOTE £9.90: £3.40, £1.40, £3.90; EX 145.80.
Owner Christopher W T Johnston **Bred** T G And Mrs Bish **Trained** Cheltenham, Gloucs

FOCUS
An exciting finish to an ordinary handicap that is rated through the runner-up to his mark.

NOTEBOOK
Personal Assurance was dropped a total of 11lb after being pulled up in his two previous starts. He bounced back to form with McCoy at his strongest. *(op 11-2)*
Gumley Gale, unsuited by the fast ground when pulled up at Exeter, lost no caste in defeat in a driving finish. *(op 9-1)*
Navarone adopted his usual tactics but the two principals were carrying too many guns for him. *(op 11-1)*
Mark Equal may have found this trip beyond him but he has never been one to find much off the bridle. *(op 10-1 tchd 9-1)*
Jacquemart Colombe(FR), never going particularly well, was in trouble a long way from home. *(op 7-2 tchd 4-1)*
Mercato(FR) *Official explanation: jockey said gelding was lame (op 6-1 tchd 7-1)*
Ankles Back(IRE) *Official explanation: jockey said gelding had breathing problem (op 6-1 tchd 7-1)*

490 SEVERN SUITE RESTAURANT STANDARD OPEN NATIONAL HUNT FLAT RACE 2m
8:55 (8:59) (Class 6) 4-6-Y-0 **£1,897** (£542; £271)

Form RPR
1 **Nocivo (FR)** 4-11-0 RJohnson 104+
(H D Daly) *hld up: hdwy 7f out: shkn up to ld wl over 1f out: rdn and r.o wl* **8/1**[3]
2 *8* **I'm Lovin It (IRE)**[22] 5-10-13 MrNWilliams[(5)] 95
(P F Nicholls) *plld hrd in tch: led over 3f out: hung lft and hdd wl over 1f out: one pce* **4/1**[2]
3 **3** *2 ½* **Ar Nos Na Gaoithe (IRE)**[10] [361] 6-10-11 ChristianWilliams 85
(Mrs A M Thorpe) *hld up in mid-div: rdn and hdwy over 3f out: styd on ins fnl f* **12/1**
0- **4** *¾* **Spring Junior (FR)**[35] [4922] 4-11-0 PJBrennan 87
(P J Hobbs) *led 6f: w ldr: led over 5f out tl over 3f out: styd on again ins fnl f* **20/1**
5 *½* **Mapuche (IRE)** 5-11-4 APMcCoy 91
(A M Balding) *hld up and bhd: hdwy 5f out: rdn and one pce fnl 3f* **7/4**[1]
653- **6** *½* **Orange Street**[44] [4801] 5-11-4 LAspell 90
(Mrs L J Mongan) *a.p: ev ch over 3f out: rdn and one pce fnl 2f* **16/1**
7 *nk* **Blue Splash (FR)** 5-11-4 JTizzard 90
(P Bowen) *hld up in mid-div: hdwy on ins over 3f out: one pce fnl 2f* **10/1**
8 *3* **Ol' Man River (IRE)** 5-10-11 MrDMansell[(7)] 87
(H D Daly) *hld up and bhd: c wd st: hdwy 3f out: edgd lft over 1f out: no imp* **25/1**
9 *shd* **Miss Mobility** 5-10-8 RWalford[(3)] 80
(A J Wilson) *hld up and bhd: rdn over 2f out: r.o fnl f: nvr nrr* **66/1**
00-2 **10** *5* **Ice Cream (FR)**[14] [277] 4-10-7 BJCrowley 71
(M E D Francis) *prom tl wknd over 3f out* **8/1**[3]
041/ **11** *¾* **Cap Classique**[622] [1334] 6-11-4 PMerrigan[(7)] 88
(Mrs H Dalton) *unruly s: mid-div: hdwy whn nt clr run bnd over 3f out: n.d after* **20/1**
1P/ **12** *nk* **Bowdens Lane**[23] 6-10-13 RStephens[(5)] 81
(D O Stephens) *prom: ev ch over 3f out: sn rdn and wknd* **50/1**
13 *3* **Indyana Run** 4-10-7 JCulloty 67
(A Hollingsworth) *a bhd* **16/1**
0- **14** *2 ½* **York Dancer**[167] [2709] 4-10-7 VSlattery 64
(A D Smith) *a bhd* **50/1**
15 *7* **Mrs White (IRE)** 5-10-4 MrMWilesmith[(7)] 61
(M S Wilesmith) *hld up in tch: wknd over 5f out* **40/1**
4 **16** *15* **Cutting Edge**[14] [277] 6-10-4 JAJenkins[(7)] 46
(A J Chamberlain) *prom: led 10f out tl over 5f out: wknd over 4f out* **50/1**
0- **17** *3 ½* **Pleased To Receive (IRE)**[58] [4589] 5-11-4 JAMcCarthy 50
(A M Hales) *t.k.h: hung rt over 5f out: a bhd* **66/1**
0 **18** *8* **Commanche Gun**[21] [179] 5-11-4 JMMaguire 42
(A E Price) *prom tl wknd over 3f out* **66/1**

3m 51.5s (3.70) **Going Correction** +0.15s/f (Yiel)
WFA 4 from 5yo 4lb 5 from 6yo 2lb **18** Ran SP% **133.3**
Speed ratings: **96,92,90,90,90 89,89,88,88,85 85,85,83,82,78 71,69,65** CSF £40.17 TOTE £11.80: £2.80, £3.30, £3.90; EX 49.20 Place 6 £8,064.40, Place 5 £1,490.17.
Owner John Hanley John Brindley **Bred** Mme Jean-Pierre Gemerec-Couteaudier **Trained** Stanton Lacy, Shropshire
■ Stewards' Enquiry : P Merrigan caution: improper riding, struck gelding in annoyance
P J Brennan three-day ban: used whip with excessive frequency and force (Jun 4-6)

FOCUS
A typical slowly-run bumper, although the winner is value for further and looks above average, with the third setting the level.

NOTEBOOK
Nocivo(FR) ◆, a springer in the market, is out of a mare who won over two miles on the Flat in France. Moving smoothly to the front, he did not give those who were in on the gamble too many anxious moments and he can go on from here. *(op 20-1)*
I'm Lovin It(IRE), who failed to complete in a couple of points, gave a good account of himself especially considering he failed to settle. *(op 7-2 tchd 5-1)*
Ar Nos Na Gaoithe(IRE) was doing her best work in the closing stages and would have preferred a stronger gallop. *(op 10-1)*
Spring Junior(FR) ran a lot better than at Towcester and eventually found a second wind after making a lot of the running.
Mapuche(IRE) is a full-brother to seven furlong and mile Group Three winner Hidden Meadow and *Imperial Cup winner Scorned. Built like a three-mile chaser, he lacked the required turn of foot. (op 9-4 tchd 6-4)*
Orange Street was another beaten for finishing speed.
Blue Splash(FR) is a full-brother to bumper winner Ungaro. *(tchd 8-1)*
Ol' Man River(IRE) ◆, a stable companion of the well-backed winner, is a half-brother to the hurdler Anns Girl. He will be better for the experience and it will be interesting to see if he is professionally ridden next time. *(op 33-1)*
T/Plt: £5,269.80 to a £1 stake. Pool: £44,035.70. 6.10 winning tickets. T/Qpdt: £671.90 to a £1 stake. Pool: £3,359.50. 3.70 winning tickets. KH

491 - 494a (Foreign Racing) - See Raceform Interactive

CARTMEL (L-H)
Wednesday, May 25

OFFICIAL GOING: Heavy changing to soft (heavy in places) after race 3 (3.25)
After a morning inspection and over 3" rain over the previous week conditions were patchy and pretty testing. Last fence omitted, leaving 5f run-in.
Wind: moderate 1/2 against Weather: mainly fine

495 BRIAN DUNN AND JOHN WADE PLAYBOYS MAIDEN HURDLE (8 hdls) 2m 1f 110y
2:15 (2:15) (Class 4) 4-Y-0+ **£3,788** (£1,165; £582; £291)

Form RPR
5-2 **1** **Bergerac (NZ)**[28] [59] 7-11-0 HOliver 105+
(R C Guest) *trckd ldrs: led between last 2: wnt clr after last: heavily eased* **5/4**[1]
03-0 **2** *9* **Petrolero (ARG)**[23] [149] 6-11-0 87 RMcGrath 93+
(James Moffatt) *nt fluent: trckd ldr: led 2 out: sn hdd 3 l down whn hit last: no ch w wnr* **9/1**
00-3 **3** *3* **Pearson Glen (IRE)**[11] [343] 6-11-0 ADobbin 87
(James Moffatt) *chsd ldrs: one pce fr 2 out* **6/1**[3]
2 **4** *15* **Rossclare (IRE)**[13] [323] 5-11-0 GLee 72
(J J Lambe, Ire) *t.k.h: led to 2 out: sn wknd* **4/1**[2]
/0-0 **5** *8* **Joe Malone (IRE)**[11] [343] 6-11-0 BHarding 64
(N G Richards) *rr-div: outpcd 5th: sn bhd* **16/1**
6 *7* **Aztec Prince (IRE)**[53] 5-10-11 MrCStorey[(3)] 57
(Miss S E Forster) *chsd ldrs: outpcd 5th: sn lost pl* **14/1**
50 **7** *16* **Ocotillo**[6] [418] 5-11-0 ADempsey 41
(James Moffatt) *chsd ldrs: reminders 4th: lost pl after next* **50/1**
8 *dist* **Mushraag (IRE)**[684] 5-10-7 PCO'Neill[(7)] —
(J J Lambe, Ire) *nt fluent: sn bhd: t.o 5th* **14/1**

0PP- **F** **Roy McAvoy (IRE)**[34] [4943] 7-10-11 ....(t) PWhelan(3) —
(M A Barnes) *chsd ldrs: 5th and pushed along whn fell 3 out* **50/1**

4m 21.6s (5.90) **Going Correction** +0.55s/f (Soft) **9** Ran SP% **111.9**
Speed ratings: **108,104,102,96,92 89,82,—,—** CSF £13.02 TOTE £1.80: £1.10, £2.80, £1.40; EX 13.70.

Owner Paul Beck **Bred** J D O'Flaherty & Mrs M L O'Flaherty **Trained** Brancepeth, Co Durham

FOCUS

A poor novices' hurdle and a heavily eased down winner who is value for more than the official margin. The time was fair for the conditions and the form looks reasonable for the grade.

NOTEBOOK

Bergerac(NZ), who looked different gear in the paddock, was kept wide of the rail. He made this look very easy and this potential chaser was value for at least 15 lengths. *(tchd 6-4)*

Petrolero(ARG), clumsy at best, but after showing head it was soon clear the winner was simply toying with him. *(op 11-1)*

Pearson Glen(IRE) kept on in his own time to finish a long way clear of the rest. This ground may not have been in his favour. *(op 9-2)*

Rossclare(IRE) would not settle in front and stopped to nothing when headed. *(op 7-2 tchd 10-3)*

Joe Malone(IRE) looks to have strictly limited ability and the one hope is that fences will improve him.

496 BURLINGTON SLATE MARES' ONLY NOVICES' (S) HURDLE (8 hdls) 2m 1f 110y

2:50 (2:50) (Class 5) 4-Y-0+ **£2,712** (£775; £387)

Form RPR

U4-0 **1** **Faraway Echo**[12] [334] 4-10-6 80.................... RMcGrath 74+
(James Moffatt) *trckd ldrs: led after 2 out: 10 l clr 1f out: tired and drvn rt out* **10/3**[1]

PP-5 **2** *2 ½* **Minster Abbi**[31] [14] 5-10-10 ....(p) NPMulholland 74
(W Storey) *chsd ldrs: kpt on to take 2nd run-in* **8/1**

4-05 **3** *2* **Noras Legacy (IRE)**[18] [214] 7-10-7 70.................... PBuchanan(3) 72
(Miss Lucinda V Russell) *chsd ldrs: outpcd between last 2: kpt on run-in* **12/1**

5-00 **4** *3* **Private Jessica**[8] [399] 4-10-6 83....................(b) HOliver 66+
(R C Guest) *trckd ldrs: led after 5th tl after 2 out: wknd fnl f* **11/2**[3]

44-0 **5** *5* **Katie Kai**[14] [302] 4-10-6 79.................... KJohnson 60
(Miss S E Forster) *w ldrs: led 3rd tl after next: wknd 3 out* **9/2**[2]

U5-4 **6** *shd* **Roadworthy (IRE)**[18] [214] 8-10-3 75.................... MrSFMagee(7) 64
(J K Magee, Ire) *led to 3rd: lost pl 5th: n.d after* **8/1**

0-02 **7** *8* **Scamp**[18] [214] 6-10-10 70....................(p) KRenwick 56
(R Shiels) *trckd ldrs: wknd 2 out* **10/1**

8 *5* **Teutonic (IRE)**[103] 4-10-3 .... PAspell(3) 47
(R F Fisher) *stdd s: hld up detached in last: hdwy 5th: wknd 2 out* **33/1**

P **Tribal Suspect (IRE)** 6-10-7 .... KJMercer(3) —
(Mrs S A Watt) *bhd: t.o 5th: p.u bef last* **14/1**

0 **P** **Daring Games**[7] [415] 4-10-3 ow4....................(p) CEddery(7) —
(B Ellison) *bhd fr 5th: t.o whn p.u bef 2 out* **33/1**

P **P** **Stylistic (IRE)**[14] [302] 4-10-6 .... GLee —
(J J Lambe, Ire) *bhd: hdwy 4th: sn wknd: bhd whn p.u bef last* **14/1**

4m 26.3s (10.60) **Going Correction** +0.55s/f (Soft)
WFA 4 from 5yo+ 4lb **11** Ran SP% **114.9**
Speed ratings: **98,96,96,94,92 92,88,86,—,—** — CSF £29.65 TOTE £5.00: £1.50, £2.60, £3.50; EX 41.20.There was no bid for the winner.

Owner Alf Chadwick **Bred** R P Williams **Trained** Cartmel, Cumbria

FOCUS

A dire event but reliable enough with the winner and third running to their marks.

NOTEBOOK

Faraway Echo, back in trip and on ground she can handle, took a decisive advantage at the elbow soon after the final flight but in the end she was begging for the line to come. *(op 3-1 tchd 7-2)*

Minster Abbi, improved by the fitting of cheekpieces, kept on to snatch second spot in the closing stages. *(op 9-1)*

Noras Legacy(IRE), tapped for toe between the last two, was staying on when it was all over and will appreciate a slightly stuffer test.

Private Jessica, with the blinkers retained, tended to do too much in front and, after showing clear second at the elbow, she was very tired at the line. *(op 7-2)*

Katie Kai, unplaced in eight previous starts, has shown she can handle the soft but, even dropped in grade, in the end she finished soundly beaten. *(op 8-1)*

Roadworthy(IRE), very keen to post, was on the retreat a long way out. *(op 9-1)*

497 ALBERT O'CONNOR'S 80TH BIRTHDAY H'CAP CHASE (12 fncs 2 omitted) 2m 5f 110y

3:25 (3:25) (Class 3) (0-115,113) 5-Y-0+ **£6,126** (£1,885; £942; £471)

Form RPR

31P **1** **Pequenita**[3] [466] 5-11-3 110....................(p) LMcGrath(3) 111+
(R C Guest) *jumpd hesitantly: chsd ldrs: reminders 6th: wnt 2nd 8th: led over 2f out: sn clr: rdn rt out: fin tired* **7/1**

1P3- **2** *2 ½* **Monita Des Bois (FR)**[39] [4867] 5-11-9 113.................... SThomas 110+
(Miss Venetia Williams) *led: 6 l clr whn blnd last: hdd over 2f out: kpt on fnl f* **7/2**[2]

0-22 **3** *1 ¾* **Galway Breeze (IRE)**[6] [427] 10-11-1 109.................... CDSharkey(7) 106+
(Mrs K Walton) *chsd ldrs: hit 2nd: outpcd 7th: rallied run-in: kpt on fnl f* **7/2**[2]

1-5P **4** *16* **Pavey Ark (IRE)**[7] [414] 7-10-5 92.................... RMcGrath 76+
(James Moffatt) *chsd ldrs: wknd last* **5/1**[3]

63-0 **5** *dist* **Stormy Beech**[25] [122] 9-10-1 88 oh4 ow1....................(p) KJohnson —
(R Johnson) *t.k.h: hdwy to chse ldrs 3rd: wknd 8th: virtually p.u run-in: t.o* **13/2**

31P- **P** **Just Sooty**[160] [2849] 10-11-12 113.................... ADobbin —
(N G Richards) *chsd ldrs: lost pl and j. slowly 8th: t.o whn p.u bef next* **10/3**[1]

5m 36.2s (5.70) **Going Correction** +0.475s/f (Soft)
WFA 5 from 7yo+ 3lb **6** Ran SP% **110.0**
Speed ratings: **108,107,106,100,—** — CSF £30.32 TOTE £11.50: £4.00, £2.70; EX 38.40.

Owner Paul Beck **Bred** Rodney Meredith **Trained** Brancepeth, Co Durham

FOCUS

Not a strong race but run at a fair gallop in the conditions. neither of the first two look that well handicapped.

NOTEBOOK

Pequenita, pulled up on totally different ground at Southwell, was very hesitant, jumped slowly and looked reluctant at time. Taking it up halfway up the extended run-in, after shooting clear in the end she struggled to last home. *(op 11-2)*

Monita Des Bois(FR), on her handicap bow, had the ground to suit but, after a blunder at the last, normally two out, she was swept aside by the winner on the run-in. To her credit she fought back all the way to the line. *(op 11-4)*

Galway Breeze(IRE), struggling to keep tabs on the first two some way out, to his credit battled hard all the way to the line on ground a good deal more testing than he prefers. *(tchd 4-1)*

Pavey Ark(IRE), back over fences, waved goodbye to the first three on the extended run-in. *(op 8-1)*

Stormy Beech, out of the handicap, is not in the best of form and this trip is probably beyond him. Even so it was a very poor effort. *(op 9-1)*

Just Sooty was already on the retreat when he jumped slowly and lost touch at the ditch, four out. *Absent since December, connections blamed the testing underfoot conditions.Official explanation: jockey said gelding had been unsuited by the heavy ground (op 11-4)*

498 R.F. MILLER HUNTERS' CHASE (FOR THE HORACE D. PAIN MEMORIAL TROPHY) (15 fncs 3 omitted) 3m 2f

4:00 (4:00) (Class 6) 5-Y-0+ **£1,568** (£448; £224)

Form RPR

23-P **1** **Victoria's Boy (IRE)**[10] 12-11-9 87.................... MrGBrewer(5) 92
(Mrs W Wild) *le to 7th: led 11th: to 3 out: styd on to ld last strides* **4/1**[2]

3-4U **2** *hd* **Ikdam Melody (IRE)**[4] [455] 9-11-11 93....................(p) MissJFoster(7) 97+
(Miss J E Foster) *jnd ldrs 5th: led 7th to 11th: led 3 out: hdd nr fin* **5/1**[3]

P0/U **3** *9* **Wilfie Wild**[24] 9-11-7 .... MrsLWard(7) 89+
(Mrs Lynne Ward) *hld up: hdwy and prom 6th: chsd ldrs fr 8th: blnd 12th: rdr hesitant appr 2 out: fdd fnl f* **6/1**

3/P- **4** *dist* **Galen (IRE)**[10] 14-11-7 67.................... MissSSharratt(7) 45
(Miss J Froggatt) *chsd ldrs to 8th: sn outpcd by first 3: btn 48 l* **33/1**

01-5 **5** *1 ¼* **Natural (IRE)**[23] [151] 8-11-13 77....................(t) MrTDavidson(5) 48
(Mrs J Williamson) *chsd ldrs to 8th: sn outpcd: bhd fr 3 out* **6/1**

55/0 **6** *23* **Hip Pocket (IRE)**[18] [221] 9-11-7 .... MrRMcCarthy(7) —
(Robert Bowling) *wnt poor 4th 11th: wknd fr 3 out* **14/1**

4/P- **P** **Gus Berry (IRE)**[25] 12-11-7 73.................... MrWKinsey(7) —
(Mrs Alison Christmas) *sn bhd: t.o 11th: p.u bef next* **20/1**

UP-3 **P** **Kilcaskin Gold (IRE)**[25] [125] 10-11-7 .... MrAJFindlay(7) —
(R A Ross) *chsd ldrs: drvn along 5th: wknd 8th: sn bhd: p.u bef 11th* **14/1**

PP3/ **P** **Over The Beck (IRE)**[3] 12-11-9 ....(p) MissAArmitage(5) —
(Mrs H D Marks) *hdwy to chse ldrs 8th: outpcd 10th: bhd fr 12th: t.o whn p.u bef last* **33/1**

240/ **U** **Venture To Fly (IRE)**[18] 11-11-8 100 ow1............ MrJamieAlexander(7) —
(N W Alexander) *mstkes: lost pl 5th: nehind fr 10th: poor 8th whn blnd and uns rdr 12th* **7/2**[1]

6m 56.8s (16.20) **Going Correction** +0.475s/f (Soft) **10** Ran SP% **111.4**
Speed ratings: **94,93,91,—,— —,—,—,—,—** CSF £23.11 TOTE £4.70: £1.60, £2.90, £2.30; EX 29.50.

Owner J J Coates **Bred** George And Mark Millar **Trained** Ross-On-Wye, H'fords

■ Stewards' Enquiry : Mr T Davidson one-day ban: used whip with excessive frequency (Jun 14)

FOCUS

A very modest hunter chase and just three in contention throughout the final circuit. The winner sets the standard.

NOTEBOOK

Victoria's Boy(IRE), winner of this two years ago and runner-up last term, would not accept defeat and snatched the spoils right on the line. *(tchd 9-2)*

Ikdam Melody(IRE) pressed home the advantage but in the end was just pipped. *(op 4-1)*

Wilfie Wild, happy to sit off the pace on the first circuit, made a mess of the ditch four out. His *rider was in two minds about which fence to miss out and he tired badly in the final home straight. (op 4-1)*

Galen(IRE), well held in points, is a pensioner with his best days a long way behind him now. *(op 28-1)*

Natural(IRE), a dual point winner, was in trouble after a circuit and the Stewards did not like his rider's use of his tick. *(op 8-1)*

Venture To Fly(IRE), in good form in points, was let down by his jumping and soon in trouble, was well behind when losing his rider at the ditch four out.

499 COOPER KENYON BURROWS H'CAP HURDLE (11 hdls) 2m 6f

4:35 (4:35) (Class 3) (0-115,110) 4-Y-0+ **£5,752** (£1,770; £885; £442)

Form RPR

02-6 **1** **Crystal Gift**[28] [64] 13-11-5 **110**.................... PCO'Neill(7) 111
(A C Whillans) *joind ldrs 6th: led after 3 out: hld on wl towards fin* **11/1**

20- **2** *¾* **Assumetheposition (FR)**[60] [4557] 5-10-5 **92**....................(p) LMcGrath(3) 92
(R C Guest) *hld up in rr: hdwy 8th: sn chsng ldrs: wnt 2nd between last 2: sn upsides: no ex nr fin* **4/1**[1]

C3-1 **3** *10* **Lanzlo (FR)**[18] [215] 8-11-7 **105**.................... RMcGrath 95
(James Moffatt) *wnt prom 7th: one pce between last 2* **13/2**

300- **4** *3* **Fantastico (IRE)**[35] [4929] 5-10-1 **92**....................(p) CDSharkey(7) 79
(Mrs K Walton) *led tl after 3 out: wknd appr last* **14/1**

-026 **5** *5* **Political Sox**[7] [410] 11-11-4 **109**.................... GThomas(7) 91
(R Nixon) *chsd ldrs: lost pl 2 out* **14/1**

165- **6** *½* **Peter's Imp (IRE)**[9] [2401] 10-10-5 **89**.................... PRobson 72+
(A Berry) *in tch: outpcd fr 3 out: 5th whn hit last* **9/2**[2]

U01- **7** *3 ½* **Leapogues Lady (IRE)**[35] [4928] 9-10-13 **97**.................... NPMulholland 75
(C A McBratney, Ire) *hdwy to chse ldrs 6th: rdn and lost pl 3 out* **11/2**[3]

0P0- **8** *7* **Green 'N' Gold**[45] [4783] 5-10-6 **90**.................... GLee 61
(M D Hammond) *hld up in rr: effrt 8th: wknd next* **7/1**

P-22 **9** *16* **Iris's Prince**[13] [317] 6-11-12 **110**.................... RGarritty 65
(A Crook) *nt fluent: w ldrs: lost pl 3 out: sn bhd* **15/2**

5m 47.8s (11.80) **Going Correction** +0.55s/f (Soft) **9** Ran SP% **112.8**
Speed ratings: **100,99,96,95,93 93,91,89,83** CSF £54.23 CT £311.76 TOTE £11.70: £3.90, £2.00, £2.00; EX 63.10.

Owner Mrs L M Whillans **Bred** Grange Stud (uk) **Trained** Newmill-On-Slitrig, Borders

FOCUS

Just a steady gallop with the whole field stacked up three from home but in the end they came home well strung out. The form looks suspect although the first two ran close to their marks.

NOTEBOOK

Crystal Gift, who last won over three years ago, likes this ground but this was his first win beyond two and a half miles. The old boy would simply not be denied and recording his eighth career win, might now retire. *(tchd 12-1)*

Assumetheposition(FR), improved since being fitted with cheekpieces, was ridden to get the extended trip. Sent in pursuit of the winner between the last two, in the end the old boy proved simply too determined. *(tchd 9-2)*

Lanzlo(FR), 7lb higher, in the end could not keep tabs on the first two on ground possibly more testing than he prefers. *(op 6-1)*

Fantastico(IRE), having his second outing after a break, took them along in his own time but he tired badly going to the final flight. He does not appreciate ground as testing at this.

Political Sox kept tabs on the leaders but his best days seem behind him now.

Peter's Imp(IRE), whose three wins over hurdles were round here, is basically just plating class. *(op 11-2)*

500 ULTRACARE PROPERTY MANAGEMENT NOVICES' HURDLE (11 hdls) 2m 6f

5:10 (5:11) (Class 4) 4-Y-0+ **£3,949** (£1,215; £607; £303)

Form RPR

10-1 **1** **Flintoff (USA)**[16] [261] 4-11-2 100.................... HOliver 101+
(R C Guest) *trckd ldrs gng wl: led on bit sn after last: v easily* **2/5**[1]

5-52 **2** *23* **Cody**[7] 417 6-11-0 78 .... ADobbin 79+
(James Moffatt) *led: qcknd 7th: rdn along next: hdd sn after last: 6 l down and wl hld whn virtually p.u last 100yds: walked over line* **11/4**[2]

0-P **3** *21* **Aba Gold (IRE)**[14] 302 5-10-2 .... DFlavin(5) 33
(Mrs L B Normile) *reminders 6th: chsng ldrs next: wknd 8th* **25/1**

0/ **4** *4* **Bella Liana (IRE)**[23] 158 5-10-4 .... PBuchanan(3) 29
(J Clements, Ire) *w ldr: rdn 8th: wknd appr last* **20/1**[3]

5 *dist* **Mill Lane** 8-10-4 ow4 .... MissSSharratt(7) —
(R Hollinshead) *bhd and pushed along 5th: t.o 8th: btn 34 l* **20/1**[3]

5m 59.1s (23.10) **Going Correction** +0.55s/f (Soft) **5** Ran SP% **111.5**
Speed ratings: **80,71,64,62,—** CSF £1.84 TOTE £1.30: £1.10, £1.10; EX 1.80 Place 6 £50.07, Place 5 £35.16.
Owner Andrew Flintoff & Paul Beck **Bred** Mill Ridge Farm Ltd & Jamm Ltd **Trained** Brancepeth, Co Durham

FOCUS
Just an amble round resulting in a very slow time, 11.3 seconds slower than the previous handicap. The winner is value for less than the official margin as the runner-up was eased.

NOTEBOOK
Flintoff(USA) made this look very one sided and with his rider keeping him under severe restraint in the end he won by a wide margin from a 78-rated plater. *(op 4-11 tchd 1-2)*
Cody, a maiden after 27 previous outings, set his own pace. He was only half a dozen lengths down on the hard-held winner when he was pulled up to a walk near the line. *(op 3-1 tchd 7-2)*
Aba Gold(IRE), who beat one home in her bumper, had been pulled up on her hurdling bow. *(op 28-1)*
Bella Liana(IRE) had shown precious little in five start in bumpers. *(op 25-1)*
T/Plt: £48.90 to a £1 stake. Pool: £33,229.20 - 495.95 winning units T/Qpdt: £10.20 to a £1 stake. Pool: £1,692.20 - 122.50 winning units WG

100 FONTWELL (L-H)
Wednesday, May 25

OFFICIAL GOING: Good to firm (good in places)
Wind: Moderate behind Weather: Sunny spells

501 GERRARD FINANCIAL SERVICES CONDITIONAL JOCKEYS' H'CAP HURDLE (11 hdls) 2m 6f 110y
2:05 (2:05) (Class 4) (0-100,100) 4-Y-0+ **£2,688** (£768; £384)

Form RPR

P00/ **1** **Spirit Of Tenby (IRE)**[912] 2130 8-10-0 **74** .... JamesDavies 75+
(W K Goldsworthy) *t.k.h in midfield: effrt appr 2 out: drvn to ld run-in: hung lft fnl 75 yds: styd on wl* **25/1**

46-1 **2** *1 ½* **Morson Boy (USA)**[15] 273 5-11-3 **99** .... RSpate(8) 98
(Mrs K Waldron) *hld up in rr: hdwy 3 out: led 2 out: hung lft and hdd run-in: nt qckn fnl 50 yds* **7/1**

66P- **3** *7* **Tass Heel (IRE)**[33] 4964 6-11-2 **90** .... JPByrne 84+
(B J Llewellyn) *in tch: j.lft and hmpd rivals 8th: drvn to chse ldng pair whn blnd 2 out: one pce* **16/1**

34/0 **4** *1 ¾* **Spider Boy**[17] 229 8-10-0 **74** oh10 ....(p) RStephens 65+
(Miss Z C Davison) *trckd ldr: led 3 out to next: sn outpcd* **66/1**

30-4 **5** *¾* **Manque Neuf**[26] 105 6-10-3 **77** ....(p) ATinkler 67
(Mrs L Richards) *in tch: mstke 3rd: bmpd 8th: no imp fr 3 out* **7/2**[2]

F2-1 **6** *¾* **The Kirk (NZ)**[19] 206 7-11-9 **100** .... RLucey-Butler(3) 90+
(M Madgwick) *hld up and bhd: mstke 1st: mod effrt 3 out: nt pce to get involved: styd on run-in* **10/3**[1]

04-P **7** *hd* **General Duroc (IRE)**[28] 54 9-11-12 **100** ....(bt) WHutchinson 89
(R T Phillips) *mid-div: hmpd 8th: rdn and no hdwy fr 3 out* **10/1**

2-05 **8** *1 ¼* **Eau Pure (FR)**[12] 329 8-10-12 **92** ....(t) EDehdashti(6) 79
(G L Moore) *trckd ldrs: n.m.r bnd appr 2 out: sn hrd rdn and btn* **11/2**[3]

0-U2 **9** *dist* **Murphy's Nails (IRE)**[16] 265 8-11-6 **94** .... MNicolls —
(K C Bailey) *led: mstke 3rd: hdd & wknd 3 out* **12/1**

00P- **10** *6* **Celestial Heights (IRE)**[40] 4853 6-10-12 **89** ....(p) ONelmes(3) —
(O Sherwood) *chsd ldrs tl hmpd and mstke 8th: nt rcvr and sn bhd* **25/1**

/P0- **11** *dist* **Jumpty Dumpty (FR)**[131] 3341 8-10-11 **85** .... RWalford —
(J C Tuck) *a towards rr: wl bhd fr 8th* **11/1**

5m 31.0s (-13.80) **Going Correction** -0.65s/f (Firm) **11** Ran SP% **113.4**
Speed ratings: **97,96,94,93,93 92,92,92,—,—** — CSF £183.16 CT £2885.05 TOTE £41.50: £10.60, £3.80, £6.40; EX 388.10.
Owner Miss Paula Hearn **Bred** Golden Vale Stud **Trained** Yerbeston, Pembrokes

FOCUS
A big shock, with the winner returning from a long layoff. The second appeared to run up to his current best but the form may not be totally reliable.

NOTEBOOK
Spirit Of Tenby(IRE), returning from a 912-day break, showed a good attitude to beat the second after jumping the last. He has acted well on quick ground in the distant past and will presumably be kept on the go during the summer if staying sound. However, he does have a history of problems and may struggle to reproduce the form.
Morson Boy(USA), making his debut for new connections, travelled easily into the lead coming to the last, but found much less than expected after. He is not the force he once was on the Flat, but is capable of picking up similar races during the summer. *(op 9-2)*
Tass Heel(IRE) ran his best race over timber on his handicap debut, despite a couple of sloppy jumps in the final circuit. He is much happier on quick ground and will be much more interesting in the coming months.
Spider Boy is still a maiden but put up his best performance for some time. The drop in trip appeared to suit him and he could improve again over slightly shorter.
Manque Neuf made a bad mistake three from home, knocking the jockey sideways, and never got back into the race. *(op 6-1)*
The Kirk(NZ) had shown improved form recently, but disappointed on his last visit to the track. He ran badly again and might be better on a more galloping track. *(op 3-1 tchd 7-2)*
Murphy's Nails(IRE) made a lot of the early running but dropped away after jumping poorly.
Jumpty Dumpty(FR) was supported in the market before the race at long odds, but never looked like repaying his investors. *(op 12-1 tchd 10-1)*

502 GERRARD INVESTMENT MANAGEMENT (S) HURDLE (9 hdls) 2m 2f 110y
2:40 (2:40) (Class 5) 4-Y-0+ **£2,359** (£674; £337)

Form RPR

-226 **1** **Borehill Joker**[10] 370 9-10-7 101 .... WKennedy(7) 93+
(J L Spearing) *hld up in rr: hdwy 6th: led 2 out: sn rdn clr: drvn out run-in* **7/4**[1]

33-4 **2** *2* **Madison Avenue (GER)**[26] 102 8-11-0 87 ....(b) AThornton 91
(T M Jones) *prom: led on bit after 3 out: hdd and outpcd by wnr next: kpt on: a hld* **9/2**[2]

00-3 **3** *21* **Sonic Sound**[17] 230 6-10-7 100 ....(t) RSpate(7) 70
(Mrs K Waldron) *chsd ldrs: led 6th tl after 3 out: sn hrd rdn and easily outpcd by ldng pair* **5/1**[3]

24-0 **4** *3* **Grand Prairie (SWE)**[27] 75 9-11-0 90 ....(p) JEMoore 67
(G L Moore) *hld up and bhd: gd hdwy to chse ldrs 3 out: sn outpcd* **6/1**

04P- **5** *¾* **Spiritual Dancer (IRE)**[127] 3402 10-11-0 95 .... LAspell 66
(L Wells) *mid-div: lost pl after 3rd: bhd and rdn 6th: styd on fr 2 out* **20/1**

0/0 **6** *8* **Philosophic**[17] 232 11-11-0 .... BHitchcott 58
(Mrs L C Jewell) *chsd ldr: j.rt 3rd: lost pl 5th: sn wl bhd and drvn along: styd on past btn horses run-in* **50/1**

00-3 **7** *½* **Final Command**[27] 75 8-11-0 87 ....(v[1]) JMogford 58
(J C Tuck) *mid-div: hdwy to ld 5th: mstke and hdd next: wknd after 3 out* **11/1**

P41- **8** *23* **Fireside Legend (IRE)**[37] 4913 6-11-0 77 ....(v) RLucey-Butler(7) 42
(Miss M P Bryant) *a towards rr: lost tch and n.d fr 6th* **20/1**

P/0- **9** *1 ¾* **Big Quick (IRE)**[66] 4484 10-10-7 93 .... MrJMorgan(7) 33
(L Wells) *chsd ldrs: racd wd in bk st fr 6th: wknd after 3 out* **25/1**

/0-0 **10** *¾* **It's Just Sally**[8] 399 8-10-7 75 .... JamesDavies 25
(B G Powell) *mid-div: rdn 5th: sn wknd* **33/1**

0-P0 **P** **Isam Top (FR)**[17] 232 9-11-0 74 .... PHide —
(M J Hogan) *led to 5th: sn wknd: t.o whn p.u bef 2 out* **40/1**

4m 25.7s (-10.30) **Going Correction** -0.65s/f (Firm) **11** Ran SP% **114.5**
Speed ratings: **94,93,84,83,82 79,79,69,68,68** — CSF £8.32 TOTE £2.50: £1.10, £1.40, £2.10; EX 11.80.The winner was bought in for 6,800gns. Sonic Sound was the subject of a friendly claim for £6,000.
Owner Mrs H M Haddock **Bred** O J Stokes **Trained** Kinnersley, Worcs

FOCUS
A very moderate seller, in which the first two pulled a long way clear and the race could be rated higher.

NOTEBOOK
Borehill Joker ◆ would have been giving lots of weight away to most of his rivals had it been a handicap, and used that advantage to win decisively. He is due to run in a selling chase over the course on Sunday, if he comes out of the race unscathed, and will be very hard to beat in his current form. *(op 13-8 tchd 2-1)*
Madison Avenue(GER), who was keen in the early stages of the race, was the only one to give the winner any kind of serious challenge in the home straight. He stays further and can pick up a similar event in the near future. *(op 8-1)*
Sonic Sound, running for his third trainer within a year, again gave the impression he would be worth a try over further as he ran on after being outpaced. *(op 10-3)*
Grand Prairie(SWE) was pushed along with a circuit to go and never got into the race at any stage. He has proved to be most disappointing recently. *(op 13-2)*
Spiritual Dancer(IRE) ran on from miles off the pace to pass a few tired rivals up the home straight. The form of the race does not look particularly strong and this effort probably amounts to very little. *(op 25-1)*
Final Command, wearing a first-time visor, ran far too freely in the early stages and never got home. *(op 9-1)*

503 GERRARD INVESTMENT MANAGEMENT H'CAP CHASE (16 fncs) 2m 6f
3:15 (3:15) (Class 4) (0-90,83) 5-Y-0+ **£4,063** (£1,250; £625; £312)

Form RPR

P0-2 **1** **Maidstone Monument (IRE)**[7] 416 10-11-0 **71** .... APMcCoy 98+
(Mrs A M Thorpe) *prom: led 7th and maintained str pce: drew clr 2 out: easily* **9/4**[1]

P6P- **2** *8* **Mollycarrsbreakfast**[40] 4856 10-10-10 **67** .... TDoyle 84+
(K Bishop) *prom: chsd wnr 9th: 2 l down whn mstke 4 out: no ex fr next* **5/1**[3]

F0-0 **3** *dist* **Honneur Fontenail (FR)**[19] 206 6-10-0 **64** .... KBurke(7) 46
(N J Hawke) *mid-div: wnt mod 4th at 11th: nt pce to trble ldng pair: tk remote 3rd 2 out* **25/1**

24-3 **4** *¾* **Tudor King (IRE)**[22] 176 11-11-12 **83** .... PJBrennan 64
(J S King) *led and set str pce to 7th: rdn in 3rd pl at 10th: steadily outpcd by ldng pair* **8/1**

0P-P **5** *nk* **Colombe D'Or**[15] 278 8-10-7 **64** ....(p) PMoloney 45
(M F Harris) *sn outpcd and bhd: modest hdwy into midfield 8th: nt pce to get involved* **25/1**

P15- **6** *hd* **Kappelhoff (IRE)**[34] 4940 8-11-5 **76** ....(v[1]) MBatchelor 57
(Mrs L Richards) *sn outpcd and bhd: passed a few btn horses fnl circ: nvr nr ldrs* **14/1**

3-60 **7** *dist* **Stopwatch (IRE)**[15] 283 10-11-2 **73** ....(p) LAspell —
(Mrs L C Jewell) *in tch to 10th* **16/1**

P2-2 **8** *14* **Alfred The Grey**[26] 101 8-11-1 **72** ....(p) PHide —
(G L Moore) *sn drvn along and bhd: t.o whn blnd 9th* **7/2**[2]

2-P4 **9** *7* **River Mere**[11] 346 11-11-3 **79** .... DLaverty(5) —
(Mrs L Williamson) *mstkes in midfield: hrd rdn 9th: sn no ch* **10/1**

P0-P **10** *dist* **Hisar (IRE)**[21] 181 12-10-11 **68** ....(t) AThornton —
(P C Ritchens) *in tch to 10th* **33/1**

5-43 **P** **Maybeseven**[15] 276 11-11-0 **71** ....(p) CLlewellyn —
(R Dickin) *sn outpcd and bhd: hrd rdn 7th: t.o whn p.u after 10th* **16/1**

5m 27.9s (-15.90) **Going Correction** -0.65s/f (Firm) **11** Ran SP% **118.9**
Speed ratings: **101,98,—,—,— —,—,—,—,—** — CSF £14.40 CT £225.75 TOTE £3.80: £1.30, £2.50, £18.80; EX 16.90.
Owner Don Jenkins **Bred** Louis Lanigan **Trained** Bronwydd Arms, Carmarthens

FOCUS
A moderate staying chase run at a very good early pace. The winner was particularly well treated, won with plenty in hand and the first two look likely to win again.

NOTEBOOK
Maidstone Monument(IRE), with McCoy taking over from a conditional jockey, kept up a fierce gallop to win very nicely. He is very well handicapped on his best form and is more than capable of following this success up, even under a penalty. *(op 2-1 tchd 11-4)*
Mollycarrsbrekfast, making his debut for the yard, gave chase to the winner without really looking likely to get on terms. A mistake four out did not help, but he kept on nicely for pressure and is not badly handicapped on his form of last spring. *(op 8-1)*
Honneur Fontenail(FR) looked very tired after jumping the last, keeping on stoutly to snatch a weary third. His only victory came over the course last March and this was his best performance since then, albeit well beaten. *(op 20-1)*
Tudor King(IRE) relinquished the lead fairly early in the race and was readily left behind afterwards. He much prefers to have his own way in front. *(op 11-2)*
Colombe D'Or was always a long way behind, but was kept going to win a minor battle for fifth. *(tchd 28-1)*
Kappelhoff(IRE), raised a massive 16lb in the weights for his last-time-out success, never figured with a chance at any stage. *(op 16-1)*
Alfred The Grey soon lost interest behind the quick pace and never got into the race. *Official explanation: trainer said gelding was unable to go the early pace and lost interest (op 9-2 tchd 5-1)*

504 GERRARD FINANCIAL SERVICES NOVICES' HURDLE (9 hdls) 2m 2f 110y
3:50 (3:50) (Class 4) 4-Y-0+ **£3,493** (£1,075; £537; £268)

Form RPR

2 **1** **Settlement Craic (IRE)**[17] 230 4-10-9 .... JimCrowley 110+
(T G Mills) *trckd ldrs: led after 3 out: easily drew clr* **6/4**[1]

440- **2** *12* **Dubai Ace (USA)**[71] 4386 4-10-9 111....................(t) JGoldstein 90
(Miss Sheena West) *chsd ldrs: hrd rdn 3 out: wnt 2nd but hld by wnr whn j.lft next* **13/8**[2]

00-1 **3** *20* **Blueberry Ice (IRE)**[27] 77 7-10-7 107.................... CMStudd(7) 75
(B G Powell) *chsd ldrs: rdn and lost pl after 4th: mod hdwy appr 2 out: n.d* **7/1**[3]

3F-P **4** *¾* **Peppershot**[16] 261 5-10-7 100....................(p) JPemberton(7) 74
(G P Enright) *led 2nd: stmbld bnd appr 4th: hdd and mstke 5th: sn bhd: styd on run-in* **20/1**

3 **5** *6* **Sound Skin (IRE)**[8] 394 7-11-0 .... LAspell 68
(A Ennis) *hld up towards rr: stmbld bdly bnd appr 4th: nvr in chalng position* **18/1**

0P-0 **6** *5* **Sean (IRE)**[17] 230 6-11-0 .... TScudamore 63
(Mrs L C Jewell) *in tch tl wknd appr 3 out* **33/1**

7 *22* **Colony Hill (IRE)** 7-11-0 .... BHitchcott 41
(R H Buckler) *wd most of way: hld up towards rr: blnd 2nd: n.d fr 6th* **33/1**

00-0 **P** **Can Can Flyer (IRE)**[26] 100 4-10-9.................... JMogford —
(J C Tuck) *hld up and bhd: mstke and reminder 4th: p.u after next* **40/1**

P0- **U** **Derwent (USA)**[14] 4756 6-10-4 .... PDavey(10) 89
(R H Buckler) *trckd ldrs: led after 5th: hit next: blnd bdly 3 out: sn hdd and outpcd: 3rd and btn whn uns rdr last* **20/1**

0- **P** **Sonderborg**[8] 1939 4-10-2 ....(p) MBatchelor —
(Miss A M Newton-Smith) *led to 2nd: hung rt bnd after next: led briefly 5th: losing pl whn stmbld next: sn p.u* **100/1**

4m 24.8s (-11.20) **Going Correction** -0.65s/f (Firm)
WFA 4 from 5yo+ 4lb **10** Ran SP% **114.7**
Speed ratings: **96,90,82,82,79 77,68,—,—,—** CSF £3.86 TOTE £2.20: £1.10, £1.30, £1.70; EX 3.90.
Owner Buxted Partnership **Bred** Pollards Stables **Trained** Headley, Surrey

FOCUS
Just a modest race but the winner was once considered good enough to have a Derby entry, and won with tons in hand. He is rated value for 20 lengths and the race could be rated higher.

NOTEBOOK
Settlement Craic(IRE) won without coming under any pressure. He was very capable on the Flat, winning handicaps from a mark of 85, so should have more than enough class to do well over hurdles. He has the size and scope to handle hurdling and will progress with experience. He is to be kept going through the summer, taking in some more novice hurdles and handicap races on the level. *(op 11-8 tchd 7-4)*
Dubai Ace(USA) took on some of the best juvenile hurdlers last jumps season, performing well on most occasions. He was readily brushed aside by the winner and looked very unenthusiastic in the final stages. Placing him will not be easy off his current official rating, and novice events are probably his best option to get his head in front. *(op 9-4 tchd 5-2 in a place)*
Blueberry Ice(IRE) was firmly put in her place against the boys. Her mares-only win probably does not amount to much and she has the option to go chasing soon. *(op 5-1 tchd 9-2)*
Peppershot made the running briefly in the early stages, but was left behind from an early stage. He ran on well in the home straight, but passed only tired horses. *(op 16-1)*
Sound Skin(IRE) did not progress from his last run and the trainer suggested the race may have *come too quickly after that effort. Official explanation: trainer said gelding ran flat and run may have come to soon after its previous run (op 25-1)*
Derwent(USA) ◆ was all set to take a fair third when losing his jockey at the last. This was a fair run and he is now qualified for handicaps. However, he will need to sharpen up his jumping technique to be fully effective over hurdles. *(tchd 16-1)*
Sonderborg *Official explanation: trainer said filly was in season (tchd 16-1)*
Can Can Flyer(IRE) *Official explanation: jockey said gelding was jumped into and never travelling thereafter (tchd 16-1)*

505 DAVID CHIVERS RETIREMENT H'CAP CHASE (13 fncs) 2m 2f
4:25 (4:25) (Class 4) (0-105,104) 5-Y-0+ **£4,065** (£1,251; £625; £312)

Form RPR

66F- **1** **French Direction (IRE)**[121] 3512 6-10-0 **78** oh3.................... PMoloney 84+
(R Rowe) *led: mstke 3 out: hdd last: rallied gamely to ld again fnl 50 yds* **20/1**

125- **2** *1¼* **Wild Power (GER)**[167] 2722 7-11-4 **99**.................... ONelmes(3) 103
(Mrs H R J Nelmes) *in tch: chsd ldr 7th: led last: hdd and no ex fnl 50 yds* **14/1**

5-65 **3** *25* **Jupon Vert (FR)**[9] 386 8-11-9 **101**.................... TScudamore 85+
(R J Hodges) *sn bhd: sme hdwy 8th: unable to chal: lft mod 3rd 2 out* **5/1**[3]

130- **4** *20* **My Galliano (IRE)**[80] 4204 9-10-12 **90**.................... JTizzard 49
(B G Powell) *nt fluent 4th and 4 out: a bhd* **15/2**

42-2 **P** **Phar City (IRE)**[19] 205 8-11-4 **96**.................... BHitchcott —
(R H Buckler) *bhd fr 4th: p.u after 7th* **9/2**[2]

4-00 **P** **Celtic Star (IRE)**[11] 360 7-10-12 **95**....................(p) DLaverty(5) —
(Mrs L Williamson) *sn bhd: t.o whn p.u bef 2 out* **16/1**

24-2 **F** **Romany Dream**[26] 103 7-10-11 **92**....................(b) DCrosse(3) 91
(R Dickin) *hdwy and prom 6th: 3 l 3rd and rdn whn fell heavily 2 out* **2/1**[1]

22-0 **U** **Walcot Lad (IRE)**[26] 103 9-10-7 **90**....................(p) RStephens(5) 74
(A Ennis) *prom: outpcd fr 9th: 4th and btn whn hit 2 out and uns rdr* **8/1**

50-3 **P** **Mount Kimble (IRE)**[26] 103 9-11-12 **104**....................(v[1]) PHide —
(P Winkworth) *prom: hrd rdn 7th: wknd next: t.o whn p.u bef 2 out* **10/1**

4m 27.8s (-7.30) **Going Correction** -0.65s/f (Firm) **9** Ran SP% **117.5**
Speed ratings: **89,88,77,68,— —,—,—,—** CSF £253.03 CT £1625.05 TOTE £20.60: £5.20, £4.30, £2.10; EX 466.70.
Owner Mrs R A Proctor **Bred** Brett Merry **Trained** Storrington, W Sussex

FOCUS
A moderate winning time for the grade. French Direction put all his previous form behind him to win nicely. The form should be solid enough at a low level.

NOTEBOOK
French Direction(IRE) showed a good attitude to regain the lead on the run to the line after being headed approaching the final fence. He lost his confidence badly when taking a crashing fall early in the year, but jumped very well in front on his own. He has time on his side to continue improving and should build on this solid effort. *(op 16-1)*
Wild Power(GER), reappearing after a 167-day break and running for new connections, looked all set to collect between the last two fences, but did not quite get home after taking the last in front. This was a fine effort and he should come on for the run.
Jupon Vert(FR), who was nibbled in the market prior to the off, only managed to secure a place *due to fallers in front of him. However, he ran well enough to suggest his turn is not too far away. (op 8-1)*
My Galliano(IRE) was never in the hunt and only got fourth due to fallers. *(op 7-1)*
Phar City(IRE) did not handle the quick ground, and was beaten at an early stage. *Official explanation: jockey said gelding was unsuited by the good to firm, good in places going and was never travelling (op 4-1 tchd 5-1)*
Mount Kimble(IRE) was a big disappointment in the first-time visor. *(op 4-1 tchd 5-1)*
Romany Dream travelled really well for most of the race, but came under pressure on entering the home straight. She would have been third at worst when ploughing through the second last, giving her jockey no chance of staying on, and should go close next time if she is none-the-worse for her heavy fall. *(op 4-1 tchd 5-1)*

506 HARDINGS BAR & CATERING NOVICES' H'CAP HURDLE (10 hdls) 2m 4f
5:00 (5:00) (Class 4) (0-90,89) 4-Y-0+ **£2,625** (£750; £375)

Form RPR

56-2 **1** **Roman Candle (IRE)**[11] 357 9-11-0 **77**.................... JPMcNamara 84+
(Lucinda Featherstone) *hld up towards rr: hdwy appr 2 out: styd on to ld run-in: drvn out* **7/1**[3]

53-3 **2** *4* **Nod's Star**[21] 185 4-11-1 **83**....................(t) LAspell 79
(Mrs L C Jewell) *mid-div: hdwy to join ldrs 3 out: led 2 out: edgd rt and hdd run-in: no ex* **10/1**

6-5U **3** *½* **Great Compton**[15] 287 5-10-7 **75**.................... LStephens(5) 77+
(B J Llewellyn) *hld up in midfield: hdwy to ld after 3 out: hdd next: hrd rdn and no ex run-in* **20/1**

23-0 **4** *shd* **Spiders Web**[22] 167 5-11-11 **88**....................(b) JEMoore 88
(G L Moore) *hld up in rr: stdy hdwy 7th: chsd ldrs appr 2 out: hrd rdn appr last: styd on same pce* **15/2**

5-06 **5** *15* **Paula Lane**[16] 265 5-11-0 **77**.................... TDoyle 62
(R Curtis) *t.k.h in rr: rdn and styd on fr 3 out: nt rch ldrs* **25/1**

U2-0 **6** *shd* **Not To Be Missed**[30] 25 7-10-13 **76**.................... WHutchinson 61
(R Dickin) *mid-div: hdwy 7th: no imp fr 3 out* **12/1**

P06- **7** *1¼* **Waverley Road**[37] 4913 8-11-5 **89**.................... RLucey-Butler(7) 73
(M Madgwick) *chsd ldrs tl wknd 3 out* **16/1**

05-1 **8** *shd* **Angie's Double**[17] 237 5-10-4 **74**.................... RSpate(7) 58
(Mrs K Waldron) *in tch tl rdn and btn 3 out* **6/1**[2]

60-0 **9** *1* **Silistra**[15] 279 6-11-9 **86**....................(p) BHitchcott 69
(Mrs L C Jewell) *led to 2nd: remained w ldrs: led briefly 3 out: hrd rdn and wknd next* **20/1**

05/5 **10** *2* **Notwhatshewanted (IRE)**[14] 295 8-11-4 **84**.................... RYoung(3) 65
(J W Mullins) *chsd ldrs to 7th* **10/1**

05-P **11** *16* **My Retreat (USA)**[22] 167 8-11-3 **85**.................... TJPhelan(5) 50
(R Fielder) *a bhd* **25/1**

44P- **12** *1¼* **Sweet Shooter**[62] 4534 5-11-5 **82**.................... PHide 46
(M Madgwick) *led 2nd to 6th: wknd next* **33/1**

00P- **13** *5* **Scarface**[76] 4289 8-11-1 **78**.................... APMcCoy 37
(Jonjo O'Neill) *in tch tl wknd 3 out* **5/2**[1]

6-FP **P** **El Hamra (IRE)**[9] 389 7-11-2 **79**.................... JMMaguire —
(T R George) *towards rr: hrd rdn 5th: t.o whn p.u bef last* **20/1**

00P- **P** **It's Got Buckleys**[155] 2927 6-10-6 **74**.................... DLaverty(5) —
(L A Dace) *hdwy and prom 3rd: wknd appr 7th: t.o whn p.u and dismntd bef last* **66/1**

0-PF **S** **China Chase (IRE)**[10] 371 6-11-0 **77**....................(b) TScudamore —
(J L Spearing) *prom: led 6th: hit next: hdd & wknd 3 out: disputing 5th and btn whn slipped up bnd sn after* **25/1**

4m 48.8s (-15.00) **Going Correction** -0.65s/f (Firm)
WFA 4 from 5yo+ 5lb **16** Ran SP% **129.1**
Speed ratings: **103,101,101,101,95 95,94,94,94,93 86,86,84,—,— —** CSF £70.58 CT £1380.19 TOTE £8.40: £1.40, £2.30, £3.60, £1.50; EX 40.40.
Owner J Roundtree **Bred** R W Huggins And P Wilkerson **Trained** Newmarket, Suffolk

FOCUS
A very weak race, probably no better than a seller, but rated through the winner back to his best.

NOTEBOOK
Roman Candle(IRE) easily gained his first win of any kind since taking a race on the Flat way back in July 1999. He was produced with a well-timed challenge to win going away and is clearly in good form at present. *(op 11-2)*
Nod's Star, a poor performer on the Flat, has shown much more promise since going hurdling. She did not quite see the trip out at Fakenham last time and that may have been the case again, although she had little chance with the winner. A small mares' race on a flat track is within her compass.
Great Compton swept into contention coming into the straight, but did not get home after and was *out-jumped at the second last. He has not won since July 2003, and that was on the Flat in* Ireland.
Spiders Web has yet to taste success under any code and has been beaten in banded events on the Flat. He will be better off back in sellers. *(op 13-2)*
Paula Lane was too keen in the early stages to get home. She kept on in the straight, and will stay further.
Angie's Double won a dreadful seller at Uttoxeter last time, for different connections, but played no part in this better grade. *(tchd 11-2)*
Scarface offered no promise on hise debut for the stable. *(op 5-1)*

507 ARUNDEL FESTIVAL 4-TUNE STANDARD OPEN NATIONAL HUNT FLAT RACE 2m 2f 110y
5:30 (5:31) (Class 6) 4-6-Y-O **£1,904** (£544; £272)

Form RPR

0 **1** **Pairtree**[30] 27 5-10-11 .... MBatchelor 95+
(Jamie Poulton) *mde all: hrd rdn over 2f out: gamely hld off chal of runner-up* **9/1**[3]

2 *1* **Silverio (GER)** 4-10-13 .... JEMoore 96+
(G L Moore) *t.k.h towards rr early: rdn after 7f: hdwy 8f out: chal fnl 2f: kpt on wl u.p: jst hld* **10/3**[1]

3 *9* **Silver Serg** 4-10-13 .... PHide 88+
(G L Moore) *hld up in rr: promising hdwy to trck ldrs 4f out: swtchd lft 2f out: rdn and one pce* **10/1**

054- **4** *7* **Letsplay (IRE)**[58] 4615 5-11-4 .... NFehily 85
(A W Carroll) *chsd ldrs: rdn 4f out: outpcd fnl 3f* **7/2**[2]

00- **5** *3½* **West Bay Storm**[73] 4349 5-10-8 .... ONelmes(3) 74
(Mrs H R J Nelmes) *chsd wnr tl 4f out: wknd over 2f out* **33/1**

- **6** *14* **Midnight Marine** 4-10-13 .... CLlewellyn 62
(J F Panvert) *mid-div: dropped to rr 1/2-way: sme hdwy 3f out: nt trble ldrs* **20/1**

0-0 **7** *8* **Megalala (IRE)**[17] 235 4-10-6 .... RLucey-Butler(7) 54
(J J Bridger) *plld hrd in rr: sme hdwy into midfield 7f out: rdn 5f out: no further prog* **33/1**

8 *4* **Florida Fiesta** 4-10-3 .... RYoung(3) 43
(Mrs H R J Nelmes) *mid-div: outpcd 7f out: sn bhd* **25/1**

-0 **9** *5* **Woolfall Princess**[22] 179 6-10-11 .... ATinkler 43
(G G Margarson) *chsd ldrs 4f: bhd fr 1/2-way* **33/1**

5- **10** *13* **Lord Leonardo (IRE)**[37] 4916 5-11-4 .... APMcCoy 37
(L Wells) *chsd ldrs: wknd 6f out: no ch whn eased fnl 3f* **7/2**[2]

0 **11** *11* **Rose Amber**[17] 235 4-10-6 .... LAspell 14
(J J Bridger) *chsd ldrs to 1/2-way* **33/1**

0- **12** *¾* **Judge'N'Thomas**[94] 3973 5-10-11 .... MrRBliss(7) 25
(M R Bosley) *hld up in rr: sme hdwy on outside after 6f: wknd 7f out* **33/1**

0 13 *22* **Mister Tibus (FR)**[22] 179 4-10-13 BJCrowley —
(J A Geake) *hld up in midfield: brief effrt 8f out: bhd fnl 5f* **16/1**

4m 22.1s (-17.20) **Going Correction** -0.65s/f (Firm)
WFA 4 from 5yo+ 4lb **13** Ran SP% **115.8**
Speed ratings: **97,96,92,89,88 82,79,77,75,69 65,64,55** CSF £34.80 TOTE £10.70: £2.20, £1.40, £4.30; EX 29.90 Place 6 £212.58, Place 5 £28.90.
Owner J W Haydon **Bred** Granham Farm **Trained** Telscombe, E Sussex

FOCUS
Probably a fair race of its type for the course. The fifth, seventh and ninth set the level.

NOTEBOOK
Pairtree clearly learnt plenty from her first run and kept on very well when challenged in the straight. She will get further in time and is due to go hurdling fairly soon. *(op 10-1)*
Silverio(GER), who is nicely bred for the Flat, came to have every chance in the final two furlongs, *but could not get past the winner. He has only recently been gelded and will improve for the race. (op 7-2 tchd 4-1 and 3-1)*
Silver Serg, a stablemate of the second, stayed on really nicely in the home straight, suggesting he will stay further in time. *(op 9-1)*
Letsplay(IRE) was very keen in the early stages and did not find a turn of foot when asked. His previous run may have flattered him a touch. *(tchd 4-1)*
West Bay Storm, who has the build of a chaser, showed plenty of pace until the race started in earnest. He will be better with more experience behind him. *(op 50-1)*
Midnight Marine *Official explanation: jockey said gelding hung left*
Lord Leonardo(IRE) was a big disappointment after a promising first run. *Official explanation: jockey said gelding hung badly right (op 3-1)*
T/Plt: £260.20 to a £1 stake. Pool: £36,314.25. 101.85 winning tickets. T/Qpdt: £34.00 to a £1 stake. Pool: £3,223.55. 70.05 winning tickets. LM

278 HUNTINGDON (R-H)

Thursday, May 26

OFFICIAL GOING: Good to firm
Wind: slight, across Weather: Warm and sunny

508 LADIES EVENING (S) HURDLE (10 hdls) 2m 5f 110y
6:10 (6:10) (Class 5) 4-Y-0+ **£2,261** (£646; £323)

Form RPR
05-2 **1** **Mantles Prince**[27] 96 11-11-0 90 ATinkler 89
(A G Juckes) *a.p: chsd ldr 6th: rdn appr 2 out: led last: styd on* **11/4**[2]
5-0P **2** *2 ½* **Shamsan (IRE)**[9] 397 8-10-7 105 (t) SWalsh(7) 87
(J Joseph) *hld up: hdwy 4th: led appr 3 out: rdn and hdd last: no ex flat* **9/1**
60-0 **3** *20* **Ashgan (IRE)**[27] 105 12-11-0 75 PFlynn 71+
(Dr P Pritchard) *led to 2nd: remained handy: led after 7th: hdd and mstke next: sn wknd* **13/2**
160- **4** *dist* **Good Thyne Johnny (IRE)**[333] 830 11-12-0 97 AO'Keeffe —
(Jennie Candlish) *mstke 1st: led next: hdd after 7th: wknd bef next* **9/2**[3]
5-PP **P** **Proper Poser (IRE)**[22] 183 9-10-11 64 ACCoyle(3) —
(M C Chapman) *hld up: wknd 6th: t.o whn p.u bef 2 out* **50/1**
P-20 **R** **Homeleigh Mooncoin**[9] 397 10-11-0 105 JamesDavies —
(B G Powell) *hld up: hdwy 4th: rdn next: wknd after 7th: bhd whn ref 2 out* **15/8**[1]
5P/P **P** **Saxon Victory (USA)**[16] 278 10-10-7 64 (v) MrRArmson(7) —
(John A Harris) *chsd ldrs: drvn along 3rd: lost pl bef next: bhd fr 5th: t.o whn p.u bef next* **33/1**

4m 59.2s (-11.60) **Going Correction** -0.65s/f (Firm) **7** Ran SP% **107.9**
Speed ratings: **95,94,86,—,— —,—** CSF £23.36 TOTE £4.80: £2.20, £2.60; EX 24.50.There was no bid for the winner
Owner Emlyn Hughes' Cleobury Golfers **Bred** Mrs Wilma Protheroe-Beynon **Trained** Abberley, Worcs

FOCUS
A dire event which saw the first two come well clear and the race is rated through the winner.

NOTEBOOK
Mantles Prince, who had done all of his previous winning on easy ground, really dug deep from two out to get on top of the runner-up and score a deserved success. He is clearly in good heart at *present, proved he can go on this ground, and looks up to winning more races at this level. (op 5-2 tchd 3-1)*
Shamsan(IRE), who missed all of 2004 due to injury, had every chance and was miles clear of the rest. This was a much more encouraging display and, while he is looked flattered by his official rating, on this evidence he still has a race or two in him at this sort of level. *(op 8-1)*
Ashgan(IRE) ran as well as could have been expected according to official ratings. *(op 9-1)*
Good Thyne Johnny(IRE) was unable to dominate on this first outing for 333 days and ran as though this race was much needed. *(tchd 5-1)*
Saxon Victory(USA) *Official explanation: jockey said gelding bled from nose (tchd 7-4)*
Homeleigh Mooncoin never looked like justifying favouritism and was already well beaten when he refused two from home. He looks one to avoid. *(tchd 7-4)*

509 ANNE FURBANK NOVICES' H'CAP HURDLE (12 hdls) 3m 2f
6:40 (6:40) (Class 4) (0-105,103) 4-Y-0+ **£3,297** (£942; £471)

Form RPR
P2-P **1** **Swifts Hill (IRE)**[27] 111 7-11-5 96 RJohnson 107+
(T R George) *chsd ldr tl led after 2nd: mde rest: drvn out* **9/1**
P04- **2** *4* **Super Road Train**[35] 4939 6-10-10 87 LAspell 94
(O Sherwood) *chsd ldrs: ev ch appr 3 out: styng on same pce whn nt fluent last* **6/1**[3]
2P-3 **3** *13* **Lord Nellsson**[14] 315 9-11-9 100 PJBrennan 97+
(J S King) *led: hdd after 2nd: remained handy: hit 6th: rdn after next: outpcd after 7th* **9/2**[2]
44-1 **4** *7* **Tickateal**[8] 417 5-11-6 97 7ex JimCrowley 84
(R D E Woodhouse) *hld up: hdwy after 7th: ev ch appr 3 out: sn wknd* **6/4**[1]
50-0 **5** *12* **Villago (GER)**[23] 167 5-10-13 90 (b) NFehily 65
(C J Mann) *chsd ldrs: rdn and wknd after 4 out* **14/1**
00-5 **6** *3 ½* **Smileafact**[12] 345 5-10-3 80 PFlynn 52
(Mrs Barbara Waring) *hld up: rdn after 7th: wknd 4 out* **33/1**
PPP- **P** **Quainton Hills**[40] 4871 11-10-2 79 WHutchinson —
(D R Stoddart) *hld up: hit 6th: wknd 4 out: t.o whn p.u bef next* **16/1**
2P-1 **P** **Nite Fox (IRE)**[18] 236 6-11-5 103 (p) PMerrigan(7) —
(Mrs H Dalton) *hld up in tch: nt fluent 3rd: dropped rr 5th: bhd fr 7th: t.o whn p.u bef 3 out* **10/1**

6m 2.70s (-19.70) **Going Correction** -0.65s/f (Firm) **8** Ran SP% **107.0**
Speed ratings: **104,102,98,96,92 91,—,—** CSF £53.95 CT £235.43 TOTE £8.30: £2.50, £1.20, £1.30; EX 87.80.
Owner Thoroughbred Ladies **Bred** Miss Ann Twomey **Trained** Slad, Gloucs
■ Stewards' Enquiry : N Fehily caution: used whip when horse was out of contention

FOCUS
A poor handicap that saw the field come home well strung out over the marathon trip. The third sets the standard and the form should work out.

NOTEBOOK
Swifts Hill(IRE) ◆ took the bull by the horns from an early stage, and made amends for a dismal effort on his handicap debut at Southwell, with a ready career-first success over this much longer distance. This sort of trip looks to be the making of him and he has the scope to win further races *in this division during the summer. Official explanation: trainer's representative said, regarding the improved form shown, gelding was better suited by this track and conventional hurdles (op 8-1)*
Super Road Train had his chance, and turned in an improved effort, but was put in his place by the winner. He clearly stays well and was clear of the rest this time. *(op 7-1)*
Lord Nellsson, consistent as he is, was again found wanting when push came to shove and looked a non-stayer over this longer distance. He remains a maiden after 29 outings over both hurdles and fences. *(tchd 5-1)*
Tickateal was found out under his 7lb penalty and disappointed for no apparent reason. *(op 13-8 tchd 11-8 and 7-4 in a place)*
Quainton Hills *Official explanation: jockey said gelding suffered a breathing problem (op 8-1)*
Nite Fox(IRE) *Official explanation: jockey said mare was never travelling (op 8-1)*

510 BIOPROGRESS NOVICES' CHASE (12 fncs) 2m 110y
7:10 (7:10) (Class 3) 5-Y-0+ **£5,421** (£1,668; £834; £417)

Form RPR
020- **1** **Stance**[47] 4768 6-11-0 JEMoore 120+
(G L Moore) *prom: chsd ldr 8th: hung lft: led appr and hit last: eased nr fin* **4/5**[1]
P5-4 **2** *4* **Medici (FR)**[4] 467 7-11-0 NFehily 110+
(Mrs Jeremy Young) *chsd ldr tl led 5th: j.lft 8th: hdd appr and hit last: styd on same pce* **9/1**
1-12 **3** *8* **Saafend Rocket (IRE)**[23] 174 7-11-12 117 RJohnson 114
(H D Daly) *hld up: hdwy 8th: wknd appr 2 out* **11/4**[2]
P-33 **4** *10* **Nopekan (IRE)**[19] 217 5-10-5 RSpate(7) 92+
(Mrs K Waldron) *hld up: hit 2nd and 4th: hdwy 8th: rdn and wknd after 3 out* **8/1**[3]
00F- **5** *17* **Husky (POL)**[28] 4444 7-11-0 JamesDavies 76+
(B G Powell) *led: j.lft: hdd 5th: mstke 7th: wknd 3 out* **50/1**
6-03 **6** *18* **Moon Shot**[16] 286 9-11-0 92 ATinkler 65+
(A G Juckes) *trckd ldrs: plld hrd: wknd 9th* **50/1**
P0P- **P** **Ela Figura**[54] 4684 5-10-5 ow3 RHobson(3) —
(M Appleby) *sn bhd: t.o whn p.u bef 6th* **150/1**

3m 58.9s (-10.40) **Going Correction** -0.65s/f (Firm)
WFA 5 from 6yo+ 2lb **7** Ran SP% **107.9**
Speed ratings: **98,96,92,87,79 71,—** CSF £7.64 TOTE £1.80: £1.80, £2.40; EX 19.90.
Owner N J Jones **Bred** Juddmonte Farms **Trained** Woodingdean, E Sussex

FOCUS
A fair event for the time of year. The winner can be rated value for further and looks set to take higher order over fences in due course.

NOTEBOOK
Stance ◆, rated 133 over hurdles, in the main jumped neatly and and ran out a clear-cut winner on this chasing bow. He had to work to get in front before the final fence, but was soon in control, and was allowed to coast home on the run-in. Given that he finished second in the County Hurdle at Cheltenham in March, he was entitled to win this comfortably, and has the scope to take much higher order in this sphere with this experience under his belt. *(op 6-5 tchd 5-4 in places)*
Medici(FR) ◆, rated 112 over hurdles, only gave way to the winner approaching the final fence and was nicely clear of the remainder at the finish. He is flattered by his proximity to the winner, but has always promised to reach greater heights over fences, and this must rate as a pleasing chase debut. A similar event looks his for the taking. *(op 17-2 tchd 10-1)*
Saafend Rocket(IRE) never threatened and was found out by his double penalty. He is not going to be the easiest to place now. *(op 2-1)*
Nopekan(IRE) did not jump as fluently as had been the case on his previous efforts this summer, but still ran close to his Ludlow form with Saafend Rocket. He may just need more cut and would benefit from a switch to handicaps now. *(op 7-1)*
Moon Shot *Official explanation: jockey said gelding suffered a breathing problem (op 33-1)*
Ela Figura *Official explanation: jockey said leather broke so he pulled up (op 100-1)*

511 BIOPROGRESS H'CAP CHASE (16 fncs) 2m 4f 110y
7:45 (7:45) (Class 4) (0-110,110) 5-Y-0+ **£3,715** (£1,143; £571; £285)

Form RPR
04-5 **1** **Celebration Town (IRE)**[27] 104 8-11-4 102 MFoley 107+
(Miss E C Lavelle) *a.p: shkn up to ld fnl 75 yds* **14/1**
/P-1 **2** *2 ½* **Gale Star (IRE)**[11] 368 12-10-1 85 7ex (t) JEMoore 88
(O Brennan) *hld up: hdwy 12th: led last: hdd fnl 75 yds* **4/1**[2]
25-6 **3** *1 ½* **Breaking Breeze (IRE)**[20] 206 10-11-3 101 PJBrennan 105+
(J S King) *chsd ldr tl hit 4th: led 11th: hdd 4 out: led next: rdn 2 out : hdd and blnd last: rdr lost iron: nt rcvr* **11/2**[3]
-656 **4** *1 ¼* **Celtic Legend (FR)**[7] 429 6-10-8 92 RMcGrath 92
(K G Reveley) *hld up: hdwy after 3 out: styd on same pce fr next* **10/3**[1]
0P-3 **5** *5* **Newick Park**[9] 395 10-10-7 91 WHutchinson 88+
(R Dickin) *chsd clr ldr 4th to 11th: wkng whn hit 2 out* **15/2**
54-P **6** *3 ½* **Father Abraham (IRE)**[18] 240 7-10-0 84 oh2 PFlynn 75
(J Akehurst) *led: clr 5th: hit 7th: j.lft 9th: hdd 11th: led 4 out: hdd next: rdn and wknd bef 2 out* **20/1**
450- **7** *9* **Dream With Me (FR)**[44] 4817 8-11-12 110 (t) BJCrowley 97+
(J A Geake) *hld up: hdwy 11th: wknd appr 2 out* **10/1**
4-63 **8** *12* **Master T (USA)**[18] 234 6-11-7 105 PHide 80+
(G L Moore) *hld up: hdwy and hit 8th: wknd 12th* **10/1**
5P-P **P** **Tails I Win**[22] 183 6-10-2 86 JGoldstein —
(Miss C J E Caroe) *hld up: a bhd: t.o whn p.u bef 4 out* **66/1**
/P-6 **P** **Boardroom Dancer (IRE)**[16] 276 8-10-6 90 PMoloney —
(Miss I E Craig) *hld up: a bhd: t.o whn p.u bef 2 out* **40/1**
00-6 **P** **Infidel (IRE)**[12] 357 5-10-7 94 NFehily —
(C J Mann) *hld up: hdwy 8th: mstke 11th (water): wkng whn hit 4 out: sn p.u* **12/1**

4m 55.8s (-10.30) **Going Correction** -0.65s/f (Firm)
WFA 5 from 6yo+ 3lb **11** Ran SP% **111.5**
Speed ratings: **93,92,91,91,89 87,84,79,—,— —** CSF £66.66 CT £343.26 TOTE £14.60: £4.90, £1.90, £2.40; EX 83.40.
Owner F S Williams **Bred** Newlands House Stud **Trained** Wildhern, Hants

FOCUS
A moderate handicap run at a decent pace. The form, rated through the third, appears fair for the class.

NOTEBOOK
Celebration Town(IRE), from a stable in decent from, showed the benefit of his recent outing at Fontwell and broke his duck over fences at the third attempt. The switch to handicap company worked the oracle, he enjoys this fast ground and can score again over this trip. *(op 9-1)*

Gale Star(IRE) came with a strong challenge to lead over the final flight, but had no answer to the winner's late surge on the run-in and was found out by his penalty. This was another soild effort on *ground that is vital to him, but the Handicapper will no doubt make life tough for him after this. (tchd 9-2)*
Breaking Breeze(IRE) showed the benefit of a recent spin over hurdles and would have finished closer but for blundering at the final fence. He can build on this again and has a race in him off this mark during the summer.
Celtic Legend(FR) , reverting to fences, could not find the change of gear to trouble the leaders and looks held by the Handicapper in this sphere. *(op 4-1 tchd 3-1)*
Newick Park failed to improve as expected for the step up in trip. *(op 8-1)*
Master T(USA) *Official explanation: jockey said gelding jumped moderately (op 9-1)*

512 BIOPROGRESS HUNTERS' CHASE (15 fncs 4 omitted) 3m
8:15 (8:18) (Class 6) 5-Y-O+ **£1,498** (£428; £214)

Form				RPR
5-5B	**1**		**Gaiac (FR)**[6] 437 11-11-7 ....(b) MissSSharratt(7) (Ms N M Hugo) *a.p: chsd ldr 11th: led appr 2 out: clr last: styd on wl* **12/1**	115+
PP-6	**2**	*16*	**Phildari (IRE)**[6] 437 9-11-7 84.......... MrDEngland(7) (Mrs Jelly O'Brien) *led and sn clr: hit 9th: hdd appr 2 out: sn wknd* **20/1**	100+
54-1	**3**	*10*	**Royal Snoopy (IRE)**[11] 374 12-12-0 100..........(b) MrRAbrahams(7) (Mrs Sarah L Dent) *chsd ldrs tl wknd appr 2 out* **9/2**[3]	98+
/1-2	**4**	*10*	**Cornish Gale (IRE)**[12] 348 11-12-7 .... MrTGreenall (D McCain Jnr) *hld up: hdwy 9th: rdn after 3 out: wknd bef next* **10/3**[2]	90+
P-32	**5**	*2 1/2*	**Teeton Priceless**[11] 374 10-11-7 .... MrNPearce(7) (Mrs Joan Tice) *chsd clr ldr: mstke 10th: rdn next: wknd after 3 out* **13/2**	77
21-2	**6**	*29*	**Find Me Another (IRE)**[16] 280 9-12-0 .... MissALStennett(7) (Mrs Caroline Bailey) *hdwy 4th: rdn 8th: wknd 12th* **9/4**[1]	75+
P6-P	**7**	*7*	**Young Tomo (IRE)**[11] 13-11-7 64..........(b) MrJJarrett(7) (Miss C J Goodall) *mstkes: prom to 6th* **66/1**	41
6P/4	**P**		**Torn Silk**[16] 280 11-11-11 .... MrCMulhall(3) (P England) *a bhd: t.o whn p.u bef 12th* **22/1**	—
4P5/	**P**		**Quango**[12] 13-11-7 ....(tp) MissJFoster(7) (Miss J E Foster) *a bhd: t.o whn p.u bef 11th* **33/1**	—
P-P6	**P**		**Good Bone (FR)**[22] 184 8-12-4 88.......... MrAWintle(3) (S Flook) *prom: mstke 3rd: lost pl after 6th: rdn next: sn bhd: t.o whn p.u bef 11th* **16/1**	—

5m 53.6s (-18.70) **Going Correction** -0.65s/f (Firm) **10** Ran SP% **112.5**
Speed ratings: **105,99,96,93,92 82,80,—,—,—** CSF £197.27 TOTE £8.40: £1.70, £4.90, £1.70; EX 277.30.
Owner K Rowlands **Bred** Comte Michel De Gigou **Trained** Malpas, Cheshire

FOCUS
An ordinary event of its type, run at a fair pace in a good time for a hunter chase, and the field finished well strung out. Two fences in back straight omitted due to the low sun.

NOTEBOOK
Gaiac(FR) , brought down at Stratford last time, relished the return to this faster ground and could hardly have run out an easier winner. He is consistent, and clearly in great heart at present, but it must be noted this was a race that took little winning. *(op 7-1)*
Phildari(IRE) found only the winner too strong and was another who relished the return to a quicker surface. He was well clear of the rest, and improved on his recent efforts, but remains vulnerable to an improver in this division.
Royal Snoopy(IRE) failed to quicken when it mattered, but ran his race nevertheless. *(op 5-1)*
Cornish Gale(IRE) was beaten by the much faster ground and is capable of better when getting his toe in once again. *(op 11-4 tchd 5-2)*
Find Me Another(IRE) , a most consistent pointer, was well backed to repeat last year's success in this event, but never threatened and has to go down as disappointing. He is probably best at shorter on slightly easier ground. *(op 3-1 tchd 4-1)*

513 BIOPROGRESS NOVICES' HURDLE (8 hdls) 2m 110y
8:45 (8:45) (Class 4) 4-Y-O+ **£3,325** (£950; £475)

Form				RPR
244-	**1**		**Resplendent Star (IRE)**[129] 3389 8-10-12 108..........(v) LAspell (Mrs L Wadham) *hld up: hdwy 5th: chsd ldr 2 out: led and hung lft flat: rdn out* **9/4**[1]	93
44-1	**2**	*1/2*	**Three Ships**[12] 279 4-10-8 104.......... MrMatthewSmith(7) (Miss J Feilden) *plld hrd and prom: led after 5th: hdd flat: styd on u.p* **11/2**	95
00-3	**3**	*3/4*	**Buttress**[13] 331 6-10-9 .... MrTGreenall(3) (M W Easterby) *hld up: hdwy appr 3 out: styd on flat* **11/4**[2]	91
6P-	**4**	*4*	**Manolo (FR)**[84] 4132 5-10-12 .... PMoloney (Ian Williams) *a.p: chsd ldr 3 out: mstke next: no ex last* **7/2**[3]	88+
00/0	**5**	*14*	**Prince Minata (IRE)**[16] 279 10-10-9 73.......... RHobson(3) (M Appleby) *led to 2nd: wknd appr 2 out* **100/1**	73
0-2	**6**	*7*	**General Smith**[12] 356 6-10-12 .... VSlattery (H J Evans) *hld up: plld hrd: nvr nr to chal* **33/1**	66
500-	**7**	*1 1/4*	**Earl Of Spectrum (GER)**[96] 3959 4-10-5 94.......... ONelmes(3) (O Sherwood) *plld hrd and sn prom: jnd ldr whn j. slowly 4th: wknd 3 out* **10/1**	61
0-U	**8**	*21*	**Grey Prince**[11] 367 4-10-8 .... JAMcCarthy (G Prodromou) *hld up: wknd appr 3 out* **66/1**	40
P0-	**9**	*6*	**Tank (IRE)**[164] 2805 4-10-8 .... JGoldstein (Miss Sheena West) *led 2nd: hdd after 5th: wknd next* **80/1**	34
00/	**10**	*dist*	**Sussex Mist**[408] 4816 6-9-12 .... RLucey-Butler(7) (J E Long) *hld up in tch: wknd appr 4th* **100/1**	—

3m 46.7s (-9.00) **Going Correction** -0.65s/f (Firm)
WFA 4 from 5yo+ 4lb **10** Ran SP% **111.8**
Speed ratings: **95,94,94,92,85 82,82,72,69,—** CSF £14.43 TOTE £4.30: £2.10, £1.90, £1.20; EX 27.10 Place 6 £93.94, Place 5 £36.76.
Owner Waterhall Racing **Bred** Airlie Stud **Trained** Newmarket, Suffolk

FOCUS
A modest novice event that saw the first four finish well clear. The form could be rated higher but looks sound for the class rated through second, fourth and fifth.

NOTEBOOK
Resplendent Star(IRE) came with a well-timed challenge to lead over the last flight, looking like scoring comfortably, but he hung and started to wander about under pressure on the run-in and had to be kept right up to his work to score. He confidence will have been boosted greatly by this, and he is entitled to improve again for this first outing for 129 days, but he is never one to place too much faith in. *(op 5-2 tchd 11-4, 10-3 in a place and 3-1 in a place)*
Three Ships deserves credit, as he took a fierce hold in the early stages, yet still went down fighting on the run-in. This was a sound effort under his penalty and he may benefit further for the move to handicaps this summer. *(op 4-1)*
Buttress ran another solid race, but again found less than looked likely when push came to shove. *He should not be long in finding a race over hurdles at this level during the summer months. (op 3-1)*
Manolo(FR) had his chance, but never really looked like justifying market support. This will have served his confidence well, however, and he should fare better now he is qualified for a handicap mark. *(op 11-2)*

T/Plt: £474.50 to a £1 stake. Pool £32,925.00. 50.65 winning units T/Qpdt: £46.20 to a £1 stake. Pool £3,184.10. 51.00 winning units CR

[384]NEWTON ABBOT (L-H)
Thursday, May 26

OFFICIAL GOING: Good (good to soft in places)
The inside rail on the bend away from the stands was reportedly at its widest point in order to preserve the ground. As a result, the times may be distorted.
Wind: Nil

514 "PREPARATION" "NATIONAL HUNT" NOVICES' HURDLE (10 hdls) 2m 6f
2:10 (2:10) (Class 4) 4-Y-O+ **£3,444** (£1,059; £529; £264)

Form				RPR
2-U	**1**		**Lease Back (FR)**[20] 201 6-11-0 .... JEMoore (L Wells) *trckd ldrs: wnt 2nd after 4th: led appr 7th: drew clr after 3 out: easily* **Evs**[1]	113+
1	**2**	*12*	**Boulevardofdreams (IRE)**[10] 384 4-11-2 .... APMcCoy (M C Pipe) *j. sltly lft thrght: led: nt fluent 4th: rdn and hdd appr 7th: no ch w wnr fr 3 out: mstke last* **Evs**[1]	98+
02-F	**3**	*10*	**Edgar Wilde (IRE)**[10] 384 7-11-0 109.......... MAFitzgerald (R Rowe) *chsd ldrs: rdn after 7th: wknd after 3 out* **7/1**[2]	84
FPP-	**4**	*4*	**Parson Ploughman**[38] 4915 10-11-0 85..........(b1) ChristianWilliams (P F Nicholls) *hld up: hdwy appr 7th: hit 3 out: sn rdn: wknd next* **28/1**[3]	80
4	**5**	*26*	**Phase Three (IRE)**[27] 110 8-11-0 .... JMMaguire (T R George) *hld up: lost tch fr 7th: t.o* **50/1**	54
6	**P**		**Sooty From Mitcham**[15] 294 5-11-0 .... RWalford (R H Alner) *t.k.h towards rr: mstke 6th: sn t.o: p.u after 3 out* **66/1**	—
6P-0	**P**		**Mevagissey (BEL)**[10] 389 8-11-0 86.......... WMarston (J D Frost) *hld up bhd: sme hdwy 7th: wknd appr 3 out: t.o and p.u bef 2 out* **40/1**	—

5m 34.3s (14.00) **Going Correction** +0.625s/f (Soft) **7** Ran SP% **121.8**
Speed ratings: **99,94,91,89,80 —,—** CSF £2.54 TOTE £2.00: £1.30, £1.10; EX 3.30.
Owner Paul Zetter **Bred** L De Bronac And Caroline De Bronac De Vazelhes **Trained** Wisborough Green, W Sussex

FOCUS
A weak novice hurdle, as one would expect for the time of year, but they went a decent pace from the start and a nice winner in the form of Ex-French chaser Lease Back, who is rated value for more than the official margin.

NOTEBOOK
Lease Back(FR) ◆, a promising second on his British debut prior to unseating when travelling well at Wincanton last time, made no mistake this time. Restrained well off the eventual runner-up early on, he readily went by that one when asked to increase the pace and was never challenged thereafter. He had some useful form to his name over fences in France as a four-year-old, but apparently got a leg problem and has benefited from stem-cell surgery. Whatever the case, looks a useful recruit and could run up a sequence. *(op 10-11 tchd 4-5 and 11-10 in a place)*
Boulevardofdreams(IRE), a winning pointer in Ireland, he was a big drifter in the market prior to getting off the mark on his Rules debut in a maiden hurdle over course and distance. Carrying a penalty for that success, it looked just like the old days when McCoy sent him to the front to make this a good test from the start, but he offered no resistance when challenged by the eventual winner and was made to look very one paced. His hurdling was not particularly fluent either, but he is open to improvement and did bump into a fair type for the time of year. *(op 7-4 tchd 15-8)*
Edgar Wilde(IRE), a faller in the maiden hurdle won by today's runner-up over course and distance on his previous start, got round this time, but lacked the pace to ever pose a threat. *(op 6-1)*
Parson Ploughman managed to win on his chasing debut last season, but he had been pulled up on his last two starts over the larger obstacles. Switched back to hurdles in first-time blinkers, he offered next to nothing and would be better off in the lowest grade on the evidence of this performance. *(op 25-1)*

515 DURALOCK FENCING SYSTEMS NOVICES' HURDLE (8 hdls) 2m 1f
2:40 (2:41) (Class 3) 4-Y-O+ **£5,525** (£1,700; £850; £425)

Form				RPR
	1		**In Media Res (FR)**[219] 4-10-3 .... CMStudd(7) (N J Henderson) *trckd ldr: led appr 3 out: shkn up appr 2 out: hung lft appr last: r.o wl: readily* **5/1**[2]	101+
1-	**2**	*5*	**Abragante (IRE)**[65] 4513 4-10-10 .... APMcCoy (M C Pipe) *hld up: hdwy appr 3 out: rdn to chse wnr appr 2 out: swtchd rt appr last: nt pce of wnr* **2/5**[1]	97+
6-F	**3**	*11*	**Skibereen (IRE)**[31] 21 5-10-9 ....(t) DLaverty(5) (Mrs A M Thorpe) *hld up: hdwy after 4th: rdn to chal after 3 out: hit next: wknd* **14/1**	88
0	**4**	*10*	**Heisse**[4] 457 5-11-0 .... RGreene (Ian Williams) *hld up: nt fluent 1st: hdwy appr 5th: rdn appr 3 out: sn wknd* **16/1**	78
PP	**5**	*19*	**Ly's West**[15] 294 5-11-0 .... JTizzard (C L Tizzard) *led: rdn and hdd appr 3 out: sn wknd* **66/1**	59
	6	*20*	**Ard Na Re (IRE)**[294] 1119 6-11-0 .... JMMaguire (Paul John Gilligan, Ire) *chsd ldrs: rdn and wknd appr 3 out* **50/1**	39
02/	**F**		**Sculptor**[748] 182 6-11-0 .... ChristianWilliams (K R Pearce) *hld up: hdwy to trck ldrs after 4th: fell next* **9/1**[3]	—
	F		**Berry Racer (IRE)**[56] 4-10-3 .... CLlewellyn (Mrs S D Williams) *mid div: losing tch whn hmpd 5th: bhd whn fell last* **50/1**	—

4m 16.6s (11.50) **Going Correction** +0.625s/f (Soft)
WFA 4 from 5yo+ 4lb **8** Ran SP% **116.1**
Speed ratings: **97,94,89,84,75 66,—,—** CSF £7.81 TOTE £5.00: £1.70, £1.10, £1.70; EX 11.00.

Owner Killinghurst Park Stud **Bred** Barron T De Zuylen De Nyevelt **Trained** Upper Lambourn, Berks

FOCUS
A weak novice hurdle and they went just a steady early pace, but the front two look fair types with the third setting the standard.

NOTEBOOK
In Media Res(FR) ◆, a winner on the Flat in France over a mile seven on soft ground, made a successful hurdling debut on his first start in this country. Given he won over so far on the level, this trip could easily have been on the short side for him, but he was never too far off the pace and always looked the stronger when sent to the front. This was the ideal start to his new career and, open to improvement with this experience under his belt, he should be able to follow up. *(op 4-1)*
Abragante(IRE) was snapped up by the Pipe/Johnson operation following his winning debut in a Wetherby bumper 65 days previously. Having his first start over hurdles, he probably bumped into a fair sort, but this was still disappointing considering the price he was eventually sent off. He should not be long in going once place better, but it is impossible to know how much improvement he could find and what his long-term prospects are. *(op 8-13 tchd 4-6 in a place)*
Skibereen(IRE), an early faller at Towcester on his second start over hurdles, ran better than he did first time up and may be progressing. *(op 12-1)*

Heisse struggled to go with the principals and gave the impression he can benefit from further experience and a step up in trip. *Official explanation: jockey said gelding had a breathing problem* *(op 14-1)*

Sculptor, returning from a 748-day absence and making his debut for new connections, was still in contention when failing to pick his front legs up at the fifth hurdle and falling. *(op 8-1 tchd 10-1)*

516 BEATRICE TURNER MEMORIAL H'CAP CHASE (20 fncs) 3m 2f 110y

3:10 (3:11) (Class 3) (0-120,118) 5-Y-0+ **£6,134** (£1,887; £943; £471)

Form				RPR
-3P2	**1**		**Gumley Gale**[2] 489 10-11-8 **114**............(t) RGreene (K Bishop) *bhd: drvn along fr 10th: hdwy after 15th to go 2nd appr 4 out: styd on dourly to ld appr last: rdn out* **10/3**[2]	127+
05-5	**2**	*5*	**Lord 'N' Master (IRE)**[20] 205 9-10-12 **104**............MBatchelor (R Rowe) *led 2nd: nt fluent 11th (water): 6 l clr whn nt fluent 3 out (water): hdd and rdn after 2 out: sn btn* **7/1**	114+
4-44	**3**	*13*	**Dear Deal**[20] 205 12-11-3 **109**............(b) JTizzard (C L Tizzard) *in tch: rdn to take clsr order after 14th: kpt on same pce fr 4 out* **8/1**	105+
/1F-	**4**	*6*	**Tremallt (IRE)**[49] 4750 14-11-12 **118**............JMMaguire (T R George) *chsd ldr: rdn after 15th: j. bdly rt 4 out: one pced after* **7/1**	108+
215/	**P**		**Slyboots (GER)**[598] 1548 6-10-2 **97**............DCrosse[(3)] (C J Mann) *led tl 2nd: chsd ldrs tl bundered bdly 13th and immediately p.u* **16/1**	—
2P5-	**P**		**Yann's (FR)**[34] 4959 9-11-12 **118**............WMarston (R T Phillips) *bhd: reminders after 10th: lost tch qckly after 13th: p.u bef next* **12/1**	—
3F5-	**P**		**Scotch Corner (IRE)**[68] 4462 7-11-0 **106**............CLlewellyn (N A Twiston-Davies) *in tch: rdn and hdwy after 14th: wknd qckly 16th: p.u bef next* **4/1**[3]	—
1-1F	**P**		**He's The Biz (FR)**[6] 439 6-10-9 **101**............ChristianWilliams (Nick Williams) *hld up rr: drvn along after 13th: wknd after 4 out: bhd and p.u bef 2 out* **5/2**[1]	—

6m 55.5s (12.10) **Going Correction** +0.55s/f (Soft) **8** Ran SP% **121.3**
Speed ratings: **104,102,98,96,**— —,—,— CSF £28.46 CT £178.46 TOTE £4.00: £1.80, £3.30, £2.30; EX 33.30.
Owner Portcullis Racing **Bred** G G A Gregson **Trained** Spaxton, Somerset
■ A first winner for Rodi Greene since he came out of retirement.

FOCUS
Slightly disappointing that half the field could not complete and just a modest handicap chase, but at least they seemed to go a decent enough gallop. The race could be rated higher.

NOTEBOOK
Gumley Gale, beaten just a short head over an extended two miles seven at Worcester only two days previously, gained compensation for that narrow defeat in game fashion, responding well to a typically strong Greene ride. A rise in the weights though, will make things much tougher. *(tchd 3-1 and 7-2 in a place)*

Lord 'N' Master(IRE) had not been at his best in recent outings, but this was more like it and he very nearly ended a losing run stretching back to March 2003. He deserves to go one place better, and is capable of doing so whilst in this sort of form. *(op 8-1)*

Dear Deal has dropped to a very reasonable mark, but he was unable to take advantage and finished well held in third. *(op 7-1)*

Tremallt(IRE), a faller in the Fox Hunters' at Aintree on his latest start, managed to complete this time and acquitted himself with credit, but connections feel he has not been given much of a chance by the Handicapper and he has now been retired. *(op 5-1)*

He's The Biz(FR) failed to bounce back from his recent Stratford fall and this performance was a little concerning. *Official explanation: trainer said gelding was unsuited by good to soft ground (op 5-1)*

Slyboots(GER), successful in a couple of novice hurdles when last seen in 2003, had no chance after making a bad mistake at the 13th and was pulled up. He should be better of the outing. *(op 5-1)*

Scotch Corner(IRE), still a maiden over fences, had been given a bit of a chance by the Handicapper, but was not at his best. *(op 5-1)*

517 "ANIMATION" H'CAP HURDLE (8 hdls) 2m 1f

3:40 (3:42) (Class 4) (0-105,101) 4-Y-0+ **£5,220** (£1,606; £803; £401)

Form				RPR
P4-1	**1**		**Miss Lehman**[10] 389 7-10-1 **83** 7ex............MissSGaisford[(7)] (J D Frost) *hld up towards rr: gd hdwy on outer after 3 out to ld next: sn clr: readily* **11/8**[1]	96+
24-4	**2**	*9*	**Delaware (FR)**[15] 298 9-10-11 **86**............JMogford (H S Howe) *led: rdn and hdd appr 5th: sn lost pl: rallied after 3 out: lft 2nd next: styd on: no ch w wnr* **7/2**[2]	87
0PP-	**3**	*14*	**Suchwot (IRE)**[34] 4956 4-9-11 **83** oh4............(vt[1]) TJMalone[(3)] (M C Pipe) *prom: rdn and ev ch after 3 out: wkng whn lft 3rd next* **7/1**[3]	66+
/4-0	**4**	*17*	**Gemini Dancer**[18] 230 6-11-10 **99**............ChristianWilliams (C L Tizzard) *hld up: hdwy appr 5th: wnt 3rd after 3 out: sn rdn: wknd qckly: lft 4th next* **14/1**	69
000-	**5**	*15*	**Blandings Castle**[194] 2189 4-10-0 **83** oh19............MBatchelor (Nick Williams) *prom tl wknd 5th* **33/1**	30
03-0	**6**	*1*	**Shaman**[18] 232 8-11-5 **101**............EDehdashti[(7)] (G L Moore) *chsd ldrs tl wknd after 5th* **8/1**	55
664-	**7**	*hd*	**King's Travel (FR)**[61] 4563 9-10-4 **86**............AGlassonbury[(7)] (J D Frost) *hld up and a bhd* **8/1**	40
	P		**Abbeymore Lady (IRE)**[196] 2158 4-9-9 **83** oh4............TJPhelan[(5)] (Paul John Gilligan, Ire) *hld up in tch: hit 4th: p.u sn after: (sddle slipped)* **20/1**	—
600-	**F**		**Olimpo (FR)**[258] 1397 4-9-9 **83** oh11............RStephens[(5)] (P J Hobbs) *hld up in tch: led 6th and pckd bdly: fnd little whn hdd appr 2 out: fell next* **9/1**	78

4m 12.2s (7.10) **Going Correction** +0.625s/f (Soft)
WFA 4 from 6yo+ 4lb **9** Ran SP% **123.4**
Speed ratings: **108,103,97,89,82 81,81,**—,— CSF £7.68 CT £26.97 TOTE £2.00: £1.40, £1.10, £3.20; EX 6.40.
Owner P A Tylor **Bred** Mrs M C Reveley **Trained** Scorriton, Devon

FOCUS
A very moderate handicap hurdle, but they went a reasonable gallop and the time was fair. The winner is rated value for more than the official margin with the second the guide to the level.

NOTEBOOK
Miss Lehman, under her penalty, was effectively 1lb lower than when successful over course and distance on her previous start because her rider put up 8lb overweight that day, and she was 9lb lower than in future handicaps. Given a well-judged ride, she took full advantage in most decisive fashion. Things will be harder off her new mark and when she is reassessed for this victory, but she is progressing and in the form of her life. *(op 6-4 tchd 5-4)*

Delaware(FR), dropped back from three miles, ran his race but just came up against an in-form, progressive rival. *(op 13-2)*

Suchwot(IRE), tried in a tongue-tie and a visor for the first time, and making his debut for Martin Pipe, ran better than on his two previous outings when he was pulled up and offered some hope. *(tchd 8-1)*

Gemini Dancer, switched to handicap company for the first time, did not last home having looked likely to pose a threat. *(op 10-1)*

Olimpo(FR), well beaten in three runs in novice company, ran better returned from a 258-day break from 11lb out of the handicap. He did not find as much as had looked likely, but would probably have been second had he not fallen two out. *(op 7-1 tchd 10-1)*

518 DURALOCK FENCING SYSTEMS H'CAP CHASE (16 fncs) 2m 5f 110y

4:10 (4:11) (Class 4) (0-110,105) 5-Y-0+ **£4,760** (£1,464; £732; £366)

Form				RPR
PL-6	**1**		**Athnowen (IRE)**[23] 170 13-11-6 **96**............ChristianWilliams (J R Payne) *a gng wl: hld up: smooth hdwy to ld after 12th: j.rt fr next but a in command: easily* **11/1**	107+
FP5-	**2**	*7*	**Alcatras (IRE)**[41] 4853 8-9-11 **84** oh9............(b) RYoung[(3)] (B J M Ryall) *hld up: hdwy fr 6th: lft 2nd 4 out: sn rdn: kpt on but a hld fr next* **7/2**[2]	79
-321	**3**	*dist*	**Paxford Jack**[11] 366 9-12-1 **105** 7ex............(v) APMcCoy (M F Harris) *j.rt: led tl 4th: prom tl 11th: sn rdn: wknd appr 4 out* **11/10**[1]	61
0-01	**4**	*16*	**Idealko (FR)**[12] 346 9-11-12 **102**............(b) RGreene (Ian Williams) *in tch tl 9th: sn t.o* **4/1**[3]	42
P1P-	**5**	*8*	**Roky Star (FR)**[119] 3556 8-11-11 **101**............SCurran (M R Bosley) *in tch: dropped rr 6th: grad lost tch: t.o* **12/1**	33
6-45	**P**		**Rutland (IRE)**[15] 296 6-10-6 **85**............(b[1]) DCrosse[(3)] (Miss K M George) *chsd ldrs tl 9th: wknd qckly and p.u bef 11th* **16/1**	—
1F-6	**U**		**Just Muckin Around (IRE)**[18] 234 9-11-6 **96**............BHitchcott (R H Buckler) *prom: led 4th: hdd after 12th: 2nd whn mstke and uns rdr 4 out* **8/1**	—

5m 32.6s (9.90) **Going Correction** +0.55s/f (Soft) **7** Ran SP% **122.9**
Speed ratings: **104,101,**—,—,— —,— CSF £54.06 TOTE £23.90: £5.60, £1.50; EX 54.40.
Owner R J Payne **Bred** Mrs A Furlong **Trained** Brompton Regis, Somerset

FOCUS
With both Paxford Jack and Idealko below form, this was a very moderate handicap chase for the grade.

NOTEBOOK
Athnowen(IRE) could not be backed with much confidence to jump off, let alone win, as he refused to race two outings previously and whipped round at the start and got well behind at Exeter on his latest run. However, back on a winning mark, he was better behaved this time and ended a year-long losing run in convincing fashion. Given his overall record, it would be unwise to take a short price about him following up. *(op 10-1)*

Alcatras(IRE) ran a very creditable race from 9lb out of the handicap, but again found one too good and remains a maiden. *(op 6-1)*

Paxford Jack, 2lb higher than in future under the penalty he picked up for winning over three miles at Fakenham on his previous outing, ran a long way below that form and was disappointing. *Official explanation: jockey said gelding was never travelling (op 5-4 tchd Evens)*

Idealko(FR), 9lb higher than when winning at Bangor on his previous outing, ran well below the level he showed there with no obvious excuse and was another to disappoint. *(op 7-2)*

Roky Star(FR), pulled up on his only previous run over fences, offered little off the back of a 119-day break. *(tchd 14-1)*

Just Muckin Around(IRE) was still in with an shout when falling four out.

519 "JUBILATION" LADY RIDERS' H'CAP HURDLE (12 hdls) 3m 3f

4:40 (4:42) (Class 4) (0-95,92) 4-Y-0+ **£3,419** (£1,052; £526; £263)

Form				RPR
622-	**1**		**Temper Lad (USA)**[75] 4325 10-10-0 **73**............MissSGaisford[(7)] (J D Frost) *chsd ldrs: sltly outpcd after 9th: rallied appr 2 out: led appr last: styd on wl* **7/2**[2]	74
PF6-	**2**	*2*	**Native Cunning**[35] 4940 7-10-6 **79** ow2............MissAGoschen[(7)] (R H Buckler) *chsd ldrs: outpcd appr 9th: rallied appr 2 out: ev ch last: no ex* **13/2**	78
5/02	**3**	*1 ¼*	**Carl's Boy**[15] 298 9-10-8 **77**............(t) MissEJJones[(3)] (D A Rees) *hld up mid div: hdwy appr 9th: led sn after 3 out: rdn and hdd appr last: no ex* **5/2**[1]	75
20-0	**4**	*4*	**Charm Offensive**[12] 358 7-10-1 **74** ow6............(v[1]) MissJMBuck[(7)] (C J Gray) *hld up rr: hdwy appr 3rd: jnd ldr after 4th: led 9th: hdd next: one pced after* **16/1**	68
-430	**5**	*17*	**Robbie On Tour (IRE)**[4] 464 6-10-6 **79**............(t) MissLucyBridges[(7)] (M C Pipe) *hld up rr: hdwy appr 9th: sn rdn: wknd after 3 out* **9/2**[3]	56
F-25	**6**	*20*	**Seeador**[16] 271 6-11-5 **92**............MissRAGreen[(7)] (J W Mullins) *in tch: rdn after 9th: sn btn* **11/2**	49
3F0/	**7**	*11*	**Rajati (USA)**[26] 10-10-5 **78**............MrsLucyRowsell[(7)] (K R Pearce) *mid div: wknd appr 9th: dismntd* **16/1**	24
P0-0	**8**	*1*	**Regal Vision (IRE)**[16] 283 8-10-9 **82**............MissCDyson[(7)] (Miss C Dyson) *led tl 9th: sn wknd* **25/1**	27
/PP-	**P**		**Polka**[8] 10-9-7 **66** oh2............(t) JemmaMarshall[(7)] (V G Greenway) *a bhd: t.o and p.u after 3 out* **10/1**	—
	P		**April Vision (IRE)**[110] 3713 6-10-6 **79**............MissCTizzard[(7)] (Paul John Gilligan, Ire) *t.k.h in tch: bmpd appr 8th and sn lost tch: t.o and p.u bef 2 out* **28/1**	—

7m 0.10s (18.10) **Going Correction** +0.625s/f (Soft) **10** Ran SP% **125.8**
Speed ratings: **98,97,97,95,90 84,81,81,**—,— CSF £29.34 CT £69.77 TOTE £4.50: £1.40, £3.60, £1.20; EX 23.80 Place 6 £21.30, Place 5 £19.23.
Owner Jack Joseph **Bred** Juddmonte Farms **Trained** Scorriton, Devon
■ A first-ever double under Rules for Sarah Gaisford.

FOCUS
A very moderate handicap hurdle for lady riders, but quite competitive and the form looks solid for the low level.

NOTEBOOK
Temper Lad(USA) has not won since October 1999 and is nowhere near as good as he was, but he has fairly tumbled in the weights since then and deserved this following his recent seconds over much shorter in selling company. All his previous wins came over two miles and he had never race over a trip this far, but he saw it out best of all. *(op 9-2)*

Native Cunning, without the blinkers on his return to hurdling, ran much better than he been doing over fences and offered some hope. *(op 6-1 tchd 7-1)*

Carl's Boy, racing over his furthest trip to date, looked the most likely winner when sent to the front before the second last, but was eventually run out of it. *(op 3-1 tchd 7-2)*

Charm Offensive, tailed off over fences on her previous outing, ran better returned to hurdles in a first-time visor, but she could not sustain her effort to the line. *(op 12-1)*

Robbie On Tour(IRE), back over hurdles, was below his best even if would have been better suited to racing in selling company. *(op 5-1 tchd 11-2)*

Seeador, back over hurdles, probably would have preferred easier ground. *(op 6-1 tchd 5-1)*

T/Plt: £51.10 to a £1 stake. Pool: £29,252.75. 417.55 winning tickets T/Qpdt: £53.50 to a £1 stake. Pool: £1,597.90. 22.10 winning tickets TM

425 WETHERBY (L-H)

Thursday, May 26

OFFICIAL GOING: Good (good to firm in places)

Wind: slight, half behind

520 VIDAL SASSOON LADY RIDERS' H'CAP HURDLE (9 hdls) 2m

6:30 (6:30) (Class 4) (0-100,96) 4-Y-O+ **£2,604** (£744; £372)

Form RPR

-626 **1** **Lone Soldier (FR)**[8] [412] 9-10-6 **83**........................ MissRachelClark(7) 88
(S B Clark) *trckd ldrs: hdwy to ld 3 out: hit next: rdn last: kpt on* **14/1**

5 **2** *hd* **Northern Friend**[11] [370] 5-10-6 **83**..........................(b) MissCMetcalfe(7) 88
(R C Guest) *trckd ldrs: hdwy 3 out: chsd wnr next: sn rdn: drvn and styd on flat: jst hld* **10/3**[2]

3P0- **3** *2 ½* **Little Task**[203] [1994] 7-10-6 **83**.. MissJRiding(7) 85
(J S Wainwright) *hld up: hdwy on inner 3 out: rdn next: kpt on fr last* **8/1**

0-42 **4** *5* **We'll Meet Again**[8] [406] 5-10-8 **85**.. MissJCoward(7) 88+
(M W Easterby) *in rr and nt fluent 1st and 2nd: hdwy 1/2-way: effrt to chse ldrs whn hmpd 3 out: sn rdn and kpt on same pce* **3/1**[1]

34-3 **5** *nk* **Cream Cracker**[19] [220] 7-11-5 **96**.............................. MissRDavidson(7) 93
(Mrs Jeremy Young) *hld up: hdwy on outer 1/2-way: effrt to chse ldrs 3 out: sn rdn and one pce fr next* **9/2**[3]

U5-0 **6** *16* **Jamorin Dancer**[26] [122] 10-9-7 **70** oh2.................(p) MissSBrotherton(7) 51
(S G Chadwick) *chsd ldr: cl up 4 out: sn rdn along and wknd appr next* **40/1**

-050 **7** *12* **Vulcan Lane (NZ)**[9] [395] 8-10-4 **81**.............................. MissTJackson(7) 50
(R C Guest) *prom: pushed along and lost pl 4th: sn bhd* **20/1**

-000 **8** *2* **Alphecca (USA)**[8] [406] 4-10-0 **77**............................(b[1]) MissPRobson(3) 40
(K G Reveley) *trckd ldrs: hdwy and cl up 5th: rdn along bef 3 out and sn wknd* **9/2**[3]

66-P **U** **Amjad**[2] [480] 8-9-7 **70** oh6...(p) MissAArmitage(7) —
(Miss Kate Milligan) *led: rdn along 4 out: hdd whn blnd and uns rdr next* **40/1**

3m 55.3s (-4.10) **Going Correction** -0.10s/f (Good)
WFA 4 from 5yo+ 4lb **9** Ran SP% **111.9**
Speed ratings: **106,105,104,102,102 94,88,87,—** CSF £58.62 CT £401.75 TOTE £9.00: £3.10, £2.50, £2.40; EX 67.90.
Owner S B Clark **Bred** Hipodromos Y Caballos S A **Trained** Sutton-on-the-Forest, N Yorks
■ Stewards' Enquiry : Miss Rachel Clark two-day ban: used whip with excessive frequency (Jun 14, Jul 17)

FOCUS
A moderate lady riders' handicap hurdle but the form looks solid enough at a moderate level.

NOTEBOOK
Lone Soldier(FR), off the same mark as when last successful, had to battle hard for his victory, but could not be begrudged the win. It is unlikely he will be capable of defying a penalty however, and is best left alone. *(op 10-1)*
Northern Friend has yet to win a race under either code, but this was his best effort to date and it will be disappointing if he can not be placed to win a races for shrewd connections. *(op 4-1 tchd 9-2 and 3-1)*
Little Task should benefit fitness wise from this first start since November and has a similar race in him.
We'll Meet Again raced lazily early on, making sight mistakes at both the first and second flight, but warmed up as the race progressed and still in with every chance when getting hampered under half a mile out. This effectively ended his chance of winning and he is worth another go. *(op 10-3)*
Cream Cracker needs to drop further in the weights before she is winning. *(op 4-1)*
Amjad was beginning to strruggle when unseating his jockey three out, but had run well for a long way and seemed to take well to the cheekpieces. *(op 33-1)*

521 "EAT & SLEEP AT THE NAGS HEAD, PICKHILL" "NATIONAL HUNT" NOVICES' HURDLE (10 hdls) 2m 4f 110y

7:00 (7:07) (Class 3) 4-Y-O+ **£5,018** (£1,544; £772; £386)

Form RPR

00-4 **1** **Shining Strand**[20] [203] 6-11-0 .... SThomas 115+
(N J Henderson) *trckd ldr: hdwy to ld appr 3 out: rdn clr next: kpt on wl* **7/2**[3]

6-41 **2** *5* **Brooklyn Brownie (IRE)**[12] [345] 6-11-6 108.............................. GLee 111
(J M Jefferson) *hld up in tch: hdwy on inner 5th: chsd wnr 3 out: rdn next and kpt on same pce* **9/4**[1]

06-2 **3** *5* **Kimono Royal (FR)**[20] [206] 7-11-0 99.................................. RThornton 100
(A King) *hld up in tch: hdwy 5th: rdn along to chse ldrs 3 out: sn drvn and one pce* **11/4**[2]

3-11 **4** *17* **Common Girl (IRE)**[11] [367] 7-11-5 110.................................. TDoyle 90+
(O Brennan) *led rdn along 4 out: hdd bef next and sn wknd* **13/2**

2-U4 **5** *28* **Fencote (IRE)**[12] [343] 8-11-0 102.. RGarritty 55
(P Beaumont) *hld up in rr: hdwy and hit 6th: rdn along 4 out: no imp fr next* **12/1**

/3P- **6** *13* **Troodos Valley (IRE)**[177] [2551] 6-11-0 .... MBradburne 42
(H D Daly) *chsd ldrs on outer: rdn along 4 out: wknd bef next* **20/1**

0-04 **7** *nk* **Rush'N'Run**[19] [209] 6-10-4 .... THalliday(10) 42
(Mrs S J Smith) *chsd ldrs: hit 4th: rdn along 6th: wknd 4 out* **66/1**

060- **8** *dist* **Tarwin**[60] [4589] 5-10-7 .... MrSFMagee(7) —
(J R Norton) *a rr: bhd fr 4 out* **100/1**

000/ **P** **Hello Mrs**[417] [4663] 7-10-7 .... DElsworth —
(Mrs S J Smith) *chsd ldr: rdn along and lost pl 5th: sn bhd and p.u bef 3 out* **100/1**

3/-2 **P** **Lago D'Oro**[11] [375] 5-10-7 .... ADobbin —
(Miss J A Camacho) *hld up in rr: hdwy 5th: rdn along next: sn wknd and bhd whn p.u bef 3 out* **25/1**

4m 59.9s (-9.00) **Going Correction** -0.10s/f (Good) **10** Ran SP% **112.8**
Speed ratings: **113,111,109,102,92 87,86,—,—,—** CSF £11.30 TOTE £5.70: £2.10, £1.70, £1.50; EX 23.60.
Owner The Queen **Bred** Queen Elizabeth **Trained** Upper Lambourn, Berks

FOCUS
A modest novice event, but the time was smart for the class of race and they finished well strung out. The form is expected to work out.

NOTEBOOK
Shining Strand, a highly-strung sort, was winning at the fifth attempt and did so with a bit to spare. He is nothing special and would never be one to place total faith in, but this was at least a step in the right direction. *(op 9-2)*
Brooklyn Brownie(IRE) faced a tougher task under his penalty and was not up to giving the weight away. He is better off back in handicaps. *(op 5-2)*
Kimono Royal(FR) was a big disappointment last season after such a promising start and he ran no more than alright here. *(op 3-1 tchd 5-2)*
Common Girl(IRE), a tough and consistent mare who has been in cracking form, did not run her race and is probably in need of a break. *(op 4-1)*
Fencote(IRE) *Official explanation: jockey said gelding was never travelling; trainer said gelding scoped dirty (tchd 11-1)*
Lago D'Oro *Official explanation: jockey said mare had a breathing problem (op 14-1)*

522 SCHOLL H'CAP CHASE (18 fncs) 2m 7f 110y

7:30 (7:32) (Class 4) (0-110,107) 5-Y-O+ **£3,916** (£1,272; £685)

Form RPR

3-06 **1** **Helvetius**[16] [283] 9-11-0 **95**.. AThornton 103
(W T Reed) *cl up: led 11th: pushed clr 4 out: rdn 2 out and styd on wl* **9/2**[3]

120- **2** *2 ½* **Penthouse Minstrel**[34] [4955] 11-11-5 **107**.......................... TJDreaper(7) 112
(R J Hodges) *hld up: hdwy 1/2-way: rdn along 5 out: chsd wnr fr next: drvn 2 out: kpt on* **9/4**[1]

/6-0 **3** *16* **Count Oski**[16] [283] 9-10-0 **88**.. WPKavanagh(7) 77
(M J Ryan) *trckd ldng pair: pushed along 6 out: drvn and wknd next* **3/1**[2]

PP-4 **P** **Cruise The Fairway (IRE)**[13] [330] 9-11-1 **96**.................. JPMcNamara —
(B G Powell) *led: hdd 11th: rdn along 5 out: wknd and p.u bef next: dismntd* **9/4**[1]

5m 54.6s (-3.90) **Going Correction** -0.10s/f (Good) **4** Ran SP% **104.7**
Speed ratings: **102,101,95,—** CSF £13.71 TOTE £3.00; EX 6.50.
Owner Mrs Anthony, Mrs Craggs, Mrs Huddlestone **Bred** Sheikh Mohammed Obaid Al Maktoum **Trained** Haydon Bridge, Northumberland

FOCUS
A tight little event with the first two to their marks in a fair time.

NOTEBOOK
Helvetius, returning to fences after a couple of spins over hurdles, raced enthusiastically and had his field beaten early in the straight. He stayed on too strongly for the runner-up, but has never won off a mark higher than this and will not be changing that statistic unless findign improvement from somewhere. *(op 10-3)*
Penthouse Minstrel is a genuine sort in the right grade and pulled well clear of the third. He kept on well all the way to the line and will continue to pay his way. *(op 3-1)*
Count Oski was beaten a long way from the finish and proved disappointing. *(op 11-4)*
Cruise The Fairway(IRE) has got problems and failed to build on his best run for a while when fourth at Aintree last time. He was struggling a long way out and was dismounted having been pulled up. *(tchd 5-2)*

523 ROCOM PLANTRONICS "NATIONAL HUNT" MAIDEN HURDLE (12 hdls) 3m 1f

8:05 (8:06) (Class 4) 4-Y-O+ **£3,416** (£976; £488)

Form RPR

6-23 **1** **Combat Drinker (IRE)**[13] [334] 7-11-0 90..............................(t) ADobbin 92+
(D McCain) *hld up towards rr: stdy hdwy 1/2-way: chal 3 out: sn led: rdn clr next: hit last: drvn flat and kpt on* **6/5**[1]

P2-2 **2** *½* **No Further Comment (IRE)**[27] [107] 5-11-0 ....(b[1]) SThomas 89
(Mrs Jeremy Young) *hld up in midfield: hdwy appr 4 out: rdn along next: drvn last: styd on wl flat* **4/1**[2]

5-P4 **3** *1 ¾* **Ladies From Leeds**[18] [236] 6-10-7 78........................(b[1]) NPMulholland 81
(A Crook) *led: rdn along after 4 out: jnd next and sn hdd: drvn 2 out and kpt on wl u.p* **33/1**

4 *11* **Dark Diva**[54] 7-10-7 .... AThornton 71+
(W T Reed) *hld up towards rr: stdy hdwy 8th: rdn to chse ldrs whn stmbld 3 out: sn rdn and kpt on same pce* **14/1**

34/4 **5** *1 ½* **Nod Ya Head**[32] [8] 9-10-0 71.. PKinsella(7) 68
(R E Barr) *cl up: rdn along 7th: drvn along appr 3 out: plugged on same pce* **16/1**

/PUP **6** *10* **Jack Weighell**[8] [414] 6-11-0 83... GLee 65
(J M Jefferson) *hld up and bhd: hdwy 4 out: rdn along bef next and nvr a factor* **40/1**

50-5 **7** *13* **Sitting Duck**[12] [356] 6-11-0 85.. JTizzard 52
(B G Powell) *in tch: hdwy to chse ldr 4 out: rdn along and wknd bef next* **9/1**

6-4 **8** *5* **Rhuna Red**[26] [124] 6-10-7 .... KRenwick 40
(J R Bewley) *chsd ldng pair: rdn along and hit 7th: sn wknd* **6/1**[3]

65-5 **9** *5* **Coyote Lakes**[12] [359] 6-11-0 80....................................(p) JPMcNamara 42
(A M McGrath) *in tch: rdn along 7th: sn wknd* **33/1**

00-0 **10** *30* **Solemn Vow**[19] [209] 4-9-8 .... SCrawford(7) —
(P Maddison) *chsd ldrs. hit 3rd and next: rdn along and lost pl 6th: mstke 8th and sn wl bhd* **100/1**

0-0 **P** **Edenderry (IRE)**[12] [355] 6-10-11 .... PAspell(3) —
(A D Brown) *a rr: t.o whn p.u bef 2 out* **66/1**

/F-6 **P** **Jockie Wells**[28] [85] 7-10-11 74.. PBuchanan(3) —
(Miss Lucinda V Russell) *a bhd: t.o whn p.u bef 3 out* **66/1**

6m 29.4s (14.90) **Going Correction** -0.10s/f (Good)
WFA 4 from 5yo+ 6lb **12** Ran SP% **114.6**
Speed ratings: **72,71,71,67,67 64,59,58,56,47 —,—** CSF £5.42 TOTE £2.30: £1.30, £1.70, £4.50; EX 7.00.
Owner B Dunn **Bred** J J Bowe **Trained** Cholmondeley, Cheshire
■ Stewards' Enquiry : S Thomas two-day ban: used whip with excessive frequency (Jun 6-7)

FOCUS
A bad race and a pedestrian winning time, rated through the winner and fifth to their marks.

NOTEBOOK
Combat Drinker(IRE) has been running better since fitted with a tongue tie and he held on well from No Further Comment who gave chase in the final furlong. He is going the right way now and will be of interest back in handicaps. *(op 6-4)*
No Further Comment(IRE), sporting the first-time blinkers, has finished second over fences the last twice and had no trouble reverting to hurdles. He kept on without ever looking likely to get to the winner and will be winning a race sooner rather than later. *(tchd 9-2)*
Ladies From Leeds, another wearing first-time blinkers, plugged on for third and was clearly helped by the headgear. *(tchd 28-1)*
Dark Diva was well adrift of the front three, but this was a promising Rules debut and she should find a small race during the summer. *(op 12-1 tchd 11-1 and 16-1)*
Nod Ya Head is not really progressing and looks very slow. *(op 14-1 tchd 12-1)*

524 GUY SALMON LAND ROVER LEEDS NOVICES' CHASE (18 fncs) 2m 7f 110y

8:35 (8:36) (Class 3) 5-Y-O+ **£5,541** (£1,705; £852; £426)

Form RPR

2-12 **1** **Ashnaya (FR)**[7] [430] 7-10-8 102..(p) DCCostello(5) 115+
(G M Moore) *trckd ldr: hdwy 5 out: chal next: sn led: rdn appr 2 out: styd on wl approahing last* **10/3**[2]

P44- **2** *8* **Shareef (FR)**[42] [4836] 8-11-0 114.. RThornton 109+
(A King) *trckd ldng pair: hdwy 5 out: cl up next: sn rdn and ev ch tl drvn and wknd appr last* **6/4**[1]

3-21 **3** *20* **Muttley Maguire (IRE)**[12] [358] 6-11-6 98.. JTizzard 99+
(B G Powell) *led: mstke 5 out: rdn next: sn hdd & wknd* **6/4**[1]

P-PP **4** *29* **Alchemystic (IRE)**[7] [419] 5-10-4 95 ....(tp) PWhelan(3) 52
(M A Barnes) *cl up: rdn along 10th: outpcd 13th: bhd fr 5 out* **40/1**[3]

5m 54.1s (-4.40) **Going Correction** -0.10s/f (Good)
WFA 5 from 6yo+ 3lb **4** Ran SP% **105.5**
Speed ratings: **103,100,93,84** CSF £8.53 TOTE £3.20; EX 7.30.
Owner B P Bradshaw **Bred** P Dane Player **Trained** Middleham Moor, N Yorks

FOCUS
The four runners finished well strung out in what was an ordinary chase.

NOTEBOOK
Ashnaya(FR), who has been running consistently well this year, pulled clear in the final furlong and won well. She ran a good race at the course last time and clearly goes well here, a fact worth bearing in mind. She is reportedly in line for a break now. *(op 3-1 tchd 11-4 and 7-2)*
Shareef(FR) has not won a race since October 2001 and failed to last out here. He is worth dropping in trip. *(op 13-8 tchd 7-4 and 15-8 in a place)*
Muttley Maguire(IRE) was the real disappointment of the race, failing to build on his first win at Worcester earlier in the month. He is better than this and worth another chance, being a six-year-old and all. *(tchd 11-8 and 13-8)*

525 HELEN OF TROY LADIES' EVENING H'CAP HURDLE (10 hdls) 2m 4f 110y
9:05 (9:06) (Class 3) (0-125,122) 4-Y-0+ **£5,037** (£1,550; £775; £387)

Form RPR

34-1 **1** **Swift Swallow**[18] [247] 7-11-11 **121** .... TDoyle 129+
(O Brennan) *hld up in rr: stdy hdwy 3 out: chsd ldrs and hit 2 out: rdn last: qckdn flat to ld last 100 yds* **11/2**[3]

01-2 **2** *1* **Enhancer**[21] [194] 7-11-10 **120** .... JCulloty 123
(M J McGrath) *trckd ldrs: hdwy 3 out: chal next: sn rdn: led last: drvn: hdd and no ex last 100 yds* **9/2**[2]

14-2 **3** *2 ½* **Dark Ben (FR)**[29] [61] 5-10-10 **111** .... DCCostello(5) 111
(Miss Kate Milligan) *in tch: gd hdwy to ld after 4 out: rdn next: j.lft 2 out: sn drvn: hdd last: one pce flat* **13/2**

U-54 **4** *1* **Why The Long Face (NZ)**[12] [347] 8-10-12 **108** ....(b¹) HOliver 108+
(R C Guest) *hld up in rr: stdy hdwy appr 3 out: chsd ldrs next: ev ch whn nt fluent last: rdn and one pce flat* **10/1**

24-P **5** *¾* **Stamparland Hill**[12] [353] 10-10-10 **106** .... GLee 104
(J M Jefferson) *led: rdn along and hdd after 4 out: outpcd next: styd on u.p appr last* **10/1**

541- **6** *1 ½* **Sovereign State (IRE)**[5] [4443] 8-11-0 **113** .... KJMercer(3) 110
(D W Thompson) *hld up in tch: hdwy 4 out: chal next: sn rdn and one pce fr 2 out* **9/1**

12-3 **7** *1* **Nick's Choice**[11] [372] 9-11-1 **116** .... LStephens(5) 112
(D Burchell) *hld up in tch: gd hdwy 4 out: cl up next: sn rdn and wknd fr 2 out* **17/2**

360- **8** *10* **After Me Boys**[40] [4868] 11-11-8 **118** .... DElsworth 104
(Mrs S J Smith) *chsd ldrs: rdn along after 4 out: wknd bef next* **4/1**[1]

00-6 **9** *17* **Rising Generation (FR)**[13] [332] 8-11-12 **122** .... ADobbin 91
(N G Richards) *chsd ldr: rdn along appr 4 out and sn wknd* **20/1**

31/P **P** **Mio Caro (FR)**[26] [127] 5-11-2 **119** ....(v¹) WKennedy(7) —
(Noel T Chance) *a rr: bhd whn p.u bef 3 out* **20/1**

5m 5.80s (-3.10) **Going Correction** -0.10s/f (Good) **10** Ran SP% **115.1**
Speed ratings: **101,100,99,99,99 98,98,94,87,—** CSF £30.60 CT £161.89 TOTE £7.80: £2.10, £1.90, £2.30; EX 33.90 Place 6 £244.50, Place 5 £20.80.
Owner Richard J Marshall **Bred** Ronald Wilkie **Trained** Worksop, Notts

FOCUS
A competitive race with most of those immediately behind the principals running to their marks and the form could work out.

NOTEBOOK
Swift Swallow does not know how to run a bad race and he showed a good change of gear after the last to deny Enhancer. This was a good performance under the weight and he is quickly making up into a useful hurdler. *(tchd 6-1)*
Enhancer is at his best on good or faster ground and only found the one too good. He may have benefited from hitting the front a bit later on and should continue to shape well. *(tchd 5-1)*
Dark Ben(FR) only gave way in the final furlong or so, but held on for third and remains in good heart. *(op 8-1)*
Why The Long Face(NZ) did himself no favours with a slight mistake at the last that cost him momentum. He may be better off back over fences. *(tchd 12-1)*
Stamparland Hill kept grinding away in fifth, but his overall profile is not one of a horse worth following. *(op 12-1)*
After Me Boys failed to run a race and has lost his form of late. *(op 5-1)*
T/Plt: £244.50 to a £1 stake. Pool £40,904.50. 122.10 winning units T/Qpdt: £20.80 to a £1 stake. Pool £2,930.00. 103.90 winning units JR

529 - 530a (Foreign Racing) - See Raceform Interactive

[394]TOWCESTER (R-H)
Friday, May 27

OFFICIAL GOING: Good to firm (good in straight)
Wind: Slight, half-against Weather: Warm and sunny

531 GG.COM "NATIONAL HUNT" NOVICES' HURDLE (8 hdls) 2m
6:25 (6:25) (Class 4) 4-Y-0+ **£4,114** (£1,266; £633; £316)

Form RPR

050- **1** **Nautic (FR)**[44] [4826] 4-10-8 .... WHutchinson 92
(R Dickin) *chsd ldrs: lft 2nd 3rd: led 2 out: rdn out* **66/1**

P-23 **2** *1 ½* **Thieves'Glen**[21] [203] 7-10-12 108 ....(b) RJohnson 95
(H Morrison) *led: hit 5th: rdn and hdd 2 out: styd on u.p* **6/5**[2]

0-0 **3** *dist* **Star Fever (IRE)**[33] [7] 4-10-8 .... JCulloty 61
(Miss H C Knight) *hld up: nvr nr to chal* **20/1**[3]

00-P **4** *23* **Roseville (IRE)**[29] [77] 5-10-2 .... DCrosse(3) —
(S T Lewis) *sn t.o* **125/1**

00/ **5** *dist* **Saxon Kingdom**[527] [2797] 6-10-5 .... JAJenkins(7) —
(M Bradstock) *sn t.o* **100/1**

0-11 **U** **Itsmyboy (IRE)**[14] [331] 5-11-12 .... APMcCoy —
(M C Pipe) *chsd ldr: nt fluent 2nd: tried to run out and uns rdr next* **5/6**[1]

3m 56.5s (-14.90) **Going Correction** -0.95s/f (Hard)
WFA 4 from 5yo+ 4lb **6** Ran SP% **108.0**
Speed ratings: **99,98,—,—,—** — CSF £140.93 TOTE £23.10: £6.30, £1.50; EX 59.40.
Owner Scrumpy Jacks **Bred** F X Cordier Et Al **Trained** Atherstone on Stour, Warwicks

FOCUS
A moderate contest and a huge shock here with 66/1 outsider Nautic landing the spoils. The form is difficult to assess with confidence.

NOTEBOOK
Nautic(FR), who had shown little over hurdles in previous attempts, plucked this effort from out of nowhere and came away from long-time leader Thieves' Glen from two out, keeping on well to cause a huge shock. Whether he can repeat this performance is open to debate, but there is no particular reason why it should go down as a fluke. *(op 50-1)*
Thieves'Glen is not the heartiest of battlers and continues to frustrate. With the favourite departing early, he should really have won and is never one to take a short price about. *(tchd 5-4)*
Star Fever(IRE) is clearly one of his stables lesser lights, but is only four and may yet be able to improve. *(op 25-1)*
Itsmyboy(IRE), on a hat-trick after a couple of cosy victories in similar races, disgraced himself in trying to run out at the third and unshipping McCoy. He has ability, but clearly has his quirks as well and is one to be wary of after this. *(op 10-11 tchd evens in places)*

532 WAYSIDE MAIDEN CHASE (14 fncs) 2m 3f 110y
6:55 (6:55) (Class 4) 5-Y-0+ **£3,553** (£1,154; £621)

Form RPR

U0-P **1** **Monty Be Quick**[13] [357] 9-10-9 74 .... MrNPearce(7) 79+
(J M Castle) *a.p: chsd ldr 6th: lft 2nd and hmpd 3 out: led bef next: sn clr* **33/1**

2 *19* **Thyne Spirit (IRE)**[19] 6-10-13 .... DCrosse(3) 58
(S T Lewis) *led to 3rd: remained handy tl outpcd 10th: hmpd by loose horse after 3 out: styd on fr last* **8/1**

20-F **3** *8* **Lough Rynn (IRE)**[7] [436] 7-11-2 106 .... SThomas 54+
(Miss H C Knight) *led 3rd: jnd whn lft clr 3 out: hdd & wknd bef next* **6/5**[1]

053- **P** **Jesnic (IRE)**[37] [4931] 5-10-13 85 .... WHutchinson —
(R Dickin) *prom to 7th: t.o whn p.u bef next* **7/1**[3]

26-P **U** **Hatsnall**[23] [181] 7-11-2 75 .... MBradburne —
(Miss C J E Caroe) *hld up: mstke and uns rdr 7th* **20/1**

40-3 **F** **Gin 'N' Fonic (IRE)**[11] [388] 5-10-6 90 .... SWalsh(7) —
(J D Frost) *chsd ldrs: 3rd and rdn whn fell 11th* **10/3**[2]

F0-5 **F** **Ultimate Limit**[21] [202] 5-10-13 69 .... PJBrennan —
(A Ennis) *hld up: hdwy 6th: chsd ldr 9th: ev ch whn fell 3 out* **17/2**

5m 7.90s (-10.30) **Going Correction** -1.20s/f (Hard) course record
WFA 5 from 6yo+ 2lb **7** Ran SP% **110.4**
Speed ratings: **72,64,61,—,—** **—,—** CSF £238.02 TOTE £21.90: £6.40, £2.90; EX 135.10.
Owner J M Castle **Bred** J M Castle **Trained** Long Crendon, Bucks

FOCUS
Another shock result with Monty Be Quick destroying the opposition. It would have been more of a race had Ultimate Limit stayed on his feet. Not a race to be confident about.

NOTEBOOK
Monty Be Quick made it two in a row for big outsiders with this resounding victory. He had never won a race prior to today in 21 starts, but it clicked on this occasion and he powered away from the field in the final couple of furlongs. He would have had much more to do had Ultimate Limit stayed on his feet, but he should have nothing taken away from him and, if holding this level of form, should be capable of following up. *(op 20-1)*
Thyne Spirit(IRE), a fair pointer in Ireland, did best of the rest and plugged on up the hill for a clear second. This was a reasonable effort and he wil improve for further. *(op 15-2 tchd 11-2)*
Lough Rynn(IRE) has never looked the strongest of finishers and he faded away in tame fashion from the home turn. *(op 11-8 tchd 6-4 and 11-10)*
Gin 'N' Fonic(IRE) did not look to be travelling overly well when coming down at the 11th and he remains winless over jumps. *(op 10-1 tchd 11-1)*
Ultimate Limit was bang there and probably looked the most likely winner when hitting the deck at the third last. He would have given the winner more to do and had he stayed on his feet, and may have even troubled him for first place. *(op 10-1 tchd 11-1)*
Jesnic(IRE) *Official explanation: jockey said gelding was unsuited by good to firm ground (op 10-1 tchd 11-1)*

533 KNIGHT FRANK NOVICES' HURDLE (10 hdls) 2m 3f 110y
7:25 (7:26) (Class 4) 4-Y-0+ **£4,143** (£1,275; £637; £318)

Form RPR

16-2 **1** **Middleham Park (IRE)**[23] [182] 5-11-3 105 .... RYoung(3) 107+
(J W Mullins) *plld hrd and prom: led after 2 out: wnt rt last: styd on wl* **2/1**[2]

6-F2 **2** *5* **Hattington**[6] [451] 7-11-6 105 .... APMcCoy 104+
(M F Harris) *hld up: racd keenly: hdwy to chse wnr appr 2 out: sn rdn: nt clr run and hit last: no ex* **10/11**[1]

2U-P **3** *26* **Lescer's Lad**[21] [201] 8-11-0 76 .... RWalford 72+
(C L Popham) *led: hit 2nd: hdd & wknd appr 2 out* **16/1**

000- **4** *21* **Legal Spy**[74] [4373] 6-11-0 .... LAspell 49
(F Jordan) *hld up: j.rt 3rd: mstke next: j. slowly 5th: mstke and hmpd 3 out: sn wknd: bhd whn tried to refuse last* **16/1**

PP- **5** *3 ½* **Regal Repose**[67] [4495] 5-10-7 ....(p) BHitchcott 39
(Miss K M George) *chsd ldr: ev ch whn pckd 3 out: sn wknd* **33/1**

4/0- **P** **Bosworth Boy**[187] [2371] 7-10-7 .... JAJenkins(7) —
(Mrs H Sweeting) *hld up: mstkes 6th and next: wknd after 3 out: bhd whn p.u bef last* **8/1**[3]

4m 56.7s (-21.40) **Going Correction** -0.95s/f (Hard)
WFA 4 from 5yo+ 4lb **6** Ran SP% **111.5**
Speed ratings: **104,102,91,83,81** — CSF £4.29 TOTE £2.80: £1.60, £1.60; EX 4.00.
Owner CPM Group Limited **Bred** Keith Wills **Trained** Wilsford-Cum-Lake, Wilts

FOCUS
As expected, the front two pulled well clear, but reliable form with the first three running to their best.

NOTEBOOK
Middleham Park(IRE), despite pulling in the early stages, found plenty under pressure and stayed on too strongly for favourite Hattington on the climb to the line. He is a fairly consistent sort who should continue to pay his way. *(tchd 15-8, 9-4 in places)*
Hattington would have given the winner more to think about had he not hit the last when a bit short of room to jump and he may prove better off on an easier circuit. *(tchd Evens, 11-10 in a place)*
Lescer's Lad ended up well beaten having made most of the running and he was simply outclassed when the tempo quickened. *(op 10-1)*
Legal Spy did his best to refuse at the last, but his jockey got him to the other side. He was well held in the end and hardly made an encouraging start to his hurdling career.

534 LADBROKES.COM H'CAP CHASE (12 fncs) 2m 110y
7:55 (7:57) (Class 3) (0-115,115) 5-Y-0+ **£6,938** (£2,135; £1,067; £533)

Form RPR

6-02 **1** **Nephite (NZ)**[10] [395] 11-10-4 **93** .... SThomas 108+
(Miss Venetia Williams) *prom: chsd clr ldr 4th: led after 3 out: rdn clr appr last* **11/2**[2]

52-0 **2** *9* **Fiery Peace**[33] [4] 8-11-9 **112** .... MBradburne 119+
(H D Daly) *hld up: hdwy 5th: chsd wnr appr 2 out: styng on same pce whn j.rt last* **13/2**[3]

31-P **3** *1 ¼* **Runner Bean**[16] [305] 11-11-4 **107** .... JPMcNamara 112
(R Lee) *chsd ldrs: styd on same pce fr 2 out* **12/1**

144- **4** *3* **James Victor (IRE)**[190] [2302] 7-10-2 **94** .... RYoung(3) 96
(N R Mitchell) *chsd ldrs: lost pl 5th: hdwy and hit 8th: wknd last* **12/1**

25-0 **5** *½* **Bobosh**[19] [248] 9-11-0 **103** .... CLlewellyn 104
(R Dickin) *chsd ldr to 4th: remained handy: rdn appr 3 out: wknd next* **15/2**

-112 **6** *6* **He's Hot Right Now (NZ)**[3] [482] 6-10-3 **95** ....(p) LMcGrath(3) 90
(R C Guest) *hld up: hit 7th: rdn and mstke 3 out: nvr trbld ldrs* **11/4**[1]

45-0	7	dist	**The Newsman (IRE)**[28] 103 13-11-8 **111** .... LAspell (G Wareham) *hld up: a bhd* **22/1**	—
-P06	P		**Auditor**[10] 395 6-9-11 **89** oh5 .... (b) DCrosse(3) (S T Lewis) *led and sn clr: j.rt: mstke 2nd: hit 8th: wknd and hdd after 3 out: p.u bef next* **33/1**	—

4m 2.80s (-16.50) **Going Correction** -1.20s/f (Hard) **8** Ran SP% **89.8**
Speed ratings: **90,85,85,83,83 80**,—,— CSF £24.68 CT £169.36 TOTE £3.90: £1.50, £2.20, £1.70; EX 16.20.
Owner Mrs H Spencer **Bred** Te Akau Thoroughbreds Syndicate **Trained** Kings Caple, H'fords
■ Lik Wood Power (11/4 JF) was withdrawn (arrived at start in undeclared cheekpieces). R4 applies, deduct 25p in the £.

FOCUS
Ordinary form, but fairly solid for the grade.

NOTEBOOK
Nephite(NZ) has been running reasonably since returning from a lay-off and, at a course his stable do well at, was able to get back to winning ways. He had dropped to a decent mark and impressed with the way he came away in the final quarter mile. He would be an obvious contender to follow up if holding this level of form. *(op 4-1)*
Fiery Peace, 7lb higher than when last winning, has recorded all his best form on easier tracks and ran well enough to suggest he is nearing a win. *(op 7-1 tchd 6-1)*
Runner Bean, racing off a career-high mark, has proved to be a really good money-spinner in the last year or so and ran another solid race in third. *(op 11-1 tchd 8-1)*
James Victor(IRE), probably the least exposed in the line-up, ran just a fair race and will need to improve on this if he is to be winning anytime soon. *(op 11-1)*
Bobosh is back on a fair mark and is entitled to be winning sooner rather than later, but needs to do better than this. *(op 7-1)*
He's Hot Right Now(NZ) was a bit disappointing and never got into the race. He is better than this and worthy of another chance. *(op 7-2 tchd 4-1)*

535 BRIAN GOODYEAR TELEBET 0808 1081122 H'CAP CHASE (18 fncs) 3m 110y
8:25 (8:25) (Class 4) (0-105,103) 5-Y-0+ **£4,926** (£1,601; £862)

Form				RPR
24-2	1		**Sir Cumference**[10] 398 9-11-0 **91** .... (b) APMcCoy (Miss Venetia Williams) *led to 12th: rdn 15th: led 2 out: styd on u.p* **15/8**[1]	100+
2-31	2	3 ½	**Petolinski**[10] 398 7-9-11 **81** 7ex .... (p) TMessenger(7) (C L Popham) *hld up in tch: chsd wnr 9th: led 12th: hdd ad hit 2 out: no ex last* **11/2**[3]	87+
14-2	3	dist	**Sissinghurst Storm (IRE)**[18] 262 7-9-11 **77** oh7 .... (p) DCrosse(3) (R Dickin) *chsd ldr: j. slowly 5th: lost pl after 9th: rdn 12th: mstke next: wknd 3 out* **13/2**	42
05-F	U		**Rose Of The Hill (IRE)**[16] 298 6-11-4 **95** .... JEMoore (M C Pipe) *hld up: blnd and uns rdr 6th* **12/1**	—
P-53	P		**Chancers Dante (IRE)**[10] 398 9-9-11 **77** oh5 .... (b) KJMercer(3) (Ferdy Murphy) *hld up: bhd fr 7th: p.u bef 13th* **5/1**[2]	—
50-2	P		**Indian Squaw (IRE)**[19] 231 6-10-4 **81** .... (t) NFehily (B De Haan) *hld up in tch: rdn and wknd 3 out: t.o whn p.u bef last* **7/1**	—
040-	R		**Garolsa (FR)**[40] 4888 11-11-12 **103** .... (bt) JTizzard (C L Tizzard) *hld up: bhd fr 8th: hmpd by loose horse and ref 14th* **11/1**	—
020-	P		**Autumn Mist (IRE)**[105] 3788 10-11-4 **95** .... (v) BJCrowley (M Scudamore) *chsd ldrs: mstke 11th: wknd 13th: t.o whn p.u bef 2 out* **16/1**	—

6m 12.3s (-34.30) **Going Correction** -1.20s/f (Hard) **8** Ran SP% **114.6**
Speed ratings: **106,104**,—,—,— —,—,— CSF £13.12 CT £54.86 TOTE £2.60: £1.40, £2.00, £2.20; EX 7.60.
Owner Mrs Nicola Moores **Bred** Richard Lissack **Trained** Kings Caple, H'fords

FOCUS
Modest form rated through the winner.

NOTEBOOK
Sir Cumference made it two in a row for his trainer and recorded his first win in over two years. He had the most solid credentials in the field and was given a simple ride by McCoy. He stays well and should still be on a fair mark after this. *(op 2-1 tchd 9-4)*
Petolinski, shouldering an 7lb penalty for his win last week, ran a good race in defeat was simply outstayed by the winner. He was a mile clear of the third, but needs to keep on improving to defy his mark.
Sissinghurst Storm(IRE) was the only other to complete, but was beaten out of sight and ran a below-par race. She was wearing first-time cheekpieces, and maybe connections will leave them off next time. *(op 8-1)*
Garolsa(FR) seemed to cry enough after being hampered by a loose horse and decided he no longer wanted to take part. *(op 9-1 tchd 8-1)*
Rose Of The Hill(IRE), a winning pointer trying out fences under Rules for the first time having been a disappointment over hurdles, got no further than the sixth and we learned nothing new about him. *(op 9-1 tchd 8-1)*
Indian Squaw(IRE), a promising second behind subsequent winner Mrs Be on her chasing debut at Plumpton, travelled well, but was running on empty from half a mile out and found this too stiff a test on the track. She may be worth another chance back on a tight circuit. *(op 9-1 tchd 8-1)*

536 SKYNET.CO.UK INTERNET SERVICES H'CAP HURDLE (8 hdls) 2m
8:55 (8:55) (Class 4) (0-105,105) 4-Y-0+ **£4,192** (£1,290; £645; £322)

Form				RPR
523-	1		**Naked Oat**[222] 1747 10-11-4 **92** .... LAspell (Mrs L Wadham) *chsd ldrs: led last: drvn out* **5/1**[3]	92
05-1	2	hd	**Sunnyarjun**[18] 265 7-11-3 **91** .... JMogford (J C Tuck) *hld up: hdwy after 5th: hung rt and led appr last: sn hdd: r.o towards fin* **4/1**[2]	93+
00-1	3	nk	**Brochrua (IRE)**[17] 284 5-11-0 **95** .... SWalsh(7) (J D Frost) *prom: rdn appr 2 out: r.o* **13/2**	95
450-	4	1 ½	**Opera Hall**[50] 4759 5-11-0 **88** .... RJohnson (H D Daly) *chsd ldr 2nd: led next: rdn: hdd and nt clr run appr last: no ex flat* **7/2**[1]	87+
-0U0	5	2	**Saorsie**[13] 357 7-11-8 **96** .... SFox (J C Fox) *hld up: styd on appr last: nvr nr to chal* **6/1**	92
50/0	6	6	**Erins Lass (IRE)**[19] 245 8-10-13 **90** .... DCrosse(3) (R Dickin) *hld up: hdwy 5th: ev ch whn pckd 3 out: wknd appr last* **9/1**	84+
-544	7	1 ¼	**Reach The Clouds (IRE)**[5] 466 13-11-1 **89** .... PFlynn (John R Upson) *hld up in tch: wknd appr 2 out* **8/1**	78
35-0	8	2	**Running Times (USA)**[19] 233 8-10-0 **81** .... (b) JAJenkins(7) (H J Manners) *led to 3rd: wknd after 3 out* **14/1**	68

4m 0.60s (-10.80) **Going Correction** -0.95s/f (Hard) **8** Ran SP% **114.3**
Speed ratings: **89,88,88,88,87 84,83,82** CSF £25.66 CT £130.47 TOTE £5.20: £1.50, £1.70, £2.40; EX 21.90 Place 6 £223.34, Place 5 £109.26.
Owner The Dyball Partnership **Bred** R B Warren **Trained** Newmarket, Suffolk

FOCUS
Another moderate race, but it did at least produce a good finish. The form is muddling but rated through the principals.

NOTEBOOK
Naked Oat, 9lb higher than when last successful, just got the better of the tight finish and received a good ride from Aspell. He had run well previously off this career-high mark, but it is doubtful whether he can defy a further rise. *(op 11-2 tchd 9-2)*
Sunnyarjun, off an 8lb higher mark than last time, ran a cracking race in defeat and just lost out in the three-way photo, the stiff climb to the line finding him out. He can win off this mark, but needs to improve again if the Handicapper raises him further. *(op 10-3)*
Brochrua(IRE), another winn last time, kept grinding away and lost out narrowly. Her wins have come at a lowly level and she does little for the form. *(op 5-1)*
Opera Hall had no more to offer in the final furlong and may be better off at a more speed-reliant track. *(op 9-2)*
Saorsie came from too far back and was never getting to the principals in time. *(op 11-2)*
T/Plt: £107.50 to a £1 stake. Pool: £35,129.85. 238.40 winning tickets. T/Qpdt: £7.20 to a £1 stake. Pool: £3,377.40. 343.95 winning tickets. CR

537 - 543a (Foreign Racing) - See Raceform Interactive

495 CARTMEL (L-H)
Saturday, May 28

OFFICIAL GOING: Good (good to soft in places, soft between last two fences on chase course)
After three fine days the ground was described as 'generally good'.
Wind: Fresh; half behind Weather: Fine and mostly sunny.

544 LANCASTER BOOKMAKERS CONDITIONAL JOCKEYS' H'CAP HURDLE (8 hdls) 2m 1f 110y
5:45 (5:45) (Class 4) (0-105,105) 4-Y-0+ **£4,113** (£1,265; £632; £316)

Form				RPR
05/3	1		**Dream Castle (IRE)**[17] 306 11-9-12 **82** .... PMerrigan(5) (Barry Potts, Ire) *trckd ldrs: led 3rd: wnt clr after 2 out: 10 l ahd whn heavily eased clsng stages* **4/1**[3]	103+
624-	2	2 ½	**Bargain Hunt (IRE)**[55] 4709 4-10-1 **89** .... PJMcDonald(5) (W Storey) *nt flunt: bhd: hdwy 6th: wnt 2nd appr last: styd on: greatly flattered* **12/1**	91
P-00	3	8	**Martin House (IRE)**[17] 306 6-10-4 **83** .... ONelmes (D W Thompson) *chsd ldrs to 6th: sn outpcd* **14/1**	81
3-02	4	12	**Petrolero (ARG)**[3] 495 6-10-8 **87** .... PAspell (James Moffatt) *chsd ldrs: wknd 6th* **7/2**[2]	73
30-2	5	½	**Dargaville (NZ)**[30] 78 6-11-2 **98** .... (p) PCO'Neill(3) (R C Guest) *chsd ldrs: wnt 2nd 5th: drvn along next: wknd between last 2* **3/1**[1]	83
UB-3	6	dist	**Dalriath**[6] 467 6-10-3 **90** .... DSwan(8) (M C Chapman) *led to 3rd: j. slowly and lost pl 5th: t.o next* **15/2**	—
2/0-	F		**Robert The Bruce**[149] 3103 10-11-9 **105** .... GBerridge(3) (L Lungo) *wnt prom 5th: 4th and wl outpcd whn fell next* **4/1**[3]	—

4m 12.5s (-3.20) **Going Correction** -0.10s/f (Good)
WFA 4 from 6yo+ 4lb **7** Ran SP% **113.3**
Speed ratings: **103,101,98,93,92** —,— CSF £45.23 CT £605.33 TOTE £6.00: £2.40, £3.90; EX 56.10.
Owner William M Brown **Bred** Miss Avril Campbell **Trained** Strabane, Co Tyrone

FOCUS
A strong pace and a heavily eased down winner who is rated value for considerably more that the official margin.

NOTEBOOK
Dream Castle(IRE), bowling along in front, stepped up the gallop and shot clear between the last two flights. Heavily eased, he was value for ten lengths plus. *(op 7-2)*
Bargain Hunt(IRE) struggled to keep up and his jumping let him down. Staying on to take second going to the final flight, the margin of defeat greatly flatters him.
Martin House(IRE), a shadow of his former self, looks set to continue to struggle. *(tchd 16-1)*
Petrolero(ARG), making a quick return on his home patch, kept tabs on the winner but was out on his feet three from home. *(op 3-1)*
Dargaville(NZ) went in pursuit of the winner but stopped to nothing between the last two. *(op 2-1)*
Robert The Bruce was being tapped for toe though still well in touch when crashing out three from home. *(op 6-1)*

545 STICKY TOFFEE PUDDING NOVICES' H'CAP HURDLE (11 hdls) 2m 6f
6:20 (6:21) (Class 4) (0-95,94) 4-Y-0+ **£3,304** (£944; £472)

Form				RPR
0-64	1		**Primitive Poppy**[21] 212 6-10-5 **76** .... PBuchanan(3) (Mrs A Hamilton) *chsd ldrs: led sn after last: sn drew clr* **11/1**	83
4P-F	2	12	**Barton Sun (IRE)**[14] 345 6-10-9 **77** .... WHutchinson (R N Bevis) *led tl sn after last: sn wknd: fin tired* **12/1**	72
F-21	3	17	**My Lady Link (FR)**[15] 329 6-11-11 **93** .... SThomas (Miss Venetia Williams) *mid-div: hdwy 7th: sn chsng ldrs: one pce fr 3 out* **3/1**[1]	71
334-	4	5	**Loscar (FR)**[102] 3871 6-10-6 **74** .... CLlewellyn (L Lungo) *rr-div: hdwy 8th: chsng ldrs next: sn wknd* **13/2**	47
2	5	4	**Mary Macs Lad (IRE)**[15] 334 6-11-1 **83** .... (b) RJohnson (John G Carr, Ire) *reluctant to go to s: chsd ldrs: mstke 5th: wknd fr 3 out* **10/3**[2]	52
06-0	6	11	**It's Harry**[34] 9 7-11-1 **93** .... THalliday(10) (Mrs S J Smith) *mid-div: outpcd 7th: no ch after* **10/1**	51
-522	7	¾	**Cody**[3] 500 6-10-12 **80** .... (vt) JTizzard (James Moffatt) *chsd ldrs: wknd 3 out* **6/1**[3]	37
045-	8	3	**Mr Prickle (IRE)**[36] 4965 5-11-12 **94** .... ATinkler (P Beaumont) *mid-div: outpcd 7th: sn lost pl* **16/1**	48
0-P6	9	4	**Sea Maize**[10] 417 7-9-11 **68** .... (b) PAspell(3) (C R Wilson) *chsd ldrs: lost pl 7th* **33/1**	18
53-6	P		**Loch Torridon**[21] 209 6-10-1 **69** .... ADempsey (James Moffatt) *sn bhd: t.o whn p.u bef 8th* **33/1**	—
PP0-	P		**Danny Leahy (FR)**[35] 4977 5-10-7 **75** .... KRenwick (M D Hammond) *in rr: t.o 7th: p.u bef 3 out* **50/1**	—
P-PU	P		**Mer Bihan (FR)**[10] 414 5-10-0 **68** .... BHarding (L Lungo) *bhd: j. slowly: t.o 7th: p.u bef 3 out* **50/1**	—
005-	P		**Lucky Piscean**[173] 2679 4-11-4 **91** .... NHannity (C W Fairhurst) *j. slowly: sn bhd: t.o whn p.u bef 2 out* **28/1**	—

5m 31.2s (-4.80) **Going Correction** -0.10s/f (Good)
WFA 4 from 5yo+ 5lb **13** Ran SP% **119.9**
Speed ratings: **104,99,93,91,90 86,85,84,83**,— —,—,— CSF £127.99 CT £500.19 TOTE £15.00: £4.90, £3.10, £1.70; EX 190.90.
Owner Ian Hamilton **Bred** Mrs Ann Hamilton **Trained** Great Bavington, Northumberland

FOCUS
A strongly-run race and in the end a runaway winner, much improved under her low weight on her handicap bow. The form could rate a lot higher.

The Form Book, Raceform Ltd, Compton, RG20 6NL

NOTEBOOK

Primitive Poppy, who is not very big and is apparently a poor traveller, was suited by the strong pace on her handicap bow and came right away on the run-in. With her it is a case of lower the weight the better and she looks to just stay. *(tchd 12-1)*

Barton Sun(IRE), unplaced in ten previous starts, took them along at a good pace but left for dead by the winner on the run-in, in the end was happy to cross the finishing line. *(op 11-1)*

My Lady Link(FR), 6lb higher, never really got competitive and has yet to prove her stamina. *(op 11-4 tchd 10-3)*

Loscar(FR), absent since February, never entered the argument. He is surely capable of better. *(op 6-1 tchd 7-1)*

Mary Macs Lad(IRE), who gave problems beforehand, looks out of love with the game. *(op 3-1 tchd 4-1)*

546 E S HARTLEY INTERMEDIATE H'CAP CHASE (18 fncs) 3m 2f

6:55 (6:55) (Class 4) (0-100,94) 5-Y-0+ **£3,425** (£1,054; £527; £263)

Form				RPR
6-14	**1**		**Billy Ballbreaker (IRE)**[11] 398 9-11-1 **83**............(tp) JTizzard (C L Tizzard) *chsd ldrs: mstke 14th: led next: 10 l clr whn idled 1/2-way up run-in: drvn out* **6/1**	99+
2P0-	**2**	*1 ½*	**Carriage Ride (IRE)**[36] 4970 7-11-12 **94**............(b[1]) BHarding (N G Richards) *disp ld to 4 out: outpcd next: rallied and upsides 1 f out: kpt on same pce* **9/1**	100
P-51	**3**	*hd*	**Lambrini Bianco (IRE)**[6] 464 7-9-8 **69** 7ex............(p) TMessenger[(7)] (Mrs L Williamson) *disp ld to 4 out: kpt on and chal 1f out: kpt on same pce* **10/3**[1]	75
2-22	**4**	*6*	**Another Club Royal**[21] 211 6-10-10 **78**............(t) GLee (D McCain) *chsd ldrs: drvn along 12th: one pce fr 4 out* **9/2**[3]	79+
F2	**5**	*27*	**Red Perk (IRE)**[21] 215 8-11-6 **88**............(p) KJohnson (R C Guest) *chsd ldrs: lost pl after 12th: bhd whn j. slowly 14th* **7/2**[2]	66+
-005	**6**	*6*	**Old Nosey (IRE)**[10] 407 9-11-6 **88**............ ADempsey (B Mactaggart) *j. slowly in rr: wnt prom 7th: drvn along 12th: sn lost pl* **14/1**	55
	F		**Kettysjames (IRE)**[5] 477 7-11-1 **83**............ RJohnson (John G Carr, Ire) *chsd ldrs: drvn along whn stmbld and fell 4 out* **5/1**	—

6m 40.1s (-0.50) **Going Correction** +0.075s/f (Yiel) 7 Ran SP% **111.1**

Speed ratings: **103,102,102,100,92 90,**— CSF £51.01 TOTE £5.80: £3.50, £4.70; EX 56.90.

Owner Blackmore Vale Syndicate **Bred** John And Philip Hore **Trained** Milborne Port, Dorset

FOCUS

A very moderate race with the winner value for approximately ten lengths and rated through the runner-up to his mark.

NOTEBOOK

Billy Ballbreaker(IRE), who has had his problems in the past, had it sewn up in a clear lead when he seemed to resent being asked to come up the home chute instead of going off for a third circuit. Putting the brakes on, in the end there was nothing to spare. *(tchd 13-2)*

Carriage Ride(IRE), in first-time blinkers, was left for dead three out but with the winner pulling himself up, he found himself level after the elbow. *(op 6-1)*

Lambrini Bianco(IRE), receiving weight all round, was taken on for the lead this time. Put back in with every chance at the elbow, he was always struggling to get there. *(op 3-1 tchd 7-2)*

Another Club Royal was in trouble with a circuit to go and was never going to find sufficient to enter the argument. *(op 3-1)*

Red Perk(IRE) dropped right out five out. It transpired that he had lost a shoe and finished lame. *Official explanation: vet said gelding lost a shoe and finished lame (op 5-1 tchd 3-1)*

Kettysjames(IRE) made hard work of it but thanks to his rider's persistence was still bang there when unluckily coming down at the final water, four out. *(tchd 11-2)*

547 BURLINGTON SLATE CARTMEL GRAND VETERANS NATIONAL H'CAP CHASE (20 fncs) 3m 6f

7:30 (7:31) (Class 3) (0-125,122) 10-Y-0+ **£8,268** (£2,544; £1,272; £636)

Form				RPR
531-	**1**		**Sir Frosty**[36] 4970 12-10-5 **101**............ RJohnson (B J M Ryall) *chsd ldrs: led 3 out: hld on wl towards fin* **9/4**[1]	113+
1-P3	**2**	*1*	**Wildfield Rufo (IRE)**[31] 62 10-10-12 **108**............(p) RMcGrath (Mrs K Walton) *chsd ldrs: wnt 2nd last: styd on: no ex last 100yds* **9/1**	117
36-1	**3**	*17*	**Uncle Mick (IRE)**[19] 262 10-10-9 **105**............(b) JTizzard (C L Tizzard) *chsd ldrs: 5th whn blnd 16th: one pce* **11/2**[3]	102+
14F-	**4**	*1*	**Harlov (FR)**[55] 4710 10-11-2 **112**............(p) ADempsey (A Parker) *chsd ldrs: led 4 out: hdd next: wknd last* **13/2**	103
P-24	**5**	*7*	**A Piece Of Cake (IRE)**[9] 423 12-11-12 **122**............ GLee (J S Goldie) *chsd ldr: led 10th to 4 out: wknd 2 out* **8/1**	106
P0P-	**6**	*¾*	**Tregastel (FR)**[36] 4970 10-10-2 **108**............(bt[1]) MissCarolineHurley[(10)] (R Ford) *in rr: hdwy and in tch 11th: lost pl 15th* **22/1**	91
303-	**7**	*18*	**Spanish Main (IRE)**[36] 4970 11-10-12 **108**............ CLlewellyn (N A Twiston-Davies) *sn drvn along in rr: sme hdwy 14th: lost pl and bhd fr next* **9/2**[2]	73
0-43	**8**	*12*	**Noshinannikin**[9] 427 11-11-9 **119**............ DElsworth (Mrs S J Smith) *in rr: hdwy 9th: lost pl 15th: sn bhd* **14/1**	72
0/	**9**	*7*	**Fanion De Neulliac (FR)**[20] 12-9-12 **101** oh8 ow5......(b) MrLRPayter[(7)] (M Sheppard) *nt fluent: a in rr: bhd fr 14th* **14/1**	47
0660	**P**		**Cromwell (IRE)**[6] 464 10-9-7 **96** oh35............(b) CMStudd[(7)] (M C Chapman) *led to 10th: sn lost pl: t.o 14th: p.u bef 4 out* **66/1**	—

7m 36.2s 10 Ran SP% **118.0**

CSF £23.62 CT £102.14 TOTE £3.40: £1.60, £2.70, £1.70; EX 35.10.

Owner J F Tucker **Bred** J F And Mrs Tucker **Trained** Rimpton, Somerset

FOCUS

A stayers' chase confined to ten-year-olds and up with the principals running to their marks.

NOTEBOOK

Sir Frosty, who has won from a 20lb higher mark in his youth, is all heart and dug deep to follow up his Perth success. He may now try his hand aginst the young pretenders in the Summer National at Uttoxeter. *(op 3-1 tchd 10-3 in places)*

Wildfield Rufo(IRE) proved suited by a return to this marathon trip and he never gave up in pursuit of the winner though in truth he was always going to be held. *(op 8-1)*

Uncle Mick(IRE), with the blinkers on again, was struggling to keep up when he got the final ditch, five out, wrong and that was the end of it as far as he was concerned. *(op 4-1)*

Harlov(FR), rested for eight weeks after his fall at Kelso, went on four out but he tired badly on the long run-in. *(op 6-1)*

A Piece Of Cake(IRE) was in the tick of things from the off but after pressing on he tired noticeably over the last two. His best days are well behind him now. *(op 9-1)*

Spanish Main(IRE) was under pressure to keep up after just four of the 20 fences and never looked like getting into the argument. *(op 5-1 tchd 11-2)*

548 CUBE247.CO.UK NOVICES' H'CAP CHASE (12 fncs) 2m 1f 110y

8:05 (8:05) (Class 4) (0-95,90) 5-Y-0+ **£3,484** (£1,072; £536; £268)

Form				RPR
5PP-	**1**		**Mikasa (IRE)**[48] 4786 5-10-1 **70**............ KJMercer[(3)] (R F Fisher) *hld up in rr: hdwy 6th: styd on run-in to ld over 1f out: hld on towards fin* **13/2**	82+
0-3S	**2**	*½*	**Parisienne Gale (IRE)**[14] 352 6-10-13 **80**............ PBuchanan[(3)] (R Ford) *set str pce: hdd 3 out: rallied after last: styd on ins fnl f: jst hld* **14/1**	94+
-22F	**3**	*6*	**College City (IRE)**[14] 357 6-11-6 **87**............(p) LMcGrath[(3)] (R C Guest) *chsd ldrs: effrt 9th: 3rd and outpcd whn blnd 2 out: kpt on one pce run-in* **11/8**[1]	97+
0-P0	**4**	*3 ½*	**Win Alot**[13] 370 7-10-4 **71**............ ACCoyle[(3)] (M C Chapman) *chsd ldr: led 3 out: hdd over 1f out: clr 3rd whn tired bdly fnl 100yds* **33/1**	75+
-54F	**5**	*25*	**Spectrum Star**[11] 395 5-10-0 **66** oh3............ BHarding (F P Murtagh) *a in rr: sme hdwy 7th: sn lost pl and bhd* **6/1**[3]	42
P0-0	**6**	*18*	**Very Tasty (IRE)**[23] 197 8-11-2 **80**............(tp) GLee (M Todhunter) *pushed along and hdwy to be in tch 7th: lost pl 9th: sn bhd: eased run-in* **7/2**[2]	60+
530-	**F**		**Rowan Castle**[41] 4872 9-11-12 **90**............ RMcGrath (Sir John Barlow Bt) *chsd ldrs: 4th and outpcd whn fell 8th* **8/1**	—

4m 26.4s (2.20) **Going Correction** +0.075s/f (Yiel)

WFA 5 from 6yo+ 2lb 7 Ran SP% **112.7**

Speed ratings: **98,97,95,93,82 74,**— CSF £76.03 TOTE £8.10: £4.10, £4.80; EX 75.70.

Owner Great Head House Estates Limited **Bred** Michael Fleming **Trained** Ulverston, Cumbria

■ Stewards' Enquiry : K J Mercer two-day ban: used whip in the incorrect place and with excessive frequency (Jun 8-9)

FOCUS

A poor race but no hanging about and the winner came from off what was a strong pace. The form is rated around the third and fourth and makes sense.

NOTEBOOK

Mikasa(IRE), suited by this much better ground, came from off the pace but he hung fire in front *and his rider had to throw everything at him to get him to hang on and break his duck.Official explanation: trainer said, regarding the improved form shown, gelding was better suited by the drop back to 2m and today's better going (op 15-2 tchd 8-1)*

Parisienne Gale(IRE), who took a maiden point in March, took them along at a very strong pace. *He came again on the run-in and switched outside at the elbow was in the end only just held. (op 12-1)*

College City(IRE) was struggling to keep up when he ploughed through the second last. After that there was no way back. *(op 10-11)*

Win Alot kept tabs on the leader. After taking charge, in the end he finished very leg-weary indeed.

Spectrum Star, a faller last time, his jumping lacked confidence and he was always out the back. *(op 5-1)*

Very Tasty(IRE), a winner of two low-grade hurdle-races here, struggled to keep in touch and his rider eventually called it a day. *(op 7-1)*

549 COBHAM MURPHY NOVICES' HURDLE (8 hdls) 2m 1f 110y

8:35 (8:36) (Class 4) 4-Y-0+ **£3,671** (£1,129; £564; £282)

Form				RPR
	1		**Diamond Cutter (NZ)**[345] 6-10-12............ HOliver (R C Guest) *t.k.h: trckd ldrs: last last: styd on wl* **5/1**[3]	98+
4-12	**2**	*3 ½*	**Malaga Boy (IRE)**[22] 201 8-11-5 107............ JTizzard (C L Tizzard) *trckd ldr: led 2 out to last: nt qckn* **11/10**[1]	101
	3	*5*	**Life Match (FR)**[16] 326 7-10-12 91............(tp) RJohnson (John G Carr, Ire) *chsd ldrs: one pce between last 2* **7/1**	89
PP-F	**4**	*5*	**Roy McAvoy (IRE)**[3] 495 7-10-9............(t) PWhelan[(3)] (M A Barnes) *a in tch: kpt on fr 2 out* **40/1**	84
PP0-	**5**	*11*	**La Folichonne (FR)**[111] 3718 6-10-2............ PAspell[(3)] (James Moffatt) *hld up: hdwy and prom 3 out: wknd next* **33/1**	66
1P-5	**6**	*4*	**Lord Rodney (IRE)**[30] 85 6-11-5 110............ RGarritty (P Beaumont) *led to 2 out: sn wknd* **11/4**[2]	76
0-0	**7**	*13*	**Rosina Copper**[14] 349 5-10-5............(t) BHarding (P Beaumont) *t.k.h in rr: nt fluent: hit 5th: t.o 2 out* **66/1**	49

4m 19.5s (3.80) **Going Correction** -0.10s/f (Good) 7 Ran SP% **110.3**

Speed ratings: **87,85,83,81,76 74,68** CSF £10.58 TOTE £5.60: £2.90, £1.10; EX 16.50 Place 6 £3,316.79, Place 5 £615.45.

Owner Gryffindor (www.racingtours.co.uk) **Bred** Mrs J L & R P Nolan & Mrs B M & T A Smith **Trained** Brancepeth, Co Durham

FOCUS

Just a steady pace and a slow time which probably flattered the third and fourth although the former sets the standard.

NOTEBOOK

Diamond Cutter(NZ), absent since running over hurdles in his native New Zealand a year ago, is a medium-sized, well-made type. Keen to get on with it, in the end he did enough. He looks ideal summer jumping material and it may not be long before he tries fences. *(op 10-1)*

Malaga Boy(IRE), dropping back in trip, was happy to get a lead. Taking charge, he did nothing wrong but the winner simply had too much basic speed for him in the closing stages. *(op 4-5)*

Life Match(FR), who has clearly had his problems, is running better now. *(op 10-1 tchd 11-1)*

Roy McAvoy(IRE), making a quick return, was probably flatttered by the modest pace at which the race was run. *(op 50-1)*

Lord Rodney(IRE), back in trip, set his own pace but he stopped to nothing when headed and something was presumably amiss. *(op 9-4 tchd 3-1)*

T/Plt: £2,101.00 to a £1 stake. Pool: £32,954.95 - 11.45 winning units T/Qpdt: £135.00 to a £1 stake. Pool: £3,468.30 - 19 winning units WG

[209]HEXHAM (L-H)

Saturday, May 28

OFFICIAL GOING: Good to firm

The meeting went ahead in very windy conditions.

Wind: Very strong, half across

550 GREATRUN.ORG NOVICES' CHASE (15 fncs) 2m 4f 110y

2:25 (2:30) (Class 3) 5-Y-0+ **£5,447** (£1,676; £628; £628)

Form				RPR
0-16	**1**		**Stan (NZ)**[28] 127 6-11-0............ HOliver (R C Guest) *keen: hld up: hdwy after 4 out: led after 2 out: pushed out fr last* **13/8**[1]	105+
3P-	**2**	*2 ½*	**Possextown (IRE)**[180] 2544 7-11-0............ ADobbin (N G Richards) *led: 2l in front whn blnd bdly 2 out: sn rcvrd: kpt on fr last: nt rch wnr* **4/1**[2]	101+
60-1	**3**	*4*	**Beat The Heat (IRE)**[10] 413 7-11-6 112............(b) BHarding (Jedd O'Keeffe) *chsd ldrs: effrt and ev ch after 2 out: no ex bef last* **9/2**[3]	99

U-55 **3** *dht* **Nomadic Blaze**[10] [413] 8-10-11 .... LMcGrath(3) 94+
(P G Atkinson) *chsd ldrs: mstke 8th: outpcd 11th: rallied between last 2: kpt on run in* **20/1**

32-2 **5** *12* **Snowy (IRE)**[17] [303] 7-11-0 102 .... PRobson 85+
(J I A Charlton) *in tch: mstke 10th: outpcd after next: no imp after* **9/2**[3]

62/2 **6** *7* **Noble House**[26] [147] 8-10-11 95 .... KJMercer(3) 74
(Mrs A Duffield) *in tch tl lost pl 7th: n.d after* **12/1**

PP0- **7** *22* **The Honey Guide**[55] [4716] 9-10-9 .... DFlavin(5) 52
(Mrs L B Normile) *hld up: hdwy to chse ldrs 10th: wknd bef 3 out* **66/1**

-PUP **8** *dist* **Mill Tower**[10] [411] 8-11-0 .... NPMulholland —
(R Nixon) *chsd ldrs to 11th: sn lost pl* **100/1**

5m 2.10s (-9.30) **Going Correction** -0.775s/f (Firm) **8** Ran SP% **109.4**
Speed ratings: **86,85,83,83,78 76,67,**—PL: Beat The Heat £0.60, Nomadic Blaze £2.10 CSF £8.60 TOTE £2.60: £1.10, £2.10; EX 11.80.
Owner Paul Beck **Bred** Mrs M A Davies **Trained** Brancepeth, Co Durham
■ Stewards' Enquiry : A Dobbin four-day ban: improper conduct (June 8-12)

FOCUS
An ordinary event that was run at just a fair pace in a modest time but could rate a bit higher form-wise.

NOTEBOOK
Stan(NZ) ◆, the pick of those with hurdles form and back on a sound surface, jumped soundly on this chasing debut and showed more than enough to suggest he can defy a penalty in a similar event. *(op 15-8 tchd 2-1)*
Possextown(IRE), who reportedly bled from the nose last time, again failed to put in a clear round but showed enough on this first start since November to suggest he can win an ordinary event in this sphere if all remains well. *(op 7-2 tchd 9-2)*
Beat The Heat(IRE) had conditions to suit and ran creditably but is likely to continue to look vulnerable against unexposed or progressive sorts in this type of event. *(op 4-1)*
Nomadic Blaze is not very consistent and got a lot closer to Beat The Heat than he had done at Sedgefield. He shaped as though a stiffer test and the step into handicap company would suit. *(op 4-1)*
Snowy(IRE) was below his best dropped in trip but should have been suited by the stiff nature of this track and is starting to look a shade disappointing. *(op 11-2)*
Noble House, from a stable among the winners, has shown ability at a modest level and has the size to make a chaser but could not get competitive on this chase debut. He may do better in due course. *(op 17-2)*

551 JUNIOR GREAT NORTH RUN H'CAP HURDLE (8 hdls) 2m 110y
3:00 (3:00) (Class 4) (0-105,104) 4-Y-0+ **£3,486** (£996; £498)

Form RPR

-145 **1** **Royal Glen (IRE)**[10] [406] 7-10-5 83 .... RMcGrath 85+
(W S Coltherd) *keen in tch: effrt 2 out: led run in: drvn and r.o wl* **9/2**[2]

00-5 **2** *¾* **Feanor**[23] [197] 7-11-9 104 .... (t) KJMercer(3) 104
(Mrs S A Watt) *hld up: smooth hdwy 2 out: effrt last: kpt on* **7/1**

3-22 **3** *nk* **Arjay**[10] [412] 7-9-7 78 .... (b) CDSharkey(7) 78
(S B Clark) *in tch: drvn bef 2 out: rallied bef last: kpt on run in* **5/1**[3]

2P3- **4** *3½* **Wyn Dixie (IRE)**[36] [4965] 6-11-3 95 .... NPMulholland 91
(P Monteith) *led: rdn after 2 out: hdd run in: sn outpcd* **9/2**[2]

UP0- **5** *6* **One Of Them**[77] [4325] 6-10-2 83 .... PWhelan(3) 73
(M A Barnes) *cl up tl rdn and wknd bef last* **20/1**

064- **6** *6* **Haadef**[15] [4969] 4-10-10 92 .... (b) GLee 72
(J Howard Johnson) *hld up in tch: rdn after 2 out: sn btn* **5/2**[1]

00-0 **7** *1½* **Test Of Faith**[16] [319] 6-9-11 80 .... DCCostello(5) 63
(J N R Billinge) *chsd ldrs to 2 out: wknd* **20/1**

4P/0 **8** *12* **Lion Guest (IRE)**[17] [306] 8-10-7 85 .... MBradburne 56
(Mrs S C Bradburne) *hld up: rdn bef 2 out: sn btn* **16/1**

3F1/ **9** *25* **Maunby Rocker**[454] [2302] 5-11-3 95 .... FKeniry 41
(P C Haslam) *keen early: chsd ldrs tl wknd qckly bef 2 out* **16/1**

0/P- **P** **Hickleton Club**[134] [3348] 7-10-0 78 oh4 .... KJohnson —
(R M Clark) *sn t.o: p.u after 5th* **80/1**

4m 8.30s (-6.90) **Going Correction** -0.50s/f (Good)
WFA 4 from 5yo+ 4lb **10** Ran SP% **116.6**
Speed ratings: **96,95,95,93,91 88,87,81,70,**— CSF £35.24 CT £164.12 TOTE £6.40: £1.80, £2.40, £1.60; EX 16.00.
Owner S Coltherd **Bred** R Goodwin **Trained** Selkirk, Borders

FOCUS
Mainly exposed sorts and an ordinary gallop to this modest handicap but the form looks reasonable on paper.

NOTEBOOK
Royal Glen(IRE), gained reward for her consistency back over a course and distance where she scored in April, travelled strongly and showed the right attitude to win an ordinary event. She should continue to give a good account. *(op 11-2)*
Feanor ◆, a course and distance winner in June last year, had conditions to suit and showed more than enough to suggest she is capable of winning a similar race in the coming weeks. *(tchd 13-2)*
Arjay again ran creditably but, although worth a try over a bit further, his losing run of three years means he is not one to place maximum faith in. *(op 11-2)*
Wyn Dixie(IRE) had the run of the race and was beaten on merit but left the impression that similar tactics on a less demanding course may see him in a better light. *(tchd 5-1)*
One Of Them had the run of the race and was not totally disgraced back over this shorter trip, but the fact he has yet to win a race under any code means he is one to tread carefully with.
Haadef, back over hurdles, offered little response once asked for an effort and looks one to have reservations about. *Official explanation: jockey said colt had a breathing problem (op 3-1)*

552 GREAT NORTH RUN H'CAP HURDLE (10 hdls) 2m 4f 110y
3:35 (3:36) (Class 4) (0-110,109) 4-Y-0+ **£3,433** (£981; £490)

Form RPR

1-50 **1** **Ramblees Holly**[13] [370] 7-10-12 102 .... TMessenger(7) 101+
(R S Wood) *keen: prom: chal 4 out: led 2 and rdn 2 out: hld on wl* **5/1**[3]

141- **2** *nk* **Izzykeen**[178] [2569] 6-11-5 102 .... DElsworth 100
(Mrs S J Smith) *chsd ldrs: chal 3rd: outpcd after 3 out: rallied between last two: edgd rt run in: kpt on u.p: jst hld* **3/1**[1]

434- **3** *3½* **Nocatee (IRE)**[25] [1476] 4-11-1 103 .... (p) FKeniry 94+
(P C Haslam) *mde most to 2 out: outpcd fr last* **7/1**

1-0P **4** *8* **Hello Baby**[21] [215] 5-10-0 83 .... (p) BHarding 69
(A C Whillans) *keen: chsd ldrs: outpcd bef 2 out: rallied bef last: no imp run in* **7/2**[2]

000- **5** *2½* **Mr Lear (USA)**[49] [4777] 6-11-11 108 .... RGarritty 92
(J J Quinn) *in tch: outpcd 3 out: rallied bef last: nt rch ldrs* **6/1**

P05- **6** *1¾* **Teme Valley**[53] [4739] 11-11-12 109 .... GLee 91
(J Howard Johnson) *hld up in tch: rdn and outpcd 3 out: sme late hdwy: nvr on terms* **14/1**

0-02 **7** *dist* **Northern Echo**[26] [152] 8-9-12 88 oh4 ow5 .... (b) GThomas(7) —
(K S Thomas) *bhd: rdn 3rd: sn struggling* **8/1**

50-0 **F** **Allez Scotia**[16] [317] 6-10-7 90 .... NPMulholland —
(R Nixon) *w ldrs whn fell 5th* **16/1**

4m 59.7s (-9.90) **Going Correction** -0.50s/f (Good)
WFA 4 from 5yo+ 5lb **8** Ran SP% **114.3**
Speed ratings: **98,97,96,93,92 91,**—,— CSF £20.88 CT £104.21 TOTE £7.30: £1.90, £1.80, £1.90; EX 24.40.
Owner R S Wood **Bred** R S Wood **Trained** Nawton, N Yorks
■ Stewards' Enquiry : D Elsworth two-day ban: used whip with excessive frequency and without giving gelding time to respond (Jun 8-9)

FOCUS
Another ordinary handicap in which the gallop was less than true. The form is rated through the winner and third.

NOTEBOOK
Ramblees Holly is not the most consistent but elected to put his best foot forward and showed the right attitude in the closing stages. His record suggests there has to be a doubt as to him putting it all in next time, though. *(op 9-2)*
Izzykeen had conditions to suit for this handicap debut and first run since December and ran right up to his best. He is well worth a try over further and looks sure to win in similar company this summer. *(op 10-3 tchd 11-4)*
Nocatee(IRE), back over hurdles, had conditions to suit and ran creditably but left the impression that an easier course would see him to better advantage. *(op 9-2)*
Hello Baby, a course and distance winner on soft ground in April, ran his best race since returned to this course but his inconsistency remains a concern. *(op 9-2 tchd 5-1)*
Mr Lear(USA), upped in trip, was not totally disgraced but did not really leave the impression that he is a winner waiting to happen. *(op 7-1 tchd 5-1)*
Teme Valley has slipped to a fair mark and, although below his best once again, will be down again in the weights and will be of more interest returned to his favoured Sedgefield. *(op 11-1)*
Northern Echo *Official explanation: trainer said gelding would not face the blinkers (op 9-1 tchd 10-1)*

553 FILM NOVA "NATIONAL HUNT" NOVICES' HURDLE (10 hdls) 2m 4f 110y
4:05 (4:09) (Class 4) 4-Y-0+ **£3,339** (£954; £477)

Form RPR

0-41 **1** **Bishop's Bridge (IRE)**[13] [369] 7-11-7 112 .... GLee 105+
(Andrew Turnell) *chsd ldrs: shkn up briefly to ld bef last: pushed out run in* **4/7**[1]

06-2 **2** *1¾* **Mooramana**[21] [209] 6-11-0 94 .... RGarritty 91
(P Beaumont) *cl up: led appr 2 out to bef last: one pce run in* **11/4**[2]

1-00 **3** *7* **Aelred**[17] [304] 12-11-0 88 .... (p) KJohnson 85+
(R Johnson) *mde most to appr 2 out: no ex bef last* **9/1**[3]

05-0 **4** *10* **Kalic D'Alm (FR)**[17] [306] 7-11-0 76 .... DO'Meara 77+
(W S Coltherd) *hld up in tch: rdn and outpcd 3 out: no imp fr next* **20/1**

P0/0 **5** *dist* **Minster Meadow**[9] [418] 6-10-7 .... (t) SGagan(7) —
(S G Chadwick) *keen: in tch to 7th: sn wknd* **100/1**

/0-5 **P** **Loch Red**[21] [209] 6-11-0 .... NPMulholland —
(C W Thornton) *bhd: lost tch fr 1/2-way: t.o whn p.u bef 2 out* **33/1**

4m 58.2s (-11.40) **Going Correction** -0.50s/f (Good) **6** Ran SP% **109.0**
Speed ratings: **101,100,97,93,**— — CSF £2.28 TOTE £1.60: £1.10, £1.50; EX 2.00.
Owner S Kimber **Bred** F Fennelly **Trained** Broad Hinton, Wilts

FOCUS
An uncompetitive race in which the pace was only fair and the winner did not have to improve to win his second race over hurdles. That said the form looks reasonable enough for the grade.

NOTEBOOK
Bishop's Bridge(IRE), with the headgear left off this time, did not have to improve to follow up over hurdles. He may look vulnerable in a more competitive race under a double penalty but may be capable of better in ordinary handicaps. *(tchd 8-13, 8-15 and 2-1in places)*
Mooramana, down in trip, had his limitations exposed once again in this company and, while not disgraced, left the impression that the step into handicap company would suit. *(op 5-2 tchd 3-1)*
Aelred was not disgraced dropped in trip on ground much quicker than ideal but he is likely to continue to look vulnerable in this type of race. *(op 12-1)*
Kalic D'Alm(FR) faced a stiff task and will be suited by the return to modest handicaps. *(op 16-1 tchd 25-1)*
Minster Meadow has still to show anything worthwhile over hurdles. *(op 80-1)*

554 NOVA INTERNATIONAL H'CAP CHASE (19 fncs) 3m 1f
4:40 (4:41) (Class 4) (0-95,95) 5-Y-0+ **£3,391** (£969; £484)

Form RPR

F4-1 **1** **Arctic Lagoon (IRE)**[21] [212] 6-10-1 70 ow1 .... (t) MBradburne 89+
(Mrs S C Bradburne) *prom: led 4 out: drew clr fr 2 out* **9/4**[1]

36/2 **2** *8* **Carnacrack**[9] [421] 11-10-12 84 .... MrCStorey(3) 95
(Miss S E Forster) *cl up: ev ch 3 out: kpt on same pce after next* **9/1**

0-P3 **3** *4* **Tee-Jay (IRE)**[21] [211] 9-11-1 84 .... FKeniry 91
(M D Hammond) *hld up: outpcd after 13th: rallied 2 out: kpt on run in: no ch w first two* **15/2**

U0-P **4** *5* **Middleway**[13] [373] 9-9-7 69 oh4 .... MJMcAlister(7) 71
(Miss Kate Milligan) *in tch: drvn along 14th: no imp fr 4 out* **16/1**

25-3 **5** *7* **Daguyda (FR)**[10] [413] 6-11-9 95 .... KJMercer(3) 90
(Ferdy Murphy) *hld up and bhd: stdy hdwy 13th: rdn and no imp bef 3 out* **15/2**

0-46 **6** *3½* **Master Jackson**[6] [464] 6-10-7 76 .... RWalford 68
(T D Walford) *led too 4th: in tch tl outpcd 1/2-way: n.d after* **6/1**[2]

30-3 **7** *2½* **Jansue Charlie**[30] [81] 11-10-0 69 oh2 .... NPMulholland 58
(R Nixon) *prom: drvn fr 13th: wknd bef 3 out* **20/1**

05-5 **8** *shd* **Now Then Sid**[28] [119] 6-11-3 86 .... PRobson 75
(Mrs S A Watt) *cl up: led 6th to 4 out: wknd bef next* **12/1**

U-15 **9** *1* **Tina's Scallywag**[6] [464] 8-10-5 74 .... DO'Meara 62
(H P Hogarth) *midfield: lost pl 1/2-way: nvr on terms* **13/2**[3]

5P-P **10** *nk* **Atomic Breeze (IRE)**[13] [373] 11-10-2 71 .... RMcGrath 59
(D M Forster) *sn towards rr: struggling fr 1/2-way* **33/1**

04-U **U** **Clawick Connection (IRE)**[30] [87] 10-9-9 69 oh5 .... DCCostello(5) —
(J N R Billinge) *cl up: led 4th to 6th: upsides whn blnd and uns rdr 12th* **16/1**

6m 11.2s (-20.70) **Going Correction** -0.775s/f (Firm) **11** Ran SP% **119.1**
Speed ratings: **102,99,98,96,94 93,92,92,92,91** — CSF £23.85 CT £134.67 TOTE £3.30: £1.30, £3.00, £4.00; EX 20.70.
Owner William A Powrie **Bred** Lord Vestey **Trained** Cunnoquhie, Fife
■ Stewards' Enquiry : D O'Meara one-day ban: used whip when out of contention (Jun 8)

FOCUS
A modest handicap but a decent gallop and this bare form looks solid and should prove reliable.

NOTEBOOK
Arctic Lagoon(IRE) ◆, back over fences from this much lower mark, won with a good deal in hand to follow up his recent hurdles win at this course and looks the type to win in similar company in this sphere, even after reassessment. *(op 3-1)*
Carnacrack is a consistent sort who ran his race and looks a good guide to the level of this form. He is vulnerable to well handicapped or progressive sorts in this sphere but should continue to give a good account. *(op 7-1)*

Tee-Jay(IRE) ran creditably over this course and distance but again did not look the most straightforward and is not one to place maximum faith in. *(op 8-1)*
Middleway, a model of inconsistency, ran his best race since winning this race last year but his record suggests he is one to tread very carefully with. *(op 14-1 tchd 12-1)*
Daguyda(FR) did not really improve in the anticipated manner returned to this longer trip and, although not knocked about, may not be one to place too much faith in. *(op 7-1)*
Master Jackson was below his recent best on ground that may have been plenty quick enough but has yet to win a race and looks another to tread carefully with. *(tchd 7-1)*

555 BRITISH HEART FOUNDATION HUNTERS' CHASE (15 fncs) 2m 4f 110y
5:15 (5:15) (Class 6) 5-Y-O+ **£1,254** (£358; £179)

Form RPR
-123 **1** **Imps Way**[8] 440 10-11-11 .... MrCMulhall(3) 109+
(Mrs T Corrigan-Clark) *hld up and bhd: smooth hdwy 10th: led gng wl between last 2: sn clr* **11/4**[2]
P3-2 **2** *26* **Bohemian Spirit (IRE)**[26] 151 7-12-2 100 .... MissRDavidson(5) 90
(Mrs R L Elliot) *keen: hld up: hdwy and prom 5th: led 9th: hdd between last two: no ex* **6/4**[1]
/UP- **3** *1 1/2* **Wynyard Dancer**[14] 11-11-2 69 ....(p) MissTJackson(5) 74
(Miss T Jackson) *cl up: rdn bef 3 out: ev ch after next: sn outpcd* **15/2**[3]
4 *11* **Suetsu (IRE)**[6] 9-11-2 .... MissCMetcalfe(5) 63
(R A Ross) *bhd: sme hdwy 4 out: no imp bef next* **12/1**
P/5- **5** *7* **Timberley**[6] 11-11-7 ....(t) MrRWGreen(7) 63
(Miss R Brewis) *sn towards rr: sme hdwy 4 out: nvr on terms* **33/1**
3P-6 **6** *12* **Nisbet**[21] 11-12-0 76 .... MissJRiding(7) 58
(Miss M Bremner) *mde most to 9th: wknd after 4 out* **9/1**
2P-0 **7** *9* **Alittlebitopower**[16] 322 8-12-0 .... MrCStorey 42
(C Storey) *hld up: hdwy and prom 5th: wknd bef 3 out* **10/1**
/F-5 **8** *dist* **Wild Edgar (IRE)**[10] 411 8-11-7 .... MrRTrotter(7) —
(A R Trotter) *prom: blnd and lost pl 5th: n.d after* **40/1**
P-P **9** *dist* **Dinan (IRE)**[26] 151 13-11-7 .... MrsJoanneBrown(7) —
(Mrs Joanne Brown) *in tch to 9th: outpcd fr next* **50/1**
P **Sandhills Boy**[6] 10-11-11 .... MJMcAlister(3) —
(E Stanners) *sn wl bhd: t.o whn p.u bef 9th* **25/1**
F-0 **P** **Jupsala (FR)**[13] 8-11-7 ....(p) MrCGillon(7) —
(J Burke) *in tch: mstke and lost pl 7th: t.o whn p.u bef 4 out* **20/1**

5m 2.60s (-8.80) **Going Correction** -0.775s/f (Firm) **11** Ran SP% **121.2**
Speed ratings: **85,75,74,70,67 63,59,—,—,—** — CSF £7.48 TOTE £3.60: £1.60, £1.20, £2.30; EX 7.80 Place 6 £8.35, Place 5 £6.43.
Owner Mrs T Corrigan-Clark **Bred** R Robinson **Trained** Scarborough, N Yorks

FOCUS
A run-of-the-mill event but a strong pace set things up to a large degree for the winner. The form looks believeable.

NOTEBOOK
Imps Way, down in trip, appreciated the strong gallop over this trip. Although the margin of victory may flatter her, she is an improved performer of late and will be interesting if allowed to compete in ordinary handicaps this summer. *(tchd 3-1 in a place)*
Bohemian Spirit(IRE) looked to have solid claims but again failed to settle and did too much too soon, conspiring only to set things up for the winner. He is better than this but a test of speed will always suit better than a test of stamina. *(op 13-8 tchd 7-4)*
Wynyard Dancer, in decent heart in points, faced a stiffish task strictly on official ratings but ran creditably and looks capable of winning more races in the point sphere next term. *(op 8-1)*
Suetsu(IRE), a point winner on her most recent outing, may be suited by the return to three miles but will have to improve to make her mark in this company next term. *(op 10-1)*
Timberley faced a stiff task on these terms and ran accordingly. *(op 25-1)*
Nisbet has yet to recapture the pick of last year's form in this sphere and was again soundly beaten. *(op 10-1 tchd 8-1)*
T/Plt: £3.60 to a £1 stake. Pool: £37,797.40. 7,603.10 winning tickets. T/Qpdt: £1.70 to a £1 stake. Pool: £2,372.20. 993.00 winning tickets. RY

556 - 562a (Foreign Racing) - See Raceform Interactive

501 FONTWELL (L-H)
Sunday, May 29

OFFICIAL GOING: Good to firm
Wind: Almost nil Weather: Overcast

563 SELBY & DOUGIE GRAY WEDDING DAY (FOUR YEARS OLD) NOVICES' HURDLE (9 hdls) 2m 2f 110y
2:25 (2:25) (Class 4) 4-Y-O **£3,380** (£1,040; £520; £260)

Form RPR
453- **1** **Maclean**[34] 4616 4-10-12 102 .... PHide 107
(G L Moore) *hld up in 5th: hdwy 6th: trckd ldr on bit appr 2 out: drvn to ld fnl 50 yds: all out* **7/2**[2]
63-B **2** *hd* **Nippy Des Mottes (FR)**[14] 367 4-10-12 106 ....(t) APMcCoy 107
(P F Nicholls) *in tch: effrt and led 3 out: hrd rdn appr next: kpt on wl whn chal run-in: hdd fnl 50 yds* **4/9**[1]
3 *20* **Mariday**[176] 4-10-12 .... LAspell 87
(L Wells) *chsd ldrs: one pce fr 3 out* **20/1**
P- **4** *9* **Hermitage Court (USA)**[9] 4826 4-10-12 ....(v[1]) JCulloty 78
(M J McGrath) *t.k.h early: trckd ldr: lft in ld 6th: hdd 3 out: wknd appr next* **16/1**[3]
-0P6 **5** *20* **Cloud Catcher (IRE)**[9] 438 4-10-2 60 ....(bt) RYoung(3) 51
(M Appleby) *hld up in rr: rdn 5th: lost tch next* **66/1**
6 *27* **Bailaora (IRE)**[12] 4-10-12 .... JEMoore 31
(B W Duke) *led: j. slowly 2nd: blnd next: blnd and hdd 6th: wknd qckly* **25/1**

4m 29.8s (-6.20) **Going Correction** -0.35s/f (Good) **6** Ran SP% **107.5**
Speed ratings: **99,98,90,86,78 66** CSF £5.20 TOTE £4.00: £1.50, £1.10; EX 6.90.
Owner Phil Collins **Bred** The Queen **Trained** Woodingdean, E Sussex

FOCUS
A weak race in which only two were serious contenders and the runner-up sets the standard. The early gallop was modest, quickening up with a circuit remaining.

NOTEBOOK
Maclean, in a weak race where only two could be taken seriously, seemed to be going better than the runner-up all the way up the straight, but in the end was flat out to get his nose in front. His resolution - which has been questioned in the past - seemed to stand up to the test. *(tchd 4-1)*
Nippy Des Mottes(FR) battled gamely under a typical McCoy drive, and in the end made the winner go all the way. He is only modest but capable of winning a little race or two during the summer. *(tchd 2-5)*
Mariday has run at distances of up to two miles on the Flat, and may need more of a stamina test over hurdles. A fair debut, but no more. *(tchd 16-1)*
Hermitage Court(USA), out of form on the Flat recently, and pulled up on his hurdling debut, did slightly better but needs to improve further. *(tchd 20-1)*
Cloud Catcher(IRE) continues to inspire little or no future confidence.
Bailaora(IRE), nothing special and winless at around a mile and a half on the Flat, also needs to learn how to jump more consistently. *(op 20-1)*

564 WEATHERBYS BANK BEGINNERS' CHASE (15 fncs) 2m 4f
3:00 (3:00) (Class 4) 5-Y-O+ **£4,478** (£1,378; £689; £344)

Form RPR
0-22 **1** **Flying Spirit (IRE)**[19] 286 6-11-0 ....(p) JEMoore 120+
(G L Moore) *chsd clr ldrs: clsd steadily to ld 4 out: grad drew clr: rdn out* **15/8**[2]
12-2 **2** *9* **Escompteur (FR)**[10] 419 5-10-11 .... APMcCoy 109+
(M C Pipe) *w.r.s and lost 15l: plld hrd: hdwy to chse clr ldr 4th: led 10th to 4 out: one pce* **6/4**[1]
PP-6 **3** *dist* **Cheeky Lad**[11] 401 5-10-7 ow3 .... MrNPearce(7) 77
(R C Harper) *led: sn 20l clr: hdd 10th: sn outpcd* **33/1**
0-U2 **4** *2* **Rigmarole**[15] 358 7-11-0 ....(bt) ChristianWilliams 75
(P F Nicholls) *sn wl bhd: remote 4th fr 1/2-way: nvr gng pce* **3/1**[3]
0-U4 **5** *30* **Kjjimmy (IRE)**[21] 231 8-10-11 .... RYoung(3) —
(J W Mullins) *chsd clr ldr to 4th: wl bhd fr 8th* **25/1**
00- **P** **Peter Parkgate**[38] 4941 6-10-7 .... TMessenger(7) —
(N R Mitchell) *sn outpcd: nt fluent 4th: wl bhd fr 6th: p.u bef 10th* **80/1**

4m 58.8s (-9.10) **Going Correction** -0.20s/f (Good)
WFA 5 from 6yo+ 3lb **6** Ran SP% **107.8**
Speed ratings: **110,106,—,—,—** — CSF £4.85 TOTE £2.80: £1.50, £1.50; EX 4.40.
Owner Richard Green (fine Paintings) **Bred** Sean Madigan **Trained** Woodingdean, E Sussex

FOCUS
A decent race for the time of year, run at a furious gallop which soon had the six runners stretched out. However, with Escompteur pulling too hard, and Rigmarole running no race at all, the form is not quite what it might have been.

NOTEBOOK
Flying Spirit(IRE) took advantage of disappointing efforts from his two market rivals, winning readily. He has now won on the Flat, over hurdles and fences. *(op 13-8)*
Escompteur(FR) ruined his chance by pulling too hard, causing him to whip round as the race began. He can win again when he behaves himself better. *(op 7-4)*
Cheeky Lad did as well as could be expected. To beat Rigmarole was a bonus, but that horse was stones below his best.
Rigmarole showed no interest and is looking a pale shadow of the top-class hurdler he used to be. *(op 11-4)*
Kjjimmy(IRE) was taking on some useful rivals and will be more at home in run-of-the-mill company around the gaffs.

565 YEOMANS HONDA (S) H'CAP CHASE (13 fncs) 2m 2f
3:35 (3:35) (Class 5) (0-90,84) 5-Y-O+ **£2,562** (£732; £366)

Form RPR
45F- **1** **River Amora (IRE)**[62] 4617 10-10-5 63 ....(p) JEMoore 77
(J J Best) *mde all: rdn 3l clr 3 out: drvn to hold on run-in* **4/1**[3]
2261 **2** *3/4* **Borehill Joker**[4] 502 9-11-5 84 .... WKennedy(7) 97
(J L Spearing) *hdwy 8th: wnt 3l 2nd 4 out: hrd rdn appr next: styd on run-in: nt catch wnr* **2/1**[1]
62-3 **3** *13* **Percipient**[30] 95 7-11-1 73 ....(v[1]) JTizzard 75+
(D R Gandolfo) *hdwy 7th: blnd 9th: no ex fr 4 out: 3rd and wl btn whn mstke last* **7/2**[2]
P5-P **4** *7* **Mr Jake**[19] 276 12-9-7 58 .... JamesWhite(7) 51
(H E Haynes) *prom: j.rt and bmpd 1st: hrd rdn and wknd 4 out* **25/1**
0-03 **5** *7* **Padamul**[20] 264 9-10-1 62 .... RYoung(3) 48
(J W Mullins) *chsd ldrs: mstke 4th: outpcd fr 8th* **16/1**
0-03 **6** *27* **Ashgan (IRE)**[3] 508 12-11-7 84 .... TJPhelan(5) 43
(Dr P Pritchard) *w wnr to 2nd: mstke 4th: rr and rdn 7th: sn lost tch* **14/1**
045- **7** *14* **Coppermalt (USA)**[41] 4915 7-10-8 66 .... BJCrowley 11
(R Curtis) *chsd ldrs: bdly bmpd 1st: j. slowly next: sn lost pl: j. slowly 4th: bhd whn blnd 9th* **8/1**
40-0 **8** *13* **Damien's Choice (IRE)**[29] 129 13-10-10 68 .... LAspell —
(Dr P Pritchard) *bhd most of way* **16/1**
060- **9** *10* **Jandal**[150] 3107 11-11-4 76 .... JAMcCarthy —
(C L Popham) *in tch: bmpd 1st: chsd ldrs 5th: blnd next: wknd 7th* **8/1**
P-0 **P** **Major Reno (IRE)**[12] 395 8-10-7 72 .... MrNPearce(7) —
(R C Harper) *mstke 3rd: a bhd: t.o whn p.u bef 8th* **50/1**

4m 34.7s (-0.40) **Going Correction** -0.20s/f (Good) **10** Ran SP% **122.0**
Speed ratings: **92,91,85,82,79 67,61,55,51,—** CSF £13.68 CT £31.77 TOTE £6.90: £1.80, £1.30, £1.70; EX 17.50.There was no bid for the winner. Borehill Joker was claimed by Mr A. Parr for £6,000.
Owner Leon Best **Bred** Donal Sheahan **Trained** Lewes, E Sussex

FOCUS
A poor race, but run at a good gallop throughout and, with the placed horses running to form, the form looks reliable for the grade.

NOTEBOOK
River Amora(IRE) dominated it from start to finish with a good round of jumping, but could not be said to have had a soft lead since he went a good gallop. Battling on gamely, he just lasted home, with the weight concession from the runner-up proving crucial. *(op 7-1)*
Borehill Joker, switching to chases this time, nearly pulled it off despite conceding plenty of weight to the winner. He is a decent performer at this level, whatever the size of the obstacles. *(op 7-4 tchd 9-4)*
Percipient has been running better of late in blinkers, and sported a first-time visor with similar results. His mistake at the fifth-last came at a crucial time. *(op 5-1)*
Mr Jake, a specialist in pulling up, showed a bit more this time, but his finishing position is not good news for those behind him. *(op 33-1)*
Padamul continues to record a low level of achievement. *(op 22-1)*
Ashgan(IRE) was soon unable to keep up with the strong early gallop. *(op 10-1)*
Damien's Choice(IRE) *Official explanation: trainer said gelding bled from nose (op 12-1 tchd 20-1)*

566 AJS GROUNDWORKS H'CAP HURDLE (11 hdls) 2m 6f 110y
4:10 (4:10) (Class 4) (0-110,115) 4-Y-O+ **£3,627** (£1,116; £558; £279)

Form RPR
32-1 **1** **Earlsfield Raider**[3] 397 5-11-10 115 ....(b) EDehdashti(7) 118+
(G L Moore) *trckd ldrs: wnt 2nd and hit 3 out: drvn to ld run-in* **13/2**
0/0- **2** *3* **Adelphi Theatre (USA)**[17] 4932 8-11-2 100 .... SThomas 101+
(R Rowe) *in tch: reminders and wnt prom after 7th: led 3 out: hrd rdn appr last: hdd and one pce run-in* **14/1**
3-62 **3** *4* **La Concha (IRE)**[14] 365 4-10-5 95 .... JCulloty 85
(M J McGrath) *hld up in rr: stdy hdwy 7th: hrd rdn appr 2 out: one pce* **12/1**
23-4 **4** *3* **Hylia**[21] 245 6-10-7 91 ....(t) JAMcCarthy 85+
(Mrs P Robeson) *chsd ldrs: led after 7th tl 3 out: one pce next: 4th and btn whn hit last* **11/2**[3]
0-02 **5** *14* **Siena Star (IRE)**[11] 410 7-10-7 91 .... RThornton 74+
(P Bowen) *hdwy 6th: mstke next: wknd appr 2 out* **5/1**[2]
03-1 **6** *3* **Wayward Melody**[21] 245 5-10-7 91 .... PHide 67
(G L Moore) *chsd ldrs: pushed along whn mstke 4th: sn lost pl: hrd rdn and n.d fr 7th* **13/2**

250- **7** *14* **Important Boy (ARG)**[222] 1769 8-9-11 **84** oh4....................(t) RYoung(3) 46
(D D Scott) *a bhd: no ch fr 8th* **50/1**

0-12 **8** *4* **Esters Boy**[15] 359 7-11-4 **102**.. JEMoore 60
(P G Murphy) *sn towards rr: rdn after 3rd: drvn along and struggling fr 7th* **13/2**

604- **9** *20* **Lahinch Lad (IRE)**[123] 3539 5-10-9 **93**.. JTizzard 31
(B G Powell) *prom tl hit 6th: wl bhd fr 8th* **18/1**

P/P- **P** **Harlequin Chorus**[40] 4918 15-9-7 **84** oh10...................... JamesWhite(7) —
(H E Haynes) *hdwy 4th: sn pushed along: losing pl in midfield whn p.u after next* **100/1**

1-3U **P** **Shower Of Hail (IRE)**[7] 468 5-11-12 **110**............................ APMcCoy —
(M C Pipe) *led: j.lft and w no fluency: hit 5th: hdd after 7th: sn wknd: wl bhd whn p.u bef 2 out* **7/2**[1]

5m 31.0s (-13.80) **Going Correction** -0.35s/f (Good)
WFA 4 from 5yo+ 5lb **11** Ran SP% **116.8**
Speed ratings: **110,108,107,106,101 100,95,94,87,—** — CSF £91.04 CT £1068.74 TOTE £8.80: £2.90, £3.50, £2.60; EX 259.90.
Owner Mrs R J Doorgachurn **Bred** Mrs R J Doorgachurn And C Stedman **Trained** Woodingdean, E Sussex

FOCUS
A typical Fontwell hurdle over this trip, run at no better than a medium pace until quickening going out onto the final circuit. The third is the best guide to the level of the form.

NOTEBOOK
Earlsfield Raider, given a very competent ride, was always ideally placed. The blinkers are working well, and helped him to defy a 10lb rise for his Towcester success. *(op 5-1)*
Adelphi Theatre(USA) needed a bit of stoking but ran well for a stable that is returning to form. His only two victories were recorded here, so it is unfortunate for his connections that the next Fontwell meeting is not until August. *(op 12-1)*
La Concha(IRE) is still a maiden but he has shown the ability to find a small race in both of his last two runs. This sort of trip suits him well but others had more experience than him. *(op 10-1)*
Hylia ran respectably but just looks a few pounds too high at present. *(op 5-1)*
Siena Star(IRE) stayed this trip at Kelso last time, so it was disappointing to see him fading so quickly in the straight.
Wayward Melody has a good record on this track but she was never travelling on this occasion. The early pace was nothing special, and she acts on fast ground, so it may just have been an off-day. *(op 5-1)*
Esters Boy was never going well. *(tchd 7-1)*
Shower Of Hail(IRE) has not got a clue about jumping, and intensive schooling will be needed. It will be one of the champion trainer's greatest achievements if he can pull it off. *(op 8-1)*

567 OFFSPEC KITCHENS H'CAP CHASE (16 fncs) 2m 6f
4:40 (4:40) (Class 4) (0-105,102) 5-Y-0+ **£4,400** (£1,354; £677; £338)

Form RPR

6P-4 **1** **Joint Authority (IRE)**[21] 234 10-11-1 **98**...................... MissLHorner(7) 108+
(D L Williams) *sn prom: led after 7th and wnt 8 to 10l clr: drvn and tired run-in: jst lasted* **7/1**

2PP- **2** *½* **Six Of One**[37] 4974 7-11-8 **98**...(p) BJCrowley 108+
(R Rowe) *hdwy 10th: wnt 7l 2nd appr 3 out: styd on u.p: catching tiring wnr nr fin* **6/1**

P-30 **3** *¾* **Blazing Batman**[9] 439 12-10-5 **86**.. TJPhelan(5) 94
(Dr P Pritchard) *hld up towards rr: drvn along 11th: wnt mod 4th 4 out: styd on u.p: nrst fin* **10/1**

05-5 **4** *2½* **Alpine Slave**[9] 439 8-11-2 **92**.. LAspell 98
(N J Gifford) *chsd ldrs: outpcd and lost pl 11th: kpt on again fr 2 out* **7/2**[2]

20-0 **5** *3½* **Sylphide**[12] 399 10-10-10 **93**... JAJenkins(7) 96+
(H J Manners) *bhd: hrd rdn 9th: styd on fr 3 out: nvr rchd ldrs* **11/2**[3]

P5-6 **6** *dist* **Multi Talented (IRE)**[23] 205 9-11-12 **102**...........................(b) AThornton —
(L Wells) *wl bhd fr 4th* **17/2**

-222 **R** **Bramblehill Duke (IRE)**[7] 461 13-11-2 **92**..........................(b) SThomas —
(Miss Venetia Williams) *prom to 7th: rr and rdn after 10th: bhd whn ref 12th* **3/1**[1]

0-03 **P** **Honneur Fontenail (FR)**[4] 503 6-9-7 **76** oh12......................... KBurke(7) —
(N J Hawke) *led tl after 7th: blnd 12th: wknd appr 3 out: 5th and btn whn blnd and nrly uns rdr next: p.u* **20/1**

5m 42.7s (-1.10) **Going Correction** -0.20s/f (Good) **8** Ran SP% **113.8**
Speed ratings: **94,93,93,92,91 —,—,—** CSF £47.68 CT £418.54 TOTE £8.70: £2.10, £1.90, £3.20; EX 59.60.
Owner Miss L Horner **Bred** G Stewart **Trained** Shefford, Berks

FOCUS
The pace was good, and the winner kept up the tempo when taking over after a circuit. The second, fourth and fifth were close to their marks, however, with Bramblehill Duke and Multi Talented running no race, the form is devalued.

NOTEBOOK
Joint Authority(IRE) won this thanks to the quick thinking of the rider, who nicked a good lead around halfway. However, the horse was legless in the last 50 yards and in another few strides *would only have finished third. Stamina is not a problem - he had just run himself into the ground. (op 15-2)*
Six Of One comes from a stable which is rediscovering its form at long last, and this run gave encouragement for a summer campaign. He would have won in another couple of strides.
Blazing Batman showed that this is the right level at which to run him. He has form over a variety of trips, but three miles suits him better than shorter these days. *(op 9-1)*
Alpine Slave appeared to find the trip a bit sharp. However, he gave the impression that he would be in with a fighting chance over three miles or more. *(op 9-2)*
Sylphide has won twice over course and distance but looked in need of more of a stamina test. *(op 5-1 tchd 6-1)*
Multi Talented(IRE) appeared to run appallingly, never remotely going the pace, but he needs at *least three miles. He will be a different proposition when back in form and returned to a longer trip. (op 9-1)*
Bramblehill Duke(IRE) did not appear to relish the prospect of going out for the final circuit, stopping to nothing passing the stands and digging his heels in when out of contention two fences later. *(op 11-4 tchd 10-3)*
Honneur Fontenail(FR)'s rider pulled off one of the recoveries of the season, but for which the partnership would have been severed. *(op 11-4 tchd 10-3)*

568 AT FONTWELL THIS AUGUST KATIE MELUA G4 H'CAP HURDLE (9 hdls) 2m 2f 110y
5:15 (5:15) (Class 4) (0-105,105) 4-Y-0+ **£3,562** (£1,096; £548; £274)

Form RPR

000- **1** **Space Cowboy (IRE)**[42] 4883 5-10-11 **90**.............................(b) JEMoore 88
(G L Moore) *hdwy 6th: led last: hrd rdn and kpt on: jst hld on* **8/1**

232- **2** *shd* **Cansalrun (IRE)**[38] 4936 6-11-5 **98**.. AThornton 96
(R H Alner) *pressed ldr: lft in ld 4th: hdd last: rallied strly: jst failed* **11/2**[3]

56-0 **3** *8* **Taranai (IRE)**[15] 357 4-10-3 **87**...(t) LAspell 73+
(B W Duke) *hld up towards rr: hdwy to chse ldr 5th: one pce fr 2 out* **20/1**

4BP- **4** *4* **Kirov King (IRE)**[52] 4759 5-11-4 **97**.. JTizzard 83
(B G Powell) *t.k.h in rr: hdwy 6th: went 2nd and j.lft 3 out: wknd appr next* **20/1**

00-0 **5** *14* **Fiddles Music**[12] 399 4-9-13 **90**.. MGoldstein(7) 59+
(Miss Sheena West) *chsd ldrs: hmpd 4th: wknd after 5th: btn whn mstke next* **14/1**

-025 **6** *3* **Blue Leader (IRE)**[13] 389 6-11-7 **100**...................................(vt) APMcCoy 69
(W K Goldsworthy) *chsd ldrs: mstke 1st: wknd after 3 out* **9/2**[2]

620- **7** *hd* **Kirkham Abbey**[14] 3926 5-11-7 **100**.. RThornton 69
(J J Quinn) *in tch: hmpd 4th: nt fluent 6th: wknd appr 2 out* **4/1**[1]

12-F **8** *1½* **Wenger (FR)**[22] 220 5-11-4 **97**...(bt) PHide 64
(P Winkworth) *hld up in tch towards rr: hmpd bnd after 5th: mstke next: hrd rdn and n.d fr 3 out* **11/2**[3]

0-11 **U** **Tinstre (IRE)**[15] 357 7-11-0 **93**... SCurran —
(P W Hiatt) *led: nt fluent 1st: blnd and uns rdr 4th* **4/1**[1]

4m 32.7s (-3.30) **Going Correction** -0.35s/f (Good)
WFA 4 from 5yo+ 4lb **9** Ran SP% **116.3**
Speed ratings: **92,91,88,86,81 79,79,79,—** CSF £52.19 CT £841.96 TOTE £9.30: £2.60, £2.00, £4.10; EX 80.70 Place 6 £212.40, Place 5 £209.09.
Owner Platt Sanderson Partnership **Bred** Kildaragh Stud **Trained** Woodingdean, E Sussex
■ Space Cowboy's victory gave trainer Gary Moore his first ever four-timer, and son Jamie a treble.
■ Stewards' Enquiry : J E Moore two-day ban: used whip with excessive frequency (Jun 9,11)

FOCUS
A routine contest, but the poor effort of one joint-favourite, and the early departure of the other one, gave the two principals less to beat. The moderate time also helps to limit the form.

NOTEBOOK
Space Cowboy(IRE) had been dropping in the weights after running poorly with what was eventually diagnosed as a back problem. With that now cured, he could be well handicapped for the time being despite the narrowness of this victory. *(op 11-1)*
Cansalrun(IRE) has been rising in the weights but continues to go well. This was a game effort, and any victory would be long overdue. *(op 5-1)*
Taranai(IRE), who acts quite well around here, showed signs of a revival. However, she was fairly handicapped and still not good enough. *(tchd 16-1)*
Kirov King(IRE) is often too keen but showed that he can do better if ever learning to be less headstrong. In the end he just failed to last home.
Fiddles Music found the quickening pace catching her out, though she did stay on better than most. The ground was plenty fast enough for her. *(op 16-1)*
Blue Leader(IRE) may be more effective on less fast ground. *(op 7-1)*
Kirkham Abbey, relatively unexposed, was disappointing. He was always struggling to maintain his *position after taking the fourth-last too slowly, though market support suggests he can do better. (op 7-2)*
Tinstre(IRE) seemed happy in front until trying to put in an extra stride at the fourth and sending his rider flying over his head. *(op 3-1)*
T/Plt: £109.00 to a £1 stake. Pool: £42,493.75. 284.55 winning tickets. T/Qpdt: £54.00 to a £1 stake. Pool: £2,667.50. 36.50 winning tickets. LM

[350]UTTOXETER (L-H)
Sunday, May 29

OFFICIAL GOING: Good to firm
The middle hurdle and the third fence in the back straight were omitted.
Wind: Slight, behind Weather: Fine

569 FIRESTORM MARES' ONLY NOVICES' HURDLE (DIV I) (9 hdls 1 omitted) 2m
2:15 (2:15) (Class 4) 4-Y-0+ **£3,035** (£934; £467; £233)

Form RPR

425- **1** **Miami Explorer**[241] 1541 5-10-10 93... TDoyle 95+
(P R Webber) *t.k.h: hdwy appr 5th: led appr 3 out: easily* **11/4**[2]

21-1 **2** *2½* **Latin Queen (IRE)**[19] 285 5-11-3 114........................... AGlassonbury(7) 101+
(J D Frost) *hld up in tch: wnt 2nd 3 out: sn rdn: kpt on same pce: no ch w wnr* **5/4**[1]

3 *5* **Aspra (FR)**[185] 5-10-10 .... MBradburne 82
(C J Down) *hld up and bhd: hdwy after 6th: one pce fr 3 out* **12/1**

54/- **4** *4* **Cheery Martyr**[406] 4881 7-10-10 .... FKeniry 78
(P Needham) *hld up: hdwy 6th: mstke 3 out: no imp* **33/1**

0-P0 **5** *hd* **Fenney Spring**[26] 178 5-10-10 66.......................................(t) CLlewellyn 79+
(W Jenks) *led 2nd tl appr 3 out: wknd appr 2 out* **22/1**

306- **6** *8* **Macchiato**[122] 3554 4-10-3 88... LVickers(3) 66
(I W McInnes) *prom tl wknd 6th* **7/1**[3]

P-P **7** *6* **La Gitana**[7] 467 5-10-10 .... JMMaguire 64
(A Sadik) *led to 2nd: wknd 6th* **100/1**

8 *2* **Bowling Along**[30] 4-10-3 .... PBuchanan(3) 58
(M E Sowersby) *a bhd* **40/1**

9 *19* **Shuil Mavourneen (IRE)**[272] 1333 6-10-10 .... NFehily 43
(D P Keane) *a bhd* **16/1**

650- **10** *9* **Princess Pea**[45] 4841 5-10-10 .... OMcPhail 34
(Mrs L Wadham) *prom: hmpd bnd appr 3 out: sn wknd* **25/1**

P- **11** *dist* **Casisle**[189] 2367 4-10-6 .... BHitchcott —
(Mary Meek) *plld hrd: short-lived effrt appr 5th: t.o fr 6th* **50/1**

3m 52.4s (-8.00) **Going Correction** -0.80s/f (Firm)
WFA 4 from 5yo+ 4lb **11** Ran SP% **113.7**
Speed ratings: **88,86,84,82,82 78,75,74,64,60** — CSF £6.09 TOTE £4.00: £1.30, £1.10, £3.20; EX 7.10.
Owner R J McAlpine **Bred** Mrs P G Wilkins And R J McAlpine **Trained** Mollington, Oxon
■ Stewards' Enquiry : T Doyle two-day ban: careless riding (Jun 9,11)

FOCUS
A modest, slowly-run affair, three seconds slower than the other division and the form, rated through the fourth, is suspect.

NOTEBOOK
Miami Explorer ◆ was back down in distance and in mares' only company for her first outing for eight months. Scoring as she pleased despite taking a good tug early on, she can defy a penalty in this sort of grade. *(op 10-3)*
Latin Queen(IRE), another reverting to two miles, proved no match for the winner under a penalty. *(op 4-5)*
Aspra(FR), four times a winner at up to nine furlongs on the Flat in France, albeit at a modest level, may well need this sort of ground to get the trip. *(op 14-1)*
Cheery Martyr already looked in trouble when missing out at the third from home on her first outing since April last year.
Fenney Spring, tried in blinkers last time, had yet to live up to her bumper win at Warwick in March last year. *(op 40-1)*

570 NEVILLE LUMB FOR BATHROOMS BEGINNERS' CHASE (14 fncs 2 omitted) 2m 6f 110y

2:45 (2:45) (Class 4) 5-Y-0+ **£4,527** (£1,393; £696; £348)

Form	Pos	Btn	Horse	Jockey	RPR
266-	**1**		**Mioche D'Estruval (FR)**[45] [4835] 5-10-10 .... RGreene (M C Pipe) *hld up: hdwy 4 out: led 2 out: drvn out* **3/1**[1]		118+
3/2-	**2**	*1 1/4*	**Peeyoutwo**[27] 10-11-3 .... BHitchcott (Mrs D A Hamer) *led: rdn and hdd 2 out: kpt on flat* **14/1**		122
22-4	**3**	*11*	**Kombinacja (POL)**[17] [318] 7-10-10 .... JMMaguire (T R George) *prom: rdn appr 4 out: wknd 2 out* **7/2**[3]		105+
15-2	**4**	*3*	**Page Point (AUS)**[27] [148] 7-11-3 116 .... HOliver (R C Guest) *hld up: hdwy 9th: rdn appr 4 out: wknd appr 3 out* **10/3**[2]		108
3-F2	**5**	*20*	**Lord Dundaniel (IRE)**[13] [386] 8-11-3 110 .... NFehily (B De Haan) *chsd ldr tl j.lft and pckd 4 out: wknd 3 out* **5/1**		93+
20-6	**6**	*15*	**Brooklyn's Gold (USA)**[21] [247] 10-11-3 .... DRDennis (Ian Williams) *hld up and bhd: hdwy 9th: wknd after 10th: blnd 2 out* **15/2**		73
3	**7**	*5*	**Prioritisation (IRE)**[17] [322] 6-10-10 .... RSpate(7) (Mrs K Waldron) *hld up in tch: reminder after 6th: wknd 10th* **20/1**		68
U/UP	**P**		**Percy Beck**[11] [413] 9-11-3 .... FKeniry (P Needham) *a bhd: t.o whn p.u bef 3 out* **100/1**		—
00-0	**P**		**Spitfire Bob (USA)**[24] [194] 6-11-0 90 .... (p) PBuchanan(3) (M E Sowersby) *blnd 2nd: sn bhd: t.o whn p.u bef 3 out* **33/1**		—

5m 32.8s
WFA 5 from 6yo+ 3lb **9** Ran SP% **114.1**
CSF £40.54 TOTE £3.10: £1.40, £2.20, £1.90; EX 79.20.
Owner Joe Moran **Bred** Mme B Le Gentil **Trained** Nicholashayne, Devon
■ Stewards' Enquiry : R Greene one-day ban: used whip without giving gelding time to respond (Jun 9)

FOCUS
A fairly interesting contest for this time of the year. The winner is value for further and the race should produce future winners.

NOTEBOOK
Mioche D'Estruval(FR), on his chasing debut, gave Martin Pipe a winner on his 60th birthday. Jumping soundly, he was not doing an awful lot in front on the run-in and Greene got a one-day ban for not giving his mount time to respond to the whip. *(tchd 10-3)*
Peeyoutwo finished alone in a match at a Welsh point at the beginning of the month. He did not go down without a fight and his jumping alone should see him off the mark in a minor event. *(tchd 12-1)*
Kombinacja(POL) jumped better this time but she had run her race at the penultimate fence. *(op 4-1)*
Page Point(AUS) was a shade disappointing his measure had been taken early in the home straight. *(op 3-1 tchd 7-2)*

571 INHOUSE BARS H'CAP HURDLE (9 hdls 1 omitted) 2m

3:20 (3:20) (Class 3) (0-115,113) 4-Y-0+ **£5,235** (£1,611; £805; £402)

Form	Pos	Btn	Horse	Jockey	RPR
6P0-	**1**		**Qabas (USA)**[105] [3843] 5-11-6 107 .... (p) RJohnson (P Bowen) *a.p: rdn 3 out: led 2 out: drvn out* **7/1**[2]		112
40-0	**2**	*nk*	**Wiscalitus (GER)**[30] [117] 6-11-12 113 .... AO'Keeffe (Miss Venetia Williams) *hld up in mid-div: hit 5th: hdwy appr 3 out: led 2 out to last: r.o* **14/1**		118
-F04	**3**	*2 1/2*	**Sir Walter (IRE)**[15] [357] 12-9-13 91 .... LStephens(5) (D Burchell) *hld up and bhd: hdwy appr 2 out: r.o flat: nrst fin* **14/1**		93
56-5	**4**	*nk*	**Kalambari (IRE)**[29] [136] 6-11-7 108 .... PJBrennan (J Joseph) *hld up: hdwy after 5th: led appr 2 out: sn hdd: one pce flat* **12/1**		111+
154-	**5**	*3*	**Bill's Echo**[203] [2064] 6-10-7 94 .... HOliver (R C Guest) *hld up: rdn 6th: hdwy appr 2 out: nvr trbld ldrs* **9/2**[1]		93
040-	**6**	*3/4*	**Castle River (USA)**[220] [1792] 6-10-13 100 .... MBatchelor (O O'Neill) *hld up and bhd: hdwy appr 2 out: nt rch ldrs* **33/1**		98
30-0	**7**	*1/2*	**Avesomeofthat (IRE)**[16] [220] 4-10-6 97 .... (t) PHolley (Mrs P N Dutfield) *hld up towards rr: mstke 2nd: hdwy appr 2 out: swtchd rt appr last: no further prog* **16/1**		91
5-65	**8**	*3*	**A Bit Of Fun**[5] [488] 4-10-11 107 .... LTreadwell(5) (J T Stimpson) *prom: rdn and ev ch 3 out: hit 2 out: sn wknd* **25/1**		98
04-2	**9**	*hd*	**Pilca (FR)**[35] [1] 5-10-13 100 .... JPMcNamara (R M Stronge) *prom tl wknd appr 2 out* **14/1**		95
504-	**10**	*1*	**Critical Stage (IRE)**[12] [4793] 6-10-13 107 .... AGlassonbury(7) (J D Frost) *nvr nr ldrs* **14/1**		101
120-	**11**	*2*	**Arm And A Leg (IRE)**[259] [1420] 10-11-1 107 .... RStephens(5) (Mrs D A Hamer) *led and mstke 1st: hdd after 6th: wknd 3 out* **14/1**		99
00-4	**12**	*3 1/2*	**New Currency (USA)**[26] [177] 5-10-12 102 .... (t) TJMalone(3) (M C Pipe) *chsd ldr: led appr 3 out: rdn and hdd appr 2 out: sn wknd* **10/1**[3]		91+
2F/P	**13**	*1 3/4*	**Dileer (IRE)**[21] [247] 6-11-5 109 .... GCarenza(3) (D J Wintle) *bhd: rdn 6th: no rspnse* **25/1**		95
33-0	**14**	*hd*	**Meadow Hawk (USA)**[29] [136] 5-10-9 96 .... (b) DRDennis (Ian Williams) *mid-div: lost pl after 5th* **16/1**		82
22-4	**15**	*shd*	**Cunning Pursuit**[30] [100] 4-11-6 111 .... MAFitzgerald (N J Henderson) *hld up in tch: wknd after 6th* **7/1**[2]		93
1P-2	**16**	*30*	**Terre De Java (FR)**[15] [343] 7-11-9 110 .... (t) TDoyle (Mrs H Dalton) *mid-div: lost pl after 6th: t.o* **12/1**		66
341-	**17**	*4*	**Hutch**[365] [554] 7-10-13 105 .... DFlavin(5) (Mrs L B Normile) *prom: rdn to ld after 6th: hdd appr 3 out: sn wknd* **16/1**		57
5P0-	**P**		**Karathaena (IRE)**[120] [3592] 5-11-7 108 .... (t) GLee (M E Sowersby) *a bhd: t.o whn p.u bef 2 out* **33/1**		—

3m 44.8s (-15.60) **Going Correction** -0.80s/f (Firm)
WFA 4 from 5yo+ 4lb **18** Ran SP% **132.2**
Speed ratings: **107,106,105,105,103 103,103,101,101,101 100,98,97,97,97 82,80,—** CSF £104.49 CT £1375.02 TOTE £8.50: £2.60, £4.70, £5.80, £4.00; EX 183.20.
Owner P Bowen **Bred** B C Jones **Trained** Little Newcastle, Pembrokes

FOCUS
A fair handicap for the time of year, and this turned out to be just as competitive as the betting suggested. The form looks solid and should work out.

NOTEBOOK
Qabas(USA), who improved when fitted with cheekpieces last year, likes a sound surface and does seem to go well when fresh.
Wiscalitus(GER), highly tried on his last two outings, lost nothing in defeat under top weight. He likes the ground good or faster.
Sir Walter(IRE), reverting to two miles, was typically doing all his best work in the closing stages. *(op 12-1)*
Kalambari(IRE) ran a sound race and would not have minded a shade further.
Bill's Echo, quite progressive over fences last year, should be all the better for this comeback over timber. *(op 4-1)*
Castle River(USA) shaped with promise on his first outing for seven months. *(tchd 40-1)*

572 WALTON HOMES H'CAP CHASE (18 fncs 2 omitted) 3m 2f

3:55 (3:55) (Class 4) (0-110,111) 5-Y-0+ **£4,485** (£1,380; £690; £345)

Form	Pos	Btn	Horse	Jockey	RPR
2PU/	**1**		**Merry Path (IRE)**[43] 11-11-12 110 .... PMoloney (Evan Williams) *hld up in tch: led 14th to 4 out: led 2 out: drvn out* **5/1**[3]		123+
2-11	**2**	*3*	**Gallik Dawn**[9] [439] 7-11-13 111 .... MAFitzgerald (A Hollingsworth) *hld up: hdwy 13th: rdn and ev ch 2 out: no ex towards fin* **2/1**[1]		119
P0-P	**3**	*3*	**Blazing Hills**[16] [330] 9-10-12 96 .... TDoyle (P T Dalton) *a.p: led 13th to 14th: rdn to ld 4 out: hdd 2 out: one pce* **14/1**		101
22P-	**4**	*16*	**Orswell Crest**[66] [4537] 11-11-8 106 .... RJohnson (P J Hobbs) *w ldr: led 11th to 13th: rdn appr 4 out: wknd 3 out* **4/1**[2]		96+
3-P4	**5**	*25*	**Judaic Ways**[26] [176] 11-10-9 93 .... MBradburne (H D Daly) *hld up: hdwy 13th: mstke 4 out: sn wknd* **7/1**		57
P03-	**P**		**Tyndarius (IRE)**[68] [4512] 14-11-5 106 .... LVickers(3) (I W McInnes) *nvr gng wl: t.o 4th: p.u bef 7th* **14/1**		—
32-2	**P**		**Were Not Stoppin**[14] [373] 10-9-13 90 .... MissJFoster(7) (R Bastiman) *a bhd: t.o whn p.u bef 3 out* **11/2**		—
6/P-	**P**		**Pharpost (IRE)**[353] [706] 10-11-8 106 .... AO'Keeffe (A G Juckes) *led to 11th: wknd qckly after 13th: t.o whn p.u bef 4 out* **40/1**		—

6m 33.0s (-32.20) **Going Correction** -1.15s/f (Hard) **8** Ran SP% **113.7**
Speed ratings: **103,102,101,96,88** —,—,— CSF £15.96 CT £129.00 TOTE £8.80: £2.70, £1.40, £2.80; EX 21.70.
Owner William Rucker **Bred** Mrs D A Merry **Trained** Cowbridge, Vale Of Glamorgan

FOCUS
A fair staying handicap for the grade and the winner is rated value for more than the official margin.

NOTEBOOK
Merry Path(IRE), a one-time decent handicap chaser, followed a facile win between the flags with a good second in the Lady Dudley Cup last month. Having his first run under Rules since the 2002 Topham, he proved he is no back-number on this sort of ground. *(op 9-2)*
Gallik Dawn, attempting a hat-trick, met his match having been raised 15lb for his latest victory and 23lb in all. *(op 13-8)*
Blazing Hills, who jumped right-handed when pulled up last time, did not put a foot wrong and produced a respectable performance. *(tchd 16-1)*
Orswell Crest ran better than when a beaten favourite at Wincanton in March but was still beaten a fair way in the end. *(op 6-1)*
Tyndarius(IRE) *Official explanation: jockey said gelding was never travelling (op 12-1)*

573 LETS LIVE RACING H'CAP HURDLE (10 hdls 2 omitted) 2m 4f 110y

4:30 (4:31) (Class 4) (0-105,105) 4-Y-0+ **£3,594** (£1,106; £553; £276)

Form	Pos	Btn	Horse	Jockey	RPR
035-	**1**		**Mick Murphy (IRE)**[307] [1049] 8-10-0 79 oh12 .... JamesDavies (V J Hughes) *mde all: rdn 3 out: drvn out* **20/1**		78+
44-3	**2**	*nk*	**Musally**[35] [5] 8-11-5 98 .... CLlewellyn (W Jenks) *hld up towards rr: hdwy 7th: hit 3 out: rdn and ev ch last: nt qckn nr fin* **7/2**[2]		95
/U-4	**3**	*1 1/4*	**Golfagent**[19] [272] 7-11-5 105 .... (t) RSpate(7) (Mrs K Waldron) *hld up and bhd: hdwy appr 3 out: rdn appr last: styd on wl flat* **14/1**		102+
006-	**4**	*9*	**Little Tobias (IRE)**[19] [3368] 6-10-11 90 .... ARoss (J S Wainwright) *prom: ev ch 3 out: wknd 2 out* **33/1**		77
P0-0	**5**	*3*	**Sunnyside Royale (IRE)**[18] [306] 6-10-4 83 .... (t) GLee (R Bastiman) *hld up: hdwy appr 6th: rdn whn n.m.r 3 out: sn wknd* **9/2**[3]		67
13-1	**6**	*11*	**Manoram (GER)**[21] [246] 6-11-0 93 .... (b) DRDennis (Ian Williams) *hld up: hdwy 5th: rdn appr 3 out: wknd appr 2 out* **11/4**[1]		66
P-0	**7**	*3*	**Ewar Bold**[7] [458] 12-9-7 79 oh1 .... (t) WPKavanagh(7) (K G Wingrove) *prom to 5th* **50/1**		49
R46-	**8**	*7*	**Del Trotter (IRE)**[49] [4786] 10-10-10 92 .... (p) PBuchanan(3) (M E Sowersby) *prom tl rdn and wknd after 7th* **33/1**		55
124/	**9**	*7*	**Die Fledermaus (IRE)**[591] [1678] 11-10-12 98 .... RCummings(7) (D J Wintle) *a bhd* **16/1**		54
P2-5	**10**	*6*	**Lancier D'Estruval (FR)**[30] [105] 6-10-0 79 .... (t) JMogford (J C Tuck) *rn in snatches: prom tl wknd appr 7th* **9/2**[3]		29
0-05	**B**		**Saxe-Coburg (IRE)**[7] [458] 8-9-7 79 oh2 .... MrTJO'Brien(7) (K G Wingrove) *hld up: hdwy 7th: wkng whn b.d 3 out* **33/1**		—
P0/P	**F**		**Wrangel (FR)**[7] [458] 11-9-13 83 .... (tp) LStephens(5) (Mrs S M Johnson) *hld up towards rr: smooth hdwy whn fell 3 out* **40/1**		—

4m 55.0s (-17.10) **Going Correction** -0.80s/f (Firm) **12** Ran SP% **115.8**
Speed ratings: **100,99,99,95,94 90,89,86,84,81** —,— CSF £84.86 CT £1038.00 TOTE £25.50: £4.40, £1.80, £2.90; EX 144.90.
Owner V J Hughes **Bred** Mrs C Roper **Trained** Bridgend, Bridgend
■ A first winner for trainer Viv Hughes.

FOCUS
A modest handicap and rated through the third, although the form is probably not strong.

NOTEBOOK
Mick Murphy(IRE), who changed hands for only 2,000 gns, gave permit holder Viv Hughes his first winner despite being no less than 12lb out of the handicap. This was his first outing since July last year and it would be reasonable to expect some further improvement. *(op 22-1)*
Musally, dropped 2lb, did nothing wrong but the winner proved just too strong. *(op 10-3)*
Golfagent was arguably a shade too confidently ridden on this switch back to hurdles. A return to a longer trip should help. *(tchd 12-1)*
Little Tobias(IRE) showed signs of a return to form but should not have been beaten for stamina, having won over just short of two miles on the Flat. *(op 28-1)*
Sunnyside Royale(IRE), another who stayed well on the level, has still yet to prove he can be effective at this sort of trip over hurdles. *(op 4-1 tchd 5-1)*
Manoram(GER), 7lb lower than his hard-fought win over fences last time, should not have been inconvenienced by the extra half-mile. *(op 5-2 tchd 3-1)*
Wrangel(FR), with the tongue tie fitted this time, was going really well and threatening a surprise when departing. He likes this ground. *(op 33-1)*

574 FIRESTORM MARES' ONLY NOVICES' HURDLE (DIV II) (9 hdls 1 omitted) 2m

5:00 (5:00) (Class 4) 4-Y-0+ **£3,035** (£934; £467; £233)

Form	Pos	Btn	Horse	Jockey	RPR
35-2	**1**		**Dewasentah (IRE)**[22] [210] 6-10-10 96 .... GLee (J M Jefferson) *chsd ldr: led 4th: lft clr 3 out: easily* **2/1**[1]		93+
33-U	**2**	*4*	**Reem Two**[16] [331] 4-10-6 100 .... JMMaguire (D McCain) *hld up: hdwy appr 2 out: r.o flat: no ch w wnr* **5/2**[2]		81
/P-5	**3**	*1 3/4*	**Bodfari Rose**[15] [343] 6-10-10 85 .... (p) JPMcNamara (A Bailey) *hld up: hdwy whn blnd 6th: wnt 2nd briefly last: one pce* **14/1**		84+
P4-0	**4**	*6*	**Celtic Romance**[21] [238] 6-10-10 78 .... JPByrne (Ms Sue Smith) *hld up: hdwy after 6th: lft 2nd 3 out: wknd last* **12/1**		78+
5	**5**	*13*	**Convent Girl (IRE)**[23] [203] 5-10-10 .... PHolley (Mrs P N Dutfield) *t.k.h in rr: hdwy whn mstke 2 out: sn wknd* **7/1**		64

	6 *1* **Rabbit**[92] 4-10-6 .... BHitchcott	59
	(Mrs A L M King) *hld up: hdwy appr 6th: wknd appr 2 out* **25/1**	
0/0-	P **Pridewood Dove**[28] 6-10-5 .... TGreenway(5)	—
	(R J Price) *led to 4th: wknd appr 6th: t.o whn p.u bef 3 out* **50/1**	
5	F **Didn't You Know (FR)**[15] [355] 4-10-6 .... RGreene	—
	(M C Pipe) *prom: wnt 2nd after 5th: ev ch whn hung rt bnd after 6th: hung lft and 2l 2nd whn fell 3 out* **4/1**[3]	

3m 49.5s (-10.90) **Going Correction** -0.80s/f (Firm)
WFA 4 from 5yo+ 4lb **8** Ran SP% **114.6**
Speed ratings: **95,93,92,89,82 82,—,—** CSF £7.43 TOTE £3.40: £1.60, £1.10, £3.20; EX 8.80.
Owner Mrs J U Hales & Mrs L M Joicey **Bred** Miss Mary O'Sullivan **Trained** Norton, N Yorks

FOCUS
A moderate event run three seconds quicker than the slowly-run first division. The winner is value for double the official margin but the form is suspect.

NOTEBOOK
Dewasentah(IRE) finally got her act together and was already assuming control when her nearest rival departed three out. She can score again in this sort of grade. *(op 7-4 tchd 9-4)*
Reem Two stuck to her task but did nothing more than finish best of the rest. *(op 2-1)*
Bodfari Rose did not help her cause when making a hash of the fourth last but she would probably have not beaten the winner under any circumstances. *(tchd 12-1)*
Celtic Romance could make no impression on the favourite and seemed to run out of steam jumping the final flight. *(op 16-1)*
Didn't You Know(FR) looked a far from straightforward ride and had just began to feel the pinch when exiting three from home. *(op 9-2 tchd 5-1 and 7-2)*

575 UTTOXETER OVERSEAS PROPERTY SHOWS 4TH/5TH JUNE CONDITIONAL JOCKEYS' H'CAP HURDLE (12 hdls 2 omitted) 3m

5:30 (5:31) (Class 4) (0-90,90) 4-Y-0+ **£3,136** (£896; £448)

Form		RPR
60-U	**1** **Over Bridge**[19] [283] 7-11-2 **80** .... JamesDavies	92+
	(Mrs S M Johnson) *a.p: led 3 out: styd on wl* **25/1**	
P-31	**2** *3* **Charlie's Double**[14] [365] 6-11-1 **79** .... DCrosse	87+
	(J R Best) *a.p: ev ch appr 3 out: mstke last: styd on one pce flat* **4/1**[1]	
114-	**3** *1* **Totheroadyouvgone**[185] [2446] 11-11-7 **85** .... (p) PCO'Neill(3)	96+
	(A E Jones) *hld up: hdwy 3rd: wnt 2nd and nt fluent 2 out: nt fluent last: one pce* **8/1**	
53-1	**4** *3/4* **Vicentio**[22] [218] 6-11-9 **87** .... ATinkler	92
	(T J Fitzgerald) *hld up in mid-div: hdwy 9th: one pce fr 2 out* **6/1**[2]	
0P-4	**5** *9* **Supreme Return**[23] [206] 6-11-9 **90** .... WHutchinson(3)	89+
	(A King) *led to 3rd: chsd ldr: lft in ld appr 5th: hdd 3 out: wknd flat* **7/1**[3]	
P42-	**6** *2 1/2* **Arctic Glow**[76] [4366] 6-10-5 **74** .... PMerrigan(5)	68
	(Mrs H Pudd) *hld up in mid-div: hdwy 5th: rdn after 9th: wknd 3 out* **7/1**[3]	
0P-B	**7** *5* **Kingscourt Lad (IRE)**[29] [133] 7-10-11 **83** .... WJones(8)	72
	(Jonjo O'Neill) *hld up and bhd: hdwy appr 9th: rdn and wkng whn hit 3 out* **10/1**	
-613	**8** *3 1/2* **Somewin (IRE)**[7] [462] 5-10-0 **72** .... (p) RSpate(8)	57
	(Mrs K Waldron) *hld up and bhd: hdwy appr 9th: rdn and wknd appr 3 out* **16/1**	
P2-5	**9** *13* **Backscratcher**[25] [181] 11-11-1 **79** .... (b) MNicolls	51
	(John R Upson) *hld up: hdwy 8th: wknd 9th* **33/1**	
40-5	**10** *1 1/4* **Silver Gift**[21] [245] 8-11-4 **87** .... PCStringer(5)	58
	(G Fierro) *a bhd* **8/1**	
05-0	**11** *5* **Nice Baby (FR)**[15] [352] 4-11-0 **87** .... TJMalone(3)	47
	(M C Pipe) *hld up in tch: lost pl 6th: bhd fr 9th* **16/1**	
0-5P	**P** **Vivre Aimer Rire (FR)**[21] [245] 4-10-1 **79** .... JKington(8)	—
	(M Scudamore) *a bhd: t.o whn p.u after 3 out* **33/1**	
00-P	**P** **Green Master (POL)**[7] [469] 5-10-12 **76** .... TGreenway	—
	(A Sadik) *chsd ldr: led 3rd tl p.u appr 5th* **33/1**	
5/3-	**P** **Noble Spy (IRE)**[27] 11-11-7 **85** .... RStephens	—
	(Mrs D A Hamer) *hld up in tch: rdn and wknd after 8th: t.o whn p.u bef 3 out* **33/1**	
05-0	**P** **Real Cracker (IRE)**[13] [389] 6-11-5 **86** .... AO'Keeffe(3)	—
	(Miss Venetia Williams) *hld up in mid-div: hdwy appr 8th: in tch whn p.u bef 3 out* **16/1**	

5m 49.3s (-15.70) **Going Correction** -0.80s/f (Firm)
WFA 4 from 5yo+ 6lb **15** Ran SP% **123.9**
Speed ratings: **94,93,92,92,89 88,86,85,81,81 79,—,—,—,—** CSF £122.92 CT £893.25 TOTE £24.00: £5.80, £1.90, £2.80; EX 160.20 Place 6 £55.62, Place 5 £45.49.
Owner I K Johnson **Bred** I K Johnson **Trained** Lulham, H'fords

FOCUS
A weak contest and the fact they went no gallop was reflected in the slow time. The fourth sets a modest standard.

NOTEBOOK
Over Bridge relished this step up to three miles and was by no means hard pressed to score.
Charlie's Double confirmed his liking for this type of surface but could not overcome a 7lb higher mark. *(op 5-1)*
Totheroadyouvgone, making his comeback over timber, found that his hurdling technique was found out when the chips were down. He will be all the better for the outing. *(op 7-1)*
Vicentio, 8lb higher than when winning from out of the handicap at Warwick, got the trip well enough albeit in a slowly-run race. *(op 11-2)*
Supreme Return appeared to get found out by this step up to three miles. *(op 11-2)*
T/Plt: £69.60 to a £1 stake. Pool: £44,115.40. 462.25 winning tickets. T/Qpdt: £22.40 to a £1 stake. Pool: £2,632.80. 86.80 winning tickets. KH

576a - 584a (Foreign Racing) - See Raceform Interactive

257 AUTEUIL (L-H)

Sunday, May 29

OFFICIAL GOING: Very soft

585a GRAS SAVOYE HIPCOVER PRIX LA BARKA (HURDLE) (GRADE 2) 2m 5f 110y

3:10 (3:09) 5-Y-0+

£51,064 (£24,965; £14,752; £10,213; £5,674; £3,972)

		RPR
	1 **Rock And Palm (FR)**[21] [257] 5-9-13 .... MDelmares	—
	(Y-M Porzier, France) **362/10**[1]	
	2 *2* **Cyrlight (FR)**[42] [4903] 5-10-6 .... CPieux	—
	(A Chaille-Chaille, France)	
	3 *6* **Rule Supreme (IRE)**[32] [68] 9-10-6 .... RWalsh	—
	(W P Mullins, Ire) *held up in mid-division, headway & 6th 3 out, 4th 2 out, ridden to take 3rd on flat, kept on*	
	4 *3* **Sphinx Du Berlais (FR)**[43] 6-10-4 .... DGallagher	—
	(F-M Cottin, France)	
	5 *2* **Cheler (FR)**[184] 6-10-4 .... LMetais	—
	(B Secly, France)	
	6 *3/4* **L'Interprete (FR)**[42] [4903] 6-10-6 .... AKondrat	—
	(T Trapenard, France)	
	7 *1 1/2* **Ennemi D'Etat (FR)**[42] [4903] 6-10-6 .... (b) RegisSchmidlin	—
	(M Rolland, France)	
	8 *hd* **Prince Dolois (FR)**[49] 7-10-4 .... CGombeau	—
	(A Bonin, France)	
	9 *15* **Geos (FR)**[43] [4860] 10-10-6 .... BGicquel	—
	(N J Henderson) *raced in mid-division on outside, weakened from 3 out*	
	10 *1/2* **Homer Wells (IRE)**[31] [90] 7-10-6 .... DJCondon	—
	(W P Mullins, Ire) *tracked leaders, 5th with a circuit to race, weakened from 3f out*	
	0 **Phonidal (FR)**[42] [4903] 9-10-6 .... (b) GAdam	—
	(M Rolland, France)	
	P **El Paradiso (FR)**[42] [4903] 8-10-6 .... (b) PMarsac	—
	(M Rolland, France)	
	P **Raikkonen (IRE)**[17] [43] 5-9-13 .... SBeaumard	—
	(W P Mullins, Ire) *always in rear, tailed off from 4 out, pulled up before 2 out*	

5m 3.00s **14** Ran SP% **2.7**
PARI-MUTUEL: WIN 37.20; PL 1.60, 1.10, 1.30; DF 11.80.
Owner Mme P Menard **Bred** Pierre Fontaine **Trained** France

NOTEBOOK
Rock And Palm(FR) sprang a surprise, but perhaps the race did not take as much winning as had looked the case beforehand, given the hot favourite's recent setback. He could run at the Galway festival in July.
Cyrlight(FR), sent off a 1-10 favourite, could never shake off his rivals and was not at his best. It was later revealed that he had recently had a minor foot problem which had resulted in him being confined to his box for a week, so in the circumstances it was not a bad effort. He should still take the beating in the French Champion Hurdle.
Rule Supreme(IRE) replicated his position in this race last year with another fine staying-on effort. This should put him spot on for a repeat bid in the French Champion Hurdle in under three weeks' time.
Geos(FR), who is more effective over a shorter trip, did not get home.
Homer Wells(IRE) was out of his depth really but he could yet join his stable companion Rule Supreme in the Grande Course de Haies d'Auteuil (French Champion Hurdle).

471 BADEN-BADEN (L-H)

Sunday, May 29

OFFICIAL GOING: Good

590a IFFEZHEIMER-JAGDRENNEN (LISTED) (CHASE) 2m 6f 110y

5:15 (5:24) 5-Y-0+ **£8,369** (£3,404; £2,553; £1,631; £780)

		RPR
	1 **Gelot (GER)** 6-10-5 .... MrOSchnakenberg	—
	(Elfi Schnakenberg, Germany)	
	2 *1/2* **Decent Fellow (GER)**[231] [1683] 10-10-10 .... JBartos	—
	(J Vana Jr, Czech Republic)	
	3 *4* **Serge (FR)**[1146] 8-10-1 .... VMoravec	—
	(W Gulcher, Germany)	
	4 *32* **Ab Und Zu (GER)**[967] 7-10-6 ow2 .... MrMRosport	—
	(O W Seiler, Germany)	
	5 *8* **Roosevelt (GER)**[588] 7-9-13 .... RMackowiak	—
	(U Stoltefuss, Germany)	
	6 *1/2* **Masamix (FR)** 7-10-1 .... JMyska	—
	(J Vana Jr, Czech Republic)	
	7 *1 1/4* **Water Quirl (GER)**[7] [471] 6-9-13 .... (b) PJohnson	—
	(M F Harris) *always behind, 5th & beaten when mistake last (20-1)* **20/1**[1]	
	8 **Liam (GER)**[973] 7-9-13 .... LSloup	—
	(J Albrecht)	

5m 37.83s **8** Ran SP% **4.8**
(including 10 euro stake) WIN 42; PL 17, 14, 22; SF 116.
Owner Frau T Basar & Frau N Gfeller **Bred** L Depken **Trained** Germany

NOTEBOOK
Water Quirl(GER) failed to build on the promise of his effort here a week earlier.

544 CARTMEL (L-H)

Monday, May 30

OFFICIAL GOING: Good (good to firm in places)
After another two dry days the going had dried out still further and was described as 'patchy but basically on the fast side of good'.
Wind: Moderate, half behind Weather: Fine, sunny and warm.

591 TOTEEXACTA MAIDEN HURDLE (11 hdls) 2m 6f

2:25 (2:29) (Class 4) 4-Y-0+ **£3,682** (£1,133; £566; £283)

Form		RPR
6/4-	**1** **Marlborough Sound**[215] [1861] 6-11-2 .... ADobbin	91+
	(N G Richards) *mid-div: hdwy 7th: styd on to ld 1f out: drvn out* **5/1**[2]	
14-0	**2** *2* **Stagecoach Diamond**[30] [133] 6-11-2 .... DElsworth	89+
	(Mrs S J Smith) *chsd ldrs: led after 8th tl 1f out: no ex* **11/1**	
2	**3** *1* **Royal Artisan (IRE)**[23] [212] 7-11-2 .... ARoss	87
	(I A Duncan, Ire) *chsd ldrs: chal last: kpt on same pce* **9/2**[1]	
	4 *shd* **Toni Alcala**[9] 6-10-13 .... KJMercer(3)	87
	(R F Fisher) *j. slowly early: bhd: gd hdwy to chse ldrs 8th: styd on run-in to snatch 3rd nr line* **5/1**[2]	
4/45	**5** *10* **Nod Ya Head**[4] [523] 9-10-2 **69** .... PKinsella(7)	70
	(R E Barr) *mid-div: hdwy 6th: outpcd fr 3 out* **33/1**	
6-	**6** *dist* **French Fashion (IRE)**[28] [154] 6-10-9 .... SThomas	—
	(I A Duncan, Ire) *w ldrs: led 7th tl after next: sn weakened: t.o:* **8/1**	
	7 *dist* **Joemanchie (IRE)**[15] [376] 7-10-9 .... OKelly(7)	—
	(Thomas O'Neill, Ire) *in tch: lost pl 6th: sn bhd: t.o* **100/1**	

P **Daggy Boy (NZ)**[232] 5-11-2 .... HOliver —
(R C Guest) *sn bhd: t.o 6th: p.u bef 8th* **22/1**

/00- P **Tandawizi**[110] 3753 8-10-4 .... DFlavin(5) —
(Mrs L B Normile) *bhd: p.u bef 3 out* **80/1**

5-42 P **The Wife's Sister**[16] 351 4-10-4 90 .... GLee —
(D McCain) *lost pl 6th: bhd whn p.u bef 3 out* **13/2**[3]

5-34 P **Uneven Line**[18] 317 9-10-6 81 .... MrCStorey(3) —
(Miss S E Forster) *sn bhd: t.o whn p.u bef 3 out* **20/1**

P **Full Kwai Ma (IRE)**[44] 5-11-2 .... (p) JPByrne —
(John G Carr, Ire) *in tch: lost pl 6th: t.o whn p.u bef 3 out* **10/1**

BPP- P **Cottage Hill**[90] 4109 6-10-6 .... PAspell(3) —
(C R Wilson) *led to 7th: wknd qckly: bhd whn p.u bef 3 out* **100/1**

0-00 P **Thepubhorse**[23] 212 5-10-11 .... DCCostello(5) —
(Mrs H O Graham) *in tch: lost pl 6th: bhd whn p.u bef 2 out* **66/1**

P **Millicent Fairways (IRE)**[383] 318 7-10-13 .... LMcGrath(3) —
(R C Guest) *t.k.h in rr: nt fluent: t.o whn p.u bef 8th* **16/1**

3 P **Life Match (FR)**[2] 549 7-11-2 .... (tp) RJohnson —
(John G Carr, Ire) *chsd ldrs: lost pl 8th: bhd whn p.u after 2 out* **10/1**

5m 22.8s (-13.20) **Going Correction** -0.325s/f (Good)
WFA 4 from 5yo+ 5lb **16** Ran SP% **125.1**
Speed ratings: **111,110,109,109,106** —,—,—,—,— —,—,—,—,— — CSF £57.88 TOTE £5.70: £2.70, £4.20, £2.20; EX 74.20.
Owner Ashleybank Investments Limited **Bred** Mrs I H Lowe **Trained** Greystoke, Cumbria

FOCUS
A decent time for the grade of contest and the race could rate higher with the fifth the best guide. There was a false start, and four of the field jumped the first flight and one of them the second flight too.

NOTEBOOK
Marlborough Sound, absent since October with a hock problem, looked booked for third and was matched at 95 on the exchanges. With his jockey at his most determined he stayed on much the best on the run-in and will make an even better chaser. *(op 3-1)*
Stagecoach Diamond, one of four who jumped off at the false start, appreciated the stamina test and after going on he fought off the challenge of the third only to find the winner too strong where it matters most. *(op 12-1 tchd 10-1)*
Royal Artisan(IRE), runner-up behind a subsequent winner at Hexham, moved upsides at the last but was simply not good enough to force his head in front.
Toni Alcala, rated 60 on the Flat where he has won seven times, was hesistant in his jumping early on but he did warm to the task. He was staying on best of all at the finish and can surely make his mark at this game. *(op 6-1 tchd 7-1 in places)*
Nod Ya Head, rated just 69, is the value to the overall level of the form. *(op 40-1)*
Daggy Boy(NZ) *Official explanation: jockey said gelding finished distressed (tchd 20-1 and 25-1)*

592 A F CONNELL (S) H'CAP HURDLE (8 hdls) 2m 1f 110y
3:00 (3:00) (Class 5) (0-90,89) 4-Y-0+ **£2,975** (£850; £425)

Form RPR

P/0- **1** **Aleemdar (IRE)**[378] 397 8-10-4 **72** .... (p) DLaverty(5) 81+
(A E Jones) *mid-div: hdwy 4th: led 3 out: hld on towards fin* **8/1**[3]

P-43 **2** *1* **Ball Games**[23] 214 7-11-4 **81** .... GLee 89+
(James Moffatt) *in rr: hdwy 3 out: mod 3rd whn hit last: styd on strly: nt quite rch wnr* **7/1**[2]

6-32 **3** *¾* **Star Trooper (IRE)**[6] 480 9-10-11 **77** .... (p) MrCStorey(3) 83+
(Miss S E Forster) *chsd ldrs: ent 2nd after 3 out: nt qckn run-in* **5/1**[1]

65-6 **4** *11* **Peter's Imp (IRE)**[5] 499 10-11-12 **89** .... PRobson 84
(A Berry) *in rr: hdwy 5th: chsng ldrs 2 out: 5th and wkng whn hit last* **5/1**[1]

0-P5 **5** *3* **Three Times A Lady**[19] 302 5-10-7 **73** .... ONelmes(3) 65
(D W Thompson) *mid-div: hdwy to chse ldrs 3 out: wknd between last 2* **28/1**

25-6 **6** *6* **Power And Demand**[23] 214 8-10-5 **73** .... DCCostello(5) 59
(C W Thornton) *mid-div: effrt 3 out: nvr rchd ldrs* **14/1**

7 *4* **Possible Gale (IRE)**[558] 2245 7-11-0 **77** .... (t) RJohnson 59
(John G Carr, Ire) *hld up in rr: hdwy 4th: wknd after 3 out* **16/1**

00-0 **8** *7* **Fortune's Fool**[12] 415 6-10-8 **74** .... DCrosse(3) 49
(I A Brown) *hld up in rr: sme hdwy 5th: nvr nr ldrs* **33/1**

-020 **9** *1¾* **Scamp**[5] 496 6-10-7 **70** .... (b[1]) KRenwick 44
(R Shiels) *w ldrs: led 3rd to 3 out: sn wknd* **25/1**

34P- **10** *hd* **Breaking Ball (IRE)**[236] 1617 5-11-7 **84** .... ADobbin 57
(N G Richards) *in tch: rdn 5th: sn btn* **7/1**[2]

11 *2* **Platium Starlight (IRE)**[17] 200 5-10-8 **78** .... (p) PCO'Neill(7) 49
(Thomas O'Neill, Ire) *led to 3rd: wknd qckly appr 2 out: eased run-in* **16/1**

00P- **12** *4* **Shady Man**[115] 3676 7-11-3 **87** .... GThomas(7) 54
(J K Hunter) *bhd fr 5th* **50/1**

-004 **13** *½* **Private Jessica**[5] 496 4-10-10 **80** .... (b) LMcGrath(3) 43
(R C Guest) *chsd ldrs: lost pl 3 out* **10/1**

3-05 **14** *4* **Stormy Beech**[5] 497 9-11-10 **87** .... (b) KJohnson 50
(R Johnson) *chsd ldrs to 5th: wknd qckly: t.o 2 out* **25/1**

POP- **15** *8* **Lady Stratagem**[12] 4106 6-10-6 **69** .... (p) BHarding 24
(E W Tuer) *bhd fr 5th* **25/1**

16 *9* **Inse Bay (IRE)**[103] 3895 6-11-0 **84** .... OKelly(7) 30
(Thomas O'Neill, Ire) *hmpd 1st: bhd fr 5th: t.o 2 out* **50/1**

640- **F** **Amber Go Go**[55] 4738 8-9-8 **67** .... MMcAvoy(10) —
(James Moffatt) *fell 1st* **14/1**

4m 9.50s (-6.20) **Going Correction** -0.325s/f (Good)
WFA 4 from 5yo+ 4lb **17** Ran SP% **125.5**
Speed ratings: **100,99,99,94,93 90,88,85,84,84 83,81,81,79,76 72,**— CSF £60.68 CT £317.57 TOTE £20.70: £5.10, £1.40, £1.70, £1.20; EX 158.90.The winner was bought in for 4,800gns.
Owner John Spence **Bred** His Highness The Aga Khan's Studs S C **Trained** Newchapel, Surrey

FOCUS
A poor race but a sound gallop and only half-a-dozen still in contention four out. The form looks pretty solid for the level.

NOTEBOOK
Aleemdar(IRE), absent for a year and pulled up on his four previous outings, took a decisive advantage but in the end he was praying for the line. *(op 7-1)*
Ball Games, dropped in at the start, made up many lengths on the run-in and would have made it with a bit further to go. *(op 8-1)*
Star Trooper(IRE) went in pursuit of the winner but was just found lacking in the final dash to the line. *(op 4-1)*
Peter's Imp(IRE) likes it here but the ground had turned against him. *(op 6-1 tchd 9-2)*

593 STANLEY LEISURE BEGINNERS' CHASE (14 fncs) 2m 5f 110y
3:35 (3:35) (Class 4) 5-Y-0+ **£4,589** (£1,412; £706; £353)

Form RPR

1-22 **1** **Pebble Bay**[12] 413 10-11-2 .... DElsworth 102+
(Mrs S J Smith) *mde all: hrd rdn fnl f: hld on towards fin* **11/8**[1]

060- **2** *1¼* **Avitta (IRE)**[46] 4837 6-10-9 .... SThomas 93+
(Miss Venetia Williams) *chsd ldrs: wnt 2nd 9th: cl up whn mstke next: styd on run-in: nt qckn last 150yds* **5/1**[3]

F20- **3** *2* **Oliverjohn (IRE)**[38] 4966 8-10-13 97 .... PBuchanan(3) 97
(Miss Lucinda V Russell) *chsd ldrs: kpt on same pce run-in* **14/1**

23/6 **4** *15* **Mounthooley**[19] 301 9-11-2 .... PRobson 82
(B Mactaggart) *in tch: effrt after 8th: 4th and one pce whn mstke 2 out: hung rt and wknd fnl 2f* **20/1**

21 **5** *2½* **Bergerac (NZ)**[5] 495 7-11-2 .... HOliver 79
(R C Guest) *hld up in rr: hit 8th: effrt 10th: nvr nr ldrs* **9/4**[2]

-P04 **6** *5* **Win Alot**[2] 548 7-10-13 71 .... ACCoyle(3) 75+
(M C Chapman) *chsd ldrs: wknd 2 out* **22/1**

-553 **7** *1½* **Nomadic Blaze**[2] 550 8-10-13 .... (p) LMcGrath(3) 74+
(P G Atkinson) *chsd ldrs: mstke 6th: sn outpcd: bhd fr 11th* **12/1**

8 *10* **Working Class Hero**[43] 6-11-2 .... GLee 63
(J M Jefferson) *a last: lost tch 9th* **25/1**

5m 19.4s (-11.10) **Going Correction** -0.25s/f (Good) **8** Ran SP% **116.9**
Speed ratings: **110,109,108,103,102 100,100,96** CSF £9.01 TOTE £2.40: £1.10, £1.90, £2.60; EX 9.90.
Owner M F Spence **Bred** Miss Rhona Brewis **Trained** High Eldwick, W Yorks

FOCUS
An ordinary beginners' chase and a decent winning time for the grade. The form looks sound enough rated through third and sixth.

NOTEBOOK
Pebble Bay jumped like an old hand and showed a very willing attitude but at the line there was nothing to spare. *(op 7-4)*
Avitta(IRE), knocked by by a blunder at the ditch four out, really put her head down and battled on the run-in but in the winner she was up against one equally determined. *(op 4-1 tchd 11-2)*
Oliverjohn(IRE), with the visor left off, ran out of his skin and deserves to pick up a maiden chase.
Mounthooley, who has clearly has had his problems, was making his chasing debut at the age of nine. Tapped for toe when clouting the second last, he hung right on the run-in as if something may have been hurting him. *(op 16-1)*
Bergerac(NZ), making his chasing debut on totally different ground, never got competitive. He can surely do a lot better than this. *(op 2-1 tchd 5-2)*

594 HOLBECK GHYLL COUNTRY HOUSE HOTEL AND RESTAURANT MAIDEN HUNTERS' CHASE (FOR THE FRASER CUP) (18 fncs) 3m 2f
4:10 (4:10) (Class 6) 5-Y-0+ **£1,495** (£460; £230; £115)

Form RPR

24-0 **1** **Buddy Girie**[16] 12-11-7 .... MrPCornforth(7) 84+
(P Cornforth) *hdwy to chse ldrs 9th: wnt 2nd 4 out: barged through on inner to ld over a f out: rdn out* **4/1**[2]

30P- **2** *5* **Lady Lambrini**[15] 5-10-7 .... TMessenger(7) 65
(Mrs L Williamson) *w ldrs: led 6th: mstke 12th: pushed wd and hdd over 1f out: no ex* **9/2**[3]

5 **3** *3* **The Unamed Man**[18] 313 9-11-7 .... MrWHill(7) 76
(J Groucott) *chsd ldrs: lost pl 7th: hdwy 4 out: styd on wl fnl 2f* **9/1**

4 *2* **Oso Tilley**[30] 6-11-0 .... MissJFoster(7) 68+
(P Grindrod) *hdwy to chse ldrs 7th: one pce fr 3 out: kpt on towards fin* **14/1**

/3F- **5** *25* **Farington Lodge (IRE)**[82] 4262 7-11-7 .... MrNSSaville(7) 49
(Niall Saville) *hld up in rr: gd hdwy 13th: wnt 3rd 2 out: wknd run-in* **7/2**[1]

/0U- **6** *13* **Barrons Pike**[49] 4809 6-11-11 .... MJMcAlister(3) 36
(B Storey) *chsd ldrs: wknd 13th* **14/1**

42-P **7** *dist* **Mollycarrs Gambul**[24] 204 6-11-2 .... MrGBrewer(5) —
(Miss Sarah Robinson) *led to 6th: chsd ldrs: wknd 4 out: sn bhd: t.o* **4/1**[2]

35-U **P** **Orleans (IRE)**[28] 151 10-11-7 .... (b) MrSimonRobinson(7) —
(S J Robinson) *virtually ref to r: p.u after 100yds* **33/1**

065/ **P** **Planet Ireland (IRE)**[8] 13-11-7 .... MrCGillon(7) —
(Mrs J L Wight) *prom: wknd 12th: t.o whn p.u after 14th* **80/1**

0/0- **U** **Beachcomber**[29] 10-11-7 .... MrAWadlow(7) —
(J Groucott) *chsd ldrs: weakaning whn blnd bdly and uns rdr 14th* **20/1**

0/P- **U** **Mystic Native (IRE)**[2] 12-11-9 59 .... WPKavanagh(5) —
(David Pearson) *mstkes: sn bhd: t.o whn blnd and uns rdr 8th* **50/1**

/P-0 **U** **Mr Cooney (IRE)**[18] 322 11-11-7 .... MrSClements(7) —
(J Clements, Ire) *nt fluent: bhd: hdwy 13th: 4th and styng on whn blnd bdly and uns rdr 4 out* **33/1**

6m 41.0s (0.40) **Going Correction** -0.25s/f (Good)
WFA 5 from 6yo+ 7lb **12** Ran SP% **117.6**
Speed ratings: **89,87,86,85,78 74,**—,—,—,— —,— CSF £21.73 TOTE £5.40: £2.00, £1.70, £3.50; EX 31.10.
Owner J Cornforth **Bred** R W Swiers **Trained** Knaresborough, N Yorks

FOCUS
A modest time, even for a maiden hunter chase, and rated cautiously through the third..

NOTEBOOK
Buddy Girie, runner-up in this race two years ago, has been in good form in points. Stalking the leader, his rider took his life in his hands barging his way through on the inner but the Stewards were in a benevolent mood. *(op 7-2 tchd 9-2)*
Lady Lambrini, off the mark in a point two weeks ago, took them along but was booked for second spot when the winner went up her inside at the elbow instead of coming round her. *(op 9-1 tchd 4-1)*
The Unamed Man, who staged a revival at Ludlow, stayed on after getting badly outpaced and was hauling the first two back at the line. *(op 8-1 tchd 10-1)*
Oso Tilley, making her debut over regulation fences, was never far away. She was keeping on in relentless fashion at the death and looks a real stayer. *(op 16-1)*
Farington Lodge(IRE), absent since falling at Catterick in March, sat way off the pace. He worked his way into a modest third at the second last fence, but he had done his running by then and faded noticeably on the flat. *(op 4-1 tchd 10-3)*
Mollycarrs Gambul stopped to nothing four out and the ground was not the sole reason. *(op 9-4)*

595 TOTESPORT.COM CONDITIONAL JOCKEYS' H'CAP HURDLE (12 hdls) 3m 2f
4:45 (4:45) (Class 4) (0-110,108) 4-Y-0+ **£4,563** (£1,404; £702; £351)

Form RPR

2/-0 **1** **Brackney Boy (IRE)**[23] 215 11-10-3 **85** .... NPMulholland 86
(I A Duncan, Ire) *hld up: outpcd 8th: hdwy 2 out: styd on to ld last 100yds* **8/1**

3-13 **2** *1¼* **Lanzlo (FR)**[5] 499 8-10-13 **105** .... MMcAvoy(10) 106+
(James Moffatt) *hld up in rr: hdwy 9th: hit 2 out: wnt 2nd between last 2: led 1f out: sn hdd and no ex* **5/1**[2]

25 **3** *5* **Mary Macs Lad (IRE)**[2] 545 6-10-1 **83** .... (p) JamesDavies 79+
(John G Carr, Ire) *a wl in tch: outpcd 3 out: styd on run-in* **7/1**

44-0 **4** *1½* **Caesar's Palace (GER)**[19] 304 8-10-11 **98** .... (p) PJMcDonald(5) 93+
(Miss Lucinda V Russell) *w ldr: outpcd and lost pl 9th: detached 3 out: poor 6th last: fin wl* **11/2**[3]

P/6- **5** ¾ **Old Rolla (IRE)**[23] 7-10-2 **84** DCCostello 78+
(Miss S E Forster) *t.k.h: trckd ldrs: led 6th: qcknd next: hdd 1f out: fdd* **9/2**[1]

1P1 **6** 7 **Pequenita**[5] [497] 5-11-6 **105** (p) PCO'Neill[(3)] 93+
(R C Guest) *mde most to 6th: wknd between last 2* **13/2**

P2-0 **7** 22 **Signed And Dated (USA)**[19] [306] 6-10-0 **82** oh1 (p) ONelmes 61+
(Mrs E Slack) *chsd ldrs: outpcd whn bdly hmpd 2 out: sn bhd: eased run-in* **16/1**

2-00 **P** **Fishki's Lad**[15] [372] 10-11-12 **108** PRobson —
(E W Tuer) *chsd ldrs: lost pl 9th: bhd whn p.u bef 2 out* **14/1**

6 **F** **Fakima (IRE)**[17] [334] 7-10-13 **95** ATinkler —
(John G Carr, Ire) *in rr: drvn along and hdwy 8th: prom 3rd and clsng whn fell 2 out* **5/1**[2]

6m 27.4s (9.40) **Going Correction** -0.325s/f (Good) **9** Ran SP% **116.4**
Speed ratings: **72,71,70,69,69 67,60,—,—** CSF £48.56 CT £297.17 TOTE £14.10: £4.70, £1.80, £2.30; EX 125.50.
Owner Dr Stephen Sinclair **Bred** Graham Duncan **Trained** Crumlin, Co Antrim

FOCUS
A modest contest that could be rated higher but probably not strong form and no gallop at all to halfway, resulting in a pedestrian winning time for the grade.

NOTEBOOK
Brackney Boy(IRE) seemed to get a second wind and he stayed on really well to pull off what had looked an unlikely victory. *(op 15-2)*
Lanzlo(FR), 7lb higher than his Hexham win, benefited from his rider's 10lb claim. He worked hard to get his head in front only be to be run out of it near the line. *(op 6-1)*
Mary Macs Lad(IRE), tried in cheekpieces this time, was persuaded to put her best foot forward when it was virtually all over. *(op 13-2)*
Caesar's Palace(GER) lost interest completely and was out with the washing until sprinting up the run-in. He seemed to finish twice as fast as the three in front of him at the line. He clearly has a mind of his own. *(op 6-1)*
Old Rolla(IRE), who has won his last four starts in points, took a keen hold. Sent on and stepping up the pace, in the end he did not truly see it out. A much stronger gallop and more patient tactics would have suited him better and with him it is a case of the softer the ground the better. *(tchd 11-2)*
Pequenita, who won over fences on totally different ground here five days earlier, was able to race from a 5lb lower mark but, even in a race run at a very steady pace to halfway, her stamina still seemed to give out. *(op 5-1 tchd 7-1 in places)*
Fishki's Lad *Official explanation: trainer said gelding pulled up lame (op 9-2)*
Fakima(IRE) was poised to take a serious hand in the finish when crashing out. *(op 9-2)*

596 MILLER HOWE HOTEL FOUR YEARS OLD NOVICES' HURDLE (8 hdls) 2m 1f 110y

5:15 (5:15) (Class 4) 4-Y-O **£3,519** (£1,082; £541; £270)

Form RPR

0-11 **1** **Flintoff (USA)**[5] [500] 4-11-5 100 PCO'Neill[(7)] 105+
(R C Guest) *led to 2nd: w ldrs: pushed along 5th: wnt 2nd between last 2: styd on run-in: led nr fin* **5/4**[1]

436- **2** nk **Smart Boy Prince (IRE)**[23] [4826] 4-10-12 95 DRDennis 91+
(C Smith) *led 2nd: hit 2 out: hdd nr fin* **12/1**

40-2 **3** 3 **Moldavia (GER)**[20] [279] 4-10-2 95 ACCoyle[(3)] 80
(M C Chapman) *hld up: stdy hdwy 5th: wnt 3rd last: kpt on same pce* **7/1**[3]

1-46 **4** 3½ **Mohawk Star (IRE)**[20] [279] 4-11-5 110 (b) SThomas 90
(Miss Venetia Williams) *chsd ldrs: one pce between last 2* **9/2**[2]

52P- **5** 1 **Aston Lad**[50] [4782] 4-10-12 103 FKeniry 83+
(M D Hammond) *in tch: effrt 3 out: one pce fr next* **9/2**[2]

643- **6** hd **Schinken Otto (IRE)**[29] [3461] 4-10-12 80 GLee 82
(J M Jefferson) *stdd s: hld up in rr: hdwy 5th: kpt on fr 2 out: nvr nrr* **20/1**

- **7** 24 **Lytham (IRE)**[18] 4-10-12 RGarritty 64+
(J J Quinn) *jnd ldrs 5th: upsides 2 out: 4th and wkng whn sn hmpd: fdd bdly sn after* **14/1**

-6 **8** 19 **Tullyhappy Lad (IRE)**[23] [210] 4-10-12 RJohnson 39
(I A Duncan, Ire) *in tch: wkng whn mstke 3 out: sn eased* **20/1**

05-P **9** 8 **Starbright**[19] [301] 4-10-5 68 MrJARichardson[(7)] 31
(W G Young) *t.k.h: trckd ldrs: lost pl 5th: t.o 3 out* **100/1**

0 **10** 1 **Air Of Supremacy (IRE)**[11] [418] 4-10-12 RMcGrath 30
(Mrs K Walton) *chsd ldrs: lost pl and reminders 4th: t.o 3 out* **25/1**

4m 8.90s (-6.80) **Going Correction** -0.325s/f (Good) **10** Ran SP% **122.0**
Speed ratings: **102,101,100,98,98 98,87,79,75,75** CSF £18.49 TOTE £2.10: £1.20, £3.30, £1.90; EX 31.80 Place 6 £79.11, Place 5 £33.11.
Owner Andrew Flintoff & Paul Beck **Bred** Mill Ridge Farm Ltd & Jamm Ltd **Trained** Brancepeth, Co Durham
■ Stewards' Enquiry : P C O'NeillR two-day ban: careless riding (Jun 11+1)

FOCUS
A modest novice event but the form looks reasonable with the placed horses close to their marks.

NOTEBOOK
Flintoff(USA), helped by his rider's 10lb claim, had to dig deep on this different ground and deserved full marks for this narrow victory. He should make a good-class novice chaser at the backend. *(op 7-4 tchd 15-8)*
Smart Boy Prince(IRE), biding his time in front, battled hard but had to give best near the line.
Moldavia(GER), ridden to stay the trip, moved up on to the heels of the first two at the final flight but she was never going to find sufficient to go head-to-head with them. *(op 8-1)*
Mohawk Star(IRE), with the blinkers back on, ran a lot better but the ground had possibly dried out too much for him.
Aston Lad, pulled up close home when looking certain to score at Hexham, was back after seven weeks on the sidelines and was not at his very best. *(op 10-3)*
Schinken Otto(IRE), absent since January, has had a run on the level since. Dropped right out, he never entered the argument but at least he kept going all the way to the line. *(op 25-1)*
Lytham(IRE), rated 68 on the level, was on the retreat when knocked out of his stride by the winner soon after two out.
T/Plt: £81.10 to a £1 stake. Pool: £35,179.55. 316.65 winning tickets. T/Qpdt: £27.70 to a £1 stake. Pool: £1,764.40. 47.05 winning tickets. WG

597 - 600a (Foreign Racing) - See Raceform Interactive

550
HEXHAM (L-H)
Tuesday, May 31

OFFICIAL GOING: Firm (good to firm in places)
Wind: Light; half across

601 GG MEDIA AMATEUR RIDERS' NOVICES' H'CAP HURDLE (8 hdls) 2m 110y

6:35 (6:36) (Class 4) (0-95,85) 4-Y-O+ **£2,716** (£776; £388)

Form RPR

P-00 **1** **Casterflo**[19] [320] 6-10-10 **69** MissPRobson 70
(W S Colthard) *hld up: hdwy and prom after 3 out: led bef last: drvn out* **7/1**

00-0 **2** ¾ **Master Nimbus**[13] [415] 5-9-12 **64** MrTJO'Brien[(7)] 64
(J J Quinn) *hld up: hdwy bef 2 out: effrt and chsd wnr run in: r.o* **16/1**

00-6 **3** 3 **Qualitair Pleasure**[13] [415] 5-11-2 **82** PKinsella[(7)] 79
(J Hetherton) *chsd ldrs: effrt 2 out: kpt on same pce fr last* **6/1**[2]

0-02 **4** 1 **Reedsman (IRE)**[16] [363] 4-10-5 **73** (b) MissCMetcalfe[(5)] 65
(R C Guest) *hld up: hdwy 2 out: kpt on fr last: nrst fin* **8/1**

4-55 **5** 3 **Northern Flash**[24] [213] 11-10-9 **71** (v) MJMcAlister[(3)] 64
(J C Haynes) *a cl up: led briefly after 2 out: outpcd run in* **13/2**[3]

04-6 **6** 2½ **Mystic Glen**[9] [469] 6-10-10 **76** MrDSlattery[(7)] 67
(P D Niven) *hld up midfield: outpcd bef 2 out: kpt on fr last: no imp* **6/1**[2]

5-06 **7** 3 **Jamorin Dancer**[5] [520] 10-10-2 **68** (p) TMessenger[(7)] 56
(S G Chadwick) *keen: led to after 2 out: wknd bef last* **28/1**

P00- **8** 2 **Vesta Flame**[51] [4782] 4-9-8 **64** (p) MissFayeBramley[(7)] 46
(P T Midgley) *hld up: hdwy bef 2 out: wknd bef last* **100/1**

00-0 **9** 5 **Huxley (IRE)**[31] [133] 6-11-12 **85** (t) MrTGreenall 66
(M G Quinlan) *keen: hld up and bhd: stdy hdwy after 3 out: rdn and no imp fr next* **3/1**[1]

/P0- **10** 3½ **Teeno Rossi (IRE)**[107] [3824] 7-10-4 **70** ow3 (b[1]) MrDAFitzsimons[(7)] 47
(J K Magee, Ire) *chsd ldrs tl wknd bef 2 out* **50/1**

/0-P **11** 6 **Northern Rambler (IRE)**[33] [81] 8-10-12 **78** JReveley[(7)] 49
(K G Reveley) *midfield tl rdn and wknd qckly 3 out* **14/1**

6- **12** 11 **Tuscany Boy (IRE)**[40] [4943] 5-11-6 **79** MrBRHamilton 42+
(C A McBratney, Ire) *in tch tl lost pl 2nd: struggling whn blnd 3 out* **16/1**

0-00 **F** **Neven**[20] [306] 6-11-2 **80** (tp) WPKavanagh[(5)] —
(Miss Lucinda V Russell) *hld up: fell 4th* **12/1**

4m 8.80s (-6.40) **Going Correction** -0.75s/f (Firm)
WFA 4 from 5yo+ 4lb **13** Ran SP% **123.0**
Speed ratings: **85,84,83,82,81 79,78,77,75,73 70,65,—** CSF £113.36 CT £725.12 TOTE £9.70: £3.00, £7.70, £3.10; EX 203.50.
Owner Alex and Janet Card **Bred** T L Robson **Trained** Selkirk, Borders

FOCUS
A low-grade event in which the pace was only fair and, not surprisingly a moderate winning time for the grade. A race that is unlikely to throw up many winners.

NOTEBOOK
Casterflo, from a stable with a good record at this course this term, showed her first worthwhile form to win a bad race but, given her record, would not be one to lump on next time.*Official explanation: trainer had no explanation for the improved form shown other than that mare had jumped a lot better on this occasion (op 9-1)*
Master Nimbus, a poor maiden, showed his first worthwhile form in a very weak event and, although in capable hands, would not be one to go in head down for in anything but the worst company next time. *(op 25-1)*
Qualitair Pleasure, a dual bumper winner, ran his best race over hurdles and, although not one for maximum faith, left the impression that the step up to two and a half miles may be in her favour. *(op 8-1)*
Reedsman(IRE), has yet to win but is from a stable in good form and again ran creditably. He too looks worth a try over further but his record suggests he is one to tread carefully with. *(op 13-2 tchd 9-1)*
Northern Flash, an inconsistent chaser with one win from 73 career starts, was not disgraced returned to hurdles but did not really shape as though one to be interested in. *(op 7-1 tchd 15-2)*
Mystic Glen left the impression that the return to further would be in her favour but she is not very consistent and the fact that she has yet to win a race has to be a worry. *(op 11-2)*
Huxley(IRE), who had shown clear signs of ability over hurdles, attracted plenty of support but failed to settle and was disappointing. A sharper course may help but he is one to tread carefully with. *(tchd 9-2)*

602 SKY BET PRESS RED TO BET MAIDEN HURDLE (8 hdls) 2m 110y

7:05 (7:06) (Class 4) 4-Y-O+ **£3,507** (£1,002; £501)

Form RPR

0-4 **1** **Longdale**[24] [210] 7-11-2 ADempsey 92+
(M Todhunter) *hld up: smooth hdwy 3 out: led whn mstke last: drvn out* **20/1**

5-32 **2** 1¼ **Sterling Guarantee (USA)**[13] [415] 7-10-9 98 CDSharkey[(7)] 90+
(N Wilson) *keen: prom: outpcd whn pckd 2 out: rallied to chse wnr last: kpt on run in* **7/2**[3]

0-20 **3** 9 **Magico (NZ)**[23] [247] 7-10-13 100 LMcGrath[(3)] 80
(R C Guest) *chsd ldrs tl rdn and outpcd between last two: kpt on fr last: no imp* **5/4**[1]

600/ **4** 2 **Now And Again**[7] [4431] 6-10-13 77 LVickers[(3)] 79+
(I W McInnes) *set stdy pce: hdd after 2 out: outpcd bef last* **33/1**

PP-0 **5** 1½ **Crofton Arch**[24] [210] 5-10-13 PWhelan[(3)] 77
(M A Barnes) *cl up: led briefly 2 out: wknd appr last* **100/1**

32-0 **6** 2½ **Quarry Island (IRE)**[21] [59] 4-10-5 96 ADobbin 63
(M Todhunter) *keen: prom tl rdn and wknd bef last* **5/2**[2]

0 **7** 3 **Si Anthony (FR)**[17] [351] 5-10-13 KJMercer[(3)] 71
(Ferdy Murphy) *bhd tl styd on fr 2 out: n.d* **20/1**

00 **8** 2½ **Penteli**[12] [418] 5-10-6 MrTGreenall[(3)] 62
(C Grant) *in tch to 1/2-way: sn lost pl* **20/1**

000/ **9** 10 **Never Forget Bowie**[21] [620] 9-11-2 58 KRenwick 59
(R Allan) *in tch tl wknd bef 2 out* **50/1**

PO-P **10** 3½ **Flashy Filly**[34] [59] 5-10-2 MJMcAlister[(7)] 48
(J C Haynes) *a bhd* **100/1**

11 8 **Shamore**[17] 6-10-9 DElsworth 40
(C Grant) *bhd: no ch fr 1/2-way* **40/1**

0- **P** **Mary Chan**[38] [4981] 6-10-2 BenOrde-Powlett[(7)] —
(C W Fairhurst) *a bhd: t.o whn p.u bef last* **66/1**

0 **P** **Galahad (FR)**[12] [418] 4-10-12 RMcGrath —
(B Storey) *in tch to 1/2-way: sn struggling: t.o whn p.u bef last* **100/1**

4m 16.3s (1.10) **Going Correction** -0.75s/f (Firm)
WFA 4 from 5yo+ 4lb **13** Ran SP% **121.3**
Speed ratings: **67,66,62,61,60 59,57,56,52,50 46,—,—** CSF £87.51 TOTE £21.90: £3.60, £1.20, £1.10; EX 60.50.
Owner David Curr **Bred** David Curr **Trained** Orton, Cumbria

FOCUS
An uncompetitive event in which the slow pace resulted in the pedestrian winning time and this bare form looks an unreliable guide.

NOTEBOOK
Longdale ◆ fully confirmed the previous bit of course and distance promise shown to win an uncompetitive event with more in hand than the winning margin suggests. He is capable of better and will be interesting in ordinary handicaps. *(op 14-1)*
Sterling Guarantee(USA) is an exposed maiden but is a fairly reliable sort who looks a good guide to the worth of this form. However, he is likely to struggle against unexposed or progressive sorts in this grade. *(op 3-1 tchd 4-1)*
Magico(NZ), from an in-form stable, has failed to get home on his two previous attempts over two and a half miles but left the impression that the return to that trip would suit. He may not be one to place maximum faith in. *(op 9-4)*
Now And Again, a poor Flat maiden, looks flattered by his proximity in this slowly-run race and is likely to continue to look vulnerable in this grade. *(op 25-1)*
Crofton Arch, who faced a stiff task at the weights is likely to fare better in very modest handicap company.

Quarry Island(IRE) looked to have fair prospects in this event but, although failing to settle, was most disappointing and is one to have reservations about. *(tchd 9-4)*

603 MENCAP NEWCASTLE NOVICES' H'CAP HURDLE (10 hdls) 2m 4f 110y
7:35 (7:35) (Class 4) (0-105,95) 4-Y-0+ **£3,496** (£999; £499)

Form				RPR
400-	**1**		**Ding Dong Belle**[188] [2428] 6-10-3 **82** ... THalliday(10)	83+
			(Mrs S J Smith) *cl up: chal 4 out: led last: kpt on gamely* **7/2**[2]	
00/P	**2**	½	**Weldman**[13] [406] 6-10-4 **73** ... RMcGrath	73
			(K G Reveley) *hld up: hdwy 3 out: effrt and ev ch run in: kpt on: hld towards fin* **16/1**	
0-00	**3**	1	**Agnese**[13] [415] 5-10-12 **81** ... WMarston	80
			(G M Moore) *cl up: led 5th to last: one pce* **5/2**[1]	
-544	**4**	4	**Sconced (USA)**[16] [365] 10-11-1 **84** ...(b) HOliver	79
			(R C Guest) *led to 5th: outpcd after next: no imp tl styd on fr last* **9/2**[3]	
60/P	**5**	2½	**Loi De Martiale (IRE)**[24] [212] 7-11-5 **88** ...(b[1]) GLee	80
			(J M Jefferson) *hld up in tch: heawday bef 4 out: rdn and outpcd bef 2 out: n.d after* **7/1**	
P0-5	**6**	dist	**One Of Them**[3] [551] 6-10-11 **83** ... PWhelan(3)	60
			(M A Barnes) *cl up tl wknd bef 2 out* **5/1**	
00P-	**P**		**Maybe She Will**[177] [2650] 7-10-5 **74** ... KRenwick	—
			(D W Whillans) *chsd ldrs to 1/2-way: sn lost pl: t.o whn p.u bef 2 out* **10/1**	

5m 1.50s (-8.10) **Going Correction** -0.75s/f (Firm) 7 Ran SP% **113.1**
Speed ratings: **85,84,84,82,81** —,— CSF £48.81 CT £161.62 TOTE £4.80: £2.10, £10.20; EX 100.40.
Owner Mrs Susan McDonald **Bred** Mrs Susan McDonald **Trained** High Eldwick, W Yorks

FOCUS
A low-grade handicap run at an ordinary gallop and a moderate winning time for the grade. The form, rated through winner and third, looks reasonable on paper.

NOTEBOOK
Ding Dong Belle, down in trip and on firm ground for the first time, showed the right attitude to win a modest event. She should stay three miles and, as she will not be going up too much for this, may be able to win a similar event. *(op 3-1)*
Weldman ran his best race over hurdles and, although unable to match the winner's tenacity, did enough to suggest a similar race can be found. A better end to end gallop may have suited. *(op 14-1)*
Agnese, a fast-ground bumper winner, had the run of the race and ran creditably with the cheekpieces left off, but her record suggests she is far from certain to reproduce this next time. *(op 9-2 tchd 9-4)*
Sconced(USA), who has yet to win over hurdles, was not totally disgraced in terms of form and will be suited by a stiffer test but does not look one to place too much faith in. *(op 9-4)*
Loi De Martiale(IRE) was not disgraced tried in blinkers but, although a stiffer test of stamina may have suited, will have to show more before he is worth a bet. *(tchd 15-2)*
One Of Them had shown a bit of promise at this course on his previous start but underlined his inconsistency with a poor effort over this longer trip (beaten before stamina became an issue) and he remains one to tread carefully with. *(op 11-2)*

604 SWINBURNE HORTICULTURAL SERVICES LTD BEGINNERS' CHASE (12 fncs) 2m 110y
8:10 (8:11) (Class 4) 5-Y-0+ **£3,731** (£1,148; £574; £287)

Form				RPR
23-3	**1**		**Cumbrian Knight (IRE)**[11] [148] 7-11-0 105 ... GLee	97+
			(J M Jefferson) *chsd ldrs: effrt and led last: rdn out* **3/1**[2]	
4-63	**2**	1	**Humid Climate**[17] [344] 5-10-9 ... PWhelan(3)	94
			(R A Fahey) *cl up: led 3 out to last: one pce run in* **3/1**[2]	
56-3	**3**	4	**Flame Phoenix (USA)**[34] [56] 6-11-0 ... JMMaguire	94+
			(D McCain) *sn chsng ldrs: ev ch 3 out: outpcd bef last* **7/4**[1]	
4-35	**4**	5	**Snooty Eskimo (IRE)**[21] [278] 13-10-10 78 ow3 ... MrHNorton(7)	90
			(W T Reed) *mde most to 3 out: outpcd between last two* **25/1**	
050/	**5**	4	**Finest Of Men**[16] 9-10-7 ... BenOrde-Powlett(7)	83
			(J B Walton) *in tch: mstke 2nd: outpcd 4 out: no imp fr next* **28/1**	
30-5	**6**	1	**Classic Calvados (FR)**[8] [9] 6-11-0 ... JimCrowley	82
			(P D Niven) *hld up: struggling 4 out: sn btn* **9/1**	
00	**U**		**Ballyboe Boy (IRE)**[31] [122] 6-11-0 84 ...(b) HOliver	—
			(R C Guest) *hmpd and uns rdr s* **8/1**[3]	
5P-P	**L**		**Gunson Hight**[9] 8-10-9 65 ...(bt[1]) DMcGann(5)	—
			(J L Gledson) *w.r.s: tk no part* **66/1**	

4m 3.50s (-5.60) **Going Correction** -0.475s/f (Good)
WFA 5 from 6yo+ 2lb 8 Ran SP% **116.3**
Speed ratings: **94,93,91,89,87 86**,—,— CSF £12.96 TOTE £3.80: £1.10, £2.10, £1.10; EX 14.70.
Owner J M Jefferson **Bred** John P A Kenny **Trained** Norton, N Yorks

FOCUS
Another uncompetitive race and an ordinary gallop resulting in a modest winning time. It could be rated higher but is limited by the steady pace.

NOTEBOOK
Cumbrian Knight(IRE), back over fences, turned in an improved effort to win an ordinary event and, given the fluency of this win, may be capable of better in ordinary handicaps. *(op 5-2)*
Humid Climate has not been very consistent since winning his maiden on the Flat, but showed enough on only this second start over fences to suggest a small race can be found. *(op 4-1 tchd 9-2)*
Flame Phoenix(USA), back on a sound surface, fared much better than on his chase debut but, although a stiffer test may help, is not going to be as good in this sphere as over hurdles on the evidence so far. *(op 9-4 tchd 5-2 and 13-8)*
Snooty Eskimo(IRE) had a stiff task at the weights but was not disgraced having enjoyed the run of the race and may fare better back in modest handicap company. *(op 14-1)*
Finest Of Men is now qualified for a handicap mark and, although only modest, may do better in that type of event when the emphasis is more on stamina. *(op 25-1)*
Classic Calvados(FR), an ordinary maiden hurdler, did not really show enough on this chase debut *to suggest he is of immediate interest over the larger obstacles.Official explanation: jockey said gelding had breathing problem (op 15-2 tchd 11-1)*

605 SHS LTD H'CAP CHASE (15 fncs) 2m 4f 110y
8:40 (8:41) (Class 4) (0-105,102) 5-Y-0+ **£3,750** (£1,154; £577; £288)

Form				RPR
31-4	**1**		**Panmure (IRE)**[19] [321] 9-11-6 **94** ... JimCrowley	100+
			(P D Niven) *chsd ldrs: effrt 3 out: led bef last: r.o wl* **5/1**[3]	
55-6	**2**	1	**Karo De Vindecy (FR)**[13] [416] 7-10-8 **82** ...(t) GLee	86
			(M D Hammond) *keen: led 2nd to bef last: kpt on run in* **4/1**[2]	
06-5	**3**	3½	**Mr Laggan**[13] [416] 10-9-7 **74** oh4 ...(p) MJMcAlister(7)	75
			(Miss Kate Milligan) *chsd ldrs: effrt and ev ch 3 out: one pce bef last* **22/1**	
-061	**4**	1½	**Helvetius**[5] [522] 9-12-0 **102** 7ex ... AThornton	101
			(W T Reed) *led to 2nd: cl up: outpcd after 4 out: rallied whn mstke last: no imp* **11/2**	
F-63	**5**	2	**Beaugency (NZ)**[13] [414] 7-11-4 **95** ... LMcGrath(3)	93+
			(R C Guest) *hld up: hdwy after 4 out: effrt 2 out: sn no imp* **10/1**	
5-33	**6**	17	**Vandante (IRE)**[21] [288] 9-10-10 **84** ... TDoyle	70+
			(R Lee) *keen: chsd ldrs: mstke and lost pl 9th: struggling fr 4 out* **7/4**[1]	
02-4	**7**	24	**Guilsborough Gorse**[16] [368] 10-11-5 **100** ... MrMWalford(7)	56
			(T D Walford) *hld up: outpcd bef 4 out: n.d* **10/1**	

4m 59.1s (-12.30) **Going Correction** -0.475s/f (Good) 7 Ran SP% **110.9**
Speed ratings: **104,103,102,101,100 94,85** CSF £24.02 CT £381.05 TOTE £6.70: £2.10, £4.10; EX 29.40.
Owner The Poppet Partnership **Bred** J J King **Trained** Barton-le-Street, N Yorks

FOCUS
A moderate handicap with no progressive sorts, but a good gallop and this form should stand up at a similar level.

NOTEBOOK
Panmure(IRE) seems suited by this trip on a sound surface and appreciated the decent gallop. His jumping was sound and he may be able to win again in ordinary company this summer. *(op 4-1)*
Karo De Vindecy(FR) ◆, a dual two mile five winner at Sedgefield last summer, ran his best race since and looks better than the bare form given he failed to settle and set a decent gallop. He is one a fair mark and is one to keep an eye on. *(op 7-1)*
Mr Laggan is an inconsistent chaser who bettered his previous efforts. He is capable of winning a small race from this mark but his recent record suggests he is not one to place maximum faith in. *(op 20-1 tchd 25-1)*
Helvetius was found out from this 7lb higher mark in a race where he was not allowed to dominate. He is likely to remain vulnerable to progressive or well handicapped types from this mark. *(op 9-2)*
Beaugency(NZ), from a stable in tremendous fettle, was far from disgraced on this chasing debut and appeals as the type to keep an eye on when upped to three miles. *(op 8-1)*
Vandante(IRE) has not won since August 2002 and, although coming here after a solid effort and *having conditions to suit, showed just why he is not the best betting proposition around.Official explanation: trainer said gelding is better suited by a flat track (op 5-2 tchd 6-4)*
Guilsborough Gorse had conditions to suit but was disappointing and looks one to tread carefully with at present. *(op 11-2)*

606 GG-BET.COM BETTING EXCHANGE H'CAP HURDLE (12 hdls) 3m
9:10 (9:10) (Class 4) (0-100,104) 4-Y-0+ **£2,590** (£740; £370)

Form				RPR
0-0F	**1**		**Pikestaff (USA)**[13] [417] 7-10-12 **83** ...(t) GLee	94+
			(M A Barnes) *cl up: led after 3 out: easily* **7/4**[1]	
0051	**2**	2½	**In Good Faith**[7] [480] 13-10-6 **84** 7ex ... PKinsella(7)	85
			(R E Barr) *hld up: hdwy 2 out: kpt on fr last: tk 2nd cl home* **9/2**[2]	
0-64	**3**	nk	**End Of An Error**[20] [304] 6-10-9 **83** ... ONelmes(3)	84
			(Mrs E Slack) *prom: chsd wnr bef 2 out: nt fluent last: kpt on run in* **7/4**[1]	
0P0-	**4**	21	**Sea Laughter (IRE)**[39] [4967] 7-11-2 **90** ... KJMercer(3)	70
			(J N R Billinge) *prom tl wknd bef 2 out* **9/1**[3]	
3/-P	**P**		**Golden Hawk (USA)**[19] [319] 10-10-2 **73** ... KJohnson	—
			(R M Clark) *plld hrd: led: clr after 4th: hdd & wknd after 3 out: sn btn: t.o whn p.u bef last* **14/1**	

5m 55.4s (-22.30) **Going Correction** -0.75s/f (Firm) 5 Ran SP% **107.6**
Speed ratings: **107,106,106,99**,— CSF £9.31 TOTE £2.80: £1.10, £2.60; EX 13.40 Place 6 £81.46, Place 5 £23.79.
Owner J M Carlyle **Bred** Juddmonte Farms **Trained** Farlam, Cumbria
■ Stewards' Enquiry : K J Mercer caution: used whip when out of contention

FOCUS
An uncompetitive race in which the gallop increased from the fourth flight. The winner is value for further.

NOTEBOOK
Pikestaff(USA), a course and distance winner on a sound surface last October, ran his best race since and won with a good deal in hand. He is capable of winning more races but his inconsistency means he is not the best betting proposition. *(tchd 11-8 and 15-8)*
In Good Faith, who returned to his best at Sedgefield last time, ran to a similar level over this longer trip and under his penalty, and should continue to give a good account on his favoured fast ground this summer. *(op 7-2)*
End Of An Error ran creditably but her losing run that stretches back to 2003 means she is not really one to be taking skinny odds about. *(op 5-2)*
Sea Laughter(IRE) has not progressed since his encouraging hurdles debut and, although more cut in the ground may help, he remains one to tread carefully with. *(op 15-2)*
Golden Hawk(USA) was again well beaten on this second start after a very lengthy absence and looks anything but straightforward. *(op 12-1 tchd 11-1)*
T/Plt: £179.70 to a £1 stake. Pool: £44,898.95. 182.35 winning tickets. T/Qpdt: £40.80 to a £1 stake. Pool: £3,433.70. 62.20 winning tickets. RY

607 - 610a (Foreign Racing) - See Raceform Interactive

569 UTTOXETER (L-H)
Thursday, June 2

OFFICIAL GOING: Soft changing to good to soft (soft in places) after race 2 (7.05)
Rain on the already watered ground resulted in a large number of withdrawals during the meeting. Third fence back straight omitted both chases.
Wind: moderate, against Weather: overcast

611 BET365 08000 322 365 MAIDEN HURDLE (14 hdls) 3m
6:30 (6:33) (Class 4) 4-Y-0+ **£2,625** (£750; £375)

Form				RPR
0-32	**1**		**Killonemoonlight (IRE)**[9] [487] 6-10-9 78 ... TDoyle	107+
			(D R Stoddart) *chsd ldrs: led 3 out: sn clr* **13/2**[3]	
OP/	**2**	16	**Boobee (IRE)**[54] 9-11-2 ... ChristianWilliams	90
			(Evan Williams) *led: hdd and hit 3 out: sn wknd* **7/2**[2]	
P20-	**3**	13	**Savannah Bay**[55] [4767] 6-11-2 120 ...(b) PJBrennan	80+
			(P J Hobbs) *chsd ldr: rdn after 4 out: wknd and blnd next: remote 3rd whn blnd last* **8/11**[1]	
PP-3	**4**	4	**Safe To Blush**[19] [359] 7-10-9 85 ... MBradburne	66
			(P A Pritchard) *mid-div: hdwy after 7th: wknd appr 4 out* **20/1**	
0-43	**5**	30	**Potts Of Magic**[24] [261] 6-11-2 87 ...(b[1]) RJohnson	43
			(R Lee) *chsd ldrs: rdn 7th: wknd bef next* **14/1**	
FP-0	**6**	18	**Selassie**[11] [458] 6-10-6 ... JKington(10)	25
			(M Scudamore) *hld up: rdn and bhd fr 7th* **66/1**	
4-35	**7**	11	**Pollensa Bay**[19] [358] 6-11-2 90 ... JCulloty	14
			(S A Brookshaw) *bhd fr 3rd* **16/1**	
00P/	**P**		**Deepritive**[775] [4641] 8-10-6 ... RHobson(3)	—
			(B D Leavy) *bhd fr 3rd: t.o whn p.u bef 4 out* **80/1**	
0-04	**P**		**Kingcombe Lane**[16] [394] 5-11-2 79 ... JPMcNamara	—
			(P W Hiatt) *hld up: rdn and wknd after 6th: t.o whn p.u bef 4 out* **66/1**	

5m 59.7s (-5.30) **Going Correction** -0.075s/f (Good) 9 Ran SP% **115.0**
Speed ratings: **105,99,95,94,84 78,74**,—,— CSF £29.26 TOTE £6.80: £1.40, £1.80, £1.10; EX 24.10.

Owner D R Stoddart **Bred** Sylvester Barrett **Trained** Adstone, Northants

FOCUS

A modest maiden run at an even pace and apart from the winner they finished very tired. The winner is value for half as much again and the race could rate higher.

NOTEBOOK

Killonemoonlight(IRE) ◆, who had been running well over shorter trips on faster ground, had won an Irish point in similar conditions and seemed to relish the stamina test. The further she went the better she travelled, and she galloped right away from her rivals in the straight. She is likely to be out before the Handicapper can re-assess her and, given similar conditions, would be a good thing even with a penalty. *(op 5-1)*

Boobee(IRE), a dual point winner on soft ground this spring, had made all on both occasions and attempted the same tactics on this return to hurdles, but was brushed aside by the winner and got very tired late on. However, he looks capable of winning a small race under Rules, be it over hurdles or fences. *(op 3-1 tchd 4-1)*

Savannah Bay, who had more than two stone in hand on official ratings, appeared to have every chance but does not appear to stay this sort of trip. He is also better on a sound surface so can be given a chance to prove he retains some of the ability that made him a Group-class stayer on the Flat. *(op 4-5 tchd 5-6, 10-11 in places)*

Safe To Blush has shown bits and pieces of form, but is only moderate and never really threatened. She will be better off in mares-only handicaps, possibly at shorter trips. *(op 25-1)*

Potts Of Magic, blinkered for the first time, was getting reminders with a circuit to go and never figured afterwards. *(tchd 16-1)*

612 FRIENDS OF ST. GILES HOSPICE NOVICES' H'CAP CHASE (16 fncs 2 omitted) 3m

7:05 (7:05) (Class 4) (0-105,100) 5-Y-0+ **£4,995** (£1,894)

Form — RPR

U6-1 **1** **Stack The Pack (IRE)**[21] 321 8-11-10 **98** .... JMMaguire 110+
(T R George) *led after 2nd: blnd 11th: lft wl clr 5 out: hit next: j. slowly last* **7/4**[2]

P4-0 **2** *20* **Luckycharm (FR)**[16] 398 6-10-2 **76** .... CLlewellyn 58
(R Dickin) *led: hdd after 2nd: chsd wnr to 9th: wknd appr 11th: lft remote 2nd 5 out* **7/1**

0-2 **B** **Assumetheposition (FR)**[8] 499 5-10-9 **92** .... (p) LMcGrath(3) —
(R C Guest) *hld up: hdwy 10th: cl 3rd whn b.d 5 out* **11/8**[1]

/5-0 **F** **Waynesworld (IRE)**[20] 334 7-10-13 **87** .... BJCrowley —
(M Scudamore) *prom: chsd wnr 9th: cl 2nd whn fell 5 out* **5/1**[3]

6m 37.9s (5.40) **Going Correction** -0.075s/f (Good)
WFA 5 from 6yo+ 6lb **4** Ran SP% **107.6**
Speed ratings: **88,81,—,—** CSF £11.42 TOTE £2.30; EX 17.50.

Owner Mrs Christine Davies **Bred** Dr J M McKelvey **Trained** Slad, Gloucs

FOCUS

A very moderate contest with the field decimated by withdrawals and halved by casualties, and a very slow time for the class.

NOTEBOOK

Stack The Pack(IRE), a winner at Perth on much faster ground, soon got to the front and had the race handed to him when his closest rival departed and brought down the favourite. He may have won anyway, but he made a couple of serious mistakes, looked quite tired in the straight and returned with a nasty cut on a hoof. He will appreciate a return to a sound surface. *(op 13-8 tchd 15-8 in a place)*

Luckycharm(FR) was well in arrears when handed second place five out, and merely completed in his own time. *(op 11-2)*

Waynesworld(IRE), returning to fences for the first time in over a year, having been absent for much of that time, was going well in the slipstream of the winner when making a complete mess of the fifth last and bringing down the favourite. He had jumped well enough to that point and may be capable of picking up a small race. *(tchd 9-2 and 11-2)*

Assumetheposition(FR), making his chasing debut, dived at the first but jumped well enough apart from that. He was going comfortably enough when given no chance by the fall of Waynesworld. He should be able to win races over fences if none the worse for this. *(tchd 9-2 and 11-2)*

613 MORGAN TIMBER AND BOARDS MARES' ONLY H'CAP HURDLE (10 hdls) 2m

7:35 (7:37) (Class 4) (0-95,90) 4-Y-0+ **£2,646** (£756; £378)

Form — RPR

-P05 **1** **Fenney Spring**[4] 569 5-10-2 **66** .... (bt) CLlewellyn 78+
(W Jenks) *led 3rd: clr 5th: hit 2 out: drvn out* **3/1**[1]

2-06 **2** *¾* **Not To Be Missed**[8] 506 7-10-12 **76** .... WHutchinson 85
(R Dickin) *a.p: chsd wnr after 3 out: styd on u.p* **10/1**

/0-0 **3** *7* **Cash Return**[29] 185 6-9-11 **64** .... (p) LVickers(3) 66
(Mrs S Lamyman) *led to 3rd: remained handy: rdn appr 3 out: styd on same pce fr next* **14/1**

55-0 **4** *12* **Margarets Wish**[39] 1 5-11-1 **79** .... RGreene 69
(T Wall) *hld up: hdwy 6th: styd on same pce fr next* **9/1**

1-03 **5** *1* **Think Quick (IRE)**[33] 134 5-10-8 **82** .... AHawkins(10) 71
(R Hollinshead) *hld up: hdwy 6th: hit next: styd on same pce* **7/2**[2]

P6-P **6** *1¾* **Gentle Warning**[19] 356 5-10-3 **70** .... RYoung(3) 57
(M Appleby) *s.s: hld up: j.rt 1st: hit 6th: n.d* **33/1**

0-6 **7** *8* **What's A Filly**[29] 185 5-11-7 **88** .... LMcGrath(3) 67
(R C Guest) *hld up: mstke 1st: hdwy 5th: sn rdn: chsd wnr next tl wknd after 3 out* **7/1**[3]

0P-0 **8** *18* **Clichy**[15] 414 5-11-7 **85** .... DElsworth 46
(Mrs S J Smith) *prom: chsd wnr 5th to next: wknd appr 3 out* **7/1**[3]

/P0- **9** *nk* **Court Empress**[121] 3635 8-10-8 **79** .... TMessenger(7) 40
(P D Purdy) *a bhd* **25/1**

60-P **10** *13* **Alethea Gee**[39] 14 7-10-12 **76** .... RMcGrath 24
(K G Reveley) *hld up: hdwy 6th: wknd bef next* **14/1**

00-6 **11** *6* **Grace Dieu**[16] 399 4-9-11 **74** .... JKington(10) 13
(M Scudamore) *s.i.s: j.rt 1st: hdwy and mstke 2nd: wknd 5th* **12/1**

PP-0 **12** *1¼* **Hayley's Pearl**[9] 487 6-10-1 **65** .... JamesDavies —
(Mrs P Ford) *prom to 6th* **66/1**

0-0P **P** **Bertie Arms**[33] 134 5-10-8 **72** .... (b[1]) GLee —
(J M Jefferson) *prom: rdn 5th: wknd next: bhd whn p.u bef 3 out* **14/1**

3m 57.8s (-2.60) **Going Correction** -0.075s/f (Good)
WFA 4 from 5yo+ 3lb **13** Ran SP% **127.3**
Speed ratings: **103,102,99,93,92 91,87,78,78,72 69,68,—** CSF £35.73 CT £387.67 TOTE £4.90: £1.90, £2.90, £8.90; EX 41.50.

Owner Michael C Stoddart & Mrs Roger Gabb **Bred** Dunchurch Lodge Stud Co **Trained** Deuxhill, Shropshire

FOCUS

A poor event and, although solid enough at for the low level, is unlikely to have much bearing on future events.

NOTEBOOK

Fenney Spring, with the blinkers reapplied, was made favourite on the strength of a fair performance at the weekend. Given a positive ride, she kicked clear after the last on the far side and then showed tenacity to hold off the second on the flat. She is on a very low rating, and whether she can take advantage of it remains to be seen. *(op 7-2)*

Not To Be Missed, whose best form has been on faster ground, made up good ground to challenge the winner after the last, but could not respond when that rival found extra. These are notoriously weak events, and she may be capable of winning one on a stiffer track. *(op 8-1)*

Cash Return, who had shown little worthwhile form prior to this, responded to the cheekpieces and was in contention for a long way. She was staying on again at the end and will appreciate a return to further.

Margarets Wish, a winner of a seller at Ludlow in January, probably appreciated a change of scene having run her previous seven races at that track. She never got into contention and merely ran on past beaten rivals. *(tchd 10-1)*

Think Quick(IRE), well backed beforehand, never got into contention but ran close to Ludlow form with the fourth. *(op 7-1)*

What's A Filly had to be ridden to get into contention on the home turn, but paid the penalty in the straight. *(tchd 13-2)*

614 IRISH POST H'CAP HURDLE (12 hdls) 2m 4f 110y

8:10 (8:10) (Class 4) (0-105,104) 4-Y-0+ **£3,412** (£975; £487)

Form — RPR

0-F5 **1** **Cannon Fire (FR)**[20] 334 4-10-9 **91** .... ChristianWilliams 92+
(Evan Williams) *hld up in tch: led 2 out: rdn out* **7/2**[1]

16-4 **2** *6* **Caper**[19] 352 5-9-11 **85** .... (p) AHawkins(10) 83
(R Hollinshead) *hld up: hdwy after 6th: outpcd appr 3 out: rallied to chse wnr last: no imp flat* **8/1**

0/0- **3** *4* **Maunsell's Road (IRE)**[41] 4969 6-11-3 **95** .... (v) BGibson 90+
(L Lungo) *chsd ldrs: rdn appr 2 out: mstke and wknd last* **6/1**[3]

36P- **4** *3½* **Rival Bidder**[136] 3391 8-11-8 **100** .... DElsworth 93+
(Mrs S J Smith) *chsd ldrs: mstke 4 out: led next: hdd and hit 2 out: wknd last* **13/2**

633- **5** *5* **Hardi De Chalamont (FR)**[47] 4871 10-10-13 **91** .... (p) AO'Keeffe 77
(Jennie Candlish) *hld up: hdwy 4 out: wknd after next* **9/2**[2]

35-1 **6** *7* **Mick Murphy (IRE)**[4] 573 8-10-0 **74** 7ex .... JamesDavies 60+
(V J Hughes) *led: hdd and hit 3 out: sn wknd* **7/2**[1]

60-5 **7** *6* **Sandywell George**[19] 357 10-10-10 **88** .... (t) TDoyle 61
(L P Grassick) *chsd ldr tl rdn and wknd appr 3 out: bhd whn hit next* **15/2**

5m 12.1s **Going Correction** -0.075s/f (Good)
WFA 4 from 5yo+ 4lb **7** Ran SP% **113.1**
Speed ratings: **97,94,93,91,89 87,85** CSF £29.55 CT £160.60 TOTE £4.30: £2.20, £3.70; EX 48.60.

Owner M J Haines **Bred** G And Mrs Forien **Trained** Cowbridge, Vale Of Glamorgan

FOCUS

An ordinary handicap but won in decisive fashion and the form could rate a little higher.

NOTEBOOK

Cannon Fire(FR), dropping back in trip, was finally able to translate some of his Flat ability to hurdles. He looks well handicapped if able to maintain this level of form. Like several other winners on the night, all his best efforts had been on a fast surface, which prompts the question as to whether the ground was as soft as the official version. *(tchd 4-1)*

Caper, who is plating class, was keeping on at the end without troubling the winner. He will be better off dropped back to sellers. *(op 12-1)*

Maunsell's Road(IRE), with the visor re-applied, appeared to have every chance until fading. He may prefer going the other way round. *(op 4-1)*

Rival Bidder, a winning chaser, moved up going well three out, but faded after the winner went past before the second last. This was not a bad effort on his return from four and a half months off. *(tchd 6-1 and 7-1)*

Hardi De Chalamont(FR) travelled well on the heels of the leaders turning in but, not for the first time, found disappointingly little in the straight and it is five years since he gained his wins in France. *(op 7-1)*

Mick Murphy(IRE), a course and distance winner here at the weekend, was 12lb out of the handicap that day and even with a penalty was off a 5lb lower mark. However, he could not repeat the dose on this easier surface. *Official explanation: trainer had no explanation for poor form shown (op 11-4)*

615 GUINNESS IRISH NIGHT H'CAP CHASE (11 fncs 1 omitted) 2m

8:40 (8:40) (Class 3) (0-125,120) 5-Y-0+ **£5,746** (£1,768; £884; £442)

Form — RPR

64-2 **1** **Papua**[19] 354 11-10-10 **104** .... (b) DRDennis 117+
(N J Hawke) *chsd ldr: led 2 out: rdn clr* **9/4**[2]

24-1 **2** *9* **Nowator (POL)**[22] 305 8-11-12 **120** .... JMMaguire 124
(T R George) *led: rdn and hdd after 4 out: wknd appr last* **4/1**[3]

24-2 **3** *2* **Amadeus (AUS)**[17] 389 8-9-7 **94** .... WKennedy(7) 97+
(M Scudamore) *prom: hit 5th: led after 4 out: hdd 2 out: wknd appr last* **2/1**[1]

0P0- **4** *dist* **Ceresfield (NZ)**[124] 3595 9-10-4 **101** .... (p) LMcGrath(3) —
(R C Guest) *hld up: hit 6th: wknd next* **10/1**

00-4 **P** **Power Unit**[12] 452 10-10-7 **106** .... RStephens(5) —
(Mrs D A Hamer) *chsd ldrs: hit 4th: wknd appr 7th: t.o whn p.u bef 3 out* **11/2**

3m 59.3s (-5.70) **Going Correction** -0.075s/f (Good) **5** Ran SP% **108.6**
Speed ratings: **111,106,105,—,—** CSF £11.05 TOTE £3.30: £1.70, £1.70; EX 10.70.

Owner Nick Quesnel **Bred** Exors Of The Late D Macrae **Trained** Hewish, Somerset

FOCUS

Another race decimated by withdrawals, but a fair winning time for the grade and the form appears reasonably sound.

NOTEBOOK

Papua, who has a terrific record at this track, gained his fourth win from five starts over fences here with a decisive victory. He is a fast-ground performer, which suggests the going had dried out quite well. *(op 3-1)*

Nowator(POL), who won well on his return from a break last month, did his best to stretch the field and rallied late on. It was no disgrace that he failed to give over a stone to a course specialist and he should find more opportunities this summer. *(op 3-1)*

Amadeus(AUS), who switched between fences and hurdles, was ridden to take the lead at the first in the straight, but the effort seemed to bottom him and he faded from the second last. *(op 15-8 tchd 9-4)*

Ceresfield(NZ) was just starting to move up from the rear when a mistake halfway down the back put her out of contention. *(op 13-2 tchd 11-1)*

Power Unit *Official explanation: vet said gelding bled from the nose (op 13-2 tchd 7-1)*

616 BRADSHAW BROS QUALITY MEAT STANDARD OPEN NATIONAL HUNT FLAT RACE 2m

9:10 (9:13) (Class 6) 4-6-Y-0 **£1,974** (£564; £282)

Form — RPR

1 **Star Shot (IRE)** 4-10-11 .... TDoyle 101+
(P R Webber) *hld up: hdwy 5f out: led over 2f out: sn rdn clr: jst hld on* **2/1**[1]

2 *shd* **Tihui Two (IRE)** 5-10-4 .... RYoung(3) 96+
(Simon Earle) *hld up: hdwy over 2f out: r.o wl: jst failed* **16/1**

3 *3½* **Silver Bow** 4-10-4 .... GLee 89
(J M Jefferson) *a.p: rdn over 3f out: styd on same pce appr fnl f* **4/1**[3]

					RPR
	4	3½	**Annie's Answer (IRE)**[11] 5-10-7 .... RJohnson (Mrs V J Makin) *led to 1/2-way: led over 5f out: hdd over 2f out: wknd fnl f* **10/1**		89
4-	5	3½	**Eight Fifty Five (IRE)**[84] 4276 5-11-0 .... WMarston (R T Phillips) *chsd ldrs: rdn over 3f out: wknd 2f out* **3/1**[2]		93+
	6	11	**Walton Way** 5-11-0 .... JPMcNamara (P W Hiatt) *swvd rt s: chsd ldr tl led 1/2-way: hdd over 5f out: wknd over 2f out* **33/1**		81
3	7	6	**Hurricane Francis**[19] 355 5-11-0 .... RWalford (T D Walford) *chsd ldrs 12f* **10/1**		75
	8	8	**Aires Rock (IRE)** 5-10-11 .... GCarenza(3) (Miss J E Foster) *hld up: rdn and wknd 7f out* **25/1**		67
	9	25	**Inch Over** 4-10-11 .... JCulloty (S A Brookshaw) *hld up in tch: plld hrd: hung rt 10f out: sn lost pl: bhd fr 1/2-way* **20/1**		39
	10	5	**Anna Gee** 5-10-7 .... RMcGrath (K G Reveley) *hld up: wknd 7f out* **8/1**		30

4m 1.00s (1.20) **Going Correction** -0.075s/f (Good)
WFA 4 from 5yo+ 3lb **10** Ran SP% **125.1**
Speed ratings: **94,93,92,90,88 83,80,76,63,61** CSF £39.81 TOTE £3.40: £1.60, £5.00, £2.00; EX 66.00 Place 6 £77.82, Place 5 £71.11.
Owner Robert Kirkland **Bred** Oliver McLoughney **Trained** Mollington, Oxon

FOCUS
An ordinary bumper with little public form to go on but dominated by jumping types and rated through the fifth for the time being.

NOTEBOOK
Star Shot(IRE), from the family of Royal Gait, was quite keen under restraint, but picked up well in the straight and looked set for a decisive win until the runner-up swooped late. He looks the type to make up into a fair hurdler when switching to jumping. *(tchd 15-8, 9-4 in places)*
Tihui Two(IRE), out of a winning hurdler, was running on steadily until picking up really strongly in the last furlong and narrowly failing to catch the winner. She should be capable of taking one of these events before going over hurdles. *(op 14-1)*
Silver Bow, a half-sister to a winning hurdler, was backed in the ring and ran quite well without ever looking likely to score. she looked in need of the experience and should do better with this under her belt. *(op 6-1 tchd 13-2)*
Annie's Answer(IRE), a point winner last month, set the gallop but was done for pace in the straight. She will appreciate longer trips in due course.
Eight Fifty Five(IRE), with previous experience in a point and a bumper, again looked as if he will appreciate a true test of stamina. *(tchd 11-4)*
Walton Way, a son of a staying hurdler and half-brother to winners over hurdles and on the Flat, showed up for a long way and should come on for the experience.
T/Plt: £138.50 to a £1 stake. Pool £57,678.30. 303.95 winning units T/Qpdt: £32.60 to a £1 stake. Pool £3,390.30. 76.90 winning units CR

617 - 628a (Foreign Racing) - See Raceform Interactive

[485]WORCESTER (L-H)

Saturday, June 4

OFFICIAL GOING: Good to firm (good in places)
A very heavy shower just before racing would have taken any sting out of the ground.
Wind: Almost nil Weather: Showers

629 HARGREAVE HALE MAIDEN HURDLE (DIV I) (10 hdls) 2m 4f
1:40 (1:40) (Class 4) 4-Y-0+ **£3,068** (£944; £472; £236)

Form				RPR
5-22	1		**Absolut Power (GER)**[23] 312 4-10-12 110 .... (p) MBradburne (J A Geake) *hld up in tch: rdn to ld last: r.o* **8/11**[1]	95
03	2	hd	**West End Wonder (IRE)**[21] 356 6-10-9 .... AScholes(7) (D Burchell) *hld up in tch: led 3 out: rdn 2 out: hdd last: r.o* **16/1**	99
	3	7	**Time Bandit (IRE)** 5-11-2 .... JEMoore (M C Pipe) *hld up towards rr: hdwy 7th: rdn 3 out: wknd flat* **10/1**	92
	4	5	**Lake Merced (IRE)**[206] 2135 5-11-2 .... APMcCoy (Jonjo O'Neill) *hld up towards rr: hdwy 5th: hit 7th: rdn and wkng whn mstke 2 out* **7/1**[2]	90+
0-04	5	5	**Cotswold Rose**[26] 261 5-10-2 .... RLucey-Butler(7) (N M Babbage) *bhd tl styd on fr 2 out: nvr nr ldrs* **20/1**	75
0-	6	8	**Monty's Salvo (USA)**[92] 4160 6-11-2 .... ATinkler (N J Henderson) *prom: led after 7th to 3 out: hung lft appr 2 out: sn wknd* **15/2**[3]	78+
60-6	7	7	**Uncle Al (IRE)**[29] 203 6-11-2 95 .... WHutchinson (K Bishop) *led to 3rd: rdn appr 6th: wknd appr 3 out* **20/1**	67
6/0-	8	7	**Takeachanceonhim**[388] 308 7-11-2 .... (t) MFoley (Mrs Barbara Waring) *t.k.h towards rr: rdn after 5th: wl bhd fr 7th* **66/1**	60
002/	9	19	**One More Stride**[604] 1593 9-11-2 75 .... SCurran (H J Manners) *hit 3rd: a bhd* **66/1**	41
0-4P	10	6	**Simiola**[18] 394 6-10-6 63 .... DCrosse(3) (S T Lewis) *t.k.h: prom: led 3rd tl after 7th: wknd 3 out* **66/1**	28
03/5	11	4	**Optimism (FR)**[21] 351 7-11-2 .... AThornton (R H Alner) *prom tl wknd after 7th* **28/1**	31
	P		**Repeat (IRE)**[81] 5-11-2 .... JPMcNamara (Lucinda Featherstone) *a bhd: lost tch 7th: t.o whn p.u bef 3 out* **66/1**	—
0-	P		**Beneking**[186] 2558 5-11-2 .... RThornton (P Bowen) *hld up in mid-div: rdn after 5th: bhd fr 7th: t.o whn p.u bef 3 out* **33/1**	—

4m 55.9s (7.90) **Going Correction** +0.20s/f (Yiel)
WFA 4 from 5yo+ 4lb **13** Ran SP% **119.0**
Speed ratings: **92,91,89,87,85 81,79,76,68,66 64,—,—** CSF £12.77 TOTE £1.90: £1.10, £3.70, £2.10; EX 15.70.
Owner Dr G Madan Mohan **Bred** H Gutschow **Trained** Kimpton, Hants

FOCUS
A moderate event and a modest time. The form is suspect and difficult to rate.

NOTEBOOK
Absolut Power(GER), settling better in the cheekpieces this time, held on well on this return to two and a half miles. *(op 10-11 tchd Evens)*
West End Wonder(IRE) ◆ appreciated the extra half-mile and stuck on gamely when collared at the last. A reproduction of this effort should see him take one of these minor events. *(tchd 20-1)*
Time Bandit(IRE), a half-brother to the winner of a point, is out of a mare who won at two and a half miles over timber. He seems likely to be one of the stable's lesser lights, at least over hurdles. *(op 11-1)*
Lake Merced(IRE) had not set the world alight in three runs in soft-ground bumpers in Ireland. *(op 11-2)*
Cotswold Rose needs a real test of stamina by the look of it. *(op 22-1)*
Simiola *Official explanation: jockey said mare hung right-handed from 2nd last (op 50-1)*

630 ANDREW GRANT NOVICES' H'CAP HURDLE (12 hdls) 3m
2:10 (2:10) (Class 4) (0-95,93) 4-Y-0+ **£3,066** (£876; £438)

Form				RPR
106-	1		**Croc An Oir (IRE)**[238] 1654 8-10-10 80 .... LMcGrath(3) (R Ford) *hld up: hdwy after 6th: mstke 9th: sn led and clr: rdn after 3 out: eased considerably flat* **11/4**[1]	108+
P-P4	2	23	**Fight The Feeling**[21] 345 7-11-8 89 .... (v) CLlewellyn (J W Unett) *hld up towards rr: hdwy after 9th: wnt 2nd 2 out: no ch w wnr* **33/1**	87+
P-60	3	7	**Twilight Dancer (IRE)**[11] 487 7-10-13 80 .... MBatchelor (Miss H E Roberts) *a.p: hit 5th: rdn 8th: one pce fr 9th* **100/1**	68
043-	4	9	**Tommy Spar**[294] 1181 5-11-12 93 .... APMcCoy (P Bowen) *prom: mstke 3rd: wknd after 9th* **4/1**[2]	72
0/	5	7	**Phar The Best (IRE)**[68] 4629 8-11-10 91 .... JTizzard (Mrs A L M King) *nvr nr ldrs* **33/1**	63
P3/6	6	½	**Harry B**[13] 457 6-10-12 86 .... MrSGray(7) (R J Price) *hld up: hdwy whn mstke 3 out: no further prog* **16/1**	58
5-54	7	2½	**Beet De Bob (IRE)**[21] 359 7-11-2 90 .... MrPCowley(7) (Mrs S E Busby) *hld up in tch: chsd wnr afer 9th: lost 2nd and wkng whn blnd 2 out* **33/1**	62+
4P-5	8	2	**Spiritual Dancer (IRE)**[10] 502 10-11-11 92 .... LAspell (L Wells) *a bhd* **33/1**	59
P60/	9	1¼	**Inagh Road (IRE)**[28] 10-10-5 72 .... RGreene (S C Burrough) *led to 7th: mstke 8th: led briefly 9th: wknd appr 3 out* **20/1**	38
5F-6	10	21	**Quel Fontenailles (FR)**[11] 295 7-11-11 92 .... MAFitzgerald (L A Dace) *a bhd: t.o* **16/1**	37
6-PP	11	8	**Francolino (FR)**[13] 464 12-10-10 77 .... JMogford (Dr P Pritchard) *hld up in tch: wknd 7th: t.o* **100/1**	14
-004	P		**Lampos (USA)**[11] 483 5-10-13 80 .... (vt) RGarritty (Miss J A Camacho) *a bhd: t.o whn p.u bef 9th* **14/1**	—
52/P	P		**Protection Money**[21] 359 5-11-4 85 .... TDoyle (L P Grassick) *a bhd: j. slowly 2nd: t.o whn p.u bef 3 out* **66/1**	—
P05-	P		**Valley Warrior**[62] 4725 8-10-5 72 .... (b) WMarston (J S Smith) *a bhd: reminder after 2nd: t.o whn p.u bef 3 out* **9/1**	—
0P-6	P		**Pendil's Princess**[21] 359 6-10-4 71 .... ATinkler (S E H Sherwood) *hld up in tch: wknd 8th: t.o whn p.u bef 3 out* **40/1**	—
5-2	P		**Squantum (IRE)**[13] 469 8-11-6 87 .... RJohnson (Mrs H Dalton) *chsd ldrs: rdn after 6th: sn wknd: t.o whn p.u bef 3 out* **9/2**[3]	—
RP-3	P		**Popsi's Cloggs**[21] 357 13-10-3 73 .... (p) DCrosse(3) (D W Lewis) *sn w ldr: led 7th to 9th: wknd qckly: bhd whn p.u bef 3 out* **10/1**	—
P00-	P		**Broomers Hill (IRE)**[114] 3765 5-10-11 78 .... (b[1]) JCulloty (L A Dace) *hld up and bhd: hdwy 7th: wkng whn mstke 3 out: p.u bef 2 out* **33/1**	—

5m 53.9s (4.70) **Going Correction** +0.20s/f (Yiel) **18** Ran SP% **127.8**
Speed ratings: **100,92,90,87,84 84,83,83,82,75 72,—,—,—,— —,—,—** CSF £105.83 CT £7511.89 TOTE £4.80: £2.00, £4.30, £9.10, £1.50; EX 147.90.
Owner Concertina Racing Four **Bred** Donal Brazil **Trained** Cotebrook, Cheshire

FOCUS
Quantity rather than quality, with the winner turning the race into a procession and value for 30 lengths. The runner-up sets the standard.

NOTEBOOK
Croc An Oir(IRE) enjoyed a successful campaign over fences last summer for Venetia Williams. He proved a revelation on this switch back to the smaller obstacles for a new yard and the Handicapper seems likely to take a dim view of this performance. *(tchd 10-3 and 7-2 in places)*
Fight The Feeling finished runner-up in a race where it was a case of the winner first and the rest nowhere.
Twilight Dancer(IRE) gave the impression he was galloping on the spot leaving the back straight.
Tommy Spar had not been seen since finishing a well-beaten third when favourite at Bangor last August. He has yet to prove he stays three miles. *(op 5-1)*
Popsi's Cloggs *Official explanation: jockey said gelding was lame (tchd 5-1)*
Squantum(IRE) *Official explanation: jockey said gelding was never travelling (tchd 5-1)*
Lampos(USA) *Official explanation: jockey said gelding had a breathing problem (tchd 5-1)*
Pendil's Princess *Official explanation: jockey said mare was never going after bad mistake (tchd 5-1)*

631 MYSON RADIATORS BEGINNERS' CHASE (18 fncs) 2m 7f 110y
2:40 (2:40) (Class 4) 5-Y-0+ **£4,270** (£1,387; £747)

Form				RPR
12-4	1		**On The Outside (IRE)**[32] 174 6-10-7 103 .... (t) JTizzard (S E H Sherwood) *hld up in tch: wnt 2nd 3 out: rdn to ld and lft clr last* **16/1**	102+
03-3	2	dist	**Hey Boy (IRE)**[13] 465 6-11-0 107 .... NFehily (C J Mann) *a.p: wknd after 3 out: lft poor 2nd last* **7/1**[3]	72
U-P3	3	1¼	**High Peak**[21] 358 8-10-11 71 .... RYoung(3) (J W Mullins) *hld up: hdwy 11th: wknd appr 4 out* **16/1**	71
600/	P		**Rostropovich (IRE)**[397] 151 8-11-0 .... (bt) APMcCoy (P F Nicholls) *j. bdly: p.u after 3rd* **3/1**[2]	—
	P		**Cool Trader (IRE)**[21] 7-10-11 .... RHobson(3) (Mrs C J Ikin) *j. slowly: sn wl bhd: t.o whn p.u bef 10th* **80/1**	—
06/6	P		**Matrix (AUS)**[21] 358 8-11-0 .... WMarston (K McAuliffe) *a bhd: rdn after 9th: t.o whn p.u bef 14th* **50/1**	—
2/2-	P		**Unleash (USA)**[31] 4823 6-11-0 .... RJohnson (P J Hobbs) *w ldr: wknd qckly appr 10th: p.u bef 11th* **10/11**[1]	—
P-3P	P		**Hardy Russian (IRE)**[13] 461 8-10-4 70 .... KBurke(10) (P R Rodford) *a bhd: rdn after 5th: t.o whn mstke 4 out: p.u bef 3 out* **80/1**	—
030-	P		**Rich Song (IRE)**[176] 2756 7-11-0 .... DElsworth (Mrs S J Smith) *hld up: hdwy 6th: led 10th to 12th: wknd after 14th: blnd 4 out: p.u bef 3 out* **20/1**	—
/F-4	P		**Pharly Star**[21] 358 11-11-0 .... MAFitzgerald (H D Daly) *led to 10th: led 12th: rdn after 2 out: hdd and stmbld last: sn p.u: broke leg: dead* **12/1**	103

5m 55.7s (0.80) **Going Correction** +0.20s/f (Yiel) **10** Ran SP% **118.5**
Speed ratings: **106,—,—,— —,—,—,—,—,—** CSF £120.11 TOTE £24.00: £3.00, £1.80, £3.10; EX 68.90.
Owner Geoffrey Vos **Bred** William O'Keeffe **Trained** Bredenbury, H'fords

FOCUS
Only three completed in an eventful contest and the form looks unreliable.

NOTEBOOK
On The Outside(IRE) built on her chasing debut at Ludlow a month ago. She had just struck the front when the only danger suffered a fatal injury at the final fence. *(op 14-1)*
Hey Boy(IRE) did not appear to be suited by the longer trip and only finished second because of the misfortune to Pharly Star. *(op 15-2 tchd 13-2)*
High Peak was in trouble on the home turn. *(op 14-1)*
Pharly Star had been narrowly headed when disaster struck at the last. *(op Evens)*

Unleash(USA) stopped as if something was amiss on his chasing debut. He was found to be in a *distressed state by the Veterinary Officer after the race.Official explanation: vet said gelding returned in distressed state (op Evens)*

632 JOHN BURKE MEMORIAL NOVICES' H'CAP CHASE (15 fncs) 2m 4f 110y
3:15 (3:15) (Class 4) (0-100,93) 5-Y-0+ **£4,221** (£1,299; £649; £324)

Form RPR
P5-2 **1** **Alcatras (IRE)**[9] 518 8-9-13 **69** ONelmes(3) 83+
(B J M Ryall) *hld up in mid-div: hdwy 9th: wnt 2nd after 11th: led 3 out: drvn out* **4/1**[2]
P24- **2** *7* **High Drama**[293] 1134 8-11-12 **93** RJohnson 105+
(P Bowen) *prom: led 4th to 5th: mstke 6th: lft in ld 11th: rdn and hdd whn mstke 3 out: eased whn btn cl home* **11/2**[3]
333- **3** *12* **Pillar Of Fire (IRE)**[42] 4976 11-10-9 **76** (v) WHutchinson 71
(Ian Williams) *hld up: hdwy 6th: no imp fr 11th* **13/2**
35P- **4** *6* **Taksina**[205] 2138 6-9-11 **69** RStephens(5) 59+
(R H Buckler) *prom tl wknd after 3 out* **16/1**
F043 **5** *17* **Sir Walter (IRE)**[6] 571 12-10-4 **71** RGreene 43
(D Burchell) *hld up and bhd: hdwy 11th: wknd 4 out* **13/2**
5/50 **6** *1 1/4* **Notwhatshewanted (IRE)**[10] 506 8-10-11 **81** RYoung(3) 52
(J W Mullins) *hld up in tch: lost pl after 6th: sn bhd: no ch whn bdly hmpd by loose horse 3 out* **20/1**
P-U4 **7** *18* **Chita's Flight**[13] 459 5-10-13 **82** (t) MBradburne 33
(S C Burrough) *a bhd: lost tch 8th* **20/1**
2P3- **8** *3/4* **Silver Dagger**[258] 1442 7-11-4 **85** (v) APMcCoy 37
(Jonjo O'Neill) *hld up: mstke 10th: struggling whn bdly hmpd 11th* **7/1**
PPP/ **P** **Wot About Me (IRE)**[33] 10-9-11 **67** oh6 LVickers(3) —
(Mrs C J Ikin) *sn t.o: p.u bef 7th* **100/1**
00-P **F** **Miss Muscat**[21] 357 5-10-0 **69** oh1 JPByrne —
(Evan Williams) *hld up in tch: led 5th: j.rt after: fell 11th* **66/1**
0/31 **P** **Multeen Gunner**[17] 416 8-11-3 **84** (p) PMoloney —
(Evan Williams) *led to 4th: prom tl wknd 8th: t.o whn p.u after 11th* **7/2**[1]
0-04 **U** **Saddler's Quest**[11] 486 8-10-12 **79** (p) JMogford —
(B P J Baugh) *hld up: hdwy 6th: rdn and wkng whn blnd and uns rdr 8th* **33/1**
5P/- **P** **Mister Moss (IRE)**[20] 12-9-11 **71** oh1 ow4 MrREGCollinson(7) —
(B P J Baugh) *hld up: hdwy after 6th: struggling whn bdly hmpd 11th: t.o whn p.u bef 4 out* **28/1**

5m 8.30s (0.80) **Going Correction** +0.20s/f (Yiel)
WFA 5 from 6yo+ 2lb **13** Ran SP% **121.1**
Speed ratings: **106,103,98,96,90 89,82,82,—,— —,—,—** CSF £25.24 CT £143.92 TOTE £6.80: £2.30, £2.50, £2.40; EX 39.60.
Owner I & Mrs K G Fawcett **Bred** Anthony O'Mahony **Trained** Rimpton, Somerset

FOCUS
A weak handicap run at a decent pace and the form could rate higher.

NOTEBOOK
Alcatras(IRE), described as excitable by his trainer, went down to the start early. Effectively 15lb lower than when running from out of the handicap last time, he did jump a shade right-handed on occasions and is flattered by the winning margin. *(op 9-2)*
High Drama would not have been beaten so far had the situation not been accepted. A step up to three miles should suit him well. *(op 9-2)*
Pillar Of Fire(IRE) had the visor back on for this return to a shorter distance. *(op 6-1 tchd 7-1 in places)*
Taksina, dropped 5lb, may not have stayed the trip but this was her first outing since November last year. *(tchd 20-1)*
Sir Walter(IRE), attempting three miles for the first time, had not run over fences for exactly three years. *(op 7-1)*
Wot About Me(IRE) *Official explanation: jockey said gelding was lame behind (op 50-1)*
Multeen Gunner ran no race at all. *Official explanation: jockey said gelding had bled from the nose (op 50-1)*

633 LOMBARD GROUP PROPERTIES H'CAP HURDLE (10 hdls) 2m 4f
3:50 (3:50) (Class 3) (0-125,125) 4-Y-0+ **£4,823** (£1,484; £742; £371)

Form RPR
32-3 **1** **Achilles Wings (USA)**[19] 387 9-10-11 **110** (p) RJohnson 117+
(Miss K M George) *hld up towards rr: hdwy appr 7th: led appr 2 out: j.rt last: drvn out* **11/1**
0-02 **2** *3 1/2* **Lupin (FR)**[11] 488 6-10-11 **110** NFehily 114+
(A W Carroll) *hld up and bhd: hdwy appr 3 out: chsd wnr fr 2 out: one pce flat* **9/2**[1]
16-P **3** *1 3/4* **Debbie**[27] 247 6-11-10 **123** LAspell 124
(B D Leavy) *hld up towards rr: hdwy appr 7th: swtchd lft 2 out: one pce* **25/1**
3-11 **4** *nk* **Kings Castle (IRE)**[19] 385 10-10-11 **110** AThornton 110
(R J Hodges) *hld up and bhd: hdwy appr 6th: sn rdn: ev ch 3 out: one pce fr 2 out* **9/1**
2-42 **5** *shd* **Alikat (IRE)**[17] 408 4-11-8 **125** JEMoore 121
(M C Pipe) *hld up in tch: rdn appr 3 out: one pce fr 2 out* **6/1**[2]
2-30 **6** *9* **Nick's Choice**[9] 525 9-10-11 **115** LStephens(5) 106
(D Burchell) *hld up in tch: wknd appr 2 out* **16/1**
00-5 **7** *4* **Count Tony**[23] 315 11-10-6 **110** (p) PCO'Neill(5) 97
(Mrs D A Hamer) *led tl after 4th: led 5th tl appr 2 out: wknd flat* **28/1**
215- **8** *1* **Waterspray (AUS)**[72] 4530 7-10-1 **100** HOliver 87+
(J L Spearing) *prom: led after 4th to 5th: ev ch 3 out: wknd appr last* **7/1**
P0-1 **9** *shd* **Cool Spice**[19] 387 8-11-7 **125** RStephens(5) 111
(P J Hobbs) *hld up towards rr: rdn whn mstke 7th: n.d* **13/2**[3]
551/ **10** *9* **Tomenoso**[420] 4729 7-11-2 **115** DElsworth 92
(Mrs S J Smith) *prom tl wknd 3 out* **10/1**
000- **11** *27* **Deferlant (FR)**[104] 3970 8-10-5 **103** ow1 (tp) MAFitzgerald 54
(K Bell) *bhd fr 6th: lost tch 7th: t.o* **25/1**
1PP- **12** *6* **Claude Greengrass**[175] 2775 9-10-8 **107** APMcCoy 51
(Jonjo O'Neill) *hld up and bhd: rdn after 6th: sn struggling: t.o* **9/1**
162/ **13** *2 1/2* **Joe Cullen (IRE)**[587] 1790 10-10-1 **110** KOlignon(10) 52
(Ian Williams) *hld up towards rr: hdwy appr 5th: wknd 7th: t.o* **11/1**
000- **P** **Saint Par (FR)**[105] 3948 7-11-7 **120** (p) AO'Keeffe —
(Jennie Candlish) *a bhd: rdn and lost tch 6th: t.o whn p.u bef 3 out* **40/1**
50-0 **U** **Pirandello (IRE)**[13] 460 7-10-13 **112** (b[1]) JPMcNamara 103
(K C Bailey) *prom: ev ch whn mstke 3 out: sn wknd: bdly hmpd and uns rdr flat* **20/1**
00-P **P** **Doce Vida (IRE)**[27] 239 7-10-12 **111** RThornton —
(A King) *hld up in tch: rdn 6th: wknd appr 3 out: no ch whn broke leg and p.u flat: dead* **40/1**

4m 48.0s **Going Correction** +0.20s/f (Yiel)
WFA 4 from 6yo+ 4lb **16** Ran SP% **130.7**
Speed ratings: **108,106,105,105,105 102,100,100,100,96 85,83,82,—,— —** CSF £60.62 CT £1265.00 TOTE £15.70: £2.30, £2.00, £3.60, £2.40; EX 101.80.
Owner David L Smith & Karen George **Bred** Juddmonte Farms Inc **Trained** Higher Easington, Devon

FOCUS
An open-looking handicap run at a modest pace but the form looks solid.

NOTEBOOK
Achilles Wings(USA), who had been raised a total of 5lb after a couple of sound efforts, was not inconvenienced by a slightly longer trip. *(op 10-1 tchd 12-1)*
Lupin(FR), another who had gone up 5lb without winning, again met one too good but was beaten more decisively than last time. *(op 6-1 tchd 7-1)*
Debbie, reported to have hung right-handed when pulled up here last time, was not beaten for stamina on her first attempt at this trip. *(op 20-1)*
Kings Castle(IRE) was racing off the same mark as when previously in a handicap prior to his back-to-back wins in sellers. *(op 8-1 tchd 10-1)*
Alikat(IRE) seems to be finding that the Handicapper just about has her measure. *(op 8-1)*
Joe Cullen(IRE) *Official explanation: jockey said gelding had a breathing problem (tchd 12-1)*

634 RON SIMS HEATING AND ELECTRICAL SERVICES H'CAP CHASE (15 fncs) 2m 4f 110y
4:35 (4:36) (Class 3) (0-125,121) 5-Y-0+ **£6,906** (£2,125; £1,062; £531)

Form RPR
1P-4 **1** **Bronzesmith**[19] 386 9-11-4 **113** JTizzard 130+
(B J M Ryall) *hld up: hdwy 7th: led appr 2 out: drvn out* **7/1**
26-1 **2** *7* **Luneray (FR)**[21] 360 6-11-2 **111** (t) APMcCoy 120
(P F Nicholls) *hld up and bhd: hdwy 9th: rdn and ev ch appr last: wknd flat* **5/2**[1]
23-3 **3** *3/4* **Deep King (IRE)**[21] 360 10-10-10 **108** RYoung(3) 116
(J W Mullins) *a.p: j.lft 2nd: nt fluent 6: pckd 11th: sn led: hdd appr 2 out: wknd last* **9/1**
151- **4** *2* **Shaadiva**[42] 4979 7-11-11 **120** RThornton 126
(A King) *hld up: hdwy 6th: ev ch 3 out: wknd appr last* **6/1**[3]
50-6 **5** *3 1/2* **Search And Destroy (USA)**[19] 386 7-11-4 **113** (b) JMMaguire 116
(T R George) *led: hdd sn after 11th: wknd appr 3 out* **13/2**
/134 **6** *1 1/4* **Galway (IRE)**[15] 437 12-10-0 **95** JamesDavies 98+
(M Scudamore) *prom tl wknd appr last* **10/1**
33-0 **7** *23* **Flahive's First**[27] 246 11-9-13 **99** LStephens(5) 78
(D Burchell) *hld up: mstke 6th: sn struggling* **25/1**
104- **8** *2 1/2* **Hors La Loi (FR)**[143] 2476 9-11-12 **121** CLlewellyn 97
(Ian Williams) *hld up in rr: nt fluent 8th: short-lived effrt 11th* **12/1**
556- **9** *6* **Palouse (IRE)**[184] 2591 9-11-2 **111** AThornton 81
(R H Buckler) *wl bhd fr 9th* **25/1**
4-12 **P** **Tamango (FR)**[14] 454 8-11-11 **120** RJohnson —
(P J Hobbs) *bhd tl p.u bef 11th* **5/1**[2]

5m 7.60s (0.10) **Going Correction** +0.20s/f (Yiel) **10** Ran SP% **119.8**
Speed ratings: **107,104,104,103,101 101,92,91,89,—** CSF £26.63 CT £161.28 TOTE £8.60: £2.40, £1.70, £2.50; EX 48.10.
Owner Mrs M E Ash **Bred** J R Ash **Trained** Rimpton, Somerset

FOCUS
A fair handicap rated through the placed horses that could figure higher. After a shower prior to the race the runners appeared to finish tired.

NOTEBOOK
Bronzesmith, dropped 2lb, had given an inclination that he was on the way back at Newton Abbot last month. Still relatively lightly-raced, there may be more improvement to come.
Luneray(FR), raised 6lb for her course and distance win, confirmed the impression that this distance stretches her to the limit. *(op 7-2)*
Deep King(IRE) was 6lb better off than when eight lengths behind Luneray here last time.
Shaadiva, who has yet to win going left-handed, found the fact she had been raised 9lb more of a problem. *(op 11-2)*
Search And Destroy(USA) has dropped to a mark only 2lb higher than when a rather fortunate winner at Bangor in April last year. *(op 6-1)*
Galway(IRE) looks quite well treated but is obviously not getting any younger. *(op 8-1)*
Tamango(FR) *Official explanation: jockey said gelding was hanging badly (op 9-2)*

635 HARGREAVE HALE MAIDEN HURDLE (DIV II) (10 hdls) 2m 4f
5:10 (5:10) (Class 4) 4-Y-0+ **£3,061** (£942; £471; £235)

Form RPR
30-6 **1** **Chase The Sunset (IRE)**[13] 459 7-11-2 98 JCulloty 100+
(Miss H C Knight) *hld up and bhd: hdwy 6th: led 3 out: j.rt last: rdn out* **5/2**[1]
P/ **2** *1 1/4* **Rebelle**[522] 3084 6-11-2 RThornton 98
(P Bowen) *chsd clr ldr: led after 7th: hdd 3 out: hit 2 out: hrd rdn flat: kpt on* **8/1**
02-2 **3** *16* **Thomo (IRE)**[19] 384 7-11-2 107 MBatchelor 82
(N E Berry) *prom: rdn appr 7th: mstke 3 out: sn wknd* **3/1**[2]
0-00 **4** *8* **On Top (IRE)**[21] 356 5-10-9 MrPCowley(7) 74
(Mrs S E Busby) *t.k.h in mid-div: hit 5th: no real prog fr 7th* **28/1**
P-P0 **5** *4* **La Gitana**[6] 569 5-10-9 JMMaguire 63
(A Sadik) *chsd ldrs: wkng whn mstkes 2 out and last* **33/1**
P-03 **6** *11* **Luristan (IRE)**[18] 396 5-10-13 74 DCrosse(3) 59
(S T Lewis) *a bhd* **20/1**
5- **7** *1/2* **Red Moor (IRE)**[177] 2731 5-10-11 RStephens(5) 59
(Mrs D A Hamer) *hld up: hdwy after 4th: wknd after 3 out* **7/2**[3]
5-6 **8** *17* **Pat Malone**[25] 277 5-11-2 JPMcNamara 42
(Lucinda Featherstone) *a bhd* **25/1**
/P-0 **9** *20* **Frazers Fortune**[13] 457 5-10-9 JAJenkins(7) 22
(H J Manners) *sn wl bhd: t.o after 4th* **50/1**
P **P** **Call Of The Seas (IRE)**[35] 133 6-11-2 TDoyle —
(J G M O'Shea) *a bhd: reminder after 2nd: t.o whn p.u bef 5th* **33/1**
40P/ **P** **Alpine Racer (IRE)**[21] 6-10-11 69 LStephens(5) —
(L J Williams) *hld up: hit 4th: sn tk clsr order: hit 5th: wknd 6th* **33/1**
P- **P** **Kerry Zulu Warrior**[194] 2395 8-11-2 DRDennis —
(M Sheppard) *led: sn clr: j.rt 6th: hdd after 7th: sn wknd: t.o whn p.u bef last* **9/1**

4m 56.7s (8.70) **Going Correction** +0.20s/f (Yiel)
WFA 4 from 5yo+ 4lb **43** Ran SP% **119.7**
Speed ratings: **90,89,83,79,78 73,73,66,58,— —,—** CSF £21.57 TOTE £3.90: £1.40, £2.50, £1.40; EX 42.20 Place 6 £123.35, Place 5 £87.58.
Owner Jim Lewis **Bred** Old Meadow Stud **Trained** West Lockinge, Oxon

FOCUS
This looked even weaker than the first division and the time was slower, so the form is suspect.

NOTEBOOK
Chase The Sunset(IRE), who had worn blinkers on his previous outing over fences, scored without Culloty having to go for his whip. *(op 3-1)*
Rebelle ◆, three times a winner at up to two miles on sand, had not been seen since pulled up at the very end of 2003. He showed the right sort of attitude and can go one better in this sort of grade especially when given a stiffer test of stamina. *(op 6-1)*
Thomo(IRE) found an error at the third last the beginning of the end. *(op 5-2 tchd 7-2)*
On Top(IRE) could have settled better over the extra half-mile. *(op 25-1 tchd 33-1)*

The Form Book, Raceform Ltd, Compton, RG20 6NL

La Gitana got tired over this longer trip. *(op 25-1 tchd 40-1)*
T/Plt: £283.20 to a £1 stake. Pool: £33,199.30. 85.55 winning tickets. T/Qpdt: £41.90 to a £1 stake. Pool: £2,320.00. 40.90 winning tickets. KH

636 - 642a (Foreign Racing) - See Raceform Interactive

[317]PERTH (R-H)

Sunday, June 5

OFFICIAL GOING: Heavy
Wind: Almost nil

643 PERTHSHIRE SOLICITORS PROPERTY CENTRE NOVICES' HURDLE (10 hdls) 2m 4f 110y

2:30 (2:30) (Class 4) 4-Y-0+ **£4,381** (£1,348; £674; £337)

Form			Horse	Jockey	RPR
43-1	**1**		**Tandava (IRE)**[39] 59 7-11-7 109 (Mrs S C Bradburne) *chsd ldrs: drvn to ld whn wandered appr last: kpt on wl run in* **5/2**[1]	KRenwick	110+
3	**2**	*1 ¼*	**Kilty Storm (IRE)**[29] 216 6-11-0 (M C Pipe) *nt fluent in rr: hdwy to chse ldrs 3 out: led after next: hdd bef last: rallied and ev ch last: kpt on u.p* **5/2**[1]	RGreene	101
5	**3**	*14*	**Sarin**[31] 192 7-11-0 (Miss Venetia Williams) *midfield: hdwy to press ldrs 2 out: rdn and outpcd bef last* **11/2**[2]	SThomas	89+
-541	**4**	*12*	**Relix (FR)**[17] 426 5-11-2 105 (A M Crow) *chsd ldr tl wknd fr 2 out* **10/1**	(t) DMcGann(5)	84+
P-31	**5**	*4*	**Supply And Fix (IRE)**[24] 319 7-11-0 100 (J J Lambe, Ire) *keen early: led to after 2 out: sn rdn and wknd* **13/2**[3]	KWhelan	74+
6-0	**6**	*3*	**Beau Peak**[36] 124 6-10-4 (D W Whillans) *in tch to 3 out: sn wknd* **50/1**	PBuchanan(3)	61
	7	*8*	**Nobodysgonanotice (IRE)**[36] 7-10-9 (J J Lambe, Ire) *chsd ldrs to 3 out: sn rdn and wknd* **40/1**	PCO'Neill(5)	60
265-	**8**	*16*	**Persian Point**[92] 4184 9-10-11 85 (Miss S E Forster) *hld up outside: struggling fr bef 3 out* **12/1**	MrCStorey(3)	44
6-66	**9**	*2 ½*	**Our Men**[17] 418 6-10-9 (N W Alexander) *chsd ldrs tl wknd after 3 out* **33/1**	TGreenway(5)	42
	10	*dist*	**Personal Impact (IRE)** 7-10-7 (J J Lambe, Ire) *a bhd: no ch fr 1/2-way* **66/1**	MrJPMcKeown(7)	—
6-00	**P**		**The Rooken (IRE)**[29] 210 6-11-0 (P Spottiswood) *a bhd: t.o whn p.u bef 2 out* **100/1**	KJohnson	—
0-P3	**P**		**Aba Gold (IRE)**[11] 500 5-10-7 (Mrs L B Normile) *sn bhd: no ch whn p.u bef last* **100/1**	NPMulholland	—
0-00	**P**		**Test Of Faith**[8] 551 6-10-9 77 (J N R Billinge) *sn bhd: t.o whn p.u bef 2 out* **100/1**	DCCostello(5)	—
P-05	**P**		**Crofton Arch**[5] 602 5-10-11 (M A Barnes) *chsd ldrs tl lost pl qckly 1/2-way: t.o whn p.u bef 2 out* **66/1**	PWhelan(3)	—

5m 28.6s (20.40) **Going Correction** +1.05s/f (Soft) **14** Ran SP% **115.9**
Speed ratings: **103,102,97,92,91 89,86,80,79,**— —,—,—,— CSF £7.57 TOTE £3.70: £1.70, £1.70, £2.30; EX 9.10.
Owner Black & White Communication (Scotland) Ltd **Bred** Newberry Stud Company **Trained** Cunnoquhie, Fife

FOCUS
A race lacking strength but a reasonable pace in the heavy conditions. The winner is the best guide to the form.

NOTEBOOK
Tandava(IRE), whose Kelso win has worked out well, turned in an improved effort to defy his penalty, despite idling in front on the run to the final hurdle. He is on good terms with himself at present and will be of interest in ordinary handicaps. *(op 2-1)*
Kilty Storm(IRE), an Irish point winner, turned in an improved effort on only this second start over hurdles and left the impression that the step up to three miles would suit. He looks capable of winning a similar race with the emphasis on stamina. *(op 7-2)*
Sarin travelled like the best horse in the race for much of the way, but did not find much when asked for an effort and looks well worth another chance in similar company back on a sounder surface. *(op 5-1 tchd 6-1)*
Relix(FR) is not the most consistent and, although effective in the ground and over this trip, was below the form of his Wetherby success and, although the step into handicaps may help, he remains one to tread carefully with. *(op 16-1)*
Supply And Fix(IRE) was below the form of his recent course runs and left the strong impression that a sounder surface is required. He was unlucky at this course last time and looks capable of winning a race this summer. *(op 6-1 tchd 11-2 and 7-1)*
Beau Peak may do better once handicapped but is likely to continue to look vulnerable in this type of event.

644 GLENVARIGILL HONDA "WIN A HONDA JAZZ" H'CAP CHASE (11 fncs 1 omitted) 2m

3:00 (3:03) (Class 4) (0-100,102) 5-Y-0+ **£6,773** (£2,084; £1,042; £521)

Form			Horse	Jockey	RPR
-021	**1**		**Nephite (NZ)**[9] 534 11-12-0 **102** (Miss Venetia Williams) *chsd ldrs: effrt bef 2 out: led run in: kpt on wl* **4/1**[3]	SThomas	108
6/	**2**	*hd*	**Jamica Plane (IRE)**[26] 292 12-10-3 **77** (J J Lambe, Ire) *led: rdn 3 out: mstke last: hdd run in: rallied: jst hld* **10/3**[1]	(p) KWhelan	84+
P-10	**3**	*16*	**Risky Way**[29] 213 9-10-7 **81** (W S Coltherd) *cl up tl outpcd bef 3 out: n.d after* **7/2**[2]	DO'Meara	71
-050	**4**	*3 ½*	**Stormy Beech**[6] 592 9-10-4 **81** (R Johnson) *hld up: effrt bef 3 out: wknd bef next* **4/1**[3]	(vt) LMcGrath(3)	67
352-	**5**	*dist*	**Bob's Buster**[64] 4689 9-11-5 **93** (R Johnson) *hld up: mstke 7th: hdwy bef 4 out: wknd bef next* **9/2**	(b[1]) KJohnson	—
22R-	**F**		**Zurs (IRE)**[211] 2055 12-10-11 **90** (J J Lambe, Ire) *prom: outpcd and 6l down whn fell 4 out* **14/1**	PCO'Neill(5)	—

4m 26.3s (23.50) **Going Correction** +1.50s/f (Heavy)
WFA 5 from 8yo+ 1lb **6** Ran SP% **110.1**
Speed ratings: **101,100,92,91,**— — CSF £17.20 CT £46.21 TOTE £5.10: £2.20, £2.30; EX 21.20.
Owner Mrs H Spencer **Bred** Te Akau Thoroughbreds Syndicate **Trained** Kings Caple, H'fords

FOCUS
An uncompetitive handicap featuring exposed types in which the pace was fair, with the winner rated to his best.

NOTEBOOK
Nephite(NZ), back on very testing ground for the first time in over two years, showed the right attitude to win an ordinary event and, given he is on good terms with himself at present, should continue to give a decent account. *(op 7-2 tchd 5-1)*
Jamica Plane(IRE) had the run of the race and performed creditably with the cheekpieces on again, despite being less than fluent at the final fence. However, his record suggests he is no good thing to reproduce this next time and his long losing run remains a concern. *(tchd 7-2)*
Risky Way was not totally disgraced given that he seems best when able to dominate on a sound surface, but his record of inconsistency means he would not be one to lump on given more suitable conditions next time. *(tchd 4-1)*
Stormy Beech had no problems with the trip or ground but, although he has slipped to a potentially favourable mark, once again showed nowhere near enough to suggest he will be capitalizing on it in the near future. *(op 9-2)*
Bob's Buster had conditions to suit on this first run for two months, but was well beaten with first-time blinkers replacing his usual cheekpieces and he is another to tread carefully with at present. *Official explanation: jockey said gelding felt wrong behind (op 11-2 tchd 4-1 and 6-1 in a place)*
Zurs(IRE), dropped in trip, looked held when coming to grief and this inconsistent sort is not one to place much faith in. *(op 10-1 tchd 9-1)*

645 STEPHEN COUNTRY HOMES NOVICES' HURDLE (8 hdls) 2m 110y

3:30 (3:33) (Class 4) 4-Y-0+ **£4,266** (£1,312; £656; £328)

Form			Horse	Jockey	RPR
43-1	**1**		**Chef De Cour (FR)**[17] 418 4-11-2 (L Lungo) *keen in midfield: smooth hdwy to ld bef last: drvn and kpt on wl run in* **4/5**[1]	ADobbin	102+
23-3	**2**	*1*	**Summer Special**[17] 418 5-10-9 105 (Mrs S C Bradburne) *in tch: effrt and ev ch run in: kpt on: jst hld* **2/1**[2]	ONelmes(3)	96
0/	**3**	*12*	**Howards Dream (IRE)**[26] 1574 7-10-12 (D A Nolan) *chsd ldrs tl outpcd fr 2 out* **50/1**	(t) RMcGrath	84
5-P0	**4**	*14*	**Starbright**[6] 596 4-10-4 68 (W G Young) *chsd ldr tl wknd between last two* **100/1**	DCCostello(5)	67
0/	**5**	*5*	**John's Treasure (IRE)**[667] 1071 5-10-9 (M A Barnes) *bhd: rdn 1/2-way: nvr on terms* **100/1**	(t) PWhelan(3)	65
00-	**6**	*1 ½*	**Moments Madness (IRE)**[14] 6-10-2 (Miss S E Forster) *led tl hdd bef last: sn btn* **100/1**	MrCStorey(3)	57
30-	**7**	*21*	**Pass Go**[212] 2025 4-10-2 (J J Lambe, Ire) *mstke 1st: a bhd* **25/1**[3]	MissJAKidd(7)	40
6-	**8**	*5*	**Killing Joke**[256] 1472 5-10-12 (J J Lambe, Ire) *bhd: rdn 1/2-way: sn btn* **25/1**[3]	AThornton	38
	9	*22*	**Honours English (IRE)**[265] 5-10-12 (J J Lambe, Ire) *bhd: blnd 3 out: nvr on terms* **33/1**	KWhelan	16
0	**10**	*2*	**Mushraag (IRE)**[11] 495 5-10-7 (J J Lambe, Ire) *a bhd* **50/1**	PCO'Neill(5)	14
	P		**Compton Earl**[633] 5-10-5 (J J Lambe, Ire) *keen: cl up to 3 out: sn btn: t.o whn p.u bef last* **25/1**[3]	MrJPMcKeown(7)	—

4m 25.8s (25.20) **Going Correction** +1.30s/f (Heavy) **11** Ran SP% **110.3**
Speed ratings: **92,91,85,79,76 76,66,64,53,52** — CSF £2.09 TOTE £1.90: £1.10, £1.10, £8.60; EX 1.70.
Owner Ashleybank Investments Limited **Bred** Andre Blee **Trained** Carrutherstown, D'fries & G'way

FOCUS
Another uncompetitive event in which the market leaders pulled clear in the closing stages but the pace was steady and this bare form does not look reliable.

NOTEBOOK
Chef De Cour(FR) looked to have bright prospects of adding to his Kelso win in this ordinary event but, although he had to be driven right out, he is probably a bit better than the bare form given he failed to settle and would have been suited by a stronger pace. He should stay further and will be interesting in ordinary handicaps. *(tchd 10-11 in place)*
Summer Special took his career record to no wins from 40 starts, but did not do a lot wrong and this consistent sort looks a good guide to the worth of this form. He should continue to perform well but that losing run has to be a worry for win-only backers. *(tchd 9-4)*
Howards Dream(IRE), a poor and inconsistent Flat performer, was not totally disgraced on this first hurdles run since October 2001 but is likely to continue to look vulnerable in this type of event.
Starbright was not disgraced in the face of a very stiff task, but is likely to continue to be held in this grade and the proximity of the third also casts doubt as to the reliability of this form.
John's Treasure(IRE) showed no immediate promise on this first start since 2003.
Moments Madness(IRE), who hinted at ability in a point last time, had the rub of this ordinary event but is another that will struggle in this type of event.

646 FAMOUS GROUSE NOVICES' CHASE (8 fncs 4 omitted) 2m

4:00 (4:00) (Class 3) 5-Y-0+ **£6,857** (£2,110; £1,055; £527)

Form			Horse	Jockey	RPR
541-	**1**		**Kid'Z'Play (IRE)**[12] 4926 9-10-12 (J S Goldie) *mde all: rdn and r.o strly fr 3 out* **3/1**[2]	RMcGrath	119+
1-11	**2**	*12*	**Tribal Dispute**[17] 419 8-11-8 127 (T D Easterby) *in tch: hdwy to chse wnr whn nt fluent 3 out: outpcd fr next* **5/4**[1]	RGarritty	114+
51-0	**3**	*15*	**Court Of Justice (USA)**[17] 425 9-10-12 (K A Morgan) *cl up tl rdn and wknd fr 3 out* **9/1**	PRobson	88
0	**4**	*13*	**Kilifi Creek (IRE)**[24] 322 8-10-7 (J J Lambe, Ire) *chsd ldrs tl wknd bef 3 out* **33/1**	PCO'Neill(5)	75
PP-5	**5**	*dist*	**Simply Da Best (IRE)**[24] 318 7-10-12 (J J Lambe, Ire) *in tch to 4 out: sn wknd* **20/1**	(b) KWhelan	—
51-6	**U**		**Sardagna (FR)**[29] 217 5-11-0 118 (M C Pipe) *in tch whn blnd and uns rdr 4th* **7/2**[3]	RGreene	—

4m 24.1s (21.30) **Going Correction** +1.50s/f (Heavy)
WFA 5 from 6yo+ 1lb **6** Ran SP% **109.4**
Speed ratings: **106,100,92,86,**— — CSF £7.15 TOTE £3.90: £1.60, £1.50; EX 5.90.
Owner Liam McGuigan **Bred** B S I Nv **Trained** Uplawmoor, E Renfrews

FOCUS
The fence before the open ditch in the straight omitted on both circuits, the open ditch on the first circuit, and the water jump. A fair contest but a decent gallop and a pleasing chase debut from the winner, who was value for further and looks sure to win again over fences.

NOTEBOOK
Kid'Z'Play(IRE) ◆, unbeaten in two hurdle runs at this course, opened his chasing account at the first time of asking with an accomplished display of jumping. He looks capable of defying a penalty in this type of event. *(op 11-4)*
Tribal Dispute had been in good heart but was a bit below his recent best under his double penalty. Better ground may suit, but he looks vulnerable to progressive or well handicapped types in handicaps from his current mark of 127. *(op 11-8 and tchd 6-4 places)*
Court Of Justice(USA), an inconstent hurdler, was again a long way below the pick of his hurdle form on only this second outing over fences and may do better in modest handicaps in due course. *(op 10-1)*
Kilifi Creek(IRE) was again soundly beaten over regulation fences and remains opposable in this type of event.
Simply Da Best(IRE), an inconsistent maiden chaser, was a long way below the form of his recent course run and remains one to tread carefully with. *(tchd 25-1)*
Sardagna(FR) looked to have solid claims in this company but her tendency to make the odd bad mistake cost her dearly before the race had started in earnest. *(op 9-2 and tchd 5-1 in places)*

647 **TOTESPORT.COM H'CAP HURDLE** (8 hdls) **2m 110y**
4:30 (4:30) (Class 3) (0-120,120) 4-Y-0+
£7,621 (£2,890; £1,445; £657; £328; £197)

Form RPR
44-2 **1** **Farne Isle**[25] 302 6-10-3 **104** (p) WKennedy(7) 110+
(G A Harker) *chsd ldrs: led 2 out: r.o strly* **10/3**[1]
44-2 **2** *7* **Kingkohler (IRE)**[17] 428 6-11-2 **110** GLee 109
(K A Morgan) *hld up: hdwy 3 out: rdn and kpt on fr last: no ch w wnr* **7/2**[2]
6F-5 **3** *7* **Spree Vision**[17] 420 9-9-7 **97** (v) DDaSilva(10) 89
(P Monteith) *hld up: hdwy to chal 2 out: rdn and outpcd bef last* **20/1**
1-03 **4** *8* **Lofty Leader (IRE)**[24] 320 6-10-3 **100** (p) ONelmes(3) 84
(Mrs H O Graham) *cl up to 2 out: sn outpcd* **6/1**
05- **5** *13* **Ali Shuffle (IRE)**[160] 3020 6-9-7 **94** oh4 MissJAKidd(7) 65
(J J Lambe, Ire) *keen: led 2nd to 2 out: sn btn* **50/1**
103- **6** *10* **Jaccout (FR)**[49] 4874 7-10-1 **95** (vt) KJohnson 56
(R Johnson) *keen: led to 2nd: lost pl next: n.d after* **9/2**[3]
245/ **7** *7* **Francies Fancy (IRE)**[85] 4337 8-10-8 **102** KWhelan 56
(J J Lambe, Ire) *hld up: short-lived effrt bef 2 out: sn btn and eased* **8/1**
-010 **P** **Border Tale**[4] 422 5-11-3 **111** JimCrowley —
(James Moffatt) *chsd ldrs tl lost pl bef 3rd: p.u bef 2 out* **13/2**

4m 22.0s (21.40) **Going Correction** +1.30s/f (Heav)
WFA 4 from 5yo+ 3lb **8** Ran SP% **108.9**
Speed ratings: **101,97,94,90,84 79,76,**— CSF £14.22 CT £173.38 TOTE £4.50: £1.50, £1.80, £4.20; EX 17.50.
Owner Steer Arms Belton Racing Club **Bred** R Brewis **Trained** Thirkleby, N Yorks
■ Stewards' Enquiry : K Whelan four-day ban: dropped hands and lost sixth place (Jun 16,18,21,22)

FOCUS
With a spate of withdrawals this did not take as much winning as seemed likely but nonetheless a fair effort from Farne Isle, who relished the conditions and is the guide to the level of the form.

NOTEBOOK
Farne Isle, who ran creditably after a short break at this course last time, proved suited by the step into handicaps and the return to a testing surface and won with plenty in hand. Life will be tougher after reassessment as the ground firms up, though. *(op 4-1 tchd 3-1)*
Kingkohler(IRE) is a consistent sort who ran creditably and looks a decent guide to the worth of *this form. Less testing conditions may suit but he looks held from his current mark in handicaps. (op 4-1and tchd 5 in a place)*
Spree Vision does not win very often and once again found less than anticipated, having looked to *be travelling as well as the winner turning for home. He remains one to tread carefully with. (op 12-1)*
Lofty Leader(IRE), tried in cheekpieces, is not the most consistent but has still to prove that very *testing conditions are ideal. However he looks worth another chance over further on better ground. (op 7-1 tchd 15-2)*
Ali Shuffle(IRE) took his career record to no wins from 31 starts and this inconsistent sort, who failed to settle, is one to have reservations about. *(op 25-1)*
Jaccout(FR), returned to hurdles, had conditions to suit but was again well beaten and, although he may be best when able to dominate, is also one to tread carefully with. *(op 5-1)*
Francies Fancy(IRE), who was not knocked about when clearly held, is an unreliable type with a very modest strike rate and is not one to place much faith in. *(op 9-2)*

648 **BARR CONSTRUCTION CITY OF PERTH GOLD CUP H'CAP CHASE** (14 fncs 4 omitted) **3m**
5:00 (5:00) (Class 2) (0-140,134) 5-Y-0+
£18,078 (£6,857; £3,428; £1,558; £779; £467)

Form RPR
F3-2 **1** **Osiris (IRE)**[37] 112 10-10-1 **109** (t) ChristianWilliams 120+
(Evan Williams) *keen: cl up: led 4 out: drew clr fr 2 out* **9/4**[1]
2-12 **2** *4* **Curtins Hill (IRE)**[24] 311 11-10-6 **121** RSpate(7) 127
(Mrs K Waldron) *hld up: effrt whn n.m.r after 3 out: kpt on fr last: no ch w wnr* **6/1**[2]
33-3 **3** *4* **Isard III (FR)**[18] 407 9-11-5 **127** RGreene 129
(M C Pipe) *in tch: effrt 3 out: hung rt next: kpt on same pce last* **13/2**[3]
4P-3 **4** *2 ½* **Parisian Storm (IRE)**[24] 311 9-10-4 **112** AThornton 114+
(Evan Williams) *in tch: hdwy and ev ch bef 3 out: rdn next: disputing 3rd and hld whn blnd last* **6/1**[2]
1-33 **5** *hd* **Kock De La Vesvre (FR)**[17] 423 7-11-12 **134** SThomas 136+
(Miss Venetia Williams) *chsd ldrs: rdn and effrt whn mstke 3 out: wknd next* **9/4**[1]
-003 **6** *dist* **Aelred**[8] 553 12-10-3 **111** (p) KJohnson —
(R Johnson) *led to 4 out: wknd bef next* **20/1**

6m 49.0s (36.40) **Going Correction** +1.50s/f (Heav) **6** Ran SP% **108.2**
Speed ratings: **99,97,96,95,95** — CSF £14.47 CT £64.25 TOTE £3.10: £1.80, £2.00; EX 13.00.
Owner Patrick Heffernan **Bred** Miss Penny Downes **Trained** Cowbridge, Vale Of Glamorgan

FOCUS
A disappointing turnout for the money and only a moderate gallop but a fair effort from the winner, who is the type to win again over fences. The form in the conditions is probably suspect, although the first two ran to their marks.

NOTEBOOK
Osiris(IRE) ◆ looked to have sound claims on his latest Punchestown run and, despite racing keenly, ran his best race over fences to beat an in-form rival. He jumped soundly and this consistent type appeals as the sort to win more races. *(op 2-1tchd 5-2 in places)*
Curtins Hill(IRE) may have preferred a stronger gallop and did not get a trouble-free run, but stuck to his task in the closing stages to register another creditable effort. A stiffer test of stamina may be in his favour. *(op 4-1)*
Isard III(FR) was not disgraced in terms of form back in handicap company, but again looked a less than easy ride and does not really appeal as one to take a short price about. *(tchd 6-1 and 7-1)*
Parisian Storm(IRE) looks a bit better than the bare form given he failed to settle and ploughed through the final fence, and he will be of more interest back on a sound surface. *(tchd 7-1)*
Kock De La Vesvre(FR), who has a good record at this course, ran creditably in conditions that would not have been ideal but he is likely to continue to look vulnerable from his current mark in handicap company. *(op 3-1tchd 10-3 in a place)*
Aelred, whose sole win over this trip came when he was allowed a soft lead in a weak race, did not get home in these conditions in this much stronger event. *(op 16-1)*

649 **PERSIMMON HOMES LADY RIDERS' MARES' ONLY H'CAP HURDLE** (8 hdls) **2m 110y**
5:30 (5:32) (Class 4) (0-90,90) 4-Y-0+ **£4,810** (£1,480; £740; £370)

Form RPR
-3S2 **1** **Parisienne Gale (IRE)**[8] 548 6-10-6 **80** MissCarolineHurley(10) 97+
(R Ford) *mde all: rdn after 2 out: styd on wl* **6/1**[3]
0-22 **2** *6* **Marathea (FR)**[19] 399 4-10-4 **76** MissNCarberry(5) 82
(Miss Venetia Williams) *hld up in tch: smooth hdwy to chse wnr after 2 out: rdn bef last: nt qckn* **6/4**[1]
-001 **3** *8* **Casterflo**[5] 601 6-10-9 **76** 7ex MissPRobson(3) 77
(W S Coltherd) *hld up in tch: hdwy 1/2-way: rdn and outpcd after 2 out* **12/1**
-34P **4** *1 ½* **Uneven Line**[6] 591 9-10-10 **81** (p) MrsNNeill(7) 82+
(Miss S E Forster) *bhd: rdn 3 out: styng on whn mstke and rdr lost iron last: no imp* **20/1**
4-05 **5** *11* **Katie Kai**[11] 496 4-10-1 **75** MissJRiding(7) 61
(Miss S E Forster) *bhd: rdn after 3 out: n.d* **25/1**
4-01 **6** *1* **Faraway Echo**[11] 496 4-10-6 **80** MissRDavidson(7) 66+
(James Moffatt) *rdr lost iron 1st: cl up tl wknd fr 2 out* **4/1**[2]
0F6- **7** *4* **Gemini Lady**[26] 4924 5-11-0 **85** MissAArmitage(7) 69
(Mrs J C McGregor) *mstke 1st: prom tl wknd 2 out* **50/1**
2-41 **8** *5* **Macreater**[19] 399 7-10-9 **76** (p) MissEJJones(3) 55
(K A Morgan) *cl up tl wknd after 2 out* **13/2**
PP/4 **9** *1 ½* **Blue Bar**[25] 302 7-11-5 **90** MissJFoster(7) 67
(G A Harker) *hld up: rdn and wknd bef 2 out* **20/1**
10 *dist* **Jailbird Rocks (IRE)**[6] 599 6-10-7 **78** (b[1]) MissJAKidd(7) —
(Hugh Paul Finegan, Ire) *sn bhd: no ch fr 1/2-way* **66/1**

4m 20.8s (20.20) **Going Correction** +1.30s/f (Heav)
WFA 4 from 5yo+ 3lb **10** Ran SP% **112.1**
Speed ratings: **104,101,97,96,91 91,89,86,86,**— CSF £13.90 CT £102.39 TOTE £8.30: £2.00, £1.30, £3.30; EX 21.30 Place 6 £5.24 Place 5 £4.35 .
Owner S J Manning **Bred** Edmond And Richard Kent **Trained** Cotebrook, Cheshire

FOCUS
A low-grade handicap in which the winner set a sound gallop and the form looks reasonable.

NOTEBOOK
Parisienne Gale(IRE), returned to hurdles, turned in her best effort yet to beat a rival that did not find as much off the bridle as seemed likely. However she showed the right attitude and looks capable of winning in similar company after reassessment.
Marathea(FR), under the excellent Nina Carberry, travelled like the best horse in the race for much of the way but found nowhere near what seemed likely when pressure was applied and, although less-testing ground may suit, she looks one to tread carefully with. *(tchd 13-8)*
Casterflo was not disgraced under a penalty given her Hexham win was gained under totally *different conditions, and she is not one to write off back on a sound surface after reassessment. (tchd 14-1)*
Uneven Line, with the cheekpieces back on, left the impression that a much stiffer test of stamina would have suited but her inconsistency means she is not really one to be interested in.
Katie Kai was again well beaten and will have to improve a fair bit to open her account over obstacles. *(op 20-1)*
Faraway Echo was not surprisingly well below the form of her recent Cartmel success and her inconsistency means she remains one to tread carefully with. *(op 5-1)*
Macreater *Official explanation: jockey said mare was unsuited by the heavy going (op 5-1)*
T/Plt: £7.90 to a £1 stake. Pool: £48,607.80. 4,453.60 winning tickets. T/Qpdt: £2.90 to a £1 stake. Pool: £2,777.80. 698.30 winning tickets. RY

[450]STRATFORD (L-H)
Sunday, June 5

OFFICIAL GOING: Chase course - good (good to firm in places); hurdle course - good to firm (good in places)
Wind: Slight, half behind Weather: Fine

650 **AVON ESTATES NOVICES' CHASE** (15 fncs) **2m 4f**
2:20 (2:20) (Class 3) 5-Y-0+ **£6,747** (£2,076; £1,038; £519)

Form RPR
4-11 **1** **Tigers Lair (IRE)**[22] 344 6-11-12 MAFitzgerald 130+
(Jonjo O'Neill) *mde all: rdn appr last: drvn out* **11/10**[1]
-221 **2** *1 ¼* **Flying Spirit (IRE)**[7] 564 6-11-6 (p) JEMoore 121+
(G L Moore) *prom: lft 2nd 6th: mstke 4 out: sn rdn: hung lft appr last: ev ch flat: nt qckn nr fin* **13/8**[2]
6P-U **3** *22* **Padre (IRE)**[28] 239 6-11-0 ATinkler 95+
(M Pitman) *hld up and bhd: hdwy 11th: wknd 3 out* **33/1**
02-U **4** *24* **Welsh Main**[22] 344 8-11-0 CLlewellyn 67
(Miss G Browne) *sn wl bhd* **33/1**
1-4P **5** *shd* **Pams Oak**[14] 459 7-11-6 100 OMcPhail 73
(P S Payne) *hld up: hdwy 8th: hit 9th: wknd 4 out* **66/1**
1-46 **F** **Grey Report (IRE)**[22] 360 8-11-6 123 (b[1]) RJohnson —
(P J Hobbs) *mstkes: chsd wnr tl fell 6th* **6/1**[3]

4m 54.2s (-5.80) **Going Correction** -0.10s/f (Good) **6** Ran SP% **107.4**
Speed ratings: **107,106,97,88,88** — CSF £3.02 TOTE £1.90: £1.50, £1.20; EX 2.60.
Owner Mrs Gay Smith **Bred** James F Whitehead **Trained** Cheltenham, Gloucs

FOCUS
A decent novice for the time of year, and the first two drew right away.

NOTEBOOK
Tigers Lair(IRE), who has taken really well to fences, put up another bold-jumping performance. He had to dig deep, but his fluent fencing made the difference. There are no suitable novice races for him now until the autumn, so he may take his chance in a handicap at Market Rasen. *(op 10-11)*
Flying Spirit(IRE) ◆ seems to have improved with experience over fences and the step up in trip. He gave the winner a real fight, and a mistake at the fourth last did not help his chance. This versatile sort look sure to win more races in this sphere. *(op 2-1)*
Padre(IRE), having just his second race over fences and fourth in all, benefited from a patient ride and was on the heels of the leaders before weakening from the third last. He has plenty of time to build on this. *(tchd 40-1)*
Pams Oak showed up until dropping out when the race began in earnest. *(op 33-1)*
Grey Report(IRE), a course and distance winner, was fitted with blinkers for the first time and jumped sketchily and to his left until departing. He has clearly lost his enthusiasm for the game and remains one to avoid. *(op 9-2)*

651 **ALLEN CARAVANS MARES' ONLY NOVICES' (S) HURDLE** (9 hdls) **2m 110y**
2:50 (2:51) (Class 5) 4-Y-0+ **£3,445** (£1,060; £530; £265)

Form RPR
0P-2 **1** **Fire Ranger**[20] 385 9-10-12 88 RJohnson 88+
(J D Frost) *hld up: hdwy 5th: mstke 6th: rdn appr 2 out: led last: all out* **4/1**[1]
P3-0 **2** *nk* **Wyoming**[33] 25 4-10-4 81 MNicolls(5) 84
(John Allen) *hld up in tch: led after 3 out: rdn and hung lft after 2 out: hdd last: r.o* **9/2**[2]
P45- **3** *12* **Go Classic**[83] 4380 5-10-12 93 JAMcCarthy 77+
(A M Hales) *led tl after 3 out: wkng whn mstke 2 out* **4/1**[1]
50-0 **4** *2* **Princess Pea**[7] 569 5-10-12 LAspell 73
(Mrs L Wadham) *prom: pckd 5th: hit 6th: wknd appr 2 out* **13/2**[3]
46-3 **5** *11* **Go Green**[6] 173 4-10-9 79 (t) SCurran 59
(P D Evans) *hld up and bhd: mstke 5th: rdn and hdwy after 6th: no further prog fr 3 out* **8/1**

The Form Book, Raceform Ltd, Compton, RG20 6NL

60-0 **6** *14* **Blue Nun**[20] 389 4-10-2 75 .... EDehdashti(7) 45
(G F H Charles-Jones) *hld up in mid-div: rdn after 4th: bhd fr 6th* **50/1**
00-0 **7** *15* **Clouds Of Gold (IRE)**[42] 14 4-10-9 75 .... ARoss 30
(J S Wainwright) *hld up in mid-div: rdn after 5th: sn struggling* **20/1**
/0-P **8** *2 ½* **Pridewood Dove**[7] 574 6-10-12 .... AO'Keeffe 40+
(R J Price) *hld up and bhd: hdwy appr 6th: stmbld and hmpd 3 out: nt rcvr* **66/1**
0 **9** *5* **She's A Terror**[22] 349 6-10-9 .... (b[1]) CRafter(3) 25
(N B King) *hld up in tch: wknd after 5th* **100/1**
P-P5 **10** *7* **Distant Romance**[24] 314 8-10-5 78 .... RLucey-Butler(7) 18
(Miss Z C Davison) *hld up in mid-div: rdn and bhd appr 5th* **40/1**
U **Seejay**[20] 5-10-12 .... MAFitzgerald —
(B R Johnson) *blnd and uns rdr 1st* **12/1**
6 **P** **Kilminchy Lady (IRE)**[12] 485 4-10-6 .... DCrosse(3) —
(B Llewellyn) *a bhd: t.o whn p.u bef 6th* **125/1**
300- **F** **La Muette (IRE)**[12] 4156 5-10-9 81 .... RYoung(3) —
(M Appleby) *hmpd s: sn prom: ev ch whn fell 3 out* **20/1**
P-4P **P** **Edgemoor Princess**[28] 236 7-10-5 64 .... MrRArmson(7) —
(R J Armson) *hmpd s: bhd fr 3rd: t.o whn p.u bef 5th* **100/1**
P **P** **Dreams Of Zena**[25] 77 6-10-12 .... WMarston —
(D Burchell) *stdd s: plld hrd in rr: mstke 3rd: t.o whn p.u bef 2 out* **33/1**
4-53 **P** **Twist N Turn**[27] 263 5-10-12 63 .... JMMaguire —
(D McCain) *wnt rt s: prom tl rn wd and lost pl bnd appr 5th: t.o whn p.u bef 2 out* **12/1**

3m 55.0s (-3.40) **Going Correction** -0.10s/f (Good)
WFA 4 from 5yo+ 3lb **16** Ran SP% **119.1**
Speed ratings: **104,103,98,97,92 85,78,77,74,71** —,—,—,—,— — CSF £19.93 TOTE £3.60: £1.90, £2.00, £2.50; EX 40.10.There was no bid for the winner. Go Classic was claimed by Richard Lee for £6,000.
Owner P A Tylor **Bred** Mrs Richard Stanley **Trained** Scorriton, Devon

FOCUS
A poor affair dominated by those at the head of the market, but the winner put up a personal best over hurdles, and the runner-up improved too.

NOTEBOOK
Fire Ranger finally got off the mark at the 20th time of asking. Proven over further, she was not that fluent at her hurdles but her stamina eventually wore down the runner-up. This was a poor contest and she will do well to add to her score in open company. *(op 3-1)*
Wyoming, claimed after winning at Leicester last month, was representing the sponsors. She looked the likely winner when taking over at the last on the far side, but was outstayed in the closing stages. She looks capable of winning a similar contest as she was well clear of the rest. *(op 11-2)*
Go Classic, highest of those with official ratings and dropped to this grade for the first time, was made plenty of use of but was quickly left behind by the principals. *(op 9-2 tchd 5-1)*
Princess Pea, having only her second try over hurdles, is not very big but ran much better in this grade. That said, connections will do well to find a race for her. *(op 7-1)*
Go Green, a dual winner on the Flat, was held up in the rear and merely stayed on past beaten rivals. *(op 7-1 tchd 9-1 in places)*
La Muette(IRE), who had been well beaten in five races on the Flat since last seen over hurdles, was going as well as any when coming down at the last on the far side. She looked sure to be involved in the finish.

652 OMAR HOMES H'CAP HURDLE (FOR THE CHARLES LEA MEMORIAL TROPHY) (14 hdls) 3m 3f

3:20 (3:22) (Class 3) (0-115,115) 4-Y-0+
£6,159 (£2,336; £1,168; £531; £265; £159)

Form RPR
5/P1 **1** **Hawthorn Prince (IRE)**[22] 353 10-11-7 110 .... WMarston 114+
(Mrs P Sly) *t.k.h: a.p: led appr last: rdn out* **9/1**
P-02 **2** *1 ½* **Brush A King**[14] 468 10-10-9 105 .... APogson(7) 106
(C T Pogson) *plld hrd in mid-div: hdwy on ins appr 10th: rdn after 2 out: styd on wl flat* **9/1**
-P26 **3** *2* **Ungaretti (GER)**[19] 397 8-10-6 95 .... DRDennis 95+
(Ian Williams) *mde most: rdn after 3 out: hdd appr last: no ex flat* **16/1**
-111 **4** *1* **Altitude Dancer (IRE)**[16] 441 5-10-9 105 .... SWalsh(7) 103
(Mrs A M Thorpe) *hld up in tch: rdn 10th: one pce fr 2 out* **9/2**[1]
4-P6 **5** *3* **Wee Danny (IRE)**[25] 298 8-9-7 89 oh1 .... RLucey-Butler(7) 84
(L A Dace) *hld up and bhd: stdy hdwy 7th: rdn appr 2 out: wknd appr last* **14/1**
25-F **6** *6* **Witness Time (IRE)**[26] 289 9-11-2 105 .... JPMcNamara 94
(B J Eckley) *w ldr: wknd 3 out* **12/1**
20-0 **7** *3 ½* **Society Buck (IRE)**[15] 450 8-11-7 115 .... MNicolls(5) 101
(John Allen) *hld up in mid-div: rdn and hdwy after 10th: wknd after 3 out* **11/1**
4-23 **8** *7* **Tell The Trees**[16] 441 4-11-0 108 .... JEMoore 82
(M C Pipe) *hld up and bhd: rdn appr 10th: hdwy appr 11th: wknd after 3 out* **5/1**[2]
-05B **9** *2* **Saxe-Coburg (IRE)**[7] 573 8-9-7 89 oh12 .... MrTJO'Brien(7) 66
(K G Wingrove) *bhd: hmpd 6th: nvr nr ldrs* **50/1**
P-00 **10** *25* **Ewar Bold**[7] 573 12-9-7 89 oh14 .... (t) JPemberton(7) 41
(K G Wingrove) *hld up in mid-div: rdn 9th: sn bhd* **100/1**
-1FP **11** *2* **He's The Biz (FR)**[10] 516 6-10-4 93 .... JCulloty 43
(Nick Williams) *j.rt 5th: a bhd* **8/1**[3]
40-0 **12** *dist* **Ice Crystal**[16] 441 8-11-12 115 .... (v[1]) CLlewellyn —
(W K Goldsworthy) *prom: lost pl after 7th: bhd appr 10th: t.o* **25/1**
0-50 **P** **Silver Gift**[7] 575 8-9-11 89 oh2 .... LVickers(3) —
(G Fierro) *a bhd: t.o whn p.u bef last* **16/1**
34-3 **F** **Wimbledonian**[26] 289 6-10-1 90 .... RJohnson —
(R T Phillips) *hld up in mid-div: fell 6th* **9/1**
3-2P **P** **Dancinginthestreet**[20] 384 5-10-5 99 .... (b) RStephens(5) —
(J L Flint) *prom tl wknd appr 10th: bhd whn p.u bef 2 out* **20/1**

6m 31.7s (-2.10) **Going Correction** -0.10s/f (Good)
WFA 4 from 5yo+ 5lb **15** Ran SP% **122.0**
Speed ratings: **99,98,97,97,96 95,93,91,91,83 83**,—,—,—,— CSF £85.95 CT £1296.61 TOTE £10.50: £4.70, £2.30, £5.60; EX 70.30.
Owner Messrs G A Libson,D L Bayliss & G Taylor **Bred** Miss Mary Rita Cahalan **Trained** Thorney, Cambs

FOCUS
A marathon affair, run at an even pace. The form is sound, with the winner back to his best novice level and the second and fourth to their marks.

NOTEBOOK
Hawthorn Prince(IRE), 6lb higher for his win at Uttoxeter, was well suited by this extreme stamina test and settled the issue with a bold leap at the last. This is his time of year and fast ground suits, so he can win more races providing he gets a decent pace. *(op 8-1 tchd 10-1)*
Brush A King, another proven stayer and last year's winner of this race, moved up to the leaders at the last flight on the far side looking like a winner. However, he took a long while to respond when asked to pick up the leaders, and by that time the winner was clear. *(op 7-1)*
Ungaretti(GER), another who stays well, dictated the pace and stuck to his task gamely, but could not find an extra gear going to the last. He deserves to pick up another race but is now a stone above his previous winning mark.
Altitude Dancer(IRE), bidding for a four-timer, having completed a hat-trick over this course and distance, is now 12lb higher than for his first win and possibly in the grip of the Handicapper.
Wee Danny(IRE), has not scored since completing a four-timer in October 2003, but he is now on a very competitive mark. He did at least show signs of a return to form, and all is not lost with him yet. *(op 16-1)*
Tell The Trees was 3lb better off with the favourite for a two and a half-length beating here last month, and clearly ran well below that effort. *(op 13-2)*

653 ALLENS CARAVANS H'CAP CHASE (18 fncs) 3m

3:50 (3:50) (Class 3) (0-125,120) 5-Y-0+ **£8,307** (£2,556; £1,278; £639)

Form RPR
1F-1 **1** **Kelly (SAF)**[32] 183 8-11-1 109 .... AO'Keeffe 126+
(Miss Venetia Williams) *a.p: led 10th: clr appr 3 out: easily* **7/2**[1]
2P/0 **2** *13* **Waterberg (IRE)**[30] 205 10-10-13 107 .... MBradburne 109+
(H D Daly) *hld up and bhd: reminder after 5th: rdn after 12th: hit 4 out: wnt 2nd appr 2 out: no ch w wnr* **7/1**
P4-0 **3** *7* **Fear Siuil (IRE)**[20] 386 12-10-8 102 .... (t) DRDennis 97+
(Nick Williams) *hdwy 3rd: chsd wnr briefly 3 out: wknd 2 out* **7/1**
11-3 **4** *¾* **Paddy The Optimist (IRE)**[14] 461 9-9-13 98 ow4 .... LStephens(5) 93+
(D Burchell) *hld up: blnd 2nd: rdn 12th: hdwy 4 out: wknd after 3 out* **4/1**[2]
45-6 **5** *9* **Montreal (FR)**[17] 423 8-11-12 120 .... (p) JEMoore 105+
(M C Pipe) *hld up and bhd: hdwy 14th: rdn after 4 out: wkng whn mstke 2 out* **5/1**[3]
2-45 **6** *6* **Killultagh Storm (IRE)**[22] 360 11-11-7 115 .... (p) TDoyle 93
(Noel T Chance) *hld up in rr: mstke 1st: hdwy 7th: wknd after 3 out* **14/1**
10-4 **7** *19* **Jazz Du Forez (FR)**[38] 76 8-9-7 94 oh25 .... AScholes(7) 53
(John Allen) *prom: lost pl 6th: wl bhd fr 13th* **33/1**
50P- **8** *1 ¼* **Saffron Sun**[106] 3955 10-10-10 104 .... JAMcCarthy 62
(J D Frost) *j.rt: led: nt fluent 6th: hdd 10th: wknd after 13th* **13/2**
F3-0 **P** **Lord Strickland**[20] 386 12-11-3 116 .... RStephens(5) —
(P J Hobbs) *prom: hit 11th: wkng whn blnd 4 out: bhd whn p.u bef 2 out* **14/1**

5m 58.3s (-3.90) **Going Correction** -0.10s/f (Good) **9** Ran SP% **113.5**
Speed ratings: **102,97,95,95,92 90,83,83**,— CSF £27.87 CT £160.67 TOTE £2.70: £1.50, £2.20, £2.80; EX 41.90.
Owner P A Deal **Bred** Litchfield Stud **Trained** Kings Caple, H'fords

FOCUS
Not the strongest form, but the progressive novice Kelly improved anpother 10lb or so in winning in good style from a couple of course specialists, and he is the type to rate higher still.

NOTEBOOK
Kelly(SAF) has taken really well to fences and has now won every chase in which he has completed. He bounced off the ground and jumped with plenty of enthusiasm and, although likely to go up a fair amount for this, is capable of winning again.
Waterberg(IRE) is well suited by a flat track and was twice a winner here in the summer of 2003. He was down to a reasonable handicap mark, having endured a long absence, and performed well enough without being able to trouble the winner. He should win again in ordinary company.
Fear Siuil(IRE), another who likes this track, has won off a 15lb higher mark in the past. He could not sustain his challenge in the closing stages. *(op 13-2)*
Paddy The Optimist(IRE) was 10lb higher than when gaining the second of two wins earlier in the year, including his rider's 4lb overweight. He is going to continue to struggle off this sort of mark. *(op 7-2)*
Montreal(FR), 10lb lower than when completing a hat-trick a year ago, had the cheekpieces re-applied but gives no indication that his losing run is about to end. *(op 13-2)*
Killultagh Storm(IRE) travelled well for a long way, but when asked for an effort had nothing in reserve. He has not won since coming to Britain.

654 WILLERBY HOLIDAY HOMES "NATIONAL HUNT" NOVICES' HURDLE (9 hdls) 2m 110y

4:20 (4:20) (Class 3) 4-Y-0+
£6,124 (£2,323; £1,161; £528; £264; £158)

Form RPR
16-1 **1** **Buena Vista (IRE)**[14] 457 4-11-3 .... JEMoore 128+
(M C Pipe) *t.k.h: j.rt: mde all: clr after 3 out: 10 l ahd last: eased considerably towards fin* **2/9**[1]
02P- **2** *3* **Good Samaritan (IRE)**[128] 3572 6-11-0 .... ATinkler 105+
(M Pitman) *chsd ldrs: mstkes 5th and 2 out: wnt 2nd appr last: r.o flat: no ch w wnr* **33/1**
01-3 **3** *6* **Zaffre (IRE)**[21] 367 6-10-6 100 .... RLucey-Butler(7) 97
(Miss Z C Davison) *hld up: hdwy appr 5th: chsd wnr after 3 out: no imp whn hit 2 out* **16/1**[2]
0-U0 **4** *13* **Breema Donna**[12] 487 7-9-11 85 .... JStevenson(10) 78
(R Dickin) *hld up: hdwy appr 5th: wknd after 6th* **100/1**
54-4 **5** *4* **Letsplay (IRE)**[11] 507 5-11-0 .... NFehily 81
(A W Carroll) *nvr nr ldrs* **33/1**
0P-4 **6** *3 ½* **Tuesday's Child**[14] 457 6-11-0 .... JCulloty 78
(Miss H C Knight) *hld up: hdwy 6th: rdn and wknd after 3 out* **20/1**[3]
20-3 **7** *1 ¼* **Benny**[28] 235 4-10-4 .... MrNKinnon(7) 74+
(R H York) *hld up: mstke 4th: sn tk clsr order: chsd wnr after 5th: mstke 3 out: sn wknd* **40/1**
/6-6 **8** *6* **Emanate**[38] 73 7-10-9 .... MNicolls(5) 70
(John Allen) *a bhd* **25/1**
0P5- **9** *dist* **Royal Maid (FR)**[34] 7-11-0 90 .... (p) DVerco —
(P R Johnson) *bhd: hmpd 2nd: t.o fr 5th* **150/1**
000- **10** *3 ½* **Will Tell**[221] 1861 7-10-11 .... LVickers(3) —
(S R Bowring) *a bhd: t.o fr 5th* **150/1**
5 **11** *3* **Mill Lane**[11] 500 8-10-4 ow4 .... MissSSharratt(7) —
(R Hollinshead) *bhd: j. slowly 1st and 2nd: reminders after 4th: sn t.o* **150/1**
0P-3 **12** *12* **Master Fox**[24] 314 7-11-0 .... JMMaguire —
(T R George) *bhd: hmpd 2nd: blnd 4th: t.o fr 5th* **33/1**
13 *14* **Dragon Blue** 5-10-0 .... EDehdashti(7) —
(G F H Charles-Jones) *nt j.w: in rr: hmpd 2nd: t.o fr 5th* **125/1**
0/0- **P** **The Bay Bridge (IRE)**[187] 2556 6-11-0 .... BJCrowley —
(Miss E C Lavelle) *a bhd: t.o whn p.u bef last* **28/1**
P **Hermano (IRE)**[372] 8-11-0 .... JAMcCarthy —
(A M Hales) *chsd wnr tl after 5th: wknd 6th: t.o whn p.u bef 2 out* **200/1**

3m 54.1s (-4.30) **Going Correction** -0.10s/f (Good) **15** Ran SP% **115.3**
Speed ratings: **106,104,101,95,93 92,91,88**,—,— —,—,—,—,— CSF £12.78 TOTE £1.20: £1.02, £5.80, £2.60; EX 16.80.

Owner M Archer & The Late Jean Broadhurst **Bred** Lodge Park Stud **Trained** Nicholashayne, Devon

FOCUS

The most uncompetitive of novice hurdles despite the size of the field. They were well strung out jumping the first flight and that situation became even more pronounced as the race progressed. The red-hot favourite won with a ton in hand and has been rated value for a 20-length win.

NOTEBOOK

Buena Vista(IRE) maintained his unbeaten record over hurdles with a facile victory and the margin could have been tripled at least had his rider wanted. His jumping was not perfect, but that is understandable given he had nothing to race with over the last mile and he should continue to make hay while the sun shines. *(op 1-4 tchd 2-7 in a place)*

Good Samaritan(IRE), withdrawn from his last intended outing due to fast ground, was allowed to take his chance this time and stayed on to finish a clear second best, though he his grossly flattered by his proximity to the winner. A return to further will suit him.

Zaffre(IRE) started second favourite despite her price, but this trip would have been too short and she was exposed for foot from the home turn. She is always going to be vulnerable under her penalty in races like this. *(op 14-1 tchd 12-1)*

Breema Donna would have preferred softer ground, but she is already exposed as moderate and probably achieved little. *(op 66-1)*

Letsplay(IRE), making his hurdling debut, probably needs further. *(op 25-1)*

655 AVON ESTATES MAIDEN OPEN NATIONAL HUNT FLAT RACE (DIV I) 2m 110y

4:50 (4:52) (Class 6) 4-6-Y-O **£3,113** (£958; £479; £239)

Form				RPR
	1		**Boomshakalaka (IRE)** 5-11-4 MAFitzgerald (N J Henderson) *hld up in mid-div: hdwy 4f out: rdn over 1f out: r.o to ld wl ins fnl f* **10/11**[1]	93+
33	**2**	½	**Ar Nos Na Gaoithe (IRE)**[12] 490 6-10-11 RJohnson (Mrs A M Thorpe) *led: hrd rdn over 1f out: hdd wl ins fnl f* **5/1**[2]	85
	3	*hd*	**Malton**[29] 5-11-1 MrTGreenall(3) (M W Easterby) *a.p: rdn over 1f out: r.o ins fnl f* **9/1**	92
	4	2	**Noble Sham** 4-11-1 JEMoore (M C Pipe) *chsd ldrs: rn green and wnt 2nd bnd over 2f out: no ex ins fnl f* **15/2**[3]	87
5/	**5**	5	**Travelling Warrior**[673] 1019 6-11-4 RThornton (M F Harris) *hld up in mid-div: hdwy over 4f out: wknd 3f out* **20/1**	86+
	6	11	**Jazz City** 5-11-4 CLlewellyn (J L Spearing) *prom: rdn whn hmpd bnd over 2f out: sn wknd* **20/1**	74
0	**7**	4	**Schindler's List**[14] 463 5-10-13 LStephens(5) (C Roberts) *nvr nr ldrs* **20/1**	70
0	**8**	1 ¾	**Lens Boy**[22] 361 6-10-11 MrRMcCarthy(7) (D Burchell) *hld up: hdwy over 7f out: wknd 4f out* **50/1**	68
	9	1 ¼	**Gwyn's Choice** 4-11-1 VSlattery (R A Harris) *n.d* **66/1**	64
	10	4	**Good Lord** 4-11-1 MFoley (J G Cann) *nvr nr ldrs* **20/1**	60
0	**11**	15	**Indyana Run**[12] 490 4-10-8 TDoyle (A Hollingsworth) *t.k.h: a bhd* **50/1**	38
	12	3 ½	**Burn Brook** 5-10-4 MrRArmson(7) (R J Armson) *hld up: hdwy after 6f: wknd over 5f out* **66/1**	37
0	**13**	6	**Mr Parson (IRE)**[25] 300 5-11-1 DCrosse(3) (S T Lewis) *prom tl wknd over 7f out* **33/1**	38
	14	½	**Crafty Glen (IRE)** 5-10-11 MrDEdwards(7) (G F Edwards) *a bhd* **66/1**	38
0-	**15**	1	**Tiasfourth**[132] 3520 4-10-8 JAMcCarthy (A M Hales) *bhd fnl 6f* **100/1**	27
	16	½	**Orions Eclipse** 4-10-8 JamesDavies (M J Gingell) *prom tl wknd 4f out* **66/1**	26

3m 58.5s (-8.20) **Going Correction** -0.10s/f (Good)

WFA 4 from 5yo+ 3lb **16** Ran SP% **123.7**

Speed ratings: **91,90,90,89,87 82,80,79,78,77 69,68,65,65,64 64** CSF £4.42 TOTE £1.90: £1.10, £2.20, £2.70; EX 5.30.

Owner The Cigar Bar Partnership **Bred** Mrs Juliet Brown **Trained** Upper Lambourn, Berks

FOCUS

A race dominated by the market principals. With nothing wanting to go on, the field stood still for a good six seconds after the tape went across, though the winning time has taken this into account. Even so, it was almost five seconds slower than the second division thanks to a moderate early pace. The form has been rated through the second.

NOTEBOOK

Boomshakalaka(IRE), out of a dam who is from the family of Travado, had been withdrawn due to a sound surface from his first two intended starts. Allowed to take his chance this time, despite the quick ground, it did not appear to suit as he looked uncomfortable on it, especially rounding the home turn, and he also ran green. Despite coming off the bridle some way out, he eventually got up near the line and, under the circumstances, this was probably a better performance than it looked. *(op 6-5 after 5-4 in places)*

Ar Nos Na Gaoithe(IRE), already placed in a couple of bumpers, tried to make her experience and her stamina count and very nearly pulled it off. Some bumpers at this time of year can be very weak and she has the ability to win one before going over hurdles. *(tchd 6-1)*

Malton, placed in one point but a faller in two others from just three starts, was always close to the pace and kept on going right to the line. He seems to possess a little bit of ability. *(op 8-1 tchd 10-1)*

Noble Sham, a half-brother to Cyanara out of the multiple winning chaser Shamana, showed up for a long way but gave the impression he would be better for the experience. *(op 9-2 tchd 8-1)*

Travelling Warrior had not been seen since his debut 22 months ago, so did not perform badly under the circumstances. *(op 16-1)*

656 AVON ESTATES MAIDEN OPEN NATIONAL HUNT FLAT RACE (DIV II) 2m 110y

5:20 (5:20) (Class 6) 4-6-Y-O **£3,107** (£956; £478; £239)

Form				RPR
06-5	**1**		**Tickers Way**[28] 241 4-10-8 APogson(7) (C Drew) *mde all: clr whn rdn over 1f out: r.o* **9/1**	95+
	2	4	**Bluecoat (USA)** 5-11-1 MrTGreenall(3) (M W Easterby) *hld up in mid-div: hdwy over 5f out: rdn over 2f out: wnt 2nd over 1f out: kpt on same pce* **7/1**[3]	93
	3	4	**Back With A Bang (IRE)**[64] 6-11-4 JMogford (Mrs N S Evans) *hld up in mid-div: hdwy over 6f out: rdn over 3f out: one pce fnl 2f* **16/1**	89
	4	¾	**Brilliant Cut** 5-11-4 ATinkler (N J Henderson) *hld up in tch: chsd wnr over 6f out tl over 1f out: one pce* **2/1**[1]	88
0	**5**	6	**Escape Wall**[28] 249 4-10-8 MrTJO'Brien(7) (K Bishop) *hld up and bhd: hdwy 5f out: wknd over 3f out* **40/1**	79
	6	1 ¾	**Supreme Nova** 5-10-6 MNicolls(5) (John Allen) *hld up in mid-div: hdwy over 8f out: wknd qckly over 1f out* **12/1**	74+
0	**7**	*nk*	**Logies Lass**[22] 361 6-10-11 WMarston (J S Smith) *nvr trbld ldrs* **33/1**	73
5	**8**	5	**Talpour (IRE)**[21] 375 5-11-1 ACCoyle(3) (M C Chapman) *prom tl wknd over 3f out* **11/1**	75
0-	**9**	3	**Lady Spur (IRE)**[63] 4720 6-10-11 ARoss (J S Wainwright) *n.d* **33/1**	65
-00	**10**	9	**Woolfall Princess**[11] 507 6-10-11 JamesDavies (G G Margarson) *hld up in tch: rdn over 6f out: wknd over 5f out* **33/1**	56
0	**11**	13	**Georgie's Lass (IRE)**[14] 463 6-10-8 RHobson(3) (C Roberts) *rdn over 6f out: a bhd* **40/1**	43
0	**12**	6	**Simplyirresistible (IRE)**[26] 277 5-10-8 DCrosse(3) (S T Lewis) *bhd fnl 6f* **66/1**	37
0	**13**	1 ½	**Country Rally**[28] 249 6-11-4 JPMcNamara (Mrs S Gardner) *w wnr: wknd over 5f out* **50/1**	43
	14	23	**The Mighty Oak** 4-11-1 OMcPhail (P S Payne) *rdn over 8f out: a bhd: t.o* **50/1**	17
3	**P**		**Oscar's Delight**[33] 179 4-10-8 CLlewellyn (J L Spearing) *hld up and bhd: hdwy over 5f out: wknd over 3f out: 7th and no ch whn p.u lame wl over 1f out* **5/2**[2]	—

3m 53.6s (-13.10) **Going Correction** -0.10s/f (Good)

WFA 4 from 5yo 3lb 5 from 6yo 1lb **61** Ran SP% **125.4**

Speed ratings: **102,100,98,97,95 94,94,91,90,86 79,77,76,65,**— CSF £69.49 TOTE £8.10: £3.00, £3.10, £4.50; EX 62.90 Place 6 £13.75 Place 5 £12.58.

Owner Peter Nicholls **Bred** Mrs S Barraclough **Trained** Rampton, Cambs

FOCUS

A fair pace from the start and the winning time was almost five seconds faster than the first division. The winner achieved a fair figure for a four-year-old.

NOTEBOOK

Tickers Way is obviously learning with experience and was much more professional on this fourth outing. Allowed an uncontested lead, he kept on winding up the pace and had established a race-winning advantage turning for home. The form may not be that strong, but there could be further improvement in him and he probably has a future. *(tchd 10-1)*

Bluecoat(USA), an American-bred debutant, stayed on to finish a clear second best but was never a threat to the winner. His yard should be able to find an opportunity for him. *(op 15-2 tchd 8-1)*

Back With A Bang(IRE), who refused in his last three outings in points, had no obstacles to worry about in this bumper debut and showed that he does possess a bit of flat speed. It will be fascinating to see how he copes with hurdles. *(op 14-1)*

Brilliant Cut, a half-brother to Altapeter and Frosty Light, kept trying to get on terms with the winner on the final circuit but he could never quite manage it and he had nothing more to offer down the home straight. He probably needs a test of stamina to bring out the best in him. *(tchd 9-4)*

Escape Wall ran a fair race at a price, but his pedigree suggests that even this sharp two miles on fast ground would probably be right on the very limit of his stamina. *(op 25-1)*

Supreme Nova ◆, a half-sister to the high-class chaser Simply Dashing, was withdrawn from her intended debut due to the fast ground. Despite the conditions, she ran with some promise until appearing to blow up and is certainly bred for the job. *(tchd 14-1)*

T/Plt: £18.90 to a £1 stake. Pool: £38,999.35. 1,503.35 winning tickets. T/Qpdt: £12.60 to a £1 stake. Pool: £2,454.60. 143.60 winning tickets. KH

657 - 663a (Foreign Racing) - See Raceform Interactive

[514]NEWTON ABBOT (L-H)

Monday, June 6

OFFICIAL GOING: Good (good to firm in places)

The ground had eased after 6mm of rain overnight.

Wind: Slight, half behind Weather: Drizzle

664 "SURFS UP" H'CAP HURDLE (8 hdls) 2m 1f

2:00 (2:01) (Class 4) (0-100,100) 4-Y-O+ **£2,646** (£756; £378)

Form				RPR
-311	**1**		**Polished**[28] 263 6-11-12 **100** (b) JCulloty (V R A Dartnall) *hld up in mid-div: hdwy appr 3 out: led 2 out: drvn out* **7/1**[3]	105+
42-0	**2**	4	**Imperial Rocket (USA)**[21] 387 8-11-6 **94** (t) MAFitzgerald (W K Goldsworthy) *chsd clr ldr: led 3 out to 2 out: no ex flat* **10/1**	94
4-35	**3**	4	**Cream Cracker**[11] 520 7-11-7 **95** JMMaguire (Mrs Jeremy Young) *hld up and bhd: hdwy after 5th: wknd appr last* **9/1**	91
6-F3	**4**	2 ½	**Skibereen (IRE)**[11] 515 5-10-10 **89** (t) DLaverty(5) (Mrs A M Thorpe) *a.p: ev ch whn mstke 2 out: 3rd and wkng whn blnd last* **12/1**	88+
P0-3	**5**	5	**Nesnaas (USA)**[34] 177 4-10-9 **86** GLee (M G Rimell) *hld up in mid-div: hdwy 5th: wknd appr 2 out* **4/1**[1]	72
00-F	**6**	8	**Olimpo (FR)**[11] 517 4-9-7 **77** MrTJO'Brien(7) (P J Hobbs) *hld up: hdwy 5th: wknd appr 2 out* **4/1**[1]	55
0P-0	**7**	13	**Phairy Storm (IRE)**[34] 167 6-9-9 **76** (b) SWalsh(7) (J D Frost) *a bhd: blnd 3 out: no ch whn blnd 2 out* **33/1**	44
00-2	**8**	3	**Virtus**[16] 456 5-10-9 **83** RJohnson (P J Hobbs) *rdn after 4th: a bhd* **9/2**[2]	48
24-F	**9**	3 ½	**Riccarton**[21] 388 12-10-6 **80** RGreene (D C Turner) *hld up in tch: lost pl after 4th: bhd fr 5th* **33/1**	41
30-P	**10**	1 ¼	**Blazeaway (USA)**[16] 456 5-10-2 **83** ow1 (b) BWharfe(7) (R S Brookhouse) *prom: ev ch 3 out: sn wknd* **33/1**	43
000-	**11**	30	**Dont Ask Me (IRE)**[130] 3554 4-10-4 **81** JEMoore (M C Pipe) *racd wd: led: sn clr: mstkes 1st and 4th: hung rt after 5th: hdd 3 out: wknd qckly: t.o* **8/1**	8

4m 5.00s (-0.10) **Going Correction** +0.075s/f (Yiel)

WFA 4 from 5yo+ 3lb **11** Ran SP% **117.4**

Speed ratings: **103,101,99,98,95 91,85,84,82,82 68** CSF £72.73 CT £629.48 TOTE £6.20: £2.10, £2.50, £2.50; EX 62.90.

Owner Cape Codders **Bred** Ewar Stud Farms **Trained** Brayford, Devon

FOCUS

A low grade handicap, but fairly competitive and the form looks solid.

NOTEBOOK

Polished was shrewdly bought at the subsequent auction after the second of his two wins in sellers in the space of a couple of days last month. He defied a 16lb rise in the ratings and top weight in this bit better company. *(op 6-1)*

Imperial Rocket(USA), tried in a tongue strap, came up against a progressive type in the winner. *(op 14-1)*

Cream Cracker has not lived up to her close third at Warwick two outings ago. *(op 8-1)*

Skibereen(IRE) was let down by his jumping late on and may only barely stay two miles over hurdles. *(tchd 14-1)*

Nesnaas(USA) disappointed after his improved effort last time and is another with stamina doubts. *(op 9-2)*

Olimpo(FR) bled from the nose. *Official explanation: trainer's representative said gelding had bled from the nose (op 5-1)*
Virtus *Official explanation: jockey said gelding was unsuited by the early pace (op 4-1)*
Dont Ask Me(IRE) *Official explanation: jockey said gelding had a breathing problem (op 7-1)*

665 WENDY GALBRAITH NINETIETH BIRTHDAY CELEBRATION H'CAP HURDLE (10 hdls) — 2m 6f

2:30 (2:33) (Class 4) (0-105,103) 4-Y-0+ **£3,571** (£1,098; £549; £274)

Form — RPR

00/1 **1** **Spirit Of Tenby (IRE)**[12] 501 8-10-3 **80** .... JamesDavies 87+
(W K Goldsworthy) *hld up: hdwy 7th: led 2 out: r.o wl* **13/2**[1]

3/0- **2** *1½* **Here Comes Harry**[45] 4956 9-9-11 **77** oh1 .... ONelmes(3) 81+
(C J Down) *hld up: hdwy 7th: ev ch whn mstke last: nt qckn* **16/1**

5P-5 **3** *5* **Celtic Ruffian (IRE)**[29] 229 7-10-0 **77** oh9 .... MBatchelor 75
(R Rowe) *a.p: led 6th: rdn after 3 out: hdd 2 out: one pce* **25/1**

50-0 **4** *1¾* **Three Lions**[27] 275 8-11-4 **95** .... JPMcNamara 92
(R S Brookhouse) *hld up and bhd: stdy hdwy 7th: rdn appr last: fnd nil* **14/1**

3-32 **5** *3½* **Classical Love**[20] 394 5-10-5 **89** ....(v) SWalsh(7) 82
(C J Down) *prom tl wknd appr last* **8/1**[3]

023- **6** *8* **Red Canyon (IRE)**[200] 2305 8-10-13 **90** .... JTizzard 75
(C L Tizzard) *hld up in tch: wknd 3 out* **9/1**

6P-2 **7** *2½* **Mollycarrsbreakfast**[12] 503 10-10-3 **80** .... TDoyle 63
(K Bishop) *led to 6th: prom tl wknd after 3 out* **16/1**

-4 **8** *hd* **Knocktemple Lass (IRE)**[37] 128 6-9-10 **80** .... DJacob(7) 62
(D P Keane) *hld up in tch: mstke 3 out: sn wknd* **8/1**[3]

P-30 **9** *3* **Wild Tempo (FR)**[21] 385 10-11-9 **100** ....(t) APMcCoy 79
(M C Pipe) *hld up in mid-div: nt fluent 3rd and 4th: bhd 5th: short-lived effrt 3 out* **15/2**[2]

4-42 **10** *4* **Delaware (FR)**[11] 517 9-10-10 **87** .... JMogford 62
(H S Howe) *prom: n.m.r bnd after 6th: sn lost pl* **9/1**

641- **11** *2½* **Herne Bay (IRE)**[84] 4369 5-11-7 **98** .... ChristianWilliams 71
(R S Brookhouse) *prom tl wknd appr 2 out* **8/1**[3]

50P- **12** *shd* **Dr Charlie**[50] 4889 7-11-5 **103** .... MissCDyson(7) 76
(Miss C Dyson) *hld up towards rr: rdn after 6th: sn struggling* **25/1**

0-04 **13** *3* **Charm Offensive**[11] 519 7-9-7 **77** oh7 ....(v) RLucey-Butler(7) 47
(C J Gray) *a bhd* **20/1**

0-04 **14** *¾* **Griffin's Legacy**[21] 384 6-10-10 **90** ....(p) DCrosse(3) 59
(N G Ayliffe) *bhd fr 7th* **16/1**

50-0 **15** *shd* **Important Boy (ARG)**[8] 566 8-10-3 **80** ....(t) RGreene 49
(D D Scott) *rdn after 3rd: a bhd* **25/1**

020/ **16** *dist* **Henry's Happiness**[415] 4873 6-10-0 **77** oh3 .... JEMoore —
(C P Morlock) *hld up in tch: wknd appr 7th: t.o* **20/1**

/P-P **17** *½* **Insurrection (IRE)**[27] 288 8-9-13 **83** ow5 ....(b[1]) MissSGaisford(7) —
(J D Frost) *a in rr: t.o* **25/1**

5m 18.3s (-2.00) **Going Correction** +0.075s/f (Yiel) **17** Ran SP% **127.7**
Speed ratings: **106,105,103,103,101 98,97,97,96,95 94,94,93,92,92** —,— CSF £99.15 CT £2421.16 TOTE £6.70: £1.70, £4.80, £9.40, £3.90; EX 205.80.
Owner Miss Paula Hearn **Bred** Golden Vale Stud **Trained** Yerbeston, Pembrokes

FOCUS
A wide-open but ordinary handicap.

NOTEBOOK
Spirit Of Tenby(IRE), raised 6lb, made it two out of two since returning from a two-and-a half-year absence and any worries about the 'bounce' factor proved to be unfounded. *(op 6-1 tchd 7-1)*
Here Comes Harry, just out of the handicap proper, pulled hard and may have found the ground too soft on his comeback at Chepstow in April. Not helped by missing out at the final flight, he may have been beaten anyway, but showed he certainly retains ability. *(op 20-1)*
Celtic Ruffian(IRE), 9lb 'wrong', began to force the pace at halfway on this drop back in distance.
Three Lions, given the kid-glove treatment, found precious little when eventually let down and may not have got the trip. *(tchd 16-1)*
Classical Love, switching to handicaps, has yet to prove she stays this sort of distance. *(tchd 10-1)*
Henry's Happiness *Official explanation: vet said mare had been jumped into behind and had lost both hind shoes*

666 ENGLISH RIVIERA H'CAP CHASE (13 fncs) — 2m 110y

3:00 (3:03) (Class 4) (0-110,110) 5-Y-0+ **£6,149** (£1,892; £946; £473)

Form — RPR

0-21 **1** **Honan (IRE)**[21] 388 6-11-4 **102** ....(v) APMcCoy 110+
(M C Pipe) *hld up: hdwy 8th: rdn 3 out: led appr last: r.o* **15/8**[1]

P4-3 **2** *1½* **The Mighty Sparrow (IRE)**[37] 126 12-10-0 **84** oh1 ....(p) MFoley 90
(A E Jones) *in rr: hit 5th: sn wl bhd: j.rt 8th and 9th: gd hdwy 4 out: sn rdn: r.o flat* **25/1**

206- **3** *½* **Half An Hour**[209] 2107 8-11-12 **110** .... RThornton 115
(A King) *hld up: hdwy after 6th: led sn after 3 out: hdd appr last: nt qckn flat* **7/1**

-653 **4** *9* **Jupon Vert (FR)**[12] 505 8-11-1 **99** .... RJohnson 95
(R J Hodges) *led 1st: hdd sn after 3 out: wknd appr last* **8/1**

/3P- **5** *2* **Smart Design (IRE)**[179] 2735 10-10-4 **88** ....(t) TDoyle 82
(K Bishop) *in rr: wl bhd 6th: hdwy appr 2 out: n.d* **20/1**

3-UP **6** *2½* **Wun Chai (IRE)**[21] 389 6-9-10 **85** oh3 ow1 ....(b) DLaverty(5) 77
(A E Jones) *prom: rdn after 7th: 5th and wkng whn blnd bdly 4 out* **10/1**

331/ **7** *7* **Jetowa Du Bois Hue (FR)**[564] 2266 8-11-6 **104** .... JMMaguire 89
(T R George) *led to 1st: chsd ldr: wknd appr 2 out* **11/2**[2]

2422 **8** *14* **Tosawi (IRE)**[13] 486 9-11-1 **99** ....(p) JEMoore 70
(R J Hodges) *a bhd: no ch whn carried rt and stmbld 9th* **13/2**[3]

L-61 **R** **Athnowen (IRE)**[11] 518 13-11-6 **104** .... ChristianWilliams —
(J R Payne) *unruly s: ref to r: tk no part* **7/1**

44-4 **U** **James Victor (IRE)**[10] 534 7-10-6 **93** .... RYoung(3) —
(N R Mitchell) *hld up: 4th and in tch whn blnd and uns rdr 5th* **8/1**

4m 9.00s (3.50) **Going Correction** +0.225s/f (Yiel) **10** Ran SP% **128.4**
Speed ratings: **100,99,99,94,93 92,89,82**,—,— CSF £49.25 CT £304.52 TOTE £1.90: £1.20, £6.40, £2.70; EX 82.50.
Owner Eminence Grise Partnership **Bred** Miss Ashling O'Connell **Trained** Nicholashayne, Devon

FOCUS
An ordinary handicap, but the form looks reasonable.

NOTEBOOK
Honan(IRE) does seem to have taken to fences and justified strong market support despite having gone up 7lb for his recent course-and-distance victory. He does not appear to be that straightforward, but McCoy knows him well. *(op 3-1 tchd 10-3)*
The Mighty Sparrow(IRE), with the cheekpieces back on, seemed likely to finish out with the washing with a circuit to go. A return to a longer trip is called for.
Half An Hour ◆ was without his usual visor for his first outing for seven months. He had not run over two miles since November 2002, so this was a first-class effort over a distance short of his best and improvement can be expected. *(op 10-1)*
Jupon Vert(FR) was back down to the mark of the second of his back-to-back soft-ground wins last November. However, he has won on this sort of surface. *(tchd 7-1)*
Smart Design(IRE), a winner over two and a half miles in Ireland, found this trip inadequate.

667 "THE RACECOURSE FOR YOUR SUMMER SOCIAL CLUB" NOVICES' HURDLE (9 hdls) — 2m 3f

3:30 (3:30) (Class 3) 4-Y-0+ **£5,525** (£1,700; £850; £425)

Form — RPR

2F- **1** **Meneur De Jeu (FR)**[108] 3927 5-11-0 .... JEMoore 116+
(M C Pipe) *hld up in tch: pckd 1st: rdn to ld 2 out: clr whn hit last: drvn out* **3/1**[2]

/5-1 **2** *4* **Amicelli (GER)**[34] 178 6-11-6 120 .... RJohnson 120+
(P J Hobbs) *a.p: led appr 7th: rdn whn hit 2 out and hdd: one pce* **4/6**[1]

25-0 **3** *11* **Loriko D'Airy (FR)**[34] 170 6-10-7 115 .... MissCDyson(7) 101
(Miss C Dyson) *t.k.h: prom: led appr 6th tl appr 7th: wknd after 3 out* **33/1**

12-6 **4** *14* **Crackleando**[38] 99 4-11-2 115 .... RThornton 89
(A King) *hld up in tch: wknd appr 6th* **11/2**[3]

03-5 **5** *dist* **Men Of Destiny (IRE)**[23] 361 4-10-10 .... JTizzard —
(B G Powell) *in rr: hit 2nd and 3rd: t.o fr 4th* **28/1**

06/ **6** *nk* **Miss Flinders**[37] 8-10-7 .... NFehily —
(D P Keane) *led tl appr 6th: wknd qckly: t.o* **33/1**

4m 35.3s (2.30) **Going Correction** +0.075s/f (Yiel)
WFA 4 from 5yo+ 3lb **6** Ran SP% **109.7**
Speed ratings: **98,96,91,85**,— — CSF £5.37 TOTE £4.30: £2.00, £1.10; EX 7.20.
Owner The Three Bobs **Bred** Haras De Saint Voir & Mme Christophe Boistier **Trained** Nicholashayne, Devon

FOCUS
They went 33/1 bar three in this uncompetitive contest.

NOTEBOOK
Meneur De Jeu(FR) ◆, whose jumping fell apart over fences when last seen back in February, appreciated this switch to hurdles. Over a trip on the short side for him, he was in command when rapping the final flight and can defy a penalty in this sort of company. *(tchd 11-4)*
Amicelli(GER) could not cope with the winner under his penalty over a shorter trip. *(op 8-13 tchd 8-11)*
Loriko D'Airy(FR) ran a bit too freely for his own good on this return to hurdling. *(op 20-1)*
Crackleando has failed to progress after his win at Hereford in March. *(op 5-1)*
Miss Flinders *Official explanation: jockey said mare hung badly right-handed (op 50-1)*

668 IRISH NIGHT, 14 JUNE (S) HURDLE (8 hdls) — 2m 1f

4:00 (4:01) (Class 5) 4-Y-0+ **£2,653** (£758; £379)

Form — RPR

04-5 **1** **Lutea (IRE)**[18] 418 5-10-12 .... APMcCoy 90+
(M C Pipe) *w ldr: j.lft 3rd: led 5th: rdn after 3 out: clr whn hit last: r.o wl* **2/1**[1]

0-S6 **2** *3½* **Blues Story (FR)**[21] 385 7-10-7 75 ....(t) MNicolls(5) 82
(N G Ayliffe) *a.p: ev ch 3 out: rdn appr 2 out: one pce* **66/1**

45 **3** *10* **Phase Three (IRE)**[11] 514 8-10-12 .... JMMaguire 72
(T R George) *hld up and bhd: hdwy appr 5th: one pce fr 2 out* **14/1**

F-56 **4** *2* **Outside Investor (IRE)**[15] 458 5-10-8 82 ....(b) KBurke(10) 76
(P R Rodford) *prom: rdn and wknd appr 2 out* **11/1**

245- **5** *nk* **Bobsleigh**[11] 3970 6-11-4 114 ....(b) RJohnson 77+
(H Morrison) *led to 5th: wknd after 3 out* **5/2**[2]

5-PP **6** *6* **Davoski**[21] 387 11-10-12 110 ....(b[1]) JAMcCarthy 64
(Dr P Pritchard) *hld up in mid-div: no hdwy fr 5th* **12/1**

050- **7** *20* **Replacement Pet (IRE)**[179] 2732 8-10-5 62 ....(bt) ATinkler 37
(Mrs S D Williams) *hld up in mid-div: struggling 5th* **40/1**

0256 **8** *2* **Blue Leader (IRE)**[8] 568 6-11-10 100 ....(t) CLlewellyn 54
(W K Goldsworthy) *a bhd* **5/1**[3]

40P/ **9** *1¾* **Silver Man**[22] 11-10-12 ....(p) RGreene 40
(D C Turner) *mstke 2nd: a bhd* **100/1**

PP5 **10** *16* **Ly's West**[11] 515 5-10-12 .... JTizzard 24
(C L Tizzard) *a bhd: mstke 3rd: lost tch fr 4th* **25/1**

P **Samara Sound**[48] 4-10-9 .... JamesDavies —
(A G Newcombe) *nt j.w: a bhd: t.o fr 4th: p.u bef 2 out* **50/1**

PPP- **P** **Dual Star (IRE)**[52] 4855 10-10-12 80 .... ChristianWilliams —
(L Waring) *prom to 4th: t.o whn p.u bef 2 out* **100/1**

PPP- **P** **Ardwelshin (FR)**[312] 1065 7-10-5 71 .... SWalsh(7) —
(C J Down) *hld up in mid-div: wknd appr 5th: t.o whn p.u bef 2 out* **50/1**

4m 7.70s (2.60) **Going Correction** +0.075s/f (Yiel)
WFA 4 from 5yo+ 3lb **13** Ran SP% **114.9**
Speed ratings: **96,94,89,88,88 85,76,75,74,67** —,—,— CSF £147.48 TOTE £2.80: £1.10, £5.30, £3.70; EX 111.80.The winner was bought in for 10,500gns. Bobsleigh was claimed by Mr H S Howe for £6,000.
Owner D A Johnson **Bred** Harry Boyle **Trained** Nicholashayne, Devon

FOCUS
Plenty of no hopers in this weak seller.

NOTEBOOK
Lutea(IRE) had failed to progress in bumpers after winning on his first two starts. Dropped in class on only his third outing over hurdles, he delivered the goods against this opposition. *(op 15-8 tchd 5-2)*
Blues Story(FR) ran by far his best race to date and came up against an above-average sort for this type of event.
Phase Three(IRE) could not raise his game in the home straight over a shorter trip. *(tchd 12-1)*
Outside Investor(IRE) failed to justify market support. *(op 16-1 tchd 10-1)*
Bobsleigh, dropped in grade, had plenty of use made of him over a trip that was short of his best. He was claimed by Stuart Howe for £6,000. *(op 9-4 tchd 15-8)*
Ly's West *Official explanation: jockey said gelding was hanging left-handed (tchd 33-1)*

669 LADIES NIGHT, 21 JUNE H'CAP CHASE (20 fncs) — 3m 2f 110y

4:30 (4:30) (Class 4) (0-110,106) 5-Y-0+ **£4,737** (£1,457; £728; £364)

Form — RPR

5-52 **1** **Lord 'N' Master (IRE)**[11] 516 9-11-12 **106** .... MBatchelor 120+
(R Rowe) *mde all: clr 4 out: rdn appr last: styd on* **7/1**[3]

51-1 **2** *2½* **Robber (IRE)**[38] 101 8-10-13 **93** .... APMcCoy 101+
(P Bowen) *hld up in tch: chsd wnr fr 15th: rdn 3 out: styd on same pce flat* **13/8**[1]

0-42 **3** *nk* **Tell Tale (IRE)**[19] 403 13-10-8 **95** .... MrTJO'Brien(7) 101
(J G Cann) *hld up: lost pl appr 7th: hdwy appr 14th: rdn 3 out: styd on one pce flat* **4/1**[2]

55P- **4** *dist* **The Sawdust Kid**[204] 2222 11-9-9 **80** oh5 .... RStephens(5) 56
(R H Buckler) *chsd wnr to 15th: wknd after 4 out* **25/1**

-PP0 **5** *29* **Francolino (FR)**[2] 630 12-10-0 **80** oh20 .... JMogford —
(Dr P Pritchard) *hld up and bhd: stdy hdwy 8th: lost pl after 13th: t.o fr 15th* **100/1**

-P3F **P** **Rings Of Power (IRE)**[15] 461 8-9-11 **80** oh3 .... RYoung(3) —
(N R Mitchell) *a bhd: rdn after 13th: mstke 15th: t.o whn p.u bef 16th* **9/1**

40-R **P** **Garolsa (FR)**[10] 535 11-11-6 **100** ....(tp) JTizzard —
(C L Tizzard) *bhd: reminders after 6th: mstkes 8th and 9th: t.o whn p.u bef 14th* **16/1**

-312 **P** **Petolinski**[10] [535] 7-9-8 **81** (p) TMessenger(7) —
(C L Popham) *hld up in tch: rdn appr 15th: wknd after 4 out: t.o whn p.u after 2 out* **4/1**[2]

2-25 **P** **Jivaty (FR)**[17] [436] 8-11-0 **101** SWalsh(7) —
(Mrs A J Hamilton-Fairley) *hld up in tch: rdn appr 14th: wknd appr 16th: t.o whn p.u bef 2 out* **16/1**

6m 44.9s (1.50) **Going Correction** +0.225s/f (Yiel) **9** Ran SP% **117.2**
Speed ratings: **106,105,105,—,—** —,—,—,— CSF £20.03 CT £53.30 TOTE £7.10: £2.00, £1.30, £1.70; EX 17.30 Place 6 £104.94 Place 5 £14.70.
Owner Dr B Alexander **Bred** Michael A McNamara **Trained** Storrington, W Sussex

FOCUS
The winner got most of these in trouble when kicking for home towards the end of the back straight. He was value for further.

NOTEBOOK
Lord 'N' Master(IRE) again enjoyed himself out in front and built on the promise of his recent second over course and distance under an enterprising ride. *(op 11-2)*
Robber(IRE) had been raised a total of 9lb for his back-to-back victories. He could not peg back the winner despite staying on willingly. *(op 7-4 tchd 6-4 and 15-8 in place)*
Tell Tale(IRE), 3lb lower than when successful over course and distance on Easter Saturday, could not get past the runner-up let alone trouble the winner. *(tchd 9-2)*
T/Plt: £51.00 to a £1 stake. Pool: £38,234.45. 546.45 winning tickets. T/Qpdt: £3.90 to a £1 stake. Pool: £3,970.80. 737.10 winning tickets. KH

[508]HUNTINGDON (R-H)

Tuesday, June 7

OFFICIAL GOING: Good to firm
Wind: nil Weather: fine and sunny

670 TOTEPLACEPOT CONDITIONAL JOCKEYS' (S) H'CAP HURDLE (8 hdls) 2m 110y

6:35 (6:37) (Class 5) (0-95,95) 4-Y-0+ **£2,296** (£656; £328)

Form RPR

003- **1** **Wardash (GER)**[45] [4975] 5-9-9 **66** oh2 (vt) PMerrigan(5) 86+
(M C Pipe) *keen trcking ldrs: led sn after 3 out: immediately drew clr: v heavily eased after last* **11/2**[3]

-P55 **2** *11* **Three Times A Lady**[8] [592] 5-10-7 **73** ONelmes 71+
(D W Thompson) *cl up: led 5th: hdd sn after 3 out: rdn and immediately wl outpcd: hit 2 out: kpt on but v flattered by proximity to wnr* **12/1**

3-42 **3** *1* **Madison Avenue (GER)**[13] [502] 8-11-9 **92** (b) RLucey-Butler(3) 90+
(T M Jones) *midfield: hrd drvn and far too much to do 3 out: styng on in 6th whn j.rt last: wnt 3rd nr fin* **4/1**[1]

P-55 **4** *nk* **Fullopep**[16] [469] 11-11-5 **88** APogson(3) 84
(J R Holt) *led tl 3rd: drvn and outpcd 3 out: plugged on fr last* **20/1**

06/4 **5** *1 ¼* **Simon's Seat (USA)**[9] [182] 6-11-5 **85** ATinkler 79
(P Howling) *chsd ldrs: u.p 5th: wnt 3rd but no ch bef 2 out: one pce after* **18/1**

0/05 **6** *nk* **Prince Minata (IRE)**[12] [513] 10-10-13 **79** MNicolls 73
(M Appleby) *t.k.h and prom: drvn in 6l 3rd 3 out: one pce and n.d after* **22/1**

-024 **7** *1 ¼* **Reedsman (IRE)**[7] [601] 4-10-1 **73** (b) PCO'Neill(3) 63
(R C Guest) *midfoield: hrd rdn 3 out: fnd nil and no ch after* **9/2**[2]

P-0B **8** *½* **Princess Stephanie**[23] [363] 7-9-9 **66** oh6 PCStringer(5) 58
(M J Gingell) *towards rr: modest prog to midfield whn bmpd last: nvr threatened ldrs* **14/1**

3/R0 **9** *7* **Estuary (USA)**[17] [451] 10-11-0 **85** ow3 NWalker(5) 70
(Ms A E Embiricos) *chsd ldrs: rdn and struggling bef 3 out* **66/1**

632- **10** *2* **Love Triangle (IRE)**[115] [2934] 4-11-9 **95** (t) SWalsh(3) 75
(N B King) *bhd and pushed along after 3rd: slt prog bef 3 out: sn struggling* **16/1**

P-53 **11** *¾* **Let's Celebrate**[23] [363] 5-11-1 **81** DCrosse 64
(F Jordan) *hld up and nvr bttr than midfield: struggling bef 3 out: blnd and nrly uns rdr next* **12/1**

-PPP **12** *nk* **Proper Poser (IRE)**[12] [508] 9-10-0 **66** oh2 (t) DMcGann 48
(M C Chapman) *bhd: rdn and lost tch after 5th* **80/1**

00/4 **13** *16* **Now And Again**[7] [602] 6-10-11 **77** AO'Keeffe 43
(I W McInnes) *chsd ldrs tl 4th: lost tch bef 3 out* **8/1**

00-0 **14** *2* **Blunham**[15] [369] 5-9-10 **70** DSwan(8) 34
(M C Chapman) *taken to post early: reluctant to line up and to r: a in rear and nvr prepared to cl* **66/1**

PP0- **15** *2* **Lord Rochester**[281] [1325] 9-11-11 **91** (p) JamesDavies 53
(K F Clutterbuck) *cl up early: lost pl and rdn 4th: t.o after next* **50/1**

200- **16** *dist* **My Ace**[44] 7-10-10 **76** (bt) GCarenza —
(Miss J E Foster) *chsd ldr: led 3rd tl 5th: fdd rapidly after 3 out: walked fnl 200 yds* **33/1**

3m 42.2s (-13.50) **Going Correction** -0.675s/f (Firm)
WFA 4 from 5yo+ 3lb **16** Ran SP% **116.1**
Speed ratings: **104,98,98,98,97 97,96,96,93,92 92,91,84,83,82** — CSF £62.14 CT £293.35 TOTE £7.50: £1.80, £3.30, £1.10, £3.50; EX 114.50.The winner was bought in for 7,900gns.
Owner D A Johnson **Bred** Gestut Rottgen **Trained** Nicholashayne, Devon

FOCUS
A fair winning time for a seller and the field came home well strung out. The winner is the type to progress further and can be rated for double his winning margin.

NOTEBOOK
Wardash(GER) , despite taking time to settle, could not have done the job any easier and should be rated for around double his winning margin. This was an overdue success, but his confidence will be sky high now and could be about to show his true ability, so looks one to follow during the summer months. He was bought back at the subsequent auction. *(op 4-1)*
Three Times A Lady ran a more encouraging race, but shaped as though she needs a stronger gallop over this trip, and is greatly flattered to have finished so close to the winner. *(op 9-1)*
Madison Avenue(GER) did not prove suited by this drop back in trip and was keeping on all too late. He is in fair form at present, and could take a race at this level when upped to a more suitable distance, but ideally needs an easier surface.
Fullopep was not disgraced over a trip patently short of his best. *(op 16-1)*
Simon's Seat(USA) *Official explanation: jockey said gelding was unsuited by the fast ground (op 16-1 tchd 20-1)*
Reedsman(IRE) met support in the betting ring, but his chance was apparent approaching the third last and he has to rate as disappointing. *(op 11-2 after 6-1 in a place)*

671 TOTESPORT.COM MAIDEN HURDLE (10 hdls) 2m 5f 110y

7:05 (7:07) (Class 4) 4-Y-0+ **£3,332** (£952; £476)

Form RPR

40-2 **1** **Dubai Ace (USA)**[13] [504] 4-10-12 **111** (t) JGoldstein 101
(Miss Sheena West) *hit 1st: midfield: effrt 7th: 3rd and rdn bef 2 out: drvn and clsd to ld after last: edgd clr cl home: all out* **11/4**[2]

4-F2 **2** *1 ¼* **Festive Chimes (IRE)**[23] [367] 4-9-12 **100** SWalsh(7) 93
(N B King) *2nd or 3rd tl jnd ldr 3 out: rdn and slt advantage last: hdd 1/2-way up run-in: nt qckn* **9/1**

3-30 **3** *10* **Mistified (IRE)**[17] [451] 4-10-9 **94** RYoung(3) 91+
(J W Mullins) *cl up: disp ld bef 3 out tl drvn and hdd last: fdd tamely* **10/1**

0-50 **4** *16* **Sitting Duck**[12] [523] 6-11-2 **80** JTizzard 80+
(B G Powell) *led: rdn and hdd bef 3 out: fdd to poor 4th next* **25/1**

P03- **5** *2 ½* **Brasilia Prince**[47] [4938] 6-10-9 **85** (p) RLucey-Butler(7) 76
(G P Enright) *detached in last pair after 5th: sme prog 7th: drvn and struggling 3 out* **50/1**

34-2 **6** *14* **Lunar Exit (IRE)**[38] [133] 4-10-9 MrTGreenall(3) 58
(Lady Herries) *midfield: rdn 6th: drvn and labouring next: no ch after* **7/4**[1]

7 *3 ½* **Internationalguest (IRE)**[15] 6-11-2 RThornton 58
(D G Bridgwater) *wnt 2nd briefly bef 6th: wknd rapidly next: t.o 3 out* **40/1**

8 *1 ½* **Tis She**[16] 7-10-6 CRafter(3) 50
(N B King) *a bhd: t.o 3 out* **100/1**

9 *10* **Bee Cee Gee**[30] 7-11-2 MFoley 47
(S J Gilmore) *j. ponderously in last: lost tch 6th: t.o 3 out* **100/1**

2 **10** *3 ½* **Musical Chord (IRE)**[29] [266] 6-11-2 TDoyle 43
(C Tinkler) *midfield: rdn 6th: sn fdd: t.o 3 out* **4/1**[3]

P- **11** *19* **Chromboy (GER)**[3] [2293] 5-10-9 MrJOwen(7) 24
(N B King) *t.k.h: pressed ldrs tl 7th: sn wknd: t.o* **100/1**

4m 57.1s (-13.70) **Going Correction** -0.675s/f (Firm)
WFA 4 from 5yo+ 4lb **11** Ran SP% **113.3**
Speed ratings: **97,96,92,87,86 81,79,79,75,74 67** CSF £24.76 TOTE £4.10: £1.50, £1.60, £2.50; EX 27.70.
Owner Mucky Duck II Partnership **Bred** Gainsborough Farm Llc **Trained** Lewes, E Sussex

FOCUS
A moderate event, run at a sedate early gallop, which saw the first two come clear.

NOTEBOOK
Dubai Ace(USA) dug deep when it mattered and ran out a gutsy winner, landing a gamble in the process. The longer trip made the difference, this was his first success over timber in six outings and he did enough to suggest he may need even further. Life will be harder under a penalty, but he can go in again on this sort of ground. *(op 7-2)*
Festive Chimes(IRE) turned in another improved effort and went down fighting. She has found her form of late, and was nicely clear of the rest this time, so can be placed to go one better at a slightly lower level. *(op 15-2)*
Mistified(IRE) found little when push came to shove and finished tired. However, this was a sound effort at the weights and he could build on this back over further. *(tchd 11-1)*
Sitting Duck understandably tried to make it a test on this drop back in trip, but lived up to his name in the straight and was made to look woefully one paced. He should do better back over further, but is one to avoid in the main.
Lunar Exit(IRE) failed to improve as expected for this longer trip and ran a stinker. He may do *better when handicapped, but still has it all to prove now.Official explanation: trainer's representative had no explanation for the poor form shown (op 6-4 tchd 15-8)*

672 TOTEQUADPOT NOVICES' CHASE (16 fncs) 2m 4f 110y

7:35 (7:35) (Class 4) 5-Y-0+ **£3,723** (£1,145; £572; £286)

Form RPR

-630 **1** **Master T (USA)**[12] [511] 6-11-0 **105** PHide 108+
(G L Moore) *t.k.h: rr early: chsd ldrs fr 8th: wnt 2nd after 3 out: rdn to cl bef last: led fnl 200 yds: kpt on* **13/2**[3]

P5-0 **2** *1 ¼* **Don Valentino (POL)**[16] [460] 6-11-0 **104** (v1) JMMaguire 106
(T R George) *pressed clr ldr: clsd 8th: led 13th: 4l clr bef 2 out: drvn bef last: hdd flat: fnd little* **9/2**[2]

6F-R **3** *6* **Althrey Dandy (IRE)**[23] 10-11-0 **105** AThornton 100
(P T Dalton) *led tl hdd and slow jump 1st: slow 2nd (water): dropped rr 7th: last 3 out: styd on after: quirky display* **10/1**

3-05 **4** *3 ½* **Turn Of Phrase (IRE)**[14] [479] 6-10-11 **105** (b) PWhelan(3) 97
(R A Fahey) *hld up midfield: mstke 11th (water): rdn next: wnt 2nd 3 out: sn demoted: wknd bef last* **11/1**

2-12 **5** *1 ¼* **Oulton Broad**[29] [264] 9-11-0 **105** (p) LAspell 96+
(F Jordan) *hld up in rr: mstke 4th: effrt bef 3 out: sn urged along: little rspnse: btn next* **7/1**

04-0 **6** *1 ¼* **Lahinch Lad (IRE)**[9] [566] 5-10-12 **93** JamesDavies 92
(B G Powell) *settled towards rr: effrt 12th: drvn and btn bef 2 out* **16/1**

0-P1 **7** *¾* **Monty Be Quick**[11] [532] 9-10-7 **80** MrNPearce(7) 93
(J M Castle) *cl up in chsng gp: lost pl 9th: rr and rdn whn mstke 3 styng on after last* **33/1**

PPP/ **8** *dist* **Breezy Betsy (IRE)**[16] 9-10-2 **79** ow2 (b) MrRArmson(7) —
(R J Armson) *tore into ld 1st and sn 10l clr: pressed fr 8th: hdd 13th: lost pl rapidly* **100/1**

40-1 **P** **Nawow**[16] [465] 5-10-12 **105** ATinkler —
(P D Cundell) *p.u and dismntd bef 3rd* **13/8**[1]

4m 56.9s (-9.20) **Going Correction** -0.675s/f (Firm)
WFA 5 from 6yo+ 2lb **9** Ran SP% **109.3**
Speed ratings: **90,89,87,85,85 84,84,—,—** CSF £33.51 TOTE £8.60: £2.20, £1.70, £3.50; EX 24.40.
Owner G L Moore **Bred** Dot Macmackin Hill Farms **Trained** Woodingdean, E Sussex
■ Stewards' Enquiry : P Hide one-day ban: used whip with excessive frequency (Jul 19)

FOCUS
A moderate winning time for the grade and the first two were nicely clear at the finish. The form looks worth treating with caution.

NOTEBOOK
Master T(USA) , despite taking a pull under restaint early on, relished the quick ground and put his best foot forward for a cosy success. This was just his second success from 14 outings over fences, and he is no certainty to follow-up, but his confidence will have been greatly boosted by this. *(op 11-2)*
Don Valentino(POL), in the first-time visor for this return to chasing, looked set for success when going clear with three to jump, but his stride soon shortened and he was powerless to resist the winner's challenge on the run-in. He is better over fences and deserves to taste success, but on this evidence, he needs to revert back down in trip. *(op 4-1)*
Althrey Dandy(IRE) ran in snatches on this return to Rules and was staying on again all too late in the day. He could prove a different proposition back over three miles, however, and is not one to write off. *(op 12-1)*
Turn Of Phrase(IRE) , with the blinkers re-applied, shaped with more encouragment, but found little when push came to shove in the straight. He can improve with further experience in this sphere, but does not look a natural. *(op 9-1)*
Nawow , off the mark on his chasing bow last time, disappointingly pulled-up early on with *something presumably amiss. Official explanation: vet said gelding was lame behind (op 7-4 tchd 2-1)*

673 TOTEEXACTA H'CAP CHASE (19 fncs) 3m
8:05 (8:05) (Class 4) (0-100,95) 5-Y-O+ **£3,580** (£1,023; £511)

Form | | | | RPR
6-03 **1** Count Oski[12] [522] 9-11-0 **83** RThornton 95+
(M J Ryan) *trckd ldrs: led 12th: rdn 3l clr bef 2 out: styd on wl: comf* **8/1**[3]
00-2 **2** *5* **Cyanara**[16] [464] 9-9-7 **69** oh7 RLucey-Butler[(7)] 77+
(Dr P Pritchard) *hld up and bhd: hit 10th: hdwy 15th: wnt 2nd after 3 out: drvn and no imp after: hld whn blnd next* **14/1**
0-00 **3** *¾* **Cyindien (FR)**[16] [464] 8-10-7 **79** (p) DCrosse[(3)] 84
(D E Cantillon) *hld up: prog 15th: rdn 3 out: wnt 3rd bef last: kpt on flat: unable to chal* **16/1**
6-P4 **4** *7* **Pangeran (USA)**[23] [366] 13-10-0 **72** oh6 ow3 CRafter[(3)] 70
(N B King) *midfield whn hit 10th: rdn and sme prog after 3 out: nt rch ldrs: hung lft flat* **40/1**
3PP- **5** *1 ½* **Presentingthecase (IRE)**[196] [2412] 7-10-0 **69** oh5 JEMoore 66
(Jonjo O'Neill) *settled midfield: hdwy 13th: drvn into 2nd after 3 out: demoted bef next: wknd steadily* **6/1**[1]
P0-0 **6** *10* **Jumpty Dumpty (FR)**[13] [501] 8-11-2 **85** JMogford 72
(J C Tuck) *hld up towards rr: smooth prog to trck ldrs 14th: pushed along bef 2 out: n.d after: far fr disgracd* **25/1**
-P40 **7** *hd* **River Mere**[13] [503] 11-10-2 **71** OMcPhail 59+
(Mrs L Williamson) *prom tl rdn and wknd appr 3 out* **14/1**
PUP/ **8** *1 ¼* **Corkan (IRE)**[589] [1816] 11-9-7 **69** oh5 WKennedy[(7)] 54
(A M Hales) *chsd ldrs tl 12th: no ch fr 15th* **16/1**
0-00 **9** *1* **Regal Vision (IRE)**[12] [519] 8-10-9 **85** MissCDyson[(7)] 69
(Miss C Dyson) *t.k.h: cl up tl 13th: no ch fr 15th* **33/1**
0-0U **10** *9* **Court Award (IRE)**[14] [486] 8-10-5 **74** JTizzard 49
(B G Powell) *hdwy to trck ldrs 8th: mstke 11th: wknd next* **25/1**
2-20 **11** *15* **Alfred The Grey**[13] [503] 8-10-3 **72** (p) LAspell 32
(G L Moore) *chsd ldrs: niggled along 10th: struggling fr 3 out: t.o* **6/1**[1]
5/4P **12** *6* **Saucynorwich (IRE)**[21] [398] 7-11-1 **84** PJBrennan 38
(J G Portman) *nt fluent and sn rdn: led tl 4th: w ldr 10th: rdn and fdd bef 13th: t.o* **25/1**
0-P3 **P** **Ballyaahbutt (IRE)**[14] [486] 6-10-8 **77** JamesDavies —
(B G Powell) *cl up: lost pl 7th: sn drvn: t.o 14th: p.u 2 out* **12/1**
PP-3 **P** **Inland Run (IRE)**[38] [137] 9-11-6 **89** RJohnson —
(R T Phillips) *sn bhd and drvn along: nvr looked keen: t.o 14th: p.u 2 out* **7/1**[2]
0-00 **P** **Farceur (FR)**[16] [466] 6-10-8 **84** (v) AGlassonbury[(7)] —
(M C Pipe) *j. stickily in last and nvr keen: struggling 11th: t.o and p.u 16th* **20/1**
0P-F **P** **Anshabil (IRE)**[18] [436] 6-11-12 **95** WHutchinson —
(A King) *mde nrly all 4th tl 12th: 5th and rdn and wkng after 3 out: p.u and dismntd bef next* **6/1**[1]

5m 52.2s (-20.10) **Going Correction** -0.675s/f (Firm) **16** Ran SP% **120.9**
Speed ratings: **106,104,104,101,101 97,97,97,97,94 89,87,—,—,—** — CSF £101.80 CT £1762.54 TOTE £8.70: £1.70, £2.00, £3.30, £6.90; EX 105.80.
Owner The Laodiceans **Bred** G W Sivell **Trained** Newmarket, Suffolk

FOCUS
A fair time for the class and the field finished failry strung out. The form is worth treating with caution.

NOTEBOOK
Count Oski readily went clear when asked to win his race and came right away from his rivals to land a decisive success. There was a lot to like about the manner of this success, and while he may not have beaten a great bunch, he should still look fairly treated on his old form when reassessed by the Handicapper. *(tchd 15-2)*
Cyanara had her chance and would have been closer but for a bad error two out, yet was firmly put in her place by the winner. This was another improved effort from 7lb out of the handicap, and she deserves to find another heat over fences.
Cyindien(FR) , with the cheekpieces re-applied, turned in a much more encouraging effort and got a lot closer to the third horse than had been the case at Southwell last time. He is fairly weighted on his hurdle form, but is still a maiden and very hard to catch right.
Pangeran(USA)'s effort proved short-lived, and he looked decididely one paced from two out, but still turned in an improved effort. He looks to have slipped to a favourable mark, but is not going to progress much more at the age of 13. *(op 33-1)*
Presentingthecase(IRE) , well backed for this return to action, shaped well enough until his lack of fitness told. He can do better with this experience under his belt, but is not one to place too much faith in. *(op 11-1)*
Alfred The Grey , back up to a more suitable trip, was never going and ran well below expectations. He looks moody. *(op 7-1)*
Anshabil(IRE) stopped as though he had been shot before two out and was disappointingly *pulled-up with something amiss. Official explanation: jockey said gelding lost its action turning into the home straight (op 5-1)*

674 TOTESPORT 0800 221 221 H'CAP CHASE (12 fncs) 2m 110y
8:35 (8:40) (Class 4) (0-95,94) 5-Y-O+ **£3,290** (£940; £470)

Form | | | | RPR
U6-P **1** **Take The Oath (IRE)**[22] [388] 8-10-1 **69** TDoyle 80+
(D R Gandolfo) *plld hrd in rr: smooth prog 3 out: wnt 2nd bef last: rdn and str run to catch ldr fnl 50 yds: readily* **12/1**
/1P- **2** *1 ¾* **Meltonian**[364] [687] 8-11-6 **88** SCurran 96+
(K F Clutterbuck) *wnt 2nd at 3rd: led sn after 3 out: 7l clr next: drvn and tired after last: ct cl home* **25/1**
0-5F **3** *5* **Ultimate Limit**[11] [532] 5-10-0 **69** PJBrennan 70
(A Ennis) *plld hrd early: sn midfield: lost pl and drvn 6th: only 7th bef last: styd on to snatch 3rd: difficult ride* **13/2**[3]
6P-0 **4** *hd* **Macgyver (NZ)**[21] [395] 9-11-1 **90** MissLHorner[(7)] 92
(D L Williams) *pressed ldrs: rdn 3 out: one pce fr next* **16/1**
/P-P **5** *3 ½* **Rash Decision (IRE)**[24] [354] 10-11-1 **86** LVickers[(3)] 84
(I W McInnes) *hld up: hdwy 7th: pressed ldrs 3 out: sn rdn: one pce next* **50/1**
-464 **6** *1 ½* **Rattina (GER)**[22] [388] 9-10-0 **71** (v) CRafter[(3)] 69+
(M F Harris) *bhd: rdn whn mstke 3 out: passed btn horses but no ch* **12/1**
5F-1 **7** *2* **River Amora (IRE)**[9] [565] 10-10-2 **70** 7ex (p) JEMoore 65
(J J Best) *prom in 2nd or 3rd tl rdn and wknd bef 2 out* **7/1**
3P4- **8** *hd* **Kicasso**[59] [4779] 6-11-10 **92** RThornton 87
(D G Bridgwater) *midfield: drvn 7th: struggling bef 3 out* **10/1**
0-25 **9** *shd* **Amptina (IRE)**[21] [395] 10-10-6 **74** DElsworth 69
(Mrs S J Smith) *hld up midfield: rdn bef 3 out: sn btn* **4/1**[1]
523- **10** *8* **Sendonthecheque (IRE)**[53] [4853] 10-10-5 **73** (v[1]) RMcGrath 60
(R Ford) *t.k.h in ld: hdd sn after 3 out: lost pl rapidly* **5/1**[2]
P-0P **11** *¾* **Major Reno (IRE)**[9] [565] 8-9-13 **72** MNicolls[(5)] 58
(R C Harper) *midfield: rdn 8th: n.d after* **100/1**
00U **12** *4* **Ballyboe Boy (IRE)**[7] [604] 6-10-11 **84** (b) PCO'Neill[(5)] 72+
(R C Guest) *mstkes and nvr gng wl in rr: blnd 7th (water) and struggling after* **10/1**
3P-P **13** *19* **Cool Dante (IRE)**[24] [354] 10-11-12 **94** JMMaguire 57
(T R George) *bhd fr 5th* **12/1**
P046 **P** **Win Alot**[8] [593] 7-10-1 **72** ow4 ACCoyle[(3)] —
(M C Chapman) *a bhd: no ch whn p.u and dismntd bef 2 out: injured* **22/1**

3m 59.6s (-9.70) **Going Correction** -0.675s/f (Firm)
WFA 5 from 6yo+ 1lb **14** Ran SP% **120.8**
Speed ratings: **95,94,91,91,90 89,88,88,88,84 84,82,73,—** CSF £270.58 CT £2124.94 TOTE £19.10: £4.60, £5.70, £2.70; EX 589.30.
Owner Starlight Racing **Bred** Bernard O'Sullivan **Trained** Wantage, Oxon

FOCUS
A modest winning time for the grade and the form looks weak. The winner can be rated value for a touch further, however.

NOTEBOOK
Take The Oath(IRE) , who shaped with promise despite being pulled up on his seasonal return 22 days previously, showed the clear benefit of that outing and won with something to spare. He took time to settle early on, but once finding his stride, he jumped with aplomb and was always going to get up on the run-in. It will be interesting to see whether he can build on this cosy success, but he *loved the ground and he is at the right end of the handicap to win more races.Official explanation: trainer had no explanation for the improved form shown (op 10-1)*
Meltonian , last seen pulling up in this event last year, had a decent advantage jumping the final fence, but he quickly tired on the run-in and had no answer to the winner's late challenge. This was a very pleasing comeback, he was nicely clear of the rest and can be placed to go one better this summer.
Ultimate Limit would have been seen to a better advantage off a stronger gallop and was doing all of his best work at the finish on this drop back in trip. He is tricky, but has age on his side and can find a race off this mark when faced with a stiffer test. *(op 9-2)*
Macgyver(NZ) failed to quicken when it mattered, but still ran his race and is slowly coming back *into form. This ground is key to him and he is one to keep an eye on when stepping back up in* trip. *(op 14-1)*
Amptina(IRE) again ran well below his best with no apparent excuses. He could be worth riding more prominently, as his only previous success came when he was allowed to dominate. *(op 6-1)*
Sendonthecheque(IRE) was lit up by the first-time visor through the early parts, and paid for that, dropping out most tamely under pressure. *(op 6-1)*

675 TOTESPORTCASINO.COM H'CAP HURDLE (10 hdls) 2m 5f 110y
9:05 (9:06) (Class 3) (0-125,118) 4-Y-O+ **£4,735** (£1,457; £728; £364)

Form | | | | RPR
55-0 **1** **Whispered Secret (GER)**[24] [353] 6-11-12 **118** APMcCoy 124+
(M C Pipe) *settled 3rd: led bef 3 out and lft in command: j.rt fnl two: easily* **6/4**[1]
6-30 **2** *6* **Joshua's Bay**[14] [488] 7-11-2 **108** RJohnson 109+
(J R Jenkins) *hld up: effrt and lft 2nd 3 out: urged along but nvr willing to overtake after: j.lft last* **11/2**[3]
5-21 **3** *9* **Mantles Prince**[12] [508] 11-10-3 **95** ATinkler 85
(A G Juckes) *chsd ldr tl 7th: sn relegated last: stuck on gamely to regain 3rd but no ch w ldrs* **11/2**[3]
10-P **4** *17* **Major Shark (FR)**[40] [92] 7-11-3 **109** (p) AO'Keeffe 82
(Jennie Candlish) *led and 6l clr tl sharp reminders after 5th: hdd bef 3 out where lft 3rd and sltly impeded: promptly downed tools* **13/2**
40-1 **F** **Travel (POL)**[26] [320] 5-11-7 **113** JMMaguire —
(T R George) *settled 4th tl effrt after 7th: 1l 2nd and chalng whn fell 3 out* **10/3**[2]

4m 57.9s (-12.90) **Going Correction** -0.675s/f (Firm) **5** Ran SP% **107.2**
Speed ratings: **96,93,90,84,—** CSF £9.22 TOTE £1.80: £1.20, £1.50; EX 7.00 Place 6 £367.02, Place 5 £163.29..
Owner David Manasseh Daniel Evans Dan Levine **Bred** G Baron Von Ullmann **Trained** Nicholashayne, Devon

FOCUS
A modest winning time for the class and the field came home strung out behind the easy winner.

NOTEBOOK
Whispered Secret(GER) ◆ , who failed to get home over three miles last time, showed his true colours over this more suitable distance and ran out an easy winner. This ground is right up his street and this will have boosted his confidence no end. Providing the Handicapper does not overreact, he could be the type to rack up a sequence this summer. *(op 5-4 tchd Evens)*
Joshua's Bay came there with a chance turning for home, but again displayed his quirks, and was put firmly in his place by the winner. He at least completed this time, and while he is a difficult ride, he is weighted to win at present. It would come as little surprise to see the headgear back on in the future. *(op 6-1 tchd 13-2)*
Mantles Prince was far from disgraced on this step up in class and on ground plenty quick enough for him. There are more prizes in plating-class to be won with him. *(op 13-2 tchd 15-2)*
Major Shark(FR) had his chance from the front, as he prefers, but quickly threw in the towel when challenged late on and ran below par. *(op 8-1 tchd 9-1)*
Travel(POL) was still in with a fighting chance prior to coming to grief and has to rate unlucky. While it cannot be confidently predicted he would have stayed all of this longer trip, he had not been asked for maximum effort at the time of his departure. *(op 11-4 tchd 7-2)*
T/Plt: £770.10 to a £1 stake. Pool: £38,033.95. 36.05 winning tickets. T/Qpdt: £85.60 to a £1 stake. Pool: £2,985.80. 25.80 winning tickets. IM

676 - 678a (Foreign Racing) - See Raceform Interactive

457 HEREFORD (R-H)
Wednesday, June 8

OFFICIAL GOING: Good to firm
Wind: almost nil Weather: sunny

679 HEREFORD JOURNAL CONDITIONAL JOCKEYS' "NATIONAL HUNT" NOVICES' HURDLE (13 hdls) 3m 2f
2:00 (2:00) (Class 4) 5-Y-O+ **£3,341** (£1,028; £514; £257)

Form | | | | RPR
0-32 **1** **Tirikumba**[19] [441] 9-10-11 103 RStephens 99
(S G Griffiths) *j.rt: mde all: rdn after 2 out: hld on wl flat* **6/4**[1]
U-F1 **2** *nk* **Bee Hawk**[25] [359] 6-11-1 105 (t) PCO'Neill[(3)] 106
(P F Nicholls) *t.k.h: hdwy after 3rd: chal on bit after 2 out: sn rdn: ev ch flat: nt qckn nr fin* **15/8**[2]
66-6 **3** *21* **Earcomesannie (IRE)**[31] [245] 5-10-5 71 TGreenway 72
(P A Pritchard) *hld up in rr: no ch fr 10th* **25/1**
05-P **4** *hd* **Valley Warrior**[4] [630] 8-10-12 72 WHutchinson 79
(J S Smith) *prom: chsd wnr fr 3rd: rdn and ev ch after 3 out: wknd after 2 out* **33/1**

000- **P** **Maximize (IRE)**[46] [4984] 11-10-9 .... TJMalone(3) —
(M C Pipe) *chsd wnr tl hmpd and lost pl 3rd: sn struggling and lost tch: t.o whn p.u after 7th* **5/2**[3]

6m 14.1s (-13.90) **Going Correction** -0.75s/f (Firm) **5** Ran SP% **110.1**
Speed ratings: **91,90,84,84,**— CSF £4.82 TOTE £3.00: £1.40, £1.10; EX 4.10.
Owner S G Griffiths **Bred** Mrs Diana Joyce **Trained** Nantgaredig, Carmarthens

FOCUS
A bad race and a moderate time for the class, but the first three have been rated as having run to their marks.

NOTEBOOK
Tirikumba, a well-exposed mare, showed a plucky attitude and, despite jumping out to her right for most of the way, got the better of Bee Hawk on the run-in. She was believed to be in season after the race and her trainer has plans to breed from her. *(op 2-1)*
Bee Hawk towered over the favourite but lacked her heart. Having travelled well, she was unable to get the better of the mare, finding little, and it is unlikely we will see the best of him until he goes chasing. *(op Evens)*
Earcomesannie(IRE), not for the first time, failed to last out this sort of trip. She will be more interesting back at two and a half miles in handicaps. *(op 20-1)*
Valley Warrior has yet to build on his decent Wincanton effort in April and was again a little disappointing. *(op 40-1)*
Maximize(IRE), better known as a chaser, is a character and, having been hampered at the third, decided he had had enough. *(op 4-1)*

680 BET365 CALL 08000 322365 NOVICES' HURDLE (10 hdls) 2m 3f 110y
2:30 (2:30) (Class 4) 4-Y-O+ **£3,750** (£1,154; £577; £288)

Form RPR

42-4 **1** **State Of Play**[39] [136] 5-11-0 108 ....(v) TDoyle 107+
(P R Webber) *a.p: wnt 2nd 5th: rdn 2 out: chalng whn bmpd appr last and flat: led cl home: r.o* **2/1**[2]

21 **2** *1* **Adjami (IRE)**[25] [343] 4-11-3 119 .... RThornton 108
(A King) *led: rdn and hung lft appr last and flat: hdd cl home* **8/11**[1]

55-1 **3** *6* **Downing Street (IRE)**[28] [301] 4-11-3 107 ....(b) AO'Keeffe 102
(Jennie Candlish) *hld up: hdwy 6th: rdn 2 out: one pce* **7/1**[3]

0P65 **4** *dist* **Cloud Catcher (IRE)**[10] [563] 4-10-0 60 ....(bt) RYoung(3) —
(M Appleby) *hld up: mstke 7th: sn struggling: t.o* **125/1**

PP **5** *15* **Call Of The Seas (IRE)**[4] [635] 6-10-4 .... ENolan(10) —
(J G M O'Shea) *a bhd: lost tch fr 5th: t.o* **80/1**

004- **6** *6* **Too Posh To Share**[125] [3667] 7-10-7 76 .... JMogford —
(D J Wintle) *chsd ldr to 5th: rdn 6th: sn wknd: t.o* **50/1**

0-04 **F** **Flurry**[25] [361] 6-10-7 .... PHide —
(C J Down) *j. bdly lft and fell 1st* **33/1**

4m 33.5s (-14.40) **Going Correction** -0.75s/f (Firm) **7** Ran SP% **110.7**
Speed ratings: **98,97,95,**—,— —,— CSF £3.70 TOTE £2.80: £1.40, £1.10; EX 4.70.
Owner Mrs C A Waters **Bred** Roland Lerner **Trained** Mollington, Oxon
■ Stewards' Enquiry : R Thornton one-day ban: careless riding (Jun 19)

FOCUS
A two horse race on paper and it was the second favourite who came out on top.

NOTEBOOK
State Of Play, who looked to be going second-best for most of the way, came close to the favourite after the last, but both jockeys seemed happy enough that it did not affect the result. He has some fair form to his name and is unexposed at this sort of trip. *(tchd 9-4)*
Adjami(IRE), an easy winner over a more suitable shorter trip at Bangor back in May, saw out this extra distance, but not as well as the winner, and he had nothing left on the run-in. He is a useful sort for the time of year and can win more races, probably back at shorter. *(tchd 4-5 in places)*
Downing Street(IRE) faced a much stiffer task than when winning at Perth and performed creditably. He ran well for a long way, but in the end was outclassed, and will be worth trying back in handicaps. *(op 15-2 tchd 8-1 and 13-2)*
Flurry got no further than the first, taking a nasty fall, and it remains to be seen how this affects her confidence. *(op 20-1)*

681 SYDNEY PHILLIPS AUCTIONEERS (S) H'CAP HURDLE (8 hdls) 2m 1f
3:00 (3:01) (Class 5) (0-90,89) 4-Y-O+ **£2,401** (£686; £343)

Form RPR

46-4 **1** **Desert Spa (USA)**[45] [1] 10-10-13 83 .... MrTJO'Brien(7) 96+
(G E Jones) *hld up in tch: led 3 out: rdn clr appr last: r.o wl* **11/2**[2]

0/5- **2** *9* **Jack Durrance (IRE)**[2] [292] 5-9-8 64 .... EDehdashti(7) 68
(G A Ham) *hld up and bhd: stdy hdwy after 4th: chsd wnr after 2 out: no imp* **50/1**

3-40 **3** *1* **Pure Brief (IRE)**[21] [412] 8-10-11 74 ....(b) RThornton 77
(J Mackie) *hld up in tch: led 4th to 3 out: one pce fr 2 out* **13/2**[3]

041- **4** *3* **Timidjar (IRE)**[62] [4754] 12-10-11 77 .... ONelmes(3) 77
(Mrs D Thomas) *hld up and bhd: hdwy after 3 out: kpt on same pce fr 2 out* **11/1**

/PP- **5** *4* **Camaraderie**[188] [2579] 9-11-3 80 .... WHutchinson 76
(A W Carroll) *hld up towards rr: hdwy 4th: wknd appr last* **5/1**[1]

50-0 **6** *½* **Baker Of Oz**[16] [238] 4-9-12 71 ....(p) AScholes(7) 64
(D Burchell) *hld up in mid-div: hdwy 4th: wknd appr last* **7/1**

5-P0 **7** *2* **My Retreat (USA)**[14] [506] 8-10-10 80 .... MrPYork(7) 74
(R Fielder) *hld up in mid-div: rdn and no real prog fr 3 out* **25/1**

006/ **8** *nk* **Assured Physique**[66] 8-9-11 65 ....(p) DLaverty(5) 58
(A E Jones) *hld up and bhd: rdn appr 5th: sme hdwy appr 2 out: n.d* **14/1**

P0/P **9** *11* **Foreman**[23] [385] 12-9-12 64 .... RYoung(3) 46
(C J Down) *a bhd* **22/1**

0-00 **10** *8* **Inducement**[9] [357] 9-10-10 80 ....(p) SWalsh(7) 54
(R M Stronge) *led after 1st to 2nd: w ldrs: ev ch 3 out: sn rdn: hit 2 out: sn wknd* **16/1**

PP-P **11** *9* **Gipsy Cricketer**[25] 9-9-13 72 ....(t) JKington(10) 37
(M Scudamore) *led 2nd to 4th: ev ch 3 out: sn rdn: wknd 2 out* **33/1**

2PP- **12** *hd* **Grimshaw (USA)**[235] [1738] 10-11-11 88 .... AO'Keeffe 53
(Mrs D A Hamer) *led tl after 1st: lost pl 3rd: sn bhd* **16/1**

54/ **13** *14* **Little Ora (IRE)**[46] 8-11-12 89 .... OMcPhail 40
(J Rudge) *prom tl nt fluent 2nd: bhd fr 3rd* **50/1**

F0/P **14** *2 ½* **Lovers Tale**[15] [486] 7-11-1 85 .... DCosgrave(7) 34
(G A Ham) *hld up in mid-div: hrd rdn whn mstke 5th: sn bhd* **100/1**

6P0- **P** **Dinofelis**[69] [4667] 7-10-9 72 ....(p) JPByrne —
(C W Moore) *prom to 3rd: t.o whn p.u bef 5th* **25/1**

6261 **U** **Lone Soldier (FR)**[13] [520] 9-11-4 88 .... CDSharkey(7) —
(S B Clark) *prom: rdn and outpcd 2 out: 4th and styng on whn blnd and uns rdr last* **13/2**[3]

/P-P **P** **Harlequin Chorus**[10] [566] 15-10-4 74 ....(bt) MrNPearce(7) —
(H E Haynes) *hld up: hdwy 3rd: rdn appr 5th: wknd after 3 out: p.u bef 2 out* **100/1**

3m 50.8s (-12.30) **Going Correction** -0.75s/f (Firm)
WFA 4 from 5yo+ 3lb **17** Ran SP% **118.9**
Speed ratings: **98,93,93,91,90 89,88,88,83,79 75,75,68,67,**— —,— CSF £263.18 CT £1828.95 TOTE £6.60: £1.30, £4.30, £1.90, £2.60; EX 223.30.There was no bid for the winner.
Owner G Elwyn Jones **Bred** Robert White & Virginia White **Trained** Bettws Bledrws, Ceredigion

FOCUS
More quantity than quality on show, but an impressive winner for the grade in the shape of Desert Spa.

NOTEBOOK
Desert Spa(USA) has been running reasonably in defeat since he scored his only previous success over hurdles here in November last year, and this was probably the weakest race he has contested since. He had them all beaten off rounding the turn for home and stayed on strongly to win impressively. He is lightly raced over hurdles and may yet be capable of a little further improvement, but that is required if he is to follow up off a higher mark. *(op 5-1 tchd 6-1)*
Jack Durrance(IRE) ◆, formerley a useful Flat racer with Mark Johnston, had shown nothing over hurdles until today and connections can take heart from this second placing. He did his best to keep tabs on the winner but was fighting a hopeless cause in the final two furlongs. He should be placed to win a similar race. *(op 40-1)*
Pure Brief(IRE) plugged on into third but achieved little and remains winless in nearly three years. *(op 11-2)*
Timidjar(IRE), who is ideally suited by further, was given plenty to do and plugged on without ever threatening. A winner over three miles last time at Taunton, this drop in trip did not suit and it is safe to assume he can do better back up in distance. *(op 12-1)*
Camaraderie shaped well on this seasonal debut and may be capable of getting his head back in front if building at all on this. *(op 11-2)*
Baker Of Oz has stamina limitations and will do better back on the Flat. *(tchd 8-1)*
Lone Soldier(FR), who has been in reasonable form, being a winner last time, looked set to battle it out for third when unseating at the last. *(op 8-1)*

682 HEREFORD JOURNAL BEGINNERS' CHASE (12 fncs) 2m
3:30 (3:32) (Class 4) 5-Y-O+ **£4,706** (£1,448; £724; £362)

Form RPR

03-5 **1** **Perouse**[32] [208] 7-11-0 ....(t) ChristianWilliams 124+
(P F Nicholls) *hld up: hdwy 6th: led 2 out: sn clr: comf* **5/4**[1]

220- **2** *11* **Dawton (POL)**[208] [2166] 7-11-0 .... JMMaguire 115+
(T R George) *chsd ldr: led 8th: rdn 3 out: hdd 2 out: sn btn* **11/2**[3]

F26- **3** *10* **Code Sign (USA)**[245] [1611] 6-11-0 .... RJohnson 108+
(P J Hobbs) *chsd ldrs: rdn and ev ch 3 out: wknd after 2 out* **10/1**

2-22 **4** *30* **Escompteur (FR)**[10] [564] 5-10-13 .... APMcCoy 71
(M C Pipe) *j.lft: led to 8th: sn wknd: t.o* **7/4**[2]

0P-P **5** *11* **Ela Figura**[13] [510] 5-10-3 .... RYoung(3) 53
(M Appleby) *blnd 2nd: sn wl bhd: t.o* **150/1**

P-63 **6** *1* **Cheeky Lad**[10] [564] 5-10-6 .... MrNPearce(7) 77+
(R C Harper) *s.v.s: a wl bhd: t.o* **40/1**

225- **L** **Dhaudeloup (FR)**[141] [3405] 10-11-0 104 .... AO'Keeffe —
(A G Juckes) *unruly s: ref to r: tk no part* **20/1**

3m 51.2s (-11.30) **Going Correction** -0.525s/f (Firm)
WFA 5 from 6yo+ 1lb **7** Ran SP% **113.1**
Speed ratings: **107,101,96,81,76 75,**— CSF £8.59 TOTE £1.70: £1.40, £2.90; EX 10.60.
Owner S McVie **Bred** Jack Iddon **Trained** Ditcheat, Somerset

FOCUS
A good beginners' chase for the track, featuring a couple of smart hurdlers in Perouse and Escompteur, although the winner has been rated two stone off his best hurdles rating.

NOTEBOOK
Perouse, whose rapid level of progress over hurdles levelled out last season, should have had nothing more than a canter around given that his chief rival Escompteur ruined his chance by going off way too fast, but he made hard enough work of getting the better of Dawton and Code Sign and, although well on top at the finish, was only a workmanlike winner. He is obviously a smart sort for the time of year and can win again, but it is highly doubtful that he can reach the heights over fences that he did over timber. *(op 11-8 tchd 13-8)*
Dawton(POL), a fast-ground lover, made a pleasing start to his chasing career, jumping soundly, and he should be capable of winning at least once this summer. *(op 5-1)*
Code Sign(USA) had previous experience of fences and he too ran well for a long way. He will find easier opportunities. *(op 8-1)*
Escompteur(FR) seems to be going the wrong way. He whipped round at the start and lost many lengths last time, and on this occasion went into a clear lead before continually losing ground by jumping out markedly to his left. He dropped away tamely some way out and, while he clearly has plenty of ability, he has a lot to prove at present. *(op 2-1 tchd 13-8)*

683 BBC HEREFORD & WORCESTER RADIO NOVICES' H'CAP HURDLE (8 hdls) 2m 1f
4:00 (4:01) (Class 4) (0-105,89) 4-Y-O+ **£3,828** (£1,178; £589; £294)

Form RPR

0-02 **1** **Master Nimbus**[8] [601] 5-9-8 64 .... MrTJO'Brien(7) 66+
(J J Quinn) *hld up in tch: led after 2 out: sn rdn clr: edgd lft flat: r.o* **4/1**[2]

-223 **2** *4* **Arjay**[11] [551] 7-10-10 80 ....(b) CDSharkey(7) 78
(S B Clark) *hld up: rdn 3 out: hdwy fr 2 out: kpt on u.p to take 2nd nr post* **4/1**[2]

-14U **3** *shd* **Storm Clear (IRE)**[19] [438] 6-11-8 85 .... WMarston 83
(D J Wintle) *hld up: hdwy appr 5th: rdn and chsd wnr after 2 out: no imp* **8/1**[3]

00-0 **4** *5* **Plantagenet Prince**[17] [457] 6-10-3 76 .... JKington(10) 69
(M Scudamore) *prom: rdn after 3 out: wknd appr last* **80/1**

6-P6 **5** *3* **Gentle Warning**[6] [613] 5-10-4 70 .... RYoung(3) 60
(M Appleby) *bhd tl hdwy on ins after 2 out: no further prog* **50/1**

P-F5 **6** *1 ½* **Queen Excalibur**[17] [457] 6-10-10 78 .... LStephens(5) 66
(C Roberts) *hld up: hdwy appr 2 out: eased whn btn appr last* **12/1**

0P0- **7** *5* **Shotacross The Bow (IRE)**[57] [4813] 8-11-10 87 ....(t) NFehily 72+
(Mrs H E Rees) *led: rdn and hdd after 2 out: eased whn btn appr last* **28/1**

P/6- **8** *8* **Transatlantic (USA)**[86] [4378] 7-11-3 80 ....(t) RJohnson 55
(H D Daly) *bhd: hit 4th: short-lived effrt 5th* **7/2**[1]

60-P **9** *1 ¾* **Claim To Fame**[18] [456] 4-11-2 82 .... PJBrennan 57+
(M Pitman) *chsd ldr tl rdn after 3 out: wkng whn hit 2 out* **25/1**

/P3- **10** *21* **Wozzeck**[76] [4529] 5-11-7 84 .... RThornton 37
(R H Buckler) *jinked lft s: bhd fr 5th* **25/1**

3-04 **R** **Spiders Web**[14] [506] 5-11-12 89 ....(b) APMcCoy —
(G L Moore) *v reluctant to s: virtually ref to r* **7/2**[1]

3m 52.6s (-10.50) **Going Correction** -0.75s/f (Firm)
WFA 4 from 5yo+ 3lb **11** Ran SP% **117.6**
Speed ratings: **94,92,92,89,88 87,85,81,80,70** — CSF £19.77 CT £123.16 TOTE £5.00: £1.50, £1.20, £2.70; EX 15.40.
Owner J H Hewitt **Bred** A H Bennett **Trained** Settrington, N Yorks

FOCUS
A poor handicap run in a modest time for the grade.

NOTEBOOK
Master Nimbus, racing off the same mark as when second at Hexham last time, made good progress around runners and gradually went clear after the second last. Clearly moderate, he can nevertheless find another small race this summer. *(op 9-2 tchd 5-1)*
Arjay battled on well for second, recording another solid effort in defeat. *(op 9-2 tchd 5-1 in places)*

Storm Clear(IRE) was unable to go with the winner and got tired in the final furlong. *(op 9-1 tchd 10-1)*
Plantagenet Prince would no doubt have delighted connections with this keeping-on fourth, showing his first real sign of ability. It was a bad race, but this was at least a step in the right direction. *(op 50-1)*
Gentle Warning shapes as though a step up in distance will help. *(op 40-1)*
Queen Excalibur *Official explanation: vet said mare bled from nose (op 10-1)*
Transatlantic(USA) has always struggled to see out his races and today was no different. He was *reported to be suffering from a breathing problem after the raceOfficial explanation: jockey said gelding had a breathing problem (op 9-2 tchd 5-1)*
Spiders Web disgraced himself at the start and clearly cannot be trusted. *(op 5-2)*

684 WEATHERBYS BANK H'CAP CHASE (14 fncs) 2m 3f
4:30 (4:30) (Class 4) (0-105,103) 5-Y-0+ **£4,459** (£1,372; £686; £343)

Form | | | | RPR
P3-1 **1** **Blakeney Coast (IRE)**[31] [234] 8-11-0 **91**.....(t) JTizzard 106+
(C L Tizzard) *mde all: rdn clr after 2 out: eased towards fin* **5/2**[1]
-050 **2** *4* **Eau Pure (FR)**[14] [501] 8-11-0 **91**..... APMcCoy 99+
(G L Moore) *hld up: hdwy 9th: rdn and outpcd after 4 out: rallied to take 2nd last: nt trble wnr* **15/2**
-00F **3** *3 ½* **Rudetski**[17] [461] 8-11-9 **100**.....(t) DRDennis 104
(M Sheppard) *hld up in tch: chsd wnr appr 9th: rdn appr 3 out: lost 2nd last: wknd* **12/1**
P35- **4** *½* **Quizzling (IRE)**[59] [4798] 7-9-11 **77** oh6..... RYoung[(3)] 80
(B J M Ryall) *hld up and bhd: mstke 2nd: outpcd 10th: hdwy appr last: styd on flat* **4/1**[3]
5-63 **5** *5* **Breaking Breeze (IRE)**[13] [511] 10-11-12 **103**..... PJBrennan 101
(J S King) *chsd wnr: rdn 7th: lost 2nd appr 9th: hit 10th: sn wknd* **10/3**[2]
F4-P **6** *2 ½* **Hi Rudolf**[40] [103] 10-9-13 **83**..... JAJenkins[(7)] 79
(H J Manners) *hld up: hdwy 7th: wknd appr 3 out* **40/1**
41-2 **P** **Solve It Sober (IRE)**[19] [436] 11-9-13 **81**..... RStephens[(5)] —
(S G Griffiths) *prom tl wknd 8th: p.u bef 9th* **13/2**
506- **P** **Tam O'Shanter**[47] [4953] 11-9-4 **77** oh19.....(v) ENolan[(10)] —
(J G M O'Shea) *bhd: blnd 5th: sn t.o: p.u bef 9th* **25/1**
F-6U **P** **Just Muckin Around (IRE)**[13] [518] 9-11-5 **96**..... RThornton —
(R H Buckler) *hld up and bhd: mstke 5th: t.o whn p.u bef 9th* **20/1**

4m 37.0s (-9.60) **Going Correction** -0.525s/f (Firm) **9** Ran SP% **115.5**
Speed ratings: **99,97,95,95,93 92,—,—,—** CSF £21.05 CT £189.28 TOTE £3.90: £1.80, £2.30, £3.00; EX 26.20.
Owner The Jam Boys **Bred** Major F B And J G B Boyd **Trained** Milborne Port, Dorset

FOCUS
A straightforward win for Blakeney Coast and the runner-up has been rated as having run to his recent best.

NOTEBOOK
Blakeney Coast(IRE), a winner last time, was given a no-nonsense ride by Tizzard and led throughout for a comfy win. He has found his form again this season and can complete the hat-trick. *(op 2-1)*
Eau Pure(FR), trying her luck over fences again, rallied well to take second and needs stepping back up in distance. *(op 7-1 tchd 8-1)*
Rudetski showed no ill-effects from his recent fall and there is a small race in him if he can manage to find some consistency.
Quizzling(IRE), well backed prior to the off, plugged on for a poor fourth and remains below the required level to win. *(op 8-1)*
Hi Rudolf, who travelled well for a long way, was not given a hard time once beaten. He ran better than his finishing position suggests and is worth watching out for in a similar race. *(op 33-1)*

685 WEATHERBYS INSURANCE STANDARD OPEN NATIONAL HUNT FLAT RACE 2m 1f
5:00 (5:02) (Class 6) 4-6-Y-0 **£1,981** (£566; £283)

Form | | | | RPR
51 **1** **Hill Forts Timmy**[17] [463] 5-11-4..... RYoung[(3)] 96
(J W Mullins) *hld up and bhd: hdwy over 7f out: rdn over 4f out: styd on to ld wl ins fnl f* **3/1**[1]
2 *½* **Mr Jawbreaker (IRE)** 6-11-0..... RThornton 90+
(J T Stimpson) *hld up in tch: rdn over 4f out: led over 2f out: hung lft over 1f out: hdd wl ins fnl f* **16/1**
00-4 **3** *1 ¼* **Show Of Hands (IRE)**[36] [179] 5-11-0..... APMcCoy 87
(J G M O'Shea) *chsd ldr: led over 3f out: rdn and hdd over 2f out: ev ch ins fnl f: nt qckn* **4/1**[2]
30-3 **4** *2* **Xcentra**[29] [277] 4-10-11..... JTizzard 82
(B G Powell) *hld up and bhd: hdwy over 8f out: rdn over 3f out: no ex ins fnl f* **11/1**
5 *9* **Ponchatrain (IRE)**[17] 5-11-0..... WMarston 77+
(D J Wintle) *sn chsng clr ldr: led 9f out: rdn and hdd over 3f out: wknd over 2f out* **20/1**
4 **6** *2* **Judy The Drinker**[17] [463] 6-9-11..... ENolan[(10)] 67
(J G M O'Shea) *bhd tl styd on fnl 2f: n.d* **11/1**
2 **7** *4* **Princess Yum Yum**[27] [316] 5-10-2..... LTreadwell[(5)] 63
(J L Spearing) *hld up towards rr: hdwy after 7f: rdn over 4f out: wknd over 3f out* **6/1**
3 **8** *4* **Silver Serg**[14] [507] 4-10-4..... EDehdashti[(7)] 63
(G L Moore) *hld up in tch: rdn over 4f out: wknd over 3f out* **5/1**[3]
0 **9** *¾* **Inch Over**[6] [616] 4-10-11..... JPByrne 63
(S A Brookshaw) *hld up and bhd: hdwy over 7f out: no imp whn hung lft bnd over 4f out* **28/1**
10 *9* **Shannon Gale Boy (IRE)** 6-11-0..... ChristianWilliams 57
(K R Pearce) *mid-div: hmpd on ins over 9f out: bhd fnl 5f* **25/1**
4 **11** *shd* **The Cliffe (IRE)**[28] [300] 6-11-0..... OMcPhail 56
(J Rudge) *hld up in tch: n.m.r on ins over 9f out: rdn over 5f out: wknd over 4f out* **14/1**
12 *27* **Dawn For The Stars (IRE)**[25] 5-10-0..... RSpate[(7)] 22
(O O'Neill) *chsd ldrs 5f* **100/1**
13 *21* **Hi Blue** 6-10-11..... RHobson[(3)] —
(M Wellings) *hld up in tch: rdn and struggling after 5f: sn bhd* **40/1**
14 *dist* **Cee Moor Biscuits**[25] 5-10-9 ow2.....(p) MrDMansell[(7)] —
(Mrs A Price) *led: sn clr: wknd and hdd 9f out: sn lost pl: t.o* **100/1**
15 *14* **Millie Boon** 6-10-0..... KBurke[(7)] —
(L J Williams) *rdn after 5f: a bhd: t.o* **66/1**

3m 52.0s (-9.10) **Going Correction** -0.75s/f (Firm)
WFA 4 from 5yo+ 3lb **15** Ran SP% **123.1**
Speed ratings: **91,90,90,89,85 84,82,80,79,75 75,62,53,—,—** CSF £52.57 TOTE £4.50: £1.40, £6.10, £1.30; EX 108.20 Place 6 £27.59, Place 5 £21.30.
Owner Mrs J C Scorgie **Bred** R L And Mrs Scorgie **Trained** Wilsford-Cum-Lake, Wilts

FOCUS
A poor bumper rated through the winner.

NOTEBOOK
Hill Forts Timmy, bidding to defy a penalty, stayed on strongest in the straight and his previous experience told in the end. He may have had to settle for second had Mr Jawbreaker not run green and, although the form is moderate, he will improve further for jumping obstacles. *(op 7-2 tchd 4-1)*
Mr Jawbreaker(IRE) was one of the more interesting outsiders and the booking of Robert Thornton for his small stable signalled a big run was expected. He travelled well throughout and quickened nicely into the lead before the turn in, only to run around under pressure and throw the race away. He would probably have won had he had the benefit of a previous outing, but he should find a similarly weak race in the coming months in which to get off the mark. *(op 11-1)*
Show Of Hands(IRE) had his chance and simply lacked a finishing kick. He will require further over hurdles. *Official explanation: jockey said gelding had a breathing problem (op 3-1)*
Xcentra is another for whom two and a half miles will help once sent hurdling. *(op 10-1 tchd 12-1)*
Ponchatrain(IRE), a recent winner of a maiden point-to-point in Ireland, was struggling from half a mile out and found this an inadequate test of stamina. He will be capable of better once tackling obstacles.
T/Plt: £18.60 to a £1 stake. Pool: £27,853.05. 1,090.05 winning tickets. T/Qpdt: £11.20 to a £1 stake. Pool: £1,639.90. 107.80 winning tickets. KH

369 MARKET RASEN (R-H)
Wednesday, June 8

OFFICIAL GOING: Good to firm
The ground was described as 'almost firm, especially in the back straight'. Third last fence omitted on each circuit in all chases.
Wind: almost nil Weather: fine and sunny, very warm

686 HYDROGEN (S) H'CAP HURDLE (10 hdls) 2m 3f 110y
2:10 (2:11) (Class 5) (0-90,85) 4-Y-0+ **£2,245** (£641; £320)

Form | | | | RPR
0-00 **1** **Sylcan Express**[17] [458] 12-10-8 **67**.....(p) MBatchelor 70
(O O'Neill) *alays handy: styd on fr 2 out: kpt on wl run-in to ld nr fin: jst hld on* **40/1**
-643 **2** *½* **End Of An Error**[8] [606] 6-11-0 **83**..... SGagan[(10)] 85
(Mrs E Slack) *in rr: rapid hdwy after last: fin wl: jst failed* **8/1**
03-2 **3** *shd* **Coxwell Cossack**[31] [237] 12-11-8 **84**..... CRafter[(3)] 86
(Mark Campion) *led tl hdd and no ex nr fin* **6/1**[3]
P-P2 **4** *½* **Kyle Of Lochalsh**[28] [306] 5-11-8 **81**..... ADempsey 82+
(J S Goldie) *chsd ldrs: kpt on wl run-in* **4/1**[1]
R0U0 **5** *2 ½* **Seemore Sunshine**[17] [469] 8-10-12 **78**..... PCStringer[(7)] 77
(M J Gingell) *hdwy 7th: chsng ldrs 2 out: one pce* **100/1**
-4PP **6** *1 ½* **Island Warrior (IRE)**[17] [458] 10-10-8 **67**.....(tp) JamesDavies 64
(B P J Baugh) *jnd ldrs 4th: one pce fr 2 out* **40/1**
6-04 **7** *2 ½* **Young Tot (IRE)**[21] [412] 7-11-12 **85**..... MAFitzgerald 80
(Mrs A Duffield) *in rr: pushed along 4th: hdwy to chse ldrs after 3 out: one pce* **7/1**
0-00 **8** *1 ¼* **Fortune's Fool**[9] [592] 6-11-1 **74**..... ATinkler 68
(I A Brown) *chsd ldrs: wknd 2 out* **40/1**
-065 **9** *nk* **Paula Lane**[14] [506] 5-11-2 **75**..... MFoley 68
(R Curtis) *hld up in rr: hdwy 3 out: one pce fr next* **10/1**
R-63 **10** *hd* **Lord Attica (IRE)**[27] [310] 6-9-12 **64**.....(v) CPoste[(7)] 57
(M F Harris) *rr-div: hdwy 3 out: nvr rchd ldrs* **14/1**
0-P0 **11** *2 ½* **Alethea Gee**[6] [613] 7-11-3 **76**..... RMcGrath 67
(K G Reveley) *hld up towards rr: sme hdwy 3 out: nvr nr ldrs* **40/1**
6-30 **12** *¾* **Lazy Lena (IRE)**[25] [345] 6-11-4 **77**..... NPMulholland 67
(Miss L C Siddall) *chsd ldrs: fdd 2 out* **14/1**
-403 **13** *¾* **Book's Way**[17] [469] 9-11-4 **77**..... GLee 66
(D W Thompson) *chsd ldrs: wknd appr 2 out* **11/2**[2]
5-40 **14** *20* **Prince Of Aragon**[25] [357] 9-11-3 **83**.....(bt) RLucey-Butler[(7)] 52
(Miss Suzy Smith) *a in rr: bhd fr 3 out: t.o* **14/1**
00-0 **P** **Super Boston**[31] [237] 5-10-11 **70**..... JimCrowley —
(Miss L C Siddall) *sn bhd: t.o whn p.u bef 7th* **22/1**
4/P0 **P** **Niciara (IRE)**[20] [429] 8-11-8 **84**..... ACCoyle[(3)] —
(M C Chapman) *nt jump wl: detached in last whn p.u after 3rd* **33/1**
04P/ **P** **Little Alfie (IRE)**[553] [2530] 8-10-8 **67**..... ARoss —
(B S Rothwell) *mid-div: lost pl 3 out: t.o whn p.u bef next* **50/1**

4m 44.6s (-5.40) **Going Correction** -0.575s/f (Firm) **17** Ran SP% **122.4**
Speed ratings: **87,86,86,86,85 84,83,83,83,83 82,81,81,73,— —,—** CSF £324.84 CT £2227.49 TOTE £42.20: £4.00, £2.30, £1.60, £2.00; EX 597.90.There was no bid for the winner.
Owner Richard Fletcher **Bred** F T Gibbon And Son **Trained** Cleeve Hill, Gloucs
■ Stewards' Enquiry : P C Stringer three-day ban: used whip with excessive frequency and without giving gelding time to respond (Jun 19, 21-22)

FOCUS
A moderate time, even for a seller with nine still well in contention at the second last flight. The winner rolled back the years and the next five home appear to have run to their marks.

NOTEBOOK
Sylcan Express, without a win for five years, sported first-time cheekpieces. He nailed the third near the line but would have been beaten himself in just two more strides.
End Of An Error was not in the first ten two out but, sprouting wings after the last, needed just a few more yards.
Coxwell Cossack, without a win for over four years, tried hard to make all and was only just found out.
Kyle Of Lochalsh, in the firing line throughout, would have been even more closely involved in the finish but for his rider losing his whip soon after the third-last flight. *(op 9-2 tchd 5-1)*
Seemore Sunshine, struggling to make any impact, ran better but he might not forget this in a hurry. *(op 80-1)*
Island Warrior(IRE), pulled up on his two most recent starts and without a win to his name for over three years, had the tongue strap back on and he ran a lot better. *(op 33-1)*
Alethea Gee *Official explanation: jockey said mare boiled over at start (op 33-1)*

687 ARGON NOVICES' HURDLE (12 hdls) 3m
2:40 (2:40) (Class 4) 4-Y-0+ **£3,234** (£924; £462)

Form | | | | RPR
5414 **1** **Relix (FR)**[3] [643] 5-11-1 105.....(t) DMcGann[(5)] 94+
(A M Crow) *chsd ldrs: led appr 2 out: styd on wl* **15/8**[1]
66-0 **2** *4* **Seattle Prince (USA)**[24] [365] 7-10-7 78..... WKennedy[(7)] 83
(S Gollings) *chsd ldrs: led after 9th: hdd appr 2 out: kpt on same pce between last 2* **8/1**
-231 **3** *8* **Combat Drinker (IRE)**[13] [523] 7-11-6 90.....(t) GLee 82+
(D McCain) *hld up: smooth hdwy 9th: w ldrs and rdn appr 2 out: sn outpcd: eased towards fin* **2/1**[2]
64-0 **4** *9* **I'm Your Man**[21] [406] 6-10-11 95..... PBuchanan[(3)] 66
(Mrs Dianne Sayer) *drvn along and hdwy 9th: sn chsng ldrs: wknd appr 2 out* **15/2**[3]

40-P **5** *16* **River Of Fire**[15] [237] 7-11-0 68 ....(v) JamesDavies 50
(C N Kellett) *led tl after 2nd: chsd ldrs: hrd rdn 3 out: lost pl appr next* **25/1**

0-00 **6** *dist* **Solemn Vow**[13] [523] 4-10-2 .... RWalford —
(P Maddison) *in tch: rdn and lost pl 9th: sn bhd: t.o* **100/1**

00-5 **7** *23* **Daily Run (IRE)**[21] [414] 7-10-9 71 ....(t) DCCostello(5) —
(G M Moore) *in tch: lost pl after 8th: sn bhd: t.o* **18/1**

0- **P** **Sirroco Wind**[115] [3830] 5-10-9 .... DFlavin(5) —
(Mrs L B Normile) *bhd and reminders 6th: t.o 9th: p.u bef 2 out* **20/1**

0-00 **P** **Hapthor**[17] [470] 6-10-8 ow1 .... DVerco —
(F Jestin) *led after 2nd: hit 7th: hdd after 9th: wknd rapidly: t.o whn p.u bef 2 out* **100/1**

30-0 **P** **Rocket Force (USA)**[24] [369] 5-11-0 99 ....(p) ATinkler —
(S Gollings) *nt fluent: in rr: rdn 8th: no rspnse: sn bhd: t.o whn p.u bef 2 out* **8/1**

5m 55.4s (-11.40) **Going Correction** -0.575s/f (Firm)
WFA 4 from 5yo+ 5lb **10** Ran SP% **118.0**
Speed ratings: **96,94,92,89,83** —,—,—,—,— CSF £17.42 TOTE £2.60: £1.10, £2.80, £1.10; EX 33.90.
Owner Stuart Taylor, David Hardy, Lee Seaton **Bred** S N C Lagardere Elevage **Trained** Bonjedward, Borders

FOCUS
A weak novices' hurdle run at just a steady pace, but in the end it produced a clear-cut winner who bounced off the fast ground.

NOTEBOOK
Relix(FR) appreciated this totally different ground and raced with real zest to keep his only pursuer at bay. *(tchd 2-1)*
Seattle Prince(USA), entered in the opening seller, went on and increased the pace, but in the end he was very much second-best. *(op 11-1)*
Combat Drinker(IRE) travelled strongly and moved into contention looking a real danger, but this point winner could only find the one pace off the bridle. *(op 15-8)*
I'm Your Man, unplaced in eight previous starts, must be wondering where his official rataing of 95 comes from. *(op 10-1)*
River Of Fire had been pulled up in selling company on his previous start.
Rocket Force(USA) looks to have lost his way completely and cheekpieces rather than a visor had no effect whatsoever. *Official explanation: jockey said gelding had a breathing problem (op 25-1)*
Sirroco Wind *Official explanation: jockey said gelding had a breathing problem (op 25-1)*

688 PARTY PERFECT (TM) BEGINNERS' CHASE (12 fncs 2 omitted) 2m 6f 110y
3:10 (3:10) (Class 4) 5-Y-O+ **£3,750** (£1,154; £577; £288)

Form RPR

520/ **1** **Bertiebanoo (IRE)**[417] [4870] 7-11-0 .... JEMoore 123+
(M C Pipe) *trckd ldr: led 4th: rdn appr 2 out: edgd lft landing last: styd on wl* **5/2**[2]

60-2 **2** *2* **Avitta (IRE)**[9] [593] 6-10-7 114 .... SThomas 113+
(Miss Venetia Williams) *trckd ldrs: wnt clr 2nd after 3 out: upsides and rdn next: j.rt and sltly hmpd last: no ex* **11/8**[1]

-003 **3** *19* **Prize Ring**[15] [479] 6-11-0 104 .... FKeniry 101+
(G M Moore) *wnt prom 5th: wl outpcd by 1st 2 appr 2 out* **6/1**[3]

P/ **4** *12* **Heather Lad**[25] 12-11-0 .... RMcGrath 88
(C Grant) *chsd ldrs: lost pl after 3 out* **11/1**

1/ **5** *10* **Kitty John (IRE)**[577] [2032] 8-10-0 90 .... WKennedy(7) 71
(J L Spearing) *chsd ldrs: wknd 3 out* **8/1**

FP0/ **6** *11* **Civil Gent (IRE)**[25] 6-11-0 55 ....(t) BHarding 67
(M E Sowersby) *nt fluent in rr: bhd fr 9th* **20/1**

-PP4 **F** **Alchemystic (IRE)**[13] [524] 5-10-5 90 ....(tp) PWhelan(3) —
(M A Barnes) *chsd ldrs: hit 1st: fell 6th* **25/1**

4/3- **P** **Darak (IRE)**[59] 9-10-7 .... PKinsella(7) —
(Mrs K J Tutty) *led to 4th: lost pl 7th: t.o whn p.u bef 9th* **28/1**

5m 26.9s (-19.50) **Going Correction** -0.575s/f (Firm)
WFA 5 from 6yo+ 2lb **8** Ran SP% **116.5**
Speed ratings: **110,109,102,98,95 91**,—,— CSF £6.66 TOTE £3.60: £1.70, £1.10, £1.80; EX 7.70.
Owner P A Newey **Bred** Edmond Cronin **Trained** Nicholashayne, Devon

FOCUS
A decent time for a race of its type and the first two look well above average by the standards of summer jumping.

NOTEBOOK
Bertiebanoo(IRE), absent for 417 days, looked as fit as a flea on his first outing for Martin Pipe. Not very big, he found the fences no problem and proved too determined for the runner-up on the run-in. *(op 9-4 tchd 11-4)*
Avitta(IRE), on much quicker ground, seemed to be just getting the worst of the argument when there was a coming together at the final fence. She jumps soundly and deserves to go on better. *(op 7-4)*
Prize Ring is basically out of sorts and did not improve one jot on his chasing debut. *(op 8-1)*
Heather Lad, a winner three times in points, had been pulled up on his only previous try under Rules. *(op 15-2)*
Kitty John(IRE), absent since winning over hurdles at Worcester in Novmber 2003, stopped to nothing starting the final turn on her chasing debut. *(tchd 9-1)*

689 MAXX (TM) GASES H'CAP HURDLE (10 hdls) 2m 3f 110y
3:40 (3:40) (Class 3) (0-120,120) 4-Y-O+ **£4,836** (£1,488; £744; £372)

Form RPR

0-33 **1** **Beseiged (USA)**[24] [370] 8-10-13 **110** .... PWhelan(3) 123+
(R A Fahey) *trckd ldrs: wnt 2nd 3 out: led appr 2 out: sn qcknd wl clr: eased towards fin* **7/2**[1]

01-0 **2** *21* **Hopbine**[26] [329] 9-10-11 **105** ....(p) GLee 95+
(J L Spearing) *hld up: hdwy 6th: wnt 2nd appr 2 out: no ch w wnr* **6/1**[2]

0054 **3** *3* **Day Du Roy (FR)**[20] [428] 7-10-9 **103** .... AThornton 89
(Miss L C Siddall) *hld up: smooth hdwy 6th: trcking ldrs 3 out: effrt appr next: kpt on to take mod 3rd nr line* **8/1**[3]

12- **4** *½* **Green Prospect (FR)**[339] [878] 5-11-7 **115** .... JEMoore 101
(M C Pipe) *led tl after 3rd: led 5th tl appr 2 out: sn wknd: lost 3rd nr line* **7/2**[1]

0/06 **5** *12* **Erins Lass (IRE)**[12] [536] 8-9-11 **94** oh5 .... DCrosse(3) 68
(R Dickin) *sn bhd: sme hdwy 7th: nvr on terms* **14/1**

0-45 **6** *½* **Half Inch**[18] [451] 5-10-4 **103** .... MNicolls(5) 76
(B I Case) *drvn along and in rr fr 5th: nvr a factor* **14/1**

3-56 **7** *¾* **Edmo Heights**[28] [305] 9-11-12 **120** .... RGarritty 92
(T D Easterby) *chsd ldrs: lost pl 7th: sn bhd* **11/1**

0-60 **8** *16* **Rising Generation (FR)**[13] [525] 8-11-12 **120** .... BHarding 76
(N G Richards) *w ldrs: wknd after 3 out: sn bhd* **12/1**

223- **9** *7* **Brave Effect (IRE)**[78] [4510] 9-10-3 **100** ....(v) PBuchanan(3) 49
(Mrs Dianne Sayer) *w ldrs: led after 3rd: hit 5th and hdd: drvn along and lost pl 7th: sn bhd* **6/1**[2]

4-4F **10** *1¾* **Siegfrieds Night (IRE)**[18] [450] 4-10-7 **115** .... DSwan(10) 59
(M C Chapman) *sn bhd and drvn along: lost tch 5th* **25/1**

00-P **P** **Saint Par (FR)**[4] [633] 7-11-12 **120** ....(p) JPMcNamara —
(Jennie Candlish) *w ldrs to 2nd: lost pl 6th: sn bhd: t.o whn p.u bef 2 out* **33/1**

4m 34.0s (-16.00) **Going Correction** -0.575s/f (Firm)
WFA 4 from 5yo+ 3lb **11** Ran SP% **120.3**
Speed ratings: **109,100,99,99,94 94,93,87,84,84** — CSF £25.87 CT £160.87 TOTE £3.90: £1.90, £2.60, £3.30; EX 30.70.
Owner Mike Caulfield **Bred** Gainsborough Farm Inc **Trained** Musley Bank, N Yorks

FOCUS
A strongly-run race and the wide-margin winner appeared to put up a personal best.

NOTEBOOK
Beseiged(USA), still 10lb higher than for his last success two years ago, was in the right frame of mind and hard on the steel when jumping clear two out. He was value for thirty lengths but what will happen to his rating after this remains to be seen.
Hopbine, an in-and-out performer, went in pursuit of the winner but was soon waving goodbye to him. *(tchd 13-2)*
Day Du Roy(FR), well backed at long odds, travelled strongly as usual but, as is his wont, his response to pressure was very limited indeed. *(op 14-1)*
Green Prospect(FR), absent since July, looked as fit as a flea. Keen to regain the lead, the winner left him for dead going to two out and he missed out on third spot near the line. *(op 3-1)*
Erins Lass(IRE), out of the handicap, never entered the argument.
Half Inch, on ground plenty lively enough for her, was struggling with a full circuit to go.
Edmo Heights *Official explanation: jockey said gelding returned lame (op 10-1 tchd 12-1)*

690 NITROGEN H'CAP CHASE (12 fncs 2 omitted) 2m 6f 110y
4:10 (4:12) (Class 4) (0-105,101) 5-Y-O+ **£3,848** (£1,184; £592; £296)

Form RPR

-513 **1** **Lanmire Tower (IRE)**[17] [464] 11-10-2 **84** ....(p) WKennedy(7) 95+
(S Gollings) *a wl in tch: drvn along 8th: styd on fr 2 out: led last 100yds* **6/1**

-0P0 **2** *1½* **Lord Of The Land**[15] [480] 12-9-11 **77** .... DCCostello(5) 85+
(Mrs E Slack) *chsd ldrs: slt ld 2 out: hdd and no ex run-in* **40/1**

200- **3** *3* **Clear Dawn (IRE)**[101] [4089] 10-11-0 **89** .... GLee 93
(J M Jefferson) *chsd ldrs: led after 3 out: sn hdd: one pce run-in* **10/1**

-635 **4** *2* **Beaugency (NZ)**[8] [605] 7-11-3 **95** ....(p) LMcGrath(3) 97
(R C Guest) *hld up wl in tch: jnd ldrs 6th: led appr 2 out: sn hdd: wknd last 150yds* **10/1**

P/P- **5** *1¾* **John Rich**[25] 9-10-0 **75** ....(tp) BHarding 75
(M E Sowersby) *a wl in tch: 7th and outpcd whn bmpd 2 out: kpt on wl* **28/1**

6564 **6** *1½* **Celtic Legend (FR)**[13] [511] 6-11-3 **92** .... RMcGrath 91
(K G Reveley) *a wl in tch: wnt prom 3 out: one pced between last 2* **7/2**[1]

F-63 **7** *9* **Raise A McGregor**[21] [416] 9-10-3 **78** .... PMoloney 72+
(Mrs S J Smith) *led 2nd: pckd 9th: hdd after 3 out: 6th and wkng whn blnd 2 out* **7/1**

-P34 **8** *4* **Benefit**[15] [481] 11-10-9 **84** .... JimCrowley 70
(Miss L C Siddall) *w ldrs: lost pl after 3 out* **11/2**[3]

5-05 **9** *2* **Bobosh**[12] [534] 9-11-12 **101** .... CLlewellyn 85
(R Dickin) *led to 2nd: lost pl 6th: sn bhd* **8/1**

3-21 **10** *dist* **Ho Ho Hill (IRE)**[29] [271] 7-11-9 **101** .... PBuchanan(3) —
(Miss Lucinda V Russell) *chsd ldrs: wknd qckly after 3 out: sn bhd: virtually p.u: t.o* **4/1**[2]

5m 34.2s (-12.20) **Going Correction** -0.575s/f (Firm) **10** Ran SP% **119.6**
Speed ratings: **98,97,96,95,95 94,91,90,89**,— CSF £174.81 CT £2364.50 TOTE £6.40: £2.00, £9.40, £3.20; EX 277.20.
Owner Mrs D Dukes **Bred** Miss Emer Carty **Trained** Scamblesby, Lincs

FOCUS
Just a steady gallop with seven still in contention two out. The first four ran to their marks and the form looks sound.

NOTEBOOK
Lanmire Tower(IRE), who is in good form, likes it here at his local track and he stayed on just the better on the run-in. His rider looks a good prospect. *(op 11-2)*
Lord Of The Land, back over fences, jumped to the front at the second-last fence but had to give best in the closing stages. *(op 28-1)*
Clear Dawn(IRE), 8lb lower than his last success, was having his first outing since February. It would be dangerous to assume that it will have improved him. *(op 11-1 tchd 12-1)*
Beaugency(NZ), tried in cheekpieces this time, travelled strongly but after going on he tired noticeably on the run-in. He is a weak finisher and probably has a problem. *(op 11-1 tchd 12-1)*
John Rich, who has been busy in points, kept on in his own time after collecting a hefty bump. It may be that the further he goes the better. *(op 25-1)*
Celtic Legend(FR) looked sure to be involved in the finish when getting into contention starting the final turn, but he did not see it out as well as some. His stamina looks doubtful. *(op 5-1)*
Raise A McGregor was on the back foot when he made a complete hash of the second-last fence. *(op 11-2)*
Ho Ho Hill(IRE), beaten off much lower marks than this prior to his Hereford success in a maiden chase, has changed stables since. He stopped to nothing starting the final turn and in the end was allowed to complete in his own time. *Official explanation: trainer said gelding ran too freely early on and suffered interference in-running (tchd 7-2)*

691 OXYGEN NOVICES' HURDLE (8 hdls) 2m 1f 110y
4:40 (4:43) (Class 4) 4-Y-O+ **£3,346** (£956; £478)

Form RPR

4-12 **1** **Three Ships**[13] [513] 4-10-11 105 .... MrMatthewSmith(7) 105+
(Miss J Feilden) *quite keen: trckd ldrs: jnd ldr 5th: slt ld 2 out: styd on wl towards fin* **10/1**

5 **2** *1½* **Constable Burton**[21] [415] 4-10-11 .... MAFitzgerald 96
(Mrs A Duffield) *w ldrs: led 3rd to 2 out: no ex last 150yds* **12/1**

1 **3** *3½* **Diamond Cutter (NZ)**[11] [549] 6-11-7 105 .... HOliver 102
(R C Guest) *trckd ldrs: t.k.h: kpt on same pce appr 2 out* **7/1**

2-24 **4** *4* **Leopold (SLO)**[15] [482] 4-10-4 99 .... CPoste(7) 88
(M F Harris) *rr-div: hdwy to chse ldrs 5th: one pce appr 2 out* **11/2**[3]

44-1 **5** *1¼* **Resplendent Star (IRE)**[13] [513] 8-11-7 108 ....(v) LAspell 98+
(Mrs L Wadham) *hld up in rr: hdwy 4th: sn trcking ldrs: effrt appr 2 out: one pce* **7/2**[2]

0-23 **6** *shd* **Moldavia (GER)**[9] [596] 4-9-11 95 .... WKennedy(7) 80
(M C Chapman) *hld up in rr: hdwy 5th: rdn after next: kpt on: nvr rchd ldrs* **8/1**

0-32 **7** *1* **King's Protector**[20] [418] 5-11-0 105 .... GLee 89
(M D Hammond) *chsd ldrs: wl outpcd appr 2 out* **9/4**[1]

F-0 **8** *dist* **Skiddaw Jones**[20] [418] 5-10-11 ....(t) PWhelan(3) —
(M A Barnes) *chsd ldrs: wknd and eased after 3 out: sn bhd: t.o* **66/1**

0 **9** *½* **Bowling Along**[10] [569] 4-10-1 .... PBuchanan(3) —
(M E Sowersby) *mid-div: lost pl 5th: sn bhd: t.o* **66/1**

The Form Book, Raceform Ltd, Compton, RG20 6NL

10 11 **Mr Pilchard**[38] 5-10-11 .... (p) LVickers[(3)] —
(Mrs S Lamyman) *led to 3rd: hit 5th: sn lost pl and bhd: t.o* **100/1**

PP- **11** 9 **Darkshape**[160] 3106 5-11-0 .... SThomas —
(Miss Venetia Williams) *s.s: a bhd: lost tch 5th: t.o* **22/1**

P **Passionate Knight (IRE)** 6-11-0 .... ARoss —
(B S Rothwell) *slowly away: bhd: reminders 3rd: t.o whn p.u bef 2 out* **50/1**

P- **F** **Young Warrior (IRE)**[196] 2430 4-10-11 .... FKeniry —
(M D Hammond) *hld up in rr: lost tch 5th: wl bhd whn fell 2 out* **50/1**

0/0 **P** **Mapilut Du Moulin (FR)**[24] 375 5-11-0 .... AThornton —
(C R Dore) *hld up towards rr: sddle slipped 3rd: p.u bef next* **40/1**

43-F **F** **Best Flight**[34] 192 5-11-0 102 .... KRenwick 89
(N Wilson) *hld up: jnd ldrs 5th: wknd appr 2 out: 7th whn fell last* **12/1**

4m 6.60s (-9.80) **Going Correction** -0.575s/f (Firm)
WFA 4 from 5yo+ 3lb **15** Ran SP% **131.1**
Speed ratings: **98,97,95,94,93 93,92,—,—,— —,—,—,—,—** CSF £128.23 TOTE £11.10: £3.80, £4.40, £3.00; EX 224.10 Place 6 £209.49, Place 5 £97.88.
Owner Ocean Trailers Ltd **Bred** Juddmonte Farms **Trained** Exning, Suffolk

FOCUS
Just a modest novices' hurdle but an improved performance from the winner and the runner-up.

NOTEBOOK
Three Ships reversed Huntingdon placings with Resplendent Star on better terms. Well handled, he was firmly in command at the line. *(op 9-1)*
Constable Burton, a dual winner on the Flat on the All-Weather, went on but in the end the winner saw it out much the better. *(op 16-1)*
Diamond Cutter(NZ) again took quite a keen grip. He ran well under his penalty. *(op 11-2)*
Leopold(SLO) keeps running well but that first win is proving elusive. *(op 7-1 tchd 15-2)*
Resplendent Star(IRE), well backed to confirm Huntingdon placings with the winner, was a shade disappointing as he did not find as much as seemed likely when popped the question. *(op 11-2)*
Moldavia(GER) kept on in her own time but never looked anything of a threat. *(op 15-2)*
King's Protector, who looked to have been found a good opportunity to make up for his Kelso misfortune, was a disappointment, finding little when the dash for home began. *(op 3-1)*
Darkshape *Official explanation: jockey said gelding reared at start (op 20-1)*
Best Flight, absent for five weeks after his Wetherby misfortune, emptied in a matter of strides and was unlucky enough to take another heavy fall at the last. *(op 33-1)*
Mapilut Du Moulin(FR) *Official explanation: jockey said saddle slipped (op 33-1)*
T/Plt: £78.80 to a £1 stake. Pool: £27,044.55. 250.30 winning tickets. T/Qpdt: £46.70 to a £1 stake. Pool: £1,595.50. 25.25 winning tickets. WG

[611]UTTOXETER (L-H)

Thursday, June 9

OFFICIAL GOING: Good to firm (good in places)
The going was described as 'good to firm at worst, good in many places'. The second last fence in the back straight has been removed until September.
Wind: Moderate, half against Weather: Fine.

692 CHRYSALIS GROUP BREAKFREE.BIZ NOVICES' H'CAP CHASE (11 fncs 1 omitted) 2m
6:40 (6:41) (Class 4) (0-105,104) 5-Y-0+ **£4,478** (£1,378; £689; £344)

Form RPR

3-41 **1** **In The Frame (IRE)**[25] 364 6-11-12 **104** .... ChristianWilliams 118
(Evan Williams) *hld up: hdwy 6th: wnt 2nd 3 out: styd on to ld last 100yds: all out* **4/1**[2]

FP1- **2** *hd* **Super Dolphin**[47] 4975 6-10-0 **78** oh2 .... PJBrennan 92
(R Ford) *chsd ldr: led 7th: hdd and no ex run-in* **10/3**[1]

52-P **3** *9* **Nazimabad (IRE)**[24] 388 6-9-9 **78** oh4 .... (t) RStephens[(5)] 83
(Evan Williams) *led to 7th: one pce fr 3 out* **8/1**

3-26 **4** *3* **Kalou (GER)**[16] 479 7-11-8 **103** .... MrTGreenall[(3)] 105
(C Grant) *hld up in rr: hdwy 6th: outpcd whn hit 8th: nvr nr ldrs* **10/1**

-404 **5** *25* **Barneys Reflection**[16] 479 5-10-13 **92** .... (b[1]) NPMulholland 68
(A Crook) *chsd ldrs: wknd 3 out* **20/1**

0-56 **6** *2* **Classic Calvados (FR)**[9] 604 6-11-2 **94** .... JimCrowley 69
(P D Niven) *a in rr: lost tch 7th* **25/1**

0F-5 **F** **Husky (POL)**[14] 510 7-10-8 **86** .... JamesDavies —
(B G Powell) *in rr whn fell 6th* **25/1**

-036 **F** **Moon Shot**[14] 510 9-11-0 **92** .... ATinkler —
(A G Juckes) *chsd ldrs: 6th and wkng whn fell 3 out* **33/1**

043- **R** **Reliance Leader**[49] 4940 9-9-11 **78** oh20 .... DCrosse[(3)] —
(D L Williams) *prom: styng on whn rn out 8th* **25/1**

2-25 **U** **Vigoureux (FR)**[18] 466 6-10-13 **98** .... (p) WKennedy[(7)] —
(S Gollings) *rr-div: bhd fr 7th: hmpd and uns rdr 3 out* **11/2**[3]

6-5U **R** **Stage Friendly (IRE)**[27] 334 6-10-11 **89** .... CLlewellyn —
(N A Twiston-Davies) *trckd ldrs: 4th whn rn out 4th* **9/1**

65-0 **U** **Bill Brown**[16] 488 7-11-0 **92** .... WHutchinson 92
(R Dickin) *mid-div: hdwy 7th: one pce fr 3 out: 4th whn blnd and uns rdr last* **9/1**

3m 53.0s (-12.00) **Going Correction** -0.80s/f (Firm)
WFA 5 from 6yo+ 1lb **12** Ran SP% **117.9**
Speed ratings: **98,97,93,91,79 78,—,—,—,— —,—** CSF £16.86 CT £102.73 TOTE £3.60: £1.70, £1.70, £3.30; EX 12.10.
Owner The Gascoigne Brookes Partnership **Bred** Mull Enterprises Ltd **Trained** Cowbridge, Vale Of Glamorgan

FOCUS
A decent event run at a break-neck gallop, with the winner improving to the level of his hurdles form. The form should work out.

NOTEBOOK
In The Frame(IRE), still 5lb lower than his hurdle-race mark, went in pursuit of the two tearaway leaders and in the end did just enough. He is right on top of his game at present in his new yard. *(op 10-3)*
Super Dolphin, held up in traffic problems, made it to the track just in time. Keeping tabs on the tearaway leader, he does not get very high at his fences. He fought back when headed and deserves to go one better. *(op 4-1)*
Nazimabad(IRE), stablemate of the winner, put an abject performance last time behind him. He set off as if it was a sprint and kept on surprisingly well all the way to the line. *(op 9-1 tchd 10-1)*
Kalou(GER), suited by the much quicker ground, was dropped in at the start. He was going nowhere when he hit four out and is hard to predict. *(op 8-1)*
Reliance Leader, 20lb wrong at the weights, might well have achieved his second placing on his seventh start over fences but for taking it into his mind to duck out four from home when presented at the fence right on the inside. *(tchd 28-1)*

693 PROACTIVE WASTE SOLUTIONS MARES' ONLY NOVICES' HURDLE (12 hdls) 2m 4f 110y
7:10 (7:13) (Class 4) 4-Y-0+ **£3,367** (£962; £481)

Form RPR

33-3 **1** **Topanberry (IRE)**[27] 329 6-10-12 97 .... APMcCoy 105+
(N G Richards) *trckd ldrs: wnt 2nd 9th: led appr next: sn clr: eased towards fin* **5/2**[1]

P-21 **2** *8* **Shady Grey**[16] 487 7-11-5 92 .... NFehily 100+
(C J Mann) *led: rdn 9th: hdd appr next: no ch w wnr* **11/4**[2]

-34F **3** *24* **Samandara (FR)**[16] 487 5-10-12 103 .... RThornton 68
(A King) *chsd ldrs: rdn appr 3 out: sn btn* **7/2**[3]

0-13 **4** *shd* **Blueberry Ice (IRE)**[15] 504 7-10-12 105 .... CMStudd[(7)] 75
(B G Powell) *trckd ldrs: rdn and wknd 9th* **7/1**

4/3- **5** *4* **Colnside Brook**[398] 204 6-10-12 98 .... MAFitzgerald 64
(B G Powell) *chsd ldrs: lost pl appr 3 out* **17/2**

6 *dist* **Daisy Fay**[460] 10-10-12 .... WMarston —
(G R I Smyly) *hld up in rr: effrt 8th: sn rdn and lost pl* **40/1**

0- **P** **Ruggtah**[21] 3141 4-10-8 .... JimCrowley —
(P D Niven) *chsd ldrs: hit 4th: lost pl 7th: sn bhd: t.o whn p.u bef 3 out* **100/1**

00-0 **P** **Another Jameson (IRE)**[40] 138 5-10-12 .... RMcGrath —
(J M Jefferson) *nt fluent: in rr: bhd fr 7th: t.o whn p.u after 3 out* **16/1**

5m 4.60s (-7.50) **Going Correction** -0.20s/f (Good)
WFA 4 from 5yo+ 4lb **8** Ran SP% **109.8**
Speed ratings: **106,102,93,93,92 —,—,—** CSF £9.05 TOTE £3.70: £1.10, £1.40, £1.70; EX 7.90.
Owner Mrs D McGawn **Bred** Miss E Hamilton **Trained** Greystoke, Cumbria

FOCUS
A weak mares' only novices hurdle but a most decisive winner, rated value for 12 lengths.

NOTEBOOK
Topanberry(IRE) went on and had this weak mares'-only race won in a matter of strides. She was value for at least 15 lengths. *(op 2-1 tchd 11-4)*
Shady Grey, checked over at the start, was picked off by the winner under her penalty but still finished clear second-best. *(op 10-3)*
Samandara(FR), who crashed out behind Shady Deal at Worcester, was on and off the bridle and, when asked a serious question, answered in the negative. *(op 3-1)*
Blueberry Ice(IRE), back against her own sex, was disapointing and dropped away four out. *(tchd 13-2 and 8-1)*
Colnside Brook was having her first outing for a year and presumably needed it. *(op 13-2)*

694 CLAYTON COSMETIC DENTAL CENTRE AND BRITESMILE H'CAP CHASE (16 fncs 2 omitted) 3m
7:40 (7:41) (Class 3) (0-115,111) 5-Y-0+ **£5,538** (£1,704; £852; £426)

Form RPR

14-3 **1** **Totheroadyouvgone**[11] 575 11-11-3 **102** .... (p) MFoley 119+
(A E Jones) *hld up: hdwy 10th: led 2 out: clr last: styd on wl* **11/1**

-2U4 **2** *6* **Mullensgrove**[19] 453 11-10-11 **103** .... MissSSharratt[(7)] 112+
(R Hollinshead) *chsd ldrs: led after 12th: hdd 2 out: kpt on same pce* **20/1**

20-2 **3** *13* **Penthouse Minstrel**[14] 522 11-11-1 **107** .... TJDreaper[(7)] 104+
(R J Hodges) *chsd ldrs: one pce fr 3 out* **8/1**[3]

4-21 **4** *13* **Emperor Ross (IRE)**[22] 411 10-11-12 **111** .... BHarding 101+
(N G Richards) *hld up: hdwy to trck ldrs 4th: wnt 2nd appr 4 out: 4th and wkng whn blnd 3 out: sn lost pl* **4/1**[1]

20-P **5** *5* **Count Campioni (IRE)**[20] 439 11-11-6 **105** .... (p) NFehily 82
(M Pitman) *in rr: reminders 8th: nvr a factor* **20/1**

F1-1 **6** *1* **Cherry Gold**[18] 468 11-11-3 **102** .... ChristianWilliams 78
(Evan Williams) *chsd ldrs: lost pl 12th: sn bhd* **4/1**[1]

4-55 **P** **Channahrlie (IRE)**[21] 430 11-10-2 **87** .... (b[1]) WHutchinson —
(R Dickin) *chsd ldrs: wknd 10th: t.o whn p.u bef 12th* **16/1**

PPF- **P** **Golden Rambler (IRE)**[54] 4864 9-11-12 **111** .... APMcCoy —
(Jonjo O'Neill) *led: blnd 12th: sn hdd: poor 5th whn p.u bef 3 out* **9/2**[2]

0-P3 **P** **Blazing Hills**[11] 572 9-10-11 **96** .... AThornton —
(P T Dalton) *chsd ldrs: blnd 5th: blnd and lost pl 9th: bhd whn p.u bef 11th* **9/2**[2]

6m 7.60s (-24.90) **Going Correction** -0.80s/f (Firm) **9** Ran SP% **111.2**
Speed ratings: **109,107,102,98,96 96,—,—,—** CSF £174.17 CT £1798.15 TOTE £11.30: £2.30, £4.30, £2.70; EX 255.80.
Owner N F Glynn **Bred** Alan & Mrs Grummit **Trained** Newchapel, Surrey

FOCUS
A sound gallop and in the end a decisive winner who looks better than ever at his advanced age.

NOTEBOOK
Totheroadyouvgone, back over fences, travelled strongly and took this in most decisive fashion. Connections are hoping he makes the cut in the Summer National here otherwise the Galway Plate beckons. *(op 10-1)*
Mullensgrove, who has changed stables, has been plying his trade in hunter chases. In the end the winner proved much too good but he ran well and should continue to give a good account of himself. *(op 16-1)*
Penthouse Minstrel keeps giving a good account of himself but he looks weighted to the limit now. *(op 10-1)*
Emperor Ross(IRE) moved up travelling best but the needle was on empty when he almost lost his rider three out. *These days he has to do everything on the bridle.Official explanation: jockey said gelding was unsuited by good to firm, good in places ground (op 7-2)*
Count Campioni(IRE) looks out of form.
Cherry Gold, back over fences, likes to dominate, and he downed tools with a mile to go.
Golden Rambler(IRE), potentially well treated, came here after a seven-week break on the back of four non-completions. Losing the advantage after a blunder, he found precious little and was eventually pulled up and dismounted. *(op 4-1)*
Blazing Hills was pulled up after a second bad mistake. *Official explanation: jockey said gelding was never travelling having made a bad mistake (op 4-1)*

695 HEWDEN TOTAL RENTAL SOLUTIONS - NATIONWIDE H'CAP HURDLE (10 hdls) 2m
8:10 (8:11) (Class 4) (0-110,108) 4-Y-0+ **£3,789** (£1,166; £583; £291)

Form RPR

0-22 **1** **Caliban (IRE)**[30] 284 7-11-9 **105** .... (v) DRDennis 110+
(Ian Williams) *j.rt: mde all: styd on u.p fr 2 out* **4/1**[3]

4-20 **2** *6* **Pilca (FR)**[11] 571 5-11-4 **100** .... JPMcNamara 99
(R M Stronge) *trckd ldrs: wnt 2nd 2 out: rdn and fnd little* **9/2**

5F/ **3** *1 ½* **Bringontheclowns (IRE)**[553] 2553 6-11-8 **104** .... PJBrennan 102
(M F Harris) *hld up: hdwy 5th: chsng ldrs 3 out: kpt on between last 2* **12/1**

4-16 **4** *shd* **Tiger Frog (USA)**[26] 347 6-11-8 **104** .... (b) WMarston 101
(J Mackie) *chsd ldrs: outpcd 3 out: styd on between last 2* **10/3**[2]

010- **5** *17* **Protocol (IRE)**[73] 4604 11-10-5 **90**..(t) LVickers(3) 70
(Mrs S Lamyman) *lost pl 3rd: sn bhd: t.o 3 out* **20/1**

33-0 **6** *dist* **Bolshoi Ballet**[33] 217 7-11-12 **108**...........................(v[1]) PMoloney —
(J Mackie) *chsd ldrs: lost pl 6th: sn bhd: t.o 3 out* **15/2**

0-13 **F** **Kentmere (IRE)**[16] 485 4-11-0 **104**.. MNicolls(5) 96
(P R Webber) *trckd ldrs: hit 5th: wnt 2nd next: reminders after 7th: wknd 2 out: 4th and wl btn whn fell last* **11/4**[1]

3m 58.4s (-2.00) **Going Correction** -0.025s/f (Good)
WFA 4 from 5yo+ 3lb **7** Ran SP% **112.1**
Speed ratings: **104,101,100,100,91** —,— CSF £21.48 CT £193.61 TOTE £5.00: £2.80, £2.20; EX 39.70.
Owner Jim Edmunds **Bred** Knocktoran Stud **Trained** Portway, Worcs

FOCUS
There was a sound pace here and the form looks solid enough.

NOTEBOOK
Caliban(IRE), with a visor this time, made every yard. He continually jumped right but kept up the gallop and in the end outbattled the runner-up.
Pilca(FR) moved up on to the heels of the winner seemingly travelling the better but, when asked to go and win the race, his response was very limited. *(op 11-2)*
Bringontheclowns(IRE), absent since pulling up in December 2003, kept on in willing fashion and has time to make up for in this yard. *(op 10-1)*
Tiger Frog(USA), 3lb higher than when successful at Warwick in May, appreciated this much quicker ground and may well be worth another try over further. *(op 9-2)*
Protocol(IRE), absent for 10 weeks after being struck into, took little interest and was soon detached in last. *(op 16-1)*
Kentmere(IRE) stopped to nothing two out and took a crashing fall at the last. Fortunately, he was none the worse. *(op 9-4)*

696 CAMERON HOMES MAIDEN HURDLE (10 hdls) 2m
8:40 (8:40) (Class 4) 4-Y-0+ **£3,437** (£982; £491)

Form RPR

3 **1** **Keep On Movin' (IRE)**[16] 487 4-10-7 .... RJohnson 96+
(T G Mills) *led 1st: styd on wl fr 2 out: eased nr fin* **3/1**[2]

6 **2** *3* **Hillcrest (NZ)**[40] 133 6-11-3 .... DRDennis 101+
(Ian Williams) *chsd ldrs: wnt 2nd 3 out: styd on no imp* **8/1**[3]

1-2 **3** *15* **Abragante (IRE)**[14] 515 4-11-0 .... APMcCoy 82
(M C Pipe) *rr-div: hdwy 6th: wnt 3rd 3 out: one pce* **3/1**[2]

4-22 **4** *4* **Text**[18] 457 4-10-7 110.. SWalsh(7) 78
(C J Down) *chsd ldrs: drvn along 6th: outpcd fr 3 out* **9/4**[1]

P **5** *7* **Felix The Fox (NZ)**[32] 242 5-11-3 .... CLlewellyn 74
(N A Twiston-Davies) *prom: outpcd and lost pl 5th: kpt on fr 3 out* **11/1**

4U6- **6** *3* **Canadian Storm**[80] 4496 4-11-0 95.. AO'Keeffe 68
(A G Juckes) *stdd s: plld v hrd in rr: kpt on fr 3 out: nvr on terms* **25/1**

000- **7** *nk* **Ice And Fire**[146] 3344 6-11-3 86.. ChristianWilliams 72+
(J T Stimpson) *hld up: hdwy 7th: sn chsng ldrs: wknd 2 out* **50/1**

0 **8** *2 ½* **Irish Playwright (IRE)**[18] 457 5-11-3 ....(v) RThornton 68
(D G Bridgwater) *led to 1st: chsd ldrs: wknd after 7th* **100/1**

9 *½* **Sinjaree**[123] 7-11-0 ....(p) LVickers(3) 68
(Mrs S Lamyman) *sn bhd: sme hdwy 3 out: nvr on terms* **100/1**

P6P **10** *22* **Sportsfield Coogee (IRE)**[24] 384 6-11-3 .... NFehily 46
(D P Keane) *hld up in rr: reminders 5th: sn bhd* **100/1**

0 **11** *2 ½* **Bobering**[18] 457 5-11-3 .... JMogford 43
(B P J Baugh) *bhd fr 5th* **100/1**

00-P **12** *26* **High Window (IRE)**[35] 192 5-10-10 .... WKennedy(7) 17
(S Gollings) *chsd ldrs: wknd 7th: sn bhd* **66/1**

04 **13** *15* **Heisse**[14] 515 5-11-3 .... PMoloney 2
(Ian Williams) *sn bhd: drvn along 4th: lost tch next* **50/1**

02P- **14** *2 ½* **Native Chancer (IRE)**[245] 1628 5-11-3 .... MAFitzgerald —
(Jonjo O'Neill) *rr-div: hdwy 6th: wknd next: sn bhd* **20/1**

00P/ **F** **Bobaway (IRE)**[888] 2945 8-11-3 .... JimCrowley —
(M G Rimell) *t.k.h: trckd ldrs: 6th and wkng whn hit 3 out: bhd whn fell last: dead* **66/1**

4m 1.60s (1.20) **Going Correction** -0.025s/f (Good)
WFA 4 from 5yo+ 3lb **15** Ran SP% **119.7**
Speed ratings: **96,94,87,85,81 80,79,78,78,67 66,53,45,44**,— CSF £25.58 TOTE £4.60: £1.50, £3.50, £1.70; EX 40.40.
Owner J E Harley **Bred** Leslie Tucker **Trained** Headley, Surrey

FOCUS
A modest novices' hurdle run at just a steady gallop but they came home well strung out.

NOTEBOOK
Keep On Movin'(IRE), dropping back in trip, was very keen to lead and, given her own way in front, never really looked in any real danger. She was value for double the official margin.
Hillcrest(NZ), absent for six weeks after being reported to have a breathing problem on his hurdling debut, did not go without market support. He stuck on in willing fashion in pursuit of the winner but the margin of defeat flatters him. Nevertheless, he still finished clear second-best. *(op 14-1)*
Abragante(IRE), settled off the pace, went in pursuit of the first two but was too slow and was never going to get anywhere near them. At 90,000gns, this Wetherby bumper winner looks an expensive buy. *(op 7-4)*
Text, in trouble a long way out, proved just too slow. *(tchd 5-2)*
Felix The Fox(NZ) kept on in his own time when it was virtually all over and looks a potential chaser. *(op 25-1 tchd 10-1)*
Canadian Storm, dropped in at the start, pulled his rider's arms out on his first outing for this stable.
Ice And Fire *Official explanation: jockey said gelding had a breathing problem (op 66-1)*
Heisse *Official explanation: jockey said gelding had a breathing problem*
Native Chancer(IRE) *Official explanation: jockey said gelding had a breathing problem*

697 P & C MORRIS H'CAP HURDLE (6 hdls 8 omitted) 3m
9:10 (9:19) (Class 4) (0-100,100) 4-Y-0+ **£2,779** (£794; £397)

Form RPR

06-1 **1** **Croc An Oir (IRE)**[5] 630 8-10-10 **87** 7ex........................ LMcGrath(3) 111+
(R Ford) *chsd ldrs: led last: drvn clr 3f out: heavily eased fnl f* **11/10**[1]

0-23 **2** *12* **Knockdoo (IRE)**[21] 429 12-11-1 **96**.. MrGGoldie(7) 95
(J S Goldie) *hld up: hdwy 4th: styd on fnl 3f: tk 2nd ins last 200yds* **14/1**

0-50 **3** *½* **Sandywell George**[7] 614 10-10-11 **88**................................(t) TJMalone(3) 87
(L P Grassick) *chsd ldrs: led appr 4th: hdd last: one pce fnl 3f* **50/1**

-FP0 **4** *1 ¾* **Greenacres Boy**[22] 412 10-10-1 **78** oh8 ow4....................(b) ACCoyle(3) 75
(M Mullineaux) *stdd s: hld up in rr: stdy hdwy 4th: wnt 2nd over 4f out: one pce fnl 3f* **50/1**

-256 **5** *1 ½* **Idlewild (IRE)**[18] 467 10-10-10 **91**.. APogson(7) 86
(C T Pogson) *chsd ldrs: outpcd 6f out: kpt on fnl 3f* **40/1**

-0F1 **6** *1 ½* **Pikestaff (USA)**[9] 606 7-11-2 **90** 7ex................................(t) JimCrowley 84
(M A Barnes) *hdwy to chse ldrs 4th: rdn next: one pce fnl 3f* **5/1**[3]

3-44 **7** *1 ¼* **Hylia**[11] 566 6-11-3 **91**..(t) JAMcCarthy 84
(Mrs P Robeson) *chsd ldrs: one pce fnl 5f* **14/1**

0-U1 **8** *5* **Over Bridge**[11] 575 7-10-6 **80**.. RJohnson 68
(Mrs S M Johnson) *chsd ldrs: wnt 2nd over 5f out: wknd over 1f out* **4/1**[2]

00-4 **9** *¾* **Fantastico (IRE)**[15] 499 5-11-2 **90**................................(p) RMcGrath 77
(Mrs K Walton) *hld up in rr: sme hdwy 6f out: nvr on terms* **20/1**

02-6 **10** *1* **Called To The Bar**[26] 353 12-11-3 **91**........................ ChristianWilliams 77
(Evan Williams) *led tl appr 4th: wknd next* **14/1**

-P44 **11** *8* **Red Nose Lady**[21] 425 8-10-12 **93**................................(b) TMessenger(7) 71
(G J Smith) *in rr: bhd fr 4th* **50/1**

000- **12** *25* **Periwinkle Lad (IRE)**[53] 4889 8-11-12 **100**........................ BJCrowley 53
(Miss Victoria Roberts) *bhd and drvn along 4th: t.o 3f out* **33/1**

01/P **13** *dist* **Bravo**[26] 352 7-10-11 **85**..(b[1]) PMoloney —
(J Mackie) *chsd ldrs: lost pl after 3rd: sn bhd: t.o 4f out* **25/1**

0P-0 **14** *dist* **Another Windfall**[40] 134 6-9-7 **74** oh11........................(t) SWalsh(7) —
(C P Morlock) *bhd: lost tch 4th: t.o 5f out: virtually p.u ins fnl f* **66/1**

6m 4.70s (-0.30) **Going Correction** -0.025s/f (Good) **14** Ran SP% **125.6**
Speed ratings: **99,95,94,94,93 93,92,91,90,90 87,79**,—,— CSF £17.48 TOTE £2.30: £1.50, £3.00, £11.50; EX 25.20 Place 6 £126.79, Place 5 £81.38.
Owner Concertina Racing Four **Bred** Donal Brazil **Trained** Cotebrook, Cheshire
■ Due to the setting sun the three hurdles in the home straight were omitted, resulting in just six being jumped instead of 14.

FOCUS
Omitting the hurdles proved a meaningless exercise as the race, which was about ten minutes late off, was run in fading light, the sun having disappeared below the horizon by the time the groundstaff had done the necessary work. There was a run of six furlongs to the first flight and a run-in of seven furlongs.

NOTEBOOK
Croc An Oir(IRE), still 19lb below his last winning chase mark, must have wondered where the obstacles had gone. Driven well clear, he strolled over the line but will have to race from a much more realistic mark in future. *(op Evens tchd 11-8)*
Knockdoo(IRE), who last won five years ago, stayed on from way off the pace on the extended run-in to snatch second spot near the line. *(op 16-1)*
Sandywell George, without a win since December 2003 and struggling over fences, ran better than of late but, with the depleted obstacles, his stamina was not truly tested.
Greenacres Boy, 8lb out of the handicap, seemed to be ridden to see out the extended trip, but in the circumstances this was not a true test. *(op 66-1)*
Idlewild(IRE), was another who did not totally prove he stays this far.
Pikestaff(USA), under pressure with a circuit to go, did not shine with hardly any hurdles to jump. *(op 8-1)*
Over Bridge, without a penalty, tried to keeb tabs on the winner but tired badly late in the night. *(op 6-1)*

T/Plt: £129.30 to a £1 stake. Pool: £47,124.50. 265.90 winning tickets. T/Qpdt: £51.60 to a £1 stake. Pool: £3,016.80. 43.20 winning tickets. WG

711 - 713a (Foreign Racing) - See Raceform Interactive

601
HEXHAM (L-H)
Saturday, June 11

OFFICIAL GOING: Good to firm

714 HADEN YOUNG LTD H'CAP CHASE (12 fncs) 2m 110y
2:30 (2:30) (Class 3) (0-125,113) 5-Y-0+ **£5,395** (£1,660; £830; £415)

Form RPR

-P21 **1** **Adjawar (IRE)**[18] 479 7-11-7 **108**.. RGarritty 127+
(J J Quinn) *w ldr: led bef 2 out: styd on strly* **7/2**[3]

5-33 **2** *4* **Gone Too Far**[24] 409 7-11-10 **111**................................(p) RThornton 122
(P Monteith) *in tch: effrt 3 out: chsd wnr bef last: kpt on: no imp* **9/4**[1]

21-P **3** *11* **Mumaris (USA)**[37] 195 11-11-9 **113**................................(p) PBuchanan(3) 114+
(Miss Lucinda V Russell) *chsd ldrs: outpcd 3 out: rallied bef last: no ch w first two* **16/1**

P-05 **4** *10* **Billie John (IRE)**[24] 409 10-11-11 **112**.. RMcGrath 102
(Mrs K Walton) *prom: outpcd 3 out: n.d after* **8/1**

211- **5** *9* **Dante's Brook (IRE)**[245] 1658 11-10-8 **95**.. GLee 79+
(B Mactaggart) *mde most to bef 2 out: wknd between last two* **13/2**

54-5 **U** **Bill's Echo**[13] 571 6-11-7 **111**.. LMcGrath(3) —
(R C Guest) *hld up in tch: blnd and uns rdr 4th* **11/4**[2]

3m 55.9s (-13.20) **Going Correction** -0.675s/f (Firm) **6** Ran SP% **110.0**
Speed ratings: **104,102,96,92,88** — CSF £11.73 TOTE £4.20: £2.00, £1.40; EX 8.10.
Owner Mrs M Taylor Mrs V stone **Bred** His Highness The Aga Khan's Studs S C **Trained** Settrington, N Yorks

FOCUS
An ordinary event in which the gallop was only fair, but the winner is going the right way and is rated value for eight lengths.

NOTEBOOK
Adjawar(IRE), back on a sound surface, maintained his unbeaten record over fences with another gutsy success. He jumps soundly and is capable of winning again in this grade after reassessment. *(tchd 4-1)*
Gone Too Far, who had conditions to suit, ran another creditable race but left the impression that he may be worth another try over two and a half miles.
Mumaris(USA) fared better than on his reappearance after a break at Wetherby last time but, while still below his best, left the impression that a stiffer test of stamina would have suited. *(op 10-1)*
Billie John(IRE) was again well beaten with no obvious excuses and he will have to show more before he is a betting proposition once again. *(op 16-1 tchd 7-1)*
Dante's Brook(IRE), 17lb higher than when last seen in October, did not run as badly as the distance beaten implies and should be better for this outing. *(op 8-1 tchd 11-2)*
Bill's Echo, a dual winner over fences at Bangor, had conditions to suit but parted company with his rider before the race began in earnest, and he is worth another chance. *(op 5-2 tchd 10-3)*

715 ST MARTIN'S CARE LTD MARES' ONLY NOVICES' HURDLE (8 hdls) 2m 110y
3:00 (3:00) (Class 4) 4-Y-0+ **£3,360** (£960; £480)

Form RPR

25-1 **1** **Miami Explorer**[13] 569 5-11-5 105.. JamesDavies 123+
(P R Webber) *keen: in tch: hdwy to ld 2 out: drew clr fr next: easily* **2/1**[2]

6-4 **2** *11* **Miss Kilkeel (IRE)**[24] 406 7-10-9 .... SMMcGovern(3) 98
(R T J Wilson, Ire) *cl up: rdn to chse wnr bef 2 out: kpt on: no imp* **6/1**[3]

5-21 **3** *7* **Dewasentah (IRE)**[13] 574 6-11-5 100.. GLee 98
(J M Jefferson) *led to 3 out: wknd fr next* **1/1**[1]

4/-4 **4** *5* **Cheery Martyr**[13] 569 7-10-12 .... FKeniry 87+
(P Needham) *prom tl outpcd bef 3 out: no imp whn blnd last* **33/1**

UP-6 **5** *1 ½* **High Class Pet**[31] 302 5-10-12 83.. PRobson 85
(F P Murtagh) *prom tl wknd bef 3 out* **25/1**

P0-5 **6** *21* **La Folichonne (FR)**[14] 549 6-10-9 .... PAspell(3) 64
(James Moffatt) *bhd: no ch fr 1/2-way* **50/1**

0-P0 **7** *10* **Flashy Filly**[11] 602 5-10-5 64.. MJMcAlister(7) 54
(J C Haynes) *midfield: rdn and wknd fr 1/2-way* **100/1**

Form	Pos	Dist	Horse	RPR
P0-0	8	shd	**Teeno Rossi (IRE)**[11] 601 7-10-5 ....(b) MrSFMagee(7) (J K Magee, Ire) *mstkes: sn bhd: no ch fr 1/2-way* **100/1**	53
406/	P		**Lady Lola (IRE)**[75] 7-10-12 .... JimCrowley (Miss J E Foster) *a bhd: t.o whn p.u 5th* **66/1**	—
	P		**Gandiloo Gully** 4-10-4 .... DFlavin(5) (Mrs L B Normile) *nt fluent in tch tl wknd 1/2-way: t.o whn p.u bef 2 out* **66/1**	—
0-	P		**Wizards Princess**[40] 332 5-10-5 .... BenOrde-Powlett(7) (D W Thompson) *hld up: sddle slipped 2nd: p.u after 4th* **100/1**	—

4m 4.30s (-10.90) **Going Correction** -0.675s/f (Firm)
WFA 4 from 5yo+ 3lb **11** Ran SP% **112.3**
Speed ratings: **98,92,89,87,86 76,71,71,—,— —** CSF £12.92 TOTE £2.60: £1.10, £1.80, £1.10; EX 18.70.
Owner R J McAlpine **Bred** Mrs P G Wilkins And R J McAlpine **Trained** Mollington, Oxon

FOCUS
An uncompetitive race in which the gallop was only ordinary. The winner has been rated value for 18 lengths.

NOTEBOOK
Miami Explorer ◆ seems an improved performer and won an uncompetitive race with plenty in hand. As her main rival disappointed, she should not go up too much for this and will be interesting in ordinary handicaps around this trip.
Miss Kilkeel(IRE) has not always been reliable and has yet to win but ran her third creditable race from her last four starts and left the impression that she will be worth another try over two and a half miles. *(op 3-1)*
Dewasentah(IRE), not for the first time, proved a disappointment in an uncompetitive race and, although she has plenty of ability, is not one to place too much faith in. *(op 6-4)*
Cheery Martyr, turned out quickly, was beaten further by the winner than at Uttoxeter. This may have come too soon but she needs to brush up her jumping and she will be suited by the step into modest handicap company.
High Class Pet is an unreliable maiden who is likely to continue to look vulnerable in this type of event. *(tchd 33-1)*
La Folichonne(FR) was again soundly beaten and is likely to remain up against it in this type of race.

716 NORTH EAST PROFILING H'CAP HURDLE (8 hdls) 2m 110y
3:35 (3:35) (Class 4) (0-100,97) 4-Y-0+ **£2,716** (£776; £388)

Form	Pos	Dist	Horse	RPR
5/31	1		**Dream Castle (IRE)**[14] 544 11-11-5 **97** .... PMerrigan(7) (Barry Potts, Ire) *mde all: kpt on strly fr 2 out* **4/1**[1]	108+
P3-4	2	8	**Wyn Dixie (IRE)**[14] 551 6-11-10 **95** .... RThornton (P Monteith) *hld up midfield: hdwy and prom 1/2-way: chsd wnr between last two: no imp* **5/1**[3]	95+
0-46	3	8	**Prince Adjal (IRE)**[31] 306 5-10-7 **83** ....(p) DCCostello(5) (G M Moore) *w wnr to bef 2 out: wknd between last two* **6/1**	74
43-6	4	8	**Schinken Otto (IRE)**[12] 596 4-10-6 **80** .... GLee (J M Jefferson) *hld up: hdwy bef 3 out: no imp fr next* **9/2**[2]	60
0512	5	1	**In Good Faith**[11] 606 13-10-5 **83** .... PKinsella(7) (R E Barr) *hld up: hdwy 2 out: kpt on: no imp* **17/2**	65
0-56	6	½	**One Of Them**[11] 603 6-10-6 **77** .... PRobson (M A Barnes) *midfield: outpcd 1/2-way: rallied 2 out: no imp* **14/1**	59
-555	7	4	**Northern Flash**[11] 601 11-10-0 **71** oh1 ....(p) JimCrowley (J C Haynes) *hld up: rdn 1/2-way: sme late hdwy: n.d* **22/1**	49
/0-P	8	2½	**Conor's Pride (IRE)**[24] 412 8-11-8 **93** .... RMcGrath (B Mactaggart) *hld up: rdn 4 out: n.d* **50/1**	68
F1/0	9	2½	**Maunby Rocker**[14] 551 5-11-7 **92** .... FKeniry (P C Haslam) *midfield: outpcd 1/2-way: n.d* **20/1**	65
-450	10	4	**Dan De Lion**[35] 213 6-10-8 **79** .... HOliver (R C Guest) *in tch to 4 out: sn btn* **12/1**	48
0P0-	11	nk	**Charlie Castallan**[85] 4439 5-9-13 **77** ow1 .... BenOrde-Powlett(7) (D W Thompson) *in tch tl wknd fr 3 out* **50/1**	45
-060	12	1	**Jamorin Dancer**[11] 601 10-9-7 **71** oh7 ....(p) TMessenger(7) (S G Chadwick) *midfield: rdn 1/2-way: sn btn* **50/1**	38
00/0	13	nk	**Never Forget Bowie**[11] 602 9-10-0 **71** oh3 .... KRenwick (R Allan) *a bhd* **66/1**	38
-P04	14	2	**Starbright**[6] 645 4-10-0 **74** oh6 .... KJohnson (W G Young) *in tch to 4th: wknd bef next* **33/1**	36
P-F4	15	3	**Roy McAvoy (IRE)**[14] 549 7-10-2 **76** ....(t) PWhelan(3) (M A Barnes) *chsd ldrs tl wknd after 3 out* **16/1**	38
-00F	16	5	**Neven**[11] 601 6-10-6 **80** ....(tp) PBuchanan(3) (Miss Lucinda V Russell) *hld up: mstke 4th: nvr on terms* **33/1**	37
P/06	F		**Blue Venture (IRE)**[30] 319 5-11-5 **90** .... ADempsey (B Mactaggart) *hld up midfield: smooth hdwy to chse ldrs whn fell 2 out* **25/1**	87

4m 4.50s (-10.70) **Going Correction** -0.675s/f (Firm)
WFA 4 from 5yo+ 3lb **17** Ran SP% **126.1**
Speed ratings: **98,94,90,86,86 86,84,82,81,79 79,79,79,78,76 74,—** CSF £22.60 CT £125.27 TOTE £4.90: £1.50, £1.40, £2.50, £1.40; EX 24.00.
Owner William M Brown **Bred** Miss Avril Campbell **Trained** Strabane, Co Tyrone
■ Stewards' Enquiry : H Oliver one-day ban: used whip when out of contention (Jun 22)

FOCUS
A decent gallop to this ordinary event but a race in which those held up were at a disadvantage. It has been rated through the runner-up.

NOTEBOOK
Dream Castle(IRE), 15lb higher than for his Cartmel win, turned in an improved effort at this completely different track and, although not many got into this, he did well given that he forced a sound pace throughout. He should continue to go well. *(op 6-1)*
Wyn Dixie(IRE), ridden with more patience this time, travelled well for a long way and showed more than enough to suggest he is capable of winning a modest event this summer. *(op 13-2)*
Prince Adjal(IRE), tried in cheekpieces, paid the price for mixing it with the winner throughout and finished further behind that one than he had done at Perth last time. He has been mainly disappointing since his debut win over hurdles. *(tchd 13-2)*
Schinken Otto(IRE), a modest maiden on the Flat and over hurdles, was not disgraced given this race suited those racing prominently, and he looks well worth a try over further. *(tchd 5-1)*
In Good Faith, back in trip, was not seen to best effect in a race where the leaders did not come back, and he will be well suited by the return to further. *(tchd 8-1)*
One Of Them shaped as though the return to further would suit but he is an unreliable maiden who is not one to place much faith in.
Blue Venture(IRE), an unreliable performer, was in the process of running creditably over this shorter trip when taking a heavy fall at the penultimate flight. *(op 20-1)*

717 LORDS TAVERNERS H'CAP CHASE (15 fncs) 2m 4f 110y
4:10 (4:10) (Class 4) (0-100,98) 5-Y-0+ **£3,332** (£952; £476)

Form	Pos	Dist	Horse	RPR
P-06	1		**Toad Hall**[24] 411 11-9-9 **72** oh3 .... DCCostello(5) (Mrs L B Normile) *midfield: outpcd 11th: rallied 3 out: styd on wl fr last to ld towards fin* **66/1**	80+
54F5	2	½	**Spectrum Star**[14] 548 5-9-11 **74** oh11 .... PAspell(3) (F P Murtagh) *bhd: blnd 10th: hdwy 4 out: led whn mstke last: kpt on: hdd towards fin* **66/1**	80+
6-53	3	3	**Mr Laggan**[11] 605 10-9-7 **72** oh1 ....(p) MJMcAlister(7) (Miss Kate Milligan) *midfield: outpcd 10th: rallied 2 out: kpt on wl fr last: no ch w first two* **16/1**	75
1-41	4	10	**Panmure (IRE)**[11] 605 9-11-12 **98** .... JimCrowley (P D Niven) *towards rr: reminders 8th: smooth hdwy to chse ldrs bef 3 out: lft in ld briefly next: sn outpcd* **3/1**[2]	95+
-354	5	10	**Snooty Eskimo (IRE)**[11] 604 13-10-9 **88** ow13 .... MrHNorton(7) (W T Reed) *chsd ldrs tl outpcd 10th: rallied 2 out: no imp* **16/1**	75+
5-50	6	4	**Now Then Sid**[14] 554 6-10-6 **78** .... PRobson (Mrs S A Watt) *chsd ldrs tl outpcd 11th: n.d after* **15/2**[3]	57
5-62	7	8	**Karo De Vindecy (FR)**[11] 605 7-10-11 **83** ....(t) GLee (M D Hammond) *keen: led to bef 3 out: led briefly after next: btn whn nt fluent last* **5/2**[1]	60+
04P-	8	3½	**French Cedar**[61] 4811 9-9-10 **78** .... DDaSilva(10) (P Monteith) *chsd ldrs tl wknd after 4 out* **25/1**	46
F5-6	9	dist	**Totland Bay (IRE)**[12] 9-10-0 **72** oh1 .... PJBrennan (B D Leavy) *chsd ldrs: outpcd whn blnd 3 out: sn btn* **10/1**	—
-5P4	P		**Pavey Ark (IRE)**[17] 497 7-11-3 **89** .... RMcGrath (James Moffatt) *sn towards rr: struggling whn p.u 10th* **12/1**	—
/4P-	P		**Atlantic Crossing (IRE)**[20] 8-11-3 **89** ....(p) RGarritty (P Beaumont) *nt fluent: a bhd: p.u bef 10th* **25/1**	—
-4U2	P		**Ikdam Melody (IRE)**[17] 498 9-11-0 **93** ....(p) MissJFoster(7) (Miss J E Foster) *a bhd: t.o whn p.u bef 4 out* **16/1**	—
1-34	P		**Winter Garden**[23] 421 11-11-9 **98** ....(p) PBuchanan(3) (Miss Lucinda V Russell) *in tch tl lost pl 1/2-way: t.o whn p.u bef 3 out* **20/1**	—
5-4	U		**Jupiter Jo**[42] 122 9-9-11 **76** ow4 .... BenOrde-Powlett(7) (J B Walton) *hld up: hdwy 7th: led bef 3 out: 2l up whn blnd and uns rdr next* **14/1**	80+

5m 3.80s (-7.60) **Going Correction** -0.675s/f (Firm)
WFA 5 from 6yo+ 2lb **14** Ran SP% **121.9**
Speed ratings: **87,86,85,81,78 76,73,72,—,— —,—,—,—** CSF £2140.00 CT £51948.75 TOTE £82.70: £14.60, £15.30, £4.60; EX 579.20.
Owner Mrs D A Whitaker **Bred** Mrs D A Whitaker **Trained** Duncrievie, Perth & Kinross

FOCUS
A strongly-run race but a moderate time for the grade and this form looks decidedly suspect.

NOTEBOOK
Toad Hall, a model of inconsistency, sprang a surprise from out of the handicap. Given his previous record and that the form of this strongly-run race looks suspect, he would not look an obvious one to follow up. *Official explanation: trainer's representative said, regarding the improved form shown, gelding appreciated the drop in trip and benefited from professional handling (op 100-1 tchd 50-1)*
Spectrum Star ran his best race in terms of form from 11lb out of the handicap but looks flattered in this strongly-run race and, as his jumping still leaves plenty to be desired, may well be one to field against at short odds next time. *(op 50-1)*
Mr Laggan seemed to run creditably but was suited by the way this race unfolded and, given he is not the most reliable, would not be certain to put his best foot forward next time. *(op 14-1 tchd 20-1)*
Panmure(IRE) was anything but disgraced from a 4lb higher mark for his recent course and distance success and he should continue to give a good account. *(op 10-3)*
Snooty Eskimo(IRE) seemed to run well from 13lb out of the handicap, especially as he was up with the strong pace throughout but, given his record of no wins from 38 starts, he would not be one to lump on from his proper mark next time. *(op 14-1)*
Now Then Sid, an inconsistent chaser, was not totally disgraced having raced close to the strong gallop, but he will have to show more before he is worth a bet in this sphere. *(op 12-1)*
Karo De Vindecy(FR) was below his best having done too much in front and, although capable of *winning from his current mark, he will have to settle better if he is to progress over fences. (op 11-4 tchd 9-4)*
Pavey Ark(IRE) *Official explanation: jockey said gelding swallowed its tongue (op 14-1)*

718 HAY & KILNER NOVICES' H'CAP HURDLE (10 hdls) 2m 4f 110y
4:40 (4:41) (Class 4) (0-105,94) 4-Y-0+ **£3,332** (£952; £476)

Form	Pos	Dist	Horse	RPR
060-	1		**Ben Britten**[166] 2994 6-11-5 **87** .... BHarding (N G Richards) *hld up: smooth hdwy after 3 out: disp ld bef last: rdr dropped whip run in: styd on to ld cl home* **8/1**	92+
0013	2	nk	**Casterflo**[6] 649 6-10-6 **74** .... GLee (W S Coltherd) *hld up: hdwy to ld bef last: rdn and kpt on: hdd towards fin* **5/2**[1]	78
6-22	3	8	**Mooramana**[14] 553 6-11-12 **94** .... RGarritty (P Beaumont) *cl up: led bef 2 out to bef last: kpt on same pce* **11/4**[2]	91+
-003	4	8	**Agnese**[11] 603 5-11-0 **82** .... WMarston (G M Moore) *chsd ldrs tl wknd fr 2 out* **4/1**[3]	72+
5-46	5	16	**Roadworthy (IRE)**[17] 496 8-10-0 **75** .... MrSFMagee(7) (J K Magee, Ire) *led to 3rd: disp ld 7th to bef 2 out: wknd* **22/1**	47
05-P	6	dist	**Lucky Piscean**[14] 545 4-11-5 **91** .... NHannity (C W Fairhurst) *hld up: rdn 4 out: wknd next* **50/1**	3
-053	F		**Noras Legacy (IRE)**[17] 496 7-10-2 **73** .... PBuchanan(3) (Miss Lucinda V Russell) *fell 1st* **14/1**	—
/455	B		**Nod Ya Head**[12] 591 9-10-4 **79** .... PKinsella(7) (R E Barr) *in tch tl wknd after 3 out: btn whn b.d next* **12/1**	66
0/P5	P		**Loi De Martiale (IRE)**[11] 603 7-11-3 **85** ....(b) JimCrowley (J M Jefferson) *in tch tl wknd 5th: p.u bef 4 out* **16/1**	—
0P-P	F		**Red Marsala**[20] 7-9-13 **70** oh4 ow2 ....(p) MrCStorey(3) (Miss S E Forster) *keen: led 3rd: jst hdd but cl up in 5th whn fell 2 out* **50/1**	50

4m 56.9s (-12.70) **Going Correction** -0.675s/f (Firm)
WFA 4 from 5yo+ 4lb **10** Ran SP% **114.9**
Speed ratings: **97,96,93,90,84 —,—,—,—,—** CSF £28.27 CT £69.06 TOTE £9.80: £3.10, £1.40, £1.60; EX 44.30.
Owner James Callow **Bred** Mrs Celia Miller **Trained** Greystoke, Cumbria

FOCUS
An ordinary handicap in which the pace was just fair but the winner appeals as the type to pick up more races.

NOTEBOOK
Ben Britten ◆ turned in a much-improved effort after a break and on this first run on very quick ground, despite his rider dropping his whip in the closing stages. He will stay three miles and appeals strongly as the type to win again. *Official explanation: trainer said, regarding the improved form shown, gelding had benefited from the good to firm ground (op 9-2)*
Casterflo, back on fast ground, showed her Perth run had not really done her justice and she turned in her best effort yet. She had no problems with the trip, pulled clear of the remainder and looks the type to win again. *(op 3-1)*
Mooramana was not disgraced on this handicap debut but, although he may benefit from the step *up to three miles, he is likely to remain vulnerable to progressive sorts from this mark. (op 3-1 tchd 5-2)*

Agnese is not the most reliable and failed to reproduce the form of her recent course and distance run. *She is capable of winning a small event from this mark but is not one to place much faith in. (op 7-1)*

Roadworthy(IRE), back up in trip and back on faster ground, was not at her best and is not one to place much faith in. *(op 20-1 tchd 25-1)*

Lucky Piscean was again soundly beaten and is of no immediate interest. *(op 40-1)*

719 POLA STANDARD OPEN NATIONAL HUNT FLAT RACE (DIV I) 2m 110y

5:15 (5:17) (Class 6) 4-6-Y-O **£1,519** (£434; £217)

Form	Pos	Dist	Horse	Jockey	SP	RPR
2	**1**		**Bluecoat (USA)**[6] [656] 5-11-1 (M W Easterby) *disp ld: led over 3f out: pushed clr fr 2f out*	MrTGreenall(3)	**7/4**[1]	90+
	2	*6*	**Bonnie Rock (IRE)** 5-10-4 (J I A Charlton) *hld up in tch: stdy hdwy 1/2-way: effrt and chsd wnr 2f out: kpt on: no imp*	GThomas(7)	**14/1**	77
4	**3**	*2*	**Mulligan's Pride (IRE)**[23] [424] 4-11-1 (G A Swinbank) *chsd ldrs: rdn and outpcd over 3f out: rallied 2f out: kpt on: no imp*	GLee	**15/8**[2]	79+
3	**4**	*1*	**Phantom Major (FR)**[18] [484] 4-10-8 (Mrs R L Elliot) *racd wd thrght: hld up: hdwy and in tch 1/2-way: effrt over 2f out: nt qckn*	MissRDavidson(7)	**5/1**[3]	78
	5	*21*	**Spa Wells (IRE)**[29] [338] 4-10-8 (Barry Potts, Ire) *slt ld to over 3f out: slipped over 2f out: sn btn*	PMerrigan(7)	**7/1**	57
	6	*11*	**Shady Baron (IRE)** 6-11-1 (J Wade) *hld up: rdn over 3f out: sn btn*	PAspell(3)	**22/1**	49
	7	*1*	**Pollensa Lady** 5-10-6 (A Crook) *in tch tl wknd over 3f out*	DMcGann(5)	**33/1**	41
0/00	**8**	*15*	**Terimons Daughter**[18] [484] 6-10-6 (E W Tuer) *keen: chsd ldrs tl wknd over 3f out*	DCCostello(5)	**40/1**	26
00-0	**9**	*dist*	**Regal Leader**[30] [323] 6-11-1 (M A Barnes) *prom tl lost pl 1/2-way: t.o*	PWhelan(3)	**100/1**	—

4m 2.10s (-10.60) **Going Correction** -0.675s/f (Firm) **9** Ran SP% **117.7**
Speed ratings: **97,94,93,92,82 77,77,70,**— CSF £26.55 TOTE £2.20: £1.10, £2.90, £1.60; EX 38.40.
Owner Lord Daresbury **Bred** M L Sefried And Rose M Sylvia **Trained** Sheriff Hutton, N Yorks

FOCUS
An ordinary event, rated through the third and fourth, in which the pace was just fair.

NOTEBOOK
Bluecoat(USA) probably did not have to improve too much on his debut run to win with something in hand and, given that he is in good hands, he appeals as the type to win races over obstacles in due course. *(op 2-1 tchd 11-4, 3-1 in places)*
Bonnie Rock(IRE), a half-sister to several winners, showed more than enough on this racecourse debut to suggest that a similar race can be found, especially when there is more of an emphasis on stamina. *(tchd 12-1)*
Mulligan's Pride(IRE) attracted support and was not disgraced, but he left the strong impression *that he is going to need a good test of stamina when sent over hurdles. (op 11-4 tchd 13-8, 3-1 in a place)*
Phantom Major(FR), who caught the eye on his debut at Sedgefield, again looked a bit better than the bare form as he raced on the outside in this ordinary event. He looks a stayer and is the type to win races over obstacles. *(tchd 9-2)*
Spa Wells(IRE) looks a bit better than the bare form as he lost his footing when headed and was *not knocked about thereafter. However he is likely to remain vulnerable in this type of event. (op 11-2 tchd 8-1)*
Shady Baron(IRE) should be better for this debut experience but is unlikely to be seen to best effect until going over obstacles in modest handicap company. *(op 14-1 tchd 25-1)*

720 POLA STANDARD OPEN NATIONAL HUNT FLAT RACE (DIV II) 2m 110y

5:50 (5:50) (Class 6) 4-6-Y-O **£1,512** (£432; £216)

Form	Pos	Dist	Horse	Jockey	SP	RPR
	1		**Lahib The Fifth (IRE)** 5-11-4 (N G Richards) *hld up: smooth hdwy to ld over 1f out: rdn and sn clr*	BHarding	**2/1**[1]	99+
0-2	**2**	*5*	**Lunar Eclipse**[28] [349] 5-10-11 (J I A Charlton) *chsd ldrs: outpcd 3 out: rallied to chse wnr 1f out: no imp*	PRobson	**4/1**[3]	85
	3	*12*	**Mae Moss** 4-10-8 (W S Coltherd) *hld up: hdwy to chse ldrs over 3f out: rdn and no ex over 1f out*	ADempsey	**25/1**	70
S	**4**	*6*	**Oscar's Lady (IRE)**[20] [470] 4-10-3 (G A Swinbank) *cl up: led 4f out to over 1f out: nt qckn*	DCCostello(5)	**11/4**[2]	66+
	5	*12*	**Little Vantage**[35] 6-10-13 (A M Crow) *in tch tl wknd over 2f out*	DMcGann(5)	**40/1**	62
5	**6**	*2 1/2*	**South Shore One**[32] [277] 4-10-1 (G A Harker) *mde most to 4f out: wknd over 2f out*	WKennedy(7)	**8/1**	50
	7	*8*	**Hard N Sharp** 5-11-4 (J M Jefferson) *chsd ldrs tl rdn and wknd over 2f out*	JimCrowley	**10/1**	52
	8	*8*	**King Amber** 4-11-1 (A Crook) *towards rr: rdn and struggling fr over 6f out*	MBradburne	**33/1**	41
0	**9**	*24*	**Over'n Out**[23] [424] 4-10-8 (A R Dicken) *w ldr tl lost pl qckly 1/2-way: sn t.o*	GLee	**16/1**	10
60-	**10**	*2*	**Norminster**[62] [4788] 4-11-1 (R Nixon) *sn bhd and detatched: nvr on terms*	NPMulholland	**50/1**	15

4m 1.20s (-11.50) **Going Correction** -0.675s/f (Firm)
WFA 4 from 5yo+ 3lb **33** Ran SP% **117.3**
Speed ratings: **100,97,92,89,83 82,78,74,63,62** CSF £9.97 TOTE £3.10: £1.10, £1.80, £11.20; EX 11.60 Place 6 £82.12, Place 5 £46.33.
Owner Jim Ennis **Bred** Denis Dunne And Thomas Phelan **Trained** Greystoke, Cumbria

FOCUS
There was an ordinary pace to this bumper, and although it was the faster of the two divisions by 0.9 seconds, it is still not strong form.

NOTEBOOK
Lahib The Fifth(IRE) ◆, a half-brother to an Irish bumper winner and to multiple hurdle scorer Bob's Gone, created a most favourable impression on this racecourse debut and, although this may not have been much of a race, he looks sure to win again. *(tchd 15-8 and 9-4)*
Lunar Eclipse has improved with every outing and ran creditably, but she is going to need a good test of stamina when sent over hurdles. *(tchd 5-1)*
Mae Moss, from a stable that has done well with its runners at this course this year, showed ability on her racecourse debut but is likely to continue to look vulnerable in this type of event.
Oscar's Lady(IRE) showed herself none the worse for her Southwell mishap, and a much stiffer test of stamina may help in future, but she will have to fare better if she is to win a race in this sphere. *(op 7-2 tchd 4-1)*
Little Vantage, who refused at the first on both starts in points, was not totally disgraced, but he is likely to continue to look vulnerable in this type of event. *(op 33-1 tchd 50-1)*
South Shore One had the run of the race and was not disgraced, but she will have to leave this form behind to make her mark in this type of event. *(op 7-1)*
T/Plt: £74.40 to a £1 stake. Pool: £38,400.45. 376.75 winning tickets. T/Qpdt: £55.70 to a £1 stake. Pool: £2,395.80. 31.80 winning tickets. RY

721 - 723a (Foreign Racing) - See Raceform Interactive

650 STRATFORD (L-H)

Sunday, June 12

OFFICIAL GOING: Good
After watering the going was slower than anticipated.
Wind: Nil Weather: Cloudy

724 HORSEPOWER NOVICES' H'CAP HURDLE (FOR THE NIGEL MUNN MEMORIAL TROPHY) (11 hdls 1 omitted) 2m 6f 110y

2:10 (2:10) (Class 4) (0-95,90) 4-Y-O+ **£3,549** (£1,092; £546; £273)

Form	Pos	Dist	Horse	Jockey	SP	RPR
-312	**1**		**Charlie's Double**[14] [575] 6-11-1 **82** (J R Best) *hld up in tch: led after 2 out: styd on wl*	DCrosse(3)	**7/2**[1]	96+
00-0	**2**	*9*	**Gondolin (IRE)**[37] [206] 5-11-2 **80** (G Brown) *hld up in mid-div: hdwy 6th: ev ch after 2 out: nt fluent last: sn btn*	(p) JEMoore	**7/2**[1]	87+
P-B0	**3**	*10*	**Kingscourt Lad (IRE)**[14] [575] 7-11-2 **80** (Jonjo O'Neill) *hld up and bhd: hdwy appr 9th: wknd after last*	RWalsh	**12/1**	75
4-15	**4**	*1 1/2*	**Little Brave**[32] [298] 10-11-7 **90** (C Roberts) *bhd tl styd on appr last: nvr nrr*	LStephens(5)	**14/1**	84
6-21	**5**	*1 1/2*	**Roman Candle (IRE)**[18] [506] 9-11-5 **83** (Lucinda Featherstone) *hld up and bhd: hdwy on ins appr 8th: wknd after last*	JPMcNamara	**5/1**[2]	75
6-42	**6**	*shd*	**Caper**[10] [614] 5-10-12 **86** (R Hollinshead) *hld up in mid-div: hdwy appr 3 out: wknd appr last*	(p) AHawkins(10)	**17/2**[3]	78
05B0	**7**	*5*	**Saxe-Coburg (IRE)**[7] [652] 8-10-6 **77** (K G Wingrove) *hld up and bhd: hdwy 7th: wknd 3 out*	JPemberton(7)	**25/1**	64
-PFS	**8**	*14*	**China Chase (IRE)**[18] [506] 6-10-10 **74** (J L Spearing) *nt fluent 5th: a bhd*	(b) PJBrennan	**40/1**	47
4P-0	**9**	*hd*	**Sweet Shooter**[18] [506] 5-10-13 **77** (M Madgwick) *mid-div: rdn after 6th: bhd fr 3 out*	ChristianWilliams	**50/1**	50
00-4	**10**	*3/4*	**Killarney Prince (IRE)**[46] [53] 6-11-3 **88** (Mrs J M Mann) *t.k.h: chsd ldr tl after 2nd: led 7th tl after 2 out: sn wknd*	MrJOwen(7)	**40/1**	60
/54-	**11**	*22*	**Jim Lad**[381] [514] 5-11-1 **79** (J W Mullins) *hld up in mid-div: rdn and wknd after 2 out*	AThornton	**20/1**	29
6P-3	**12**	*3 1/2*	**Tass Heel (IRE)**[18] [501] 6-11-5 **90** (B J Llewellyn) *bhd fr 3 out*	MrRMcCarthy(7)	**9/1**	36
6/6P	**P**		**Matrix (AUS)**[8] [631] 8-11-5 **83** (K McAuliffe) *led to 5th: led 6th to 7th: wknd appr 8th: bhd whn p.u bef 9th*	(v[1]) NFehily	**40/1**	—
30P-	**P**		**Heatherlea Squire (NZ)**[117] [3859] 7-11-3 **84** (D J Wintle) *hld up in tch: wknd appr 3 out: bhd whn p.u after 2 out*	GCarenza(3)	**40/1**	—
P-10	**P**		**Miss Jessica (IRE)**[25] [414] 5-11-6 **84** (Miss M E Rowland) *chsd ldr after 2nd: led 5th to 6th: wknd appr 8th: t.o whn p.u bef 9th*	JMogford	**25/1**	—

5m 28.0s (-1.70) **Going Correction** +0.025s/f (Yiel) **15** Ran SP% **120.2**
Speed ratings: **103,99,96,95,95 95,93,88,88,88 80,79,**—,—,— CSF £14.36 CT £135.15 TOTE £4.60: £2.20, £1.80, £5.00; EX 32.70.
Owner The Highly Hopeful Club **Bred** J R Heatley **Trained** Hucking, Kent

FOCUS
The final flight was omitted in an event where not many came into the race in form.

NOTEBOOK
Charlie's Double is turning into a progressive staying hurdler. He won going away despite the ground being slower than he prefers and the trip being the bare minimum for him.
Gondolin(IRE), dropped 5lb, was the subject of an old-fashioned gamble having been available at 33/1 in the morning. Leaving all his previous form behind, one can only hope that those in the know were on each way. *(op 11-2 tchd 13-2 and 6-1 in places)*
Kingscourt Lad(IRE) was 6lb better off than when 18 lengths behind the winner at Uttoxeter last time. Given a fair bit to do, he could not sustain what at one time was a promising-looking run and may have failed to stay. *(op 11-1)*
Little Brave only got going when the race was as good as over.
Roman Candle(IRE), raised 6lb, seemed to find this longer trip just beyond him. *(tchd 11-2 in places)*
Caper is another with stamina doubts over this distance. *(op 9-1)*

725 HOSPICE AT HOME NURSES H'CAP CHASE (15 fncs) 2m 4f

2:40 (2:40) (Class 4) (0-110,110) 5-Y-O+ **£4,784** (£1,472; £736; £368)

Form	Pos	Dist	Horse	Jockey	SP	RPR
036-	**1**		**Calon Lan (IRE)**[128] [3687] 14-9-8 **85** oh3 ow1 (B J Llewellyn) *hld up: hdwy 8th: led 3 out: clr last: hrd rdn flat: fin tired*	SWalsh(7)	**9/1**	100+
4-52	**2**	*3/4*	**Kind Sir**[29] [360] 9-11-3 **101** (A W Carroll) *w ldr: led 4th to 3 out: rallied flat*	WHutchinson	**3/1**[1]	112
3-00	**3**	*25*	**Flahive's First**[8] [634] 11-10-8 **97** (D Burchell) *bhd tl styd on fr 2 out: nvr nr ldrs*	LStephens(5)	**14/1**	83
P-41	**4**	*2 1/2*	**Joint Authority (IRE)**[14] [567] 10-11-0 **105** (D L Williams) *prom: mstke 2nd: hmpd 6th: wknd 8th*	MissLHorner(7)	**5/1**[2]	94+
2-61	**5**	*20*	**Burning Truth (USA)**[21] [458] 11-11-12 **110** (M Sheppard) *led to 4th: prom tl wknd 4 out*	PJBrennan	**13/2**[3]	74
2-40	**6**	*3 1/2*	**Guilsborough Gorse**[12] [605] 10-10-7 **98** (T D Walford) *hld up and bhd: mstke 3rd: short-lived effrt 10th: mstke 11th*	MrMWalford(7)	**16/1**	58
664-	**7**	*29*	**Snipe**[202] [2394] 7-11-6 **104** (Ian Williams) *hld up in mid-div: hdwy 8th: wknd 11th*	DRDennis	**7/1**	35
40-4	**F**		**Barnards Green (IRE)**[29] [354] 7-10-0 **84** oh3 (R H Alner) *prom: 3rd whn fell 6th*	(b[1]) RWalford	**10/1**	—
PP2-	**P**		**Andy's Lad (IRE)**[63] [4792] 13-9-12 **89** (D Burchell) *mstkes: bhd fr 8th: t.o whn p.u bef 11th*	(p) AScholes(7)	**20/1**	—
4P-0	**P**		**Get The Point**[40] [170] 11-10-6 **90** (Dr P Pritchard) *a towards rr: t.o whn p.u bef 3 out*	JamesDavies	**22/1**	—
41-0	**P**		**Harik**[19] [103] 11-11-12 **110** (G L Moore) *bhd: hdwy after 9th: wknd appr 11th: t.o whn p.u bef 3 out*	(bt) JEMoore	**12/1**	—

4m 58.7s (-1.30) **Going Correction** +0.15s/f (Yiel) **11** Ran SP% **115.9**
Speed ratings: **108,107,97,96,88 87,75,**—,—,— — CSF £36.95 CT £382.20 TOTE £11.30: £2.90, £1.80, £4.30; EX 52.60.
Owner R Williams **Bred** J And Mrs Harold-Barry **Trained** Fochriw, Caerphilly

FOCUS
A modest handicap run at a decent clip with the winner, who could be rated value for a bit further, finishing leg weary.

NOTEBOOK
Calon Lan(IRE), who had only been with his new stable a month, has gone well fresh in the past. Three times a winner last summer, lack of a recent outing did seem to be catching up with him at the end. *(op 10-1 tchd 12-1 in a place)*

Kind Sir was able to get to the front earlier this time and had shaken off all bar the winner four out. He fought back on the run-in but could not quite overhaul the tiring winner. *(op 4-1)*
Flahive's First just plugged on to finish a very modest third. *(op 12-1)*
Joint Authority(IRE), up 7lb, likes genuinely fast ground and did not get that here. *(op 6-1)*
Burning Truth(USA) has only ever won on good to firm so this watered ground would have been against him. *(op 6-1)*

726 PARKRIDGE H'CAP HURDLE (9 hdls) 2m 110y
3:15 (3:16) (Class 3) (0-120,120) 4-Y-0+
£6,322 (£2,398; £1,199; £545; £272; £163)

Form RPR
4B-0 **1** **Monticelli (GER)**[35] [247] 5-11-6 **114** .... RJohnson 119+
(P J Hobbs) *hld up in mid-div: hdwy appr 5th: led 2 out: drvn out* **7/1**[2]
53-1 **2** *3* **Maclean**[14] [563] 4-10-10 **107** .... JEMoore 107+
(G L Moore) *hld up and bhd: hdwy after 3 out: hit 2 out: one pce flat* **8/1**[3]
30-1 **3** *1 ½* **Hilltime (IRE)**[20] [370] 5-10-12 **111** .... DCCostello[(5)] 114+
(J J Quinn) *hld up in tch: led briefly appr 2 out: btn whn hung rt and lost 2nd cl home* **12/1**
3P-2 **4** *1 ¼* **Figaro Du Rocher (FR)**[25] [409] 5-10-4 **105** .... (t) AGlassonbury[(7)] 107+
(M C Pipe) *led: j.rt 5th: rdn whn hung rt and hdd bnd appr 2 out: hit last: one pce* **9/2**[1]
12-0 **5** *nk* **Golden Chalice (IRE)**[43] [136] 6-10-7 **106** .... PCO'Neill[(5)] 105
(Miss E C Lavelle) *hld up and bhd: hdwy appr 6th: one pce fr 2 out* **18/1**
3-06 **6** *4* **Shaman**[17] [517] 8-10-6 **100** .... LAspell 95
(G L Moore) *hld up and bhd: rdn and hdwy appr 2 out: nvr trbld ldrs* **66/1**
40-6 **7** *9* **Castle River (USA)**[14] [571] 6-10-6 **100** .... MBatchelor 86
(O O'Neill) *hld up and bhd: hdwy appr 6th: rdn after 3 out: sn wknd* **8/1**[3]
23-5 **8** *1 ½* **Dominican Monk (IRE)**[22] [450] 6-11-12 **120** .... MAFitzgerald 107+
(C Tinkler) *hld up in mid-div: hit 2 out: sn wknd* **14/1**
-F22 **9** *3* **Hattington**[16] [533] 7-11-0 **108** .... NFehily 89
(M F Harris) *nvr nr ldrs* **20/1**
0210 **10** *8* **Forzacurity**[22] [450] 6-10-9 **108** .... LStephens[(5)] 81
(M Sheppard) *prom tl wknd after 6th* **33/1**
133- **11** *7* **Scalloway (IRE)**[227] [1709] 5-11-4 **112** .... CLlewellyn 78
(D J Wintle) *hld up in tch: wnt 2nd briefly 4th: wknd appr 6th* **25/1**
20-0 **12** *2* **Arm And A Leg (IRE)**[14] [571] 10-10-13 **107** .... AO'Keeffe 71
(Mrs D A Hamer) *prom: mstke 3rd: wknd after 5th* **50/1**
6-54 **R** **Kalambari (IRE)**[14] [571] 6-11-2 **110** .... PJBrennan —
(J Joseph) *ref to r: tk no part* **16/1**
114- **R** **Brave Dane (IRE)**[11] [1715] 7-10-1 **100** .... DLaverty[(5)] —
(L A Dace) *ref to r: tk no part* **33/1**
6-33 **U** **Lord Lington (FR)**[35] [247] 6-11-0 **108** .... WMarston —
(D J Wintle) *in rr: last whn blnd and uns rdr 4th* **18/1**
P0-1 **P** **Qabas (USA)**[14] [571] 5-11-4 **112** .... (p) RThornton —
(P Bowen) *hld up in tch: wknd 3 out: bhd whn p.u bef last* **9/1**
P-23 **P** **Odagh Odyssey (IRE)**[22] [452] 11-11-6 **114** .... JMMaguire —
(Miss E C Lavelle) *chsd ldr to 4th: wkng whn hit 6th: bhd whn p.u bef 2 out* **40/1**
P **Room To Room Gold (IRE)**[364] [741] 9-11-2 **110** .... AThornton —
(R H Alner) *hld up and bhd: hdwy appr 6th: wknd 3 out: bhd whn p.u bef 2 out* **8/1**[3]

3m 56.5s (-1.90) **Going Correction** +0.025s/f (Yiel)
WFA 4 from 5yo+ 3lb **18** Ran SP% **125.2**
Speed ratings: **105,103,102,102,102 100,96,95,93,90 86,85,—,—,— —,—,—** CSF £59.42 CT £681.40 TOTE £9.70: £2.90, £2.50, £3.30, £2.00; EX 72.20.
Owner Mrs M Findlay **Bred** Mrs I Bodewein **Trained** Withycombe, Somerset

FOCUS
A competitive handicap.

NOTEBOOK
Monticelli(GER) benefited from the fact that the ground had been well watered and saw it out well to the finish. *(op 9-1)*
Maclean ran a sound race on his handicap debut and his attitude could again not be faulted. *(op 10-1)*
Hilltime(IRE), raised 8lb for winning a race at Uttoxeter in which the form has worked out well, threw away second place after hanging like a gate at the death. *(op 16-1)*
Figaro Du Rocher(FR), back over hurdles, stuck to his task despite giving the distinct impression that he would have preferred to have been going right-handed. *(op 11-2 tchd 6-1)*
Golden Chalice(IRE) put a disappointing effort at Worcester last time behind him without ever really making his presence felt. *(op 14-1)*
Qabas(USA) *Official explanation: jockey said good ground was too soft (op 8-1 tchd 10-1)*

727 SANDAL HOUSE STUD H'CAP CHASE (18 fncs) 3m
3:50 (3:50) (Class 3) (0-135,127) 5-Y-0+
£8,961 (£3,399; £1,699; £772; £386; £231)

Form RPR
43-3 **1** **Little Big Horse (IRE)**[35] [248] 9-11-3 **118** .... DElsworth 129
(Mrs S J Smith) *mde most to 12th: rdn appr 2 out: rallied to ld last strides* **7/2**[2]
400- **2** *nk* **Dark Room (IRE)**[60] [4821] 8-10-7 **108** .... JEMoore 120+
(Jonjo O'Neill) *w ldr: led 12th: rdn appr 2 out: 3 l clr last: ct last strides* **7/1**
56-1 **3** *5* **Moving Earth (IRE)**[31] [311] 12-11-4 **119** .... CLlewellyn 126+
(A W Carroll) *hld up in rr: hdwy 13th: rdn appr 2 out: one pce* **5/1**[3]
3-P2 **4** *10* **Montifault (FR)**[31] [313] 10-11-5 **120** .... (t) RWalsh 116
(P F Nicholls) *racd wd: hld up in tch: wknd after 3 out* **3/1**[1]
-213 **5** *8* **Sky Warrior (FR)**[22] [454] 7-11-12 **127** .... ChristianWilliams 123+
(Evan Williams) *prom tl stmbld bdly 14th: nt rcvr* **5/1**[3]
5-65 **6** *29* **Montreal (FR)**[7] [653] 8-11-2 **120** .... (p) TJMalone[(3)] 79
(M C Pipe) *hld up: hdwy 13th: wknd 3 out: t.o* **10/1**
F20- **P** **Happy Hussar (IRE)**[65] [4766] 12-9-7 **101** oh8 .... RLucey-Butler[(7)] —
(Dr P Pritchard) *hld up in rr: j. slowly 6th and 7th: sn lost tch: t.o whn p.u bef 14th* **20/1**

6m 2.00s (-0.20) **Going Correction** +0.15s/f (Yiel) **7** Ran SP% **106.9**
Speed ratings: **106,105,104,100,98 88,—** CSF £23.72 CT £100.45 TOTE £4.90: £1.90, £3.90; EX 27.80.
Owner Paul J Dixon **Bred** A D C Cathers **Trained** High Eldwick, W Yorks

FOCUS
Not a great contest considering the prize money on offer.

NOTEBOOK
Little Big Horse(IRE) duly relished the return to three miles and fought back to pull what had looked an unlikely victory out of the fire. *(op 4-1)*
Dark Room(IRE) may have been edging left on the run-in and his rider certainly appeared to become unbalanced near the finish. This was definitely a case of defeat being snatched from the jaws of victory. *(op 8-1 tchd 17-2)*
Moving Earth(IRE) ran his race off a 3lb higher mark. *(op 7-2 tchd 11-2 in places)*
Montifault(FR) was taken wide in search of the fastest ground but the game was up after the third last. *(op 11-4 tchd 5-2 and 10-3)*
Sky Warrior(FR) was possibly just beginning to feel the pinch when a bad stumble five out put all doubts to rest. *(op 15-2)*

728 CABLESANDSTUFF.COM NOVICES' CHASE (18 fncs) 3m
4:20 (4:20) (Class 3) 5-Y-0+ **£5,483** (£1,782; £959)

Form RPR
31P- **1** **Sweet Diversion (IRE)**[51] [4961] 6-11-6 122 .... (t) RWalsh 124+
(P F Nicholls) *a.p: w ldr whn blnd and lft clr 2 out: drvn out* **9/4**[2]
66-1 **2** *8* **Mioche D'Estruval (FR)**[14] [570] 5-11-0 .... RGreene 109+
(M C Pipe) *keen early: hld up: mstke 10th: hdwy 11th: rdn after 14th: lft 8 l 2nd whn stmbld and sltly hmpd 2 out: blnd last* **6/4**[1]
3-U1 **3** *dist* **Celtic Boy (IRE)**[19] [486] 7-11-6 117 .... RJohnson 125+
(P Bowen) *chsd ldr fr 3rd: led 13th: slt ld whn fell 2 out: rmntd* **5/2**[3]
P **P** **Cool Trader (IRE)**[8] [631] 7-10-9 .... DLaverty[(5)] —
(Mrs C J Ikin) *nt jump wl: a bhd: rdn 4th: p.u bef 9th* **100/1**
6U-2 **F** **Blaze On**[25] [401] 6-10-7 .... MrPYork[(7)] —
(R H York) *chsd ldr to 3rd: pckd 10th: wknd 11th: mstke 13th: last whn fell 14th* **18/1**
F-R3 **F** **Althrey Dandy (IRE)**[5] [672] 10-11-4 105 .... AThornton 100
(P T Dalton) *led to 13th: ev ch whn mstke 3 out: sn wknd: 10 l 4th whn fell 2 out* **25/1**

6m 2.50s (0.30) **Going Correction** +0.15s/f (Yiel)
WFA 5 from 6yo+ 6lb **6** Ran SP% **109.4**
Speed ratings: **105,102,—,—,— —** CSF £6.01 TOTE £3.40: £2.00, £1.50; EX 7.50.
Owner Ian Marshall **Bred** Con O'Keeffe **Trained** Ditcheat, Somerset

FOCUS
The tricky penultimate fence had a big say in the outcome of this novice chase.

NOTEBOOK
Sweet Diversion(IRE) had shown the benefit of a wind operation when successful over this course and distance in April. His trainer reported he still choked a bit in the mud at Newton Abbot last time and was fitted with a tongue strap here. Possibly going fractionally better than Celtic Boy when left clear, the faster the ground the better for him. *(tchd 85-40)*
Mioche D'Estruval(FR) was fortunate to finish second after being a bit too keen early on. *(tchd 7-4 in places)*
Celtic Boy(IRE) was being strongly pressed by the winner when crumpling on landing two from home. *(op 11-4)*
Althrey Dandy(IRE) looked booked for fourth when coming to grief.

729 PREMIER CRU NOVICES' HURDLE (9 hdls) 2m 110y
4:50 (4:51) (Class 3) 4-Y-0+
£6,310 (£2,393; £1,196; £544; £272; £163)

Form RPR
1-11 **1** **Darrias (GER)**[22] [450] 4-11-5 132 .... RWalsh 115+
(P F Nicholls) *hld up towards rr: smooth hdwy appr 6th: rdn to ld 2 out: r.o* **4/5**[1]
21 **2** *2 ½* **Settlement Craic (IRE)**[18] [504] 4-11-3 .... JimCrowley 110
(T G Mills) *hld up in tch: led 5th to 2 out: nt qckn* **15/8**[2]
3 *7* **Screenplay**[31] 4-10-11 .... JGoldstein 97
(Miss Sheena West) *hld up in tch: ev ch after 3 out: sn rdn: wknd after 2 out* **33/1**
-4P0 **4** *23* **Simiola**[8] [629] 6-10-4 63 .... DCrosse[(3)] 70
(S T Lewis) *hld up and bhd: hdwy appr 6th: wknd after 3 out* **100/1**
P-0 **5** *5* **Desert Image (IRE)**[28] [369] 4-10-11 .... (t) WHutchinson 69
(C Tinkler) *hld up in mid-div: short-lived effrt 3 out* **66/1**
P-22 **6** *5* **Lyricist's Dream**[31] [314] 6-10-7 76 .... JPByrne 60
(R L Brown) *led tl after 4th: sn wknd: hmpd 3 out* **50/1**
7 *hd* **Doris Souter (IRE)**[34] 5-10-7 .... WMarston 60
(D J Wintle) *hld up in mid-div: hdwy 5th: hit 3 out: sn wknd* **50/1**
8 *11* **Rio De Janeiro (IRE)**[31] 4-10-11 .... MAFitzgerald 53
(P R Chamings) *hld up in tch: wknd appr 3 out* **50/1**
9 *3 ½* **Iffy**[10] 4-10-11 .... LAspell 49
(P D Cundell) *a bhd* **25/1**
10 *5* **Firebird Rising (USA)**[26] 4-10-4 .... PJBrennan 37
(R Brotherton) *stdd s: a in rr* **100/1**
3- **11** *½* **Weet A Head (IRE)**[19] [1794] 4-10-11 .... DRDennis 44
(R Hollinshead) *hdwy 3rd: disp ld 5th: wknd 3 out: mstke last* **25/1**
4 **12** *13* **Alekhine (IRE)**[19] [485] 4-10-11 .... RJohnson 31
(P J Hobbs) *hld up in mid-div: hdwy after 4th: wknd appr 3 out* **16/1**[3]
00 **F** **Weet An Haul**[21] [457] 4-10-4 .... PMerrigan[(7)] —
(T Wall) *prom: hit 5th: wkng whn fell 3 out* **100/1**
0/6- **P** **Lord Thomas (IRE)**[207] [2275] 7-11-0 .... AThornton —
(A J Wilson) *a bhd: t.o whn p.u after 3 out* **100/1**
00 **P** **Scary Night (IRE)**[21] [467] 5-10-4 .... CareyWilliamson[(10)] —
(M J Gingell) *t.k.h: a bhd: hit 6th: t.o whn p.u after 3 out* **100/1**
50/ **P** **Just Magical**[49] 8-10-7 .... CLlewellyn —
(Mrs C A Dunnett) *chsd ldr: led after 4th to 5th: sn wknd: t.o whn p.u after 3 out* **100/1**

4m 0.10s (1.70) **Going Correction** +0.025s/f (Yiel) **16** Ran SP% **120.2**
Speed ratings: **97,95,92,81,79 77,76,71,70,67 67,61,—,—,— —** CSF £2.17 TOTE £1.70: £1.10, £1.30, £6.10; EX 2.60 Place 6 £21.00, Place 5 £12.73.
Owner Peter Hart **Bred** Gestut Rottgen **Trained** Ditcheat, Somerset

FOCUS
A modest winning time for the grade, 3.6 seconds slower than the earlier handicap.

NOTEBOOK
Darrias(GER) continues to go from strength to strength and completed a four-timer back in novice company. *(op 5-6 tchd Evens in places)*
Settlement Craic(IRE) did nothing wrong but could not cope with the progressive winner. *(op 2-1 tchd 7-4)*
Screenplay has been running well on the Flat having developed into an out-and-out stayer. He made sure the two major players did not have the script to themselves despite running over a trip and course that would have been plenty sharp enough for him. He can get off the mark when given a stiffer test of stamina. *(op 25-1)*
Simiola is exposed as extremely moderate over hurdles and achieved nothing in finishing a remote fourth.
Scary Night(IRE) *Official explanation: jockey said gelding had a breathing problem*
T/Plt: £86.60 to a £1 stake. Pool: £49,352.15. 415.90 winning tickets. T/Qpdt: £12.40 to a £1 stake. Pool: £3,665.50. 218.70 winning tickets. KH

730 - 741a (Foreign Racing) - See Raceform Interactive

679 **HEREFORD** (R-H)

Tuesday, June 14

OFFICIAL GOING: Good to firm

Wind: Moderate, across Weather: Fine

742 HFT FORKLIFTS LTD 21ST ANNIVERSARY NOVICES' HURDLE (10 hdls) 2m 3f 110y

6:45 (6:45) (Class 4) 4-Y-O+ £4,241 (£1,305; £652; £326)

Form					RPR
	1		**Grey Tune (IRE)**[465] 4201 6-10-2 ... JKington[(10)] (M Scudamore) *hld up and bhd: hdwy appr 6th: rdn to ld 2 out: drvn out* **50/1**		100
12	2	½	**Boulevardofdreams (IRE)**[19] 514 4-10-12 ... DCrosse[(3)] (M C Pipe) *a.p: led and mstke 7th: rdn and hdd 2 out: ev ch last: r.o* **8/1**		102
3-13	3	¾	**Kilindini**[23] 457 4-11-1 114 ... BJCrowley (Miss E C Lavelle) *led to 2nd: a.p: hrd rdn after 2 out: ev ch last: nt qckn* **5/2[2]**		102+
0/0P	4	dist	**Mapilut Du Moulin (FR)**[6] 691 5-10-12 ... PJBrennan (C R Dore) *hld up and bhd: hdwy 6th: wknd 3 out: lft poor 4th last* **66/1**		—
06-P	P		**Old Golden Bay**[45] 138 5-10-9 ... RHobson[(3)] (M Wellings) *a bhd: t.o whn p.u bef 7th* **100/1**		—
	P		**Impulsivo**[36] 5-10-12 ... AThornton (Simon Earle) *nt j.w: a in rr: t.o whn p.u bef 7th* **50/1**		—
00P-	P		**Ms Freebee**[22] 4527 6-10-5 ... AO'Keeffe (M Mullineaux) *a bhd: t.o whn p.u after 2 out* **100/1**		—
36	P		**Mr Dip**[28] 394 5-10-7 ... DLaverty[(5)] (L A Dace) *a behing: j.rt 1st: rdn after 6th: sn t.o: p.u bef last* **25/1**		—
	P		**Final Melody**[65] 5-10-5 ... RThornton (P Bowen) *hld up: blnd 1st: sn in tch: wknd 3 out: t.o whn p.u bef last* **22/1**		—
-232	P		**Thieves'Glen**[18] 531 7-10-12 105 ... MAFitzgerald (H Morrison) *prom: led after 6th to 7th: wknd appr 2 out: bhd whn p.u bef last* **7/2[3]**		—
P-P	P		**Kerry Zulu Warrior**[10] 635 8-10-12 ... DRDennis (M Sheppard) *t.k.h: led 2nd tl after 6th: wknd after 3 out: t.o whn p.u after 2 out* **50/1**		—
5-31	F		**Tom Bell (IRE)**[23] 460 5-10-12 110 ... (v) NCarter[(7)] (J G M O'Shea) *hld up: sltly hmpd 1st: hdwy appr 5th: ev ch 2 out: 4th and wkng whn fell last* **2/1[1]**		94
00-	P		**A Monk Swimming (IRE)**[116] 3678 4-10-8 ... JGoldstein (Miss J S Davis) *hld up in tch: lost pl and j. path after 4th: sn bhd: t.o whn p.u bef last* **50/1**		—

4m 42.8s (-5.10) **Going Correction** -0.225s/f (Good) **13** Ran SP% **114.7**

Speed ratings: **101,100,100,**—,— —,—,—,—,— —,—,— CSF £373.87 TOTE £106.60: £17.00, £2.30, £1.10; EX 78.90.

Owner Mrs N M Watkins **Bred** Patrick Halvey **Trained** Bromsash, Herefordshire

FOCUS

Plenty of dead wood in this ordinary event.

NOTEBOOK

Grey Tune(IRE) was well beaten in a bumper and a maiden hurdle on soft ground in Ireland early last year. His shock win on this faster surface apparently came as a big surprise to his new connections.

Boulevardofdreams(IRE) stuck to his task over a trip that would have been on the short side for him, especially on this quicker ground. *(op 13-2)*

Kilindini put a disappointing effort here last time behind him over this longer trip. *(op 11-4 tchd 9-4 and 3-1 in places)*

Thieves'Glen *Official explanation: jockey said gelding was lame and lost a front shoe (op 5-2)*

Tom Bell(IRE) has yet to show he gets this sort of distance over hurdles despite the fact that he stayed pretty well on the Flat. *(op 5-2)*

Ms Freebee *Official explanation: jockey said mare had a breathing problem (op 5-2)*

743 HFT - NISSAN MOTOR (GB) LTD - INDUSTRIAL MACHINERY (S) HURDLE (8 hdls) 2m 1f

7:15 (7:15) (Class 5) 4-6-Y-O £2,219 (£634; £317)

Form				RPR
2560	1		**Blue Leader (IRE)**[8] 668 6-11-8 98 ... (bt[1]) CLlewellyn (W K Goldsworthy) *led tl after 1st: led after 4th: rdn after 2 out: r.o wl* **11/2**	102+
46-0	2	5	**Rumbling Bridge**[51] 5 4-10-9 93 ... MBradburne (H D Daly) *hld up in tch: rdn to chse wnr appr 2 out: no imp* **9/4[1]**	82+
62F-	3	6	**Gabor**[253] 1592 6-11-4 110 ... (b) ChristianWilliams (B J Llewellyn) *hld up in tch: chsd wnr appr 5th tl appr 2 out: wknd appr last* **3/1[2]**	84
0-10	4	1¼	**Trickstep**[27] 412 4-11-1 97 ... JMMaguire (D McCain) *hld up: hdwy appr 5th: rdn after 3 out: wknd appr last* **7/2[3]**	80
0P-4	5	13	**Makandy**[42] 173 6-10-5 ... MrRArmson[(7)] (R J Armson) *led after 1st tl after 4th: hung lft 5th: wknd 3 out* **33/1**	64
55P-	6	10	**Magenta Rising (IRE)**[11] 1859 5-10-5 74 ... RThornton (W M Brisbourne) *hld up: hdwy 3rd: wknd 2 out* **9/1**	47
-036	7	15	**Luristan (IRE)**[10] 635 5-10-9 73 ... (p) DCrosse[(3)] (S T Lewis) *hld up and bhd: hdwy 4th: hrd rdn and wknd after 5th* **16/1**	39
/PP-	8	1¾	**Saposcat (IRE)**[9] 918 5-10-5 ... MrDavidTurner[(7)] (Dr P Pritchard) *a bhd: lost tch appr 5th* **66/1**	37
000/	9	dist	**Cash 'n Carrots**[31] 6-10-7 ... MNicolls[(5)] (R C Harper) *prom: lost pl 3rd: sn rdn and struggling: t.o* **50/1**	—

3m 59.4s (-3.70) **Going Correction** -0.225s/f (Good)

WFA 4 from 5yo+ 3lb **9** Ran SP% **115.7**

Speed ratings: **99,96,93,93,87 82,75,74,**— CSF £18.74 TOTE £7.20: £2.10, £1.20, £1.80; EX 13.90.There was no bid for the winner. Rumbling Bridge was claimed by Miss J. Davis for £6,000.

Owner Ms Diane Morgan **Bred** Gainsborough Stud Management Ltd **Trained** Yerbeston, Pembrokes

FOCUS

A modest seller.

NOTEBOOK

Blue Leader(IRE), who had the visor left off last time, found the first-time blinkers working the oracle. *(op 9-2)*

Rumbling Bridge was a rare runner for his stable in a seller having become disappointing. He was subsequently claimed for £6,000. *(tchd 5-2)*

Gabor, previously trained by Gary Moore, was dropped into a seller with the blinkers refitted for this comeback over hurdles. *(op 7-2 tchd 11-4)*

Trickstep could not take advantage of being back in the right sort of grade. *(op 9-2)*

744 HFT - NISSAN FORKTRUCK FINANCE CLASSIFIED CHASE (14 fncs) 2m 3f

7:45 (7:45) (Class 4) 5-Y-O+ £3,711 (£1,142; £571; £285)

Form				RPR
00F3	1		**Rudetski**[6] 684 8-10-12 100 ... (t) DRDennis (M Sheppard) *hld up: mstke and lost pl 2nd: hdwy 7th: led 2 out: clr appr last: r.o wl* **11/2**	104+
/0-F	2	6	**Kavi (IRE)**[46] 106 5-10-10 100 ... AThornton (Simon Earle) *a.p: mstke 3 out: sn outpcd: rallied and wnt 2nd whn pckd bdly last: nt rcvr* **5/1**	98+
121-	3	5	**Woodenbridge Dream (IRE)**[85] 4497 8-10-12 82 ... RThornton (R Lee) *chsd ldr: led 3rd: hdd and hit 2 out: wknd last* **5/2[1]**	94+
6534	4	19	**Jupon Vert (FR)**[8] 666 8-10-12 99 ... SThomas (R J Hodges) *hld up: hdwy 4th: wknd 4 out* **7/2[2]**	73
4-P6	5	3½	**Hi Rudolf**[6] 684 10-10-5 83 ... JAJenkins[(7)] (H J Manners) *hld up: hdwy 8th: rdn and wknd appr 3 out* **33/1**	70
3P-5	6	dist	**Smart Design (IRE)**[8] 666 10-10-12 88 ... (t) JPMcNamara (K Bishop) *a bhd: mstke 10th: t.o* **14/1**	—
5-P4	7	1¾	**Mr Jake**[16] 565 12-10-7 55 ... JHarris[(5)] (H E Haynes) *led to 3rd: w ldr to 6th: sn rdn: wknd 8th: t.o* **66/1**	—
353-	U		**Bobsbest (IRE)**[55] 4934 9-10-12 85 ... WHutchinson (R J Price) *stmbld and uns rdr bnd after 2nd* **4/1[3]**	—

4m 45.2s (-1.40) **Going Correction** -0.225s/f (Good)

WFA 5 from 8yo+ 1lb **8** Ran SP% **113.9**

Speed ratings: **93,90,88,80,78** —,—,— CSF £33.15 TOTE £5.00: £1.60, £1.50, £1.70; EX 25.20.

Owner M J Jordan and J N Jordan **Bred** Matthews Breeding And Racing Ltd **Trained** Eastnor, H'fords

FOCUS

A modest time for the grade.

NOTEBOOK

Rudetski was thought by his trainer to have suffered from the bounce factor when third over course and distance last time. He goes on fast ground and will carry on during the summer. *(op 4-1)*

Kavi(IRE) had found a second wind and was closing quite fast on the winner when landing on his nose at the final fence. We will never know whether he would have bustled up Rudetski. *(op 4-1 tchd 11-2)*

Woodenbridge Dream(IRE) had a bit to find at the weights and did not get his own way out in front this time on a return to a longer trip. *(op 11-4 tchd 10-3)*

Mr Jake *Official explanation: vet said gelding bled from the nose*

745 HFT - MANITOU (SITELIFT) LTD NOVICES' H'CAP HURDLE (13 hdls) 3m 2f

8:15 (8:16) (Class 4) (0-100,96) 4-Y-O+ £3,828 (£1,178; £589; £294)

Form				RPR
3121	1		**Charlie's Double**[2] 724 6-11-2 **89** 7ex ... DCrosse[(3)] (J R Best) *hld up in mid-div: hdwy 7th: led sn after 3 out: sn rdn: styd on* **6/4[1]**	104+
PU-4	2	1¼	**Bustisu**[46] 96 8-10-0 **77** ... RLucey-Butler[(7)] (D J Wintle) *hld up and bhd: hdwy 9th: chsd wnr appr 2 out: hung rt appr last: nt qckn flat* **20/1**	87
04-2	3	6	**Super Road Train**[19] 509 6-11-6 **90** ... LAspell (O Sherwood) *hld up in mid-div: lost pl 6th: rdn and hdwy appr 2 out: styd on flat* **11/2[3]**	94
-435	4	5	**Potts Of Magic**[12] 611 6-11-3 **87** ... (b) RThornton (R Lee) *hld up in tch: rdn and wknd after 3 out* **25/1**	86
60-5	5	12	**Cracow (IRE)**[29] 385 8-10-5 **75** ... CLlewellyn (W K Goldsworthy) *nvr nr ldrs* **16/1**	62
P-06	6	5	**Selassie**[12] 611 6-9-6 **72** oh6 ow2 ... JKington[(10)] (M Scudamore) *prom: led appr 8th: rdn and hdd sn after 3 out: wknd 2 out* **50/1**	54
5-16	7	25	**Mick Murphy (IRE)**[12] 614 8-10-12 **82** ... JamesDavies (V J Hughes) *led: nt fluent and hdd 3rd: led 6th tl appr 8th: rdn appr 10th: sn wknd* **14/1**	39
0P/2	8	21	**Boobee (IRE)**[12] 611 9-11-12 **96** ... ChristianWilliams (Evan Williams) *hld up: hmpd 2nd: hdwy after 6th: rdn and wknd appr 2 out* **10/1**	32
5-FU	9	18	**Rose Of The Hill (IRE)**[18] 535 6-11-11 **95** ... PJBrennan (M C Pipe) *hld up: hdwy after 7th: sn rdn: wknd appr 10th: t.o* **8/1**	13
0/5	10	¾	**Phar The Best (IRE)**[10] 630 8-11-6 **90** ... (v[1]) AThornton (Mrs A L M King) *a bhd* **25/1**	—
P-32	P		**Mead (IRE)**[23] 458 8-11-6 **90** ... (t) WMarston (D J Wintle) *hld up: hmpd 2nd: bhd whn rdn after 7th: t.o whn p.u and dismntd after 2 out* **5/1[2]**	—
05P	P		**Madhahir (IRE)**[31] 352 5-9-7 **70** ... (v) PCStringer[(7)] (M J Gingell) *prom: led 3rd to 6th: blnd 7th: wknd qckly after 9th: t.o whn p.u after 2 out* **66/1**	—

6m 22.8s (-5.20) **Going Correction** -0.225s/f (Good) **12** Ran SP% **120.7**

Speed ratings: **99,98,96,95,91 90,82,75,70,70** —,— CSF £38.54 CT £143.50 TOTE £2.00: £1.10, £6.30, £1.60; EX 73.50.

Owner The Highly Hopeful Club **Bred** J R Heatley **Trained** Hucking, Kent

FOCUS

This stamina test played to the strengths of the in-form winner.

NOTEBOOK

Charlie's Double, with both ground and distance back in his favour, continued on the crest of a wave on this quick reappearance. *(op 7-4 tchd 15-8 and 2-1 in places)*

Bustisu found the combination of a marathon distance and a sound surface just what the doctor ordered. Not for the first time she showed a tendency to hang right and was inclined to duck in behind the winner once in the short home straight. However, she did stay on willingly to the end. *(op 16-1)*

Super Road Train, up 3lb, again showed that all he does is stay. *(tchd 5-1)*

Potts Of Magic, a flop in blinkers last time, seemed to find the extended trip beyond him, although he was not beaten that far in the end.

746 HFT - COLLINS ENGINEERING LTD H'CAP CHASE (19 fncs) 3m 1f 110y

8:45 (8:46) (Class 4) (0-110,109) 5-Y-O+ £4,764 (£1,466; £733; £366)

Form				RPR
054-	1		**Excellent Vibes (IRE)**[243] 1712 7-10-0 **83** ... CLlewellyn (N A Twiston-Davies) *a.p: chsd ldr fr 7th: led 2 out: styd on wl* **12/1**	101+
PP/4	2	5	**Keltic Lord**[24] 455 9-10-0 **83** ... VSlattery (P W Hiatt) *hld up and bhd: hit 11th: hdwy 4 out: 3 l 2nd whn mstke last: no imp* **25/1**	92+
FRP-	3	14	**Mazileo**[60] 4856 12-11-8 **105** ... (p) DRDennis (Ian Williams) *led 3rd: clr 8th: hdd 2 out: 3rd and wkng whn mstke last* **16/1**	101+

1-34 **4** *16* **Paddy The Optimist (IRE)**[9] 653 9-10-6 **94** .... LStephens(5) 72
(D Burchell) *hld up and bhd: mstke 7th: hdwy appr 14th: wknd appr 15th* **11/2**[2]

-12P **5** *1 ½* **Silver Samuel (NZ)**[23] 461 8-10-6 **89** ....(t) JPByrne 66+
(S A Brookshaw) *prom: lost pl 8th: bhd whn mstke and bdly hmpd 12th: n.d after* **16/1**

-PF5 **6** *9* **Pete The Painter (IRE)**[23] 461 8-10-1 **85** oh3 ow1........(b) MBradburne 52
(J W Tudor) *hld up and bhd: hdwy 8th: rdn 14th: wknd appr 15th* **15/2**

-303 **7** *1 ½* **Blazing Batman**[16] 567 12-9-12 **86** .... TJPhelan(5) 52
(Dr P Pritchard) *bhd fr 13th* **12/1**

-031 **F** **Count Oski**[7] 673 9-10-7 **90** 7ex... AThornton —
(M J Ryan) *hld up in mid-div: fell 10th* **13/2**[3]

44- **P** **Connemara Mist (IRE)**[82] 4539 10-9-7 **83** oh14..........(b) MrGTumelty(7) —
(Mrs N S Evans) *a bhd: t.o whn p.u bef 12th* **100/1**

0-05 **P** **Sylphide**[16] 567 10-10-1 **91** .... JAJenkins(7) —
(H J Manners) *a bhd: rdn after 8th: t.o whn p.u bef 12th* **25/1**

1/P **U** **Windy Spirit (IRE)**[27] 413 10-11-2 **99** .... ChristianWilliams —
(Evan Williams) *bhd tl hmpd and uns rdr 10th* **20/1**

5P-1 **P** **Team Captain**[35] 276 11-10-8 **98** .... SWalsh(7) —
(C J Down) *prom tl wknd appr 14th: t.o whn p.u bef 2 out* **14/1**

2P-4 **F** **Orswell Crest**[16] 572 11-11-7 **104** .... PJBrennan —
(P J Hobbs) *hld up in tch: rdn after 10th: fell 12th* **16/1**

1-12 **P** **Robber (IRE)**[8] 669 8-10-10 **93** ....(b[1]) RThornton —
(P Bowen) *hld up in mid-div: hdwy 8th: wknd 4 out: bhd whn p.u bef last* **4/1**[1]

P-13 **U** **Presence Of Mind (IRE)**[25] 439 7-11-12 **109** .... BJCrowley —
(Miss E C Lavelle) *hld up in mid-div: mstke 6th: hmpd and uns rdr 13th* **10/1**

1-PP **P** **Ankles Back (IRE)**[21] 489 8-11-10 **107** .... MAFitzgerald —
(H D Daly) *led to 3rd: prom tl wknd after 13th: t.o whn p.u after 13th* **12/1**

6m 22.0s (-12.20) **Going Correction** -0.225s/f (Good) **16** Ran SP% **130.4**
Speed ratings: **109,107,103,98,97 95,94,—,—,— —,—,—,—,— —** CSF £291.06 CT £4795.14 TOTE £18.20: £4.10, £7.80, £3.80, £1.50; EX 830.30.
Owner Thomas D Goodman **Bred** Gainsborough Stud Management Ltd **Trained** Naunton, Gloucs

FOCUS
This did not turn out to be as competitive as the betting suggested but it was a fair time for the grade of contest.

NOTEBOOK
Excellent Vibes(IRE) ◆, who won three staying hurdles in 2003 for his present trainer, was returning after a spell with Peter Pritchard. Making a successful chasing debut on his first outing since last October, he is at the right end of the handicap and could be set for a profitable summer.
Keltic Lord, a dual winner between the flags, gave a good account of himself on this switch from hunter chases. Lightly raced, he may be capable of further improvement now he is being handled by a professional trainer.
Mazileo, 7lb higher than was easily landing this race last year, eventually paid the penalty for doing too much once in the lead. He at least showed he retains ability. *(op 14-1)*
Sylphide *Official explanation: jockey said mare bled from the nose (op 9-2)*
Robber(IRE) did not find the application of blinkers to be a successful experiment. *(op 9-2)*

747 HFT - HEREFORD LOW LOADERS H'CAP HURDLE (8 hdls) 2m 1f
9:15 (9:17) (Class 4) (0-105,105) 4-Y-0+ **£4,153** (£1,278; £639; £319)

Form RPR

10-1 **1** **Kims Pearl (IRE)**[23] 462 7-11-0 **98** .... LStephens(5) 104+
(D Burchell) *a.p: led after 2 out: rdn out* **5/1**[2]

000- **2** *1 ¼* **Titian Flame (IRE)**[83] 4514 5-10-6 **92** .... MrRMcCarthy(7) 94+
(D Burchell) *hld up and bhd: hdwy 3 out: rdn after 2 out: r.o flat: nt rch wnr* **12/1**

2-02 **3** *1 ½* **Imperial Rocket (USA)**[8] 664 8-11-1 **94** ....(t) MAFitzgerald 94
(W K Goldsworthy) *led tl after 1st: led 3rd tl after 2 out: sn rdn: kpt on flat* **4/1**[1]

4-04 **4** *1 ¼* **Celtic Romance**[16] 574 6-10-0 **79** oh1 .... JPByrne 78
(Ms Sue Smith) *hld up and bhd: hdwy on outside 5th: rdn after 2 out: hit last: one pce* **20/1**

-F34 **5** *4* **Skibereen (IRE)**[8] 664 5-10-10 **89** ....(t) DRDennis 85+
(Mrs A M Thorpe) *hld up in tch: rdn and wkng whn mstke last* **9/1**

3F0- **6** *8* **Mr Whizz**[23] 1420 8-11-8 **101** .... JGoldstein 88
(A P Jones) *hld up in tch: rdn and no hdwy fr 3 out* **25/1**

23-1 **7** *10* **Naked Oat**[18] 536 10-11-2 **95** .... LAspell 72
(Mrs L Wadham) *hld up in tch: wknd appr 5th* **7/1**[3]

PP0- **8** *3* **Bearaway (IRE)**[168] 3040 8-11-11 **104** ....(t) JMMaguire 78
(Mrs H Dalton) *mid-div: wknd after 3 out* **20/1**

50-0 **9** *hd* **Viva Forever (FR)**[37] 238 6-10-9 **88** ....(bt) BJCrowley 62
(A M Hales) *hld up towards rr: hdwy after 4th: wknd appr 2 out* **40/1**

04-5 **10** *1 ½* **Maharaat (USA)**[46] 100 4-11-8 **104** ....(b[1]) PJBrennan 73
(P J Hobbs) *hld up in tch: rdn appr 4th: wknd 3 out* **7/1**[3]

3/66 **11** *shd* **Harry B**[10] 630 6-10-6 **85** .... WHutchinson 57
(R J Price) *hld up in mid-div: hdwy appr 5th: rdn and wknd after 3 out* **9/1**

21F/ **12** *7* **Knight's Emperor (IRE)**[1004] 1235 8-11-2 **95** .... CLlewellyn 60
(J L Spearing) *a bhd* **12/1**

3P-5 **13** *dist* **Black Bullet (NZ)**[34] 305 12-11-2 **95** ....(t) AO'Keeffe —
(Jennie Candlish) *prom to 5th: t.o* **12/1**

31/ **14** *15* **Hakim (NZ)**[673] 1105 11-10-9 **88** .... WMarston —
(J L Spearing) *led after 1st to 3rd: wknd 5th: t.o* **20/1**

14-R **F** **Brave Dane (IRE)**[2] 726 7-11-2 **100** .... DLaverty(5) —
(L A Dace) *hld up and bhd: hdwy appr 5th: wknd appr 2 out: fell last* **20/1**

22P- **U** **Heavenly Stride**[57] 4914 9-11-12 **105** .... RThornton —
(P Bowen) *mid-div: rdn appr 5th: sn bhd: hmpd and uns rdr last* **11/1**

3m 55.6s (-7.50) **Going Correction** -0.225s/f (Good)
WFA 4 from 5yo+ 3lb **16** Ran SP% **138.4**
Speed ratings: **108,107,106,106,104 100,95,94,94,93 93,90,—,—,— —** CSF £65.50 CT £282.29 TOTE £6.50: £3.00, £4.30, £1.10, £3.80; EX 120.70 Place 6 £95.34, Place 5 £27.08.
Owner John Richards **Bred** Mrs D McDonogh **Trained** Briery Hill, Blaenau Gwent

FOCUS
A wide-open handicap with Dai Burchell responsible for the first two home.

NOTEBOOK
Kims Pearl(IRE), 11lb higher than when successful over slightly further here last month, showed that she can handle fast ground and does seem to be settling much better. *(op 6-1 tchd 9-2)*
Titian Flame(IRE), another who has previously shown her best form on soft ground, stays further and could not peg back her in-form stable companion. She seems to have come to hand. *(op 10-1 tchd 14-1)*
Imperial Rocket(USA) is knocking on the door and was in no mood to throw in the towel once headed. *(op 9-2 tchd 5-1)*
Celtic Romance gave a good account of herself on this return to handicap company. *(tchd 22-1)*
Skibereen(IRE) had finished a similar distance behind Imperial Rocket on exactly the same terms at Newton Abbot last time. *(op 12-1)*
T/Plt: £81.50 to a £1 stake. Pool: £44,661.95. 399.80 winning tickets. T/Qpdt: £31.20 to a £1 stake. Pool: £3,648.70. 86.30 winning tickets. KH

[664] NEWTON ABBOT (L-H)
Tuesday, June 14
OFFICIAL GOING: Good to firm (good in places)
Wind: Moderate, against

748 LEINSTER MAIDEN HURDLE (10 hdls) 2m 6f
6:30 (6:30) (Class 4) 4-Y-0+ **£3,435** (£1,057; £528; £264)

Form RPR

1 **Lawyer Des Ormeaux (FR)**[638] 6-11-2 .... RJohnson 108+
(P Bowen) *t.k.h early: sn trckd ldr: led sn after 3 out: rdn next: drvn out run-in* **2/1**[2]

2 *1 ½* **Getoutwhenyoucan (IRE)**[24] 5-11-2 .... APMcCoy 107+
(M C Pipe) *trckd ldrs: rdn 3 out: wnt 2nd appr 2 out: no imp under hrd driving after* **11/8**[1]

-256 **3** *6* **Seeador**[19] 519 6-10-13 92 .... RYoung(3) 99
(J W Mullins) *led: nt fluent first 2: rdn and hdd sn after 3 out: one pce after* **9/2**[3]

-244 **4** *1 ¼* **Leopold (SLO)**[6] 691 4-10-5 99 .... CPoste(7) 94
(M F Harris) *hld up in rr: hdwy appr 4 out: no imp appr 2 out* **7/1**

P **Duke's View (IRE)**[264] 4-10-12 .... RGreene —
(D C Turner) *bhd: j. slowly 4th: t.o whn p.u bef 2 out* **50/1**

50- **P** **One For Terry (IRE)**[145] 3445 5-10-9 .... JTizzard —
(Mrs S D Williams) *a bhd: t.o whn p.u bef 2 out* **33/1**

P **Holmwood Jack (IRE)** 4-10-7 ....(p) RStephens(5) —
(Miss C J Williams) *mid-div: lost tch 6th: t.o whn p.u bef 4 out* **50/1**

5m 19.8s (-0.50) **Going Correction** -0.30s/f (Good)
WFA 4 from 5yo+ 4lb **7** Ran SP% **113.0**
Speed ratings: **88,87,85,84,— —,—** CSF £5.20 TOTE £2.70: £2.80, £1.60; EX 6.40.
Owner David M Williams **Bred** Pierre Bourdon **Trained** Little Newcastle, Pembrokes

FOCUS
A modest pace let to a very moderate time for the grade, 9.7 seconds slower than the later handicap. The third and fourth set the standard for the form and the principals could be reasonable types.

NOTEBOOK
Lawyer Des Ormeaux(FR), placed over hurdles in France, was racing for the first time in 21 months over a longer trip on the fastest ground he has encountered. After racing close to the pace, he was always holding the favourite over the final half-mile but the way he was looking sideways between the last two flights suggested he would prefer easier ground. *(op 11-4)*
Getoutwhenyoucan(IRE), a dual winning pointer making his hurdling debut, did his best to get to the winner but lacked the pace to do so. He is nothing special, but would probably prefer a stiffer test or easier ground. *(op 11-10)*
Seeador, well backed, was able to set his own modest pace but was still comfortably picked off. Like many of the others, this ground probably did not suit him. *(op 7-1 tchd 15-2)*
Leopold(SLO) tried to get amongst the front trio on the final circuit, but could never make any real impression. This trip was half a mile further than he has attempted before and it did not have the desired result. *(op 5-1)*

749 KILDARE AMATEUR RIDERS' (S) H'CAP HURDLE (8 hdls 1 omitted) 2m 3f
7:00 (7:00) (Class 5) (0-95,89) 4-Y-0+ **£2,590** (£740; £370)

Form RPR

F0-3 **1** **Lucky Do (IRE)**[35] 284 8-11-5 **89** .... AngharadFrieze(7) 94+
(A E Jones) *hld up: stdy hdwy fr 5th: led appr 2 out: pushed out run-in* **25/1**

344- **2** *1* **Indian Beat**[300] 1206 8-10-7 **75** .... TMessenger(5) 77+
(C L Popham) *hld up: hdwy 5th: pressed ldr and ev ch 2 out: rdn and nt qckn run-in* **20/1**

5-00 **3** *1 ¾* **Nice Baby (FR)**[16] 575 4-10-11 **85** .... MrFelixDeGiles(7) 80
(M C Pipe) *hld up in rr: hdwy fr 6th: ev ch appr 2 out: one pce after* **33/1**

22-1 **4** *8* **Temper Lad (USA)**[19] 519 10-10-10 **76** .... MissSGaisford(3) 67
(J D Frost) *racd wd: hld up towards rr: sme hdwy appr 2 out: nvr on terms* **11/4**[1]

50-4 **5** *½* **Club Royal**[29] 389 8-10-12 **80** .... MrTJO'Brien(5) 71
(N E Berry) *hld up in rr: hdwy appr 6th: rdn and wknd appr 2 out* **11/2**[2]

P-06 **6** *2 ½* **Earn Out**[31] 352 4-10-13 **83** .... MrJMorgan(3) 67
(M C Pipe) *chsd ldrs: tl rdn and wknd appr 2 out* **14/1**

-023 **7** *1 ½* **Spectacular Hope**[23] 458 5-11-0 **84** .... MrMWalford(7) 71
(J W Mullins) *in rr: styd on bef 2 out: nvr nr to chal* **7/1**

P-P4 **8** *hd* **Beyond Borders (USA)**[30] 363 7-10-10 **78** ow1.....(v[1]) MrDEdwards(5) 65
(G F Edwards) *in tch: rdn appr 6th: bef 2 out* **16/1**

-630 **9** *1 ½* **Lord Attica (IRE)**[6] 686 6-9-8 **64** ....(b) MissBPDonnelly(7) 49
(M F Harris) *towards rr: nvr nr to chal* **20/1**

/5-2 **10** *2 ½* **Jack Durrance (IRE)**[6] 681 5-10-2 **72** ow8 .... MrNPearce(7) 58+
(G A Ham) *a in rr* **6/1**[3]

-00P **11** *1 ¾* **Farceur (FR)**[7] 673 6-11-3 **87** ....(v) MrRQuinn(7) 68
(M C Pipe) *in front rnk: led appr 6th: hdd & wknd appr 2 out* **33/1**

065- **12** *13* **The Footballresult**[279] 1393 4-10-0 **74** ....(b) LHeard(7) 38
(Miss G Browne) *hit 1st: a bhd* **16/1**

/0-P **13** *9* **Bosworth Boy**[18] 533 7-10-1 **71** .... MrFBrennan(7) 30
(Mrs H Sweeting) *a wl in rr* **33/1**

06-0 **14** *9* **Impero**[31] 356 7-10-4 **74** ....(b) MrDanielChinn(7) 24
(G F Bridgwater) *a bhd* **33/1**

PP-0 **15** *28* **Grimshaw (USA)**[6] 681 10-11-4 **88** ....(p) MrJoshuaHarris(7) 10
(Mrs D A Hamer) *led: blnd 3rd: rdn and hdd appr 6th: wknd qckly sn after* **20/1**

PP-P **B** **Polka**[19] 519 10-9-8 **64** .... MissRAGreen(7) —
(V G Greenway) *mid-div whn b.d 6th* **20/1**

F0/0 **F** **Rajati (USA)**[19] 519 10-10-10 **78** ....(b) MrsLucyRowsell(5) —
(K R Pearce) *w ldrs and cl 2nd whn fell 6th* **25/1**

0PP/ **P** **Miss Man**[80] 11-9-9 **63** oh9 .... LNewnes(5) —
(N E Berry) *bhd: making sme hdwy whn bdly hmpd 6th: nt rcvr: t.o whn p.u bef 2 out* **33/1**

4m 30.7s (-2.30) **Going Correction** -0.30s/f (Good)
WFA 4 from 5yo+ 3lb **18** Ran SP% **128.7**
Speed ratings: **92,91,90,87,87 86,85,85,84,83 83,77,73,70,58 —,—,—** CSF £433.25 CT £15291.68 TOTE £58.50: £9.70, £4.20, £6.70, £1.10; EX 346.20.There was no bid for the winner.
Owner D A N Ross **Bred** Mrs S Hanly **Trained** Newchapel, Surrey
■ A first winner under Rules for Angharad Frieze.

FOCUS
A big field for this poor seller and a modest pace meant that the bulk of the field were still close together half a mile from home. The runner-up sets the level but the form does not appear that solid.

NOTEBOOK

Lucky Do(IRE), dropped 6lb since finishing a well-beaten third of five here last month, was having only his second start for the yard and won this fairly comfortably under a hands-and-heels ride. This was a poor race though and the moderate pace makes the form a bit suspect. *(op 16-1)*

Indian Beat, dropping back from three miles and returning from a ten-month break, had every chance but lacked a change of gear over this trip in a moderately-run race. He is a reliable sort in this grade, but is still looking for his first win of any description after 37 tries under both codes. *(tchd 25-1)*

Nice Baby(FR), who had never got within 24 lengths of winning in seven previous outings over hurdles and a bumper, did much better this time but the pace of the race meant that she probably did not achieve much and her proximity does nothing for the form. *(op 20-1)*

Temper Lad(USA), who relished the longer trip when winning over a mile further here last month, found this moderately-run race completely against him and he was never nearer than at the line. It also transpired that he had finished lame so deserves another chance under more suitable conditions. *Official explanation: vet said gelding was lame on his right hind leg (op 7-2)*

Club Royal ran a similar race to last time on his second outing for his new yard. *(op 7-1)*

Rajati(USA), dropping in trip, was given a positive ride over possibly an inadequate trip and was still in the firing line when toppling over three from home. *(op 20-1)*

750 MUNSTER NOVICES' CHASE (16 fncs) 2m 5f 110y

7:30 (7:30) (Class 3) 5-Y-0+ **£6,163** (£1,896; £948; £474)

Form / RPR

P0-1 **1** **Chivite (IRE)**[23] [459] 6-11-6 .... RJohnson 106+
(P J Hobbs) *trckd ldr: stmbld on landing 6th: led 5 out: rdn clr appr 2 out: eased run-in* **4/7**[1]

05-2 **2** *7* **Milord Lescribaa (FR)**[23] [465] 5-10-12 .... RGreene 85
(M C Pipe) *hld up in rr: hdwy 9th: wnt 2nd appr 2 out: no ch w wnr* **15/2**[3]

60/0 **3** *16* **Inagh Road (IRE)**[10] [630] 10-10-7 .... JamesWhite(7) 75+
(S C Burrough) *led tl hdd 5 out: rdn and wknd after 3 out* **33/1**

06-3 **4** *20* **Papillon De Iena (FR)**[23] [459] 5-10-12 .... APMcCoy 58+
(M C Pipe) *hld up in rr: hdwy whn hit 10th: sn struggling and lost tch 4 out* **5/2**[2]

60-0 **5** *25* **Jandal**[16] [565] 11-10-7 71 .... TMessenger(7) 26
(C L Popham) *chsd ldng paor tl wknd 8th: t.o* **50/1**

06/6 **P** **Miss Flinders**[8] [667] 8-10-7 .... NFehily —
(D P Keane) *a bhd: lost tch 7th: t.o whn p.u bef 5 out* **33/1**

5m 18.0s (-4.70) **Going Correction** -0.05s/f (Good)
WFA 5 from 6yo+ 2lb **6** Ran SP% **111.8**
Speed ratings: **106,103,97,90,81** — CSF £5.51 TOTE £1.60: £1.20, £2.30; EX 3.80.
Owner I Russell **Bred** B Kennedy **Trained** Withycombe, Somerset

FOCUS

A small field, but thanks to Inagh Road a decent pace and the form looks reliable.

NOTEBOOK

Chivite(IRE), under an 8lb penalty for his Hereford chasing debut success, was always travelling well and once he had finally got the better of the long-time leader rounding the home turn, the race was over. He is a 130-rated hurdler and there seems no reason why he should not be at least as good over fences, especially on a sound surface like this. *(op 8-11)*

Milord Lescribaa(FR) made progress on the final circuit and went in pursuit of the winner starting up the home straight, but it was all to no avail. He appreciated cut over hurdles and will not always run into a decent sort like the winner in races like this. *(op 7-1 tchd 8-1)*

Inagh Road(IRE), a winning pointer making a belated debut over regulation fences, made sure there was no hanging about but had to concede his young rivals had the better of him from the home bend. A shorter trip might help, but he is always going to be vulnerable to a progressive youngster in races like this.

Papillon De Iena(FR), just over seven lengths behind the winner at Hereford, was beaten out of sight this time and cannot blame the ground as he won on it over hurdles. *(op 9-4)*

Miss Flinders *Official explanation: jockey said mare hung badly left*

751 GUINNESS H'CAP HURDLE (10 hdls) 2m 6f

8:00 (8:00) (Class 3) (0-120,125) 4-Y-0+ **£5,408** (£1,664; £832; £416)

Form / RPR

1UP- **1** **Mr Fluffy**[61] [4835] 8-11-5 **116** .... RStephens(5) 121+
(P J Hobbs) *hld up in rr: hdwy 4 out: led appr 2 out: in command after* **6/1**

5-01 **2** *4* **Whispered Secret (GER)**[7] [675] 6-12-5 **125** 7ex .... APMcCoy 124
(M C Pipe) *hld up in tch: hdwy to ld sn after 3 out: rdn and hdd appr next: no imp after* **2/1**[1]

-416 **3** *4* **Alva Glen (USA)**[23] [460] 8-10-12 **104** .... OMcPhail 101+
(B J Llewellyn) *t.k.h: hld up in rr: keeping on past btn horses whn wnt 3rd and blnd last: one pce* **8/1**

265- **4** *3/4* **Baloo**[187] [2734] 9-11-0 **106** .... RJohnson 100
(J D Frost) *disp 2nd for most of way tl rdn appr 4 out: wknd appr 2 out* **11/2**[3]

21-3 **5** *27* **Kadam (IRE)**[35] [275] 5-10-13 **105** ....(b) JTizzard 72
(P F Nicholls) *disp 2nd tl mstke 4 out: wknd bef next* **9/4**[2]

6-21 **P** **Middleham Park (IRE)**[18] [533] 5-11-1 **110** .... RYoung(3) —
(J W Mullins) *hld up in tch: lost pl 6th: t.o whn p.u bef 2 out: lame* **12/1**

30-P **P** **Fireball Macnamara (IRE)**[29] [387] 9-11-4 **110** ....(v[1]) NFehily —
(M Pitman) *led: hit 3rd: hdd sn after 3 out: wknd rapidly and t.o whn p.u bef next* **20/1**

5m 10.1s (-10.20) **Going Correction** -0.30s/f (Good) **7** Ran SP% **117.3**
Speed ratings: **106,104,103,102,93** —,— CSF £19.78 TOTE £7.10: £3.30, £2.30; EX 64.80.
Owner The Cockpit Crew **Bred** Miss S Bannatyne **Trained** Withycombe, Somerset

FOCUS

A fair little handicap and a true pace which resulted in a time 9.7 seconds quicker than the opener. The form looks reasonable with the winner well treated on his old form.

NOTEBOOK

Mr Fluffy ◆ has not enjoyed much luck since returning to hurdles, but was taking on much less-taxing opposition this time and had little difficulty in forging away from his rivals down the home straight. These conditions are ideal and there should be more opportunities for him this summer. *(op 7-1)*

Whispered Secret(GER), under his ideal conditions and carrying a 7lb penalty for his Huntingdon victory, went to the front exiting the back straight but was firmly put in his place by the winner afterwards. It would be harsh to say the penalty beat him as the winner was taking a big drop in class and he will not always come across a rival like him. *(tchd 9-4)*

Alva Glen(USA), trying his longest trip to date, did not appear to be beaten through lack of stamina and a monumental blunder at the last made no difference to his final placing. *(op 6-1)*

Baloo probably needs at least three miles these days and was entitled to need this first run in six months. *(op 8-1 tchd 5-1)*

Kadam(IRE) should have had no problem with the trip or the ground so this was just plain disappointing. *(op 5-2 tchd 2-1)*

Fireball Macnamara(IRE) *Official explanation: jockey said gelding pulled up lame (op 14-1)*

Middleham Park(IRE) *Official explanation: trainer said gelding spread a plate (op 14-1)*

752 LIMERICK H'CAP CHASE (13 fncs) 2m 110y

8:30 (8:31) (Class 4) (0-110,109) 5-Y-0+ **£4,737** (£1,457; £728; £364)

Form / RPR

4-4U **1** **James Victor (IRE)**[8] [666] 7-11-0 **93** .... RYoung(3) 104+
(N R Mitchell) *j.w: mde all: in command fr 2 out* **13/2**

6-P1 **2** *1 1/2* **Take The Oath (IRE)**[7] [674] 8-10-0 **76** 7ex .... TDoyle 83
(D R Gandolfo) *hld up in rr: hdwy to go 2nd 3 out: sn rdn and no imp fr next* **9/4**[1]

25-2 **3** *12* **Wild Power (GER)**[20] [505] 7-11-9 **102** .... ONelmes(3) 100+
(Mrs H R J Nelmes) *hld up: hdwy 7th: wknd 3 out* **9/2**[3]

60-6 **4** *1/2* **Saby (FR)**[37] [246] 7-11-12 **102** .... RJohnson 98+
(P J Hobbs) *trckd wnr tl sn after 4 out: wknd next* **11/2**

-211 **5** *1/2* **Honan (IRE)**[8] [666] 6-12-5 **109** 7ex ....(v) APMcCoy 103
(M C Pipe) *hld up in tch: chsd wnr sn after 4 out tl next: wknd bef 2 out* **5/2**[2]

4-F0 **6** *13* **Riccarton**[8] [664] 12-10-0 **76** oh4 .... RGreene 59+
(D C Turner) *hld up in tch: rdn 7th: wknd 4 out* **33/1**

4220 **P** **Tosawi (IRE)**[8] [666] 9-11-9 **99** ....(p) JTizzard —
(R J Hodges) *in rr: hit 4th: losing tch whn p.u bef 6 out* **16/1**

4m 6.90s (1.40) **Going Correction** -0.05s/f (Good) **7** Ran SP% **115.1**
Speed ratings: **94,93,87,87,87 81**,— CSF £22.66 TOTE £9.00: £3.10, £1.50; EX 30.10.
Owner Barry R Burke **Bred** Antakiya Partnership **Trained** Piddletrenthide, Dorset

FOCUS

With the winner able to set his own pace the winning time was moderate for the grade and the form does not appear strong.

NOTEBOOK

James Victor(IRE), proven on this sort of ground, was able to establish an uncontested lead and crucially jumped really well, which played a big part in him being able to keep his rivals at bay. He will not always enjoy that luxury and this form probably amounts to little. *(op 6-1)*

Take The Oath(IRE), carrying a 7lb penalty for his win at Huntingdon the previous week, was the only one to get anywhere near the winner in the latter stages, but could never quite get on top of him and a stronger pace would almost certainly have suited him better. *(op 11-4 tchd 2-1)*

Wild Power(GER) only barely gets the trip, even on a sharp track, but despite this race not being at all strongly run he finished rather weakly after looking likely to get involved at one point. *Official explanation: jockey said gelding lost a shoe (op 5-1)*

Saby(FR), in such great heart last year especially at this track, has been in nothing like the same form this year and this was another mediocre performance. *(op 5-1 tchd 9-2)*

Honan(IRE), unbeaten in two previous outings over fences, probably found this faster ground as big a handicap as his welter burden under a penalty. *(op 3-1 tchd 7-2)*

753 DUBLIN CITY NOVICES' H'CAP HURDLE (8 hdls) 2m 1f

9:00 (9:01) (Class 4) (0-105,105) 4-Y-0+ **£3,435** (£1,057; £528; £264)

Form / RPR

4-04 **1** **Gemini Dancer**[19] [517] 6-11-4 **97** .... JTizzard 104+
(C L Tizzard) *wl bhd and nt a fluent: hdwy on ins to go 2nd appr 2 out: led bef last: drvn clr run-in* **33/1**

03-1 **2** *4* **Wardash (GER)**[7] [670] 5-9-11 **79** oh15 ....(vt) TJMalone(3) 85+
(M C Pipe) *a in tch: wnt 2nd after 3 out: led bef hit 2 out: sn hdd and wandered: no imp run-in* **10/11**[1]

00-6 **3** *1/2* **Thai Town**[29] [389] 6-9-7 **79** oh2 .... MrTJO'Brien(7) 81
(A E Jones) *wl in rr tl styd on appr 2 out: styd on strly u.p run-in: nvr nrr* **10/1**

5-03 **4** *nk* **Compton Star**[24] [456] 5-9-7 **79** .... JamesWhite(7) 81
(R J Hodges) *a.p: rdn after 3 out: fdd after next* **20/1**

00-1 **5** *shd* **Space Cowboy (IRE)**[16] [568] 5-11-2 **95** ....(b) JEMoore 97
(G L Moore) *mid-div: hdwy to chse ldrs 3 out: one pce form 2 out* **7/1**[3]

6-10 **6** *17* **Beechwood**[23] [460] 7-11-2 **105** .... KBurke(10) 90
(P R Rodford) *trckd ldrs mstke 3 out: sn rdn and wknd* **25/1**

2-46 **7** *shd* **Separated (USA)**[21] [487] 4-11-1 **97** .... RJohnson 79
(P J Hobbs) *mstke 5th: a towards rr* **11/1**

6-00 **8** *1 1/2* **Twentytwosilver (IRE)**[23] [460] 5-10-8 **90** .... ONelmes(3) 73
(N J Hawke) *led after 2nd: hdd after 3 out: wknd rapidly* **20/1**

4-11 **9** *3 1/2* **Miss Lehman**[19] [517] 7-10-9 **95** .... MissSGaisford(7) 75
(J D Frost) *in tch on outside tl wknd 4 out* **4/1**[2]

0-5F **10** *1 1/2* **Bottom Drawer**[24] [456] 5-10-5 **89** .... RStephens(5) 67
(Mrs D A Hamer) *hld up: effrt 4 out: sn wknd* **25/1**

0-1P **11** *1* **Fallout (IRE)**[23] [462] 4-10-10 **95** .... RYoung(3) 69
(J W Mullins) *t.k.h: mid-div tl wknd appr 3 out* **33/1**

U-P3 **12** *20* **Lescer's Lad**[18] [533] 8-10-0 **79** oh3 .... RWalford 36
(C L Popham) *led tl after 2nd: prom tl wknd qckly 5th* **50/1**

0-00 **F** **Avesomeofthat (IRE)**[16] [571] 4-11-0 **96** ....(t) PHolley 89
(Mrs P N Dutfield) *hld up: hdwy 4 out: rdn and hel in 5th whn fell last* **16/1**

4m 2.60s (-2.50) **Going Correction** -0.30s/f (Good)
WFA 4 from 5yo+ 3lb **13** Ran SP% **133.2**
Speed ratings: **93,91,90,90,90 82,82,81,80,79 79,69**,— CSF £69.14 CT £407.77 TOTE £26.90: £6.40, £1.30, £3.80; EX 174.10 Place 6 £21.60, Place 5 £17.15.
Owner R G Tizzard **Bred** Mrs Georgette Baroudji **Trained** Milborne Port, Dorset

FOCUS

A modest contest in which an ordinary pace resulted in a moderate winning time for the class. The form could be rated higher but confidence is limited.

NOTEBOOK

Gemini Dancer, who did hint at a little ability in his most recent outing here, came from well off the pace to collar the favourite between the last two flights and found plenty, despite paddling through the final obstacle. The winning time puts a doubt over the value of the form, but he is still relatively lightly raced and has room for improvement in the jumping department. *Official explanation: trainer had no explanation for the improved form shown (tchd 40-1)*

Wardash(GER), easy winner of a Huntingdon seller the previous week, was nonetheless 15lb out of the handicap yet started an odds-on favourite. He looked likely to succeed in getting to the front at the second last, but did not jump it very well and then started to hang which handed the advantage to the eventual winner. He is due to go up to a mark of 87 from Saturday which demonstrates just how hard life is going to get for him. *(op 13-8 tchd 7-4)*

Thai Town is progressing slowly over hurdles and the way he was staying on suggests a longer trip will suit him. *(op 12-1 tchd 14-1)*

Compton Star ran his race, but always finds one or two to beat him and is still looking for his first win of any sort after 19 attempts under both codes.

Space Cowboy(IRE), raised 5lb for his Fontwell victory, did not build on that success under conditions that should have suited. *(op 8-1)*

Avesomeofthat(IRE) was held when coming down at the last.

T/Plt: £26.90 to a £1 stake. Pool: £38,425.30. 1,042.00 winning tickets. T/Qpdt: £11.10 to a £1 stake. Pool: £2,698.80. 179.70 winning tickets. JS

754 - 757a (Foreign Racing) - See Raceform Interactive

629 WORCESTER (L-H)

Wednesday, June 15

OFFICIAL GOING: Good

The ground had eased after 5mm of rain during the morning.

Wind: Moderate across Weather: Fine

758 PUNTERSLOUNGE.COM BETTING FORUM NOVICES' CLAIMING HURDLE (8 hdls) 2m

2:20 (2:22) (Class 4) 4-Y-0+ **£3,080** (£880; £440)

Form				RPR
2-33	1		**Percipient**[17] [565] 7-10-12 82 (v) TDoyle	84+
			(D R Gandolfo) *a.p: rdn to ld flat: drvn out* 13/2[3]	
0-04	2	3	**Princess Pea**[10] [651] 5-10-3 LAspell	71+
			(Mrs L Wadham) *j.rt: hld up in mid-div: mstke 3rd: hdwy 5th: rdn to ld appr last: hdd flat: one pce* 5/1[2]	
F	3	1	**Berry Racer (IRE)**[20] [515] 4-10-0 WHutchinson	66
			(Mrs S D Williams) *t.k.h in rr: hdwy after 5th: nt fluent last: one pce* 66/1	
35	4	¾	**Sound Skin (IRE)**[21] [504] 7-11-4 94 MAFitzgerald	83
			(A Ennis) *hld up in tch: rdn and ev ch appr last: no ex flat* 7/1	
50-0	5	7	**Replacement Pet (IRE)**[9] [668] 8-10-3 62 (bt) RGreene	62+
			(Mrs S D Williams) *a.p: rdn after 5th: led 3 out to 2 out: wknd flat* 40/1	
P5	6	5	**Felix The Fox (NZ)**[6] [696] 5-11-8 CLlewellyn	76+
			(N A Twiston-Davies) *led to 3 out: led 2 out: sn hdd: wknd last* 13/2[3]	
	7	5	**Magic Warrior**[11] 5-11-0 SFox	62
			(J C Fox) *plld hrd in rr: hdwy appr 3 out: wknd appr last* 40/1	
6P	8	12	**Sooty From Mitcham**[20] [514] 5-10-10 AThornton	46
			(R H Alner) *prom: racd wd bk st: rdn and wknd appr 3 out* 50/1	
3-00	9	20	**Meadow Hawk (USA)**[17] [571] 5-11-6 95 (b) DRDennis	36
			(Ian Williams) *mid-div: rdn after 5th: no ch whn hmpd 2 out* 2/1[1]	
0-P0	10	3½	**Pridewood Dove**[10] [651] 6-10-5 AO'Keeffe	18
			(R J Price) *a bhd: mstke last* 40/1	
	11	9	**Buchanan Street (IRE)**[58] 4-10-9 (tp) JMMaguire	13
			(R Ford) *bhd fr 4th* 40/1	
0-0	12	dist	**Tiasfourth**[10] [655] 4-10-5 ow1 MBradburne	—
			(A M Hales) *nt jump wl in rr: t.o fr 5th* 66/1	
43-5	F		**Hunter Pudding**[30] [384] 5-10-0 TMessenger(7)	—
			(C L Popham) *t.k.h in tch: wkng whn fell 2 out* 16/1	
P	P		**Hermano (IRE)**[10] [654] 8-11-0 BJCrowley	—
			(A M Hales) *t.k.h towards rr: mid-div whn p.u bef 3rd* 33/1	

3m 53.1s (4.70) **Going Correction** +0.175s/f (Yiel)

WFA 4 from 5yo+ 3lb **14** Ran SP% **112.7**

Speed ratings: **95,93,93,92,89 86,84,78,68,66 61,—,—,—** CSF £34.89 TOTE £6.30: £1.70, £2.00, £59.70; EX 29.50.Princess Pea was claimed by Martin Pipe for £5,000

Owner Nigel Stafford **Bred** Aston House Stud **Trained** Wantage, Oxon

FOCUS

A modest winning time for the class, almost two seconds slower than the seller.

NOTEBOOK

Percipient, returning to hurdles after a spell over fences, travelled nicely for most of the race, and was produced with a perfectly timed challenge after the last. He is clearly very moderate and possibly quirky, as the jockey was keen to keep him away from the other runners during the race. *(op 5-1 tchd 7-1)*

Princess Pea, a half-sister to Spunkie and Three Lions, was beaten in a mares-only seller last time, but held every chance jumping the last. She is not very big and probably lacks scope, but was claimed by Martin Pipe after the race.

Berry Racer(IRE), only banded class on the Flat, ran well enough to suggest she can win an ordinary race at some stage.

Sound Skin(IRE) ran much better than she had done last time - the trainer suggested the race had come too quickly - and kept on through beaten horses. A stiffer course might be more of an advantage. *(op 13-2 tchd 6-1)*

Replacement Pet(IRE) led briefly at the top of the straight after being under pressure a long way from home, and did well to finish as close as she did.

Felix The Fox(NZ), who was pulled up in a bumper first time out, led the field for most of the race until weakening after jumping the second-last. He does have more scope for improvement than others, but is clearly not very good at this stage. *(op 11-2)*

Magic Warrior did not shape too badly on his hurdling debut, creeping into contention before stamina gave way. A less-demanding track will help in the future.

Meadow Hawk(USA), well supported before the race, showed nothing and is disappointing. *(op 3-1)*

Buchanan Street(IRE) *Official explanation: jockey said gelding had a breathing problem (op 33-1)*

Hermano(IRE) *Official explanation: jockey said saddle slipped (op 28-1)*

759 PUNTERSLOUNGE.COM BETTING FORUM BEGINNERS' CHASE (18 fncs) 2m 7f 110y

2:55 (2:55) (Class 4) 5-Y-0+ **£4,173** (£1,284; £642; £321)

Form				RPR
60-0	1		**After Me Boys**[20] [525] 11-11-0 DElsworth	112+
			(Mrs S J Smith) *a.p: wnt 2nd 7th: led appr 4 out: rdn after 3 out: idled appr last: r.o* 11/2[3]	
P-3P	2	8	**Inland Run (IRE)**[8] [673] 9-11-0 89 RJohnson	97+
			(R T Phillips) *led: rdn and hdd appr 4 out: one pce fr 3 out* 14/1	
-3PP	3	11	**Hardy Russian (IRE)**[11] [631] 8-10-4 70 (p) KBurke(10)	82
			(P R Rodford) *wl bhd 6th: lft 3rd last: nvr nrr* 80/1	
-P33	4	dist	**High Peak**[11] [631] 8-10-11 71 RYoung(3)	76
			(J W Mullins) *mstkes: hld up and bhd: hdwy 14th: wkng whn lft 3rd and sltly hmpd 4 out: no ch whn mstke and uns rdr last: re* 20/1	
53U-	F		**Jacks Jewel (IRE)**[61] [4853] 8-11-0 80 JTizzard	—
			(C J Down) *hld up and bhd: sme hdwy whn fell 10th* 25/1	
0P-2	P		**Lady Lambrini**[16] [594] 5-9-8 TMessenger(7)	—
			(Mrs L Williamson) *hld up in tch: hit 10th: mstke 11th: sn wknd: 5th whn p.u bef 14th* 9/1	
P-	P		**St Helier**[11] 10-10-2 RStephens(5)	—
			(D O Stephens) *hld up in tch: reminder after 6th: wkng whn mstke 9th: t.o whn p.u bef 11th* 33/1	
04-0	P		**Quick**[20] [207] 5-10-8 (v) APMcCoy	—
			(M C Pipe) *w ldr to 7th: reminders and swtchd rt appr 8th: wknd after 9th: hmpd 10th: p.u bef 11th* 1/1[1]	
32-3	U		**Good Man Again (IRE)**[35] [298] 7-11-0 ChristianWilliams	—
			(Evan Williams) *hld up and bhd: hdwy 9th: hit 10th: mstke 14th: 4 l 3rd and hld whn blnd and uns rdr 4 out* 4/1[2]	

6m 5.70s (10.80) **Going Correction** +0.175s/f (Yiel)

WFA 5 from 7yo+ 2lb **9** Ran SP% **114.8**

Speed ratings: **89,86,82,—,— —,—,—,—** CSF £65.12 TOTE £6.10: £1.90, £4.40, £20.70; EX 59.50.

Owner Keith Nicholson **Bred** R F And Mrs Knipe **Trained** High Eldwick, W Yorks

FOCUS

A moderate time for the grade.

NOTEBOOK

After Me Boys, making his chasing debut as an 11-year-old, idled when getting to the front and made harder work of winning than looked likely. Relatively lightly raced for his age, he should win more races over fences if getting to the track a bit more often. *(op 5-1 tchd 6-1)*

Inland Run(IRE) made a lot of the running until passed by the eventual winner exiting the back straight. He can win a race over fences, especially if dropped in distance.

Hardy Russian(IRE) was being pushed along after jumping one fence and never figured. *(op 66-1)*

High Peak was well beaten when unseating the rider at the last. The jockey remounted to claim the place money. *(tchd 22-1)*

Good Man Again(IRE) still had a chance when coming down three out, and it remains to be seen whether his confidence has taken a knock after this. *(op 9-2 tchd 7-2)*

Quick does not looked a natural over fences, but was reported to have finished distressed after the race. *Official explanation: trainer said gelding was distressed (op 9-2 tchd 7-2)*

760 FREEBETSGALORE.COM (S) H'CAP HURDLE (8 hdls) 2m

3:30 (3:30) (Class 5) (0-85,90) 4-Y-0+ **£3,122** (£892; £446)

Form				RPR
6-41	1		**Desert Spa (USA)**[7] [681] 10-11-12 90 7ex MrTJO'Brien(7)	99+
			(G E Jones) *hld up in mid-div: hdwy 3rd: led appr 2 out: rdn and hung lft flat: r.o* 9/2[2]	
00-3	2	1¾	**Not Amused (UAE)**[28] [412] 5-11-8 79 (v) DRDennis	86+
			(Ian Williams) *hld up in tch: rdn and ev ch 2 out: swtchd rt flat: nt qckn* 7/2[1]	
0U05	3	8	**Seemore Sunshine**[7] [686] 8-11-0 78 PCStringer(7)	77
			(M J Gingell) *hld up in mid-div: hdwy 3 out: nt clr run after 2 out: mstke last: r.o flat* 25/1	
-024	4	3½	**Dunkerron**[24] [469] 8-11-2 80 SWalsh(7)	76
			(J Joseph) *led tl after 2nd: prom: rdn after 5th: wknd appr 2 out: hung lft flat* 14/1	
60/1	5	shd	**Reverse Swing**[46] [134] 8-11-7 78 APMcCoy	73
			(Mrs H Dalton) *racd wd: prom tl wknd 3 out* 5/1[3]	
P-P0	6	2½	**Gipsy Cricketer**[7] [681] 9-10-5 72 (t) JKington(10)	65
			(M Scudamore) *prom: led appr 5th tl appr 2 out: wknd appr last* 33/1	
P552	7	5	**Three Times A Lady**[8] [670] 5-10-12 72 ONelmes(3)	60
			(D W Thompson) *prom tl rdn and wknd 3 out* 9/1	
-04P	8	hd	**Kingcombe Lane**[13] [611] 5-11-4 75 JPMcNamara	63
			(P W Hiatt) *mid-div: bhd fr 4th* 33/1	
-P00	9	1	**My Retreat (USA)**[7] [681] 8-11-2 80 MrPYork(7)	67
			(R Fielder) *nvr nr ldrs* 33/1	
2/0-	10	9	**Sofisio**[19] [1623] 8-11-6 77 (tp) NFehily	55
			(Miss S J Wilton) *hld up in tch: wknd 3 out* 20/1	
0-00	11	shd	**Damien's Choice (IRE)**[17] [565] 13-11-0 71 JMogford	49
			(Dr P Pritchard) *a bhd* 66/1	
-564	12	6	**Outside Investor (IRE)**[9] [668] 5-11-1 82 (b) KBurke(10)	54
			(P R Rodford) *mid-div: bhd fr 4th* 12/1	
0360	13	8	**Luristan (IRE)**[1] [743] 5-10-13 73 (p) DCrosse(3)	37
			(S T Lewis) *prom: led after 2nd tl appr 5th: sn wknd* 33/1	
641-	14	17	**Donatus (IRE)**[336] [949] 9-11-3 74 (p) AThornton	21
			(Miss K M George) *pckd 1st: a bhd* 25/1	
4500	15	10	**Dan De Lion**[4] [716] 6-11-5 79 LMcGrath(3)	16
			(R C Guest) *a bhd* 25/1	
06-P	16	½	**Waterline Blue (IRE)**[38] [237] 4-11-2 76 RJohnson	9
			(P Bowen) *a bhd* 8/1	
/5-5	P		**Vrubel (IRE)**[43] [173] 6-10-8 72 (bt) APogson(7)	—
			(J R Holt) *dropped rr 3rd: t.o whn p.u bef 5th* 100/1	
-P05	P		**La Gitana**[11] [635] 5-11-0 71 JMMaguire	—
			(A Sadik) *hld up in tch: wknd 4th: t.o whn p.u bef 3 out* 25/1	

3m 51.2s (2.80) **Going Correction** +0.175s/f (Yiel)

WFA 4 from 5yo+ 3lb **18** Ran SP% **126.9**

Speed ratings: **100,99,95,93,93 92,89,89,88,84 84,81,77,68,63 63,—,—** CSF £18.80 CT £375.25 TOTE £2.70: £1.20, £1.90, £6.70, £2.70; EX 27.50.There was no bid for the winner.

Owner G Elwyn Jones **Bred** Robert White & Virginia White **Trained** Bettws Bledrws, Ceredigion

■ Stewards' Enquiry : Mr T J O'Brien caution: careless riding

FOCUS

A big field of disappointing sorts for this moderate seller.

NOTEBOOK

Desert Spa(USA) moved easily throughout the race and looked like winning easily approaching the last hurdle. However, he did not find a great deal off the bridle and drifted across the course under pressure. After this win, he may not be easy to place.

Not Amused(UAE), who was supported in the market before the race, had every chance but did not get home as well as the winner. This was a sound effort in the grade and he can go close in similar races in the summer. *(op 7-1)*

Seemore Sunshine got slightly squeezed up before jumping the last, causing him to make a mistake. He was staying on slowly and will appreciate being stepped up in trip. *(tchd 33-1)*

Dunkerron, dropping back in trip, stayed on in the latter stages after being outpaced. He is not particularly well handicapped over hurdles and is probably best in this type of race at the moment.

Reverse Swing never picked up when the jockey asked her to quicken. She has not progressed from her last race despite being given time to get over it following a long layoff. *(op 4-1 tchd 6-1 in places)*

Gipsy Cricketer ran well for most of the race until weakening badly after jumping the last.

Damien's Choice(IRE) *Official explanation: jockey said gelding finished lame*

Waterline Blue(IRE), who ran in the 2003 Coventry Stakes at Royal Ascot, is an unlikely type to win a race over hurdles given the fact that he was a sprinter on the Flat. His starting price reflected the weakness of the race. *Official explanation: jockey said gelding had a breathing problem*

761 PUNTERSLOUNGE.COM BETTING FORUM H'CAP CHASE (15 fncs) 2m 4f 110y

4:05 (4:05) (Class 3) (0-120,120) 5-Y-0+ **£5,499** (£1,692; £846; £423)

Form				RPR
P-41	1		**Bronzesmith**[11] [634] 9-11-12 120 JTizzard	136+
			(B J M Ryall) *hld up and bhd: hdwy 9th: led 2 out: drvn clr flat* 7/1[3]	
3-33	2	7	**Deep King (IRE)**[11] [634] 10-10-10 107 RYoung(3)	115
			(J W Mullins) *w ldr: led 9th: rdn and hdd 2 out: wknd flat* 10/1	
40-0	3	1	**Rheindross (IRE)**[30] [390] 10-11-9 117 NFehily	124
			(C J Mann) *prom: j. slowly 7th: outpcd 11th: styd on flat* 10/1	
4-22	4	1¼	**Xaipete (IRE)**[32] [346] 13-10-4 101 LMcGrath(3)	109+
			(R C Guest) *hld up: hdwy on ins appr 7th: lft 3rd and bdly hmpd 3 out: no ex flat* 14/1	
3-11	5	10	**Silence Reigns**[26] [437] 11-11-7 115 (bt) RWalsh	111
			(P F Nicholls) *hld up in tch: lost pl after 6th: n.d after* 2/1[1]	
P0-0	6	dist	**Heart Midoltian (FR)**[34] [311] 8-11-3 111 (vt) JEMoore	—
			(M C Pipe) *a bhd: t.o* 33/1	
-223	7	¾	**Galway Breeze (IRE)**[21] [497] 10-11-0 108 RMcGrath	—
			(Mrs K Walton) *a bhd: t.o* 18/1	

-014 **8** *2* **Idealko (FR)**[20] [518] 9-10-8 **102** .... DRDennis —
(Dr P Pritchard) *prom: lost pl appr 6th: t.o* **33/1**

0-23 **9** *8* **Penthouse Minstrel**[6] [694] 11-10-6 **107** .... TJDreaper(7) —
(R J Hodges) *a bhd: rdn 5th: t.o fr 9th* **18/1**

00/0 **P** **Wave Rock**[52] [4] 10-10-7 **101** .... (b) JCulloty —
(A W Carroll) *j.rt: mde most to 9th: wknd after 11th: p.u bef 4 out* **14/1**

P1-2 **P** **Croix De Guerre (IRE)**[32] [344] 5-11-10 **120** .... (b) RJohnson —
(P J Hobbs) *prom tl wknd 11th: blnd 3 out: j. bdly rt 2 out: t.o whn p.u bef last* **6/1**[2]

-123 **U** **Saafend Rocket (IRE)**[20] [510] 7-11-9 **117** .... MBradburne 124
(H D Daly) *hld up in mid-div: hdwy 11th: 2 l 3rd and rdn whn blnd and uns rdr 3 out* **14/1**

P/P- **P** **Colonel Bradley (IRE)**[360] [789] 11-11-6 **114** .... APMcCoy —
(Jonjo O'Neill) *hld up in tch: nt fluent 8th: sn struggling: mstke 10th: t.o whn p.u bef 4 out* **25/1**

5m 7.00s (-0.50) **Going Correction** +0.175s/f (Yiel)
WFA 5 from 7yo+ 2lb **13** Ran SP% **118.6**
Speed ratings: **107,104,103,103,99** —,—,—,—, —,—,— CSF £73.12 CT £700.03 TOTE £8.20: £2.70, £3.40, £4.10; EX 77.10.
Owner Mrs M E Ash **Bred** J R Ash **Trained** Rimpton, Somerset

FOCUS
A fairly decent, competitive race over jumps for the middle of June. The winner was value for much more than the winning distance.

NOTEBOOK
Bronzesmith was always travelling really well during the race and won easily. He can expect another hefty rise in the weights after this, but is clearly progressing the right way. *(op 13-2 tchd 6-1)*
Deep King(IRE) is a model of consistency and ran another solid race in defeat. He was legless after the last but had enough in hand to secure another placing. He remains in good form. *(op 12-1)*
Rheindross(IRE), having his first run for the stable, really found his stride after the last, and was closing on the second really quickly as the line approached. He should be capable of winning a race soon but his overall profile is not that of a horse who wins that often. *(op 14-1)*
Xaipete(IRE) still shows plenty of enthusiasm for his age and clearly still loves his racing. However, he is without a win for a long time and will need a much weaker race to get his head in front again before retiring. *(op 12-1)*
Silence Reigns, who was nicely handicapped on his old form, should have been a lot more competitive than he was, and is clearly not as good as he once was in this grade. *(tchd 9-4)*
Saafend Rocket(IRE) was in the process of running well until crashing out of the race three from home. A Ludlow specialist, he does not look particularly well handicapped at present. *(op 12-1)*
Croix De Guerre(IRE) is not particularly well handicapped on his hurdling form, and was pulled up after making a couple of costly jumping errors. *(op 12-1)*

762 JANET LODGE BIRTHDAY H'CAP HURDLE (10 hdls) 2m 4f
4:40 (4:41) (Class 4) (0-110,110) 4-Y-O+ **£3,516** (£1,082; £541; £270)

Form RPR

00-4 **1** **Blue Hawk (IRE)**[39] [220] 8-10-3 **94** .... JPritchard(7) 102
(R Dickin) *a.p: led 7th: clr appr 3 out: hrd rdn flat: r.o* **25/1**

4/F- **2** *1 ¼* **Stocks 'n Shares**[410] [126] 9-10-4 **88** .... (t) MFoley 95
(Miss E C Lavelle) *hld up in tch: hdwy after 7th: chsd wnr fr 3 out: sn rdn: r.o flat* **15/2**

23-6 **3** *5* **Red Canyon (IRE)**[9] [665] 8-10-6 **90** .... (b) JTizzard 92
(C L Tizzard) *led tl after 4th: rdn appr 5th: mstke 3 out: styd on same pce fr 2 out* **16/1**

-11U **4** *¾* **Tinstre (IRE)**[17] [568] 7-10-9 **93** .... SCurran 94
(P W Hiatt) *hld up: hdwy 6th: rdn appr 2 out: one pce* **9/1**

040- **5** *3* **Touch Of Ebony (IRE)**[133] [3645] 6-10-13 **102** .... LStephens(5) 100
(C Roberts) *hld up and bhd: stdy hdwy appr 3 out: nvr nr to chal* **40/1**

3P2- **6** *13* **Like A Lord (IRE)**[190] [2691] 7-11-6 **104** .... DElsworth 89
(Mrs S J Smith) *hld up in mid-div: hdwy appr 6th: wknd appr 3 out* **7/1**[3]

0-54 **7** *3 ½* **Burundi (IRE)**[34] [315] 11-11-6 **104** .... JCulloty 86
(A W Carroll) *hld up and bhd: hdwy after 7th: wknd appr 2 out* **14/1**

00-1 **8** *1 ¼* **Bob's Gone (IRE)**[28] [410] 7-10-13 **104** .... TMessenger(7) 84
(B P J Baugh) *prom: led 2nd tl after 4th: rdn 7th: wknd 3 out* **11/2**[2]

-0P2 **9** *hd* **Shamsan (IRE)**[20] [508] 8-10-4 **95** .... (tp) SWalsh(7) 75
(J Joseph) *hld up: short-lived effrt after 7th* **33/1**

6P-4 **10** *27* **Manolo (FR)**[20] [513] 5-10-11 **95** .... RThornton 48
(Ian Williams) *hld up: hdwy after 7th: wknd after 3 out* **9/1**

300- **11** *6* **Irishkawa Bellevue (FR)**[221] [2038] 7-11-0 **101** .... (b) DCrosse(3) 48
(Jean-Rene Auvray) *bhd: reminders after 4th: t.o fr 6th* **40/1**

P-62 **12** *nk* **Phildari (IRE)**[20] [512] 9-10-3 **94** .... MrDEngland(7) 41
(N A Twiston-Davies) *prom tl j. slowly 5th: t.o* **14/1**

3 **13** *3 ½* **Mantras (FR)**[25] [451] 6-11-12 **110** .... APMcCoy 53
(M C Pipe) *prom: rdn after 4th: sn struggling: t.o* **3/1**[1]

14 *dist* **Brendar (IRE)**[248] [1671] 8-11-1 **99** .... (b1) JEMoore —
(J J Best) *rdn appr 6th: a bhd: t.o* **33/1**

0-40 **P** **Antigiotto (IRE)**[25] [451] 4-10-12 **100** .... (b) RJohnson —
(P Bowen) *hld up in tch: led after 4th to 7th: sn wknd: bhd whn plld bef 2 out* **11/1**

4m 47.6s (-0.40) **Going Correction** +0.175s/f (Yiel)
WFA 4 from 5yo+ 4lb **15** Ran SP% **126.8**
Speed ratings: **107,106,104,104,103 97,96,95,95,85 82,82,81**,—,— CSF £206.12 CT £3132.50 TOTE £43.50: £9.60, £2.70, £5.30; EX 325.00.
Owner Miss Michelle Thomas **Bred** Pat Dowling **Trained** Atherstone on Stour, Warwicks

FOCUS
A competitive race for the grade, stolen by the winner, who sped clear off the far turn.

NOTEBOOK
Blue Hawk(IRE) was given a well-judged ride from the front, stealing an advantage leaving the back straight. He won with a shade more in hand than the winning distance suggests, but will do well to take a race again in similar fashion.
Stocks 'n Shares, having her first start for Emma Lavelle, had every chance after jumping the last, but could not catch the winner. She is attractively handicapped over hurdles and can be found an opportunity if not regressing from this race. *(tchd 8-1)*
Red Canyon(IRE) shaped much better than of late but remains without a win since 2002. He has run well in the summer before, and may find a weak staying hurdle somewhere. *(op 14-1)*
Tinstre(IRE), who fell at the first last time when trying to land a three-timer, ran well for a horse who has been raised nearly a stone in the weights since the beginning of May. *(op 8-1)*
Touch Of Ebony(IRE) shaped well after a layoff and stays further than this trip. However, he is still without a win of any description. *(op 25-1)*
Like A Lord(IRE) ran well on his first run after a break. He can be reasonably expected to improve from this effort, whether he stays hurdling or goes chasing. *(op 8-1 tchd 13-2)*
Burundi(IRE) *Official explanation: jockey said gelding had a breathing problem (tchd 16-1)*
Bob's Gone(IRE) did not show a great deal on his first run for new connections. *(op 13-2 tchd 9-1)*
Manolo(FR) *Official explanation: jockey said gelding hung right throughout (op 10-1)*
Mantras(FR) was well backed before the race but showed nothing during it. *(op 6-1 tchd 13-2)*

763 CANNONS HEALTH CLUB MAIDEN HURDLE (12 hdls) 3m
5:15 (5:16) (Class 4) 4-Y-O+ **£3,445** (£1,060; £530; £265)

Form RPR

F-F **1** **Caspers Case**[25] 12-11-2 .... RWalsh 100
(P F Nicholls) *w ldr: led 4th to 8th: led 9th: rdn appr last: drvn out* **11/4**[2]

P **2** *3 ½* **Hi Tech Man (IRE)**[36] [281] 7-11-2 .... (b1) JCulloty 97
(D E Cantillon) *hld up in mid-div: hdwy 7th: ev ch whn mstke 3 out: sn rdn: edgd lft flat: no ex* **9/1**

040- **3** *24* **Flying Druid (FR)**[69] [4756] 5-11-2 **99** .... ChristianWilliams 76+
(Evan Williams) *hld up: hdwy after 6th: wknd appr 3 out* **10/1**

0-4 **4** *5* **Victree (IRE)**[38] [235] 6-11-2 .... JEMoore 68
(L Wells) *hld up and bhd: reminders after 4th: hdwy whn mstke 6th: wknd after 9th: hmpd 3 out* **12/1**

5 *17* **Pharshu (IRE)**[44] 8-10-2 .... MrJSnowden(7) 44
(C L Tizzard) *hld up towards rr: hdwy whn mstke 7th: wknd appr 3 out* **33/1**

P-34 **6** *dist* **Safe To Blush**[13] [611] 7-10-6 **85** .... (b1) ONelmes(3) —
(P A Pritchard) *led to 2nd: w ldrs tl wknd 7th: t.o whn j.lft 3 out* **14/1**

F **Teddy's Song** 7-11-2 .... MBradburne —
(P A Pritchard) *mstkes: bhd tl fell 9th* **66/1**

P/0- **P** **Samson Des Galas (FR)**[213] [2225] 7-11-2 .... JMMaguire —
(R Ford) *a bhd: t.o whn p.u after 7th* **33/1**

0 **P** **Tis She**[8] [671] 7-10-6 .... (p) CRafter(3) —
(N B King) *prom: lost pl and rdn appr 7th: t.o whn p.u bef 9th* **100/1**

F-P4 **P** **Peppershot**[21] [504] 5-10-9 **100** .... JPemberton(7) —
(G P Enright) *prom tl wknd 7th: t.o whn p.u bef 3 out* **16/1**

UPP/ **P** **Lord Castle (IRE)**[396] 9-11-2 .... SCurran —
(P W Hiatt) *reminders after 3rd: sn bhd: t.o whn p.u bef 7th* **100/1**

40 **P** **Cutting Edge**[22] [490] 6-10-2 .... SWalsh(7) —
(A J Chamberlain) *a bhd: j. slowly 1st: rdn after 5th: t.o whn p.u after 7th* **66/1**

6-0S **F** **Bally's Bak**[33] [329] 7-9-13 **100** .... THalliday(10) —
(Mrs S J Smith) *mid-div: nt fluent 3rd: wnt 4th and styng on whn fell 3 out: dead* **5/2**[1]

3P-6 **P** **Troodos Valley (IRE)**[20] [521] 6-11-2 **100** .... RJohnson —
(H D Daly) *led and pckd 2nd: hdd 4th: led 8th to 9th: wknd appr 3 out: bhd whn p.u bef last* **6/1**[3]

5m 51.2s (2.00) **Going Correction** +0.175s/f (Yiel) **14** Ran SP% **119.7**
Speed ratings: **103,101,93,92,86** —,—,—,—,— —,—,—,— CSF £27.06 TOTE £3.60: £1.80, £3.20, £3.70; EX 19.50 Place 6 £1,328.54, Place 5 £468.82.
Owner Sir Richard Cooper **Bred** Sir Richard Cooper **Trained** Ditcheat, Somerset

FOCUS
A poor staying maiden hurdle dominated by two ex-pointers.

NOTEBOOK
Caspers Case, having his first run over hurdles at the age of 12, kept plugging away up the home straight to win nicely. He would be no sure thing to follow up next time as he has his problems staying upright. *(op 9-4 tchd 3-1)*
Hi Tech Man(IRE) held every chance up the straight but looked slightly reluctant about going past. He had shown that tendency between the flags, although he has won races, and may no be one to trust implicitly. *(op 25-1)*
Flying Druid(FR) did not appear to stay the extra distance and was beaten a long way out. *(op 11-1 tchd 12-1)*
Victree(IRE) looked both green and pretty slow. He will need more time. *(op 10-1)*
Pharshu(IRE) was easily dropped when the principals went for home, and finished well beaten. *(op 25-1)*
Bally's Bak was starting to stay on when taking a fatal fall three from home. *(op 13-2 tchd 11-2)*
Troodos Valley(IRE) stopped very quickly when put under pressure. He does not appear to have a trip. *(op 13-2 tchd 11-2)*
T/Plt: £2,468.70 to a £1 stake. Pool: £29,252.65. 8.65 winning tickets. T/Qpdt: £327.20 to a £1 stake. Pool: £2,122.90. 4.80 winning tickets. KH

329 AINTREE (L-H)
Thursday, June 16

OFFICIAL GOING: Good
Wind: Fresh; half against Weather: Fine

764 MATALAN MAIDEN HURDLE (9 hdls) 2m 110y
6:30 (6:31) (Class 4) 4-Y-O+ **£4,202** (£1,293; £646; £323)

Form RPR

1 **Whispered Promises (USA)**[326] 4-10-13 .... JPMcNamara 89
(R S Brookhouse) *a.p: led last: hrd rdn flat: r.o* **16/1**

2 *shd* **Predator (GER)**[305] 4-10-13 .... APMcCoy 89
(Jonjo O'Neill) *hld up: hdwy after 6th: led 2 out to last: hrd rdn: r.o* **10/11**[1]

-660 **3** *2* **Our Men**[11] [643] 6-10-13 .... PBuchanan(3) 90
(Miss Lucinda V Russell) *hld up and bhd: hdwy 4th: rdn appr 2 out: styd on flat* **40/1**

4 *11* **Millicent Cross (IRE)** 7-11-2 .... GLee 80+
(R Ford) *plld hrd: sn prom: led 3 out to 2 out: sn wknd* **7/1**[3]

5 *1 ¾* **Menai Straights**[20] 4-10-10 .... KJMercer(3) 74
(R F Fisher) *hld up and bhd: smooth hdwy appr 3 out: wknd 2 out* **50/1**

P- **6** *4* **Uncle John**[18] [2288] 4-10-13 .... (p) DRDennis 70
(Ian Williams) *hld up in tch: rdn and wknd 2 out* **16/1**

0UP/ **7** *14* **Optimistic Harry**[431] [4756] 6-11-2 .... RMcGrath 59
(R Ford) *bhd: reminders after 3rd: nvr nr ldrs* **50/1**

1-23 **8** *7* **Abragante (IRE)**[7] [696] 4-10-13 .... JEMoore 49
(M C Pipe) *a bhd* **5/1**[2]

9 *17* **Melograno (IRE)**[59] 5-10-13 .... CRafter(3) 35
(Mark Campion) *w ldr: led 2nd to 3 out: sn wknd* **50/1**

0-0P **10** *2 ½* **Dumfries**[39] [238] 4-10-6 **87** .... BWharfe(7) 30
(T H Caldwell) *led to 2nd: w ldr to 5th: sn wknd* **33/1**

400- **11** *dist* **Ndola**[77] [2705] 6-11-2 .... PMoloney —
(B J Curley) *hld up in tch: rdn and wknd 6th: t.o* **14/1**

4m 9.00s (4.40) **Going Correction** +0.15s/f (Yiel)
WFA 4 from 5yo+ 3lb **11** Ran SP% **111.2**
Speed ratings: **95,94,94,88,88 86,79,76,68,67** — CSF £29.90 TOTE £20.60: £2.80, £1.10, £5.10; EX 37.50.
Owner Mrs S J Brookhouse **Bred** Springwood Llc And Morgan's Ford Farm **Trained** Wixford, Warwicks

FOCUS
They went no great pace in what was quite an interesting maiden for this time of the year, although there was not much to go on in order to rate the form.

NOTEBOOK

Whispered Promises(USA) ◆, a dual seven-furlong juvenile winner for Mark Johnston, stayed a mile and a half on the Flat. Nibbled at in the ring, he showed the right sort of attitude to hold on gamely. He can defy a penalty. *(op 25-1)*

Predator(GER) ◆, the winner of a ten-furlong maiden at Baden-Baden, looked well tuned up for his hurdling debut. He did nothing wrong against a rival who refused to be beaten and can go one better in this sort of company. *(op 8-11 tchd 4-6)*

Our Men ◆ showed tremendous improvement for his new trainer against a couple of above-average newcomers for this time of the season. A reproduction of this effort will see him take a similar event. *Official explanation: trainer said gelding finished lame*

Millicent Cross(IRE) eventually paid the penalty for refusing to settle and would have preferred a more strongly-run race. *(op 5-1)*

Menai Straights, a seven-furlong winner at Carlisle nearly a year ago, was ridden as if stamina *could be a problem and one cannot help thinking that connection's reservations were proved right.* *(op 40-1)*

Uncle John was pulled up on soft ground on his only previous venture over hurdles. His only win on the Flat came over seven furlongs but he does stays in excess of a mile and a half. *(op 20-1)*

765 LITTLEWOODS BET DIRECT SUPPORTS MARINA DALGLISH APPEAL H'CAP CHASE (19 fncs) 3m 1f (Mildmay)

7:00 (7:00) (Class 3) (0-120,119) 5-Y-0+ **£5,759** (£1,772; £886; £443)

Form — RPR

2U42 **1** **Mullensgrove**[7] 694 11-10-3 **103** ..... MissSSharratt[(7)] 112+
(R Hollinshead) *hld up and bhd: mstke 5th: hit 12th: hdwy appr 3 out: led 2 out: sn clr: rdn out* **9/1**

-430 **2** *1 1/4* **Noshinannikin**[19] 547 11-11-12 **119** ..... DElsworth 127
(Mrs S J Smith) *hld up and bhd: hdwy 15th: rdn and swtchd lft 2 out: r.o flat: nt rch wnr* **16/1**

2-P3 **3** *8* **Cassia Heights**[34] 330 10-11-5 **112** ..... (t) JCulloty 112
(S A Brookshaw) *hld up: hdwy 14th: ev ch appr 2 out: wknd flat* **10/1**

3-45 **4** *3* **Jacquemart Colombe (FR)**[23] 489 8-11-6 **113** ..... MAFitzgerald 110
(P Bowen) *hld up in tch: rdn after 12th: hmpd 15th: wknd 4 out* **8/1**[3]

P3-2 **5** *2 1/2* **Monita Des Bois (FR)**[22] 497 5-11-1 **114** ..... SThomas 103
(Miss Venetia Williams) *hld up in tch: lft in ld 15th: rdn and hdd 2 out: sn wknd* **12/1**

52-1 **6** *8* **Iverain (FR)**[34] 330 9-10-12 **105** ..... RMcGrath 93+
(Sir John Barlow Bt) *hld up: hdwy appr 12th: wknd 2 out* **8/1**[3]

PP-1 **P** **Personal Assurance**[23] 489 8-11-10 **117** ..... (b) APMcCoy —
(Jonjo O'Neill) *j. bdly: sn bhd: p.u bef 14th* **9/2**[2]

1PP- **P** **Clever Thyne (IRE)**[84] 4528 8-11-5 **112** ..... (t) RJohnson —
(H D Daly) *led to 3rd: chsd ldr tl wnt lame and p.u after 14th* **16/1**

P **Oh My Lord (IRE)**[34] 341 7-10-2 **95** ..... (t) GLee —
(A J Martin, Ire) *t.k.h: w ldr: led 3rd tl blnd bdly and sddle slipped 15th: sn p.u and dismntd* **5/4**[1]

6m 31.9s (1.50) **Going Correction** +0.075s/f (Yiel) **9** Ran SP% **123.4**
WFA 5 from 7yo+ 6lb
Speed ratings: **100,99,97,96,95 92,—,—,—** CSF £136.36 CT £1486.32 TOTE £9.20: £1.50, £3.80, £2.40; EX 152.20.
Owner Mrs Jane Lowe **Bred** D J Lowe **Trained** Upper Longdon, Staffs

FOCUS

A fair handicap rated through the second, but the form of this race was devalued by the fact that the front two in the betting failed to complete.

NOTEBOOK

Mullensgrove soon took command after leading at the penultimate fence and managed to hold on with his rider throwing the kitchen sink at him towards the finish. *(op 12-1)*

Noshinannikin got the trip well but it was rather a case of the winner getting first run.

Cassia Heights was on his best behaviour this time but perhaps an extended three miles stretches his stamina to the limit. *(op 9-1)*

Jacquemart Colombe(FR) was not beaten so far this time but is still not quite firing on all cylinders. *(tchd 9-1)*

Clever Thyne(IRE) *Official explanation: vet said gelding pulled up lame (op 15-8 tchd 2-1 in places)*

Personal Assurance, raised 8lb, was let down big time by his jumping. *(op 15-8 tchd 2-1 in places)*

Oh My Lord(IRE), a heavily-backed Irish raider, gave the impression that his saddle may have *slipped forward a little prior to him completely losing his back end five from home.Official explanation: jockey said saddle slipped (op 15-8 tchd 2-1 in places)*

766 LADBROKESPOKER.COM H'CAP HURDLE (11 hdls) 2m 4f

7:30 (7:36) (Class 3) (0-125,124) 4-Y-0+ **£5,512** (£1,696; £848; £424)

Form — RPR

0F/1 **1** **Kristoffersen**[33] 352 5-10-8 **106** ..... DRDennis 109+
(Ian Williams) *hld up: hdwy 8th: led 3 out to 2 out: led last: all out* **5/1**[2]

002- **2** *shd* **Silver Charmer**[63] 4837 6-11-6 **118** ..... GLee 120
(H S Howe) *hld up and plld hrd: hdwy appr 3 out: ev ch last: hrd rdn: r.o* **5/1**[2]

1-22 **3** *2 1/2* **Enhancer**[21] 525 7-11-12 **124** ..... JCulloty 124
(M J McGrath) *hld up: hdwy 4th: led 5th to 7th: led briefly appr 3 out: led 2 out to last: no ex flat* **4/1**[1]

F220 **4** *3 1/2* **Hattington**[4] 726 7-10-10 **108** ..... PJBrennan 104
(M F Harris) *a.p: swtchd lft appr 3 out: rdn appr 2 out: swtchd rt appr last: wknd flat* **12/1**

100- **5** *12* **Anatar (IRE)**[54] 4982 7-11-12 **124** ..... JEMoore 108
(M C Pipe) *hld up: rdn after 8th: nvr trbld ldrs* **9/1**

30-4 **6** *2* **Castleshane (IRE)**[9] 99 8-11-11 **123** ..... RJohnson 107+
(S Gollings) *plld hrd in rr: hdwy 6th: led briefly after 8th: wknd 2 out* **6/1**[3]

000- **7** *8* **Prince Among Men**[246] 1704 8-11-8 **120** ..... ADobbin 94
(N G Richards) *plld hrd: led to 3rd: w ldrs: led 7th tl after 8th: wknd 3 out* **16/1**

P-33 **8** *1* **Hugo De Perro (FR)**[28] 425 10-10-7 **108** ..... (p) PBuchanan[(3)] 81
(Miss Lucinda V Russell) *v rel to r: hdwy after 2nd: jnd ldrs 5th: wknd 8th* **20/1**

F64- **9** *2 1/2* **Big Wheel**[261] 1536 10-10-7 **112** ..... GThomas[(7)] 83
(N G Richards) *led 2nd to 3rd: prom tl wknd appr 3 out* **20/1**

11F- **10** *18* **Masters Of War (IRE)**[319] 1088 8-11-8 **120** ..... APMcCoy 73
(Jonjo O'Neill) *w ldr: led 3rd to 5th: sn wknd* **5/1**[2]

5m 24.0s (20.30) **Going Correction** +0.15s/f (Yiel) **10** Ran SP% **117.4**
Speed ratings: **65,64,63,62,57 56,53,53,52,45** CSF £30.93 CT £107.94 TOTE £6.30: £2.10, £1.80, £1.90; EX 40.80.
Owner Ian Williams **Bred** Five Horses Ltd **Trained** Portway, Worcs

FOCUS

With no one wanting to get on with it it took around half a minute to get to the first flight in this slowly-run affair. Not surprisingly the time was pedestrian and the form is suspect, although the first three ran close to their marks.

NOTEBOOK

Kristoffersen claimed after falling in a Taunton seller in March last year, was subsequently found to have fractured both a hock and his knee. Raised 6lb for winning a valuable seller, he has returned better than ever and just got the better of a tremendous battle in what can only be called a 'mickey mouse' affair. *(op 11-2 tchd 6-1)*

Silver Charmer proved a handful because of the funereal pace. She had a real set-to with the winner and the fact that she would have preferred more of a test of stamina makes this effort all the more praiseworthy. *(op 4-1)*

Enhancer, up 4lb, was totally unsuited by the way things panned out as he seems at his best when held up for a late run off a decent pace. *(op 5-1)*

Hattington had to be switched twice after the race had developed into a sprint. *(op 11-1)*

Castleshane(IRE) might just as well have adopted his usual front-running tactics given the way things worked out. *(op 7-1)*

767 CARPENTERS SHAMROCK NOVICES' H'CAP CHASE (14 fncs 2 omitted) 2m 4f (Mildmay)

8:05 (8:07) (Class 3) (0-110,108) 5-Y-0+ **£6,186** (£2,010; £1,082)

Form — RPR

5-U1 **1** **Lonesome Man (IRE)**[27] 436 9-11-1 **97** ..... RJohnson 118+
(Tim Vaughan) *mde all: sn clr: blnd 10th: unchal* **13/2**

-350 **2** *22* **Pollensa Bay**[14] 611 6-10-0 **82** oh1 ..... (b[1]) MFoley 71
(S A Brookshaw) *hld up: hmpd and pckd 2nd: chsd wnr after 4th: hit 10th: no imp* **16/1**

414- **3** *29* **Baikaline (FR)**[59] 4915 6-11-0 **96** ..... APMcCoy 56
(Ian Williams) *hld up: hmpd 2nd: hdwy 8th: wknd 9th: mstke 11th* **3/1**[1]

6354 **U** **Beaugency (NZ)**[8] 690 7-10-6 **91** ..... (p) LMcGrath[(3)] —
(R C Guest) *blnd and uns rdr 2nd* **10/3**[2]

P **Liberty Boy (IRE)**[682] 1104 7-10-0 **82** oh1 ..... JEMoore —
(Jonjo O'Neill) *a bhd: t.o whn p.u bef 11th* **10/1**

40/4 **P** **Pristeen Spy**[33] 348 8-10-0 **82** oh1 ..... GLee —
(R Ford) *chsd wnr: mstke 1st: j.lft 2nd: mstke 7th: sn rdn and wknd: t.o whn p.u bef 10th* **7/1**

-611 **P** **Moscow Dancer (IRE)**[29] 409 8-11-12 **108** ..... NPMulholland —
(P Monteith) *mstkes in rr: hdwy 10th: wknd after 11th: t.o whn p.u after 3 out* **7/2**[3]

5m 5.90s (-3.00) **Going Correction** +0.075s/f (Yiel) **7** Ran SP% **111.1**
Speed ratings: **109,100,88,—,— —,—** CSF £80.79 TOTE £6.70: £2.90, £4.30; EX 90.00.
Owner T Vaughan **Bred** James Wilson **Trained** Bridgend
■ The first winner under Rules for permit holder Tim Vaughan.

FOCUS

A very moderate race in which the winner was value for more than the official margin. The cross fence was omitted because of a low sun and the Mildmay fences took their toll on these novices.

NOTEBOOK

Lonesome Man(IRE), raised 5lb, ran what remained of the field ragged and even then he was lucky to survive his one jumping error. His trainer thinks he need to go left-handed. *(op 6-1)*

Pollensa Bay did not find the first-time blinkers working the oracle and the chase was in vain from a long way out.

Baikaline(FR) again out the value of her win at Plumpton into context. *(op 7-2 tchd 4-1 in places)*

Moscow Dancer(IRE) made a string of jumping errors on this step up in distance. *Official explanation: jockey said gelding ran flat (op 9-4)*

768 LIVERPOOL FC EUROPEAN CHAMPIONS H'CAP HURDLE (13 hdls) 3m 110y

8:40 (8:40) (Class 4) (0-110,108) 4-Y-0+ **£3,757** (£1,156; £578; £289)

Form — RPR

-213 **1** **My Lady Link (FR)**[19] 545 6-10-13 **93** ..... SThomas 101+
(Miss Venetia Williams) *hld up in mid-div: hdwy 10th: led 3 out: clr 2 out: easily* **5/1**[2]

1/0- **2** *4* **Zygomatic**[191] 2693 7-10-7 **90** ..... KJMercer[(3)] 90
(R F Fisher) *hld up and bhd: hdwy fr 3 out: styd on to take 2nd post: no ch w wnr* **25/1**

00R- **3** *shd* **Swansea Bay**[69] 4764 9-11-6 **100** ..... MAFitzgerald 100
(P Bowen) *hld up in tch: ev ch 3 out: rdn and one pce fr 2 out* **13/2**[3]

-230 **4** *1 1/4* **Tell The Trees**[11] 652 4-11-9 **108** ..... (p) APMcCoy 103+
(M C Pipe) *hld up: hdwy 10th: rdn and ev ch 3 out: one pce fr 2 out* **5/1**[2]

0-04 **5** *1 3/4* **Three Lions**[10] 665 8-11-1 **95** ..... JPMcNamara 92
(R S Brookhouse) *hld up: hdwy after 10th: eased whn btn cl home* **12/1**

-022 **6** *8* **Brush A King**[11] 652 10-11-4 **105** ..... APogson[(7)] 94
(C T Pogson) *t.k.h in mid-div: hdwy 5th: ev ch 3 out: wknd 2 out* **7/2**[1]

-055 **7** *3/4* **Al Mabrook (IRE)**[23] 480 10-10-5 **85** ..... GLee 74
(N G Richards) *hld up in mid-div: rdn after 10th: no hdwy* **12/1**

-623 **8** *1/2* **La Concha (IRE)**[18] 566 4-10-10 **95** ..... JCulloty 78
(M J McGrath) *t.k.h in rr: hdwy appr 3 out: rdn and wknd after 2 out* **8/1**

-501 **9** *nk* **Ramblees Holly**[19] 552 7-11-5 **106** ..... TMessenger[(7)] 94
(R S Wood) *hld up: hdwy after 7th: rdn appr 3 out: wknd 2 out* **14/1**

4-04 **10** *15* **Caesar's Palace (GER)**[17] 595 8-11-0 **97** ..... (p) PBuchanan[(3)] 70
(Miss Lucinda V Russell) *led to 7th: wknd after 10th* **10/1**

22-P **11** *1 1/2* **Fabrezan (FR)**[33] 353 6-11-8 **102** ..... (p) RThornton 73
(B D Leavy) *w ldr: led 7th to 3 out: sn wknd* **20/1**

-50P **12** *23* **Silver Gift**[11] 652 8-9-13 **84** ..... DLaverty[(5)] 32
(G Fierro) *hld up in mid-div: hdwy 7th: wknd 10th: t.o* **25/1**

5-63 **P** **Magical Liaison (IRE)**[23] 488 7-11-1 **95** ..... (b) CLlewellyn —
(W Jenks) *prom tl p.u after 4th* **14/1**

45-P **P** **Phase Eight Girl**[25] 468 9-10-3 **83** ..... WHutchinson —
(J Hetherton) *a bhd: rdn after 7th: t.o whn p.u bef 2 out* **33/1**

P5P- **P** **Dajazar (IRE)**[182] 2848 9-10-6 **93** ..... CDSharkey[(7)] —
(Mrs K Walton) *prom tl rdn and wknd after 10th: t.o whn p.u bef 2 out* **50/1**

6m 14.5s (-1.90) **Going Correction** +0.15s/f (Yiel) **15** Ran SP% **135.2**
Speed ratings: **109,107,107,107,106 104,103,103,103,98 98,91,—,—,—** CSF £138.44 CT £866.25 TOTE £6.80: £2.10, £9.80, £3.90; EX 293.00.
Owner Six Diamonds Partnership **Bred** P Joubert **Trained** Kings Caple, H'fords

FOCUS

A competitive staying handicap with the winner value for double the official margin and solid form.

NOTEBOOK

My Lady Link(FR) found no difficulty in supplementing her win over two and a half miles here last *month despite running off a 6lb higher mark. A switch back to hurdling has been the making of* her. *Official explanation: trainer had no explanation for the improved form shown (op 11-2 tchd 6-1)*

Zygomatic ◆ certainly proved he stayed this longer trip on his first outing for six months. He can be ridden a bit closer to the pace in future and improvement is expected. *(op 20-1)*

Swansea Bay, who blotted his copybook when left at the start in the Topham, could not take full advantage of being 27lb lower than his mark over fences. This should at least have sweetened him up.

Tell The Trees was 4lb better off than when three and a half lengths behind the winner over an inadequate two and a half miles here last month.

Three Lions, trying an even longer trip, is not one who finds an awful lot when push comes to shove. *(op 14-1)*

Brush A King again took a strong hold and it appeared to eventually catch up with him. *(op 13-2 tchd 7-1)*
Magical Liaison(IRE) *Official explanation: trainer said gelding pulled up lame having hit a flight of hurdles, but subsequently returned sound (op 16-1)*

769 LIVER BIRD DEVELOPMENTS STANDARD OPEN NATIONAL HUNT FLAT RACE — 2m 1f
9:15 (9:15) (Class 6) 4-6-Y-O — **£2,261** (£646; £323)

Form — RPR

1 **Zumrah (IRE)** 4-11-1 .... APMcCoy 101+
(P Bowen) *hld up and bhd: stdy hdwy over 3f out: led over 1f out: qcknd clr ins fnl f: readily* **2/1**[1]

0-1 2 *4* **Lindbergh Law (USA)**[23] [484] 5-11-11 .... ADobbin 104
(G A Swinbank) *hld up towards rr: hdwy over 4f out: rdn and ev ch over 1f out: one pce* **4/1**[3]

3 *1 ¼* **Livingonaknifedge (IRE)**[32] 6-11-4 .... DRDennis 96
(Ian Williams) *hld up: hdwy 6f out: led 3f out: rdn and hdd over 1f out: one pce* **10/1**

2 4 *9* **Silverio (GER)**[22] [507] 4-10-8 .... EDehdashti(7) 84
(G L Moore) *a.p: rdn and ev ch over 2f out: wknd over 1f out* **4/1**[3]

03-1 5 *1 ½* **Master Marmalade**[39] [241] 4-11-8 .... JEMoore 89
(D Morris) *t.k.h: a.p: led over 4f out to 3f out: wknd over 2f out* **10/3**[2]

6 *13* **Bobble**[80] 5-10-4 .... MrGTumelty(7) 65
(R N Bevis) *hld up in tch: wknd 5f out* **25/1**

0- 7 *5* **Palace Pett**[149] [3407] 5-10-8 .... DCrosse(3) 60
(J R Best) *w ldr: led 8f out tl over 4f out: sn wknd* **25/1**

50- 8 *5* **Rocky Agenda (IRE)**[180] [2886] 4-11-1 .... NHannity 59
(G A Harker) *hld up and bhd: rdn and hdwy over 3f out: wknd over 2f out* **16/1**

9 *13* **Scolboa Arctic (IRE)**[60] 5-10-11 .... DElsworth 42
(Mrs S J Smith) *led: hdd 8f out: wknd over 4f out* **12/1**

4m 28.6s (11.00) **Going Correction** +0.15s/f (Yiel)
WFA 4 from 5yo+ 3lb — **9 Ran SP% 126.8**
Speed ratings: **80,78,77,73,72 66,64,61,55** CSF £11.54 TOTE £3.30: £2.40, £1.70, £1.90; EX 14.80 Place 6 £1,207.97, Place £726.90.
Owner David A Smith **Bred** Shadwell Estate Company Limited **Trained** Little Newcastle, Pembrokes

FOCUS
A typically slowly-run bumper nearly 20 seconds slower than the opening novice hurdle with the fifth the best guide to the value of the form.

NOTEBOOK
Zumrah(IRE), a half-brother to seven furlong to mile and a half Group Three winner Rabah and eight and ten furlong winner Muhtafel, never made it to the racecourse for Ed Dunlop. He won this nicely and showed a turn of foot off a slow pace. *(tchd 9-4 and 5-2 in places)*
Lindbergh Law(USA) probably beat nothing of the calibre of the winner at Sedgefield and eventually got well outpointed under a penalty. *(op 7-2)*
Livingonaknifedge(IRE) has started favourite in all three of his points and finally managed to complete when winning in modest company at Tabley last month. *(tchd 12-1)*
Silverio(GER) was a shade disappointing after his second at Fontwell and may not have found this a sufficient test of stamina. *(op 13-2)*
Master Marmalade proved difficult to settle because of the lack of pace and his form could be best forgotten. *(op 4-1)*
T/Plt: £649.80 to a £1 stake. Pool: £41,616.80 - 46.75 winning units T/Qpdt: £148.60 to a £1 stake. Pool: £3,634.90 - 18.10 winning units KH

770 - 776a (Foreign Racing) - See Raceform Interactive

583 AUTEUIL (L-H)
Saturday, June 18

OFFICIAL GOING: Very soft

777a PRIX AGUADO (LISTED) (HURDLE) (C&G) — 2m 1f 110y
1:10 (1:15) 3-Y-O — **£37,447** (£18,723; £10,922; £7,411; £3,511)

RPR

1 **Sunny Winner (FR)**[20] [583] 3-10-1 .... PMarsac —
(G Cherel, France)

2 *¾* **Tidal Fury (IRE)**[62] [4900] 3-9-13 .... SLeloup —
(J Jay) *jumped left, led to 7th (of 11th), led 9th to flat, unable to quicken closing stages (51/10)*

3 *2* **Chiaro (FR)**[20] [583] 3-10-1 .... (b) FEstrampes —
(J-L Pelletan, France)

4 *2* **Full Magic (FR)**[15] 3-9-13 .... RegisSchmidlin —
(M Rolland, France)

5 *2 ½* **Roi Du Val (FR)**[15] 3-9-13 ow2 .... BChameraud —
(H Hosselet, France)

6 *4* **El Cascador (FR)**[32] 3-9-13 ow2 .... AKondrat —
(T Trapenard, France)

7 *4* **Duc De Regniere (FR)**[32] 3-9-11 .... EChazelle —
(G Cherel, France)

8 *10* **Merci Papi (FR)**[4] 3-9-13 .... SDupuis —
(T Trapenard, France)

4m 23.0s — **10 Ran**
PARI-MUTUEL (including one euro stakes): WIN 5.60 (coupled with Ducde Regniere); PL 2.20, 1.90, 1.60; DF 21.60.
Owner J-P H Dubois **Bred** Ecurie Winning **Trained** France

NOTEBOOK
Tidal Fury(IRE) was soon ten lengths clear but forfeited more than half that advantage with a very slow jump at the second. Headed for a furlong or so down the back straight, he was soon back at the head of affairs and, challenged after the last, battled back gamely and only admitted defeat in the last 30 yards. Rarely fluent and jumping to his left, his hurdling did improve as the race wore on. Undoubtedly a talented individual, he has a real future at this game if his jumping kinks can be ironed out.

778a PRIX ALAIN DU BREIL - COURSE DE HAIES D'ETE (GRADE 1) (HURDLE) — 2m 3f 110y
2:45 (2:46) 4-Y-O — **£73,404** (£35,887; £21,206; £14,681; £8,156; £5,709)

RPR

1 **Strangely Brown (IRE)**[51] [88] 4-10-6 .... RWalsh 137
(E McNamara, Ire) *raced in 4th, went 3rd at 7th (of 11), 2nd & ridden 2 out, driven to lead 100yds out, ran on (66/10)* **66/10**[1]

2 *3* **Royale Athenia (FR)**[20] [584] 4-10-1 .... (b) CGombeau 129
(B Barbier, France)

3 *15* **Aroldo (FR)**[20] [584] 4-10-6 .... RegisSchmidlin 119
(J Bertran De Balanda, France)

4 *3* **Kiko (FR)**[20] [584] 4-10-6 .... JacquesRicou 116
(A Chaille-Chaille, France)

5 *3* **Sol Roc (FR)**[41] [258] 4-10-6 .... BChameraud 113
(J Bertran De Balanda, France)

6 *4* **Icarro (FR)**[11] 4-10-6 .... HGallorini 109
(J-P Gallorini, France)

7 *2* **Bonbon Rose (FR)**[20] [586] 4-10-6 .... CPieux 107
(A Chaille-Chaille, France)

8 *10* **King's Daughter (FR)**[20] [584] 4-10-1 .... DGallagher 92
(F-M Cottin, France)

P **Gerfaut (FR)**[20] [584] 4-10-6 .... SBeaumard —
(T Civel, France)

P **Nooska Tivoli (FR)**[20] [584] 4-10-6 .... (b) SLeloup —
(P Tual, France)

4m 38.0s — **11 Ran SP% 13.2**
PARI-MUTUEL: WIN 7.60; PL 3.20, 2.40, 2.90; DF 35.60.
Owner We Didn't Name Him Syndicate **Bred** Barry Noonan **Trained** Rathkeale, Co. Limerick

NOTEBOOK
Strangely Brown(IRE) jumped really well given that he was encountering these solid French hurdles for the first time. Always to the fore, he went in pursuit of the leader at the second last and, switched to the stands' rail after the last, responded well to a strong drive to get on top in the closing stages. Softer ground and the longer trip undoubtedly brought about an improved run from this tough campaigner, although with the red-hot favourite Bonbon Rose running no kind of race, this may turn out to have been a surprisingly weak contest for such a large first prize.

779a GRANDE COURSE DE HAIES D'AUTEUIL (GRADE 1) (HURDLE) — 3m 1f 110y
4:00 (4:02) 5-Y-O+
£95,745 (£46,809; £27,660; £19,150; £10,638; £7,447)

RPR

1 **Lycaon De Vauzelle (FR)**[62] [4903] 6-10-8 .... BChameraud 140
(J Bertran De Balanda, France)

2 *4* **Rule Supreme (IRE)**[20] [585] 9-10-8 .... RWalsh 136
(W P Mullins, Ire) *a cl up bhd slow pce, led 3rd, mstke & hdd 4th, wnt 2nd 4 out, rdn nxt, ran on under pressure flat, no chance with wnr*

3 *3* **Double Car (FR)**[20] [587] 9-10-8 .... CCheminaud 133
(B De Watrigant, France)

4 *¾* **Sphinx Du Berlais (FR)**[20] [585] 6-10-8 .... DGallagher 132
(F-M Cottin, France)

5 *2 ½* **Cheler (FR)**[20] [585] 6-10-8 .... CPieux 130
(B Secly, France)

6 *3* **Ennemi D'Etat (FR)**[20] [585] 6-10-8 .... (b) RegisSchmidlin 127
(M Rolland, France)

7 *dist* **Prince Dolois (FR)**[20] [585] 7-10-8 .... BThelier —
(A Bonin, France)

P **Mister Gyor (FR)**[20] [589] 5-10-4 .... CGombeau —
(B Barbier, France)

6m 31.0s — **8 Ran**
PARI-MUTUEL: WIN 4.60; PL 1.30, 1.10, 1.60; DF 3.00.
Owner F Wintz **Bred** Mme F Beaudot **Trained** France

NOTEBOOK
Lycaon De Vauzelle(FR) led two from home and was soon in command.
Rule Supreme(IRE) was odds-on to give his trainer a third consecutive win in this staying contest, but a farcical early pace did not help his cause and contributed to him jumping clumsily in the early stages. Coming under pressure two out, he looked well beaten, but rallied to take second when stamina came into play on the run-in. Mullins felt that the heatwave may also have played its part in this below-par effort.

714 HEXHAM (L-H)
Sunday, June 19

OFFICIAL GOING: Good to firm
Second last flight omitted on each circuit. Hexham's richest day's racing, but there were 18 non-runners due to the ground.
Wind: fresh against

780 TOTEPLACEPOT NOVICES' HURDLE (6 hdls 2 omitted) — 2m 110y
2:20 (2:20) (Class 3) 4-Y-O+
£6,072 (£2,303; £1,151; £523; £261; £157)

Form — RPR

5-11 1 **Miami Explorer**[8] [715] 5-11-1 113 .... TDoyle 119+
(P R Webber) *keen: in tch: smooth hdwy to ld between last two: sn clr: easily* **4/7**[1]

-315 2 *10* **Supply And Fix (IRE)**[14] [643] 7-10-7 .... MissJAKidd(7) 98+
(J J Lambe, Ire) *led to between last two: kpt on: no ch w wnr* **7/1**[3]

-322 3 *½* **Sterling Guarantee (USA)**[19] [602] 7-10-7 98 .... CDSharkey(7) 92
(N Wilson) *midfield: rdn 2 out: rallied bef last: kpt on: no imp* **11/2**[2]

06-6 4 *8* **Macchiato**[21] [569] 4-10-1 88 .... LVickers(3) 74
(I W McInnes) *in tch: rdn 2 out: sn one pce* **25/1**

-566 5 *10* **One Of Them**[8] [716] 6-10-11 76 .... PBuchanan(3) 74
(M A Barnes) *chsd ldrs: drvn along 2 out: sn no ex* **66/1**

00 6 *11* **Si Anthony (FR)**[19] [602] 5-10-11 .... KJMercer(3) 63
(Ferdy Murphy) *hld up: rdn 3 out: nvr rchd ldrs* **33/1**

0/3 7 *4* **Howards Dream (IRE)**[4] [645] 7-11-0 .... (t) RMcGrath 59
(D A Nolan) *a bhd* **50/1**

P040 8 *5* **Starbright**[8] [716] 4-10-6 68 .... DCCostello(5) 51
(W G Young) *prom to 2 out: sn rdn and wknd* **200/1**

/0-F 9 *8* **Lady Godson**[52] [82] 6-10-7 .... GLee 39
(B Mactaggart) *bhd: rdn 3 out: nvr on terms* **100/1**

0-P 10 *8* **Wizards Princess**[8] [715] 5-10-4 .... ONelmes(3) 31
(D W Thompson) *mstkes: a bhd* **100/1**

0- 11 *12* **Miss Ocean Monarch**[85] [4547] 5-10-7 .... DO'Meara 19
(N Waggott) *sn bhd: no ch fr 1/2-way* **200/1**

P **Kaysglory**[697] 6-11-0 .... PRobson —
(F P Murtagh) *a bhd: t.o whn p.u bef last* **200/1**

30-0 P **Pass Go**[6] [738] 4-10-11 .... JLCullen —
(J J Lambe, Ire) *a bhd: t.o whn p.u bef last* **50/1**

0-41 **P** **Longdale**[19] 602 7-11-6 ADobbin —
(M Todhunter) *hld up in tch: effrt to chse clr ldrs after 2 out: wknd qckly and p.u bef last* **10/1**

(-15.20) **Going Correction** -0.90s/f (Hard)
WFA 4 from 5yo+ 3lb **14** Ran SP% **116.3**
Speed ratings: **99,94,94,90,85 80,78,76,72,68 63,—,—,—** CSF £4.70 TOTE £1.30: £1.10, £2.30, £1.50; EX 5.80.

Owner R J McAlpine **Bred** Mrs P G Wilkins And R J McAlpine **Trained** Mollington, Oxon

FOCUS
A race lacking strength but a fair gallop and an impressive winner, who was value for twice the official margin and may be able to hold his own in better company.

NOTEBOOK
Miami Explorer ◆ did not have to improve too much to win with plenty more in hand than the winning margin suggests and, although reportedly finishing sore, looks the type to hold her own in stronger company. She will be very much of interest back on the Flat from only a 45 rating. *(op 1-2)*
Supply And Fix(IRE), back in trip, had conditions to suit and ran creditably. He will be suited by the return to two and a half miles and can win a similar event this summer away from progressive sorts. *(op 5-1)*
Sterling Guarantee(USA), from a stable among the winners, was not disgraced and shaped as though the return to further and the step into handicap company would suit. *(op 7-1 tchd 5-1)*
Macchiato finished a similar distance behind the eased down winner as at Uttoxeter and is likely to remain vulnerable in this type of event.
One Of Them, a modest and inconsistent maiden, was not totally disgraced in the face of a very stiff task but his record suggests he would not be one to look out for returned to handicaps.
Si Anthony(FR), only lightly raced in recent times, again left the strong impression that the step up to two and a half miles and beyond would suit and he will be interesting in modest handicaps. *(tchd 40-1)*

781 CATHERINE BRIGHOUSE MEMORIAL CONDITIONAL JOCKEYS' (S) H'CAP HURDLE (8 hdls 2 omitted) 2m 4f 110y
2:50 (2:52) (Class 5) (0-95,90) 4-Y-0+ **£3,066** (£876; £438)

Form RPR
P/3- **1** **Plenty Courage**[63] 4872 11-10-9 **79** MJMcAlister[(6)] 95+
(B Storey) *chsd ldrs: rdn 3 out: rallied to ld bef last: kpt on strly* **11/1**
-300 **2** *12* **Lazy Lena (IRE)**[11] 686 6-10-8 **75** StephenJCraine[(3)] 79+
(Miss L C Siddall) *midfield: hdwy bef 3 out: led between last 2: kpt on same pce* **16/1**
4-30 **3** *7* **Howaboys Quest (USA)**[40] 283 8-11-3 **89** (p) PJMcDonald[(8)] 84
(Ferdy Murphy) *rn in snatches: midfield: hdwy and prom 3 out: outpcd after next: rallied bef last: kpt on* **14/1**
-323 **4** *½* **Star Trooper (IRE)**[20] 592 9-10-13 **82** (p) TMessenger[(5)] 77
(Miss S E Forster) *midfield: drvn fr 3 out: rallied between last 2: kpt on: no imp* **5/1**[2]
4030 **5** *½* **Book's Way**[11] 686 9-10-13 **77** ONelmes 71
(D W Thompson) *chsd ldrs: rdn 3 out: one pce after next* **12/1**
10-P **6** *1* **Wally Wonder (IRE)**[42] 237 7-11-2 **85** (b) LBerridge[(5)] 78
(R Bastiman) *nt fluent: mde most to between last two: sn outpcd* **14/1**
4-04 **7** *3* **Frankincense (IRE)**[26] 480 9-11-4 **82** (p) PRobson 72
(A J Lockwood) *prom tl rdn and wknd between last two* **14/1**
-020 **8** *5* **Northern Echo**[22] 552 8-10-12 **79** (p) EDehdashti[(3)] 64
(K S Thomas) *bhd: rdn after 4 out: nvr on terms* **20/1**
0200 **9** *1¾* **Scamp**[20] 592 6-10-4 **68** (p) KJMercer 51
(R Shiels) *a bhd* **33/1**
-PF0 **10** *14* **Step In Line (IRE)**[26] 480 13-9-12 **65** ow1 BenOrde-Powlett[(3)] 34
(D W Thompson) *bhd: rdn 4 out: nvr on terms* **33/1**
0/40 **11** *24* **Now And Again**[12] 670 6-10-13 **77** DCrosse 22
(I W McInnes) *chsaed ldrs tl rdn and wknd after 2 out* **22/1**
053F **P** **Noras Legacy (IRE)**[8] 718 7-10-9 **73** DMcGann —
(Miss Lucinda V Russell) *sn bhd: lost tch fr 4th: p.u bef 2 out* **16/1**
/UPP **P** **Percy Beck**[21] 570 9-10-9 **76** CDSharkey[(3)] —
(P Needham) *bhd and early reminders: no ch fr 4 out: p.u bef last* **40/1**
60-5 **P** **Just Sal**[50] 120 9-10-13 **77** NPMulholland —
(R Nixon) *in tch to 3 out: wknd after next: t.o whn p.u bef last* **16/1**
P5-5 **P** **Western Bluebird (IRE)**[32] 417 7-10-6 **70** (b) DCCostello —
(Miss Kate Milligan) *sn bhd: no ch fr 1/2-way: p.u nr finish* **14/1**
5-P3 **P** **Comfortable Call**[26] 480 7-11-12 **90** (t) AO'Keeffe —
(H Alexander) *midfield: hdwy 1/2-way: rdn and wknd after 2 out: p.u after last* **9/1**[3]
5 **R** **Greenfort Brave (IRE)**[38] 317 7-11-4 **85** PCO'Neill[(3)] —
(J J Lambe, Ire) *hld up: hdwy into midfield 1/2-way: wknd 3 out: t.o. when ran out last* **16/1**
6432 **F** **End Of An Error**[11] 686 6-10-11 **85** SGagan[(10)] 89
(Mrs E Slack) *bhd: drvn 4 out: hdwy between last 2: styng on wl and disputing 4th whn fell last* **4/1**[1]

4m 54.7s (-14.90) **Going Correction** -0.90s/f (Hard) **18** Ran SP% **130.3**
Speed ratings: **92,87,84,84,84 84,82,80,80,74 65,—,—,—,— —,—,—** CSF £173.41 CT £2516.73 TOTE £9.10: £1.80, £6.90, £3.00, £1.80; EX 269.40.There was no bid for the winner

Owner K Ferguson **Bred** Mrs E R Courage **Trained** Kirklinton, Cumbria
■ A first winner as a trainer for ex-jockey Brian Storey and a first winner on his first ride as a professional for Michael McAlister.

FOCUS
A field comprising exposed sorts and a decent pace but, although the winner could score again and the placed horses ran to form, a race that is unlikely to be throwing up too many winners.

NOTEBOOK
Plenty Courage, who missed last year, returned to hurdles and showed he retains much of his old ability when beating a poor lot with plenty in hand to give his current trainer his first winner. Life will be tougher after reassessment, though. *(op 7-1 tchd 12-1)*
Lazy Lena(IRE) ran arguably her best race over hurdles but, given she has yet to win and that she is not the most consistent, would not be certain to reproduce this next time.
Howaboys Quest(USA) is not very reliable and, although not disgraced in terms of form, did not look the most straightforward and, given his losing run, is not one to be placing too much faith in.
Star Trooper(IRE), back up in trip, was not disgraced but left the impression that easier ground would have been in his favour. *(op 11-2)*
Book's Way was not totally disgraced but did not leave the impression that a return to winning ways was imminent.
Wally Wonder(IRE), well beaten of late, ran a bit better than the bare form suggests as he helped force a decent gallop and his jumping was less than fluent on occasions. He is not one to write off yet back on easier ground. *(op 16-1)*
Comfortable Call *Official explanation: jockey said gelding pulled up lame (op 5-1)*
End Of An Error has not won since 2003 and is not the easiest of rides but was in the process of running creditably when coming to grief. She may be suited by the return to three miles but does need things to go her way. *(op 5-1)*

782 TOTEQUADPOT NOVICES' CHASE (15 fncs) 2m 4f 110y
3:20 (3:20) (Class 3) 5-Y-0+ **£6,890** (£2,120; £1,060; £530)

Form RPR
-233 **1** **Wet Lips (AUS)**[31] 419 7-10-11 (p) LMcGrath[(3)] 108+
(R C Guest) *mde most to 7th: mstke next: wnt 2nd 3 out: led appr last: styd on* **7/4**[2]
62-2 **2** *3½* **Dad's Elect (GER)**[28] 459 6-11-0 DRDennis 104+
(Ian Williams) *chsd ldrs: led 3 out: hdd and hit last: no ex* **13/8**[1]
P/4 **3** *7* **Heather Lad**[11] 688 12-11-0 RMcGrath 96
(C Grant) *chsd ldrs: one pce fr 2 out* **9/1**
0033 **4** *24* **Prize Ring**[11] 688 6-11-0 99 FKeniry 72
(G M Moore) *in tch: drvn along 6th: outpcd and lost pl 12th* **11/2**[3]
PP4F **5** *½* **Alchemystic (IRE)**[11] 688 5-10-5 90 (t) GThomas[(7)] 70
(M A Barnes) *w ldrs: wknd 3 out* **22/1**
P0-P **P** **Danny Leahy (FR)**[22] 545 5-10-12 70 KRenwick —
(M D Hammond) *sn bhd: t.o 6th: p.u after 8th* **50/1**
P0-0 **P** **Charlie Castallan**[8] 716 5-10-9 ONelmes[(3)] —
(D W Thompson) *bhd fr 6th: t.o 12th: p.u bef last* **28/1**
P/P- **P** **Alfie Bright**[202] 2544 7-10-9 DFlavin[(5)] —
(Mrs L B Normile) *lost tch 6th: t.o whn p.u bef 8th* **66/1**
04 **P** **Kilifi Creek (IRE)**[14] 646 8-11-0 87 (p) JLCullen —
(J J Lambe, Ire) *w ldrs: led 7th to 3 out: poor 4th whn p.u bef last* **16/1**

5m 1.90s (-9.50) **Going Correction** -0.40s/f (Good)
WFA 5 from 6yo+ 2lb **9** Ran SP% **117.0**
Speed ratings: **102,100,98,88,88 —,—,—,—** CSF £5.18 TOTE £3.00: £1.60, £1.90, £1.40; EX 6.90.

Owner Concertina Racing Three **Bred** Woodlands Stud Nsw **Trained** Brancepeth, Co Durham

FOCUS
An ordinary event in which the pace was only fair at best in the first half of the contest. The runner-up sets a reasonable standard.

NOTEBOOK
Wet Lips(AUS) ◆, back over a more suitable trip, was ridden more prominently this time and showed the right attitude to win an ordinary event. His jumping was sound in the main and he appeals as the type to win again over fences. *(op 9-4)*
Dad's Elect(GER) looked to have decent claims in this company and ran creditably on ground that may have been plenty quick enough. He looks capable of winning in similar company this summer. *(op 6-4 tchd 7-4 in places)*
Heather Lad ran his best race to date over regulation fences but left the impression that a much stiffer test of stamina over this trip would have suited. *(op 16-1 tchd 8-1)*
Prize Ring is essentially a disappointing type these days and once again showed that he is not the most reliable betting proposition around. *(tchd 6-1)*
Alchemystic(IRE), who has a poor completion record over obstacles this year, was soundly beaten and is of little immediate interest. *(op 20-1)*
Kilifi Creek(IRE) had the run of a modest race but stopped very quickly and will have to show more before he is worth a bet.

783 LIZ AND MARGARUERITE'S GREAT ESCAPE NOVICES' H'CAP CHASE (19 fncs) 3m 1f
3:50 (3:50) (Class 4) (0-105,102) 5-Y-0+ **£3,818** (£1,175; £587; £293)

Form RPR
F-06 **1** **Inglewood**[32] 413 5-9-8 **83** MJMcAlister[(7)] 96+
(Miss Kate Milligan) *mde most: rdn and kpt on strly fr 3 out* **33/1**
22R- **2** *9* **Starbuck**[28] 11-9-9 **76** oh1 DMcGann[(5)] 86
(A M Crow) *a cl up: drvn bef 3 out: chsd wnr bef last: kpt on: no imp* **11/2**[3]
-P33 **3** *4* **Tee-Jay (IRE)**[22] 554 9-10-6 **82** FKeniry 90+
(M D Hammond) *chsd ldrs tl rdn and one pce fr 2 out* **4/1**[2]
4-11 **4** *nk* **Arctic Lagoon (IRE)**[22] 554 6-10-4 **80** (t) MBradburne 88+
(Mrs S C Bradburne) *prominent: niggled along 4 out: effrt after next: one pce between last two* **5/4**[1]
-003 **5** *¾* **Cyindien (FR)**[12] 673 8-10-0 **79** (p) DCrosse[(3)] 84
(D E Cantillon) *hld up in tch: effrt bef 3 out: wknd fr next* **8/1**
26-3 **6** *dist* **Litron (IRE)**[38] 319 8-11-10 **100** JLCullen —
(J J Lambe, Ire) *hld up: hdwy bef 9th: chsd ldrs bef 3 out: rdn and wknd qckly bef next* **12/1**
5-F3 **F** **Ornella Speed (FR)**[26] 481 5-9-11 **82** oh6 (t) KJMercer[(3)] —
(Ferdy Murphy) *bhd: no ch whn fell heavily 4 out* **9/1**
50/5 **P** **Finest Of Men**[19] 604 9-9-12 **81** ow5 BenOrde-Powlett[(7)] —
(J B Walton) *hld up in tch: hit 5th: p.u bef next* **20/1**
0P-P **P** **Killer (FR)**[43] 212 7-9-11 **76** oh12 (vt[1]) PBuchanan[(3)] —
(Miss Lucinda V Russell) *cl up to 1/2-way: sn struggling: blnd bdly 4 out: sn p.u* **66/1**

6m 17.9s (-14.00) **Going Correction** -0.40s/f (Good)
WFA 5 from 6yo+ 6lb **9** Ran SP% **117.8**
Speed ratings: **106,103,101,101,101 —,—,—,—** CSF £207.20 CT £906.57 TOTE £34.50: £7.10, £1.70, £2.10; EX 271.40.

Owner The Aunts **Bred** Guy Reed And Mrs A H Daniels **Trained** Middleham Moor, N Yorks
■ A double for Michael McAlister on his first two rides as a professional. He rode 16 winners as an amateur.

FOCUS
A modest handicap run at an ordinary pace but with the second to fifth close to their marks the form might work out.

NOTEBOOK
Inglewood, an inconsistent hurdler, turned in a much-improved effort on only this third start over fences. He had the run of the race and it remains to be seen whether this can be reproduced from a higher mark next time.
Starbuck, in winning form in points on his last two starts, had conditions to suit and showed enough to suggest a similar race can be found this summer. *(tchd 5-1)*
Tee-Jay(IRE) had the run of the race and reversed recent placings with Arctic Lagoon but a stiffer test of stamina would have suited and there is still room for improvement with his fencing. *(op 9-2 tchd 3-1)*
Arctic Lagoon(IRE), up 10lb for his course and distance win, was still well treated on the pick of his hurdles form but did not go through the race with the same zest as last time and proved a shade disappointing. He is worth another chance over fences. *(op 11-10 tchd 6-4)*
Cyindien(FR), with the cheekpieces on again, did not find much for pressure and his record of no wins from 19 starts and his inconsistency means he is one to tread carefully with.
Litron(IRE), who is not the most consistent, had still to prove that he stays this sort of trip, but the way he capitulated in a race run at just an ordinary pace suggested it was more than just stamina to blame. *(op 14-1 tchd 16-1 and 11-1)*
Finest Of Men *Official explanation: jockey said gelding pulled up lame*

784 TOTESPORT 0800 221 221 H'CAP HURDLE (6 hdls 2 omitted) 2m 110y
4:20 (4:22) (Class 4) (0-110,107) 4-Y-0+
£7,247 (£2,748; £1,374; £624; £312; £187)

Form RPR

45/0 **1** **Francies Fancy (IRE)**14 647 8-11-7 **102** JLCullen 123+
(J J Lambe, Ire) *hld up: smooth hdwy after 2 out: rdn to ld appr last: kpt on wl* **6/1**2

4-5U **2** *6* **Bill's Echo**8 714 6-10-10 **94** LMcGrath(3) 109+
(R C Guest) *hld up: hdwy 1/2-way: led briefly between last two: kpt on: no ch w wnr* **11/2**1

261U **3** *6* **Lone Soldier (FR)**11 681 9-9-13 **87** CDSharkey(7) 95
(S B Clark) *prom: rdn after 2 out: kpt on fr last: nt rch first two* **12/1**

00-5 **4** *3 1/2* **Mr Lear (USA)**22 552 6-11-6 **106** (v1) DCCostello(5) 111
(J J Quinn) *prom: drvn and disp ld between last two: one pce* **16/1**

1451 **5** *4* **Royal Glen (IRE)**22 551 7-10-7 **88** RMcGrath 89
(W S Colthered) *hld up: hdwy to chse ldrs between last two: wknd bef last* **7/1**3

3065 **6** *13* **Mister Moussac**39 304 6-10-10 **91** (p) GLee 79
(Miss Kariana Key) *prom tl rdn and outpcd after 2 out: n.d after* **12/1**

0-P0 **7** *nk* **Conor's Pride (IRE)**8 716 8-10-9 **90** NPMulholland 77
(B Mactaggart) *mde most to between last two: sn btn* **50/1**

5125 **8** *4* **In Good Faith**8 716 13-10-2 **83** RWalford 66
(R E Barr) *midfield: lost pl 1/2-way: n.d after* **14/1**

23-0 **9** *1 1/2* **Brave Effect (IRE)**11 689 9-10-10 **98** SGagan(7) 80
(Mrs Dianne Sayer) *prom to 2 out: sn lost pl* **20/1**

0-01 **10** *3* **Acceleration (IRE)**32 406 5-10-6 **87** (t) ADobbin 66
(R Allan) *hld up in tch: drvn 2 out: sn btn* **11/2**1

0-0P **11** *nk* **Valuable (IRE)**26 480 8-10-0 **81** oh1 KJohnson 59
(R Johnson) *sn wl bhd: nvr on terms* **33/1**

5453 **12** *1/2* **Merryvale Man**26 482 8-11-3 **103** DMcGann(5) 81
(Miss Kariana Key) *in tch to 3 out: sn wknd* **20/1**

34-3 **13** *4* **Nocatee (IRE)**22 552 4-11-5 **103** (p) FKeniry 74
(P C Haslam) *chsd ldrs: reminders and lost pl 1/2-way: sn n.d* **11/2**1

F-53 **14** *13* **Spree Vision**4 647 9-10-5 **96** (v) DDaSilva(10) 57
(P Monteith) *hld up: hdwy and prom 1/2-way: weaklened between last two* **25/1**

U0P- **F** **Garw Valley**179 2939 6-9-12 **86** MrSRees(7) —
(M Wigham) *hld up: fell 3 out* **33/1**

0-52 **P** **Feanor**22 551 7-11-9 **107** (t) KJMercer(3) —
(Mrs S A Watt) *bhd: hmpd 3 out: p.u next* **8/1**

/22- **P** **Sandabar**390 495 12-10-2 **83** DO'Meara —
(N Waggott) *keen: cl up tl wknd 2 out: t.o whn p.u bef last* **20/1**

164- **P** **Tunes Of Glory (IRE)**64 4867 9-11-3 **103** StephenJCraine(5) —
(D McCain) *in tch to 1/2-way: sn lost pl: p.u after 2 out* **33/1**

3m 57.8s (-17.40) **Going Correction** -0.90s/f (Hard) course record
WFA 4 from 5yo+ 3lb **18** Ran SP% **140.9**
Speed ratings: **104,101,98,96,94 88,88,86,85,84 84,84,82,76,—** —,—,— CSF £41.13 CT £418.69 TOTE £9.20: £2.70, £2.40, £3.80, £3.00; EX 125.60.
Owner Mike Futter **Bred** Michael Munnelly **Trained** Dungannon, Co. Tyrone

FOCUS
A run-of-the-mill handicap in which the pace was only fair. the third and fourth were to their marks and the form should work out.

NOTEBOOK
Francies Fancy(IRE), back on a sound surface, justified the market support to win in authoritative fashion but, given his recent record is one of inconsistency, may not be one to take too short a price about next time. *(op 8-1)*
Bill's Echo, back over hurdles from a much lower mark, showed enough on ground he handles to suggest a similar event can be found this summer. *(op 6-1)*
Lone Soldier(FR) had conditions to suit and ran creditably but left the impression that a stiffer test of stamina over this trip would have been to his liking. *(op 11-1)*
Mr Lear(USA), who is back on a fair mark, ran creditably but was another that left the impression that a stiffer test of stamina would have suited.
Royal Glen(IRE), a dual course and distance winner, was not disgraced back at her favourite *course but is likely to look vulnerable to progressive or well-handicapped types from this mark. (op 8-1)*
Mister Moussac, who has not won for a year, was again below his best and his form is far too patchy at present for him to be a reliable betting proposition.

785 TOTESPORTCASINO.COM NOVICES' HURDLE (8 hdls 2 omitted) 2m 4f 110y
4:50 (4:52) (Class 4) 4-Y-0+ £3,391 (£969; £484)

Form RPR

1 **Fourth Dimension (IRE)**82 6-10-12 KRenwick 86+
(D Nicholls) *chsd clr ldrs: smooth hdwy to ld bef last: r.o wl* **11/4**1

-00P **2** *8* **Thepubhorse**20 591 5-10-7 DCCostello(5) 76
(Mrs H O Graham) *chsd clr ldr: led after 5th to bef last: kpt on same pce* **25/1**

3 *21* **True Temper (IRE)**133 8-10-0 77 DMcGann(5) 48
(A M Crow) *in tch: outpcd 3 out: no imp after next* **16/1**

-00P **4** *dist* **The Rooken (IRE)**14 643 6-10-5 GThomas(7) —
(P Spottiswood) *hmpd 1st: nvr on terms* **50/1**

00-6 **5** *3 1/2* **Moments Madness (IRE)**14 645 6-10-5 KJohnson —
(Miss S E Forster) *midfield: wknd fr 1/2-way* **16/1**

0-1 **F** **Poor Tactic's (IRE)**39 306 9-11-5 JLCullen —
(J J Lambe, Ire) *fell 1st* **11/4**1

-00P **P** **Hapthor**11 687 6-10-9 ow4 DVerco —
(F Jestin) *a bhd: t.o whn p.u bef last* **33/1**

06/P **U** **Lady Lola (IRE)**8 715 7-11-4 ow20 MrNSSaville(7) —
(Miss J E Foster) *led tl j. awkwardly and uns rdr 1st* **40/1**

P **Whisky In The Jar (IRE)** 4-10-1 MJMcAlister(7) —
(S J Marshall) *hmpd 1st: a bhd: mstke 4th: p.u after next* **11/1**3

P-65 **P** **High Class Pet**8 715 5-10-5 83 ADobbin —
(F P Murtagh) *hld up: wknd fr 3 out: t.o whn p.u bef last* **9/1**2

1P-P **P** **Just Sooty**25 497 10-10-5 95 CDSharkey(7) —
(S B Clark) *led and clr: hdd after 5th: sn btn: p.u between last two* **11/4**1

4m 59.9s (-9.70) **Going Correction** -0.90s/f (Hard)
WFA 4 from 5yo+ 4lb **11** Ran SP% **121.3**
Speed ratings: **82,78,70,—,—** —,—,—,—,— — CSF £80.96 TOTE £3.50: £1.40, £8.00, £3.50; EX 55.30 Place 6 £84.79, Place 5 £79.03.
Owner The McCauley Boys **Bred** Milton Park Stud Partnership **Trained** Sessay, N Yorks

FOCUS
A race lacking any strength, but even though the gallop was sound throughout the winning time was over five seconds slower than the conditional jockeys' event over the same trip.

NOTEBOOK
Fourth Dimension(IRE), a fair staying handicapper at best on the Flat, had conditions to suit and the race teed up for him on this hurdles debut. What he achieved is debatable but he could do no more than win easily and is entitled to improve for the experience. *(op 3-1 tchd 2-1)*
Thepubhorse ran easily his best race over hurdles in a contest lacking any strength, and his future surely lies in low-grade handicaps. *(op 14-1)*
True Temper(IRE) is a poor and inconsistent hurdler whose proximity is further confirmation that this bare form is modest at best and, although not disgraced, is likely to continue to look vulnerable in this grade. *(op 10-1)*
The Rooken(IRE) showed nothing in the face of a stiff task. *(tchd 66-1)*
Moments Madness(IRE) will be suited by the step into low-grade handicaps in due course. *Official explanation: jockey said mare finished distressed (op 12-1)*
Just Sooty, disappointing over fences on his last two starts, did too much too soon back over hurdles on this first start for his new stable but he does not look one to place much faith in at present. *(op 4-1)*
T/Plt: £4,974.30 to a £1 stake. Pool: £43,951.05. 6.45 winning tickets. T/Qpdt: £2,044.50 to a £1 stake. Pool: £2,762.90. 0.80 winning tickets. RY

786 - 800a (Foreign Racing) - See Raceform Interactive

748 NEWTON ABBOT (L-H)
Tuesday, June 21

OFFICIAL GOING: Good to firm (good in places)
Wind: nil Weather: fine

801 HERALD EXPRESS LADIES DAY H'CAP HURDLE (10 hdls) 2m 6f
6:40 (6:40) (Class 4) (0-95,96) 4-Y-0+ £2,716 (£776; £388)

Form RPR

6-03 **1** **Taranai (IRE)**23 568 4-11-0 **85** (t) APMcCoy 86
(B W Duke) *hld up towards rr: hdwy after 6th: led sn after 2 out: r.o wl* **12/1**

-5U3 **2** *3* **Great Compton**27 506 5-10-4 **76** LStephens(5) 78
(B J Llewellyn) *hld up towards rr: hdwy after 6th: led after 3 out tl sn after 2 out: swtchd rt jst bef last: one pce* **6/1**3

64-5 **3** *1 1/2* **Vivante (IRE)**46 206 7-10-6 **73** WMarston 74
(A J Wilson) *chsd ldrs: rdn after 6th: one pce fr 2 out* **7/1**

4-51 **4** *shd* **Lutea (IRE)**15 668 5-11-12 **93** TJMurphy 93
(M C Pipe) *plld hrd in rr: stdy hdwy appr 7th: rdn appr 2 out: one pce* **7/2**1

41-4 **5** *10* **Timidjar (IRE)**13 681 12-10-7 **77** ONelmes(3) 67
(Mrs D Thomas) *hld up and bhd: hdwy after 3 out: no further prog fr 2 out* **17/2**

044- **6** *2 1/2* **Moorlands Return**165 3263 6-11-11 **92** (p) ChristianWilliams 80
(Evan Williams) *prom: reminders after 4th: rdn after 6th: wknd appr 2 out* **5/1**2

-0U0 **7** *3/4* **Court Award (IRE)**14 673 8-10-9 **76** JTizzard 63
(B G Powell) *led: hdd after 3 out: wknd 2 out* **40/1**

-045 **8** *nk* **Cotswold Rose**17 629 5-10-8 **80** TJPhelan(5) 67
(N M Babbage) *towards rr: rdn after 3rd: short-lived effrt after 3 out* **20/1**

6-63 **9** *1 3/4* **Earcomesannie (IRE)**13 679 5-9-13 **71** TGreenway(5) 56
(P A Pritchard) *hld up in tch: rdn and wknd appr 2 out* **12/1**

-040 **10** *8* **Charm Offensive**15 665 7-10-5 **75** ow5 (v) RHobson(3) 52
(C J Gray) *a bhd* **33/1**

PP6- **11** *15* **Goss Hawk (NZ)**85 4621 5-11-9 **90** JEMoore 52
(Jonjo O'Neill) *hld up in mid-div: hdwy 5th: rdn after 3 out: wkng whn mstke 2 out* **25/1**

-036 **12** *dist* **Ashgan (IRE)**23 565 12-10-8 **75** RGreene —
(Dr P Pritchard) *w ldrs: rdn appr 5th: wknd appr 7th: t.o* **33/1**

/0-0 **P** **Big Quick (IRE)**27 502 10-11-2 **90** MrJMorgan(7) —
(L Wells) *bhd fr 7th: t.o whn p.u bef 2 out* **33/1**

P23- **P** **Sundawn Lady**62 4929 7-10-13 **80** (b) MBradburne —
(C P Morlock) *prom tl wknd after 6th: t.o whn p.u bef 2 out* **9/1**

P0-0 **P** **Court Empress**19 613 8-10-1 **75** JamesWhite(7) —
(P D Purdy) *hld up in tch: rdn and wknd appr 5th: t.o whn p.u bef 2 out* **66/1**

5m 13.0s (-7.30) **Going Correction** -0.30s/f (Good)
WFA 4 from 5yo+ 4lb **15** Ran SP% **122.9**
Speed ratings: **101,99,99,99,95 94,94,94,93,90 85,—,—,—,—** CSF £79.17 CT £559.07 TOTE £11.10: £2.80, £3.70, £2.40; EX 155.50.
Owner The Southern Lights **Bred** J Davison **Trained** Lambourn, Berks

FOCUS
A very modest handicap, but with the runner-up and fourth close to their marks the for appears solid.

NOTEBOOK
Taranai(IRE), who shaped with promise at Fontwell yet was another 2lb lower here, showed the right attitude. She goes well on fast ground and this step up in trip suited her. *(op 10-1)*
Great Compton took it up on the home turn, but wandered in front and was collared after the second last. He is running well since the Handicapper has given him a chance but he is not a straightforward ride. *(op 7-1 tchd 15-2)*
Vivante(IRE) had ground and trip to suit and turned in another solid effort from a pound lower mark. *(op 15-2 tchd 13-2)*
Lutea(IRE) was back up in class having landed a seller last time. Taking a tug in rear through the early part of the race, he closed going well to reach the heels of the leaders but had no more to offer from the second last. This trip just found him out. *(op 4-1)*
Timidjar(IRE) ran respectably back over this more suitable trip but was beaten before the home turn. *(op 9-1 tchd 8-1)*
Moorlands Return, off the track since January, was the subject of support in the ring on this handicap debut and first run since leaving Colin Tizzard's yard. Wearing cheekpieces for the first *time, he was being pushed along from some way out and may well need easier ground. (op 6-1 tchd 13-2)*
Court Award(IRE), back over hurdles, cut out the running until collared going into the final turn. *(op 33-1)*
Goss Hawk(NZ), without the tongue tie for this first run since March, was close enough three from home but soon faded out of contention. *(op 20-1)*
Court Empress *Official explanation: vet said mare bled from nose (op 50-1)*

802 HOOPERS NOVICES' HURDLE (9 hdls 1 omitted) 2m 6f
7:10 (7:11) (Class 3) 4-Y-0+ £5,421 (£1,668; £834; £417)

Form RPR

3 **1** **Time Bandit (IRE)**17 629 5-11-0 TJMurphy 96+
(M C Pipe) *hld up and bhd: hdwy 3 out: led 2 out: hung rt and lft clr last: r.o* **5/2**2

0 **2** *10* **Colony Hill (IRE)**27 504 7-11-0 BHitchcott 86
(R H Buckler) *hld up in mid-div: hdwy appr 7th: wkng whn lft 2nd last* **33/1**

2-23 **3** *6* **Thomo (IRE)**17 635 7-11-0 100 MBatchelor 80
(N E Berry) *prom: rdn after 6th: wknd after 3 out* **4/1**3

4 *9* **Cherrywood (IRE)**44 6-11-0 (vt1) JEMoore 71
(M C Pipe) *mde most: hit 3rd: rdn appr 5th: hdd after 3 out: sn wknd* **7/1**

PP-0 **5** *26* **Saposcat (IRE)**[7] 743 5-10-7 ..... MrDavidTurner(7) 45
(Dr P Pritchard) *t.k.h: prom tl wknd 6th* **100/1**
0-55 **6** *10* **Cracow (IRE)**[7] 745 8-11-0 75 ..... (b) CLlewellyn 35
(W K Goldsworthy) *bhd fr 6th: sn lost tch* **14/1**
R/ **U** **Sutton Lion**[551] 2818 13-10-7 ..... JamesWhite(7) —
(P D Purdy) *tried to refuse and uns rdr 1st* **100/1**
032- **P** **Cedar Rangers (USA)**[357] 833 7-10-9 86 ow2 ..... MrDEdwards(7) —
(G F Edwards) *t.k.h in rr: hdwy 6th: prom whn p.u lame bef 3 out* **16/1**
P/2 **U** **Rebelle**[17] 635 6-11-0 ..... APMcCoy 94
(P Bowen) *w ldr: n.m.r after 3 out: sn led: hdd 2 out: 1 l down whn sltly hmpd and blnd and uns rdr last* **7/4**[1]

5m 19.4s (-0.90) **Going Correction** -0.30s/f (Good) **9** Ran SP% **114.9**
Speed ratings: **89,85,83,79,70 66**,—,—,— CSF £63.65 TOTE £2.50: £1.40, £9.60, £1.30; EX 116.30.
Owner D A Johnson **Bred** Miss Mary Murphy **Trained** Nicholashayne, Devon
■ A winner on his first day back for Timmy Murphy, who broke his arm at Punchestown on April 26th.

FOCUS
Aa moderate event but the pace only really lifted on the final circuit and the time was very moderate time for the grade, 6.4 seconds slower than the opener and the form looks dubious. The fourth last flight was bypassed.

NOTEBOOK
Time Bandit(IRE) ◆ did well to win this, as he is a big gelding who was not suited by this sharp track. He appeared held turning out of the back straight, but stayed on to lead at the second last and was left clear after jumping across his nearest pursuer at the final flight. Well regarded by connections, who landed the last two runnings of this event with Therealbandit and Vodka Bleu, he is one to keep on the right side. *(op 7-2 tchd 9-4)*
Colony Hill(IRE) showed a considerable improvement on his hurdles debut a month ago and only cried enough between the final two flights. He was fortunate to pick up second prize, however. *(op 25-1)*
Thomo(IRE) made the frame again but does look a limited performer. *(op 6-1)*
Cherrywood(IRE) was sold for 15,000 euros after a string of placed runs in Irish point-to-points. A stablemate of the winner, visored for this debut under Rules, he made much of the running but was quickly beaten once headed after the third from home. *(tchd 8-1)*
Cedar Rangers(USA) was close enough when appearing to go wrong in the back straight. *(op 11-1)*
Rebelle ran a good race, but appeared held in second when blundering away his rider at the final flight when unsighted by the winner. He should be capable of finding compensation. *(op 11-1)*

803 BOYCE HATTON NOVICES' CHASE (13 fncs) 2m 110y
7:40 (7:40) (Class 3) 5-Y-0+ **£6,119** (£1,882; £941; £470)

Form RPR
603- **1** **One Cornetto (IRE)**[73] 4777 6-11-1 ..... LAspell 124+
(L Wells) *hld up: hdwy 7th: led on bit after 3 out: rdn clr appr last: drvn out* **11/1**
60-U **2** *11* **Mister Flint**[30] 459 7-11-1 ..... RJohnson 113
(P J Hobbs) *led to 6th: led 7th: hdd after 3 out: one pce* **4/1**[3]
500- **3** *3 ½* **Nawamees (IRE)**[17] 4438 7-11-1 ..... APMcCoy 109
(G L Moore) *hld up: hdwy 7th: hrd rdn appr 4 out: lft 3rd 3 out: one pce* **11/4**[2]
6-34 **4** *15* **Papillon De Iena (FR)**[7] 750 5-11-0 ..... JEMoore 93
(M C Pipe) *chsd ldr: led 6th to 7th: rdn appr 9th: wknd appr 4 out* **16/1**
5 **5** *4* **Pharshu (IRE)**[6] 763 8-10-1 ..... (t) MrJSnowden(7) 83
(C L Tizzard) *bhd: hit 6th: nvr nr ldrs* **50/1**
-F06 **6** *5* **Riccarton**[7] 752 12-11-1 72 ..... (t) RGreene 85
(D C Turner) *wl bhd fr 6th* **66/1**
335- **7** *dist* **Artane Boys**[210] 2410 8-11-1 105 ..... MAFitzgerald —
(Jonjo O'Neill) *hld up: nt fluent 3rd: struggling whn mstke 7th: t.o* **8/1**
0-3F **F** **Gin 'N' Fonic (IRE)**[25] 532 5-10-7 90 ..... SWalsh(7) —
(J D Frost) *last whn fell 3rd* **16/1**
63-F **F** **Fontanesi (IRE)**[45] 208 5-11-0 ..... TJMurphy 108
(M C Pipe) *hld up: hdwy appr 8th: 4 l 3rd whn fell 3 out (water)* **13/8**[1]

4m 3.60s (-1.90) **Going Correction** -0.125s/f (Good)
WFA 5 from 6yo+ 1lb **9** Ran SP% **119.4**
Speed ratings: **99,93,92,85,83 80**,—,—,— CSF £57.87 TOTE £18.60: £2.90, £2.20, £1.30; EX 61.60.
Owner Mrs Carrie Zetter-Wells **Bred** Mrs Mary Phelan **Trained** Wisborough Green, W Sussex

FOCUS
Quite a competitive novice chase for this time of year, and although the winner was impressive the form is held down by the fifth and sixth.

NOTEBOOK
One Cornetto(IRE) had plenty to find with some of these on hurdles ratings, but he scored in good style and is going to make a better chaser than he was a hurdler. He likes fast ground and he looks well capable of winning again. *(tchd 12-1)*
Mister Flint, reverting to front-running tactics for this second crack at fences, jumped pretty well but was a spent force once headed. He is capable of landing a small race over fences. *(op 6-1)*
Nawamees(IRE) made a respectable enough chasing debut, keeping on after starting to struggle in the back straight. He wore cheekpieces last time over hurdles and on a recent spin on the Flat, and may need the headgear again. *(op 2-1)*
Papillon De Iena(FR), ridden more prominently than on his two previous attempts over fences, ran better than he had on this track a week earlier but still has plenty to prove. *(op 14-1)*
Artane Boys, out of action since his chasing debut back in November, steadily lost his pitch after a third-fence error. *(op 7-1)*
Fontanesi(IRE), winner of the County Hurdle in March and rated 136 over the smaller obstacles, jumped well enough on this chase debut but was under pressure and appeared held when coming down at the water jump, three from home. He does lack a bit of scope for fences. *(op 2-1 tchd 9-4 and 6-4)*

804 DARTINGTON TECH WOMEN ON TOP NOVICES' HURDLE (8 hdls) 2m 1f
8:15 (8:16) (Class 3) 4-Y-0+ **£5,538** (£1,704; £852; £426)

Form RPR
6-11 **1** **Buena Vista (IRE)**[16] 654 4-11-7 ..... APMcCoy 126+
(M C Pipe) *mde all: clr appr last: easily* **2/13**[1]
55 **2** *5* **Convent Girl (IRE)**[23] 574 5-10-2 ..... RYoung(3) 95
(Mrs P N Dutfield) *hld up: hdwy appr 5th: chsd wnr appr 2 out: no imp* **12/1**[2]
2P-0 **3** *19* **Native Chancer (IRE)**[12] 696 5-10-12 ..... MAFitzgerald 83
(Jonjo O'Neill) *hld up in tch: rdn and wknd appr 2 out* **20/1**
40 **4** *hd* **Alekhine (IRE)**[9] 729 4-10-9 ..... RJohnson 80
(P J Hobbs) *hld up: j.lft 3rd: hdwy appr 5th: hit 3 out: rdn and wknd appr 2 out* **14/1**[3]
P **5** *dist* **Duke's View (IRE)**[7] 748 4-10-9 ..... RGreene —
(D C Turner) *a bhd: t.o fr 5th* **100/1**
0F-P **6** *24* **Thespian Lady**[44] 243 4-9-11 ..... MNicolls(5) —
(Mrs A J Hamilton-Fairley) *prom to 4th: t.o* **66/1**
F **Don Argento**[309] 4-10-9 ..... ATinkler —
(Mrs A J Bowlby) *last whn fell 3rd* **50/1**

00/5 **P** **Saxon Kingdom**[25] 531 6-10-5 ..... JBunsell(7) —
(M Bradstock) *prom tl wknd appr 5th: t.o whn p.u bef 2 out* **100/1**
P **Big Tom (IRE)**[255] 4-10-9 ..... JamesDavies —
(B G Powell) *plld hrd: hdwy after 2nd: rdn and wknd qckly after 4th: t.o whn p.u bef 5th* **50/1**

3m 57.9s (-7.20) **Going Correction** -0.30s/f (Good) **9** Ran SP% **113.2**
Speed ratings: **104,101,92,92**,— —,—,—,— CSF £2.52 TOTE £1.10: £1.10, £1.10, £1.60; EX 3.00.
Owner M Archer & The Late Jean Broadhurst **Bred** Lodge Park Stud **Trained** Nicholashayne, Devon

FOCUS
An uncompetitive event and another easy winner, value for three times the official margin.

NOTEBOOK
Buena Vista(IRE) made it three from three over hurdles with another effortless success. Now likely to be given a break before coming back in the autumn, he can handle a step up in class. *(op 2-11)*
Convent Girl(IRE) had little problem picking off the eventual third and fourth rounding the home turn but the winner proved much too good for her. She is now eligible for a mark and it will be interesting to see how literal an interpretation the handicapper takes of this form. *(op 14-1)*
Native Chancer(IRE), who showed little on two previous tries over hurdles, was well held in the end but did get the better of a duel for third spot. *(tchd 25-1)*
Alekhine(IRE) appeared third best on merit but was pipped for that placing on the line. He is not coming up to expectations but is now qualified for handicaps. *(op 16-1 tchd 12-1)*

805 YEARS YOUNGER H'CAP CHASE (16 fncs) 2m 5f 110y
8:45 (8:46) (Class 4) (0-105,104) 5-Y-0+ **£4,807** (£1,479; £739; £369)

Form RPR
0-21 **1** **Maidstone Monument (IRE)**[27] 503 10-10-3 81 ..... RJohnson 98+
(Mrs A M Thorpe) *mde all: rdn clr 2 out: r.o wl* **7/2**[2]
32P- **2** *9* **Sunshan**[310] 1193 9-10-8 86 ..... RGreene 93
(R J Hodges) *a.p: chsd wnr appr 11th: sn rdn: no imp fr 3 out* **33/1**
4-03 **3** *3 ½* **Fear Siuil (IRE)**[16] 653 12-11-7 99 ..... (t) DRDennis 103
(Nick Williams) *hld up in mid-div: hdwy 8th: one pce fr 3 out* **9/1**
0502 **4** *2* **Eau Pure (FR)**[13] 684 8-10-13 91 ..... (t) JEMoore 93
(G L Moore) *hld up in mid-div: hdwy 8th: rdn and one pce fr 4 out* **9/1**
5-21 **5** *15* **Alcatras (IRE)**[17] 632 8-9-11 78 oh1 ..... ONelmes(3) 65
(B J M Ryall) *nvr nr ldrs* **9/2**[3]
2612 **6** *1 ¾* **Borehill Joker**[23] 565 9-10-8 86 ..... AThornton 71
(Miss K M George) *hld up in mid-div: hdwy whn mstke 12th: no further prog* **16/1**
0-06 **7** *4* **Jumpty Dumpty (FR)**[14] 673 8-10-0 78 ..... (t) JMogford 59
(J C Tuck) *hld up and bhd: sme hdwy 9th: j.rt 10th: sn struggling* **16/1**
2-2P **8** *15* **Phar City (IRE)**[27] 505 8-11-4 96 ..... BHitchcott 62
(R H Buckler) *prom to 11th* **25/1**
0UP- **9** *21* **Jabiru (IRE)**[31] 12-11-5 104 ..... (b) MrDEdwards(7) 49
(Mrs K M Sanderson) *chsd wnr: j.lft 2nd: lost 2nd 10th: sn wknd: t.o* **33/1**
4-06 **10** *8* **Lahinch Lad (IRE)**[14] 672 5-10-13 93 ..... JamesDavies 28
(B G Powell) *hld up in mid-div: bhd whn rdn appr 10th: t.o* **40/1**
P6P0 **P** **Sportsfield Coogee (IRE)**[12] 696 6-9-8 79 ow1 ..... (b[1]) DJacob(7) —
(D P Keane) *a bhd: hmpd 3rd: t.o whn p.u bef 12th* **100/1**
-25P **P** **Jivaty (FR)**[15] 669 8-11-2 94 ..... ATinkler —
(Mrs A J Hamilton-Fairley) *a bhd: rdn appr 5th: t.o whn p.u bef 4 out* **50/1**
644- **F** **River Quoile**[17] 9-10-1 79 ..... RWalford —
(R H Alner) *hld up in tch: rdn appr 11th: sn wknd: no ch whn fell last* **25/1**
U/-2 **P** **Romantic Hero (IRE)**[44] 240 9-10-9 87 ..... (b) APMcCoy —
(C R Egerton) *prom: n.m.r 2nd: mstke 9th: wknd 11th: t.o whn p.u bef 2 out* **10/3**[1]
54-1 **P** **Excellent Vibes (IRE)**[7] 746 7-10-12 90 7ex ..... CLlewellyn —
(N A Twiston-Davies) *hld up towards rr: mstke 3rd: sn struggling: t.o whn p.u bef 12th* **5/1**

5m 15.5s (-7.20) **Going Correction** -0.125s/f (Good)
WFA 5 from 6yo+ 2lb **15** Ran SP% **130.9**
Speed ratings: **108,104,103,102,97 96,95,89,82,79** —,—,—,—,— CSF £122.32 CT £1020.98 TOTE £4.80: £2.30, £8.10, £2.40; EX 103.70.
Owner Don Jenkins **Bred** Louis Lanigan **Trained** Bronwydd Arms, Carmarthens

FOCUS
A fair time for the class, the winner setting a decent pace and capable of better, with the runner-up setting the standard.

NOTEBOOK
Maidstone Monument(IRE) made all at a sound pace and stayed on really strongly. He went up 10lb for his recent Fontwell victory, but has won off no less than 20lb higher than this in the past and he can score again if allowed his own way up front. *(op 9-2)*
Sunshan chased the winner throughout the final circuit but was unable to get past him. This was an encouraging return to action on his first run since August. *(op 25-1)*
Fear Siuil(IRE) is slipping down the handicap and this was a decent run, although after moving into third spot with six to jump he was unable to make any real impression on the two in front of him. *(op 8-1 tchd 10-1)*
Eau Pure(FR), who had the tongue tie back on, was held with four to jump. She is a winner over fences in France but this was only her second run in a chase over here. *(op 12-1)*
Alcatras(IRE), put up 9lb after winning at Worcester, was never in the hunt. *(op 5-1)*
Excellent Vibes(IRE), under a 7lb penalty, was soon in trouble after an early mistake. He found *things happening too quickly for him and needs further.Official explanation: jockey said gelding ran flat and race may had come too soon for it - ran seven days previous (tchd 9-2)*
Romantic Hero(IRE), who made a promising return to the track at Uttoxeter, ran well enough up to *a point but dropped out of contention in the back straight. He needs three miles plusOfficial explanation: trainer said gelding lost both hind shoes and was lame behind (tchd 9-2)*
Jivaty(FR) *Official explanation: jockey said gelding had a breathing problem (tchd 9-2)*

806 WELLYBUTE H'CAP HURDLE (7 hdls 1 omitted) 2m 1f
9:15 (9:16) (Class 4) (0-105,102) 4-Y-0+ **£3,452** (£1,062; £531; £265)

Form RPR
634- **1** **Englishtown (FR)**[199] 2636 5-11-9 96 ..... APMcCoy 105+
(Jonjo O'Neill) *hld up and bhd: smooth hdwy after 5th: led 2 out: rdn out* **11/4**[2]
0U05 **2** *1 ¾* **Saorsie**[25] 536 7-11-3 95 ..... RStephens(5) 100
(J C Fox) *hld up: hdwy 5th: rdn and ev ch 2 out: nt qckn* **12/1**
0-32 **3** *hd* **Not Amused (UAE)**[6] 760 5-10-6 79 ..... (v) DRDennis 84
(Ian Williams) *hld up: hdwy appr 5th: led briefly appr 2 out: rdn and nt qckn* **9/4**[1]
000- **4** *19* **Isleofhopeantears (IRE)**[9] 4442 6-9-7 73 oh6 ..... MrTJO'Brien(7) 62+
(A E Jones) *t.k.h: a.p: led appr 5th tl appr 2 out: sn wknd* **25/1**
P-0P **5** *3 ½* **Mevagissey (BEL)**[26] 514 8-10-7 80 ..... ChristianWilliams 62
(J D Frost) *hld up in mid-div: hdwy appr 5th: wknd appr 2 out* **25/1**
-S62 **6** *1 ¾* **Blues Story (FR)**[15] 668 7-10-9 87 ..... (t) MNicolls(5) 68
(N G Ayliffe) *led to 2nd: wknd appr 5th: wl btn whn mstke 2 out* **25/1**
33-3 **7** *26* **Classic Croco (GER)**[42] 279 4-11-12 102 ..... (b[1]) SThomas 54
(Mrs Jeremy Young) *prom tl rdn and wknd after 5th* **8/1**

21-P **8** *3 ½* **Jayed (IRE)**[36] 389 7-10-12 **92** .... JBunsell(7) 43
(M Bradstock) *t.k.h: led 2nd tl hdd and slipped bnd appr 5th: wknd rapidly* **20/1**
3-12 **9** *29* **Wardash (GER)**[7] 753 5-11-0 **87** .... (vt) TJMurphy 9
(M C Pipe) *a bhd: t.o* **7/2**[3]
/P-P **P** **Loramore**[49] 167 8-10-0 **73** oh2 .... RWalford —
(J C Tuck) *a bhd: t.o whn p.u after 4th* **50/1**
0-45 **P** **Club Royal**[7] 749 8-10-7 **80** .... (p) JamesDavies —
(N E Berry) *hld up: rdn after 4th: sn bhd: t.o whn p.u bef 2 out* **16/1**

3m 57.8s (-7.30) **Going Correction** -0.30s/f (Good) **11** Ran SP% **122.6**
Speed ratings: **105,104,104,95,93 92,80,78,65,— —** CSF £33.33 CT £89.21 TOTE £4.10: £2.20, £2.90, £1.10; EX 30.30 Place 6 £62.28, Place 5 £19.66..
Owner John P McManus **Bred** Darley Stud Management Co Ltd **Trained** Cheltenham, Gloucs

FOCUS
This moderate handicap was run at a sound pace. The winner was value for a bit further and, with those in the frame behind close to their marks, the form looks solid. The third last flight was bypassed as it was damaged.

NOTEBOOK
Englishtown(FR), having his first outing for six months, ran out a comfortable winner. He obviously goes well on fast ground and, still a novice, there should be plenty of options for him in the coming weeks. *(op 3-1 tchd 5-2)*
Saorsie was one of three in line at the second last but could not quicken up. He has put in a couple of better efforts of late and he was a winner off 5lb higher than this at Towcester in the autumn. *(op 11-1 tchd 10-1)*
Not Amused(UAE) struck the front on the turn into the home straight but was quickly tackled and did not find a great deal. He is running well at present but might not be one to place too much faith in. *(op 3-1 tchd 10-3)*
Isleofhopeanteears(IRE), quickly beaten once collared leaving the back straight, was third on the Flat in Jersey eaerlier this month. *(op 20-1)*
Jayed(IRE) *Official explanation: jockey said gelding slipped on bend turning into back straight (op 16-1)*
Wardash(GER), soon niggled along in rear, made a short-lived effort going to the fourth last. He looks held by the Handicapper. *Official explanation: jockey said gelding was never travelling*
T/Plt: £94.90 to a £1 stake. Pool: £49,836.65. 383.35 winning tickets. T/Qpdt: £10.00 to a £1 stake. Pool: £3,893.10. 288.00 winning tickets. KH

807 - 810a (Foreign Racing) - See Raceform Interactive

758 WORCESTER (L-H)
Wednesday, June 22

OFFICIAL GOING: Good to firm (firm in home straight on hurdle course)
Almost unbroken sunshine meant the ground was quickening throughout the afternoon.
Wind: Nil Weather: Warm and sunny

811 WINTERFOLD HOUSE SCHOOL NOVICES' HURDLE (8 hdls) 2m
2:30 (2:34) (Class 4) 4-Y-0+ **£3,419** (£1,052; £526; £263)

Form RPR
31 **1** **Rajayoga**[29] 485 4-11-4 .... LAspell 100
(M H Tompkins) *t.k.h towards rr: hdwy 5th: led and hit 2 out: drvn out* **5/4**[1]
-062 **2** *1* **Not To Be Missed**[20] 613 7-10-7 81 .... WHutchinson 88
(R Dickin) *uns rdr and bolted bef s: hld up: hdwy appr 4th: carried rt 3 out: rdn and ev ch last: nt qckn* **10/1**[3]
4 **3** *1 ¼* **Double Aspect (IRE)**[53] 133 4-10-11 .... APMcCoy 91
(Jonjo O'Neill) *w ldr: hrd rdn and hung lft appr 2 out: ev ch last: no ex towards fin* **7/4**[2]
4 *5* **Fleetwood Bay**[200] 5-11-0 .... JCulloty 89
(V R A Dartnall) *plld hrd: hdwy to ld after 2nd: j.rt 3 out: hdd 2 out: wkng whn j.rt last* **10/1**[3]
00-0 **5** *5* **Ice And Fire**[13] 696 6-11-0 86 .... (t) ChristianWilliams 84
(J T Stimpson) *hld up: hdwy and j.rt 3 out: wkng whn j.rt 2 out and last* **40/1**
41/0 **6** *8* **Cap Classique**[29] 490 6-11-0 .... RJohnson 76
(Mrs H Dalton) *led into s: hld up: hdwy 5th: rdn and wknd appr 3 out* **20/1**
3/50 **7** *15* **Optimism (FR)**[18] 629 7-11-0 .... AThornton 61
(R H Alner) *led tl after 2nd: prom tl wknd 5th* **80/1**
4P04 **8** *19* **Simiola**[10] 729 6-10-4 63 .... DCrosse(3) 35
(S T Lewis) *pckd 1st: a bhd* **40/1**
P-0 **9** *dist* **Casisle**[24] 569 4-9-11 .... CMStudd(7) —
(Mary Meek) *prom tl wknd 4th: t.o* **150/1**
00 **P** **Irish Playwright (IRE)**[13] 696 5-11-0 .... RThornton —
(D G Bridgwater) *hld up in tch: wknd 5th: bhd whn p.u bef 3 out* **100/1**

3m 43.0s (-5.40) **Going Correction** -0.425s/f (Good) **10** Ran SP% **111.5**
Speed ratings: **96,95,94,92,89 85,78,68,—,—** CSF £13.00 TOTE £2.40: £1.10, £2.70, £1.10; EX 12.30.
Owner Mystic Meg Limited **Bred** Mystic Meg Limited **Trained** Newmarket, Suffolk

FOCUS
This was quite competitive despite the fact the bookmakers went 10/1 bar two. The form looks fair and solid enough.

NOTEBOOK
Rajayoga is proving to be better over hurdles than he was on the Flat but had to work harder this time under a penalty for his course and distance win. He is now likely to switch to handicaps. *(op Evens tchd 11-8)*
Not To Be Missed ◆ completed a circuit of the course after getting rid of his rider on the way to the start. This was a fine effort in the circumstances and she deserves to go one better. *(op 9-1 tchd 11-1)*
Double Aspect(IRE) got run out of it in the closing stages after again looking to be not that straightforward. *(op 9-4)*
Fleetwood Bay, who won the six-furlong St Leger Yearling Stakes at two, never tackled beyond a mile for Rod Millman. Jumping right once the chips were down, he is going to have to learn to settle. *(op 12-1 tchd 14-1)*
Ice And Fire, fitted with a tongue strap, is another who did not help his cause by jumping right-handed in the home straight. *(op 28-1)*

812 JP SEAFOODS NOVICES' CHASE (18 fncs) 2m 7f 110y
3:00 (3:00) (Class 4) 5-Y-0+ **£4,134** (£1,272; £636; £318)

Form RPR
2-3U **1** **Good Man Again (IRE)**[7] 759 7-11-0 99 .... ChristianWilliams 89+
(Evan Williams) *hld up: hdwy 4 out: hrd rdn to ld last: drvn out* **5/1**[2]
-R3F **2** *1 ¾* **Althrey Dandy (IRE)**[10] 728 10-11-0 102 .... AThornton 85
(P T Dalton) *j.rt: prom: lost pl 6th: hdwy appr 10th: hit 14th: sn outpcd: rallied appr last: edgd lft last: styd on* **10/1**
35-4 **3** *hd* **Quizzling (IRE)**[14] 684 7-10-11 74 .... RYoung(3) 85
(B J M Ryall) *a.p: rdn to ld 2 out: hdd last: nt qckn* **9/1**[3]
P/3- **4** *5* **The Croppy Boy**[271] 1497 13-11-0 74 .... JMogford 80
(Mrs N S Evans) *led: j.rt 3 out: sn rdn: j.rt and hdd 2 out: wknd flat* **66/1**
1-35 **5** *2* **Kadam (IRE)**[8] 751 5-10-8 105 .... (b) RWalsh 73+
(P F Nicholls) *hld up: hdwy 11th: rdn and ev ch appr 2 out: sn wknd* **9/4**[1]
0/P0 **F** **Lovers Tale**[14] 681 7-10-7 80 .... EDehdashti(7) —
(G A Ham) *hld up and bhd: hit 13th: no ch whn fell 4 out* **80/1**
0-05 **P** **Jandal**[8] 750 11-10-7 71 .... TMessenger(7) —
(C L Popham) *prom to 5th: bhd whn rdn 8th: t.o whn mstke 11th: sn p.u* **80/1**
-4P5 **P** **Pams Oak**[17] 650 7-11-0 100 .... OMcPhail —
(P S Payne) *t.k.h: hdwy 4th: hit 7th: wknd 11th: t.o whn p.u after 14th* **14/1**
350- **P** **Harbour Bound (IRE)**[263] 1556 6-11-0 104 .... PMoloney —
(Evan Williams) *j. slowly 1st and 2nd: sn wl bhd: t.o whn p.u bef 8th* **14/1**
2-41 **P** **On The Outside (IRE)**[18] 631 6-10-7 105 .... (t) JTizzard —
(S E H Sherwood) *hld up in tch: ev ch appr 4 out: rdn and wknd appr 3 out: p.u bef 2 out* **9/4**[1]

5m 55.4s (0.50) **Going Correction** 0.0s/f (Good)
WFA 5 from 6yo+ 2lb **10** Ran SP% **114.6**
Speed ratings: **99,98,98,96,96 —,—,—,—,—** CSF £51.51 TOTE £5.40: £1.30, £3.30, £2.70; EX 51.80.
Owner Mrs D L O'Sullivan **Bred** Alan Inglis **Trained** Cowbridge, Vale Of Glamorgan

FOCUS
An ordinary novice chase with stamina still proving to be an issue despite the fast ground. The form could rate higher but the third and fourth limit confidence.

NOTEBOOK
Good Man Again(IRE), who stays well, put unseating his rider at the final ditch when possibly looking held here last week behind him. He finally got his act together on only his second outing over fences. *(op 7-1)*
Althrey Dandy(IRE) was inclined to jump a shade right-handed and edged over to the far rail on the run-in after finding a second wind.
Quizzling(IRE), who again came in for market support, turned in a decent performance especially considering he would have been 23lb and 26lb respectively better off with the first two in a handicap. *(op 16-1)*
The Croppy Boy, lightly-raced since winning a couple of points five years ago, jumped right when the chips were down on his first outing for nine months. *(op 50-1)*
Kadam(IRE), who improved over hurdles for the fitting of blinkers, gave the impression that this trip is beyond his best on this chasing debut. *(tchd 5-2)*
On The Outside(IRE) was reported by her jockey to have had a breathing problem. *Official explanation: jockey said mare had a breathing problem (op 15-8 tchd 5-2)*

813 RUPERT ANTON, "BIG BIRTHDAY" NOVICES' H'CAP HURDLE (10 hdls) 2m 4f
3:30 (3:33) (Class 4) (0-100,93) 4-Y-0+ **£3,510** (£1,080; £540; £270)

Form RPR
U00- **1** **Court One**[17] 2656 7-11-2 **83** .... WHutchinson 93
(R J Price) *hld up towards rr: stdy hdwy appr 6th: chal on bit appr 2 out: rdn and hung lft flat: r.o to ld post* **14/1**
11U4 **2** *shd* **Tinstre (IRE)**[7] 762 7-11-12 **93** .... SCurran 103
(P W Hiatt) *led 2nd to 5th: w ldr: led 7th: hrd rdn and edgd rt flat: hdd post* **12/1**
P-64 **3** *20* **Delphine**[29] 487 6-11-2 **83** .... JMMaguire 73
(T R George) *hld up in mid-div: lost pl 5th: hdwy whn n.m.r appr 3 out: wknd appr 2 out* **11/1**
-025 **4** *3* **Siena Star (IRE)**[24] 566 7-11-10 **91** .... RThornton 78
(P Bowen) *prom tl wknd appr 3 out* **5/1**[2]
F345 **5** *4* **Skibereen (IRE)**[8] 747 5-11-8 **89** .... (t) DRDennis 72
(Mrs A M Thorpe) *prom: led 5th to 7th: ev ch 3 out: wkng whn lft 3rd 2 out* **14/1**
0-4 **6** *26* **City Affair**[42] 295 4-10-11 **82** .... (p) JPMcNamara 35
(C J Down) *played up s: hld up and bhd: nvr nr ldrs* **14/1**
60-5 **7** *1 ¼* **Fairmorning (IRE)**[22] 237 6-10-3 **73** .... DCrosse(3) 29
(C N Kellett) *prom tl wknd appr 6th* **25/1**
0-20 **8** *8* **Virtus**[16] 664 5-11-1 **82** .... RJohnson 40+
(P J Hobbs) *prom: wkng whn hmpd 2 out* **9/1**
000- **9** *2* **Oscars Vision (IRE)**[94] 4484 5-11-6 **87** .... MAFitzgerald 33
(B W Duke) *led to 2nd: prom tl rdn and wknd 6th* **7/1**[3]
P **10** *1* **Liberty Boy (IRE)**[6] 767 7-11-0 **81** .... (b1) APMcCoy 26
(Jonjo O'Neill) *hld up in mid-div: rdn after 6th: wkng whn nt fluent and sddle slipped 3 out* **20/1**
604/ **P** **Red Tyrant**[23] 7-10-7 **81** .... (b1) DCosgrave(7) —
(R Flint) *bhd fr 4th: rdn 5th: t.o whn p.u after 7th* **40/1**
00/ **P** **Roscam**[557] 2748 8-10-9 **76** .... WMarston —
(G A Ham) *t.k.h in rr: hdwy after 4th: prom whn p.u after 7th* **8/1**
0-02 **F** **Gondolin (IRE)**[10] 724 5-10-13 **80** .... JEMoore 87
(G Brown) *hld up and bhd: hdwy 7th: 2 l 3rd and rdn whn fell 2 out* **5/2**[1]

4m 43.0s (-5.00) **Going Correction** -0.425s/f (Good)
WFA 4 from 5yo+ 4lb **13** Ran SP% **125.9**
Speed ratings: **93,92,84,83,82 71,71,68,67,66 —,—,—** CSF £175.03 CT £1943.71 TOTE £14.60: £6.70, £4.30, £3.50; EX 245.80.
Owner Derek & Cheryl Holder **Bred** Mrs C R Holder **Trained** Lugwardine, H'fords

FOCUS
The form could rate higher but a modest time for the grade in the conditions with the top weight only rated 93.

NOTEBOOK
Court One, fit from the Flat, stepped up on his previous form over hurdles and the more trouble he finds in a race the better according to his trainer. He did just manage to pull it out of the fire after *lugging in behind the second on the run-in.Official explanation: trainer said, regarding the improved form shown, gelding had benefited from the good to firm ground on this occasion*
Tinstre(IRE), who went up 13lb for his back-to-back victories last month, drew right away from the rest with the winner in the home straight. He did come off a true line in the closing stages but *hardly deserved to be pipped on the line.Official explanation: owner said gelding lost a front plate after last*
Delphine, switching to handicaps, appeared to have plenty of weight for what she has actually achieved and has also yet to prove she stays this sort of trip. *(op 9-1)*
Siena Star(IRE) again showed that he is not the most consistent of animals. *(op 7-1)*
Skibereen(IRE) got found out by the longer distance. *(op 11-1)*
Roscam *Official explanation: jockey said gelding pulled up lame (op 9-4)*
Gondolin(IRE), set to go up 5lb in future handicaps, had the cheekpieces left off and was just beginning to look held when taking a heavy fall at the penultimate flight. *(op 9-4)*

814 TOTESPORT.COM H'CAP HURDLE (12 hdls) 3m
4:00 (4:02) (Class 2) (0-140,131) 4-Y-0+
£12,696 (£4,815; £2,407; £1,094; £547; £328)

Form			Horse	Jockey	RPR
U5-1	**1**		**Ballycassidy (IRE)**[34] [423] 9-11-5 **124** ... RJohnson (P Bowen) *a.p: led 3rd: rdn appr 2 out: styd on wl* **13/8**[1]		131+
2-11	**2**	*7*	**Earlsfield Raider**[24] [566] 5-11-3 **122** ...(b) JEMoore (G L Moore) *hld up in mid-div: hdwy 7th: chsd wnr and hit 2 out: no imp: fin lame* **16/1**		122+
1114	**3**	*shd*	**Altitude Dancer (IRE)**[17] [652] 5-10-0 **105** ... RThornton (Mrs A M Thorpe) *a.p: rdn appr 3 out: one pce fr 2 out* **11/1**		104
P0-3	**4**	*6*	**Mondial Jack (FR)**[34] [422] 6-11-1 **120** ... RGreene (M C Pipe) *hld up and bhd: hdwy appr 9th: rdn appr 3 out: wknd 2 out* **20/1**		113
-425	**5**	*¾*	**Alikat (IRE)**[18] [633] 4-11-1 **125** ... TJMurphy (M C Pipe) *hld up and bhd: hdwy 9th: rdn and no imp fr 3 out* **16/1**		112
P0-0	**6**	*dist*	**Champagne Harry**[46] [207] 7-11-9 **128** ...(t) CLlewellyn (N A Twiston-Davies) *hld up in tch: rdn and wknd 3 out: mstke 2 out: t.o* **28/1**		—
21-2	**7**	*dist*	**Global Challenge (IRE)**[50] [168] 6-11-6 **125** ...(b) APMcCoy (Jonjo O'Neill) *hld up in mid-div: mstke 6th: bhd fr 9th: t.o* **11/1**		—
5-F6	**8**	*11*	**Witness Time (IRE)**[17] [652] 9-9-9 **105** ... MNicolls[(5)] (B J Eckley) *led to 3rd: wknd 8th: t.o* **33/1**		—
-F12	**P**		**Bee Hawk**[14] [679] 6-10-4 **109** ...(t) RWalsh (P F Nicholls) *bhd tl p.u after 6th* **9/2**[2]		—
2P/0	**P**		**Jollyolly**[34] [422] 6-11-12 **131** ...(p) ChristianWilliams (P Bowen) *hld up in tch: p.u lame after 6th* **66/1**		—
P-P4	**P**		**Reasonable Reserve (IRE)**[31] [468] 8-10-5 **110** ...(b) JamesDavies (B G Powell) *prom to 9th: t.o whn p.u bef 2 out* **50/1**		—
0-F5	**P**		**It's Definite (IRE)**[34] [422] 6-10-12 **117** ...(p) MAFitzgerald (P Bowen) *prom: rdn 7th: sn wknd: t.o whn p.u bef 3 out* **16/1**		—
01-6	**P**		**Openide**[55] [88] 4-11-0 **124** ... NFehily (B W Duke) *hld up in mid-div: rdn after 6th: sn bhd: t.o whn p.u after 8th* **14/1**		—
6P-P	**P**		**Columbus (IRE)**[55] [92] 8-11-4 **123** ...(b) AO'Keeffe (Jennie Candlish) *a bhd: lost tch 6th: t.o whn p.u and dismntd after 2 out* **100/1**		—
UP-1	**U**		**Mr Fluffy**[8] [751] 8-10-12 **122** 6ex ... RStephens[(5)] (P J Hobbs) *hld up in mid-div: hdwy appr 8th: rdn after 9th: 7th and wkng whn blnd and uns rdr 3 out* **10/1**[3]		—

5m 34.2s (-15.00) **Going Correction** -0.425s/f (Good)
WFA 4 from 5yo+ 5lb **15** Ran SP% **121.9**
Speed ratings: **108,105,105,103,103** —,—,—,—,— —,—,—,—,— CSF £27.49 CT £235.23 TOTE £2.40: £1.90, £3.30, £4.50; EX 42.20.
Owner R Owen & P Fullagar **Bred** Michael Griffin **Trained** Little Newcastle, Pembrokes

FOCUS
A valuable handicap for this time of the year and the form looks solid and can rate higher.

NOTEBOOK
Ballycassidy(IRE), reverting to hurdles, took advantage of a mark a stone lower than when bolting up to win another good prize over fences at Kelso last month. He is now likely to go back over fences at Market Rasen's big summer jumping meeting in July. *(op 9-4)*
Earlsfield Raider has undoubtedly improved since being fitted with blinkers. However, he could not cope with the well-handicapped winner having been raised a total of 17lb. He was reported to have finished lame. *Official explanation: jockey said gelding pulled up lame (op 14-1)*
Altitude Dancer(IRE), again running off a career-high mark, was certainly not disgraced in this stronger company. *(op 12-1 tchd 14-1, 16-1 in a place)*
Mondial Jack(FR) was remaining over hurdles on ground that may have been plenty quick enough for him. *(op 16-1 tchd 25-1)*
Alikat(IRE), taking on her elders on this first attempt at three miles, again ran as if she has more than her fair share of weight.
Columbus(IRE) *Official explanation: jockey said gelding pulled up lame*
It's Definite(IRE) *Official explanation: jockey said gelding pulled up lame*

815 SAVILLS H'CAP CHASE (15 fncs) 2m 4f 110y
4:30 (4:33) (Class 4) (0-110,110) 5-Y-0+ **£5,138** (£1,581; £790; £395)

Form			Horse	Jockey	RPR
53-U	**1**		**Bobsbest (IRE)**[8] [744] 9-10-1 **85** ... AO'Keeffe (R J Price) *hld up in mid-div: hdwy 9th: hrd rdn to ld appr last: all out* **5/1**[3]		96+
-5U0	**2**	*nk*	**Stage Friendly (IRE)**[13] [692] 6-10-5 **89** ... CLlewellyn (N A Twiston-Davies) *t.k.h: hld up: hdwy 3rd: blnd 8th: mstke 9th: swtchd rt appr 2 out: ev ch last: r.o* **11/1**		102+
4P-3	**3**	*6*	**Navarone**[29] [489] 11-11-7 **105** ... PMoloney (Ian Williams) *led: rdn and hdd appr last: wknd flat* **9/2**[2]		109
00-2	**4**	*1 ¼*	**Dark Room (IRE)**[10] [727] 8-11-10 **108** ... APMcCoy (Jonjo O'Neill) *a.p: rdn after 11th: one pce fr 4 out* **5/1**[3]		111+
0-65	**5**	*18*	**Search And Destroy (USA)**[18] [634] 7-11-11 **109** ...(b) JMMaguire (T R George) *chsd ldr tl after 11th: mstke 4 out: sn wknd* **4/1**[1]		98+
P55-	**6**	*1 ¼*	**Moral Justice (IRE)**[269] [1520] 12-10-0 **84** oh14 ... JamesDavies (S J Gilmore) *prom tl wknd 4 out* **66/1**		67
00-0	**7**	*6*	**Deferlant (FR)**[18] [633] 8-11-12 **110** ...(tp) MAFitzgerald (K Bell) *hld up: mstke 8th: j. slowly 9th: sn bhd* **25/1**		87
4-51	**8**	*1*	**Celebration Town (IRE)**[27] [511] 8-11-12 **110** ... MFoley (Miss E C Lavelle) *a bhd* **8/1**		86
0F31	**9**	*dist*	**Rudetski**[8] [744] 8-11-7 **105** 7ex ...(t) DRDennis (M Sheppard) *hld up: hdwy after 6th: mstke 10th: sn wknd: t.o* **11/1**		—
P4-0	**P**		**Kicasso**[15] [674] 6-10-2 **86** ... RThornton (D G Bridgwater) *mid-div: lost pl 4th: bhd whn p.u after 6th* **12/1**		—
0-3P	**P**		**Mount Kimble (IRE)**[28] [505] 9-11-1 **99** ... PHide (P Winkworth) *hld up in tch: lost pl 4th: bhd fr 7th: t.o whn p.u bef 4 out* **25/1**		—

5m 3.80s (-3.70) **Going Correction** 0.0s/f (Good) **11** Ran SP% **116.2**
Speed ratings: **107,106,104,104,97 96,94,94,**—,— — CSF £55.88 CT £265.93 TOTE £7.30: £2.00, £7.10, £1.40; EX 79.30.
Owner R A Jefferies **Bred** Patrick Stanley **Trained** Lugwardine, H'fords

FOCUS
They went 4/1 the field in what looked like being a pretty competitive affair but the form does not look that great.

NOTEBOOK
Bobsbest(IRE), who enjoyed this genuinely fast ground, is as tough as teak and simply refused to be beaten. He is reasonably handicapped and should not go up too much for this. *(op 13-2)*
Stage Friendly(IRE) ◆ had another eventful outing over fences and did not have time to recover by the next fence after nearly unseating his rider at the second ditch. He will win races once he really gets his act together. *Official explanation: jockey said gelding pulled up sore (op 9-1)*
Navarone did not find a return to a shorter distance the answer and is proving difficult to win with despite having slipped to a mark 11lb lower than when he last scored. *(op 6-1)*
Dark Room(IRE), another dropping back from three miles, was set to go up 5lb at the weekend after his narrow defeat last time. He may have found this ground a bit lively. *(op 4-1)*
Search And Destroy(USA) was just beginning to feel the pinch when missing out at the last ditch proved the final nail in the coffin. *(op 5-1)*
Mount Kimble(IRE) *Official explanation: jockey said gelding was lame*

816 CANNONS HEALTH CLUB MAIDEN OPEN NATIONAL HUNT FLAT RACE (DIV 1) 2m
5:00 (5:02) (Class 6) 4-6-Y-0 **£1,506** (£430; £215)

Form			Horse	Jockey	RPR
05-4	**1**		**Shakerattleandroll (IRE)**[45] [242] 4-11-1 ... MAFitzgerald (J Nicol) *hld up and bhd: hdwy over 4f: hrd rdn to ld over 1f out: all out* **8/1**[3]		94
2	**2**	*½*	**I'm Lovin It (IRE)**[29] [490] 5-11-4 ... RWalsh (P F Nicholls) *hld up: hdwy over 6f: led over 2f out: rdn and hdd over 1f out: r.o* **5/4**[1]		96
0	**3**	*6*	**Blue Splash (FR)**[29] [490] 5-11-4 ... APMcCoy (P Bowen) *hld up in tch: led 6f out: rdn and hdd over 2f out: wknd fnl f* **9/4**[2]		90
	4	*3 ½*	**Liamos (IRE)**[24] 5-10-11 ... MrPYork[(7)] (R H York) *plld hrd early: in tch: rdn over 2f out: edgd lft and wknd over 1f out* **20/1**		87
0-	**5**	*15*	**Redlynch Spirit (IRE)**[129] [3837] 5-11-4 ... JTizzard (C L Tizzard) *plld hrd early: prom: wkng whn n.m.r over 4f out* **16/1**		72
	6	*14*	**The Boobi (IRE)** 4-10-8 ... AO'Keeffe (Miss M E Rowland) *hld up: hdwy 8f out: wknd over 3f out* **66/1**		48
0	**7**	*4*	**Alotdone (IRE)**[31] [463] 6-11-4 ...(p) JMogford (Mrs N S Evans) *led 3f: prom tl rdn and wknd over 4f out* **50/1**		54
	8	*7*	**Kong King** 5-10-11 ... MrCPHuxley[(7)] (A E Jones) *hld up: slipped bnd over 5f out: a bhd* **40/1**		47
46	**R**		**Judy The Drinker**[14] [685] 6-10-1 ... ENolan[(10)] (J G M O'Shea) *hung bdly rt and rn out after 2f* **16/1**		—
	P		**Just Freya** 4-10-8 ... WHutchinson (R Dickin) *led after 3f to 6f out: sn wknd: t.o whn p.u ins fnl f* **66/1**		—
	R		**True Venture** 5-10-4 ... CMStudd[(7)] (R Curtis) *hld up: hdwy over 6f out: wkng whn hung bdly rt bnd and rn out over 3f out* **33/1**		—
6	**P**		**Walton Way**[20] [616] 5-11-4 ... JPMcNamara (P W Hiatt) *hld up in mid-div: dropped to rr over 5f out: t.o whn p.u over 1f out* **12/1**		—

3m 41.6s (-6.20) **Going Correction** -0.425s/f (Good)
WFA 4 from 5yo+ 3lb **12** Ran SP% **120.9**
Speed ratings: **98,97,94,93,85 78,76,73,**—,— —,— CSF £18.02 TOTE £9.50: £1.80, £1.10, £1.60; EX 31.80.
Owner Miss Anita Farrell **Bred** The Thoroughbred Corporation **Trained** Newmarket, Suffolk
■ Stewards' Enquiry : R Walsh two-day ban: used whip with excessive frequency (Jul 3,5)

FOCUS
This modest bumper was the faster of the two divisions by a second and the form looks reasonably solid for the grade.

NOTEBOOK
Shakerattleandroll(IRE), whose previous best effort had been on the Polytrack at Lingfield back in February, was suited by the fact that the ground had quickened up during the afternoon. *(op 10-1)*
I'm Lovin It(IRE) settled better this time and did nothing wrong but could not quite pull out as much as the winner when let down. *(op 7-4)*
Blue Splash(FR) had more use made of him than when just under five lengths behind the runner-up here last time. *(op 5-2 tchd 3-1)*
Liamos(IRE) looked set to be concerned in the finish when falling in a weak point-to-point last month. *(tchd 25-1)*
Judy The Drinker *Official explanation: jockey said, regarding failing to pull up having taken the wrong course, mare hung badly right and he was unable to pull her up until she ran out again in the home straight (op 50-1)*
Walton Way *Official explanation: jockey said gelding was unsuited by good to firm, firm in places ground (op 50-1)*
Just Freya *Official explanation: jockey said filly lost her action (op 50-1)*
True Venture *Official explanation: jockey said mare lost her action (op 50-1)*

817 CANNONS HEALTH CLUB MAIDEN OPEN NATIONAL HUNT FLAT RACE (DIV 2) 2m
5:30 (5:32) (Class 6) 4-6-Y-0 **£1,506** (£430; £215)

Form			Horse	Jockey	RPR
	1		**Houlihans Free (IRE)**[18] 6-11-4 ...(t) RWalsh (P F Nicholls) *hld up and bhd: hdwy 5f out: rdn to ld ins fnl f: r.o wl* **10/3**[2]		96+
2	**2**	*3 ½*	**Mr Jawbreaker (IRE)**[14] [685] 6-11-4 ... RThornton (J T Stimpson) *a.p: led on bit over 3f out: rdn and hdd ins fnl f: one pce* **7/2**[3]		90
06-5	**3**	*3 ½*	**Be Positive**[42] [300] 5-11-4 ... PHide (C J Down) *plld hrd in tch: rdn and ev ch over 1f out: one pce fnl f* **20/1**		86
	4	*8*	**Seymour Weld** 5-10-13 ... DLaverty[(5)] (A E Jones) *chsd ldr tl over 4f out: hung rt and rn wd bnd over 3f out: sn btn* **33/1**		78
	5	*1*	**Daihannah (IRE)**[18] 5-10-11 ... ChristianWilliams (Miss H E Roberts) *hld up and bhd: rdn and hdwy 3f out: wknd wl over 1f out* **40/1**		70
0	**6**	*5*	**Berkeley Court**[53] [138] 4-11-1 ... JEMoore (C A Cyzer) *hld up in mid-div: rdn and hdwy ins over 4f out: ev ch 3f out: wknd over 1f out* **8/1**		69
0-0	**7**	*4*	**Just Ruby**[39] [349] 4-10-8 ... LAspell (F Jordan) *mid-div: lost pl 8f out: n.d after* **40/1**		58
	8	*1 ¼*	**Playing Dirty** 5-11-4 ... APMcCoy (M C Pipe) *hld up in mid-div: hdwy over 6f out: rdn over 4f out: wknd 3f out* **11/8**[1]		67
	9	*½*	**Dontelldonandgerry** 5-10-11 ... SCurran (P D Evans) *plld hrd: prom tl wknd 6f out* **18/1**		59
6	**10**	*10*	**Clintos**[44] [266] 4-11-1 ...(t) WMarston (G R I Smyly) *hld up and bhd: hdwy 9f out: rdn over 5f out: sn wknd* **66/1**		53
/P0-	**11**	*6*	**Claydon Cavalier**[337] [1019] 6-11-4 ... JPMcNamara (P A Trueman) *led: rdn and hdd over 3f out: sn wknd* **66/1**		50

3m 42.6s (-5.20) **Going Correction** -0.425s/f (Good)
WFA 4 from 5yo+ 3lb **11** Ran SP% **119.3**
Speed ratings: **96,94,92,88,88 85,83,82,82,77 74** CSF £14.86 TOTE £5.90: £1.80, £1.20, £3.90; EX 16.00 Place 6 £134.72, Place 5 £119.65.
Owner H B Geddes **Bred** Peadar Devereux **Trained** Ditcheat, Somerset

FOCUS
Another moderate affair a second slower than the first division although the form looks reasonable and the winner can rate higher.

NOTEBOOK

Houlihans Free(IRE), the winner of a maiden Irish point last year, had seemingly struggled to get home in his two completed points in this country. Perhaps the fitting of a tongue tie helped as he has already had a soft-palate operation. *(op 7-2 tchd 4-1)*

Mr Jawbreaker(IRE) got beaten for finishing speed after travelling well and perhaps more of an end-to-end gallop would have helped. *(tchd 3-1)*

Be Positive ran his best race to date despite proving difficult to settle. *(op 14-1)*

Seymour Weld had just lost second when he shot himself in the foot on the home turn.

Daihannah(IRE), who has twice rather thrown away his chance in maiden open points, may not be one who relishes a battle. *(op 33-1)*

Playing Dirty comes from the same family as Morley Street and Granville Again but favourite backers knew their fate early in the home straight. *(tchd 6-4)*

T/Plt: £176.90 to a £1 stake. Pool: £33,588.50. 138.60 winning tickets. T/Qpdt: £59.20 to a £1 stake. Pool: £2,556.10. 31.90 winning tickets. KH

818 - 821a (Foreign Racing) - See Raceform Interactive

686 MARKET RASEN (R-H)

Friday, June 24

OFFICIAL GOING: Good

The top couple of inches soon turned soft but it was still firm underneath and the riders reckoned it was 'basically good to soft'. Third last fence omitted.

Wind: Light, half behind Weather: Persistent rain until after race two.

822 MARKETRASENRACES.CO.UK (S) H'CAP HURDLE (8 hdls) 2m 1f 110y

2:10 (2:10) (Class 5) (0-90,87) 4-Y-0+ **£2,296** (£656; £328)

Form				RPR
61U3	1		**Lone Soldier (FR)**[5] [784] 9-11-5 **87** CDSharkey(7) (S B Clark) *mid-field: hdwy 4th: wnt 2nd 3 out: sn led: clr between last 2: rdn out* **9/2**[1]	97+
-P00	2	*12*	**Alethea Gee**[16] [686] 7-10-11 **72** RMcGrath (K G Reveley) *hld up: hdwy 4th: wnt mod 3rd after 3 out: hrd rdn and kpt on: tk 2nd nr line* **14/1**	69
-463	3	*½*	**Prince Adjal (IRE)**[13] [716] 5-11-8 **83** (p) ARoss (G M Moore) *led: clr 4th: hit next 2: hdd after 3 out: kpt on same pce* **9/2**[1]	81+
U053	4	*8*	**Seemore Sunshine**[9] [760] 8-10-9 **77** PCStringer(7) (M J Gingell) *in tch: hdwy 5th: outpcd fr next* **5/1**[2]	66
PF00	5	*9*	**Step In Line (IRE)**[5] [781] 13-10-0 **64** PBuchanan(3) (D W Thompson) *chsd ldrs: one pce fr 3 out* **25/1**	44
-003	6	*½*	**Martin House (IRE)**[27] [544] 6-11-2 **80** ONelmes(3) (D W Thompson) *chsd ldrs: wknd fr 3 out* **9/2**[1]	59
-F40	7	*4*	**Nutley Queen (IRE)**[33] [467] 6-9-7 **61** (t) TMessenger(7) (M Appleby) *in rr: sme hdwy 5th: nvr a factor* **25/1**	36
0240	8	*2½*	**Reedsman (IRE)**[17] [670] 4-10-8 **72** (b) HOliver (R C Guest) *t.k.h: trckd ldrs: lost pl after 3 out* **8/1**[3]	42
/P-0	9	*3*	**Hidden Smile (USA)**[55] [134] 8-11-0 **75** (t) LAspell (F Jordan) *bhd: sme hdwy 3 out: sn wknd* **20/1**	45
-P00	10	*12*	**Flashy Filly**[13] [715] 5-9-11 **65** ow1 MJMcAlister(7) (J C Haynes) *a in rr: bhd fr 5th* **40/1**	23
506/	11	*4*	**Red September**[2] 8-10-4 **72** CaptLHorner(7) (D L Williams) *a in rr: bhd fr 5th* **20/1**	26
PPP0	12	*nk*	**Proper Poser (IRE)**[17] [670] 9-10-0 **64** ow3 ACCoyle(3) (M C Chapman) *a bhd* **66/1**	17
00-0	13	*2½*	**Vesta Flame**[24] [601] 4-9-11 **64** (p) KJMercer(3) (P T Midgley) *prom: lost pl 3rd: sn bhd* **20/1**	12
0-56	P		**La Folichonne (FR)**[13] [715] 6-11-0 **75** JimCrowley (James Moffatt) *chsd ldrs: lost pl 5th: sn bhd: p.u bef 2 out* **20/1**	—

4m 14.6s (-1.80) **Going Correction** +0.025s/f (Yiel)
WFA 4 from 5yo+ 3lb **14 Ran SP% 119.7**
Speed ratings: **105,99,99,95,91 91,89,88,87,82 80,80,79,—** CSF £55.28 CT £304.54 TOTE £5.30: £2.20, £3.80, £1.80; EX 106.30.There was no bid for the winner.
Owner S B Clark **Bred** Hipodromos Y Caballos S A **Trained** Sutton-on-the-Forest, N Yorks

FOCUS
A poor handicap but run at a decent pace and rated through the runner-up to her mark.

NOTEBOOK

Lone Soldier(FR) is in good form at present and defied top-weight with a wide margin success. This was his best effort for a long time.

Alethea Gee, kept away from the other runners at the start, was much more settled beforehand this time. She worked hard to snatch second spot near the line and will be suited by a return to two and a half miles.

Prince Adjal(IRE) took them along but the persistent rain had turned the ground against him and his jumping rather let him down. *(op 4-1)*

Seemore Sunshine, a maiden after 11 previous starts, basically looks paceless. *(op 6-1 tchd 13-2)*

Step In Line(IRE), now in his 14th year, last visited the winner's enclosure fives year ago. *(tchd 28-1)*

Martin House(IRE), dropped into selling company for the first time, continues on the downgrade. *(tchd 4-1)*

Vesta Flame *Official explanation: jockey said filly was unsuited by good ground (op 16-1)*

823 WEATHERBYS INSURANCE H'CAP CHASE (12 fncs 2 omitted) 2m 6f 110y

2:40 (2:41) (Class 3) (0-135,126) 5-Y-0+ **£7,473** (£2,299; £1,149; £574)

Form				RPR
-522	1		**Kind Sir**[12] [725] 9-10-1 **101** WHutchinson (A W Carroll) *trckd ldrs: led 3 out: blnd next: styd on* **9/2**[1]	112+
0-21	2	*7*	**Giorgio (IRE)**[36] [427] 7-10-10 **113** (b) PBuchanan(3) (Miss Lucinda V Russell) *w ldr: led 4th to 3 out: kpt on same pce fr next* **9/2**[1]	116
521-	3	*19*	**The Pennys Dropped (IRE)**[327] [1091] 8-10-9 **109** APMcCoy (Jonjo O'Neill) *t.k.h: wnt prom 5th: 4th and struggling whn blnd 3 out: tk remote 3rd last* **11/2**[2]	100+
4-2F	4	*8*	**Romany Dream**[30] [505] 7-9-11 **100** oh8 (b) DCrosse(3) (R Dickin) *blnd 2nd: wnt prom 5th: wknd 3 out* **20/1**	76
41-	5	*26*	**Benrajah (IRE)**[68] [4880] 8-11-6 **120** PRobson (M Todhunter) *led to 4th: drvn along 7th: lost pl after 9th: sn bhd* **7/1**	70
110-	F		**Farlington**[134] [3767] 8-11-8 **122** WMarston (P Bowen) *chsd ldrs: fell 5th* **7/1**	—
U421	P		**Mullensgrove**[8] [765] 11-10-3 **110** 7ex MissSSharratt(7) (R Hollinshead) *hld up: prom whn bdly hmpd 5th: sn p.u lame* **11/2**[2]	—
F4-4	P		**Marked Man (IRE)**[34] [454] 9-11-12 **126** TDoyle (R Lee) *hld up in last: blnd 5th: wl hld whn blnd 9th: p.u bef next* **13/2**[3]	—

5m 39.3s (-7.10) **Going Correction** -0.125s/f (Good) **8 Ran SP% 110.2**
Speed ratings: **107,104,97,95,86 —,—,—** CSF £23.63 CT £104.85 TOTE £5.70: £1.60, £2.00, £2.10; EX 24.70.
Owner Layton T Cheshire **Bred** Belgrave Bloodstock Ltd **Trained** Cropthorne, Worcs

FOCUS
A fair handicap for the time of year run at a sound pace and the race could be rated slightly higher.

NOTEBOOK

Kind Sir found this extended trip no problem and, though doing his best to throw it away two out, he thoroughly deserved this first success for over a year. *(op 4-1)*

Giorgio(IRE), 6lb higher, did not have the firm ground he relishes this time and in the end was very much second best. *(op 5-1)*

The Pennys Dropped(IRE), absent since winning here ten months ago, was already struggling when he almost demolished the last in the back straight. *(op 4-1)*

Romany Dream, 8lb 'wrong', has yet to show she stays this far. *(op 16-1)*

Benrajah(IRE), 8lb higher, did not enjoy an uncontested lead and the ground was not in his favour either. *(tchd 8-1)*

Mullensgrove was nearly brought down at an early stage and, lame behind, had to be removed *from the course in a horse ambulance. Official explanation: vet said gelding was lame (op 6-1 tchd 13-2)*

824 KIERAN KELLY AND SEAN CLEARY CELEBRATORY H'CAP HURDLE (8 hdls) 2m 1f 110y

3:10 (3:11) (Class 3) (0-135,129) 4-Y-0+ **£6,545** (£2,014; £1,007; £503)

Form				RPR
56-6	1		**Xellance (IRE)**[34] [450] 8-11-2 **119** RJohnson (P J Hobbs) *w ldrs: led 2 out: hrd rdn and r.o gamely run-in* **4/1**[2]	122
33-3	2	*½*	**Borora**[42] [332] 6-11-12 **129** TDoyle (R Lee) *hld up in tch: jnd ldrs 3 out: rdn next: hit last: no ex towards fin* **7/2**[1]	133+
4-15	3	*1¾*	**Resplendent Star (IRE)**[16] [691] 8-10-5 **108** (v) LAspell (Mrs L Wadham) *trckd ldrs: effrt 3 out: nt qckn between last 2* **9/1**	109
0-46	4	*¾*	**Castleshane (IRE)**[8] [766] 8-11-6 **123** MAFitzgerald (S Gollings) *led to 2 out: kpt on same pce* **15/2**	123
-4F0	5	*4*	**Siegfrieds Night (IRE)**[7] [689] 4-10-0 **109** ACCoyle(3) (M C Chapman) *chsd ldrs: outpcd after 3 out: styd on between last 2* **22/1**	102
26-0	6	*9*	**All Bleevable**[40] [370] 8-9-11 **103** oh3 LVickers(3) (Mrs S Lamyman) *jumpd rt: w ldrs: lost pl after 3 out* **20/1**	93+
/P5-	7	*7*	**Ballykettrail (IRE)**[403] [395] 9-10-9 **112** JEMoore (Jonjo O'Neill) *in tch towards rr: lost pl 3 out: sn bhd* **25/1**	92
2-05	8	*3*	**Golden Chalice (IRE)**[12] [726] 6-9-12 **106** PCO'Neill(5) (Miss E C Lavelle) *hld up in rr: effrt 5th: wknd next* **5/1**[3]	89+
0-1P	9	*12*	**Qabas (USA)**[12] [726] 5-10-9 **112** (p) APMcCoy (P Bowen) *chsd ldrs: lost pl 5th: bhd fr next* **4/1**[2]	77

4m 16.1s (-0.30) **Going Correction** +0.025s/f (Yiel)
WFA 4 from 5yo+ 3lb **9 Ran SP% 113.6**
Speed ratings: **101,100,100,99,97 93,90,89,84** CSF £17.91 CT £116.45 TOTE £5.30: £2.60, £1.50, £2.10; EX 22.60.
Owner The Five Nations Partnership **Bred** T Harris **Trained** Withycombe, Somerset

FOCUS
A fair handicap but the time was ordinary and the form, rated through the third, does not look that solid.

NOTEBOOK

Xellance(IRE) took a narrow advantage and simply would not be denied. This versatile type is really better suited by a stiffer test these days. *(op 7-2)*

Borora went head-to-head with the winner but, after a clumsy jump at the final flight, just missed out to a very tough and determined opponent. *(tchd 4-1)*

Resplendent Star(IRE), on his handicap debut, ran a lot better than last time and fought hard all the way to the line. *(op 12-1)*

Castleshane(IRE), who last won over two years ago, reverted to front-running tactics and to his credit fought back all the way to the line. *(op 6-1 tchd 8-1)*

Siegfrieds Night(IRE), at last dropping in the weights, ran a lot better than of late. *(op 20-1)*

Golden Chalice(IRE) ran poorly. *(op 11-2)*

Qabas(USA), pulled up two weeks earlier, again had the ground against him and dropped out in a *matter of strides. Official explanation: trainer was unable to offer any explanation for poor form shown (op 7-2)*

825 CLUGSTON NOVICES' CHASE (10 fncs 2 omitted) 2m 1f 110y

3:40 (3:40) (Class 3) 5-Y-0+ **£5,434** (£1,672; £836; £418)

Form				RPR
1-2P	1		**Croix De Guerre (IRE)**[9] [761] 5-11-5 120 (b) RJohnson (P J Hobbs) *w ldr: led 3rd: jumpd lft and lft clr 2 out: rdn out* **9/4**[2]	120
2P-1	2	*9*	**Space Star**[56] [104] 5-11-5 123 TDoyle (P R Webber) *trckd ldrs: wnt 2nd 7th: rdn after next: chalng whn hmpd: blnd and rdr lost irons 2 out: kpt on wl* **8/13**[1]	118+
-25U	3	*26*	**Vigoureux (FR)**[15] [692] 6-10-7 95 (p) WKennedy(7) (S Gollings) *trckd ldrs: blnd 4th: wknd after 3 out* **8/1**[3]	85+
P5/	4	*dist*	**Triple Crown (IRE)**[25] 12-11-0 64 JPMcNamara (P W Hiatt) *led to 3rd: wknd 7th: sn bhd: t.o 2 out* **40/1**	—

4m 22.9s (-8.20) **Going Correction** -0.125s/f (Good) **4 Ran SP% 106.2**
Speed ratings: **113,109,97,—** CSF £4.12 TOTE £2.80; EX 3.80.
Owner Jack Joseph **Bred** T Wada **Trained** Withycombe, Somerset

FOCUS
An uncompetitive novices' chase but a decent time for the type of contest.

NOTEBOOK

Croix De Guerre(IRE), pulled up just nine days earlier, sealed the issue when going left-handed and almost putting the challenging runner-up on the deck two out. He could struggle back in handicap company. *(op 2-1)*

Space Star, 9lb inferior to the winner over hurdles, was less than a length down when left with no room at all on the outside two out. His rider performed miracles to keep the partnership intact, but the impression was that on the day he was only second best anyway. He looks harshly treated on 123 on what he has actually achieved over fences so far. *(op 4-6)*

Vigoureux(FR) had a lot to find and was left behind starting the home turn. *(tchd 9-1)*

Triple Crown(IRE), placed in three of his 14 starts in points, looks a lost cause under Rules. *(op 25-1)*

826 HAPPY BIRTHDAY BARBARA, LOVE YOU LOTS NOVICES' H'CAP HURDLE (8 hdls) 2m 1f 110y

4:10 (4:10) (Class 4) (0-100,100) 4-Y-0+ **£3,609** (£1,031; £515)

Form				RPR
0-63	1		**Qualitair Pleasure**[24] [601] 5-10-6 **83** KJMercer(3) (J Hetherton) *hld up in rr: hdwy after 3 out: wnt 2nd appr 2 out: styd on to ld run-in* **11/1**	88+
40-0	2	*2*	**Jimmy Byrne (IRE)**[55] [120] 5-11-7 **95** (v[1]) HOliver (R C Guest) *w ldrs: led 4th: clr 3 out: hit next: hdd and no ex run-in* **7/1**	98+
/0P-	3	*3*	**Zarakash (IRE)**[403] [397] 5-11-1 **89** APMcCoy (Jonjo O'Neill) *hld up in rr: hdwy 5th: wnt 2nd after 3 out: hung rt between last 2: kpt on same pce* **6/1**[3]	89+
2232	4	*7*	**Arjay**[16] [683] 7-10-0 **81** (b) CDSharkey(7) (S B Clark) *chsd ldrs: hit 3 out: wknd appr next* **9/2**[1]	73

50-4 **5** *1 ½* **That's Racing**^{37} [414] 5-10-2 **76** .... JEMoore 67
(J Hetherton) *in rr: hdwy 4th: outpcd and lost pl 3 out: styd on between last 2* **8/1**
55-3 **6** *6* **Given A Chance**^{18} [369] 4-11-5 **99** .... LVickers$^{(3)}$ 81
(Mrs S Lamyman) *led to 4th: outpcd 3 out: n.d after* **16/1**
006- **7** *8* **Slalom (IRE)**^{113} [4141] 5-10-13 **87** .... RJohnson 69+
(P Bowen) *w ldrs: mstke 4th: blnd next: wknd qckly after 3 out* **5/1**^{2}
-035 **8** *1 ½* **Think Quick (IRE)**^{22} [613] 5-9-12 **82** .... AHawkins$^{(10)}$ 57
(R Hollinshead) *in rr fr 4th* **16/1**
-236 **P** **Moldavia (GER)**^{7} [691] 4-11-4 **95** .... MAFitzgerald —
(M C Chapman) *bhd fr 5th: p.u bef 2 out* **14/1**
350/ **P** **King Claudius (IRE)**^{800} [4608] 9-11-2 **90** .... TDoyle —
(M C Banks) *bhd and drvn along 5th: t.o 3 out: p.u bef next* **11/1**
2-0P **P** **Six Pack (IRE)**^{41} [354] 7-11-4 **92** .... GLee —
(Andrew Turnell) *chsd ldrs: wknd qckly 3 out: wl bhd whn p.u bef next* **16/1**
220/ **P** **Buz Kiri (USA)**^{19} [2710] 7-10-12 **86** .... WHutchinson —
(A W Carroll) *w ldrs: lost pl 5th: sn bhd: t.o whn p.u bef 2 out* **22/1**

4m 18.1s (1.70) **Going Correction** +0.025s/f (Yiel)
WFA 4 from 5yo+ 3lb **12** Ran SP% **118.1**
Speed ratings: **97,96,94,91,91 88,84,84,—,— —,—** CSF £86.32 CT £513.28 TOTE £15.50: £4.10, £2.60, £2.40; EX 217.00.
Owner Qualitair Holdings Limited **Bred** Qualitair Stud Ltd **Trained** Norton, N Yorks

FOCUS
A very moderate handicap and, despite the slow time, the runner-up and fifth ran to their marks so the form looks reasonable.

NOTEBOOK
Qualitair Pleasure ◆, a dual bumper winner, was given a much more patient ride and stayed on on willing fashion to gain the upper hand on the run-in. Even from her revised mark she will still look leneiently treated. *(op 10-1 tchd 12-1)*
Jimmy Byrne(IRE), who has changed stables, stole a useful advantage and in the end only the winner proved capable of overhauling him. *(op 8-1 tchd 17-2)*
Zarakash(IRE), unplaced in four previous starts, was having his first outing for over a year. A winner on the Flat at three in Ireland, this was better but his attitude did not altogether impress. *(op 4-1)*
Arjay has yet to win over hurdles yet his rating keeps going up.
That's Racing found this drop in trip against him. Putting in all his best work at the finish, he is still inexperienced. *(op 10-1)*
Buz Kiri(USA) *Official explanation: jockey said gelding was unsuited by good ground (op 14-1)*

827 SMART & COOK INSURANCE BROKERS NOVICES' H'CAP CHASE (12 fncs 2 omitted) 2m 6f 110y
4:40 (4:40) (Class 4) (0-105,95) 5-Y-0+ **£4,180** (£1,286; £643; £321)

Form RPR
-5F3 **1** **Ultimate Limit**^{17} [674] 5-10-0 **75** oh6 .... PJBrennan 92+
(A Ennis) *in rr: drvn along 8th: gd hdwy 3 out: sn chsng ldr: led appr 2 out: styd on wl* **4/1**^{2}
P-P1 **2** *9* **Seaniethesmuggler (IRE)**^{40} [371] 7-11-5 **95** .... WKennedy$^{(7)}$ 109
(S Gollings) *chsd ldrs: wnt 2nd 2 out: wandered: kpt on same pce* **4/1**^{2}
/P-5 **3** *10* **John Rich**^{16} [690] 9-10-0 **72** ....(tp) PBuchanan$^{(3)}$ 76
(M E Sowersby) *chsd ldrs: wl outpcd appr 2 out* **10/1**^{3}
4-02 **4** *2 ½* **Luckycharm (FR)**^{22} [612] 6-10-3 **75** ....(v) DCrosse$^{(3)}$ 76
(R Dickin) *in rr: hdwy 7th: sn chsng ldrs: j.rt 9th: 4th and wkng whn hit 2 out* **16/1**
054/ **5** *5* **The Nobleman (USA)**^{391} 9-9-7 **69** .... TMessenger$^{(7)}$ 65
(D Shaw) *led: hit 3rd: hdd appr 2 out: sn wknd* **28/1**
2R-2 **6** *14* **Starbuck**^{5} [783] 11-10-1 **75** .... DMcGann$^{(5)}$ 63+
(A M Crow) *chsd ldrs: lost pl appr 2 out* **10/3**^{1}
PP-5 **7** *7* **Presentingthecase (IRE)**^{17} [673] 7-10-0 **69** oh5 .... JEMoore 49+
(Jonjo O'Neill) *in tch: wknd qckly 3 out: sn bhd* **4/1**^{2}
PP-5 **P** **Camaraderie**^{16} [681] 9-10-10 **79** .... WHutchinson —
(A W Carroll) *chsd ldrs: hit 5th: lost pl 8th: bhd whn p.u bef 3 out* **12/1**
0P4- **P** **Kalexandro (FR)**^{88} [4619] 7-10-1 **77** .... MissJFoster$^{(7)}$ —
(Miss J E Foster) *chsd ldrs: lost pl and hit 6th: t.o 9th: j. slowly next: sn p.u* **20/1**

5m 44.9s (-1.50) **Going Correction** -0.125s/f (Good)
WFA 5 from 6yo+ 2lb **9** Ran SP% **114.0**
Speed ratings: **97,93,90,89,87 82,80,—,—** CSF £20.73 CT £147.08 TOTE £4.90: £1.90, £1.60, £1.80; EX 30.00.
Owner Lady Wates **Bred** D And Mrs Holmes **Trained** Beare Green, Surrey

FOCUS
A very moderate contest but those in the frame behind the winner were close to their marks giving the form a solid appearance.

NOTEBOOK
Ultimate Limit, 6lb out of the handicap, is on the up and stuck to his guns in willing fashion to in the end pull right away. *(op 7-2 tchd 9-2,5-1 in places)*
Seaniethesmuggler(IRE), given plenty of weight, ducked and dived and in the end proved no match. *(op 7-2)*
John Rich, with all the aids again, continues to struggle to make an impact under Rules. *(op 12-1)*
Luckycharm(FR), with a visor on again, is a hesitant jumper and he had no more to give when missing out the second last.
The Nobleman(USA), last seen in a point a year ago, gave his fences plenty of air but stopped quickly when headed. *(op 25-1 tchd 33-1)*
Starbuck, making a quick return to action, was below his best the easy ground in part to blame. *Official explanation: jockey said gelding was unsuited by good ground (op 7-2)*
Presentingthecase(IRE) stopped to nothing starting the final turn. *(op 9-2 tchd 5-1)*

828 RACING UK ON CHANNEL 432 STANDARD OPEN NATIONAL HUNT FLAT RACE 2m 1f 110y
5:10 (5:11) (Class 6) 4-6-Y-0 **£1,827** (£522; £261)

Form RPR
0-12 **1** **Lindbergh Law (USA)**^{8} [769] 5-11-6 .... DCCostello$^{(5)}$ 109+
(G A Swinbank) *hld up: hdwy to join ldrs 7f out: led over 3f out: drvn clr 1f out: styd on wl* **9/4**^{1}
0- **2** *6* **Melrose**^{190} [2852] 6-10-11 .... JEMoore 89+
(J Hetherton) *hld up: hdwy to chse ldrs 6f out: wnt 2nd over 2f out: no real imp* **10/1**^{3}
3 *5* **Silver Sparrow (IRE)**^{61} 4-11-1 .... APMcCoy 88
(P Bowen) *trckd ldrs: rdn over 3f out: outpcd over 2f out: kpt on* **11/4**^{2}
3 **4** *nk* **Silver Bow**^{22} [616] 4-10-8 .... GLee 81
(J M Jefferson) *trckd ldrs: led 6f out: hdd over 3f out: sn outpcd: kpt on fnl f* **11/4**^{2}
5 *10* **Thorn Of The Rose (IRE)** 4-10-8 .... JimCrowley 71+
(James Moffatt) *set slow pce 1f: lost pl 6f out: n.d after* **22/1**
0 **6** *23* **Double Measure**^{40} [375] 5-11-4 .... RWalford 58
(T D Walford) *t.k.h: led after 1f: qckned 10f out: hdd 6f out: lost pl 4f out* **20/1**
0 **7** *½* **Aires Rock (IRE)**^{22} [616] 5-11-1 .... GCarenza$^{(3)}$ 57
(Miss J E Foster) *chsd ldrs: lost pl over 5f out: sn bhd* **25/1**
5 **8** *1 ¾* **Little Vantage**^{13} [720] 6-10-13 .... DMcGann$^{(5)}$ 55
(A M Crow) *plld hrd in rr: lost pl 6f out: sn bhd* **80/1**

4m 27.7s (11.20) **Going Correction** +0.025s/f (Yiel)
WFA 4 from 5yo+ 3lb **8** Ran SP% **107.4**
Speed ratings: **76,73,71,70,66 56,56,55** CSF £21.09 TOTE £2.80: £1.10, £2.00, £1.20; EX 19.50 Place 6 £114.40, Place 5 £57.56.
Owner Mrs F H Crone & Mrs J A Lawson **Bred** Caboodee Stud **Trained** Melsonby, N Yorks

FOCUS
A moderate bumper made worse by the funereal pace; they stood still for over ten seconds at the start and took two minutes to cover the first three quarters of a mile. The second is the best guide but the form looks suspect.

NOTEBOOK
Lindbergh Law(USA), warm beforehand, came right away in the end but the opposition was mediocre. *(tchd 5-2)*
Melrose, whose one previous outing was in December, stayed on in willing fashion to finish clear second best.
Silver Sparrow(IRE) a well-made type, is a good walker. Third in an Irish point in April, he looks to have a lot more stamina than speed. *(tchd 5-2 and 3-1)*
Silver Bow, on edge beforehand, went on and stepped up the gallop but this hardly represented an improvement on her debut effort. *(op 5-2 tchd 9-4)*
T/Plt: £193.10 to a £1 stake. Pool: £30,222.65. 114.25 winning tickets. T/Qpdt: £56.90 to a £1 stake. Pool: £2,331.60. 30.30 winning tickets. WG

829 - 837a (Foreign Racing) - See Raceform Interactive

692 UTTOXETER (L-H)
Sunday, June 26

OFFICIAL GOING: Good to firm (good in places)
The jockeys reported no jar in ground that was drying out all the time. Third last fence omitted.
Wind: Almost nil Weather: Sunny

838 LETS LIVE RACING CLUB NOVICES' HURDLE (10 hdls) 2m
2:15 (2:16) (Class 4) 4-Y-0+ **£3,622** (£1,035; £517)

Form RPR
-213 **1** **Dewasentah (IRE)**^{15} [715] 6-11-0 97 .... GLee 110+
(J M Jefferson) *hld up in mid-div: hdwy 5th: led 2 out: shkn up and sn clr: pushed out* **10/1**
31 **2** *12* **Keep On Movin' (IRE)**^{17} [696] 4-10-11 .... TDoyle 96+
(T G Mills) *led: rdn and hdd and whn mstke 2 out: btn whn hit last* **4/1**^{3}
62 **3** *13* **Hillcrest (NZ)**^{17} [696] 6-11-0 .... DRDennis 85
(Ian Williams) *chsd wnr fr 2nd to 6th: wknd after 7th* **7/2**^{2}
4 *¾* **Anko (POL)**^{203} 6-11-0 .... RJohnson 86+
(P J Hobbs) *bhd: nt fluent 2nd: styd on fr 3 out: nvr nr ldrs* **22/1**
00-0 **5** *3* **Dorans Lane**^{59} [77] 7-10-7 .... RThornton 75
(W M Brisbourne) *hld up towards rr: short-lived effrt 7th* **100/1**
4 **6** *3 ½* **Lake Merced (IRE)**^{22} [629] 5-11-0 .... APMcCoy 78+
(Jonjo O'Neill) *hld up in tch: chsd ldr 6th tl rdn appr 3 out: sn wknd* **16/1**
P-6 **7** *3* **Uncle John**^{10} [764] 4-10-11 .... WHutchinson 73+
(Ian Williams) *hld up in mid-div: hdwy appr 6th: wknd after 7th* **40/1**
20-0 **8** *2 ½* **Kirkham Abbey**^{28} [568] 5-11-0 98 .... RGarritty 73
(J J Quinn) *hld up in mid-div: rdn after 5th: bhd fr 7th* **25/1**
1-22 **9** *hd* **Argent Ou Or (FR)**^{33} [485] 4-10-11 .... TJMurphy 69
(M C Pipe) *a bhd* **9/1**
00 **10** *7* **Bobering**^{17} [696] 5-11-0 .... JMogford 65
(B P J Baugh) *hit 2nd: a bhd* **100/1**
3-P **11** *14* **Beaver (AUS)**^{38} [418] 6-11-0 ....(t) HOliver 51
(R C Guest) *hld up in tch: rdn after 6th: wknd 7th* **9/4**^{1}
2/0- **12** *½* **Amir Zaman**^{67} [22] 7-11-0 .... PMoloney 51
(J R Jenkins) *hld up in mid-div: mstke 4th: bhd fr 7th* **25/1**
00/P **P** **Double Emblem (IRE)**^{16} [8] 8-10-2 ....(b^{1}) LStephens$^{(5)}$ —
(B R Foster) *a bhd: t.o whn p.u bef 3 out* **100/1**
P- **P** **Costa Del Sol (IRE)**^{16} [2703] 4-10-11 ....(t) CLlewellyn —
(Miss Victoria Roberts) *a bhd: t.o whn p.u bef 3 out* **100/1**
5-60 **P** **Pat Malone**^{22} [635] 5-11-0 .... JPMcNamara —
(Lucinda Featherstone) *chsd ldr to 2nd: prom tl wknd appr 6th: mstke 7th: t.o whn p.u bef 3 out* **66/1**

3m 42.3s (-18.10) **Going Correction** -1.15s/f (Hard)
WFA 4 from 5yo+ 3lb **15** Ran SP% **117.9**
Speed ratings: **99,93,86,86,84 82,81,80,80,76 69,69,—,—,—** CSF £46.57 TOTE £14.00: £2.70, £2.00, £1.60; EX 35.30.
Owner Mrs J U Hales & Mrs L M Joicey **Bred** Miss Mary O'Sullivan **Trained** Norton, N Yorks

FOCUS
An ordinary contest and there were plenty available at long odds in this modest novice hurdle. The race could be rated a little higher with the first two coming away from the rest.

NOTEBOOK
Dewasentah(IRE), who may well have paid the penalty for having too much use made of her over the stiff course at Hexham last time, bounced back to the form that saw her win here last month. *(tchd 9-1)*
Keep On Movin'(IRE) confirmed the recent course form with Hillcrest in no uncertain manner despite the penalty but she had no answer to the winner. *(op 7-2)*
Hillcrest(NZ) may have been flattered by his proximity to Keep On Movin' here last time but this was still disappointing especially considering he was meeting his old rival on 7lb better terms. *Official explanation: jockey said gelding hung left-handed (op 11-2)*
Anko(POL), six times a winner at up to a mile and a quarter in Poland, did show a little promise for the future. *(op 16-1)*
Argent Ou Or(FR) *Official explanation: jockey said gelding hung slightly right-handed (op 10-1)*
Beaver(AUS), reported to have had a breathing problem last time, did not find the fitting of a tongue tie the answer. *(op 11-4 tchd 2-1)*
Costa Del Sol(IRE) *Official explanation: jockey said gelding had a breathing problem (op 66-1)*

839 QUALITEL MOBILE PHONES FOR BUSINESS CONDITIONAL JOCKEYS' (S) H'CAP HURDLE (12 hdls) 2m 6f 110y
2:45 (2:47) (Class 5) (0-90,90) 4-Y-0+ **£2,401** (£686; £343)

Form RPR
2565 **1** **Idlewild (IRE)**^{17} [697] 10-11-6 **90** .... APogson$^{(6)}$ 90+
(C T Pogson) *a.p: chsd ldr 2 out: led last: styd on wl* **12/1**
0-05 **2** *6* **Fiddles Music**^{28} [568] 4-11-1 **89** .... MGoldstein$^{(5)}$ 78
(Miss Sheena West) *hld up: hdwy 9th: styd on same pce fr last* **9/1**^{3}

041/ **3** ½ **Astronaut**[29] 8-11-1 **87** AGlassonbury(8) 83+
(M C Pipe) *hld up: hdwy and mstke 8th: rdn to go 2nd flat: eased and lost 2nd 30 yds fr line* **5/2**[1]

04P0 **4** 2 **Kingcombe Lane**[11] [760] 5-10-10 **74** MNicolls 67+
(P W Hiatt) *led: hdd and mstke 3rd: remained w ldr tl led 8th: rdn and hdd last: wknd flat* **66/1**

5-10 **5** 1 **Angie's Double**[32] [506] 5-10-10 **74** TJMalone 65
(Mrs K Waldron) *hld up: styd on fr 2 out: nvr nr to chal* **7/1**[2]

5-UP **6** ½ **Nimvara (IRE)**[40] [399] 9-10-6 **73** PCO'Neill(3) 63
(Evan Williams) *hld up: stmbld after 3rd: hdwy 9th: wknd appr last* **20/1**

0360 **7** 6 **Ashgan (IRE)**[5] [801] 12-10-11 **75** TJPhelan 61+
(Dr P Pritchard) *chsd ldr tl led 3rd: hdd 8th: wknd appr last* **40/1**

33-5 **8** 3½ **Hardi De Chalamont (FR)**[24] [614] 10-11-12 **90** (v) AO'Keeffe 71
(Jennie Candlish) *hld up: hdwy whn nt fluent 2 out: sn rdn: wkng whn mstke last* **10/1**

P0-0 **9** 1¼ **Gebora (FR)**[16] [9] 6-11-4 **87** TMessenger(5) 66
(B R Foster) *prom: rdn whn mstke 3 out: sn wknd* **50/1**

46-0 **10** 3½ **Del Trotter (IRE)**[28] [573] 10-11-7 **85** (p) PAspell 61
(M E Sowersby) *hld up: hdwy after 6th: wknd 3 out* **33/1**

0305 **11** 5 **Book's Way**[7] [781] 9-10-13 **77** KJMercer 48
(D W Thompson) *prom: hit 9th: wknd next* **10/1**

3002 **12** dist **Lazy Lena (IRE)**[7] [781] 6-10-11 **75** NPMulholland —
(Miss L C Siddall) *hld up in tch: wknd after 3 out* **7/1**[2]

6130 **13** 5 **Somewin (IRE)**[28] [575] 5-9-13 **71** (v1) RSpate(8) —
(Mrs K Waldron) *hld up: hdwy after 6th: wknd 8th* **7/1**[2]

/3-P **P** **Noble Spy (IRE)**[28] [575] 11-11-3 **81** (p) RStephens —
(Mrs D A Hamer) *hld up: a bhd: t.o whn p.u bef 3 out* **22/1**

5-P0 **P** **Oro Street (IRE)**[36] [451] 9-11-8 **86** (p) TGreenway —
(G F Bridgwater) *chsd ldrs: lost pl after 3rd: t.o whn p.u bef 8th* **50/1**

-554 **P** **Fullopep**[19] [670] 11-11-10 **88** JamesDavies —
(J R Holt) *chsd ldrs: mstke 7th: sn rdn: wknd next: t.o whn p.u bef 3 out* **16/1**

5m 19.6s (-25.10) **Going Correction** -1.15s/f (Hard)
WFA 4 from 5yo+ 4lb **16** Ran SP% **127.7**
Speed ratings: **97,94,94,94,93 93,91,90,89,88 86,—,—,—,— —** CSF £114.87 CT £367.82 TOTE £14.20: £2.30, £1.50, £1.20, £21.20; EX 184.10.The winner was bought in for 4,000gns. Astronaut was claimed by Richard Guest for £6,000. Fiddles Music was claimed by Donald Gould for £6,000.
Owner C T Pogson **Bred** Donal Turner **Trained** Farnsfield, Notts

FOCUS
A very ordinary selling handicap with the fourth limiting the form.

NOTEBOOK
Idlewild(IRE) could be named the winner some way from home and this trip proved no problem on his return to selling company. *(op 11-1)*
Fiddles Music, stepping up in distance for this drop into a seller, proved no match for the winner *and was lucky to finish second. She was subsequently claimed by Richard Guest for £6,000. (op 8-1 tchd 10-1)*
Astronaut ran away with a similar event over slightly shorter here when last seen under Rules in August 2003. The winner of his last two points, he had worked hard to secure second place when *his rider apparently mistook the winning post. However, it turned out that his mount was very lame. Official explanation: jockey said gelding lost its action close home; vet said gelding finished lame (op 11-4 tchd 3-1)*
Kingcombe Lane ran by far his best race to date over a trip that may have stretched him to the limit. *(op 50-1)*
Angie's Double was 9lb higher than when a convincing winner of a similar contest over a quarter of a mile less here last month. *(tchd 8-1)*
Nimvara(IRE) settled better in this lower grade and perhaps two and a half miles is as far as she wants to go.

840 CITY OF STOKE ON TRENT CELEBRATION PLATE H'CAP CHASE (11 fncs 1 omitted) 2m
3:20 (3:21) (Class 3) (0-135,130) 5-Y-0+ **£10,186** (£3,134; £1,567; £783)

Form RPR

12-1 **1** **Danish Decorum (IRE)**[43] [354] 6-10-7 **111** ChristianWilliams 125+
(Evan Williams) *chsd ldr: led 3rd to 5th: led after 4 out: rdn after 2 out: r.o wl* **3/1**[1]

36P- **2** 2½ **Duke Of Buckingham (IRE)**[80] [4751] 9-11-12 **130** TDoyle 141
(P R Webber) *hld up in mid-div: hdwy 7th: chsd wnr 3 out: mstke 2 out: rdn and r.o one pce* **12/1**

123U **3** 3½ **Saafend Rocket (IRE)**[11] [761] 7-10-13 **117** RJohnson 124
(H D Daly) *hld up and bhd: hdwy appr 7th: sn rdn: kpt on same pce fr 2 out* **8/1**[3]

-224 **4** nk **Escompteur (FR)**[18] [682] 5-10-10 **115** TJMurphy 122+
(M C Pipe) *hld up in mid-div: hdwy appr 7th: ev ch 4 out: one pce fr 3 out* **8/1**[3]

4-21 **5** 2 **Papua**[24] [615] 11-10-7 **111** (b) DRDennis 116
(N J Hawke) *chsd ldrs: rdn and no hdwy fr 3 out* **9/1**

054 **6** 7 **Billie John (IRE)**[15] [714] 10-10-5 **109** RMcGrath 107
(Mrs K Walton) *chsd ldrs tl rdn and wknd after 3 out* **28/1**

05-2 **7** 2 **Lord Of The Hill (IRE)**[49] [246] 10-10-3 **107** JEMoore 105+
(G Brown) *led to 3rd: led 5th: mstke 7th: rdn and hdd after 4 out: wknd after 3 out* **16/1**

-23P **8** dist **Odagh Odyssey (IRE)**[14] [726] 11-11-4 **122** (v) BJCrowley —
(Miss E C Lavelle) *j.rt 1st: a bhd: t.o* **33/1**

06-3 **P** **Half An Hour**[20] [666] 8-10-6 **110** (v) RThornton —
(A King) *a bhd: t.o whn p.u bef 7th* **10/1**

P16 **P** **Pequenita**[27] [595] 5-10-10 **115** (p) HOliver —
(R C Guest) *bhd: rdn 3rd: t.o 5th: p.u bef 7th* **40/1**

0211 **P** **Nephite (NZ)**[21] [644] 11-10-7 **111** ow1 SThomas —
(Miss Venetia Williams) *a bhd: t.o whn p.u bef 4 out* **10/1**

/41- **P** **Orinocovsky (IRE)**[25] [1373] 6-10-4 **108** PMoloney —
(N P Littmoden) *chsd ldrs to 5th: t.o whn p.u bef 3 out* **12/1**

U **Magic Sky (FR)**[105] 5-11-5 **124** (t) RWalsh —
(P F Nicholls) *hld up in mid-div: hdwy appr 7th: prom whn tried to run out and uns rdr 4 out* **5/1**[2]

3m 44.1s (-20.90) **Going Correction** -1.15s/f (Hard)
WFA 5 from 6yo+ 1lb **13** Ran SP% **122.2**
Speed ratings: **106,104,103,102,101 98,97,—,—,— —,—,—** CSF £39.45 CT £272.33 TOTE £3.80: £2.00, £2.70, £2.80; EX 60.90.
Owner W Ralph Thomas **Bred** Michael Doyle And Christy Ryan **Trained** Cowbridge, Vale Of Glamorgan

FOCUS
A strongly-run race resulted in a fast time with several front-runners in the field. The form looks solid with the placed horses running to their marks.

NOTEBOOK
Danish Decorum(IRE) shrugged off an 11lb hike in the ratings for his course and distance win last month. He is a progressive two-mile chaser. *(op 10-3 tchd 7-2)*
Duke Of Buckingham(IRE) was returning after being pulled up at the Grand National meeting. He gave a very good account of himself but could not cope with an improving type at these weights.
Saafend Rocket(IRE), who has yet to win going left-handed, stuck to his task on a drop back to the minimum trip. *(op 9-1)*
Escompteur(FR) seemed to have his fair share of weight based on what he has actually achieved over fences.
Papua, raised 7lb for his course and distance win, had finished five lengths behind Danish Decorum on 2lb worse terms here last month. *(tchd 10-1)*
Half An Hour *Official explanation: jockey said gelding was never travelling (op 6-1)*
Magic Sky(FR), three times a winner on soft ground over fences in France, blotted his copy book when around three lengths down at the fourth last. *(op 6-1)*

841 WEATHERBYS BANK H'CAP HURDLE (12 hdls) 2m 4f 110y
3:55 (3:55) (Class 4) (0-110,110) 4-Y-0+ **£4,595** (£1,414; £707; £353)

Form RPR

41-0 **1** **Herne Bay (IRE)**[20] [665] 5-11-0 **98** JPMcNamara 103+
(R S Brookhouse) *hld up in tch: led 2 out: rdn out* **20/1**

41-2 **2** 3 **Izzykeen**[29] [552] 6-11-7 **105** DElsworth 107+
(Mrs S J Smith) *led to 7th: led appr 3 out: rdn and hdd next: styd on same pce flat* **5/1**[1]

1 **3** 1¾ **Lawyer Des Ormeaux (FR)**[12] [748] 6-11-7 **105** RJohnson 104
(P Bowen) *a.p: rdn 2 out: styd on same pce last* **11/2**[2]

-202 **4** 7 **Pilca (FR)**[17] [695] 5-11-2 **100** (p) RThornton 92
(R M Stronge) *mid-div: hdwy 7th: rdn and wknd appr last* **14/1**

00-2 **5** 1¾ **Titian Flame (IRE)**[12] [747] 5-10-8 **97** LStephens(5) 87+
(D Burchell) *hld up: styd on fr 2 out: nt rch ldrs* **8/1**

U-43 **6** 3 **Golfagent**[28] [573] 7-11-1 **106** (t) RSpate(7) 93
(Mrs K Waldron) *hld up: hdwy 7th: wknd 2 out* **16/1**

-302 **7** 3 **Joshua's Bay**[19] [675] 7-11-10 **108** GLee 92
(J R Jenkins) *hld up: hdwy 9th: wknd 3 out* **12/1**

13 **8** 3½ **Diamond Cutter (NZ)**[18] [691] 6-11-4 **107** PCO'Neill(5) 88
(R C Guest) *chsd ldrs: ev ch 3 out: wknd after next* **13/2**[3]

00- **9** 3½ **Ingres**[45] [18] 5-11-3 **101** RWalsh 78
(B G Powell) *hld up: a in rr* **12/1**

1PP- **10** 1¾ **Spike And Divel (IRE)**[250] [1774] 7-10-13 **97** APMcCoy 75+
(Jonjo O'Neill) *chsd ldr tl led 7th: mstke next: hdd appr 3 out: sn wknd* **9/1**

2100 **11** 17 **Forzacurity**[14] [726] 6-11-8 **106** DRDennis 65
(M Sheppard) *hld up: wknd 4 out* **25/1**

-00P **12** 8 **Celtic Star (IRE)**[7] [505] 7-11-9 **110** (b) DCrosse(3) 61
(Mrs L Williamson) *mid-div: hdwy 6th: wknd after 9th* **50/1**

4-32 **13** shd **Musally**[28] [573] 8-11-2 **100** CLlewellyn 50
(W Jenks) *mid-div: mstke 1st: wknd 7th* **10/1**

-54R **R** **Kalambari (IRE)**[14] [726] 6-11-5 **110** (p) SWalsh(7) —
(J Joseph) *ref to r* **25/1**

BP-4 **P** **Kirov King (IRE)**[28] [568] 5-10-11 **95** JTizzard —
(B G Powell) *bhd fr 6th: t.o whn p.u bef 2 out* **33/1**

-PP6 **P** **Davoski**[20] [668] 11-11-5 **103** (b) JAMcCarthy —
(Dr P Pritchard) *chsd ldrs: lost pl 5th: mstke and wknd 7th: t.o whn p.u bef 3 out* **40/1**

-20R **P** **Homeleigh Mooncoin**[31] [508] 10-11-1 **99** JamesDavies —
(B G Powell) *chsd ldrs: rdn 4th: sn lost pl: bhd fr 7th: t.o whn p.u bef 9th* **66/1**

4m 50.1s (-22.00) **Going Correction** -1.15s/f (Hard) **17** Ran SP% **124.8**
Speed ratings: **95,93,93,90,89 88,87,86,84,84 77,74,74,—,— —,—** CSF £115.28 CT £650.63 TOTE £35.90: £8.00, £1.40, £1.70, £4.50; EX 298.50.
Owner R S Brookhouse **Bred** Roland H Alder **Trained** Wixford, Warwicks

FOCUS
A moderate affair with the winner having only landed a seller two outings ago. However, the first three all have the potential to rate higher.

NOTEBOOK
Herne Bay(IRE), disappointing when stepped up in distance at Newton Abbot last time, returned to *the form that saw him bolt up in a Stratford seller in March.Official explanation: trainer said, regarding the improved form shown, gelding was better suited by today's ground (tchd 22-1)*
Izzykeen, back up in distance, found the winner too much of a handful off a 3lb higher mark. *(op 9-2)*
Lawyer Des Ormeaux(FR) is lightly-raced and ought to be capable of improvement but on this occasion the Handicapper did appear to have his measure. *(op 9-2)*
Pilca(FR) seemed to get found out by the longer trip.
Titian Flame(IRE), raised 5lb, found she had given the leaders too much rope on this return to a longer distance. *(op 9-1)*

842 BRITANNIA BUILDING SOCIETY ENGLISH SUMMER NATIONAL (A H'CAP CHASE) (21 fncs 3 omitted) 4m 110y
4:25 (4:30) (Class 2) (0-140,140) 5-Y-0+
£43,500 (£16,500; £8,250; £3,750; £1,875; £1,125)

Form RPR

0-03 **1** **Rheindross (IRE)**[11] [761] 10-10-3 **117** NFehily 135+
(C J Mann) *a gng wl: led 16th: clr appr last: easily* **25/1**

-15P **2** 7 **Caught At Dawn (IRE)**[15] 11-10-6 **120** RThornton 130
(M H Weston) *hld up in mid-div: hdwy 8th: rdn and ev ch 3 out: one pce fr 2 out* **25/1**

3P21 **3** 10 **Gumley Gale**[31] [516] 10-10-9 **123** (t) RGreene 123
(K Bishop) *hld up in tch: rdn and wknd 3 out* **25/1**

0R-3 **4** 2½ **Swansea Bay**[10] [768] 9-10-13 **127** MAFitzgerald 125
(P Bowen) *hld up in tch: rdn after 17th: wknd 3 out* **12/1**

F10- **5** 2 **Comanche War Paint (IRE)**[65] [4967] 8-10-6 **120** RWalsh 116
(P F Nicholls) *hld up in mid-div: rdn appr 17th: no real prog fr 4 out* **4/1**[1]

U4-2 **6** shd **Double Honour (FR)**[38] [423] 7-11-12 **140** (b) PJBrennan 137+
(P J Hobbs) *w ldr: led 15th to 16th: rdn after 17th: ev ch whn mstke 4 out: sn wknd* **8/1**

3-33 **7** 9 **Isard III (FR)**[21] [648] 9-10-13 **127** TJMurphy 113
(M C Pipe) *hld up and bhd: mstke 5th: hdwy 15th: wknd appr 3 out* **20/1**

-122 **8** 1 **Curtins Hill (IRE)**[21] [648] 11-10-1 **122** RSpate(7) 110+
(Mrs K Waldron) *mstke 1st: blnd 2nd: a bhd* **28/1**

PU/1 **9** ½ **Merry Path (IRE)**[28] [572] 11-10-1 **115** PMoloney 100
(Evan Williams) *mid-div: lost pl 13th: in rr whn mstke 14th: n.d after* **8/1**

00/1 **10** 13 **Pay It Forward**[42] [379] 7-11-1 **129** RMPower 103+
(Mrs John Harrington, Ire) *hld up and bhd: mstkes 7th and 11th: hdwy whn mstke 15th: wknd after 4 out* **9/2**[2]

2F-1 **11** 8 **Meneur De Jeu (FR)**[20] [667] 5-10-9 **129** APMcCoy 87
(M C Pipe) *a bhd* **10/1**

-335 **P** **Kock De La Vesvre (FR)**[21] [648] 7-11-5 **133** SThomas —
(Miss Venetia Williams) *a bhd: t.o whn p.u bef 2 out* **25/1**

4F-F **P** **Lord Noelie (IRE)**[38] [423] 12-11-10 **138** JMMaguire —
(Mrs Jeremy Young) *led to 15th: wknd qckly 16th: p.u bef 17th* **22/1**

/0- **P** **Royal Tir (FR)**[414] [224] 9-10-13 **127** RJohnson —
(P J Hobbs) *hld up in tch: lost pl after 14th: t.o whn p.u bef 17th* **40/1**

260- **P** **French Executive (IRE)**[74] [4821] 10-10-13 **127** ChristianWilliams —
(P F Nicholls) *hld up towards rr: hdwy appr 17th: wkng whn blnd 4 out: bhd whn p.u bef 2 out* **22/1**

4/P- **P** **Bassett Tiger (IRE)**[15] [721] 9-10-7 **121** (t) JCulloty —
(W P Mullins, Ire) *t.k.h in rr: hdwy after 10th: lost pl 13th: rallied 17th: wknd appr 4 out: bhd whn p.u bef 2 out* **7/1**[3]

8m 16.1s
WFA 5 from 7yo+ 6lb **16** Ran SP% **124.4**
CSF £507.44 CT £14657.65 TOTE £37.10: £6.10, £7.30, £6.40, £2.50; EX 780.20 TRIFECTA Not won..
Owner Brian Walsh (Co Kildare) **Bred** Brian Neilan and John Hanly **Trained** Upper Lambourn, Berks

FOCUS
They went no great pace despite the fast ground in this stamina contest, but with the placed horses close to their marks the race might work out.

NOTEBOOK
Rheindross(IRE) was a turn up for the books on this big step up in distance and there was no one more surprised than his trainer. He is now suddenly considered a Velka Pardubicka type.
Caught At Dawn(IRE), switching to handicaps from hunter chases, was another who proved to be a bit of a revelation but not quite as much as the winner. *(op 33-1)*
Gumley Gale seemed to have plenty to do off a 9lb higher mark and did not see out this marathon distance as well as the first two. *(tchd 33-1 in places)*
Swansea Bay, attempting four miles for the first time on this switch back to fences, was another who did not seem to get home. *(tchd 14-1)*
Comanche War Paint(IRE), one of the few proven stayers in the field, was rather going up and down on the spot in the home straight.
Double Honour(FR) was another who was more or less guaranteed to stay but his error at the first in the home straight spelt the beginning of the end. *(op 9-1)*
Pay It Forward was let down by his jumping. *(op 4-1)*

843 BELLHOUSERACING.COM MAIDEN HURDLE (12 hdls) 2m 4f 110y
4:55 (5:04) (Class 4) 4-Y-0+ **£4,023** (£1,238; £619; £309)

Form RPR

4-02 **1** **Stagecoach Diamond**[27] [591] 6-11-2 DElsworth 103
(Mrs S J Smith) *hld up: hdwy 6th: nt fluent 3 out: sn rdn: ev ch whn lft in ld flat: all out* **9/4**[1]

2 **2** *shd* **Getoutwhenyoucan (IRE)**[12] [748] 5-11-2 TJMurphy 103
(M C Pipe) *hld up: hdwy 6th: rdn and ev ch flat: styd on* **5/2**[2]

5 **3** *9* **Ponchatrain (IRE)**[18] [685] 5-11-2 WMarston 101+
(D J Wintle) *chsd ldrs: led 4 out: slt ld whn blnd last: sn hdd and nt rcvr* **25/1**

P/ **4** *8* **Incorporation**[8] [2059] 6-10-13 RHobson(3) 86
(M Appleby) *hld up: hdwy after 8th: wkng whn hit 3 out* **100/1**

1/0- **5** *14* **Aide De Camp (FR)**[191] [2873] 6-11-2 GLee 72
(M Todhunter) *trckd ldr: plld hrd: led 4th: hdd 4 out: wknd next* **12/1**

6 *1 3/4* **Scarrabus (IRE)**[40] 4-10-12 RWalsh 66
(B G Powell) *hld up: hdwy 9th: wknd next* **11/2**[3]

450- **7** *10* **Moscow Executive**[199] [2730] 7-10-9 ATinkler 53
(W M Brisbourne) *hld up: hdwy and blnd 8th: sn wknd* **50/1**

8 *7* **Dubai Dreams**[61] 5-10-13 LVickers(3) 53
(S R Bowring) *led: j. slowly and hdd 4th: wknd 9th* **25/1**

000/ **9** *15* **Lolanita**[738] [4180] 7-10-4 RStephens(5) 31
(Tim Vaughan) *prom to 9th* **100/1**

/0P4 **10** *1 1/2* **Mapilut Du Moulin (FR)**[12] [742] 5-11-2 PJBrennan 37
(C R Dore) *prom: mstke and wknd 7th* **40/1**

F **The Sneakster (IRE)** 7-10-9 MFoley —
(S A Brookshaw) *hld up: fell 3rd* **50/1**

0-00 **P** **Slight Hiccup**[43] [343] 5-10-9 AO'Keeffe —
(C W Moore) *a bhd: t.o whn p.u bef 8th* **100/1**

/10- **P** **Saxon Mist**[71] [4865] 6-11-2 RThornton —
(A King) *hld up: rdn 5th: sn wknd: t.o whn p.u bef 8th* **13/2**

3-55 **P** **Men Of Destiny (IRE)**[20] [667] 4-10-12 JTizzard —
(B G Powell) *prom: rdn and lost pl 5th: sn bhd: t.o whn p.u bef 8th* **50/1**

4m 54.7s (-17.40) **Going Correction** -1.15s/f (Hard)
WFA 4 from 5yo+ 4lb **14** Ran SP% **114.7**
Speed ratings: **87,86,83,80,75 74,70,68,62,61** —,—,—,— CSF £7.19 TOTE £3.10: £1.60, £1.30, £4.70; EX 8.80.
Owner Mrs Jacqueline Conroy **Bred** R Russell **Trained** High Eldwick, W Yorks

FOCUS
Quantity rather than quality in this maiden hurdle, the time was slow and could be suspect.

NOTEBOOK
Stagecoach Diamond, who won his bumper on this sort of ground, held on by the skin of his teeth after taking advantage of Ponchatrain's blunder at the last. *(op 5-2 tchd 15-8)*
Getoutwhenyoucan(IRE) went down by the narrowest of margins with all guns blazing over a trip that would have been short of his best. He should soon go one better. *(op 7-4)*
Ponchatrain(IRE) ◆ was being strongly pressed but still looked the one to catch on this hurdling debut when making a real nonsense of the last. He deserves another chance. *(tchd 33-1)*
Incorporation, pulled up on his only previous try over hurdles in November 2002, would have been fit enough after four outings on the Flat.
Saxon Mist *Official explanation: jockey said gelding lost its confidence (op 15-2)*

844 RACECOURSE VIDEO SERVICES STANDARD OPEN NATIONAL HUNT FLAT RACE 2m
5:30 (5:33) (Class 6) 4-6-Y-O **£2,002** (£572; £286)

Form RPR

150- **1** **Don And Gerry (IRE)**[106] [4333] 4-10-5 AntonyEvans(3) 94+
(P D Evans) *led 2f: a.p: led on bit 3f out: clr over 1f out: easily* **9/2**[3]

2 *6* **Super Revo** 4-11-1 GLee 93
(Miss J A Camacho) *prom: rdn 5f out: outpcd over 3f out: rallied to take 2nd ins fnl f: no ch w wnr* **8/1**

3 *1* **Coeur D'Alene** 4-11-1 AThornton 92
(Dr J R J Naylor) *hld up and bhd: hdwy over 3f out: styd on fnl f* **6/1**

4 *5* **Zen Garden** 4-10-8 APMcCoy 80
(W M Brisbourne) *hld up and bhd: rdn and hdwy over 3f out: one pce fnl 2f* **3/1**[1]

5 *1 1/2* **Lady Roania (IRE)** 5-10-11 RGreene 82
(S C Burrough) *w ldr: led 5f out: rdn and hdd 3f out: wknd fnl f* **40/1**

6 *14* **Thenford Lad (IRE)** 4-11-1 MBradburne 72
(D J S Ffrench Davis) *led after 2f to 5f out: wknd over 3f out* **20/1**

7 *hd* **Pretty Lady Rose**[43] 5-10-4 MrMWall(7) 67
(T Wall) *hld up in mid-div: wknd over 3f out* **66/1**

8 *1* **According To Plan (IRE)** 5-10-11 CPoste(7) 73
(A E Jones) *prom: rdn over 4f out: hung rt bnd and wknd over 3f out* **25/1**

3 **9** *1* **Snargate**[35] [470] 5-11-4 RWalford 72
(T D Walford) *hld up: short-lived effrt over 9f out* **8/1**

10 *3 1/2* **Bugle**[27] 5-11-4 ChristianWilliams 69
(Evan Williams) *hld up: rdn and short-lived effrt over 3f out* **7/2**[2]

11 *29* **Ciarans Lass** 6-10-5 ow1 MrRHodges(7) 34
(C Roberts) *a bhd* **33/1**

12 *dist* **Must Be Mistaken** 4-10-1 MrPCollington(7) —
(A L Forbes) *hld up in tch: lost pl 8f out: t.o* **40/1**

3m 50.0s (-9.80) **Going Correction** -1.15s/f (Hard)
WFA 4 from 5yo+ 3lb **12** Ran SP% **119.8**
Speed ratings: **78,75,74,72,71 64,64,63,63,61 46,**— CSF £37.64 TOTE £6.10: £2.50, £2.20, £1.70; EX 48.10 Place 6 £271.74, Place 5 £104.01..
Owner D Healy **Bred** Pat Jones **Trained** Pandy, Abergavenny

FOCUS
This bumper was very slowly run and, dominated by newcomers, may not have taken much winning.

NOTEBOOK
Don And Gerry(IRE) came back to the sort of form that saw her win a weak Ludlow bumper on her debut. She seemed to relish the sounder surface. *(op 7-2)*
Super Revo, six times a winner at up to a mile and a quarter in Poland, did show a little promise for the future. *(op 9-1 tchd 10-1)*
Coeur D'Alene shaped well enough on his debut and will have hopefully learnt a lot. *(op 13-2 tchd 11-2)*
Zen Garden, a Khalid Abdulla cast-off, is a half-brother to a mile and three-quarter Fibresand winner and six and seven-furlong Polytrack winner Roman Maze. *(op 11-4 tchd 4-1)*
Lady Roania(IRE) is out of a winning Irish pointer.
T/Jkpt: Not won. T/Plt: £194.70 to a £1 stake. Pool: £70,204.10. 263.20 winning tickets. T/Qpdt: £41.40 to a £1 stake. Pool: £4,448.40. 79.50 winning tickets. KH

LE TOUQUET (L-H)
Sunday, June 26

OFFICIAL GOING: Good

845a PRIX JACQUES GELIOT (CROSS-COUNTRY CHASE) 3m 2f
3:00 (12:00) 5-Y-0+ **£6,809** (£3,404; £1,986; £1,348; £638)

RPR

1 **Karine Des Ongrais (FR)**[63] 10-10-5 MrPBrechet —
(P Chemin, France)

2 *3/4* **Dulcigris (FR)**[754] 9-10-5 LDeschamps —
(J-P Carnel, France)

3 *dist* **Dekatell Le Dun (FR)**[364] 14-10-5 LHoubron —
(A Sannier, France)

4 *dist* **Bidou (FR)**[1558] 10-10-5 (b) PBigot —
(P Cottin, France)

5 *dist* **Joie Du Manoir (FR)**[991] 8-9-13 MrPPaysan —
(Mme L Bellet, France) *refused, continued to finish 5th*

6 *dist* **Kirless (FR)** 7-10-1 ALeCourtois —
(P Quinton, France) *refused, continued to finish 6th*

F **Kasbimy (FR)**[1361] 6-10-3 BLombart —
(J-P Carnel, France)

P **Joint Authority (IRE)**[14] [725] 10-10-10 CaptLHorner —
(D L Williams)

8 Ran
PARI-MUTUEL (including 1 Euro Stake): WIN 3.40; PL 1.50, 2.00, 1.90; DF 46.60.
Owner Mme P Chemin **Bred** Marc & Mme Odile Trincot **Trained** France

NOTEBOOK
Joint Authority(IRE) faced little chance of winning and never threatened to land a blow.

846a PRIX OFFICE DU TOURISME CAMIERS SAINTE-CECILE (CLAMING HURDLE) 2m 1f
4:00 (12:00) 5-Y-0+ **£3,745** (£1,872; £1,092; £741; £351)

RPR

1 **Don De Matha (FR)**[28] 5-10-8 (b) LHoubron —
(D Grandin, France)

2 *1* **Leviathan De Brule (FR)** 5-10-3 GDerat —
(J P Delbe, France)

3 *7* **Princess Morgane (USA)**[32] 5-9-13 J-LBeaunez —
(P Alexanian, France)

4 *3/4* **Bercaldoun (FR)**[105] 6-10-12 JeremyLobel —
(P Chatelain, France)

5 *3* **Dianica (FR)**[49] 6-10-8 (b) ACordelet —
(R Le Gal, France)

6 *1/2* **Maradamo (FR)**[91] 5-10-3 (b) CSanterne —
(R Le Gal, France)

7 *1 1/2* **Kurbani (FR)**[1182] 7-10-8 SDrillot —
(H Billot, France)

8 *dist* **Petit Owen (FR)**[19] 5-10-3 RHouchard —
(F Weisgerber, France)

9 *dist* **Le Pacha De Cercy (FR)** 6-10-8 CECayeux —
(H Billot, France)

10 *dist* **Macgyver (NZ)**[19] [674] 9-10-12 CaptLHorner —
(D L Williams)

0 **Guinelia (FR)** 6-10-3 RMercey —
(C Bertrand, France)

0 **Dream Seeker (USA)**[60] 8-10-8 MRegainaz —
(F Weisgerber, France)

0 **Star De Lambre (FR)**[1010] 6-10-12 PBigot —
(J-P Cordonnier, France)

R **Loi Martiale (FR)**[743] 7-10-3 LDeschamps —
(P Quinton, France) *refused to race*

F **Jolie Mome Deux (FR)** 5-10-3 RBonnet —
(F Bellenger, France)

P **La Petite Lulu (FR)**[747] 5-10-3 BLombart —
(J-P Carnel, France)

16 Ran
PARI-MUTUEL: WIN 4.90; PL 2.10, 7.50, 2.00; DF 26.70.
Owner D Grandin **Bred** P Dibatista & Gaec La Vastine **Trained** France

NOTEBOOK
Macgyver(NZ) was tailed off and offered little.

847 - 853a (Foreign Racing) - See Raceform Interactive

643 PERTH (R-H)

Wednesday, June 29

OFFICIAL GOING: Good to firm (firm in places in back straight)

Wind: almost nil

854 DEVIL'S HORSEMEN JOUSTING SATURDAY JULY 10TH MARES' ONLY MAIDEN HURDLE (10 hdls) 2m 4f 110y

2:20 (2:20) (Class 4) 4-Y-0+ **£3,542** (£1,090; £545; £272)

Form				RPR
/-44	**1**		**Cheery Martyr**[18] 715 7-11-0 85 FKeniry (P Needham) *hld up: hdwy and prom 3 out: drvn bef next: styd on wl to ld nr fin* **10/1**	86
	2	*shd*	**Ring Street Roller (IRE)**[12] 774 5-11-0 RJohnson (J J Lambe, Ire) *in tch on outside: led after 3 out: wandered bdly u.p between last two: hung bdly lft run in: kpt on: hdd cl home* **6/1**[2]	89+
455-	**3**	*5*	**Tea's Maid**[335] 1069 5-11-0 80 GLee (Mrs A M Thorpe) *chsd ldrs tl rdn and nt qckn fr 2 out* **10/1**	81
000	**4**	*3 ½*	**Penteli**[29] 602 5-10-11 74 MrTGreenall(3) (C Grant) *in tch: outpcd bef 3 out: rallied next: no imp* **25/1**	78
0	**5**	*14*	**Staff Nurse (IRE)**[37] 192 5-11-0 KRenwick (N Wilson) *hld up: hdwy bef 3 out: no imp fr next* **8/1**[3]	64
34P4	**6**	*¾*	**Uneven Line**[24] 649 9-10-11 81 (p) MrCStorey(3) (Miss S E Forster) *prom tl wknd bef 2 out* **8/1**[3]	63
0/4	**7**	*5*	**Bella Liana (IRE)**[35] 500 5-10-9 ow2 MrSClements(7) (J Clements, Ire) *bhd: rdn whn hmpd bef 3 out: no ch whn hmpd last* **50/1**	65+
0-65	**8**	*29*	**Moments Madness (IRE)**[10] 785 6-11-0 KJohnson (Miss S E Forster) *bhd: rdn 1/2-way: nvr on terms* **50/1**	29
-465	**9**	*1 ½*	**Roadworthy (IRE)**[18] 718 8-10-7 MrSFMagee(7) (J K Magee, Ire) *led to 4 out: wknd next* **40/1**	27
110-	**10**	*12*	**Arctic Moss (IRE)**[109] 4333 6-11-0 JPMcNamara (E W Tuer) *nt fluent in rr: mstke and nrly uns rdr 2nd: no imp whn sltly hmpd bef 3 out* **15/8**[1]	15
-P3P	**P**		**Aba Gold (IRE)**[24] 643 5-10-9 DFlavin(5) (Mrs L B Normile) *a bhd: p.u bef 7th* **50/1**	—
P/40	**P**		**Blue Bar**[24] 649 7-11-0 85 (p) RMcGrath (G A Harker) *chsd ldrs: hit 4 out: broke down and p.u bef next* **8/1**[3]	—
0-00	**P**		**Clouds Of Gold (IRE)**[24] 651 4-10-10 72 ARoss (J S Wainwright) *in tch to 1/2-way: sn lost pl: t.o whn p.u bef 2 out* **50/1**	—
F6-0	**F**		**Gemini Lady**[6] 649 5-10-11 81 PBuchanan(3) (Mrs J C McGregor) *cl up: mstke but led 4 out: hdd after next: sn outpcd: btn whn fell last* **33/1**	64

4m 57.1s (-11.10) **Going Correction** -0.50s/f (Good)
WFA 4 from 5yo+ 4lb **14** Ran SP% **117.7**
Speed ratings: **101,100,99,97,92 92,90,79,78,74** —,—,—,— CSF £64.89 TOTE £10.80: £2.30, £2.10, £2.90; EX 87.50.
Owner P Needham **Bred** P Aconley **Trained** Marwood, Co Durham

FOCUS
A low-grade and uncompetitive race in which the market leader disappointed on her hurdling debut. The third is the best guide to the form.

NOTEBOOK
Cheery Martyr appreciated the step up to this trip and showed the right attitude to beat a wayward rival. She will find life tougher under a penalty in this type of race, though, and modest handicaps will be the way forward. *(tchd 8-1)*
Ring Street Roller(IRE) bettered the form of her hurdles debut over this longer trip but looked a hard ride in this modest event and, given she would almost certainly have won had she kept straight, would not be one to take a short price about. *(op 11-2)*
Tea's Maid was not disgraced on this first start for a year but is exposed as modest and, although worth a try over three miles, is likely to continue to look vulnerable in this type of event. *(op 14-1)*
Penteli seemed to run her best race to date over hurdles and left the strong impression that the step up to three miles and the move into handicaps would suit. *(op 20-1)*
Staff Nurse(IRE), a Banded Flat winner, had her limitations exposed in this modest race and is likely to continue to look vulnerable in this grade.
Uneven Line is a modest and inconsistent performer who was well beaten back over this longer trip. She is not the best betting proposition around. *(op 10-1)*
Arctic Moss(IRE), a triple bumper winner, looked sure to go well in this company on this hurdles *debut, but she ran poorly and will have to brush up her jumping if she is to progress in this sphere. Official explanation: jockey said mare was never travelling; vet said mare finished slightly lame on the right fore (op 2-1 tchd 9-4)*

855 FAMOUS GROUSE NOVICES' CHASE (12 fncs) 2m

2:50 (2:51) (Class 3) 5-Y-0+ **£6,734** (£2,072; £1,036; £518)

Form				RPR
41-1	**1**		**Kid'Z'Play (IRE)**[24] 646 9-11-4 RMcGrath (J S Goldie) *mde all: rdn and hld on wl fr 2 out* **3/1**[2]	118+
20-2	**2**	*2 ½*	**Dawton (POL)**[21] 682 7-10-12 JMMaguire (T R George) *pressed wnr: mstke 4 out: sn rdn: kpt on fr 2 out* **7/4**[1]	109+
611P	**3**	*3*	**Moscow Dancer (IRE)**[13] 767 8-11-10 108 NPMulholland (P Monteith) *hld up: hdwy after 7th: effrt 2 out: one pce last* **8/1**	116
	4	*13*	**Glenfolan (IRE)**[60] 7-10-12 BHarding (A J Martin, Ire) *prom tl rdn and wknd bef 2 out* **28/1**	91
P-55	**5**	*18*	**Simply Da Best (IRE)**[24] 646 7-10-12 (b) RJohnson (J J Lambe, Ire) *hld up in tch: hdwy and prom 1/2-way: wknd bef 3 out* **16/1**	73
0P-0	**6**	*3 ½*	**Seeyaaj**[41] 428 5-10-8 (t) PBuchanan(3) (Miss Lucinda V Russell) *hld up: hdwy and prom 1/2-way: blnd and wknd 4 out* **66/1**	69
3545	**7**	*7*	**Snooty Eskimo (IRE)**[18] 717 13-10-7 77 ow2 MajorHNorton(7) (W T Reed) *chsd ldrs tl wknd fr 8th* **100/1**	65
110-	**8**	*15*	**Manoubi**[59] 1640 6-10-12 ADobbin (M Todhunter) *in tch: lost pl 6th: n.d after* **9/2**[3]	48
-264	**U**		**Kalou (GER)**[20] 692 7-10-9 101 (p) MrTGreenall(3) (C Grant) *hld up in tch: mstke and uns rdr 4th* **12/1**	—

3m 53.0s (-9.80) **Going Correction** -0.50s/f (Good)
WFA 5 from 6yo+ 1lb **9** Ran SP% **110.2**
Speed ratings: **104,102,101,94,85 84,80,73,**— CSF £8.36 TOTE £3.70: £1.30, £1.50, £2.60; EX 4.60.
Owner Liam McGuigan **Bred** B S I Nv **Trained** Uplawmoor, E Renfrews

FOCUS
A reasonable contest in which the pace was sound and this bare form is solid and should stand up at a similar level.

NOTEBOOK
Kid'Z'Play(IRE) ◆ turned in an improved effort to maintain his unbeaten record over obstacles at this course on this much quicker ground. His jumping was sound, he has the right attitude, is best *when able to dominate, and he will be interesting in ordinary handicaps around tight tracks. (op 9-4 tchd 7-2 in places)*
Dawton(POL) had shaped well on his chasing debut and again ran creditably, especially as he made a mistake at a crucial stage. He is best on a sound surface and looks sure to win a similar race. *(op 9-4 tchd 5-2 in places)*
Moscow Dancer(IRE), who ran poorly upped to two and a half miles last time, jumped with more fluency and fared much better under his double penalty back over this trip. He is likely to remain *vulnerable in this type of event and will be of more interest in handicaps against exposed rivals. (op 10-1)*
Glenfolan(IRE), an Irish point winner when last seen in April, left the impression that this trip was very much on the sharp side and he may fare better over further and in modest handicaps in due course. *(op 25-1 tchd 33-1)*
Simply Da Best(IRE) is an inconsistent sort who again had his limitations exposed in this type of event. His lack of consistency means he is not a reliable betting proposition.
Seeyaaj faced a stiff task on this chasing debut and offered little immediate promise.
Snooty Eskimo(IRE) *Official explanation: jockey said gelding lost a front shoe*
Manoubi, a dual hurdles winner at this course, proved most disappointing on this chase debut and looks one to tread carefully with. *(op 7-2)*

856 CHRISTMAS PARTIES IN THE NELSON STAND NOVICES' H'CAP HURDLE (10 hdls) 2m 4f 110y

3:20 (3:21) (Class 4) (0-100,100) 4-Y-0+ **£4,290** (£1,320; £660; £330)

Form				RPR
50P-	**1**		**Red Chief (IRE)**[140] 3764 5-10-6 80 GLee (Mrs A M Thorpe) *hld up: hdwy 3 out: rdn to ld last: kpt on wl* **8/1**[3]	89+
0-6P	**2**	*2 ½*	**Olympic Storm (IRE)**[42] 414 7-10-11 85 BHarding (N G Richards) *hld up: smooth hdwy to ld 2 out: hdd run in: kpt on same pce* **10/1**	92+
5665	**3**	*4*	**One Of Them**[10] 780 6-9-13 76 PBuchanan(3) (M A Barnes) *cl up: ev ch 2 out: one pce* **12/1**	78
3223	**4**	*2*	**Sterling Guarantee (USA)**[10] 780 7-11-3 98 CDSharkey(7) (N Wilson) *bhd: rdn 3 out: kpt on fr next: no imp* **10/1**	98
-P24	**5**	*½*	**Kyle Of Lochalsh**[9] 686 5-10-8 82 ADempsey (J S Goldie) *hld up in tch: rdn after 3 out: outpcd fr next* **7/2**[1]	82
3152	**6**	*3 ½*	**Supply And Fix (IRE)**[10] 780 7-11-12 100 RJohnson (J J Lambe, Ire) *led to 2 out: sn btn* **5/1**[2]	98+
00U0	**7**	*shd*	**Ballyboe Boy (IRE)**[22] 674 6-10-9 83 (b) HOliver (R C Guest) *hld up: hdwy 4 out: wknd bef 2 out* **14/1**	79
00	**8**	*24*	**Mushraag (IRE)**[12] 776 5-9-7 74 oh7 (t) MissJAKidd(7) (J J Lambe, Ire) *bhd: drvn after 4 out: nvr rchd ldrs* **50/1**	46
611-	**9**	*16*	**Glinger (IRE)**[347] 988 12-11-2 90 ADobbin (N G Richards) *chsd ldrs to 3 out: sn btn* **7/2**[1]	46
0/	**10**	*8*	**Native Guide (IRE)**[80] 10-10-4 85 MrRMPMcNally(7) (Noel C Kelly, Ire) *prom to 4 out: lost tch next* **14/1**	33
P6-P	**U**		**Muller (IRE)**[58] 147 5-9-9 74 oh10 DCCostello(5) (R W Thomson) *bhd whn uns rdr 1st* **100/1**	—
P-PF	**P**		**Red Marsala**[18] 718 7-9-12 75 oh10 ow1 (p) MrCStorey(3) (Miss S E Forster) *a bhd: lost tch 1/2-way: t.o whn p.u bef 2 out* **66/1**	—

4m 57.4s (-10.80) **Going Correction** -0.50s/f (Good) **12** Ran SP% **115.9**
Speed ratings: **100,99,97,96,96 95,95,86,79,76** —,— CSF £82.77 CT £956.68 TOTE £13.10: £2.60, £2.70, £2.40; EX 124.90.
Owner Mrs A M Thorpe **Bred** Tom Deane **Trained** Bronwydd Arms, Carmarthens

FOCUS
An ordinary event in which those held up had the edge. The form looks solid enough with those in the frame behind the winner running close to form.

NOTEBOOK
Red Chief(IRE) has not been very consistent but turned in an improved effort on this first run for *new connections. He should stay three miles and may be able to win again after reassessment. (op 9-1 tchd 10-1)*
Olympic Storm(IRE) looked exposed as modest and unreliable but travelled strongly for much of the way and turned in an improved effort on this first run for his new stable. He looks sure to win a similar event. *(op 16-1)*
One Of Them ran creditably back in handicap company and back over this longer trip. He fared *best of those racing close to the strong gallop and looks capable of winning a similar event. (op 11-1)*
Sterling Guarantee(USA) ran a similar race back over this trip in handicap company as he had been doing over two miles and, although capable of winning a modest event, does not look one to place maximum faith in. *(tchd 12-1)*
Kyle Of Lochalsh was not totally disgraced returned to hurdles but his record of one Flat win from 33 career runs suggests he is not one to be taking single-figure odds about. *(tchd 4-1)*
Supply And Fix(IRE) was below his recent best back up in trip but he may be a little better than the bare form given that he ensured a decent gallop. He is not one to write off yet. *(op 11-2 tchd 4-1)*

857 PRESTIGE SCOTLAND H'CAP CHASE (18 fncs) 3m

3:50 (3:50) (Class 3) (0-120,119) 5-Y-0+ **£8,141** (£2,505; £1,252; £626)

Form				RPR
-U13	**1**		**Celtic Boy (IRE)**[17] 728 7-11-12 119 RJohnson (P Bowen) *cl up: led 4th: styd on strly fr 3 out* **4/1**[3]	142+
P	**2**	*5*	**Oh My Lord (IRE)**[13] 765 7-10-2 95 (t) RMcGrath (A J Martin, Ire) *keen: led to 4th: pressed wnr: rdn and nt qckn fr 3 out* **7/4**[1]	100
-214	**3**	*2 ½*	**Emperor Ross (IRE)**[20] 694 10-11-4 111 ADobbin (N G Richards) *hld up: hdwy 14th: rdn and no imp fr 3 out* **7/2**[2]	114
5U5/	**4**	*30*	**Pessimistic Dick**[572] 2578 12-10-5 98 BHarding (Mrs J C McGregor) *chsd ldrs tl lost pl 14th: sn btn* **33/1**	71
4P3-	**5**	*nk*	**Verchoyles Lad (IRE)**[9] 799 8-11-7 114 PACarberry (John G Carr, Ire) *chsd ldrs: mstke and lost pl 11th: n.d after* **13/2**	96+
/2-P	**U**		**Madam's Man**[52] 240 9-11-1 108 CLlewellyn (N A Twiston-Davies) *in tch tl mstke and uns rdr 5th* **7/1**	—

6m 4.10s (-8.50) **Going Correction** -0.50s/f (Good) **6** Ran SP% **107.4**
Speed ratings: **94,92,91,81,81** — CSF £10.90 TOTE £5.20: £2.80, £1.70; EX 11.10.
Owner Walters Plant Hire Ltd **Bred** William G Corrigan **Trained** Little Newcastle, Pembrokes

FOCUS
A decent event in which the pace was even throughout, and this form could be rated higher and should prove reliable.

NOTEBOOK
Celtic Boy(IRE) ◆, whose better display of jumping resulted in an improved display of form, took a fair event with plenty in hand. This right-handed course seemed to suit and he will be of interest against exposed performers after reassessment. *(tchd 9-2)*
Oh My Lord(IRE), who caught the eye at Aintree before his saddle slipped, was not disgraced in terms of form but proved a bit disappointing under ideal conditions. However, he is in good hands, open to improvement and is worth another chance. *(op 11-8)*

Emperor Ross(IRE) had conditions to suit and was not disgraced in terms of form but, although he did not find as much off the bridle as seemed likely for much of the way, it transpired he was struck into. *Official explanation: vet said gelding was struck into (op 4-1 tchd 9-2)*
Pessimistic Dick shaped as though this first start for new connections on this first run since December 2003 was needed, but he will have to show more before he is worth a bet. *(op 25-1)*
Verchoyles Lad(IRE) had conditions to suit but ruined his chance with a bad mistake at the water jump, and he will have to brush up his fencing if he is to win again in this sphere. *(op 7-1)*

858 BET WITH THE DEWHURST RING BOOKMAKERS NOVICES' H'CAP CHASE (15 fncs) 2m 4f 110y

4:20 (4:21) (Class 4) (0-105,105) 5-Y-0+ **£6,903** (£2,124; £1,062; £531)

Form				RPR
54-4	1		**Goodbadindiferent (IRE)**62 [83] 9-9-11 **79** oh3 .... KJMercer(3)	95+
			(Mrs J C McGregor) *prom: rdn 4 out: rallied to ld run in: kpt on wl* **11/1**	
3P-2	2	2 ½	**Possextown (IRE)**32 [550] 7-11-12 **105** .... ADobbin	115
			(N G Richards) *j.w: led to run in: kpt on same pce* **5/2**[1]	
5-4U	3	7	**Jupiter Jo**18 [717] 9-9-11 **83** oh3 ow4 .... BenOrde-Powlett(7)	90+
			(J B Walton) *keen: chsd ldrs: disputing 2nd whn blnd bdly 3 out: sn one pce* **12/1**	
5-02	4	5	**Don Valentino (POL)**22 [672] 6-11-11 **104** .... (v) JMMaguire	102
			(T R George) *cl up tl rdn and wknd between last two* **8/1**	
/3-1	5	*shd*	**Plenty Courage**10 [781] 11-9-7 **79** oh2 .... MJMcAlister(7)	79+
			(B Storey) *in tch: lost pl 5th: rallied 10th: effrt bef 3 out: wknd next* **9/2**[3]	
3/64	6	15	**Mounthooley**30 [593] 9-10-11 **90** .... GLee	76+
			(B Mactaggart) *hld up: blnd 11th: n.d* **16/1**	
-054	7	22	**Turn Of Phrase (IRE)**22 [672] 6-11-4 **100** .... (v) PWhelan(3)	61
			(R A Fahey) *in tch: drvn and wknd fr 4 out* **25/1**	
22F-	8	15	**York Rite (AUS)**98 [4525] 9-10-0 **79** oh1 .... (p) HOliver	25
			(R C Guest) *hld up: slipped bnd after 4th: nvr on terms* **4/1**[2]	
/00-	9	7	**Ballistic Boy**389 [642] 8-10-11 **90** .... PRobson	29
			(R W Thomson) *a bhd* **100/1**	
43-P	10	5	**Matmata De Tendron (FR)**66 [8] 5-10-10 **91** .... NPMulholland	23
			(A Crook) *a bhd* **33/1**	
-	P		**Partners Choice (IRE)**94 [4599] 8-10-0 **79** oh5 .... (t) PACarberry	—
			(John G Carr, Ire) *chsd ldrs to 10th: sn btn: p.u bef 4 out* **66/1**	
20-3	P		**Oliverjohn (IRE)**30 [593] 8-11-1 **97** .... PBuchanan(3)	—
			(Miss Lucinda V Russell) *prom to 11th: sn btn: t.o whn p.u bef 2 out* **16/1**	

5m 4.30s (-11.00) **Going Correction** -0.50s/f (Good)
WFA 5 from 6yo+ 2lb **12** Ran SP% **114.9**
Speed ratings: **100,99,96,94,94 88,80,74,71,70** —,— CSF £38.31 CT £343.38 TOTE £16.70: £3.60, £1.70, £3.20; EX 62.30.
Owner The Good To Soft Firm **Bred** Mrs M Brophy **Trained** Milnathort, Perth & Kinross

FOCUS
An ordinary handicap in which the pace was sound. The winner is value for further and the form should work out, with those just outside the places running to their marks.

NOTEBOOK
Goodbadindiferent(IRE) has not proved reliable but he attracted support and turned in an improved effort on this first run on a quick surface. The ground may be the key to him, he should stay three miles and may be capable of further success over fences. *(op 12-1)*
Possextown(IRE) ◆ turned in an improved display of jumping and ran his best race over regulation fences on this handicap debut. He pulled clear of the remainder and looks more than capable of winning a similar event. *(op 11-4 tchd 3-1 in places)*
Jupiter Jo ran creditably in terms of form but once again a bad mistake at a crucial time effectively ended his chance. He is going to have to jump better if he is to win races over regulation fences.
Don Valentino(POL) travelled strongly for much of the way but left the impression that he did not stay this trip in a truly-run race. He should prove suited by a return to shorter. *(op 7-1)*
Plenty Courage is probably a bit better than the bare form suggests as he tended to go in snatches and enjoyed anything but the run of the race. He may be best when able to dominate and is worth another chance over fences. *(op 4-1 tchd 5-1)*
Mounthooley looks on a stiff mark over fences and never looked like getting competitive after a blunder when the race was starting to take shape. He will have to show more before he is worth a bet in this sphere.

859 GG.COM BETTING EXCHANGE H'CAP HURDLE (12 hdls) 3m 110y

4:50 (4:50) (Class 4) (0-110,108) 4-Y-0+ **£5,626** (£1,731; £865; £432)

Form				RPR
/30-	1		**September Moon**395 [571] 7-10-13 **95** .... RJohnson	101
			(Mrs A M Thorpe) *midfield: hdwy bef 3 out: led next: styd on wl* **10/1**	
3-14	2	2	**Vicentio**31 [575] 6-10-6 **88** .... GLee	92
			(T J Fitzgerald) *keen: hld up: hdwy and prom 3 out: kpt on fr next: nt rch wnr* **10/3**[1]	
60-1	3	1 ½	**Ben Britten**18 [718] 6-10-11 **93** .... ADobbin	96
			(N G Richards) *hld up midfield: hdwy and ev ch bef 2 out: one pce last* **7/2**[2]	
24-P	4	6	**Cill Uird (IRE)**12 [774] 7-9-7 **82** oh4 .... (p) MissJAKidd(7)	80+
			(J J Lambe, Ire) *cl up: led briefly bef 2 out: sn outpcd* **66/1**	
P/00	5	7	**Lion Guest (IRE)**32 [551] 8-9-11 **82** .... KJMercer(3)	73+
			(Mrs S C Bradburne) *prom tl wknd bef 2 out* **66/1**	
F6-4	6	8	**She's My Girl (IRE)**8 [809] 10-10-11 **93** .... (p) PACarberry	75
			(John G Carr, Ire) *led to bef 2 out: sn btn* **6/1**[3]	
0F16	7	3 ½	**Pikestaff (USA)**20 [697] 7-10-8 **90** .... (t) PRobson	68
			(M A Barnes) *hld up: rdn 4 out: n.d* **16/1**	
0265	8	*nk*	**Political Sox**35 [499] 11-11-5 **108** .... GThomas(7)	86
			(R Nixon) *bhd: drvn 4 out: nvr on terms* **20/1**	
06-4	9	29	**Little Tobias (IRE)**31 [573] 6-10-6 **88** .... ARoss	37
			(J S Wainwright) *chsd ldrs tl rdn and wknd fr 3 out* **14/1**	
0-	10	5	**Woody Glen (IRE)**17 [730] 8-10-6 **88** .... (t) BHarding	32
			(A J Martin, Ire) *hld up: stdy hdwy and in tch after 3 out: rdn and wknd bef next* **9/1**	
132-	11	10	**No Sam No**297 [1374] 7-10-3 **88** .... (p) PBuchanan(3)	22
			(Miss Lucinda V Russell) *chsd ldrs to 4 out: sn lost pl* **14/1**	
0-5P	12	*dist*	**Divet Hill**41 [423] 11-11-5 **108** .... EWhillans(7)	—
			(Mrs A Hamilton) *sn bhd: no ch fr 1/2-way* **20/1**	
	P		**Cathkin Lad (IRE)**27 [621] 6-10-9 **91** .... ATinkler	—
			(John G Carr, Ire) *hld up: broke down and p.u after 7th* **33/1**	
5P-P	P		**Dajazar (IRE)**13 [768] 9-10-4 **93** .... (p) CDSharkey(7)	—
			(Mrs K Walton) *towards rr: struggling fr 1/2-way: p.u bef 3 out* **100/1**	

5m 54.9s (-16.00) **Going Correction** -0.50s/f (Good) **14** Ran SP% **114.3**
Speed ratings: **105,104,103,101,99 97,96,95,86,85 81**,—,—,— CSF £39.57 CT £141.83 TOTE £9.30: £3.00, £1.70, £2.70; EX 54.20 Place 6 £140.64, Place 5 £23.91.
Owner J H Lee **Bred** Queen Elizabeth **Trained** Bronwydd Arms, Carmarthens

FOCUS
Another ordinary handicap but a race that suited those ridden with a degree of patience. The form looks fairly solid.

NOTEBOOK
September Moon, off the course since May last year, proved suited by the test of stamina and turned in an improved effort. She showed the right attitude and it will be interesting to see if this can be reproduced next time.
Vicentio, who comes out of a race that has thrown up winners, ran creditably given that he failed *to settle early on. He looks capable of winning in similar company away from progressive sorts. (op 4-1)*
Ben Britten ran creditably upped to this trip from his higher mark and, given he is only relatively *lightly raced over hurdles and is in good hands, may be capable of a little better in due course. (op 3-1)*
Cill Uird(IRE), 4lb out of the handicap, was not disgraced in the first-time cheekpieces, having raced up with the decent pace throughout. This modest and inconsistent maiden would not be one to lump on next time. *(op 50-1 tchd 100-1)*
Lion Guest(IRE), who missed last year, ran his best race of this year upped to this trip for the first time. Stamina was not a problem and he looks up to winning a small race this summer. *(op 50-1)*
She's My Girl(IRE) was not disgraced given she helped to ensure a decent gallop and will be equally effective returned to shorter on this evidence. *(op 5-1 tchd 13-2)*
T/Plt: £456.00 to a £1 stake. Pool: £37,545.80. 60.10 winning tickets. T/Qpdt: £104.80 to a £1 stake. Pool: £2,889.20. 20.40 winning tickets. RY

811 WORCESTER (L-H)

Wednesday, June 29

OFFICIAL GOING: Good (good to soft in places)
The ground, already watered, took a further 10mm of rain overnight, but jockeys reported it to be more good than good to soft.
Wind: Nil Weather: Light rain for last two races

860 SEVERN SUITE RESTAURANT FOR EXCELLENT SERVICE CONDITIONAL JOCKEYS' NOVICES' H'CAP HURDLE (10 hdls) 2m 4f

2:10 (2:10) (Class 4) (0-105,100) 4-Y-0+ **£3,031** (£866; £433)

Form				RPR
-066	1		**Earn Out**15 [749] 4-10-1 **82** .... DJacob(3)	84+
			(M C Pipe) *sn bhd: hdwy appr 3 out: rdn to ld flat: r.o* **10/1**	
354	2	*nk*	**Sound Skin (IRE)**14 [758] 7-11-3 **91** .... (p) RStephens	96
			(A Ennis) *hld up in mid-div: hdwy 6th: lft in ld after 3 out: rdn and hdd flat: r.o* **14/1**	
0/6-	3	3	**Smiling Applause**80 [4797] 6-10-2 **76** .... JamesDavies	80+
			(Mrs Barbara Waring) *hld up in mid-div: hdwy appr 6th: rdn appr 2 out: ev ch last: 3rd and hld whn wnt lame and eased nr fin* **14/1**	
4P-2	4	1 ½	**Good Heart (IRE)**48 [322] 10-9-10 **78** .... (t) MissCarolineHurley(8)	79
			(R Ford) *hld up and bhd: rapid hdwy appr 5th: kpt on same pce flat* **4/1**[1]	
0-02	5	4	**Jimmy Byrne (IRE)**5 [826] 5-11-4 **95** .... (p) PCO'Neill(3)	94+
			(R C Guest) *hld up and bhd: hdwy whn pckd 7th: rdn appr 2 out: wknd flat* **11/2**[2]	
0-56	6	½	**Smileafact**34 [509] 5-9-10 **75** .... MGoldstein(5)	71
			(Mrs Barbara Waring) *hld up: hdwy 7th: sn rdn: wknd 3 out* **40/1**	
000-	7	3	**Ice Rain (IRE)**227 [2223] 5-9-12 **75** .... WKennedy(3)	68
			(Evan Williams) *hld up and bhd: mstkes 5th and 6th: hdwy whn n.m.r on ins appr 3 out: wknd appr 2 out* **16/1**	
-303	8	*hd*	**Mistified (IRE)**22 [671] 4-11-2 **94** .... DLaverty	83
			(J W Mullins) *hld up and bhd: mstke 5th: rdn 6th: hdwy 7th: wknd 2 out* **13/2**	
P-FP	9	10	**Caucasian (IRE)**50 [288] 7-10-6 **80** .... TJPhelan	63
			(Ian Williams) *prom tl wknd 3 out* **33/1**	
P040	10	26	**Simiola**7 [811] 6-10-8 **82** .... DCrosse	39
			(S T Lewis) *t.k.h: hdwy 3rd: wknd 3 out* **100/1**	
	11	10	**Mr Wonderful (IRE)**417 [236] 7-9-12 **77** .... PCStringer(5)	24
			(P O'Connor) *rdn 6th: a bhd* **125/1**	
	12	8	**Fencethegap (IRE)**39 8-10-5 **79** .... ONelmes	18
			(A E Price) *prom: lost pl 3rd: rallied after 4th: wknd 5th* **22/1**	
-3FF	P		**Gin 'N' Fonic (IRE)**8 [803] 5-10-13 **90** .... (p) SWalsh(3)	—
			(J D Frost) *chsd ldr tl appr 5th: wknd and p.u bef 3 out* **16/1**	
P/0-	P		**Lady At Leisure (IRE)**16 [518] 5-9-9 **74** oh6 .... KBurke(5)	—
			(M J Ryan) *prom tl rdn and wknd after 7th: p.u bef 3 out* **66/1**	
042-	P		**Smith's Tribe**223 [2290] 7-11-12 **100** .... MNicolls	—
			(B J Eckley) *led tl pckd and wnt lame 3 out: p.u sn after 2 out* **6/1**[3]	
-P30	P		**Lescer's Lad**15 [753] 8-9-10 **75** .... TMessenger(5)	—
			(C L Popham) *j.rt: prom tl rdn and wknd after 7th: p.u after 3 out* **66/1**	
/660	P		**Harry B**15 [747] 6-10-11 **85** .... (v1) AO'Keeffe	—
			(R J Price) *mid-div: hdwy after 5th: rdn and wknd after 7th: p.u bef 3 out* **14/1**	

4m 51.2s (3.20) **Going Correction** +0.175s/f (Yiel)
WFA 4 from 5yo+ 4lb **17** Ran SP% **118.4**
Speed ratings: **100,99,98,98,96 96,95,95,91,80 76,73**,—,—,— —,— CSF £131.59 CT £1962.05 TOTE £11.70: £2.30, £2.90, £3.70, £2.10; EX 249.90.
Owner M C Pipe **Bred** Mrs W Smith **Trained** Nicholashayne, Devon

FOCUS
A distinctly moderate event and not strong form, but competitive enough.

NOTEBOOK
Earn Out was last and a few lengths detached with a circuit to run, but he steadily worked his way into the picture under a good ride from substitute jockey Daryl Jacob. Striking the front on the run-in, if anything he was ahead too early as the runner-up was coming back at him near the finish. *He can be rated as value for a little further than this but may not be one to rely upon for a follow up. (op 18-1)*
Sound Skin(IRE) ◆, equipped with sheepskin cheekpieces for the first time, was well positioned throughout and lost nothing in defeat. This is probably his optimum trip and he should be placed to land a similar event over the summer. *(op 12-1)*
Smiling Applause was suited by this drop in trip and he only gave best on the run-in, but unfortunately he appeared to break down quite badly close home.
Good Heart(IRE) ran respectably on this return to hurdles but this winning pointer is probably best over three miles. *(op 5-1)*
Jimmy Byrne(IRE), with cheekpieces in place of the visor, was held up out the back. He made an error at the fourth from home when in the process of closing and lacked the pace to challenge thereafter. A quirky individual, he is due to race off a 4lb higher mark in the future and could struggle. *(op 7-2)*
Smileafact, who has been given a chance by the handicapper, is a very limited performer but showed slightly more on this occasion.
Mistified(IRE) *Official explanation: jockey said gelding had been unsuited by the good, good to soft in places ground (op 6-1)*
Harry B *Official explanation: jockey said gelding had been lame (op 7-1 tchd 15-2)*
Smith's Tribe, having his first run since November, was in front and still travelling well when he went wrong soon after the third last. His rider had to let him pop over the next before being able to pull up. *(op 7-1 tchd 15-2)*

861 TONY SPEER NOVICES' HURDLE (12 hdls) 3m
2:40 (2:41) (Class 4) 4-Y-0+ **£3,484** (£1,072; £536; £268)

Form RPR
P2-6 **1** **Like A Lord (IRE)**[14] 762 7-10-12 104 DElsworth 110+
(Mrs S J Smith) *mde all: clr 3 out: unchal* **10/3**[2]
2563 **2** *8* **Seeador**[15] 748 6-10-12 92 AThornton 95
(J W Mullins) *chsd ldrs: outpcd after 4 out: rallied to chse wnr 2 out: no imp* **9/1**
P2 **3** *14* **Hi Tech Man (IRE)**[14] 763 7-10-12 (b) TJMurphy 83+
(D E Cantillon) *hld up: hdwy appr 3 out: n.d* **10/3**[2]
0-21 **4** *11* **Dubai Ace (USA)**[22] 671 4-10-13 111 (t) JGoldstein 76+
(Miss Sheena West) *hld up: rdn 7th: hdwy after next: chsd wnr 3 out: wknd next* **5/2**[1]
4 **5** *3 ½* **Oso Tilley**[30] 594 6-9-12 MissJFoster(7) 60
(Miss J E Foster) *chsd ldrs: rdn after 8th: wknd appr 3 out* **50/1**
0-30 **6** *9* **Benny**[24] 654 4-10-0 MrNKinnon(7) 58+
(R H York) *hld up: hdwy 8th: chsd wnr next tl wknd 3 out: hmpd next* **40/1**
0/ **7** *6* **Slave's Adventure**[18] 11-10-2 ow4 MrRHodges(7) 49
(R J Price) *prom: chsd wnr 4th to 4 out: sn wknd* **100/1**
P- **P** **Days Of Gold**[17] 6-9-12 TMessenger(7) —
(C L Popham) *hld up: wknd after 8th: t.o whn p.u bef 3 out* **125/1**
PP5 **P** **Call Of The Seas (IRE)**[21] 680 6-10-2 ENolan(10) —
(J G M O'Shea) *hld up: bhd fr 5th: t.o whn p.u bef last* **125/1**
00 **F** **Thiseldo Us**[38] 458 10-10-12 SCurran 67
(M B Shears) *hld up: hdwy after 8th: 4th and wkng whn fell 2 out* **125/1**
/3-5 **F** **Colnside Brook**[20] 693 6-10-5 98 JamesDavies —
(B G Powell) *hld up: plld hrd: hdwy 5th: wkng whn fell 3 out: dead* **8/1**[3]
0 **P** **Internationalguest (IRE)**[22] 671 6-10-12 (p) RThornton —
(D G Bridgwater) *hld up: rdn 7th: a in rr: t.o whn p.u bef 3 out* **40/1**
0 **P** **Scolboa Arctic (IRE)**[13] 769 5-9-10 ow1 THalliday(10) —
(Mrs S J Smith) *hld up: hdwy after 6th: wknd appr 3 out: bhd whn p.u bef next* **50/1**
1 **P** **Grey Tune (IRE)**[15] 742 6-10-8 110 JKington(10) —
(M Scudamore) *chsd wnr 2nd to 4th: lost pl next: sn bhd: tailed fr 7th: p.u bef 4 out* **10/1**
0- **P** **Royal Upstart**[29] 1625 4-10-7 PJBrennan —
(M B Shears) *hld up: j. slowly 2nd: sme hdwy appr 9th: sn wknd: t.o whn p.u bef 3 out* **125/1**
00/ **P** **Mr Eye Popper (IRE)**[443] 4783 6-10-12 ChristianWilliams —
(J T Stimpson) *prom: stmbld and lost pl 5th: sn bhd: t.o whn p.u bef 3 out* **100/1**

5m 56.2s (7.00) **Going Correction** +0.175s/f (Yiel) **16** Ran SP% **118.9**
Speed ratings: **95,92,87,84,82 79,77,—,—,— —,—,—,—,— —** CSF £31.99 TOTE £4.90: £2.30, £2.70, £1.70; EX 35.90.
Owner Billy McCullough **Bred** G McCourt And John Hussey **Trained** High Eldwick, W Yorks
■ Stewards' Enquiry : J Kington three-day ban: improper riding - continued when gelding appeared to be exhausted (Jul 10-11, 13)

FOCUS
Few got home in this weakly contested maiden event but the winner is value for almost double the official margin and could rate higher.

NOTEBOOK
Like A Lord(IRE) made every yard and ran out a very easy winner. Fitter for his recent return to action here after a six-month absence, he liked the ground and was clear with the race in the bag by the third from home. The step up to three miles proved no problem at all and he may carry his penalty over hurdles before switching to fences. *(op 9-4 tchd 7-2 in places)*
Seeador stays well and he passed beaten rivals from the penultimate flight to claim a pretty remote second. *(op 12-1)*
Hi Tech Man(IRE) stayed on from the rear of the field without ever getting to grips with the leaders. He is not the easiest of rides but could be capable of a little better. *(op 9-2)*
Dubai Ace(USA) responded to pressure to go after the winner at the third last, but he did not get home over this longer trip. *(op 3-1 tchd 10-3)*
Oso Tilley, a winning pointer, was keeping on past beaten horses on this debut over hurdles.
Benny has ability but looks to need time to strengthen.
Thiseldo Us jumped the second last well but came down a couple of strides after the flight. He was keeping on and might have made the frame. *(op 14-1)*

Grey Tune(IRE), well behind when pulled up, unfortunately collapsed having suffered an internal haemorrhage. *(op 14-1)*

862 TO SPONSOR A RACE CALL 0870 220 2772 NOVICES' H'CAP CHASE (12 fncs) 2m
3:10 (3:12) (Class 4) (0-95,95) 5-Y-0+ **£3,818** (£1,175; £587; £293)

Form RPR
030- **1** **Appach (FR)**[78] 4813 6-11-7 **90** AThornton 118+
(J W Mullins) *hld up: stdy hdwy fr 5th: led on bit last: v easily* **28/1**
453 **2** *7* **Phase Three (IRE)**[23] 668 8-11-4 **87** RThornton 95
(T R George) *chsd ldr: led 2 out to last: no ch w wnr* **25/1**
5F31 **3** *3* **Ultimate Limit**[5] 827 5-10-6 **76** 7ex PJBrennan 80
(A Ennis) *a.p: rdn 4 out: one pce fr 3 out* **11/4**[1]
6F-1 **4** *nk* **French Direction (IRE)**[35] 505 6-11-0 **83** PMoloney 89+
(R Rowe) *led: hit 6th: rdn and hdd 2 out: no ex flat* **6/1**[3]
5 *21* **Tarbuck (IRE)**[25] 12-10-13 **87** RStephens(5) 71
(Mrs D A Hamer) *prom: mstke 4th: rdn and wknd 4 out* **16/1**
5640 **6** *2 ½* **Outside Investor (IRE)**[14] 760 5-10-0 **80** KBurke(10) 61
(P R Rodford) *bhd: blnd 5th: nvr nr ldrs* **40/1**
1126 **7** *5* **He's Hot Right Now (NZ)**[33] 534 6-11-7 **95** (p) PCO'Neill(5) 72
(R C Guest) *a bhd* **7/1**
8 *14* **Shuil Monty (IRE)**[18] 9-10-7 **83** MrPYork(7) 46
(R H York) *bhd fr 8th* **18/1**
P-PP **9** *1 ½* **Tails I Win**[34] 511 6-10-4 **76** ACCoyle(3) 37
(Miss C J E Caroe) *bhd fr 6th* **100/1**
20P- **10** *15* **Plain Chant**[343] 1026 8-10-5 **74** ChristianWilliams 20
(C Roberts) *j.rt: bhd fr 7th* **33/1**
0-60 **P** **What's A Filly**[27] 613 5-11-1 **84** JMogford —
(R C Guest) *a bhd: t.o whn p.u bef 4 out* **50/1**
P-30 **P** **Master Fox**[24] 654 7-10-10 **79** NFehily —
(T R George) *in tch to 6th: t.o whn p.u bef 4 out* **33/1**
0-P0 **P** **Blazeaway (USA)**[23] 664 5-10-9 **79** (p) BJCrowley —
(R S Brookhouse) *bhd fr 6th: t.o whn p.u bef 4 out* **50/1**
-566 **P** **Classic Calvados (FR)**[20] 692 6-11-2 **85** (t) JimCrowley —
(P D Niven) *j.rt: sn bhd: t.o whn p.u bef 4 out* **16/1**
/065 **P** **Erins Lass (IRE)**[21] 689 8-11-6 **89** WHutchinson —
(R Dickin) *j. bdly rt: bhd fr 6th: t.o whn p.u bef 4 out* **25/1**
3-00 **P** **Off The Edge (AUS)**[48] 320 6-10-9 **78** DRDennis —
(Ian Williams) *hld up: hdwy 7th: wknd appr 4 out: bhd whn p.u bef last* **11/1**
-P12 **P** **Take The Oath (IRE)**[15] 752 8-10-8 **77** TDoyle —
(D R Gandolfo) *bhd: pushed along and short-lived effrt appr 4 out: bhd whn p.u bef last* **7/2**[2]

3m 57.1s (3.50) **Going Correction** +0.275s/f (Yiel)
WFA 5 from 6yo+ 1lb **17** Ran SP% **125.4**
Speed ratings: **102,98,97,96,86 85,82,75,74,67 —,—,—,—,— —,—** CSF £560.23 CT £2559.51 TOTE £31.10: £5.30, £3.40, £2.00, £1.80; EX 327.40.
Owner Adam Day **Bred** A Aubry And Michel Aubry **Trained** Wilsford-Cum-Lake, Wilts

FOCUS
A very moderate contest, but the winner is value for nearly three times the winning margin and with the time reasonable, although not many got into this novice handicap from off the pace, the form should work out.

NOTEBOOK
Appach(FR) was a poignant winner, as he was previously trained by the late Helen Bridges who was killed when he bolted and threw her in April. He had not shown much in two runs over fences in the French provinces in the spring of last year, but he jumped with aplomb on this debut for the Mullins yard and, after cruising up to the leaders on the home turn, went on to score without turning a hair. This was no fluke and he is clearly on the upgrade. *(tchd 25-1)*
Phase Three(IRE) is a winning pointer but he is effective at this trip. He ran a solid race on this debut over regulation fences but was no match for the winner on these terms. *(op 33-1)*
Ultimate Limit found this too sharp, having won over three-quarters of a mile further last time, but kept on having come under pressure on the turn out of the back straight. He was 10lb well in compared with future handicaps and may not prove easy to place now, although a step back up in trip will obviously help. *(op 10-3 tchd 7-2)*
French Direction(IRE), who set a strong pace, was headed at the second last but only cried enough on the flat. This was a respectable effort off a 5lb higher mark than when successful under similar tactics at Fontwell, even more so when it transpired that he had hurt himself when making an error in the back straight. *(op 11-2)*
Tarbuck(IRE), successful in a restrcited point-to-point earlier in the month, showed up well until fading on the home turn. He needs further.
He's Hot Right Now(NZ) *Official explanation: jockey said, regarding the running and riding, his orders had been to hold gelding up and give it a good view of the fences, adding that gelding jumped the early fences very deliberately and so he tried to give it confidence throughout but it was atill slow at many of the fences; he further added that having asked gelding for an effort in back straight without any response he felt it prudent to allow gelding to come home in its own time (op 17-2 tchd 9-1)*
Take The Oath(IRE) came into the race in good form but he was never able to get into the action. *(op 10-3)*

863 TANKSHARE (S) HURDLE (8 hdls) 2m
3:40 (3:41) (Class 5) 4-Y-0+ **£3,024** (£864; £432)

Form RPR
-615 **1** **Burning Truth (USA)**[17] 725 11-11-5 110 DRDennis 110+
(M Sheppard) *mde all: clr 3 out: styd on wl* **11/8**[1]
005- **2** *17* **Captain Cloudy**[20] 4362 5-10-12 84 TJMurphy 87+
(D Flood) *hld up: plld hrd: hdwy appr 3 out: rdn whn hmpd after next: wnt 2nd but no ch w wnr last* **8/1**[3]
P440 **3** *3* **Red Nose Lady**[20] 697 8-10-12 90 (b) TMessenger(7) 92+
(G J Smith) *chsd wnr: rdn appr 3 out: wkng whn swvd lft after next* **12/1**
0PP- **4** *2* **Who Cares Wins**[71] 4918 9-10-12 93 (v) MAFitzgerald 80
(J R Jenkins) *hld up: hdwy 4th: rdn appr 3 out: sn wknd* **20/1**
2F-3 **4** *dht* **Gabor**[15] 743 6-11-5 107 (p) ChristianWilliams 87
(B J Llewellyn) *mid-div: rdn 4th: styd on appr last: n.d* **5/1**[2]
05P/ **6** *3 ½* **Brief Decline (IRE)**[32] 10-10-5 95 SWalsh(7) 76
(J D Frost) *hld up: sme hdwy after 3 out: n.d* **10/1**
5-20 **7** *4* **Jack Durrance (IRE)**[15] 749 5-10-12 65 WMarston 72
(G A Ham) *hld up: stmbld 4 out: sme hdwy next: n.d* **11/1**
0-65 **8** *1 ¾* **Prince Valentine**[8] 180 4-10-2 83 WKennedy(7) 67
(D B Feek) *chsd ldrs tl wknd appr 3 out* **50/1**
0-05 **9** *10* **Replacement Pet (IRE)**[14] 758 8-10-5 68 (bt) RGreene 53
(Mrs S D Williams) *chsd ldrs: rdn 4th: wknd appr 3 out* **50/1**
P0 **10** *6* **Liberty Boy (IRE)**[7] 813 7-10-12 81 (b) APMcCoy 54
(Jonjo O'Neill) *hld up in tch: rdn 4th: wknd after next* **12/1**
0 **11** *14* **Magic Warrior**[14] 758 5-10-12 SCurran 40
(J C Fox) *hld up: sme hdwy appraoching 3 out: sooon wknd* **33/1**
0U00 **12** *13* **Court Award (IRE)**[8] 801 8-10-12 76 JTizzard 27
(B G Powell) *chsd ldrs to 5th* **20/1**
P-05 **13** *dist* **Saposcat (IRE)**[8] 802 5-10-5 MrDavidTurner(7) —
(Dr P Pritchard) *mid-div: sn drvn along: wknd 3rd* **100/1**
PP **P** **Hermano (IRE)**[14] 758 8-10-12 BJCrowley —
(A M Hales) *hld up: a in rr: t.o whn p.u bef 3 out* **100/1**
600- **P** **Croker (IRE)**[146] 3664 10-10-9 76 DCrosse(3) —
(S T Lewis) *prom: lost pl appr 3rd: t.o whn p.u bef 5th* **50/1**
P0/ **P** **Harry The Hoover (IRE)**[13] 2331 5-10-5 PCStringer(7) —
(M J Gingell) *mstke 1st: a in rr: t.o whn p.u bef 3 out* **100/1**

3m 49.0s (0.60) **Going Correction** +0.175s/f (Yiel)
WFA 4 from 5yo+ 3lb **16** Ran SP% **124.0**
Speed ratings: **105,96,95,94,94 92,90,89,84,81 74,67,—,—,— —** CSF £12.04 TOTE £2.20: £1.50, £3.20, £4.50; EX 23.80.The winner was bought in for 5,500gns. Captain Cloudy was the subject of a friendly claim.
Owner G Jones **Bred** Juddmonte Farms **Trained** Eastnor, H'fords
■ Stewards' Enquiry : T Messenger one-day ban: careless riding (Jul 10)

FOCUS
Not the most competitive of sellers despite the size of field and the form looks weak.

NOTEBOOK
Burning Truth(USA), who had scored when dropped into this grade at Hereford two starts ago, found this straightforward. He was well held over fences last time at Stratford, where they had *over-watered in his trainer's opinion, but this ground was fine and he routed the opposition. (op 13-8 tchd 7-4)*
Captain Cloudy won the battle for the runner-up spot despite being badly hampered by the third before the final flight. He was having only his fourth run over hurdles and could improve, but he only just gets this trip and his career record of no wins from 32 attempts under both codes sounds a warning. *(tchd 9-1)*
Red Nose Lady, dropped in trip, ran a better race on the return to this grade but was beaten when swerving badly to her left on the approach to the final flight.
Who Cares Wins does not look the horse he was but did show a bit more than of late. *(tchd 11-2)*
Gabor, who looked the principal danger to the winner based on official figures, was fitted with cheekpieces instead of the usual blinkers. He was being shoved along from halfway and could merely plug on to force a dead-heat for fourth. *(tchd 11-2)*
Brief Decline(IRE) , without a win since the summer of 1999, came into this fit from *point-to-pointing. Official explanation: jockey said gelding had a breathing problem (op 11-1 tchd 9-1)*

864 ARENA LEISURE H'CAP HURDLE (10 hdls) 2m 4f

4:10 (4:14) (Class 3) (0-130,124) 4-Y-0+ **£6,942** (£2,136; £1,068; £534)

Form				RPR
61-0	**1**		**Schapiro (USA)**[52] [247] 4-11-6 **122** .... APMcCoy (Jonjo O'Neill) *hld up: hdwy 4th: mstke 5th: led appr 3 out: hrd rdn and hung rt flat: jst hld on* **4/1**[2]	122+
2-31	**2**	*shd*	**Achilles Wings (USA)**[25] [633] 9-11-4 **116** .... (p) AThornton (Miss K M George) *hld up in mid-div: nt clr run and swtchd rt after 7th: sn rdn: hdwy 2 out: r.o wl u.p flat: jst failed* **8/1**	118
-221	**3**	*2 ½*	**Absolut Power (GER)**[25] [629] 4-10-7 **109** .... (p) MBradburne (J A Geake) *hld up in mid-div: hdwy 7th: rdn appr 2 out: hit last: no ex towards fin* **5/1**[3]	105+
-041	**4**	*4*	**Gemini Dancer**[15] [753] 6-10-6 **104** .... JTizzard (C L Tizzard) *hld up and bhd: t.k.h whn hdwy 6th: rdn after 2 out: hung lft flat: wknd towards fin* **14/1**	101+
00-5	**5**	*14*	**Anatar (IRE)**[13] [766] 7-11-11 **123** .... TScudamore (M C Pipe) *hld up and bhd: hdwy appr 5th: wkng whn pckd 7th* **12/1**	104
0-00	**6**	*1 ¼*	**Arm And A Leg (IRE)**[17] [726] 10-10-6 **104** .... (p) AO'Keeffe (Mrs D A Hamer) *led tl appr 5th: wknd appr 3 out* **33/1**	84
606-	**7**	*nk*	**Atum Re (IRE)**[68] [4972] 8-11-0 **112** .... RWalsh (P F Nicholls) *hld up and bhd: rdn and hdwy after 7th: wknd 3 out* **6/4**[1]	91
51/0	**8**	*1 ½*	**Tomenoso**[25] [633] 7-11-3 **115** .... DElsworth (Mrs S J Smith) *prom tl rdn and wknd after 7th* **11/1**	93
-21P	**9**	*1 ½*	**Middleham Park (IRE)**[15] [751] 5-10-9 **110** .... RYoung(3) (J W Mullins) *j.rt: hld up in tch: led briefly 7th: wknd 3 out* **20/1**	86
1F-0	**10**	*dist*	**Masters Of War (IRE)**[13] [766] 8-11-8 **120** .... MAFitzgerald (Jonjo O'Neill) *a bhd: t.o* **25/1**	—
PP-P	**P**		**Dual Star (IRE)**[23] [668] 10-9-10 **101** oh25 ow3 .... SWalsh(7) (L Waring) *a bhd: rdn after 4th: p.u bef 5th* **100/1**	—
20/P	**P**		**Gigs Bounty**[38] [465] 7-10-12 **110** .... NFehily (C C Bealby) *hld up in tch: lost pl after 4th: in rr whn mstke 5th: p.u bef 6th* **22/1**	—
P16P	**P**		**Pequenita**[3] [840] 5-10-0 **103** .... (b) PCO'Neill(5) (R C Guest) *w ldr: reminders after 1st: led appr 5th to 7th: wknd qckly: p.u bef 3 out* **25/1**	—

4m 48.3s (0.30) **Going Correction** +0.175s/f (Yiel)
WFA 4 from 5yo+ 4lb **13** Ran SP% **131.2**
Speed ratings: **106,105,104,103,97 97,97,96,95,— —,—,—** CSF £36.67 CT £174.45 TOTE £4.70: £1.70, £2.20, £2.40; EX 29.80 Trifecta £141.90 Part won. Pool: £199.90 - 0.30 winning tickets..
Owner John P McManus **Bred** Midhurst Farm Inc Et Al **Trained** Cheltenham, Gloucs

FOCUS
This was run at a good clip, but the three leaders had gone off too fast and played no part in the finish. The third and fourth set the standard and the race could rate a bit higher.

NOTEBOOK
Schapiro(USA) was a disappointing favourite over two miles here last month, but the step back up in trip suited. Having seen off the challenges of the eventual third and fourth, he was clear at the final flight but he hung right on the run-in and was all out at the line as the runner-up finished strongly. *He has the ability but does not look one to trust implicitly.Official explanation: trainer's representative said, regarding the improved form shown, gelding had been able to dominate over this longer trip (old market op 6-1)*
Achilles Wings(USA), attempting to follow up his course and distance win off this 6lb higher mark, hit a flat spot early in the home straight and was still only fourth jumping the last, but he ran on strongly for pressure and nearly snatched the race. *(old market tchd 9-1 new market op 7-1 tchd 10-1)*
Absolut Power(GER), a consistent sort, ran a solid race but appeared to have no excuses. *(old market op 7-1)*
Gemini Dancer, 7lb higher than at Newton Abbot, travelled strongly under restraint and looked a big danger until putting in an awkward jump at the second last. Immediately coming under pressure, he could only stick on at the same pace and it could well be that he failed to stay. *(old market op 20-1 new market op 16-1)*
Arm And A Leg(IRE) finished well beaten in the end after setting a strong pace. *(old market op 50-1)*
Atum Re(IRE), having his first run since leaving Paul Webber's yard, is currently rated 10lb lower over hurdles than he is over fences. After closing from the rear leaving the back straight he lacked the pace to land a blow. *(old market tchd 3-1 and 10-3 in places, new market op 7-4)*
Masters Of War(IRE) *Official explanation: jockey said gelding had a breathing problem (old market op 40-1 tchd 50-1 new market op 20-1)*

865 SUCKLING TRANSPORT H'CAP CHASE (18 fncs) 2m 7f 110y

4:40 (4:43) (Class 4) (0-110,109) 5-Y-0+ **£4,163** (£1,281; £640; £320)

Form				RPR
0/1-	**1**		**Ross Comm**[297] [1372] 9-10-7 **90** .... DElsworth (Mrs S J Smith) *chsd ldrs: led 12th: j.rt 2 out: styd on wl* **15/8**[1]	114+
-215	**2**	*8*	**Alcatras (IRE)**[8] [805] 8-9-11 **83** oh6 .... ONelmes(3) (B J M Ryall) *hld up: j.rt: hdwy 9th: chsd wnr 14th: styd on same pce fr 2 out* **10/3**[2]	97+
1/PU	**3**	*29*	**Windy Spirit (IRE)**[15] [746] 10-11-2 **99** .... ChristianWilliams (Evan Williams) *hld up: j.rt 6th: mstke 11th: nvr trbld ldrs* **22/1**	82
0035	**4**	*18*	**Cyindien (FR)**[10] [783] 8-9-11 **83** oh4 .... (p) DCrosse(3) (D E Cantillon) *prom: rdn 10th: wknd 14th* **11/1**	60+
PP05	**5**	*dist*	**Francolino (FR)**[23] [669] 12-10-0 **83** oh23 .... JMogford (Dr P Pritchard) *chsd ldrs: lost pl 3rd: bhd fr 5th* **66/1**	—
-443	**P**		**Dear Deal**[34] [516] 12-11-7 **104** .... (b) JTizzard (C L Tizzard) *bhd fr 5th: t.o whn p.u bef 10th* **10/1**	—
-P10	**P**		**Monty Be Quick**[22] [672] 9-9-7 **83** .... TMessenger(7) (J M Castle) *chsd ldrs to 10th: t.o whn p.u bef 4 out* **22/1**	—
031F	**P**		**Count Oski**[15] [746] 9-10-8 **91** .... RThornton (M J Ryan) *bhd: sme hdwy 10th: sn wknd: t.o whn p.u bef 12th* **7/1**[3]	—
PP-2	**P**		**Six Of One**[25] [567] 7-11-2 **99** .... (p) MAFitzgerald (R Rowe) *hld up: hdwy 10th: wknd 12th: t.o whn p.u bef 4 out* **10/1**	—
PF-P	**P**		**Golden Rambler (IRE)**[20] [694] 9-11-6 **103** .... (b¹) APMcCoy (Jonjo O'Neill) *led 2nd to 6th: mstke and wknd 14th: t.o whn p.u bef next* **11/1**	—
PU0-	**P**		**Wrens Island (IRE)**[70] [4934] 11-10-3 **86** .... WHutchinson (R Dickin) *led tyo 2nd: led 6th to 12th: wknd qckly: t.o whn p.u bef 5 out* **33/1**	—

6m 0.40s (5.50) **Going Correction** +0.275s/f (Yiel) **11** Ran SP% **118.3**
Speed ratings: **101,98,88,82,— —,—,—,—,— —** CSF £8.68 CT £103.37 TOTE £3.00: £1.80, £2.00, £3.60; EX 16.70.
Owner Kevin G Treanor **Bred** A Dawson **Trained** High Eldwick, W Yorks

FOCUS
This handicap turned out to be pretty uncompetitive and those that completed came home at lengthy intervals. The form is understandably far from strong.

NOTEBOOK
Ross Comm, absent since winning here last September having sustained a minor fracture to a hind leg, stayed on much too well for his only serious challenger up the straight and was in command when idling on the run-in. A versatile sort who is effective at any trip from two and a half to three miles, he won despite the ground having gone against him. *(op 2-1)*
Alcatras(IRE) performed respectably from out of the weights at a course he goes well at, although not for the first time he showed a proclivity to jump out to his right. *(op 11-2)*
Windy Spirit(IRE) did not jump too well but he kept going to secure third place rather by default. *(op 20-1)*
Cyindien(FR) weakened after chasing the pace and finished tired. *(op 20-1)*
Golden Rambler(IRE), dropped 8lb and tried in first-time headgear, showed up for a long way but was a beaten fourth when pulled up four from home. He still has a good deal to prove. *(op 7-1 tchd 13-2)*
Count Oski did not jump fluently and his confidence could well have been adversely affected by his fall at Hereford. *(op 7-1 tchd 13-2)*
Monty Be Quick *Official explanation: jockey said gelding had a breathing problem (op 7-1 tchd 13-2)*

866 CANNONS HEALTH CLUB STANDARD OPEN NATIONAL HUNT FLAT RACE 2m

5:10 (5:11) (Class 6) 4-6-Y-0 **£1,873** (£535; £267)

Form				RPR
2	**1**		**Tihui Two (IRE)**[27] [616] 5-10-11 .... MAFitzgerald (Simon Earle) *mde all: clr 3f out: r.o wl* **9/4**[1]	103+
	2	*14*	**Haloo Baloo**[73] 5-11-4 .... APMcCoy (Jonjo O'Neill) *hld up: hdwy 5f out: wnt 2nd over 1f out: no ch w wnr* **8/1**[3]	95
1	**3**	*8*	**Houlihans Free (IRE)**[7] [817] 6-11-11 .... (t) RWalsh (P F Nicholls) *hld up and bhd: hdwy on ins over 4f out: chsd wnr over 3f out: rdn over 2f out: wknd over 1f out* **9/4**[1]	95+
0	**4**	*7*	**Pumpkin Pickle**[38] [463] 4-9-12 .... KBurke(10) (P R Rodford) *hld up towards rr: rdn 6f out: hdwy over 3f out: sn no imp* **25/1**	70
6	**5**	*24*	**Bobble**[13] [769] 5-10-4 .... MrGTumelty(7) (R N Bevis) *prom: rdn 5f out: wknd 3f out* **50/1**	49
0-5	**6**	*3 ½*	**Redlynch Spirit (IRE)**[7] [816] 5-11-4 .... JTizzard (C L Tizzard) *plld hrd: prom tl wknd over 3f out* **12/1**	53
U-	**7**	*2*	**Amyroseisuppose**[212] [2542] 6-10-11 .... JAMcCarthy (C P Morlock) *t.k.h in tch: rdn over 5f out: wknd over 3f out* **50/1**	44
00	**8**	*1*	**Indyana Run**[24] [655] 4-10-1 .... TMessenger(7) (A Hollingsworth) *swvd bdly lft and lost pl sn after s: rdn over 5f out: a bhd* **33/1**	40
	9	*1 ½*	**Swift Water (IRE)** 5-11-4 .... RThornton (T R George) *hld up in tch: rdn over 3f out: sn wknd* **4/1**[2]	48
0	**10**	*10*	**Crafty Glen (IRE)**[24] [655] 5-10-11 .... MrDEdwards(7) (G F Edwards) *prom tl rdn and wknd over 5f out* **66/1**	38
	11	*3 ½*	**Just Gabby (IRE)** 6-10-11 .... SCurran (M B Shears) *a bhd* **50/1**	28
	12	*dist*	**Double Belle** 5-10-11 .... RGreene (S C Burrough) *hld up in tch: lost pl after 6f: t.o fnl 8f: fin lame* **25/1**	—

3m 51.3s (3.50) **Going Correction** +0.175s/f (Yiel)
WFA 4 from 5yo 3lb 5 from 6yo 1lb **12** Ran SP% **118.4**
Speed ratings: **98,91,87,83,71 69,68,68,67,62 60,—** CSF £20.73 TOTE £2.80: £1.50, £3.00, £1.80; EX 18.00 Place 6 £37.45, Place 5 £15.17.
Owner Ms Gillian Metherell **Bred** J F C Maxwell **Trained** Sutton Veny, Wilts

FOCUS
A steadily-run bumper in which the third sets the standard.

NOTEBOOK
Tihui Two(IRE) ◆ confirmed the promise of her debut effort with an impressive victory, in front after half a furlong following a tardy start and quickening right away in the final quarter mile. She is evidently a quirky mare who is nervous around other horses, but she certainly has an engine and it would be no surprise to see her win again. *(tchd 2-1, 5-2 in places)*
Haloo Baloo, who had a couple of runs in Irish point-to-points in the spring, stayed on steadily for second and looks a chasing type for the future. *(op 9-1 tchd 7-1)*
Houlihans Free(IRE), penalised for his course and distance win, went after the winner early in the home straight but could make no impression. In all probability the ground had gone against him. *(op 2-1 tchd 5-2)*
Pumpkin Pickle was keeping on in the latter stages and obviously has a bit of ability.
Swift Water(IRE) is out of an Irish bumper winner who is a half-sister to useful staying chaser Unholy Allliance and Jolly Green Giant. She should be capable of better with this run behind her. *(op 5-1)*

T/Jkpt: Not won. T/Plt: £51.10 to a £1 stake. Pool: £44,542.55. 636.00 winning tickets. T/Qpdt: £12.20 to a £1 stake. Pool: £2,854.80. 171.80 winning tickets. KH

867 - 869a (Foreign Racing) - See Raceform Interactive

[854] PERTH (R-H)

Thursday, June 30

OFFICIAL GOING: Good to soft (good in places)

870 GG.COM NOVICES' HURDLE (8 hdls) 2m 110y

2:10 (2:11) (Class 4) 4-Y-0+ **£4,280** (£1,317; £658; £329)

Form				RPR
050-	**1**		**Rajam**[80] [4810] 7-10-5 99 .... (p) WKennedy(7) (G A Harker) *in tch: smooth hdwy to ld 2 out: sn clr* **11/2**[2]	120+
030-	**2**	*6*	**Va Vavoom (IRE)**[104] [4434] 7-10-12 118 .... CLlewellyn (N A Twiston-Davies) *led to 2 out: kpt on same pce* **10/11**[1]	105
2444	**3**	*½*	**Leopold (SLO)**[16] [748] 4-10-9 98 .... PJBrennan (M F Harris) *keen: prom: disp ld 3 out to next: one pce* **14/1**	101
0/40	**4**	*11*	**Bella Liana (IRE)**[1] [854] 5-10-2 .... PBuchanan(3) (J Clements, Ire) *midfield: effrt bef 3 out: no imp fr next* **100/1**	86
3-32	**5**	*1 ¾*	**Summer Special**[25] [645] 5-10-12 105 .... (p) MBradburne (Mrs S C Bradburne) *in tch: effrt 3 out: no imp next* **6/1**[3]	91
05-5	**6**	*3*	**Ali Shuffle (IRE)**[25] [647] 6-10-7 .... PCO'Neill(5) (J J Lambe, Ire) *hld up: shkn up after 2 out: nvr nrr* **100/1**	88
F-00	**7**	*1 ¾*	**Skiddaw Jones**[22] [691] 5-10-9 80 .... (t) PWhelan(3) (M A Barnes) *hld up: effrt after 3 out: wknd next* **100/1**	87
0-	**8**	*13*	**So Determined (IRE)**[17] [738] 4-10-9 .... RJohnson (J J Lambe, Ire) *w ldr tl rdn and wknd after 3 out* **9/1**	71
	9	*1 ¾*	**Dyneburg (POL)**[297] 5-10-12 .... JMMaguire (T R George) *keen: prom to 3 out: sn btn* **16/1**	72
	10	*¾*	**Captain Saif**[9] 5-10-12 .... (t) KRenwick (N Wilson) *bhd: struggling fr 1/2-way* **66/1**	71
	11	*dist*	**Dalkeys Lass**[22] 4-10-2 .... NPMulholland (Mrs L B Normile) *cl up tl lost pl after 3rd: mstke and struggling next* **100/1**	—

45-0 **12** *10* **Alfie's Connection**[49] [323] 4-10-9 .... RMcGrath **50/1**
(K G Reveley) *hld up: struggling fr 1/2-way*
13 *2 1/2* **Power Strike (USA)**[607] 4-10-4 .... DFlavin(5) —
(Mrs L B Normile) *nt fluent towards rr: wknd fr 4th* **100/1**
14 *17* **Drumossie (AUS)**[379] 5-10-9 .... LMcGrath(3) —
(R C Guest) *nt fluent: a bhd* **25/1**
143/ **P** **Rockanroll**[13] [786] 9-10-12 89 .... ADobbin —
(C A McBratney, Ire) *towards rr: struggling 4th: t.o whn p.u bef last* **100/1**

3m 58.7s (-1.90) **Going Correction** +0.10s/f (Yiel)
WFA 4 from 5yo+ 3lb **15** Ran SP% **117.8**
Speed ratings: **108,105,104,99,98 97,96,90,89,89** —,—,—,—,— CSF £10.70 TOTE £6.90: £1.60, £1.20, £2.80; EX 20.10.
Owner Our Emerald Club **Bred** Shadwell Estate Company Limited **Trained** Thirkleby, N Yorks

FOCUS
An ordinary event in which the pace seemed sound. The winner is value for 15l and should rate higher, with the third setting the standard.

NOTEBOOK
Rajam ◆ turned in easily his best effort over hurdles tried in the first-time cheekpieces to win with plenty in hand and, on this evidence, could be up to defying a penalty in ordinary company this summer. *(op 15-2)*
Va Vavoom(IRE) looked the one to beat, even dropped markedly in trip, but proved disappointing. Although the return to further will be in his favour, he does not look one to be taking a short price about in this grade. *(op Evens tchd 11-10 in places)*
Leopold(SLO) is a consistent sort who looks the best guide to the level of this form but, although the return to further is going to be in his favour, he is likely to continue to look vulnerable in this type of event. *(op 12-1)*
Bella Liana(IRE), dropped in trip, ran creditably in the face of a stiff task but left the impression that the return to further and the step into modest handicaps would suit.
Summer Special has been a model of consistency but proved disappointing and may still have been feeling the effects of a hard race in bad ground at the last meeting here. This run does not do *him justice but his record suggests he is not one to place much faith in.Official explanation: jockey said gelding did not face the cheekpieces (op 11-2)*
Ali Shuffle(IRE) is a modest and inconsistent maiden who left the impression that a stiffer test will suit, but he is likely to continue to struggle in this grade. *(op 50-1)*
Power Strike(USA) *Official explanation: trainer said colt scoped dirty post-race (op 66-1)*

871 NORTHERN MARINE UNDERWRITERS CLAIMING HURDLE (10 hdls) 2m 4f 110y
2:40 (2:40) (Class 4) 4-Y-0+ **£3,653** (£1,124; £562; £281)

Form RPR
0-06 **1** **Champagne Harry**[8] [814] 7-11-12 128 .... CLlewellyn 111+
(N A Twiston-Davies) *in tch: hdwy bef 3 out: led after next: styd on wl* **5/2**[2]
24-2 **2** *1 3/4* **High Drama**[26] [632] 8-11-8 110 .... APMcCoy 105
(P Bowen) *cl up: led 3 out: hdd next: rallied last: kpt on same pce run in* **7/4**[1]
-232 **3** *11* **Knockdoo (IRE)**[21] [697] 12-10-13 96 .... MrGGoldie(7) 92
(J S Goldie) *bhd: hdwy bef 2 out: kpt on: nt rch first two* **8/1**
0 **4** *9* **Possible Gale (IRE)**[31] [592] 7-10-12 77 ....(tp) ATinkler 75
(John G Carr, Ire) *cl up: led 5th to 3 out: sn outpcd* **50/1**
6-P1 **5** *24* **Mr Fernet**[53] [232] 8-10-11 99 .... CPoste(7) 57
(M F Harris) *hld up: effrt 4 out: btn after next* **14/1**
6-40 **6** *12* **Little Tobias (IRE)**[1] [859] 6-11-4 88 .... ARoss 45
(J S Wainwright) *led to 5th: reminders next: wknd fr 3 out* **25/1**
-530 **7** *3* **Spree Vision**[11] [784] 9-10-4 96 ....(v) DDaSilva(10) 38
(P Monteith) *bhd: struggling fr 4 out: t.o* **25/1**
123- **P** **Minivet**[45] [1504] 10-11-3 114 .... KJMercer(3) —
(R Allan) *chsd ldrs tl wknd 7th: t.o whn p.u bef 2 out* **9/2**[3]

5m 7.70s (-0.50) **Going Correction** +0.10s/f (Yiel) **8** Ran SP% **110.5**
Speed ratings: **104,103,99,95,86 82,80,**— CSF £6.95 TOTE £3.50: £1.70, £1.10, £1.90; EX 7.00.Champagne Harry was the subject of a friendly claim.
Owner H R Mould **Bred** H R Mould And G M Macechern **Trained** Naunton, Gloucs

FOCUS
An uncompetitive event in which the pace was fair. The fourth sets the level in a weak race.

NOTEBOOK
Champagne Harry proved well suited by the drop in grade and showed the right attitude to break his losing run. Whether he will be able to prove competitive from his current mark back in handicaps is another matter, though. *(tchd 11-4, 3-1 in places)*
High Drama, back over hurdles, gave it his best shot after getting the run of the race and looks the best guide to the level of this form. He will be of interest back over fences from his lower handicap mark. *(op 15-8 tchd 2-1)*
Knockdoo(IRE) has not won since 2000 and had a stiff task at the weights, but fared the best of those to come from off the pace. He will be suited by the return to further but his record suggests he is not one to be lumping on. *(op 10-1)*
Possible Gale(IRE), who had a stiff task at the weights, had the run of the race and may be flattered by his proximity. His record suggests he would be no good thing to reproduce this back in handicaps next time. *(op 33-1)*
Mr Fernet had a stiff task at the weights but was one of the few to come here in much form and so *was disappointing over a trip which he seems to stay. He looks one to have reservations about. (op 12-1)*
Little Tobias(IRE), turned out quickly and dropped in trip, is an inconsistent sort who did not show anywhere near enough to suggest he is of immediate interest. *(op 20-1)*
Minivet *Official explanation: jockey said gelding lost a front shoe (op 4-1)*

872 SATELLITE INFORMATION SERVICES NOVICES' CHASE (18 fncs) 3m
3:10 (3:10) (Class 3) 5-Y-0+ **£6,773** (£2,084; £1,042; £521)

Form RPR
02-2 **1** **Mr Ed (IRE)**[16] [207] 7-11-0 ....(p) APMcCoy 118+
(P Bowen) *hld up: smooth hdwy bef 4 out: led 2 out: readily* **2/7**[1]
2 *8* **Lord Of Gortmerron (IRE)**[32] 6-11-0 .... JPMcNamara 98
(C J Cosgrave, Ire) *cl up: rdn bef 4 out: kpt on fr 2 out: no ch w wnr* **16/1**[3]
P/43 **3** *2 1/2* **Heather Lad**[11] [782] 12-11-0 .... RMcGrath 96+
(C Grant) *mde most to 2 out: kpt on same pce* **10/1**[2]
P-0U **4** *30* **Mr Cooney (IRE)**[31] [594] 11-10-8 ow1 .... MrSClements(7) 66
(J Clements, Ire) *hld up in tch: outpcd 13th: n.d after* **25/1**
0 **5** *5* **Personal Impact (IRE)**[25] [643] 7-10-9 .... PCO'Neill(5) 60
(J J Lambe, Ire) *cl up tl outpcd bef 4 out: btn whn mstke next* **100/1**
PUP0 **P** **Mill Tower**[33] [550] 8-10-7 .... GThomas(7) —
(R Nixon) *a bhd: struggling 13th: t.o whn p.u bef 2 out* **100/1**
-P **P** **Partners Choice (IRE)**[1] [858] 8-11-0 74 ....(t) ATinkler —
(John G Carr, Ire) *hld up in tch: blnd 8th: p.u bef next* **33/1**
P **Sweet Sabastion**[41] [447] 7-11-0 .... BHarding —
(C A McBratney, Ire) *chsd ldrs tl wknd fr 14th: t.o whn p.u bef 2 out* **50/1**
P **Derrinraw (IRE)**[13] [776] 6-10-7 .... MrRMPMcNally(7) —
(Stephen McConville, Ire) *a bhd: struggling 13th: t.o whn plld bef last* **50/1**

6m 26.0s (13.40) **Going Correction** +0.10s/f (Yiel) **9** Ran SP% **105.4**
Speed ratings: **81,78,77,67,65** —,—,—,— CSF £3.69 TOTE £1.20: £1.20, £2.00, £1.10; EX 5.80.
Owner Gwilym J Morris **Bred** P E Banahan **Trained** Little Newcastle, Pembrokes

FOCUS
An uncompetitive event in which the pace was sound and a bloodless victory to start to his chasing career from the long odds-on favourite. He was value for 20l and is sure to rate higher.

NOTEBOOK
Mr Ed(IRE) ◆, a 149-rated hurdler who ran creditably on the Flat last time, won an ordinary event on his chase debut with a good deal in hand. His jumping was sound and he left the impression he would be able to hold his own in stronger company. *(tchd 1-3 in places)*
Lord Of Gortmerron(IRE), an Irish point winner making his debut over regulation fences, left the impression that a stiffer test of stamina and the step into handicap company would be ideal in due course. *(tchd 14-1 and 20-1)*
Heather Lad jumped soundly and ran creditably and, although advancing in years, will be of interest in ordinary handicaps when the emphasis is on stamina. *(op 7-1 tchd 6-1)*
Mr Cooney(IRE) was again well beaten over regulation fences and continues to look opposable in this sphere.
Personal Impact(IRE) achieved little on this debut over regulation fences. *(op 66-1)*
Partners Choice(IRE) *Official explanation: jockey said his leg had become caught in the breast girth and he had to pull up (tchd 40-1)*

873 DM HALL H'CAP HURDLE (8 hdls) 2m 110y
3:40 (3:41) (Class 3) (0-125,120) 4-Y-0+
£7,516 (£2,851; £1,425; £648; £324; £194)

Form RPR
0-1F **1** **Travel (POL)**[23] [675] 5-11-5 113 .... JMMaguire 125+
(T R George) *chsd ldrs: smooth hdwy and led bef 2 out: sn clr* **6/1**[3]
6-2U **2** *8* **Bodfari Signet**[10] [422] 9-11-2 110 .... MBradburne 109
(Mrs S C Bradburne) *hld up: effrt bef 3 out: kpt on fr next: no ch w wnr* **12/1**
14-1 **3** *2* **Millagros (IRE)**[15] [302] 5-11-5 113 .... JimCrowley 110
(I Semple) *hld up: hdwy bef 3 out: hung lft bef next: one pce* **9/2**[1]
/311 **4** *4* **Dream Castle (IRE)**[19] [716] 11-10-11 110 .... PCO'Neill(5) 103
(Barry Potts, Ire) *keen: mde most to bef 2 out: sn btn* **5/1**[2]
-34P **5** *1 3/4* **Winter Garden**[19] [717] 11-9-11 94 oh1 .... PBuchanan(3) 85
(Miss Lucinda V Russell) *bhd: drvn 1/2-way: kpt on fr 2 out: nvr on terms* **50/1**
3-42 **6** *11* **Wyn Dixie (IRE)**[19] [716] 6-10-3 97 .... TJMurphy 77
(P Monteith) *hld up: effrt 3 out: sn no imp* **9/2**[1]
00-0 **7** *6* **Prince Among Men**[14] [766] 8-11-12 120 .... ADobbin 94
(N G Richards) *prom tl rdn and wknd after 4 out* **8/1**
F2F/ **8** *10* **Loy's Lad (IRE)**[579] [2457] 9-9-11 94 oh1 .... KJMercer(3) 58
(Miss V Scott) *bhd: drvn bef 4 out: nvr on terms* **40/1**
-600 **9** *4* **Rising Generation (FR)**[22] [689] 8-11-10 118 .... BHarding 78
(N G Richards) *cl up tl rdn and wknd fr 3 out* **20/1**
5- **10** *30* **Oyez (IRE)**[235] [2087] 8-10-10 104 .... RJohnson 34
(J J Lambe, Ire) *cl up tl wknd after 4 out* **10/1**
03P- **F** **Drift Away (USA)**[281] [1477] 5-9-8 95 .... MissJAKidd(7) —
(J J Lambe, Ire) *hld up: fell 2nd* **40/1**
5F/3 **B** **Bringontheclowns (IRE)**[21] [695] 6-10-10 104 .... PJBrennan —
(M F Harris) *hld up: b.d 2nd* **12/1**
-P00 **P** **Conor's Pride (IRE)**[11] [784] 8-10-0 94 oh4 .... NPMulholland —
(B Mactaggart) *keen: cl up tl wknd 1/2-way: t.o whn p.u bef 3 out* **33/1**

3m 58.7s (-1.90) **Going Correction** +0.10s/f (Yiel) **13** Ran SP% **117.4**
Speed ratings: **108,104,103,101,100 95,92,87,86,71** —,—,— CSF £69.37 CT £356.86 TOTE £7.80: £2.10, £3.20, £1.90; EX 78.30.
Owner Mrs Sharon C Nelson **Bred** Adam Milewski **Trained** Slad, Gloucs

FOCUS
An ordinary event in which the pace was sound and this bare form should prove reliable. The third looks the best guide to the level.

NOTEBOOK
Travel(POL), unbeaten in three starts at this course, showed himself none the worse for his Huntingdon fall. He will find things tougher after reassessment but, given the way he went through this race, may well be capable of better. *(op 5-1)*
Bodfari Signet is a reliable sort who ran creditably and is worth another try over two and a half miles, but left the impression that he would be vulnerable to progressive or well handicapped types from his current mark.
Millagros(IRE) was not disgraced on this handicap debut but did not look the easiest of rides and is likely to find things difficult against progressive types from this mark. *(tchd 5-1)*
Dream Castle(IRE) was found out by the 13lb rise in the weights and the fact that he was not allowed an uncontested lead. He is high enough in the weights but will be of more interest when allowed his own way in front. *(op 9-2 tchd 6-1 in place)*
Winter Garden was not disgraced back over hurdles but, although leaving the impression that a stiffer test of stamina would suit, remains one to tread carefully with, especially as his stable is very quiet at present. *(op 40-1)*
Wyn Dixie(IRE) was a long way below his recent best but was disappointing, even allowing for the fact that those held up never got into the race. He is not one to write off despite this below-par effort, but is not one for maximum faith either. *(op 5-1 tchd 4-1, 6-1 in a place)*

874 NORTHERN MARINE UNDERWRITERS H'CAP CHASE (12 fncs) 2m
4:10 (4:15) (Class 4) (0-100,94) 5-Y-0+ **£7,104** (£2,186; £1,093; £546)

Form RPR
-103 **1** **Risky Way**[25] [644] 9-10-13 81 .... GLee 95
(W S Coltherd) *hld up midfield: rdn bef 3 out: rallied to ld run in: edgd rt: kpt on wl* **8/1**
P1-2 **2** *2 1/2* **Super Dolphin**[21] [692] 6-11-1 83 .... ADobbin 95+
(R Ford) *cl up: hit 7th: nt fluent 4 out: effrt and ev ch fr next: kpt on run in* **7/2**[1]
6/2 **3** *2 1/2* **Jamica Plane (IRE)**[25] [644] 12-11-2 84 ....(p) RJohnson 93
(J J Lambe, Ire) *mde most to run in: kpt on same pce* **4/1**[2]
60/ **4** *10* **Loulou Nivernais (FR)**[20] [706] 6-11-0 82 .... ARoss 81
(J G Cosgrave, Ire) *hld up midfield: smooth hdwy to chse ldrs bef 3 out: rdn and wknd fr next* **40/1**
U-14 **5** *14* **Apadi (USA)**[53] [246] 9-11-6 91 .... LMcGrath(3) 78+
(R C Guest) *hld up: hdwy bef 4 out: rdn and no imp bef next* **7/1**[3]
14P/ **6** *13* **Dottie Digger (IRE)**[577] [2511] 6-10-2 73 ....(p) PBuchanan(3) 45
(Miss Lucinda V Russell) *chsd ldrs: drvn along whn blnd 3 out: sn btn* **20/1**
4646 **7** *16* **Rattina (GER)**[23] [674] 9-10-0 68 ....(b[1]) PJBrennan 24
(M F Harris) *chsd ldrs tl rdn and wknd fr 4 out* **7/1**[3]
2R-F **P** **Zurs (IRE)**[25] [644] 12-11-8 90 .... TJMurphy —
(J J Lambe, Ire) *sn bhd: t.o whn p.u bef 2 out* **16/1**
P0-3 **P** **Little Task**[30] [520] 7-11-12 94 .... BHarding —
(J S Wainwright) *a bhd: t.o whn p.u 4 out* **16/1**

The Form Book, Raceform Ltd, Compton, RG20 6NL

505- **P** **Salvage**[71] 4927 10-11-0 **82** .... PRobson —
(Mrs J C McGregor) *sn bhd: t.o whn p.u bef 2 out* **10/1**

5550 **P** **Northern Flash**[19] 716 11-10-0 **68** oh1 .... (p) FKeniry —
(J C Haynes) *mstke 1st: a bhd: t.o whn p.u 4 out* **25/1**

41P- **P** **Ratty's Band**[351] 952 11-10-4 **77** .... DFlavin(5) —
(Mrs L B Normile) *loose bef s: a bhd: t.o whn p.u 4 out* **20/1**

P0-0 **P** **The Honey Guide**[33] 550 9-10-0 **68** oh4 .... NPMulholland —
(Mrs L B Normile) *in tch: effrt bef 3 out: 5th and hld whn nrly fell next: sn p.u* **50/1**

4m 3.20s (0.40) **Going Correction** +0.10s/f (Yiel) **13** Ran SP% **117.0**
Speed ratings: **103,101,100,95,88 82,74,—,—,— —,—,—** CSF £34.17 CT £130.98 TOTE £9.30: £2.50, £2.10, £1.90; EX 34.30.
Owner Mrs L J McLeod **Bred** Mrs N A Ward And W J Musson **Trained** Selkirk, Borders

FOCUS
A modest event but a strongly-run race meant those racing up with the pace had little extra to give in the closing stages. The form appears reasonable.

NOTEBOOK
Risky Way is not renowned for his consistency and was wisely ridden with a bit more patience than is usually the case but, with the leaders going off quickly, he did have things teed up for him to a certain degree and would not be one to take a short price about next time.
Super Dolphin fared the best of those that raced up with the strong pace and looks better than the bare form given he was less than fluent on occasions. He looks sure to win a race in similar company over fences.
Jamica Plane(IRE) has not won for some time but confirmed the promise of his recent course and distance run and will be of more interest when it looks as though he will be able to get an uncontested lead. He looks sure to win a similar race. *(op 11-2)*
Loulou Nivernais(FR) had been disappointing over fences but ran his best race over the larger obstacles. However, he did not find as much as seemed likely when asked for his effort and would not be one to lump on at much shorter odds next time. *(op 33-1)*
Apadi(USA) had the race run to suit but was disappointing and remains one to tread carefully with. *(op 6-1)*
Dottie Digger(IRE), with the cheekpieces back on, shaped as though a bit better than the bare form on this chase debut and first run for well over a year and should be better for the experience.
Zurs(IRE) *Official explanation: jockey said gelding had never been travelling (op 20-1)*
Salvage *Official explanation: jockey said gelding pulled up lame (op 20-1)*

875 DM HALL NOVICES' HURDLE (12 hdls) 3m 110y
4:40 (4:42) (Class 4) 4-Y-0+ **£4,153** (£1,278; £639; £319)

Form RPR

P/2U **1** **Rebelle**[9] 802 6-10-12 .... APMcCoy 87+
(P Bowen) *chsd ldrs: led appr 2 out: kpt on strly* **6/4**[1]

1 **2** *4* **Fourth Dimension (IRE)**[11] 785 6-11-4 .... KRenwick 86
(D Nicholls) *prom: effrt after 3 out: kpt on fr next: nt rch wnr* **11/4**[2]

2000 **3** *3/4* **Scamp**[11] 781 6-10-2 68 .... (p) KJMercer(3) 72
(R Shiels) *led to 5th: led 4 out to appr 2 out: kpt on same pce* **33/1**

2204 **4** *11* **Hattington**[14] 766 7-11-4 107 .... PJBrennan 77+
(M F Harris) *hld up: hdwy to chse ldrs after 3 out: rdn and wknd next* **4/1**[3]

3P- **5** *8* **Right Direction (IRE)**[13] 786 7-10-7 .... PCO'Neill(5) 60
(J J Lambe, Ire) *hld up: drvn 4 out: no imp fr next* **33/1**

6-0 **6** *26* **Tuscany Boy (IRE)**[10] 796 5-10-12 77 .... ADobbin 34
(C A McBratney, Ire) *hld up: rdn 4 out: n.d* **16/1**

0 **7** *dist* **Nobodysgonanotice (IRE)**[25] 643 7-10-12 .... RJohnson —
(J J Lambe, Ire) *w ldr: led 5th to 4 out: wknd next* **25/1**

543- **P** **Quizzical**[197] 2839 7-10-12 87 .... (p) ATinkler —
(John G Carr, Ire) *in tch to 1/2-way: sn lost pl: t.o whn p.u bef 3 out* **10/1**

6m 18.2s (7.30) **Going Correction** +0.10s/f (Yiel) **8** Ran SP% **111.4**
Speed ratings: **92,90,90,86,84 76,—,—** CSF £5.50 TOTE £2.50: £1.10, £1.50, £5.50; EX 6.10.
Owner P Bowen **Bred** Christopher Shankland **Trained** Little Newcastle, Pembrokes

FOCUS
A race lacking strength and one in which the gallop was only fair. The proximity of the third limits the form.

NOTEBOOK
Rebelle ♦, who missed last year, ran his best race over hurdles and appreciated the step up to this trip. Although this was not much of a contest, he showed the right attitude and appeals as the type to win again over hurdles. *(op 7-4)*
Fourth Dimension(IRE), who took an uncompetitive race on his hurdling debut, ran at least as well under a penalty in this stronger event and had no problem with the longer trip. He should be placed to best advantage. *(op 2-1)*
Scamp, a poor and inconsistent hurdler, had the run of the race over this longer trip and her proximity confirms that this bare form is not reliable. She is likely to continue to look vulnerable in this type of event.
Hattington proved disappointing as he had looked worth a chance over this trip and, although the return to two and a half miles may suit, he looks one to continue to field against at shortish odds in this type of event. *(op 9-2 tchd 5-1 in a place)*
Right Direction(IRE), having his third run for a handicap mark, left the impression that a stiffer test and the step into handicaps would suit. *(op 25-1)*
Tuscany Boy(IRE) faced a stiff task at the weights and ran accordingly. *(op 20-1 tchd 25-1 in a place)*

876 GG.COM INTERMEDIATE OPEN NATIONAL HUNT FLAT RACE 2m 110y
5:15 (5:19) (Class 6) 4-6-Y-0 **£2,226** (£636; £318)

Form RPR

0-22 **1** **Lunar Eclipse**[19] 720 5-10-5 .... PRobson 85
(J I A Charlton) *prom: effrt 3f out: styd on wl fnl f to ld towards fin* **9/2**[2]

2/5- **2** *nk* **Dalawan**[152] 3584 6-10-9 .... PAspell(3) 92
(Mrs J C McGregor) *cl up: led over 4f out: styd on wl: hdd towards fin* **16/1**[3]

1 **3** *7* **Zumrah (IRE)**[14] 769 4-11-2 .... APMcCoy 89
(P Bowen) *racd wd: hld up: hdwy and prom 4f out: rdn 3f out: one pce fr 2f out* **4/9**[1]

3 **4** *3* **Mae Moss**[19] 720 4-10-2 .... ADempsey 72
(W S Coltherd) *cl up: ev ch over 4f out: rdn and outpcd fr over 2f out: b.b.v* **20/1**

0- **5** *4* **Saddlers' Harmony (IRE)**[194] 2886 4-10-9 .... RMcGrath 75
(K G Reveley) *hld up: hdwy over 5f out: rdn and no imp fr 3f out* **16/1**[3]

6 *16* **Brickland (IRE)**[28] 623 4-9-9 .... MrNMcKnight(7) 52
(Mayne Kidd, Ire) *prom tl wknd over 4f out* **50/1**

5 **7** *2 1/2* **Spa Wells (IRE)**[19] 719 4-10-4 .... PCO'Neill(5) 57
(Barry Potts, Ire) *led to over 4f out: sn btn* **20/1**

8 *6* **Magic Brook** 6-10-12 .... KRenwick 54
(R Allan) *in tch tl rdn and wknd over 4f out* **50/1**

0 **9** *hd* **Pollensa Lady**[19] 719 5-10-5 .... GLee 46
(A Crook) *keen: in tch tl wknd over 4f out* **33/1**

04- **10** *3/4* **End Of Saga**[309] 1287 6-10-5 .... BenOrde-Powlett(7) 53
(J B Walton) *hld up: rdn 6f out: sn btn* **50/1**

00- **11** *19* **Beau Saddler**[110] 4323 4-10-6 .... PBuchanan(3) 31
(A R Dicken) *hld up: rdn over 5f out: sn btn* **50/1**

4m 2.50s (1.70) **Going Correction** +0.10s/f (Yiel) **11** Ran SP% **119.5**
Speed ratings: **100,99,96,95,93 85,84,81,81,81 72** CSF £65.44 TOTE £6.40: £1.90, £3.40, £1.10; EX 111.40 Place 6 £4.93, Place 5 £3.81.
Owner J W Robson **Bred** J W Robson **Trained** Stocksfield, Northumberland

FOCUS
A modest gallop in the first half of the race and, with the favourite disappointing, this form looks nothing special although solid enough with most of the principals close to their marks.

NOTEBOOK
Lunar Eclipse turned in her best effort yet to get off the mark and again left the impression that a good test of stamina is going to suit when sent over hurdles. *(op 11-2)*
Dalawan ran his best race yet, finishing clear of the remainder, and looks sure to go close in similar company this summer. *(op 20-1)*
Zumrah(IRE) very much looked the one to beat judged on his facile Aintree success but proved a big disappointment on only this second racecourse outing. Given that initial promise though, he would not be one to write off just yet. *(op 2-5 tchd 1-2 in places)*
Mae Moss again showed ability, despite breaking a blood-vessel, but is likely to continue to struggle in this type of event. *Official explanation: jockey said filly bled from the nose*
Saddlers' Harmony(IRE) was not disgraced on only this second racecourse outing but left the impression that a much stiffer test would suit when sent over obstacles.
Brickland(IRE) was again well beaten and is not one to be interested in in this type of event.
T/Plt: £7.20 to a £1 stake. Pool: £35,836.75. 3,604.80 winning tickets. T/Qpdt: £2.80 to a £1 stake. Pool: £2,284.40. 603.30 winning tickets. RY

877 - 890a (Foreign Racing) - See Raceform Interactive

822 MARKET RASEN (R-H)
Sunday, July 3

OFFICIAL GOING: Good to firm
Between 1' and 3' water had been put on the track. The going was described as 'good to firm, firm in the back straight'.
Wind: moderate, half-against. Weather: fine and sunny

891 DON NOBLE CONDITIONAL JOCKEYS' (S) HURDLE (10 hdls) 2m 6f
2:15 (2:16) (Class 5) 4-Y-0+ **£2,296** (£656; £328)

Form RPR

-105 **1** **Angie's Double**[7] 839 5-10-5 74 .... RSpate(8) 89+
(Mrs K Waldron) *trckd ldrs: led bef 3 out: clr between last 2: easily* **9/2**[3]

6-00 **2** *8* **Del Trotter (IRE)**[7] 839 10-11-0 85 .... (p) KJMercer 77
(M E Sowersby) *prom: chsd wnr fr 3 out: no imp* **25/1**

P-01 **3** *dist* **Greencard Golf**[50] 351 4-11-3 100 .... AO'Keeffe 39
(Jennie Candlish) *bhd: hdwy 7th: lft poor 3rd 2 out: btn 42 l* **7/1**

0-PP **4** *8* **Saragann (IRE)**[50] 346 10-12-1 105 .... SWalsh(3) 46
(N B King) *w ldrs: wknd 3 out* **25/1**

1/00 **5** *2 1/2* **Dilsaa**[56] 238 8-11-12 96 .... PRobson 37
(K A Ryan) *j. slowly 2nd: mid-div: hdwy 5th: wknd after 7th: bhd whn blnd last* **7/2**[2]

-60P **6** *4* **Pat Malone**[7] 838 5-11-0 .... DLaverty 21
(Lucinda Featherstone) *nt jump wl: sn bhd: lost tch 7th* **40/1**

-001 **7** *shd* **Sylcan Express**[25] 686 12-11-12 71 .... (p) TJPhelan —
(O O'Neill) *bhd: drvn along 6th: nvr on terms* **14/1**

000- **F** **Dover Creek**[140] 3838 5-10-2 .... KBurke(5) —
(Miss M E Rowland) *in rr whn fell 4th* **80/1**

P654 **F** **Cloud Catcher (IRE)**[25] 680 4-9-13 60 .... (bt) TMessenger(5) —
(M Appleby) *bhd whn fell 3rd* **40/1**

2P-U **R** **Heavenly Stride**[19] 747 9-11-12 104 .... RStephens —
(P Bowen) *trckd ldrs: racd wd and rn out 3 out* **3/1**[1]

4PP6 **P** **Island Warrior (IRE)**[25] 686 10-11-12 66 .... (t) JamesDavies —
(B P J Baugh) *prom: lost pl 5th: t.o whn p.u bef 2 out* **28/1**

U **Munaawesh (USA)**[13] 4-10-8 .... CDSharkey(3) 54
(D W Chapman) *nt fluent: bhd: hdwy 7th: poor 3rd whn swvd rt and uns rdr 2 out* **7/1**

P **P** **Passionate Knight (IRE)**[25] 691 6-10-11 .... (v[1]) PAspell(3) —
(B S Rothwell) *t.k.h: led tl after 5th: wknd qckly: t.o 7th: p.u bef next* **80/1**

PP-P **P** **Soroka (IRE)**[42] 469 6-11-6 85 .... (bt[1]) JPByrne —
(Jennie Candlish) *w ldrs: led after 5th: hung bdly rt and hdd bef 3 out: sn lost pl: bhd whn p.u bef 2 out* **18/1**

5m 18.4s (-9.90) **Going Correction** -0.45s/f (Good)
WFA 4 from 5yo+ 3lb **14** Ran SP% **120.8**
Speed ratings: **100,97,—,—,— —,—,—,—,— —,—,—,—** CSF £112.69 TOTE £5.30: £1.70, £6.00, £2.30; EX 99.90.The winner was bought in for 5,000gns.
Owner Nick Shutts **Bred** P And Mrs Wafford **Trained** Stoke Bliss, Worcs
■ A first winner under her married name for Karen Waldron, previously Karen Marks.

FOCUS
A weak seller but the easy winner seemed to turn in a much improved performance and is rated value for more than the official margin and the race could rate higher. There was some confusion amongst the riders whether or not the third last flight should be by-passed.

NOTEBOOK
Angie's Double had plenty to find judged on official ratings but, bursting clear, took this with a fair *amount in hand. She will be out soon under a penalty, her rating is bound to shoot up after this. (op 11-2)*
Del Trotter(IRE), who has not tasted success for over two years, is getting long in the tooth but was the only one to finish within hailing distance of the winner.
Greencard Golf, top-rated on official figures, is better going left-handed but even so this was still a poor effort. *(op 6-1)*
Saragann(IRE), pulled up on three of his previous four starts, looks bang out of form.
Dilsaa, absent for eight weeks, was on the retreat when his rider thought twice about missing out the third last flight. *(tchd 10-3 and 4-1)*
Heavenly Stride found the quick ground no problem and was bang in the argument when his rider went to by-pass the third last then changed his mind at the last moment and found himself outside the wing. The arrows indicating the flight should be by-passed were still there on the approach and there was definitely a misunderstanding among the groundstaff. *(op 12-1)*
Munaawesh(USA), a maiden after 31 starts on the Flat where he is rated just 45, was in third spot, *about ten lengths behind the runner-up, when he jinked and parted company with his rider two out. (op 12-1)*

892 DON NOBLE BOOKMAKER "PAYS DOUBLE RESULT" NOVICES' HURDLE (10 hdls) 2m 3f 110y
2:45 (2:46) (Class 3) 4-Y-0+ **£4,940** (£1,520; £760; £380)

Form RPR

-223 **1** **Enhancer**[17] 766 7-11-5 125 .... TJMurphy 117+
(M J McGrath) *trckd ldrs: hdwy on ins to ld last: drvn clr: readily* **10/11**[1]

-412 **2** *3 1/2* **Brooklyn Brownie (IRE)**[38] 521 6-11-5 108 .... GLee 111+
(J M Jefferson) *w ldrs: led after 3 out: j.lft and hdd last: nt pce of wnr* **3/1**[2]

-F22 **3** *4* **Festive Chimes (IRE)**[26] [671] 4-9-10 100............................. SWalsh(7) 90
(N B King) *led: qckknd 6th: hdd after 3 out: one pce appr last* **12/1**

1 **4** *3* **Whispered Promises (USA)**[17] [764] 4-11-2 .... JPMcNamara 100
(R S Brookhouse) *trckd ldrs: effrt and outpcd 2 out: kpt on run-in* **9/1**

0-61 **5** *1* **Chase The Sunset (IRE)**[29] [635] 7-11-5 100............................. JCulloty 102
(Miss H C Knight) *hld up towards rr: stdy hdwy 3 out: effrt 2 out: sn outpcd: kpt on run-in* **8/1**[3]

6 **6** *18* **Shady Baron (IRE)**[22] [719] 6-10-10 .... PAspell(3) 78
(J Wade) *chsd ldrs: rdn 3 out: lost pl appr 2 out* **200/1**

PP-0 **7** *1 1/2* **Darkshape**[25] [691] 5-10-13 .... SThomas 77
(Miss Venetia Williams) *hld up in rr: kpt on fr 3 out: nvr a factor* **33/1**

8 *28* **Southern Bazaar (USA)**[12] 4-10-10 .... RMcGrath 46
(M E Sowersby) *a in rr: detached fr 3 out* **200/1**

06 **9** *17* **Double Measure**[9] [828] 5-10-13 .... JimCrowley 32
(T D Walford) *in rr: pushed along 5th: t.o 3 out* **66/1**

00 **10** *24* **Bowling Along**[25] [691] 4-10-3 .... BHarding —
(M E Sowersby) *in tch: lost pl after 7th: sn bhd* **200/1**

0/ **P** **Knight General Mac**[41] [1599] 6-10-6 .... CDSharkey(7) —
(N Bycroft) *chsd ldrs: lost pl 7th: sn bhd: t.o whn p.u between last 2* **200/1**

4m 39.1s (-10.90) **Going Correction** -0.45s/f (Good)
WFA 4 from 5yo+ 2lb **11 Ran SP% 112.6**
Speed ratings: **103,101,100,98,98 91,90,79,72,63** — CSF £3.58 TOTE £1.80: £1.10, £1.30, £2.50; EX 3.50.
Owner Gallagher Equine Ltd **Bred** Juddmonte Farms **Trained** Maidstone, Kent

FOCUS
A fair novices' hurdle for the time of the year run in a reasonable time but the winner did not need to be at his best to win.

NOTEBOOK
Enhancer had plenty in hand and, sneaking through on the inner to lead at the last, had only to be kept up to his work. A winner of three bumpers and two hurdle races now, he will try his hand over fences later this year. *(op 5-4 tchd 5-6)*
Brooklyn Brownie(IRE), who had 17lb to find with the winner on official ratings, continues in good form but this potential chaser simply met one too good. *(op 9-4)*
Festive Chimes(IRE), 11lb behind the winner but 6lb ahead of the runner-up on official figures, was dropping back in trip. She stepped up the gallop from the front but, when asked for maximum effort, she could only keep on in her own time. *(op 10-1)*
Whispered Promises(USA) travelled strongly but tapped for toe two out, he could only keep on in *his own time. The step up in trip did not seem a problem. Official explanation: jockey said gelding was unsuited by good to firm ground (op 17-2)*
Chase The Sunset(IRE), who failed to make the grade over fences, travelled supremely well but his response to pressure was disappointing. *(op 9-1)*

893 DON NOBLE BOOKMAKER "GIVES GUARANTEED ODDS" BEGINNERS' CHASE (14 fncs) 2m 4f
3:15 (3:19) (Class 4) 5-Y-0+ **£3,926** (£1,208; £604; £302)

Form RPR

40-0 **1** **Touch Closer**[66] [92] 8-10-12 .... APMcCoy 113+
(P Bowen) *chsd ldr: hit 5th: reminders 7th: led after 4 out: kpt on run-in* **6/4**[1]

06-B **2** *1 3/4* **The Glen**[42] [465] 7-10-12 .... TDoyle 109
(R Lee) *in tch: jnd ldrs 8th: chal 3 out: kpt on same pce run-in* **5/1**[3]

14-F **3** *11* **Bushido (IRE)**[42] [465] 6-10-12 .... DElsworth 103+
(Mrs S J Smith) *jnd ldrs 8th: upsides 3 out: wknd between last 2: eased run-in* **11/4**[2]

-334 **4** *8* **Nopekan (IRE)**[38] [510] 5-10-4 105............................. RSpate(7) 92+
(Mrs K Waldron) *hmpd 5th: wnt prom 9th: outpcd 11th: sn struggling* **10/1**

5450 **5** *1/2* **Snooty Eskimo (IRE)**[4] [855] 13-10-6 75 ow1............................. MajorHNorton(7) 90
(W T Reed) *led 2nd: hit 10th: hdd after next: wknd appr 3 out* **50/1**

6 *28* **Offalevel**[21] 7-10-12 .... RGreene 61
(R J Hodges) *hld up in rr: hdwy 8th: lost pl after next* **22/1**

7 *dist* **Broadspeed**[406] 9-9-12 .... PCStringer(7) —
(M J Gingell) *wnt prom 7th: lost pl 9th: sn bhd: t.o* **100/1**

P **Floritchel (FR)**[57] 8-10-12 .... BHarding —
(W McKeown) *blnd 4th: sn bhd: t.o whn p.u bef 11th* **50/1**

-045 **P** **Three Lions**[17] [768] 8-10-12 .... JPMcNamara —
(R S Brookhouse) *nt fluent: bhd tl p.u after 7th* **10/1**

P-P **P** **Box On (IRE)**[56] [239] 8-10-12 107............................. ChristianWilliams —
(Miss V Scott) *in rr: bhd fr 8th: p.u bef 3 out* **16/1**

30 **P** **Prioritisation (IRE)**[35] [570] 6-10-7 .... DLaverty(5) —
(Mrs K Waldron) *led to 2nd: lost pl after 8th: sn bhd: t.o whn p.u bef 2 out* **33/1**

4m 55.8s (-6.90) **Going Correction** -0.45s/f (Good)
WFA 5 from 6yo+ 1lb **11 Ran SP% 119.6**
Speed ratings: **95,94,89,86,86 75,—,—,—,—** — CSF £9.58 TOTE £2.50: £1.40, £1.90, £1.50; EX 15.10.
Owner Donttellthewife Partnership **Bred** I W T And Mrs Loftus **Trained** Little Newcastle, Pembrokes

FOCUS
A moderate race in which Touch Closer did not look to be enjoying himself, but the race should work out at a modest level.

NOTEBOOK
Touch Closer, whose previous run over fences was in March 2004, was having his first outing for this trainer. Looking very fit indeed he did not look a natural but the champion was at his most determined. Three miles will suit him better though. *(op 2-1)*
The Glen ◆, out of luck on his chasing debut, is rated a stone and a half inferior to the winner over hurdles. He pushed him hard and deserves to go one better. *(op 11-2)*
Bushido(IRE), rated almost the equal of the winner over hurdles and another out of luck on his first try over fences at Southwell, ran as if just in need of the outing after six weeks absence and, with his chance gone but third place assured, he was sensibly given as easy time as possible. There will be another day. *(op 2-1)*
Nopekan(IRE) was going nowhere four out and is finding the transition to fences difficult. *(tchd 11-1)*
Snooty Eskimo(IRE), who brings his pension book to the races, was making a quick return after losing a shoe at Perth. Jumping boldly in front and, rated just 75, a novices' handicap is surely his only option. *(tchd 66-1)*

894 DON NOBLE BOOKMAKER H'CAP CHASE (12 fncs) 2m 1f 110y
3:45 (3:48) (Class 4) (0-110,110) 5-Y-0+ **£3,770** (£1,160; £580; £290)

Form RPR

0/ **1** **Ceannairceach (IRE)**[267] [1669] 12-11-0 98............................. GLee 117+
(J M Jefferson) *trckd ldrs: led 6th: styd on wl fr 2 out: readily* **11/2**

-411 **2** *3 1/2* **In The Frame (IRE)**[24] [692] 6-11-12 110............................. ChristianWilliams 124+
(Evan Williams) *chsd ldrs: drvn along 8th: upsides 3 out: nt qckn run-in* **13/8**[1]

P-0P **3** *2* **Get The Point**[21] [725] 11-10-2 86............................. JamesDavies 97
(Dr P Pritchard) *chsd ldrs 3rd: one pce fr 2 out* **12/1**

1-P3 **4** *10* **Runner Bean**[37] [534] 11-11-8 106............................. RThornton 109+
(R Lee) *lft in ld 3rd: hdd 6th: wknd appr 3 out* **3/1**[2]

-0PP **B** **Six Pack (IRE)**[9] [826] 11-7-3 101.............................(t) MFoley —
(Andrew Turnell) *chsd ldrs: bdly hmpd and b.d 3rd* **14/1**

1-P3 **F** **Mumaris (USA)**[22] [714] 11-11-12 110.............................(p) RJohnson —
(Miss Lucinda V Russell) *led: clr whn fell 3rd* **5/1**[3]

4m 22.7s (-8.40) **Going Correction** -0.45s/f (Good) **6 Ran SP% 109.5**
Speed ratings: **100,98,97,93,—** — CSF £14.82 TOTE £6.10: £3.70, £2.00; EX 24.50.
Owner D Traynor **Bred** D Traynor **Trained** Norton, N Yorks

FOCUS
A modest contest but a decisive winner who was value for further. The race is rated through the runner-up.

NOTEBOOK
Ceannairceach(IRE), a winner three times over fences in Ireland, was fresh and well on his first outing since October. As befits a son of Strong Gale, he bounced off the fast ground and, pressing home the advantage, in the end scored in most decisive fashion. He looks set to continue to give a good account of himself here this summer. *(op 13-2)*
In The Frame(IRE), 6lb higher, was being niggled early on the final circuit. He worked his way upsides three out but on the run-in the winner proved much the stronger. *(op 11-8 tchd 7-4)*
Get The Point, only 1lb higher than his last success at Fontwell in March, stuck on in his own time *and never really threatened the first two. He might not appreciate the ground as quick as this. (op 9-1)*
Runner Bean, competing in this event for the third year running, may not have appreciated being left in front at an early stage. *(op 7-2)*

895 BET WITH DON NOVICES' H'CAP HURDLE (8 hdls) 2m 1f 110y
4:15 (4:17) (Class 4) (0-105,100) 4-Y-0+ **£3,444** (£984; £492)

Form RPR

0-26 **1** **General Smith**[38] [513] 6-11-0 88............................. VSlattery 93+
(H J Evans) *bhd: hdwy after 5th: upsides whn hit last: edgd lft and styd on to ld nr fin* **40/1**

0P-3 **2** *nk* **Zarakash (IRE)**[9] [826] 5-11-2 90............................. APMcCoy 93+
(Jonjo O'Neill) *trckd ldrs: styd on to ld last 75yds: hdd nr fin* **2/1**[1]

34P- **3** *1 1/4* **Neckar Valley (IRE)**[20] [2832] 6-11-12 100............................. RThornton 102+
(R M Whitaker) *w ldrs: led 5th: nt fluent last: hdd and no ex run-in* **14/1**

36-2 **4** *2* **Smart Boy Prince (IRE)**[34] [596] 4-11-10 100............................. DRDennis 97
(C Smith) *led to 5th: kpt on same pce run-in* **7/1**[3]

FP0- **5** *2 1/2* **Ground Breaker**[167] [3393] 5-11-6 97............................. MrTGreenall(3) 95+
(M W Easterby) *hld up in rr: hdwy 4th: sn chsng ldrs: kpt on same pce between last 2* **9/1**

-000 **6** *13* **Meadow Hawk (USA)**[18] [758] 5-11-2 90.............................(v[1]) PMoloney 74
(Ian Williams) *mid-div: outpcd after 5th: n.d after* **12/1**

0-00 **7** *1 1/2* **Silistra**[39] [506] 6-10-2 86.............................(p) CMessenger(10) 68
(Mrs L C Jewell) *in tch: outpcd 5th: n.d after* **25/1**

400- **8** *14* **Weston Rock**[171] [3330] 6-11-11 99............................. JimCrowley 67
(T D Walford) *sn bhd and drvn along: nvr a factor* **25/1**

400- **9** *27* **Rathlin Island**[170] [3350] 7-10-9 83............................. MFoley 24
(Miss V Scott) *bhd and reminders 3rd: nvr on terms* **16/1**

P-PP **10** *27* **Just Sooty**[14] [785] 10-10-10 91............................. MissRachelClark(7) 5
(S B Clark) *bhd fr 4th* **33/1**

P-06 **P** **Sean (IRE)**[39] [504] 6-11-2 90............................. TScudamore —
(Mrs L C Jewell) *bhd: p.u bef 2 out* **40/1**

06-0 **P** **Mamore Gap (IRE)**[12] [9] 7-11-2 90............................. GLee —
(M E Sowersby) *in rr: eased after 6th: p.u lame bef next* **12/1**

-040 **F** **Rush'N'Run**[38] [521] 6-9-11 81............................. THalliday(10) —
(Mrs S J Smith) *chsd ldrs: hrd rdn whn swvd bdly lft and fell 6th* **18/1**

32-0 **P** **Love Triangle (IRE)**[26] [670] 4-10-9 92............................. SWalsh(7) —
(N B King) *chsd ldrs: lost pl whn hmpd 3 out: sn bhd: p.u bef last* **33/1**

-40P **P** **Antigiotto (IRE)**[18] [762] 4-11-8 98............................. RJohnson —
(P Bowen) *chsd ldrs: lost pl appr 6th: eased and bhd whn p.u bef last* **5/1**[2]

00P- **P** **Sweet Chariot**[97] [4614] 6-10-9 83............................. PJBrennan —
(Mrs H Dalton) *in tch: lost pl and eased after 6th: bhd whn p.u bef last* **50/1**

4m 8.40s (-8.00) **Going Correction** -0.45s/f (Good)
WFA 4 from 5yo+ 2lb **16 Ran SP% 126.1**
Speed ratings: **99,98,98,97,96 90,89,83,71,59 —,—,—,—,—** — CSF £121.59 CT £1289.10 TOTE £36.00: £6.60, £1.90, £3.80, £1.20; EX 170.30.
Owner Mrs Jane Evans **Bred** D And Mrs Holmes **Trained** Honeybourne, Worcs
■ Tom Halliday, 20, and attached to Sue Smith's yard, tragically died as a result of his injuries. He had ridden four winners in all.

FOCUS
A very moderate affair that produced a close finish with the third and fourth setting the level. This was James Evans's first winner as a trainer.

NOTEBOOK
General Smith, a sprinter on the Flat, was put to sleep on his handicap bow over hurdles. He saw out the trip really well and forced his head in front near the line. *(op 28-1)*
Zarakash(IRE), with the champ at his best, was persuaded to put his head in front late on only to be touched off near the line. *(op 3-1)*
Neckar Valley(IRE), fit from the Flat, was hanging on to a narrow lead when he fluffed his lines at the last and in the end he was collared on the flat. *(op 12-1)*
Smart Boy Prince(IRE), hoisted 5lb after Cartmel, took them along to halfway and was only found lacking on the run-in. *(op 15-2)*
Ground Breaker, on his handicap debut, was having his first outing since January. He had been *unlucky when taking a heavy fall here three outings ago and can surely find a novices' hurdle. (op 8-1)*
Sweet Chariot *Official explanation: jockey said gelding hung left (op 9-2)*
Antigiotto(IRE) was pulled up for the second successive time and has a lot to prove now. *(op 9-2)*

896 RICHARD NOBLE H'CAP CHASE (14 fncs) 2m 6f 110y
4:45 (4:52) (Class 4) (0-105,98) 5-Y-0+ **£3,848** (£1,184; £592; £296)

Form RPR

P/42 **1** **Keltic Lord**[19] [746] 9-10-13 85............................. VSlattery 112+
(P W Hiatt) *hld up: hdwy 9th: led after 11th: sn clr* **12/1**

33-3 **2** *12* **Pillar Of Fire (IRE)**[29] [632] 11-10-2 74.............................(v) WHutchinson 86+
(Ian Williams) *chsd ldrs: one pce appr 3 out: lft clr 2nd last* **11/2**[2]

-620 **3** *22* **Phildari (IRE)**[18] [762] 9-10-5 84............................. MrDEngland(7) 79+
(N A Twiston-Davies) *led to 6th: hit next: hit 8th: 5th and wkng whn blnd 3 out* **8/1**

P6P- **4** *1 3/4* **Hehasalife (IRE)**[71] [4980] 8-11-11 97............................. TJMurphy 84
(Mrs H Dalton) *w.r.s: bhd: blnd 4th: hdwy 8th: chsng ldrs 11th: wknd appr next* **16/1**

-533 **5** *nk* **Mr Laggan**[22] [717] 10-9-8 73.............................(p) MJMcAlister(7) 60
(Miss Kate Milligan) *chsd ldrs: blnd 5th: lost pl 10th* **16/1**

2P-2 **6** ½ **Sunshan**[12] 805 9-11-0 **86** .... RGreene 72
(R J Hodges) *chsd ldrs: led 6th: blnd 8th: hdd after 11th: wknd next* **8/1**

-406 **7** 16 **Guilsborough Gorse**[21] 725 10-11-0 **93** .... MrMWalford(7) 63
(T D Walford) *in rr: drvn along 8th: bhd fr 11th* **20/1**

P2-2 **8** 6 **Balla D'Aire (IRE)**[49] 368 10-10-2 **74** .... SCurran 38
(K F Clutterbuck) *chsd ldrs: lost pl 8th: sn bhd* **22/1**

0P02 **9** 12 **Lord Of The Land**[25] 690 12-10-8 **80** .... BHarding 32
(Mrs E Slack) *in rr and drvn along 6th: bhd fr 8th* **16/1**

0614 **P** **Helvetius**[33] 605 9-11-12 **98** .... AThornton —
(W T Reed) *bhd whn p.u after 7th* **12/1**

00-3 **P** **Clear Dawn (IRE)**[25] 690 10-11-3 **89** .... GLee —
(J M Jefferson) *in rr: bhd fr 8th: p.u bef 3 out* **13/2**[3]

-303 **P** **Howaboys Quest (USA)**[14] 781 8-10-12 **87** ....(p) KJMercer(3) —
(Ferdy Murphy) *sn in rr: t.o 8th: p.u bef 3 out* **20/1**

P-53 **R** **John Rich**[9] 827 9-9-7 **72** oh1 ....(tp) PJMcDonald(7) 81
(M E Sowersby) *hdwy 8th: sn chsng ldrs: disputing 2nd whn rn out last* **25/1**

21-3 **P** **Woodenbridge Dream (IRE)**[19] 744 8-11-1 **87** .... RJohnson —
(R Lee) *chsd ldrs: hit 7th: mstke 9th: sn wknd: bhd whn p.u bef 2 out* **4/1**[1]

222R **P** **Bramblehill Duke (IRE)**[35] 567 13-11-4 **90** ....(b) SThomas —
(Miss Venetia Williams) *hld up in tch: lost pl 10th: bhd whn p.u bef 2 out* **12/1**

5m 35.2s (-11.20) **Going Correction** -0.45s/f (Good) **15** Ran SP% **129.4**
Speed ratings: **101,96,89,88,88 88,82,80,76,—** —,—,—,—,— CSF £79.40 CT £586.06 TOTE £12.60: £3.00, £2.80, £4.20; EX 104.10 Trifecta £404.20 Part won. Pool £569.30. 0.50 winning units. Place 6 £39.69, Place 5 £8.51..
Owner Paul Porter **Bred** Miss H Day **Trained** Hook Norton, Oxon

FOCUS
A low-grade handicap run at a strong pace and a potentially leniently treated wide-margin winner.

NOTEBOOK
Keltic Lord, a winner of three points, shot clear rounding the final turn and fast ground is clearly in his favour. *(op 9-1)*
Pillar Of Fire(IRE), in a visor this time, has not won for over two years and he looked only third best. *(op 13-2 tchd 7-1)*
Phildari(IRE), back over fences, was dropping away when he made one mistake too many at the third last. *(op 10-1 tchd 11-1)*
Hehasalife(IRE), who has a history of breathing problems, did a twirl at the gate after one false start. After a bad mistake early on he did well to get on to the coat tails of the five leaders on the turn for home, but his exertions then took their toll.
Sunshan, having his second race in less than two weeks after a year off, stopped to nothing three out and the word 'bounce' was being mumbled afterwards. *(op 9-1)*
Clear Dawn(IRE) *Official explanation: jockey said gelding was never travelling (op 8-1)*
John Rich, moody at times in points, looked likely to claim second spot when deciding he did not fancy jumping the last at all. *(op 8-1)*
Woodenbridge Dream(IRE), who anticipated the start first time, was 12lb higher than when winning at Hereford two outings ago. Keen to get on with it after two jumping errors, he dropped tamely away before calling it a day. Even though this extended trip may be beyond him, it was still a disappointing effort. *Official explanation: jockey said gelding was never going (op 8-1)*
T/Jkpt: Not won. T/Plt: £51.60 to a £1 stake. Pool: £61,801.10. 874.00 winning tickets. T/Qpdt: £25.50 to a £1 stake. Pool: £3,644.10. 105.70 winning tickets. WG

897 - 900a (Foreign Racing) - See Raceform Interactive

838 UTTOXETER (L-H)

Tuesday, July 5

OFFICIAL GOING: Good to soft
Persistent rain saw the ground turn markedly softer than had been expected.
Middle flight in back straight and third fence in back straight omitted.
Wind: virtually nil Weather: overcast

901 GRANT THORNTON PRIVATE CLIENTS SERVICES NOVICES' HURDLE (SERIES QUALIFIER) (9 hdls 1 omitted) 2m
6:40 (6:41) (Class 4) 4-Y-0+ **£3,412** (£975; £487)

Form RPR

5-0 **1** **Red Moor (IRE)**[31] 635 5-11-0 .... BHitchcott 103+
(Mrs D A Hamer) *hld up midfield: effrt 6th: lft 2nd and hmpd 3 out: led next: clr last: drvn out* **6/1**[3]

F/11 **2** 7 **Kristoffersen**[19] 766 5-11-10 111 .... DRDennis 109+
(Ian Williams) *trckd ldrs: effrt 6th: lft in ld and hmpd 3 out: sn hrd drvn: hdd next: outpcd bef last* **9/4**[2]

00-P **3** 16 **A Monk Swimming (IRE)**[21] 742 4-10-12 .... JGoldstein 76
(Miss J S Davis) *t.k.h: pressed ldr tl 6th: rdn and wknd bef 3 out: mod 3rd after* **50/1**

5-03 **4** 1¾ **Loriko D'Airy (FR)**[29] 667 6-10-7 105 .... MissCDyson(7) 77+
(Miss C Dyson) *t.k.h: led tl hdd and poor jump 6th: rapidly lost tch* **15/2**

P-03 **5** 3 **Native Chancer (IRE)**[14] 804 5-11-0 .... JEMoore 73
(Jonjo O'Neill) *impeded 2nd: bhd: last after 4th: lost tch tamely 6th* **12/1**

0UP- **6** 6 **Un Autre Espere**[137] 2456 6-10-11 71 .... LVickers(3) 67
(C C Bealby) *bhd: impeded 2nd: lost tch qckly after 6th* **50/1**

F **Jubilee Prince**[23] 5-10-7 .... TO'Brien(7) —
(A E Jones) *4th whn fell 2nd* **33/1**

F **P** **Don Argento**[14] 804 4-10-12 .... ATinkler —
(Mrs A J Bowlby) *prom tl reminders 4th: dropped himself bk to last bef 6th: crawled over and p.u* **100/1**

122/ **F** **Alpine Fox**[583] 2488 8-10-7 .... MissJCWilliams(7) —
(T R George) *settled handy: led gng v strly 6th: 4l clr and in control whn fell next: dead* **2/1**[1]

P-4 **P** **Hermitage Court (USA)**[18] 563 4-10-12 ....(v) TJMurphy —
(M J McGrath) *plld hrd early: hld up and bhd: v relucant fr 6th and sn tailed himself off: p.u next* **16/1**

4m 4.60s (4.20) **Going Correction** +0.25s/f (Yiel) **10** Ran SP% **111.6**
WFA 4 from 5yo+ 2lb
Speed ratings: **99,95,87,86,85 82,—,—,—,—** CSF £19.30 TOTE £12.40: £2.80, £1.30, £4.30; EX 19.30.
Owner Hanford's Chemist Ltd **Bred** Camogue Stud Ltd **Trained** Nantycaws, Carmarthens

FOCUS
A moderate novices' hurdle, which saw the field come home strung out behind the ready winner. The first two ran to their marks but overall the form looks suspect.

NOTEBOOK
Red Moor(IRE) relished the drop in trip and came right away from his rivals in the straight to record a first success over timber at the third attempt. He clearly enjoyed the recent ease in the gound and appeals as the type who could prove better over hurdles than he was on the Flat, so further success this summer is on the cards. *(op 11-2)*
Kristoffersen , bidding for the hat-trick, was put in his place by the winner from two out and did not appear overly suited by the drop in trip. This was still a fair effort under his double penalty and he is happier on a faster surface, so is not one to write off on this display. *(tchd 2-1)*
A Monk Swimming(IRE) again had his limitations fully exposed, but still turned in his most encouraging display over hurdles to date.
Loriko D'Airy(FR) again took a keen hold through the early parts and ultimately paid the price on *this rain-softened ground. He can do better, but is not one to place too much faith in over hurdles. (op 7-1)*
Native Chancer(IRE) *(tchd 14-1)*
Alpine Fox , making his return from a 583-day layoff and having his first outing over hurdles, was still going best of all prior to his tragic fall. *(op 15-8)*

902 SPINAL INJURIES ASSOCIATION NOVICES' H'CAP CHASE (14 fncs 1 omitted) 2m 4f
7:10 (7:10) (Class 4) (0-100,97) 5-Y-0+ **£4,507** (£1,387; £693; £346)

Form RPR

UP/0 **1** **Optimistic Harry**[19] 764 6-10-0 **71** oh2 .... PJBrennan 87+
(R Ford) *j.rt early: keen and green in rr: stdy prog 9th: 6th next: cl qckly to ld bef 2 out: sn clr: heavily eased after last* **11/1**

P-2P **2** 8 **Lady Lambrini**[20] 759 5-9-10 **73** .... DLaverty(5) 75
(Mrs L Williamson) *keen: led 4th: jnd and hit 10th: hdd bef 2 out: one pce and sn no ch w wnr* **15/2**

P334 **3** 7 **High Peak**[20] 759 8-9-11 **71** .... RYoung(3) 68+
(J W Mullins) *hld up towards rr: effrt 9th: struggling to get on terms whn blnd 3 out: no imp after: mstke last* **11/2**[1]

4-32 **4** hd **The Mighty Sparrow (IRE)**[29] 666 12-11-0 **85** ....(p) MFoley 81
(A E Jones) *hmpd 1st: chsd ldrs: mstke 8th: rdn 10th: sn outpcd: plugged on flat* **6/1**[2]

-PP0 **5** ¾ **Tails I Win**[6] 862 6-10-2 **76** .... ACCoyle(3) 71
(Miss C J E Caroe) *settled 3rd bhd clr ldng pair: clsd and nt fluent 6th: sn 2nd: jnd ldr 10th tl hdd bef 2 out: rdn and sn fdd* **50/1**

6 5 **On The Forty**[83] 4832 8-10-12 **83** .... JEMoore 73
(Jonjo O'Neill) *nt jump wl: hld up: effrt to chse ldrs 7th: hit 9th: rdn and outpcd next: blnd 3 out* **7/1**[3]

-04U **7** 4 **Saddler's Quest**[31] 632 8-10-1 **72** .... JMogford 58
(B P J Baugh) *bhd: hmpd 3rd: j. slowly 6th: lost tch 9th* **20/1**

1/5 **8** nk **Kitty John (IRE)**[27] 688 8-10-9 **85** .... WKennedy(5) 71
(J L Spearing) *midfield: effrt to chse ldrs 7th tl 9th: wknd next: no ch whn mstke 2 out* **12/1**

/06- **9** dist **Combined Venture (IRE)**[423] 220 9-9-11 **71** oh2 .... DCrosse(3) —
(P O'Connor) *keen early: midfield tl lost pl and j. slowly 7th: lost tch and mstke 9th: btn 63l* **33/1**

R3F2 **R** **Althrey Dandy (IRE)**[13] 812 10-11-12 **97** .... AThornton —
(P T Dalton) *led rnd at s: whipped rnd and ref to r* **6/1**[2]

0-PF **U** **Miss Muscat**[31] 632 5-10-0 **72** oh4 .... JPByrne —
(Evan Williams) *j.lft 1st: 5th whn blnd and uns rdr 8th* **9/1**

54/5 **P** **The Nobleman (USA)**[11] 827 9-10-0 **71** oh6 .... JamesDavies —
(D Shaw) *plld hrd: led tl 4th: wkng whn j. slowly 7th: t.o after 9th: p.u 3 out* **10/1**

5m 13.5s (-7.10) **Going Correction** -0.15s/f (Good) **12** Ran SP% **113.0**
WFA 5 from 6yo+ 1lb
Speed ratings: **108,104,102,101,101 99,98,97,—,—** —,— CSF £85.87 CT £503.90 TOTE £17.50: £4.20, £2.50, £2.60; EX 142.50.
Owner bellhouseracing.com **Bred** Ford Farm Bloodstock **Trained** Cotebrook, Cheshire

FOCUS
A very weak novices' handicap, run at a modest gallop, and the field came home strung out. The form may be suspect, but the winner can be rated for more than the winning margin.

NOTEBOOK
Optimistic Harry , making his chasing and handicap debut, finally put his best foot forward and ran out a facile winner, being value for a lot further than his already wide winning margin. Chasing is clearly going to bring out his potential and, while he could be in trouble should the Handicapper *reacts literally to this form, he will take some beating if turned out under a penalty in this sphere. Official explanation: trainer said, regarding the improved form shown, gelding was very green in its previous race over hurdles and has since benefited from extensive schooling (op 16-1)*
Lady Lambrini finished clear of the rest and posted a more encouraging effort. However, she was greatly flattered by her proximity to the winner. *(op 6-1)*
High Peak again lacked fluency over his fences and looked unsuited by the drop in trip. He is not *one to write off from this mark when faced with faster ground back over a longer trip, however. (op 5-1)*
The Mighty Sparrow(IRE) failed to see out this longer trip on the deteriorating ground and ran well below his recent level of form. He is better on fast ground, but is never one to place all that much faith in. *(op 4-1)*

903 TARGET EXCEL (S) HURDLE (9 hdls 1 omitted) 2m
7:40 (7:41) (Class 5) 4-Y-0+ **£2,317** (£662; £331)

Form RPR

4403 **1** **Red Nose Lady**[6] 863 8-11-3 90 ....(p) JMogford 101+
(G J Smith) *3rd bhd clr ldng pair after 4th: clsd to 2nd after next: rdn to ld and nt fluent 3 out: edgd clr bef last: plugged on* **17/2**

220- **2** 5 **Lightning Star (USA)**[309] 1329 10-11-10 102 ....(b) JEMoore 102
(G L Moore) *midfield: u.p and reluctant bef 6th: clsd to chal 3 out: ev ch tl fnd nil between last two* **11/2**[2]

F-34 **3** 1¼ **Gabor**[6] 863 6-11-4 107 ....(b) RJohnson 95
(B J Llewellyn) *chsd clr ldr tl 4th and clr of rest: downed tools and rdn after 5th: kpt on again 2 out but no ch* **8/1**

64-0 **4** 7 **Big Wheel**[19] 766 10-10-12 110 .... ADobbin 82
(N G Richards) *hld up midfield: effrt 6th: chal and ev ch 3 out: rdn and fdd 2 out* **5/1**[1]

555- **5** 6 **Dante's Battle (IRE)**[45] 13-10-11 97 .... RSpate(7) 82
(Mrs K Waldron) *midfield: outpcd 6th: n.d after* **25/1**

405- **6** 4 **Saif Sareea**[34] 2393 5-11-4 93 .... MBradburne 80+
(A L Forbes) *settled midfield: clsd after 5th: led after next: rdn and hdd 3 out: wknd rapidly: mstke last* **5/1**[1]

00P- **7** dist **Friedhelmo (GER)**[6] 4926 9-11-10 112 ....(t) JimCrowley —
(P D Niven) *rr and drvn 5th: nvr gng wl after: t.o 3 out: eased and btn 63l* **7/1**

6-02 **8** 5 **Rumbling Bridge**[6] 743 4-10-10 90 ....(p) JGoldstein —
(Miss J S Davis) *midfield: lost tch u.str.p after 6th: sn t.o: eased and btn 68l* **9/1**

P00/ **P** **Wotan (IRE)**[851] 4032 7-10-12 .... TDoyle —
(R Curtis) *t.k.h in rr: lost tch 6th: t.o and p.u 3 out* **66/1**

P-F **P** **Young Warrior (IRE)**[27] 691 4-10-10 .... FKeniry —
(M D Hammond) *struggling in rr after 4th: t.o and p.u 6th* **50/1**

P- **P** **Peruvian Breeze (IRE)**[318] 1230 4-10-10 .... ChristianWilliams —
(Evan Williams) *keen and prom in chsng gp tl mstke 5th: stopped to nil: p.u next* **13/2**[3]

-P0P **P** **Blazeaway (USA)**[6] 862 5-10-12 79..............................(b) JPMcNamara —
(R S Brookhouse) *led and str hold: sn 8l clr: rdn and hdd after 6th: immediately gave up and wl bhd whn p.u next* **50/1**

4m 2.70s (2.30) **Going Correction** +0.25s/f (Yiel)
WFA 4 from 5yo+ 2lb **12** Ran SP% **115.4**
Speed ratings: **104,101,100,97,94 92,—,—,—,— —,—** CSF £52.79 TOTE £7.30: £1.90, £2.40, £2.10; EX 78.30.The winner was bought in for 5,000gns.

Owner Slow Donkey Partnership **Bred** R J And Mrs D M L Weston **Trained** Six Hills, Leics

FOCUS
A weak event, featuring largely out of form hurdlers, rated through the winner and the third.

NOTEBOOK
Red Nose Lady , with the blinkers left off in favour of the cheekpieces, stuck to her task under pressure and outstayed her rivals to score a deserved success. She is not easy to predict - and is vulnerable outside of this grade - but is versatile as regards ground and is clearly in good form at present. *(op 8-1)*

Lightning Star(USA) had every chance on this first run for 309 days, but lacked the resolution of the winner from two out and found little for maximum pressure. In his defence, he could have needed the outing and is entitled to improve fitness-wise. *(op 9-2)*

Gabor again looked reluctant when asked for an effort and merely plugged on at his own pace in the straight. He would have found this ground against him, however. *(tchd 9-1)*

Big Wheel , best in according to official figures, fell in a hole when push came to shove and has to rate a disappointing. He is evidently regressing fast. *(op 4-1)*

Saif Sareea , popular in the betting on this first outing over hurdles for 225 days, hit the front four out but ultimately his effort proved short-lived. He is at best on quicker ground. *(op 13-2)*

904 JOBS @ PERTEMPS H'CAP CHASE (11 fncs 1 omitted) 2m
8:10 (8:12) (Class 4) (0-110,109) 5-Y-0+ **£4,871** (£1,499; £749; £374)

Form RPR

22F3 **1** **College City (IRE)**[38] 548 6-10-3 **86**..............................(p) FKeniry 102+
(R C Guest) *hld up: effrt after 7th: wnt 2nd next: led bef 2 out but drvn and immediately jnd: sn lft clr: eased flat* **7/2**[2]

-332 **2** *8* **Deep King (IRE)**[20] 761 10-11-8 **108**.............................. RYoung(3) 115
(J W Mullins) *led: drvn and hdd bef 2 out where lft 2nd: immediately outpcd by wnr* **7/2**[2]

64-0 **3** *5* **Snipe**[23] 725 7-11-4 **101**.............................. DRDennis 104+
(Ian Williams) *keen chsng ldr: rdn after 7th: lost 2nd at next: btn whn lft 3rd 2 out: blnd last* **13/2**[3]

4-23 **4** *8* **Amadeus (AUS)**[33] 615 8-10-9 **92**.............................. TScudamore 88+
(M Scudamore) *chsd ldrs: rdn and outpcd 8th: 5th and btn whn hit 3 out* **3/1**[1]

35-0 **5** *dist* **Artane Boys**[14] 803 8-11-5 **102**.............................. JEMoore —
(Jonjo O'Neill) *plld v hrd early: last whn hit 2nd: stl v keen whn mstke 6th: sn rdn and fnd nil: lost tch 8th: btn 67l* **10/1**

1-0P **6** *1* **Harik**[23] 725 11-11-12 **109**..............................(bt) PHide —
(G L Moore) *hld up and bhd: hmpd 7th: sn t.o: btn 68l* **14/1**

1F/0 **U** **Knight's Emperor (IRE)**[21] 747 8-10-11 **94**.............................. RThornton —
(J L Spearing) *midfield: 5l 5th whn blnd bdly and uns rdr 7th* **11/1**

60P **U** **What's A Filly**[6] 862 5-10-2 **85**.............................. HOliver 102+
(R C Guest) *hld up in rr: smooth prog 8th: jnd ldr gng strly whn blnd and uns rdr 2 out: unlucky* **16/1**

4m 3.60s (-1.40) **Going Correction** -0.15s/f (Good) **8** Ran SP% **112.8**
Speed ratings: **97,93,90,86,— —,—,—** CSF £16.24 CT £73.86 TOTE £5.40: £1.70, £1.50, £1.70; EX 17.90.

Owner Mrs Anna Kenny **Bred** P J Hannon **Trained** Brancepeth, Co Durham

FOCUS
A moderate event, but the form is reasonably solid and it could throw up its share of future winners during the summer.

NOTEBOOK
College City(IRE) , well backed, found the soft ground very much to his liking and duly got back to winning ways, but has to rate a fortunate winner. He was left in the clear two out after his stablemate, What's A Filly, unseated when travelling just as well and he may well have played second fiddle but for that.

Deep King(IRE) is a much better horse on a quick surface and should be forgiven this form. He is a winner waiting to happen over fences when reverting to fast ground. *(tchd 4-1)*

Snipe is flattered by his finishing position and never rated a threat, after running too freely through the early stages. He needs better ground, but is yet to really convince over fences. *(op 8-1)*

Amadeus(AUS) was well supported as the rain fell in his favour, but showed little and has to rate as very disappointing. *(op 4-1)*

What's A Filly , pulled up on her chase debut six days previously, looked to be going better than her eventual winning stablemate prior to unseating two out and was an unlucky loser. It is hard to know what to make of this improved form, but the suspicion is that it was no fluke and she could find a race this summer on similarly easy ground. *(op 14-1)*

905 GRANT THORNTON EXECUTIVE CLUB MARES' ONLY H'CAP HURDLE (10 hdls 2 omitted) 2m 4f 110y
8:40 (8:41) (Class 4) (0-105,105) 4-Y-0+ **£3,896** (£1,199; £599; £299)

Form RPR

P50- **1** **Lilac**[99] 4613 6-10-0 **79**.............................. WHutchinson 84+
(R J Price) *hld up towards rr: hdwy gng wl bef 3 out: led bef next and hit it: sn clr: v easily* **20/1**

-631 **2** *12* **Qualitair Pleasure**[11] 826 5-10-9 **91**.............................. KJMercer(3) 83
(J Hetherton) *wl bhd: prog in 6th but rdn bef 3 out: styd on to go 2nd bef last: no ch w wnr* **5/1**[2]

P051 **3** *5* **Fenney Spring**[33] 613 5-10-0 **79** oh2..............................(t) CLlewellyn 67+
(W Jenks) *chsd ldrs: 4th whn blnd 7th: wkng whn hit 2 out* **13/2**

0P0- **4** *1* **Blue Yonder**[236] 2146 5-10-0 **79** oh2.............................. PMoloney 66+
(Evan Williams) *plld hrd: led after 1st: sn 6l clr: mstke 3 out: sn hdd and drvn: lost 2nd bef last* **14/1**

00-0 **5** *9* **Oscars Vision (IRE)**[13] 813 5-10-5 **84**..............................(v[1]) NFehily 63+
(B W Duke) *led tl after 1st: chsd clr ldr: clsd 7th: ev ch 3 out: sn fdd* **12/1**

1051 **6** *10* **Angie's Double**[2] 891 5-9-7 **79** oh5.............................. RSpate(7) 46
(Mrs K Waldron) *chsd ldng pair after 4th tl rdn bef 7th: wknd bef next* **7/2**[1]

-456 **7** *13* **Half Inch**[27] 689 5-11-2 **100**..............................(p) CHonour(5) 54
(B I Case) *4th and drvn after 5th: dropped rr 7th: t.o* **11/1**

0-03 **8** *17* **Cash Return**[33] 613 6-9-11 **79** oh12..............................(p) LVickers(3) 16
(Mrs S Lamyman) *mstke 4th: nvr bttr than midfield: wknd 7th: eased bef 2 out: t.o* **25/1**

5-PP **P** **Phase Eight Girl**[19] 768 9-9-10 **80**.............................. RStephens(5) —
(J Hetherton) *wl bhd: t.o after 5th: p.u 7th* **25/1**

0230 **P** **Spectacular Hope**[21] 749 5-10-1 **83**.............................. RYoung(3) —
(J W Mullins) *rr and u.p after 5th: t.o and p.u after 7th* **12/1**

P0P- **P** **Halfajobjones**[80] 4866 6-10-0 **79** oh15..............................(v[1]) JPByrne —
(C W Moore) *v slow jump 1st: a reluctant after and sn drvn: t.o 5th: p.u after next* **66/1**

3-32 **P** **Nod's Star**[41] 506 4-10-3 **85**..............................(t) LAspell —
(Mrs L C Jewell) *hld up and bhd: hdwy to trck ldrs bef 3 out: wkng whn hit next: p.u last* **6/1**[3]

-355 **P** **Rose Of York (IRE)**[49] 399 5-9-9 **79** oh6..............................(t) DLaverty(5) —
(Mrs A M Thorpe) *hit 2nd: chsd ldrs: 4th whn j. slowly 6th: lost tch qckly and p.u next* **9/1**

5m 21.3s (9.20) **Going Correction** +0.25s/f (Yiel)
WFA 4 from 5yo+ 3lb **13** Ran SP% **120.8**
Speed ratings: **92,87,85,85,81 77,72,66,—,— —,—,—** CSF £116.63 CT £744.39 TOTE £29.20: £4.70, £3.00, £2.00; EX 323.20.

Owner Derek & Cheryl Holder **Bred** Derek Collett Holder And Mrs Cheryl Regi **Trained** Lugwardine, H'fords

FOCUS
A poor mares-only contest, with half the field out of the handicap proper, and the form looks worth treating with caution.

NOTEBOOK
Lilac , having her first outing for 99 days, could hardly have won any easier and should be rated value for even further. She did well to handle this ground, having previously shown her best form on a fast surface, and has clearly resumed this season in grand form. However, while this advertised the current decent form of her yard, she is going to find life difficult when reassessed in the future. *(op 25-1)*

Qualitair Pleasure , raised 8lb for her recent Market Rasen success, stayed on stoutly after jumping three out only to find the winner gone beyond recall. She may not be weighted out of winning just yet and is happier on faster ground. *(op 11-2)*

Fenney Spring , with the blinkers left off, failed to see out this longer trip and never seriously threatened. She will be better back at shorter, and probably needs the headgear re-applied, but does look high in the weights now. *(op 7-1)*

Blue Yonder paid the price late on for running too keen through the early stages. He should at least come on physically for the outing and this was a slight improvement on his previous efforts. *(op 12-1)*

Oscars Vision(IRE) showed a bit more in the first-time visor, was unsuited by the deteriorating surface and looks to be falling to a realistic mark now.

Angie's Double , a facile winner at Stratford 48 hours previously, failed to quicken on this slower ground and disappointed. *(op 10-3)*

Cash Return *Official explanation: jockey said mare had a breathing problem*

906 PERTEMPS PEOPLE DEVELOPMENT GROUP H'CAP HURDLE (12 hdls 2 omitted) 3m
9:10 (9:16) (Class 4) (0-110,110) 4-Y-0+ **£4,260** (£1,311; £655; £327)

Form RPR

045P **1** **Three Lions**[2] 893 8-10-10 **94**.............................. JPMcNamara 101+
(R S Brookhouse) *t.k.h in midfield: clsd gng wl after 9th: led after 3 out: clr bef last: comf* **14/1**

U0-P **2** *7* **Wild Spice (IRE)**[47] 421 10-11-12 **110**.............................. SThomas 110
(Miss Venetia Williams) *led tl after 1st: j. slowly 3rd: prom: wnt 2nd at 9th: rdn and carried lft after 3 out: wandering bef last: no ch w wnr* **20/1**

6-11 **3** *1 1/2* **Croc An Oir (IRE)**[26] 697 8-11-7 **105**.............................. TJMurphy 104+
(R Ford) *hld up: effrt to midfield and racing wd fr 8th: chal 3 out: sn rdn: outpcd 2 out: nt fluent last* **2/1**[1]

136- **4** *3 1/2* **Koumba (FR)**[214] 2608 7-10-13 **97**.............................. ChristianWilliams 92
(Evan Williams) *prom: ev ch 3 out: sn drvn: kpt on steadily at one pce fr next* **7/1**[3]

0/11 **5** *5* **Spirit Of Tenby (IRE)**[29] 665 8-10-2 **86**.............................. JamesDavies 76
(W K Goldsworthy) *hld up and bhd: sme prog 9th: sn u.p: btn whn nt fluent 3 out* **9/2**[2]

-212 **6** *7* **Shady Grey**[26] 693 7-11-2 **100**.............................. NFehily 85+
(C J Mann) *led after 1st: rdn and hung lft and hdd after 3 out: wkng whn hit next* **7/1**[3]

PP-0 **7** *3 1/2* **Spike And Divel (IRE)**[9] 841 7-10-13 **97**.............................. JEMoore 80+
(Jonjo O'Neill) *keen in midfield: rdn 9th: ev ch next: sn dropped out* **20/1**

P263 **8** *22* **Ungaretti (GER)**[30] 652 8-10-12 **96**.............................. DRDennis 54
(Ian Williams) *prom tl drvn and wknd bef 3 out* **7/1**[3]

50P0 **9** *dist* **Silver Gift**[19] 768 8-9-9 **84** oh3..............................(p) DLaverty(5) —
(G Fierro) *midfield tl 7th: t.o bef 3 out: btn 84l* **25/1**

FP04 **P** **Greenacres Boy**[26] 697 10-10-0 **87** oh9 ow3..............................(b) ACCoyle(3) —
(M Mullineaux) *hld up and a last: hit 8th and lost tch: p.u next* **33/1**

-436 **F** **Golfagent**[9] 841 7-11-1 **106**..............................(t) RSpate(7) —
(Mrs K Waldron) *hld up and bhd: shortlived effrt 3 out: sn rdn: 6l 7th and wkng whn fell next* **12/1**

6m 35.5s (30.50) **Going Correction** +0.25s/f (Yiel) **11** Ran SP% **119.7**
Speed ratings: **59,56,56,55,53 51,49,42,—,— —** CSF £255.21 CT £804.72 TOTE £18.40: £3.90, £6.00, £1.90; EX 159.00 Place 6 £207.13, Place 5 £101.30.

Owner R S Brookhouse **Bred** Jim Short **Trained** Wixford, Warwicks

FOCUS
A fair event for the class. However, the ground had gone against many of the principals the time was slow and the form may be suspect.

NOTEBOOK
Three Lions , pulled up on his chasing bow just two days previously at Market Rasen, showed no ill-effects of that effort and could have been called the winner with two to jump. This proved he stays three miles, and is better over hurdles than fences, but the pace was not strong and he is not certain to confirm this form off a higher mark in the future. *(op 11-1)*

Wild Spice(IRE) , another reverting to hurdles having been pulled up last time, turned in his best effort for some time yet had no chance with the winner. He is tricky, looks too high in the weights over timber and it would be no surprise to see the headgear back on in the future. *(op 16-1 tchd 22-1)*

Croc An Oir(IRE) , bidding for the hat-trick, was found out by his 18lb rise in the weights and looked unsuited by the slower ground. He remains in good form and may be capable of getting closer back on a quick surface. *(op 11-4)*

Koumba(FR) , having his first outing for 214 days, shaped with encouragement and had every chance until tiring late on. He is entitled to improve on this and can be placed to advantage by connections off this mark and probably wants a faster surface. *(op 8-1)*

Spirit Of Tenby(IRE) , another bidding for the hat-trick, looked a non-stayer over this longer trip and was not helped by the softer ground. He still looks fairly treated at present and may be able to get closer when reverting to his ideal conditions. *(tchd 5-1)*

T/Plt: £265.40 to a £1 stake. Pool £59,112.95. 162.55 winning units T/Qpdt: £76.00 to a £1 stake. Pool £4,213.50. 41.00 winning units IM

907 - 910a (Foreign Racing) - See Raceform Interactive

860WORCESTER (L-H)

Wednesday, July 6

OFFICIAL GOING: Chase course - good (good to soft in places); hurdle course - good (good to firm in places)

Wind: Light, behind Weather: Fine

911 DOVE HOMES MAIDEN HURDLE (8 hdls) 2m

6:10 (6:10) (Class 4) 4-Y-0+ £3,444 (£984; £492)

Form RPR

0/ **1** **Decisive**[18] [3392] 6-11-2 .... TDoyle 113+
(P R Webber) *mde all: clr whn rdn appr last: r.o wl* **8/1**

3 **2** *10* **Screenplay**[24] [729] 4-11-0 .... JGoldstein 98
(Miss Sheena West) *hld up in tch: rdn appr 3 out: kpt on to take 2nd flat: no ch w wnr* **15/8**[1]

46 **3** *3* **Lake Merced (IRE)**[10] [838] 5-11-2 .... APMcCoy 97
(Jonjo O'Neill) *hld up in mid-div: hdwy appr 5th: rdn to chse wnr 2 out: no ex flat* **16/1**

3 **4** *4* **Aspra (FR)**[38] [569] 5-10-9 .... MBradburne 86
(C J Down) *hld up in mid-div: rdn and hdwy after 5th: styd on one pce flat* **14/1**

3 **5** *1 1/4* **Mariday**[38] [563] 4-11-0 .... LAspell 90
(L Wells) *t.k.h: prom tl rdn and wknd appr 2 out* **25/1**

30- **6** *1 1/2* **Hatch A Plan (IRE)**[13] [3899] 4-11-0 .... RJohnson 88
(Mrs A J Hamilton-Fairley) *sn chsng wnr: rdn and lost 2nd 2 out: wknd last* **9/2**[2]

650- **7** *13* **Idle Journey (IRE)**[132] [4022] 4-11-0 104........ TScudamore 75
(M Scudamore) *hld up towards rr: hdwy after 5th: wknd appr last* **7/1**[3]

5F **8** *1 3/4* **Didn't You Know (FR)**[38] [574] 4-10-7 .... GSupple 67
(M C Pipe) *t.k.h in rr: hdwy 4th: wknd after 5th: mstke 3 out* **22/1**

9 *3* **Court Alliance**[30] 6-11-2 .... WHutchinson 73
(R J Price) *hld up in mid-div: rdn and short-lived effrt after 5th* **16/1**

P56 **10** *5* **Felix The Fox (NZ)**[21] [758] 5-11-2 .... CLlewellyn 68
(N A Twiston-Davies) *hld up in tch: lost pl appr 3rd: bhd fr 4th* **16/1**

11 *7* **Shaaban (IRE)**[7] 4-11-0 ....(p) AO'Keeffe 59
(R J Price) *hit 4th: a bhd* **20/1**

F3 **12** *10* **Berry Racer (IRE)**[21] [758] 4-10-7 .... RGreene 42
(Mrs S D Williams) *a bhd* **40/1**

13 *2 1/2* **Secluded**[35] [2981] 5-10-11 .... MNicolls(5) 48
(N G Ayliffe) *hld up: hdwy appr 3rd: wknd 5th* **50/1**

0 **14** *1 1/4* **Melograno (IRE)**[20] [764] 5-10-13 .... CRafter(3) 47
(Mark Campion) *a bhd* **66/1**

50/ **15** *19* **Tallison**[102] 7-10-13 .... RYoung(3) 28
(N R Mitchell) *prom tl wknd 4th* **100/1**

16 *12* **Brazil Nut**[348] 4-10-7 .... RSpate(7) 14
(Mrs K Waldron) *rdn 4th: a bhd* **100/1**

PP-P **17** *dist* **Spreejinsky**[53] 7-10-9 ....(t) WPKavanagh(7) —
(K G Wingrove) *a bhd: nt fluent 3rd: t.o 5th: j. bdly rt last* **150/1**

3m 47.7s (-0.70) **Going Correction** +0.10s/f (Yiel)
WFA 4 from 5yo+ 2lb **17** Ran SP% **122.4**
Speed ratings: **105,100,98,96,95 95,88,87,86,83 80,75,74,73,63 57,57** CSF £22.21 TOTE £13.00: £3.30, £1.20, £3.40; EX 51.40.

Owner Peter S Jensen **Bred** Shutford Stud **Trained** Mollington, Oxon

FOCUS

Not many got into this. Fairly solid form.

NOTEBOOK

Decisive has only run once before over hurdles, back in February 2003. Making the running like he *usually does on the Flat, he was never seriously challenged and ran out a comfortable winner.* *(op 10-1)*

Screenplay ran a second good race over hurdles and again shaped as if a step up in trip would prove beneficial. *(op 9-4)*

Lake Merced(IRE) went after the winner at the second last but did not find much when the pressure was on. He is now eligible for handicaps. *(op 12-1)*

Aspra(FR) was staying on well at the end and on this evidence she will get a bit further than this. *(op 10-1)*

Mariday was in third place for much of the way until fading going to the second last.

Hatch A Plan(IRE), fit from the Flat, raced in close attendance to the eventual winner until dropping away from the second last. *(op 13-2)*

Court Alliance *Official explanation: jockey said he pulled up gelding believing it to be lame but it subsequently returned sound*

912 SENAD GROUP NOVICES' HURDLE (10 hdls) 2m 4f

6:40 (6:41) (Class 4) 4-Y-0+ £3,471 (£1,068; £534; £267)

Form RPR

032 **1** **West End Wonder (IRE)**[32] [629] 6-10-5 100........ AScholes(7) 111+
(D Burchell) *hld up: hdwy 6th: led sn after next: drvn clr flat* **9/1**

1-6P **2** *8* **Openide**[14] [814] 4-11-2 124........ APMcCoy 105
(B W Duke) *chsd ldrs: pushed along fr 5th: sltly outpcd 7th and sn rdn: styd on to chse wnr appr last: no imp flat* **13/8**[1]

51-6 **3** *19* **Cantgeton (IRE)**[64] [178] 5-11-5 .... TJMurphy 93+
(M C Pipe) *in tch: clsd 5th: chsd wnr bef 3 out: rdn after next: wknd appr last* **5/1**[2]

232P **4** *9* **Thieves'Glen**[22] [742] 7-10-12 105........ TScudamore 73
(H Morrison) *trckd ldr: chal 5th to 7th: sn rdn and wknd* **11/1**

5 *11* **Porto (IRE)**[24] 10-10-12 .... JTizzard 62
(B J M Ryall) *chsd ldrs tl rdn and wknd bef 7th* **28/1**

6 *11* **Lost In The Snow (IRE)**[46] 7-10-12 .... DRDennis 51
(M Sheppard) *in tch tl wknd 7th* **25/1**

000- **7** *12* **It's Gwendolene**[79] [4911] 5-10-5 .... JGoldstein 32
(Miss Sheena West) *a towards rr* **100/1**

-003 **8** *4* **The Langer (IRE)**[58] [266] 5-10-9 .... DCrosse(3) 35
(S T Lewis) *bhd fr 5th: t.o* **50/1**

P-51 **9** *1 1/2* **Walsingham (IRE)**[45] [469] 7-10-12 90........ RJohnson 34
(R Lee) *led: hit 7th and hdd: sn wknd: t.o* **7/1**[3]

021- **10** *3* **Rash Moment (FR)**[100] [4611] 6-10-12 115........ RSpate(7) 38
(Mrs K Waldron) *trckd ldrs: rdn 6th: mstke 7th: sn wknd: t.o* **7/1**[3]

00-4 **11** *3* **Legal Spy**[40] [533] 6-10-12 .... LAspell 28
(F Jordan) *hld up: mstke 1st: a bhd: t.o* **80/1**

-55P **12** *8* **Men Of Destiny (IRE)**[10] [843] 4-9-13 .... JBunsell(10) 17
(B G Powell) *nt jump wl: a bhd: t.o fr 5th* **66/1**

5- **13** *6* **Iris's Dream**[286] [1489] 5-10-12 .... MAFitzgerald 14
(Jonjo O'Neill) *hld up bhd ldrs: 3rd whn mstke and lost pl 5th: nt fluent next: sn wknd: t.o* **20/1**

P **Kateseliie**[66] 5-10-5 .... PJBrennan —
(J L Spearing) *a bhd: t.o whn p.u bef 3 out* **100/1**

-04F **P** **Flurry**[28] [680] 6-9-12 .... SWalsh(7) —
(C J Down) *t.k.h: a bhd: mstke 6th: t.o whn p.u bef 3 out* **66/1**

P/4 **P** **Incorporation**[10] [843] 6-10-9 .... RHobson(3) —
(M Appleby) *in tch tl wknd 5th: t.o whn p.u bef 7th* **33/1**

P **Imtouchingwood**[408] 4-10-2 .... MBatchelor —
(L Wells) *in tch tl rdn and wknd 4th: t.o whn p.u bef 3 out* **50/1**

4m 48.9s (0.90) **Going Correction** +0.10s/f (Yiel)
WFA 4 from 5yo+ 3lb **17** Ran SP% **123.2**
Speed ratings: **102,98,91,87,83 78,74,72,71,70 69,66,63,—,— —,—** CSF £23.04 TOTE £12.70: £2.50, £1.10, £2.00; EX 32.40.

Owner Mouse Racing **Bred** Lucayan Stud Ltd **Trained** Briery Hill, Blaenau Gwent

FOCUS

A modest novice hurdle in which the winner was value for 10l.

NOTEBOOK

West End Wonder(IRE), who has been running well here this summer, came clear on the run-in *for a comprehensive victory. There is no reason why he cannot continue to progress.* *(op 10-1 tchd 8-1)*

Openide, disappointing in a handicap here last time, was being pushed along from an early stage. He eventually responded to presure and stayed on, but found the winner much too good. *(op 9-4)*

Cantgeton(IRE), who had been off the track for two months, ran respectably under his penalty but was beaten a fair way in the end. *(op 11-2 tchd 9-2)*

Thieves'Glen, not as keen since the visor was left off, raced prominently until fading on the home turn. He does not appear to stay. *(op 9-1)*

Porto(IRE), who made all in an intermediate point-to-point last month, was making his debut for this yard. *(op 25-1)*

Walsingham(IRE), who has changed stables since winning at Southwell, dropped away once headed at the last flight in the back straight. *(op 11-1)*

Rash Moment(FR), formerly with Henry Daly, may have been in need of this first start since March. *(op 9-2)*

Iris's Dream *Official explanation: jockey said gelding ran roo free*

Incorporation *Official explanation: jockey said gelding had bled from the nose*

913 VAILLANT BOILERS NOVICES' H'CAP HURDLE (12 hdls) 3m

7:10 (7:11) (Class 4) (0-95,95) 4-Y-0+ £3,136 (£896; £448)

Form RPR

6-22 **1** **Fu Fighter**[49] [414] 4-11-0 87........(t) ChristianWilliams 90
(Evan Williams) *hld up and bhd: hdwy appr 9th: rdn and edgd lft appr last: styd on u.p to ld nr fin* **4/1**[1]

00-1 **2** *1/2* **Court One**[14] [813] 7-11-8 91........ WHutchinson 97
(R J Price) *hld up in mid-div: hdwy appr 9th: led appr 3 out: rdn flat: hdd nr fin* **9/1**

/0-3 **3** *6* **Maunsell's Road (IRE)**[19] [614] 6-11-9 92........(v) ADobbin 93+
(L Lungo) *hld up in tch: rdn appr 2 out: one pce* **15/2**[3]

0661 **4** *7* **Earn Out**[7] [860] 4-10-9 82........ TJMurphy 71
(M C Pipe) *hld up and bhd: hdwy on ins appr 3 out: no real prog fr 2 out* **9/2**[2]

5 *13* **Case Equal (IRE)**[47] [446] 5-11-3 86........ APMcCoy 69+
(Jonjo O'Neill) *hld up in mid-div: hdwy appr 8th: n.m.r on ins after 9th: sn rdn: ev ch 3 out: wknd appr last* **10/1**

-P42 **6** *18* **Fight The Feeling**[32] [630] 7-11-5 88........(v) CLlewellyn 50
(J W Unett) *prom tl rdn and wknd appr 9th* **14/1**

4-23 **7** *2 1/2* **Super Road Train**[22] [745] 6-11-7 90........(b[1]) LAspell 50
(O Sherwood) *prom: led 9th tl appr 3 out: sn wknd* **8/1**

36P **8** *3 1/2* **Mr Dip**[22] [742] 5-10-12 86........ DLaverty(5) 42
(L A Dace) *t.k.h in tch: rdn and wknd appr 3 out* **33/1**

2/26 **9** *dist* **Noble House**[39] [550] 8-11-12 95........ MAFitzgerald —
(Mrs A Duffield) *led to 4th: w ldr: led 7th to 8th: wknd after 9th: t.o* **33/1**

-FP0 **10** *30* **Caucasian (IRE)**[7] [860] 7-10-11 80........ DRDennis —
(Ian Williams) *a bhd: t.o fr 3 out* **40/1**

0/ **U** **Needtoknow (IRE)**[32] 6-10-1 77........(p) PCStringer(7) —
(M J Gingell) *bhd tl j.big and uns rdr 4th* **33/1**

F-60 **P** **Quel Fontenailles (FR)**[32] [630] 7-11-2 85........ AThornton —
(L A Dace) *a bhd: t.o whn p.u bef 3 out* **28/1**

P6-0 **F** **Goss Hawk (NZ)**[15] [801] 5-11-4 87........(t) JEMoore —
(Jonjo O'Neill) *reluctant to go to post and line up: bhd tl fell 5th* **66/1**

/P2- **P** **Avadi (IRE)**[262] [1752] 7-11-6 89........ TDoyle —
(P T Dalton) *chsd ldr: led 4th to 7th: wknd 9th: t.o whn p.u bef 3 out* **22/1**

U-42 **F** **Bustisu**[22] [745] 8-10-6 82........ RLucey-Butler(7) 65
(D J Wintle) *hld up and bhd: hdwy 9th: sn rdn: wknd 2 out: 12l 6th whn fell last* **8/1**

006- **P** **Peggy's Prince**[102] [4565] 7-10-11 85........ CHonour(5) —
(J D Frost) *prom: pushed along after 3rd: wknd appr 7th: t.o whn p.u bef 3 out* **50/1**

/P5P **P** **Loi De Martiale (IRE)**[25] [718] 7-11-0 83........(b) GLee —
(J M Jefferson) *prom: reminders after 7th: led 8th to 9th: wknd qckly and p.u bef 3 out* **25/1**

5m 55.0s (5.80) **Going Correction** +0.10s/f (Yiel)
WFA 4 from 5yo+ 4lb **17** Ran SP% **124.3**
Speed ratings: **94,93,91,89,85 79,78,77,—,— —,—,—,—,— —,—** CSF £36.43 CT £270.23 TOTE £6.40: £1.70, £1.30, £2.20, £2.50; EX 33.00.

Owner The Boyz R Uz Partnership **Bred** R P Williams **Trained** Cowbridge, Vale Of Glamorgan

■ Stewards' Enquiry : M A Fitzgerald one-day ban: improper riding - tried to prevent a rival passing on the inside (Jul 17)

A P McCoy one-day ban: careless riding (Jul 17)

FOCUS

A low-grade novices' handicap.

NOTEBOOK

Fu Fighter was tongue tied for the first time. He showed the right attitude to get the better of a keen tussle from the last and had no problem with this longer trip. *(op 11-2)*

Court One was 8lb higher than when successful over half a mile shorter here last time. He took up *the running travelling well, but was tackled on the run-in and just missed out after a good battle.* *(op 13-2)*

Maunsell's Road(IRE), well beaten on the Flat last time, ran a decent race on this second try at three miles but could not get in a blow at the first two. *(tchd 7-1)*

Earn Out, unpenalised for his win in a conditionals' race here a week earlier, did not shape as if he really needed this longer trip. He goes up 5lb now and could struggle. *(op 6-1)*

Case Equal(IRE), who did not show much in three runs for Arthur Moore in Ireland, looked a potential threat at the first in the home straight but did not get home. *(op 9-1)*

Bustisu was a spent force in sixth place when coming down at the second last. *(op 15-2)*

914 RICHARD WRIGHT MEMORIAL BEGINNERS' CHASE (12 fncs) 2m

7:40 (7:41) (Class 4) 5-Y-0+ **£4,104** (£1,263; £631; £315)

Form RPR

5-22 **1** **Milord Lescribaa (FR)**[22] [750] 5-10-12 .... RGreene 113
(M C Pipe) *chsd ldrs: briefly outpcd 7th: rdn after 4 out: chal 2 out: led sn after last: all out* **6/1**[3]

2FU- **2** *1 1/4* **Tonic Du Charmil (FR)**[75] [4966] 5-10-12 111 ....(t) TJMurphy 113+
(M C Pipe) *hld up: racd wd: stdy hdwy 7th: slt mstke next: led and j.rt 2 out: j.rt last and hdd: r.o u.p* **11/4**[2]

/2-2 **3** *1* **Peeyoutwo**[38] [570] 10-10-12 120 .... BHitchcott 111
(Mrs D A Hamer) *chsd ldr: mstke 5th: led 7th to 2 out: no ex flat* **5/2**[1]

54-0 **4** *25* **Jim Lad**[24] [724] 5-10-12 79 .... AThornton 86
(J W Mullins) *chsd ldrs to 4th: no ch fr 8th* **20/1**

P30- **5** *3 1/2* **Ela Re**[77] [4932] 6-10-12 .... MAFitzgerald 82
(C R Dore) *led: nt fluent 6th: hdd next: rdn after 8th: wknd 3 out* **9/1**

0-05 **6** *6* **Ice And Fire**[14] [811] 6-10-12 ....(t) RThornton 76
(J T Stimpson) *tended to jump rt: in rr: hdwy 4th: wknd 8th* **40/1**

6-33 **7** *15* **Flame Phoenix (USA)**[36] [604] 6-10-12 .... JMMaguire 61
(D McCain) *towards rr: rdn 6th: lost tch next: t.o* **7/1**

43-0 **8** *13* **Reliance Leader**[27] [692] 9-10-9 58 .... DCrosse(3) 48
(D L Williams) *chsd ldrs tl mstke and lost pl 4th: rdn 6th: sn no ch: t.o* **66/1**

2-U4 **9** *5* **Welsh Main**[31] [650] 8-10-12 .... CLlewellyn 43
(Miss G Browne) *in tch: dropped rr 5th: t.o fr 7th* **20/1**

P-P5 **10** *9* **Ela Figura**[28] [682] 5-10-2 .... RYoung(3) 27
(M Appleby) *chsd ldrs tl hit 5th: bhd fr next: t.o* **100/1**

50-P **P** **Harbour Bound (IRE)**[14] [812] 6-10-12 104 .... ChristianWilliams —
(Evan Williams) *reminders 1st: sn wl bhd: j. slowly 4th: p.u bef next* **9/1**

3m 53.8s (0.20) **Going Correction** -0.025s/f (Good) **11** Ran SP% **116.5**
Speed ratings: **98,97,96,84,82 79,72,65,63,58** — CSF £22.46 TOTE £7.80: £2.00, £1.60, £1.20; EX 26.20.
Owner M C Pipe **Bred** Louis Lafitte, And Marcel Barreyat **Trained** Nicholashayne, Devon
■ Stewards' Enquiry : R Greene two-day ban: used whip with excessive frequency (Jul 17, 20)

FOCUS
A modest event that was run at a decent pace. The first three finished well clear.

NOTEBOOK
Milord Lescribaa(FR), runner-up on his two previous chasing attempts, got off the mark under a strong ride from Greene. The result might have been different had his stablemate kept straight over the last two fences. *(op 12-1)*
Tonic Du Charmil(FR), off the track since April, would probably have won had he not jumped out badly to his right at the last two fences. He jumped well enough otherwise and, as horses often jump right-handed in the home straight at Worcester, it could pay to forgive him this. *(op 3-1)*
Peeyoutwo, back in trip following a promising initial effort over fences, only conceded defeat on the run-in. He can win a minor race over fences but could do with brushing up his jumping. *(op 9-4)*
Jim Lad, who has been beaten in selling company over hurdles, was never in the hunt on this chase bow. *(op 18-1)*
Ela Re took the field along at a decent pace on this chase debut but was headed in the back straight and the game was soon up once in line for home. *(op 6-1)*
Reliance Leader *Official explanation: jockey said gelding was lame (op 50-1)*
Harbour Bound(IRE) appears to have lost his enthusiasm. *(op 14-1 tchd 16-1)*

915 MAZAK AND POWER PANELS "TOGETHER SUCCESS" H'CAP HURDLE (8 hdls) 2m

8:15 (8:16) (Class 4) (0-110,106) 4-Y-0+ **£3,432** (£1,056; £528; £264)

Form RPR

50/2 **1** **Sunnyland**[45] [462] 6-10-2 82 .... RJohnson 90+
(P J Hobbs) *a.p: hung rt fr 3 out: led last: hrd rdn flat: r.o* **3/1**[1]

P-24 **2** *1 1/4* **Figaro Du Rocher (FR)**[24] [726] 5-11-11 105 ....(t) TScudamore 112
(M C Pipe) *led: rdn appr 2 out: hdd last: nt qckn towards fin* **5/1**[2]

34-1 **3** *3* **Englishtown (FR)**[15] [806] 5-11-10 104 .... APMcCoy 108
(Jonjo O'Neill) *hld up and bhd: smooth hdwy after 5th: rdn 2 out: nt fluent last: no ex* **3/1**[1]

PP-3 **4** *9* **Suchwot (IRE)**[41] [517] 4-9-11 82 oh5 ....(vt) TJMalone(3) 75
(M C Pipe) *hld up and bhd: mstke 3rd: hdwy appr 5th: rdn appr 3 out: wknd appr 2 out* **40/1**

1000 **5** *2 1/2* **Forzacurity**[10] [841] 6-11-7 106 .... LStephens(5) 99
(M Sheppard) *w ldr: rdn after 5th: wknd 2 out* **40/1**

4-RF **6** *1 1/4* **Brave Dane (IRE)**[22] [747] 7-11-0 99 .... DLaverty(5) 91+
(L A Dace) *hld up and bhd: hdwy after 5th: mstke 3 out: wkng whn mstke 2 out* **50/1**

2324 **7** *6* **Arjay**[12] [826] 7-10-1 81 ....(b) GLee 66
(S B Clark) *nvr nr ldrs* **10/1**[3]

1U31 **8** *3/4* **Lone Soldier (FR)**[12] [822] 9-10-11 98 .... CDSharkey(7) 83
(S B Clark) *hld up in tch: rdn and wknd after 5th* **14/1**

00-0 **9** *3 1/2* **Ingres**[10] [841] 5-11-0 101 .... CMStudd(7) 82
(B G Powell) *hld up in mid-div: lost pl 4th: n.d after* **18/1**

U052 **10** *shd* **Saorsie**[15] [806] 7-11-1 100 .... RStephens(5) 81
(J C Fox) *hld up: hdwy after 4th: rdn and wknd after 5th* **10/1**[3]

5601 **11** *8* **Blue Leader (IRE)**[22] [743] 6-11-8 102 ....(bt) CLlewellyn 75
(W K Goldsworthy) *hld up in tch: wknd after 5th* **16/1**

41-0 **12** *8* **Donatus (IRE)**[21] [760] 9-10-0 80 oh6 ....(p) BHitchcott 45
(Miss K M George) *hld up in mid-div: mstke 3rd: bhd fr 5th* **100/1**

6126 **13** *2* **Borehill Joker**[15] [805] 9-11-6 100 .... AThornton 63
(Miss K M George) *hld up in tch: wknd 4th* **20/1**

6P6- **14** *13* **Stonewall George (NZ)**[218] [2558] 7-11-1 95 .... MAFitzgerald 45
(Jonjo O'Neill) *hld up in mid-div: mstke 5th: sn bhd* **33/1**

1644 **15** *14* **Little Rort (IRE)**[50] [397] 6-10-4 87 .... DCrosse(3) 23
(S T Lewis) *prom: j.rt 1st: rdn appr 4th: wknd appr 5th* **25/1**

3m 48.8s (0.40) **Going Correction** +0.10s/f (Yiel)
WFA 4 from 5yo+ 2lb **15** Ran SP% **122.0**
Speed ratings: **103,102,100,96,95 94,91,91,89,89 85,81,80,73,66** CSF £17.36 CT £50.27 TOTE £3.80: £1.90, £2.30, £1.70; EX 26.40.
Owner D H Smith **Bred** C D Harrison **Trained** Withycombe, Somerset

FOCUS
Quite a competitive handicap.

NOTEBOOK
Sunnyland, dropped in trip, was always well placed and got to the front at the final flight. She hung *to her right in the latter stages but that was as much through greenness as anything. (op 4-1 tchd 11-4 and 9-2 in a place)*
Figaro Du Rocher(FR) is an excellent jumper and these brush hurdles suited him. Attempting to make all, he only gave best on the run-in. *(op 9-2 tchd 11-2)*
Englishtown(FR) improved from the rear to rate a danger but could only keep on at the same pace once let down. This was a solid run from an 8lb higher mark. *(tchd 11-4 and 10-3)*
Suchwot(IRE) does not look entirely straightforward but this was a second improved run since switching to the Pipe yard.
Forzacurity could only plug on at the same pace once coming under pressure at the last flight in the back straight. He has struggled with the handicapper since scoring off a mark of 96 four runs ago.
Brave Dane(IRE) was chasing the leaders when untidy at the first two flights in the home straight. This was at least a bit more encouraging.

916 MYSON RADIATORS H'CAP CHASE (12 fncs 6 omitted) 2m 7f 110y

8:45 (8:57) (Class 4) (0-100,100) 5-Y-0+ **£3,562** (£1,096; £548; £274)

Form RPR

4-1P **1** **Excellent Vibes (IRE)**[15] [805] 7-11-4 92 .... CLlewellyn 101
(N A Twiston-Davies) *in tch: rdn bef 7th: chsd ldrs 4 out: styd on wl u.p flat to ld nr fin* **8/1**

4-34 **2** *nk* **Tudor King (IRE)**[42] [503] 11-10-7 81 .... PJBrennan 90
(J S King) *trckd ldr: disp ld 3rd tl led 7th: hdd 2 out: rallied u.p to ld last: hdd nr fin* **14/1**

PF56 **3** *5* **Pete The Painter (IRE)**[22] [746] 8-10-6 80 ....(p) MBradburne 87+
(J W Tudor) *chsd ldrs: rdn 4 out: j.rt next: tk slt ld 2 out: hdd and blnd last: no ex flat* **14/1**

3600 **4** *15* **Ashgan (IRE)**[10] [839] 12-9-9 74 oh2 .... TJPhelan(5) 63
(Dr P Pritchard) *chsd ldrs tl lost pl after 6th: rdn after 8th: styd on fr 3 out* **66/1**

2152 **5** *1/2* **Alcatras (IRE)**[7] [865] 8-10-3 77 ....(p) RJohnson 70+
(B J M Ryall) *chsd ldrs: tended to jump rt: rdn and wknd 4 out: blnd 2 out* **3/1**[1]

/506 **6** *dist* **Notwhatshewanted (IRE)**[32] [632] 8-9-13 76 ....(p) RYoung(3) —
(J W Mullins) *mstkes 4th and 6th: lost tch bef next: t.o* **20/1**

0P2- **P** **Adalie**[114] [4377] 11-10-6 87 .... SWalsh(7) —
(J D Frost) *hld up in rr: lost tch after 6th: t.o whn p.u bef 4 out* **25/1**

3-U1 **P** **Bobsbest (IRE)**[14] [815] 9-11-4 92 .... AO'Keeffe —
(R J Price) *midfield: mstkes 6th and next: sn wknd: t.o whn p.u bef 4 out* **8/1**

-336 **P** **Vandante (IRE)**[36] [605] 9-10-7 81 .... TDoyle —
(R Lee) *hld up in rr: mstke 2nd: rdn and wknd after 6th: wl bhd whn p.u bef 3 out* **7/1**[3]

-141 **P** **Billy Ballbreaker (IRE)**[39] [546] 9-11-4 92 ....(t) JTizzard —
(C L Tizzard) *in tch tl rdn and wknd after 6th: t.o whn p.u bef 4 out* **11/2**[2]

0P-0 **P** **Plain Chant**[7] [862] 8-10-0 74 ....(v[1]) OMcPhail —
(C Roberts) *mstke 2nd: a in rr: rdn and lost tch after 6th: t.o whn p.u bef 4 out* **33/1**

03-P **P** **Khaladjistan (IRE)**[64] [176] 7-10-0 74 oh1 ....(tp) MBatchelor —
(Miss S J Wilton) *led to 7th: pckd next: sn rdn and wknd: wl bhd whn p.u bef 2 out* **40/1**

04-U **P** **Murat (FR)**[47] [436] 5-11-6 99 ....(v[1]) TJMurphy —
(M C Pipe) *towards rr: hdwy after 6th: j.rt next: wknd qckly after 8th: no ch whn p.u bef 4 out* **9/1**

-060 **F** **Lahinch Lad (IRE)**[15] [805] 5-10-6 85 .... JamesDavies 75
(B G Powell) *in rr: reminders after 6th: rdn and hdwy after 8th: disp 3rd and styng on whn fell 2 out* **20/1**

5m 50.9s (-4.00) **Going Correction** -0.025s/f (Good)
WFA 5 from 7yo+ 1lb **14** Ran SP% **118.7**
Speed ratings: **105,104,103,98,98** —,—,—,—,— —,—,—,— CSF £99.33 CT £1549.10 TOTE £8.30: £2.30, £4.00, £4.70; EX 100.60.
Owner Thomas D Goodman **Bred** Gainsborough Stud Management Ltd **Trained** Naunton, Gloucs

FOCUS
The first three fences in the back straight were omitted on both circuits due to the low sun. This left a long run to the first fence they jumped and an even longer one between fences six and seven. The form should be treated with a degree of caution.

NOTEBOOK
Excellent Vibes(IRE), who had excuses for his flop at Newton Abbot, returned to form but needed every almost every yard of this longer trip to get on top. *(op 15-2)*
Tudor King(IRE), always up with the pace, regained the lead at the final fence but was just caught. This was a brave effort and he remains capable of scoring off this mark. *(op 12-1 tchd 10-1)*
Pete The Painter(IRE), dropped 5lb, ran a better race with cheekpieces on in place of the visor, but a last-fence blunder did for his chance. His sole win under Rules came at this track. *(op 16-1)*
Ashgan(IRE) stayed on past beaten opponents over the last few fences. *(op 50-1)*
Alcatras(IRE), wearing cheekpieces for the first time, did his usual trick of jumping out to the right and had been seen off before the third last. *(tchd 10-3)*
Bobsbest(IRE), raised 7lb for his win here a fortnight earlier, did not jump very well and was beaten too far out for this longer trip to be blamed. *(tchd 9-2)*
Billy Ballbreaker(IRE), 9lb higher than at Cartmel and with the cheekpieces left off, lost touch with *the leaders on the very long run between the sixth and seventh fences.Official explanation: jockey said gelding hung right and was never travelling (tchd 9-2)*
Murat(FR), a first-fence casualty on his only previous venture over fences, was visored for the first time. He made good headway to join the leaders in the back straight but his stamina appeared to ebb away on the home turn and he was pulled up. *(tchd 9-2)*
Lahinch Lad(IRE), given a chance by the handicapper, was keeping on for pressure and was set to make the frame when coming down at the second last. *(tchd 9-2)*

917 POWER PANELS,"GOING FOR GOLD" STANDARD OPEN NATIONAL HUNT FLAT RACE 2m

9:15 (9:24) (Class 6) 4-6-Y-0 **£1,856** (£530; £265)

Form RPR

0/ **1** **Acushnet**[440] [4934] 6-11-4 .... GLee 112+
(J M Jefferson) *hld up in mid-div: hdwy over 5f out: led on bit over 1f out: v easily* **13/2**[3]

4 **2** *4* **Noble Sham**[31] [655] 4-11-2 .... TJMurphy 90
(M C Pipe) *hld up in mid-div: hdwy on ins 6f out: rdn over 2f out: wnt 2nd ins fnl f: no ch w wnr* **13/8**[1]

22 **3** *1 3/4* **Mr Jawbreaker (IRE)**[14] [817] 6-11-4 .... RThornton 90
(J T Stimpson) *a.p: led over 3f out: rdn and hdd over 1f out: one pce* **3/1**[2]

0 **4** *12* **So Cloudy**[53] [349] 4-10-9 .... JMMaguire 69
(D McCain) *hld up and bhd: hdwy 5f out: rdn over 3f out: wknd 2f out* **9/1**

0 **5** *1 1/4* **Hard N Sharp**[25] [720] 5-11-4 .... AThornton 77
(J M Jefferson) *hld up towards rr: hdwy 6f out: wknd over 2f out* **20/1**

6 *1/2* **Balmoral Star** 4-10-9 .... ADobbin 67
(D McCain) *hld up and bhd: rdn and styd on fnl 3f: n.d* **14/1**

S4 **7** *5* **Oscar's Lady (IRE)**[25] [720] 4-10-9 .... JimCrowley 62
(G A Swinbank) *hld up in tch: led over 5f out: rdn and hdd over 3f out: wknd over 2f out* **8/1**

00- **8** *6* **Milli Wizz**[209] [2730] 5-10-11 .... ATinkler 58
(W M Brisbourne) *hld up and bhd: short-lived effrt 5f out* **40/1**

0 **9** *dist* **April Rose**[45] [463] 5-10-6 ow2 .... MrSJGraham(7) —
(K G Wingrove) *led: hdd and hung rt 5f out: sn lost pl: t.o* **80/1**

00 **10** *3 1/2* **Mr Parson (IRE)**[31] [655] 5-11-1 .... DCrosse(3) —
(S T Lewis) *a bhd: rdn 9f out: t.o fnl 7f* **50/1**

The Form Book, Raceform Ltd, Compton, RG20 6NL

0 **11** *5* **Millie Boon**[28] 685 6-10-6 .... LStephens(5) —
(L J Williams) *prom tl wknd 5f out: t.o* **66/1**
0 **12** *30* **Gwyn's Choice**[31] 655 4-11-2 .... VSlattery —
(R A Harris) *prom: rdn 8f out: sn wandered and wknd qckly: t.o* **25/1**
0 **13** *6* **Must Be Mistaken**[10] 844 4-10-2 .... MrPCollington(7) —
(A L Forbes) *w ldr: rdn and wknd 5f out: t.o* **100/1**

3m 51.0s (3.20) **Going Correction** +0.10s/f (Yiel)
WFA 4 from 5yo+ 2lb **13** Ran SP% **120.9**
Speed ratings: **96,94,93,87,86 86,83,80,—,— —,—,—** CSF £16.91 TOTE £5.90: £1.50, £1.40, £1.90; EX 22.50 Place 6 £25.49, Place 5 £12.06.
Owner Dean Bostock And Raymond Bostock **Bred** J R Bostock **Trained** Norton, N Yorks

FOCUS
Only an ordinary bumper but a facile winner in Acushnet, rated value for 20l.

NOTEBOOK
Acushnet was well beaten on his only run for Neil King in April of last year. He won this very easily indeed, value for twice the winning margin and, while it was a moderate contest, he obviously has plenty of ability and should be kept on the right side. *(op 7-1)*
Noble Sham was flattered to finish only four lengths off the eased-down winner, but will not always bump into one so good and he can land an ordinary bumper. A longer trip will suit him when he goes hurdling. *(op 2-1)*
Mr Jawbreaker(IRE), runner-up on his two previous runs, again ran his race but was no match whatsoever for the impressive winner and lost out for second too inside the final furlong. *(op 10-3 tchd 7-2)*
So Cloudy showed a little more than she had when too keen on her debut in May.
Hard N Sharp, a stablemate of the easy winner, had finished behind today's seventh at Hexham. *(tchd 18-1)*
T/Plt: £46.00 to a £1 stake. Pool: £52,814.90. 836.75 winning tickets. T/Qpdt: £19.40 to a £1 stake. Pool: £4,127.10. 157.10 winning tickets. KH/RL

918 - 935a (Foreign Racing) - See Raceform Interactive

870 PERTH (R-H)

Sunday, July 10

OFFICIAL GOING: Good to firm (good in places in back straight)
Wind: virtually nil

936 FAMOUS GROUSE EXPERIENCE MAIDEN HURDLE (DIV I) (8 hdls) 2m 110y
2:20 (2:20) (Class 4) 4-Y-O+ **£3,779** (£1,163; £581; £290)

Form RPR
1 **1** **Lahib The Fifth (IRE)**[29] 720 5-11-2 .... ADobbin 99+
(N G Richards) *hld up in rr: hit 4th: hdwy 1/2-way: cl up 3 out: rdn to ld between last 2: drvn out* **4/6**[1]
-325 **2** *3/4* **Summer Special**[10] 870 5-11-2 105 .... MBradburne 96
(Mrs S C Bradburne) *trckd ldrs: led 3 out: rdn next: sn hdd: drvn and rallied flat: kpt on* **15/2**[3]
2 **3** *3 1/2* **Ring Street Roller (IRE)**[11] 854 5-10-4 .... PCO'Neill(5) 87+
(J J Lambe, Ire) *s.s and bhd: hdwy to chse ldrs 1/2-way: rdn along 3 out and ev ch tl drvn and one pce fr next* **12/1**
0-33 **4** *1* **Buttress**[45] 513 6-10-13 98 .... MrTGreenall(3) 92
(M W Easterby) *in tch: hdwy and cl up 3 out: ev ch tl rdn along next and hld whn hit last* **4/1**[2]
235- **5** *27* **Blackthorn**[13] 1552 6-10-6 99 .... MissCarolineHurley(10) 65
(R Ford) *chsd ldrs: effrt and cl up 3 out: sn rdn and wknd bef next* **14/1**
0/30 **6** *1 1/2* **Howards Dream (IRE)**[21] 780 7-11-2 .... (t) RMcGrath 63
(D A Nolan) *chsd ldrs: rdn along appr 3 out and sn wknd* **100/1**
06P- **7** *5* **Another Superman (IRE)**[194] 3045 6-11-2 .... (v[1]) MFoley 58
(Lindsay Woods, Ire) *hit 1st: chsd ldrs tl rdn along appr 3 out and sn wknd* **66/1**
000- **8** *4* **Inmate (IRE)**[123] 4263 4-11-0 .... BHarding 52
(Mrs E Slack) *hld up in rr: hit 4th: rdn along 4 out and wknd bef next* **100/1**
9 *9* **Jordans Spark**[32] 4-10-11 .... PAspell(3) 43
(P Monteith) *a rr: bhd fr 3 out* **50/1**
0/00 **10** *17* **Never Forget Bowie**[29] 716 9-11-2 66 .... KRenwick 28
(R Allan) *led and c lear: rdn along 4 out: hdd next and sn wknd* **100/1**

3m 53.5s (-7.10) **Going Correction** -0.525s/f (Firm)
WFA 4 from 5yo+ 2lb **10** Ran SP% **112.5**
Speed ratings: **95,94,93,92,79 79,76,74,70,62** CSF £6.20 TOTE £1.70: £1.02, £1.80, £4.10; EX 4.80.
Owner Jim Ennis **Bred** Denis Dunne And Thomas Phelan **Trained** Greystoke, Cumbria

FOCUS
A modest maiden hurdle in which the pace was steady and the form looks suspect, despite the placed horses running to form, but the winner is unexposed and looks the type to go on.

NOTEBOOK
Lahib The Fifth(IRE), who was impressive in his bumper, did not score easily, but the runner-up is a difficult horse to win with and he always looked like doing enough on his hurdling debut. He looks the type to progress. *(op Evens tchd 5-4 in a place and 11-10 in places)*
Summer Special is a very difficult horse to win with and, while he ran well in defeat to an unexposed sort, experience tells us that this is not a sign that he is likely to go one better next time. *(op 7-1)*
Ring Street Roller(IRE), dropping back in trip having not looked an easy ride last time, did not get away on terms but she came to have her chance from the third last. She is now eligible for a handicap mark. *(op 8-1)*
Buttress is another who has had a number of chances to break his duck. He might be better employed in handicap company. *(op 7-2)*
Blackthorn was having his first outing over hurdles since October but that absence was no excuse as he came here fit from the Flat. *(op 9-1)*
Howards Dream(IRE) was out of his depth and needs dropping in grade. *(op 66-1)*

937 SUNDAY MAIL NOVICES' CHASE (15 fncs) 2m 4f 110y
2:50 (2:51) (Class 3) 5-Y-O+ **£6,825** (£2,100; £1,050; £525)

Form RPR
1-11 **1** **Kid'Z'Play (IRE)**[11] 855 9-11-12 .... RMcGrath 131+
(J S Goldie) *led: hit 6th: pushed along 3 out: rdn and hdd appr next: rallied last: drvn and styd on wl flat* **2/1**[2]
1P-1 **2** *3* **Native Coral (IRE)**[60] 303 7-11-6 115 .... ADobbin 122
(N G Richards) *trckd ldrs gng wl: smooth hdwy 4 out: led appr 2 out: rdn last: drvn flat: sn hdd and no ex* **3/1**[3]
2-43 **3** *20* **Kombinacja (POL)**[42] 570 7-10-7 .... JMMaguire 94+
(T R George) *cl up: effrt 4 out and sn pushed along: rdn next: drvn and wknd appr 2 out* **7/4**[1]
P-06 **4** *16* **Seeyaaj**[11] 855 5-10-10 .... (t) PBuchanan(3) 85+
(Miss Lucinda V Russell) *in tch: rdn along appr 4 out and sn outpcd* **40/1**
0/0- **P** **Maitre Levy (GER)**[32] 7-10-11 .... PAspell(3) —
(D A Nolan) *in tch whn mstke 6th and p.u after* **12/1**
UP0P **U** **Mill Tower**[10] 872 8-10-7 .... GThomas(7) —
(R Nixon) *in tch: pushed along whn blnd and uns rdr 11th* **100/1**

5m 2.40s (-12.90) **Going Correction** -0.525s/f (Firm)
WFA 5 from 6yo+ 1lb **6** Ran SP% **105.8**
Speed ratings: **103,101,94,88,—** — CSF £7.63 TOTE £2.40: £1.40, £1.80; EX 4.00.
Owner Liam McGuigan **Bred** B S I Nv **Trained** Uplawmoor, E Renfrews

FOCUS
Not a bad little novice chase for the time of year. The first two were close to their marks and the race could rate higher.

NOTEBOOK
Kid'Z'Play(IRE), successful on each of his previous four visits to this venue, showed admirable battling qualities to rally having been headed by the eventual runner-up going to two out. A splendidly versatile type, he is effective on any ground and, on this evidence, appreciated returning to two and a half miles. *(op 15-8)*
Native Coral(IRE), previously unbeaten when completing, travelled well in behind the leading pair and jumped to the front two out, but he could not shake off the attentions of the winner, from whom he was receiving 6lb, and had no answer when the that rival joined him again at the last and drew clear on the run-in. The drop back in trip may not have been to his advantage. *(op 11-4)*
Kombinacja(POL), who enjoyed a very handy weight allowance, was backed into favouritism. She kept the winner company out in front for most of the way but was outpaced from three out. *(op 2-1)*
Seeyaaj was a long way behind Kid'z'play here last time over two miles, and this longer distance made no difference whatsoever. *(op 33-1)*

938 FAMOUS GROUSE NOVICES' HURDLE (10 hdls) 2m 4f 110y
3:20 (3:20) (Class 3) 4-Y-O+ **£4,764** (£1,466; £733; £366)

Form RPR
4122 **1** **Brooklyn Brownie (IRE)**[7] 892 6-11-4 108 .... GLee 96+
(J M Jefferson) *hld up in tch: effrt and pushed along to cl 3 out: led and hit next: sn rdn and edgd rt: drvn last: kpt in u.p flat* **4/7**[1]
6653 **2** *3/4* **One Of Them**[11] 856 6-10-5 80 .... GThomas(7) 88
(M A Barnes) *led and sn clr: pushed along 3 out: rdn and hdd next: sn drvn and edgd lft: ev ch last: kpt on u.p flat* **40/1**
0004 **3** *5* **Penteli**[11] 854 5-10-5 79 .... RMcGrath 76
(C Grant) *chsd ldr: rdn along 3 out: kpt on same pce fr next* **25/1**
3-11 **4** *6* **Tandava (IRE)**[35] 643 7-11-10 112 .... MBradburne 91+
(Mrs S C Bradburne) *hld up in tch: effrt and pushed along appr 3 out: sn rdn and kpt on same pce fr 2 out* **9/4**[2]
0-1F **5** *dist* **Poor Tactic's (IRE)**[21] 785 9-10-13 87 .... PCO'Neill(5) —
(J J Lambe, Ire) *hld up in tch: rdn along after 4 out: sn drvn and outpcd* **11/1**[3]

5m 0.30s (-7.90) **Going Correction** -0.525s/f (Firm) **5** Ran SP% **109.0**
Speed ratings: **94,93,91,89,—** CSF £17.32 TOTE £1.60: £1.10, £6.80; EX 26.30.
Owner P Gaffney & J N Stevenson **Bred** John P A Kenny **Trained** Norton, N Yorks

FOCUS
There was only a steady early pace to this novice hurdle and the performances of the second and third cast doubt over the value of the form.

NOTEBOOK
Brooklyn Brownie(IRE) made hard work of landing the odds in what was a steadily-run affair. He needed almost every yard of this trip to get the better of the enterprisingly-ridden runner-up, who on official ratings had 22lb to find with him at the weights. *(op 4-6 tchd 8-11 in places)*
One Of Them took advantage of the steady early pace to grab an uncontested lead and, given a good ride from the front, made the winner pull out all the stops. He had 22lb to find with the winner at these weights so this was a great effort, but the form should probably not be taken literally. *(tchd 33-1)*
Penteli also had a mountain to climb at these weights. She was staying on again at the finish, though, and shapes as though she will get further in time.
Tandava(IRE) was chasing a hat-trick but this steadily-run affair on much quicker ground than he encountered on his previous two starts found him out. He can be forgiven this and will be a much better proposition back on easier ground. *(op 2-1 tchd 5-2 in places)*

939 LANGVALE HOMES H'CAP CHASE (12 fncs) 2m
3:50 (3:53) (Class 4) (0-105,105) 5-Y-O+ **£8,346** (£2,568; £1,284; £642)

Form RPR
6/23 **1** **Jamica Plane (IRE)**[10] 874 12-10-0 84 .... (p) PCO'Neill(5) 93
(J J Lambe, Ire) *led: rdn along 4 out: hdd next: drvn and rallied to ld last: kpt on gamely* **9/1**
4532 **2** *1* **Phase Three (IRE)**[11] 862 8-10-8 87 .... JMMaguire 95
(T R George) *a.p: effrt to ld 3 out: rdn next: hdd last: drvn and rallied flat: kpt on* **11/2**[2]
1031 **3** *1* **Risky Way**[10] 874 9-10-9 88 .... DO'Meara 95
(W S Coltherd) *in tch: hdwy 4 out: rdn along next: styd on u.p fr 2 out: drvn and ch flat: kpt on* **6/1**[3]
264U **4** *5* **Kalou (GER)**[11] 855 7-11-5 101 .... (p) MrTGreenall(3) 104+
(C Grant) *towards rr: hdwy 5 out: rdn along and in tch whn hit 2 out: kpt on same pce u.p appr last* **14/1**
-PU6 **5** *4* **Javelot D'Or (FR)**[49] 466 8-10-1 80 .... ARoss 78
(Mrs B K Thomson) *in tch: hdwy to chse ldrs appr 4 out: drvn next: wknd appr last* **50/1**
-4U3 **6** *8* **Jupiter Jo**[11] 858 9-9-10 82 ow2 .... BenOrde-Powlett(7) 72
(J B Walton) *bhd: hdwy appr 4 out: styd on fr next: nt rch ldrs* **12/1**
42P- **7** *1 1/4* **Ideal Du Bois Beury (FR)**[120] 4320 9-10-7 89 .... PAspell(3) 78
(P Monteith) *a rr* **16/1**
1260 **8** *1* **He's Hot Right Now (NZ)**[11] 862 6-11-2 95 .... (p) HOliver 83
(R C Guest) *midfield: rdn along appr 4 out and sn btn* **7/1**
130- **9** *6* **Influential (IRE)**[374] 856 9-10-5 84 .... MFoley 66
(J J Lambe, Ire) *a rr* **25/1**
1P-P **10** *4* **Ratty's Band**[10] 874 11-10-0 79 oh3 .... NPMulholland 57
(Mrs L B Normile) *chsd ldrs: rdn along 4 out: wknd next* **25/1**
3-31 **11** *10* **Cumbrian Knight (IRE)**[13] 604 7-11-12 105 .... GLee 73
(J M Jefferson) *towards rr: pushed along and sme hdwy whn nt fluent 7th: rdn along next and sn bhd* **10/1**
/FF- **P** **Young Chevalier**[106] 4555 8-11-5 98 .... KRenwick —
(J R Adam) *s.i.s: a rr: bhd whn p.u bef 4 out* **20/1**
1-22 **P** **Super Dolphin**[10] 874 6-10-6 85 .... ADobbin —
(R Ford) *trckd ldrs: hdwy to chse wnr 5th: pushed along 8th: rdn and blnd 4 out: sn p.u* **7/2**[1]

3m 53.5s (-9.30) **Going Correction** -0.525s/f (Firm) **13** Ran SP% **118.1**
Speed ratings: **102,101,101,98,96 92,91,91,88,86 81,—,—** CSF £55.93 CT £326.58 TOTE £9.40: £3.10, £2.20, £2.60; EX 61.10.
Owner J P Kearney **Bred** Jerry Keegan **Trained** Dungannon, Co. Tyrone
■ Stewards' Enquiry : A Dobbin caution: careless riding
J M Maguire one-day ban: used whip with excessive force (Jul 21)

FOCUS
A low-grade handicap but the first three all ran to their marks and the form looks sound enough for the level.

NOTEBOOK

Jamica Plane(IRE) enjoyed himself in front and, while he was headed at the third last, he rallied well to regain the lead and win all out. He has been running well in this country this summer and should continue to acquit himself with credit, especially when he is allowed to dominate. *(op 8-1)*

Phase Three(IRE), having his second start over fences, looked to have taken the leader's measure at the third last, only to find his rival in no mood to give in over the final two. He remains open to improvement over fences. *(op 13-2)*

Risky Way, raised 7lb for his recent course and distance success, was still potentially well treated as has won over fences off a 2lb higher mark than this in the past. He had his chance but the first two always had his measure on the run-in. *(op 15-2)*

Kalou(GER) did best of those that were held up at the back of the field. The cheekpieces did not appear to have an impact one way or the other.

Javelot D'Or(FR) is very well handicapped on his best form but although he ran one of his better races since moving to his current stable, this was still a fair way short of what is required for him to get his head in front again. *(op 40-1)*

Jupiter Jo was unsuited by the drop in trip. *(tchd 14-1)*

Super Dolphin hit the fourth-last pretty hard but he was weakening at the time. This was a disappointing effort given the promise of his last two starts and he simply seemed to have an off-day. *(op 4-1)*

940 CONTRACT SCOTLAND 15 YEARS IN CONSTRUCTION RECRUITMENT H'CAP HURDLE (8 hdls) 2m 110y

4:20 (4:24) (Class 4) (0-110,110) 4-Y-0+ **£6,877** (£2,116; £1,058; £529)

Form — RPR

4515 **1** **Royal Glen (IRE)**[21] 784 7-10-4 **88** ... RMcGrath 99+
(W S Coltherd) *hld up: smooth hdwy appr 3 out: led next and qcknd clr: easily* **8/1**

B21- **2** *7* **Another Deckie (IRE)**[133] 4088 7-11-12 **110** ... ADobbin 106
(L Lungo) *hld up: hdwy 1/2-way: effrt to join ldrs 3f out: cl up next: sn rdn and kpt on same pce* **11/4**[1]

4-12 **3** *1 ½* **Nowator (POL)**[38] 615 8-11-7 **105** ... JMMaguire 100
(T R George) *cl up: led 2nd: pushed along and hit 5th: rdn after 3 out: hdd next: sn drvn and kpt on same pce* **3/1**[2]

P245 **4** *2 ½* **Kyle Of Lochalsh**[6] 856 5-10-0 **84** oh2 ... ADempsey 76
(J S Goldie) *trckd ldrs: hdwy and cl up 1/2-way: pushed along and mstke 5th rdn 3 out: drvn and one pce fr 2 out* **7/2**[3]

3-00 **5** *8* **Brave Effect (IRE)**[21] 784 9-10-13 **97** ... (v) BHarding 81
(Mrs Dianne Sayer) *prom: effrt 3 out and ev ch tl rdn and outpcd next: blnd bdly last* **20/1**

34P5 **6** *1 ¼* **Winter Garden**[10] 873 11-10-6 **93** ... PBuchanan(3) 76
(Miss Lucinda V Russell) *towards rr: pushed along 3 out: rdn and sme hdwy next: sn drvn along and blnd last: nvr a factor* **33/1**

1526 **7** *5* **Supply And Fix (IRE)**[11] 856 7-10-10 **99** ... PCO'Neill(5) 77
(J J Lambe, Ire) *led to 2nd: chsd ldrs tl rdn along and wknd apprpoaching 3 out* **10/1**

05-6 **8** *12* **Teme Valley**[43] 552 11-11-8 **106** ... GLee 72
(J Howard Johnson) *bhd fr 1/2-way* **20/1**

5300 **9** *6* **Spree Vision**[10] 871 9-10-3 **90** ... PAspell(3) 50
(P Monteith) *a rr: bhd fr 1/2-way* **25/1**

3m 49.5s (-11.10) **Going Correction** -0.525s/f (Firm) **9** Ran SP% **110.4**
Speed ratings: **105,101,101,99,96 95,93,87,84** CSF £28.03 CT £76.48 TOTE £8.60: £2.00, £1.90, £1.20; EX 26.80.
Owner S Coltherd **Bred** R Goodwin **Trained** Selkirk, Borders

FOCUS
A modest handicap but the winner won with authority and appears to be improving, and the placed horses were close to their marks.

NOTEBOOK

Royal Glen(IRE) did not look obviously well handicapped, but the form of her Hexham fifth had been boosted by the subsequent success of the third so that effort may have been better than at first glance. She drew clear between the final two flights and won easily, being value for about double the official winning margin, and if she can translate this improvement back to the Flat she could get off the mark in that sphere in the near future. *(tchd 9-1)*

Another Deckie(IRE) took part despite there being a notice in the morning paper suggesting he would not take part if the ground was very firm. Returning from over four months off, he appeared to run to near his mark. *(op 5-2)*

Nowator(POL) could not take advantage of being rated a stone lower over hurdles than he is over fences. *(op 11-4 tchd 5-2)*

Kyle Of Lochalsh, a winner on the Flat six days earlier, failed to translate that good form back over timber. *(op 4-1 tchd 9-2)*

Brave Effect(IRE) appears to run his best races when allowed an uncontested lead. *(tchd 25-1)*

Winter Garden again looked to find this trip an inadequate test of stamina.

Teme Valley *Official explanation: jockey said gelding was never travelling*

941 TOTAL E & P U.K PLC H'CAP HURDLE (12 hdls) 3m 110y

4:50 (4:50) (Class 4) (0-100,96) 4-Y-0+ **£5,752** (£1,770; £885; £442)

Form — RPR

0-13 **1** **Ben Britten**[11] 859 6-11-11 **95** ... ADobbin 104+
(N G Richards) *hld up towards rr: smooth hdwy on inner 4 out: trckd ldr next: led 2 out: rdn appr last: styd on wl flat* **4/1**[1]

-6P2 **2** *3* **Olympic Storm (IRE)**[11] 856 7-11-6 **90** ... BHarding 94+
(N G Richards) *hld up towards rr: stdy hdwy appr 3 out: trckd ldrs next: rdn to chal last: drvn and one pce flat* **8/1**[3]

F160 **3** *3 ½* **Pikestaff (USA)**[11] 859 7-10-12 **89** ... (t) BenOrde-Powlett(7) 90
(M A Barnes) *a.p: led 8th: rdn along after 3 out: hdd next: sn drvn and kpt on same pce* **25/1**

2323 **4** *1 ¾* **Knockdoo (IRE)**[10] 871 12-11-5 **96** ... MrGGoldie(7) 95
(J S Goldie) *bhd: hdwy 4 out: rdn along next: styd on fr 2 out* **14/1**

432F **5** *1 ¼* **End Of An Error**[21] 781 6-10-5 **85** ... SGagan(10) 84+
(Mrs E Slack) *bhd and nt fluent: pushed along and mstke 6th: rdn along 3 out: styd on fr 2 out: nrst fin* **7/1**[2]

0200 **6** *14* **Northern Echo**[21] 781 8-10-1 **78** ... (p) GThomas(7) 62
(K S Thomas) *towards rr: hdwy appr 3 out: sn rdn along and no imp appr next* **50/1**

-441 **7** *6* **Cheery Martyr**[11] 854 7-10-12 **89** ... CDSharkey(7) 67
(P Needham) *in tch: hdwy to trck ldrs 4th: rdn along and lost pl 9th: bhd after next* **12/1**

-P43 **8** *5* **Ladies From Leeds**[45] 523 6-10-7 **80** ... (b) MrTGreenall(3) 53
(A Crook) *cl up: led 5th to 8th: pushed along and hit 3 out: sn wknd* **20/1**

P-P0 **9** *7* **Cool Dante (IRE)**[33] 674 10-11-7 **91** ... JMMaguire 57
(T R George) *a rr* **20/1**

/005 **10** *dist* **Lion Guest (IRE)**[11] 859 8-10-11 **81** ... MBradburne —
(Mrs S C Bradburne) *in tch: hdwy to chse ldrs 1/2-way: rdn along and wkng whn hit 3 out and sn bhd* **12/1**

0-45 **11** *13* **That's Racing**[16] 826 5-10-0 **75** ... DCCostello(5) —
(J Hetherton) *chsd ldrs: cl up 1/2-way: rdn along 9th: sn wknd* **10/1**

00P2 **P** **Thepubhorse**[21] 785 5-10-12 **85** ... ONelmes(3) —
(Mrs H O Graham) *bhd fr 1/2-way: p.u bef 2 out* **16/1**

3P-5 **P** **Right Direction (IRE)**[10] 875 7-10-4 **79** ... PCO'Neill(5) —
(J J Lambe, Ire) *bhd fr 1/2-way: p.u bef 2 out* **7/1**[2]

0-3P **P** **Clear Dawn (IRE)**[7] 896 10-11-8 **92** ... GLee —
(J M Jefferson) *chsd ldrs: rdn along whn hit 4 out and sn p.u* **12/1**

0003 **P** **Scamp**[10] 875 6-10-7 **80** ... (p) KJMercer(3) —
(R Shiels) *chsd ldrs: rdn along and lost pl 8th: bhd whn p.u bef last* **20/1**

32-0 **P** **No Sam No**[11] 859 7-10-13 **86** ... (p) PBuchanan(3) —
(Miss Lucinda V Russell) *led to 5th: rdn along and lost pl 8th: bhd whn p.u lame after 4 out* **20/1**

5m 56.5s (-14.40) **Going Correction** -0.525s/f (Firm) **16** Ran SP% **125.7**
Speed ratings: **102,101,99,99,98 94,92,90,88,—** —,—,—,—,— — CSF £32.84 CT £737.81 TOTE £3.40: £2.00, £2.20, £4.40, £2.70; EX 21.10.
Owner James Callow **Bred** Mrs Celia Miller **Trained** Greystoke, Cumbria

FOCUS
A modest contest run at a good pace and eventually fought out by the Nicky Richards trained pair.

NOTEBOOK

Ben Britten, one of the lighter-raced runners in the field, looks to be improving as he won off a 2lb higher mark than when beaten over course and distance last time. His stable companion made him pull out all the stops, but he was nicely on top at the finish. *(tchd 9-2)*

Olympic Storm(IRE) made a race of it with his better-fancied stable companion, jumping the last upsides, only to lose the battle on the run-in. He has improved for a change of stable and saw this longer trip out well. *(op 11-1)*

Pikestaff(USA) helped set a decent pace and did well to cling on for third place. He is not the most consistent type around but this was a good effort off what was a 6lb higher mark than when last successful. *(op 33-1)*

Knockdoo(IRE) is running with credit at present but at his age he is always going to be vulnerable to rivals with a bit more scope for progress. *(tchd 12-1)*

End Of An Error did his usual thing of staying on when it was all over. *(tchd 8-1 in places)*

Northern Echo is a poor performer handicapped up to the hilt at present.

Clear Dawn(IRE) *Official explanation: jockey said gelding lost its action (tchd 8-1 in a place and 6-1 in places)*

Right Direction(IRE) *Official explanation: jockey said gelding swallowed its tongue (tchd 8-1 in a place and 6-1 in places)*

942 FAMOUS GROUSE EXPERIENCE MAIDEN HURDLE (DIV II) (8 hdls) 2m 110y

5:20 (5:21) (Class 4) 4-Y-0+ **£3,770** (£1,160; £580; £290)

Form — RPR

52 **1** **Constable Burton**[19] 691 4-10-11 ... KJMercer(3) 102+
(Mrs A Duffield) *mde all: sn clr: rdn and blnd 2 out: styd on strly appr last* **2/1**[1]

-000 **2** *9* **Skiddaw Jones**[10] 870 5-10-13 80 ... (t) PWhelan(3) 89
(M A Barnes) *in tch: hdwy to chse wnr 3 out: rdn and clsd up next: sn drvn and no imp appr last* **16/1**

24 **3** *3 ½* **Rossclare (IRE)**[46] 495 5-10-11 ... PCO'Neill(5) 86
(J J Lambe, Ire) *prom: chsd wnr fr 3rd: rdn along 3 out: sn one pce* **4/1**[3]

000- **4** *½* **Winslow Boy (USA)**[23] 2171 4-10-11 72 ... PAspell(3) 84+
(P Monteith) *hld up towards rr: hdwy 3 out: drvn along next: 4th and wl hld whn blnd last* **9/1**

P0-5 **5** *8* **Ground Breaker**[7] 895 5-10-13 97 ... MrTGreenall(3) 77
(M W Easterby) *hld up towards rr: effrt and sme hdwy 3 out: sn rdn and wknd next* **9/4**[2]

6 *12* **Templet (USA)**[12] 5-11-2 ... BHarding 65
(W G Harrison) *a rr* **10/1**

04-0 **P** **End Of Saga**[10] 876 6-10-9 ... BenOrde-Powlett(7) —
(J B Walton) *a rr: bhd whn p.u bef 2 out* **50/1**

400/ **P** **Eyes Dont Lie (IRE)**[55] 2556 7-11-2 ... RMcGrath —
(D A Nolan) *in topucxh to 1/2-way: sn outpcd and bhd whn p.u 2 out* **50/1**

0400 **P** **Starbright**[21] 780 4-10-9 68 ... DCCostello(5) —
(W G Young) *chsd ldrs: rdn along and outpcd fr 4th: bhd whn p.u bef 2 out* **100/1**

/P-P **P** **Hickleton Club**[43] 551 7-10-11 71 ... (p) DMcGann(5) —
(R M Clark) *chsd wnr to 3rd: rdn along next: sn lost pl and bhd whn p.u bef 2 out* **100/1**

3m 51.0s (-9.60) **Going Correction** -0.525s/f (Firm)
WFA 4 from 5yo+ 2lb **41** Ran SP% **115.0**
Speed ratings: **101,96,95,94,91 85,—,—,—,—** CSF £32.83 TOTE £2.60: £1.60, £4.50, £1.60; EX 22.10 Place 6 £32.73, Place 5 £25.08.
Owner Middleham Park Racing Xv **Bred** D R Botterill **Trained** Constable Burton, N Yorks

FOCUS
An enterprising ride on the favourite, who dominated throughout, and the quicker of the two divisions by 2.5sec.

NOTEBOOK

Constable Burton was found a weak affair and, given an uncontested lead, made every yard to win at the third time of asking. He made a hash of jumping the second last but was nicely clear at the time and came home unchallenged. *(op 15-8 tchd 9-4)*

Skiddaw Jones posted his best effort over hurdles to date by winning the separate race for second. *(tchd 20-1)*

Rossclare(IRE), who had an excuse for running poorly at Cartmel on account of the ground, had no such excuse this time and was disappointing. *(op 9-2)*

Winslow Boy(USA), a firm-ground winner on the Flat, appreciated these quicker conditions and stayed on from off the pace. *(op 10-1)*

Ground Breaker failed to build on his encouraging reappearance outing at Market Rasen last time, and perhaps the race came too soon. *(tchd 5-2)*

T/Plt: £11.00 to a £1 stake. Pool: £43,190.70. 2,855.55 winning tickets. T/Qpdt: £7.70 to a £1 stake. Pool: £2,638.90. 253.25 winning tickets. JR

724 STRATFORD (L-H)

Sunday, July 10

OFFICIAL GOING: Good to firm

Wind: nil Weather: hot & sunny

943 LE GRAND PRIX DE BRIAN WALKER NOVICES' (S) HURDLE (9 hdls) 2m 110y

2:00 (2:01) (Class 5) 4-6-Y-0 **£3,094** (£884; £442)

Form — RPR

-120 **1** **Wardash (GER)**[19] 806 5-11-0 84 ... (vt) TJMurphy 90+
(M C Pipe) *a.p: wnt 2nd 4th: led 6th: in command whn lft clr 2 out: eased flat* **10/3**[1]

6-53 **2** *5* **Charlie Chapel**[61] 273 6-11-0 92 ... JPMcNamara 80+
(N J Hawke) *hld up and bhd: hdwy after 3 out: lft 2nd and hmpd 2 out: no ch w wnr* **6/1**

0 **3** *5* **Firebird Rising (USA)**[28] [729] 4-10-5 .... AntonyEvans 64
(R Brotherton) *t.k.h towards rr: mstke 2nd: hdwy after 6th: one pce fr 3 out* **50/1**

P/6 **4** *6* **Raheel (IRE)**[38] [232] 5-11-0 .... TScudamore 67
(M R Hoad) *hld up and bhd: hdwy appr 3 out: nvr trbld ldrs* **18/1**

5 *1 ¾* **Tshukudu**[41] 4-10-5 .... MBatchelor 56
(Mrs A L M King) *t.k.h: hdwy appr 6th: wknd appr 2 out* **50/1**

0/4 **6** *15* **Kilrossanty (IRE)**[49] [458] 6-11-0 .... ChristianWilliams 50
(R Flint) *hld up and bhd: stdy hdwy 5th: wknd after 3 out* **11/2**[3]

00/ **7** *7* **Dancing Hill**[482] [4375] 6-10-7 .... RGreene 36
(K Bishop) *hld up in tch: rdn whn mstke 5th: sn wknd* **25/1**

00/ **8** *2 ½* **Behan**[520] [2361] 6-10-7 .... JAJenkins[(7)] 41
(A J Chamberlain) *hld up in mid-div: bhd whn mstke 5th* **50/1**

9 *8* **Rosemount King (USA)**[29] 6-11-0 .... BHitchcott 33
(Mrs D A Hamer) *hld up in tch: mstke 5th: sn wknd* **20/1**

F **10** *13* **Jubilee Prince**[5] [901] 5-11-0 .... AO'Keeffe 20
(A E Jones) *sn wl bhd* **33/1**

00 **P** **Georgie's Lass (IRE)**[25] [656] 6-10-2 .... LStephens[(5)] —
(C Roberts) *sn t.o: p.u after 5th* **66/1**

P **Superclean**[68] 5-10-7 .... JTizzard —
(Mrs A L M King) *a bhd: mstke 3rd: t.o whn p.u bef 2 out* **66/1**

P/ **P** **Arthur Pendragon**[531] [3511] 5-10-9 .... RStephens[(5)] —
(Mrs S M Johnson) *hld up in tch: wknd 3 out: t.o whn p.u bef 2 out* **40/1**

P-F **F** **Zuleta**[11] [3] 4-10-5 .... JamesDavies 74
(B D Leavy) *w ldr: led after 2nd: hdd 6th: rdn after 3 out: 4 l 2nd and hld whn fell 2 out* **33/1**

-104 **P** **Trickstep**[26] [743] 4-11-4 95 .... (p) RJohnson —
(D McCain) *led tl after 2nd: chsd ldr to 4th: wknd after 3 out: bhd whn p.u bef 2 out* **11/2**[3]

14U3 **P** **Storm Clear (IRE)**[32] [683] 6-11-6 86 .... WMarston —
(D J Wintle) *hld up in mid-div: hdwy on ins after 5th: 4th and wkng whn wnt lame and p.u bef 2 out* **7/2**[2]

3m 53.1s (-5.30) **Going Correction** -0.65s/f (Firm)
WFA 4 from 5yo+ 2lb **16** Ran SP% **121.4**
Speed ratings: **86,83,81,78,77 70,67,66,62,56** —,—,—,—,— — CSF £21.68 TOTE £4.50: £1.90, £2.30, £7.20; EX 17.20.The winner was bought in for 13,000gns. Raheel was claimed by Mr R. Williams for £6,000.

Owner D A Johnson **Bred** Gestut Rottgen **Trained** Nicholashayne, Devon

FOCUS
A very weak event, run at a steady pace, which saw the field finish strung out behind the easy winner.

NOTEBOOK
Wardash(GER) relished the drop back to this level and ran out a facile winner, being value for nearly double his winning margin. Granted he was aided by Zuleta's fall two out, but he was well in command of that rival at the time, and he has now won on his last two outings at this level. He is not one to place too much faith in, but may be able to give a better showing back up in grade with this confidence-booster under his belt. *(op 3-1)*

Charlie Chapel, making his debut for new connections and best in at the weights according to official figures, kept on at his own pace from three out and is flattered by his finishing position. He was clear of the rest, however, and may be able to get closer in this grade in the future when faced with a stiffer test on easier ground. *(op 9-2)*

Firebird Rising(USA), dropping in grade after showing little on his hurdling debut over course and distance last time, again refused to settle through the early stages and never rated a serious threat. This was a slight improvement but, on this evidence, she will struggle outside of plating company in this sphere.

Raheel(IRE), returning to hurdles, was doing all of his best work too late in the day and never seriously figured. *(op 20-1)*

Kilrossanty(IRE) ran a tame race and failed to build on his recent effort in this grade at Hereford. *(op 8-1)*

Storm Clear(IRE) *Official explanation: jockey said gelding was lame (tchd 9-2)*

Zuleta was in the process of running a personal best over hurdles when she came to grief two out. She would most likely have finished second with a clear round, but whether she can build on this much depends on how severely her confidence will have been dented by this second consecutive fall. *(tchd 9-2)*

944 BIRMINGHAM EVENING MAIL NOVICES' CHASE (18 fncs) 3m

2:30 (2:30) (Class 3) 5-Y-0+ **£5,586** (£1,815; £977)

Form RPR

1P-1 **1** **Sweet Diversion (IRE)**[28] [728] 6-11-13 127 .... (t) ChristianWilliams 117+
(P F Nicholls) *hld up: wnt 2nd 3rd: led 2 out: lft clr last* **9/4**[2]

000/ **2** *15* **Mr Mighty (IRE)**[773] [483] 9-10-8 .... MrGPewter[(7)] 80
(G R Pewter) *j.rt: led: sn wl clr: wknd and hdd after 3 out: sn wknd: lft 2nd last* **50/1**[3]

-050 **3** *dist* **Saposcat (IRE)**[11] [863] 5-10-3 .... MrDavidTurner[(7)] —
(Dr P Pritchard) *chsd ldr to 3rd: wknd after 10th: sn lost tch: t.o* **66/1**

2-21 **F** **Mr Ed (IRE)**[10] [872] 7-11-7 .... (p) APMcCoy 111
(P Bowen) *hld up: disp 2nd fr 10th: led after 3 to 2 out: ev ch whn fell last* **4/11**[1]

6m 12.0s (9.80) **Going Correction** -0.75s/f (Firm)
WFA 5 from 6yo+ 5lb **4** Ran SP% **107.5**
Speed ratings: **53,48**,—,— CSF £28.16 TOTE £2.90; EX 16.40.

Owner Ian Marshall **Bred** Con O'Keeffe **Trained** Ditcheat, Somerset

FOCUS
A match race on paper, and so it proved, but the winner is clearly flattered by his winning margin. The slow, uneven pace did not see Mr Ed at his best.

NOTEBOOK
Sweet Diversion(IRE) was just about winning the battle with Mr Ed prior to that rival coming to grief at the final fence, and he was then allowed to coast home and record his second straight success. He has been improved for the recent application of a tongue tie, deserves credit for giving away weight to a decent performer and, while he is greatly flattered by his winning margin, he is clearly at the top of his game at present. He will not be the easiest to place now, however. *(op 5-2)*

Mr Mighty(IRE) did not look suited by racing on this left-handed track, as he continually jumped right over his fences, and he is vastly-flattered by his finishing position. That said, he should improve plenty for this outing and could fare better when qualified for handicaps this summer. *(op 40-1)*

Mr Ed(IRE), who took time to find his stride before winning on his chasing bow at Perth ten days previously, was still bang in contention prior to meeting the last fence all wrong and coming to grief. It could be deemed slightly disappointing that he could not shake off the eventual winner - who he is rated 24lb higher than over hurdles - but he was not suited by the tactical gallop and is far from one to write off on the back of this display. *(tchd 2-5)*

945 BIRMINGHAM EVENING MAIL JUVENILE NOVICES' HURDLE (8 hdls 1 omitted) 2m 110y

3:00 (3:03) (Class 3) 3-Y-O **£5,434** (£1,672; £836; £418)

Form RPR

1 **Polar Passion**[289] 3-10-5 .... DRDennis 74+
(R Hollinshead) *hld up: hdwy 3 out: rdn to ld last: drvn out* **33/1**

2 *¾* **Shingle Street (IRE)**[17] 3-10-12 .... SThomas 80+
(Miss Venetia Williams) *w ldr: lft in ld 2 out: hdd last: kpt on* **8/1**[3]

3 *nk* **Dramatic Review (IRE)**[33] 3-10-12 .... FKeniry 79
(P C Haslam) *a.p: rdn and ev ch last: kpt on* **9/1**

4 *5* **Compton Quay**[27] 3-10-12 .... RThornton 74
(A King) *hld up in tch: hit 2nd: rdn appr 5th: mstke 2 out: one pce* **12/1**

5 *3* **Mr Kalandi (IRE)**[15] 3-10-12 .... (t) PMoloney 71
(P W D'Arcy) *t.k.h: prom tl wknd appr last* **14/1**

6 *7* **John Forbes**[15] 3-10-12 .... APMcCoy 66+
(B Ellison) *led: nt fluent 1st: mstke 5th: hdd after 3 out: wknd appr 2 out* **5/2**[1]

7 *¾* **Kinfayre Boy**[30] 3-10-12 .... PRobson 63
(K W Hogg) *hld up in mid-div: hdwy after 5th: wknd after 3 out* **50/1**

8 *7* **Magdelaine**[62] 3-10-0 .... WKennedy[(5)] 49
(A M Hales) *a bhd: rdn appr 5th: no ch whn hmpd 2 out* **40/1**

R **Vracca**[13] 3-10-5 .... TJMurphy 4
(M C Pipe) *unruly s: ref to r: tk no part* **4/1**[2]

P **Mabella (IRE)**[28] 3-10-5 .... ChristianWilliams 4
(B Llewellyn) *a bhd: lost tch 4th: t.o whn p.u bef 3 out* **33/1**

P **Blinis (IRE)**[55] 3-10-2 .... KBurke[(10)] —
(P R Rodford) *t.k.h in mid-div: bhd fr 3 out: t.o whn p.u bef 2 out* **20/1**

P **Miss Dinamite**[69] 3-10-5 .... BHitchcott —
(Mrs C J Ikin) *hld up in tch: rdn 4th: sn wknd: t.o whn p.u bef 3 out* **66/1**

F **Champagne Rossini (IRE)**[37] 3-10-9 .... ACCoyle[(3)] 63
(M C Chapman) *hld up and bhd: mstke 2nd: hdwy appr 3 out: no imp whn fell 2 out* **33/1**

P **Nelson (POL)**[232] 3-10-12 .... RJohnson —
(P J Hobbs) *hld up in tch: nt fluent 2nd: lost pl after 3rd: sn bhd: t.o whn p.u bef 3 out* **8/1**[3]

P **Imperial Miss (IRE)**[178] 3-10-5 .... NFehily —
(B W Duke) *hld up in mid-div: mstke 4th: rdn appr 3 out: sn bhd: t.o whn p.u bef 2 out* **40/1**

F **Strathtay**[33] 3-10-2 .... TJMalone[(3)] 77+
(M C Pipe) *hld up in tch: slipped through on ins to ld after 3 out: 4 l clr whn j.lft and fell 2 out* **10/1**

3m 54.2s (-4.20) **Going Correction** -0.65s/f (Firm) **16** Ran SP% **126.2**
Speed ratings: **83,82,82,80,78 75,75,71**,—,— —,—,—,—,— — CSF £276.29 TOTE £49.90: £10.00, £3.10, £2.70; EX 736.80.

Owner Tim Leadbeater **Bred** Longdon Stud Ltd **Trained** Upper Longdon, Staffs

■ The first juvenile hurdle of the season.

FOCUS
The first juvenile hurdle of the season, albeit a moderate one, and the first three came clear. The form is suspect as the time was slower than the seller and Strathtay should have won but for falling two out. The third-last flight was bypassed.

NOTEBOOK
Polar Passion, out the back in two outings on the Flat, dug deep when it mattered and got off the mark at the first attempt over timber with a hard-fought success. However, she has to rate a fortunate winner and, while she is entitled to improve for this, will not be prove easy to place in the future. *(op 28-1)*

Shingle Street(IRE), just denied over 12 furlongs in a claimer at Newcastle last time, turned in a respectable debut for new connections and will most probably need a stiffer test to be seen at his best over hurdles. He could be placed to go one better at this level during the summer. *(op 9-1 tchd 10-1)*

Dramatic Review(IRE), a maiden and rated 49 on the Flat, did little wrong in defeat and turned in a fair debut effort. He is limited, but was clear of the rest at the finish and may be the type to prove better in this sphere than he was on the level. *(tchd 8-1)*

Compton Quay, an All-Weather nursery winner off a mark of 68 in 2004, was not all that fluent at his hurdles and never looked a serious threat. He seems to have lost his way of late, and while he should come on for the experience, looks only moderate.

Mr Kalandi(IRE), a consistent maiden on the Flat and rated 55, ran too keen on this first attempt at hurdling and ultimately paid the price.

John Forbes, rated 71 on the Flat, was none to fluent over his hurdles and failed to get home. He may need to be ridden more patiently and will have to brush up his jumping if he is to taste success in this sphere. *(tchd 11-4)*

Vracca, winner of a nine furlong Longchamp claimer 13 days previously, played up at the start and it was not the biggest surprise when she refused to take part. She has it all to prove now. *(op 5-1 tchd 7-2)*

Strathtay, winner of a seller in 2004 and rated 56 on the Flat, was booked for a comfortable success prior to falling two out and has to rate unlucky. On this evidence, she should soon be making amends and looks likely to rate higher over timber than she did on the Flat. *(op 9-1 tchd 11-1)*

946 BIRMINGHAM EVENING MAIL H'CAP CHASE (FOR THE STRATFORD SUMMER CUP) (14 fncs 1 omitted) 2m 4f

3:30 (3:33) (Class 3) (0-120,119) 5-Y-0+
£9,152 (£3,471; £1,735; £789; £394; £236)

Form RPR

3-11 **1** **Blakeney Coast (IRE)**[32] [684] 8-10-6 99 .... (t) JTizzard 123+
(C L Tizzard) *a.p: hit 10th: led after 4 out: clr 2 out: easily* **5/1**[1]

2244 **2** *14* **Escompteur (FR)**[14] [840] 5-11-7 115 .... TJMurphy 119+
(M C Pipe) *a.p: led 4th tl after 4 out: one pce fr 3 out* **11/2**[2]

-4U1 **3** *hd* **James Victor (IRE)**[26] [752] 7-10-5 101 .... RYoung[(3)] 107+
(N R Mitchell) *a.p: sltly hmpd 10th: ev ch 3 out: sn rdn: one pce* **20/1**

6-12 **4** *6* **Luneray (FR)**[36] [634] 6-11-5 112 .... (t) ChristianWilliams 111
(P F Nicholls) *hld up: hdwy 8th: wknd after 3 out* **8/1**[3]

PP1/ **5** *19* **Noble Justice (IRE)**[610] [2018] 9-10-11 111 .... JamesWhite[(7)] 98+
(R J Hodges) *hld up in mid-div: in tch whn bdly hmpd 10th: sn wknd* **40/1**

3-16 **6** *4* **Manoram (GER)**[42] [573] 6-10-13 106 .... (b) MAFitzgerald 85+
(Ian Williams) *w ldr: blnd 3rd: lost pl 6th: rdn after 7th: sn bhd* **14/1**

25-0 **7** *1* **Dun An Doras (IRE)**[55] [386] 9-11-5 112 .... JAMcCarthy 87
(J D Frost) *nvr nr ldrs* **16/1**

0140 **8** *5* **Idealko (FR)**[25] [761] 9-10-8 101 .... RGreene 71
(Dr P Pritchard) *a bhd* **66/1**

04-0 **9** *3 ½* **Hors La Loi (FR)**[36] [634] 9-11-12 119 .... CLlewellyn 86
(Ian Williams) *a bhd* **16/1**

3P-0 **U** **Nick The Jewel**[68] [178] 10-11-7 114 .... JEMoore —
(J S King) *bdly bmpd and uns rdr 1st* **33/1**

-12P **B** **Tamango (FR)**[36] [634] 8-11-12 119 .... RJohnson —
(P J Hobbs) *hld up: hdwy after 8th: prom whn b.d 10th* **17/2**

23-3 **F** **Silvergino (IRE)**[66] 193 5-10-11 **105**.. PJBrennan —
(Mrs Jeremy Young) *led to 4th: w ldr whn fell 10th* **10/1**
11-0 **P** **Renvyle (IRE)**[63] 248 7-11-1 **108**..(b) APMcCoy —
(Jonjo O'Neill) *mid-div: hmpd 1st: j. slowly 4th: sn bhd: t.o whn p.u bef 11th* **8/1**[3]
6-3P **P** **Half An Hour**[14] 840 8-11-3 **110**...(v) RThornton —
(A King) *s.i.s: sme hdwy 5th: hit 8th: sn struggling: t.o whn p.u bef 4 out* **16/1**

4m 40.3s (-19.70) **Going Correction** -0.75s/f (Firm) course record
WFA 5 from 6yo+ 1lb **14** Ran SP% **109.8**
Speed ratings: **109,103,103,100,93 91,91,89,87,— —,—,—,—** CSF £26.83 CT £374.37 TOTE £5.40: £1.70, £2.10, £8.00; EX 27.30.
Owner The Jam Boys **Bred** Major F B And J G B Boyd **Trained** Milborne Port, Dorset
■ Fear Siuil (13/2) was withdrawn on vet's advice. R4 applies, deduct 10p in the £.

FOCUS
A fair chase for the time of year, run at a strong pace, and the winner broke the previous course record by nearly 2 seconds. The form is solid. The first fence on the side of the course was bypassed on the second circuit.

NOTEBOOK
Blakeney Coast(IRE) ◆ landed the hat-trick with another imperious display of fencing, can be rated value for more than his already wide winning margin and broke the previous course record by nearly two seconds. He has been rejuvenated by the recent application of a tongue tie, loves this fast ground and looks well up to defying another inevitable rise in the weights this summer. *(op 9-2)*
Escompteur(FR) was put firmly in his place by the winner at the weights, but stuck to his task under pressure and again emerged with credit in defeat. He may benefit from a more patient ride over this trip and it could be that he ideally needs easier ground, but it is disappointing that he has yet to win over fences. *(op 7-1)*
James Victor(IRE) , raised 8lb for winning at Newton Abbot last time, turned in another improved effort yet was found out by this longer trip. He looks progressive and could resume winning ways when reverting to shorter on this sort of ground.
Luneray(FR)produced only a short-lived effort and, while she remains in fair form, she does look to be in the Handicapper's grip on this evidence. *(op 7-1 tchd 9-1)*
Noble Justice(IRE) , last seen winning off this mark at Wincanton 610 days previously, was not disgraced and looks sure to improve for the outing. *(op 33-1)*
Hors La Loi(FR) *Official explanation: vet said gelding bled from the nose (op 14-1)*

947 BIRMINGHAM EVENING MAIL SUMMER H'CAP HURDLE (FOR THE STRATFORD SUMMER SALVER) (9 hdls) 2m 110y
4:00 (4:03) (Class 3) (0-125,122) 4-Y-0+
£7,377 (£2,798; £1,399; £636; £318; £190)

Form RPR
-023 **1** **Imperial Rocket (USA)**[26] 747 8-10-1 **97**..........................(t) CLlewellyn 104+
(W K Goldsworthy) *a.p: wnt 2nd 6th: rdn to ld 2 out: r.o* **10/1**
-13F **2** 1½ **Kentmere (IRE)**[31] 695 4-10-6 **104**.. TDoyle 107
(P R Webber) *hld up in tch: outpcd after 5th: rdn and rallied 3 out: r.o flat* **12/1**
-464 **3** ¾ **Castleshane (IRE)**[16] 824 8-11-12 **122**................................... APMcCoy 127+
(S Gollings) *led: rdn after 3 out: hdd 2 out: kpt on same pce flat* **4/1**[2]
4F05 **4** 5 **Siegfrieds Night (IRE)**[16] 824 4-10-6 **107**.......................... ACCoyle(3) 104
(M C Chapman) *hld up in mid-div: rdn and hdwy after 6th: one pce fr 3 out* **33/1**
6P-5 **5** 1 **Sachsenwalzer (GER)**[19] 99 7-10-9 **105**............................ TJMurphy 103
(C Grant) *hld up in tch: mstke 3rd: one pce fr 3 out* **16/1**
-022 **6** 6 **Lupin (FR)**[36] 633 6-11-2 **112**.. NFehily 104
(A W Carroll) *hld up and bhd: stdy hdwy fr 3 out: nvr nr to chal* **6/1**[3]
014- **7** 2½ **Sigwells Club Boy**[147] 3836 5-9-12 **99**............................ RStephens(5) 88
(J L Flint) *no hdwy fr 6th* **14/1**
-420 **8** 2 **Delaware (FR)**[34] 665 9-10-0 **96** oh9.................................. JMogford 83
(H S Howe) *bhd 2nd: rdn after 4th: nvr nr ldrs* **33/1**
3-10 **9** nk **Naked Oat**[26] 747 10-9-7 **96** oh2....................................... SWalsh(7) 83
(Mrs L Wadham) *hld up in tch: wknd appr 3 out* **16/1**
10P- **10** ½ **Border Tale**[4] 647 5-11-0 **110**.. JimCrowley 96
(James Moffatt) *bhd: reminders after 4th: n.d* **11/1**
-550 **11** ¾ **Reservoir (IRE)**[49] 460 4-11-2 **114**.................................... RJohnson 98
(P J Hobbs) *hld up in mid-div: reminders after 4th: mstke 5th: n.d after* **16/1**
10-2 **12** 2½ **Genuine Article (IRE)**[50] 450 9-11-4 **114**...................... MAFitzgerald 97
(M Pitman) *chsd ldr tl after 4th: sn pushed along: wknd appr 3 out* **7/2**[1]
-044 **13** 5 **Celtic Romance**[26] 747 6-10-0 **96** oh16................................ JPByrne 74
(Ms Sue Smith) *a bhd* **66/1**
400- **14** ½ **Le Gris (GER)**[91] 4799 6-9-6 **98** oh10 ow2.......................... KBurke(10) 76
(P R Rodford) *a bhd* **33/1**
-021 **P** **Ton-Chee**[6] 482 6-10-7 **103**... PRobson —
(K W Hogg) *prom: chsd ldr after 4th to 6th: wknd 3 out: sn eased: p.u bef 2 out* **14/1**

3m 44.8s (-13.60) **Going Correction** -0.65s/f (Firm)
WFA 4 from 5yo+ 2lb **15** Ran SP% **122.9**
Speed ratings: **106,105,104,102,102 99,98,97,97,96 96,95,92,92,—** CSF £122.67 CT £570.31 TOTE £11.80: £3.40, £2.90, £1.80; EX 96.30.
Owner Mrs L A Goldsworthy **Bred** Ralph C Wilson Jnr Trustee **Trained** Yerbeston, Pembrokes

FOCUS
A modest handicap, but run at a decent pace and the form appears solid enough for the class.

NOTEBOOK
Imperial Rocket(USA) , raised for finishing third last time, proved the Handicapper correct and gained a deserved success in ready fashion. This was his first victory since 2001 and he has clearly improved for the recent application of a tongue tie, so while he will go up again in the weights for this further progression cannot be totally ruled out. *(tchd 9-1)*
Kentmere(IRE) found the decent gallop much to his liking and turned in a personal best over hurdles in defeat. He may have a little more improvement left in him, but is not the easiest of rides.
Castleshane(IRE) again set a decent gallop, as he prefers, but his fate was apparent approaching two out and he could offer no more under his big weight when challenged. He was still clear of the rest, however, and this rates an improvement on his most recent efforts.
Siegfrieds Night(IRE) ran another improved race, but failed to quicken when it mattered. He could get closer if encountering easier ground in the near future.
Lupin(FR) was given a fair bit to do from off the pace and did not look to fully let himself down on this fast ground when asked for maximum effort. He can be rated slightly better than the bare form and has the scope to win more races over timber when reverting to a softer ground. *(op 7-1)*
Genuine Article(IRE) dropped out quickly when push came to shove and this has to rate a most *disappointing effort. He has plenty to prove now. Official explanation: vet said gelding had a cut on its left fore (tchd 3-1)*

948 BIRMINGHAM EVENING MAIL NOVICES' H'CAP CHASE (16 fncs) 2m 5f 110y
4:30 (4:32) (Class 4) (0-105,98) 5-Y-0+ **£4,134** (£1,272; £636; £318)

Form RPR
/421 **1** **Keltic Lord**[7] 896 9-11-6 **92** 7ex.. RThornton 115+
(P W Hiatt) *hld up: hdwy 6th: led on bit 3 out: clr appr last: easily* **11/10**[1]
/31P **2** 22 **Multeen Gunner**[36] 632 8-10-12 **84**....................................(p) PMoloney 88+
(Evan Williams) *led: hdd 3 out: sn rdn: no ch w wnr* **15/2**[2]
4-P **3** 6 **Mantilla**[51] 436 8-11-3 **89**..(b) DRDennis 77
(Ian Williams) *prom tl rdn and wknd approching 3 out* **12/1**[3]
3F2R **4** 8 **Althrey Dandy (IRE)**[5] 902 10-11-11 **97**............................ AThornton 82+
(P T Dalton) *led into s: s.i.s: hdwy 9th: hmpd 11th: 5th and wkng whn blnd 12th* **14/1**
220P **5** 21 **Tosawi (IRE)**[26] 752 9-11-12 **98**..................................(p) TScudamore 57
(R J Hodges) *a bhd* **20/1**
5 **6** 9 **Tarbuck (IRE)**[11] 862 12-10-10 **82**.. PJBrennan 32
(Mrs D A Hamer) *hld up in tch: mstke 5th: rdn and wknd appr 12th* **16/1**
P10P **7** 3 **Monty Be Quick**[11] 865 9-10-1 **80**..................................... MrTJO'Brien(7) 27
(J M Castle) *hld up in mid-div: stmbld after 9th: sn bhd* **22/1**
-024 **U** **Luckycharm (FR)**[16] 827 6-10-0 **72**..............................(v) WHutchinson —
(R Dickin) *j.rt and uns rdr 1st* **12/1**[3]
54U **F** **Beaugency (NZ)**[24] 767 7-11-2 **93**.................................... WKennedy(5) —
(R C Guest) *hld up in mid-div: fell 11th* **12/1**[3]
0- **P** **Baden Vugie (IRE)**[103] 8-10-7 **86** oh8 ow14........................ MrNPearce(7) —
(S T Lewis) *a bhd: t.o whn p.u bef 7th* **100/1**
141P **P** **Billy Ballbreaker (IRE)**[4] 916 9-11-6 **92**................................(tp) JTizzard —
(C L Tizzard) *bhd tl p.u bef 11th* **15/2**[2]
256- **P** **Pure Steel (IRE)**[53] 11-10-5 **82**...................................... LStephens(5) —
(Miss L Day) *bhd: rdn after 8th: p.u bef 11th* **50/1**
15/P **P** **Slyboots (GER)**[45] 516 6-11-11 **97**.. NFehily —
(C J Mann) *prom tl wknd 12th: t.o whn p.u bef 2 out* **18/1**
50-F **P** **Mvezo**[54] 398 7-10-0 **72** oh8.. JPByrne —
(Evan Williams) *hld up in mid-div: hdwy 10th: wknd appr 12th: bhd whn p.u bef 3 out* **40/1**

5m 3.00s (-11.40) **Going Correction** -0.75s/f (Firm) course record **14** Ran SP% **126.5**
Speed ratings: **90,82,79,76,69 66,64,—,—,— —,—,—,—** CSF £10.78 CT £76.79 TOTE £2.20: £1.10, £2.80, £4.80; EX 12.60.
Owner Paul Porter **Bred** Miss H Day **Trained** Hook Norton, Oxon

FOCUS
A weak handicap that saw the field well strung out at the finish. The winner equalled the course record, is clearly progressing and could rate higher.

NOTEBOOK
Keltic Lord again advertised his preference for fast ground with a facile success under his penalty, equalling the course record in the process. He did not need to obviously improve to take this, but there was an awful lot to like about the manner of this success and he is clearly in the form of his life at present, helped by the recent good form of his yard. *(op 11-8 tchd 6-4 in a place)*
Multeen Gunner turned in one of his better efforts and, whilst outclassed by the winner, ran to the form which saw him score at Sedgfield in May. He can find easier opportunities off this mark, but has an inconsistent profile and is not one to place much faith in. *(op 7-1)*
Mantilla , with blinkers replacing the visor, at least completed this time, but continues to run well below her previous best.
Althrey Dandy(IRE) again looked less than fluent over his fences and is not one to trust. *(op 16-1)*
Monty Be Quick *Official explanation: jockey said gelding clipped heels and stumbled with a circuit to run (op 20-1)*
Billy Ballbreaker(IRE) *Official explanation: jockey said gelding was never travelling (op 8-1)*

949 BIRMINGHAM EVENING MAIL H'CAP HURDLE (12 hdls) 2m 6f 110y
5:00 (5:01) (Class 4) (0-105,106) 4-Y-0+ **£3,601** (£1,108; £554; £277)

Form RPR
1-01 **1** **Herne Bay (IRE)**[14] 841 5-11-13 **106**................................... JPMcNamara 114+
(R S Brookhouse) *hld up and bhd: hdwy after 7th: led 2 out: sn rdn: styd on wl* **10/1**[3]
0P-1 **2** 6 **Red Chief (IRE)**[11] 856 5-10-9 **88**....................................... RJohnson 91+
(Mrs A M Thorpe) *hld up in mid-div: hdwy after 7th: led after 3 out to 2 out: one pce* **5/1**[1]
-F51 **3** 3 **Cannon Fire (FR)**[38] 614 4-11-1 **98**.............................. ChristianWilliams 93
(Evan Williams) *hld up: hdwy 8th: one pce fr 2 out* **13/2**[2]
6230 **4** 3½ **La Concha (IRE)**[24] 768 4-10-12 **95**.................................. RThornton 86
(M J McGrath) *hld up: hdwy 8th: wkng whn nt fluent last* **12/1**
/115 **5** 8 **Spirit Of Tenby (IRE)**[5] 906 8-10-7 **86**.............................. TJMurphy 73
(W K Goldsworthy) *hld up in mid-div: hdwy after 8th: wknd appr 3 out* **5/1**[1]
500- **6** 13 **Dantes Venture (IRE)**[171] 3435 8-11-5 **98**..........................(v) TDoyle 72
(Miss I E Craig) *chsd ldrs: led after 7th tl after 3 out: wknd appr 2 out* **50/1**
3-63 **7** shd **Red Canyon (IRE)**[25] 762 8-10-11 **90**...............................(b) JTizzard 64
(C L Tizzard) *led to 4th: wknd appr 3 out* **10/1**[3]
0-10 **8** 12 **Bob's Gone (IRE)**[25] 762 7-11-5 **103**............................ TJPhelan(5) 65
(B P J Baugh) *w ldr: led 4th tl after 7th: wknd after 8th* **14/1**
0-31 **P** **Nifty Roy**[8] 152 5-11-2 **95**.. PRobson —
(K W Hogg) *bhd: mstke 6th: t.o whn p.u bef 2 out* **16/1**
0006 **P** **Meadow Hawk (USA)**[7] 895 5-10-11 **90**..........................(v) MAFitzgerald —
(Ian Williams) *a bhd: t.o whn p.u bef 9th* **18/1**
-031 **P** **Taranai (IRE)**[19] 801 4-10-7 **90**...(t) NFehily —
(B W Duke) *hld up in tch: wknd after 8th: t.o whn p.u bef 2 out* **10/1**[3]
-2PP **P** **Dancinginthestreet**[35] 652 5-10-13 **97**..........................(t) LStephens(5) —
(J L Flint) *hld up in tch: j.rt 4th: wknd 7th: sn p.u* **33/1**
0-25 **F** **Titian Flame (IRE)**[14] 841 5-10-13 **97**............................ WKennedy(5) —
(D Burchell) *hld up and bhd: hdwy after 7th: in tch whn fell 8th* **10/1**[3]
05-6 **P** **Georgian Harry (IRE)**[64] 218 8-11-2 **95**............................ WMarston —
(R T Phillips) *hld up: hdwy appr 6th: wnt lame and p.u after 8th* **16/1**
/P-P **P** **Colonel Bradley (IRE)**[25] 761 11-11-2 **95**............................ APMcCoy —
(Jonjo O'Neill) *nvr gng wl towards rr: struggling fr 8th: t.o whn p.u bef 2 out* **14/1**

5m 10.7s (-19.00) **Going Correction** -0.65s/f (Firm)
WFA 4 from 5yo+ 3lb **15** Ran SP% **126.0**
Speed ratings: **107,104,103,102,99 95,95,91,—,— —,—,—,—,—** CSF £62.54 CT £364.80 TOTE £9.40: £3.30, £2.20, £2.90; EX 48.80 Place 6 £387.77, Place 5 £149.25.
Owner R S Brookhouse **Bred** Roland H Alder **Trained** Wixford, Warwicks

FOCUS
A fair handicap for the class, run at a sound pace and the field finished fairly strung out behind the in-form winner. The form looks reasonable with the third and fourth close to their marks.

NOTEBOOK
Herne Bay(IRE) comfortably defied top weight and followed up his recent Uttoxeter success off an 8lb higher mark. The step back to this trip was in his favour, he clearly likes this track and is clearly back in top form at present. However, he will need to keep progressing as the Handicapper is sure to make life tough after this. *(op 8-1)*
Red Chief(IRE) was found out more by the longer trip, rather than his latest 8lb rise in the weights. *He remains on the upgrade and could well taste success once again when reverting to shorter. (tchd 9-2)*
Cannon Fire(FR) ran his race, but may not have been totally suited by this step back up in trip and *does now look in the Handicapper's grip after being raised 7lb for his previous Uttoxeter success. (op 11-2)*

La Concha(IRE) improved on his latest effort, but despite the drop back in trip, dropped out rather tamely at the business end of the race. He is really struggling to find his optimum trip. *(op 10-1)*
Spirit Of Tenby(IRE) failed to improve as expected for this drop back in trip and return to a faster surface. He may well have found this coming too soon after his recent Uttoxeter effort, but this still leaves him with a bit to prove in the future. *(op 11-2)*
Georgian Harry(IRE) *Official explanation: jockey said gelding was lame*
Dancinginthestreet *Official explanation: jockey said gelding was unsuited by the good to firm ground*
T/Plt: £207.00 to a £1 stake. Pool: £41,996.75. 148.05 winning tickets. T/Qpdt: £34.80 to a £1 stake. Pool: £3,285.30. 69.70 winning tickets. KH

950 - 953a (Foreign Racing) - See Raceform Interactive

879 TIPPERARY

Sunday, July 10

OFFICIAL GOING: Flat course - good to firm (firm in places); jumps courses - good to firm (good in places)

954a BETDAQ.COM HURDLE (GRADE 3) 2m

3:45 (3:45) 4-Y-0+ **£32,319** (£9,482; £4,517; £1,539)

			RPR
1		**Accordion Etoile (IRE)**[92] [4771] 6-11-8 161 ... JLCullen (Paul Nolan, Ire) *chsd ldrs in mod 4th: clsr order fr 3 out: chal and led appr last: rdn out and styd on wl run-in* **1/3**[1]	133+
2	1 ½	**Red Square Lady (IRE)**[8] [703] 7-11-0 113 ...20 AndrewJMcNamara (Michael John Phillips, Ire) *chsd clr ldr in 2nd: clsr order fr bef st: rdn to* **chal and ld bef 2 out: strly pressed and hdd wl bef last: kpt on same pce** **25/1**	124
4	shd	**Ansar (IRE)**[11] [4397] 9-11-10 140 ... BJGeraghty (D K Weld, Ire) *chsd ldrs in mod 3rd: clsr order bef st: rdn and no imp in 4th whn mstke last: kpt on run-in* **9/1**[3]	132
5	3	**Sky's The Limit (FR)**[14] [3963] 4-10-8 123 ... JCulloty (E J O'Grady, Ire) *racd mod 6th: rdn and no imp appr st: kpt on* **25/1**	113
6	1	**More Rainbows (IRE)**[14] [703] 5-11-7 126 ... PFlynn (Noel Meade, Ire) *towards rr thrght: mod 8th 4 out: no imp and kpt on fr next* **10/1**	125
7	3	**Anno Jubilo (GER)**[8] [1009] 8-11-5 ... CO'Dwyer (C F Swan, Ire) *led and clr: slt mstke 3rd: reduced ld fr bef st: strly pressed and hdd bef 2 out: sn lost pl and no ex* **16/1**	120?
8	25	**In The Forge**[562] [2970] 8-11-5 ...(t) RMPower (M Halford, Ire) *towards rr thrght: nvr a factor: t.o* **16/1**	95
9	dist	**Dujareva**[17] [820] 4-10-3 94 ... JFLevins (J P Broderick, Ire) *a towards rr: nvr a danger: completely t.o* **100/1**	—

3m 38.7s
WFA 4 from 5yo+ 2lb **9** Ran SP% **127.1**
CSF £17.43 TOTE £1.60: £1.10, £4.20, £2.30; DF 39.00.
Owner Banjo Syndicate **Bred** John McKeever **Trained** Enniscorthy, Co. Wexford

NOTEBOOK
Accordion Etoile(IRE) only did the minimum to win this on his reappearance, quickening up nicely after leading just before the last flight. He won the race last year and, officially 52lb superior to the runner-up and conceding just 8lb here, one just might have wished for a more authoritative style of performance but the fact is none of the bigger names wanted to finish any closer. He certainly relishes this fast ground and could carry top weight in the Galway Hurdle or possibly switch to fences at that meeting. *(op 2/5)*
Red Square Lady(IRE) ran a career best and looked a possibility to give the winner something to do before being readily outpaced from the last. *(op 20/1)*
Calorando(IRE) move smoothly enough into third place before the last flight but progress was *limited on the run-in. He will be meeting the winner on advantageous terms in the Galway Hurdle. (op 6/1)*
Ansar(IRE) showed something of a return to form here and will go back over fences now, bidding for a repeat of last year's success in the Galway Plate. *(op 7/1)*
Sky's The Limit(FR) ran as good a trial for the big hurdle at Galway as could be imagined.
More Rainbows(IRE) was out of contention for most of the way but stayed on in the straight and is capable of leaving this well behind him.
Anno Jubilo(GER) ran in front and weakened from two out. *(op 14/1)*

955 - 957a (Foreign Racing) - See Raceform Interactive

801 NEWTON ABBOT (L-H)

Monday, July 11

OFFICIAL GOING: Good to firm (good in places)

There were 18 non-runners, due mainly to problems on the M5.
Wind: Almost nil Weather: Sunny and warm

958 WESTCOUNTRY H'CAP CHASE (13 fncs) 2m 110y

2:00 (2:01) (Class 4) (0-100,100) 5-Y-0+ **£3,376** (£964; £482)

Form				RPR
-324	1		**The Mighty Sparrow (IRE)**[6] [902] 12-10-11 85 ...(p) MFoley (A E Jones) *a.p: led appr 9th: rdn clr appr 2 out: eased flat* **7/2**[2]	99+
F/0U	2	14	**Knight's Emperor (IRE)**[6] [904] 8-11-6 94 ... RThornton (J L Spearing) *hld up: hdwy 4th: wnt 2nd 4 out: rdn 3 out: no ch w wnr* **11/2**	90
0-64	3	2 ½	**Saby (FR)**[27] [752] 7-11-11 99 ... RJohnson (P J Hobbs) *chsd ldr: mstke 9th: one pce fr 4 out* **2/1**[1]	93+
F066	4	3	**Riccarton**[20] [803] 12-10-0 74 oh6 ... RGreene (D C Turner) *hld up: outpcd appr 7th: styd on fr 2 out* **20/1**	64
0-4F	5	9	**Barnards Green (IRE)**[29] [725] 7-10-7 81 ...(v) AThornton (R H Alner) *led: hdd appr 9th: rdn appr 4 out: wknd 3 out* **5/1**[3]	62
1-00	6	5	**Donatus (IRE)**[5] [915] 9-10-13 90 ...(p) RYoung[(3)] (Miss K M George) *mstke 3rd: a bhd* **16/1**	66
F-50	7	12	**Johnny Grand**[55] [395] 8-10-0 74 oh2 ... JMogford (D W Lewis) *pushed along after 6th: a bhd* **8/1**	38
00P0	8	21	**Farceur (FR)**[27] [749] 6-9-12 75 ...(v) TJMalone[(3)] (M C Pipe) *hld up in tch: lost pl and rdn 5th: t.o fr 8th* **14/1**	18

4m 8.00s (2.50) **Going Correction** -0.10s/f (Good) **8** Ran SP% **116.0**
Speed ratings: **90,83,82,80,76 74,68,58** CSF £23.70 CT £47.94 TOTE £4.30: £1.70, £1.50, £1.20; EX 24.60.
Owner Graham Brown **Bred** P J Donovan **Trained** Newchapel, Surrey

FOCUS
A moderate handicap chase in which the field was decimated by withdrawals due to traffic problems. It produced a poor winning time.

NOTEBOOK
The Mighty Sparrow(IRE) had shown signs of a return to form here last month, but had disappointed over a longer trip on softer ground since. He clearly relished this ground and, once taking over at the middle fence on the far side, had the race in safe keeping. Surprisingly, this was his first success over fences, and may not be his last on this evidence. *(tchd 10-3)*
Knight's Emperor(IRE) is only recently returned from the best part of three years off, and is gradually finding some form, although he had no chance with the winner and was tiring near the end. *(op 9-2)*
Saby(FR) has a good record here, but has been struggling for form of late and was left behind down the far side before staying on again. This was his easiest assignment for some time and clearly he cannot be supported with any confidence at present. *(op 9-4)*
Riccarton was never in contention and merely stayed on past beaten horses. *(op 25-1 tchd 33-1)*
Barnards Green(IRE) had the visor re-applied and set the pace, but was soon in trouble once the winner went on. He has slipped back to a decent mark, but is never easy to catch right and his record of just one success from 23 outings tells it's own tale. *(op 6-1)*
Johnny Grand *Official explanation: jockey said gelding was never travelling (op 7-1 tchd 9-1)*

959 VICTOR GOORD 40TH BIRTHDAY H'CAP HURDLE (8 hdls) 2m 1f

2:30 (2:32) (Class 3) (0-115,107) 4-Y-0+ **£4,854** (£1,493; £746; £373)

Form				RPR
P-32	1		**Zarakash (IRE)**[8] [895] 5-10-9 90 ... APMcCoy (Jonjo O'Neill) *w ldr: led appr 5th: rdn and hdd appr 2 out: rallied last: sn led: drvn out* **9/4**[1]	93+
552	2	1	**Convent Girl (IRE)**[20] [804] 5-10-10 94 ... RYoung[(3)] (Mrs P N Dutfield) *hld up and bhd: hdwy appr 5th: led appr 2 out: sn rdn and carried hd high: hdd flat: nt qckn* **11/2**[3]	95+
0414	3	1	**Gemini Dancer**[12] [864] 6-11-9 104 ... JTizzard (C L Tizzard) *hld up: hdwy after 4th: rdn appr 2 out: kpt on flat* **5/2**[2]	104
0-40	4	11	**New Currency (USA)**[43] [571] 5-11-5 100 ...(t) TJMurphy (M C Pipe) *chsd ldrs: outpcd 3 out: rallied appr 2 out: sn ev ch imp* **7/1**	89
P	5	6	**Room To Room Gold (IRE)**[29] [726] 9-11-12 107 ... AThornton (R H Alner) *hld up in rr: hdwy appr 5th: wknd appr 2 out* **7/1**	90
26-0	6	1 ¼	**Hamadeenah**[51] [451] 7-11-5 105 ... MNicolls[(5)] (C J Down) *led tl appr 5th: rdn and wknd after 3 out* **11/1**	88+
PPU-	P		**Thrashing**[87] [4853] 10-11-5 100 ...(p) ATinkler (A E Jones) *a bhd: lost tch fr 4th: t.o whn p.u bef 2 out* **33/1**	—

3m 59.6s (-5.50) **Going Correction** -0.10s/f (Good)
WFA 4 from 5yo+ 2lb **7** Ran SP% **111.0**
Speed ratings: **108,107,107,101,99 98,—** CSF £14.19 CT £30.39 TOTE £2.60: £1.50, £2.70; EX 12.50.
Owner John P McManus **Bred** His Highness The Aga Khan's Studs S C **Trained** Cheltenham, Gloucs

FOCUS
Another moderate race affected by non-runners. It was run at a decent gallop and the first three came clear, suggesting the form is solid.

NOTEBOOK
Zarakash(IRE) looked like throwing in the towel when headed before the second last, but responded to his rider's urgings and rallied to get back in front on the run-in and win going away. He had looked reluctant on both his previous outings at Market Rasen, but his attitude could not be faulted this time and he clearly loves this racing on fast ground. While a rise in the weights will make life tough, he may have more to offer this summer. *(tchd 2-1)*
Convent Girl(IRE) , making her handicap debut, looked the winner when hitting the front full of running, but her stride shortened dramatically as soon as she was asked for maximum effort and she could do no more when Zarakash came back at her on the run-in. The awkward head carriage she displayed late on is definite cause for concern, but she has yet to truly prove she gets even this trip over timber.
Gemini Dancer , a good winner over course and distance last month but beaten off this mark over a longer trip since, was still travelling extremely well after jumping three out but then got caught flat-footed before staying on again to finish on the heels of the front pair. There was a suggestion that he failed to stay the two and a half miles at Worcester last time, but this effort suggests he does indeed need further. *(op 3-1)*
New Currency(USA) ran another lifeless race and continues to frustrate. *(op 8-1 tchd 9-1)*
Hamadeenah *Official explanation: jockey said mare had a breathing problem (op 10-1)*

960 NORTH DEVON CANCER CARE H'CAP CHASE (20 fncs) 3m 2f 110y

3:00 (3:01) (Class 3) (0-135,123) 5-Y-0+
£6,656 (£2,524; £1,262; £573; £286; £172)

Form				RPR
21-3	1		**The Pennys Dropped (IRE)**[17] [823] 8-10-10 107 ... APMcCoy (Jonjo O'Neill) *chsd ldr: led 4 out: rdn and styd on wl fr 2 out* **8/1**	123+
4-31	2	6	**Totheroadyouvgone**[32] [694] 11-11-2 113 ...(p) MFoley (A E Jones) *hld up in rr: rdn and rapid hdwy after 4 out: ev ch 2 out: one pce* **9/2**[3]	122+
-211	3	7	**Maidstone Monument (IRE)**[20] [805] 10-10-0 97 oh4 ... RJohnson (Mrs A M Thorpe) *led: mstke 12th (water): rdn and hdd 4 out: wknd appr 2 out* **7/2**[2]	98
5U-1	4	3 ½	**Dead-Eyed Dick (IRE)**[50] [461] 9-11-2 113 ... PJBrennan (Nick Williams) *hld up and bhd: hdwy on ins 12th: cl 3rd whn mstke 4 out: btn whn mstke 2 out (water)* **11/2**	112+
10-5	5	1	**Comanche War Paint (IRE)**[15] [842] 8-11-5 116 ... RWalsh (P F Nicholls) *chsd ldrs: reminders after 7th and 8th: rdn and wknd 15th* **10/3**[1]	113
60-P	6	dist	**French Executive (IRE)**[15] [842] 10-11-5 123 ...(t) MissCTizzard[(7)] (P F Nicholls) *hld up: mstke 2nd: rdn after 10th: lost tch 13th: t.o whn blnd bdly 4 out* **20/1**	—
-P24	P		**Montifault (FR)**[29] [727] 10-10-6 113 ...(bt[1]) LHeard[(10)] (P F Nicholls) *t.k.h: prom tl wknd appr 15th: t.o whn p.u bef 2 out* **10/1**	—
20/1	P		**Bertiebanoo (IRE)**[33] [688] 7-11-7 118 ... TJMurphy (M C Pipe) *hld up in tch: pushed along after 13th: wknd after 14th: t.o whn p.u bef 3 out* **6/1**	—

6m 35.4s (-8.00) **Going Correction** -0.10s/f (Good) **8** Ran SP% **118.1**
Speed ratings: **107,105,103,102,101 —,—,—** CSF £45.82 CT £151.67 TOTE £7.80: £2.10, £2.20, £1.30; EX 59.30.
Owner John P McManus **Bred** Niall Flynn **Trained** Cheltenham, Gloucs

FOCUS
A fair staying handicap for the time of year, run at a sound gallop and not surprisingly the field came home fairly strung out. The form looks reasonable.

NOTEBOOK
The Pennys Dropped(IRE) ◆ was handy throughout and finally showed his true colours over fences with a ready success under yet another typically strong ride from McCoy. This was by far his best display to date in this sphere, it was his most polished round of fencing to date, he can be rated value for further and looked well suited by this step back up in trip. He could well go on from this now. *(tchd 10-1)*
Totheroadyouvgone came from a long way off the pace to challenge in the straight, but the energy he used to make up that ground soon told and he was ultimately put in his place from two out. This was a decent effort off his new mark and, when dropping back to three miles, may be able to get his head back in front. *(tchd 4-1 and 5-1)*

Maidstone Monument(IRE) , raised 16lb for winning for winning over shorter at this track last time yet still racing from 4lb out of the handicap, ran a brave race over this longer trip yet proved a sitting duck approaching the turn for home. He can find easier opportunities off this new mark, will appreciate reverting to shorter and clearly remains in good heart at present. *(tchd 10-3)*

Dead-Eyed Dick(IRE) looked a big threat when joining the leaders down the back straight, but his effort ultimately proved short-lived and he was well held at the finish. He ideally needs an easier surface, but still has to prove he can mix it off this career-high mark. *(op 5-1)*

Comanche War Paint(IRE) ran in snatches throughout the first circuit and never posed a serious threat to the principals. This has to rate as disappointing and he has not looked totally happy in this sphere since winning over hurdles in the spring. *(op 4-1)*

Bertiebanoo(IRE) *Official explanation: jockey said gelding was never travelling (tchd 8-1)*

961 JEWSON MARES' ONLY NOVICES' HURDLE (SERIES QUALIFIER)
(10 hdls) **2m 6f**
3:30 (3:30) (Class 3) 4-Y-0+ **£4,690** (£1,443; £721; £360)

Form RPR
643- **1** **Leroy's Sister (FR)**84 [4914] 5-11-0 93 .... RWalsh 101+
(P F Nicholls) *a.p: led appr 2 out: clr whn pckd 2 out: easily* **13/8**2
55-3 **2** *24* **Tea's Maid**12 [854] 5-11-0 83 .... APMcCoy 76
(Mrs A M Thorpe) *chsd ldr: led 3 out: rdn and hdd appr 2 out: sn btn* **9/2**3
2126 **3** *19* **Shady Grey**6 [906] 7-11-6 100 .... NFehily 67+
(C J Mann) *led: rdn and hdd 3 out: sn wknd* **6/5**1
00P- **4** *13* **Trefoilalight**193 [3111] 6-10-9 64 .... CHonour(5) 44
(J D Frost) *hld up: hdwy 4th: rdn and wknd appr 7th* **100/1**
3-5F **5** *3* **Hunter Pudding**26 [758] 5-11-0 79 .... RGreene 41
(C L Popham) *hld up and bhd: j.rt 5th: hdwy after 6th: sn rdn: wknd 7th* **25/1**
/0F- **P** **Silkie Pekin**197 [2973] 6-10-11 .... RYoung(3) —
(N R Mitchell) *a in rr: t.o whn p.u and dismntd bef 3 out: lame* **66/1**
0P0- **P** **Kilmucklin Girl (IRE)**42 6-10-7 .... MrTJO'Brien(7) —
(A S T Holdsworth) *hld up in tch: lost pl and mstke 5th: bhd fr 6th: t.o whn p.u bef 3 out* **125/1**

5m 14.6s (-5.70) **Going Correction** -0.10s/f (Good)
WFA 4 from 5yo+ 3lb **7** Ran SP% **108.9**
Speed ratings: **106,97,90,85,84** —,— CSF £8.21 TOTE £2.70: £1.50, £2.20; EX 8.10.
Owner W A Bromley **Bred** S Peneau **Trained** Ditcheat, Somerset

FOCUS
A very poor event for the class, with the top-rated horse only rated 100. The winner was full value for her winning margin and she and the runner-up set the standard.

NOTEBOOK
Leroy's Sister(FR) finally put her best foot forward and opened her account over timber at the seventh attempt with a decisive success. She has been refreshed by a recent break, and while her jumping is still not particularly fluent, this was an improved effort and she could be a bit better than she showed last season. However, it should be noted this took little winning. *(op 2-1)*

Tea's Maid , badly treated on official figures, travelled smoothly for most of the race before being passed by the winner after the third-last flight. She had no answer to that rival's finishing kick but was still well clear of the third. A shorter trip might suit as she showed plenty of pace during the race. *(op 3-1)*

Shady Grey set a decent pace and had an uncontested lead for much of the early part of the race. However, she came under pressure well before the fourth-last flight and was easily disposed of when joined. The race may have come too quickly after her last outing, but even so it was still a weak effort from the only previous winner in the field. *(op 5-4 tchd 11-8)*

Silkie Pekin *Official explanation: jockey said mare was lame, but subsequently returned sound (op 50-1)*

962 MARSH BEGINNERS' CHASE (16 fncs) 2m 5f 110y
4:00 (4:00) (Class 3) 5-Y-0+ **£5,546** (£1,802; £970)

Form RPR
3-FF **1** **Fontanesi (IRE)**20 [803] 5-10-13 .... TJMurphy 127+
(M C Pipe) *hld up: hdwy appr 8th: led on bit whn j.lft and bmpd 12th: drew clr fr 3 out: easily* **11/8**2
/2-P **2** *7* **Unleash (USA)**37 [631] 6-11-0 .... RJohnson 118+
(P J Hobbs) *hld up: hdwy whn nt fluent 8th: ev ch 4 out: rdn and one pce fr 3 out* **5/4**1
F/ **3** *dist* **River Dante (IRE)**23 8-11-0 ....(t) MAFitzgerald 88
(L G Cottrell) *led: hdd and bmpd 12th: wknd 4 out* **16/1**
0-6P **P** **Infidel (IRE)**46 [511] 5-10-13 89 .... NFehily —
(C J Mann) *j. bdly rt: bhd fr 5th: t.o whn p.u after 9th* **12/1**
F **Penthouse Melody**37 7-10-7 .... RGreene —
(R J Hodges) *hld up in tch: lost pl after 7th: bhd fr 9th: poor 4th whn fell 2 out* **50/1**
P **Shanbally Lad (IRE)**121 6-10-7 .... DJacob(7) —
(D P Keane) *w ldr tl nt fluent 3rd: mstke 11th: wkng whn mstke 12th: t.o whn p.u bef 3 out* **10/1**3

5m 21.0s (-1.70) **Going Correction** -0.10s/f (Good)
WFA 5 from 6yo+ 1lb **6** Ran SP% **111.2**
Speed ratings: **99,96**,—,—,—,— — CSF £3.58 TOTE £2.10: £1.30, £1.40; EX 4.00.
Owner D A Johnson **Bred** John R Gaines Thoroughbreds L L C And Orpendal **Trained** Nicholashayne, Devon

FOCUS
Yet another race weakened by withdrawals. The time was modest for a race of its type and the market leaders dominated from a long way out.

NOTEBOOK
Fontanesi(IRE) , who looked beaten when coming to grief at the water jump here last month, did not appear to put a foot wrong this time and was always holding Unleash over the last three fences. He could well build on this now that he has completed and, as a County Hurdle winner, he is clearly an above-average performer for this time of year. However, with Unleash probably performing below his best over the larger obstacles just now, this probably took little winning and he will need to improve again if he is to truly make his mark over fences. *(op 7-4)*

Unleash(USA) , rated 7lb superior to his market rival over hurdles, finished distressed on his chasing debut at Worcester last month, but even though this was an improvement on that effort he was readily dismissed by the winner and it remains to be seen whether chasing is going to be his game. *(op 4-5)*

River Dante(IRE) , a faller in a maiden hunter chase in his only previous outing under Rules 15 months ago, was fit from the pointing field and made much of the running before finding himself outclassed by the big two over the last half-mile. What he actually achieved this time is debatable. *(op 20-1)*

Infidel(IRE) compromised any chance he might have had by jumping badly to his right several times and he was pulled up with a circuit left. *(op 12-1)*

Shanbally Lad(IRE) *Official explanation: jockey said gelding was unsuited by the good to firm (good in places) ground (op 12-1)*

963 NORTH DEVON CANCER CARE MAIDEN OPEN NATIONAL HUNT FLAT RACE 2m 1f
4:30 (4:31) (Class 6) 4-6-Y-0 **£1,848** (£528; £264)

Form RPR
1 **Twelve Paces** 4-11-0 .... TJMurphy 100+
(M C Pipe) *hld up: stdy hdwy after 4f: rdn and sltly outpcd 3f out: rallied to ld over 1f out: rdn out* **11/4**2
2 *2 ½* **Silver Sister** 4-10-2 .... CHonour(5) 87
(J D Frost) *plld hrd: led after 3f: rdn 3f out: hdd over 1f out: nt qckn* **6/1**
3 **3** *2* **Coeur D'Alene**15 [844] 4-11-0 .... AThornton 92
(Dr J R J Naylor) *prom: lost pl 4f out: rdn and rallied 3f out: one pce fnl 2f* **13/8**1
6 **4** *12* **Jazz City**36 [655] 5-11-2 .... APMcCoy 82
(J L Spearing) *hld up in rr: hdwy 5f out: ev ch over 3f out: sn rdn: wknd 2f out* **3/1**3
0 **5** *3 ½* **According To Plan (IRE)**15 [844] 5-10-11 .... DLaverty(5) 79
(A E Jones) *led 3f: chsd ldr: wknd over 3f out* **16/1**

4m 2.80s (-2.50) **Going Correction** -0.10s/f (Good)
WFA 4 from 5yo+ 2lb **5** Ran SP% **109.9**
Speed ratings: **101,99,98,93,91** CSF £18.21 TOTE £3.10: £1.90, £3.00; EX 16.20 Place 6 £31.59, Place 5 £21.89.
Owner D A Johnson **Bred** J W Haydon **Trained** Nicholashayne, Devon

FOCUS
An uncompetitive bumper run at a steady early pace which resulted in something of a sprint finish. The third sets the level and the winner can rate higher in due course.

NOTEBOOK
Twelve Paces ◆ , a half-brother to three winners including smart performer Crocadee, was very weak in the market and was clearly expected to need this debut. He still did the job well, despite not having the race run to suit and proving green under pressure, and looked better the further he went. This was his yard's first bumper winner of the current campaign, and this son of Double Trigger looks likely to appreciate further in time and should jump a fence in due course. *(op 2-1 tchd 3-1)*

Silver Sister , well backed on course, did not do a lot wrong on her debut although she did enjoy the run of the race. A sister to a couple of hurdles winners, she will do better when consenting to settle and should make her mark in time. *(op 8-1)*

Coeur D'Alene failed to build on his recent debut effort at Uttoxeter and has to rate as disappointing. He may do better in time, but has a deal to prove now. *(op 7-4)*

Jazz City came there to have every chance leaving the back straight, but could not match the speed of the principals in the closing stages. He looks in need of a stiffer test. *(op 11-4)*

According To Plan(IRE) , who finished over 20 lengths behind Coeur D'Alene at Uttoxeter on his debut, only made up a little of that deficit at this sharper track.

T/Plt: £12.60 to a £1 stake. Pool: £40,924.40. 2,352.80 winning tickets. T/Qpdt: £10.00 to a £1 stake. Pool: £2,432.20. 179.80 winning tickets. KH

969 - 970a (Foreign Racing) - See Raceform Interactive

901 UTTOXETER (L-H)
Wednesday, July 13

OFFICIAL GOING: Good (good to soft in back straight)
Wind: Light, against Weather: Hot and sunny

971 SUNWIN RENAULT MANSFIELD NOVICES' HURDLE (10 hdls) 2m
2:10 (2:10) (Class 4) 4-Y-0+ **£3,381** (£966; £483)

Form RPR
52- **1** **Catchthebug (IRE)**230 [2448] 6-10-12 .... APMcCoy 106+
(Jonjo O'Neill) *led 2nd: clr 5th: jnd 2 out: drvn out* **10/11**1
40- **2** *3 ½* **Pirouettes (IRE)**30 [4444] 5-10-5 .... JEMoore 93
(Ernst Oertel) *hld up: hdwy 6th: chsd wnr 3 out: ev ch next: rdn whn blnd last: styd on same pce* **7/1**3
50-0 **3** *dist* **Idle Journey (IRE)**7 [911] 4-10-10 104 ....(t) TScudamore 66
(M Scudamore) *hld up: hdwy to chse wnr 6th: wknd 3 out* **9/2**2
-PP0 **4** *12* **The Yellow Earl (IRE)**56 [415] 5-10-12 .... GLee 54
(J M Jefferson) *hit 2nd: a bhd* **33/1**
P0-0 **5** *23* **Tank (IRE)**32 [513] 4-10-10 .... JGoldstein 29
(Miss Sheena West) *led to 2nd: chsd wnr tl mstke and wknd 6th* **66/1**
0 **P** **River Iris**74 [138] 4-9-10 .... RSpate(7) —
(Lucinda Featherstone) *a bhd: t.o whn p.u bef 3 out* **50/1**
/P6- **F** **Ragasah**78 [4439] 7-10-5 .... MFoley —
(Ernst Oertel) *chsd ldrs: 4th and wkng whn fell 3 out* **25/1**
P **Opera Knight**48 5-10-5 ....(p) AScholes(7) —
(G H Yardley) *nt jump wl: a bhd: t.o whn p.u bef 3 out* **50/1**
P **Revolve**28 5-10-12 .... LAspell —
(O Sherwood) *mid-div: mstke 5th: sn wknd: t.o whn p.u bef 3 out* **10/1**
0-05 **P** **Dorans Lane**17 [838] 7-10-5 77 .... RThornton —
(W M Brisbourne) *chsd ldrs to 6th: t.o whn p.u bef 3 out* **14/1**
060- **P** **Royaltea**121 [4367] 4-9-12 87 .... LTreadwell(5) —
(J T Stimpson) *mid-div: sddle slipped 2nd: p.u after 4th* **14/1**

3m 52.8s (53.20) **Going Correction** -0.325s/f (Good)
WFA 4 from 5yo+ 2lb **11** Ran SP% **117.7**
Speed ratings: **106,104**,—,—,—,—,—,—,—,—,— — CSF £7.57 TOTE £1.80: £1.10, £2.10, £1.50; EX 8.10.
Owner John P McManus **Bred** B Kennedy **Trained** Cheltenham, Gloucs

FOCUS
A modest novices' hurdle, which lost any strength in depth due to the three withdrawals and, although the winner is value for further, the form is ordinary.

NOTEBOOK
Catchthebug(IRE) , last seen finishing runner-up over course and distance 230 days previously, duly went one better with a ready display and got off the mark over timber at the third time of asking. He enjoyed the rain-softened ground, shaped as though he will get further and, while he could be placed to score again under a penalty this summer, his long-term future looks to lie very much with the Handicapper. *(op 11-10 tchd 6-5 in places)*

Pirouettes(IRE) gradually eased into contention to join the leader at the top of the straight but, while she briefly hit the front, always looked like playing second fiddle to the winner and was eventually well held. This was much her best display to date over hurdles, she jumped well in the main and it will be no surprise to see her placed to advantage during the summer now she is eligible for handicaps.

Idle Journey(IRE) failed to really build on his recent effort at Worcester and was put in his place a long way from the finish. He is not without hope, but has yet to truly prove he stays this trip. *(op 4-1)*

The Yellow Earl(IRE) was never in contention and looks merely plating class.

Royaltea *Official explanation: jockey said saddle slipped*

972 SUNWIN RENAULT DERBY BEGINNERS' CHASE (15 fncs) 2m 4f
2:40 (2:40) (Class 4) 5-Y-O+ **£4,715** (£1,451; £725; £362)

Form				RPR
0-22	**1**		**Avitta (IRE)**[35] 688 6-10-5 109 SThomas (Miss Venetia Williams) *a.p: chsd ldr 3rd: led 5th to 8th: led 9th: mstke and lft clr 3 out: eased flat* **11/10**[1]	99+
52-P	**2**	*10*	**Mylo**[60] 353 7-10-12 (p) APMcCoy (Jonjo O'Neill) *hld up: hdwy 7th: styd on same pce fr 4 out: lft mod 2nd next* **2/1**[2]	89
30-P	**3**	*18*	**Rich Song (IRE)**[39] 631 7-10-12 88 DElsworth (Mrs S J Smith) *prom to 9th: lft remote 3rd 3 out* **6/1**[3]	71
	4	*8*	**Lost Treasure (IRE)**[44] 8-10-12 JMogford (Mrs M Evans) *chsd ldr to 3rd: remained handy tl wknd 9th* **25/1**	63
0P0	**5**	*20*	**Major Reno (IRE)**[36] 674 8-10-7 54 MNicolls[(5)] (R C Harper) *rr 3rd: rdn 6th: wknd appr 9th* **50/1**	43
PP05	**U**		**Tails I Win**[8] 902 6-10-9 62 ACCoyle[(3)] (Miss C J E Caroe) *led to 5th: led 8th to next: cl 2nd and rdn whn blnd and uns rdr 3 out* **14/1**	85+

5m 5.50s (-15.10) **Going Correction** -0.60s/f (Firm) **6** Ran SP% **107.7**
Speed ratings: **106,102,94,91,83** — CSF £3.45 TOTE £1.70: £1.10, £1.90; EX 3.30.
Owner P A Deal, A Hirschfeld & M Graham **Bred** Sheikh Mohammed Bin Rashid Al Maktoum **Trained** Kings Caple, H'fords

FOCUS
An ordinary beginners' chase that saw the field finish strung out behind the easy winner, who is rated value for nearly double the official margin.

NOTEBOOK
Avitta(IRE) ◆ deservedly opened her account over fences at the third attempt with a facile success. Always handily placed, she did not need to be fully extended to settle the issue turning for home and can be rated value for further then her already wide-winning margin. She could be the type to run up a sequence in novice company during the summer, with her mares' allowance sure to come in handy. *(op 5-4 tchd 11-8 in places)*
Mylo , with first-time cheekpieces replacing blinkers for this chase debut, jumped well enough yet was never a serious threat to the winner. While he may do better with further experience over fences, and probably wants further, he is never one to place any faith in. *(op 13-8)*
Rich Song(IRE) was made to look very one paced approaching the final bend and merely plugged on at his own pace in the straight. He at least completed this time, will be better suited by a step back up in trip and should be of more interest when going handicapping. *(op 13-2 tchd 11-2)*
Tails I Win was in the process of running a personal best prior to unseating three out, and while she certainly would not have won, she would have been placed with a clear round.

973 GORDON LAMB LTD CONDITIONAL JOCKEYS' (S) H'CAP HURDLE (10 hdls) 2m
3:10 (3:10) (Class 5) (0-95,93) 4-Y-O+ **£2,317** (£662; £331)

Form				RPR
5-04	**1**		**Margarets Wish**[30] 613 5-10-10 77 ONelmes (T Wall) *hld up: hdwy 5th: led next: mstke 2 out: styd on wl* **14/1**	84+
05-2	**2**	*5*	**Captain Cloudy**[14] 863 5-11-3 84 DCrosse (D Flood) *hld up: hdwy 3 out: nt rch wnr* **7/1**[3]	84
0/15	**3**	*½*	**Reverse Swing**[28] 760 8-10-3 78 PMerrigan[(8)] (Mrs H Dalton) *hld up in tch: chsd wnr 3 out: rdn next: styng on same pce whn mstke last* **6/1**[1]	77
-200	**4**	*1*	**Jack Durrance (IRE)**[14] 863 5-10-0 72 KBurke[(5)] (G A Ham) *hld up: hdwy after 5th: rdn 3 out: styd on same pce appr last* **20/1**	71+
-403	**5**	*5*	**Pure Brief (IRE)**[35] 681 8-10-0 74 (b) TBurrows[(7)] (J Mackie) *chsd ldr to 3 out: sn rdn: wknd last* **6/1**[1]	67
355P	**6**	*1¼*	**Rose Of York (IRE)**[8] 905 5-10-6 73 (t) DLaverty (Mrs A M Thorpe) *prom: rdn after 4 out: wknd appr 2 out* **7/1**[3]	65
21-0	**7**	*9*	**Luminoso**[52] 458 13-11-7 93 AHawkins[(5)] (J D J Davies) *chsd ldrs to appr 6th* **12/1**	76
2-0P	**8**	*3*	**Love Triangle (IRE)**[10] 895 4-11-6 92 (t) SWalsh[(3)] (N B King) *a in rr* **50/1**	70
P0-0	**9**	*12*	**Little Villain (IRE)**[79] 25 7-10-4 71 (p) JamesDavies (T Wall) *chsd ldrs: ev ch 4 out: wknd bef next* **33/1**	39
F400	**10**	*dist*	**Nutley Queen (IRE)**[2] 822 6-10-0 67 oh8 (t) MNicolls (M Appleby) *a bhd* **25/1**	—
-042	**P**		**Princess Pea**[28] 758 5-10-9 79 TJMalone[(3)] (M C Pipe) *prom tl p.u after 4th: lame* **13/2**[2]	—
0-00	**P**		**Gebora (FR)**[17] 839 6-11-2 83 AO'Keeffe (B R Foster) *led: rdn and hdd 6th: wknd qckly and p.u bef next* **50/1**	—
05-6	**U**		**Saif Sareea**[8] 903 5-11-7 93 DCosgrave[(5)] (A L Forbes) *hld up: hdwy 5th: cl up whn mstke and uns rdr next* **9/1**	—
00P-	**P**		**Dinarelli (FR)**[82] 4962 6-11-1 90 (t) AGlassonbury[(8)] (M C Pipe) *a in rr: bhd whn hmpd bnd after 4th: t.o whn p.u bef 6th* **12/1**	—

3m 56.8s (-3.60) **Going Correction** -0.325s/f (Good)
WFA 4 from 5yo+ 2lb **14** Ran SP% **114.4**
Speed ratings: **96,93,93,92,90 89,85,83,77,—** —,—,—,— CSF £98.86 CT £653.85 TOTE £12.50: £3.20, £2.20, £2.80; EX 70.50.The winner was bought in for 5,200gns. Captain Cloudy was claimed by Miss Sheena West for £6,000. Saif Sareea was claimed by Mr S. L. Walker for £6,000.
Owner A H Bennett **Bred** A H Bennett **Trained** Harton, Shropshire

FOCUS
This was a weak, yet fairly competitive selling handicap, run at a fair gallop and the form makes sense rated through the placed horses.

NOTEBOOK
Margarets Wish , reverting to hurdles, relished this drop down in class and got back to winning ways with a dogged success. Once she hit the front full of running on the final bend she never really looked like being caught, despite some less then fluent jumps over the final two flights. She had dropped back to her last winning mark for this, and while her confidence will have been boosted, she is not one to lump on for a follow-up bid. *(op 16-1)*
Captain Cloudy , making his handicap debut, took too long to find his full stride from off the pace and was staying on all too late in the day. He has a race in him at this level, but looks in need of a stiffer test. *(op 13-2)*
Reverse Swing lacked the necessary change of gears when it mattered, but stuck to her task well under pressure and turned in an improved effort. She should continue to pay her way at this level during the summer. *(op 9-2)*
Jack Durrance(IRE) found less then looked likely when push came to shove and was ultimately well held. He is hard to predict and remains winless over timber from nine outings.
Pure Brief(IRE) ran to his recent level and shows no real sign of ending his long losing run. *(op 5-1)*
Luminoso *Official explanation: trainer said gelding's blood was wrong (op 20-1)*
Princess Pea *Official explanation: vet said mare pulled up lame (op 7-1)*

974 SUNWIN RENAULT NOTTINGHAM H'CAP HURDLE (14 hdls) 3m
3:40 (3:40) (Class 3) (0-120,110) 4-Y-O+ **£6,097** (£1,876; £938; £469)

Form				RPR
5-13	**1**		**Downing Street (IRE)**[35] 680 4-11-7 109 (b) AO'Keeffe (Jennie Candlish) *hld up: hdwy 8th: chsd ldr and hit 2 out: led last: rdn out* **12/1**	113+
30-1	**2**	*8*	**September Moon**[14] 859 7-11-2 100 RJohnson (Mrs A M Thorpe) *chsd ldrs tl led 4 out: rdn and hdd last: no ex flat* **7/2**[2]	101+
1/00	**3**	*11*	**Tomenoso**[14] 864 7-11-12 110 DElsworth (Mrs S J Smith) *led: hit 6th: hung rt bnd after next: hdd 4 out: rdn next: wknd last* **12/1**	103+
2630	**4**	*3½*	**Ungaretti (GER)**[8] 906 8-10-12 96 DRDennis (Ian Williams) *chsd ldr to 4 out: wknd bef next* **20/1**	81
2024	**5**	*5*	**Pilca (FR)**[17] 841 5-11-2 100 JPMcNamara (R M Stronge) *mid-div: hdwy 8th: wknd 3 out* **14/1**	80
00-0	**6**	*nk*	**Weston Rock**[10] 895 6-11-1 99 JimCrowley (T D Walford) *hld up: rdn 8th: n.d* **25/1**	78
/41-	**7**	*3*	**Around Before (IRE)**[395] 734 8-11-3 101 (t) APMcCoy (Jonjo O'Neill) *prom tl rdn and wknd appr 3 out* **5/2**[1]	77
0-P2	**8**	*20*	**Wild Spice (IRE)**[8] 906 10-11-12 110 SThomas (Miss Venetia Williams) *mid-div: rdn 5th: wknd after next* **7/1**[3]	66
40P-	**9**	*15*	**Pass Me By**[109] 4549 6-11-12 110 RWalford (T D Walford) *a in rr: lost tch 8th* **25/1**	51
-300	**10**	*shd*	**Wild Tempo (FR)**[37] 665 10-10-12 96 (t) TJMurphy (M C Pipe) *hld up: reminders 3rd: effrt after 8th: sn wknd* **8/1**	37
53F-	**P**		**Canon Barney (IRE)**[127] 4239 10-11-12 110 (b[1]) JEMoore (Jonjo O'Neill) *hld up: hdwy and mstke 7th: sn rdn and wknd: t.o whn p.u bef 2 out: lame* **20/1**	—

6m 2.30s (-2.70) **Going Correction** -0.325s/f (Good)
WFA 4 from 5yo+ 4lb **11** Ran SP% **113.7**
Speed ratings: **91,88,84,83,81 81,80,74,69,69** — CSF £50.15 CT £518.09 TOTE £11.50: £3.30, £2.00, £4.50; EX 43.10 Trifecta £137.20 Pool: £464.04 - 2.40 winning units.
Owner Reuben Fielding **Bred** M Stewkesbury And The Luna Wells Syndicate **Trained** Basford Green, Staffs

FOCUS
A modest event for the grade, but the winner looks progressive. It was a slow time for the class, but the field again came home fairly strung out at the finish.

NOTEBOOK
Downing Street(IRE) ◆ dug deep to get on top over the final flight and returned to winning ways with a comfortable success on his handicap debut. While he again did not appear the easiest of rides, he relished this step up to three miles and was full value for his winning margin. Still only four, he is progressing nicely over hurdles and looks one to follow.
September Moon , raised 5lb for winning on her seasonal bow at Perth, did nothing wrong in defeat and only gave way on the run-in. While the Handicapper may have her in his sights at present, she was clear of the rest and could find another race at this level. *(op 10-3)*
Tomenoso , stepping up in trip, would have finished closer but for attempting to run out at the bend on the far side near the racecourse stables, but he deserves credit for sticking to his task once headed and was not disgraced off top weight. He may just need to drop back in trip to be seen at his best, however.
Ungaretti(GER) was again not totally disgraced and ran to his recent level. He can find easier opportunities, but is never one to place any real faith in.
Pilca(FR) , taking another step up in trip, again travelled well through his race only to find less than looked likely when push came to shove. He remains winless since switching from France, but may be worth chancing with a more prominent ride back over a shorter trip and he may just need softer ground. *(op 16-1)*
Around Before(IRE) ran very much as though this seasonal debut was needed and can be given another chance back on a faster surface. *(tchd 11-4)*
Canon Barney(IRE) *Official explanation: vet said gelding pulled up lame (op 25-1)*

975 EZRA SUGDEN H'CAP CHASE (16 fncs) 2m 5f
4:10 (4:10) (Class 4) (0-110,107) 5-Y-O+ **£5,174** (£1,592; £796; £398)

Form				RPR
-003	**1**		**Flahive's First**[31] 725 11-10-10 96 LStephens[(5)] (D Burchell) *hld up in tch: led 3 out: styd on wl* **9/1**	109+
/1-1	**2**	*9*	**Ross Comm**[14] 865 9-11-8 103 DElsworth (Mrs S J Smith) *chsd ldrs: hit 7th: led 4 out: rdn and hdd next: wknd last* **2/1**[1]	109+
U0-P	**3**	*1*	**Wrens Island (IRE)**[14] 865 11-10-0 81 WHutchinson (R Dickin) *prom: chsd ldr 5 out: ev ch 3 out: styd on same pce fr next* **16/1**	83
36-1	**4**	*½*	**Calon Lan (IRE)**[31] 725 14-10-6 94 SWalsh[(7)] (B J Llewellyn) *hld up: hit 5th: bhd next: hit 5 out: hdwy next: rdn 3 out: styd on same pce fr next* **13/2**[3]	98+
P-33	**5**	*11*	**Navarone**[21] 815 11-11-10 105 APMcCoy (Ian Williams) *led: rdn and hdd 4 out: ev ch next: wknd 2 out* **2/1**[1]	99+
-655	**6**	*5*	**Search And Destroy (USA)**[21] 815 7-11-12 107 (b) JMMaguire (T R George) *chsd ldr to 5 out: wknd bef next* **6/1**[2]	93

5m 14.7s (-12.80) **Going Correction** -0.60s/f (Firm) **6** Ran SP% **110.2**
Speed ratings: **100,96,96,96,91 89** CSF £27.33 CT £267.51 TOTE £11.60: £4.30, £1.50; EX 38.30.
Owner Don Gould **Bred** Flahive Brick Work Ltd **Trained** Briery Hill, Blaenau Gwent

FOCUS
A modest handicap chase in which five of the six runners were still in with a shout three from home. The second and fourth were close to their marks and the form should work out well enough.

NOTEBOOK
Flahive's First put his best foot forward under pressure and came right away in the closing stages to record his first success away from Cartmel for more than six years. Turning around Stratford form with Calon Lan, he had dropped down to a winning mark for this and was given a decent ride by Stephens. *Official explanation: trainer had no explanation for the improved form shown (op 10-1)*
Ross Commsurvived an error at the last fence with a circuit to run. He showed narrowly ahead at the fourth last but was soon made to look pedestrian, the 13lb rise for his recent Worcester victory appearing to tell. *(op 11-8)*
Wrens Island(IRE)was unable to adopt his favoured front-running role, but he did not seem to mind and this was an improvement on his recent efforts, a drop in the weights having helped. *(op 20-1)*
Calon Lan(IRE) had finished a long way ahead of today's winner when scoring at Stratford last time. He dropped to the rear with more than a circuit to run, but rallied to have a chance going to the third last only to clout that obstacle. Held from that point, he is currently rated higher than he has been for three years and is surely not getting better at his age. *(op 5-1)*
Navaronedropped to the rear with more than a circuit to run, but rallied to have a chance going to the third last only to clout that obstacle. Held from that point, he is currently rated higher than he has been for three years and is surely not getting better at his age.*Official explanation: jockey said gelding had a breathing problem (op 3-1)*
Search And Destroy(USA)continues to fall in the weights but was the first beaten. *(op 7-1)*

976 RENAULT VANS THAT RUN AND RUN AND RUN MAIDEN HURDLE (12 hdls) 2m 4f 110y
4:40 (4:40) (Class 4) 4-Y-0+ £3,465 (£990; £495)

Form RPR

F223 **1** **Festive Chimes (IRE)**[10] [892] 4-9-13 100 .... SWalsh(7) 98+
(N B King) *hld up and bhd: hdwy to chse ldr 3 out: led next: rdn out* **9/4**[2]

P-26 **2** *6* **Rifleman (IRE)**[50] [488] 5-11-2 106 .... (v) APMcCoy 102+
(P Bowen) *a.p: jnd ldr 4 out: led and clr next: hdd 2 out: no ex last* **11/8**[1]

50-0 **3** *30* **Moscow Executive**[17] [843] 7-10-9 .... ATinkler 65
(W M Brisbourne) *hld up: hdwy and hit 6th: rdn and wknd appr 3 out* **16/1**

00-0 **4** *9* **It's Gwendolene**[7] [912] 5-10-9 .... JGoldstein 56
(Miss Sheena West) *prom: rdn 6th: wknd after next* **50/1**

53 **5** *dist* **Ponchatrain (IRE)**[17] [843] 5-11-2 .... WMarston —
(D J Wintle) *prom: jnd ldr 5th: led next: hdd & wknd 3 out* **9/2**[3]

6 *dist* **Grande Cascade** 4-9-13 .... AScholes(7) —
(Lucinda Featherstone) *hld up: a bhd: lost tch 6th* **50/1**

7 *27* **Girlie Power** 8-10-4 .... MNicolls(5) —
(P W Hiatt) *chsd ldrs tl wknd after 6th* **20/1**

P-30 **F** **Tass Heel (IRE)**[31] [724] 6-11-2 88 .... RJohnson —
(B J Llewellyn) *led tl fell 4th* **9/1**

P05P **P** **La Gitana**[20] [760] 5-10-9 67 .... JMMaguire —
(A Sadik) *chsd ldr tl lft in ld 4th: hdd 6th: wknd after next: t.o whn p.u bef 2 out* **50/1**

5m 8.10s (-4.00) **Going Correction** -0.325s/f (Good)
WFA 4 from 5yo+ 3lb **9** Ran SP% **117.6**
Speed ratings: **94,91,80,76,—** —,—,—,— CSF £5.92 TOTE £3.40: £1.10, £1.30, £4.20; EX 8.70 Place 6 £19.99, Place 5 £17.32.
Owner Nolan Catterwell & P Persse **Bred** Burton Agnes Stud Co Ltd **Trained** Newmarket, Suffolk

FOCUS
Another moderate event, weakened by the withdrawal of debutant Star Member, that produced a poor winning time for the grade and the form may prove unreliable.

NOTEBOOK
Festive Chimes(IRE) deservedly got off the mark at the eighth attempt over hurdles, under well-judged ride from Walsh. Full value for her winning margin, she is a model of consistency, is still only four and could well progress on this during the summer now she has finally got her head in front. *(op 11-4 tchd 3-1)*
Rifleman(IRE) looked to be set for his first success when going clear at the top of the home straight, but he was clearly running on empty approaching two out, as he found just the same pace when challenged by the winner. It has to be considered bitterly disappointing that remains winless from ten outings over timber, and while it may well be that he is happier over shorter, he remains one to avoid nevertheless. *(op 6-5 tchd 6-4)*
Moscow Executive simply plugged on best of the rest to finish a never-dangerous third. She will no doubt fare better when qualified for handicaps. *(op 14-1)*
Ponchatrain(IRE) dropped out tamely when headed at the top of the straight and disappointed. This former winning pointer probably needs further.
T/Jkpt: £143,910.20 to a £1 stake. Pool: £202,690.50. 1.00 winning ticket. T/Plt: £14.90 to a £1 stake. Pool: £43,396.95. 2,113.55 winning tickets. T/Qpdt: £12.70 to a £1 stake. Pool: £1,804.30. 104.40 winning tickets. CR

911 WORCESTER (L-H)
Wednesday, July 13

OFFICIAL GOING: Good to firm (firm in places)
The watered ground had dried out during a hot day.
Wind: almost nil Weather: fine and warm

977 APOLLO SECURITY MAIDEN HURDLE (12 hdls) 3m
6:35 (6:40) (Class 4) 4-Y-0+ £2,639 (£754; £377)

Form RPR

1 **Charango Star**[81] 7-11-2 .... RJohnson 104
(W K Goldsworthy) *hld up: hdwy after 6th: led after 9th: sn rdn: edgd lft flat: all out* **7/1**

22 **2** *½* **Getoutwhenyoucan (IRE)**[17] [843] 5-11-2 .... TJMurphy 103
(M C Pipe) *a.p: ev ch whn bmpd flat: hrd rdn: nt qckn* **2/1**[2]

6-23 **3** *3* **Kimono Royal (FR)**[48] [521] 7-11-2 99 .... RThornton 100
(A King) *hld up: sn in tch: rdn 2 out: one pce flat* **15/8**[1]

3 **4** *11* **Silver Sparrow (IRE)**[19] [828] 4-10-12 .... JEMoore 87+
(P Bowen) *hld up and bhd: hdwy 7th: rdn appr 2 out: wknd appr last* **20/1**

00F **5** *12* **Thiseldo Us**[14] [861] 10-11-2 .... SCurran 77
(M B Shears) *prom: lost pl after 6th: no hdwy whn hit 3 out* **100/1**

5U4- **6** *dist* **Ashfield Orchestra (IRE)**[143] [3979] 9-10-2 .... MissIsabelTompsett(7) —
(M Brown) *led tl after 3rd: prom tl wknd appr 8th: t.o* **33/1**

5 **7** *dist* **Porto (IRE)**[7] [912] 10-11-2 .... JTizzard —
(B J M Ryall) *prom: led after 3rd tl after 9th: wknd qckly 3 out: t.o* **25/1**

44-6 **8** *24* **Moorlands Return**[22] [801] 6-11-2 92 .... (p) ChristianWilliams —
(Evan Williams) *bhd fr 3rd: t.o* **9/2**[3]

1/06 **U** **Cap Classique**[21] [811] 6-10-9 .... PMerrigan(7) —
(Mrs H Dalton) *hld up: hdwy appr 8th: 6th and in tch whn blnd and uns rdr 9th* **40/1**

0-P0 **P** **Bosworth Boy**[29] [749] 7-11-2 67 .... WHutchinson —
(Mrs H Sweeting) *hld up in mid-div: mstke 3rd: rdn after 4th: bhd whn mstkes 7th and 8th: t.o whn p.u bef 9th* **100/1**

5m 50.2s (1.00) **Going Correction** -0.05s/f (Good)
WFA 4 from 5yo+ 4lb **10** Ran SP% **114.8**
Speed ratings: **96,95,94,91,87** —,—,—,—,— CSF £20.66 TOTE £8.30: £2.10, £1.10, £1.10; EX 23.40.
Owner Cliff Johnson **Bred** Mrs Joanna Cross **Trained** Yerbeston, Pembrokes

FOCUS
A modest maiden with the finish fought out by a couple of winning pointers. The placed horses were close to their marks and the form looks pretty solid.

NOTEBOOK
Charango Star was pretty consistent between the flags but never really lived up to the promise of his maiden point win. His trainer thinks he will be better for the experience of this successful debut under Rules. *(op 9-1 tchd 6-1)*
Getoutwhenyoucan(IRE) had the longer trip to help this time but yet again he found one just too good. *(op 15-8 tchd 5-2)*
Kimono Royal(FR), another stepping up to three miles, lacked the required turn of foot when the chips were really down. *(op 7-4 tchd 13-8 and 2-1)*
Silver Sparrow(IRE) did not get home after being given a test of stamina on this graduation from a bumper. *(op 18-1 tchd 25-1)*

978 LADBROKESCASINO.COM (S) H'CAP HURDLE (10 hdls) 2m 4f
7:05 (7:10) (Class 5) (0-90,90) 4-Y-0+ £2,702 (£772; £386)

Form RPR

6004 **1** **Ashgan (IRE)**[7] [916] 12-10-4 73 .... TJPhelan(5) 80+
(Dr P Pritchard) *a.p: led appr 6th: rdn clr after 3 out: drvn out* **33/1**

0-P6 **2** *2* **Wally Wonder (IRE)**[24] [781] 7-11-5 83 .... (b) GLee 87
(R Bastiman) *led tl after 4th: ev ch after 7th: rdn whn j.lft last: no ex* **10/1**

UP6 **3** *3* **Nimvara (IRE)**[17] [839] 9-10-8 72 .... ChristianWilliams 73
(Evan Williams) *hld up and bhd: hdwy whn mstke 7th: rdn and outpcd appr 2 out: styd on flat: fin lame* **12/1**

0244 **4** *4* **Dunkerron**[28] [760] 8-10-9 80 .... SWalsh(7) 77
(J Joseph) *prom: led after 4th tl appr 6th: wknd 2 out* **10/1**

44-2 **5** *1½* **Indian Beat**[29] [749] 8-11-2 80 .... TJMurphy 77+
(C L Popham) *hld up towards rr: hdwy appr 6th: j.rt 3 out: wknd last: fin lame* **6/1**[2]

0-P5 **6** *7* **River Of Fire**[35] [687] 7-10-4 68 .... (v) JamesDavies 57
(C N Kellett) *hld up in mid-div: hdwy after 6th: hrd rdn after 7th: wknd 3 out* **25/1**

-003 **7** *4* **Nice Baby (FR)**[29] [749] 4-10-11 88 .... AGlassonbury(10) 70
(M C Pipe) *hld up and bhd: hmpd 1st: sme hdwy appr 3 out: n.d* **8/1**[3]

5B00 **8** *½* **Saxe-Coburg (IRE)**[31] [724] 8-10-2 73 .... (t) MrTJO'Brien(7) 57
(K G Wingrove) *hld up in tch: wknd 7th* **12/1**

3-50 **9** *½* **Hardi De Chalamont (FR)**[17] [839] 10-11-12 90 .... (v) AO'Keeffe 74
(Jennie Candlish) *hld up and bhd: hdwy appr 7th: wnt lft and wknd appr 2 out* **25/1**

3600 **10** *9* **Luristan (IRE)**[28] [760] 5-10-7 71 .... ATinkler 46
(S T Lewis) *prom tl wknd 7th* **100/1**

0534 **11** *nk* **Seemore Sunshine**[19] [822] 8-10-7 76 .... CHonour(5) 50
(M J Gingell) *prom tl rdn and wknd qckly after 7th* **12/1**

U000 **12** *¾* **Court Award (IRE)**[14] [863] 8-10-5 69 .... (b[1]) JTizzard 42
(B G Powell) *t.k.h: a bhd* **33/1**

3-PP **13** *19* **Khaladjistan (IRE)**[7] [916] 7-11-7 85 .... (tp) NFehily 39
(Miss S J Wilton) *mid-div: reminders after 4th: rdn appr 7th: sn bhd* **25/1**

00/P **14** *8* **Wotan (IRE)**[8] [903] 7-10-6 70 .... TDoyle 16
(R Curtis) *t.k.h in tch: lost pl after 4th: sn bhd* **50/1**

6-00 **15** *dist* **Impero**[29] [749] 7-10-5 69 .... (v) JGoldstein —
(G F Bridgwater) *prom: rdn after 4th: wknd appr 6th: t.o* **66/1**

5 **F** **Case Equal (IRE)**[7] [913] 5-11-8 86 .... (b[1]) APMcCoy —
(Jonjo O'Neill) *fell 1st* **10/3**[1]

0-0P **P** **Fairtoto**[32] 9-11-12 90 .... (b) JMogford —
(Mrs N S Evans) *a bhd: t.o 5th: p.u bef 3 out* **50/1**

F-10 **P** **River Amora (IRE)**[36] [674] 10-10-5 69 .... (p) JEMoore —
(J J Best) *mid-div: stmbld 5th: p.u bef 6th* **16/1**

20-6 **P** **Serious Position (IRE)**[74] [129] 10-11-12 90 .... LAspell —
(F Jordan) *hld up in tch: p.u lame after 5th* **16/1**

4m 46.9s (-1.10) **Going Correction** -0.05s/f (Good)
WFA 4 from 5yo+ 3lb **19** Ran SP% **125.3**
Speed ratings: **100,99,98,96,95 93,91,91,91,87 87,86,79,76,—** —,—,—,— CSF £321.79 CT £4196.94 TOTE £29.20: £3.70, £2.90, £3.00, £1.90; EX 362.00.There was no bid for the winner. Case Equal (no.4) was claimed by C. E. Handford for £6,000.
Owner Timber Pond Racing Club **Bred** C O'Brennan **Trained** Purton, Gloucs

FOCUS
Quantity rather than quality in this seller which took even less winning after the favourite crashed out at the first. However, those immediately behind the winner were close to their marks and the form looks pretty solid at a low level.

NOTEBOOK
Ashgan(IRE), reverting back to hurdes, was no less than 40lb lower than when he registered his last victory under Rules which came over course and distance exactly three years ago.
Wally Wonder(IRE), whose bumper win at Downpatrick came on pretty fast ground, confirmed he does not mind hearing his feet rattle. *(op 12-1)*
Nimvara(IRE) showed why connections have been trying her over further. *Official explanation: vet said mare finished lame (op 10-1)*
Dunkerron should not have been inconvenienced by a return to a longer trip. *(op 11-1 tchd 9-1)*
Indian Beat could have been feeling the ground when jumping right-handed at the third last and eventually finished lame. *Official explanation: jockey said gelding finished lame (op 7-1 tchd 5-1)*
Serious Position(IRE) *Official explanation: jockey said gelding was lame (op 12-1)*

979 BMS CONTRACTS LTD NOVICES' H'CAP CHASE (12 fncs) 2m
7:35 (7:42) (Class 4) (0-95,86) 5-Y-0+ £3,785 (£1,164; £582; £291)

Form RPR

2-P3 **1** **Nazimabad (IRE)**[34] [692] 6-11-0 74 .... (t) ChristianWilliams 99+
(Evan Williams) *j.w: mde all: clr appr 4th: unchal* **3/1**[2]

-331 **2** *11* **Percipient**[28] [758] 7-10-12 72 .... (v) TDoyle 80
(D R Gandolfo) *a.p: chsd wnr fr 5th: no imp fr 4 out* **11/4**[1]

/500 **3** *15* **Optimism (FR)**[21] [811] 7-11-5 79 .... AThornton 76+
(R H Alner) *hld up in mid-div: hmpd 3rd: no real prog fr 4 out* **16/1**

-PFU **4** *6* **Miss Muscat**[8] [902] 5-10-8 68 .... JPByrne 58+
(Evan Williams) *hld up and bhd: mstke 6th: sme hdwy 4 out: 4th and no ch whn mstke last* **20/1**

06-0 **5** *19* **Combined Venture (IRE)**[8] [902] 9-10-6 69 .... (t) DCrosse(3) 37
(P O'Connor) *chsd wnr to 5th: wknd appr 7th* **33/1**

0-0P **6** *17* **The Honey Guide**[13] [874] 9-10-4 64 .... NPMulholland 15
(Mrs L B Normile) *hld up in tch: 3rd and wkng whn blnd 4 out* **14/1**

/44- **7** *10* **Dark Island**[274] [1693] 10-9-11 64 .... CMStudd(7) 5
(Mary Meek) *prom tl wknd appr 5th: t.o* **66/1**

P/01 **7** *dht* **Optimistic Harry**[8] [902] 6-11-2 76 7ex .... PJBrennan 17
(R Ford) *j.rt: a bhd: blnd bdly 8th: sn t.o* **7/2**[3]

6 **F** **On The Forty**[8] [902] 8-11-9 83 .... (b[1]) APMcCoy —
(Jonjo O'Neill) *hld up in tch: fell 3rd* **11/1**

444- **P** **Karakum**[184] [3300] 6-11-3 84 .... SWalsh(7) —
(A J Chamberlain) *hld up and bhd: p.u bef 4th* **33/1**

-P50 **U** **Ela Figura**[7] [914] 5-10-9 72 .... (t) RYoung(3) —
(M Appleby) *bhd: sltly hmpd 5th: blnd and uns rdr 10th* **50/1**

F-5F **P** **Husky (POL)**[34] [692] 7-11-3 77 .... JamesDavies —
(B G Powell) *hld up and bhd: t.o whn p.u after 8th: bbv* **16/1**

-056 **P** **Ice And Fire**[7] [914] 6-11-12 86 .... RThornton —
(J T Stimpson) *mid-div: j.rt and mstke 5th: t.o whn p.u bef 7th* **40/1**

3m 49.4s (-4.20) **Going Correction** -0.25s/f (Good) **13** Ran SP% **117.2**
Speed ratings: **100,94,87,84,74 66,61,61,—,—** —,—,— CSF £11.12 CT £112.12 TOTE £3.80: £1.50, £1.70, £3.50; EX 9.70.
Owner Fox And Hounds Racing **Bred** His Highness The Aga Khan's Studs S C **Trained** Cowbridge, Vale Of Glamorgan

FOCUS
There was no hanging about in this low-grade affair with the winner dominating throughout. He is rated value for more than the official margin and the second sets the level for the form.

NOTEBOOK

Nazimabad(IRE) had turned this into a procession some way from home and recorded a fast time despite coming home at his leisure. *(tchd 11-4 and 10-3)*

Percipient was never really any threat to the winner on this return to fences. *(op 5-1)*

Optimism(FR) was hardly thrown in at the deep end on this chasing bow.

Miss Muscat at least managed to complete the course for the first time over fences. *(tchd 22-1)*

Optimistic Harry would have had another 10lb to carry had his new mark been in force. Jumping right more or less throughout this time on this faster ground, why his rider did not pull him up after an horrendous blunder five out only he knows. *(op 11-4)*

Karakum *Official explanation: trainer said jockey's stirrup leather had broken during the race (op 10-1)*

Husky(POL) *Official explanation: jockey said gelding bled from the nose (op 10-1)*

980 LADBROKES.COM H'CAP HURDLE (10 hdls) 2m 4f
8:10 (8:10) (Class 4) (0-110,110) 4-Y-0+ **£4,153** (£1,278; £639; £319)

Form					RPR
4-13	1		**Englishtown (FR)**[7] 915 5-11-6 **104** (t) APMcCoy (Jonjo O'Neill) *hld up: hdwy 6th: led 3 out: clr whn j.lft last: readily* **7/4**[1]		116+
311	2	3	**Rajayoga**[21] 811 4-11-4 **105** LAspell (M H Tompkins) *hld up in tch: rdn appr 2 out: chsd wnr appr last: one pce* **4/1**[2]		107
6151	3	5	**Burning Truth (USA)**[14] 863 11-11-12 **110** DRDennis (M Sheppard) *led to 3 out: sn rdn: wknd flat* **10/1**		110
5-05	4	2 ½	**Artane Boys**[8] 904 8-11-9 **107** JEMoore (Jonjo O'Neill) *hld up and bhd: hdwy appr 3 out: mstke 2 out: styd on flat* **25/1**		107+
6-5R	5	3	**Sninfia (IRE)**[52] 458 5-11-0 **98** WMarston (G A Ham) *t.k.h towards rr: nt fluent 5th: hdwy 6th: mstke 3 out: sn wknd* **25/1**		95+
0P20	6	2 ½	**Shamsan (IRE)**[28] 762 8-10-1 **92** (tp) SWalsh[(7)] (J Joseph) *hld up and bhd: hdwy 6th: lost pl 7th: no real prog fr 3 out* **28/1**		84
30	7	1 ½	**Mantras (FR)**[28] 762 6-11-5 **110** MrRQuinn[(7)] (M C Pipe) *prom: wnt 2nd after 6th: ev ch appr 3 out: sn rdn: wknd appr last* **16/1**		101
1U42	8	2 ½	**Tinstre (IRE)**[21] 813 7-11-2 **100** SCurran (P W Hiatt) *chsd ldr tl after 6th: wknd after 7th* **6/1**[3]		89+
-320	9	6	**Musally**[17] 841 8-11-2 **100** (b[1]) CLlewellyn (W Jenks) *hld up in tch: wknd 6th* **12/1**		82
0-05	P		**Sunnyside Royale (IRE)**[25] 573 6-10-0 **84** oh3 (t) GLee (R Bastiman) *a bhd: t.o whn p.u bef 2 out* **9/1**		—
3P0-	P		**Blaise Wood (USA)**[6] 3676 4-10-1 **88** ow1 OMcPhail (A L Forbes) *t.k.h: lost pl 3rd: bhd whn j. slowly 5th: t.o whn p.u bef 3 out* **50/1**		—

4m 45.8s (-2.20) **Going Correction** -0.05s/f (Good)
WFA 4 from 5yo+ 3lb **11** Ran SP% **116.4**
Speed ratings: **102,100,98,97,96 95,95,94,91,— —** CSF £8.85 CT £53.64 TOTE £2.60: £1.10, £2.30, £2.70; EX 11.20.
Owner John P McManus **Bred** Darley Stud Management Co Ltd **Trained** Cheltenham, Gloucs
■ Stewards' Enquiry : H Oliver £200 fine: passport irregularity

FOCUS
Quite a competitive handicap run at a fair pace and the form is reasonably solid.

NOTEBOOK

Englishtown(FR), set to go up 2lb at the weekend, did not mind a return to two and a half miles and scored with something in hand. *(op 2-1 tchd 9-4)*

Rajayoga, taking on his elders on this transition to handicaps, did seem to get the extra half a mile well enough. *(op 9-2)*

Burning Truth(USA) eventually found his big weight anchoring him having only landed sellers on his last two outings over hurdles. *(op 7-1)*

Artane Boys, who pulled too hard over fences last time, was switched off nicely and should find this acting as something of a confidence booster. *(op 20-1 tchd 16-1)*

Sninfia(IRE) proved difficult to settle but did behave herself this time. *(op 16-1)*

981 LADBROKESPOKER.COM H'CAP CHASE (18 fncs) 2m 7f 110y
8:40 (8:40) (Class 4) (0-100,100) 5-Y-0+ **£3,906** (£1,202; £601; £300)

Form					RPR
060F	1		**Lahinch Lad (IRE)**[7] 916 5-10-6 **85** TJMurphy (B G Powell) *hld up: hdwy 9th: rdn to ld flat: r.o* **11/2**[3]		92+
44-F	2	nk	**River Quoile**[22] 805 9-9-7 **74** DJacob[(7)] (R H Alner) *chsd ldrs: rdn to ld 2 out: hdd flat: r.o* **8/1**		85
F563	3	15	**Pete The Painter (IRE)**[7] 916 8-10-6 **80** (p) MBradburne (J W Tudor) *hld up: hdwy 9th: j.rt 11th and 13th: wkng whn j. bdly rt last* **4/1**[1]		79+
4-22	4	2	**High Drama**[13] 871 8-11-9 **97** APMcCoy (P Bowen) *hld up in tch: lost pl after 9th: styd on fr 3 out: n.d* **4/1**[1]		91
RP-3	5	¾	**Mazileo**[29] 746 12-11-12 **100** (p) DRDennis (Ian Williams) *j.rt: led tl appr 4 out: wknd 2 out* **8/1**		93
-342	6	8	**Tudor King (IRE)**[7] 916 11-10-7 **81** PJBrennan (J S King) *chsd ldr: led appr 4 out: nt fluent 3 out: hdd and mstke 2 out: sn wknd* **9/2**[2]		70+
UP/0	7	1	**Corkan (IRE)**[36] 673 11-9-9 **74** oh15 WKennedy[(5)] (A M Hales) *hld up and bhd: rdn 10th: nvr nr ldrs* **33/1**		58
-000	8	7	**Regal Vision (IRE)**[36] 673 8-9-12 **79** ow1 MissCDyson[(7)] (Miss C Dyson) *chsd ldrs: rdn 11th: wknd 12th: bhd whn bmpd 4 out* **33/1**		56
P/0-	9	7	**Illineylad (IRE)**[385] 809 11-10-0 **74** oh7 JMogford (Mrs N S Evans) *chsd ldrs tl wknd 14th* **25/1**		44
3030	10	5	**Blazing Batman**[29] 746 12-10-6 **85** TJPhelan[(5)] (Dr P Pritchard) *mid-div: mstke 2nd: bhd fr 8th* **16/1**		50
05PP	U		**Madhahir (IRE)**[29] 745 5-9-9 **79** oh12 TGreenway[(5)] (M J Gingell) *bhd: rdn 6th: last whn blnd and uns rdr 9th* **50/1**		—
P-1P	P		**Team Captain**[29] 746 11-11-1 **96** SWalsh[(7)] (C J Down) *a bhd: j.rt 2nd and 3rd: t.o whn p.u bef 12th: bbv* **16/1**		—

5m 48.2s (-6.70) **Going Correction** -0.25s/f (Good)
WFA 5 from 6yo+ 1lb **12** Ran SP% **119.2**
Speed ratings: **101,100,95,95,94 92,91,89,87,85 —,—** CSF £47.80 CT £198.01 TOTE £4.80: £2.50, £2.90, £2.20; EX 73.30.
Owner Robert Gunn **Bred** David Allan **Trained** Morestead, Hants

FOCUS
A very moderate contest run at a fast early pace with the two leaders taking each other on and the form is probably not strong.

NOTEBOOK

Lahinch Lad(IRE) built on the promise of his run over course and distance a week earlier when he fell at the penultimate fence. Set to go up 4lb in future handicaps, he ran out a narrow winner under a very confident ride. *(op 7-1)*

River Quoile, the winner of a fast-ground point in May, lost little in defeat and can take a similar event off this sort of mark. *(op 9-1 tchd 10-1)*

Pete The Painter(IRE) was plagued by his old problem of jumping right-handed. *(op 7-1)*

High Drama, reverting to fences, could never get competitive after losing his pitch at halfway.

Mazileo, dropped 5lb, set a strong pace despite jumping right and eventually had to give best. *(op 7-1)*

Tudor King(IRE), set to rise 2lb at the weekend, appeared to pay the penalty for trying to go the pace set by Mazileo. *(op 7-2)*

Team Captain *Official explanation: jockey said gelding bled from the nose (op 14-1)*

982 LADBROKES FREEPHONE 0800 524 524 MAIDEN HURDLE (8 hdls) 2m
9:10 (9:12) (Class 4) 4-Y-0+ **£3,402** (£972; £486)

Form					RPR
-353	1		**Cream Cracker**[37] 664 7-10-9 95 JMMaguire (Mrs Jeremy Young) *hld up: hdwy appr 3 out: led appr last: r.o wl* **15/8**[1]		98+
50-1	2	5	**Don And Gerry (IRE)**[17] 844 4-10-7 WMarston (P D Evans) *hld up: hdwy approching 5th: led on bit 2 out: sn hdd: hit last: rdn and one pce* **3/1**[2]		89+
4	3	3 ½	**Anko (POL)**[17] 838 6-11-2 RJohnson (P J Hobbs) *hld up: hdwy appr 4th: led 3 out to 2 out: one pce* **10/3**[3]		93
0/4	4	7	**Tubber Streams (IRE)**[16] 24 8-11-2 BHitchcott (B A Pearce) *led: nt fluent 1st: hdd after 2nd: prom: wkng whn nt fluent last* **40/1**		87+
-F56	5	nk	**Queen Excalibur**[35] 683 6-10-9 78 AThornton (C Roberts) *hld up: hdwy appr 5th: wknd 2 out* **14/1**		79
	6	3 ½	**Shandrani (GER)**[36] 6-10-11 TGreenway[(5)] (D G Bridgwater) *prom: led appr 3rd to 3 out: wknd 2 out* **33/1**		82
0400	7	9	**Simiola**[14] 860 6-10-9 77 ATinkler (S T Lewis) *hld up: hdwy appr 4th: rdn and ev ch 3 out: wknd appr last* **50/1**		66
6	8	2 ½	**Lost In The Snow (IRE)**[7] 912 7-11-2 DRDennis (M Sheppard) *w ldr: led after 2nd tl appr 3rd: wknd 3 out* **10/1**		71
0	9	14	**Shaaban (IRE)**[7] 911 4-11-0 (p) AO'Keeffe (R J Price) *a bhd* **20/1**		55
042/	10	11	**Master Ellis (IRE)**[833] 4445 6-11-2 SThomas (R L Brown) *hld up: mstke 1st: hdwy appr 3 out: wknd appr 2 out* **20/1**		46
0-P	11	19	**Royal Upstart**[14] 861 4-11-0 PJBrennan (M B Shears) *mstke 1st: a bhd* **66/1**		25
	12	4	**Thornton Bridge**[32] 7-10-9 CMStudd[(7)] (D L Williams) *j.rt: a bhd* **50/1**		23
P-00	P		**Casisle**[21] 811 4-10-0 SWalsh[(7)] (Mary Meek) *sn wl bhd: t.o whn p.u bef 3rd* **100/1**		—

3m 46.2s (-2.20) **Going Correction** -0.05s/f (Good)
WFA 4 from 6yo+ 2lb **13** Ran SP% **119.9**
Speed ratings: **103,100,98,95,95 93,88,87,80,75 65,63,—** CSF £7.05 TOTE £2.70: £1.40, £1.50, £1.60; EX 9.40 Place 6 £18.36, Place 5 £14.48..
Owner Ridge Racing **Bred** T C Frost **Trained** Charlton Mackrell, Somerset
■ Stewards' Enquiry : B Hitchcott one-day ban: used whip excessive frequency (Jul 25)

FOCUS
A poor event in which the bookmakers went 10/1 bar three in a race which lacked strength in depth. The third and fifth set a reasonable standard for the grade.

NOTEBOOK

Cream Cracker ◆ took full advantage of a return to novice company and ran out a convincing winner. She can defy a penalty in this sort of class. *(op 9-4 tchd 7-4)*

Don And Gerry(IRE) did not find as much as seemed likely on her hurdling debut and the fact she clouted the last made not the slightest difference to the result. *(tchd 7-2)*

Anko(POL) duly stepped up on his Uttoxeter debut but he failed to raise his game when the race was on in earnest. *(op 3-1)*

Tubber Streams(IRE) was dropping back in distance having lost all chance at the start in an outing on the Flat last month. *(op 33-1)*

Queen Excalibur is only modest by the look of it. *(op 12-1)*

Shandrani(GER), three times a winner on the Flat in Germany, may find that stamina is going to be a problem.

T/Plt: £28.00 to a £1 stake. Pool: £44,448.45. 1,158.75 winning tickets. T/Qpdt: £9.80 to a £1 stake. Pool: £3,184.00. 239.80 winning tickets. KH

983 - 986a (Foreign Racing) - See Raceform Interactive

[591] CARTMEL (L-H)
Thursday, July 14

OFFICIAL GOING: Hurdle course - good to firm (good in places); chase course - good (good to firm in places)
Wind: Almost nil Weather: Overcast

987 WEATHERBYS INSURANCE NOVICES' H'CAP HURDLE (8 hdls) 2m 1f 110y
2:30 (2:31) (Class 4) (0-90,90) 4-Y-0+ **£3,073** (£878; £439)

Form					RPR
0U00	1		**Ballyboe Boy (IRE)**[15] 856 6-11-0 **81** (b) LMcGrath[(3)] (R C Guest) *sn chsng ldr: hrd drvn fr bef 3 out: looked hld whn lft clr last: styd on u.p: all out* **11/1**		90+
/404	2	7	**Bella Liana (IRE)**[14] 870 5-10-9 **80** MrSClements[(7)] (J Clements, Ire) *chsd ldrs: pushed along bef 5th: chsd ldng pair fr next: no imp after: lft 2nd after last: one pced* **11/1**		82
3S21	3	¾	**Parisienne Gale (IRE)**[39] 649 6-11-2 **90** MissCarolineHurley[(10)] (R Ford) *led: reminders bef 3 out where nt fluent: pressed whn blnd last: lost all ch but kpt trying* **7/1**[3]		95+
3240	4	5	**Arjay**[8] 915 7-10-10 **81** (b) CDSharkey[(7)] (S B Clark) *hld up midfield: sme prog after 5th: no ch w ldrs fr next* **8/1**		77
660-	5	5	**Rockerfella Lad (IRE)**[52] 4414 5-10-10 **74** (b) GLee (M Todhunter) *j. slowly 1st: bhd: drvn after 5th: passed btn horses after 2 out: no ch* **16/1**		65
-021	6	5	**Master Nimbus**[27] 683 5-10-0 **71** MrTJO'Brien[(7)] (J J Quinn) *settled towards rr: hdwy 5th: rdn next: fnd nil after and nvr on terms* **4/1**[1]		57
0350	7	13	**Think Quick (IRE)**[20] 826 5-10-6 **80** AHawkins[(10)] (R Hollinshead) *bhd: rdn 3rd: nvr gng wl* **14/1**		53
200-	8	12	**Two Steps To Go (USA)**[270] 1747 6-10-9 **73** PJBrennan (E A Elliott) *bhd: rdn and struggling after 5th* **16/1**		34
-0P0	9	15	**Dumfries**[28] 764 4-10-10 **83** BWharfe[(7)] (T H Caldwell) *towards rr: rdn and no rspnse after 5th* **28/1**		27
P00/	10	dist	**Known Maneuver (USA)**[15] 4512 7-10-7 **74** ACCoyle[(3)] (M C Chapman) *towards rr: lost tch after 5th: btn 89l* **33/1**		—
P002	11	½	**Alethea Gee**[20] 822 7-10-8 **72** RMcGrath (K G Reveley) *prom: rdn and wknd bef 3 out: virtually p.u flat: btn 90l* **8/1**		—

-016 **P** **Faraway Echo**[39] 649 4-10-12 **78** ADobbin —
(James Moffatt) *chsd ldrs tl rdn and fdd after 5th: t.o and p.u 2 out* **6/1**[2]

4m 8.00s (-7.70) **Going Correction** -0.30s/f (Good)
WFA 4 from 5yo+ 2lb **12** Ran SP% **110.5**
Speed ratings: **105,101,101,99,97 94,89,83,77,— —,—** CSF £117.30 CT £865.40 TOTE £16.50: £4.70, £3.10, £2.40; EX 150.10.

Owner Fly By Night Syndicate **Bred** Matt Carr **Trained** Brancepeth, Co Durham

■ Stewards' Enquiry : Mr S Clements four day ban: used whip with excessive frequency (Aug 5, Sep 11,22,24)

FOCUS

A very moderate handicap, run at a strong gallop and few managed to land a blow from off the pace. The form looks solid rated through the winner and fourth.

NOTEBOOK

Ballyboe Boy(IRE) was always racing up with the generous pace and kept finding plenty for his rider under pressure, en route to a first success over timber at the seventh attempt. He looked well suited by the undulations of this track, and this was by far his best display to date for current connections, although he is flattered by his winning margin. It would be little surprise to see him build on this now he has got his head in front. *(tchd 12-1)*

Bella Liana(IRE) , making her handicap debut, kept to her task gamely under pressure and turned in another fair effort. She is slowly going the right way and, while only moderate, can find a race off this mark when reverting to further.

Parisienne Gale(IRE) set the decent pace from the off, and was still just about on top prior to meeting the last flight all wrong and thus losing any chance. She remains in good heart, can be rated better than the bare form and may not be weighted out of winning just yet. *(op 11-2)*

Arjay ran his race and reversed his Hereford form with Mr Nimbus, but never rated a serious threat. He looks to need a drop back into plating-company and remains winless over hurdles from 14 outings. *(op 15-2 tchd 9-1)*

Master Nimbus looked a brief threat from off the pace down the back straight, but found very little *when asked for his effort and this must rate a disappointing performance. He has it to prove now.* *(op 9-2 tchd 5-1)*

Faraway Echo *Official explanation: jockey said filly had bled from the nose (op 8-1)*

988 STICKY TOFFEE PUDDING (S) H'CAP HURDLE (10 hdls 1 omitted) 2m 6f

3:00 (3:00) (Class 5) (0-90,90) 4-Y-0+ **£2,723** (£778; £389)

Form RPR

5-64 **1** **Peter's Imp (IRE)**[17] 592 10-11-6 **87** KJMercer(3) 97+
(A Berry) *settled rr of midfield: prog gng strly fr 8th: led bef last: sn clr: eased cl home: easily* **9/2**[1]

32F5 **2** *1 ¾* **End Of An Error**[4] 941 6-10-11 **85** SGagan(10) 89+
(Mrs E Slack) *wl bhd tl 8th: prog next: 3rd and rdn whn nt fluent last: styd on wl but wnr was easing nr fin* **6/1**[2]

FP-0 **3** *5* **Top Pack (IRE)**[68] 209 6-11-1 **79** (v[1]) BHarding 77
(N G Richards) *prom: pressed ldr fr 5th tl led passing omitted 2 out: hdd bef last: rdn and wknd flat* **33/1**

0-3P **4** *3 ½* **Little Task**[10] 874 7-11-5 **83** DO'Meara 78+
(J S Wainwright) *wl bhd tl 8th: styd on stoutly fr appr last: too much to do* **14/1**

3234 **5** *3 ½* **Star Trooper (IRE)**[25] 781 9-10-13 **80** MrCStorey(3) 71
(Miss S E Forster) *prom: bmpd along fr omitted 2 out: weakend bef last* **6/1**[2]

1/P0 **6** *1* **Bravo**[35] 697 7-11-2 **80** (v) PMoloney 70
(J Mackie) *chsd ldrs: rdn after 3 out: no rspnse and sn btn* **33/1**

2006 **7** *nk* **Northern Echo**[4] 941 8-10-7 **78** (p) GThomas(7) 68
(K S Thomas) *nvr bttr than midfield: nt rch ldrs fr 3 out: mstke last* **33/1**

1/00 **8** *6* **Maunby Rocker**[33] 716 5-11-11 **89** FKeniry 73
(P C Haslam) *last whn blnd bdly 3rd: rdn 6th: nvr gng wl* **25/1**

P020 **9** *shd* **Lord Of The Land**[11] 896 12-11-2 **85** (p) DCCostello(5) 69
(Mrs E Slack) *chsd ldrs: j. slowly 4th: rdn 8th: sn btn* **20/1**

P3-0 **10** *½* **Silver Dagger**[40] 632 7-11-10 **88** (v) APMcCoy 75+
(Jonjo O'Neill) *midfield: shkn up bef 6th: disputing 4th but u.p whn blnd bdly 8th: no ch after* **8/1**[3]

3050 **11** *¾* **Book's Way**[18] 839 9-10-8 **75** PAspell(3) 58+
(D W Thompson) *led: rdn and hdd passing omitted 2 out: sn fdd* **16/1**

P-PP **12** *17* **Dajazar (IRE)**[15] 859 9-11-5 **90** CDSharkey(7) 55
(Mrs K Walton) *chsd ldrs: rdn 8th: wknd after next: checked on bnd between last two: eased fnl 100 yds* **66/1**

14-P **13** *23* **Diamond Joshua (IRE)**[51] 352 7-11-12 **90** (v) RJohnson 32
(J Gallagher) *a wl bhd: no ch fr 8th* **10/1**

15/0 **14** *20* **Kilbride Lad (IRE)**[64] 304 11-11-7 **90** PCO'Neill(5) 12
(J J Lambe, Ire) *chsd ldrs tl drvn and wknd 3 out: virtually p.u ent st* **33/1**

0-06 **P** **Very Tasty (IRE)**[47] 548 8-11-2 **80** (tp) GLee —
(M Todhunter) *bhd and racing on outside: struggling 7th: p.u 3 out* **16/1**

0550 **P** **Al Mabrook (IRE)**[28] 768 10-11-5 **83** (p) ADobbin —
(N G Richards) *midfield whn mstke 6th and reminders: nt gng wl after: p.u after 8th* **17/2**

5m 27.4s (-8.60) **Going Correction** -0.30s/f (Good) **16** Ran SP% **117.8**
Speed ratings: **103,102,100,99,98 97,97,95,95,95 94,88,80,73,— —** CSF £27.76 CT £799.14 TOTE £4.60: £1.80, £1.80, £7.60, £3.40; EX 27.90.There was no bid for the winner. End of An Error was claimed by Dennis Deacon for £6,000.

Owner Ian & Arthur Bolland **Bred** Don Kelly **Trained** Cockerham, Lancs

FOCUS

A poor event run at a generous gallop and the winner can be rated for at least treble his winning margin. The second-last flight was bypassed.

NOTEBOOK

Peter's Imp(IRE) , who posted an improved effort on the Flat last time, was allowed to bide his time off the pace before smoothly cutting through the pack to lead and ultimately ran out a facile winner. He loves this venue - this was his fourth success from ten outings at the track - and can be rated value for much further than his winning margin. *(op 5-1)*

End Of An Error , as on her only other start at the track back in 2003, took too long to get going and was staying on dourly at the finish. This was another creditable effort, but she is on a long losing run and is flattered by her proximity to the eased-down winner. *(op 13-2)*

Top Pack(IRE) , equipped with the a first-time visor for this handicap bow, paid for racing up with the strong pace and could only plug on at the one pace in the straight. This was much his best display to date, however, and he can get closer over this trip with more patient tactics.

Little Task would have been closer with a more prominent ride and can be rated better than the bare form. *(tchd 16-1)*

Star Trooper(IRE) dropped out late and ran a little below expectations. He was another who paid for racing up with the generous gallop. *(tchd 11-2)*

Silver Dagger , down in class, turned in a moody effort and looks one to avoid at all costs on this evidence. *(tchd 17-2)*

989 E S HARTLEY H'CAP CHASE (18 fncs) 3m 2f

3:35 (3:34) (Class 4) (0-105,100) 5-Y-0+ **£4,485** (£1,380; £690; £345)

Form RPR

6/22 **1** **Carnacrack**[47] 554 11-10-7 **84** MrCStorey(3) 95+
(Miss S E Forster) *2nd or 3rd tl led 15th: drvn along fr last: all out in fnl f but kpt battling in tremendous style* **9/2**[1]

213- **2** *2 ½* **Be The Tops (IRE)**[334] 1179 7-11-12 **100** (b) APMcCoy 108
(Jonjo O'Neill) *cl up: rdn to go 2nd 3 out: hrd drvn fr last: outbattled by wnr and no imp fnl f* **11/2**[2]

PPP- **3** *1 ½* **Tierkely (IRE)**[323] 1284 10-10-11 **85** ARoss 91
(J J Lambe, Ire) *bhd: 7th and rdn after 12th: outpcd tl gd prog to go 3rd at last: styng on v strly up st* **40/1**

-12P **4** *13* **Robber (IRE)**[30] 746 8-11-6 **94** (p) RJohnson 90+
(P Bowen) *prom: rdn after 12th: wknd bef 15th* **11/2**[2]

660P **5** *16* **Cromwell (IRE)**[47] 547 10-9-7 **74** oh15 (b) CMStudd(7) 51
(M C Chapman) *led: rdn bef 13th: hdd 15th: lost 3rd at last and wknd* **66/1**

00P0 **6** *8* **Celtic Star (IRE)**[18] 841 7-10-13 **90** (b) DCrosse(3) 59
(Mrs L Williamson) *hld up midfield: nt fluent 11th and 12th: wknd after 14th* **40/1**

4P-P **7** *nk* **Iron Express**[81] 12 9-11-6 **94** (p) FKeniry 63
(G M Moore) *chsd ldrs tl rdn and wknd tamely 11th: sn wl bhd* **12/1**

P0-2 **P** **Carriage Ride (IRE)**[47] 546 7-11-6 **94** (b) BHarding —
(N G Richards) *sn bhd and nvr gng wl: lost tch 11th: t.o and p.u 13th* **9/2**[1]

4-P4 **P** **Cill Uird (IRE)**[15] 859 7-10-11 **90** (p) PCO'Neill(5) —
(J J Lambe, Ire) *midfield: mstke 4th: blnd 8th: wknd 11th: t.o and p.u 15th* **25/1**

R-FP **P** **Zurs (IRE)**[14] 874 12-11-2 **90** (p) JPMcNamara —
(J J Lambe, Ire) *last and rdn 7th: nvr gng wl: lost tch 11th: t.o and p.u 13th* **25/1**

-513 **P** **Lambrini Bianco (IRE)**[47] 546 7-9-12 **74** oh5 ow3 (p) DLaverty(5) —
(Mrs L Williamson) *sn bhd: nt fluent: j. slowly 7th and drvn: t.o and p.u 13th* **6/1**[3]

5P4P **P** **Pavey Ark (IRE)**[33] 717 7-11-1 **89** RMcGrath —
(James Moffatt) *hld up midfield: 5th and effrt whn mstke 13th: sn outpcd: t.o whn p.u and dismntd ent st* **20/1**

4U2P **U** **Ikdam Melody (IRE)**[33] 717 9-10-12 **93** (p) MissJFoster(7) —
(Miss J E Foster) *nvr bttr than midfield: lost tch 11th: disputing remote 7th whn blnd bdly and uns rdr 3 out* **14/1**

6m 31.2s (-9.40) **Going Correction** -0.15s/f (Good) **13** Ran SP% **114.6**
Speed ratings: **108,107,106,102,97 95,95,—,—,— —,—,—** CSF £26.38 CT £869.03 TOTE £5.60: £2.30, £2.00, £15.60; EX 21.60.

Owner C Storey **Bred** Mrs R Brewis **Trained** Kirk Yetholm, Borders

■ This race went off 25 seconds before the appointed time.

FOCUS

A moderate handicap, run at a sound pace, and the form looks fair for the class with the first two running to their marks. The first three came clear.

NOTEBOOK

Carnacrack , racing off the same mark as when successful in this event in 2003, showed a wonderful attitude under pressure, jumped superbly and never really looked like being headed once hitting the front. He has now landed three of his four career wins at this venue, relishes this decent ground and has clearly resumed this season in great heart.

Be The Tops(IRE) , making his return from a 334-day layoff, ran a brave race yet never quite looked like getting to the winner try as he might. This was a very respectable effort off top weight, *he got the trip well enough and this consistent gelding can be expected to improve for the outing.* *(op 6-1)*

Tierkely(IRE) , pulled up on his last three outings in 2004 and having his first run for 323 days, flew up the run-in and turned in his best effort since 2003. He looks to need a stiffer track to be seen at best and, while his next outing should reveal more, he may not be too badly treated at present. *(op 33-1)*

Robber(IRE) , with first-time cheekpieces replacing blinkers, improved on his latest dismal effort yet his fate was on the cards a fair way out this time. He probably wants softer ground, but has a bit to prove off this mark at present.

Carriage Ride(IRE), runner-up over course and distance on his seasonal bow last time, ran in snatces throughout and was disappointingly pulled up. *(tchd 5-1)*

Cill Uird(IRE) *Official explanation: jockey said mare made a bad mistake in the back straight and was never travelling thereafter (tchd 5-1)*

990 EUROPEAN BREEDERS FUND BEGINNERS' CHASE (12 fncs) 2m 1f 110y

4:10 (4:10) (Class 4) 5-Y-0+ **£4,429** (£1,363; £681; £340)

Form RPR

43-0 **1** **Salinas (GER)**[72] 177 6-10-12 PJBrennan 96+
(M F Harris) *prom: led 6th: rdn clr after last: a in command after* **7/2**[2]

-223 **2** *4* **Mooramana**[33] 718 6-10-12 RGarritty 89
(P Beaumont) *led tl 6th: rdn and outpcd in 3rd at 8th: rallied to go 2nd after last: styd on: nt rch wnr* **5/2**[1]

00-0 **3** *4* **My Ace**[37] 670 7-9-12 (bt) MissJFoster(7) 78
(Miss J E Foster) *cl up: chsd wnr fr 7th tl rdn and demoted after last:looked to be wkng but kpt plugging on* **66/1**

0-0 **4** *2* **Manoubi**[15] 855 6-10-12 ADobbin 85+
(M Todhunter) *mstke 4th: nvr looked gng wl: drvn 6th: struggling befpre 9th* **5/1**

-555 **5** *13* **Simply Da Best (IRE)**[15] 855 7-10-7 (p) PCO'Neill(5) 71+
(J J Lambe, Ire) *towards rr: last and losing tch 8th* **15/2**

3-0P **6** *5* **Earl Sigurd (IRE)**[57] 416 7-10-5 MrSFMagee(7) 70+
(J K Magee, Ire) *hld up and bhd: effrt 8th: rdn and disputing 4th next: blnd bdly 2 out and bridle bec dislodged: lost all ch* **14/1**

-330 **7** *1 ½* **Flame Phoenix (USA)**[8] 914 6-10-12 (p) GLee 66+
(D McCain) *j. slowly and nvr looked keen: rdn most of way: lost tch bef 9th* **9/2**[3]

PP00 **U** **Proper Poser (IRE)**[20] 822 9-10-5 62 CMStudd(7) —
(M C Chapman) *blnd and uns rdr 2nd* **80/1**

0-06 **F** **Waziya**[62] 331 6-9-9 82 CDThompson(10) —
(Mrs L Williamson) *out of control and flyjumping gng to s: s.s: fell 1st* **66/1**

3-6P **P** **Loch Torridon**[47] 545 6-10-12 RMcGrath —
(James Moffatt) *chsd ldrs: nt fluent 8th: rdn and sn outpcd: 6th and no ch whn pckd last: p.u lame ent st* **40/1**

4m 22.8s (-1.40) **Going Correction** -0.15s/f (Good) **10** Ran SP% **110.7**
Speed ratings: **97,95,93,92,86 84,83,—,—,—** CSF £12.32 TOTE £5.20: £1.80, £1.40, £7.10; EX 15.70.

Owner Prevention & Detection (Holdings) Ltd **Bred** Stiftung Gestut Fahrhof **Trained** Edgcote, Northants

FOCUS

A moderate beginners' chase. The field finished strung out and the form makes sense, with the first three all close to their hurdles form.

NOTEBOOK

Salinas(GER) bounced right back to his best under a positive ride from Brennan, and got off the mark at the first time of asking over fences. He is at best on fast ground, jumped fluently throughout and could strike again under a penalty during the summer. *(op 4-1)*

Mooramana ◆ , rated 4lb lower than Salinas over hurldes, was not suited by the drop in trip on this chasing debut and was doing all of his best work up the run-in. This was very close to the level of his hurdling form, but he has always appealed as the type to prove better over the larger obstacles and he should not be long in getting off the mark when stepping back up in trip. *(op 11-4 tchd 9-4)*

My Ace , pulled up in a point on her only previous attempt over fences, turned a much-improved race and stuck to her task well under pressure. She will be suited by a stiffer test, and on her previous best efforts over hurdles, there was no fluke about this effort. *(op 50-1)*

Manoubi , easy to back, ran in snatches after an early mistake and again ran well below expectations. He has yet to convince that he is a natural over fences. *(op 3-1)*

Simply Da Best(IRE) *Official explanation: jockey said saddle slipped (op 8-1 tchd 9-1)*

Earl Sigurd(IRE) ran an improved race and can be rated better than the bare form, as he blundered *all chance away at the penultimate fence. Official explanation: jockey said gelding lost its bridle after a bad mistake at the second-last fence (tchd 12-1 and 16-1)*

Flame Phoenix(USA) , as on his previous outing at Worcester, turned in a very moody effort and is going the wrong way over fences. *(op 11-2 tchd 6-1)*

Loch Torridon *Official explanation: jockey said gelding pulled up distressed (tchd 50-1)*

991 FRANK WHITTLE PARTNERSHIP MAIDEN HURDLE (8 hdls) 2m 1f 110y
4:40 (4:40) (Class 4) 4-Y-0+ **£3,532** (£1,087; £543; £271)

Form				RPR
236-	**1**		**Crathorne (IRE)**[19] 3751 5-10-12 98 ... ADobbin (M Todhunter) *prom: led gng wl 3 out: mstke next: rdn between last two: clr after last: eased cl home* **4/1**[2]	114+
	2	*1 ¾*	**Spuradich (IRE)**[299] 5-10-12 ... APMcCoy (Jonjo O'Neill) *nt fluent towards rr: effrt and hit 5th: chsd wnr after 3 out: sn drvn: nt qckn bef last: a hld flat* **4/5**[1]	109+
6-24	**3**	*10*	**Smart Boy Prince (IRE)**[11] 895 4-10-10 100 ... DRDennis (C Smith) *led: drvn and hdd 3 out: btn next* **10/1**	97
4443	**4**	*6*	**Leopold (SLO)**[14] 870 4-10-3 98 ... CPoste[(7)] (M F Harris) *chsd ldrs: rdn bef 5th: one pce and n.d fr next* **14/1**	91
50	**5**	*10*	**Greenfort Brave (IRE)**[25] 781 7-10-12 ... JPMcNamara (J J Lambe, Ire) *handy early: dropped to rr after 4th: hrd drvn to make sme late prog* **100/1**	83
-024	**6**	*1*	**Petrolero (ARG)**[12] 544 6-10-2 87 ... MMcAvoy[(10)] (James Moffatt) *chsd ldrs: rdn 5th: struggling fr next: nt fluent 2 out* **25/1**	83+
03-5	**7**	*dist*	**The Connor Fella**[21] 424 4-10-5 ... DCCostello[(5)] (F P Murtagh) *bhd: lost tch bef 5th: btn 60l* **100/1**	—
	P		**Campbells Lad**[10] 4-10-10 ... GLee (A Berry) *midfield: wknd after 5th: wl bhd whn p.u 2 out* **50/1**	—
0-P0	**P**		**Wizards Princess**[25] 780 5-10-5 ... ARoss (D W Thompson) *plld hrd in last pair: pckd 4th: sn t.o: p.u 2 out* **100/1**	—
P	**P**		**Whisky In The Jar (IRE)**[25] 785 4-10-3 ... MJMcAlister[(7)] (S J Marshall) *last pair: rdn and lost tch 4th: sn t.o: p.u after next* **100/1**	—
	P		**Troodos Jet**[36] 4-10-7 ... PBuchanan[(3)] (K W Hogg) *nt fluent 3rd: hld up in rr: lost tch bef 5th: t.o and p.u after 2 out* **100/1**	—
023/	**P**		**Corries Wood (IRE)**[671] 1348 6-10-7 ... PCO'Neill[(5)] (J J Lambe, Ire) *chsd ldrs tl rdn and wknd 3 out: disputing poor 6th whn p.u last* **50/1**	—
4P-3	**P**		**Neckar Valley (IRE)**[11] 895 6-10-12 100 ... RThornton (R M Whitaker) *pressed ldr tl 3 out: rdn whn mstke next: wknd: 4th whn p.u last* **13/2**[3]	—

4m 9.80s (-5.90) **Going Correction** -0.30s/f (Good)
WFA 4 from 5yo+ 2lb **13** Ran SP% **117.4**
Speed ratings: **101,100,95,93,88 88,—,—,—,— —,—,—** CSF £7.53 TOTE £4.40: £1.50, £1.50, £2.10; EX 14.40.
Owner FF Racing Services Partnership XVII **Bred** Shirley Blue Syndicate **Trained** Orton, Cumbria

FOCUS

Little strength in depth to this novice event and the first two came well clear. Both could rate higher, but the overall form is suspect.

NOTEBOOK

Crathorne(IRE) , who showed modest form in three outings over hurdles last season, was given a fine ride by Dobbin and readily got off the mark at the fourth attempt. He has been in good heart on the Flat this year and looked the part this time, putting in by far his best round of jumping to date. While he will be vulnerable under a penalty when the better novice hurdlers come out to play, he could nick another race this summer and remains open to further improvement over a longer trip in this sphere. *(op 3-1)*

Spuradich(IRE) , rated 93 on the Flat and having his first outing for 299 days, was well backed for this hurdling bow yet always looked like playing second fiddle from two out. He took time to get into a rhythm over his hurdles, but improved as the race went on and it would be a surprise if he did not prove better than this form with further experience under his belt. *(op 11-10 tchd 6-5)*

Smart Boy Prince(IRE) turned in a brave effort from the front, but had his limitations exposed by the front pair from three out. He is a fair benchmark for this form, was clear of the rest and deserves to find a race over timber. *(op 9-1 tchd 8-1)*

Leopold(SLO) ran near to his recent level and was not disgraced. He may do better back over further, but is hard to win with nevertheless.

Greenfort Brave(IRE) was doing all of his best work at the finish and showed his first worthwhile form over hurdles to date. However, he does hold down this form somewhat. *(op 80-1)*

Neckar Valley(IRE) *Official explanation: jockey said gelding was unsuited by the good to firm, good in places ground (op 6-1)*

992 BADGER PRESS NOVICES' HURDLE (11 hdls) 2m 6f
5:15 (5:15) (Class 4) 4-Y-0+ **£3,513** (£1,081; £540; £270)

Form				RPR
-1F2	**1**		**Romany Prince**[53] 467 6-11-5 115 ... TScudamore (S Gollings) *settled towards rr: wnt 2nd bef 7th: led gng best 3 out: drew clr after next: in command after* **11/10**[1]	110+
-021	**2**	*8*	**Stagecoach Diamond**[18] 843 6-11-5 103 ... DElsworth (Mrs S J Smith) *cl up: drvn and outpcd bef 3 out: styd on after last to go 2nd 50 yds out: no ch w wnr* **4/1**[3]	100
/2U1	**3**	*1 ¾*	**Rebelle**[14] 875 6-11-5 99 ... (p) APMcCoy (P Bowen) *set stdy pce: drvn and hdd 3 out: ev ch next: sn outpcd: lost 2nd nr fin* **7/4**[2]	98
	4	*dist*	**Protecting Heights (IRE)**[72] 4-10-6 ... PBuchanan[(3)] (M E Sowersby) *j. slowly 1st: bhd: lost tch 6th: soldiered on: v slow jump 8tl wnr fin: btn 120l* **66/1**	—
0	**P**		**Magic Brook**[14] 876 6-10-12 ... KRenwick (R Allan) *rdn 4th: lost tch 6th: wl t.o whn p.u 8th* **66/1**	—
06/	**P**		**Night Mail**[306] 2528 5-10-10 ow1 ... GCarenza[(3)] (Miss J E Foster) *prom: j. slowly 4th: wknd 5th: mmstke next: wl t.o whn p.u 8th* **80/1**	—

5m 29.2s (-6.80) **Going Correction** -0.30s/f (Good)
WFA 4 from 5yo+ 3lb **6** Ran SP% **108.2**
Speed ratings: **100,97,96,—,—** — CSF £5.60 TOTE £2.30: £1.50, £1.90; EX 8.30 Place 6 £42.46, Place 5 £8.50.
Owner J B Webb **Bred** P And Mrs Venner **Trained** Scamblesby, Lincs

FOCUS

A modest novice event, run at an ordinary gallop, and the winner did the job nicely. The form is sound with the first three close to their marks.

NOTEBOOK

Romany Prince simply had to be kept up to his work up the run-in and got back to winning way with a bloodless success. He was entitled to win as he did according to official ratings, but this was his most accomplished round of jumping to date and there was a lot to like about the manner of this success. The trip looked ideal and he is one to keep on the right side of if turned out again during the summer. *(op 5-4)*

Stagecoach Diamond ran on well enough after hitting a flat spot before three out and will surely better this form when reverting to a more galloping track. *(op 7-2 tchd 5-1)*

Rebelle , sporting first-time cheekpieces, had the run of the race in front and was a sitting duck for the winner from three out. However, he stuck to his task once headed and was not disgraced as he had a fairly stiff task at these weights. *(tchd 6-4)*

Protecting Heights(IRE) was predictably outclassed. *(op 33-1)*

T/Plt: £26.90 to a £1 stake. Pool: £38,817.80 - 1,051.20 winning tickets T/Qpdt: £5.50 to a £1 stake. Pool: £2,441.40 - 323.80 winning tickets IM

993 - 996a (Foreign Racing) - See Raceform Interactive

464 SOUTHWELL (L-H)
Friday, July 15

OFFICIAL GOING: Good (good to firm in places)

Wind: Nil Weather: Sunny

997 BETFREDCASINO.COM H'CAP CHASE (16 fncs) 2m 5f 110y
2:20 (2:21) (Class 4) (0-95,93) 5-Y-0+ **£4,251** (£1,308; £654; £327)

Form				RPR
P-24	**1**		**Good Heart (IRE)**[16] 860 10-11-5 86 ... (t) GLee (R Ford) *hld up and bhd: stdy prog 12th: rdn after next: chal and lft in ld last: drvn clr after hanging both directions st* **13/2**	93
-630	**2**	*1 ¾*	**Raise A McGregor**[37] 690 9-10-9 76 ... DElsworth (Mrs S J Smith) *keen and prom: rdn bef 3 out: led next: rdn whn wnt bdly lft last and hdd: one pce and nt rcvr* **7/2**[2]	83+
4060	**3**	*6*	**Guilsborough Gorse**[12] 896 10-11-5 93 ... MrMWalford[(7)] (T D Walford) *hld up and nt bttr than midfield tl drvn 12th: effrt bef 3 out: sn outpcd: plugged on again to go 3rd but no ch last* **20/1**	92
55-5	**4**	*1 ¼*	**Dante's Battle (IRE)**[10] 903 13-9-9 69 ... RSpate[(7)] (Mrs K Waldron) *hld up and bhd: mstke 8th: hdwy 11th: chal 13th: rdn and wknd bef 2 out* **14/1**	68+
55-6	**5**	*1*	**Moral Justice (IRE)**[23] 815 12-10-3 70 ... JamesDavies (S J Gilmore) *led: rdn bef 3 out: hdd next: stl 3rd at last: plodded on* **16/1**	67
-44	**6**	*5*	**Nosam**[58] 416 15-11-7 88 ... (tp) HOliver (R C Guest) *bhd: rdn and outpcd 12th: styng on fr after next: no ch* **16/1**	80
PP-0	**7**	*5*	**Claude Greengrass**[41] 633 9-11-10 91 ... APMcCoy (Jonjo O'Neill) *prom: shkn up 9th: drvn 12th: remained w ev ch tl reluctant and nt run on after 3 out* **12/1**	79+
-250	**8**	*20*	**Amptina (IRE)**[38] 674 10-10-4 71 ... JimCrowley (Mrs S J Smith) *nvr bttr than midfield: rdn and lost tch after 13th* **11/2**[3]	38
50-4	**P**		**Pink Harbour**[64] 314 7-11-1 87 ... StephenJCraine[(5)] (D McCain) *hmpd 1st: wl in tch tl 9th: dropped bk last and mstke 11th: t.o 13th: p.u 2 out* **20/1**	—
0/0-	**F**		**Son Of Flighty**[153] 7-10-2 69 ... ChristianWilliams (Evan Williams) *plld hrd on outside: nt fluent and several positions: dropped rr 11th: struggling whn fell heavily 3 out: winded but rcvrd* **10/3**[1]	—

Owner M J Caldwell **Bred** Timothy Dunne **Trained** Cotebrook, Cheshire

FOCUS

A moderate handicap contested largely by out-of-form chasers. The pace was not strong.

NOTEBOOK

Good Heart(IRE), patiently ridden, got on top at the final fence and scored in workmanlike style. Gaining his first win under Rules since his debut in a bumper back in 1999, he has improved since joining Richard Ford's yard and had run well over hurdles last time. *(op 7-1)*

Raise A McGregor took a slight lead at the second last but forfeited the advantage when jumping out to his left at the final fence. His strike rate is not good but he is probably up to winning a similar event if things go right for him. *(op 4-1)*

Guilsborough Gorse, who is due to be dropped 8lb, plugged on for pressure over the last couple of fences and may need further these days. *(tchd 25-1)*

Dante's Battle(IRE), beaten in a selling hurdle last time, looked a danger on the home turn before fading. *(op 16-1)*

Moral Justice(IRE) jumped soundly out in front. He wound up the pace on the final circuit but stopped to nothing when tackled at the second last. *(tchd 20-1)*

Son Of Flighty, a winning pointer earlier in the year, was well supported on his debut for the in-form Williams yard, but he jumped out to his right throughout and was well adrift when taking a heavy fall. There was not much encouragement to be gleaned from this but he may be worth another chance going the other way round. *(op 3-1 tchd 11-4)*

Pink Harbour *Official explanation: jockey said mare gurgled (op 3-1 tchd 11-4)*

998 BETFREDPOKER.COM MAIDEN CHASE (19 fncs) 3m 2f
2:55 (2:56) (Class 4) 5-Y-0+ **£4,439** (£1,366; £683; £341)

Form				RPR
	1		**Nick Junior (IRE)**[100] 4744 6-11-2 ... ChristianWilliams (Evan Williams) *pressed ldrs gng wl: led 16th: drew clr after next and effectively lft solo 2 out: heavily eased flat: impressive* **10/3**[2]	116+
3F-5	**2**	*25*	**Farington Lodge (IRE)**[46] 594 7-11-2 ... DElsworth (Mrs S J Smith) *lft in ld 4th: hdd 12th: hrd drvn and wknd after 16th: lft remote 2nd 2 out and flattered by proximity to wnr* **11/2**	86+
2-22	**3**	*4*	**No Further Comment (IRE)**[50] 523 5-10-11 ... (b) SThomas (Mrs Jeremy Young) *chsd ldrs: nt fluent 10th: drvn 13th: fnd nthing after: wl btn 16th: lft remote 3rd by two departures two out* **2/1**[1]	70
	4	*3*	**Sarahs Quay (IRE)**[100] 4740 6-10-9 ... PJBrennan (K J Burke) *mstkes in rr: rdn 9th: hdwy to midfield and mstke 12th: wknd next and hanging lft after: remote fr 16th* **40/1**	65
0	**U**		**Broadspeed**[12] 893 9-10-4 ... TGreenway[(5)] (M J Gingell) *led tl lunged at 4th and uns rdr* **100/1**	—

P4-P **P** **Kalexandro (FR)**[21] 827 7-10-9 72 MissJFoster(7) —
(Miss J E Foster) *sn bhd: struggling 12th: t.o and p.u 3 out* **66/1**
040- **P** **Lambrini Mist**[176] 3437 7-11-2 69 OMcPhail —
(Mrs L Williamson) *dropped bk last 12th: t.o and p.u next* **40/1**
/433 **F** **Heather Lad**[15] 872 12-11-2 100 RMcGrath 94
(C Grant) *hld up: stdy prog 9th: wnt 2nd bef 3 out: 8l 2nd and wkng whn fell heavily 2 out* **10/1**
30P **P** **Prioritisation (IRE)**[12] 893 6-10-9 RSpate(7) —
(Mrs K Waldron) *reminder 3rd: bhd and nvr gng wl: drvn and lost tch after 12th: t.o and p.u 15th* **40/1**
P23 **P** **Hi Tech Man (IRE)**[16] 861 7-11-2 (b) PMoloney —
(D E Cantillon) *mstkes 5th and 9th: lost pl bef 10th: drvn and no rspnse after 12th: t.o and p.u 3 out* **8/1**
0-P0 **P** **Northern Rambler (IRE)**[45] 601 8-11-2 66 (b) JimCrowley —
(K G Reveley) *rdn 5th: nvr looked happy: in tch tl 12th: wkng tamely whn blnd 14th: t.o and p.u next* **50/1**
3- **U** **High Gear (IRE)**[297] 1466 7-11-2 95 APMcCoy 97
(Jonjo O'Neill) *prom: led 12th: hdd 16th: sn hrd rdn: 3rd bef 2 out: wnt 7l 2nd and no ch w wnr whn blnd and uns 2 out* **9/2**[3]

6m 34.6s (-4.70) **Going Correction** -0.175s/f (Good)
WFA 5 from 6yo+ 5lb **12** Ran SP% **121.9**
Speed ratings: **100,92,91,90,—** —,—,—,—,— —,— CSF £22.40 TOTE £4.20: £1.70, £2.00, £1.10; EX 18.10.

Owner Ian Brice **Bred** Fred Williams **Trained** Cowbridge, Vale Of Glamorgan

FOCUS
An ordinary maiden chase with the runner-up setting the standard and the winner could rate higher.

NOTEBOOK
Nick Junior(IRE) ◆, successful in three point-to-points in Ireland, made an impressive debut for Evan Williams. Still on the bridle when taking it up four from home, he made his only real error at the next and was in command when left clear at the second last. Bogged down in the mud in a Gowran hunter chase on his most recent start, he wants good, fast ground and looks the sort to go on to better things. *(op 3-1 tchd 5-2)*

Farington Lodge(IRE) made a good deal of the running on his first start for this stable, but was a spent force with four to jump and was fortunate to inherit a remote second. *(op 9-1)*

No Further Comment(IRE), back over fences, was beaten with five to jump. He is better than this. *(op 9-4 tchd 5-2)*

Sarahs Quay(IRE), a winning pointer in Ireland, is going to have to jump regulation fences better than she did here. *(op 33-1)*

Heather Lad was in the process of running another sound race when he took a heavy fall at the second last. *(op 4-1)*

High Gear(IRE) was staying on and disputing second, but no threat to the winner, when coming down at the penultimate fence. He has the ability to win a race of this nature. *(op 4-1)*

999 CARTWRIGHT KING H'CAP CHASE (13 fncs) 2m 1f
3:25 (3:28) (Class 4) (0-100,100) 5-Y-O+ **£4,231** (£1,302; £651; £325)

Form RPR
2F31 **1** **College City (IRE)**[10] 904 6-11-2 **93** 7ex (p) LMcGrath(3) 105+
(R C Guest) *hld up and bhd: smooth prog 7th: mstke 9th: wnt 3rd bef 3 out: led next: rdn and kpt on wl flat* **13/2**[2]
-500 **2** *1 ½* **Johnny Grand**[4] 958 8-9-11 **74** oh2 (p) DCrosse(3) 83
(D W Lewis) *hit 1st: towards rr: stdy prog 8th: 6th and hrd rdn after 10th: styd on to go 2nd at last: nt rch wnr* **33/1**
-P31 **3** *3* **Nazimabad (IRE)**[2] 979 6-10-7 **81** 7ex (t) ChristianWilliams 87
(Evan Williams) *t.k.h: w ldr tl 3rd: prom tl led bef 3 out: rdn and hdd next: one pced* **5/6**[1]
P12P **4** *nk* **Take The Oath (IRE)**[16] 862 8-10-3 **77** TDoyle 83+
(D R Gandolfo) *hld up: hdwy 8th: 4th and ch bef 3 out: sn rdn and no imp: disputing 3rd whn nt fluent last* **9/1**[3]
-P06 **5** *7* **Gipsy Cricketer**[30] 760 9-10-0 **74** oh5 (t) TScudamore 75+
(M Scudamore) *keen: led 4th: hdd bef 3 out: tired rapidly next* **25/1**
6460 **6** *19* **Rattina (GER)**[15] 874 9-9-7 **74** oh7 (v) CPoste(7) 53
(M F Harris) *chsd ldrs: rdn 9th: lost tch next* **14/1**
-040 **7** *nk* **Macgyver (NZ)**[19] 846 9-10-9 **90** CaptLHorner(7) 69
(D L Williams) *chsd ldrs tl 7th: wl bhd after 10th* **20/1**
PP-P **P** **Pharbeitfrome (IRE)**[69] 221 11-9-9 **74** (t) DCCostello(5) —
(W B Stone) *immediately labouring: lost tch 5th: t.o 6th: p.u 10th* **66/1**
6F **P** **On The Forty**[2] 979 8-10-9 **83** APMcCoy —
(Jonjo O'Neill) *hld up: hdwy 7th: drvn and wknd after 10th: poor 6th whn p.u 3 out* **14/1**
P5/4 **P** **Triple Crown (IRE)**[21] 825 12-9-11 **76** oh15 ow2 MNicolls(5) —
(P W Hiatt) *mstkes and struggling bdly fr s: rdn 3rd: t.o 6th: p.u 9th* **100/1**
554P **P** **Fullopep**[19] 839 11-11-5 **100** APogson(7) —
(J R Holt) *mstke 4th: already outpcd whn j.lft and mstke 5th: t.o and p.u 3 out* **50/1**
2P2- **P** **Master Henry (GER)**[283] 1604 11-11-12 **100** DRDennis —
(Ian Williams) *keen: disp ld tl 4th: rdn and wknd 7th: mstke 10th: t.o and p.u next* **12/1**
PU65 **P** **Javelot D'Or (FR)**[5] 939 8-10-6 **80** RJohnson —
(Mrs B K Thomson) *chsd ldrs: brief effrt in 3rd and j. slowly 7th: wknd next: t.o and p.u 2 out* **14/1**

4m 7.30s (-4.30) **Going Correction** -0.175s/f (Good) **13** Ran SP% **121.6**
Speed ratings: **103,102,100,100,97 88,88,—,—,— —,—,—** CSF £199.17 CT £360.17 TOTE £5.90: £2.00, £15.30, £1.30; EX 296.70.

Owner Mrs Anna Kenny **Bred** P J Hannon **Trained** Brancepeth, Co Durham

FOCUS
A very modest contest run at a good gallop and the form looks pretty solid.

NOTEBOOK
College City(IRE), a pound well in under the penalty for his win at Uttoxeter, came from off the pace to score decisively. Connections had been worried that the ground might be too fast for him but he had no problem with the underfoot conditions. *(op 6-1)*

Johnny Grand ran a better race in the cheekpieces, but in truth he was merely staying on past beaten horses from the second last. On this evidence he needs further.

Nazimabad(IRE) had enjoyed an uncontested lead when hacking up in a weak race at Worcester two days earlier, but this time he was taken on firstly by Master Henry and then by Gipsy Cricketer. That factor, and his 7lb penalty, eventually combined to cause his downfall. *(op evens tchd 11-10)*

Take The Oath(IRE) ran better than he had on his latest start but faded over the final three fences. He could be in the Handicapper's grip. *(op 11-1 tchd 8-1)*

Gipsy Cricketer, reverting to fences, was not discredited from 5lb out of the weights. *(op 20-1)*

On The Forty, soon on the deck in Nazimabad's race at Worcester two days earlier, showed a hint of ability and can race off 5lb lower in future handicaps. *(tchd 12-1)*

1000 MIDLANDS RACING NOVICES' (S) HURDLE (11 hdls) 2m 5f 110y
3:55 (3:58) (Class 5) 4-Y-0+ **£2,695** (£770; £385)

Form RPR
0516 **1** **Angie's Double**[10] 905 5-10-7 74 RSpate(7) 89+
(Mrs K Waldron) *prom in chsng gp fr 4th: clsd 3 out: rdn to ld bef next: clr and ears pricked last: easily* **7/2**[2]
U **2** *12* **Munaawesh (USA)**[12] 891 4-10-5 PKinsella(7) 72+
(D W Chapman) *prom in chsng gp fr 4th: effrt 3 out: rdn to ld briefly bef next: one pce and no ch w wnr bef last* **14/1**
PP- **3** *2 ½* **Golly (IRE)**[401] 697 9-10-8 JAJenkins(7) 73+
(D L Williams) *prom in chsng gp: wnt 2nd bef 5th: clsd 3 out: sn hrd drvn: racd awkwardly and fnd nil fr next: mstke last* **6/1**
61-P **4** *½* **Doof (IRE)**[77] 111 5-11-0 115 MrRQuinn(7) 77
(M C Pipe) *keen and sn wl clr: 24l ahd 6th: wknd 3 out: sn passed by 3 rivals and looked wl btn: plodded on again fr last* **9/2**[3]
-000 **5** *6* **Impero**[2] 978 7-11-1 69 JGoldstein 65
(G F Bridgwater) *lost pl 5th: struggling fr 7th* **33/1**
0-0P **6** *10* **Super Boston**[37] 686 5-11-1 68 (b) AThornton 55
(Miss L C Siddall) *mounted crse: nvr bttr than midfield: rdn and struggling after 7th* **28/1**
06/0 **7** *7* **Red September**[21] 822 8-10-8 69 (p) CaptLHorner(7) 48
(D L Williams) *midfield: rdn 7th: sn lost tch* **40/1**
8 *½* **In Ainm De (IRE)**[69] 9-10-8 64 KRenwick 41
(N Wilson) *a wl bhd: lost tch after 6th* **20/1**
-013 **9** *19* **Greencard Golf**[12] 891 4-11-4 100 AO'Keeffe 32
(Jennie Candlish) *mstkes in rr: last whn pckd bdly 4th: sn drvn: remote fr 7th and nt keen* **12/1**
0-50 **P** **Daily Run (IRE)**[37] 687 7-10-10 68 (t) DCCostello(5) —
(G M Moore) *struggling in rr: t.o and p.u 7th* **25/1**
0P-0 **P** **Red Autumn**[57] 426 8-11-1 70 (b[1]) JimCrowley —
(K G Reveley) *midfield: mstke 5th: lost tch after next: t.o and p.u 3 out* **40/1**
6-06 **P** **It's Harry**[48] 545 7-11-1 90 DElsworth —
(Mrs S J Smith) *mstke 2nd: nvr looked keen: rdn and lost tch after 6th: t.o and p.u 2 out* **3/1**[1]
6/PU **P** **Lady Lola (IRE)**[26] 785 7-10-1 MissJFoster(7) —
(Miss J E Foster) *last away: bolted into 2nd bhd long ldr after 2nd tl bef 5th: stopped to nil: t.o and p.u 7th* **40/1**
0P40 **F** **Mapilut Du Moulin (FR)**[19] 843 5-11-1 MAFitzgerald 65
(C R Dore) *hld up: sme prog 7th: last of five w ch and rdn after 3 out: 10l 5th and btn whn stmbld and fell 2 out* **12/1**

5m 18.1s (-4.20) **Going Correction** -0.175s/f (Good) **14** Ran SP% **124.1**
Speed ratings: **100,95,94,94,92 88,86,86,79,— —,—,—,—** CSF £48.29 TOTE £3.70: £1.80, £4.70, £2.50; EX 84.10.The winner was bought in for 8,000gns.

Owner Nick Shutts **Bred** P And Mrs Wafford **Trained** Stoke Bliss, Worcs

FOCUS
A weak race in which the pack were content to let the clear leader come back to them. However, the winner is on the upgrade and can score again

NOTEBOOK
Angie's Double, gaining her third win of the campaign, is a decent sort in this grade and she stayed on strongly to shrug off the runner-up from the second last. The ground had been too soft for her in a better contest on her latest start. *(op 3-1 tchd 4-1 in a place)*

Munaawesh(USA) was just getting the worse of his tussle with the mare when he was awkward *two from home. This was only his second run over hurdles and a seller should come his way. (op 16-1 tchd 20-1)*

Golly(IRE), not seen since pulling up in a chase over a year ago, appeared to blow up on the home turn after looking sure to be involved in the finish. *(op 7-1)*

Doof(IRE), the pick on BHB figures, quickly compiled a clear lead, tactics which paid off two starts ago, and was some 25 lengths to the good setting out on the final circuit. His stride shortened in the back straight and he was swallowed up, but he did stick on again and is capable of better back on easy ground. *(tchd 5-1)*

It's Harry, down in grade, was never in the hunt. *(op 4-1)*

1001 MOELLER CONTROL GEAR H'CAP HURDLE (8 hdls, 1 omitted) 2m 1f
4:30 (4:30) (Class 3) (0-125,120) 4-Y-0+ **£5,408** (£1,664; £832; £416)

Form RPR
-242 **1** **Figaro Du Rocher (FR)**[9] 915 5-10-11 **105** (t) TScudamore 112+
(M C Pipe) *set brisk pce: pushed clr bef last: easily* **11/10**[1]
-52P **2** *10* **Feanor**[26] 784 7-10-10 **107** (t) KJMercer(3) 104
(Mrs S A Watt) *hld up last tl 3 out: effrt to chse ldng pair bef omitted next: urged and fnd little after: lft 2nd at last* **5/1**[3]
3-06 **3** *7* **Bolshoi Ballet**[36] 695 7-10-11 **105** (b) GLee 95
(J Mackie) *lft 3rd at 3rd: j. slowly 5th and drvn: nvr gng wl after: no ch fr 3 out* **9/1**
-153 **4** *3 ½* **Resplendent Star (IRE)**[21] 824 8-11-0 **108** (v) LAspell 96+
(Mrs L Wadham) *hld up: rdn and j. slowly 5th: nvr gng wl after: last after 3 out* **4/1**[2]
6-06 **F** **All Bleevable**[21] 824 8-10-6 **100** JEMoore —
(Mrs S Lamyman) *disputing 2nd whn tk off too sn and fell 3rd* **16/1**
00-6 **U** **Migration**[45] 372 9-11-9 **120** LVickers(3) —
(Mrs S Lamyman) *taken to post v early: plld hrd towards rr tl hmpd and uns rdr 3rd* **33/1**
0005 **F** **Forzacurity**[9] 915 6-10-5 **104** LStephens(5) 103
(M Sheppard) *mounted crse and taken down early: pressed wnr tl rdn and outpcd after 2 out: 6l 2nd whn fell last* **11/1**

3m 57.3s (-7.60) **Going Correction** -0.175s/f (Good) **7** Ran SP% **111.4**
Speed ratings: **110,105,102,100,— —,—** CSF £6.96 CT £30.08 TOTE £1.60: £2.00, £3.20; EX 9.20.

Owner Pipe Monkees **Bred** S Aulert And Daniel Pepin **Trained** Nicholashayne, Devon

FOCUS
Not the most competitive of events, bu the time was fair and the form looks pretty solid. The second last flight was bypassed due to an injured jockey.

NOTEBOOK
Figaro Du Rocher(FR) had run a big race off this mark on his return to hurdles last time and was due to race off 5lb higher in future handicaps. Setting a decent pace, he stayed on too strongly for his only serious challenger on the extended run to the final flight. A versatile and likeable sort, he will still be well treated compared with his chase rating after this. *(tchd 6-5)*

Feanor won this event two years ago but was 13lb higher. Held up in rear, she closed travelling well leaving the back straight, but the effort flattened out before the last flight where she was left in second. *(op 6-1)*

Bolshoi Ballet, back in blinkers, was toiling early on the final circuit and remains out of sorts. *(tchd 10-1)*

Resplendent Star(IRE), who has his quirks, did not look happy from halfway. *(op 9-2)*

Forzacurity chased the winner, but was held on the long run to the final flight, where he came down. He remains high enough in the weights. *(op 10-1 tchd 12-1)*

1002 LADIES DAY SUNDAY 21ST AUGUST NOVICES' H'CAP HURDLE (13 hdls) 3m 2f

5:00 (5:03) (Class 4) (0-90,94) 4-Y-0+ **£3,360** (£960; £480)

Form				RPR
-221	1		**Fu Fighter**[9] 913 4-11-12 **94** 7ex ....(t) ChristianWilliams (Evan Williams) *taken steadily towards rr: stdy prog 7th: chal after 3 out: led next: sn clr and on bit: hrd hld* **2/1**[1]	103+
4-53	2	6	**Vivante (IRE)**[24] 801 7-10-9 **73** ....(p) WMarston (A J Wilson) *prom: drvn and outpcd bef 2 out: 4th appr last: rallied and styd on wl: no ch w wnr* **5/1**[2]	71
0034	3	¾	**Agnese**[34] 718 5-11-4 **82** .... RJohnson (G M Moore) *sn pressing ldr: led 8th: drvn after 3 out: hdd next: sn outpcd: mstke last and wnt lft: lost 2nd cl home* **9/1**	80+
05P-	4	3	**Follow Up**[88] 4914 7-11-4 **89** .... CDSharkey(7) (S B Clark) *prom: drvn and ev ch bef 2 out: nt qckn appr last* **40/1**	84+
6614	5	dist	**Earn Out**[9] 913 4-10-12 **87** .... MrRQuinn(7) (M C Pipe) *a wl bhd: detached fr reat after 6th and nvr looked like clsng: btn 42l* **12/1**	—
0/P2	P		**Weldman**[45] 603 6-10-4 **75** .... PKinsella(7) (K G Reveley) *midfield: rdn and wknd 10th: t.o and p.u 2 out* **8/1**	—
-340	P		**Waydale Hill**[54] 469 6-11-2 **80** ....(p) RWalford (T D Walford) *rdn 6th: lost tch after 8th: t.o and p.u 2 out* **12/1**	—
-5PP	P		**Vivre Aimer Rire (FR)**[47] 575 4-10-7 **75** .... TScudamore (M Scudamore) *wl in rr: lost tch after 8th: t.o and p.u 10th* **50/1**	—
5220	P		**Cody**[48] 545 6-11-2 **80** ....(vt) JimCrowley (James Moffatt) *chsd ldrs: rdn 7th: lost tch 3 out: t.o and p.u last* **20/1**	—
6/0-	P		**Derry Dice**[244] 2198 9-11-3 **88** ....(b) APogson(7) (C T Pogson) *nt fluent 4th: sn rdn: rr 7th: last whn blnd 8th: sn p.u* **40/1**	—
000-	P		**Lady Shanan (IRE)**[159] 3719 5-10-13 **80** .... ONelmes(3) (D A Rees) *bhd: brief effrt to midfield after 8th: wknd 10th: t.o and p.u 2 out* **40/1**	—
6-02	P		**Seattle Prince (USA)**[37] 687 7-11-7 **90** .... WKennedy(5) (S Gollings) *chsd ldrs: j. slowly 5th: drvn 9th: sn lost tch: t.o and p.u 2 out* **14/1**	—
0	P		**Mr Wonderful (IRE)**[16] 860 7-10-7 **74** ....(p) DCrosse(3) (P O'Connor) *bhd: stdy prog 8th: chsd ldrs 10th: lost tch u.p after 3 out: poor 6th whn p.u next* **66/1**	—
60P-	P		**Roman Consul (IRE)**[210] 2872 7-11-12 **90** .... APMcCoy (Jonjo O'Neill) *set slow pce: hdd 8th: sn rdn: lost tch tamely u.p 3 out: sn eased: p.u next* **6/1**[3]	—

6m 28.5s (-0.90) **Going Correction** -0.175s/f (Good)
WFA 4 from 5yo+ 4lb **14** Ran SP% **123.0**
Speed ratings: **94,92,91,91,**— —,—,—,— —,—,—,— CSF £12.04 CT £77.85 TOTE £2.90: £2.60, £2.10, £2.40; EX 16.20 Place 6 £24.99, Place 5 £6.72.
Owner The Boyz R Uz Partnership **Bred** R P Williams **Trained** Cowbridge, Vale Of Glamorgan

FOCUS
A low-grade handicap run at a very steady pace, but the placed horses were close to their marks, the winner is value for more than double the official margin and can rate higher.

NOTEBOOK
Fu Fighter has improved as he has stepped up in trip and he ran out a very easy winner. *Progressing well, he was a pound well in under his penalty compared with future handicaps. (tchd 15-8 and 9-4)*
Vivante(IRE), tried in cheekpieces, was in fourth and going nowhere turning for home, but she began to stay on going to the final flight and finished well. She really needs even further but things should click for her one day. *(tchd 9-2)*
Agnese, who lost second spot after a mistake at the final flight, still has to prove she truly stays this sort of trip. *(op 11-1)*
Follow Up travelled well until coming off the bridle on the home turn. This was an encouraging run *on his first outing since leaving Nicky Henderson's care and he should be sharper next time. (op 33-1)*
Earn Out, racing from a 5lb higher mark, was always at the back of the field and looks to have *ideas of his own. Official explanation: jockey said, regarding the apparent tender ride, his orders were to drop gelding in, cover it up and kid it throughout as gelding does not respond to strong handling, adding that gelding jumped moderately and never travelled well after halfway, staying on at one pace past beaten horses in the latter stages; trainer's representative added that gelding is indeed a character and a difficult ride who seems to go better for inexperienced riders; vet said gelding had lost a hind shoe (tchd 14-1)*
T/Plt: £16.70 to a £1 stake. Pool: £36,120.55. 1,574.05 winning tickets. T/Qpdt: £5.40 to a £1 stake. Pool: £2,472.20. 334.80 winning tickets. IM

1003 - 1009a (Foreign Racing) - See Raceform Interactive

891 MARKET RASEN (R-H)

Saturday, July 16

OFFICIAL GOING: Good (good to firm in places)
After nine dry days 5" water was put on the track. 'Perfect ground, a good job well done' was one top rider's verdict.
Wind: almost nil Weather: fine and sunny

1010 TOTESCOOP6 SUMMER HURDLE (H'CAP) (8 hdls) 2m 1f 110y

2:10 (2:10) (Class 2) (0-145,131) 4-Y-0+
£20,300 (£7,700; £3,850; £1,750; £875; £525)

Form				RPR
-111	1		**Buena Vista (IRE)**[25] 804 4-11-7 **128** .... APMcCoy (M C Pipe) *led to last: sn led again: styd on wl* **2/1**[1]	135+
0-13	2	1¼	**Hilltime (IRE)**[11] 726 5-10-3 **113** .... DCCostello(5) (J J Quinn) *chsd ldrs: wnt 2nd after 3 out: upsides next: led fractionally last: sn hdd and no ex* **20/1**	119
3-32	3	2½	**Borora**[22] 824 6-11-7 **131** .... WKennedy(5) (R Lee) *hld up: hdwy 4th: chsng ldrs 3 out: nt qckn fr next* **20/1**	134
105-	4	1¼	**Tulipa (POL)**[38] 2624 6-11-2 **121** .... JMMaguire (T R George) *hld up and bhd: hdwy 5th: chsng ldrs after next: nt qckn fr 2 out* **17/2**[3]	123
-332	5	shd	**Gone Too Far**[12] 714 7-10-7 **112** ....(v) TJMurphy (P Monteith) *a in tch: outpcd 3 out: styd on fr next* **16/1**	114
4-14	6	3½	**Donovan (NZ)**[64] 332 6-10-0 **108** ....(v[1]) LMcGrath(3) (R C Guest) *bhd: reminders 5th: hdwy next: 7th and styng on whn blnd 2 out: nt rcvr* **40/1**	109+
3-50	7	1¾	**Dominican Monk (IRE)**[34] 726 6-11-0 **119** .... MAFitzgerald (C Tinkler) *chsd ldrs: one pce appr 2 out* **40/1**	115
11-0	8	7	**Zonergem**[56] 450 7-11-10 **129** .... RThornton (Lady Herries) *hld up in last pair. hdwy 3 out: kpt on fr next: nvr a factor* **14/1**	118
0-02	9	3	**Wiscalitus (GER)**[48] 571 6-10-12 **117** .... AO'Keeffe (Miss Venetia Williams) *chsd ldrs: wknd appr 2 out* **16/1**	103
000-	10	5	**King Eider**[32] 4768 6-11-1 **120** .... ADobbin (B Ellison) *bhd: hdwy 5th: chsng ldrs after 3 out: btn appr next* **7/1**[2]	101
6P-2	11	4	**Duke Of Buckingham (IRE)**[20] 840 9-10-13 **118** .... TDoyle (P R Webber) *mid-div: hdwy u.p 3 out: lost pl appr next* **16/1**	95
-2U2	12	shd	**Bodfari Signet**[16] 873 9-10-9 **114** .... MBradburne (Mrs S C Bradburne) *bhd and drvn along 3rd: nvr on terms* **100/1**	91
6-61	13	½	**Xellance (IRE)**[22] 824 8-10-13 **123** .... RStephens(5) (P J Hobbs) *chsd ldrs: lost pl after 4th* **14/1**	100
/P4-	14	2½	**Overstrand (IRE)**[32] 4862 6-11-11 **130** .... GLee (M Todhunter) *hld up in rr: nvr on terms* **33/1**	104
0-00	15	dist	**Prince Among Men**[16] 873 8-10-12 **117** .... BHarding (N G Richards) *bhd: t.o 5th* **80/1**	—
-1F1	P		**Travel (POL)**[16] 873 5-10-12 **127** .... WMcCarthy(10) (T R George) *chsd ldrs: lost pl appr 2 out: p.u bef last* **16/1**	—
603-	P		**Jake Black (IRE)**[22] 3206 5-10-9 **114** .... RGarritty (J J Quinn) *chsd ldrs: lost pl after 5th: bhd whn p.u bef last* **16/1**	—
B-01	P		**Monticelli (GER)**[34] 726 5-11-2 **121** .... RJohnson (P J Hobbs) *mid-div: drvn along 4th: hdwy and in tch next: eased and p.u sn after 3 out* **12/1**	—

4m 9.40s (-7.00) **Going Correction** -0.15s/f (Good)
WFA 4 from 5yo+ 2lb **18** Ran SP% **126.4**
Speed ratings: **109,108,107,106,106 105,104,101,99,97 95,95,95,94,**— —,—,— CSF £49.93 CT £678.45 TOTE £3.10: £1.10, £5.30, £3.70, £2.60; EX 70.10 TRIFECTA Not won..
Owner M Archer & The Late Jean Broadhurst **Bred** Lodge Park Stud **Trained** Nicholashayne, Devon

FOCUS
A decent handicap run at a sound pace. It looks rock solid summer form with the third and fourth to their marks.

NOTEBOOK
Buena Vista(IRE), on his handicap bow, was given a typically attacking ride. Headed fractionally at the last, the champion, who never left the inside, soon had him back in front and he was firmly in command at the line. He has come an awful long way in a relatively short time. *(tchd 9-4)*
Hilltime(IRE), 10lb higher than his win here, has been in good form on the level in the meantime. Stalking the winner, he went a neck up jumping the last but he could not sustain the advantage for very long. He deserves full marks for this. *(op 16-1)*
Borora is not that big to be shouldering top weight. As usual he ran out of his skin, but he is now 19lb higher than for his last success.
Tulipa(POL), a sick horse after Galway last year, came here fit from the Flat. She ran a highly respectable race and this will have helped get her eye in. *(op 9-1 tchd 8-1)*
Gone Too Far, twice a winner on the Flat recently, is already a winner over fences. He kept on after being tapped for toe and is worth a try over a bit further. *(op 14-1)*
Donovan(NZ), the last to make the cut, wore a first-time visor and was unlucky not to finish a fair bit closer.
Dominican Monk(IRE) keeps running well but as a result get no relief.

1011 COBELFRET JUVENILE NOVICES' HURDLE (8 hdls) 2m 1f 110y

2:40 (2:43) (Class 3) 3-Y-0 **£4,784** (£1,472; £736; £368)

Form				RPR
	1		**Dan's Heir**[45] 3-10-12 .... APMcCoy (P C Haslam) *trckd ldrs: led 5th: styd on wl run-in* **9/4**[1]	103+
	2	3	**Goldstar Dancer (IRE)**[12] 3-10-12 .... RGarritty (J J Quinn) *trckd ldrs: wnt 2nd appr 2 out: almost upsides sn after last: no ex* **33/1**	99
1-2	3	13	**Tidal Fury (IRE)**[28] 777 3-11-5 .... GLee (J Jay) *j.lft: sn trcking ldrs: led 4th to next: j. bdly lft and wknd 2 out* **9/4**[1]	94+
6	4	2½	**John Forbes**[6] 945 3-10-12 .... ADobbin (B Ellison) *hld up: hdwy to chse ldrs 3rd: wknd appr 2 out* **9/2**[2]	84
	5	dist	**Cold Play**[30] 3-10-12 .... NFehily (C J Mann) *bhd and reminders 3rd: lost tch 3 out: btn 37 l* **16/1**	—
	6	hd	**Good Investment**[19] 3-10-12 .... FKeniry (P C Haslam) *in rr: drvn along 4th: lost tch 3 out* **12/1**[3]	—
	7	1¾	**Haenertsburg (IRE)**[14] 3-10-5 .... MAFitzgerald (A L Forbes) *led to 4th: lost pl 3 out: sn bhd* **66/1**	—
	8	6	**Giant's Rock (IRE)**[84] 3-10-12 ....(t) PJBrennan (B J Llewellyn) *chsd ldrs: lost pl 5th: sn bhd* **12/1**[3]	—
	P		**Hunipot**[12] 3-10-2 .... PBuchanan(3) (M E Sowersby) *j. bdly: sn bhd: t.o whn tried refuse 3rd: p.u after next* **100/1**	—

4m 15.7s (-0.70) **Going Correction** -0.15s/f (Good) **9** Ran SP% **106.4**
Speed ratings: **95,93,87,86,**— —,—,—,— CSF £56.61 TOTE £3.20: £1.20, £6.30, £1.30; EX 81.80.
Owner Blue Lion Racing V **Bred** R P Williams **Trained** Middleham, N Yorks
■ Vracca (9/1) was withdrawn (refused to line up). R4 applies, deduct 10p in the £.

FOCUS
With the third, a French-import, running way below expectations this was probably just a very ordinary juvenile hurdle.

NOTEBOOK
Dan's Heir, rated 59 and a dual winner on the level, is from a stable that excels in this department. *Jumping like an old hand, he simply would not be denied and in the end was drawing away. (op 2-1)*
Goldstar Dancer(IRE), rated 11lb inferior to the winner on the level, went in pursuit but after getting almost upsides, he had to concede defeat on the run-in. *(op 25-1)*
Tidal Fury(IRE), a winner and runner-up in a Listed hurdle in France, continually gave away ground jumping to his right. He went sideways two out and stopped to almost nothing. He was reported *to have a breathing problem. Official explanation: jockey said gelding had a breathing problem (tchd 5-2)*
John Forbes, rated 11lb ahead of the winner on the Flat, did not improve on his initial try over *hurdles. He looks to have a mind of his own and he has yet to prove his stamina for this game. (op 11-2 tchd 6-1)*

1012 GILBERT AND MOLLY KING MEMORIAL HBLB H'CAP CHASE (12 fncs) 2m 1f 110y

3:15 (3:17) (Class 3) (0-120,120) 5-Y-0+ **£5,557** (£1,710; £855; £427)

Form				RPR
1-6U	1		**Sardagna (FR)**[41] 646 5-11-10 **118** .... TJMurphy (M C Pipe) *hdwy 8th: cl 3rd whn hit 3 out: led last: r.o* **12/1**	131+
0/1	2	1½	**Ceannairceach (IRE)**[13] 894 12-10-12 **106** .... GLee (J M Jefferson) *wnt mod 3rd 7th: w ldrs 9th: upsides last: kpt on wl* **8/1**[3]	117
5U2	3	2½	**Bill's Echo**[27] 784 6-11-0 **111** .... LMcGrath(3) (R C Guest) *hld up in rr: smooth hdwy 8th: led 3 out tl last: no ex* **9/1**	120+
-P34	4	13	**Runner Bean**[13] 894 11-10-11 **105** .... RThornton (R Lee) *hdwy to chse ldrs 7th: led 9th to next: wknd between last 2* **25/1**	103+
2-02	5	7	**Fiery Peace**[50] 534 8-11-4 **112** .... MBradburne (H D Daly) *in rr: hdwy 8th: sn chsng ldrs: 4th and btn whn blnd 2 out* **6/1**[2]	104+

-2F4 **6** *12* **Romany Dream**[22] [823] 7-9-11 **94** oh2..............................(b) DCrosse[(3)] 70
(R Dickin) *w ldrs: led 5th tl 9th: wknd next* **14/1**
62-0 **7** *1 ¼* **Duchamp (USA)**[69] [248] 8-11-12 **120**..............................(p) RJohnson 95
(A M Balding) *hld up in rr: bhd fr 8th* **14/1**
2115 **8** *14* **Honan (IRE)**[32] [752] 6-11-0 **108**..............................(v) APMcCoy 69
(M C Pipe) *hdwy to chse ldrs 7th: sn rdn: lost pl after next: bhd fr 3 out* **8/1**[3]
11P3 **U** **Moscow Dancer (IRE)**[17] [855] 8-11-7 **115**.............................. JPMcNamara —
(P Monteith) *last whn blnd bdly and uns rdr 5th* **10/1**
321- **P** **Musical Stage (USA)**[402] [695] 6-11-7 **115**..............................(t) TDoyle —
(P R Webber) *mstkes: in rr: bhd whn p.u bef 3 out* **11/2**[1]
-212 **P** **Giorgio (IRE)**[22] [823] 7-11-2 **113**..............................(b) PBuchanan[(3)] —
(Miss Lucinda V Russell) *chsd ldng pair: wknd 7th: bhd whn p.u bef 2 out* **8/1**[3]
205- **P** **Latalomne (USA)**[93] [4838] 11-11-6 **119**.............................. PCO'Neill[(5)] —
(N Wilson) *racd wd: led to 5th: wknd qckly 7th: sn bhd: p.u bef 2 out* **8/1**[3]

4m 21.9s (-9.20) **Going Correction** -0.325s/f (Good) **12** Ran SP% **118.1**
Speed ratings: **107,106,105,99,96 91,90,84,—,— —,—** CSF £104.95 CT £915.84 TOTE £12.10: £5.10, £3.00, £3.10; EX 200.00.
Owner D A Johnson **Bred** Suc Herve De La Heronniere **Trained** Nicholashayne, Devon

FOCUS
Another decent handicap in which they went off at a suicidal pace and the two tearaway leaders dropped away before the home turn. The third and fourth set the standard and the form should work out.

NOTEBOOK
Sardagna(FR), given a most patient ride, jumped much better apart from tapping the third last. Really thrown at the last, she responded in ultra-game style and was always doing enough on the run-in.
Ceannairceach(IRE), 8lb higher, ran out of his skin but in the winner met a slightly un-exposed type over fences. *(op 7-1)*
Bill's Echo, back over fences, came there strongly to take charge three out but in the end the first two proved simply too tough. *(op 10-1 tchd 11-1)*
Runner Bean, still 2lb higher than his last success, ran a shade better than last time but is still not exactly firing on all cylinders. *(op 20-1)*
Fiery Peace, absent for seven weeks, came from off the pace but had no more to give when getting the second last all wrong. *(op 5-1)*
Romany Dream helped set a suicidal pace and she fell in a heap three out. More patient tactics over further are what is needed. *(op 12-1 tchd 16-1)*
Musical Stage(USA), absent for a year, clattered his way round on his handicap debut and never on terms, eventually wisely called it a day. *(op 6-1 tchd 13-2)*

1013 TOTESPORT SUMMER PLATE (A H'CAP CHASE) (LISTED RACE) (13 fncs 1 omitted) 2m 6f 110y
3:45 (3:48) (Class 1) (0-150,148) 5-Y-0+
£37,700 (£14,300; £7,150; £3,250; £1,625; £975)

Form RPR
F62- **1** **Tango Royal (FR)**[92] [4848] 9-10-8 **133**..............................(t) TJMalone[(3)] 149+
(M C Pipe) *hld up: hmpd 5th: hdwy to chse ldrs 9th: led after 11th: lft clr last* **25/1**
552- **2** *12* **Impek (FR)**[85] [4972] 9-11-7 **143**.............................. JCulloty 147+
(Miss H C Knight) *hld up: smooth hdwy 9th: chsng ldrs after 11th: lft 2nd last: no ch w wnr* **15/2**[3]
5-11 **3** *1 ¼* **Ballycassidy (IRE)**[24] [814] 9-11-12 **148**.............................. APMcCoy 152+
(P Bowen) *nt fluent: chsd ldrs: 4th and styng on same pce whn j.lft 2 out* **5/2**[1]
31-1 **4** *½* **Good Lord Louis (IRE)**[61] [386] 7-10-1 **123**.............................. PJBrennan 130+
(P J Hobbs) *chsd ldrs: led 11th: sn hdd: 5 l 2nd whn blnd bdly last: nt rcvr* **7/1**[2]
4-4P **5** *4* **Marked Man (IRE)**[22] [823] 9-10-3 **125**.............................. TDoyle 122
(R Lee) *in rr: hdwy 10th: kpt on same pce fr next* **40/1**
-330 **6** *3 ½* **Isard III (FR)**[20] [842] 9-10-3 **125**.............................. TJMurphy 119
(M C Pipe) *bhd: sme hdwy 10th: kpt on fr 2 out: nvr nrr* **11/1**
3-31 **7** *1* **Little Big Horse (IRE)**[34] [727] 9-10-2 **124**.............................. DElsworth 117
(Mrs S J Smith) *in tch: outpcd 10th: kpt on fr 2 out* **12/1**
101- **8** *5* **Liverpool Echo (FR)**[94] [4824] 5-10-1 **135**.............................. RSpate[(7)] 118
(Mrs K Waldron) *bhd: sme hdwy 11th: nvr on terms* **14/1**
05P- **9** *21* **Jakari (FR)**[98] [4772] 8-11-1 **137**.............................. RJohnson 104
(H D Daly) *led to 11th: wknd bef next* **10/1**
-411 **10** *5* **Bronzesmith**[31] [761] 9-10-7 **129**.............................. JTizzard 91
(B J M Ryall) *bhd: hdwy 8th: wknd 10th* **16/1**
/0-P **11** *16* **Royal Tir (FR)**[20] [842] 9-10-0 **122**.............................. JEMoore 68
(P J Hobbs) *in tch: bdly hmpd 5th: n.d after* **66/1**
41-5 **12** *8* **Benrajah (IRE)**[22] [823] 8-10-0 **122** oh3.............................. GLee 60
(M Todhunter) *w ldr: wknd 9th: sn bhd* **33/1**
U131 **F** **Celtic Boy (IRE)**[17] [857] 7-10-6 **128**.............................. MAFitzgerald —
(P Bowen) *chsd ldrs: 5th whn fell 5th* **9/1**
U **U** **Magic Sky (FR)**[20] [840] 5-10-0 **127** oh3..............................(t) ChristianWilliams —
(P F Nicholls) *bhd whn blnd and uns rdr 3rd* **20/1**
102- **P** **Ebinzayd (IRE)**[40] [4846] 9-10-8 **130**.............................. ADobbin —
(L Lungo) *chsd ldrs: blnd 7th: lost pl 9th: t.o whn p.u after 11th* **14/1**
P213 **U** **Gumley Gale**[20] [842] 10-10-0 **122**..............................(t) RGreene 119
(K Bishop) *bhd: sme hdwy 8th: lost pl after 11th: bhd whn blnd and uns rdr last* **25/1**

5m 30.1s (-16.30) **Going Correction** -0.325s/f (Good)
WFA 5 from 7yo+ 1lb **16** Ran SP% **126.5**
Speed ratings: **115,110,110,110,108 107,107,105,98,96 90,88,—,—,— —** CSF £201.53 CT £655.65 TOTE £33.90: £5.30, £2.30, £1.70, £2.00; EX 281.60 Trifecta £1189.60 Pool £4,858.94. 2.90 winning units.
Owner B A Kilpatrick **Bred** Patrice Metenier **Trained** Nicholashayne, Devon
■ Impek was Best Mate's partner Jim Culloty's final ride before he announced his retirement.

FOCUS
A high-class renewal of this rich prize, run in a smart time, and a wide-margin winner completing a 1013/1 three-timer for Martin Pipe and the race could rate higher. The third-last fence had to be omitted with Mick Fitzgerald still being treated on the landing side for what turned out to be a broken neck.

NOTEBOOK
Tango Royal(FR), knocked out of his stride early on, was in no hurry to join issue. In front starting the home turn, he was about five lengths up when his victory was sealed at the final fence. *(op 20-1)*
Impek(FR), suited by the right-handed track, went round in cruise control. His response to pressure was not for the first time limited to say the very least and he was handed second spot at the last. *(op 7-1)*
Ballycassidy(IRE) took this two years ago when it was run over two and a half miles. He was rather let down by his jumping but deserves full praise for the way he battled on all the way to the line. *(op 3-1 tchd 7-2 in a place)*
Good Lord Louis(IRE), 12lb higher and up in grade, jumped to the front at the last in the back straight but he was clinging on to second spot when he met the last all wrong, his rider making a remarkable recovery. He was having only his fourth start over fences and there should be even better to come. *(op 6-1)*
Marked Man(IRE), pulld up last time, ran a lot better and the extended trip did not seem to be a problem. *(op 33-1 tchd 50-1)*
Isard III(FR), happier over this much shorter trip, jumped better but never really got competitive. *(op 10-1 tchd 12-1)*

1014 JEWSON NOVICES' HURDLE (SERIES QUALIFIER) (8 hdls) 2m 1f 110y
4:20 (4:21) (Class 3) 4-Y-0+ **£4,836** (£1,488; £744; £372)

Form RPR
50-1 **1** **Rajam**[16] [870] 7-11-1 112..............................(p) WKennedy[(5)] 111+
(G A Harker) *smooth hdwy to go 2nd 3 out: led on bit after next: eased fnl 75yds: easily* **4/6**[1]
5-36 **2** *4* **Given A Chance**[22] [826] 4-10-9 97.............................. LVickers[(3)] 91+
(Mrs S Lamyman) *led and sn clr: hdd after 2 out: no ch w wnr* **17/2**[3]
0 **3** *2 ½* **Dyneburg (POL)**[16] [870] 5-11-0.............................. JMMaguire 87
(T R George) *hld up in last pl: hdwy 5th: mod 3rd 2 out: kpt on* **20/1**
0 **4** *13* **Drumossie (AUS)**[16] [870] 5-10-11.............................. LMcGrath[(3)] 77+
(R C Guest) *reminders 5th: outpcd fr next* **33/1**
5 *24* **Repent At Leisure**[315] 5-10-9.............................. PCO'Neill[(5)] 50
(R C Guest) *hld up: lost tch 5th* **25/1**
40-0 **6** *26* **Olympian Time**[63] [349] 5-10-2.............................. MNicolls[(5)] 17
(Miss J E Foster) *4th whn mstke 4th: mstke and wknd next: sn bhd* **150/1**
00/0 **7** *½* **Known Maneuver (USA)**[2] [987] 7-10-7 74.............................. CMStudd[(7)] 23
(M C Chapman) *chsd clr ldrs: wknd 3 out* **100/1**
8 *30* **Durba (AUS)**[379] 5-11-0.............................. HOliver —
(R C Guest) *hld up: sme hdwy 5th: sn wknd and bhd: t.o 2 out* **16/1**
1-33 **P** **Zaffre (IRE)**[41] [654] 6-10-13 100.............................. JEMoore —
(Miss Z C Davison) *mstke 3rd: reminders next: poor 6th whn p.u after 3 out* **7/2**[2]

4m 19.0s (2.60) **Going Correction** -0.15s/f (Good)
WFA 4 from 5yo+ 2lb **9** Ran SP% **111.8**
Speed ratings: **88,86,85,79,68 57,56,43,—** CSF £6.44 TOTE £1.70: £1.10, £1.90, £3.20; EX 6.60.
Owner Our Emerald Club **Bred** Shadwell Estate Company Limited **Trained** Thirkleby, N Yorks

FOCUS
A moderate contest a slow time and very much a one-sided contest with the runner-up the best guide to the form.

NOTEBOOK
Rajam, with the cheekpieces on again, was happy to bide his time. He moved up on the bridle to shadow the leader and in the end scored with any amount in hand. His confidence must be sky high. *(op 8-13)*
Given A Chance stole a march at the start and was soon in a clear lead. However, the winner was only playing with him and he was left for dead when the button was pressed. *(op 8-1 tchd 15-2)*
Dyneburg(POL), a winner five times on the Flat in his native Poland, showed a bit more than he had done on his debut behind the winner at Perth. *(op 16-1)*
Drumossie(AUS), a winner on the level in his homeland, had beaten just one on his debut behind the winner at Perth. *(op 28-1 tchd 40-1)*
Repent At Leisure had finished unplaced in five starts on the Flat. *(op 28-1)*
Zaffre(IRE), third behind Buena Vista at Stratford, was never happy and was going nowhere when pulled up on the home turn. *(op 4-1)*

1015 MORTONS PRINT NOVICES' H'CAP CHASE (14 fncs) 2m 6f 110y
4:50 (4:54) (Class 4) (0-100,93) 5-Y-0+ **£3,740** (£1,151; £575; £287)

Form RPR
54UF **1** **Beaugency (NZ)**[6] [948] 7-11-7 **93**.............................. PCO'Neill[(5)] 112+
(R C Guest) *hld up: hdwy 8th: led appr 3 out: r.o wl run-in* **10/1**
23-0 **2** *7* **Sendonthecheque (IRE)**[39] [674] 10-10-0 **67**.............................. PJBrennan 79+
(R Ford) *j.rt: led: clr to 8th: hdd appr 3 out: one pce run-in* **9/2**[2]
-530 **3** *8* **John Rich**[13] [896] 9-10-1 **71**..............................(tp) PBuchanan[(3)] 74
(M E Sowersby) *in tch: hdwy to chse ldrs 11th: one pce fr next* **10/1**
P333 **4** *4* **Tee-Jay (IRE)**[27] [783] 9-10-13 **80**.............................. FKeniry 80+
(M D Hammond) *chsd clr ldr: mstke 11th: one pce fr next* **5/1**[3]
06-0 **5** *1 ¾* **Swallow Magic (IRE)**[75] [152] 7-10-12 **82**.............................. KJMercer[(3)] 79
(Ferdy Murphy) *bhd: sme hdwy 10th: kpt on fr 3 out: nvr nr ldrs* **8/1**
P-10 **6** *½* **Make It Easy (IRE)**[60] [398] 9-9-7 **67** oh1.............................. CaptLHorner[(7)] 64
(D L Williams) *in rr: t.o 11th: kpt on fr next* **5/1**[3]
3-P0 **7** *½* **Matmata De Tendron (FR)**[17] [858] 5-11-0 **86**.............................. MBradburne 77
(A Crook) *chsd ldrs: outpcd 10th: no ch after* **33/1**
P0OU **8** *dist* **Proper Poser (IRE)**[2] [990] 9-9-7 **67** oh5.............................. CMStudd[(7)] —
(M C Chapman) *in rr: drvn along 7th: t.o 11th* **33/1**
P0/6 **P** **Civil Gent (IRE)**[38] [688] 6-10-0 **67** oh12..............................(t) BHarding —
(M E Sowersby) *bhd and reminders 5th: t.o 11th: p.u bef next* **25/1**
5-43 **P** **Quizzling (IRE)**[24] [812] 7-10-9 **76**.............................. JTizzard —
(B J M Ryall) *chsd ldrs: hit 5th: reminders 7th: lost pl and p.u bef 9th* **10/3**[1]

5m 41.3s (-5.10) **Going Correction** -0.325s/f (Good)
WFA 5 from 6yo+ 1lb **10** Ran SP% **113.6**
Speed ratings: **95,92,89,88,87 87,87,—,—,—** CSF £53.36 CT £461.77 TOTE £12.20: £3.30, £1.90, £2.20; EX 85.90.
Owner Gryffindor (www.racingtours.co.uk) **Bred** D M Kerr **Trained** Brancepeth, Co Durham

FOCUS
Quite a competitive low-grade handicap run at a sound early gallop, but the winning time was 11.2 seconds slower than the Summer Plate and the form is unlikely to prove strong.

NOTEBOOK
Beaugency(NZ), who failed to get round on his two most recents starts, jumped with aplomb and running away when taking charge, he scored in most decisive fashion. His rider looks full value for his claim. *(op 8-1)*
Sendonthecheque(IRE), placed four times in 16 previous starts, had the visor left off. Keen to lead, he continually jumped right-handed and in the end the winner proved much too good. *(op 5-1 tchd 4-1)*
John Rich at least behaved himself this time but he clearly has his limitations. *(op 9-1 tchd 8-1)*
Tee-Jay(IRE) kept tabs on the leader but over this slightly shorter trip he proved simply too slow.
Swallow Magic(IRE), making his chasing debut, sat way out of his ground and did quite well to finish as close as he did. *(op 7-1 tchd 13-2)*
Make It Easy(IRE), a prolific point winner, found himself in an impossible position and only stayed on late in the day. *(op 11-2)*
Quizzling(IRE) looked in trouble the minute he clattered the fifth fence. He never looked to be moving properly afterwards and was well in arrears when calling it a day. Official explanation: jockey said gelding was never travelling in final circuit *(op 4-1)*

1016 LYS-LINE H'CAP HURDLE (10 hdls) 2m 6f
5:20 (5:23) (Class 3) (0-125,122) 4-Y-O+ **£4,810** (£1,480; £740; £370)

Form RPR
1-21 **1** **Rift Valley (IRE)**[65] 315 10-10-13 **109**..............(v) RJohnson 114+
(P J Hobbs) *led 2nd: qcknd 6th and after 3 out: styd on wl run-in* **7/4**[1]
-1P0 **2** *3 ½* **Qabas (USA)**[22] 824 5-11-2 **112**..............(p) ADobbin 112+
(P Bowen) *trckd ldrs: wnt 2nd appr 2 out: nt qckn appr last* **11/1**
1-22 **3** *7* **Izzykeen**[20] 841 6-11-0 **110**.............. DElsworth 105+
(Mrs S J Smith) *w ldrs: handy 3rd whn hit 2 out: hung lft appr last: one pce* **4/1**[2]
F-00 **4** *2* **Masters Of War (IRE)**[17] 864 8-11-10 **120**..............(t) APMcCoy 110
(Jonjo O'Neill) *hld up: hdwy and hit 6th: rdn appr 2 out: one pce* **8/1**
-050 **5** *4* **Bobosh**[38] 690 9-10-0 **96** oh3.............. WHutchinson 82
(R Dickin) *led to 2nd: w wnr: drvn along 6th: wknd appr 2 out* **33/1**
4163 **6** *shd* **Alva Glen (USA)**[32] 751 8-10-8 **104**.............. PJBrennan 90
(B J Llewellyn) *in rr: effrt 7th: nvr trbld ldrs* **7/1**[3]
5010 **7** *13* **Ramblees Holly**[30] 768 7-10-5 **106**.............. DMcGann(5) 79
(R S Wood) *hit 4th: rdn and lost tch 7th* **25/1**
F054 **8** *1 ¾* **Siegfrieds Night (IRE)**[6] 947 4-10-1 **107**.............. CMStudd(7) 75
(M C Chapman) *prom: blnd 5th: bhd fr 7th* **10/1**
P-1U **P** **Mr Fluffy**[24] 814 8-11-7 **122**.............. RStephens(5) —
(P J Hobbs) *in rr: lost pl 7th: bhd whn p.u bef 2 out* **9/1**

5m 25.0s (-3.30) **Going Correction** -0.15s/f (Good)
WFA 4 from 5yo+ 3lb **9** Ran SP% **114.2**
Speed ratings: **100,98,96,95,94 93,89,88,—** CSF £21.26 CT £68.42 TOTE £2.60: £1.40, £2.20, £1.90; EX 16.50 Place 6 £120.70, Place 5 £54.59.
Owner Mrs Kathy Stuart **Bred** Mrs Anne Macdermott **Trained** Withycombe, Somerset

FOCUS
A fair handicap and a fine ride from the front by Richard Johnson. The winner is value for more than the official margin with the runner-up setting the standard.

NOTEBOOK
Rift Valley(IRE), stepping up the pace with a circuit to go, put his foot on the pedal again starting the home turn. He was never seriously challenged and was right on top at the line. *(op 13-8 tchd 15-8)*
Qabas(USA), who needs fast ground, worked his way on to the winner's quarters but he was never going to finish any better than runner-up.
Izzykeen moved almost upsides and hit the second last. He hung violently between the last two and though wayward, this trip looks to stretch him to the very limit.
Masters Of War(IRE), bang out of form on his two most recent starts, wore a tongue strap this time but his effort still looked to lack commitment. *(tchd 7-1)*
Bobosh, back over hurdles, was 3lb 'wrong'. He struggled to keep up with the winner with a full circuit to go and threw in the towel going to the second last flight. *(op 25-1)*
Alva Glen(USA) seemed to run a moody race and his response to pressure was half-hearted at best.
T/Plt: £66.80 to a £1 stake. Pool: £53,597.60. 585.00 winning tickets. T/Qpdt: £29.90 to a £1 stake. Pool: £1,995.50. 49.30 winning tickets. WG

958 NEWTON ABBOT (L-H)
Sunday, July 17

OFFICIAL GOING: Good to firm (good in places)
Wind: virtually nil

1017 SOUTH WEST RACING CLUB CLASSIFIED HURDLE (9 hdls) 2m 3f
2:00 (2:00) (Class 4) 4-Y-O+ **£2,618** (£748; £374)

Form RPR
-630 **1** **Red Canyon (IRE)**[7] 949 8-11-2 90..............(p) JTizzard 98
(C L Tizzard) *chsd ldr: led appr 3 out: sn rdn: hdd appr 2 out: rallied to ld appr last: r.o wl: rdn out* **4/1**[2]
560/ **2** *4* **Glenfield Heights**[1607] 3758 10-10-9 90.............. MrTJO'Brien(7) 96+
(W G M Turner) *hld up in tch: mstke 4th: tk clsr order after next: led on bit appr 2 out: sn rdn: hdd after 2 out: blnd last: no ex* **20/1**
0254 **3** *5* **Siena Star (IRE)**[25] 813 7-11-2 90.............. TScudamore 89
(P Bowen) *hld up mid div: stdy hdwy to go 4th after 6th: rdn after 3 out: kpt on same pce* **10/3**[1]
031P **4** *16* **Taranai (IRE)**[7] 949 4-10-10 90..............(t) AThornton 67
(B W Duke) *hld up mid div: hdwy appr 6th: 5th whn stmbld 3 out: sn rdn: one pced* **11/2**
-261 **5** *6* **General Smith**[14] 895 6-11-3 94.............. RHobson(3) 71
(H J Evans) *hld up towards rr: hdwy appr 3 out: sn rdn: no imp after* **5/1**[3]
230P **6** *3* **Spectacular Hope**[12] 905 5-10-10 79.............. RYoung(3) 61
(J W Mullins) *hld up towards rr and n.d* **12/1**
P-4P **7** *5* **Kirov King (IRE)**[21] 841 5-11-2 90.............. JPMcNamara 59
(B G Powell) *led: nt fluent 1st: sn clr: rdn and hdd appr 3 out: wknd appr 2 out* **9/1**
64-0 **8** *24* **King's Travel (FR)**[52] 517 9-10-11 84.............. CHonour(5) 35
(J D Frost) *a towards rr* **14/1**
P6/P **9** *12* **Contemporary Art**[43] 7-10-9 90..............(b[1]) KBurke(7) 23
(N J Dawe) *chsd ldrs: mstke 4th: wknd appr 6th* **66/1**
/00- **10** *dist* **Daisy Dale**[203] 2973 7-10-10 80.............. TJMalone(3) —
(S C Burrough) *hld up towards rr: sme hdwy after 5th: wknd after next: t.o* **100/1**
F60- **P** **Great Game**[354] 1058 5-11-2 65..............(t) BHitchcott —
(A S T Holdsworth) *bhd fr 5th: t.o and p.u bef 3 out* **100/1**
20-P **P** **Floranz**[54] 487 9-10-13 85.............. JMogford —
(Mrs M Evans) *a towards rr: lost tch fr 5th: t.o and p.u bef 3 out* **20/1**

4m 28.3s (-4.70) **Going Correction** -0.15s/f (Good)
WFA 4 from 5yo+ 2lb **12** Ran SP% **112.5**
Speed ratings: **103,101,99,92,89 88,86,76,71,— —,—** CSF £79.55 TOTE £5.30: £1.60, £8.80, £1.40; EX 217.60.
Owner Miss Jayne Brace & Gwyn Brace **Bred** C J Foy **Trained** Milborne Port, Dorset

FOCUS
A seller in disguise and the form is therefore very ordinary but the time was reasonable.

NOTEBOOK
Red Canyon(IRE), without a win in three years, was never far off the lead, but looked beaten when passed quarter of a mile out. However, Tizzard coaxed another run out of him and he finished strongly to win going away. This would have done his confidence good and he may now be worth switching to fences. *(tchd 9-2)*
Glenfield Heights ran a remarkable race on this first outing for nearly five years. He came there cantering on the run to the second last, but found little under pressure and it is highly likely the lack of a recent run cost him. There is a strong possibility of him bouncing, but if he somehow managed to avoid it and is given a break to recover from these exertions, then maybe he can pick up a small race during the summer months. *(op 16-1)*
Siena Star(IRE) ran one of his better races, plugging on into third. Selling company is likely to represent his best chance of winning. *(op 7-2 tchd 4-1)*
Taranai(IRE) was adrift of the front three and was unsuited by this drop in trip, having won here over further latest. She is worth another chance. *(op 6-1 tchd 5-1)*
General Smith ran just an ordinary race and found little for pressure in the straight. *(op 4-1)*
Great Game *Official explanation: jockey said gelding had a breathing problem (op 66-1)*

1018 SOUTH WEST RACING CLUB MAIDEN HURDLE (10 hdls) 2m 6f
2:30 (2:52) (Class 3) 4-Y-O+ **£4,877** (£1,500; £750; £375)

Form RPR
4-50 **1** **Maharaat (USA)**[33] 747 4-10-8 101.............. RStephens(5) 93
(P J Hobbs) *trckd ldrs: shkn up to chal aproaching 2 out: led last: pushed out* **4/1**[3]
0L0- **2** *1* **Kentucky King (USA)**[192] 3232 5-11-2.............. BHitchcott 95
(Mrs D A Hamer) *trckd ldrs: led 3 out: sn hrd rdn: hdd last: kpt on* **25/1**
3030 **3** *½* **Mistified (IRE)**[18] 860 4-10-10 94.............. RYoung(3) 91
(J W Mullins) *mid div: hdwy after 6th: pressed ldr and ev ch fr 3 out : hrd rdn appr next: no ex run-in* **11/4**[2]
4/04 **4** *dist* **Spider Boy**[53] 501 8-11-2 70.............. JMogford 58
(Miss Z C Davison) *led: rdn and hdd 3 out: sn wknd* **25/1**
0-4R **5** *1 ¼* **Fille Detente**[74] 182 5-10-6 75.............. RHobson(3) 50
(C J Gray) *hld up towards rr: sme late hdwy: nvr a danger* **25/1**
3/0- **6** *1 ½* **Aruba Dam (IRE)**[143] 4029 7-10-9.............. JPMcNamara 48
(B G Powell) *hld up towards rr: hdwy appr 7th: rdn after 3 out: sn btn* **14/1**
0P/0 **7** *½* **Silver Man**[41] 668 11-10-9..............(p) MrRQuinn(7) 52
(D C Turner) *mid div: rdn appr 7th: wknd 3 out* **100/1**
P/ **8** *1 ½* **Mardereil (IRE)**[50] 8-10-6.............. ONelmes(3) 43
(N J Hawke) *hld up mid div: hdwy to trck ldrs after 6th: rdn after next: wknd* **40/1**
0-00 **9** *8* **Important Boy (ARG)**[41] 665 8-11-2 78..............(t) TScudamore 42
(D D Scott) *prom tl 6th: sn bhd* **20/1**
4 **10** *30* **Cherrywood (IRE)**[26] 802 6-11-2.............. GSupple —
(M C Pipe) *mid div tl 5th: sn bhd: t.o* **14/1**
11 *½* **Award Me An Oscar (IRE)**[71] 5-10-13.............. TJMalone(3) —
(M C Pipe) *prom: hit 2nd: rdn and wknd qckly 3 out* **13/8**[1]
5 **P** **Daihannah (IRE)**[25] 817 5-10-9.............. JPByrne —
(Miss H E Roberts) *a towards rr: t.o and p.u bef 2 out* **25/1**
0 **P** **Dragon Blue**[42] 654 5-10-4.............. CHonour(5) —
(G F H Charles-Jones) *a towards rr: t.o and p.u after 6th* **100/1**
P30P **P** **Lescer's Lad**[18] 860 8-11-2 72..............(t) RWalford —
(C L Popham) *chsd ldrs tl after 6th: sn bhd: t.o and p.u bef 2 out* **50/1**

5m 18.1s (-2.20) **Going Correction** -0.15s/f (Good)
WFA 4 from 5yo+ 3lb **14** Ran SP% **124.6**
Speed ratings: **98,97,97,—,— —,—,—,—,— —,—,—,—** CSF £101.99 TOTE £5.80: £2.30, £11.60, £1.20; EX 182.70.
Owner Mrs Belinda Harvey **Bred** Shadwell Farm LLC **Trained** Withycombe, Somerset
■ The race was delayed after newcomer Off My Toes (50/1) was fatally injured going to post.

FOCUS
Modest maiden hurdle form with the third setting the standard.

NOTEBOOK
Maharaat(USA) was allowed to race without the blinkers on this occasion and ran out a good winner. The extra distance clearly suited the gelding and, as a four-year-old, he is entitled to improve further. He did, however, look an awkward ride and it would no surprise to see the headgear reapplied in future. *(op 7-2 tchd 9-2)*
Kentucky King(USA) improved for the increase in distance and kept battling right the way to the line. He should have little trouble finding a similar race in the coming months.
Mistified(IRE) can be used as a yardstick and he recorded a fair placed effort. He finds winning hard, however, and cannot be relied upon. *(op 3-1 tchd 10-3)*
Award Me An Oscar(IRE), a winning pointer, was understandably made a short-priced favourite but offered little and will no doubt have disappointed connections. Looking at how quickly he stopped it would not surprise to learn in future that he had a problem and he has to be worth another chance. *(op 11-4 tchd 3-1)*

1019 SOUTH WEST RACING CLUB BEGINNERS' CHASE (13 fncs) 2m 110y
3:00 (3:17) (Class 4) 5-Y-O+ **£4,046** (£1,245; £622; £311)

Form RPR
0-22 **1** **Dawton (POL)**[18] 855 7-11-0.............. JMMaguire 115+
(T R George) *led tl 5th: w ldr: led 3 out: sn rdn: wnt lft and mstke last: kpt on: rdn out* **13/8**[2]
-012 **2** *2* **Whispered Secret (GER)**[33] 751 6-11-0.............. TScudamore 114+
(M C Pipe) *in tch: wnt 3rd after 6th: hit 8th: rdn and effrt approachng 2 out: swtchd lft and ev ch whn hmpd after last: no ex* **5/4**[1]
33-0 **3** *7* **Scalloway (IRE)**[35] 726 5-11-0.............. CLlewellyn 104+
(D J Wintle) *prom: led 5th tl 3 out: sn rdn: kpt on same pce* **14/1**
F/3 **4** *10* **River Dante (IRE)**[6] 962 8-11-0..............(t) JTizzard 94
(L G Cottrell) *chsd ldrs tl outpcd appr 8th: nt a danger after* **20/1**
4-04 **5** *23* **Jim Lad**[11] 914 5-11-0 79.............. AThornton 71
(J W Mullins) *hld up towards rr: nvr trbld ldrs* **25/1**
2044 **6** *9* **Hattington**[17] 875 7-11-0..............(v[1]) BHitchcott 62
(M F Harris) *chsd ldrs: hit 6th: grad fdd fr next* **10/1**[3]
20P5 **7** *2 ½* **Tosawi (IRE)**[7] 948 9-10-9 98.............. JHarris(5) 60
(R J Hodges) *sn drvn along in rr: nvr a factor* **25/1**
6406 **8** *8* **Outside Investor (IRE)**[18] 862 5-10-4 75.............. KBurke(10) 52
(P R Rodford) *a towards rr* **33/1**
PP4- **9** *24* **Droumleigh Lad (IRE)**[112] 4578 10-11-0 85.............. JMogford 28
(Miss Z C Davison) *a towards rr* **66/1**

4m 3.30s (-2.20) **Going Correction** -0.05s/f (Good) **9** Ran SP% **115.2**
Speed ratings: **103,102,98,94,83 79,77,74,62** CSF £3.92 TOTE £2.50: £1.10, £1.60, £2.30; EX 4.30.
Owner B A Kilpatrick **Bred** Pan Andrzej Zielinski **Trained** Slad, Gloucs
■ Stewards' Enquiry : J M Maguire one-day ban: careless riding (Jul 28)

FOCUS
An ordinary beginners' chase, but two fair hurdlers pulled clear of the remainder as expected. The winner sets the level and the form could rate higher.

NOTEBOOK
Dawton(POL) had only the one rival to beat on the book and he ran out a workmanlike winner. He looked set to battle out a close finish until hampering the runner-up and leaving him short of racing room. He may have been a fortunate winner, but he is a fair sort and can probably defy a penalty in novice company. *(op 6-4)*
Whispered Secret(GER) made a pleasing start to his fencing career and may have been an unlucky loser. He was rallying bravely when shut out by the winner, but connections should have little trouble getting him to win a race or two in the summer months. *(op 11-8 tchd 6-4, 13-8 in a place)*
Scalloway(IRE) is the other to take from the race as he went with the front pair for a long way before eventually being left behind. He was far inferior to them over hurdles and will find easier opportunities.
River Dante(IRE) may be helped by further in handicaps. *(tchd 16-1)*
Droumleigh Lad(IRE) *Official explanation: trainer's representative said gelding had finished sore (op 50-1)*

1020 SOUTH WEST RACING CLUB H'CAP HURDLE (9 hdls) 2m 3f

3:30 (3:41) (Class 3) (0-125,124) 4-Y-0+ **£4,784** (£1,472; £736; £368)

Form RPR

P5 **1** **Room To Room Gold (IRE)**[6] [959] 9-10-9 **107**.................... AThornton 111+
(R H Alner) *trckd ldrs: hit 3 out: led on bit next: r.o wl: readily* **10/1**

33F- **2** *6* **Toi Express (IRE)**[245] [2216] 9-11-8 **120**........................ JTizzard 118
(R J Hodges) *hld up: tk clsr order 6th: rdn after 3 out: styd on to go 2nd run-in: no ch w wnr* **12/1**

506- **3** *½* **Goss**[218] [2772] 8-10-0 **108**.. WJones(10) 105
(Jonjo O'Neill) *w ldr: led 5th tl after 3 out: sn rdn: kpt on same pce* **12/1**

-133 **4** *hd* **Kilindini**[33] [742] 4-10-13 **114**.. BJCrowley 109+
(Miss E C Lavelle) *in tch: tk clsr order 6th: rdn and effrt appr 2 out: kpt on same pce* **11/2[3]**

-006 **5** *1* **Arm And A Leg (IRE)**[18] [864] 10-10-4 **102**........................(p) BHitchcott 99+
(Mrs D A Hamer) *led at gd pce: hdd 5th: prom: led after 3 out: hdd and mstke 2 out: kpt on same pce* **16/1**

0231 **6** *½* **Imperial Rocket (USA)**[7] [947] 8-10-6 **104** 7ex..................(t) CLlewellyn 100
(W K Goldsworthy) *in tch: rdn and effrt appr 2 out: kpt on same pce* **7/4[1]**

0-10 **7** *1* **Cool Spice**[43] [633] 8-11-7 **124**.. RStephens(5) 119
(P J Hobbs) *a towards rr: nvr on terms* **7/2[2]**

0-55 **8** *14* **Anatar (IRE)**[18] [864] 7-11-9 **121**.. TScudamore 102
(M C Pipe) *a towards rr: nvr on terms* **11/2[3]**

4m 26.2s (-6.80) **Going Correction** -0.15s/f (Good)
WFA 4 from 7yo+ 2lb **8** Ran SP% **119.7**
Speed ratings: **108,105,105,105,104 104,104,98** CSF £118.99 CT £1466.68 TOTE £12.30: £2.70, £2.70, £2.20; EX 109.30.
Owner D Brennan **Bred** Fintan Farrell **Trained** Droop, Dorset

FOCUS
Modest form, but an impressive winner for the grade with the second and fourth being the benchmarks for the form.

NOTEBOOK
Room To Room Gold(IRE) made short work of some modest opposition and left behind his two previous efforts in Britain. Never far off the pace - has been restrained in past - it was clear from around half a mile out he was going to win and he strode away under pressure to score with any amount in hand. He is sure to go up in the handicap for this, but is surely capable of defying a *penalty if arriving in this form again. Official explanation: trainer said, regarding the improved form shown, gelding was better suited by being ridden more prominently today (op 8-1)*
Toi Express(IRE) got the better of Goss on the run-in to claim second and shaped as though this first run for some time was need. He is an obvious one to watch out for in future, but may need to drop a few pounds before winning again. *(op 10-1)*
Goss was another returning from a break and he ran well for a long way, just losing second on the *run-in. He is not as good as he was, but is evidently still capable of winning at a modest level. (op 9-1)*
Kilindini continues to run well, but could ideally do with dropping a few pounds. *(op 9-2)*
Imperial Rocket(USA) appeared to have no excuses and simply seemed to run flat. He was well supported and may be worth another chance. *(op 11-4)*

1021 SOUTH WEST RACING CLUB NOVICES' HURDLE (8 hdls) 2m 1f

4:00 (4:08) (Class 4) 4-Y-0+ **£3,334** (£952; £476)

Form RPR

430- **1** **Theocritus (GER)**[167] [3624] 4-10-12 85.................................. AThornton 90
(Nick Williams) *trckd ldrs: lost pl and dropped rr appr 3 out: rdn and gd hdwy appr 2 out: led sn after last: r.o wl* **9/2[2]**

1-12 **2** *1¾* **Latin Queen (IRE)**[18] [569] 5-11-2 114................................ CHonour(5) 99+
(J D Frost) *prom: led 3rd: edgd lft 2 out and last: hdd sn after last: no ex* **4/7[1]**

0 **3** *2* **Doris Souter (IRE)**[35] [729] 5-10-7 .... WMarston 81
(D J Wintle) *keen trcking ldrs: mstke 4th: rdn to chse ldr appr 2 out: kpt on* **12/1**

40-6 **4** *4* **Giust In Temp (IRE)**[75] [173] 6-10-7 77.......................... MrTJO'Brien(7) 84
(Mrs K M Sanderson) *hld up: smooth hdwy 3 out: sn rdn: kpt on same pce* **66/1**

5F0 **5** *8* **Didn't You Know (FR)**[11] [911] 4-10-5 .... GSupple 67
(M C Pipe) *hld up: hdwy appr 3 out to chse ldrs: sn rdn: one pced* **16/1**

6/ **6** *7* **The Cute Won (USA)**[45] [622] 7-11-0 ....(t) CLlewellyn 69
(W K Goldsworthy) *led tl 3rd: w ldr: rdn after 3 out: wknd next* **10/1[3]**

P5 **7** *10* **Duke's View (IRE)**[26] [804] 4-10-5 .... MrRQuinn(7) 57
(D C Turner) *in tch tl sddle slipped appr 5th* **200/1**

P6-0 **8** *5* **Bebe Factual (GER)**[64] [343] 4-10-9 .... TJMalone(3) 52
(J D Frost) *bhd fr 4th* **66/1**

9 *shd* **Brown Fox (FR)**[71] 4-10-2 .... ONelmes(3) 45
(C J Down) *mid div tl 5th: sn bhd* **33/1**

00-5 **10** *13* **Blandings Castle**[52] [517] 4-10-12 64..................................(v[1]) JPMcNamara 39
(Nick Williams) *hld up and n.d* **100/1**

11 *9* **Chanfron**[289] 4-10-12 .... BHitchcott 30
(R H Buckler) *chsd ldrs tl 4th: sn bhd* **33/1**

4m 1.90s (-3.20) **Going Correction** -0.15s/f (Good)
WFA 4 from 5yo+ 2lb **11** Ran SP% **114.9**
Speed ratings: **101,100,99,97,93 90,85,83,83,77 72** CSF £7.43 TOTE £6.10: £1.80, £1.02, £3.00; EX 11.80.
Owner Gale Force Three **Bred** Gestut Berg Eberstein **Trained** George Nympton, Devon

FOCUS
A two-horse race on paper but it was the second favourite who emerged victorious. The winner, fourth and fifth set the level for the form.

NOTEBOOK
Theocritus(GER) caused a minor surprise in landing this novices' hurdle, overturning odds-on favourite Latin Queen. He looked set to have to settle for second for much of the way, but was helped by the favourite continually edging left at her hurdles and he came through with a strong late run. His current lowly rating should allow him to enjoy further success at handicap level.
Latin Queen(IRE) spurned a great opportunity and was basically disappointing. She arguably threw *victory away in edging left and is clearly one to have reservations about in future. (op 4-6 tchd 8-11 in a place)*
Doris Souter(IRE) improved on her previous hurdling form and kept on well into third. Races at selling level will be more up her street. *(op 10-1)*
Giust In Temp(IRE) ran well, but is a poor performer and does little for the form. *(op 33-1)*
Didn't You Know(FR) is evidently one of her powerful stable's lesser lights. *(op 20-1)*
Duke's View(IRE) *Official explanation: trainer said saddle slipped (op 100-1)*

1022 SOUTH WEST RACING CLUB H'CAP CHASE (20 fncs) 3m 2f 110y

4:30 (4:34) (Class 4) (0-110,109) 5-Y-0+ **£3,738** (£1,150; £575; £287)

Form RPR

/1U- **1** **Rolfes Delight**[264] [1850] 13-10-5 **88**.. MFoley 100+
(A E Jones) *in tch: bmpd 5th: led after next: mde rest: in commamd fr 3 out: comf* **11/2[3]**

-13U **2** *5* **Presence Of Mind (IRE)**[33] [746] 7-11-12 **109**.................... BJCrowley 117+
(Miss E C Lavelle) *hld up: hdwy after 10th: rdn to go 2nd 3 out: kpt on but a hld by wnr fr next* **5/1[2]**

-2P0 **3** *12* **Phar City (IRE)**[26] [805] 8-10-12 **95**.. BHitchcott 89
(R H Buckler) *trckd ldrs: chsd wnr fr 10th: rdn after 4 out: one pced* **10/1**

6-13 **4** *7* **Uncle Mick (IRE)**[50] [547] 10-11-8 **105**................................(bt) JTizzard 92
(C L Tizzard) *chsd ldrs tl outpcd appr 16th: nt a danger after* **5/2[1]**

F/0- **U** **Major Sharpe (IRE)**[296] [1496] 13-9-11 **83** oh1.............................. RYoung(3) —
(B J M Ryall) *led tl blnd and uns rdr 2nd* **25/1**

3PP3 **P** **Hardy Russian (IRE)**[32] [759] 8-9-6 **85** oh13 ow2..............(p) KBurke(10) —
(P R Rodford) *bhd fr 6th: t.o and p.u bef 13th* **28/1**

0/3- **F** **Chief Predator (USA)**[48] 11-10-0 **88** oh8 ow5.................. LStephens(5) —
(B J Llewellyn) *trcking ldrs whn blkd and fell 5th* **7/1**

6010 **P** **Blue Leader (IRE)**[11] [915] 6-10-5 **88**................................(bt) CLlewellyn —
(W K Goldsworthy) *bhd fr 9th: t.o and p.u after 13th* **15/2**

5P-4 **P** **The Sawdust Kid**[41] [669] 11-9-9 **83** oh13........................ RStephens(5) —
(R H Buckler) *in tch: tk clsr order after 6th: rdn and wknd appr 4 out: bhd and p.u bef 2 out* **16/1**

UP-0 **P** **Jabiru (IRE)**[26] [805] 12-10-9 **99**.......................................(b) MrTJO'Brien(7) —
(Mrs K M Sanderson) *trckd ldr: lft in ld 2nd tl after 6th: chsd ldr: blnd 10th: sn bhd: p.u bef 13th* **12/1**

6m 40.3s (-3.10) **Going Correction** -0.05s/f (Good) **10** Ran SP% **114.8**
Speed ratings: **102,100,96,94,—,—,—,—,—,—** CSF £33.39 CT £267.58 TOTE £6.90: £2.00, £1.40, £4.00; EX 37.40 Place 6 £95.55, Place 5 £52.20.
Owner Graham Brown **Bred** N J Barrowclough **Trained** Newchapel, Surrey

FOCUS
A weak race and only four of the ten managed to complete in what was a real stamina test. The winner looks on a fair mark.

NOTEBOOK
Rolfes Delight, who was clearly ready for this test on his return from a nine-month break, dominated the opposition once taking it up and powered away for an easy success. Despite being a 13-year-old, he is evidently still a capable performer. *(op 13-2)*
Presence Of Mind(IRE) is far from consistent, but this was one of his better efforts. Unfortunately for his followers, he cannot be guaranteed to build on the run. *(op 9-2)*
Phar City(IRE) was a bit adrift of the front two and increased his already poor strike rate. *(op 11-1)*
Uncle Mick(IRE) was the only other to complete and gets a mention for no other reason. *(op 3-1)*
T/Plt: £56.80 to a £1 stake. Pool £40,241.40. 516.85 winning tickets T/Qpdt: £21.60 to a £1 stake. Pool £2,592.20. 88.40 winning tickets TM

[943]STRATFORD (L-H)

Sunday, July 17

OFFICIAL GOING: Good to firm (good in places)
With the ground drying out some fast times were recorded and the going may well have been quicker than the original description.
Wind: almost nil Weather: sunny & hot

1023 CLAYDON HORSE EXERCISERS JUVENILE NOVICES' HURDLE (9 hdls) 2m 110y

2:10 (2:14) (Class 3) 3-Y-O

£6,043 (£2,292; £1,146; £521; £260; £156)

Form RPR

1 **Federstar (GER)**[14] 3-10-12 .... PJBrennan 95+
(M F Harris) *j.rt: led tl after 4th: w ldr: rdn appr 2 out: led cl home: all out* **15/8[2]**

2 *hd* **Royal Master**[30] 3-10-12 .... FKeniry 93
(P C Haslam) *a.p: rdn to ld 2 out: hdd cl home* **8/1[3]**

3 *dist* **Ferrara Flame (IRE)**[9] 3-10-5 .... RJohnson 58
(R Brotherton) *hld up: rdn and struggling fr 5th: lft poor 3rd last* **9/1**

P **4** *6* **Imperial Miss (IRE)**[7] [945] 3-10-5 .... LAspell 48
(B W Duke) *prom tl wknd 3 out* **20/1**

5 *shd* **Shugula (IRE)**[24] 3-10-5 .... TDoyle 48
(Ms J S Doyle) *hld up in tch: j.rt 2nd: wknd after 4th: nt fluent 5th* **80/1**

P **6** *16* **Mabella (IRE)**[7] [945] 3-10-2 .... TJPhelan(3) 32
(B Llewellyn) *t.k.h towards rr: t.o fr 5th* **33/1**

7 *8* **Robmantra**[36] 3-10-12 .... OMcPhail 31
(B J Llewellyn) *t.k.h in rr: t.o fr 6th* **66/1**

U **Fair Along (GER)**[123] 3-10-12 .... RThornton —
(J L Flint) *hld up: mstke 1st: ref and uns rdr 3rd* **14/1**

2 **F** **Shingle Street (IRE)**[7] [945] 3-10-12 ....(b) SThomas 89
(Miss Venetia Williams) *w ldr: led after 4th: mstke 6th: rdn and hdd 2 out: 4 l 3rd and wkng whn fell last* **7/4[1]**

3m 52.0s (-6.40) **Going Correction** -0.375s/f (Good) **9** Ran SP% **109.4**
Speed ratings: **100,99,—,—,— —,—,—,—** CSF £15.20 TOTE £2.40: £1.10, £2.20, £2.40; EX 15.90.
Owner The Piranha Partnership **Bred** R Paulick **Trained** Edgcote, Northants

FOCUS
A poor contest for the grade and with little to go on is rated through time.

NOTEBOOK
Federstar(GER), a dual winner on the Flat in Germany for Christian Von der Recke, only recently arrived in this country. Showing a tendency to jump right, he was particularly bad at the second last and did well to score on fast ground that was not thought to be in his favour. *(op 2-1 tchd 7-4)*
Royal Master ◆, a maiden at up to a mile on the Flat, seemed set to score when the winner jumped badly right at the penultimate hurdle. It was not a lack of stamina that beat him and he looks a ready-made future winner before the competition hots up. *(tchd 17-2)*
Ferrara Flame(IRE), who finally got off the mark in a seven-furlong Chepstow seller last month, was fortunate to finish third.
Shingle Street(IRE), fitted with the blinkers he had worn for his last two starts on the level, probably had more on his plate than when narrowly beaten over course and distance a week earlier. *(op 15-8)*

1024 CLAYDON HORSE EXERCISERS NOVICES' CHASE (13 fncs) 2m 1f 110y

2:40 (2:44) (Class 3) 5-Y-0+ **£5,434** (£1,672; £836; £418)

Form RPR

-2P1 **1** **Croix De Guerre (IRE)**[23] [825] 5-11-12 123...........................(b) RJohnson 135+
(P J Hobbs) *w ldr: led 9th: rdn clr appr last: r.o wl* **9/1**

03-1 **2** *8* **One Cornetto (IRE)**[26] [803] 6-11-6 132.. LAspell 120
(L Wells) *hld up: hit 4th: hdwy 9th: chsd wnr appr 4 out: rdn appr 2 out: no imp* **4/1[2]**

P-12 **3** *9* **Space Star**[23] [825] 5-11-6 123.. TDoyle 113+
(P R Webber) *hld up: hdwy 9th: rdn and wknd after 3 out* **13/2[3]**

0/44 **4** *25* **Tubber Streams (IRE)**[4] [982] 8-10-7 .... PTGallagher(7) 87+
(B A Pearce) *j.lft: led: hit 1st: hdd and hit 9th: sn wknd* **100/1**

30-5 **P** **Ela Re**[11] [914] 6-11-0 .... PJBrennan —
(C R Dore) *a bhd: mstke 3rd: t.o fr 8th: p.u bef 3 out* **50/1**
3-51 **P** **Perouse**[39] [682] 7-11-6 .... (t) ChristianWilliams —
(P F Nicholls) *a bhd: rdn appr 9th: t.o whn p.u bef 3 out* **4/6**[1]
4m 3.20s (-9.30) **Going Correction** -0.55s/f (Firm) **6** Ran SP% **106.3**
Speed ratings: **98,94,90,79,**— — CSF £39.53 TOTE £7.30: £2.40, £1.90; EX 27.90.
Owner Jack Joseph **Bred** T Wada **Trained** Withycombe, Somerset

FOCUS
A fair novice chase for the time of year and a good pace resulted in a fast time. The winner is likely to go up a fair amount for this.

NOTEBOOK
Croix De Guerre(IRE) appears something of a reformed character these days and his attitude could not be faulted under a double penalty. *(op 8-1)*
One Cornetto(IRE) tried to make a race of it but had to admit he got licked by the winner as his chance melted away on a hot day. *(op 7-2)*
Space Star would probably not have beaten the winner when unlucky at Market Rasen and had no excuses this time on 6lb better terms. *(op 7-1 tchd 8-1)*
Perouse was never travelling according to his rider. *Official explanation: jockey said gelding was never travelling (tchd 4-7 and 4-11 in places)*

1025 CLAYDON HORSE EXERCISERS H'CAP CHASE (FOR THE CLAIREFONTAINE CHALLENGE TROPHY) (18 fncs) 3m

3:10 (3:13) (Class 3) (0-125,119) 5-Y-£9,182 (£3,512; £1,779; £834; £441)

Form RPR
4211 **1** **Keltic Lord**[7] [948] 9-10-11 **104** 7ex .... RThornton 119+
(P W Hiatt) *hld up: hdwy 6th: led 14th tl blnd 4 out: rdn to ld appr 2 out: clr appr last: r.o wl* **5/4**[1]
0-24 **2** *4* **Dark Room (IRE)**[25] [815] 8-11-6 **113** .... JEMoore 120
(Jonjo O'Neill) *led to 2nd: remained prom: rdn 13th: outpcd after 3 out: styd on flat: nt trble wnr* **16/1**
/F5- **3** *nk* **Harry's Dream**[256] [1985] 8-11-3 **110** .... RJohnson 118+
(P J Hobbs) *hld up: hdwy 13th: outpcd 3 out: styd on flat* **15/2**[3]
033 **4** *½* **Fear Siuil (IRE)**[26] [805] 12-10-5 **98** .... (t) DRDennis 104
(Nick Williams) *hld up: hdwy 12th: rdn appr 14th: led 4 out tl appr 2 out: one pce* **8/1**
6-13 **5** *25* **Moving Earth (IRE)**[35] [727] 12-11-12 **119** .... TJMurphy 107+
(A W Carroll) *hld up and bhd: rdn and lost tch fr 4 out* **11/1**
-PP0 **P** **Just Sooty**[14] [895] 10-10-13 **113** .... CDSharkey(7) —
(S B Clark) *a bhd: blnd 11th: sn t.o: p.u after 13th* **50/1**
2-16 **P** **Iverain (FR)**[31] [765] 9-10-11 **104** .... SThomas —
(Sir John Barlow Bt) *a bhd: mstke 1st: rdn 13th: t.o whn p.u bef 2 out* **25/1**
2-25 **P** **Lodestar (IRE)**[66] [321] 8-10-13 **106** .... (b) ChristianWilliams —
(Ian Williams) *prom: rdn after 13th: wknd 4 out: bhd whn p.u after 2 out* **4/1**[2]
-521 **P** **Lord 'N' Master (IRE)**[41] [669] 9-11-5 **112** .... MBatchelor —
(R Rowe) *led 2nd: hit 7th and 8th: hit 14th and hdd: sn wknd: bhd whn p.u bef 2 out* **11/1**
5m 41.8s (-20.40) **Going Correction** -0.55s/f (Firm) course record **9** Ran SP% **115.7**
Speed ratings: **112,110,110,110,102** —,—,—,— CSF £21.63 CT £113.07 TOTE £2.10: £1.40, £2.60, £2.00; EX 20.60 Trifecta £67.20 Pool £341.20. 3.60 winning units.
Owner Paul Porter **Bred** Miss H Day **Trained** Hook Norton, Oxon

FOCUS
A fair handicap run in a decent time for the grade and a course record. the winner is value for twice the winning margin and the form looks solid.

NOTEBOOK
Keltic Lord completed a hat-trick on consecutive Sundays despite being 12lb higher than when defying a 7lb penalty here last week. He did well to overcome a bad mistake at the final ditch and will be given a break now. *(op 11-10 tchd Evens in a place)*
Dark Room(IRE) certainly appreciated the return to three miles and found a second wind to secure thwe runner-up spot after looking held at the end of the back straight.
Harry's Dream, having his first start since last November, showed no signs of the jumping errors that have cost him dear in the past. He could have blown up three from home before staying on again and may be capable of improvement. *(op 8-1 tchd 17-2)*
Fear Siuil(IRE) was 19lb lower than when completing a Stratford hat-trick in 2003. One of those victories did come over this three miles but he only barely gets the trip. *(op 10-1)*
Lord 'N' Master(IRE) *Official explanation: trainer said gelding pulled up slightly sore (op 8-1)*

1026 STRATFORD OPERATIC SOCIETY 42ND STREET H'CAP HURDLE (12 hdls) 2m 6f 110y

3:40 (3:40) (Class 3) (0-115,113) 4-Y-0+
£6,322 (£2,398; £1,199; £545; £272; £163)

Form RPR
1211 **1** **Charlie's Double**[33] [745] 6-10-6 **96** .... DCrosse(3) 97
(J R Best) *a.p: rdn 9th: led after 3 out: drvn out* **3/1**[1]
2213 **2** *¾* **Absolut Power (GER)**[18] [864] 4-11-5 **110** .... (p) MBradburne 107+
(J A Geake) *hld up: hdwy after 8th: chal 2 out: rdn and ev ch whn nt fluent last: nt qckn* **15/2**
1143 **3** *¾* **Altitude Dancer (IRE)**[25] [814] 5-11-4 **105** .... RThornton 104
(Mrs A M Thorpe) *a.p: rdn and kpt on same pce fr 2 out* **11/2**
2-15 **4** *7* **Azzemour (FR)**[58] [441] 6-10-4 **101** .... (t) LHeard(10) 93
(P F Nicholls) *hld up: hdwy appr 8th: wknd after 3 out* **7/2**[2]
0226 **5** *3* **Brush A King**[17] [768] 10-10-13 **107** .... APogson(7) 97+
(C T Pogson) *w ldr: led 3rd: hit 3 out: sn rdn and hdd: wknd appr 2 out* **12/1**
22P- **6** *6* **The Sister**[120] [4459] 8-11-5 **109** .... (v) TJPhelan(3) 92
(Jonjo O'Neill) *prom: rdn after 8th: wknd 3 out* **12/1**
0-00 **7** *6* **Society Buck (IRE)**[42] [652] 8-11-7 **113** .... MNicolls(5) 90
(John Allen) *hld up: rdn appr 8th: wknd appr 9th* **16/1**
-000 **8** *dist* **Ewar Bold**[42] [652] 12-9-9 **89** oh12 ow2 .... (t) MrMWall(7) —
(K G Wingrove) *led to 3rd: rdn after 7th: wknd 8th* **50/1**
/112 **P** **Kristoffersen**[12] [901] 5-11-9 **110** .... DRDennis —
(Ian Williams) *a bhd: t.o whn p.u bef 2 out* **5/1**[3]
/F3- **P** **Glencoyle (IRE)**[424] [418] 5-11-12 **113** .... PMoloney —
(Miss L Day) *bhd: rdn 6th: sn lost tch: t.o whn p.u after 3 out* **50/1**
5m 16.2s (-13.50) **Going Correction** -0.375s/f (Good)
WFA 4 from 5yo+ 3lb **10** Ran SP% **116.2**
Speed ratings: **108,107,107,105,104 101,99,**—,—,— CSF £26.06 CT £117.06 TOTE £3.90: £1.50, £2.30, £1.90; EX 29.10.
Owner The Highly Hopeful Club **Bred** J R Heatley **Trained** Hucking, Kent

FOCUS
A well-contested handicap with the first three pretty much to their marks.

NOTEBOOK
Charlie's Double continues on the crest of a wave and made it four out of six despite having been raised a total of 22lb. He may now go to the Galway Festival before having a break and switching to fences where his trainer reckons he will do even better. *(tchd 11-4)*
Absolut Power(GER), tackling this trip for the first time, was going better than the winner at the second last. However, being outjumped at the final flight proved vital with such a short run-in. *(op 7-1 tchd 8-1)*
Altitude Dancer(IRE) was racing over three miles three furlongs when completing a hat-trick in the month of May here. He will not mind a return to further on this evidence. *(op 7-1)*
Azzemour(FR) had no excuses on account of the distance this time. *(op 9-2)*
Brush A King, dropping back in trip, settled better than he had done in his two previous outings. *(op 11-1)*
Ewar Bold *Official explanation: jockey said gelding finished lame*
Kristoffersen jumped poorly according to his rider. *Official explanation: jockey said gelding jumped poorly (op 9-2)*

1027 GAY KINDERSLEY 75TH BIRTHDAY FEGENTRI INVITATION H'CAP HURDLE (GENTLEMAN AMATEUR RIDERS) (9 hdls) 2m 110y

4:10 (4:11) (Class 4) (0-105,105) 4-Y-0+ **£5,024** (£1,546; £773; £386)

Form RPR
-P15 **1** **Mr Fernet**[17] [871] 8-11-7 **98** .... MrHEngblom 98+
(M F Harris) *hld up: hdwy 4th: rdn to ld and blnd 2 out: drvn out* **16/1**
-100 **2** *nk* **Naked Oat**[7] [947] 10-11-3 **94** .... MrJSnowden 92
(Mrs L Wadham) *a.p: led after 3 out: rdn and hdd 2 out: r.o flat* **11/2**[3]
0435 **3** *½* **Sir Walter (IRE)**[43] [632] 12-11-2 **93** .... EWhillans 91
(D Burchell) *hld up and bhd: hdwy after 3 out: rdn 2 out: r.o flat* **13/2**
-052 **4** *3* **Fiddles Music**[21] [839] 4-10-11 **90** .... MrATDuff 84+
(D Burchell) *hld up: hdwy 5th: one pce fr 2 out* **8/1**
U310 **5** *2½* **Lone Soldier (FR)**[11] [915] 9-11-6 **97** .... LNewnes 89
(S B Clark) *bhd tl styd on fr 3 out: nvr nrr* **12/1**
14-0 **6** *6* **Sigwells Club Boy**[7] [947] 5-11-8 **99** .... MrMLesage 85
(J L Flint) *led 2nd to 4th: wknd after 3 out* **10/1**
03-0 **7** *½* **Wages**[75] [177] 5-11-1 **92** .... (p) MrJPO'Farrell 79+
(A M Hales) *prom: led 4th tl after 3 out: wknd appr 2 out* **16/1**
20-P **8** *1¼* **Happy Hussar (IRE)**[35] [727] 12-11-4 **95** .... MrLoekVanDerHam 79
(Dr P Pritchard) *in rr: struggling 4th: nvr nr ldrs* **25/1**
-411 **9** *2½* **Desert Spa (USA)**[32] [760] 10-11-7 **98** .... MrCVonBallmoos 80
(G E Jones) *prom tl rdn and wknd after 5th* **5/1**[2]
31- **10** *11* **Fille D'Honfleur**[49] 4-11-12 **105** .... MrDEdwards 74
(M C Pipe) *hld up: hdwy 5th: wknd after 3 out* **9/2**[1]
PP6P **11** *7* **Davoski**[21] [841] 11-11-8 **99** .... MrJOwen 63
(Dr P Pritchard) *led to 2nd: wknd after 4th* **20/1**
0P-F **12** *1¼* **Garw Valley**[9] [784] 6-10-9 **86** .... MrBKing 49
(M Wigham) *hld up in tch: wknd 4th* **33/1**
3m 56.4s (-2.00) **Going Correction** -0.375s/f (Good) **12** Ran SP% **114.8**
Speed ratings: **89,88,88,87,86 83,82,82,81,76 72,72** CSF £97.44 CT £638.94 TOTE £18.80: £5.50, £2.10, £2.10; EX 109.90.
Owner M Harris **Bred** Cliveden Stud Ltd **Trained** Edgcote, Northants
■ A first winner over jumps in Britain for Swedish rider Henrik Engblom, but he has won the big amateurs' race at Epsom.

FOCUS
A low-grade affair for European amateur riders run at a modest pace.

NOTEBOOK
Mr Fernet, despite being very awkward at the second last, found the combination of being back on a sound surface and a return to two miles doing the trick. *(op 14-1)*
Naked Oat did nothing wrong but could not take advantage of the winner's error at the penultimate hurdle. *(op 13-2)*
Sir Walter(IRE), reverting to hurdles, was another who ran his race. *(op 6-1)*
Fiddles Music needed softer ground to put more of an emphasis on stamina on such a sharp course.
Lone Soldier(FR), 10lb higher than when winning a Market Rasen seller last month, would have preferred a stronger-run race.
Fille D'Honfleur, a French import, found the ground totally different to when he crossed the channel to win at Lingfield back in February. *(op 6-1)*

1028 CLAYDON HORSE EXERCISERS NOVICES' H'CAP HURDLE (10 hdls) 2m 3f

4:40 (4:40) (Class 4) (0-105,100) 4-Y-0+ **£4,134** (£1,272; £636; £318)

Form RPR
-035 **1** **Native Chancer (IRE)**[12] [901] 5-10-8 **82** .... JEMoore 101+
(Jonjo O'Neill) *hld up in mid-div: hdwy 6th: lft in ld after 3 out: clr 2 out: eased considerably flat* **14/1**
0-00 **2** *6* **Kirkham Abbey**[21] [838] 5-11-7 **95** .... (v) RGarritty 100+
(J J Quinn) *hld up in tch: ev ch appr 2 out: sn rdn: one pce* **12/1**
0-05 **3** *4* **Oscars Vision (IRE)**[12] [905] 5-10-8 **82** .... (v) LAspell 82
(B W Duke) *hld up in tch: rdn 6th: one pce fr 3 out* **10/1**[3]
-160 **4** *1½* **Mick Murphy (IRE)**[33] [745] 8-10-8 **82** .... ChristianWilliams 80
(V J Hughes) *a.p: no hdwy fr 7th* **16/1**
-426 **5** *1* **Caper**[35] [724] 5-10-2 **86** .... (p) AHawkins(10) 83
(R Hollinshead) *bhd tl r.o appr 2 out: n.d* **12/1**
5221 **6** *5* **Kind Sir**[23] [823] 9-11-12 **100** .... WHutchinson 93+
(A W Carroll) *led: clr after 3rd: hit 7th and hdd: hit 3 out: sn wknd* **11/2**[2]
/6-0 **7** *9* **Transatlantic (USA)**[39] [683] 7-10-6 **80** .... (t) RJohnson 63
(H D Daly) *a bhd* **14/1**
6-60 **8** *dist* **Emanate**[42] [654] 7-9-13 **78** .... MNicolls(5) —
(John Allen) *a bhd: t.o* **40/1**
1201 **9** *dist* **Wardash (GER)**[7] [943] 5-11-3 **91** 7ex .... (vt) TJMurphy —
(M C Pipe) *hld up and bhd: short-lived effrt 4th: eased whn no ch after 3 out: t.o* **7/2**[1]
0-FP **P** **Spring Bee**[56] [462] 5-9-11 **74** oh5 .... (v) DCrosse(3) —
(T Wall) *bhd tl p.u bef 6th* **50/1**
600- **P** **Oh Sunny Boy (IRE)**[283] [1631] 4-10-0 **77** oh1 .... JamesDavies —
(B G Powell) *a bhd: t.o whn p.u bef 2 out* **20/1**
-410 **P** **Macreater**[42] [649] 7-9-9 **76** .... (p) SWalsh(7) —
(K A Morgan) *a bhd: rdn after 5th: t.o whn p.u bef 7th* **20/1**
/PP- **P** **La Rose**[113] 5-10-2 **81** .... TGreenway(5) —
(Paul Morris) *a bhd: rdn 5th: t.o whn p.u bef 6th* **50/1**
0-21 **P** **Dash For Cover (IRE)**[67] [295] 5-11-0 **88** .... RThornton —
(J G Portman) *chsd ldr: led 7th: stl gng wl whn lost action and p.u after 3 out* **7/2**[1]
4m 23.0s (-12.30) **Going Correction** -0.375s/f (Good)
WFA 4 from 5yo+ 2lb **14** Ran SP% **119.4**
Speed ratings: **110,107,105,105,104 102,98,**—,—,— —,—,—,— CSF £159.35 CT £1761.17 TOTE £16.30: £4.60, £3.60, £2.90; EX 202.00 Place 6 £319.03, Place 5 £178.89.
Owner Big Boys Club **Bred** William J Noonan **Trained** Cheltenham, Gloucs

FOCUS
A strong pace led to a decent time for the class of race.

NOTEBOOK
Native Chancer(IRE), taking full advantage of Dash For Cover's misfortune, was ten lengths clear jumping the last and was eased to a walk on the short run-in. *(op 12-1)*

Kirkham Abbey was fitted with the visor he had worn for four of his victories on the Flat. He could not live with the winner in the short home straight. *(op 10-1 tchd 14-1)*
Oscars Vision(IRE) appreciated the return to faster ground but could not take advantage of having slipped a total of 10lb in the ratings. *(op 12-1)*
Mick Murphy(IRE) was back to the right sort of trip having found three and a quarter miles beyond him at Hereford.
Caper could never get competitive in a strongly-run race. *(tchd 14-1 in a place)*
Kind Sir, having a rare run over hurdles, paid the penalty for tearing off in the lead under top weight. *(op 5-1)*
Wardash(GER) did not seem to be having one of his going days. *(tchd 3-1)*
Dash For Cover(IRE) was travelling as well as the winner when it looked as if he may well have broken down at the end of the back straight. *Official explanation: jockey said gelding lost its action (op 4-1 tchd 9-2)*
T/Jkpt: Not won. T/Plt: £282.00 to a £1 stake. Pool: £51,004.35. 132.00 winning tickets. T/Qpdt: £42.80 to a £1 stake. Pool: £4,009.32. 69.30 winning tickets. KH

1029 - 1035a (Foreign Racing) - See Raceform Interactive

[977] WORCESTER (L-H)
Wednesday, July 20

OFFICIAL GOING: Good to firm (firm in places on hurdle course)
Wind: Fresh behind Weather: Fine

1036 3663 FIRST FOR FOOD SERVICE NOVICES' HURDLE (10 hdls) 2m 4f
2:10 (2:11) (Class 4) 4-Y-0+ **£3,406** (£1,048; £524; £262)

Form					RPR
-615	1		**Chase The Sunset (IRE)**[17] [892] 7-11-5 100 .... (Miss H C Knight) *hld up: hdwy and j.rt 4th: led on bit 2 out: clr whn j. bdly rt last: v easily* **11/8**[2]	TJMurphy	104+
/0-P	2	2 ½	**The Bay Bridge (IRE)**[45] [654] 6-10-12 .... (Miss E C Lavelle) *hld up and bhd: nt fluent 2nd: hdwy fr 3 out: rdn and r.o flat: no ch w wnr* **33/1**[3]	BJCrowley	82
-6P2	3	2 ½	**Openide**[14] [912] 4-11-2 121 .... (B W Duke) *led: rdn 6th: hdd and mstke 2 out: no ex flat* **4/5**[1]	APMcCoy	86+
0	4	dist	**Secluded**[14] [911] 5-10-7 84 ....(b) (N G Ayliffe) *hld up: wnt 2nd 4th: rdn and ev ch appr 3 out: wknd appr 2 out* **33/1**[3]	MNicolls[(5)]	—
04FP	5	22	**Flurry**[14] [912] 6-10-5 .... (C J Down) *chse ldr to 4th: wknd 5th: t.o* **66/1**	MBradburne	—
0	6	26	**Thornton Bridge**[7] [982] 7-10-5 .... (D L Williams) *hld up: j.rt fr 5th: sn wknd: t.o* **80/1**	CMStudd[(7)]	—
0	7	dist	**Pretty Lady Rose**[24] [844] 5-9-12 .... (T Wall) *t.k.h in tch: lost pl after 4th: t.o* **50/1**	MrMWall[(7)]	—

4m 44.1s (-3.90) **Going Correction** -0.45s/f (Good)
WFA 4 from 5yo+ 3lb **7 Ran SP% 108.2**
Speed ratings: **89,88,87,—,— —,—** CSF £26.98 TOTE £2.90: £1.10, £8.20; EX 27.10.
Owner Jim Lewis **Bred** Old Meadow Stud **Trained** West Lockinge, Oxon

FOCUS
An uncompetitive affair with a moderate winning time, almost six seconds slower than the later handicap. The winner is value for 15 lengths but is rated to his mark.

NOTEBOOK
Chase The Sunset(IRE) is the type who needs to do everything on the bridle. He appreciated the quick ground and enjoyed not having to come under pressure. His rider let him run down the final flight before cruising home, but this told us nothing new and he would be one to take on in better company. *(op 13-8)*
The Bay Bridge(IRE) made no show on his hurdling debut at Stratford but this was a lot more promising. The extra half mile brought him into the picture after he had looked highly unlikely to be involved leaving the back straight, and this chasing type, who was not given a hard race, is open to further improvement. *(op 25-1 tchd 22-1)*
Openide was the pick on the figures, but he is not an easy ride and was under pressure a long way out. Down on his nose at the second last when upsides the eventual winner, that error may have cost him the runner-up spot, but the overall impression is that he is going the wrong way. *(op 8-11 tchd 5-6 in places)*
Secluded ran a bit better than his finishing position suggests. The re-application of blinkers brought about an improved show and he was keeping the main two company leaving the back straight. He soon beat a retreat when pressure was applied though, and his trainer later reported *that the gelding had a breathing problem.Official explanation: trainer said gelding had a breathing problem (op 25-1)*

1037 FRANCHISE YOUR BUSINESS WITH HORWATH FRANCHISING NOVICES' HURDLE (8 hdls) 2m
2:40 (2:40) (Class 4) 4-Y-0+ **£3,393** (£1,044; £522; £261)

Form					RPR
3531	1		**Cream Cracker**[7] [982] 7-10-12 95 .... (Mrs Jeremy Young) *hld up: hdwy 4th: led 2 out: sn rdn: all out* **3/1**[2]	JMMaguire	105+
26P-	2	2	**Harrycat (IRE)**[26] [3851] 4-10-10 105 ....(p) (V Smith) *chsd ldr: led 5th to 2 out: sn hrd rdn and sddle slipped: nt qckn flat* **11/4**[1]	APMcCoy	102+
0-12	3	10	**Don And Gerry (IRE)**[7] [982] 4-10-3 .... (P D Evans) *hld up in tch: ev ch 3 out: sn rdn: wknd flat* **4/1**[3]	WMarston	87+
34	4	5	**Aspra (FR)**[14] [911] 5-10-5 .... (C J Down) *in rr tl styd on flat: n.d* **12/1**	MBradburne	81
60-P	5	½	**Royaltea**[7] [971] 4-9-12 87 .... (J T Stimpson) *plld hrd: in tch: rdn appr 4th: wknd after 5th* **66/1**	LTreadwell[(5)]	79
/444	6	½	**Tubber Streams (IRE)**[3] [1024] 8-10-5 .... (B A Pearce) *led: clr appr 4th: hdd 5th: wknd appr 2 out* **50/1**	PTGallagher[(7)]	87
6	7	27	**Scarrabus (IRE)**[24] [843] 4-10-10 .... (B G Powell) *hld up towards rr: hdwy after 4th: rdn and wknd after 5th* **13/2**	TJMurphy	58
13	8	¾	**Houlihans Free (IRE)**[21] [866] 6-10-12 ....(t) (P F Nicholls) *hld up in rr: short-lived effrt 5th* **10/1**	ChristianWilliams	59
35	9	2 ½	**Mariday**[14] [911] 4-10-10 .... (L Wells) *blnd 5th: a bhd* **28/1**	LAspell	55
60	10	19	**Lost In The Snow (IRE)**[7] [982] 7-10-12 .... (M Sheppard) *a bhd: t.o* **66/1**	DRDennis	38
4000	P		**Simiola**[7] [982] 6-10-5 77 .... (S T Lewis) *a bhd: t.o whn p.u bef 3 out* **100/1**	ATinkler	—
00-	P		**Bertocelli**[20] [3517] 4-10-3 ....(p) (K F Clutterbuck) *hld up in tch: wknd appr 4th: t.o whn p.u bef 3 out* **80/1**	SWalsh[(7)]	—

3m 40.4s (-8.00) **Going Correction** -0.45s/f (Good)
WFA 4 from 5yo+ 2lb **12 Ran SP% 112.4**
Speed ratings: **102,101,96,93,93 93,79,79,77,68 —,—** CSF £10.99 TOTE £4.20: £1.10, £1.40, £2.20; EX 18.20.
Owner Ridge Racing **Bred** T C Frost **Trained** Charlton Mackrell, Somerset

FOCUS
A modest novice hurdle run at a decent pace and, with those immediately behind the winner all running close to their marks, the form looks reasonably solid.

NOTEBOOK
Cream Cracker, despite being burdened with a penalty, followed up her recent course and distance success and confirmed form with Don And Gerry and three other rivals. She looks to be going the right way. *(tchd 7-2)*
Harrycat(IRE), wearing cheekpieces for the first time on his return to hurdling, did not look very *willing under pressure but he might have finished a little closer had his saddle not slippedOfficial explanation: jockey said saddle slipped (op 5-2)*
Don And Gerry(IRE) had a 7lb pull with Cream Cracker for a beating of five lengths here last time, and given that was her hurdling debut it was reasonable to expect some improvement. She blundered at the fourth last, though, and while she kept on fairly well, she never looked capable of challenging the first two. *(op 7-2)*
Aspra(FR) stayed on under a considerate ride. She is now eligible for a handicap mark and should be seen to better effect in that sphere. *(tchd 14-1)*
Royaltea failed to settle.
Tubber Streams(IRE), having his third start within the space of eight days, set a good pace in front and, as he had done here a week earlier, paid for his efforts in the closing stages. *(op 66-1)*
Scarrabus(IRE) had a breathing problem according to Murphy. *Official explanation: jockey said gelding had a breathing problem (op 8-1 tchd 6-1)*
Houlihans Free(IRE) finished sore according to his rider. *Official explanation: jockey said gelding finished sore (op 7-1)*
Simiola finished lame according to her rider. *Official explanation: jockey said mare was lame*

1038 CHARLES CLEGHORN BIRTHDAY BEGINNERS' CHASE (18 fncs) 2m 7f 110y
3:10 (3:10) (Class 4) 5-Y-0+ **£4,124** (£1,269; £634; £317)

Form					RPR
-F5P	1		**It's Definite (IRE)**[28] [814] 6-10-12 ....(p) (P Bowen) *led to 2nd: a.p: led 4 out: sn rdn: drvn out* **13/2**[3]	RJohnson	111+
30-1	2	2	**Snoopy Loopy (IRE)**[82] [117] 7-10-12 .... (P Bowen) *hld up: mstke 1st: hdwy to ld 11th: hdd 4 out: hrd rdn appr 2 out: rallied and edgd lft flat: no ex* **8/15**[1]	APMcCoy	109+
6/5-	3	26	**Cedar Chief**[6] 8-10-5 65 ....(b) (B A Pearce) *led 2nd: hit 10th: mstke and hdd 11th: wkng whn mstke 12th* **50/1**	PTGallagher[(7)]	88+
-134	4	14	**Blueberry Ice (IRE)**[41] [693] 7-9-12 .... (B G Powell) *prom tl wknd 13th* **16/1**	CMStudd[(7)]	61
2-23	5	hd	**Peeyoutwo**[14] [914] 10-10-12 120 .... (Mrs D A Hamer) *hld up: hdwy 9th: wknd 4 out* **4/1**[2]	BHitchcott	68
4	P		**Lost Treasure (IRE)**[7] [972] 8-10-12 .... (Mrs M Evans) *hld up: rdn and lost tch 8th: t.o whn p.u and dismntd bef 10th* **100/1**	JMogford	—

5m 45.6s (-9.30) **Going Correction** -0.225s/f (Good) **6 Ran SP% 107.4**
Speed ratings: **106,105,96,92,91** — CSF £10.19 TOTE £9.40: £3.00, £1.10; EX 11.70.
Owner R Owen & P Fullagar **Bred** Yeomanstown Stud **Trained** Little Newcastle, Pembrokes

FOCUS
An interesting beginners' chase which revolved around two chasing debutants from the Peter Bowen yard. The race could be rated higher but makes sense on time.

NOTEBOOK
It's Definite(IRE), rated 18lb inferior to Snoopy Loopy over hurdles, was kept wide by Johnson and jumped appreciably better than his stablemate. In command over the last three fences, he should be able to add to this while the ground rides fast. *(op 8-1 tchd 9-1 and 6-1)*
Snoopy Loopy(IRE), sold out of Vicky Scott's yard for 120,000gns after scoring at the Punchestown Festival, stumbled on landing over the first fence and put in a rather novicey round afterwards. After being administered with a reminder when becoming a little detached from the leading quartet with a circuit to run, he moved up stylishly to lead at the end of the back straight, but he was shaded by his stablemate at the fourth last and soon fighting a losing battle. While this was disappointing, the fast ground can be put down as a reason and he should do better when he *can get his toe in. Official explanation: jockey said gelding was unsuited by good to firm ground; vet said gelding finished lame (op 8-13 tchd 1-2, 4-6 in places)*
Cedar Chief has won his share of point-to-points but is nothing special in that field. His jumping deteriorated after he lost the lead but he did stay on again in the latter stages. *(op 33-1)*
Blueberry Ice(IRE), a winner on fast ground over hurdles, was left toiling as the pace lifted in the final mile on this chase debut. *(tchd 20-1)*
Peeyoutwo had the best previous chase form on offer but, after turning into the straight in a close third, he was soon left behind by the leading pair. A trip of around two and a half miles could be what he needs. *Official explanation: jockey said gelding was unsuited by good to firm ground (op 5-2)*
Lost Treasure(IRE) *Official explanation: jockey said gelding was never travelling (op 66-1)*

1039 HYLTON HYUNDAI H'CAP HURDLE (12 hdls) 3m
3:40 (3:40) (Class 3) (0-125,125) 4-Y-0+ **£4,686** (£1,442; £721; £360)

Form					RPR
-131	1		**Downing Street (IRE)**[7] [974] 4-10-13 116 7ex ....(b) (Jennie Candlish) *hld up in rr: hdwy after 9th: rdn to ld flat: r.o* **11/2**[3]	AO'Keeffe	113+
4255	2	hd	**Alikat (IRE)**[28] [814] 4-11-8 125 .... (M C Pipe) *hld up: hdwy to ld after 3 out: j. bdly rt 2 out: hrd rdn and hdd flat: r.o* **9/1**	TJMurphy	123+
1-20	3	2 ½	**Global Challenge (IRE)**[28] [814] 6-11-12 125 ....(v[1]) (Jonjo O'Neill) *hld up: sn in tch: ev ch whn carried rt 2 out: one pce flat* **20/1**	JEMoore	124+
01-5	4	6	**Thyne For Intersky (IRE)**[82] [109] 6-10-11 110 ....(b) (Jonjo O'Neill) *hld up: hdwy 3 out: rdn and wknd after 2 out* **4/1**[2]	APMcCoy	102
R-34	5	¾	**Swansea Bay**[24] [842] 9-10-2 101 .... (P Bowen) *prom: rdn appr 3 out: wknd appr last* **5/2**[1]	TScudamore	93
-061	6	3	**Champagne Harry**[20] [871] 7-11-9 122 .... (N A Twiston-Davies) *prom tl wknd 9th* **10/1**	CLlewellyn	111
P-34	7	¾	**Parisian Storm (IRE)**[45] [648] 9-11-2 115 .... (Evan Williams) *hld up: hdwy 7th: wknd appr 2 out* **6/1**	ChristianWilliams	103
1-0P	8	8	**Renvyle (IRE)**[10] [946] 7-11-2 118 .... (Jonjo O'Neill) *w ldr: led 9th tl after 3 out: sn wknd* **25/1**	TJPhelan[(3)]	98
PPP-	9	9	**Prokofiev (USA)**[82] [4692] 9-11-0 120 ....(b) (Jonjo O'Neill) *led to 9th: wkng whn pckd 3 out* **100/1**	ECooper[(7)]	91
3020	P		**Joshua's Bay**[24] [841] 7-10-9 108 .... (J R Jenkins) *hld up: bhd tl p.u lame bef 8th: dead* **16/1**	RJohnson	—

5m 37.1s (-12.10) **Going Correction** -0.45s/f (Good)
WFA 4 from 6yo+ 4lb **10 Ran SP% 113.8**
Speed ratings: **102,101,101,99,98 97,97,94,91,—** CSF £50.85 CT £913.59 TOTE £7.20: £2.20, £3.20, £6.30; EX 55.30.
Owner Reuben Fielding **Bred** M Stewkesbury And The Luna Wells Syndicate **Trained** Basford Green, Staffs

FOCUS
A fair handicap in which the four-year-olds came out on top. The race could be rated higher but the form is a little suspect.

NOTEBOOK
Downing Street(IRE) has been in good form in novice company and looked a rare thing in this handicap - a potential improver. Held up in the early stages, he came with a late challenge to score, and this fairly lightly-raced gelding could be capable of further improvement. *(op 4-1 tchd 6-1 in places)*

Alikat(IRE) made her bid for glory heading for the second last, but she ran right down the flight, taking Global Challenge with her and, although in front on the run-in, found the relatively unexposed *winner just too strong. This performance will not help her with regards to her already stiff mark.* *(tchd 10-1)*

Global Challenge(IRE), who normally wears blinkers, wore a visor for the first time. He was being delivered with his effort when carried right at the second last but, although he would have finished a bit closer, he was third best on the day.

Thyne For Intersky(IRE) may have needed this first outing since April, but he has a record of running well fresh so it might not be wise to assume there will be bags of improvement to come next time. *(op 9-2)*

Swansea Bay had recorded six wins from six starts at this track prior to this, but although he remains theoretically well handicapped over hurdles, he has shown on a number of occasions that he struggles over timber off marks in three figures. *(op 7-2)*

Champagne Harry won a weak claimer last time and this proved a lot more competitive. *(tchd 12-1)*

1040 COUNTY AIR AMBULANCE H'CAP HURDLE (10 hdls) 2m 4f

4:10 (4:11) (Class 4) (0-100,98) 4-Y-O+ **£3,087** (£882; £441)

Form RPR

43-4 **1** **Tommy Spar**[46] 630 5-11-7 **92** RJohnson 102
(P Bowen) *hld up in rr: rdn 7th: hdwy 3 out: edgd lft and led flat: r.o wl* **5/1**[2]

F513 **2** *1 ½* **Cannon Fire (FR)**[10] 949 4-11-10 **98** ChristianWilliams 104
(Evan Williams) *hld up: hdwy 7th: hrd rdn and led briefly flat: nt qckn* **3/1**[1]

06-0 **3** *2 ½* **Slalom (IRE)**[26] 826 5-10-11 **87** WKennedy(5) 94+
(D Burchell) *hld up and bhd: hdwy appr 5th: led 7th: sn rdn clr: hdd and no ex flat* **20/1**

-PPP **4** *8* **Phase Eight Girl**[15] 905 9-10-6 **77** WHutchinson 76+
(J Hetherton) *hld up: rdn 7th: hdwy appr last: nt rch ldrs* **20/1**

5 *¾* **Suits Me Fine (IRE)**[58] 474 5-11-5 **90** APMcCoy 87
(Jonjo O'Neill) *hld up and bhd: hdwy appr 7th: wknd appr last* **5/1**[2]

36P0 **6** *5* **Mr Dip**[14] 913 5-10-8 **84** DLaverty(5) 76
(L A Dace) *hld up and bhd: sme hdwy fr 2 out: n.d* **33/1**

333- **7** *2* **What You Know (IRE)**[286] 1630 11-11-5 **90** (p) BHitchcott 80
(Mrs D A Hamer) *hld up: hdwy whn n.m.r appr 7th: wknd 2 out* **20/1**

5651 **8** *12* **Idlewild (IRE)**[24] 839 10-11-5 **97** APogson(7) 75
(C T Pogson) *hld up and bhd: hdwy appr 5th: wknd 2 out* **10/1**

0041 **9** *2 ½* **Ashgan (IRE)**[7] 978 12-10-6 **80** 7ex TJPhelan(3) 56
(Dr P Pritchard) *chsd ldrs tl wknd 7th* **11/1**

P5PP **10** *15* **Loi De Martiale (IRE)**[14] 913 7-10-9 **80** (b) AThornton 41
(J M Jefferson) *hld up: hdwy 5th: wknd 7th* **33/1**

P/0- **11** *dist* **Lago Nam (FR)**[357] 1056 6-10-0 **71** oh7 (vt[1]) TJMurphy —
(M C Pipe) *chsd ldr: reminders sn after s and bnd after 4th: nt fluent 5th: wkng whn n.m.r appr 7th: t.o* **6/1**[3]

-06P **P** **Sean (IRE)**[17] 895 6-11-0 **85** TScudamore —
(Mrs L C Jewell) *hld up: mstke 5th: bhd whn p.u bef 7th* **66/1**

PP/P **P** **Miss Man**[36] 749 11-9-7 **71** oh17 LNewnes(7) —
(N E Berry) *wl bhd: mstke 2nd: t.o whn p.u bef 3 out* **66/1**

0656 **P** **Mister Moussac**[31] 784 6-11-4 **89** (p) BJCrowley —
(Miss Kariana Key) *led to 7th: sn wknd: bhd whn p.u bef 3 out* **14/1**

4m 38.2s (-9.80) **Going Correction** -0.45s/f (Good) **14** Ran SP% **119.9**
Speed ratings: **101,100,99,96,95 93,93,88,87,81** —,—,—,— CSF £19.05 CT £280.32 TOTE £6.20: £2.70, £1.20, £7.20; EX 17.50.

Owner Ralph Morgans **Bred** R Morgans **Trained** Little Newcastle, Pembrokes

FOCUS

An ordinary handicap but another race dominated by the youngsters. The form looks pretty solid with the fourth to sixth close to their marks.

NOTEBOOK

Tommy Spar has struggled to get home over three miles on a couple of occasions, including on his reappearance last time out, and he appreciated this drop back to two and a half miles, seeing it out more strongly than the two who looked like fighting it out jumping the last. He is likely to go chasing sooner rather than later. *(op 6-1)*

Cannon Fire(FR) had just mastered Slalom when the winner appeared on the scene. He ran better in this lesser grade than when third at Stratford, but this effort will not help his cause with the Handicapper. *(tchd 7-2)*

Slalom(IRE), making his debut for his new stable, was enterprisingly kicked into a clear lead running out of the back straight and looked likely to be difficult to peg back, but in hindsight he probably went a bit too soon. This was still his best effort over hurdles to date, though.

Phase Eight Girl stayed on without ever looking a threat to the first three. She needs this quick ground and is back on a fair mark, so she could be one to keep in mind when she gets a chance to run over three miles plus again. *(tchd 22-1)*

Suits Me Fine(IRE), debuting for his new yard having previously raced in Ireland, had never before run on ground as quick as this. He struggled to go the pace when things hotted up. *(op 10-1)*

Lago Nam(FR) was never travelling according to his rider. *Official explanation: jockey said gelding was never travelling (op 9-2)*

1041 CHELTENHAM AND GLOUCESTER CLADDING SWISH H'CAP CHASE (18 fncs) 2m 7f 110y

4:40 (4:44) (Class 4) (0-100,98) 5-Y-O+ **£3,816** (£1,174; £587; £293)

Form RPR

-03P **1** **Honneur Fontenail (FR)**[52] 567 6-10-0 **72** oh15 (p) PJBrennan 80+
(N J Hawke) *hld up and bhd: reminders after 4th and 5th: hdwy 9th: outpcd 13th: rallied appr 4 out: led appr 2 out: r.o* **66/1**

203- **2** *¾* **Oh So Brave**[277] 1732 8-11-9 **95** ChristianWilliams 101
(Evan Williams) *led to 2nd: chsd ldr: ev ch last: hrd rdn: r.o* **9/2**[3]

44-P **3** *8* **Connemara Mist (IRE)**[36] 746 10-10-0 **72** oh6 (b) JMogford 72+
(Mrs N S Evans) *j.rt: led 2nd tl appr 13th: wknd appr 4 out: lft 3rd 2 out* **100/1**

F-PP **4** *dist* **Fearless Mel (IRE)**[67] 346 11-11-6 **92** (p) AO'Keeffe —
(Mrs H Dalton) *j.rt: hdwy after 9th: wknd after 4 out* **28/1**

4305 **5** *dist* **Robbie On Tour (IRE)**[55] 519 6-10-4 **79** (vt) TJMalone(3) —
(M C Pipe) *sn t.o* **10/1**

P **Corston Jigthyme (IRE)**[68] 335 7-11-0 **86** RJohnson —
(P Bowen) *a bhd: t.o 9th: p.u bef last* **5/1**

/1-P **P** **Mustang Molly**[84] 51 13-10-0 **77** MNicolls(5) —
(P W Hiatt) *a bhd: t.o whn p.u bef 11th* **18/1**

-1P1 **U** **Excellent Vibes (IRE)**[14] 916 7-11-12 **98** CLlewellyn —
(N A Twiston-Davies) *hmpd and uns rdr 2nd* **3/1**[1]

0-P3 **P** **Wrens Island (IRE)**[7] 975 11-10-9 **81** WHutchinson —
(R Dickin) *bhd: hmpd 4th: t.o 9th: p.u bef 4 out* **7/1**

/-2P **R** **Romantic Hero (IRE)**[29] 805 9-11-1 **87** (b) APMcCoy —
(C R Egerton) *prom: led 11th tl after 3 out: 3rd and wkng whn ref 2 out: lame* **4/1**[2]

-P3P **P** **Ballyaahbutt (IRE)**[43] 673 6-10-0 **72** oh4 JamesDavies —
(B G Powell) *chsd ldrs: mstke 11th: sn wknd: mstke 13th: t.o whn p.u bef 4 out* **50/1**

F2R4 **P** **Althrey Dandy (IRE)**[10] 948 10-11-11 **97** (p) AThornton —
(P T Dalton) *hld up and bhd: sme hdwy whn j.rt 10th: bhd whn p.u bef 13th* **20/1**

5m 50.4s (-4.50) **Going Correction** -0.225s/f (Good) **12** Ran SP% **119.4**
Speed ratings: **98,97,95**,—,— —,—,—,—,— —,— CSF £347.99 CT £26657.15 TOTE £59.60: £12.60, £2.40, £22.90; EX 1624.60.

Owner Wags To Riches Partnership **Bred** S Dupuy **Trained** Hewish, Somerset

■ Stewards' Enquiry : Christian Williams one-day ban: charged tape and caused starter to fall from rostrum (Jul 31)

FOCUS

Only five finished in this low-grade handicap, a strong pace being partly to blame, and the form means little with the third the best guide.

NOTEBOOK

Honneur Fontenail(FR), with the cheekpieces back on, caused a real shock from more than a stone out of the handicap although much of the credit goes to his rider, who was shoving him along with more than a circuit to run. He plugged on to jump ahead at the second last and found enough after idling on the run-in. He is only six and this was much his best run to date, so he is entitled to more improvement when the emphasis is on stamina.

Oh So Brave blundered at the first ditch, but generally jumped well on this second run over fences. A winning pointer and hurdler, he was in the front rank all the way and was renewing his challenge on the run-in. *(op 4-1)*

Connemara Mist(IRE), another who was out of the weights, ran better than on his three previous runs in this country but showed a tendency to jump out to his right. *(op 66-1)*

Fearless Mel(IRE) at least completed this time but was beaten a long way in the end. *(op 33-1 tchd 25-1)*

Robbie On Tour(IRE), having another crack at fences, just did not want to know and trailed throughout. *(op 14-1)*

Excellent Vibes(IRE) was out of the race at the first open ditch. *(op 7-2)*

Romantic Hero(IRE) looked sure to win when facing up to the final four fences in front, but he was *soon showing signs of distress and was beaten when refusing at the second last. Official explanation: jockey said gelding was lame (op 7-2)*

Althrey Dandy(IRE) *Official explanation: jockey said gelding was lame (op 7-2)*

1042 3663 FIRST FOR FOOD SERVICE HBLB STANDARD OPEN NATIONAL HUNT FLAT RACE 2m

5:10 (5:13) (Class 6) 4-6-Y-O **£1,946** (£556; £278)

Form RPR

0/- **1** **Youlbesolucky (IRE)**[488] 4447 6-11-4 APMcCoy 94+
(Jonjo O'Neill) *hld up in tch: rdn to ld 2f out: r.o* **2/1**[1]

2 *½* **Fountain Crumble** 4-10-9 ChristianWilliams 84
(P F Nicholls) *hld up and bhd: hdwy 5f out: nt clr run and swtchd rt over 3f out: ev ch over 1f out: rdn and r.o ins fnl f* **6/1**[3]

223 **3** *3 ½* **Mr Jawbreaker (IRE)**[14] 917 6-11-4 RThornton 90
(J T Stimpson) *hld up in tch: ev ch 2f out: sn rdn: one pce fnl f* **4/1**[2]

4 *¾* **Creagh Bay (IRE)**[380] 886 6-11-4 WMarston 89
(R T Phillips) *s.s: hld up and bhd: hdwy over 5f out: rdn and one pce fnl 2f* **11/1**

04 **5** *8* **Pumpkin Pickle**[21] 866 4-9-13 KBurke(10) 72
(P R Rodford) *hld up and bhd: rdn 8f out: hdwy over 3f out: one pce fnl 2f* **25/1**

000- **6** *¾* **Needle Prick (IRE)**[101] 4801 4-11-2 CLlewellyn 78
(N A Twiston-Davies) *hld up in mid-div: hdwy 4f out: hrd rdn over 2f out: no imp* **8/1**

7 *5* **Sunny South East (IRE)**[105] 4746 5-10-11 TScudamore 68
(S Gollings) *w ldr: led 4f out: rdn and hdd 2f out: wknd 1f out* **7/1**

60-5 **8** *9* **Mialyssa**[59] 463 5-10-6 JDiment(5) 59
(M R Bosley) *led after 2f to 4f out: wknd 3f out* **50/1**

9 *3* **Its A Classic** 4-11-2 JMogford 61
(Mrs N S Evans) *plld hrd in tch: swtchd rt over 3f out: sn wknd* **100/1**

0- **10** *7* **Hypark (IRE)**[336] 1212 6-10-6 LStephens(5) 49
(C Roberts) *led 2f: prom tl wknd over 5f out* **33/1**

05 **11** *29* **Hard N Sharp**[14] 917 5-11-4 AThornton 27
(J M Jefferson) *plld hrd: a bhd* **20/1**

12 *1 ½* **Counsellor Tim** 5-11-4 MBradburne 26
(C J Down) *a bhd* **33/1**

00- **13** *6* **Pacharan Queen**[239] 2413 4-10-9 PMoloney 11
(V Smith) *t.k.h in mid-div: rdn and bhd fnl 5f* **66/1**

14 *28* **Cardi Lyn** 5-11-4 BHitchcott —
(Mrs D A Hamer) *mid-div: rdn 8f out: sn struggling: t.o* **33/1**

0- **15** *6* **Nearly A Breeze**[256] 2051 5-10-11 JamesDavies —
(C J Down) *a bhd: t.o whn virtually p.u fnl f* **66/1**

3m 38.1s (-9.70) **Going Correction** -0.45s/f (Good)
WFA 4 from 5yo+ 2lb **15** Ran SP% **122.9**
Speed ratings: **106,105,104,103,99 99,96,92,90,87 72,72,69,55,52** CSF £12.97 TOTE £2.10: £1.20, £3.20, £2.00; EX 21.90 Place 6 £98.85, Place 5 £43.98.

Owner Mrs Gay Smith **Bred** M W And Mrs M Doran **Trained** Cheltenham, Gloucs

FOCUS

Not a great bumper but easy to rate with the majority of the first five close to their marks. The winner looks capable of improving on the bare form.

NOTEBOOK

Youlbesolucky(IRE), a big, scopey type, had not run for 488 days, but this success was not unexpected as he was backed in the market beforehand. He needed plenty of rousting to assert but the impression left was that there was more in the locker. He could well go in again under a penalty, but he is out of a half-sister to high-class staying chaser Kingsmark, so will not come into his own until given a test of stamina over obstacles. *(op 3-1 tchd 10-3)*

Fountain Crumble was dwarfed by the winner and lacks that one's scope, but she is a speedier type and clearly has some ability. She would not have to step up much on this effort to go one better in similar company. *(op 9-2)*

Mr Jawbreaker(IRE) keeps running well in these bumpers and once again ran alright, but he did not find a lot off the bridle and is the type who will continue to struggle when pitched against potential improvers from the bigger yards. *(tchd 9-2)*

Creagh Bay(IRE), absent for over a year since his last outing, made a fairly promising start to his career with his new stable. He is entitled to come on for the run. *(tchd 10-1)*

Pumpkin Pickle, who was having her third start, did not show any obvious improvement. *(op 50-1)*

Needle Prick(IRE) was more patiently ridden this time but it made little difference. *(tchd 7-1)*

Sunny South East(IRE), another making her debut for a new stable, was up there throughout and had every chance. *(op 5-1)*

T/Plt: £214.60 to a £1 stake. Pool: £42,479.15. 144.50 winning tickets. T/Qpdt: £93.30 to a £1 stake. Pool: £2,737.90. 21.70 winning tickets. KH

1043 - (Foreign Racing) - See Raceform Interactive

[971]UTTOXETER (L-H)

Thursday, July 21

OFFICIAL GOING: Good to firm

Wind: Light, against Weather: Overcast

1044 STAFFORDSHIRE LIFE AND OUR TIME H'CAP CHASE (16 fncs) 2m 5f
2:35 (2:36) (Class 4) (0-90,89) 5-Y-O+ £3,510 (£1,080; £540; £270)

Form				RPR
40/1	1		**Bell Rock**[64] [404] 7-11-7 **84** RThornton (Mrs T J Hill) *hld up: hdwy 8th: led appr and j.rt 2 out: rdn out* **9/2**[1]	95+
0/4P	2	1	**Pristeen Spy**[35] [767] 8-10-7 **70** PJBrennan (R Ford) *led: rdn and hdd appr 2 out: styd on* **11/2**[2]	78+
12P4	3	½	**Take The Oath (IRE)**[6] [999] 8-11-0 **77** TDoyle (D R Gandolfo) *hld up in tch: rdn to chse wnr last: no ex nr fin* **7/1**	83
5-54	4	3 ½	**Dante's Battle (IRE)**[6] [997] 13-9-13 **69** RSpate(7) (Mrs K Waldron) *hld up: hdwy after 9th: rdn whn hmpd 3 out: styd on same pce flat* **10/1**	73+
2F-0	5	17	**York Rite (AUS)**[22] [858] 9-11-1 **78** (p) HOliver (R C Guest) *hld up: mstke 5th: n.d* **13/2**	64
60-	6	6	**Mister Kingston**[90] [4953] 14-9-7 **63** oh2 (v) JPritchard(7) (R Dickin) *mstke 2nd: bhd fr 4th* **40/1**	43
P0-0	7	6	**Jo's Sale (IRE)**[76] [203] 6-11-8 **85** ChristianWilliams (Evan Williams) *hld up: hdwy 9th: wknd appr 4 out* **9/1**	59
10P0	8	3	**Monty Be Quick**[11] [948] 9-10-10 **80** MrTJO'Brien(7) (J M Castle) *hld up: hit 8th: effrt appr 5 out: sn wknd* **16/1**	51
P3	P		**Mantilla**[11] [948] 8-11-12 **89** (b) DRDennis (Ian Williams) *chsd ldrs tl wknd after 9th: bhd whn p.u bef 3 out* **6/1**[3]	—
00P-	P		**Maunby Roller (IRE)**[155] [3886] 6-9-9 **65** oh6 ow2 (v) SWalsh(7) (K A Morgan) *chsd ldrs tl wknd appr 8th: bhd whn p.u bef 10th* **50/1**	—
-2P2	F		**Lady Lambrini**[16] [902] 5-10-4 **73** DLaverty(5) (Mrs L Williamson) *prom: chsd ldr 6th: cl 3rd but rdn whn fell 3 out* **9/1**	—
P-PP	P		**Pharbeitfrome (IRE)**[6] [999] 11-10-4 **74** (t) TMessenger(7) (W B Stone) *chsd ldrs: rdn 9th: wknd next: behins whn p.u bef 3 out* **100/1**	—

5m 20.3s (-7.20) **Going Correction** -0.70s/f (Firm)
WFA 5 from 6yo+ 1lb **12 Ran SP% 114.0**
Speed ratings: **85,84,84,83,76 74,72,70,—,— —,—** CSF £28.79 CT £169.55 TOTE £4.60: £1.80, £1.60, £2.10; EX 35.10.
Owner Alan Hill **Bred** A J Struthers **Trained** Chinnor, Oxon

■ The first winner since taking out a full licence for Lawney Hill.

FOCUS
A poor handicap which saw the first three come clear. The form appears sound with the third setting the level.

NOTEBOOK
Bell Rock followed up his win in a maiden hunter chase at Folkestone in May with a fairly straightforward success under a fine ride from Thornton. He jumps well and, while he was placed in points over three miles, this is likely to prove his optimum trip under Rules. He has clearly started handicap life on a decent mark, should not go up too much in the weights and can win again on this sort of ground.
Pristeen Spy stuck gamely to his task once headed and turned in a much-improved display. He can build on this and looks capable of going one better from this mark, yet looks to be crying out for return to three miles. *(op 6-1 tchd 13-2)*
Take The Oath(IRE), ridden to get this trip, ran a sound race in defeat yet found this a trip too far. With a sharper test, he could certainly get back to winning ways. *(op 6-1 tchd 15-2)*
Dante's Battle(IRE) turned in another sound effort, and may be better suited by a drop in trip over fences, but is basically on the downgrade.
York Rite(AUS) *(op 7-1)*
Maunby Roller(IRE) *Official explanation: jockey said gelding was unsuited by the good to firm ground (op 8-1)*
Lady Lambrini was still in contention when coming to grief at the third last fence, and would most likely have filled a place has she stayed on her feet. *(op 8-1)*

1045 WEATHERBYS BANK H'CAP HURDLE (FOR THE KEN BOULTON TROPHY) (12 hdls) 2m 6f 110y
3:05 (3:05) (Class 4) (0-110,105) 4-Y-O+ £4,468 (£1,375; £687; £343)

Form				RPR
0-06	1		**Weston Rock**[8] [974] 6-11-3 **96** RWalford (T D Walford) *hld up: hdwy after 8th: chsd ldr 3 out: led next: sn clr* **16/1**	110+
436F	2	14	**Golfagent**[16] [906] 7-11-5 **105** (t) RSpate(7) (Mrs K Waldron) *hld up: hdwy 9th: styd on same pce fr 2 out* **14/1**	102
36-4	3	shd	**Koumba (FR)**[16] [906] 7-11-4 **97** ChristianWilliams (Evan Williams) *chsd ldr to 9th: rdn appr 2 out: styd on same pce* **9/2**[3]	94
-142	4	3	**Vicentio**[22] [859] 6-10-12 **91** GLee (T J Fitzgerald) *hld up: mstke 4th: hdwy 7th: rdn 3 out: styd on same pce fr next* **3/1**[2]	85
16PP	5	4	**Pequenita**[22] [864] 5-11-7 **100** (p) HOliver (R C Guest) *led: hdd whn blnd 2 out: sn wknd* **22/1**	92+
40PP	6	½	**Antigiotto (IRE)**[18] [895] 4-10-13 **96** APMcCoy (P Bowen) *hld up: hdwy 7th: wknd 3 out* **16/1**	81
0-12	7	17	**September Moon**[8] [974] 7-11-7 **100** RJohnson (Mrs A M Thorpe) *chsd ldrs: ev chnace appr 3 out: sn rdn and wknd* **11/4**[1]	77+
P-U0	P		**Heavenly Stride**[18] [891] 9-11-11 **104** RThornton (P Bowen) *chsd ldrs to 9th: bhd whn p.u bef next* **14/1**	—
P06	P		**Bravo**[7] [988] 7-10-1 **80** (v) PMoloney (J Mackie) *hld up: effrt appr 8th: sn wknd: bhd whn p.u bef 3 out* **20/1**	—
-FU0	P		**Rose Of The Hill (IRE)**[37] [745] 6-11-1 **94** (v[1]) TJMurphy (M C Pipe) *in rr: reminders 6th: wknd after next: t.o whn p.u bef 3 out* **11/1**	—

5m 29.8s (-14.90) **Going Correction** -0.60s/f (Firm)
WFA 4 from 5yo+ 3lb **10 Ran SP% 112.4**
Speed ratings: **101,96,96,95,93 93,87,—,—,—** CSF £205.57 CT £1175.03 TOTE £18.30: £4.30, £4.10, £1.50; EX 236.20.
Owner Mrs H Spath **Bred** H A Shone **Trained** Sheriff Hutton, N Yorks

FOCUS
A moderate handicap, run at a fair gallop, and the winner could hardly have won any easier. The runner-up is the best guide to the form which could rate a little higher.

NOTEBOOK
Weston Rock finally got off the mark at the 11th attempt over timber and ran out a wide-margin winner. He looked well suited by this trip, has clearly come right of late and it would be little surprise to see him go in again under a penalty. However, connections will be no doubt praying the *Handicapper does not take this form too literally. Official explanation: trainer had no explanation for the improved form shown (tchd 20-1)*
Golfagent, while fully put in his place by the winner, he was not disgraced off top weight and stuck to his task well under pressure. He needs some respite from the Handicapper before getting back to winning ways over hurdles.
Koumba(FR) was made to look very one paced by the winner from two out and failed to really improve for this return to faster ground. *(op 4-1)*
Vicentio was never really going at any stage and turned in a tame effort. This leaves him with a fair bit to prove off this career-high mark. *(tchd 10-3)*
September Moon, who came into this in grand form, dropped out very quickly at the top of the home straight as though something may have been amiss. She was later reported to have injured her off-fore. *Official explanation: vet said mare injured its off-foreleg (op 9-4)*
Bravo *Official explanation: jockey said gelding lost its action*

1046 DRAYTON BEAUMONT GROUP NOVICES' H'CAP HURDLE (10 hdls) 2m
3:40 (3:40) (Class 4) (0-95,88) 4-Y-O+ £2,723 (£778; £389)

Form				RPR
F565	1		**Queen Excalibur**[8] [982] 6-11-3 **78** AThornton (C Roberts) *hld up: hdwy 6th: led after next: clr last: rdn out* **12/1**	85+
0020	2	1 ½	**Alethea Gee**[7] [987] 7-10-11 **72** GLee (K G Reveley) *hld up: hdwy appr 3 out: styd on wl: nt rch wnr* **20/1**	77
0-F6	3	½	**Olimpo (FR)**[45] [664] 4-11-0 **77** RJohnson (P J Hobbs) *hld up: hdwy 3 out: chsd wnr and j.rt next: styd on* **11/2**[2]	81+
040	4	8	**Young Tot (IRE)**[43] [686] 7-11-6 **84** KJMercer(3) (Mrs A Duffield) *hld up: hdwy appr 3 out: styd on same pce fr next* **12/1**	80
5-22	5	3	**Captain Cloudy**[5] [973] 5-11-9 **84** JGoldstein (Miss Sheena West) *hld up: hdwy 5th: rdn appr 3 out: wkng whn hit last* **7/1**[3]	80+
P-05	6	5	**Desert Image (IRE)**[39] [729] 4-11-11 **88** TDoyle (C Tinkler) *hld up: hdwy 3 out: wknd next* **10/1**	74
P-60	7	¾	**Uncle John**[25] [838] 4-11-6 **83** (p) DRDennis (Ian Williams) *chsd ldrs: led 7th: sn hdd: rdn and wknd appr 2 out* **12/1**	68
U001	8	shd	**Ballyboe Boy (IRE)**[7] [987] 6-11-8 **88** 7ex (b) PCO'Neill(5) (R C Guest) *chsd ldrs: led and mstke 5th: hdd 7th: wknd qckly* **7/1**[3]	75
0P-0	9	½	**Debatable**[76] [203] 6-11-5 **87** KBurke(7) (N J Hawke) *hld up: hdwy 5th: wknd appr 3 out* **33/1**	74
5340	10	3 ½	**Seemore Sunshine**[8] [978] 8-10-8 **76** JAJenkins(7) (M J Gingell) *hld up in tch: hmpd bnd after 4th: wkng whn hit 3 out* **33/1**	59
5-32	11	2	**Tea's Maid**[10] [961] 5-11-8 **83** APMcCoy (Mrs A M Thorpe) *chsd ldr to 3rd: remained handy tl wknd appr 2 out: bhd whn blnd last: eased* **4/1**[1]	64
00F	12	5	**Weet An Haul**[39] [729] 4-10-13 **79** DCrosse(3) (T Wall) *hld up: a in rr: bhd whn hit 2 out* **66/1**	53
/056	13	dist	**Prince Minata (IRE)**[44] [670] 10-11-0 **78** RHobson(3) (M Appleby) *chsd ldrs tl wknd after 6th* **20/1**	—
-06F	14	1 ¼	**Waziya**[7] [990] 6-11-2 **82** DLaverty(5) (Mrs L Williamson) *bhd fr 4th* **66/1**	—
P0-4	15	½	**Blue Yonder**[16] [905] 5-11-2 **77** ChristianWilliams (Evan Williams) *led: racd keenly: hdd 5th: wknd appr 7th* **7/1**[3]	—
0P00	P		**Dumfries**[7] [987] 4-10-13 **83** BWharfe(7) (T H Caldwell) *bhd whn p.u after 4th* **50/1**	—

3m 54.7s (-5.70) **Going Correction** -0.60s/f (Firm) **16 Ran SP% 125.4**
Speed ratings: **90,89,89,85,83 81,80,80,80,78 77,75,—,—,— —** CSF £232.76 CT £1486.37 TOTE £14.80: £3.90, £4.60, £2.40, £2.20; EX 273.40.
Owner Dr Simon Clarke **Bred** George Joseph Hicks **Trained** Newport, Newport

FOCUS
A poor novice event in which the third and fifth set the standard for the form.

NOTEBOOK
Queen Excalibur, who did not go unbacked for this, found the generous early pace to her liking and ultimately ran out a ready winner. This was her first success of any kind, it was her best round *of jumping to date and she can build on this if able to maintain her current mood. Official explanation: trainer's representative had no explanation for the improved form shown other than that mare is leaning to settle in her races*
Alethea Gee was given a fair bit to do from off the pace and stayed on stoutly, only to find the winner gone beyond recall. This was much more like her true form and, with a more positive ride, she could go one better at this lowly level. *(op 22-1)*
Olimpo(FR) turned in a much more encouraging effort and would have given the winner more to think about, but for jumping badly out to his right at the penultimate flight. There is a race to be won with him off this mark. *(op 5-1)*
Young Tot(IRE)
Dumfries *Official explanation: jockey said gelding pulled up lame (op 40-1)*

1047 102.8 RAM FM NOVICES' HURDLE (12 hdls) 2m 6f 110y
4:15 (4:16) (Class 4) 4-Y-O+ £3,325 (£950; £475)

Form				RPR
P-	1		**Explosive Fox (IRE)**[12] [3978] 4-10-10 TDoyle (C P Morlock) *plld hrd: a.p: chsd ldr 6th: led after 3 out: clr last: styd on wl* **14/1**	105+
2231	2	4	**Festive Chimes (IRE)**[8] [976] 4-10-3 98 SWalsh(7) (N B King) *hld up and bhd: hdwy after 3 out: rdn to chse wnr appr last: too much to do* **9/4**[2]	98+
21-0	3	10	**Rash Moment (FR)**[15] [912] 6-11-0 112 RSpate(7) (Mrs K Waldron) *a.p: rdn 8th: chsd wnr appr 2 out tl wknd bef last* **9/1**	100+
F-10	4	2 ½	**Meneur De Jeu (FR)**[25] [842] 5-11-7 (v[1]) APMcCoy (M C Pipe) *led: rdn and hdd after 3 out: sn wknd* **13/8**[1]	97
10-P	5	13	**Saxon Mist**[25] [843] 6-11-0 RThornton (A King) *chsd ldrs tl wknd 3 out* **12/1**	82+
0U	6	dist	**Broadspeed**[6] [998] 9-10-0 (p) JAJenkins(7) (M J Gingell) *hld up: a bhd* **100/1**	—
0P-P	P		**Ms Freebee**[37] [742] 6-10-4 ACCoyle(3) (M Mullineaux) *hld up: t.o whn p.u bef 8th* **100/1**	—
/2P-	P		**Inch'Allah (FR)**[239] [2428] 9-11-0 100 AO'Keeffe (Jennie Candlish) *hld up: bhd whn p.u after 7th* **7/1**[3]	—
/0-P	P		**Samson Des Galas (FR)**[36] [763] 7-11-0 PJBrennan (R Ford) *chsd ldrs tl wknd appr 3 out: bhd whn p.u bef next* **33/1**	—
/0-P	P		**Derry Dice**[6] [1002] 9-10-7 88 (b) APogson(7) (C T Pogson) *chsd ldr to 6th: wknd bef next: t.o whn p.u bef 4 out* **33/1**	—

5m 34.5s (-10.20) **Going Correction** -0.60s/f (Firm)
WFA 4 from 5yo+ 3lb **10 Ran SP% 113.6**
Speed ratings: **93,91,88,87,82 —,—,—,—,—** CSF £45.44 TOTE £18.50: £2.60, £1.10, £1.80; EX 61.60.
Owner L M Power **Bred** Swettenham Stud, Caradale Trading Co And T Stack **Trained** Kingston Lisle, Oxon

■ Stewards' Enquiry : S Walsh seven-day ban: riding an ill-judged race (Aug 1,5,8-9,13-14,17)

FOCUS
A moderate novice event, run at a fair pace, and the field were strung out at the finish. The form may be reasonable and the race could produce winners.

NOTEBOOK

Explosive Fox(IRE) , fit from racing on the Flat, jumped neatly throughout on this return to hurdling and ran on strongly when asked to win his race, ultimately running out a ready winner. He stayed the trip well, clearly likes this sort of surface and could prove better in this sphere than he was on the level. *(op 25-1)*

Festive Chimes(IRE) , patiently ridden when getting off the mark at this track a week previously, was this time given too much ground to make up and was never going to reach the winner try as she might. She remains in good form, is capable of further success and will surely be given a more positive ride next time. *(op 15-8 tchd 7-4)*

Rash Moment(FR) improved on his latest effort and again advertised his liking for quick ground. This should have restored his confidence and he could well build on this in such events during the summer. *(op 8-1)*

Meneur De Jeu(FR) , in the first-time visor on this return to hurdling, set off at a decent clip yet proved a sitting duck from three out and has to rate disappointing. He is not one of his powerful yard's leading lights, but is surely capable of better then this. *(op 11-8 tchd 7-4, 15-8 in a place)*

Inch'Allah(FR) *Official explanation: jockey said gelding pulled up lame (tchd 8-1)*

Derry Dice *Official explanation: jockey said gelding finished lame (tchd 8-1)*

1048 RACINGFIXTURES.CO.UK WITH PHOTOGRAPHIX INTERMEDIATE OPEN NATIONAL HUNT FLAT RACE 2m

4:50 (4:50) (Class 6) 4-6-Y-O **£1,981** (£566; £283)

Form	Pos	Dist	Horse	Jockey	SP	RPR
	1		**Ericas Charm**^{448} [83] 5-10-9	APMcCoy		89
			(P Bowen) *hld up: hdwy 7f out: led 3f out: rdn over 1f out: all out*		**11/4**^{2}	
3	2	*nk*	**Back With A Bang (IRE)**^{46} [656] 6-11-2	JMogford		96
			(Mrs N S Evans) *chsd ldrs: outpcd over 4f out: rallied and n.m.r 3f out: styd on u.p*		**14/1**	
	3	*6*	**Sevens Delight** 5-10-9	DElsworth		85+
			(Mrs S J Smith) *chsd ldrs: rdn over 3f out: wknd over 1f out*		**16/1**	
	4	*3 1/2*	**Sweep Home** 5-11-2	RJohnson		86
			(P Bowen) *hld up: styd on fnl 2f: nvr nrr*		**10/1**	
0-	5	*4*	**Firion King (IRE)**^{300} [1500] 5-10-9	BWharfe(7)		82
			(T H Caldwell) *led 13f: wknd 2f out*		**66/1**	
60-	6	*5*	**Soviet Committee**^{173} [3598] 5-10-13	PWhelan(3)		77
			(T J Fitzgerald) *hld up in tch: rdn 6f out: wknd over 2f out*		**20/1**	
0	7	*8*	**Burn Brook**^{46} [655] 5-10-4 ow2	MrRArmson(7)		64
			(R J Armson) *bhd: r.o ins fnl f: nvr nrr*		**50/1**	
0/1	8	*1 3/4*	**Acushnet**^{15} [917] 6-11-9	GLee		78+
			(J M Jefferson) *plld hrd and prom: trckd ldr over 12f out: rdn over 3f out: sn wknd*		**11/8**^{1}	
00-0	9	*8*	**Milli Wizz**^{15} [917] 5-10-9	TScudamore		52
			(W M Brisbourne) *hld up: n.d*		**50/1**	
0	10	*24*	**Anna Gee**^{49} [616] 5-10-2	PKinsella(7)		28
			(K G Reveley) *hld up in tch: plld hrd: wknd over 5f out*		**33/1**	
	11	*2 1/2*	**Bryans Bach (IRE)** 4-11-0	ATinkler		31
			(C Tinkler) *a in rr*		**7/1**^{3}	
000-	12	*4*	**Simonstown**^{167} [3682] 5-11-2	NPMulholland		29
			(M D Hammond) *hld up: hdwy 1/2-way: wknd 4f out*		**100/1**	
00/	13	*3 1/2*	**Freindlypersuasion**^{459} [4886] 5-10-11	TGreenway(5)		25
			(Paul Morris) *chsd ldrs: rdn 7f out: sn lost pl*		**50/1**	

3m 52.8s (-7.00) **Going Correction** -0.60s/f (Firm)

WFA 4 from 5yo+ 2lb **13** Ran SP% **119.0**

Speed ratings: **93,92,89,88,86 83,79,78,74,62 61,59,57** CSF £38.63 TOTE £4.10: £1.80, £2.90, £3.30; EX 47.30.

Owner N Elliott **Bred** A Munnis And K Helliwell **Trained** Little Newcastle, Pembrokes

FOCUS

An ordinary bumper, typically run at a steady early pace and the first two came clear. The winner is the best guide to the form.

NOTEBOOK

Ericas Charm , making her British debut for a new stable, travelled nicely into contention at the top of the straight and proved game when push came to shove to get off the mark at the third attempt. She is clearly versatile as regards underfoot conditions, will be suited by further in due course and looks an interesting prospect for novice hurdling. *(op 5-2)*

Back With A Bang(IRE) was staying on stoutly in the closing stages and was only just denied. He really needs further, so this was a solid effort and he has a future under Rules. *(op 16-1 tchd 12-1)*

Sevens Delight made a pleasing debut and was only found wanting approaching the last furlong. She handled the fast ground, will be sharper next time and can find a race in this sphere. *(op 20-1)*

Sweep Home , half-brother to modest staying hurdler Prince Des Galles, was doing all of his best work from two out and shaped with promise under a largely educational ride. *(op 12-1)*

Acushnet , comfortably off the mark at Worcester 15 days previously, spoilt his chances of getting home by running too keenly throughout the first half of the contest. He is almost certainly capable of better, and while he may look vulnerable under his penalty in this sphere, he is not one to write *off yet. Official explanation: jockey said gelding was too keen early in the race (op 5-4 tchd 6-4, 13-8 in places)*

Bryans Bach(IRE) *Official explanation: jockey said gelding was never travelling and hung right-handed throughout (op 11-2)*

1049 MOTIVA H'CAP CHASE (12 fncs) 2m

5:20 (5:21) (Class 3) (0-115,114) 5-Y-O+ **£6,123** (£1,884; £942; £471)

Form	Pos	Dist	Horse	Jockey	SP	RPR
FU-2	1		**Tonic Du Charmil (FR)**^{15} [914] 5-11-9 **111**	(t) TJMurphy		125+
			(M C Pipe) *hld up: hdwy and mstke 4 out: led last: rdn out*		**9/2**^{3}	
5U23	2	*1 1/2*	**Bill's Echo**^{5} [1012] 6-11-4 **111**	PCO'Neill(5)		123+
			(R C Guest) *hld up: hdwy 4 out: led 2 out: hdd last: styd on same pce flat*		**7/2**^{1}	
0546	3	*8*	**Billie John (IRE)**^{25} [840] 10-11-4 **106**	JimCrowley		111+
			(Mrs K Walton) *hld up: hdwy 4 out: led next: hdd 2 out: wkng whn mstke last*		**10/1**	
-310	4	*5*	**Cumbrian Knight (IRE)**^{11} [939] 7-11-3 **105**	GLee		103
			(J M Jefferson) *hld up: hdwy 4 out: wknd next*		**10/1**	
-224	5	*4*	**Xaipete (IRE)**^{36} [761] 13-10-11 **99**	HOliver		93
			(R C Guest) *hld up: hdwy appr 5 out: wknd after 3 out*		**10/1**	
-215	6	*1 3/4*	**Papua**^{25} [840] 11-11-8 **110**	(b) DRDennis		103+
			(N J Hawke) *chsd ldrs: led appr 4 out: hdd 3 out: wknd next*		**9/2**^{3}	
0PPB	7	*10*	**Six Pack (IRE)**^{18} [894] 7-10-13 **101**	(t) ADempsey		83
			(Andrew Turnell) *bhd fr 6th*		**25/1**	
P-0U	8	*16*	**Nick The Jewel**^{11} [946] 10-11-12 **114**	PJBrennan		80
			(J S King) *chsd ldr: chal and mstke 5 out: wknd next*		**33/1**	
P0-0	P		**Bearaway (IRE)**^{37} [747] 8-11-6 **108**	(t) RThornton		—
			(Mrs H Dalton) *led: mstke 5 out: hdd & wknd bef next: p.u bef 3 out*		**16/1**	
-024	P		**Don Valentino (POL)**^{22} [858] 6-11-1 **103**	(v) APMcCoy		—
			(T R George) *chsd ldrs: rdn appr 4 out: wkng whn mstke 3 out: p.u bef next*		**4/1**^{2}	

3m 51.4s (-13.60) **Going Correction** -0.70s/f (Firm) **10** Ran SP% **118.5**

Speed ratings: **106,105,101,98,96 95,90,82,—,—** CSF £21.79 CT £151.84 TOTE £7.30: £2.90, £1.60, £3.70; EX 19.40 Place 6 £252.71, Place 5 £145.29.

Owner Roger Stanley & Yvonne Reynolds **Bred** Mme Guilhaine Le Borgne **Trained** Nicholashayne, Devon

FOCUS

A modest handicap, run at a decent clip and the first two pulled clear. The form appears sound and should work out.

NOTEBOOK

Tonic Du Charmil(FR) finally showed his true colours and, under a fine ride from Murphy, landed his first race over fences at the 11th time of asking. While this was his finest round of jumping to date, he was still not foot perfect, and he is clearly still learning with every run. He can be rated value for further and has more races in him this summer. *(op 5-1)*

Bill's Echo had every chance, but proved powerless to resist the winner's late challenge. He was clear in second, and no doubt he deserves to go one better, yet will always be vulnerable to an improver over fences. *(op 5-2)*

Billie John(IRE) , winner of this event in 2004 off an identical mark, turned in a more encouraging *display even though his effort was only short-lived. He can continue to pay his way off this mark. (op 14-1)*

Cumbrian Knight(IRE) ran a moody race and has gone the wrong way since winning his beginners' chase at Hexham in May. *(op 14-1)*

Papua , a course specialist, dropped out tamely under pressure and must rate disappointing. *(tchd 5-1)*

Don Valentino(POL) *(op 5-1)*

T/Plt: £544.70 to a £1 stake. Pool: £45,893.50. 61.50 winning tickets. T/Qpdt: £44.20 to a £1 stake. Pool: £3,339.50. 55.90 winning tickets. CR

1050 - 1061a (Foreign Racing) - See Raceform Interactive

479 SEDGEFIELD (L-H)

Monday, July 25

OFFICIAL GOING: Firm (good to firm in places)

After no rain for two and a half weeks the ground was described as 'very firm', with an ever growing list of casualties. Third last fence omitted both chases.

Wind: Moderate; half against Weather: Overcast and cool

1062 TOTEPLACEPOT BEGINNERS' CHASE (14 fncs 2 omitted) 2m 5f

2:30 (2:30) (Class 4) 5-Y-O+ **£4,182** (£1,287; £643; £321)

Form	Pos	Dist	Horse	Jockey	SP	RPR
03-2	1		**Oh So Brave**^{5} [1041] 8-10-12 95	ChristianWilliams		97+
			(Evan Williams) *j.rt: led to 3rd: chsd ldr: mstke last: styd on to ld nr fin: lame*		**13/8**^{1}	
433F	2	*hd*	**Heather Lad**^{10} [998] 12-10-12 100	GLee		96
			(C Grant) *chsd ldrs: styd on to r upsides run-in: no ex nr fin*		**11/1**	
-005	3	*1/2*	**Brave Effect (IRE)**^{15} [940] 9-10-12 89	BHarding		95
			(Mrs Dianne Sayer) *chsd ldr: led 3rd: edgd rt run-in: hdd nr fin*		**12/1**	
5/00	4	*4*	**Kilbride Lad (IRE)**^{11} [988] 11-10-12	(b) JPMcNamara		91
			(J J Lambe, Ire) *chsd ldrs: outpcd 9th: styd on fr 2 out*		**40/1**	
0334	5	*5*	**Prize Ring**^{36} [782] 6-10-12 93	FKeniry		86
			(G M Moore) *chsd ldrs: one pce fr 3 out*		**8/1**^{3}	
6532	6	*hd*	**One Of Them**^{15} [938] 6-10-5 79	GThomas(7)		86
			(M A Barnes) *in tch: outpcd 9th: kpt on fr 3 out*		**18/1**	
0500	7	*dist*	**Book's Way**^{11} [988] 9-10-9	PAspell(3)		—
			(D W Thompson) *sn bhd: t.o 8th*		**66/1**	
00	8	*19*	**Nobodysgonanotice (IRE)**^{16} [930] 7-10-7	PCO'Neill(5)		—
			(J J Lambe, Ire) *sn bhd: t.o fr 8th*		**100/1**	
0060	P		**Northern Echo**^{11} [988] 8-10-5	(p) CDSharkey(7)		—
			(K S Thomas) *sn bhd: t.o whn p.u bef 10th*		**150/1**	
0100	P		**Ramblees Holly**^{9} [1016] 7-10-7	DMcGann(5)		—
			(R S Wood) *nt fluent: sn bhd: t.o 8th: p.u bef 2 out*		**7/2**^{2}	
5-5P	U		**Western Bluebird (IRE)**^{36} [781] 7-10-5 70	(b) MJMcAlister(7)		—
			(Miss Kate Milligan) *in rr whn blnd and uns rdr 1st*		**100/1**	
250-	P		**Dead Mans Dante (IRE)**^{241} [2462] 7-10-9	KJMercer(3)		—
			(Ferdy Murphy) *stdd s: hld up in rr: rn wd bnd and p.u bef 5th*		**10/1**	
0-3P	P		**Oliverjohn (IRE)**^{26} [858] 8-10-9 92	PBuchanan(3)		—
			(Miss Lucinda V Russell) *in tch: outpcd 7th: bhd fr 10th: t.o whn p.u bef 2 out*		**14/1**	

5m 7.30s (-16.10) **Going Correction** -0.80s/f (Firm) **13** Ran SP% **115.0**

Speed ratings: **98,97,97,96,94 94,—,—,—,— —,—,—** CSF £20.08 TOTE £2.10: £1.10, £1.20, £5.50; EX 15.30.

Owner Mrs J M Hegarty **Bred** Mrs J Hegarty **Trained** Cowbridge, Vale Of Glamorgan

FOCUS

A modest beginners' chase and a brave winner but at a cost. The form is not strong but looks sound enough, with the placed horses to their marks.

NOTEBOOK

Oh So Brave, a winning pointer, continually gave away ground jumping to his right. After clouting the last he stayed on to take what looked an unlikely victory. How long he will be on the sidelines remains to be seen. *(op 6-4 tchd 2-1)*

Heather Lad, none the worse for his heavy fall at Southwell, just missed out in the end. *(op 9-1)*

Brave Effect(IRE), who last ran over fences on this card a year ago, stepped up the gallop early on the final circuit and in the end just missed out. This marked an improved effort from him. *(op 14-1)*

Kilbride Lad(IRE), a winning pointer, has cut little ice over hurdles of late including selling company. His last win over hurdles was over five years ago now and three miles might be his trip in his advancing years. *(op 50-1 tchd 33-1)*

Prize Ring, who did not stride out going to post, is struggling to make any impact over fences. *(op 9-1)*

One Of Them, having just his fourth start over fences, will have a better chance of breaking his duck in a three-mile novices' handicap chase. *(op 20-1)*

Ramblees Holly, rated 105 over hurdles, would not have a cut at his fences on his chasing debut and was soon struggling. *Official explanation: jockey said gelding jumped poorly early (tchd 9-1)*

Dead Mans Dante(IRE) *Official explanation: jockey said saddle slipped (tchd 9-1)*

1063 JOHN WADE FOR EQUESTRIAN FIBRE AND RUBBER (S) H'CAP HURDLE (QUALIFIER) (8 hdls) 2m 1f

3:00 (3:07) (Class 5) (0-90,90) 4-Y-O+ **£2,317** (£662; £331)

Form	Pos	Dist	Horse	Jockey	SP	RPR
00-0	1		**Two Steps To Go (USA)**^{11} [987] 6-9-13 **70**	MrTJO'Brien(7)		77+
			(E A Elliott) *hld up: hdwy 5th: styd on to ld between last 2: rdn out*		**10/1**^{3}	
-0P0	2	*2 1/2*	**Valuable (IRE)**^{36} [784] 8-10-13 **77**	KJohnson		82+
			(R Johnson) *hld up: hdwy to chse ldr 5th: led after next: hdd between last 2: no ex*		**25/1**	
-000	3	*7*	**Fortune's Fool**^{47} [686] 6-10-8 **72**	ATinkler		70+
			(I A Brown) *hld up: hdwa 5th: one pce fr 2 out*		**14/1**	
3-15	4	*5*	**Plenty Courage**^{26} [858] 11-11-5 **90**	MJMcAlister(7)		83+
			(B Storey) *chsd ldrs: chal after 3 out: one pce fr next*		**8/1**^{2}	
3400	5	*7*	**Seemore Sunshine**^{4} [1046] 8-10-4 **75**	JAJenkins(7)		60
			(M J Gingell) *mid-div: hdwy 3 out: one pce*		**12/1**	

P00P **6** *9* **Conor's Pride (IRE)**[25] [873] 8-11-10 **88** .... NPMulholland 64
(B Mactaggart) *led tl after 3 out: sn wknd* **50/1**

000 **7** *2 ½* **Dan De Lion**[40] [760] 6-10-13 **77** .... (b[1]) HOliver 50
(R C Guest) *in tch: rdn 3 out: sn outpcd* **16/1**

-PP0 **8** *nk* **Dajazar (IRE)**[11] [988] 9-11-0 **85** .... CDSharkey[(7)] 58
(Mrs K Walton) *in tch: wknd 3 out* **66/1**

55P6 **9** *1 ¾* **Rose Of York (IRE)**[12] [973] 5-10-4 **73** .... (t) DLaverty[(5)] 44
(Mrs A M Thorpe) *chsd ldrs: lost pl appr 2 out* **11/1**

2404 **10** *5* **Arjay**[11] [987] 7-10-10 **79** .... (b) DCCostello[(5)] 45
(S B Clark) *in rr fr 5th* **9/2**[1]

0036 **11** *2 ½* **Martin House (IRE)**[10] [822] 6-10-11 **78** .... (p) PBuchanan[(3)] 41
(D W Thompson) *w ldrs: hit 3 out: sn lost pl* **12/1**

000 **12** *shd* **Mushraag (IRE)**[26] [856] 5-10-0 **67** .... (t) TJPhelan[(3)] 30
(J J Lambe, Ire) *in tch to 5th: sn lost pl* **16/1**

00-0 **13** *5* **Ice Rain (IRE)**[26] [860] 5-10-9 **73** .... ChristianWilliams 65+
(Evan Williams) *bhd: hdwy 5th: 5th whn heavily eased last: virtually p.u: lame* **9/2**[1]

000 **P** **Bowling Along**[22] [892] 4-10-3 **69** .... (t) BHarding —
(M E Sowersby) *stdd s: bhd: t.o whn p.u bef 2 out* **25/1**

3m 52.6s (-13.90) **Going Correction** -0.75s/f (Firm)
WFA 4 from 5yo+ 2lb **14** Ran SP% **109.9**
Speed ratings: **102,100,97,95,91 87,86,86,85,83 81,81,79,—** CSF £195.99 CT £2551.91 TOTE £13.80: £4.30, £6.10, £6.20; EX 366.40.The winner was sold to A.Singer for 7,000gns.
Owner Eric A Elliott **Bred** Twilite Farm Inc **Trained** Rushyford, Co Durham
■ Stewards' Enquiry : D Laverty one-day ban: careless riding (Aug 5)

FOCUS
A strongly-run selling handicap with the first two coming from off the pace. The third sets the level and the race could rate higher.

NOTEBOOK
Two Steps To Go(USA) looked in good nick and, given a patient ride, was always doing more than enough. He was sold at the auction and joins Maurice Barnes. *(op 12-1)*
Valuable(IRE), bang out of form, went on but in the end the winner saw it out the better.
Fortune's Fool, unplaced in a dozen previous starts, shaped as if a return to a longer trip will be in his favour. *(op 16-1 tchd 20-1)*
Plenty Courage, 11lb higher than Hexham, did well considering he raced up with what was a *strong pace. However, he was struck into and was dismounted after the line. Official explanation: jockey said the gelding was struck into (op 11-2)*
Seemore Sunshine, a maiden after 14 previous starts, at least showed a bit more than he had done on his two previous outings. *(op 16-1)*
Arjay was disappointing and never figured. *(tchd 5-1)*
Ice Rain(IRE), running in a seller for the first time, was fifth and well held when he looked to break *down soon after the final flight. Official explanation: jockey said the gelding finished lame (op 5-1 tchd 11-2)*

1064 JOHN SMITH'S EXTRA SMOOTH MARES' ONLY NOVICES' HURDLE (8 hdls) 2m 1f
3:30 (3:33) (Class 4) 4-Y-0+ **£3,406** (£1,048; £524; £262)

Form RPR

3-U2 **1** **Reem Two**[57] [574] 4-10-10 99 .... JMMaguire 92+
(D McCain) *in rr: reminders after 3rd: hdwy next: w ldrs 3 out: slt ld appr last: kpt on wl nr fin* **6/4**[1]

6-42 **2** *1* **Miss Kilkeel (IRE)**[17] [926] 7-11-2 .... SMMcGovern[(3)] 98
(R T J Wilson, Ire) *trckd ldrs: led 5th: hdd appr last: kpt on: no ex nr fin* **6/4**[1]

600/ **3** *30* **Yellow Soil Star (IRE)**[702] [1188] 6-10-7 .... PCO'Neill[(5)] 61
(J J Lambe, Ire) *chsd ldrs: wknd appr 2 out* **22/1**

P000 **4** *7* **Flashy Filly**[31] [822] 5-10-5 61 .... MJMcAlister[(7)] 54
(J C Haynes) *prom: lost pl after 5th* **150/1**

F26- **5** *8* **Sylvie D'Orthe (FR)**[113] [4709] 4-10-5 78 .... (v) DMcGann[(5)] 44
(A C Wilson) *chsd ldrs: lost pl after 5th* **25/1**

3-0 **6** *12* **Zahunda (IRE)**[92] [14] 6-10-2 .... CareyWilliamson[(10)] 34
(M J Gingell) *in rr fr 5th* **16/1**[3]

000- **7** *10* **Compton Princess**[232] [2649] 5-10-9 66 .... MrCStorey[(3)] 24
(Miss S E Forster) *t.k.h: led to 5th: sn lost pl and bhd* **66/1**

0-P5 **P** **Royaltea**[5] [1037] 4-10-5 87 .... LTreadwell[(5)] —
(J T Stimpson) *t.k.h: w ldrs: p.u bef 3rd* **15/2**[2]

00- **P** **Dawn Frolics**[229] [2709] 4-10-3 .... JAJenkins[(7)] —
(M J Gingell) *blnd and lost pl 4th: sn bhd: t.o whn p.u bef 2 out* **100/1**

3m 54.2s (-12.30) **Going Correction** -0.75s/f (Firm)
WFA 4 from 5yo+ 2lb **9** Ran SP% **109.0**
Speed ratings: **98,97,83,80,76 70,66,—,—** CSF £3.38 TOTE £2.10: £1.10, £1.10, £4.90; EX 2.90.
Owner Dave Ellis **Bred** Darley **Trained** Cholmondeley, Cheshire

FOCUS
A weak mares-only novices' hurdle and they bet 16/1 bar three. The runner-up is the best guide to the form.

NOTEBOOK
Reem Two looked to have been found a good opportunity but she made very hard work of it. Given reminders with a full circuit to go in the end she was persuaded to do just enough. *(op 11-8)*
Miss Kilkeel(IRE), on the back of a Wexford win, went on and fought back hard pressing the winner all the way to the line. *(tchd 13-8)*
Yellow Soil Star(IRE), absent for almost two years, like the rest was left for dead by the first two. *(op 20-1)*
Flashy Filly had finished unplaced in seven previous tries including in selling company. Flashy she is not!
Royaltea took a fierce grip and her saddle went on the downhill run to the third flight. *Official explanation: jockey said saddle slipped (op 13-2 tchd 9-1)*

1065 TOTESPORT.COM H'CAP CHASE (14 fncs 2 omitted) 2m 5f
4:00 (4:01) (Class 4) (0-110,93) 5-Y-0+ **£4,459** (£1,372; £686; £343)

Form RPR

-506 **1** **Now Then Sid**[44] [717] 6-10-5 **75** .... PBuchanan[(3)] 99+
(Mrs S A Watt) *hdwy to chse ldrs 7th: led 3 out: styd on between last 2* **6/1**[3]

6-05 **2** *7* **Swallow Magic (IRE)**[9] [1015] 7-10-8 **78** .... KJMercer[(3)] 96+
(Ferdy Murphy) *hdwy to chse ldrs 7th: chal 2 out: one pce between last 2* **6/1**[3]

2113 **3** *dist* **Maidstone Monument (IRE)**[14] [960] 10-11-12 **93** .... APMcCoy 81
(Mrs A M Thorpe) *led to 2nd: drvn along 9th: wknd 11th: btn 31 l* **2/1**[1]

PPP- **4** *12* **Danteco**[364] [1048] 10-10-9 **83** .... MJMcAlister[(7)] 59
(Miss Kate Milligan) *mstkes: led 3rd to 5th: blnd 8th: wknd appr 3 out* **22/1**

/44- **5** *13* **Taleban**[285] [1703] 10-10-12 **82** .... PAspell[(3)] —
(J Wade) *reminders 7th: sn outpcd and bhd* **16/1**

F-05 **U** **York Rite (AUS)**[4] [1044] 9-10-11 **78** .... (p) HOliver —
(R C Guest) *mstke and uns rdr 1st* **6/1**[3]

565/ **P** **Little John**[92] 9-10-8 **75** .... GLee —
(W S Coltherd) *reminders 7th: sn bhd: p.u after next* **50/1**

0200 **P** **Lord Of The Land**[11] [988] 12-10-7 **79** .... DCCostello[(5)] —
(Mrs E Slack) *last whn hmpd 1st: bhd: t.o whn p.u bef 9th* **12/1**

/231 **P** **Jamica Plane (IRE)**[15] [939] 12-11-3 **89** .... (p) PCO'Neill[(5)] —
(J J Lambe, Ire) *chsd ldrs: led 7th: hdd and eased 3 out: sn p.u* **11/2**[2]

-FPP **P** **Zurs (IRE)**[11] [989] 12-11-1 **82** .... (p) JPMcNamara —
(J J Lambe, Ire) *led 2nd to 3rd: led 5th to 7th: sn lost pl: bhd whn p.u bef 9th* **22/1**

5m 2.70s (-20.70) **Going Correction** -0.80s/f (Firm) **10** Ran SP% **115.8**
Speed ratings: **107,104,—,—,— —,—,—,—,—** CSF £41.00 CT £97.05 TOTE £7.10: £2.00, £3.10, £1.10; EX 43.50.
Owner Mrs S A Watt **Bred** Mrs J Jackson **Trained** Brompton-on-Swale, N Yorks
■ A first success as a full licence holder for Sharon Watt.

FOCUS
A fair time for the grade, 4.6 seconds faster than the beginners' chase. The leaders went off far too fast for their own good and the winner did not need to run to his best to score.

NOTEBOOK
Now Then Sid, almost two stone better treated than over hurdles, was well supported on the morning line to make it tenth time lucky over fences. Happy to sit off the pace, in the end he did it *in workmanlike style. Suited by quick ground, he might well be capable of a follow up. Official explanation: trainer said, regarding the improved form shown, gelding had benfitted from a change in bedding following suspicion that it was suffering from a dust allergy (op 8-1 tchd 11-2)*
Swallow Magic(IRE), a point and hurdle-race winner in Ireland, has struggled to make an impact here. On just his second start over fences, he jumped the second last upsides but it was soon evident that he was booked for second spot. *(op 8-1)*
Maidstone Monument(IRE), stepping back in trip, helped make sure this was a true test but he *only succeeded in running himself to a near standstill with four fences still left to be jumped. (op 13-8 tchd 9-4)*
Danteco, pulled up on his three most recent starts, blundered his way round before calling it a day. *(op 28-1)*
Taleban, absent since October, never got competitive. *(op 25-1)*
Jamica Plane(IRE) was in the thick of things until going lame three from home. *(op 9-2)*

1066 TOTEEXACTA CONDITIONAL JOCKEYS' NOVICES' H'CAP HURDLE (10 hdls) 2m 5f 110y
4:30 (4:33) (Class 4) (0-95,94) 4-Y-0+ **£2,667** (£762; £381)

Form RPR

4UF1 **1** **Beaugency (NZ)**[9] [1015] 7-11-12 **94** .... WKennedy 100+
(R C Guest) *hld up: hdwy 7th: lft in ld appr 2 out: styd on run-in* **5/2**[1]

0043 **2** *2* **Penteli**[15] [938] 5-10-1 **79** .... MrBenHamilton[(10)] 82
(C Grant) *chsd ldrs: lft upsides gng to 2 out: nt qckn run-in* **14/1**

P-12 **3** *3* **Red Chief (IRE)**[15] [949] 5-11-8 **90** .... DLaverty 90
(Mrs A M Thorpe) *rr-div: hdwy 7th: styd on fr 2 out: nt rch 1st 2* **3/1**[2]

505 **4** *17* **Greenfort Brave (IRE)**[11] [991] 7-11-3 **85** .... PCO'Neill 68
(J J Lambe, Ire) *rr-div: sme hdwy 7th: nvr nr ldrs* **20/1**

424- **5** *1* **Destino**[316] [1413] 6-11-0 **87** .... TMessenger[(5)] 69
(Mrs S J Smith) *chsd ldrs: lost pl appr 2 out* **10/1**

F005 **6** *5* **Step In Line (IRE)**[31] [822] 13-9-11 **68** oh6 .... BenOrde-Powlett[(3)] 47+
(D W Thompson) *rr-div: sme hdwy 7th: wknd 3 out* **100/1**

5PPU **7** *dist* **Madhahir (IRE)**[12] [981] 5-9-13 **70** oh1 ow2 .... JAJenkins[(3)] —
(M J Gingell) *sn drvn along: bhd fr 6th: t.o* **100/1**

-00P **8** *8* **Test Of Faith**[50] [643] 6-10-7 **75** .... (b[1]) PAspell —
(J N R Billinge) *led to 1st: chsd ldrs: wknd after 7th: sn bhd: t.o* **33/1**

53FP **9** *dist* **Noras Legacy (IRE)**[36] [781] 7-10-3 **71** .... NPMulholland —
(Miss Lucinda V Russell) *prom: drvn along 5th: lost pl and mstke 7th: sn bhd: wl t.o* **33/1**

55/P **P** **Redouble**[76] [282] 9-10-5 **73** .... ONelmes —
(W B Stone) *sn bhd: t.o 7th: p.u bef 2 out* **50/1**

6-PU **P** **Muller (IRE)**[26] [856] 5-10-0 **68** oh4 .... DCCostello —
(R W Thomson) *in tch: lost pl 5th: p.u bef next* **125/1**

0-00 **P** **Diamond Vein**[67] [428] 6-10-12 **85** .... MrJEClare[(5)] —
(S P Griffiths) *bhd fr 6th: t.o whn p.u bef 3 out* **25/1**

46-4 **P** **Kippour (FR)**[84] [148] 7-11-5 **92** .... LBerridge[(5)] —
(S B Clark) *reluctant to go to s: rel to r: t.o whn p.u bef 4th* **16/1**

5P-4 **P** **Follow Up**[10] [1002] 7-11-3 **88** .... CDSharkey[(3)] 88
(S B Clark) *led 1st: qckd 7th: 4 l clr whn p.u appr 2 out: dead* **15/2**

006 **U** **Si Anthony (FR)**[36] [780] 5-10-7 **78** .... KJMercer[(3)] 60
(Ferdy Murphy) *chsd ldrs: 5th and wl outpcd whn mstke and uns rdr 2 out* **7/1**[3]

4m 58.2s (-17.50) **Going Correction** -0.75s/f (Firm) **15** Ran SP% **118.7**
Speed ratings: **101,100,99,93,92 90,—,—,—,— —,—,—,—,—** CSF £34.14 CT £112.08 TOTE £3.00: £1.60, £4.20, £1.70; EX 40.10.
Owner Gryffindor (www.racingtours.co.uk) **Bred** D M Kerr **Trained** Brancepeth, Co Durham

FOCUS
A poor race run at a fair pace and the complexion changed altogether going to two out. The third sets the standard.

NOTEBOOK
Beaugency(NZ) took advantage of a much lower mark over hurdles, biding his time and finding himself left in charge going to two out. If turning out again over the next eleven days he will be able to run without a penalty. *(op 10-3)*
Penteli is steadily improving and did well on her handicap bow, keeping on all the way to the line after racing up with what was quite a strong pace.
Red Chief(IRE), 10lb higher than Perth, seemed to give the first two a little too much rope. He stayed on well from the second last but was never going to get on terms. *(op 5-2 tchd 10-3)*
Greenfort Brave(IRE), unplaced in ten previous starts, had run out in a seller two outings ago. *(tchd 22-1)*
Destino, absent since September, paid the penalty for racing up with what was quite a strong pace. *(op 15-2)*
Follow Up, well supported, was taking a big drop back in trip. He stepped up the gallop early on the final circuit and looked like taking some catching when he went horribly wrong at the top of the hill. He had to be put down. *(op 12-1)*

1067 TOTESPORT 0800 221 221 H'CAP HURDLE (13 hdls) 3m 3f 110y
5:00 (5:00) (Class 4) (0-110,110) 4-Y-0+ **£3,347** (£1,030; £515; £257)

Form RPR

1603 **1** **Pikestaff (USA)**[15] [941] 7-9-13 **90** .... (t) BenOrde-Powlett[(7)] 99+
(M A Barnes) *w ldrs: led 4th: clr appr 2 out: eased nr fin* **7/2**[2]

21-1 **2** *20* **Graffiti Tongue (IRE)**[76] [289] 12-11-12 **110** .... (p) APMcCoy 97
(Evan Williams) *sn pushed along: nvr gng wl: all out to go mod 3rd 10th: wnt mod 2nd after 3 out: hrd rdn and no imp* **7/2**[2]

0343 **3** *17* **Agnese**[10] [1002] 5-9-9 **84** oh2 .... DCCostello[(5)] 54
(G M Moore) *w ldrs: rdn along 8th: wknd after 3 out* **4/1**[3]

O/P- **4** *15* **Tioga Gold (IRE)**[24] 11 6-9-12 **85**.......................... ONelmes(3) 40
(L R James) *in tch: wknd after 9th: sn bhd* **66/1**
PP-3 **5** *10* **Tierkely (IRE)**[11] 989 10-10-2 **86**.......................... ChristianWilliams 31
(J J Lambe, Ire) *reminders 5th: sn bhd: lost tch 10th* **5/2**[1]
-061 **P** **Inglewood**[36] 783 5-9-11 **88**.......................... MJMcAlister(7) —
(Miss Kate Milligan) *led to 4th: lost pl 8th: t.o 3 out: p.u bef next* **5/1**

6m 19.7s (-44.20) **Going Correction** -0.75s/f (Firm) course record **6** Ran SP% **111.2**
Speed ratings: **103,97,92,88,85** — CSF £15.88 TOTE £4.70: £2.10, £1.50; EX 23.90 Place 6 £62.47, Place 5 £38.54.
Owner J M Carlyle **Bred** Juddmonte Farms **Trained** Farlam, Cumbria

FOCUS
An end-to-end gallop resulting in a new record time over a distance not used that often here. The race could be rated higher.

NOTEBOOK
Pikestaff(USA), 7lb higher than his last success at Hexham in May, stays all day and bounces off fast ground. He had this won some way from home and was able to ease off near the line. If the Handicapper takes this at face value he will have a lot more on his plate in future. *(tchd 4-1)*
Graffiti Tongue(IRE), 3lb higher and on a career-high mark, tested the champion's resolve to the full. Picking them off one by one, in the end the winner proved one too many. *(op 2-1)*
Agnese mixed it from the off but under pressure with a full circuit to go, she finally cracked. *(op 9-2)*
Tioga Gold(IRE), pulled up when last seen over hurdles over a year ago, has been bang out of form on the level since. *(tchd 80-1)*
Tierkely(IRE), making his hurdling bow, was soon under pressure and he seemed to lose all interest early on the final circuit. *Official explanation: jockey said the gelding never travelled (op 9-2)*
Inglewood, back over hurdles, went off like a scalded cat. In the end he was pulled up having been struck into, the final casualty on a bad day which was no advert for summer jumping when the ground was as firm as it was here. *Official explanation: vet said gelding was struck into (op 6-1 tchd 9-2)*
T/Plt: £282.40 to a £1 stake. Pool: £49,398.25. 127.65 winning tickets. T/Qpdt: £2.40 to a £1 stake. Pool: £4,458.20. 1,348.00 winning tickets. WG

1068 - 1072a (Foreign Racing) - See Raceform Interactive

DIEPPE (R-H)
Tuesday, July 26

OFFICIAL GOING: Very soft

1073a GRAND STEEPLE-CHASE DE DIEPPE (CHASE) 2m 5f
2:55 (2:55) 5-Y-0+ **£11,574** (£5,787; £3,376; £2,291; £1,085)

RPR
1 **Domirome (FR)**[118] 7-10-10 .... JacquesRicou —
(G Macaire, France)
2 *2* **Anna's Blue (FR)**[53] 10-10-5 .... LGerard —
(J-L Henry, France)
3 *1 1/2* **Apanal (GER)**[254] 2239 5-10-3 .... ADuchene —
(H Hack, Germany)
4 *5* **Karine Des Ongrais (FR)**[30] 845 10-10-8 .... MrPBrechet —
(P Chemin, France)
5 *1 1/2* **Viana (FR)**[100] 5-10-3 .... SJuteau —
(E Lecoiffier, France)
6 *3/4* **Sworovski (IRE)**[32] 5-10-3 .... PMarsac —
(C Aubert, France)
7 *8* **Marchand De Reve (FR)**[38] 9-10-10 .... BThelier —
(P Briard, France)
8 *20* **Golly (IRE)**[11] 1000 9-10-4 ow3.......................... JAJenkins —
(D L Williams) *mistake 1st, jumped well after, went 2nd 8th, lost place steadily throughout final circuit*
9 *2 1/2* **Kasbimy (FR)**[30] 845 6-10-1 .... LDeschamps —
(J-P Carnel, France)
P **River Groom (FR)**[1157] 6-10-1 .... RFlament —
(J-P Carnel, France)
P **Don De Matha (FR)**[30] 846 5-10-5 ....(b) LHoubron —
(D Grandin, France)
R **Ginko Biloba (FR)**[375] 6-10-12 .... VSuscosse —
(F-M Cottin, France)
P **Monsieur Le Chouan (FR)**[67] 5-10-5 .... SDupuis —
(T Trapenard, France) **23/1**[1]

5m 19.6s
WFA 5 from 6yo+ 1lb **14** Ran SP% **4.2**
PARI-MUTUEL (including 1 euro stake): WIN 1.20 PL 1.10, 4.30, 4.00;DF 22.20.
Owner Mme Y Shen **Bred** J Gandre **Trained** France

NOTEBOOK
Golly(IRE)jumped well enough and was prominent early, but could not go the pace and was well beaten.

1074a GRAND STEEPLE-CHASE CROSS COUNTRY DE LA VILLE DIEPPE (CHASE) (CROSS-COUNTRY) 3m 5f
3:30 (3:33) 5-Y-0+ **£14,979** (£7,489; £4,369; £2,965; £1,404)

RPR
1 **Jungle Fever (FR)**[492] 8-10-5 ow2.......................... MrPBrechet —
(P Chemin, France)
2 *3/4* **Le Cluzeau (FR)**[1346] 10-10-8 .... JacquesRicou —
(G Macaire, France)
3 *1 1/2* **Hawaii (FR)** 10-10-3 .... DDelorme —
(Mme L Bellet, France)
4 *4* **Dulcigris (FR)**[30] 845 9-10-1 .... LDeschamps —
(J-P Carnel, France)
5 *1 1/2* **Jojo I (FR)** 8-10-3 .... SHamon —
(S Hamon, France)
6 *dist* **Joint Authority (IRE)**[30] 845 10-10-3 .... CaptLHorner —
(D L Williams) *nt fluent, towards rr, mstke 13th, just in tch when almost fell 5 out, t.o when another terrible blunder 3 out*
F **Jo D'Alco (FR)** 8-10-1 .... SDrillot —
(P Briard, France)
P **Dekatell Le Dun (FR)**[30] 845 14-10-1 .... RFlament —
(A Sannier, France)

8m 56.5s **9** Ran
PARI-MUTUEL: WIN 2.00; PL 1.20, 1.40, 1.40; DF 3.60.
Owner Mme P Chemin **Bred** G Ferte **Trained** France

NOTEBOOK
Joint Authority(IRE) struggled with these fences, and was already starting to struggle when couple of bad mistakes late on finished his chance.

1017 NEWTON ABBOT (L-H)
Wednesday, July 27

OFFICIAL GOING: Good to soft (soft in places)
The going had eased after rain. The first fence in the home straight was omitted in all chases.
Wind: Nil Weather: Raining

1075 SUMMER CONDITIONAL JOCKEYS' H'CAP HURDLE (8 hdls 1 omitted) 2m 3f
2:05 (2:05) (Class 4) (0-100,97) 4-Y-0+ **£2,632** (£752; £376)

Form RPR
-222 **1** **Marathea (FR)**[52] 649 4-10-4 **79**.......................... PCO'Neill(3) 82+
(Miss Venetia Williams) *hld up: hdwy 4th: led 6th: r.o wl* **10/3**[1]
0524 **2** *1 1/2* **Fiddles Music**[10] 1027 4-10-13 **90**.......................... LHeard(5) 91+
(D Burchell) *hld up and bhd: hdwy after 6th: wnt 2nd and pckd 2 out: kpt on flat* **6/1**
6301 **3** *1 3/4* **Red Canyon (IRE)**[10] 1017 8-11-11 **97** 7ex..........................(p) DJacob(3) 98
(C L Tizzard) *prom: outpcd 6th: rallied appr 2 out: styd on flat* **14/1**
0/21 **4** *6* **Sunnyland**[21] 915 6-11-2 **90**.......................... DPO'Dwyer(5) 86+
(P J Hobbs) *hld up and bhd: nt fluent and rdr lost iron briefly 1st: hdwy 5th: wknd after 2 out* **4/1**[2]
-45P **5** *2* **Club Royal**[36] 806 8-10-9 **78**..........................(p) JamesDavies 71
(N E Berry) *hld up: hdwy 4th: mstke 6th: wknd appr 2 out* **25/1**
P3-0 **6** *2* **Wozzeck**[49] 683 5-10-2 **81**..........................(p) PDavey(10) 72
(R H Buckler) *w ldr: led 4th to 6th: wknd 2 out* **50/1**
0351 **7** *10* **Native Chancer (IRE)**[10] 1028 5-11-3 **89** 7ex.......................... TJPhelan(3) 70
(Jonjo O'Neill) *hld up: hdwy 4th: wknd after 6th* **9/2**[3]
0-40 **F** **Blue Yonder**[6] 1046 5-10-3 **77**.......................... WMcCarthy(5) —
(Evan Williams) *bhd tl fell last* **25/1**
150- **P** **Faddad (USA)**[305] 1508 9-11-1 **84**..........................(t) WKennedy —
(P Bowen) *a bhd: t.o whn p.u bef 2 out* **9/1**
5P/6 **P** **Brief Decline (IRE)**[28] 863 10-11-9 **95**.......................... SWalsh(3) —
(J D Frost) *bhd fr 6th: t.o whn p.u bef 2 out* **66/1**
P-34 **P** **Suchwot (IRE)**[21] 915 4-10-2 **77**..........................(vt) TJMalone(3) —
(M C Pipe) *prom: mstke 3rd: wknd after 6th: t.o whn p.u bef 2 out* **9/1**
6/P0 **P** **Contemporary Art**[10] 1017 7-11-2 **90**..........................(vt[1]) KBurke(5) —
(N J Dawe) *led to 4th: sn rdn and lost pl: t.o appr 6th: p.u bef 2 out* **100/1**

4m 49.5s (16.50) **Going Correction** +0.90s/f (Soft)
WFA 4 from 5yo+ 2lb **12** Ran SP% **114.3**
Speed ratings: **101,100,99,97,96 95,91,—,—,— —,—** CSF £22.04 CT £244.30 TOTE £3.60: £1.30, £3.10, £4.50; EX 18.90.
Owner Sir Clement Freud **Bred** J Biraben And Robert Labeyrie **Trained** Kings Caple, H'fords

FOCUS
This was a moderate conditional jockeys' handicap to open proceedings. The pace was fair in the conditions and the form appears to make sense with the first three pretty much to marks. The third-last flight was bypassed.

NOTEBOOK
Marathea(FR) finally got off the mark over timber, at the sixth attempt, under a well-judged ride from O'Neill. She is well suited by this sort of ground, and this probably represented her easiest assignment to date, but further improvement cannot be ruled out during the summer while at this end of the handicap. *(op 4-1)*
Fiddles Music could only manage the same pace under pressure in the straight, but was eating into the winner's advantage on the run-in and may have benefited from a more positive ride. She helps set the level of this form. *(op 7-1 tchd 8-1)*
Red Canyon(IRE) , under a penalty for his recent course and distance success, was doing his best work in the home straight after looking to get outpaced down the back. This was a fair effort under top weight on ground he would have found plenty soft enough, but he is never one to trust implicitly. *(op 12-1)*
Sunnyland , whose rider momentarily lost an iron after the first hurdle, failed to quicken on this testing ground and was made to look very one paced. Her latest 8lb rise in the weights looks harsh on this evidence, but she may do better back on a quicker surface. *(op 7-2)*
Native Chancer(IRE) proved very disappointing under his penalty and will probably leave this form behind when reverting to faster ground. *(op 10-3)*
Contemporary Art *Official explanation: vet said gelding finished lame*

1076 TAXIFAST CLASSIFIED CHASE (13 fncs 3 omitted) 2m 5f 110y
2:35 (2:35) (Class 4) 5-Y-0+ **£3,267** (£933; £466)

Form RPR
110- **1** **Philippa Yeates (IRE)**[111] 4754 6-10-8 86..........................(p) TJMalone(3) 95+
(M C Pipe) *a.p: wnt 2nd 4th: rdn to ld 3 out: sn clr: r.o wl* **7/2**[2]
1260 **2** *8* **Borehill Joker**[21] 915 9-11-0 86.......................... AThornton 90+
(Miss K M George) *hld up: stdy hdwy 5th: mstke 10th: wnt 2nd last: no ch w wnr* **4/1**[3]
P-26 **3** *8* **Sunshan**[24] 896 9-11-0 85.......................... RGreene 82+
(R J Hodges) *hld up: sn in tch: chsd wnr fr 3 out: wknd flat* **4/1**[3]
1PP/ **4** *8* **Silent Sound (IRE)**[570] 3201 9-11-0 85..........................(p) JTizzard 73
(C L Tizzard) *hld up: struggling after 7th: n.d after* **33/1**
P-00 **5** *7* **Debatable**[6] 1046 6-11-0 87.......................... PJBrennan 66
(N J Hawke) *hld up: hdwy after 7th: wknd 3 out* **16/1**
P-PP **P** **Gordy's Joy**[66] 459 5-10-10 65.......................... SCurran —
(G A Ham) *a bhd: mstke 7th: sn lost tch: p.u bef 8th* **100/1**
P-0P **P** **Plain Chant**[21] 916 8-11-0 66..........................(p) ChristianWilliams —
(C Roberts) *bhd fr 7th: t.o 8th: p.u after 2 out* **50/1**
P-56 **P** **Smart Design (IRE)**[43] 744 10-11-0 79..........................(t) JPMcNamara —
(K Bishop) *chsd ldr to 4th: wknd 8th: t.o whn p.u after 2 out* **8/1**
31P2 **P** **Multeen Gunner**[17] 948 8-11-0 84..........................(p) PMoloney —
(Evan Williams) *led: j.rt 2nd: hdd 3 out: sn wknd: bhd whn p.u after 2 out* **11/4**[1]

5m 52.2s (29.50) **Going Correction** +1.25s/f (Heav)
WFA 5 from 6yo+ 1lb **9** Ran SP% **111.8**
Speed ratings: **96,93,90,87,84** —,—,—,— CSF £17.52 TOTE £4.80: £1.80, £1.70, £1.70; EX 21.80.
Owner B A Kilpatrick **Bred** B A Kilpatrick **Trained** Nicholashayne, Devon

FOCUS
A tight, yet low-grade classified chase run at a modest gallop and the field finished well strung out. The form could rate higher but is probably weak.

NOTEBOOK
Philippa Yeates(IRE) , returning from a 111-day break, got off the mark at the first time of asking over fences with a clear-cut success. Given that two of her best displays over hurdles were on a testing surface, it was no surprise she relished this deteriorating ground and she jumped neatly for a debutante. She can be hard to predict, but should be placed to win again over fences.

Borehill Joker had no chance with the winner, yet still turned in an improved effort and reversed recent course form with Sunshan on this softer ground. He is very hard to win with over fences, despite being rated 12lb lower than he is over hurdles. *(op 10-3 tchd 9-2)*
Sunshan went in pursuit of the winner at the top of the straight, but never looked a threat and paid for those exertions by losing second late in the day. He really needs faster ground. *(tchd 7-2)*
Silent Sound(IRE) merely plugged on at his own pace throughout, but is entitled to improve for this first outing in 570 days. *(op 25-1)*
Debatable, an most impressive bumper winner when with Paul Webber in 2003, is evidently a tricky customer. However, he did not jump badly on this chase bow and is worth perservering with on this evidence. *(tchd 14-1)*
Multeen Gunner stopped quickly once headed and can surely do better when reverting to quick ground. *(op 3-1)*

1077 JEWSON MAIDEN HURDLE (SERIES QUALIFIER) (8 hdls) 2m 1f
3:10 (3:12) (Class 3) 4-Y-0+ **£4,795** (£1,475; £737; £368)

Form RPR
1 **Gold Guest**[6] 6-11-2 ....(t) RThornton 95+
(P D Evans) *hld up in tch: led and wnt rt 2 out: r.o wl* **4/1**[2]
00-0 **2** *3* **Le Gris (GER)**[17] [947] 6-11-2 86 .... AThornton 89
(P R Rodford) *chsd ldr: led briefly appr 2 out: nt qckn flat* **13/2**
P-P **3** *7* **Peruvian Breeze (IRE)**[22] [903] 4-11-0 .... ChristianWilliams 81+
(Evan Williams) *hld up and bhd: hdwy after 3 out: one pce fr 2 out* **14/1**
4 *9* **Fine Palette**[35] 5-11-2 .... PJBrennan 76+
(B J Llewellyn) *hld up in tch: led 3 out tl appr 2 out: 4th and wkng whn mstke 2 out* **11/2**[3]
P04- **5** *1* **Shalati Princess**[32] [4918] 4-10-7 80 .... SCurran 63
(J C Fox) *racd wd: led to 3rd: wknd after 3 out* **12/1**
6 *5* **Port Sodrick**[239] 4-10-7 .... KBurke(7) 65
(R H Alner) *hld up: hdwy 5th: ev ch 3 out: 5th and wkng whn blnd 2 out* **8/1**
P-00 **7** *1 3/4* **Darkshape**[24] [892] 5-11-2 .... SThomas 65
(Miss Venetia Williams) *hld up: hdwy 5th: rdn and wknd after 3 out* **12/1**
00-0 **P** **Daisy Dale**[10] [1017] 7-10-9 80 .... RGreene —
(S C Burrough) *hld up and bhd: hdwy 5th: wknd after 3 out: t.o whn p.u bef 2 out* **50/1**
6 **P** **Tog Go Boge (IRE)**[74] [356] 7-11-2 .... WMarston —
(R T Phillips) *t.k.h: mstke 1st: hdwy 5th: wknd after 3 out: t.o whn p.u bef 2 out* **16/1**
P **Bold Trump**[20] 4-10-11 ....(t) DCrosse(3) —
(M Salaman) *prom: j. slowly 1st and 2nd: led after 4th to 3 out: sn wknd: t.o whn p.u bef 2 out* **33/1**
22 **P** **Treacysdream (IRE)**[66] [463] 5-10-9 .... RSpate(7) —
(Mrs K Waldron) *hld up: blnd 1st: hdwy to ld 3rd: hdd after 4th: wknd after 3 out: t.o whn p.u bef 2 out* **11/4**[1]

4m 34.4s (29.30) **Going Correction** +0.90s/f (Soft)
WFA 4 from 5yo+ 2lb **11 Ran SP% 119.3**
Speed ratings: **67,65,62,58,57 55,54,—,—,— —** CSF £31.17 TOTE £6.80: £2.40, £2.80, £4.50; EX 39.00.
Owner Mrs S Clifford **Bred** The Hon D K And Mrs Oliver **Trained** Pandy, Abergavenny

FOCUS
This already moderate conteat was weakened by the withdrawal of Dyneburg and hurdling debutant Barking Mad. It was run at a farcical early gallop and the form is very ordinary despite the placed horses running close to their marks.

NOTEBOOK
Gold Guest, who landed a seller at Bath six days previously on firm ground, dug deep to see off the runner-up and came right away on the run-in to make a winning debut over timber. His jumping was fluent throughout, he was not at all inconvenienced by this much softer ground and is entitled to improve with a stiffer test in this sphere. *(op 10-3)*
Le Gris(GER), rated just 86 over hurdles, only gave way on the run-in and turned in a much more encouraging effort. This is clearly his preferred ground and it would come as little surprise to see the headgear back on in the future. *(tchd 7-1)*
Peruvian Breeze(IRE) fared the best of those to be held up off the steady pace and turned in by far his best display to date over hurdles. He was put in his place late on, but looked to make up his ground too quickly and can build on this now his confidence should have been restored.
Fine Palette, rated 70 on the Flat and whose stable won this in 2004, hit the front three out yet failed to sustain his gallop and was ultimately made to look very one paced. He has been struggling for form on the Flat of late and this has to rate a disappointing start to his hurdling career. *(op 4-1)*
Treacysdream(IRE) ran well below expectations on this hurdling bow and looked unsuited by the tacky ground. However, he needs further and will need to improve his jumping if he is to progress in this sphere. *(op 4-1)*

1078 NEWTON ABBOT RACECOURSE NOVICES' CHASE (13 fncs 3 omitted) 2m 5f 110y
3:45 (3:45) (Class 3) 5-Y-0+ **£5,356** (£1,648; £824)

Form RPR
-FF1 **1** **Fontanesi (IRE)**[16] [962] 5-11-5 .... TJMurphy 133+
(M C Pipe) *w ldr: led after 2 out: easily* **4/7**[1]
/PU3 **2** *5* **Windy Spirit (IRE)**[28] [865] 10-11-0 97 .... ChristianWilliams 108
(Evan Williams) *hld up: outpcd 9th: styd on to take 2nd flat: no ch w wnr* **12/1**[3]
013- **3** *5* **Fool On The Hill**[102] [4859] 8-11-12 137 .... PJBrennan 117+
(P J Hobbs) *led: hdd after 2 out: wknd flat* **15/8**[2]

5m 57.9s (35.20) **Going Correction** +1.25s/f (Heav)
WFA 5 from 8yo+ 1lb **3 Ran SP% 106.1**
Speed ratings: **86,84,82** CSF £4.95 TOTE £1.40; EX 8.70.
Owner D A Johnson **Bred** John R Gaines Thoroughbreds L L C And Orpendal **Trained** Nicholashayne, Devon

FOCUS
Despite there only being the three runners, this was an above-average novice event for the time of year with the winner value for four times the winning margin. The pace was moderate, however.

NOTEBOOK
Fontanesi(IRE) followed-up his recent course and distance success with a facile display under his penalty. He did well to perform as he did on this ground, as he has shown all of his previous best form on a quicker surface, and is value for more than his already-wide winning margin. Despite lacking size for chasing, he is really getting his act together now over fences and will no doubt be very hard to beat in his quest for the hat-trick despite a double penalty. In the long term, however, he is likely to prove vulnerable to the better novices in this sphere. *(op 8-13)*
Windy Spirit(IRE) ◆, who faced an impossible task at these weights, stayed on with real purpose from two out and turned in a fair effort, considering he would have been totally unsuited by the moderate gallop over this trip. Connections will no doubt be keen to turn him out in a handicap off his current official mark and this former winning pointer is one to note when reverting to three miles. *(op 14-1 tchd 16-1)*
Fool On The Hill dropped right away from the penultimate fence and was found out by his penalties in this testing ground. He can do better, but is not going to be the easiest to place this term. *(op 7-4)*

1079 GILL AKESTER H'CAP HURDLE (12 hdls) 3m 3f
4:20 (4:21) (Class 4) (0-105,105) 4-Y-0+ **£3,292** (£940; £470)

Form RPR
222 **1** **Getoutwhenyoucan (IRE)**[14] [977] 5-11-12 102 .... TJMurphy 120+
(M C Pipe) *mde all: clr after 3 out: easily* **7/4**[1]
2-14 **2** *7* **Temper Lad (USA)**[43] [749] 10-10-0 76 .... RJohnson 82+
(J D Frost) *a.p: wnt 2nd after 8th: rdn after 3 out: no ch w wnr* **11/4**[2]
3000 **3** *25* **Wild Tempo (FR)**[14] [974] 10-10-8 94 ....(t) AGlassonbury(10) 73
(M C Pipe) *hld up in rr: hit 1st: hdwy 9th: rdn and wknd appr 2 out* **14/1**
-120 **4** *7* **Esters Boy**[59] [566] 7-11-12 102 .... LAspell 74
(P G Murphy) *hld up: hit 2nd: mstke 9th: sn struggling* **14/1**
4PP- **5** *6* **Cresswell Gold**[255] [2223] 8-9-11 76 oh7 .... ONelmes(3) 42
(D A Rees) *hld up: hdwy 7th: wknd after 3 out* **28/1**
0303 **P** **Mistified (IRE)**[10] [1018] 4-11-0 94 .... AThornton —
(J W Mullins) *prom: sltly hmpd 8th: wknd 3 out: t.o whn p.u bef 2 out* **8/1**
1P1U **P** **Excellent Vibes (IRE)**[7] [1041] 7-10-7 83 .... CLlewellyn —
(N A Twiston-Davies) *w wnr tl after 8th: rdn and wknd appr 9th: t.o whn p.u after 3 out* **10/3**[3]

7m 16.1s (34.10) **Going Correction** +0.90s/f (Soft)
WFA 4 from 5yo+ 4lb **7 Ran SP% 114.0**
Speed ratings: **85,82,75,73,71 —,—** CSF £7.23 CT £47.10 TOTE £2.10: £1.30, £1.50; EX 5.80.
Owner D A Johnson **Bred** M J Halligan **Trained** Nicholashayne, Devon

FOCUS
A modest staying handicap hurdle, run at a steady pace and the first two came clear. The winner is trated value for nearly double the winning margin and can rate higher.

NOTEBOOK
Getoutwhenyoucan(IRE) ◆ relished this much softer ground and made a winning handicap debut, getting off the mark over hurdles at the fourth attempt in the process. This imposing son of Old Vic had no trouble with the longer trip, jumped very neatly throughout and was not at all fully extended to score by a wide margin. He should go on from this now, and is more than capable of winning further prizes over hurdles while at this end of the handicap, but will not come into his own until eventually going novice chasing. *(tchd 6-4)*
Temper Lad(USA) was well backed, and ran a fair race, yet was ultimately fully put in his place by the winner. He was nicely clear of the rest at the finish, clearly enjoys it at this venue and will not always run into such a well-handicapped rival as the winner. *(op 9-2)*
Wild Tempo(FR) turned in a more encouraging effort than his recent efforts, yet was never a threat at any stage. He has two ways of running and remains one to avoid. *(op 12-1)*
Esters Boy *(op 12-1)*
Excellent Vibes(IRE) found nothing when asked for his effort and, as expected, looked totally unsuited by this testing ground. He is a different proposition on a faster surface. *(tchd 7-2)*

1080 NEWTONABBOTRACING.COM H'CAP CHASE (11 fncs 2 omitted) 2m 110y
4:55 (4:56) (Class 3) (0-125,124) 5-Y-0+ **£5,343** (£1,644; £822; £411)

Form RPR
12PB **1** **Tamango (FR)**[17] [946] 8-11-7 119 .... RJohnson 127
(P J Hobbs) *chsd ldr: rdn to ld and wnt lft last: drvn out* **5/2**[2]
2421 **2** *1/2* **Figaro Du Rocher (FR)**[12] [1001] 5-11-12 124 ....(t) TScudamore 132
(M C Pipe) *led: rdn and hdd last: sn swtchd rt: r.o* **5/6**[1]
P1/5 **3** *27* **Noble Justice (IRE)**[17] [946] 9-10-3 108 .... JamesWhite(7) 89
(R J Hodges) *hld up: 3rd and wkng whn hit 2 out (water)* **12/1**
0031 **4** *4* **Flahive's First**[14] [975] 11-10-2 105 .... LStephens(5) 82
(D Burchell) *hld up: rdn whn mstke 8th: sn struggling* **9/2**[3]

4m 24.0s (18.50) **Going Correction** +1.25s/f (Heav) **4 Ran SP% 109.0**
Speed ratings: **106,105,93,91** CSF £5.29 TOTE £3.70; EX 5.30 Place 6 £71.55, Place 5 £33.18.
Owner The Brushmakers **Bred** Mme Dominique Le Drans **Trained** Withycombe, Somerset

FOCUS
Despite the small field this was a fair handicap, run at a sound pace and the first two, who ran to their marks, coming well clear.

NOTEBOOK
Tamango(FR) really dug deep to get on top in the home straight and got back to winning ways with a workmanlike success. He would have found this ground plenty soft enough, so deserves credit for giving his all, and can be rated value for slightly further as he was idling when in front on the run-in. The drop in trip proved to his liking. *(op 9-4)*
Figaro Du Rocher(FR), a winner over hurdles off a 19lb lower mark 12 days previously, could not cope under his big weight when the winner challenged at the top of the straight, but he stuck to his task gamely when headed and lost little in defeat. He can resume winning ways off this mark when reverting to faster ground and clearly remains in decent form. *(op 10-11 tchd 4-5)*
Noble Justice(IRE) was put in his place when the race got serious down the back straight, but is another who ideally prefers a sounder surface and is entitled to come on again for the outing. *(op 11-1 tchd 14-1)*
Flahive's First found nothing when the tempo increased and was beaten too far out for his latest 9lb rise in the weights to become an issue. He has a bit to prove now. *(op 5-1 tchd 4-1)*
T/Plt: £115.90 to a £1 stake. Pool: £37,089.95. 233.50 winning tickets. T/Qpdt: £48.70 to a £1 stake. Pool: £2,318.10. 35.20 winning tickets. KH

1081 - 1082a (Foreign Racing) - See Raceform Interactive

1071
GALWAY (R-H)
Wednesday, July 27

OFFICIAL GOING: Good to firm

1083a HEWLETT-PACKARD GALWAY PLATE (HANDICAP CHASE) (GRADE A) 2m 6f
3:40 (3:40) 4-Y-0+
£86,382 (£27,304; £13,120; £4,609; £3,191; £1,773)

RPR
1 **Ansar (IRE)**[17] [954] 9-11-11 135 .... DFO'Regan(3) 141
(D K Weld, Ire) *settled 4th: 5th after 3 out: hdwy on inner 2 out: led after last: rdn clr st: styd on strly* **10/1**
2 *7* **Ursumman (IRE)**[17] [955] 6-10-8 115 .... NPMadden 114
(Niall Madden, Ire) *trckd ldrs: 6th 1/2-way: 3rd 3 out: cl 2nd and chal after last: outpcd ent st: no ex fnl f* **14/1**
3 *3/4* **Light On The Broom (IRE)**[86] [156] 9-10-10 120 ....(t) MPWalsh(3) 118
(Gerard Stack, Ire) *towards rr: 8th and hdwy appr 3 out: led next: hdd after last: kpt on same pce st* **25/1**
4 *hd* **Junior Fontaine (FR)**[91] [69] 8-11-3 124 ....(b[1]) CO'Dwyer 122
(A L T Moore, Ire) *mid-div: plld hrd early: 9th after 4 out: 7th whn slt mstke last: rdn and kpt on* **11/1**
5 *2 1/2* **Warrens Castle (IRE)**[38] [792] 8-10-11 118 .... RWalsh 114
(W P Mullins, Ire) *rr of mid-div: 9th 3 out: hdwy next: 4th after last: kpt on u.p st* **11/2**[1]

6 2 **Banasan (IRE)**[18] 930 7-12-0 135 PCarberry 129
(M J P O'Brien, Ire) *hld up in tch: 10th 1/2-way: 6th 3 out: 3rd and hdwy bef 2 out: 5th after last: sn no ex* **8/1**[3]

7 3 **Ball O Malt (IRE)**[80] 248 9-11-1 122 PWhelan 113
(R A Fahey) *mid-div: 9th 1/2-way: 7th bef 3 out: no imp fr next: kpt on one pce* **25/1**

8 3 **Look Between Us (IRE)**[46] 722 8-10-8 115 RGeraghty 103
(L J Archdeacon, Ire) *hld up in rr: kpt on one pce fr 3 out* **16/1**

9 1 **Prince Of Pleasure (IRE)**[18] 932 11-10-12 119 BMCash 106
(D Broad, Ire) *towards rr: impr into mid-div 6 out: no imp after 3 out* **33/1**

10 2 1/2 **Berkley (IRE)**[79] 269 8-10-8 118 (b) JMAllen[(3)] 102
(Patrick Michael Verling, Ire) *trckd ldrs in 5th: impr into 2nd 5 out: led 3 out: hdd next: wknd fr last* **14/1**

11 3 **Wests Awake (IRE)**[17] 955 9-10-7 114 PFlynn 95
(I Madden, Ire) *a towards rr* **33/1**

12 2 **Mutakarrim**[31] 3029 8-11-9 130 (b) RMPower 109
(D K Weld, Ire) *nvr a factor* **20/1**

13 13 **Mirpour (IRE)**[31] 4770 6-11-3 124 (b) BJGeraghty 90
(Eoin Griffin, Ire) *mid-div: impr into 7th 1/2-way: 5th 3 out: wknd next* **8/1**[3]

14 2 **Totheroadyouvgone**[16] 960 11-10-3 113 (p) RCColgan[(3)] 77
(A E Jones) *a bhd* **33/1**

15 4 1/2 **Glynn Dingle (IRE)**[38] 792 12-10-12 119 BHarding 79
(A J Martin, Ire) *a bhd* **25/1**

16 dist **Roi Six (FR)**[27] 880 7-11-3 124 JLCullen 45
(Mrs S A Bramall, Ire) *led: hdd 3rd: led again 8th: hdd 3 out: wknd qckly: t.o* **25/1**

F **Il En Reve (FR)**[12] 1007 7-10-1 111 (b) MDarcy[(3)] —
(S J Treacy, Ire) *fell 1st* **20/1**

F **Kickham (IRE)**[46] 722 9-11-1 122 APMcCoy —
(E J O'Grady, Ire) *fell 1st* **15/2**[2]

P **Hume Castle (IRE)**[65] 476 9-11-2 123 GCotter —
(Mrs John Harrington, Ire) *mid-div: mstke 7 out: p.u bef 5 out* **25/1**

U **Quadco (IRE)**[17] 955 11-11-2 126 (b) TGMRyan[(3)] —
(P A Fahy, Ire) *sn cl up in 2nd: led 3rd: hdd 8th: remained cl up tl uns rdr 5 out* **16/1**

P **Splendour (IRE)**[25] 886 10-11-7 128 JPElliott —
(Miss S Cox, Ire) *in tch early: dropped to rr and reminders bef 1/2-way: p.u bef 2 out* **33/1**

P **Kid'Z'Play (IRE)**[17] 937 9-11-9 130 ADempsey —
(J S Goldie) *chsd ldrs in 3rd: mstke 5th: wknd bef 6 out: bhd whn bad mstke 4 out: sn p.u* **25/1**

5m 23.2s **22** Ran SP% **136.3**
CSF £127.56 CT £3426.84 TOTE £10.90: £2.80, £3.90, £12.50, £2.50; DF 253.50.
Owner Mrs K Devlin **Bred** Hh Aga Khan's Studs Sc **Trained** The Curragh, Co Kildare

NOTEBOOK
Ansar(IRE) gave a repeat of last year's win and in doing so achieved his seventh course success. Allowed an unimpeded passage through on the inner, he took control of the race after the last and made light of his big weight on the long uphill run-in. He is a small horse and conditions might suit him in the big chase in Japan next April, which is the long-term target. *(op 9/1)*
Ursumman(IRE) is a consistent handicapper in his own class, but even at a difference of 20lb was no match for the winner. *(op 12/1)*
Light On The Broom(IRE) put up a career-best performance, but was just keeping on at the one pace.
Junior Fontaine(FR), wearing first-time blinkers, had a half-dozen in front of him when clipping the top of the last but he stayed on well enough uphill. *(op 10/1 tchd 12/1)*
Warrens Castle(IRE) improved to track the leaders on the run down to the second last, but could not get into a challenging position although staying on at the end. He would prefer further. *(op 6/1)*
Banasan(IRE) ran well on ground that was too quick for him. *(op 7/1)*
Ball O Malt(IRE) made a forward move on the downhill run to the second last, but could never get close enough to challenge although staying on late.
Mirpour(IRE) *Official explanation: vet said gelding broke a blood vessel*
Totheroadyouvgone was always towards the rear
Kid'Z'Play(IRE) had lost all chance when blundering badly four out and was quickly pulled up

[1023]STRATFORD (L-H)
Thursday, July 28

OFFICIAL GOING: Good to soft
The ground had softened considerably after half an inch of rain overnight and further showers before racing.
Wind: Moderate across Weather: Late showers

1084 RENATE VIDEO SERVICES MAIDEN HURDLE (10 hdls) 2m 3f
2:25 (2:25) (Class 3) 4-Y-0+ **£5,408** (£1,664; £832; £416)

Form RPR
463 1 **Lake Merced (IRE)**[22] 911 5-11-0 100 JEMoore 93+
(Jonjo O'Neill) *mid-div: hdwy 6th: rdn to ld 2 out: hit last: drvn out* **13/8**[1]

5-5P 2 3 1/2 **Earls Rock**[67] 469 7-11-0 77 DRDennis 89
(J K Cresswell) *a.p: led 6th: rdn and hdd 2 out: one pce* **14/1**

4434 3 13 **Leopold (SLO)**[14] 991 4-10-4 98 (v[1]) CPoste[(7)] 74+
(M F Harris) *hld up and bhd: hdwy 6th: rdn and ev ch after 3 out: 3rd and wkng whn hit 2 out* **15/8**[2]

42-0 4 25 **Tyup Pompey (IRE)**[78] 295 4-10-11 85 JGoldstein 48
(Miss J S Davis) *led to 2nd: prom tl wknd appr 3 out* **16/1**

5 5 **Keep Asking (IRE)**[81] 9-11-0 RJohnson 46
(Mrs D A Hamer) *hld up and bhd: hit 1st and 6th: no ch fr 7th* **9/1**[3]

P-0P 6 21 **Brother Ted**[67] 465 8-10-7 85 (t) TMessenger[(7)] 25
(J K Cresswell) *prom: 4th and wkng whn mstke 3 out: t.o* **16/1**

0 7 5 **Durba (AUS)**[12] 1014 5-10-11 LMcGrath[(3)] 20
(R C Guest) *hld up and bhd: struggling whn mstke 3 out: t.o* **20/1**

44-0 P **Dark Island**[15] 979 10-10-7 64 CMStudd[(7)] —
(Mary Meek) *hld up: rdn 4th: sn bhd: t.o whn p.u after 6th* **100/1**

4446 P **Tubber Streams (IRE)**[8] 1037 8-10-7 85 (p) PTGallagher[(7)] —
(B A Pearce) *t.k.h: led 2nd to 6th: wknd qckly: t.o whn p.u after 3 out* **11/1**

4m 42.8s (7.50) **Going Correction** +0.45s/f (Soft)
WFA 4 from 5yo+ 2lb **9** Ran SP% **115.4**
Speed ratings: **102,100,95,84,82 73,71,—,—** CSF £25.55 TOTE £2.40: £1.30, £4.40, £1.50; EX 29.70.
Owner John P McManus **Bred** Aidan Sexton **Trained** Cheltenham, Gloucs

FOCUS
A weak novice event, rated through the winner.

NOTEBOOK
Lake Merced(IRE), shaping like a stayer, was rather on and off the bridle on this sharp course. He appreciated being back up in distance and on soft ground for the first time since he came over from Ireland. *(op 9-4)*
Earls Rock, rated 23lb inferior to the winner, was finishing in the prize money for the first time which does put the value of this form into context. *(op 16-1)*
Leopold(SLO), tried in a visor for this return to a longer trip, was a shade disappointing having already shown he could handle this sort of ground. *(op 13-8)*
Tubber Streams(IRE) *Official explanation: vet said gelding bled from the nose*

1085 BRYANT HOMES (S) HURDLE (9 hdls) 2m 110y
3:00 (3:00) (Class 5) 4-7-Y-0 **£2,947** (£842; £421)

Form RPR
-0P0 1 **Love Triangle (IRE)**[15] 973 4-10-9 88 (tp) ONelmes[(3)] 80
(N B King) *hld up: hdwy appr 6th: mstke 3 out: sn led and rdn: j.lft and bmpd whn hdd 2 out: sn btn: fin 2nd, 10l: awrdd r* **25/1**

F3-P 2 17 **Glencoyle (IRE)**[11] 1026 5-11-6 113 PMoloney 81
(Miss L Day) *a.p: led 3rd tl after 3 out: wknd appr 2 out: fin 3rd, 10l & 7l: plcd 2nd* **8/1**

6/45 3 10 **Simon's Seat (USA)**[6] 670 6-11-0 85 ATinkler 65
(P Howling) *hld up in tch: lost pl 4th: sn rdn: hdwy 5th: ev ch 3 out: sn wknd: fin 4th, plcd 3rd* **11/2**[3]

0- 4 2 1/2 **Regulated (IRE)**[10] 1217 4-10-5 JAJenkins[(7)] 61
(H J Manners) *bhd: hit 2nd: nvr nr ldrs: fin 5th, plcd 4th* **33/1**

5 20 **Gameset'N'Match**[19] 4-10-12 PJBrennan 41
(W G M Turner) *hld up and bhd: hdwy 5th: wknd after 3 out: fin 6th, plcd 5th* **20/1**

6 18 **Vonadaisy**[10] 4-10-5 VSlattery 16
(R A Harris) *mid-div: mstke 5th: sn bhd: fin 7th, plcd 6th* **25/1**

3-00 7 9 **Wages**[11] 1027 5-11-0 92 (p) RJohnson 16
(A M Hales) *hld up in mid-div: mstke 5th: rdn and wknd 3 out: fin 8th, plcd 7th* **7/2**[2]

P/P 8 11 **Arthur Pendragon**[18] 943 5-10-9 LStephens[(5)] 5
(Mrs S M Johnson) *a bhd: t.o: fin 9th, plcd 8th* **50/1**

03 9 1/2 **Firebird Rising (USA)**[18] 943 4-10-5 WMarston —
(R Brotherton) *t.k.h: in tch: rdn and wknd appr 3 out: t.o: fin 10th, plcd 9th* **8/1**

-00P 10 9 **Casisle**[15] 982 4-9-12 59 CMStudd[(7)] —
(Mary Meek) *prom to 5th: t.o: fin 11th, plcd 10th* **80/1**

234 D **Sterling Guarantee (USA)**[29] 856 7-10-7 98 (p) CDSharkey[(7)] 92+
(N Wilson) *hld up mid-div: hdwy 4th: led 2 out: clr last: rdn out: fin 1st, 10l: disq* **15/8**[1]

P **Confuzed**[93] 5-11-0 JGoldstein —
(A P Jones) *a bhd: t.o whn p.u bef 2 out* **20/1**

000- P **Just Midas**[319] 1420 7-11-11 86 SWalsh[(7)] —
(N M Babbage) *led to 3rd: rdn after 5th: wkng whn stmbld 3 out: sn p.u* **33/1**

4m 9.00s (10.60) **Going Correction** +0.45s/f (Soft)
WFA 4 from 5yo+ 2lb **13** Ran SP% **120.9**
Speed ratings: **88,85,80,79,69 61,57,51,51,47 93,—,—** CSF £58.16 TOTE £2.80: £1.30, £5.10, £2.40; EX 51.10.The winner was bought in for 11,000gns - annulled when horse was disqualified. Sterling Guarantee disq: procaine in urine sample. Wilson fined £700.
Owner St Gatien Racing Club **Bred** Peter Kelly **Trained** Newmarket, Suffolk

FOCUS
A weak seller won in a modest time. The winner stood out on form.

NOTEBOOK
Love Triangle(IRE), another wearing cheekpieces for the first time over jumps, would have been meeting the winner on 10lb better terms in a handicap. *(op 20-1)*
Glencoyle(IRE) was dropping into a seller for the first time having been pulled up over much further here on his comeback. The ground may have been on the soft side for him.
Sterling Guarantee(USA) was fitted with cheekpieces for this second start in a seller. Bought in for 11,000gns despite having broken both his pelvis and blood-vessels in the past, but that sale was rendered invalid when he was disqualified due to a prohibited substance. *(op 2-1 tchd 9-4)*

1086 JENKINSONS CATERERS NOVICES' H'CAP CHASE (18 fncs) 3m
3:35 (3:35) (Class 4) (0-105,99) 5-Y-0+ **£5,321** (£2,018)

Form RPR
-230 1 **Super Road Train**[22] 913 6-11-3 **90** (b) LAspell 97+
(O Sherwood) *hld up: sltly hmpd 9th: wnt 2nd 10th: led 4 out: lft clr 2 out* **10/1**

P12 2 13 **Seaniethesmuggler (IRE)**[34] 827 7-11-3 **95** WKennedy[(5)] 94+
(S Gollings) *hld up: lft 2nd and hmpd 9th: lost 2nd 10th: lft 4 l 2nd whn mstke 2 out: no imp* **11/4**[1]

/5-3 F **Cedar Chief**[8] 1038 8-10-0 **73** oh8 (b) PJBrennan —
(B A Pearce) *led tl fell 9th* **4/1**[3]

3-U U **High Gear (IRE)**[13] 998 7-11-8 **95** (v[1]) JEMoore —
(Jonjo O'Neill) *hld up: pckd 1st: j. slowly 6th and 7th: cl 3rd whn bdly hmpd and uns rdr 9th* **3/1**[2]

-3U1 F **Good Man Again (IRE)**[36] 812 7-11-12 **99** ChristianWilliams 103
(Evan Williams) *j.lft: chsd ldr: jnd ldr 8th: lft in ld 9th: hdd 4 out: rdn and ev ch whn fell 2 out* **11/4**[1]

6m 8.00s (5.80) **Going Correction** +0.175s/f (Yiel) **5** Ran SP% **107.4**
Speed ratings: **97,92,—,—,—** CSF £35.33 TOTE £12.00: £4.10, £1.90; EX 33.70.
Owner David Knox **Bred** David Knox Textiles Ltd **Trained** Upper Lambourn, Berks

FOCUS
The first fence in the home straight proved as tricky as ever for these novices all three times it was jumped. Hard to assess this form, with the winner rated to a level similar to his best bumper/hurdles form.

NOTEBOOK
Super Road Train remained in the blinkers he had worn last time on this switch to fences. He appeared to be going that vital bit better than Good Man Again when presented the race two out. *(op 12-1 tchd 14-1)*
Seaniethesmuggler(IRE) looked fortunate to finish second. *(tchd 5-2)*
Good Man Again(IRE), inclined to jump left-handed, was not travelling quite as well as the winner when caught out by the trappy penultimate fence. *(op 9-4)*

1087 JOHN SMITH H'CAP HURDLE (9 hdls) 2m 110y
4:10 (4:10) (Class 3) (0-120,118) 4-Y-0+
£6,130 (£2,325; £1,162; £528; £264; £158)

Form RPR
-500 1 **Dominican Monk (IRE)**[12] 1010 6-11-11 **117** TDoyle 122
(C Tinkler) *hld up: hdwy 5th: rdn to ld after 2 out: drvn out* **8/1**

2316 2 3 **Imperial Rocket (USA)**[11] 1020 8-10-10 **102** (t) RJohnson 104
(W K Goldsworthy) *w ldr: led appr 5th: rdn after 3 out: hdd after 2 out: no ex towards fin* **6/1**

16-2 3 15 **Old Marsh (IRE)**[68] 452 9-11-7 **118** MrCJSweeney[(5)] 105
(A W Carroll) *hld up: hdwy appr 6th: rdn after 3 out: sn wknd* **3/1**[1]

005F 4 1 1/4 **Forzacurity**[13] 1001 6-10-7 **104** LStephens[(5)] 90
(M Sheppard) *chsd ldrs tl rdn and wknd after 3 out* **16/1**

-RF6 5 29 **Brave Dane (IRE)**[13] 915 7-9-12 **97** CMStudd[(7)] 54
(L A Dace) *led into s: a bhd* **33/1**

-146 6 8 **Donovan (NZ)**[12] 1010 6-10-13 **108** (v) LMcGrath[(3)] 57
(R C Guest) *chsd ldrs: hit 5th: wknd appr 6th* **10/3**[2]

5151 P **Royal Glen (IRE)**[18] 940 7-10-7 **99** GLee —
(W S Coltherd) *bhd fr 5th: t.o whn p.u after 3 out* **5/1**[3]

10-P **P** **Broke Road (IRE)**[8] [99] 9-11-4 **115**................................ WKennedy(5) —
(Mrs H Dalton) *led tl appr 5th: rdn and wknd 3 out: t.o whn p.u bef 2 out* **8/1**

F/3B **U** **Bringontheclowns (IRE)**[28] [873] 6-10-12 **104**.................(v[1]) PJBrennan —
(M F Harris) *hld up: 6th and struggling whn blnd and uns rdr 3 out* **14/1**

4m 2.70s (4.30) **Going Correction** +0.45s/f (Soft) **9** Ran SP% **116.7**
Speed ratings: **107,105,98,97,84 80,—,—,—** CSF £56.06 CT £178.31 TOTE £8.50: £2.10, £2.30, £2.00; EX 59.30.

Owner George Ward **Bred** Mrs Joan And Jimmy Doran **Trained** Compton, Berks

FOCUS
They went a decent pace in what was a fairly competitive handicap. This was a personal best from the winner and the form could be rated higher.

NOTEBOOK
Dominican Monk(IRE) took advantage of being back in the right sort of class. He is not that big but the intention is to send him chasing.

Imperial Rocket(USA) helped force the good pace and came out of the race with plenty of credit for one who likes the top of the ground. *(op 5-1)*

Old Marsh(IRE), reverting to hurdles for the first time since February 2003, could not sustain a promising-looking run. *(op 4-1)*

Forzacurity may have paid the penalty for going in pursuit of the leading pair. *(op 14-1)*

Donovan(NZ), remaining in a visor, handles soft ground but was never travelling according to his rider. *Official explanation: jockey said gelding was never travelling (op 7-2)*

1088 MARLBOROUGH TILES H'CAP CHASE (FOR THE GAY, EVE AND TIM SHEPPARD MEMORIAL TROPHY) (13 fncs) 2m 1f 110y

4:45 (4:45) (Class 4) (0-105,105) 5-Y-O+ **£4,960** (£1,612; £868)

Form RPR

31/0 **1** **Hakim (NZ)**[44] [747] 11-10-9 **88**.. PJBrennan 114+
(J L Spearing) *mde all: rdn clr appr 2 out: mstke last: eased flat* **13/2**[3]

0-4P **2** *25* **Power Unit**[56] [615] 10-11-7 **100**.......................................(p) BHitchcott 106+
(Mrs D A Hamer) *chsd wnr: mstke 1st: mstke and lost 2nd 4 out: lft 2nd 3 out: sn btn* **12/1**

0/0P **3** *20* **Wave Rock**[43] [761] 10-11-4 **97**..(b) NFehily 74
(A W Carroll) *prom: mstke 4th: wknd 9th* **10/1**

FF-P **P** **Young Chevalier**[18] [939] 8-11-2 **95**...................................... KRenwick —
(J R Adam) *hld up: rdn after 7th: sn lost tch: t.o whn p.u bef 4 out* **14/1**

F311 **P** **College City (IRE)**[13] [999] 6-11-4 **100**.......................(p) LMcGrath(3) —
(R C Guest) *hld up: blnd 2nd: pckd 7th: wkng whn mstke 9th: p.u bef 4 out* **11/10**[1]

/0U2 **F** **Knight's Emperor (IRE)**[17] [958] 8-11-1 **94**......................... RThornton —
(J L Spearing) *hld up: reminders 6th: hdwy appr 9th: wnt 2nd 4 out: 2 l down whn fell 3 out* **11/4**[2]

4m 11.9s (-0.60) **Going Correction** +0.175s/f (Yiel) **6** Ran SP% **111.1**
Speed ratings: **108,96,88,—,—** — CSF £64.10 CT £743.91 TOTE £6.10: £2.40, £3.80; EX 58.10.

Owner T N Siviter **Bred** Mrs B C Hennessy **Trained** Kinnersley, Worcs

FOCUS
A weak race which took little winning with the favourite turning out to be a flop, but it was a fair time for the grade.

NOTEBOOK
Hakim(NZ) ◆, given a pipe-opener over hurdles last month, had also made all in a novices' handicap chase at Southwell off this mark when previously seen in August 2003. The time was very respectable and he looks well handicapped. *(op 9-1)*

Power Unit did not exactly find the refitting of cheekpieces reviving his fortunes over fences. *(op 7-1)*

Wave Rock was reverting to a shorter trip but continues on the decline. *(op 7-1)*

College City(IRE) was let down by his jumping on this hat-trick bid having gone up a stone in all. *(op 6-5 tchd 5-4)*

1089 LUDDINGTON NOVICES' HURDLE (12 hdls) 2m 6f 110y

5:20 (5:20) (Class 3) 4-Y-O+
£6,078 (£2,305; £1,152; £524; £262; £157)

Form RPR

5-12 **1** **Amicelli (GER)**[52] [667] 6-11-4 117.. RJohnson 123+
(P J Hobbs) *led 2nd: hit 3 out: rdn clr 2 out: r.o wl* **7/4**[2]

F21 **2** *5* **Romany Prince**[14] [992] 6-11-8 115.................................. TScudamore 122
(S Gollings) *hld up: chsd wnr after 5th: rdn after 3 out: no imp fr 2 out* **1/1**[1]

2312 **3** *23* **Festive Chimes (IRE)**[7] [1047] 4-10-0 103.............................. SWalsh(7) 92+
(N B King) *hld up and bhd: hdwy after 7th: rdn after 3 out: wknd 2 out* **9/2**[3]

0-0P **4** *dist* **Court Empress**[37] [801] 8-9-12 75.................................. JamesWhite(7) —
(P D Purdy) *hld up in tch: rdn appr 8th: sn wknd: t.o* **100/1**

4P **5** *dist* **Lost Treasure (IRE)**[8] [1038] 8-10-12 .... ChristianWilliams —
(Mrs M Evans) *led to 2nd: wknd after 7th: t.o* **66/1**

0/0- **6** *3 ½* **Mcmahon's Brook**[165] [3837] 6-10-12 .... JMogford —
(Mrs N S Evans) *chsd wnr tl after 5th: wknd after 7th: t.o* **125/1**

/00- **P** **Expensive Folly (IRE)**[210] [3110] 7-10-5 .... JAJenkins(7) —
(A J Chamberlain) *a bhd: hit 5th: lost tch 6th: t.o whn p.u bef 2 out* **100/1**

5m 40.4s (10.70) **Going Correction** +0.45s/f (Soft)
WFA 4 from 6yo+ 3lb **7** Ran SP% **108.8**
Speed ratings: **99,97,89,—,— —,—** CSF £3.61 TOTE £3.60: £1.60, £1.10; EX 4.10 Place 6 £104.35, Place 5 £82.55.

Owner Jack Joseph **Bred** Gestut Brummerhof **Trained** Withycombe, Somerset

FOCUS
A three-horse race to all intents and purposes and a modest time for a race of its class. The winner was the clear form choice. The runner-up ran to his mark.

NOTEBOOK
Amicelli(GER) appreciated the return to a longer trip and made sure it would be a reasonable test of stamina. *(op 6-4 tchd 15-8)*

Romany Prince was beginning to fight a losing battle at the end of the back straight. *(op 5-4 tchd 10-11, 11-8 in places)*

Festive Chimes(IRE) may well have found the ground too soft. *(op 7-2)*

T/Plt: £264.00 to a £1 stake. Pool: £34,143.90 - 94.40 winning units T/Qpdt: £112.20 to a £1 stake. Pool: £2,094.00 - 13.80 winning units KH

1090 - 1092a (Foreign Racing) - See Raceform Interactive

1081 GALWAY (R-H)
Thursday, July 28

OFFICIAL GOING: Good to firm

1093a GUINNESS GALWAY HURDLE H'CAP (GRADE A) (9 hdls) 2m

3:45 (3:45) 4-Y-O+
£81,702 (£25,886; £12,411; £4,326; £2,978; £1,631)

RPR

1 **More Rainbows (IRE)**[11] [954] 5-9-10 125......................... NPMadden 127
(Noel Meade, Ire) *settled 3rd: impr into 2nd 3 out: chal and led after 2 out: rdn clr last: styd on wl u.p* **33/1**

2 *1* **Tiger Cry (IRE)**[61] [560] 7-9-11 126.. PACarberry 127
(A L T Moore, Ire) *trckd ldrs: 5th 1/2-way: 6th after 3 out: sltly hmpd next: 4th appr st: styd on u.p fr last* **16/1**

3 *1 ½* **Callow Lake (IRE)**[32] [252] 5-9-10 125....................................... MDGrant 125
(Mrs John Harrington, Ire) *mid-div: impr into 7th 1/2-way: 4th after 3 out: 2nd and rdn after next: no ex fr last* **14/1**

4 *1* **Calorando (IRE)**[18] [954] 6-10-3 131.. RWalsh 131
(Anthony Mullins, Ire) *mid-div: 9th 1/2-way: 7th after 3 out: sltly hmpd next: kpt on fr last* **12/1**

5 *9* **Portant Fella**[14] [995] 6-9-10 125...(p) JPElliott 115
(Ms Joanna Morgan, Ire) *cl up: led bef 3rd: strly pressed after 3 out: hdd after 2 out: no ex fr last* **33/1**

6 *2* **Accordion Etoile (IRE)**[18] [954] 6-11-11 159...................... RMMoran(7) 149
(Paul Nolan, Ire) *hld up in rr: kpt on fr after 3 out* **8/1**[3]

7 *¾* **Native Stag (IRE)**[14] [995] 7-9-7 125 4ex............................. TGMRyan(3) 112
(P A Fahy, Ire) *mid-div: 8th 1/2-way: kpt on u.p fr 2 out* **25/1**

8 *3 ½* **Athlumney Lad (IRE)**[3] [3288] 6-9-5 125.............................. RJMolloy(5) 108
(Noel Meade, Ire) *bhd early: 10th 1/2-way: no imp fr bef 2 out* **14/1**

9 *¾* **Say What You See (IRE)**[110] [4768] 5-9-12 127............................ TJMurphy 110
(M C Pipe) *led: hdd bef 3rd: remained prom: 2nd 4 out: 3rd appr 2 out: sn no ex* **14/1**

10 *10* **Akshar (IRE)**[24] [735] 6-9-12 127..(b) DTEvans 100
(D K Weld, Ire) *towards rr: hmpd 3 out: no ex* **20/1**

11 *5* **Dabiroun (IRE)**[15] [65] 4-9-7 125............................... MissNCarberry(3) 93
(Paul Nolan, Ire) *hld up: bdly hmpd 3 out: sn no ex* **16/1**

12 *shd* **Moratorium (USA)**[39] [787] 10-9-10 125.. APCrowe 92
(Noel Meade, Ire) *towards rr thrght* **20/1**

13 *25* **Sky's The Limit (FR)**[18] [954] 4-9-7 125................................. PWFlood(3) 67
(E J O'Grady, Ire) *trckd ldrs in 5th: 4th 4 out: wknd qckly after next: eased bef last* **14/1**

14 *shd* **Mags Benefit (IRE)**[43] [252] 5-9-10 125..(t) PFlynn 67
(T Hogan, Ire) *rr of mid-div: dropped towards rr 4 out: sltly hmpd next: no ex* **50/1**

B **Emmpat (IRE)**[20] [818] 7-9-3 125... MPWatts(7) —
(Anthony Mullins, Ire) *towards rr: rdn and no imp after 3 out: b.d next* **20/1**

F **Cloone River (IRE)**[32] [1383] 9-10-7 135... JLCullen —
(Paul Nolan, Ire) *towards rr early: prog 1/2-way: 8th and in tch whn fell 3 out* **2/1**[1]

F **Definate Spectacle (IRE)**[15] [208] 5-10-5 133........................ PCarberry —
(Noel Meade, Ire) *trckd ldrs: 7th early: 5th 4 out: 4th and in tch whn fell 2 out* **13/2**[2]

3m 36.4s
WFA 4 from 5yo+ 2lb **20** Ran SP% **129.9**
CSF £480.28 CT £7556.64 TOTE £37.80: £6.70, £3.10, £3.70, £2.10; DF 646.00.
Owner Neighbours Racing Club **Bred** Dr A J O'Reilly **Trained** Castletown, Co Meath
■ Stewards' Enquiry : P A Carberry two-day ban: used whip with excessive force and frequency (Aug 6,7)

NOTEBOOK
More Rainbows(IRE), never out of the leading trio, led before the second last and had gone clear over the final flight.He stayed on gamely, really relishing the fast ground. Under these ideal conditions there is more improvement in him, a fact appreciated by the Handicapper who raised him 8lb. *(op 20/1)*
Tiger Cry(IRE), very much prepared for the race, was one of those hampered by Definate Specatacle's fall two out but stayed on strongly from the last.
Callow Lake(IRE) was chasing the winner with little avail after two out but kept on bravely to the end. *(op 12/1)*
Calorando(IRE) was progressing nicely on the heels of the leaders when hampered by the faller at the second last. *(op 10/1)*
Portant Fella was only 1 lb out but is well in the handicapper's grip. *(op 25/1)*
Accordion Etoile(IRE) never got competitive under the weight and a chasing career beckons, sooner rather than later. *(op 9/1)*
Say What You See(IRE) raced prominently until weakening after jumping the second last in third place. *(op 12/1)*
Cloone River(IRE), last year's winner, took a crashing fall at the third from home and came back a very sore horse. *(op 9/4)*
Definate Spectacle(IRE) was making smooth progress when falling at the second last and would almost certainly have been concerned in the finish. *(op 9/4)*

1094 - (Foreign Racing) - See Raceform Interactive

343 BANGOR-ON-DEE (L-H)
Friday, July 29

OFFICIAL GOING: Good to soft (good in places on chase course)
Wind: Almost nil Weather: Overcast

1095 AZURE CATERERS JUVENILE NOVICES' HURDLE (9 hdls) 2m 1f

2:05 (2:05) (Class 4) 3-Y-O **£3,413** (£1,050; £525; £262)

Form RPR

U **1** **Fair Along (GER)**[12] [1023] 3-10-12 .... ChristianWilliams 103+
(J L Flint) *a cl up: led appr 4 out: sn wl clr: easily* **33/1**

2 *dist* **Millquista D'Or**[11] 3-10-5 .... WMarston 63
(G A Ham) *midfield: mstke 3rd: hdwy appr 5th: wnt 2nd bef 2 out: no ch w wnr* **40/1**

3 *3 ½* **Sharp N Frosty**[28] 3-10-12 .... ATinkler 58
(W M Brisbourne) *midfield: hdwy appr 4 out: wknd after 3 out* **14/1**

F **4** *1 ¼* **Strathtay**[19] [945] 3-10-5 .... TJMurphy 50
(M C Pipe) *in rr: sme hdwy appr 5th: no imp whn j.rt 3 out: n.d* **2/1**[1]

5 *10* **Golden Feather**[27] 3-10-12 .... HOliver 47
(R C Guest) *mstkes: prom: 2nd appr 3 out tl bef 2 out: sn wknd* **11/4**[2]

6 2 ½ **First Fought (IRE)**[19] 3-10-12 .... JMMaguire 44
(D McCain) *hld up: mstke 1st: hdwy after 4th: blnd next: wkng whn mstke 3 out* **16/1**

7 1 **Fransiscan**[11] 3-10-12 .... FKeniry 43
(P C Haslam) *in tch tl wknd after 3 out* **14/1**

P4 8 15 **Imperial Miss (IRE)**[12] [1023] 3-10-5 .... PJBrennan 21
(B W Duke) *led: hdd appr 4 out: rdn bef next: sn wknd: wl btn whn mstke 2 out* **25/1**

9 1 ½ **Winter Coral (FR)**[67] 3-10-5 .... JMogford 20
(Mrs N S Evans) *in tch: rdn after 4th: wknd next* **66/1**

P6 P **Mabella (IRE)**[12] [1023] 3-10-2 .... TJPhelan(3) —
(B Llewellyn) *a bhd: t.o whn p.u bef 3 out* **50/1**

P P **Nelson (POL)**[19] [945] 3-10-12 .... RJohnson —
(P J Hobbs) *bhd: mstke 3rd: sn reminders: t.o whn p.u bef 2 out* **16/1**

P P **Miss Dinamite**[19] [945] 3-9-12 .... TMessenger(7) —
(Mrs C J Ikin) *mstke 1st: a bhd: t.o whn p.u bef 2 out* **100/1**

5 P **Cold Play**[13] [1011] 3-10-12 ....(b) NFehily —
(C J Mann) *prom tl rdn and wknd appr 4 out: t.o whn p.u bef 2 out* **25/1**

P **Tiffin Brown**[11] 3-10-12 ....(t) APMcCoy —
(P C Haslam) *midfield: struggling appr 5th: sn btn: t.o whn p.u bef 2 out* **3/1**[3]

4m 7.50s (-3.40) **Going Correction** -0.225s/f (Good) **14** Ran SP% **127.6**
Speed ratings: **99**,—,—,—,— —,—,—,—,— —,—,—,— CSF £948.28 TOTE £68.90: £16.90, £14.40, £6.80; EX 1464.70.
Owner J L Flint **Bred** Gestut Harzburg **Trained** Kenfig Hill, Bridgend

FOCUS
A difficult race to assess, it has been rated at around the level expected for this time of year.

NOTEBOOK
Fair Along(GER), an early casualty on his hurdles debut, jumped well on this occasion and the race was quickly over once he had moved to the front. A modest perfomer on the level, successful twice on the All-Weather, he looks likely to prove better than that over hurdles but it has to be said that he beat little here.
Millquista D'Or, a plater on the Flat, merely plugged on to finish best of the rest on this hurdles debut.
Sharp N Frosty, well beaten on this hurdles debut, won a ten-furlong handicap in easy ground in April but has shown little on the Flat since. *(op 25-1)*
Strathtay, unlucky in a similar race on her hurdling debut, was being scrubbed along from some way out and was never in the hunt. *(tchd 9-4)*
Golden Feather, rated 80 on the Flat for John Gosden, was beaten a neck at Sandown by subsequent Glorious Goodwood winner Group Captain earlier this month. He showed prominently on this hurdles debut, but did not get home after racing too freely and hardly jumped a flight properly. *(op 5-2 tchd 3-1)*
First Fought(IRE) was a modest maiden on the Flat. Closing when having to be picked up off the floor at the fifth, he may do a bit better with this initial experience of hurdling behind him. *(op 18-1)*
Imperial Miss(IRE) *Official explanation: trainer said filly had breathing problem*
Tiffin Brown was a poor performer on the Flat although he did manage to win a bad race last time out. *He was sent off at a short enough price for this hurdles debut and was soon in trouble.Official explanation: jockey said gelding had breathing problem (op 4-1 tchd 11-4)*
Cold Play *Official explanation: vet said gelding bled from nose (op 4-1 tchd 11-4)*

1096 RIPPLEFFECT NOVICES' CHASE (15 fncs) 2m 4f 110y
2:35 (2:35) (Class 3) 5-Y-0+ **£5,408** (£1,664; £832; £416)

Form RPR

0-U2 1 **Mister Flint**[38] [803] 7-11-0 .... RJohnson 133
(P J Hobbs) *mde all: mstke 2nd: clr tl after 9th: j.lft last: drvn out* **4/1**[2]

-21F 2 1 ¼ **Mr Ed (IRE)**[19] [944] 7-11-6 ....(p) APMcCoy 138
(P Bowen) *hld up: hdwy after 9th: rdn after next: wnt 2nd 4 out: cl up whn hit 2 out: nt qckn run-in* **1/2**[1]

/ 3 dist **Slooghy (FR)**[881] [3880] 9-11-0 116............ ATinkler 108
(N J Henderson) *chsd clr ldr: clsd after 9th: rdn and lost 2nd 4 out: wknd next* **9/2**[3]

6-66 4 dist **Bentyheath Lane**[72] [414] 8-10-11 62............(b) ACCoyle(3) —
(M Mullineaux) *a bhd: lost tch after 7th: t.o* **66/1**

P P **Shanbally Lad (IRE)**[18] [962] 6-11-0 .... NFehily —
(D P Keane) *hld up: niggled along after 5th: lost tch after 7th: t.o whn p.u bef 3 out* **25/1**

4m 57.5s (-15.00) **Going Correction** -0.475s/f (Good) **5** Ran SP% **110.2**
Speed ratings: **109,108**,—,—,— CSF £6.89 TOTE £4.70: £1.80, £1.10; EX 9.40.
Owner Alan Peterson **Bred** M H Ings **Trained** Withycombe, Somerset

FOCUS
A fair novice chase, much the fastest race on the card, and it has been rated positively. The winner is rated as having run to his hurdles mark.

NOTEBOOK
Mister Flint ♦, back up in trip, survived a blunder at the second and a low jump at the next to make all. A half-brother to Gold Cup runner-up Go Ballistic, he should stay further than this should connections choose to take that route and he looks to be on the upgrade. *(op 5-1 tchd 11-2)*
Mr Ed(IRE) ran his best race so far over fences but was still a stone and a half off his best hurdles form. He closed under pressure on the home turn, but got in too close to the second last and was always being held from then on. The return to three miles, and a bigger field, should suit him. *(op 4-7)*
Slooghy(FR) had not been seen since being brought down over hurdles in March 2003, but he was a late withdrawal from a race two months later and was a non-runner three times this May due to the ground being too fast. Finally making his chasing debut, he jumped well enough but seemed to blow up four from home. *(op 3-1)*

1097 JEWSON NOVICES' HURDLE (SERIES QUALIFIER) (9 hdls) 2m 1f
3:10 (3:10) (Class 3) 4-Y-0+ **£4,870** (£1,498; £749; £374)

Form RPR

52-1 1 **Catchthebug (IRE)**[16] [971] 6-11-6 107............ APMcCoy 112+
(Jonjo O'Neill) *mde all: rdn appr last: styd on wl to draw clr run-in* **10/11**[1]

312 2 6 **Keep On Movin' (IRE)**[33] [838] 4-10-11 108............ RJohnson 98+
(N A Callaghan) *chsd wnr: rdn after 3 out: no ex run-in* **15/8**[2]

00-4 3 10 **Winslow Boy (USA)**[19] [942] 4-10-9 83............ PAspell(3) 87
(P Monteith) *midfield: hdwy after 4th: rdn and wknd appr last* **14/1**[3]

0-03 4 dist **Moscow Executive**[16] [976] 7-10-7 .... ATinkler —
(W M Brisbourne) *midfield: wknd 4 out* **28/1**

04 5 hd **Drumossie (AUS)**[13] [1014] 5-10-11 .... LMcGrath(3) —
(R C Guest) *towards rr: sme hdwy appr 5th: wknd 4 out* **25/1**

P **Beveller**[20] 6-11-0 .... TScudamore —
(W M Brisbourne) *a bhd: t.o whn p.u bef 2 out* **33/1**

00 P **Shaaban (IRE)**[16] [982] 4-10-12 ....(p) AO'Keeffe —
(R J Price) *bhd: rdn and lost tch 4th: blnd 5th: sn p.u* **40/1**

P-PP P **Ms Freebee**[8] [1047] 6-10-4 ....(b) ACCoyle(3) —
(M Mullineaux) *chsd ldrs tl wknd appr 4th: t.o whn p.u bef 5th* **66/1**

P **Giunchiglio**[14] 6-11-0 .... RThornton —
(W M Brisbourne) *chsd ldrs: mstke 5th: wknd 4 out: t.o whn p.u bef 2 out* **14/1**[3]

P **Royal Lustre**[161] 4-10-12 .... GLee —
(M Todhunter) *midfield: hit 3rd: mstke 4th: wknd 4 out: t.o whn p.u bef 3 out* **33/1**

4m 4.50s (-6.40) **Going Correction** -0.225s/f (Good)
WFA 4 from 5yo+ 2lb **10** Ran SP% **117.6**
Speed ratings: **106,103,98**,—,— —,—,—,—,— CSF £2.65 TOTE £1.80: £1.10, £1.10, £3.40; EX 2.80.
Owner John P McManus **Bred** B Kennedy **Trained** Cheltenham, Gloucs

FOCUS
A modest novice but straightforward to rate, with the winner and third running to form.

NOTEBOOK
Catchthebug(IRE) defied the penalty for his Uttoxeter win in workmanlike style. He could have more improvement in him over a longer trip. *(op Evens tchd 11-10 and 5-6)*
Keep On Movin'(IRE) was formerly with Terry Mills. Chasing the favourite all the way, she kept trying but was always being held. *(op 7-4 tchd 2-1)*
Winslow Boy(USA), who faced a stiff task on official ratings, ran a respectable race and finished a mile clear of the rest.
Moscow Executive, who probably needs further, did best of the three Brisbourne representatives but that is not saying a lot. *(op 33-1 tchd 25-1)*
Drumossie(AUS) has not shown much over hurdles yet but is now eligible for handicaps.
Giunchiglio, a regressive performer on the level, showed up prominently up to a point on this hurdles debut but was a remote fifth when pulling up. *(tchd 28-1)*
Royal Lustre *Official explanation: jockey said gelding bled from nose (tchd 28-1)*

1098 DAVID MANNING ASSOCIATES NOVICES' H'CAP CHASE (12 fncs) 2m 1f 110y
3:45 (3:45) (Class 4) (0-105,103) 5-Y-0+ **£4,104** (£1,263; £631; £315)

Form RPR

4035 1 **Pure Brief (IRE)**[16] [973] 8-10-0 77 oh3............(p) PMoloney 86
(J Mackie) *in tch: led appr 2 out: drvn out* **14/1**

0- 2 nk **Who Dares (IRE)**[57] [619] 7-10-10 87............ APMcCoy 96
(Jonjo O'Neill) *hld up in tch: hdwy 4 out: rdn to chse wnr appr last: r.o u.p towards fin* **4/1**[2]

PP-1 3 5 **Mikasa (IRE)**[62] [548] 5-9-11 77............ KJMercer(3) 81+
(R F Fisher) *hld up in rr: hmpd 4 out: hdwy appr 2 out: styd on run-in: nt trble ldng pair* **8/1**

1/50 4 nk **Kitty John (IRE)**[24] [902] 8-9-9 77 oh3............ WKennedy(5) 81
(J L Spearing) *prom: led 2nd: rdn and hdd appr 2 out: no ex run-in* **12/1**

0010 5 ½ **Ballyboe Boy (IRE)**[8] [1046] 6-10-1 81 oh2 ow4............(b) LMcGrath(3) 84
(R C Guest) *racd keenly: led to 2nd: remained cl up: rdn appr 2 out: no ex after last* **7/1**

532- 6 3 **Forest Chief (IRE)**[120] [4668] 9-11-8 99............(t) ChristianWilliams 99
(Evan Williams) *hld up: hdwy 3 out: rdn appr 2 out: one pce bef last* **15/2**

2P-0 7 13 **Ideal Du Bois Beury (FR)**[19] [939] 9-10-7 87............ PAspell(3) 74
(P Monteith) *midfield: stmbld whn wkng 4 out: mstke whn bhd next* **9/1**

/0-0 8 4 **Gentle Beau**[87] [177] 7-11-12 103............ RJohnson 90+
(P J Hobbs) *hld up: mstke 8th and 4 out: 7th and no imp whn blnd 2 out: n.d* **9/2**[3]

4-03 9 17 **Snipe**[24] [904] 7-11-8 99............ DRDennis 65
(Ian Williams) *prom tl wknd 4 out* **7/2**[1]

4m 18.0s (-8.40) **Going Correction** -0.475s/f (Good) **9** Ran SP% **120.1**
Speed ratings: **99,98,96,96,96 94,89,87,79** CSF £73.65 CT £495.02 TOTE £20.90: £4.80, £1.50, £3.10; EX 122.80.
Owner Mrs V D Gandola-Gray **Bred** John B O'Connor **Trained** Church Broughton, Derbys

FOCUS
A very modest novices' handicap, run at a reasonable pace.

NOTEBOOK
Pure Brief(IRE), who showed little in two tries over fences in the summer of 2003, was beaten in a selling hurdle on his penultimate start. Racing from 3lb out of the handicap, he was good enough to land this weak event and might have won with a bit more to spare but for idling in front.
Who Dares(IRE) was placed just once from 11 starts for Tommy Carmody in Ireland. Not always fluent on this first run from Jackdaws Castle, he was doing his best work at the end and needs to return to further. *(op 7-2)*
Mikasa(IRE) was raised 7lb after his Cartmel win. In rear when hampered with four to jump, he stayed on steadily from the next and will be suited by a return to further.
Kitty John(IRE), down in trip and ridden from the front, showed more than she had in two previous attempts over fences this summer.
Ballyboe Boy(IRE) could not take advantage of his lower mark over fences. *(op 8-1)*
Gentle Beau, making his chasing debut after nearly three months' absence, made several errors with one at the final ditch ending what chance he may have had. *(op 4-1)*
Snipe *Official explanation: jockey said gelding was struck into from behind (op 5-1)*

1099 DWF SOLICITORS H'CAP HURDLE (11 hdls) 2m 4f
4:20 (4:20) (Class 3) (0-115,110) 4-Y-0+ **£4,826** (£1,485; £742; £371)

Form RPR

5132 1 **Cannon Fire (FR)**[9] [1040] 4-10-11 98............ ChristianWilliams 107+
(Evan Williams) *trckd ldrs: wnt 2nd 7th: rdn to ld appr last: drew clr run-in: comf* **5/2**[1]

3114 2 6 **Dream Castle (IRE)**[29] [873] 11-11-5 110............ PMerrigan(7) 113
(Barry Potts, Ire) *led: rdn appr 2 out: hdd bef last: no ex run-in* **11/1**

0-04 3 6 **Manoubi**[15] [990] 6-11-7 105............(b[1]) GLee 102
(M Todhunter) *midfield: hdwy after 6th: rdn after 3 out: wknd appr last* **12/1**

245 4 17 **Xaipete (IRE)**[8] [1049] 13-11-8 106............ HOliver 86
(R C Guest) *hmpd s: hld up: hdwy whn mstke 4 out: no imp after* **12/1**

13 5 11 **Lawyer Des Ormeaux (FR)**[33] [841] 6-11-10 108............ APMcCoy 77
(P Bowen) *chsd ldr to 7th: wknd appr 3 out* **3/1**[2]

50-1 6 1 ½ **Lilac**[24] [905] 6-10-7 91............ WHutchinson 59
(R J Price) *hld up: niggled along appr 6th: wknd 7th* **6/1**[3]

/003 7 19 **Tomenoso**[16] [974] 7-11-10 108............ NFehily 57
(Mrs S J Smith) *in tch: rdn after 6th: sn wknd* **7/1**

-5R5 8 17 **Sninfia (IRE)**[16] [980] 5-10-12 96............ WMarston 28
(G A Ham) *rel to r: in rr: midfield after 5th: rdn after 6th: wknd next* **20/1**

5500 P **Reservoir (IRE)**[19] [947] 4-11-9 110............ RJohnson —
(P J Hobbs) *j. slowly 3rd: sn wl bhd: t.o whn p.u bef 4 out* **14/1**

P04P P **Greenacres Boy**[24] [906] 10-10-1 88 oh9 ow4............(b) ACCoyle(3) —
(M Mullineaux) *rel to r: a wl bhd: t.o whn p.u bef 4 out* **40/1**

/0P- **P** **Severn Air**[397] [830] 7-10-13 **97** .... RThornton —
(J L Spearing) *midfield: rdn after 6th: wknd next: t.o whn p.u bef 4 out* **16/1**

4m 50.3s (-7.30) **Going Correction** -0.225s/f (Good)
WFA 4 from 5yo+ 3lb **11** Ran SP% **123.8**
Speed ratings: **105,102,100,93,89 88,80,74,—,—** — CSF £32.59 CT £294.49 TOTE £3.30: £1.20, £3.60, £3.00; EX 35.70.

Owner M J Haines **Bred** G And Mrs Forien **Trained** Cowbridge, Vale Of Glamorgan

FOCUS
A pretty weak handicap in which the first two both ran to form.

NOTEBOOK
Cannon Fire(FR), officially 2lb well in, got to the front-runner between the last two flights and was in control when landing on all fours at the final flight. Although value for a slightly greater margin of victory, he did not need to improve on his previous form to win this. *(op 3-1)*

Dream Castle(IRE) is Northern Ireland-trained but his last five races have been in Britain. Running the only way he knows, he was collared between the last two flights and was unable to counter. This longer trip did stretch his stamina.

Manoubi, back over hurdles and tried in blinkers, travelled strongly but found less than he had promised once coming off the bridle on the home turn.

Xaipete(IRE), over hurdles for the first time since October, ran respectably considering he both lost ground at the start and made a serious error at the fourth last. *(op 11-1)*

Lawyer Des Ormeaux(FR) was below par, and the ground should not have been a problem as he coped with easy conditions in France. *(op 10-3 tchd 7-2)*

1100 BROWNS OF CHESTER CONDITIONAL JOCKEYS' H'CAP HURDLE (12 hdls) 3m
4:55 (4:52) (Class 4) (0-95,94) 4-Y-0+ **£3,045** (£870; £435)

Form RPR

-3P4 **1** **Little Task**[2] [988] 7-11-0 **82** .... PAspell 95+
(J S Wainwright) *hld up: hdwy appr 3 out: led bef 2 out: sn clr: eased towards fin* **12/1**

F-52 **2** *3 ½* **Farington Lodge (IRE)**[14] [998] 7-10-9 **82** .... TMessenger(5) 85
(Mrs S J Smith) *in tch: rdn appr 4 out: wnt 2nd 2 out: no ch w wnr* **9/1**

-320 **3** *5* **Tea's Maid**[8] [1046] 5-11-1 **83** .... WKennedy 81
(Mrs A M Thorpe) *midfield: reminders after 3rd: rdn appr 7th: hdwy next: one pce fr bef 2 out* **10/1**

6145 **4** *1 ¼* **Earn Out**[14] [1002] 4-10-7 **87** .... AGlassonbury(8) 83+
(M C Pipe) *hld up: stdy hdwy 5th: rdn and outpcd bef 8th: keeping on steadily in 4th whn mstke last: no imp* **10/1**

-053 **5** *7* **Oscars Vision (IRE)**[12] [1028] 5-11-0 **82** ....(v) DCrosse 72+
(B W Duke) *prom: led 7th: hit 4 out: rdn and hdd appr 2 out: wknd bef last* **7/1**[3]

0-00 **6** *15* **Little Villain (IRE)**[16] [973] 7-10-1 **69** ....(b[1]) ONelmes 44
(T Wall) *towards rr: hdwy after 6th: wknd 8th* **16/1**

0-33 **7** *1* **Maunsell's Road (IRE)**[23] [913] 6-11-12 **94** ....(v) NPMulholland 68
(L Lungo) *in tch: hdwy after 6th: rdn appr 4 out: wkng whn mstke next* **5/1**[2]

6300 **8** *8* **Lord Attica (IRE)**[45] [749] 6-9-8 **68** oh6........(b) CPoste(6) 34
(M F Harris) *midfield: hdwy appr 6th: rdn after 7th: wknd bef 4 out* **25/1**

2313 **9** *dist* **Combat Drinker (IRE)**[51] [687] 7-11-2 **90** ....(t) StephenJCraine(6) —
(D McCain) *hld up: hdwy 3rd: 2nd whn blnd 8th: rdn appr 3 out: wknd bef next: t.o* **5/2**[1]

043- **P** **Kyber**[10] [4782] 4-11-6 **92** .... KJMercer —
(R F Fisher) *led: hdd 7th: wknd 4 out: t.o whn p.u bef 2 out* **16/1**

0P-P **P** **Firstflor**[81] [261] 6-10-2 **70** .... AO'Keeffe —
(F Jordan) *prom tl wknd appr 4 out: t.o whn p.u bef 3 out* **25/1**

0P **P** **Mr Wonderful (IRE)**[14] [1002] 7-9-13 **70** ....(p) SWalsh(3) —
(P O'Connor) *a bhd: rdn after 5th: t.o whn p.u bef 3 out* **40/1**

-05P **U** **Dorans Lane**[16] [971] 7-10-9 **77** .... TGreenway —
(W M Brisbourne) *t.k.h: chsd ldrs tl blnd bdly and uns rdr 5th* **28/1**

2- **P** **Alaipour (IRE)**[21] [839] 6-11-6 **93** .... PMerrigan(5) —
(Barry Potts, Ire) *prom early: lost pl 3rd: sn bhd: t.o whn p.u bef 2 out* **14/1**

40-F **P** **Amber Go Go**[60] [592] 8-9-8 **68** oh1 ow4........ MMcAvoy(10) —
(James Moffatt) *midfield: lost pl appr 5th: sn bhd: t.o whn p.u bef 3 out* **25/1**

0005 **P** **Impero**[14] [1000] 7-9-12 **69** .... EDehdashti(3) —
(G F Bridgwater) *towards rr: niggled along after 3rd: t.o whn p.u bef 3 out* **25/1**

5m 56.9s (0.10) **Going Correction** -0.225s/f (Good)
WFA 4 from 5yo+ 4lb **16** Ran SP% **133.3**
Speed ratings: **90,88,87,86,84 79,79,76,—,— —,—,—,—,—** — CSF £117.36 CT £1161.43 TOTE £13.40: £2.80, £2.70, £3.20, £1.50; EX 238.70 Place 6 £522.45, Place 5 £27.18.

Owner Keith Jackson **Bred** Stetchworth Park Stud Ltd **Trained** Kennythorpe, N Yorks
■ Due to an error by the starter this race went off nearly three minutes early.

FOCUS
A poor event but still a moderate time for the class of contest. Ordinary form, but the winner was value for a bit extra.

NOTEBOOK
Little Task, sharper for a spin on the Flat two days earlier, was tackling this trip for the first time. Under a patient ride, he stayed on steadily from the third last to pick off his rivals and was value for a greater margin of victory as he was eased down with his race won.

Farington Lodge(IRE), reverting to hurdles, was flattered to finish as close as he did to the eased winner. He lacks anything in the way of a gear change but he does stay well. *(op 17-2)*

Tea's Maid, beaten favourite over an inadequate two miles on her latest start, ran better over this more suitable trip but was held from the second last. *(op 9-1)*

Earn Out is not the most consistent and is one to be wary of, but this was a respectable effort. *(op 8-1)*

Oscars Vision(IRE), without a win since her racecourse debut in a bumper, went for home three out but failed to see out this longer trip. *(op 13-2)*

Combat Drinker(IRE) weakened quickly on the home turn and a bad blunder at the eighth flight could have left its mark. *(op 4-1)*

T/Plt: £1,303.60 to a £1 stake. Pool: £29,464.95 - 16.50 winning units T/Qpdt: £27.20 to a £1 stake. Pool: £3,479.51 - 94.35 winning units DO

1010 MARKET RASEN (R-H)
Sunday, July 31

OFFICIAL GOING: Good to firm (good in places)
After just 4mm of rain over the previous 36 hours the ground was basically good, easy on the hurdle track and good to soft in places on the chase course.
Wind: Almost nil Weather: Fine and eventually sunny and warm.

1107 BUY YOUR TICKETS ONLINE@MARKETRASENRACES.CO.UK (S) H'CAP HURDLE (8 hdls) 2m 1f 110y
2:10 (2:10) (Class 5) (0-95,87) 4-7-Y-0 **£2,282** (£652; £326)

Form RPR

00-0 **1** **Seafire Lad (IRE)**[85] [210] 4-10-6 69........(p) KJohnson 67
(R Johnson) *trckd ldrs: t.k.h: led appr 2 out: hld on nr fin* **20/1**

-406 **2** *hd* **Little Tobias (IRE)**[31] [871] 6-11-5 85........(b[1]) DCCostello(5) 85
(J S Wainwright) *chsd ldr: upsides last: no ex nr fin* **17/2**

404 **3** *4* **Young Tot (IRE)**[10] [1046] 7-11-6 84........ KJMercer(3) 80
(Mrs A Duffield) *hld up in mid-div: stdy hdwy 3 out: kpt on same pce appr last* **11/4**[1]

U/0- **4** *1 ¼* **Coachman (IRE)**[119] 7-10-0 61 oh4........ DO'Meara 56
(A J Lockwood) *bhd: hdwy after 3 out: styd on wl run-in* **66/1**

UP-6 **5** *2 ½* **Un Autre Espere**[26] [901] 6-10-7 71........ LVickers(3) 63
(C C Bealby) *mid-div: hdwy 5th: sn chsng ldrs: one pce fr 2 out* **11/1**

2400 **6** *16* **Reedsman (IRE)**[2] [822] 4-10-7 70........(v) HOliver 44
(R C Guest) *mid-div: hdwy 5th: sn chsng ldrs: wknd appr 2 out* **13/2**[3]

6-PP **7** *1* **Longstone Lass**[18] [480] 5-11-9 87........(v) TJPhelan(3) 65+
(D Carroll) *led: j.lft: hdd appr 2 out: 5th and wkng whn mstke 2 out* **6/1**[2]

/454 **8** *1 ¼* **Simon's Seat (USA)**[3] [1085] 6-11-10 85........ ATinkler 66+
(P Howling) *chsd ldrs: lost pl appr 2 out* **7/1**

P40F **9** *2* **Mapilut Du Moulin (FR)**[16] [1000] 5-11-2 77........(t) PJBrennan 49
(C R Dore) *bhd whn blnd 4th* **14/1**

050/ **10** *5* **La Maestra (FR)**[70] 7-11-1 81........(b[1]) LStephens(5) 48
(Miss L Day) *mid-div: drvn along and wknd 3 out* **33/1**

/0-P **11** *hd* **Lady At Leisure (IRE)**[32] [860] 5-10-0 68........ KBurke(7) 35
(M J Ryan) *hld up in rr: effrt u.p 3 out: sn wknd* **33/1**

0/00 **12** *1 ½* **Known Maneuver (USA)**[15] [1014] 7-10-3 71........ CMStudd(7) 36
(M C Chapman) *mid-div: lost pl after 5th: sn bhd* **40/1**

00 **13** *nk* **Dan De Lion**[6] [1063] 6-10-11 77........(b) WKennedy(5) 42
(R C Guest) *chsd ldrs: rdn and wknd after 3 out* **12/1**

00-P **P** **Bertocelli**[11] [1037] 4-10-2 72........(b) SWalsh(7) —
(K F Clutterbuck) *bhd fr 4th: t.o whn p.u bef 2 out* **25/1**

PP5P **P** **Call Of The Seas (IRE)**[32] [861] 6-9-7 64........(t) ENolan(10) —
(J G M O'Shea) *sn bhd: t.o 4th: p.u after 3 out* **33/1**

4m 24.3s (7.90) **Going Correction** +0.325s/f (Yiel)
WFA 4 from 5yo+ 2lb **15** Ran SP% **121.4**
Speed ratings: **95,94,93,92,91 84,83,83,82,80 80,79,79,—,—** CSF £173.37 CT £626.67 TOTE £29.30: £5.90, £2.90, £1.90; EX 264.70.There was no bid for the winner.

Owner Robert Johnson **Bred** J Meaney **Trained** Newburn, Tyne & Wear

FOCUS
A poor seller run at just a steady gallop and in the end the first five came clear. The form makes sense but is very weak.

NOTEBOOK
Seafire Lad(IRE), fitted with cheekpieces on his handicap bow, took a keen grip but in the end was *persuaded to do just enough. Official explanation: trainer said, regarding the improved form shown, gelding may have benefited from the fitting of cheekpieces*

Little Tobias(IRE), down in trip and fitted with blinkers, showed a lot more than he has done of late both on the Flat and over hurdles. He looked likely to get his head in front when upsides at the last but could never quite manage it. *(op 9-1)*

Young Tot(IRE) keeps threatening to make his mark but, after travelling strongly, off the bridle he could only stay on in his own time. *(op 3-1 tchd 10-3)*

Coachman(IRE), out of luck in points, was racing from out of the handicap. Only tenth three out, he finished to some purpose and will appreciate a stiffer test.

Un Autre Espere, dropped into selling company, has now finished out of the places in a dozen *starts over hurdles. However, he was some way clear of the others. Official explanation: jockey said gelding hung badly right (op 16-1)*

Reedsman(IRE), who ran on the level two days earlier, lacks size and has yet to hit the target in 13 starts over hurdles now. *(op 6-1 tchd 7-1)*

Bertocelli *Official explanation: jockey said gelding was never travelling*

1108 ALMOST WORLD FAMOUS BRAMALL CONSTRUCTION NOVICES' HURDLE (10 hdls) 2m 6f
2:40 (2:42) (Class 3) 4-Y-0+ **£4,784** (£1,472; £736; £368)

Form RPR

-061 **1** **Weston Rock**[10] [1045] 6-11-3 105........ RWalford 112
(T D Walford) *chsd ldrs fr 4th: drvn along 6th: wnt 2nd appr 2 out: slt ld last: styd on towards fin* **10/3**[3]

212 **2** *1 ¼* **Romany Prince**[3] [1089] 6-11-9 115........ TScudamore 117
(S Gollings) *trckd ldrs: led after 3 out: hdd last: nt qckn last 100yds* **15/8**[1]

02-0 **3** *13* **Miss Merenda**[82] [279] 4-10-1 94........ PJBrennan 82
(J F Panvert) *trckd ldr: led and qcknd 6th: hdd after 3 out: one pce fr next* **20/1**

-262 **4** *1* **Rifleman (IRE)**[18] [976] 5-10-11 105........(bt[1]) APMcCoy 91
(P Bowen) *hdwy to chse ldrs 4th: 4th and outpcd whn hit 2 out* **9/4**[2]

P-1 **5** *30* **Explosive Fox (IRE)**[10] [1047] 4-11-0........ TDoyle 75+
(C P Morlock) *trckd ldrs: t.k.h: rdn and wknd after 3 out* **13/2**

P/PP **6** *14* **Primitive Jean**[92] [124] 6-10-1........ PAspell(3) 40
(C R Wilson) *s.s: a bhd* **100/1**

4-0P **7** *6* **End Of Saga**[21] [942] 6-10-4........ TMessenger(7) 41
(J B Walton) *chsd ldrs: outpcd 3 out: sn lost pl* **100/1**

PP0- **8** *10* **Crown Agent (IRE)**[45] [4284] 5-10-11........ DO'Meara 31
(M E Sowersby) *hld up in rr: bhd fr 7th* **80/1**

4 **9** *2* **Protecting Heights (IRE)**[17] [992] 4-10-5........ PBuchanan(3) 26
(M E Sowersby) *bhd fr 6th* **80/1**

06 **10** *dist* **Thornton Bridge**[11] [1036] 7-10-4........ CMStudd(7) —
(D L Williams) *jnd ldrs 4th: lost pl after next: sn bhd: t.o 2 out* **100/1**

00/0 **P** **Lolanita**[35] [843] 7-10-4........ RJohnson —
(Tim Vaughan) *led to 6th: lost pl appr 3 out: t.o next: p.u bef last* **50/1**

5m 33.1s (4.80) **Going Correction** +0.325s/f (Yiel)
WFA 4 from 5yo+ 3lb **11** Ran SP% **114.1**
Speed ratings: **104,103,98,98,87 82,80,76,75,—** — CSF £9.80 TOTE £4.90: £1.50, £1.20, £3.50; EX 10.10.

Owner Mrs H Spath **Bred** H A Shone **Trained** Sheriff Hutton, N Yorks

FOCUS

A fair novice with three previous winners in the line-up, but even so it lacked in strength in depth and in the end it was just a two-horse race run at a steady pace to past halfway. The form appears reliable with the first two to form.

NOTEBOOK

Weston Rock, nursed back to full fitness, was making hard work of it some way out but he stuck to his guns and was firmly in command at the line. He will definitely make a chaser. *(op 3-1 tchd 7-2)*

Romany Prince, making a quick return under a double penalty, went on travelling the better but at the line was very much second best. Considering he is rated 105 on the Flat, he has not really fulfilled expectations over hurdles. *(op 9-4 tchd 7-4)*

Miss Merenda, absent for almost three months, was having her first race for new connections. *She went on and stepped up the pace but in the end was totally outclassed by the first two. (op 16-1)*

Rifleman(IRE), stepping up in trip with a change of aids, never looked that happy and seemed to have accepted defeat in very ready fashion when he clouted the second last. *(tchd 5-2)*

Explosive Fox(IRE) would not settle in this stronger event and he dropped away in a matter of strides going to two out. With him it might be a case of the firmer the ground the better. *(op 6-1)*

1109 UK OIL AND GAS FOR BOILERS H'CAP CHASE (14 fncs) 2m 4f

3:15 (3:15) (Class 4) (0-90,89) 5-Y-0+ **£3,552** (£1,093; £546; £273)

Form					RPR
6203	1		**Phildari (IRE)**^{28} [896] 9-10-5 **75** ... MrDEngland$^{(7)}$		93+
			(N A Twiston-Davies) *led 4th to 8th: led 4 out: lft clr next*	7/1^{3}	
P-00	2	9	**Claude Greengrass**^{16} [997] 9-11-8 **85** ... (b) APMcCoy		94
			(Jonjo O'Neill) *in rr: hdwy 10th: styd on fr 3 out: tk mod 2nd run-in*	9/1	
-620	3	1 1/4	**Karo De Vindecy (FR)**^{50} [717] 7-11-6 **83** ... GLee		91
			(M D Hammond) *hld up in rr: hdwy 8th: lft 2nd 3 out: j.lft last: one pce*	11/1	
3-32	4	hd	**Pillar Of Fire (IRE)**^{28} [896] 11-10-10 **73** ... (v) WHutchinson		81
			(Ian Williams) *chsd ldrs: outpcd and lost pl 4 out: styd on fr 2 out*	4/1^{1}	
6302	5	4	**Raise A McGregor**^{16} [997] 9-11-2 **79** ... WMarston		83
			(Mrs S J Smith) *chsd ldrs: 5th and wl outpcd whn hmpd 3 out*	6/1^{2}	
4U36	6	4	**Jupiter Jo**^{21} [939] 9-11-0 **80** ... PBuchanan$^{(3)}$		80
			(J B Walton) *chsd ldrs: 4th and outpcd whn hmpd 3 out: sn wknd*	12/1	
5002	7	9	**Johnny Grand**^{16} [999] 8-10-11 **77** ... (p) DCrosse$^{(3)}$		68
			(D W Lewis) *chsd ldrs: reminders 8th: sn lost pl*	14/1	
/1-P	8	5	**Gray Knight (IRE)**^{63} 8-10-12 **75** ... (p) RThornton		61
			(Mrs T J Hill) *j.rt: w ldrs: led 8th to 4 out: sn wknd*	25/1	
2-20	9	6	**Balla D'Aire (IRE)**^{28} [896] 10-10-9 **72** ... SCurran		52
			(K F Clutterbuck) *led to 4th: lost pl 10th*	33/1	
-05U	10	shd	**York Rite (AUS)**^{6} [1065] 9-11-1 **78** ... (p) HOliver		58
			(R C Guest) *bhd and drvn along 8th*	11/1	
P05U	11	9	**Tails I Win**^{18} [972] 6-10-3 **69** ... ACCoyle$^{(3)}$		40
			(Miss C J E Caroe) *bhd: sme hdwy 9th: lost pl 4 out*	7/1^{3}	
1PP/	12	dist	**Alpha Romana (IRE)**^{480} [4701] 11-11-5 **89** ... (p) MrPCowley$^{(7)}$		—
			(Mrs S E Busby) *bhd fr 8th: t.o*	40/1	
56-P	P		**Pure Steel (IRE)**^{21} [948] 11-10-11 **79** ... LStephens$^{(5)}$		—
			(Miss L Day) *bhd: t.o whn p.u bef 4 out*	66/1	
PPP-	P		**Palais (IRE)**^{8} [3057] 10-10-12 **78** ... LVickers$^{(3)}$		—
			(John A Harris) *nt fluent: bhd: t.o 4 out: p.u bef next*	50/1	
	F		**Castle Oliver (IRE)**^{241} [2597] 7-10-0 **70** ... SWalsh$^{(7)}$		80
			(A J Chamberlain) *rr-div: gd hdwy 10th: 4 l 2nd whn fell 3 out*	11/1	
5633	U		**Pete The Painter (IRE)**^{18} [981] 8-10-10 **80** ... (p) MrJETudor$^{(7)}$		—
			(J W Tudor) *mid-div and drvn along whn mstke and uns rdr 6th*	14/1	

5m 5.70s (3.00) **Going Correction** +0.175s/f (Yiel) **16** Ran SP% **128.0**

Speed ratings: **101,97,96,96,95 93,90,88,85,85 81,—,—,—,— —** CSF £70.18 CT £711.50 TOTE £10.70: £2.60, £1.90, £2.90, £1.90; EX 105.70.

Owner J C England **Bred** F Murray **Trained** Naunton, Gloucs

FOCUS

A low-grade handicap run at a sound pace and in the end a wide-margin winner. The third and fifth set the standard and the winner looks well handicapped.

NOTEBOOK

Phildari(IRE), potentially leniently treated on the best of his hunter chase form, jumped for fun and looked to have it won when left out on his own at the third-last fence. In this sort of mood another success is very much on the cards. *(op 9-1)*

Claude Greengrass is a bit reluctant but the champion eventually persuaded him to do just enough to secure second spot. *(op 8-1 tchd 15-2)*

Karo De Vindecy(FR) tried different tactics but, after being left in second spot, he found little and went sideways at the last.

Pillar Of Fire(IRE) had finished a long away ahead of the winner here last time but he has yet to break his duck over fences and ran a moody sort of race. *(op 9-2)*

Raise A McGregor was struggling to keep on terms when he became tangled with the faller three out. *(op 13-2)*

Gray Knight(IRE) *Official explanation: jockey said gelding had breathing problem*

Castle Oliver(IRE), unplaced in nine starts over fences in Ireland, was having his first outing since December. He was booked for second spot when crashing out three from home. *(op 10-1)*

1110 EMBERS OF SLEAFORD H'CAP CHASE (16 fncs 1 omitted) 3m 1f

3:50 (3:51) (Class 3) (0-115,112) 5-Y-0+ **£5,655** (£1,740; £870; £435)

Form					RPR
13-2	1		**Be The Tops (IRE)**^{17} [989] 7-11-3 **102** ... (b) APMcCoy		112+
			(Jonjo O'Neill) *chsd ldr: led 11th: kpt on fr 3 out: rdn rt out*	9/4^{1}	
-113	2	1 3/4	**Croc An Oir (IRE)**^{26} [906] 8-11-12 **111** ... GLee		119
			(R Ford) *hld up in rr: hdwy and mod 3rd 11th: jnd wnr appr 3 out: swtchd rt between last 2: no ex run-in*	7/2^{2}	
P4-2	3	27	**Tommy Carson**^{97} [22] 10-11-3 **102** ... MBatchelor		83
			(Jamie Poulton) *chsd ldrs: drvn along 10th: sn wl outpcd: tk remote 3rd last*	9/1	
-106	4	1 3/4	**Make It Easy (IRE)**^{15} [1015] 9-9-11 **85** oh20 ... KJMercer$^{(3)}$		64
			(D L Williams) *chsd ldrs: outpcd 10th: sn detached: kpt on fr 3 out*	16/1	
P-35	5	21	**Mazileo**^{18} [981] 12-10-13 **98** ... (p) DRDennis		56
			(Ian Williams) *led: hdd 11th: wknd appr 3 out*	13/2^{3}	
-414	6	18	**Panmure (IRE)**^{50} [717] 9-10-12 **97** ... JimCrowley		37
			(P D Niven) *a in rr: bhd fr 11th*	14/1	
15B-	F		**Field Roller (IRE)**^{106} [4868] 5-11-8 **112** ... TJMurphy		—
			(M C Pipe) *hld up: fell 3rd*	7/2^{2}	
5303	P		**John Rich**^{15} [1015] 9-9-11 **85** oh15 ... (tp) PBuchanan$^{(3)}$		—
			(M E Sowersby) *racd wd: bhd fr 10th: t.o whn p.u bef 12th*	20/1	

6m 20.9s (-16.50) **Going Correction** +0.175s/f (Yiel)

WFA 5 from 7yo+ 5lb **8** Ran SP% **115.9**

Speed ratings: **108,107,98,98,91 85,—,—** CSF £11.24 CT £58.27 TOTE £2.60: £1.30, £1.70, £1.90; EX 7.80.

Owner John P McManus **Bred** John J M Power **Trained** Cheltenham, Gloucs

FOCUS

A modest handicap run at a sound gallop with the somewhat reluctant winner persuaded to do enough to keep his head in front. The runner-up sets the level but the winner has the ability to rate higher. The last fence was bypassed on the second circuit.

NOTEBOOK

Be The Tops(IRE) went on looking to have the race in the bag but he suddenly put the brakes on halfway round the final turn. Despite looking reluctant the champion made sure he kept his head in *front all the way to the line. He does not lack ability but clearly has something of a mind of his* own. *(new market tchd 15-8)*

Croc An Oir(IRE), back over fences, had finished runner-up in this last year from a stone lower mark. Allowed to get on level terms on the final turn, he could never find quite enough to worry the winner out of it. *(new market op 3-1 tchd 11-4)*

Tommy Carson, who prefers much more give underfoot, struggled to keep up early on the final circuit. *(new market op 10-1)*

Make It Easy(IRE), 20lb out of the handicap, is a prolific winner in points but he struggles hopelessly to make an impact under Rules. *(new market tchd 14-1 in places)*

Mazileo, back on a winning mark, as usual made the running but he seemed to give up rather too easily when challenged. *(new market op 10-1)*

Field Roller(IRE), making his chase debut from his hurdle-race mark, was on deck at the final fence with two circuits to go. *(new market op 5-1)*

1111 EMBERS FOR ALL YOUR GAS APPLIANCES H'CAP HURDLE (10 hdls) 2m 3f 110y

4:25 (4:26) (Class 3) (0-125,119) 4-Y-0+ **£4,849** (£1,492; £746; £373)

Form					RPR
UF11	1		**Beaugency (NZ)**^{6} [1066] 7-9-10 **94** ... WKennedy$^{(5)}$		112+
			(R C Guest) *in rr: hdwy and drvn along 3 out: led appr 2 out: clr last: kpt rt up to work*	2/1^{1}	
41-6	2	19	**Sovereign State (IRE)**^{4} [525] 8-11-2 **112** ... (p) ONelmes$^{(3)}$		109+
			(D W Thompson) *chsd ldrs: led after 3 out: hdd appr next: j.lft last 2: no ch w wnr*	14/1	
0PF-	3	nk	**Turkama (FR)**^{34} 8-11-12 **119** ... RJohnson		114
			(L A Dace) *hld up in rr: hdwy 7th: kpt on same pce fr 2 out: hit last*	14/1	
3105	4	4	**Lone Soldier (FR)**^{14} [1027] 9-9-10 **96** ... CDSharkey$^{(7)}$		87
			(S B Clark) *chsd ldrs: rdn and outpcd 7th: styd on fr 2 out*	25/1	
P51	5	8	**Room To Room Gold (IRE)**^{14} [1020] 9-11-7 **114** ... AThornton		97
			(R H Alner) *in tch: hit 5th: effrt 3 out: sn btn*	5/1^{3}	
4-06	6	nk	**Sigwells Club Boy**^{14} [1027] 5-10-4 **97** ... JamesDavies		79
			(J L Flint) *chsd ldrs: led 3 out: sn hdd: wknd appr next*	12/1	
-011	7	3	**Herne Bay (IRE)**^{21} [949] 5-11-6 **113** ... JPMcNamara		92
			(R S Brookhouse) *in tch: effrt 3 out: sn wknd*	7/2^{2}	
0540	8	1 3/4	**Siegfrieds Night (IRE)**^{15} [1016] 4-10-1 **104** ... CMStudd$^{(7)}$		79
			(M C Chapman) *chsd ldr: led 7th: hdd after next: sn lost pl*	12/1	
021P	9	9	**Ton-Chee**^{3} [947] 6-10-6 **102** ... KJMercer$^{(3)}$		71
			(K W Hogg) *chsd ldrs: lost pl after 3 out*	33/1	
242-	P		**Alpine Hideaway (IRE)**^{30} [1747] 12-10-2 **95** ... GLee		—
			(J S Wainwright) *in rr: bhd fr 6th: t.o whn p.u bef 2 out*	14/1	
0-5P	P		**Ela Re**^{14} [1024] 6-10-13 **106** ... PJBrennan		—
			(C R Dore) *handful bef s: led to 7th: wknd rapidly: t.o whn p.u bef 2 out*	25/1	
0P-0	P		**Friedhelmo (GER)**^{3} [903] 9-11-2 **109** ... (t) JimCrowley		—
			(P D Niven) *chsd ldrs: lost pl after 6th: sn bhd: t.o whn p.u bef 2 out*	12/1	

4m 51.3s (1.30) **Going Correction** +0.325s/f (Yiel)

WFA 4 from 5yo+ 2lb **12** Ran SP% **125.9**

Speed ratings: **110,102,102,100,97 97,96,95,91,— —,—** CSF £32.56 CT £338.23 TOTE £3.20: £1.50, £4.90, £4.10; EX 44.20.

Owner Gryffindor (www.racingtours.co.uk) **Bred** D M Kerr **Trained** Brancepeth, Co Durham

FOCUS

A sound pace in this modest handicap and in the end a wide-margin winner who will not be resting on his laurels. The runner-up is the best guide to the form.

NOTEBOOK

Beaugency(NZ), without a penalty, came right away, kept right up to his work. He will be out again at Sedgefield on Friday. *(op 9-4 tchd 11-4)*

Sovereign State(IRE), in action on the level just three days earlier, had the cheekpieces back on but in the end all he had was a distant view of the in-form winner.

Turkama(FR), a winner over hurdles and fences in France, the latest two months ago, would have *edged the runner-up out of second spot but for his saddle slipping slightly.Official explanation: jockey said saddle slipped (op 16-1)*

Lone Soldier(FR), stepping up in trip, was only ninth three out and he may be worth a try over even further. *(op 20-1)*

Room To Room Gold(IRE), 7lb higher, would have appreciated much faster ground but even so it was a disappointing effort.

Sigwells Club Boy ran better than on his two most recent starts which came after a break but stamina does not look his strong suit. *(tchd 14-1)*

Herne Bay(IRE), 7lb higher, really needs further but even so this was a poor effort. *(op 4-1 tchd 9-2)*

1112 UK OIL AND GAS FOR PLUMBING NOVICES' HURDLE (DIV I) (8 hdls) 2m 1f 110y

4:55 (4:57) (Class 3) 4-Y-0+ **£4,446** (£1,368; £684; £342)

Form					RPR
2131	1		**Dewasentah (IRE)**^{35} [838] 6-11-3 110 ... GLee		93+
			(J M Jefferson) *hld up: stdy hdwy 4th: chsng ldrs and shkn up 3 out: led appr next: r.o wl: eased towards fin*	4/7^{1}	
-030	2	4	**Cash Return**^{26} [905] 6-9-12 67 ... (p) CMStudd$^{(7)}$		73
			(Mrs S Lamyman) *chsd ldrs: led 5th: hdd appr 2 out: kpt on: no ch w wnr*	16/1	
	3	3 1/2	**Western Roots**^{9} 4-10-7 ... LVickers$^{(3)}$		75
			(I W McInnes) *hld up in rr: gd hdwy to chse ldrs 3 out: one pce fr next*	8/1^{2}	
-31P	4	6	**Nifty Roy**^{21} [949] 5-11-4 ... JimCrowley		80+
			(K W Hogg) *w ldrs: outpcd appr 2 out*	8/1^{2}	
00-P	5	17	**Dawn Frolics**^{6} [1064] 4-10-3 ... JamesDavies		45
			(M J Gingell) *t.k.h: trckd ldrs: wknd 3 out*	80/1	
0-	6	4	**Jollys Pride**^{74} [2129] 4-10-10 ... SCurran		48
			(K F Clutterbuck) *hld up in rr: hdwy to chse ldrs 3 out: sn wknd*	50/1	
06-	7	7	**The Needler (IRE)**^{130} [4526] 5-10-5 ... TMessenger$^{(7)}$		43
			(B N Pollock) *t.k.h: trckd ldrs: mstke and lost pl 5th: sn bhd*	9/1^{3}	
P/P-	8	5	**Irish Prince (IRE)**^{452} [171] 9-10-9 72 ow4 ... MrMLurcock$^{(7)}$		42
			(Robert Gray) *led: t.k.h: hdd 5th: lost pl next*	66/1	
FP-	9	5	**Mandhoor (IRE)**^{134} [4457] 5-10-9 93 ... (t) PAspell$^{(3)}$		33
			(J Wade) *chsd ldrs 2nd: drvn along 5th: sn lost pl and bhd*	12/1	

4m 23.5s (7.10) **Going Correction** +0.325s/f (Yiel)

WFA 4 from 5yo+ 2lb **9** Ran SP% **114.1**

Speed ratings: **97,95,93,91,83 81,78,76,74** CSF £11.62 TOTE £1.40: £1.02, £4.40, £3.00; EX 9.10.

Owner Mrs J U Hales & Mrs L M Joicey **Bred** Miss Mary O'Sullivan **Trained** Norton, N Yorks

FOCUS

A weak novices' hurdle run at no great pace with the 67-rated runner-up the only one to trouble the winner. The form looks sound but limited, with the runner-up holding it down.

NOTEBOOK

Dewasentah(IRE), in no hurry to join issue, had to be put about her business but in the end it was *plain sailing. She is much improved and, strengthening all the time, should make a chaser. (op 8-15 tchd 1-2 8-13 in places)*

Cash Return, lightly backed at long odds, had 31lb to find with the winner but the difference between the two was nowhere near that amount at the line. *(op 25-1)*

Western Roots, a winner at up to a mile and rated just 56 on the level, was held up to get the trip but his stamina looks suspect. *(op 12-1)*

Nifty Royis basically just a stayer and when the pace was stepped up he was left flat-footed. *(tchd 9-1)*

Dawn Frolics, pulled up six days earlier, is headstrong and almost devoid of ability. *(op 66-1)*

1113 UK OIL AND GAS FOR PLUMBING NOVICES' HURDLE (DIV II) (8 hdls) 2m 1f 110y

5:25 (5:26) (Class 3) 4-Y-0+ **£4,433** (£1,364; £682; £341)

Form				RPR
/-2P	1		**Lago D'Oro**[66] [521] 5-10-5 .... GLee (Miss J A Camacho) *chsd ldrs: led appr 2 out: j.lft last 2: forged clr run-in* 4/1[2]	89+
-31F	2	8	**Tom Bell (IRE)**[47] [742] 5-11-4 110 .... (v) APMcCoy (J G M O'Shea) *led: stmbld landing 3 out: hdd appr next: 3 l down and hld whn hit last* 8/13[1]	97+
-P5P	3	13	**Royaltea**[6] [1064] 4-9-12 84 .... LTreadwell(5) (J T Stimpson) *stdd s: hld up in rr: hdwy 4th: wnt mod 3rd appr 2 out* 8/1[3]	66
P	4	9	**Troodos Jet**[17] [991] 4-10-7 .... KJMercer(3) (K W Hogg) *sn bhd: t.o 4th: sme hdwy 3 out: nvr on terms* 50/1	64
3-06	5	hd	**Zahunda (IRE)**[6] [1064] 6-9-9 .... CareyWilliamson(10) (M J Gingell) *trckd ldrs: lost pl after 3 out* 28/1	59
	6	1	**Maria Bonita (IRE)**[46] 4-10-3 .... JamesDavies (C N Kellett) *tk fierce hold: trckd ldrs: wknd after 3 out: mod 4th and tired whn mstke 2 out* 25/1	56
00	7	18	**Durba (AUS)**[3] [1084] 5-10-12 .... HOliver (R C Guest) *mod 6th and wkng whn mstke 3 out: sn wl bhd* 20/1	47
	P		**Rossall Point**[44] 4-10-10 .... KRenwick (R Allan) *in rr fr 4th: t.o 3 out: p.u bef next* 18/1	—
50-	P		**Frenchgate**[27] [3395] 4-10-7 .... PBuchanan(3) (M E Sowersby) *bhd and pushed along 3rd: sn t.o: p.u bef 2 out* 50/1	—

4m 25.0s (8.60) **Going Correction** +0.325s/f (Yiel)

WFA 4 from 5yo+ 2lb **33** Ran SP% **114.3**

Speed ratings: **93,89,83,79,79 79,71,—,—** CSF £6.70 TOTE £6.10: £2.00, £1.10, £1.70; EX 10.00 Place 6 £17.65, Place 5 £7.76.

Owner Mrs S Camacho **Bred** Mrs S Camacho **Trained** Norton, N Yorks

FOCUS

The slower of the two divisions although the form looks better on paper, but the race is not all that solid.

NOTEBOOK

Lago D'Oro, who has had a wind operation, jumped sideways over the last two but still came clear of the favourite. *(tchd 9-2)*

Tom Bell(IRE) had the roll of pacemaker thrust upon him and, after stumbling on landing three out, he seemed to have accepted defeat when hitting the last. When he won at Hereford he came from off the pace. *(op 4-6)*

Royaltea, pulled up with a slipped saddle six days earlier, basically struggles to see out the two-mile trip. *(op 7-1)*

Troodos Jet, an out-of-form sprinter on the Flat, had been pulled up on his hurdling debut two weeks earlier.

Zahunda(IRE) has gone backwards since finishing third on her debut over hurdles at Stratford in April. *(op 25-1)*

Maria Bonita(IRE), a winner of an All-Weather claimer on the level, pulls far too hard to give herself any chance of lasting out the trip over hurdles. *(tchd 28-1)*

T/Plt: £18.20 to a £1 stake. Pool: £44,214.45. 1,766.35 winning tickets. T/Qpdt: £4.70 to a £1 stake. Pool: £3,376.00. 529.30 winning tickets. WG

1114 - 1115a (Foreign Racing) - See Raceform Interactive

1103

GALWAY (R-H)

Sunday, July 31

OFFICIAL GOING: Good to firm

1116a CORRIB VILLAGE H'CAP HURDLE (14 hdls) 3m

3:20 (3:20) (88-130,119) 4-Y-0+ **£9,234** (£2,709; £1,290; £439)

			RPR
1		**Millanymare (IRE)**[19] [968] 6-10-2 99 ow1 .... RWalsh (A J Martin, Ire) *hld up towards rr: impr into mid-div 1/2-way: smooth hdwy into 3rd bef 2 out: led appr last: rdn clr run-in* 10/3[1]	107
2	6	**Matt Wood (IRE)**[23] [921] 6-10-5 108 .... RMMoran(7) (Paul Nolan, Ire) *cl up in 2nd: slt mstke 3 out: sn led: hit next: rdn and hdd bef last: kpt on same pce* 8/1	111
3	10	**Dow Jones (GER)**[4] [1082] 7-11-8 117 .... CO'Dwyer (M Halford, Ire) *attempted to make all: slt mstke 4 out: hdd after 3 out: sn rdn: 3rd and no ex after next* 7/1	111
4	9	**Mesmeric (IRE)**[5] [3795] 7-11-10 119 .... DNRussell (B G Powell) *rr of mid-div: 10th 1/2-way: hdwy after 3 out: 5th bef next: mod 4th and no imp bef last* 14/1	104
5	3 1/2	**Cupla Cairde**[18] [984] 5-10-9 108 .... (b) PWFlood(3) (D T Hughes, Ire) *mid-div: prog into mod 3rd bef 8th: rdn after 3 out: 5th and no ex after next* 16/1	89
6	3 1/2	**Florida Belle (IRE)**[5] [1071] 6-10-4 101 .... RGeraghty (P A Fahy, Ire) *mid-div: 6th 6 out: rdn and no imp fr 3 out* 16/1	77
7	3 1/2	**Noleens Moon (IRE)**[26] [908] 7-10-1 98 .... MDGrant (P J Rothwell, Ire) *towards rr: sme prog after 3 out: no imp fr next* 8/1	71
8	9	**Wests Awake (IRE)**[4] [1083] 9-9-13 99 .... APLane(3) (I Madden, Ire) *nvr a factor* 20/1	63
9	4 1/2	**Coccinelle (IRE)**[77] [379] 7-10-4 101 .... (p) JPElliott (Michael Cunningham, Ire) *mid-div: hmpd 5 out: no imp fr next* 16/1	60
10	6	**Open Range (IRE)**[77] [379] 5-10-6 103 .... PCarberry (Noel Meade, Ire) *mid-div: 7th and pushed along 6 out: wknd fr 4 out* 5/1[3]	56
11	20	**Cantbeatheyouth (IRE)**[12] [1033] 6-9-10 94 .... NPMadden (Noel Meade, Ire) *a towards rr* 14/1	26
12	1	**Hume Theatre (IRE)**[37] [830] 6-10-3 100 .... GTHutchinson (Mrs John Harrington, Ire) *4th to 1/2-way: rdn after 4 out: sn wknd: eased fr last* 12/1	32
F		**Laragh House (IRE)**[18] [985] 6-9-13 99 .... MPWalsh(3) (E J O'Grady, Ire) *3rd early: slow 5th: fell 5 out* 9/2[2]	—

5m 40.1s **17** Ran SP% **136.1**

CSF £35.65 CT £193.83 TOTE £3.20: £1.60, £2.60, £1.90; DF 21.30.

Owner V P Walsh **Bred** Noel Murphy **Trained** Kildalkey, Co Meath

NOTEBOOK

Mesmeric(IRE) was turning out for a second time at the meeting following a lacklustre effort on the Flat five days previously. He stayed on from three out to go a moderate fourth in the straight but was never going to get on terms.

1117 - 1120a (Foreign Racing) - See Raceform Interactive

1075

NEWTON ABBOT (L-H)

Monday, August 1

OFFICIAL GOING: Good to soft (soft in places)

The first fence in the home straight was omitted.

Wind: Almost nil

1121 NEWTONABBOTRACING.COM CLAIMING HURDLE (8 hdls) 2m 1f

2:00 (2:01) (Class 4) 4-Y-0+ **£2,702** (£772; £386)

Form				RPR
0-31	1		**Lucky Do (IRE)**[48] [749] 8-11-2 97 .... APMcCoy (A E Jones) *hld up: hdwy appr 5th: wnt 2nd appr 3 out: led next: clr whn pckd last: easily* 7/2[1]	107+
4353	2	4	**Sir Walter (IRE)**[15] [1027] 12-10-5 95 .... LStephens(5) (D Burchell) *t.k.h: trckd ldrs: led appr 5th: hdd 2f out: one pce after* 5/1[3]	94
0-13	3	11	**Brochrua (IRE)**[66] [536] 5-10-4 96 .... CHonour(5) (J D Frost) *hld up in tch: hdwy appr 5th: one pce appr 2 out* 13/2	82
0520	4	nk	**Saorsie**[26] [915] 7-11-0 100 .... RStephens(5) (J C Fox) *hld up: hdwy appr 5th:: wnt 3rd after 3f out: but no imp on first 2 and lost 3rd cl home* 7/1	92
4200	5	3 1/2	**Delaware (FR)**[22] [947] 9-10-13 87 .... (b) JMogford (H S Howe) *led to 3rd: rdn after next: no hdwy fr 3 out* 14/1	82
S626	6	18	**Blues Story (FR)**[41] [806] 7-11-0 85 .... (t) MNicolls(5) (N G Ayliffe) *mid-div: lost tch after 4th* 28/1	70
/3-0	7	5	**Better Moment (IRE)**[93] [129] 8-10-10 98 .... (v) GSupple (M C Pipe) *trckd ldrs: rdn appr 5th: sn bhd* 10/1	56
0P00	8	9	**Farceur (FR)**[21] [958] 6-10-0 85 .... (v) AGlassonbury(10) (M C Pipe) *a bhd and nvr gng wl* 33/1	47
P/00	9	7	**Silver Man**[15] [1018] 11-10-9 64 .... (p) MrRQuinn(7) (D C Turner) *prom tl rdn and wknd appr 5th* 100/1	46
4606	10	11	**Rattina (GER)**[17] [999] 9-10-6 106 .... (b) PJBrennan (M F Harris) *a in rr: t.o* 20/1	25
P/PP	P		**Miss Man**[12] [1040] 11-10-6 54 .... MBatchelor (N E Berry) *a bhd: p.u after 4th* 100/1	—
0P	P		**Dragon Blue**[15] [1018] 5-10-0 .... ONelmes(3) (G F H Charles-Jones) *a bhd: p.u after 4th* 100/1	—
	P		**Smith N Allan Oils**[136] 6-10-13 .... RHobson(3) (P A Blockley) *a bhd: t.o whn p.u bef 2 out* 33/1	—
360/	P		**Raneen Nashwan**[698] [1268] 9-10-10 .... VSlattery (R J Baker) *hld up: a bhd: t.o whn p.u bef 2 out* 25/1	—
300	P		**Mantras (FR)**[19] [980] 6-11-2 109 .... (v[1]) RGreene (M C Pipe) *trckd ldr: led 3rd: hdd appr 5th: sn wknd: t.o whn p.u bef 2 out* 4/1[2]	—

4m 15.3s (10.20) **Going Correction** +0.675s/f (Soft) **15** Ran SP% **121.4**

Speed ratings: **103,101,95,95,94 85,83,79,75,70 —,—,—,—,—** CSF £19.74 TOTE £4.30: £1.60, £2.10, £2.90; EX 24.50.

Owner D A N Ross **Bred** Mrs S Hanly **Trained** Newchapel, Surrey

FOCUS

A very weak event, run at a fair gallop and the field finished well strung out. The runner-up sets the level.

NOTEBOOK

Lucky Do(IRE) , last seen winning a selling handicap at this venue 48 days previously, followed up under a well-judged ride from McCoy and had no trouble with the drop back in trip. Versatile as regards underfoot conditions, he has improved plenty since joining his current yard and, on this evidence, looks sure to make a bold bid in his quest for the hat-trick. *(op 9-2 tchd 5-1)*

Sir Walter(IRE) , back down in class, turned in another solid effort yet was put in his place by the winner in the home straight. He remains in good form, and was well clear of the rest this time, yet will continue to be vulnerable in whatever grade to anything progressive. *(tchd 4-1)*

Brochrua(IRE) failed by some way to confirm her course and distance form with the winner on this *much easier ground and was never a factor. She is a different proposition on a quick surface. (op 5-1)*

Saorsiemade a short-lived effort and he failed to improve for the drop into this grade. He really is proving hard to predict and his stable has yet to have a winner in 2005.

Blues Story(FR) *Official explanation: trainer said gelding bled from nose (op 25-1 tchd 33-1)*

Mantras(FR) dropped out very tamely and was disappointingly pulled up. He is clearly one to have *reservations about. Official explanation: trainer was unable to offer any explanation for poor form shown (tchd 9-2)*

1122 PARTYFARECATERERS.CO.UK CONDITIONAL JOCKEYS' H'CAP CHASE (17 fncs 3 omitted) 3m 2f 110y

2:30 (2:30) (Class 4) (0-90,89) 5-Y-0+ **£3,326** (£950; £475)

Form				RPR
P/00	1		**Corkan (IRE)**[19] [981] 11-10-0 63 oh4 .... (p) TJMalone (A M Hales) *trckd ldr: led 12th: rdn whn chal appr last: kpt on gamely* 7/1	73
02-4	2	1/2	**Southerndown (IRE)**[71] [464] 12-11-1 78 .... WKennedy (R Lee) *hld up: stdy hdwy fr 11th: wnt 2nd after 2 out and chal bef last: kpt on but no imp run-in* 11/4[1]	87
PP4/	3	dist	**Alabaster**[510] [4247] 10-9-6 63 .... KBurke(5) (N J Hawke) *in tch: hit 5th: wnt 2nd 4 out: tl wknd qckly after 2 out: t.o* 40/1	—
0-22	4	25	**Cyanara**[55] [673] 9-10-6 69 .... JamesDavies (Dr P Pritchard) *hld up: tk clsr oreder 7th: wknd 3 out: t.o* 3/1[2]	—
P055	5	23	**Francolino (FR)**[33] [865] 12-10-0 63 oh5 .... DCrosse (Dr P Pritchard) *in tch to 10th: sn bhd: t.o* 20/1	—
0300	6	6	**Blazing Batman**[19] [981] 12-11-6 83 .... TJPhelan (Dr P Pritchard) *hld up: lost tch 11th: t.o* 12/1	—
PP3P	P		**Hardy Russian (IRE)**[15] [1022] 8-10-7 70 .... ONelmes (P R Rodford) *a bhd: t.o whn p.u after 11th* 12/1	—
000-	P		**Shellin Hill (IRE)**[323] [1414] 11-10-1 64 .... (p) MNicolls (R J Baker) *in tch: tl wknd qckly and p.u after 11th* 20/1	—

The Form Book, Raceform Ltd, Compton, RG20 6NL

0-FP **P** **Mvezo**22 948 7-10-1 64 (v1) JPByrne —
(Evan Williams) *trckd ldrs: hmpd 3rd: rdn 11th: sn wknd: p.u bef next* **10/1**

22RP **R** **Bramblehill Duke (IRE)**29 896 13-11-9 89 (b) AO'Keeffe(3) —
(Miss Venetia Williams) *led: hit 2nd: hdd 12th: wkng whn ref 3 out* **9/2**3

7m 10.3s (26.90) **Going Correction** +0.825s/f (Soft) **10** Ran SP% **118.8**
Speed ratings: **93,92**,—,—,— —,—,—,—,— CSF £27.51 CT £735.59 TOTE £11.90: £3.00, £1.50, £5.90; EX 40.50.
Owner Alan Spargo **Bred** Miss A And Miss Bridget Daly **Trained** Quainton, Bucks

FOCUS
A poor handicap and a moderate winning time, even allowing for the conditions, and the first two came miles clear. The form is weak.

NOTEBOOK
Corkan(IRE), 4lb out of the handicap and with the cheekpieces re-applied, looked a sitting duck when the runner-up came to challenge approaching the final fence, but dug deep and gamely outbattled that rival to score. This was his first success since 2002, and he has tumbled in the weights as a result, but this dour stayer is far from certain to follow-up on this. *(op 8-1)*
Southerndown(IRE) was given a fine ride by Kennedy, looking all over the winner approaching the final fence, yet failed to find as much as looked likely when push came to shove and was eventually outbattled on the run-in. While this was another decent effort, he has not got his head in front for the best part of two years now, and it is not the first time he has flattered to deceive off the bridle. *(op 3-1)*
Alabaster ran a fair race, until her lack of fitness kicked in at the top of the straight, on this handicap bow and return from a 510-day absence. She has clearly had her problems, yet is at least entitled to improve for the outing and probably for a drop in trip. *(op 33-1)*
Cyanara turned in a moody effort and was way below the level of her recent efforts. *(op 7-2)*
Bramblehill Duke(IRE) was beating a retreat prior to refusing at the third last fence. He really does look out of love with racing now.

1123 SUMMER FESTIVAL IN THREE WEEKS NOVICES' HURDLE (9 hdls) 2m 3f
3:00 (3:00) (Class 3) 4-Y-0+ **£4,854** (£1,493; £746; £373)

Form RPR
1-63 **1** **Cantgeton (IRE)**26 912 5-11-6 108 TJMurphy 105
(M C Pipe) *trckd ldr: led 3 out: hdd briefly bef next: rdn and in command whn edgd rt appr last* **7/4**2

4143 **2** 3 1/2 **Gemini Dancer**21 959 6-11-6 107 JTizzard 104+
(C L Tizzard) *trckd ldrs: wnt 2nd 3 out: chal bef next: hld in 2nd whn awkward and slipped on landing last* **5/4**1

56P/ **3** 28 **Prince On The Ter**810 10-10-7 LHeard(7) 67
(B Scriven) *led to 3 out: wknd rapidly* **50/1**

P50 **4** 1 1/2 **Duke's View (IRE)**15 1021 4-10-12 RGreene 64
(D C Turner) *in tch to 4th: sn bhd: t.o* **80/1**

0PP- **5** 7 **Past Heritage**181 3634 6-10-9 DLaverty(5) 59
(A E Jones) *in tch: but no hdwy after 5th: t.o* **66/1**

4- **6** 17 **Sweet Az**356 1166 5-10-7 TDoyle 35
(S C Burrough) *a bhd: t.o* **25/1**

7 12 **Silver Emperor (IRE)**557 4-10-12 ChristianWilliams 28
(P A Blockley) *nt fluent first: a bhd: t.o* **33/1**

R **Grey Court** 10-10-7 JamesWhite(7) —
(P D Purdy) *awkwards 1st: wl bhd whn ref 2nd* **100/1**

P **Norman's Glories**862 7-11-0 APMcCoy —
(A E Jones) *t.k.h: in tch: wkng whn j.rt 6th: t.o whn p.u bef 2 out* **9/2**3

4m 53.6s (20.60) **Going Correction** +0.675s/f (Soft)
WFA 4 from 5yo+ 15lb **9** Ran SP% **111.5**
Speed ratings: **83,81,69,69,66 59,53**,—,— CSF £4.13 TOTE £3.60: £1.30, £1.02, £11.00; EX 5.00.
Owner D A Johnson **Bred** John Murphy **Trained** Nicholashayne, Devon

FOCUS
A pedestrian winning time for the class of race and the first two came well clear. Despite this the form is sound enough.

NOTEBOOK
Cantgeton(IRE), easy to back, showed his true colours with a dogged success under a positive ride from Murphy. He again gave the impression that he is yet to reach his peak, and is well worth another try over further on this evidence, yet may be better off in handicaps now, as he looks likely to be vulnerable under a double penalty in this division. *(op 11-8)*
Gemini Dancer came with a strong challenge at the top of the straight, yet surprisingly failed to sustain his effort over this longer trip and was readily held at the finish. He was miles clear of the rest in second, and it may well be that he is just a strong finisher over two miles, so is not one to write off just yet. *(tchd 11-8)*
Prince On The Ter, last seen in a point 810 days previously, shaped well enough until his lack of fitness became an issue before the turn for home. He has his limitations, but is at least entitled to *improve for the outing and really needs a stiffer test.Official explanation: trainer said gelding lost a front shoe (op 66-1)*
Duke's View(IRE) *Official explanation: trainer said gelding lost a shoe (op 66-1 tchd 100-1)*
Norman's Glories, having his first run for 862 days, gave himself little chance of getting home by *failing to settle and was disappointingly pulled up. He should be capable of better.Official explanation: jockey said gelding hung badly right-handed (op 5-1 tchd 11-2 and 4-1)*

1124 RACECOURSE FOR CONFERENCES NOVICES' CHASE (11 fncs 2 omitted) 2m 110y
3:30 (3:30) (Class 3) 5-Y-0+ **£5,317** (£1,636; £818; £409)

Form RPR
-U21 **1** **Mister Flint**3 1096 7-11-4 RJohnson 135+
(P J Hobbs) *led: sn clr: sme times j.rt: hit 4th: in total command fr 8th: hit last: eased run-in: unchal* **11/10**1

U-21 **2** 26 **Tonic Du Charmil (FR)**11 1049 5-11-4 117 (t) TJMurphy 107+
(M C Pipe) *frequent mstkes: chsd wnr thrght: no ch after 8th* **11/8**2

4560 **3** 10 **Half Inch**27 905 5-10-0 98 CHonour(5) 80
(B I Case) *last tl wnt 3rd 5th: a wl bhd: t.o* **14/1**

P313 **4** dist **Nazimabad (IRE)**17 999 6-11-4 88 (t) ChristianWilliams —
(Evan Williams) *racd 3rd to 5th: sn t.o* **6/1**3

4m 16.8s (11.30) **Going Correction** +0.825s/f (Soft) **4** Ran SP% **110.7**
Speed ratings: **106,93,89**,— CSF £3.21 TOTE £1.80; EX 3.00.
Owner Alan Peterson **Bred** M H Ings **Trained** Withycombe, Somerset

FOCUS
a fair novice chase for the time of year that concerned the first pair in the betting and the field came home well strung out. The runner-up lost any chance with his sloppy jumping and the winner is value for more than the official margin.

NOTEBOOK
Mister Flint, who lowered the colours of Mr Ed when opening his account over fences at Bangor three days previously, maintained his progression with an imperious display under his penalty. He totally lost the plot over hurdles last season after taking a heavy fall at Kempton when fancied to beat the smart Marcel, but is clearly getting his act together over fences and is settling much better through the early parts of his races. Further improvement cannot be ruled out, even though life will now be tougher under double penalty in this sphere. *(op 5-4)*
Tonic Du Charmil(FR) was let down by his jumping and disappointingly failed to build on his recent Uttoxeter handicap success. He cannot be followed until his fencing shows signs of improvement, but should he eventually iron out his problems, there are further races to be won with him in this sphere. *(op 11-10 tchd 6-4 in a place)*
Half Inch, making his chase debut, merely kept on at his own pace throughout and was never a *factor. He can find easier opportunities, however, and may be better off in low-grade handicaps. (op 12-1 tchd 16-1)*
Nazimabad(IRE) failed to run his race and was later reported to have suffered a breathing problem. *Official explanation: jockey said gelding had a breathing problem (op 8-1)*

1125 "ALMAPA" FATHER JOHN WRENN MEMORIAL H'CAP HURDLE (9 hdls 1 omitted) 2m 6f
4:00 (4:00) (Class 4) (0-110,110) 4-Y-0+ **£3,301** (£943; £471)

Form RPR
00-0 **1** **Irishkawa Bellevue (FR)**47 762 7-10-13 100 (b) DCrosse(3) 110+
(Jean-Rene Auvray) *trckd ldrs: led after 2 out: sn clr: comf* **25/1**

1U-6 **2** 12 **Mac Hine (IRE)**94 111 8-11-0 98 (t) APMcCoy 91
(Jonjo O'Neill) *hld up: hdwy bef rdn to chse wnr after 2 out: sn no ch w wnr* **11/8**1

65-4 **3** 1 3/4 **Baloo**48 751 9-11-2 105 CHonour(5) 96
(J D Frost) *chsd ldr: led 3rd: hdd after 3 out: sn one pce* **8/1**

F00- **4** 1/2 **Yourman (IRE)**101 4960 5-11-8 106 TJMurphy 97
(M C Pipe) *hld p: blnd 2nd: hdwy appr 6th: rdn 2 out: wknd qckly* **3/1**2

1-P4 **5** 15 **Doof (IRE)**17 1000 5-11-12 110 GSupple 86
(M C Pipe) *racd wd and t.k.h: hit 1st: led to 3rd: wknd qckly after 7th* **6/1**

101- **P** **Mrs Philip**140 4380 6-10-13 97 PJBrennan —
(P J Hobbs) *hld up in tch: nt much toom after 7th: wknd rapidly and p.u bef next (2 out)* **5/1**3

5m 33.4s (13.10) **Going Correction** +0.675s/f (Soft) **6** Ran SP% **113.0**
Speed ratings: **103,98,98,97,92** — CSF £63.00 TOTE £47.70: £8.70, £1.30; EX 113.20.
Owner The Magpie Partnership **Bred** G Leveque **Trained** Upper Lambourn, Berks

FOCUS
A modest event, run at a sound gallop but the form is not altogether solid and the third is the best guide to the form. The second last flight was bypassed.

NOTEBOOK
Irishkawa Bellevue(FR) was given an enterprising ride by Crosse, taking the race by the scruff of the neck approaching the penultimate flight, and found plenty when in front en-route to a surprise success. He has clearly improved for a recent break, this is his optimum trip and his confidence will be high now. However, he does look flattered by this form and may struggle if the Handicapper *reacts literally. Official explanation: trainer said, regarding the improved form shown, gelding appreciated today's better ground (op 16-1)*
Mac Hine(IRE), with the tongue tie re-applied and well backed for this return from a 940-day break, was again found wanting under pressure and has to rate as disappointing. He has yet to win over hurdles, and despite being currently rated 10lb higher over fences, shows little sign of taking advantage. *(op 13-8)*
Baloo was not totally disgraced over a trip short of his best and on ground he would have found *plenty soft enough. A return to three miles on quick ground ought to see him in a much better* light. *(op 7-1)*
Yourman(IRE), making his seasonal return after a 101-day break, never convinced after an early error and turned in a disappointing effort. He has managed just the one success from 16 outings over hurdles to date and really has it all to prove now. *(tchd 7-2)*
Doof(IRE) again turned in a moody effort and has gone markedly backwards since winning over course and distance on soft ground in April. *(op 7-1)*
Mrs Philip failed to really act on this ground - as all of her previous best efforts suggested - and should be given another chance off this mark when reverting to a quick surface. *(op 4-1)*

1126 YOUR COMPANY NAME HERE H'CAP CHASE (11 fncs 2 omitted) 2m 110y
4:30 (4:30) (Class 4) (0-105,104) 5-Y-0+ **£3,747** (£1,153; £576; £288)

Form RPR
-0P3 **1** **Get The Point**29 894 11-10-8 86 JamesDavies 93
(Dr P Pritchard) *hld up in tch: wnt 2nd 3 out: rdn to ld bef last: drvn out run-in* **5/1**3

P065 **2** 4 **Gipsy Cricketer**17 999 9-9-5 79 oh9 ow1 JKington(10) 82
(M Scudamore) *mde most tl rdn and hdd bef last: kpt on one pce* **7/1**

-234 **3** 17 **Amadeus (AUS)**27 904 8-10-10 88 TScudamore 80+
(M Scudamore) *racd 3rd tl wnt 2nd after 5th: rdn and wknd qckly 3 out* **11/8**1

3-3F **4** dist **Silvergino (IRE)**22 946 5-11-12 104 PJBrennan —
(Mrs Jeremy Young) *trckd ldr tl after 5th: rdn appr 6th: sn wknd: t.o* **7/4**2

4m 25.9s (20.40) **Going Correction** +0.825s/f (Soft) **4** Ran SP% **107.6**
Speed ratings: **85,83,75**,— CSF £28.61 TOTE £5.80; EX 17.20 Place 6 £81.79, Place 5 £49.39.
Owner Norwester Racing Club **Bred** Stilvi Compania Financiera S A **Trained** Purton, Gloucs

FOCUS
A very moderate handicap and a poor winning time, more than nine seconds slower than the earlier novice chase, and the form is weak.

NOTEBOOK
Get The Point was given a well-judged ride and came right away on the run-in to score. This easier ground was much to his liking, but it must be noted this probably took little winning and he is likely to struggle off a higher mark in the future. *(op 9-2)*
Gipsy Cricketer, 9lb out of the handicap yet aided by his rider's claim, turned in a brave effort from the front. His last success came in a point in 2004, however, and he is fully exposed under Rules. *(op 11-2 tchd 15-2)*
Amadeus(AUS) was well backed, but never rated a threat and is struggling for form at present. *(op 13-8)*
Silvergino(IRE) proved very disappointing and did not look suited by this ground. *(tchd 15-8)*
T/Plt: £103.80 to a £1 stake. Pool: £41,240.85. 289.85 winning tickets. T/Qpdt: £20.40 to a £1 stake. Pool: £2,481.30. 90.00 winning tickets. JS

1127 - 1145a (Foreign Racing) - See Raceform Interactive

1062 SEDGEFIELD (L-H)
Friday, August 5

OFFICIAL GOING: Good to firm (firm in places)
After 2 1/2mm overnight rain the ground was described as 'quick but even'. Third last fence omitted on each circuit.
Wind: Fresh, half against Weather: Mainly fine but blustery

1146 WEATHERBYS BANK JUVENILE NOVICES' HURDLE (8 hdls) 2m 1f
2:30 (2:30) (Class 4) 3-Y-O **£3,380** (£1,040; £520; £260)

Form RPR
1 **Wembury Point (IRE)**62 3-10-11 GLee 80+
(B G Powell) *trckd ldrs: led between last 2: forged clr run-in* **4/1**2

6 **2** 8 **Good Investment**20 1011 3-10-11 FKeniry 77+
(P C Haslam) *chsd ldrs: led and mstke 3 out: 2l down and hld whn sddle slipped bdly last: eased* **11/2**3

3 *6* **Ignotus** 3-10-11 .... JimCrowley 65
(G A Swinbank) *hld up in last: hdwy 5th: wnt mod 3rd after 3 out: sn rdn: one pce* **7/2**[1]
4 *7* **Snow Tempest (USA)**[170] 3-10-11 .... ADobbin 59+
(T G Mills) *chsd ldrs: rdn 3 out: one pce* **4/1**[2]
5 *11* **Forest Viking (IRE)**[32] 3-10-11 .... ARoss 47
(J S Wainwright) *chsd ldrs: wknd after 3 out* **7/1**
6 *1 1/4* **Sergeant Small (IRE)**[41] 3-10-8 ow4 .... MrMatthewSmith(7) 50
(John Berry) *in rr: sme hdwy 3 out: nvr on terms* **50/1**
7 *5* **French Gold**[10] 3-10-4 .... KRenwick 34
(N Wilson) *mid-div: lost pl 3 out* **12/1**
8 *1 3/4* **Midnight In Moscow (IRE)**[66] 3-10-11 .... BHarding 39
(P C Haslam) *led to 3 out: sn wknd* **25/1**
9 *9* **Swallow Falls (IRE)**[16] 3-9-13 .... StephenJCraine(5) 23
(D McCain) *chsd ldrs: wknd 3 out* **33/1**
10 *9* **Diktatit**[9] 3-10-1 .... LMcGrath(3) 14
(R C Guest) *hld up in rr: blnd 4th: sn bhd* **33/1**
11 *4* **Oblivious**[23] 3-10-8 .... GCarenza(3) 17
(K J Burke) *a bhd* **33/1**
PP **F** **Miss Dinamite**[7] [1095] 3-9-11 .... TMessenger(7) —
(Mrs C J Ikin) *chsd ldrs: rdn along whn fell 4th* **100/1**

3m 55.7s (-10.80) **Going Correction** -0.975s/f (Hard) **12** Ran SP% **113.4**
Speed ratings: **86,82,79,76,70 70,68,67,62,58 56,**— CSF £23.68 TOTE £5.80: £2.00, £2.30, £1.30; EX 29.20.
Owner Mr & Mrs D A Gamble **Bred** Philip Brady **Trained** Morestead, Hants

FOCUS
Probably just a very ordinary early-season juvenile hurdle run in a modest time.

NOTEBOOK
Wembury Point(IRE), a maiden and rated just 55 on the level, is quite a tall type. With the second in trouble, he was able to pull clear on the run-in. *(tchd 7-2)*
Good Investment, a winner on the Flat and rated 60, showed a lot more than first time. Clattering the third last as he took the lead, his measure had been taken when his saddle slipped right round at the last and his rider did well to cling on and finish. *(op 6-1 tchd 13-2)*
Ignotus, bred to be a jumper, has plenty of size and scope and looked in top trim. In no hurry to join issue, when pushed along he could not get near the first two. The experience will not be lost on him. *(op 9-2)*
Snow Tempest(USA), a maiden rated 60 on the level, is a keen type. Flat out three from home, he proved woefully one paced. *(op 7-2 tchd 9-2)*
Forest Viking(IRE), placed on the Flat and rated just 49, has been out of form of late and he was going backwards three out. *(op 8-1)*

1147 WEATHERBYS INSURANCE BEGINNERS' CHASE (11 fncs 2 omitted) 2m 110y
3:00 (3:00) (Class 4) 5-Y-0+ **£4,075** (£1,254; £627; £313)

Form RPR
00-0 **1** **King Eider**[20] [1010] 6-10-12 .... ADobbin 117+
(B Ellison) *w ldr: led 6th: styd on wl run-in* **7/2**[3]
50-P **2** *3 1/2* **Dead Mans Dante (IRE)**[11] [1062] 7-10-9 .... KJMercer(3) 113
(Ferdy Murphy) *hld up in rr: gd hdwy 8th: wnt 2nd after next: rdn between last 2: chal last: no ex* **16/1**
3-03 **3** *12* **Scalloway (IRE)**[19] [1019] 5-10-12 .... CLlewellyn 101
(D J Wintle) *trckd ldrs: effrt 9th: one pce* **5/2**[1]
33F2 **4** *5* **Heather Lad**[11] [1062] 12-10-12 100 .... GLee 96
(C Grant) *outpcd and lost pl 4th: hdwy 8th: one pce fr next* **8/1**
0053 **5** *1 1/4* **Brave Effect (IRE)**[11] [1062] 9-10-12 89 .... BHarding 95
(Mrs Dianne Sayer) *chsd ldrs: outpcd fr 3 out* **9/1**
-221 **6** *7* **Caliban (IRE)**[14] [695] 7-10-12 .... (v) WHutchinson 88
(Ian Williams) *j.rt: led: mstke and hdd 9th: sn wknd* **10/3**[2]
5326 **7** *10* **One Of Them**[11] [1062] 6-10-5 79 .... GThomas(7) 78
(M A Barnes) *in tch: outpcd 7th: sn lost pl* **25/1**
5-0 **8** *4* **Oyez (IRE)**[36] [873] 8-10-12 .... JPMcNamara 74
(J J Lambe, Ire) *in rr: sme hdwy 6th: sn lost pl* **25/1**
0-03 **P** **My Ace**[22] [990] 7-9-12 .... (bt) MissJFoster(7) —
(Miss J E Foster) *bhd fr 5th: t.o 7th: p.u bef 2 out* **40/1**
-0P6 **P** **The Honey Guide**[23] [979] 9-10-8 61 ow1 .... DFlavin(5) —
(Mrs L B Normile) *in rr: sme hdwy 8th: sn lost pl: last whn p.u bef last* **100/1**

3m 54.5s (-19.70) **Going Correction** -0.975s/f (Hard) **10** Ran SP% **112.0**
Speed ratings: **107,105,99,97,96 93,88,86,—,—** CSF £48.27 TOTE £4.50: £2.20, £2.00, £2.20; EX 63.30.
Owner Angela Rix & Partners **Bred** Sir Thomas Pilkington **Trained** Norton, N Yorks

FOCUS
A fair beginners' chase run at a strong pace with the winner a decent recruit and a vastly improved effort from the unexposed runner-up. Those in the frame behind the winner ran close to their marks.

NOTEBOOK
King Eider, a winner on the Flat and twice over hurdles, jumped well and, kept right up to his work, proved much too good for this lot. He bounces off fast ground such as he encountered here and looks a decent recruit. *(op 3-1)*
Dead Mans Dante(IRE) went in pursuit of the winner but, after landing upsides at the last, he found the winner too quick. He should find a maiden chase all right. *(op 20-1 tchd 22-1)*
Scalloway(IRE), rated 9lb inferior to the winner over hurdles, was easily left behind by the first two.
Heather Lad jumped round in his own time but over this trip lacked the speed to take a hand.
Brave Effect(IRE), with the visor left off, was readily left behind in the final half mile.
Caliban(IRE), last seen in action on the Flat, continually lost ground jumping to his right. After *losing the lead when making a mistake, his stamina seemed to drain away. (tchd 3-1 and 7-2 in a place)*
My Ace *Official explanation: trainer said mare bled from the nose*

1148 JOHN WADE FOR EQUESTRIAN FIBRE AND RUBBER (S) H'CAP HURDLE (QUALIFIER) (8 hdls) 2m 1f
3:30 (3:31) (Class 5) (0-95,90) 4-Y-0+ **£2,275** (£650; £325)

Form RPR
-P62 **1** **Wally Wonder (IRE)**[23] [978] 7-11-7 85 .... (b) GLee 96+
(R Bastiman) *chsd ldr: led after 3 out: drvn out* **9/4**[1]
0P02 **2** *7* **Valuable (IRE)**[11] [1063] 8-10-13 77 .... KJohnson 81
(R Johnson) *hld up: hdwy 5th: lft 2nd between last 2: kpt on same pce* **7/2**[2]
0003 **3** *1 3/4* **Fortune's Fool**[11] [1063] 6-10-5 72 .... PWhelan(3) 74
(I A Brown) *hld up: hdwy 5th: kpt on one pce fr 2 out* **9/2**[3]
0600 **4** *20* **Jamorin Dancer**[55] [716] 10-9-7 64 .... (p) TMessenger(7) 46
(S G Chadwick) *chsd ldrs: lost pl after 3 out* **16/1**
-PP0 **5** *1 1/4* **Longstone Lass**[5] [1107] 5-11-2 87 .... (v) SCrawford(7) 73+
(D Carroll) *led tl after 3 out: 5th and wkng whn bdly hmpd between last 2* **12/1**
3-0P **6** *nk* **Mersey Mirage**[8] [180] 8-10-1 65 .... (be) HOliver 45
(R C Guest) *t.k.h: trckd ldrs to 3 out: sn lost pl* **25/1**
0004 **7** *5* **Flashy Filly**[11] [1064] 5-9-10 67 oh3 ow3 .... (p) MJMcAlister(7) 42
(J C Haynes) *chsd ldrs: drvn along and lost pl 4th* **28/1**
/0-4 **8** *8* **Coachman (IRE)**[5] [1107] 7-10-0 64 oh7 .... JimCrowley 31
(A J Lockwood) *in rr: lost tch 4th* **10/1**
0-00 **9** *9* **Vesta Flame**[42] [822] 4-9-9 67 oh1 ow2 .... CDSharkey(7) 24
(P T Midgley) *in rr and reminders after 4th: sn bhd* **33/1**
5555 **P** **Simply Da Best (IRE)**[22] [990] 7-11-12 90 .... (b) JPMcNamara —
(J J Lambe, Ire) *in rr fr 5th: wl bhd whn p.u bef 2 out* **12/1**
22-P **U** **Sandabar**[47] [784] 12-11-2 80 .... (t) DO'Meara 82
(Miss Tracy Waggott) *hld up: hdwy 4th: wnt 2nd appr 2 out: 4 l down whn virtually p.u, bdly hmpd and uns rdr between last 2* **12/1**

3m 52.2s (-14.30) **Going Correction** -0.975s/f (Hard)
WFA 4 from 5yo+ 15lb **11** Ran SP% **119.5**
Speed ratings: **94,90,89,80,79 79,77,73,69,—,—** CSF £10.79 CT £33.23 TOTE £3.70: £1.50, £1.80, £1.30; EX 8.80.There was no bid for the winner.
Owner Richard Long **Bred** T W Nicholson **Trained** Cowthorpe, N Yorks
■ Sandabar was Tracy Waggott's first runner after taking over the trainer's licence from her father Norman.

FOCUS
A selling handicap run at a strong pace and not without some drama. With the placed horses running to thir previous marks, the form looks sound at a very modest level.

NOTEBOOK
Wally Wonder(IRE), suited by the strong gallop over this half-mile shorter trip, was better than ever and looked to be in command when his nearest pursuer went out of the contest on the downhill run to the final flight. *(op 11-4 tchd 2-1)*
Valuable(IRE), dropped in, was handed second spot between the last two but he was never doing anything like enough to trouble the winner. *(tchd 4-1)*
Fortune's Fool at least finished closer to Valuable this time. Even so this trip looks on the sharp side for him. *(op 7-1)*
Jamorin Dancer, without a win for over two years, continues largely out of form. *(op 14-1)*
Longstone Lass, much better behaved, took them along at a strong gallop but all chance had gone when she was almost knocked over. *(op 8-1)*
Sandabar, who last won over four years ago, was pulled up when last seen out six weeks ago. He was booked for second when he hung right and completely lost his action between the last two. With Longstone Lass cannoning into him, his rider had no chance. He was reported none the worse afterwards. *Official explanation: jockey said gelding lost action (op 8-1)*

1149 JEWSON NOVICES' HURDLE (SERIES QUALIFIER) (8 hdls) 2m 1f
4:00 (4:00) (Class 4) 4-Y-0+ **£3,380** (£1,040; £520; £260)

Form RPR
5260 **1** **Supply And Fix (IRE)**[26] [940] 7-10-12 .... JPMcNamara 98+
(J J Lambe, Ire) *mde all: qcknd after 3 out: styd on wl* **11/4**[2]
2 *4* **United Nations**[13] 4-10-11 .... KRenwick 93
(N Wilson) *hld up: stdy hdwy 5th: wnt 2nd after 3 out: rdn between last 2: no imp* **15/2**
-U21 **3** *2 1/2* **Reem Two**[11] [1064] 4-10-10 99 .... JMMaguire 89
(D McCain) *chsd ldrs: reminders 5th: one pce fr 2 out* **5/4**[1]
66 **4** *16* **Shady Baron (IRE)**[33] [892] 6-10-9 .... PAspell(3) 75
(J Wade) *in tch: wnt prom 3 out: sn wknd* **33/1**
0-01 **5** *18* **Two Steps To Go (USA)**[11] [1063] 6-11-1 70 .... PBuchanan(3) 63
(M A Barnes) *chsd ldrs: outpcd 5th: sn lost pl* **11/1**
P4 **6** *1 1/2* **Troodos Jet**[5] [1113] 4-10-8 .... KJMercer(3) 55
(K W Hogg) *hld up and bhd: sme hdwy 3 out: sn wknd* **66/1**
31P4 **7** *15* **Nifty Roy**[5] [1112] 5-11-4 95 .... JimCrowley 47
(K W Hogg) *prom: drvn along 5th: lost pl next* **6/1**[3]
P **8** *12* **Marton Mere**[77] [437] 9-10-5 .... MissJFoster(7) 29
(Miss J E Foster) *chsd ldrs: rdn and lost pl after 5th: sn bhd* **100/1**

3m 50.1s (-16.40) **Going Correction** -0.975s/f (Hard)
WFA 4 from 5yo+ 15lb **8** Ran SP% **110.9**
Speed ratings: **99,97,95,88,79 79,72,66** CSF £21.56 TOTE £4.60: £1.10, £2.20, £1.02; EX 35.40.
Owner J J Lambe **Bred** Michael L Flynn **Trained** Dungannon, Co. Tyrone

FOCUS
A fair novice but the two likely favourites were withdrawn on account of the fast ground. It was a strong pace and the winner deserved his change of luck in what was just a fair novice but overall the form looks sound.

NOTEBOOK
Supply And Fix(IRE) took them along at a strong gallop and, stepping up the ante three out, never *looked in any real danger. After his Perth mishap he richly deserved this.Official explanation: trainer had no explanation for the improved form shown (op 9-4 tchd 3-1)*
United Nations, useful at three on the level, went in pursuit of the winner but was never making any real impression. His stamina looks suspect. *(op 8-1 tchd 7-1)*
Reem Two, who made hard work of getting off the mark here, found the penalty all too much and was struggling soon after halfway. *(op 13-8 tchd 7-4 in places)*
Shady Baron(IRE) still looks some way short of the finished article. *(op 25-1)*
Two Steps To Go(USA), who changed hands after his selling-race success, found this much too tough. *(op 16-1 tchd 10-1)*
Nifty Roy, making a quick return, continues way off the boil. *(op 9-2)*

1150 LJJ CONTRACTORS 01642 617517 H'CAP CHASE (13 fncs 3 omitted) 2m 5f
4:30 (4:31) (Class 4) (0-105,96) 5-Y-0+ **£4,124** (£1,269; £634; £317)

Form RPR
-052 **1** **Swallow Magic (IRE)**[11] [1065] 7-10-5 78 .... KJMercer(3) 93+
(Ferdy Murphy) *hld up in rr: stdy hdwy 8th: led last: r.o wl: readily* **9/4**[2]
05U0 **2** *4* **York Rite (AUS)**[5] [1109] 9-10-8 78 .... (p) HOliver 88
(R C Guest) *trckd ldr: led 9th to last: nt qckn* **20/1**
5061 **3** *1 1/2* **Now Then Sid**[11] [1065] 6-10-9 82 7ex .... PBuchanan(3) 93+
(Mrs S A Watt) *chsd ldrs: pushed along 8th: chal and hit 2 out: one pce* **5/4**[1]
P4PP **4** *3* **Pavey Ark (IRE)**[22] [989] 7-10-10 80 .... GLee 86
(James Moffatt) *in tch: effrt 9th: one pce fr 2 out* **16/1**
00-0 **5** *20* **Ballistic Boy**[37] [858] 8-10-10 85 .... DCCostello(5) 81+
(R W Thomson) *chsd ldrs: wknd between last 2: heavily eased run-in* **40/1**
P-35 **6** *5* **Tierkely (IRE)**[11] [1067] 10-11-2 86 .... ARoss 67
(J J Lambe, Ire) *in rr: drvn along after 6th: t.o 9th* **25/1**
44-5 **7** *1 1/4* **Taleban**[11] [1065] 10-10-9 82 .... (p) PAspell(3) 61
(J Wade) *j.rt: led to 9th: sn lost pl and bhd* **14/1**
454 **P** **Xaipete (IRE)**[7] [1099] 13-11-9 96 .... LMcGrath(3) —
(R C Guest) *hld up in rr: stdy hdwy 8th: cl 2nd and travelling strly whn broke hind leg and p.u after 3 out: dead* **7/1**[3]

5m 6.60s (-16.80) **Going Correction** -0.975s/f (Hard) **8** Ran SP% **111.3**
Speed ratings: **93,91,90,89,82 80,79,**— CSF £39.62 CT £74.25 TOTE £3.30: £1.30, £4.10, £1.10; EX 56.50.

Owner J D Gordon **Bred** Foreneish Racing **Trained** West Witton, N Yorks

FOCUS

A poor handicap but sound enough form with the placed horses running to their marks. Just 12 fences were jumped instead of the normal 15.

NOTEBOOK

Swallow Magic(IRE), 7lb better off with Now Then Sid, travelled sweetly and readily outpaced the runner-up on the run-in. Whether he can build on this remains to be seen. *(op 3-1 tchd 10-3)*

York Rite(AUS), a maiden after 16 previous tries over fences, shook off the favourite but was then outspeeded by the winner up the hill. *(op 16-1)*

Now Then Sid did not jump as well this time and was in trouble early on the final circuit. Working his way upsides at the second last, from that point on he could only find the one pace. He will bounce back. *(op Evens tchd 10-11)*

Pavey Ark(IRE), pulled up on his two most recent starts, ran a whole lot better. He has slipped to a lenient mark. *(op 12-1)*

Ballistic Boy, who clearly has had his problems, was having just his second outing for this yard. *(tchd 50-1)*

Xaipete(IRE), running his 130th race, enjoyed 17 career victories and earned over £143,000. It was a sad end but at least he died in action giving his all and looking to be enjoying himself until disaster struck. *(op 6-1)*

1151 CALVERTS CARPETS H'CAP HURDLE (10 hdls) 2m 5f 110y

5:00 (5:04) (Class 4) (0-110,110) 4-Y-0+ **£3,386** (£1,042; £521; £260)

Form				RPR
/P-0	**1**		**Mocharamor (IRE)**[84] [340] 7-11-12 **110** JPMcNamara (J J Lambe, Ire) *chsd ldrs: led 3 out: clr whn hit 2 out: j.lft and blnd last: rdn out* **16/1**	114+
3P41	**2**	2 1/2	**Little Task**[7] [1100] 7-9-11 **84** oh2 PAspell(3) (J S Wainwright) *hld up in last: hdwy 7th: wnt 2nd 2 out: styd on: nvr able chal* **3/1**[2]	84
0P2P	**3**	3 1/2	**Thepubhorse**[26] [941] 5-9-10 **85** DCCostello(5) (Mrs H O Graham) *chsd ldrs: one pce fr 2 out* **12/1**[3]	81
4PP-	**4**	8	**Michaels Dream (IRE)**[17] [1411] 6-10-11 **95** KRenwick (N Wilson) *wnt prom 4th: rdn 7th: outpcd fr next* **12/1**[3]	83
F111	**5**	4	**Beaugency (NZ)**[5] [1111] 7-11-0 **101** 7ex LMcGrath(3) (R C Guest) *hld up: hdwy and prom 6th: hrd drvn 3 out: lost pl after next* **4/5**[1]	85
23/P	**6**	1 3/4	**Corries Wood (IRE)**[22] [991] 6-10-6 **90** ARoss (J J Lambe, Ire) *in tch: outpcd whn mstke 7th: kpt on fr next* **33/1**	72
00P6	**7**	17	**Conor's Pride (IRE)**[11] [1063] 8-10-4 **88** NPMulholland (B Mactaggart) *led to 3 out: wknd between last 2: 6th whn blnde last* **33/1**	53
0050	**8**	4	**Lion Guest (IRE)**[26] [941] 8-9-7 **84** oh5 TMessenger(7) (Mrs S C Bradburne) *chsd ldrs: lost pl 3 out: sn bhd* **20/1**	45

4m 56.7s (-19.00) **Going Correction** -0.975s/f (Hard) **8** Ran SP% **112.5**

Speed ratings: **95,94,92,89,88 87,81,80** CSF £62.60 CT £605.28 TOTE £17.40: £4.90, £1.20, £3.00; EX 109.40 Place 6 £8.46, Place 5 £5.50.

Owner Andrew Wishart **Bred** Miss Kelly Hazzard **Trained** Dungannon, Co. Tyrone

FOCUS

Not strong form with the winner back to his Irish form of two years ago and the runner-up finding this trip on the sharp side.

NOTEBOOK

Mocharamor(IRE), who did not go unbacked, was awkward at the last two but was never in any danger of being caught. *(op 18-1 tchd 14-1)*

Little Task, 2lb out of the handicap, was happy to sit at the back. He went in pursuit of the winner but was never going to get close enough to land a blow. This shorter trip did not play to his strengths. *(op 7-2)*

Thepubhorse, a springer in the market, had been pulled up on his previous start. Dropping back in trip, this is probably as good as he is. *(op 22-1)*

Michaels Dream(IRE), having his first outing over hurdles for over a year, had shown little in two recent outings on the level. He ran a rather moody race here. *(op 10-1)*

Beaugency(NZ) moved up on the bridle with a circuit to go but, suddenly coming under pressure three out, dropped away in tired fashion after the next. *(op 8-11 tchd 4-6)*

T/Plt: £13.00 to a £1 stake. Pool: £33,581.05. 1,877.20 winning tickets. T/Qpdt: £4.90 to a £1 stake. Pool: £2,881.80. 435.00 winning tickets. WG

1036 WORCESTER (L-H)

Friday, August 5

OFFICIAL GOING: Good to firm (good in places on chase course)

The first flight in the home straight was omitted in all hurdle races.

Wind: Fresh, behind

1152 BETFREDPOKER.COM AMATEUR RIDERS' H'CAP HURDLE (10 hdls 2 omitted) 3m

2:20 (2:20) (Class 4) (0-95,94) 4-Y-0+ **£3,516** (£1,082; £541; £270)

Form				RPR
2221	**1**		**Marathea (FR)**[9] [1075] 4-10-3 **79** MrTJO'Brien(5) (Miss Venetia Williams) *a in tch: led 2 out: hrd rdn run-in: all out* **3/1**[1]	82+
-532	**2**	hd	**Vivante (IRE)**[21] [1002] 7-9-13 **74** (p) MrDEngland(7) (A J Wilson) *a in tch: ev ch fr 2 out: pressed wnr and kpt on run-in* **9/1**[2]	80+
23-P	**3**	11	**Sundawn Lady**[45] [801] 7-10-4 **79** (b) MrGTumelty(7) (C P Morlock) *mid-div: hdwy appr 6th: swtchd rt appr 2 out: sn hung lft: kpt on one pce after* **33/1**	75+
45-0	**4**	4	**Coppermalt (USA)**[68] [565] 7-10-1 **74** LNewnes(5) (R Curtis) *in rr tl hdwy fr 7th: hrd rdn appr 2 out: one pce after* **50/1**	65
-241	**5**	1 1/4	**Good Heart (IRE)**[21] [997] 10-10-5 **78** (t) MissSSharratt(5) (R Ford) *hld up: hdwy on ins appr 2 out: styd on: nt rch ldrs* **9/1**[2]	68
60F1	**6**	3/4	**Lahinch Lad (IRE)**[23] [981] 5-11-4 **93** MrSPJones(7) (B G Powell) *in rr: rdn appr 6th: hdwy appr 2 out: fdd sonn after* **11/1**[3]	82
1155	**7**	4	**Spirit Of Tenby (IRE)**[26] [949] 8-10-10 **85** MissPMHearn(7) (W K Goldsworthy) *hld up: hdwy appr 6th: wknd bef 2 out* **16/1**	70
4354	**8**	3	**Potts Of Magic**[52] [745] 6-11-3 **85** (b) MrDHDunsdon (R Lee) *chsd ldrs tl wknd 2 out* **33/1**	67
0535	**9**	1 3/4	**Oscars Vision (IRE)**[7] [1100] 5-11-0 **82** (v) MrCJSweeney (B W Duke) *bhd tl hdwy appr 6th: wknd bef 2 out* **9/1**[2]	62
503	**10**	6	**Sandywell George**[57] [697] 10-10-12 **87** (vt[1]) MrFelixDeGiles(7) (L P Grassick) *mid-div: hdwy after 5th: hrd rdn and wknd appr 2 out* **40/1**	61
-U1P	**11**	3	**Bobsbest (IRE)**[30] [916] 9-10-12 **87** ow3 MrSGray(7) (R J Price) *bhd: hdwy appr 2 out: sn wknd* **14/1**	58
040-	**12**	2 1/2	**Marki (FR)**[139] [4463] 5-10-10 **83** MrAJBerry(5) (Jonjo O'Neill) *prom: wnt 2nd 6th tl wknd appr 2 out* **12/1**	52
3055	**13**	dist	**Robbie On Tour (IRE)**[16] [1041] 6-10-2 **77** (tp) MrCHughes(7) (M C Pipe) *mistake 1st: a bhd: t.o* **25/1**	—
P06-	**14**	26	**Miss Lewis**[150] [4240] 7-10-12 **87** (t) MrDGreenway(7) (C J Down) *led to 2nd: led again 4th tl hdd appr 2 out: wknd rapidly* **66/1**	—
P000	**P**		**Farceur (FR)**[4] [1121] 6-10-10 **85** (p) MrRQuinn(7) (M C Pipe) *a bhd: t.o whn p.u after 5th* **50/1**	—
02/F	**P**		**Sculptor**[71] [515] 6-11-3 **90** MrsLucyRowsell(5) (K R Pearce) *in tch tl wknd after 6th: p.u bef 8th* **33/1**	—
PPP4	**P**		**Phase Eight Girl**[16] [1040] 9-10-3 **76** EWhillans(5) (J Hetherton) *a bhd: rdn appr 6th: t.o whn p.u bef 2 out* **14/1**	—
6304	**P**		**Ungaretti (GER)**[23] [974] 8-11-12 **94** MissEJJones (Ian Williams) *led 2nd to 4th: rdn and wknd 6th: t.o whn p.u bef 2 out* **33/1**	—
2F52	**U**		**End Of An Error**[22] [988] 6-10-12 **87** MrsEJSmith(7) (A W Carroll) *wl bhd tl hdwy and clsng on ldrs whn blnd and uns rdr 2 out* **12/1**	87+
-223	**P**		**No Further Comment (IRE)**[21] [998] 5-11-8 **90** (p) MrNWilliams (Mrs Jeremy Young) *trckd ldrs tl wknd after 7th: t.o whn p.u bef 2 out* **14/1**	—

5m 40.2s (-9.00) **Going Correction** -0.225s/f (Good)

WFA 4 from 5yo+ 17lb **20** Ran SP% **128.1**

Speed ratings: **106,105,102,100,100 100,98,97,97,95 94,93,—,—,— —,—,—,—,—** CSF £27.49 CT £792.54 TOTE £3.90: £1.70, £2.20, £5.40, £10.80; EX 29.90.

Owner Sir Clement Freud **Bred** J Biraben And Robert Labeyrie **Trained** Kings Caple, H'fords

■ Stewards' Enquiry : Mr C Hughes caution: used whip when out of contention

FOCUS

A moderate race in which the first two came clear in the latter stages. The winner has been rated to the level of her recent win.

NOTEBOOK

Marathea(FR) was officially 6lb well in, having escaped a penalty for her win in a conditionals' race at Newton Abbot. She had no trouble with the different underfoot conditions or five-furlong longer trip, and showed commendable gameness to edge out the runner-up after a good tussle. *(op 4-1)*

Vivante(IRE) was locked together with the eventual winner from the second last and only gave best in the last few strides. The pair pulled well clear of the rest and her luck should change soon. *(op 8-1)*

Sundawn Lady, still to win a race, ran respectably following a break but she hung left up the home straight and was left behind by the first two in the final quarter-mile. *(tchd 40-1)*

Coppermalt(USA), beaten in a selling chase when last seen at the end of May, is still a maiden but ran an improved race on this step up in trip.

Good Heart(IRE), successful over fences last time, was able to race off an 8lb lower mark here. He was never in a challenging position but was staying on steadily at the end.

Lahinch Lad(IRE), winner of a chase at this course last time, could never land a blow under his inexperienced rider but was not disgraced. There should be a bit more improvement in him back over fences. *(op 12-1)*

Marki(FR) showed little in three runs in this country for Thierry Doumen last season. Stepped up in trip for this handicap debut, he was travelling well in second place turning into the home straight but soon came under pressure and dropped away. The drop back to two and a half miles could pay dividends and he looks one to keep an eye on. *(op 10-1)*

End Of An Error was running her usual sort of race, and was staying on from the rear, when she blundered away her rider at the penultimate flight. *(op 11-1)*

1153 CANNONS HEALTH CLUB CLAIMING HURDLE (8 hdls 2 omitted) 2m 4f

2:50 (2:50) (Class 4) 4-Y-0+ **£3,045** (£870; £435)

Form				RPR
-115	**1**		**Silence Reigns**[51] [761] 11-11-0 (bt) LHeard(10) (P F Nicholls) *hld up in mid-div and gng wl: hdwy appr 6th: shkn up to ld run-in: cleverly* **10/3**[2]	116+
300P	**2**	3/4	**Mantras (FR)**[4] [1121] 6-10-8 109 MrRQuinn(7) (M C Pipe) *hld up in mid-div: outpcd 6th: styd on to lead last: rdn and hdd run-in* **16/1**	101
4110	**3**	3 1/2	**Desert Spa (USA)**[19] [1027] 10-10-2 97 MrTJO'Brien(7) (G E Jones) *a.p: wnt 2nd appr 2 out: ev ch tl wknd run-in* **12/1**	92
010P	**4**	10	**Blue Leader (IRE)**[19] [1022] 6-10-12 101 (tp) JEMoore (W K Goldsworthy) *prom: rdn to chse ldrs 2 out: wknd bef last* **33/1**	85
P206	**5**	7	**Shamsan (IRE)**[23] [980] 8-11-1 90 (tp) RJohnson (J Joseph) *mid-div: hdwy 5th: one pce fr 2 out* **33/1**	81
36F2	**6**	1 3/4	**Golfagent**[15] [1045] 7-11-3 103 (t) RSpate(7) (Mrs K Waldron) *mid-div: rdn 5th: wknd after 3 out* **16/1**	88
000/	**7**	1	**Whose Line Is It**[549] [3654] 7-11-1 PJBrennan (N J Hawke) *in tch tl rdn and wknd appr 2 out* **40/1**	78
4265	**8**	1	**Caper**[19] [1028] 5-10-5 85 (p) AHawkins(10) (R Hollinshead) *mid-div: hdwy to chse ldrs 5th: wknd 2 out* **33/1**	77
1513	**9**	11	**Burning Truth (USA)**[23] [980] 11-11-4 110 DRDennis (M Sheppard) *led tl hdd appr 2 out: sn wknd* **3/1**[1]	69
-125	**10**	15	**Oulton Broad**[59] [672] 9-10-13 104 (p) JDiment(5) (F Jordan) *mstke 1st: a bhd* **20/1**	54
250-	**11**	dist	**Russian Court**[309] [1546] 9-11-0 107 MrRHodges(7) (S E H Sherwood) *a bhd: t.o* **25/1**	—
200-	**12**	shd	**Miss Skippy**[315] [1498] 6-10-11 97 AThornton (A G Newcombe) *mid-div tl wknd 6th: t.o* **28/1**	—
3-00	**13**	1 3/4	**Better Moment (IRE)**[4] [1121] 8-10-12 98 (v) RGreene (M C Pipe) *trckd ldrs: tl rdn and lost pl 4th: t.o* **40/1**	—
-063	**14**	8	**Bolshoi Ballet**[21] [1001] 7-11-13 102 (b) PMoloney (J Mackie) *prom tl lost pl appr 4th: t.o* **25/1**	—
0130	**P**		**Greencard Golf**[21] [1000] 4-10-10 94 (v[1]) AO'Keeffe (Jennie Candlish) *a bhd: t.o whn p.u bef 2 out* **66/1**	—
0-PP	**P**		**Harbour Bound (IRE)**[30] [914] 6-10-9 104 (tp) ChristianWilliams (Evan Williams) *bhd: t.o 4th: p.u bef 2 out* **25/1**	—
-224	**P**		**High Drama**[23] [981] 8-11-7 109 APMcCoy (P Bowen) *mid-div: rdn 5th: snn bhd: p.u and dismntd bef 2 out* **5/1**[3]	—
0-5	**F**		**Regulated (IRE)**[8] [1085] 4-10-0 (p) JAJenkins(7) (H J Manners) *trckd ldrs: led appr 2 out: rdn and hdd whn fell last* **66/1**	85
60/	**P**		**Le Cavalier (USA)**[1352] [2274] 8-11-5 TGreenway(5) (Mrs L Williamson) *prom tl wknd after 3rd: t.o whn p.u bef 5th* **100/1**	—
5P60	**P**		**Rose Of York (IRE)**[11] [1063] 5-10-5 73 (t) RThornton (Mrs A M Thorpe) *sn trckd ldr: rdn and wknd 6th: bhd whn mstke 2 out: p.u bef last* **50/1**	—

4m 40.47s (-7.53) **Going Correction** -0.225s/f (Good)

WFA 4 from 5yo+ 16lb **20** Ran SP% **123.6**

Speed ratings: **106,105,104,100,97 96,96,96,91,85 —,—,—,— —,—,—,—,—** CSF £45.43 TOTE £4.20: £2.30, £4.00, £3.80; EX 72.40. The winner was claimed by Nick Shutts for £10,000. Golfagent was claimed by Mrs P. Tollit for £10,000. Regulated was claimed by Paul Blockley for £5,000.

Owner Mrs M Findlay **Bred** Cheveley Park Stud Ltd **Trained** Ditcheat, Somerset

FOCUS

A fair claimer in which the winner was value for further with the placed horses setting the level.

NOTEBOOK
Silence Reigns, best known as a hunter chaser these days, was appearing over hurdles for only the second time in more than five years. After travelling strongly, he was slightly outpaced when coming off the bit before the final flight and was only third over the obstacle, but he soon asserted on the run-in. He now joins Karen Waldron, who ironically lost two of her runners on the card to claims. *(op 3-1 tchd 5-2)*
Mantras(FR) responded to pressure to show ahead at the final flight, but he idled markedly in front and the favourite soon cut him down. He does have his quirks but this was a more encouraging effort. *(op 14-1)*
Desert Spa(USA), successful twice in selling company in June, bounced back to form after a disappointing effort last time. He stayed this longer trip well enough. *(op 14-1)*
Blue Leader(IRE), well beaten in a chase last time, ran a better race back over hurdles and with cheekpieces replacing the blinkers, although he never threatened to get his head in front. *(op 25-1)*
Shamsan(IRE) kept plugging away without being able to get into the action. *(op 25-1)*
Golfagent was claimed after the race and a return to point-to-pointing looks likely in the spring. *(op 14-1)*
Burning Truth(USA) had a decent chance at the weights but, after making the running as usual, he could not counter when headed on the approach to the home straight. *(op 4-1)*
Rose Of York(IRE) *(op 33-1)*
Regulated(IRE) is exposed as a poor performer on the Flat but this was only his third run over hurdles. Equipped with cheekpieces for the first time, he ran a good race and would probably have finished fourth had he not fallen at the last. He now joins Paul Blockley. *(op 33-1)*

1154 PETER "MR PERFECT" BURNS 70TH BIRTHDAY NOVICES' HURDLE (8 hdls 2 omitted) 2m 4f
3:20 (3:21) (Class 4) 4-Y-0+ £3,332 (£952; £476)

Form					RPR
344	1		**Aspra (FR)**[16] [1037] 5-10-5 89 ... MBradburne (C J Down) *hld up in tch: wnt 2nd 6th: rdn to ld run-in* **7/2**[3]		90
1334	2	1 ½	**Kilindini**[19] [1020] 4-11-3 114 ... BJCrowley (Miss E C Lavelle) *led tl after 1st: led again after 6th: rdn: hung lft and hdd run-in* **7/4**[2]		101+
-104	3	11	**Meneur De Jeu (FR)**[15] [1047] 5-11-5 115 ...(v) APMcCoy (M C Pipe) *hld up in tch: pushed along fr 5th: nvr nr to chal after* **13/8**[1]		91
/0-0	4	6	**Takeachanceonhim**[62] [629] 7-10-12 ...(t) BHitchcott (Mrs Barbara Waring) *t.k.h: in rr: tk clsr order 3rd: bhd fr 5th* **33/1**		78
-034	5	6	**Loriko D'Airy (FR)**[31] [901] 6-10-5 100 ... MissCDyson(7) (Miss C Dyson) *t.k.h: frequently j.rt: led after 1st: hdd after 6th: wknd appr 2 out* **20/1**		72
045	6	14	**Pumpkin Pickle**[16] [1042] 4-10-3 ... RGreene (P R Rodford) *trckd ldrs: mstke 1st: bhd fr 5th* **25/1**		49
/00-	7	14	**Across The Water**[248] [2550] 11-10-0 64 ... TGreenway(5) (G H Jones) *a in rr* **100/1**		37
0-40	P		**Legal Spy**[30] [912] 6-10-8 ow1 ... JDiment(5) (F Jordan) *t.k.h: p.u lame after 3rd: dismntd* **100/1**		—

4m 45.1s (-2.90) **Going Correction** -0.225s/f (Good)
WFA 4 from 5yo+ 16lb **8** Ran SP% **110.2**
Speed ratings: **96,95,91,88,86 80,75,—** CSF £9.47 TOTE £5.60: £1.40, £1.10, £1.40; EX 11.70.

Owner P D Holland & C Hackett **Bred** Paul Hilger **Trained** Mutterton, Devon

FOCUS
An ordinary event and the form does not look strong and has been rated negatively.

NOTEBOOK
Aspra(FR) was well suited by the step up to this trip. Going better than the runner-up from the turn in, she had a bit to do after an awkward jump at the final flight but rallied to assert on the run-in.. *(op 10-3)*
Kilindini was a length or so to the good landing over the last, but he hung on the flat and could not contain the mare who in truth had looked to have his measure from the home turn. He continues to run with credit but may remain vulnerable under his penalty. *(op 6-4)*
Meneur De Jeu(FR), reverting to the tactics which brought him success at Newton Abbot, was being chased along from halfway and never looked happy. He should be left alone at present. *(op 2-1 tchd 9-4)*
Takeachanceonhim showed a bit more than on his hurdles debut in June but all evidence points to him being a very modest performer. *(op 40-1)*
Loriko D'Airy(FR) has ability, but was again too keen and he faded after being collared on the home turn. He probably needs easier ground.

1155 BOB LOVE "KING OF THE DIRT" MEMORIAL BEGINNERS' CHASE (15 fncs) 2m 4f 110y
3:50 (3:51) (Class 4) 5-Y-0+ £4,104 (£1,263; £631; £315)

Form				RPR
2-P2	1		**Unleash (USA)**[25] [962] 6-10-12 ... RJohnson (P J Hobbs) *hld up in rr: hdwy whn mstke 4 out: sn rdn and 3rd last: styd on strly to ld run-in* **5/2**[2]	124+
/2P-	2	1 ¾	**Bold Bishop (IRE)**[146] [4332] 8-10-12 ... APMcCoy (Jonjo O'Neill) *a in tch: wnt 2nd 11th: led appr 4 out: j.rt next: all out and hdd run-in* **10/3**[3]	122+
0122	3	½	**Whispered Secret (GER)**[19] [1019] 6-10-12 ... RThornton (M C Pipe) *hld up: hdwy after 11th: rdn 3 out: ev ch last: one pce whn swtchd lft run-in* **2/1**[1]	120
6-B2	4	12	**The Glen**[33] [893] 7-10-12 ... TDoyle (R Lee) *chsd ldrs: mstke 3rd and again whn making hdwy 9th: pressed ldrs 3 out: wknd appr last* **9/1**	110+
44-P	5	3	**Karakum**[23] [979] 6-10-12 84 ... SCurran (A J Chamberlain) *t.k.h and often j.rt: clr 6th: wknd and hdd appr 4 out: mstke next* **100/1**	106+
-223	6	dist	**Izzykeen**[20] [1016] 6-10-12 ... DElsworth (Mrs S J Smith) *disp ld early: t.k.h: wknd 11th: t.o whn blnd 4 out* **9/1**	—
1-03	P		**Rash Moment (FR)**[15] [1047] 6-10-5 ... RSpate(7) (Mrs K Waldron) *mid-div: wknd 9th: t.o whn p.u after 11th* **33/1**	—
50/0	P		**Tallison**[30] [911] 7-10-9 ... RYoung(3) (N R Mitchell) *a bhd: lost tch 7th: t.o whn p.u after 11th* **100/1**	—
-PPP	P		**Gordy's Joy**[9] [1076] 5-9-12 65 ... EDehdashti(7) (G A Ham) *prom: j.rt 5th: wkng whn mstke 7th: p.u bef 11th* **150/1**	—

5m 1.50s (-6.00) **Going Correction** -0.225s/f (Good) **9** Ran SP% **110.6**
Speed ratings: **102,101,101,96,95 —,—,—,—** CSF £10.81 TOTE £3.40: £1.60, £1.40, £1.20; EX 12.00.

Owner M G St Quinton **Bred** Cheveley Park Stud **Trained** Withycombe, Somerset

FOCUS
Not a bad race but the winner and second were both some way below their hurdling form. The proximity of the fifth is a concern.

NOTEBOOK
Unleash(USA) looked an unlikely winner for much of the way, but he eventually began to motor between the last two fences and scored well in the end. Now he has got off the mark over the larger obstacles he could improve, especially when given the chance to tackle three miles. *(op 10-3)*
Bold Bishop(IRE), pulled up in the Imperial Cup when last in action in March, had been runner-up on his only previous run over fences. Jumping soundly, he moved to the front early in the home straight and looked set to score until edging right and conceding defeat on the run-in. He should not be long in going one better, especially on better ground. *(op 2-1 tchd 7-2)*
Whispered Secret(GER), who made his chasing debut over half a mile shorter, ran a solid race especially as he was rated some way inferior to the first two over hurdles. His turn will come. *(op 5-2 tchd 7-4)*
The Glen did not jump as well as the placed horses but only faded out of contention between the last two fences. *(op 8-1 tchd 10-1)*
Karakum, a plater over hurdles who did not get far on his recent chasing debut, was certainly not disgraced but lack of stamina is going to remain a problem. *(op 66-1)*

1156 RACING BY THE RIVER (S) H'CAP HURDLE (7 hdls 1 omitted) 2m
4:20 (4:23) (Class 5) (0-85,85) 4-Y-0+ £3,094 (£884; £442)

Form				RPR
50-P	1		**Faddad (USA)**[9] [1075] 9-11-11 84 ...(t) APMcCoy (P Bowen) *a.p: led after 2nd to next: outpcd after 5th: styd on to ld last: drvn out* **5/1**[2]	93
3500	2	1 ¼	**Think Quick (IRE)**[22] [987] 5-10-10 79 ... AHawkins(10) (R Hollinshead) *hld up: hdwy appr 2 out: rdn and styd on to go 2nd run-in* **12/1**	87
-200	3	4	**Virtus**[44] [813] 5-11-6 79 ...(b[1]) RJohnson (P J Hobbs) *led 3rd tl rdn and hdd last: no ex and lost 2nd run-in* **11/2**[3]	83
1300	4	3 ½	**Somewin (IRE)**[40] [839] 5-10-4 70 ...(p) RSpate(7) (Mrs K Waldron) *hld up in rr: hdwy appr 5th: wnt 2nd appr 2 out tl no ex and mstke last* **20/1**	71
2004	5	2 ½	**Jack Durrance (IRE)**[23] [973] 5-10-6 72 ... EDehdashti(7) (G A Ham) *hld up: hdwy appr 2 out: one pce bef last: edgd lft run-in* **9/2**[1]	70
0410	6	3 ½	**Ashgan (IRE)**[16] [1040] 12-11-1 77 ... TJPhelan(3) (Dr P Pritchard) *led tl after 2nd: sn lost pl but styd in tch: no imp fr 2 out* **8/1**	72
04-5	7	¾	**Shalati Princess**[9] [1077] 4-11-6 80 ... SCurran (J C Fox) *mid-div: rdn and hdwy appr 2 out: wknd bef last* **16/1**	73
P-00	8	1 ½	**Hidden Smile (USA)**[42] [822] 8-11-0 73 ...(t) LAspell (F Jordan) *t.k.h: hdwy 3rd: wknd fr 2 out* **16/1**	65
10P	9	3 ½	**River Amora (IRE)**[23] [978] 10-10-9 68 ...(p) JEMoore (J J Best) *in tch tl wknd appr 2 out* **16/1**	57
0560	10	3	**Prince Minata (IRE)**[15] [1046] 10-10-13 75 ... RHobson(3) (M Appleby) *racd wd in tch: rdn after 4th: wknd appr 2 out* **33/1**	61
	11	13	**Kevins View (IRE)**[13] [236] 9-11-4 77 ... PMoloney (A W Carroll) *chsd ldrs tl lost pl 3rd: nvr on terms after* **20/1**	50
0400	12	1	**Macgyver (NZ)**[21] [999] 9-11-5 85 ... CaptLHorner(7) (D L Williams) *hld up in tch: wknd 4th* **20/1**	57
-40F	13	8	**Blue Yonder**[9] [1075] 5-11-2 75 ...(p) ChristianWilliams (Evan Williams) *a towards rr* **14/1**	39
50/0	14	7	**La Maestra (FR)**[5] [1107] 7-11-3 81 ...(b) LStephens(5) (Miss L Day) *prom tl wknd appr 5th* **100/1**	38
0PP-	15	11	**Coctail Lady (IRE)**[383] [1004] 5-11-9 82 ...(t) NFehily (B W Duke) *a bhd* **33/1**	28
050-	16	1 ¾	**Highlight Girl**[18] [1992] 4-11-2 76 ... PJBrennan (A W Carroll) *chsd ldrs: mstke 2nd: wknd next* **25/1**	19
6/6	17	hd	**The Cute Won (USA)**[19] [1021] 7-11-10 83 ...(bt) RThornton (W K Goldsworthy) *mid-div: bhd fr 4th* **14/1**	27
00F0	18	dist	**Weet An Haul**[15] [1046] 4-11-1 75 ... RGreene (T Wall) *a bhd: t.o* **40/1**	—
6000	P		**Luristan (IRE)**[23] [978] 5-10-10 69 ... ATinkler (S T Lewis) *sn t.o: p.u after 2nd* **50/1**	—

3m 44.0s (-4.40) **Going Correction** -0.225s/f (Good)
WFA 4 from 5yo+ 15lb **19** Ran SP% **129.4**
Speed ratings: **102,101,99,97,96 94,94,93,91,90 83,83,79,75,70 69,69,—,—** CSF £58.97 CT £358.00 TOTE £4.90: £2.20, £3.20, £2.00, £4.30; EX 70.80.The winner was bought by Mrs A. M. Thorpe for 7,000gns. Somewin was claimed by Mr M. A. Lloyd for £6,000.
Owner Don Jones **Bred** Minstrel Gbr **Trained** Little Newcastle, Pembrokes

FOCUS
A run-of-the-mill seller, run in a fair time and the form looks sound with the placed horses to their best.

NOTEBOOK
Faddad(USA), fitter for his recent return to action, rallied to challenge at the final flight and was well on top on the run-in. This is his ground. *(tchd 4-1)*
Think Quick(IRE) looked set for a midfield finish until suddenly picking up from the second last and flying home. She gave a swish of the tail on the run-in and is obviously not straightforward. *(op 14-1)*
Virtus showed more in the first-time blinkers on this drop into the bottom grade, but he was inclined to hang in the straight and was cut down at the final flight. *(op 13-2)*
Somewin(IRE) ran a decent race over a trip some way short of her best. She changed hands after the race.
Jack Durrance(IRE) ran his race with no apparent excuses. *(op 5-1 tchd 6-1)*
Ashgan(IRE) was 4lb higher than when a shock winner over half a mile further here last month. *(op 9-1 tchd 11-1)*
Kevins View(IRE) *Official explanation: jockey said gelding bled from the nose (op 16-1)*
Luristan(IRE) *Official explanation: jockey said gelding was never travelling*

1157 WEATHERBYS INSURANCE H'CAP CHASE (18 fncs) 2m 7f 110y
4:50 (4:54) (Class 3) (0-125,123) 5-Y-0+ £6,825 (£2,100; £1,050; £525)

Form				RPR
1-12	1		**Ross Comm**[23] [975] 9-10-6 103 ... DElsworth (Mrs S J Smith) *a.p: wnt 2nd 1/2-way: led 13th: j.rt 2 out and again whn clr last* **10/3**[2]	120+
/66-	2	5	**Master Tern (USA)**[279] [1906] 10-10-12 109 ... APMcCoy (Jonjo O'Neill) *hld up in mid-div: hdwy to trck ldrs 13th: wnt 2nd 3 out: rdn and no imp fr next* **12/1**	118
-345	3	6	**Swansea Bay**[16] [1039] 9-11-12 123 ... LAspell (P Bowen) *mid-div: hdwy 10th: mstke 14th: wknd 4 out: lft poor 3rd last* **3/1**[1]	126
1400	4	1	**Idealko (FR)**[26] [946] 9-10-1 98 ... RGreene (Dr P Pritchard) *bhd and mstkes: styd on one pce fr 4 out: nvr on terms* **25/1**	100
12-	5	2 ½	**Native Daisy (IRE)**[107] [4931] 10-10-4 101 ... RThornton (C J Down) *trckd ldr to 1/2-way: sn rdn: wknd 14th* **9/2**[3]	101
0-P0	6	dist	**Royal Tir (FR)**[20] [1013] 9-11-5 116 ...(bt) RJohnson (P J Hobbs) *in tch tl rdn and wknd 14th: t.o* **22/1**	—
P/02	7	22	**Waterberg (IRE)**[61] [653] 10-10-9 106 ... MBradburne (H D Daly) *mstkes and in rr: lost tch 14th: t.o* **11/2**	—
F06-	8	8	**Smile Pleeze (IRE)**[114] [4821] 13-11-6 117 ...(p) DRDennis (M Sheppard) *prom tl blnd 7th: lost tch 11th: sn t.o* **16/1**	—

32P4 **F** **Thieves'Glen**[30] 912 7-10-13 **110** .... TScudamore —
(H Morrison) *led tl blnd and hdd 13th: wkng and 3rd whn fell last* **10/1**

5m 46.9s (-8.00) **Going Correction** -0.225s/f (Good) **9** Ran SP% **112.5**
Speed ratings: **104,102,100,100,99** —,—,—,— CSF £39.97 CT £130.08 TOTE £3.50: £1.60, £2.90, £1.40; EX 43.40.

Owner Kevin G Treanor **Bred** A Dawson **Trained** High Eldwick, W Yorks

FOCUS
A fair handicap and not an easy race to assess, but the winner can probably rate higher.

NOTEBOOK
Ross Comm, unsuited by the sticky ground when beaten off this mark at Uttoxeter last time, likes it here and gained his third course win in comfortable fashion. *(op 5-2)*

Master Tern(USA), well beaten in two starts in the autumn when his yard was under a cloud, ran a better race on this return to action but was no match for the winner. He is certainly well handicapped at present, having gained his last victory in 2003 off a 20lb higher mark. *(op 14-1)*

Swansea Bay, reverting to fences, is not the force of old and was unable to give the weight away. He has not won a chase since taking the Edward Hanmer at Haydock in November 2003 off a mark of 146. *(op 4-1 tchd 9-2)*

Idealko(FR), having his third run for this yard, was never in the hunt but did seem to stay this longer trip. *(op 20-1)*

Native Daisy(IRE), twice taken out due to fast ground since her last run in April, made a satisfactory return to the track without proving that she stays this far. *(op 4-1)*

Thieves'Glen, back over fences, held a clear lead for a time, but this longer trip eventually told and he was beaten in third when coming down at the last. *(op 12-1 tchd 14-1)*

1158 BETFREDCASINO.COM MAIDEN HURDLE (7 hdls 1 omitted) 2m
5:20 (5:24) (Class 4) 4-Y-0+ **£3,555** (£1,094; £547; £273)

Form RPR

03 **1** **Doris Souter (IRE)**[19] 1021 5-10-9 .... WMarston 81
(D J Wintle) *nvr worse than 3rd: wnt 2nd 5 out: led appr 2 out: drvn out run-in* **12/1**

6-03 **2** ¾ **Slalom (IRE)**[16] 1040 5-10-11 87........ WKennedy(5) 88
(D Burchell) *bhd: styd on appr 2 out and kpt on to go 2nd run-in: nvr nrr* **9/4**[1]

0- **3** 1½ **Lucky Arthur (IRE)**[53] 4029 4-10-5 .... ONelmes(3) 78
(J G M O'Shea) *hld up: hdwy appr 2 out: styd on one pce* **80/1**

0-64 **4** 5 **Giust In Temp (IRE)**[19] 1021 6-10-9 84........ MrTJO'Brien(7) 81
(Mrs K M Sanderson) *hld up: hdwy 5th: chal 2 out to last: hung lft and wknd run-in* **33/1**

4- **5** 1¾ **Bronco Charlie (IRE)**[314] 1510 7-11-2 .... APMcCoy 79
(Jonjo O'Neill) *in chsng gp: hdwy to go 2nd briefly appr 2 out: rdn and wknd bef last* **5/2**[2]

-P65 **6** 1¼ **Gentle Warning**[58] 683 5-10-6 67........ RYoung(3) 71
(M Appleby) *hld up: mstke 5th: hdwy appr 2 out: nvr nr to chal* **50/1**

0-02 **7** 6 **Le Gris (GER)**[9] 1077 6-11-2 86........ AThornton 72
(P R Rodford) *hld up: hdwy 4th: wkng whn mstke last* **12/1**

235- **8** 1½ **Holly Walk**[171] 3455 4-10-8 85........(p) ATinkler 63
(A G Juckes) *hld up: hdwy 2 out: styd on but nvr on terms* **25/1**

6 **9** 10 **Port Sodrick**[9] 1077 4-10-8 .... KBurke(7) 60
(R H Alner) *mstke 1st: mid-div: rdn 3rd: nvr on terms* **50/1**

3-30 **10** 2½ **Classic Croco (GER)**[45] 806 4-11-1 99........ SThomas 57
(Mrs Jeremy Young) *in rr: hdwy 5th: rdn and wknd appr 2 out* **11/2**[3]

0- **11** 6 **Sean Nos (IRE)**[205] 3319 4-11-1 .... JamesDavies 51
(W K Goldsworthy) *led: sn clr: hdd & wknd rapidly appr 2 out* **33/1**

12 15 **Bally Hall (IRE)**[26] 5-11-2 .... JEMoore 37
(J M Bradley) *t.k.h: in chsng gp: wkng whn mstke 2 out* **40/1**

6P **13** 7 **Tog Go Boge (IRE)**[9] 1077 7-11-2 .... RJohnson 30
(R T Phillips) *a bhd* **50/1**

0/ **F** **Abbey Hill**[61] 3345 8-10-9 .... RGreene —
(W S Kittow) *fell 1st* **100/1**

P **P** **Bold Trump**[9] 1077 4-10-12 ....(t) DCrosse(3) —
(M Salaman) *a bhd: t.o whn p.u bef 2 out* **100/1**

2233 **U** **Mr Jawbreaker (IRE)**[16] 1042 6-11-2 .... RThornton —
(J T Stimpson) *reluctant to s: hmpd and uns rdr 1st* **8/1**

00 **U** **April Rose**[30] 917 5-10-2 ....(t) JPemberton(7) —
(K G Wingrove) *bhd whn j.lft: stmbld on landing and uns rdr 2nd* **100/1**

U66- **P** **Uncle Batty**[334] 1371 5-10-11 .... TGreenway(5) —
(Mrs L Williamson) *chsd ldr tl wknd rapidly bef 5th: p.u and dismntd sn after* **100/1**

3m 46.8s (-1.60) **Going Correction** -0.225s/f (Good)
WFA 4 from 5yo+ 15lb **18** Ran SP% **124.5**
Speed ratings: **95,94,93,91,90 89,86,86,81,79 76,69,65,**—,— —,—,— CSF £38.55 TOTE £15.50: £3.50, £1.40, £18.10; EX 54.40 Place 6 £33.03, Place 5 £11.25.

Owner A F Merritt **Bred** R C Snaith **Trained** Naunton, Gloucs

■ Stewards' Enquiry : W Marston caution: used whip with excessive frequency

FOCUS
A very weak event which has been rated through the fourth.

NOTEBOOK
Doris Souter(IRE) got off the mark on her third run over hurdles, but in truth this was a poor event. She is likely to struggle under a penalty. *(tchd 14-1)*

Slalom(IRE), third over half a mile further here last month, found this too sharp but was staying on at the end. *(op 4-1)*

Lucky Arthur(IRE), strangely named for a filly, was well beaten on her one previous try over hurdles back in February and has been beaten in banded company on the Flat since. Staying on from the second last, she probably needs a greater test of stamina. *(op 66-1)*

Giust In Temp(IRE), behind today's winner last time, had every chance from the second last but threw it away by hanging on the run-in.

Bronco Charlie(IRE), having his first run since September, was a little disappointing on this hurdling debut. He was close enough on the home turn but his challenge petered out between the last two obstacles. *(op 6-4)*

Gentle Warning again looked in need of a longer trip.

Uncle Batty *Official explanation: jockey said gelding lost its action*

T/Plt: £26.10 to a £1 stake. Pool: £38,842.45. 1,082.95 winning tickets. T/Qpdt: £4.50 to a £1 stake. Pool: £2,325.70. 377.50 winning tickets. JS

1159 - 1175a (Foreign Racing) - See Raceform Interactive

[997] SOUTHWELL (L-H)
Monday, August 8

OFFICIAL GOING: Good to firm
Wind: Light, behind Weather: Fine and sunny

1176 ECA AND EDMUNDSON ELECTRICAL NOVICES' H'CAP CHASE (12 fncs 1 omitted) 2m 1f
2:15 (2:18) (Class 4) (0-100,93) 5-Y-0+ **£4,163** (£1,281; £640; £320)

Form RPR

0351 **1** **Pure Brief (IRE)**[10] 1098 8-11-2 **83**........(p) PMoloney 93
(J Mackie) *a.p: led 2 out: drvn out* **11/2**[3]

-045 **2** *nk* **Jim Lad**[22] 1019 5-10-9 **79**........(p) RYoung(3) 89
(J W Mullins) *a.p: ev ch fr 2 out: styd on* **14/1**

3134 **3** *8* **Nazimabad (IRE)**[7] 1124 6-11-7 **88**........(t) ChristianWilliams 90
(Evan Williams) *led: clr 4th: hdd appr 3 out: wknd bef last* **5/1**[2]

5003 **4** *shd* **Optimism (FR)**[26] 979 7-10-11 **78**........ AThornton 80
(R H Alner) *chsd ldrs tl wknd appr 2 out* **12/1**

06-F **5** *3* **Lascar De Ferbet (FR)**[100] 126 6-11-9 **90**........ JMMaguire 92+
(R Ford) *chsd ldr: led appr 3 out: hdd whn hit next: sn wknd* **8/1**

/000 **6** *6* **Known Maneuver (USA)**[8] 1107 7-9-13 **71**........ TGreenway(5) 64
(M C Chapman) *bhd tl styd on fr 2 out: nvr nrr* **100/1**

4045 **7** *3½* **Barneys Reflection**[60] 692 5-11-2 **83**........(v) MBradburne 73
(A Crook) *mid-div: wknd 9th* **20/1**

00U0 **8** *3½* **Proper Poser (IRE)**[23] 1015 9-9-7 **67** oh14........ CMStudd(7) 53
(M C Chapman) *hld up: a in rr* **100/1**

00 **9** *dist* **Dan De Lion**[8] 1107 6-10-6 **76**........(b) LMcGrath(3) —
(R C Guest) *hld up: hdwy 6th: wknd 9th* **25/1**

0-2 **B** **Who Dares (IRE)**[10] 1098 7-11-11 **92**........(b[1]) APMcCoy —
(Jonjo O'Neill) *hld up: b.d 3rd* **9/2**[1]

3345 **F** **Prize Ring**[14] 1062 6-11-12 **93**........(p) FKeniry —
(G M Moore) *prom tl fell 3rd: dead* **8/1**

4633 **F** **Prince Adjal (IRE)**[45] 822 5-11-2 **83**........ HOliver —
(R C Guest) *hld up: hdwy whn fell 8th* **9/2**[1]

6/00 **P** **Red September**[24] 1000 8-9-9 **69**........(p) CaptLHorner(7) —
(D L Williams) *a bhd: t.o whn p.u bef last* **50/1**

4m 4.50s (-7.10) **Going Correction** -0.40s/f (Good) course record **13** Ran SP% **117.5**
Speed ratings: **100,99,96,96,94 91,90,88,**—,— —,—,— CSF £72.26 CT £411.06 TOTE £6.20: £2.20, £6.70, £1.50; EX 100.80.

Owner Mrs V D Gandola-Gray **Bred** John B O'Connor **Trained** Church Broughton, Derbys

FOCUS
A poor contest but fair form for the grade. The third-last flight was bypassed.

NOTEBOOK
Pure Brief(IRE), off the mark over fences from a 6lb lower mark at Bangor most recently, was to the fore throughout and battled on gamely under a good ride from Moloney. Evidently on the up, he may well be able to complete the hat trick. *(op 5-1)*

Jim Lad, sporting the first-time cheekpieces, made the winner pull out all the stops and, although just denied, connections can take heart from the fact he beat the remainder cosily. *(op 16-1)*

Nazimabad(IRE) had every chance but struggled off this 14lb higher mark than when last successful. He needs some help from the Handicapper. *(op 9-2 tchd 4-1)*

Optimism(FR) just failed to get the better of Nazimabad for third, but this was a reasonable effort and he is in the right hands to win races. *(op 11-1)*

Lascar De Ferbet(FR) failed to last home having taken it up before three out and in the end was disappointing. *(tchd 17-2, 9-1 in places)*

Prince Adjal(IRE) fell too early to say how he would have fared. *(op 7-2 tchd 10-3)*

Who Dares(IRE) was in the wrong place at the wrong time and was unable to avoid being brought down after Prize Ring fell. *(op 7-2 tchd 10-3)*

1177 LADBROKES.COM NOVICES' CHASE (19 fncs) 3m 2f
2:45 (2:48) (Class 3) 5-Y-0+ **£5,447** (£1,676; £838; £419)

Form RPR

F3 **1** **Bushido (IRE)**[36] 893 6-11-0 .... DElsworth 114+
(Mrs S J Smith) *chsd ldrs: led 7th to 11th: led next: nt fluent 2 out: drvn out* **11/4**[3]

PU32 **2** *1¼* **Windy Spirit (IRE)**[12] 1078 10-11-0 99........ ChristianWilliams 108
(Evan Williams) *hld up: hdwy 12th: rdn to chse wnr last: styd on* **8/1**

12/P **3** *5* **Phar From Frosty (IRE)**[82] 413 8-11-0 .... APMcCoy 104+
(C R Egerton) *a.p: mstke 13th: rdn appr 3 out: styd on same pce fr next* **9/4**[2]

F5P1 **4** *30* **It's Definite (IRE)**[19] 1038 6-11-6 ....(p) RJohnson 89+
(P Bowen) *prom: mstkes 4th and 12th: rdn 15th: sn wknd* **15/8**[1]

006U **5** *dist* **Si Anthony (FR)**[14] 1066 5-10-7 .... KJMercer(3) —
(Ferdy Murphy) *a bhd* **33/1**

4/5P **P** **The Nobleman (USA)**[34] 902 9-10-7 65........ TMessenger(7) —
(D Shaw) *plld hrd: led to 7th: wknd 12th: t.o whn p.u bef 4 out* **100/1**

0-P3 **P** **Rich Song (IRE)**[26] 972 7-11-0 83........ NFehily —
(Mrs S J Smith) *hld up: hdwy 7th: rdn 9th: wknd next: t.o whn p.u bef 13th* **25/1**

552- **P** **Bang And Blame (IRE)**[303] 1662 9-10-11 81........ PAspell(3) —
(M W Easterby) *chsd ldrs: led 11th to next: wknd 4 out: hit next: t.o whn p.u bef 2 out* **25/1**

6m 26.8s (-12.50) **Going Correction** -0.40s/f (Good)
WFA 5 from 6yo+ 4lb **8** Ran SP% **115.0**
Speed ratings: **103,102,101,91,**— —,—,— CSF £22.45 TOTE £3.90: £1.20, £2.50, £1.50; EX 22.50.

Owner Mrs B Ramsden **Bred** Mrs George Robinson **Trained** High Eldwick, W Yorks

FOCUS
A fair novice event for the time of year and the winner can rate higher.

NOTEBOOK
Bushido(IRE) has been getting the hang of things over fences and followed his recent third with a workmanlike winning performance. A tough little gelding, he should prove to be a good money-spinner over fences, as he was over the smaller obstacles. *(op 3-1 tchd 5-2)*

Windy Spirit(IRE) was always being held by the winner, but made him work for his victory. He can find a small race, possibly back in handicaps off his current mark. *(tchd 7-1)*

Phar From Frosty(IRE) had his chance and was simply not good enough. This was another relatively disappointing effort and as yet he does not look as good as he was over hurdles. *(op 10-3)*

It's Definite(IRE), off the mark on his chasing debut at Worcester, was unable to confirm the promise of that effort and failed to run to form. *Official explanation: jockey said gelding lost its action (op 6-4 tchd 9-4)*

1178 LADBROKESPOKER.COM H'CAP CHASE (16 fncs) 2m 5f 110y

3:15 (3:18) (Class 4) (0-90,88) 5-Y-0+ **£3,926** (£1,208; £604; £302)

Form RPR
3343 **1** **High Peak**34 [902] 8-10-6 **71** RYoung(3) 86+
(J W Mullins) *hld up: hdwy 9th: led appr 3 out: rdn out* **13/2**2
2P5- **2** *1 ½* **Old Buddy (IRE)**139 [4503] 9-11-10 **86** JTizzard 97
(B G Powell) *hld up: hdwy 7th: outpcd after 4 out: hdwy after next: styd on* **25/1**
336P **3** *16* **Vandante (IRE)**33 [916] 9-11-5 **81** TDoyle 79+
(R Lee) *mid-div: dropped rr 8th: hdwy and hit 3 out: n.d* **18/1**
2500 **4** *9* **Amptina (IRE)**24 [997] 10-10-6 **68** DElsworth 61+
(Mrs S J Smith) *mid-div: sme hdwy 5 out: n.d* **22/1**
5000 **5** *26* **Book's Way**14 [1062] 9-9-11 **62** oh4 PAspell(3) 22
(D W Thompson) *a bhd* **33/1**
-0PP **U** **Plain Chant**12 [1076] 8-9-13 **66** (p) LStephens(5) —
(C Roberts) *blnd and uns rdr 2nd* **80/1**
2031 **P** **Phildari (IRE)**8 [1109] 9-10-13 **82** 7ex MrDEngland(7) —
(N A Twiston-Davies) *a in rr: t.o whn p.u bef 3 out* **7/2**1
2P2F **P** **Lady Lambrini**18 [1044] 5-10-11 **73** RJohnson —
(Mrs L Williamson) *bhd fr 7th: t.o whn p.u bef 4 out* **20/1**
-P3P **P** **Wrens Island (IRE)**19 [1041] 11-11-3 **79** WHutchinson —
(R Dickin) *chsd ldrs to 10th: t.o whn p.u bef 3 out* **40/1**
-002 **P** **Claude Greengrass**8 [1109] 9-11-9 **85** APMcCoy —
(Jonjo O'Neill) *prom: mstke 4th: lost pl next: bhd whn p.u bef 10th* **15/2**
0- **P** **Marmot D'Estruval (FR)**87 [335] 5-11-1 **82** MrGBarfoot-Saunt(5) —
(Mrs Tracey Barfoot-Saunt) *bhd whn j.rt 7th: t.o whn p.u bef 9th* **100/1**
/3-4 **P** **The Croppy Boy**47 [812] 13-10-12 **74** JMogford —
(Mrs N S Evans) *prom: riden whn mstke 8th: wknd 10th: t.o whn p.u bef 3 out* **33/1**
0/11 **P** **Bell Rock**18 [1044] 7-11-12 **88** RThornton —
(Mrs T J Hill) *hld up: mstke 3rd: rdn appr 10th: wknd next: t.o whn p.u bef 3 out* **7/2**1
33/ **P** **Noaff (IRE)**471 11-11-8 **84** ChristianWilliams —
(Evan Williams) *led after 2nd: hdd appr 3 out: wkng whn p.u and dismntd bef 2 out* **9/1**
/4P2 **P** **Pristeen Spy**18 [1044] 8-10-9 **71** (p) PJBrennan —
(R Ford) *led: hdd after 2nd: mstke next: blnd 11th: wknd next: t.o whn p.u bef 3 out* **7/1**3

5m 24.5s (-2.70) **Going Correction** -0.40s/f (Good) **15** Ran SP% **120.8**
Speed ratings: **88,87,81,76,68** —,—,—,—,— —,—,—,—,— CSF £155.19 CT £2788.59 TOTE £9.70: £2.30, £9.90, £3.80; EX 186.30.
Owner Mrs Dinah Webb-Bowen **Bred** S R Hope **Trained** Wilsford-Cum-Lake, Wilts

FOCUS
A weak race and a case of survival of the fittest with only a third of the 15 runners managing to complete. The first two ran to recent marks but the rest were nowhere near.

NOTEBOOK
High Peak, back on his favoured fast surface, was made to work pretty hard for it in the end having gone clear three furlongs out, but he was always holding the resolute runner-up and was probably value for double the official winning margin, as he got a little lonely out in front in the final furlong. He should continue to be a threat under similar conditions. *(op 11-1)*
Old Buddy(IRE), whose sole win came in soft ground, handled these faster conditions well and rallied gamely to re-challenge the winner in the final furlong or so. This was a good effort under his big weight, but this fragile sort could never be backed with conviction.
Vandante(IRE) has yet to win since coming to this country, but he ran well to a point and deserves a little credit, albeit he was ultimately well beaten. *(op 16-1)*
Amptina(IRE) is on a reasonable mark, but failed to do enough to suggest he is ready to take advantage of it. *(op 20-1)*
Book's Way has never convinced over regulation fences and, although deserving some credit for at least finishing, was hopelessly tailed off. *(op 50-1)*
Noaff(IRE) *Official explanation: jockey said gelding lost its action (op 10-1 tchd 8-1)*
Phildari(IRE) was never going at any point and his 7lb penalty could not be put forward as an excuse. *Official explanation: jockey said gelding was never travelling (op 10-1 tchd 8-1)*
Bell Rock failed to confirm the promise of his Uttoxeter win and was struggling from a long way out. *Official explanation: vet said gelding pulled up sore (op 10-1 tchd 8-1)*

1179 LADBROKESCASINO.COM H'CAP HURDLE (9 hdls) 2m 1f

3:45 (3:48) (Class 3) (0-125,125) 4-Y-0+ **£5,109** (£1,572; £786; £393)

Form RPR
3112 **1** **Rajayoga**14 [980] 4-10-10 **110** LAspell 124+
(M H Tompkins) *hld up: hdwy 3 out: led next: rdn clr appr last* **3/1**1
4643 **2** *7* **Castleshane (IRE)**29 [947] 8-11-7 **120** TScudamore 127+
(S Gollings) *led: rdn and hdd 2 out: sn outpcd* **7/2**2
0065 **3** *12* **Arm And A Leg (IRE)**22 [1020] 10-10-3 **102** (p) RJohnson 96
(Mrs D A Hamer) *chsd ldrs: rdn 5th: wknd after next* **8/1**
0-11 **4** *4* **Kims Pearl (IRE)**55 [747] 7-10-2 **106** LStephens(5) 97+
(D Burchell) *chsd ldr 3rd tl wknd appr 2 out* **5/1**3
46U- **5** *8* **Gabla (NZ)**170 [3327] 9-10-3 **102** (p) HOliver 84
(R C Guest) *hld up: bhd fr 5th* **33/1**
P-55 **6** *¾* **Sachsenwalzer (GER)**14 [947] 7-10-3 **102** PJBrennan 83
(C Grant) *chsd ldrs tl wknd after 3 out* **14/1**
1054 **7** *¾* **Lone Soldier (FR)**8 [1111] 9-9-9 **101** oh3 ow2 CDSharkey(7) 82
(S B Clark) *hld up: wknd 5th* **28/1**
05F4 **8** *10* **Forzacurity**11 [1087] 6-9-13 **103** WKennedy(5) 74
(M Sheppard) *hld up: hdwy 4th: wknd 3 out* **14/1**
21-P **P** **Musical Stage (USA)**23 [1012] 6-11-2 **115** (t) TDoyle —
(P R Webber) *a in rr: t.o whn p.u bef 2 out* **10/1**
1F1P **F** **Travel (POL)**23 [1010] 5-11-12 **125** JMMaguire 107
(T R George) *chsd ldrs: lost pl 4th: rdn 3 out: wknd bef next: poor 5th whn fell last: dead* **9/1**

3m 53.0s (-11.90) **Going Correction** -0.40s/f (Good)
WFA 4 from 5yo+ 15lb **10** Ran SP% **113.8**
Speed ratings: **112,108,103,101,97 97,96,92**,—,— CSF £13.89 CT £73.95 TOTE £4.40: £1.90, £1.30, £3.00; EX 12.90.
Owner Mystic Meg Limited **Bred** Mystic Meg Limited **Trained** Newmarket, Suffolk

FOCUS
A reasonable handicap hurdle for the time of year, won impressively and in a good time.

NOTEBOOK
Rajayoga has enjoyed a fruitful time of it since going hurdling, this being his third win in five attempts. Fourth on the Flat the other day, he relished this return to obstacles and travelled sweetly before getting the better of Castleshane and going clear. He is progressing well and should be capable of defying a higher mark. *(op 7-2 tchd 4-1)*
Castleshane(IRE) is a game old stick and he ran another honest race from the front. 12 lengths clear of the third, he not on a bad mark now and may be capable of winning a similar race. *(op 9-4)*
Arm And A Leg(IRE) was left behind when the pace really quickened and is still a few pounds above a winning rating. *(tchd 9-1)*
Kims Pearl(IRE), up 8lb from her last win at Hereford, found the extra weight her undoing and was below her best. She clearly needs to improve to defy this mark.
Gabla(NZ) did not shape without promise on this first start since February and slight improvement is to be expected. *(op 40-1)*
Travel(POL) had run his race and was well held when falling fatally at the last. *(tchd 11-1)*

1180 LADBROKESGAMES.COM (S) HURDLE (9 hdls) 2m 1f

4:15 (4:17) (Class 5) 4-Y-0+ **£2,632** (£752; £376)

Form RPR
550- **1** **Harry Potter (GER)**132 [4640] 6-10-12 (tp) ChristianWilliams 103+
(Evan Williams) *hld up: hdwy and mstke 5th: led after 2 out: rdn clr* **13/8**1
25-L **2** *4* **Dhaudeloup (FR)**61 [682] 10-10-12 **106** JMogford 93
(A G Juckes) *chsd ldr tl led 5th: hdd after 2 out: sn outpcd* **9/1**
-544 **3** *10* **Dante's Battle (IRE)**18 [1044] 13-10-12 **94** RSpate(7) 90
(Mrs K Waldron) *chsd ldrs: ev ch appr 2 out: sn wknd* **12/1**
/P- **4** *4* **Governor Daniel**367 [1133] 14-10-5 DJBoland(7) 81+
(Ian Williams) *prom: rdn 5th: wknd appr 2 out* **8/1**3
6510 **5** *20* **Idlewild (IRE)**19 [1040] 10-10-12 **97** APogson(7) 66
(C T Pogson) *hld up: nvr trbld ldrs* **7/2**2
-PP4 **6** *10* **Saragann (IRE)**36 [891] 10-10-12 **95** RJohnson 49
(N B King) *hld up: hdwy 5th: wknd 3 out* **9/1**
0P6 **7** *¾* **Super Boston**24 [1000] 5-10-12 **68** (b) AThornton 48
(Miss L C Siddall) *msiatke 1st: rdn 3rd: a bhd* **40/1**
PP05 **8** *6* **Longstone Lass**3 [1148] 5-10-5 **87** (v) SCrawford(7) 42
(D Carroll) *chsd ldrs tl led after 2nd: hdd 5th: wknd appr 3 out* **16/1**
04PP **9** *2 ½* **Greenacres Boy**10 [1099] 10-11-2 **75** (p) ACCoyle(3) 47
(M Mullineaux) *hld up: a in rr* **33/1**
P **P** **Confuzed**11 [1085] 5-10-12 JGoldstein —
(A P Jones) *bhd fr 5th: t.o whn p.u bef 2 out* **40/1**
-PPP **P** **Pharbeitfrome (IRE)**18 [1044] 11-10-9 **62** (bt1) GCarenza(3) —
(W B Stone) *bhd fr 3rd: t.o whn p.u bef 5th* **66/1**
P/P0 **P** **Arthur Pendragon**11 [1085] 5-10-7 (t) LStephens(5) —
(Mrs S M Johnson) *hld up: bhd fr 5th: t.o whn p.u bef 2 out* **66/1**
P-50 **P** **Black Bullet (NZ)**55 [747] 12-10-12 **92** (t) AO'Keeffe —
(Jennie Candlish) *j.rt: led tl after 2nd: wknd 6th: t.o whn p.u bef 2 out* **10/1**

3m 57.9s (-7.00) **Going Correction** -0.40s/f (Good) **13** Ran SP% **124.9**
Speed ratings: **100,98,93,91,82 77,77,74,73**,— —,—,— CSF £18.17 TOTE £2.10: £1.20, £2.80, £4.20; EX 26.90.The winner was bought in for 4,000gns.
Owner F Jeffers **Bred** Wilh Jackson **Trained** Cowbridge, Vale Of Glamorgan

FOCUS
A modest contest and the winner can rate higher, but the form looks just average.

NOTEBOOK
Harry Potter(GER), dropping into this grade for the first time, proved good enough to break his duck over hurdles, striding away to win with plenty in hand. The first-time tongue tie, cheekpieces combination appeared to help and it is not hard to envisage him winning back at a slightly higher level. *(op 2-1 after early 11-4 and 5-2 in places, tchd 11-8)*
Dhaudeloup(FR) is a decent sort at this level, albeit he is nowhere near as good as he used to be, and he ran a sound race without proving to be a match for the winner. A return to further may help.
Dante's Battle(IRE), who has been running over fences the last twice, appreciated this return to hurdles and ran well for one of his age.
Governor Daniel was below his best on this first start in over a year, but the outing should bring him on and better can be expected next time. *(op 6-1)*
Idlewild(IRE) found this an inadequate test of stamina and lacked the pace to reach a challenging position. *(op 4-1 tchd 10-3)*

1181 LADBROKES.COM H'CAP HURDLE (11 hdls) 2m 5f 110y

4:45 (4:45) (Class 4) (0-110,106) 4-Y-0+ **£3,445** (£1,060; £530; £265)

Form RPR
0030 **1** **Tomenoso**10 [1099] 7-11-12 **106** DElsworth 110+
(Mrs S J Smith) *chsd ldr tl led 4th: rdn and hdd last: rallied to ld fnl 50 yds* **15/2**
3510 **2** *hd* **Native Chancer (IRE)**12 [1075] 5-11-2 **96** JEMoore 99
(Jonjo O'Neill) *a.p: mstke 3rd: hrd rdn to ld last: rdr dropped whip and hdd fnl 50 yds: nt run on* **8/1**
-123 **3** *3* **Red Chief (IRE)**14 [1066] 5-10-10 **90** RJohnson 91+
(Mrs A M Thorpe) *hld up: mstke 6th: sn rdn: hdwy 7th: hit 3 out: styd on same pce fr next* **85/40**1
1321 **4** *shd* **Cannon Fire (FR)**10 [1099] 4-11-10 **106** ChristianWilliams 104
(Evan Williams) *chsd ldrs: rdn appr 2 out: styd on same pce* **11/4**2
5161 **5** *25* **Angie's Double**24 [1000] 5-10-8 **95** RSpate(7) 70
(Mrs K Waldron) *hld up: hdwy 7th: wknd 3 out* **10/1**
5FP- **6** *24* **Glashedy Rock (IRE)**139 [4503] 8-11-1 **95** PMoloney 46
(M F Harris) *hld up: a in rr: bhd fr 7th* **20/1**
-6PP **7** *27* **Infidel (IRE)**28 [962] 5-11-0 **94** (p) NFehily 18
(C J Mann) *hld up in tch: wknd 8th* **33/1**
2265 **P** **Brush A King**22 [1026] 10-11-4 **105** APogson(7) —
(C T Pogson) *led to 4th: wknd after 8th: t.o whn p.u bef 2 out* **6/1**3

5m 13.3s (-9.00) **Going Correction** -0.40s/f (Good)
WFA 4 from 5yo+ 16lb **8** Ran SP% **112.6**
Speed ratings: **100,99,98,98,89 80,71**,— CSF £62.22 CT £170.52 TOTE £11.00: £2.90, £2.40, £1.10; EX 89.70.
Owner Keith Nicholson **Bred** Mrs J Glover **Trained** High Eldwick, W Yorks

FOCUS
A modest handicap hurdle and a game winner. The form looks sound enough with the third and fourth to their marks.

NOTEBOOK
Tomenoso ◆, who has been shaping well since returning from over a year off, was racing here off a 9lb lower mark than when returning and both he and jockey deserve credit for a gutsy display. Always towards the fore, he had them all beaten off apart from Native Chancer who appeared to be travelling best. However, the seven-year-old relished the battle and having been headed jumping the last, he responded instantly to Elsworth's urgings and nosed his way back to the front, probably winning with more in hand that it looked. His chase-orientated stable tends to get the most out of *their horses and he looks a decent handicap prospect for the larger obstacles.Official explanation: trainer's representative had no explanation for the improved form shown (op 9-1 tchd 7-1)*
Native Chancer(IRE), 14lb higher than when winning at Stratford last month, had since been beaten and appeared to face a stiff task, but he showed that last running to be all wrong and just lost out to the resolute victor. His rider dropped his whip close home, but it did not appear to make much difference and he will not find winning easy off this sort of mark. *(op 5-1)*
Red Chief(IRE) has yet to run a bad race since returning at Perth in June, but he was beaten fair and square here and needs to improve to defy a mark of 90. *(op 11-4)*
Cannon Fire(FR) just lost out in a tight finish for third, but was upwards of 25 lengths clear of the remainder. This was not a bad effort, but he is another who looks to be a tad high in the weights at present. *(op 9-4)*

1182 LADBROKES FREEPHONE 0800 524 524 NOVICES' HURDLE (9 hdls) 2m 1f
5:15 (5:15) (Class 4) 4-Y-0+ **£3,393** (£1,044; £522; £261)

Form					RPR
	1		**Irish Wolf (FR)**[57] 5-10-12	RJohnson	110+
			(P Bowen) *hld up: hdwy 6th: rdn after 3 out: led last: drvn out*	9/4[2]	
5-01	2	3	**Red Moor (IRE)**[34] [901] 5-11-5	BHitchcott	113+
			(Mrs D A Hamer) *chsd ldrs: led 2 out: hung rt and hdd whn mstke last: no ex*	9/1[3]	
2	3	6	**Spuradich (IRE)**[25] [991] 5-10-12	APMcCoy	99
			(Jonjo O'Neill) *hld up: hdwy 4th: outpcd bef 2 out: styd on appr last*	5/6[1]	
3-P0	4	9	**Beaver (AUS)**[43] [838] 6-10-12 103	(p) HOliver	92+
			(R C Guest) *led: blnd 2nd: hdd & wknd 2 out*	14/1	
03	5	3	**Dyneburg (POL)**[23] [1014] 5-10-12	JMMaguire	87
			(T R George) *hld up: wknd 6th*	16/1	
60	6	1	**Scarrabus (IRE)**[19] [1037] 4-10-11	JTizzard	85
			(B G Powell) *chsd ldr to 6th: wknd after 3 out*	66/1	
	P		**Weresmimum** 5-10-9	LVickers[(3)]	—
			(Mrs S Lamyman) *hld up: bhd fr 4th: t.o whn p.u bef 6th*	100/1	
0PP-	P		**Copyerselfon (IRE)**[176] [3835] 6-10-7	(p) WKennedy[(5)]	—
			(A M Hales) *hld up: rdn 3rd: wknd 6th: t.o whn p.u bef 2 out*	100/1	

4m 1.80s (-3.10) **Going Correction** -0.40s/f (Good)
WFA 4 from 5yo+ 15lb **8** Ran SP% **111.3**
Speed ratings: **91,89,86,82,81 80,—,—** CSF £20.76 TOTE £3.70: £1.50, £2.20, £1.02; EX 14.80 Place 6 £121.77, Place 5 £42.59.
Owner The Hacking Partnership **Bred** Mrs Magalen Bryant **Trained** Little Newcastle, Pembrokes

FOCUS
A fair novice event for the time of year that could be rated higher but limited by the slow time.

NOTEBOOK
Irish Wolf(FR), making his British/hurdling debut, had to be given a forceful ride by Johnson, but he was well on top at the line and may improve for the step up to two and a half miles. His stable do exceptionally well during the summer and it would not surprise to see him follow up. *(tchd 7-4)*
Red Moor(IRE) is now getting his act together over hurdles and followed his Uttoxeter win with a sound effort under his penalty. *(tchd 10-1)*
Spuradich(IRE) was a big disappointment, failing to build on his hurdling debut second and basically looking slow. Two and a half miles may be the answer, but he has something to prove now. *(op 8-11 tchd evens)*
Beaver(AUS) ran well for a long way and it was only in the final quarter mile that he began to feel the pinch. He is the type connections will do well with once handicapping. *(op 16-1 tchd 20-1)*
T/Plt: £235.10 to a £1 stake. Pool: £40,190.65. 124.75 winning tickets. T/Qpdt: £71.60 to a £1 stake. Pool: £2,867.10. 29.60 winning tickets. CR

1183 - 1186a (Foreign Racing) - See Raceform Interactive

[1121]NEWTON ABBOT (L-H)
Tuesday, August 9

OFFICIAL GOING: Good to firm (good in places)
The first fence in the home straight was omitted in all chases. The running rail on the bend past the stands was out to its furthest extent.
Wind: virtually nil Weather: sunny

1187 "ELEVEN DAYS TO GO" (S) HURDLE (8 hdls 1 omitted) 2m 3f
2:00 (2:00) (Class 5) 4-Y-0+ **£2,625** (£750; £375)

Form					RPR
00/0	1		**Dancing Hill**[30] [943] 6-10-7 68	PJBrennan	82
			(K Bishop) *hld up and bhd: hdwy appr 6th: sn rdn: wnt 2nd appr 2 out: led flat: r.o*	100/1	
P-21	2	1	**Fire Ranger**[65] [651] 9-10-13 92	RJohnson	88+
			(J D Frost) *hld up: sltly hmpd 3rd: hdwy appr 6th: led appr 2 out: hrd rdn appr last: hdd and nt qckn flat*	11/4[2]	
P/6P	3	7	**Brief Decline (IRE)**[13] [1075] 10-11-7 90	CHonour[(5)]	93
			(J D Frost) *hld up in tch: reminders after 5th: wknd appr last*	33/1	
4060	4	17	**Outside Investor (IRE)**[23] [1019] 5-11-6 80	(p) AThornton	70
			(P R Rodford) *prom: lft in ld 3rd: hdd 4th: led appr 6th tl appr 2 out: sn wknd*	20/1	
00P2	5	hd	**Mantras (FR)**[4] [1153] 6-11-5 109	MrRQuinn[(7)]	76
			(M C Pipe) *chsd ldrs: reminders appr 4th: wknd after 6th*	5/2[1]	
PU-P	6	8	**Thrashing**[29] [959] 10-11-12 100	(tp) ATinkler	68
			(A E Jones) *bhd: rdn after 5th: nvr nr ldrs*	25/1	
6266	7	5	**Blues Story (FR)**[8] [1121] 7-10-9 85	(t) MNicolls[(5)]	51
			(N G Ayliffe) *prom: led 4th tl appr 6th: sn wknd*	20/1	
3-06	8	6	**Wozzeck**[13] [1075] 5-11-0 79	(p) BHitchcott	45
			(R H Buckler) *prom tl wknd appr 2 out*	16/1	
45P5	9	10	**Club Royal**[13] [1075] 8-11-6 77	(p) MBatchelor	41
			(N E Berry) *prom: sltly hmpd 3rd: wknd appr 6th*	16/1	
0	10	7	**Silver Emperor (IRE)**[8] [1123] 4-10-12	ChristianWilliams	26
			(P A Blockley) *a bhd*	66/1	
-P45	F		**Doof (IRE)**[8] [1125] 5-11-3 110	TJMalone[(3)]	—
			(M C Pipe) *led tl fell 3rd*	4/1[3]	
/P0F	U		**Lovers Tale**[48] [812] 7-10-11 82	RHobson[(3)]	—
			(G A Ham) *bhd tl hmpd and uns rdr 3rd*	100/1	
F-	P		**Garrigon**[15] [3791] 4-10-12	(p) VSlattery	—
			(P A Blockley) *hld up in tch: rdn and wknd appr 6th: t.o whn p.u bef 2 out*	25/1	
PP/4	P		**Silent Sound (IRE)**[13] [1076] 9-11-6 83	(p) JTizzard	—
			(C L Tizzard) *hld up in mid-div: v bdly hmpd 3rd: sn t.o: p.u after 5th*	9/1	

4m 32.7s (-0.30) **Going Correction** +0.175s/f (Yiel)
WFA 4 from 5yo+ 15lb **14** Ran SP% **120.6**
Speed ratings: **107,106,103,96,96 93,90,88,84,81** —,—,—,— CSF £354.57 TOTE £76.50: £12.10, £1.20, £12.60; EX 500.20.There was no bid for the winner.
Owner Ed Byrne **Bred** I W T And Mrs Loftus **Trained** Spaxton, Somerset

FOCUS
A weak seller with the runner-up the best guide but the form is very moderate.

NOTEBOOK
Dancing Hill seemed to appreciate the return to a longer trip but even her owner was shocked by the win.
Fire Ranger could not hold the surprise winner after looking set to follow up her Stratford win in similar company. *(tchd 3-1)*
Brief Decline(IRE), reported to have had a breathing problem in a similar event in Worcester in June, was pulled up in better company over this course and distance last time. *(tchd 25-1)*
Outside Investor(IRE) did not find being back up to this distance the answer after a couple of outings over fences. *(op 25-1 tchd 16-1)*
Mantras(FR), making a quick reappearance, was not on one of his going days. *(tchd 11-4)*
Thrashing *Official explanation: jockey said gelding had a breathing problem (op 16-1)*
Silent Sound(IRE) *Official explanation: jockey said gelding was badly hampered by a faller (op 16-1)*

1188 HOLD YOUR EXHIBITION HERE H'CAP HURDLE (8 hdls) 2m 1f
2:30 (2:32) (Class 4) (0-110,108) 4-Y-0+ **£3,326** (£950; £475)

Form					RPR
06-3	1		**Goss**[23] [1020] 8-11-2 **108**	WJones[(10)]	111
			(Jonjo O'Neill) *t.k.h: w ldr: led 2 out: rdn out*	6/1[3]	
04-0	2	1 1/4	**Critical Stage (IRE)**[72] [571] 6-11-4 **105**	CHonour[(5)]	107
			(J D Frost) *a.p: rdn appr 2 out: ev ch last: nt qckn*	7/1	
5F05	3	1 1/2	**Didn't You Know (FR)**[23] [1021] 4-9-11 **83**	TJMalone[(3)]	82
			(M C Pipe) *hld up in mid-div: hdwy after 3 out: kpt on same pce flat*	7/1	
-F63	4	2	**Olimpo (FR)**[19] [1046] 4-10-0 **83** oh3	RJohnson	80
			(P J Hobbs) *hld up and bhd: hdwy 3 out: ev ch 2 out: sn rdn: fnd nil*	10/3[2]	
06-P	5	2 1/2	**Chakra**[85] [389] 11-10-11 **96**	RHobson[(3)]	92
			(C J Gray) *hld up in rr: gd hdwy to ld 5th: hdd 2 out: sn wknd*	25/1	
23/	6	1 3/4	**Stars Delight (IRE)**[801] [517] 8-11-9 **105**	PHide	100+
			(J J Best) *prom tl: wknd 2 out*	10/1	
P504	7	5	**Duke's View (IRE)**[8] [1123] 4-9-11 **83** oh9	ONelmes[(3)]	71
			(D C Turner) *mde most to 5th: wknd appr 2 out*	50/1	
1150	8	2	**Honan (IRE)**[24] [1012] 6-10-13 **95**	(v) APMcCoy	82
			(M C Pipe) *prom tl wknd after 3 out*	3/1[1]	
3312	9	20	**Percipient**[27] [979] 7-10-8 **90**	(v) TDoyle	57
			(D R Gandolfo) *w ldrs: wknd after 3 out*	15/2	
10U/	10	8	**Investment Force (IRE)**[633] [2153] 7-10-7 **96** ow1	MrMHooper[(7)]	55
			(M Sheppard) *bhd: mstke 1st: struggling fr 5th*	33/1	

4m 9.80s (4.70) **Going Correction** +0.175s/f (Yiel)
WFA 4 from 6yo+ 15lb **10** Ran SP% **117.0**
Speed ratings: **95,94,93,92,91 90,88,87,78,74** CSF £46.89 CT £302.86 TOTE £5.40: £2.00, £2.50, £2.50; EX 61.10.
Owner John P McManus **Bred** Juddmonte Farms **Trained** Cheltenham, Gloucs

FOCUS
A modest handicap that could be rated higher but is limited by the time.

NOTEBOOK
Goss obviously goes well for his young rider and ran out a decisive winner with the help of Jones' 10lb allowance. *(op 5-1)*
Critical Stage(IRE), whose course and distance win came on testing ground, bounced back to form having been given a chance by the Handicapper.
Didn't You Know(FR) ran her best race to date on this switch to handicaps despite not looking that straightforward a ride. *(tchd 8-1)*
Olimpo(FR), 3lb 'wrong', was going as well as any at the penultimate hurdle but only flattered to deceive. *(op 4-1 tchd 3-1)*
Chakra eventually paid the penalty for his rider apparently having a rush of blood once in the back straight for the final time. *(op 16-1)*
Stars Delight(IRE) ◆, previously trained by Gary Moore, was not knocked about once his chance had gone. *He really wants further and should be all the better for his first outing for over two years. (op 7-1)*

1189 CAVANNA GROUP H'CAP CHASE (13 fncs 3 omitted) 2m 5f 110y
3:00 (3:00) (Class 3) (0-120,118) 5-Y-0+ **£5,421** (£1,668; £834; £417)

Form					RPR
51-4	1		**Shaadiva**[66] [634] 7-11-12 **118**	RThornton	125+
			(A King) *hld up in tch: led last: rdn out*	7/1	
-6UP	2	1 1/2	**Just Muckin Around (IRE)**[62] [684] 9-10-1 **93**	BHitchcott	100+
			(R H Buckler) *hld up in tch: led after 3 out to last: nt qckn*	50/1	
-656	3	8	**Montreal (FR)**[58] [727] 8-11-3 **112**	(p) TJMalone[(3)]	111+
			(M C Pipe) *hld up in rr: mstke 1st: hdwy 9th: one pce fr 2 out*	6/1	
2111	4	6	**Keltic Lord**[23] [1025] 9-11-7 **113**	VSlattery	106+
			(P W Hiatt) *hld up in mid-div: hdwy 7th: wknd after 3 out*	7/2[1]	
1133	5	9	**Maidstone Monument (IRE)**[15] [1065] 10-10-1 **93**	TScudamore	76
			(Mrs A M Thorpe) *chsd ldrs: led 10th tl after 3 out: sn wknd*	7/1	
334	6	5	**Fear Siuil (IRE)**[23] [1025] 12-10-4 **96**	(t) DRDennis	74
			(Nick Williams) *hld up and bhd: stdy hdwy 6th: wknd after 2 out*	4/1[2]	
3-0P	7	8	**Lord Strickland**[65] [653] 12-10-10 **109**	MrTJO'Brien[(7)]	79
			(P J Hobbs) *bhd: hit 5th: mstke 8th: nvr nr ldrs*	9/1	
-0U0	8	12	**Nick The Jewel**[19] [1049] 10-11-0 **106**	PJBrennan	64
			(Andrew Turnell) *chsd ldr: led after 7th to 10th: wknd after 3 out*	50/1	
5-00	9	shd	**Dun An Doras (IRE)**[30] [946] 9-10-13 **110**	CHonour[(5)]	67
			(J D Frost) *bhd fr 8th*	20/1	
-0P6	10	dist	**Harik**[35] [904] 11-11-1 **107**	(bt) JEMoore	—
			(G L Moore) *bhd: pushed along after 5th: t.o 8th*	40/1	
-U11	P		**Lonesome Man (IRE)**[54] [767] 9-11-4 **110**	RJohnson	—
			(Tim Vaughan) *led tl after 7th: wkng whn mstke 10th: bhd whn p.u bef 3 out*	11/2[3]	

5m 21.3s (-1.40) **Going Correction** +0.175s/f (Yiel) **11** Ran SP% **118.0**
Speed ratings: **109,108,105,103,100 98,95,91,90,—** — CSF £287.44 CT £2209.33 TOTE £9.30: £2.30, £9.80, £2.40; EX 219.50.
Owner Cheltenham Racing Ltd **Bred** Cliffe Rowlands And Khalifa Dasmal **Trained** Barbury Castle, Wilts

FOCUS
There was plenty of pace early on in this competitive handicap and the form looks solid and could rate higher.

NOTEBOOK
Shaadiva defied top weight with a clear-cut victory and put any doubts to rest about her ability to win going left-handed. *(op 6-1)*
Just Muckin Around(IRE), a real in-and-out performer, put some dimal performances behind him and lost nothing in defeat in this slightly stronger company. *(op 40-1)*
Montreal(FR), given time to recover from an error at the first, could not take advantage of an 8lb drop in the ratings over this shorter trip. *(op 9-1)*
Keltic Lord, bidding for a four-timer, had duly been given three weeks off but had gone up another 9lb. *(op 3-1)*
Maidstone Monument(IRE) is at his best when able to dominate and could not do that on this occasion.
Fear Siuil(IRE) had no excuses on account of the distance this time. *(tchd 7-2)*

1190 HAPPY 75TH BIRTHDAY COLIN WILLCOCKS JUVENILE NOVICES' HURDLE (8 hdls) 2m 1f
3:30 (3:31) (Class 3) 3-Y-O **£4,807** (£1,479; £739; £369)

Form					RPR
	1		**Election Seeker (IRE)**[47] 3-10-12	PHide	90+
			(G L Moore) *hld up: hdwy appr 3 out: led 2 out: clr last: r.o wl*	6/1	
	2	6	**The Castilian (FR)**[25] 3-10-9	TJMalone[(3)]	85+
			(M C Pipe) *w ldr: led after 4th: hdd whn sltly hmpd and mstke 2 out: sn btn*	9/4[1]	

3 *5* **Double Kudos (FR)**[19] 3-10-12 .... MBatchelor 78
(Jamie Poulton) *a.p: rdn after 3 out: one pce fr 2 out* **4/1**[2]

4 *7* **Dream Along**[181] 3-10-12 .... JimCrowley 71
(Mrs A J Perrett) *prom: reminders after 3rd and 4th: rdn appr 5th: wknd appr 2 out* **16/1**

P40 5 *10* **Imperial Miss (IRE)**[11] 1095 3-9-12 ....(t) DJacob(7) 54
(B W Duke) *bhd fr 5th* **33/1**

6 *¾* **Forfeiter (USA)**[12] 3-10-12 .... PJBrennan 60
(M F Harris) *hld up: hdwy after 4th: wknd appr 3 out* **10/1**

P **Gortumblo**[24] 3-10-5 .... MrTJO'Brien(7) —
(K Bishop) *a bhd: t.o whn p.u bef 2 out* **16/1**

P **Stock Exchange (IRE)** 3-10-12 .... RJohnson —
(P Bowen) *nt jump wl: a in rr: hung bdly rt and p.u bnd after 4th* **9/2**[3]

P **Penny Island (IRE)**[17] 3-10-12 .... RThornton —
(A King) *hld up and bhd: hdwy whn hit 5th: sn wknd: t.o whn p.u bef 2 out* **6/1**

P **Weet N Measures**[274] 3-10-12 .... ChristianWilliams —
(P A Blockley) *t.k.h: led: hit 2nd: hdd after 4th: sn wknd: t.o whn p.u bef 2 out* **33/1**

4m 6.40s (1.30) **Going Correction** +0.175s/f (Yiel) **10** Ran SP% **124.3**
Speed ratings: **103,100,97,94,89 89,**—,—,—,— CSF £21.88 TOTE £8.30: £2.70, £1.40, £1.90; EX 29.30.
Owner Pleasure Palace Racing **Bred** Mrs Cherry Faeste **Trained** Woodingdean, E Sussex

FOCUS
There were some fair Flat recruits in this juvenile event and the form looks above average for the time of year.

NOTEBOOK
Election Seeker(IRE) ◆, successful over a mile on fast ground at Salisbury in June, looks to have taken well to hurdling and came home a convincing winner. He can score again. *(op 4-1 tchd 13-2)*
The Castilian(FR) ◆, the winner of a nine-furlong claimer on good ground at Longchamp in June, was subsequently tried in blinkers. He did enough to suggest that his able trainer can find him a suitable opening. *(op 3-1)*
Double Kudos(FR), a fair maiden on the Flat, could not raise his game despite some strong driving. *(op 5-1)*
Dream Along twice got rid of his rider leaving the stalls in three outings on the Flat. Woken up a couple of times before halfway, he eventually gave best on the long run to the second last. *(op 11-1)*

1191 CAR BOOT SALE HERE 28 AUGUST H'CAP CHASE (17 fncs 3 omitted) 3m 2f 110y

4:00 (4:01) (Class 4) (0-100,100) 5-Y-0+ **£3,395** (£970; £485)

Form RPR

-134 **1** **Uncle Mick (IRE)**[23] 1022 10-11-12 **100**........(p) JTizzard 106+
(C L Tizzard) *prom: hit 9th: rdn and outpcd 12th: rallied 2 out: led last: styd on wl* **5/1**[3]

4-P3 **2** *6* **Connemara Mist (IRE)**[20] 1041 10-10-0 **74** oh5........(b) JMogford 72
(Mrs N S Evans) *led to 2nd: led 4th to 3 out: sn rdn: ev ch last: no ex* **33/1**

3-UU **3** *1 ¼* **High Gear (IRE)**[12] 1086 7-11-7 **95**........(b) APMcCoy 110+
(Jonjo O'Neill) *nt jump wl: hld up: hdwy 12th: mstke 13th: lft in ld whn reluctant and hdd and mstke last: nt run on* **8/1**

1064 **4** *3* **Make It Easy (IRE)**[9] 1110 9-9-7 **74** oh9........ CaptLHorner(7) 68
(D L Williams) *hld up and bhd: hdwy 2 out: one pce flat* **16/1**

4-F2 **5** *3 ½* **River Quoile**[27] 981 9-9-13 **80**........ DJacob(7) 71
(R H Alner) *led 2nd to 4th: prom: wknd after 2 out* **7/2**[1]

2P43 **P** **Take The Oath (IRE)**[19] 1044 8-10-3 **77**........ TDoyle —
(D R Gandolfo) *bhd fr 12th: t.o whn p.u bef 2 out* **15/2**

4P **P** **The Sawdust Kid**[23] 1022 11-10-0 **74** oh13........ BHitchcott —
(R H Buckler) *prom tl wknd after 12th: t.o whn p.u bef 3 out* **25/1**

PPP- **P** **Yassar (IRE)**[135] 4586 10-11-1 **89**........ WMarston —
(D J Wintle) *hld up and bhd: hdwy 10th: wknd 12th: bhd whn p.u bef 14th* **25/1**

03P1 **P** **Honneur Fontenail (FR)**[20] 1041 6-10-6 **80**........(p) PJBrennan —
(N J Hawke) *chsd ldrs: rdn appr 10th: wknd 11th: t.o whn p.u bef 12th* **12/1**

12P4 **P** **Robber (IRE)**[26] 989 8-11-6 **94**........ RThornton —
(P Bowen) *hld up: lost pl 7th: rdn after 10th: sn struggling: t.o whn p.u bef 13th* **5/1**[3]

101- **P** **Sparkling Spring (IRE)**[317] 1520 14-11-7 **95**........ ChristianWilliams 107
(Evan Williams) *hld up and bhd: hdwy 11th: led 3 out: rdn whn wnt lame and p.u jst bef last* **9/2**[2]

6m 51.6s (8.20) **Going Correction** +0.175s/f (Yiel) **11** Ran SP% **120.8**
Speed ratings: **94,92,91,90,89** —,—,—,—,— — CSF £166.16 CT £1318.00 TOTE £7.00: £2.50, £9.50, £2.40; EX 186.30.
Owner D J Hinks **Bred** J L Rothwell **Trained** Milborne Port, Dorset

FOCUS
A very eventful staying handicap and the form has been adjusted accordingly.

NOTEBOOK
Uncle Mick(IRE) was a fortunate winner coming through to take advantage of the misfortune of Sparkling Spring and the antics of High Gear.
Connemara Mist(IRE), 5lb out of the handicap, gave a decent account of himself but was still lucky to finish second. *(op 25-1)*
High Gear(IRE), back in blinkers having tried a visor last time, never seemed to be having a cut at his fences. He really blotted his copybook when apparently presented the race at the last and is one to be wary of. *(tchd 9-1)*
Make It Easy(IRE), 9lb out of the handicap, began to stay on at the water jump but could not take advantage of all the incident up front.
River Quoile, raised 6lb after his good second at Worcester, may have been found out by the extended trip. *(op 6-1)*
Sparkling Spring(IRE) was in fine form last summer winning twice over hurdles and hacking up over fences when last seen in September. He appeared set to make a winning comeback until breaking down going to the final fence. *(op 3-1 tchd 5-1)*

1192 ANTIQUES FAIR HERE 27 AUGUST H'CAP HURDLE (12 hdls) 3m 3f

4:30 (4:32) (Class 4) (0-110,108) 4-Y-0+ **£3,334** (£952; £476)

Form RPR

-42F **1** **Bustisu**[34] 913 8-9-7 **82**........ RCummings(7) 88+
(D J Wintle) *hld up and bhd: hdwy 9th: led appr 2 out: rdn and r.o flat* **16/1**

0003 **2** *¾* **Wild Tempo (FR)**[13] 1079 10-9-12 **90**........(t) AGlassonbury(10) 94
(M C Pipe) *hld up: rdn appr 9th: hdwy after 3 out: chsd wnr and carried hd high fr 2 out: nt qckn flat* **14/1**

135 **3** *7* **Lawyer Des Ormeaux (FR)**[11] 1099 6-11-12 **108**........ JEMoore 105
(P Bowen) *hld up in tch: rdn after 3 out: wknd appr last* **9/1**

41-0 **4** *½* **Around Before (IRE)**[27] 974 8-11-5 **101**........(t) APMcCoy 98
(Jonjo O'Neill) *hld up in tch: led 8th: rdn and hdd appr 2 out: wknd appr last* **2/1**[2]

2211 **5** *dist* **Fu Fighter**[25] 1002 4-11-6 **105**........(t) ChristianWilliams —
(Evan Williams) *hld up: hdwy appr 9th: wknd appr 2 out* **7/4**[1]

3013 **6** *½* **Red Canyon (IRE)**[13] 1075 8-11-1 **97**........(p) JTizzard —
(C L Tizzard) *led tl after 2nd: led 5th to 8th: rdn and wknd 9th* **7/1**[3]

-000 **7** *dist* **Important Boy (ARG)**[23] 1018 8-9-11 **82** oh7........(t) ONelmes(3) —
(D D Scott) *led after 2nd to 5th: rdn and wknd appr 9th: t.o* **66/1**

5/PP **8** *6* **Slyboots (GER)**[30] 948 6-11-1 **97**........ NFehily —
(C J Mann) *w ldrs: wknd after 3 out: t.o* **33/1**

/000 **P** **Silver Man**[8] 1121 11-9-7 **82** oh18........(p) MrCHughes(7) —
(D C Turner) *hld up towards rr: p.u lame after 3rd* **100/1**

4-3F **P** **Wimbledonian**[65] 652 6-10-8 **90**........ WMarston —
(R T Phillips) *hld up: rdn 6th: sn bhd: t.o whn p.u after 8th* **9/1**

6m 42.8s (0.80) **Going Correction** +0.175s/f (Yiel)
WFA 4 from 6yo+ 17lb **10** Ran SP% **120.2**
Speed ratings: **105,104,102,102,**— —,—,—,—,— CSF £211.86 CT £2149.14 TOTE £19.50: £4.50, £4.00, £2.40; EX 138.20 Place 6 £2,326.51, Place 5 £693.80.
Owner John W Egan **Bred** M J Roberts **Trained** Naunton, Gloucs

FOCUS
A moderate handicap and the marathon trip really sorted these out. The third sets the level for the form.

NOTEBOOK
Bustisu relished the stamina test and only really came off the bridle in the short run-in. *(op 20-1)*
Wild Tempo(FR), not for the first time, looked rather reluctant but did stay on to the end. *(op 16-1 tchd 20-1)*
Lawyer Des Ormeaux(FR) eventually appeared to get found out by the combination of a big step up in distance and a welter burden. *(op 8-1)*
Around Before(IRE), on faster ground this time, should not have been beaten on the grounds of stamina. *(op 5-2)*
Fu Fighter was disappointing on his hat-trick bid but he had gone up a total of 18lb. *(tchd 2-1)*
T/Jkpt: Not won. T/Plt: £5,211.30 to a £1 stake. Pool: £56,039.75. 7.85 winning tickets. T/Qpdt: £152.90 to a £1 stake. Pool: £4,631.20. 22.40 winning tickets. KH

1193 - 1200a (Foreign Racing) - See Raceform Interactive

1095 BANGOR-ON-DEE (L-H)

Saturday, August 13

OFFICIAL GOING: Chase course - good; hurdle course - good (good to soft in places) changing to good to soft after race 2 (3.00)
Wind: Light across Weather: Heavy rain prior to racing, turning fine; shower during race 5.

1201 ABS CONSULTING JUVENILE NOVICES' HURDLE (DIV I) (9 hdls) 2m 1f

2:25 (2:26) (Class 4) 3-Y-0 **£3,034** (£933; £466; £233)

Form RPR

U1 **1** **Fair Along (GER)**[15] 1095 3-11-5 .... ChristianWilliams 106+
(J L Flint) *mde all: clr after 3rd: unchal* **13/8**[1]

0 **2** *25* **Diktatit**[8] 1146 3-10-2 .... LMcGrath(3) 59
(R C Guest) *plld hrd: bhd: hdwy appr 5th: wnt 2nd bef 2 out: no ch w wnr* **66/1**

3 *4* **Maunby Reveller**[15] 3-10-12 .... APMcCoy 62
(P C Haslam) *swtg: hld up in tch: outpcd 5th: nvr on terms after* **6/1**[3]

6 **4** *2 ½* **First Fought (IRE)**[15] 1095 3-10-12 .... JMMaguire 60
(D McCain) *hld up: hdwy 4th: chsd clr wnr fr 3 out tl appr next: sn wknd* **25/1**

2 **5** *dist* **Millquista D'Or**[15] 1095 3-10-5 .... WMarston —
(G A Ham) *chsd ldrs: rdn appr 5th: mstke whn wkng 4 out: t.o* **20/1**

6 *nk* **Heres The Plan (IRE)**[308] 3-10-5 .... PMoloney —
(M G Quinlan) *t.k.h: midfield: hdwy appr 4th: chsd clr wnr bef 4 out tl next: sn wknd: t.o whn mstke last* **7/2**[2]

3 **P** **Sharp N Frosty**[15] 1095 3-10-12 ....(t) ATinkler —
(W M Brisbourne) *a bhd: t.o whn p.u bef 3 out* **12/1**

P **P** **Tiffin Brown**[15] 1095 3-10-12 ....(t) FKeniry —
(P C Haslam) *midfield: wknd 4 out: t.o whn p.u bef 2 out* **20/1**

P **Irish Hawk (GER)**[323] 3-10-12 .... PJBrennan —
(M F Harris) *chsd clr wnr tl wknd appr 4 out: t.o whn p.u bef 2 out* **16/1**

0 **P** **Midnight In Moscow (IRE)**[8] 1146 3-10-12 .... BHarding —
(P C Haslam) *t.k.h: mstke 1st: a bhd: t.o whn p.u bef 2 out* **66/1**

P **Don Pasquale**[138] 3-10-7 .... LTreadwell(5) —
(J T Stimpson) *sweating: t.k.h: trckd ldrs tl wknd 4th: t.o whn p.u bef 5th* **12/1**

4m 14.2s (3.30) **Going Correction** +0.175s/f (Yiel) **11** Ran SP% **112.2**
Speed ratings: **99,87,85,84,**— —,—,—,—,— — CSF £150.10 TOTE £2.30: £1.20, £11.70, £2.40; EX 145.60.
Owner J L Flint **Bred** Gestut Harzburg **Trained** Kenfig Hill, Bridgend

FOCUS
A seemingly truly-run affair on rain-softened ground with winner running his rivals ragged to ultimately score with some ease and is value for more than the official margin.

NOTEBOOK
Fair Along(GER), a winner over course and distance a fortnight ago, sweated up a little beforehand and was keen early on. However, that did not stop him defying a penalty in great style and he could be above average for the time of year. *(tchd 7-4)*
Diktatit, a maiden sprint winner on the level, pulled fiercely early on and was put in the race two flights from home before plugging on to take second. This was a step up on her first effort.
Maunby Reveller, from a stable that enjoys good success in this sphere, got warm pre-race and was never competitive. He took third late on, but may need a drop in class. *(op 13-2 tchd 7-1)*
First Fought(IRE) threatened to get competitive on the home turn, but faded rapidly.
Millquista D'Or was sketchy at her hurdles before dropping away after breaking a blood-vessel. *Official explanation: trainer said filly bled from the nose*
Heres The Plan(IRE) was well-backed to make a winning debut at his new vocation, but folded when his jumping deteriorated from the third last. *(op 11-4 tchd 5-2)*
Don Pasquale *Official explanation: jockey said gelding lost its action (op 50-1)*
Sharp N Frosty was a major disappointment and his breathing problems failed to be resolved by the first-time tongue tie. *Official explanation: jockey said gelding had a breathing problem (op 50-1)*
Midnight In Moscow(IRE) *Official explanation: jockey said gelding had a breathing problem (op 50-1)*
Tiffin Brown *Official explanation: jockey said gelding had a breathing problem (op 50-1)*

1202 GENESIS WEALTH MANAGEMENT NOVICES' H'CAP HURDLE (9 hdls) 2m 1f

3:00 (3:01) (Class 4) (0-105,99) 4-Y-0+ **£4,270** (£1,314; £657; £328)

Form RPR

2003 **1** **Virtus**[8] 1156 5-10-6 **79**........(b) RJohnson 85+
(P J Hobbs) *midfield: hdwy 4th: rdn to ld 2 out: mstke last: drvn out* **6/1**[3]

5 **2** 2½ **Keep Asking (IRE)**[16] [1084] 9-10-8 **81** .... BHitchcott 81
(Mrs D A Hamer) *chsd ldr appr 2nd: led 4 out: rdn and hdd 2 out: nt fluent last: styd on same pce* **25/1**

0-43 **3** 3 **Winslow Boy (USA)**[15] [1097] 4-10-10 **87** .... PAspell(3) 84+
(P Monteith) *midfield: hdwy 4th: rdn after 3 out: kpt on same pce* **7/1**

0513 **4** 2½ **Fenney Spring**[39] [905] 5-10-4 **77** ....(t) CLlewellyn 72
(W Jenks) *chsd ldrs: rdn appr 2 out: one pce* **10/1**

-034 **5** 4 **Moscow Executive**[15] [1097] 7-10-0 **73** oh2 .... ATinkler 64
(W M Brisbourne) *hld up: hdwy 4 out: rdn appr 2 out: wknd bef last* **16/1**

03-0 **6** 4 **West Hill (IRE)**[9] [238] 4-9-9 **74** oh3 ....(t) StephenJCraine(5) 60
(D McCain) *midfield: mstke 5th: hdwy 4 out: rdn and wknd after next* **20/1**

U232 **7** dist **Bill's Echo**[23] [1049] 6-11-9 **99** .... LMcGrath(3) —
(R C Guest) *rdn after 4th: a bhd: t.o* **7/2**[2]

66-P **8** 3 **Uncle Batty**[8] [1158] 5-9-10 **74** .... DLaverty(5) —
(Mrs L Williamson) *a bhd: mstke 5th and 4 out: t.o* **40/1**

000 **P** **Bobering**[48] [838] 5-10-1 **74** .... JMogford —
(B P J Baugh) *a bhd: t.o whn p.u bef 2 out* **66/1**

30-0 **P** **Diagon Alley (IRE)**[105] [120] 5-10-0 **73** oh4 .... FKeniry —
(K W Hogg) *a bhd: t.o whn p.u bef 2 out* **50/1**

P46 **P** **Troodos Jet**[8] [1149] 4-10-9 **83** .... GLee —
(K W Hogg) *rdn appr 5th: a bhd: t.o whn p.u bef 4 out* **33/1**

0-60 **P** **Grace Dieu**[72] [613] 4-9-4 **74** .... JKington(10) —
(M Scudamore) *w.r.s: a wl bhd: t.o whn p.u bef 2 out* **25/1**

-321 **P** **Zarakash (IRE)**[33] [959] 5-11-9 **96** .... APMcCoy —
(Jonjo O'Neill) *chsd ldrs: rdn appr 4 out: wknd next: t.o whn p.u bef 2 out* **3/1**[1]

211/ **P** **Newsplayer (IRE)**[669] [1658] 9-10-13 **86** ....(t) WMarston —
(R T Phillips) *led to 4 out: wknd qckly next: t.o whn p.u bef 2 out* **10/1**

4m 14.8s (3.90) **Going Correction** +0.175s/f (Yiel)
WFA 4 from 5yo+ 15lb **14** Ran SP% **119.4**
Speed ratings: **97,95,94,93,91 89,—,—,—,— —,—,—,—** CSF £145.44 CT £1081.81 TOTE £7.70: £2.30, £9.50, £2.10; EX 327.70.
Owner P R Bateman **Bred** Cheveley Park Stud Ltd **Trained** Withycombe, Somerset

FOCUS
A moderate handicap with neither Zarakash or Bill's Echo running their races. The winner was beaten in a seller last time and this was a race that did not take much winning.

NOTEBOOK
Virtus took advantage of the failings of others to score under a typically forceful ride. He has been beaten in sellers and his performance underlines the level of the contest. *(op 13-2)*
Keep Asking(IRE), an ex-pointer, was close up throughout and kept to his task. He could pick up a little race over further.
Winslow Boy(USA) posted another solid effort at the track on his first dip into handicap company, reversing recent placings with Moscow Executive. *(op 9-1)*
Fenney Spring was nibbled at in the market pre-race and probably ran up to her mark. *(op 16-1)*
Moscow Executive spread a plate after stumbling with a circuit to run, but ran respectably in the circumstances. *Official explanation: jockey said mare spread a plate having stumbled with a circuit to go*
Bill's Echo was very disappointing as he was never in the hunt despite having conditions to suit. *(op 3-1)*
Zarakash(IRE) was reported lame after being pulled up two from home. *Official explanation: vet said gelding was lame (op 7-2)*

1203 CHILDREN'S FUNDAY H'CAP CHASE (15 fncs) 2m 4f 110y
3:30 (3:30) (Class 4) (0-100,99) 5-Y-0+ **£4,173** (£1,284; £642; £321)

Form RPR

PFU4 **1** **Miss Muscat**[31] [979] 5-10-0 **73** oh7 .... JPByrne 89+
(Evan Williams) *hld up: hdwy 8th: led after 3 out: edgd lft appr last: edgd rt run-in: drvn out* **20/1**

04U0 **2** 2 **Saddler's Quest**[39] [902] 8-10-0 **73** oh5 .... JMogford 87+
(B P J Baugh) *a.p: chsd wnr after 3 out: kpt on u.p tl eased whn hld towards fin* **25/1**

3025 **3** 18 **Raise A McGregor**[13] [1109] 9-10-5 **78** .... WMarston 76+
(Mrs S J Smith) *led: hdd after 3 out: wknd next* **4/1**[1]

5U02 **4** 6 **York Rite (AUS)**[8] [1150] 9-10-5 **78** ....(p) HOliver 67
(R C Guest) *midfield: outpcd 10th: kpt on fr bef last: nvr on terms* **9/2**[2]

P-00 **5** 1½ **Ideal Du Bois Beury (FR)**[15] [1098] 9-10-7 **83** .... PAspell(3) 71
(P Monteith) *bhd: hmpd sltly 6th: effrt appr 11th: no imp on ldrs* **14/1**

/504 **6** 9 **Kitty John (IRE)**[15] [1098] 8-10-4 **77** .... RThornton 60+
(J L Spearing) *trckd ldrs tl rdn and wknd appr 2 out* **9/2**[2]

633U **7** 1¼ **Pete The Painter (IRE)**[13] [1109] 8-10-7 **80** ....(p) MBradburne 62+
(J W Tudor) *trckd ldrs tl wknd 10th* **17/2**

0-4P **8** dist **Pink Harbour**[29] [997] 7-10-4 **82** .... StephenJCraine(5) —
(D McCain) *prom tl wknd 10th: t.o* **14/1**

P2FP **9** 10 **Lady Lambrini**[5] [1178] 5-9-10 **74** ow1 .... DLaverty(5) —
(Mrs L Williamson) *j. slowly 1st: chsd ldrs: rdn and lost pl bef 6th: wknd 10th: t.o* **16/1**

-664 **U** **Bentyheath Lane**[15] [1096] 8-10-0 **73** oh11 ....(b) FKeniry —
(M Mullineaux) *midfield: mstke and uns rdr 6th* **28/1**

002P **P** **Claude Greengrass**[5] [1178] 9-10-13 **86** ....(v[1]) APMcCoy —
(Jonjo O'Neill) *towards rr: rdn after 5th: t.o whn p.u bef 9th* **5/1**[3]

5m 7.90s (-4.60) **Going Correction** -0.25s/f (Good) **11** Ran SP% **114.8**
Speed ratings: **98,97,90,88,87 84,83,—,—,— —** CSF £377.76 CT £2395.62 TOTE £24.10: £6.60, £8.40, £1.70; EX 263.30.
Owner Red & Black Racing **Bred** J Huckle And Miss E Saunders **Trained** Cowbridge, Vale Of Glamorgan

FOCUS
A weak event which provided a surprise winner who posted a virtually error-free round for once and won accordingly. The race is probably best rated through the third.

NOTEBOOK
Miss Muscat, 7lb out of the handicap, normally blights her chance with some poor fencing, but posted a clear round to score. She could be ahead of the Handicapper providing this level of jumping can be repeated.
Saddler's Quest was 5lb out of the handicap but probably still ran his best race over fences. This was the first time he has been competitive at this trip from seven attempts. *(op 20-1)*
Raise A McGregor is without a win in two years and faded when headed at the third last. He has ability, as he displayed over course and distance two years ago, but it has paid to oppose him in recent times. *(op 7-2)*
York Rite(AUS) is still a maiden over fences and is fully exposed as limited.
Ideal Du Bois Beury(FR) is extremely well handicapped these days but cannot be relied on. *(tchd 12-1 and 16-1)*
Kitty John(IRE), from a stable in good form, weakened disappointingly and may require faster conditions.
Claude Greengrass is another moody customer and not even the first-time visor could induce some honesty. *(op 6-1)*

1204 CORBETT BOOKMAKERS DEE HURDLE (H'CAP) (9 hdls) 2m 1f
4:05 (4:05) (Class 2) (0-145,144) 4-Y-0+ **£19,500** (£6,000; £3,000; £1,500)

Form RPR

-311 **1** **Yes Sir (IRE)**[86] [420] 6-11-12 **144** .... APMcCoy 152+
(P Bowen) *mde all: sn clr: unchal* **5/1**[3]

-111 **2** 8 **Darrias (GER)**[62] [729] 4-10-13 **132** .... RWalsh 129+
(P F Nicholls) *chsd ldrs: wnt 2nd appr 4 out: rdn bef 2 out: mstke last: no ch w wnr* **9/4**[1]

3300 **3** 8 **Flame Phoenix (USA)**[30] [990] 6-10-2 **120** .... GLee 109+
(D McCain) *hld up: sme hdwy after 3 out: one pce* **25/1**

UU **4** 7 **Magic Sky (FR)**[28] [1013] 5-10-0 **125** .... LHeard(7) 106
(P F Nicholls) *hld up: sme hdwy after 4th: no imp: wknd 3 out* **25/1**

21-2 **5** 1 **Another Deckie (IRE)**[34] [940] 7-10-0 **118** oh8 .... PMoloney 100+
(L Lungo) *midfield: sme hdwy whn mstke 4th: wkng whn mstke 3 out* **12/1**

40-5 **6** 14 **Portant Fella**[12] [1093] 6-10-1 **122** ....(p) MissNCarberry(3) 88
(Ms Joanna Morgan, Ire) *midfield: wknd 3 out* **15/2**

34 **7** 5 **Calorando (IRE)**[16] [1093] 6-10-8 **133** .... MPWatts(7) 94
(Anthony Mullins, Ire) *bhd fr 4th* **7/2**[2]

6FF- **8** 21 **Spectrometer**[20] [2637] 8-11-12 **144** .... DRDennis 84
(Ian Williams) *bhd fr 3rd* **33/1**

P4-0 **9** 10 **Overstrand (IRE)**[12] [1010] 6-10-9 **127** ....(b) ADobbin 57
(M Todhunter) *chsd wnr tl appr 4 out: wkng whn blnd next* **20/1**

05-4 **10** 18 **Tulipa (POL)**[28] [1010] 6-10-3 **121** .... JMMaguire 33
(T R George) *mstke 5th: a bhd* **11/2**

4m 9.00s (-1.90) **Going Correction** +0.175s/f (Yiel)
WFA 4 from 5yo+ 15lb **10** Ran SP% **119.9**
Speed ratings: **111,107,103,100,99 93,90,80,76,67** CSF £16.88 CT £263.58 TOTE £4.90: £2.60, £1.70, £4.10; EX 10.10.
Owner Ms Y M Hill **Bred** Louis Hill **Trained** Little Newcastle, Pembrokes

FOCUS
A good handicap for the tracka dna decisive winner with the runner-up setting the standard.

NOTEBOOK
Yes Sir(IRE) is beginning to look the finished article and relished an aggressive ride to score in style. The Handicapper will probably take a dim view of this effort, but he is a versatile, progressive type who acts on any ground while also boasting winning form over further. He looks booked for future success and will make a smashing chaser. *(op 4-1 tchd 11-2)*
Darrias(GER) lost nothing in defeat as he threatened to get on terms four from home before the winner kicked again. The German recruit has improved all summer and probably met a smart rival here. *(op 10-3)*
Flame Phoenix(USA) has been a disappointing recruit to fences, but was much happier on his return to hurdles and posted his best effort for some time.
Magic Sky(FR), a recruit from France, has shown some temperament in the past, but did little wrong back over hurdles. He relished the underfoot conditions.
Another Deckie(IRE) made a bad mistake three out which halted him in his tracks just as he was getting into the race. He should not be written off and he would be interesting back on faster ground. *(op 11-1 tchd 14-1)*
Calorando(IRE), a creditable fourth in the Galway Hurdle last time, was never travelling and probably found conditions too testing. *(op 10-3)*

1205 MAPLE LEAF FINANCIAL SERVICES GROUP H'CAP CHASE (18 fncs) 3m 110y
4:40 (4:42) (Class 3) (0-120,116) 5-Y-0+ **£8,073** (£2,484; £1,242; £621)

Form RPR

-340 **1** **Parisian Storm (IRE)**[24] [1039] 9-11-8 **112** .... ChristianWilliams 130+
(Evan Williams) *mde all: clr appr 3 out: easily* **5/1**

1132 **2** 20 **Croc An Oir (IRE)**[13] [1110] 8-11-11 **115** .... GLee 103+
(R Ford) *bhd: hit 12th: tk poor 2nd towards fin* **10/3**[1]

3-21 **3** 2 **Be The Tops (IRE)**[13] [1110] 7-11-6 **110** ....(b) APMcCoy 99+
(Jonjo O'Neill) *prom: mstke 12th: rdn 14th: wknd appr 3 out* **9/2**[3]

-121 **4** 1 **Ross Comm**[8] [1157] 9-11-12 **116** .... DElsworth 101
(Mrs S J Smith) *midfield: wknd 4 out* **4/1**[2]

-P45 **5** 1½ **Judaic Ways**[76] [572] 11-10-0 **90** .... RJohnson 77+
(H D Daly) *hld up: hdwy after 10th: chsd wnr 14th: j.lft whn wkng last: sn lost 2nd* **16/1**

-3PP **6** 19 **Half An Hour**[34] [946] 8-11-4 **108** .... WHutchinson 73
(A King) *prom tl wknd 4 out* **22/1**

44-2 **P** **Shareef (FR)**[79] [524] 8-11-8 **112** .... RThornton —
(A King) *hld up: struggling after 13th: p.u bef next* **13/2**

6P-4 **P** **Hehasalife (IRE)**[41] [896] 8-9-9 **92** .... PMerrigan(7) —
(Mrs H Dalton) *w.r.s: hdwy to midfield after 3rd: lost pl after 9th: hdwy bef 13th: wknd bef 4 out: t.o whn p.u befoe* **7/1**

6m 11.6s (-11.60) **Going Correction** -0.25s/f (Good) **8** Ran SP% **114.0**
Speed ratings: **108,101,100,100,100 94,—,—** CSF £22.59 CT £79.51 TOTE £5.60: £1.60, £1.60, £2.00; EX 31.60.
Owner Mark Glastonbury Grant Lewis **Bred** Sean Hennessy **Trained** Cowbridge, Vale Of Glamorgan

FOCUS
A fair handicap with the winner value for half as much again as the winning margin, but not an easy race to rate.

NOTEBOOK
Parisian Storm(IRE), returned to fences after a below-par effort over hurdles last time, was a second winner on the card for his handler. He arguably needed his last run and, although he is thought best on top of the ground, he enjoyed the ease in the ground to rout his rivals. *(op 4-1)*
Croc An Oir(IRE), 4lb better off with Be The Tops for a one and a half length beating last time, is paying for a profitable summer and the Handicapper may have his measure. *(op 4-1)*
Be The Tops(IRE), up 8lb for his narrow win at Market Rasen, has never been one to trust implicitly and failed to build on his victory. He continues to be a hard ride. *(op 10-3)*
Ross Comm, something of a Worcester specialist, did not appear to handle the softer ground and was always well held. *(op 7-2)*
Judaic Ways faded dramatically at the last when jumping left and may have needed his first run in 11 weeks. Three of his four career wins have come at Ludlow.
Hehasalife(IRE), well-backed pre-race, is a frustrating individual who whipped round at the start before jumping poorly. He is undeniably well handicapped, but his temperament may prevent him from taking advantage. *(op 12-1)*

1206 WREXHAM MAIDEN HURDLE (11 hdls) 2m 4f
5:10 (5:12) (Class 4) 4-Y-0+ **£3,460** (£1,064; £532; £266)

Form RPR

-002 **1** **Kirkham Abbey**[9] [1028] 5-11-2 98 ....(v) RGarritty 116+
(J J Quinn) *trckd ldrs: led 4 out: clr whn blnd 2 out: sn rdn: eased run-in* **5/1**[2]

23P- **2** 15 **Incursion**[13] [2454] 4-11-0 .... RThornton 95+
(A King) *led to 1st: led again 4th: blnd and hdd 4 out: wknd appr 2 out* **11/8**[1]

L0-2 **3** *3/4* **Kentucky King (USA)**[27] 1018 5-11-2 95 .... BHitchcott 94
(Mrs D A Hamer) *trckd ldrs: rdn and wknd appr 2 out* **8/1**[3]

320- **4** *dist* **Treaty Stone**[248] 2708 6-11-2 .... APMcCoy —
(Jonjo O'Neill) *midfield: sme hdwy 6th: blnd next: sn wknd* **9/1**

P5P3 **5** *11* **Royaltea**[13] 1113 4-10-2 85 .... LTreadwell(5) —
(J T Stimpson) *a bhd* **20/1**

0-P5 **6** *19* **Saxon Mist**[23] 1047 6-11-2 .... RJohnson —
(P Bowen) *a bhd* **9/1**

00-0 **7** *3 1/2* **It's Ej**[91] 345 7-11-2 100 .... DElsworth —
(Mrs S J Smith) *in tch: wknd 6th* **12/1**

8 *dist* **Air Guitar (IRE)**[58] 773 5-11-2 .... PMoloney —
(M G Quinlan) *midfield: wknd appr 6th: t.o* **14/1**

0P **R** **River Iris**[31] 971 4-10-7 .... VSlattery —
(Lucinda Featherstone) *a bhd: ref 6th* **66/1**

60/P **P** **Le Cavalier (USA)**[8] 1153 8-11-2 80 .... ADobbin —
(Mrs L Williamson) *a bhd: t.o whn p.u bef 6th* **50/1**

0/ **P** **Babarullah**[856] 4542 7-10-9 .... TMessenger(7) —
(B R Foster) *midfield: wknd appr 6th: t.o whn p.u bef next* **66/1**

05PU **F** **Dorans Lane**[15] 1100 7-10-9 77 .... ATinkler —
(W M Brisbourne) *midfield: hdwy 7th: 4th and 8 l off pce whn fell 3 out* **33/1**

03-0 **P** **Dunston Durgam (IRE)**[83] 458 11-10-13 64 .... TJPhelan(3) —
(Ms Sue Smith) *led 1st to 4th: remained prom: mstke whn wkng 6th: t.o whn p.u bef next* **66/1**

P **Honourable Collins (IRE)**[97] 5-11-2 .... HOliver —
(Mrs Tracey Barfoot-Saunt) *midfield: rdn after 4th: mstke 5th: wknd appr 6th: t.o whn p.u bef 2 out* **20/1**

5m 3.90s (6.30) **Going Correction** +0.175s/f (Yiel)
WFA 4 from 5yo+ 16lb **14 Ran SP% 123.1**
Speed ratings: **94,88,87**,—,— —,—,—,—,— —,—,—,— CSF £12.20 TOTE £5.00: £1.90, £1.40, £2.70; EX 15.90.

Owner Mrs Marie Taylor **Bred** Highclere Stud Ltd **Trained** Settrington, N Yorks

FOCUS
A moderate maiden hurdle but the winner is value for more than the official margin and the third sets the level for the form.

NOTEBOOK
Kirkham Abbey, rated 70 on the level in his prime, was thought to require a faster surface, but got off the mark at the eighth time of asking over hurdles. However, he is already rated 98 over timber and any over-reaction by the assessor may make life tough. *(op 6-1)*

Incursion was ridden aggressively in a bid to get his head in front for the first time over hurdles. Fit *from a Flat campaign, this was another tame effort and he is not one to take a short price about. (tchd 6-4)*

Kentucky King(USA) has looked reluctant in the past, however this was a second consecutive effort where he has reached the frame and he may be a transformed character. *(op 12-1)*

Treaty Stone, extremely easy to back, had shown promise in a couple of bumpers last term but failed to build on those efforts. *(op 9-2)*

1207 ABS CONSULTING JUVENILE NOVICES' HURDLE (DIV II) (9 hdls) 2m 1f
5:40 (5:41) (Class 4) 3-Y-O **£3,026** (£931; £465; £232)

Form RPR

2 **1** **Goldstar Dancer (IRE)**[28] 1011 3-10-12 .... RGarritty 91+
(J J Quinn) *t.k.h: prom: led 2nd: clr appr 2 out: eased towards fin* **3/1**[1]

4 **2** *10* **Compton Quay**[34] 945 3-10-12 .... RThornton 78
(A King) *trckd ldrs: rdn to take 2nd after 3 out: no ch w wnr* **3/1**[1]

3 *22* **Optimum (IRE)**[164] 3-10-12 .... AThornton 56
(J T Stimpson) *trckd ldrs: wnt 2nd 4 out tl wknd after next* **12/1**

4 *6* **Time For You**[32] 3-10-5 .... AO'Keeffe 43
(J M Bradley) *mstkes: a bhd* **25/1**

5 **5** *8* **Golden Feather**[15] 1095 3-10-12 .... HOliver 42
(R C Guest) *hld up: hmpd 2nd: sme hdwy 4 out: wknd next* **11/2**[3]

P **Crazy Flirt (IRE)**[12] 3-10-5 .... BHitchcott —
(A E Jones) *prom to 3rd: t.o whn p.u bef 5th* **16/1**

P **Smemi An Nada** 3-10-12 .... RJohnson —
(P Bowen) *j.lft 2nd and 3rd: a bhd: t.o whn p.u bef 5th* **12/1**

P **Blushing Russian (IRE)**[3] 3-10-12 .... FKeniry —
(P C Haslam) *hld up: sme hdwy after 4th: wkng whn mstke 3 out: t.o whn p.u bef 2 out* **20/1**

P **Kerry's Blade (IRE)**[7] 3-10-12 .... APMcCoy —
(P C Haslam) *t.k.h: led to 2nd: remained prom: stmbld 5th: wknd appr 3 out: t.o whn p.u bef 2 out* **7/2**[2]

4m 23.6s (12.70) **Going Correction** +0.175s/f (Yiel) **9 Ran SP% 117.5**
Speed ratings: **77,72,61,59,55** —,—,—,— CSF £12.64 TOTE £4.10: £1.60, £1.70, £2.90; EX 14.40 Place 6 £51.04, Place 5 £30.32.

Owner Double Eight Syndicate **Bred** D Maher **Trained** Settrington, N Yorks

FOCUS
A very moderate time, even allowing for the ground The first two ran close to their marks but there was little encouragement for those that finished in behind.

NOTEBOOK
Goldstar Dancer(IRE) had run well on his first start over hurdles and confirmed that impression to give his predominantly Flat yard a double on the card. He did not beat much, but was hardly troubled to do so and could defy a penalty if well placed. *(op 5-2 tchd 9-4 and 10-3)*

Compton Quay, a seven-furlong winner on the level, plugged on to take second without ever truly threatening. *(op 4-1)*

Optimum(IRE), a recruit from the David Loder stable, travelled well enough until a lack of peak fitness told. He could do better with this experience behind him. *(op 14-1 tchd 11-1)*

Time For You was a sprinter on the Flat and jumped like one. *(op 20-1)*

Golden Feather had looked an obvious recruit to this sphere prior to his debut, but was again disappointing, albeit after being slightly hampered at the second flight. *(op 13-2 tchd 7-1)*

Kerry's Blade(IRE) appeared a likely type for juvenile hurdles and was backed accordingly. However, he was keen early on and stumbled at the fifth before weakening badly. *(op 11-4 tchd 4-1)*

T/Plt: £55.90 to a £1 stake. Pool: £32,500.95. 423.80 winning tickets. T/Qpdt: £6.40 to a £1 stake. Pool: £1,866.30. 214.95 winning tickets. DO

1107 MARKET RASEN (R-H)
Saturday, August 13

OFFICIAL GOING: Soft (heavy in places)
Wind: Moderate across Weather: Heavy rain early

1208 MERCEDES-BENZ OF HULL & LINCOLNSHIRE (S) HURDLE (8 hdls) 2m 1f 110y
5:35 (5:36) (Class 5) 4-Y-O+ **£2,247** (£642; £321)

Form RPR

12-4 **1** **Green Prospect (FR)**[66] 689 5-11-6 113 .... TScudamore 84+
(M C Pipe) *mde all: sn clr: 20l ahd 4th: hrd drvn and wknd flat: hung on gamely nr fin* **8/11**[1]

10-5 **2** *nk* **Protocol (IRE)**[65] 695 11-11-10 88 .... (t) LVickers(3) 89
(Mrs S Lamyman) *chsd wnr tl 5th: drvn into 2nd briefly bef 2 out: lft 8l 2nd at last: styd on to get win nk of wnr 50yds out: n.g.t* **12/1**

20U- **3** *16* **Chariot (IRE)**[112] 4975 4-10-12 82 .... SCurran 58
(M R Bosley) *chsng gp: wnt 2nd 5th: rdn and lost pl after next: lft poor 3rd at last* **16/1**

4 *1* **Glenviews Surlami (IRE)**[14] 4-10-5 .... KJohnson 50
(R C Guest) *20l last at 1st: bhd: reminder 3 out: sn lost tch* **12/1**

50- **5** *30* **Forbearing (IRE)**[185] 3758 8-11-13 105 .... (p) TDoyle 52+
(F Jordan) *a bhd: lost tch 3 out: t.o next* **10/1**

4005 **P** **Seemore Sunshine**[19] 1063 8-10-6 73 .... PCStringer(7) —
(M J Gingell) *lost tch 4th: t.o 3 out: p.u next* **16/1**

0P02 **P** **Love Triangle (IRE)**[16] 1085 4-10-9 88 .... (tp) ONelmes(3) —
(N B King) *nt fluent: towards rr: lost tch 3 out: t.o and p.u last* **8/1**[3]

4062 **F** **Little Tobias (IRE)**[5] 1107 6-10-8 90 .... (b) DCCostello(5) 77+
(J S Wainwright) *settled 3rd or 4th: rdn to go 2nd bef 2 out: 6l 2nd and plugging on whn fell last* **9/2**[2]

4m 35.7s (19.30) **Going Correction** +1.075s/f (Soft)
WFA 4 from 5yo+ 15lb **8 Ran SP% 123.4**
Speed ratings: **100,99,92,92,78** —,—,— CSF £12.78 TOTE £2.00: £1.10, £2.80, £5.50; EX 16.50.The winner was bought by P.Watney for 8,400gns.

Owner Stuart M Mercer **Bred** J Brion Et Al **Trained** Nicholashayne, Devon

■ Stewards' Enquiry : T Scudamore four-day ban: using whip with excessive force and frequency, and without regard to gelding's stride pattern (August 24-25,27,29)

FOCUS
Bad stuff and hot favourite Green Prospect made much harder work of winning than he should have done. The runner-up is the best guide to the form.

NOTEBOOK
Green Prospect(FR) appreciated this drop back down in trip and supplemented May's course and distance win. However, he had to work harder than anticipated for his win, as he was entitled to beat Protocol easily at the weights, and it remains to be seen if he will be as effective back up in grade. *(op 4-6 tchd 5-6)*

Protocol(IRE) has seen his best days and is approaching the end of his career, but he still made the hot favourite pull out the stops. He was clear of the third, and may be capable of winning again at this lowly level. *(op 9-1)*

Chariot(IRE) was a well beaten and fortunate third, being left to claim a place after the last-flight fall of Little Tobias. *(op 14-1)*

Glenviews Surlami(IRE) was detached before the first hurdle had been jumped and never got into it. *(op 16-1 tchd 20-1)*

Little Tobias(IRE) had run well and was keeping on in second when coming down at the last. He would have been third had he stood on his feet, but it remains to be seen how this affects confidence. *(op 5-1 tchd 11-2)*

1209 GALA CASINOS NOVICES' H'CAP HURDLE (10 hdls) 2m 3f 110y
6:05 (6:07) (Class 4) (0-100,96) 4-Y-O+ **£4,875** (£1,500; £750; £375)

Form RPR

060 **1** **Thornton Bridge**[13] 1108 7-9-7 70 oh6 .... CMStudd(7) 73
(D L Williams) *20l clr 1st: pressed fr 6th: rdn after 3 out: forged clr next: drvn rt out* **14/1**

PP04 **2** *8* **The Yellow Earl (IRE)**[31] 971 5-9-9 70 .... DCCostello(5) 65
(J M Jefferson) *settled chsng gp: 3rd and rdn and struggling 3 out: plodded into 2nd after last: no ch w wnr* **4/1**[3]

0040 **3** *6* **Private Jessica**[75] 592 4-10-5 77 .... KJohnson 65+
(R C Guest) *chsd wnr: chal fr 6th: nt fluent next: almost upsides 3 out: looked gng best tl floundered bdly 2 out: lost 2nd after last* **11/4**[2]

06/P **4** *dist* **Night Mail**[30] 992 5-10-7 80 .... GCarenza(3) —
(Miss J E Foster) *last and rdn after 5th: t.o 3 out: p.u last* **13/2**

0202 **P** **Alethea Gee**[23] 1046 7-9-13 76 .... PKinsella(7) —
(K G Reveley) *hld up in rr: lost tch rapidly 3 out: btn 64l* **2/1**[1]

-065 **P** **Zahunda (IRE)**[13] 1113 6-10-1 81 .... CareyWilliamson(10) —
(M J Gingell) *t.k.h in chsng gp: wknd 7th: bdly t.o whn p.u last* **8/1**

5m 24.0s (34.00) **Going Correction** +1.075s/f (Soft)
WFA 4 from 5yo+ 15lb **6 Ran SP% 111.1**
Speed ratings: **75,71,69**,—,— — CSF £66.12 CT £196.07 TOTE £19.10: £5.90, £2.50; EX 100.20.

Owner R J Hewitt **Bred** Mrs M Armstrong **Trained** Shefford, Berks

FOCUS
A pedestrian winning time and the runners once again finished tired. The form is difficult to rate with the first two having little form.

NOTEBOOK
Thornton Bridge stole the race at the start as he found himself a long way clear, around 20 lengths, jumping the first and never looked back. There was an element of fluke about the win, and it remains to be seen how well the form works out. *(op 12-1 tchd 10-1 and 16-1)*

The Yellow Earl(IRE) plugged on into second, but was never getting anywhere near the winner. This was not a bad effort and there may be a poor race in him, possibly over further. *(op 6-1)*

Private Jessica stopped to nothing having travelled well and appeared to get bogged down in the conditions. She may be worth another chance back on faster ground. *(tchd 9-4 and 3-1)*

Night Mail was the only other to complete, but was beaten out of sight and achieved little. *(op 5-1)*

Alethea Gee found the change in the going against her and was never going. *(op 9-4 tchd 15-8)*

1210 MERCHANT RENTALS PLC NOVICES' CHASE (14 fncs) 2m 4f
6:35 (6:35) (Class 3) 5-Y-O+ **£5,492** (£1,690; £845; £422)

Form RPR

0-01 **1** **Touch Closer**[41] 893 8-10-11 126 .... (p) TGreenway(5) 121+
(P Bowen) *prom: lft in ld 11th: sn rdn: hdd 3 out: led briefly next: drvn to regain advantage fnl stride* **2/1**[1]

-212 **2** *shd* **Tonic Du Charmil (FR)**[12] 1124 5-11-2 117 .... (t) TScudamore 119
(M C Pipe) *settled handy: nt fluent 9th and 10th: lft 2nd next: led 3 out tl next: sn led again: small advantage and drvn after tl pip* **9/4**[2]

The Form Book, Raceform Ltd, Compton, RG20 6NL

122 **3** *11* **Seaniethesmuggler (IRE)**[16] [1086] 7-10-11 94................ WKennedy(5) 109+
(S Gollings) *hld up: wnt 3rd after 11th: sn rdn and nvr got in a blow at ldng pair* **7/2**[3]

0/5- **4** *13* **Tickton Flyer**[132] [4716] 7-10-7 ....(b) KJMercer(3) 89
(M W Easterby) *hld up last tl 8th: rdn 11th: nvr nr ldrs after but styng on flat* **6/1**

654- **5** *17* **Worlaby Dale**[38] [4507] 9-10-7 ....(p) LVickers(3) 82+
(Mrs S Lamyman) *j.rt: chsd clr ldr tl clsd to ld 7th: blnd 11th and immediately dropped rt out* **20/1**

00/2 **P** **Mr Mighty (IRE)**[34] [944] 9-10-3 87.................................... MrGPewter(7) —
(G R Pewter) *j.rt: led and clr tl 5th: hdd 7th: last by next: p.u 9th* **16/1**

5m 14.4s (11.70) **Going Correction** +0.70s/f (Soft) **6** Ran SP% **111.3**
Speed ratings: **104,103,99,94,87** — CSF £7.05 TOTE £2.70: £1.60, £1.60; EX 8.20.
Owner Donttellthewife Partnership **Bred** I W T And Mrs Loftus **Trained** Little Newcastle, Pembrokes

FOCUS
A tight finish to this fair novice event in which the lead was swapped on several occasions inside the final quarter mile. The form is rated through the third and should work out.

NOTEBOOK
Touch Closer, off the mark on his chase debut at the course last month, had the cheekpieces reapplied here and it appeared to make him concentrate a bit more as he rallied bravely under pressue to regain the lead in the dying strides. He looked set to come off second best for most of the straight, but he is developing in to a fair sort for the time of year and may complete a hat trick. *(op 5-4)*
Tonic Du Charmil(FR) travelled strongly into the straight, but a mistake at the second last appeared to hand Touch Closer the advantage, only for him to battle back into the lead before being nailed on the line again. His remains open to further improvement and will be interesting back handicaps. *(op 7-2)*
Seaniethesmuggler(IRE) was well adrift of the front two and basically lacked a change of gear. He needs a stiffer test. *(op 4-1)*
Tickton Flyer has fared only moderately since going fencing and, like Seaniethesmuggler, he was found wanting for pace. *(op 10-1)*

1211 IRISH NIGHT CONDITIONAL JOCKEYS' H'CAP HURDLE (10 hdls) 2m 6f
7:10 (7:10) (Class 4) (0-110,110) 4-Y-0+ **£3,259** (£931; £465)

Form RPR

013- **1** **Friendly Request**[403] [892] 6-9-9 **82**.. KBurke(5) 96+
(N J Hawke) *settled handy: chal 3 out: led on bit next: immediately burst clr: drvn out* **9/1**

6PP5 **2** *13* **Pequenita**[23] [1045] 5-11-1 **97**..(b) WKennedy 98
(R C Guest) *set stdy pce: rdn and hdd 2 out: no ch w wnr after: all out to keep 2nd pl* **4/1**[3]

P412 **3** *½* **Little Task**[8] [1151] 7-10-8 **90**... PAspell 90
(J S Wainwright) *hld up: effrt outside 3 out: sn pushed along and outpcd: kpt on after last: unable to chal* **3/1**[1]

0432 **4** *nk* **Penteli**[19] [1066] 5-9-4 **82**... MrBenHamilton(10) 82
(C Grant) *chsd ldr tl rdn bef 2 out: styd on same pce after* **7/2**[2]

0-40 **5** *½* **Fantastico (IRE)**[65] [697] 5-9-13 **87**................................(p) CDSharkey(6) 86
(Mrs K Walton) *mostly last: rdn and lost tch 3 out: plugging on again whn nt fluent last* **4/1**[3]

12-0 **6** *½* **Wilfred (IRE)**[81] [488] 4-11-4 **110**... WJones(8) 107
(Jonjo O'Neill) *t.k.h: cl up tl rdn after 3 out: one pce and n.d fr next* **11/2**

5m 58.6s (30.30) **Going Correction** +1.075s/f (Soft) **6** Ran SP% **112.6**
Speed ratings: **87,82,82,81,81 81** CSF £44.14 CT £133.64 TOTE £10.30: £5.30, £1.90; EX 76.10.
Owner W E Donohue **Bred** W E Donohue **Trained** Hewish, Somerset

FOCUS
A moderate handicap and a slow time but the winner destroyed the opposition, who came home well bunched and close to their marks.

NOTEBOOK
Friendly Request ran out an easy winner in receipt of plenty of weight from the second and third, clearing away in impressive fashion having travelled extremely well. This was her first start in over a year and, as long as she avoids the dreaded 'bounce' factor, will be entitled to follow up. *(tchd 8-1)*
Pequenita had no chance with the winner and was always fighting for second best in the home straight. Time may show she faced a very stiff task attempting to give the winner so much weight. *(op 7-2)*
Little Task has been in pretty decent form but may have preferred more of a test of stamina as he was unable to quicken sufficiently. *(op 7-2)*
Penteli was untried on this sort of ground and, although handling it, did not look altogether comfortable on it. *(tchd 4-1)*
Fantastico(IRE) is not the quickest about, but she plodded on and was ultimately not beaten far. *(op 11-2 tchd 6-1)*
Wilfred(IRE) brought up the rear but again, but was not beaten far at all and a return to better ground may help. *(op 7-2)*

1212 MERCHANT RENTALS PLC H'CAP CHASE (12 fncs) 2m 1f 110y
7:45 (7:45) (Class 4) (0-105,105) 5-Y-0+ **£3,779** (£1,163; £581; £290)

Form RPR

633F **1** **Prince Adjal (IRE)**[5] [1176] 5-10-1 **83**..............................(e[1]) LMcGrath(3) 100+
(R C Guest) *mde all: qcknd clr bef 3 out: heavily eased after last* **11/4**[2]

0-2B **2** *21* **Who Dares (IRE)**[5] [1176] 7-10-13 **92**......................................(p) JEMoore 81
(Jonjo O'Neill) *plld hrd tl 1/2-way: hld up in tch: u.p after 9th: no ch w wnr fr next: tk 2nd 2 out: mstke last* **13/8**[1]

0-00 **3** *5* **Gentle Beau**[15] [1098] 7-11-5 **98**... PJBrennan 84+
(P J Hobbs) *hld up towards rr: rdn 7th: wnt mod 2nd and mstke 3 out: relegated 3rd and no ch next* **10/3**[3]

/P2- **4** *9* **Minster York**[77] 11-10-13 **99**.. MrJOwen(7) 76+
(H H G Owen) *cl up: j. slowly 6th and rdn: mstke 9th: rdn and fnd nil bef next: no ch after: mstke last* **16/1**

00P/ **P** **Stantons Church**[91] 8-10-0 **79** oh1.................................... JamesDavies —
(Mrs P Ford) *dropped rr 6th: lost tch and j.rt 8th and 9th: t.o and p.u sn after* **20/1**

065P **U** **Erins Lass (IRE)**[45] [862] 8-10-2 **84**...................................... DCrosse(3) 62
(R Dickin) *mstke 4th: slow next: sn drvn into 2nd: nt fluent 9th: lost pl: 12l 4th but jst bhd 2nd horse whn lunged at 2 out and uns* **7/1**

4m 41.8s (10.70) **Going Correction** +0.70s/f (Soft) **6** Ran SP% **111.0**
Speed ratings: **104,94,92,88,**— — CSF £7.84 CT £13.13 TOTE £3.70: £1.60, £1.40; EX 9.50.
Owner J W Andrews **Bred** Adjalisa Syndicate **Trained** Brancepeth, Co Durham

FOCUS
A poor handicpa but an easy winner, value for more than the official margin and can rate higher.

NOTEBOOK
Prince Adjal(IRE), as with the previous winner, gave his field a good beating and the first-time eyeshield really seemed to help. His previous form in soft ground was not great, but he proved his effectiveness on it here and, if the headgear has the same affect next time, is sure to go close in a follow-up bid. *(op 9-4)*
Who Dares(IRE) was no match for the winner and was basically disappointing. Top connections will have to work their magic to get a win out of him, as he has been disappointing to date. *(op 7-4 tchd 6-4)*
Gentle Beau has been running poorly of late over both hurdles and fences and this was another moderate effort. *(op 9-2)*
Erins Lass(IRE) has not run a decent race for nearly two years, but she was in the process of running well here, only to unseat at a crucial stage. *(op 8-1)*

1213 GALA CASINOS MARES' ONLY NOVICES' HURDLE (8 hdls) 2m 1f 110y
8:15 (8:17) (Class 4) 4-Y-0+ **£3,391** (£969; £484)

Form RPR

1 **Gaelic Roulette (IRE)**[5] 5-10-5 .... TBailey(7) 97+
(J Jay) *settled towards rr: stdy prog 5th: wnt 2nd gng wl after next: led 2 out: hrd pressed to line but hld on gamely* **8/1**

3123 **2** *nk* **Festive Chimes (IRE)**[16] [1089] 4-11-1 103........................... ONelmes(3) 103
(N B King) *hld up midfield: clsd to ld after 3 out: hdd next: drvn and kpt battling tl no ex nr fin* **5/4**[1]

0- **3** *23* **Langdon Lane**[128] [4753] 4-10-11 .... TDoyle 76+
(P R Webber) *cl up in chsng gp: wnt 2nd at 5th tl rdn and tired bdly bef 2 out: mstke last* **7/1**[3]

0302 **4** *7* **Cash Return**[13] [1112] 6-10-5 85..(tp) CMStudd(7) 67
(Mrs S Lamyman) *led briefly 1st: chsd ldr tl 5th: drvn and lost pl next: sn wl bhd* **7/2**[2]

0-P5 **5** *22* **Dawn Frolics**[13] [1112] 4-10-11 .... JamesDavies 44
(M J Gingell) *led after 1st: nt jump wl but sn 8l clr: hdd after 3 out and sn labouring: fin v tired and t.o* **33/1**

0 **6** *10* **Sunny South East (IRE)**[24] [1042] 5-10-12 .... TScudamore 35
(S Gollings) *chsd ldrs: rdn bef 5th: t.o after 3 out* **12/1**

04 **P** **So Cloudy**[38] [917] 4-10-11 .... JMMaguire —
(D McCain) *racd in last pl: struggling 5th: t.o and p.u 2 out* **20/1**

P **Magic Verse**[45] 4-10-8 .... LVickers(3) —
(I W McInnes) *hld up and bhd: mstke 4th: drvn and lost tch after 3 out: t.o and p.u next* **16/1**

4m 34.3s (17.90) **Going Correction** +1.075s/f (Soft)
WFA 4 from 5yo+ 15lb **8** Ran SP% **111.6**
Speed ratings: **103,102,92,89,79 75**,—,— CSF £18.18 TOTE £8.90: £1.60, £1.10, £2.00; EX 24.30 Place 6 £85.15, Place 5 £51.90.
Owner Graham & Lynn Knight **Bred** J F Tuthill **Trained** Newmarket, Suffolk

FOCUS
A typically modest mares-only race with the runner-up setting the standard.

NOTEBOOK
Gaelic Roulette(IRE), a 50-rated Flat performer, will no doubt have delighted connections with this successful switch to hurdling, battling on gamely to deny Festive Chimes. She will struggle once the better horses start to emerge, so connections may be wise to try and find her another race in the coming weeks. *(tchd 9-1)*
Festive Chimes(IRE) set a good standard and went down fighting, but the winner just had too much for her. She was clear of the third and will find a race eventually. *(op Evens)*
Langdon Lane, who made her debut in a Listed prize at the Aintree Grand National meeting, made a moderate start to her hurdling career, but deserves to be given another chance on a faster surface. *(op 5-1 tchd 8-1)*
Cash Return has never run well in soft ground and found this change in going against her. She is worthy of another chance. *(op 9-2)*
T/Plt: £1,489.40 to a £1 stake. Pool: £28,259.45. 13.85 winning tickets. T/Qpdt: £15.30 to a £1 stake. Pool: £3,193.90. 153.50 winning tickets. IM

1214 - 1217a (Foreign Racing) - See Raceform Interactive

[1084]STRATFORD (L-H)
Sunday, August 14

OFFICIAL GOING: Good to firm (good in places)
Wind: Almost nil Weather: Sunny

1218 HOOK NORTON VETS CLAIMING HURDLE (10 hdls) 2m 3f
2:20 (2:20) (Class 4) 4-Y-0+ **£3,610** (£1,111; £555; £277)

Form RPR

4031 **1** **Red Nose Lady**[40] [903] 8-10-9 97...(b) JMogford 97
(G J Smith) *chsd clr ldr: clsd 4th: led after next: drvn and kpt on flat* **12/1**

3532 **2** *¾* **Sir Walter (IRE)**[13] [1121] 12-10-5 96.................................... LStephens(5) 97
(D Burchell) *keen in rr: hdwy 7th: wnt 2nd bef 2 out: sn ev ch: rdn and a hld fr last* **7/1**

040- **3** *1 ¼* **Nightwatchman (IRE)**[164] [4132] 6-10-3 102....................... CDSharkey(7) 96
(S B Clark) *hld up in rr: prog 7th: rdn bef 2 out: styd on steadily but no imp fr last* **20/1**

1103 **4** *9* **Desert Spa (USA)**[9] [1153] 10-10-3 98.............................. MrTJO'Brien(7) 88+
(G E Jones) *hdwy 5th: pressed ldrs after 3 out: rdn and wknd bef next where mstke* **11/2**[3]

-4P2 **5** *4* **Power Unit**[17] [1088] 10-11-2 110... BHitchcott 90+
(Mrs D A Hamer) *prom: rdn and ev ch whn racd awkwardly on bnd bef 2 out: sn wknd* **10/3**[1]

-133 **6** *6* **Brochrua (IRE)**[13] [1121] 5-10-4 96.. CHonour(5) 76
(J D Frost) *j. slowly 3rd: dropped rr and rdn after 5th: lost tch after 3 out* **9/1**

1250 **7** *hd* **Oulton Broad**[9] [1153] 9-11-2 102..(p) APMcCoy 83
(F Jordan) *t.k.h in midfield: effrt bef 7th: flattered after 3 out: gave up tamely bef next* **14/1**

P3P **8** *dist* **Mantilla**[24] [1044] 8-10-8 115...(v) DJBoland(7) —
(Ian Williams) *chsd ldrs: rdn 5th: sn dropped out: no ch 7th: btn 51l* **16/1**

02-6 **9** *dist* **Cybele Eria (FR)**[112] [1] 8-9-12 92.. MNicolls(5) —
(John Allen) *lost tch 6th: t.o 3 out: btn 83l* **18/1**

400- **P** **Perfect Venue (IRE)**[177] [3920] 12-10-10 88.......................... WMarston —
(A J Wilson) *rdn after 5th: sn bhd: t.o and p.u 2 out* **66/1**

P-F0 **P** **Garw Valley**[28] [1027] 6-10-2 84... MrBKing(7) —
(M Wigham) *j.rt: handy tl rdn and fdd bef 6th: t.o and p.u 3 out* **66/1**

5130 **P** **Burning Truth (USA)**[9] [1153] 11-10-10 110............................ DRDennis —
(M Sheppard) *rdn to ld: clr tl 4th: hdd after next: wknd after 7th: p.u after 3 out* **4/1**[2]

0 **P** **Rosemount King (USA)**[35] [943] 6-10-10 .... AO'Keeffe —
(Mrs D A Hamer) *j. slowly 2nd: last and already struggling and drvn whn mstke 3rd: t.o and p.u after 5th* **66/1**

4m 35.6s (0.30) **Going Correction** +0.225s/f (Yiel) **13** Ran SP% **115.7**
Speed ratings: **108,107,107,103,101 99,99**,—,—,— —,—,— CSF £89.45 TOTE £9.10: £2.50, £2.10, £4.00; EX 35.90.Nightwatchman was the subject of a friendly claim.
Owner Slow Donkey Partnership **Bred** R J And Mrs D M L Weston **Trained** Six Hills, Leics

FOCUS
A fair winning time for a claimer and the form looks solid enough with the winner rated to his best.

NOTEBOOK

Red Nose Lady, under a positive ride from Mogford, was able to step up on her recent Uttoxeter win and outbattled weak finisher Sir Walter after the last. She is clearly on the up and has every chance of completing the hat-trick.

Sir Walter(IRE) does not find winning easy, but he ran a solid race and should continue to perform well at this sort of level. A return to two miles may help. *(op 13-2)*

Nightwatchman(IRE) ran an improved race, the rise in distance and drop in grade appearing to help. He should have little trouble finding a race at this level.

Desert Spa(USA) was a bit adrift of the front three and did not appear to see out the trip. *(op 5-1)*

Power Unit folded tamely from two out and was ultimately disappointing. He ran well to a point, but now has a few questions to answer. *(op 9-2)*

Brochrua(IRE) did not offer much and was another who seemed to struggle to last out. *(tchd 10-1)*

Burning Truth(USA) *Official explanation: jockey said gelding was lame*

1219 CHEQUERS AT ETTINGTON H'CAP CHASE (18 fncs) 3m

2:50 (2:51) (Class 4) (0-105,105) 5-Y-O+ **£5,486** (£1,688; £844; £422)

Form RPR

/P1- **1** **Music To My Ears (IRE)**[301] [1752] 7-11-3 **96**................ APMcCoy 113+
(Jonjo O'Neill) *pressed ldr: led 6th: shkn up to go clr 2 out: idled bef last: unchal* **3/1**[1]

P/4- **2** *10* **Yakareem (IRE)**[441] [578] 9-9-9 **79** oh5................ TGreenway[(5)] 84
(D G Bridgwater) *sn chsng ldrs: wnt 2nd bef 13th: rdn 15th: chal briefly next: wknd 2 out* **25/1**

5-3F **3** *20* **Cedar Chief**[17] [1086] 8-8-8 **80** oh14 ow1................(b) PTGallagher[(7)] 65
(B A Pearce) *mstke 4th: chsd wnr 8th tl bef 13th: drvn and lost pl qckly: plugged on into poor 3rd after last* **33/1**

3346 **4** *3* **Fear Siuil (IRE)**[5] [1189] 12-11-3 **96**................(t) DRDennis 78
(Nick Williams) *hdwy 8th: sn niggled along: wnt 3rd at 13th: rdn and wknd 15th: lost poor 3rd after last* **11/2**[2]

3P1P **5** *24* **Honneur Fontenail (FR)**[5] [1191] 6-10-1 **80**................(v[1]) PJBrennan 38
(N J Hawke) *sn rdn along in rr: sme prog in midfield whn nrly fell 9th: in hopeless pursuit of ldrs fr 13th: t.o* **12/1**

-324 **6** *5* **Pillar Of Fire (IRE)**[14] [1109] 11-10-0 **79** oh6................(b[1]) WHutchinson 32
(Ian Williams) *effrt to chse ldrs 8th: rdn 12th: lost tch and blnd 14th: fnd nil after: t.o* **8/1**[3]

40-P **7** *18* **Lambrini Mist**[30] [998] 7-9-9 **79** oh10................ DLaverty[(5)] 14
(Mrs L Williamson) *j. modly in rr: sn getting reminders: lost tch 6th: t.o 9th* **50/1**

4000 **U** **Macgyver (NZ)**[9] [1156] 9-9-10 **82**................ CaptLHorner[(7)] —
(D L Williams) *2nd whn uns rdr 7th* **25/1**

PP0P **P** **Just Sooty**[28] [1025] 10-11-4 **104**................ CDSharkey[(7)] —
(S B Clark) *bhd: losing tch whn mstke 10th: p.u next* **50/1**

5-54 **F** **Alpine Slave**[77] [567] 8-10-11 **90**................ RThornton —
(N J Gifford) *j. slowly 5th: nt fluent 6th: towards rr tl fell 7th* **3/1**[1]

0-40 **F** **Jazz Du Forez (FR)**[70] [653] 8-9-7 **79** oh10................ JPritchard[(7)] —
(John Allen) *reminders 3rd: nvr travelling wl: rr and rdn whn fell 10th* **33/1**

0PP- **P** **Mr Nemo (IRE)**[206] [3442] 9-11-12 **105**................ ChristianWilliams —
(Evan Williams) *keen in ld tl 6th: qckly lost pl: t.o and p.u 12th* **9/1**

P60- **P** **Sunday Habits (IRE)**[273] [2216] 11-10-0 **82**................ DCrosse[(3)] —
(Dr P Pritchard) *j. modly in rr: drvn and lost tch 7th: t.o 10th: p.u 3 out* **16/1**

5m 55.7s (-6.50) **Going Correction** -0.10s/f (Good) **13** Ran SP% **117.6**
Speed ratings: **106,102,96,95,87 85,79,—,—,— —,—,—** CSF £80.04 CT £2061.85 TOTE £3.20: £1.90, £6.30, £7.50; EX 80.70.

Owner John P McManus **Bred** Eamonn McCarthy **Trained** Cheltenham, Gloucs

FOCUS

A moderate race with not much strength in depth and they were strung out like washing, but Music To My Ears ran out a tidy winner.

NOTEBOOK

Music To My Ears(IRE), last seen in October when he was winning for the first time over fences, had the tongue tie he wore for the first time that day left off. However, it did not affect his perfomance and he ran out a tidy winner, albeit from a couple of moderate performers. His trainer is keen to get him out again rather soon before the soft ground is upon us, and as long as he is not put up too much, he would be entitled to go close in a follow-up bid. *(op 7-2 tchd 11-4)*

Yakareem(IRE) ran a bit better last time and confirmed the promise of that run with a clear-cut second to an unexposed rival. He was getting plenty of weight, but is probably capable of winning a small race. *(op 20-1)*

Cedar Chief plodded on through beaten rivals and ran well considering he was quite a way out of the handicap. *(op 50-1)*

Fear Siuil(IRE) has not won since October 2003 and he did not do enough to suggest he is about to end that barren run. *(op 5-1)*

Honneur Fontenail(FR) lost all chance when making a mistake at the ninth and nearly coming down. His jockey was wisely not too hard on him afterwards and he deserves another chance. *(tchd 14-1)*

Alpine Slave is a lazy character and not for the first time his sloppy jumping let him down. *(op 7-2 tchd 4-1)*

1220 LEW BARCLAY BOOKMAKERS STAYERS NOVICES' HURDLE (12 hdls) 2m 6f 110y

3:20 (3:20) (Class 3) 4-Y-O+

£6,182 (£2,345; £1,172; £533; £266; £159)

Form RPR

122 **1** **Romany Prince**[14] [1108] 6-11-8 115................ TScudamore 121+
(S Gollings) *mstke 1st: settled in 3rd pl tl led 6th: rdn 2 out: a holding rival fr last* **2/1**[2]

2132 **2** *1 ½* **Absolut Power (GER)**[28] [1026] 4-11-1 114................(p) MBradburne 112
(J A Geake) *trckd ldrs: wnt 2nd 3 out: rdn and ev ch next: nt qckn after last* **15/8**[1]

40-F **3** *9* **Redspin (IRE)**[20] [394] 5-10-9 104................ DCrosse[(3)] 104+
(J S Moore) *hld up: impr to 2nd pl 6th tl 3 out: sn hrd drvn: effrt to dispute cl whn blnd 2 out: nt rcvr* **14/1**

112P **4** *6* **Kristoffersen**[28] [1026] 5-11-8 110................ DRDennis 105+
(Ian Williams) *hld up tl effrt 6th: cl up 3 out: sn cajoled along: wknd next* **9/1**

6151 **5** *18* **Chase The Sunset (IRE)**[25] [1036] 7-11-8 107................ WMarston 86
(Miss H C Knight) *towards rr: rdn 7th and nvr looked to be gng wl after: lost tch tamely 3 out* **5/1**[3]

56- **6** *11* **Fast Cindy (USA)**[336] [1416] 6-10-5................ PJBrennan 58
(Paul Morris) *towards rr but in tch tl rdn and wknd 3 out* **50/1**

-566 **7** *½* **Smileafact**[46] [860] 5-10-12 73................ BHitchcott 65
(Mrs Barbara Waring) *midfield tl rdn and lost tch 8th* **100/1**

6/ **8** *18* **Scarlet Dawn (IRE)**[700] [1378] 7-10-5................ ChristianWilliams 40
(D A Rees) *nt fluent 3rd: bhd: outpcd 8th: t.o after 3 out* **66/1**

P-15 **9** *9* **Explosive Fox (IRE)**[14] [1108] 4-11-1 107................ TDoyle 41
(C P Morlock) *led 3rd tl 5th: prom tl drvn 8th: dropped out rapidly: t.o* **16/1**

050- **P** **Slinky Malinky**[264] [2411] 7-10-0................ TGreenway[(5)] —
(D G Bridgwater) *led at slow pce tl 3rd: led 5th tl next: losing pl whn p.u and dismntd 8th* **66/1**

5m 37.72s (8.02) **Going Correction** +0.225s/f (Yiel)
WFA 4 from 5yo+ 16lb **10** Ran SP% **113.3**
Speed ratings: **95,94,91,89,83 79,79,72,69,—** CSF £6.10 TOTE £3.00: £1.20, £1.10, £3.10; EX 6.00.

Owner J B Webb **Bred** P And Mrs Venner **Trained** Scamblesby, Lincs

FOCUS

A fair novices' hurdle for the time of year and easy to rate with the first three pretty much to form.

NOTEBOOK

Romany Prince has got his act together over hurdles in recent months and he put up a fine performance, battling on gamely to hold the favourite. He was conceding 7lb to the runner up and it will be interesting to see how he fares in better races once the 'proper' jumpers appear. *(op 7-4)*

Absolut Power(GER) never runs a bad race, but he does not have a great win record and he was outbattled by the winner. He seems honest enough, but could not really be put up as one to follow. *(op 2-1 tchd 7-4)*

Redspin(IRE) was a tad unfortunate as he looked certain to play a hand in the finish when hitting the second last. This ended all chance and he had to make do with third. There should be a similar race in him if in the same sort of form. *(op 16-1)*

Kristoffersen jumped a lot more fluently than when pulled up at the course last time, but was simply outclassed by the front three and was ultimately well beaten. *(op 17-2)*

Chase The Sunset(IRE) once again demonstrated his inability to run two races alike, but due to his inconsistency it would be hard to rule out a much better effort next time. *(op 6-1)*

Slinky Malinky *Official explanation: jockey said mare lost its action but returned sound (tchd 100-1)*

1221 MID-WARWICKSHIRE CLEANING SUPPLIES H'CAP CHASE (13 fncs) 2m 1f 110y

3:50 (3:51) (Class 3) (0-125,125) 5-Y-O+ **£6,929** (£2,132; £1,066; £533)

Form RPR

/12- **1** **East Tycoon (IRE)**[323] [1504] 6-11-12 **125**................ APMcCoy 144+
(Jonjo O'Neill) *settled midfield: hdwy 7th: led gng wl 3 out: clr next: easily: impressive* **9/4**[1]

5463 **2** *6* **Billie John (IRE)**[24] [1049] 10-10-4 **103**................ JimCrowley 107+
(Mrs K Walton) *hld up towards rr: effrt 9th: qcknd ahd bef 3 out where hdd and mstke: one pce and no ch w wnr after* **14/1**

3F-2 **3** *6* **Toi Express (IRE)**[28] [1020] 9-11-6 **119**................ RJohnson 118+
(R J Hodges) *t.k.h in rr: prog 9th: chal and rdn 3 out: sn outpcd by wnr: 3rd and wl hld fr next* **7/1**

21P- **4** *13* **Young Owen**[290] [1866] 7-10-4 **103**................ JMogford 88+
(A G Juckes) *taken to post early: hld up and nvr bttr than midfield: kpt on go modest 4th bef 2 out* **50/1**

1-43 **5** *8* **Fiori**[95] [305] 9-10-9 **108**................ RThornton 84
(P C Haslam) *cl up in 3rd or 4th tl rdn and wknd 7th: n.d after* **11/1**

0/12 **6** *nk* **Ceannairceach (IRE)**[29] [1012] 12-10-10 **109**................ GLee 87+
(J M Jefferson) *hit 6th: chsd ldrs tl wknd and nt fluent 10th* **6/1**[3]

2-11 **7** *2 ½* **Danish Decorum (IRE)**[49] [840] 6-11-8 **121**................ ChristianWilliams 95+
(Evan Williams) *set decent pce: nt fluent 9th and 10th where hdd: eased fr next* **3/1**[2]

0314 **8** *¾* **Flahive's First**[18] [1080] 11-10-0 **104**................ LStephens[(5)] 76
(D Burchell) *last and rdn 4th: nvr gng wl: no ch fr 7th* **25/1**

-123 **9** *4* **Nowator (POL)**[35] [940] 8-11-4 **117**................ JMMaguire 85
(T R George) *pressed ldr and 8l clr of rest early: led briefly 10th: wknd next and eased* **12/1**

4U13 **U** **James Victor (IRE)**[35] [946] 7-9-13 **101**................ RYoung[(3)] —
(N R Mitchell) *uns rdr 1st* **14/1**

4m 9.90s (-2.60) **Going Correction** -0.10s/f (Good) **10** Ran SP% **117.7**
Speed ratings: **101,98,95,89,86 86,85,84,82,—** CSF £33.61 CT £196.33 TOTE £1.60: £1.60, £4.10, £1.70; EX 41.40.

Owner Mrs Gay Smith **Bred** Mrs D Tsui **Trained** Cheltenham, Gloucs

FOCUS

A fair handicap that was strongly run and looks solid, and a good winner who was value for 15 lengths.

NOTEBOOK

East Tycoon(IRE) made it two from two over fences and was quite impressive considering this was his first start in some time, having been off with a fractured shinbone. He is a useful type for the time of year and looks capable of holding his own against the better types in the jump season 'proper'. *(tchd 5-2)*

Billie John(IRE) had his chance and kept on well into second without proving anywhere good enough to trouble the winner. He is not getting any better, but is evidently still capable of winning off this sort of mark. *(op 12-1)*

Toi Express(IRE) was readily outpaced as the winner went on and in the end could only manage a one-paced third. He may soon be ready to win again. *(op 12-1)*

Young Owen never got into it having been held up, running on through beaten horses late to claim fourth. He will find life easier down in grade. *(op 40-1)*

Ceannairceach(IRE) ensured the pace was true, but paid the price for it late on and he was beaten some way out. This was disappointing and he now has a bit to prove. *(op 11-2)*

Flahive's First also suffered as he tried to keep tabs on Danish Decorum early and like that one, was a spent force when the race began to heat up.

1222 J.P. SEAFOODS NOVICES' HURDLE (9 hdls) 2m 110y

4:20 (4:21) (Class 3) 4-Y-O+

£6,322 (£2,398; £1,199; £545; £272; £163)

Form RPR

6P-2 **1** **Harrycat (IRE)**[25] [1037] 4-10-11 105................(p) PHide 107
(V Smith) *mde all: hit 3rd: qcknd clr 6th: 3l ahd whn hit 2 out: flagged after last: all out* **7/1**[3]

1311 **2** *½* **Dewasentah (IRE)**[14] [1112] 6-11-1 110................ GLee 110
(J M Jefferson) *settled 3rd or 4th: pushed along and outpcd whn wnr qcknd 6th: rallied and styd on gamely fr 2 out: snatched 2nd* **4/1**[2]

1112 **3** *nk* **Darrias (GER)**[1] [1204] 4-11-7 132................ ChristianWilliams 116
(P F Nicholls) *settled trcking ldrs: effrt 6th: drvn to chse wnr after 3 out: kpt on u.p fr next: lost 2nd nr fin* **1/1**[1]

4-5 **4** *14* **Bronco Charlie (IRE)**[9] [1158] 7-10-12................ APMcCoy 95+
(Jonjo O'Neill) *nt a fluent: pressed wnr tl after 5th: rdn and lost 2nd after 3 out: fdd tamely* **8/1**

-644 **5** *13* **Giust In Temp (IRE)**[9] [1158] 6-10-5 84................ MrTJO'Brien[(7)] 80
(Mrs K M Sanderson) *hld up and nvr bttr than midfield: lost tch 6th: plodded on* **33/1**

00P **6** *25* **Irish Playwright (IRE)**[53] [811] 5-10-12................ JMogford 55
(D G Bridgwater) *prom tl drvn and wknd bef 5th: t.o whn mstke 2 out* **100/1**

The Form Book, Raceform Ltd, Compton, RG20 6NL

0 7 1 **Bally Hall (IRE)**[9] 1158 5-10-12 ....(t) JEMoore 54
(J M Bradley) *towards rr: lost tch 5th: t.o after 3 out* **100/1**
P **Super Dominion**[48] 8-10-12 .... DRDennis —
(R Hollinshead) *towards rr: struggling 6th: t.o and p.u 2 out* **50/1**
6 P **Maria Bonita (IRE)**[14] 1113 4-10-4 .... JamesDavies —
(C N Kellett) *lft last after 3rd: t.o 6th: p.u after next* **100/1**
0 P **Brown Fox (FR)**[28] 1021 4-10-1 .... ONelmes(3) —
(C J Down) *handy tl after 4th: fading whn mstke 3 out: t.o and p.u next* **100/1**
P **Nashaab (USA)**[8] 8-10-12 .... RThornton —
(P D Evans) *plld hrd in midfield: brief effrt 6th: fdd qckly next: t.o and p.u 2 out* **12/1**
0- P **Ben Lomand**[8] 2705 5-10-12 .... NFehily —
(B W Duke) *t.k.h early: struggling whn jumed slowly 5th: looked irresolute whn slow 3 out: t.o and p.u next* **66/1**
233U P **Mr Jawbreaker (IRE)**[9] 1158 6-10-12 .... AThornton —
(J T Stimpson) *almost ref 1st and jockey had both legs on same side of horse briefly: last whn slow 2nd: struggled over next and p.u* **33/1**

4m 2.40s (4.00) **Going Correction** +0.225s/f (Yiel) 13 Ran SP% **114.6**
Speed ratings: **99,98,98,92,85 74,73,—,—,— —,—,—** CSF £33.42 TOTE £10.80: £2.00, £1.80, £1.10; EX 33.50.
Owner The S.I.R. Partnership **Bred** Piercetown Stud **Trained** Exning, Suffolk
■ The first jumps winner for trainer Vince Smith.

FOCUS
An ordinary contest in which the pace was modest, but it did produce a good finish as a result. The runner-up and fifth set the level for the form.

NOTEBOOK
Harrycat(IRE) was given a good ride and he was able to gain a big enough advantage to hang on from the late challenge of the runner-up. He was probably a bit flattered, having made all at a steady gallop, but this win will do him good and it will be interesting to see how he gets on in handicaps.
Dewasentah(IRE) would have appreciated a stronger gallop and may have won had the pace been solid. She was readily outpaced as the winner kicked, but saw her race out strongly and a return to further will help. *(op 9-2 tchd 5-1)*
Darrias(GER) rallied bravely and kept going right the way to the line, but he was unable to concede the weight in the end and he may have found the race coming too soon, having won at Bangor the previous day. *(op 10-11 tchd 11-10 in places)*
Bronco Charlie(IRE) has shown little since joining current connections and remains one to avoid on this evidence. *(op 6-1)*
Nashaab(USA) gave himself little chance of getting home in pulling hard and he needs to learn to settle better. *Official explanation: jockey said gelding knocked itself (op 10-1)*
Super Dominion *Official explanation: jockey said gelding had a breathing problem (op 10-1)*
Maria Bonita(IRE) *Official explanation: jockey said saddle slipped (op 10-1)*
Brown Fox(FR) *Official explanation: trainer said mare lost a plate in running and was found to be sore on returning home (op 10-1)*

1223 GG.COM CONDITIONAL JOCKEYS' H'CAP HURDLE (9 hdls) 2m 110y
4:50 (4:50) (Class 4) (0-105,105) 4-Y-0+ £3,581 (£1,102; £551; £275)

Form RPR
341 1 **Sterling Guarantee (USA)**[17] 1085 7-11-3 **99**....(p) CDSharkey(3) 98
(N Wilson) *trckd ldrs: coaxed along in 4th after 3 out: hanging lft up st: led 2 out: kpt on steadily fr last* **6/1**
5242 2 1 1/2 **Fiddles Music**[18] 1075 4-10-7 **92**.... LHeard(5) 89
(D Burchell) *prom tl led 5th: rdn and hdd 2 out: ev ch last: nt qckn* **4/1**[1]
0045 3 1 3/4 **Jack Durrance (IRE)**[9] 1156 5-9-11 **79** oh7.... EDehdashti(3) 76+
(G A Ham) *trckd ldrs: rdn into 2nd after 3 out tl bef next: reluctant and one pced after* **33/1**
52P2 4 8 **Feanor**[30] 1001 7-11-12 **105**....(t) KJMercer 93
(Mrs S A Watt) *dropped out wl bhd: effrt 6th: one pce and nt rch ldrs fr bef 2 out* **9/1**
0540 5 11 **Lone Soldier (FR)**[6] 1179 9-11-2 **95**.... PAspell 72
(S B Clark) *chsd ldrs tl rdn and lost pl bef 6th: n.d after* **25/1**
-041 6 3 **Margarets Wish**[32] 973 5-10-7 **86**.... ONelmes 60
(T Wall) *hld up towards rr: effrt to go 2nd at 6th tl rdn after next: wknd bef 2 out* **12/1**
-323 7 7 **Not Amused (UAE)**[54] 806 5-10-0 **84**....(v) DJBoland(5) 51
(Ian Williams) *chsd ldrs tl drvn and wknd 3 out* **11/2**[3]
5204 8 3 1/2 **Saorsie**[13] 1121 7-11-5 **98**.... RStephens 61
(J C Fox) *bhd: rdn 3rd: nvr gng wl after: no ch fr 6th* **10/1**
6U-5 9 21 **Gabla (NZ)**[6] 1179 9-11-1 **102**....(b) JMoorman(8) 44
(R C Guest) *cl 2nd tl led 4th: hdd next: rdn and dropped out qckly: t.o* **20/1**
6-P5 10 22 **Chakra**[5] 1188 11-11-3 **96**.... TJMalone 16
(C J Gray) *hld up and bhd: lost tch after 5th: t.o* **22/1**
5651 F **Queen Excalibur**[24] 1046 6-10-6 **85**.... JamesDavies —
(C Roberts) *hld up: 8th whn fell 4th* **5/1**[2]
446P P **Tubber Streams (IRE)**[17] 1084 8-10-1 **85**.... PTGallagher(5) —
(B A Pearce) *t.k.h: led tl 4th: wknd rapidly 6th: t.o and p.u 2 out* **33/1**
0U2F P **Knight's Emperor (IRE)**[17] 1088 8-10-13 **92**.... WKennedy —
(J L Spearing) *mstke 2nd: nt fluent 3rd: midfield tl rdn 5th: sn wknd: t.o and p.u 2 out* **10/1**

4m 4.10s (5.70) **Going Correction** +0.225s/f (Yiel)
WFA 4 from 5yo+ 15lb 13 Ran SP% **121.0**
Speed ratings: **95,94,93,89,84 83,79,78,68,57 —,—,—** CSF £29.05 CT £740.18 TOTE £7.80: £2.50, £2.00, £6.10; EX 28.70 Place 6 £92.52, Place 5 £12.12.
Owner Ian W Glenton Peter Whinham Keith Benson **Bred** P W Freedman **Trained** Upper Helmsley, N Yorks

FOCUS
A bad race to round off proceedings with the winner to his mark and a slight improvement from the third.

NOTEBOOK
Sterling Guarantee(USA) ran out a workmanlike winner of this bad race, plugging on well under a decent ride. He tended to edge to his left under pressure and is not straightforward, so cannot be backed with confidence to follow up. *(op 11-2)*
Fiddles Music, not for the first time this season, had to settle for the runner-up spot. She did nothing wrong but just lacks that extra bit of pace at the end of her races. *(op 9-2)*
Jack Durrance(IRE) has definitely got a race in him and, although anything but consistent, may be worth perservering with at a lowly level. *(tchd 28-1)*
Feanor came from a long way back under an over-confident ride and may have been closer had he been ridden more positively. *(op 11-1)*
Lone Soldier(FR) is a poor performer and needs dropping into selling company before winning again.
T/Plt: £119.40 to a £1 stake. Pool: £40,445.05. 247.25 winning tickets. T/Qpdt: £5.60 to a £1 stake. Pool: £3,314.50. 431.10 winning tickets. IM

1224 - 1230a (Foreign Racing) - See Raceform Interactive

[1152] WORCESTER (L-H)
Wednesday, August 17

OFFICIAL GOING: Good to firm
First flight in home straight omitted.
Wind: Nil Weather: Sunny and hot

1231 WORCESTER FESTIVAL NOVICES' HURDLE (10 hdls 2 omitted) 3m
1:40 (1:40) (Class 4) 4-Y-0+ £3,373 (£1,038; £519; £259)

Form RPR
1 **Moscow Blue**[64] 4-10-9 ....(t) PMoloney 105+
(Evan Williams) *hld up in rr: mstke 2nd: nt fluent 4th: hdwy 7th: led appr last: rdn and styd on wl* **33/1**
F0-0 2 6 **Ballynattin Buck (IRE)**[18] 1104 9-10-12 104....(t) DRDennis 100
(M Sheppard) *t.k.h: a.p: led 5th: clr 6th: rdn appr 2 out: hdd appr last: one pce* **12/1**
0611 3 7 **Weston Rock**[17] 1108 6-11-3 111.... MrMWalford(7) 106+
(T D Walford) *hld up: hdwy 6th: rdn after 8th: wknd after 2 out* **11/8**[1]
1 4 3/4 **Charango Star**[35] 977 7-11-4 108.... RJohnson 98
(W K Goldsworthy) *led to 5th: rdn appr 8th: wknd appr 2 out* **7/4**[2]
15- 5 dist **That's For Sure**[364] 1212 5-10-12 .... ChristianWilliams —
(Evan Williams) *led after 1st to 5th: rdn and wknd appr 2 out: t.o* **8/1**[3]
6 6 18 **Grande Cascade**[35] 976 4-9-11 .... MNicolls(5) —
(Lucinda Featherstone) *hld up: lost tch 6th: sn t.o: fin lame* **125/1**
U-0 P **Amyroseisuppose**[49] 866 6-10-5 .... TDoyle —
(C P Morlock) *bhd fr 4th: t.o whn p.u bef 8th* **80/1**
000- P **Morgan Be**[200] 3598 5-10-7 .... DLaverty(5) —
(Mrs L Williamson) *prom tl wknd appr 4th: t.o 6th: p.u bef 8th* **100/1**
634/ F **Countess Kiri**[129] 7-10-5 ....(p) JEMoore —
(P Bowen) *nt jump wl: prom: reminders after 3rd: wknd 6th: t.o whn fell 8th* **16/1**

5m 37.2s (-12.00) **Going Correction** -0.525s/f (Firm)
WFA 4 from 5yo+ 17lb 9 Ran SP% **109.1**
Speed ratings: **99,97,94,94,— —,—,—,—** CSF £328.54 TOTE £41.30: £6.30, £2.90, £1.10; EX 214.00.
Owner George Houghton **Bred** Juddmonte Farms **Trained** Cowbridge, Vale Of Glamorgan

FOCUS
An ordinary novices' hurdle. The penalised third and fourth ran to their marks and the winner is an above-average newcomer.

NOTEBOOK
Moscow Blue, who failed to win on the Flat for John Gosden and latterly Howard Johnson, appeared the stable's second string on this hurdling debut. He was less than fluent in rear through the first part of the race, but steadily worked his way into the picture and ran out a ready winner in the end. The tongue tie and crossed noseband benefited him but it remains to be seen if they work next time. *(op 25-1)*
Ballynattin Buck(IRE), who won a Listed handicap chase for Arthur Moore at Wexford in November, was making his debut for this yard. Racing rather keenly and in front before halfway on this return to hurdles, he was reeled in between the last two flights and finished sore. He could be interesting back over fences. *(op 11-1)*
Weston Rock, who was kept a little wide of his rivals, was anchored by his double penalty. He seems more effective at slightly shorter. *(op 13-8)*
Charango Star, penalised for his win over course-and-distance, was in trouble with five to jump, but this thorough stayer did keep on for pressure. *(op 6-4 tchd 15-8)*
That's For Sureis a stablemate of the winner. A bumper scorer at this venue who was making his hurdling debut, he ran as if this first start for a year was needed. *(tchd 9-1)*

1232 BETFREDCASINO.COM BEGINNERS' CHASE (18 fncs) 2m 7f 110y
2:15 (2:15) (Class 4) 5-Y-0+ £4,036 (£1,242; £621; £310)

Form RPR
0/4- 1 **Splash Out Again**[346] 1370 7-11-2 .... RJohnson 107+
(P Bowen) *prom: mstke 1st: led 4th: rdn appr last: styd on wl* **4/1**[3]
2-P2 2 1 1/2 **Mylo**[35] 972 7-11-2 .... APMcCoy 104
(Jonjo O'Neill) *hld up: hdwy 12th: chsd wnr 4 out: rdn appr 2 out: styd on same pce flat* **9/4**[1]
P/20 3 8 **Boobee (IRE)**[64] 745 9-11-2 .... ChristianWilliams 96
(Evan Williams) *led 2nd to 4th: prom tl wknd appr 3 out* **13/2**
1344 4 dist **Blueberry Ice (IRE)**[28] 1038 7-10-2 103.... CMStudd(7) —
(B G Powell) *bhd fr 4th: hdwy 8th: mstke 14th: sn wknd: t.o* **14/1**
-03P 5 dist **Rash Moment (FR)**[12] 1155 6-10-9 .... RSpate(7) —
(Mrs K Waldron) *j. bdly rt: a in rr: t.o fr 9th* **16/1**
60-6 P **Mister Kingston**[27] 1044 14-10-6 56....(b) JStevenson(10) —
(R Dickin) *a bhd: t.o 9th: p.u after 14th* **100/1**
00-6 P **Dantes Venture (IRE)**[38] 949 8-11-2 .... TDoyle —
(Miss I E Craig) *bhd fr 5th: mstke 7th: t.o whn p.u bef 10th* **10/1**
25PP P **Jivaty (FR)**[57] 805 8-11-2 94.... RThornton —
(Mrs A J Hamilton-Fairley) *led to 4th: prom tl wknd 13th: t.o whn p.u bef 4 out* **20/1**
-522 P **Farington Lodge (IRE)**[19] 1100 7-11-2 86.... DElsworth —
(Mrs S J Smith) *hld up: hdwy 10th: nt fluent 12th: 4th whn p.u appr 4 out* **7/2**[2]

5m 46.5s (-8.40) **Going Correction** -0.35s/f (Good) 9 Ran SP% **113.7**
Speed ratings: **100,99,96,—,— —,—,—,—** CSF £13.80 TOTE £4.30: £2.40, £1.10, £2.10; EX 15.20.
Owner R Owen & P Fullagar **Bred** K And Mrs Magee **Trained** Little Newcastle, Pembrokes

FOCUS
A modest event of its type. The winner ran to the level of his hurdles form and the runner-up to the form of his recent chase \n\x\x debut.

NOTEBOOK
Splash Out Again was fit enough for this first run for 11 months. Making much of the running, he put in a rather novicey round of jumping on this chasing debut but stayed on willingly to hold off the favourite. He only ran four times over hurdles and is entitled to improve as he gathers experience. *(op 7-2)*
Mylo, without the usual headgear, did not do a great deal wrong on this step back up in trip, but this frustrating individual again found one to beat him. *(tchd 11-4)*
Boobee(IRE) made virtually all the running to land two point-to-points in the spring but was unable to dominate. He was not disgraced on this debut over regulation fences but would probably prefer easier ground. *(op 5-1)*
Dantes Venture(IRE) *Official explanation: jockey said gelding lost its action (op 11-1 tchd 12-1)*
Farington Lodge(IRE) had dropped out of contention and looked set to finish fourth when he was suddenly pulled up before the fourth last. *(op 11-1 tchd 12-1)*

1233 CANNONS HEALTH CLUB (S) HURDLE (8 hdls 2 omitted) 2m 4f
2:50 (2:50) (Class 5) 4-Y-O+ **£2,940** (£840; £420)

Form RPR
0604 **1** **Outside Investor (IRE)**8 [1187] 5-11-7 80 (p) RThornton 91
(P R Rodford) *hld up: hdwy 6th: rdn after 2 out: led sn after last: drvn out* **14/1**
/36- **2** *2* **Winding River (IRE)**205 [3514] 8-11-0 APMcCoy 83+
(C R Egerton) *hld up in tch: led appr 2 out: rdn whn swvd rt and hdd sn after last: nt run on* **1/1**1
-P00 **3** *1 1/4* **Cool Dante (IRE)**38 [941] 10-11-7 88 JMMaguire 88
(T R George) *hld up: hdwy 7th: rdn appr 2 out: one pce flat* **12/1**
P560 **4** *6* **Felix The Fox (NZ)**42 [911] 5-11-0 87 CLlewellyn 76+
(N A Twiston-Davies) *hld up: hdwy 4th: led 5th: hdd appr 2 out: rdn appr last: wknd flat* **10/1**3
P0FU **5** *24* **Lovers Tale**8 [1187] 7-10-7 82 EDehdashti(7) 51
(G A Ham) *hld up and bhd: hdwy 5th: pckd 6th: sn rdn: wknd appr 2 out* **80/1**
00-P **6** *dist* **Shellin Hill (IRE)**16 [1122] 11-11-0 75 (p) VSlattery —
(R J Baker) *led to 2nd: led 4th to 5th: wknd 6th: t.o* **40/1**
000- **7** *8* **Welsh Doll (IRE)**117 [4954] 6-10-7 TScudamore —
(D Brace) *hld up in tch: wknd 5th: t.o* **50/1**
30P6 **8** *22* **Spectacular Hope**31 [1017] 5-11-0 79 (p) AThornton —
(J W Mullins) *hld up in tch: wknd 5th: t.o* **10/1**3
U **Zeis (IRE)**303 5-10-11 (t) ONelmes(3) —
(Miss J R Gibney) *hld up: hdwy appr 5th: prom whn blnd and uns rdr 6th* **16/1**
0U/0 **P** **Investment Force (IRE)**8 [1188] 7-11-0 95 (p) MrMHooper(7) —
(M Sheppard) *prom: jnd ldrs after 3rd: wknd 5th: t.o whn p.u bef 2 out* **40/1**
4PP0 **P** **Greenacres Boy**9 [1180] 10-11-7 75 (p) AO'Keeffe —
(M Mullineaux) *hld up and bhd: hdwy after 3rd: wknd 6th: t.o whn p.u bef 2 out* **40/1**
3-P3 **P** **Glencoyle (IRE)**20 [1085] 5-11-7 105 (p) PMoloney —
(Miss L Day) *w ldr: reminders after 1st: led 2nd to 4th: sn rdn: wknd after 5th: p.u after 6th: lame* **5/1**2

4m 40.3s (-7.70) **Going Correction** -0.525s/f (Firm) **12** Ran SP% **115.6**
Speed ratings: **94,93,92,90,80** —,—,—,—,— —,— CSF £28.18 TOTE £18.90: £3.90, £1.10, £4.10; EX 49.70.The winner was bought in for 3,250gns. Winding River was claimed by Dr R. D. P. Newland for £6,000.
Owner Les Trott **Bred** Moyglare Stud Farm Ltd **Trained** Ash, Somerset

FOCUS
A very modest affair. The winner set a personal best and the third and fourth ran to their marks.

NOTEBOOK
Outside Investor(IRE) has been found wanting in this sort of event plenty of times in the past and had the least chance on official figures. He had appeared not to get home over a furlong less when returned to hurdles last time, but he stayed on to catch the flagging favourite on the run-in. *(op 16-1)*
Winding River(IRE), off the track since running in a handicap chase in January, moved to the front going best, but he jinked soon after landing over the final flight and threw away the advantage. He has looked a weak finisher before and it would be no surprise to see the headgear on again for his new yard. *(op 11-8 tchd 10-11)*
Cool Dante(IRE) has not sparkled since landing a handicap chase at Perth a year ago but ran a better race on this drop in grade. *(op 9-1)*
Felix The Fox(NZ), in a seller for the first time, had his chance but was found out in the end by this longer trip. *(op 15-2)*
Glencoyle(IRE) *Official explanation: jockey said gelding was lame (op 11-2 tchd 6-1)*
Zeis(IRE), a winner of two 12-furlong claimers for Hughie Morrison in 2004, was just behind the leaders on this hurdles bow and debut for this yard when blundering away his rider. *(op 11-2 tchd 6-1)*

1234 BETFREDPOKER.COM H'CAP HURDLE (10 hdls 2 omitted) 3m
3:25 (3:25) (Class 3) (0-125,124) 4-Y-O+ **£4,745** (£1,460; £730; £365)

Form RPR
131F **1** **Celtic Boy (IRE)**32 [1013] 7-11-9 **121** RJohnson 125
(P Bowen) *hld up: hdwy appr 6th: rdn appr 2 out: led last: all out* **5/2**1
0616 **2** *2* **Champagne Harry**28 [1039] 7-11-8 **120** CLlewellyn 122
(N A Twiston-Davies) *chsd ldr: led appr 7th: rdn after 2 out: hdd last: nt qckn* **9/1**
00P- **3** *11* **Majestic (IRE)**126 [4823] 10-11-5 **124** (bt) DJBoland(7) 115
(Ian Williams) *led: clr 2nd: hdd appr 7th: wknd appr 2 out* **25/1**
P515 **4** *1 1/4* **Room To Room Gold (IRE)**17 [1111] 9-11-1 **113** AThornton 104+
(R H Alner) *racd wd: hld up in tch: mstke 6th: wknd appr 2 out* **12/1**
1311 **5** *23* **Downing Street (IRE)**28 [1039] 4-11-4 **119** (b) AO'Keeffe 98+
(Jennie Candlish) *hld up in rr: hdwy appr 7th: wknd appr 2 out* **5/2**1
0-01 **6** *dist* **After Me Boys**63 [759] 11-11-3 **115** DElsworth —
(Mrs S J Smith) *bhd fr 6th: t.o* **13/2**2
/F-2 **P** **Stocks 'n Shares**63 [762] 9-10-0 **98** oh5 MFoley —
(Miss E C Lavelle) *a bhd: t.o whn p.u bef 2 out* **7/1**3
-004 **P** **Masters Of War (IRE)**32 [1016] 8-11-6 **118** (t) APMcCoy —
(Jonjo O'Neill) *hld up: hit 2nd: blnd 5th: sn bhd: t.o whn p.u bef 8th* **10/1**

5m 33.5s (-15.70) **Going Correction** -0.525s/f (Firm)
WFA 4 from 7yo+ 17lb **8** Ran SP% **113.6**
Speed ratings: **105,104,100,100,92** —,—,— CSF £24.56 CT £449.16 TOTE £4.00: £1.20, £3.00, £6.20; EX 32.80.
Owner Walters Plant Hire Ltd **Bred** William G Corrigan **Trained** Little Newcastle, Pembrokes

FOCUS
A fair handicap hurdle which could be rated a bit higher.

NOTEBOOK
Celtic Boy(IRE) has become too high in the handicap over fences but was able to race off a mark only 2lb higher than when landing a chase in June. He had to work hard to get to the front and there was nothing to spare at the end. *(op 4-1)*
Champagne Harry has yet to win a handicap but he continues to slide down the weights and went down fighting, finishing clear of the remainder. *(op 15-2)*
Majestic(IRE), who is without a win since early 2001, soon held a clear lead on this first run since the spring. He was collared in the back straight but did keep on again for pressure. *(op 16-1)*
Room To Room Gold(IRE), who was kept wide for most of the way in search of the best ground, did not get home over this longer trip. He has now been beaten twice off higher marks since scoring at Newton Abbot. *(op 10-1 tchd 9-1)*
Downing Street(IRE), bidding for his fourth win of the campaign, was 3lb higher than when scoring over course and distance a month ago when he had Champagne Harry behind. He moved into third place leaving the back straight but was soon on the retreat again. *(op 10-3)*
Stocks 'n Shares *Official explanation: trainer said mare was unsuited by good to firm ground (op 8-1)*

1235 DROITWICH LANDROVER MAIDEN HURDLE (7 hdls 1 omitted) 2m
4:00 (4:01) (Class 4) 4-Y-O+ **£3,445** (£1,060; £530; £265)

Form RPR
1 **Compton Drake**10 6-10-9 (t) SCrawford(7) 116+
(G A Butler) *plld hrd: sn prom: led 3rd: r.o wl* **14/1**
-123 **2** *11* **Don And Gerry (IRE)**28 [1037] 4-10-8 RThornton 91+
(P D Evans) *hld up: hdwy 3rd: rdn appr 2 out: kpt on one pce flat* **11/4**2
43 **3** *2 1/2* **Anko (POL)**35 [982] 6-11-2 RJohnson 95
(P J Hobbs) *hld up and bhd: rdn and hdwy appr 2 out: one pce flat* **10/1**
0622 **4** *1 1/2* **Not To Be Missed**56 [811] 7-10-9 89 WHutchinson 87
(R Dickin) *hld up: hdwy 3rd: one pce fr 2 out* **7/1**3
6445 **5** *2 1/2* **Giust In Temp (IRE)**3 [1222] 6-10-9 84 MrTJO'Brien(7) 91
(Mrs K M Sanderson) *hld up: hdwy 3rd: no imp fr 2 out* **33/1**
0-3 **6** *11* **Lucky Arthur (IRE)**12 [1158] 4-10-5 ONelmes(3) 72
(J G M O'Shea) *bhd: rdn 5th: nvr trbld ldrs* **25/1**
3- **7** *1 1/4* **Corrib Drift (USA)**63 [3946] 5-11-2 MBatchelor 79
(Jamie Poulton) *led: nt fluent and hdd 3rd: rdn and wknd appr 2 out* **16/1**
35-0 **8** *7* **Holly Walk**12 [1158] 4-10-8 85 (p) ATinkler 64
(A G Juckes) *a bhd* **40/1**
13 **9** *18* **Zumrah (IRE)**48 [876] 4-11-1 APMcCoy 53
(P Bowen) *hld up: hdwy appr 4th: wknd appr 2 out* **2/1**1
10 *21* **Barking Mad (USA)**9 7-11-2 LAspell 33
(J R Boyle) *prom: mstke 1st: wknd appr 5th* **15/2**
4FP5 **11** *26* **Flurry**28 [1036] 6-10-9 MBradburne —
(C J Down) *hld up: rdn after 4th: sn bhd: t.o* **100/1**
12 *3* **Grey Admiral (USA)**404 4-11-1 PJBrennan —
(B R Johnson) *a bhd: mstke 4th: t.o* **66/1**

3m 38.3s (-10.10) **Going Correction** -0.525s/f (Firm)
WFA 4 from 5yo+ 15lb **12** Ran SP% **117.6**
Speed ratings: **104,98,97,96,95 89,89,85,76,66 53,51** CSF £52.03 TOTE £16.20: £5.20, £1.60, £3.70; EX 84.30.
Owner Erik Penser **Bred** Meon Valley Stud **Trained** Blewbury, Oxon

FOCUS
Probably a decent race of its type. The winner was value for further and the second and third ran to their marks achieved over course-and-distance.

NOTEBOOK
Compton Drake ◆, a six-times winner on the Flat at up to a mile and a quarter, was impressive in the context of this event despite showing signs of greenness on his hurdling debut. He has plenty of size about him and ought to be able to handle a step up in grade. *(op 10-1 tchd 16-1)*
Don And Gerry(IRE), placed in similar company over course and distance, came up against an opponent with far more scope than her but looks a fair guide to the form. *(op 5-1)*
Anko(POL), one place behind Don And Gerry here on his latest start, was set a fair deal to do but might have been a little nearer had he not got in a bit close to the second last. *(op 9-1 tchd 12-1)*
Not To Be Missed, who held a clear chance on official figures, appeared to run her race with no apparent excuse on this first run for two months. *(op 11-2)*
Giust In Temp(IRE) ran his race again but is an exposed performer. *(op 40-1)*
Holly Walk *Official explanation: jockey said filly was unsuited by good to firm ground (op 33-1)*
Zumrah(IRE) disappointed in her second bumper and it was a similar story on this hurdles debut as she faded rather tamely after looking likely to take a hand in the finish. *(op 15-8 tchd 9-4)*
Barking Mad(USA), a prolific winner on the Flat, was too keen on this hurdles bow and did not get home. *(op 7-1)*

1236 ENTERTAINMENT FREE FOR CHILDREN H'CAP CHASE (15 fncs) 2m 4f 110y
4:35 (4:35) (Class 4) (0-105,105) 5-Y-O+ **£4,212** (£1,296; £648; £324)

Form RPR
25P- **1** **Sacrifice**230 [3112] 10-10-12 **91** MFoley 101
(K Bishop) *hld up and bhd: stdy hdwy 7th: led 2 out: drvn clr flat* **16/1**
3-41 **2** *5* **Tommy Spar**28 [1040] 5-11-7 **100** APMcCoy 106+
(P Bowen) *hld up in mid-div: hdwy 8th: led 11th: rdn and hdd 2 out: no ex flat* **3/1**1
600 **3** *5* **Lost In The Snow (IRE)**28 [1037] 7-10-0 **79** oh1 PMoloney 79
(M Sheppard) *hld up in mid-div: hdwy 10th: wknd last* **20/1**
-643 **4** *8* **Saby (FR)**37 [958] 7-11-6 **99** RJohnson 93+
(P J Hobbs) *bhd tl styd on fr 2 out: n.d* **8/1**
1/53 **5** *11* **Noble Justice (IRE)**21 [1080] 9-11-3 **103** JamesWhite(7) 84
(R J Hodges) *hld up in tch: lost pl 8th: rallied 11th: wknd appr 4 out* **14/1**
50-0 **6** *9* **Dream With Me (FR)**83 [511] 8-11-11 **104** (t) MBradburne 76
(J A Geake) *bhd: short-lived effrt appr 4 out* **20/1**
166 **7** *6* **Manoram (GER)**38 [946] 6-11-12 **105** (v) DRDennis 71
(Ian Williams) *prom tl wknd appr 3 out* **20/1**
-005 **P** **Debatable**21 [1076] 6-10-0 **79** oh1 PJBrennan —
(N J Hawke) *a bhd: mstke 9th: p.u bef 11th* **15/2**3
/0-6 **R** **Aruba Dam (IRE)**31 [1018] 7-10-0 **79** oh1 JamesDavies —
(B G Powell) *a bhd: blnd 4 out: t.o whn ref last* **22/1**
12-5 **P** **Native Daisy (IRE)**12 [1157] 10-11-6 **99** RThornton —
(C J Down) *prom tl wknd 11th: t.o whn p.u bef last* **4/1**2
/0P3 **P** **Wave Rock**20 [1088] 10-10-10 **89** (v1) NFehily —
(A W Carroll) *led to 11th: wkng whn mstke 3 out: bhd whn p.u bef last* **18/1**
5-23 **P** **Wild Power (GER)**64 [752] 7-11-6 **102** (p) ONelmes(3) —
(Mrs H R J Nelmes) *hld up in tch: wknd appr 4 out: bhd whn p.u bef 2 out* **8/1**
/P-P **P** **Pharpost (IRE)**80 [572] 10-11-8 **101** (v1) AO'Keeffe —
(A G Juckes) *hld up in tch: rdn 8th: wknd 9th: t.o whn p.u bef 4 out* **40/1**
0505 **P** **Bobosh**32 [1016] 9-11-6 **99** WHutchinson —
(R Dickin) *prom: blnd 1st: rdn appr 5th: sn lost pl: bhd whn p.u bef 9th* **16/1**

4m 56.7s (-10.80) **Going Correction** -0.35s/f (Good) **14** Ran SP% **123.8**
Speed ratings: **106,104,102,99,94 91,89**,—,—,— —,—,—,— CSF £62.93 CT £1016.14 TOTE £23.10: £5.60, £1.90, £10.10; EX 222.80.
Owner K Bishop **Bred** Michael James Cornish **Trained** Spaxton, Somerset

FOCUS
Quite a competitive if low-grade handicap. A personal best from the winner, with the second improving on his recent hurdles win.

NOTEBOOK
Sacrifice has never previously scored outside hunter chases and had been beaten in 17 handicaps, but he came good on this first start since December. He obviously goes well fresh and could struggle to reproduce this form next time.
Tommy Spar, a recent winner over hurdles at this venue, ran a good race on this chasing debut but was gunned down after jumping out to his right when the pressure was on. *(op 7-2 tchd 4-1)*
Lost In The Snow(IRE), a winning pointer, has been struggling over hurdles, but he ran a better race on his first run over fences. There could be a chase in him if the Handicapper drops him a few pounds. *(op 16-1)*
Saby(FR) is back on a decent mark now, but although he stayed on in the latter stages he never looked like troubling the principals. *(op 9-1)*

The Form Book, Raceform Ltd, Compton, RG20 6NL

Noble Justice(IRE) has become well handicapped if he can recapture the form he was showing a couple of years ago.
Debatable *Official explanation: jockey said gelding was lame* *(op 14-1 tchd 7-1)*

1237 K.D.T.C. 35TH ANNIVERSARY HBLB STANDARD OPEN NATIONAL HUNT FLAT RACE 2m

5:05 (5:10) (Class 6) 4-6-Y-O **£1,906** (£544; £272)

Form RPR

2 **1** **Fountain Crumble**[28] 1042 4-10-8 ChristianWilliams 94+
(P F Nicholls) *hld up in mid-div: hdwy 6f out: led over 2f out: rdn over 1f out: r.o* **5/2**[2]

0/-1 **2** *1 ½* **Youlbesolucky (IRE)**[28] 1042 6-11-9 APMcCoy 108+
(Jonjo O'Neill) *a.p: led 5f out: rdn and hdd over 2f out: nt qckn ins fnl f* **6/4**[1]

0 **3** *5* **Dontelldonandgerry**[56] 817 5-10-9 RThornton 89
(P D Evans) *led 3f: led 6f out to 5f out: kpt on one pce ins fnl f* **12/1**

3 **4** *3 ½* **Sevens Delight**[27] 1048 5-10-9 DElsworth 85
(Mrs S J Smith) *hld up in tch: rdn and wknd over 1f out* **7/1**[3]

5 *¾* **Rising Tempest** 4-10-1 TMessenger[(7)] 83
(Mrs S J Smith) *hld up in mid-div: rdn and hdwy 4f out: wknd over 2f out* **20/1**

6 *5* **Must Be Keen** 6-11-2 LAspell 87+
(Ernst Oertel) *hld up towards rr: hdwy 5f out: rdn whn swtchd lft over 2f out: sn wknd* **33/1**

60-6 **7** *3* **Soviet Committee**[27] 1048 5-11-2 (t) ARoss 83
(T J Fitzgerald) *hld up in tch: lost pl 6f out: n.d after* **16/1**

8 *1 ¼* **Mr Cee** 5-10-6 ARAdams[(10)] 82
(Mrs S J Smith) *prom tl wknd 3f out* **20/1**

0-0 **9** *11* **Hypark (IRE)**[28] 1042 6-10-4 LStephens[(5)] 64
(C Roberts) *a mid-div* **33/1**

10 *7* **Dovers Venture** 4-10-8 JMogford 56
(Miss M E Rowland) *nvr nr ldrs* **66/1**

0-5 **11** *5* **Firion King (IRE)**[27] 1048 5-10-9 BWharfe[(7)] 59
(T H Caldwell) *prom tl wknd over 4f out* **25/1**

12 *25* **Canis Lupus** 4-10-8 MrPMason[(7)] 33
(J A T De Giles) *a bhd* **33/1**

0-5 **13** *dist* **Keen Royal**[106] 179 4-10-8 BHitchcott —
(Miss Suzy Smith) *uns rdr bef s: hld up towards rr: sme hdwy 10f out: wl bhd fnl 5f: t.o* **28/1**

000- **14** *1* **Home Rule**[118] 4941 5-10-2 JPemberton[(7)] —
(G P Enright) *a bhd: t.o fnl 8f* **50/1**

15 *2 ½* **Ben Gorm (IRE)** 5-10-11 (t) TGreenway[(5)] —
(P A Pritchard) *bhd: rn wd bnd after 5f: t.o fnl 8f* **50/1**

16 *26* **Busy Man (IRE)**[101] 6-11-2 TScudamore —
(J R Jenkins) *plld hrd: led after 3f to 6f out: sn wknd: t.o* **50/1**

P **Willhebemyguy** 6-10-13 ONelmes[(3)] —
(Mrs H R J Nelmes) *bhd tl p.u 5f out* **40/1**

3m 36.7s (-11.10) **Going Correction** -0.525s/f (Firm)
WFA 4 from 5yo+ 1lb **17** Ran SP% **130.1**
Speed ratings: **106,105,102,101,100 98,96,96,90,87 84,72,—,—,— —,—** CSF £6.01 TOTE £2.90: £1.20, £1.10, £3.70; EX 5.80 Place 6 £57.10, Place 5 £27.75.
Owner The Fountains Partnership **Bred** A And S Franklin **Trained** Ditcheat, Somerset

FOCUS
A fair time for a bumper when compared with the earlier hurdle over the same trip. The first two both improved on their debut runs here but there was not much strength in depth.

NOTEBOOK
Fountain Crumble went down by half a length to Youlbesolucky here a month ago, but was able to turn the tables on these 6lb better terms. She is not very big, but showed a good attitude to hold off her much larger opponent and she may be able to defy the penalty in a mares-only race. *(op 2-1 tchd 11-4)*
Youlbesolucky(IRE) made a bold bid to follow up his course win under a penalty but found the filly just too strong at the weights this time. *(op 3-1)*
Dontelldonandgerry settled better than on her debut and obviously has some ability. *(op 10-1 tchd 9-1)*
Sevens Delight probably ran up to the form of her third at Uttoxeter on her debut when she had two of these behind. *(tchd 6-1)*
Rising Tempest, a stablemate of the fourth, is not very big but this was a pleasing start to her career. *(tchd 14-1)*
Willhebemyguy *Official explanation: jockey said gelding was distressed* *(op 25-1)*
T/Plt: £131.80 to a £1 stake. Pool: £29,422.90. 162.85 winning tickets. T/Qpdt: £31.10 to a £1 stake. Pool: £2,229.40. 52.90 winning tickets. KH

1238 - 1244a (Foreign Racing) - See Raceform Interactive

563 FONTWELL (L-H)

Thursday, August 18

OFFICIAL GOING: Good to firm
Wind: Nil

1245 JEWSON NOVICES' HURDLE (SERIES QUALIFIER) (8 hdls 1 omitted) 2m 2f 110y

5:30 (5:30) (Class 4) 4-Y-0+ **£3,373** (£1,038; £519; £259)

Form RPR

1 **Almizan (IRE)**[68] 5-10-12 PHide 109+
(G L Moore) *keen: trckd ldrs: effrt to go 2nd bef 2 out: rdn to ld near omitted last: steadily drew clr* **9/2**[2]

1534 **2** *5* **Resplendent Star (IRE)**[34] 1001 8-11-4 108 (v) LAspell 109+
(Mrs L Wadham) *cl up: led 6th: drvn whn swtchd rt to miss omitted last: sn hdd: wknd fnl 100 yds* **7/1**[3]

-33P **3** *3 ½* **Zaffre (IRE)**[33] 1014 6-10-4 100 RLucey-Butler[(7)] 97
(Miss Z C Davison) *rr but wl in tch: rdn 3 out: sn outpcd: plugged into 3rd nr fin* **16/1**

P-4P **4** *hd* **Hermitage Court (USA)**[44] 901 4-10-10 RThornton 96
(M J McGrath) *set modest pce: hdd 6th: drvn and lost 2nd bef 2 out: fnd little and v one pced: lost 3rd nr line* **33/1**

5 *7* **Flotta**[48] 6-10-12 TJMurphy 92+
(B G Powell) *plld hrd and cl up: rdn to go 2nd briefly bef 2 out: sn racing w awkward hd carriage: wknd wl bef omitted last* **5/2**[1]

6 *4* **Ring Of Destiny**[5] 6-10-12 ChristianWilliams 87
(J Jay) *nt fluent 2nd: cl up tl drvn and wknd appr 3 out* **7/1**[3]

13F2 **7** *6* **Kentmere (IRE)**[39] 947 4-11-2 105 TDoyle 86+
(P R Webber) *cl up: rdn 5th: lost tch tamely wl bef 2 out* **5/2**[1]

654F **8** *dist* **Cloud Catcher (IRE)**[46] 891 4-10-0 60 (tp) RYoung[(3)] —
(M Appleby) *j. stickily in last and sn getting reminders: lost tch bef 3rd: t.o 5th: btn 114l* **100/1**

4m 22.4s (-13.60) **Going Correction** -1.00s/f (Hard)
WFA 4 from 5yo+ 15lb **8** Ran SP% **110.1**
Speed ratings: **88,85,84,84,81 79,77,—** CSF £32.87 TOTE £5.60: £2.00, £2.00, £2.40; EX 37.10.
Owner G L Moore **Bred** Sheikh Ahmed Bin Rashid Al Maktoum **Trained** Woodingdean, E Sussex

FOCUS
They did not go a great gallop early on and the final time was moderate for the grade. The form is not the most solid depite the placed horses being close to their marks. The final flight was bypassed.

NOTEBOOK
Almizan(IRE) was a useful stayer on the Flat at his best but he has been below that level over the past two years. Making his hurdling debut, his stamina kicked in during the closing stages and he drew clear for a comfortable success. He will get further than this, will be suited by a stronger pace and can win again. *(op 7-1)*
Resplendent Star(IRE) ran up to his best but looked to be outstayed from the omitted final flight. *(op 13-2 tchd 6-1)*
Zaffre(IRE), a course and distance winner, is fairly exposed. Her staying-on effort does not do a lot for the value of the form. *(op 12-1)*
Hermitage Court(USA), well beaten over course and distance in a similar contest back in May, enjoyed the benefit of setting his own modest gallop. He was rather keen, though, and his final placing also suggests the form is not that strong. *(tchd 40-1)*
Flotta, a fairly useful middle-distance performer on the Flat, looked sure to be involved in the finish turning for home, but he weakened very quickly and clearly something was amiss. The vet later *reported that the gelding was suffering from synchronous diaphramatic flutter.Official explanation: jockey said gelding tired; vet said gelding was suffering from synchronous diaphramatic flutter* *(op 15-8 tchd 7-4)*
Kentmere(IRE), who was keen, ran poorly on this return to novice company. This was not his true running. *(op 11-4)*

1246 WEATHERBYS BANK MAIDEN HURDLE (11 hdls) 2m 6f 110y

6:00 (6:03) (Class 4) 4-Y-0+ **£3,284** (£938; £469)

Form RPR

-225 **1** **Captain Cloudy**[5] 1046 5-11-2 85 JGoldstein 89+
(Miss Sheena West) *keen in last: 25l fr ldr after 1st: stdy prog 8th: rdn bef last: sn led flat: styd on wl to go clr* **9/2**[2]

P-P3 **2** *5* **Peruvian Breeze (IRE)**[22] 1077 4-10-13 ChristianWilliams 80+
(Evan Williams) *hld up towards rr: effrt 8th: led bef 2 out where j.rt: drvn and hdd flat: outstyd by wnr* **7/2**[1]

0-20 **3** *8* **Martovic (IRE)**[96] 349 6-10-9 JPMcNamara 70+
(K C Bailey) *prom: stmbld after 3 out: one pced fr next: nt fluent last: tk 3rd nr fin* **5/1**[3]

60 **4** *½* **Port Sodrick**[13] 1158 4-10-13 RWalford 72
(R H Alner) *midfield: j. slowly 4th: lost pl after 7th: stl only 9th and rdn bef 2 out: kpt on wl wout threatening* **9/1**

03-5 **5** *½* **Brasilia Prince**[72] 671 6-11-2 85 RThornton 74
(G P Enright) *nt a fluent: chsd ldrs: rdn and one pced after 3 out: btn 6th whn mstke next: plugged on* **8/1**

/044 **6** *3* **Spider Boy**[32] 1018 8-10-9 70 (p) RLucey-Butler[(7)] 71
(Miss Z C Davison) *cl 2nd and clr of rest tl led 5th: hdd 7th: led again 3 out: drvn and hdd bef next: fdd to lose 3 pls fr last* **7/1**

00P- **7** *10* **Lyrical Lily**[210] 3438 7-10-4 LStephens[(5)] 54
(B J Llewellyn) *sloppy jumping thrght: midfield early: last by 6th: blnd next: no ch after* **33/1**

8 *22* **The Boro Man (IRE)**[61] 7-11-2 PJBrennan 39
(Mrs Jeremy Young) *keen towards rr: prog 6th: 4th whn blnd 8th: rdn and fdd bef 2 out* **33/1**

06PP **9** *19* **Sean (IRE)**[29] 1040 6-11-2 83 (t) TScudamore 20
(Mrs L C Jewell) *hld up towards rr: lost tch after 7th: t.o* **25/1**

0 **10** *1* **Award Me An Oscar (IRE)**[32] 1018 5-11-2 (t) GSupple 19
(M C Pipe) *set slow pce: hdd 5th: led again 7th tl rdn and hdd 3 out: eased fr next: t.o* **12/1**

22P **P** **Treacysdream (IRE)**[22] 1077 5-10-9 RSpate[(7)] —
(Mrs K Waldron) *keen in rr: hdwy 8th: rdn and wknd bef 2 out: 7th whn broke down and p.u after last* **7/1**

5m 28.2s (-16.60) **Going Correction** -1.00s/f (Hard)
WFA 4 from 5yo+ 16lb **11** Ran SP% **120.6**
Speed ratings: **88,86,83,83,83 82,78,70,64,64** — CSF £21.32 TOTE £5.70: £1.70, £1.70, £2.80; EX 17.30.
Owner Michael Moriarty **Bred** J P Coggan **Trained** Lewes, E Sussex

FOCUS
Plating-class form rated through the winner, and a moderate time for a race of this class.

NOTEBOOK
Captain Cloudy, who raced too free on the Flat last time, was keen here as well but he was ridden with more restraint. Brought with a steady challenge to lead on the run-in, he won in good style, but the form is weak. *(op 4-1)*
Peruvian Breeze(IRE), another held up off the pace, built on the promise of his Newton Abbot effort but found the winner just too strong over this longer trip. *(op 5-2 tchd 9-4 in a place)*
Martovic(IRE), making her hurdling debut, is bred to stay well and jump a fence in time. She travelled smoothly but clipped heels and stumbled after the third last, and in the circumstances did well to recover and finish third. She is entitled to improve, but she will have to because this was a poor race. *(op 6-1)*
Port Sodrick, stepping up from two miles, kept on but never looked a danger to the first two. *(op 12-1)*
Brasilia Prince did not jump that well and never looked a threat to the principals. *(op 9-1)*
Spider Boy, who is exposed as poor, continues to run as though finding this trip too far. *(op 10-1)*
The Boro Man(IRE) *Official explanation: trainer's representative said gelding lost a front shoe* *(tchd 40-1)*

1247 T WARE DEVELOPMENTS H'CAP CHASE (19 fncs) 3m 2f 110y

6:30 (6:30) (Class 4) (0-100,98) 5-Y-0+ **£4,686** (£1,442; £721; £360)

Form RPR

P44 **1** **Pangeran (USA)**[72] 673 13-9-11 72 oh7 ONelmes[(3)] 78
(N B King) *enthusiastic in ld: hdd briefly after 13th: hdd again 16th: 4l 2nd and looked hld whn lft in ld 3 out: edgd clr flat: gamel* **11/1**

-F25 **2** *1 ¾* **River Quoile**[9] 1191 9-10-1 80 DJacob[(7)] 85+
(R H Alner) *trckd ldrs: hit 11th: 5th and rdn whn nt fluent 15th: effrt and lft 2nd 3 out: pressed wnr tl no ex fnl 100 yds* **3/1**[2]

2301 **3** *13* **Super Road Train**[21] 1086 6-11-12 98 (b) LAspell 92+
(O Sherwood) *handy: wnt 2nd after 10th: led after 13th tl slow jump next and relegated 3rd: drvn bef 3 out: fnd nthing after* **3/1**[2]

003/ **4** *22* **Autumn Fantasy (USA)**[10] 4406 6-11-4 90 (t) PHide 69+
(G L Moore) *cl up tl 15th: rdn and wknd after next* **7/1**[3]

0PPU **5** *10* **Plain Chant**[10] 1178 8-9-7 **72** oh6 (p) MrTJO'Brien[(7)] 31
(C Roberts) *bhd but in tch: blnd 13th: struggling next: lost tch and blnd 16th: continued wl bhd* **22/1**

/0-U **6** *24* **Major Sharpe (IRE)**[32] 1022 13-10-10 **82** JTizzard 17
(B J M Ryall) *blnd 2nd: tended to jump rt in last pair: lost tch u.p 13th: t.o whn blnd 15th* **16/1**

0F16 **F** **Lahinch Lad (IRE)**[13] 1152 5-11-3 **93** TJMurphy 95+
(B G Powell) *settled handy: j. slowly 10th: lft 2nd at 14th: led 16th: 4l clr and looked wnr whn fell 3 out* **5/2[1]**

7m 4.20s (3.10) **Going Correction** +0.10s/f (Yiel)
WFA 5 from 6yo+ 4lb **7** Ran SP% **109.6**
Speed ratings: **99,98,94,88,85 78,—** CSF £41.46 TOTE £7.40: £3.60, £2.20; EX 38.20.
Owner Neil King **Bred** Heronwood Farm Inc **Trained** Newmarket, Suffolk

FOCUS
A very moderate contest run at a steady early gallop resulted in the pace picking up quite a bit over the final five fences as the race developed into something of a test of speed. The runner-up sets the standard.

NOTEBOOK
Pangeran(USA) benefited from the fall of the leader three out and showed the greater resolution over the final two fences to grab an unlikely victory from 7lb out of the handicap. His success says a lot about the poor quality of this race, however. *(op 12-1 tchd 10-1)*
River Quoile had every chance when the leader crashed out at the third last, but he did not show as much resolve as his veteran rival and had to settle for second. He has yet to win a race under Rules. *(op 11-4)*
Super Road Train, put up 8lb for winning a novice handicap on his chase debut in which he was one of only two to complete, was unable to respond when the pace quickened up from the fourth last. The way the race developed probably did not suit him. *(tchd 7-2)*
Autumn Fantasy(USA), who was almost pulled up in a pipe-opener on Polytrack ten days earlier, was making his chasing debut. He began to lose touch from the sixth last and he might be happier over shorter - his best effort over hurdles came over two and a half miles. *(op 15-2 tchd 13-2)*
Lahinch Lad(IRE) took it up going well and looked to have the race at his mercy when crashing out at the third last. Although this was a bad race, he remains capable of winning despite an 8lb rise for his Worcester success last month. *(op 11-4)*

1248 HARBEN'S EQUINE CARE CENTRE CLAIMING HURDLE (10 hdls) 2m 4f
7:00 (7:00) (Class 4) 4-Y-0+ **£2,604** (£744; £372)

Form RPR

20-2 **1** **Lightning Star (USA)**[44] 903 10-11-0 102 (b) APMcCoy 102+
(G L Moore) *trckd ldrs: wnt 2nd after 3 out: coaxed ahd last: hung bdly rt but sn clr: rdn out* **7/2[2]**

-343 **2** *1½* **Gabor**[7] 903 6-11-0 94 (b) RJohnson 101+
(B J Llewellyn) *led and up to 8l clr: hit 5th: rdn after next: hit 3 out and hrd drvn: jnd and blnd last: sn btn* **10/1**

1151 **3** *3* **Silence Reigns**[13] 1153 11-10-13 120 (bt) RSpate[(7)] 106+
(Mrs K Waldron) *hld up in rr: smooth prog bef 2 out: rdn and ev ch whn nt fluent last: no ex* **11/4[1]**

-135 **4** *5* **Moving Earth (IRE)**[32] 1025 12-11-9 117 NFehily 101
(A W Carroll) *bhd: last and rdn 7th: rchd midfield bef 2 out: hrd drvn and no imp after* **11/2[3]**

F0-6 **5** *23* **Mr Whizz**[15] 747 8-11-0 99 (p) JGoldstein 69
(A P Jones) *chsd ldrs: j. slowly 7th: drvn after 3 out: btn whn mstke next* **16/1**

2065 **6** *9* **Shamsan (IRE)**[13] 1153 8-10-7 90 (tp) SWalsh[(7)] 60
(J Joseph) *cl up: nt fluent 6th: drvn and fdd bef 2 out* **33/1**

0F-4 **7** *9* **La Lambertine (FR)**[88] 460 4-11-3 113 TJMurphy 54
(M C Pipe) *sn niggled: chsd ldrs but nvr keen: lost tch u.p 3 out* **11/4[1]**

0-05 **8** *dist* **Tank (IRE)**[36] 971 4-10-11 MGoldstein[(7)] —
(Miss Sheena West) *chsd ldr tl hrd rdn and lost pl bef 7th: t.o after 3 out: btn 99l* **66/1**

4m 44.5s (-19.30) **Going Correction** -1.00s/f (Hard)
WFA 4 from 6yo+ 16lb **8** Ran SP% **110.3**
Speed ratings: **98,97,96,94,85 81,77,—** CSF £34.32 TOTE £4.10: £1.60, £2.60, £1.30; EX 22.60.
Owner Phil Collins **Bred** Runnymede Farm Inc **Trained** Woodingdean, E Sussex

FOCUS
A fair claimer for the time of year, but with several unreliable types, rated through the winner.

NOTEBOOK
Lightning Star(USA) travelled strongly but, like the third, is the type who needs to do everything on the bridle. He did not find a good deal once hitting the front but had enough in reserve to hold off the runner-up, who had been off the bridle for a long way. *(op 5-1)*
Gabor was under pressure a long way out but in fairness he kept responding and, although unable to shake off the attentions of the easy winner, finished nicely clear of the rest. He is hard work but can be relied upon to run his race. *(op 14-1)*
Silence Reigns, best in at these weights, looked to be going as well as the winner running towards the final flight, but he is the type who needs to do everything on the bridle, and a minor blunder at the last was all he needed to throw in the towel. *(op 5-2 tchd 3-1)*
Moving Earth(IRE), dropping back in trip on this return to hurdles, kept on without getting competitive, but he shaped well enough. *(op 5-1)*
La Lambertine(FR) was missing the headgear on this big drop in grade, but the ground was quicker than ideal and she was weak in the market beforehand. She was never travelling for Murphy in the race itself and remains one to have reservations about. *(op 2-1)*

1249 COCA COLA BEGINNERS' CHASE (13 fncs) 2m 2f
7:30 (7:30) (Class 4) 5-Y-0+ **£4,361** (£1,342; £671; £335)

Form RPR

00-3 **1** **Nawamees (IRE)**[58] 803 7-11-0 (b[1]) APMcCoy 97+
(G L Moore) *cl up: hit 7th: mstke 9th: nt fluent next and rdn: led 3 out: hrd drvn last: all out* **4/6[1]**

4-P0 **2** *1½* **Diamond Joshua (IRE)**[35] 988 7-10-11 ONelmes[(3)] 90
(N B King) *mstke 2nd: outpcd by ldng trio after 7th: rallied after 10th: rdn into 2nd at last: fnd little and a hld* **20/1**

5603 **3** *1¾* **Half Inch**[17] 1124 5-10-2 98 CHonour[(5)] 82+
(B I Case) *chsd ldr: ev ch 3 out: looked hld whn blnd next: styd on at one pce after* **11/2[3]**

50U **4** *18* **Ela Figura**[6] 979 5-10-4 69 (t) RYoung[(3)] 63
(M Appleby) *hld up: lost tch w ldng trio after 7th: struggling to get on terms whn indifferent jumps at fnl three fences* **50/1**

P6-6 **5** *3* **L'Etang Bleu (FR)**[102] 233 7-10-7 64 (tp) RLucey-Butler[(7)] 67
(P Butler) *j. slowly 2nd: slow 4th and continued last: t.o 8th: slt late prog* **28/1**

32-6 **6** *18* **Forest Chief (IRE)**[20] 1098 9-11-0 96 (vt[1]) ChristianWilliams 49
(Evan Williams) *set brisk pce but lacked fluency: j.rt fr 8th: hdd 3 out: j. wildly rt and eased over fnl two* **11/4[2]**

4m 34.7s (-0.40) **Going Correction** +0.10s/f (Yiel) **6** Ran SP% **112.2**
Speed ratings: **104,103,102,94,93 85** CSF £13.36 TOTE £1.70: £1.20, £3.30; EX 12.30.
Owner Paul Stamp **Bred** Kilfrush Stud Ltd **Trained** Woodingdean, E Sussex

FOCUS
A moderate contest and the favourite should have won easily on his hurdling efforts and this hard-fought victory looks weak form.

NOTEBOOK
Nawamees(IRE), who had the blinkers on for the first time, made very hard work of what should have been a relatively simple task, especially in view of the disappointing effort of the second favourite. On his hurdling form he should have won easily, and he will need to improve a good deal on this performance if he is to defy a penalty. *(tchd 8-11, 4-5 in places)*
Diamond Joshua(IRE), missing the visor on his chasing debut, was given a patient ride and steadily got himself into contention going to three out. He kept on to go second but ducked in behind the winner on the run-in and looked happy to finish where he did. He has always been a difficult horse to win with. *(tchd 25-1)*
Half Inchtook the race to the odds-on favourite but lost that battle over the third and second last, and lost second place jumping the last. It was not a bad effort on ground quicker than ideal. *(op 8-1)*
Ela Figura is a poor performer and once again she had plenty on her plate. *(tchd 40-1)*
Forest Chief(IRE), visored for the first time, jumped out to his right, and this became more and more marked as the race went on. *He could have been feeling something.Official explanation: vet said gelding lost a front shoe (op 5-2)*

1250 AUTO FINANCE DIRECT 01329 220221 H'CAP HURDLE (9 hdls) 2m 2f 110y
8:00 (8:00) (Class 4) (0-110,110) 4-Y-0+ **£3,360** (£960; £480)

Form RPR

0-15 **1** **Space Cowboy (IRE)**[10] 753 5-10-11 **95** (p) PHide 107+
(G L Moore) *trckd ldrs: a gng wl fnl circ: chal after 3 out: mstke 2 out: led bef last: rdn clr* **10/3[1]**

5-13 **2** *7* **Red Dahlia**[93] 399 8-10-0 **84** oh2 ATinkler 86
(M Pitman) *bhd: 7th and rdn at 5th: clsd next: led bef 3 out tl hdd u.p bef last: sn outpcd* **6/1**

-066 **3** *3* **Sigwells Club Boy**[18] 1111 5-10-5 **96** LHeard[(7)] 97
(J L Flint) *settled in rr: prog after 6th: chal 2 out: rdn and hld whn hit last* **10/1**

0653 **4** *19* **Arm And A Leg (IRE)**[10] 1179 10-11-4 **102** RJohnson 82
(Mrs D A Hamer) *t.k.h: lft in ld 2nd: hdd 5th: lost pl next: no ch after: blnd last* **6/1**

10P4 **5** *13* **Blue Leader (IRE)**[13] 1153 6-11-2 **100** (tp) RThornton 67
(W K Goldsworthy) *pressed ldr 2nd tl bef 6th: rdn and fdd ent st: blnd 2 out and last* **12/1**

040- **6** *13* **Sheer Guts (IRE)**[94] 392 6-10-4 **88** ChristianWilliams 42
(Evan Williams) *mstkes in last: reminders 3rd: lost tch 5th: t.o and eased 2 out* **16/1**

20P- **7** *8* **Statley Raj (IND)**[122] 4914 6-10-9 **93** TJMurphy 39
(B G Powell) *racd on outside and rn in snatches: rdn bef 6th: hit next and fdd: eased after 2 out: t.o* **7/2[2]**

0-60 **8** *8* **Castle River (USA)**[7] 726 6-11-0 **98** (p) MBatchelor 36
(O O'Neill) *t.k.h: prom tl led 5th: hdd and hrd rdn bef 3 out: sn fdd: t.o* **11/2[3]**

23P0 **P** **Odagh Odyssey (IRE)**[53] 840 11-11-12 **110** (v) APMcCoy —
(Miss E C Lavelle) *led tl broke down 2nd: p.u* **14/1**

4m 20.0s (-16.00) **Going Correction** -1.00s/f (Hard) **9** Ran SP% **118.6**
Speed ratings: **93,90,88,80,75 69,66,63,—** CSF £24.70 CT £183.94 TOTE £4.40: £1.60, £2.00, £3.30; EX 16.10 Place 6 £76.09, Place 5 £17.77.
Owner Platt Sanderson Partnership **Bred** Kildaragh Stud **Trained** Woodingdean, E Sussex

FOCUS
A modest handicap and an ordinary winning time for the grade, but the early pace was good and it looks solid enough form, with the winner value for more than the official margin.

NOTEBOOK
Space Cowboy(IRE) travelled well and, taking over approaching the final flight, drew clear on the run-in for a very comfortable success. The steady pace may have beaten him at Newton Abbot and off this better gallop he bounced back to his best. He remains capable of improving further. *(op 4-1)*
Red Dahlia was suited by the way the race was run and, although she could do nothing to hold off the cosy winner, she finished a clear second off what had looked a stiff enough mark beforehand.
Sigwells Club Boy likes a decent pace in his races and he got that here, even if the ground was perhaps on the quick side for him. Together with the front two, he pulled clear of the rest, and he might be able to find a race when the cards fall right.
Arm And A Leg(IRE), missing the cheekpieces, continues to look held off his current mark. *(tchd 7-1)*
Blue Leader(IRE) usually struggles in handicap company and is more at home in selling grade. *(op 10-1)*
Statley Raj(IND), having his first outing for his new stable, came under pressure leaving the back straight and dropped out tamely. He is entitled to come on for this first run since April. *(op 4-1)*
Odagh Odyssey(IRE) *Official explanation: jockey said gelding pulled up lame (op 12-1)*
T/Plt: £101.90 to a £1 stake. Pool: £36,562.75. 261.75 winning tickets. T/Qpdt: £11.60 to a £1 stake. Pool: £3,422.10. 217.40 winning tickets. IM

1251 - 1261a (Foreign Racing) - See Raceform Interactive

1187 NEWTON ABBOT (L-H)
Saturday, August 20

OFFICIAL GOING: Good (good to firm in places)
First fence in home straight omitted.
Wind: Slight, behind

1262 TOTEPLACEPOT H'CAP HURDLE (12 hdls) 3m 3f
2:00 (2:01) (Class 4) (0-90,95) 4-Y-0+ **£2,782** (£856; £428; £214)

Form RPR

0-0P **1** **Big Quick (IRE)**[60] 801 10-11-0 **85** MrJMorgan[(7)] 85+
(L Wells) *hld up towards rr: nt fluent 5th: hit 8th: hdwy next: rdn to chse ldrs after 3 out: led appr last: rdn out* **28/1**

3203 **2** *1* **Tea's Maid**[22] 1100 5-10-13 **82** WKennedy[(5)] 81+
(Mrs A M Thorpe) *mid div: hdwy 7th: led 3 out: sn rdn: wnt lft and pckd 2 out and hdd: ev ch last: no ex* **13/2[3]**

PP-5 **3** *6* **Cresswell Gold**[24] 1079 8-10-5 **69** TScudamore 61
(D A Rees) *hld up towards rr: hdwy appr 9th: rdn after 3 out: ev ch 2 out: sn wknd* **11/1**

0644 **4** *1½* **Make It Easy (IRE)**[11] 1191 9-9-10 **67** CaptLHorner[(7)] 58
(D L Williams) *in tch: jnd ldrs 5th: led appr 9th: hdd 3 out: sn one pced* **13/2[3]**

0032 **5** *1* **Wild Tempo (FR)**[11] 1192 10-11-7 **95** (t) AGlassonbury[(10)] 85
(M C Pipe) *hld up bhd: hdwy appr 9th: chsd ldrs 3 out: sn rdn and btn* **11/2[2]**

P1UP **6** *15* **Excellent Vibes (IRE)**[24] 1079 7-11-4 **82** APMcCoy 57
(N A Twiston-Davies) *trckd ldrs: wnt prom 9th: sn rdn: ev ch 3 out: wknd appr next* **11/4[1]**

1454 **7** *10* **Earn Out**[22] 1100 4-10-12 **86** MrCHughes[(7)] 48
(M C Pipe) *hld up and a towards rr* **7/1**

-3FP **8** *23* **Wimbledonian**[11] 1192 6-11-11 **89** .... RJohnson 31
(R T Phillips) *a bhd* **8/1**

000P **9** *dist* **Farceur (FR)**[15] 1152 6-11-2 **80** .... (v) RGreene —
(M C Pipe) *sn stuggling: t.o fr 8th* **50/1**

0550 **10** *20* **Robbie On Tour (IRE)**[15] 1152 6-10-9 **76** .... (t) TJMalone(3) —
(M C Pipe) *led tl 2nd: prom: wknd appr 9th* **14/1**

0P-4 **P** **Trefoilalight**[40] 961 6-10-0 **69** ow5 .... CHonour(5) —
(J D Frost) *mid div tl 8th: sn bhd: p.u bef 2 out* **25/1**

6-PP **P** **Pure Steel (IRE)**[20] 1109 11-9-12 **67** .... (p) LStephens(5) —
(Miss L Day) *led 2nd tl after 8th: sn wknd: p.u bef 2 out* **40/1**

0-P **P** **Marmot D'Estruval (FR)**[12] 1178 5-10-13 **82** .... MrGBarfoot-Saunt(5) —
(Mrs Tracey Barfoot-Saunt) *chsd ldrs tl 7th: sn bhd: p.u bef 2 out* **100/1**

6m 38.3s (-3.70) **Going Correction** -0.40s/f (Good)
WFA 4 from 5yo+ 17lb **13** Ran SP% **120.0**
Speed ratings: **89,88,86,86,86 81,78,71,—,— —,—,—** CSF £198.47 CT £2158.21 TOTE £26.30: £5.50, £2.40, £3.00; EX 1186.20.
Owner R A Gadd **Bred** Wainbody Estates **Trained** Wisborough Green, W Sussex

FOCUS
A pretty weak handicap hurdle, and the winning time was slow.

NOTEBOOK
Big Quick(IRE) had been lightly raced and out of form since last winning in April 2003 but, off the back of a 60-day break, he returned to his best despite looking far from straightforward. Not jumping that well, he received a fine ride form Morgan, who kidded him along for most of the way before very much making his mind up for him when the race got serious. His wins-to-runs record *suggests he is one to take on next time. Official explanation: trainer's representative said, regarding the improved form shown, gelding had benefited from a lay off and from running over today's extended trip (op 20-1)*
Tea's Maid is still a maiden, but this was an improved effort and she should find a similar race before too much longer. *(op 6-1 tchd 7-1)*
Cresswell Gold gained her only win under Rules in the corresponding race in 2004. She had no excuse, but this was one of her better efforts. *(tchd 10-1)*
Make It Easy(IRE), racing over hurdles for the first time since 2003, has since won in point-to-points and over fences under Rules. This was respectable and he could go on. *(op 6-1)*
Wild Tempo(FR) had not been running badly in defeat recently, but he was below his best this time and remains winless in this country. *(op 5-1)*
Excellent Vibes(IRE), as when pulled up over course and distance on his previous start, ran below expectations and may prefer genuinely fast ground. *(op 7-2)*
Robbie On Tour(IRE) *Official explanation: vet said gelding finished lame (op 20-1)*

1263 TOTESPORT 0800 221 221 H'CAP HURDLE (7 hdls 1 omitted) 2m 1f
2:30 (2:31) (Class 3) (0-125,121) 4-Y-O+ **£5,434** (£1,672; £836; £418)

Form RPR

-01P **1** **Monticelli (GER)**[35] 1010 5-11-12 **121** .... RJohnson 128+
(P J Hobbs) *in tch: wnt 3rd appr 5th: led appr 2 out: rdn appr last: kpt on wl* **13/2**

4-02 **2** *3* **Critical Stage (IRE)**[11] 1188 6-10-8 **108** .... CHonour(5) 110
(J D Frost) *mid div: lost pl and dropped rr 4th: rdn and hdwy after 3 out: chal for 2nd 2 out: kpt on: nt rch wnr* **10/1**

-054 **3** *3/4* **Artane Boys**[38] 980 8-10-11 **106** .... APMcCoy 107
(Jonjo O'Neill) *nvr fluent: hld up: hdwy appr 3 out: chsd wnr and rdn appr 2 out: lost 2nd run-in* **7/1**

5311 **4** *6* **Cream Cracker**[31] 1037 7-10-10 **105** .... JMMaguire 100
(Mrs Jeremy Young) *hld up bhd: hdwy appr 3 out: rdn to chal for 2nd 2 out: wknd appr last* **5/1**[2]

4212 **5** *10* **Figaro Du Rocher (FR)**[24] 1080 5-11-6 **115** .... (t) TScudamore 100
(M C Pipe) *led tl 3rd: w ldr tl wknd after 3 out* **4/1**[1]

0/0- **6** *8* **Silver Prophet (IRE)**[26] 4777 6-10-13 **108** .... SCurran 85
(M R Bosley) *in tch tl 4th: sn bhd* **25/1**

4/F- **7** *17* **Wait For The Will (USA)**[8] 1814 9-11-6 **115** .... (b) PHide 75
(G L Moore) *hld up and a towards rr* **5/1**[2]

1-PP **P** **Musical Stage (USA)**[12] 1179 6-11-1 **110** .... (bt[1]) TDoyle —
(P R Webber) *chsd ldrs tl wknd qckly after 4th: t.o and p.u bef 2 out* **33/1**

3162 **P** **Imperial Rocket (USA)**[23] 1087 8-10-9 **104** .... (t) RThornton —
(W K Goldsworthy) *w ldr: led 3rd: rdn and hdd appr 2 out: wknd qckly: p.u bef last* **6/1**[3]

3m 56.0s (-9.10) **Going Correction** -0.40s/f (Good) **9** Ran SP% **109.3**
Speed ratings: **105,103,103,100,95 91,83,—,—** CSF £62.20 CT £427.79 TOTE £7.90: £2.20, £2.60, £2.60; EX 60.90.
Owner Mrs M Findlay **Bred** Mrs I Bodewein **Trained** Withycombe, Somerset

FOCUS
A fair handicap hurdle and solid form, with the runner-up back to his course and distance best and the third right up to form too. The first flight in the back straight was bypassed on the final circuit.

NOTEBOOK
Monticelli(GER), pulled up in the Summer Hurdle at Stratford on his previous start, would have found this easier and returned to form with a decisive success. He is unexposed still and ought to *remain competitive when reassessed. Official explanation: trainer had no explanation for the improved form shown (op 8-1)*
Critical Stage(IRE) ran well off a mark 3lb higher than when second over course and distance on his previous start and remains in good form. *(op 11-1 tchd 9-1)*
Artane Boys's hurdling was not great, and while he still reproduced the form of his recent Worcester fourth, he failed to build on the promise shown there. *(op 11-2)*
Cream Cracker was chasing the hat-trick following a couple of wins in maiden and novice *company, but he was 10lb higher than when last seen in a handicap as a result and was well held. (op 9-2 tchd 4-1)*
Figaro Du Rocher(FR), turned over at odds on over fences last time, proved most disappointing back over hurdles off a mark 10lb higher than when winning at Southwell two starts ago. *(op 7-2)*
Wait For The Will(USA), returned to hurdles for the first time since 2003, never really threatened and was a little disappointing. *(op 6-1)*

1264 TOTEQUADPOT NOVICES' CHASE (11 fncs 2 omitted) 2m 110y
3:05 (3:05) (Class 3) 5-Y-O+ **£7,956** (£2,448; £1,224; £612)

Form RPR

-033 **1** **Scalloway (IRE)**[15] 1147 5-10-12 109 .... CLlewellyn 125+
(D J Wintle) *j.w: set gd pce: mde most: hdd briefly 7th: rdn 6 l clr after 2 out: eased fnl 30yds* **7/1**

-6U1 **2** *1 1/4* **Sardagna (FR)**[35] 1012 5-11-1 125 .... TJMurphy 123
(M C Pipe) *outpcd early: tk clsr order 5th: jnd ldrs 8th: sltly outpcd 3 out: rallied to go 2nd appr last: no ch w wnr* **15/8**[1]

2P11 **3** *6* **Croix De Guerre (IRE)**[34] 1024 5-11-8 137 .... (b) RJohnson 127+
(P J Hobbs) *chsd wnr tl 5th: sn niggled along: wnt 2nd 3 out: rdn bef next: wknd appr last* **2/1**[2]

-221 **4** *25* **Dawton (POL)**[34] 1019 7-11-4 .... (b[1]) JMMaguire 99+
(T R George) *chsd wnr: led: mstke and hdd 7th: wknd appr 3 out* **5/2**[3]

3m 58.1s (-7.40) **Going Correction** -0.40s/f (Good) **4** Ran SP% **109.2**
Speed ratings: **101,100,97,85** CSF £20.20 TOTE £10.80; EX 24.00.
Owner Lady Blyth **Bred** Hugh Kelly **Trained** Naunton, Gloucs

FOCUS
Just the four runners and not easy to fix the level of the form, but a competitive novice chase nonetheless and Scalloway appeared to produce a career-best effort.

NOTEBOOK
Scalloway(IRE) had quite a bit to find on official ratings with both Sardagna and Croix De Guerre, and he was nine lengths behind Dawton on his chasing debut two starts ago but, given a good, positive ride, he put up by far his best effort to date. This did not appear to be a fluke, but a penalty with make things much tougher. *(op 8-1 tchd 9-1 and 13-2)*
Sardagna(FR), successful in a handicap off a mark of 118 on her previous start, was never really going that well and just seemed to find things happening a bit quick for her. She is better than this, but probably wants slightly easier ground. *(op 7-4 tchd 2-1)*
Croix De Guerre(IRE) was the highest rated of these, but was just found out under his penalties. *(op 7-4)*
Dawton(POL) had today's winner nine lengths behind when winning over course and distance on his previous start, but he never really recovered after making a mistake at the seventh and was well below form. *(op 3-1)*

1265 LORD MILDMAY MEMORIAL H'CAP CHASE (13 fncs 3 omitted) 2m 5f 110y
3:35 (3:35) (Class 2) (0-145,142) 5-Y-O+
£27,436 (£10,406; £5,203; £2,365; £1,182; £709)

Form RPR

2PB1 **1** **Tamango (FR)**[24] 1080 8-10-7 **123** .... RJohnson 137
(P J Hobbs) *mid div: smooth hdwy after 9th: led appr last: styd on wl: rdn out* **20/1**

P-11 **2** *1 3/4* **Sweet Diversion (IRE)**[41] 944 6-10-11 **127** .... (t) ChristianWilliams 139
(P F Nicholls) *trckd ldr: led 8th: hrd pressed fr 3 out: rdn and hdd appr last: kpt on* **12/1**

P-20 **3** *1 1/4* **Duke Of Buckingham (IRE)**[35] 1010 9-11-2 **132** .... TDoyle 143
(P R Webber) *hld up bhd: stdy hdwy fr 9th: trckd ldrs after 3 out: rdn and effrt after 2 out: kpt on same pce* **33/1**

4110 **4** *3/4* **Bronzesmith**[35] 1013 9-10-12 **128** .... RThornton 138
(B J M Ryall) *mid div: hdwy 9th: rdn to ld after 2 out: sn hdd: no ex* **50/1**

21F2 **5** *6* **Mr Ed (IRE)**[22] 1096 7-11-4 **134** .... (p) ADobbin 140+
(P Bowen) *mid div: hdwy 10th: cl up a travelling wl 2 out: sn rdn: one pced* **11/2**[2]

62-1 **6** *1* **Tango Royal (FR)**[35] 1013 9-11-9 **142** .... (t) TJMalone(3) 146+
(M C Pipe) *hld up bhd: j.rt 10th: styd on fr 3 out: nvr on terms* **12/1**

UU4 **7** *1 3/4* **Magic Sky (FR)**[7] 1204 5-10-1 **124** .... LHeard(7) 125
(P F Nicholls) *hld up towards rr: hdwy 9th: cl up 2 out: sn rdn: one pced* **40/1**

12-1 **8** *1* **East Tycoon (IRE)**[6] 1221 6-11-0 **130** 5ex .... APMcCoy 133+
(Jonjo O'Neill) *mid div: making stdy hdwy whn blnd 10th: nt a danger after* **5/2**[1]

6563 **9** *11* **Montreal (FR)**[11] 1189 8-9-7 **116** oh5 .... (p) PMerrigan(7) 105
(M C Pipe) *a towards rr* **16/1**

20F- **10** *3/4* **Cameron Bridge (IRE)**[217] 3358 9-11-0 **130** .... PJBrennan 119+
(P J Hobbs) *mid div: hdwy appr 7th: w ldr after 8th: ev ch whn nt fluent 2 out (water): wknd* **20/1**

-111 **11** *5* **Blakeney Coast (IRE)**[41] 946 8-10-0 **116** oh1 .... (t) JTizzard 99
(C L Tizzard) *led tl nt fluent and hdd 8th: sn bhd* **7/1**[3]

605- **12** *13* **Mouseski**[129] 4822 11-11-12 **142** .... CLlewellyn 112
(P F Nicholls) *mid div tl 7th: sn t.o* **40/1**

3306 **13** *dist* **Isard III (FR)**[35] 1013 9-10-6 **122** .... RGreene —
(M C Pipe) *a bhd: t.o fr 9th* **20/1**

FF11 **14** *3 1/2* **Fontanesi (IRE)**[24] 1078 5-11-6 **136** .... TJMurphy —
(M C Pipe) *hmpd 10th: a in rr* **11/1**

-263 **P** **Sunshan**[24] 1076 9-9-7 **116** oh32 .... JamesWhite(7) —
(R J Hodges) *in tch tl 10th: t.o and p.u after 2 out* **150/1**

1-14 **P** **Good Lord Louis (IRE)**[35] 1013 7-10-2 **125** .... MrTJO'Brien(7) —
(P J Hobbs) *chsd ldrs tl 8th: sn lost tch: p.u after 2 out* **9/1**

5m 8.40s (-14.30) **Going Correction** -0.40s/f (Good) **16** Ran SP% **120.8**
Speed ratings: **110,109,108,108,106 106,105,105,101,100 99,94,—,—,— —** CSF £222.89 CT £7673.37 TOTE £22.20: £3.90, £1.90, £4.60, £6.10; EX 92.20.
Owner The Brushmakers **Bred** Mme Dominique Le Drans **Trained** Withycombe, Somerset

FOCUS
A decent renewal of this valuable handicap chase and very competitive. Sound form overall.

NOTEBOOK
Tamango(FR) did well to win over an inadequate two miles here on his previous start and, back up to a more suitable trip, he defied a 4lb higher mark in this much better contest. Phillip Hobbs said he fancied him the least out of his three runners, but he won decisively under a determined ride and is clearly on the upgrade. The plan was going to be to return to hurdles for a race at Perth in September, but that may now be reviewed. *(op 16-1)*
Sweet Diversion(IRE), chasing the hat-trick following a couple of wins in small field novice chases, would have found this much tougher and ran a fine race in defeat. Progressing nicely, he should have a good season and is one to keep on the right side of. *(op 14-1)*
Duke Of Buckingham(IRE), well beaten in the Summer Hurdle on his previous start, ran a big race returned to fences and stepped back up in trip. He is not the easiest to win with these days, but is worth having on your side when in this form. *(op 25-1)*
Bronzesmith, well beaten in the Summer Plate on his previous start, returned to the sort of form that saw him win twice at Worcester earlier in the year and emerges with plenty of credit.
Mr Ed(IRE) did not pick up as one might have expected under pressure, but he did keep on and this still represented a very useful level of form. Given this was just his fourth run over fences, he is open to improvement and is one to keep on the right side of this season. *(tchd 6-1)*
Tango Royal(FR), 9lb higher than when winning the Summer Plate on his previous start, was not *quite in the same sort of form this time and his wins tend to be quite spaced out these days. (op 10-1)*
East Tycoon(IRE), upped to his furthest trip to date off a mark 5lb higher than when winning at Stratford on his previous start, seemed to lose his chance when making a bad mistake at the tenth and can be forgiven this.
Blakeney Coast(IRE) had been in great form lately, but he was 17lb higher than when winning at Stratford last time and would have found this much tougher. *(op 8-1)*
Fontanesi(IRE) had been progressing well in novice company recently, but put up no show this *time and was disappointing. Official explanation: jockey said gelding was never travelling (op 10-1 tchd 12-1)*

1266 TOTEPOOL AWAYBET NOVICES' HURDLE (9 hdls) 2m 3f
4:10 (4:14) (Class 3) 4-Y-O+ **£5,473** (£1,684; £842; £421)

Form RPR

0/1 **1** **Decisive**[45] 911 6-11-4 .... RJohnson 123
(P Bowen) *mde all: rdn whn chal appr 2 out: kpt on wl: rdn out* **11/8**[2]

2231 **2** *2 1/2* **Enhancer**[48] 892 7-11-10 124 .... TJMurphy 126
(M J McGrath) *in tch: chsd wnr fr 5th: rdn and ev ch 2 out: no ex appr last* **6/5**[1]

3 *dist* **Persian Genie (IRE)**[26] 4-10-3 ....(t) MBradburne 53
(J A Geake) *mid div: chsd ldng pair in distant 3rd after 6th: no further imp* **14/1**[3]

4-6 **4** *23* **Sweet Az**[19] 1123 5-10-5 ....(p) TDoyle 37
(S C Burrough) *chsd wnr tl 5th: wkng whn hit next: t.o* **33/1**

00 **5** *17* **Silver Emperor (IRE)**[11] 1187 4-10-10 .... ChristianWilliams 25
(P A Blockley) *a bhd: t.o fr 6th* **100/1**

0/F **6** *4* **Abbey Hill**[15] 1158 8-9-12 .... AGlassonbury(7) 16
(W S Kittow) *j. slowly wl in rr: sme hdwy appr 6th: wknd bef 3 out: t.o* **50/1**

00 **7** *dist* **Award Me An Oscar (IRE)**[2] 1246 5-10-5 ....(t) MrCHughes(7) —
(M C Pipe) *w wnr tl 5th: wknd qckly and sn t.o* **14/1**[3]

P **Foreign Field (FR)**[153] 6-10-9 .... RYoung(3) —
(Mrs Tracey Barfoot-Saunt) *a bhd: t.o and p.u bef 2 out* **33/1**

P **P** **Honourable Collins (IRE)**[7] 1206 5-10-12 .... JTizzard —
(Mrs Tracey Barfoot-Saunt) *a bhd: t.o and p.u bef 2 out* **50/1**

0456 **F** **Pumpkin Pickle**[15] 1154 4-9-10 .... KBurke(7) 53
(P R Rodford) *hld up: sme hdwy after 3 out: chalng for distant 3rd whn fell 2 out* **33/1**

4m 22.4s (-10.60) **Going Correction** -0.40s/f (Good)
WFA 4 from 5yo+ 15lb **10** Ran SP% **114.6**
Speed ratings: **106,104,—,—,—,— —,—,—,—,—** CSF £3.24 TOTE £2.50: £1.10, £1.10, £2.60; EX 4.00.
Owner R Owen & P Fullagar **Bred** Shutford Stud **Trained** Little Newcastle, Pembrokes

FOCUS
Very little strength in depth, but the front two pulled a mile clear and are fair novices.

NOTEBOOK
Decisive, successful in a maiden hurdle at Worcester for Paul Webber on his previous start, improved on the form of that success to follow up under his penalty on his debut for Peter Bowen. This was a weak race, but the runner-up set a fair standard and he could win again. *(op 5-4)*
Enhancer, successful in a similar event at Market Rasen on his previous start, had to give 6lb to the unexposed winner and emerges with plenty of credit in defeat. *(op 5-4 tchd 11-8)*
Persian Genie(IRE), a 46-rated maiden on the Flat, proved no match for the front two on her hurdling debut, but is entitled to improve for the experience. *(op 12-1)*
Sweet Az, with the cheekpieces back on, was well beaten but is now qualified for a handicap mark. *(op 40-1 tchd 25-1)*
Award Me An Oscar(IRE) *Official explanation: vet said gelding was lame (tchd 11-1)*

1267 TOTESPORT.COM H'CAP CHASE (17 fncs 3 omitted) 3m 2f 110y
4:45 (4:47) (Class 3) (0-125,126) 5-Y-0+ **£6,014** (£1,850; £925; £462)

Form RPR

3453 **1** **Swansea Bay**[15] 1157 9-11-4 **117** .... ADobbin 126
(P Bowen) *j. sltly rt thrght: chsd ldng trio: j. slowly and reminders 10th: styd on u.p fr 2 out: led fnl strides* **2/1**[1]

1-04 **2** *½* **Around Before (IRE)**[11] 1192 8-11-3 **116** ....(t) APMcCoy 124
(Jonjo O'Neill) *trckd ldr: led 15th: sn rdn: 2 l clr last: hrd rdn and no ex whn ct fnl strides* **5/2**[2]

3401 **3** *4* **Parisian Storm (IRE)**[7] 1205 9-11-13 **126** .... ChristianWilliams 130
(Evan Williams) *led: blnd 3rd: hdd 15th: sn rdn: kpt on same pce* **2/1**[1]

0P06 **4** *16* **Celtic Star (IRE)**[37] 989 7-9-11 **99** oh16 ....(v) DCrosse(3) 89+
(Mrs L Williamson) *hld up: rdn after 13th: sn lost tch* **20/1**

4004 **5** *6* **Idealko (FR)**[15] 1157 9-10-0 **99** oh5 .... RGreene 85+
(Dr P Pritchard) *chsd ldrs in 3rd: rdn after 15th: wknd appr 3 out* **9/1**[3]

6m 28.5s (-14.90) **Going Correction** -0.40s/f (Good) **5** Ran SP% **110.0**
Speed ratings: **106,105,104,99,98** CSF £7.60 TOTE £2.90: £1.70, £1.50; EX 7.70 Place 6 £3,225.80, Place 5 £639.93.
Owner Peter Bowling **Bred** D L Morgan **Trained** Little Newcastle, Pembrokes

FOCUS
Just the five runners, but the first three all ran to form.

NOTEBOOK
Swansea Bay had not won over fences since November 2003, but this was the lowest mark he has raced off over the larger obstacles since 2002 and he ended that losing run under a very strong ride from Tony Dobbin. *(tchd 9-4)*
Around Before(IRE), back over fences, ran right up to his best but was just unable to resist the winners's strong challenge. *(op 11-4)*
Parisian Storm(IRE), 14lb higher than when winning at Bangor on his previous start, seemed to run close to his best in defeat. *(op 13-8)*
Celtic Star(IRE) ran a little better with the visor replacing the blinkers, but he was still well held. *(op 25-1)*
Idealko(FR), upped to his furthest trip to date, was well beaten. *(op 12-1)*
T/Plt: £1,070.40 to a £1 stake. Pool: £41,132.35. 28.05 winning tickets. T/Qpdt: £82.70 to a £1 stake. Pool: £2,727.20. 24.40 winning tickets. TM

1262 NEWTON ABBOT (L-H)
Sunday, August 21

OFFICIAL GOING: Good to firm (firm in places)
Wind: Nil

1268 TOTEPLACEPOT JUVENILE NOVICES' HURDLE (7 hdls 1 omitted) 2m 1f
2:10 (2:10) (Class 3) 3-Y-0 **£5,356** (£1,648; £824; £412)

Form RPR

4 **1** **Dream Along**[12] 1190 3-10-12 ....(b) JimCrowley 90
(Mrs A J Perrett) *chsd ldr: rdn to ld after 3 out: j.lft fr next: mstke last: drvn out* **9/1**[3]

2F **2** *¾* **Shingle Street (IRE)**[35] 1023 3-10-12 .... APMcCoy 89
(Miss Venetia Williams) *chsd ldr: rdn after 3 out: wnt 2nd appr 2 out: hrd rdn to chal appr last: kpt on* **5/2**[2]

2 **3** *15* **The Castilian (FR)**[12] 1190 3-10-12 .... TJMurphy 74
(M C Pipe) *led: slipped: sn rdn and reluctant on bnd after 4th: hdd after 3 out: sn btn* **8/11**[1]

P **4** *dist* **Crazy Flirt (IRE)**[8] 1207 3-10-0 .... DLaverty(5) —
(A E Jones) *mstke 1st: nt fluent 2nd: t.o fr next* **100/1**

4 **B** **Time For You**[8] 1207 3-9-12 .... CJDavies(7) —
(J M Bradley) *b.d 1st* **40/1**

F **Obstreperous Way**[18] 3-10-12 .... JAMcCarthy —
(P R Chamings) *fell 1st* **25/1**

B **Alphun (IRE)**[12] 3-10-12 .... PHide —
(G L Moore) *plld hrd: hld up: b.d 1st* **16/1**

4m 1.20s (-3.90) **Going Correction** -0.35s/f (Good) **7** Ran SP% **109.6**
Speed ratings: **95,94,87,—,—,—,—** CSF £29.65 TOTE £8.20: £3.90, £1.50; EX 20.90.
Owner Hesmonds Stud **Bred** Hesmonds Stud Ltd **Trained** Pulborough, W Sussex
■ Stewards' Enquiry : T J Murphy one-day ban: used whip with excessive force (Sep 3)

FOCUS
The first flight in the back straight was bypassed on the second circuit. A moderate juvenile contest in which three of the seven runners exited at the first, but they were outsiders and it is unlikely the outcome would have been different. The runner-up is the best guide to the level of the form.

NOTEBOOK
Dream Along, who raced lazily when a creditable fourth on his hurdling debut, had shown himself to be a quirky character when twice unseating on the Flat, but the re-application of blinkers seemed to help and he stayed on strongly to reverse form with The Castilian. This was a modest race, but he is open to a certain amount of improvement with this being only his fifth-ever racecourse outing. *(op 8-1)*
Shingle Street(IRE) ran another solid race in defeat, but has yet to win under either code despite having had several good chances. He will find a race eventually and gives the impression a greater distance may help. *(op 11-4)*
The Castilian(FR), two places ahead of Dream Along on his debut at Fontwell, was unable to confirm the form. The combination of him under-performing and Dream Along improving for the blinkers led to his defeat. A worrying factor for the future is that he did not look too keen and he is clearly not one to take short odds on again. *(tchd 4-5)*

1269 TOTESPORT.COM BEGINNERS' CHASE (17 fncs 3 omitted) 3m 2f 110y
2:40 (2:49) (Class 3) 5-Y-0+ **£6,014** (£1,850; £925; £462)

Form RPR

2221 **1** **Getoutwhenyoucan (IRE)**[25] 1079 5-10-8 112 .... TJMurphy 114+
(M C Pipe) *j.w: mde all: in command fr 13th: comf* **5/6**[1]

U322 **2** *3* **Windy Spirit (IRE)**[13] 1177 10-10-12 110 .... ChristianWilliams 108
(Evan Williams) *hld up: tk clsr order 9th: wnt 2nd after 3 out: kpt on but no ch w wnr* **6/4**[2]

4 **3** *25* **Sarahs Quay (IRE)**[37] 998 6-10-5 .... PJBrennan 76
(K J Burke) *hld up bhd ldng pair: chsd wnr after 12th: hit next: rdn appr 3 out: sn wknd* **18/1**

06F- **4** *dist* **Kings Linen (IRE)**[377] 1157 9-10-7 .... CHonour(5) —
(B I Case) *chsd ldrs tl 9th: reminders after next: hit 12th: sn lost tch: t.o whn lft remote 4th run-in* **14/1**[3]

0-P0 **5** *dist* **Lambrini Mist**[7] 1219 7-10-7 69 .... DLaverty(5) —
(Mrs L Williamson) *w wnr tl 12th: sn bhd: v tired in distant 4th whn p.u run-in* **40/1**

6m 28.7s (-14.70) **Going Correction** -0.35s/f (Good)
WFA 5 from 6yo+ 4lb **5** Ran SP% **108.9**
Speed ratings: **107,106,98,—,—** CSF £2.48 TOTE £2.00: £1.50, £1.10; EX 2.80.
Owner D A Johnson **Bred** M J Halligan **Trained** Nicholashayne, Devon

FOCUS
An uncompetitive race weakened by the withdrawal of Phar From Frosty. The form is modest with the runner-up setting the standard, but the winner is value for more than the winning margin.

NOTEBOOK
Getoutwhenyoucan(IRE) ◆, making his chase debut, had his task simplified by the withdrawal of Phar From Frosty and appreciated the positive ride from Murphy, jumping like an experienced handicapper and winning with plenty in hand. Still only a five-year-old, he looks a useful sort for the time of year and it will be surprising if he does not rack-up a sequence before the better horses emerge. *(op 10-11 tchd Evens)*
Windy Spirit(IRE) ran yet another good race in defeat, but had to give way to a younger, unexposed rival. His trainer should be able to get a win out of him whilst in this sort of form. *(op 11-8)*
Sarahs Quay(IRE) was no match for the front two and will find life easier in low-grade handicaps. *(op 16-1)*

1270 TOTESPORT SUMMER FESTIVAL H'CAP HURDLE (10 hdls) 2m 6f
3:10 (3:19) (Class 2) (0-140,138) 4-Y-0+
£24,777 (£9,398; £4,699; £2,136; £1,068; £640)

Form RPR

531- **1** **Goblet Of Fire (USA)**[122] 4938 6-11-0 **126** ....(b) RWalsh 130
(P F Nicholls) *a travelling wl: trckd ldrs: led on bit appr 2 out: rdn appr last: kpt on: rdn out* **11/2**[2]

-131 **2** *1¼* **Englishtown (FR)**[39] 980 5-10-3 **115** ....(t) APMcCoy 118
(Jonjo O'Neill) *mid div: hdwy appr 3 out: swtchd lft: rdn to press wnr appr 2 out: kpt on but no ex run-in* **7/2**[1]

54RR **3** *shd* **Kalambari (IRE)**[56] 841 6-9-9 **114** oh2 ow2 .... SWalsh(7) 117
(J D Frost) *in tch: rdn after 3 out: styd on wl run-in: nt rch wnr* **100/1**

/2-P **4** *1¾* **Mumbling (IRE)**[7] 397 7-10-0 **112** oh1 .... JamesDavies 113
(B G Powell) *in tch: rdn after 3 out: no imp tl styd on appr last* **16/1**

1-54 **5** *1* **Mcbain (USA)**[32] 387 6-10-11 **123** .... PJBrennan 123
(P J Hobbs) *hld up towards rr: hdwy after 6th: rdn to chse ldrs after 3 out: kpt on same pce* **12/1**

2552 **6** *3* **Alikat (IRE)**[32] 1039 4-10-10 **127** .... TJMalone(3) 122+
(M C Pipe) *in tch: rdn after 3 out: kpt on same pce* **20/1**

2-02 **7** *shd* **Penny Pictures (IRE)**[46] 422 6-11-12 **138** .... RThornton 135
(M C Pipe) *hld up towards rr: hdwy after 6th:rdn to chse ldrs after 3 out : one pced after* **16/1**

-610 **8** *3½* **Xellance (IRE)**[36] 1010 8-10-11 **123** .... RJohnson 117
(P J Hobbs) *in tch: lost pl after 6th: rdn after next: nt a danger after* **12/1**

0110 **9** *2½* **Herne Bay (IRE)**[21] 1111 5-9-10 **113** .... MNicolls(5) 104
(R S Brookhouse) *chsd ldrs tl 3 out: sn wknd* **14/1**

033- **10** *2* **Football Crazy (IRE)**[19] 4765 6-11-6 **132** .... WMarston 123+
(P Bowen) *led: mstke and hdd 5th: nvr travelling after* **7/2**[1]

PF-3 **11** *1* **Turkama (FR)**[21] 1111 8-10-2 **119** .... DLaverty(5) 107
(L A Dace) *plld hrd: mid div: hdwy 3rd: led 5th: rdn and hdd appr 2 out: wknd* **50/1**

122 **12** *24* **Boulevardofdreams (IRE)**[68] 742 4-10-1 **115** .... TJMurphy 77
(M C Pipe) *mid div tl wknd appr 3 out* **10/1**[3]

F00- **13** *½* **Grave Doubts**[156] 4438 9-11-1 **127** ....(t) TDoyle 91
(K Bishop) *hld up: sme hdwy appr 3 out: sn wknd* **25/1**

-550 **14** *1¼* **Anatar (IRE)**[35] 1020 7-10-8 **120** .... TScudamore 82
(M C Pipe) *a in rr* **33/1**

34F- **15** *26* **Milligan (FR)**[207] 3541 10-10-10 **125** .... TJPhelan(3) 61
(Dr P Pritchard) *dwlt: a bhd* **66/1**

-1UP **P** **Mr Fluffy**[36] 1016 8-10-4 **121** .... RStephens(5) —
(P J Hobbs) *mid div: mstke 4th: wknd appr 7th: t.o and p.u bef 2 out* **33/1**

5m 12.0s (-8.30) **Going Correction** -0.35s/f (Good)
WFA 4 from 5yo+ 16lb **16** Ran SP% **121.7**
Speed ratings: **101,100,100,99,99 98,98,97,96,95 95,86,86,85,76** — CSF £23.95 CT £1769.92 TOTE £6.40: £1.70, £1.50, £16.00, £4.80; EX 37.40 TRIFECTA Not won..
Owner Mrs Angela Tincknell **Bred** Compagnia Generale **Trained** Ditcheat, Somerset

FOCUS
A good handicap with a valuable prize for the time of year that went the way of the fancied runners. However, the form is limited by proximity of the third and fourth.

NOTEBOOK

Goblet Of Fire(USA), up 7lb from last time, has been transformed by the re-application of blinkers and, having travelled fluently, he found plenty under pressure to win with a bit in hand in the end. He is really starting to get his act together now and is likely to head to Market Rasen next for a similarly valuable race. *(op 6-1)*

Englishtown(FR) was taking a marked rise in grade and was up to the task, making the winner pull out the stops. He was receiving 11lb, but is gradually improving and is also likely to head to Market Rasen *(tchd 4-1)*

Kalambari(IRE) was rightly made 100/1, having refused to take part the last twice, but he was in the mood on this occasion and he kept on strongly to pick up some valuable place money. He is quite a bit higher in the weights than when last successful, but showed he is up to winning at a slightly lower level. *(op 66-1)*

Mumbling(IRE) ran well on this return to hurdles, but simply lacked the pace of the winner and it may take a step up to three miles before he is winning again.

Mcbain(USA) showed improved form on this step up in distance and, if anything, shaped as though an extra quarter mile would suit. He is likely to continue to run well in similar races, but probably without winning.

Alikat(IRE), racing off her highest-ever mark, kept battling away and just got the better of her stable companion for sixth. This was the highest-ever mark she has raced off and she needs to improve to win off it. *(op 16-1)*

Penny Pictures(IRE) has recorded most of his wins at a slightly lower level and his current mark of 138 will continue to make life hard for him.

Football Crazy(IRE) never looked comfortable and ran a rare below-par race. For some reason he *lacked his usual zip, but there is still the possibility he may have needed this.Official explanation: vet said gelding was lame (tchd 10-3)*

1271 TOTEPOOL NOVICES' H'CAP CHASE (13 fncs 3 omitted) 2m 5f 110y

3:40 (3:44) (Class 3) (0-120,111) 5-Y-0+ **£6,816** (£2,215; £1,192)

Form				RPR
5-43	1		**Baloo**[20] 1125 9-10-3 **93** ... CHonour(5) (J D Frost) *hld up in 3rd: hdwy to ld 6th: drew 6l clr appr 9th: a in command after* **11/8**[1]	110+
-3F3	2	8	**Cedar Chief**[7] 1219 8-9-7 **85** oh20 ... (b) PTGallagher(7) (B A Pearce) *led tl 6th: chsd wnr: rdn appr 3 out: kpt on but no further imp on wnr* **13/2**	88
0136	3	19	**Red Canyon (IRE)**[12] 1192 8-10-12 **97** ... (p) JTizzard (C L Tizzard) *nvr fluent in rr: reminders after 4th: sn lost tch: lft poor 3rd at the 9th* **10/3**[3]	83+
10-1	F		**Philippa Yeates (IRE)**[25] 1076 6-10-9 **97** ... (p) TJMalone(3) (M C Pipe) *chsd ldrs: rdn after 8th: fell next: dead* **11/4**[2]	—

5m 14.8s (-7.90) **Going Correction** -0.35s/f (Good) 4 Ran SP% **105.2**

Speed ratings: **100,97,90,**— CSF £8.61 TOTE £2.40; EX 10.60.

Owner Cloud Nine-Premier Cru **Bred** R G Frost **Trained** Scorriton, Devon

FOCUS

A race that took little winning and an ideal opportunity for Baloo. The runner-up is the best guide to the level but the form is not that solid.

NOTEBOOK

Baloo, whose chase rating is 11lb lower than his mark over hurdles, was able to take full advantage and ran out an authoritative winner. This was a bad race, so he will have to up his game off a higher mark, but this should have done his confidence good. *(tchd 5-4 and 6-4 in a place)*

Cedar Chief has been performing well since returned to racing under Rules, but he was no match for the winner, despite being in receipt of weight. *Official explanation: vet said gelding was lame (op 8-1)*

Red Canyon(IRE) did not show a great deal on this chase debut, his indifferent jumping letting him down. He was a tough and genuine performer over hurdles, and will win races over the larger obstacles if getting his jumping together. *(op 4-1)*

Philippa Yeates(IRE), a drifter in the market beforehand, did not look to be going particularly well when coming down at the eighth, sadly for connections taking a fatal fall. *(op 7-4)*

1272 TOTEEXACTA NOVICES' H'CAP HURDLE (8 hdls) 2m 1f

4:10 (4:12) (Class 3) (0-110,107) 4-Y-0+ **£5,434** (£1,672; £836; £418)

Form				RPR
-151	1		**Space Cowboy (IRE)**[3] 1250 5-11-7 **102** 7ex ... (b) PHide (G L Moore) *trckd ldrs: led on bit appr 2 out: r.o wl: readily* **7/2**[2]	111+
F634	2	1 ½	**Olimpo (FR)**[12] 1188 4-10-1 **83** ... RJohnson (P J Hobbs) *hld up: smooth hdwy after 3 out: pressed wnr fr 2 out: nt qckn run-in* **5/1**	84
1432	3	6	**Gemini Dancer**[20] 1123 6-11-12 **107** ... JTizzard (C L Tizzard) *t.k.h in tch: blnd 3 out: sn rcvrd: rdn appr next: kpt on* **4/1**[3]	104+
031	4	3 ½	**Doris Souter (IRE)**[16] 1158 5-10-4 **85** ... WMarston (D J Wintle) *chsd ldrs: rdn to ld appr 2 out: sn hdd: one pced after* **3/1**[1]	78
-000	5	1 ¼	**Twentytwosilver (IRE)**[13] 753 5-10-7 **88** ... PJBrennan (N J Hawke) *hld up: hdwy after 3 out: sn rdn: wknd appr last* **16/1**	79
2615	6	6	**General Smith**[35] 1017 6-10-13 **94** ... VSlattery (H J Evans) *hld up mid div: rdn after 3 out: sn wknd* **25/1**	79
1604	7	6	**Mick Murphy (IRE)**[35] 1028 8-10-0 **81** ... JamesDavies (V J Hughes) *w ldr: rdn after 3 out: sn wknd* **14/1**	60
-110	8	¾	**Miss Lehman**[68] 753 7-10-6 **94** ... MissSGaisford(7) (J D Frost) *hld up and a bhd* **12/1**	73
2010	9	¾	**Wardash (GER)**[35] 1028 5-10-9 **90** ... (vt) TJMurphy (M C Pipe) *led: rdn and hdd appr 2 out: sn btn: eased run-in* **16/1**	68

3m 56.2s (-8.90) **Going Correction** -0.35s/f (Good)

WFA 4 from 5yo+ 15lb 9 Ran SP% **113.9**

Speed ratings: **106,105,102,100,100 97,94,94,93** CSF £21.40 CT £71.53 TOTE £4.80: £1.10, £2.40, £2.30; EX 28.50.

Owner Platt Sanderson Partnership **Bred** Kildaragh Stud **Trained** Woodingdean, E Sussex

FOCUS

An ordinary handicap but a tidy performance from the in-form Space Cowboy. The third ran to his recent mark with the first two both showing improved form.

NOTEBOOK

Space Cowboy(IRE), shouldering a 7lb penalty for his Fontwell victory, made it three from his last four starts over hurdles and had the cheekpieces replaced by the blinkers. He is evidently in cracking form at present and it will be interesting to see if he is turned out quickly in his bid for a hat-trick. *(op 3-1)*

Olimpo(FR) continues to find at least one too good and he was no match for Space Cowboy as that one quickened. He was clear of the third and is capable of better in time, with him being only a four-year-old. *(op 11-2)*

Gemini Dancer was always going to struggle to give weight to the other principals, but he made a good fist of it and is a fair prospect for fences. *(op 9-2)*

Doris Souter(IRE) appeared to hold good chances of supplementing her maiden hurdling success on this handicap debut and she looked set to be involved in the finish when nosing ahead with quarter of a mile to run. However, she was eclipsed late on and simply did not look good enough, even in receipt of so much weight. *(op 10-3 tchd 11-4)*

Twentytwosilver(IRE) is without a win in a long time under both codes and he did not do enough to suggest he is about to end the barren spell.

Miss Lehman *Official explanation: jockey said mare was unsuited by the fast ground*

1273 TOTESPORT 0800 221 221 H'CAP CHASE (11 fncs 2 omitted) 2m 110y

4:40 (4:41) (Class 4) (0-110,108) 5-Y-0+ **£5,473** (£1,684; £842; £421)

Form				RPR
U2FP	1		**Knight's Emperor (IRE)**[7] 1223 8-10-12 **94** ... RThornton (J L Spearing) *hld up: stdy prog fr 8th: rdn after 2 out: styd on strly: hung lft run-in: led fnl 75yds* **10/1**	103
3322	2	1 ¼	**Deep King (IRE)**[47] 904 10-11-9 **108** ... RYoung(3) (J W Mullins) *trckd ldr: led 7th: 6l clr after 2 out: sn rdn: narrow advantage whn hit last: no ex whn hdd fnl 75yds* **3/1**[2]	117+
P2-P	3	8	**Master Henry (GER)**[37] 999 11-10-13 **95** ... DRDennis (Ian Williams) *led at gd pce tl 7th: w ldr: rdn after 3 out: kpt on same pce* **14/1**	95
U13U	4	3	**James Victor (IRE)**[7] 1221 7-11-5 **101** ... TScudamore (N R Mitchell) *chsd ldrs: jnd ldrs briefly 6th: rdn after 3 out: one pced* **11/2**[3]	98
2156	5	3	**Papua**[31] 1049 11-11-12 **108** ... (b) RJohnson (N J Hawke) *in tch tl 8th: sn rdn: one pced after* **8/1**	102
-514	6	1	**Lutea (IRE)**[61] 801 5-10-11 **93** ... TJMurphy (M C Pipe) *t.k.h early: hld up: niggled along after 5th: nvr trbld ldrs* **5/2**[1]	86
0P31	7	15	**Get The Point**[20] 1126 11-10-9 **91** ... JamesDavies (Dr P Pritchard) *mstke 5th: a towards rr* **12/1**	69
1500	P		**Honan (IRE)**[12] 1188 6-11-10 **106** ... (v) APMcCoy (M C Pipe) *bhd fr 5th: t.o and p.u bef 3 out* **10/1**	—
464-	P		**Just Reuben (IRE)**[198] 3685 10-9-7 **82** oh14 ... MrTJO'Brien(7) (C L Tizzard) *in tch tl 6th: t.o and p.u bef 3 out* **25/1**	—

3m 56.8s (-8.70) **Going Correction** -0.35s/f (Good) 9 Ran SP% **116.5**

Speed ratings: **106,105,101,100,98 98,91,**—,— CSF £41.93 CT £429.65 TOTE £13.30: £4.10, £1.10, £3.00; EX 46.70.

Owner Mrs P Joynes **Bred** S W D Mcllveen **Trained** Kinnersley, Worcs

FOCUS

A moderate contest but the form, rated through the runner-up, looks reliable and is backed up by a decent time.

NOTEBOOK

Knight's Emperor(IRE) has been difficult to train in the past two or three seasons and as a result this was only his seventh start since last winning in September of 2002. Given a confident ride by Thornton, he crept through the field and, although looking far from comfortable under pressure, he did enough. Whether he can go on from this is open to debate. *(tchd 11-1)*

Deep King(IRE) was finishing in the first three for the 12th consecutive occasion and is a model of consistency. He made a bold attempt and lost little in defeat and can hopefully find another race. *(op 7-2)*

Master Henry(GER) took them along at a good clip and had his chance, simply being unable to raise his game when the front two went by. *(op 12-1 tchd 16-1)*

James Victor(IRE) was readily tapped for speed once the tempo quickened and he ideally needs a stiffer test. *(op 5-1)*

Papua was always likely to struggle under top weight and he needs to drop a few pounds. *(op 7-1)*

Lutea(IRE) was the big disappointment of the race, failing to improve as much as anticipated for this switch to fences. *(op 10-3)*

1274 TOTESPORTCASINO.COM STANDARD OPEN NATIONAL HUNT FLAT RACE 2m 1f

5:10 (5:11) (Class 6) 4-6-Y-0 **£2,583** (£738; £369)

Form				RPR
	1		**Long Road Home (IRE)** 6-10-13 ... MrJPMagnier(5) (Jonjo O'Neill) *a.p: led 1/2-way: shkn up over 2f out: comf* **5/2**[2]	97+
42	2	2 ½	**Noble Sham**[46] 917 4-11-3 ... TJMurphy (M C Pipe) *trckd ldrs: rdn and sltly outpcd 3f out: styd on fr 2f out: wnt 2nd ins fnl f: no ch w wnr* **9/2**[3]	90
	3	1 ¼	**Mr Ex (ARG)** 4-10-6 ... LAspell (G L Moore) *trckd ldrs: rdn to chse wnr 2f out: no imp after: lost 2nd ins fnl f* **10/1**	78
	4	6	**Moonshine Vixen** 4-10-5 ... MNicolls(5) (P W Hiatt) *hld up: rdn and hung lft fr over 2f out: kpt on same pce fnl f* **20/1**	76
0-	5	1	**Daramoon (IRE)**[123] 4935 4-10-10 ... RThornton (D J S Ffrench Davis) *hld up: tk clsr order 5f out: rdn 3f out: wknd over 1f out* **40/1**	75
	6	7	**Our Girl Kaz (IRE)** 5-10-11 ... JAMcCarthy (M Hill) *hld up in tch: rdn and effrt 4f out: wknd over 2f out* **7/1**	69
1	7	nk	**Ericas Charm**[31] 1048 5-11-4 ... APMcCoy (P Bowen) *led tl 1/2-way: w wnr: rdn over 2f out: wknd qckly* **2/1**[1]	75
	8	dist	**Bizarre Native**[78] 5-11-4 ... RJohnson (W K Goldsworthy) *mid div tl wknd over 4f out* **20/1**	—
	9	4	**Holmwood Legend** 4-10-10 ... LHeard(7) (Miss C J Williams) *a towards rr* **40/1**	—
	R		**Jane's Rug Rat** 6-10-11 ... MrTJO'Brien(7) (C L Popham) *in tch tl rn off crse on bnd 7f out and p.u* **33/1**	—

3m 59.0s (-6.30) **Going Correction** -0.35s/f (Good)

WFA 4 from 5yo+ 1lb 10 Ran SP% **119.0**

Speed ratings: **100,98,98,95,94 91,91,**—,—,— CSF £13.55 TOTE £3.50: £1.10, £1.10, £4.40; EX 17.80 Place 6 £63.98, Place 5 £23.58.

Owner Mrs John Magnier **Bred** Mrs Kathleen Duff **Trained** Cheltenham, Gloucs

FOCUS

Ordinary bumper form as is to be expected for the time of year, rated through the second.

NOTEBOOK

Long Road Home(IRE) did it nicely on this racecourse debut, coming clear under a collected ride from Magnier and winning with something in hand. This was not a strong race, but he may be capable of defying a penalty in similarly modest company. *(op 3-1 tchd 10-3)*

Noble Sham is steadily progressing and he stayed on all the way to the line without being able to match the winner's speed. He will appreciate further once sent hurdling and is sure to win races for top connections. *(op 4-1)*

Mr Ex(ARG), whose trainer is sending out plenty of winners at present, made a pleasing debut and gave the impression he will improve for the experience. He can find a similar race.*Official explanation: vet said gelding was jarred up post-race (op 9-1)*

Moonshine Vixen made a pleasing debut and may find life easier in mares-only company. *(op 22-1)*

Daramoon(IRE) stepped up on her initial effort, but may need hurdles before being able to win. *(op 33-1)*

Our Girl Kaz(IRE) failed to live up to market expectations and did not appear to get home. *(tchd 5-1)*

Ericas Charm failed to build on her Uttoxeter win and the way she tied up under pressure suggests there may have been something amiss. *Official explanation: jockey said mare lost its action (op 5-2)*

T/Jkpt: Not won. T/Plt: £73.40 to a £1 stake. Pool: £52,282.10. 519.70 winning tickets. T/Qpdt: £28.40 to a £1 stake. Pool: £3,691.20. 96.00 winning tickets. TM

[1176]SOUTHWELL (L-H)

Sunday, August 21

OFFICIAL GOING: Good

Wind: Almost nil Weather: Sunny

1275 RIVA BINGO OF NEWARK BEGINNERS' CHASE (16 fncs) 2m 5f 110y

2:30 (2:30) (Class 4) 5-Y-0+ **£4,173** (£1,284; £642; £321)

Form RPR

1223 **1** **Whispered Secret (GER)**[16] 1155 6-11-0 .... RGreene 120+
(M C Pipe) *a.p: led after 4 out: clr next: comf* **4/5**[1]

2236 **2** *14* **Izzykeen**[16] 1155 6-11-0 .... DElsworth 105+
(Mrs S J Smith) *led 2nd: rdn and hdd after 4 out: styng on same pce whn mstke next* **11/2**[2]

5350 **3** *12* **Oscars Vision (IRE)**[16] 1152 5-10-7 80 .... NFehily 82
(B W Duke) *prom to 11th* **12/1**

3F24 **4** *5* **Heather Lad**[16] 1147 12-11-0 100 .... GLee 84
(C Grant) *chsd ldr 2nd: ev ch 4 out: sn rdn and wknd* **11/2**[2]

0452 **5** *6* **Jim Lad**[13] 1176 5-11-0 85 ....(p) AThornton 81+
(J W Mullins) *led to 2nd: remained handy: ev ch 4 out: wknd bef next* **7/1**[3]

-10P **6** *dist* **Miss Jessica (IRE)**[70] 724 5-10-7 .... JMogford —
(Miss M E Rowland) *hld up: hdwy 5th: wknd 10th* **25/1**

0006 **U** **Known Maneuver (USA)**[13] 1176 7-10-9 64 .... TGreenway(5) —
(M C Chapman) *hld up: mstke and uns rdr 4th* **50/1**

0U00 **F** **Proper Poser (IRE)**[13] 1176 9-10-7 52 .... CMStudd(7) —
(M C Chapman) *hld up: wknd 9th: t.o whn fell 3 out* **66/1**

0503 **P** **Saposcat (IRE)**[42] 944 5-10-7 .... MrDavidTurner(7) —
(Dr P Pritchard) *prom: j. slowly and dropped rr 4th: bhd and reluctant fr next: t.o whn p.u bef 2 out* **66/1**

5m 25.0s (-2.20) **Going Correction** -0.075s/f (Good) **9** Ran SP% **115.3**

Speed ratings: **101,95,91,89,87** —,—,—,— CSF £5.76 TOTE £1.50: £1.10, £2.80, £4.40; EX 6.90.

Owner David Manasseh Daniel Evans Dan Levine **Bred** G Baron Von Ullmann **Trained** Nicholashayne, Devon

FOCUS

A weak beginners' chase and the field came home well strung out. The form looks pretty sound rated through the winner with the placed horses to their hurdles marks.

NOTEBOOK

Whispered Secret(GER) gained a deserved first success over fences and won as his short price entitled him to. His jumping improves with each outing, he stays this trip well and will no doubt be high on confidence now. He ought to be placed to strike again in this sphere before the ground turns softer. *(tchd 5-6)*

Izzykeen was firmly put in his place by the winner, but still turned in a more encouraging display and was well clear of the rest. He should be capable of better with further experience over fences. *(tchd 5-1)*

Oscars Vision(IRE) , with the visor left off on this chasing bow, jumped adequately yet was never a threat at any stage. She is at least entitled to improve for this experience, and should find her feet when switching to handicaps, but remains one to have reservations about.

Heather Lad failed to improve as expected for the return to this longer trip and faded disappointingly from three out. *(op 13-2 tchd 5-1)*

Jim Lad looked a non-stayer of this longer trip and can get closer again when reverting to shorter. He is yet to win a race of any description from 28 outings.

1276 TRAVAIL EMPLOYMENT GROUP H'CAP CHASE (19 fncs) 3m 2f

3:00 (3:01) (Class 4) (0-110,110) 5-Y-0+ **£4,160** (£1,280; £640; £320)

Form RPR

-UU3 **1** **High Gear (IRE)**[12] 1191 7-10-11 95 ....(b) NFehily 107+
(Jonjo O'Neill) *hld up in tch: rdn after 4 out: lft 2nd next: styd on u.p to ld towards fin* **9/2**[2]

136/ **2** *3* **Aegean**[822] 383 11-11-5 103 .... DElsworth 112+
(Mrs S J Smith) *mde most tl after 9th: chsd ldr: ev ch whn mstke 4 out: lft in ld next: rdn and hdd towards fin* **7/1**

30-4 **3** *11* **Tipsy Mouse (IRE)**[93] 439 9-11-12 110 ....(p) HOliver 108+
(R C Guest) *hld up: hdwy 10th: wkng whn lft 3rd 3 out: blnd next* **4/1**[1]

/020 **4** *nk* **Waterberg (IRE)**[16] 1157 10-11-6 104 .... MBradburne 100
(H D Daly) *in rr: reminders 3rd: mstke 6th: hdwy 13th: outpcd fr 15th* **9/1**

P-P0 **5** *15* **Iron Express**[38] 989 9-10-5 89 ....(p) FKeniry 70
(G M Moore) *chsd ldrs to 11th* **5/1**[3]

52-P **6** *dist* **Bang And Blame (IRE)**[13] 1177 9-9-11 84 oh7 .... APSpell(3) —
(M W Easterby) *hld up: rdn 10th: a bhd* **17/2**

0P2- **P** **Lost In Normandy (IRE)**[360] 1296 8-9-11 84 oh9 .... DCrosse(3) —
(Mrs L Williamson) *chsd ldrs: rdn and wknd after 12th: bhd whn p.u bef 14th* **10/1**

60-P **P** **Sunday Habits (IRE)**[7] 1219 11-9-7 84 oh2 .... MrDavidTurner(7) —
(Dr P Pritchard) *sn pushed along and prom: wknd 9th: t.o whn p.u bef 13th* **14/1**

P-4P **U** **Hehasalife (IRE)**[8] 1205 8-9-7 84 ....(b) PMerrigan(7) 93+
(Mrs H Dalton) *mstke 1st: prom: led after 9th: mstke 12th: slt ld whn mstke and uns rdr 3 out* **13/2**

6m 37.5s (-1.80) **Going Correction** -0.075s/f (Good) **9** Ran SP% **117.0**

Speed ratings: **99,98,94,94,89** —,—,—,— CSF £36.50 CT £137.00 TOTE £5.40: £1.40, £2.40, £1.50; EX 53.60.

Owner John P McManus **Bred** Oliver And Salome Brennan **Trained** Cheltenham, Gloucs

FOCUS

A modest staying handicap, run at a sound gallop, and the form looks fair.

NOTEBOOK

High Gear(IRE) finally showed his true colours and gained a career-first success at the 16th time of asking, with a dour performance. He responded gamely under pressure, put in by far his best round of jumping to date and clearly stays very well. While he is clearly a very tricky ride, he may have more to offer now he has got his head in front. *(tchd 4-1)*

Aegean , returning from a 822-day layoff, posted a very encouraging return to action and was only run out of it close home. His next outing should reveal more, but he looks to have retained enthusiasm and all of his ability. *(op 13-2)*

Tipsy Mouse(IRE) , making his debut for new connections, ran lazily throughout and merely plugged on for third. He has lost the plot this year, but he is on a fair mark if his new yard can get him in the mood once again, and would ideally prefer softer ground in the future. *(tchd 9-2)*

Waterberg(IRE) was another who ran in snatches and never threatened. He is happier with more cut in the ground, but has a fair bit to prove now nevertheless. *(op 8-1)*

Iron Express , who won this in 2004 off a 6lb higher mark, found little when push came to shove and continues to look out of sorts. *(op 15-2)*

Hehasalife(IRE) has to go down as unlucky, as he was still bang in contention prior to unshipping his rider three out and would have gone very close. The first-time blinkers clearly had the desired effect and he is undoubtedly on a decent mark at present. *(op 7-1 tchd 15-2)*

1277 OLE INTERNATIONAL H'CAP CHASE (16 fncs) 2m 5f 110y

3:30 (3:31) (Class 4) (0-100,98) 5-Y-0+ **£4,192** (£1,290; £645; £322)

Form RPR

2415 **1** **Good Heart (IRE)**[16] 1152 10-11-5 91 ....(t) GLee 100
(R Ford) *hld up: hdwy 10th: chsd ldr 4 out: led 2 out: styd on wl* **5/1**[2]

-2B2 **2** *5* **Who Dares (IRE)**[8] 1212 7-11-6 92 .... NFehily 96
(Jonjo O'Neill) *hld up in tch: led after 6th: j.rt 9th: rdn and hdd 2 out: styd on same pce last* **8/1**

P-13 **3** *9* **Mikasa (IRE)**[23] 1098 5-10-2 77 .... KJMercer(3) 72
(R F Fisher) *hld up: hdwy 9th: hmpd bnd sn after: wknd 2 out* **6/1**[3]

-215 **4** *8* **Roman Candle (IRE)**[70] 724 9-10-11 83 .... JPMcNamara 70
(Lucinda Featherstone) *chsd ldrs: mstke 5th: sn lost pl: hdwy 10th: wknd 3 out* **10/1**

3P/P **5** *26* **Beaver Lodge (IRE)**[43] 488 8-11-12 98 .... JMogford 59
(B P J Baugh) *chsd ldr: led appr 3rd: hdd 6th: hmpd 9th: wknd after 4 out* **33/1**

U024 **6** *½* **York Rite (AUS)**[8] 1203 9-10-6 78 ....(p) HOliver 39
(R C Guest) *chsd ldrs to 10th* **5/1**[2]

5004 **U** **Amptina (IRE)**[13] 1178 10-10-0 72 oh9 .... DElsworth —
(Mrs S J Smith) *hld up: blnd and uns rdr 5th* **9/1**

2-50 **F** **Backscratcher**[84] 575 11-9-9 72 oh7 ....(b) WKennedy(5) —
(John R Upson) *prom: led 6th: sn hdd: w ldr whn hmpd and fell 9th* **12/1**

UPP- **P** **Never Awol (IRE)**[208] 3523 8-9-13 78 .... TMessenger(7) —
(B N Pollock) *led to appr 3rd: lost pl 5th: bhd whn hmpd 9th: t.o whn p.u bef 3 out* **14/1**

FU41 **F** **Miss Muscat**[8] 1203 5-10-7 79 .... JPByrne 51
(Evan Williams) *hld up: nt fluent: hdwy 9th: wknd 3 out: in rr whn tried to refuse and fell last* **10/3**[1]

5m 27.8s (0.60) **Going Correction** -0.075s/f (Good) **10** Ran SP% **118.2**

Speed ratings: **95,93,89,87,77 77**,—,—,—,— CSF £45.34 CT £248.16 TOTE £6.00: £2.10, £2.60, £2.50; EX 21.70.

Owner M J Caldwell **Bred** Timothy Dunne **Trained** Cotebrook, Cheshire

FOCUS

A moderate handicap, run at a fair gallop, and the form looks sound for the class with the placed horses setting the level.

NOTEBOOK

Good Heart(IRE) , not disgraced over hurdles last time, ran out a ready winner under a strong ride from Lee. He has now won his last two outings over fences - both over course and distance - and is clearly still improving. He should go very close in his quest for the hat-trick, despite another inevitable rise in the weights, and connections cited the Becher Chase at Aintree in November as a possible future target. *(op 11-2)*

Who Dares(IRE) , with the headgear abandoned, turned in another fair effort yet was again found wanting at the business end of the race. He got the longer trip well enough, and finished clear of the rest, but he has still to win race so can never be backed with any confidence.

Mikasa(IRE) did not appear that suited by the longer trip, and is not without hope off this mark when reverting to shorter, as he has developed into a consistent performer of late.

Roman Candle(IRE) , making his belated chasing debut, shaped with a degree of promise and should learn from this experience. *(op 9-1)*

Beaver Lodge(IRE) *Official explanation: jockey said gelding finished lame*

Miss Muscat , raised 6lb for her surprise victory at Bangor eight days previously, again saw her jumping problems materialise and she was well beaten prior to falling at the final fence. She is one to have reservations about. *(op 3-1)*

1278 T W SAMPSON CENTENARY (S) HURDLE (9 hdls) 2m 1f

4:00 (4:02) (Class 5) 4-7-Y-0 **£2,632** (£752; £376)

Form RPR

-5PP **1** **Ela Re**[21] 1111 6-11-5 105 .... AThornton 107+
(C R Dore) *mde all: sn clr: unchal* **11/4**[1]

05 **2** *3½* **Staff Nurse (IRE)**[27] 854 5-10-5 ....(p) KRenwick 85
(N Wilson) *settled in 3rd: chsd wnr 3 out: sn rdn and no imp* **3/1**[2]

024- **3** *21* **Scippit**[406] 918 6-10-12 89 .... DO'Meara 71
(Miss Tracy Waggott) *hld up: nvr nr to chal* **5/1**

0/00 **4** *shd* **La Maestra (FR)**[16] 1156 7-10-5 77 ....(bt) PMoloney 64
(Miss L Day) *hld up: nvr nr to chal* **25/1**

U2 **5** *7* **Munaawesh (USA)**[25] 1000 4-10-4 .... PKinsella(7) 63
(D W Chapman) *hld up: sme hdwy 6th: wknd 3 out* **4/1**[3]

4006 **6** *3½* **Reedsman (IRE)**[21] 1107 4-10-11 68 ....(p) HOliver 59
(R C Guest) *hld up: a bhd* **12/1**

-000 **7** *¾* **Wages**[24] 1085 5-10-7 87 ....(p) WKennedy(5) 60
(A M Hales) *hld up: wknd appr 3 out* **15/2**

0/P **P** **Knight General Mac**[49] 892 6-10-5 .... CDSharkey(7) —
(N Bycroft) *chsd wnr tl wknd 3 out: t.o whn p.u bef next* **40/1**

4m 2.80s (-2.10) **Going Correction** -0.075s/f (Good)

WFA 4 from 5yo+ 15lb **8** Ran SP% **114.1**

Speed ratings: **101,99,89,89,86 84,84**,— CSF £11.50 TOTE £3.70: £1.80, £1.40, £1.40; EX 9.80.The winner was sold to Mrs S Smith for 10,200gns.

Owner L Cohen **Bred** Side Hill Stud **Trained** West Pinchbeck, Lincs

FOCUS

A dire contest and the first two came well clear. The form is pretty weak.

NOTEBOOK

Ela Re relished the drop to this lowly grade and made all for a clear-cut success. He can be rated value for further and, while he only scored as his official rating entitled him to, his confidence should have been nicely boosted for an impending return to a higher level. *(op 5-2)*

Staff Nurse(IRE) appreciated the combination of a drop to this class and the application of first-time cheekpieces, showing her best form over timber to date. She has clearly found her level and is now eligible for handicaps in this sphere. *(op 7-2 tchd 11-4)*

Scippit , making his seasonal debut, merely plugged on at the same pace and shaped as though the outing was needed. *(op 4-1)*

La Maestra(FR) , tried in a first-time tongue tie, ran near to her recent level and never threatened.

Munaawesh(USA)'s effort proved short-lived and he never looked like justifying on-course support in the betting. He is not one to rely on, but is capable of better and probably requires a stiffer test. *(op 11-2)*

1279 NEWARK ADVERTISER LADIES DAY CLAIMING HURDLE (13 hdls) 3m 2f

4:30 (4:32) (Class 4) 4-Y-0+ **£2,961** (£846; £423)

Form RPR

0P60 **1** **Super Boston**[13] 1180 5-10-10 68 ....(b) AThornton 81
(Miss L C Siddall) *mstke 1st: bhd: hdwy 8th: rdn to chse ldr appr 2 out: styd on u.p to ld last: sn clr* **8/1**

304P **2** *6* **Ungaretti (GER)**[16] 1152 8-11-5 93 ....(p) PMoloney 84
(Ian Williams) *chsd ldr tl led 4th: hdd 8th: led next: clr 2 out: rdn and hdd last: sn btn* **6/4**[1]

0-P0 **3** *10* **Happy Hussar (IRE)**[35] 1027 12-10-8 92 .... DrPPritchard(5) 68
(Dr P Pritchard) *led to 4th: lost pl appr 7th: rallied 3 out: wknd next* **2/1**[2]

0-50 **4** *17* **Fairmorning (IRE)**[10] 813 6-10-7 70..................................(p) DCrosse(3) 55+
(C N Kellett) *hld up: hdwy to ld 8th: hdd next: ev ch 3 out: wknd bef next* **7/1**[3]
PP6P **5** *dist* **Island Warrior (IRE)**[49] 891 10-10-13 66..........................(tp) JMogford —
(B P J Baugh) *chsd ldrs to 10th* **14/1**
P0-P **P** **Broughton Boy**[91] 465 5-10-12 .... TMessenger(7) —
(G J Smith) *prom: blnd and wknd 7th: p.u bef next* **40/1**
0 **P** **In Ainm De (IRE)**[37] 1000 9-10-3 64.. KRenwick —
(N Wilson) *chsd ldr 3rd: rdn 6th: wknd 9th: t.o whn p.u after 3 out* **12/1**

6m 24.3s (-5.10) **Going Correction** -0.075s/f (Good) **7** Ran SP% **113.7**
Speed ratings: **104,102,99,93,— —,—** CSF £20.97 TOTE £12.30: £3.30, £1.50; EX 24.80.
Owner M K Oldham **Bred** M K Oldham **Trained** Colton, N Yorks

FOCUS
A weak event, which proved a real stamina test, and the field came home strung out. The form is suspect.

NOTEBOOK
Super Boston, despite running in snatches, clearly relished this markedly longer trip as he ultimately ran out a decisive winner. This was his first-ever success at the 17th atttempt, and a vastly-improved performance at these weights, but his overall profile indicates he is not one to lump on for a follow-up bid. *(op 9-1)*
Ungaretti(GER) looked booked to finally end his long losing run when pulling clear at the top of the straight, but his stride shortened soon after jumping the penultimate flight, and he proved powerless to resist the winner's late challenge. He appreciated the re-application of cheekpieces and, although fully exposed, still retains the ability to find a race at this level. *(tchd 11-8, 13-8 and 7-4 in places)*
Happy Hussar(IRE), down in class and best in according to official figures, failed to improve for the step back up to a suitably longer distance and disappointed. He is happier over fences these days, but is struggling for form and should never be totally relied upon. *(tchd 7-4)*
Fairmorning(IRE) showed a bit more encouragement in the first-time cheekpieces, but again threw in the towel under maximum pressure and remains impossible to win with. *(op 9-1)*

1280 EXPERIENCE NOTTINGHAMSHIRE H'CAP HURDLE (11 hdls) 2m 5f 110y
5:00 (5:01) (Class 4) (0-100,96) 4-Y-0+ **£3,562** (£1,096; £548; £274)

Form RPR
-032 **1** **Slalom (IRE)**[16] 1158 5-11-2 **91**..(p) WKennedy(5) 94+
(D Burchell) *hld up: hdwy 8th: led 2 out: styd on wl* **5/1**[2]
/0-2 **2** *3 1/2* **Zygomatic**[66] 768 7-11-4 **91**.. KJMercer(3) 91+
(R F Fisher) *hld up: hdwy 8th: stmbld after 3 out: sn outpcd: styd on u.p appr last* **4/1**[1]
0-P5 **3** *5* **Miniballist (IRE)**[96] 397 7-11-11 **95**...............................(t) WHutchinson 92+
(R T Phillips) *hld up: hdwy 8th: led appr 2 out: sn hdd: blnd and wknd last* **16/1**
44-4 **4** *5* **Ipledgeallegiance (USA)**[15] 370 9-11-11 **95**....................... DO'Meara 84
(Miss Tracy Waggott) *hld up: sme hdwy appr 2 out: nvr trbld ldrs* **8/1**
5 **5** *nk* **Suits Me Fine (IRE)**[32] 1040 5-11-4 **88**.. NFehily 77
(Jonjo O'Neill) *hld up: hdwy appr 2 out: n.d* **7/1**
6312 **6** *1 1/4* **Qualitair Pleasure**[47] 905 5-11-4 **91**...................................... PAspell(3) 78
(J Hetherton) *hld up: hdwy appr 2 out: n.d* **8/1**
4146 **7** *12* **Panmure (IRE)**[21] 1110 9-11-3 **87**... GLee 62
(P D Niven) *mid-div: hdwy 7th: wknd appr 2 out* **6/1**[3]
PP4P **8** *9* **Phase Eight Girl**[16] 1152 9-10-5 **75**.................................... MBradburne 41
(J Hetherton) *a bhd* **11/1**
5105 **9** *1 3/4* **Idlewild (IRE)**[13] 1180 10-11-5 **96**.. APogson(7) 61
(C T Pogson) *chsd clr ldrs: lft 2nd appr 7th: wknd bef 2 out* **12/1**
5PPP **10** *14* **Vivre Aimer Rire (FR)**[37] 1002 4-9-4 **72** oh2........................ JKington(10) 21
(M Scudamore) *mid-div: wknd 7th* **50/1**
555 **11** *3 1/2* **Francolino (FR)**[20] 1122 12-10-0 **70**.. RGreene 17
(Dr P Pritchard) *chsd clr ldrs: rdn 5th: wknd 7th* **50/1**
5-0B **12** *14* **Amber Dawn**[96] 394 6-10-8 **78**... OMcPhail 11
(J Gallagher) *j.lft: chsd clr ldr tl lft in ld after 6th: sn clr: wknd and hdd appr 2 out* **50/1**
2650 **U** **Caper**[16] 1153 5-10-5 **85**...(p) AHawkins(10) —
(R Hollinshead) *hld up: hdwy whn blnd and uns rdr 3 out* **10/1**
-36 **P** **Dalriath**[30] 544 6-10-11 **88**... CMStudd(7) —
(M C Chapman) *led and sn clr: wknd and hdd after 6th: sn p.u* **25/1**

5m 16.9s (-5.40) **Going Correction** -0.075s/f (Good)
WFA 4 from 5yo+ 16lb **14** Ran SP% **126.4**
Speed ratings: **106,104,102,101,100 100,96,92,92,87 85,80,—,—** CSF £26.64 CT £308.32 TOTE £6.00: £2.20, £2.00, £7.30; EX 24.60 Place 6 £21.69, Place 5 £16.46.
Owner W M Gorman **Bred** Mrs D Hutch **Trained** Briery Hill, Blaenau Gwent

FOCUS
A moderate handicap run at a strong gallop and suiting those restrained at the back early on. The form looks straightforward and sound for the grade.

NOTEBOOK
Slalom(IRE), with the cheekpieces re-applied, found the longer distance playing to his strengths and gained a much-deserved first success over hurdles at the seventh attempt. The recent change of stable has clearly had the desired effect and, on this evidence, he can be placed to strike again now connections have seemingly found his optimum trip.
Zygomatic ◆ did not prove suited by the drop to this trip, as he got badly outpaced at a crucial stage, but still turned in another creditable display. A return to three miles on a similar surface can see him gain compensation. *(op 9-2)*
Miniballist(IRE) had her chance, but was put in her place approaching the final flight. This must rate a more encouraging effort, but consistency is far from her strong suit and she remains one to have reservations about.
Ipledgeallegiance(USA), not disgraced on the Flat 15 days previously, never threatened over a trip that does stretch his stamina. He is regressive, but ought to appreciate a drop back in trip. *(op 7-1)*
T/Plt: £21.90 to a £1 stake. Pool: £39,366.35. 1,310.70 winning tickets. T/Qpdt: £12.50 to a £1 stake. Pool: £2,273.00. 134.50 winning tickets. CR

1281 - 1290a (Foreign Racing) - See Raceform Interactive

936 PERTH (R-H)
Tuesday, August 23

OFFICIAL GOING: Good to firm
Wind: almost nil

1291 ORION ALL STARS NOVICES' HURDLE (8 hdls) 2m 110y
5:45 (5:45) (Class 4) 4-Y-0+ **£3,115** (£1,214; £633; £316)

Form RPR
11 **1** **Lahib The Fifth (IRE)**[44] 936 5-11-5 .... ADobbin 101+
(N G Richards) *hld up: hdwy 1/2-way: rdn along to chse ldr and 4 l down whn lft in ld 2 out: drvn out* **4/6**[1]
0002 **2** *3* **Skiddaw Jones**[26] 942 5-10-9 88...(t) PWhelan(3) 89
(M A Barnes) *hld up in midfield: hdwy 1/2-way: rdn along appr 2 out: drvn and ch last: one pce flat* **10/1**
6 **3** *10* **Templet (USA)**[19] 942 5-10-12 ....(b) BHarding 79
(W G Harrison) *chsd clr ldr: rdn along 3 out: sn drvn and wknd bef next* **100/1**
0-0P **4** *11* **King's Envoy (USA)**[35] 320 6-10-9 95............................. PBuchanan(3) 68
(Mrs J C McGregor) *a rr: bhd fr 1/2-way* **33/1**
0/0- **F** **Lanhel (FR)**[200] 3682 6-10-9 .... PAspell(3) 62
(J Wade) *chsd ldrs: rdn along 4 out: wknd bef next and bhd whn fell last* **66/1**
-034 **P** **Lofty Leader (IRE)**[79] 647 6-11-5 99.................................. MBradburne —
(Mrs H O Graham) *a rr: rdn along and bhd whn mstke 5th: sn t.o and p.u bef 2 out* **5/1**[2]
F **Millennium Hall**[45] 6-10-2 .... DDaSilva(10) 97+
(P Monteith) *led: clr 1/2-way: pushed along and hit 3 out: 4 l clr whn stmbld on landing and fell next* **13/2**[3]
P **Inch High**[27] 7-10-12 .... GLee —
(J S Goldie) *in tch: nt fluent 1st: j.rt 2nd: sn rdn along and lost pl next: bhd fr 1/2-way: t.o whn p.u bef 2 out* **33/1**

3m 55.5s (-5.10) **Going Correction** -0.125s/f (Good) **8** Ran SP% **107.4**
Speed ratings: **107,105,100,95,— —,—,—** CSF £6.86 TOTE £1.70: £1.10, £1.20, £6.30; EX 9.00.
Owner Jim Ennis **Bred** Denis Dunne And Thomas Phelan **Trained** Greystoke, Cumbria

FOCUS
Lahib The Fifth was a fortunate winner as Millennium Hall would have won had he stayed upright. The winner has scope for improvement but the second, third and fourth hold the form down badly.

NOTEBOOK
Lahib The Fifth(IRE) was probably a fortunate winner as he was starting to struggle before the leader fell two out. He looks ready for a step up in trip now as he does not appear to have natural pace, but he does possess scope for improvement. *(op 4-7 tchd 11-8 in places)*
Skiddaw Jones is rated only 88 and gives the form a poor look. He is another in the race that may well be better suited by further over hurdles. *(tchd 9-1)*
Templet(USA) was third by default as the long-time leader and probable winner fell two out, and so he achieved very little. *(op 50-1)*
King's Envoy(USA) has managed only one second - a decent effort behind a talented Flat perfomer/hurdler - in ten runs to date over hurdles, and looks harshly handicapped on the other efforts. He will find it difficult in handicap company off his current mark.
Millennium Hall was most unfortunate not to win after over-jumping the second-last flight. As long as his confidence has not been affected he ought to win next time in similar company. *(op 13-2)*
Inch High showed very little on his belated hurdling debut. *(op 13-2)*
Lofty Leader(IRE), without the cheekpieces, showed nothing and is regressing. *(op 13-2)*

1292 INVERALMOND RENAULT NOVICES' CHASE (15 fncs) 2m 4f 110y
6:15 (6:17) (Class 3) 5-Y-0+ **£5,257** (£2,277)

Form RPR
13-3 **1** **Fool On The Hill**[27] 1078 8-11-10 137.................................... PJBrennan 122+
(P J Hobbs) *mde all: rdn appr last: drvn and hung rt run in: kpt on* **8/15**[1]
1P3U **2** *1 1/2* **Moscow Dancer (IRE)**[38] 1012 8-11-10 115.............................. TJMurphy 120
(P Monteith) *trckd wnr: effrt 2 out: rdn to chal last: ev ch whn n.m.r and hmpd flat: kpt on* **15/8**[2]
4P56 **P** **Winter Garden**[44] 940 11-11-1 95.................................... PBuchanan(3) —
(Miss Lucinda V Russell) *sn rdn along: lost pl 3rd: bhd whn p.u bef 8th* **14/1**[3]

5m 17.2s (1.90) **Going Correction** +0.125s/f (Yiel) **3** Ran SP% **106.7**
Speed ratings: **101,100,—** CSF £1.91 TOTE £1.50; EX 1.40.
Owner Louisville Syndicate **Bred** Mrs M Fairbairn And E Gadsden **Trained** Withycombe, Somerset
■ Stewards' Enquiry : P J Brennan three-day ban: careless riding (Sep 3,4,7) interf. to Moscow Dancer

FOCUS
A poor turnout for a reasonable prize. With forecast favourite Kid'Z'Play withdrawn in the morning and Winter Garden showing no interest from an early stage, the race developed into a match, won by the highest-rated of the two. The form is dubious.

NOTEBOOK
Fool On The Hill, rated 22lb higher over fences than the second, won nicely enough despite his jockey not appearing to know which way to go after jumping the last. He was in front for a long time and possibly idled in front. Paddy Brennan received a three-day ban for careless riding. Official explanation: vet said gelding was lame on right fore *(op 2-5 tchd 4-7)*
Moscow Dancer(IRE) had a stiff task with the winner on official figures and ran respectably. His jumping was not as quick as the winner's and he was a shade unlucky not to win after suffering interference after the last which nearly took him on to the wrong course. *(op 5-2)*
Winter Garden slowed into the first fence and did not jump with much fluency afterwards. He does not look interested in racing and could not even finish for third-place money. *(op 10-1 tchd 16-1 in a place)*

1293 REG VARDY EDINBURGH RENAULT CLAIMING HURDLE (8 hdls) 2m 110y
6:45 (6:48) (Class 4) 4-6-Y-0
£3,596 (£1,364; £682; £310; £155; £93)

Form RPR
4-00 **1** **Overstrand (IRE)**[10] 1204 6-11-12 124....................................(b) ADobbin 104+
(M Todhunter) *hld up: hdwy 3 out: rdn to ld next: drvn clr last: styd on* **11/8**[1]
0- **2** *5* **Cadeaux Rouge (IRE)**[21] 1397 4-10-0 ....(t) KJMercer(3) 74
(D W Thompson) *hld up in rr: pushed along and outpcd appr 3 out: gd hdwy next: rdn to chse wnr last: no imp flat* **25/1**
35-5 **3** *1* **Blackthorn**[31] 936 6-11-3 95.. GLee 87
(R Ford) *led to 5th: pushed along after next: rdn 2 out and kpt on same pce* **4/1**[3]
5520 **4** *2 1/2* **Three Times A Lady**[69] 760 5-9-13 72.............................. DCCostello(5) 72
(D W Thompson) *prom: led 5th: rdn along and hdd 2 out: sn drvn and wknd last* **10/1**
0-01 **5** *4* **Seafire Lad (IRE)**[23] 1107 4-10-13 75...................................(p) KJohnson 77
(R Johnson) *chsd ldrs: rdn along after 3 out: drvn and one pce fr next* **16/1**
00F0 **6** *2 1/2* **Neven**[27] 716 6-10-8 75.. PBuchanan(3) 72
(Miss Lucinda V Russell) *in tch: rdn along and wknd bef 3 out* **50/1**
-433 **7** *3* **Winslow Boy (USA)**[10] 1202 4-11-2 87.................................. PAspell(3) 77
(P Monteith) *chsd ldrs: rdn along 5th: drvn 3 out and sn wknd* **3/1**[2]

4m 0.30s (-0.30) **Going Correction** -0.125s/f (Good)
WFA 4 from 5yo+ 15lb **7** Ran SP% **107.9**
Speed ratings: **95,92,92,91,89 87,86** CSF £30.09 TOTE £2.10: £1.10, £9.10; EX 42.00.The winner was claimed by Naughty Diesel Ltd for £15,000
Owner F F Racing Services Partnership IV **Bred** Airlie Stud **Trained** Orton, Cumbria

FOCUS
A modest time even for a claiming hurdle, 4.8 seconds slower than the opener. The winner was thought to be badly handicapped over hurdles and was subsequently sold after the race for £15,000 to new owners.

NOTEBOOK

Overstrand(IRE) was rated well in advance of his rivals on official figures and did it fairly easily in the end. We learnt nothing new about him, although his trainer suggested that he was badly handicapped after the race and was performing like a 90-rated horse, and he was sold to new connections after the race for £15,000. *(op 11-10 tchd 6-4)*

Cadeaux Rouge(IRE) was a very poor performer on the Flat and did well after being quite a way behind at one point. He could need further than this over hurdles as he performed over extended trips on the Flat. *(tchd 33-1)*

Blackthorn made a lot of the early running until caught with two flights to jump. He was fairly promising early in his hurdling career and should find a small handicap off his current handicap mark. *(op 6-1)*

Three Times A Lady almost certainly ran to her form and finished where she was entitled to.

Seafire Lad(IRE) won a seller last time in first-time cheekpieces but found this company too much. *(op 20-1 tchd 14-1)*

Winslow Boy(USA) ran below his recent fair form and looked very laboured in the home straight. *(op 11-4)*

1294 PARKS RENAULT NOVICES' H'CAP HURDLE (12 hdls) 3m 110y

7:15 (7:18) (Class 4) (0-105,105) 4-Y-O **£4,197** (£1,605; £813; £381; £201)

Form				RPR
063-	**1**		**Drumbeater (IRE)**[130] 4854 5-10-4 **83** .... PJBrennan (P J Hobbs) *hld up: hdwy 1/2-way: cl up whn mstke 3 out: sn rdn: led after 2 out: drvn clr last: styd on* **2/1**[2]	94+
3260	**2**	*6*	**One Of Them**[18] 1147 6-9-10 **82** .... BenOrde-Powlett(7) (M A Barnes) *a.p: led 8th: rdn along and hdd after 2 out: drvn and one pce last* **7/1**[3]	85
P2P3	**3**	*3*	**Thepubhorse**[18] 1151 5-10-1 **85** .... DCCostello(5) (Mrs H O Graham) *cl up: rdn along 3 out: drvn and one pce fr next* **8/1**	85
P-03	**4**	*21*	**Top Pack (IRE)**[40] 988 6-10-0 **79** ....(b[1]) BHarding (N G Richards) *led: rdn along and hdd 8th: wknd bef 3 out* **8/1**	61+
-P00	**5**	*dist*	**Matmata De Tendron (FR)**[38] 1015 5-10-12 **91** .... MBradburne (A Crook) *chsd ldrs: rdn along 8th: sn lost pl and bhd fr 4 out* **25/1**	—
1322	**P**		**Croc An Oir (IRE)**[10] 1205 8-11-12 **105** .... GLee (R Ford) *hld up in rr: niggled along 1/2-way: rdn along 4 out: sn outpcd and bhd whn p.u bef 2 out* **13/8**[1]	—

6m 5.40s (-5.50) **Going Correction** -0.125s/f (Good) **6** Ran SP% **110.0**
Speed ratings: **103,101,100,93,**— — CSF £15.09 TOTE £2.70: £1.60, £3.90; EX 19.30.

Owner D Allen **Bred** Paul McDonnell **Trained** Withycombe, Somerset

FOCUS

A poor event in which Drumbeater won despite some sloppy jumps at the last three hurdles. This is unlikely to be strong form.

NOTEBOOK

Drumbeater(IRE), taking a big step up in trip, jumped the last three appallingly but still won with plenty in hand. He will be handicapped by his hurdling fluency against better horses. *(tchd 7-4)*

One Of Them is thoroughly exposed over timber but ran a decent race behind the easy winner. Without a win to date over obstacles, a seller is within his grasp in his current form. *(op 10-1)*

Thepubhorse is of very limited ability and ran as well as could have been expected. *(op 12-1)*

Top Pack(IRE), in first-time blinkers, dropped away badly after making some of the early running. His jumping was not fluent either. *(op 7-1)*

Croc An Oir(IRE), returned to hurdles after a couple of tries over fences, ran very badly and is one to leave alone at present. *Official explanation: jockey said gelding ran flat (tchd 2-1)*

1295 ARNOLD CLARK RENAULT H'CAP CHASE (15 fncs) 2m 4f 110y

7:45 (7:47) (Class 3) (0-120,120) 5-Y-O+

£6,017 (£2,282; £1,141; £518; £259; £155)

Form				RPR
P-12	**1**		**Native Coral (IRE)**[44] 937 7-11-12 **120** .... ADobbin (N G Richards) *hld up in toucnh: hdwy whn hit 4 out: cl up next: swtchd rt and rdn to chal last: led flat and styd on wl* **3/1**[1]	132+
052-	**2**	*3*	**Jallastep (FR)**[228] 3257 8-10-5 **99** .... GLee (J S Goldie) *trckd ldrs: cl 4 out: effrt next: rdn and ev ch 2 out tl drvn and nt qckn flat* **10/3**[2]	107
4632	**3**	*1 ½*	**Billie John (IRE)**[9] 1221 10-10-9 **103** .... JimCrowley (Mrs K Walton) *trckd ldrs: hdwy to ld 8th: rdn along 4 out: drvn 2 out: hdd and one pce flat* **5/1**[3]	110
F-20	**4**	*nk*	**Ball O Malt (IRE)**[27] 1083 9-11-9 **120** .... PWhelan(3) (R A Fahey) *hld up: hdwy 1/2-way: chsd ldrs whn hit 4 out: cl up next: rdn and ev ch 2 out tl drvn last and one pce flat* **3/1**[1]	127+
01-5	**5**	*½*	**Jordan's Ridge (IRE)**[6] 423 9-10-13 **110** .... PAspell(3) (P Monteith) *in tch: pushed along 8th: rdn along 4 out: one pce fr 2 out* **12/1**	116
16F-	**6**	*28*	**Jefertiti (FR)**[221] 3343 8-10-5 **102** .... PBuchanan(3) (Miss Lucinda V Russell) *led to 8th: cl up tl rdn along appr 3 out and sn wknd* **8/1**	80

5m 13.4s (-1.90) **Going Correction** +0.125s/f (Yiel) **6** Ran SP% **108.5**
Speed ratings: **108,106,106,106,105 95** CSF £12.70 TOTE £3.10: £2.60, £1.70; EX 12.70.

Owner City Rovers Partnership **Bred** P Fitzgerald **Trained** Greystoke, Cumbria

■ Stewards' Enquiry : P Buchanan two-day ban: careless riding (Sep 3-4)

FOCUS

A decent contest for the track and pretty solid form. Native Coral looks a horse to follow until beaten after winning comfortably.

NOTEBOOK

Native Coral(IRE) ◆ was the least exposed in the field and moved smoothly for most of the race. Switched for a run before the last, he stayed on well after getting to the front, and he looks a horse to stay with until beaten again. *(op 5-2 tchd 10-3)*

Jallastep(FR) was another in the race to travel with ease, and was just outpaced by the winner after jumping the last. He looks more than capable of adding to his only win over fences soon. *(op 9-2)*

Billie John(IRE) ◆ ran really well against some decent rivals and should make use of his favourable handicap mark given a slightly easier task. The step back up in trip appeared to pose few problems and more options should be available to his connections as a result. *(op 11-2)*

Ball O Malt(IRE), who ran well in the Galway Plate last time, was travelling well enough until a mistake at the fourth-last slowed his progress. He did not get home as well as the first three and is 10lb higher in the handicap than for his last win over fences. *(op 5-2)*

Jordan's Ridge(IRE) made ground from the rear of the field but gave the impression he never quite wanted to get that close. He had plenty of time to get to the leaders but never got past another horse and probably needs easier company to be effective.

Jefertiti(FR) raced keenly for most of the race and did not get home. *(tchd 9-1)*

1296 MACKIE MOTORS RENAULT H'CAP HURDLE (10 hdls) 2m 4f 110y

8:15 (8:16) (Class 3) (0-115,114) 4-Y-O+

£5,405 (£2,050; £1,025; £466; £233; £139)

Form				RPR
000-	**1**		**Just In Time**[225] 3297 10-11-5 **114** .... MrSClements(7) (J Clements, Ire) *cl up: led after 1st: rdn along 3 out: styd on wl u.p fr next* **25/1**	124
4631	**2**	*1 ½*	**Lake Merced (IRE)**[26] 1084 5-10-12 **100** .... GLee (Jonjo O'Neill) *trckd ldrs: effrt 3 out: ev ch next: sn rdn and kpt on same pce flat* **7/2**[2]	108
3325	**3**	*1*	**Gone Too Far**[6] 1010 7-11-10 **112** ....(v) TJMurphy (P Monteith) *keen: hld up towards rr: hdwy 4 out: rdn along after next: drvn appr last and kpt on* **3/1**[1]	119
0535	**4**	*6*	**Brave Effect (IRE)**[6] 1147 9-10-7 **95** .... BHarding (Mrs Dianne Sayer) *led to after 1st: cl up tl rdn 2 out: wknd and eased last* **9/1**	98+
1-62	**5**	*2 ½*	**Sovereign State (IRE)**[23] 1111 8-11-7 **112** ....(p) PAspell(3) (D W Thompson) *hld up in tch: effrt 4 out: rdn along next and sn one pce* **10/1**	111
043	**6**	*½*	**Manoubi**[25] 1099 6-11-2 **104** ....(b) ADobbin (M Todhunter) *hld up towards rr: hit 8th: rdn along 4 out and btn after next* **4/1**[3]	102
3-33	**7**	*1 ½*	**Speed Kris (FR)**[97] 410 6-11-5 **107** ....(p) MBradburne (Mrs S C Bradburne) *chsd ldrs: rdn along 3 out: sn wknd* **5/1**	104
100-	**P**		**Time To Roam (IRE)**[123] 4969 5-10-12 **103** ....(p) PBuchanan(3) (Miss Lucinda V Russell) *a rr: rdn along and bhd appr 3 out: p.u bef next* **20/1**	—

5m 3.00s (-5.20) **Going Correction** -0.125s/f (Good) **8** Ran SP% **111.6**
Speed ratings: **104,103,103,100,99 99,99,**— CSF £107.16 CT £342.14 TOTE £28.70: £6.20, £1.80, £1.90; EX 485.10 Place 6 £19.30, Place 5 £13.29.

Owner James Clements **Bred** Albert Steigenberger **Trained** Scarva, Co. Down

FOCUS

This was run at a slow pace and the winner quickened away from the field before the second-last flight. The third sets the standard for the form.

NOTEBOOK

Just In Time set the pace at a steady gallop and, under a well-judged ride, strode clear of his rivals between the last two hurdles. He was a decent horse in the dim and distant past but this success owed as much to his jockey's skill as any upturn in form.

Lake Merced(IRE) taking a slight rise in trip, clipped the last quite hard and was never getting to the leader. He is at the right end of the handicap at the moment for further success.

Gone Too Far was travelling reasonably well until entering the home straight, but did not get home as well as the first two. That said, he was not beaten far considering he was giving weight to them. *(op 11-4)*

Brave Effect(IRE) ◆ looked the eventual winner's biggest challenger coming into the home straight but faded on the run for the line. He has not won for over two years but is becoming nicely handicapped and travelled well for most of the race, and will be better suited by two miles. *(op 12-1)*

Sovereign State(IRE) was last jumping the penultimate hurdle and ran on through beaten horses. *(op 9-1)*

Manoubi would not have been suited by the way the race was run and is almost certainly more effective in a strongly-run race rather than one with a gradual increase in pace. *(op 7-2 tchd 9-2)*

T/Plt: £63.80 to a £1 stake. Pool £42,455.35. 485.55 winning tickets T/Qpdt: £66.70 to a £1 stake. Pool £2606.60. 28.90 winning tickets JR

1231 WORCESTER (L-H)

Tuesday, August 23

OFFICIAL GOING: Good to firm

The first hurdle in the home straight was again omitted because of fire damage.
Wind: almost nil Weather: fine

1297 PETER THOMAS MEMORIAL CONDITIONAL JOCKEYS' H'CAP HURDLE (7 hdls 1 omitted) 2m

5:30 (5:30) (Class 4) (0-90,88) 4-Y-O+ **£3,381** (£966; £483)

Form				RPR
366-	**1**		**Norton Sapphire**[148] 4602 6-10-0 **62** .... TJPhelan (V R A Dartnall) *a.p: led appr 2 out: clr appr last: easily* **7/2**[1]	82+
5002	**2**	*13*	**Think Quick (IRE)**[18] 1156 5-10-13 **83** .... AHawkins(8) (R Hollinshead) *hld up and bhd: rdn and hdwy appr 2 out: r.o wl flat: no ch w wnr* **9/1**	85
-056	**3**	*2*	**Desert Image (IRE)**[5] 1046 4-11-8 **85** ....(b[1]) ONelmes (C Tinkler) *hld up in mid-div: hdwy 4th: rdn and one pce fr 2 out* **16/1**	84
P-65	**4**	*2 ½*	**Un Autre Espere**[23] 1107 6-10-3 **70** .... TMessenger(5) (C C Bealby) *led to 2nd: a.p: rdn after 5th: one pce fr 2 out* **25/1**	68
651F	**5**	*1 ½*	**Queen Excalibur**[9] 1223 6-11-4 **85** .... LHeard(5) (C Roberts) *hld up: hdwy 5th: 2 l 2nd whn pckd 2 out: sn hung lft and btn: wknd flat* **10/1**	82+
-P55	**6**	*3 ½*	**Dawn Frolics**[10] 1213 4-10-1 **64** .... JamesDavies (M J Gingell) *bhd: hdwy 2 out: n.d* **66/1**	56
P-PP	**7**	*hd*	**Firstflor**[25] 1100 6-10-5 **70** .... JDiment(3) (F Jordan) *hld up towards rr: hdwy after 5th: wknd appr last* **66/1**	62
-34P	**8**	*1 ¾*	**Suchwot (IRE)**[27] 1075 4-10-9 **75** ....(vt) TJMalone(3) (M C Pipe) *hld up in mid-div: hdwy on ins appr 4th: wknd appr 2 out* **11/1**	65
60/P	**9**	*1 ½*	**Raneen Nashwan**[22] 1121 9-11-4 **83** .... SWalsh(3) (R J Baker) *bhd: rdn and sme hdwy appr 2 out: nvr nr ldrs* **66/1**	72
2543	**10**	*2*	**Siena Star (IRE)**[37] 1017 7-11-12 **88** ....(p) TGreenway (P Bowen) *mid-div: nt fluent 3rd: rdn after 5th: sn no imp* **8/1**	75
5600	**11**	*9*	**Prince Minata (IRE)**[18] 1156 10-10-5 **72** .... RSpate(5) (M Appleby) *prom: mstke 5th: sn rdn and wknd* **50/1**	50
P/0-	**12**	*3 ½*	**Homebred Buddy**[233] 3177 6-10-2 **64** .... DCrosse (P Bowen) *led 2nd tl appr 2 out: wknd qckly: no ch whn j.rt last* **25/1**	39
33F1	**13**	*1*	**Prince Adjal (IRE)**[10] 1212 5-11-1 **83** ....(e) CEddery(6) (R C Guest) *a bhd* **4/1**[2]	57
00-0	**14**	*9*	**Will Tell**[79] 654 7-10-12 **74** ....(t) DLaverty (S R Bowring) *bhd fr 5th* **25/1**	39
0031	**15**	*20*	**Virtus**[10] 1202 5-11-6 **85** ....(b) RStephens(3) (P J Hobbs) *mid-div: lost pl and hit 3rd: sn bhd* **5/1**[3]	30
065P	**16**	*13*	**Zahunda (IRE)**[10] 1209 6-10-6 **78** .... CareyWilliamson(10) (M J Gingell) *a bhd* **66/1**	10
-60P	**R**		**Grace Dieu**[10] 1202 4-10-3 **74** ....(v[1]) JKington(8) (M Scudamore) *ref to r: tk no part* **50/1**	—

3m 41.4s (-7.00) **Going Correction** -0.225s/f (Good)
WFA 4 from 5yo+ 15lb **17** Ran SP% **124.7**
Speed ratings: **108,101,100,99,98 96,96,95,95,94 89,87,87,82,72 66,**— CSF £33.45 CT £455.69 TOTE £4.00: £1.60, £2.00, £4.20, £4.40; EX 53.50.

Owner Miracle In Mind Partnership **Bred** Miss Sara Davies And David Lewis **Trained** Brayford, Devon

FOCUS
Pretty straightforward form and solid enough. A fair time for the type of race, 3.6 seconds quicker than the later maiden hurdle.

NOTEBOOK
Norton Sapphire, bought for just 2,600gns at Ascot Sales in May, looks a bargain on the evidence of this performance. She can score again in this sort of company. *(op 9-2)*
Think Quick(IRE), raised 4lb for her second over course and distance, again got going late in the day but would not have beaten the winner under any circumstances. *(op 8-1)*
Desert Image(IRE), tried in blinkers, could only plug on at the same pace despite having been dropped 3lb. *(op 20-1)*
Un Autre Espere was another unable to raise his game sufficiently. *(op 20-1)*
Queen Excalibur, again 7lb higher for her Uttoxeter win, found disappointingly little and hung after nodding on landing at the penultimate hurdle. *(op 9-1)*
Dawn Frolics adopted totally different tactics and ran her best race to date. *(op 50-1)*
Virtus *Official explanation: jockey said gelding was never travelling (op 9-2 tchd 11-2)*

1298 BETFREDCASINO.COM NOVICES' HURDLE (8 hdls 2 omitted) 2m 4f
6:00 (6:01) (Class 4) 4-Y-0+ **£3,373** (£1,038; £519; £259)

Form RPR
3342 **1** **Kilindini**[18] 1154 4-11-3 114 .... BJCrowley 110+
(Miss E C Lavelle) *mde all: drew clr 2 out: 12 l ahd last: eased considerably flat* **7/4**[1]
-150 **2** *4* **Explosive Fox (IRE)**[9] 1220 4-11-3 107 .... (p) TDoyle 95
(C P Morlock) *chsd wnr: ev ch appr 2 out: sn hrd rdn and btn* **7/1**
20-4 **3** *16* **Treaty Stone**[10] 1206 6-10-12 .... APMcCoy 74
(Jonjo O'Neill) *chsd ldrs tl rdn and wknd appr 2 out* **11/2**[3]
4 *7* **Dark Rum** 9-10-12 .... TScudamore 67
(M Scudamore) *hld up and bhd: sme hdwy appr 2 out: n.d* **28/1**
5-F **5** *1 ½* **Pure Pleasure (NZ)**[101] 356 6-10-12 .... AThornton 66
(N M Babbage) *plld hrd in rr: sme hdwy 2 out: n.d* **7/1**
00U- **6** *17* **Mr Fisher (IRE)**[80] 8-10-7 73 .... (p) LStephens(5) 49
(D Burchell) *hld up: reminders after 3rd: j.rt 6th: sn wknd* **25/1**
P **7** *26* **Foreign Field (FR)**[3] 1266 6-10-5 .... LHeard(7) 23
(Mrs Tracey Barfoot-Saunt) *hld up: rdn 4th: sn struggling: t.o* **50/1**
00-P **8** *1 ¾* **Expensive Folly (IRE)**[26] 1089 7-10-5 .... SWalsh(7) 21
(A J Chamberlain) *hld up in tch: lost pl after 3rd: sn bhd: t.o* **100/1**
9 *23* **Paulinski**[767] 4-10-3 .... AO'Keeffe —
(F Jordan) *a bhd: t.o* **66/1**
15-5 **P** **That's For Sure**[6] 1231 5-10-12 .... (t) ChristianWilliams —
(Evan Williams) *hld up: hdwy and mstke 5th: sn wknd: j.rt 6th: bhd whn sn p.u* **3/1**[2]

4m 43.8s (-4.20) **Going Correction** -0.225s/f (Good) **10** Ran SP% **113.5**
Speed ratings: **99,97,91,88,87 80,70,69,60,—** CSF £13.78 TOTE £2.30: £1.10, £2.20, £2.20; EX 14.40.
Owner Nigel Foster **Bred** C N H Foster **Trained** Wildhern, Hants

FOCUS
A modest event run at a decent pace. The winner has been rated value for 15 lengths.

NOTEBOOK
Kilindini has been pretty consistent at this level since his win at Plumpton in May and proved far too good for this opposition. *(op 2-1 tchd 85-40 and 9-4 in a place)*
Explosive Fox(IRE), in cheekpieces for the first time over jumps, stays further and proved no match for the winner at this trip. *(op 8-1)*
Treaty Stone has yet to translate his two placed efforts in bumpers to hurdles. *(op 7-2 tchd 6-1)*
Dark Rum was making a very belated racecourse debut. *(op 25-1 tchd 33-1)*
Pure Pleasure(NZ) could have settled a lot better over this extra half a mile. *(op 13-2)*
That's For Sure *Official explanation: jockey said gelding was lame (op 7-2 tchd 11-4)*

1299 HYGIENE SOLUTIONS H'CAP CHASE (12 fncs) 2m
6:30 (6:31) (Class 4) (0-90,90) 5-Y-0+ **£3,354** (£1,032; £516; £258)

Form RPR
2-40 **1** **Jazz Night**[95] 437 8-11-12 90 .... APMcCoy 107
(S Lycett) *a.p: rdn appr 3 out: hit 2 out: led flat: r.o wl* **4/1**[1]
5443 **2** *5* **Dante's Battle (IRE)**[15] 1180 13-9-11 68 ow2 .... RSpate(7) 80
(Mrs K Waldron) *hld up and bhd: mstke 4th: hdwy 8th: rdn appr last: kpt on same pce flat* **7/1**
0652 **3** *½* **Gipsy Cricketer**[22] 1126 9-11-0 78 .... TScudamore 89
(M Scudamore) *led 2nd: j.rt 3 out and last: hrd rdn and hdd flat: wknd* **6/1**[3]
-22P **4** *3* **Super Dolphin**[44] 939 6-11-7 85 .... JMMaguire 93
(R Ford) *led to 2nd: a.p: rdn appr 4 out: one pce fr 2 out* **4/1**[1]
0-P1 **5** *10* **Faddad (USA)**[18] 1156 9-11-12 90 .... (t) RThornton 88
(Mrs A M Thorpe) *hld up mid-div: rdn 5th: sn lost pl: n.d after* **11/2**[2]
-4F5 **6** *¾* **Barnards Green (IRE)**[43] 958 7-10-13 77 .... (v) AThornton 74
(R H Alner) *t.k.h: a.p: chsd wnr fr 6th: hit 3 out: wknd appr last* **9/1**
00-P **7** *2 ½* **Just Midas**[26] 1085 7-11-4 85 .... TJPhelan(3) 80
(N M Babbage) *plld hrd in rr: short-lived effrt 4 out* **66/1**
-200 **8** *5* **Balla D'Aire (IRE)**[23] 1109 10-10-1 65 .... SCurran 55
(K F Clutterbuck) *a bhd* **9/1**
5440 **9** *16* **Reach The Clouds (IRE)**[88] 536 13-11-7 90 .... MNicolls(5) 64
(John R Upson) *mstke 4th: a bhd* **20/1**
600/ **U** **Royal Racer (FR)**[54] 4669 7-10-13 80 .... (b) DCrosse(3) —
(J R Best) *hld up: hdwy after 3rd: 7th and wkng whn blnd and uns rdr 4 out* **20/1**

3m 49.2s (-4.40) **Going Correction** -0.225s/f (Good) **10** Ran SP% **113.2**
Speed ratings: **102,99,99,97,92 92,91,88,80,—** CSF £30.48 CT £164.24 TOTE £4.90: £2.20, £2.00, £3.20; EX 45.50.
Owner The Berryman Lycett Experience **Bred** R G Percival **Trained** Naunton, Gloucs
■ Shaun Lycett's first winner since taking out a full licence.

FOCUS
There was no hanging around in this competitive-looking handicap. It looks a straightforward race to rate, suggesting solid form.

NOTEBOOK
Jazz Night, better known as a two-mile hunter chaser, won going away on this switch to handicaps. *(op 9-2 tchd 5-1)*
Dante's Battle(IRE), reverting back to fences, had been dropped 3lb and ran his race under a patient ride. *(tchd 15-2)*
Gipsy Cricketer did not help his cause by jumping right-handed at two fences in the home straight and hit a brick wall on the run-in. *(op 8-1)*
Super Dolphin put a disappointing performance at Perth last time behind him. *(tchd 9-2)*

1300 BETFREDPOKER.COM H'CAP HURDLE (8 hdls 2 omitted) 2m 4f
7:00 (7:01) (Class 3) (0-135,122) 4-Y-0+ **£6,792** (£2,090; £1,045; £522)

Form RPR
-540 **1** **Burundi (IRE)**[69] 762 11-10-8 104 .... NFehily 106
(A W Carroll) *hld up in rr: hdwy appr 2 out: hrd rdn to ld nr fin* **11/1**
1100 **2** *¾* **Herne Bay (IRE)**[2] 1270 5-11-3 113 .... JPMcNamara 114
(R S Brookhouse) *hld up: hdwy 6th: hrd rdn and ev ch flat: nt qckn cl home* **7/2**[3]
P113 **3** *shd* **Croix De Guerre (IRE)**[3] 1264 5-11-12 122 .... (b) RJohnson 123
(P J Hobbs) *chsd ldr: rdn to ld and j.lft 2 out: sn hung lft: hrd rdn and hdd nr fin* **3/1**[2]
-114 **4** *1 ¼* **Kims Pearl (IRE)**[15] 1179 7-10-4 105 .... LStephens(5) 105
(D Burchell) *t.k.h: led to 2 out: hrd rdn and nt qckn flat* **7/2**[3]
1-54 **5** *dist* **Thyne For Intersky (IRE)**[34] 1039 6-10-13 109 .... (b) APMcCoy 97
(Jonjo O'Neill) *hld up: pushed along after 3rd: rdn 5th: sn struggling: t.o: fin lame* **15/8**[1]

4m 37.7s (-10.30) **Going Correction** -0.225s/f (Good) **5** Ran SP% **112.6**
Speed ratings: **111,110,110,110,—** CSF £47.86 TOTE £9.80: £2.80, £2.30; EX 60.30.
Owner R G Owens **Bred** Olympic Bloodstock Ltd And Swettenham Stud **Trained** Cropthorne, Worcs

FOCUS
Only a small field but a tremendous finish.

NOTEBOOK
Burundi(IRE) justified some market support by getting up in a driving finish with the help of the stands' rail. *(old market tchd 14-1 new market op 14-1)*
Herne Bay(IRE), making a quick reappearance, was travelling best early in the home straight and it could be that his exertions at Newton Abbot had taken the edge off him. *(new market op 4-1 tchd 9-2)*
Croix De Guerre(IRE), another who ran at Newton Abbot at the weekend, was switching back to hurdles. He did not go down without a fight despite hanging left after jumping that way two out. *(old market op 3-1 new market op 11-4)*
Kims Pearl(IRE) turned in a fine effort and this was arguably her best performance so far. *(old market op 9-2 new market op 4-1 tchd 10-3)*
Thyne For Intersky(IRE), dropping back in distance, seems to have his own ideas about the game and it may be foolish to simply put this performance down to the fact that he finished lame. *Official explanation: vet said gelding was lame (new market op 7-4 tchd 2-1)*

1301 HAPPY 40TH BIRTHDAY, BRIAN MURNAGHAN H'CAP CHASE (18 fncs) 2m 7f 110y
7:30 (7:31) (Class 3) (0-125,120) 5-Y-0+ **£5,516** (£1,792; £965)

Form RPR
/535 **1** **Noble Justice (IRE)**[6] 1236 9-10-2 103 .... JamesWhite(7) 113
(R J Hodges) *hld up: hdwy 11th: led 3 out: hung rt 2 out: drvn out* **6/1**
66-2 **2** *1* **Master Tern (USA)**[18] 1157 10-11-1 109 .... (p) APMcCoy 118
(Jonjo O'Neill) *chsd ldr to 4th: hld up: hdwy after 14th: rdn appr 2 out: r.o flat* **9/4**[2]
-011 **3** *nk* **Touch Closer**[10] 1210 8-11-11 119 .... (p) RJohnson 128
(P Bowen) *led to 7th: led 14th to 3 out: rdn and hdd 3 out: ev ch flat: nt qckn* **5/4**[1]
1220 **P** **Curtins Hill (IRE)**[58] 842 11-11-5 120 .... RSpate(7) —
(Mrs K Waldron) *t.k.h: j.rt: wnt 2nd 4th: led 7th to 14th: 4th whn p.u lame appr 4 out* **5/1**[3]

6m 15.7s (20.80) **Going Correction** -0.225s/f (Good) **4** Ran SP% **106.2**
Speed ratings: **56,55,55,—** CSF £18.49 TOTE £9.50; EX 28.20.
Owner Fieldspring Racing **Bred** C Ronaldson **Trained** Charlton Adam, Somerset

FOCUS
The form looks pretty sound but they stood still for 20 seconds at the start when no-one wanted to lead.

NOTEBOOK
Noble Justice(IRE), supported in the ring, bounced back to form and held on well after being inclined to hang right-handed. *(op 10-1 tchd 11-1)*
Master Tern(USA) has never really looked a natural over fences but turned in a sound effort. *(op 13-8)*
Touch Closer, a reluctant leader over this longer trip, looked fairly treated on this graduation to handicaps and would not have minded a stiffer test of stamina. *(op 11-8)*

1302 WORCESTER ROWING CLUB MAIDEN HURDLE (7 hdls 1 omitted) 2m
8:00 (8:01) (Class 4) 4-Y-0+ **£3,406** (£1,048; £524; £262)

Form RPR
4455 **1** **Giust In Temp (IRE)**[6] 1235 6-10-9 84 .... MrTJO'Brien(7) 85
(Mrs K M Sanderson) *hld up in tch: led 2 out: rdn and r.o flat* **4/1**[2]
130 **2** *nk* **Zumrah (IRE)**[6] 1235 4-11-1 .... RJohnson 84
(P Bowen) *hld up and bhd: hdwy appr 2 out: rdn appr last: r.o flat* **9/2**[3]
0 **3** *4* **Dubai Dreams**[58] 843 5-10-13 .... (b) LVickers(3) 81
(S R Bowring) *led to 5th: led 2 out: hit last and hdd: no ex flat* **20/1**
U **4** *¾* **Zeis (IRE)**[6] 1233 5-10-13 .... (t) ONelmes(3) 80
(Miss J R Gibney) *hld up: hdwy 4th: rdn and one pce fr 2 out* **6/1**
PPP/ **5** *1 ¼* **Golders Green**[499] 4762 8-10-11 .... MNicolls(5) 79
(P W Hiatt) *chsd ldr: led 5th to 2 out: wknd flat* **40/1**
00- **6** *9* **Honest Injun**[255] 2367 4-11-1 .... ATinkler 69
(A G Juckes) *hld up and bhd: hdwy appr 2 out: no further prog* **16/1**
0/ **7** *1* **Mary's Baby**[19] 2205 5-10-9 .... VSlattery 62
(Mrs A M Thorpe) *hld up in mid-div: nt fluent 3rd: hdwy appr 2 out: rdn and wknd appr last* **16/1**
8 *½* **Urban Dream (IRE)**[302] 4-11-1 .... TScudamore 67
(R A Farrant) *hld up and bhd: hdwy after 5th: rdn and wknd 2 out* **16/1**
4-54 **9** *2 ½* **Bronco Charlie (IRE)**[9] 1222 7-11-2 .... APMcCoy 66
(Jonjo O'Neill) *prom tl wknd after 5th* **15/8**[1]
45/ **10** *4* **Broughton Knows**[139] 507 8-10-9 .... TMessenger(7) 62
(Mrs C J Ikin) *bhd fr 4th* **20/1**
11 *11* **Woolstone Boy (USA)**[79] 4-10-8 .... TBailey(7) 50
(J Jay) *hld up in tch: hit 2nd and 4th: rdn appr 2 out: sn wknd* **33/1**
000 **12** *21* **Durba (AUS)**[23] 1113 5-11-2 .... HOliver 30
(R C Guest) *hld up in mid-div: wkng whn mstke 5th* **33/1**
00U **13** *8* **April Rose**[18] 1158 5-10-2 .... (t) MrTCollier(7) 15
(K G Wingrove) *j.rt: a bhd* **100/1**

3m 45.0s (-3.40) **Going Correction** -0.225s/f (Good)
WFA 4 from 5yo+ 15lb **13** Ran SP% **123.7**
Speed ratings: **99,98,96,96,95 91,90,90,89,87 81,71,67** CSF £21.98 TOTE £6.10: £1.90, £2.00, £6.30; EX 30.70 Place 6 £1,026.59, Place 5 £373.79.
Owner Mrs K M Sanderson **Bred** Azienda Agricola Il Tiglio Di Amelia Prevedello **Trained** Tiverton, Devon

FOCUS
A weak maiden hurdle and the form looks far from solid.

NOTEBOOK
Giust In Temp(IRE) finally found a suitable opportunity to get off the mark and travelled best for much of the race. *Official explanation: trainer said, regarding the improved form shown, gelding was better suited by being ridden more prominently today (op 5-2)*
Zumrah(IRE) had finished a long way behind the winner on his hurdling debut here last week. He would appear to be going the right way and can take a similar event. *(op 5-1 tchd 4-1)*
Dubai Dreams, three times a winner at up to 11 furlongs in Banded company on Fibresand, was another to improve considerably on his hurdling debut. Perhaps the fitting of the blinkers he usually wore on the Flat combined with the shorter trip helped.
Zeis(IRE), a springer in the market, showed that he seems to have taken to hurdling. *(op 12-1 tchd 14-1)*
Golders Green, pulled up on his three previous starts over hurdles, was dropping back to two miles on this first outing since April 2004. *(op 20-1)*
Bronco Charlie(IRE) was in trouble at the end of the back straight. *(op 2-1 tchd 9-4)*
T/Plt: £2,617.20 to a £1 stake. Pool £36,032.20. 10.05 winning tickets T/Qpdt: £461.80 to a £1 stake. Pool £2,964.70. 4.75 winning tickets KH

1303 - 1306a (Foreign Racing) - See Raceform Interactive

1291 **PERTH** (R-H)
Wednesday, August 24

OFFICIAL GOING: Good (good to firm in places)
Wind: Fresh, behind

1307 AT THE RACES MAIDEN HURDLE (10 hdls) 2m 4f 110y
2:20 (2:23) (Class 4) 4-Y-O+ **£3,089** (£1,181; £598; £280; £148)

Form | | | | RPR
320- **1** **Ostfanni (IRE)**[19] 4087 5-10-7 101 ... GLee 85+
(M Todhunter) *trckd ldrs: hdwy and cl up whn hit 3 out: led appr next: sn clr* **4/6**[1]
034- **2** *6* **Hestherelad (IRE)**[358] 1336 6-11-0 90 ... KJohnson 82
(R Johnson) *led: hit 4th: hdd 7th: cl nup tl rdn along and one pce appr 2 out* **25/1**
4343 **3** *7½* **Leopold (SLO)**[27] 1084 4-10-12 98 ... PJBrennan 75+
(M F Harris) *trckd ldrs: effrt appr 3 out: sn rdn along: drvn bef 2 out and sn btn: fin 4th, 6l, 2½l & 5l: plcd 3rd* **4/1**[2]
05- **4** *10* **Shulmin**[211] 3532 5-10-4 ... PAspell(3) 60
(J Wade) *hld up: hdwy to chse ldrs whn hit 4 out: sn rdn and wknd: fin 5th, plcd 4th* **33/1**
400P **5** *dist* **Starbright**[45] 942 4-10-7 68 ... DCCostello(5) —
(W G Young) *midfield: rdn along bef 4 out and sn bhd: fin 6th, plcd 5th* **100/1**
3 **D** **True Temper (IRE)**[66] 785 8-10-2 77 ... DMcGann(5) 72
(A M Crow) *a.p: led 7th: rdn along and hdd appr 2 out: sn drvn and one pce. fin 3rd, 6l & 2½l: disq and plcd last* **12/1**
PP0/ **P** **Feeling Fizzical**[669] 1763 7-11-0 ... ADempsey —
(Mrs J C McGregor) *bolted bef s: a rr: bhd whn p.u bef 5th* **100/1**
F50- **P** **Bubba Boy (IRE)**[246] 2927 5-11-0 ... TJMurphy —
(P Monteith) *hld up in rr: lost tch 1/2-way: t.o whn p.u after 2 out* **15/2**[3]
P/6- **P** **Safe Shot**[51] 330 6-11-0 72 ... (p) JimCrowley —
(Mrs J C McGregor) *a rr: lost tch and bhd fr 1/2-way: t.o whn p.u bef 2 out* **40/1**
00P- **P** **Wee Sean (IRE)**[143] 4713 5-10-11 ... PBuchanan(3) —
(Miss Lucinda V Russell) *keen: chsd ldrs tl lost pl 1/2-way: sn bhd and p.u bef 2 out* **100/1**

5m 10.0s (1.80) **Going Correction** +0.15s/f (Yiel)
WFA 4 from 5yo+ 16lb **10** Ran SP% **111.6**
Speed ratings: **102,99,96,93,— 98,—,—,—,—** CSF £22.68 TOTE £1.40: £1.10, £4.40, £1.50; EX 19.70.
Owner FF Racing Services Partnership XVI **Bred** Mrs Brigitte Schlueter **Trained** Orton, Cumbria
■ Stewards' Enquiry : D McGann seven-day ban: failed to weigh-in (Sep 4,7,9,11,18,21-22)

FOCUS
A weak maiden that proved a straightforward task for the warm favourite. The form is limited by the proximity of the disqualified third.

NOTEBOOK
Ostfanni(IRE) justified strong support at the head of the market and broke her duck over timber at the sixth time of asking. Ther recent easing of the ground was much in her favour and, while this represented her most straightforward task to date, her confidence will have been greatly boosted by this. *(op 5-6 tchd 10-11 in places)*
Hestherelad(IRE), making his return from a 358-day break, showed up well at the head of affairs for a long way yet was ultimately no match for the winner. He still held off the remainder of the field, is entitled to improve for the outing and this must rate a sound effort at the weights.
Leopold(SLO), with the visor abandoned, turned in a moody effort and never rated a serious threat. He is capable of better, but really is a very frustrating sort and remains a maiden over hurdles after 17 outings now. *(op 7-2 tchd 9-2)*
True Temper(IRE) ran slightly above herself according to official ratings and looks to have resumed this season in fair form. She would be of interest in low-grade handicaps off this current mark. However, she was later disqualified as her rider failed to weigh in after the race. *(op 14-1 tchd 16-1 in a place)*
Bubba Boy(IRE), having his first outing since leaving Martin Pipe, again showed little and was disappointingly pulled up. He has badly regressed since his bumper days, and while his new trainer is often adept at rejuvenating such characters, his main hope of improvement may rest on a switch to fences. *(op 11-2)*

1308 RUSSEL + AITKEN (S) H'CAP HURDLE (10 hdls) 2m 4f 110y
2:50 (2:53) (Class 5) (0-90,90) 4-Y-O+
£3,155 (£1,196; £598; £272; £136; £81)

Form | | | | RPR
260 **1** **Noble House**[49] 913 8-11-9 90 ... KJMercer(3) 94
(Mrs A Duffield) *mde all: rdn along 3 out: drvn appr last and styd on wl* **9/2**[3]
0500 **2** *5* **Lion Guest (IRE)**[19] 1151 8-11-1 79 ... MBradburne 78
(Mrs S C Bradburne) *in tch: hdwy to trck ldrs 1/2-way: effrt to chse wnr after 3 out: rdn and ev ch next tl drvn last and one pce flat* **10/3**[1]
0056 **3** *5* **Step In Line (IRE)**[30] 1066 13-9-9 64 oh2 ... DCCostello(5) 58
(D W Thompson) *chsd ldrs: hdwy and cl up 1/2-way: pushed along whn hit 3 out: drvn next: kpt on same pce* **10/1**
32 **4** *¾* **Ball Games**[36] 592 7-11-7 85 ... GLee 79+
(James Moffatt) *hld up: hdwy 4 out: rdn to chse ldng pair2 out: sn drvn and wknd appr last* **7/2**[2]
26-5 **5** *1* **Sylvie D'Orthe (FR)**[30] 1064 4-10-4 75 ... DMcGann(5) 66
(A C Wilson) *prom: pushed along and lost pl 6th: styd on u.p fr 2 out* **20/1**
-0P6 **6** *2½* **Earl Sigurd (IRE)**[17] 1173 7-11-5 90 ... MrSFMagee(7) 80
(J K Magee, Ire) *hld up towards rr: hdwy and hit 4 out: chsd ldrs next: sn rdn and no imp* **10/1**
0040 **7** *24* **Flashy Filly**[19] 1148 5-9-8 65 oh3 ow1 ... (p) MJMcAlister(7) 31
(J C Haynes) *hld up: hdwy on outer to chse ldrs 4 out: sn rdn and wknd* **33/1**
0403 **8** *½* **Private Jessica**[11] 1209 4-10-9 75 ... (p) HOliver 39
(R C Guest) *chsd ldrs: rdn along 3 out: sn wknd* **7/1**
00F- **P** **Grafton Truce (IRE)**[420] 844 8-10-7 74 ... (t) PBuchanan(3) —
(Miss Lucinda V Russell) *nt fluent: a bhd: t.o whn p.u after 3 out* **25/1**
U65P **P** **Javelot D'Or (FR)**[40] 999 8-11-2 85 ... TGreenway(5) —
(Mrs B K Thomson) *chsd ldrs: rdn along and outpcd 4 out: bhd whn p.u and dismntd after next* **14/1**

5m 11.0s (2.80) **Going Correction** +0.15s/f (Yiel)
WFA 4 from 5yo+ 16lb **10** Ran SP% **112.4**
Speed ratings: **100,98,96,95,95 94,85,85,—,—** CSF £19.03 CT £139.01 TOTE £5.80: £1.30, £2.10, £3.80; EX 21.10.The winner was sold to Mr A.Normile for 5,000gns.
Owner R Renny **Bred** Conduit Farm Partnership **Trained** Constable Burton, N Yorks

FOCUS
A very poor event, run at a sound pace, and the field came home strung out. The form looks weak with the placed horses setting the level.

NOTEBOOK
Noble House rightly put his stamina to great effect on this drop in trip, making all for a career-first success over hurdles at the sixth attempt. The drop in class worked the oracle, but his confidence will be high now so he may be able to do better back at a higher level under simlarly postive tactics at this distance. *(op 7-1)*
Lion Guest(IRE), whose sole success over hurdles came over course and distance in 2003 off a mark of 85, looked very one-paced when push came to shove and was well held. He was not disgraced at the weights, however, and finished nicely clear of the rest. *(op 7-2)*
Step In Line(IRE) would have been a bit closer but for making a mistake three out and ran a fair race. This is his level, but as a 13-year-old he is always going to prove vulnerable over hurdles. *(op 12-1)*
Ball Games, having his first run over hurdles for 86 days, was ridden to get the longer trip and patently failed to get home. This was disappointing, but he should be capable of getting closer when reverting to a sharper test. *(op 10-3 tchd 3-1)*
Javelot D'Or(FR) *Official explanation: jockey said gelding failed to handle the bend out of the straight (op 10-1)*

1309 DAILY RECORD H'CAP CHASE (18 fncs) 3m
3:20 (3:20) (Class 4) (0-110,107) 5-Y-O+ **£6,145** (£2,437; £1,304)

Form | | | | RPR
P-22 **1** **Possextown (IRE)**[56] 858 7-11-12 107 ... ADobbin 125+
(N G Richards) *mde all: j.w: clr whn hit 3 out: kpt on* **13/8**[2]
U5/4 **2** *14* **Pessimistic Dick**[56] 857 12-10-12 93 ... GLee 92
(Mrs J C McGregor) *in tch: mstke 8th: pushed along and mstke 12th: sn outpcd and wl bhd: styd on fr 2 out: tk 2nd on run-in* **16/1**
P1-1 **3** *11* **Music To My Ears (IRE)**[10] 1219 7-11-8 103 7ex ... BHarding 98+
(Jonjo O'Neill) *trckd wnr: mstke 9th: rdn along 5 out: mstke next: sn drvn and wknd: lost 2nd run-in* **5/4**[1]
1U2- **F** **Ryminster**[155] 4509 6-9-13 83 ... PAspell(3) —
(J Wade) *blnd 1st and in rr tl fell 5th* **5/1**[3]

6m 13.6s (1.00) **Going Correction** +0.05s/f (Yiel) **4** Ran SP% **105.1**
Speed ratings: **100,95,91,—** CSF £15.38 TOTE £2.40; EX 15.40.
Owner Jimmy Dudgeon **Bred** Mrs M E Foster **Trained** Greystoke, Cumbria

FOCUS
A modest handicap but, with the favourite disappointing, the winner scored as he pleased and is rated as having improved slightly.

NOTEBOOK
Possextown(IRE) ◆ put in a fine round of fencing throughout the first half of the contest and already had his rivals well beaten when making an error three out, which caused him to tire. He may be a touch flattered by this, but it was a greatly-deserved success, and he does look to be progressive. A drop back to two and a half miles can see him win more races now his confidence has been greatly boosted. *(tchd 7-4 in a place)*
Pessimistic Dick, whose fate was on the cards a long way out after some sloppy mistakes, merely plugged on past the tiring Music To My Ears on the run-in. An even stiffer test will be to his advantage. *(op 14-1)*
Music To My Ears(IRE), an impressive winner on his comeback ten days previously, again saw his jumping problems materialise and tired rapidly from two out. Life will be tougher in the future as he is due to go up another 3lb shortly, but he may well have bounced this time and he is not one to write off just yet. *Official explanation: trainer's representative had no explanation for the poor form shown (tchd 6-5)*
Ryminster jumped erratically and it was no real surprise when he came to grief. *(tchd 11-2 in places)*

1310 OSSIAN'S ALE CONDITIONAL JOCKEYS' H'CAP HURDLE (12 hdls) 3m 110y
3:50 (3:50) (Class 4) (0-90,88) 5-Y-O+
£4,268 (£1,619; £809; £368; £184; £110)

Form | | | | RPR
405 **1** **Fantastico (IRE)**[11] 1211 5-11-3 85 ... (p) CDSharkey(6) 94+
(Mrs K Walton) *hld up in rr: stdy hdwy 9th: rdn 2 out: styd on to chal last: sn led and drvn out* **4/1**[1]
4042 **2** *8* **Bella Liana (IRE)**[20] 1136 5-11-4 80 ... DFlavin 83+
(J Clements, Ire) *a.p: led 7th: hdd briefly 9th: sn led again: hit 3 out and rdn along: drvn whn blnd last: sn hdd & wknd* **4/1**[1]
3 *1¼* **Astronaut**[59] 839 8-11-6 88 ... (p) CEddery(6) 89+
(R C Guest) *trckd ldrs: hdwy 4 out: clsd up whn hit next: drvn along 2 out and ev ch tl wknd appr last* **9/2**[2]
POP- **4** *1* **Mags Two**[176] 4106 8-10-5 72 ... PMerrigan(5) 71
(I McMath) *hld up towards rr: hdwy 4 out: rdn along next: styd on fr 2 out: nrst fin* **33/1**
3-00 **5** *12* **Silver Dagger**[41] 988 7-11-6 85 ... (p) MJMcAlister(3) 72
(J C Haynes) *chsd ldrs: rdn along 4 out: drvn and wknd after next* **25/1**
2602 **6** *14* **One Of Them**[1] 1294 6-11-3 82 ... BenOrde-Powlett(3) 55
(M A Barnes) *prom: led briefly 9th: sn hdd and rdn:wknd after 3 out* **13/2**
00P0 **7** *9* **Test Of Faith**[30] 1066 6-10-8 70 ... PAspell 34
(J N R Billinge) *a rr* **33/1**
0005 **8** *5* **Book's Way**[16] 1178 9-10-10 72 ... KJMercer 31
(D W Thompson) *cl up: led 5th to 7th: rdn along 8th: sn lost pl and bhd* **10/1**
/PP6 **9** *13* **Primitive Jean**[24] 1108 6-10-2 64 ... NPMulholland 10
(C R Wilson) *a rr* **66/1**
40/0 **P** **Mr Cavallo (IRE)**[98] 417 13-10-8 78 ... NWalker(8) —
(Miss Lucinda V Russell) *led to 5th: rdn along and lost pl 7th: sn bhd and p.u bef 9th* **33/1**
P042 **P** **The Yellow Earl (IRE)**[11] 1209 5-10-8 70 ... DCCostello —
(J M Jefferson) *hld up: effrt and sme hdwy 7th: rdn along next: sn wknd and p.u bef 3 out* **5/1**[3]

6m 9.90s (-1.00) **Going Correction** +0.05s/f (Yiel) **11** Ran SP% **111.4**
Speed ratings: **103,100,100,99,95 91,88,86,82,— —** CSF £18.48 CT £71.22 TOTE £4.00: £1.60, £1.60, £1.60; EX 18.90.

Owner The Suffolk Punch Syndicate **Bred** John And Mark Bourke **Trained** Middleham, N Yorks

FOCUS

A poor handicap run at a decent gallop, and the form looks fair for the grade with the first two the best guides.

NOTEBOOK

Fantastico(IRE) was given a fine ride by her conditional rider and came right away from her rivals on the run-in to score a welcome success. She had dropped back to her last winning mark for this - her only previous victory also came at this course - but she was later found to have struck into *herself and could be off the track for some time as a result.Official explanation: vet said mare was struck into (tchd 7-2)*

Bella Liana(IRE) was hard at it from some way out, yet stuck to her task under pressure and would have been closer but for making crucial mistakes late on. She has developed a habit of finding one too good, but looked suited by the longer trip and her turn should come at this level before long. *(op 7-2)*

Astronaut , with the cheekpieces applied for the first-time over hurdles, had every chance yet failed to see out the longer trip as well as the first two. He had a decent spell in point-to-points earlier this year, so he might be worth sending over regulation fences now, but even so he would have better *claims when reverting to shorter. Official explanation: vet said gelding finished lame but returned sound (op 4-1)*

Mags Two may have been closer with a more positive ride over this longer trip, as he was doing all of his best work late on. He is entitled to improve for this seasonal bow and could be on a fair mark at present. *(op 25-1)*

Silver Dagger , with first-time cheekpieces replacing the visor on this debut for new connections, showed a bit more this time and appreciated the longer trip. *(op 20-1)*

One Of Them , runner-up over course and distance just 24 hours previously, clearly found this coming too soon. *(op 7-1)*

The Yellow Earl(IRE) *Official explanation: jockey said gelding lost its action (tchd 11-2)*

1311 SCOTTISH WIDOWS INVESTMENT SOLUTIONS H'CAP CHASE (12 fncs) 2m

4:20 (4:23) (Class 4) (0-100,100) 5-Y-0+

£5,405 (£2,050; £1,025; £466; £233; £139)

Form				RPR
432-	**1**		**Kniaz (FR)**[37] [1029] 7-11-12 **100** ... ADobbin *(A J Martin, Ire) hld up: hdwy 8th: rdn along to chse ldrs 3 out: drvn next: styd on flat to ld nr line* **15/8**[1]	108
F-PP	**2**	*nk*	**Young Chevalier**[27] [1088] 8-11-1 **89** ... KRenwick *(J R Adam) led: rdn along and hit 4 out: clr 2 out: hung rt flat: drvn and hdd nr line* **25/1**	98+
0313	**3**	*3*	**Risky Way**[45] [939] 9-11-2 **90** ... GLee *(W S Coltherd) hld up in rr: hdwy 5 out: rdn along to chse ldrs 3 out: drvn next: styd on flat* **3/1**[2]	95
6-F5	**4**	*1*	**Lascar De Ferbet (FR)**[16] [1176] 6-11-1 **89** ... JMMaguire *(R Ford) chsd ldrs: hdwy whn hmpd 4 out: rdn next: styng on whn blnd last: one pce flat* **6/1**[3]	94+
P-P0	**5**	*6*	**Ratty's Band**[45] [939] 11-10-2 **76** ... NPMulholland *(Mrs L B Normile) chsd ldrs: hit 8th: rdn along to chse ldr whn mstke 3 out: sn drvn and grad wknd* **25/1**	75+
U-50	**6**	*6*	**Gabla (NZ)**[10] [1223] 9-11-5 **93** ... (b) HOliver *(R C Guest) a.p: rdn along whn blnd 4 out: drvn next and sn wknd* **20/1**	85
4PP4	**7**	*14*	**Pavey Ark (IRE)**[19] [1150] 7-10-3 **77** ... JimCrowley *(James Moffatt) in tch: hdwy to chse ldrs 5 out: rdn along next and sn wknd* **6/1**[3]	55
50P	**8**	*15*	**Northern Flash**[55] [874] 11-10-0 **74** oh8 ... (p) FKeniry *(J C Haynes) chsd ldrs on outer: rdn along 5 out and sn wknd* **25/1**	37
4P/6	**P**		**Dottie Digger (IRE)**[55] [874] 6-9-11 **74** oh6 ... (p) PBuchanan(3) *(Miss Lucinda V Russell) prom: rdn along 7th: lost pl next: bhd whn p.u bef 2 out* **16/1**	—

3m 57.6s (-5.20) **Going Correction** -0.275s/f (Good) **9** Ran SP% **110.5**

Speed ratings: **102,101,100,99,96 93,86,79,—** CSF £47.16 CT £128.11 TOTE £3.00: £1.50, £7.10, £1.30; EX 74.60.

Owner Dewsweepers Syndicate **Bred** Haras De La Faisanderie And Luc Bouillette **Trained** Kildalkey, Co Meath

FOCUS

A moderate handicap run at a true pace and producing a cracking finish. The form is sound with the third and fourth setting the standard.

NOTEBOOK

Kniaz(FR) looked held jumping the final fence but found extra on the run-in and just did enough to get up near the line. He was placed twice over hurdles in June 2004 at this track off a 13lb higher mark, so he was entitled to score, despite the burden of top weight. This was his first ever success over fences and it added to his trainer's fine record on such British raids. *(op 9-4)*

Young Chevalier looked booked for success jumping the final fence but his stride shortened on the run-in and he could offer no more when the winner swooped in the dying strides. Having failed to complete on his previous four outings, this was a vastly-improved effort, and he should be capable of gaining compensation off this mark providing he can maintain this current mood. *(op 20-1)*

Risky Way , easy to back, stayed on without ever rating a serious threat. This was another sound effort over a course and distance he enjoys, but he does look weighted near to his best over fences at present. He would be quite interesting if switched back to hurdles as he is currently rated 2lb lower than his last winning mark in that sphere. *(op 9-4)*

Lascar De Ferbet(FR) failed to find as much as looked likely when push came to shove and was beaten when belting the final fence. He has yet to truly prove he stays even the minimum trip over either hurdles or fences.

Pavey Ark(IRE) ran well below par on this drop back in trip and was disappointing. He is on a declining mark and may do better when upped again in trip. *(op 8-1)*

1312 SIS H'CAP HURDLE (8 hdls) 2m 110y

4:50 (4:50) (Class 3) (0-120,115) 4-Y-0+

£4,860 (£1,843; £921; £419; £209; £125)

Form				RPR
0-11	**1**		**Rajam**[22] [1014] 7-11-4 **112** ... (p) WKennedy(5) *(G A Harker) hld up in rr: pusahed along and hdwy 3 out: cl up next: rdn to ld appr last: drvn and styd on wl flat* **9/4**[1]	120+
320	**2**	*1 1/2*	**Bill's Echo**[11] [1202] 6-10-7 **99** ... LMcGrath(3) *(R C Guest) hld up in rr: hit 5th: hdwy 3 out: rdn to challenge next and ev ch tl drvn and nt qckn flat* **4/1**[2]	105
1142	**3**	*7*	**Dream Castle (IRE)**[26] [1099] 11-11-2 **112** ... PMerrigan(7) *(Barry Potts, Ire) led and sn clr: rdn along 3 out: drvn next: hdd appr last: hit last and sn wknd* **6/1**	112+
5354	**4**	*8*	**Brave Effect (IRE)**[1] [1296] 9-10-6 **95** ... JimCrowley *(Mrs Dianne Sayer) prominent: effrt to chse ldr 3 out: rdn along appr next and sn wknd* **20/1**	86
21P0	**5**	*shd*	**Ton-Chee**[24] [1111] 6-10-9 **101** ... KJMercer(3) *(K W Hogg) in tch: hdwy to chse ldrs 3 out: sn rdn and wknd bef next* **33/1**	92
151P	**6**	*13*	**Royal Glen (IRE)**[27] [1087] 7-10-9 **98** ... GLee *(W S Coltherd) hld up in tch: hdwy on outer appr 4 out: rdn along next and sn wknd* **8/1**	76
6000	**7**	*9*	**Rising Generation (FR)**[55] [873] 8-11-11 **114** ... BHarding *(N G Richards) chsd ldr: hit 3rd: rdn along and wknd appr 3 out* **20/1**	83
246-	**8**	*19*	**South Bronx (IRE)**[139] [4752] 6-11-9 **112** ... (t) MBradburne *(Mrs S C Bradburne) chsd ldrs: rdn along and outpcd appr 3 out* **14/1**	62
-000	**P**		**Prince Among Men**[39] [1010] 8-11-12 **115** ... ADobbin *(N G Richards) hld up: rdn along and lost tch 4 out: bhd whn p.u bef 2 out* **5/1**[3]	—

3m 54.5s (-6.10) **Going Correction** -0.275s/f (Good) **9** Ran SP% **112.0**

Speed ratings: **103,102,99,95,95 89,84,75,—** CSF £11.19 CT £45.04 TOTE £3.40: £1.50, £1.10, £2.00; EX 17.10 Place 6 £11.22, Place 5 £9.29.

Owner Miss J S Dollan **Bred** Shadwell Estate Company Limited **Trained** Thirkleby, N Yorks

FOCUS

A fair handicap run at a strong pace throughout, and the first two came clear. The form, rated through the third, looks pretty sound.

NOTEBOOK

Rajam , winner of his previous two outings in novice grade, translated that form to handicap company and landed the hat-trick in game fashion. He has been transformed by the recent application of cheekpieces and is clearly in the form of his life at present. It is possible he may improve again for a step up in trip as he has scored over 12 furlongs on the Flat.

Bill's Echo had every chance and came from a similar position as the winner, but he lacked the same finishing kick. He did little wrong in defeat, finished clear of the rest, and is certainly weighted to win over both hurdles and fences at present. However, he does have a habit of finding one or two too good. *(op 7-2 tchd 9-2)*

Dream Castle(IRE) gained the early lead, as he prefers, but was a sitting duck for the first pair approaching the final flight. While he remains in good heart and may prefer a slightly stiffer test, he still has to prove he is up to this career-high mark. *(op 5-1)*

Brave Effect(IRE) raced handily yet was firmly put in his place when the race got serious. His effort over further at this track just 24 hours previously suggested he should have been suited by the drop back in trip, but he clearly found this coming too soon. *(tchd 25-1)*

South Bronx(IRE) , who had some fair form as a novice last season, proved unsuited by the drop to this trip and shaped as though the race was needed. Better should be expected when he is faced with a stiffer test once again.

Prince Among Men ran poorly and is badly struggling for form at present.

T/Plt: £22.50 to a £1 stake. Pool: £40,670.00. 1,319.25 winning tickets. T/Qpdt: £3.90 to a £1 stake. Pool: £2,899.20. 544.40 winning tickets. JR

1313 - 1316a (Foreign Racing) - See Raceform Interactive

1201 BANGOR-ON-DEE (L-H)

Thursday, August 25

OFFICIAL GOING: Chase course - good; hurdles course - good to soft (good in places)

Wind: Moderate, across Weather: Sunshine and showers

1317 BANGORONDEERACES.CO.UK MARES' ONLY NOVICES' HURDLE (11 hdls) 2m 4f

2:10 (2:10) (Class 4) 4-Y-0+ **£3,786** (£1,165; £582; £291)

Form				RPR
-460	**1**		**Separated (USA)**[72] [753] 4-10-10 95 ... RJohnson *(P J Hobbs) midfield: hdwy appr 7th: led bef 3 out: hung lft between last 2: mstke last: drvn out* **3/1**[1]	90+
U213	**2**	*1 1/2*	**Reem Two**[20] [1149] 4-10-12 99 ... StephenJCraine(5) *(D McCain) t.k.h: a.p: ev ch fr 3 out: rdn bef 2 out: nt qckn towards fin* **9/2**[2]	94
0345	**3**	*17*	**Moscow Executive**[12] [1202] 7-10-12 71 ... ATinkler *(W M Brisbourne) hld up: hdwy after 6th: rdn after 3 out: sn wknd: tk mod 3rd 2 out* **8/1**[3]	72
6/0	**4**	*2*	**Scarlet Dawn (IRE)**[11] [1220] 7-10-12 ... ChristianWilliams *(D A Rees) in rr: effrt 4 out: no imp on ldrs* **50/1**	70
0-3	**5**	*3 1/2*	**Langdon Lane**[12] [1213] 4-10-10 ... TDoyle *(P R Webber) trckd ldrs: rdn appr 3 out: wknd bef next* **9/2**[2]	65
5P35	**6**	*nk*	**Royaltea**[12] [1206] 4-10-10 85 ... RThornton *(J T Stimpson) plld hrd: hld up: hdwy appr 7th: rdn whn chsng ldrs bef 3 out: wknd appr next* **12/1**	64
06	**7**	*7*	**Sunny South East (IRE)**[12] [1213] 5-10-12 ... JPMcNamara *(S Gollings) led: hdd appr 3 out: sn wknd* **25/1**	59
00-0	**8**	*8*	**Across The Water**[20] [1154] 11-10-7 64 ... (p) TGreenway(5) *(G H Jones) midfield: hdwy appr 6th: rdn bef 4 out: wknd appr next* **80/1**	51
-00P	**F**		**Slight Hiccup**[60] [843] 5-10-7 ... LTreadwell(5) *(C W Moore) a bhd: fell 7th* **80/1**	—
0	**P**		**Girlie Power**[43] [976] 8-10-7 ... MNicolls(5) *(P W Hiatt) in tch: lost pl 5th: rdn appr next: sn t.o: p.u bef 3 out* **80/1**	—
50-	**P**		**Go Gwenni Go**[372] [1212] 6-10-12 ... BHitchcott *(Mrs D A Hamer) in tch: wkng whn hmpd 7th: t.o whn p.u bef 3 out* **33/1**	—
P3P-	**P**		**Fields Of Home (IRE)**[159] [4461] 7-10-12 ... (t) AO'Keeffe *(Jennie Candlish) prom tl rdn and wknd appr 4 out: t.o whn p.u bef 2 out* **3/1**[1]	—

5m 0.50s (2.90) **Going Correction** -0.15s/f (Good)

WFA 4 from 5yo+ 16lb **12** Ran SP% **117.6**

Speed ratings: **88,87,80,79,78 78,75,72,—,— —,—** CSF £16.20 TOTE £4.30: £1.60, £1.80, £2.80; EX 14.20.

Owner J L N **Bred** Cheveley Park Stud **Trained** Withycombe, Somerset

FOCUS

Typically ordinary mares-only hurdle form and a modest time.

NOTEBOOK

Separated(USA) made harder work of winning than had looked likely at one stage, but she showed the right sort of attitude and appreciated the less competitive nature of this race, having disappointing in a novices' handicap latest. She will need to up her game if she is to defy a penalty and a return to handicaps may be the wiser option. *(op 7-2)*

Reem Two appreciated this rise in distance and kept going right the way to the line. She had run *well previously under a penalty and this genuine mare will no doubt continue to pay her way. (op 4-1)*

Moscow Executive faced an uphill task at the weights and ran as well as could have been expected. She may find life easier at selling level. *(tchd 10-1)*

Scarlet Dawn(IRE) hinted at her first sign of ability and will find opportunities in low-grade selling handicaps.

Langdon Lane, who made her debut in a Listed bumper at Aintree, has not lived up to expectations and she once again failed to see out her race. Genuine fast ground may see her in a better light, but she has plenty to prove.

1318 ROSE HILL BEGINNERS' CHASE (12 fncs) 2m 1f 110y
2:40 (2:40) (Class 4) 5-Y-0+ **£4,704** (£1,447; £723; £361)

Form RPR
-556 **1** **Sachsenwalzer (GER)**[17] 1179 7-10-12 .... PJBrennan 106+
(C Grant) *t.k.h: in tch: led and edgd lft after 2 out: styd on wl to draw clr run-in* **11/2**[3]
/F2- **2** *8* **Never (FR)**[366] 1274 8-10-12 ....(t) APMcCoy 98
(Jonjo O'Neill) *t.k.h: hld up: mstke 2nd: hdwy appr 7th: led bef 3 out: rdn and hdd 2 out: wknd run-in* **5/2**[2]
02-5 **3** *2* **Low Cloud**[47] 332 5-10-12 .... RGarritty 98+
(J J Quinn) *t.k.h: led: hdd appr 3 out: regained ld and mstke next: sn hdd: n.m.r and swtchd rt between last 2: blunder* **2/1**[1]
4U02 **4** *9* **Saddler's Quest**[12] 1203 8-10-12 76.............................. JMogford 87
(B P J Baugh) *prom tl rdn and wknd appr 3 out* **10/1**
2P0- **5** *hd* **True Mariner (FR)**[195] 3792 5-10-12 114.............................. JAMcCarthy 87
(B I Case) *hld up: effrt appr 7th: wknd 4 out* **11/2**[3]
63-P **U** **Cool Carroll (IRE)**[117] 122 7-10-5 91.............................. GLee —
(J Howard Johnson) *prom tl blnd bdly and uns rdr 4 out* **12/1**
0/P- **P** **Mountsorrel (IRE)**[131] 6-10-5 64.............................. PMerrigan(7) —
(T Wall) *in tch early: j. slowly 4th and sn bhd: t.o whn p.u bef 2 out* **66/1**

4m 16.9s (-9.50) **Going Correction** -0.85s/f (Firm) **7** Ran SP% **110.9**
Speed ratings: **87,83,82,78,78** —,— CSF £19.14 TOTE £5.20: £2.90, £2.10; EX 29.10.
Owner Mrs A Meller **Bred** H -H Grunhagen **Trained** Newton Bewley, Co Durham

FOCUS
Modest form and a modest time, so the race is unlikely to produce many winners.

NOTEBOOK
Sachsenwalzer(GER), a fair hurdler who has never found winning easy, seemed to enjoy every moment of this chase debut and quickened up best to leave the regressive Never trailing on the run-in. He had reportedly been schooled over the 'mini' fences at Southwell and that practice has clearly not been lost on him. He may have further improvement in him and could defy a penalty if placed well. *(op 7-1)*
Never(FR), who has been in steady decline in recent years, warmed to his tasked after a few sloppy early jumps and made smooth headway to come through and take a narrow lead jumping three out. However, McCoy began to get serious with him as they turned for home and he was basically done for speed by the winner. He probably has a small race in him, but is a risky betting proposition. *(tchd 11-4 in places)*
Low Cloud got really lit up on this fencing debut and did well to hang in there for as long as he did. He made several mistakes, but can find a small race if brushing up his jumping. *(op 11-4)*
Saddler's Quest has yet to convince as a chaser and he was struggling from half a mile out. *Official explanation: jockey said gelding bled from the nose (op 12-1)*
True Mariner(FR), who was taking a significant drop in grade, was given plenty to do and never got into it. He is better than this and will come on for the run. *(op 4-1 tchd 6-1)*
Cool Carroll(IRE) was not out of it when coming down, but her overall chasing form is modest. *(op 8-1)*

1319 ALFA AGGREGATES PRODUCTS H'CAP HURDLE (11 hdls) 2m 4f
3:10 (3:10) (Class 4) (0-110,105) 4-Y-0+ **£3,710** (£1,141; £570; £285)

Form RPR
6534 **1** **Arm And A Leg (IRE)**[7] 1250 10-11-1 101.............................. LHeard(7) 107
(Mrs D A Hamer) *t.k.h: hld up: hdwy appr 7th: led after 3 out: sn rdn: r.o* **10/1**
50-1 **2** *3* **Harry Potter (GER)**[17] 1180 6-11-12 105.................(tp) ChristianWilliams 109+
(Evan Williams) *hld up: hdwy 7th: chsd wnr appr 2 out: rdn and hung lft bef last: no ex run-in* **9/2**[2]
2624 **3** *14* **Rifleman (IRE)**[25] 1108 5-11-12 105.............................. APMcCoy 94
(P Bowen) *trckd ldrs: mstke 3 out: wknd next* **3/1**[1]
PP52 **4** *3 1/2* **Pequenita**[12] 1211 5-11-4 97..............................(b) HOliver 83
(R C Guest) *led to 6th: led again next: hdd after 3 out: wknd 2 out* **15/2**
-5P2 **5** *24* **Earls Rock**[28] 1084 7-10-9 88.............................. DRDennis 61+
(J K Cresswell) *prom: led 6th to 7th: rdn appr 3 out: sn wknd* **9/2**[2]
0PP6 **6** *8* **Antigiotto (IRE)**[35] 1045 4-10-12 93.............................. RJohnson 45
(P Bowen) *midfield: hdwy whn hit 5th: rdn appr 7th: wknd 4 out* **13/2**[3]
510/ **7** *3* **Donie Dooley (IRE)**[615] 2838 7-11-7 100.............................. AThornton 51
(P T Dalton) *a bhd* **20/1**
006- **8** *1 1/2* **Kaid (IRE)**[212] 3528 10-9-7 79.............................. MrTCollier(7) 28
(R Lee) *in tch: lost pl 4th: bhd after* **18/1**
PP0- **P** **Wise Tale**[20] 1568 6-10-8 87.............................. JimCrowley —
(P D Niven) *trckd ldrs: rdn and wknd after 6th: t.o whn p.u bef 2 out* **12/1**

4m 57.4s (-0.20) **Going Correction** -0.15s/f (Good)
WFA 4 from 5yo+ 16lb **9** Ran SP% **113.3**
Speed ratings: **94,92,87,85,76 73,71,71,**— CSF £54.22 CT £168.90 TOTE £13.20: £4.20, £1.70, £1.10; EX 61.90.
Owner H L Davies **Bred** Martyn J McEnery **Trained** Nantycaws, Carmarthens

FOCUS
A moderate handicap and a race made up of horses who have either yet to win or find winning hard these days.

NOTEBOOK
Arm And A Leg(IRE) had a little bit to prove at the trip, but he saw it out better than anything in the end and he was simply too good for the favourite. His rider's 7lb allowance would have helped as he is not the best handicapped horse, but he hit a rich vein of form around this time last year so maybe he can defy a rise. *(op 9-1)*
Harry Potter(GER), who is reportedly not the biggest, battled his way back to challenge the winner and this has to go down as a good performance under joint top weight. He only won a seller last time and will continue to be hard to place off his current mark. *(op 10-3)*
Rifleman(IRE) is a frustrating charatcer and he could only plod on to claim a well-beaten third. He remains one to avoid. *(op 4-1)*
Pequenita took them along for a long way, but was left trailing in the home straight and it may take a drop into selling company before she is winning again. *(op 7-1 tchd 8-1)*
Earls Rock hinted at better to come when runner-up last time, but this was a step back in the right direction.
Antigiotto(IRE) was never jumping with any great fluency and he dropped out tamely. He continues to disappoint. *(op 8-1)*

1320 HALLOWS ASSOCIATES H'CAP CHASE (11 fncs 1 omitted) 2m 1f 110y
3:40 (3:45) (Class 3) (0-125,125) 5-Y-0+ **£8,151** (£2,508; £1,254; £627)

Form RPR
1/01 **1** **Hakim (NZ)**[28] 1088 11-10-0 99 oh3.............................. PJBrennan 111
(J L Spearing) *led to 2nd: remained prom: led again after 3 out: drew clr run-in: styd on wl* **10/1**
110 **2** *8* **Danish Decorum (IRE)**[11] 1221 6-11-8 121.............. ChristianWilliams 125
(Evan Williams) *led 2nd tl after 3 out: stl ev ch next: no ex run-in* **9/1**[3]
141- **3** *5* **Specular (AUS)**[182] 4031 9-11-2 115.............................. APMcCoy 114
(Jonjo O'Neill) *hld up: hdwy 6th: rdn to chse ldrs appr 2 out: wknd last* **7/4**[1]
P05- **4** *13* **Log On Intersky (IRE)**[131] 4863 9-11-12 125.............................. ADobbin 111
(J Howard Johnson) *cl up tl wknd 3 out* **14/1**
P344 **5** *3/4* **Runner Bean**[40] 1012 11-10-5 104.............................. RThornton 89
(R Lee) *midfield: rdn appr 4 out: nvr trbld ldrs* **20/1**
F-23 **6** *1/2* **Toi Express (IRE)**[11] 1221 9-11-6 119.............................. RJohnson 104
(R J Hodges) *a bhd* **9/1**[3]
311P **7** *12* **College City (IRE)**[28] 1088 6-9-12 100..............................(b) LMcGrath(3) 73
(R C Guest) *hld up: effrt 4 out: sn btn* **12/1**
2122 **8** *9* **Tonic Du Charmil (FR)**[12] 1210 5-11-4 117.............................. (t) TJMurphy 81
(M C Pipe) *a bhd* **4/1**[2]
U06/ **P** **Ichi Beau (IRE)**[468] 346 11-11-8 121..............................(t) JPMcNamara —
(A J Martin, Ire) *prom tl wknd 7th: t.o whn p.u bef 2 out* **11/1**
-P3F **P** **Mumaris (USA)**[53] 894 11-10-8 110.............................. PBuchanan(3) —
(Miss Lucinda V Russell) *midfield: niggeld along after 4th: sn bhd: t.o whn p.u after 3 out* **40/1**

4m 8.00s (-18.40) **Going Correction** -0.85s/f (Firm) **10** Ran SP% **115.3**
Speed ratings: **106,102,100,94,94 93,88,84,**—,— CSF £94.32 CT £232.38 TOTE £12.40: £2.80, £2.20, £1.50; EX 177.40.
Owner T N Siviter **Bred** Mrs B C Hennessy **Trained** Kinnersley, Worcs

FOCUS
A fair handicap run at a good pace, as was to be expected with four recognised front-runners in the line up. The winner has returned to action in good form. The open ditch in the back straight was omitted.

NOTEBOOK
Hakim(NZ), who has returned from injury in good form this season, kept up the gallop off his feather weight and came away from the tiring Danish Decorum. The rain the course had seen was a big plus for the gelding and connections will now aim to find a race in which he can bid for his hat-trick. *(op 8-1)*
Danish Decorum(IRE) has really improved since being switched to fences and left behind a recent disappointing effort at Stratford. The weight concession to the winner began to tell in the final quarter mile, but he beat the remainder easily enough and remains progressive. *(op 8-1 tchd 10-1)*
Specular(AUS) began to get his act together over fences towards the end of last season and he was evidently well fancied to make a winning return off what seemed a fair mark. He looked as though the run would do him good on paddock inspection, so it was no surprise to see him 'blow up' once coming under pressure. He travelled strongly and is worthy of another chance. *(op 11-4 tchd 3-1 in places)*
Log On Intersky(IRE) has been keeping top handicap company for the past two seasons and much better was expected on this drop in grade. However, he was unable to lead and raced with little enthusiasm, eventually trailing in well-beaten. *(op 8-1)*
Runner Bean kept on from the rear to claim fifth but was never involved.
Toi Express(IRE), who has been most progressive this season. In a race where it paid to race prominently, his hold up tactics were no good and he may be worth another chance. *(op 10-1)*
Tonic Du Charmil(FR) *Official explanation: jockey said gelding was never travelling (tchd 9-2)*

1321 CARLSBERG UK H'CAP CHASE (16 fncs 2 omitted) 3m 110y
4:10 (4:12) (Class 4) (0-100,95) 5-Y-0+ **£4,056** (£1,248; £624; £312)

Form RPR
-PP4 **1** **Fearless Mel (IRE)**[36] 1041 11-11-5 88..............................(p) AO'Keeffe 110+
(Mrs H Dalton) *t.k.h: midfield: hdwy 10th (water): led 12th: clr 3 out: rdn appr last: eased towards fin* **14/1**
446 **2** *18* **Nosam**[41] 997 15-10-11 83..............................(tp) LMcGrath(3) 84
(R C Guest) *in tch: hdwy 8th: wnt 2nd 4 out: no ch w wnr* **10/1**
223 **3** *1 3/4* **Seaniethesmuggler (IRE)**[12] 1210 7-11-7 95.................. WKennedy(5) 95+
(S Gollings) *hld up: hdwy appr 11th: rdn bef 3 out: btn whn pckd 2 out* **4/1**[3]
0354 **4** *5* **Cyindien (FR)**[57] 865 8-10-9 78..............................(p) ChristianWilliams 72
(Evan Williams) *hld up: effrt appr 3 out: no imp* **7/2**[2]
5 *nk* **Killy Lass (IRE)**[47] 934 9-10-5 74.............................. TJMurphy 68
(A J Martin, Ire) *chsd ldrs: hit 11th: sn wknd* **3/1**[1]
PP0P **6** *15* **Greenacres Boy**[8] 1233 10-9-9 69 oh5....................(p) StephenJCraine(5) 48
(M Mullineaux) *bhd: mstke 1st: hdwy 11th: rdn and wknd 3 out* **33/1**
3-13 **P** **Over Zealous (IRE)**[108] 262 13-10-7 81..............................(b) MNicolls(5) —
(John R Upson) *led 2nd (water) to 3rd: in 2nd whn sn p.u* **8/1**
P2-P **P** **Lost In Normandy (IRE)**[4] 1276 8-10-3 75.............................. DCrosse(3) —
(Mrs L Williamson) *led to 2nd (water): remained handy: wknd 8th: t.o whn p.u bef 13th* **8/1**
P3PP **P** **Wrens Island (IRE)**[17] 1178 11-10-2 71..............................(v[1]) WHutchinson —
(R Dickin) *t.k.h: prom: led 3rd: sn clr: hdd 12th: wknd 4 out: t.o whn p.u bef next* **14/1**

6m 1.50s (-21.70) **Going Correction** -0.85s/f (Firm) **9** Ran SP% **114.8**
Speed ratings: **100,94,93,92,91 87,**—,—,— CSF £139.20 CT £668.67 TOTE £25.60: £4.80, £2.20, £2.10; EX 127.10.
Owner The Leppington Partnership **Bred** T J Kennedy **Trained** Norton, Shropshire

FOCUS
The open ditch in the back straight was omitted. Weak form, but Fearless Mel spreadeagled the opposition with his new 'hanging bit' preventing him from jumping as far right as usual.

NOTEBOOK
Fearless Mel(IRE), who has a habit of jumping/hanging right, had a 'hanging bit' applied to counter that and was always travelling strongly. He found himself in a clear lead rounding the turn for home and, despite getting a little tired in the final quarter mile, always had the race in the bag. He had shown nothing since winning his first race at Taunton last December and as a result was 3lb lower *here, so it will be interesting to see if this lightly-raced 11-year-old is capable of going on from this. Official explanation: trainer said, regarding the improved form shown, gelding was fitted with a new type of bit today, in order to correct its tendency to hang (op 12-1)*
Nosam does the form little favours and it will be surprising if the veteran is still up to winning races. *(op 9-1)*
Seaniethesmuggler(IRE) is possibly better at slightly shorter and he was unable to raise his game when asked. *(op 3-1)*
Cyindien(FR) is a long-standing maiden and a switch to the Evan William's stable has clearly done little for him. *(op 4-1)*
Killy Lass(IRE) never seemed to be jumping or travelling with any real fluency and looks very slow. *(op 7-2)*

1322 CHESHIRE LIFE CONDITIONAL JOCKEYS' NOVICES' H'CAP HURDLE (9 hdls) 2m 1f
4:40 (4:43) (Class 4) (0-105,102) 3-Y-0+ **£3,710** (£1,141; £570; £285)

Form RPR
0216 **1** **Master Nimbus**[5] 987 5-9-11 76 oh6.............................. DCCostello(3) 88+
(J J Quinn) *t.k.h: chsd ldr to 4th and wnt 2nd again 4 out: led appr 2 out: drew clr after last: r.o wl* **7/2**[2]
0-23 **2** *5* **Kentucky King (USA)**[12] 1206 5-11-0 95.............................. LHeard(5) 99+
(Mrs D A Hamer) *hld up: hdwy 4th: wnt 2nd whn hit 2 out: sn rdn: no ch w wnr after last* **4/1**[3]
1 **3** *3 1/2* **Gaelic Roulette (IRE)**[12] 1213 5-11-2 97.............................. TBailey(5) 97
(J Jay) *hld up: hit 2nd: hdwy 6th: one pce fr 2 out* **5/1**

3-06 **4** *12* **West Hill (IRE)**[12] 1202 4-9-8 **77** oh6 (t) StephenJCraine(6) 64
(D McCain) *led: rdn and hdd appr 2 out: wknd between last 2* **9/1**
40-3 **5** *3* **Nightwatchman (IRE)**[11] 1218 6-11-9 **102** CDSharkey(3) 87
(S B Clark) *in tch: lost pl after 3rd: rdn and no imp whn mstke 3 out* **8/1**
-0P6 **6** *28* **Brother Ted**[28] 1084 8-9-13 **80** (t) TMessenger(5) 37
(J K Cresswell) *t.k.h: in tch: chsd ldr 4th to 4 out: wknd next* **20/1**
-025 **7** *9* **Jimmy Byrne (IRE)**[57] 860 5-11-2 **98** (p) CEddery(6) 46
(R C Guest) *hld up: hdwy 5th: rdn and wknd 3 out* **3/1**[1]
0/PP **U** **Le Cavalier (USA)**[12] 1206 8-10-4 **80** TGreenway —
(Mrs L Williamson) *chsd ldrs: rdn and lost pl 4th: blnd and uns rdr next* **33/1**

4m 12.2s (1.30) **Going Correction** -0.15s/f (Good)
WFA 4 from 5yo+ 15lb **8** Ran SP% **112.7**
Speed ratings: **90,87,86,80,78 65,61,—** CSF £17.70 CT £67.77 TOTE £4.40: £1.30, £2.00, £1.70; EX 22.50.
Owner J H Hewitt **Bred** A H Bennett **Trained** Settrington, N Yorks

FOCUS
The steady early gallop, resulting in a modest time, scuppered the chance of many and the form does not look strong.

NOTEBOOK
Master Nimbus, unsuited by the ease in the ground when disappointing at Cartmel back in July, had subsequently run well when second on the Flat only five days prior to this and he ran out an easy winner off his feather weight. The slow pace was of no hindrance and, as he is evidently in good form at present, may be able to follow up. *(op 5-1)*
Kentucky King(USA) saw his race out better on this drop back in trip, but was always having to play second fiddle to the winner. *(op 11-2)*
Gaelic Roulette(IRE) would not have been suited by the slow gallop and was unable to quicken sufficiently back in third. This was not a bad effort and she deserves another chance to build on her winning debut. *(op 10-3)*
West Hill(IRE) was responsible for the steady gallop, but this poor performer was unable to capitalise on the easy lead and he faded into fourth. *(op 11-1)*
Nightwatchman(IRE), who shaped as though in need of three miles when a staying on third at Stratford last time, was bizarrely dropped in trip and would have been least-best suited by the slow pace. He should have the run ignored and is not one to give up on yet.
Jimmy Byrne(IRE) ran below form and was struggling from a long way out. *(op 5-2 tchd 10-3, 7-2 in places)*

1323 COUNTRYSIDE DAY INTERMEDIATE OPEN NATIONAL HUNT FLAT RACE 2m 1f
5:10 (5:12) (Class 6) 4-6-Y-0 **£1,946** (£556; £278)

Form RPR
1 **Jeremy Cuddle Duck (IRE)** 4-10-10 MGoldstein(7) 100+
(N A Twiston-Davies) *prom: led after 5f: hdd after 6f: regained ld 1/2-way: rdn and hung rt over 2f out: clr over 1f out: styd on wl* **7/2**[1]
2 *10* **Bonchester Bridge** 4-10-10 MFoley 83
(N J Henderson) *midfield: hdwy 5f out: wnt 2nd over 1f out: no ch w wnr* **13/2**
050 **3** *1* **Hard N Sharp**[36] 1042 5-11-4 RJohnson 90
(Mrs A M Thorpe) *midfield: hdwy 5f out: rdn over 3f out: one pce fnl f* **25/1**
4 *hd* **Constantius** 4-11-3 JPMcNamara 89
(K C Bailey) *in tch: rdn and ev ch over 2f out: one pce fnl f* **14/1**
5 *9* **Solway Willy** 4-11-3 ADobbin 80
(N G Richards) *hld up: hdwy over 6f out: rdn whn chsng ldrs over 2f out: wknd over 1f out* **4/1**[2]
6 *3 ½* **Two Good (IRE)** 5-10-11 JimCrowley 70
(P D Niven) *towards rr: kpt on fr 2f out: nvr trbld ldrs* **50/1**
006- **7** *3* **Petrovka (IRE)**[133] 4841 5-10-11 RThornton 67
(S Gollings) *in tch: rdn over 3f out: wknd over 2f out* **28/1**
8 *3* **Cresswell Willow (IRE)** 5-10-11 TJMurphy 64
(W K Goldsworthy) *hld up: rdn and rn green 5f out: nvr trbld ldrs* **25/1**
9 *½* **Aaron's Run** 5-11-4 SCurran 71
(M R Bosley) *hld up: hdwy 1/2-way: pushed along over 6f out: wknd over 2f out* **66/1**
32 **10** *11* **Back With A Bang (IRE)**[35] 1048 6-11-4 JMogford 60
(Mrs N S Evans) *prom: rdn over 4f out: wknd over 3f out* **10/1**
11 *9* **Sir Harry Hall (IRE)** 4-11-3 APMcCoy 50
(P Bowen) *midfield: hdwy 9f out: rdn and j. road over 4f out: wknd over 3f out* **13/2**
12 *nk* **Chaga** 4-10-10 CLlewellyn 43
(W Jenks) *a bhd* **18/1**
0-50 **13** *3 ½* **Firion King (IRE)**[8] 1237 5-10-11 BWharfe(7) 47
(T H Caldwell) *prom tl wknd over 6f out* **33/1**
00- **14** *dist* **Times Up Barney**[159] 4451 5-11-4 SThomas —
(C W Moore) *a bhd: t.o* **66/1**
P **15** *dist* **Just Freya**[64] 816 4-10-10 WHutchinson —
(R Dickin) *t.k.h: hld up: gd hdwy to ld after 6f: hdd 1/2-way: sn wknd: t.o* **66/1**
16 *1* **Bobe Brick** 4-11-3 OMcPhail —
(B R Foster) *led: hdd after 5f: wknd qckly bef 1/2-way: t.o* **50/1**
F **Cloudy Club (IRE)** 6-11-4 TDoyle —
(P R Webber) *prom to 1/2-way: sn wknd: fell over 1f out* **6/1**[3]

4m 5.40s (-5.70) **Going Correction** -0.15s/f (Good)
WFA 4 from 5yo+ 1lb **17** Ran SP% **126.7**
Speed ratings: **107,102,101,101,97 95,94,93,92,87 83,83,81,—,— —,—** CSF £25.07 TOTE £4.20: £1.50, £2.40, £10.00; EX 33.20 Place 6 £64.96, Place 5 £24.19.
Owner N A Twiston-Davies **Bred** C Kenneally **Trained** Naunton, Gloucs

FOCUS
Probably a decent bumper for the time of year and the time was good for the grade.

NOTEBOOK
Jeremy Cuddle Duck(IRE), strong in the market beforehand, created a good impression on this winning debut, powering away in impressive fashion. His stable does well in this sphere and he may bid to defy a penalty, albeit that is not always easy in bumpers. He looks a nice hurdling prospect and is one to keep on the right side of. *(op 5-1 tchd 3-1)*
Bonchester Bridge, in contrast to the winner was weak in the market before the race and she ran as though today was not the day. Given a considerate ride, she should have little trouble finding a similar race. *(op 5-1 tchd 7-1)*
Hard N Sharp had shown little previously and does little for the form, but there is the possibility he is progressing and he should be given the benefit of the doubt.
Constantius is an interesting one for the future as, having travelled strongly for a mile and a half, he appeared to get tired in the final two furlongs as a lack of fitness began to tell. Although his future lies over fences, the way he travelled suggested he is up to winning a race in this sphere and he is worth siding with in future. *(op 12-1)*
Solway Willy, whose stable had sent out three of their four previous bumper runners to win this season, could not improve that statistic, but he shaped promisingly with the future in mind and he is another who will appreciate a sterner test over hurdles. *(op 3-1)*
Just Freya *Official explanation: jockey said filly ran keenly and hung badly right*

Cloudy Club(IRE), a big, rangy son of Moscow Society, simply looked in need of more time and was beginning to weaken when appearing to stumble and hit the deck over a furlong out. He should leave this running behind as long as his confidence has not been affected. *(op 8-1 tchd 10-1)*
T/Plt: £32.50 to a £1 stake. Pool: £38,978.15. 875.05 winning tickets. T/Qpdt: £14.90 to a £1 stake. Pool: £2,554.20. 126.35 winning tickets. DO

1329 - 1331a (Foreign Racing) - See Raceform Interactive

[987] CARTMEL (L-H)
Saturday, August 27

OFFICIAL GOING: Good (good to firm on bottom bend; good to soft in places along wood side on chase course)
Wind: Almost nil Weather: Sunny

1332 GRANT THORNTON UK LLP JUVENILE NOVICES' HURDLE (DIV I) (8 hdls) 2m 1f 110y
2:10 (2:10) (Class 4) 3-Y-0 **£3,760** (£1,157; £578; £289)

Form RPR
21 **1** **Goldstar Dancer (IRE)**[14] 1207 3-11-5 RGarritty 91+
(J J Quinn) *led tl after 3rd: prom and gng wl tl led again 2 out: sn in command: easily* **1/1**[1]
2 *5* **Negas (IRE)**[30] 3-10-12 GLee 77+
(J Howard Johnson) *prom: chsd wnr fr 2 out: kpt on steadily but a hld* **16/1**
3 *2* **Dennick**[5] 3-10-12 FKeniry 75+
(P C Haslam) *plld v hrd: j. slowly 1st: led after 3rd: hdd 2 out: rdn and nt qckn after* **22/1**
4 *7* **Sound And Vision (IRE)**[23] 3-10-12 BHarding 67
(M Dods) *nvr beter than midfield: rdn 3 out: n.d fr after next* **9/1**
5 *¾* **Backstreet Lad**[39] 3-10-12 ChristianWilliams 66
(Evan Williams) *keen pressing ldrs: rdn bef 2 out: sn btn* **13/2**[3]
6 *17* **Bellalou**[61] 3-10-5 MBradburne 49+
(Mrs S A Watt) *hld up in midfield: rdn and wknd bef 2 out* **25/1**
7 *dist* **Procrastinate (IRE)**[11] 3-10-9 KJMercer(3) —
(R F Fisher) *j. poorly in last pair: sn lost tch: t.o 3 out: btn 75l* **33/1**
P **8** *3 ½* **Irish Hawk (GER)**[14] 1201 3-10-5 CPoste(7) —
(M F Harris) *towrds rr: lost tch after 5th: t.o 3 out: btn 78l* **33/1**
9 *½* **Scorpio Sally (IRE)**[29] 3-10-5 KRenwick —
(M D Hammond) *nt fluent and sn in rr: rdn and lost tch bef 5th: t.o next: btn 79l* **25/1**
3P **B** **Sharp N Frosty**[14] 1201 3-10-12 (t) ATinkler 58
(W M Brisbourne) *chsd ldrs tl rdn and wknd bef 2 out: poor 7th whn b.d last* **20/1**
P **Keepasharplookout (IRE)**[150] 3-10-12 KJohnson —
(C W Moore) *v keen and nvr fluent: sn detached fr rest: blnd 3rd and 4th and continued t.o tl p.u 2 out* **50/1**
02 **F** **Diktatit**[14] 1201 3-10-2 LMcGrath(3) 56
(R C Guest) *plld hrd in rr: effrt bef 3 out: threatened briefly in 3rd next: drvn and sn wknd: 5th and btn whn fell last* **11/2**[2]

4m 13.4s (-2.30) **Going Correction** -0.225s/f (Good) **12** Ran SP% **119.2**
Speed ratings: **96,93,92,89,89 81,—,—,—,— —,—** CSF £17.14 TOTE £1.90: £1.10, £3.30, £6.40; EX 22.50.
Owner Double Eight Syndicate **Bred** D Maher **Trained** Settrington, N Yorks

FOCUS
A weak juvenile contest but a straightforward success for recent Bangor winner Goldstar Dancer, who is value for a little more than the official margin.

NOTEBOOK
Goldstar Dancer(IRE) has created a good impression since being switched to hurdles and supplemented his recent success with another smooth display. Always travelling strongly, he quickened away as they turned for home and soon put the result beyond doubt. This was probably a fair effort under a penalty, but he will need to continue to progress to defy a double penalty. *(op 11-10)*
Negas(IRE), a moderate Flat performer, was always likely to improve for a switch to hurdles and he kept on nicely for second without ever looking a serious threat to the winner. He can find small race in the coming weeks.
Dennick, who was in a similar league to Negas on the level, did remarkably well to finish as close as he did considering he pulled so hard in the early stages, but maybe that reflects on how poor those behind were. His stable does well in this type of race and he too can pick up a small contest if learning to settle better. *(op 18-1)*
Sound And Vision(IRE) did not shape with a great deal of promise on this hurdles debut, but is entitled to improve for the experience. *(tchd 17-2)*
Backstreet Lad had similar claims to the placed horses on Flat form, but he failed to last out having raced a tad keenly. *(tchd 7-1)*
Diktatit had run her race and was struggling when coming down at the last. Her recent second showed she has got ability, but she may not be up to winning until racing in low-grade handicaps. *(op 8-1)*

1333 PETER'S IMP CONDITIONAL JOCKEYS' (S) H'CAP HURDLE (11 hdls) 2m 6f
2:45 (2:47) (Class 5) (0-90,90) 4-Y-0+ **£3,083** (£881; £440)

Form RPR
P0-0 **1** **Green 'N' Gold**[25] 499 5-11-7 **85** NPMulholland 91
(M D Hammond) *keen in midfield: effrt 8th: wnt cl 3rd 3 out: rdn to ld between last two: clr last: kpt on* **7/2**[2]
4123 **2** *6* **Little Task**[14] 1211 7-11-12 **90** PAspell 90
(J S Wainwright) *wl bhd: rr and rdn and plenty to do bef 8th: styd on fr 2 out to go 2nd after last: kpt on but nvr rchd wnr* **5/2**[1]
40-6 **3** *6* **Sheer Guts (IRE)**[9] 1250 6-11-7 **85** (b) PCO'Neill 79
(Evan Williams) *cl 2nd tl led gng wl 3 out: rdn and hdd between last two: fnd little and sn btn* **10/1**
0563 **4** *2 ½* **Step In Line (IRE)**[3] 1308 13-9-9 **64** oh2 PJMcDonald(5) 57+
(D W Thompson) *chsd ldrs: rdn and outpcd bef 3 out: plugged on* **7/1**
/0-F **5** *9* **Son Of Flighty**[43] 997 7-10-8 **72** (p) WKennedy 55
(Evan Williams) *j.rt: nt fluent early: led: rdn and hdd 3 out: 3rd and btn next: fdd after* **13/2**[3]
0-FP **6** *5* **Amber Go Go**[29] 1100 8-9-8 **68** ow1 MMcAvoy(10) 46
(James Moffatt) *bhd: blnd 7th: no ch after* **9/1**
PPU0 **7** *1 ½* **Madhahir (IRE)**[33] 1066 5-10-3 **67** (v) JamesDavies 43
(M J Gingell) *cl up tl rdn and lost pl 6th: nvr gng wl after* **20/1**
40F0 **8** *26* **Mapilut Du Moulin (FR)**[27] 1107 5-10-7 **74** (b1) StephenJCraine(3) 24
(C R Dore) *keen: chsd ldrs tl wknd qckly bef 3 out: fin v slowly: t.o* **25/1**
6-P0 **9** *dist* **Uncle Batty**[14] 1202 5-10-8 **72** DLaverty —
(Mrs L Williamson) *tk frntic hold: nvr bttr than midfield: lost tch 7th: t.o 3 out: btn 125l* **25/1**

0-0P **P** **Diagon Alley (IRE)**[14] [1202] 5-10-2 **69** MJMcAlister(3) —
(K W Hogg) *j. slowly 4th: sn rdn in last: struggling 6th: t.o and p.u 2 out* **16/1**

5m 26.4s (-9.60) **Going Correction** -0.225s/f (Good) **28** Ran SP% **114.1**
Speed ratings: **108,105,103,102,99 97,97,87,—,—** CSF £12.33 CT £75.88 TOTE £3.60: £1.40, £1.50, £2.40; EX 6.60.The winner was bought in for 6,000gns.
Owner E Whalley **Bred** Micky Hammond Racing Ltd And S Branklin **Trained** Middleham, N Yorks

FOCUS
A fair time for a seller and five seconds quicker than the later maiden hurdle over the same trip. The form looks sound enough with those in the frame behind the winning running to their marks.

NOTEBOOK
Green 'N' Gold has steadily been dropping in the weights and was racing off an 11lb lower mark than when last successful. The ground was in her favour and, having travelled nicely, she was sent into a winning lead after the second last. This is about her level these days and it will be interesting to see of she is turned out under a penalty. *(tchd 4-1)*
Little Task came from an impossible position on a track where it pays to race handy and never gave his backers a realistic chance. He was putting in some good late work and deserves another chance. *(op 3-1 tchd 9-4)*
Sheer Guts(IRE) has been out of sorts of late and, although this was a better effort, it was disappointing how he 'fell in a hole' once maximum pressure was applied. *(op 7-1 tchd 12-1)*
Step In Line(IRE) lacked the speed of the younger horses and ran as well as could have been expected. *(op 15-2)*
Son Of Flighty spoiled his chance with several sloppy jumps and faded out of it disappointingly. *(op 7-1 tchd 8-1)*

1334 CONCEPT TILES BEGINNERS' CHASE (14 fncs) 2m 5f 110y
3:20 (3:21) (Class 4) 5-Y-O+ **£4,550** (£1,400; £700; £350)

Form RPR

P-01 **1** **Mocharamor (IRE)**[22] [1151] 7-10-12 JPMcNamara 99
(J J Lambe, Ire) *led tl 5th: j.lft next: prom tl chsd ldr bef 11th: led 2f out: rdn clr and styd on stoutly* **8/1**

F244 **2** 2 ½ **Heather Lad**[6] [1275] 12-10-12 100 GLee 96
(C Grant) *trckd ldrs: effrt 11th: chal last: w wnr 2f out: drvn and nt qckn after* **16/1**

206/ **3** 4 **Darina's Boy**[854] [4789] 9-10-12 KJohnson 92+
(Mrs S J Smith) *plld hrd: led 5th: clr next: stl gng wl after last: hdd 2f out: sn btn but kpt on gamely* **10/1**

3222 **4** 4 **Windy Spirit (IRE)**[6] [1269] 10-10-12 110 ChristianWilliams 89+
(Evan Williams) *hld up and bhd: sltly hmpd 3rd: effrt in 8l 4th 3 out: rdn and no imp after* **10/3**[2]

053/ **5** 9 **Rolling River (IRE)**[988] [2474] 8-10-9 PAspell(3) 79
(J Wade) *bhd: mstkes 4th and whn making prog 5th (water): effrt 9th: rdn and wknd 11th* **50/1**

5-24 **6** 2 **Page Point (AUS)**[90] [570] 7-10-12 116 (p) HOliver 78+
(R C Guest) *plld hrd: mstke 10th: chsd ldr tl bef 11th: wknd qckly 2 out* **4/1**[3]

116- **7** dist **Count Fosco**[175] [4169] 7-10-12 ADobbin —
(M Todhunter) *mstkes: hld up towards rr: consistent errors whn asked to improve fnl circ: rdn 9th: btn whn blnd 3 out: eased: btn 92l* **11/4**[1]

8 1 **Devondale (IRE)**[796] [728] 9-10-9 (t) KJMercer(3) —
(Ferdy Murphy) *hld up and bhd: lost tch 10th: btn 93l* **25/1**

-641 **F** **Peter's Imp (IRE)**[30] [988] 10-10-12 95 NPMulholland —
(A Berry) *settled midfield tl fell 3rd* **7/1**

5m 26.0s (-4.50) **Going Correction** -0.225s/f (Good) **9** Ran SP% **114.1**
Speed ratings: **99,98,96,95,91 91,—,—,—** CSF £114.57 TOTE £9.60: £2.20, £2.50, £3.10; EX 201.10.
Owner Andrew Wishart **Bred** Miss Kelly Hazzard **Trained** Dungannon, Co. Tyrone

FOCUS
A moderate contest but a good effort by the progressive Mocharamor, who could be rated much higher if the fourth and sixth were used as yardsticks for the form.

NOTEBOOK
Mocharamor(IRE), a winner over hurdles at Sedgefield earlier in the month, had won a point-to-point earlier in his career and ran out a workmanlike winner on this return to fences. A progressive gelding, he remains open to further improvement and will eventually do well in handicap chases. *(tchd 9-1)*
Heather Lad, who spent many years running in points, has done extremely well since being switched to racing under Rules and, although he has yet to get his head in front, the gallant 12-year-old's consistency should see him rewarded sooner or later.
Darina's Boy spoiled his chance by racing keenly on this return from a break, but he kept plugging away once headed and improvement can be expected on this initial outing over fences.
Windy Spirit(IRE) continues to run well without winning and simply found this trip on the sharp side. A return to further will help, especially in handicaps. *(op 3-1 tchd 7-2)*
Page Point(AUS) is an inconsistent character and threw in one of his 'lesser' efforts. *(op 7-2 tchd 9-2)*
Count Fosco made too many mistakes and was never really travelling on this chase debut. He is worth another chance, but some work clearly needs to be done on his jumping. *(op 3-1 tchd 10-3 in places)*

1335 LAKELAND VINTNERS - LAURENT PERRIER NOVICES' H'CAP CHASE (12 fncs) 2m 1f 110y
3:50 (3:54) (Class 4) (0-95,90) 5-Y-O+ **£4,215** (£1,297; £648; £324)

Form RPR

S213 **1** **Parisienne Gale (IRE)**[44] [987] 6-11-7 **85** GLee 101+
(R Ford) *j.w: mde all: gng bttr than two chalrs after last and r.o strly: readily* **3/1**[1]

U366 **2** 7 **Jupiter Jo**[27] [1109] 9-10-12 **76** BHarding 82
(J B Walton) *prom: chsd wnr bef 9th: rdn two out: no match for wnr after last* **6/1**

5322 **3** 1 ¼ **Sir Walter (IRE)**[13] [1218] 12-10-2 **66** ChristianWilliams 71
(D Burchell) *plld hrd towards rr: effrt 9th: 6th and rdn last: kpt on to chse ldng pair over 1f out: one pce and unable to chal* **7/2**[2]

36P **4** ¾ **Dalriath**[6] [1280] 6-11-3 **88** CMStudd(7) 92
(M C Chapman) *plld hrd: sn midfield: rdn and pressing ldrs whn mstke 3 out: btn next* **33/1**

60/4 **5** 4 **Loulou Nivernais (FR)**[58] [874] 6-11-3 **81** ADempsey 81
(M Todhunter) *plld hrd in rr: rapid hdwy 9th: disp 2nd and rdn after last: fdd fnl 2f* **9/1**

-133 **6** 1 ½ **Mikasa (IRE)**[6] [1277] 5-10-10 **77** (p) KJMercer(3) 76
(R F Fisher) *j. slowly 4th: pushed along bef 7th: nvr bttr than midfield: rdn and btn 3 out* **9/2**[3]

-03P **7** 6 **My Ace**[22] [1147] 7-10-12 **83** (bt) MissJFoster(7) 76
(Miss J E Foster) *chsd ldr tl appr 7th: ev ch bef 9th: wknd next* **33/1**

555P **8** 2 **Simply Da Best (IRE)**[22] [1148] 7-11-9 **87** JPMcNamara 78
(J J Lambe, Ire) *hld up towards rr: mstke 8th: sn rdn: n.d fr next* **16/1**

0246 **9** 2 ½ **Petrolero (ARG)**[44] [991] 6-11-7 **85** JamesDavies 75+
(James Moffatt) *midfield: prog to 2nd bef 7th tl appr 9th: rdn and sn lost pl* **25/1**

2600 **10** 7 **He's Hot Right Now (NZ)**[48] [939] 6-11-7 **90** (p) PCO'Neill(5) 73+
(R C Guest) *pressed ldrs tl mstke 7th: rdn next: last and struggling bef 9th* **8/1**

006U **U** **Known Maneuver (USA)**[6] [1275] 7-9-9 **64** TGreenway(5) —
(M C Chapman) *bhd: last and rdn 8th: struggling whn mstke and uns rdr 2 out* **50/1**

4m 18.9s (23.80) **Going Correction** -0.225s/f (Good) **11** Ran SP% **118.4**
Speed ratings: **102,98,98,98,96 95,92,92,90,87** — CSF £21.24 CT £66.39 TOTE £3.60: £1.80, £2.40, £1.50; EX 22.90.
Owner S J Manning **Bred** Edmond And Richard Kent **Trained** Cotebrook, Cheshire

FOCUS
Moderate stuff, but it was a joy to see the unexposed winner going about her business with a certain relish. The time was reasonable and the form looks pretty solid.

NOTEBOOK
Parisienne Gale(IRE), whose only previous effort over fences resulted in a second placing at this course, made mincemeat of some exposed rivals and really seemed to enjoy herself. Sent straight into the lead, she threw in several excellent leaps and came clear after the last to win stylishly. She is evidently on the up and it will be disappointing if she fails to follow up. *(tchd 10-3)*
Jupiter Jo ran a solid race and stuck with the winner for as long as he could, but was left trailing on the run-in and simply lacked the pace. *(tchd 13-2)*
Sir Walter(IRE) is much happier over hurdles than fences, but this was not a bad effort from the 12-year-old, although he makes little appeal with the future in mind. *(op 4-1)*
Dalriath failed to get home having pulled hard early, but was far from disgraced on this chase debut and should improve with experience. *(op 20-1)*
Loulou Nivernais(FR) has hardly set the world alight since coming from Ireland and probably needs to drop a further few pounds before he could be considered as a likely winner. *(tchd 10-1)*

1336 LADBROKES NOVICES' H'CAP HURDLE (FOR THE ARMY BENEVOLENT CHALLENGE CUP) (8 hdls) 2m 1f 110y
4:25 (4:27) (Class 4) (0-100,90) 4-Y-O+ **£4,173** (£1,284; £642; £321)

Form RPR

053- **1** **Baawrah**[283] [2268] 4-10-7 **72** GLee 77+
(M Todhunter) *hld up midfield: wnt cl up after 5th: drvn ahd bef last: styd on but all out* **8/1**

306- **2** 1 **Rare Coincidence**[2] [3461] 4-11-4 **86** KJMercer(3) 88+
(R F Fisher) *chsd ldr tl led after 3rd: rdn and hdd 2 out: pressed wnr and ev ch fr bef last: kpt on but a hld* **11/2**[3]

0105 **3** 1 ¼ **Ballyboe Boy (IRE)**[29] [1098] 6-11-10 **88** (b) HOliver 89
(R C Guest) *led tl after 3rd: sn rdn: lost interest 5th and sn detached fr ldng quartet: rallied bef last: styng on for driving cl home* **9/2**[2]

0FU- **4** ¾ **Alpha Juliet (IRE)**[179] [4108] 4-11-6 **85** FKeniry 85+
(G M Moore) *mstkes 1st and 3rd: prom: led 2 out: rdn and hdd bef last: no ex fnl f* **14/1**

-P32 **5** nk **Peruvian Breeze (IRE)**[9] [1246] 4-11-7 **86** (t) ChristianWilliams 85
(Evan Williams) *hld up: wnt prom 5th: rdn and outpcd after 2 out: tried to rally last: one pce u.p flat* **4/1**[1]

24-2 **6** 3 ½ **Bargain Hunt (IRE)**[30] [544] 4-11-4 **90** PJMcDonald(7) 87+
(W Storey) *chsd ldrs tl lost pl and j. slowly 5th: n.d after but sme late prog* **7/1**

5134 **7** 20 **Fenney Spring**[14] [1202] 5-10-12 **76** (bt) CLlewellyn 53
(W Jenks) *bhd: rdn bef 5th: nvr gng wl: btn bef 3 out* **9/2**[2]

0-F0 **8** 1 ¼ **Lady Godson**[69] [780] 6-10-0 **64** oh4 NPMulholland 39
(B Mactaggart) *pressed ldrs early: rdn and wknd 4th: wl bhd after next* **66/1**

1P40 **9** 23 **Nifty Roy**[22] [1149] 5-11-12 **90** ADobbin 42
(K W Hogg) *nvr bttr than midfield: rdn 5th: sn lost tch: virtually p.u ent st* **12/1**

P46P **10** dist **Troodos Jet**[14] [1202] 4-11-4 **83** MBradburne —
(K W Hogg) *stdd s: a lagging: t.o bef 3 out: btn 50l* **66/1**

6/P4 **P** **Night Mail**[14] [1209] 5-10-10 **77** (p) GCarenza(3) —
(Miss J E Foster) *dwlt: reluctant and rdn fr s: trailed along tl p.u after 5th* **50/1**

4m 10.9s (-4.80) **Going Correction** -0.225s/f (Good)
WFA 4 from 5yo+ 15lb **11** Ran SP% **114.7**
Speed ratings: **101,100,100,99,99 97,89,88,78,—** — CSF £50.64 CT £222.06 TOTE £7.90: £2.60, £2.00, £1.90; EX 56.50.
Owner J D Gordon **Bred** Darley **Trained** Orton, Cumbria
■ Stewards' Enquiry : K J Mercer four-day ban: used whip with excessive frequency (Sep 7,9,11,18)

FOCUS
Modest form but the winner is value for further and could score again. The third, fourth and fifth ran close to their marks, giving the form a solid appearance.

NOTEBOOK
Baawrah, who showed his first real sign of ability over hurdles in the first-time cheekpieces at Hexham last time, had the headgear left off but was still able to confirm that promise and received a strong ride from Lee to break his duck. Racing here off a measly mark of 72, it will be surprising if there is not more to come and he should be capable of defying a higher rating.
Rare Coincidence had not raced over hurdles since January, but he seemed to appreciate the change and ran the winner, who was in receipt of plenty of weight, close. He can find a race at a similar level. *(op 9-2)*
Ballyboe Boy(IRE) has been mixing hurdling and fencing and he ran a creditable race in defeat. A stiffer track may help. *(op 5-1)*
Alpha Juliet(IRE) had every chance and is not really progressing. It may take a drop into selling company to see her get her head in front. *(op 11-1)*
Peruvian Breeze(IRE) was always likely to struggle on this drop back in trip and, although he had the aid of a tongue tie, he was always struggling to keep tabs on the leaders. Two and a half miles is probably his ideal trip. *(tchd 9-2)*
Bargain Hunt(IRE) kept plugging away but looked as though he would be more at home on a galloping track. *(op 9-1)*

1337 MAHOOD MARQUEES MAIDEN HURDLE (11 hdls) 2m 6f
4:55 (4:57) (Class 4) 4-Y-O+ **£3,770** (£1,160; £580; £290)

Form RPR

000- **1** **Melmount Star (IRE)**[171] [4259] 7-11-2 GLee 84+
(J Howard Johnson) *chsd ldr bef 4th tl led 2 out: rdn last: kpt on steadily and a holding rivals* **8/1**

664 **2** 2 **Shady Baron (IRE)**[22] [1149] 6-10-13 PAspell(3) 80
(J Wade) *handy: j. slowly 4th: wnt prom 7th: rdn and chsd wnr between last two: no imp* **11/1**

4324 **3** 5 **Penteli**[14] [1211] 5-10-9 82 ADobbin 70+
(C Grant) *kpt hanging rt: rdn fr 5th: mstke 6th: midfield tl wl outpcd bef 3 out: kpt on fr last: hung violently rt: nt run on* **13/8**[1]

000 **4** *3* **Nobodysgonanotice (IRE)**[33] [1062] 7-10-11 81................. PCO'Neill(5) 72
(J J Lambe, Ire) *set slow pce tl bef 4th: last and struggling 7th: remote 3 out: styng on again fr last: no ch* **25/1**

5054 **5** *1 ¼* **Greenfort Brave (IRE)**[20] [1174] 7-11-2 83........................ JPMcNamara 71
(J J Lambe, Ire) *t.k.h: mstke 1st: led bef 4th tl hdd 2 out: rdn and fdd bef last* **11/2**[2]

FP-6 **6** *24* **Glashedy Rock (IRE)**[19] [1181] 8-11-2 91................................ SThomas 61+
(M F Harris) *cl up: rdn 3 out: dropped out rapidly next* **14/1**

U00- **7** *17* **City Palace**[102] [3568] 4-11-0 ....(tp) ChristianWilliams 58+
(Evan Williams) *t.k.h in rr: effrt to go cl up 5th: ev ch tl stopped to nil 2 out: t.o* **6/1**[3]

-0P0 **8** *26* **End Of Saga**[27] [1108] 6-11-2 .... KJohnson —
(J B Walton) *keen and cl up: wkng whn j. slowly 8th: t.o next* **66/1**

43-P **P** **Kyber**[29] [1100] 4-10-11 90.. KJMercer(3) —
(R F Fisher) *t.k.h in last: j. slowly 4th: brief effrt after 7th: rdn and fnd nil bef next: sn t.o: p.u last* **11/2**[2]

5m 31.4s (-4.60) **Going Correction** -0.225s/f (Good)
WFA 4 from 5yo+ 16lb **9** Ran SP% **114.6**
Speed ratings: **99,98,96,95,94 86,80,70,—** CSF £88.45 TOTE £9.60: £2.00, £2.50, £1.40; EX 158.70.
Owner Mrs Lucy Forbes **Bred** J O'Keeffe **Trained** Billy Row, Co Durham

FOCUS
An awful contest that is unlikely to produce winners and the runner-up is probably the best guide to the form.

NOTEBOOK
Melmount Star(IRE) came into this having shown little in three previous outings and the fact he was able to win underlines the strength of the contest. He should get a mark in the high 80s, low 90s for this and it will be interesting to see how or if he progresses. *(op 10-1)*
Shady Baron(IRE) is gradually getting better over hurdles he kept on into second without ever seriously threatening the winner. He may be able to find a small race, probably in handicaps. *(op 12-1)*
Penteli lost her chance as she continually hung to her right on this sharp left-handed track and it may have been that she was feeling something. If choosing to not give her the benefit of the doubt then she is one to avoid. *(op 7-4)*
Nobodysgonanotice(IRE) kept going right to the line and would be of more interest in handicaps. *(op 33-1)*
Greenfort Brave(IRE) did not put up much of a fight once headed and was most disappointing. *(op 13-2)*
Glashedy Rock(IRE) is a regressive gelding and he continues to shape without any promise at all. *(op 12-1)*

1338 GRANT THORNTON UK LLP JUVENILE NOVICES' HURDLE (DIV II) (8 hdls) 2m 1f 110y
5:25 (5:28) (Class 4) 3-Y-0 **£3,760** (£1,157; £578; £289)

Form RPR

1 **Aviation**[23] 3-10-12 .... FKeniry 94+
(G M Moore) *cl up: mstke 2nd: wnt 2nd bef 2 out: rdn to ld last: hld on wl* **11/4**[2]

2 *1 ¼* **Moonfleet (IRE)**[23] 3-9-12 .... CPoste(7) 83
(M F Harris) *keen: hld up towards rr: prog 4th: led bef 2 out: rdn and hdd last: kpt on but a jst hld* **11/1**

3 *9* **Verstone (IRE)**[25] 3-10-2 .... KJMercer(3) 74
(R F Fisher) *v free to post: t.k.h in rr: mstke 3rd: prog 3 out: wnt 3rd bef last: drvn and sn wl hld* **16/1**

4 *14* **Truckle**[9] 3-10-12 .... ADobbin 67
(C W Fairhurst) *plld hrd: mstke 3rd: trckd ldrs tl fdd u.p bef 2 out* **11/1**

0 **5** *½* **Kinfayre Boy**[40] [945] 3-10-12 .... MBradburne 66
(K W Hogg) *hld up towards rr: effrt bef 3 out: rdn and wknd next* **33/1**

6 *½* **Ansells Legacy (IRE)**[13] 3-10-12 .... NPMulholland 71+
(A Berry) *midfield: blnd bdly 4th: slt prog whn blnd again 2 out: wl btn after* **14/1**

7 *13* **Madge**[54] 3-10-5 .... GLee 46
(W Storey) *mstke 1st: hld up: prog 5th: wnt 2nd 3 out: lost pl bef next and fdd bdly* **16/1**

55 **8** *11* **Golden Feather**[14] [1207] 3-10-12 .... HOliver 42
(R C Guest) *chsd ldr tl 3rd: bhd fr 5th* **9/1**[3]

62 **9** *8* **Good Investment**[17] [1146] 3-10-12 .... SThomas 34
(P C Haslam) *led tl 3rd and again bef 5th: hdd bef 2 out: stopped to nil: t.o* **9/4**[1]

64 **P** **First Fought (IRE)**[14] [1201] 3-10-12 .... JMMaguire —
(D McCain) *bhd: drvn after 5th: no rspnse: t.o and p.u last* **11/1**

P **Time To Succeed**[356] 3-10-9 .... PAspell(3) —
(J S Wainwright) *keen to s: sn 8l bhd rest: drvn and labouring bdly after 4th: t.o and p.u after next* **66/1**

F **P** **Champagne Rossini (IRE)**[5] [945] 3-10-5 .... CMStudd(7) —
(M C Chapman) *mounted crse: uns bef s: plld hrd: led 3rd tl bef 5th: fading rapidly whn blnd next: p.u 2 out* **33/1**

4m 11.4s (-4.30) **Going Correction** -0.225s/f (Good) **12** Ran SP% **118.2**
Speed ratings: **100,99,95,89,89 88,83,78,74,— —,—** CSF £32.83 TOTE £3.70: £1.70, £3.70, £3.90; EX 29.90 Place 6 £109.26, Place 5 £64.46.
Owner G R Orchard **Bred** D J And Mrs Deer **Trained** Middleham Moor, N Yorks

FOCUS
The stronger of the two divisions and the race should produce the occasional winner.

NOTEBOOK
Aviation, a modest Flat performer, was always to the fore and was given a well-judged ride by Keniry. He battled on from the persistent Moonfleet and, with the pair pulling nine lengths clear of the third, the form is probably decent for the time of year. *(tchd 3-1)*
Moonfleet(IRE), who was rather inconsistent on the Flat, made a pleasing start to her hurdling career and kept pushing right the way to the line. A race will come her way if she can build on this. *(op 9-1)*
Verstone(IRE) was poor on the Flat, but always looked the sort who would do better over hurdles and she made a pleasing if not spectacular start to her hurdling career. She can win races, even if it has to be at a lower level. *(op 12-1)*
Truckle, who did not progress on the Flat, made too may mistakes on this hurdling debut and did not get home having raced far too keenly. He deserves another chance and should do better if learning to settle. *(op 14-1)*
Kinfayre Boy has shown little in two starts and needs a drop in grade.
Good Investment failed to build on his second from earlier in the month and there may well have been something amiss judging by how quickly he stopped. He is better than this, but now has something to prove. *(op 11-4 tchd 2-1)*
T/Plt: £90.80 to a £1 stake. Pool: £34,333.40. 275.80 winning tickets. T/Qpdt: £76.20 to a £1 stake. Pool: £1,783.50. 17.30 winning tickets. IM

[1208] MARKET RASEN (R-H)
Saturday, August 27

OFFICIAL GOING: Good (good to firm in places)
6mm water was put on the track over the two previous days and the going was described as'mainly good but patchy, on the soft side in places'.
Wind: virtually nil Weather: fine

1339 LINCOLNSHIRE MOTORS JUVENILE NOVICES' HURDLE (8 hdls) 2m 1f 110y
5:00 (5:02) (Class 4) 3-Y-0 **£3,469** (£991; £495)

Form RPR

2 **1** **Royal Master**[24] [1023] 3-10-12 .... APMcCoy 85+
(P C Haslam) *trckd ldrs: led after last: hrd rdn and edgd lft: jst hld on* **5/4**[1]

2 *nk* **Whirling**[32] 3-10-5 .... TJMurphy 78
(M C Pipe) *in tch: reminders 4th: jnd ldrs 2 out: n.m.r and swtchd lft run-in: styd on wl: jst failed* **2/1**[2]

3 *shd* **Pseudonym (IRE)**[7] 3-10-12 ....(t) PJBrennan 85
(M F Harris) *w.r.s: reluctant ldr: qcknd 5th: hdd after last: wandered and no ex nr line* **9/1**[3]

4 *8* **Azahara**[20] 3-10-5 .... JimCrowley 72+
(K G Reveley) *chsd ldrs: 4th and wl btn whn blnd last* **28/1**

5 *24* **Eborarry (IRE)**[30] 3-10-12 .... DO'Meara 58+
(T D Easterby) *chsd ldrs: blnd 3 out: wknd next: 5th and wl btn whn stmbld landing last* **16/1**

6 *nk* **Dishdasha (IRE)**[23] 3-10-12 .... NFehily 52
(C R Dore) *in rr: kpt on fr 3 out: nvr on terms* **33/1**

7 *1 ¾* **Asteem**[59] 3-10-9 .... LVickers(3) 51
(M E Sowersby) *in tch: lost pl 5th: no ch after* **50/1**

8 *shd* **Folly Mount**[110] 3-10-12 .... PMoloney 50
(M W Easterby) *hld up in rr: bhd fr 5th* **33/1**

9 *4* **Tiffin Deano (IRE)**[28] 3-10-12 .... SCurran 46
(H J Manners) *mstkes: a in rr* **50/1**

PPF **10** *½* **Miss Dinamite**[22] [1146] 3-9-12 .... TMessenger(7) 39
(Mrs C J Ikin) *in rr: wknd 3 out: sn bhd* **100/1**

11 *12* **Final Overture (IRE)**[52] 3-10-0 .... DCCostello(5) 27
(J S Wainwright) *a in rr: bhd fr 5th* **100/1**

3 **12** *7* **Optimum (IRE)**[14] [1207] 3-10-12 .... AThornton 27
(J T Stimpson) *chsd ldrs: wkd 3 out: bhd whn blnd next* **9/1**[3]

4m 31.2s (14.80) **Going Correction** +0.375s/f (Yiel) **12** Ran SP% **118.9**
Speed ratings: **82,81,81,78,67 67,66,66,64,64 59,56** CSF £3.74 TOTE £2.10: £1.10, £1.80, £2.40; EX 5.50.
Owner Vyas Ltd & Kary-On Racing Partnership **Bred** Dunchurch Lodge Stud Co **Trained** Middleham, N Yorks

FOCUS
They stood still for about six seconds when the tape went up and Pseudonym, who did a pirouette, was still able to jump off in front eventually. A low-grade early season juvenile hurdle, the first three in close contention clear of the rest. The race is ratred through the winner but without much confidence.

NOTEBOOK
Royal Master, runner-up at Pontefract since Stratford, travelled strongly but in the end it took all the champions' strength to keep his head in front. *(op 11-8 tchd 11-10)*
Whirling, picked up for 10,000gns after winning a seller at Beverley, looked very fit indeed. She took plenty of stoking up but, after being forced to change position on the run-in, in the end she just missed out. *(op 5-2 tchd 11-4 in a place)*
Pseudonym(IRE), rated 5lb ahead of the winner on the Flat, is now with his third trainer this year. He did a twirl at the start but with no one else keen to lead, still set off in front. He came off a true line on the run-in yet still only just missed out in the end. *(op 15-2)*
Azahara, rated 49 on the level and bang out of form this time, was well held when flattening the last. Stamina could be an issue at this game. *(op 25-1)*
Eborarry(IRE), a winner and rated 51 on the level, was the biggest horse in the field but he had been hung out to dry when crossing his legs on landing at the final flight. *(op 12-1)*
Dishdasha(IRE), a banded winner on the Flat and rated just 45, was never in contention.

1340 ST BARNABAS HOSPICE MAIDEN HURDLE (8 hdls) 2m 1f 110y
5:30 (5:31) (Class 4) 4-Y-0+ **£3,427** (£979; £489)

Form RPR

-243 **1** **Smart Boy Prince (IRE)**[19] [991] 4-11-1 100.......................... DRDennis 103+
(C Smith) *mde all: clr whn mstke 2 out: heavily eased towards fin* **9/4**[2]

2 *14* **Sharaab (USA)**[16] 4-11-1 .... PMoloney 85
(D E Cantillon) *hld up towards rr: stdy hdwy 5th: wnt 3rd appr 2 out: styd on to take mod 2nd nr fin* **25/1**

3 *½* **Always Esteemed (IRE)**[50] 5-11-2 .... TJMurphy 86
(K A Ryan) *trckd ldrs: wnt 2nd 4th: hung lft appr 2 out: sn btn: lost 2nd nr line* **15/8**[1]

S40 **4** *5* **Oscar's Lady (IRE)**[52] [917] 4-10-8 .... JimCrowley 73
(G A Swinbank) *hld up in rr: gd hdwy 5th: chsng ldrs appr 2 out: one pce* **40/1**

5 *5* **Rarefied (IRE)**[7] 4-11-1 .... DO'Meara 80+
(T D Easterby) *chsd ldrs: 5th and wl btn whn bdly hmpd after 2 out* **16/1**

6 *12* **Hugs Destiny (IRE)**[23] 4-10-8 .... BenOrde-Powlett(7) 63
(M A Barnes) *mid-div: blnd 4th: nvr on terms* **20/1**

236- **7** *11* **Blue Wing**[197] [3653] 4-11-1 .... RJohnson 58+
(R Flint) *prom: lost pl after 3 out* **20/1**

3 **8** *3* **Western Roots**[27] [1112] 4-10-12 .... LVickers(3) 49
(I W McInnes) *in rr fr 4th* **12/1**

0- **9** *nk* **Humdinger (IRE)**[16] [2501] 5-10-6 .... ONelmes(3) 42
(John A Harris) *in rr fr 4th* **100/1**

10 *9* **Thesaurus**[647] 6-11-2 .... DElsworth 40
(Mrs S J Smith) *chsd ldrs: lost pl appr 3 out: sn bhd* **13/2**[3]

0/0- **P** **Getaway Girl**[461] [485] 7-10-9 .... RThornton —
(O Brennan) *bhd: t.o whn p.u bef 5th* **50/1**

/05- **P** **Seraph**[67] [1253] 5-11-2 82.. NFehily —
(O Brennan) *chsd ldrs: wknd 5th: mstke next: t.o whn p.u bef 2 out* **40/1**

PP0- **P** **Risk Factor**[222] [3389] 6-11-2 .... WHutchinson —
(Ian Williams) *in tch: lost pl after 4th: t.o whn p.u bef 2 out* **80/1**

050- **U** **Glowing Ember**[154] [4560] 5-10-9 88.. PJBrennan 77
(J F Panvert) *hld up: hdwy 5th: 4th and styng on same pce whn stmbld bdly and uns rdr after 2 out* **14/1**

4m 19.9s (3.50) **Going Correction** +0.375s/f (Yiel)
WFA 4 from 5yo+ 15lb **14** Ran SP% **121.6**
Speed ratings: **107,100,100,98,96 90,85,84,84,80 —,—,—,—** CSF £63.57 TOTE £4.10: £1.30, £8.90, £1.60; EX 101.30.

Owner Phil Martin **Bred** J Kennedy **Trained** Temple Bruer, Lincs

FOCUS

A weak novices' hurdle and in the end very much a one horse race with the winner value for more than the official margin.

NOTEBOOK

Smart Boy Prince(IRE) already had it in the bag when getting the second last wrong and, able to take things easily near the line, was full value for 20 lengths. No one could say that he was breaking his duck over hurdles out of turn. *(op 5-2)*

Sharaab(USA), placed twice from 14 starts on the Flat, seemed to be ridden with one eye on getting the trip and he kept on from off the pace to snatch a remote second spot near the line.

Always Esteemed(IRE), rated two stone better than the first two on the level, went in pursuit of the winner but he hung when asked a question and looked anything but keen. *(tchd 13-8 and 2-1 in places)*

Oscar's Lady(IRE), who showed a glimmer of ability in bumpers, sat way off the pace but she was making no inroads at all over the last two. *(op 33-1)*

Rarefied(IRE), rated 12lb higher than the winner on the level, ran without his usual blinkers and had been hung out to dry when almost put out of the contest after the second-last flight.

1341 HENDERSON INSURANCE H'CAP HURDLE (12 hdls) 3m

6:00 (6:00) (Class 3) (0-120,120) 4-Y-O+ **£4,758** (£1,464; £732; £366)

Form				RPR
F00-	1		**Midnight Creek**[16] 2946 7-11-2 **110** ... JimCrowley (G A Swinbank) *hld up: effrt to chse ldrs 8th: 3rd and outpcd 3 out: styd on to ld run-in: all out* **16/1**	112
1221	2	nk	**Romany Prince**[13] 1220 6-11-12 **120** ... RThornton (S Gollings) *trckd ldrs: j.rt and slt ld 3 out: hdd run-in: no ex nr fin* **10/3**[1]	122
0301	3	2 ½	**Tomenoso**[19] 1181 7-11-2 **110** ... DElsworth (Mrs S J Smith) *led to 3rd: led 6th: hdd and bmpd 3 out: nt qckn run-in: hld whn eased nr fin* **8/1**	110+
-211	4	16	**Rift Valley (IRE)**[42] 1016 10-11-8 **116** ... (v) RJohnson (P J Hobbs) *dropped rr and drvn along 5th: t.o and eased 3 out: styd on between last 2: snatched remote 4th nr line* **7/2**[2]	103+
-120	5	½	**September Moon**[37] 1045 7-10-8 **102** ... TJMurphy (Mrs A M Thorpe) *trckd ldrs: hmpd bnd after 5th: hdwy to chse ldrs 3 out: sn outpcd: mstke last: lost 4th nr line* **9/2**[3]	86+
6031	6	5	**Pikestaff (USA)**[33] 1067 7-9-13 **100** ... (t) BenOrde-Powlett(7) (M A Barnes) *chsd ldrs: lost pl after 9th* **12/1**	78
5P14	7	½	**It's Definite (IRE)**[19] 1177 6-11-9 **117** ... (p) APMcCoy (P Bowen) *chsd ldrs: reminders 4th: rdn 8th: lost pl next* **5/1**	94
U4-3	8	16	**Celtic Blaze (IRE)**[36] 397 6-10-6 **100** ... (vt) ARoss (B S Rothwell) *hld up in rr: hdwy to chse ldrs 9th: lost pl after next: sn bhd* **14/1**	67+
323-	9	21	**Esterelle (USA)**[9] 1972 10-10-0 **94** oh1 ... SCurran (H J Manners) *led 3rd to 6th: lost pl 8th: t.o 3 out* **33/1**	34

6m 8.90s (2.10) **Going Correction** +0.375s/f (Yiel) **9** Ran SP% **114.4**

Speed ratings: **111,110,110,104,104 102,102,97,90** CSF £69.67 CT £468.95 TOTE £17.30: £5.30, £1.50, £2.70; EX 58.00.

Owner A Butler **Bred** T E Pocock **Trained** Melsonby, N Yorks

FOCUS

A sound gallop resulting in a decent time for a fair handicap and the first three had it to themselves starting the home turn. The form looks solid enough, rated through the winner and third.

NOTEBOOK

Midnight Creek, back with his former handler and fit after a recent spin on the level, ambled round in the rear for over a circuit. Kept right up to his work, he looked in two minds on the run-in but eventually did just enough. *(op 14-1)*

Romany Prince, on his handicap debut, went on three out and stepped up the pace. He battled hard all the way to the line and was only just denied. He has become a model of consistency. *(op 4-1 tchd 3-1)*

Tomenoso, 4lb higher, was knocked out of the way by the runner-up. He never gave up trying but, with third place the best he could hope for, his rider wisely accepted it near the line. *(op 9-1)*

Rift Valley(IRE), 7lb higher, was unsuited by the well watered track. He took little interest and, after his rider gave up, he decided to stay on with the winning line in sight. *(op 10-3)*

September Moon, who injured her off-fore when last seen five weeks previously, was knocked back on the paddock bend with a circuit to go. Tapped for toe three out, she missed out on third spot near the line. *(op 13-2)*

Pikestaff(USA), 10lb higher, was another unsuited by the false ground. *(op 10-1)*

It's Definite(IRE), back over hurdles, was never happy and the champ was soon pushing and shoving. *(op 9-2)*

1342 CROSSROADS TRUCK & BUS H'CAP CHASE (17 fncs) 3m 1f

6:30 (6:34) (Class 3) (0-120,123) 5-Y-O+ **£5,343** (£1,644; £822; £411)

Form				RPR
2P-6	1		**The Sister**[41] 1026 8-11-0 **108** ... (v) APMcCoy (Jonjo O'Neill) *in tch: mstke 2nd: jnd ldr 4 out: led next: rdn out* **9/2**[3]	126+
2233	2	4	**Seaniethesmuggler (IRE)**[2] 1321 7-9-10 **95** ... (p) WKennedy(5) (S Gollings) *trckd ldrs: led 11th: hdd 3 out: kpt on same pce fr next* **11/4**[1]	107+
4531	3	17	**Swansea Bay**[7] 1267 9-12-1 **123** ... (p) RJohnson (P Bowen) *chsd ldrs: reminders 7th and 10th: outpcd fr 4 out* **9/2**[3]	120+
31	4	dist	**Bushido (IRE)**[19] 1177 6-11-6 **114** ... DElsworth (Mrs S J Smith) *led to 3rd: hit 8th: wknd after 4 out: t.o* **4/1**[2]	91
6UP2	5	12	**Just Muckin Around (IRE)**[18] 1189 9-10-0 **94** oh1 ... BHitchcott (R H Buckler) *chsd ldrs: wknd 4 out: t.o next* **8/1**	—
120-	P		**Barton Hill**[127] 4974 8-10-12 **106** ... (b) NFehily (D P Keane) *in rr: lost tch 12th: t.o whn p.u bef 3 out* **14/1**	—
1460	S		**Panmure (IRE)**[6] 1280 9-10-3 **97** ... JimCrowley (P D Niven) *last but in tch tl slipped bnd and uns rdr after 3rd* **16/1**	—
3/0-	P		**Pauntley Gofa**[473] 280 9-10-11 **105** ... RThornton (J L Spearing) *led 3rd to 11th: wkng whn hit next: bhd whn p.u bef 13th* **28/1**	—

6m 22.4s (-15.00) **Going Correction** -0.50s/f (Good) **8** Ran SP% **110.1**

Speed ratings: **104,102,97,—,— —,—,—** CSF £16.61 CT £53.39 TOTE £5.20: £1.90, £1.20, £1.40; EX 16.20.

Owner Mrs R H Thompson **Bred** Mrs R Thompson **Trained** Cheltenham, Gloucs

FOCUS

A modest contest but an improved performance by the winner, improved since being fitted with the headgear, and the runner-up back at his favourite track.

NOTEBOOK

The Sister, back after a sharpener over hurdles, made hard work of it and gave her supporters a fright, guessing at the last. Improved by the fitting of a visor, she does not look straightforward by any means. *(tchd 4-1)*

Seaniethesmuggler(IRE), making a quick return on his happy hunting ground, had cheekpieces fitted this time. He went on and stepped up the gallop but in the end the winner saw it out much the better. *(op 4-1)*

Swansea Bay, tried in cheepieces again, had to be put about his job and seemed quite happy to let the first two leave him behind. *(op 7-2)*

Bushido(IRE), who still has plenty to prove over fences, stopped to nothing starting the home turn. He will continue to struggle from thius sort of mark. *(tchd 7-2)*

Just Muckin Around(IRE), hard to predict, stopped to nothing in a matter of strides four out. *(op 9-1)*

1343 DIXON JOHNSTONE FINANCIAL SERVICES LTD H'CAP CHASE (14 fncs) 2m 4f

7:00 (7:02) (Class 4) (0-90,90) 5-Y-O+ **£3,343** (£955; £477)

Form				RPR
65PU	1		**Erins Lass (IRE)**[14] 1212 8-11-1 **79** ... WHutchinson (R Dickin) *hld up: hdwy 9th: led appr 3 out: j.rt last 3: styd on wl* **12/1**	96+
54-5	2	7	**Worlaby Dale**[14] 1210 9-11-9 **90** ... (p) LVickers(3) (Mrs S Lamyman) *chsd ldrs: led 10th: hdd and blnd 3 out: kpt on same pce: no ch w wnr* **33/1**	103+
6060	3	6	**Rattina (GER)**[26] 1121 9-10-3 **67** ... PJBrennan (M F Harris) *led to 5th: chsd ldrs: hit 7th: one pce fr 3 out* **22/1**	70
5P-4	4	shd	**Taksina**[84] 632 6-10-1 **65** ... BHitchcott (R H Buckler) *chsd ldrs: upsides gng to 3 out: one pce* **10/1**[3]	68
-061	5	¾	**Toad Hall**[77] 717 11-10-9 **78** ... DFlavin(5) (Mrs L B Normile) *hld up in tch: hdwy and prom 8th: rdn next: 4th and one pce whn blnd 2 out* **12/1**	82+
0253	6	2	**Raise A McGregor**[14] 1203 9-10-12 **76** ... DElsworth (Mrs S J Smith) *chsd ldrs: mstke 5th: outpcd appr 3 out: no threat after* **10/3**[2]	78+
0521	7	5	**Swallow Magic (IRE)**[22] 1150 7-11-2 **87** ... TJDreaper(7) (Ferdy Murphy) *in rr: outpcd 7th: sme hdwy whn blnd 4 out: nvr on terms* **15/8**[1]	84+
PP46	8	5	**Saragann (IRE)**[19] 1180 10-10-6 **73** ... ONelmes(3) (N B King) *chsd ldrs: outpcd appr 3 out: sn btn* **33/1**	63
/11P	9	9	**Bell Rock**[19] 1178 7-11-10 **88** ... RThornton (Mrs T J Hill) *in rr: blnd 2nd: bhd fr 9th* **10/3**[2]	69
324-	10	22	**Noble Colours**[307] 1827 12-9-7 **64** oh3 ... TMessenger(7) (Mrs C J Ikin) *t.k.h: trckd ldrs: led 5th to 10th: sn lost pl and bhd* **40/1**	23
0P-P	P		**Maunby Roller (IRE)**[37] 1044 6-9-9 **66** oh7 ow2 ... (v) SWalsh(7) (K A Morgan) *chsd ldrs: lost pl 5th: bhd whn p.u bef 8th* **100/1**	—

5m 2.60s (-0.10) **Going Correction** -0.50s/f (Good) **11** Ran SP% **119.1**

Speed ratings: **80,77,74,74,74 73,71,69,66,57** — CSF £316.01 CT £8286.56 TOTE £15.70: £4.00, £9.50, £4.90; EX 252.50.

Owner Stratford Members Club **Bred** M Brassil **Trained** Atherstone on Stour, Warwicks

■ Trainer Robin Dickin's 300th career winner.

■ Stewards' Enquiry : B Hitchcott two-day ban: used whip with excessive force (Sep 7,9)

FOCUS

A moderate contest with the first four having failed to win over fences previously and the first three in the betting were well below par. However, the form looks believable with the third to sixth close to their marks.

NOTEBOOK

Erins Lass(IRE), whose two hurdle-race wins were round here, was having just her third start over fences from a mark 10lb lower than her hurdle-race mark. She dived left in front over the last three fences but was never in any danger.

Worlaby Dale, who has yet to win a race of any sort, carried topweight on just his second start over fences. He had handed the advantage to the winner when making a hash of the third last and from there on was never going to be anything but second best. *(op 20-1)*

Rattina(GER), who has not won for over three years, had the headgear left off and is not a certain stayer. *(op 20-1)*

Taksina, a long standing maiden under jumping rules, was bang in contention but, under severe pressure, even lost out on third spot on the line. *(op 15-2)*

Toad Hall, 6lb higher, travelled strongly but was going nowhere when he hit the second last fence hard.

Raise A McGregor has not tasted success for over two years and the watered ground was not exactly in his favour. *(op 4-1)*

Swallow Magic(IRE), 9lb higher, was never on terms and his chance was slim to say the least when he almost demolished the final ditch, four out. The watered ground was not in his favour but that is clutching at straws. *(op 9-4)*

Bell Rock, back on a right-handed track, barged through the second and was out of contention throughout the final circuit. *(op 4-1)*

Maunby Roller(IRE) *Official explanation: trainer said gelding was unsuited by good ground and prefers a firmer surface (op 50-1)*

1344 MISS MARKET RASEN RACECOURSE H'CAP HURDLE (6 hdls 4 omitted) 2m 3f 110y

7:30 (7:35) (Class 4) (0-95,94) 4-Y-O+ **£3,393** (£969; £484)

Form				RPR
P621	1		**Wally Wonder (IRE)**[22] 1148 7-11-12 **94** ... (b) JimCrowley (R Bastiman) *wnt 2nd 4th: led 3f out: hrd rdn: all out* **10/3**[1]	99
600-	2	shd	**Vicky Bee**[236] 3204 6-11-2 **84** ... AThornton (M G Quinlan) *hld up: wnt prom last: swtchd rt 1f out: sn upsides: jst failed* **4/1**[2]	89
2F46	3	5	**Romany Dream**[42] 1012 7-10-5 **76** ... (b) DCrosse(3) (R Dickin) *hld up: hdwy to chse ldrs last: one pce fnl 2f* **4/1**[2]	76
P60P	4	1	**Rose Of York (IRE)**[22] 1153 5-10-4 **72** ... (t) RJohnson (Mrs A M Thorpe) *chsd ldr: led last: hdd 3f out: one pce* **15/2**	71
5405	5	8	**Lone Soldier (FR)**[13] 1223 9-11-5 **94** ... TJDreaper(7) (S B Clark) *hdwy and in tch last: sn wl outpcd* **7/1**[3]	85
005-	6	6	**Everytime**[282] 2298 5-11-1 **83** ... DO'Meara (M W Easterby) *in rr fr 5th: nvr a factor* **33/1**	68
0-52	7	½	**Protocol (IRE)**[14] 1208 11-11-5 **90** ... (t) LVickers(3) (Mrs S Lamyman) *led: clr 4th: hdd and hit last: sn wknd* **7/1**[3]	74
062F	8	1	**Little Tobias (IRE)**[14] 1208 6-11-3 **90** ... (b) DCCostello(5) (J S Wainwright) *outpcd and drvn along 4th: bhd fr next* **9/1**	73
2-04	9	6	**Tyup Pompey (IRE)**[30] 1084 4-10-13 **83** ... JGoldstein (Miss J S Davis) *in rr fr 4th: sn bhd* **20/1**	58
6-4P	10	dist	**Kippour (FR)**[33] 1066 7-11-3 **92** ... CDSharkey(7) (S B Clark) *prom: drvn along 4th: sn lost pl and bhd: t.o and virtually p.u fnl 2f* **25/1**	—

4m 59.4s (9.40) **Going Correction** +0.375s/f (Yiel)

WFA 4 from 5yo+ 15lb **10** Ran SP% **121.4**

Speed ratings: **96,95,93,93,90 87,87,87,84,—** CSF £17.87 CT £56.59 TOTE £4.00: £1.30, £1.60, £2.30; EX 33.50 Place 6 £91.43, Place 5 £79.40.

Owner Richard Long **Bred** T W Nicholson **Trained** Cowthorpe, N Yorks

FOCUS

Due to the setting sun the two flights in the home straight were taken out. Just six instead of the standard ten flights were jumped with a run-in of about three quarters of a mile. By the time the groundstaff had done their work the sun had disappeared over the horizon! The form looks ordinary, with the third the best guide to the level.

NOTEBOOK

Wally Wonder(IRE) made it four wins from his last 11 starts defying a 9lb weight rise in a race that counts for little with only six hurdles jumped and a run-in of about six furlongs. *(tchd 11-4)*

Vicky Bee, absent since January, has changed stables. On her handicap bow, she was switched inside the winner a furlong out and just missed out. With so few hurdles to jump the form must be taken with a pinch of salt. *(op 5-1)*
Romany Dream, a winner of two chases, was back over hurdles from a much lower mark but *jumping hardly entered the equation and in the circumstances it was a highly creditable effort. (tchd 9-2)*
Rose Of York(IRE), pulled up in a claiming hurdle just three weeks earlier, has had plenty of experience on the flat and the lack of hurdles to jump probably helped her. *(op 17-2 tchd 9-1)*
Lone Soldier(FR), 7lb higher than his last selling race success, worked hard to get on to the heels of the leaders at the final flight but with another three quarters of a mile still to run, he must have been wondering what was happening. *(op 13-2 tchd 15-2)*
Tyup Pompey(IRE) *Official explanation: jockey said mare finished distressed*
T/Plt: £210.20 to a £1 stake. Pool: £24,108.05. 83.70 winning tickets. T/Qpdt: £133.20 to a £1 stake. Pool: £2,233.30. 12.40 winning tickets. WG

1345 - 1355a (Foreign Racing) - See Raceform Interactive

[1332]CARTMEL (L-H)
Monday, August 29

OFFICIAL GOING: Good
Wind: Nil Weather: Sunny

1356 E S HARTLEY MARES' ONLY NOVICES' HURDLE (11 hdls) 2m 6f
2:20 (2:20) (Class 4) 4-Y-0+ **£4,075** (£1,254; £627; £313)

Form				RPR
20-1	1		**Ostfanni (IRE)**[5] [1307] 5-11-5 101 GLee (M Todhunter) *trckd ldrs: wnt 2nd 7th: led appr last: sn lft clr: eased heavily run in* **5/6**[1]	113+
0422	2	22	**Bella Liana (IRE)**[5] [1310] 5-10-5 MrSClements[(7)] (J Clements, Ire) *in tch: hdwy appr 3 out: no imp on ldrs: lft poor 2nd bef last: no ch w wnr* **7/2**[2]	76+
00/3	3	4	**Yellow Soil Star (IRE)**[22] [1171] 6-10-12 JPMcNamara (J J Lambe, Ire) *hld up: rdn after 2 out: no imp: wl btn whn blnd last* **33/1**	66
0-36	4	1 1/4	**Lucky Arthur (IRE)**[12] [1235] 4-10-10 82 JAMcCarthy (J G M O'Shea) *hld up: effrt appr 3 out: nvr on terms* **16/1**	63
000-	5	27	**Night Pearl (FR)**[140] [4807] 4-10-10 BHarding (B Storey) *chsd ldr to 7th: wknd appr 3 out: t.o* **100/1**	36
1263	P		**Shady Grey**[49] [961] 7-11-5 100 NFehily (C J Mann) *led: rdn appr 3 out: hdd and p.u bef last: dead* **4/1**[3]	—
4	U		**Glenviews Surlami (IRE)**[16] [1208] 4-10-10 HOliver (R C Guest) *hld up: in last pl whn stmbld and uns rdr 3 out* **33/1**	—

5m 31.1s (-4.90) **Going Correction** -0.40s/f (Good)
WFA 4 from 5yo+ 16lb **7** Ran SP% **109.5**
Speed ratings: **92,84,82,82,72** —,— CSF £3.72 TOTE £1.80: £1.30, £1.90; EX 3.00.
Owner FF Racing Services Partnership XVI **Bred** Mrs Brigitte Schlueter **Trained** Orton, Cumbria

FOCUS
A modest time, 6.4 seconds slower than the later handicap. This ended up a virtual non-event when long-time leader Shady Grey suffered a fatal injury before the last. However, the winner is progressive and rated value for more than the official margin.

NOTEBOOK
Ostfanni(IRE) was always travelling supremely well and won very easily after her only challenger broke down badly before the last. She will now have a double penalty in novice events and will do well to find such weak company again, although she clearly has plenty of ability. It was reported after the race she had a cut to her hind leg. *(op 4-5)*
Bella Liana(IRE) would have been a poor third and only managed to grab second after Shady Grey suffered a fatal injury. *(op 9-2)*
Yellow Soil Star(IRE), trying the trip for the first time, failed to get competitive at any stage.
Lucky Arthur(IRE), stepping up in trip, was another in the field that did not get involved at any stage. On the plus side, she will now be handicapped and should not get a bad mark given her form. *(op 14-1)*
Shady Grey was beaten after making the running when suffering a fatal injury before jumping the last. *(op 28-1)*
Glenviews Surlami(IRE) still appeared to have something to give when coming down three out. Whilst she is clearly very moderate and would not have troubled the winner, she can win a small race at some stage. *(op 28-1)*

1357 BEETHAM ORGANISATION (S) H'CAP HURDLE (8 hdls) 2m 1f 110y
2:55 (2:55) (Class 5) (0-90,85) 4-Y-0+ **£3,104** (£887; £443)

Form				RPR
0-	1		**Diamond Jack (IRE)**[12] [1242] 7-11-2 75 (p) JPMcNamara (J J Lambe, Ire) *prom: led on bit 2 out: drew clr at the last: eased towards fin* **11/2**[3]	82+
06UU	2	6	**Known Maneuver (USA)**[2] [1335] 7-10-3 67 TGreenway[(5)] (M C Chapman) *in tch: hdwy 4 out: led after 3 out to next: sn rdn: no ch w wnr run-in* **25/1**	66+
0-PP	3	17	**Samson Des Galas (FR)**[39] [1047] 7-9-9 64 MissCarolineHurley[(10)] (R Ford) *prom 2nd: mstke 4 out: sn lost pl: n.d after* **8/1**	45
5U4-	4	1	**Free Will**[388] [1128] 8-11-11 84 (p) DElsworth (R C Guest) *in tch: cl up 2 out: lost pl and eased appr last: n.d after* **7/2**[2]	66+
-0P6	5	3	**Mersey Mirage**[24] [1148] 8-10-5 64 (v) KJohnson (R C Guest) *hld up: rdn whn hit 3 out: n.d* **14/1**	41
-4P0	6	2	**Pink Harbour**[16] [1203] 7-10-12 76 (b[1]) StephenJCraine[(5)] (D McCain) *led: hdd after 3 out: wknd next* **7/1**	51
000-	7	17	**Thornton Charlotte**[173] [4257] 4-10-1 64 PAspell[(3)] (B S Rothwell) *cl up: rdn appr 3 out: wknd next* **25/1**	21
-00P	P		**Clouds Of Gold (IRE)**[61] [854] 4-10-9 69 (b[1]) ARoss (J S Wainwright) *hld up: pushed along appr 4 out: t.o whn p.u bef last* **20/1**	—
24	F		**Ball Games**[5] [1308] 7-11-12 85 GLee (James Moffatt) *hld up: hdwy appr 3 out: rdn after next: 3rd and 3 l down whn fell last* **2/1**[1]	87

4m 15.6s (-0.10) **Going Correction** -0.40s/f (Good)
WFA 4 from 7yo+ 15lb **9** Ran SP% **113.7**
Speed ratings: **84,81,73,73,72 71,63**,—,— CSF £121.89 CT £1081.98 TOTE £6.30: £1.70, £6.80, £2.30; EX 103.10.The winner was bought in for 4,000gns.
Owner J P Kearney **Bred** Seamus King **Trained** Dungannon, Co. Tyrone

FOCUS
A pedestrian time, even for a race like this. The form is poor and is unlikely to be reliable, with the runner-up the best guide.

NOTEBOOK
Diamond Jack(IRE) moved easily throughout the race and won with plenty in hand. The race amounts to very little and it remains to be seen whether he will run in this country again. *(op 13-2)*
Known Maneuver(USA), who had unseated his rider the last twice over fences, travelled nicely for a lot of the race but was readily outpaced by the winner. He has yet to win a race under National Hunt rules.
Samson Des Galas(FR) had pulled up on his last two efforts, over further, and at least managed to finish this time. The fact his starting price was fairly short shows how bad the race was. *(op 15-2)*
Free Will, returning after a year off the track, travelled well before weakening after jumping the last. The Stewards enquired into his running as he did not appear to come under sufficient pressure to hang on for a place. The jockey reported the horse needs kidding along and finds nothing off the bridle. He also reported that the horse gurgled, so it would be something of a surprise if he is not fitted with a tongue tie next time. The trainer's representative also reported the horse was blowing hard and been struck into on his near hind, even though he had travelled noticeably wide *throughout the race. Official explanation: jockey said, regarding the apparent tender ride in the closing stages, his orders were to jump off handy and take gelding wide for the better ground, adding that gelding needs to be kidded along as it finds nothing off the bridle, and that it gurgled after jumping the final hurdle; trainer's representative said gelding blew hard after race and had also been struck into on its near hind*
Pink Harbour, fitted with first-time blinkers, made most of the running until passed three from home. She weakened very quickly afterwards despite setting only a sedate pace. *(op 8-1)*
Ball Games would not have beaten the winner when coming down at the last. *(tchd 9-4 in places)*

1358 CHAS KENDALL H'CAP CHASE (18 fncs) 3m 2f
3:30 (3:31) (Class 4) (0-110,104) 5-Y-0+ **£4,680** (£1,440; £720; £360)

Form				RPR
005/	1		**Infini (FR)**[906] [4027] 9-11-5 97 DElsworth (Mrs S J Smith) *led: clr to 12th: lft clr again next: mstke 14th: 12 l ahd last: sn rdn: all out* **4/1**[3]	105+
-356	2	1/2	**Tierkely (IRE)**[24] [1150] 10-10-7 85 JPMcNamara (J J Lambe, Ire) *chsd ldr to 7th: rdn appr 11th: outpcd bef 13th: styd on wl towards fin* **10/3**[2]	88
/PP0	3	1 3/4	**Slyboots (GER)**[20] [1192] 6-11-0 92 NFehily (C J Mann) *chsd ldrs: lost pl 6th: bhd whn hmpd 13th: sn outpcd: styd on towards fin* **7/1**	95+
3140	4	3/4	**Flahive's First**[15] [1221] 11-11-5 104 LHeard[(7)] (D Burchell) *hld up: lft chsng clr ldr 13th tl no ex towards fin* **10/3**[2]	104
3U1F	F		**Good Man Again (IRE)**[32] [1086] 7-11-7 99 ChristianWilliams (Evan Williams) *hld up: hdwy 4th: chsd ldr 7th: cl 2nd whn fell 13th* **5/2**[1]	—

6m 34.9s (-5.70) **Going Correction** -0.40s/f (Good) **5** Ran SP% **107.2**
Speed ratings: **92,91,91,91**,— CSF £16.39 TOTE £5.80: £2.30, £1.90; EX 8.60.
Owner Mrs S Smith **Bred** Henry-Georges Boutin **Trained** High Eldwick, W Yorks

FOCUS
A very modest race and a moderate winning time, with the winner rated value for further, but the form is suspect.

NOTEBOOK
Infini(FR) produced a fine display after such a long time off the track. After setting a quick pace early, he finished pretty tired and would be no sure thing to reproduce this effort next time. *(op 9-2)*
Tierkely(IRE) never looked like being involved in the finish until the favourite departed on the last circuit and the winner weakened late on. His second placing probably amounts to very little *(op 3-1 tchd 7-2)*
Slyboots(GER) was another who benefited from the winner weakening late on, and finished closer than looked likely after being hampered by the faller. This was slightly better effort than his other recent efforts and he is gradually finding form again. *(op 8-1)*
Flahive's First has an excellent record at the track but failed to fire on any cylinder this time. *(op 11-4 tchd 7-2)*
Good Man Again(IRE) is becoming a very frustrating horse to punters. He has more than enough ability to win races - he has already won over fences - but has also developed a bad habit of not finishing races. Almost certainly unlucky not to have won this race given the way things panned out, he remains a dodgy betting proposition while his jumping is so erratic. *(op 9-4 tchd 11-4 in places)*

1359 CUBE247.CO.UK H'CAP CHASE (14 fncs) 2m 5f 110y
4:05 (4:07) (Class 4) (0-100,100) 5-Y-0+ **£3,828** (£1,178; £589; £294)

Form				RPR
6203	1		**Karo De Vindecy (FR)**[29] [1109] 7-10-9 83 GLee (M D Hammond) *in tch: led 9th: in command after: easily* **5/2**[1]	101+
PP40	2	3 1/2	**Pavey Ark (IRE)**[5] [1311] 7-10-0 77 PBuchanan[(3)] (James Moffatt) *in tch: wnt 2nd after 10th: rdn appr 2 out: no ch w wnr fnl 200 yds* **13/2**[3]	89+
-005	3	7	**Ideal Du Bois Beury (FR)**[16] [1203] 9-10-4 81 PAspell[(3)] (P Monteith) *hld up: rdn and hdwy appr 4 out (water): 3rd whn blnd 2 out: wknd last* **9/1**	87+
4151	4	7	**Good Heart (IRE)**[8] [1277] 10-11-10 98 7ex (t) ADobbin (R Ford) *bhd 5th (water): sn niggled along: hdwy appr 9th: wknd bef 4 out (water)* **10/3**[2]	97+
004U	5	dist	**Amptina (IRE)**[8] [1277] 10-10-0 74 oh11 DElsworth (Mrs S J Smith) *prom: rdn after 10th: sn wknd: t.o* **12/1**	—
PP-P	6	24	**Mr Nemo (IRE)**[15] [1219] 9-11-12 100 (p) PMoloney (Evan Williams) *led: hdd 9th: wknd qckly next: t.o* **14/1**	—
0-00	7	2 1/2	**Jo's Sale (IRE)**[39] [1044] 6-10-6 80 ChristianWilliams (Evan Williams) *prom: mstke 3rd: wknd 10th: blnd 3 out: t.o* **9/1**	—
2442	U		**Heather Lad**[2] [1334] 12-11-2 100 MrBenHamilton[(10)] (C Grant) *hld up: mstke 1st: blnd and uns rdr 4th* **7/1**	—

5m 17.7s (-12.80) **Going Correction** -0.40s/f (Good) **8** Ran SP% **111.8**
Speed ratings: **107,105,103,100**,— —,—,— CSF £18.42 CT £121.65 TOTE £3.80: £1.40, £1.60, £2.50; EX 18.80.
Owner Racing Management & Training Ltd **Bred** A Grue **Trained** Middleham, N Yorks

FOCUS
A fair winning time for the grade. The winner has the scope to be quite a bit better than his current mark, while the second was well handicapped on his winning form and the form could work out.

NOTEBOOK
Karo De Vindecy(FR) had shaped a bit better when ridden with more restraint last time, and did the job very nicely after hitting the front six from home. If he can be kept settled during his races, he has the potential to win a few races at this level given his lowly mark. *(op 11-4 tchd 3-1 in places)*
Pavey Ark(IRE) ◆ shaped much better than of recent and connections will presumably look for a race at Sedgefield for him, as he has gone well at that course before. *(op 8-1)*
Ideal Du Bois Beury(FR) was already under some pressure when sloppy jumps at the final three fences sealed his fate. *(op 7-1)*
Good Heart(IRE) kept on for strong pressure and probably found his penalty against him after a good recent spell. *(op 3-1)*
Heather Lad has been in good form this season but did not get any further than the fourth. *(op 6-1)*

1360 DARK HORSE RACING MAIDEN HURDLE (8 hdls) 2m 1f 110y
4:40 (4:40) (Class 4) 4-Y-0+ **£4,270** (£1,314; £657; £328)

Form				RPR
30-0	1		**Dubonai (IRE)**[119] [149] 5-10-11 97 (t) DCCostello[(5)] (G M Moore) *in tch: led run-in: r.o to draw clr towards fin* **8/1**	100+
243	2	6	**Rossclare (IRE)**[50] [942] 5-11-2 JPMcNamara (J J Lambe, Ire) *hld up: hdwy 4th: rdn whn chsng ldrs appr last: wnt 2nd towards fin: nt trble wnr* **7/2**[2]	91
63	3	1 1/2	**Templet (USA)**[6] [1291] 5-11-2 (b) JAMcCarthy (W G Harrison) *chsd ldrs: led 3 out: hdd run-in: wknd towards fin* **25/1**	90

	4	10	**Coronado's Gold (USA)**[66] 4-11-1 ... PMoloney (V Smith) *chsd ldr: ev ch 3 out: rdn whn hmpd appr last: sn wknd* **7/2**[2]	81+
2	5	6	**United Nations**[24] [1149] 4-11-1 ... KRenwick (N Wilson) *in tch: rdn after 2 out: sn wknd* **4/1**[3]	76+
0	6	1 ½	**Teutonic (IRE)**[7] [496] 4-10-5 ... PBuchanan(3) (R F Fisher) *t.k.h: midfield: rdn appr 2 out: wknd bef last* **100/1**	64
350-	7	14	**Mr Twins (ARG)**[142] [4776] 4-10-8 86 ... BenOrde-Powlett(7) (M A Barnes) *midfield: rdn appr 2 out: sn wknd* **33/1**	57
	8	4	**Senor Bond (USA)**[10] 4-11-1 ... FKeniry (P C Haslam) *bolted for half a circ bef s: chsd ldrs tl wknd 2 out* **10/1**	53
360-	9	3 ½	**Obay**[154] [4611] 4-11-1 105 ... ADobbin (M Todhunter) *led: hdd 3 out: rdn whn hit rail appr last: sn wknd* **11/4**[1]	55+
	10	30	**Peggy Naylor**[889] 4-10-5 ... PAspell(3) (Miss J E Foster) *a bhd* **66/1**	13
060	11	30	**Tin Healy's Pass**[103] [415] 5-11-2 ... BHarding (I McMath) *a bhd: t.o* **50/1**	—
00/	P		**La Mago**[58] [4482] 5-10-9 ... KJohnson (Mrs A M Naughton) *a bhd: t.o whn p.u bef 3 out* **100/1**	—
P	F		**Beveller**[31] [1097] 6-11-2 ... ATinkler (W M Brisbourne) *hld up: no imp whn fell 2 out* **100/1**	—
P	P		**Royal Lustre**[7] [1097] 4-11-1 ... (p) ADempsey (M Todhunter) *in tch: wknd after 4 out: t.o whn p.u bef last* **66/1**	—

4m 13.4s (-2.30) **Going Correction** -0.40s/f (Good)
WFA 4 from 5yo+ 15lb **14** Ran SP% **126.0**
Speed ratings: **89,86,85,81,78 77,71,69,68,55 41,—,—,—** CSF £37.81 TOTE £10.80: £3.00, £1.70, £6.00; EX 23.60.
Owner Geoff Jewson **Bred** Paradime Ltd **Trained** Middleham Moor, N Yorks

FOCUS
A moderate winning time for this weak maiden. The winner scored nicely and looks capable of holding his own in lowly handicap company and the runner-up sets the standard.

NOTEBOOK
Dubonai(IRE), having his first run for the stable, put up a pleasing performance to quicken clear of his rivals after the last. He looks more than capable of making his mark in handicap company off his mark when reassessed. *(op 10-1)*

Rossclare(IRE) stalked the pace for much of the race but was slightly outpaced as the principals quickened. He only secured second late on and will probably need further to be at his best. *(tchd 5-1 early)*

Templet(USA) led exiting the far straight but could not hold his final two challengers. He should do better now handicapped and might be worth a try over slightly further, or on a stiff track at this distance.

Coronado's Gold(USA) has not had much racing but looked to enjoy himself until weakening three from home. He looks capable of winning a race over hurdles. *(op 9-2)*

United Nations moved nicely for much of the race but, as had been the case first time over hurdles, he did not seem to truly get home. *(tchd 9-2)*

Teutonic(IRE) did not shape without promise in behind the leaders. *(op 80-1)*

Senor Bond(USA) gave his chance away before the race, bolting with the jockey for almost half the track.

Obay found very little after making the running until three out. He is becoming frustrating over hurdles. *(op 3-1)*

1361 HADWINS AUDI H'CAP HURDLE (11 hdls) 2m 6f
5:15 (5:19) (Class 4) (0-110,108) 4-Y-O+ **£4,550** (£1,400; £700; £350)

Form				RPR
PP-4	1		**Michaels Dream (IRE)**[24] [1151] 6-10-11 **93** ... (b) KRenwick (N Wilson) *prom: led appr 4th: clr bef 3 out tl bef last: clr again run-in: r.o wl* **9/1**	101+
2422	2	11	**Fiddles Music**[15] [1223] 4-10-3 **94** ... LHeard(7) (D Burchell) *hld up: hdwy 4 out: wnt 2nd appr 2 out: sn rdn: one pce run-in* **10/3**[2]	89
0321	3	2 ½	**Slalom (IRE)**[8] [1280] 5-10-11 **98** 7ex ... (p) WKennedy(5) (D Burchell) *hld up: rdn appr 3 out: hdwy bef 2 out: 3rd whn blnd last: one pce after* **5/2**[1]	94+
656P	4	6	**Mister Moussac**[40] [1040] 6-10-0 **85** ... PBuchanan(3) (Miss Kariana Key) *led: hdd appr 4th: remained cl up: rdn bef 2 out: wknd bef last* **10/1**	73
0436	5	6	**Manoubi**[6] [1296] 6-11-8 **104** ... (b) GLee (M Todhunter) *hld up: hdwy appr 4 out: rdn bef 2 out: sn wknd* **9/2**[3]	86
5400	6	hd	**Siegfrieds Night (IRE)**[29] [1111] 4-10-13 **102** ... TGreenway(5) (M C Chapman) *prom tl rdn and wknd after 2 out* **9/1**	82
210/	7	dist	**Backcraft (IRE)**[788] [794] 7-11-12 **108** ... DElsworth (Mrs S J Smith) *trckd ldrs tl wknd after 4 out: t.o* **6/1**	—
4P-6	P		**The Masareti Kid (IRE)**[122] [110] 8-10-0 **82** oh2 ... (v[1]) BHarding (I McMath) *plld hrd: in tch: rdn after 6th: sn wknd: t.o whn p.u bef 3 out* **16/1**	—

5m 24.7s (-11.30) **Going Correction** -0.40s/f (Good)
WFA 4 from 5yo+ 16lb **8** Ran SP% **119.1**
Speed ratings: **104,100,99,96,94 94,—,—** CSF £41.51 CT £100.31 TOTE £11.70: £3.00, £1.10, £1.40; EX 55.10 Place 6 £100.74, Place 5 £86.84.
Owner Mrs Michael John Paver **Bred** M J Paver **Trained** Upper Helmsley, N Yorks

FOCUS
A reasonable low-grade handicap with the placed horses running to form. Michaels Dream benefited from having the blinkers refitted and won nicely.

NOTEBOOK
Michaels Dream(IRE), with the blinkers reapplied after a slightly moody run last time, made just about all the running to win with plenty in hand. This was his first success over timber but he has had plenty of racing, with a record that suggests he does not win very often. *(op 12-1)*

Fiddles Music, stepping up by six furlongs from her last run, has been in fair form this season but could not reel in the leader, despite getting weight. *(tchd 3-1)*

Slalom(IRE), a stablemate of the second, found his penalty enough to stop him and a slight blunder at the last finished his efforts for second. *(op 11-4)*

Mister Moussac is very moderate indeed, and did not achieve a great deal after racing prominently. *(op 12-1)*

Manoubi is becoming very disappointing over hurdles. The slight step up in trip did not help and is probably not well handicapped on his current ability. *(op 5-1)*

Backcraft(IRE), off the track for 788 days, ran very much as though the race was needed and as yet it is not clear what ability he retains. *(op 5-1)*

T/Plt: £139.20 to a £1 stake. Pool: £27,218.60. 142.70 winning tickets. T/Qpdt: £15.80 to a £1 stake. Pool: £1,166.80. 54.60 winning tickets. DO

[670]HUNTINGDON (R-H)
Monday, August 29

OFFICIAL GOING: Good to firm
Wind: Fresh, across Weather: Sunny

1362 SAXONGATE APPEAL CONDITIONAL JOCKEYS' (S) HURDLE (10 hdls) 2m 4f 110y
2:05 (2:06) (Class 5) 4-Y-O+ **£2,240** (£640; £320)

Form				RPR
0656	1		**Shamsan (IRE)**[11] [1248] 8-10-9 89 ... (t) SWalsh(3) (J Joseph) *hld up: hit 7th: hdwy appr 3 out: chsd ldr next: led last: hung lft flat: rdn out* **7/1**[3]	89+
/6P3	2	6	**Brief Decline (IRE)**[20] [1187] 10-10-12 95 ... JamesDavies (J D Frost) *chsd ldrs: led appr 3 out: rdn and hdd last: no ex flat* **9/2**[1]	82
U4	3	shd	**Zeis (IRE)**[6] [1302] 5-10-12 ... (t) ONelmes (Miss J R Gibney) *hld up: hdwy to chse ldr 3 out: styd on same pce fr next* **9/2**[1]	83+
P-4	4	½	**Governor Daniel**[21] [1180] 14-10-7 105 ... DJBoland(5) (Ian Williams) *hld up: rdn 5th: hdwy next: styd on same pce fr 2 out* **9/2**[1]	81
13P-	5	17	**Dunowen (IRE)**[131] [4932] 10-11-3 96 ... MNicolls (J M P Eustace) *hld up: rdn 5th: hdwy 7th: wknd appr 2 out* **7/1**[3]	74+
6-62	6	6	**Relative Hero (IRE)**[37] [273] 5-10-12 75 ... (p) TJPhelan (Miss S J Wilton) *chsd ldrs: rdn and lost pl 6th: wknd after 3 out* **9/1**	58
1-P0	7	2 ½	**Gray Knight (IRE)**[29] [1109] 8-10-7 ... (b[1]) TMessenger(5) (Mrs T J Hill) *mde most to appr 3 out: wknd qckly* **25/1**	56
0F00	8	10	**Mapilut Du Moulin (FR)**[2] [1333] 5-10-12 74 ... (b) GCarenza (C R Dore) *chsd ldr: mstke 3rd: ev ch after 7th: wknd next* **66/1**	46
6000	9	7	**Prince Minata (IRE)**[6] [1297] 10-10-7 72 ... (t) RSpate(5) (M Appleby) *hld up: a in rr* **50/1**	39
P6P5	10	6	**Island Warrior (IRE)**[8] [1279] 10-10-12 66 ... (b) DCrosse (B P J Baugh) *chsd ldrs tl wknd appr 3 out* **40/1**	33
F-40	11	13	**La Lambertine (FR)**[11] [1248] 4-11-1 110 ... (b) TJMalone(3) (M C Pipe) *chsd ldrs: rdn and lost pl 3rd: bhd fr next* **11/2**[2]	26

4m 38.3s (-17.00) **Going Correction** -1.175s/f (Hard)
WFA 4 from 5yo+ 16lb **11** Ran SP% **114.7**
Speed ratings: **85,82,82,82,76 73,72,68,66,64 59** CSF £37.23 TOTE £8.50: £2.10, £2.00, £1.80; EX 50.60.There was no bid for the winner. La Lambertine was claimed by Mr J. L. Flint for £6,000.
Owner Jack Joseph **Bred** Burton Agnes Stud Co Ltd **Trained** Coleshill, Bucks

FOCUS
A very modest time given the conditions, even for a seller, and although the first and third ran to their marks, the form does not look strong.

NOTEBOOK
Shamsan(IRE) had a bit to find with some at the weights, but he was given a good ride by his young pilot and ran out a tidy winner. This was his first success in nearly three years and he may be capable of winning again at this level. *(op 15-2)*
Brief Decline(IRE) has been performing respectably since returning from a spell pointing, but he was no match for the winner. He just held on for second and can win a small race if repeating this effort to this level in future. *Official explanation: vet said gelding pulled up lame (op 4-1)*
Zeis(IRE) is relatively unexposed over hurdles and he kept on well from the rear to challenge for second. A more positive ride in future may see him winning. *(op 11-2)*
Governor Daniel is a solid performer at this level, but he is getting on in years now and he lacked the pace of some when the race really began to heat up. He may be worth a try at three miles.
Dunowen(IRE) was well adrift of the front four and is not in the best of form at present. *(tchd 13-2)*
La Lambertine(FR) ran too bad to be true and there is clearly something not quite right with her at present. *(op 5-1)*

1363 LITE FM 106-108 H'CAP CHASE (12 fncs) 2m 110y
2:40 (2:40) (Class 4) (0-100,97) 5-Y-O+ **£3,311** (£946; £473)

Form				RPR
-401	1		**Jazz Night**[6] [1299] 8-12-1 **97** 7ex ... APMcCoy (S Lycett) *hld up in tch: chsd clr ldr 6th: rdn after 3 out: led flat: hung rt: drvn out* **10/3**[1]	112+
4-P5	2	2	**Karakum**[24] [1155] 6-11-2 **91** ... TMessenger(7) (A J Chamberlain) *led: mstke 3rd: clr next: pckd 2 out: hdd flat: hung rt: styd on same pce* **12/1**	106+
4525	3	9	**Jim Lad**[8] [1275] 5-11-3 **85** ... (p) AThornton (J W Mullins) *mstke 1st: hld up: hdwy 9th: styd on same pce fr 3 out* **11/2**[3]	89
1P-2	4	12	**Meltonian**[83] [674] 8-11-11 **93** ... SCurran (K F Clutterbuck) *chsd ldrs: rdn after 3 out: wkng whn blnd last* **13/2**	90+
P223	5	6	**Kercabellec (FR)**[99] [466] 7-11-4 **93** ... APogson(7) (J R Cornwall) *plld hrd and prom: blnd 2nd: wknd 8th* **10/1**	81+
0100	6	14	**Wardash (GER)**[8] [1272] 5-11-8 **90** ... (vt) TJMurphy (M C Pipe) *chsd ldrs: j. slowly 4th: blnd and wknd 8th* **14/1**	66+
0P-0	P		**Statley Raj (IND)**[11] [1250] 6-11-8 **90** ... RThornton (B G Powell) *p.u after 1st* **10/1**	—
-003	P		**Gentle Beau**[16] [1212] 7-11-12 **94** ... RJohnson (P J Hobbs) *hld up: bhd fr 6th: t.o whn p.u bef 9th* **4/1**[2]	—
0U4	P		**Ela Figura**[11] [1249] 5-9-8 **69** ... (t) RSpate(7) (M Appleby) *hld up: a in rr: hit 3 out: t.o whn p.u bef next* **50/1**	—
0601	F		**Thornton Bridge**[16] [1209] 7-10-0 **75** ... CMStudd(7) (D L Williams) *chsd ldr: blnd 3rd: wknd after 6th: t.o whn fell 3 out* **12/1**	—

3m 58.9s (-10.40) **Going Correction** -0.575s/f (Firm) **10** Ran SP% **114.0**
Speed ratings: **101,100,95,90,87 80,—,—,—,—** CSF £41.11 CT £213.05 TOTE £3.50: £1.30, £4.60, £1.80; EX 75.90.
Owner The Berryman Lycett Experience **Bred** R G Percival **Trained** Naunton, Gloucs

FOCUS
Moderate handicap form, but the in-form Jazz Night made it two wins in six days. The placed horses ran close to their marks and the form looks solid

NOTEBOOK
Jazz Night, up 7lb for his Worcester win, needed all of McCoy's strength to follow up, but he was on top at the line and gave a good performance considering he had plenty of weight to shoulder. He will need to progress again to complete the hat-trick. *(op 7-2)*
Karakum gave the winner most to think about and made him pull out all the stops, but he was left behind close home and remains winless. *(op 9-1)*
Jim Lad plugged on from the rear to claim a place, but was never really in the hunt and may have benefited from a more positive ride. *(op 5-1)*
Meltonian has been running reasonably, but he was struggling from half a mile out and got left behind. *(op 7-1)*
Kercabellec(FR) has never been one to trust and not for the first time he spoiled his chance by racing keenly. He remains winless over fences.
Wardash(GER) was the only other to complete and deserves a mention just for doing so. *(op 16-1)*

Gentle Beau, who came into this as the least exposed, was a real disappointment and never at any stage looked as though he was going to oblige. He is better than this but now has a few questions to answer. *(op 9-2 tchd 5-1 in places)*

1364 BIDWELLS MAIDEN HURDLE (8 hdls) 2m 110y
3:15 (3:17) (Class 4) 4-Y-0+ **£2,681** (£766; £383)

Form RPR
035 **1** **Dyneburg (POL)**[21] [1182] 5-11-2 .... JMMaguire 105+
(T R George) *hld up: nt fluent 5th: hdwy 3 out: led next: drvn out* **25/1**
32 **2** *3* **Screenplay**[9] [911] 4-11-1 .... JGoldstein 101
(Miss Sheena West) *chsd ldrs: led after 5th: rdn and hdd 2 out: styd on same pce flat* **10/3**[2]
00- **3** *1* **Resonance**[219] [3485] 4-10-8 .... CLlewellyn 93
(N A Twiston-Davies) *chsd ldrs: led 3 out: rdn and hdd next: no ex flat* **18/1**
0 **4** *6* **Air Guitar (IRE)**[16] [1206] 5-11-2 .... AThornton 95
(M G Quinlan) *hld up: hdwy appr 3 out: styng on same pce whn hit next* **50/1**
/3U- **5** *½* **Gallant Hero**[466] [434] 6-11-2 .... RJohnson 99+
(P J Hobbs) *led tl after 1st: led appr 4th: hit next: sn hdd: wknd bef last* **7/4**[1]
615/ **6** *4* **Rome (IRE)**[37] [4788] 6-11-2 .... RThornton 91
(G P Enright) *hld up: hdwy appr 4th: wkng whn hit last* **18/1**
50-U **7** *1½* **Glowing Ember**[2] [1340] 5-10-9 88 .... PJBrennan 82
(J F Panvert) *hld up: effrt appr 3 out: wknd bef next* **33/1**
606 **8** *3½* **Scarrabus (IRE)**[21] [1182] 4-11-1 90 .... TJMurphy 85
(B G Powell) *chsd ldrs: lost pl 4th: wknd after 3 out* **66/1**
/03- **9** *14* **Danebank (IRE)**[24] [2846] 5-11-2 103 .... DRDennis 79+
(J Mackie) *chsd ldrs tl wknd appr 2 out* **5/1**[3]
-362 **10** *3½* **Given A Chance**[44] [1014] 4-10-12 97 .... LVickers(3) 67
(Mrs S Lamyman) *led after 1st: hdd appr 4th: wknd 3 out* **14/1**
11 *dist* **Bahamian Breeze**[469] 4-10-8 .... MrJOwen(7) —
(Mrs D Haine) *hld up and a bhd* **66/1**
00/0 **P** **Behan**[50] [943] 6-11-2 .... SCurran —
(A J Chamberlain) *a bhd: t.o whn p.u bef 2 out* **150/1**
6P **P** **Maria Bonita (IRE)**[15] [1222] 4-10-8 .... JamesDavies —
(C N Kellett) *mstke 1st: a bhd: t.o whn p.u bef 2 out* **150/1**
P **Zonic Boom (FR)**[14] 5-11-2 .... APMcCoy —
(Mrs H Dalton) *hld up: hdwy 5th: wknd bef next: bhd whn p.u bef 2 out* **13/2**

3m 36.3s (-19.40) **Going Correction** -1.175s/f (Hard)
WFA 4 from 5yo+ 15lb **14** Ran SP% **119.7**
Speed ratings: **98,96,96,93,93 91,90,88,82,80** —,—,—,— CSF £107.61 TOTE £22.40: £3.90, £1.60, £5.90; EX 138.80.
Owner Mrs Sharon C Nelson **Bred** Sk Moszna Sp Z O O **Trained** Slad, Gloucs

FOCUS
Weak maiden hurdle form but the form looks solid enough with the second the best guide.

NOTEBOOK
Dyneburg(POL) has hardly been setting the world alight since arriving fom abroad, but he pulled a performance from out of nowhere and left all previous efforts behind to run out a clear-cut winner. His jumping is not the sharpest, but he clearly has an engine and he was always holding the placed horses once getting to the lead. It will be interesting to see what mark he gets for handicaps as *there should be more to come. Official explanation: jockey said, regarding the improved form shown, horse appreciated today's faster ground having found it rather "dead" at Southwell, adding that horse jumped better today and after struggling to halfway was able - due to the leaders stopping in front - to get his second wind and run on in the latter stages (op 20-1)*
Screenplay has a consistent profile over hurdles and he ran another solid race, keeping on right the way to the line. He has a race in him and should be winning shortly if found a suitable opportunity. *(op 4-1)*
Resonance had shown very little in two previous tries over hurdles, but she is not all that bad on the Flat and this faster ground helped. She was given a positive ride by Llewellyn and was trying her best right the way to the line so is entitled to win a small race on this evidence, possibly in mares-only company. *(op 16-1)*
Air Guitar(IRE) stepped up on his initial effort over hurdles and was another who appeared to appreciate the faster conditions. *Official explanation: jockey said gelding lost its off fore shoe*
Gallant Hero set the standard and was rightly made favourite, but he did not look happy from some way out faded disappointingly into fifth. He is one to avoid on this evidence. *(tchd 13-8)*
Danebank(IRE) had been heading the right way over hurdles until this, but he now has a few questions to answer after what can only be described as a shocking display. *(op 6-1)*

1365 HUNTS POST BEGINNERS' CHASE (16 fncs) 2m 4f 110y
3:50 (3:51) (Class 4) 5-Y-0+ **£3,740** (£1,151; £575; £287)

Form RPR
20-3 **1** **Savannah Bay**[88] [611] 6-10-12 ....(b) PJBrennan 115+
(P J Hobbs) *mde all: sn clr: drvn out* **7/2**[2]
5342 **2** *1¼* **Resplendent Star (IRE)**[11] [1245] 8-10-12 ....(v) LAspell 112
(Mrs L Wadham) *chsd wnr troughout: rdn 2 out: styd on* **17/2**[3]
1515 **3** *3½* **Chase The Sunset (IRE)**[15] [1220] 7-10-12 102 .... TJMurphy 110+
(Miss H C Knight) *chsd ldrs: rdn appr 2 out: styd on same pce* **7/2**[2]
0-P2 **4** *24* **Dead Mans Dante (IRE)**[24] [1147] 7-10-9 117 .... KJMercer(3) 89+
(Ferdy Murphy) *hld up: mstke 6th: hit 3 out: sn wknd* **7/2**[2]
-P02 **5** *7* **Diamond Joshua (IRE)**[11] [1249] 7-10-9 .... ONelmes(3) 78
(N B King) *hld up: wknd 3 out* **20/1**
3444 **6** *dist* **Blueberry Ice (IRE)**[12] [1232] 7-9-12 98 ....(b[1]) CMStudd(7) —
(B G Powell) *reluctant to s: a t.o* **40/1**
-P22 **P** **Mylo**[12] [1232] 7-10-12 .... APMcCoy —
(Jonjo O'Neill) *chsd ldrs: mstke 5th: wknd 3 out: p.u bef next* **3/1**[1]

4m 52.2s (-13.90) **Going Correction** -0.575s/f (Firm) **7** Ran SP% **109.4**
Speed ratings: **103,102,101,92,89** —,— CSF £28.62 TOTE £5.10: £2.90, £5.00; EX 43.40.
Owner Brian Walsh **Bred** Pegasus Racing Ltd **Trained** Withycombe, Somerset

FOCUS
A fair chase for the time of year and a good winner in Savannah Bay, who appeared to enjoy the challenge of jumping fences. The placed horses suggest the form is solid enough.

NOTEBOOK
Savannah Bay is not without his quirks, but he was a useful hurdler and this first attempt at fences appeared to make a man of him. Given a good, positive ride by Johnson, he had the race won some way out and was always holding the runner-up. This was a fair effort and he has obvious chances of following up under a penalty. *(tchd 4-1 in places)*
Resplendent Star(IRE) had a bit to find with the winner on hurdle ratings and made a promising start to his chasing career. He beat the third well enough and is capable of improving on this first effort over fences. *(op 7-1)*
Chase The Sunset(IRE) has yet to win over fences, but he has run many good races in defeat and may find life easier back in handicaps. *(op 4-1 tchd 9-2 in places)*
Dead Mans Dante(IRE) was given a good, confident ride by Mercer but, having given the third last a whack, his effort petered out. *(op 11-4)*
Mylo, who has been performing consistently well in recent starts, did not look that keen after an early mistake which seemed to knock his enthusiasm. *(op 7-2)*

1366 JANUARYS COMMERCIAL PROPERTY H'CAP HURDLE (8 hdls) 2m 110y
4:25 (4:26) (Class 4) (0-110,107) 4-Y-0+ **£3,346** (£956; £478)

Form RPR
/00- **1** **Mexican Pete**[15] [2221] 5-11-8 103 .... TJMurphy 105+
(A W Carroll) *hld up: hdwy 5th: led 2 out: r.o wl* **9/2**[2]
0543 **2** *1¾* **Artane Boys**[9] [1263] 8-11-12 107 .... APMcCoy 107
(Jonjo O'Neill) *hld up: hdwy 3 out: chsd wnr last: r.o* **10/1**
6342 **3** *3½* **Olimpo (FR)**[8] [1272] 4-10-1 83 .... RJohnson 79
(P J Hobbs) *hld up and bhd: hdwy and n.m.r appr 2 out: styd on same pce flat* **11/4**[1]
005- **4** *3* **Sir Night (IRE)**[25] [3144] 5-10-13 94 .... AThornton 88
(Jedd O'Keeffe) *chsd ldrs: rdn appr 2 out: styd on same pce* **33/1**
2P24 **5** *shd* **Feanor**[15] [1223] 7-11-6 104 ....(t) KJMercer(3) 98+
(Mrs S A Watt) *hld up: hdwy after 2 out: no imp last* **25/1**
-050 **6** *2* **Golden Chalice (IRE)**[23] [824] 6-11-6 106 .... PCO'Neill(5) 97
(Miss E C Lavelle) *hld up: hdwy and hit 5th: wknd last* **11/2**[3]
30-4 **7** *nk* **My Galliano (IRE)**[12] [505] 9-10-12 93 .... JTizzard 85+
(B G Powell) *hld up: plld hrd: hdwy 4th: chsd ldr next: rdn appr 2 out: wknd last* **12/1**
-164 **8** *6* **Tiger Frog (USA)**[28] [695] 6-11-8 103 ....(b) WMarston 89+
(J Mackie) *chsd ldrs: hit 3 out: sn wknd* **8/1**
5F40 **9** *2½* **Forzacurity**[21] [1179] 6-11-0 100 .... LStephens(5) 85+
(M Sheppard) *led: hdd after 1st: led appr 4th: hdd whn hmpd 2 out: sn wknd* **28/1**
5604 **10** *14* **Felix The Fox (NZ)**[12] [1233] 5-10-4 85 .... CLlewellyn 54
(N A Twiston-Davies) *plld hrd: led after 1st: hdd appr 4th: wknd after next* **14/1**
3122 **11** *5* **Keep On Movin' (IRE)**[31] [1097] 4-11-7 103 .... RThornton 66
(N A Callaghan) *prom to 3 out* **15/2**

3m 39.3s (-16.40) **Going Correction** -1.175s/f (Hard)
WFA 4 from 5yo+ 15lb **11** Ran SP% **116.8**
Speed ratings: **91,90,88,87,87 86,85,83,81,75 73** CSF £47.17 CT £146.76 TOTE £4.10: £1.10, £3.90, £2.20; EX 91.20.
Owner First Chance Racing **Bred** First Chance Racing **Trained** Cropthorne, Worcs

FOCUS
An ordinary handicap run in a modest time for the grade, three seconds slower than the maiden hurdle. The form looks a bit suspect with the runner-up the best guide.

NOTEBOOK
Mexican Pete, whose last win under either code came two years ago, was given a confident ride by Murphy and he was delivered with a well-timed run to win going away. He is on a fair mark and can win further races if remaining in this kind of form. *(op 5-1)*
Artane Boys has seemed happier since reverting to hurdles and he put up a good performance in second. He may need a little help from the Handicapper however, as he will remain vulnerable. *(op 8-1)*
Olimpo(FR) continues to frustrate. He is consistent, but finds winning hard and it may take a switch to fences before he wins. *(op 10-3)*
Sir Night(IRE) ran well on this return to hurdles and is well enough weighted to win a lesser contest. *(op 25-1)*
Feanor has not been in the best of form and ran better than the market suggested she would. She is another who may need some help from the Handicapper.

1367 THANK YOU FOR SUPPORTING SAXONGATE H'CAP HURDLE (12 hdls) 3m 2f
5:00 (5:00) (Class 4) (0-95,95) 4-Y-0+ **£2,618** (£748; £374)

Form RPR
UU31 **1** **High Gear (IRE)**[8] [1276] 7-11-12 95 ....(b) APMcCoy 100+
(Jonjo O'Neill) *a.p: led last: drvn out* **2/1**[1]
F52U **2** *1¼* **End Of An Error**[24] [1152] 6-11-4 87 .... RThornton 92+
(A W Carroll) *hld up: outpcd 3 out: r.o flat: nt rch wnr* **5/2**[2]
3-P3 **3** *¾* **Sundawn Lady**[24] [1152] 7-10-2 78 ....(b) MrGTumelty(7) 79
(C P Morlock) *a.p: chsd ldr 6th: led next: hdd appr 3 out: ev ch fr 2 out: no ex flat* **13/2**[3]
F0-P **4** *2* **L'Orage Lady (IRE)**[113] [245] 7-11-5 95 ....(p) PMerrigan(7) 94
(Mrs H Dalton) *led to 5th: mstke 7th: rdn appraoching 2 out: styd on same pce last* **14/1**
604 **5** *nk* **Port Sodrick**[11] [1246] 4-10-3 82 .... KBurke(7) 78
(R H Alner) *hld up: hdwy 5th: led appr 3 out: rdn and hdd last: no ex* **9/1**
3FP0 **6** *21* **Wimbledonian**[9] [1262] 6-11-2 85 .... RJohnson 63
(R T Phillips) *hld up: rdn 5th: wknd after 9th* **9/1**
-P56 **7** *1½* **River Of Fire**[37] [978] 7-10-0 69 oh3 ....(v) JamesDavies 45
(C N Kellett) *chsd ldrs tl wknd appr 3 out* **40/1**
00-P **8** *dist* **Perfect Venue (IRE)**[15] [1218] 12-11-2 85 .... WMarston —
(A J Wilson) *chsd ldr tl led 5th: hdd 7th: wknd appr 2 out* **50/1**
4U4/ **P** **Your My Angel (IRE)**[773] [910] 9-10-0 72 ....(p) KJMercer(3) —
(J A Supple) *hld up: wknd appr 3 out: bhd whn p.u bef next* **10/1**

6m 4.70s (-17.70) **Going Correction** -1.175s/f (Hard)
WFA 4 from 6yo+ 17lb **9** Ran SP% **115.4**
Speed ratings: **80,79,79,78,78 72,71**,—,— CSF £7.69 CT £25.96 TOTE £3.10: £1.30, £1.30, £1.90; EX 6.10 Place 6 £82.74, Place 5 £44.26.
Owner John P McManus **Bred** Oliver And Salome Brennan **Trained** Cheltenham, Gloucs

FOCUS
A low-grade contest and a pedestrian winning time given the conditions. The third and fourth ran close to their marks suggesting the form is reasonably solid.

NOTEBOOK
High Gear(IRE), a quirky sort who was reverting to hurdles having won over fences latest, was given a strong ride by McCoy and won with a bit to spare. He is not one to trust, but is clearly in good form at present. *(op 9-4)*
End Of An Error may have been an unfortunate loser, as a mistake at the fifth last cost her ground and momentum and the winner got first run as a result. She was finishing to good effect and is entitled to win a similar event if remaining in this sort of form. *(tchd 11-4 and 3-1 in places)*
Sundawn Lady remains a maiden and, although running another reasonable race in defeat, remains below a winning standard. *(op 7-1 tchd 6-1)*
L'Orage Lady(IRE) kept plugging on having raced prominently throughout and the first-time cheekpieces appeared to help. *(tchd 16-1)*
Port Sodrick is the one to take from the race. Always travelling strongly, he was well suited by this step up in trip and showed improved form. He was still there with every chance jumping two out, but got a little tired in the final furlong. There is definitely a similar race in him and, as a four-year-old, further improvement is to be expected. *(op 10-1)*
T/Plt: £115.70 to a £1 stake. Pool: £23,218.85. 146.45 winning tickets. T/Qpdt: £16.00 to a £1 stake. Pool: £737.70. 34.00 winning tickets. CR

1368 - 1371a (Foreign Racing) - See Raceform Interactive

GRANVILLE-ST-PAIR-SUR-MER

Sunday, August 28

OFFICIAL GOING: Good to firm

1372a PRIX DE GRANVILLE (CLAIMING CHASE) 2m 5f 110y

2:30 (12:00) 5-Y-0+ **£3,064** (£1,532; £894; £606; £287)

RPR

1 **Nonita (FR)**[277] 5-10-8 (b) AdelineGadras —
(T Civel, France)

2 *nse* **Golly (IRE)**[33] [1073] 9-10-12 CaptLHorner —
(D L Williams) *always in touch, progress 4 out, mistake 3 out, 2nd at last, stayed on strongly flat, just failed*

3 *2* **Cehix Des Mottes (FR)**[172] 8-10-12 (b) JMorel —
(L Viel, France)

4 *10* **Frou Frou Bere (FR)**[3222] 12-10-8 JRoyer —
(P Montfort, France)

5 *4* **Mister Du Bois (FR)** 5-10-12 DBidet —
(L Bellet, France)

6 *3* **Marie Noune (FR)**[471] 5-10-8 CECayeux —
(T Civel, France)

7 *15* **Furioso (FR)**[65] 12-10-8 CGabard —
(T Yon, France)

8 *dist* **Lac Leman (FR)**[172] 6-10-8 (b) RGeraghty —
(X Puleo, France)

P **Or Passion (FR)** 7-10-8 DDelorme —
(L Bellet, France)

P **Saint Shabby (FR)**[659] 9-10-8 MrCHerpin —
(P Chemin, France)

10 Ran

PARI-MUTUEL (including 1 Euro stake): WIN 6.70 (coupled with LacLeman); PL 3.60, 3.30, 3.70; DF 84.90.

Owner Jean-Paul Senechal **Bred** G Vaillant **Trained** France

NOTEBOOK

Golly(IRE) appreciated the quicker ground and only just failed to get up in the dying strides.

1373a PRIX ULTIMATE (CROSS-COUNTRY CHASE) 3m

3:30 (12:00) 5-Y-0+ **£3,404** (£1,702; £993; £674; £319)

RPR

1 **Prudencio (FR)** 7-10-5 DDelorme —
(L Bellet, France)

2 *1 1/2* **Leod'Or (FR)** 6-11-9 JPlouganou —
(P Cottin, France)

3 *4* **Le Maraudeur (FR)**[1854] 9-11-5 DGouard —
(J-C Obellianne, France)

4 *15* **Marine Des Ongrais (FR)** 8-10-5 MrCHerpin —
(P Chemin, France) *fin 5th, plcd 4th*

5 *dist* **Joint Authority (IRE)**[33] [1074] 10-11-7 CaptLHorner —
(D L Williams) *not always fluent, always towards rear, fin 6th, plcd 5th*

6 *10* **Kaola Du Houx (FR)** 7-11-3 TBoivin —
(E Lecoiffier, France) *finished 7th, placed 6th*

D *15* **Marco Bonheur (FR)** 11-10-10 ALeCourtois —
(D Lenfant, France) *fin 4th, disqualified, placed last*

F **July Bleue (FR)** 8-10-10 DBidet —
(L Bellet, France)

F **Blue Chip (FR)** 9-10-5 JZuliani —
(P Quinton, France)

F **Faline Du Rocher (FR)** 8-10-8 CGabard —
(D Lenfant, France)

10 Ran

PARI-MUTUEL: WIN 3.30 (coupled with July Bleue); PL 2.10, 3.20, 2.80;DF 6.30.

Owner Mme L Bellet **Bred** J-P Leseigneur **Trained** France

NOTEBOOK

Joint Authority(IRE) had his ground but he was let down by his jumping.

[1146] SEDGEFIELD (L-H)

Tuesday, August 30

OFFICIAL GOING: Good to firm

The well watered ground was described as 'beautiful' after the first race, but it dried out considerably and ended up 'quick' and taking its toll.

Wind: Moderate; half-behind Weather: Fine and sunny.

1374 GALAXY NORTH EAST ENGLAND MAIDEN HURDLE (10 hdls) 2m 5f 110y

2:00 (2:00) (Class 4) 4-Y-0+ **£2,961** (£846; £423)

Form RPR

1 **High Country (IRE)**[27] 5-11-2 GLee 93+
(M D Hammond) *hld up: wnt prom 5th: led after 3 out: j.lft last 2: 6 l clr whn stmbld landing last and bridle worked loose: coasted home* **9/4**[1]

0545 2 *1 3/4* **Greenfort Brave (IRE)**[3] [1337] 7-10-11 83 PCO'Neill[(5)] 83+
(J J Lambe, Ire) *hld up towards rr: gd hdwy 3 out: wnt 2nd next: styd on run-in: flattered* **13/2**

3/P6 3 *10* **Corries Wood (IRE)**[25] [1151] 6-11-2 JPMcNamara 74+
(J J Lambe, Ire) *led to 3rd: led after 5th: hdd after 3 out: one pce* **11/2**[3]

33 4 *1* **True Temper (IRE)**[6] [1307] 8-10-4 77 DMcGann[(5)] 64
(A M Crow) *chsd ldrs: outpcd appr 2 out* **11/2**[3]

0-40 5 *21* **Coachman (IRE)**[25] [1148] 7-11-2 61 FKeniry 50
(A J Lockwood) *in tch: wl outpcd fr 3 out* **40/1**

00-F 6 *19* **Dover Creek**[58] [891] 5-10-9 JMogford 24
(Miss M E Rowland) *in rr: bhd fr 7th* **100/1**

00P- 7 *26* **Bullies Acre (IRE)**[204] [3740] 5-10-13 PBuchanan[(3)] 5
(F P Murtagh) *chsd ldrs: wknd 3 out* **100/1**

8 *26* **Fighter Command**[50] 4-11-0 ChristianWilliams —
(Evan Williams) *t.k.h: led 3rd tl after 5th: lost pl 3 out: sn bhd* **12/1**

/0-F U **Lanhel (FR)**[7] [1291] 6-10-13 PAspell[(3)] —
(J Wade) *stdd s: wnt prom 5th: blnd and uns rdr 7th* **50/1**

P **Fairly Glorious**[557] 4-10-7 PKinsella[(7)] —
(Mrs K J Tutty) *bhd fr 7th: t.o whn p.u bef 2 out* **100/1**

-42F F **Approaching Land (IRE)**[107] [363] 10-11-2 90 DO'Meara —
(M W Easterby) *sn trcking ldrs: fell 7th* **4/1**[2]

0/U- P **Victoria's Pet**[245] [3039] 9-10-9 EWhillans[(7)] —
(F P Murtagh) *mstkes: sn bhd: t.o after 5th: p.u bef 7th* **100/1**

5m 1.20s (-14.50) **Going Correction** -0.90s/f (Hard)

WFA 4 from 5yo+ 16lb **12** Ran SP% **110.9**

Speed ratings: **90,89,85,85,77 70,61,51,—,— —,—** CSF £16.05 TOTE £2.90: £1.10, £2.10, £2.10; EX 19.10.

Owner Frank Hanson **Bred** Barronstown Stud And Orpendale **Trained** Middleham, N Yorks

FOCUS

A modest winning time, 2.1 seconds slower than the later handicap over the same trip. The winner was value for a good deal more, the 83-rated runner-up sets the standard.

NOTEBOOK

High Country(IRE) ◆, a maiden on the Flat, was well backed to make a winning debut over hurdles. He travelled easily and was in total command when he stumbled on landing at the last, causing the bridle to come loose. With his rider only able to sit still up the hill, he was value for ten lengths. He should win again. *(op 11-4)*

Greenfort Brave(IRE), unplaced in 13 previous starts, is greatly flattered by his proximity to the winner but even so it seemed an improved effort. *(op 6-1)*

Corries Wood(IRE), who has lost time to make up for, found the first two drawing right away from him on the downhill run to the last. *(tchd 5-1 and 6-1)*

True Temper(IRE), rated just 77, is still a maiden now after 17 attempts. *(op 5-1 tchd 9-2)*

Approaching Land(IRE), absent since May, hit the deck for the second time in a row. *(op 7-2)*

1375 JOHN WADE FOR EQUINE FIBRE AND RUBBER (S) H'CAP HURDLE (QUALIFIER) (8 hdls) 2m 1f

2:30 (2:35) (Class 5) (0-90,90) 4-Y-0+ **£2,317** (£662; £331)

Form RPR

04 1 **Possible Gale (IRE)**[11] [1256] 7-11-2 80 (tp) RJohnson 90
(John G Carr, Ire) *chsd ldrs: led 3 out: styd on wl between last 2: rdn rt out* **4/1**[2]

504- 2 *2 1/2* **Dalida**[22] [2868] 4-11-2 81 FKeniry 87
(P C Haslam) *mid-div: hdwy to chse wnr 2 out: kpt on wl: no imp* **16/1**

P022 3 *7* **Valuable (IRE)**[25] [1148] 8-11-3 81 KJohnson 81
(R Johnson) *hld up in rr: hdwy 5th: one pce fr 2 out* **13/2**[3]

0033 4 *3/4* **Fortune's Fool**[25] [1148] 6-10-8 72 ATinkler 71
(I A Brown) *chsd ldrs: kpt on one pce fr 3 out* **9/1**

/000 5 *4* **Maunby Rocker**[47] [988] 5-11-7 85 (p) BHarding 80
(P C Haslam) *in tch: effrt 3 out: one pce* **25/1**

2-PU 6 *3 1/2* **Sandabar**[25] [1148] 12-11-5 83 (t) HOliver 75
(Miss Tracy Waggott) *in tch: jnd ldrs 5th: wknd appr 2 out* **20/1**

F01- 7 *2* **Compton Eagle**[23] [1173] 5-11-0 78 JPMcNamara 70+
(J J Lambe, Ire) *hld up towards rr: hdwy 5th: sn chsng ldrs: wknd appr 2 out* **7/1**

202P 8 *3/4* **Alethea Gee**[17] [1209] 7-10-12 76 GLee 65
(K G Reveley) *hld up: hdwy 5th: rdn and wknd next* **7/2**[1]

0P-P 9 *1 3/4* **Sweet Chariot**[58] [895] 6-10-10 81 PMerrigan[(7)] 68
(Mrs H Dalton) *hld up and bhd: hdwy on ins whn bdly hmpd after 3 out: no ch after* **33/1**

/P-0 10 *16* **Irish Prince (IRE)**[30] [1112] 9-10-5 76 ow4 MrMLurcock[(7)] 47
(Robert Gray) *t.k.h and racd wd: led to 4th: lost pl after next: sn bhd* **100/1**

-000 U **Hidden Smile (USA)**[25] [1156] 8-10-7 71 (t) LAspell —
(F Jordan) *chsd ldrs: stmbld landing after 3rd and uns rdr* **14/1**

1P2P P **Multeen Gunner**[34] [1076] 8-11-5 83 (v[1]) PMoloney —
(Evan Williams) *chsd ldr: led 4th to 3 out: hung lft and wknd qckly: bhd whn p.u bef next* **9/1**

3m 52.6s (-13.90) **Going Correction** -0.90s/f (Hard)

WFA 4 from 5yo+ 15lb **12** Ran SP% **113.1**

Speed ratings: **96,94,91,91,89 87,86,86,85,78 —,—** CSF £58.31 CT £404.15 TOTE £4.80: £1.80, £3.80, £1.60; EX 65.60.There was no bid for the winner

Owner P J Lohan **Bred** Miller's Bloodstock Ltd **Trained** Maynooth, Co. Kildare

FOCUS

A run-of-the-mill seller run at a sound pace. The third and fourth set the standard.

NOTEBOOK

Possible Gale(IRE), a maiden after 16 previous starts, left nothing to chance. He will struggle outside selling company. *(op 5-1)*

Dalida, last seen in action on the Flat three weeks earlier, chased the winner hard but was never going to find enough to get in a blow. *(op 12-1)*

Valuable(IRE), on a long losing run, keeps running respectably without threatening to get his head back in front. *(op 7-1)*

Fortune's Fool, awash with sweat at the start, ran another creditable race but that first success is proving elusive. *(tchd 10-1)*

Maunby Rocker, with the cheekpieces re-fitted, ran better without ever threateing to find sufficient to take a real hand. *(op 20-1)*

Sandabar, clearly none the worse, has not tasted success for over four years now. *(op 11-1)*

Alethea Gee, taken last to post, was not helped by the delay caused the the loose horse. She looks to live on her nerves. *(op 9-2 tchd 10-3)*

Multeen Gunner *Official explanation: jockey said gelding suffered interference, as a result lost its action and was pulled up (op 17-2 tchd 8-1)*

1376 BP CATS NOVICES' H'CAP CHASE (16 fncs) 2m 5f

3:00 (3:02) (Class 4) (0-95,95) 5-Y-0+ **£4,173** (£1,284; £642; £321)

Form RPR

5U3- 1 **Red Flyer (IRE)**[217] [3528] 6-11-4 87 FKeniry 100+
(P C Haslam) *hdwy to chse ldrs 8th: styd on to ld between last 2: kpt on* **12/1**

0613 2 *2* **Now Then Sid**[25] [1150] 6-10-12 84 PBuchanan[(3)] 95
(Mrs S A Watt) *chsd ldrs: outpcd 3 out: styd on between last 2: tk 2nd last 50 yds* **10/3**[1]

3662 3 *3 1/2* **Jupiter Jo**[3] [1335] 9-10-7 76 BHarding 84
(J B Walton) *wnt prom 8th: styd on same pce between last 2* **4/1**[3]

-PP 4 *3/4* **Partners Choice (IRE)**[18] [1199] 8-10-2 71 (t) JamesDavies 79+
(John G Carr, Ire) *hdwy 6th: chsng ldrs 8th: one pce between last 2* **50/1**

5210 5 *3 1/2* **Swallow Magic (IRE)**[3] [1343] 7-11-1 87 KJMercer[(3)] 91+
(Ferdy Murphy) *last whn blnd 1st: wl bhd: hdwy 4 out: styd on: nt rch ldrs* **7/2**[2]

F5P/ 6 *9* **Stallone**[82] [1765] 8-10-10 79 KRenwick 77+
(N Wilson) *trckd ldrs: led on bit 12th: hdd between last 2: wknd bdly: eased run-in* **14/1**

0246 7 *11* **York Rite (AUS)**[9] [1277] 9-10-9 78 (p) HOliver 61
(R C Guest) *lft in ld 1st: hdd 3rd: 2nd whn blnd 10th: lost pl 12th* **14/1**

060P 8 *15* **Northern Echo**[36] [1062] 8-10-2 78 ow3 (p) GThomas[(7)] 46
(K S Thomas) *sn bhd: detached fr 8th* **100/1**

4P2P U **Pristeen Spy**[22] [1178] 8-10-1 70 GLee —
(R Ford) *led tl blnd bdly and uns rdr 1st* **6/1**

The Form Book, Raceform Ltd, Compton, RG20 6NL

5-00 **P** **Oyez (IRE)**25 [1147] 8-11-12 **95** ... JPMcNamara —
(J J Lambe, Ire) *led 3rd: hdd 13th: 4th and wkng whn blnd 3 out: p.u bef next* **40/1**
4P5 **P** **Lost Treasure (IRE)**33 [1089] 8-10-7 **76** ... (vt1) ChristianWilliams —
(Evan Williams) *mstkes: sn lost pl and bhd: reluctant and t.o 8th: p.u bef 2 out* **14/1**

5m 8.00s (-15.40) **Going Correction** -0.90s/f (Hard) **11** Ran SP% **112.7**
Speed ratings: **93,92,90,90,89 85,81,75,—,—** — CSF £51.18 CT £190.65 TOTE £10.40: £2.80, £1.90, £1.30; EX 38.90.
Owner Mrs C Barclay **Bred** Scuderia Cesare Turri **Trained** Middleham, N Yorks

FOCUS
A low-grade handicap rated through the second and third and an unexposed winner over fences.

NOTEBOOK
Red Flyer(IRE), having just his second start over fences, was racing from a mark 4lb lower than his hurdle-race mark. Weak in the market, he seeme to relish this stiffer test of stamina. *(op 7-1)*
Now Then Sid, 9lb higher than his win here two outings ago, kept on after being tapped for toe to take second spot up the final hill. He is well worth a try over three miles. *(op 7-2 tchd 3-1)*
Jupiter Jo, having his second outing in three days, tried hard but looks woefully one paced. *(op 5-1)*
Partners Choice(IRE), unplaced in a dozen previous starts, seemed to show improved form even if it was at a very low level. *(op 40-1)*
Swallow Magic(IRE), 9lb higher than for his win here, was out of contention after almost going at the very first fence. He made up a fair amount of ground from four out and was motoring to some purpose up the final hill. *(tchd 4-1)*
Stallone, fit from the Flat, was coming to fences comparitively late in life. He took it up running away five out, but when headed stopped to nothing and in the end struggled to get up the final hill.

1377 OLIVER WENDELS MEMORIAL NOVICES' HURDLE (8 hdls) 2m 1f
3:30 (3:30) (Class 4) 4-Y-0+ **£3,675** (£1,050; £525)

Form RPR
2601 **1** **Supply And Fix (IRE)**25 [1149] 7-11-5 ... JPMcNamara 98+
(J J Lambe, Ire) *wl away: clr ld to 2nd: qcknd 5th: styd on fr 2 out* **2/1**1
520- **2** *4* **Coming Again (IRE)**145 [4756] 4-10-11 108 ... (t) GLee 83
(D McCain) *chsd wnr: kpt on fr 3 out: no real imp* **9/4**2
034P **3** *1 1/4* **Lofty Leader (IRE)**7 [1291] 6-11-2 99 ... ONelmes(3) 91+
(Mrs H O Graham) *in rr: reminders 3rd: hdwy 3 out: kpt on one pce* **14/1**3
-015 **4** *8* **Two Steps To Go (USA)**25 [1149] 6-10-12 78 ... (t) BenOrde-Powlett(7) 83+
(M A Barnes) *chsd wnr: rdn and wknd 3 out* **16/1**
5-00 **5** *28* **Alfie's Connection**61 [870] 4-10-4 ... PKinsella(7) 46
(K G Reveley) *outpcd 4th: sn lost pl: bhd fr 3 out* **50/1**
P **Dextrous**527 8-10-9 ... ACCoyle(3) —
(P T Midgley) *stdd s: bhd: sme hdwy 5th: wknd next: bhd whn p.u bef 2 out: lame* **100/1**
0-06 **F** **Olympian Time**45 [1014] 5-9-12 ... MissJFoster(7) 40
(Miss J E Foster) *hdwy to chse ldrs 2nd: outpcd 5th: poor 5th whn fell 2 out* **100/1**
411 **P** **Sterling Guarantee (USA)**16 [1223] 7-10-12 104 ... (p) CDSharkey(7) —
(N Wilson) *chsd ldrs: rdn and lost pl 5th: t.o whn p.u lame bef 2 out* **9/4**2

3m 53.9s (-12.60) **Going Correction** -0.90s/f (Hard)
WFA 4 from 5yo+ 15lb **8** Ran SP% **111.4**
Speed ratings: **93,91,90,86,73** —,—,— CSF £6.64 TOTE £2.00: £1.10, £1.30, £2.60; EX 6.60.
Owner D J McCormack **Bred** Michael L Flynn **Trained** Dungannon, Co. Tyrone
■ Stewards' Enquiry : C D Sharkey seven-day ban: failed to pull up a lame horse (Sep 11,18,21-25)

FOCUS
The winner was gifted a big lead at the start and under a tactical ride from the front was never going to be caught. He looked the best horse on the day anyway and is value for more than the official margin.

NOTEBOOK
Supply And Fix(IRE), gifted a useful lead at the start, ambled round in front until picking up the pace at the first down the back. He never looked like being caught and his rider deserves full marks. *(op 7-4 tchd 13-8)*
Coming Again(IRE), absent since suffering an overreach at Taunton in April, looked fighting fit but he could not summon the pace to get in a serious blow at the winner. *(op 11-4)*
Lofty Leader(IRE), pulled up a week earlier on his return from a break, was soon making hard work of it and, though keeping on all the way to the line, never threatened. *(tchd 16-1)*
Two Steps To Go(USA) will continue to struggle outside selling company. *(op 25-1)*
Dextrous *Official explanation: jockey said gelding lost its action (op 66-1)*
Sterling Guarantee(USA) suddenly dropped back at the first down the back straight but was not finally pulled up until two more hurdles had been jumped. It turned out he had damaged a tendon *and the lad was handed a seven-day suspension for not immediately pulling up a lame horse. (op 66-1)*

1378 SEDGEFIELD PADDOCK BOOKMAKERS H'CAP CHASE (21 fncs) 3m 3f
4:00 (4:00) (Class 4) (0-105,90) 5-Y-0+ **£4,647** (£1,430; £715; £357)

Form RPR
1 **Innisfree (IRE)**9 [1285] 7-11-5 **86** ... (tp) KJMercer(3) 99
(John G Carr, Ire) *wnt prom 6th: led 13th: styd on wl fr 2 out* **13/2**
3334 **2** *10* **Tee-Jay (IRE)**45 [1015] 9-11-1 **79** ... GLee 86+
(M D Hammond) *jnd ldrs 13th: chsd wnr fr 15th: hld whn eased sn after last: fin lame* **2/1**1
441 **3** *dist* **Pangeran (USA)**12 [1247] 13-10-9 **76** ... ONelmes(3) —
(N B King) *wnt pominent 13th: outpcd 15th: hung rt and tk poor 3rd run-in: btn 36 l* **7/1**
2F3- **4** *7* **Rag Week (IRE)**356 [1391] 8-11-12 **90** ... ChristianWilliams —
(Evan Williams) *led to 4th: drvn along 13th: sn wknd* **4/1**2
PP-4 **5** *13* **Danteco**36 [1065] 10-10-11 **80** ... DCCostello(5) —
(Miss Kate Milligan) *chsd ldr: led 4th: blnd 12th: hdd next: hit 16th: sn lost tch w 1st 2: mod 3rd whn blnd 3 out: weakend bdly run-in* **12/1**
3562 **P** **Tierkely (IRE)**1 [1358] 10-11-7 **85** ... JPMcNamara —
(J J Lambe, Ire) *in tch: sn pushed along: lost pl and p.u after 13th: lame* **10/1**
-P05 **P** **Iron Express**9 [1276] 9-11-11 **89** ... (p) FKeniry —
(G M Moore) *chsd ldrs: reminders 8th: dropped rr 11th: bhd whn p.u bef 13th* **5/1**3

6m 39.0s (-27.80) **Going Correction** -0.90s/f (Hard) **7** Ran SP% **112.6**
Speed ratings: **105,102,—,—,—** — —,— CSF £20.16 TOTE £7.00: £2.40, £2.10; EX 23.80.
Owner Coleman Country Syndicate **Bred** E J O'Sullivan **Trained** Maynooth, Co. Kildare

FOCUS
A staying handicap 15lb below the race ceiling, not run at a strong pace and in the end the winner left to come clear. a difficult race to rate with the runner-up finishing lame.

NOTEBOOK
Innisfree(IRE), on his first try in handicap company over fences, bounced off the quick ground and in the end was left to come clear up the final hill for a bloodless first success over fences. *(op 8-1)*
Tee-Jay(IRE), still awaiting his first success over fences, travelled marginally better than the winner but he looked held when he went lame soon after the final fence and he was sensibly nursed up the hill. *(op 11-4)*
Pangeran(USA), who took this a year ago from a 5lb higher mark, was 4lb higher than Fontwell *and was left trailing from the first down the back. At his age he should be at home with his feet up! (op 11-2)*
Rag Week(IRE), absent for almost a year, has finished well beaten on both his starts since his crashing fall at Southwell this time last year.
Danteco, not the best of jumpers, seems to have basically lost the plot.
Iron Express looks to have gone right off the boil. *(op 11-2)*
Tierkely(IRE) *Official explanation: jockey said gelding lost its action (op 11-2)*

1379 JOHN SMITH'S EXTRA SMOOTH H'CAP HURDLE (10 hdls) 2m 5f 110y
4:30 (4:31) (Class 4) (0-100,100) 4-Y-0+ **£2,940** (£840; £420)

Form RPR
43-P **1** **Quizzical**23 [1174] 7-10-10 **84** ... (b) JamesDavies 84
(John G Carr, Ire) *chsd ldrs: drvn along 3 out: wnt 2nd next: hrd rdn and styd on to ld post* **11/2**
-P53 **2** *shd* **Miniballist (IRE)**9 [1280] 7-11-7 **95** ... (t) RJohnson 95
(R T Phillips) *hld up: wnt prom 5th: jnd ldr 7th: led next: hdd post* **9/4**1
6-36 **3** *1 1/2* **Litron (IRE)**72 [783] 8-11-12 **100** ... JPMcNamara 99+
(J J Lambe, Ire) *hld up off the pce. stdy hdwy 7th: effrt appr 2 out: styd on run-in: nt rch 1st 2* **4/1**2
-P0P **4** *5* **Northern Rambler (IRE)**46 [998] 8-9-7 **74** ... (p) PKinsella(7) 68
(K G Reveley) *chsd ldrs: one pce fr 3 out* **25/1**
P400 **5** *13* **Nifty Roy**3 [1336] 5-11-2 **90** ... (b1) GLee 71
(K W Hogg) *chsd ldrs: lft in ld after 6th: hdd 3 out: wknd and eased between last 2* **12/1**
0004 **6** *dist* **Nobodysgonanotice (IRE)**3 [1337] 7-10-7 **81** ... ChristianWilliams —
(J J Lambe, Ire) *led to 3rd: drvn along 5th: lost pl next: sn bhd: t.o: btn 36 l* **8/1**
2P33 **P** **Thepubhorse**7 [1294] 5-10-6 **85** ... DCCostello(5) —
(Mrs H O Graham) *led 3rd: p.u after 6th: lame* **5/1**3
PP00 **P** **Dajazar (IRE)**36 [1063] 9-10-1 **82** ... (b) CDSharkey(7) —
(Mrs K Walton) *reluctant: sn drvn along: in tch tl dropped bk 6th: t.o whn p.u after next* **20/1**

4m 59.1s (-16.60) **Going Correction** -0.90s/f (Hard) **8** Ran SP% **110.2**
Speed ratings: **94,93,93,91,86** —,—,— CSF £17.44 CT £50.36 TOTE £6.90: £1.90, £1.40, £1.60; EX 19.10 Place 6 £18.35, Place 5 £10.75.
Owner James Hepburn **Bred** Side Hill Stud **Trained** Maynooth, Co. Kildare
■ A fourth Irish-trained winner on the card, and a first-ever treble for County Kildare trainer John Carr.
■ Stewards' Enquiry : James Davies caution: used whip without giving gelding time to respond

FOCUS
A weak event in which the third ought to have given the first two more to do and the narrow runner-up sets the level. By now the ground had firmed up appreciably.

NOTEBOOK
Quizzical stuck to his task under a most determined ride and put his head in front on the line to record his first win on his 36th attempt. No one could say he did not deserve it. *(op 6-1 tchd 13-2)*
Miniballist(IRE) went on three out and looked to have things under control, only to be caught out right on the line. *(tchd 15-8)*
Litron(IRE), back over hurdles, was given a ride the late Paul Kelleway on Bula would have been proud of. In no hurry at all to pick up the leaders, some solid work up the final hill was much too *late. In defence, he gave the impression that he would have been happier going right-handed. (op 10-3)*
Northern Rambler(IRE), back over hurdles and with the blinkers left off, may have to descend to selling-race company if he is to break his duck. *(op 18-1)*
Nifty Roy, in first-time blinkers, was left in charge but when collared he found nothing at all and in the end simply completed in his own time. *(op 8-1)*
Thepubhorse was bowling along in front enjoying himself when sadly he broke down. *(op 13-2 tchd 7-1)*

T/Plt: £43.10 to a £1 stake. Pool: £34,070.05. 576.75 winning tickets. T/Qpdt: £6.70 to a £1 stake. Pool: £2,222.00. 244.30 winning tickets. WG

1268 NEWTON ABBOT (L-H)
Wednesday, August 31

OFFICIAL GOING: Good to firm (good in places)
First fence in home straight omitted.
Wind: Light becoming moderate; ahead

1380 SMIRNOFF VODKA JUVENILE NOVICES' HURDLE (7 hdls 1 omitted) 2m 1f
2:00 (2:00) (Class 4) 3-Y-0 **£3,057** (£940; £470; £235)

Form RPR
P **1** **Gortumblo**22 [1190] 3-10-12 ... JPMcNamara 76+
(K Bishop) *lft in ld 1st: carried wd and hdd after 4th: styd cl up: led again sn after 3 out: rdn appr next: blunderd last: kpt on* **25/1**
F4 **2** *1 1/2* **Strathtay**33 [1095] 3-10-5 ... TJMurphy 67
(M C Pipe) *trckd wnr 1st: trckd styd in cl tch: wnt 2nd after 3 out: rdn appr next: kpt on but no imp run-in* **7/2**1
23 **3** *20* **The Castilian (FR)**10 [1268] 3-10-12 ... TScudamore 54
(M C Pipe) *in tch: led after 4th: hdd sn after 3 out: wknd qckly* **9/2**2
4 *dist* **Darko Karim**72 3-10-5 ... JamesWhite(7) —
(R J Hodges) *hmpd 1st: hit next: t.o after j. slowly 4th* **7/1**
5 *11* **Moonside**41 3-10-5 ... BHitchcott —
(J A Geake) *hmpd 1st: behin whn j. slowly 3rd: sn t.o* **25/1**
R **Josear**65 3-10-12 ... MBradburne —
(C J Down) *bhd whn ref 2nd* **8/1**
U **Mount Arafat**40 3-10-9 ... DCrosse(3) —
(M Salaman) *led tl wnt bdly lft and uns rdr 1st* **66/1**
U **Spence Appeal (IRE)**28 3-10-7 ... LStephens(5) —
(C Roberts) *wnt lft: blnd and uns rdr 1st* **7/2**1
U **Southern Shore (IRE)**13 3-10-12 ... (t) ChristianWilliams —
(D Burchell) *wnt bdly lft and uns rdr 1st* **11/2**3

4m 13.1s (8.00) **Going Correction** +0.15s/f (Yiel) **9** Ran SP% **110.8**
Speed ratings: **87,86,76,—,—** —,—,—,— CSF £106.52 TOTE £30.60: £7.20, £1.40, £1.20; EX 177.60.
Owner Mrs A E Baker **Bred** London Thoroughbred Services Ltd **Trained** Spaxton, Somerset

FOCUS
A very dramatic juvenile hurdle, with three horses unseating at the first, one refusing at the second, and the loose horses continually causing interference thereafter. As a result, the form is worth next to nothing. The first flight in the back straight was bypassed on the final circuit.

NOTEBOOK
Gortumblo completely lost his way on the Flat after winning over five furlongs on his debut, and was pulled up on his first start over hurdles in a similar event over course and distance but, in a farce of a race, he proved best of the depleted field, despite meeting trouble himself and looking *very awkward going toward the last. Official explanation: trainer's representative said, regarding the improved form shown, gelding was hampered at the first hurdle last time out (op 20-1)*

Strathtay, although running better than at Bangor on her previous start, did not appear to achieve a great deal in second. *(op 9-4)*
The Castilian(FR) was well beaten in third and was seems to be regressing. *(op 4-1 tchd 5-1)*
Darko Karim, a 66-rated maiden on the Flat, can be forgiven this as he was badly hampered during the trouble at the first and could not get back into it thereafter. *(tchd 13-2 and 15-2)*
Moonside, a 35-rated maiden on the Flat, also met with trouble at the first.
Spence Appeal(IRE), twice a winner in selling company on the Flat, was another to get rid of his pilot in the trouble at the first. *(tchd 6-1)*
Josear, a moderate Flat performer whose only success came over a mile on Fibresand, refused at the second and did not offer much hope for the future. *(tchd 6-1)*
Southern Shore(IRE), successful in a mile and a half seller on the Flat for Clive Cox on his previous start, got caught up in the trouble at the first and unseated his rider. *(tchd 6-1)*
Mount Arafat, a 30-rated maiden on the Flat, was very awkward going to the first before unseating and causing lots of trouble in behind. *(tchd 6-1)*

1381 BAILEY'S IRISH CREAM CONDITIONAL JOCKEYS' H'CAP HURDLE (8 hdls) 2m 1f
2:30 (2:30) (Class 4) (0-105,100) 4-Y-0+ **£3,088** (£950; £475; £237)

Form RPR
0453 **1** **Jack Durrance (IRE)**[17] [1223] 5-10-2 **79** EDehdashti(3) 82+
(G A Ham) *hld up: gd hdwy to go 2nd 5th: led appr 2 out: rdn out run-in* **8/1**[3]
2040 **2** *2 ½* **Saorsie**[17] [1223] 7-11-8 **96** WKennedy 95
(J C Fox) *mid-div: hdwy appr 5th: styd on to chse wnr run-in* **9/1**
000/ **3** *2* **Sunset King (USA)**[27] [4489] 5-9-13 **81** JamesWhite(8) 78
(R J Hodges) *hld up: hdwy appr 5th: sn rdn: styd on fr 2 out: nvr nrr* **16/1**
F053 **4** *hd* **Didn't You Know (FR)**[22] [1188] 4-10-7 **85** TJMalone(3) 82+
(M C Pipe) *in tch: hdwy to ld appr 3 out: rdn and hdd bef next: wnt lft bef last: no ex run-in* **7/4**[1]
-000 **5** *½* **Better Moment (IRE)**[26] [1153] 8-11-2 **95** (v) PMerrigan(5) 91
(M C Pipe) *led tl hdd appr 3 out: rdn bef next: nt qckn after* **33/1**
0005 **6** *2* **Twentytwosilver (IRE)**[10] [1272] 5-10-9 **88** KBurke(5) 82
(N J Hawke) *bhd tl hdwy 5th: wnt 3rd after 3 out: stmbld next: sn btn* **9/1**
6434 **7** *nk* **Saby (FR)**[14] [1236] 7-10-5 **82** RStephens(3) 76
(P J Hobbs) *trckd ldrs to 5th: no hdwy after 3 out* **3/1**[2]
4540 **8** *¾* **Simon's Seat (USA)**[31] [1107] 6-10-9 **83** DCrosse 76
(S C Burrough) *trckd ldr to 5th: rdn and no hdwy after* **20/1**
550 **9** *22* **Francolino (FR)**[10] [1280] 12-10-0 **74** oh4 TJPhelan 45
(Dr P Pritchard) *mid-div to 4th: sn bhd* **66/1**
10-0 **10** *19* **Tizi Ouzou (IRE)**[107] [389] 4-11-6 **95** (v) RWalford 46
(M C Pipe) *hld up: reminders after 4th: sn wl bhd* **14/1**
-P50 **11** *6* **Chakra**[17] [1223] 11-11-3 **94** RLucey-Butler(3) 40
(C J Gray) *a struggling in rr* **20/1**

4m 3.60s (-1.50) **Going Correction** +0.15s/f (Yiel)
WFA 4 from 5yo+ 15lb **11** Ran SP% **119.0**
Speed ratings: **109,107,106,106,106 105,105,105,94,85 83** CSF £74.26 CT £1135.04 TOTE £9.20: £3.00, £2.70, £5.80; EX 50.80.
Owner Rose Farm Developments (UK) Ltd **Bred** Atlantic Racing Limited **Trained** Rooks Bridge, Somerset

FOCUS
Not a bad event for the grade and the race is likely to produce winners with the runner-up, fourth and fifth setting a solid standard. The winning time was 9.5 seconds quicker than the juvenile hurdle.

NOTEBOOK
Jack Durrance(IRE) has been threatening to win a race for a while now and he flew in off his feather weight. Always travelling strongly, he had the race won turning for home and, although not streaking clear, he found what was required to win a shade comfortably. There should be more to come from the five-year-old who seems to have found his form again and is worth sticking with in his follow-up bid. *(op 6-1)*
Saorsie came away from the rest to claim a clear second and is on a winning mark. He was giving plenty of weight away to the winner and is one to watch out for next time. *(op 10-1)*
Sunset King(USA) has been running poorly both on the Flat and over hurdles so this keeping-on *third will no doubt have delighted connections. There is a small race in him if building on this. (tchd 20-1)*
Didn't You Know(FR) looked likely to test the winner at one stage, but her effort petered out in the final furlong or so and she was unable to hang on for a place. Her trainer will find her a race eventually. *(op 11-4)*
Better Moment(IRE) ran his best race to date this season and his masterful trainer may be able to coax a win out of him, albeit he is not the best handicapped horse around. *(op 20-1)*
Twentytwosilver(IRE) ran better than his finishing position suggests, but is without a win in nearly three years under both codes and is not doing enough at present to suggest he is about to end that run. *(op 8-1)*
Saby(FR) was the disappointment of the race, failing to run to form on this return to hurdles. *(tchd 7-2)*
Chakra *Official explanation: jockey said gelding had a breathing problem (op 16-1)*

1382 ERNEST & JULIO GALLO NOVICES' CHASE (11 fncs 2 omitted) 2m 110y
3:05 (3:05) (Class 4) 5-Y-0+ **£3,684** (£1,133; £566)

Form RPR
2231 **1** **Whispered Secret (GER)**[10] [1275] 6-11-5 APMcCoy 137+
(M C Pipe) *trckd ldr: led appr 6th: clr fr next: eased run-in: nt extended* **5/6**[1]
006- **2** *14* **Kings Brook**[158] [4561] 5-10-12 DRDennis 115
(Nick Williams) *racd in 3rd tl chsd easy wnr fr 4 out* **10/1**[3]
0331 **3** *12* **Scalloway (IRE)**[11] [1264] 5-11-5 122 CLlewellyn 110
(D J Wintle) *led tl hdd appr 6th: rdn and sn wknd* **11/8**[2]

3m 57.3s (-8.20) **Going Correction** -0.225s/f (Good) **3** Ran SP% **105.8**
Speed ratings: **110,103,97** CSF £5.82 TOTE £1.70; EX 6.90.
Owner David Manasseh Daniel Evans Dan Levine **Bred** G Baron Von Ullmann **Trained** Nicholashayne, Devon

FOCUS
With Scalloway failing to give his true running, this was a straightforward task for Whispered Secret. The winning time was still fair for the class. The runner-up is the best guide to the form.

NOTEBOOK
Whispered Secret(GER), off the mark over fences in a beginners' chase over two miles five at Southwell on his previous start, had his chance made much easier with his main market rival running below form and defied his penalty on this drop in trip in good style. He is going the right way, but will find things tougher from now on. *(op 4-5)*
Kings Brook, a 99-rated maiden over hurdles, made a promising debut over fences. His jumping was slow on occasions, so there is room for improvement and he could do better. *(op 8-1 tchd 11-1)*
Scalloway(IRE), under his penalty, was well below the form he showed to win a reasonable novice event over course and distance on his previous start and now looks a touch flattered by the bare result of that victory. *(op 5-4 tchd 6-4)*

1383 SCHWEPPES "NATIONAL HUNT" NOVICES' HURDLE (9 hdls) 2m 3f
3:35 (3:35) (Class 3) 4-Y-0+ **£4,702** (£1,446; £723; £361)

Form RPR
-212 **1** **Fire Ranger**[22] [1187] 9-10-12 92 RJohnson 100
(J D Frost) *hld up in tch: hdwy to go 2nd after 3 out: rdn to ld appr last: r.o wl* **9/2**
1232 **2** *5* **Don And Gerry (IRE)**[14] [1235] 4-10-3 90 RThornton 87+
(P D Evans) *led tl rdn and hdd appr last: no ex run-in* **5/2**[1]
30-1 **3** *7* **Theocritus (GER)**[45] [1021] 4-11-3 93 AThornton 93
(Nick Williams) *hld up in tch: hdwy to chse ldr 5th tl rdn 3 out: one pce after* **10/3**[2]
2PP- **4** *6* **Smart Mover**[136] [4887] 6-10-12 107 TJMurphy 82
(Miss H C Knight) *trckd ldr to 4th: styd prom tl rdn 3 out: sn btn* **7/2**[3]
-2P1 **5** *12* **Lago D'Oro**[31] [1113] 5-10-9 TJPhelan(3) 70
(Dr P Pritchard) *hld up: wknd 3 out* **10/1**
0-6R **6** *nk* **Aruba Dam (IRE)**[14] [1236] 7-10-5 78 PJBrennan 63
(B G Powell) *hld up in rr: effrt appr 6th: wknd 3 out* **33/1**
7 *nk* **Impatient Lady**[143] 8-10-5 JTizzard 62
(J D Frost) *trckd ldrs to 5th: sn bhd* **16/1**
00- **8** *dist* **Barum Belle**[161] [4519] 5-10-5 ChristianWilliams —
(Mrs S D Williams) *trckd ldrs: wnt 2nd 4th: wknd next: t.o* **25/1**

4m 40.0s (7.00) **Going Correction** +0.15s/f (Yiel) **8** Ran SP% **113.8**
Speed ratings: **91,88,85,83,78 78,78,—** CSF £16.47 TOTE £6.70: £1.70, £2.00, £1.20; EX 10.20.
Owner P A Tylor **Bred** Mrs Richard Stanley **Trained** Scorriton, Devon

FOCUS
A moderate novices' hurdle run in a modest time and runners finished strung out. The form looks somewhat suspect with the third setting the level.

NOTEBOOK
Fire Ranger has been building up a more consistent profile of late and she benefited from a mistake by the runner-up at the second last which allowed her to nip through and in the end win going away. She should continue in good form and would be of interest if pitched into a handicap off this sort of mark. *(op 5-1 tchd 11-2)*
Don And Gerry(IRE) took them along for most of the way and looked set to really ask a question of the eventual winner as they turned for home, but an error at the second last knocked her out of her stride and in the end she had no more to give. *(op 11-4 tchd 3-1 in places)*
Theocritus(GER), 8lb higher than when successful at the course in July, appeared to run his race but was simply unable to give weight to the front two. *(op 7-2 tchd 3-1)*
Smart Mover travelled well but, as with many of his stable companions last season, he appeared to blow up. He will not be at his best until tackling fences. *(op 3-1 tchd 4-1)*

1384 BELL'S SCOTCH WHISKY (S) HURDLE (10 hdls) 2m 6f
4:10 (4:10) (Class 5) 4-7-Y-0 **£2,569** (£734; £367)

Form RPR
00-0 **1** **Miss Skippy**[26] [1153] 6-10-12 97 AThornton 100
(A G Newcombe) *trckd ldr to 4th: wnt 2nd again 6th: led 3 out: in command by next: comf* **14/1**
3432 **2** *7* **Gabor**[13] [1248] 6-11-5 100 (b) RJohnson 101+
(B J Llewellyn) *j.lft thrght: led: clr 3rd: hdd 3 out: sn rdn and no hdwy fr next* **3/1**[2]
0P25 **3** *5* **Mantras (FR)**[22] [1187] 6-10-12 107 TJMurphy 88
(M C Pipe) *a in tch: rdn to go 3rd: appr last: no ch w first 2* **4/1**[3]
500P **4** *2* **Honan (IRE)**[10] [1273] 6-10-12 93 (v) TScudamore 86
(M C Pipe) *bhd: hdwy whn hit 6th: rdn appr 2 out: wknd sn after* **14/1**
/004 **5** *15* **La Maestra (FR)**[10] [1278] 7-10-5 77 (b) PMoloney 64
(Miss L Day) *a bhd: nvr on terms* **66/1**
6243 **6** *6* **Rifleman (IRE)**[6] [1319] 5-10-12 105 (t) APMcCoy 65
(P Bowen) *in tch tl rdn and wknd qckly 3 out* **11/8**[1]
P **Delgany Gale (IRE)**[89] [627] 6-10-12 JTizzard —
(M Hill) *a bhd: t.o whn p.u bef 2 out* **50/1**
P **French Risk (IRE)**[43] 5-10-12 (vt) ChristianWilliams —
(Evan Williams) *a bhd: t.o whn p.u bef 2 out* **14/1**
P-4P **P** **Trefoilalight**[11] [1262] 6-10-1 64 ow1 (p) CHonour(5) —
(J D Frost) *chsd ldrs: wnt 2nd 4th tl wknd fr 6th: taile off whn p.u bef 2 out* **50/1**

5m 19.8s (-0.50) **Going Correction** +0.15s/f (Yiel) **9** Ran SP% **112.5**
Speed ratings: **106,103,101,100,95 93,—,—,—** CSF £55.40 TOTE £13.40: £3.00, £1.10, £1.70; EX 47.80.The winner was bought in for 6,000gns. Gabor was claimed by Mr P. G. Airey for £6,000.
Owner Steadshaw Partnership 4 **Bred** Mrs C R M Pugh **Trained** Yarnscombe, Devon

FOCUS
As is to be expected with sellers, very moderate form, rated through the runner-up, though the winning time was not bad for the type of race.

NOTEBOOK
Miss Skippy, upped to her furthest trip to date and dropped into selling company for the first time, *ran out a convincing winner. On the evidence of this performance, she should get three miles. Official explanation: trainer said, regarding the improved form shown, mare was having her first run for the stable at Worcester last time and she had had training problems, but she came on for that run (op 11-1 tchd 16-1)*
Gabor made his jockey work very hard almost throughout and was no match for the winner late on. He is on a losing run stretching back to May 2004. *(op 7-2)*
Mantras(FR), a beaten favourite in a similar race over two miles three round here on his previous start, ran a little better upped to his furthest trip to date, but he was still well below his official rating (he was best off at the weights) and is not doing enough to warrant following. *(op 9-2 tchd 5-1)*
Honan(IRE), returned to hurdling having been pulled up over fences on his previous start, did not exactly run badly, but he was still well held and is unproven over a trip this far. *(op 10-1 tchd 16-1)*
Rifleman(IRE), with the tongue-tie re-fitted on this drop into selling company, had an obvious chance at the weights but ran no sort of race and was most disappointing. He looks like one to keep avoiding. *(op 6-4)*

1385 20TH ANNIVERSARY OF THE TOM HOLT AND REALITY H'CAP CHASE (17 fncs 3 omitted) 3m 2f 110y
4:40 (4:42) (Class 4) (0-110,106) 5-Y-0+ **£3,675** (£1,130; £565; £282)

Form RPR
2-42 **1** **Southerndown (IRE)**[30] [1122] 12-9-9 **80** oh2 WKennedy(5) 87
(R Lee) *bhd: rdn and hdwy fr 12th: styd on to ld appr last: kpt on wl* **5/2**[2]
1341 **2** *1 ½* **Uncle Mick (IRE)**[22] [1191] 10-11-12 **106** (p) JTizzard 112
(C L Tizzard) *trckd ldrs: outpcd 12th: styd on to go 2nd appr last: no imp run-in* **3/1**[3]
1U-1 **3** *8* **Rolfes Delight**[45] [1022] 13-11-3 **97** APMcCoy 99+
(A E Jones) *hld up: hit 9th: hdwy to go 2nd 12th: bmpd 3 out: led after next: rdn: wknd and hdd appr last* **9/4**[1]
3544 **4** *10* **Cyindien (FR)**[6] [1321] 8-10-0 **80** oh2 (b) PMoloney 72+
(Evan Williams) *trckd ldr: smetimes j.rt: led 5th: clr 7th: hdd after 2 out: sn wknd* **13/2**

-P32 **5** *dist* **Connemara Mist (IRE)**[22] 1191 10-10-0 80 oh8..................(b) JMogford —
(Mrs N S Evans) *j.rt thrght: led tl hdd 5th: wknd after 12th: t.o* **13/2**
6m 39.5s (-3.90) **Going Correction** -0.225s/f (Good) **5** Ran SP% **111.0**
Speed ratings: **96,95,93,90,—** CSF £10.55 TOTE £3.70: £1.30, £2.30; EX 12.70.
Owner Mrs Bill Neale And John Jackson **Bred** Robert Kenny Jnr **Trained** Byton, H'fords

FOCUS
A race made up of slow, exposed performers and Southerndown recorded his first win in over two years. The first and third set the standard for the form.

NOTEBOOK
Southerndown(IRE) is a consistent and genuine performer at this sort of level and he came from off the pace to quickly cut down leader Rolfes Delight. He was always holding runner-up Uncle Mick and this first win in over two years should do his confidence the world of good. He will remain on a winning mark. *(op 7-2)*
Uncle Mick(IRE), a fortunate winner at the course earlier in the month, went in pursuit of the winner in the straight, but was always struggling to get to him and the massive weight concession told. *(tchd 7-2)*
Rolfes Delight has been in great form of late and he looked set to go close when being sent on by McCoy. However, he began to tire on the run down towards the last and ended up fading disappointingly into third. He is 13, and is not getting any better, but there may be another small race in him. *(op 13-8)*
Cyindien(FR) is slow and will continue to find winning hard. *(op 7-1 tchd 8-1)*
Connemara Mist(IRE) has been heading the right way, but this was a poor effort and the way he stopped suggested he may well have gone too quick. *Official explanation: jockey said gelding jumped right and was never travelling* *(op 7-1 tchd 6-1)*

1386 GROLSCH INTERMEDIATE OPEN NATIONAL HUNT FLAT RACE 2m 1f
5:10 (5:10) (Class 6) 4-6-Y-O **£1,813** (£518; £259)

Form				RPR
	1		**Flying Spur (IRE)** 4-11-3 .... TJMurphy (M C Pipe) *trckd ldrs: wnt 2nd 7f out: rdn to ld 2f out: hrd pressed fnl f: jst hld on* **15/8**[1]	91
03	**2**	*hd*	**Dontelldonandgerry**[14] 1237 5-10-11 .... RThornton (P D Evans) *led tl rdn and hdd 2f out: rallied gamely fnl f: jst failed* **2/1**[2]	85
	3	*17*	**Milanshan (IRE)** 5-10-4 .... WPKavanagh[(7)] (J W Mullins) *bhd: wl in rr 1/2-way: styd on past btn horses to go 3rd fnl f: n.d* **7/2**[3]	68
0-00	**4**	*4*	**Hypark (IRE)**[14] 1237 6-10-6 .... LStephens[(5)] (C Roberts) *trckd ldr to 7f out: rdn over 4f out: one pce and wknd over 1f out* **16/1**	64
0	**5**	*2 1/2*	**Its A Classic**[42] 1042 4-11-3 .... JMogford (Mrs N S Evans) *a bhd* **16/1**	68
0	**6**	*23*	**Holmwood Legend**[10] 1274 4-10-10 .... LHeard[(7)] (Miss C J Williams) *trckd ldrs tl wknd over 4f out* **33/1**	45
0	**7**	*3/4*	**Bryans Bach (IRE)**[41] 1048 4-11-3 .... ATinkler (C Tinkler) *in tch: rdn 1/2-way: wknd over 4f out* **8/1**	44

4m 4.10s (-1.20) **Going Correction** +0.15s/f (Yiel) **7** Ran SP% **116.2**
Speed ratings: **108,107,99,98,96 86,85** CSF £6.15 TOTE £3.00: £1.50, £1.30; EX 7.30 Place 6 £86.79, Place 5 £47.18.
Owner Stuart M Mercer **Bred** Mrs Aileen Duggan **Trained** Nicholashayne, Devon

FOCUS
A very creditable winning time for a bumper and the first two came well clear with the second the best guide to the level of the form.

NOTEBOOK
Flying Spur(IRE) , half-brother to winning hurdlers Crookstown Castle and Mattys Joy, got his career off to a perfect start with a game success. He looks as though he will appreciate further over hurdles in time and, while he does not appeal as one of his stable's leading lights, nevertheless remains open to plenty of improvement. *(op 11-8 tchd 2-1)*
Dontelldonandgerry looked like folding when headed in the straight, but responded well to maximum pressure to rally and was only just denied at the finish. She is clearly up to winning a similar race before the ground turns soft, but is vulnerable to an improver. *(op 7-4 tchd 13-8)*
Milanshan(IRE) , strongly backed on course, ran distinctly green through the early stages and was keeping on all too late. She should improve for this debut experience and, as a half-sister to staying chaser Even More, may do better over further when faced with hurdles. *(op 8-1)*
Hypark(IRE) , although made to look very one paced when the race became serious, kept on and is slowly going the right way. She does appear little better than plating class, however. *(op 12-1)*
T/Plt: £54.10 to a £1 stake. Pool: £36,238.70. 488.25 winning tickets. T/Qpdt: £8.60 to a £1 stake. Pool: £2,761.10. 236.10 winning tickets. JS

1387 - 1393a (Foreign Racing) - See Raceform Interactive

SARATOGA (R-H)
Friday, September 2

OFFICIAL GOING: Yielding

1394a NEW YORK TURF WRITERS CUP H'CAP HURDLE (GRADE 1) 2m 3f
6:00 (6:00) 4-Y-0+ **£46,875** (£15,625; £7,813; £3,906; £2,344)

			RPR
1		**Hirapour (IRE)**[314] 1839 9-11-4 .... MOMcCarron (Doug Fout, U.S.A) **5/4**[1]	135
2	*3 3/4*	**Three Carat (USA)** 5-10-0 .... DanielleHodsdon (J E Sheppard, U.S.A) **18/1**	113
3	*1 3/4*	**Party Airs (USA)**[855] 64 6-10-2 .... CyrilMurphy (T Voss, U.S.A) **23/1**	114
4	*1*	**Understood (USA)**[1546] 9-10-4 ....(b) ADobbin (R Valentine, U.S.A) **102/10**	115
5	*8 1/2*	**Paradise's Boss (USA)** 5-11-0 .... XAizpuru (J R S Fisher, U.S.A) **2/1**[2]	116
6	*6 1/4*	**Mulahen**[1529] 10-10-2 .... RMassey (Katherine McKenna, U.S.A) **34/1**	98
7	*2 3/4*	**Praise The Prince (NZ)**[1413] 10-10-8 .... JodyPetty (Sanna Hendriks, U.S.A) **16/1**	101
8	*2*	**Mauritania (USA)** 8-10-0 .... ZMiller (R Valentine, U.S.A) **102/10**	91
P		**Say What You See (IRE)**[36] 1093 5-10-6 .... DBentley (M C Pipe) *led early, close up until 3 out, pulled up before 2 out* **73/10**[3]	—

4m 24.9s **8** Ran SP% **125.9**
PARI-MUTUEL (including $2 stakes): WIN 4.50; PL (1-2) 3.10, 10.40;SHOW (1-2-3) 2.60, 6.20, 7.50; SF 61.00.
Owner Eldon Farm Racing Stable **Bred** His Highness The Aga Khan's Studs S C **Trained** USA

[1218] STRATFORD (L-H)
Saturday, September 3

OFFICIAL GOING: Good (good to firm in places)
Wind: Nil Weather: Warm and sunny

1395 LAFARGE PLASTERBOARD CONDITIONAL JOCKEYS' (S) H'CAP HURDLE (12 hdls) 2m 6f 110y
2:25 (2:25) (Class 5) (0-95,90) 4-Y-0+ **£2,704** (£832; £416; £208)

Form				RPR
5-04	**1**		**Coppermalt (USA)**[29] 1152 7-10-9 73 .... DCrosse (R Curtis) *settled rr: nt fluent 5th: prog 9th: qcknd to ld after 3 out: sn 3l clr: rdn and kpt on wl flat* **11/2**[2]	77+
60P4	**2**	*1 1/2*	**Rose Of York (IRE)**[7] 1344 5-10-8 72 ....(t) WKennedy (Mrs A M Thorpe) *keen in chsng gp: effrt 9th: hit next: sn chsng wnr: hit 2 out: rdn and kpt on: a hld* **13/2**[3]	73+
P003	**3**	*1*	**Cool Dante (IRE)**[17] 1233 10-11-2 88 .... WMcCarthy[(8)] (T R George) *chsd ldrs: rdn and sltly outpcd after 3 out: wnt 3rd next: styd on flat but a hld* **11/2**[2]	88+
-006	**4**	*8*	**Little Villain (IRE)**[36] 1100 7-9-12 67 ....(p) PMerrigan[(5)] (T Wall) *chsd ldr tl 3rd: prom in chsng gp after tl drvn after 3 out: sn btn* **12/1**	58
1-45	**5**	*13*	**Timidjar (IRE)**[74] 801 12-10-12 76 .... ONelmes (Mrs D Thomas) *towards rr: rdn 9th: sn outpcd: n.d fr next* **4/1**[1]	54
0010	**6**	*2*	**Sylcan Express**[62] 891 12-10-7 71 ....(p) TJPhelan (O O'Neill) *bhd: drvn 8th: sn lost tch* **18/1**	47
-40F	**7**	*3*	**Jazz Du Forez (FR)**[20] 1219 8-10-5 69 .... MNicolls (John Allen) *set mod pce tl after 3rd: nt fluent 8th: chsd ldr tl after 3 out: rdn and fnd nil: sn fdd* **16/1**	42
2444	**8**	*2 1/2*	**Dunkerron**[52] 978 8-10-12 79 .... SWalsh[(3)] (J Joseph) *towards rr: nt fluent 5th: rdn bef 9th: sn struggling* **8/1**	50
45/0	**9**	*6*	**Broughton Knows**[11] 1302 8-10-10 79 .... TMessenger[(5)] (Mrs C J Ikin) *bhd: drvn whn nt fluent 8th: sn lost tch* **18/1**	44
3P0-	**P**		**Audiostreetdotcom**[200] 3858 8-11-12 90 ....(p) RStephens (R A Harris) *nvr nr ldrs: rdn 8th: nt keen: t.o whn climbed next: sn p.u* **16/1**	—
20/0	**P**		**Henry's Happiness**[89] 665 6-10-5 74 .... RSpate[(5)] (C P Morlock) *prom in chsng gp: rdn whn hit 8th: 7th and fading whn mstke next: p.u and dismntd 2 out* **12/1**	—
0FU5	**F**		**Lovers Tale**[17] 1233 7-10-12 79 .... EDehdashti[(3)] (G A Ham) *str hold: rushed into ld after 3rd: sn 10l clr: hdd after 3 out: 7l 4th and wkng whn fell heavily last* **33/1**	74

5m 35.5s (5.80) **Going Correction** -0.15s/f (Good) **12** Ran SP% **115.8**
Speed ratings: **83,82,82,79,74 74,73,72,70,— —,—** CSF £40.65 CT £206.51 TOTE £6.30: £2.30, £2.40, £2.00; EX 38.30.There was no bid for the winner.
Owner Collective Dreamers **Bred** Pendley Farm **Trained** Lambourn, Berks

FOCUS
A moderate event of its type and a slow time but the first three were all close to their marks.

NOTEBOOK
Coppermalt(USA), finally getting off the mark, gave his trainer his first winner for more than 500 days. He stays well and a step up to three miles could suit him. *(op 5-1)*
Rose Of York(IRE), reverting to a longer trip, landed awkwardly over the second last and could not bridge the gap to the winner. *(tchd 6-1)*
Cool Dante(IRE) was staying on stoutly after the first two had got away from him at the end of the back straight. *(op 6-1 tchd 5-1)*
Little Villain(IRE) had cheekpieces back in place of the blinkers and ran a slightly more encouraging race.
Timidjar(IRE), who won this event a year ago, could never land a blow after being caught out as the tempo increased early on the final circuit. *(tchd 7-2)*
Jazz Du Forez(FR) showed prominently on this return to hurdles but dropped away from the third last. *(op 20-1)*
Lovers Tale, much too keen, was soon in a clear lead. He was inevitably reeled in and was a beaten fourth when falling at the final flight. *(op 25-1)*

1396 WALLS AND CEILINGS INTERNATIONAL BEGINNERS' CHASE (16 fncs) 2m 5f 110y
3:00 (3:00) (Class 3) 5-Y-0+ **£6,210** (£2,337; £1,200; £581)

Form				RPR
/203	**1**		**Boobee (IRE)**[17] 1232 9-11-0 99 .... ChristianWilliams (Evan Williams) *chsd ldr: clsd to ld 10th: mstke 13th: 4l clr whn hit next: pckd 2 out: in command after: gamely* **10/3**[3]	114+
P22P	**2**	*13*	**Mylo**[5] 1365 7-11-0 .... APMcCoy (Jonjo O'Neill) *settled chsng ldrs: j. slowly 3rd: chsd wnr fr 11th: rdn whn nt fluent 3 out: hld next: blnd last: rdr lost iron briefly* **11/4**[2]	104+
235	**3**	*27*	**Peeyoutwo**[45] 1038 10-11-0 120 .... BHitchcott (Mrs D A Hamer) *chsd ldrs: effrt to dispute 2nd briefly 11th: rdn next: fdd qckly 3 out* **2/1**[1]	74
4F-0	**4**	*14*	**Milligan (FR)**[13] 1270 10-10-11 115 .... TJPhelan[(3)] (Dr P Pritchard) *j. poorly in last: struggling 10th: t.o whn blnd 13th* **12/1**	60
0446	**F**		**Hattington**[48] 1019 7-10-7 .... CPoste[(7)] (M F Harris) *keen: hld up in rr: 7l 5th whn fell 9th* **10/1**	—
50P-	**P**		**Tumbleweed Glen (IRE)**[202] 3842 9-11-0 57 .... JMMaguire (P Kelsall) *towards rr: mstke 5th: hit 7th: last next: t.o 10th: p.u 12th* **50/1**	—
0/0-	**P**		**Kaikovra (IRE)**[485] 191 9-11-0 102 .... TScudamore (M F Harris) *keen: led and sn 6l clr: pressed fr 7th: hdd and mstke 10th: 4th and tiring whn p.u after next* **12/1**	—

5m 7.40s (-7.00) **Going Correction** -0.15s/f (Good) **7** Ran SP% **109.5**
Speed ratings: **106,101,91,86,— —,—** CSF £12.24 TOTE £4.00: £2.00, £1.60; EX 7.90.
Owner Ms H D Oakes **Bred** Mrs F Kingston **Trained** Cowbridge, Vale Of Glamorgan

FOCUS
This was run at a decent pace and could be higher, but has been rated conservatively through the runner-up..

NOTEBOOK
Boobee(IRE), down in trip, was ridden with more restraint before taking up the running early on the final circuit. Pulling away from his pursuers, his jumping became somewhat ragged as he began to tire but he kept going to score by a wide margin. *(op 11-4)*
Mylo returned to form after pulling up last time, but never appeared likely to catch the winner and his chance had already gone when he belted the last. *(tchd 3-1)*
Peeyoutwo was again rather disappointing, and although he has won on a sound surface he might be happier with cut in the ground. *(op 9-4 tchd 5-2 in places)*
Kaikovra(IRE), making his chasing debut following a four-month break, was free to post. Racing keenly and soon clear, he was headed at the tenth and his rider quickly drew stumps. *(op 20-1)*
Hattington, upped in trip and without the visor for this second try over fences, was well in touch when coming down early on the final circuit. *(op 20-1)*

1397 LAFARGE PLASTERBOARD JUVENILE NOVICES' HURDLE (9 hdls) 2m 110y
3:35 (3:35) (Class 3) 3-Y-O

£6,235 (£2,365; £1,182; £537; £268; £161)

Form RPR
2 **1** **Moonfleet (IRE)**[7] [1338] 3-10-5 ..... RJohnson 85
(M F Harris) *cl up: led bef 2 out: rdn and hanging lft after: drvn and all out but hld on wl* **9/1**[3]
2 ¾ **Knightsbridge Hill (IRE)**[45] 3-10-12 ..... RThornton 91
(A King) *settled midfield: effrt after 3 out: rdn bef next: styd on flat to snatch 2nd: encouraging effrt* **20/1**
3 *hd* **Fu Manchu**[126] 3-10-12 ..... APMcCoy 91
(Jonjo O'Neill) *keen chsng ldrs: rdn to go 2nd 2 out: sn flashed tail: j. deliberately last: no imp after and demoted cl home* **6/5**[1]
2F2 **4** 1 ¾ **Shingle Street (IRE)**[13] [1268] 3-10-12 .....(t) AO'Keeffe 89
(Miss Venetia Williams) *pressed ldr tl led after 3 out: hdd bef next: drvn and nt qckn after* **14/1**
1 **5** 2 ½ **Polar Passion**[55] [945] 3-10-11 ..... DRDennis 86
(R Hollinshead) *midfield: effrt after 6th: rdn after 3 out: btn next* **18/1**
6 ¾ **Royal Wedding**[98] 3-10-12 ..... LAspell 86
(N J Gifford) *keen in midfield: effrt 6th: pressed ldrs after 3 out: onepced bef next* **16/1**
1 **7** 3 **Election Seeker (IRE)**[25] [1190] 3-11-4 ..... PHide 89
(G L Moore) *unruly paddock and mounted crse: pressed ldrs: rdn and effrt after 3 out: wknd next* **4/1**[2]
P **8** 1 ¼ **Kerry's Blade (IRE)**[21] [1207] 3-10-12 ..... FKeniry 82
(P C Haslam) *keen chsng ldrs: rdn 5th: outpcd bef 3 out: n.d after* **66/1**
9 *nk* **Voir Dire**[58] 3-10-9 .....(t) RYoung(3) 81
(Mrs P N Dutfield) *in tch: effrt after 6th: handy on outside after 3 out: wkng whn blnd next* **28/1**
3 **10** 3 ½ **Double Kudos (FR)**[14] [1190] 3-10-12 ..... MBatchelor 78
(Jamie Poulton) *mstkes in rr: rdn 5th: lost tch next* **16/1**
11 *shd* **Discomania**[28] 3-10-12 ..... GLee 78
(J A Glover) *keen: prom: led after 3 out: rdn and hdd bef next where mstke whn wkng* **33/1**
4 **12** 24 **Azahara**[7] [1339] 3-10-5 ..... JimCrowley 47
(K G Reveley) *a bhd: rdn and lost bef 6th* **25/1**
13 13 **Pippilongstocking**[69] 3-10-5 ..... TDoyle 34
(E G Bevan) *stdd in last pl: lost tch bef 6th: t.o* **50/1**
14 1 ½ **Tyson Returns**[103] 3-10-12 ..... SCurran 39
(A J Chamberlain) *keen: led tl rdn and hdd after 3 out: fdd rapidly: t.o* **150/1**
4B **P** **Time For You**[13] [1268] 3-10-0 ..... RStephens(5) —
(J M Bradley) *bhd: lost tch bef 6th: t.o and p.u 2 out* **80/1**
P **P** **Don Pasquale**[21] [1201] 3-10-12 .....(t) JMogford —
(J T Stimpson) *plld hrd in rr: rapid hdwy 4th: pressed ldrs briefly 6th: fdd rapidly: t.o and p.u 2 out* **66/1**

4m 6.40s (8.00) **Going Correction** -0.15s/f (Good) **16** Ran SP% **121.0**
Speed ratings: **75,74,74,73,72 72,70,70,70,68 68,57,50,50,—** — CSF £173.62 TOTE £8.70: £2.10, £6.00, £1.40; EX 139.80.
Owner Moonfleet Racing **Bred** Tsarina Stud **Trained** Edgcote, Northants

FOCUS
Quite a competitive juvenile event. The pace was very modest and as a consequence there were plenty in with a chance on the home turn. The final time was pedestrian and the form may be suspect, with the fourth the best guide.

NOTEBOOK
Moonfleet(IRE) raced close to the modest pace and, kicked on rounding the home turn, had built up enough momentum to hold on. This was an improvement on her debut second but the lack of a true gallop casts doubts over the form. *(op 8-1)*
Knightsbridge Hill(IRE) ◆, a disappointing sort for this yard on the Flat, shaped well on his hurdles debut, finishing fast but foiled by the short run-in. He is capable of going one better. *(op 16-1)*
Fu Manchu, previously with David Loder, was third in a Listed race at the Newmarket Guineas meeting when last seen. He showed ability on this hurdles debut and can get off the mark in a truly-run race, but his attitude does not look the best and he might not be one to place too much faith in. *(op 6-4)*
Shingle Street(IRE), equipped with a tongue tie for the first time, ran his race again but his limitations are now apparent.
Polar Passion was found wanting under the penalty for her debut win over track and trip. She gave the impression that she might prefer a stiffer track. *(op 20-1)*
Royal Wedding, regressive on the Flat for David Loder, was not disgraced on this hurdles debut but he is going to have to settle better. *(op 14-1)*
Election Seeker(IRE), who accounted for a couple of subsequent winners at Newton Abbot, gave problems in the preliminaries. He was one of several who could have done with a stronger pace. *(op 7-2 tchd 3-1)*

1398 MCMAHON HOLDINGS H'CAP CHASE (18 fncs) 3m
4:10 (4:10) (Class 3) (0-120,120) 5-Y-O+

£8,961 (£3,399; £1,699; £772; £386; £231)

Form RPR
-41P **1** **On The Outside (IRE)**[73] [812] 6-10-11 **105** .....(t) JTizzard 116+
(S E H Sherwood) *disp 2nd tl led 9th: gng wl after: 4l clr 2 out: rdn flat: kpt on gamely* **20/1**
F5-3 **2** *nk* **Harry's Dream**[48] [1025] 8-11-1 **109** ..... RJohnson 118
(P J Hobbs) *hld up and bhd: effrt 14th: wnt 2nd 3 out: rdn and sltly outpcd next: rallied and kpt on stoutly flat* **11/4**[1]
-042 **3** 4 **Around Before (IRE)**[14] [1267] 8-11-12 **120** .....(t) APMcCoy 125
(Jonjo O'Neill) *prom: wnt 2nd 12th tl rdn and hit 3 out: one pced and wl hld fr next* **4/1**[2]
1114 **4** 2 ½ **Keltic Lord**[25] [1189] 9-11-5 **113** ..... RThornton 119+
(P W Hiatt) *hld up: effrt 14th: wnt 3rd and hit next: sn rdn: nt fluent next: unable qck after* **6/1**
-124 **5** 1 ½ **Luneray (FR)**[55] [946] 6-11-3 **111** .....(t) RWalsh 112
(P F Nicholls) *midfield: hit 6th: nt fluent 15th and qckly lost grnd: kpt on again after 2 out* **9/2**[3]
-54F **6** ½ **Alpine Slave**[20] [1219] 8-10-0 **94** oh4 ..... JamesDavies 95
(N J Gifford) *disp 2nd tl 9th: rdn and outpcd 14th: kpt on steadily but n.d after* **12/1**
4-23 **7** ¾ **Tommy Carson**[34] [1110] 10-10-4 **98** ..... MBatchelor 98
(Jamie Poulton) *hit 1st and 4th: led tl hdd and reminder 9th: rdn after: wknd bef 3 out* **14/1**
5P-1 **8** 2 **Sacrifice**[17] [1236] 10-10-3 **97** ..... MFoley 95
(K Bishop) *effrt to midfield 8th: rdn and outpcd 15th: kpt plugging on fr 2 out* **12/1**
3013 **9** 20 **Super Road Train**[16] [1247] 6-10-1 **95** ow1 .....(b) LAspell 81+
(O Sherwood) *rdn 3rd: continued last and nvr looked happy: hit 11th: lost tch 13th* **11/1**
1-PP **P** **Mustang Molly**[45] [1041] 13-9-11 **96** oh22 ow2 ..... MNicolls(5) —
(P W Hiatt) *keen in rr: mstke 9th: rdn 12th: lost tch next: t.o and p.u 3 out* **50/1**

5m 52.0s (-10.20) **Going Correction** -0.15s/f (Good) **10** Ran SP% **116.2**
Speed ratings: **111,110,109,108,108 108,107,107,100,—** CSF £77.35 CT £275.28 TOTE £22.90: £3.60, £1.50, £2.20; EX 102.80.
Owner Geoffrey Vos **Bred** William O'Keeffe **Trained** Bredenbury, H'fords

FOCUS
Quite a well contested handicap and a fair time for the class, and with those in the frame behind the winner running to their marks, the form looks solid.

NOTEBOOK
On The Outside(IRE) ◆ has reportedly had an operation on her breathing since her last run. Always up with the pace, she scooted clear on the home turn and although her lead was being reduced, scored with a bit up her sleeve. There should be more improvement in her and she can win again. *(op 16-1 tchd 25-1)*
Harry's Dream was fitter for his reappearance. He was slightly outpaced with three to jump, and although he stayed on willingly to close on the winner he is perhaps flattered to have only been beaten a neck. *(op 3-1)*
Around Before(IRE) travelled well for a long way but was in trouble after hitting the third from home. A 4lb rise for a defeat last time took him to a mark 16lb higher than when last successful. *(tchd 9-2 in places)*
Keltic Lord looks held by the Handicapper now, although his jumping let him down when the heat was on. *(op 7-1)*
Luneray(FR), upped in trip, was slightly hampered turning into the back straight on the final circuit and lost further ground at the final ditch. She was keeping on in the latter stages and on this evidence is worth another try over three miles on a sharp track like this. *(tchd 5-1)*
Alpine Slave jumped well enough but, while he has won here, he may be suited by a more galloping track. *(op 10-1)*

1399 WALLS AND CEILINGS INTERNATIONAL H'CAP CHASE (13 fncs) 2m 1f 110y
4:45 (4:45) (Class 3) (0-120,116) 5-Y-**£6,253** (£2,312; £1,156; £525; £262)

Form RPR
146/ **1** **Joey Tribbiani (IRE)**[706] [1465] 8-10-10 **100** ..... WHutchinson 112+
(T Keddy) *hld up towards rr: lost tch w ldng quartet bef 9th: 8l 5th whn mstke 3 out: rdn and lft 4th 2 out: str run to ld flat* **7/1**
-236 **2** 3 **Toi Express (IRE)**[9] [1320] 9-11-5 **116** ..... JamesWhite(7) 125+
(R J Hodges) *settled 3rd: wnt 2nd at 10th: cl up and rdn whn lft in ld 2 out: hdd 100 yds out: immediately outpcd* **9/1**
6323 **3** 5 **Billie John (IRE)**[11] [1295] 10-10-12 **102** ..... JimCrowley 105
(Mrs K Walton) *hld up and towards rr: outpcd bef 9th: passed two rivals flat but nvr able to chal* **4/1**[2]
4P25 **4** ½ **Power Unit**[20] [1218] 10-10-6 **96** .....(p) BHitchcott 103+
(Mrs D A Hamer) *cl up: 4th and ev ch whn cannoned into bk of Deep King 10th: sn drvn: racd awkwardly and lft 3rd and mstke 2 out: no ex* **14/1**
31/0 **5** 1 **Jetowa Du Bois Hue (FR)**[89] [666] 8-10-9 **99** ..... JMMaguire 107+
(T R George) *led tl after 2nd: chsd ldr tl 10th: sn rdn: looked btn whn lft 2nd but hmpd 2 out: eased after* **6/1**[3]
F463 **6** ½ **Romany Dream**[7] [1344] 7-9-12 **91** .....(b) DCrosse(3) 92
(R Dickin) *dwlt: 15l fr ldr 1st: a bhd: struggling 8th: n.d after* **10/1**
3/5- **F** **Montevideo**[492] [76] 5-11-4 **108** ..... APMcCoy —
(Jonjo O'Neill) *midfield: outpcd after 5th: rdn 7th: struggling next: fell 10th* **6/1**[3]
3222 **U** **Deep King (IRE)**[13] [1273] 10-11-1 **108** ..... RYoung(3) 117
(J W Mullins) *led after 2nd: narrow advantage but rdn whn blnd and uns rdr 2 out* **7/2**[1]
PP/5 **P** **Golders Green**[11] [1302] 8-9-11 **92** oh1 ow2 ..... MNicolls(5) —
(P W Hiatt) *t.k.h: mstke 1st: j. slowly 3rd: nvr bttr than midfield: dropped bk last at 8th: t.o and p.u 3 out* **33/1**

4m 6.60s (-5.90) **Going Correction** -0.15s/f (Good) **9** Ran SP% **112.0**
Speed ratings: **107,105,103,103,102 102,—,—,—** CSF £64.09 CT £283.62 TOTE £9.30: £2.60, £2.50, £1.60; EX 103.60.
Owner NewmarketConnections.com **Bred** Peter Henley Jnr **Trained** Newmarket, Suffolk

FOCUS
An ordinary handicap chase and although slightly muddling, it could throw up winners.

NOTEBOOK
Joey Tribbiani(IRE), formerly with Ian Williams, was running for the first time in nearly two years. He was still only fifth over the second last, but the picture then changed and he came with a good run after the last to win going away. *(op 9-1)*
Toi Express(IRE) was 6lb higher than when landing this event a year ago for the Philip Hobbs yard. He looked to have been handed the prize when the leader departed at the second last, but he was cut down quite easily on the run-in. *(op 10-1)*
Billie John(IRE) made late gains without getting into the action and looks worth another try over two and a half miles.
Power Unit had the cheekpieces refitted for this return to fences. He was right in the mix when he was hampered at the fifth from home and could never get back on terms afterwards. *(op 11-1)*
Jetowa Du Bois Hue(FR) had been dropped 5lb since his comeback three months ago from a lengthy absence. Held when left in second place at the penultimate fence, he was hampered by the faller and was quickly back-pedalling. *(op 15-2)*
Romany Dream gave away ground with a slow start and was never nearer than at the end. *(op 9-1)*
Deep King(IRE), just ahead when surviving a mistake at the fifth last, was not so lucky at the tricky penultimate fence. He was under pressure at the time and might have had to settle for place money again. *(tchd 4-1 in places)*
Montevideo, making his chasing debut on his first start since April 2004, was well beaten when coming down. *(tchd 4-1 in places)*

1400 LAFARGE PLASTERBOARD H'CAP HURDLE (9 hdls) 2m 110y
5:15 (5:15) (Class 3) (0-125,123) 4-Y-O+

£6,200 (£2,351; £1,175; £534; £267; £160)

Form RPR
313/ **1** **Black De Bessy (FR)**[499] [4930] 7-10-13 **110** ..... RWalford 121+
(D R C Elsworth) *settled trcking ldrs: wnt 2nd 3 out: led bef next: rdn and a holding rival flat* **6/1**[3]
1133 **2** ½ **Croix De Guerre (IRE)**[11] [1300] 5-11-12 **123** .....(b) RJohnson 130
(P J Hobbs) *settled 3rd: wnt 2nd after 5th: rdn to ld 3 out: hdd bef next: kpt on flat but a hld* **11/4**[1]
-600 **3** 14 **Castle River (USA)**[16] [1250] 6-10-0 **97** oh1 ..... JamesDavies 90
(O O'Neill) *hld up and bhd: effrt 6th: hit next: sn drvn: wknd bef 2 out* **10/1**
/F-0 **4** 3 **Wait For The Will (USA)**[14] [1263] 9-11-1 **112** .....(b) PHide 102
(G L Moore) *hld up midfield: hdwy after 5th: flattered after 3 out: sn rdn and reluctant: wl btn bef next* **7/1**
0-41 **5** 5 **Blue Hawk (IRE)**[80] [762] 8-9-11 **101** ..... JPritchard(7) 86
(R Dickin) *set str pce: led tl after 4th: sn rdn: lost tch 3 out* **7/2**[2]

The Form Book, Raceform Ltd, Compton, RG20 6NL

2-41 **6** *16* **Green Prospect (FR)**[21] [1208] 5-10-13 **110** .... VSlattery 79
(M J McGrath) *pressed ldr tl led after 4th: j.rt next two: hdd 3 out: fdd qckly* **8/1**

4/0- **7** *28* **My Sharp Grey**[474] [397] 6-10-1 **98** .... OMcPhail 39
(J Gallagher) *bhd: struggling 5th: t.o 3 out* **33/1**

P/F- **P** **Per Amore (IRE)**[475] [380] 7-10-13 **110** .... SThomas —
(Miss H C Knight) *bhd: lost tch after 4th: t.o next: p.u 2 out* **11/1**

0/U- **P** **Private Benjamin**[42] [1440] 5-10-6 **103** .... MBatchelor —
(Jamie Poulton) *midfield: wknd bef 6th: t.o and p.u 2 out* **12/1**

3m 51.6s (-6.80) **Going Correction** -0.15s/f (Good) 9 Ran SP% **114.8**
Speed ratings: **110,109,103,101,99 91,78,—,—** CSF £23.32 CT £162.59 TOTE £7.40: £2.00, £1.40, £3.00; EX 28.20.

Owner Mrs Derek Fletcher **Bred** A D'Agnese **Trained** Newmarket, Suffolk

FOCUS
A modest handicap but the winner was value for further. It was run at a good pace and the first two pulled a long way clear, and the form could be rated higher.

NOTEBOOK
Black De Bessy(FR), returning from a 17-month absence, was running over hurdles for the first time in Britain but he has won over them in France. After taking the lead going best on the home turn, he was steadied into the last two flights but was always holding the favourite. *(tchd 7-1)*
Croix De Guerre(IRE) is a consistent sort these days and ran his race again, worrying away at the winner from the second last without being able to get by. *(op 3-1 tchd 10-3 and 7-2 in a place)*
Castle River(USA) ran his best race for some time, but after moving into third place on the home turn he was soon left well behind by the principals. *(tchd 9-1)*
Wait For The Will(USA) travelled better this time, but found little once coming off the bridle and remains one to be wary of. *(op 11-2 tchd 8-1)*
Blue Hawk(IRE), 7lb higher for his win at Worcester, made the running at a good clip but did not last much beyond halfway. *(op 4-1 tchd 9-2 and 10-3)*
Green Prospect(FR), sold out of Martin Pipe's yard after winning a seller, probably prefers easier ground. Not for the first time he showed a tendency to jump out to his right. *(op 9-1)*

1401 WALLS AND CEILINGS INTERNATIONAL STANDARD OPEN NATIONAL HUNT FLAT RACE 2m 110y
5:45 (5:47) (Class 6) 4-6-Y-O **£3,108** (£1,149; £574; £261; £130)

Form RPR

1 **Finns Cross (IRE)**[106] [444] 6-11-4 .... JimCrowley 92
(K G Reveley) *mde all: rdn 2f out: sn forged clr: styd on* **11/2**[3]

2 *6* **Granite Man (IRE)**[135] [4951] 5-11-4 .... APMcCoy 86
(Jonjo O'Neill) *w wnr tl rdn 4f out: rn green ent st: wl outpcd fnl 2f* **1/1**[1]

3 *8* **Opera Singer** 4-11-1 .... PWhelan(3) 78
(R A Fahey) *keen trcking ldng pair: rdn 4f out: wknd over 2f out* **2/1**[2]

0 **4** *10* **Cresswell Willow (IRE)**[9] [1323] 5-10-11 .... RJohnson 61
(W K Goldsworthy) *midfield: pushed along and struggling 7f out* **14/1**

6 **5** *11* **The Boobi (IRE)**[73] [816] 4-10-11 .... JMogford 50
(Miss M E Rowland) *rdn and lost tch 1/2-way: remote through fnl 6f* **20/1**

6 *26* **Fertility** 5-10-11 .... OMcPhail 24
(B J Llewellyn) *lost tch 1/2-way: t.o fnl 6f* **16/1**

0 **P** **Dovers Venture**[17] [1237] 4-10-6 .... MNicolls(5) —
(Miss M E Rowland) *rdn 1/2-way: sn t.o: p.u and dismntd 6f out* **33/1**

3m 53.7s (-13.00) **Going Correction** -0.15s/f (Good) 7 Ran SP% **119.0**
Speed ratings: **94,91,87,82,77 65,—** CSF £12.13 TOTE £6.70: £3.20, £1.60; EX 11.50 Place 6 £57.46, Place 5 £25.16.

Owner James P O'Keeffe **Bred** William O'Keeffe **Trained** Lingdale, N Yorks

FOCUS
An ordinary bumper in which the pace only lifted from halfway. The fourth and fifth set the standard for the form.

NOTEBOOK
Finns Cross(IRE) did not show a great deal in three runs in Ireland. Staying on too strongly for the favourite from the home turn, he looks to have plenty of stamina. *(op 4-1 tchd 6-1)*
Granite Man(IRE) was third at Gowran in April on his only start for Timothy Doyle. On this faster ground, he was put in his place from the home turn. *(op 5-6 tchd 11-8)*
Opera Singer, whose dam won at up to two miles on the Flat and was a winning hurdler, was well supported on this debut. He never really settled behind the leading pair and was soon in trouble once brought under pressure. *(op 7-2 tchd 7-4)*
Cresswell Willow(IRE) was merely best of the rest.
T/Plt: £105.40 to a £1 stake. Pool: £35,954.40. 248.85 winning tickets. T/Qpdt: £35.40 to a £1 stake. Pool: £2,722.00. 56.80 winning tickets. IM

1402 - 1403a (Foreign Racing) - See Raceform Interactive

1245 FONTWELL (L-H)
Sunday, September 4

OFFICIAL GOING: Good to firm
There was only one steeplechase on the card.
Wind: Almost nil Weather: Sunny and warm

1404 BETTERWARE JUVENILE NOVICES' HURDLE (9 hdls) 2m 2f 110y
2:35 (2:35) (Class 4) 3-Y-O **£3,421** (£1,052; £526; £263)

Form RPR

1 **1** **Wembury Point (IRE)**[30] [1146] 3-11-5 .... TJMurphy 94+
(B G Powell) *hld up in tch: drvn to press ldrs appr last: swtchd rt run-in: styd on wl to ld fnl 50 yds* **7/2**[3]

42 **2** *1 1/2* **Compton Quay**[22] [1207] 3-10-12 .... RThornton 83
(A King) *trckd ldrs: j.lft 1st: drvn to slt ld run-in: hdd and no ex fnl 50 yds* **11/4**[1]

25 **3** *1/2* **Millquista D'Or**[22] [1201] 3-10-5 .... (t) JAMcCarthy 76
(G A Ham) *towards rr: rdn and lost tch 5th: rallied 3 out: drvn to chal run-in: one pce* **14/1**

4 *hd* **Trigger Guard** 3-10-12 .... PHide 85+
(G L Moore) *hld up in tch: j. slowly and lost pl 3 out: rallied next: led and blnd last: sn hdd: one pce fnl 100 yds* **9/2**

3 **5** *21* **Pseudonym (IRE)**[8] [1339] 3-10-12 .... (t) TScudamore 67+
(M F Harris) *set modest pce: nt a fluent: rdn 6th: hdd & wknd appr 2 out* **3/1**[2]

0 **6** *6* **Tiffin Deano (IRE)**[8] [1339] 3-10-5 .... TMessenger(7) 55
(H J Manners) *sn bhd: nt fluent 4th and 5th: nvr rchd ldrs* **33/1**

P405 **7** *7* **Imperial Miss (IRE)**[26] [1190] 3-10-2 .... (t) DCrosse(3) 41
(B W Duke) *prom tl hrd rdn and wknd 3 out* **40/1**

6 **8** *12* **Sergeant Small (IRE)**[30] [1146] 3-10-7 ow2 .... MrMatthewSmith(7) 38
(John Berry) *t.k.h: prom tl wknd 3 out* **25/1**

F **Amaya Silva**[225] 3-10-5 .... JamesDavies —
(S Dow) *hld up towards rr: hmpd and blnd 1st: fell next* **33/1**

4m 28.0s (-8.00) **Going Correction** -0.60s/f (Firm) 9 Ran SP% **110.9**
Speed ratings: **92,91,91,91,82 79,76,71,—** CSF £12.79 TOTE £4.30: £1.30, £1.40, £2.40; EX 13.50.

Owner Mr & Mrs D A Gamble **Bred** Philip Brady **Trained** Morestead, Hants

FOCUS
Not a bad juvenile hurdle and it should produce winners, with the winner capable of rating higher.

NOTEBOOK
Wembury Point(IRE), who did it quite nicely on his recent hurdles debut, defied a penalty in workmanlike fashion and appreciated the extra distance. He is evidently going to make a better hurdler than Flat performer and, with further progress expected, there is every chance he can complete the hat-trick, even under a double penalty. *(op 10-3)*
Compton Quay is gradually progressing over hurdles and it was only in the final half furlong that he began to struggle, Wembury Point finishing too strongly for him. A sharp two miles will suit ideally at present and he has a similar race in him. *(op 10-3)*
Millquista D'Or failed to build on her hurdling debut when only fifth at Bangor, but the first-time tongue tie enabled her to put in an improved effort. She needs to up her game if she is to be winning, but that is is possible. *(tchd 12-1)*
Trigger Guard, a full-brother to the stable's winning hurdler Earlsfield Raider, shaped promisingly on this racecourse debut and would have been third had his jumping been a bit slicker. There should be improvement to come and he too can find a race at this level. *(tchd 5-1)*
Pseudonym(IRE) failed to build on a promising hurdles debut and the way he stopped under pressure suggested there may have been something amiss.

1405 WORTHING FOOTBALL CLUB CLAIMING HURDLE (10 hdls) 2m 4f
3:10 (3:10) (Class 4) 4-Y-O+ **£2,569** (£734; £367)

Form RPR

6041 **1** **Outside Investor (IRE)**[18] [1233] 5-10-12 88 .... (p) RThornton 102
(P R Rodford) *hld up: hdwy and swtchd outside appr 2 out: jnd ldrs last: styd on to ld fnl 50 yds* **6/1**[3]

0311 **2** *1/2* **Red Nose Lady**[21] [1218] 8-10-9 99 .... (p) JMogford 100+
(G J Smith) *led: rdn appr 2 out: edgd lft and hdd fnl 50 yds: dismntd after line* **3/1**[2]

0-21 **3** *1/2* **Lightning Star (USA)**[17] [1248] 10-10-12 102 .... (b) PHide 101
(G L Moore) *hld up in tch: mstke 3rd: chal on bit appr last: rdn and fnd little run-in* **2/1**[1]

2500 **4** *1 1/4* **Oulton Broad**[21] [1218] 9-11-0 100 .... (p) LAspell 102
(F Jordan) *t.k.h: a.p: no ex run-in* **9/1**

5PPP **5** *12* **Jivaty (FR)**[18] [1232] 8-10-12 115 .... JamesDavies 88
(Mrs A J Hamilton-Fairley) *prom: hrd rdn 3 out: wknd next* **10/1**

50-5 **6** *1* **Forbearing (IRE)**[22] [1208] 8-10-3 100 .... JDiment(5) 83
(F Jordan) *plld hrd and hung lft thrght: nt fluent: in tch tl outpcd appr 3 out* **14/1**

2602 **7** *28* **Borehill Joker**[39] [1076] 9-11-1 98 .... WKennedy(5) 83+
(Miss K M George) *in rr: nt fluent 5th: hrd rdn and lost tch 7th* **15/2**

4m 52.4s (-11.40) **Going Correction** -0.60s/f (Firm) 7 Ran SP% **110.1**
Speed ratings: **98,97,97,97,92 91,80** CSF £22.94 TOTE £7.90: £2.90, £1.90; EX 29.90.

Owner Les Trott **Bred** Moyglare Stud Farm Ltd **Trained** Ash, Somerset

FOCUS
Moderate form that could be rated higher through placed horses, but they were below their best and the form is somewhat suspect.

NOTEBOOK
Outside Investor(IRE), 8lb higher than when winning at Worcester last month, got on top in the final half furlong but was made to work mighty hard for the win and it subsequently transpired that the runner-up had finished lame, whih detracts a little from his effort. He will need to improve again to defy a further rise. *(op 11-2 tchd 13-2)*
Red Nose Lady was lame on pulling up and ran mightily well considering. She was always to the *fore and kept battling away, but the winner was too strong on the climb for the line.Official explanation: vet said mare was lame (tchd 10-3)*
Lightning Star(USA) has always been a quirky sort and not for the first time he did not deliver the goods once coming under maximum pressure. He remains one to be wary of. *(op 9-4)*
Oulton Broad ran better than he has of late and had every chance. He is gradually slipping in the weights, but is still a few pounds higher than ideal. *(op 12-1)*
Jivaty(FR) has become disappointing and has not shown much for current connections. *(op 8-1)*
Forbearing(IRE) *Official explanation: jockey said gelding hung left in straight (op 12-1 tchd 16-1)*
Borehill Joker *(tchd 8-1)*

1406 ISABELLA HARRIS MEMORIAL H'CAP CHASE (16 fncs) 2m 6f
3:45 (3:45) (Class 4) (0-110,107) 5-Y-O+ **£5,397** (£1,660; £830; £415)

Form RPR

2-5P **1** **Native Daisy (IRE)**[18] [1236] 10-11-2 97 .... JamesDavies 109+
(C J Down) *chsd ldng pair: rdn along fr 11th: led appr last: drvn clr: styd on* **7/1**

P064 **2** *3 1/2* **Celtic Star (IRE)**[15] [1267] 7-9-13 83 .... (b) DCrosse(3) 93+
(Mrs L Williamson) *chsd ldr: led 9th: j.rt fr next: hdd 11th: led 3 out tl appr last: no ex run-in* **13/2**[3]

3464 **3** *5* **Fear Siuil (IRE)**[21] [1219] 12-10-13 94 .... (t) TJMurphy 99+
(Nick Williams) *patiently rdn: hld up and wl bhd: hdwy 3 out: pressed ldrs next: no ex run-in* **7/2**[1]

3/3- **4** *3* **Wild Knight (IRE)**[127] 8-11-10 105 .... JPMcNamara 109+
(R J Hodges) *mstkes: mod 4th most of way: effrt 3 out: wknd next* **6/1**[2]

2P4F **5** *10* **Thieves'Glen**[30] [1157] 7-11-9 104 .... TScudamore 99+
(H Morrison) *led to 9th and set gd pce: nt fluent fnl circ: led 11th to 3 out: sn wknd* **15/2**

0P60 **6** *24* **Harik**[26] [1189] 11-11-5 107 .... (bt) EDehdashti(7) 74
(G L Moore) *sn wl bhd: dismntd after line* **16/1**

03/4 **7** *18* **Autumn Fantasy (USA)**[17] [1247] 6-10-4 85 .... (t) PHide 34
(G L Moore) *sn outpcd: wl bhd whn mstke 6th* **7/2**[1]

33U0 **P** **Pete The Painter (IRE)**[22] [1203] 8-9-9 81 oh7 .... (p) RStephens(5) —
(J W Tudor) *mid-div to 4th: mstke and dropped rr 6th: sn wl bhd: t.o whn p.u bef 11th* **10/1**

5m 34.6s (-9.20) **Going Correction** -0.325s/f (Good) 8 Ran SP% **111.3**
Speed ratings: **103,101,99,98,95 86,79,—** CSF £48.46 CT £180.52 TOTE £8.00: £1.90, £2.10, £1.60; EX 41.00.

Owner W R Baddiley **Bred** Monatrim Stud **Trained** Mutterton, Devon

FOCUS
An ordinary handicap chase in which the pace was true and Native Daisy ran out a comfy winner.

NOTEBOOK
Native Daisy(IRE), whose last win came at Cheltenham in April, was one of many in with a chance jumping two out, but she found an extra gear and stayed on strongly up the hill. This was a return to form and she may be capable of following up, as long as the Handicapper does not put her up too much. *Official explanation: trainer had no explanation for the improved form shown (op 8-1)*
Celtic Star(IRE) kept on again to give chase to the winner, but was always being held. He is on a *fair mark and, as this was a step back in the right direction, may soon be capable of winning* again. *(op 8-1)*
Fear Siuil(IRE) is getting no better and has not won for over two years now. He was well to the fore in the betting nonetheless and appeared to run his race, but was vulnerable at the business end and will continue to be so. *(op 4-1)*
Wild Knight(IRE) has been in good form in points, finding the slower tempo of racing to his liking, but he struggled back under Rules and his jumping was not up to the task. *(tchd 11-2)*
Thieves'Glen is an inconsistent performer who continues to frustrate. *(op 6-1 tchd 8-1)*

Harik *Official explanation: vet said gelding was lame (op 14-1)*
Autumn Fantasy(USA) ran too bad to be true, failing to build on a mildly promising chase debut. He is better than this, but now has a bit to prove. *(op 3-1)*

1407 LAURA WALSHAM NOVICES' HURDLE (9 hdls) 2m 2f 110y

4:20 (4:21) (Class 4) 4-Y-0+ **£3,360** (£1,034; £517; £258)

Form RPR

322 **1** **Screenplay**[6] [1364] 4-10-11 .... JGoldstein 109+
(Miss Sheena West) *chsd ldr: mstke 1st: led after 5th: drvn to hold on run-in* **7/4**[2]

345- **2** ¾ **Hathlen (IRE)**[12] [4616] 4-10-11 101..(b) PHide 106
(G L Moore) *hld up in midfield: stdy hdwy to chse ldr appr 2 out: chal last: rdn and kpt on: jst hld* **11/2**[3]

3-0 **3** 22 **Corrib Drift (USA)**[18] [1235] 5-10-12 .... MBatchelor 85
(Jamie Poulton) *prom: wnt 2nd appr 3 out: 3rd and btn whn mstke next* **33/1**

-040 **4** 21 **Tyup Pompey (IRE)**[8] [1344] 4-10-11 83............................ JamesDavies 63
(Miss J S Davis) *led: blnd bdly 5th: sn hdd: hrd rdn and wknd 3 out* **66/1**

212 **5** ½ **Adjami (IRE)**[88] [680] 4-11-4 116.. RThornton 70
(A King) *prom tl wknd appr 2 out* **6/5**[1]

00- **6** dist **Indigo Sky (IRE)**[58] [4496] 4-10-11 .... JPMcNamara —
(B G Powell) *hld up towards rr: lost tch appr 3 out* **50/1**

00-0 **P** **Cadtauri (FR)**[124] [179] 4-10-11 .... TJMurphy —
(Miss H C Knight) *a bhd: t.o whn p.u bef 3 out* **33/1**

0503 **P** **Hard N Sharp**[10] [1323] 5-10-12 .... TScudamore —
(Mrs A M Thorpe) *a towards rr: t.o 6th: p.u bef 3 out* **33/1**

4m 21.1s (-14.90) **Going Correction** -0.60s/f (Firm) **8** Ran SP% **109.5**
Speed ratings: **107,106,97,88,88** —,—,— CSF £10.08 TOTE £3.00: £1.10, £1.70, £5.80; EX 13.60.
Owner The Horse Players **Bred** Juddmonte Farms **Trained** Lewes, E Sussex

FOCUS
Ordinary novice hurdle form and, with Adjami disappointing, the front pair had their task made easier. The winner is rated better than the bare result.

NOTEBOOK
Screenplay was made to work hard for this maiden victory over hurdles, but he showed the right sort of attitude and much of the credit has to go to Goldstein, who gave him a good, positive ride. He will need to up his game to defy a penalty, but connections also have the option on handicaps and that appeals as the more favourable route. *(op 2-1)*
Hathlen(IRE) has gone well over a year without a win under either code and he again found one too good. He travelled well, but is not the heartiest of characters and is another who may be better off in handicaps. *(op 15-2)*
Corrib Drift(USA) was well adrift of the front two and achieved little in finishing third. Low-grade handicaps are likely to represent his best chance of success.
Tyup Pompey(IRE) remains winless and may need a drop into selling company. *(tchd 50-1)*
Adjami(IRE) set a strong standard and was really entitled to win. However, he soon folded once coming under strong pressure and faded disappointingly. He is better than this, but now has a bit to prove. *(op 10-11)*

1408 OLDWICK SADDLERY & LIVERY YARD H'CAP HURDLE (11 hdls) 2m 6f 110y

4:50 (4:50) (Class 4) (0-110,102) 4-Y-0+ **£3,993** (£1,228; £614; £307)

Form RPR

2251 **1** **Captain Cloudy**[17] [1246] 5-11-0 **90**.. JGoldstein 97+
(Miss Sheena West) *patiently rdn: hld up and bhd: hdwy on bit 3 out: led next: shkn up and responded wl run-in: rdn out* **3/1**[2]

5102 **2** 1¾ **Native Chancer (IRE)**[27] [1181] 5-11-9 **99**................................ TJMurphy 101
(Jonjo O'Neill) *prom: led briefly appr 2 out: hrd rdn and nt pce of wnr run-in* **9/4**[1]

/3BU **3** 11 **Bringontheclowns (IRE)**[38] [1087] 6-11-5 **102**........................ CPoste[(7)] 93
(M F Harris) *hld up towards rr: hdwy 8th: one pce fr 3 out* **16/1**

1205 **4** 6 **September Moon**[8] [1341] 7-11-6 **101**................................ WKennedy[(5)] 86
(Mrs A M Thorpe) *prom: jnd ldr 3 out: wknd appr next* **11/2**[3]

-4P4 **5** 11 **Hermitage Court (USA)**[17] [1245] 4-11-6 **98**.......................... RThornton 70
(M J McGrath) *t.k.h: led tl wknd appr 2 out* **10/1**

350 **6** 13 **Mariday**[46] [1037] 4-11-3 **95**... LAspell 54
(L Wells) *t.k.h on outside: hld up in tch: rdn after 7th: sn wknd* **11/1**

23-0 **7** ½ **Esterelle (USA)**[8] [1341] 10-10-9 **92**................................ TMessenger[(7)] 53
(H J Manners) *in tch tl wknd 8th* **20/1**

31P4 **8** 8 **Taranai (IRE)**[49] [1017] 4-10-11 **89**......................................(t) JamesDavies 40
(B W Duke) *hld up in 6th: rdn 8th: sn wknd* **7/1**

5m 31.1s (-13.70) **Going Correction** -0.60s/f (Firm)
WFA 4 from 5yo+ 15lb **8** Ran SP% **111.7**
Speed ratings: **99,98,94,92,88 84,83,81** CSF £9.99 CT £85.26 TOTE £4.10: £1.40, £1.20, £3.60; EX 7.50.
Owner Michael Moriarty **Bred** J P Coggan **Trained** Lewes, E Sussex

FOCUS
A steady gallop, but Goldstein excelled on the winner, this time under hold-up tactics. The winner is value for more than the official margin with the runner-up setting the standard.

NOTEBOOK
Captain Cloudy, whose rider excelled with a positive ride in the previous race, showed his versatility and gave the gelding a perfect waiting ride. Having travelled fluently, he found what was required under pressure and won with a bit to spare. He has now won his last two starts and clearly acts well at this course. *(op 10-3)*
Native Chancer(IRE) made the winner work hard and was clear of the third. He probably faced a stiff task giving 9lb to the in-form winner and will no doubt find easier opportunities. *(op 11-4)*
Bringontheclowns(IRE) has been a bit in-and-out since arriving from Ireland and may need some further help from the Handicapper.
September Moon ideally wants further than this, but should could still have been expected to fare better. *(op 5-1)*
Hermitage Court(USA) again spoiled his chance by racing keenly and he will not be winning until learning to settle better.

1409 TOTEPOOL FREE £5 BET H'CAP HURDLE (9 hdls) 2m 2f 110y

5:20 (5:22) (Class 4) (0-110,107) 4-Y-0+ **£3,354** (£1,032; £516; £258)

Form RPR

3434 **1** **Leopold (SLO)**[11] [1307] 4-10-6 **95**.. CPoste[(7)] 101+
(M F Harris) *hld up in rr: rdn 7th: gd hdwy 3 out: led appr next: rdn clr: styd on* **13/2**

5432 **2** 4 **Artane Boys**[6] [1366] 8-11-2 **107**.. WJones[(10)] 107
(Jonjo O'Neill) *hld up in tch: effrt appr 2 out: kpt on to take 2nd nr fin* **15/8**[1]

-04R **3** nk **Spiders Web**[88] [683] 5-10-8 **89**..(be) PHide 89
(G L Moore) *in tch: effrt 3 out: chsd wnr last: hrd rdn and nt qckn: lost 2nd nr fin* **6/1**

-02F **4** 13 **Gondolin (IRE)**[74] [813] 5-10-4 **85**.................................... JamesDavies 74+
(G Brown) *chsd ldrs: led 3 out tl appr next: sn btn* **7/2**[2]

0P45 **5** nk **Blue Leader (IRE)**[17] [1250] 6-11-3 **98**..................................(bt) TJMurphy 84
(W K Goldsworthy) *prom tl wknd after 3 out* **11/2**[3]

4P/P **6** 7 **Sungio**[119] [237] 7-10-1 **87**.. LStephens[(5)] 66
(B P J Baugh) *chsd ldr: led 2nd to 3 out: sn wknd* **14/1**

6-65 **7** dist **L'Etang Bleu (FR)**[17] [1249] 7-9-7 **81** oh3....................(vt) RLucey-Butler[(7)] —
(P Butler) *led to 2nd: prom tl wknd qckly 3 out* **33/1**

4m 26.9s (-9.10) **Going Correction** -0.60s/f (Firm)
WFA 4 from 5yo+ 14lb **7** Ran SP% **109.6**
Speed ratings: **95,93,93,87,87 84,**— CSF £18.08 TOTE £7.80: £2.40, £1.80; EX 17.30 Place 6 £43.77, Place 5 £25.42.
Owner A J Duffield **Bred** Gestut Guthler Hof - Kuchyna **Trained** Edgcote, Northants

FOCUS
A welcome first win for Leopold, who came away to win with something in hand. The placed horses ran to form and the race should work out.

NOTEBOOK
Leopold(SLO), a long-standing maiden who has had many good chances, was finally getting off the mark at the 20th attempt and did it in tidy fashion. It is hoped he can go on from this and he should follow up. *(tchd 7-1)*
Artane Boys has been performing well since reverting to hurdles and he stayed on well up the hill to claim second. He was never in with a chance of getting to the winner, but will find a race if holding this level of form. *(op 2-1)*
Spiders Web was unable to go on with the winner after the last and he remains winless after 23 starts. He may find a race eventually, but is hardly one to follow.
Gondolin(IRE) is a quirky sort and cannot be relied upon, but he has plenty of ability and he will pop up at a price one day.
Blue Leader(IRE) is back on a winning mark, but he is not in the best of form at present and it may take a few more runs before he is ready to strike. *(op 9-2)*
T/Plt: £48.10 to a £1 stake. Pool: £43,689.15. 662.25 winning tickets. T/Qpdt: £12.40 to a £1 stake. Pool: £3,004.10. 177.90 winning tickets. LM

1297 WORCESTER (L-H)

Sunday, September 4

OFFICIAL GOING: Good to firm
The first flight in the home straight was omitted all circuits in all hurdle races.
Wind: Light, ahead

1410 BETFREDPOKER.COM NOVICES' HURDLE (10 hdls 2 omitted) 3m

2:20 (2:20) (Class 4) 4-Y-0+ **£3,399** (£1,046; £523; £261)

Form RPR

531- **1** **Classical Ben**[171] [4415] 7-11-4 107.. GLee 104+
(R A Fahey) *hld up in mid-div: hdwy 6th: wnt 2nd appr 2 out: led sn after: ridde out: comf* **5/2**[1]

6026 **2** 6 **One Of Them**[11] [1310] 6-10-5 84................................ BenOrde-Powlett[(7)] 88
(M A Barnes) *trckd ldrs: rdn and lost pl appr 2 out: styd on: hung lft run-in but kpt on to go 2nd* **12/1**

/06U **3** 1 **Cap Classique**[53] [977] 6-10-5 .... PMerrigan[(7)] 87+
(Mrs H Dalton) *hld up in rr: hit 4th: hdwy 7th: led appr 2 out: hdd sn after: no ex and lost 2nd run-in* **14/1**

3540 **4** 11 **Potts Of Magic**[30] [1152] 6-10-12 82..(b) RJohnson 76
(R Lee) *mde most tl rdn and hdd appr 2 out: wknd bef last* **7/1**

5322 **5** ½ **Vivante (IRE)**[30] [1152] 7-10-5 81... WMarston 69
(A J Wilson) *plld hrd: trckd ldr: rdn appr 2 out: wknd sn after* **11/4**[2]

0-P0 **6** dist **Expensive Folly (IRE)**[12] [1298] 7-10-5 ....(v[1]) SWalsh[(7)] —
(A J Chamberlain) *a bhd: t.o* **100/1**

1 **7** hd **Moscow Blue**[18] [1231] 4-11-2 ....(t) PMoloney —
(Evan Williams) *bhd tl hdwy 6th: rdn and lost tch after 3 out: t.o* **7/2**[3]

0-PP **8** 20 **Marmot D'Estruval (FR)**[15] [1262] 5-10-12 77.......................... JTizzard —
(Mrs Tracey Barfoot-Saunt) *trckd ldrs: rdn appr 7th: sn wknd: t.o* **100/1**

P0 **9** 8 **Foreign Field (FR)**[12] [1298] 6-10-5 ....(b[1]) LHeard[(7)] —
(Mrs Tracey Barfoot-Saunt) *mid-div: rdn 1/2-way: sn bhd: t.o* **100/1**

50-P **P** **Slinky Malinky**[21] [1220] 7-10-0 .... TGreenway[(5)] —
(D G Bridgwater) *chsd ldrs to 1/2-way: sn bhd: t.o whn p.u bef 2 out* **66/1**

000- **P** **Kiev (IRE)**[17] [4611] 5-10-12 .... RGreene —
(D G Bridgwater) *j. slowly 1st: mid-visiion: wknd qckly 3 out: t.o whn p.u bef next* **66/1**

5m 38.0s (-11.20) **Going Correction** -0.275s/f (Good)
WFA 4 from 5yo+ 16lb **11** Ran SP% **110.3**
Speed ratings: **107,105,104,101,100** —,—,—,—,— — CSF £29.90 TOTE £3.80: £1.40, £4.20, £3.00; EX 42.10.
Owner J D Clark And Partners **Bred** J D Clark And Partners **Trained** Musley Bank, N Yorks

FOCUS
A moderate novice hurdle, run at a solid gallop and the winner can be rated value for further with the runner-up setting the standard.

NOTEBOOK
Classical Ben , last seen winning over this trip at Hexham on soft ground in March, followed-up with a decisive success under his penalty, and can be rated value for slightly further. Clearly versatile as regards underfoot conditons, he looks to be getting his act together now over timber and in the right hands hands to progress further. However, life will be a lot tougher under a double penalty in the future. *(op 10-3)*
One Of Them turned in an improved effort and is clearly happier on a genuinely fast surface. He is fully exposed, and remains without success over timber from 19 outings, so his proximity does hold down the strength of this form somewhat. However, a drop into plating-class can see him get closer to that elusive first victory.
Cap Classique , popular on the betting exchanges, had still to be posed a serious question approaching the penultimate flight yet found little for pressure and was ultimately well held. He clearly has ability, and loves this ground, so may be capable of tasting success over hurdles when faced with a sharper test in the future. *(op 16-1)*
Potts Of Magic cut out the donkey work until being readily brushed aside by the principals from two out. He may find life easier in low-grade handicaps off his current mark. *(op 10-1)*
Vivante(IRE) spoilt his chance when refusing to settle through the first half of the contest and ran well below her recent level. She can do better. *(op 3-1 tchd 5-2)*
Moscow Blue , a debut winner over course and distance 18 days previously, proved easy to back and his fate was clear from a long way out. He has plenty to prove now. *(op 2-1)*

1411 BETFREDCASINO.COM BEGINNERS' CHASE (12 fncs) 2m

2:55 (2:55) (Class 4) 5-Y-0+ **£4,085** (£1,257; £628; £314)

Form RPR

220- **1** **Tighe Caster**[134] [4982] 6-10-12 .... TDoyle 115+
(P R Webber) *hld up rr: hdwy 8th: rdn appr 2 out: styd on to ld run-in* **3/1**[1]

050- **2** 1½ **Demi Beau**[141] [4860] 7-10-12 .... ChristianWilliams 114
(Evan Williams) *hld up in mid-div: wnt 2nd 5th: j.rt next: led 3 out: rdn appr last no ex and hdd run-in* **4/1**[2]

F2-2 **3** 1¾ **Never (FR)**[10] [1318] 8-10-12 ....(t) APMcCoy 112
(Jonjo O'Neill) *hld up: hdwy after 8th: cl 3rd last: no imp run-in* **7/1**

1-05 **4** *11* **Queen Soraya**[112] [372] 7-10-5 SThomas 97+
(Miss H C Knight) *mde most tl hdd run-in: wknd appr last* **9/2**[3]
-P15 **5** *12* **Faddad (USA)**[12] [1299] 9-10-12 86 (t) RJohnson 95+
(Mrs A M Thorpe) *trckd ldr tl lost pl after 6th: sn bhd* **14/1**
0-P0 **6** *26* **Just Midas**[12] [1299] 7-10-9 76 TJPhelan(3) 63
(N M Babbage) *trckd ldrs tl wknd 8th* **100/1**
503P **7** *dist* **Saposcat (IRE)**[14] [1275] 5-10-5 MrDavidTurner(7) —
(Dr P Pritchard) *sn wl bhd: t.o* **125/1**
3112 **P** **Dewasentah (IRE)**[21] [1222] 6-10-5 GLee —
(J M Jefferson) *mid-div: hdwy 7th: 5th whn p.u bef 2 out* **3/1**[1]
U/0P **P** **Investment Force (IRE)**[18] [1233] 7-10-12 (p) DRDennis —
(M Sheppard) *trckd ldrs tl hit 7th: sn rdn and wknd: t.o whn p.u bef 4 out* **66/1**

3m 46.3s (-7.30) **Going Correction** -0.275s/f (Good) **9** Ran SP% **110.6**
Speed ratings: **107,106,105,99,93 80,—,—,—** CSF £14.67 TOTE £4.10: £1.50, £1.20, £2.10; EX 17.80.
Owner D P Barrie & M J Rees **Bred** Lingbourne Stud **Trained** Mollington, Oxon

FOCUS
A fair beginners' chase which saw the first three come clear. The form looks solid and should work out.

NOTEBOOK
Tighe Caster, rated 120 over hurdles, dug deep on the run-in to get up and score at the first time of asking over fences. As was the case numerous times over hurdles last season, he took time to settle through the early parts, but his jumping was sound and he showed the right attitude under pressure when it mattered. He is starting life over fences at the right time and could rate higher before the season's end. *(op 11-4 tchd 7-2)*
Demi Beau, rated 139 at his peak over hurdles with Charlie Mann before losing his way after an injury last term, made a promising debut over fences for his new connections and was only denied on the run-in. He jumped neatly, is entitled to improve for this experience and, if his new yard can rekindle his enthusiasm, could well prove a decent aquisition. *(op 11-2 tchd 6-1)*
Never(FR), easy to back, again flattered to deceive when off the bridle, yet still turned in an improved effort. He has regressed in the last year, and remains one to have reservations about, but certainly has a small race in him over fences before the classy novice chases come out to play. *(op 11-2 tchd 5-1)*
Queen Soraya, rated 120 over hurdles, jumped neatly and showed up encouragingly for a long way at the head of affairs before finding her lack of fitness an issue. She appeals as the type to do better in this sphere and, considering it may take her a few outings to reach peak fitness, is one to be with when the ground is on the quick side. *(tchd 4-1 and 5-1)*
Faddad(USA) *(op 20-1)*
Dewasentah(IRE), progressive over hurdles during the summer, shaped well enough until stopping quickly approaching the penultimate fence. She has a bit to prove now, but is not one to write off on the back of this fencing bow. *Official explanation: jockey said mare was lame (tchd 11-4)*

1412 BETFREDCASINO.COM NOVICES' H'CAP CHASE (15 fncs) 2m 4f 110y
3:30 (3:30) (Class 4) (0-105,104) 5-Y-O+ **£4,134** (£1,272; £636; £318)

Form RPR
6312 **1** **Lake Merced (IRE)**[12] [1296] 5-11-12 104 APMcCoy 110
(Jonjo O'Neill) *trckd ldr: led 4th: rdn and hdd 2 out: responded to forceful handling to ld again run-in: all out* **6/1**[3]
6003 **2** *hd* **Lost In The Snow (IRE)**[18] [1236] 7-10-0 78 PMoloney 84
(M Sheppard) *hld up: hdwy appr 4 out: stongly rdn and fin fast run-in: jst failed* **9/1**
412 **3** *1 1/4* **Tommy Spar**[18] [1236] 5-11-9 101 RJohnson 106
(P Bowen) *trckd ldrs: rdn appr 4 out: kpt on: wnt briefly 2nd run-in but edgd lft and no ex nr fin* **2/1**[1]
3431 **4** *3/4* **High Peak**[27] [1178] 8-9-11 78 oh1 RYoung(3) 83+
(J W Mullins) *hld up: hdwy 7th: led 2 out: hung rt sn after last and no ex* **7/2**[2]
0034 **5** *4* **Optimism (FR)**[27] [1176] 7-10-0 78 RWalford 79+
(R H Alner) *trckd ldrs gng wl: ev ch 2 out tl wknd run-in* **15/2**
4P5P **6** *4* **Lost Treasure (IRE)**[5] [1376] 8-10-0 78 oh2 SCurran 74
(Evan Williams) *led to 4th: wknd appr 2 out* **33/1**
3104 **7** *8* **Cumbrian Knight (IRE)**[18] [1049] 7-11-8 100 GLee 88
(J M Jefferson) *hld up in rr: mstke 10th: sn bhd* **7/1**
F45- **8** *1/2* **Fantastic Champion (IRE)**[140] [4879] 6-9-12 81 MNicolls(5) 69
(J R Cornwall) *hld up: rdn 11th: nvr on terms* **18/1**

5m 16.2s (8.70) **Going Correction** -0.275s/f (Good) **8** Ran SP% **112.3**
Speed ratings: **72,71,71,71,69 68,65,64** CSF £54.16 CT £143.60 TOTE £5.20: £1.80, £2.00, £1.40; EX 64.30.
Owner John P McManus **Bred** Aidan Sexton **Trained** Cheltenham, Gloucs
■ Stewards' Enquiry : P Moloney one-day ban: used whip with excessive frequency (Sep 18)
A P McCoy one-day ban: used whip with excessive frequency (Sep 18)

FOCUS
A moderate novices' handicap, run at a steady early pace, which resulted in five horses all holding a chance at the penultimate fence. The form looks suspect but the third sets the level.

NOTEBOOK
Lake Merced(IRE), making his chasing bow, responded to all of McCoy's typically never-say-die urgings in the straight and just did enough land the spoils, despite the burden of top weight. Considering this was his first attempt at the bigger obstacles, he did really well to jump as he did under pressure and could prove to be better than the bare form. *(op 5-1)*
Lost In The Snow(IRE) took time to hit full stride from off the pace, but was motoring on the run-in and just found the line coming a stride or two too soon. He reversed course and distance form with Tommy Spar and is clearly going the right way. *(tchd 8-1)*
Tommy Spar, a well-backed favourite, had his chance yet failed to see out his race as well as the first two. This was another sound effort, and he remains capable of opening his account over fences, granted similarly fast ground in the future. *(op 11-4)*
High Peak, raised 7lb for finally getting off the mark at Southwell 27 days previously, proved very easy in the betting ring beforehand. However, he still ran another improved race and only tired on jumping the final fence. While he still has to prove he is up to this higher mark, he remains in good form and is a consistent sort at this level. *(op 3-1)*
Optimism(FR) ◆, well backed, was travelling best of all and had yet to be posed a serious question approaching two out. However, his stride soon shortened when push came to shove and he patently failed to see out the longer trip. Granted a sharper test, he should be placed to strike before too long. *(op 10-1)*

1413 BETFREDPOKER.COM H'CAP HURDLE (8 hdls 2 omitted) 2m 4f
4:05 (4:05) (Class 4) (0-110,108) 4-Y-O+ **£4,192** (£1,290; £645; £322)

Form RPR
56P4 **1** **Mister Moussac**[6] [1361] 6-10-4 85 GLee 97+
(Miss Kariana Key) *mid-divisin: hdwy 6th: lost pl appr 3 out: rallied to ld 2 out: wnt bdly rt last: lft clr run-in* **13/2**
U420 **2** *8* **Tinstre (IRE)**[4] [980] 7-11-5 100 SCurran 103+
(P W Hiatt) *trckd ldr tl lost pl appr 2 out: rallied after 2 out: lft poor 2nd last* **9/1**
0/01 **3** *1 1/4* **Dancing Hill**[26] [1187] 6-10-3 84 RGreene 82
(K Bishop) *wl bhd tl mde late hdwy: styng on fr 2 out* **9/1**
-0B0 **4** *5* **Amber Dawn**[14] [1280] 6-10-0 81 oh7 OMcPhail 74
(J Gallagher) *hld up: hdwy 5th: ev ch appr 2 out: wknd appr last* **33/1**
P00- **5** *1* **Reflex Blue**[17] [4759] 8-10-6 87 (v) AO'Keeffe 79
(R J Price) *hld up: hdwy 3rd: rdn appr 2 out: lft 3rd and sltly hmpd least: wknd run-in* **14/1**
2-06 **6** *10* **Wilfred (IRE)**[22] [1211] 4-11-12 108 (b) APMcCoy 89
(Jonjo O'Neill) *prom tl wknd appr 2 out* **11/2**[2]
1363 **7** *5* **Red Canyon (IRE)**[14] [1271] 8-11-2 97 (p) JTizzard 81+
(C L Tizzard) *trckd ldr: led 4th: hdd 2 out: btn whn hmpd last* **6/1**[3]
0416 **8** *2* **Margarets Wish**[21] [1223] 5-10-1 85 ONelmes(3) 60
(T Wall) *a bhd* **14/1**
0-02 **D** *7* **Ballynattin Buck (IRE)**[18] [1231] 9-11-9 104 (t) DRDennis 72
(M Sheppard) *led to 5th: wknd appr 2 out* **9/2**[1]
-650 **F** **A Bit Of Fun**[98] [571] 4-11-4 105 LTreadwell(5) 112+
(J T Stimpson) *chsd ld 3f out: hdd next: cl 2nd whn impeded and fell last* **16/1**
0663 **F** **Sigwells Club Boy**[17] [1250] 5-10-8 96 LHeard(7) 94
(J L Flint) *hld up: hdwy after 3f out: swtchd rt and clsng on ldrs whn fell next* **7/1**

4m 37.2s (-10.80) **Going Correction** -0.275s/f (Good) **11** Ran SP% **115.8**
Speed ratings: **110,106,106,104,103 99,97,97,94,—** — CSF £62.76 CT £528.84 TOTE £8.60: £2.80, £3.30, £2.50; EX 66.60.
Owner Arthur Symons Key **Bred** Miss Carrie Key-Forestal **Trained** Knaresborough, N Yorks

FOCUS
A poor handicap, run at a strong gallop, and the field finished fairly strung out behind the decisive winner. The form is worth treating with caution, although the placed horses ran to their marks.

NOTEBOOK
Mister Moussac finally took advantage of his declining official rating and ultimately ran out a clear-cut winner. He looked like folding when coming under heavy pressure three out, but responded gamely for pressure and was already in command when jumping markedly right and hampering A Bit Of Fun at the final flight. A follow-up bid depends on whether he can maintain this current mood. *(op 8-1)*
Tinstre(IRE), 14th of 15 in a maiden on the Flat four days previously, plugged on under pressure and is clearly flattered by his finishing position. That said, this was an improved effort and he seems to like this venue. *(op 8-1 tchd 10-1)*
Dancing Hill, the shock 100/1 winner of a Newton Abbot seller last time, got going all too late in the day. However, she stuck to her task under pressure and is clearly not without hope off her official mark. *(op 10-1 tchd 8-1)*
Amber Dawn emerged with every chance two out, but was readily brushed aside therafter. This was not a bad effort from 7lb out of the handicap, so a drop to plating company may see her finally get closer to breaking her duck. *(op 25-1)*
Wilfred(IRE) looked to have a chance on his previous efforts, despite the burden of top weight, but weakened tamely when push came to shove in the straight. He is probably capable of better back at two miles, however. *(tchd 5-1 and 6-1)*
Red Canyon(IRE) *(op 7-1)*
Ballynattin Buck(IRE) had his chance, yet looked to go off too fast for his own good, as he had *nothing left in the tank when challenged in the straight. He has a fair bit to prove now.Official explanation: trainer had no explanation for the poor form shown (tchd 5-1)*
Sigwells Club Boy was still in with a place chance when coming to grief. *(op 9-1)*
A Bit Of Fun was just held by the winner prior to coming to grief at the final hurdle, but still this must rate an improved effort and he enjoyed the return to the longer trip. He would have been second but for falling. *(op 9-1)*

1414 BETFREDPOKER.COM H'CAP CHASE (18 fncs) 2m 7f 110y
4:40 (4:41) (Class 4) (0-90,89) 5-Y-O+ **£4,231** (£1,302; £651; £325)

Form RPR
3426 **1** **Tudor King (IRE)**[53] [981] 11-11-9 83 GLee 96+
(Andrew Turnell) *a.p: led appr last: r.o gamely: p.u after line and dismntd: lame* **9/1**
36P3 **2** *1 1/4* **Vandante (IRE)**[27] [1178] 9-11-6 80 RJohnson 91
(R Lee) *hld up: hdwy after 9th: styd on to go 2nd run-in: no ch w wnr* **11/1**
P2PU **3** *4* **Pristeen Spy**[5] [1376] 8-10-10 70 JMMaguire 77
(R Ford) *chsd ldrs: led appr 4 out: hung lft and hdd appr last: no ex and lost 2nd run-in* **14/1**
4 *4* **Cool Present (IRE)**[42] [1057] 6-11-5 79 FKeniry 83+
(K R Burke) *hld up in tch: rdn 3 out: styd on one pce* **16/1**
P-20 **5** *2 1/2* **Mollycarrsbrekfast**[90] [665] 10-10-9 69 TDoyle 71+
(K Bishop) *led to 4th: led 7th tl hdd appr 4 out: wknd 2 out* **6/1**[1]
0020 **6** *12* **Johnny Grand**[35] [1109] 8-11-3 77 (p) MFoley 66
(D W Lewis) *bhd: mde sme late hdwy but nvr on terms* **33/1**
P50- **7** *1* **Just Jolly (IRE)**[154] [4718] 10-11-2 83 APogson(7) 71
(J R Cornwall) *mid-div: hdwy appr 11th: wknd 4 out* **33/1**
3503 **8** *8* **Oscars Vision (IRE)**[14] [1275] 5-11-12 89 (v) NFehily 66
(B W Duke) *sn towards rr: nvr on terms* **28/1**
F252 **9** *5* **River Quoile**[17] [1247] 9-10-13 80 DJacob(7) 55
(R H Alner) *prom whn mstke 5th: lost pl 5th: bhd after* **7/1**[3]
0-PP **10** *23* **Sunday Habits (IRE)**[14] [1276] 11-10-4 71 MrDavidTurner(7) 23
(Dr P Pritchard) *led 4th to 7th: wknd 13th* **66/1**
-224 **11** *21* **Cyanara**[34] [1122] 9-10-5 68 TJPhelan(3) —
(Dr P Pritchard) *sn bhd and styd there* **18/1**
64-P **12** *5* **Just Reuben (IRE)**[14] [1273] 10-10-8 68 (b) JTizzard —
(C L Tizzard) *in tch: hdwy 9th: wknd appr 11th* **25/1**
/4-2 **P** **Yakareem (IRE)**[21] [1219] 9-10-9 74 TGreenway(5) —
(D G Bridgwater) *a rr: t.o whn p.u bef 13th: dismntd* **13/2**[2]
66-6 **P** **Hill Forts Henry**[121] [202] 7-10-10 73 RYoung(3) —
(J W Mullins) *nt jump wl bhd and t.o whn p.u bef 13th* **8/1**
P1P5 **P** **Honneur Fontenail (FR)**[21] [1219] 6-11-2 76 (v) RGreene —
(N J Hawke) *nvr gng wl: lost tch 11th: p.u bef 13th* **16/1**
55 **P** **Suits Me Fine (IRE)**[14] [1280] 5-11-10 87 APMcCoy —
(Jonjo O'Neill) *chsd ldrs: rdn 14th and wknd qckly: p.u bef next* **7/1**[3]

5m 49.4s (-5.50) **Going Correction** -0.275s/f (Good) **16** Ran SP% **120.4**
Speed ratings: **98,97,96,94,94 90,89,87,85,77 70,69,—,—,—** — CSF £97.92 CT £1389.98 TOTE £9.70: £2.30, £2.40, £3.70, £5.10; EX 89.90.
Owner J R Kinloch **Bred** Capt D Foster And B Corscadden **Trained** Broad Hinton, Wilts

FOCUS
A seller in disguise but the form looks reasonable. The pace was fair and the big field finished well strung out.

NOTEBOOK
Tudor King(IRE), a habitual front-runner, was this time given a more patient ride by Lee and the tactics duly paid off in some style. This was a much-deserved success, yet his overall record suggests he will struggle off a higher mark in the future. *(op 17-2 tchd 8-1)*
Vandante(IRE) stayed on well, despite never rating a serious threat to the winner, and posted another sound effort. He looks to be running into form now. *(op 12-1 tchd 10-1)*

Pristeen Spy posted a return to form, and may have gone for home too soon this time, as he did not look to be helping his rider when hanging towards the final fence. He would be very interesting in future off this mark if the cheekpieces were re-applied, granted a similarly fast ground, and given a slightly more patient ride. *(op 12-1)*
Cool Present(IRE), making her British debut for a new yard, could only keep on at the same pace *when it mattered and was well held. She may be able to build on this over further, however.* *(op 14-1)*
Mollycarrsbrekfast, whose previous success came over course and distance in 2003, was not disgraced on this return to chasing. However, while he is well-treated at present in this sphere and capable of better, he is not one to place any great faith in. *(op 5-1)*
River Quoile *Official explanation: jockey said gelding jumped badly throughout (op 9-1)*
Yakareem(IRE) *Official explanation: jockey said gelding pulled up feelingly (tchd 6-1 and 7-1)*

1415 BETFREDCASINO.COM MAIDEN HURDLE (6 hdls 2 omitted) 2m
5:10 (5:21) (Class 4) 4-Y-0+ **£3,388** (£968; £484)

Form RPR
2 **1** **Sharaab (USA)**[8] [1340] 4-11-2 ....(t) PMoloney 85
(D E Cantillon) *hld up: hdwy fr 3 out: led next: r.o wl run-in* **5/1**[2]
23 **2** *1 1/2* **Spuradich (IRE)**[27] [1182] 5-11-2 .... APMcCoy 85+
(Jonjo O'Neill) *hld up: hdwy whn stmbld 2 out: rdn and wnt 2nd appr last: no imp run-in* **8/11**[1]
6 **3** *2* **Hugs Destiny (IRE)**[8] [1340] 4-10-9 .... BenOrde-Powlett(7) 82
(M A Barnes) *hld up in tch: rdn and ev ch 2 out: one pce run-in* **8/1**
5P25 **4** *9* **Earls Rock**[10] [1319] 7-11-2 88.... DRDennis 73
(J K Cresswell) *led tl hdd appr 2 out: wknd appr last* **15/2**[3]
00 **5** *8* **Bally Hall (IRE)**[21] [1222] 5-11-2 ....(t) WHutchinson 67+
(J M Bradley) *trckd ldr: led briefly appr 2 out: wekened appr last* **66/1**
P- **6** *5* **Pollys Angel**[147] [4795] 6-10-4 .... DLaverty(5) 53
(C N Kellett) *nt jump wl: a bhd* **125/1**
P- **7** *17* **Marsh Orchid**[69] [3403] 4-11-2 .... NFehily 43
(C C Bealby) *mid-div: wknd after 3 out* **33/1**
/6-P **8** *dist* **Lord Thomas (IRE)**[84] [729] 7-11-2 .... WMarston —
(A J Wilson) *chsd ldng pair tl wknd qckly after 3 out: t.o* **80/1**
056P **P** **Ice And Fire**[53] [979] 6-10-11 86.... LTreadwell(5) —
(J T Stimpson) *j. slowly 3rd: a bhd: t.o whn p.u bef last* **16/1**

3m 44.9s (-3.50) **Going Correction** -0.275s/f (Good) **9** Ran SP% **109.8**
Speed ratings: **97,96,95,90,86 84,75,—,—** CSF £8.62 TOTE £6.10: £2.00, £1.10, £1.70; EX 10.50 Place 6 £119.29, Place 5 £44.98.
Owner Mrs E M Clarke,Mrs J Hart,Mrs C Reed **Bred** Shadwell Farm LLC **Trained** Newmarket, Suffolk

FOCUS
A modest maiden, run at a moderate pace, and the form appears suspect with the runner-up well below previous form.

NOTEBOOK
Sharaab(USA) showed the benefit of his recent hurdling bow at Market Rasen eight days previously, digging deep to get the better of the runner-up and score at the second time of asking. The tongue tie he wore on the Flat was re-applied for this, he jumped neatly throughout and is clearly going to prove better in this sphere. *(op 11-2)*
Spuradich(IRE) again lacked resolution at the business end of his race and was ultimately well held by the winner. This has to rate a missed opportunity, he has failed to progress on his Cartmel debut and really does look one to have reservations about. However, he now qualifies for handicaps and can hardly be too harshly treated on his form to date. *(tchd 4-5)*
Hugs Destiny(IRE) held every chance until lacking the necessary change of gears two out, and improved on his recent Market Rasen debut, getting a lot closer to the winner this time. He is one to keep an eye on when qualified for handicaps and stepping up in trip. *(op 10-1 tchd 7-1)*
Earls Rock set the modest pace and was a sitting duck approaching the penultimate flight. He probably wants easier ground, but remains winless from 12 outings over timber and is merely plating-class. *(op 7-1)*
Ice And Fire *Official explanation: jockey said gelding hung right throughout (op 12-1)*
T/Plt: £186.10 to a £1 stake. Pool: £42,319.45. 165.95 winning tickets. T/Qpdt: £36.30 to a £1 stake. Pool: £3,162.30. 64.45 winning tickets. JS

1416 - 1419a (Foreign Racing) - See Raceform Interactive

1114 GALWAY (R-H)
Sunday, September 4

OFFICIAL GOING: Good to firm

1420a SMIRNOFF H'CAP CHASE (LISTED RACE) 2m 6f
4:30 (4:30) (0-135,133) 4-Y-0+ **£16,159** (£4,741; £2,258; £769)

RPR
1 **Rocking Ship (IRE)**[51] [1007] 7-9-10 105.... JPElliott 114
(Ms Joanna Morgan, Ire) *mde all: slt mstke 4th: strly pressed and jnd bef 2 out: rdn and clr appr st: reduced ld and kpt on wl u.p ins fnl f* **12/1**
2 *3 1/2* **Golden Storm (IRE)**[10] [1325] 8-10-9 121....(b) JMAllen(3) 126
(Joseph Crowley, Ire) *trckd ldrs: mainly 2nd: dropped to 3rd appr 2 out: rdn to chal in 2nd ins fnl f: kpt on same pce* **11/1**
3 *4* **Curfew Tolls (IRE)**[30] [1162] 9-9-10 105.... DJCondon 106
(Henry De Bromhead, Ire) *chsd ldrs: impr to dispute ld travelling wl bef 2 out where slow: sn rdn: dropped to 3rd and kpt on one pce ins fnl f* **8/1**
4 *2* **Light On The Broom (IRE)**[39] [1083] 9-10-11 123....(t) MPWalsh(3) 122
(Gerard Stack, Ire) *towards rr: 7th and hdwy fr bef 2 out: wnt 4th appr st: kpt on same pce u.p* **5/1**[2]
5 *8* **The Culdee (IRE)**[10] [1325] 9-10-4 113.... PACarberry 104
(F Flood, Ire) *mid-div: sme slt mstkes: 6th and rdn appr 2 out: sn no imp* **6/1**[3]
6 *13* **Blitzy Boy (IRE)**[7] [1354] 11-9-10 105.... NPMadden 83
(G T Lynch, Ire) *towards rr: prog into 4th appr 2 out: 5th and no imp u.p fr bef st* **10/1**
7 *15* **Trotsky (IRE)**[29] [1167] 7-9-11 106.... GCotter 69
(D T Hughes, Ire) *cl up: slt mstke 4th: dropped to 6th bef 5 out: sn no imp* **10/1**
8 *12* **Quadco (IRE)**[10] [1325] 11-11-3 126.... DNRussell 77
(P A Fahy, Ire) *trckd ldrs: 5th and rdn appr 2 out: sn no ex* **8/1**
9 *3* **Il En Reve (FR)**[14] [1283] 7-10-11 120....(b) JLCullen 68
(S J Treacy, Ire) *chsd ldrs early: mid-div and rdn fr 7 out: sn n.d* **7/1**
10 *12* **Fatherofthebride (IRE)**[10] [1104] 9-10-2 114....(b) TGMRyan(3) 50
(Joseph Crowley, Ire) *bhd and rdn fr early: nvr a factor* **7/2**[1]
F **Satco Express (IRE)**[227] [3450] 9-10-11 123.... MDarcy(3) —
(E Sheehy, Ire) *towards rr tl fell 5th* **14/1**
P **Wests Awake (IRE)**[35] [1116] 9-10-3 112.... PFlynn —
(I Madden, Ire) *towards rr: mstke 7 out and p.u sn after* **16/1**

5m 21.0s **16** Ran SP% **134.7**
CSF £152.38 CT £1158.98 TOTE £38.80: £10.10, £4.50, £3.90; DF 336.20.
Owner Clare Connection Syndicate **Bred** John White **Trained** Ballivor, Co Meath

NOTEBOOK
Rocking Ship(IRE) needs this fast ground but is inconsistent at best. He made all and held on well under pressure. *Official explanation: trainer said, regarding the improved form shown, gelding was at times moody and difficult to predict, adding that it may have benefited from having a small break since its last run having been campaigned quite often prior to that to avail of its preference for fast ground*
Golden Storm(IRE) has not won since taking this race 12 months ago. He rarely runs on firm ground but put up his best performance for a long time on it here. *(op 10/1)*
Curfew Tolls(IRE) has only soft ground form to his credit and was point-to-pointing earlier in the year. *(op 8/1)*
Light On The Broom(IRE) finished third in the Galway Plate here in July but, 3lb higher, could not reproduce that form. He flattered briefly after the last but found little uphill.
The Culdee(IRE) needs totally different underfoot conditions but this was not a bad prep for the Kerry National at Listowel. *(op 5/1)*
Quadco(IRE) showed little sparkle.
Fatherofthebride(IRE) ran badly after showing enthusiasm on the Flat last time. *Official explanation: jockey said gelding missed the break and never travelled thereafter (op 7/2 tchd 4/1)*

1421 - 1427a & 1429a-1430a (Foreign Racing) - See Raceform Interactive

851 AUTEUIL (L-H)
Tuesday, September 6

OFFICIAL GOING: Very soft

1428a PRIX DES PLATANES (HURDLE) (C&G) 2m 2f
1:50 (1:52) 3-Y-O **£19,745** (£9,872; £5,759; £3,908; £1,851)

RPR
1 **Tidal Fury (IRE)**[52] [1011] 3-10-3 .... SLeloup 123
(J Jay) *led to 5 out, led again before 2 out, ridden after last, ran on strongly*
2 *5* **Oh Calin (FR)**[29] 3-10-1 .... DGallagher 116
(A Chaille-Chaille, France) **4/1**[1]
3 *6* **Chiaro (FR)**[80] [777] 3-10-5 ....(b) FEstrampes 114
(J-L Pelletan, France) **9/2**[2]
4 *3* **Royals Darling (GER)**[10] 3-9-12 ....(b) VKorytar 104
(W Baltromei, Germany) **12/1**[3]
5 *2 1/2* **Un Nononito (FR)**[100] [583] 3-10-3 .... JacquesRicou 106
(G Macaire, France)
6 *2* **Sasso Lungo (FR)**[100] [583] 3-10-1 .... GDerat 102
(Mme C De La Soudiere-Niault, France)

4m 7.00s **6** Ran SP% **45.9**
PARI-MUTUEL: WIN 4.20; PL 2.50, 2.60; SF 19.50.
Owner Twelfth Night **Bred** Robert De Vere Hunt **Trained** Newmarket, Suffolk

NOTEBOOK
Tidal Fury(IRE), who finished second in a Listed hurdle here back in June, adopted his favoured front-running tactics and ran out a clear winner.

1044 UTTOXETER (L-H)
Wednesday, September 7

OFFICIAL GOING: Good to firm
The third fence in the back straight and third last fence were omitted in all chases.
Wind: Almost nil. Weather: Warm & sunny.

1431 A & S ENTERPRISES NOVICES' HURDLE (12 hdls) 2m 4f 110y
2:00 (2:00) (Class 4) 4-Y-0+ **£3,412** (£975; £487)

Form RPR
1322 **1** **Absolut Power (GER)**[24] [1220] 4-11-3 114....(p) APMcCoy 113+
(J A Geake) *chsd clr ldr: hit 4th: clsd 8th: led next: hit 3 out: sn wl in command: heavily eased flat* **8/13**[1]
1502 **2** *11* **Explosive Fox (IRE)**[15] [1298] 4-11-3 105....(p) TDoyle 100
(C P Morlock) *led and sn 8l clr: hit 6th: blnd next: pressed 8th: hdd next: relegated 3rd and drvn 3 out: mstke next: plodded into 2nd at* **6/1**[3]
1 **3** *1* **Irish Wolf (FR)**[30] [1182] 5-10-13 110.... TGreenway(5) 100
(P Bowen) *nvr looked gng wl and sme errors: clsd bef 7th: drvn 9th: hanging lft after: chsd wnr vainly 3 out tl last* **3/1**[2]
-000 **4** *dist* **Vesta Flame**[33] [1148] 4-10-3 64.... AO'Keeffe —
(Miss L V Davis) *racd in last: hrd drvn and lost tch after 6th: t.o next: btn 78l* **100/1**
60-P **P** **Blazing The Trail (IRE)**[25] [384] 5-10-11 ....(p) NFehily —
(C J Mann) *bhd: rdn and lost tch bef 7th: t.o and p.u next* **25/1**
0-33 **P** **Sonic Sound**[105] [502] 6-10-4 96....(t) RSpate(7) —
(Mrs K Waldron) *chsd ldng pair tl 5th: drvn after next: hopelessly t.o fr 7th tl p.u 3 out: dismntd but later rdn bk* **28/1**

5m 1.40s (-10.70) **Going Correction** -0.60s/f (Firm) **6** Ran SP% **109.5**
Speed ratings: **96,91,91,—,— —** CSF £4.64 TOTE £1.60: £1.10, £2.20; EX 3.50.
Owner Dr G Madan Mohan **Bred** H Gutschow **Trained** Kimpton, Hants
■ Stewards' Enquiry : T Doyle two-day ban: used whip with excessive frequency (Sep 18, 21)

FOCUS
A modest novice event, run at a decent pace. The winner won as he pleased and probably ran to the level of his last run.

NOTEBOOK
Absolut Power(GER) tracked the leader before taking up the running approaching the home turn, and once in front never looked like being caught at any stage. He was entitled to win according to official figures, but this was richly-deserved, as he really is a model of consistency. Still only four, he loves this sort of ground and can add further to his tally now his confidence will have been greatly-boosted. *(op 4-5)*
Explosive Fox(IRE) set off at a brisk early gallop, but the winner always had him in his sights, and he was ultimately a sitting duck coming out of the back straight. However, he still deserves credit for sticking to his task when headed and may be worth another shot over a bit further now. *(op 8-1)*
Irish Wolf(FR) was ridden to get this longer trip and never really looked happy at any stage. He was less than fluent over his hurdles early on, and took some driving to get to the leaders on the second circuit, before ultimately finding just the same pace under maximum pressure when it really mattered. He may do better back over shorter, and it is interesting that he used to sport blinkers on *the Flat in France, so is not one to write off just yet. Official explanation: jockey said horse hung left-handed throughout (op 9-4)*
Vesta Flame never threatened at any stage and is merely plating class.
Blazing The Trail(IRE) *Official explanation: jockey said gelding pulled up lame*

1432 BCA VEHICLE REMARKETING (S) HURDLE (10 hdls) 2m

2:35 (2:36) (Class 5) 4-6-Y-O £2,275 (£650; £325)

Form RPR

1 **Euro Route (IRE)**[31] [4568] 4-10-12 JMogford 93+
(G J Smith) *mod 4th after 4th: stdy prog 7th: wnt 2nd 2 out: drvn ahd last: sn forged clr* **66/1**

052 **2** *4* **Staff Nurse (IRE)**[17] [1278] 5-10-5 85 (p) KRenwick 82
(N Wilson) *25l 3rd after 4th bhd tearaway pair: clsd 7th: chsd ldr 3 out tl next: regained 2nd and ch last: drvn and nt qckn after* **7/2**[1]

26-0 **3** *nk* **Always Flying (USA)**[4] [369] 4-10-5 93 CDSharkey[(7)] 90+
(N Wilson) *sn setting furious gallop: 20l clr 5th: stl 7l ahd 3 out: edging lft after: mstke next: hdd last: drvn and nt qckn* **7/1**[3]

2U3- **4** *½* **Double Royal (IRE)**[30] [4369] 6-10-12 83 DCrosse 89
(J G M O'Shea) *prom in chsng gp: effrt 7th: sn hrd rdn: outpcd after 2 out: plugged on again flat* **11/1**

P356 **5** *13* **Royaltea**[13] [1317] 4-10-0 82 LTreadwell[(5)] 69
(J T Stimpson) *plld hrd and nvr bttr than midfield: lost tch after 7th* **7/1**[3]

00P4 **6** *2 ½* **Honan (IRE)**[7] [1384] 6-10-12 93 (v) APMcCoy 74+
(M C Pipe) *midfield: pushed along to go 3rd at 6th: blnd next: nt run on: wl btn bef 3 out* **9/2**[2]

0 **7** *2 ½* **Urban Dream (IRE)**[15] [1302] 4-10-12 TScudamore 71
(R A Farrant) *nvr nr ldrs: struggling after 7th: mstke next* **20/1**

00-P **8** *8* **Oh Sunny Boy (IRE)**[4] [1028] 4-10-12 74 TJMurphy 63
(B G Powell) *nvr nr ldrs: struggling whn hit 7th* **16/1**

P02P **9** *2* **Love Triangle (IRE)**[19] [1208] 4-10-9 88 (bt) ONelmes[(3)] 61
(N B King) *hld up towards rr: nvr nr ldrs: wl bhd 7th* **20/1**

10 *9* **Sososimple (IRE)**[9] [1369] 5-9-12 KHClarke[(7)] 45
(D Broad, Ire) *nvr nr ldrs: lost tch u.p bef 3 out* **20/1**

P-0 **11** *4* **Chromboy (GER)**[92] [671] 5-10-7 CHonour[(5)] 48
(N B King) *t.k.h: nvr bttr than midfield and no threat: lost tch 7th* **100/1**

0 **12** *1* **Senor Bond (USA)**[9] [1360] 4-10-12 FKeniry 47
(P C Haslam) *hld up and nvr nr ldrs: wl bhd fr 7th* **8/1**

0 **13** *dist* **Power Strike (USA)**[69] [870] 4-10-7 DFlavin[(5)] —
(Mrs L B Normile) *midfield and off pce of ldrs whn hit 6th: no ch after: eased 3 out: btn 87l* **100/1**

24-3 **14** *5* **Scippit**[17] [1278] 6-10-12 85 DO'Meara —
(Miss Tracy Waggott) *racd in last: no ch fr 6th: eased 3 out: btn 92l* **12/1**

0-0 **P** **Sean Nos (IRE)**[33] [1158] 4-10-12 JamesDavies —
(W K Goldsworthy) *sent to post v early: w tearaway ldr tl flattened 2nd and nrly fell: immediately p.u but bolted on flat all the way to fin* **25/1**

3m 50.3s (-10.10) **Going Correction** -0.60s/f (Firm) 15 Ran SP% **120.0**
Speed ratings: **101,99,98,98,92 90,89,85,84,80 78,77,—,—,—** CSF £278.55 TOTE £146.70: £30.00, £1.80, £2.10; EX 1567.20.The winner was bought in for 5,600gns. Double Royal (IRE) was claimed by Mrs T. J. Hill for £6,000.
Owner K G Kitchen **Bred** Frit Von Ballmoos **Trained** Six Hills, Leics
■ Stewards' Enquiry : K Renwick one-day ban: used whip with excessive frequency (Sep 18)

FOCUS
A very weak event, even by selling standards, and like the first race it was run at a strong pace. The overall form looks sound enough.

NOTEBOOK
Euro Route(IRE) , at one time rated 87 as a juvenile sprinter in Ireland, enjoyed the decent gallop and dug deep when it mattered in the home straight to land his first success over hurdles at the third attempt. The manner in which he travelled before being asked to win his race, suggests this was no fluke, and a recent change of scenery has clearly had the desired effect.
Staff Nurse(IRE) chased the pace throughout, and was staying on again at the death, having hit a flat spot turning out of the back straight. She is clearly not straightforward, but remains capable of success in this grade and may be worth trying over further again now. *(op 4-1)*
Always Flying(USA) was a distance clear at one stage, and ultimately went off too fast for his own good, as he tired quickly approaching the final flight and had no more to offer once headed. He is not without hope in this grade over hurdles and will surely be given a slightly more patient ride next time. *(op 8-1)*
Double Royal(IRE) turned in a fair effort on ground he would have found plenty fast enough. He is reliable in this grade, albeit still a maiden over hurdles. *(op 10-1)*
Royaltea failed to really land a blow back over this more suitably shorter trip, having refused to settle through the early stages. *(op 8-1 tchd 17-2)*
Honan(IRE) , the only runner in the field to have previously won a race over jumps, looked to make up his ground too quickly and found nothing under maximum pressure. *(op 7-2)*
Sean Nos(IRE) *Official explanation: jockey said gelding became uncontrollable after making a mistake at the first (tchd 33-1)*

1433 LOMBARD VEHICLE MANAGEMENT H'CAP CHASE (10 fncs 2 omitted) 2m

3:05 (3:05) (Class 4) (0-100,100) 5-Y-0+ £3,486 (£996; £498)

Form RPR

0/45 **1** **Loulou Nivernais (FR)**[11] [1335] 6-10-6 80 ADempsey 93+
(M Todhunter) *hld up towards rr: stl 6th but making smooth prog bef 3 out: chal last: carried hd high but styd on to ld fnl 50 yds* **9/1**

0- **2** *nk* **Mattys Joy (IRE)**[13] [1324] 6-11-3 91 (p) RThornton 102+
(Daniel Mark Loughnane, Ire) *chsd clr ldr: clsd to ld 4th: 8l ahd 6th where swished tail: mstke 3 out: sn drvn: ct and no ex 50 yds out* **12/1**

-F54 **3** *6* **Lascar De Ferbet (FR)**[14] [1311] 6-11-0 88 JMMaguire 94+
(R Ford) *hld up midfield: effrt 6th: wnt 2nd and blnd 3 out: sn rdn: lost 2nd bef last: wknd* **5/1**[1]

6000 **4** *10* **He's Hot Right Now (NZ)**[11] [1335] 6-10-11 85 (p) HOliver 79
(R C Guest) *t.k.h: chsd ldrs: rdn and looking hld whn mstke 3 out: sn btn* **8/1**

1343 **5** *8* **Nazimabad (IRE)**[30] [1176] 6-11-0 88 (t) ChristianWilliams 82+
(Evan Williams) *racd freely: settled 3rd: blnd 5th: wnt 2nd next tl rdn and lost pl bef 3 out: sn eased* **11/2**[2]

P0P4 **6** *3 ½* **Northern Rambler (IRE)**[8] [1379] 8-9-7 74 oh8 (p) PKinsella[(7)] 57
(K G Reveley) *wl bhd: out of tch after 4th: slt prog to midfield whn mstke 6th: nvr gng wl after* **20/1**

24-0 **7** *16* **Noble Colours**[11] [1343] 12-9-7 74 oh13 TMessenger[(7)] 41
(Mrs C J Ikin) *midfield: lost tch bef 6th: sn wl bhd* **50/1**

11/P **8** *18* **Newsplayer (IRE)**[25] [1202] 9-11-10 98 (t) RJohnson 47
(R T Phillips) *led and clr tl mstke 3rd: hdd next: lost tch qckly after 6th: wl btn whn mstke 2 out: t.o* **5/1**[1]

0/ **9** *dist* **Just Different (IRE)**[83] [770] 8-11-12 100 LAspell —
(P G Murphy) *keen early: poor last after 4th: t.o bef 3 out: btn 99l* **14/1**

0P6P **P** **The Honey Guide**[33] [1147] 9-9-9 74 oh13 DCCostello[(5)] —
(Mrs L B Normile) *rr tl p.u bef 2nd* **66/1**

0-43 **P** **Treaty Stone**[15] [1298] 6-11-10 98 APMcCoy —
(Jonjo O'Neill) *j. slowly 4th: chsd ldrs tl struggling and mstke 6th: t.o and p.u 3 out* **7/1**[3]

-P05 **P** **Ratty's Band**[14] [1311] 11-10-0 74 oh1 NPMulholland —
(Mrs L B Normile) *terrible mstke 3rd: sn lost tch u.p: blnd again 5th: continued t.o tl p.u 3 out* **12/1**

3m 48.3s (-16.70) **Going Correction** -1.15s/f (Hard) 12 Ran SP% **112.6**
Speed ratings: **95,94,91,86,82 81,73,64,—,— —,—** CSF £102.81 CT £597.65 TOTE £10.50: £3.30, £1.80, £2.10; EX 205.50.
Owner F G Steel **Bred** J Dufour **Trained** Orton, Cumbria

FOCUS
As expected, this moderate handicap was run at a solid pace, and the field were again strung out at an early stage. The first two came clear on the run-in. The winner produced a big step up on his previous chase runs to the level of his best hurdles form. Solid enough form.

NOTEBOOK
Loulou Nivernais(FR) produced a remarkable display to score a first success over fences at the ninth attempt. He ran in snatches at the rear throughout the first circuit, before finally responding to his rider's urgings and arriving on the scene with three to jump. He came back onto the bridle thereafter and, despite showing a high head carriage when asked for maximum effort on the run-in, was always going to get up. He can win again, but is clearly a very tricky ride.
Mattys Joy(IRE) ran a solid race in defeat, having cut out much of the running from halfway, and was only denied in the dying strides. He is a likeable sort, despite only having been successful once to date, and this must rate an improved effort.
Lascar De Ferbet(FR) enjoyed the decent pace and would have probably been closer but for making a mistake three out. However, he would still not have beaten the front pair.
He's Hot Right Now(NZ) turned in his best effort over fences to date, despite always being held by the principals. He is potentially well treated on his hurdle form and could build on this, perhaps over a touch further. *(op 11-1)*

Newsplayer(IRE) went off too fast for his own good and could do nothing when Mattys Joy took him on down the back straight. He is better than this. *(op 9-2)*

1434 ALLIED IRISH BANK (GB) H'CAP HURDLE (12 hdls) 2m 4f 110y

3:40 (3:40) (Class 3) (0-125,122) 4-Y-0+ £6,825 (£2,100; £1,050; £525)

Form RPR

6100 **1** **Xellance (IRE)**[17] [1270] 8-11-5 122 MrTJO'Brien[(7)] 128+
(P J Hobbs) *settled 3rd: wnt 2nd and mstke 7th: rdn 3 out: ev ch whn mstke 2 out: 2l down last: drvn and rallied to ld fnl 50 yds* **9/2**[3]

040- **2** *1 ¼* **Mister Arjay (USA)**[7] [3592] 5-10-13 109 ADobbin 113
(B Ellison) *led: drew clr w wnr after 9th: rdn next: looked lft in command 2 out and 2l ahd last: wknd and hdd clsng stages* **11/1**

3214 **3** *9* **Cannon Fire (FR)**[30] [1181] 4-10-9 106 ChristianWilliams 100
(Evan Williams) *chsd ldrs: niggled after 6th: sn outpcd by ldrs: kpt on steadily to go modest 3rd bef 2 out* **11/2**

1232 **4** *10* **Festive Chimes (IRE)**[25] [1213] 4-10-3 103 ONelmes[(3)] 87
(N B King) *settled towards rr: effrt 8th: wnt 3rd after next: rdn and nt rch ldrs: lost 3rd bef 2 out* **9/1**

2UP- **5** *7* **Take The Stand (IRE)**[144] [4861] 9-11-12 122 APMcCoy 102+
(P Bowen) *pressed ldr tl nt fluent 7th: sn rdn: wknd after 9th: nt fluent 3 out* **10/3**[1]

0F-0 **6** *5* **Cameron Bridge (IRE)**[18] [1265] 9-11-0 110 RJohnson 86+
(P J Hobbs) *hld up: effrt 7th: chsng ldrs whn mstke next: sn rdn: btn after 9th* **4/1**[2]

0245 **7** *10* **Pilca (FR)**[56] [974] 5-9-9 98 SWalsh[(7)] 61
(R M Stronge) *hld up in last pair: lost tch after 8th* **12/1**

42-0 **P** **Sully Shuffles (IRE)**[111] [422] 10-11-12 122 GLee —
(M Todhunter) *bhd: last and struggling after 6th: p.u next* **14/1**

4m 56.5s (-15.60) **Going Correction** -0.60s/f (Firm)
WFA 4 from 5yo+ 15lb 8 Ran SP% **109.3**
Speed ratings: **105,104,101,97,94 92,88,—** CSF £45.99 CT £251.83 TOTE £3.90: £1.10, £4.00, £2.10; EX 71.50.
Owner The Five Nations Partnership **Bred** T Harris **Trained** Withycombe, Somerset

FOCUS
A fair handicap, run at a solid pace, and the first two had it two themselves in the home straight. The form looks sound, with the winner back to the level of his best 2004 form.

NOTEBOOK
Xellance(IRE) dug deep to get the better of the runner-up close home and resume winning ways. He appeared held when making an error at the penultimate flight, but responded to maximum pressure and his superior stamina ultimately told. The decent pace was to his liking, as was the drop to this grade, and he again displayed battling qualities when it mattered. Versatile as regards trip, he relishes a fast surface, but this was his highest winning mark to date and he is not at all certain to follow-up back in a higher grade.
Mister Arjay(USA) ◆, fit from the Flat yet having his first outing over hurdles for 221 days, has to rate unlucky, as he made a bold bid from the front only to be mugged in the final 25 yards. He saw out every yard of this trip and, providing he can maintain this current mood, should be placed to go one better before too long. *(op 8-1)*
Cannon Fire(FR) was never quite on terms, yet stuck to his task throughout and ran to his best. He is a decent benchmark for this form and does have another race within his compass from his current rating. *(op 9-2)*
Festive Chimes(IRE), whose only success in this sphere came over course and distance in July, ran her race and remains in good heart. She is consistent and can find easier opportunities in the future. *(op 10-1)*
Take The Stand(IRE), last season's Gold Cup runner-up, found things happening all too quickly on this return to hurdling and his fate was apparent from some way out. He is capable of much better over further and should be seen in a totally different light when resuming over fences in due course. *(op 3-1)*
Cameron Bridge(IRE)travelled sweetly off the pace for a long way, but made an error at a crucial stage when easing into contention and was held thereafter. He can do better over hurdles, but is not one to rely on. *(op 7-2)*

1435 ALLIED IRISH BANK (GB) H'CAP CHASE (11 fncs 4 omitted) 2m 4f

4:15 (4:15) (Class 3) (0-125,124) 5-Y-0+ £8,043 (£2,475; £1,237; £618)

Form RPR

-204 **1** **Ball O Malt (IRE)**[15] [1295] 9-11-7 119 APMcCoy 129+
(R A Fahey) *settled off pce: stdy prog after 7th: wnt 2nd 3 out: led next: drvn and edgd lft last: styd on wl* **11/4**[1]

0-13 **2** *1 ½* **Beat The Heat (IRE)**[102] [550] 7-10-11 109 (b) BHarding 118+
(Jedd O'Keeffe) *chsd ldrs: mstke 6th: effrt 8th: rdn 3 out: ev ch fr next: wnt lft last: no imp after* **8/1**

0-00 **3** *1 ¼* **Prince Of Pleasure (IRE)**[13] [1325] 11-11-5 117 RThornton 123
(D Broad, Ire) *led tl 4th and again after 7th: drvn and hdd 2 out: one pce but kpt on gamely flat* **11/1**

102 **4** *10* **Danish Decorum (IRE)**[13] [1320] 6-11-10 122 ChristianWilliams 120+
(Evan Williams) *wnt 2nd at 3rd: led next: hdd after 7th: hit next: rdn and wknd after 3 out* **5/1**[2]

6U12 **5** *6* **Sardagna (FR)**[18] 1264 5-11-12 **124** .... TJMurphy 114
(M C Pipe) *settled off pce: blnd 7th: hit 8th: brief effrt bef next but nvr able to rch ldrs* **7/1**[3]

05-4 **6** *8* **Log On Intersky (IRE)**[13] 1320 9-11-10 **122** .... GLee 104
(J Howard Johnson) *taken to post early: chsd ldrs: niggled after 5th: nt fluent 8th: drvn and lost tch bef next* **7/1**[3]

1-55 **7** *dist* **Jordan's Ridge (IRE)**[15] 1295 9-10-11 **109** .... KRenwick —
(P Monteith) *detached in last pair: rdn after 5th: struggling after: t.o 3 out: btn 67l* **10/1**

1565 **8** *9* **Papua**[17] 1273 11-10-8 **106** ....(b) DRDennis —
(N J Hawke) *chsd ldrs tl wknd u.p after 7th: t.o 3 out: btn 76l* **14/1**

1513 **P** **Silence Reigns**[20] 1248 11-10-3 **108** ....(bt) RSpate(7) —
(Mrs K Waldron) *nt fluent and detached in last pair: struggling whn blnd 7th: t.o and p.u next* **7/1**[3]

4m 51.9s (-28.70) **Going Correction** -1.15s/f (Hard) **9** Ran SP% **116.0**
Speed ratings: **111,110,109,105,103 100,—,—,—** CSF £25.31 CT £210.22 TOTE £3.70: £2.10, £1.10, £3.90; EX 31.70.
Owner Declan Kinahan **Bred** Con O'Connell **Trained** Musley Bank, N Yorks

FOCUS
Another fair handicap and another race run at a strong gallop, thus ensuring the field were strung out early. It produced a creditable winning time for a race of its class. The first two showed improved form and the third ran to his mark.

NOTEBOOK
Ball O Malt(IRE) ◆ relished the early pace and deservedly scored his second success over fences in dogged fashion. He needed all of McCoy's strength to hold off his rivals on the run-in, but he jumped well throughout and there was a fair bit to like about the manner in which he cruised into contention. While a rise in the weights will make life harder now, he appeals as the type who may be able to progress further over fences this term and is in the right hands to do so. *(op 10-3 tchd 7-2)*
Beat The Heat(IRE) ◆ made a pleasing return from his 102-day break and did little wrong in defeat. He should have little trouble finding another race off this sort of rating over fences. *(op 9-1)*
Prince Of Pleasure(IRE) fared the best of those to force the early pace and ran close to his Galway Plate form with the winner. He is another who can be placed to resume winning ways off his current mark if able to maintain this current mood. *(op 20-1)*
Danish Decorum(IRE), previously unbeaten in three outings at this track, produced another fair effort without rating a serious threat. He gives the form a sound look, but the Handicapper looks to have his measure now. *(op 4-1)*
Sardagna(FR) merely kept on at the same pace throughout and was unable to land a blow at any stage. This was some way below her recent level and she does look too high in the weights at present. *(op 5-1)*
Log On Intersky(IRE) is struggling for form at present and continues to look out of sorts. *(op 9-1)*

1436 KATHARINE HOUSE HOSPICE H'CAP HURDLE (14 hdls) 3m
4:50 (4:50) (Class 4) (0-110,107) 4-Y-0+ **£4,133** (£1,181; £590)

Form RPR

1353 **1** **Lawyer Des Ormeaux (FR)**[29] 1192 6-11-12 **107** .... RJohnson 112+
(P Bowen) *settled midfield: effrt 10th: wnt 2nd and rdn 3 out: led and wandered bef last: drvn out* **7/1**[3]

00-4 **2** *2* **Yourman (IRE)**[37] 1125 5-11-10 **105** .... TJMurphy 108
(M C Pipe) *wl in rr: stl plenty to do and drvn bef 3 out: styd on to go 2nd last: one pce and nt rch wnr* **7/1**[3]

1204 **3** *2 ½* **Esters Boy**[42] 1079 7-11-5 **100** .... LAspell 100
(P G Murphy) *chsd ldrs: rdn and effrt whn rn wd bef 3 out: kpt on steadily after but unable to chal* **25/1**

1424 **4** *1* **Vicentio**[48] 1045 6-10-12 **93** .... GLee 92
(T J Fitzgerald) *settled midfield: effrt 11th: drvn into 3rd 2 out: wknd after last* **8/1**

0 **5** *2 ½* **Coccinelle (IRE)**[14] 1116 7-11-3 **98** ....(p) NFehily 96+
(K A Morgan) *prom: led after 11th and tried to get clr: rdn and hdd bef last: fdd tamely* **25/1**

3R-2 **6** *2 ½* **Pardon What**[113] 397 9-10-13 **94** .... APMcCoy 88
(S Lycett) *rn in snatches and nvr looked v keen on jumping: midfield: rdn and brief effrt bef 3 out: fnd little after* **7/1**[3]

1232 **7** *½* **Little Task**[11] 1333 7-10-6 **90** ....(p) PAspell(3) 84
(J S Wainwright) *hld up and bhd: prog to midfield after 11th: sn rdn: nt trble ldrs fr next* **11/1**

1615 **8** *nk* **Angie's Double**[30] 1181 5-10-6 **94** .... RSpate(7) 87
(Mrs K Waldron) *bhd: rdn 9th: sn outpcd: sme late prog: n.d* **20/1**

0325 **9** *3 ½* **Wild Tempo (FR)**[18] 1262 10-10-4 **95** ....(t) AGlassonbury(10) 85
(M C Pipe) *bhd: rdn 9th: btn after 11th: racd awkwardly after* **20/1**

300- **10** *28* **Accepting**[14] 3765 8-11-8 **103** ....(b) PMoloney 65
(J Mackie) *prom: hrd drvn 11th: dropped out v tamely* **12/1**

6-43 **11** *9* **Koumba (FR)**[48] 1045 7-11-0 **95** .... ChristianWilliams 48
(Evan Williams) *2nd or 3rd tl led 11th: sn rdn and hdd: wknd bef next: eased appr 2 out: t.o* **6/1**[2]

P524 **12** *4* **Pequenita**[13] 1319 5-11-0 **95** ....(b) HOliver 44
(R C Guest) *led tl rdn and hdd 11th: sn fdd: eased after 3 out: t.o* **20/1**

0-PP **13** *4* **Floranz**[52] 1017 9-10-4 **85** .... SCurran 30
(Mrs M Evans) *cl up tl drvn after 8th: rr next: t.o 3 out* **66/1**

12 **14** *6* **Fourth Dimension (IRE)**[42] 875 6-10-13 **94** .... KRenwick 33
(N Wilson) *chsd ldrs: reminder 4th: wknd u.p 10th: eased bef 3 out: t.o* **11/2**[1]

5m 58.8s (-6.20) **Going Correction** -0.60s/f (Firm) **14** Ran SP% **117.8**
Speed ratings: **86,85,84,84,83 82,82,82,81,71 68,67,66,64** CSF £48.77 CT £1165.60 TOTE £10.70: £3.50, £3.00, £8.00; EX 58.10 Place 6 £201.81, Place 5 £147.43.
Owner D M Williams & C B Brookes **Bred** Pierre Bourdon **Trained** Little Newcastle, Pembrokes

FOCUS
A modest, yet fairly competitive handicap for the class, run at a steady gallop. The two at the top of the handicap duly came home first and second and it produced a pedestrian winning time for a race of its type.

NOTEBOOK
Lawyer Des Ormeaux(FR) got his head back in front with a brave effort under top weight. He has stamina in abundance, enjoyed this fast ground and does possess a willing attitude. While he may have a little more to offer over this sort of trip over hurdles, and would be entitled to plenty of respect if turned out under a penalty, he will only reach his peak when going chasing in due course. *(op 8-1 tchd 9-1)*
Yourman(IRE) took time to pick up from the back of the pack, but when doing so he stayed on with purpose and at one stage on the run-in looked as if he may get to the eventual winner. He hard to win with, but is worth another chance over this trip and, like the winner, will probably come into his own when tackling fences. *(op 15-2 tchd 6-1)*
Esters Boy posted an improved effort and was not at all disgraced in defeat. He looks best at this distance and can find easier opportunities.
Vicentio had his chance and turned in another fair effort. He just looks a touch high in the weights at present. *(op 10-1)*
Coccinelle(IRE), reverting to hurdles, went clear at the top of the straight, yet her effort proved short-lived and she was ultimately well held. It was still a much-improved effort, however, and she can build on this. *(op 20-1)*
Pardon What failed to improve on his recent efforts, and not even the champion jockey could get him in the mood, which has to be worrying for his connections. *(op 15-2 tchd 8-1)*
Fourth Dimension(IRE) was handy before dropping out very quickly under pressure and was *heavily eased thereafter. He has it all to prove now. Official explanation: trainer had no explanation for the poor form shown (op 4-1)*
T/Plt: £360.50 to a £1 stake. Pool: £36,741.75. 74.40 winning tickets. T/Qpdt: £69.50 to a £1 stake. Pool: £2,708.30. 28.80 winning tickets. IM

1437 - 1439a (Foreign Racing) - See Raceform Interactive

1317 BANGOR-ON-DEE (L-H)
Friday, September 9

OFFICIAL GOING: Chase course - good (good to soft in places); hurdle course - good to soft (soft in places)
There was 15mm of rain the night before racing and the ground rode slower than forecast.
Wind: Almost nil Weather: overcast

1440 BETDAQ - THE BETTING EXCHANGE JUVENILE NOVICES' HURDLE (DIV I) (9 hdls) 2m 1f
1:55 (1:56) (Class 4) 3-Y-O **£3,057** (£940; £470; £235)

Form RPR

1 **Etoile Russe (IRE)**[37] 3-10-12 .... APMcCoy 82+
(P C Haslam) *nt fluent: keen: mde virtually all: rdn whn blnd 2 out: awkward last: drvn and all out* **10/3**[2]

5 **2** *1 ½* **Backstreet Lad**[13] 1332 3-10-12 .... ChristianWilliams 77
(Evan Williams) *nt fluent: cl up tl rdn and outpcd 3 out: rallied to go 2nd and mstke next: drvn and styd on flat* **10/3**[2]

3 **3** *10* **Verstone (IRE)**[13] 1338 3-10-5 .... GLee 60
(R F Fisher) *keen: pressed wnr: wandered bef 2nd: drvn and relegated 3rd 2 out: wandering again and sn wknd* **2/1**[1]

0 **4** *14* **Swallow Falls (IRE)**[35] 1146 3-10-0 .... StephenJCraine(5) 48+
(D McCain) *chsd ldrs: 3rd and effrt 3 out: sn drvn: wknd bef next* **22/1**

5 *30* **Pitsi Kahtoh**[20] 3-10-0 .... MNicolls(5) 16
(P W Hiatt) *mstke 3rd: chsd ldrs tl wknd and mstke 6th: mstke next: continued t.o* **14/1**

6 *9* **Top Pursuit**[432] 3-10-9 .... PWhelan(3) 14
(J L Spearing) *midfield: lost tch rapidly bef 5th: sn t.o* **33/1**

PPF0 **7** *1 ½* **Miss Dinamite**[13] 1339 3-9-12 .... TMessenger(7) —
(Mrs C J Ikin) *keen and stdd wl in rr: lost tch rapidly 5th and continued t.o* **100/1**

8 *dist* **Ardasnails (IRE)**[108] 3-10-12 ....(bt[1]) SCurran —
(K G Wingrove) *keen in rr: mstke 4th: sn struggling: continued hopelessly t.o: btn 130l* **50/1**

U **9** *15* **Southern Shore (IRE)**[9] 1380 3-10-5 ....(t) AScholes(7) —
(D Burchell) *inordinately clumsy: lost tch and rdn 3rd: fs bhd fr 5th: btn 145l* **8/1**[3]

P **P** **Time To Succeed**[13] 1338 3-10-9 .... ACCoyle(3) —
(J S Wainwright) *keen early: midfield: mstke 3rd: u.p and j. slowly next: t.o and p.u 5th* **66/1**

4m 19.5s (8.60) **Going Correction** +0.325s/f (Yiel) **10** Ran SP% **109.0**
Speed ratings: **92,91,86,80,65 61,60,—,—,—** CSF £13.49 TOTE £2.80: £1.70, £1.10, £1.10; EX 17.20.
Owner M C Mason **Bred** Roland H Alder **Trained** Middleham, N Yorks

FOCUS
A weak juvenile hurdle run at a slow early pace and best rated through the runner-up. The slower of the two divisions by two seconds.

NOTEBOOK
Etoile Russe(IRE), rated 61 on the Flat, was given an astute ride from the front and jumped pretty well in the main. He might not have beaten much however and was getting tired after the last even though the gallop was pedestrian early on. *(op 7-2)*
Backstreet Lad appeared as though he was going to be left behind when the pace quickened, but stuck on gamely to threaten after the last. He settled better than on his debut and should find an opening. *(tchd 3-1)*
Verstone(IRE), a creditable third on debut in a race which is working out quite well, helped cut out the ordinary early gallop. She had no answer to the injection of pace and may not have enjoyed the softer conditions. *(op 7-4)*
Swallow Falls(IRE) displayed some promise as she travelled nicely before fading. This was an improvement on her debut effort and she may appreciate less of a test of stamina. *(op 20-1)*
Pitsi Kahtoh looked to possess some stamina given her breeding, but dropped away tamely from four out. *(op 16-1)*

1441 BETDAQ - THE BETTING EXCHANGE JUVENILE NOVICES' HURDLE (DIV II) (9 hdls) 2m 1f
2:25 (2:29) (Class 4) 3-Y-O **£3,049** (£938; £469; £234)

Form RPR

2F24 **1** **Shingle Street (IRE)**[6] 1397 3-10-12 ....(t) AO'Keeffe 89+
(Miss Venetia Williams) *led tl after 1st: cl up tl led again 3 out: sn rdn clr: in n.d after 2 out: eased flat* **3/1**[1]

4 **2** *18* **Sound And Vision (IRE)**[13] 1332 3-10-12 .... BHarding 69+
(M Dods) *hld up in midfield: stdy prog 5th: chsd wnr after 3 out: rdn and sn no ch w wnr nt fluent next: nt fluent last* **5/1**[2]

3 *19* **Naval Force**[31] 3-10-12 .... DRDennis 55+
(Ian Williams) *prom: nt fluent 4th: blnd next: lost tch w ldng pair after 3 out: blnd bdly next* **11/1**

0 **4** *1* **Procrastinate (IRE)**[13] 1332 3-10-12 .... ADobbin 47
(R F Fisher) *hld up and bhd: effrt after 4th: chsd ldrs briefly 6th: fdd after next* **33/1**

5 *19* **Vocative (GER)**[42] 3-10-5 .... FKeniry 21
(P C Haslam) *chsd ldrs:mstke 3rd: swished tail 4th: rdn bef 6th where j. slowly: sn tired: t.o after mstke 3 out* **13/2**[3]

PP **6** *6* **Don Pasquale**[6] 1397 3-10-12 ....(t) JMogford 22
(J T Stimpson) *keen: led after 1st: mstkes 4th and 6th: drvn and hdd next: stopped to nil: t.o* **33/1**

U **7** *5* **Spence Appeal (IRE)**[9] 1380 3-10-7 .... LStephens(5) 17
(C Roberts) *mstkes in rr: struggling bef 5th: t.o 3 out* **7/1**

P **8** *1 ¾* **Keepasharplookout (IRE)**[13] 1332 3-10-12 .... JPByrne 15
(C W Moore) *plld hrd in last: a detached: t.o 6th* **66/1**

P **Lara's Girl**[293] 3-10-5 .... SCurran —
(K G Wingrove) *bhd: rdn and lost tch 5th: blnd next: t.o and p.u 3 out* **66/1**

The Form Book, Raceform Ltd, Compton, RG20 6NL

0 **P** **Final Overture (IRE)**[13] [1339] 3-10-0 .... DCCostello(5) —
(J S Wainwright) *wl bhd: rdn and labouring after 3rd: t.o and p.u 5th*
100/1

3 **P** **Dennick**[13] [1332] 3-10-12 .... APMcCoy —
(P C Haslam) *plld v hrd: wnt 2nd and mstke 3rd: lost pl 5th: 7th and fading whn blnd 6th: p.u next*
3/1[1]

4m 17.5s (6.60) **Going Correction** +0.325s/f (Yiel) **33** Ran SP% **110.7**
Speed ratings: **97,88,79,79,70 67,65,64,—,— —** CSF £16.69 TOTE £4.00: £1.60, £1.60, £2.60; EX 13.60.
Owner Richard Abbott & Mario Stavrou **Bred** Sean O'Keeffe **Trained** Kings Caple, H'fords

FOCUS
Another juvenile hurdle lacking in depth and won by an exposed three-year-old. The form is rated through the winner. The faster of the two divisions by two seconds.

NOTEBOOK
Shingle Street(IRE), the clear pick on the ratings, could hardly be accused of being unexposed and took advantage of a good opportunity to score over hurdles at the fifth time of asking. He may find life tougher under a penalty. *(op 5-2)*
Sound And Vision(IRE), fourth on his debut over hurdles, probably ran a similar race and could pick up an event of this nature early season. *(op 11-2 tchd 6-1)*
Naval Force was held when blundering badly two from home. This was a reasonable effort first time over hurdles, although he was inconsistent on the level and cannot be replied upon to reproduce this run. *(op 9-1)*
Procrastinate(IRE) was moderate on the Flat and his presence in fourth ensures the form is not to be trusted implicitly. *(op 25-1)*
Vocative(GER), backed from 8/1 into 13/2, flashed her tail under pressure and weakened tamely. *(op 8-1)*
Keepasharplookout(IRE) *Official explanation: jockey said, regarding the running and riding, his orders were to start off in rear, settle gelding and creep his way into the race, adding that gelding pulled hard, jumped sketchily early on, and subsequently tired in the closing stages on soft ground*
Dennick was in contention before blundering at the fourth last, which led to him being pulled up. *Official explanation: jockey said gelding had a breathing problem (tchd 11-4 and 10-3)*

1442 BET EACHWAY AT BETDAQ.CO.UK NOVICES' CHASE (15 fncs) 2m 4f 110y
3:00 (3:00) (Class 4) 5-Y-0+ £4,433 (£1,364; £682; £341)

Form RPR
U211 **1** **Mister Flint**[39] [1124] 7-11-12 132 .... RJohnson 127+
(P J Hobbs) *sn wl clr: 30l ahd 5th: stdd after next: pressed 2 out tl last: drvn to pull away fr rival flat*
4/11[1]

4112 **2** *4* **In The Frame (IRE)**[68] [894] 6-11-12 115 .... ChristianWilliams 124+
(Evan Williams) *hld up: wnt 2nd at 6th: clsd next: nt fluent 10th: rdn to chal 2 out: ch but no imp whn swtchd rt and pckd last: eased*
7/1[3]

-016 **3** *26* **After Me Boys**[23] [1234] 11-11-5 115 .... DElsworth 96+
(Mrs S J Smith) *chsd clr ldr tl 6th: in tch fr next tl rdn and fdd bef 3 out*
6/1[2]

6033 **4** *11* **Half Inch**[22] [1249] 5-10-5 98 .... RThornton 65
(B I Case) *hld up and nvr looked dangerous: lost tch bef 10th*
16/1

P0P6 **5** *dist* **Greenacres Boy**[15] [1321] 10-10-9 56 .... (p) ACCoyle(3) —
(M Mullineaux) *j. tentatively in last: rdn and nt keen after 10th: sn t.o: btn 84l*
66/1

5m 6.30s (-6.20) **Going Correction** -0.175s/f (Good) **5** Ran SP% **107.5**
Speed ratings: **104,102,92,88,—** CSF £3.41 TOTE £1.20: £1.10, £1.90; EX 2.30.
Owner Alan Peterson **Bred** M H Ings **Trained** Withycombe, Somerset

FOCUS
This was dominated by the winner who established a healthy lead from the off and never looked like being caught. Decent novice form, rated through the second.

NOTEBOOK
Mister Flint is getting his act together over fences and, although this victory was ultimately hard work, he duly completed the hat-trick. A headstrong character, his fencing has improved with experience which was a necessity given his rise in the ratings. *(op 1-3 tchd 2-5)*
In The Frame(IRE) has found some consistency with his current connections and would have pressurised the winner but for a mistake at the last. This was a fair effort on ground softer than ideal. *(op 13-2 tchd 15-2)*
After Me Boys was nibbled at in the pre-race market, but was a shade disappointing for the second successive outing and looks out of form at present. He has seemed to save his better efforts for flatter left-handed tracks than this. *(op 8-1)*
Half Inch is exposed and a little high in the handicap for what she has achieved. *(op 14-1)*
Greenacres Boy is unreliable and remains a risky betting proposition.

1443 BETDAQ 24 HOUR TELEBET H'CAP HURDLE (11 hdls) 2m 4f
3:35 (3:35) (Class 4) (0-110,109) 4-Y-0+ £3,412 (£1,050; £525; £262)

Form RPR
P-41 **1** **Michaels Dream (IRE)**[11] [1361] 6-11-4 100 7ex .... (b) KRenwick 107+
(N Wilson) *pressed ldr: drew level 6th tl relegated 3rd at next: sn drvn: stl 3rd but rallying 2 out: led bef last: forged clr*
9/2[3]

-U20 **2** *5* **Murphy's Nails (IRE)**[107] [501] 8-10-12 94 .... JPMcNamara 97+
(K C Bailey) *j. awkwardly at times: mde most tl 7th: drvn ahd again 2 out: sn hdd: tired and plodded on*
20/1

2211 **3** *11* **Marathea (FR)**[35] [1152] 4-9-13 87 .... PCO'Neill(5) 79+
(Miss Venetia Williams) *hld up in tch: clsd to ld 7th: rdn and hdd 2 out: tired and btn whn blnd last*
11/4[1]

P6P- **4** *1* **Calomeria**[189] [4156] 4-11-7 109 .... StephenJCraine(5) 97
(D McCain) *keen pressing ldrs: mstke 3rd: rdn bef 7th: lost tch next: plugged on*
14/1

2132 **5** *6* **Reem Two**[15] [1317] 4-11-3 100 .... JMMaguire 82
(D McCain) *handy: rdn after 5th: nt gng wl after: 4th whn mstke 7th: no ch after: eased bef 2 out*
6/1

13-1 **F** **Friendly Request**[27] [1211] 6-10-2 91 .... KBurke(7) —
(N J Hawke) *cl up tl 5th: 6th and wkng whn fell next*
4/1[2]

3126 **P** **Qualitair Pleasure**[19] [1280] 5-10-8 90 .... GLee —
(J Hetherton) *hld up last: struggling whn swvd to avoid faller 6th: continued t.o: p.u 3 out*
4/1[2]

5m 6.50s (8.90) **Going Correction** +0.325s/f (Yiel) **7** Ran SP% **110.6**
Speed ratings: **95,93,88,88,85 —,—** CSF £68.36 CT £275.66 TOTE £4.30: £2.80, £5.70; EX 46.70.
Owner Mrs Michael John Paver **Bred** M J Paver **Trained** Upper Helmsley, N Yorks

FOCUS
An ordinary handicap run in a modest time for a race of its class, and with only the winner seeming to handle conditions. The runner-up displayed promise until a lack of condition found him out.

NOTEBOOK
Michaels Dream(IRE), in good heart following a recent Cartmel win, relished the cut in the ground to outstay his rivals and defy a 7lb penalty in style. He appears to be a revitalised character in the blinkers. *(op 5-1)*
Murphy's Nails(IRE), off the track since May, posted one of his better efforts and coped well with the ground. He has been difficult to train, but he should soon be winning off his current mark if he can stay sound. *(op 18-1)*
Marathea(FR) has been quietly progressive on quicker ground, but found the overnight rain nullified her effectiveness. She should not be written off back on a faster surface. *(op 10-3)*
Calomeria faced a tough task off top weight on her first start for six months. Keen early on, she plugged on well enough and can step up on this encouraging reappearance. *(op 12-1)*
Reem Two has been well placed this summer, but was well beaten on her return to handicaps. The change in conditions probably worked against her. *(op 5-1)*
Qualitair Pleasure *Official explanation: jockey said mare was unsuited by the good to soft (soft in places) ground (op 5-1)*

1444 GLOBAL BETTING EXCHANGE H'CAP HURDLE (9 hdls) 2m 1f
4:10 (4:11) (Class 3) (0-135,135) 4-Y-0+ £10,227 (£3,147; £1,573; £786)

Form RPR
4-22 **1** **Kingkohler (IRE)**[33] [647] 6-10-1 110 .... PJBrennan 112
(K A Morgan) *keen: hld up and bhd: clsd after 5th: led 3 out: rdn bef next: hld on wl in driving fin*
9/2[2]

FF-0 **2** *½* **Spectrometer**[27] [1204] 8-11-12 135 .... DRDennis 137+
(Ian Williams) *chsd clr ldr: clsd to ld 5th: hdd 3 out: sn rdn: stl pressing wnr last: kpt on cl home*
20/1

0-54 **3** *¾* **Mr Lear (USA)**[12] [784] 6-9-9 109 oh3 .... DCCostello(5) 111+
(J J Quinn) *off pce in midfield: nt fluent 4th: sn clsd on ldrs: rdn after 3 out: ch but kpt hanging lft fr next: no imp flat*
6/1

3003 **4** *3 ½* **Flame Phoenix (USA)**[27] [1204] 6-10-9 118 .... (t) GLee 116
(D McCain) *swishing tail and drvn bef 1st: hit 3rd: bhd tl gradual prog 5th: 4th whn nt fluent next: styd on steadily wout zest fr 2 o*
15/2

/50- **5** *17* **Rooster's Reunion (IRE)**[188] [4188] 6-10-6 115 .... TDoyle 103+
(D R Gandolfo) *hld up last tl prog 5th: brief effrt whn nt fluent 3 out: rdn and sn wknd*
5/1[3]

4-22 **6** *dist* **Salute (IRE)**[11] [332] 6-10-5 114 .... LAspell —
(P G Murphy) *hld up towards rr: lost tch 5th: t.o 3 out: sn eased: btn 68l*
4/1[1]

10/0 **7** *7* **Backcraft (IRE)**[11] [1361] 7-10-0 109 oh1 .... DElsworth —
(Mrs S J Smith) *20l 3rd after 3rd: effrt bef 5th: wknd qckly next: t.o 3 out: sn eased: btn 75l*
16/1

16-2 **8** *dist* **Top Achiever (IRE)**[133] [99] 4-10-0 109 oh1 .... JPByrne —
(C W Moore) *led and sn 8l clr: hit 3rd and 4th: hdd and mstke 5th: stopped to nil and sn t.o: btn 110l*
12/1

100- **P** **Dancing Pearl**[139] [4982] 7-11-0 123 .... WHutchinson —
(C J Price) *midfield: brief effrt bef 5th: rdn bef next: sn fdd: remote 6th whn p.u 2 out*
13/2

4m 12.5s (1.60) **Going Correction** +0.325s/f (Yiel)
WFA 4 from 5yo+ 14lb **9** Ran SP% **112.6**
Speed ratings: **109,108,108,106,98 —,—,—,—** CSF £79.76 CT £538.65 TOTE £4.30: £1.30, £6.00, £2.60; EX 122.70.
Owner Jo Champion, H Morgan, E Barlow **Bred** J F Tuthill **Trained** Waltham-On-The-Wolds, Leics
■ Stewards' Enquiry : P J Brennan one-day ban: used whip without allowing sufficient time for response (Sep 21)

FOCUS
A decent event run at a fair gallop in a time by far the fastest of the four races run over the trip on the day, five seconds quicker than division two of the juvenile hurdle. It was only a fair time for the class of contest, though, and the form is rated through the winner. Solid form.

NOTEBOOK
Kingkohler(IRE) had looked exposed off this mark in previous handicaps, but battled on gamely to hold on after the last. He is a game, genuine type who deserved this success. *(op 5-1)*
Spectrometer is a light of former years, but recaptured some form after a sequence of below-par runs. He appreciated this return to hurdles and could be placed to advantage.
Mr Lear(USA) had the visor removed and bounced back to form on more suitable ground than he had encountered of late. This was a creditable effort and he remains competitive off his mark. *(op 7-1)*
Flame Phoenix(USA) did not take to fences and showed some temperament here before staying on late. He had looked to be on the way back on his previous start, but this was a mulish display. *(op 8-1 tchd 7-1)*
Rooster's Reunion(IRE) has displayed glimpses of ability in a stop-start career and shaped with a little promise. He should be better for the outing. *(op 6-1)*
Salute(IRE), given a warm-up on the Flat, was a major disappointment and was eased after losing touch mid race. *This was surely not his running. Official explanation: jockey said gelding was unsuited by the good to soft (soft in places) ground*

1445 BETDAQ TELEBET 0870 178 1221 "NATIONAL HUNT" NOVICES' HURDLE (9 hdls) 2m 1f
4:45 (4:46) (Class 4) 4-Y-0+ £3,474 (£1,069; £534; £267)

Form RPR
-631 **1** **Cantgeton (IRE)**[39] [1123] 5-11-12 111 .... TJMurphy 123+
(M C Pipe) *led after 1st: v slow pce: hdd after 2nd: led again 5th: drew clr on bridle bef 2 out: heavily eased flat*
1/2[1]

5/0- **2** *10* **Aces Four (IRE)**[309] [1998] 6-10-12 .... GLee 84+
(W McKeown) *hld up midfield: effrt to chse wnr 6th: hit next: sn wl btn: tired fr 2 out*
8/1[3]

-0P4 **3** *5* **Court Empress**[43] [1089] 8-10-5 75 .... CLlewellyn 66
(P D Purdy) *dropped rr after 3rd: stl poor 7th and sltly impeded 3 out: sn wnt 3rd and kpt plugging on gamely: no hope of rching ldrs*
40/1

500- **4** *dist* **Moorlands Milly**[190] [4138] 4-10-0 .... LStephens(5) —
(D Burchell) *bhd: struggling bef 5th: no ch after mstke next: btn 48l* **25/1**

5 *17* **Nearly Never** 10-10-5 .... NCarter(7) —
(Mrs S J Smith) *chsd ldrs: rdn 5th: fdd next: t.o after 3 out: btn 65l* **20/1**

P **Its Mick (IRE)** 8-10-12 .... DElsworth —
(Mrs S J Smith) *cl up tl 4th: wkng whn j. slowly next: exhausted whn climbed 6th and p.u*
11/1

00- **P** **Wizzical Lad**[322] [1802] 5-10-5 .... (p) TMessenger(7) —
(B N Pollock) *towards rr: rdn 5th: nvr gng wl after: btn whn mstke 3 out: t.o and p.u next*
40/1

0- **P** **Bollitree Bob**[251] [3153] 4-10-12 .... TScudamore —
(M Scudamore) *plld hrd: clsd fr rr to ld after 2nd: hit 3rd: hdd 5th: stopped to nil: t.o and p.u 2 out*
15/2[2]

4m 25.8s (14.90) **Going Correction** +0.325s/f (Yiel)
WFA 4 from 5yo+ 14lb **8** Ran SP% **111.4**
Speed ratings: **77,72,69,—,— —,—,—** CSF £4.53 TOTE £1.50: £1.02, £1.70, £6.20; EX 5.40.
Owner D A Johnson **Bred** John Murphy **Trained** Nicholashayne, Devon

FOCUS
An uncompetitive novices' hurdle, won in a time 11 seconds slower than division one of the juvenile hurdle. Very difficult to rate, the winner value for 25l but he might not have needed to improve.

NOTEBOOK
Cantgeton(IRE) barely came out of a canter to rout some limited rivals. This was little more than an exercise canter and told us nothing knew about him. *(op 4-7 tchd 8-13 in places and 4-6 in a place)*
Aces Four(IRE), placed in a bumper, plugged on take second, but was grossly flattered to finish so close to the winner. *(op 6-1 tchd 11-2)*
Court Empress reached the frame due more to her gameness than any latent natural ability.

Moorlands Milly is already confirmed as modest and was beaten 48 lengths into fourth. *(op 20-1)*
Its Mick(IRE) *Official explanation: vet said gelding bled from the nose (op 12-1 tchd 14-1)*

1446 BETDAQ.CO.UK H'CAP CHASE (18 fncs) 3m 110y
5:15 (5:15) (Class 4) (0-105,100) 5-Y-0+ **£4,422** (£1,360; £680; £340)

Form | | | | RPR
PP41 **1** **Fearless Mel (IRE)**[15] [1321] 11-11-12 **100** .... AO'Keeffe 114+
(Mrs H Dalton) *a gng wl: trckd ldrs: led bef 14th and sn clr: 10l ahd 2 out: rdn and nt hrd pressed to hold dwindling ld flat* **5/2**[1]
2-PP **2** *3* **Lost In Normandy (IRE)**[15] [1321] 8-10-0 **74** oh7 ....(b) DCrosse 82+
(Mrs L Williamson) *hld up: midfield whn slipped bef 10th and rdr lost iron briefly: effrt 15th: chsd wnr u.p after 3 out: kpt on: a hld* **16/1**
P-66 **3** *8* **Glashedy Rock (IRE)**[13] [1337] 8-11-4 **92** .... PMoloney 92+
(M F Harris) *nt a fluent: last tl 9th: hdwy 14th: mstke next: rdn and disputing mod 3rd whn mstke 2 out: hit last: n.d* **12/1**
P455 **4** *1 ¼* **Judaic Ways**[27] [1205] 11-10-12 **86** .... RJohnson 83
(H D Daly) *settled in rr: sme hdwy 15th: rdn and disputing poor 3rd 2 out: n.d* **4/1**[2]
5-0F **5** *18* **Waynesworld (IRE)**[99] [612] 7-10-13 **87** .... TScudamore 74+
(M Scudamore) *mde most tl hdd bef 14th: sn rdn: lost tch qckly fr 3 out* **5/1**[3]
500 **6** *20* **Francolino (FR)**[9] [1381] 12-9-11 **74** oh28 .... TJPhelan(3) 33
(Dr P Pritchard) *w ldr and led for short periods to 12th: wknd 14th: toiled on: t.o* **40/1**
2-P6 **7** *3 ½* **Bang And Blame (IRE)**[19] [1276] 9-9-11 **74** oh1 .... PAspell(3) 29
(M W Easterby) *prom early: lost pl and niggled 7th: rdn 11th: hit 14th and lost tch: t.o* **8/1**
PP0- **8** *dist* **Rufius (IRE)**[205] [3884] 12-10-0 **74** oh14 .... CLlewellyn —
(P Kelsall) *sn towards rr: hit 9th: lost tch after 12th: sn wl t.o: btn 110l* **20/1**
F **P** **Castle Oliver (IRE)**[40] [1109] 7-9-8 **75** oh4 ow1 .... SWalsh(7) —
(A J Chamberlain) *towards rr tl prog to trck ldrs 12th: handy whn nt fluent next: sn p.u* **6/1**

6m 18.0s (-5.20) **Going Correction** -0.175s/f (Good) **9** Ran SP% **111.4**
Speed ratings: **101,100,97,97,91 84,83,—,—** CSF £37.50 CT £390.50 TOTE £2.30: £1.40, £4.40, £3.70; EX 31.80 Place 6 £60.42, Place 5 £52.43.
Owner The Leppington Partnership **Bred** T J Kennedy **Trained** Norton, Shropshire

FOCUS
A poor contest won by the one horse with recent winning form, who has been rated as value for 6l. Not a strong race.

NOTEBOOK
Fearless Mel(IRE), up 12lb for a facile win at the track a fortnight ago, followed up and had a little more in hand than the winning margin suggested. The application of a hanging bit has brought about a revitalisation in his fortunes and he coped with the easier conditions better than expected.
Lost In Normandy(IRE), pulled up on his last two starts, overcame a bad slip before the 10th fence to stay on into second. This was a more encouraging performance and he is worth considering at this favourite track in the future.
Glashedy Rock(IRE) rarely posts an error-free round and this outing was no exception. His proximity in third ensures the form is modest. *(op 10-1)*
Judaic Ways looked fit enough for his reappearance but was well held in fourth. His best efforts have come at Ludlow. *(op 7-2)*
Waynesworld(IRE) set a strong gallop but paid for his early exertions. *(op 11-2)*
Castle Oliver(IRE) *Official explanation: trainer said gelding was unsuited by the good (good to soft in places) ground*
T/Plt: £57.10 to a £1 stake. Pool: £32,793.10. 418.75 winning tickets. T/Qpdt: £22.50 to a £1 stake. Pool: £2,296.90. 75.50 winning tickets. IM

1447 - 1453a (Foreign Racing) - See Raceform Interactive

[1395]STRATFORD (L-H)
Sunday, September 11

OFFICIAL GOING: Soft (good to soft in places)
The ground changed from Good and there were 15 non-runners.
Wind: nil Weather: cloudy

1454 BBC COVENTRY AND WARWICKSHIRE MAIDEN HURDLE (12 hdls) 2m 6f 110y
2:25 (2:27) (Class 3) 4-Y-0+ **£5,564** (£1,712; £856; £428)

Form | | | | RPR
1 **Star Member (IRE)**[25] 6-11-0 .... DRDennis 100
(Ian Williams) *chsd ldr: led 6th: rdn 2 out: drvn out* **2/1**[1]
04 **2** *1 ¼* **Air Guitar (IRE)**[13] [1364] 5-11-0 .... PMoloney 99
(M G Quinlan) *hld up in mid-div: hdwy 5th: chsd wnr appr 8th: rdn after 3 out: hung lft appr last: styd on flat* **5/1**[3]
3 *9* **Cirrus (FR)** 6-11-0 .... GLee 90
(K G Reveley) *hld up in tch: wknd after 3 out* **7/2**[2]
0/ **4** *4* **Rhossili (IRE)**[785] [919] 5-11-0 .... LAspell 87+
(Mrs L Wadham) *hld up: hdwy 5th: wknd after 3 out* **20/1**
5 *24* **Aljoash (IRE)**[106] 9-10-2 .... LStephens(5) 55
(C Roberts) *nvr nr ldrs* **20/1**
5 **6** *5* **Menai Straights**[12] [764] 4-10-12 .... TScudamore 55
(P S Payne) *hld up in mid-div: mstke 1st: nt fluent 7th: hdwy 8th: hit 3 out: sn wknd* **16/1**
7 *19* **Land Sun's Legacy (IRE)**[9] 4-10-9 ....(p) ACCoyle(3) 36
(J S Wainwright) *hld up and bhd: hdwy appr 6th: wknd 9th* **40/1**
4 **8** *3* **Dark Rum**[19] [1298] 9-10-4 .... JKington(10) 35
(M Scudamore) *a bhd* **14/1**
PP **9** *½* **Honourable Collins (IRE)**[22] [1266] 5-11-0 .... HOliver 35
(Mrs Tracey Barfoot-Saunt) *t.k.h in tch: wknd after 7th* **100/1**
36-0 **10** *dist* **Blue Wing**[15] [1340] 4-10-12 ....(t) ChristianWilliams —
(R Flint) *a towards rr: t.o* **16/1**
6P- **P** **Woodstock Express**[401] [1137] 5-11-0 .... RJohnson —
(P Bowen) **11/1**
P **Alto Bold**[911] 7-10-7 .... JMogford —
(P S Payne) *plld hrd in rr: t.o whn p.u bef 8th* **66/1**
P **Pips Assertive Way**[35] 4-10-5 .... VSlattery —
(A W Carroll) *nt jump wl: plld hrd in rr: t.o whn p.u bef 2 ouy* **33/1**
00U0 **P** **April Rose**[19] [1302] 5-10-7 ....(t) SCurran —
(K G Wingrove) *t.k.h: led to 6th: rdn and wknd 8th: t.o whn p.u bef 3 out* **100/1**

5m 46.0s (16.30) **Going Correction** +0.625s/f (Soft)
WFA 4 from 5yo+ 15lb **14** Ran SP% **117.4**
Speed ratings: **96,95,92,91,82 80,74,73,73,— —,—,—,—** CSF £10.85 TOTE £3.10: £1.80, £1.50, £1.70; EX 23.50.
Owner A L R Morton **Bred** Killeen Castle Stud **Trained** Portway, Worcs

FOCUS
Modest hurdle form, but Star Member did it nicely enough and may have more to offer. Difficult to rate with very little form on offer.

NOTEBOOK
Star Member(IRE), a useful Flat performer who has lost his way, was revitalised by this switch to hurdling and ran out a ready winner. He did not have much to beat, but will no doubt have delighted connections with this successful transition and there may well be more to come. *(op 9-4 tchd 5-2)*
Air Guitar(IRE) is improving with hurdling experience and he pulled clear of the third. He will find a race, probably a handicap, and three miles will help. *(op 7-2 tchd 11-2)*
Cirrus(FR) was clearly expected to make a show on this hurdling debut, being sent off at 7/2, and he was not discredited. Improvement can be expected on this and, in time, he can win races. *(op 8-1)*
Rhossili(IRE) appeared to be suited by the cut in the ground and improved on previous efforts.He will fare better in low-grade handicaps. *Official explanation: jockey said gelding lost a shoe (op 16-1)*
Woodstock Express failed to improve for the step up in trip and looks to be going the wrong way. *(op 15-2)*

1455 ROBIN DICKIN PARTNERSHIP OWNERS NOVICES' CHASE (18 fncs) 3m
3:00 (3:00) (Class 3) 5-Y-0+ **£6,318** (£2,444; £1,308)

Form | | | | RPR
14 **1** **Charango Star**[25] [1231] 7-11-0 .... TJMurphy 118+
(W K Goldsworthy) *chsd ldr: hit 3 out: sn rdn to ld: r.o* **9/4**[2]
2/P3 **2** *2* **Phar From Frosty (IRE)**[34] [1177] 8-11-0 120 .... APMcCoy 115
(C R Egerton) *j.lft: led: rdn and hdd after 3 out: nt qckn flat* **10/11**[1]
43 **3** *dist* **Sarahs Quay (IRE)**[21] [1269] 6-10-7 .... PJBrennan —
(K J Burke) *j.lft and mstkes: hld up: lost tch fr 8th: t.o* **11/2**[3]
U **Our Mr Navigator (IRE)**[189] 7-11-0 .... TScudamore —
(N R Mitchell) *blnd 1st: blnd and uns rdr 2nd* **14/1**

6m 4.00s (1.80) **Going Correction** +0.325s/f (Yiel) **4** Ran SP% **105.2**
Speed ratings: **110,109,—,—** CSF £4.67 TOTE £2.60; EX 4.90.
Owner Cliff Johnson **Bred** Mrs Joanna Cross **Trained** Yerbeston, Pembrokes

FOCUS
A good chase debut by Charango Star, who had too much for Phar From Frosty in the closing stages and was stepping up by a stone on the form of his recent hurdles win. The runner-up improved by 11lb on this second run over fences but was still well below his hurdles best.

NOTEBOOK
Charango Star, a dual point winner, made a successful switch to the larger obstacles and won with a bit to spare. Given a nice introductory ride, it was a good effort to beat the 120-rated winner and he should defy a penalty *(op 2-1)*
Phar From Frosty(IRE) is getting the hang of fences and he kept plugging on despite being unable to match the winner. He will pick up a race eventually, but the way he continued to jump out to the left was slightly offputting. *(tchd 5-6, Evens in places)*
Sarahs Quay(IRE) ruined any chance she had by jumping sloppily and a return to a faster surface may help. *(op 8-1)*

1456 103.7 FM H'CAP HURDLE (12 hdls) 2m 6f 110y
3:30 (3:30) (Class 3) (0-115,115) 4-Y-0+ **£5,404** (£1,663; £831; £415)

Form | | | | RPR
2320 **1** **Little Task**[4] [1436] 7-9-12 **90** .... PAspell(3) 91
(J S Wainwright) *hld up: stdy hdwy 7th: rdn to ld after 2 out: r.o wl* **7/1**
0-35 **2** *2* **Nightwatchman (IRE)**[17] [1322] 6-10-11 **100** .... GLee 99
(S B Clark) *w ldr: led appr 3rd: hit 4th: rdn and hdd after 2 out: nt qckn flat* **4/1**[2]
10/ **3** *20* **Good Potential (IRE)**[546] [4339] 9-10-3 **92** ....(t) AntonyEvans 76+
(D J Wintle) *led tl appr 3rd: chsd ldr: rdn and ev ch after 3 out: sn wknd* **5/1**[3]
2511 **4** *5* **Captain Cloudy**[7] [1408] 5-10-9 **98** 7ex .... JGoldstein 72
(Miss Sheena West) *t.k.h in rr: wl bhd 6th: nvr nr ldrs* **5/2**[1]
03-B **5** *2 ½* **Penny's Crown**[135] [96] 6-9-8 **90** oh3 ow1 .... EDehdashti(7) 62
(G A Ham) *hld up: hdwy 8th: wknd 9th* **16/1**
5030 **6** *7* **Sandywell George**[37] [1152] 10-9-11 **89** oh2 ....(vt) TJMalone(3) 54
(L P Grassick) *hld up in tch: wknd appr 9th* **16/1**
030- **P** **Beauchamp Prince (IRE)**[180] [4386] 4-11-8 **113** .... TScudamore —
(M Scudamore) *prom tl wknd appr 9th: t.o whn p.u bef 2 out* **4/1**[2]
4-64 **P** **Sweet Az**[22] [1266] 5-10-0 **89** oh24 ....(b[1]) TDoyle —
(S C Burrough) *hld up in tch: lost pl 3rd: reminders appr 4th and 6th: sn t.o: p.u after 7th* **66/1**

5m 41.0s (11.30) **Going Correction** +0.625s/f (Soft)
WFA 4 from 5yo+ 15lb **8** Ran SP% **111.0**
Speed ratings: **105,104,97,95,94 92,—,—** CSF £33.48 CT £146.53 TOTE £8.40: £2.00, £1.70, £1.50; EX 19.90.
Owner Keith Jackson **Bred** Stetchworth Park Stud Ltd **Trained** Kennythorpe, N Yorks

FOCUS
The front two pulled well clear in what was a modest handicap hurdle. Probably not strong form.

NOTEBOOK
Little Task, who had disappointed only four days previously at Uttoxeter, bounced right back to his best and was clearly none the worse for the outing. He was always going to win once taking the lead off Nightwatchman jumping two out, but he remains quite high in the weights and will be doing well to defy an even higher mark. *(op 8-1)*
Nightwatchman(IRE) has been crying out for this sort of trip and he stepped up on previous efforts, pulling well clear of the third. A faster surface would have been preferable and he definitely has a race in him at this level. *(op 9-2)*
Good Potential(IRE) was below par on this return from a break, folding disappointingly in the final quarter mile, but he is better than this and may have needed the run. *(op 7-1 tchd 15-2 in places)*
Captain Cloudy has been in cracking form, winning three of his last four starts, but he was unable to run to form in this ground and never really picked up. He deserves another chance, but his new higher mark will not make life easy. *Official explanation: jockey said gelding was unsuited by the soft (good to soft in places) ground (tchd 11-4)*
Beauchamp Prince(IRE), last seen finishing 13th when out of his depth in a Listed juvenile handicap at the Cheltenham Festival, showed very little, but is capable of much better and may well have needed the outing. *(op 5-2)*

1457 BBC COVENTRY AND WARWICKSHIRE OPEN CENTRE H'CAP CHASE (13 fncs) 2m 1f 110y
4:05 (4:05) (Class 3) (0-120,115) 5-Y-0+ **£7,681** (£3,035; £1,672)

Form | | | | RPR
342- **1** **Glengarra (IRE)**[190] [4187] 8-10-5 **94** .... TDoyle 118+
(D R Gandolfo) *prom: led 4th: drew clr fr 3 out: 15 l ahd whn nrest rival fell 2 out* **3/1**[2]
13U4 **2** *dist* **James Victor (IRE)**[21] [1273] 7-10-8 **97** .... TScudamore 81
(N R Mitchell) *led to 4th: chsd wnr tl wkng whn mstke 4 out: lft poor 2nd 2 out* **7/1**

1P-4 **3** *4* **Young Owen**[28] 1221 7-10-10 **99** .... JMogford —
(A G Juckes) *wl bhd fr 5th* **16/1**
41-3 **F** **Specular (AUS)**[17] 1320 9-11-12 **115** .... APMcCoy —
(Jonjo O'Neill) *hld up: 5th and in tch whn fell 4th* **6/4**[1]
-PP2 **P** **Young Chevalier**[18] 1311 8-10-3 **92** .... KRenwick —
(J R Adam) *w ldrs: rdn and wknd 8th: t.o whn p.u bef last* **8/1**
2FP1 **F** **Knight's Emperor (IRE)**[21] 1273 8-10-8 **97** .... RThornton 96
(J L Spearing) *hld up in tch: reminders 6th: chsd wnr appr 4 out: 15 l 2nd and btn whn fell 2 out* **5/1**[3]

4m 18.4s (5.90) **Going Correction** +0.325s/f (Yiel) **6** Ran SP% **111.2**
Speed ratings: **99,—,—,—,—** — CSF £22.16 CT £272.92 TOTE £4.30: £1.60, £2.50; EX 22.80.

Owner Starlight Racing **Bred** T J Whitley **Trained** Wantage, Oxon

FOCUS
A messy race with only three of the six runners managing to complete, and Glengarra ran out an easy winner, value for 40 lengths. Knight's Emperor has been rated as 25l second.

NOTEBOOK
Glengarra(IRE), without a win in 16 previous attempts, may have benefited from the mishap to the favourite, but he could not have won any easier and was already clear when Knight's Emperor came down two out. He may be open to further improvement and is entitled to go close in a follow-up bid. *(op 10-3 tchd 7-2)*
James Victor(IRE) was struggling in third when left clear by Knight's Emperor's fall, but he was beaten too far for it to matter and achieved little. *(tchd 13-2)*
Young Owen was the only other to finish and fortunate to pick up third prize. *Official explanation: jockey said gelding was unsuited by the soft (good to soft in places) ground (op 11-1)*
Knight's Emperor(IRE) is not the most consistent, but he was in the process of running a fair race when coming down at the second last. It remains to be seen how this affects confidence. *(tchd 7-4)*
Young Chevalier failed to build on his surprise Perth second and his inconsistency was once again in evidence. *(tchd 7-4)*
Specular(AUS), who shaped with promise before getting tired on his reappearance at Bangor, was rightly made favourite and was, as you would expect, still going nicely when coming down at the fourth. *(tchd 7-4)*

1458 SHELDON BOSLEY MEMORIAL H'CAP HURDLE (9 hdls) 2m 110y
4:40 (4:40) (Class 4) (0-110,108) 4-Y-0+ **£4,163** (£1,281; £640; £320)

Form RPR
6P41 **1** **Mister Moussac**[7] 1413 6-10-9 **91** 7ex........ RThornton 101+
(Miss Kariana Key) *mde all: hung rt fr after 3 out: clr last: r.o wl* **4/1**[2]
PU-0 **2** *8* **Looks The Business (IRE)**[22] 78 4-11-1 **97** .... PJBrennan 98
(W G M Turner) *t.k.h: a.p: rdn and one pce fr 2 out* **16/1**
612- **3** *2 ½* **Buffalo Bill (IRE)**[274] 2772 9-11-10 **106** .... RJohnson 105
(A M Hales) *hld up in tch: wnt 2nd 5th: rdn and ev ch appr 2 out: one pce* **4/1**[2]
3111 **4** *½* **Polished**[97] 664 6-11-12 **108** ....(b) ATinkler 108+
(V R A Dartnall) *hld up: rdn and hdwy after 3 out: kpt on same pce fr 2 out* **3/1**[1]
6003 **5** *20* **Castle River (USA)**[8] 1400 6-11-0 **96** .... JamesDavies 74
(O O'Neill) *hld up: stdy hdwy 4th: rdn after 6th: wknd after 3 out* **10/1**
4551 **6** *7* **Giust In Temp (IRE)**[19] 1302 6-10-8 **97** .... MrTJO'Brien(7) 68
(Mrs K M Sanderson) *hld up in tch: wknd after 5th* **14/1**
23P- **7** *10* **Sunley Future (IRE)**[147] 4883 6-11-3 **99** .... MFoley 60
(N J Henderson) *plld hrd: sn prom: lost pl appr 5th: n.d after* **5/1**[3]
4055 **8** *1 ½* **Lone Soldier (FR)**[15] 1344 9-10-11 **93** .... KRenwick 53
(S B Clark) *w wnr: rdn 5th: sn wknd* **25/1**
-4P0 **9** *hd* **Kippour (FR)**[15] 1344 7-10-2 **87** .... PAspell(3) 46
(S B Clark) *rdn 5th: a bhd* **33/1**
30-U **10** *30* **Bestam**[113] 456 6-10-11 **93** .... JMogford 22
(Mrs A V Roberts) *a bhd: t.o* **16/1**

4m 5.90s (7.50) **Going Correction** +0.625s/f (Soft)
WFA 4 from 5yo+ 14lb **10** Ran SP% **116.0**
Speed ratings: **107,103,102,101,92 89,84,83,83,69** CSF £63.24 CT £272.96 TOTE £4.80: £1.50, £3.30, £2.60; EX 112.50.

Owner Arthur Symons Key **Bred** Miss Carrie Key-Forestal **Trained** Knaresborough, N Yorks

FOCUS
Mister Moussac defied a penalty with something in hand and is clearly at the top of his game at present. The form looks pretty solid.

NOTEBOOK
Mister Moussac, shouldering a 7lb penalty for his recent Worcester victory, led throughout and cleared away under pressure after the last to eventually win cosily. He is clearly in top form at the minute and may well complete the hat-trick. *(op 7-2)*
Looks The Business(IRE), who was reverting to hurdles, was never far from the pace and kept plugging away to claim second. He was always being held by the winner however and shaped as though a bit further would not go amiss. *(op 14-1)*
Buffalo Bill(IRE) has been in decent form of late, but was always going to find it tough to give weight to the winner and he faded in the final quarter mile. He may need to drop a few pounds before winning again. *(op 7-2)*
Polished completed the quartet that pulled clear, but he never actually looked like winning and seemed to find this new 8lb higher mark a bit too much on a return from a break. *(op 7-2 tchd 4-1)*
Sunley Future(IRE) is a quirky sort who has spoiled his chance on many an occasion by pulling hard and, although he was supported in the market beforehand, his early exertions began to tell from some way out. He is not one to make a habit of backing. *(op 8-1)*

1459 FREE BETS @GG.COM STANDARD NATIONAL HUNT FLAT RACE 2m 110y
5:10 (5:10) (Class 6) 4-6-Y-0 **£3,532** (£1,087; £543; £271)

Form RPR
1 **Fourty Acers (IRE)**[134] 5-11-1 .... TJMalone(3) 112+
(M C Pipe) *hld up and bhd: hdwy on ins 8f out: led 3f out: sn clr* **4/1**[3]
40- **2** *13* **Magical Legend**[157] 4753 4-10-4 .... MrTJO'Brien(7) 92
(L Corcoran) *a.p: rdn and ev ch 3f out: sn btn* **10/3**[2]
3 *11* **Mister Zaffaran (IRE)**[99] 6-10-11 .... MrPCallaghan(7) 88
(Mrs N S Evans) *led after 1f: rdn and hdd 3f out: sn wknd* **10/1**
4 *5* **Thenford Lord (IRE)** 4-11-1 .... ONelmes(3) 83
(D J S Ffrench Davis) *hld up in mid-div: rdn 9f out: sn struggling: n.d after* **14/1**
5 *7* **Mr Tee Pee (IRE)**[161] 5-10-11 .... MissLucyBridges(7) 76
(M C Pipe) *hld up in rr: hdwy 7f out: ev ch 3f out: sn wknd* **5/4**[1]
6 *9* **Pitton Prince** 6-10-11 .... MrDavidTurner(7) 67
(N R Mitchell) *a bhd* **20/1**
00/0 **7** *dist* **Freindlypersuasion**[52] 1048 5-11-4 .... DCrosse —
(Paul Morris) *a bhd: t.o* **80/1**
8 *5* **Double Grace (IRE)** 5-10-4 .... MissLGardner(7) —
(Mrs S Gardner) *a bhd: t.o* **16/1**
0 **9** *nk* **Jane's Rug Rat**[21] 1274 6-10-11 .... TMessenger(7) —
(C L Popham) *hld up in mid-div: rdn 9f out: sn bhd: t.o* **25/1**
00- **10** *¾* **Discord**[218] 3710 4-10-11 .... BWharfe(7) —
(T H Caldwell) *prom: rdn and wknd qckly 4f out: t.o* **40/1**
0-0 **11** *dist* **Lady Spur (IRE)**[98] 656 6-10-6 .... DCCostello(5) —
(J S Wainwright) *hld up in mid-div: rdn 9f out: bhd fnl 5f: virtually p.u fnl 3f: t.o* **33/1**
00 **12** *dist* **Millie Boon**[67] 917 6-10-6 .... LTreadwell(5) —
(L J Williams) *led 1f: wknd qckly 5f out: virtually p.u fnl 3f: t.o* **80/1**

4m 1.60s (-5.10) **Going Correction** +0.625s/f (Soft)
WFA 4 from 5yo+ 14lb **12** Ran SP% **125.6**
Speed ratings: **104,97,92,90,87 82,—,—,—,— —,—** CSF £17.95 TOTE £6.10: £2.40, £1.20, £2.90; EX 10.50 Place 6 £91.76, Place 5 £76.57.

Owner M C Pipe **Bred** Greg Lawler **Trained** Nicholashayne, Devon

FOCUS
Modest bumper form, but Fourty Acers ran out a tidy winner and is worth siding with in future. The race has been rated through the second.

NOTEBOOK
Fourty Acers(IRE), winner of an Irish point in April, ran out quite a tidy winner of this ordinary bumper and really stretched clear once given his head. He looks a potentially useful sort and, with further improvement anticipated once he tackles obstacles/a greater distance, he looks one to keep on the right side of. *(op 10-3)*
Magical Legend, last seen finishing down the field in the Listed bumper at Aintree, was no match for the winner, but beat the remainder well enough and should prove capable of winning a mares' bumper. *(op 4-1 tchd 3-1)*
Mister Zaffaran(IRE), last seen finishing second in an Irish point, was unable to match the front pair as they went on, but is going to appreciate further once sent hurdling and is capable of better.
Thenford Lord(IRE) did not show a great deal on ths racecourse debut, but is likely to appreciate a bit further over hurdles. *(op 16-1)*
Mr Tee Pee(IRE), winner of his only point-to-point back in April, appeared to be the Pipe first string if the betting was to be believed, but he was well and truly put in the shade by his stable companion and could only manage a well-beaten fifth. He is surely better than this, but now has something to prove. *(op 7-4 tchd 2-1)*
T/Plt: £123.10 to a £1 stake. Pool: £50,825.45. 301.40 winning tickets. T/Qpdt: £29.30 to a £1 stake. Pool: £3,062.00. 77.20 winning tickets. KH

1475 - 1477a (Foreign Racing) - See Raceform Interactive

[229]PLUMPTON (L-H)
Sunday, September 18

OFFICIAL GOING: Good to firm
Wind: almost nil Weather: fine but cloudy

1478 POSIT JUVENILE NOVICES' HURDLE (9 hdls) 2m
2:10 (2:11) (Class 3) 3-Y-0 **£4,784** (£1,472; £736; £368)

Form RPR
1 **Toss The Caber (IRE)**[20] 3-10-12 .... JimCrowley 93+
(K G Reveley) *prom in chsng gp: pushed along and outpcd 6th: modest 6th 3 out: styd on bef next: led sn after last: rdn clr* **8/1**
21 **2** *2 ½* **Moonfleet (IRE)**[15] 1397 3-10-11 .... RJohnson 90+
(M F Harris) *hld up: prog 5th: chsd clr ldr next: clsd to ld bef 2 out: hdd and hung lft after last: nt qckn* **11/4**[2]
6 **3** *5* **Royal Wedding**[15] 1397 3-10-12 .... LAspell 86+
(N J Gifford) *in tch: prog 6th: clsd on ldr 3 out: w new ldr 2 out: stl nrly upsides last: wknd flat* **3/1**[3]
4 *5* **Piran (IRE)**[338] 3-10-12 .... JPMcNamara 82+
(R H Alner) *hld up in rr: outpcd 6th: rdn and prog to chse clr ldng trio 3 out: keeping on whn blnd 2 out: fdd* **14/1**
4BP **5** *11* **Time For You**[10] 1397 3-10-5 .... WMarston 62
(J M Bradley) *wl in tch: sltly hmpd 5th: outpcd fr next: n.d after* **100/1**
6 *2 ½* **Atacama Star**[34] 3-10-12 .... TJMurphy 70+
(B G Powell) *racd freely: nt fluent: led and sn 15l clr: hdd & wknd bef 2 out: no ch whn blnd last* **5/2**[1]
7 *5* **Ghaill Force**[15] 3-10-5 .... RLucey-Butler(7) 62
(P Butler) *prom in chsng gp: chsd ldr 5th to 6th: wknd 3 out* **100/1**
R **8** *½* **Josear**[18] 1380 3-10-12 .... MBradburne 61
(C J Down) *chsd ldr tl tried to refuse 2nd: mstkes after: wknd after 6th* **16/1**
F **Vino Venus**[24] 3-10-5 .... JGoldstein —
(Miss Sheena West) *chsd clr ldr fr 2nd tl fell 5th* **66/1**
6 **P** **Dishdasha (IRE)**[22] 1339 3-10-12 .... JTizzard —
(C R Dore) *hld up: p.u bef 3rd: sddle slipped* **33/1**
F **Arno River** 3-10-5 .... MrJAJenkins(7) —
(D Brace) *a in rr: reminder 3rd: wknd after 6th: poor last whn fell last* **40/1**
P **Loitokitok**[6] 3-10-12 .... ATinkler —
(P D Cundell) *j. slowly 1st: in tch to 5th: outpcd after next: wl bhd whn p.u bef 2 out* **50/1**

3m 41.0s (-20.20) **Going Correction** -1.35s/f (Hard) **12** Ran SP% **114.7**
Speed ratings: **96,94,92,89,84 83,80,80,—,— —,—** CSF £29.44 TOTE £8.10: £1.90, £1.50, £1.60; EX 22.80.

Owner P D Savill **Bred** P D Savill **Trained** Lingdale, N Yorks

FOCUS
A moderate juvenile hurdle, run at a decent pace, and the field were strung out at the finish. The third sets the standard for the form.

NOTEBOOK
Toss The Caber(IRE) , a dual winner on the Flat and rated 57, got his National Hunt career off to a perfect start with a decisive success. He jumped well enough, responded positively after hitting a flat spot at halfway, and looked better the further he went. A stiffer test should suit him in due course and he will most likely prove better in this sphere than he was on the level. *(op 9-1 tchd 7-1)*
Moonfleet(IRE) just hung fire when in front on the run-in and was always going to be caught by the winner. This was a sound effort under penalty, however, and she has made a bright start to her hurdling career. *(tchd 10-3)*
Royal Wedding settled better this time and ran very close to his debut form with the runner-up. He may be better suited by a less undulating track and could pick up a race or two in this sphere as he gains further experience. *(op 11-4)*
Piran(IRE) who, despite being rated 65 on the Flat still showed little in four outings for Brian Meehan, would have finished a bit closer but for blundering the penultimate flight and posted a satisfactory debut. He is at least entitled to improve for this return from a 338-day layoff. *(op 20-1)*
Time For You shaped more encouragingly, but still failed to get into contention at any stage. *(op 66-1)*
Atacama Star , a winner off a mark of 65 on the Flat in July, proved too keen at the head of affairs and ultimately was a sitting duck turning into the home straight. He will not only need to settle better, but also improve his jumping, if he is to progress in this sphere. *(op 11-4)*
Dishdasha(IRE) *Official explanation: jockey said saddle slipped (op 25-1)*

1479 TRITON NOVICES' H'CAP CHASE (14 fncs) 2m 4f
2:40 (2:40) (Class 4) (0-105,104) 4-Y-0+

£3,390 (£1,285; £642; £292; £146; £87)

Form				RPR
/40-	1		**Corporate Player (IRE)**[263] [3079] 7-11-7 **104**.................... WKennedy(5) (Noel T Chance) *trckd ldrs: wnt 2nd bef 10th: led 3 out: 4 l clr 2 out: tired after last: jst hld on* **15/2**	112
4314	2	½	**High Peak**[14] [1412] 8-9-11 **78**.................... RYoung(3) (J W Mullins) *hld up: last tl 8th: outpcd fr 10th but stl gng wl: rdn 2 out: styng on whn mstke last: clsd flat: too much to do* **3/1**[2]	86+
P155	3	shd	**Faddad (USA)**[14] [1411] 9-10-8 **86**....................(t) RJohnson (Mrs A M Thorpe) *trckd ldr: led 9th to 3 out: sn rdn: kpt on flat as wnr tired* **9/2**[3]	93
0F5	4	nk	**Waynesworld (IRE)**[9] [1446] 7-10-4 **82**.................... JamesDavies (M Scudamore) *cl up: w ldng pair 10th: drvn and outpcd in 3rd bef 2 out: styd on again flat* **7/1**	89
446F	5	7	**Hattington**[15] [1396] 7-11-1 **100**.................... CPoste(7) (M F Harris) *hld up: nt fluent 4th: rdn to chse ldrs 4 out: no imp next: mstke 2 out: fdd* **8/1**	101+
0/0	6	dist	**Just Different (IRE)**[11] [1433] 8-11-3 **95**.................... LAspell (P G Murphy) *led to 9th: losing pl whn blnd next: sn t.o: btn 76l* **20/1**	—
0-01	P		**Irishkawa Bellevue (FR)**[48] [1125] 7-10-7 **85**....................(b) DCrosse (Jean-Rene Auvray) *nt fluent: dropped to last and drvn 8th: sn t.o: p.u bef 4 out: bbv* **5/2**[1]	—

4m 58.6s (-19.85) **Going Correction** -1.15s/f (Hard) **7 Ran SP% 111.9**
Speed ratings: **93,92,92,92,89** —,— CSF £29.69 CT £111.99 TOTE £6.60: £3.60, £2.60; EX 20.80.

Owner A D Weller **Bred** Robert Robinson **Trained** Upper Lambourn, Berks

FOCUS
A moderate novices' handicap that saw the first four closely covered at the finish. A steady early pace resulted in a modest winning time for the class, but the form makes sense with the first four all close to their marks.

NOTEBOOK
Corporate Player(IRE) , despite drifting badly in the betting ring, made a winning return from a 263-day layoff and broke his duck over fences at the third time of asking. He took up the running three out, having jumped fluently throughout, and never looked in danger thereafter despite tiring in the final 100 yards. Despite the fact he has clearly had his share of problems, he has always been well regarded by current connections, and has started handicap life on a decent mark. *(op 10-3 tchd 8-1)*

High Peak was doing all of his best work at the finish, having been set a fair bit to do from off the pace by Young. He is right at home on this sort of surface, has become a consistent sort over fences, and is clearly not without hope off his current official rating. *(op 7-2)*

Faddad(USA) again appeared one paced, but clearly enjoyed the step up in trip and turned in his best effort to date over fences. He still looks weighted to around his best, however. *(tchd 5-1)*

Waynesworld(IRE) kept on under pressure and showed the benefit of a recent 5lb drop in the weights. Off this mark, he may be capable of finally landing an event under Rules when reverting to further. *(op 11-1)*

Just Different(IRE) *Official explanation: trainer said gelding bled from nose*

Irishkawa Bellevue(FR) was well backed to follow-up his recent hurdling success, which came off a 15lb higher mark, yet never jumped with any fluency and was disappointingly pulled up. He was later found to have bled from the nose. *Official explanation: jockey said gelding bled from nose (op 10-3)*

1480 TCA NOVICES' HURDLE (9 hdls) 2m
3:10 (3:12) (Class 4) 4-Y-0+ **£3,360** (£960; £480)

Form				RPR
	1		**Anticipating**[36] 5-10-12.................... PHide (G L Moore) *patiently rdn: hld up in rr: prog 3 out: chsd ldr bef 2 out where mstke: rdn to ld flat: jst hld on* **7/2**[1]	110+
40P-	2	shd	**Turbo (IRE)**[27] [3492] 6-10-12 106....................(p) JPMcNamara (T G Mills) *hld up in rr: rapid prog 3 out: led bef next and sn clr: rdn and hdd flat: rallied nr fin* **6/1**	109
B3F-	3	11	**La Dolfina**[313] [2102] 5-10-5.................... RJohnson (P J Hobbs) *hld up wl in rr: prog after 3 out: chsd clr ldng pair 2 out: no imp* **4/1**[2]	91
	4	2	**Carte Sauvage (USA)**[15] 4-10-12.................... SThomas (M F Harris) *pressed ldr tl bef 3 out: sn drvn: outpcd bef 2 out* **15/2**	96
4323	5	¾	**Gemini Dancer**[28] [1272] 6-11-5 107.................... JTizzard (C L Tizzard) *hld up wl in rr: in tch whn blnd 3 out: sn rdn and outpcd: no ch after* **5/1**[3]	104+
351	6	1½	**Dyneburg (POL)**[20] [1364] 5-11-5 110.................... JMMaguire (T R George) *prom: nt fluent 4th and 5th: chsd ldr briefly after 3 out: sn rdn and wknd* **7/1**	102+
20-5	7	1¾	**Whistling Fred**[133] [230] 6-10-12.................... TJMurphy (B De Haan) *hld up wl in rr and racd on outer: mstke 4th: nudged along fr 3 out: nvr nr ldrs: do bttr* **14/1**	93+
01-0	8	4	**Atlantic City**[10] [100] 4-11-5.................... MBatchelor (Mrs L Richards) *nt fluent 1st and 6th: settled midfield: outpcd and rdn after 3 out: wknd* **16/1**	95
0-5F	9	hd	**Regulated (IRE)**[44] [1153] 4-10-2 90.................... AngharadFrieze(10) (P A Blockley) *nt jump wl: prom to 6th: sn u.p and struggling* **80/1**	88
	10	nk	**Head Boy**[29] 4-10-12.................... JamesDavies (S Dow) *prom: led 3 out: rdn and hdd bef next: wknd rapidly* **66/1**	87
0-	11	14	**Pick Of The Crop**[61] [2577] 4-10-12.................... LAspell (J R Jenkins) *hld up: effrt 6th: chsd ldrs bef 3 out: sn rdn and wknd: eased bef 2 out* **100/1**	73
00-0	12	1¼	**Welsh Doll (IRE)**[32] [1233] 6-9-12.................... MrJAJenkins(7) (D Brace) *racd awkwardly: mde most to 3 out: wknd rapidly* **100/1**	65
6	13	3	**Gameset'N'Match**[26] [1085] 4-10-5.................... RLucey-Butler(7) (Miss M P Bryant) *lost pl 3rd: sn struggling in rr: bhd fr 6th* **100/1**	69
	P		**Corton Denham**[57] 4-10-5.................... JPemberton(7) (G P Enright) *s.s: a last: lost tch 3rd: t.o whn p.u bef 3 out* **100/1**	—

3m 40.3s (-20.90) **Going Correction** -1.35s/f (Hard)
WFA 4 from 5yo+ 14lb **14 Ran SP% 116.7**
Speed ratings: **98,97,92,91,91 90,89,87,87,87 80,79,78,**— CSF £24.18 TOTE £4.00: £1.60, £2.00, £2.30; EX 31.60.

Owner D R Hunnisett **Bred** George Strawbridge **Trained** Woodingdean, E Sussex

■ Stewards' Enquiry : J P McNamara caution: careless riding

FOCUS
No great strength in depth, but the two principals were useful on the Flat at their best and came well clear. The form looks reasonable for the time of year and both could rate higher.

NOTEBOOK
Anticipating , rated 85 at his best on the Flat, was well backed to open his account at the first time of asking and duly did so with a narrow success. Ridden to get the trip, he jumped well enough until blundering at the penultimate flight, and then looked to have it all to do, but his Flat ability came into play on the run-in and he did well to pick off the runner-up. He can be rated better than the bare form and, if hurdling can rekindle his enthusiasm, he could have a lot more to offer. *(op 4-1 tchd 10-3, 3-1 in places and 9-2 in a place)*

Turbo(IRE) , last seen over hurdles 239 days previously, did nothing wrong in defeat and can be considered a touch unlucky to have bumped into the winner, as he was well clear of the rest. This was more encouraging than his recent efforts on the Flat and, if able to maintain this current mood, should have little trouble in finding a similar event. *(tchd 7-1)*

La Dolfina , off since falling at Huntingdon 313 days previously, was given a fairly considerate ride and finished her race well enough. She did enough to suggest she has improvement in her. *(op 7-2 tchd 9-2 in places)*

Carte Sauvage(USA) , who lost his way on the Flat when with Mark Johnston yet was rated 101 at his best, fared the best of those to race up with the early gallop and made a satisfactory debut. He should improve for this experience and should be suited by a longer trip in due course. *(op 7-1)*

Gemini Dancer lost momentum after a bad error three out and was well held. He should be rated slightly better than the bare result and helps set the level of this form. *(op 11-2)*

Dyneburg(POL) did not really impress with his hurdling this time and failed to make use of his previous experience. He does look vulnerable under his penalty, but is capable of better than this. *(op 6-1)*

Head Boy

1481 ITG EUROPE H'CAP HURDLE (9 hdls) 2m
3:45 (3:45) (Class 3) (0-125,121) 4-Y-0+

£8,943 (£3,392; £1,696; £771; £385; £231)

Form				RPR
3221	1		**Screenplay**[14] [1407] 4-10-12 **107**.................... JGoldstein (Miss Sheena West) *trckd ldng pair: effrt to ld sn after 3 out: drvn next: jnd last: styd on wl flat* **7/1**[3]	112
030-	2	1½	**Frontier**[27] [2516] 8-11-7 **116**....................(t) RJohnson (B J Llewellyn) *hld up in tch: effrt 3 out: chsd wnr bef next: upsides last: nt qckn flat* **9/2**[2]	119
F-04	3	6	**Wait For The Will (USA)**[15] [1400] 9-11-1 **110**....................(bt) PHide (G L Moore) *hld up: clsd on ldrs gng wl 3 out: rdn and fnd nil next: one pce* **8/1**	107
4341	4	1¾	**Leopold (SLO)**[14] [1409] 4-10-0 **102**.................... CPoste(7) (M F Harris) *hld up: effrt 3 out: rdn whn hmpd on bnd sn after: nt rcvr but kpt on fr last* **14/1**	101+
5-40	5	1½	**Tulipa (POL)**[36] [1204] 6-11-2 **121**.................... WMcCarthy(10) (T R George) *hld up: wl in tch 5th: j. slowly next and outpcd: nvr on terms w ldrs after: plugged on* **9/2**[2]	115
6311	6	6	**Cantgeton (IRE)**[9] [1445] 5-11-6 **115**.................... TJMurphy (M C Pipe) *disp ld to 3 out: sn wknd* **11/4**[1]	103
/U-P	7	3	**Private Benjamin**[15] [1400] 5-10-5 **100**.................... MBatchelor (Jamie Poulton) *chsd ldrs: rdn fr 6th: outpcd u.p fr 3 out* **33/1**	86+
0506	8	½	**Golden Chalice (IRE)**[20] [1366] 6-10-11 **106** ow1.................... BJCrowley (Miss E C Lavelle) *disp ld to 3 out: wkng whn mstkes 2 out and last* **11/1**	92+
014-	9	2½	**Mount Vettore**[6] [3461] 4-10-2 **97**.................... JimCrowley (K G Reveley) *plld hrd: hld up: stl in rr but wl in tch whn blnd bdly 3 out: nt rcvr* **14/1**	84+
F-04	10	1¼	**Milligan (FR)**[15] [1396] 10-11-8 **120**.................... TJPhelan(3) (Dr P Pritchard) *prom whn j. slowly 1st: wl in rr by 3rd: lost tch 6th: plugged on flat* **50/1**	101
00-0	U		**Domenico (IRE)**[26] [218] 7-9-7 **95** oh7.................... RLucey-Butler(7) (J R Jenkins) *hld up: prog on inner after 3 out: cl 3rd and gng wl whn mstke and uns rdr 2 out* **14/1**	94+

3m 35.9s (-25.30) **Going Correction** -1.35s/f (Hard)
WFA 4 from 5yo+ 14lb **11 Ran SP% 119.9**
Speed ratings: **109,108,105,104,103 100,99,98,97,97** — CSF £40.01 CT £263.65 TOTE £9.70: £2.70, £2.20, £2.30; EX 66.30.

Owner The Horse Players **Bred** Juddmonte Farms **Trained** Lewes, E Sussex

FOCUS
A fair handicap and the form looks solid for the class. A strong early gallop helped produce a decent winning time for the grade and much the fastest of the four races run over the trip on the card.

NOTEBOOK
Screenplay , off the mark over hurdles at Fontwell last time, followed up with another dogged display on this handicap bow. He is evidently progressing nicely, has a very likeable attitude when under pressure and appeals as one to follow while in this sort of mood. If turned out under a penalty, he will be very hard to beat, especially if reverting to a stiffer test. *(op 6-1)*

Frontier ◆ travelled smoothly throughout, and looked at one point as if he may do the business, but was ultimately unable to concede the weight to the determined winner. This was a promising return to the hurdling arena and a reproduction of this form really ought to see him get back to winning ways. *(op 11-2)*

Wait For The Will(USA) , with the tongue strap re-applied, once again flattered to deceive and threw in the towel when asked for maximum effort. He needs all to fall right in his races, and while he is capable on his day, remains a hard horse to catch right. *(op 9-1 tchd 15-2)*

Leopold(SLO) would have probably finished a lot closer to the front pair but for meeting trouble on the home turn, as he finished strongly on the run-in. His recent success at Fontwell has clearly boosted his confidence and he may still be on a fair mark at present. *(op 12-1 tchd 16-1)*

Tulipa(POL) never looked particularly happy at any stage and, while she was not disgraced, does look in need of some respite from the Handicapper. *(op 5-1)*

Cantgeton(IRE) , making his handicap debut having won his previous two starts in novice company, helped set the decent gallop and ultimately dropped out disappointingly in this quest for the hat-trick. He may have found this ground too lively and is not one to write off on the back of this effort. *(op 3-1 tchd 10-3 in a place)*

Mount Vettore , despite refusing to settle early on, made a promising return to hurdling and had yet to be asked a serious question prior to losing his chance when meeting the third last all wrong.

Domenico(IRE) had claims of being placed prior to unseating his rider.

1482 ITG SMARTSERVERS H'CAP HURDLE (PART OF THE AUSTRALIA V GB/IRELAND JUMP JOCKEYS CHALLENGE) (12 hdls) 2m 5f
4:20 (4:21) (Class 4) (0-105,103) 4-Y-0+ **£3,262** (£932; £466)

Form				RPR
-132	1		**Red Dahlia**[31] [1250] 8-10-9 **86**.................... ATinkler (M Pitman) *cl up: led 9th: mde rest: drvn and hld on flat* **7/2**[1]	87
05	2	½	**Coccinelle (IRE)**[11] [1436] 7-11-7 **98**....................(p) BMcLean (K A Morgan) *cl up: rdn 3 out: prog to chse wnr 2 out: chal flat: jst hld* **11/2**	99
01-P	3	3½	**Mrs Philip**[13] [1125] 6-11-5 **96**.................... RJohnson (P J Hobbs) *racd wd: cl up: chsd wnr 3 out to next: one pce* **9/2**[2]	93
0-F3	4	2½	**Redspin (IRE)**[15] [1220] 5-11-12 **103**.................... PHamblin (J S Moore) *hld up: rdn and outpcd after 9th: kpt on fr 2 out: n.d* **5/1**[3]	98

0446 **5** 5 **Spider Boy**[31] 1246 8-9-7 **77** oh7..............(p) RLucey-Butler(7) 67
(Miss Z C Davison) *mde most to 9th: wknd bef 2 out* **14/1**

6060 **6** shd **Scarrabus (IRE)**[13] 1364 4-10-12 **90**.............. TJMurphy 78
(B G Powell) *hld up: in tch and gng wl 3 out: wknd bef next* **5/1**[3]

0-P0 **7** 10 **Oh Sunny Boy (IRE)**[11] 1432 4-9-9 **83** oh4 ow5.............. JBunsell(10) 61
(B G Powell) *prog to join ldr 6th: hit next: wkng whn blnd 3 out: no ch after* **33/1**

3630 **8** 12 **Red Canyon (IRE)**[14] 1413 8-11-4 **95**..............(p) BScott 62
(C L Tizzard) *in tch: pushed along bef 9th: wknd 3 out* **8/1**

00-6 **P** **Moon Catcher**[128] 329 4-11-11 **103**..............(t) JTizzard —
(D Brace) *last and rdn after 5th: t.o 9th: p.u bef 2 out* **16/1**

4m 53.2s (-31.60) **Going Correction** -1.35s/f (Hard)
WFA 4 from 5yo+ 15lb **9** Ran SP% **115.7**
Speed ratings: **106,105,104,103,101 101,97,93,—** CSF £23.49 CT £87.72 TOTE £3.40: £1.60, £1.80, £2.00; EX 29.30.
Owner John Goodman **Bred** T G And Mrs Bish **Trained** Upper Lambourn, Berks

FOCUS
A moderate handicap which saw the first two come clear. The form makes sense but is not strong.

NOTEBOOK
Red Dahlia, raised another 2lb for finishing second at Fontwell last time, got back to winning ways in game fashion under a positive ride over this longer trip. She has really found her form of late, *loves a fast surface and may well be able to defy another rise in the weights on this evidence. (op 4-1 tchd 9-2)*
Coccinelle(IRE) was ridden with slightly more restraint over this shorter trip and only gave way on the run-in. She has clearly improved for the recent switch to her current yard and is capable of resuming winning ways off this sort of mark. *(op 9-2)*
Mrs Philip posted a much more encouraging effort and can build on this, provided similarly fast ground in the coming weeks. She may appreciate a drop back in trip, however. *(op 4-1)*
Redspin(IRE) does not do anything quickly and again advertised that. He is very hard to catch right *(op 9-2)*
Scarrabus(IRE) was going as well as any three out, yet dropped away tamely when asked for maximum effort. The fact he has yet to taste success from 20 outings on both the Flat and over hurdles rather sums him up. *(op 8-1 tchd 17-2)*

1483 ITG LOGIC (S) H'CAP HURDLE (9 hdls) 2m
4:55 (4:56) (Class 5) (0-95,94) 4-Y-0+ **£2,254** (£644; £322)

Form RPR

0P46 **1** **Honan (IRE)**[11] 1432 6-10-10 **88**..............(v) AGlassonbury(10) 92
(M C Pipe) *hld up: rr of main gp and drvn 3 out: prog u.p bef next: led bef last: drvn out* **11/1**

-530 **2** 1 ½ **Let's Celebrate**[103] 670 5-10-11 **79**.............. LAspell 81
(F Jordan) *hld up in rr: stdy prog 3 out: n.m.r bnd sn after: rdn to chal and w wnr last: nt qckn* **14/1**

02P0 **3** 4 **Alethea Gee**[19] 1375 7-10-6 **74**.............. JimCrowley 72
(K G Reveley) *hld up in rr: stdy prog fr 3 out: rdn to chal bef last: fnd nil* **15/2**

/153 **4** shd **Reverse Swing**[67] 973 8-10-11 **79**.............. RJohnson 77
(Mrs H Dalton) *hld up: prog to dispute 2nd 3 out: sn rdn: effrt u.p and cl up after 2 out: fdd* **4/1**[2]

000U **5** ½ **Hidden Smile (USA)**[19] 1375 8-10-3 **71**..............(t) DCrosse 69
(F Jordan) *prom in chsng gp: hit 3rd: chsd clr ldr 3 out to after next: wknd last* **25/1**

0000 **6** 2 ½ **Prince Minata (IRE)**[10] 1362 10-10-1 **72**.............. RYoung(3) 67
(M Appleby) *led and sn wl clr: c bk to field fr 3 out: hdd & wknd bef last* **40/1**

330/ **7** 3 **Mighty Pip (IRE)**[26] 880 9-10-4 **79**.............. MrJAJenkins(7) 71
(M R Bosley) *hld up in rr: effrt 3 out: sn rdn: wknd 2 out* **33/1**

04R3 **8** hd **Spiders Web**[14] 1409 5-11-9 **91**..............(be) PHide 83+
(G L Moore) *t.k.h: hld up in rr: sme prog 3 out: no real imp whn stmbld bdly bnd bef 2 out: nt rcvr* **6/1**[3]

0 **9** ½ **Tuckerman**[41] 925 4-11-3 **85**.............. JPMcNamara 76
(A J Martin, Ire) *hld up in rr: sme prog after 3 out: shkn up and nt qckn bef 2 out* **10/3**[1]

4106 **10** 1 ½ **Ashgan (IRE)**[44] 1156 12-10-4 **77**.............. DrPPritchard(5) 67
(Dr P Pritchard) *chsd ldr to after 2nd: sn lost pl: t.o 6th: plugged on fr 2 out* **20/1**

005 **11** 11 **Bally Hall (IRE)**[14] 1415 5-10-10 **78**..............(t) WMarston 57
(J M Bradley) *plld hrd: chsd clr ldr after 2nd tl wknd 3 out* **14/1**

34P0 **12** 19 **Suchwot (IRE)**[26] 1297 4-10-5 **73**..............(vt) TJMurphy 33
(M C Pipe) *hld up: lost tch after 5th: t.o next* **6/1**[3]

P4-0 **13** 7 **Droumleigh Lad (IRE)**[63] 1019 10-11-5 **94**.............. RLucey-Butler(7) 47
(Miss Z C Davison) *in tch in chsng gp to 6th: wknd rapidly: t.o* **50/1**

3m 40.7s (-20.50) **Going Correction** -1.35s/f (Hard)
WFA 4 from 5yo+ 14lb **13** Ran SP% **121.0**
Speed ratings: **97,96,94,94,93 92,91,91,90,90 84,75,71** CSF £143.85 CT £1240.79 TOTE £17.60: £3.30, £5.50, £3.00; EX 347.00.There was no bid for the winner
Owner Eminence Grise Partnership **Bred** Miss Ashling O'Connell **Trained** Nicholashayne, Devon

FOCUS
A very poor event, run at a sound gallop and the first two were clear at the finish. The runner-up and fourth are the best guides to the level of the form.

NOTEBOOK
Honan(IRE) finally put his best foot forward again and was well on top at the finish. This was his first success over timber, but while he is capable on his day, he has two ways of running and the fact he scored as he did sums up the low level of this form. *(tchd 12-1)*
Let's Celebrate made a pleasing return to action and only tired on the run-in. He was clear of the rest at the finish, and is entitled to improve for the outing, but consistency has never been his strong suit.
Alethea Gee produced one of her better efforts and looked a threat until tiring badly after the final flight. *(op 7-1 tchd 8-1)*
Reverse Swing was put in her place after the penultimate hurdle and ran below the level of her recent efforts. *(op 7-2 tchd 9-2)*
Spiders Web looked held prior to getting the penultimate flight all wrong and paid for running too freely through the early parts. He has his quirks, but is capable of better on his day. *(op 7-1 tchd 5-1)*
Tuckerman, whose yard has a fine record on their raids to Britain, was set too much to do from off the pace and never figured. *(op 7-2 tchd 3-1)*

1484 ITG ACE H'CAP CHASE (18 fncs) 3m 2f
5:25 (5:26) (Class 4) (0-110,106) 5-Y-0+
£3,303 (£1,252; £626; £284; £142; £85)

Form RPR

/2-1 **1** **Mr Splodge**[112] 11-10-12 **99**.............. MrJETudor(7) 120+
(Mrs T J Hill) *t.k.h: hld up tl prog to ld 8th: drew clr after 13th: in n.d after: 10l ahd last: eased nr fin* **7/2**[2]

-230 **2** 6 **Tommy Carson**[15] 1398 10-10-11 **94**.............. CBolger(3) 100
(Jamie Poulton) *chsd ldr to 7th: rdn 12th: effrt u.p to chse clr wnr 14th: kpt on but no real imp* **7/2**[2]

413 **3** 15 **Pangeran (USA)**[19] 1378 13-9-7 **80** oh6.............. RLucey-Butler(7) 71
(N B King) *hld up: outpcd fr 13th: wnt v modest 3rd 3 out: n.d* **16/1**

3412 **4** 3 **Uncle Mick (IRE)**[18] 1385 10-11-12 **106**..............(p) JTizzard 94
(C L Tizzard) *prom: chsd wnr 12th: nt run on after next and sn dropped wl bk: kpt on again fr 2 out* **4/1**[3]

0045 **5** 14 **Idealko (FR)**[29] 1267 9-11-0 **94**.............. RGreene 68
(Dr P Pritchard) *hld up: nt fluent 10th: pushed along 12th: sn wl outpcd: wnt v modest 3rd 14th to 3 out: wknd* **14/1**

-PP0 **6** 3 ½ **Sunday Habits (IRE)**[14] 1414 11-9-7 **80** oh15.............. MrDavidTurner(7) 51
(Dr P Pritchard) *led: j. slowly and hdd 8th: chsd wnr to 12th: wknd 14th* **20/1**

U311 **F** **High Gear (IRE)**[20] 1367 7-11-7 **101**..............(b) TJMurphy —
(Jonjo O'Neill) *hld up: wl in tch whn stmbld on landing and fell 8th* **5/2**[1]

6m 33.45s (-20.55) **Going Correction** -1.15s/f (Hard) **7** Ran SP% **110.3**
Speed ratings: **85,83,78,77,73 72,—** CSF £15.37 CT £156.84 TOTE £4.90: £2.80, £2.50; EX 17.70 Place 6 £176.85, Place 5 £112.28.
Owner Alan Hill **Bred** Mrs P J Fairbarns **Trained** Chinnor, Oxon

FOCUS
A very impressive display by the winner, who is value for nearly treble his winning margin, and the field finished well strung out. However, it was pedestrian winning time for the grade given the conditions.

NOTEBOOK
Mr Splodge ◆, who has carried all before him in points this year, translated that form to Rules and made a winning handicap bow in effortless fashion. He is still improving at the age of 11, rarely makes a mistake over his fences and loves this sort of ground. While the Handicapper will no doubt take a dim view of this, it is hard to say just how good he may be in this sphere and he could well bag a decent prize before the season is out.
Tommy Carson, a three-time winner at the track, was made to look pedestrian when the winner asserted down the back straight and is greatly flattered by his proximity at the finish. He can be considered unlucky to have bumped into such a progressive rival, however, and was well clear of the rest.
Pangeran(USA) turned in a fair effort from out of the handicap, yet was never in the hunt at any stage. *(op 14-1)*
Uncle Mick(IRE) turned in a moody effort and performed below the form of his recent runs. *(op 7-2)*
High Gear(IRE), reverting to fences in his quest for the hat-trick, fell too early to tell how he would have fared, yet it is safe to assume he would not have lived with the winner. *(op 11-4)*
T/Plt: £172.60 to a £1 stake. Pool: £42,126.10. 178.10 winning tickets. T/Qpdt: £52.10 to a £1 stake. Pool: £2,602.80. 36.90 winning tickets. JN

1431 UTTOXETER (L-H)
Sunday, September 18

OFFICIAL GOING: Good to firm
The open ditch in the home straight was omitted.
Wind: nil Weather: cloudy

1485 MAKE MONEY @ MARKHOLDER.COM NOVICES' HURDLE (DIV I) (12 hdls) 2m 4f 110y
2:20 (2:20) (Class 4) 4-Y-0+ **£2,978** (£851; £425)

Form RPR

2324 **1** **Festive Chimes (IRE)**[11] 1434 4-10-8 103.............. ONelmes(3) 91+
(N B King) *hld up in tch: led appr 3 out: stmbld 2 out: rdn and r.o wl flat* **7/4**[1]

5660 **2** 2 ½ **Smileafact**[35] 1220 5-10-12 73..............(v[1]) BHitchcott 87
(Mrs Barbara Waring) *a.p: rdn and ev ch appr 3 out: r.o one pce flat* **25/1**

503P **3** nk **Hard N Sharp**[14] 1407 5-10-12.............. RThornton 87
(Mrs A M Thorpe) *chsd ldr: rdn and outpcd appr 3 out: rallied and ev ch last: no ex flat* **9/1**

3213 **4** 2 **Slalom (IRE)**[20] 1361 5-11-0 100..............(p) LStephens(5) 94+
(D Burchell) *hld up and bhd: hdwy after 9th: chsd wnr 3 out tl nt fluent 2 out: one pce flat* **15/8**[2]

0P/ **5** 28 **Paradise Garden (USA)**[471] 1346 8-10-10 ow8.............. TBurrows(10) 65
(P L Clinton) *led tl appr 3 out: sn wknd* **40/1**

4FP- **6** ½ **Yes Ses Les**[359] 1495 6-10-7.............. DLaverty(5) 57
(G Fierro) *plld hrd: nt fluent: a bhd* **25/1**

/56- **7** 6 **Munny Hill**[469] 665 5-10-5.............. TMessenger(7) 51
(M Appleby) *bhd: rdn after 8th: sn struggling* **40/1**

06F **8** dist **Olympian Time**[19] 1377 5-10-0.............. MNicolls(5) —
(Miss J E Foster) *hld up in mid-div: rdn 8th: sn bhd: t.o* **33/1**

00-0 **9** ½ **Times Up Barney**[24] 1323 5-10-12.............. JPByrne —
(C W Moore) *j. slowly 1st: a bhd: t.o fr 8th:* **50/1**

03P5 **P** **Rash Moment (FR)**[32] 1232 6-10-12 110.............. RSpate(7) —
(Mrs K Waldron) *hld up in tch: rdn after 9th: sn eased and p.u* **7/1**[3]

5m 2.80s (-9.30) **Going Correction** -0.525s/f (Firm)
WFA 4 from 5yo+ 15lb **10** Ran SP% **111.1**
Speed ratings: **96,95,94,94,83 83,81,—,—,—** CSF £46.33 TOTE £2.70: £1.20, £4.60, £2.30; EX 66.70.
Owner Nolan Catterwell & P Persse **Bred** Burton Agnes Stud Co Ltd **Trained** Newmarket, Suffolk

FOCUS
There were not many to enthuse about in this modest event with the fourth setting the level for the form.

NOTEBOOK
Festive Chimes(IRE) quickly recovered from a hiccup at the penultimate hurdle and scored fairly readily. She goes on the soft but is at her best on a fast surface. *(op 13-8)*
Smileafact showed significant improvement in the first-time visor and kept on to secure the runner-up spot. *(op 33-1)*
Hard N Sharp, pulled up on his hurdling debut, showed his third in a Bangor bumper to be no flash in the pan.
Slalom(IRE), back in novice company, was fighting a losing battle after an untidy jump at the second last.

1486 TRENT COMMUNICATIONS (S) H'CAP HURDLE (12 hdls) 2m 6f 110y
2:50 (2:52) (Class 5) (0-90,90) 4-Y-0+ **£2,289** (£654; £327)

Form RPR

P0-P **1** **Wise Tale**[8] 1319 6-11-7 **85**..............(v) GLee 91+
(P D Niven) *chsd ldr: led 6th: clr appr last: comf* **6/1**[1]

-04F **2** 6 **Gold Quest (IRE)**[119] 8-11-2 **90**.............. DJBoland(10) 86
(Ian Williams) *a.p: chsd wnr after 6th: rdn appr 2 out: no imp* **8/1**[3]

P0-P **3** 3 **Audiostreetdotcom**[15] 1395 8-11-5 **90**..............(b) MrJoshuaHarris(7) 84+
(R A Harris) *hld up in mid-div: mstke 7th: hdwy 8th: rdn and hmpd after 9th: styd on one pce flat* **20/1**

3-B5	4	1 ¾	**Penny's Crown**[7] [1456] 6-11-1 **86**........ EDehdashti(7) (G A Ham) *hld up in mid-div: lost pl 8th: sme hdwy appr 3 out: styd on fr 2 out* **12/1**	77
P/P6	5	1	**Sungio**[14] [1409] 7-11-1 **84**........ LStephens(5) (B P J Baugh) *hld up in tch: mstke 8th: rdn and one pce fr 3 out* **25/1**	75+
42FF	6	2 ½	**Approaching Land (IRE)**[19] [1374] 10-11-9 **90**........ MrTGreenall(3) (M W Easterby) *hld up towards rr: hdwy 6th: hit 9th: wknd appr last* **7/1**[2]	80+
00/0	7	7	**Whose Line Is It**[44] [1153] 7-11-8 **86**........ PJBrennan (N J Hawke) *hld up and bhd: hdwy appr 8th: rdn appr 3 out: sn wknd* **17/2**	67
1250	8	*nk*	**In Good Faith**[91] [784] 13-10-11 **82**........ PKinsella(7) (R E Barr) *bhd: rdn after 6th: nvr nr ldrs* **9/1**	62
P/0-	9	3 ½	**Banningham Blaze**[27] [242] 5-11-10 **88**........(v) ADobbin (A W Carroll) *hld up and bhd: hdwy 8th: wknd after 2 out* **20/1**	65
130P	10	*nk*	**Greencard Golf**[44] [1153] 4-11-10 **90**........ AO'Keeffe (Jennie Candlish) *hld up and bhd: hdwy whn hmpd after 9th: wknd appr 2 out: blnd last* **20/1**	70+
-005	11	½	**Silver Dagger**[25] [1310] 7-11-5 **83**........(p) FKeniry (J C Haynes) *mid-div: rdn after 5th: bhd fr 9th* **14/1**	59
06-0	12	12	**Kaid (IRE)**[24] [1319] 10-10-8 **79**........ MrTCollier(7) (R Lee) *bhd fr 9th* **25/1**	43
-06P	13	9	**It's Harry**[65] [1000] 7-11-9 **87**........ DElsworth (Mrs S J Smith) *hld up in tch: rdn and wknd appr 3 out* **6/1**[1]	42
50	P		**Porto (IRE)**[67] [977] 10-11-7 **85**........ RThornton (B J M Ryall) *prom to 8th: t.o whn p.u bef 3 out* **20/1**	—
0603	P		**Rattina (GER)**[22] [1343] 9-11-6 **84**........ NFehily (M F Harris) *led to 6th: wknd appr 7th: t.o whn p.u bef 9th* **11/1**	—
4P00	P		**Kippour (FR)**[7] [1458] 7-11-4 **87**........ DCCostello(5) (S B Clark) *mid-div: lost pl 4th: mstke 5th: sn bhd: t.o whn p.u bef 3 out* **25/1**	—

5m 28.5s (-16.20) **Going Correction** -0.525s/f (Firm) **16** Ran SP% **126.0**
Speed ratings: **107,104,103,103,102 102,99,99,98,98 98,93,90,—,—** — CSF £48.98 CT £909.83 TOTE £6.30: £1.80, £2.50, £5.90, £3.60; EX 48.50.The winner was bought in for 6,600gns.

Owner B Ll Parry **Bred** Gainsborough Stud Management Ltd **Trained** Barton-le-Street, N Yorks

FOCUS
A wide-open selling handicap with the winner value for more than the official margin and the time decent for the grade.

NOTEBOOK
Wise Tale was unsuited by the soft ground when pulled up at Bangor last month. He took advantage of a drop in grade off a mark only a pound higher than when he scored at Market Rasen in July last year. *(op 13-2)*

Gold Quest(IRE), who finished fourth in a Sedgefield hunter chase in May, tried his best but had to be content to play second fiddle. *(op 10-1)*

Audiostreetdotcom had one of his going days and stuck on to the end. *(op 22-1)*

Penny's Crown had faster ground to help her get the trip this time. *(op 14-1)*

Sungio stays very well and this step up in distance was never going to be a problem.

Approaching Land(IRE) should at least have had his confidence restored following a couple of falls. *(op 11-2)*

1487 BETTERWARE NOVICES' CHASE (10 fncs 2 omitted) 2m

3:25 (3:27) (Class 3) 5-Y-0+ **£5,434** (£1,672; £836; £418)

Form				RPR
1220	1		**Tonic Du Charmil (FR)**[24] [1320] 5-11-4 117........(t) TScudamore (M C Pipe) *hld up in tch: led 2 out: drvn out* **4/1**[2]	122+
-B24	2	½	**The Glen**[44] [1155] 7-10-12........ RThornton (R Lee) *a.p: hit 2 out: kpt on flat* **8/1**	116+
50-2	3	1 ¾	**Demi Beau**[14] [1411] 7-10-12........ ChristianWilliams (Evan Williams) *hld up: hdwy after 7th: led after 3 out to 2 out: no ex flat* **13/8**[1]	114+
06-2	4	¾	**Kings Brook**[18] [1382] 5-10-12........ ADobbin (Nick Williams) *hld up: hdwy after 7th: hung lft towards fin: one pce* **10/1**	112
2-23	5	2	**Never (FR)**[14] [1411] 8-10-12........(t) NFehily (Jonjo O'Neill) *hld up and bhd: hdwy 3 out: one pce flat* **11/2**[3]	112+
03-2	6	5	**Your Advantage (IRE)**[144] [60] 5-10-9 103........(t) PBuchanan(3) (Miss Lucinda V Russell) *a.p: led briefly 3 out: wknd appr last* **20/1**	105
0B04	7	1	**Amber Dawn**[14] [1413] 6-10-5........ OMcPhail (J Gallagher) *w ldr: led 7th to 3 out: sn wknd* **66/1**	97
0-6U	8	11	**Migration**[41] [1001] 9-10-9........(p) LVickers(3) (Mrs S Lamyman) *hit 1st: a bhd: no ch whn j.rt 2 out* **33/1**	93
/0-P	9	10	**Kaikovra (IRE)**[15] [1396] 9-10-12 102........ BHitchcott (M F Harris) *led to 7th: sn wknd* **50/1**	83
P2-P	10	3 ½	**Avadi (IRE)**[74] [913] 7-10-12 90........ AThornton (P T Dalton) *bhd fr 6th: mstke last* **33/1**	80
	P		**Cappacurry (IRE)**[185] [4420] 6-10-12........ AntonyEvans (Evan Williams) *a bhd: hit 6th: p.u bef last* **33/1**	—
5561	P		**Sachsenwalzer (GER)**[24] [1318] 7-11-4........ PJBrennan (C Grant) *hld up: hdwy 4th: blnd 5th: wknd 8th: bhd whn j.rt 2 out: p.u bef last* **8/1**	—

3m 49.5s (-15.50) **Going Correction** -0.725s/f (Firm) **12** Ran SP% **121.8**
Speed ratings: **109,108,107,107,106 104,103,98,93,91** —,— CSF £34.08 TOTE £5.70: £1.70, £2.00, £1.80; EX 30.10.

Owner Roger Stanley & Yvonne Reynolds **Bred** Mme Guilhaine Le Borgne **Trained** Nicholashayne, Devon

FOCUS
With the first five home covered by only five lengths, the value of this form remains to be seen, although it should work out.

NOTEBOOK
Tonic Du Charmil(FR), taken off his legs in a strongly-run Bangor handicap last time, jumped much better than has often been the case and held on under pressure. *(op 9-2 tchd 5-1)*

The Glen, dropping back in distance, was helped by the fact they went a decent gallop. He deserves to go one better and a return to further will help. *(op 15-2)*

Demi Beau ◆ confirmed he has taken to fences and ought to be able to find a suitable opening. *Official explanation: trainer said gelding was struck into from behind (tchd 7-4, 15-8 in places)*

Kings Brook benefited from the experience gained at Newton Abbot although Dobbin was unable to get to the bottom of him in the closing stages. *(op 8-1)*

Never(FR) had finished a length closer to Demi Beau at Worcester last time. *(op 6-1 tchd 13-2)*

Your Advantage(IRE) would not have minded softer ground for his first outing since April.

Sachsenwalzer(GER) *Official explanation: jockey said gelding pulled up after mistake at second-last*

1488 EXCLOOSIVE EVENT HIRE H'CAP HURDLE (12 hdls) 2m 4f 110y

4:00 (4:00) (Class 3) (0-115,108) 4-Y-0+ **£5,265** (£1,620; £810; £405)

Form				RPR
5401	1		**Burundi (IRE)**[26] [1300] 11-11-10 **106**........ WHutchinson (A W Carroll) *hld up and bhd: hdwy after 9th: rdn to ld last: r.o wl: fin lame* **8/1**[3]	115
-411	2	2	**Michaels Dream (IRE)**[9] [1443] 6-11-10 **106**........(b) ADobbin (N Wilson) *a.p: led 9th: clr appr 3 out: hdd last: nt qckn* **11/2**[2]	113
/03-	3	11	**Navado (USA)**[460] [755] 6-11-12 **108**........ NFehily (Jonjo O'Neill) *hld up and bhd: hdwy 7th: rdn 9th: wknd appr last* **8/1**[3]	104
2-15	4	*nk*	**Brigadier Benson (IRE)**[127] [353] 5-11-5 **101**........ AThornton (R H Alner) *hld up: hdwy 6th: rdn appr 3 out: wknd appr last* **5/1**[1]	97
4222	5	3	**Fiddles Music**[20] [1361] 4-10-4 **94**........ LHeard(7) (D Burchell) *hld up: lost pl 7th: n.d after* **5/1**[1]	86
1P05	6	9	**Ton-Chee**[25] [1312] 6-11-1 **100**........ PBuchanan(3) (K W Hogg) *t.k.h: prom: hit 6th and 9th: ev ch appr 3 out: sn rdn: wknd after 2 out* **25/1**	84
4202	7	7	**Tinstre (IRE)**[14] [1413] 7-11-3 **99**........ SCurran (P W Hiatt) *w ldr to 8th: wknd 9th* **11/2**[2]	76
6-20	8	*dist*	**Top Achiever (IRE)**[9] [1444] 4-11-11 **108**........ JPByrne (C W Moore) *a in rr: virtually p.u flat* **22/1**	—
-352	P		**Nightwatchman (IRE)**[7] [1456] 6-11-4 **100**........ GLee (S B Clark) *led to 9th: wknd qckly appr 3 out: p.u bef 2 out* **5/1**[1]	—
54P-	P		**Monti Flyer**[148] [4976] 7-11-3 **104**........ DCCostello(5) (S B Clark) *t.k.h in tch: wknd after 7th: bhd whn p.u bef 3 out* **25/1**	—

4m 58.1s (-14.00) **Going Correction** -0.525s/f (Firm)
WFA 4 from 5yo+ 15lb **10** Ran SP% **115.0**
Speed ratings: **105,104,100,99,98 95,92,—,—,—** CSF £49.93 CT £361.58 TOTE £8.90: £2.60, £1.80, £3.00; EX 16.40.

Owner R G Owens **Bred** Olympic Bloodstock Ltd And Swettenham Stud **Trained** Cropthorne, Worcs

FOCUS
A competitive-looking handicap with the finish fought out by the two who had won on their previous starts. The time was reasonable and the fourth sets the level for the form.

NOTEBOOK
Burundi(IRE) followed up his Worcester victory having only gone up 2lb. He unfortunately finished lame after banging his off-fore knee at the second last.

Michaels Dream(IRE) appeared set to complete a hat-trick early in the home straight. However, he had been raised a total of 13lb and could not hold the in-form winner. *(op 7-2)*

Navado(USA) has yet to show he can be effective at this trip but this was his first start since June last year. *(tchd 9-1)*

Brigadier Benson(IRE) came in for support in the ring on this first outing for four months. *(op 8-1)*

Fiddles Music was nearly a stone better off than when beaten 11 lengths by Michaels Dream at Cartmel. *(op 13-2)*

Nightwatchman(IRE) *Official explanation: trainer said gelding had a breathing problem (op 9-2)*

1489 WILLIAM TWIGG (MATLOCK) LTD CENTENARY H'CAP CHASE (14 fncs 2 omitted) 2m 5f

4:35 (4:37) (Class 3) (0-120,119) 5-Y-0+ **£6,256** (£1,925; £962; £481)

Form				RPR
U-14	1		**Dead-Eyed Dick (IRE)**[69] [960] 9-11-6 **113**........ PJBrennan (Nick Williams) *hld up and bhd: hdwy and bmpd 9th: mstke 11th: led 2 out: drvn out* **7/1**[3]	122+
212P	2	¾	**Giorgio (IRE)**[64] [1012] 7-11-1 **111**........(b) PBuchanan(3) (Miss Lucinda V Russell) *a.p: rdn 3 out: r.o flat* **14/1**	118
2362	3	2 ½	**Toi Express (IRE)**[15] [1399] 9-11-5 **119**........ JamesWhite(7) (R J Hodges) *hld up in tch: rdn 3 out: kpt on same pce fr 2 out* **10/1**	124
UP25	4	5	**Just Muckin Around (IRE)**[22] [1342] 9-10-0 **93**........ BHitchcott (R H Buckler) *prom: hit 2nd: stmbld bnd appr 5th: j.lft 9th: led appr 11th to 2 out: wknd last* **20/1**	95+
3060	5	9	**Isard III (FR)**[29] [1265] 9-11-12 **119**........ TScudamore (M C Pipe) *hld up in mid-div: lost pl 7th: sme hdwy appr 3 out: n.d* **8/1**	110
-132	6	*nk*	**Beat The Heat (IRE)**[11] [1435] 7-11-5 **112**........(b) BHarding (Jedd O'Keeffe) *hld up and bhd: hdwy appr 8th: rdn 9th: wknd after 10th* **7/1**[3]	102
460S	7	2	**Panmure (IRE)**[22] [1342] 9-10-4 **97**........ GLee (P D Niven) *bhd: mstke 4th: reminders after 5th: short-lived effrt 11th* **12/1**	85
40-3	8	1 ½	**Strong Magic (IRE)**[126] [366] 13-9-11 **93** oh1........ LVickers(3) (J R Cornwall) *w ldr to 7th: wknd 8th* **33/1**	80
3PP6	9	23	**Half An Hour**[36] [1205] 8-10-13 **106**........(v) WHutchinson (A King) *led tl appr 11th: rdn and wknd appr 3 out* **12/1**	70
2-11	F		**Catchthebug (IRE)**[51] [1097] 6-11-4 **111**........ NFehily (Jonjo O'Neill) *hld up: hit 2nd: fell 8th* **6/1**[2]	—
1404	P		**Flahive's First**[20] [1358] 11-10-6 **104**........ LStephens(5) (D Burchell) *a bhd: mstke 6th: p.u bef 2 out* **16/1**	—
120-	P		**Free Gift**[184] [4436] 7-11-2 **109**........ AThornton (R H Alner) *t.k.h: prom: hit 10th: sn wknd: bhd whn p.u bef 3 out* **3/1**[1]	—

5m 11.4s (-16.10) **Going Correction** -0.725s/f (Firm) **12** Ran SP% **120.1**
Speed ratings: **101,100,99,97,94 94,93,92,84,—** —,— CSF £99.65 CT £989.43 TOTE £8.10: £2.20, £3.50, £3.10; EX 131.50.

Owner Mrs Jane Williams **Bred** Edward And Teresa Forde **Trained** George Nympton, Devon

■ Stewards' Enquiry : P J Brennan caution: used whip in an incorrect place

FOCUS
A decent event for this time of year with the first three close to the marks, making the form look sound.

NOTEBOOK
Dead-Eyed Dick(IRE) goes well when fresh and had to dig deep to score off a career-high mark. He still has not got that many miles on the clock. *(tchd 8-1)*

Giorgio(IRE) was back to a more suitable trip and made sure the winner had to work hard for victory. *(op 16-1)*

Toi Express(IRE) appeared to get the longer distance well enough but could not overcome a 3lb rise in the ratings. *(op 12-1)*

Just Muckin Around(IRE) was back down in distance having failed to stay the extended three miles at Market Rasen last time. *(op 16-1)*

Free Gift failed to settle properly on his graduation from hunter chases. *Official explanation: trainer said gelding may have been in need of the race (op 7-2)*

1490 LEAMORE CONTRACTS NOVICES' H'CAP HURDLE (10 hdls) 2m

5:05 (5:07) (Class 4) (0-95,94) 4-Y-0+ **£2,681** (£766; £383)

Form				RPR
2161	1		**Master Nimbus**[24] [1322] 5-10-13 **86**........ DCCostello(5) (J J Quinn) *hld up in tch: hung lft after 7th: swtchd rt and rdn to ld flat: r.o wl* **11/2**[1]	91+

2322 **2** *3* **Don And Gerry (IRE)**[18] [1383] 4-11-8 **90** AntonyEvans 91+
(P D Evans) *t.k.h in tch: led appr 3 out: clr whn j.rt 2 out: sn rdn: j.rt last: hdd and no ex flat* **11/2**[1]

650- **3** *1 ½* **Secret's Out**[313] [2108] 9-11-10 **92** TScudamore 90
(F Lloyd) *hld up towards rr: hdwy after 7th: rdn 3 out: one pce flat* **25/1**

554- **4** *2* **Rainbow Tree**[197] [4166] 5-11-12 **94** NFehily 91+
(C C Bealby) *hld up: hdwy whn mstke 5th: rdn appr 3 out: one pce fr 2 out* **6/1**[2]

51F5 **5** *1 ½* **Queen Excalibur**[26] [1297] 6-10-12 **85** LStephens(5) 80
(C Roberts) *bhd tl hdwy 2 out: nt rch ldrs* **7/1**

20/P **6** *5* **Buz Kiri (USA)**[46] [826] 7-11-4 **86** WHutchinson 77+
(A W Carroll) *bhd tl hdwy 2 out: n.d* **33/1**

531 **7** *nk* **Jack Durrance (IRE)**[18] [1381] 5-10-11 **86** EDehdashti(7) 75
(G A Ham) *hld up in mid-div: hit 2nd: rdn after 7th: no hdwy* **9/1**

00P- **8** *2* **Greatest By Phar**[230] [3620] 4-11-8 **90** AThornton 77
(J Akehurst) *hld up in mid-div: no imp whn mstke 3 out* **12/1**

4005 **9** *¾* **Nifty Roy**[19] [1379] 5-11-5 **87** (b) ADobbin 73
(K W Hogg) *hld up in tch: wknd appr 3 out* **25/1**

006/ **10** *2 ½* **Rust En Vrede**[14] [895] 6-11-6 **88** ADempsey 72
(D Carroll) *a bhd* **25/1**

3024 **11** *17* **Cash Return**[36] [1213] 6-11-0 **85** (p) LVickers(3) 52
(Mrs S Lamyman) *led: j.lft and bmpd 1st: sn hdd: prom tl wknd 3 out* **22/1**

56PP **12** *½* **Ice And Fire**[14] [1415] 6-11-4 **86** (v[1]) ChristianWilliams 52
(J T Stimpson) *led after 1st: j.rt 7th: hdd appr 3 out: sn wknd* **20/1**

0522 **P** **Staff Nurse (IRE)**[11] [1432] 5-11-3 **85** (p) GLee —
(N Wilson) *prom tl wknd after 7th: bhd whn p.u bef 3 out* **7/1**

-P24 **R** **Dead Mans Dante (IRE)**[20] [1365] 7-10-13 **88** PJMcDonald(7) —
(Ferdy Murphy) *hld up and bhd: stdy hdwy and in tch whn rn out 3 out* **13/2**[3]

3m 52.6s (-7.80) **Going Correction** -0.525s/f (Firm)
WFA 4 from 5yo+ 14lb **14** Ran SP% **124.7**
Speed ratings: **98,96,95,94,94 91,91,90,89,88 80,79,—,—** CSF £33.78 CT £722.92 TOTE £6.50: £2.40, £2.30, £9.70; EX 31.70.

Owner J H Hewitt **Bred** A H Bennett **Trained** Settrington, N Yorks

FOCUS
A competitive low-grade handicap, but the form looks pretty solid and should work out.

NOTEBOOK
Master Nimbus continues on the upgrade and came through to overcome a 10lb hike in the ratings having already shown he can handle this faster ground. *(op 9-2)*

Don And Gerry(IRE) gave the impression he was going to take some catching until he jumped right at the last two hurdles and got swamped by the winner. *(op 7-1)*

Secret's Out gave a very good account of himself after a ten-month absence and will strip fitter next time.

Rainbow Tree should find this first run since March putting an edge on him. *(op 13-2)*

Queen Excalibur was doing all her best work quite late in the day. *(op 8-1)*

Staff Nurse(IRE) *Official explanation: trainer's representative had no explanation for the poor form shown (op 9-1)*

Dead Mans Dante(IRE), reverting to hurdles, was creeping into contention apparently going well when blotting his copybook at the third last. *(op 9-1)*

1491 MAKE MONEY @ MARKHOLDER.COM NOVICES' HURDLE (DIV II) (12 hdls) 2m 4f 110y

5:35 (5:37) (Class 4) 4-Y-0+ **£2,978** (£851; £425)

Form RPR

1 **Thedublinpublican (IRE)**[140] 5-10-12 NFehily 103+
(C C Bealby) *plld hrd: led appr 2nd: hit 3rd: j.lft and hdd 4th: lft in ld 9th: rdn whn mstke last: r.o* **13/2**

4 **2** *1 ¾* **Toni Alcala**[8] [591] 6-10-12 ADobbin 98
(R F Fisher) *hld up in mid-div: reminders after 5th: hdwy whn sltly hmpd 9th: hung lft 3 out: sn outpcd: rallied and hung lft flat: r.o* **5/2**[2]

32-2 **3** *1* **Cansalrun (IRE)**[112] [568] 6-10-5 102 RWalford 90
(R H Alner) *led tl after 1st: prom: chsd wnr fr 9th: one pce flat* **7/4**[1]

6PP **4** *24* **Maria Bonita (IRE)**[20] [1364] 4-9-13 TGreenway(5) 65
(C N Kellett) *hld up and bhd: bdly hmpd 9th: n.d* **50/1**

5 *dist* **Xila Fontenailles (FR)**[329] 4-10-4 PJBrennan —
(N J Hawke) *hld up and bhd: sltly hmpd 7th: sn struggling: blnd last: virtually p.u flat* **16/1**

0/ **P** **Saddlers Boy**[37] [1923] 7-10-12 KJohnson —
(R Johnson) *a in rr: lost tch 6th: t.o whn p.u bef 3 out* **40/1**

1 **F** **Gold Guest**[2] [1077] 6-11-5 (t) AntonyEvans —
(P D Evans) *plld hrd: hdwy after 3rd: led 4th: clr appr 7th: 2l ahd whn fell 9th* **5/1**[3]

0 **U** **Mr Cee**[32] [1237] 5-10-5 NCarter(7) —
(Mrs S J Smith) *plld hrd: chsd ldrs: lost pl and nt fluent 6th: rdn after 7th: rallied whn bdly hmpd 9th: no ch whn blnd and uns rdr last* **16/1**

5m 5.10s (-7.00) **Going Correction** -0.525s/f (Firm)
WFA 4 from 5yo+ 15lb **8** Ran SP% **111.1**
Speed ratings: **92,91,90,81,— —,—,—** CSF £22.39 TOTE £7.00: £1.10, £1.80, £1.10; EX 18.40 Place 6 £331.70, Place 5 £157.99.

Owner Ady Boughen **Bred** Michael A Walsh **Trained** Barrowby, Lincs

FOCUS
A moderate winning time for the class and the slowest of the three races run over the trip on the day. The form looks suspect with the third the best guide.

NOTEBOOK
Thedublinpublican(IRE) was apparently the subject of an old-fashioned gamble but his trainer claimed that neither he nor his owner had backed him. It is thought he had not been getting home over three miles in Irish points. *(op 22-1)*

Toni Alcala, a winner at up to two miles on the Flat, did not turn out to be that easy a ride. He eventually found a second wind and is crying out for further. *(op 11-4 tchd 9-4)*

Cansalrun(IRE) lacked the required acceleration despite the return to a longer trip. *(op 6-5)*

Gold Guest had run creditably when getting no luck in running over a mile and a quarter at Nottingham two days earlier. His lead had shrunk considerably when he capsized four out and he will need to learn to settle to get this trip. *(op 4-1 tchd 7-2)*

T/Plt: £325.60 to a £1 stake. Pool: £45,655.15. 102.35 winning tickets. T/Qpdt: £26.60 to a £1 stake. Pool: £3,544.80. 98.45 winning tickets. KH

1492 - 1507a (Foreign Racing) - See Raceform Interactive

1307 PERTH (R-H)

Wednesday, September 21

OFFICIAL GOING: Good (good to firm in places)
Wind: Breezy, half-against

1508 STRONACHS MAIDEN HURDLE (10 hdls) 2m 4f 110y

2:20 (2:21) (Class 4) 4-Y-0+ **£3,653** (£1,124; £562; £281)

Form RPR

212- **1** **Harry Blade**[308] [2275] 6-11-2 CLlewellyn 97
(N A Twiston-Davies) *midfield: lost pl 4th: sn drvn along: sme hdwy after 4 out: outpcd after next: rallied to ld bef last: styd on wl* **10/11**[1]

5-3 **2** *4* **L'Eau Du Nil (FR)**[150] [3] 4-11-1 RJohnson 93+
(P J Hobbs) *hld up: hdwy and prom 3 out: outpcd bef next: rallied to chse wnr whn hit last: one pce* **9/4**[2]

633 **3** *5* **Templet (USA)**[23] [1360] 5-11-2 89 (b) JAMcCarthy 88
(W G Harrison) *hld up: hdwy and prom 3rd: effrt and led briefly between last two: sn outpcd* **16/1**

0046 **4** *1* **Nobodysgonanotice (IRE)**[22] [1379] 7-11-2 (b[1]) JPMcNamara 87
(J J Lambe, Ire) *led to bef 2 out: sn one pce* **50/1**

5/6- **5** *2 ½* **Handa Island (USA)**[8] [2967] 6-10-13 MrTGreenall(3) 85
(M W Easterby) *chsd ldrs: led bef 2 out: hdd & wknd between last two* **20/1**

0-FU **6** *dist* **Lanhel (FR)**[22] [1374] 6-10-9 MrCDawson(7) —
(J Wade) *plld hrd: chsd ldrs to 3 out: sn btn* **100/1**

00P6 **7** *16* **Starbright**[28] [1307] 4-10-12 68 PBuchanan(3) —
(W G Young) *cl up tl wknd bef 3 out* **100/1**

000- **8** *10* **Culbann (IRE)**[183] [4507] 6-10-2 81 (t) TJDreaper(7) —
(C Rae) *a bhd* **100/1**

P **Remus Lupin**[232] 4-11-1 ADobbin —
(F P Murtagh) *a bhd: t.o whn p.u bef 2 out* **66/1**

P **Books Delight** 5-10-6 PAspell(3) —
(J Wade) *sn bhd: struggling fnl circ: no ch whn p.u bef 2 out* **66/1**

/6-P **P** **Safe Shot**[28] [1307] 6-10-11 72 (p) DCCostello(5) —
(Mrs J C McGregor) *prom to 4 out: sn wknd: p.u bef 2 out* **100/1**

3- **P** **Ardynagh (IRE)**[280] [2838] 6-11-2 (t) GLee —
(J Howard Johnson) *midfield: rdn 4 out: struggling bef next: p.u bef 2 out* **9/1**[3]

5m 7.30s (-0.90) **Going Correction** +0.05s/f (Yiel)
WFA 4 from 5yo+ 15lb **12** Ran SP% **112.7**
Speed ratings: **103,101,99,99,98 —,—,—,—,— —,—** CSF £2.74 TOTE £1.90: £1.20, £1.20, £2.10; EX 2.90.

Owner N A Twiston-Davies **Bred** H R Mould And G M Macechern **Trained** Naunton, Gloucs

FOCUS
A modest maiden on paper but won by a potentially decent hurdler. The race is probably best rated through the third, who appeared to run to form, but the first two should leave this form well behind.

NOTEBOOK
Harry Blade ◆ took a long time to get going and still raced green during the race. He has plenty of potential and will be a nice chaser in time, but there are more hurdle races to be won with him en route, and is the type his trainer could aim for the Persian War Hurdle at Chepstow - a race he won *last year with a similarly inexperienced type - as a galloping track will suit this horse much more. (tchd Evens)*

L'Eau Du Nil(FR), stepping up in trip by half a mile, moved nicely towards the leaders approaching the home bend but found a lot less than looked likely off the bridle and was a shade disappointing. He does not seem to be getting home over hurdles at this stage of his career. *(op 5-2 tchd 2-1)*

Templet(USA) is a low-grade sort over hurdles but ran another respectable race, suggesting he can win an ordinary handicap this autumn/winter. *(op 14-1)*

Nobodysgonanotice(IRE), wearing first-time blinkers, set a reasonable pace and stayed on fairly well when headed.

Handa Island(USA) raced prominently for much of the race before weakening up the straight. He has been regressing on the Flat recently and, although he will now be handicapped over hurdles, it remains to see how much ability he retains. *(op 16-1)*

Ardynagh(IRE), very much a chasing type, did not improve for the fitting of a tongue tie and *disappointed after travelling freely in the early stages.Official explanation: jockey said gelding had a breathing problem (tchd 10-1 in places)*

1509 D M HALL CHARTERED SURVEYORS NOVICES' CHASE (12 fncs) 2m

2:55 (2:55) (Class 3) 5-Y-0+ **£6,808** (£2,095; £1,047; £523)

Form RPR

P5P- **1** **Cyborg De Sou (FR)**[188] [4414] 7-10-7 WKennedy(5) 112+
(G A Harker) *hld up and bhd: smooth hdwy 4 out: led 2 out: pushed out* **14/1**

64U4 **2** *¾* **Kalou (GER)**[73] [939] 7-10-9 100 MrTGreenall(3) 110
(C Grant) *hld up in tch: hdwy to chse ldrs 8th: rdn 3 out: chsd wnr last: kpt on* **8/1**[3]

1P1 **3** *8* **Monticelli (GER)**[32] [1263] 5-10-12 RJohnson 104+
(P J Hobbs) *nt fluent: chsd clr ldrs: hdwy to ld 4 out: hdd 2 out: outpcd last* **8/11**[1]

303- **4** *10* **Dalaram (IRE)**[158] [4860] 5-10-12 GLee 95+
(J Howard Johnson) *hld up in tch: hdwy and cl up whn nt fluent 4 out: rdn next: wknd fr 2 out* **11/4**[2]

P/6P **5** *23* **Dottie Digger (IRE)**[28] [1311] 6-10-2 63 (v) PBuchanan(3) 62
(Miss Lucinda V Russell) *nt fluent: keen: led 1st to 4 out: wknd next* **66/1**

-00P **P** **Oyez (IRE)**[22] [1376] 8-10-12 JPMcNamara —
(J J Lambe, Ire) *keen: led to 1st: cl up tl wknd 7th: p.u bef 4 out* **50/1**

4m 0.90s (-1.90) **Going Correction** +0.05s/f (Yiel) **6** Ran SP% **105.8**
Speed ratings: **106,105,101,96,85** — CSF £94.91 TOTE £12.30: £3.60, £3.00; EX 79.30.

Owner John J Maguire **Bred** Thierry Picard **Trained** Thirkleby, N Yorks

FOCUS
A decent-looking novice event that resulted in a surprise. Two horses with previous experience dominated the finish but they are only modest at best. Of the newcomers, Monticelli jumped indifferently, while Dalaram ran like a horse that needed the race.

NOTEBOOK
Cyborg De Sou(FR) scythed through his rivals jumping the third last after being detached for much of the race. He has already been fairly exposed over fences, but this was a good performance and he should pick up more races if he reproduces his best. *(op 9-1)*

Kalou(GER) is fully exposed over fences but travelled nicely throughout the race and looked a real danger between the last two fences. He appeared to run up to his best and can win a small handicap somewhere. *(op 7-1 tchd 9-1)*

Monticelli(GER), making his chasing debut, spoilt his chances with some indifferent jumping and was well beaten by a horse only rated 100 over fences. He was well supported before the race and is clearly thought capable of better. *(op 11-10 tchd 6-5 in a place)*

Dalaram(IRE) made a promising start over fences without immediately suggesting he is about to transfer all of his hurdling ability to the bigger obstacles. He did little wrong during the race, but was fairly weak in the market and can reasonably be expected to improve for the run. *(op 2-1)*

Dottie Digger(IRE) is a poor type and did not get home after racing too keenly in the early stages. *(op 33-1)*

1510 BETFAIR.COM CLAIMING HURDLE (8 hdls) 2m 110y

3:30 (3:30) (Class 4) 4-Y-0+ **£4,212** (£1,296; £648; £324)

Form | | | | RPR

04-2 **1** **Dalida**[9] 1375 4-10-7 87........ APMcCoy 94+
(P C Haslam) *prom: led after 4 out: drew clr fr 2 out* **4/1**[3]

-210 **2** *3 1/2* **Talarive (USA)**[120] 480 9-10-11 101........(tp) JimCrowley 91
(P D Niven) *cl up: led briefly 4 out: rdn and outpcd after next: kpt on to chse wnr run in: no imp* **7/2**[2]

04 **3** *6* **Big Wheel**[78] 903 10-10-8 100........ ADobbin 82
(N G Richards) *hld up: hdwy and pressed wnr 3 out: sn rdn: no ex bef last* **2/1**[1]

4322 **4** *6* **Gabor**[21] 1384 6-11-5 100........(b) EWhillans(7) 96+
(M Todhunter) *keen: led to 4 out: mstke and wknd next* **8/1**

P **Obe One**[35] 5-11-9........ GLee —
(J Howard Johnson) *bhd: rdn after 4 out: p.u after next* **20/1**

23-P **F** **Minivet**[38] 871 10-10-5 114........ KJMercer(3) 78
(R Allan) *chsd ldrs tl outpcd after 3 out: 14l down in 4th whn fell last* **7/1**

0-2 **U** **Cadeaux Rouge (IRE)**[29] 1293 4-9-13........(t) DCCostello(5) 65
(D W Thompson) *hld up in tch: hit 4th: wknd 3 out: wl btn whn hmpd and uns rdr last* **25/1**

4m 0.20s (-0.40) **Going Correction** +0.05s/f (Yiel)
WFA 4 from 5yo+ 14lb **7** Ran SP% **107.8**
Speed ratings: **102,100,97,94,—** —,— CSF £16.48 TOTE £5.00: £1.90, £2.90; EX 22.50.
Owner Mrs C Barclay **Bred** Mrs S J Brasher **Trained** Middleham, N Yorks

FOCUS
A moderate claimer full of disappointing types. However, it was the reasonably unexposed filly Dalida that won nicely and she can pick up a small handicap. Talarive probably ran up to his best while Big Wheel continues to disappoint.

NOTEBOOK
Dalida crept around the inside of the track and won nicely after travelling well. She is open to more improvement and can win a handicap off her revised mark. *(op 7-2)*
Talarive(USA), returning from a break, ran on quite well after being outpaced in the back straight. He does not win very often but suggested a return to further would help. *(op 3-1 tchd 4-1, 9-2 in places)*
Big Wheel settled nicely for his rider in midfield and looked to have every chance. However, he found very little off the bridle when asked to chase the eventual winner and was re-passed by the second between the last two. *(op 11-4 tchd 15-8, 3-1 in a place)*
Gabor, making his debut for the yard, raced with plenty of zest in the early stages before making a mistake when coming under pressure. He is hard to win with but had plenty to do on official figures and should be found easier chances in the future.
Minivet was staying on behind the leaders when tipping over at the last. He has become very frustrating but needs a stiffer test of stamina over hurdles than two miles. *(op 6-1)*
Obe One did not shape with any promise on his hurdling debut. *(op 6-1)*

1511 ROYAL BANK OF SCOTLAND H'CAP CHASE (FOR THE DUKE OF ATHOLL CHALLENGE CUP) (18 fncs) 3m

4:05 (4:06) (Class 3) (0-115,115) 5-Y-0+ **£8,190** (£2,520; £1,260; £630)

Form | | | | RPR

-221 **1** **Possextown (IRE)**[28] 1309 7-11-12 115........ ADobbin 128+
(N G Richards) *j.w: mde all at decent gallop: styd on strly fr 3 out* **7/4**[1]

-011 **2** *10* **Mocharamor (IRE)**[25] 1334 7-11-3 106........ JPMcNamara 107+
(J J Lambe, Ire) *chsd wnr thrght: rdn and edgd rt fr 3 out: no ex next* **9/2**[3]

5/42 **3** *17* **Pessimistic Dick**[28] 1309 12-10-0 89 oh6........ GLee 68
(Mrs J C McGregor) *bhd: hdwy 7th: no imp fnl circ* **16/1**

05-1 **4** *5* **Ta Ta For Now**[125] 421 8-10-3 92 ow3........ MBradburne 66
(Mrs S C Bradburne) *sn bhd: no ch fnl circ* **13/2**

P411 **5** *1/2* **Fearless Mel (IRE)**[12] 1446 11-11-4 107........ AO'Keeffe 81
(Mrs H Dalton) *chsd ldrs tl wknd fr 4 out: btn whn j.rt next* **4/1**[2]

562P **6** *29* **Tierkely (IRE)**[22] 1378 10-10-0 89 oh4........(p) ARoss 34
(J J Lambe, Ire) *a bhd: no ch fr 1/2-way* **25/1**

1UP6 **7** *1* **Excellent Vibes (IRE)**[32] 1262 7-10-9 98........ CLlewellyn 42
(N A Twiston-Davies) *towards rr: outpcd fr 7th: nvr on terms after* **11/2**

6m 12.5s (-0.10) **Going Correction** +0.05s/f (Yiel) **7** Ran SP% **113.0**
Speed ratings: **102,98,93,91,91 81,81** CSF £10.17 TOTE £2.30: £2.10, £3.10; EX 8.50.
Owner The Folly Racing Club **Bred** Mrs M E Foster **Trained** Greystoke, Cumbria

FOCUS
Very much a one-sided affair with the winner being the most progressive in the race. Mocharamor and Fearless Mel both came into the race on the back of two wins, but were readily outclassed.

NOTEBOOK
Possextown(IRE) was always in control of his rivals, despite his big weight, and won in pleasing style. He reportedly does not want the ground too soft and will be given a break when the winter weather starts, but he is a grand type who jumps nicely and can move on to better things. A race such as the Becher Chase at Aintree in November might suit him if the ground remains good. *(tchd 2-1 in places)*
Mocharamor(IRE) was unlucky to bump into such a progressive sort but probably ran up to his best. He remains in good heart and beat the third-placed horse with ease. *(op 11-2 tchd 6-1 in places)*
Pessimistic Dick is on the decline and was beaten further by the winner than on their meeting in August, despite meeting him on much better terms. *(op 20-1)*
Ta Ta For Now, given a break after his win last time and raised 8lb in the weights, did not show a great deal despite being proven under the conditions, and will be better suited by lesser competition. *(op 15-2 tchd 8-1)*
Fearless Mel(IRE) has risen markedly in the weights for his last two wins and looks now be in the Handicapper's grip. *(op 3-1)*
Excellent Vibes(IRE) is not a consistent sort and ran particularly badly. He is still 6lb above his last winning handicap mark. *(op 6-1 tchd 5-1)*

1512 STERLING ASSURANCE JUVENILE NOVICES' HURDLE (8 hdls) 2m 110y

4:40 (4:41) (Class 4) 3-Y-0 **£4,199** (£1,292; £646; £323)

Form | | | | RPR

1 **1** **Aviation**[25] 1338 3-11-5........ FKeniry 102+
(G M Moore) *trckd ldrs: rdn to ld 2 out: styd on strly* **11/4**[1]

2 *2 1/2* **Jackadandy (USA)**[16] 3-10-12........ GLee 90
(J Howard Johnson) *nt fluent: cl up: led briefly bef 2 out: mstke last: kpt on u.p* **9/2**[3]

3 *2* **Comical Errors (USA)**[20] 3-10-5........ PMerrigan(7) 89+
(P C Haslam) *in tch: hdwy and ev ch 2 out: kpt on same pce run in* **14/1**

3 **4** *13* **Dramatic Review (IRE)**[73] 945 3-10-12........(t) APMcCoy 75
(P C Haslam) *mde most to bef 2 out: sn btn* **7/2**[2]

5 *1/2* **Jenkins Lane (IRE)**[28] 3-10-12........ JPMcNamara 75
(J J Lambe, Ire) *hld up: hdwy and in tch after 3 out: rdn and wknd next* **8/1**

6 *2* **Casalese**[28] 3-10-12........ ADobbin 73
(M D Hammond) *towards rr: drvn after 4 out: wkng whn checked after next* **33/1**

7 *nk* **Countrywide Sun**[17] 3-10-12........ JimCrowley 72
(A C Whillans) *bhd: rdn bef 3 out: nvr on terms* **33/1**

8 *6* **Hawksbury Heights**[92] 3-10-12........ RJohnson 66
(J J Lambe, Ire) *nt fluent in midfield: mstke 5th: outpcd whn hmpd bnd after 3 out* **5/1**

P **Lerida**[513] 3-10-9........ PBuchanan(3) —
(Miss Lucinda V Russell) *bhd: struggling 1/2-way: t.o whn p.u bef last* **100/1**

6 **S** **Bellalou**[25] 1332 3-10-2........ KJMercer(3) —
(Mrs S A Watt) *cl up: disp ld 3rd: 4th and outpcd whn slipped up bnd after 3 out* **16/1**

4m 10.4s (9.80) **Going Correction** +0.05s/f (Yiel) **10** Ran SP% **114.3**
Speed ratings: **78,76,75,69,69 68,68,65,—,—** CSF £15.05 TOTE £4.20: £1.60, £2.10, £4.10; EX 18.90.
Owner G R Orchard **Bred** D J And Mrs Deer **Trained** Middleham Moor, N Yorks

FOCUS
A pedestrian winning time even for a race likes this, more than ten seconds slower than the claiming hurdle.

NOTEBOOK
Aviation has not looked back since being bought out of a Flat claimer by current connections. Under a 7lb penalty, he bounded clear of his rivals and won nicely despite pricking his ears in front. Things will get much more difficult for him but the Wensleydale Juvenile Hurdle at Wetherby in October would seem the logical race for him in the early part of the season. *(op 9-4 tchd 3-1 in places)*
Jackadandy(USA), who has shaped like a stayer on the Flat, kept on well after being passed in the straight. He has not had much racing and can improve with experience. *(op 11-2 tchd 6-1)*
Comical Errors(USA) did not show a great deal on the Flat but shaped much better on his first start over hurdles. *(op 25-1)*
Dramatic Review(IRE) cut out a lot of the running before fading in the straight. He can be given another chance to confirm his first effort over hurdles when tried in easier company. *(op 4-1)*
Jenkins Lane(IRE) was making headway when slightly hampered by Bellalou slipping over on the final turn. He found little when asked to close on the leaders and shaped like a horse that did not stay.
Hawksbury Heights was just starting to weaken when badly hampered by a horse slipping over on the final bend. *(op 4-1)*

1513 A C MANAGEMENT CONSULTING LTD H'CAP HURDLE (12 hdls) 3m 110y

5:15 (5:15) (Class 3) (0-115,114) 4-Y-0+ **£5,434** (£1,672; £836; £418)

Form | | | | RPR

63-1 **1** **Drumbeater (IRE)**[29] 1294 5-10-4 92........ RJohnson 102+
(P J Hobbs) *nt fluent: in tch: led after 3 out: mstke last: styd on wl* **11/4**[2]

/4-1 **2** *1 1/2* **Marlborough Sound**[114] 591 6-11-3 105........ ADobbin 113+
(N G Richards) *keen: hld up in tch: effrt and chsd wnr after 3 out: sn rdn: kpt on fr last* **5/1**[3]

443- **3** *12* **Russian Sky**[163] 4812 6-10-13 101........ LFletcher 96
(Mrs H O Graham) *chsd ldrs: outpcd 4 out: rallied bef 2 out: no ch w first two* **20/1**

342- **4** *16* **Tynedale (IRE)**[164] 4785 6-11-5 114........ TJDreaper(7) 93
(Mrs A Hamilton) *chsd ldrs tl wknd fr 3 out* **10/1**

P61- **5** *30* **Gazump (FR)**[200] 4187 7-11-3 105........ CLlewellyn 54
(N A Twiston-Davies) *led to after 3 out: sn rdn and wknd* **7/4**[1]

-330 **6** *20* **Speed Kris (FR)**[29] 1296 6-11-3 105........(p) MBradburne 34
(Mrs S C Bradburne) *hld up: rdn bef 4 out: sn btn* **12/1**

-132 **P** **Lanzlo (FR)**[114] 595 8-11-6 108........ JimCrowley —
(James Moffatt) *a bhd: t.o whn p.u 3 out* **20/1**

425- **P** **Culcabock (IRE)**[230] 3658 5-11-6 111........ PBuchanan(3) —
(Miss Lucinda V Russell) *a bhd: t.o whn p.u bef 2 out* **33/1**

-545 **P** **Thyne For Intersky (IRE)**[29] 1300 6-11-7 109........(p) APMcCoy —
(Jonjo O'Neill) *prom: drvn 1/2-way: wknd 4 out: t.o whn p.u bef 2 out* **11/1**

6m 5.40s (-5.50) **Going Correction** +0.05s/f (Yiel) **9** Ran SP% **117.3**
Speed ratings: **110,109,105,100,90 84,—,—,—** CSF £17.02 CT £229.99 TOTE £4.10: £1.50, £2.00, £5.20; EX 13.90 Place 6 £152.54, Place 5 £133.82.
Owner D Allen **Bred** Paul McDonnell **Trained** Withycombe, Somerset

FOCUS
A moderate handicap that only involved two in the home straight.

NOTEBOOK
Drumbeater(IRE), running off a 9lb higher mark than his last course and distance success, still struggles in the jumping department but made full use of his low weight to hold the second. He is progressive but his jumping will cause him problems as he rises through the grades. *(tchd 7-2 in places)*
Marlborough Sound, returning from a break, found the combination of giving weight away and racing keenly in the early stages too much after jumping the second last. He is, however, progressing in the right direction and should be capable of winning more races. *(op 9-2)*
Russian Sky shaped nicely on his return to action but was easily left behind up the straight and will need less-competitive races to have a serious chance.
Tynedale(IRE) ran well for a long way on his seasonal debut but did not get home. *(tchd 12-1 in places)*
Gazump(FR) was well supported in the market prior to the race but ran poorly. He has yet to prove he stays this trip and possibly did not get home. *(op 9-4)*
Speed Kris(FR) has not won since his days in France and does not look like reversing that trend soon.

T/Plt: £118.20 to a £1 stake. Pool: £40,680.55. 251.10 winning tickets. T/Qpdt: £11.90 to a £1 stake. Pool: £3,601.30. 223.65 winning tickets. RY

1514 - (Foreign Racing) - See Raceform Interactive

1504 LISTOWEL (L-H)

Wednesday, September 21

OFFICIAL GOING: Good

1515a GUINNESS KERRY NATIONAL H'CAP CHASE (GRADE A) 3m

4:10 (4:10) 4-Y-0+

£64,095 (£20,478; £9,840; £3,457; £2,393; £1,329)

RPR

1 **Euro Leader (IRE)**[27] 1325 7-12-0 133........ RWalsh 151+
(W P Mullins, Ire) *hld up towards rr: hdwy into 6th after 4 out: cl 3rd after 3 out: chal and led 2 out: slt mstke last: styd on wl u.p: all out* **11/2**[2]

2 *nk* **Monterey Bay (IRE)**[10] 1464 9-10-3 108 6ex........ TJMurphy 124+
(Ms F M Crowley, Ire) *cl up: led fr 9th: rdn and strly pressed after 3 out: slt mstke next: j.rt last: styd on wl u.p* **5/1**[1]

3 *4 1/2* **Pearly Jack**[27] 1325 7-10-11 119........ MDarcy(3) 129
(D E Fitzgerald, Ire) *hld up early: prog 1/2-way: 5th 6 out: 3rd next: 2nd bef 3 out: rdn to chal bef 2 out: 3rd and no ex bef last* **7/1**[3]

4 4 **Howaya Pet (IRE)**[144] 143 9-11-6 125 ....(t) BJGeraghty 131
(Gerard Keane, Ire) *trckd ldrs: 6th 1/2-way: 4th after 4 out: kpt on same pce u.p fr next* 14/1

5 3 ½ **Randwick Roar (IRE)**[27] 1325 6-10-12 117 .... DNRussell 120
(P M J Doyle, Ire) *in tch: 9th 1/2-way: 8th 3 out: kpt on u.p* 9/1

6 shd **Garvivonnian (IRE)**[10] 1463 10-11-7 133 .... MJFerris(7) 135
(Edward P Mitchell, Ire) *mid-div: 8th 1/2-way: 10th bef 5 out: kpt on same pce fr 3 out* 33/1

7 3 ½ **Light On The Broom (IRE)**[17] 1420 9-11-1 123 ....(t) MPWalsh(3) 122
(Gerard Stack, Ire) *towards rr: styd on fr 3 out* 16/1

8 hd **Bizet (IRE)**[147] 71 9-11-6 125 .... JLCullen 124
(F Flood, Ire) *trckd ldrs on inner: 7th 5 out: 5th 3 out: no ex fr 2 out* 12/1

9 4 **Berkley (IRE)**[27] 1325 8-10-11 116 ....(b) DFO'Regan 111
(Patrick Michael Verling, Ire) *mid-div: 6th 5 out: 7th and no ex 3 out: wknd bef next* 16/1

10 12 **Oh So Lively (IRE)**[31] 1283 7-10-5 113 ....(t) PWFlood(3) 96
(E J O'Grady, Ire) *cl up: 3rd bef 1/2-way: 2nd 6 out: 3rd and rdn 3 out: sn wknd* 8/1

11 nk **Il En Reve (FR)**[17] 1420 7-10-11 119 ....(b) TGMRyan(3) 101
(S J Treacy, Ire) *cl up: 2nd 1/2-way: 4th 6 out: wknd fr next* 20/1

12 6 **Danaeve (IRE)**[10] 1464 10-10-5 110 .... PFlynn 86
(Gerard Keane, Ire) *a towards rr* 33/1

13 shd **Totheroadyouvgone**[56] 1083 11-10-2 110 ....(p) RCColgan(3) 86
(A E Jones) *a towards rr* 25/1

14 20 **Eskimo Jack (IRE)**[27] 1325 9-10-12 117 .... CO'Dwyer 73
(A L T Moore, Ire) *a bhd* 20/1

15 4 ½ **Junior Fontaine (FR)**[27] 1083 8-11-2 126 .... RMMoran(5) 78
(A L T Moore, Ire) *hld up towards rr: no ex after 5 out* 14/1

16 9 **Piercing Sun (IRE)**[28] 1313 6-11-2 121 ....(p) PCarberry 64
(Anthony Mullins, Ire) *a bhd* 11/1

F **Andy Higgins (IRE)**[33] 1260 8-9-8 106 ....(b1) DFFlannery(7) —
(E J O'Grady, Ire) *mid-div: prog 1/2-way: 5th 7 out: 4th and in tch whn fell 4 out* 14/1

P **Fatherofthebride (IRE)**[17] 1420 9-10-8 113 ....(b) DJCasey —
(Joseph Crowley, Ire) *led: hdd 9th: remained cl up to 6 out: wkng whn mstke 4 out: t.o whn p.u bef 2 out* 14/1

5m 43.3s **18** Ran SP% **139.4**
CSF £36.39 CT £212.08 TOTE £6.10: £2.40, £1.80, £2.00, £2.00; DF 20.20.
Owner John Cox **Bred** Mrs Maureen Mullins **Trained** Muine Beag, Co Carlow

NOTEBOOK
Euro Leader(IRE) allayed fears that three miles would be too far and coped with the 13lb rise. *(op 11/2 tchd 6/1)*

[1404]FONTWELL (L-H)

Thursday, September 22

OFFICIAL GOING: Good to firm
Wind: Nil Weather: sunny and warm

1519 REDBANK LONG PADDOCK WINES JUVENILE NOVICES' HURDLE (9 hdls) 2m 2f 110y
2:10 (2:10) (Class 4) 3-Y-O **£3,577** (£1,022; £511)

Form RPR

4 1 **Snow Tempest (USA)**[26] 1146 3-10-12 ....(b) TDoyle 103+
(T G Mills) *racd freely: mde all: drew rt away fr 3 out: hit last: easily* 12/1

253 2 14 **Millquista D'Or**[18] 1404 3-10-5 87 ....(t) JAMcCarthy 76
(G A Ham) *in tch in rr: rdn after 4th: plugged on fr 6th: wnt 2nd last: no ch w wnr* 8/1

4 3 4 **Trigger Guard**[18] 1404 3-10-12 .... PHide 80+
(G L Moore) *hld up in rr: prog 6th: chsd wnr 3 out: no imp: wknd and lost 2nd last* 3/1[1]

4 25 **Water Pistol**[26] 3-10-12 .... JimCrowley 54
(Mrs A J Perrett) *prom: chsd wnr 5th to 3 out: wknd: t.o* 3/1[1]

R0 5 1 ½ **Josear**[4] 1478 3-10-12 .... MBradburne 53
(C J Down) *prom to 6th: wkng whn mstke 3 out: t.o* 50/1

06 6 6 **Tiffin Deano (IRE)**[18] 1404 3-10-5 .... MrJAJenkins(7) 47
(H J Manners) *hit 1st: a in rr: lost tch 5th: t.o fr next* 66/1

7 27 **Palace Walk (FR)**[208] 3-10-12 .... TJMurphy 20
(B G Powell) *in tch: chsd ldng pair briefly after 5th: wknd rapidly 3 out: t.o* 7/1[3]

P **Smart Tiger (GER)**[74] 3-10-12 .... PMoloney —
(N P Littmoden) *mostly chsd wnr to 5th: sn wknd: t.o whn p.u bef 2 out* 10/3[2]

F P **Amaya Silva**[18] 1404 3-10-5 .... JamesDavies —
(S Dow) *w wnr whn blnd 1st: last whn mstke 2nd: sn t.o: p.u after 5th* 50/1

PF00 P **Miss Dinamite**[13] 1440 3-9-12 .... TMessenger(7) —
(Mrs C J Ikin) *chsd ldrs: rdn bef 4th: wknd next: t.o whn p.u bef 2 out* 100/1

4m 23.1s (-12.90) **Going Correction** -0.575s/f (Firm) **10** Ran SP% **110.8**
Speed ratings: **104,98,96,85,85 82,71,—,—,—** CSF £95.42 TOTE £15.40: £3.40, £2.00, £1.30; EX 44.30.
Owner Ian West **Bred** Diamond A Racing Corp **Trained** Headley, Surrey

FOCUS
Weak juvenile hurdle form and, although Snow Tempest did it nicely, he beat very little. The third sets the level for the form.

NOTEBOOK
Snow Tempest(USA), sporting blinkers for the first time over hurdles, left his previous effort at Sedgefield behind and, having travelled strongly, he began to stretch clear. This was a bad race, but there may be more to come and he will now head to the sales. *(op 14-1)*
Millquista D'Or confirmed recent course form with Trigger Guard, but she never got anywhere near the winner and remains exposed. *(tchd 7-1)*
Trigger Guard failed to build on a mildly promising debut and needs to improve if he is to be winning anytime soon. *(op 5-2)*
Water Pistol, a disappointing sort on the Flat, is bred to stay all day, being by top-class Flat-stayer Double Trigger out of a winning hurdler, but he made a poor start to his hurdling career and had nothing left to offer from three out. He is not the biggest and does not look to have much of a future. *(op 7-2)*
Palace Walk(FR), a superbly-bred gelding who showed little on the Flat, travelled well but stopped quickly once coming under pressure and may have needed this first outing since February. He is worthy of another chance. *(op 8-1)*
Smart Tiger(GER), twice a winner in Germany, was reported to have lost his action and can be *given another chance to show what he can do. Official explanation: jockey said gelding lost its action (op 3-1 tchd 11-4)*

1520 LOUIS LATOUR (S) H'CAP HURDLE (9 hdls) 2m 2f 110y
2:40 (2:41) (Class 5) (0-85,84) 4-Y-0+ **£2,254** (£644; £322)

Form RPR

0-63 1 **Sheer Guts (IRE)**[26] 1333 6-11-7 84 ....(vt1) PCO'Neill(5) 95+
(Evan Williams) *prom in chsng gp: chsd ldr 6th: clsd fr 2 out: led last: drvn clr* 6/1[3]

-P00 2 8 **Gray Knight (IRE)**[24] 1362 8-11-4 76 ....(b) RThornton 77
(Mrs T J Hill) *prom in chsng gp: rdn 3 out: clsd next: in tch last: one pce flat* 14/1

-P00 3 8 **Oh Sunny Boy (IRE)**[4] 1482 4-11-1 74 ....(p) TJMurphy 69+
(B G Powell) *pressed ldr and sn clr of rest: led 5th and sn clr: blnd 3 out: hit 2 out: hdd & wknd last: fin tired* 7/1

-P50 4 6 **Distant Romance**[109] 651 8-10-6 71 .... RLucey-Butler(7) 58
(Miss Z C Davison) *in tch in chsng gp: rdn bef 3 out: no real imp bef next* 40/1

0U-3 5 5 **Chariot (IRE)**[40] 1208 4-11-2 82 .... MrJAJenkins(7) 63
(M R Bosley) *hld up in rr: prog 6th: drvn bef 3 out: no further hdwy and wl btn bef 2 out: mstke last* 12/1

-364 6 6 **Lucky Arthur (IRE)**[24] 1356 4-11-6 82 .... ONelmes(3) 57
(J G M O'Shea) *in tch in midfield: rdn after 6th: btn whn blnd 3 out* 5/1[2]

06F0 7 nk **Waziya**[63] 1046 6-11-3 75 ....(p) DCrosse 51
(Mrs L Williamson) *nvr on terms w ldrs: u.p and struggling fr 6th: wknd 3 out* 50/1

5/00 8 9 **Broughton Knows**[19] 1395 8-10-10 75 ....(p) TMessenger(7) 42
(Mrs C J Ikin) *in tch: rdn 4th: wknd next: bhd fr 6th: t.o* 16/1

4440 P **Dunkerron**[19] 1395 8-10-13 78 .... SWalsh(7) —
(J Joseph) *in tch tl wknd u.p after 4th: p.u bef 6th* 10/1

/0-1 P **Aleemdar (IRE)**[115] 592 8-11-0 77 ....(p) DLaverty(5) —
(A E Jones) *hld up in rr: pushed along 5th: wknd next: t.o whn p.u bef 2 out* 4/1[1]

60P/ P **Jeune Premier (FR)**[528] 8-10-6 64 ....(t) ChristianWilliams —
(Evan Williams) *led at fast pce to 5th: wknd rapidly: p.u bef next* 5/1[2]

0045 P **La Maestra (FR)**[22] 1384 7-11-5 77 ....(b) PMoloney —
(Miss L Day) *nvr on terms: last and drvn after 5th: sn wl bhd: poor 9th whn p.u and dismntd flat* 40/1

4m 26.2s (-9.80) **Going Correction** -0.575s/f (Firm)
WFA 4 from 6yo+ 14lb **12** Ran SP% **116.3**
Speed ratings: **97,93,90,87,85 83,82,79,—,— —,—** CSF £82.53 CT £602.55 TOTE £6.40: £2.40, £4.60, £2.20; EX 90.10.There was no bid for the winner. Lucky Arthur was claimed by Mrs Lisa Williamson for £6,000
Owner Fox And Hounds Racing **Bred** E Tynan **Trained** Cowbridge, Vale Of Glamorgan

FOCUS
A poor selling in which they went a decent early pace and the runners were well strung out at the line. The winner was improved for the fitting of the aids.

NOTEBOOK
Sheer Guts(IRE), who was always travelling extremely well, was given a fine ride by his young pilot and picked up well once asked to go on and win. He appeared to find two and three quarter miles beyond him at Cartmel, but this trip was much more to his liking and he may be capable of scoring again at a similarly lowly level. *(op 8-1)*
Gray Knight(IRE) left behind a poor effort at Huntingdon and kept on well for a clear second. He shaped as though a return to further will help. *(op 16-1)*
Oh Sunny Boy(IRE) held a clear advantage at one stage, but it was evident from three out that he was beginning to weaken and a tired lunge at the second last sealed his fate. He is still only four and capable of better yet. *(tchd 15-2)*
Distant Romance ran one of her better races, making some good late headway, but she makes little appeal as a likely future winner. *(op 33-1)*
Lucky Arthur(IRE) never got into it after his pilot lost her iron following a mistake at the first, and she may be worthy of another chance. *(tchd 11-2)*
Waziya *Official explanation: jockey said mare hung right (op 33-1)*
Aleemdar(IRE) ran most disappointingly on this first start since May and he never got into it after *being hampered at the top bend.Official explanation: jockey said gelding was hampered top of hill final circuit and lost action (op 33-1)*
La Maestra(FR) *Official explanation: vet said mare finished lame (op 33-1)*

1521 CHAMPAGNE JOSEPH PERRIER MAIDEN CHASE (13 fncs) 2m 2f
3:10 (3:10) (Class 4) 4-Y-0+ **£3,993** (£1,228; £614; £307)

Form RPR

0606 1 **Scarrabus (IRE)**[4] 1482 4-10-7 90 .... TJMurphy 91+
(B G Powell) *hld up in tch: quick move on inner to ld 3 out: clr next: pushed out* 5/2[2]

55 2 5 **Pharshu (IRE)**[93] 803 8-10-7 ....(t) MrJSnowden(7) 90
(C L Tizzard) *wl in tch: nt fluent 5th: effrt after 4 out: w wnr next: sn outpcd* 10/1

4-4P 3 1 ½ **Lightin' Jack (IRE)**[121] 486 7-11-7 104 .... MFoley 96
(Miss E C Lavelle) *led to 3rd: steadily lost pl 6th: effrt again gng wl 10th: outpcd fr 3 out* 9/4[1]

6P-0 4 ½ **Down The Stretch**[146] 104 5-11-7 99 .... LAspell 95
(A Ennis) *t.k.h: hld up in cl tch: pressed ldr 7th to 10th: easily outpcd 3 out: plugged on* 8/1

-P52 5 18 **Karakum**[24] 1363 6-11-0 94 .... MrJAJenkins(7) 80+
(A J Chamberlain) *prom: nt fluent 6th: led 7th to 3 out: wknd rapidly* 9/2[3]

6 6 10 **Tellem Noting (IRE)**[116] 8-11-7 ....(t) JTizzard 67
(B G Powell) *led 4th to 7th: lost pl after next: wknd 10th: t.o* 10/1

P **Thorny Issue**[145] 6-11-7 ....(p) SCurran —
(M J Gingell) *j. slowly: struggling in last fr 6th: p.u bef 9th* 20/1

4m 31.0s (-4.10) **Going Correction** -0.575s/f (Firm)
WFA 4 from 5yo+ 14lb **7** Ran SP% **111.6**
Speed ratings: **86,83,83,82,74 70,—** CSF £24.57 TOTE £2.90: £2.00, £3.60; EX 25.10.
Owner I S Smith **Bred** Michael And Fiona O'Connor **Trained** Morestead, Hants

FOCUS
A moderate winning time, even for a race like this. The winner is value for further with the fourth setting the standard.

NOTEBOOK
Scarrabus(IRE) has never been the strongest of finishers, but this switch to fences may well be the making of him and this time, having travelled strongly, he found plenty. He will be doing well to find as weaker race in future, but being a four-year-old may have further improvement in him and his current mark of 90 gives him a chance in handicaps. *(op 11-4 tchd 3-1 in a place and 9-4 in a place)*
Pharshu(IRE) kept on well for second without having the pace of the winner and ran her best race yet under Rules. A return to further will help and she may find a suitable opportunity in mares-only company. *(op 12-1 tchd 14-1 and 9-1)*
Lightin' Jack(IRE), not seen since disappointing at Worcester in May, has displayed more than enough ability to suggest winning a race of this nature should be a formality, but he again disappointed and is becoming a bit of a liability. *(op 2-1 tchd 5-2)*
Down The Stretch had every chance and recorded one of his better efforts. He is only a five-year-old and may yet have some improvement in him. *(op 7-1)*

Karakum failed to build on his recent Huntingdon second and took a step back in the wrong direction. *Official explanation: jockey said gelding was unsuited by the good to firm ground (op 4-1)*

1522 HILDON.COM NOVICES' HURDLE (11 hdls) 2m 6f 110y

3:40 (3:40) (Class 4) 4-Y-O+ **£3,334** (£1,026; £513; £256)

Form				RPR
2-03	1		**Miss Merenda**[53] [1108] 4-10-3 94... PJBrennan (J F Panvert) *trckd ldr: upsides 3 out: rdn and outpcd by new ldr bef next: kpt on wl flat to ld last 75yds* **4/1**[2]	86
3241	2	2 ½	**Festive Chimes (IRE)**[4] [1485] 4-11-0 103........................... ONelmes(3) (N B King) *hld up in tch: prog 8th: led after 3 out: kicked 4l clr next: hung rt flat: hdd last 75yds* **3/1**[1]	98+
	3	10	**Oh So Hardy**[19] 4-9-12 ....(t) DLaverty(5) (M A Allen) *settled in last pair: rdn after 7th: mstke next: outpcd 3 out: n.d after: plugged on* **50/1**	73
0-P2	4	1 ¾	**The Bay Bridge (IRE)**[64] [1036] 6-10-12 .... MFoley (Miss E C Lavelle) *mstke 2nd: hld up in last pair: lft bhd bef 3 out: modest effrt bef 2 out: shkn up bef last: nvr nr ldrs* **6/1**	80+
5022	5	20	**Explosive Fox (IRE)**[15] [1431] 4-11-3 105..................................(p) TDoyle (C P Morlock) *led: hdd and btn sn after 3 out: no ch whn mstke last* **9/2**[3]	70+
-5F0	6	dist	**Regulated (IRE)**[4] [1480] 4-10-0 90.................... AngharadFrieze(10) (P A Blockley) *chsd ldng pair to 8th: sn wknd u.p: t.o* **25/1**	—
15/6	P		**Rome (IRE)**[24] [1364] 6-10-12 .... RThornton (G P Enright) *in tch tl wknd after 8th: t.o last whn p.u bef 2 out* **3/1**[1]	—

5m 30.5s (-14.30) **Going Correction** -0.575s/f (Firm) **7** Ran SP% **108.3**
Speed ratings: **101,100,96,96,89** —,— CSF £14.94 TOTE £4.90: £2.30, £1.60; EX 20.60.
Owner J F Panvert **Bred** Ian Moss **Trained** Hildenborough, Kent

FOCUS
A moderate contest but the outcome of this changed quickly in the last furlong, with Festive Chimes hanging badly right and handing Miss Merenda victory. The principals are rated as having run to their marks.

NOTEBOOK
Miss Merenda, a game mare who often wants for a bit of pace when it matters, was swept aside by the runner-up rounding for home, but she stuck to the task admirably and powered up the hill to take full advantage of the winner hanging badly to her right. She will stay three miles and her current mark of 94 looks a fair one for handicaps. *(tchd 9-2)*
Festive Chimes(IRE) is highly consistent filly and she looked set to go on and score when racing ahead before the second last, but she threw it away after the last, hanging badly to her right. This was out of character and it is safe to assume to will continue to pay her way. *(op 11-4)*
Oh So Hardy, rated just 35 on the Flat, appeared to run above expectations on this hurdles debut and plodded on down the straight to claim an admirable third. He looked to be struggling badly at one point, but stuck to his task well and should prove good enough to score at selling level.
The Bay Bridge(IRE) stayed on after the race was all over and may have benefited from a more positive ride. He is the type to do better in handicaps and definitely has more to give. *(op 11-2 tchd 5-1)*
Explosive Fox(IRE)has been running well in similar events under a penalty and looked to hold every chance here. Allowed to take them along at a steady gallop, he really had no excuse for this poor showing and it was disappointing how quickly he dropped away once headed three out. He is better than this, but consistency is hardly his strong point. *(op 4-1)*
Rome(IRE), supported in the market beforehand, was evidently expected to step up on his reappearance effort over this trip, but he again showed little and it remains to be seen how much ability he retains. *Official explanation: trainer said gelding didn't stay the trip (op 7-2 tchd 4-1 in a place)*

1523 3663 FIRST FOR FOOD SERVICE CONDITIONAL JOCKEYS' NOVICES' H'CAP HURDLE (10 hdls) 2m 4f

4:10 (4:10) (Class 4) (0-100,98) 4-Y-O+ **£3,393** (£1,044; £522; £261)

Form				RPR
2154	1		**Roman Candle (IRE)**[32] [1277] 9-10-8 83............................ PMerrigan(3) (Lucinda Featherstone) *hld up in last pair: mstkes 2nd and 6th: prog 3 out: hrd rdn bef next: styd on to chse ldr last: drvn to ld fnl 75yds* **4/1**[2]	84+
0PP-	2	½	**Rhetorical**[19] [4910] 4-9-9 74.. RLucey-Butler(6) (P Butler) *w ldr: led 4th: narrow advantage but gng best after 3 out: rdn bef last: hdd fnl 75yds* **66/1**	73
200-	3	4	**Atlantis (HOL)**[229] [3703] 6-10-13 91.................................. EDehdashti(6) (G L Moore) *in tch: pushed along 6th: effrt on inner bef 3 out: w wnr bef 2 out: nt qckn u.p last* **7/2**[1]	87
-232	4	3	**Kentucky King (USA)**[28] [1322] 5-11-7 98.............................(t) LHeard(5) (Mrs D A Hamer) *rel to r: sn in tch towards rr: prog to press ldrs whn blnd 3 out: sn rdn: one pce next* **4/1**[2]	92+
00/P	5	5	**Roscam**[92] [813] 8-9-13 76.. KBurke(5) (G A Ham) *t.k.h: cl up: jnd ldr on outer 3 out tl rdn and fdd bef 2 out* **17/2**	64
P556	6	3	**Dawn Frolics**[30] [1297] 4-10-0 73 oh11.. DCrosse (M J Gingell) *hld up in last pair: effrt 7th: cl up but rdn 3 out: no hdwy fr 2 out* **33/1**	57
00/3	7	10	**Sunset King (USA)**[22] [1381] 5-10-2 82.............................. JamesWhite(8) (R J Hodges) *t.k.h: prom: w ldr 3 out tl wknd bef next* **13/2**[3]	60+
P325	8	dist	**Peruvian Breeze (IRE)**[26] [1336] 4-10-13 86.............................. PCO'Neill (Evan Williams) *prom: lost pl 6th: wknd bef 3 out: sn t.o* **4/1**[2]	—
-020	P		**Rumbling Bridge**[79] [903] 4-10-13 86.. ONelmes (Miss J S Davis) *led to 4th: wknd 7th: sn t.o: p.u bef 2 out* **16/1**	—

4m 51.1s (-12.70) **Going Correction** -0.575s/f (Firm)
WFA 4 from 5yo+ 15lb **9** Ran SP% **116.4**
Speed ratings: **102,101,100,99,97 95,91**,—,— CSF £161.75 CT £1014.20 TOTE £3.60: £1.90, £10.40, £2.00; EX 203.50.
Owner J Roundtree **Bred** R W Huggins And P Wilkerson **Trained** Newmarket, Suffolk

FOCUS
Poor form, but the winner sets the level and the race may produce the odd winner.

NOTEBOOK
Roman Candle(IRE), whose most recent efforts have been poor, including when tried over fences latest, bounced back to form returned to the smaller obstacles and showed a good attitude to edge ahead in the dying strides. However, it is has to be debatable whether he can defy a rise. *(op 10-3)*
Rhetorical, who had shown nothing in five previous starts, was well held back on the Flat recently and this effort came as something of a surprise. He found plenty for pressure having raced prominently throughout and, if this was no flash in the pan, he can surely find a race at selling level. *(tchd 50-1)*
Atlantis(HOL), well supported in the market beforehand, was struggling from some way out, but to his credit he kept going and held every chance in the straight. He is not straightforward, but can find a race at a moderate level. *(op 5-1)*
Kentucky King(USA) ran another reasonable race, but remains vulnerable to something less exposed. *(op 10-3)*
Peruvian Breeze(IRE) was well below par and there was surely something amiss. *(tchd 5-1)*

1524 HENNINGS WINE MERCHANTS H'CAP CHASE (15 fncs) 2m 4f

4:40 (4:40) (Class 4) (0-105,105) 5-Y-O+ **£4,793** (£1,475; £737; £368)

Form				RPR
131/	1		**Thalys (GER)**[187] 7-11-2 95... TDoyle (P R Webber) *nt fluent early: hld up in rr: prog 10th: led 4 out: in command fr next: drvn out* **9/4**[1]	107+
5024	2	7	**Eau Pure (FR)**[93] [805] 8-10-12 91.......................................(bt[1]) JEMoore (G L Moore) *settled midfield: clsd fr 10th: rdn to chse wnr 3 out: no imp* **5/1**[3]	97+
4-P0	3	4	**Just Reuben (IRE)**[18] [1414] 10-10-0 79 oh21...................... TScudamore (C L Tizzard) *led to 4 out: lost 2nd next: kpt on to hold on for 3rd* **33/1**	80
4636	4	1	**Romany Dream**[19] [1399] 7-10-12 91....................................(b) BHitchcott (R Dickin) *t.k.h: trckd ldrs: rdn and outpcd 11th: chsd ldng trio after 4 out: no imp u.p* **9/2**[2]	91
0642	5	11	**Celtic Star (IRE)**[18] [1406] 7-10-4 83......................................(b) DCrosse (Mrs L Williamson) *trckd ldrs: j.rt 7th: drvn and lost tch fr 12th: n.d after* **9/2**[2]	75+
-600	6	4	**Stopwatch (IRE)**[120] [503] 10-9-11 79 oh13............................ TJMalone(3) (Mrs L C Jewell) *a wl in rr: lost tch fr 10th: no ch after* **33/1**	64
4340	7	1	**Saby (FR)**[22] [1381] 7-11-4 97... PJBrennan (P J Hobbs) *settled in midfield: rdn and struggling 11th: nvr on terms after* **10/1**	81
6301	8	¾	**Master T (USA)**[107] [672] 6-11-12 105... PHide (G L Moore) *hld up in last pair: already losing tch whn mstke 10th: bhd after* **11/1**	88
0206	9	7	**Johnny Grand**[18] [1414] 8-10-0 79 oh2..................................(b) JMogford (D W Lewis) *mostly chsd ldr to 11th: wknd rapidly* **25/1**	55
P6-F	10	dist	**Quiet Millfit (USA)**[137] [234] 9-10-2 81 oh1 ow2.......................... LAspell (R Ingram) *hld up in last pair: nt fluent 4th: nudged along and lost tch 10th: sn wl bhd: t.o and virtually p.u flat* **16/1**	—

4m 56.8s (-11.10) **Going Correction** -0.575s/f (Firm) **10** Ran SP% **116.8**
Speed ratings: **99,96,94,94,89 88,87,87,84**,— CSF £14.22 CT £282.10 TOTE £3.80: £1.60, £2.20, £4.40; EX 21.20.
Owner Miss P Theobald **Bred** L Eisele **Trained** Mollington, Oxon

FOCUS
A moderate race but a good performance by the well-supported Thalys with the runner-up the guide to the value of the form.

NOTEBOOK
Thalys(GER), who was most progressive a couple seasons back, had not been seen since disappointing in a point at Cottenham back in March (reportedly failing to stay three miles). Always travelling strongly, he went on four out and came away to win nicely. He may now head off to the sales, but whoever he reappears for, he is likely to follow up if not raised too much for this. *(op 5-2 tchd 3-1 in places and 11-4 in places)*
Eau Pure(FR) has largely struggled since winning at the course back in March, but she went in pursuit of the winner and gave it her all. She may need to drop a few pounds before winning again, however. *(tchd 9-2 and 11-2)*
Just Reuben(IRE) was racing from some way out of the weights and ran much better than could have been expected. He is 5lb lower than when last scoring and may return to winning ways once dropped in grade.
Romany Dream has yet to win in handicap company and will need to improve on this if she is to do so. *(op 5-1 tchd 11-2)*
Celtic Star(IRE) was a bit adrift of the front four, but is on a decent mark and may soon be ready to strike. *(op 5-1)*

1525 GONZALEZ BYASS CROFT H'CAP HURDLE (11 hdls) 2m 6f 110y

5:10 (5:10) (Class 4) (0-110,108) 4-Y-O+ **£4,024** (£1,238; £619; £309)

Form				RPR
0-42	1		**Yourman (IRE)**[15] [1436] 5-11-12 108....................................... TJMurphy (M C Pipe) *racd wd and hld up in tch: prog to chse ldr 3 out: mstke next and looked hld: kpt on wl to ld flat* **2/1**[1]	114+
2054	2	4	**September Moon**[18] [1408] 7-11-3 99.. RThornton (Mrs A M Thorpe) *disp ld tl def advantage 8th: blnd 3 out: rdn 3 l clr 2 out: hdd and no ex flat* **6/1**	101+
0-00	3	14	**Ingres**[78] [915] 5-10-10 99.. CMStudd(7) (B G Powell) *trckd ldrs: gng wl 3 out: lost pl but stl gng wl sn after: nudged along to take 3rd 2 out: nvr nr ldng pair* **20/1**	86
3506	4	6	**Mariday**[18] [1408] 4-10-9 93... LAspell (L Wells) *settled in rr: pushed along and lost tch in last bef 8th: nvr on terms after: plugged on fr 2 out* **16/1**	72
5341	5	2	**Arm And A Leg (IRE)**[28] [1319] 10-11-5 108.............................. LHeard(7) (Mrs D A Hamer) *settled in rr: pushed along after 7th: outpcd next: blnd 3 out and rdr lost iron briefly: nt rcvr* **9/1**	95+
1022	6	4	**Native Chancer (IRE)**[18] [1408] 5-10-13 105............................. WJones(10) (Jonjo O'Neill) *trckd ldrs: gng wl 3 out: drvn and fnd nil bef 2 out: wknd* **4/1**[2]	80
-0P1	7	5	**Big Quick (IRE)**[33] [1262] 10-10-4 93 ow1........................... MrJMorgan(7) (L Wells) *nt fluent in rr: reminders and prog 6th: drvn 8th: wknd 3 out* **12/1**	63
-440	8	20	**Hylia**[105] [697] 6-10-8 90...(t) JAMcCarthy (Mrs P Robeson) *disp ld to 8th: wknd rapidly after 3 out* **9/2**[3]	40

5m 30.35s (-14.45) **Going Correction** -0.575s/f (Firm)
WFA 4 from 5yo+ 15lb **8** Ran SP% **114.1**
Speed ratings: **102,100,95,93,92 91,89,82** CSF £14.69 CT £181.85 TOTE £2.80: £1.60, £1.50, £4.10; EX 16.30 Place 6 £186.82, Place 5 £71.70.
Owner D A Johnson **Bred** Matt Carr **Trained** Nicholashayne, Devon

FOCUS
A modest hurdle in which the complexion of this changed quickly after the last with Yourman in the end winning going away. The form does not look strong.

NOTEBOOK
Yourman(IRE), a staying-on second over three miles at Uttoxeter last time, needed all of that extra stamina here and came through strongly after the last to win going away. He will need to find improvement to defy a higher mark however. *(op 5-2 tchd 11-4 and 3-1 in a place)*
September Moon, a slight disappointment over course and distance earlier in the month, showed that running to be all wrong and ran a fine race in second, just being found out by the stiff finish. She is on a reasonable mark and can find another contest at this sort of level, possibly back over two and a half miles.
Ingres is the one to take from the race. Given a strange ride, he travelled supremely well for most of the way but was allowed to drop back and give away ground turning in. It did not affect his finishing position, but the Stewards did look into this and the only explanation his rider could offer was that he was unsuited by the fast ground. There is definitely more to come from this five-year-old and he is one to watch out for in a similar event. *Official explanation: jockey said gelding was unsuited by the good to firm ground*
Mariday stayed on all too late in the day, coming through to claim a never-nearer fourth. He looked quirky at times during the race, but is only a four-year-old and deserves the benefit of the doubt for the time being. *(op 25-1)*

Arm And A Leg(IRE) was never really travelling and could do no more than plod on through tiring rivals. His rider momentarily lost an iron after a mistake at the third last, but if did not affect his chance of reaching a place. *(op 8-1 tchd 7-1)*

Native Chancer(IRE) was unable to confirm recent course form with either September Moon or Mariday and was clearly below par, albeit there was no obvious excuse. *(op 7-2)*

T/Plt: £458.10 to a £1 stake. Pool: £39,880.05. 63.55 winning tickets. T/Qpdt: £45.80 to a £1 stake. Pool: £3,292.20. 53.10 winning tickets. JN

1508 PERTH (R-H)

Thursday, September 22

OFFICIAL GOING: Good to soft (good in places)

Wind: fresh, against

1526 BRACEWELL STIRLING ARCHITECTS 80TH ANNIVERSARY NOVICES' HURDLE (12 hdls) 3m 110y

2:20 (2:20) (Class 4) 4-Y-0+ **£3,536** (£1,088; £544; £272)

Form			Horse	Jockey	RPR
0/11	1		**Decisive**[33] 1266 6-11-9 122	RJohnson	136+
			(P Bowen) *mde all: drew clr fr 3 out: easily*	1/1[1]	
22-3	2	19	**Catch The Perk (IRE)**[133] 321 8-11-0 110	(p) PBuchanan[(3)]	108+
			(Miss Lucinda V Russell) *cl up: pushed along 1/2-way: outpcd 4 out: rallied to chse wnr after next: no imp fr next*	7/2[2]	
0021	3	22	**Kirkham Abbey**[40] 1206 5-11-3 108	(v) RGarritty	81
			(J J Quinn) *prom: rdn 4 out: outpcd fr next*	4/1[3]	
/P63	4	2	**Corries Wood (IRE)**[23] 1374 6-10-11 86	JPMcNamara	73
			(J J Lambe, Ire) *chsd ldrs tl wknd fr 4 out*	20/1	
05-6	5	5	**Everytime**[26] 1344 5-10-5 80 ow1	MrOGreenall[(7)]	69
			(M W Easterby) *bhd: no ch fr 1/2-way*	66/1	
5634	P		**Step In Line (IRE)**[26] 1333 13-10-6 62	DCCostello[(5)]	—
			(D W Thompson) *in tch to 7th: sn wknd: t.o whn p.u bef 2 out*	100/1	
36-	P		**Sergio Coimbra (IRE)**[195] 4299 6-10-11	ADobbin	—
			(N G Richards) *hld up in tch: hdwy to chse wnr 4 out to after next: wknd qckly and p.u bef 2 out*	8/1	

6m 21.8s (10.90) **Going Correction** +0.50s/f (Soft) **7** Ran SP% **110.6**

Speed ratings: **102,95,88,88,86** —,— CSF £4.51 TOTE £2.00: £1.10, £2.70; EX 4.40.

Owner R Owen & P Fullagar **Bred** Shutford Stud **Trained** Little Newcastle, Pembrokes

FOCUS

A fair pace and another step in the right direction from Decisive, who won with much more in hand than the winning margin suggests. The runner-up sets the standard for the form.

NOTEBOOK

Decisive ◆, up in trip and on easier ground than for his two previous hurdle wins, maintained his unbeaten record in this sphere with a very fluent performance. His jumping was sound and he appeals as the type to hold his own in stronger company. *(op 10-11 tchd 11-10)*

Catch The Perk(IRE), back after a break, is suited by a test and was far from disgraced for a stable that has found winners hard to come by this term. He is vulnerable in this grade but will be of interest granted a sufficient test back in handicaps. *(op 4-1)*

Kirkham Abbey, off the mark over hurdles in an ordinary event last time, was found out under his penalty against a useful sort over this longer trip. The handicap route looks the best option now, but he has never been one for maximum faith. *(op 9-2, tchd 5-1 in places)*

Corries Wood(IRE) looked to have a stiff task in this company and was well beaten on this rain-softened ground. He has yet to win but he travelled strongly for a long way and the return to handicaps and better ground will suit.

Everytime faced a very stiff task.

Sergio Coimbra(IRE), who had shown ability in a bumper and on his hurdle debut, stopped quickly in the end after taking a grip over this longer trip following a break, but showed more than enough to suggest he can win a small race when qualified for a handicap mark. *(tchd 9-1)*

1527 JEWSON NOVICES' HURDLE (SERIES QUALIFIER) (8 hdls) 2m 110y

2:50 (2:51) (Class 4) 4-Y-0+ **£4,303** (£1,324; £662; £331)

Form			Horse	Jockey	RPR
521	1		**Constable Burton**[28] 942 4-11-1 104	KJMercer[(3)]	101+
			(Mrs A Duffield) *poached 8l ld s: nt fluent: mde all: hld on wl fr 2 out: unchal*	8/1	
0-01	2	1 3/4	**Dubonai (IRE)**[24] 1360 5-10-13 98	(t) DCCostello[(5)]	98
			(G M Moore) *prom chsng gp: wnt 2nd after 3 out: kpt on fr last: nt rch wnr*	7/1	
	3	3 1/2	**Motorway (IRE)**[410] 4-10-12	RJohnson	89
			(P J Hobbs) *hld up: hdwy bef 3 out: rdn next: kpt on fr last*	7/2[2]	
-0P4	4	7	**King's Envoy (USA)**[30] 1291 6-10-9 88	PAspell[(3)]	82
			(Mrs J C McGregor) *prom: drvn and outpcd after 3 out: kpt on fr last: no imp*	100/1	
0-1	5	5	**Diamond Jack (IRE)**[24] 1357 7-11-4 82	(p) JPMcNamara	83
			(J J Lambe, Ire) *hld up: hdwy and prom 3 out: wknd appr next*	33/1	
	6	nk	**Majorca**[80] 4-10-12	GLee	76
			(J Howard Johnson) *hld up: stdy hdwy after 4 out: rdn and wknd bef 2 out*	20/1	
00-3	7	hd	**Resonance**[24] 1364 4-10-5 99	CLlewellyn	69
			(N A Twiston-Davies) *chsd clr ldr tl hit 3 out and wknd*	5/1[3]	
0	8	7	**Jordans Spark**[31] 936 4-10-12	KRenwick	69
			(P Monteith) *a bhd*	100/1	
F	9	19	**Millennium Hall**[30] 1291 6-10-9	PBuchanan[(3)]	50
			(Miss Lucinda V Russell) *keen: mstke 1st: prom to 4 out: wknd*	8/1	
	10	6	**Nuzzle**[41] 5-10-5	BHarding	37
			(N G Richards) *a bhd*	100/1	
	11	9	**Compton Dragon (USA)**[27] 6-10-12	KJohnson	35
			(R Johnson) *nvr on terms*	25/1	
5	P		**Solway Willy**[28] 1323 4-10-12	ADobbin	—
			(N G Richards) *a bhd: t.o whn p.u bef 3 out*	25/1	
	P		**Tashkandi (IRE)**[136] 5-10-12	APMcCoy	—
			(P Bowen) *midfield: hdwy 1/2-way: wknd 3 out: p.u next*	11/4[1]	

4m 11.7s (11.10) **Going Correction** +0.50s/f (Soft)

WFA 4 from 5yo+ 14lb **13** Ran SP% **118.6**

Speed ratings: **93,92,90,87,84 84,84,81,72,69 65**,—,— CSF £59.16 TOTE £9.10: £2.60, £3.00, £3.00; EX 66.10.

Owner Middleham Park Racing Xv **Bred** D R Botterill **Trained** Constable Burton, N Yorks

FOCUS

A decent gallop set by the winner but, a modest winning time for the grade. The form looks sound with the first two and fifth running to their marks.

NOTEBOOK

Constable Burton was allowed a sizeable advantage at the start and never looked like being pegged back in the last half a mile. This result may flatter him given that leeway at the start but he has scope for further progress and there is room for improvement in the jumping department, so he may be capable of a bit better. *(op 7-1)*

Dubonai(IRE) off the mark over hurdles at Cartmel in the first time tongue-tie last time, ran at least as well in defeat against a rival who poached a big lead at the start. He should continue to go well in ordinary company. *(op 9-1)*

Motorway(IRE) ◆, a Flat winner for Roger Charlton last year, shaped with promise on his hurdling debut and first run of the year. He left the impression that two and a half miles will suit and he looks well up to winning a race. *(op 11-4)*

King's Envoy(USA), exposed as an ordinary maiden on the Flat and over obstacles, was not disgraced in the face of a stiff task and left the impression that he would be worth a try over two and a half miles. *(op 66-1)*

Diamond Jack(IRE), the winner of a poor event at Cartmel last time, was found out under his penalty in this stronger event and the handicap option looks the most realistic one.

Majorca, a dual Flat winner for John Gosden last year, was easy to back and not totally disgraced on this hurdles debut. He should do better in ordinary handicaps in due course.

Resonance had form on easy ground on the Flat but has become disappointing and dropped out tamely once again. She looks one to have reservations about. *(tchd 11-2)*

1528 MORRIS LESLIE GROUP NOVICES' H'CAP HURDLE (10 hdls) 2m 4f 110y

3:20 (3:20) (Class 3) (0-110,110) 4-Y-0+ **£4,810** (£1,480; £740; £370)

Form			Horse	Jockey	RPR
324-	1		**Miss Shakira (IRE)**[155] 4924 7-10-4 88	CLlewellyn	100+
			(N A Twiston-Davies) *sn chsng ldr: led after 3 out: rdn next: kpt on wl*	7/2[2]	
-113	2	2 1/2	**Mr Mischief**[108] 312 5-11-12 110	APMcCoy	120
			(P C Haslam) *hld up: smooth hdwy 4 out: chsng wnr whn hung lft u.p bef 2 out: kpt on same pce fr last*	7/4[1]	
2436	3	16	**Rifleman (IRE)**[22] 1384 5-10-9 100	MrTJO'Brien[(7)]	94
			(P Bowen) *chsd ldrs tl outpcd 3 out: n.d after*	10/1[3]	
3243	4	shd	**Penteli**[26] 1337 5-9-9 84 oh2	DCCostello[(5)]	77
			(C Grant) *hld up: hdwy 5th: wknd bef 3 out*	10/1[3]	
6-0F	5	21	**Gemini Lady**[85] 854 5-9-11 84 oh6	PAspell[(3)]	56
			(Mrs J C McGregor) *led to after 3 out: sn wknd*	66/1	
0-05	L		**Joe Malone (IRE)**[120] 495 6-10-0 84 oh1	BHarding	—
			(N G Richards) *w.r.s: ref to r*	12/1	
2454	P		**Kyle Of Lochalsh**[9] 940 5-10-0 84 oh2	GLee	—
			(J S Goldie) *prom to 4 out: sn wknd: p.u after next*	7/2[2]	
34-2	P		**Hestherelad (IRE)**[29] 1307 6-10-6 90	(p) KJohnson	—
			(R Johnson) *prom to 4 out: sn wknd: p.u after next*	14/1	
0P-P	P		**Wee Sean (IRE)**[29] 1307 5-9-11 84 oh5	PBuchanan[(3)]	—
			(Miss Lucinda V Russell) *plld hrd: chsd ldrs: lost pl 1/2-way: t.o whn p.u bef 3 out*	100/1	

5m 14.8s (6.60) **Going Correction** +0.50s/f (Soft) **9** Ran SP% **115.8**

Speed ratings: **107,106,99,99,91** —,—,—,— CSF £10.39 CT £54.36 TOTE £5.00: £1.60, £1.50, £2.70; EX 13.90.

Owner F J Mills & W Mills **Bred** Tom Fitzgerald **Trained** Naunton, Gloucs

FOCUS

An ordinary event in which the winner and second pulled clear of the remainder from the third last. The form does not look particularly solid.

NOTEBOOK

Miss Shakira(IRE) ◆ returned from a break in better form than ever and, although she had the run of the race to a larger degree than the runner-up, looked the more resolute of the pair and appeals as the type to win more races.

Mr Mischief ran well against a well-handicapped rival but did not look the easiest of rides for pressure as he persistently hung to his left. A more end-to-end gallop would have suited better and he is the type to win again. *(op 15-8 tchd 2-1)*

Rifleman(IRE) was not disgraced against a couple of rivals that are almost certainly better than their marks, but the fact that he has yet to win over hurdles and has not won on the Flat for well over two years means he is one to tread carefully with. *(op 9-1)*

Penteli was not totally disgraced but may need a lesser grade than this one if she is to get off the mark over obstacles.

Gemini Lady had the run of the race but took her career record to no wins from 31 starts and is not one to place much faith in. *(op 50-1)*

Kyle Of Lochalsh was disappointing back over hurdles and may need a sound surface to be seen to best advantage. *Official explanation: jockey said gelding was unsuited by the good to soft (good in places) going (op 9-2)*

1529 BRACEWELL STIRLING H'CAP CHASE (12 fncs) 2m

3:50 (3:50) (Class 3) (0-115,115) 5-Y-0+ **£8,209** (£2,526; £1,263; £631)

Form			Horse	Jockey	RPR
3253	1		**Gone Too Far**[30] 1296 7-11-9 112	(v) RJohnson	128+
			(P Monteith) *prom: led after 6th: mde rest: styd on strly fr 3 out*	8/1	
6F-6	2	8	**Jefertiti (FR)**[30] 1295 8-10-5 97	PBuchanan[(3)]	105+
			(Miss Lucinda V Russell) *cl up: led briefly 6th: rdn whn j.rt and bmpd 3 out: kpt on fr next: nt rch wnr*	9/1	
-145	3	4	**Apadi (USA)**[84] 874 9-10-0 89 oh1	HOliver	94+
			(R C Guest) *keen: hld up: hmpd 7th: hdwy whn hit 4 out: rdn next: kpt on fr last: no imp*	20/1	
52-2	4	4	**Jallastep (FR)**[30] 1295 8-10-10 99	ADobbin	98
			(J S Goldie) *hld up: hdwy bef 3 out: rdn and no ex fr next*	4/1[2]	
/451	5	1/2	**Loulou Nivernais (FR)**[15] 1433 6-10-0 89 oh2	ADempsey	88
			(M Todhunter) *prom: mstke 3 out: sn rdn and btn*	5/1[3]	
2-66	6	2 1/2	**Kids Inheritance (IRE)**[127] 409 7-11-10 113	GLee	112+
			(J M Jefferson) *cl up: j.lft 7th: j.lft and bdly bmpd 3 out: sn btn*	14/1	
3133	7	1 1/4	**Risky Way**[29] 1311 9-10-1 90	DO'Meara	85
			(W S Coltherd) *towards rr: rdn 4 out: sn btn*	9/1	
1-3F	8	1 3/4	**Specular (AUS)**[11] 1457 9-11-12 115	APMcCoy	108
			(Jonjo O'Neill) *hld up: rdn bef 4 out: sn btn*	11/4[1]	
-50P	P		**Black Bullet (NZ)**[45] 1180 12-11-5 108	(t) AO'Keeffe	—
			(Jennie Candlish) *led to 6th: sn p.u*	25/1	
-025	U		**Fiery Peace**[68] 1012 8-11-3 109	MrTGreenall[(3)]	—
			(C Grant) *hld up: hit: blkd and uns rdr 7th*	14/1	

4m 6.10s (3.30) **Going Correction** +0.45s/f (Soft) **10** Ran SP% **116.4**

Speed ratings: **109,105,103,101,100 99,98,98**,—,— CSF £76.75 CT £1390.66 TOTE £10.60: £2.80, £1.90, £9.70; EX 83.10.

Owner D A Johnson **Bred** Worksop Manor Stud Farm **Trained** Rosewell, Midlothian

FOCUS

A competitive handicap run at a decent gallop but it paid to race up with the pace. The race could be rated higher.

NOTEBOOK

Gone Too Far, a versatile sort with a fair strike rate under all codes, jumped soundly and showed the right attitude in the closing stages under a typically strong ride. His jumping was sound but life will be tougher after reassessment. *(tchd 9-1)*

Jefertiti(FR), a dual winner over fences last year, ran his best race since his latest win in November and may be a bit better than the bare form given he was baulked at the third last. He will be of interest when his yard returns to form. *(op 8-1)*

Apadi(USA) was not disgraced in terms of form but again looked less than straightforward and he is not really one to be placing maximum faith in. *(op 16-1)*

Jallastep(FR) was below the level of his latest run over two and a half miles at Perth and his lack of consistency means he is rarely the best betting proposition around. *(op 9-2)*
Loulou Nivernais(FR), off the mark over fences at Uttoxeter last month, folded quickly after a third-last fence error having looked to be travelling better than anything at the time. He looks the sort that needs things to fall right. *(op 13-2 tchd 7-1 in places)*
Kids Inheritance(IRE), who showed a tendency to jump to his left, may be a bit better than the bare form given he took a hefty bump at the third last, but he does look vulnerable from his current mark at present. *(op 12-1)*
Specular(AUS) again proved a disappointment and is unlikely to reach the level of form over fences that he showed over hurdles. Although capable of winning again, he looks one to tread carefully with. *(op 3-1 tchd 10-3 in places)*

1530 ANDERSON ANDERSON AND BROWN H'CAP HURDLE (8 hdls) 2m 110y
4:20 (4:20) (Class 3) (0-115,112) 4-Y-0+ **£5,616** (£1,728; £864; £432)

Form RPR
43-P **1** **Top Style (IRE)**[10] [120] 7-10-4 **95** (p) WKennedy(5) 107
(G A Harker) *in tch: drvn 3 out: rallied and led next: styd on wl* **3/1**[1]
0000 **2** *9* **Rising Generation (FR)**[29] [1312] 8-11-12 **112** ADobbin 115
(N G Richards) *led to bef 2 out: rdn and hung lft: kpt on same pce* **5/1**[3]
34P3 **3** *4* **Lofty Leader (IRE)**[23] [1377] 6-10-11 **97** (p) LFletcher 98+
(Mrs H O Graham) *hld up: outpcd bef 3 out: rallied next: no imp last* **5/1**[3]
0022 **4** *1 ¾* **Skiddaw Jones**[21] [1291] 5-10-3 **92** (t) PWhelan(3) 89
(M A Barnes) *keen: cl up: led briefly bef 2 out: sn outpcd* **13/2**
10F- **5** *7* **Silver Sedge (IRE)**[164] [4810] 6-9-13 **88** PBuchanan(3) 78
(Mrs A Hamilton) *chsd ldrs tl rdn and wknd bef 2 out* **7/2**[2]
51P6 **6** *½* **Royal Glen (IRE)**[29] [1312] 7-10-11 **97** ADempsey 87
(W S Coltherd) *prom tl rdn and wknd bef 2 out* **16/1**
245 **P** **Feanor**[24] [1366] 7-11-0 **103** (t) KJMercer(3) —
(Mrs S A Watt) *hld up: rdn after 3 out: sn btn: t.o whn p.u bef last* **7/1**

4m 12.2s (11.60) **Going Correction** +0.50s/f (Soft) **7** Ran SP% **112.3**
Speed ratings: **92,87,85,85,81 81**,— CSF £17.72 CT £70.38 TOTE £4.10: £2.00, £2.40; EX 20.00.
Owner J B Stead **Bred** Jordan Fogarty **Trained** Thirkleby, N Yorks

FOCUS
An ordinary handicap resulted in a moderate winning time for a race of its type, seven seconds slower than the bumper, and the form is probably not strong.

NOTEBOOK
Top Style(IRE) returned to winning ways back over hurdles tried in cheekpieces. He is effective on quicker ground and, although he will be up in the weights for this, may improve again for two and a half miles and may be capable of winning another ordinary event. *(op 4-1)*
Rising Generation(FR) had the run of the race and produced his best effort for some time but, although he has slipped in the weights this year, this result showed he is still vulnerable to progressive or unexposed sorts from his current mark. *(op 4-1)*
Lofty Leader(IRE) is not the most consistent but ran creditably with the cheekpieces back on and left the impression that the step up to two and a half miles would be in his favour. *(op 13-2)*
Skiddaw Jones left the impression that less of a test over this trip would have suited, but a career record of one (Flat) win from 27 starts means he is not one to get heavily involved in from a punting perspective. *(op 11-2)*
Silver Sedge(IRE) ran as though the race was needed after a break of over five months, but his lack of consistency means he is not really one to be placing too much faith in. *(tchd 4-1)*
Royal Glen(IRE) found the ground against her once again and she was below her best for the third consecutive time. However, she should be down in the weights again and will be of more interest back on a sound surface. *(op 12-1)*

1531 ALBION DRILLING SERVICES LTD NOVICES' CHASE (15 fncs) 2m 4f 110y
4:50 (4:50) (Class 3) 5-Y-0+ **£6,808** (£2,095; £1,047; £523)

Form RPR
31F1 **1** **Celtic Boy (IRE)**[36] [1234] 7-11-10 **128** RJohnson 136+
(P Bowen) *pressed ldr: led 10th: styd on wl fr 3 out: clr whn mstke last* **10/11**[1]
2 **2** *16* **Lord Of Gortmerron (IRE)**[34] [1260] 6-10-12 JPMcNamara 109+
(C J Cosgrave, Ire) *chsd clr ldrs: hdwy to press wnr 4 out: rdn and one pce fr next* **16/1**
111P **3** *18* **Kid'Z'Play (IRE)**[57] [1083] 9-12-2 **130** GLee 117+
(J S Goldie) *led: hit and hdd 10th: nt fluent after: wknd bef 3 out* **11/8**[2]
4-41 **4** *dist* **Goodbadindiferent (IRE)**[85] [858] 9-11-4 **86** BHarding —
(Mrs J C McGregor) *bhd: no ch fr 6th* **12/1**[3]

5m 24.5s (9.20) **Going Correction** +0.45s/f (Soft) **4** Ran SP% **108.1**
Speed ratings: **100,93,87**,— CSF £10.55 TOTE £1.90; EX 13.60.
Owner Walters Plant Hire Ltd **Bred** William G Corrigan **Trained** Little Newcastle, Pembrokes

FOCUS
Only two with a chance on paper and, with the second favourite disappointing, this did not take as much winning as seemed likely and the winner did not need to run to his best to score.

NOTEBOOK
Celtic Boy(IRE), a typical improver from this yard, did not have to improve to win his fourth race from his last six starts with his main rival disappointing. He is a useful sort but his jumping is still a *bit hit and miss and he may be off for a while having returned with a nasty overreach.* *(op Evens tchd 11-10 and 6-5 in a place)*
Lord Of Gortmerron(IRE) had plenty to find at the weights but this winning Irish pointer travelled strongly for a long way and showed more than enough to suggest he could win a race back in a more realistic grade. *(op 20-1 tchd 25-1)*
Kid'Z'Play(IRE) lost his unbeaten record at this course and, although he had a bit to find with the winner at the weights, proved a disappointment. His jumping fell apart once headed and, given his rating of 130, may not be the easiest to place successfully from now on. *(op 6-5 tchd 11-10)*
Goodbadindiferent(IRE), an inconsistent chaser, faced a stiff task on these terms and never threatened. *(tchd 14-1 and 16-1 in a place)*

1532 GREGGS OF SCOTLAND LONG SERVICE STANDARD NATIONAL HUNT FLAT RACE 2m 110y
5:20 (5:20) (Class 6) 4-6-Y-0 **£2,275** (£650; £325)

Form RPR
1 **Balamory Dan (IRE)** 4-10-11 WKennedy(5) 106+
(G A Harker) *prom: led 3f out: r.o strly* **11/2**
/5-2 **2** *7* **Dalawan**[84] [876] 6-10-9 TJDreaper(7) 96
(Mrs J C McGregor) *hld up: smooth hdwy over 4f out: effrt and chsd wnr over 2f out: kpt on: no imp* **9/2**[3]
3 *7* **Persian Prince (IRE)** 5-10-10 ow1 MrCDawson(7) 90
(J Wade) *hld up: hdwy and prom over 6f out: rdr lost iron briefly over 3f out: kpt on same pce fr 2f out* **50/1**
0-33 **4** *3* **Chief Dan George (IRE)**[126] [424] 5-10-11 TGreenway(5) 88+
(D R MacLeod) *hld up: hdwy over 3f out: rdn and hung bdly lft over 2f out: edgd rt and sn no imp* **12/1**
30- **5** *6* **Hialeah**[184] [4513] 4-10-13 MrTGreenall(3) 80
(M W Easterby) *keen: chsd ldr tl rdn and outpcd over 2f out* **6/1**
6 **6** *3 ½* **Two Good (IRE)**[28] [1323] 5-10-4 DCCostello(5) 70
(P D Niven) *prom: drvn fr over 4f out: sn no imp* **20/1**
0- **7** *1 ¾* **Boxclever**[153] [4971] 4-10-13 KJMercer(3) 75
(J M Jefferson) *hld up: hdwy 4f out: rdn and outpcd fr 3f out* **7/2**[1]
0- **8** *5* **Brundeanlaws**[225] [3757] 4-10-2 BenOrde-Powlett(7) 63
(Mrs H O Graham) *led: reminders 1/2-way: hdd 3f out: sn btn* **100/1**
5 **9** *13* **Thorn Of The Rose (IRE)**[90] [828] 4-9-13 MMcAvoy(10) 50
(James Moffatt) *bhd: outpcd 1/2-way: n.d* **25/1**
10 *5* **Broadband** 6-10-13 MrCStorey(3) 52
(Miss S E Forster) *bhd: hdwy on outside over 4f out: rdn and wknd fr over 3f out* **50/1**
11 *28* **Intersky Emerald (IRE)** 4-10-9 MrAJBerry(7) 24
(Jonjo O'Neill) *prom: rdn 4f out: sn btn* **4/1**[2]
12 *1 ½* **Dark Rebel (IRE)** 5-10-13 PAspell(3) 22
(J Wade) *hld up: rdn over 4f out: nvr on terms* **20/1**
0- **13** *26* **Lost And Found**[340] [1753] 5-10-9 MrOGreenall(7) —
(C Grant) *prom to 1/2-way: sn lost pl* **66/1**
14 *2 ½* **Yankee Holiday (IRE)** 5-11-2 NPMulholland —
(Mrs S C Bradburne) *hld up midfield: struggling over 5f out: sn btn* **20/1**
15 *11* **Ardent Number** 5-10-9 PJMcDonald(7) —
(D W Thompson) *a bhd: struggling fr 1/2-way* **25/1**

4m 5.20s (4.40) **Going Correction** +0.50s/f (Soft)
WFA 4 from 5yo+ 14lb **15** Ran SP% **126.1**
Speed ratings: **109,105,102,101,98 96,95,93,87,84 71,71,58,57,52** CSF £28.38 TOTE £6.50: £2.80, £1.80, £12.20; EX 23.60 Place 6 £80.41, Place 5 £66.81.
Owner D K Woods **Bred** Desmond Woods **Trained** Thirkleby, N Yorks

FOCUS
A decent gallop resulted in a useful winning time for a bumper, significantly quicker than both hurdle races over the same trip. The form looks above average with the majority of those immediately behind the winner close to their marks.

NOTEBOOK
Balamory Dan(IRE) ◆, a half-brother to a Flat winner in this country and in Japan, created a most favourable impression on this racecourse debut and looks the type to hold his own in better company. *(op 9-2)*
Dalawan again ran his race after a near three-month break and looks a good guide to the worth of this form. He looks capable of winning an ordinary race over obstacles in due course. *(op 6-1)*
Persian Prince(IRE) related to an Irish bumper and a hurdle winner, shaped with a modicum of promise on this debut but left the impression that the best will not be seen of him until he tackles further over obstacles.
Chief Dan George(IRE) seemed to run his race after a break of over four months but, although he may do better over hurdles granted a stiffer test, it was disconcerting to see him hang so badly for pressure in the straight.
Hialeah fared a bit better than the bare form given he took a good hold at the head of this truly-run race. He may do better over hurdles when learning to settle. *(op 5-1 tchd 7-1)*
Two Good(IRE) showed only modest form but left the impression that a decent test of stamina would be in her favour when sent over hurdles. *(op 16-1)*
Boxclever travelled strongly for a long way but dropped out tamely and was some way below even the modest level he showed at this course on his only previous run in April. *(op 5-1)*
T/Plt: £71.40 to a £1 stake. Pool: £44,585.25. 455.55 winning tickets. T/Qpdt: £46.50 to a £1 stake. Pool: £3,069.50. 48.80 winning tickets. RY

1533 - 1537a (Foreign Racing) - See Raceform Interactive

1410 WORCESTER (L-H)
Friday, September 23

OFFICIAL GOING: Good to firm (good in places on chase course)
The first flight in the home straight was omitted in all hurdle races.
Wind: Slight across Weather: Fine

1538 BETFREDCASINO.COM NOVICES' HURDLE (8 hdls 2 omitted) 2m 4f
2:10 (2:10) (Class 4) 4-Y-0+ **£3,451** (£1,062; £531; £265)

Form RPR
422 **1** **Noble Sham**[33] [1274] 4-10-11 TJMurphy 102+
(M C Pipe) *j. sltly lft: mde all: hit 6th: mstke 2 out: rdn and edgd rt flat: r.o* **15/8**[1]
12P4 **2** *2 ½* **Kristoffersen**[40] [1220] 5-11-2 **109** DJBoland(10) 109
(Ian Williams) *hld up in tch: rdn appr 2 out: wnt 2nd last: one pce* **5/2**[2]
63 **3** *6* **Hugs Destiny (IRE)**[19] [1415] 4-10-4 BenOrde-Powlett(7) 88
(M A Barnes) *chsd wnrs: nt fluent 6th: rdn appr 2 out: wknd flat* **8/1**
2134 **4** *14* **Slalom (IRE)**[5] [1485] 5-11-0 **100** (v[1]) LStephens(5) 87+
(D Burchell) *a.p: stmbld 6th: rdn whn nt fluent 2 out: wkng whn mstke last* **10/3**[3]
56 **5** *7* **Menai Straights**[12] [1454] 4-10-11 TScudamore 67
(P S Payne) *hld up: hdwy appr 5th: wknd appr 2 out* **25/1**
5P **6** *dist* **Daihannah (IRE)**[68] [1018] 5-10-5 ChristianWilliams —
(Miss H E Roberts) *bhd fr 4th: t.o* **40/1**
7 *8* **Tia Marnie** 7-10-5 AntonyEvans —
(S Lycett) *a bhd: rdn 4th: t.o* **66/1**
535 **U** **Ponchatrain (IRE)**[72] [976] 5-10-12 WMarston —
(D J Wintle) *rrd and uns rdr s* **12/1**
000/ **P** **Fact Cat**[1292] [4180] 7-10-12 AO'Keeffe —
(Ernst Oertel) *hld up in mid-div: lost pl and pckd 6th: t.o whn p.u bef 2 out* **66/1**

4m 46.8s (-1.20) **Going Correction** -0.175s/f (Good)
WFA 4 from 5yo+ 15lb **9** Ran SP% **114.5**
Speed ratings: **95,94,91,86,83** —,—,—,— CSF £6.74 TOTE £3.20: £1.80, £1.10, £2.60; EX 7.30.
Owner D A Johnson **Bred** Lord Northampton **Trained** Nicholashayne, Devon

FOCUS
An ordinary event but the runner-up sets the standard and the winner is rated value for further than the official margin.

NOTEBOOK
Noble Sham ◆ made a successful transition to hurdles after being placed in three ordinary *bumpers. His jumping has room for improvement and he is in the right hands to go on from here. (op 9-4 tchd 11-4)*
Kristoffersen, given a short break, had his rider's big allowance to offset some of his double penalty but could still not cope with the winner. *(tchd 9-4)*
Hugs Destiny(IRE) stayed fairly well on the Flat but did not seem to quite see out this longer trip. *(tchd 7-1)*
Slalom(IRE) did not find a switch from cheekpieces to a visor the answer. *(op 3-1 tchd 7-2)*
Menai Straights *Official explanation: jockey said gelding finished sore (op 33-1)*

1539 HYGIENE SOLUTIONS H'CAP HURDLE (10 hdls 2 omitted) 3m
2:40 (2:40) (Class 4) (0-100,94) 4-Y-0+ **£3,458** (£1,064; £532; £266)

Form RPR
5404 **1** **Potts Of Magic**[19] [1410] 6-11-0 **82** (b) RThornton 86
(R Lee) *hld up in tch: rdn to ld last: drvn out* **11/2**[2]

5/- **2** *2* **Aston (USA)**[55] 1104 5-11-7 **94**...(p) WKennedy(5) 96
(R C Guest) *hld up in mid-div: hdwy 7th: rdn and ev ch last: one pce* **13/2**[3]

0000 **3** *2 ½* **Regal Vision (IRE)**[72] 981 8-10-2 **77**............................. MissCDyson(7) 77
(Miss C Dyson) *hld up in tch: led 7th: rdn and hdd last: no ex* **33/1**

650U **4** *1 ½* **Caper**[33] 1280 5-10-7 **85**..(p) AHawkins(10) 83
(R Hollinshead) *hld up and bhd: hdwy after 8th: ev ch 2 out: wknd flat* **10/1**

3250 **5** *2 ½* **Wild Tempo (FR)**[16] 1436 10-11-2 **94**........................(t) AGlassonbury(10) 90
(M C Pipe) *hld up and bhd: hdwy 7th: rdn 8th: one pce fr 2 out* **13/2**[3]

5400 **6** *16* **Simon's Seat (USA)**[23] 1381 6-10-12 **80**...............................(p) RGreene 60
(S C Burrough) *j.rt: bhd: rdn 6th: hdwy appr 2 out: wknd appr last* **12/1**

P-53 **7** *½* **Cresswell Gold**[34] 1262 8-9-13 **70**.................................. ONelmes(3) 49
(D A Rees) *hld up in mid-div: hdwy 7th: wknd appr 2 out* **7/1**

5006 **8** *26* **Francolino (FR)**[14] 1446 12-9-11 **68** oh1............................. TJPhelan(3) 21
(Dr P Pritchard) *chsd ldr: rdn 7th: wknd after 8th* **66/1**

0U-6 **9** *22* **Mr Fisher (IRE)**[31] 1298 8-10-0 **73**...................................(v[1]) LStephens(5) 4
(D Burchell) *hld up in tch: wknd after 8th* **25/1**

0-P6 **10** *7* **Shellin Hill (IRE)**[37] 1233 11-10-7 **75**...................................(b[1]) VSlattery —
(R J Baker) *hld up in tch: wknd 8th* **50/1**

P0-0 **11** *5* **Rufius (IRE)**[14] 1446 12-10-0 **68** oh4...................................... CLlewellyn —
(P Kelsall) *prom tl wknd 6th* **40/1**

1P5P **12** *7* **Honneur Fontenail (FR)**[19] 1414 6-10-0 **68** oh4..............(b) PJBrennan —
(N J Hawke) *hld up in mid-div: rdn after 5th: hdwy 6th: wknd 8th* **14/1**

0306 **13** *13* **Sandywell George**[12] 1456 10-11-2 **87**...........................(vt) TJMalone(3) —
(L P Grassick) *hld up in mid-div: rdn 7th: sn bhd* **20/1**

/0-0 **P** **Illineylad (IRE)**[72] 981 11-10-0 **68** oh1.................................. JMogford 60
(Mrs N S Evans) *led to 7th: wkng whn blnd 2 out: p.u bef last* **33/1**

06U3 **P** **Cap Classique**[19] 1410 6-11-2 **91**.. PMerrigan(7) —
(Mrs H Dalton) *a bhd: carried rt 3rd and 5th: t.o whn p.u bef 2 out* **4/1**[1]

5m 46.2s (-3.00) **Going Correction** -0.175s/f (Good) **15** Ran SP% **118.4**
Speed ratings: **98,97,96,95 89,89,81,73,71 69,67,63,—,—** CSF £37.79 CT £1087.12 TOTE £5.90: £2.10, £4.00, £6.20; EX 56.20.
Owner J E Potter **Bred** J E Potter **Trained** Byton, H'fords

FOCUS
A modest contest with the joint top weights only rated 94. The form is weak with the fourth the best guide to the level.

NOTEBOOK
Potts Of Magic found the blinkers doing the trick at the fifth time of asking. His trainer thinks he still needs to grow up both mentally and physically. *(op 10-1)*
Aston(USA) was a winner over both hurdles and fences at around this trip on firm ground in Ireland. He is still young and lost little in defeat on his first outing for his new connections. *(tchd 7-1)*
Regal Vision(IRE), reverting back to hurdles, ran his best race for some time having slipped considerably down the handicap. *(op 28-1)*
Caper may have found this trip just beyond his best. *(op 14-1)*
Wild Tempo(FR) remains difficult to win with even for Martin Pipe. *(op 7-1 tchd 15-2)*
Cap Classique is not a straightforward customer, so twice being carried right by the *wayward-jumping Simon's Seat would not have helped. Official explanation: jockey said gelding had breathing problem and was struck into (op 7-2)*

1540 SWANSEA BAY BEGINNERS' CHASE (18 fncs) 2m 7f 110y
3:10 (3:10) (Class 4) 5-Y-0+ **£4,071** (£1,252; £626; £313)

Form RPR

-430 **1** **Koumba (FR)**[16] 1436 7-11-2 .... ChristianWilliams 106
(Evan Williams) *hld up: hdwy 7th: bmpd 9th: led appr 10th: hdd after 14th: sn rdn rallied to ld after 2 out: drvn out* **7/2**[3]

22P2 **2** *1 ½* **Mylo**[20] 1396 7-11-2 .... APMcCoy 104
(Jonjo O'Neill) *a.p: led 7th tl appr 10th: led after 14th: rdn and j.rt fr 4 out: hdd after 2 out: styd on same pce flat* **7/4**[2]

-PP0 **3** *dist* **Floranz**[16] 1436 9-10-9 .... SCurran —
(Mrs M Evans) *bhd: blnd 2nd: mstke 4th: wnt modest 3rd 11th: no ch whn mstke 14th* **33/1**

P02 **4** *4* **Qabas (USA)**[69] 1016 5-10-13 ....(p) RJohnson —
(P Bowen) *blnd 2nd: a bhd: t.o fr 11th* **13/8**[1]

0P-P **5** *dist* **Tumbleweed Glen (IRE)**[20] 1396 9-11-2 57......................(b) CLlewellyn —
(P Kelsall) *prom: led and bmpd 6th: hdd 7th: wknd appr 10th: sn t.o* **33/1**

0/P- **U** **Bruern (IRE)**[279] 2896 8-11-2 .... WMarston —
(Mrs Mary Hambro) *blnd and uns rdr 2nd* **18/1**

P00 **P** **Foreign Field (FR)**[19] 1410 6-11-2 64.......................................(b) RGreene —
(Mrs Tracey Barfoot-Saunt) *j.rt: led to 6th: wknd appr 8th: t.o 11th: mstke 14th: sn p.u* **33/1**

5m 53.4s (-1.50) **Going Correction** -0.125s/f (Good) **7** Ran SP% **110.8**
Speed ratings: **97,96,—,—,— —,—** CSF £9.82 TOTE £4.50: £1.90, £1.10; EX 13.60.
Owner Mr and Mrs Glynne Clay **Bred** Herve D'Armaille **Trained** Cowbridge, Vale Of Glamorgan

FOCUS
This uncompetitive event did not take much winning and could be too high, but has been rated through the runner-up.

NOTEBOOK
Koumba(FR), who had schooled well at home, made a successful start to his chasing career, beating a frustrating horse rated far superior to him over hurdles. *(op 4-1)*
Mylo was going best on the home turn but seems to keep finding a way to get beaten. *(tchd 15-8 and 2-1 in a place)*
Floranz could never get competitive on her chasing debut after a couple of early errors. *(op 28-1)*
Qabas(USA) was another always fighting a losing battle on this switch to fences after making a mess of the first ditch. *(tchd 7-4 and 15-8 in places)*

1541 BETFREDPOKER.COM NOVICES' H'CAP HURDLE (7 hdls 1 omitted) 2m
3:45 (3:45) (Class 4) (0-105,105) 4-Y-0+ **£4,231** (£1,302; £651; £325)

Form RPR

/214 **1** **Sunnyland**[58] 1075 6-10-11 **90**... RJohnson 100
(P J Hobbs) *hld up in tch: rdn 2 out: led last: edgd rt flat: all out* **7/2**[1]

2431 **2** *¾* **Smart Boy Prince (IRE)**[27] 1340 4-11-12 **105**......................... DRDennis 114
(C Smith) *chsd ldr: led 4th: rdn 2 out: hdd last: r.o* **6/1**[3]

00-0 **3** *½* **Dont Ask Me (IRE)**[109] 664 4-10-2 **81**..................................(t) TJMurphy 90
(M C Pipe) *hld up and bhd: j. slowly 3rd: hdwy after 5th: ev ch 2 out: sn rdn: kpt on flat* **7/1**

3222 **4** *8* **Don And Gerry (IRE)**[5] 1490 4-10-11 **90**........................... AntonyEvans 92+
(P D Evans) *hld up and bhd: hdwy appr 2 out: sn rdn: btn whn rdr dropped whip last* **11/2**[2]

5516 **5** *1 ½* **Giust In Temp (IRE)**[12] 1458 6-10-11 **97**....................... MrTJO'Brien(7) 97+
(Mrs K M Sanderson) *hld up in tch: rdn appr 2 out: wknd flat* **28/1**

0-35 **6** *1 ¾* **Nesnaas (USA)**[109] 664 4-10-6 **85**... GLee 83
(M G Rimell) *hld up and bhd: hdwy appr 2 out: wknd appr last* **15/2**

0563 **7** *¾* **Desert Image (IRE)**[31] 1297 4-10-6 **85**.................................(b) TDoyle 82
(C Tinkler) *hld up in mid-div: sme hdwy after 5th: wknd 2 out* **16/1**

1611 **8** *5* **Master Nimbus**[5] 1490 5-10-9 **93** 7ex................................ DCCostello(5) 86+
(J J Quinn) *hld up in mid-div: hdwy appr 2 out: wknd appr last* **6/1**[3]

0/P0 **9** *nk* **Raneen Nashwan**[31] 1297 9-10-0 **79**.. VSlattery 70
(R J Baker) *nvr nr ldrs* **33/1**

1 **10** *1* **Euro Route (IRE)**[16] 1432 4-11-3 **96**.. JMogford 86
(G J Smith) *nvr bttr than mid-div* **25/1**

550- **11** *6* **Orion Express**[28] 1702 4-10-5 **84**.. JAMcCarthy 68
(M Hill) *j. slowly 3rd: a bhd* **33/1**

U6-6 **12** *6* **Canadian Storm**[106] 696 4-10-13 **92**.. AO'Keeffe 70
(A G Juckes) *t.k.h in rr: short-lived effrt 5th* **40/1**

1F55 **13** *¾* **Queen Excalibur**[5] 1490 6-10-1 **85**................................ LStephens(5) 63
(C Roberts) *hld up in mid-div: j. slowly 3rd: bhd fr 5th* **16/1**

46P- **P** **Stokesies Boy**[465] 751 5-10-2 **81**... OMcPhail —
(C Roberts) *bhd fr 5th: p.u bef 2 out* **66/1**

00P/ **P** **Bellino Empresario (IRE)**[673] 2250 7-9-11 **79** oh15........... TJPhelan(3) —
(B Llewellyn) *a bhd: p.u bef 2 out* **100/1**

/0-0 **P** **Homebred Buddy**[31] 1297 6-10-0 **79** oh18.............................. DCrosse —
(P Bowen) *led to 4th: wknd qckly and p.u bef 2 out* **66/1**

3m 41.4s (-7.00) **Going Correction** -0.175s/f (Good) **16** Ran SP% **121.8**
Speed ratings: **110,109,109,105,104 103,103,100,100,100 97,94,93,—,—** — CSF £23.12 CT £144.19 TOTE £4.20: £1.50, £2.00, £2.80, £1.10; EX 27.90.
Owner D H Smith **Bred** C D Harrison **Trained** Withycombe, Somerset
■ Stewards' Enquiry : D R Dennis two-day ban: used whip with excessive frequency (Oct 4-5)
R Johnson caution: used whip with excessive frequency

FOCUS
Plenty of no hopers in what was still a competitive affair run at a decent pace and producing a fair time. The form looks moderate but solid enough.

NOTEBOOK
Sunnyland had also shown a tendency to go right-handed when successful over course and distance in June. To his credit, he held on gamely with nothing to spare. *(op 5-1)*
Smart Boy Prince(IRE), 5lb higher than when previously in a handicap, lost no caste in defeat under top weight. *(op 7-1)*
Dont Ask Me(IRE) ◆ showed tremendous improvement for the fitting of a tongue tie. There are races to be won with him off this sort of mark assuming this was not a flash in the pan. *(op 9-1)*
Don And Gerry(IRE) settled better on a return to more patient tactics but it was a case of the end not justifying the means.
Giust In Temp(IRE) did not have the excuse of soft ground this time and looks harshly treated. *(op 25-1)*
Nesnaas(USA) was unable to sustain his effort. *(op 10-1)*

1542 ARENA LEISURE H'CAP CHASE (12 fncs) 2m
4:15 (4:15) (Class 3) (0-125,125) 5-Y-0+ **£8,190** (£2,520; £1,260; £630)

Form RPR

UU40 **1** **Magic Sky (FR)**[34] 1265 5-11-2 **122**... LHeard(7) 136+
(P F Nicholls) *hld up in mid-div: stdy hdwy appr 4 out: rdn appr last: led flat: r.o wl* **12/1**

222U **2** *1 ¾* **Deep King (IRE)**[20] 1399 10-10-6 **108**...................................... RYoung(3) 117
(J W Mullins) *a.p: led 7th: rdn appr 2 out: hdd and nt qckn last* **14/1**

1F4- **3** *10* **Another Joker**[293] 2625 10-11-9 **122**...................................... JMMaguire 122+
(J L Needham) *chsd ldr: rdn appr 2 out: wknd appr last* **20/1**

410- **4** *¾* **Multeen River (IRE)**[190] 4410 9-11-11 **124**.............................. APMcCoy 122
(Jonjo O'Neill) *hld up in mid-div: hdwy 7th: rdn appr 4 out: wknd flat* **8/1**

6-24 **5** *nk* **Kings Brook**[5] 1487 5-10-0 **99**... PJBrennan 97
(Nick Williams) *hld up and bhd: stdy hdwy 7th: wknd 3 out* **4/1**[1]

2125 **6** *21* **Figaro Du Rocher (FR)**[34] 1263 5-11-12 **125**...................(t) TScudamore 102
(M C Pipe) *prom: rdn appr 8th: sn wknd* **9/1**

4011 **7** *1* **Jazz Night**[25] 1363 8-10-6 **105**... TJMurphy 81
(S Lycett) *prom tl rdn and wknd after 8th* **10/1**

3006 **8** *14* **Blazing Batman**[53] 1122 12-9-11 **99** oh21............................. TJPhelan(3) 61
(Dr P Pritchard) *a bhd* **125/1**

02 **U** **Bill's Echo**[30] 1312 6-10-9 **113**.. WKennedy(5) —
(R C Guest) *blnd bdly and uns rdr 1st* **11/2**[3]

660 **P** **Manoram (GER)**[37] 1236 6-10-2 **101**..(v) GLee —
(Ian Williams) *mid-div: bhd fr 6th: p.u bef 4 out* **20/1**

42-1 **P** **Glengarra (IRE)**[12] 1457 8-10-2 **101** 7ex...................................... TDoyle —
(D R Gandolfo) *led tl blnd 7th: blnd 8th: sn p.u* **9/2**[2]

514- **P** **Progressive (IRE)**[279] 2880 7-10-5 **104**...................................... TSiddall —
(Jonjo O'Neill) *j. bdly: a bhd: t.o whn p.u bef 7th* **14/1**

3m 47.4s (-6.20) **Going Correction** -0.125s/f (Good) **12** Ran SP% **115.1**
Speed ratings: **110,109,104,103,103 93,92,85,—,— —,—** CSF £155.17 CT £3291.83 TOTE £11.20: £3.10, £5.20, £8.50; EX 196.90.
Owner Mrs Kathy Stuart **Bred** J C Mugain **Trained** Ditcheat, Somerset

FOCUS
A fair handicap run in a fast time with the runner-up setting the standard and the winner value for further.

NOTEBOOK
Magic Sky(FR) ◆ was very confidently ridden on this return to a shorter trip. He really got his act together and would appear to be on the upgrade.
Deep King(IRE) is a model of consistency and again did nothing wrong, but he keeps finding one too good.
Another Joker could never get to his favourite front-running position and is entitled to come on for his first outing since December last year. *(op 16-1)*
Multeen River(IRE) failed to get home on this comeback after a six-month layoff. *(op 10-1)*
Kings Brook looked well handicapped based on his recent run at Uttoxeter but this could have come too soon. *(op 9-2)*
Glengarra(IRE) was let down by his jumping. *Official explanation: jockey said gelding made two bad mistakes (op 7-2)*

1543 MET AND COBBETTS STANDARD OPEN NATIONAL HUNT FLAT RACE 2m
4:50 (4:54) (Class 6) 4-6-Y-0 **£2,037** (£582; £291)

Form RPR

1 **Briscoe Place (IRE)**[159] 5-11-4 .... APMcCoy 106+
(Jonjo O'Neill) *t.k.h in mid-div: hdwy after 4f: led 3f out: r.o wl* **9/2**[3]

2 *3 ½* **Valassini** 5-10-8 .... TJPhelan(3) 92
(J L Needham) *t.k.h in mid-div: hdwy 6f out: rdn over 2f out: chsd wnr and swtchd lft over 1f out: no imp* **66/1**

3 *3* **Busy Henry** 5-10-11 .... MrTJO'Brien(7) 96
(Mrs K M Sanderson) *a.p: ev ch 3f out: one pce fnl 2f* **40/1**

032 **4** *4* **Dontelldonandgerry**[23] 1386 5-10-11 .... AntonyEvans 85
(P D Evans) *led: hdd 5f out: led briefly over 3f out: wknd over 1f out* **6/1**

3 **5** *1 ½* **Mister Zaffaran (IRE)**[12] 1459 6-11-4 .... JMogford 91
(Mrs N S Evans) *w ldr: led 5f out tl over 3f out: rdn over 2f out: sn wknd* **33/1**

6 **6** *½* **Must Be Keen**[37] 1237 6-10-13 .... MrSWalker(5) 90
(Ernst Oertel) *t.k.h in mid-div: hdwy 6f out: wknd over 2f out* **14/1**

1 **7** *nk* **Flying Spur (IRE)**[23] 1386 4-11-11 .... TJMurphy 97
(M C Pipe) *prom: ev ch over 3f out: wknd over 1f out* **6/1**

0/10 **8** *3/4* **Acushnet**[64] 1048 6-11-11 .... GLee 96
(J M Jefferson) *hld up and bhd: stdy hdwy on ins over 5f out: no further prog fnl 4f* **7/2**[1]

9 *6* **Presentforyou (IRE)** 6-11-4 .... PJBrennan 83
(R Ford) *bhd: rdn over 4f out: nvr nr ldrs* **33/1**

10 *1 3/4* **Graham (IRE)** 5-11-4 .... RJohnson 81
(P Bowen) *hld up in mid-div: hdwy 7f out: wknd 3f out* **4/1**[2]

6 **11** *6* **Our Girl Kaz (IRE)**[33] 1274 5-10-11 .... JAMcCarthy 68
(M Hill) *a bhd* **20/1**

12 *nk* **North Roc** 4-11-4 .... TScudamore 75
(M Scudamore) *hld up and bhd: hdwy on outside 6f out: wknd over 3f out* **33/1**

13 *2* **Alderley Girl** 6-10-11 .... RGreene 66
(Dr P Pritchard) *a bhd* **100/1**

0-0 **14** *12* **Silly Miss Off (IRE)**[152] 7 4-10-1 .... JKington[(10)] 54
(M Scudamore) *bhd most of way* **66/1**

0- **P** **Fashion Shoot**[204] 4138 4-10-11 .... CLlewellyn —
(P Kelsall) *prom 6f: t.o whn p.u over 4f out* **80/1**

3m 44.8s (-3.00) **Going Correction** -0.175s/f (Good) **15** Ran SP% **116.9**
Speed ratings: **100,98,96,94,94 93,93,93,90,89 86,86,85,79,—** CSF £289.21 TOTE £6.00: £2.70, £13.00, £14.80; EX 626.50 Place 6 £376.89, Place 5 £272.05.
Owner Mrs Jonjo O'Neill **Bred** Michael Croke **Trained** Cheltenham, Gloucs

FOCUS
This was probably only an ordinary bumper but the winner can rate higher, with the fourth the best guide to the level.

NOTEBOOK
Briscoe Place(IRE), who slipped up in his only point in Ireland, is built like a chaser and scored nicely. Connections will be hopeful that he can go on to better things. *(op 5-1 tchd 4-1)*
Valassini made no appeal on breeding and her starting price suggests that she ran well above expectations. *(op 50-1)*
Busy Henry, who changed hands for 5,500 gns earlier this year, was another who probably surprised connections on his debut. *(op 33-1)*
Dontelldonandgerry duly reversed the form of her narrow defeat by Flying Spur at Newton Abbot on 7lb better terms. *(op 7-1 tchd 5-1)*
Mister Zaffaran(IRE) again had plenty of use made of him and lasted longer on this faster surface. *(op 25-1 tchd 22-1)*
Must Be Keen showed signs of ability but lived up to his name. *(tchd 16-1)*
Flying Spur(IRE) had no excuses under his penalty. *(op 7-2)*
Acushnet did not have the excuse of failing to settle on this occasion. *(op 4-1 tchd 9-2)*
T/Plt: £685.00 to a £1 stake. Pool: £42,231.30. 45.00 winning tickets. T/Qpdt: £214.70 to a £1 stake. Pool: £3,742.80. 12.90 winning tickets. KH

1544 - 1547a (Foreign Racing) - See Raceform Interactive

1339 MARKET RASEN (R-H)

Saturday, September 24

OFFICIAL GOING: Good
After 5mm rain the previous day on top of 20mm water put on the track over the previous three days the ground was described as 'good, slow in places'.
Wind: Light; half behind Weather: Fine and sunny

1548 BLUESQCASINO.COM H'CAP HURDLE (10 hdls) 2m 3f 110y

2:10 (2:11) (Class 2) (0-145,141) 4-Y-0+
£27,232 (£10,329; £5,164; £2,347; £1,173; £704)

Form RPR

5/5- **1** **Rooftop Protest (IRE)**[6] 1353 8-9-9 **117** ....(tp) DFFlannery[(7)] 132+
(T Hogan, Ire) *w ldr: led 3rd: wnt clr appr 2 out: styd on strly* **9/2**[1]

00-0 **2** *9* **Grave Doubts**[34] 1270 9-10-10 **125** ....(t) RGreene 130+
(K Bishop) *in rr: hdwy 6th: styd on to take 2nd between last 2: hit last: no ch w wnr* **66/1**

02-2 **3** *3 1/2* **Silver Charmer**[100] 766 6-10-6 **121** .... GLee 122
(H S Howe) *in rr: hdwy 6th: styd on wl fr 2 out* **18/1**

1001 **4** *1/2* **Xellance (IRE)**[17] 1434 8-10-6 **128** .... MrTJO'Brien[(7)] 128
(P J Hobbs) *chsd ldrs: hit 7th: one pce fr next* **20/1**

-001 **5** *1 3/4* **Overstrand (IRE)**[32] 1293 6-10-2 **120** ....(b) ONelmes[(3)] 118
(Robert Gray) *mid-div: hdwy to chse ldrs 7th: one pce fr 3 out* **40/1**

5526 **6** *hd* **Alikat (IRE)**[34] 1270 4-10-11 **127** .... TJMurphy 124
(M C Pipe) *bhd and drvn along 6th: styd on fr 3 out: nvr nrr* **16/1**

33-0 **7** *3 1/2* **Football Crazy (IRE)**[34] 1270 6-11-3 **132** .... APMcCoy 130+
(P Bowen) *led to 3rd: chsd wnr: wknd between last 2* **6/1**[2]

/0-1 **8** *5* **Mr Cool**[140] 207 11-11-2 **141** .... AGlassonbury[(10)] 131
(M C Pipe) *in rr: sme hdwy 6th: nvr nr ldrs* **14/1**

F-02 **9** *nk* **Spectrometer**[15] 1444 8-10-13 **138** .... DJBoland[(10)] 127
(Ian Williams) *chsd ldrs: drvn along 7th: lost pl next* **16/1**

2331 **10** *6* **Wet Lips (AUS)**[97] 782 7-10-4 **119** ....(bt) HOliver 102
(R C Guest) *chsd ldrs: lost pl 7th* **25/1**

31-1 **11** *11* **Goblet Of Fire (USA)**[34] 1270 6-11-3 **132** ....(b) RWalsh 107+
(P F Nicholls) *trckd ldrs: wknd 3 out: sn bhd and eased* **9/2**[1]

-111 **12** *11* **Rajam**[31] 1312 7-10-0 **120** ....(v) WKennedy[(5)] 81
(G A Harker) *rr-div: sme hdwy on outside whn hit 3 out: sn wknd* **8/1**

1466 **13** *5* **Donovan (NZ)**[58] 1087 6-9-7 **115** oh7 ....(v) PMerrigan[(7)] 71
(R C Guest) *a in rr: t.o 2 out* **50/1**

F-30 **14** *29* **Turkama (FR)**[34] 1270 8-10-3 **118** .... CLlewellyn 45
(L A Dace) *nt fluent: a bhd: t.o 7th* **50/1**

-545 **U** **Mcbain (USA)**[34] 1270 6-10-8 **123** .... RJohnson —
(P J Hobbs) *in tch: stmbld landing 4th and uns rdr* **7/1**[3]

205- **P** **Samsaam (IRE)**[282] 2857 8-10-6 **121** ....(vt) TScudamore —
(M C Pipe) *in rr and reluctant 5th: t.o whn p.u bef next* **25/1**

10U- **S** **Forager**[170] 4752 6-11-3 **132** .... RThornton —
(M J Ryan) *in tch: reminders after 4th: sn lost pl: bhd whn hmpd and fell bnd after 5th* **14/1**

4m 41.3s (-8.70) **Going Correction** +0.05s/f (Yiel) **17** Ran SP% **124.9**
WFA 4 from 6yo+ 14lb
Speed ratings: **119,115,114,113,113 113,111,109,109,107 102,98,96,84,— —,—** CSF £313.28 CT £4916.47 TOTE £5.70: £1.10, £30.10, £3.70, £4.10; EX 285.50.
Owner M G Byrne **Bred** J Costelloe **Trained** Nenagh, Co. Tipperary
■ David Flannery's first winner in Britain.

FOCUS
A smart winning time, even for a competitive race like this. This went a strong gallop and the winner deserves full mraks. The form looks rock solid.

NOTEBOOK
Rooftop Protest(IRE), third on the Flat a week earlier, likes going right-handed. He went on and keeping up the gallop in relentless fashion, he came right away. A tilt at the Irish Cesarewitch is now on the cards. *(op 6-1)*
Grave Doubts, who has been out of sorts, returned to form and seemed to benefit from the step up in trip. *(op 50-1)*
Silver Charmer, absent for over three months, has gone well when fresh in the past. *(op 16-1)*
Xellance(IRE), 6lb higher, found a career-high mark beyond him.
Overstrand(IRE), his confidence restored by his success in a claimer, gave a good account of himself on his first outing for his new trainer. *(op 33-1)*
Alikat(IRE) was struggling with a circuit to go but to her credit she stuck to her task. *(tchd 14-1)*
Football Crazy(IRE), who took this a year ago from a 3lb lower mark, kept tabs on the winner but became very leg-weary indeed between the last two flights. *(tchd 11-2)*
Goblet Of Fire(USA), 6lb higher, lay a lot handier than usual and dropped out in a matter of strides *starting the home turn. His rider soon called it a day.Official explanation: trainer had no explanation for the poor form shown (op 4-1)*
Rajam *Official explanation: jockey said gelding shortened its stride after last flight*

1549 BLUE SQUARE NOVICES' CHASE (14 fncs) 2m 6f 110y

2:45 (2:45) (Class 2) 5-Y-0+ **£14,118** (£4,344; £2,172; £1,086)

Form RPR

/25- **1** **Iris's Gift**[217] 3942 8-10-13 .... APMcCoy 141+
(Jonjo O'Neill) *trckd ldr: hit 3rd and 6th: led 7th: hit 3 out: blnd last: styd on wl* **1/2**[1]

-112 **2** *4* **Sweet Diversion (IRE)**[35] 1265 6-11-7 129 ....(t) RWalsh 141
(P F Nicholls) *chsd ldrs: wnt 2nd 7th: kpt on wl fr 3 out: no imp run-in* **11/4**[2]

4-52 **3** *30* **Worlaby Dale**[9] 1343 9-10-13 90 ....(p) LVickers 103
(Mrs S Lamyman) *led to 7th: outpcd next: kpt on to take remote 3rd last* **66/1**

3-31 **4** *2 1/2* **Fool On The Hill**[32] 1292 8-11-7 137 .... PJBrennan 109
(P J Hobbs) *chsd ldrs: drvn along 8th: wknd 4 out* **8/1**[3]

1144 **5** *4* **Keltic Lord**[21] 1398 9-11-7 111 .... GLee 105
(P W Hiatt) *prom: outpcd 8th: sn lost tch: kpt on fr 3 out* **14/1**

45-0 **P** **Fantastic Champion (IRE)**[8] 1412 6-10-13 76 .... APogson —
(J R Cornwall) *nt jump wekk: sn detached and t.o in rr: p.u bef 8th* **80/1**

5m 39.3s (-7.10) **Going Correction** -0.15s/f (Good) **6** Ran SP% **113.8**
Speed ratings: **106,104,94,93,91** — CSF £2.51 TOTE £1.60: £1.50, £1.10; EX 2.50.
Owner Robert Lester **Bred** Mrs R Crank **Trained** Cheltenham, Gloucs

FOCUS
Iris's Gift, the 2004 Stayers' Hurdle winner, was having just his second outing over fences but he looks to have plenty to learn. The runner-up, rated 47lb inferior over hurdles, deserves plenty of credit.

NOTEBOOK
Iris's Gift, a flop on his only previous start over fences, looked in grand trim after his summer off. His jumping was far from fault free but he always looked in command despite a blunder at the last. Basically just a galloper, he is possibly better going left-handed and he will need plenty more experience before he is ready for a step up in grade. At this stage the 2006 Cheltenham Gold Cup can only be a dream. *(op 4-6 tchd 8-11)*
Sweet Diversion(IRE), having his eighth start over fences and rated just 129, did well to bustle up a 172-rated hurdler. *(op 3-1 tchd 10-3)*
Worlaby Dale, who has yet to win a race of any description, had a mountain to climb but kept going well enough to secure a remote third place.
Fool On The Hill, ridden with more restraint than usual, ran way below form and the extended trip was not the sole reason. *(op 7-1)*
Keltic Lord ran a stale sort of race and his busy and rewarding summer may have caught up with him for the time being at least. *(op 10-1)*

1550 BLUE SQUARE "DIAL 64555" H'CAP CHASE (14 fncs) 2m 6f 110y

3:15 (3:17) (Class 2) (0-145,145) 5-Y-0+
£23,906 (£9,067; £4,533; £2,060; £1,030; £618)

Form RPR

-310 **1** **Little Big Horse (IRE)**[70] 1013 9-10-4 **123** .... DElsworth 140+
(Mrs S J Smith) *chsd ldr: led 3rd: drew clr appr last: styd on wl* **20/1**

52-2 **2** *11* **Impek (FR)**[70] 1013 9-11-8 **141** .... TJMurphy 147
(Miss H C Knight) *hld up in tch: lft cl 2nd 3 out: kpt on same pce between last 2* **6/1**[2]

521- **3** *2* **Ladalko (FR)**[161] 4862 6-10-1 **120** .... RWalsh 128+
(P F Nicholls) *in tch: hdwy whn blnd 10th: effrt appr 3 out: kpt on same pce* **7/4**[1]

4013 **4** *1 1/2* **Parisian Storm (IRE)**[35] 1267 9-10-7 **126** .... ChristianWilliams 129
(Evan Williams) *led to 3rd: chsd ldrs: one pce fr 3 out* **50/1**

PB11 **5** *7* **Tamango (FR)**[35] 1265 8-10-10 **129** .... RJohnson 126+
(P J Hobbs) *hld up in rr: hdwy 8th: 4th and one pce whn mstke 3 out* **15/2**

-121 **6** *4* **Native Coral (IRE)**[32] 1295 7-10-6 **125** .... ADobbin 119+
(N G Richards) *prom: outpcd 7th: hdwy 9th: wknd 3f out: hit last* **13/2**[3]

2-10 **7** *10* **East Tycoon (IRE)**[35] 1265 6-11-0 **133** ....(b) APMcCoy 115
(Jonjo O'Neill) *in tch: pushed along 8th: nvr on terms* **7/1**

6/4- **8** *nk* **Virgin Soldier (IRE)**[29] 12 9-10-2 **121** .... GLee 102
(G A Swinbank) *chsd ldrs: wknd after 4 out* **40/1**

2-16 **9** *nk* **Tango Royal (FR)**[35] 1265 9-11-5 **141** ....(t) TJMalone[(3)] 125+
(M C Pipe) *hld up in tch: hit 4th: sme hdwy whn hmpd 10th: nvr on terms* **16/1**

5630 **10** *16* **Montreal (FR)**[35] 1265 8-9-7 **119** oh8 ....(p) PMerrigan[(7)] 84
(M C Pipe) *bhd: drvn along 8th: no rspnse* **40/1**

213U **11** *dist* **Gumley Gale**[70] 1013 10-10-2 **121** ....(t) RGreene —
(K Bishop) *chsd ldrs: lost pl after 7th: sn bhd: t.o 3 out* **25/1**

3F1- **F** **Full House (IRE)**[155] 4974 6-10-10 **129** .... TDoyle 143+
(P R Webber) *trckd ldrs: cl 2nd whn fell 3 out* **10/1**

0FU- **P** **Risk Accessor (IRE)**[139] 253 10-11-12 **145** .... NFehily —
(Jonjo O'Neill) *hld up in rr: bhd whn p.u bef 3 out* **22/1**

5m 36.5s (-9.90) **Going Correction** -0.15s/f (Good) **13** Ran SP% **123.0**
Speed ratings: **111,107,106,105,103 102,98,98,98,92 —,—,—** CSF £133.35 CT £328.07 TOTE £20.00: £3.50, £2.10, £1.40; EX 91.80.
Owner Paul J Dixon **Bred** A D C Cathers **Trained** High Eldwick, W Yorks

FOCUS
A good handicap for the time of year with a career-best effort from the winner who reserves his best for here. The runner-up and fourth set the standard.

NOTEBOOK
Little Big Horse(IRE), who reserves his best for here, looked at his very best after a ten-week break. Soon setting the pace, he went right away between the last two and the Handicapper will not overlook this. *(tchd 25-1 in a place)*
Impek(FR), ridden by Murphy for the first time, as usual travelled strongly but, left second on the heels of the winner three out, he was left for dead between the last two. Significantly he has yet to win a handicap over fences. *(tchd 13-2)*
Ladalko(FR), much improved over hurdles, returned to fences from a mark 17lb lower than his chase rating. He travelled smoothly but a bad blunder five out left him with plenty to do. He kept on in his own time over the last three and should not be given up on yet. *(op 13-8)*
Parisian Storm(IRE), 14lb higher than his last win, was unable to dominate yet still ran with credit.

Tamango(FR), 6lb higher, workd his way on to the heels of the leaders but was going nowhere when he met the third last all wrong.
Native Coral(IRE), 5lb higher, found this much too tough. *(op 7-1 tchd 15-2)*
Full House(IRE), 9lb higher tan when successful at Sandown in April, was still on the heels of the winner when crashing out three from home but at that point his stamina had not been truly tested. Second best was the most that could have been achieved. *(op 11-1)*

1551 BLUESQPOKER.COM JUVENILE NOVICES' HURDLE (8 hdls) 2m 1f 110y
3:50 (3:50) (Class 3) 3-Y-O **£8,346** (£2,568; £1,284; £642)

Form				RPR
2	**1**		**Whirling**[28] [1339] 3-10-5 (v[1]) TJMurphy (M C Pipe) *chsd ldrs: led 3rd: clr 2 out: 10l up whn blnd last: kpt on* **5/1**[3]	106+
	2	*7*	**Finland (UAE)**[12] 3-10-9 KJMercer[(3)] (Mrs A Duffield) *chsd ldrs: lft 2nd 5th: no imp and hit last 2* **20/1**	104+
	3	*7*	**Patxaran (IRE)**[10] 3-10-5 APMcCoy (P C Haslam) *chsd ldrs: effrt 3 out: one pce* **9/4**[1]	89
211	**4**	*24*	**Goldstar Dancer (IRE)**[14] [1332] 3-11-6 106 RGarritty (J J Quinn) *mid-div: kpt on to take remote 3rd after 3 out* **7/1**	80
	5	*4*	**Emerald Destiny (IRE)**[31] 3-10-12 ADempsey (D Carroll) *hld up and bhd: kpt on fr 3 out: nvr on terms* **66/1**	68
	6	*1 ¾*	**Dock Tower (IRE)**[75] 3-10-12 DO'Meara (M E Sowersby) *in rr: sme hdwy whn hmpd 5th: nvr a factor* **100/1**	66
PP	**7**	*6*	**Tiffin Brown**[42] [1201] 3-10-12 (t) FKeniry (P C Haslam) *in rr: sme hdwy 5th: nvr a factor* **66/1**	60
35	**8**	*6*	**Pseudonym (IRE)**[20] [1404] 3-10-12 (t) PJBrennan (M F Harris) *led to 3rd: lost pl 5th* **20/1**	54
	9	*15*	**Three Boars**[31] 3-10-7 WKennedy[(5)] (S Gollings) *rea-div whn hmpd 5th: nvr a factor* **20/1**	39
2	**10**	*3*	**Knightsbridge Hill (IRE)**[21] [1397] 3-10-12 WHutchinson (A King) *in tch: drvn along after 3rd: bhd fr 5th* **5/2**[2]	36
15	**11**	*hd*	**Polar Passion**[21] [1397] 3-10-9 DRDennis (R Hollinshead) *in tch to 4th: sn lost pl and bhd* **20/1**	33
	12	*22*	**Hamburg Springer (IRE)**[25] 3-10-12 SThomas (M J Polglase) *bhd fr 4th: t.o* **66/1**	14
	P		**Crimson Bow (GER)**[11] 3-10-2 LVickers[(3)] (J G Given) *mstkes: bhd fr 4th: t.o whn p.u bef 2 out* **80/1**	—
	F		**Ellerslie Tom**[26] 3-10-12 JMMaguire (T P Tate) *trckd ldrs: erratic 1st: cl 2nd whn fell 5th* **14/1**	—

4m 15.6s (-0.80) **Going Correction** +0.05s/f (Yiel) **14** Ran SP% **120.9**
Speed ratings: **103,99,96,86,84 83,80,78,71,70 70,60,—,—** CSF £98.77 TOTE £5.90: £1.30, £5.60, £1.70; EX 179.80.
Owner Roger Stanley & Yvonne Reynolds II **Bred** Limestone Stud **Trained** Nicholashayne, Devon

FOCUS
A sound pace and an improved effort from the winner but the form looks limited.

NOTEBOOK
Whirling, sharpened up by a visor, had this won two out and a blunder at the last hardly stopped her. *(op 6-1)*
Finland(UAE), unplaced in eight starts on the level, is rated 60 in that sphere. He was making no impression at all on the winner when hitting the last two flights. *(tchd 18-1)*
Patxaran(IRE), a dual winner on the Flat and rated 73, was making hard work of it some way out and never threatened to trouble the winner let alone the second. *(op 2-1)*
Goldstar Dancer(IRE), under a double penalty, has since been beaten in banded company on the Flat. *(op 6-1)*
Emerald Destiny(IRE), unplaced in eight starts on the Flat, is rated just 35 and was never in contention.
Knightsbridge Hill(IRE) was struggling to kept up with a full circuit to go. This was too bad to be true. *Official explanation: jockey said colt never travelled (op 11-4 tchd 3-1 and 9-4)*
Ellerslie Tom, a big type, came here after success in a very modest maiden at Ripon. Rated 67 and with no starting stalls to worry him, he ducked and dived at the first but was almost upsides the winner when crashing out four from home. All he needs is some fine tuning. *(op 20-1)*

1552 AUDREY BUTTERY REUNION H'CAP HURDLE (10 hdls) 2m 6f
4:25 (4:27) (Class 4) (0-110,110) 4-Y-O+ **£3,376** (£964; £482)

Form				RPR
0-P1	**1**		**Wise Tale**[6] [1486] 6-10-8 92 7ex (v) GLee (P D Niven) *chsd ldrs: led appr 2 out: drvn rt out* **7/1**	101+
052	**2**	*2*	**Coccinelle (IRE)**[6] [1482] 7-11-0 98 (p) PJBrennan (K A Morgan) *mid-div: hdwy to chse ldrs 7th: wnt 2nd appr last: kpt on: no real imp* **6/1**	103
321-	**3**	*6*	**Prairie Sun (GER)**[7] [2567] 4-10-12 100 KJMercer[(3)] (Mrs A Duffield) *w ldr: led 3rd: hdd appr 2 out: one pce between last 2* **7/2**[1]	100+
0-P	**4**	*3 ½*	**Karathaena (IRE)**[9] [571] 5-11-7 105 ADobbin (M E Sowersby) *hld up: hdwy to chse ldrs 6th: one pce fr 3 out* **20/1**	101
2115	**5**	*1*	**Fu Fighter**[46] [1192] 4-11-6 105 (t) ChristianWilliams (Evan Williams) *hld up: hdwy 7th: sn chsng ldrs: outpcd appr 2 out* **9/2**[3]	99
PP-U	**6**	*dist*	**Nick The Silver**[140] [218] 4-10-12 97 (p) TJMurphy (M C Pipe) *chsd ldrs: wknd 3 out: sn bhd: t.o: btn 45 l* **12/1**	—
5240	**7**	*1 ½*	**Pequenita**[17] [1436] 5-10-9 93 (p) HOliver (R C Guest) *led to 3rd: wknd rapidly 6th: sn bhd: t.o* **16/1**	—
100P	**8**	*7*	**Ramblees Holly**[61] [1062] 7-11-2 105 DMcGann[(5)] (R S Wood) *sn in rr and drvn along: t.o fr 5th* **33/1**	—
33P-	**P**		**Rookery Lad**[332] [1853] 7-11-6 104 DCrosse (C N Kellett) *sn in rr: t.o 7th: p.u bef 2 out* **33/1**	—
0540	**P**		**Turn Of Phrase (IRE)**[23] [858] 6-11-7 105 (b) AThornton (Robert Gray) *dropped rr 3rd: sn t.o: p.u bef 6th* **16/1**	—
P2P-	**P**		**Countback (FR)**[167] [4798] 6-10-0 84 oh1 (p) WHutchinson (C C Bealby) *reminders 3rd: sn bhd: t.o whn p.u bef 2 out* **28/1**	—
3121	**P**		**Lake Merced (IRE)**[20] [1412] 5-11-6 104 APMcCoy (Jonjo O'Neill) *chsd ldrs: rdn and lost pl 6th: sn bhd: t.o whn p.u bef 2 out* **4/1**[2]	—

5m 31.6s (3.30) **Going Correction** +0.05s/f (Yiel)
WFA 4 from 5yo+ 15lb **12** Ran SP% **120.7**
Speed ratings: **96,95,93,91,91 —,—,—,—,— —,—** CSF £48.00 CT £173.93 TOTE £8.80: £2.40, £2.20, £2.00; EX 46.00.
Owner B Ll Parry **Bred** Gainsborough Stud Management Ltd **Trained** Barton-le-Street, N Yorks

FOCUS
Just a modest pace and an improved effort from the winner but overall the form does not look strong at all.

NOTEBOOK
Wise Tale, under his penalty for his selling races success, was ridden a lot handier than on some occasions in the past. He had to be kept right up to his work. *(op 11-2)*
Coccinelle(IRE), having her third outing, stuck on to push the winner hard but she looks weighted to the limit. *(op 8-1)*
Prairie Sun(GER), improved and a winner four times on the level this year, was soon setting the pace but it was rather a jaded effort. *(op 10-3)*
Karathaena(IRE), who has been skipping classes, has been out of form and this was a better effort but she is still not exactly sparkling. *(tchd 25-1)*
Fu Fighter, re-vitalised in this yard, is 11lb higher than his last win and this trip looks on the sharp side for him. *(op 5-1)*
Lake Merced(IRE), back over hurdles, was in trouble setting out on to the final circuit. *(tchd 5-1)*

1553 EASIBED NOVICES' H'CAP HURDLE (8 hdls) 2m 1f 110y
4:55 (4:56) (Class 4) (0-100,100) 4-Y-O+ **£3,427** (£979; £489)

Form				RPR
600	**1**		**Uncle John**[10] [1046] 4-9-11 81 (v[1]) DJBoland[(10)] (Ian Williams) *chsd ldrs fr 3rd: styd on fr 2 out: wnt 2nd last 75yds: led post* **8/1**	82
-654	**2**	*shd*	**Un Autre Espere**[32] [1297] 6-9-7 74 oh5 TMessenger[(7)] (C C Bealby) *chsd ldr: led 5th: faltered and hdd last stride* **10/1**	75
/46-	**3**	*1 ¼*	**Night Sight (USA)**[21] [2370] 8-11-3 94 (p) LVickers[(3)] (Mrs S Lamyman) *hld up in rr: stdy hdwy 4th: effrt and chsng ldrs 2 out: edgd lft run-in: styd on wl towards fin* **11/2**[3]	94
0250	**4**	*¾*	**Jimmy Byrne (IRE)**[30] [1322] 5-11-7 95 HOliver (R C Guest) *chsd ldrs: chal last: no ex* **5/1**[2]	95+
06/0	**5**	*2 ½*	**Rust En Vrede**[6] [1490] 6-11-0 88 ADempsey (D Carroll) *hld up in rr: hdwy 4th: chsng ldrs appr 2 out: one pce whn j.lft last* **20/1**	86+
6156	**6**	*19*	**General Smith**[34] [1272] 6-11-5 93 VSlattery (H J Evans) *hld up in rr: hdwy 5th: sn chsng ldrs: wknd appr 2 out* **12/1**	71
63F-	**7**	*2*	**Movie King (IRE)**[8] [3326] 6-11-7 100 (p) WKennedy[(5)] (S Gollings) *led to 5th: lost pl after next: soo bhd* **14/1**	76
05-P	**8**	*nk*	**Seraph**[28] [1340] 5-10-8 82 JEMoore (O Brennan) *mid-div: hdwy 5th: wknd after next* **20/1**	57
4030	**9**	*6*	**Private Jessica**[31] [1308] 4-10-0 74 oh1 (p) KJohnson (R C Guest) *in rr: effrt 5th: sn bhd* **12/1**	43
4-30	**P**		**Scippit**[17] [1432] 6-10-11 85 DO'Meara (Miss Tracy Waggott) *in rr: bhd whn p.u bef 2 out* **20/1**	—
P0-0	**U**		**Crown Agent (IRE)**[3] [1108] 5-9-9 74 oh10 (p) DCCostello[(5)] (M E Sowersby) *in rr whn blnd and uns rdr 2nd* **40/1**	—
213-	**P**		**Game On (IRE)**[202] [4211] 9-11-8 96 AThornton (B N Pollock) *chsd ldrs: lost pl after 4th: sn bhd: t.o whn p.u bef 2 out* **2/1**[1]	—
00-U	**P**		**Alfadora**[152] [21] 5-10-12 86 PJBrennan (M F Harris) *in rr: hdwy 4th: chsng ldrs 3 out: sn wknd: poor 8th whn p.u bef next* **20/1**	—

4m 22.5s (6.10) **Going Correction** +0.05s/f (Yiel)
WFA 4 from 5yo+ 14lb **13** Ran SP% **129.1**
Speed ratings: **88,87,87,87,85 77,76,76,73,— —,—,—** CSF £84.21 CT £494.96 TOTE £10.40: £2.60, £4.90, £2.50; EX 125.60.
Owner Mrs John Lee **Bred** Aramstone Stud **Trained** Portway, Worcs
■ The first winner in Britain for David Boland, to go with two in Ireland.

FOCUS
A moderate contest, in effect just a seller, and a very slow winning time, nearly seven seconds slower than the juvenile novice hurdle over the same trip. Although the first two ran to their marks the form looks shaky.

NOTEBOOK
Uncle John, a winner in selling company on the Flat, kept on to snatch the prize right on the line. *Official explanation: trainer had no explanation for the improved form shown other than that gelding may have benefited from having a visor on for the first time (op 15-2)*
Un Autre Espere, unplaced in 13 previous starts over hurdles, was 5lb out of the handicap. He went on at the middle hurdle down the back and looked in charge until hanging fire and throwing it away near the line. *(op 12-1)*
Night Sight(USA), not as good as he once was on the Flat this year, moved up from the rear travelling strongly but he seemed to hit a flat spot two out. Diving left on the run-in, he was fast reeling in the first two at the line. *(op 5-1)*
Jimmy Byrne(IRE), with the headgear left off, landed upides at the last but he attitude did not totally convince. *(op 6-1)*
Rust En Vrede, dual winner on the All-Weather, has achieved little over hurdles and he looked to be doing his best to duck out of a battle. *(tchd 22-1)*
General Smith did not revive on his return to the scene of his sole win over hurdles.
Game On(IRE), returning to hurdles after a six-month break from a mark a stone lower than over fences, was in trouble at halfway and was hopelessly in arrears when calling it a day. *(op 4-1)*

1554 DUCKWORTH LANDROVER STANDARD NATIONAL HUNT FLAT RACE 2m 1f 110y
5:25 (5:25) (Class 6) 4-6-Y-O **£1,960** (£560; £280)

Form				RPR
3-	**1**		**Don't Push It (IRE)**[293] [2662] 5-10-11 MrAJBerry[(7)] (Jonjo O'Neill) *trckd ldrs: led 2f out: rdn out* **8/11**[1]	102+
21	**2**	*6*	**Bluecoat (USA)**[105] [719] 5-11-8 MrTGreenall[(3)] (M W Easterby) *led: clr after 3f: hdd 2f out: no ex* **4/1**[2]	100
	3	*3 ½*	**Network Oscar (IRE)** 4-10-11 MrOGreenall[(7)] (M W Easterby) *bhd: hdwy on outside 6f out: sn chsng ldrs: one pce fnl 3f* **25/1**	89
	4	*nk*	**Redditzio** 4-10-6 DCCostello[(5)] (C W Thornton) *trckd ldrs: drvn along and outpcd 7f out: styd on fnl 3f* **40/1**	82
	5	*3 ½*	**Stroom Bank (IRE)** 5-11-4 DCrosse (C C Bealby) *mid-div: hdwy 6f out: one pce fnl 3f* **12/1**	86
	6	*5*	**Goldsmeadow** 6-10-13 MNicolls[(5)] (O Brennan) *mid-div: hdwy 6f out: wknd over 2f out* **50/1**	81
	7	*4*	**City Music (IRE)** 4-10-11 NCarter[(7)] (Mrs S J Smith) *sn in rr and drvn along: styd on fnl 3f: nvr on terms* **16/1**	77
	8	*½*	**Fairlight Express (IRE)** 5-10-13 PCO'Neill[(5)] (P L Gilligan) *stdd s: hdwy 6f out: wknd over 2f out* **7/1**[3]	76
	9	*3 ½*	**Tickhill Tom** 5-11-1 KJMercer[(3)] (C W Fairhurst) *staedied s: bhd: kpt on fnl 4f: nvr a factor* **40/1**	73
6	**10**	*3 ½*	**Silent Age (IRE)**[132] [375] 4-10-13 WKennedy[(5)] (S Gollings) *hld up in mid-div: effrt u.p 6f out: nvr on terms* **20/1**	69
65	**11**	*12*	**The Boobi (IRE)**[21] [1401] 4-10-6 LTreadwell[(5)] (Miss M E Rowland) *chsd ldrs: lost pl over 5f out: sn bhd* **66/1**	50
	12	*12*	**Defenceoftherealm (IRE)** 5-10-11 (p) MissJFoster[(7)] (Miss J E Foster) *chsd ldrs: lost pl over 3f out: sn bhd* **50/1**	45
	13	*11*	**Crystal Haven** 4-10-4 MissJCoward[(7)] (M W Easterby) *staedied s: bhd and pushed along 6f out* **40/1**	27

4m 21.5s (5.00) **Going Correction** +0.05s/f (Yiel)
WFA 4 from 5yo+ 14lb **13** Ran SP% **125.3**
Speed ratings: **90,87,85,85,84 81,80,79,78,76 71,66,61** CSF £3.54 TOTE £1.80: £1.10, £1.70, £6.50; EX 4.20 Place 6 £54.41, Place 5 £14.26.

Owner John P McManus **Bred** Dominick Valley **Trained** Cheltenham, Gloucs

FOCUS

A modest time, even for a bumper. Although the winner is better than average for the time of year, the form looks weak with those behind the first two flattered.

NOTEBOOK

Don't Push It(IRE), third at Warwick in December on his only previous start, was the paddock pick. He had the leader covered and made this looks very straightforward. *(op 11-10)*

Bluecoat(USA), on his toes beforehand, took them along at his own pace but when the winner was asked a question he was very soon put in his place. *(op 9-2)*

Network Oscar(IRE), one his his trainer's three representatives, stands over plenty of ground. He made a satisfactory bow but looks to have more stamina than speed. *(tchd 28-1)*

Redditzio, jumped bred, kept on in her own time after struggling to keep up and stamina looks her forte.

Stroom Bank(IRE), a half-brother to three Flat winners, stands over plenty of ground. He showed a glimmer of ability but has a lot more stamina than speed. *(op 7-1)*

T/Plt: £142.10 to a £1 stake. Pool: £61,995.40. 318.40 winning tickets. T/Qpdt: £48.60 to a £1 stake. Pool: £3,196.50. 48.60 winning tickets. WG

1555 - 1558a (Foreign Racing) - See Raceform Interactive

[1362]HUNTINGDON (R-H)

Sunday, September 25

OFFICIAL GOING: Good to firm (good in places)

1559 "HEARTS FIRST" H'CAP HURDLE (10 hdls) 2m 4f 110y

2:10 (2:12) (Class 3) (0-120,120) 4-Y-0+ **£4,803** (£1,478; £739; £369)

Form					RPR
360-	1		**Fire Dragon (IRE)**[194] 4386 4-11-10 **119**	APMcCoy	125+
			(Jonjo O'Neill) *hld up: hmpd 3rd: hdwy 7th: rdn to ld 2 out: r.o wl* **8/1**		
0-40	2	5	**My Galliano (IRE)**[27] 1366 9-10-0 **94** oh2	TJMurphy	93
			(B G Powell) *plld hrd: in tch: hmpd 3rd: led after 7th: rdn and hdd 2 out: one pce* **10/1**		
3221	3	2 ½	**Absolut Power (GER)**[18] 1431 4-11-9 **118**	(p) MBradburne	113
			(J A Geake) *hld up: hdwy 4th: rdn and ev ch 2 out: one pce* **4/1**[1]		
3414	4	3 ½	**Leopold (SLO)**[7] 1481 4-10-0 **102**	CPoste[(7)]	94
			(M F Harris) *hld up and bhd: sltly hmpd 3rd: hdwy 7th: no further prog fr 3out* **7/1**[3]		
35U-	5	¾	**Royal Atalza (FR)**[23] 4764 8-11-12 **120**	PMoloney	112
			(G A Huffer) *hld up and bhd: sltly hmpd 3rd: nt fluent 6th: hdwy whn n.m.r on ins bend after 7th: nvr trbld ldrs* **12/1**		
3421	6	28	**Kilindini**[33] 1298 4-11-5 **114**	BJCrowley	77
			(Miss E C Lavelle) *led until jmpd slowly 1st: lft in ld 3rd: hdd after 7th: wkng when hit 3 out* **11/2**[2]		
-416	7	2	**Green Prospect (FR)**[22] 1400 5-10-7 **108**	SWalsh[(7)]	70
			(M J McGrath) *prom: hmpd 3rd: rdn and wknd after 7th* **28/1**		
6P0R	8	dist	**Dabus**[126] 466 10-10-2 **103**	AnnStokell[(7)]	—
			(M C Chapman) *plld hrd: prom tl wknd appr 6th: sn t.o* **66/1**		
4006	B		**Siegfrieds Night (IRE)**[10] 1361 4-9-12 **100**	CMStudd[(7)]	—
			(M C Chapman) *b.d 3rd* **20/1**		
P411	F		**Mister Moussac**[14] 1458 6-10-5 **99**	RThornton	—
			(Miss Kariana Key) *led 1st tl fell 3rd* **4/1**[1]		
30-0	P		**Stolen Song**[8] 218 5-9-9 **94** oh4	(b) LTreadwell[(5)]	—
			(M J Ryan) *bhd: rdn after 2nd: lost tch and mstke 7th: sn plld up* **11/1**		

4m 39.6s **Going Correction** -0.625s/f (Firm)

WFA 4 from 5yo+ 15lb **11** Ran SP% **113.8**

Speed ratings: **104,102,101,99,99 88,88,—,—,—** — CSF £79.96 CT £366.90 TOTE £6.80: £3.00, £4.10, £1.10; EX 115.30.

Owner Mrs Gay Smith **Bred** Juddmonte Farms **Trained** Cheltenham, Gloucs

FOCUS

This looked a tight race on paper, but Fire Dragon won quite impressively and looks sure to go on to better things. The placed horses ran to their marks, suggesting the form is reasonable.

NOTEBOOK

Fire Dragon(IRE), last seen finishing down the field at the Cheltenham Festival; put up a good weight-carrying performance and settled the outcome of this rather quickly. A tough and progressive sort, he has a decent handicap in him and is sure to play a prominent role at Cheltenham's Paddy Power meeting in November. *(op 6-1)*

My Galliano(IRE) has steadily been falling in the weights and this return to two and a half miles helped the nine-year-old. He was receiving plenty of weight from the winner and was not in the same league, but beat the remainder well and has a race in him off this sort of mark. *(op 9-1)*

Absolut Power(GER) has only finished out of the first three once in 11 starts since arriving from Germany and he ran another fine race in defeat. He had every chance, but lacked that turn of speed, so maybe a return to further will help. *(op 9-2)*

Leopold(SLO) has found life tougher off this new mark since winning at Fontwell, but he was not discredited back in fourth and may be helped by a drop back in trip. *(op 8-1 tchd 17-2)*

Royal Atalza(FR), who has been performing creditably on the Flat, was always going to be vulnerable under top-weight and he ran pretty much as expected. A stiffer test will help, but he probably needs some further help from the Handicapper.

Kilindini ran too badly to be true and was unable to build on his Worcester victory. He is better than this and is worthy of another chance. *(tchd 13-2)*

Mister Moussac, in good form and on a hat-trick, came down too early to gauge how he would have fared, but the likelihood is he would have been battling it out for a place at least. *(tchd 7-2)*

1560 INTERNET MARKETING AT OXYGENMAD.CO.UK NOVICES' H'CAP CHASE (19 fncs) 3m

2:45 (2:45) (Class 4) (0-105,95) 5-Y-0+ **£3,723** (£1,145; £572; £286)

Form					RPR
F313	1		**Ultimate Limit**[88] 862 5-11-0 **86**	PJBrennan	100+
			(A Ennis) *t.k.h: hld up: hdwy 13th: led last: styd on wl* **9/2**[2]		
4	2	7	**Cool Present (IRE)**[21] 1414 6-10-9 **78**	FKeniry	87+
			(K R Burke) *a.p: hit 3 out: sn rdn and outpcd: rallied 2 out: styd on same pce flat* **4/1**[1]		
603P	3	1 ¾	**Rattina (GER)**[7] 1486 9-10-0 **69** oh4	TScudamore	74
			(M F Harris) *led: rdn appr 2 out: hdd last: wknd* **20/1**		
04F2	4	15	**Gold Quest (IRE)**[7] 1486 8-11-2 **85**	DRDennis	77+
			(Ian Williams) *hld up in tch: rdn and ev ch appr 2 out: wknd appr last* **11/2**[3]		
2520	5	8	**River Quoile**[21] 1414 9-10-4 **80**	DJacob[(7)]	65+
			(R H Alner) *w ldr to 4th: j.rt 10th: mstke and lost pl 11th: sn struggling* **6/1**		
2332	6	18	**Seaniethesmuggler (IRE)**[29] 1342 7-11-7 **95**	(p) WKennedy[(5)]	64+
			(S Gollings) *bhd: reminders after 5th: hmpd 11th: no ch fr 13th* **4/1**[1]		
5030	P		**Oscars Vision (IRE)**[21] 1414 5-10-9 **81**	(b[1]) NFehily	—
			(B W Duke) *a bhd: blnd 10th: t.o whn p.u after 12th* **16/1**		
PU00	P		**Madhahir (IRE)**[29] 1333 5-9-7 **72** oh5	(v) PCStringer[(7)]	—
			(M J Gingell) *nt j.w: a in rr: t.o 7th: p.u bef 12th* **66/1**		
P	P		**Cappacurry (IRE)**[7] 1487 6-10-8 **77**	ChristianWilliams	—
			(Evan Williams) *mid-div: blnd 15th: t.o whn p.u bef 2 out* **10/1**		
-P05	F		**Lambrini Mist**[35] 1269 7-9-10 **70** oh4 ow1	DLaverty[(5)]	67
			(Mrs L Williamson) *prom: outpcd 3 out: rallied 2 out: 5 l 4th whn fell last* **40/1**		

5m 59.5s (-12.80) **Going Correction** -0.50s/f (Good)

WFA 5 from 6yo+ 3lb **10** Ran SP% **111.5**

Speed ratings: **101,98,98,93,90 84,—,—,—,—** CSF £22.06 CT £313.44 TOTE £3.60: £1.60, £1.80, £4.00; EX 18.00.

Owner Lady Wates **Bred** D And Mrs Holmes **Trained** Beare Green, Surrey

FOCUS

Moderate stuff, but a reasonable gallop and a good winner, who came away after the last and could rate higher.

NOTEBOOK

Ultimate Limit, last seen finishing third over two miles at Worcester in June, appreciated this return to a more suitable distance and ran out a ready winner, defying a career-high mark in the process. Open to further improvement being a five-year-old, this is definitely his distance and he will have realistic chances of following up. *(op 7-2)*

Cool Present(IRE) has performed well since arriving from Ireland and she gave her all in trying to get to the winner, but she was always being held and could do no more than plug on for second. She will pick up a race shortly off this sort of mark. *(op 9-2 tchd 5-1)*

Rattina(GER) is 21lb lower than when starting out handicap life over fences and is evidently *well-handicapped. She has run a bit better the last twice and may soon be ready to win. (op 18-1 tchd 16-1)*

Gold Quest(IRE) ran a bit better than his finishing position suggests on this fencing debut and a drop back in trip may enable him to pick up a similar race.

River Quoile is hardly a frequent winner and, not for the first time, he ran below expectations. *(op 15-2)*

Seaniethesmuggler(IRE) was not going from an early stage he failed to run to form. He is better *than this and is usually consistent, but now has a bit to prove. Official explanation: jockey said gelding never travelled (op 7-2)*

1561 INSIDE EDGE MAGAZINE H'CAP CHASE (16 fncs) 2m 4f 110y

3:20 (3:20) (Class 3) (0-135,134) 5-Y-0+ **£6,987** (£2,150; £1,075; £537)

Form					RPR
-203	1		**Duke Of Buckingham (IRE)**[36] 1265 9-11-11 **133**	TDoyle	149+
			(P R Webber) *hld up and bhd: hit 5th: hdwy 11th: led appr 2 out: hit 2 out: clr whn mstke last: r.o wl* **11/4**[1]		
2311	2	14	**Whispered Secret (GER)**[25] 1382 6-11-12 **134**	APMcCoy	137+
			(M C Pipe) *sn chsng ldr: led after 11th: rdn and hdd appr 2 out: hit 2 out: 5 l 2nd and btn whn hit last* **4/1**[3]		
F-06	3	4	**Cameron Bridge (IRE)**[18] 1434 9-11-7 **129**	RJohnson	127+
			(P J Hobbs) *hld up and bhd: 4th whn mstke 12th: wnt 3rd 2 out: mstke last: nvr nr ldrs* **15/2**		
3623	4	3 ½	**Toi Express (IRE)**[7] 1489 9-10-4 **119**	JamesWhite[(7)]	113
			(R J Hodges) *hld up: hit 10th: nt fluent 11th (water): n.d* **9/1**		
P0-5	5	3	**True Mariner (FR)**[31] 1318 5-10-1 **109**	JAMcCarthy	101+
			(B I Case) *t.k.h: led: hdd after 11th: pckd 12th: sn wknd* **28/1**		
1104	6	8	**Bronzesmith**[36] 1265 9-11-6 **128**	JTizzard	114+
			(B J M Ryall) *hld up: hit 5th and 6th: no ch fr 11th: mstke last* **11/2**		
665-	P		**Peccadillo (IRE)**[197] 4331 11-11-3 **125**	AThornton	—
			(R H Alner) *chsd ldr early: lost pl 7th: bhd whn mstke 9th: sn p.u* **3/1**[2]		

4m 51.4s (-14.70) **Going Correction** -0.50s/f (Good) **7** Ran SP% **112.3**

Speed ratings: **108,102,101,99,98 95,—** CSF £13.96 TOTE £3.40: £1.80, £2.20; EX 13.60.

Owner The Dream On Partnership **Bred** Mrs C M Hurley **Trained** Mollington, Oxon

FOCUS

This decent handicap looked tricky on paper, but Duke Of Buckingham was on song and ran out an easy winner.

NOTEBOOK

Duke Of Buckingham(IRE), whose last win over fences came off an 8lb lower mark, has been running well over fences this summer and, although his jumping was far from fluent, he proved far too strong for novice Whispered Secret. A useful sort on his day, he should continue to pay his way, but will go up in the weights for this. *(op 10-3)*

Whispered Secret(GER) faced no easy task giving 1lb to the winner, especially being a novice, and he ran pretty much as well as could have been expected. He is firmly in the Handicapper's grip and will find life easier back in novice events. *(op 7-2)*

Cameron Bridge(IRE) has not been in the best of form, but this was a better effort and he may soon be ready to win again, especially with a little further help from the Handicapper. *(op 7-1)*

Toi Express(IRE) is a consistent sort and he again appeared to run his race, but is not obviously well-handicapped and does not appeal as a likely future winner. *(op 10-1)*

Bronzesmith has found life difficult off this sort of mark of late and he remains out of sorts.

Peccadillo(IRE) usually does well at this time of year, but he was most disappointing on this return *and something was presumably amiss. He is better than this and worthy of another chance. Official explanation: jockey said gelding never travelled (op 10-3)*

1562 BETTINGJOBS.COM RECRUITMENT CONSULTANCY NOVICES' HURDLE (DIV I) (8 hdls) 2m 110y

3:55 (3:55) (Class 4) 4-Y-0+ **£3,073** (£878; £439)

Form					RPR
4-	1		**Dr Cerullo**[294] 2658 4-10-12	TDoyle	107+
			(C Tinkler) *hld up in tch: led appr 3 out: rdn clr 2 out: eased towards fin* **4/1**[3]		
	2	10	**Sunday City (JPN)**[21] 4-10-12	APMcCoy	95
			(R A Fahey) *hld up and bhd: hdwy 5th: chsd wnr appr 3 out: rdn appr 2 out: no imp* **2/1**[1]		
0-U0	3	8	**Glowing Ember**[27] 1364 5-10-5 88	PJBrennan	80
			(J F Panvert) *hld up: hdwy 4th: rdn and one pce fr 3 out* **9/1**		
0-0	4	4	**Pick Of The Crop**[7] 1480 4-10-12	LAspell	83
			(J R Jenkins) *hld up and bhd: hdwy and nt fluent 5th: no further prog fr 3 out* **80/1**		
0	5	8	**Woolstone Boy (USA)**[33] 1302 4-10-12	(t) JPMcNamara	75
			(J Jay) *bhd tl styd on fr 3 out: n.d* **66/1**		
0-0	6	12	**Adalar (IRE)**[15] 279 5-10-12	SThomas	63
			(P W D'Arcy) *nvr nr ldrs* **16/1**		
21	7	nk	**Sharaab (USA)**[21] 1415 4-11-5 95	(t) PMoloney	70
			(D E Cantillon) *nvr nr ldrs* **11/4**[2]		
P/5P	8	2 ½	**Golders Green**[22] 1399 8-10-7 89	MNicolls[(5)]	60
			(P W Hiatt) *chsd clr ldrs: wknd 5th* **50/1**		
0-U0	9	11	**Bestam**[14] 1458 6-10-12 91	(e) JMogford	49
			(Mrs A V Roberts) *t.k.h: led tl appr 5th: wknd appr 3 out* **33/1**		
	10	6	**Davy's Luck**[58] 5-10-5	WMarston	36
			(J M Bradley) *mstkes: bhd fr 4th* **40/1**		
2	11	dist	**Granite Man (IRE)**[22] 1401 5-10-12	JEMoore	—
			(Jonjo O'Neill) *a bhd: t.o* **8/1**		

The Form Book, Raceform Ltd, Compton, RG20 6NL

00-6 **12** *12* **Indigo Sky (IRE)**[21] 1407 4-10-12 ....(b) TJMurphy —
(B G Powell) *t.k.h: w ldr: led appr 5th: hdd and wkng whn mstke 3 out: t.o* **28/1**
P **Lady Ellendune**[33] 4-10-0 .... JDiment[(5)] —
(Andrew Turnell) *t.k.h: a bhd: hit 3rd: blnd 4th: t.o whn p.u bef 3 out* **66/1**

3m 43.0s (-12.70) **Going Correction** -0.625s/f (Firm) **13** Ran SP% **122.0**
Speed ratings: **104,99,95,93,89 84,84,82,77,74** —,—,— CSF £12.64 TOTE £5.30: £2.20, £1.60, £2.10; EX 19.50.
Owner Doubleprint **Bred** Eurostrait Ltd **Trained** Compton, Berks

FOCUS
Moderate stuff, but the winner did it nicely and looks capable of further progress. The third is the best guide to the level of the form.

NOTEBOOK
Dr Cerullo, who did not shape with a great amount of promise on his debut at Warwick back in December, has clearly improved for a break and he made quite a taking reappearance. The form is nothing special and he will need to improve to defy a penalty, but that is entirely possible. *(op 5-1)*
Sunday City(JPN), who is still without a win under either code, performed well on this hurdles debut, but evidently failed to live up to market expectations and proved no match for the winner. However, he can find a race on this evidence. *(op 5-2)*
Glowing Ember, compared to the front two, is well exposed and she ran as well as she was entitled to. Handicaps are likely to represent her best chance of winning. *(op 8-1)*
Pick Of The Crop ran his best race to date over hurdles, but is probably going to need a drop into selling company to score.
Woolstone Boy(USA) stepped up on his initial effort, but was still beaten too far to be of interest anytime soon.
Sharaab(USA) set a standard of sorts, but he never featured and was clearly below par. He is better than this, but now has a few questions to answer. *(op 7-2 tchd 4-1 in a place)*
Granite Man(IRE) *Official explanation: jockey said gelding off bridle early, unsuited by fast pace & mistake 1st hurdle back straight (op 5-1)*
Indigo Sky(IRE) *Official explanation: jockey said the colt was too keen (op 25-1)*

1563 M. A. R. S. (SOUTH WEST) LTD JUVENILE NOVICES' HURDLE (8 hdls) 2m 110y
4:30 (4:31) (Class 4) 3-Y-O **£3,452** (£986; £493)

Form RPR
6P **1** **Dishdasha (IRE)**[7] 1478 3-10-12 .... NFehily 73
(C R Dore) *hld up in rr: hdwy after 5th: hrd rdn to ld flat: r.o* **40/1**
4BP5 **2** *1 1/4* **Time For You**[7] 1478 3-10-5 .... WMarston 65
(J M Bradley) *a.p: led 4th: j.lft 2 out: hdd and nt qckn flat* **25/1**
3 *1* **Outside Half (IRE)**[8] 3-10-12 ....(t) TJMurphy 71
(W J Musson) *hld up and bhd: hdwy after 3 out: fin wl* **8/1**[3]
4 *hd* **Just Beware**[8] 3-9-12 ....(p) RLucey-Butler[(7)] 64
(Miss Z C Davison) *hld up and bhd: hdwy appr 2 out: fin fast* **50/1**
U0 **5** *3/4* **Spence Appeal (IRE)**[16] 1441 3-10-7 .... LStephens[(5)] 71+
(C Roberts) *led to 4th: ev ch 2 out: no ex flat* **20/1**
U0 **6** *nk* **Southern Shore (IRE)**[16] 1440 3-10-12 ....(b) AntonyEvans 71+
(D Burchell) *hld up and bhd: hdwy 5th: ev ch whn hit last: wknd* **33/1**
7 *11* **Bold Pursuit (IRE)**[28] 3-10-9 .... KJMercer[(3)] 59
(Mrs A Duffield) *hld up in mid-div: no hdwy fr 3 out* **11/1**
P1 **8** *1 1/2* **Gortumblo**[25] 1380 3-11-5 .... JPMcNamara 66+
(K Bishop) *prom: j.lft 2nd: wknd 2 out* **8/1**[3]
9 *6* **Galaxy Dancer (IRE)** 3-10-12 .... LAspell 51
(Mrs L Wadham) *plld hrd in mid-div: hmpd 2nd: mstke 3rd: short-lived effrt 3 out* **6/1**[2]
066 **10** *2* **Tiffin Deano (IRE)**[3] 1519 3-10-5 ....(b[1]) MrJAJenkins[(7)] 49
(H J Manners) *plld hrd: j.rt: prom: mstke 1st: wknd after 5th* **66/1**
11 *6* **Gogetter Girl**[8] 3-10-5 ....(b) OMcPhail 36
(J Gallagher) *plld hrd: prom tl mstke 4th* **66/1**
P **12** *2 1/2* **Lara's Girl**[16] 1441 3-9-12 .... WPKavanagh[(7)] 34
(K G Wingrove) *rdn 5th: a bhd* **100/1**
5 **13** *1 3/4* **Pitsi Kahtoh**[16] 1440 3-10-0 .... MNicolls[(5)] 32
(P W Hiatt) *hld up in mid-div: hdwy on ins approachin 4th: wknd after 5th* **33/1**
0 **14** *1/2* **Ardasnails (IRE)**[16] 1440 3-10-12 .... SCurran 38
(K G Wingrove) *a bhd* **80/1**
F241 **15** *6* **Shingle Street (IRE)**[16] 1441 3-11-5 105..(t) AO'Keeffe 45+
(Miss Venetia Williams) *w ldr: mstkes 4th and 5th: sn rdn: wkng whn mstke 3 out* **11/8**[1]
16 *dist* **Diatonic**[15] 3-10-12 .... ADempsey —
(D Carroll) *plld hrd in mid-div: hmpd 2nd and 3rd: bhd fr 5th: t.o* **20/1**
U **Bainoona**[141] 3-10-5 .... ChristianWilliams —
(Evan Williams) *stmbld bdly and uns rdr 1st* **11/1**

3m 49.0s (-6.70) **Going Correction** -0.625s/f (Firm) **17** Ran SP% **124.1**
Speed ratings: **90,89,88,88,88 88,83,82,79,78 75,74,73,73,70** —,— CSF £780.85 TOTE £60.50: £11.00, £6.80, £2.30; EX 504.50.
Owner W Lunn Haulage **Bred** Locsot S R L **Trained** West Pinchbeck, Lincs

FOCUS
Weak juvenile hurdle form rated through the runner-up, and the race is unlikely to produce many future winners.

NOTEBOOK
Dishdasha(IRE), who was unable to build on a mildly promising first effort over hurdles when his saddle slipped at Plumpton, in hindsight was sent off a particularly big price here and he found plenty under pressure to get the better of fellow outsider Time For You. There was no fluke about the performance, but he will need to improve further to defy a penalty. *(op 33-1)*
Time For You was bang there throughout and had every chance, but she was unable to hold off the winner after the last. This was her best effort yet over hurdles.
Outside Half(IRE), a lowly-rated Flat performer, came home well having been held up and would have pressed the winner with a slightly more prominent ride. He can win races at a moderate level on this evidence. *(tchd 9-1)*
Just Beware is evidently going to make a better hurdler than Flat-racer and she finished to good effect. A more positive ride will benefit in future, as will a greater distance in time.
Spence Appeal(IRE) is gradually getting the hang of things, but makes little appeal as a likely future winner on this evidence. *(op 18-1 tchd 22-1)*
Shingle Street(IRE), off the mark at Bangor last time following a string off decent efforts in defeat, *was beaten too easily for this to be his true running and now has his well-being to prove.Official explanation: trainer had no explanation for the poor form shown (tchd 5-4, 6-4 in places)*

1564 HAZEL CASEY 50TH BIRTHDAY H'CAP HURDLE (12 hdls) 3m 2f
5:05 (5:09) (Class 4) (0-90,90) 4-Y-O+ **£2,674** (£764; £382)

Form RPR
0P-4 **1** **Mags Two**[32] 1310 8-10-1 72.. PMerrigan[(7)] 79+
(I McMath) *hdwy 3rd: led 3 out: nt fluent 2 out: sn clr: comf* **9/2**[1]
-P33 **2** *5* **Sundawn Lady**[27] 1367 7-10-9 80..(b) MrGTumelty[(7)] 79
(C P Morlock) *led to 2nd: led 3rd tl after 9th: one pce fr 2 out* **15/2**[3]
0450 **3** *4* **Cotswold Rose**[96] 801 5-10-11 78.. TJPhelan[(3)] 73
(N M Babbage) *hld up and bhd: hdwy after 8th: rdn appr 3 out: nt fluent last: one pce* **14/1**
-041 **4** *4* **Coppermalt (USA)**[22] 1395 7-11-0 78.. TDoyle 69
(R Curtis) *hld up and bhd: hdwy after 7th: rdn after 9th: no imp fr 3 out* **11/2**[2]
0P00 **5** *3 1/2* **Silver Gift**[82] 906 8-10-10 79.. DLaverty[(5)] 67
(G Fierro) *hld up and bhd: hdwy 9th: sn rdn: wknd appr 2 out* **12/1**
P4P0 **6** *1 3/4* **Phase Eight Girl**[35] 1280 9-10-9 73.. WHutchinson 59
(J Hetherton) *mid-div: rdn appr 9th: no real prog fr 3 out* **10/1**
6-55 **7** *3/4* **Sylvie D'Orthe (FR)**[32] 1308 4-10-2 73.. DMcGann[(5)] 56
(A C Wilson) *hld up and bhd: hdwy appr 8th: wknd appr 3 out* **33/1**
/P0- **8** *4* **Magic Red**[25] 1911 5-11-6 84.. JEMoore 65
(M J Ryan) *w ldrs: led after 9th to 3 out: sn wknd* **10/1**
6-6P **9** *13* **Hill Forts Henry**[21] 1414 7-11-0 78.. AThornton 46
(J W Mullins) *hld up towards rr: hdwy 9th: hit 3 out: sn wknd* **11/1**
3250 **10** *3/4* **Peruvian Breeze (IRE)**[3] 1523 4-11-6 86.. ChristianWilliams 51
(Evan Williams) *a bhd* **8/1**
3-00 **11** *7* **Esterelle (USA)**[21] 1408 10-11-5 90.. MrJAJenkins[(7)] 50
(H J Manners) *prom tl wknd 8th* **25/1**
05P- **12** *shd* **Lantern Leader (IRE)**[224] 10-11-12 90.. TScudamore 50
(M J Gingell) *hld up in tch: wknd appr 8th* **40/1**
3-0P **13** *12* **Dunston Durgam (IRE)**[43] 1206 11-10-0 64.. JPByrne 12
(Ms Sue Smith) *hld up in mid-div: hdwy 7th: wknd after 9th* **50/1**
60P5 **14** *24* **Cromwell (IRE)**[73] 989 10-11-1 86..(b) CMStudd[(7)] 10
(M C Chapman) *prom tl wknd 7th* **25/1**
FPP- **15** *dist* **Mid Summer Lark (IRE)**[183] 4551 9-11-5 90.. MrDJewett[(7)] —
(I McMath) *led 2nd to 3rd: w ldrs to 8th: sn wknd: t.o* **50/1**
P06P **P** **Bravo**[66] 1045 7-11-0 78..(tp) NFehily —
(J Mackie) *in tch tl p.u lame bef 8th* **14/1**
0-P3 **U** **Audiostreetdotcom**[7] 1486 8-11-5 90..(b) MrJoshuaHarris[(7)] 81+
(R A Harris) *hld up in mid-div: hdwy after 7th: cl 4th whn sddle slipped and uns rdr 3 out* **14/1**

6m 13.4s (-9.00) **Going Correction** -0.625s/f (Firm)
WFA 4 from 5yo+ 16lb **17** Ran SP% **127.6**
Speed ratings: **88,86,85,84,82 82,82,80,76,76 74,74,70,63,**— —,— CSF £37.46 CT £455.96 TOTE £6.20: £1.50, £2.30, £3.80, £2.00; EX 37.40.
Owner Mrs A J McMath **Bred** D A Harrison **Trained** Cumwhinton, Cumbria

FOCUS
Weak form rated through the runner-up with the winner looking value for a bit further.

NOTEBOOK
Mags Two, who has been running no more than respectably over shorter, improved a good deal for this extra distance and stayed on strongly to win cosily. He looks capable of further improvement over this sort of trip and may well be capable of following up. *(op 15-2)*
Sundawn Lady is generally a consistent sort and she appeared to run her race in second. She has still to win her first race however and does not make any great appeal as a future winner. *(op 9-1)*
Cotswold Rose was well served by this rise in distance and she may well be capable of scoring at a similarly low level. *(op 16-1)*
Coppermalt(USA), 5lb higher than when winning at Stratford, had every chance and may well have found this trip a shade too far. *(op 6-1 tchd 5-1)*
Silver Gift left several poor efforts behind and took a step back in the right direction. However, whether he will be able to progress again and get his head in front is doubtful. *(op 14-1 tchd 16-1)*
Peruvian Breeze(IRE) *Official explanation: jockey said, regarding the running and riding, his orders were to drop gelding in last and creep into the race, adding that gelding jumped well but did not pick up when asked for an effort coming out of the top bend and had nothing left prior to jumping the penultimate hurdle; trainer said gelding, running over the trip for the first time, had no chance when they quickened in the latter stages (op 15-2)*
Audiostreetdotcom *Official explanation: jockey said saddle slipped (op 12-1)*

1565 BETTINGJOBS.COM RECRUITMENT CONSULTANCY NOVICES' HURDLE (DIV II) (8 hdls) 2m 110y
5:35 (5:38) (Class 4) 4-Y-O+ **£3,073** (£878; £439)

Form RPR
1 **United Spirit (IRE)**[12] 4-10-5 .... BHarding 95+
(Jedd O'Keeffe) *hld up: hdwy 4th: led 2 out: rdn and r.o flat* **14/1**
042 **2** *3* **Air Guitar (IRE)**[14] 1454 5-10-12 103.. PMoloney 96
(M G Quinlan) *a.p: ev ch 2 out: sn rdn: one pce* **2/1**[2]
U-02 **3** *2 1/2* **Looks The Business (IRE)**[14] 1458 4-11-5 97.. PJBrennan 101
(W G M Turner) *w ldr: led 3 out: rdn and hdd 2 out no ex flat* **11/2**[3]
0 **4** *13* **Head Boy**[7] 1480 4-10-12 .... JamesDavies 81
(S Dow) *hld up and bhd: hdwy appr 3 out: no imp fr 2 out* **40/1**
5P/ **5** *shd* **Sarn**[51] 2182 6-10-9 .... ACCoyle[(3)] 80
(M Mullineaux) *bhd tl styd on flat: nvr nrr* **66/1**
0P/- **6** *5* **Buster (IRE)**[546] 4588 6-10-12 .... WHutchinson 75
(M J Ryan) *prom: lost pl after 3rd: n.d after* **33/1**
7 *7* **Listen To Reason (IRE)**[15] 4-10-9 .... LVickers[(3)] 68
(J G Given) *hld up: hdwy after 5th: wknd after 3 out* **16/1**
0 **8** *10* **Busy Man (IRE)**[39] 1237 6-10-12 .... LAspell 58
(J R Jenkins) *hld up and bhd: hdwy after 5th: wknd after 3 out* **66/1**
3U-5 **9** *1/2* **Gallant Hero**[27] 1364 6-10-12 102.. RJohnson 76+
(P J Hobbs) *led tl mstke 3 out: wknd 2 out: eased flat* **6/4**[1]
56F- **10** *8* **Gold For Me (FR)**[156] 4956 6-10-7 95.. DMcGann[(5)] 50
(A C Wilson) *hld up: rdn after 5th: sn bhd* **20/1**
00F- **11** *6* **Chiqitita (IRE)**[156] 4958 4-10-5 .... JMogford 37
(Miss M E Rowland) *prom: rdn after 4th: wknd after 5th* **100/1**
00-P **12** *1/2* **Wizzical Lad**[16] 1445 5-10-5 ....(p) TMessenger[(7)] 43
(B N Pollock) *a towards rr* **100/1**

3m 44.0s (-11.70) **Going Correction** -0.625s/f (Firm) **12** Ran SP% **116.4**
Speed ratings: **102,100,99,93,93 90,87,82,82,78 76,75** CSF £41.65 TOTE £14.00: £3.40, £1.20, £1.80; EX 51.70 Place 6 £140.59, Place 5 £54.28..
Owner Colin And Melanie Moore **Bred** Atlantic Racing Limited **Trained** Middleham Moor, N Yorks

FOCUS
Ordinary novice form, but the winner is value for double the official margin.

NOTEBOOK
United Spirit(IRE), a 55-rated Flat performer whose last effort on the level was a poor one, clearly appreciated the challenge of jumping an obstacle and put up a fair effort in disposing of the *103-rated winner. He will need to step up on this to defy a penalty, but that is entirely possible. (op 16-1)*
Air Guitar(IRE) set a fair standard having finished a decent second last time, but the combination of this drop in trip/faster ground did not appear to suit and he was outspeeded by the winner. He definitely has a race of this nature in him, but needs more of a test. *(op 9-4 tchd 5-2 in a place)*
Looks The Business(IRE) faced a stiff task giving weight to the front pair and time may show this to be a decent effort. He should continue to pay his way. *(op 5-1)*
Head Boy stepped up on his initial effort over hurdles and the way he kept on suggests he will prove suited to trips beyond this. *(op 33-1)*
Sarn ran above market expectations and was only just denied fourth. He may find a race at selling level. *(op 50-1)*

Gallant Hero looked an 'iffy' favourite, but he should surely have run better than he did and it is safe to assume there was something amiss. However, he is clearly unreliable and can never be backed with confidence.

T/Plt: £565.90 to a £1 stake. Pool: £43,068.35. 55.55 winning tickets. T/Qpdt: £120.10 to a £1 stake. Pool: £2,687.30. 16.55 winning tickets. KH

1374 SEDGEFIELD (L-H)

Tuesday, September 27

OFFICIAL GOING: Good to firm (good in places)

Wind: Fairly strong, behind

1566 GOSFORTH BUILDING & DECORATING SERVICES CONDITIONAL JOCKEYS' NOVICES' H'CAP HURDLE (10 hdls) 2m 5f 110y

2:20 (2:20) (Class 4) (0-90,89) 4-Y-0+ **£2,681** (£766; £383)

Form				RPR
0334	**1**		**Fortune's Fool**[28] 1375 6-10-9 **72** ... DCrosse (I A Brown) *midfield: hdwy 1/2-way: led bef 2 out: sn rdn: hdd towards fin: fin 2nd: btn 1¼l: awrdd r* **11/2**[3]	73
/P-4	**2**	4¼	**Tioga Gold (IRE)**[64] 1067 6-11-3 **80** ... ONelmes (L R James) *hld up: drvn along and effrt bef 3 out: kpt on same pce after next: fin 3rd, 1½l & 3l: plcd 2nd* **20/1**	78
FU-4	**3**	*3*	**Alpha Juliet (IRE)**[31] 1336 4-11-7 **85** ... DCCostello (G M Moore) *chsd clr ldrs: hdwy to ld 7th: hdd bef 2 out: no ex: fin 4th, plcd 3rd* **7/1**	79
5452	**4**	*3*	**Greenfort Brave (IRE)**[11] 1477 7-11-8 **85** ... PCO'Neill (J J Lambe, Ire) *bhd: struggling 6th: styd on fr 2 out: nrst fin: fin 5th, plcd 4th* **9/2**[2]	78
P240	**5**	*6*	**Dead Mans Dante (IRE)**[9] 1490 7-11-8 **88** ... KJMercer(3) (Ferdy Murphy) *nt fluent towards rr: hmpd 5th: drvn along and effrt bef 3 out: sn n.d: fin 6th, plcd 5th* **10/3**[1]	76+
	6	*5*	**Tornado Alley (IRE)**[30] 1352 6-11-4 **81** ... (p) WKennedy (J J Lambe, Ire) *led to after 1st: led 4th to 7th: ev ch tl wknd bef 2 out: fin 7th, plcd sixth* **14/1**	63
00-0	**D**		**Rathlin Island**[86] 895 7-11-3 **80** ... (p) PAspell (Miss V Scott) *chsd ldrs: outpcd 6th: rallied to press ldr bef 2 out: styd on to ld towards fin: fin 1st, 1¼l: disq (failed to draw correct weight)* **16/1**	82
050-	**P**		**Awwal Marra (USA)**[12] 2846 5-11-2 **79** ... NPMulholland (E W Tuer) *a bhd: t.o whn p.u 6th* **22/1**	—
-405	**F**		**Coachman (IRE)**[28] 1374 7-9-9 **63** oh2 ... PJMcDonald(5) (A J Lockwood) *a bhd: struggling whn fell 6th* **16/1**	—
00-2	**P**		**Vicky Bee**[31] 1344 6-11-4 **89** ... TBailey(8) (M G Quinlan) *bhd: struggling whn bdly hmpd 6th: p.u next* **9/2**[2]	—
P-PP	**R**		**Wee Sean (IRE)**[5] 1528 5-10-9 **80** ow1 ... NWalker(8) (Miss Lucinda V Russell) *led briefly after 1st: rn out appr next* **66/1**	—
300/	**F**		**Good Time Bobby**[96] 12 8-11-0 **80** ... MJMcAlister(3) (Miss Kate Milligan) *cl up: led 2nd to 4th: fell heavily next* **50/1**	—

5m 1.80s (-13.90) **Going Correction** -0.875s/f (Firm)
WFA 4 from 5yo+ 15lb **12** Ran SP% **118.3**
Speed ratings: **89,88,87,86,84 82,90,**—,—,— —,— CSF £108.77 CT £785.60 TOTE £8.00: £3.00, £4.20, £3.20; EX 88.20.
Owner I A Brown **Bred** Mrs P A Clark **Trained** Great Edstone, N Yorks

FOCUS
A dire event, run at an ordinary gallop and the form is supect. The winner was disqualified as his rider lost his weight cloth approaching the penultimate flight and failed to draw the correct weight.

NOTEBOOK
Fortune's Fool, up in trip, had no more to offer when challenged two out, but stuck to his task and finished nicely clear of the rest. Although he may be considered lucky to have eventually have been awarded the race, he may well have held Rathlin Island had that rival carried the correct weight anyway. *(op 13-2 tchd 7-1)*
Tioga Gold(IRE) improved for the drop back in trip, and was in turn clear in third place, but never really threatened to get his head in front. The return to plating-class over this trip looks in order now. *(op 16-1)*
Alpha Juliet(IRE) failed to improve for the longer trip and was well beaten. *(op 8-1 tchd 11-2)*
Greenfort Brave(IRE), well backed, gave himself too much to do from off the pace and was staying on all too late. He is capable of better. *(op 7-1)*
Dead Mans Dante(IRE) did not impress with his jumping throught the first circuit and never looked like getting to the leaders at any stage. He is probably happier over a shorter trip, but is not one to *place any confidence in. Official explanation: trainer's representative said gelding scoped dirty post race (op 11-4)*
Rathlin Island finally put his best foot forward and gamely got off the mark over hurdles at the fourth attempt. The first-time cheekpieces had the desired effect, as did the longer trip, and his stable has clearly hit a bit of form now. However, he was subsequently disqualified, as his rider lost his weight cloth approaching the penultimate flight and failed to draw the correct weight (4lb light).
Awwal Marra(USA) *Official explanation: trainer said saddle slipped (op 4-1)*
Vicky Bee *(op 4-1)*

1567 COORS BREWERY CLAIMING HURDLE (8 hdls) 2m 1f

2:55 (2:55) (Class 4) 4-Y-0+ **£2,625** (£750; £375)

Form				RPR
5-60	**1**		**Teme Valley**[79] 940 11-10-8 105 ... GLee (J Howard Johnson) *in tch: pushed along 4 out: ev ch next: rdn to ld bef last: styd on strly* **2/1**[2]	93+
01-0	**2**	*7*	**Compton Eagle**[28] 1375 5-12-0 ... JPMcNamara (J J Lambe, Ire) *w ldr: led 4 out to bef last: one pce* **40/1**	103
0223	**3**	*5*	**Valuable (IRE)**[28] 1375 8-10-5 81 ... KJohnson (R Johnson) *hld up: hdwy to chal 3 out: one pce bef next* **8/1**[3]	75
4-21	**4**	*2 1/2*	**Dalida**[6] 1510 4-10-7 87 ... APMcCoy (P C Haslam) *chsd ldrs: hmpd and stmbld bdly 3 out: n.d after* **7/4**[1]	80+
P	**5**	*4*	**Dextrous**[28] 1377 8-10-9 ... ACCoyle(3) (P T Midgley) *bhd: hdwy and prom after 3 out: rdn and outpcd fr next* **20/1**	76+
P-00	**6**	*5*	**Irish Prince (IRE)**[28] 1375 9-11-1 72 ... ONelmes(3) (Robert Gray) *prom: outpcd 4 out: n.d after* **100/1**	76
6-03	**7**	*hd*	**Always Flying (USA)**[20] 1432 4-10-10 91 ... KRenwick (N Wilson) *keen: mde most to 4 out: wknd next* **9/1**	68
0154	**8**	*1 1/4*	**Two Steps To Go (USA)**[28] 1377 6-10-3 78 ... (t) BenOrde-Powlett(7) (M A Barnes) *towards rr: outpcd 4 out: nvr on terms* **22/1**	67
00-6	**F**		**Sunridge Fairy (IRE)**[26] 428 6-10-11 89 ... ADobbin (L R James) *midfield: fell 4th* **12/1**	—
0P-0	**P**		**Lady Stratagem**[120] 592 6-10-5 64 ... BHarding (E W Tuer) *a bhd: t.o whn p.u bef 2 out* **66/1**	—

3m 51.7s (-14.80) **Going Correction** -0.875s/f (Firm)
WFA 4 from 5yo+ 14lb **10** Ran SP% **112.5**
Speed ratings: **99,95,93,92,90 87,87,87,**—,— CSF £80.64 TOTE £2.70: £1.40, £9.30, £2.80; EX 120.50.Teme Valley (no.7) was claimed by R. C. Guest for £5,000.
Owner Chris Heron **Bred** Juddmonte Farms **Trained** Billy Row, Co Durham

FOCUS
A typically weak heat for the grade and the course specialist Teme Valley won as he was entitled to at the weights.

NOTEBOOK
Teme Valley, having his first-ever outing at this lowly level, ultimately ran out a most decisive winner and posted his 11th success at the track in the process. Despite the fact he had looked on the downgrade previously this term and was by some way the oldest in this line-up, he was entitled *to win at the weights. He was rather surprisingly claimed at the subsequent auction for £5000. (tchd 15-8 in a place)*
Compton Eagle turned in a fair effort from the front and, despite holding no chance with the winner *at the weights, finished nicely clear of the rest. This track looks to bring the best out in him. (op 33-1 tchd 50-1)*
Valuable(IRE) failed to to sustain his effort from two out and was well beaten in the end. He is at least consistent in this grade and helps set the level for this form. *(tchd 9-1)*
Dalida, an easy winner in this class at Perth six days previously, would have finished a lot closer but for losing all chance when almost coming down at the third-last flight. She remains in good heart and can be rated better than the bare form. *(op 15-8 tchd 2-1)*

1568 CASTLEMAINE XXXX NOVICES' CHASE (16 fncs) 2m 5f

3:30 (3:31) (Class 3) 5-Y-0+ **£5,512** (£1,696; £848; £424)

Form				RPR
314	**1**		**Bushido (IRE)**[31] 1342 6-11-4 112 ... DElsworth (Mrs S J Smith) *cl up: led 2 out: hit last: styd on wl* **9/2**[2]	123+
2211	**2**	*5*	**Possextown (IRE)**[6] 1511 7-11-10 115 ... ADobbin (N G Richards) *led to 2 out: sn rdn: hit last: sn no ex* **8/13**[1]	124+
34-P	**3**	*5*	**Deja Vu (IRE)**[150] 121 6-10-12 ... GLee (J Howard Johnson) *prom tl rdn and outpcd after 3 out* **15/2**[3]	105
43	**4**	*dist*	**Sort It Out (IRE)**[132] 415 8-10-9 ... KJMercer(3) (Ferdy Murphy) *chsd ldrs to 12th: sn wknd* **20/1**	85
0P65	**5**	*dist*	**Greenacres Boy**[18] 1442 10-10-9 53 ... ACCoyle(3) (M Mullineaux) *cl up to 12th: wknd: t.o* **200/1**	—
-220	**6**	*3 1/2*	**Iris's Prince**[125] 499 6-10-5 ... TJDreaper(7) (A Crook) *sn bhd: no ch fnl circ* **33/1**	—
PP60	**P**		**Primitive Jean**[34] 1310 6-10-2 ... PAspell(3) (C R Wilson) *a bhd: t.o whn p.u bef 2 out* **200/1**	—
/40-	**P**		**Noel's Pride**[240] 9-10-12 ... NFehily (C C Bealby) *sn towards rr: t.o whn p.u bef 3 out* **25/1**	—
P025	**P**		**Diamond Joshua (IRE)**[29] 1365 7-10-9 107 ... ONelmes(3) (N B King) *sn bhd: no ch fr 1/2-way: p.u bef 3 out* **40/1**	—
00-P	**P**		**Honest Endeavour**[156] 13 6-10-12 ... DO'Meara (J M Jefferson) *hld up: shortlived effrt after 8th: no imp fr next: t.o whn p.u bef 3 out* **33/1**	—

5m 5.60s (-17.80) **Going Correction** -0.725s/f (Firm) **10** Ran SP% **109.8**
Speed ratings: **104,102,100,**—,— —,—,—,—,— CSF £7.26 TOTE £6.70: £1.60, £1.10, £2.50; EX 10.50.
Owner Mrs B Ramsden **Bred** Mrs George Robinson **Trained** High Eldwick, W Yorks

FOCUS
A modest novice chase, run at a fair gallop, and the form looks sound.

NOTEBOOK
Bushido(IRE) enjoyed the drop back in trip and, despite making an error at the final fence, already had the race safely in the bag at that point. This has to rate a personal best over fences and, considering he won off a mark of 122 over timer in 2004, he would be of interest back in handicaps from his current mark while in this vein of form. *(op 5-1 tchd 11-2 in a place)*
Possextown(IRE), returning to novice company in search of the hat-trick, proved anchored by his double penalty when pressed by the winner and was well held at the finish. However, he is not one to write off over fences on the back of this display, as this was his third outing in fairly quick *succession and all his previous best form has come on a left-handed track over a longer trip. (tchd 4-7 and 4-6)*
Deja Vu(IRE), pulled up on his latest outing 150 days previously, jumped well enough on this chasing bow and was not disgraced. He should improve for the experience and may prove happier over a longer trip in this sphere. *(op 8-1)*
Sort It Out(IRE), making his chasing bow under Rules, did not jump all that well early on and never rated a serious threat to the principals. He is entitled to improve for the outing and should find his feet once going handicapping over fences. *(op 14-1)*

1569 CAMERONS STRONGARM NOVICES' HURDLE (7 hdls 1 omitted) 2m 1f

4:05 (4:05) (Class 4) 4-Y-0+ **£3,388** (£968; £484)

Form				RPR
-441	**1**		**Snow's Ride**[132] 415 5-11-4 100 ... GLee (M D Hammond) *in tch: hdwy to ld bef 2 out: styd on wl fr last* **7/2**[2]	109+
	2	*4*	**George Stubbs (USA)**[34] 7-10-11 ... ADobbin (B Ellison) *hld up: hdwy and prom bef 2 out: ev ch appr last: kpt on same pce* **13/2**	100+
	3	*5*	**Spring Breeze**[34] 4-10-11 ... (v) BHarding (M Dods) *w ldr: led 4th to bef 2 out: sn no ex* **4/1**[3]	93
005-	**4**	*5*	**Apsara**[10] 4110 4-10-4 90 ... FKeniry (G M Moore) *hld up: hdwy after 3 out: outpcd fr next* **12/1**	81
	5	*8*	**Oldenway**[31] 6-10-11 ... APMcCoy (R A Fahey) *nt fluent: keen: hld up in tch: rdn and wknd bef 2 out* **9/4**[1]	83+
660-	**6**	*1/2*	**Noble Pursuit**[26] 4257 8-10-4 80 ... PKinsella(7) (R E Barr) *prom: outpcd after 3 out: n.d after* **40/1**	80
6011	**7**	*13*	**Supply And Fix (IRE)**[28] 1377 7-11-11 ... JPMcNamara (J J Lambe, Ire) *led to 4th: cl up tl wknd bef 2 out* **7/1**	81
-FU6	**8**	*10*	**Lanhel (FR)**[6] 1508 6-10-8 ... PAspell(3) (J Wade) *plld hrd: prom to 1/2-way: sn wknd* **50/1**	57
/60-	**9**	*1 1/2*	**Lorio Du Misselot (FR)**[307] 2432 6-10-8 ... KJMercer(3) (Ferdy Murphy) *hmpd 1st: a bhd* **33/1**	55
04P	**10**	*30*	**So Cloudy**[45] 1213 4-9-13 ... StephenJCraine(5) (D McCain) *keen: hld up: wknd fr 1/2-way* **100/1**	18
56	**U**		**South Shore One**[108] 720 4-10-4 ... DElsworth (C Grant) *uns rdr 1st* **66/1**	—
00-0	**P**		**Inmate (IRE)**[79] 936 4-10-11 ... KJohnson (Mrs E Slack) *sn wl bhd: t.o whn p.u bef 2 out* **100/1**	—

3m 51.5s (-15.00) **Going Correction** -0.875s/f (Firm)
WFA 4 from 5yo+ 14lb **12** Ran SP% **117.3**
Speed ratings: **100,98,95,93,89 89,83,78,77,63** —,— CSF £25.56 TOTE £5.40: £1.90, £1.40, £1.60; EX 29.00.
Owner Belarus Partnership **Bred** Biddestone Stud And Partner **Trained** Middleham, N Yorks

FOCUS
Not a bad little event and it should produce the odd winner. The third last was bypassed.

The Form Book, Raceform Ltd, Compton, RG20 6NL

NOTEBOOK

Snow's Ride, off the mark over hurdles at the course in May, could have been expected to improve for this first outing since, but he was far too good for his field and ran on strongly to win with something to spare. Clearly progressive, he may well go on to complete the hat-trick and deserves his place in a better-class race. *(op 9-2)*

George Stubbs(USA), a 58-rated Flat performer, came through to challenge in the final two furlongs, but he lacked the speed of the winner. This was a pleasing first effort and he looks capable of winning at a similar level, with a rise in distance unlikely to be a problem. *(op 10-1)*

Spring Breeze, a fair Flat racer, is the type to make a decent hurdler and he made a pleasing start. His best form on the level was over this sort of trip, so maybe trips in excess of this will see him in a better light. *(op 5-1 tchd 7-2)*

Apsara again found a few too good and she will find life easier once contesting handicaps. *(op 9-1)*

Oldenway was most disappointing on this hurdling debut, failing to jump with any fluency. He was a useful sort on the Flat and should be given another chance. *(tchd 5-2)*

Supply And Fix(IRE), on a hat-trick having won twice at this course in August, faced a stiff task shouldering a double penalty, but he should still have fared better than he did and it was disappointing how quickly he stopped. *(op 9-2)*

1570 BLACK SHEEP BREWERY H'CAP CHASE (16 fncs) 2m 5f

4:40 (4:40) (Class 4) (0-110,104) 5-Y-O+ **£4,410** (£1,357; £678; £339)

Form | | | | RPR

6132 **1** **Now Then Sid**[28] 1376 6-10-3 **84** KJMercer(3) 99+
(Mrs S A Watt) *hld up: pushed along 10th: hdwy and prom 3 out: led between last 2: styd on wl* **11/4**[1]

3233 **2** *9* **Billie John (IRE)**[24] 1399 10-11-9 **101** ADobbin 108+
(Mrs K Walton) *cl up: effrt and ev ch 2 out: one pce last* **6/1**[2]

P-45 **3** *4* **Danteco**[28] 1378 10-9-7 **78** oh7 MJMcAlister(7) 82+
(Miss Kate Milligan) *mstke 1st: sn chsng ldrs: hit 7th and 3 out: edgd lft next: one pce* **40/1**

2031 **4** *10* **Karo De Vindecy (FR)**[29] 1359 7-10-13 **91** GLee 83
(M D Hammond) *hld up midfield: rdn 4 out: one pce bef 2 out* **11/4**[1]

3544 **5** *4* **Brave Effect (IRE)**[12] 1312 9-11-4 **96** BHarding 88+
(Mrs Dianne Sayer) *led to between last 2: wknd qckly last* **16/1**

0615 **6** *5* **Toad Hall**[31] 1343 11-9-9 **78** oh2 DCCostello(5) 61
(Mrs L B Normile) *bhd tl sme late hdwy: nvr on terms* **16/1**

0 **7** *18* **Devondale (IRE)**[31] 1334 9-10-4 **89** TJDreaper(7) 54
(Ferdy Murphy) *bhd: struggling 1/2-way: n.d after* **20/1**

4-50 **8** *13* **Taleban**[53] 1150 10-9-11 **78** oh3 (p) PAspell(3) 30
(J Wade) *sn bhd: t.o fr 1/2-way* **25/1**

60S0 **F** **Panmure (IRE)**[9] 1489 9-11-5 **97** (p) JimCrowley —
(P D Niven) *prom: 7l 6th and wkng whn fell 3 out* **8/1**

3-PU **P** **Cool Carroll (IRE)**[33] 1318 7-10-6 **91** LBerridge(7) —
(J Howard Johnson) *sn wl bhd: t.o whn p.u bef 6th* **33/1**

P402 **P** **Pavey Ark (IRE)**[29] 1359 7-9-11 **78** oh1 PBuchanan(3) —
(James Moffatt) *in tch to 11th: sn wknd: t.o whn p.u bef 2 out* **7/1**[3]

5m 6.10s (-17.30) **Going Correction** -0.725s/f (Firm) **11** Ran SP% **117.0**

Speed ratings: **103,99,98,94,92 90,83,79,—,—** — CSF £19.04 CT £538.96 TOTE £4.60: £2.00, £1.60, £8.10; EX 25.80.

Owner Mrs S A Watt **Bred** Mrs J Jackson **Trained** Brompton-on-Swale, N Yorks

FOCUS

Modest stuff and the field finished strung out.

NOTEBOOK

Now Then Sid has found his form in the last month or so and, under a typically-confident Mercer ride, he came through to win easily. A progressive gelding, there may well be more to come and he remains open to improvement off this sort of mark. *(op 10-3 tchd 4-1)*

Billie John(IRE) ran yet another good race in defeat and was not inconvenienced by the step back up in trip. *(tchd 13-2)*

Danteco returned to a bit of form and ran better than the market suggested he would. A further drop in the weights should see him capable of winning at a similarly lowly level. *(op 25-1)*

Karo De Vindecy(FR) seemed unable to cope with his 8lb rise for winning at Cartmel and he was readily brushed aside by the leaders. *(op 9-4 tchd 2-1)*

Brave Effect(IRE) set a good clip, but he suffered towards the end as a consequence and stopped sharply inside the final quarter mile. *(op 12-1)*

1571 WEATHERBYS MESSAGING SERVICE H'CAP HURDLE (10 hdls) 2m 5f 110y

5:15 (5:15) (Class 4) (0-110,110) 4-Y-O+ **£3,789** (£1,166; £583; £291)

Form | | | | RPR

1132 **1** **Mr Mischief**[5] 1528 5-11-12 **110** APMcCoy 116+
(P C Haslam) *hld up: hdwy bef 3 out: led next: drvn out* **6/5**[1]

-363 **2** *2* **Litron (IRE)**[28] 1379 8-11-3 **101** JPMcNamara 104+
(J J Lambe, Ire) *hld up: hdwy 1/2-way: led briefly bef 2 out: kpt on fr last* **3/1**[2]

6211 **3** *7* **Wally Wonder (IRE)**[31] 1344 7-11-2 **100** (b) JimCrowley 96
(R Bastiman) *led to bef 2 out: sn no ex* **10/1**

26P **4** *¾* **Qualitair Pleasure**[18] 1443 5-10-3 **90** KJMercer(3) 85
(J Hetherton) *hld up: smooth hdwy and ev ch bef 2 out: sn rdn and btn* **16/1**

4-30 **5** *3 ½* **Nocatee (IRE)**[100] 784 4-11-4 **103** FKeniry 94
(P C Haslam) *prom: lost pl 3rd: n.d after* **40/1**

3224 **6** *2* **Gabor**[6] 1510 6-11-2 **100** ADobbin 90
(M Todhunter) *cl up: reminder 3rd: wknd fr 3 out* **20/1**

2500 **7** *6* **In Good Faith**[9] 1486 13-9-7 **84** oh2 PKinsella(7) 68
(R E Barr) *bhd: rdn bef 3 out: nvr on terms* **50/1**

0-01 **8** *¾* **Green 'N' Gold**[31] 1333 5-10-6 **90** GLee 76+
(M D Hammond) *keen: hdwy to chse ldrs 3rd: rdn and wknd 3 out* **8/1**[3]

00P0 **9** *1* **Ramblees Holly**[3] 1552 7-11-2 **105** DMcGann(5) 87
(R S Wood) *chsd ldrs to 4 out: sn lost pl* **20/1**

-506 **10** *2 ½* **Gabla (NZ)**[34] 1311 9-11-0 **98** (p) HOliver 78
(R C Guest) *hld up midfield: hdwy 4 out: wknd qckly 2 out* **40/1**

(-15.70) **Going Correction** -0.875s/f (Firm)

WFA 4 from 5yo+ 15lb **10** Ran SP% **112.9**

Speed ratings: **93,92,89,89,88 87,85,85,84,83** CSF £4.71 CT £21.74 TOTE £1.80: £1.10, £1.70, £2.80; EX 6.10 Place 6 £42.20, Place 5 £8.78..

Owner Middleham Park Racing I & Mrs C Barclay **Bred** Mrs Maureen Barbara Walsh **Trained** Middleham, N Yorks

FOCUS

Another good effort by the bang in form Mr Mischief.

NOTEBOOK

Mr Mischief is very consistent and he ground out his third win over hurdles. He has been in good form back on the Flat and now deserves to take his in a better race. *(op 11-8 tchd 6-4 in a place)*

Litron(IRE) had every chance and was clear of the third, simply being unlucky to bump into the in-form winner. He should remain on a winning mark. *(op 9-2)*

Wally Wonder(IRE) was bidding for a hat-trick and appeared to hold obvious claims, but he was a spent force from over two out and he was unable to go on with the front two. *(tchd 11-1 in places)*

Qualitair Pleasure has lost her a bit of late, but this was a better effort and she may soon be ready to strike. *(op 11-1)*

Nocatee(IRE) ran better than his price suggested he would and is entitled to come on for this first outing since June. *(tchd 50-1)*

T/Plt: £81.60 to a £1 stake. Pool: £45,854.60. 409.95 winning tickets. T/Qpdt: £7.20 to a £1 stake. Pool: £4,505.20. 459.10 winning tickets. RY

1572 - 1576a (Foreign Racing) - See Raceform Interactive

742 HEREFORD (R-H)

Thursday, September 29

1577 Meeting Abandoned - track damaged while being prepared

1584 - 1586a (Foreign Racing) - See Raceform Interactive

780 HEXHAM (L-H)

Friday, September 30

OFFICIAL GOING: Good to firm

Wind: Strong, against

1587 G G MEDIA HEXHAM NOVICES' HURDLE (12 hdls) 3m

2:00 (2:10) (Class 4) 4-Y-O+ **£3,430** (£980; £490)

Form | | | | RPR

2-32 **1** **Catch The Perk (IRE)**[8] 1526 8-11-1 110 (p) PBuchanan(3) 99+
(Miss Lucinda V Russell) *led: rdn 2 out: hdd briefly last: kpt on gamely* **6/5**[1]

0-01 **2** *hd* **Rathlin Island**[3] 1566 7-10-12 80 (p) RJohnson 93
(Miss V Scott) *cl up: rdn to ld briefly last: kpt on: hld cl home* **5/1**[3]

3130 **3** *7* **Combat Drinker (IRE)**[63] 1100 7-11-4 90 (t) JMMaguire 92
(D McCain) *hld up in tch: hdwy between last 2: no ex run in* **11/2**

4 *7* **Alghaazy (IRE)**[25] 4-10-10 GLee 77
(M D Hammond) *nt fluent: in tch: effrt 2 out: wknd bef last* **5/2**[2]

F/ **P** **Amanpuri (GER)**[293] 3901 7-10-12 MBradburne —
(P A Blockley) *in tch tl wknd 4 out: p.u 2 out* **50/1**

005 **P** **Silver Emperor (IRE)**[41] 1266 4-10-0 68 (p) AngharadFrieze(10) —
(P A Blockley) *keen: cl up tl wknd qckly bef 2 out: p.u after 2 out* **100/1**

5m 50.4s (-27.30) **Going Correction** -1.05s/f (Hard)

WFA 4 from 7yo+ 16lb **6** Ran SP% **109.0**

Speed ratings: **103,102,100,98,—** — CSF £7.39 TOTE £2.00: £1.10, £3.30; EX 5.50.

Owner A A Bissett **Bred** Miss Yvonne McClintock And Mrs Jean O'Brien **Trained** Milnathort, Perth & Kinross

FOCUS

An uncompetitive event in which the pace was fair. The winner was 9lb off his best and the runner-up showed improved form.

NOTEBOOK

Catch The Perk(IRE) is a gutsy sort who had a good chance at the weights and showed the right attitude on ground probably quicker than ideal to break a losing run for the stable. He should not be going up for this win and will be of interest on easier ground back in handicaps. *(op 10-11 tchd 5-6 and 11-8, 6-4 in a place)*

Rathlin Island, who turned in an improved effort in first-time cheekpieces at Sedgefield earlier in the week, fully confirmed that promise. A good test seems to suit and he looks sure to pick up a small event. *(op 11-2 tchd 6-1 and 9-2)*

Combat Drinker(IRE) may be better on a sound surface and put a poor run behind him after this break. He is likely to remain vulnerable in this grade but may do better back in ordinary handicap company. *(op 15-2)*

Alghaazy(IRE), a modest Flat maiden, was fairly well supported on this hurdles debut and ran with a modicum of promise. There is plenty of room for improvement in the jumping department but he should be better for this experience. *(op 3-1 tchd 9-4)*

Amanpuri(GER) faced a stiff task and is likely to continue to look vulnerable in this type of event.

Silver Emperor(IRE), tried in cheekpieces, again showed nothing. *Official explanation: vet said gelding was lame*

1588 DURHAM COUNTY CRICKET CLUB (S) HURDLE (8 hdls) 2m 110y

2:30 (2:37) (Class 5) 4-Y-O+ **£2,436** (£696; £348)

Form | | | | RPR

041 **1** **Possible Gale (IRE)**[31] 1375 7-11-5 90 (tp) RJohnson 89+
(John G Carr, Ire) *hld up midfield: hdwy and cl up 5th: led 2 out: edgd lft last: kpt on run in* **85/40**[1]

-015 **2** *3 ½* **Seafire Lad (IRE)**[38] 1293 4-11-5 75 (p) KJohnson 83
(R Johnson) *a.p: effrt and chsd wnr between last two: kpt on same pce fr last* **33/1**

3 *3 ½* **Titus Salt (USA)**[8] 4-10-12 GLee 73
(M D Hammond) *hld up: hdwy 3 out: outpcd between last two: no imp run in* **16/1**

-030 **4** *8* **Always Flying (USA)**[3] 1567 4-10-5 91 CDSharkey(7) 65
(N Wilson) *keen: led to 2 out: wknd bef last* **7/1**

U4-4 **5** *hd* **Free Will**[32] 1357 8-10-12 84 (p) HOliver 65+
(R C Guest) *keen: chsd ldrs tl wknd fr 2 out* **9/1**

1540 **6** *12* **Two Steps To Go (USA)**[3] 1567 6-10-12 78 (t) BenOrde-Powlett(7) 59
(M A Barnes) *prom tl drvn and wknd bef 2 out* **33/1**

522P **7** *½* **Staff Nurse (IRE)**[12] 1490 5-10-5 85 (p) KRenwick 45
(N Wilson) *cl up to 1/2-way: sn lost pl* **11/2**[3]

4F **P** **Ball Games**[32] 1357 7-11-5 85 JimCrowley —
(James Moffatt) *a bhd: t.o whn p.u bef 5th* **8/1**

60-0 **P** **Obay**[32] 1360 4-10-12 100 (t) ADobbin —
(M Todhunter) *hld up: lost tch and p.u bef 5th* **4/1**[2]

00-5 **P** **Night Pearl (FR)**[32] 1356 4-10-5 BHarding —
(B Storey) *in tch to 4th: sn struggling: t.o whn p.u bef 2 out* **66/1**

-5PU **P** **Western Bluebird (IRE)**[13] 1062 7-10-5 65 (p) MJMcAlister(7) —
(Miss Kate Milligan) *chsd ldrs to 4th: sn lost pl: p.u next* **100/1**

4m 4.10s (-11.10) **Going Correction** -0.675s/f (Firm) **11** Ran SP% **115.2**

Speed ratings: **99,97,95,91,91 86,85,—,—,—** — CSF £76.09 TOTE £2.60: £1.30, £3.20, £4.50; EX 41.40.The winner was bought in for 8,200gns.

Owner P J Lohan **Bred** Miller's Bloodstock Ltd **Trained** Maynooth, Co. Kildare

FOCUS

A modest event in which the pace was sound. The winner was value for further and ran pretty much to his mark. The overall form is probably not strong.

NOTEBOOK

Possible Gale(IRE), one of the few that came into this in top form, had the run of the race and ran up to his best to notch his second successive win over hurdles. He stays further and should continue to give a good account. *(op 9-4 tchd 5-2 and 2-1)*

Seafire Lad(IRE) looked to have plenty to find on these terms but turned in an improved effort and looks the type to be placed to best advantage in the coming months. *(op 40-1 tchd 50-1)*

Titus Salt(USA), who showed ability at up to a mile and a quarter on the Flat, is not one to place maximum faith in but was not disgraced on this hurdle debut and is entitled to be better for this experience. *(op 14-1)*

Always Flying(USA) was not at his best but did leave the impression that this trip on a track such as Catterick or Musselburgh would be much more to his liking. While only modest, he looks capable of winning a small race. *(op 15-2 tchd 8-1)*
Free Will, with the cheekpieces on again, failed to build on his recent run after a lengthy break at this much stiffer track. He may not be one for maximum faith. *(tchd 10-1)*
Two Steps To Go(USA) is not very consistent and, although having a bit to find on these terms, was again some way below his best.
Staff Nurse(IRE) *Official explanation: jockey said mare pulled up lame (op 6-1 tchd 13-2)*
Western Bluebird(IRE) *Official explanation: jockey said gelding pulled up lame (op 66-1)*
Obay *Official explanation: jockey said gelding was never travelling (op 66-1)*

1589 YOUNGS CHARTERED SURVEYORS H'CAP CHASE (19 fncs) 3m 1f
3:05 (3:06) (Class 4) (0-100,95) 5-Y-0+ **£3,304** (£944; £472)

Form					RPR
3342	**1**		**Tee-Jay (IRE)**[31] 1378 9-10-11 **79**	GLee	97+
			(M D Hammond) *hld up in tch: hdwy 1/2-way: led 2 out: drvn clr* **7/2**[1]		
R-26	**2**	*2 ½*	**Starbuck**[98] 827 11-10-2 **75**	DMcGann[(5)]	83
			(A M Crow) *cl up: led 14th to 2 out: kpt on fr last: no ch w wnr* **11/1**		
5/-2	**3**	*7*	**Aston (USA)**[7] 1539 5-11-5 **95**	(p) PCO'Neill[(5)]	93
			(R C Guest) *hld up: nt fluent 14th: outpcd 3 out: kpt on fr last: no imp* **4/1**[2]		
1	**4**	*1 ¼*	**Innisfree (IRE)**[21] 1451 7-11-12 **94**	(tp) RJohnson	95+
			(John G Carr, Ire) *mstkes: prom tl drvn and outpcd between last two* **7/2**[1]		
0-P4	**5**	*4*	**Middleway**[125] 554 9-9-7 **68** oh4	MJMcAlister[(7)]	64
			(Miss Kate Milligan) *led to 10th: cl up tl rdn and outpcd fr 3 out* **16/1**		
6156	**6**	*1 ¾*	**Toad Hall**[3] 1570 11-10-5 **78** ow2	DFlavin[(5)]	73+
			(Mrs L B Normile) *cl up: led 10th to 14th: rallied: no ex whn hit last* **12/1**		
2105	**7**	*¾*	**Swallow Magic (IRE)**[31] 1376 7-11-0 **85**	KJMercer[(3)]	78
			(Ferdy Murphy) *hld up: sme hdwy bef 3 out: sn rdn and no imp fr next* **9/2**[3]		
5-14	**8**	*3 ½*	**Ta Ta For Now**[9] 1511 8-11-7 **89**	MBradburne	79
			(Mrs S C Bradburne) *chsd ldrs to 1/2-way: sn lost pl: n.d after* **9/1**		
60P0	**9**	*dist*	**Northern Echo**[31] 1376 8-10-1 **76** ow6	(p) GThomas[(7)]	—
			(K S Thomas) *prom tl lost pl after 13th: sn struggling* **100/1**		

6m 14.0s (-17.90) **Going Correction** -0.675s/f (Firm)
WFA 5 from 7yo+ 3lb **9** Ran SP% **115.5**
Speed ratings: **101,100,97,97,96 95,95,94,—** CSF £40.37 CT £160.30 TOTE £3.90: £1.70, £4.00, £1.20; EX 27.10.
Owner T J Equestrian Ltd **Bred** James Rabbitte **Trained** Middleham, N Yorks

FOCUS
A run-of-the-mill handicap in which the pace was sound. The form is fairly solid for the level, with the winner rated value for around 9l.

NOTEBOOK
Tee-Jay(IRE) is rarely one for maximum faith but he seems to go well at this course and appreciated the decent gallop before winning with more in hand than the margin suggests. This was his first win over fences and he may be capable of better at a modest level. *(op 5-2)*
Starbuck had conditions to suit and ran well on this first run for just over three months. He looks sure to pick up a similar event in the coming months providing he gets his ground. *(op 10-1)*
Aston(USA) ◆, back over fences, again showed enough for his current stable to suggest there are races to be won either over hurdles or in this sphere. *(op 5-1)*
Innisfree(IRE), who beat today's winner at Sedgefield over three miles and three furlongs last month, was again below his best and, on this evidence, there is still room for improvement in the jumping department. *(op 9-2)*
Middleway was not totally disgraced on this first start since May but his record of inconsistency means he remains one to tread carefully with. *(op 20-1)*
Toad Hall, who has won over three miles and on fast ground, was not totally disgraced but, given *his lack of consistency, is not the best betting proposition around.Official explanation: vet said gelding was lame (op 14-1)*

1590 TARMAC NORTHERN MARES' ONLY NOVICES' HURDLE (10 hdls) 2m 4f 110y
3:40 (3:42) (Class 4) 4-Y-0+ **£3,479** (£994; £497)

Form					RPR
0-11	**1**		**Ostfanni (IRE)**[19] 1356 5-11-10 103	GLee	112+
			(M Todhunter) *keen: cl up: led after 6th: styd on strly to go clr after 2 out: eased nr fin* **4/6**[1]		
1325	**2**	*6*	**Reem Two**[21] 1443 4-10-11 100	StephenJCraine[(5)]	92
			(D McCain) *led to after 6th: cl up tl no ex between last two* **10/3**[2]		
S404	**3**	*11*	**Oscar's Lady (IRE)**[34] 1340 4-10-9	JimCrowley	74
			(G A Swinbank) *hld up: outpcd 4 out: kpt on fr 2 out: no ch w first two* **6/1**[3]		
	4	*7*	**Entre Amis** 5-10-10	FKeniry	68
			(G M Moore) *prom tl rdn and outpcd after 3 out* **25/1**		
0-2U	**5**	*nk*	**Cadeaux Rouge (IRE)**[9] 1510 4-10-6 78	(t) KJMercer[(3)]	67
			(D W Thompson) *hld up tch: outpcd 4 out: rallied appr 2 out: btn last* **12/1**		
	6	*dist*	**Solway Cloud** 5-10-3	MJMcAlister[(7)]	—
			(B Storey) *prom to 6th: wknd next* **50/1**		
/000	**7**	*20*	**Terimons Daughter**[111] 719 6-10-10	NPMulholland	—
			(E W Tuer) *keen: chsd ldrs tl wknd after 3 out* **150/1**		

5m 14.4s (4.80) **Going Correction** -0.175s/f (Good)
WFA 4 from 5yo+ 15lb **7** Ran SP% **111.5**
Speed ratings: **83,80,76,73,73 —,—** CSF £3.07 TOTE £1.70: £1.10, £1.70; EX 3.30.
Owner Ian Hall Racing **Bred** Mrs Brigitte Schlueter **Trained** Orton, Cumbria

FOCUS
A slow gallop resulted in a very slow winning time for the class. The winner was value for around 12l and the form looks pretty sound.

NOTEBOOK
Ostfanni(IRE) ◆ is in tremendous form over hurdles and turned in her best effort yet to win this uncompetitive event. She should have no problems staying three miles and will be of interest in ordinary handicap company. *(tchd 5-6)*
Reem Two looked the main danger in this uncompetitive event but, although not disgraced, was flattered to finish as close as she did to the easy winner. She is likely to remain vulnerable to progressive sorts in this grade. *(op 7-2 tchd 4-1)*
Oscar's Lady(IRE) has only reached a modest level over hurdles to date but left the impression that the step up to three miles and the switch into handicap company in due course will be to her advantage. *(op 13-2 tchd 5-1)*
Entre Amis looks flattered by her proximity on this debut and she was quickly left behind when the pace increased on the run to the penultimate flight. She is likely to remain vulnerable in this type of event. *(op 16-1)*
Cadeaux Rouge(IRE) looked to have a stiff task on these terms and was well beaten over this *longer trip. Modest handicaps at around two miles may provide the best chance of success. (op 16-1)*
Solway Cloud offered no immediate promise on this racecourse debut. *(tchd 40-1)*

1591 SIS NOVICES' HURDLE (8 hdls) 2m 110y
4:15 (4:15) (Class 4) 4-Y-0+ **£3,507** (£1,002; £501)

Form					RPR
36-1	**1**		**Crathorne (IRE)**[59] 991 5-11-5 108	ADobbin	100+
			(M Todhunter) *mde all: rdn and r.o strly fr 2 out* **6/4**[1]		
0224	**2**	*2 ½*	**Skiddaw Jones**[8] 1530 5-10-9 92	(t) PWhelan[(3)]	86
			(M A Barnes) *in tch: effrt bef 2 out: chsd wnr between last two: kpt on run in* **9/1**[3]		
1	**3**	*shd*	**High Country (IRE)**[31] 1374 5-11-5	GLee	93
			(M D Hammond) *chsd ldrs: effrt and rdn after 3 out: kpt on u.p fr last* **7/4**[2]		
-P04	**4**	*2 ½*	**Beaver (AUS)**[53] 1182 6-10-12 100	(t) HOliver	84+
			(R C Guest) *prom: outpcd 3 out: rallied bef last: kpt on: no imp* **9/1**[3]		
50-0	**5**	*4*	**Mr Twins (ARG)**[32] 1360 4-10-5 86	(t) BenOrde-Powlett[(7)]	79
			(M A Barnes) *cl up tl rdn and outpcd after 2 out* **50/1**		
6/	**6**	*hd*	**Loner**[423] 1934 7-10-12	DO'Meara	79
			(W S Coltherd) *bhd: outpcd 3 out: n.d after* **100/1**		
0-33	**7**	*8*	**Pearson Glen (IRE)**[128] 495 6-10-12 100	JimCrowley	71
			(James Moffatt) *hld up: sme hdwy after 3 out: no imp fr next* **9/1**[3]		
4-	**8**	*25*	**Timbuktu**[209] 4180 4-10-12	BHarding	46
			(B Storey) *prom: outpcd after 3 out: btn next* **20/1**		
6-	**9**	*16*	**Ontario Sunset**[160] 4981 4-10-7	DCCostello[(5)]	30
			(G M Moore) *j.rt: rdr lost iron first: prom tl wknd fr 4 out* **40/1**		

4m 8.60s (-6.60) **Going Correction** -0.175s/f (Good)
WFA 4 from 5yo+ 14lb **9** Ran SP% **116.5**
Speed ratings: **108,106,106,105,103 103,99,88,80** CSF £15.52 TOTE £2.30: £1.10, £2.40, £1.80; EX 15.60.
Owner FF Racing Services Partnership XVII **Bred** Shirley Blue Syndicate **Trained** Orton, Cumbria

FOCUS
Another uncompetitive event in which the gallop was only fair. The winner was rated value for further and the second, third and fifth all ran close to their marks.

NOTEBOOK
Crathorne(IRE) ◆ is at the top of his game at present and was a decisive winner of this uncompetitive event. He should prove equally effective over two and a half miles and may be capable of better in ordinary company. *(op 7-4 tchd 2-1)*
Skiddaw Jones ran creditably in the face of a stiffish task but left the impression that the step back into ordinary handicap company would offer his best chance of success. *(op 17-2 tchd 10-1)*
High Country(IRE), the easy winner of an ordinary event over two miles and five furlongs on his hurdle debut last month, was found out over this shorter trip but is worth another chance in this company when returned to further. *(op 2-1 tchd 13-8)*
Beaver(AUS) was not disgraced and, although he may not be entirely straightforward, looks capable of notching a small event in handicap company in due course. On this evidence, he looks worth a try over further. *(op 11-1 tchd 8-1)*
Mr Twins(ARG), tried in a tongue-tie, had a stiff task at the weights and looks flattered by his proximity in a race run at just an ordinary gallop.
Loner, returning after a lengthy break, did not do anywhere near enough to suggest he is of any interest in the short term. *(op 80-1)*

1592 ALAN MERRIGAN H'CAP CHASE (12 fncs) 2m 110y
4:50 (4:52) (Class 4) (0-100,98) 5-Y-0+ **£3,304** (£944; £472)

Form					RPR
2F/0	**1**		**Loy's Lad (IRE)**[92] 873 9-11-12 **98**	SStronge	105
			(Miss V Scott) *prom: rdn 3 out: rallied to ld last: kpt on u.p* **25/1**		
1330	**2**	*1 ¼*	**Risky Way**[8] 1529 9-11-4 **90**	GLee	96
			(W S Coltherd) *led: rdn 2 out: hdd last: rallied: hld towards fin* **4/1**[1]		
52-5	**3**	*1*	**Bob's Buster**[117] 644 9-11-7 **93**	KJohnson	98
			(R Johnson) *hld up: hdwy bef 3 out: rdn after next: kpt on fr last* **12/1**		
F543	**4**	*nk*	**Lascar De Ferbet (FR)**[23] 1433 6-11-2 **88**	JMMaguire	92
			(R Ford) *hld up: hdwy 8th: chsd ldr 2 out to bef last: one pce run in* **9/2**[2]		
0004	**5**	*7*	**He's Hot Right Now (NZ)**[23] 1433 6-10-11 **83**	(bt[1]) HOliver	81+
			(R C Guest) *cl up tl outpcd after 2 out* **13/2**		
3/	**6**	*13*	**Moss Bawn (IRE)**[239] 3673 9-11-3 **89**	ADobbin	73
			(B Storey) *cl up tl outpcd 3 out: n.d after* **6/1**		
4515	**7**	*½*	**Loulou Nivernais (FR)**[8] 1529 6-11-1 **87**	ADempsey	71
			(M Todhunter) *hld up: drvn bef 3 out: n.d* **5/1**[3]		
P05P	**8**	*23*	**Ratty's Band**[23] 1433 11-10-0 **72** oh3	NPMulholland	33
			(Mrs L B Normile) *prom: hit 8th: blnd next: sn btn* **28/1**		
/6P5	**U**		**Dottie Digger (IRE)**[9] 1509 6-9-11 **72** oh9	(v) PBuchanan[(3)]	—
			(Miss Lucinda V Russell) *cl up whn pckd and uns rdr after 1st* **33/1**		
-PP4	**P**		**Partners Choice (IRE)**[31] 1376 8-10-0 **72** oh2	(t) JamesDavies	—
			(John G Carr, Ire) *hld up in tch: rdn and wknd fr 7th: p.u bef 3 out* **11/2**		

4m 5.70s (-21.90) **Going Correction** -0.175s/f (Good) **10** Ran SP% **115.8**
Speed ratings: **101,100,99,99,96 90,90,79,—,—** CSF £123.13 CT £1290.30 TOTE £30.60: £6.10, £2.00, £3.30; EX 231.70.
Owner Miss Victoria Scott Jnr **Bred** J And Mrs Liggett **Trained** Elsdon, Northumberland

FOCUS
A run-of-the-mill handicap but they went a decent gallop and the form looks pretty solid at this level.

NOTEBOOK
Loy's Lad(IRE) ◆, a three-mile winner at this course, proved suited by the decent gallop back over this trip and did enough when stamina came into play to win a modest event. He should not be up too much for this win and may be capable of better. *(op 16-1)*
Risky Way had the run of the race and ran creditably. He seems much more consistent these days, knows how to win and, on this evidence, may be able to pick up another modest event before the year is out. *(op 9-2)*
Bob's Buster was without the headgear. He is not very reliable and has not won for some time, but had the race run to suit and showed he retains enough ability to win a similar event in the near future when things fall for him. *(op 10-1)*
Lascar De Ferbet(FR) is proving a consistent sort over fences and, although yet to win a race, looks worth a try over further than this trip. *(tchd 5-1)*
He's Hot Right Now(NZ) failed to improve for the fitting of first-time blinkers and has yet to reach the level of form he showed over hurdles in May. *(op 7-1 tchd 8-1, 6-1 in a place)*
Moss Bawn(IRE), having his first start for his new stable and dropped back in trip, shaped as though this first run since February was needed and he is not one to write off just yet. *(tchd 13-2)*
Partners Choice(IRE) *Official explanation: jockey said gelding lost its action (op 13-2)*

1593 METRO CENTRE INTERMEDIATE NATIONAL HUNT FLAT RACE 2m 110y
5:20 (5:20) (Class 6) 4-6-Y-0 **£1,911** (£546; £273)

Form					RPR
5	**1**		**Rising Tempest**[44] 1237 4-10-1	ARAdams[(10)]	87+
			(Mrs S J Smith) *prom: hdwy to ld over 2f out: edgd lft ins fnl f: styd on wl* **7/2**[2]		
42-	**2**	*3*	**Amalfi Storm**[180] 4720 4-10-8	MrTGreenall[(3)]	84+
			(M W Easterby) *cl up: ev ch tl outpcd over 2f out: rallied over 1f out: kpt on: nt rch wnr* **4/5**[1]		

3 ½ **Topwell** 4-10-13 ... PCO'Neill(5) 87
(R C Guest) *hld up: shkn up and hdwy over 2f out: effrt and rdn over 1f out: no ex ins fnl f* **8/1**[3]
4 3 **Stoneferry** 5-10-11 ... MrTCollier(7) 84
(R Johnson) *hld up in tch: hdwy and ev ch over 2f out: hung lft and outpcd ins fnl f* **25/1**
050- 5 6 **Now Then Auntie (IRE)**[237] [3710] 4-10-8 ... KJMercer(3) 71
(Mrs S A Watt) *cl up: led over 6f out to over 2f out: wknd over 1f out* **14/1**
6 1 ¼ **Laertes** 4-10-8 ... MrBenHamilton(10) 77
(C Grant) *hld up: outpcd over 4f out: n.d after* **25/1**
00- 7 1 ½ **Rosedale Gardens**[317] [2271] 5-10-11 ... MissJCoward(7) 75
(M W Easterby) *led to over 6f out: wknd over 3f out* **25/1**
8 19 **Whitsun** 5-10-11 ... MissAArmitage(7) 56
(Miss Kate Milligan) *hld up: hdwy to chal over 6f out: wknd over 3f out* **20/1**
9 dist **Thegirlfromclapham (IRE)** 5-10-6 ... WKennedy(5) —
(D Carroll) *bhd: struggling over 6f out: t.o* **9/1**

4m 10.7s (-2.00) **Going Correction** -0.175s/f (Good) **9** Ran SP% **121.9**
Speed ratings: **97,95,95,93,91 90,89,80,—** CSF £6.72 TOTE £4.90: £1.30, £1.10, £2.30; EX 12.40 Place 6 £16.68, Place 5 £10.40.
Owner ownaracehorse.co.uk (Panama) **Bred** D A Wales **Trained** High Eldwick, W Yorks
■ A first winner on his third ride for Andrew Adams.

FOCUS
An ordinary gallop to what looks almost certainly an ordinary event. The first two are better than the bare result.

NOTEBOOK
Rising Tempest is not very big but showed improved form to win a modest event on only her second start. Two and a half miles plus is going to suit her when sent over obstacles and she may be capable of winning a race in that sphere. *(tchd 4-1)*
Amalfi Storm was well supported on this first start for six months and, although finding one too good again, looks a good guide to the worth of this form. She is sure to be placed to best advantage over obstacles in due course. *(op 11-8 tchd 6-4 in a place)*
Topwell ◆, related to a couple of Flat winners, showed more than enough having been set a bit to do in a steadily-run race on this racecourse debut to suggest he is capable of winning a similar event. *(op 11-2)*
Stoneferry, related to a couple of bumper winners, was easy to back but showed ability, despite hanging, on this racecourse debut. He is entitled to improve for this experience. *(op 20-1)*
Now Then Auntie(IRE) had the run of the race and was not totally disgraced but her proximity confirms this form is nothing special. *(op 12-1)*
Laertes is likely to need time and a distance of ground before he is seen to best advantage.
T/Plt: £15.20 to a £1 stake. Pool: £40,194.15. 1,927.25 winning tickets. T/Qpdt: £7.60 to a £1 stake. Pool: £3,312.80. 322.30 winning tickets. RY

1519 FONTWELL (L-H)
Saturday, October 1

OFFICIAL GOING: Good
Wind: Moderate, across

1594 DENMANS GARDEN JUVENILE MAIDEN HURDLE (9 hdls) 2m 2f 110y
2:00 (2:00) (Class 4) 3-Y-0 **£2,583** (£738; £369)

Form RPR
43 1 **Trigger Guard**[9] [1519] 3-10-12 ... (b[1]) PHide 88+
(G L Moore) *in tch: rdn to ld appr 2 out: clr last: rdn out* **4/1**[2]
2 2 ½ **Looking Great (USA)**[75] 3-10-12 ... ATinkler 83
(R F Johnson Houghton) *hld up towards rr: hdwy after 6th: nt clr run after 3 out: styd on to go 2nd after last* **33/1**
0 3 ¾ **Palace Walk (FR)**[9] [1519] 3-10-12 ... TJMurphy 82
(B G Powell) *mid div: swtchd to outer and niggled along appr 3 out: rdn after 2 out: styd on* **16/1**
R05 4 1 ¾ **Josear**[9] [1519] 3-10-12 ... MBradburne 80
(C J Down) *mid div: hdwy after 3 out to chse ldr: sn rdn: kpt on same pce* **100/1**
4 5 3 **Just Beware**[6] [1563] 3-9-12 ... (p) RLucey-Butler(7) 70
(Miss Z C Davison) *hld up towards rr: stdy hdwy after 3 out: rdn after next: kpt on same pce* **14/1**
6 2 ½ **Carraig (IRE)**[32] 3-10-5 ... ChristianWilliams 68
(Evan Williams) *hld up towards rr: styd on fr 2 out: nvr trbld ldrs* **33/1**
63 7 4 **Royal Wedding**[13] [1478] 3-10-12 ... (t) LAspell 71
(N J Gifford) *mid div: blnd 3rd: hdwy to ld after 3 out: hdd next: sn wknd* **11/4**[1]
4 8 ½ **Piran (IRE)**[13] [1478] 3-10-12 ... (b[1]) AThornton 71+
(R H Alner) *in tch: hdwy after 6th to chse ldrs: rdn and pckd 2 out: one pced run-in* **7/1**
3 9 15 **Naval Force**[22] [1441] 3-10-12 ... (p) DRDennis 55
(Ian Williams) *trckd ldrs: jnd ldr 6th: rdn and wknd after 3 out* **10/1**
10 10 **Jamaaron**[114] 3-10-12 ... PJBrennan 45
(W G M Turner) *trckd ldrs: mstke 6th: ev ch 3 out: sn rdn and btn* **16/1**
U 11 dist **Bainoona**[6] [1563] 3-10-5 ... PMoloney —
(Evan Williams) *a towards rr* **66/1**
12 3 ½ **Cross My Shadow (IRE)**[12] 3-10-5 ... (t) CPoste(7) —
(M F Harris) *prom tl 6th: sn wknd* **20/1**
F 13 1 ¾ **Obstreperous Way**[41] [1268] 3-10-12 ... JAMcCarthy —
(P R Chamings) *towards rr: mstke 2nd and rdr lost iron: sn t.o* **66/1**
P **Goose Chase**[89] 3-10-12 ... NFehily —
(C J Mann) *led tl 3 out: wknd qckly and p.u bef next* **11/2**[3]
U P **Mount Arafat**[31] [1380] 3-10-12 ... (t) WHutchinson —
(M Salaman) *towards rr: rn wd on bnd appr 6th: sn bhd: t.o and p.u bef 2 out* **100/1**

4m 38.5s (2.50) **Going Correction** -0.10s/f (Good) **15** Ran SP% **117.7**
Speed ratings: **89,87,87,86,85 84,82,82,76,72 —,—,—,—,—** CSF £131.05 TOTE £4.90: £2.10, £5.90, £5.10; EX 203.10.
Owner The Harlequin Walk Partnership **Bred** Mrs R J Doorgachurn And C Stedman **Trained** Woodingdean, E Sussex

FOCUS
A weak juvenile hurdle race run in a moderate time, even for a race like this, slower than both the seller and bumper run over the same trip later on the card.

NOTEBOOK
Trigger Guard, blinkered for the first time, looked like winning by a decent margin after taking it up two out, but he was doing little on the run-in and may have been fortunate that none of his rivals was able to take advantage. He does not look at all straightforward. *(op 7-2 tchd 9-2 in places)*
Looking Great(USA), rated just 45 on the Flat, was tried over as far as 14 furlongs on the level and this performance was that of a stayer. He has already shown himself to be better over hurdles by finishing second here, but his proximity does little for the form.
Palace Walk(FR) ran better than on his hurdling debut here last month, but will need to improve again to find a race. *(tchd 20-1)*
Josear has shown nothing over hurdles so far, though he is a winner on the Flat, and almost certainly did not achieve much in reaching his final position. *(tchd 66-1)*
Just Beware never looked like winning and this effort rather suggests the Huntingdon race she had finished fourth in on her hurdling debut was very poor. *(tchd 12-1)*
Royal Wedding, with the tongue-tie applied, was in front turning for home but stopped as if finding this slightly longer trip too far. *(op 10-3)*

1595 FOCUS ON FLORA, CREATIVE FLORISTS BEGINNERS' CHASE (15 fncs) 2m 4f
2:35 (2:35) (Class 3) 5-Y-0+ **£5,317** (£1,636; £818; £409)

Form RPR
260/ 1 **Detonateur (FR)**[86] [1454] 7-11-0 ... DRDennis 111+
(Ian Williams) *hld up but in tch: hdwy after 9th: hit 11th: led next: in command whn mstke last: styd on wl* **9/2**
2P22 2 8 **Mylo**[8] [1540] 7-11-0 ... APMcCoy 104+
(Jonjo O'Neill) *rn in snatches: in tch: rdn appr 11th: lft 4th 4 out: styd on u.p to go 2nd 2 out: hld whn hit last* **11/4**[1]
025P 3 21 **Diamond Joshua (IRE)**[4] [1568] 7-10-11 107 ... (v) ONelmes(3) 82
(N B King) *mid div tl dropped rr 5th: bdly hmpd 12th: styd on to go distant 3rd run-in: nvr trbld ldrs* **20/1**
0-P0 4 3 ½ **Kaikovra (IRE)**[13] [1487] 9-11-0 97 ... BHitchcott 80+
(M F Harris) *led: nt fluent 7th: rdn and hdd 12th: wknd next* **25/1**
6006 5 23 **Stopwatch (IRE)**[9] [1524] 10-11-0 66 ... (p) LAspell 65+
(Mrs L C Jewell) *chsd ldr: rdn and lft 3rd 4 out: sn wknd* **50/1**
PPP5 F **Jivaty (FR)**[27] [1405] 8-11-0 93 ... PHide —
(Mrs A J Hamilton-Fairley) *chsd ldrs tl fell 9th* **16/1**
45-3 U **Vingis Park (IRE)**[151] [172] 7-11-0 ... (t) ATinkler —
(V R A Dartnall) *in tch: mstke 11th: blnd and uns rdr 12th* **10/3**[3]
03F- U **Balladeer (IRE)**[386] [1400] 7-11-0 ... TJMurphy —
(Miss H C Knight) *trckd ldrs: cl 3rd whn blnd and uns rdr 12th* **3/1**[2]
055- U **Minnie The Moocher**[162] [4964] 5-10-4 ... RYoung(3) —
(J W Mullins) *hld up towards rr: bdly hmpd and uns rdr 9th* **50/1**

5m 5.40s (-2.50) **Going Correction** -0.025s/f (Good) **9** Ran SP% **111.3**
Speed ratings: **104,100,92,91,81 —,—,—,—** CSF £16.59 TOTE £7.00: £2.10, £1.10, £2.90; EX 21.70.
Owner Ian Williams **Bred** Georges Halphen And Myriam Bollack-Badel **Trained** Portway, Worcs

FOCUS
Plenty of grief in this beginners' chase, but the pace looked decent enough. The winner has been rated to the level of his best hurdling form.

NOTEBOOK
Detonateur(FR), given a break since returning from a much longer layoff on the Flat in July, was making his chasing debut and landed his first race of any description. His jumping was not that convincing, especially down the final line of fences, but he never looked like being beaten and that aspect of his game should improve with experience. *(op 5-1)*
Mylo has plenty of experience of fences now, but he never looked happy at any stage and the Champion jockey did wonders to get him into any sort of contention. He has now finished runner-up in his last six completed starts and looks very much one to avoid. *(op 3-1 tchd 9-4 and 10-3 in places)*
Diamond Joshua(IRE), with the visor back on for the first time over fences, is not progressing over the larger obstacles and his final position owes much to the misfortune of others. *(op 16-1)*
Kaikovra(IRE) was given a positive ride as usual but he does not seem to be getting home over this trip over fences. *(op 16-1)*
Balladeer(IRE) was still in with every chance when hitting the top of the fourth last and losing his rider. He has the ability, but work is required on the jumping front. *(op 7-2 tchd 9-2)*
Vingis Park(IRE) was not completely out of it when appearing to swerve to avoid the stricken Balladeer after jumping the fourth last and sending his rider out the side door. *(op 7-2 tchd 9-2)*

1596 SYLVIA STALL BIRTHDAY NOVICES' HURDLE (10 hdls) 2m 4f
3:10 (3:10) (Class 4) 4-Y-0+ **£3,500** (£1,000; £500)

Form RPR
5 1 **Flotta**[15] [1245] 6-10-12 ... TJMurphy 125+
(B G Powell) *racd wd: a.p: led 4th: mde rest: drew clr after 3 out: v easily* **3/1**[2]
1 2 14 **Almizan (IRE)**[34] [1245] 5-11-5 ... JEMoore 114+
(G L Moore) *hld up towards rr: hdwy after 6th: rdn to chse wnr after 3 out : no ch w wnr fr next: blnd last* **2/1**[1]
2-23 3 6 **Cansalrun (IRE)**[13] [1491] 6-10-5 102 ... RWalford 91
(R H Alner) *led tl 4th: chsd wnr: rdn after 7th: one pced* **5/1**[3]
2P42 4 2 ½ **Kristoffersen**[8] [1538] 5-11-2 109 ... DJBoland(10) 109
(Ian Williams) *chsd ldrs: rdn after 7th: one pced fr next: hung lft run-in* **11/2**
3-03 5 13 **Corrib Drift (USA)**[27] [1407] 5-10-9 ... CBolger(3) 85+
(Jamie Poulton) *mid div: hdwy after 6th: rdn after next: sn wknd* **16/1**
04-0 6 13 **He's The Gaffer (IRE)**[148] [201] 5-10-12 ... BHitchcott 69
(R H Buckler) *mid div: rdn after 7th: sn wknd* **50/1**
6-51 7 dist **It's My Party**[57] [235] 4-10-12 ... PJBrennan —
(W G M Turner) *mid div: rdn after 6th: bhd fr next: t.o* **12/1**
8 20 **Lyes Green**[325] 4-10-12 ... LAspell —
(O Sherwood) *hld up towards rr: making hdwy whn virtually fell 7th: nt rcvr* **40/1**
400- 9 29 **Westcraft (IRE)**[166] [4916] 5-10-12 ... ChristianWilliams —
(A Ennis) *mid div tl 6th: sn t.o* **25/1**
43-2 P **Maarees**[57] [235] 4-9-12 ... JPemberton(7) —
(G P Enright) *sn struggling in rr: t.o fr 4th: p.u after 6th* **40/1**
34-0 P **Code (IRE)**[120] [242] 4-10-5 ... RLucey-Butler(7) —
(Miss Z C Davison) *mid div tl 6th: sn bhd: t.o and p.u after 2 out* **100/1**

4m 51.8s (-12.00) **Going Correction** -0.10s/f (Good)
WFA 4 from 5yo+ 14lb **11** Ran SP% **115.6**
Speed ratings: **103,97,95,94,88 83,—,—,—,— —** CSF £9.20 TOTE £4.00: £2.00, £1.60, £1.70; EX 11.70.
Owner G Hatchard,R Gunn,L Gilbert & R Williams **Bred** W G R Wightman **Trained** Morestead, Hants

FOCUS
An ordinary novice hurdle, but the winner scored with a ton in hand and could be useful. He has been rated as value for an 18-length success.

NOTEBOOK
Flotta, who showed some aptitude for this game on his hurdling debut here back in August, was kept noticeably wide the whole way, presumably in search of better ground. He was always travelling supremely well and could have won by double the winning margin had his rider so wished. Provided the problems that afflicted him on his debut do not reoccur, there should be more to come from him over timber. *(tchd 7-2 and 4-1 in a place)*
Almizan(IRE) had Flotta almost 16 lengths behind him when winning on his hurdling debut here back in August, but that was probably misleading in view of the problems his opponent had. He was sent in pursuit of his old rival jumping the last on the far side, but was never travelling as well and he was very tired when completely flattening the last. *(op 9-4)*

Cansalrun(IRE) has plenty of experience of hurdling, but she lacks pace and was comfortably seen off over the last half-mile. This was her sixth consecutive placing, but she is not progressing and will do well to win a race in the near future. *(op 4-1)*
Kristoffersen was easily disposed of late on and his double penalty for his two victories early in the summer continue to prove too much of a burden. *(tchd 5-1)*
Corrib Drift(USA) did not seem to appreciate stepping up in trip again.
Lyes Green, making his hurdling debut and racing for the first time in 11 months, was just beginning to creep closer when appearing to overjump at the fourth last and ending up sprawled on his belly. It was too early to say how he would have fared, but as he only raced three times on the Flat he remains relatively unexposed. *(op 25-1)*
Westcraft(IRE) *Official explanation: trainer said gelding was unsuited by good going (tchd 33-1)*
Code(IRE) *Official explanation: jockey said gelding had breathing problem*

1597 RICHARD DUNWOODY THERACINGSITE.CO.UK CONDITIONAL JOCKEYS' (S) H'CAP HURDLE (9 hdls) 2m 2f 110y

3:45 (3:45) (Class 5) (0-85,91) 4-Y-0+ **£2,394** (£684; £342)

Form | | | | RPR
P504 **1** **Distant Romance**[9] 1520 8-10-9 **71** ... RLucey-Butler[(3)] 72
(Miss Z C Davison) *hld up bhd: styd on fr 3 out: led last: drvn out* **25/1**
-P0P **2** *1 3/4* **Isam Top (FR)**[129] 502 9-11-1 **74** ... DLaverty 73
(M J Hogan) *chsd ldrs: j.rt 5th: rdn after 3 out: ev ch last: no ex* **22/1**
04F- **3** *1/2* **Dontnock'Er (IRE)**[187] 4617 7-9-9 **64** ... PDavey[(10)] 63
(R H Buckler) *mid div: tk clsr order 3rd: rdn after 3 out: ev ch last: kpt on same pce* **8/1**
0P60 **4** *6* **Spectacular Hope**[45] 1233 5-10-12 **79** ... (v[1]) WPKavanagh[(8)] 74+
(J W Mullins) *hld up: hdwy 5th: led next: rdn after 2 out: hdd last: one pced* **6/1**[3]
P002 **5** *14* **Gray Knight (IRE)**[9] 1520 8-10-12 **76** ... (b) TMessenger[(5)] 55
(Mrs T J Hill) *mid div tl dropped rr after 5th: sn rdn: nt a danger after* **7/2**[2]
-631 **6** *shd* **Sheer Guts (IRE)**[9] 1520 6-12-4 **91** ... (vt) PCO'Neill 70
(Evan Williams) *hld up: rdn and short lived effrt after 3 out: wknd next* **3/1**[1]
00U5 **7** *dist* **Hidden Smile (USA)**[13] 1483 8-10-9 **71** ... (t) JDiment[(3)] —
(F Jordan) *led tl 5th: sn wknd* **8/1**
P003 **8** *1/2* **Oh Sunny Boy (IRE)**[9] 1520 4-10-13 **72** ... (b[1]) TJMalone —
(B G Powell) *chsd ldrs: rdn after 3 out: wknd qckly* **7/2**[2]

4m 37.6s (1.60) **Going Correction** -0.10s/f (Good)
WFA 4 from 5yo+ 13lb **8** Ran SP% **114.1**
Speed ratings: **91,90,90,87,81 81,—,—** CSF £405.18 CT £4719.29 TOTE £25.70: £3.50, £4.30, £2.40; EX 1607.50.The winner was bought in for 6,400gns. Sheer Guts was claimed by Naughty Diesel Ltd for £6,000
Owner A A Goldson **Bred** Mrs J E McGetrick **Trained** Hammerwood, E Sussex

FOCUS
A low-grade selling hurdle run in a modest time, even for a seller, and the run from the second-last flight to the winning post seemed to be in slow motion.

NOTEBOOK
Distant Romance, who finished fourth behind Sheer Guts, Gray Knight and Oh Sunny Boy in a similar contest here last month, turned the form completely on its head. Given a patient ride, she picked up the flagging leaders between the last two flights and even though she was travelling very slowly on the run-in, she was at least decelerating at a lesser rate than her rivals. She will do very well to add to this. *(op 12-1)*
Isam Top(FR), off since May, was never far away and had every chance but had nothing left on the run-in. His only previous win in August 2002 came here, but he has been running particularly poorly this year. *(op 16-1 tchd 25-1 in places)*
Dontnock'Er(IRE), returning from a seven-month break, did not achieve much in finishing third and was presumably using this as a pipe-opener before returning to fences. *(op 11-1)*
Spectacular Hope, visored for the first time, does not seem to stay much beyond two miles. *(op 10-1)*
Gray Knight(IRE) was disappointing with no obvious excuses. *(tchd 4-1)*
Sheer Guts(IRE), who had three of these behind him when winning here last month, not for the first time seemed to stop very quickly. *(op 5-2)*

1598 HARBEN'S EQUINE CARE CENTRE SALMON SPRAY H'CAP HURDLE (9 hdls) 2m 2f 110y

4:20 (4:20) (Class 3) (0-135,127) 4-Y-0+
£9,030 (£3,425; £1,712; £778; £389; £233)

Form | | | | RPR
061- **1** **Fait Le Jojo (FR)**[48] 8-11-7 **127** ... HEphgrave[(5)] 134+
(L Corcoran) *chsd ldrs: led after 5th: rdn and hdd appr last: lft clr last: rdn out* **33/1**
2211 **2** *5* **Screenplay**[13] 1481 4-10-12 **113** ... JGoldstein 113
(Miss Sheena West) *chsd ldrs: hit 3 out: sn rdn to press ldrs: kpt on same pce: lft 2nd last* **3/1**[1]
002- **3** *dist* **Nathos (GER)**[185] 4666 8-11-4 **119** ... NFehily 87
(C J Mann) *in tch tl 5th: sn rdn: lft 4th and sltly hmpd on bnd after 3 out: no further imp: lft 3rd last* **11/2**[3]
3-00 **4** *1* **Keepthedreamalive**[155] 116 7-11-8 **123** ... BHitchcott 90
(R H Buckler) *chsd ldrs tl 5th: sn bhd: lft 4th at the last* **16/1**
032- **5** *11* **Forever Dream**[191] 4535 7-11-4 **119** ... RJohnson 75
(P J Hobbs) *hld up towards rr: hdwy after 6th: wknd after 3 out* **8/1**
-226 **6** *15* **Salute (IRE)**[22] 1444 6-10-13 **114** ... LAspell 55
(P G Murphy) *hld up and a towards rr* **20/1**
/46- **P** **Fundamental**[307] 2516 6-11-12 **127** ... APMcCoy —
(W K Goldsworthy) *led tl 4th: sn bhd: p.u bef 6th* **8/1**
3-12 **P** **Maclean**[8] 726 4-10-9 **110** ... (p) JEMoore —
(G L Moore) *hld up: sme hdwy after 6th: hit next: sn wknd: p.u bef 2 out* **9/2**[2]
1511 **F** **Space Cowboy (IRE)**[41] 1272 5-10-7 **108** ... (b) PHide 116+
(G L Moore) *hld up in tch: trckd ldr after 3 out: slt advantage whn fell last: unlucky* **11/2**[3]
1P1- **P** **Gan Eagla (IRE)**[191] 4531 6-10-7 **108** ... (b) SThomas —
(Miss Venetia Williams) *prom: hit 3rd: led after 4th tl after next: sn bhd: p.u bef 2 out* **14/1**
U-P0 **S** **Private Benjamin**[13] 1481 5-10-0 **101** oh3 ... MBatchelor —
(Jamie Poulton) *mid div: hdwy after 6th: 4th and rdn whn stmbld and fell on bnd after 3 out* **66/1**

4m 28.1s (-7.90) **Going Correction** -0.10s/f (Good)
WFA 4 from 5yo+ 13lb **11** Ran SP% **117.9**
Speed ratings: **111,108,—,—,— —,—,—,—,— —** CSF £132.10 CT £656.10 TOTE £36.10: £5.60, £1.40, £1.90; EX 168.10.
Owner M Ephgrave **Bred** Marchant International Ltd **Trained** Kingsbridge, Devon
■ The first training success for former jockey Liam Corcoran.

FOCUS
A decent handicap in which the winner has been rated as having returned to the best of his 2003 chase form, and the unlucky Space Cowboy has been rated as value for a length success. A decent pace found out a few and resulted in a creditable winning time, by far the fastest race over the trip on the day.

NOTEBOOK
Fait Le Jojo(FR), a winner on his last start on the British mainland at Plumpton a year ago for Philip Hobbs, had landed the Jersey Champion Hurdle in the meantime. Another to benefit from racing wide, he was always up with the pace but looked to be getting the worst of the argument with Space Cowboy when gifted the race at the last. *(op 25-1)*
Screenplay, raised 6lb in his bid for a hat-trick, had every chance but would only have finished third had the leader not crashed out at the last. *(op 7-2)*
Nathos(GER) was beaten a long way despite finishing third, but would probably only have finished fifth had grief not befallen a couple of rivals during the last half-mile. *(op 10-1 tchd 11-1)*
Keepthedreamalive, who faced some very stiff tasks after winning his first two outings over hurdles last season, was entitled to need this following a six-month break but will need to improve to be competitive off this mark.
Forever Dream was returning from a seven-month break and ran as though needing it. *(op 9-1)*
Private Benjamin, comparatively lightly raced over hurdles, was in the process of running a decent race at a huge price when losing his footing on the home bend. *(tchd 5-1)*
Fundamental *Official explanation: jockey said gelding was never travelling (tchd 5-1)*
Maclean *Official explanation: jockey said gelding was never travelling (tchd 5-1)*
Space Cowboy(IRE), raised 6lb in his bid for a hat-trick, did everything right and it seemed a question of how far when he cruised to the front coming to the last. He seemed to jump the flight alright, but crumpled on landing and can be considered extremely unlucky. *(tchd 5-1)*

1599 S.D.S. GROUP CUP H'CAP CHASE (19 fncs) 3m 2f 110y

4:50 (4:50) (Class 3) (0-125,118) 5-Y-0+ **£6,147** (£2,313; £1,188; £575)

Form | | | | RPR
3/6- **1** **Snowy Ford (IRE)**[204] 4313 8-11-8 **114** ... LAspell 131
(N J Gifford) *hld up: tk clsr order after 13th: jnd ldr 15th: led after 4 out: rdn after 2 out: edgd rt cl home: styd on wl: rdn out* **12/1**
11-F **2** *1 1/4* **Tom Sayers (IRE)**[148] 205 7-11-5 **116** ... RStephens[(5)] 132
(P J Hobbs) *trckd ldr: led 13th tl after 4 out: rdn after 3 out: rallied and ev ch last: no ex* **13/8**[1]
PP-0 **3** *dist* **Prokofiev (USA)**[73] 1039 9-11-9 **115** ... (b) APMcCoy 95
(Jonjo O'Neill) *prom: rdn appr 14th: one pced fr next: wnt 3rd run-in* **11/2**[3]
0242 **4** *3* **Eau Pure (FR)**[9] 1524 8-10-0 **92** oh1 ... (p) JEMoore 69
(G L Moore) *hld up: hdwy appr 14th: wnt 3rd after next: sn rdn: one pced: lost 3rd run-in* **9/2**[2]
61-6 **P** **Twisted Logic (IRE)**[134] 439 12-11-12 **118** ... RWalford —
(R H Alner) *lost tch fr 9th: t.o and p.u bef 13th* **11/1**
P04- **P** **Rollo (IRE)**[185] 4655 7-10-3 **95** ... (v[1]) PJBrennan —
(M F Harris) *led tl pckd and hdd 13th: sn bhd: t.o and p.u bef 4 out* **6/1**
3-25 **P** **Monita Des Bois (FR)**[107] 765 5-11-5 **113** ... SThomas —
(Miss Venetia Williams) *chsd ldrs: nt fluent 8th: lost tch after 13th: t.o and p.u after 4 out* **12/1**

6m 56.8s (-4.30) **Going Correction** -0.025s/f (Good)
WFA 5 from 7yo+ 2lb **7** Ran SP% **109.7**
Speed ratings: **105,104,—,—,— —,—** CSF £30.85 TOTE £15.00: £4.20, £1.90; EX 35.60.
Owner R V Shaw **Bred** Thomas Hatton **Trained** Findon, W Sussex

FOCUS
An ordinary handicap chase that only concerned the front pair from a long way out. The winner was at least as good as this at his best over hurdles and the runner-up remains well handicapped.

NOTEBOOK
Snowy Ford(IRE) ◆, making his debut for the yard, had dropped to a very reasonable mark on the pick of his Irish form and he showed a good attitude at the end of what became a virtual match with the runner-up. Considering this was his first outing since March and his best form had been shown on much softer ground, this was a fair effort and there could be other opportunities for him. *(op 16-1)*
Tom Sayers(IRE), racing for the first time since May and off a 12lb higher mark than for his last win, did very little wrong and just bumped into a well-handicapped rival. He beat the others soundly enough and should be able to return to winning ways with this outing under his belt. *(op 11-8 and 7-4 in a place)*
Prokofiev(USA), pulled up in his last three outings over fences, was again not on a going day and achieved little in finishing a remote third. *(op 5-1)*
Eau Pure(FR), with the cheekpieces back on, had race fitness on her side but ran as though not staying this longer trip. *(op 5-1 tchd 11-2)*
Twisted Logic(IRE) *Official explanation: jockey said gelding was never travelling (op 10-1 tchd 9-1)*

1600 ALLSTAFF INTERMEDIATE OPEN NATIONAL HUNT FLAT RACE 2m 2f 110y

5:20 (5:21) (Class 6) 4-6-Y-0 **£1,869** (£534; £267)

Form | | | | RPR
40-2 **1** **Magical Legend**[20] 1459 4-10-4 ... MrTJO'Brien[(7)] 100+
(L Corcoran) *trckd ldrs: led 5f out: rdn over 1f out: edgd rt ins fnl f: styd on wl* **10/1**[3]
2 *9* **Castle Dargan (IRE)**[148] 6-11-4 ... RJohnson 98
(Mrs A M Thorpe) *in tch: hdwy 6f out: rdn to chse wnr over 1f out: kpt on but no ch w wnr* **25/1**
3 **3** *3* **Mr Ex (ARG)**[41] 1274 4-11-4 ... JEMoore 95
(G L Moore) *hld up: tk clsr order 8f out: rdn to chse ldrs 4f out: kpt on same pce* **4/1**[2]
42P- **4** *1 1/4* **Ballyhoo (IRE)**[254] 3445 5-10-11 ... AThornton 87
(J W Mullins) *hld up: hdwy over 4f out: rdn over 3f out: kpt on same pce* **10/1**[3]
5 *1/2* **Heynewboy** 5-10-11 ... MissRAGreen[(7)] 93
(J W Mullins) *hld up: stmbld on bnd over 7f out: hdwy over 4f out: rdn 3f out: kpt on same pce* **28/1**
2- **6** *16* **Money Line (IRE)**[304] 2576 6-11-4 ... APMcCoy 77
(Jonjo O'Neill) *prom: led 8f out: rdn and hdd 5f out: wknd over 2f out* **8/11**[1]
7 *20* **Rhapsody In Bloom** 4-10-11 ... MrJMorgan[(7)] 57
(L Wells) *in tch: hdwy 6f out: wknd over 3f out* **16/1**
44 **8** *dist* **Allez Melina**[145] 266 4-10-11 ... ATinkler —
(Mrs A J Hamilton-Fairley) *led tl 8f out: wknd 5f out* **20/1**

4m 37.3s (-2.00) **Going Correction** -0.10s/f (Good) **8** Ran SP% **114.0**
Speed ratings: **99,95,93,93,93 86,78,—** CSF £216.32 TOTE £13.50: £2.40, £5.40, £1.40; EX 136.40 Place 6 £371.73, Place 5 £70.07.
Owner R H Kerswell **Bred** R H And Mrs Kerswell **Trained** Kingsbridge, Devon

FOCUS
A moderate bumper and the form probably amounts to little. Even though the time was quicker than the juvenile maiden hurdle and the seller, it was substantially slower than the handicap.

NOTEBOOK
Magical Legend probably only had to repeat her Stratford effort to win this the way she did, but she will find things tough under a penalty and might be best going straight over hurdles. *(op 9-1)*

Castle Dargan(IRE), pulled up in three out of four Irish points in the spring, was comfortably beaten by the winner but he was conceding race fitness to the filly and shaped as though in need of a greater test of stamina. *(tchd 28-1)*
Mr Ex(ARG) was a bit disappointing and did not build on the promise of his Newton Abbot debut. *(op 9-2)*
Ballyhoo(IRE), not seen since pulling up in January, had previously shown some ability but the break did not result in a return to form. Perhaps the ground was too quick, but she still has questions to answer. *(op 8-1)*
Money Line(IRE) dropped away tamely over the last quarter-mile and was very disappointing in view of the promise of his Plumpton debut, even allowing for that being ten months ago and the *ground being much faster this time. Official explanation: trainer was unable to offer any explanation for poor form shown (op 4-6 tchd 4-5 and 5-6 in a place)*
Allez Melina *Official explanation: jockey said filly had breathing problem (op 16-1)*
T/Plt: £1,903.70 to a £1 stake. Pool: £37,161.50. 14.25 winning tickets. T/Qpdt: £699.90 to a £1 stake. Pool: £3,026.60. 3.20 winning tickets. TM

[418]KELSO (L-H)

Sunday, October 2

OFFICIAL GOING: Good to firm
Wind: Breezy, half against

1601 GG.COM JUVENILE NOVICES' HURDLE (8 hdls) 2m 110y

2:20 (2:20) (Class 3) 3-Y-O **£4,914** (£1,512; £756; £378)

Form RPR
P0 **1** **Kerry's Blade (IRE)**[17] 1397 3-10-10 FKeniry 94+
(P C Haslam) *prom: effrt and led last: hung lft: nrly uns rdr (lost irons) run in: rdn and hld on wl* **14/1**[3]
3 **2** *1 ¾* **Comical Errors (USA)**[11] 1512 3-10-3 MrTJO'Brien[(7)] 89
(P C Haslam) *trckd ldrs: led 4th to last: ev ch run in: kpt on: hld towards fin* **9/2**[2]
3 *3* **Desert Buzz (IRE)**[20] 3-10-7 PAspell[(3)] 87+
(J Hetherton) *midfield: effrt 3 out: kpt on fr last: no imp* **66/1**
4 *1 ¼* **Devils Delight (IRE)**[15] 3-10-3 NPMulholland 78
(C W Thornton) *hld up: effrt u.p bef 2 out: kpt on fr last: nvr rchd ldrs* **100/1**
2 **5** *2* **Jackadandy (USA)**[11] 1512 3-10-10 GLee 86+
(J Howard Johnson) *keen: cl up: led whn mstke and hdd 4th: cl up tl rdn and outpcd fr last* **4/7**[1]
0 **6** *5½* **Countrywide Sun**[11] 1512 3-10-3 EWhillans[(7)] 76
(A C Whillans) *in tch tl rdn and wknd fr 2 out: fin 7th, ½l & 5l: plcd 6th* **28/1**
40 **7** *½* **Azahara**[11] 1397 3-9-7 PKinsella[(10)] 68
(K G Reveley) *cl up: led 3rd to bef next: ev ch tl wknd bef last: fin 8th: plcd 7th* **14/1**[3]
05 **8** *3* **Kinfayre Boy**[7] 1338 3-10-10 JAMcCarthy 72
(K W Hogg) *led to 3rd: wknd next: n.d after: fin 9th: plcd 8th* **33/1**
9 *16* **Tudor Oak (IRE)**[16] 3-10-10 MBradburne 56
(Mark Campion) *hld up: effrt u.p bef 3 out: sn no imp: fin 10th: plcd 9th* **100/1**
0 **10** *7* **Madge**[36] 1338 3-10-3 ADobbin 44
(W Storey) *towards rr: drvn 1/2-way: nvr on terms: fin 11th: plcd 10th* **16/1**
11 *3 ½* **Dantor** 3-10-3 BenOrde-Powlett[(7)] 46
(M A Barnes) *a bhd: fin 12th: plcd 11th* **66/1**
12 *6* **Coola Tagula (IRE)**[121] 3-10-5 DCCostello[(5)] 40
(C W Thornton) *a bhd: struggling fr 1/2-way: fin 13th: plcd 12th* **100/1**
5 **D** **Emerald Destiny (IRE)**[8] 1551 3-10-10 ADempsey 81
(D Carroll) *in tch: effrt bef 2 out: hung lft and outpcd last: fin 6th, ½l: disq: lost weight cloth* **20/1**

3m 51.6s (-12.10) **Going Correction** -1.00s/f (Hard) **13** Ran SP% **118.2**
Speed ratings: **88,87,85,85,84 81,81,80,72,69 67,64,84** CSF £72.95 TOTE £18.90: £4.20, £2.00, £16.00; EX 48.10.
Owner G Chapman **Bred** D H W Dobson **Trained** Middleham, N Yorks

FOCUS
A low-grade event rated through the runner-up and, despite the quick ground, a very moderate winning time for the type of contest.

NOTEBOOK
Kerry's Blade(IRE), who seems suited by a sound surface, improved to win his first race and may be a bit better than the bare form given that he nearly unshipped his rider on the run-in. However, it was only a modest event and, given his previous inconsistency, he would be no good thing to follow up under a penalty.
Comical Errors(USA) ran to a similar level as on his hurdling debut at Perth recently and, although no good thing for a similar event next time, looks sure to pick up a small race in this sphere in due course. *(op 4-1 tchd 5-1 and 7-2 in a place)*
Desert Buzz(IRE), exposed as a poor and inconsistent Flat maiden, was not disgraced on this hurdling debut. He shaped as though a stiffer test would suit but his Flat record suggests he would not be one to lump on next time. *(op 40-1)*
Devils Delight(IRE), who showed precious little in three Flat starts, was another whose proximity on this hurdling debut casts a doubt over the worth of the form. A stiffer test may suit but she is likely to remain vulnerable in this grade.
Jackadandy(USA), in front of the runner up at Perth, was disappointing and again left the impression that this represented too much of a test of speed. There is room for improvement with his jumping but he does not look one for maximum faith. *(op 5-6 tchd 10-11 in places)*
Emerald Destiny(IRE), a poor and inconsistent Flat maiden, was not totally disgraced on only this second start over hurdles but faced inevitable disqualification after his rider weighed in light (lost weight cloth).

1602 DOUBLE FIVE BAR NOVICES' H'CAP CHASE (17 fncs) 2m 6f 110y

2:50 (2:50) (Class 4) (0-100,100) 5-Y-0+ **£4,225** (£1,300; £650; £325)

Form RPR
2-25 **1** **Snowy (IRE)**[127] 550 7-11-12 **100** GLee 111
(J I A Charlton) *chsd ldrs: effrt 2 out: led run in: styd on wl* **10/3**[2]
PP4P **2** *1 ¼* **Partners Choice (IRE)**[2] 1592 8-10-0 **74** oh4 (t) NPMulholland 85+
(John G Carr, Ire) *cl up: mstke 10th: led last to run in: kpt on same pce* **12/1**
0053 **3** *1* **Ideal Du Bois Beury (FR)**[34] 1359 9-10-2 **79** PAspell[(3)] 89+
(P Monteith) *hld up: blnd 5th: rdn 4 out: no imp tl styd on strly fr last: nt rch first two* **9/1**
U3-1 **4** *¾* **Red Flyer (IRE)**[33] 1376 6-11-4 **92** FKeniry 100
(P C Haslam) *in tch: effrt 3 out: kpt on fr last* **3/1**[1]
-414 **5** *4* **Goodbadindiferent (IRE)**[10] 1531 9-10-12 **86** BHarding 90
(Mrs J C McGregor) *cl up: led 9th to last: wknd run in* **8/1**
6623 **6** *3* **Jupiter Jo**[33] 1376 9-9-10 **77** ow2 BenOrde-Powlett[(7)] 78
(J B Walton) *hld up: hdwy 1/2-way: outpcd fr 4 out* **5/1**[3]
2460 **7** *¾* **York Rite (AUS)**[33] 1376 9-10-1 **75** (tp) KJohnson 77+
(R C Guest) *hld up: effrt u.p whn hit 3 out: sn no imp* **12/1**
0P46 **8** *12* **Northern Rambler (IRE)**[25] 1433 8-9-5 **75** oh8 ow1 (p) PKinsella[(10)] 65+
(K G Reveley) *led to 9th: cl up tl wknd 3 out* **20/1**
0-05 **9** *24* **Ballistic Boy**[58] 1150 8-10-2 **81** DCCostello[(5)] 45
(R W Thomson) *in tch tl rdn and wknd fr 2 out* **16/1**
0-FP **P** **Silent Voice (IRE)**[142] 334 8-9-11 **74** oh2 PBuchanan[(3)] —
(Sir John Barlow Bt) *bhd: t.o whn p.u bef 2 out* **33/1**

5m 35.5s (-21.10) **Going Correction** -0.75s/f (Firm) **10** Ran SP% **114.8**
Speed ratings: **106,105,105,104,103 102,102,98,89,—** CSF £41.44 CT £329.10 TOTE £3.20: £1.60, £3.60, £2.30; EX 85.60.
Owner Mr & Mrs Raymond Anderson Green **Bred** Mrs Mary Clarke **Trained** Stocksfield, Northumberland

FOCUS
An ordinary handicap, rated through the fourth, in which the pace was just fair.

NOTEBOOK
Snowy(IRE), who goes well here and is unbeaten under Graham Lee, ran right up to his best after a break of over four months. His three wins over obstacles have been at this course and he may well be capable of a bit better on decent ground. *(op 3-1)*
Partners Choice(IRE) ran well from 4lb out of the handicap back over this more suitable trip but his inconsistency and the fact he has yet to win a race prevent him from being a betting proposition next time. *(op 11-1)*
Ideal Du Bois Beury(FR) ran creditably in terms of form after an early blunder. He has slipped to a potentially favourable mark and is capable of winning a race of this nature but his losing run of over three years means he is one to tread carefully with. *(op 12-1)*
Red Flyer(IRE), upped 5lb for his Sedgefield win, ran creditably and left the impression that he would have been suited by a stiffer test of stamina over this trip. He looks worth a try over three miles. *(op 7-2 tchd 4-1 in a place)*
Goodbadindiferent(IRE) was not disgraced in terms of form back on a sound surface but it is worth remembering that he had the run of the race and, given his inconsistency, is not really the best betting proposition around. *(op 15-2 tchd 7-1)*
Jupiter Jo has yet to win over regulation fences and did not leave the impression things would be changing in the near future judged on this run. *(op 6-1)*
Ballistic Boy *Official explanation: vet said gelding pulled up lame (op 12-1)*

1603 SUNDAY MAIL H'CAP CHASE (19 fncs) 3m 1f

3:25 (3:25) (Class 3) (0-115,115) 5-Y-0+ **£5,434** (£1,672; £836; £418)

Form RPR
322P **1** **Croc An Oir (IRE)**[40] 1294 8-11-11 **114** ADobbin 122+
(R Ford) *in tch: hit 15th: hdwy to ld 2 out: kpt on wl* **3/1**[1]
4P-4 **2** *1 ½* **Primitive Way**[137] 411 13-10-0 **89** oh2 (p) BHarding 93
(Miss S E Forster) *cl up: led 14th to 16th: outpcd 2 out: kpt on fr last: nt rch wnr* **7/1**
124- **3** *nk* **Interdit (FR)**[318] 2297 9-11-9 **112** KRenwick 115
(Mrs B K Thomson) *j.rt: mde most to 12th: led 4 out to 2 out: rallied: kpt on run in* **3/1**[1]
/423 **4** *4* **Pessimistic Dick**[11] 1511 12-10-0 **89** oh6 GLee 89+
(Mrs J C McGregor) *cl up: led 12th to 14th: outpcd 3 out: kpt on u.p fr last* **10/1**
-P32 **5** *¾* **Wildfield Rufo (IRE)**[127] 547 10-11-1 **111** CDSharkey[(7)] 110+
(Mrs K Walton) *chsd ldrs: j. slowly and lost pl 5th: j. slowly next: drvn 14th: no imp fr 3 out* **7/2**[2]
0316 **U** **Pikestaff (USA)**[36] 1341 7-10-4 **100** (t) BenOrde-Powlett[(7)] —
(M A Barnes) *prom: mstke and outpcd 12th: sixth and hld whn blnd and uns rdr 3 out* **13/2**[3]

6m 9.00s (-20.60) **Going Correction** -0.75s/f (Firm) **6** Ran SP% **107.1**
Speed ratings: **102,101,101,100,99** — CSF £20.58 CT £55.84 TOTE £3.30: £2.00, £3.20; EX 26.60.
Owner Concertina Racing Four **Bred** Donal Brazil **Trained** Cotebrook, Cheshire

FOCUS
An ordinary handicap, rated through the fourth, in which the pace was once again only fair.

NOTEBOOK
Croc An Oir(IRE), back over fences, returned to something like his best. He is best around this trip on a sound surface but a further rise in the weights is going to leave him vulnerable in better company. *(tchd 11-4 and 7-2)*
Primitive Way, back in handicap company and after a break, ran creditably with the cheekpieces back on. A stiffer test of stamina would have been preferable and he could pick up a modest handicap from his current mark. *(op 6-1 tchd 8-1)*
Interdit(FR) has a good record at this course and ran creditably on this first run after a break, despite showing a tendency to jump to his right. He should be better for this run but may be vulnerable to progressive or well-handicapped sorts from his current mark. *(tchd 5-2)*
Pessimistic Dick was not disgraced from 6lb out of the handicap and is another that would have been suited by a stiffer test of stamina. He will be of more interest when dropped in grade. *(tchd 11-1)*
Wildfield Rufo(IRE), the winner of this race from a 13lb lower mark last year, was not beaten that far but never threatened to get competitive after a couple of sloppy earlier jumps. Easier ground may suit but he does look vulnerable from his current mark. *(op 9-4)*
Pikestaff(USA), making his chasing debut, was far from foot perfect and was already held when coming to grief. It remains to be seen how this will have affected his confidence and he will have to jump better before he is a betting proposition over fences. *(op 8-1 tchd 10-1)*

1604 NSPCC FULL STOP H'CAP HURDLE (8 hdls) 2m 110y

4:00 (4:00) (Class 3) (0-120,115) 4-Y-0+ **£5,499** (£1,692; £846; £423)

Form RPR
05-4 **1** **Sir Night (IRE)**[31] 1366 5-10-5 **94** BHarding 102
(Jedd O'Keeffe) *chsd ldrs: effrt 2 out: led after last: hld on wl* **12/1**
2531 **2** *nk* **Gone Too Far**[10] 1529 7-11-12 **115** (v) KRenwick 123
(P Monteith) *chsd ldr: pushed along bef 3 out: led appr last to after last: rallied: jst hld* **2/1**[1]
043 **3** *1 ½* **Big Wheel**[11] 1510 10-10-6 **95** ADobbin 101
(N G Richards) *in tch: effrt bef 2 out: drvn and kpt on run in* **7/2**[2]
4-26 **4** *6* **Bargain Hunt (IRE)**[20] 1336 4-9-7 **89** PJMcDonald[(7)] 89
(W Storey) *bhd: detached 1/2-way: kpt on fr 2 out: nvr rchd ldrs* **14/1**
1453 **5** *9* **Apadi (USA)**[10] 1529 9-10-10 **99** KJohnson 90
(R C Guest) *keen: hld up: hdwy to chse ldrs after 4 out: wknd fr 2 out* **25/1**
1P66 **6** *hd* **Royal Glen (IRE)**[10] 1530 7-10-6 **95** GLee 86
(W S Coltherd) *in tch: outpcd bef 3 out: n.d after* **15/2**
P056 **7** *7* **Ton-Chee**[14] 1488 6-10-11 **100** FKeniry 84
(K W Hogg) *led to appr last: sn btn* **14/1**
4P33 **8** *10* **Lofty Leader (IRE)**[10] 1530 6-10-6 **95** (p) LFletcher 69
(Mrs H O Graham) *bhd: outpcd 1/2-way: nvr on terms* **9/1**
14-0 **R** **Mount Vettore**[14] 1481 4-9-12 **97** PKinsella[(10)] —
(K G Reveley) *ref to r* **12/1**

-543 **P** **Mr Lear (USA)**^{23} [1444] 6-11-3 **111**..............(v) DCCostello$^{(5)}$ 111+
(J J Quinn) *hld up in tch: drvn 3 out: cl 4th and keeping on whn broke down and p.u after last* **13/2**^{3}

3m 45.1s (-18.60) **Going Correction** -1.00s/f (Hard)
WFA 4 from 5yo+ 13lb **10** Ran SP% **123.2**
Speed ratings: **103,102,102,99,95 95,91,87,—,—** CSF £39.50 CT £109.72 TOTE £17.10: £2.90, £2.10, £1.30; EX 84.30 Trifecta £259.40 Part won. Pool £365.44 - 0.80 winning units..
Owner Highbeck Racing **Bred** Mrs Kate And Patrick Tobin **Trained** Middleham Moor, N Yorks

FOCUS
Another run-of-the-mill handicap in which it paid to race up with the pace, but the form should work out alright.

NOTEBOOK
Sir Night(IRE) had the run of the race and turned in his best effort over hurdles. He is worth a try over a bit further and may be capable of better still. *(op 11-1 tchd 14-1)*
Gone Too Far is a consistent and versatile sort who had the run of the race and ran up to his best back over hurdles. Effective over further, he should continue to give a good account. *(op 5-2 tchd 11-4 in places)*
Big Wheel fared better back in handicap company on his favoured fast ground than he had done in a Perth claimer and, although not one for maximum faith, may be capable of winning another race on a sound surface in the near future. *(op 11-2)*
Bargain Hunt(IRE) did well to finish as close as he did given the unpromising position he was in at halfway, but his record of no wins from 36 career starts means he remains one to tread carefully with. *(op 12-1)*
Apadi(USA) was not totally disgraced back over hurdles but he is the type that needs things to fall right and did not do enough to suggest he is a winner waiting to happen in this sphere. *(op 20-1)*
Royal Glen(IRE) was a bit of a disappointment back on her favoured fast ground and she looks to have gone off the boil for the time being. *(op 14-1)*
Mr Lear(USA) has not won for some time but was in the process of running creditably when pulling up feelingly after the last. He has always looked happiest on easier ground. *(op 7-2)*

1605 RADIO BORDERS NOVICES' H'CAP HURDLE (10 hdls) 2m 2f
4:35 (4:37) (Class 4) (0-95,97) 3-Y-0+ **£3,146** (£899; £449)

Form RPR
620 **1** **Good Investment**^{36} [1338] 3-9-7 **84** oh1..............(p) MrTJO'Brien$^{(7)}$ 74
(P C Haslam) *chsd ldrs: effrt bef 2 out: led run in: styd on strly* **4/1**^{2}
53-1 **2** *4* **Baawrah**^{36} [1336] 4-10-10 **77**.............. GLee 80
(M Todhunter) *midfield: drvn and reminders 4th: rdn fr 1/2-way: kpt on fr 2 out: nt rch wnr* **2/1**^{1}
6110 **3** *nk* **Master Nimbus**^{9} [1541] 5-11-7 **93**.............. DCCostello$^{(5)}$ 96
(J J Quinn) *trckd ldrs: effrt bef 2 out: led last to run in: edgd lft: one pce* **13/2**^{3}
6333 **4** *2 1/2* **Templet (USA)**^{11} [1508] 5-11-9 **90**..............(b) JAMcCarthy 90
(W G Harrison) *hld up midfield: outpcd 4 out: rallying whn blnd 2 out: kpt on run in* **10/1**
0P60 **5** *1 1/4* **Starbright**^{11} [1508] 4-10-1 **68**.............. KRenwick 67
(W G Young) *cl up: led 3 out to last: sn no ex* **50/1**
PP-0 **6** *5* **Sandy Bay (IRE)**^{7} [306] 6-10-11 **78**..............(v) MBradburne 72
(W G Harrison) *hld up: outpcd and hung lft 4 out: rallied bef 2 out: no imp fr last* **22/1**
-0F5 **7** *2 1/2* **Gemini Lady**^{10} [1528] 5-10-8 **78**.............. PAspell$^{(3)}$ 70
(Mrs J C McGregor) *led to 3 out: wknd bef next* **25/1**
3-64 **8** *4* **The Miner**^{137} [407] 7-11-6 **90**..............(p) MrCStorey$^{(3)}$ 78
(Miss S E Forster) *keen: cl up: ev ch 3 out: wknd after next* **16/1**
2P03 **9** *4* **Alethea Gee**^{14} [1483] 7-9-11 **74**.............. PKinsella$^{(10)}$ 58
(K G Reveley) *hld up: rdn after 4 out: nvr on terms* **9/1**
600- **10** *1 1/2* **Okayman (FR)**^{305} [2567] 4-10-3 **70**.............. ADempsey 52
(A Parker) *a bhd* **18/1**
0050 **11** *17* **Nifty Roy**^{14} [1490] 5-11-4 **85**.............. ADobbin 50
(K W Hogg) *a bhd* **12/1**
-F00 **P** **Lady Godson**^{36} [1336] 6-10-0 **67** oh7.............. NPMulholland —
(B Mactaggart) *in tch to 4th: sn lost pl: t.o whn p.u bef 2 out* **50/1**

4m 12.9s (-27.00) **Going Correction** -1.00s/f (Hard)
WFA 3 from 4yo 17lb 4 from 5yo+ 13lb **12** Ran SP% **116.7**
Speed ratings: **101,99,99,97,97 95,94,92,90,89 82,—** CSF £12.05 CT £49.71 TOTE £5.60: £2.20, £1.90, £3.30; EX 15.90.
Owner Dennis Rogers **Bred** Milton Park Stud **Trained** Middleham, N Yorks

FOCUS
An ordinary gallop but the winner appeals as the type to win again in a similar grade and the form looks pretty solid for the level.

NOTEBOOK
Good Investment ◆, who ran as though something was amiss last time, ran right up to his best on this handicap debut in the first-time cheekpieces and left the impression that he should prove effective over further. He appeals as the type to win another similar event. *(tchd 9-2)*
Baawrah who beat a subsequent winner at Cartmel, was higher in the weights but, although running creditably, turned in a very laboured performance. He should be suited by two and a half miles on a more galloping course. *(tchd 7-4 and 9-4, 5-2 in places)*
Master Nimbus put a below-par effort firmly behind him but, although running creditably, is 29lb higher than for his Hereford win in June and is likely to remain vulnerable to progressive or well-handicapped sorts. *(op 11-2 tchd 7-1)*
Templet(USA) ran another fair race and would have finished closer had he not ploughed through the penultimate flight. He looks capable of winning a small event but remains one to tread carefully with. *(op 8-1)*
Starbright, an inconsistent maiden, had the run of the race and ran creditably but his record suggests he would be anything but certain to reproduce this next time. *(op 20-1)*
Sandy Bay(IRE) left the impression that a stiffer test of stamina would have been in his favour but, given that he has yet to win a race under any code, he does not look one to place much faith in. *(op 20-1 tchd 25-1)*

1606 CANTORODDS.COM H'CAP HURDLE (11 hdls) 2m 6f 110y
5:05 (5:08) (Class 4) (0-105,105) 4-Y-0+ **£3,513** (£1,081; £540; £270)

Form RPR
2434 **1** **Penteli**^{10} [1528] 5-9-12 **82**.............. DCCostello$^{(5)}$ 86
(C Grant) *midfield: hdwy bef 3 out: led last: drvn and styd on wl* **10/1**
-P11 **2** *3 1/2* **Wise Tale**^{8} [1552] 6-11-5 **98**..............(v) GLee 98
(P D Niven) *cl up: drvn along bef 2 out: kpt on fr last: nt rch wnr* **10/3**^{2}
43-3 **3** *nk* **Russian Sky**^{11} [1513] 6-11-8 **101**.............. LFletcher 101
(Mrs H O Graham) *cl up: led 2 out to last: kpt on u.p* **11/4**^{1}
3306 **4** *1* **Speed Kris (FR)**^{11} [1513] 6-11-11 **104**..............(v) MBradburne 103
(Mrs S C Bradburne) *midfield: drvn fr 4 out: kpt on fr 2 out: nvr rchd ldrs* **12/1**
3201 **5** *3/4* **Little Task**^{21} [1456] 7-11-1 **97**.............. PAspell$^{(3)}$ 95
(J S Wainwright) *hld up: hdwy bef 3 out: kpt on fr last: no imp* **9/1**
0056 **6** *3 1/2* **Old Nosey (IRE)**^{127} [546] 9-10-9 **88**.............. ADempsey 84+
(B Mactaggart) *led to 2 out: outpcd last* **16/1**
5002 **7** *24* **Lion Guest (IRE)**^{39} [1308] 8-10-0 **79**.............. KRenwick 65+
(Mrs S C Bradburne) *prom tl rdn and wknd fr 2 out: eased whn btn run in* **18/1**
-330 **8** *14* **Hugo De Perro (FR)**^{108} [766] 10-11-9 **105**..............(p) PBuchanan$^{(3)}$ 62
(Miss Lucinda V Russell) *rel to r and wl bhd: hdwy 1/2-way: wknd 4 out* **16/1**
4365 **9** *29* **Manoubi**^{34} [1361] 6-11-9 **102**..............(p) ADobbin 30
(M Todhunter) *hld up: rdn whn mstke 4 out: sn btn* **8/1**^{3}
UPF/ **P** **Eyze (IRE)**^{533} [4861] 9-11-6 **99**.............. NPMulholland —
(B Mactaggart) *cl up: lost pl qckly and p.u after 6th* **40/1**
F-43 **P** **Kidithou (FR)**^{148} [215] 7-11-12 **105**.............. BHarding —
(W T Reed) *mifield: lost pl 1/2-way: t.o whn p.u bef 2 out* **10/1**
P **Winds Supreme (IRE)**^{220} [4040] 6-10-11 **90**.............. KJohnson —
(M A Barnes) *keen: prom tl dropped rr 1/2-way: t.o whn p.u bef 2 out* **40/1**

5m 16.5s (-21.20) **Going Correction** -1.00s/f (Hard) **12** Ran SP% **118.6**
Speed ratings: **96,94,94,94,94 92,84,79,69,— —,—** CSF £44.23 CT £119.11 TOTE £10.70: £2.40, £1.80, £1.80; EX 46.40 Place 6 £74.15, Place 5 £14.30.
Owner Girsonfield Stud Racing **Bred** Mrs Maureen Barbara Walsh **Trained** Newton Bewley, Co Durham
■ Stewards' Enquiry : D C Costello one-day ban: used whip with excessive frequency (Oct 13)

FOCUS
A run-of-the-mill handicap in which the pace was only fair.

NOTEBOOK
Penteli showed the right attitude and improved back on a sound surface to notch her first win. She should have no problems staying three miles and, given she is only relatively lightly raced, may be capable of better. *(tchd 11-1)*
Wise Tale, 6lb higher than when successful at Market Rasen, ran equally as well. He is in the form of his life at present and left the impression that he will be well worth a try over three miles. *(op 9-4)*
Russian Sky showed the benefit of a recent spin at Perth and returned to something like his best. He is essentially a consistent sort who stays three miles and should continue to give a good account in this sort of company. *(op 9-2)*
Speed Kris(FR), who last won in France nearly two years ago, ran creditably in terms of form but, while a stronger overall gallop would have suited, he is not really one to place too much faith in. *(op 14-1)*
Little Task was not disgraced given this race suited those that raced close to the pace.His style means that he needs things to fall just right but he should continue to give a good account.
Old Nosey(IRE) had the run of the race and ran creditably returned to hurdles but his recent inconsistency means he is not really one to place much faith in. *(op 18-1 tchd 20-1)*
T/Plt: £77.80 to a £1 stake. Pool: £31,949.10. 299.75 winning tickets. T/Qpdt: £3.90 to a £1 stake. Pool: £2,708.00. 506.60 winning tickets. RY

1548 MARKET RASEN (R-H)
Sunday, October 2

OFFICIAL GOING: Good (good to soft in places)
After a showery week the ground was described as 'just on the slow side of good, perfect jumping ground'. The rails had been moved to freshen things.
Wind: Almost nil Weather: Fine and sunny

1607 DBS BUILDERS MERCHANT CONDITIONAL JOCKEYS' H'CAP HURDLE (8 hdls) 2m 1f 110y
2:10 (2:11) (Class 4) (0-100,97) 4-Y-0+ **£2,611** (£746; £373)

Form RPR
06-2 **1** **Rare Coincidence**^{21} [1336] 4-11-4 **89**..............(p) KJMercer 100+
(R F Fisher) *led after 1st: hdd 2nd: hit 3 out: led appr next: rdn clr run-in* **10/3**^{1}
54-4 **2** *6* **Rainbow Tree**^{14} [1490] 5-11-4 **94**..............(b^{1}) TMessenger$^{(5)}$ 97+
(C C Bealby) *trckd ldrs: led 5th tl appr 2 out: kpt on same pce* **4/1**^{2}
/6-5 **3** *2 1/2* **Handa Island (USA)**^{11} [1508] 6-11-2 **87**.............. GBerridge 88+
(M W Easterby) *in rr: hdwy to chse ldrs 3 out: kpt on same pce fr next* **5/1**^{3}
3F-0 **4** *2 1/2* **Movie King (IRE)**^{8} [1553] 6-11-9 **97**.............. SWalsh$^{(3)}$ 94
(S Gollings) *reluctant to line-up: bhd: hdwy to chse ldrs 3 out: hung lft and one pce fr next* **14/1**
0240 **5** *6* **Cash Return**^{14} [1490] 6-10-11 **82**..............(tp) LTreadwell 73
(Mrs S Lamyman) *in rr: outpcd 5th: kpt on fr 2 out: nvr on terms* **28/1**
0550 **6** *7* **Lone Soldier (FR)**^{21} [1458] 9-11-1 **91**.............. SMarshall$^{(5)}$ 75
(S B Clark) *trckd ldrs: led 2nd to 5th: wknd next* **9/1**
0-03 **7** *3 1/2* **Idle Journey (IRE)**^{81} [971] 4-11-3 **93**..............(t) MDarcy$^{(5)}$ 74
(M Scudamore) *hld up: hdwy 5th: sn chsng ldrs: wknd 2 out* **11/1**
3542 **8** *2 1/2* **Sound Skin (IRE)**^{95} [860] 7-11-10 **95**..............(p) CBolger 73
(A Ennis) *outpcd and n.d fr 5th* **15/2**
62F0 **9** *30* **Little Tobias (IRE)**^{36} [1344] 6-10-13 **87**..............(b) TJDreaper$^{(3)}$ 35
(J S Wainwright) *chsd ldrs: wknd after 5th: sn bhd: t.o* **16/1**
1050 **P** **Idlewild (IRE)**^{42} [1280] 10-11-4 **95**.............. APogson$^{(6)}$ —
(C T Pogson) *led tl after 1st: dropped rr 3rd: t.o next: p.u bef 5th* **22/1**
6-64 **P** **Macchiato**^{105} [780] 4-10-11 **85**.............. EDehdashti$^{(3)}$ —
(I W McInnes) *trckd ldrs: hung lft and lost pl after 5th: t.o whn p.u bef 2 out* **12/1**

4m 22.4s (6.00) **Going Correction** +0.475s/f (Soft)
WFA 4 from 5yo+ 13lb **11** Ran SP% **117.9**
Speed ratings: **105,102,101,100,97 94,92,91,78,— —** CSF £17.47 CT £66.33 TOTE £4.10: £1.40, £1.70, £2.10; EX 16.90.
Owner A Kerr **Bred** D R Tucker **Trained** Ulverston, Cumbria

FOCUS
A low-grade handicap with the first two were one-two from four out. A big step up in form from the winner, with the second rated to his best.

NOTEBOOK
Rare Coincidence, in good form on the Flat this year, broke his duck over hurdles in most convincing fashion on just his sixth attempt. *(op 4-1)*
Rainbow Tree, better for his return outing, sported blinkers for the first time. He went on but in the end the winner simply had too much speed for this past bumper winner. *(tchd 9-2)*
Handa Island(USA), a smart stayer on the Flat at three, is but a shadow of his former self. On his handicap debut, he proved simply too slow to take a real hand. *(op 15-2)*
Movie King(IRE), in a mulish mood at the start, jumped better, but it was disconcerting the way he refused to go forward in a straight line on the run-in. *(op 12-1)*
Cash Return, placed just twice in fifteen previous starts, struggled badly before keeping on in her own time, plenty of it! *(op 25-1)*
Sound Skin(IRE) *Official explanation: jockey said gelding hung badly left (op 7-1)*

1608 A J GLASSFIBRE NOVICES' HURDLE (12 hdls) 3m

2:40 (2:41) (Class 3) 4-Y-O+ **£4,810** (£1,480; £740; £370)

Form RPR

-121 **1** **Amicelli (GER)**^{66} [1089] 6-11-10 117 RJohnson 120+
(P J Hobbs) *j.lft: trckd ldrs: led 8th: qcknd 3 out: hrd rdn and hld on* **6/4**^{1}

2 ½ **Restart (IRE)**^{87} 4-10-11 JPMcNamara 107+
(Lucinda Featherstone) *hld up: wnt prom 7th: chsd wnr appr 2 out: hit last: styd on towards fin* **14/1**

42 **3** 6 **Toni Alcala**^{6} [1491] 6-10-9 (p) KJMercer$^{(3)}$ 101
(R F Fisher) *trckd ldrs: effrt appr 2 out: kpt on same pce* **11/2**^{3}

/35- **4** 11 **Millenaire (FR)**^{289} [2874] 6-10-12 TSiddall 91+
(Jonjo O'Neill) *hld up in tch: wnt prom 7th: outpcd fr 3 out* **7/2**^{2}

334 **5** 7 **True Temper (IRE)**^{33} [1374] 8-10-0 80 DMcGann$^{(5)}$ 76
(A M Crow) *trckd ldrs: lost pl after 3 out* **16/1**

5-P0 **6** 7 **Seraph**^{8} [1553] 5-10-5 78 MrDAFitzsimmons$^{(7)}$ 76
(O Brennan) *wnt prom 7th: wknd 3 out* **50/1**

32U- **7** 8 **River Marshal (IRE)**^{194} [4509] 7-10-12 NFehily 91+
(C C Bealby) *hdwy to chse ldrs 5th: fdd 2 out: 5th whn heavily eased last: virtually p.u: lame* **9/1**

0- **P** **Runshan (IRE)**^{165} [4935] 5-10-12 RThornton —
(D G Bridgwater) *j.lft: led to 8th: lost pl 3 out: t.o whn p.u bef next* **25/1**

352P **P** **Nightwatchman (IRE)**^{14} [1488] 6-10-12 105 (t) DO'Meara —
(S B Clark) *wnt prom 7th: lost pl 3 out: t.o whn p.u bef next* **12/1**

0-0U **P** **Crown Agent (IRE)**^{8} [1553] 5-10-5 64 (p) TJDreaper$^{(7)}$ —
(M E Sowersby) *j.lft: w ldr: rdn and lost pl appr 3 out: tailed of whn p.u bef 2 out* **66/1**

6m 17.4s (10.60) **Going Correction** +0.475s/f (Soft)
WFA 4 from 5yo+ 15lb **10** Ran SP% **115.1**
Speed ratings: **101,100,98,95,92 90,87,—,—,—** CSF £24.33 TOTE £2.20: £1.40, £3.80, £1.90; EX 23.10.
Owner Jack Joseph **Bred** Gestut Brummerhof **Trained** Withycombe, Somerset

FOCUS
Just a steady gallop until the final mile. The winner did not need to be at his best to score and the race has been rated through the third.

NOTEBOOK
Amicelli(GER), who looked in tip-top trim, defied a double penalty, digging deep and given every possible assistance from the saddle. *(tchd 13-8)*
Restart(IRE), a 58-rated stayer on the Flat, went in pursuit of the winner and was closing the gap all the way to the line. An even stronger gallop would have suited him better and he can surely find an opening.
Toni Alcala, if anything suited by the step up in trip, keeps running well but the winning habit seems something in the past in his case.
Millenaire(FR), absent since flopping in December, was on his toes beforehand. He was hopelessly outpaced in the final straight and this leggy type may not recapture the sparkle he showed in bumper company until he goes over fences.
True Temper(IRE) was simply not up to the task and low-grade handicaps offer her a better opportunity. *(op 20-1)*
River Marshal(IRE), absent since March and back over hurdles, seemed to go badly wrong and *left the course in the horse ambulance.* *Official explanation: jockey said filly finished lame (tchd 10-1)*

1609 TESCO MARKET RASEN H'CAP CHASE (14 fncs) 2m 6f 110y

3:15 (3:15) (Class 4) (0-110,108) 4-Y-O+ **£3,770** (£1,160; £580; £290)

Form RPR

3326 **1** **Seaniethesmuggler (IRE)**^{7} [1560] 7-10-13 95 (p) RThornton 107+
(S Gollings) *trckd ldrs: led 9th: qcknd appr 3 out: r.o wl* **5/2**^{1}

366- **2** 3½ **Moustique De L'Isle (FR)**^{201} [4387] 5-11-1 99 NFehily 103
(C C Bealby) *prom: outpcd 8th: hdwy 4 out: styd on to go 2nd aftewr last: no imp* **8/1**

560- **3** 2 **Penalty Clause (IRE)**^{6} [3920] 5-9-9 86 oh1 ow2 AScholes$^{(7)}$ 89+
(Lucinda Featherstone) *hdwy to chse ldrs 8th: 2nd whn hit last: one pce* **66/1**

P24- **4** 2½ **Roschal (IRE)**^{182} [4725] 7-11-11 107 RJohnson 110+
(P J Hobbs) *hld up: hdwy to trck ldrs 4th: 4 l 2nd and rdn whn hit 3 out: fdd last 150yds* **3/1**^{2}

35U- **5** ¾ **Runaway Bishop (USA)**^{290} [2849] 10-10-0 89 APogson$^{(7)}$ 89
(J R Cornwall) *in tch: outpcd 8th: one pce fr 4 out* **14/1**

P-12 **6** dist **Gale Star (IRE)**^{129} [511] 12-10-6 88 JEMoore 62
(O Brennan) *t.k.h in rr: hdwy 10th: sn chsng ldrs: wknd appr 3 out: sn bhd and eased: t.o* **9/1**

-213 **7** dist **Be The Tops (IRE)**^{50} [1205] 7-11-12 108 (b) TSiddall —
(Jonjo O'Neill) *chsd ldrs: lost pl after 7th: t.o 3 out: eventually completed* **7/1**

4P-P **P** **Monti Flyer**^{14} [1488] 7-11-3 99 DO'Meara —
(S B Clark) *in tch: lost pl 8th: sn bhd: t.o whn p.u bef 4 out* **33/1**

05/1 **F** **Infini (FR)**^{34} [1358] 9-11-8 104 DElsworth —
(Mrs S J Smith) *led to 9th: lost pl and swtchd outside: bhd whn fell heavily 4 out* **11/2**^{3}

5m 50.7s (4.30) **Going Correction** +0.15s/f (Yiel) **9** Ran SP% **113.7**
Speed ratings: **98,96,96,95,94** —,—,—,— CSF £22.63 CT £1024.59 TOTE £3.20: £1.70, £2.70, £8.10; EX 53.00.
Owner J B Webb **Bred** Mrs Grace Bracken **Trained** Scamblesby, Lincs

FOCUS
An improved performance by the well backed winner, who was followed home by two chasing debutants. The winner has been rated as value to further and the second to his chasing mark, but the third holds the form down a bit.

NOTEBOOK
Seaniethesmuggler(IRE), who has fallen in love with this place, put a poor effort last week behind him and justified the market support in most convincing fashion. *(op 9-2)*
Moustique De L'Isle(FR), absent since March, was making his chasing bow and he stuck on in *grim fashion to follow the winner home. With him it is a case of the softer the ground the better. (op 9-1)*
Penalty Clause(IRE), last seen in banded company on the Flat a week earlier, was making his chasing bow. An error at the last soon saw him forfeit second spot. He really prefers quicker ground and it seems fences could be the making of him. *(op 40-1)*
Roschal(IRE), absent since April, looked very fit but he was getting the worst of the argument with the winner when he went through the third last. It would be dangerous to assume he will improve for the outing. *(op 5-2)*
Runaway Bishop(USA), absent since December, just jumps and stays and the outing will not be lost on him. *(op 12-1)*
Be The Tops(IRE) seemed to lose all interest setting out on to the final circuit. *(op 6-1)*
Infini(FR), who finished in some distress at Cartmel, seemed to lose all interest when headed. *Pulling him wide had no effect and he took a crashing fall. He has questions to answer now. (op 5-1)*

1610 A J GLASSFIBRE H'CAP HURDLE (8 hdls) 2m 1f 110y

3:50 (4:00) (Class 3) (0-120,115) 4-Y-O+ **£4,849** (£1,492; £746; £373)

Form RPR

P4 **1** **Karathaena (IRE)**^{8} [1552] 5-10-12 104 KJMercer$^{(3)}$ 111+
(M E Sowersby) *trckd ldrs: led appr 2 out: clr last: comf* **6/1**^{3}

-221 **2** 7 **Kingkohler (IRE)**^{23} [1444] 6-11-11 114 PJBrennan 114+
(K A Morgan) *wnt prom 4th: hrd drvn 3 out: styd on to take mod 2nd last: no ch w wnr* **7/2**^{1}

215- **3** 8 **Iberus (GER)**^{28} [2481] 7-11-3 106 RThornton 97
(S Gollings) *w ldr: rdn appr 2 out: wknd last* **9/2**^{2}

006B **4** ¾ **Siegfrieds Night (IRE)**^{7} [1559] 4-10-4 100 (t) CMStudd$^{(7)}$ 90
(M C Chapman) *in tch: dropped rr 3 out: sn bhd: styd on appr last: fin strly* **18/1**

6-31 **5** nk **Goss**^{54} [1188] 8-11-2 115 WJones$^{(10)}$ 105
(Jonjo O'Neill) *mde most: hdd appr 2 out: wknd last* **13/2**

42-P **6** 1½ **Alpine Hideaway (IRE)**^{17} [1111] 12-10-3 95 (p) MrTGreenall$^{(3)}$ 83
(J S Wainwright) *in rr and drvn along 4th: sme hdwy appriaching 2 out: nvr a threat* **22/1**

-544 **7** 18 **Why The Long Face (NZ)**^{129} [525] 8-10-9 108 JMoorman$^{(10)}$ 78
(R C Guest) *a in rr: bhd and drvn along 5th* **12/1**

-33U **8** 1 **Lord Lington (FR)**^{112} [726] 6-11-5 108 WMarston 77
(D J Wintle) *trckd ldrs: lost pl appr 3 out* **8/1**

P0R0 **9** 30 **Dabus**^{7} [1559] 10-10-7 103 AnnStokell$^{(7)}$ 42
(M C Chapman) *t.k.h: trckd ldrs: dropped rr 4th: sn wl bhd: t.o 3 out* **50/1**

4m 21.1s (4.70) **Going Correction** +0.475s/f (Soft)
WFA 4 from 5yo+ 13lb **9** Ran SP% **98.4**
Speed ratings: **108,104,101,101,100 100,92,91,78** CSF £20.63 CT £63.17 TOTE £8.00: £2.50, £1.40, £1.80; EX 26.70.
Owner The Southwold Set **Bred** John Flynn And Mrs Eimear Mulhern **Trained** Goodmanham, E Yorks
■ Ela Re (9/2) was withdrawn (bolted before start). Rule 4 applies, deduct 15p in the £.

FOCUS
No great gallop but in the end an improved performance from the winner who had plenty in hand. The race could be rated a fair bit higher but is probably not one to get carried away with.

NOTEBOOK
Karathaena(IRE), who has a history of wind problems, found the drop back in distance no problem at all. She went on travelling well within herself and never really had to be asked a question. *(op 15-2)*
Kingkohler(IRE), 4lb higher, was running from a career-high mark. Hard at work three out, he kept on to finish clear second best but was no match whatsoever for the winner. *(op 4-1 tchd 9-2)*
Iberus(GER), a negative on the morning line, has had two recent outings this year on the Flat. He tired badly on the run-in and his stamina is suspect. *(op 6-1 after early 15-2 in a place)*
Siegfrieds Night(IRE), with his tongue tied down for the first time, seemed to lose all interest before making up many lengths on the run-in. He has a mind of his own. *(op 16-1)*
Goss, absent since August and running from a 7lb higher mark, was quite keen in front and he tired noticeably on the run-in. Now may be the time to put him back over fences. *(op 6-1 tchd 11-2)*

1611 BM&J "NATIONAL HUNT" NOVICES' HURDLE (10 hdls) 2m 3f 110y

4:25 (4:29) (Class 4) 4-Y-O+ **£3,311** (£946; £473)

Form RPR

11- **1** **Square Mile (IRE)**^{458} [858] 5-11-0 JEMoore 112+
(Jonjo O'Neill) *in tch: wnt 2nd after 3 out: rdn appr next: led last: styd on* **3/1**^{2}

555- **2** 1½ **Emmasflora**^{235} [3753] 7-10-0 85 APogson$^{(7)}$ 103
(C T Pogson) *led to last: no ex* **40/1**

042- **3** 10 **Monsieur Delage**^{217} [4090] 5-11-0 RThornton 101+
(S Gollings) *trckd ldrs: rdn appr 2 out: one pced 3rd whn mstke last* **7/1**

1 **4** 12 **Thedublinpublican (IRE)**^{14} [1491] 5-11-7 NFehily 95
(C C Bealby) *trckd ldrs: wknd appr 2 out* **4/1**^{3}

535U **5** 8 **Ponchatrain (IRE)**^{9} [1538] 5-11-0 WMarston 81+
(D J Wintle) *chsd ldrs: lost pl appr 2 out* **12/1**

P/ **6** 2½ **Sealed Orders**^{161} 8-10-4 LVickers$^{(3)}$ 71
(Mrs S Lamyman) *in rr fr 6th: sme hdwy appr 2 out: nvr on terms* **100/1**

0- **7** 3½ **Over The Blues (IRE)**^{291} [2829] 5-10-7 MrAJBerry$^{(7)}$ 74
(Jonjo O'Neill) *nt jump wl: bhd fr 5th: sme hdwy 2 out: nvr on terms* **12/1**

00- **8** 13 **Hidden Storm (IRE)**^{188} [4611] 6-10-7 MFoley 54
(Mrs S J Humphrey) *a in rr: bhd fr 6th* **80/1**

P **9** ¾ **Its Mick (IRE)**^{23} [1445] 8-11-0 DElsworth 60
(Mrs S J Smith) *chsd ldrs: lost pl after 6th: bhd fr 3 out* **28/1**

30-5 **10** nk **Hialeah**^{10} [1532] 4-10-11 MrTGreenall$^{(3)}$ 60
(M W Easterby) *t.k.h in rr: bhd fr 6th* **22/1**

11 ¾ **Casalani (IRE)**^{536} 6-10-7 WHutchinson 52
(C C Bealby) *unruly and uns rdr paddock: in rr: bhd fr 6th* **25/1**

1- **P** **My Skipper (IRE)**^{185} [4673] 4-11-0 SThomas —
(Miss H C Knight) *in raer: drvn along 5th: sn bhd: t.o 7th: p.u bef next* **9/4**^{1}

4m 57.9s (7.90) **Going Correction** +0.475s/f (Soft)
WFA 4 from 5yo+ 13lb **12** Ran SP% **120.0**
Speed ratings: **103,102,98,93,90 89,88,82,82,82 82,—** CSF £124.20 TOTE £4.40: £2.10, £6.70, £2.20; EX 140.60.
Owner John P McManus **Bred** Mrs K Purfield **Trained** Cheltenham, Gloucs

FOCUS
Just a steady gallop but with the favourite flopping this probably took little winning. Not an easy race to assess, the winner rated to the level of his bumper form.

NOTEBOOK
Square Mile(IRE), unbeaten in two bumpers, was reappearing after fifteen months on the sidelines. He made very hard work of it but was in command at the line and basically looks just a stayer. *(tchd 7-2)*
Emmasflora, well beaten on her three previous starts, seems much improved in her new quarters. She settled well in front and made the winner dig deep.
Monsieur Delage, absent since February and making his hurdling bow, was well supported but he had been hung out to dry when getting the last all wrong. *(op 12-1)*
Thedublinpublican(IRE), very edgy beforehand, dropped away in a matter of strides turning for home. *(op 3-1)*
Ponchatrain(IRE), a winning pointer in Ireland, behaved himself at the start this time but he had his limitations ruthlessly exposed. *(tchd 14-1)*
My Skipper(IRE), a winning favourite on his debut in a a bumper at Ludlow in March, had two handlers in the paddock. He never went a yard and, driven along with a full circuit to go, just got *further and further behind before calling it a day. Something was clearly badly amiss here. (op 11-4 tchd 3-1)*

1612 KATIE LOUISE BREWIN MEMORIAL H'CAP CHASE (12 fncs) 2m 1f 110y
4:55 (4:58) (Class 4) (0-100,98) 5-Y-0+ £3,349 (£957; £478)

Form RPR
11P0 1 **College City (IRE)**[38] 1320 6-11-5 **98**....(p) PMerrigan(7) 114+
(R C Guest) *hld up: hdwy to chse ldr 8th: led 2 out: stmbld landing last: r.o strly: readily* **5/1**
6542 2 *5* **Un Autre Espere**[8] 1553 6-10-4 **76**.... NFehily 82+
(C C Bealby) *trckd ldr: led 3rd to 2 out: kpt on same pce run-in* **9/2**[3]
1534 3 *15* **Reverse Swing**[14] 1483 8-10-7 **79**....(t) RJohnson 72+
(Mrs H Dalton) *in rr: hdwy and in tch whn mstke 7th: one pce fr 3 out* **4/1**[2]
P-24 4 *6* **Meltonian**[34] 1363 8-11-6 **92**.... SCurran 78+
(K F Clutterbuck) *in rr: hdwy 8th: mod 3rd 3 out: sn fdd* **14/1**
1336 5 *6* **Mikasa (IRE)**[36] 1335 5-10-1 **76**.... KJMercer(3) 54
(R F Fisher) *nt fluent: in rr: sme hdwy 8th: wl outpcd appr 3 out* **10/3**[1]
2235 6 *17* **Kercabellec (FR)**[34] 1363 7-10-12 **91**.... APogson(7) 62+
(J R Cornwall) *t.k.h: trckd ldrs: lost pl appr 3 out: sn bhd* **8/1**
6523 P **Gipsy Cricketer**[40] 1299 9-10-6 **78**.... SThomas —
(M Scudamore) *led: mstke 2nd: hdd next: dropped rr 7th: t.o 4 out: sn p.u* **9/2**[3]

4m 31.3s (0.20) **Going Correction** +0.15s/f (Yiel) **7** Ran SP% **113.9**
Speed ratings: **105,102,96,93,90 83,**— CSF £27.52 CT £97.72 TOTE £4.60: £3.00, £3.40; EX 46.10.
Owner Mrs Anna Kenny **Bred** P J Hannon **Trained** Brancepeth, Co Durham

FOCUS
A low-grade handicap run at a sound pace and a ready winner, value for 10l. The race could be rated up to 8lb higher but that looks dubious given the level of the runner-up's hurdling form.

NOTEBOOK
College City(IRE), with the cheekpieces back on, travelled strongly and, making light of a stumble at the last, ran out a ready winner to give his trainer his first success for seven weeks. *(op 11-2)*
Un Autre Espere, making his chasing debut, jumped soundly in front but in the end the winner was much too good. *(op 4-1)*
Reverse Swing, wearing a tongue strap on her debut over fences, made a couple of minor jumping errors before being left well behind over the final three fences.
Meltonian ran a moderate race and faded noticeably over the last three fences. *(op 9-1)*
Mikasa(IRE), absent for five weeks, wouldn't really have a cut at his fences and never entered the argument. *(op 9-2)*
Gipsy Cricketer, absent for six weeks, last tasted success under Rules over three years ago and he was in trouble early on the final circuit here. *(op 4-1 tchd 5-1)*

1613 SPECIAL EVENTS COUNTRYSIDE STANDARD OPEN NATIONAL HUNT FLAT RACE 2m 1f 110y
5:25 (5:25) (Class 6) 4-6-Y-0 £1,918 (£548; £274)

Form RPR
1/ 1 **Spirit Of New York (IRE)**[575] 4199 6-11-4.... MrAJBerry(7) 93+
(Jonjo O'Neill) *trckd ldrs: wnt 2nd 9f out: led 3f out: sn rdn: styd on wl fnl f* **9/4**[1]
1- 2 *1 ¼* **Dancing Partner (USA)**[225] 3953 4-11-8.... MrTGreenall(3) 92+
(M W Easterby) *trckd ldrs: chal 2f out: sn rdn: no ex ins last* **9/4**[1]
3 *3* **Schumann** 4-11-4.... ATinkler 82+
(M Pitman) *trckd ldrs: effrt and cl up 2f out: kpt on same pce* **11/4**[2]
4 *5* **Try**[140] 6-10-13.... DMcGann(5) 77
(A M Crow) *set slow pce: qcknd 9f out: hdd 3f out: edgd rt and outpcd fnl 2f* **50/1**
60 5 *6* **Silent Age (IRE)**[8] 1554 4-11-4....(t) RThornton 71
(S Gollings) *chsd ldrs: drvn along 6f out: rallied over 3f out: wknd over 2f out* **25/1**
6 *13* **Cottam Phantom** 4-10-11.... MissJCoward(7) 58
(M W Easterby) *prom: lost pl over 5f out: sn bhd* **14/1**[3]
7 *27* **Barneys Joy** 6-10-11.... MrDAFitzsimmons(7) 31
(O Brennan) *trckd ldrs: t.k.h: drvn along 6f out: wknd over 3f out: sn bhd* **20/1**
P **Cisco (GER)** 5-11-1.... KJMercer(3) —
(M E Sowersby) *last but in tch: drvn along 10f out: lost pl 6f out: sn t.o: p.u over 3f out* **25/1**

4m 30.5s (14.00) **Going Correction** +0.475s/f (Soft) **8** Ran SP% **109.3**
Speed ratings: **87,86,85,82,80 74,62,**— CSF £6.65 TOTE £2.80: £1.10, £1.30, £1.60; EX 7.10 Place 6 £68.93, Place 5 £49.78.
Owner John P McManus **Bred** D Mitchell **Trained** Cheltenham, Gloucs

FOCUS
A moderate time, even for a bumper. They stood still when the tapes went up and there was no pace at all to the halfway mark. The first three are all capable of better than the bare form.

NOTEBOOK
Spirit Of New York(IRE), absent since winning at Newbury in March 2004, looked fit and was on his toes. He took time to assert but was firmly in command at the line and this half-brother to Native Emperor will waste no time before he goes over fences. *(op 7-4)*
Dancing Partner(USA), who won in soft ground at Uttoxeter in February, did not go down without a struggle and can surely make his mark over hurdles. *(tchd 2-1 and 5-2 in a place)*
Schumann, who cost 380,000gns as a yearling, was off-cast for just 22,000gns last year. He moved into contention once in line for home but when the dash began he was made to look very slow. *(op 10-3 tchd 7-2)*
Try, pulled up in a maiden point in May, ambled round in front before getting left behind when the dash for home began in earnest. *(op 40-1)*
Silent Age(IRE), having his third outing, could have done with a much stronger pace, but really this looks as good as he is. *Official explanation: jockey said gelding had breathing problem (tchd 20-1)*
T/Plt: £138.30 to a £1 stake. Pool: £26,403.30. 139.35 winning tickets. T/Qpdt: £68.60 to a £1 stake. Pool: £1,373.50. 14.80 winning tickets. WG

[1485] UTTOXETER (L-H)
Sunday, October 2

OFFICIAL GOING: Good
Wind: Slight, against Weather: light shower after race 5 (4.15)

1614 STRATSTONE JAGUAR STOKE NOVICES' HURDLE (FOR THE STAFFORDSHIRE REGIMENT CHALLENGE CUP) (10 hdls) 2m
2:00 (2:02) (Class 4) 4-Y-0+ £3,395 (£970; £485)

Form RPR
1 **Crow Wood**[29] 6-10-10.... RGarritty 113+
(J J Quinn) *t.k.h: led after 2nd: clr after 4th: hit 2 out: rdn flat: eased towards fin* **2/1**[2]
3- 2 *5* **Barton Flower**[168] 4885 4-10-3.... TJMurphy 94+
(D P Keane) *hld up in tch: chsd wnr fr 3 out: no imp: bttr for r* **9/1**[3]
10 3 *12* **Euro Route (IRE)**[9] 1541 4-11-3 95.... JMogford 94
(G J Smith) *led tl after 2nd: chsd wnr to 3 out: wknd 2 out* **22/1**
0- 4 *shd* **The Real Deal (IRE)**[197] 4463 4-10-10.... DRDennis 87
(Nick Williams) *mstke 1st: mid-div: styd on fr 2 out: nvr trbld ldrs* **50/1**
5 *12* **Mikado**[365] 4-10-10.... APMcCoy 77+
(Jonjo O'Neill) *hld up: hdwy appr 6th: wknd 3 out* **13/8**[1]
2P15 6 *1 ¾* **Lago D'Oro**[32] 1383 5-10-10.... RGreene 73
(Dr P Pritchard) *prom: hit 7th: rdn appr 3 out: sn wknd* **25/1**
0- 7 *¾* **Theatre Tinka (IRE)**[6] 1541 6-10-10.... CLlewellyn 72
(R Hollinshead) *hld up and bhd: sme hdwy 7th: nvr nr ldrs* **25/1**
8 *4* **Tytheknot**[345] 4-10-10.... LAspell 68
(O Sherwood) *mid-div: nt fluent 7th: sn struggling* **16/1**
9 *6* **Shergael (IRE)**[15] 4-10-10.... AntonyEvans 62
(J L Spearing) *bhd fr 6th* **66/1**
10 *2* **Spanish Tan (NZ)** 5-10-7.... TJPhelan(3) 60
(Jonjo O'Neill) *a in rr* **22/1**
0 11 *2 ½* **Land Sun's Legacy (IRE)**[21] 1454 4-10-7....(p) ACCoyle(3) 58
(J S Wainwright) *a bhd* **66/1**
400- 12 *4* **Pauls Plain**[148] 3953 4-10-10.... MBatchelor 54
(P W Hiatt) *bhd fr 6th* **66/1**
P **Dictator (IRE)**[392] 4-10-10....(t) TDoyle —
(D R Gandolfo) *prom tl p.u bef 6th* **16/1**
P- P **Jarvo**[22] 1849 4-10-5.... DLaverty(5) —
(Mark Campion) *bhd fr 6th: p.u after 7th* **66/1**
0 P **Bahamian Breeze**[34] 1364 4-10-10.... PMoloney —
(G Haine) *a bhd: t.o whn p.u bef 3 out* **66/1**
P **Melford Red (IRE)**[142] 5-10-10....(t) OMcPhail —
(R F Marvin) *a bhd: t.o whn p.u bef 3 out* **100/1**

3m 47.3s (-13.10) **Going Correction** -0.55s/f (Firm) **16** Ran SP% **120.0**
Speed ratings: **110,107,101,101,95 94,94,92,89,88 86,84,**—,—,— — CSF £18.02 TOTE £3.10: £1.50, £1.70, £5.70; EX 18.80.
Owner Mrs Marie Taylor **Bred** C Humphris **Trained** Settrington, N Yorks

FOCUS
Little strength in depth, but the winner was an impressive on his debut and should be rated for at least double his winning margin. It was also fair winning time for the grade.

NOTEBOOK
Crow Wood , a progressive performer on the Flat at around ten to twelve furlongs and rated 99 in that sphere, ran out an impressive winner on his hurdling bow and should be rated value for a lot further than his winning margin. He ran freely early on, but that can be forgiven as he would have found things happening a lot slower than he is used to in big handicaps on the Flat, and there was a lot to like about the overall manner in which he went about his business. He has all the right attributes to rate highly over hurdles, and should appreciate a stiffer test in due course, so could well bag a decent prize before the season is out. *(op 7-4)*
Barton Flower was doing all of her best work at the finish and made a pleasing return to action, but must rate flattered by her proximity to the winner. This was an improvement on her debut back in April, she is going the right way and should find a race in due course, perhaps when eligible for handicaps in this sphere. *(op 10-1)*
Euro Route(IRE) , who took a seller in good fashion over course and distance on his penultimate outing, ran close to his best in defeat and gives the form a sound look. He may be better off in handicaps, however. *(op 20-1)*
The Real Deal(IRE) , who showed little on his only previous outing last season, lost confidence after a mistake at the first flight yet was staying on well enough at the finish and turned in a much more encouraging effort. He could be on the upgrade. *(op 40-1)*
Mikado , a former Ballydoyle inmate rated 115 on the Flat and who took a Listed race at the Curragh when last seen exactly a year ago, failed to translate that ability on this hurdling bow and was most disappointingly beaten a long way out. Considering he was fifth in the St Leger and third in the Ebor in 2004, he is surely capable of better in this sphere, and may well be in need of a longer trip to show his best. However, he still has it all to prove after this. *(tchd 7-4)*
Dictator(IRE) *Official explanation: jockey said gelding lost its action (op 50-1)*
Jarvo *Official explanation: vet said gelding bled from nose (op 50-1)*

1615 SENTINEL CONDITIONAL JOCKEYS' H'CAP CHASE (18 fncs) 3m
2:30 (2:30) (Class 4) (0-100,100) 5-Y-0+ £3,325 (£950; £475)

Form RPR
0F54 1 **Waynesworld (IRE)**[14] 1479 7-10-8 **82**.... TJMalone 107+
(M Scudamore) *hld up in rr: hdwy appr 13th: led 3 out: clr 2 out: easily* **9/1**
-PP2 2 *21* **Lost In Normandy (IRE)**[23] 1446 8-10-0 **74** oh3....(b) DLaverty 79+
(Mrs L Williamson) *prom: mstke 8th: rdn and outpcd 12th: styd on to take 2nd post: no ch w wnr* **7/1**
4-21 3 *shd* **Sir Cumference**[128] 535 9-11-6 **97**....(b) PCO'Neill(3) 100
(Miss Venetia Williams) *w ldr: led 4 out to 3 out: sn btn* **4/1**[1]
0060 4 *2 ½* **Francolino (FR)**[9] 1539 12-10-0 **74** oh28.... TJPhelan 74
(Dr P Pritchard) *led to 4 out: wknd appr 2 out* **80/1**
P6P- 5 *5* **Buzybakson (IRE)**[172] 4824 8-11-8 **96**.... MNicolls 91
(J R Cornwall) *prom to 10th* **33/1**
P655 6 *1 ¾* **Greenacres Boy**[5] 1568 10-9-11 **74** oh21....(p) StephenJCraine(3) 68
(M Mullineaux) *t.k.h: hdwy 4th: wknd appr 3 out* **66/1**
5131 7 *dist* **Lanmire Tower (IRE)**[116] 690 11-11-2 **90**....(p) WKennedy —
(S Gollings) *mstke 4th: sn bhd: t.o* **8/1**
-P3P F **Rich Song (IRE)**[55] 1177 7-10-6 **83**.... NCarter(3) —
(Mrs S J Smith) *prom: cl 3rd whn fell 11th* **14/1**
0F4/ P **Whispering John (IRE)**[667] 2569 9-11-9 **100**.... RLucey-Butler(3) —
(W G M Turner) *j.rt: a in rr: t.o whn p.u bef 7th* **8/1**
6P32 P **Vandante (IRE)**[28] 1414 9-10-5 **84**.... LHeard(5) —
(R Lee) *hld up: rdn 12th: sn bhd: no ch whn blnd and rdr lost irons: p.u bef 2 out* **9/2**[2]
50P- U **Randolph O'Brien (IRE)**[186] 4655 5-11-2 **98**.... MGoldstein(6) —
(N A Twiston-Davies) *hld up: hdwy 8th: 4 l 4th whn mstke and uns rdr 14th* **6/1**[3]

6m 8.70s (-23.80) **Going Correction** -0.55s/f (Firm)
WFA 5 from 7yo+ 2lb **11** Ran SP% **109.5**
Speed ratings: **101,94,93,93,91 90,**—,—,—,— — CSF £65.51 CT £269.83 TOTE £10.00: £1.80, £1.70, £2.20; EX 61.50.
Owner F J Mills & W Mills **Bred** A W Buller **Trained** Bromsash, Herefordshire

FOCUS
A weak handicap, run at a fair gallop and the winner won as he pleased. A big improvement in form for the winner, but the next three home were all fairly close to their pre-race marks.

NOTEBOOK
Waynesworld(IRE) , back up in trip, ran out a facile winner, under a fine ride by his improving jockey, to open his account under Rules at the 16th attempt. Having bided his time off the pace, he made smooth headway through the pack to join the leaders on the turn for home and was far from fully extended to go clear of his rivals from three out. He clearly enjoyed the chance to be held up over this longer trip, and would be very hard to stop on this evidence if turned out quickly before he is re-assessed. However, his connections will be praying the Handicapper does not react literally to this much-improved form. *(tchd 8-1)*
Lost In Normandy(IRE) , well ahead of the winner at Bangor last time, never looked like confirming that form and appeared to throw in a fairly moody effort. He was staying on at the death, and has at least found some form of late, but he is clearly not one to rely on. *(op 15-2 tchd 8-1)*

Sir Cumference was still going well at the top of the straight, but failed to find a change of pace when the winner challenged three out and was ultimately well beaten. He is entitled to improve a good deal for this first outing for 128 days, however. *(op 10-3)*
Francolino(FR) was found wanting when push came to shove at the top of the straight, but still turned in a much-improved effort, considering he was running from two stone out of the handicap. It remains to be seen whether he can build on this, however. *(op 50-1)*
Vandante(IRE) was well held prior to being pulled up two out. *(op 5-1)*
Whispering John(IRE) *Official explanation: jockey said gelding finished distressed (op 5-1)*

1616 MEUC - MERLIN RACING TO SAVE LIVES (S) HURDLE (14 hdls) 3m

3:05 (3:05) (Class 5) 4-7-Y-0 **£2,205** (£630; £315)

Form RPR
00-1 **1** **Midnight Creek**[15] 1341 7-11-5 116 JimCrowley 107+
(G A Swinbank) *t.k.h: hdwy 5th: led 3 out: comf* **11/8**[1]
U1FF **2** *2 ½* **Good Man Again (IRE)**[34] 1358 7-10-12 99 (vt[1]) ChristianWilliams 93+
(Evan Williams) *plld hrd: hdwy appr 10th: chsd wnr fr 3 out: rdn and one pce fr 2 out* **5/2**[2]
0/4 **3** *8* **Rhossili (IRE)**[21] 1454 5-10-12 LAspell 86+
(Mrs L Wadham) *led 2nd to 3 out: sn wknd* **6/1**[3]
30P0 **4** *3 ½* **Greencard Golf**[14] 1486 4-11-4 87 AO'Keeffe 87
(Jennie Candlish) *hld up and bhd: hdwy after 11th: wknd after 3 out* **14/1**
56-0 **5** *22* **Munny Hill**[14] 1485 5-10-9 RYoung[(3)] 59
(M Appleby) *hld up in tch: wknd after 11th* **33/1**
0 **6** *15* **Alderley Girl**[9] 1543 6-10-5 RGreene 37
(Dr P Pritchard) *t.k.h in tch: hit 10th: sn wknd* **80/1**
7 *dist* **Room Enough**[155] 5-10-5 (b[1]) MrRHodges[(7)] —
(S E H Sherwood) *led to 2nd: prom: rdn after 8th: wknd appr 10th: virtually p.u flat* **10/1**
0 **P** **King Amber**[113] 720 4-10-8 ONelmes[(3)] —
(A Crook) *prom: j.rt 7th: mstke 10th: sn wknd bhd whn p.u after 11th* **80/1**
PP0- **P** **Great Expense**[362] 1599 6-10-12 AEvans —
(G R Pewter) *t.k.h: lost pl 4th: bhd fr 6th: t.o whn p.u bef 10th* **100/1**

6m 7.80s (2.80) **Going Correction** -0.55s/f (Firm)
WFA 4 from 5yo+ 15lb **9** Ran SP% **107.1**
Speed ratings: **73,72,69,68,61 56,—,—,—** CSF £4.25 TOTE £2.30: £1.30, £1.10, £1.80; EX 4.90.The winner was sold to A Sadik for 7,200gns. Good Man Again was claimed by A Sadik for £6,000.
Owner A Butler **Bred** T E Pocock **Trained** Melsonby, N Yorks

FOCUS

A pedestrian time, even for a seller, due to the sedate early gallop. The form is suspect, but the winner can be rated value for further.

NOTEBOOK

Midnight Creek, who took a handicap at Market Rasen on his previous outing over hurdles, did not have to be at his best to follow up in this lowly class and duly scored with a fair bit in hand. He should remain a force to be reckoned with if kept to this level and will not be fussed when the ground turns soft. *(op Evens)*
Good Man Again(IRE), reverting to hurdles after falling on his previous two outings over fences, was the only one to make a real race of it with the winner and was not at all disgraced at the weights. The fitting of a tongue tie and visor for the first time looked to have a positive effect and *his confidence should have been restored now. Official explanation: vet said gelding finished distressed (op 9-4 tchd 2-1)*
Rhossili(IRE) set the sedate early gallop and was a sitting duck for the first two when the race got serious. He is flattered by this form, but still looked to run near to his recent Stratford form.
Greencard Golf again looked woefully one-paced when push came to shove, yet still ran very close to his official rating. *(op 20-1)*
Great Expense *Official explanation: vet said gelding had a breathing problem (op 80-1)*

1617 SCOTT WILSON H'CAP HURDLE (12 hdls) 2m 4f 110y

3:40 (3:40) (Class 3) (0-130,123) 4-Y-0+ **£8,593** (£2,644; £1,322; £661)

Form RPR
545U **1** **Mcbain (USA)**[8] 1548 6-11-7 **123** RStephens[(5)] 129+
(P J Hobbs) *hld up and bhd: hdwy appr 2 out: led last: rdn out* **5/1**[2]
-11U **2** *2* **Itsmyboy (IRE)**[128] 531 5-11-9 **120** TJMurphy 124+
(M C Pipe) *hld up in tch: rdn and ev ch appr last: edgd lft flat: nt qckn* **4/1**[1]
3013 **3** *3 ½* **Tomenoso**[36] 1341 7-10-13 **113** PWhelan[(3)] 112
(Mrs S J Smith) *chsd ldr: rdn to ld appr 3 out: hdd appr 2 out: one pce* **7/1**
-161 **4** *¾* **Stan (NZ)**[127] 550 6-11-11 **122** HOliver 121+
(R C Guest) *hld up: hdwy appr 8th: led appr 2 out: hit and hdd last: wknd* **6/1**
P/1- **5** *26* **Rainbows Aglitter**[378] 1448 8-11-7 **118** TDoyle 90
(D R Gandolfo) *hld up: hdwy 9th: hit 3 out: sn wknd* **11/2**[3]
/F-P **6** *dist* **Per Amore (IRE)**[29] 1400 7-10-10 **107** (b) PMoloney —
(Miss H C Knight) *prom: mstke 2nd: jnd ldr 5th: wknd after 8th: t.o* **25/1**
44-1 **P** **Nonantais (FR)**[155] 127 8-11-12 **123** MBatchelor —
(M Bradstock) *t.k.h: led: clr to 4th: hdd 8th: wknd after 9th: t.o whn p.u bef last* **5/1**[2]
03-3 **P** **Navado (USA)**[14] 1488 6-10-11 **108** APMcCoy —
(Jonjo O'Neill) *hld up in tch: led whn j.lft and mstke 8th: j.lft 9th: hdd appr 3 out: sn wknd: p.u bef 2 out* **13/2**

4m 56.4s (-15.70) **Going Correction** -0.55s/f (Firm) **8** Ran SP% **112.7**
Speed ratings: **107,106,104,104,94 —,—,—** CSF £24.92 CT £137.90 TOTE £7.00: £2.00, £1.60, £2.30; EX 18.00.
Owner Hill, Trembath, Bryan and Outhart **Bred** Lazy Lane Stables Inc **Trained** Withycombe, Somerset

FOCUS

A fair handicap and the form looks sound for the grade. The race has been rated through the third. The first two are capable of rating higher in due course.

NOTEBOOK

Mcbain(USA) looked to have it all to do three out, but kept gamely to his task and eventually wore down his rivals to lead at the final flight and win this in ready fashion. While this may be his first handicap success over timber, he boasts some strong placed form in this sphere, and really did deserve to resume winning ways. His rider's claim proved a big advantage this time, but he is *certainly capable of further progression now his confidence should have been fully restored. (op 4-1 tchd 11-2 in places)*
Itsmyboy(IRE), who was left with plenty of questions to answer after trying to run out and then unseating his rider on his previous outing 128 days ago, showed his true colours and had every chance on this handicap debut. He just looked a touch one-paced when it mattered over this longer trip, yet still finished a clear second best, and is not one to write off by any means. *(op 5-1)*
Tomenoso had his chance, but was just found wanting for pace from two out and did not look suited by this drop back from three miles. He remains in decent heart, and helps set the level of this form, but will surely be seen back over further before too long. *(op 9-1)*
Stan(NZ), last seen winning on his chase debut 127 days previously, failed to find as much as looked likely when push came to shove after the penultimate flight and then lost any chance when blundering at the last hurdle. He can be given another chance to atone from his current mark with this outing under his belt and he remains open to further progression this season. *(op 13-2)*
Rainbows Aglitter, having his first outing since winning over course and distance off a 5lb lower mark 378 days previously, ran as though this was needed and was not given a hard time after making an error three out. *(tchd 5-1)*
Navado(USA) *(op 11-2)*
Nonantais(FR) ran too freely on this return from a 155-day break and should be seen in a totally different light when getting his favoured soft ground in the future. *(op 11-2)*

1618 P M HARRIS BEGINNERS' CHASE (FOR THE ROYAL LANCASTRIAN & MERCIAN YEOMANRY CHALLENGE CUP)(16 fncs) 2m 5f

4:15 (4:16) (Class 4) 4-Y-0+ **£3,799** (£1,169; £584; £292)

Form RPR
210- **1** **Darkness**[200] 4394 6-11-7 APMcCoy 142+
(C R Egerton) *a.p: pckd 1st: hit 6th: pckd 9th: led after 9th: lft wl clr 2 out: hit last* **9/4**[2]
06/3 **2** *dist* **Darina's Boy**[36] 1334 9-11-4 PWhelan[(3)] 97
(Mrs S J Smith) *w ldr to 9th: rdn 11th: wknd appr 4 out: lft poor 2nd 2 out* **11/2**[3]
3U3- **3** *23* **The Holy Bee (IRE)**[188] 4611 6-11-7 PMoloney 67
(Miss H C Knight) *bhd fr 8th* **17/2**
060 **4** *2 ½* **Sunny South East (IRE)**[38] 1317 5-10-9 WKennedy[(5)] 58
(S Gollings) *a bhd* **33/1**
5 *2 ½* **Honor And Glory**[141] 5-11-7 DRDennis 63
(Nick Williams) *bhd fr 8th* **14/1**
0-PP **P** **Broughton Boy**[42] 1279 5-11-0 (t) MrNPearce[(7)] —
(G J Smith) *nt jump wl: a bhd: t.o whn p.u bef 9th* **66/1**
0PP **P** **Mr Wonderful (IRE)**[65] 1100 7-11-7 67 VSlattery —
(P O'Connor) *nt jump wl: a bhd: t.o whn p.u bef 9th* **100/1**
5-L2 **P** **Dhaudeloup (FR)**[55] 1180 10-11-7 104 JMogford —
(A G Juckes) *led: clr 6th: hdd after 9th: hit 10th: sn p.u* **12/1**
240- **F** **Lady Zephyr (IRE)**[198] 4434 7-11-0 CLlewellyn 132+
(N A Twiston-Davies) *a.p: chsd wnr fr 10th: rdn appr 3 out: 2 l 2nd whn fell 2 out* **13/8**[1]

5m 9.10s (-18.40) **Going Correction** -0.55s/f (Firm) **9** Ran SP% **114.6**
Speed ratings: **113,—,—,—,— —,—,—,—** CSF £15.22 TOTE £3.10: £1.40, £1.60, £2.10; EX 18.10.
Owner Lady Lloyd-Webber **Bred** Heatherwold Stud **Trained** Chaddleworth, Berks

FOCUS

A smart winning time for the grade, 8.7 seconds quicker than the later handicap over the same trip, and the winner looks a decent recruit for novice chasing. He is flattered by his winning margin, however.

NOTEBOOK

Darkness ◆, who disappointed in first-time blinkers in the Royal & SunAlliance Hurdle when last seen, got his chase career off to a perfect start and recorded a smart winning time. However, he did not totally convince with his jumping, and was greatly aided by Lady Zephyr falling two out, so is flattered by his wide winning margin. That said, he appeared to be holding that rival at the time of her departure, is entitled to improve for the experience and has to rate an exciting recruit to the novice chase division. He will also be suited by a softer surface in the future. *(op 2-1)*
Darina's Boy was put in his place when the market leaders asserted with four to jump and has to rate as flattered by his eventual finishing position. He is likely to fare better as he gains further experience and when going handicapping in this sphere. *(op 7-1)*
The Holy Bee(IRE), who has always promised to do better over fences, was never a serious factor on this chasing bow and was well beaten. He is nothing special, but as is the case with many of his yard's runners, he should strip a lot fitter for this comeback run. *(op 8-1 tchd 9-1)*
Dhaudeloup(FR) *Official explanation: jockey said gelding pulled up lame (op 2-1)*
Lady Zephyr(IRE), who had some excellent novice hurdle form last term and is rated 126 in that division, tended to run in snatches on this chasing bow and was just looking held by the winner prior to taking a very tired fall two out. She jumped well in the main, however, and should put this experience behind her in due course, especially when encountering softer ground. *(op 2-1)*

1619 LES SWANWICK ELECTRICAL "NATIONAL HUNT" NOVICES' HURDLE (12 hdls) 2m 6f 110y

4:45 (4:45) (Class 4) 4-Y-0+ **£3,360** (£960; £480)

Form RPR
11- **1** **Black Jack Ketchum (IRE)**[438] 1027 6-10-12 APMcCoy 122+
(Jonjo O'Neill) *hld up: stdy hdwy after 6th: lft in ld 8th: v easily* **9/4**[2]
PP-4 **2** *3* **Smart Mover**[32] 1383 6-10-12 104 TJMurphy 107
(Miss H C Knight) *hld up: hdwy 4th: ev ch 3 out: rdn after 2 out: one pce* **5/1**[3]
2 **3** *2* **Bally's Bro (IRE)**[152] 179 6-10-12 CLlewellyn 107+
(N A Twiston-Davies) *sn chsng ldr: bdly hmpd 8th: rdn appr 2 out: one pce* **6/1**
0PF **4** *dist* **Slight Hiccup**[38] 1317 5-9-12 79 MrJAJenkins[(7)] —
(C W Moore) *hld up and bhd: sme hdwy after 9th: n.d* **40/1**
0PP/ **5** *9* **Chocolate Bombe (IRE)**[147] 8-10-12 RGreene —
(S Lycett) *prom: nt fluent 7th: sn wknd: t.o* **25/1**
0-00 **F** **Lady Spur (IRE)**[21] 1459 6-10-2 ACCoyle[(3)] —
(J S Wainwright) *bhd tl fell 6th* **66/1**
P **P** **Thorny Issue**[10] 1521 6-10-12 AO'Keeffe —
(M J Gingell) *sn bhd: t.o whn p.u after 7th* **50/1**
PPP- **P** **Jacks Helen**[165] 4933 8-10-5 JMogford —
(G J Smith) *bhd fr 7th: t.o whn p.u bef 3 out* **50/1**
0/ **P** **Spud's Fancy**[722] 1622 6-10-5 JPByrne —
(D A Rees) *prom tl wknd 4th: t.o whn p.u bef 9th* **40/1**
123- **F** **Heltornic (IRE)**[178] 4753 5-10-5 TScudamore —
(M Scudamore) *j.rt: led: 3 l clr whn fell 8th* **2/1**[1]
P430 **P** **Ladies From Leeds**[84] 941 6-10-2 80 (b) ONelmes[(3)] —
(A Crook) *in tch: lost pl 3rd: t.o whn p.u after 7th* **14/1**

5m 30.4s (-14.30) **Going Correction** -0.55s/f (Firm) **11** Ran SP% **115.9**
Speed ratings: **102,100,100,—,— —,—,—,—,— —** CSF £13.17 TOTE £2.50: £1.70, £1.20, £1.40; EX 9.70.
Owner Mrs Gay Smith **Bred** E Morrissey **Trained** Cheltenham, Gloucs

FOCUS

Little strength in depth to this novice event, but the form amongst the principals is fair, and the winner looks potentially very useful. He can be rated value for around 15 lengths.

NOTEBOOK

Black Jack Ketchum(IRE) ◆, a clear-cut winner of two bumpers in 2004, made a winning debut over hurdles in great style and can be rated value for at least five times his official winning distance. Granted his task was made easier when Heltornic fell down the back straight, but he was still travelling with ease in behind at the time and would most likely have beaten that rival in any case. He jumped neatly, looked well suited by the longer trip and is clearly a very useful novice hurdler in the making. Although he has yet to prove himself on a soft surface, his dam won numerous races with cut in the ground *(op 2-1)*

Smart Mover, who failed to really progress last term after winning a bumper on his debut, had every chance yet was firmly put in his place from two out and is flattered by his proximity to the winner. The return to this longer trip helped and, while he will surely only peak when sent over fences in the future, it will come as a surprise if he cannot find a race over timber from his current rating this season. *(tchd 11-2)*
Bally's Bro(IRE), a staying-on second on his debut in a bumper when last seen 152 days previously, was not helped by the fall of Heltornic yet would not have finished much closer in any case on this hurdling bow. However, he can improve for this outing and should be suited by farther in due course. *(op 7-1 tchd 15-2)*
Heltornic(IRE), who showed decent form in three mares-only bumpers last season, was still going nicely prior to coming down at the eighth and would most likely have finished second with a clear round. Providing her confidence is not dented after this, she can maintain her progression and should prove a force to be reckoned with amongst her own sex in this division. *(tchd 9-4)*

1620 BTC EVENTS FOURSEASONSMARQUEEHIRE.COM H'CAP CHASE (FOR QUEEN'S ROYAL LANCERS CHALL. CUP) (16 fncs) 2m 5f

5:15 (5:15) (Class 4) (0-105,104) 5-Y-0+ **£4,114** (£1,266; £633; £316)

Form / RPR

04P- **1** **Icy Prospect (IRE)**[204] 4324 7-11-12 **104**.................. CLlewellyn 119+
(N A Twiston-Davies) *hld up in tch: led after 12th: drvn out* **11/4**[1]

0-30 **2** *3 ½* **Strong Magic (IRE)**[14] 1489 13-10-9 **92**.................. MNicolls(5) 99
(J R Cornwall) *led to 3rd: a.p: chsd wnr fr 2 out: one pce* **12/1**

20-P **3** *4* **Barton Hill**[36] 1342 8-11-5 **104**..................(b) DJacob(7) 107
(D P Keane) *hld up and bhd: pckd 1st: hdwy appr 4 out: one pce fr 3 out* **9/2**[2]

P-43 **4** *½* **Young Owen**[21] 1457 7-11-5 **97**.................. JMogford 100
(A G Juckes) *hld up and bhd: stdy hdwy appr 9th: ev ch whn j.lft 4 out: wknd appr last* **14/1**

-203 **5** *8* **Magico (NZ)**[124] 602 7-11-5 **97**.................. HOliver 95+
(R C Guest) *bhd: hmpd 4 out: nvr trbld ldrs* **6/1**[3]

6425 **6** *nk* **Celtic Star (IRE)**[10] 1524 7-10-5 **83**..................(v) DCrosse 77
(Mrs L Williamson) *prom: pckd 9th: rdn after 12th: wknd after 4 out* **7/1**

2-P0 **7** *3 ½* **Avadi (IRE)**[14] 1487 7-10-12 **90**.................. AThornton 82+
(P T Dalton) *w ldr: led 3rd: rdn and hdd after 12th: wknd appr 2 out* **16/1**

4-2P **8** *hd* **Tirley Storm**[140] 368 10-10-0 **78** oh3.................. PMoloney 69
(J S Smith) *t.k.h in mid-div: short-lived effrt on ins 12th* **12/1**

6-14 **F** **Calon Lan (IRE)**[81] 975 14-11-1 **93**.................. TJMurphy —
(B J Llewellyn) *hld up in mid-div: hdwy and cl up whn hmpd and fell 4 out* **7/1**

5m 17.8s (-9.70) **Going Correction** -0.55s/f (Firm) **9** Ran SP% **112.1**
Speed ratings: **96,94,93,92,89 89,88,88,**— CSF £33.18 CT £141.62 TOTE £3.20: £1.70, £3.30, £1.80; EX 53.30 Place 6 £33.32, Place 5 £15.20.
Owner David Mason **Bred** Thomas Earney **Trained** Naunton, Gloucs

FOCUS
A modest time for the grade, 8.7 seconds slower than the beginners' chase over the same trip, and the field were strung out at the finish. The winner could rate higher but this is probably modest form.

NOTEBOOK
Icy Prospect(IRE), a former point, bumper and hurdles winner, got back to winning ways with a ready success on this chasing debut. He has clearly begun handicap life on a decent mark, and while this was a weak event, it would be a surprise were he not to add to this despite an inevitable weight rise in the future. *(op 5-2)*
Strong Magic(IRE) turned in his best effort of the current campaign, and while holding no chance with the winner, gamely stuck to his task to finish a clear second. He is a good benchmark for this form.
Barton Hill, back in trip, failed to sustain his effort from off the pace and really does look in need of further respite from the Handicapper at present. *(op 6-1)*
Young Owen failed to get home over this longer trip and can get closer off this mark when reverting to shorter. *(op 12-1)*
T/Plt: £19.60 to a £1 stake. Pool: £33,749.35. 1,256.40 winning tickets. T/Qpdt: £4.90 to a £1 stake. Pool: £1,903.50. 284.45 winning tickets. KH

1471 TIPPERARY

Sunday, October 2

OFFICIAL GOING: Flat course - soft to heavy; hurdle course - soft (yielding to soft in places); chase course- yielding to soft (soft in places)

1621a JOHN JAMES MCMANUS MEMORIAL HURDLE (GRADE 1) 2m

3:15 (3:15) 4-Y-0+ **£46,170** (£13,546; £6,453; £2,198)

RPR

1 **Harchibald (FR)**[156] 114 6-11-12 166.................. PCarberry 146+
(Noel Meade, Ire) *a.p: 3rd 4 out: impr into 2nd travelling wl after 3 out: chal appr 2 out: 2L down and no imp whn lft in clr ld last: eased* **13/8**[1]

2 *2* **Ansar (IRE)**[36] 1083 9-11-12 138..................(b) DFO'Regan 135
(D K Weld, Ire) *hld up in tch: 4th 4 out: rdn and no imp next: lft mod 2nd last: styd on wout threatening wnr* **14/1**[3]

3 *4* **Calorando (IRE)**[10] 1534 6-11-12 132..................(b) MPWatts 131
(Anthony Mullins, Ire) *hld up: 5th 4 out: lost tch next: kpt on same pce fr 2 out: lft mod 3rd fr last* **25/1**

4 *3 ½* **Hasty Prince**[288] 2901 7-11-12 .... BJGeraghty 128+
(Jonjo O'Neill) *prom: 2nd fr 4th: 3rd and rdn after 3 out: sn no ex* **14/1**[3]

5 *dist* **Red Square Lady (IRE)**[24] 1438 7-11-7 123.......... AndrewJMcNamara —
(Michael John Phillips, Ire) *prom: 3rd appr 1/2-way: wknd 4 out: t.o* **33/1**

6 *3 ½* **Royal Paradise (FR)**[200] 4394 5-11-12 .... CO'Dwyer —
(Thomas Foley, Ire) *2nd early: dropped to rr and drvn along 1/2-way: trailing fr 3 out: t.o* **9/2**[2]

F **Solerina (IRE)**[154] 90 8-11-7 158.................. DJCasey 141+
(James Bowe, Ire) *attempted to make all: rdn and strly pressed bef 2 out: 2L advantage and in command whn fell last* **13/8**[1]

3m 51.1s **7** Ran SP% **114.5**
CSF £26.29 TOTE £2.70: £2.00, £3.10; DF 41.50.
Owner D P Sharkey **Bred** S N C Ecurie Bouchard Jean-Lo **Trained** Castletown, Co Meath

FOCUS
Solerina would probably have won had she not fallen and the race has been rated through the the horses in the frame whom Harchibald beat easily enough.

NOTEBOOK
Harchibald(FR) was in second place, over two lengths down and making absolutely no impact, when presented with the race at the last by Solerina's fall. He'll come on physically from this but remains a thinker. *(op 2/1 tchd 6/4)*
Ansar(IRE) was beginning to struggle four hurdles out but stayed on with some purpose, but all to late, after Solerina's departure. *(op 12/1)*
Calorando(IRE) was beginning to trail from three out and had no chance when gifted with third place at the last and then running on. *(op 20/1)*
Hasty Prince weakened after the third last and wasn't any sort of threat after. *(op 12/1)*
Royal Paradise(FR), having his first outing since Cheltenham, dropped right away before four out *and finished completely tailed off. Official explanation: trainer said gelding was scoped by the racecourse vet and found to have a lot of mucus on its lungs (op 5/1 tchd 11/2)*
Solerina(IRE), easy to back, went off in front but never attempted to build her customary long lead. Travelling best before the straight, she had her race won until a slight mistake at the last and a bad landing saw her come down. Unscathed, she might revert to the Flat for her next outing. *(op 4/5)*

1622a KEVIN MCMANUS BOOKMAKER GRIMES NOVICE CHASE (GRADE 3) 2m 4f

4:15 (4:15) 4-Y-0+ **£20,776** (£6,095; £2,904; £989)

RPR

1 **Church Island (IRE)**[23] 1452 6-11-2 .... DFO'Regan 123+
(Michael Hourigan, Ire) *trckd ldrs in 5th: 3rd fr 1/2-way: 2nd 3 out: sn rdn: chal next: led bef last: styd on wl* **5/1**[3]

2 *7* **Waltons Mountain (IRE)**[13] 1502 7-11-2 .... RWalsh 116
(Anthony Mullins, Ire) *attempted to make all: hit 7th: mstke 4 out: rdn appr 2 out: hdd and no ex bef last* **7/2**[2]

3 *6* **Mamouna Gale (IRE)**[86] 921 7-11-0 .... BJGeraghty 108
(E J O'Grady, Ire) *prom: 2nd bef 1/2-way: rdn 4 out: 3rd and no imp after next* **7/1**

4 *dist* **Lord Archie (IRE)**[20] 1468 7-11-2 .... AndrewJMcNamara —
(Cecil Ross, Ire) *hld up: mod 6th 1/2-way: no ex fr 4 out: t.o* **10/1**

5 *20* **Matt Wood (IRE)**[27] 1423 6-10-11 .... JLCullen —
(Paul Nolan, Ire) *chsd ldrs: 4th appr 1/2-way: no ex after 4 out: t.o* **10/1**

6 *dist* **Dromlease Express (IRE)**[540] 4741 7-11-2 .... GTHutchinson —
(C Byrnes, Ire) *a bhd: trailing thrght: completely t.o* **9/1**

P **Gortinard (IRE)**[27] 1423 7-11-5 .... PCarberry —
(C Byrnes, Ire) *bhd: sn trailing: completely t.o whn p.u bef 8th* **6/1**[4]

P **Present Company (IRE)**[13] 1502 7-10-11 .... DJCasey —
(Edward U Hales, Ire) *prom to 1/2-way: drvn along and lost pl whn bad mstke 8th: sn wknd: t.o whn p.u bef 4 out* **25/1**

4m 55.5s **8** Ran SP% **123.4**
CSF £25.51 TOTE £6.50: £1.60, £1.10, £2.10; DF 18.60.
Owner B J Craig **Bred** J S Bolger **Trained** Patrickswell, Co Limerick

FOCUS
Improved form for the winner with the second running to his winning mark.

NOTEBOOK
Church Island(IRE) has nothing in the way of a turn of foot but was travelling best from a long way out. He led before the last and drew away on the run-in. *(op 5/1 tchd 11/2)*
Waltons Mountain(IRE) ran in front but his tally of mistakes left him vulnerable and he was done with once headed on the run to the last.
Mamouna Gale(IRE) wasn't able to make any impressive from the third last. *(op 5/1)*
Dromlease Express(IRE) was detached from an early stage. *Official explanation: jockey said, regarding the poor form shown, gelding was never travelling and had to pushed along from the start just to keep in touch, adding that gelding had not run since April 2004 and felt a bit rusty (op 6/1)*
Gortinard(IRE) trailed after appearing to slip going into the first fence and was tailed off until being *pulled up before the eighth. Official explanation: jockey said, regarding the poor form shown, gelding slipped on take-off at the first fence and lost its confidence thereafter (op 6/4 tchd 11/8)*
Present Company(IRE) *Official explanation: jockey said mare made a respiratory noise in running (op 6/4 tchd 11/8)*

1623a KEVIN MCMANUS BOOKMAKER JOE MAC NOVICE HURDLE (GRADE 3) 2m

4:55 (4:55) 4-Y-0+ **£20,776** (£6,095; £2,904; £989)

RPR

1 **French Accordion (IRE)**[136] 433 5-11-1 112.................. BJGeraghty 118+
(Paul Nolan, Ire) *trckd ldrs in 3rd: impr to dispute ld after 5th: led bef 4 out: edgd clr next: rdn and strly pressed bef last: styd on wl* **5/1**[2]

2 *1 ½* **Carthalawn (IRE)**[10] 1537 4-10-10 .... DJCondon 112
(C Byrnes, Ire) *mid-div: 5th 4 out: impr into 3rd after 3 out: 2nd bef next: rdn to chal appr last: kpt on u.p* **8/1**

3 *7* **Name For Fame (USA)**[14] 1495 6-10-10 103.................. NPMadden 105
(R Donohoe, Ire) *towards rr: 9th 4 out: hdwy after next: 6th bef 2 out: kpt on wl* **12/1**

4 *½* **Grand Lili**[12] 1505 4-10-9 96.................. BCByrnes 103
(John Charles McConnell, Ire) *hld up in tch: impr into 5th 4 out: 4th after 3 out: kpt on* **20/1**

5 *4 ½* **Sauterelle (IRE)**[17] 1471 5-10-10 100.................. RMPower 100+
(Thomas Mullins, Ire) *mid-div: 7th 4 out: mod 5th after 3 out: kpt on same pce* **10/1**

6 *1* **Hardwick**[11] 1516 6-11-1 .... RWalsh 104+
(Adrian Maguire, Ire) *trckd ldrs: 3rd after 1/2-way: 2nd 3 out: rdn and no imp bef next: wknd bef last* **6/4**[1]

7 *4 ½* **Rights Of Man (IRE)**[14] 1461 6-11-5 111.................. JLCullen 103
(D E Fitzgerald, Ire) *led: clr early: jnd after 5th: hdd bef next: rdn and wknd 3 out* **6/1**[3]

8 *¾* **Sundeck (FR)**[59] 1138 5-11-5 .... DGHogan 102
(Ronald O'Leary, Ire) *trckd ldrs: 4th 4 out: wknd next* **14/1**

9 *10* **Royal Man (FR)**[185] 4677 4-10-10 .... DJCasey 83
(C F Swan, Ire) *a towards rr* **20/1**

10 *4* **Dantys Hampshire (IRE)**[112] 733 8-11-1 106..................(t) DFO'Regan 84
(Sean Aherne, Ire) *settled 2nd: 4th 1/2-way: wknd bef 4 out* **8/1**

11 *9* **My Native Lad (IRE)**[28] 1416 7-11-1 110.................. PCarberry 75
(Noel Meade, Ire) *mid-div: rdn and wknd 4 out* **9/1**

12 *25* **Bunmahon (IRE)**[14] 1494 5-11-1 ....(t) TPTreacy 50
(Mrs John Harrington, Ire) *a bhd: t.o* **20/1**

3m 53.0s
WFA 4 from 5yo+ 13lb **12** Ran SP% **140.9**
CSF £52.55 TOTE £6.00: £3.50, £2.90, £3.20; DF 107.40.
Owner Padraig Brady **Bred** John McKeever **Trained** Enniscorthy, Co. Wexford

FOCUS
A good novice hurdle in which the winner has been rated back to his best.

NOTEBOOK
French Accordion(IRE), a brother to Accordion Etoile, was impressive here when gaining his second course win. He was allowed go on before the fourth last and then had to pull out something to contain the runner-up from the last. The response was solid and he looks above average. Cheltenham in November is mooted. *(op 3/1)*
Carthalawn(IRE), with a win and three seconds from five starts in bumpers, was making his hurdling bow. He came with a well timed effort before the last but couldn't match the winner although finishing clear of the third. *(op 6/1)*
Hardwick looked useful at Listowel but this ex-pointer needs further and was readily outpaced here from before the second last. *(op 6/4 tchd 7/4)*

1624 - 1625a (Foreign Racing) - See Raceform Interactive

1467 ROSCOMMON (R-H)

Monday, October 3

OFFICIAL GOING: Flat & hurdle course - soft; chase course - soft to heavy

1626a KILBEGNET EUROPEAN BREEDERS FUND NOVICE CHASE (GRADE 3) — 2m

4:45 (4:45) 5-Y-0+ **£20,776** (£6,095; £2,904; £989)

			RPR
1		**Master Ofthe Chase (IRE)**[15] [1494] 7-11-1 .... DJCasey (C F Swan, Ire) *trckd ldrs: impr into 2nd travelling wl 3 out: shkn up to ld appr last: r.o wl: easily* **3/1[3]**	134+
2	3 ½	**Kahuna (IRE)**[147] [270] 8-11-1 133........................ JRBarry (E Sheehy, Ire) *attempted to make all: drvn along bef 2 out: rdn and hdd appr last: kpt on without troubling wnr* **15/8[1]**	127
3	20	**Cash And Carry (IRE)**[9] [1555] 7-11-1 117........................ PWFlood (E J O'Grady, Ire) *prom: 2nd 1/2-way: mstke 4 out: 4th and rdn next: lost tch bef 2 out: one pce* **9/1**	107
4	1 ½	**Top Strategy (IRE)**[103] [67] 5-10-11 .... RWalsh (T M Walsh, Ire) *hld up in tch: 5th 3 out: mod 4th bef 2 out: sn no ex* **7/1**	102
5	2	**Runfar (IRE)**[21] [1469] 9-10-10 93........................(tp) DFO'Regan (John Monroe, Ire) *hld up in tch: slt mstke 1st: last 4 out: kpt on same pce fr next* **25/1**	99
6	25	**Zum See (IRE)**[145] [309] 6-11-1 .... PCarberry (Noel Meade, Ire) *settled 2nd: 3rd 1/2-way: rdn and no imp bef 2 out: sn wknd: eased fr last: t.o* **11/4[2]**	79
R		**Inch Island (IRE)**[12] [950] 5-10-11 .... RCColgan (G M Lyons, Ire) *w.r.s and ref to r* **20/1**	—

4m 6.50s **7** Ran SP% **117.6**

CSF £9.97 TOTE £4.40: £2.00, £2.00; DF 11.70.

Owner Thomas Keane **Bred** Thomas Keane **Trained** Cloughjordan, Co Tipperary

NOTEBOOK

Master Ofthe Chase(IRE), who would not want the ground any worse than this, had the benefit of race-fitness over the favourite and he made that tell. *(op 11/4)*

Kahuna(IRE), having his first outing since May, looked the one to beat on form, but Master Ofthe Chase had the edge in fitness and that proved the decisive factor here. *(op 6/4)*

Cash And Carry(IRE) hurt his chances with a mistake at the fourth last. *(op 8/1)*

Top Strategy(IRE) ran a promising first race over fences. He was a decent juvenile hurdler and there should be better to come from him over fences. *(op 8/1)*

Zum See(IRE) *Official explanation: jockey said gelding felt sore on pulling up; vet said gelding was blowing hard post race (op 7/2)*

1627 - 1629a (Foreign Racing) - See Raceform Interactive

1559 HUNTINGDON (R-H)

Tuesday, October 4

OFFICIAL GOING: Good (good to firm in places)

Wind: Nil Weather: fine

1630 DEBBIE LORD IS 40 H'CAP HURDLE (12 hdls) — 3m 2f

2:30 (2:31) (Class 4) (0-110,108) 4-Y-0+ **£3,286** (£939; £469)

Form				RPR
2043	1		**Esters Boy**[27] [1436] 7-11-5 101........................ LAspell (P G Murphy) *a.p: wnt 2nd 3rd: rdn appr 2 out: led flat: drvn out* **7/1**	102
311F	2	nk	**High Gear (IRE)**[16] [1484] 7-11-4 100........................(b) APMcCoy (Jonjo O'Neill) *hld up: hdwy 9th: rdn appr 2 out: styd on flat* **11/4[1]**	101+
42F1	3	nk	**Bustisu**[56] [1192] 8-9-13 88........................ RCummings[(7)] (D J Wintle) *hld up and bhd: hdwy whn nt fluent 3 out: sn rdn: styd on flat* **7/1**	89+
0542	4	½	**September Moon**[12] [1525] 7-11-5 101........................ RJohnson (Mrs A M Thorpe) *led: rdn appr 2 out: hdd flat: no ex towards fin* **4/1[2]**	101
10-5	5	2 ½	**Diletia**[146] [297] 8-11-6 102........................ AThornton (R H Alner) *hld up: hdwy 6th: rdn after 9th: outpcd after 3 out: styd on flat* **5/1[3]**	99
4160	6	6	**Green Prospect (FR)**[9] [1559] 5-11-5 108........................ SWalsh[(7)] (M J McGrath) *hld up and bhd: hdwy appr 3 out: rdn appr 2 out: wkng whn hit last* **33/1**	100+
P005	7	21	**Silver Gift**[9] [1564] 8-9-9 82 oh3........................ DLaverty[(5)] (G Fierro) *a bhd* **11/1**	58+
R-26	8	8	**Pardon What**[27] [1436] 9-10-12 94........................ JTizzard (S Lycett) *nt fluent: chsd ldr to 3rd: prom: rdn 9th: wknd 3 out* **10/1**	68+
-000	P		**Esterelle (USA)**[9] [1564] 10-10-1 90........................ MrJAJenkins[(7)] (H J Manners) *a bhd: t.o whn p.u bef 2 out* **28/1**	—

6m 26.2s (3.80) **Going Correction** -0.50s/f (Good) **9** Ran SP% **112.1**

Speed ratings: **74,73,73,73,72 71,64,62,—** CSF £26.24 CT £138.72 TOTE £10.40: £2.70, £1.70, £2.60.

Owner J Cooper **Bred** Bram Davis And Mrs Louise A Murphy **Trained** East Garston, Berks

■ Stewards' Enquiry : A P McCoy caution: used whip with excessive frequency

FOCUS

A pedestrian winning time for the grade due to the sedate pace set until approaching the final turn. The form must be treated with slight caution as a result.

NOTEBOOK

Esters Boy, back up in trip, proved most suited to the real lack of pace over this stiffer test and showed guts to fend off his challengers on the run-in and resume winning ways. He still has to conclusively prove that he stays this far however, but has developed some consistency of late and should continue to pay his way despite a future weight rise. *(op 15-2 tchd 13-2)*

High Gear(IRE), who fell early in his quest for the hat-trick over fences at Plumpton last time, hit a flat spot when the tempo increased turning for home and, despite all of McCoy's urgings, just failed to reel in the winner on the run-in. He would have most likely have scored with a stronger pace and remains one to keep on your side at this level. *(tchd 3-1)*

Bustisu, raised 6lb for winning over slightly further at Newton Abbot previously, was another to be totally unsuited by the sedate gallop and deserves credit in the circumstances. She is clearly capable of winning off this new mark when getting the true pace she requires at this distance. *(tchd 13-2)*

September Moon set the sedate gallop for most of the way - which would have suited her on this marked step up in trip - yet still failed to get home as well as the principals. She is a consistent mare, and while she holds few secrets from the Handicapper, may still be able to find a race when reverting to shorter. *(op 9-2 tchd 5-1)*

Diletia got markedly outpaced when the race got serious approaching the final turn and was always playing catch-up thereafter. She is another who is requires a stronger gallop at this trip and can do better. *(op 9-2)*

1631 LITE FM 106.8 NOVICES' H'CAP CHASE (16 fncs) — 2m 4f 110y

3:00 (3:03) (Class 4) (0-105,104) 4-Y-0+ **£3,731** (£1,148; £574; £287)

Form				RPR
6/0-	1		**Galtee View (IRE)**[51] [1226] 7-10-10 88........................(p) PMoloney (Evan Williams) *hld up in mid-div: hdwy 10th: led 4 out tl after 3 out: led 2 out: drvn out* **6/1[3]**	97+
-4P3	2	1 ¾	**Lightin' Jack (IRE)**[12] [1521] 7-11-12 104........................ MFoley (Miss E C Lavelle) *led to 4 out: led after 3 out: j.lft and hdd 2 out: kpt on same pce flat* **11/1**	109
22P-	3	14	**Lucky Sinna (IRE)**[236] [3775] 9-11-7 99........................ TJMurphy (B G Powell) *hld up in mid-div: smooth hdwy 3 out: sn btn* **13/2**	90
554-	4	1 ½	**Bob The Builder**[213] [4191] 6-11-11 103........................ CLlewellyn (N A Twiston-Davies) *j.lft: sn chsng wnr: wknd after 3 out* **11/4[1]**	96+
B040	5	8	**Amber Dawn**[16] [1487] 6-11-3 95........................ OMcPhail (J Gallagher) *hld up in tch: mstke 9th: rdn 12th: wknd 4 out* **20/1**	77
-433	6	2 ½	**Kombinacja (POL)**[86] [937] 7-11-10 102........................ JMMaguire (T R George) *prom: rdn 9th: blnd 3 out: sn wknd* **5/1[2]**	84+
PPP-	7	5	**Master Brew**[228] [3922] 7-10-0 78 oh13........................ DCrosse (J R Best) *hld up in mid-div: mstke 6th: lost pl 8th: hdwy 11th: wknd 3 out* **25/1**	52
0334	8	2 ½	**Half Inch**[25] [1442] 5-11-1 98........................(b[1]) CHonour[(5)] (B I Case) *prom tl wknd 4 out* **33/1**	72+
0345	P		**Optimism (FR)**[30] [1412] 7-10-0 78........................ RWalford (R H Alner) *a bhd: t.o whn p.u bef 2 out* **6/1[3]**	—
FP	P		**Castle Oliver (IRE)**[25] [1446] 7-9-7 78 oh8........................ SWalsh[(7)] (A J Chamberlain) *a bhd: blnd and sddle slipped 4 out: p.u bef 3 out* **14/1**	—
/5P-	P		**Charliemoore**[236] [3766] 9-10-12 90........................ JEMoore (G L Moore) *a bhd: nt fluent 2nd: rdn 7th: blnd 4 out: p.u bef 3 out* **40/1**	—

5m 0.30s (-5.80) **Going Correction** -0.425s/f (Good) **11** Ran SP% **114.2**

Speed ratings: **94,93,88,87,84 83,81,80,—,— —** CSF £62.64 CT £441.30 TOTE £6.10: £2.00, £3.20, £2.60; EX 73.00.

Owner R E R Williams **Bred** E Tynan **Trained** Cowbridge, Vale Of Glamorgan

FOCUS

A modest winning time for the class and the first two came well clear.

NOTEBOOK

Galtee View(IRE), equipped with cheekpieces on this British debut for his new connections, showed the benefit of a recent change of scenery and got off the mark over fences at the eighth attempt in dogged fashion. His trainer is proving adept to transforming such characters and, considering he won off a mark of 99 over hurdles in Ireland, may still be head of the Handicapper in this sphere despite an inevitable weight rise. *(op 7-1)*

Lightin' Jack(IRE) made a brave bid from the front and stuck to his task gamely enough when headed, but ultimately found the weight concession to the winner beyond him. This was much his best effort for some time, he was well clear of the rest and appreciated the step back up to this trip. *(op 8-1)*

Lucky Sinna(IRE) found less than looked likely when push came to shove turning out of the back straight and merely plugged on at the same pace from two out. Granted, he may have been in need of this first outing for 236 days, but the fact he has yet to find a race of any description now in 16 attempts dictates that he is one to avoid. *(op 7-1)*

Bob The Builder, returning from a 213-day break and popular in the betting for this chase and handicap debut, tended to jump to his left throughout and was ultimately well beaten after looking like playing a part in the finish until jumping three out. He will be more suited to a left-handed track in the future and was not given at all a hard time in the home straight, yet still does not look obviously well handicapped on this evidence. *(op 5-2 tchd 3-1)*

Castle Oliver(IRE) *Official explanation: jockey said saddle slipped (op 12-1)*

1632 H2ONATIONWIDE.CO.UK NOVICES' HURDLE (10 hdls) — 2m 4f 110y

3:30 (3:34) (Class 3) 4-Y-0+ **£4,888** (£1,504; £752; £376)

Form				RPR
	1		**Cruzspiel**[49] 5-10-11 ....(v) APMcCoy (J R Fanshawe) *a.p: hit 5th: led 6th: clr whn hit last: comf* **4/5[1]**	109+
41-P	2	4	**Orinocovsky (IRE)**[73] [840] 6-10-11 .... TDoyle (N P Littmoden) *led to 6th: chsd wnr: rdn appr 2 out: no imp* **22/1**	97+
0-1	3	1 ¼	**Ponderon**[152] [194] 5-11-3 .... JAMcCarthy (Mrs P Robeson) *hld up: hdwy 6th: rdn after 7th: one pce fr 3 out: fin lame* **2/1[2]**	102+
03P3	4	2 ½	**Hard N Sharp**[16] [1485] 5-10-11 .... RJohnson (Mrs A M Thorpe) *hld up: 5 l 5th whn blnd 3 out: nvr trbld ldrs* **25/1**	94+
5/6P	5	¾	**Rome (IRE)**[12] [1522] 6-10-11 .... RThornton (G P Enright) *hld up: hdwy appr 6th: mstke 7th: rdn after 3 out: one pce* **40/1**	93+
14-	P		**Billyandi (IRE)**[187] [4673] 5-10-11 .... CLlewellyn (N A Twiston-Davies) *t.k.h: chsd ldr tl after 5th: wknd appr 6th: t.o whn p.u bef 2 out* **14/1[3]**	—

4m 42.1s (-13.20) **Going Correction** -0.50s/f (Good)

WFA 4 from 5yo+ 14lb **6** Ran SP% **106.2**

Speed ratings: **105,103,103,102,101** — CSF £16.33 TOTE £1.70: £1.50, £5.90; EX 12.40.

Owner P Garvey **Bred** Old Mill Stud **Trained** Newmarket, Suffolk

FOCUS

A fair novice event, run at a decent pace and the form looks sound. The winner can be rated value for further and should rate higher in due course.

NOTEBOOK

Cruzspiel, rated 102 on the Flat and who made all to take the Queen Alexandra Stakes over two miles and six furlongs at Royal Ascot at York in June, sweated profusely prior to and during the race, a trait he has shown in the past on the Flat. That did not stop him from making a winning debut however, and he jumped neatly in the main despite a mistake over the final flight. He really ought to defy a penalty in this class, is starting life over hurdles at the right age, and has the scope to rate higher in this sphere. *(op 10-11)*

Orinocovsky(IRE), returning from a 73-day break, did his best from the front yet was a sitting duck for the winner throughout. He kept to his task once headed and did enough to suggest he should pick up a race when going handicapping in this sphere, plus he always has the option of reverting to chasing where has has a rating of 106. *(op 20-1)*

Ponderon, last seen getting off the mark in this sphere at Wetherby 152 days previously, took time to get going on this return to action and never seriously threatened. He lost his action late on and was found to have finished lame, but is capable of better than he showed this time. *(tchd 15-8)*

Hard N Sharp would have finished a touch closer but for making an error three out and posted another improved effort. He looks to type to find his feet once eligible for handicaps over timber. *(op 20-1)*

Billyandi(IRE), a bumper winner on debut at Towcester in March, ran very freely on this return from a 187-day break and never looked happy at any stage. This was a disappointing start to his hurdling career. *(op 10-1)*

1633 RACING UK H'CAP HURDLE (8 hdls) 2m 110y

4:00 (4:02) (Class 3) (0-130,125) 4-Y-0+ **£6,435** (£1,980; £990; £495)

Form RPR

00-1 **1** **Mexican Pete**[36] [1366] 5-10-11 **110** TJMurphy 125+
(A W Carroll) *hld up and bhd: smooth hdwy appr 3 out: led after 2 out: mstke last: v easily* **6/4**[1]

0-0U **2** *7* **Pirandello (IRE)**[122] [633] 7-10-9 **108** JPMcNamara 113+
(K C Bailey) *hld up: hdwy appr 4th: led 3 out: sn rdn: hdd after 2 out: no ch w wnr whn eased flat* **7/1**

40-2 **3** *1 1/2* **Mister Arjay (USA)**[27] [1434] 5-11-0 **113** ADobbin 112
(B Ellison) *led tl after 1st: lost pl 4th: rallied 5th: sn rdn: one pce fr 3 out* **10/3**[2]

-405 **4** *2 1/2* **Tulipa (POL)**[16] [1481] 6-11-7 **120** JMMaguire 118+
(T R George) *hld up: hdwy 4th: rdn and ev ch 2 out: sn wknd* **5/1**[3]

3313 **5** *6* **Scalloway (IRE)**[34] [1382] 5-10-10 **109** CLlewellyn 100
(D J Wintle) *led after 1st tl appr 4th: wknd after 3 out* **14/1**

5-10 **6** *2* **Ziggy Zen**[108] [332] 6-11-4 **117** NFehily 106
(C J Mann) *prom: led appr 4th to 3 out: sn wknd* **20/1**

000- **7** *dist* **Candarli (IRE)**[208] [4286] 9-10-13 **112** TDoyle —
(D R Gandolfo) *a bhd: lost tch: 5th: t.o* **18/1**

3m 42.6s (-13.10) **Going Correction** -0.50s/f (Good) **7** Ran SP% **108.9**
Speed ratings: **110,106,106,104,102 101,**— CSF £11.26 CT £26.14 TOTE £2.10: £1.50, £2.70; EX 18.50.
Owner First Chance Racing **Bred** First Chance Racing **Trained** Cropthorne, Worcs

FOCUS
A fair handicap run at a decent pace and the winner can be rated value for further. The form appears solid for the grade.

NOTEBOOK
Mexican Pete followed-up his previous success over course and distance in September under a typically confident ride from Murphy and easily defied a 7lb higher mark. He has been rejuvenated since joining his new stable and reverting to hurdling, as he has now won three times in as many starts over course and distance and there was an awful lot to like about the manner in which he went about his business. Having always threatened to prove better over timber, he could be finally be about to come good and could well strike again despite the Handicapper being sure to have his say after this. *(op 7-4 tchd 15-8)*
Pirandello(IRE) ◆ was a sitting duck for the winner after hitting the front with three to jump and was ultimately firmly put in his place. He was not given too hard a time when beaten on the run-in however, and this was much his best effort for some time. His stable endured a torrid time last season and this could be an indication that they may be about to turn the corner. *(op 8-1 tchd 17-2)*
Mister Arjay(USA) , raised 4lb for finishing second on his hurdling comeback at Plumpton last time, lacked the pace to rate a serious threat over this shorter trip. He still ran close to his new mark in defeat however, and can be given another chance to atone when reverting to further. *(op 3-1 tchd 11-4)*
Tulipa(POL) was in with every chance jumping the penultimate flight, yet failed to sustain her effort and dropped out rather tamely thereafter. She is worth a try over further, but still looks too high in the weights in any case. *(tchd 9-2)*

1634 HUNTINGDON RACECOURSE FOR CONFERENCES NOVICES' CHASE (19 fncs) 3m

4:30 (4:31) (Class 3) 5-Y-0+ **£5,343** (£1,644; £822; £411)

Form RPR

41P1 **1** **On The Outside (IRE)**[31] [1398] 6-10-5 113 (t) JTizzard 120+
(S E H Sherwood) *hld up: wnt 2nd 9th: led 15th: hit 3 out: clr appr last: styd on* **9/4**[2]

F2-1 **2** *5* **Bob Ar Aghaidh (IRE)**[163] [10] 9-10-12 115 TDoyle 117+
(C Tinkler) *chsd ldr to 9th: mstke 10th: outpcd 11th: rdn 4 out: rallied after 3 out: one pce fr 2 out* **5/2**[3]

0-31 **3** *3 1/2* **Savannah Bay**[36] [1365] 6-10-12 117 (b) PJBrennan 118+
(P J Hobbs) *led: rdn and hdd 15th: 4 l 2nd and btn whn blnd and rdr lost iron briefly 2 out* **15/8**[1]

/0P- **4** *dist* **Moss Campian**[177] 7-10-5 64 TBailey[(7)] —
(Mrs A V Roberts) *a in rr: hmpd 2nd: t.o fr 8th* **100/1**

61-U **F** **Stanway**[152] [193] 6-10-12 110 CLlewellyn —
(Mrs Mary Hambro) *fell 2nd* **9/1**

5m 54.8s (-17.50) **Going Correction** -0.425s/f (Good) **5** Ran SP% **105.1**
Speed ratings: **112,110,109,—,—** CSF £7.66 TOTE £3.30: £1.50, £1.70; EX 9.80.
Owner Geoffrey Vos **Bred** William O'Keeffe **Trained** Bredenbury, H'fords

FOCUS
A decent time for the class of contest and it appears to be solid form for the division. The winner is most progressive.

NOTEBOOK
On The Outside(IRE) ◆ , reverting to novice company, took up the running down the back straight and, despite a mistake at the third last, never looked in serious danger from that point on. She has now scored on three of her four outings over fences, is clearly progressing fast and again advertised her liking for a quick surface. It always pays to follow a mare in form and her female allowance will always be an advantage in this division. *(op 2-1)*
Bob Ar Aghaidh(IRE) , last seen breaking his duck over fences 163 days previously, ran very much as though he needed this outing and was not given a hard time when his fate became apparent at the top of the straight. He seemed to get this longer trip and is entitled to improve for the outing. *(op 2-1)*
Savannah Bay , who made all when making a winning chase debut at this track over shorter last time, tired to repeat the feat yet was found out by the longer trip. His rider did remarkably well to get him back in contention for the runner-up spot after losing his irons after an error two out and this one-time Group-class stayer on the Flat ought to be seen in a better light when reverting to shorter in due course. *(op 5-2)*
Moss Campian was predictably totally outclassed. *(op 66-1)*
Stanway departed way too early to tell how he would have fared. *(op 8-1)*

1635 HINCHINGBROOKE INTERMEDIATE OPEN NATIONAL HUNT FLAT RACE 2m 110y

5:00 (5:02) (Class 6) 4-6-Y-0 **£1,816** (£519; £259)

Form RPR

321- **1** **Brave Rebellion**[190] [4615] 6-11-11 JimCrowley 90+
(K G Reveley) *mde all: rdn 2f out: sn clr: r.o wl* **30/100**[1]

05- **2** *9* **Chunky Lad**[355] [1714] 5-11-4 PJBrennan 71
(W G M Turner) *hld up in tch: rdn over 2f out: wnt 2nd over 1f out: sn edgd lft: no ch w wnr* **6/1**[2]

0/0- **3** *5* **Jeepers Creepers**[292] [2852] 5-11-4 RJohnson 66
(Mrs A M Thorpe) *chsd wnr: rdn and ev ch over 2f out: wknd over 1f out* **16/1**[3]

4 *4* **Viennchee Run** 4-11-4 SCurran 62
(K F Clutterbuck) *hld up: rdn over 2f out: no rspnse* **20/1**

5 *25* **Aitchjayem**[157] 5-10-11 MrJAJenkins[(7)] 37
(H J Manners) *a bhd: lost tch 6f out: t.o* **50/1**

6 *dist* **Trizzy**[157] 5-10-4 MissJRiding[(7)] —
(H J Manners) *bhd fnl 4f: t.o* **33/1**

3m 51.3s (-5.20) **Going Correction** -0.50s/f (Good)
WFA 4 from 5yo+ 13lb **6** Ran SP% **106.8**
Speed ratings: **92,87,85,83,71** — CSF £1.98 TOTE £1.30: £1.10, £1.70; EX 2.20 Place 6 £31.69, Place 5 £16.37 .
Owner Cristiana's Crew **Bred** A G Knowles **Trained** Lingdale, N Yorks

FOCUS
A dire event, mainly due to the two late withdrawls, which provided a simple task for the winner under his penalty.

NOTEBOOK
Brave Rebellion was left with a straightforward task after the withdrawls of his two main rivals and duly made a winning return to action in easy fashion. He may not have beaten much, but he settled better than when winning over course and distance when last seen 190 days previously and will be high on confidence now for an impending switch to novice hurdles. *(op 2-5)*
Chunky Lad emerged as a clear second best, without ever holding a chance with the winner, and was not disgraced on this return from a 355-day break. *(op 5-1 tchd 9-2)*
Jeepers Creepers paid for trying to go with the winner from two out and had nothing left in the tank when pressed by the eventual runner-up. He is at least entitled to come on for this outing. *(op 12-1 tchd 20-1)*
Viennchee Run , out of a winning pointer, failed to find anything when asked to improve approaching two out and was well beaten. He will no doubt be seen in a better light over further in due course, but is clearly only modest. *(op 16-1 tchd 25-1)*
T/Plt: £30.20 to a £1 stake. Pool: £42,724.20. 1,031.15 winning tickets. T/Qpdt: £9.40 to a £1 stake. Pool: £3,138.10. 246.80 winning tickets. KH

[294] EXETER (R-H)

Wednesday, October 5

OFFICIAL GOING: Firm (good to firm in places)
Wind: Light against.

1636 DEAN & DYBALL CONDITIONAL JOCKEYS' (S) H'CAP HURDLE (10 hdls) 2m 3f

2:10 (2:10) (Class 5) (0-95,95) 4-Y-0+ **£3,083** (£881; £440)

Form RPR

6P50 **1** **Island Warrior (IRE)**[37] [1362] 10-10-0 **69** oh3 (tp) TJPhelan 77+
(B P J Baugh) *chsd ldrs: led sn after 5th: jnd beford 3 out: rdn and hit 2 out: kpt on and in command run-in* **66/1**

4P00 **2** *1 1/2* **Suchwot (IRE)**[17] [1483] 4-9-12 **70** (vt) TJMalone[(3)] 75
(M C Pipe) *w.w: rdn and hdwy appr 5th: jnd wnr bef 3 out: wnt lft last 2 and no imp run-in* **13/2**

4006 **3** *20* **Simon's Seat (USA)**[12] [1539] 6-10-6 **80** (p) JamesWhite[(5)] 65
(S C Burrough) *mid-div: hdwy and rdn to chse first 2 appr 3 out: sn btn* **4/1**[1]

0-00 **4** *shd* **Tizi Ouzou (IRE)**[35] [1381] 4-11-6 **92** PMerrigan[(3)] 77
(M C Pipe) *bhd: railed off 3rd: mstke next: styd on past btn horses fr 3 out* **9/1**

-455 **5** *1 3/4* **Timidjar (IRE)**[32] [1395] 12-10-1 **75** RSpate[(5)] 58
(Mrs D Thomas) *bhd and nvr nr to chal* **8/1**

1-00 **6** *5* **Luminoso**[84] [973] 13-11-4 **92** AHawkins[(5)] 70
(J D J Davies) *hld up in mid-div: sme hdwy after 7th: nvr on terms* **16/1**

-B54 **7** *7* **Penny's Crown**[17] [1486] 6-10-12 **84** EDehdashti[(3)] 55
(G A Ham) *mid-div: wknd 3 out* **5/1**[2]

P-44 **8** *14* **Governor Daniel**[37] [1362] 14-11-4 **95** DJBoland[(8)] 52
(Ian Williams) *chsd ldrs tl wknd after 7th* **9/1**

PP **9** *2 1/2* **Cappacurry (IRE)**[10] [1560] 6-10-8 **77** (vt[1]) PCO'Neill 32
(Evan Williams) *chsd ldr tl wknd appr 3 out* **20/1**

6-00 **10** *24* **Bebe Factual (GER)**[58] [1021] 4-10-10 **82** (b) SWalsh[(3)] 13
(J D Frost) *led sn clr: wkng whn hit 5th: sn hdd* **25/1**

PP-5 **P** **Past Heritage**[65] [1123] 6-10-3 **72** DLaverty —
(A E Jones) *a bhd: t.o whn p.u after 7th* **11/2**[3]

020P **P** **Rumbling Bridge**[13] [1523] 4-10-11 **80** (b[1]) TGreenway —
(Miss J S Davis) *mid-div: wknd appr 7th: t.o whn p.u bef 2 out* **20/1**

4m 18.7s (-22.20) **Going Correction** -1.075s/f (Hard) **12** Ran SP% **117.2**
Speed ratings: **103,102,93,93,93 91,88,82,81,71** —,— CSF £441.23 CT £2147.66 TOTE £57.30: £12.30, £3.90, £1.90; EX 633.50.
Owner D N Longstaff **Bred** Hugh Harley **Trained** Audley, Staffs

FOCUS
The ground was lightening fast for this meeting and some times were very quick, including this race. A very poor seller and a complete shock. The form does not look sound.

NOTEBOOK
Island Warrior(IRE) travelled nicely for much of the race from 3lb out of the weights. He completely reversed form with Governor Daniel on his last run but, as this was his first win since April 2002, a repeat of this effort is far from guaranteed.Official explanation: trainer said, regarding the improved form shown, yard was suffering from a virus when gelding ran poorly last time *(op 50-1)*
Suchwot(IRE) weaved his own route around the track and received a reminder in the dip on the far side. He jumped out to his left at the last, which probably cost him any chance of victory, and it was also noticeable that his ears were firmly back under pressure. *(op 10-1)*
Simon's Seat(USA) was well backed before the race but never threatened to get involved. He is without a win over hurdles and has regularly been beaten heavily in all previous attempts. *(op 7-1)*
Tizi Ouzou(IRE), who was well behind at a very early stage, did well to get as close as she did. *(op 8-1)*
Timidjar(IRE) is possibly a little better than his finishing position suggests. *(op 13-2)*
Penny's Crown was extremely disappointing for no apparent reason. *(op 6-1)*
Governor Daniel who was being niggled from an early stage and ran no race at all. *(op 5-1)*

1637 NASH AND CO NOVICES' H'CAP HURDLE (11 hdls) 2m 6f 110y

2:40 (2:40) (Class 4) (0-100,90) 3-Y-0+ **£3,818** (£1,175; £587; £293)

Form RPR

0P-3 **1** **Glacial Delight (IRE)**[152] [201] 6-11-12 **90** BFenton 104+
(Miss E C Lavelle) *hld up in rr: smooth hdwy fr 7th: led 3 out: clr next: comf* **7/2**[2]

25-4 **2** *8* **Moorland Monarch**[160] [74] 7-11-0 **83** CHonour[(5)] 82
(J D Frost) *mid-div: hdwy: 7th: wnt 2nd after 2 out: no ch w wnr* **16/1**

1445 **3** *1 1/2* **Keltic Lord**[11] [1549] 9-11-10 **88** RThornton 86
(P W Hiatt) *mid-div: rdn and hdwy after 5th: kpt on one pce fr 3 out* **2/1**[1]

50-0 **4** *4* **Orion Express**[12] [1541] 4-10-11 **83** LHeard[(7)] 76
(M Hill) *chsd ldrs: rdn appr 3 out: sn btn* **20/1**

-6P0 **5** *1 1/2* **Hill Forts Henry**[10] [1564] 7-10-11 **78** (p) RYoung[(3)] 70
(J W Mullins) *trckd ldr: led after 8th: rdn and hdd 3 out: wknd* **14/1**

0404 **6** *1 3/4* **Tyup Pompey (IRE)**[31] [1407] 4-11-4 **83** JamesDavies 72
(Miss J S Davis) *hld up: a in rr* **40/1**

-205 **7** *8* **Mollycarrsbrekfast**[31] 1414 10-10-13 **77** TDoyle 59
(K Bishop) *led tl hdd after 8th: wknd rapidly sn after* **15/2**[3]

0030 **8** *30* **Nice Baby (FR)**[84] 978 4-11-9 **88** (vt) GSupple 39
(M C Pipe) *a in rr: rdn appr 6th: t.o* **11/1**

P00- **P** **Oasis Banus (IRE)**[198] 4496 4-10-7 **72** TJMurphy —
(M C Pipe) *hld up in rr: rdn and lost tch 7th: t.o whn p.u bef last* **7/2**[2]

5m 18.9s (-20.40) **Going Correction** -1.075s/f (Hard) course record
WFA 4 from 6yo+ 14lb **9** Ran SP% **117.6**
Speed ratings: **92,89,88,87,86 86,83,72,**— CSF £55.82 CT £141.61 TOTE £4.80: £2.10, £3.80, £1.10; EX 39.30.
Owner The Friday Night Racing Club **Bred** Patrick Tarrant **Trained** Wildhern, Hants
■ A winner for Barry Fenton on his first ride since breaking his leg in January.

FOCUS
Not a strong race and a modest winning time for the grade, but the winner did it well and is value for 15 lengths.

NOTEBOOK
Glacial Delight(IRE) was going much the best of the leaders and, as the gaps opened up in front of him along the rail, he moved nicely into the lead and came home smoothly. This was his handicap debut after a layoff, and he looks fairly well treated. A winner between the flags in Ireland, he has the size to go on and make a nice chaser under Rules, but will probably stay over the smaller obstacles until the Handicapper gets hold of him. *(op 10-3 tchd 3-1)*
Moorland Monarch was well beaten by the time he passed the line but did not shape without promise on his return to the track after a 160-day absence. He was tried over fences last season and will presumably be sent over them again in the near future.
Keltic Lord was 16lb better off over timber compared with his winning form over fences, but he never looked like making that advantage tell. He has had plenty of racing since the spring and is probably ready for a nice break. *(op 15-8 tchd 9-4)*
Orion Express probably ran his best race to date after travelling well for a lot of the race. *(op 28-1)*
Mollycarrsbrekfast faded right out of contention after making a lot of the early running. *(op 8-1)*
Oasis Banus(IRE) was subject to market support before the race but showed very little again. He will struggle to win a race of any description unless he finds improvement from somewhere. *(op 6-1)*

1638 DEAN & DYBALL CHALLENGE TROPHY BEGINNERS' CHASE (17 fncs) 2m 7f 110y
3:10 (3:10) (Class 4) 5-Y-0+ **£4,761** (£1,465; £732; £366)

Form RPR

12-6 **1** **Castlemore (IRE)**[150] 244 7-11-0 RJohnson 110+
(P J Hobbs) *trckd ldrs: lft in ld 8th: clr 12th: blnd 3 out: heavily eased run-in* **10/11**[1]

U **2** *18* **Our Mr Navigator (IRE)**[24] 1455 7-11-0 SCurran 75
(N R Mitchell) *j.lft thrght: hld up bhd ldrs: wnt 2nd 11th: no imp fr next* **16/1**

P3FP **3** *2* **Rings Of Power (IRE)**[121] 669 8-10-11 68 RYoung(3) 73
(N R Mitchell) *hld up in rr: wnt 3rd 12th but no hdwy after* **4/1**[2]

PP **4** *10* **Box On (IRE)**[94] 893 8-10-9 102 LStephens(5) 63
(B J Llewellyn) *a bhd: lost tch 8th* **6/1**[3]

04-P **5** *18* **Rollo (IRE)**[4] 1599 7-10-7 95 (v) CPoste(7) 51+
(M F Harris) *mstkes: chsd wnr 8th to 11th: wkng whn hit 12th* **6/1**[3]

30PP **F** **Lescer's Lad**[80] 1018 8-10-7 76 CMStudd(7) —
(C L Popham) *trckd ldr: led 3rd tl fell 8th* **25/1**

5m 46.4s (-132.2) **Going Correction** -0.55s/f (Firm) **6** Ran SP% **110.7**
Speed ratings: **98,92,91,88,82** — CSF £14.35 TOTE £1.60: £1.50, £5.00; EX 12.60.
Owner Castlemore Securities Limited **Bred** Malachy Hanley **Trained** Withycombe, Somerset

FOCUS
A very moderate novice chase, easily won by the winner, who looked value for 35 lengths. Those in behind did not show anything to suggest that they are about to win.

NOTEBOOK
Castlemore(IRE) had more trouble with the fences and a fallen horse than he did with any of his rivals, and walked across the winning line a long way clear of the runner-up. He did well to get past Lescer's Lad when that one fell at the eighth, and a mistake at the third last were his only real problems. Reported to have finished lame last time, connections will be delighted to have collected this sizeable winning prize for little more than a schooling session. *(op 6-5 tchd 4-5)*
Our Mr Navigator(IRE) has had his fair share of problems getting around the track, but he jumped pretty well this time and will hopefully derive confidence for the run. However, he was completely outclassed and will need his sights considerably lowered. *(op 14-1)*
Rings Of Power(IRE) never got close and is only rated 68. *(op 7-2)*
Box On(IRE) was always in rear and was another never to pose any threat. *(op 5-1 tchd 13-2)*
Rollo(IRE) made a bad error in front of the stands first time around and looked to lose his confidence just after. However, he was still in contention on the far side before fading right out of it up the home straight. *(tchd 7-1)*
Lescer's Lad was seen walking away after the race looking reasonably sound after a horrible-looking fall. *(tchd 33-1)*

1639 DEAN & DYBALL H'CAP CHASE (19 fncs) 3m 1f 110y
3:40 (3:40) (Class 4) (0-110,106) 5-Y-0+ **£5,427** (£1,670; £835; £417)

Form RPR

0P-0 **1** **Saffron Sun**[122] 653 10-11-5 **99** RJohnson 112+
(J D Frost) *trckd ldr: led 7th to 8th: j. slowly 14th: led and j.rt fr 4 out: rdn out run-in* **2/1**[1]

/0-1 **2** *1 ½* **Galtee View (IRE)**[1] 1631 7-11-1 **95** 7ex (p) PMoloney 104+
(Evan Williams) *hld up in rr: hdwy appr 4 out: wnt 2nd bef 2 out: styd on* **9/2**

5205 **3** *13* **River Quoile**[10] 1560 9-10-0 **80** RWalford 78+
(R H Alner) *a.p: led 8th to 12th: one pce fr 4 out* **4/1**[3]

4124 **4** *2 ½* **Uncle Mick (IRE)**[17] 1484 10-11-12 **106** (p) JTizzard 100
(C L Tizzard) *trckd ldrs: led 12th: rdn after 15th: hdd & wknd 4 out* **10/3**[2]

PP06 **5** *11* **Sunday Habits (IRE)**[17] 1484 11-9-7 **80** oh15 MrDavidTurner(7) 63
(Dr P Pritchard) *a in tch: led 8th to 12th: one pce fr 4 out* **33/1**

F3-4 **6** *5* **Rag Week (IRE)**[36] 1378 8-10-0 **85** PCO'Neill(5) 63
(Evan Williams) *chsd ldrs: rdn and lost position 8th: a bhd after* **6/1**

6m 8.30s (-19.70) **Going Correction** -0.55s/f (Firm) course record **6** Ran SP% **111.8**
Speed ratings: **108,107,103,102,99 97** CSF £11.42 TOTE £2.40: £1.20, £4.30; EX 15.80.
Owner Mrs J F Bury **Bred** G Blight **Trained** Scorriton, Devon

FOCUS
A very moderate chase, but the first two are probably capable of a bit better. Saffron Sun likes it around Exeter and gained another win here after getting first run.

NOTEBOOK
Saffron Sun has run well after a break before and was returning after being absent for 122 days here. Extremely well handicapped on the best of his form, he completed his fifth course success with the minimum of fuss. Travelling keenly just behind the leaders, he jumped well, albeit markedly out to the right up the straight, and got first run on his rivals to win nicely. The winning distance should not see him raised too much in the handicap and he can win again. *(op 9-4 tchd 15-8)*
Galtee View(IRE) was making a quick reappearance after his win the previous day. Penalised 7lb for that victory and running over about half-a-mile further, he stalked the pace at the rear of the field and was probably beaten by the winner's injection of pace three from home. *(op 7-2)*
River Quoile moved nicely for much of the race but was readily left behind as they entered the straight. He remains a maiden under Rules and is becoming disappointing. *(op 5-1)*
Uncle Mick(IRE) was being pushed along passing the stands for the first time, but did manage to get to the lead by the halfway point. He has had plenty of racing during the summer and weakened in the final stages. *(op 7-2)*
Sunday Habits(IRE) did well to get around after being under pressure almost from flag fall.
Rag Week(IRE), the stable's second string, never threatened to take a hand in proceedings and was most disappointing.

1640 DEAN & DYBALL NOVICES' HURDLE (8 hdls) 2m 1f
4:10 (4:11) (Class 4) 4-Y-0+ **£4,290** (£1,320; £660; £330)

Form RPR

1 **Boychuk (IRE)**[86] 966 4-10-12 RJohnson 101+
(P J Hobbs) *a in tch: led after 5th: qcknd clr whn chal 2 out: readily: promising* **4/11**[1]

0P **2** *10* **Brown Fox (FR)**[52] 1222 4-10-5 MBradburne 74
(C J Down) *hld up in rr: hdwy after 5th: wnt 2nd after 2f out: nt pce of wnr* **50/1**

/P00 **3** *2 ½* **Raneen Nashwan**[12] 1541 9-10-12 77 (p) VSlattery 78
(R J Baker) *led 4th tl after 5th: sn rdn and one pce fr 3 out* **14/1**

1006 **4** *3* **Wardash (GER)**[37] 1363 5-11-5 88 (vt) TJMurphy 82
(M C Pipe) *led tl after 2nd: styd prom tl rdn appr 3 out: one pce after* **7/1**[2]

00-0 **5** *5* **Barum Belle**[35] 1383 5-10-5 (t) ATinkler 66+
(R A Farrant) *mid-div: hung lft approaching 3 out: sn btn* **50/1**

6 *13* **Life Estates**[137] 5-10-7 CHonour(5) 57
(J D Frost) *hld up: a bhd* **50/1**

0- **7** *hd* **Oasis Blue (IRE)**[316] 2413 4-10-9 TJMalone(3) 57
(M C Pipe) *led after 2nd: hdd 4th: wknd qckly appr 3 out* **12/1**[3]

0 **8** *dist* **Impatient Lady**[35] 1383 8-10-5 JTizzard —
(J D Frost) *virtually ref to r: a t.o* **20/1**

(-9.20) **Going Correction** -1.075s/f (Hard)
WFA 4 from 5yo+ 13lb **8** Ran SP% **110.8**
Speed ratings: **78,73,72,70,68 62,62,**— CSF £30.46 TOTE £1.30: £1.10, £8.80, £2.20; EX 32.10.
Owner Mrs D L Whateley **Bred** Robert Donaldson **Trained** Withycombe, Somerset

FOCUS
A very modest novice hurdle run in a slow time for the conditions. The winner, rated value for 20 lengths, will probably leave this form well behind in due course.

NOTEBOOK
Boychuk(IRE), sold out of the John Kiely stable for 36,000gns, won very easily and found the obstacles his only challenge. He will need to become more fluent as he rises in class, but he looks money well spent by the same owners who secured Gold Medallist last season. *(tchd 8-15 in a place)*
Brown Fox(FR) momentarily looked a danger approaching two out but folded quickly under pressure and was ultimately well beaten. She collected a couple of wins in her native France over six and seven furlongs, and is more than capable of winning an ordinary maiden as long as stamina does not become an issue. *(op 33-1)*
Raneen Nashwan is a 77-rated maiden over hurdles and gives those behind him little cause for enthusiasm in the near future. *(op 16-1)*
Wardash(GER) had an impossible task giving the winner weight having only won two sellers. He is not that consistent and is difficult to predict. *(op 5-1)*
Barum Belle appeared to have problems negotiating the home turn but was never causing the leader any problems. *(op 33-1)*
Oasis Blue(IRE) should not be totally dismisssed in the future as he showed a modicum of ability. *(tchd 14-1)*
Impatient Lady started well behind the rest of the field and is not to be trusted. *(op 16-1 tchd 14-1)*

1641 HARRIET HALF CENTURY H'CAP HURDLE (10 hdls) 2m 3f
4:40 (4:40) (Class 3) (0-125,114) 4-Y-0+ **£5,148** (£1,584; £792; £396)

Form RPR

-421 **1** **Yourman (IRE)**[13] 1525 5-11-12 **114** TJMurphy 120+
(M C Pipe) *hld up: smooth hdwy after 7th: led appr 2 out: hung lft and strly rdn: all out run-in* **9/4**[1]

2121 **2** *1 ¼* **Fire Ranger**[35] 1383 9-10-10 **98** RJohnson 100
(J D Frost) *hld up: hdwy to go 2nd after 7th: ev ch last but nt qckn run-in* **11/4**[2]

035/ **3** *4* **Quintus (USA)**[54] 1127 10-10-11 **99** RThornton 97
(A King) *hld up: hadway after 7th: no imp fr 3 out* **7/2**[3]

6300 **4** *½* **Red Canyon (IRE)**[17] 1482 8-10-5 **93** (v) JTizzard 92+
(C L Tizzard) *led: lft wl clr 4th: rdn appr 3 out: hdd & wknd bef next* **8/1**

0411 **5** *3* **Outside Investor (IRE)**[31] 1405 5-10-8 **103** (p) KBurke(7) 98
(P R Rodford) *in tch: lft 2nd 4th: wknd appr 3 out* **12/1**

3/1- **6** *2* **Noble Calling (FR)**[58] 49 8-11-1 **110** JamesWhite(7) 103
(R J Hodges) *hld up: wknd after 7th* **8/1**

3415 **F** **Arm And A Leg (IRE)**[13] 1525 10-11-1 **108** RStephens(5) —
(Mrs D A Hamer) *trakce ldr tl fell 4th* **12/1**

4m 21.5s (-19.40) **Going Correction** -1.075s/f (Hard) **7** Ran SP% **117.3**
Speed ratings: **97,96,94,94,93 92,**— CSF £9.61 CT £20.64 TOTE £2.90: £1.80, £1.60; EX 8.10 Place 6 £11.79, Place 5 £4.31.
Owner D A Johnson **Bred** Matt Carr **Trained** Nicholashayne, Devon
■ Stewards' Enquiry : T J Murphy caution: used whip down the shoulder in the forehand position

FOCUS
This was run in a considerably slower time than the opening seller. The winner is probably value for more than the winning margin, and the second continues to improve at her level.

NOTEBOOK
Yourman(IRE), dropping three furlongs in trip and raised 6lb since scoring at Fontwell, was given a really patient waiting ride and hit the front just before the second last. It was very noticeable that the jockey wanted to keep him close to his rivals but, despite his best efforts, he hung left under pressure and nearly gave away his advantage. No doubt there was more left in the locker than looked apparent, but he clearly needs a really confident ride to be seen at his very best. *(op 5-2 tchd 3-1)*
Fire Ranger is a consistent sort at her level and almost completed a double on the day for her small stable. She may have been slightly flattered to finish so close but appeared to run up to her best and can be placed to win another race during the season. *(op 3-1)*
Quintus(USA) had form in similar conditions in Ireland and, on his first start for the Alan King stable, stayed on well from the rear after getting outpaced in the back straight. *(op 5-1)*
Red Canyon(IRE) set off at a quick pace in front and did not have a lot left in reserve at the end of the race. *(op 11-1)*
Outside Investor(IRE) was racing off a 23lb higher mark than for his win back in August, and shaped accordingly. *(op 9-1)*
Noble Calling(FR) has a good record at this track but was most disappointing.
T/Plt: £22.30 to a £1 stake. Pool: £40,011.40. 1,305.80 winning tickets. T/Qpdt: £4.50 to a £1 stake. Pool: £2,812.70. 456.60 winning tickets. JS

531 TOWCESTER (R-H)

Wednesday, October 5

OFFICIAL GOING: Good to firm

Wind: Almost nil Weather: Overcast

1642 JEWSON NOVICES' HURDLE (SERIES QUALIFIER) (8 hdls) 2m

2:30 (2:30) (Class 3) 4-Y-0+ **£5,512** (£1,696; £848; £424)

Form RPR

4312 **1** **Smart Boy Prince (IRE)**[12] [1541] 4-11-4 110 .... WHutchinson 110+
(C Smith) *mde all: rdn appr last: r.o wl* **11/4**[3]

1 **2** *3 ½* **Anticipating**[17] [1480] 5-11-4 .... PHide 106
(G L Moore) *hld up: hdwy 5th: chsd wnr 2 out: sn rdn: no imp* **5/2**[2]

46-3 **3** *4* **Night Sight (USA)**[11] [1553] 8-10-9 94 ....(v[1]) LVickers(3) 96
(Mrs S Lamyman) *hld up in rr: hdwy 3 out: rdn 2 out: 3rd and btn whn no fluent last* **18/1**

4 **4** *7* **Carte Sauvage (USA)**[17] [1480] 4-10-12 .... PJBrennan 90+
(M F Harris) *chsd wnr: bmpd 4th: sn rdn: wknd 2 out* **7/1**

0P/P **5** *20* **Brandeston Ron (IRE)**[160] [79] 6-10-12 ....(t) CLlewellyn 74+
(M Pitman) *t.k.h: prom: wknd 3 out: bhd whn hmpd 2 out* **66/1**

12-F **F** **Mister Mustard (IRE)**[153] [194] 8-11-8 120 .... APMcCoy 95
(Ian Williams) *hld up: hdwy appr 3 out: 6 l 5th and wkng whn fell 2 out* **15/8**[1]

3m 42.3s (-29.10) **Going Correction** -1.70s/f (Hard)
WFA 4 from 5yo+ 13lb **6** Ran SP% **109.3**
Speed ratings: **104,102,100,96,86** — CSF £9.72 TOTE £3.50: £1.60, £1.50; EX 10.10.
Owner Phil Martin **Bred** J Kennedy **Trained** Temple Bruer, Lincs

FOCUS
Just an ordinary novices' hurdle, but third-placed Night Sight should not really be used to hold the form down too much as he is probably a little better than his previous form over obstacles would suggest.

NOTEBOOK
Smart Boy Prince(IRE) is developing into a fair hurdler and made it two wins from his last three starts with a decisive success. This was a moderate race, but he is still improving and could go well in the Jewson series final at Cheltenham. *(op 3-1 tchd 5-2, 7-2 in a place and 10-3 in a place)*
Anticipating, a fair middle-distance handicapper on the Flat who got off the mark on his hurdling debut at Plumpton, ran well under his penalty but just bumped into a progressive sort with more experience over obstacles. He should continue to go the right way. *(op 3-1)*
Night Sight(USA) ◆, fitted with a visor for the first time instead of cheekpieces, never really threatened the front two but still posted a very creditable effort in second. He could be interesting in low-grade handicap company. *Official explanation: trainer said gelding was struck into (op 14-1)*
Carte Sauvage(USA), a one-time smart Flat performer, failed to build on the promise he showed *on his hurdling debut at Plumpton and made just finishing fourth look very hard work. (op 9-1 tchd 13-2)*
Mister Mustard(IRE), well held when falling at Wetherby when last seen 153 days previously, was again beaten when coming down. He had no easy task giving weight away all round, but was still well below the form he showed when rattling up a hat-trick last season. He could do better stepped back up in trip and switched to soft ground. *(op 13-8 tchd 2-1)*

1643 EPSON (S) HURDLE (10 hdls) 2m 3f 110y

3:00 (3:03) (Class 5) 4-7-Y-0 **£2,891** (£826; £413)

Form RPR

/0-0 **1** **Banningham Blaze**[17] [1486] 5-10-5 85 ....(v) WHutchinson 82+
(A W Carroll) *hld up and bhd: hdwy appr 2 out: led last: rdn out* **4/1**[2]

P-U6 **2** *1* **Nick The Silver**[11] [1552] 4-10-8 95 ....(p) AGlassonbury(10) 94
(M C Pipe) *a.p: rdn to ld after 2 out: hdd last: r.o* **5/1**[3]

6316 **3** *10* **Sheer Guts (IRE)**[4] [1597] 6-11-4 91 ....(vt) AThornton 84
(Robert Gray) *hld up in mid-div: led after 3 out: rdn and hdd after 2 out: wknd last* **7/2**[1]

-626 **4** *3* **Relative Hero (IRE)**[37] [1362] 5-10-12 75 ....(p) NFehily 76+
(Miss S J Wilton) *prom: lost pl appr 3 out: btn whn mstke 2 out* **8/1**

5F06 **5** *3 ½* **Regulated (IRE)**[13] [1522] 4-10-9 89 ....(p) CBolger(3) 72
(P A Blockley) *led: hung lft 3rd: rdn and hdd after 3 out: sn wknd* **11/2**

P-PP **6** *1 ¼* **Maunby Roller (IRE)**[39] [1343] 6-10-12 70 ....(p) LAspell 70
(K A Morgan) *w ldr: rdn and ev ch appr 2 out: sn wknd* **33/1**

2PP- **7** *18* **Jug Of Punch (IRE)**[258] [3433] 6-10-7 86 .... MNicolls(5) 55+
(S T Lewis) *hld up in tch: wknd appr 2 out* **18/1**

P0P- **8** *dist* **Zadok The Priest (IRE)**[403] [1304] 5-10-12 82 ....(t) WMarston —
(B S Rothwell) *a bhd: hit 2nd: t.o fr 3 out* **14/1**

6F-0 **9** *1 ¼* **Gold For Me (FR)**[10] [1565] 6-10-7 95 .... DMcGann(5) —
(A C Wilson) *a bhd: t.o fr 3 out* **8/1**

4m 45.1s (-33.00) **Going Correction** -1.70s/f (Hard)
WFA 4 from 5yo+ 13lb **9** Ran SP% **111.4**
Speed ratings: **98,97,93,92,91 90,83,—,—** CSF £23.37 TOTE £4.60: £1.80, £2.10, £1.80; EX 19.00.The winner was bought in for 6,000gns. Nick The Silver was claimed by Naughty Diesel Ltd for £6,000.
Owner Dennis Deacon **Bred** D J And Mrs Deer **Trained** Cropthorne, Worcs

FOCUS
A typically moderate seller but the first three appear to have run to their marks and the form might work out alright.

NOTEBOOK
Banningham Blaze had not shown much in three runs on the Flat this year and was well beaten on his return to hurdles in a similar event over two miles six at Uttoxeter last time but, dropped in distance, she was well backed and stepped up significantly on her recent efforts under a fine waiting from Wayne Hutchinson. She was, though, best off at the weights. *(tchd 7-2)*
Nick The Silver, whose only previous win came in a claimer over three miles two, had the speed to cope with this shorter trip and ran well behind the clearly well-fancied Banningham Blaze on his *first run in selling company. Well ahead of the remainder, he looks up to winning a similar race. (op 6-1 tchd 9-2)*
Sheer Guts(IRE), twice a course winner, ran better than at Fontwell just four days earlier on his debut for a new trainer, but he did not quite see out his race and this may have come a little too soon. *(op 11-4 tchd 4-1)*
Relative Hero(IRE) had it all to do at the weights so this was probably not that bad an effort. *(op 14-1)*
Regulated(IRE), dropped in grade with the cheekpieces re-fitted, did not offer a great deal. *(op 6-1)*

1644 EPSON BEGINNERS' CHASE (12 fncs) 2m 110y

3:30 (3:32) (Class 3) 4-Y-0+ **£5,460** (£1,680; £840; £420)

Form RPR

05-3 **1** **Winsley**[159] [104] 7-11-6 .... LAspell 115+
(O Sherwood) *hld up: stmbld appr 6th: hdwy 7th: led appr 4 out: clr fr 3 out: easily* **7/4**[1]

3P-P **2** *9* **Rookery Lad**[11] [1552] 7-11-6 100 .... DCrosse 103
(C N Kellett) *hld up in tch: led after 5th tl appr 4 out: one pce fr 3 out* **7/1**

2-53 **3** *11* **Low Cloud**[41] [1318] 5-11-6 .... APMcCoy 93+
(J J Quinn) *t.k.h: mstkes: hdwy 7th: wknd after 3 out* **2/1**[2]

4-00 **4** *23* **Noble Colours**[28] [1433] 12-10-13 61 .... TMessenger(7) 69
(Mrs C J Ikin) *w ldrs to 6th* **50/1**

0-55 **F** **True Mariner (FR)**[10] [1561] 5-11-6 109 .... JAMcCarthy —
(B I Case) *in tch whn fell 4th* **5/1**[3]

66 **U** **Tellem Noting (IRE)**[13] [1521] 8-11-6 76 ....(t) JPMcNamara —
(B G Powell) *led: hdd whn blnd and uns rdr 4th* **22/1**

PP- **P** **Kim Buck (FR)**[318] [2369] 7-11-6 .... PJBrennan —
(K A Morgan) *a bhd: hmpd 4th: hung lft after 7th: t.o whn p.u bef 2 out* **33/1**

P-P5 **F** **Tumbleweed Glen (IRE)**[12] [1540] 9-11-6 57 ....(b) CLlewellyn —
(P Kelsall) *prom: led 4th tl after 5th: 4 l 4th whn fell 4 out* **66/1**

4m 6.90s (-12.40) **Going Correction** -0.725s/f (Firm) **8** Ran SP% **109.6**
Speed ratings: **100,95,90,79,— —,—,—** CSF £12.70 TOTE £2.10: £1.10, £1.70, £1.50; EX 16.40.
Owner Absolute Solvents Ltd **Bred** P K Gardner **Trained** Upper Lambourn, Berks

FOCUS
A weak beginners' chase won comfortably by Winsley, but his performance has been rated as still 9lb off his best hurdling form so there could be better still to come.

NOTEBOOK
Winsley, a 119-rated hurdler, offered promise on his chasing debut when third at Wetherby on his last start 159 days ago and stepped up on that on his return from a break to run out a comfortable winner. Oliver Sherwood thinks he is best when kept fresh, so he could find more opportunities if given the right amount of time between races. *(op 6-4 tchd 15-8)*
Rookery Lad had been pulled up on his two latest starts, including back over hurdles on his previous outing, but he is not that bad on his day and, returned to fences, fared best behind the easy winner. *(op 9-1 tchd 10-1 in places)*
Low Cloud, just as when third on his chasing debut at Bangor, raced keenly and did not always jump that well. He has the ability, but still appears to have a fair bit to learn. *(op 5-2)*
Tumbleweed Glen(IRE) was still close up when falling, but there was still a long way to go. *(tchd 11-2)*
True Mariner(FR) fell too early to know how he might have fared and remains winless over fences. *(tchd 11-2)*

1645 EPSON H'CAP HURDLE (8 hdls) 2m

4:00 (4:01) (Class 4) (0-95,95) 4-Y-0+ **£3,601** (£1,108; £554; £277)

Form RPR

043 **1** **Young Tot (IRE)**[66] [1107] 7-11-2 85 .... PJBrennan 88+
(M Sheppard) *mde virtually all: j.lft 2 out and last: drvn out* **10/1**

U202 **2** *1* **Murphy's Nails (IRE)**[26] [1443] 8-11-12 95 ....(p) JPMcNamara 97
(K C Bailey) *w wnr: rdn appr 2 out: r.o flat* **9/1**

P461 **3** *nk* **Honan (IRE)**[17] [1483] 6-11-1 94 ....(v) AGlassonbury(10) 96
(M C Pipe) *hld up: hdwy appr 5th: rdn appr 2 out: kpt on flat* **11/1**

/56- **4** *nk* **Treasure Trail**[181] [4759] 6-11-7 90 .... WHutchinson 91
(Ian Williams) *a.p: rdn appr 2 out: nt qckn flat* **12/1**

4465 **5** *6* **Spider Boy**[17] [1482] 8-9-8 70 ....(p) RLucey-Butler(7) 65
(Miss Z C Davison) *prom: 5th and btn whn hit last* **25/1**

6 *¾* **Hi Laurie (IRE)**[17] [1493] 10-11-1 84 .... TScudamore 79
(M Scudamore) *bhd tl styd on fr 2 out: nvr trbld ldrs* **11/2**[1]

00-0 **7** *1 ½* **City Palace**[39] [1337] 4-10-3 72 .... ChristianWilliams 65
(Evan Williams) *hld up towards rr: hdwy appr 2 out: nvr trbld ldrs* **6/1**[2]

00-5 **8** *1* **Reflex Blue**[31] [1413] 8-11-2 85 ....(v) AO'Keeffe 77
(R J Price) *chsd ldrs tl wknd appr 2 out* **25/1**

U3-4 **9** *8* **Double Royal (IRE)**[28] [1432] 6-11-6 89 .... DCrosse 73
(Mrs T J Hill) *nvr nr ldrs* **25/1**

/55- **10** *¾* **Libre**[59] [1446] 5-10-10 79 .... LAspell 62
(F Jordan) *hld up and bhd: hdwy into mid-div appr 3 out: wknd appr 2 out* **15/2**[3]

0- **11** *2 ½* **Kinkeel (IRE)**[195] [4536] 6-11-7 90 .... NFehily 71
(A W Carroll) *t.k.h in mid-div: rdn appr 2 out: sn wknd* **8/1**

-540 **12** *4* **Bronco Charlie (IRE)**[43] [1302] 7-11-9 92 .... APMcCoy 69
(Jonjo O'Neill) *a bhd* **8/1**

000U **13** *shd* **Macgyver (NZ)**[52] [1219] 9-10-6 82 .... CaptLHorner(7) 59
(D L Williams) *a bhd* **66/1**

1340 **14** *8* **Fenney Spring**[39] [1336] 5-10-5 74 ....(bt) CLlewellyn 43
(W Jenks) *hld up: hdwy appr 4: wknd 3 out* **16/1**

/0-0 **15** *9* **My Sharp Grey**[32] [1400] 6-11-12 95 .... OMcPhail 55
(J Gallagher) *a bhd* **66/1**

3m 45.6s (-25.80) **Going Correction** -1.70s/f (Hard)
WFA 4 from 5yo+ 13lb **15** Ran SP% **119.2**
Speed ratings: **96,95,95,95,92 91,91,90,86,86 84,82,82,78,74** CSF £91.21 CT £1015.77 TOTE £14.00: £3.70, £3.90, £3.90; EX 79.20.
Owner Out Of Bounds Racing Club **Bred** James Patrick Kelly **Trained** Eastnor, H'fords

FOCUS
A moderate handicap hurdle run at an ordinary pace early on. The race has been rated through the second and fourth.

NOTEBOOK
Young Tot(IRE) was still a maiden going into this following two runs in bumpers, 13 over hurdles, and four runs over fences, and he was beaten in a seller when last seen but, making his debut for a new trainer on the back of a 66-day break, he was ridden much more positively than was usually the case and responded well to the tactics. He should not go up too much for this and could progress now he has finally got his head in front.
Murphy's Nails(IRE), with the cheekpieces back on, confirmed the promise he showed on his return from a break over two and a half miles at Bangor on his previous start, but made hard work of securing second and gave the impression he can do better back up in trip. *(op 8-1 tchd 10-1)*
Honan(IRE), 6lb higher, would have found this tougher than the Plumpton seller he won on his previous start, but the conditions were in his favour and he ran creditably. *(op 10-1)*
Treasure Trail ran well in fourth on the back of a 181-day break and could build on this.
Spider Boy ran very respectably but he remains a maiden and must be dropped into selling company to have a realistic chance of finally winning.
Hi Laurie(IRE), the winner of one race over hurdles from 23 starts (the first 11 were in bumpers) in Ireland, proved pretty disappointing on her English debut. *(op 7-1)*
City Palace, without the tongue-tie and cheekpieces this time, and dropped six furlongs in trip, was well held and offered little. *(op 13-2)*

1646 EPSON H'CAP CHASE (18 fncs) 3m 110y

4:30 (4:33) (Class 4) (0-90,84) 5-Y-0+ **£3,523** (£1,084; £542; £271)

Form RPR

2P6- **1** **Ashgreen**[196] [4516] 8-11-9 81 .... SThomas 101+
(Miss Venetia Williams) *led tl after 1st: a.p: lft in ld 13th: clr appr 2 out: v easily* **9/2**[2]

5 **2** *2 ½* **Killy Lass (IRE)**[41] [1321] 9-11-2 74 .... APMcCoy 81+
(B J Llewellyn) *hld up and bhd: hdwy whn hmpd appr 12th: rdn 4 out: wnt 2nd flat: no ch w wnr* **9/2**[2]

133 **3** *1 ¼* **Pangeran (USA)**[17] 1484 13-10-13 **74** .... ONelmes(3) 78
(N B King) *a.p: w wnr 4 out: rdn appr 2 out: one pce* **16/1**

6444 **4** *8* **Make It Easy (IRE)**[46] 1262 9-10-3 **68** .... CaptLHorner(7) 64
(D L Williams) *chsd ldrs: lost pl appr 6th: hdwy 13th: wknd after 3 out* **13/2**[3]

P-44 **5** *11* **Taksina**[39] 1343 6-10-5 **63** .... BHitchcott 51+
(R H Buckler) *hld up and bhd: hdwy 8th: hit 3 out: sn rdn and wknd* **9/1**

0-00 **6** *18* **Rufius (IRE)**[12] 1539 12-10-0 **58** oh3 .... CLlewellyn 25
(P Kelsall) *bhd: short-lived effrt appr 3 out* **33/1**

4F56 **F** **Barnards Green (IRE)**[43] 1299 7-11-2 **74** .... AThornton —
(R H Alner) *sn bhd: fell 10th* **16/1**

PP-P **R** **Never Awol (IRE)**[45] 1277 8-10-9 **74** .... (p) TMessenger(7) —
(B N Pollock) *led after 1st tl rn out 13th* **16/1**

4-23 **S** **Sissinghurst Storm (IRE)**[131] 535 7-10-10 **68** .... WHutchinson —
(R Dickin) *prom: disputing 3rd whn slipped up appr 12th* **4/1**[1]

P06P **P** **Auditor**[131] 534 6-11-7 **84** .... MNicolls(5) —
(S T Lewis) *hld up and bhd: hdwy 7th: wknd appr 14th: t.o whn p.u bef 3 out* **50/1**

6m 25.1s (-21.50) **Going Correction** -0.725s/f (Firm) **10** Ran SP% **102.2**
Speed ratings: **105,104,103,101,97 91,—,—,—,—** CSF £20.57 CT £207.73 TOTE £5.20: £1.30, £1.20, £4.40; EX 27.60.
Owner C J Green **Bred** C J And T L Green **Trained** Kings Caple, H'fords
■ Cyindien (7/1) was withdrawn (kicked at start). R4 applies, deduct 10p in the £.

FOCUS
A very moderate handicap chase rated through the third, who appeared to run to the best of his recent form.

NOTEBOOK
Ashgreen, a winner of three point-to-points in 2003, did not really progress as one might have expected last season but, without the headgear this time and ridden much more positively, he defied a 196-day break to gain his first win under Rules pretty easily. This was a very moderate race, but connections appear to have found the key to him and he looks up to winning again. *(op 11-2 tchd 6-1)*
Killy Lass(IRE) is incredibly one-paced so her chance would not have been helped at all when she was hampered down the back straight by the favourite, but she responded well to strong pressure from the Champion to take second. She would probably get another three miles, so maybe soft ground will suit. *(op 5-1 tchd 4-1)*
Pangeran(USA) had conditions to suit and ran another solid race. He is a fine servant. *(op 12-1)*
Make It Easy(IRE), back over fences following a creditable fourth over hurdles at Newton Abbot on his previous start, could not a hold a position and was never a danger. *(op 7-1 tchd 15-2)*
Taksina, back up in trip, was well beaten and remains winless. *(op 10-1 tchd 11-1 and 8-1)*
Sissinghurst Storm(IRE), without the cheekpieces this time, was still in contention when slipping up down the back straight.

1647 EPSON "NATIONAL HUNT" NOVICES' H'CAP HURDLE (11 hdls) 2m 5f
5:00 (5:04) (Class 4) (0-105,100) 3-Y-0+ **£3,445** (£1,060; £530; £265)

Form RPR

00P- **1** **New Time (IRE)**[218] 4113 6-11-1 **89** .... APMcCoy 91
(Jonjo O'Neill) *hld up in rr: hdwy 8th: led appr 3 out: all out* **13/8**[1]

6364 **2** *nk* **Romany Dream**[13] 1524 7-10-2 **76** .... (b) BHitchcott 77
(R Dickin) *hld up in tch: rdn appr 2 out: ev ch last: r.o* **5/1**

-154 **3** *5* **Brigadier Benson (IRE)**[17] 1488 5-11-12 **100** .... AThornton 96
(R H Alner) *hld up in tch: rdn 3 out: pckd 2 out: one pce* **7/2**[3]

4-43 **4** *nk* **The Gangerman (IRE)**[143] 365 5-11-5 **93** .... CLlewellyn 89
(N A Twiston-Davies) *w ldr: led 6th to 7th: ev ch 3 out: sn rdn: hung lft and hit last: wknd* **5/2**[2]

6-05 **5** *11* **Munny Hill**[3] 1616 5-9-7 **74** oh10 .... TMessenger(7) 59
(M Appleby) *led to 6th: led 7th: rdn and hdd appr 3 out: sn wknd* **33/1**

5m 37.0s (-4.20) **Going Correction** -1.70s/f (Hard) **5** Ran SP% **108.5**
Speed ratings: **40,39,37,37,33** CSF £9.54 TOTE £2.10: £1.70, £2.90; EX 10.90 Place 6 £65.88, Place 5 £34.71.
Owner John P McManus **Bred** Mrs Noreen McManus **Trained** Cheltenham, Gloucs

FOCUS
They just hacked along early and then went a steady pace for most of the way, so the winning time is completely meaningless and the form of this moderate handicap hurdle for novices could be suspect.

NOTEBOOK
New Time(IRE) did not really progress after winning his bumper last season and was pulled up on his chasing debut when last seen 218 days previously but, back over hurdles for his reappearance, he just proved good enough. While it is hard to know what to make of the form, he did not appear suited by the slow pace and can probably step up on this in a more strongly-run affair. *(op 9-4)*
Romany Dream does most of her racing over fences these days, but she is 14lb lower over hurdles and was just held. With the pace slow, she may be a touch flattered to get so close to the winner, but she still looks capable of finding a race over the smaller obstacles. *(tchd 9-2)*
Brigadier Benson(IRE) did not really build on the promise he showed on his return from a break at Uttoxeter, but he was still not beaten that far. *(op 5-2)*
The Gangerman(IRE), dropped slightly in trip on his return from a 143-day break, would probably have been seen to better effect finishing off a strong pace. *(op 11-4)*
T/Plt: £61.60 to a £1 stake. Pool: £45,165.85. 534.50 winning tickets. T/Qpdt: £26.80 to a £1 stake. Pool: £3,326.70. 91.70 winning tickets. KH

201 WINCANTON (R-H)
Thursday, October 6

OFFICIAL GOING: Firm
Wind: Virtually nil

1648 MIRAGE SIGNS H'CAP HURDLE (11 hdls) 2m 6f
2:30 (2:30) (Class 4) (0-95,92) 4-Y-0+ **£3,031** (£866; £433)

Form RPR

1 **Habitual (IRE)**[20] 1477 4-11-12 **92** .... APMcCoy 97+
(John A Quinn, Ire) *hld up: trckd ldrs: driven to take slt ld 2 out: kpt on strly run-in: readily* **2/1**[2]

122- **2** *2* **Saucy Night**[210] 4287 9-10-0 **66** oh1 .... GLee 69+
(Simon Earle) *slt ld tl def advantage fr 5th: shkn up and narrowly hdd 2 out: styd on same pce appr last* **1/1**[1]

PP-2 **3** *4* **Rhetorical**[14] 1523 4-10-5 **78** .... RLucey-Butler(7) 77
(P Butler) *w ldr to 5th: styd cl 2nd: rdn after 3 out: wknd after next* **14/1**

50U4 **4** *4* **Caper**[13] 1539 5-10-9 **85** .... (p) AHawkins(10) 80
(R Hollinshead) *hld up rr but wl in tch: hdwy to trck ldrs 4 out: rdn appr 2 out: sn btn* **5/1**[3]

5P-0 **5** *dist* **Lantern Leader (IRE)**[11] 1564 10-11-10 **90** .... (p) WMarston —
(M J Gingell) *chsd ldrs tl j. slowly and wknd 4 out: t.o* **40/1**

5m 22.2s (-2.90) **Going Correction** -0.70s/f (Firm) **5** Ran SP% **109.1**
Speed ratings: **78,77,75,74,—** CSF £4.48 TOTE £2.90: £1.30, £1.10; EX 5.20.
Owner P F Kilmartin **Bred** Rathasker Stud **Trained** Blackmiller Hill, Co. Kildare

FOCUS
A moderate handicap, run at a sedate early gallop in a pedestrian time and the form is worth treating with caution.

NOTEBOOK
Habitual(IRE) kept Saucy Night in his sights throughout, appreciated the tactical nature of the race and was perfectly placed by McCoy to pounce when the tempo got serious. He has improved since being upped in trip in this sphere - as could have been expected considering his sole success on the level came over two miles last year - and his confidence will have been nicely boosted now. He should have a bit more to offer in this sphere and clearly enjoys a fast surface. *(tchd 9-4)*
Saucy Night was not all that fluent early on, but his hurdling improved as the race progressed, and he would surely have been better suited by setting a stronger gallop and trying to burn off his younger rivals. While this must rate a fair way below his progressive chase form of last season, he is still entitled to improve for this first outing for 210 days and certainly has the ability to win races in this sphere when things go his way. *(op 11-10 tchd 10-11)*
Rhetorical got markedly outpaced when the race got serious and was merely keeping on at the same pace at the finish. He is very modest, but is at least he seems to be trying his best at present. *(op 10-1)*
Caper was not suited by being restrained off the ordinary gallop on this drop back from three miles, but still found less than looked likely when push came to shove and can be considered disappointing. He needs a stiffer test, but is one to have reservations about all the same. *(op 6-1 tchd 13-2)*

1649 STABLEYARD BY HARLOW JUVENILE NOVICES' HURDLE (8 hdls) 2m
3:00 (3:02) (Class 4) 3-Y-0 **£3,360** (£960; £480)

Form RPR

03 **1** **Palace Walk (FR)**[5] 1594 3-10-12 .... GLee 89+
(B G Powell) *lft in ld 3rd: hdd next: sn led again: pushed clr appr last: comf* **4/1**[3]

233 **2** *4* **The Castilian (FR)**[36] 1380 3-10-12 100 .... (v[1]) RGreene 85+
(M C Pipe) *plld hrd early:prom: chsd wnr after 3 out: rdn and mstke next: one pce and readily hld whn hit last* **15/2**

U05 **3** *7* **Spence Appeal (IRE)**[11] 1563 3-10-7 .... LStephens(5) 75
(C Roberts) *led and hit 1st: hdd appr 3rd: rdn to stay chsng ldrs 4 out: wknd appr 2 out* **3/1**[2]

0 **4** *1* **Ghaill Force**[18] 1478 3-10-5 .... (t) RLucey-Butler(7) 74
(P Butler) *j. slowly 1st: in tch: hdwy to chsd ldrs 4 out: wnt 2nd 3 out: sn rdn: wknd 2 out* **16/1**

6 **5** *12* **Top Pursuit**[27] 1440 3-10-9 .... PWhelan(3) 62
(J L Spearing) *chsd ldrs: hit 4th: wknd 3 out: no ch whn hit last* **50/1**

6 *dist* **Dizzy Lizzy**[26] 3-10-6 ow1 .... DRDennis —
(Nick Williams) *chsd ldrs: hit 4th and sn wknd: t.o* **14/1**

6 **P** **Atacama Star**[18] 1478 3-10-12 .... RThornton —
(B G Powell) *plld way to ld appr 3rd: veered bdly lft and hdd: slt ld again next: sn hdd: wknd 3 out: t.o whn p.u next* **7/4**[1]

3m 40.3s (-8.80) **Going Correction** -0.70s/f (Firm) **7** Ran SP% **107.6**
Speed ratings: **95,93,89,89,83 —,—** CSF £28.86 TOTE £5.10: £2.40, £2.60; EX 9.90.
Owner Winterbeck Manor Stud **Bred** Elevage Haras De Bourgeauville **Trained** Morestead, Hants

FOCUS
A weak juvenile hurdle, run at an uneven gallop, and the field came home strung out.

NOTEBOOK
Palace Walk(FR) confirmed the promise of his recent improved effort at Fontwell five days previously and ultimately broke his duck over hurdles in decisive fashion. He jumped well in the main and, on this evidence, will no doubt enjoy reverting to a stiffer test in the future. Sure to prove better over hurdles than he was on the Flat, he may not have beaten a great deal, but could defy a penalty in the coming weeks before this division warms up. *(tchd 10-3)*
The Castilian(FR) was lit up by the first-time visor throughout the first half of the race, yet still emerged as the clear danger to the eventual winner at the top of the straight and would have finished slightly closer but for an error at the penultimate flight. He should do better as he learns to settle and, while he is clearly modest, helps set the level of this form. *(op 9-2)*
Spence Appeal(IRE) lost his place at halfway before staying on again, albeit at the same pace, and ultimately proved disappointing. He looks one to avoid. *(op 7-2 tchd 11-4)*
Ghaill Force improved on his recent debut at Plumpton, yet failed to see out his race was well as the principals and was well held. He is yet to win a race of any description from 13 outings now. *(op 25-1)*
Atacama Star, whose rider attempted to restrain him this time, found it backfiring as he ultimately pulled his way to the front and then proved intractable turning into the back straight towards the horse boxes. He eventually paid for those exertions and is clearly a very headstrong character, so it would come as little surprise to see him reverting to the Flat after this disappointing display. *(op 2-1)*

1650 WESTERN DAILY PRESS RACEGOERS CLUB H'CAP CHASE (17 fncs) 2m 5f
3:30 (3:30) (Class 4) (0-110,109) 5-Y-0+ **£4,777** (£1,470; £735; £367)

Form RPR

-635 **1** **Breaking Breeze (IRE)**[120] 684 10-11-5 **102** .... PJBrennan 113+
(Andrew Turnell) *led: hit 10th: hdd appr 3 out and sn hrd drvn: styd chsng ldrs and rallied gamely u.p to ld again nr fin* **10/3**[2]

263P **2** *1 ¼* **Sunshan**[47] 1265 9-9-8 **84** .... JamesWhite(7) 93
(R J Hodges) *chsd ldrs: wnt 2nd 12th: chal fr 4 out tl led last: rdn run-in: hdd nr fin* **3/1**

5351 **3** *1 ¾* **Noble Justice (IRE)**[44] 1301 9-11-9 **106** .... RThornton 113
(R J Hodges) *hld up rr but in tch: hdwy 13th: trckd ldrs 4 out: slt ld fr next: hdd last: no ex run-in* **3/1**[1]

3U42 **4** *8* **James Victor (IRE)**[25] 1457 7-10-11 **97** .... RYoung(3) 96
(N R Mitchell) *rr but in tch: hdwy to chal fr 12th: wknd fr 3 out* **13/2**

-P03 **5** *12* **Just Reuben (IRE)**[14] 1524 10-10-0 **83** oh8 .... RGreene 72+
(C L Tizzard) *chsd wnr to 12th: sn rdn: wknd appr 3 out* **14/1**

4643 **P** **Fear Siuil (IRE)**[32] 1406 12-10-10 **93** .... (t) DRDennis —
(Nick Williams) *chsd ldrs: hit 13th: stl travelling wl whn hmpd and slipped bdly sn after 4 out: nt rcvr: p.u bef next* **9/2**[3]

5m 5.40s (-17.70) **Going Correction** -0.70s/f (Firm) **6** Ran SP% **111.3**
Speed ratings: **105,104,103,100,96 —** CSF £13.78 TOTE £5.40: £2.00, £2.10; EX 26.90.
Owner V Askew **Bred** Michael Griffin **Trained** Broad Hinton, Wilts

FOCUS
This modest handicap lost a fair amount of its interest due to the late withdrawal of top weight Free Gift. It was run at a decent gallop and the first three came clear, and the form looks sound with the placed horses running to their marks.

NOTEBOOK
Breaking Breeze(IRE) got back to winning ways in tremendously game fashion under a strong ride. He set a decent tempo until the turn for home, and looked like being held as he was headed three out, but was not to be denied and rallied to get back on top close home. This was his first success since taking a seller just over a year ago, and he has clearly benefited from a recent break, but he has been beaten off higher marks in the past and is not at all certain to follow-up. *(tchd 7-2)*
Sunshan had every chance, and looked like scoring after jumping the final fence, yet proved powerless to resist the winner's renewed challenge when it mattered. This is much more his level and he should be capable of resuming winning ways off this current mark before too long if kept to this grade. *(op 4-1)*

Noble Justice(IRE), despite getting a touch outpaced down the back straight, emerged travelling best of all three from home, but he failed to quicken from there on and was ultimately found out by *his latest 3lb rise for winning at Worcester last time. He is a decent benchmark for this form. Official explanation: vet said gelding was lame (op 11-4 tchd 4-1)*

James Victor(IRE) was put in his place at the top of the straight and was well beaten. *(op 11-2)*

Fear Siuil(IRE) was still travelling as well as any prior to jumping into the back of his rivals after the fourth last and then losing his hind legs when slipping up turning into the bend soon after. That put an end to any chance he may have had and, although he has not managed to score for two *years, he is certainly weighted to win at present. Official explanation: jockey said gelding lost its hind legs on final bend (tchd 4-1, 5-1 in places)*

1651 MRS RICKMAN IS 40 H'CAP HURDLE (8 hdls) 2m

4:00 (4:00) (Class 4) (0-110,107) 4-Y-O+ **£3,110** (£957; £478; £239)

Form RPR

-023 **1** **Looks The Business (IRE)**[11] [1565] 4-10-9 **97**.............. MrTJO'Brien(7) 100+
(W G M Turner) *chsd ldrs: drvn to chal 2 out: sn led: styd on u.p run-in* **3/1**[2]

4115 **2** *3 ½* **Outside Investor (IRE)**[1] [1641] 5-11-1 **103**..........................(p) KBurke(7) 102
(P R Rodford) *bhd: drvn along fr 4 out: styd on u.p appr last to take 2nd cl home but no imp on wnr* **14/1**

314- **3** *nk* **Tignasse (FR)**[190] [4660] 4-11-3 **98**.. JEMoore 97
(G L Moore) *chsd ldrs: rdn 2 out: wandered and no imp appr last: wknd and lost 2nd nr fin* **9/1**

0035 **4** *2 ½* **Castle River (USA)**[25] [1458] 6-11-0 **95**............................... JamesDavies 92+
(O O'Neill) *bhd: rdn fr 3 out: styd on u.p fr 2 out but nvr gng pce to rch ldrs* **12/1**

3235 **5** *1 ¾* **Gemini Dancer**[18] [1480] 6-11-12 **107**... JTizzard 102+
(C L Tizzard) *led: 5l clr after 4th: rdn and chal 2 out: sn hdd: wknd run-in* **6/1**

3F-3 **6** *4* **La Dolfina**[18] [1480] 5-11-5 **100**.. PJBrennan 98+
(P J Hobbs) *bhd: stdy hdwy whn bdly hmpd and hit rail bnd appr 2 out: nt rcvr* **11/4**[1]

024- **7** *28* **Berengario (IRE)**[186] [4723] 5-11-11 **106**.. JAMcCarthy 76+
(S C Burrough) *chsd ldrs tl wknd qckly 3 out* **4/1**[3]

3m 36.1s (-13.00) **Going Correction** -0.70s/f (Firm)
WFA 4 from 5yo+ 13lb **7** Ran SP% **110.3**
Speed ratings: **105,103,103,101,100 98,84** CSF £36.76 TOTE £3.10: £1.80, £4.80; EX 27.40.

Owner M J B Racing **Bred** Mrs M O'Callaghan **Trained** Sigwells, Somerset

■ Stewards' Enquiry : P J Brennan one-day ban: careless riding (Oct 17)

FOCUS

This modest handicap was run at a generous pace, thanks to the free-running Gemini Dancer, and form is reasonable for the grade.

NOTEBOOK

Looks The Business(IRE) gained a deserved success in ready fashion and clearly appreciated the claim of his capable amateur rider. He jumped with fluency throughout, showed a willing attitude when asked to win his race and had no trouble with this much quicker surface. Having resumed life *over hurdles in decent form, he should continue to pay his way, despite a future weight rise. (op 11-4 tchd 7-2)*

Outside Investor(IRE) , fifth of seven at Exeter just 24 hours previously, was doing all of his best work at the finish and turned in an improved effort. He was not really suited by the drop back to this trip on such a sharp track, however. *(op 16-1)*

Tignasse(FR) , returning from a 190-day break and making her handicap debut, had every chance at the top of the straight, but ultimately found her lack of fitness an issue and lost second close home. She ought to improve a deal for this outing, appreciated the faster ground and can find a *race off her current mark. Official explanation: trainer's representative said filly returned with cuts on its hind legs (op 10-1 tchd 8-1)*

Castle River(USA) improved a deal for this return to a faster surface and, while never rating a serious threat, managed to get a lot closer to the winner than had been the case at Stratford last time. *(tchd 14-1)*

Gemini Dancer ran too freely at the head of affairs through the first half of the contest and ultimately paid the price. *(op 5-1)*

La Dolfina got badly checked on the rail when attempting to challenge on the inside turning for home and lost any chance thereafter. While it is not certain she would have won, she has to rate very unlucky, and has clearly begun handicap life on a fair mark. *(op 3-1)*

Berengario(IRE) was well backed on this return from a 186-day break, but he dropped out very *quickly approaching the back straight as though something may well have been amiss. Official explanation: trainer said gelding was unsuited by the firm ground (tchd 9-2)*

1652 WINCANTONRACECOURSE.CO.UK CONDITIONAL JOCKEYS' H'CAP CHASE (21 fncs) 3m 1f 110y

4:30 (4:30) (Class 4) (0-100,91) 5-Y-O+ **£4,108** (£1,264; £632)

Form RPR

4261 **1** **Tudor King (IRE)**[32] [1414] 11-11-12 **91**.................................... JDiment 100+
(Andrew Turnell) *mde all: j.w: c clr after 4 out: easily* **5/4**[1]

0-2P **2** *25* **Indian Squaw (IRE)**[132] [535] 6-10-11 **76**...........................(t) WKennedy 65+
(B De Haan) *racd in 3rd: hit 8th: pressed ldrs 14th: chsd wnr next: no ch after 4 out: mstke and slipped on landing 2 out* **6/4**[2]

P5P0 **3** *28* **Honneur Fontenail (FR)**[13] [1539] 6-10-3 **73**...................(p) KBurke(5) 29
(N J Hawke) *hit 1st: rdr lost iron: chsd wnr: rdn 13th: chal next to 15th: wknd qckly fr 17th* **7/2**[3]

6m 35.9s (-4.00) **Going Correction** -0.70s/f (Firm) **3** Ran SP% **106.7**
Speed ratings: **78,70,61** CSF £3.42 TOTE £1.80; EX 2.30.

Owner J R Kinloch **Bred** Capt D Foster And B Corscadden **Trained** Broad Hinton, Wilts

FOCUS

This was weakened by the withdrawals of the two at the foot of the handicap, but it made no difference to the likeable Tudor King. The form is virtually unrateable and weak, however, and it produced a very slow winning time indeed.

NOTEBOOK

Tudor King(IRE) , who made all in great fashion to follow-up his recent Worcester success off an 8lb higher mark. He has always been capable of holding his form well, does jump his fences very well and really is a very likeable old performer. However, while this officially has to rate as a personal best, he simply beat two very unreliable rivals, and connections will no doubt be praying the Handicapper does not take this form literally. *(op 6-4)*

Indian Squaw(IRE) again displayed her quirks and was well beaten prior to blundering at the penultimate fence. She is obviously not going to live up to her decent pedigree, and remains a maiden after nine career starts, but she may just be happier on softer ground and a stiffer track in the future. *(op 5-4)*

Honneur Fontenail(FR) failed to jump with any fluency, and ran in snatches before finally throwing in the towel approaching four from home. He is one to avoid, despite appearing to be on a fair mark at present. *(tchd 4-1)*

1653 FIREWORKS HERE 5TH NOVEMBER NOVICES' H'CAP HURDLE (8 hdls) 2m

5:00 (5:01) (Class 4) (0-100,98) 3-Y-O+ **£3,762** (£1,075; £537)

Form RPR

356 **1** **Nesnaas (USA)**[13] [1541] 4-10-13 **85**.. GLee 95+
(M G Rimell) *in tch: chsd ldrs 3 out: led appr 2 out: pushed clr last: comf* **7/2**[2]

1F **2** *3 ½* **Gold Guest**[18] [1491] 6-11-8 **94**..(t) RThornton 98+
(P D Evans) *hld up rr but in tch: hdwy to chse ldrs 3 out: chsd wnr after 2 out: sn no imp* **7/2**[2]

2324 **3** *6* **Kentucky King (USA)**[14] [1523] 5-11-12 **98**..........................(t) BHitchcott 96
(Mrs D A Hamer) *chsd ldrs: drvn to chal 3 out: led sn after: hdd appr 2 out: btn sn after* **11/1**[3]

/23- **4** *5* **Rojabaa**[371] [1545] 6-10-7 **86**.. RLucey-Butler(7) 79
(W G M Turner) *in tch: hdwy to chse ldrs 3 out: rdn bhd next and sn btn* **16/1**

404 **5** *shd* **Alekhine (IRE)**[107] [804] 4-10-10 **82**.. PJBrennan 75
(P J Hobbs) *hld up rr but in tch: hdwy 3 out: chsd ldrs appr next: sn wknd* **11/8**[1]

310 **6** *2 ½* **Jack Durrance (IRE)**[18] [1490] 5-10-6 **85**........................... EDehdashti(7) 76+
(G A Ham) *bhd but in tch: hdwy to chse ldrs 3 out: sn rdn: wknd next* **20/1**

0006 **7** *13* **Prince Minata (IRE)**[18] [1483] 10-10-0 **72** oh1.......................(t) OMcPhail 54+
(M Appleby) *led: rdn and hdd after 3 out: wknd u.p next* **40/1**

0/30 **8** *1 ¾* **Sunset King (USA)**[14] [1523] 5-10-3 **82**............................ JamesWhite(7) 58
(R J Hodges) *bhd fr 4th* **20/1**

/0F- **9** *18* **Salim**[443] [1017] 8-10-2 **74**.. JGoldstein 32
(Miss J S Davis) *chsd ldr: challnged 3 out: wknd qckly bef next* **66/1**

3m 34.5s (-14.60) **Going Correction** -0.70s/f (Firm)
WFA 4 from 5yo+ 13lb **9** Ran SP% **114.2**
Speed ratings: **109,107,104,101,101 100,93,93,84** CSF £15.59 CT £119.52 TOTE £4.70: £1.90, £1.70, £2.00; EX 19.70 Place 6 £96.71, Place 5 £85.56.

Owner Mark Rimell **Bred** Shadwell Farm LLC **Trained** Leafield, Oxon

FOCUS

A moderate novices' handicap, run at a fair pace that produced a fair winning time for the grade of contest, and the first two were clear at the finish. The third sets the standard and the winner can rate higher.

NOTEBOOK

Nesnaas(USA) was allowed to go on by his rider two out, having travelled smoothly and jumped neatly up to that point, and ultimately ran out a clear-cut winner to break his duck at the seventh attempt over hurdles. He had struggled to fully see out his races over timber previously, but this sharp two miles proved right up his street, as did the fast surface, and he can be rated value for slightly further. He looks an improving sort and, as long as the Handicapper is not too harsh, is certainly capable adding to his tally this season. *(op 4-1 tchd 9-2)*

Gold Guest proved hard to settle under restraint through the early parts, but still emerged to have every chance approaching two from home, and simply met a much better handicapped rival this *time. He was nicely clear of the rest and remains up to winning again off this mark in the future. (op 11-4)*

Kentucky King(USA) showed no signs of trouble at the start this time and ran close to his recent level in defeat. *(op 14-1 tchd 10-1)*

Rojabaa made a pleasing return from a 371-day layoff and should improve a fair bit for the outing. *(op 14-1 tchd 18-1)*

Alekhine(IRE) , making his handicap debut in this sphere after a 107-day break, was very well backed and had his chance, yet ultimately found very little when push came to shove. This was disappointing. *(op 7-4 tchd 5-4)*

T/Plt: £92.40 to a £1 stake. Pool: £40,903.50. 322.85 winning tickets. T/Qpdt: £43.70 to a £1 stake. Pool: £2,281.20. 38.60 winning tickets. ST

1538 WORCESTER (L-H)

Thursday, October 6

OFFICIAL GOING: Chase course - good (good to firm in places); hurdle course - good to firm

Wind: Nil Weather: overcast with some drizzle

1654 ANDYLOOS MAIDEN HURDLE (8 hdls) 2m

2:20 (2:21) (Class 4) 4-Y-O+ **£3,708** (£1,141; £570; £285)

Form RPR

522- **1** **Allumee**[172] [4885] 6-11-2 113.. RJohnson 109+
(P J Hobbs) *chsd ldrs: led after 5th: clr appr last: eased flat* **10/11**[1]

0P-2 **2** *¾* **Turbo (IRE)**[18] [1480] 6-11-2 110..(p) JPMcNamara 106+
(T G Mills) *hld up and bhd: hdwy 3 out: rdn and r.o wl flat: nt rch eased wnr* **9/4**[2]

1302 **3** *9* **Zumrah (IRE)**[44] [1302] 4-11-2 .... CLlewellyn 99+
(P Bowen) *hld up in tch: chsd wnr appr 3 out: rdn appr 2 out: one pce* **12/1**

4 **4** *4* **Coronado's Gold (USA)**[19] [1360] 4-11-2 .... PMoloney 93
(V Smith) *hld up towards rr: hdwy 5th: rdn appr 2 out: wknd appr last* **25/1**

5 *nk* **It's The Limit (USA)**[61] 6-11-2 .... TJMurphy 92
(W K Goldsworthy) *hld up in tch: hdwy 4th: rdn appr 2 out: wknd flat* **8/1**[3]

6 *1 ¼* **Sgt Pepper (IRE)**[187] 4-11-2 .... LAspell 91
(O Sherwood) *hld up and bhd: hdwy appr 3 out: nvr trbld ldrs* **20/1**

3565 **7** *7* **Royaltea**[29] [1432] 4-10-4 79.. LTreadwell(5) 79+
(J T Stimpson) *chsd ldrs: wknd 3 out: 6th and btn whn blnd 2 out* **80/1**

466- **8** *2* **Courageous Dove**[21] [4451] 4-11-2 .... VSlattery 82
(A Bailey) *mid-div: rdn after 5th: sn struggling* **66/1**

PPP- **9** *18* **Forest Rail (IRE)**[214] [4208] 5-10-9 64... SCurran 57
(L Corcoran) *plld hrd: j.rt: led tl after 5th: wknd after 3 out: no ch whn mstke last* **200/1**

0/P- **10** *12* **Supershot (IRE)**[117] [2549] 7-11-2 .... TDoyle 52
(O Brennan) *a bhd* **66/1**

6P0/ **11** *1 ¾* **Only For Gold**[41] [3355] 10-10-13 .... TJPhelan(3) 50
(Dr P Pritchard) *a bhd* **200/1**

P-0 **12** *dist* **Marsh Orchid**[32] [1415] 4-11-2 .... NFehily —
(C C Bealby) *a bhd: t.o* **100/1**

P **Arnbi Dancer**[201] 6-11-2 ....(t) JMogford —
(Mrs N S Evans) *hld up in tch: j. slowly and lost pl 3rd: sn bhd: t.o whn p.u bef 3 out* **150/1**

0U0P **P** **April Rose**[25] [1454] 5-10-2 .... MrJAJenkins(7) —
(K G Wingrove) *t.k.h towards rr: j. slowly 3rd: sn toiling: t.o whn p.u bef 3 out* **200/1**

3m 44.9s (-3.50) **Going Correction** -0.025s/f (Good) **14** Ran SP% **117.9**
Speed ratings: **107,106,102,100,99 99,95,94,85,79 78,—,—,—** CSF £2.86 TOTE £1.50: £1.10, £1.10, £1.50; EX 4.10.

Owner High Spirits **Bred** Mrs H J Houghton **Trained** Withycombe, Somerset

FOCUS
Plenty of dead wood in this ordinary maiden hurdle, but the time was ordinary and the form, rated through the third, looks believable.

NOTEBOOK
Allumee finally got off the mark on ground plenty quick enough for him. He could have won by a wider margin and can defy a penalty in this sort of grade. *(op 5-4)*
Turbo(IRE) finished with a flourish but is still flattered by his proximity to the winner. He is knocking on the door in this type of event. *(op 11-4 tchd 3-1)*
Zumrah(IRE) had more to do this time and was unable to go with the winner. *(tchd 14-1)*
Coronado's Gold(USA) was another to have his limitations exposed in this slightly better company. *(op 20-1)*
It's The Limit(USA), a dual mile and a half winner for Amanda Perrett, stayed further and should not have been beaten on the grounds of stamina. *(op 7-1 tchd 6-1)*
Sgt Pepper(IRE), a pretty useful juvenile for Richard Hannon, only twice attempted a mile and a quarter and stamina could be an issue. *(op 14-1)*
April Rose *Official explanation: jockey said mare bled from the nose*
Arnbi Dancer *Official explanation: jockey said gelding was never travelling and may have resented the tongue strap*

1655 PUNTERSLOUNGE.COM BETTING FORUM (S) H'CAP HURDLE (12 hdls) 3m

2:50 (2:50) (Class 5) (0-95,93) 4-Y-0+ **£2,996** (£856; £428)

Form | | | | RPR
046- **1** Southerncrosspatch[182] 4754 14-10-9 **76** MFoley 83
(Mrs Barbara Waring) *hld up: rdn and hdwy appr 3 out: styd on to ld fnl 100 yds* **25/1**
2505 **2** 1 3/4 **Wild Tempo (FR)**[13] 1539 10-11-2 **93** (t) AGlassonbury(10) 98+
(M C Pipe) *hld up and bhd: hdwy 8th: led 2 out: hrd rdn and edgd lft flat: hdd and no ex fnl 100 yds* **11/2**[2]
F03- **3** 6 **Anflora**[274] 3228 8-10-3 **70** ChristianWilliams 69
(B J Llewellyn) *a.p: led after 9th: rdn and hdd 2 out: wknd flat* **5/1**[1]
0033 **4** 1 1/4 **Cool Dante (IRE)**[33] 1395 10-11-9 **90** JMMaguire 88
(T R George) *hld up in tch: rdn appr 3 out: wknd appr last* **5/1**[1]
25P3 **5** 3 **Diamond Joshua (IRE)**[5] 1595 7-11-3 **87** (v) ONelmes(3) 82
(N B King) *prom: j. slowly 1st: mstke 2nd: sn lost pl: styd on fr 2 out: nvr trbld ldrs* **10/1**
0-0P **6** 6 **Illineylad (IRE)**[13] 1539 11-10-0 **67** JMogford 56
(Mrs N S Evans) *led tl after 3rd: led appr 8th: hdd after 9th: sn rdn: wknd appr 2 out* **16/1**
0P-0 **7** 11 **Greatest By Phar**[18] 1490 4-11-8 **90** RJohnson 67
(J Akehurst) *hld up and bhd: hdwy after 9th: wknd appr 2 out* **13/2**[3]
0-F5 **8** 8 **Son Of Flighty**[40] 1333 7-10-3 **70** (b[1]) AntonyEvans 40
(Evan Williams) *hld up: hdwy appr 9th: wknd appr 3 out* **10/1**
/000 **9** 19 **Broughton Knows**[14] 1520 8-9-12 **72** (v) TMessenger(7) 23
(Mrs C J Ikin) *prom: mstke 1st: rdn 7th: sn wknd* **50/1**
00P **10** dist **Shaaban (IRE)**[17] 1097 4-10-0 **68** (v[1]) AO'Keeffe —
(R J Price) *hld up in mid-div: blnd 9th: sn bhd: t.o* **14/1**
-P3U **U** **Audiostreetdotcom**[11] 1564 8-11-1 **89** (b) MrJoshuaHarris(7) —
(R A Harris) *hld up in tch: ev ch whn tried to refuse and uns rdr 3 out* **7/1**
0P/P **P** **Jeune Premier (FR)**[14] 1520 8-9-9 **67** oh3 (vt) LTreadwell(5) —
(Evan Williams) *led after 3rd: hdd appr 8th: sn rdn: wknd appr 9th: t.o whn p.u bef 3 out* **25/1**

5m 51.4s (2.20) **Going Correction** -0.025s/f (Good) **12** Ran SP% **114.9**
WFA 4 from 6yo+ 15lb
Speed ratings: **95,94,92,92,91 89,85,82,76,— —,—** CSF £152.74 CT £813.46 TOTE £30.10: £6.70, £2.00, £2.20; EX 252.10.There was no bid for the winner.
Owner E S Chivers **Bred** Mrs Patricia Morgan **Trained** Welford-on-Avon, Warwicks

FOCUS
A poor staying seller rated through the placed horses to their marks.

NOTEBOOK
Southerncrosspatch was brought back into training after refusing to accept retirement at one stage. It was good to see that there was no bid for this grand old servant. *(tchd 22-1)*
Wild Tempo(FR) appeared finally set to score in this country when striking the front but he could *not hold the winner and unfortunately finished lame. Official explanation: trainer's representative said gelding finished lame (op 5-1)*
Anflora finally gave best on the run-in with the ground plenty fast enough for her. *(op 7-1)*
Cool Dante(IRE) had shaped as though he would be suited by this slightly longer trip when running in a similar contest at Stratford last month. *(tchd 11-2)*
Diamond Joshua(IRE) was attempting this trip for the first time on his return to hurdles. *(op 15-2)*

1656 IAN VALENTINE 37 TODAY HA-HA BIRTHDAY NOVICES' H'CAP CHASE (18 fncs) 2m 7f 110y

3:20 (3:20) (Class 4) (0-105,103) 5-Y-0+ **£4,160** (£1,280; £640; £320)

Form | | | | RPR
F541 **1** **Waynesworld (IRE)**[4] 1615 7-10-5 **82** TScudamore 101+
(M Scudamore) *hld up in tch: wnt 2nd 11th: hmpd 13th: led on bit 3 out: clr 2 out: easily* **1/1**[1]
5-P4 **2** 7 **Valley Warrior**[120] 679 8-10-0 **77** oh7 PMoloney 84
(J S Smith) *hld up in rr: hdwy after 14th: wnt 2nd 2 out: no ch w wnr* **16/1**
/3P- **3** 12 **House Warmer (IRE)**[193] 4580 6-10-7 **84** (t) LAspell 82+
(A Ennis) *hld up in tch: hmpd 13th: rdn and outpcd after 14th: 4th and btn whn mstke 2 out* **11/1**
3060 **4** 3 **Sandywell George**[13] 1539 10-9-11 **77** oh3 (vt) TJMalone(3) 69
(L P Grassick) *chsd ldr: led after 14th to 3 out: wknd appr last* **25/1**
2PU3 **5** nk **Pristeen Spy**[32] 1414 8-9-9 **77** oh7 StephenJCraine(5) 78+
(R Ford) *led tl blnd bdly and lost pl 13th: nt rcvr* **11/2**[3]
1-P3 **6** dist **Mrs Philip**[18] 1482 6-11-6 **97** RJohnson —
(P J Hobbs) *hld up: hdwy 11th: lft in ld 13th: hdd after 14th: sn rdn and wknd: virtually p.u flat* **10/3**[2]

5m 58.9s (4.00) **Going Correction** +0.175s/f (Yiel) **6** Ran SP% **106.5**
Speed ratings: **100,97,93,92,92** — CSF £13.66 CT £88.53 TOTE £2.10: £1.20, £6.00; EX 20.60.

Owner F J Mills & W Mills **Bred** A W Buller **Trained** Bromsash, Herefordshire

FOCUS
An uncompetitive event but the winner is value for more than the official margin.

NOTEBOOK
Waynesworld(IRE) ◆, unpenalised for his recent win in a conditional jockeys' event at Uttoxeter, confirmed that he has really got his act together. A hat-trick looks on the cards. *(op 4-5 tchd 8-11)*
Valley Warrior, 7lb out of the handicap on his chasing debut, proved no match for a winner in top form. *(tchd 25-1)*
House Warmer(IRE), pulled up when last seen back in March, does not look like becoming hot in the near future on this evidence. *(op 12-1)*
Sandywell George did not find a return to fences the answer. *(op 16-1)*
Pristeen Spy was lucky to survive an horrendous error at the sixth from home. *(op 13-2 tchd 8-1)*
Mrs Philip ran as if something was amiss on her chasing bow. *(op 3-1 tchd 7-2)*

1657 BETFREDPOKER.COM "NATIONAL HUNT" NOVICES' HURDLE (12 hdls) 3m

3:50 (3:50) (Class 4) 4-Y-0+ **£3,464** (£1,066; £533; £266)

Form | | | | RPR
5-32 **1** **Harry's Dream**[33] 1398 8-10-12 100 RJohnson 105+
(P J Hobbs) *hld up in tch: wnt 2nd 7th: led appr 3 out: sn clr: v easily* **1/6**[1]
35 **2** 15 **Mister Zaffaran (IRE)**[13] 1543 6-10-12 JMogford 75+
(Mrs N S Evans) *chsd ldr: led 6th tl appr 3 out: sn btn: hung bdly rt to paddock exit sn after last* **8/1**[2]
3 3 **Great Escape (IRE)**[172] 9-10-12 SCurran 63
(L Corcoran) *led to 6th: wknd 9th: hit 2 out* **20/1**[3]
4 dist **Weldiva** 5-9-12 TMessenger(7) —
(B N Pollock) *a last: lost tch appr 7th: t.o* **40/1**

5m 59.3s (10.10) **Going Correction** -0.025s/f (Good) **4** Ran SP% **104.0**
Speed ratings: **82,77,76,—** CSF £1.80 TOTE £1.10; EX 1.60.
Owner Peter Partridge **Bred** P Partridge And R M Kellow **Trained** Withycombe, Somerset

FOCUS
A pedestrian winning time for what was something of a non-event. The winner is value for twice the winning margin.

NOTEBOOK
Harry's Dream made light of this simple task. Considered to have matured and strengthened since last term, he will now return to fences. *(op 2-11 tchd 1-7, 1-5 in places)*
Mister Zaffaran(IRE), graduating from bumpers, had already conceded that the winner was in a different league before his antics on the run-in. *(op 10-1)*
Great Escape(IRE) had been placed in all three of his completed points in Ireland. *(op 12-1)*

1658 PUNTERSLOUNGE.COM BETTING FORUM MARES' ONLY H'CAP HURDLE (10 hdls) 2m 4f

4:20 (4:20) (Class 3) (0-120,118) 4-Y-0+ **£4,823** (£1,484; £742; £371)

Form | | | | RPR
511- **1** **Penneyrose Bay**[187] 4694 6-11-3 **109** MBradburne 122+
(J A Geake) *mde all: clr whn j.rt 2 out and last: comf* **3/1**[1]
0-01 **2** 8 **Miss Skippy**[36] 1384 6-10-7 **99** BJCrowley 102+
(A G Newcombe) *t.k.h: a.p: chsd wnr appr 3 out: sn rdn: no imp* **8/1**
4601 **3** 8 **Separated (USA)**[42] 1317 4-10-3 **95** RJohnson 90+
(P J Hobbs) *hld up: mstke 6th: hdwy 7th: rdn 3 out: wknd appr last* **9/2**[3]
6P-4 **4** 5 **Calomeria**[27] 1443 4-10-12 **109** StephenJCraine(5) 97
(D McCain) *chsd wnr tl after 4th: wnt 2nd briefly 7th: sn rdn: wknd appr last* **14/1**
2225 **5** 1 1/4 **Fiddles Music**[18] 1488 4-10-2 **94** ChristianWilliams 81
(D Burchell) *hld up: hdwy 5th: wknd appr 2 out* **11/2**
U125 **6** 10 **Sardagna (FR)**[29] 1435 5-11-12 **118** TJMurphy 95
(M C Pipe) *a bhd* **10/3**[2]
0-6P **7** 13 **Moon Catcher**[18] 1482 4-10-8 **100** TScudamore 64
(D Brace) *hld up in tch: wnt 2nd after 4th: j. slowly 6th: sn rdn: wknd appr 3 out: mstke last* **25/1**
0-30 **8** 9 **Resonance**[14] 1527 4-10-7 **99** CLlewellyn 54
(N A Twiston-Davies) *a bhd: mstke 2 out* **20/1**
P3U- **9** 1 1/2 **Prayerful**[179] 4790 6-10-0 **92** DCrosse 45
(J G M O'Shea) *a bhd* **33/1**

4m 43.3s (-4.70) **Going Correction** -0.025s/f (Good)
WFA 4 from 5yo+ 14lb **9** Ran SP% **111.0**
Speed ratings: **108,104,101,99,99 95,89,86,85** CSF £25.01 CT £100.62 TOTE £3.40: £1.50, £3.20, £1.30; EX 29.80 Trifecta £107.20 Pool: £559.10 - 3.70 winning tickets..
Owner Sir Christopher Wates **Bred** Sir Christopher Stephen Wates **Trained** Kimpton, Hants

FOCUS
A fair winning time for the type of contest with the winner value for more than the official margin and the third to form.

NOTEBOOK
Penneyrose Bay, who failed to get in-foal when covered by Generous, will be given another chance at motherhood at the end of the season. Finding little difficulty overcoming a 9lb rise in the weights for winning the mares-only final at Newbury, she will eventually go chasing. *(tchd 10-3)*
Miss Skippy was not disgraced considering she only won a seller at Newton Abbot last time. *(op 9-1 tchd 10-1)*
Separated(USA), 2lb lower than when last in a handicap, had hung left when winning at Bangor. Again giving the impression that she might not be that straightforward, it is possible she may have been feeling the faster ground. *(op 4-1)*
Calomeria has done all her winning on soft ground. *(op 9-1)*
Fiddles Music is fully exposed. *(op 7-1 tchd 15-2)*
Sardagna(FR) was never travelling according to her rider. *Official explanation: jockey said mare was never travelling (op 7-2 tchd 4-1)*

1659 BETFREDCASINO.COM CONDITIONAL JOCKEYS' H'CAP CHASE (12 fncs) 2m

4:50 (4:51) (Class 4) (0-105,105) 5-Y-0+ **£5,161** (£1,588; £794; £397)

Form | | | | RPR
0U00 **1** **Nick The Jewel**[58] 1189 10-11-8 **101** GCarenza 111
(Andrew Turnell) *chsd ldr: j.rt 1st: led 8th: rdn appr 2 out: drvn out* **8/1**
3435 **2** 3/4 **Nazimabad (IRE)**[29] 1433 6-10-7 **86** (t) PCO'Neill 96+
(Evan Williams) *a.p: hit 8th: ev ch last: hrd rdn: r.o* **10/3**[2]
0-0P **3** 8 **Bearaway (IRE)**[77] 1049 8-11-6 **105** (t) PMerrigan(6) 110+
(Mrs H Dalton) *hld up: hdwy 6th: mstkes 8th and 2 out: sn wknd* **12/1**
1553 **4** 2 1/2 **Faddad (USA)**[18] 1479 9-10-7 **86** (t) DLaverty 87+
(Mrs A M Thorpe) *prom: lost pl 5th: rallied after 8th: pckd 3 out: sn wknd* **4/1**[3]
P310 **5** 14 **Get The Point**[46] 1273 11-10-12 **91** TJPhelan 80+
(Dr P Pritchard) *hld up: hdwy 6th: rdn appr 3 out: wknd appr 2 out* **25/1**
P525 **6** 21 **Karakum**[14] 1521 6-10-12 **94** MrJAJenkins(3) 58
(A J Chamberlain) *nt jump wl: hdwy appr 7th: wknd appr 4 out* **20/1**
2-P3 **7** 4 **Master Henry (GER)**[46] 1273 11-10-4 **91** DJBoland(8) 51
(Ian Williams) *led to 8th: sn wknd* **8/1**
0032 **8** 10 **Lost In The Snow (IRE)**[32] 1412 7-10-1 **80** ONelmes 30
(M Sheppard) *nvr gng wl: sn struggling in rr* **5/2**[1]

3m 53.8s (0.20) **Going Correction** +0.175s/f (Yiel) **8** Ran SP% **110.2**
Speed ratings: **106,105,101,100,93 82,80,75** CSF £33.26 CT £298.94 TOTE £9.10: £2.20, £1.20, £3.30; EX 38.30.
Owner Marlborough Racing Partnership **Bred** Mrs C Janaway **Trained** Broad Hinton, Wilts

FOCUS
A moderate handicap but the time was reasonable and the placed horses set a reasonable standard.

NOTEBOOK
Nick The Jewel bounced back to form having dropped down the weights and held on well under pressure. *(op 10-1 tchd 12-1)*
Nazimabad(IRE) lost little in defeat having only been dropped a couple of pounds. *(op 7-2 tchd 3-1)*
Bearaway(IRE), returning after a break, could not overcome a second mistake. *(op 14-1)*
Faddad(USA) only ever won in the selling grade over hurdles. *(op 9-2 tchd 7-2)*

Lost In The Snow(IRE) soon had favourite backers knowing their fate. *Official explanation: jockey said gelding was never travelling (op 10-3 tchd 7-2)*

1660 PUNTERSLOUNGE.COM BETTING FORUM INTERMEDIATE OPEN NATIONAL HUNT FLAT RACE — 2m

5:20 (5:27) (Class 6) 4-6-Y-O **£1,946** (£556; £278)

Form					RPR
001-	**1**		**Sun Pageant**[168] 4941 4-11-4 ... APMcCoy (M G Rimell) *led after 3f: clr over 1f out: pushed out*	**8/11**[1]	95+
	2	*8*	**Waldo's Dream** 5-11-4 ... RJohnson (P Bowen) *chsd wnr after 5f: rdn and hung lft 3f out: eased whn btn ins fnl f*	**3/1**[2]	85+
6	**3**	*3*	**Goldsmeadow**[12] 1554 6-10-13 ... MNicolls(5) (O Brennan) *hld up in tch: wknd over 3f out*	**14/1**	81
	4	*½*	**Phriapatius** 4-10-11 ... WPKavanagh(7) (Dr J R J Naylor) *hld up: hdwy and hung rt over 6f out: rdn 5f out: wknd 4f out*	**40/1**	81
0-	**5**	*5*	**Chapel Bay**[207] 4349 5-10-4 ... PMerrigan(7) (Mrs H Dalton) *led 3f: wknd over 4f out*	**7/1**[3]	69
05	**6**	*1*	**Its A Classic**[36] 1386 4-10-11 ... MrPCallaghan(7) (Mrs N S Evans) *hld up: hdwy on ins over 4f out: wknd 3f out*	**66/1**	75
	7	*23*	**Penarwel**[152] 6-11-4 ... LAspell (F Jordan) *bhd fnl 5f*	**20/1**	52

3m 48.5s (0.70) **Going Correction** -0.025s/f (Good)
WFA 4 from 5yo+ 13lb **7** Ran **SP% 110.8**
Speed ratings: **97,93,91,91,88 88,76** CSF £2.79 TOTE £1.60: £1.40, £2.60; EX 3.70 Place 6 £15.25, Place 5 £13.24.
Owner J & L Wetherald - M & M Glover **Bred** R W Huggins **Trained** Leafield, Oxon

FOCUS
A weak bumper rated through the third.

NOTEBOOK
Sun Pageant readily defied her penalty against some modest opposition. *(op Evens)*
Waldo's Dream, out of a mare who won over hurdles, showed signs of inexperience when let down. *(op 4-1)*
Goldsmeadow is flattered by his proximity to the runner-up let alone the winner. *(op 8-1)*
Phriapatius proved a difficult ride and is also flattered to have finished so close to the first two. *(op 14-1)*
T/Plt: £49.30 to a £1 stake. Pool: £43,029.25. 636.30 winning tickets. T/Qpdt: £22.30 to a £1 stake. Pool: £2,472.00. 82.00 winning tickets. KH

CARLISLE (R-H)

Friday, October 7

OFFICIAL GOING: Good to firm (good in places down the back straight)
The first hurdle in the home straight was omitted on both circuits in all hurdle races.
Wind: Almost nil

1661 CUMBRIA LOCAL ENTERPRISE AGENCY NETWORK NOVICES' HURDLE (7 hdls 2 omitted) — 2m 1f

2:10 (2:12) (Class 4) 4-Y-O+ **£3,423** (£978; £489)

Form					RPR
	1		**Darasim (IRE)**[56] 7-10-11 ... APMcCoy (Jonjo O'Neill) *nt fluent: mstke 1st: prom: drvn 3 out: rallied and ev ch next: led last: edgd rt: drvn out*	**1/1**[1]	106+
P0-F	**2**	*2*	**Hollywood Critic (USA)**[162] 82 4-10-1 ... DDaSilva(10) (P Monteith) *hld up and bhd: smooth hdwy to ld 2 out: hdd last: kpt on same pce run in*	**100/1**	99
	3	*14*	**Lord Baskerville**[39] 4-10-4 ... PJMcDonald(7) (W Storey) *bhd tl styd on fr 2 out: n.d*	**100/1**	85
23-6	**4**	*3½*	**Bywell Beau (IRE)**[166] 8 6-10-4 97 ... GThomas(7) (J I A Charlton) *keen: led to after 2nd: lft clr next: hdd 2 out: sn btn*	**12/1**[3]	82
0-	**5**	*1¼*	**Water Taxi**[216] 4180 4-10-8 ... KJMercer(3) (Ferdy Murphy) *hld up: hdwy to chse ldr briefly bef 2 out: sn rdn and btn*	**25/1**	80
	6	*26*	**Polyarnoe Bay**[173] 5-10-4 ... RWalford (T D Walford) *a bhd: no ch fr 1/2-way*	**20/1**	47
P	**7**	*4*	**Books Delight**[16] 1508 5-10-1 ... PAspell(3) (J Wade) *prom tl wknd bef 2 out*	**100/1**	43
46P-	**8**	*6*	**Bodkin Boy (IRE)**[168] 4965 5-10-11 ... MBradburne (Mrs S C Bradburne) *hld up: rdn 3 out: sn btn*	**33/1**	44
	9	*4*	**River Line (USA)**[24] 4-10-11 ... FKeniry (C W Fairhurst) *blnd 1st: prom: lft 2nd 3rd: rdn and wknd bef 2 out*	**100/1**	40
-012	**10**	*14*	**Dubonai (IRE)**[15] 1527 5-10-13 100 ... (t) DCCostello(5) (G M Moore) *hld up in tch: rdn after 3 out: sn btn*	**13/8**[2]	33
0/P	**P**		**Saddlers Boy**[19] 1491 7-10-11 ... KJohnson (R Johnson) *a bhd: t.o whn p.u bef last*	**100/1**	—
5P/	**F**		**Gollyhott (IRE)**[576] 4256 10-10-11 ... DElsworth (Mrs S J Smith) *prom tl fell 4th: dead*	**20/1**	—
5-	**R**		**New Wish (IRE)**[69] 1232 5-10-4 ... CDSharkey(7) (S B Clark) *keen: led after 2nd: rn out next*	**20/1**	—

4m 6.70s (-19.00) **Going Correction** -1.10s/f (Hard)
WFA 4 from 5yo+ 13lb **13** Ran **SP% 121.8**
Speed ratings: **100,99,92,90,90 78,76,73,71,64** —,—,— CSF £152.14 TOTE £2.00: £1.10, £14.70, £22.40; EX 161.90.
Owner Markus Graff **Bred** His Highness The Aga Khan's Studs S C **Trained** Cheltenham, Gloucs

FOCUS
An unsatisfactory result with former high-class Flat stayer Darasim being all out to beat a couple of 100/1 shots. The time is the best basis for the rating.

NOTEBOOK
Darasim(IRE), a high-class stayer on the Flat until losing his form this season, has always been a quirky sort and was renowned for throwing in the towel if things did not go his way. However, he stuck to his guns on this first crack at hurdling and battled on well to justify short odds despite failing to jump with any fluency. For one so talented, he should have been winning on the bridle and in being all out to beat a couple of 100/1 shots, this has to go down as a disappointing effort. Further is going to suit, but he lacks the size and scope to improve over obstacles and, whilst he has an engine, it would be most surprising if he were to reach the top over hurdles. *(op 4-5 tchd 11-10)*
Hollywood Critic(USA) had shown next to nothing in three previous tries over hurdles and this came as something of a shock. He was travelling much the best throughout the final half mile, but his inexperienced jockey was unable to try and get first run on the favourite and in the end he was done for a bit of speed. He has a future at a lowly level if this proves to be no fluke.
Lord Baskerville, a poor Flat-performer, kept on from some way back to claim a place, but was well held and it is debatable exactly when he achieved.
Bywell Beau(IRE) appeared to hold sound place claims and he had his chance having led for most of the way, but he was not good enough in the end and failed to see his out. *(op 10-1)*
Water Taxi, who showed little on his only previous outing over hurdles, made good headway from the rear to reach a challenging position, but he had done all his running by the second-last and in the end faded into fifth. There was plenty of promise to be taken from this and he can win races at a modest level.
Dubonai(IRE) set the standard, but he never got into it having been held up and ran a lifeless race. *He is better than this, but now has a few questions to answer. Official explanation: trainer said gelding bled from the nose (op 11-4)*

1662 HONISTER SLATE MINE BEGINNERS' CHASE (16 fncs) — 2m 4f

2:40 (2:40) (Class 4) 4-Y-O+ **£4,202** (£1,293; £646; £323)

Form					RPR
0P-0	**1**		**Pass Me By**[86] 974 6-11-7 110 ... (e1) HOliver (R C Guest) *cl up: led 10th: mde rest: styd on wl*	**7/1**	103+
	2	*4*	**Wee William**[166] 5-11-7 ... RWalford (T D Walford) *keen: prom: outpcd 4 out: kpt on fr last: nt rch wnr*	**33/1**	93
1303	**3**	*1¾*	**Combat Drinker (IRE)**[7] 1587 7-11-2 88 ... (t) StephenJCraine(5) (D McCain) *hld up: hdwy 10th: chsd wnr between last two: no ex run in*	**6/1**	92+
46-0	**4**	*5*	**South Bronx (IRE)**[44] 1312 6-11-7 ... (t) MBradburne (Mrs S C Bradburne) *chsd ldrs: led 9th to next: drvn 4 out: outpcd fr 2 out*	**10/3**[2]	88+
144-	**5**	*5*	**Northern Minster**[180] 4787 6-11-7 ... ADobbin (F P Murtagh) *prom: effrt and ev ch 4 out: rdn whn hit 2 out: sn no ex*	**3/1**[1]	85+
244-	**6**	*10*	**Spring Gamble (IRE)**[216] 4171 6-11-7 ... FKeniry (G M Moore) *hld up: reminders after 9th and hdwy bef next: rdn and wknd fr 4 out*	**7/2**[3]	71
	P		**Port Natal (IRE)**[176] 2562 7-11-4 ... PAspell(3) (J Wade) *sn bhd: lost tch and p.u bef 12th*	**40/1**	—
-FPP	**P**		**Silent Voice (IRE)**[5] 1602 8-11-0 72 ... TJDreaper(7) (Sir John Barlow Bt) *a bhd: t.o whn p.u bef 12th*	**66/1**	—
	P		**Sandy Gold (IRE)**[138] 7-11-7 ... PMoloney (Miss J E Foster) *led to 9th: lost pl after next: t.o whn p.u bef 2 out*	**15/2**	—

5m 4.30s (-15.60) **Going Correction** -1.10s/f (Hard) **9** Ran **SP% 115.7**
Speed ratings: **87,85,84,82,80 76,**—,—,— CSF £161.76 TOTE £10.30: £2.70, £4.00, £2.10; EX 108.30.
Owner Paul Beck **Bred** Miss Coreen McGregor **Trained** Brancepeth, Co Durham

FOCUS
Modest form and a slow time, but Pass Me By did it nicely is value for more than the official margin and may have more to offer.

NOTEBOOK
Pass Me By, pulled up on his only previous try over fences, was a different proposition today and and ran out quite a tidy winner. The first-time eyeshield appeared to make a difference and, being an unexposed sort, may well have more to offer. *(op 9-1 tchd 10-1)*
Wee William, a winner in points, could hardly have made a more pleasing start to his Rules career and stayed on nicely to claim second. A return to three miles is going to help and, with improvement anticipated, he can be expected to win races at this sort of level. *(op 16-1)*
Combat Drinker(IRE), who failed to complete in either of his two previous tries over fences, jumped adequately and put in an improved performance. He is only modest, but will be capable of winning once handicapping. *(op 11-2)*
South Bronx(IRE) did not shape without promise on this fencing debut and may have more to offer once stepping up to three miles. *(op 7-2)*
Northern Minster was the main disappointment of the race, failing to improve for this switch to fences. He has always looked the type to do better over the larger obstacles, so can probably be given another chance.
Spring Gamble(IRE) is a frustrating sort who has yet to win in 13 starts and this was another modest effort. *(op 4-1)*

1663 BUSINESS LINK OF CUMBRIA NOVICES' H'CAP HURDLE (9 hdls 2 omitted) — 2m 4f

3:15 (3:15) (Class 4) (0-90,90) 3-Y-O+ **£3,416** (£976; £488)

Form					RPR
005-	**1**		**Saucy King**[202] 4457 5-11-5 **86** ... MrTGreenall(3) (M W Easterby) *hld up: hdwy bef 2 out: led between last two: jnd and edgd rt run in: jst hld on*	**12/1**	91
6P4	**2**	*shd*	**Qualitair Pleasure**[10] 1571 5-11-9 **90** ... KJMercer(3) (J Hetherton) *hld up: hdwy bef 2 out: disp ld run in: kpt on: jst failed*	**13/2**	95
P4-0	**3**	*2½*	**Lord Rosskit (IRE)**[163] 59 5-11-12 **90** ... FKeniry (G M Moore) *chsd ldrs: led whn mstke 2 out: sn hdd: one pce run in*	**4/1**[2]	93+
653-	**4**	*7*	**Not A Trace (IRE)**[168] 4969 6-11-7 **85** ... MBradburne (Mrs S C Bradburne) *chsd ldrs: hit 3 out: one pce next*	**11/2**[3]	80
3342	**5**	*2*	**Fortune's Fool**[10] 1566 6-10-8 **72** ... ATinkler (I A Brown) *hld up: hdwy ins after 3 out: rdn and one pce next*	**7/2**[1]	65
045	**6**	*11*	**Drumossie (AUS)**[70] 1097 5-11-6 **84** ... (b1) HOliver (R C Guest) *keen: hld up: hdwy to press ldrs 2 out: sn rdn and outpcd*	**11/1**	68+
-034	**7**	*6*	**Top Pack (IRE)**[45] 1294 6-10-12 **76** ... BHarding (N G Richards) *prom tl rdn and wknd bef 2 out*	**8/1**	56+
U25	**8**	*5*	**Munaawesh (USA)**[47] 1278 4-10-6 **77** ... PKinsella(7) (Mrs Marjorie Fife) *in tch tl wknd fr 3 out*	**14/1**	48
0500	**9**	*8*	**Nifty Roy**[5] 1605 5-11-7 **85** ... ADobbin (K W Hogg) *led to bef 2 out: sn wknd*	**12/1**	48
0P-0	**10**	*2½*	**Bullies Acre (IRE)**[38] 1374 5-9-11 **64** ... PAspell(3) (F P Murtagh) *hld up: rdn 3 out: sn btn*	**40/1**	25
0PP-	**11**	*7*	**Minster Brig**[179] 4806 6-10-0 **64** ... ADempsey (A Parker) *chsd ldrs: lost pl bef 3 out: t.o*	**33/1**	18
-PUP	**12**	*29*	**Muller (IRE)**[74] 1066 5-9-9 **64** ... DCCostello(5) (R W Thomson) *a bhd: t.o fr 3 out*	**66/1**	—
	P		**Leonia's Rose (IRE)**[119] 701 6-10-13 **80** ... PBuchanan(3) (Miss Lucinda V Russell) *keen: cl up tl wknd after 4 out: t.o whn p.u bef 2 out*	**20/1**	—

4m 57.6s (-19.50) **Going Correction** -1.10s/f (Hard)
WFA 4 from 5yo+ 14lb **13** Ran **SP% 124.1**
Speed ratings: **95,94,93,91,90 85,83,81,78,77 74,62,**— CSF £89.55 CT £379.19 TOTE £17.10: £4.20, £2.10, £2.10; EX 104.70.
Owner Lord Daresbury **Bred** Wyck Hall Stud Ltd **Trained** Sheriff Hutton, N Yorks
■ Stewards' Enquiry : Mr T Greenall two-day ban: used whip with excessive frequency (Oct 18,20)

FOCUS
A close finish to a moderate event, with the first two rated on their bumper form and the fourth close to previous hurdles form.

NOTEBOOK

Saucy King looked the sort to show improved form for this switch to handicaps and, having travelled strongly in rear, he made smooth headway to come through and challenge. Locked in a tooth and nail battle with the runner-up from the last, he looked to be coming off second best, but just shaded it and Greenall deserves much credit. There may well be more to come from the *gelding and he can handle a rise. Official explanation: trainer's representative said, regarding the improved form shown, gelding had strengthened up over the summer and may have benefited from today's good ground (op 11-1)*

Qualitair Pleasure has found her form again and followed a fair effort at Sedgefield with a battling display in an agonisingly close defeat. She can find a race if going on from this, albeit she is still 7lb higher than when last winning. *(op 15-2 tchd 6-1)*

Lord Rosskit(IRE) had not shown a great deal in four previous attempts, but he was clearly expected to put in an improved performance on this handicap debut and duly did so. This seems to be his trip for the time being and he remains open to improvement. *(op 5-1 tchd 6-1)*

Not A Trace(IRE), although suited by stiff tracks like this, finds two and a half miles on the sharp side and he ran pretty much as expected. A return to further will allow him to show better form. *(op 5-1 tchd 6-1)*

Fortune's Fool, somewhat fortunately off the mark at the 20th attempt at Sedgefield last time when the original winner lost his weight cloth, was allowed to race off the same mark but never really got into it having been held up and was disappointing. He may benefit from a more positive ride in future. *(op 10-3)*

Leonia's Rose(IRE) *Official explanation: jockey said mare was unsuited by the good to firm (good in places) ground (op 25-1 tchd 16-1)*

1664 ENVIRONMENT4BUSINESS H'CAP CHASE (18 fncs) 3m

3:45 (3:45) (Class 3) (0-115,114) 5-Y-0+ **£5,365** (£1,651; £825; £412)

Form | | | | RPR

1214 **1** **Ross Comm**[55] 1205 9-11-11 **113** DElsworth 130+
(Mrs S J Smith) *j.w: chsd ldrs: led 12th: drew clr fr 4 out* **11/4**[1]

-16P **2** *11* **Iverain (FR)**[82] 1025 9-11-1 **103** GLee 108+
(Sir John Barlow Bt) *cl up: led 9th to 12th: pressed wnr: one pce fr 4 out* **12/1**

/-23 **3** *5* **Aston (USA)**[7] 1589 5-10-5 **95** (p) HOliver 94+
(R C Guest) *in tch: hit 7th: effrt u.p 13th: no imp fr next* **4/1**[3]

-121 **4** *1* **Ashnaya (FR)**[134] 524 7-11-0 **107** DCCostello(5) 102
(G M Moore) *in tch: outpcd 13th: n.d after* **7/2**[2]

32-P **5** *dist* **Heidi III (FR)**[163] 62 10-11-10 **112** (p) ADobbin —
(M D Hammond) *led to 9th: outpcd next: sn n.d* **9/2**

3-52 **6** *20* **World Vision (IRE)**[148] 321 8-11-9 **114** KJMercer(3) —
(Ferdy Murphy) *prom tl wknd 12th* **6/1**

6m 3.20s (-26.70) **Going Correction** -1.10s/f (Hard)
WFA 5 from 7yo+ 2lb **6** Ran SP% **109.0**
Speed ratings: **100,96,94,94,—** — CSF £28.23 TOTE £3.50: £2.60, £3.50; EX 29.60.
Owner Kevin G Treanor **Bred** A Dawson **Trained** High Eldwick, W Yorks

FOCUS

Ross Comm made short work of these and remains progressive while the third sets the standard.

NOTEBOOK

Ross Comm ran out an authoritative winner, jumping as one would expect a Smith horse to jump, and he surged clear in the straight. A progressive gelding, there looks to be more to come and he may well defy yet another rise in the weights. *(tchd 3-1)*

Iverain(FR), last seen pulling up at Stratford in July, has evidently returned in good heart and ran well despite proving to be no match for the winner. He should remain on a decent mark. *(op 10-1)*

Aston(USA) had some improving to do to mix it with the winner, but he was not disgraced off his low weight and will find easier opportunities. *(op 9-2 tchd 5-1)*

Ashnaya(FR), 5lb higher than when winning at Wetherby back in May, had not been seen since and it was reasonable to expect her to need this. She is one to watch out for next time with the cheekpieces reapplied. *(op 4-1)*

Heidi III(FR), who signed off last season with a poor effort at Kelso, did not do much better on this reappearance and was beaten a very long way. *(op 11-2 tchd 4-1)*

World Vision(IRE), although in need of some help from the Handicapper, ran too bad to be true and there was presumably something amiss. *(op 4-1)*

1665 ACTIV8 BUSINESS SOLUTIONS CONDITIONAL JOCKEYS' H'CAP HURDLE (7 hdls 2 omitted) 2m 1f

4:20 (4:20) (Class 4) (0-110,107) 4-Y-0+ **£3,325** (£950; £475)

Form | | | | RPR

P330 **1** **Lofty Leader (IRE)**[5] 1604 6-10-9 **95** AGlassonbury(5) 104+
(Mrs H O Graham) *hld up: hdwy to ld bef 2 out: hung lft: kpt on strly: eased towards fin* **10/1**

-264 **2** *7* **Bargain Hunt (IRE)**[5] 1604 4-10-3 **89** PJMcDonald(5) 88
(W Storey) *bhd: detached 1/2-way: kpt on wl fr 2 out: no ch w wnr* **7/1**

03-4 **3** *1/2* **Vicario**[166] 5 4-11-6 **107** StephenJCraine(6) 108+
(D McCain) *cl up: effrt and ev ch bef 2 out: one pce whn blnd last* **9/1**

00-P **4** *3 1/2* **Time To Roam (IRE)**[45] 1296 5-10-11 **100** (v) NWalker(8) 95
(Miss Lucinda V Russell) *prom tl rdn and one pce fr 2 out* **16/1**

0F-5 **5** *1/2* **Silver Sedge (IRE)**[15] 1530 6-10-3 **87** TJDreaper(3) 83+
(Mrs A Hamilton) *chsd ldrs: rdn 3 out: rallied next: sn outpcd* **11/2**[2]

0045 **6** *10* **He's Hot Right Now (NZ)**[7] 1592 6-11-6 **101** (tp) PCO'Neill 86
(R C Guest) *hld up: effrt bef 3 out: sn n.d* **11/2**[2]

0560 **7** *nk* **Ton-Chee**[5] 1604 6-11-5 **100** (t) DCCostello 84
(K W Hogg) *led to bef 2 out: sn btn* **18/1**

-426 **8** *2 1/2* **Wyn Dixie (IRE)**[99] 873 6-11-0 **95** GBerridge 77
(W Amos) *chsd ldrs: effrt bef 2 out: sn btn* **6/1**[3]

1-0U **9** *3 1/2* **Polyphon (FR)**[149] 306 7-10-3 **84** KJMercer 62
(P Monteith) *hld up: rdn bef 2 out: nvr on terms* **7/2**[1]

0/00 **P** **Backcraft (IRE)**[28] 1444 7-11-7 **105** NCarter(3) —
(Mrs S J Smith) *chsd ldrs: outpcd whn hit 3 out: sn btn: t.o whn p.u bef next* **14/1**

4m 12.0s (-13.70) **Going Correction** -1.10s/f (Hard)
WFA 4 from 5yo+ 13lb **10** Ran SP% **116.7**
Speed ratings: **88,84,84,82,82 77,77,76,74,—** CSF £78.39 CT £659.43 TOTE £11.60: £2.70, £2.10, £3.70; EX 83.60.
Owner L H Gilmurray **Bred** John Redmond **Trained** Philip Law, Borders

FOCUS

Ordinary stuff, a moderate time, and although the form appears sound enough it will be surprising if the race produces anything other than the occasional winner.

NOTEBOOK

Lofty Leader(IRE), who is hardly consistent, had little trouble disposing of some modest opposition and despite running around, was able to come clear. He cannot be relied up on to *repeat to effort next time however, and he is one to be wary of. Official explanation: trainer had no explanation for the improved form shown (tchd 12-1)*

Bargain Hunt(IRE), some way ahead of the winner at Kelso five days previously, was unable to confirm the form and caught the winner on a going day. He has been running reasonably, but not well enough to suggest a win is imminent. *(op 6-1)*

Vicario shaped with mild promise on this return from a break and naturally can be expected to improve for it. *(op 7-1)*

Time To Roam(IRE) remains out of form and needs further help from the Handicapper. *(op 14-1)*

Silver Sedge(IRE) has failed to go on from his win back in February and this was another poor display. *(op 5-1 tchd 9-2 and 6-1)*

Polyphon(FR) could have been expected to need this first run since May, but he was heading up the market and clearly ran below expectations. He is better known as a chaser and should do better returned to the larger obstacles. *(op 5-1)*

1666 DAVID ALLEN & CO H'CAP CHASE (12 fncs) 2m

4:50 (4:50) (Class 3) (0-125,119) 5-Y-0+ **£5,443** (£1,675; £837; £418)

Form | | | | RPR

3310 **1** **Wet Lips (AUS)**[13] 1548 7-11-5 **119** (bt) PMerrigan(7) 136+
(R C Guest) *chsd ldrs: rdn 4 out: rallied and ev ch 2 out: led run in: pushed out* **7/1**

2U **2** *2 1/2* **Bill's Echo**[14] 1542 6-11-1 **113** PCO'Neill(5) 125
(R C Guest) *hld up: smooth hdwy to ld after 2 out: rdn and hdd run in: no ex* **7/2**[2]

5-46 **3** *6* **Log On Intersky (IRE)**[30] 1435 9-11-11 **118** GLee 124
(J Howard Johnson) *led to after 2 out: sn no ex* **5/1**[3]

F-62 **4** *3 1/2* **Jefertiti (FR)**[15] 1529 8-10-1 **97** PBuchanan(3) 101+
(Miss Lucinda V Russell) *cl up: effrt bef 3 out: ev ch next: sn outpcd* **11/4**[1]

/126 **5** *7* **Ceannairceach (IRE)**[54] 1221 12-11-2 **109** DO'Meara 105
(J M Jefferson) *prom: drvn and outpcd bef 4 out: n.d after* **6/1**

5445 **6** *7* **Brave Effect (IRE)**[10] 1570 9-10-3 **96** BHarding 85
(Mrs Dianne Sayer) *hld up: hit 5 out: nvr on terms* **7/1**

3/6- **7** *nk* **The Tinker**[520] 184 10-10-11 **104** MBradburne 92
(Mrs S C Bradburne) *prom tl wknd bef 5 out* **14/1**

3m 56.6s (-20.50) **Going Correction** -1.10s/f (Hard) **7** Ran SP% **111.5**
Speed ratings: **107,105,102,101,97 94,93** CSF £30.61 CT £130.28 TOTE £6.70: £3.10, £1.70; EX 14.00.
Owner Concertina Racing Three **Bred** Woodlands Stud Nsw **Trained** Brancepeth, Co Durham

FOCUS

A fair contest in which they went a true gallop throughout and it was the extra stamina of Wet Lips that won him the day. The runner-up is the best guide to the level of the form.

NOTEBOOK

Wet Lips(AUS), the supposed Guest second-string, made it two wins from four outings over fences with a strong-galloping display, seeing his race out better than any other on this drop in trip. He remains unexposed and, but will need to progress further to defy a rise. *(op 13-2)*

Bill's Echo was found out by the stiff finish and had no answer to his stablemate as stamina began to kick in. He does not find winning easy, but is still only six and has time to improve. *(tchd 4-1)*

Log On Intersky(IRE) would have won this with three legs a couple of seasons back, but he continues in steady decline and even getting his own way out in front for the first-time since last winning in November 2003 failed to bring about any real improvement. *(op 9-2)*

Jefertiti(FR) is on a winning mark again, but he was unable to cling on to the leaders after jumping the second last and was left trailing.

Ceannairceach(IRE) is starting to go the wrong way having made a promising start when arriving in England and he now has a bit to prove.

1667 UK TRADE & INVESTMENT STANDARD OPEN NATIONAL HUNT FLAT RACE 2m 1f

5:20 (5:20) (Class 6) 4-6-Y-0 **£1,932** (£552; £276)

Form | | | | RPR

/ **1** **Linda's Theatre** 5-11-4 ADobbin 96+
(N G Richards) *hld up: hdwy to ld over 1f out: wandered u.p: hld on wl fnl f* **6/4**[2]

2 *3/4* **Another Lord (IRE)**[166] 6-11-4 KRenwick 94
(Mrs B K Thomson) *cl up: led over 2f out to over 1f out: kpt on fnl f* **33/1**

212 **3** *1* **Bluecoat (USA)**[13] 1554 5-11-8 MrTGreenall(3) 100
(M W Easterby) *led to over 2f out: sn outpcd: kpt on fnl f* **5/4**[1]

2 **4** *2 1/2* **Bonnie Rock (IRE)**[118] 719 5-10-4 GThomas(7) 84
(J I A Charlton) *cl up: ev ch over 2f out: one pce over 1f out* **7/1**[3]

0 **5** *dist* **Intersky Emerald (IRE)**[15] 1532 4-11-4 APMcCoy —
(Jonjo O'Neill) *hld up in tch: outpcd 4f out: sn btn* **9/1**

4m 12.5s (-16.80) **Going Correction** -1.10s/f (Hard)
WFA 4 from 5yo+ 13lb **5** Ran SP% **109.9**
Speed ratings: **95,94,94,93,—** CSF £33.70 TOTE £2.10: £1.50, £5.50; EX 42.20 Place 6 £1,118.67, Place 5 £534.89.
Owner John Wills **Bred** J R Wills **Trained** Greystoke, Cumbria
■ Stewards' Enquiry : A Dobbin one-day ban: used whip with excessive frequency (Oct 18)

FOCUS

A weak bumper rated through the third, with only the front two making any real appeal with the future in mind.

NOTEBOOK

Linda's Theatre, a half-brother to a couple of sprint winners, saw out this stiff two miles one in great fashion and held on grittily despite evident signs of greeness. He shaped as though a true gallop would help in future and will probably stay further once going hurdling. *(op 7-4 tchd 11-8)*

Another Lord(IRE), a winning pointer, exceeded expectations and made the winner pull out all the stops. A greater test is obviously going to suit in future and it will be disappointing if he does not go on from this. *(op 25-1)*

Bluecoat(USA) was left vulnerable by his penalty and was unable to cope with the small weight concession. He will appreciate two and a half miles plus once jumping obstacles. *(op 6-5 tchd 6-4)*

Bonnie Rock(IRE) improved on her Hexham outing and closed the gap with Bluecoat. She will find things easier against her own sex. *(tchd 6-1)*

Intersky Emerald(IRE) has shown nothing now in two starts and is clearly one of his trainer's lesser beasts. *(op 8-1)*

T/Plt: £808.40 to a £1 stake. Pool: £38,870.05. 35.10 winning tickets. T/Qpdt: £74.40 to a £1 stake. Pool: £4,589.40. 45.60 winning tickets. RY

1440 BANGOR-ON-DEE (L-H)

Saturday, October 8

OFFICIAL GOING: Good to soft (good in places on chase course)

The ground had eased following persistent rain before and at the start of the meeting.

Wind: Nil Weather: Rain during first race.

1668 NUMARK H'CAP HURDLE (9 hdls) 2m 1f

2:20 (2:23) (Class 3) (0-120,119) 4-Y-0+ **£10,332** (£3,179; £1,589; £794)

Form | | | | RPR

21-3 **1** **Prairie Sun (GER)**[14] 1552 4-10-7 **100** JTizzard 123+
(Mrs A Duffield) *hld up: hdwy 4th: rdn appr 3 out: led appr 2 out: in command whn lft wl clr last* **4/1**[1]

50-3 **2** *22* **Secret's Out**[20] 1490 9-10-1 **94** AO'Keeffe 90
(F Lloyd) *hld up and bhd: hdwy 5th: hrd rdn appr 2 out: lft poor 2nd last* **33/1**

0034 **3** *4* **Flame Phoenix (USA)**[29] 1444 6-11-6 **118**..............(t) StephenJCraine(5) 110
(D McCain) *hld up and bhd: hdwy 4th: wknd appr 3 out* **22/1**

12-3 **4** *6* **Buffalo Bill (IRE)**[27] 1458 9-10-13 **106**.................................... PJBrennan 98+
(A M Hales) *hld up: hdwy 4th: wknd appr 2 out: bdly hmpd last* **11/2**[2]

135- **5** *4* **Fortune Point (IRE)**[66] 2502 7-10-7 **100**.......................... WHutchinson 82
(A W Carroll) *prom to 6th* **25/1**

41 **6** *1 1/4* **Karathaena (IRE)**[6] 1610 5-10-11 **111** 7ex........................... PKinsella(7) 92
(M E Sowersby) *mid-div: struggling fr 5th* **7/1**

5440 **7** *8* **Why The Long Face (NZ)**[6] 1610 8-11-1 **108**..........................(p) HOliver 81
(R C Guest) *bhd: hmpd after 3rd: rdn appr 4th: no rspnse* **33/1**

315 **8** *6* **Goss**[6] 1610 8-11-8 **115**.. APMcCoy 82
(Jonjo O'Neill) *led tl after 3rd: wknd 6th* **12/1**

000- **9** *7* **Its Crucial (IRE)**[171] 4926 5-11-12 **119**................................ AntonyEvans 79
(N A Twiston-Davies) *rdn after 4th: a bhd* **25/1**

0- **10** *13* **Twist 'n Shout**[203] 4469 8-10-7 **110**.. WJones(10) 57
(Jonjo O'Neill) *bhd fr 5th* **16/1**

1144 **11** *hd* **Kims Pearl (IRE)**[46] 1300 7-10-6 **106**.............................. TMessenger(7) 56+
(S Lycett) *prom tl blnd 4th* **25/1**

F45- **S** **Cutthroat**[233] 3907 5-10-9 **107**... RStephens(5) —
(P J Hobbs) *bhd whn slipped up bnd after 3rd* **13/2**

650F **U** **A Bit Of Fun**[34] 1413 4-10-10 **108**.. LTreadwell(5) 99
(J T Stimpson) *hdwy 4th: wknd appr 2 out: lft poor 2nd whn hmpd and uns rdr last* **25/1**

1423 **P** **Dream Castle (IRE)**[19] 1501 11-10-12 **112**.............................. PMerrigan(7) —
(Barry Potts, Ire) *led after 1st tl after 3rd: wknd appr 5th: t.o whn p.u bef 2 out* **6/1**[3]

5PP1 **F** **Ela Re**[48] 1278 6-10-12 **105**.. DElsworth 112
(Mrs S J Smith) *broke tape and bolted bef s: sn prom: led after 3rd tl appr 2 out: 10l 2nd and btn whn fell last* **9/1**

4m 12.6s (1.70) **Going Correction** +0.225s/f (Yiel) **15** Ran SP% **124.7**
WFA 4 from 5yo+ 13lb
Speed ratings: **105,94,92,89,88 87,83,80,77,71 71,—,—,—,—** CSF £142.32 CT £2619.18 TOTE £5.60: £2.00, £11.10, £8.00; EX 310.80 TRIFECTA Not won..
Owner Miss Helen Wynne **Bred** Gestut Isarland **Trained** Constable Burton, N Yorks

FOCUS
The change in the ground may have led to this handicap not being as competitive as expected. The runner-up is the best guide to the level of the form.

NOTEBOOK
Prairie Sun(GER) found the combination of give in the ground and a significant drop back in distance just what the doctor ordered. She was already ten lengths ahead when her two closest pursuers departed at the last. *(op 6-1)*
Secret's Out was up in class and should only be considered fourth best on merit.
Flame Phoenix(USA) only finished in the money because of the misfortune of others. *(op 20-1 tchd 25-1)*
Buffalo Bill(IRE) would not have been beaten quite so far had he not been brought to a standstill at the final flight. *(op 6-1)*
Dream Castle(IRE) *Official explanation: jockey said gelding lost its action (op 11-2 tchd 5-1)*
Ela Re repeated the sort of antics that led to him being withdrawn at the start last time. He probably did too much in the lead on the rain-softened ground and had no answer to the winner. *(op 11-2 tchd 5-1)*
A Bit Of Fun should be considered third best on merit. *(op 11-2 tchd 5-1)*

1669 BRIGHT FUTURE NOVICES' CHASE (15 fncs) 2m 4f 110y
2:55 (2:55) (Class 3) 5-Y-0+ **£7,198** (£2,215; £1,107; £553)

Form RPR

25-1 **1** **Iris's Gift**[14] 1549 8-11-10 .... APMcCoy 144+
(Jonjo O'Neill) *mde all: rdn appr 2 out: styd on* **8/11**[1]

222- **2** *4* **Montgermont (FR)**[196] 4554 5-11-0 .... AThornton 130+
(Mrs L C Taylor) *t.k.h: mstkes: chsd wnr fr 2nd: one pce fr 2 out* **20/1**

1614 **3** *12* **Stan (NZ)**[6] 1617 6-11-6 122.. HOliver 124
(R C Guest) *hld up in rr: hdwy 10th: styd on fr 3 out: n.d* **25/1**

511- **4** *3 1/2* **Olney Lad**[231] 3948 6-11-0 .... RGarritty 115
(Mrs P Robeson) *bhd fr 9th* **7/1**[3]

442- **U** **Easter Present (IRE)**[194] 4611 6-11-0 .... SThomas —
(Miss H C Knight) *mstke 1st: mstke and uns rdr 2nd* **25/1**

P **Irish Raptor (IRE)**[209] 6-11-0 .... AntonyEvans —
(N A Twiston-Davies) *prom: stmbld bdly 2nd: wknd 9th: bhd whn p.u bef 11th* **16/1**

2/2- **P** **Mount Karinga**[329] 2185 7-11-0 .... ChristianWilliams —
(P F Nicholls) *hld up in tch: wknd 10th: bhd whn p.u bef 2 out* **7/2**[2]

5m 7.20s (-5.30) **Going Correction** -0.125s/f (Good) **7** Ran SP% **111.0**
Speed ratings: **105,103,98,97,— —,—** CSF £16.39 TOTE £1.40: £1.40, £7.10; EX 12.90 Trifecta £109.90 Part won. Pool: £154.80 - 0.60 winning units..
Owner Robert Lester **Bred** Mrs R Crank **Trained** Cheltenham, Gloucs

FOCUS
An interesting novice chase which obviously centred around the winner, but the other three finishers can all win chases.

NOTEBOOK
Iris's Gift jumped much better this time. He produced a workmanlike performance with the give in the ground helping him overcome a trip and course on the sharp side for him. He will be kept to novice company for the time being. *(op 4-6 tchd 4-5 in places)*
Montgermont(FR), on his chasing debut, certainly made sure that the winner did not have things all his own way. He does need to brush up his jumping but looks a ready-made future winner. *(tchd 22-1 tchd 25-1 in places)*
Stan(NZ), reverting back to fences, was by no means knocked about under his penalty. The fact he appears to have learnt to settle should stand him in good stead. *(op 20-1)*
Olney Lad would have appreciated even softer ground for his first start over fences. He should at least be better for the experience. *(op 8-1 tchd 17-2)*
Mount Karinga was disappointing having not been seen since making a promising chasing debut at Cheltenham last November. *(op 4-1 tchd 9-2)*

1670 TOTESCOOP6 H'CAP CHASE (18 fncs) 3m 110y
3:25 (3:25) (Class 3) (0-125,124) 5-Y-0+**£13,845** (£4,260; £2,130; £1,065)

Form RPR

323- **1** **Ebony Light (IRE)**[175] 4869 9-10-9 **112**..................(p) StephenJCraine(5) 128
(D McCain) *w ldr: led 6th to 9th: led 10th: j.rt 3 out: sn rdn: styd on wl flat* **7/1**[3]

2-12 **2** *3 1/2* **Mckelvey (IRE)**[143] 407 6-11-12 **124**.. AThornton 137+
(P Bowen) *hld up: reminders after 4th: hdwy 12th: sn rdn: outpcd 3 out: rallied appr last: styd on u.p* **5/1**[1]

1245 **3** *1 3/4* **Luneray (FR)**[35] 1398 6-10-13 **111**..............................(t) ChristianWilliams 122
(P F Nicholls) *racd wd: hld up: hdwy 8th: rdn and ev ch last: no ex* **12/1**

31F- **4** *9* **Radcliffe (IRE)**[230] 3974 8-10-5 **103**... SThomas 107+
(Miss Venetia Williams) *led to 6th: led 9th to 10th: rdn after 3 out: wkng whn hit 2 out* **9/1**

10-6 **5** *5* **Caribbean Cove (IRE)**[159] 150 7-10-3 **101**..............................(p) HOliver 98
(R C Guest) *hld up and bhd: hdwy appr 14th: wknd 4 out* **16/1**

6-22 **6** *hd* **Master Tern (USA)**[46] 1301 10-10-11 **109**........................(p) APMcCoy 106
(Jonjo O'Neill) *hld up and bhd: hdwy appr 14th: wknd 4 out* **11/2**[2]

20-2 **7** *hd* **Koquelicot (FR)**[148] 330 7-11-8 **120**.. PJBrennan 117
(P J Hobbs) *prom: rdn after 12th: wknd 13th* **11/2**[2]

P-61 **8** *dist* **The Sister**[42] 1342 8-11-4 **116**...(v) TSiddall —
(Jonjo O'Neill) *hld up: hdwy appr 8th: rdn appr 12th: mstke 13th: sn wknd: t.o* **7/1**[3]

6/0- **U** **Cill Churnain (IRE)**[525] 110 12-11-5 **117**................................... DElsworth —
(Mrs S J Smith) *prom: wknd 12th: bhd whn blnd and uns rdr 4 out* **14/1**

123/ **P** **Russian Gigolo (IRE)**[596] 3922 8-11-3 **115**....................... AntonyEvans —
(N A Twiston-Davies) *hld up and bhd: hit 6th: rdn 11th: short-lived effrt after 12th: t.o whn mstke 4 out: p.u bef 3 out* **7/1**[3]

6m 15.8s (-7.40) **Going Correction** -0.125s/f (Good) **10** Ran SP% **115.2**
Speed ratings: **106,104,104,101,99 99,99,—,—,—** CSF £42.30 CT £414.74 TOTE £9.30: £2.20, £2.40, £4.40; EX 41.80 Trifecta £158.60 Part won. Pool: £223.50 - 0.10 wining units..
Owner Roger Bellamy **Bred** J Boylson **Trained** Cholmondeley, Cheshire

FOCUS
A fair handicap although several of these had something to prove. The third sets the level for the form.

NOTEBOOK
Ebony Light(IRE), a consistent sort, was always willing to help force the pace and turned in a good staying performance. His trainer wants to get him up the weights so he can qualify for the Grand National and in the meantime the Welsh version could well be on the agenda. *(op 8-1)*
Mckelvey(IRE) found a second wind under top weight and shapes like an out-and-out stayer. *(op 4-1)*
Luneray(FR) apparently went in search of better ground with doubts about her stamina. Still travelling well going to the penultimate fence, she may not quite have got home. *(tchd 14-1)*
Radcliffe(IRE) adopted his usual front-running tactics but the winner would not leave him alone. He was still not disgraced on his first start since February. *(op 12-1)*
Caribbean Cove(IRE), returning after a summer break, remains unproven at three miles. *(op 14-1)*
Master Tern(USA) found this more competitive than when twice finishing second at Worcester in August. *(tchd 5-1)*

1671 GORDON MYTTON HOMES NOVICES' HURDLE (11 hdls) 2m 4f
4:00 (4:00) (Class 3) 4-Y-0+ **£4,914** (£1,512; £756; £378)

Form RPR

2P-2 **1** **Good Samaritan (IRE)**[125] 654 6-10-11 .... ATinkler 112+
(M Pitman) *a.p: led after 3 out: sn rdn: nt fluent last: drvn out* **7/1**[3]

203 **2** *nk* **Martovic (IRE)**[51] 1246 6-10-4 .... JAMcCarthy 103
(K C Bailey) *hld up and bhd: hdwy on ins 5th: rdn appr 2 out: ev ch flat: nt qckn cl home* **16/1**

534- **3** *9* **Armariver (FR)**[239] 3785 5-10-11 .... ChristianWilliams 103+
(P F Nicholls) *hld up: hdwy appr 7th: ev ch appr 2 out: sn rdn: wknd last* **6/4**[1]

/-12 **4** *16* **Youlbesolucky (IRE)**[52] 1237 6-10-11 .... APMcCoy 86+
(Jonjo O'Neill) *led to 4th: led 8th: mstke 3 out: sn hdd & wknd* **3/1**[2]

5- **5** *7* **Sandmartin (IRE)**[179] 4819 5-10-11 .... PJBrennan 80+
(P J Hobbs) *hld up in tch: rdn appr 7th: hit 3 out: sn wknd* **16/1**

/FP- **6** *13* **Allez Mousson**[349] 1822 7-10-4 87.......................................(p) BWharfe(7) 65
(A Bailey) *w ldrs: led after 6th: hdd 8th: wknd appr 2 out* **33/1**

5P/5 **7** *hd* **Sarn**[13] 1565 6-10-8 .... ACCoyle(3) 65
(M Mullineaux) *a bhd* **40/1**

P **8** *21* **Daggy Boy (NZ)**[131] 591 5-10-11 .... BJCrowley 44
(R C Guest) *a bhd* **66/1**

06- **9** *dist* **Gaining Ground (IRE)**[340] 1979 5-10-6 .... MNicolls(5) —
(John R Upson) *w ldrs: led 4th tl after 6th: rdn and wkng whn bdly hmpd 7th: t.o* **100/1**

10 *7* **Shem Dylan (NZ)**[377] 6-10-11 .... HOliver —
(R C Guest) *a bhd: t.o* **40/1**

00-5 **F** **Imperial Royale (IRE)**[146] 369 4-10-6 84 ow5................ TBurrows(10) —
(P L Clinton) *towards rr tl fell 7th* **100/1**

/P-3 **P** **The Muratti**[147] 351 7-10-11 .... JTizzard —
(Miss I E Craig) *a bhd: t.o 7th: p.u bef 2 out* **25/1**

P **Kiss The Girls (IRE)**[203] 4468 6-10-11 77.................................. AO'Keeffe —
(Jennie Candlish) *a bhd: t.o whn p.u bef 2 out* **66/1**

13 **P** **Irish Wolf (FR)**[31] 1431 5-11-4 110...(p) AThornton —
(P Bowen) *prom tl wknd after 3 out: p.u bef 2 out* **8/1**

P **Gustavo**[158] 4-10-11 .... SThomas —
(Miss Venetia Williams) *hld up: hdwy appr 6th: wknd after 3 out: p.u bef 2 out* **12/1**

5m 9.60s (12.00) **Going Correction** +0.525s/f (Soft) **15** Ran SP% **124.7**
WFA 4 from 5yo+ 14lb
Speed ratings: **97,96,93,86,84 78,78,70,—,— —,—,—,—,—** CSF £106.88 TOTE £6.90: £2.00, £4.00, £1.30; EX 121.90.
Owner Malcolm C Denmark **Bred** Mrs Christine Kelly **Trained** Upper Lambourn, Berks

FOCUS
Several of these had more experience of bumpers than hurdles, but despite the winner being value for further the third sets an ordinary standard.

NOTEBOOK
Good Samaritan(IRE) appreciated the longer trip and showed the right sort of attitude after being untidy at the final flight. *(op 13-2)*
Martovic(IRE) ◆ appeared to be delivering a winning challenge on the run-in but the winner pulled out that vital bit more. She appears to be going the right way.
Armariver(FR) ◆ seemed a big danger turning for home and can get off the mark when back down in distance. *(op 7-4 tchd 15-8 and 2-1 in places)*
Youlbesolucky(IRE), graduating from bumpers, found an error at the third last the beginning of the end. The ease in the ground may not have been in his favour. *(op 11-4 tchd 100-30 in places)*
Sandmartin(IRE) ran well on his hurdling debut until rapping the third from home. *(op 20-1)*
Daggy Boy(NZ) *Official explanation: jockey said gelding was unsuited by the good to soft ground*
Irish Wolf(FR) *Official explanation: jockey said horse lost a front shoe (op 9-1)*

1672 TOTEPOOL AWAYBET "NATIONAL HUNT" NOVICES' HURDLE (9 hdls) 2m 1f
4:35 (4:35) (Class 4) 4-Y-0+ **£4,470** (£1,375; £687; £343)

Form RPR

1 **1** **Jeremy Cuddle Duck (IRE)**[44] 1323 4-10-11 .... AntonyEvans 120+
(N A Twiston-Davies) *chsd ldr: led appr 2 out: rdn appr last: r.o* **15/8**[1]

2 *2* **Private Be** 6-10-11 .... PJBrennan 115
(P J Hobbs) *led: rdn and hdd appr 2 out: ev ch last: no ex towards fin* **16/1**

3 *16* **Nor'Nor'East (IRE)** 7-10-11 .... APMcCoy 105+
(Jonjo O'Neill) *hld up in mid-div: hdwy appr 5th: cl 4th whn blnd 3 out: nt rcvr: lft 3rd last* **6/1**[3]

/0-2 **4** *6* **Aces Four (IRE)**[29] [1445] 6-10-11 .... WHutchinson 93
(W McKeown) *hld up and bhd: sme hdwy appr 6th: nvr trbld ldrs* **11/1**

FP0- **5** *26* **Jolly Boy (FR)**[218] [4158] 6-10-11 .... AO'Keeffe 67
(Miss Venetia Williams) *bhd fr 6th* **11/1**

2-3 **6** *3 ½* **Nevada Red**[153] [242] 4-10-6 .... StephenJCraine(5) 64
(D McCain) *prom tl rdn and wknd appr 6th* **14/1**

0-P **7** *4* **Bollitree Bob**[29] [1445] 4-10-11 .... BJCrowley 60
(M Scudamore) *plld hrd: a bhd* **33/1**

20 **8** *9* **Granite Man (IRE)**[13] [1562] 5-10-11 .... TSiddall 51
(Jonjo O'Neill) *a bhd* **33/1**

0- **P** **Sunny Daze**[531] [7] 5-10-11 .... JTizzard —
(D McCain) *bhd fr 6th: t.o whn p.u bef 2 out* **66/1**

230- **P** **Charming Fellow (IRE)**[182] [4774] 5-10-11 .... SThomas —
(Miss H C Knight) *bhd fr 6th: t.o whn p.u bef 2 out* **4/1**[2]

3P-0 **F** **Sunley Future (IRE)**[27] [1458] 6-10-11 99........ ATinkler 100
(N J Henderson) *plld hrd: a.p: hit 6th: wknd appr 2 out: 15l 3rd whn fell last* **6/1**[3]

4m 18.3s (7.40) **Going Correction** +0.525s/f (Soft)
WFA 4 from 5yo+ 13lb **11** Ran SP% **119.9**
Speed ratings: **103,102,94,91,79 77,75,71,—,—** — CSF £35.78 TOTE £2.40: £1.60, £4.10, £1.90; EX 52.10.
Owner Trevor Hemmings **Bred** C Kenneally **Trained** Naunton, Gloucs

FOCUS
Most of these lacked previous hurdling experience and the fourth sets the standard for the form.

NOTEBOOK
Jeremy Cuddle Duck(IRE) followed up his victory in a bumper on similar ground here in August. Jumping soundly, he found what was required when eventually let down despite still showing signs of inexperience. *(op 11-4 tchd 3-1 in places)*
Private Be ◆, out of a winning chaser, did not have the bumper experience of the winner and normal improvement should see him go one better.
Nor'Nor'East(IRE), a half-brother to a winning Irish hurdler, is out of a smart staying chaser. He effectively lost his chance when making a hash of the third last. *(op 11-2)*
Aces Four(IRE) could never get to grips with the principals. *(op 12-1 tchd 10-1)*

1673 MILES MACADAM H'CAP CHASE (12 fncs) 2m 1f 110y
5:10 (5:11) (Class 4) (0-110,109) 4-Y-0+ **£4,715** (£1,451; £725; £362)

Form RPR

P254 **1** **Power Unit**[35] [1399] 10-10-13 **96**........ BHitchcott 108
(Mrs D A Hamer) *a.p: rdn to ld last: edgd rt flat: drvn out* **11/2**[3]

34P- **2** *2* **New Bird (GER)**[377] [1518] 10-11-9 **106**........ WHutchinson 116
(Ian Williams) *w ldr: led 8th to last: nt qckn* **12/1**

4660 **3** *shd* **Donovan (NZ)**[14] [1548] 6-10-1 **84**........(p) HOliver 94
(R C Guest) *hld up: hdwy 8th: rdn appr 3 out: kpt on flat* **7/4**[1]

025U **4** *18* **Fiery Peace**[16] [1529] 8-11-12 **109**........ SThomas 101
(C Grant) *j.rt: nvr trbld ldrs* **12/1**

FP1F **5** *nk* **Knight's Emperor (IRE)**[27] [1457] 8-11-0 **97**........ APMcCoy 91+
(J L Spearing) *hld up in tch: rdn and wknd appr 2 out* **7/2**[2]

00-6 **6** *12* **Ready To Rumble (NZ)**[143] [406] 8-10-7 **90**........ BJCrowley 76+
(R C Guest) *bhd fr 4 out* **6/1**

500- **P** **Superior Weapon (IRE)**[180] [4808] 11-10-0 **83** oh2........(t) PJBrennan —
(A Robson) *led: hdd and hit 8th: sn wknd: t.o whn p.u bef 2 out* **20/1**

0F5- **P** **Special Agenda (IRE)**[498] [532] 11-9-13 **87**........ StephenJCraine(5) —
(M J M Evans) *hld up: blnd 3rd: bhd fr 8th: t.o whn p.u bef 2 out* **14/1**

4m 24.8s (-1.60) **Going Correction** 0.0s/f (Good) **8** Ran SP% **115.1**
Speed ratings: **103,102,102,94,93 88,—,—** CSF £64.06 CT £160.86 TOTE £6.50: £2.10, £2.40, £1.30; EX 54.40.
Owner C A Hanbury **Bred** Mrs M E Nolan **Trained** Nantycaws, Carmarthens

FOCUS
A moderate handicap and the form is not easy to rate, although the principals were some 7lb better than this at best.

NOTEBOOK
Power Unit, with the cheekpieces left off, had been given a bit of a chance by the Handicapper and showed that he may well have been unlucky last time. *(op 7-1)*
New Bird(GER), returning after an absence of a year, had a good battle with the winner before being forces to admit defeat. He is now 7lb lower than when he last won. *(op 10-1)*
Donovan(NZ), pulled up on his only previous start over fences, ran well and is very well handicapped compared with his hurdles rating. *(op 15-8 tchd 2-1 in places)*
Fiery Peace kept shooting himself in the foot by jumping right-handed. *(op 10-1)*
Knight's Emperor(IRE) has never won on ground this soft. *(op 3-1 tchd 11-4)*

1674 TOTESPORT.COM MARES' ONLY STANDARD OPEN NATIONAL HUNT FLAT RACE 2m 1f
5:40 (5:40) (Class 6) 4-6-Y-0 **£1,873** (£535; £267)

Form RPR

2 **1** **Bonchester Bridge**[44] [1323] 4-11-0 .... ATinkler 93+
(N J Henderson) *mde all: clr whn rdn over 1f out: r.o* **2/1**[1]

2 *8* **Bella Bonkers** 5-10-4 .... BWharfe(10) 83
(N A Twiston-Davies) *hld up in tch: rdn over 3f out: chsd wnr over 2f out: hung lft over 1f out: one pce* **11/1**

3 **3** *2* **Milanshan (IRE)**[38] [1386] 5-10-7 .... WPKavanagh(7) 81
(J W Mullins) *a.p: rdn over 5f out: kpt on same pce fnl 2f* **20/1**

51 **4** *1* **Rising Tempest**[8] [1593] 4-10-11 .... ARAdams(10) 87
(Mrs S J Smith) *a.p: chsd wnr 8f out tl over 2f out: one pce* **7/1**[3]

5- **5** *9* **Shuil Bob (IRE)**[209] [4349] 5-11-0 .... WHutchinson 73+
(C Tinkler) *mid-div: rdn and hdwy over 4f out: wknd over 2f out* **5/2**[2]

6 *dist* **Wellfield**[146] 5-10-7 .... MGoldstein(7) —
(N A Twiston-Davies) *a bhd* **20/1**

0 **7** *1 ¾* **Chaga**[44] [1323] 4-11-0 .... PJBrennan —
(W Jenks) *mid-div: short-lived effrt over 3f out* **40/1**

8 *15* **Eastender**[148] [338] 4-11-0 .... SThomas —
(Miss Venetia Williams) *t.k.h towards rr: hdwy 7f out: wknd over 4f out* **25/1**

0-5 **9** *8* **Daramoon (IRE)**[48] [1274] 4-11-0 .... ChristianWilliams —
(D J S Ffrench Davis) *hld up: hdwy over 8f out: wknd over 5f out* **33/1**

00 **10** *dist* **Logies Lass**[125] [656] 6-11-0 .... AntonyEvans —
(J S Smith) *mid-div: rdn over 7f out: sn bhd* **40/1**

34 **11** *4* **Silver Bow**[106] [828] 4-11-0 .... AThornton —
(J M Jefferson) *a bhd* **7/1**[3]

12 *7* **Four Kisses (IRE)** 5-10-11 .... TJPhelan(3) —
(Ms Sue Smith) *a bhd* **25/1**

13 *dist* **Bally Abbie** 4-11-0 .... ARoss —
(P Beaumont) *a bhd: t.o* **28/1**

000- **14** *dist* **Davnic**[391] [1421] 5-11-0 .... DVerco —
(Paul Morris) *plld hrd in mid-div: bhd fnl 6f: t.o* **66/1**

15 *1 ½* **Commaover**[181] 6-10-9 .... StephenJCraine(5) —
(R Ford) *a bhd: t.o* **50/1**

4m 19.1s (8.00) **Going Correction** +0.525s/f (Soft) **15** Ran SP% **127.2**
Speed ratings: **102,98,97,96,92 —,—,—,—,— —,—,—,—,—** CSF £23.81 TOTE £2.50: £1.50, £3.60, £4.90; EX 29.70 Place 6 £34.22, Place 5 £9.72.
Owner W H Ponsonby **Bred** W H F Carson **Trained** Upper Lambourn, Berks

FOCUS
A weak mares' bumper and the change in the ground appeared to take its toll on most of these. The fourth is the best guide to the form.

NOTEBOOK
Bonchester Bridge could do nothing more than run this field ragged and only time will show the value of the form. *(op 6-5)*
Bella Bonkers, a half-sister to staying hurdlers Sau-Mynde and Oh So Wisley, would in theory have been helped by the rain that had got into the ground. *(op 12-1)*
Milanshan(IRE) kept plugging away after being the first of the leading group under pressure. *(op 25-1)*
Rising Tempest could not defy a penalty on this slower ground. *(op 8-1 tchd 13-2)*
Shuil Bob(IRE), a full-sister to the winning hurdler and chaser Bob Ar Aghaidh, had shaped well on her debut at Warwick last March. *(op 7-2)*
T/Plt: £39.20 to a £1 stake. Pool: £48,429.40. 901.70 winning tickets. T/Qpdt: £9.00 to a £1 stake. Pool: £2,081.10. 170.20 winning tickets. KH

CHEPSTOW (L-H)
Saturday, October 8

OFFICIAL GOING: Good (good to soft in places) changing to good to soft after race 2 (1.55)
Wind: Moderate, behind Weather: Wet and misty, poor visibility, clearing last 2 races

1675 BETFAIRGAMES.COM H'CAP HURDLE (11 hdls) 2m 4f
1:25 (1:26) (Class 3) (0-120,120) 4-Y-0+
£6,252 (£2,371; £1,185; £539; £269; £161)

Form RPR

05-0 **1** **Mouseski**[49] [1265] 11-10-8 **102**........ RWalsh 112+
(P F Nicholls) *prom: chsd ldr 7th: led appr 4 out: drew clr between last 2: drvn out flat* **11/2**[1]

343- **2** *2 ½* **Shalako (USA)**[200] [4504] 7-11-11 **119**........ RJohnson 124
(P J Hobbs) *never far away: rdn 4 out: sn outpcd by ldrs: styd on to go 2nd flat* **8/1**

3116 **3** *1 ¾* **Cantgeton (IRE)**[20] [1481] 5-11-7 **115**........ TJMurphy 118
(M C Pipe) *hld up in tch: hdwy after 7th: upsides wnr 3 out: nt fluent next & sn one pce: lost 2nd flat* **13/2**[3]

2143 **4** *1* **Cannon Fire (FR)**[31] [1434] 4-10-12 **106**........ PMoloney 108
(Evan Williams) *prom: rdn 4 out: outpcd by ldrs next: styd on fr 2 out* **14/1**

114- **5** *2* **Mel In Blue (FR)**[188] [4717] 7-10-13 **114**........ MrSWaley-Cohen(7) 114
(R Waley-Cohen) *hld up midfield: hdwy after 7th: wknd 2 out* **6/1**[2]

4RR3 **6** *¾* **Kalambari (IRE)**[48] [1270] 6-11-4 **119**........ SWalsh(7) 118
(J D Frost) *towards rr: stdy hdwy 7th: kpt on one pce fr 3 out* **28/1**

32-2 **7** *3 ½* **Jockser (IRE)**[145] [387] 4-11-4 **115**........ RYoung(3) 111
(J W Mullins) *mid-div: rdn & sme hdwy 4 out: nvr rchd ldrs* **10/1**

5500 **8** *9* **Anatar (IRE)**[48] [1270] 7-11-10 **118**........ TScudamore 105
(M C Pipe) *nvr beyond mid-div* **16/1**

112- **9** *5* **Tresor Preziniere (FR)**[424] [1167] 7-10-12 **116**........ DPO'Dwyer(10) 98
(P J Hobbs) *in tch tl wknd appr 3 out* **25/1**

4322 **10** *22* **Artane Boys**[34] [1409] 8-11-1 **109**........ JEMoore 69
(Jonjo O'Neill) *t.k.h in rr: stdy hdwy 7th: wknd 4 out: t.o* **12/1**

45-5 **11** *6* **Bobsleigh**[33] [668] 6-11-4 **112**........ JMogford 66
(H S Howe) *a towards rr: lost tch after 7th: t.o* **20/1**

10/0 **12** *8* **Donie Dooley (IRE)**[44] [1319] 7-10-6 **100**........ JamesDavies 46
(P T Dalton) *hld up in rr: lost tch 7th: t.o whn hmpd 4 out* **50/1**

P52- **13** *dist* **Jonanaud**[141] [4518] 6-11-5 **120**........ MrJAJenkins(7) —
(H J Manners) *a towards rr: t.o fr 7th* **40/1**

2-16 **F** **The Kirk (NZ)**[136] [501] 7-9-13 **100**........ RLucey-Butler(7) —
(M Madgwick) *a bhd: t.o whn fell 4 out* **20/1**

2-14 **F** **Water King (USA)**[147] [353] 6-11-0 **108**........ BFenton 104
(R M Stronge) *hld up in tch: rdn 4 out: 8th and btn whn fell 2 out* **10/1**

2-35 **P** **Nuit Sombre (IRE)**[15] [460] 5-11-4 **112**........ DCrosse —
(J G M O'Shea) *led tl appr 4 out: sn wknd: wl bhd whn p.u bef 2 out* **22/1**

0PP- **P** **Dat My Horse (IRE)**[415] [1220] 11-10-5 **106**........ LHeard(7) —
(Tim Vaughan) *hld up: rdn 5th: sn lost tch: t.o whn p.u bef 4 out* **100/1**

-415 **P** **Blue Hawk (IRE)**[35] [1400] 8-9-13 **100**........ JPritchard(7) —
(R Dickin) *trckd ldr: clr of remainder to 5th: lost pl whn mstke 7th: wknd qckly: t.o whn p.u bef 4 out* **20/1**

4m 48.8s (-13.90) **Going Correction** -0.55s/f (Firm)
WFA 4 from 5yo+ 14lb **18** Ran SP% **123.9**
Speed ratings: **105,104,103,102,102 101,100,96,94,86 83,80,—,—,— —,—,—** CSF £42.68 CT £301.67 TOTE £5.20: £2.50, £2.20, £2.10, £3.40; EX 49.20 Trifecta £98.20 Part won. Pool: £138.37 - 0.30 winning units..
Owner M H Dare **Bred** M H Dare **Trained** Ditcheat, Somerset

FOCUS
A fair handicap and the form looks solid enough. The winner can do better.

NOTEBOOK
Mouseski had not run over hurdles since April 2002, when with Ron Hodges, but has made great strides over fences since. Reappearing off a mark no less than 40lb lower than in his latest chase, he shook off the challenge of Cantgeton and was then always holding Shalako. He is probably too old to ever match his chase mark now, but it will be surprising if he can not win another handicap hurdle or two. *(op 9-2 tchd 6-1)*
Shalako(USA) was reverting to hurdles from a good mark but had the blinkers left off on this first run since March. He could not go with the leaders early in the home straight but was staying on well at the end. *(op 11-1)*
Cantgeton(IRE) looked a big threat at the third last, but he was a little awkward at the next and could not go with the winner. Run out of second place on the flat, he did not quite home in this rain-softened ground. *(op 11-2 tchd 7-1)*
Cannon Fire(FR) ran another solid race but has now been held three times from this mark since scoring at Bangor off 8lb lower in July. *(op 16-1)*
Mel In Blue(FR) was right in the thick of things turning for home but the lack of a recent run then began to tell. He is likely to go chasing before long and should do well in that sphere. *(op 8-1)*
Kalambari(IRE) moved into third place at the first flight in the home straight but was left behind by the two leaders from the next. *(op 25-1 tchd 33-1)*
Jockser(IRE), effectively making his seasonal debut, ran an encouraging race from a career-high mark. *(op 8-1)*

1676 BETFAIR.COM H'CAP CHASE (18 fncs) 3m
1:55 (1:57) (Class 2) (0-145,140) 5-Y-O+
£14,964 (£5,676; £2,838; £1,290; £645; £387)

Form — RPR

412- **1** **I Hear Thunder (IRE)**[218] 4162 7-10-0 **114** oh3 .... BHitchcott 124+
(R H Buckler) *nvr far away: rdn after 4 out: led 2 out: drvn out* **9/1**

1FP- **2** 1 1/4 **Colourful Life (IRE)**[175] 4861 9-11-9 **137** .... RWalsh 146+
(P F Nicholls) *in tch: rdn 4 out: ev ch 2 out: sn hung lft: swtchd rt flat: r.o* **3/1**[1]

100- **3** 7 **Torche (IRE)**[205] 4411 7-10-7 **121** ....(v) TScudamore 124+
(M Scudamore) *prom: led 5th: rdn 10th: hdd next: led 5 out to 3 out: wknd after 2 out* **25/1**

111 **4** 1 1/4 **Tigers Lair (IRE)**[125] 650 6-11-3 **131** .... JEMoore 132+
(Jonjo O'Neill) *lft in ld 1st: hdd next: lft 2nd 7th: led 11th to 5 out: led 3 out to 2 out: n.m.r & switched rt bef last: wknd flat* **6/1**[3]

21F- **5** 17 **Le Jaguar (FR)**[174] 4886 5-9-11 **120** oh3 ow4 ....(t) LHeard(7) 101
(P F Nicholls) *in tch to 12th* **13/2**

FU-P **6** 18 **Risk Accessor (IRE)**[14] 1550 10-11-12 **140** .... NFehily 105
(Jonjo O'Neill) *a in rr: t.o fr 13th* **25/1**

-160 **7** 12 **Tango Royal (FR)**[14] 1550 9-11-9 **140** ....(t) TJMalone(3) 93
(M C Pipe) *in tch: hit 4th: rdn 9th: wknd 12th: t.o* **20/1**

110- **8** 3/4 **Philson Run (IRE)**[175] 4861 9-11-4 **132** .... DRDennis 84
(Nick Williams) *towards rr: sme hdwy 12th: wknd appr 5 out: t.o* **9/1**

400- **P** **Amberleigh House (IRE)**[182] 4772 13-11-7 **135** .... GLee —
(D McCain) *in tch tl wknd 11th: t.o whn p.u bef 4 out* **40/1**

3P-P **P** **The Bandit (IRE)**[140] 454 8-10-11 **125** .... BFenton —
(Miss E C Lavelle) *hld up in rr: hdwy 12th: wknd 5 out: t.o whn p.u bef 3 out* **7/2**[2]

0134 **P** **Parisian Storm (IRE)**[14] 1550 9-10-12 **126** .... PMoloney —
(Evan Williams) *led: slipped, j. slowly & hdd 1st: led 2nd to 5th: 2nd whn p.u bef 7th: dismntd* **14/1**

6m 9.90s (-5.00) **Going Correction** +0.025s/f (Yiel)
WFA 5 from 6yo+ 2lb **11** Ran SP% **116.4**
Speed ratings: **109,108,106,105,100 94,90,89,—,—** — CSF £35.51 CT £663.10 TOTE £10.40: £2.30, £2.30, £5.10; EX 47.30 Trifecta £168.40 Part won. Pool: £237.20 - 0.30 winning units..
Owner Nick Elliott **Bred** D H Lalor **Trained** Melplash, Dorset

FOCUS
A decent handicap chase, and reasonably solid form, with the second, third and fourth all within a few pounds of their marks.

NOTEBOOK
I Hear Thunder(IRE), a consistent novice last term, was 3lb out of the handicap. One of four in with a chance at the second last, he stayed on well to assert. The Handicapper is going to step in now but he has further improvement in him over this trip. *(op 10-1)*
Colourful Life(IRE) operates well when fresh and ran a good race on this seasonal bow, but had to settle for second best after hanging to his left from the penultimate fence. *(op 11-4 tchd 7-2)*
Torche(IRE), having his first run since the Cheltenham Festival, was in and out of the lead to the third last and finally faded with two to jump. He should pay his way this season when the emphasis is on stamina.
Tigers Lair(IRE) ◆, unbeaten in three novice chases in the summer, ran a cracker against these seasoned handicappers. Jumping really well, he looked set to score when moving back to the front three from home but he nodded on landing over the next and was soon on the retreat. He did not quite see out the trip in the softening ground but can win a decent race over slightly shorter. *(op 11-2 tchd 5-1)*
Le Jaguar(FR), 3lb out of the weights for this seasonal bow, was left behind by the principals before the end of the back straight but should come on for the run. *(op 8-1)*
Risk Accessor(IRE), again without the tongue tie, has shown little in two starts since leaving Christy Roche's yard. *Official explanation: vet said gelding returned lame on left fore*
Amberleigh House(IRE), rising 14, made a satisfactory start to what is likely to be his final season. *Official explanation: jockey said gelding had bled from nose (op 33-1)*
The Bandit(IRE) *Official explanation: jockey said gelding had a breathing problem (op 33-1)*
Parisian Storm(IRE) *Official explanation: jockey said gelding had struck into itself (op 33-1)*

1677 BETFAIR H'CAP HURDLE (8 hdls) 2m 110y
2:25 (2:30) (Class 2) 4-Y-O
£20,300 (£7,700; £3,850; £1,750; £875; £525)

Form — RPR

011- **1** **Admiral (IRE)**[16] 4858 4-11-7 **134** .... PCO'Neill(5) 148+
(R C Guest) *mde all: rdn 2 out: styd on wl* **16/1**

030- **2** 4 **Zalda**[207] 4386 4-10-1 **116** .... MrTJO'Brien(7) 125
(P J Hobbs) *hld up towards rr: hdwy after 4th: chsd wnr bef 2 out: no imp flat* **9/1**

416- **3** 10 **Nanga Parbat (FR)**[198] 4538 4-10-2 **110** ....(t) RWalsh 109
(P F Nicholls) *chsd ldrs: rdn 3 out: kpt on same pce fr next* **5/2**[1]

1123 **4** shd **Darrias (GER)**[55] 1222 4-11-3 **132** ....(t) LHeard(7) 131
(P F Nicholls) *in tch: rdn 5th: sn no ch w ldrs: styd on appr last* **14/1**

1- **5** 3 **Ursis (FR)**[318] 2430 4-10-9 **117** .... NFehily 113
(Jonjo O'Neill) *hld up midfield: rdn 3 out: sn wknd* **11/2**[3]

42-0 **6** 6 **Double Dizzy**[164] 65 4-9-9 **108** oh5 .... WKennedy(5) 98
(R H Buckler) *prom: rdn 4 out: nt fluent next: sn wknd* **66/1**

305- **7** 1/2 **Noble Request (FR)**[172] 4920 4-11-0 **122** .... RJohnson 112+
(P J Hobbs) *chsd wnr tl after 3 out: sn rdn: wknd bef last* **20/1**

-6P0 **8** 12 **Moon Catcher**[2] 1658 4-9-7 **108** oh8 .... KBurke(7) 85
(D Brace) *a in rr: rdn along 4th: sn lost tch* **100/1**

520- **9** hd **Regal Setting (IRE)**[42] 4386 4-10-10 **118** .... GLee 95
(J Howard Johnson) *rdn after 2nd: bhd fr 4th* **7/1**

521- **10** 8 **Arrayou (FR)**[171] 4930 4-11-2 **124** ....(b) LAspell 93
(O Sherwood) *a in rr: lost tch 4 out: t.o* **20/1**

60-1 **P** **Fire Dragon (IRE)**[13] 1559 4-11-4 **126** .... JEMoore —
(Jonjo O'Neill) *midfield whn slipped bdly on landing 2nd and sn p.u* **5/1**[2]

15P- **P** **Etendard Indien (FR)**[204] 4433 4-10-12 **120** .... MFoley —
(N J Henderson) *hld up mid-div: sme hdwy 5th: wknd after next: t.o whn p.u bef last* **10/1**

4m 2.10s (-8.30) **Going Correction** -0.25s/f (Good) **12** Ran SP% **116.8**
Speed ratings: **109,107,102,102,100 98,97,92,92,88** —,— CSF £144.49 CT £487.31 TOTE £15.30: £3.40, £3.70, £1.60; EX 241.40 Trifecta £191.30 Part won. Pool: £269.56 - 0.10 winning units..
Owner Willie McKay **Bred** R Lee **Trained** Brancepeth, Co Durham
■ This event was previously known as the Free Handicap Hurdle.

FOCUS
A competitive renewal and the form looks particularly solid. Those finishing from third to seventh all seemed to run within a few pounds of their marks, so no reason to doubt the much improved displays from both of the first two.

NOTEBOOK
Admiral(IRE) ◆, fit from a spin on the Flat, was given a good ride by O'Neill and made every yard. The form of last season's Ayr win has been upgraded, but this was still another big step up. Likely to stay further and still highly progressive, he can win again. *(op 12-1)*
Zalda moved into second place after the third from home but could not get to the winner. This was a very pleasing return to action nevertheless, and she shaped as if she would stay a bit further than this. *(op 11-1)*
Nanga Parbat(FR) was ante-post favourite for the Fred Winter Handicap at the Cheltenham Festival only to be balloted out. Tongue-tied for the first time, he had his chance three out but was unable to quicken up. He could perhaps have done with the rain staying away. *(op 3-1)*
Darrias(GER), tongue tied for the first time, could not go with the leaders early in the home straight but did keep on for pressure in the latter stages. He looks held off his current mark.
Ursis(FR) had not run since making an impressive hurdles debut at Wetherby last November and can be expected to come on for this return to action. *(op 9-2 tchd 6-1)*
Double Dizzy ran respectably from 5lb out of the handicap. *(op 50-1)*
Noble Request(FR), a stablemate of the runner-up, chased the winner until fading from the second last.
Regal Setting(IRE), who had a run on the Flat in August, did not look keen from an early stage. *Official explanation: jockey said gelding had a breathing problem (op 15-2)*
Fire Dragon(IRE), 7lb higher, was wisely pulled up after almost coming down at the second. *(op 6-1)*

1678 BETFAIR.COM NOVICES' CHASE (18 fncs) 3m
3:00 (3:03) (Class 3) 5-Y-O+ **£5,681** (£1,748; £874; £437)

Form — RPR

2-41 **1** **State Of Play**[122] 680 5-10-10 110 .... PMoloney 122+
(Evan Williams) *hld up: blnd 2nd: hdwy after 7th: wnt 2nd 4 out: 2 l down whn lft in ld 2 out: sn clr: eased cl home* **11/1**

4301 **2** 7 **Koumba (FR)**[15] 1540 7-10-12 109 .... LAspell 112
(Evan Williams) *hld up: hdwy appr 8th: lft 2nd 2 out: one pce after* **16/1**

1FP0 **3** 10 **He's The Biz (FR)**[125] 652 6-10-12 101 .... DRDennis 102
(Nick Williams) *hld up: hdwy appr 4 out: mstke 2 out: no imp after* **33/1**

P00/ **4** 6 **One Day (NZ)**[567] 4455 7-10-7 100 .... PCO'Neill(5) 99+
(R C Guest) *hld up: j. slowly 6th: mstke 11th: hdwy appr 14th: mstke 3 out: sn wknd* **20/1**

P140 **5** 19 **It's Definite (IRE)**[42] 1341 6-10-12 112 ....(p) GLee 77
(P Bowen) *in tch tl wknd 12th* **10/1**[3]

000- **6** 15 **Florida Dream (IRE)**[189] 4687 6-10-12 112 .... CLlewellyn 62
(N A Twiston-Davies) *nt jump wl: led after 2nd to 3rd: remained cl up tl wknd 14th* **5/2**[1]

6P/3 **7** 3/4 **Prince On The Ter**[68] 1123 10-10-9 65 .... CBolger(3) 61
(B Scriven) *led: hdd after 2nd: led again 3rd: hdd appr 14th: wknd bef next* **100/1**

005- **F** **Jiver (IRE)**[189] 4687 6-10-12 110 .... TScudamore —
(M Scudamore) *prom tl fell 4th* **16/1**

2F-1 **F** **Moscow Whisper (IRE)**[150] 296 8-10-12 115 .... RJohnson 120+
(P J Hobbs) *in tch: hdwy 4th: mstke 9th: led appr 14th: 2 l up whn fell 2 out* **5/2**[1]

141 **C** **Charango Star**[27] 1455 7-10-12 110 .... TJMurphy —
(W K Goldsworthy) *midfield: hmpd 4th: lost pl 7th: hdwy 13th: ev ch whn carried out by loose horse 14th* **4/1**[2]

6m 27.4s (12.50) **Going Correction** +0.65s/f (Soft)
WFA 5 from 6yo+ 2lb **10** Ran SP% **115.0**
Speed ratings: **105,102,99,97,91 86,85,—,—,—** CSF £152.88 TOTE £16.00: £3.00, £3.00, £4.10; EX 168.60.
Owner William Rucker **Bred** Roland Lerner **Trained** Cowbridge, Vale Of Glamorgan

FOCUS
Difficult to assess, but the winner has been rated as value for 12l, and the faller as a 2l second.

NOTEBOOK
State Of Play ◆ won a novice hurdle at Hereford in June on his final run for Paul Webber. Without the visor for this chasing debut, he survived an early blunder and steadily worked his way into the picture. Travelling well when left in front at the second last, he might well have won in any case. He stayed this longer trip well and can win more races over fences. *(op 9-1)*
Koumba(FR) stayed on well in the latter stages but his stablemate was much too strong. This was a decent effort on ground that was softer than he would have liked. *(op 14-1)*
He's The Biz(FR), back over the larger obstacles, looked held turning for home but stayed on past beaten horses in the straight. He has done all his winning on better ground. *(op 20-1)*
One Day(NZ) was having his first run for over eighteen months. He made several mistakes on this chasing debut but showed ability before weakening over the last three fences. *(op 16-1)*
It's Definite(IRE), reverting to fences, was not best suited by the rain-softened ground. *(op 9-1)*
Florida Dream(IRE) has the scope to make a chaser but he is going to have to jump better than he did on this debut over fences. *(op 3-1 tchd 9-4)*
Moscow Whisper(IRE), having his first run for five months, moved to the front on the home turn, but jumped out to his right up the home straight and came down after getting in too close to the second last. The winner was going just as well at the time and may well have prevailed anyway, but he can win again over fences provided his jumping holds up. *(op 3-1)*
Charango Star, successful in a moderate event on his chasing debut, closed right up on the long turn and was very much in contention when a loose horse took him out at the first fence in the straight. *(op 3-1)*

1679 BETFAIRPOKER.COM JUVENILE NOVICES' HURDLE (8 hdls) 2m 110y
3:35 (3:40) (Class 4) 3-Y-O **£3,614** (£1,112; £556; £278)

Form — RPR

1 **Vale De Lobo**[56] 3-10-3 .... RWalsh 95+
(P F Nicholls) *mstke 1st: trckd ldrs: wnt 2nd after 4th: led 3 out: rdn clr after last* **7/4**[1]

2 8 **Double Spectre (IRE)**[41] 3-10-10 .... DCrosse 94+
(Jean-Rene Auvray) *prom: led appr 2nd: hdd 3 out: stl ev ch whn blnd 2 out: one pce fr last* **20/1**

3 nk **Dusty Dane (IRE)**[173] 3-10-3 .... MrTJO'Brien(7) 94+
(W G M Turner) *in tch: effrt to chse ldrs 4 out: disputing 2nd but no ch w wnr whn stmbld last: one pce after* **28/1**

4 1 **Inchcape Rock**[5] 3-10-10 .... VSlattery 91
(J G M O'Shea) *hld up: styd on wl fr bef last: nvr nrr* **100/1**

5 5 **Barnbrook Empire (IRE)**[21] 3-10-3 .... OMcPhail 79
(B J Llewellyn) *towards rr: hdwy appr 4 out: no imp whn blnd last* **66/1**

6 16 **Theflyingscottie**[30] 3-10-5 .... CHonour(5) 70
(J D Frost) *in tch: hdwy appr 4 out: wknd bef 2 out* **66/1**

52 **7** 1 1/4 **Backstreet Lad**[29] 1440 3-10-10 ....(tp) PMoloney 69
(Evan Williams) *midfield: rdn appr 3 out: sn wknd* **12/1**

8 18 **Lorna Dune**[25] 3-10-0 .... ONelmes(3) 44
(J G M O'Shea) *sn bhd* **66/1**

3 **9** 27 **Fu Manchu**[35] 1397 3-10-10 .... JEMoore 24
(Jonjo O'Neill) *a bhd: t.o* **4/1**[3]

P **Harry's Simmie (IRE)**[366] 3-9-11 ow1 .... SWalsh(7) —
(R C Harper) *a bhd: t.o 4th: p.u bef 4 out* **40/1**

P **Pennestamp (IRE)**[5] 3-10-7 .... TJMalone(3) —
(J G M O'Shea) *mstke 2nd: a bhd: t.o whn p.u bef 4 out* **50/1**

F P **Arno River**[20] [1478] 3-10-10 .... TScudamore —
(D Brace) *prom tl wknd after 4th: t.o whn p.u bef 3 out* **100/1**

2 P **Negas (IRE)**[42] [1332] 3-10-10 .... GLee —
(J Howard Johnson) *cl up tl rdn and wknd after 4th: t.o whn p.u bef 3 out* **10/1**

21 P **Whirling**[14] [1551] 3-10-10 ....(v) TJMurphy —
(M C Pipe) *led: hdd appr 2nd and mstke: wknd 4th: t.o whn p.u bef 3 out* **3/1**[2]

P **Leprechaun's Maite**[177] 3-10-0 .... AngharadFrieze(10) —
(P A Blockley) *midfield: wknd appr 3 out: t.o whn p.u bef 2 out* **66/1**

P **Cloonavery (IRE)**[65] 3-10-10 .... JamesDavies —
(B Llewellyn) *trckd ldrs: effrt after 4th: wknd appr 3 out: t.o whn p.u bef 2 out* **50/1**

4m 15.8s (5.40) **Going Correction** +0.40s/f (Soft) **16** Ran SP% **120.7**
Speed ratings: **103,99,99,98,96 88,88,79,66,— —,—,—,—,— —** CSF £40.47 TOTE £2.80: £1.50, £4.30, £5.20; EX 47.20.
Owner Mrs M Findlay **Bred** J B Haggas **Trained** Ditcheat, Somerset

FOCUS
Not many got into the action in what is a very difficult race to assess. It has been rated around the 4th, 5th and 6th's Flat form, but a fair bit of guesswork is involved.

NOTEBOOK
Vale De Lobo was a fair filly on the Flat over middle distances, latterly for William Haggas. Drawing clear with the runner-up over the last three flights, she stayed on well to assert on the run-in. This was not a great race but she should be able to win again. *(op 9-4 tchd 5-2)*
Double Spectre(IRE), a lightly raced maiden on the Flat for this yard, showed plenty of promise on *this hurdles debut but a blunder at the penultimate flight ended his chanceOfficial explanation: jockey said gelding hung right in home straight (op 25-1)*
Dusty Dane(IRE), a maiden on the Flat, stayed on resolutely up the straight and, although no threat *to the winner, was disputing second spot when losing his back legs on landing over the last. (op 33-1)*
Inchcape Rock, beaten in a Windsor seller in cheekpieces five days earlier, passed a number of *floundering rivals in the latter stages and obviously possesses a bit of aptitude for this game. (op 66-1)*
Barnbrook Empire(IRE) was exposed as a plating-class maiden on the Flat.
Theflyingscottie, beaten in sellers on the Flat, made good headway to move into third place on the *long home turn but never had a chance with the first two and faded going to the second last. (op 50-1)*
Backstreet Lad *Official explanation: jockey said gelding had a breathing problem (tchd 14-1)*
Fu Manchu *Official explanation: vet said gelding finished distressed (op 7-2)*
Cloonavery(IRE), a winner over a mile on Polytrack for Jamie Osborne, failed to get home on this hurdling debut. *(tchd 66-1)*
Whirling did not last long in the lead and was being administered reminders before halfway. She *dropped right out of contention on the home turn and the ground was probably to blameOfficial explanation: trainer's representative said filly returned lame (tchd 66-1)*

1680 JEWSON NOVICES' HURDLE (SERIES QUALIFIER) (8 hdls) 2m 110y
4:05 (4:11) (Class 4) 4-Y-0+ **£3,601** (£1,108; £554; £277)

Form RPR

210- **1** **Rimsky (IRE)**[182] [4774] 4-10-12 .... CLlewellyn 112+
(N A Twiston-Davies) *led: awkward jump and hdd 3rd: remained prom: narrow ld appr 2 out to last: rallied to ld nr fin* **9/2**[3]

2 *1* **Desert Quest (IRE)**[113] 5-10-12 .... RWalsh 108
(P F Nicholls) *midfield: stdy hdwy 4th: chal 2 out: led last: hung lft u.p flat: hdd nr fin* **2/1**[1]

1 **3** *3* **Twelve Paces**[89] [963] 4-10-12 .... TJMurphy 108+
(M C Pipe) *trckd ldrs: chal whn mstke 2 out: sn hung lft and one pce* **3/1**[2]

31F2 **4** *2 1/2* **Tom Bell (IRE)**[69] [1113] 5-11-4 107 .... DCrosse 108
(J G M O'Shea) *towards rr: hdwy 4th: rdn after 3 out: kpt on one pce fr next* **16/1**

0-13 **5** *12* **Theocritus (GER)**[38] [1383] 4-11-4 93 .... DRDennis 97+
(Nick Williams) *in tch: outpcd by ldrs 5th: n.d after* **33/1**

6 *5* **Archduke Ferdinand (FR)**[128] 7-10-12 .... RThornton 89+
(A King) *keen in midfield: blnd 2nd: stdy hdwy fr 4th: led gng wl after 4 out: hdd bef 2 out: sn wknd* **14/1**

00-4 **7** *1 1/4* **Moorlands Milly**[29] [1445] 4-10-0 .... LStephens(5) 77
(D Burchell) *towards rr: styd on past btn horses fr 2 out* **100/1**

344/ **8** *1 1/4* **Freeline Fantasy (IRE)**[154] 8-10-5 .... LHeard(7) 83
(Tim Vaughan) *w ldr: led 3rd tl after 4th: sn wknd* **50/1**

0 **9** *5* **Davy's Luck**[13] [1562] 5-10-5 .... WMarston 71
(J M Bradley) *a towards rr* **100/1**

0321 **10** *1 1/4* **West End Wonder (IRE)**[94] [912] 6-10-11 110 .... AScholes(7) 82
(D Burchell) *trckd ldrs: led after 4th: jinked into next: sn hdd & wknd* **8/1**

1P3/ **11** *2* **Before The Mast (IRE)**[672] [2589] 8-10-5 .... CPoste(7) 74
(M F Harris) *in rr: sme hdwy 5th: wkng whn mstke next* **66/1**

6 **12** *12* **Glide**[126] [243] 4-10-12 .... MBradburne 62
(J A B Old) *in tch tl wknd bef 5th: t.o* **100/1**

4- **13** *29* **Man Ray (USA)**[193] [4640] 4-10-12 .... JEMoore 33
(Jonjo O'Neill) *hld up mid-div: hdwy after 4th: rdn bef 3 out: wkng whn mstke 2 out: t.o* **9/1**

P **Mount Benger**[22] 5-10-12 .... JamesDavies —
(Mrs A J Hamilton-Fairley) *a bhd: t.o whn p.u bef 3 out* **50/1**

P **Ganymede**[71] 4-10-12 .... VSlattery —
(J G M O'Shea) *in rr: pushed along 3rd: lost tch next: t.o whn p.u bef 2 out* **22/1**

P **Limogos (GER)**[546] 5-10-5 .... MissLGardner(7) —
(Mrs S Gardner) *midfield: rdr lost whip 2nd: bhd fr 4th: t.o whn p.u bef last* **100/1**

4m 17.2s (6.80) **Going Correction** +0.40s/f (Soft) **16** Ran SP% **126.8**
Speed ratings: **100,99,98,96,91 88,88,87,85,84 83,78,64,—,— —** CSF £14.37 TOTE £6.60: £2.00, £1.80, £1.60; EX 17.50.
Owner D J & S A Goodman **Bred** J Duggan **Trained** Naunton, Gloucs

FOCUS
A fair novice hurdle, rated around the fourth and fifth. It should produce winners.

NOTEBOOK
Rimsky(IRE) was a useful bumper horse last term. He rather ran in snatches on this hurdles debut and did not always jump fluently, but fought his way back to the front on the run-in and looks capable of better, especially when he steps up in distance. *(op 3-1)*
Desert Quest(IRE), very useful for David Loder on the level, looked set to make a winning debut over hurdles when taking a narrow lead at the last, but he hung on the run-in and was outbattled by *the winner. He is able but quirky, and it would be no surprise to see some headgear back on soon. (op 9-4)*
Twelve Paces, green when successful on his bumper debut three months ago, again showed his *inexperience when the pressure was on. He should have no problem winning in ordinary company. (op 13-2)*
Tom Bell(IRE), without the visor, ran a decent race under the penalty he picked up when landing a handicap back in May.
Theocritus(GER), back down in trip, was unable to go with the leaders early in the home straight but kept on steadily from the third last. He could be interesting when returning to handicaps.
Archduke Ferdinand(FR) was once a smart stayer on the Flat for Paul Cole, winner of the Northumberland Plate in 2001, but he was well beaten on his only start on the level this year. After taking quite a hold in the early part of this hurdles debut, he eased to the front at the third last, but was quickly tackled and dropped away. He needs to settle better.
West End Wonder(IRE), returning after a summer break, tried to get clear of his field on the home turn but was run down after wandering going into the first flight in the straight. *(tchd 17-2)*
Man Ray(USA) finished last in the end, but he certainly did not shape without promise and is entitled to strip fitter for the run. *(op 8-1)*

1681 BETFAIRPOKER.COM STANDARD OPEN NATIONAL HUNT FLAT RACE () 2m 110y
4:40 (4:41) (Class 6) 4-6-Y-0 **£1,960** (£560; £280)

Form RPR

1 **Leading Contender (IRE)** 4-11-4 .... RJohnson 125+
(P J Hobbs) *hld up: hdwy 6f out: led over 3f out: drew clr fnl f: r.o wl* **9/2**[2]

2 *9* **Asudo (IRE)** 4-10-11 .... SCrawford(7) 114+
(N A Twiston-Davies) *trckd ldrs: wnt 2nd over 3f out: no ch w wnr fnl f* **25/1**

2- **3** *3 1/2* **Scalini'S (IRE)**[379] [1500] 5-10-11 .... MrAJBerry(7) 110
(Jonjo O'Neill) *midfield: hdwy 6f out: rdn to chse ldrs over 2f out: one pce over 1f out* **8/1**

2- **4** *12* **Could Be Alright (IRE)**[193] [4644] 6-10-13 .... WKennedy(5) 98
(Noel T Chance) *in tch: ev ch 4f out: rdn and wknd over 2f out* **11/4**[1]

5/3- **5** *1 1/2* **The Baillie (IRE)**[290] [2940] 6-11-4 .... RThornton 96
(C R Egerton) *t.k.h: in tch: effrt to chse ldrs ef out: wknd over 2f out* **14/1**

6 *16* **Supremely Smart (IRE)** 5-11-4 .... CLlewellyn 80
(N A Twiston-Davies) *bhd: hdwy 7f out: rdn over 4f out: wknd over 2f out* **6/1**

51- **7** *6* **Arumun (IRE)**[196] [4559] 4-11-11 .... TScudamore 81
(M Scudamore) *led: hdd over 3f out: wknd over 2f out* **10/1**

8 *1/2* **Little Word**[126] 6-10-4 .... MrJCook(7) 67
(P D Williams) *t.k.h: prom tl wknd 7f out* **66/1**

4 **9** *nk* **Thenford Lord (IRE)**[27] [1459] 4-11-4 .... MBradburne 73
(D J S Ffrench Davis) *towards rr: rdn over 4f out: nvr on terms* **50/1**

10 *5* **Cornish Jack** 5-10-13 .... CHonour(5) 68
(J D Frost) *in tch: lost pl after 4f: no imp after* **25/1**

11 *20* **Graig Hill Cracker (IRE)** 6-11-4 .... JPByrne 48
(R L Brown) *prom: rn wd and lost pl after 2f: hdwy 1/2-way: wknd 6f out* **100/1**

12 *14* **Brave Jo (FR)** 4-10-11 .... KBurke(7) 34
(N J Hawke) *a bhd* **50/1**

23- **13** *5* **Here We Go (IRE)**[297] [2831] 6-11-4 .... TJMurphy 29
(W K Goldsworthy) *prom tl wknd qckly over 4f out* **5/1**[3]

14 *5* **Gold Vic (IRE)** 5-11-4 .... GLee 24
(P Bowen) *midfield unitl wknd 6f out* **12/1**

460 **P** **Judy The Drinker**[108] [816] 6-10-1 .... ENolan(10) —
(J G M O'Shea) *midfield: lost pl after 4f: p.u after 6f* **66/1**

4m 5.60s (-4.60) **Going Correction** +0.40s/f (Soft) **15** Ran SP% **126.0**
Speed ratings: **104,99,98,92,91 84,81,81,81,78 69,62,60,57,—** CSF £123.11 TOTE £6.30: £2.10, £8.20, £3.80; EX 224.20 Place 6 £299.41, Place 5 £137.69.
Owner Mrs Joanna Peppiatt **Bred** Noel Walsh **Trained** Withycombe, Somerset

FOCUS
A very good bumper, run in a fast time. The winner looks a high-class recruit and the next two should have no problem winning races.

NOTEBOOK
Leading Contender(IRE) ◆, who cost 13,500gns at three, is out of a mare who was fourth in an Irish bumper on her only run. He drew right away against the stands' rail in the final three furlongs and looks a very good prospect. The graded race at Cheltenham's Open meeting looks a suitable target. *(op 4-1)*
Asudo(IRE) is a half-brother to three minor winners, out of a successful Irish pointer. He was second best in the last three furlongs but had run up against a smart rival. He stuck to his task well and should have no problem landing a bumper. *(op 14-1)*
Scalini'S(IRE) ◆ has been off for more than a year after being beaten at odds-on on his debut. He shaped with plenty of promise in what looks a decent race and is well up to winning in ordinary company. *(op 7-1)*
Could Be Alright(IRE), runner-up on his debut here in the spring, ran his race but was found wanting in what looked a hot event of its type. *(op 5-2 tchd 3-1)*
The Baillie(IRE) ran respectably on this first outing since Christmas. He was withdrawn from a novice hurdle over an extended two and three-quarter miles last month and looks to have plenty of stamina. *(op 12-1)*
Supremely Smart(IRE), whose dam won over hurdles and fences at two miles, is a half-brother to bumper winner Icy Blast. *(op 4-1)*
Arumun(IRE), penalised for his win at Haydock in March, made the running at a decent pace until the winner eased past. *(op 12-1 tchd 14-1)*
Here We Go(IRE), previously with Jonjo O'Neill, ran as if in need of this first start since December. *(op 8-1)*
T/Plt: £812.20 to a £1 stake. Pool: £52,405.10. 47.10 winning tickets. T/Qpdt: £102.00 to a £1 stake. Pool: £2,068.60. 15.00 winning tickets. DO/RL

[1587] HEXHAM (L-H)
Saturday, October 8

OFFICIAL GOING: Good to firm
Wind: Breezy 1/2 against

1682 NORTHERN RAIL NOVICES' CHASE (12 fncs) 2m 110y
2:05 (2:06) (Class 4) 4-Y-0+ **£4,290** (£1,320; £660; £330)

Form RPR

3-26 **1** **Your Advantage (IRE)**[20] [1487] 5-11-3 103 ....(t) PBuchanan(3) 109+
(Miss Lucinda V Russell) *chsd ldrs: drvn to ld between last two: styd on wl* **14/1**

1P01 **2** *3/4* **College City (IRE)**[6] [1612] 6-11-8 98 ....(p) DCCostello(5) 114
(R C Guest) *hld up in tch: hdwy to press ldrs between last two: kpt on fr last: hld towards fin* **11/2**[3]

1P4- **3** *5* **Silver Jack (IRE)**[241] [3755] 7-11-6 94 .... ADobbin 102
(M Todhunter) *bhd: reminders 5th: struggling after next: kpt on fr 2 out: no ch w first two* **10/1**

3F10 **4** *4* **Prince Adjal (IRE)**[46] [1297] 5-11-3 97 ....(e) LMcGrath(3) 98
(R C Guest) *cl up: hit 3rd: led 5th to between last two: wknd run in* **16/1**

0 **5** 2 **Tornado Alley (IRE)**[11] 1566 6-11-6 JPMcNamara 96
(J J Lambe, Ire) *hld up: hdwy bef 3 out: rdn and outpcd next: n.d after* **50/1**
43P- **6** 7 **Gaelic Flight (IRE)**[182] 4777 7-11-6 103 TDoyle 92+
(Noel T Chance) *in tch: effrt whn hit 3 out: rallied and chal between last two: wknd run in* **6/4**[1]
2131 **F** **Parisienne Gale (IRE)**[42] 1335 6-10-13 97 KRenwick 89
(R Ford) *led: hit and hdd 5th: 2l down whn fell 2 out* **2/1**[2]
3m 58.7s (-10.40) **Going Correction** -0.60s/f (Firm) 7 Ran SP% **112.3**
Speed ratings: **100,99,97,95,94 91,**— CSF £83.28 TOTE £12.20: £2.10, £3.10; EX 45.20.
Owner Mr and Mrs T P Winnell **Bred** Janus Bloodstock Inc **Trained** Milnathort, Perth & Kinross

FOCUS
An ordinary event but one in which the pace was sound and this form should stand up at a similar level.

NOTEBOOK
Your Advantage(IRE), from a stable back among the winners, turned in his best effort over fences to win his first race over the larger obstacles. He should stay two and a half miles and may be capable of a bit better. *(op 12-1 tchd 16-1)*
College City(IRE) had won three of his previous five races and turned in another solid effort to pull clear of the remainder. A truly-run race over this trip seems to suit and he remains the type to win again when things fall right. *(op 4-1)*
Silver Jack(IRE) ran creditably in terms of form on this chase debut but left the impression that much easier ground and a step up in trip would have been to his liking. He jumped soundly in the main and looks sure to win a race over fences. *(op 15-2)*
Prince Adjal(IRE), back over fences after a poor run over hurdles, is not the most reliable but seemed to be anchored by his 14lb rise for his previous wide margin Market Rasen success over the larger obstacles. *(op 10-1)*
Tornado Alley(IRE) is an inconsistent performer who is a maiden under all codes and, although not totally disgraced, did not leave the impression that he was a winner waiting to happen. *(op 33-1)*
Gaelic Flight(IRE), a fast-ground bumper and hurdle winner, fared better than the distance beaten suggests on this first run for six months, but the way he dropped out in the closing stages means he is one to be wary of at short odds. *(op 9-4)*
Parisienne Gale(IRE), 12lb higher than when successful at Cartmel, was in the process of running creditably when coming to grief. There are more races to be won with the mare if this has not affected her confidence. *(op 5-2)*

1683 S.I.T.A. MARES' ONLY NOVICES' HURDLE (8 hdls) 2m 110y
2:35 (2:36) (Class 4) 4-Y-O+ **£3,708** (£1,141; £570; £285)

Form RPR
1 **1** **United Spirit (IRE)**[13] 1565 4-11-3 BHarding 95+
(Jedd O'Keeffe) *in tch: hdwy to ld between last two: kpt on wl* **11/4**[2]
U2- **2** 3 **Tingshaw Ring (IRE)**[7] 1403 5-11-10 ADobbin 99+
(Eoin Doyle, Ire) *hld up midfield: hdwy bef 2 out: pressed wnr bef last: kpt on same pce run in* **7/2**[3]
0R-0 **3** 3½ **August Rose (IRE)**[150] 302 5-10-7 PBuchanan(3) 82
(Miss Lucinda V Russell) *prom: outpcd bef 2 out: rallied bef last: nt rch first two* **50/1**
4 7 **Omas Leader (IRE)**[62] 1171 7-10-10 JPMcNamara 75
(J J Lambe, Ire) *hld up: hdwy and prom appr 2 out: outpcd between last two* **20/1**
05-4 **5** 6 **Apsara**[11] 1569 4-10-10 90 FKeniry 69
(G M Moore) *chsd ldr to bef 2 out: sn rdn and btn* **10/1**
0/P- **6** shd **Ro Eridani**[26] 722 5-10-7 MrCStorey(3) 68
(Miss S E Forster) *keen: led: hit 3rd: hdd between last two: sn btn* **100/1**
7 dist **Auburn Lodge (IRE)**[37] 4-10-10 KRenwick —
(J J Lambe, Ire) *bhd: rdn after 3 out: nvr on terms* **20/1**
0000 **8** 3½ **Terimons Daughter**[8] 1590 6-10-10 NPMulholland —
(E W Tuer) *bhd: struggling fr 1/2-way* **100/1**
13- **F** **Boberelle (IRE)**[210] 4333 5-10-10 TDoyle —
(C Tinkler) *hld up: fell 2nd* **13/8**[1]
56U **P** **South Shore One**[11] 1569 4-10-5 DCCostello(5) —
(C Grant) *in tch to 3 out: sn wknd: t.o whn p.u run in* **20/1**
0 **U** **Nuzzle**[16] 1527 5-10-3 SMarshall(7) —
(N G Richards) *hld up: hdwy and in tch whn wnt lft and uns rdr 3 out* **50/1**
000- **P** **Kokopelli Mana (IRE)**[181] 4788 5-10-10 DO'Meara —
(J M Jefferson) *prom to 4 out: sn wknd: t.o whn p.u bef last* **33/1**
4m 8.50s (-6.70) **Going Correction** -0.60s/f (Firm)
WFA 4 from 5yo+ 13lb 12 Ran SP% **119.2**
Speed ratings: **91,89,87,84,81 81,**—,—,—,— —,— CSF £12.04 TOTE £3.70: £1.10, £2.10, £3.30; EX 7.80.
Owner Colin And Melanie Moore **Bred** Atlantic Racing Limited **Trained** Middleham Moor, N Yorks
■ Stewards' Enquiry : Mr C Storey caution: used whip when out of contention

FOCUS
An ordinary event that could be rated too high although the proximity of the minor placed horses holds the form down. However, the winner kept her unbeaten record and looks the type to progress again.

NOTEBOOK
United Spirit(IRE) ◆ turned in an improved effort to maintain her unbeaten record over hurdles. She travelled strongly before showing the right attitude to pull clear and appeals as the type to win again in this sphere. *(op 3-1 tchd 10-3)*
Tingshaw Ring(IRE) is vulnerable to progressive sorts under a double penalty in this grade but she ran with credit and looks a good guide to the level of this form. She will not mind the return to two and a half miles and should continue to run well. *(op 4-1)*
August Rose(IRE) seemed to turn in a much-improved effort on this first run for five months and on only this second start for current connections. Her proximity holds the form down but she may do better in modest handicaps.
Omas Leader(IRE), who needs one more run for a handicap mark, was not disgraced in an ordinary event and looks the type to do better when upped to two and a half miles.
Apsara, whose sole win came on her second start on the Flat last year, again had her limitations *exposed in this type of event and is likely to continue to look vulnerable in this grade.Official explanation: jockey said filly bled from nose (op 8-1)*
Ro Eridani was not totally disgraced given she was very keen but her record suggests she is not really one to be interested in.
Boberelle(IRE), who showed fair form in two outings in bumpers, was an early casualty on this hurdle debut but is worth another chance over obstacles. *(op 7-4 tchd 2-1 and 15-8 in places)*

1684 METROCENTRE H'CAP CHASE (15 fncs) 2m 4f 110y
3:05 (3:06) (Class 4) (0-110,117) 5-Y-O+ **£4,329** (£1,332; £666; £333)

Form RPR
3PP- **1** **Alfy Rich**[241] 3752 9-10-10 94 ADobbin 94+
(M Todhunter) *chsd ldrs: led 10th: mde rest: styd on strly fr 3 out* **11/4**[1]
5335 **2** 8 **Mr Laggan**[97] 896 10-9-7 84 oh12 MJMcAlister(7) 75
(Miss Kate Milligan) *w ldr: lft in ld 7th: hdd 10th: cl up: rdn 3 out: kpt on fr last: no ch w wnr* **12/1**
-0P0 **3** 2½ **Renvyle (IRE)**[80] 1039 7-11-4 105 (p) LMcGrath(3) 96+
(R C Guest) *hld up in tch: hdwy bef 3 out: wnt 2nd bef last to run in: no ex* **9/2**[3]
0S0F **4** 8 **Panmure (IRE)**[11] 1570 9-10-11 95 (tp) TDoyle 76
(P D Niven) *chsd ldrs: outpcd 4 out: n.d after* **4/1**[2]
402P **5** 16 **Pavey Ark (IRE)**[11] 1570 7-9-11 84 oh9 PAspell(3) 49
(James Moffatt) *hld up in tch: effrt whn hit 3 out: sn btn* **17/2**
3302 **U** **Risky Way**[8] 1592 9-10-8 92 DO'Meara —
(W S Coltherd) *mde most tl blnd bdly and uns rdr 7th* **11/4**[1]
5m 0.40s (-11.00) **Going Correction** -0.60s/f (Firm) 6 Ran SP% **109.7**
Speed ratings: **96,92,92,88,82** — CSF £28.57 TOTE £3.90: £1.40, £4.10; EX 59.40.
Owner The Carlisle Cavaliers **Bred** Paul M Rich **Trained** Orton, Cumbria
■ A milestone for Tony Dobbin, who became only the tenth jump jockey to reach 1000 winners in Britain.

FOCUS
An uncompetitive race rated through the runner-up and the winner proved well suited by these much quicker conditions.

NOTEBOOK
Alfy Rich, down in trip, proved suited by this much quicker ground and recorded his best effort over fences. Although this was an ordinary race, his jumping was sound and he may be capable of further success granted suitable conditions. *(tchd 5-2 and 3-1)*
Mr Laggan reserves some of his better efforts for this course and ran well from 12lb out of the handicap. However his record of inconsistency and his wins-to-runs ratio means he is not one to be taking shortish odds about next time. *(op 10-1)*
Renvyle(IRE), a fair but quirky sort for Jonjo O'Neill, shaped much better than on his three previous runs on this first start after a break and first run for Richard Guest, who is just the man to get the best out of him. He is not one to write off yet. *(op 13-2 tchd 7-1)*
Panmure(IRE), a fast-ground course and distance winner, is still higher in the weights than his last success and did not really do enough to suggest he is a winner waiting to happen. *(op 7-2)*
Pavey Ark(IRE) is an inconsistent performer who was again below his best and he remains one to tread carefully with at present. *(op 8-1 tchd 9-1)*
Risky Way, who has been running more consistently of late than has sometimes been the case, *gave his rider no chance of staying aboard before the race started in earnest over this longer trip. (op 5-2 tchd 9-4)*

1685 ST JAMES SECURITY H'CAP HURDLE (12 hdls) 3m
3:40 (3:41) (Class 4) (0-100,99) 4-Y-O+ **£3,185** (£910; £455)

Form RPR
1 **1** **Habitual (IRE)**[2] 1648 4-11-4 99 7ex MrRQuinn(7) 106+
(John A Quinn, Ire) *in tch: hdwy to ld after 2 out: drvn out fr last* **11/8**[1]
-0P4 **2** 5 **Hello Baby**[133] 552 5-10-2 82 EWhillans(7) 82
(A C Whillans) *chsd ldrs: effrt and chal 2 out: drifted lft fr last: kpt on same pce* **12/1**
-010 **3** 10 **Green 'N' Gold**[11] 1571 5-11-3 90 NPMulholland 80
(M D Hammond) *keen: hld up: hdwy to chse ldrs bef 2 out: outpcd between last two* **6/1**[2]
4P06 **4** 5 **Phase Eight Girl**[13] 1564 9-9-11 73 oh3 (b[1]) PAspell(3) 58
(J Hetherton) *bhd: outpcd 4 out: sme late hdwy: nvr on terms* **14/1**
-05L **5** 1 **Joe Malone (IRE)**[16] 1528 6-10-10 83 BHarding 67
(N G Richards) *keen: hld up: hdwy bef 4 out: rdn and wknd bef 2 out* **12/1**
4600 **6** 11 **York Rite (AUS)**[6] 1602 9-10-1 74 (v[1]) KJohnson 47
(R C Guest) *hld up: hdwy 1/2-way: led briefly appr 2 out: wknd between last two* **9/1**
2246 **7** 4 **Gabor**[11] 1571 6-11-12 99 ADobbin 68
(M Todhunter) *in tch: j. slowly 4th: rallied 4 out: wknd after next* **14/1**
0464 **8** 4 **Nobodysgonanotice (IRE)**[17] 1508 7-11-2 89 (b) JPMcNamara 54
(J J Lambe, Ire) *led to appr 2 out: sn btn* **12/1**
5000 **P** **In Good Faith**[11] 1571 13-10-8 81 FKeniry —
(R E Barr) *cl up tl wknd 4 out: t.o whn p.u bef 2 out* **25/1**
4525 **P** **Greenfort Brave (IRE)**[11] 1566 7-10-12 85 KRenwick —
(J J Lambe, Ire) *in tch tl lost pl 4 out: sn btn: t.o whn p.u bef 2 out* **7/1**[3]
5m 57.7s (-20.00) **Going Correction** -0.60s/f (Firm)
WFA 4 from 5yo+ 15lb 10 Ran SP% **119.1**
Speed ratings: **109,107,104,102,102 98,97,95,**—,— CSF £19.63 CT £81.32 TOTE £2.70: £1.20, £2.20, £2.30; EX 25.60.
Owner P F Kilmartin **Bred** Rathasker Stud **Trained** Blackmiller Hill, Co. Kildare
■ Robert Quinn's second winner; since his first two years ago he has suffered a broken neck in a point-to-point fall.

FOCUS
An ordinary contest in which the pace was decent but the winner was value for more and looks a progressive sort on a sound surface.

NOTEBOOK
Habitual(IRE) ◆ is progressing well over fences and ran his best race in this sphere turned out quickly after his Wincanton win earlier in the week. He seemed suited by this three-mile trip and is the sort to win again on a sound surface. *(op 7-4)*
Hello Baby ran creditably against a progressive sort on this first run for over four months and, although not the most consistent so far, looks capable of winning another small race in this sphere. *(op 10-1)*
Green 'N' Gold was not disgraced, especially as she failed to settle in the first half of the race and she not surprisingly had little to offer in the closing stages. She is not the most reliable betting proposition around. *(op 10-1)*
Phase Eight Girl was not totally disgraced from 3lb out of the handicap but never looked likely to take a hand and her record suggests she is one to tread very carefully with from a punting point of view. *(op 12-1)*
Joe Malone(IRE), who refused to race last time, consented to jump off this time but did not look the most straightforward given he failed to settle and, on this evidence, will be suited by the return to two and a half miles. *(op 8-1)*
York Rite(AUS), who had not been at his best over fences in recent times, was again disappointing on this first hurdle run in over a year. *(op 8-1)*

1686 JOHN BRYSON MEMORIAL CLASSIFIED CHASE (19 fncs) 3m 1f
4:15 (4:15) (Class 4) 5-Y-O+ **£3,640** (£1,120; £560; £280)

Form RPR
3421 **1** **Tee-Jay (IRE)**[8] 1589 9-11-0 90 FKeniry 97
(M D Hammond) *in tch: hdwy 14th: rdn 3 out: rallied to ld run in: styd on* **13/8**[1]
1050 **2** 3½ **Swallow Magic (IRE)**[8] 1589 7-10-7 83 (v[1]) TJDreaper(7) 93
(Ferdy Murphy) *led to 5th: led 8th: rdn 2 out: hdd run in: one pce* **8/1**
0533 **3** 13 **Ideal Du Bois Beury (FR)**[6] 1602 9-10-11 79 PAspell(3) 80
(P Monteith) *bhd: hit 11th: hdwy u.p bef 3 out: no imp fr next* **11/2**[2]
-262 **4** 3½ **Starbuck**[8] 1589 11-10-9 80 DMcGann(5) 77
(A M Crow) *chsd ldrs: outpcd 15th: no imp fr 3 out* **11/2**[2]
P634 **5** 8 **Corries Wood (IRE)**[16] 1526 6-11-0 85 JPMcNamara 69
(J J Lambe, Ire) *midfield: effrt 15th: no imp bef 3 out* **17/2**

0P00 **6** *dist* **Northern Echo**[8] 1589 8-10-7 64............(p) GThomas(7) —
(K S Thomas) *bhd: drvn 1/2-way: nvr on terms* **50/1**

025/ **7** *2* **Some Trainer (IRE)**[22] 1477 9-11-0 67............(tp) BHarding —
(J G Cromwell, Ire) *prom tl wknd fr 14th* **16/1**

3/6 **P** **Moss Bawn (IRE)**[8] 1592 9-11-0 89............(b) ADobbin —
(B Storey) *chsd ldrs: blnd 11th: wknd fr 4 out: t.o whn p.u bef last* **15/2**[3]

510/ **P** **Minsgill Glen**[538] 4882 9-10-11 67............ ADempsey —
(Mrs J K M Oliver) *chsd ldrs to 15th: sn struggling: t.o whn p.u bef last* **33/1**

634P **P** **Step In Line (IRE)**[16] 1526 13-10-7 69............ CDSharkey(7) —
(D W Thompson) *cl up: led 5th to 8th: lost pl 14th: t.o whn p.u bef last* **100/1**

PP-0 **P** **Mid Summer Lark (IRE)**[13] 1564 9-10-9 90............ DCCostello(5) —
(I McMath) *chsd ldrs tl lost pl 6th: struggling 1/2-way: t.o whn p.u bef 3 out* **16/1**

6m 15.6s (-16.30) **Going Correction** -0.60s/f (Firm) **11** Ran SP% **119.9**
Speed ratings: **102,100,96,95,93** —,—,—,—,— — CSF £15.98 TOTE £2.10: £1.50, £2.50, £1.70; EX 25.70.
Owner T J Equestrian Ltd **Bred** James Rabbitte **Trained** Middleham, N Yorks

FOCUS
An ordinary contest run at a fair pace and this bare form should prove reliable with the first two to their marks.

NOTEBOOK
Tee-Jay(IRE), who goes well at this course, turned in an improved effort to follow up his latest success. Stamina is very much his strong suit and, given his jumping has improved, may be able to win again in this sphere. *(tchd 6-4)*
Swallow Magic(IRE), tried in a first-time visor and adopting very different tactics, ran creditably against a course specialist and pulled well clear of the remainder. He is not one for maximum faith but can win again on this evidence. *(op 9-1)*
Ideal Du Bois Beury(FR), who has yet to win over fences and is without a hurdle success since 2002, was not disgraced but was again far from foot perfect and his lack of consistency means he is not really one to be interested in at single-figure odds. *(op 7-1 tchd 15-2)*
Starbuck finished much further behind the winner than he had done over the same course and distance last time and consistency does not look to be his strongest suit. *(op 15-2 tchd 8-1)*
Corries Wood(IRE), an inconsistent maiden hurdler, was well beaten on this first run over regulation fences and will have to fare better to get off the mark in this sphere. *(op 15-2 tchd 9-1)*
Northern Echo, a poor and inconsistent hurdler, again showed nothing over fences.
Moss Bawn(IRE) *Official explanation: jockey said gelding had a breathing problem (op 10-1)*

1687 INSITU CLEANING NOVICES' HURDLE (10 hdls) 2m 4f 110y
4:50 (4:51) (Class 4) 4-Y-0+ **£3,640** (£1,120; £560; £280)

Form RPR

6- **1** **Key To The Kingdom (IRE)**[10] 1575 5-11-5............(p) TDoyle 106
(Eoin Doyle, Ire) *trckd ldrs: led appr 2 out: edgd lft bef last: kpt on wl* **13/8**[1]

36-P **2** *½* **Sergio Coimbra (IRE)**[16] 1526 6-10-12............ ADobbin 99
(N G Richards) *hld up in tch: outpcd after 3 out: rallied to chse wnr bef last: kpt on run in* **9/2**[3]

P044 **3** *dist* **Beaver (AUS)**[8] 1591 6-10-9 97............(p) LMcGrath(3) —
(R C Guest) *keen: cl up: led 3 out to appr next: sn btn* **15/8**[2]

0-15 **4** *25* **Diamond Jack (IRE)**[16] 1527 7-11-5............(p) JPMcNamara —
(J J Lambe, Ire) *hld up in tch: hdwy and chsng ldrs whn stmbld 2 out: sn btn* **16/1**

P **Em'Sgem**[154] 11-10-3 ow1............ GBerridge(3) —
(W Amos) *a bhd: struggling and p.u bef 4 out* **100/1**

/3- **P** **Rosslare (FR)**[248] 3653 6-10-9............ PWhelan(3) —
(R A Fahey) *led to 3 out: wknd bef next: t.o whn p.u bef last* **15/2**

P **Master Farrier**[168] 5-10-9............ PBuchanan(3) —
(Miss Lucinda V Russell) *chsd ldrs tl lost pl bef 4 out: sn btn: t.o whn p.u bef last* **28/1**

5m 1.10s (-8.50) **Going Correction** -0.60s/f (Firm) **7** Ran SP% **113.1**
Speed ratings: **92,91**,—,—,—,—,— CSF £9.48 TOTE £2.60: £2.60, £2.60; EX 13.70.
Owner Paul Holden **Bred** E) Ennistown Stud **Trained** Mooncoin, Co. Kilkenny

FOCUS
A low-grade event in which the pace was modest and the winner is the best guide but the form looks less than reliable.

NOTEBOOK
Key To The Kingdom(IRE), returned to hurdles, did not have to improve to notch his second win in this sphere. He stays three miles but will be vulnerable under a double penalty from now on in this type of event. *(op Evens tchd 7-4)*
Sergio Coimbra(IRE), down in trip and having his first run on a sound surface, ran creditably in this ordinary event and is sure to be placed to best advantage in due course. *(op 11-2 tchd 6-1)*
Beaver(AUS) pulled too hard in a steadily-run race to give himself any real chance of lasting home over this longer trip. He does not look straightforward and is not one to take too short a price about. *(op 7-2)*
Diamond Jack(IRE) did not seem to get home, even in a race run at only a fair pace, and he is likely to continue to look vulnerable under a penalty in this type of event. *(op 12-1 tchd 20-1 in a place)*
Rosslare(FR), who showed ability on his debut in a soft-ground bumper, failed to match that level on this hurdle debut over this longer trip and on this different ground but he is not one to write off just yet. *(op 8-1 tchd 7-1)*

1688 HEXHAM STANDARD NATIONAL HUNT FLAT RACE (CONDITIONAL JOCKEYS' AND AMATEUR RIDERS' RACE) 2m 110y
5:20 (5:20) (Class 6) 4-6-Y-O **£1,904** (£544; £272)

Form RPR

1 **One More Step** 4-10-11............ MrRTierney(7) 115+
(J J Quinn) *hld up: gd hdwy and prom 1/2-way: led over 3f out: drew clr fr 2f out: v easily* **11/4**[2]

42-2 **2** *17* **Amalfi Storm**[8] 1593 4-10-8............ MrTGreenall(3) 84
(M W Easterby) *led to over 3f out: kpt on same pce fr over 2f out* **1/1**[1]

3 *3 ½* **Overnight** 5-10-11............ EWhillans(7) 88
(Mrs A C Hamilton) *hld up: hdwy 1/2-way: disp 2nd over 2f out: no imp* **25/1**

4 **4** *24* **Redditzio**[14] 1554 4-10-6............ DCCostello(5) 57
(C W Thornton) *in tch: drvn after 6f: outpcd 7f out: n.d after* **11/2**[3]

5 *8* **Moonshine Gap** 5-10-11............ PJMcDonald(7) 56
(R Ford) *hld up: hdwy over 6f out: sn no imp* **25/1**

6 *6* **Alisons Treasure (IRE)** 6-10-11............ MrPLishman(7) 50
(R Johnson) *bhd: detatched after 6f: n.d* **25/1**

0 **7** *1* **Broadband**[16] 1532 6-11-1............ MrCStorey(3) 49
(Miss S E Forster) *hld up: outpcd 1/2-way: nvr on terms* **50/1**

0P **8** *nk* **Dovers Venture**[35] 1401 4-10-4............ MrsKLDarmody(7) 41
(Miss M E Rowland) *in tch tl wknd over 6f out* **50/1**

9 *dist* **Redeswire Ruby** 4-10-4............ SMarshall(7) —
(Mrs H O Graham) *sn wl bhd: nvr on terms* **20/1**

P0- **10** *11* **Bodfari Sauvage**[312] 2556 5-11-1............ GBerridge(3) —
(J J Lambe, Ire) *keen: in tch tl wknd over 5f out* **16/1**

50 **U** **Thorn Of The Rose (IRE)**[16] 1532 4-10-8............ PAspell(3) —
(James Moffatt) *cl up: clipped heels and uns rdr 6f out* **20/1**

4m 1.00s (-11.70) **Going Correction** -0.60s/f (Firm)
WFA 4 from 5yo+ 13lb **11** Ran SP% **122.9**
Speed ratings: **103,95,93,82,78 75,75,74**,—,— — CSF £5.59 TOTE £3.90: £1.20, £1.10, £8.90; EX 8.20 Place 6 £179.60, Place 5 £13.79.
Owner Roger J Marley **Bred** R And Mrs S Edwards **Trained** Settrington, N Yorks

FOCUS
Ordinary form from the placed horses downwards but plenty to like about the way the winner demolished this field and he is one to keep on the right side with the runner-up setting the standard.

NOTEBOOK
One More Step ◆, who is from the family of Buck House, created a very favourable impression on this racecourse debut and, given the manner of this win, appeals strongly as the type to hold his own in stronger company. *(tchd 3-1)*
Amalfi Storm had her limitations exposed against a potentially fair sort but she has been fairly consistent and looks a good guide to the worth of this form. She should be placed to best advantage over obstacles. *(op 5-4)*
Overnight, who is out of a poor hurdler and related to another poor hurdler, hinted at ability on this racecourse debut but is likely to continue to look vulnerable in this type of event.
Redditzio, who was not disgraced on her debut at Market Rasen in September, looked slow on this quicker ground and is likely to continue to look vulnerable in this type of event. *(op 7-1)*
Moonshine Gap achieved little on this racecourse debut.
Alisons Treasure(IRE) was soundly beaten after getting a long way behind early on and is likely to remain vulnerable in bumpers. *(tchd 22-1)*
T/Plt: £38.40 to a £1 stake. Pool: £29,754.50. 564.25 winning tickets. T/Qpdt: £7.50 to a £1 stake. Pool: £1,577.10. 153.70 winning tickets. RY

1689 - 1690a (Foreign Racing) - See Raceform Interactive

[918] GOWRAN PARK (R-H)
Saturday, October 8

OFFICIAL GOING: Good to firm

1691a LANGTONS HOUSE H'CAP HURDLE (LISTED RACE) 3m
3:00 (3:00) 5-Y-0+ **£17,313** (£5,079; £2,420; £824)

RPR

1 **Red Square Lady (IRE)**[6] 1621 7-10-9 123............ AndrewJMcNamara(3) 125
(Michael John Phillips, Ire) *trckd ldrs in 3rd: impr into 2nd 6 out: chal and led 2 out: sn wandered abt: jnd after last: kpt on wl to ld again nr fin* **6/1**[2]

3 *2* **Rory Sunset (IRE)**[14] 1556 7-9-11 108............ DJCasey 108
(C F Swan, Ire) *hld up towards rr: impr into 5th bef 3 out: mod 3rd 2 out: kpt on* **6/1**[2]

4 *1* **Nassaro (IRE)**[16] 1536 5-9-11 108............(t) PCarberry 107
(M Halford, Ire) *hld up in rr: slt mstke 4 out: hdwy after 3 out: mod 4th 2 out: kpt on* **10/3**[1]

5 *8* **Limerick Lord (IRE)**[34] 1416 8-9-10 107............ DJCondon 98
(T J Taaffe, Ire) *trckd ldrs in 5th: impr into 3rd 6 out: pushed along after 4 out: no ex fr 2 out* **7/1**[3]

6 *11* **Hurry Bob (IRE)**[10] 1575 10-10-7 118............ RMPower 98
(Thomas Mullins, Ire) *in tch: 5th 5 out: 6th 3 out: no ex bef next* **16/1**

7 *1 ½* **Matt Wood (IRE)**[6] 1622 6-9-6 111............ RMMoran(5) 90
(Paul Nolan, Ire) *prom: 4th to 3 out: no ex bef next* **9/1**

8 *12* **Harithabad (FR)**[178] 4830 10-9-10 107............ NPMadden 73
(Noel Meade, Ire) *hld up: reminders 4th: rdn 5 out: no imp whn slt mstke next: sn wknd* **20/1**

9 *shd* **Florida Coast (IRE)**[314] 2523 10-11-3 135............ MrNMcParlan(7) 102
(James Bowe, Ire) *settled 2nd: pckd 1st: slt mstke 4th: lost pl bef 5 out: sn no ex* **8/1**

10 *10* **Black Ouzel (IRE)**[10] 1572 5-9-7 107............ RCColgan(3) 63
(H Rogers, Ire) *chsd ldrs: 6th and rdn 5 out: sn wknd: t.o* **16/1**

5m 34.2s **11** Ran SP% **111.8**
CSF £56.09 CT £332.21 TOTE £4.00: £1.80, £3.30, £1.90; DF 55.60.
Owner T Egan **Bred** Mrs Una M T Heffernan **Trained** Fethard, Co Tipperary

NOTEBOOK
Red Square Lady(IRE), who was out of her depth against Harchibald and company last time, appreciated returning to this lower grade and, back on her favoured fast ground, gained a narrow victory. Her trainer is now considering bringing her over to Cheltenham next month for a two-mile-five-furlong handicap. *(op 5/1)*
Dow Jones(GER), another who is at his best on fast ground, did not go down without a fight. *(op 8/1)*
Rory Sunset(IRE), whose two wins to date have come on firm ground, showed the benefit of his recent return from a four-month break at Listowel. *(op 8/1)*
Nassaro(IRE) is now running off a mark 9lb higher than for his last win. *(op 3/1)*

1692a NATIONAL LOTTERY AGENT CHAMPION CHASE (GRADE 2) 2m 4f
3:30 (3:30) 5-Y-0+ **£31,854** (£8,804; £4,195)

RPR

1 **Always**[71] 1102 6-11-6 123............(b) PCarberry 144
(Noel Meade, Ire) *cl up in 2nd: rdn to chal after 3 out: led after next: styd on wl u.p fr last* **9/1**[3]

2 *nk* **Strong Project (IRE)**[15] 1544 9-11-6 138............ DJCasey 144
(C F Swan, Ire) *attempted to make all: rdn and strly pressed 3 out: hdd after next: kpt on u.p fr last* **2/1**[2]

3 *3* **Ansar (IRE)**[6] 1621 9-11-6 148............ DFO'Regan 141
(D K Weld, Ire) *cl up in 3rd: bad mstke 2nd: rdn to chal 3 out: no imp after 2 out: eased after last* **1/2**[1]

4m 53.2s **3** Ran SP% **110.0**
CSF £23.20 TOTE £6.50; DF 10.50.
Owner D P Sharkey **Bred** Newgate Stud Co **Trained** Castletown, Co Meath

NOTEBOOK
Always had plenty to find at the weights, as he is officially rated 15lb inferior to the runner-up and 25lb inferior to Ansar, but he was better suited to the steady pace in this small field than the other two and just held on in a tight finish. The favourite returned with an injury and the form should not be taken literally.
Strong Project(IRE), who has had leg trouble in the past, would not have been ideally suited by these quick conditions. *(op 7/4 tchd 2/1)*
Ansar(IRE) was best in at the weights but a mistake at the second fence, which resulted in him cutting his stifle, resulted in a below-par effort. He will now be rested for the winter and brought *back next year with a view to winning a third Galway Plate. Official explanation: jockey said gelding felt flat throughout; vet said gelding received a prod wound to its right stifle and was slightly stiff post race (op 1/2 tchd 8/13)*

1693 - 1699a (Foreign Racing) - See Raceform Interactive

[1050]LIMERICK (R-H)

Sunday, October 9

OFFICIAL GOING: Yielding changing to yielding to soft after race 1 (2.10)

1700a ANGLO IRISH BANK MUNSTER NATIONAL H'CAP CHASE (GRADE A) 3m

3:45 (4:15) 4-Y-0+ **£43,971** (£13,475; £6,382; £2,127; £709)

RPR

1 **Star Clipper**[164] [91] 8-10-2 119 .... PCarberry 128
(Noel Meade, Ire) *rr of mid-div: clsr in 6th bef 3 out: sn 5th: rdn to go 2nd and chal after last: led on inner run-in: styd on wl* **16/1**

2 *1 ½* **Pearly Jack**[18] [1515] 7-10-0 120 ow1 .... MDarcy(3) 128
(D E Fitzgerald, Ire) *chsd ldrs: impr to ld sn after 3 out: clr appr next where nt fluent: sn strly pressed: hdd and kpt on same pce run-in* **10/3**[2]

3 *1 ½* **Mariah Rollins (IRE)**[10] [89] 7-11-1 135 .... SGMcDermott(3) 141
(P A Fahy, Ire) *mid-div: impr into 2nd bef st: sn rdn: no imp and kpt on same pce fr bef last* **7/1**[3]

4 *2* **Banasan (IRE)**[16] [1544] 7-11-4 135 .... BJGeraghty 139
(M J P O'Brien, Ire) *chsd ldrs: 4th and kpt on same pce u.p st* **7/1**[3]

5 *5* **Garvivonnian (IRE)**[18] [1515] 10-10-8 132 .... MJFerris(7) 131
(Edward P Mitchell, Ire) *a.p: led fr 6 out: hdd sn after 3 out: sn no imp u.p* **20/1**

6 *20* **Bizet (IRE)**[18] [1515] 9-10-8 125 .... JLCullen 104
(F Flood, Ire) *towards rr: sme slt mstkes: prog into 8th appr 3 out: sn no imp u.p* **8/1**

7 *5* **Alcapone (IRE)**[16] [1544] 11-11-2 133 .... CO'Dwyer 107
(M F Morris, Ire) *cl up: led fr 4th: hdd fr 6 out: no ex fr 3 out: n.d whn bad mstke 2 out* **14/1**

8 *2 ½* **Lincam (IRE)**[163] [115] 9-9-12 120 .... JFLevins(5) 92
(C F Swan, Ire) *chsd ldrs: no imp u.p in 9th fr bef 3 out* **14/1**

9 *dist* **Montayral (FR)**[16] [1544] 8-11-5 136 .... JPElliott —
(P Hughes, Ire) *chsd ldrs: dropped to 10th fr 10th: sn n.d: t.o* **25/1**

10 *5* **Snob Wells (IRE)**[6] [1627] 8-9-10 113 .... (t) NPMadden —
(Noel Meade, Ire) *mid-div best: dropped to rr fr 10th: sn n.d: t.o* **16/1**

P **Light On The Broom (IRE)**[18] [1515] 9-10-6 123 .... (t) RMPower —
(Gerard Stack, Ire) *a towards rr: t.o whn p.u bef 2 out* **16/1**

P **Ransboro (IRE)**[45] [91] 6-9-10 113 .... DJCasey —
(C F Swan, Ire) *cl up: 6th whn slt mstke 6 out: sn no imp and wknd: p.u bef 3 out* **12/1**

F **Euro Leader (IRE)**[18] [1515] 7-11-10 141 8ex .... RWalsh 140
(W P Mullins, Ire) *mid-div: wnt 6th fr 3 out: rdn and sn no imp: n.d whn fell last* **11/4**[1]

P **The Wipper (IRE)**[165] [72] 9-9-10 113 .... (b) PACarberry —
(Sean Aherne, Ire) *sn led: j.lft and hdd 4th: dropped towards 10th: p.u bef 7 out* **25/1**

U **Berkley (IRE)**[18] [1515] 8-9-10 116 .... (b) JMAllen(3) —
(Patrick Michael Verling, Ire) *mid-div: rdn to chse ldrs appr 7 out: no imp and trailing whn uns rdr 3 out* **16/1**

6m 12.1s **15** Ran SP% **142.9**

CSF £81.60 CT £445.85 TOTE £48.00: £11.00, £1.60, £3.00; DF 219.80.

Owner D P Sharkey **Bred** Bottisham Heath Stud **Trained** Castletown, Co Meath

NOTEBOOK

Star Clipper, making his seasonal debut after a 164-day break, was given a fine ride by Carberry and sealed the race with a superb leap at the final fence. This was by far his best effort to date, it was also his first success since 2003, and indeed his first to date over three miles. If he can maintain this current mood, he could be set for greater heights this term, and should still look on a fair mark despite an inevitable rise in the weights.

Pearly Jack, third in the Kerry National at Listowel last time, produced another solid effort and was only denied on the run-in. He is a decent benchmark for this form, and he has only finished once out of the frame at this track from six outings, but still he is still to get his head in front over this trip and may just be at his best when reverting to shorter. *(op 7/2 tchd 3/1)*

Mariah Rollins(IRE), a Grade One winning novice over fences last season, had the benefit of a recent spin on the Flat over two miles at Thurles coming into this. She had never previously run over this far, or indeed in a handicap, yet she seemed to get home well enough and turned in a very respectable effort. This gives connections plenty of options now they know she stays the trip and she looks set for another profitable campaign.

Banasan(IRE) had his chance ran to his recent level back over this longer trip. He just looks a touch high in the weights at present. *(op 6/1)*

Euro Leader(IRE), who landed his third consecutive success when defying top weight in the Kerry National 18 days previously, was just starting to tread water under his 8lb penalty and was held prior to coming down at the final fence. He may have found this rain-softened ground against him, but he was more likely to have been feeling the effects of his hard-fought success at Listowel last time, and is not one to write off just yet. *(op 3/1 tchd 7/2)*

1702a SHERRY FITZGERALD O'MALLEY CHASE 2m 1f

4:50 (5:15) 4-Y-0+ **£12,465** (£3,657; £1,742; £593)

RPR

1 **Watson Lake (IRE)**[164] [89] 7-11-12 146 .... PCarberry 148+
(Noel Meade, Ire) *mde all: clr appr st: reduced ld whn lft further in front 2 out: nt extended and eased run-in* **4/5**[1]

2 *2 ½* **Accordion Etoile (IRE)**[73] [1093] 6-10-11 .... JLCullen 126
(Paul Nolan, Ire) *trckd ldrs: j. sltly lft 6 out: mod 3rd appr st: clsd and 2nd whn bad mstke 2 out: no imp after* **9/4**[2]

3 *3 ½* **Arteea (IRE)**[166] [40] 6-10-8 .... AndrewJMcNamara(3) 122
(Michael Hourigan, Ire) *racd mainly 5th: rdn in mod 4th appr st: kpt on wout threatening fr bef 2 out* **11/2**[3]

4 *4 ½* **Vic Ville (IRE)**[153] [270] 6-10-11 .... DFO'Regan 118
(Michael Hourigan, Ire) *trckd ldr: mainly 2nd: no imp u.p st* **20/1**

5 *5* **Barrack Buster**[72] [1102] 6-10-6 110 .... RWalsh 108
(Martin Brassil, Ire) *racd mainly 6th: no imp and kpt on wout threatening fr 5 out* **20/1**

6 *25* **Green Belt Flyer (IRE)**[134] [560] 7-11-2 121 .... BJGeraghty 93
(Mrs John Harrington, Ire) *trckd ldrs: rdn and dropped to 5th appr st: sn no ex* **9/1**

P **San Angelo (IRE)**[190] [4701] 8-10-13 .... (t) MFMooney(3) —
(Patrick Mooney, Ire) *a in rr: t.o whn p.u bef 2 out* **33/1**

4m 17.2s **7** Ran SP% **124.2**

CSF £3.51 TOTE £2.10: £2.10, £1.70; DF 3.60.

Owner John Corr **Bred** Thomas F O'Brien **Trained** Castletown, Co Meath

NOTEBOOK

Watson Lake(IRE), a high-class novice over fences last term, got his second season chasing off to a perfect start with a ready success under top weight. He was just about on top of the runner-up, prior to that rival making a bad error two out, and put in a fine round of jumping throughout. This showed the benefit of a recent breathing operation - carried out in an attempt to help him see out his races properly - and is certainly one to respect in all the top events over fences at this trip and up to two and a half miles. *(op 1/1)*

Accordion Etoile(IRE) ◆, fourth in the Champion Hurdle at Cheltenham last season and making his eagerly anticipated chase debut, proved easy to back on account of the deteriorating ground. However, he still shaped with clear promise and was yet to be asked a serious question prior to losing all chance with a bad error at the penultimate fence. This marks him out to be one of the leading Irish novice chase prospects for this season, he will no doubt derive plenty of experience from this, and will enjoy the return to a faster surface in the future. *(op 7/4)*

1701 - 1704a (Foreign Racing) - See Raceform Interactive

[1547]AUTEUIL (L-H)

Sunday, October 9

OFFICIAL GOING: Very soft

1705a PRIX GEORGES DE TALHOUET-ROY (HURDLE) (GRADE 2) 2m 2f

1:15 (1:15) 3-Y-0 **£51,064** (£24,965; £14,752; £10,213; £5,674; £3,972)

RPR

1 **Tidal Fury (IRE)**[33] [1428] 3-10-6 .... SLeloup 120
(J Jay) *led til headed 5th, led again next, narrow leader when left clear by faller close home (23/10)* **23/10**[1]

2 *2 ½* **King Foraday (FR)**[16] 3-10-2 .... (b) XHondier 114
(F Doumen, France)

3 *1 ½* **Kasbah Bliss (FR)**[24] 3-10-2 .... ADuchene 112
(F Doumen, France) **43/10**[2]

4 *snk* **Etoile Des Iles (FR)**[19] 3-9-11 .... LGerard 107
(M Nigge, France)

5 *6* **Golden Silver (FR)**[11] 3-10-2 .... OSauvaget 106
(H Hosselet, France)

6 *4* **Chiaro (FR)**[16] 3-10-6 .... (b) FEstrampes 106
(J-L Pelletan, France) **18/1**[3]

F **Gold Heart (FR)**[30] 3-10-2 .... BGicquel —
(G Macaire, France)

F **Sunny Winner (FR)**[15] [777] 3-10-6 .... CPieux —
(G Cherel, France)

4m 21.0s **8** Ran SP% **54.4**

PARI-MUTUEL: WIN 3.30; PL 1.70, 4.90, 2.30; SF 47.60.

Owner Twelfth Night **Bred** Robert De Vere Hunt **Trained** Newmarket, Suffolk

NOTEBOOK

Tidal Fury(IRE) recorded another win on his travels in France and his first in Graded company. He seems to be progressing well and clearly thrives in testing ground.

PARDUBICE (L-H)

Sunday, October 9

OFFICIAL GOING: Good to firm

1710a VELKA PARDUBICKA CESKE POJISTOVNY (CROSS-COUNTRY CHASE) 4m 2f 110y

2:40 (2:47) 7-Y-0+ **£52,484** (£24,143; £15,745; £7,348; £5,248)

RPR

1 **Maskul (USA)**[364] [1683] 11-10-7 .... DFuhrmann —
(F Holcak, Czech Republic)

2 *½* **Decent Fellow (GER)**[133] [590] 10-10-7 .... JBartos —
(J Vana Jr, Czech Republic)

3 *19* **Laneret (CZE)**[364] [1683] 9-10-7 .... PTuma —
(C Olehla, Czech Republic)

4 *9* **Kedon (CZE)**[728] [1652] 10-10-7 .... JVanaJr —
(J Vana Jr, Czech Republic)

5 *dist* **Belovodsk (RUS)** 13-10-7 .... JPlzak —
(Dr R Vitek, Czech Republic)

6 *dist* **Red Dancer (FR)**[1059] [1940] 9-10-7 .... DusanAndres —
(C Olehla, Czech Republic)

7 *15* **Ascot (POL)** 8-10-7 .... ZMatysik —
(Z Matysik, Czech Republic)

R **Luzcadou (FR)**[148] [362] 12-10-7 .... KJMercer —
(Ferdy Murphy)

U **Odyseusz (POL)** 7-10-7 .... MStromsky —
(F Zobal, Czech Republic)

U **Iraklion (POL)**[2934] 10-10-7 .... RHavelka —
(J Votava, Czech Republic)

P **Nostalgia (POL)**[386] 8-10-3 .... JKamenicek —
(R Holcak, Czech Republic)

U **Hastaven (FR)**[364] [1683] 10-10-7 .... TomasHurt —
(C Olehla, Czech Republic)

F **Registana (GER)**[331] [2167] 9-10-3 .... JimCrowley —
(C Olehla, Czech Republic)

U **Jack De Traou Land (FR)**[1526] 8-10-7 .... VLuka —
(J Vana Jr, Czech Republic)

U **Takagi (IRE)**[17] [1536] 10-10-7 .... JMMaguire —
(Miss Clare Judith Macmahon, Ire)

U **Chailand (CZE)** 8-10-7 .... MartinaRuzickova —
(Martina Ruzickova, Czech Republic)

9m 11.25s **18** Ran

PARI-MUTUEL (including 1 krouna stake): WIN 17.60; PL 3.20, 1.60,23.70; DF 278.20.

Owner Staj Nyznerov **Bred** Shadwell Estate Co Ltd **Trained** Czechoslavakia

NOTEBOOK

Maskul(USA), who won this race back in 2002, was running in the race for the fifth time. Placed behind Registana in the last two renewals, he had to jump over that mare when she fell at the second obstacle, and in a battle to the line, just got the better of Decent Fellow, whom he beat into second back in 2002, too.

Decent Fellow(GER), who was beaten into second by Maskul in this event back in 2002, had to settle for the same again. He is a consistent performer in this race, having now been finished second or third in the last four renewals.

Luzcadou(FR) refused at the same obstacle (the sixth last) he refused at last year.

Takagi(IRE) sustained a fatal injury.

Registana(GER), winner of the last two renewals, exited early on when falling at the second obstacle. She has now been retired.

[1614]UTTOXETER (L-H)

Wednesday, October 12

OFFICIAL GOING: Good to soft(good in places)

The ground had eased after 8mm of rain overnight.

Wind: Slight behind Weather: Rain after race 4.

1711 WEATHERBYS MESSAGING SERVICE NOVICES' HURDLE (12 hdls) 2m 6f 110y

2:10 (2:11) (Class 4) 4-Y-0+ **£3,507** (£1,002; £501)

Form	Pos	Btn	Horse	Jockey	RPR	Trainer / comment	SP
11-2	**1**		**The Cool Guy (IRE)**[168] 70 5-10-12	CLlewellyn	129+	(N A Twiston-Davies) *chsd ldr: led appr 3 out: clr appr 2 out: easily*	**4/7**[1]
C25-	**2**	*6*	**Moorlands Again**[332] 2212 10-10-7 116	LStephens(5)	112+	(M Sheppard) *led: rdn and hdd appr 3 out: sn btn*	**8/1**[2]
-321	**3**	*3 ½*	**Killonemoonlight (IRE)**[132] 611 6-10-7 104	MNicolls(5)	107	(D R Stoddart) *hld up in tch: rdn and hung lft appr 3 out: one pce*	**17/2**[3]
	4	*9*	**Random Quest**[53] 7-10-12	RJohnson	99+	(B J Llewellyn) *prom: mstke 3rd: j.lft 9th: rdn appr 3 out: wknd last*	**12/1**
214-	**5**	*15*	**Classic Quart (IRE)**[214] 4333 4-10-4	TScudamore	79+	(M Scudamore) *hld up in mid-div: hdwy 6th: rdn and wknd 3 out*	**16/1**
220-	**6**	*16*	**Midnight Gold**[182] 4825 5-10-9 103	TJPhelan(3)	67	(L P Grassick) *nvr nr ldrs*	**50/1**
6602	**7**	*15*	**Smileafact**[24] 1485 5-10-12 89	(v) BHitchcott	52	(Mrs Barbara Waring) *hld up in mid-div: hdwy 6th: rdn and wknd 7th*	**40/1**
UPP/	**8**	*dist*	**Youpeeveecee (IRE)**[663] 2841 9-10-12 88	AO'Keeffe	—	(Miss L V Davis) *a bhd: t.o fr 9th*	**100/1**
	P		**Lead Role (IRE)**[577] 7-10-12	JTizzard	—	(D R Gandolfo) *a bhd: t.o whn p.u bef 3 out*	**66/1**
0/P	**P**		**Spud's Fancy**[10] 1619 6-10-5	ChristianWilliams	—	(D A Rees) *a bhd: t.o whn p.u bef 3 out*	**150/1**
31-4	**P**		**Ravenscar**[166] 106 7-10-5 95	APogson(7)	—	(C T Pogson) *prom tl wknd 7th: t.o whn p.u bef 3 out*	**20/1**
55-2	**P**		**Lord Jay Jay (IRE)**[151] 345 5-10-12 97	SThomas	—	(Miss H C Knight) *a bhd: t.o whn p.u bef 3 out*	**33/1**

5m 32.0s (-12.70) **Going Correction** -0.10s/f (Good)

WFA 4 from 5yo+ 14lb **12** Ran SP% **114.1**

Speed ratings: **110,107,106,103,98 92,87,—,—,— —,—** CSF £4.91 TOTE £1.40: £1.10, £2.60, £2.70; EX 6.10.

Owner Frosty's Four **Bred** Kieran Strain **Trained** Naunton, Gloucs

FOCUS

An interesting novice hurdle in which the impressive winner has been rated value for 17 lengths. He recorded a decent winning time for a race of its type, too, and the form looks solid.

NOTEBOOK

The Cool Guy(IRE) ◆, one of last season's top bumper performers, was hot favourite to make a winning debut over timber. He tracked the leader for most of the race before being asked to go to the front at the third last, and quickly drew clear of the rest going to the next and winning with a good deal in hand. An embryo chaser, he jumped these hurdles well enough and looks an exciting prospect for the season ahead, with the Royal & SunAlliance Hurdle perhaps a suitable long-term target. *He is well regarded at home and will not be risked on fast ground. (tchd 8-15 and 8-13 in places)*

Moorlands Again, a ten-year-old returning from an 11-month absence, set a fair hurdling standard on his performances at Cheltenham last autumn, but having made most to three out he was left for dead when the favourite was asked to quicken. He has clearly not been the easiest to train but he has the ability to win a modest race, perhaps back over fences. *(op 7-1)*

Killonemoonlight(IRE), the winner of a weak race over three miles on soft ground here back in June, had a penalty to overcome on her first outing since, and found that all too much, but she was keeping on well enough at the finish. *(op 9-1 tchd 8-1)*

Random Quest, very useful on the Flat in his prime, has not won for over three years and was making a move to the winter game fairly late in his career. He stayed two miles well on the Flat so this distance should be ideal over hurdles, but he did not see it out as well as one would have expected. Nevertheless, he is entitled to come on for the experience. *(op 16-1)*

Classic Quart(IRE), another bumper winner making her hurdling debut and seasonal reappearance, is out of a mare who was a useful staying hurdler, and she should make her mark in time. *(op 14-1)*

Smileafact *Official explanation: jockey said gelding would not face the visor*

1712 ADVANCED PLUMBING & HEATING (CHESTERFIELD 01246 551537) CONDITIONAL JOCKEYS' (S) HURDLE (12 hdls) 2m 4f 110y

2:40 (2:40) (Class 5) 4-7-Y-0 **£2,184** (£624; £312)

Form	Pos	Btn	Horse	Jockey	RPR	Trainer / comment	SP
B540	**1**		**Penny's Crown**[7] 1636 6-10-12 84	EDehdashti(3)	90+	(G A Ham) *chsd ldrs: led on bit appr 3 out: sn clr: easily*	**5/2**[1]
2P-P	**2**	*6*	**Countback (FR)**[18] 1552 6-10-5 83	(p) TMessenger(5)	72+	(C C Bealby) *led to 2nd: a.p: mstke 9th: hrd rdn appr 3 out: wnt 2nd appr 2 out: no ch w wnr*	**9/2**
0P04	**3**	*9*	**Greencard Golf**[10] 1616 4-11-2 87	LTreadwell	69+	(Jennie Candlish) *hld up in rr: hdwy 8th: nt clr run and lost pl after 9th: no real prog whn blnd last*	**11/4**[2]
-33P	**4**	*20*	**Sonic Sound**[35] 1431 6-10-2 94	(t) RSpate(8)	41	(Mrs K Waldron) *t.k.h: hdwy 6th: led after 9th: rdn and hdd appr 3 out: wknd appr 2 out*	**7/2**[3]
6F00	**5**	*dist*	**Waziya**[20] 1520 6-10-3 75	(p) TJMalone	—	(Mrs L Williamson) *led 2nd tl after 9th: sn wknd: t.o*	**12/1**
00-P	**P**		**Kiev (IRE)**[16] 1410 5-10-10 75	(t) TGreenway	—	(D G Bridgwater) *bhd fr 3rd: hit 4th: t.o whn p.u bef 8th*	**12/1**

5m 14.9s (2.80) **Going Correction** +0.125s/f (Yiel) **6** Ran SP% **111.0**

Speed ratings: **99,96,93,85,—** — CSF £13.77 TOTE £3.70: £2.10, £2.80; EX 16.00.The winner was bought in for 6,600gns.

Owner The Browns And Brats **Bred** D J And Mrs Deer **Trained** Rooks Bridge, Somerset

FOCUS

A weak affair but they went a fair pace as Waziya and Countback, who both wore cheekpieces, took each other on for the lead in the early stages. The winner has been rated as value for 13 lengths.

NOTEBOOK

Penny's Crown had the race set up nicely for her as she tracked the pacesetters and came through to win in good style. She did not let herself down on the firm ground at Exeter last time, but her previous form gave her every chance in this grade and the ground had come in her favour. *(op 7-2)*

Countback(FR) stayed on again having been left behind by the winner and Sonic Sound on the turn into the straight. He had shown nothing on his seasonal reappearance but, down in grade, returned to form, and as he has run quite well on Polytrack in the past, a switch back to the Flat must remain an option. *(op 7-2)*

Greencard Golf has a course and distance win to his name but he finished behind Penny's Crown over an extended two miles six here last month and, in addition to the ground turning in his opponent's favour, he was also 1lb worse off at the weights with her. *(op 7-2)*

Sonic Sound was best in at the weights by a fair margin but his current wellbeing was of concern. He looked a danger on the turn into the straight but his best form has been on quicker ground and he just did not get home. *(op 3-1)*

1713 ACE EUROPEAN GROUP LTD H'CAP CHASE (18 fncs) 3m

3:15 (3:15) (Class 4) (0-90,89) 5-Y-0+ **£3,536** (£1,088; £544; £272)

Form	Pos	Btn	Horse	Jockey	RPR	Trainer / comment	SP
/	**1**		**Mill Bank (IRE)**[51] 1289 10-10-11 74	PMoloney	98+	(Evan Williams) *chsd ldr: lft in ld 8th: clr 3 out: 12l ahd last: eased flat*	**16/1**
/05-	**2**	*7*	**Cool Song**[238] 3884 9-10-2 68	CBolger(3)	78	(Miss Suzy Smith) *hdwy 3rd: wnt 2nd after 2 out: no ch w wnr*	**33/1**
5U-5	**3**	*3*	**Runaway Bishop (USA)**[10] 1609 10-11-7 89	MNicolls(5)	96	(J R Cornwall) *hld up towards rr: hmpd 8th: rdn and hdwy appr 14th: styd on same pce fr 3 out*	**14/1**
P4/3	**4**	*6*	**Alabaster**[72] 1122 10-9-7 63 oh5	KBurke(7)	65+	(N J Hawke) *hld up in tch: mstke 6th: lost pl 14th: no real prog whn mstke 2 out*	**40/1**
P6-1	**5**	*6*	**Ashgreen**[7] 1646 8-11-11 88 7ex	SThomas	86+	(Miss Venetia Williams) *hld up in tch: chsd wnr 12th: hrd rdn 3 out: wknd after 2 out*	**3/1**[2]
5411	**6**	*11*	**Waynesworld (IRE)**[6] 1656 7-11-12 89 7ex	TScudamore	78+	(M Scudamore) *bhd: j.rt 1st: nvr nr ldrs*	**5/2**[1]
45P-	**7**	*12*	**Indian Laburnum (IRE)**[204] 4509 8-11-4 81	(p) NFehily	53	(C C Bealby) *mid-div: mstke 3rd: sn lost pl: rdn after 11th: hdwy appr 13th: wknd appr 3 out*	**9/1**
6556	**8**	*4*	**Greenacres Boy**[10] 1615 10-10-0 66 oh10 ow3	(p) ACCoyle(3)	34	(M Mullineaux) *t.k.h in mid-div: wknd after 14th*	**66/1**
3502	**9**	*dist*	**Pollensa Bay**[118] 767 6-10-12 75	(b) LAspell	—	(S A Brookshaw) *bhd: hdwy 7th: mstke 13th: wknd 14th: t.o*	**22/1**
0P-0	**F**		**Agincourt (IRE)**[167] 81 9-10-4 67	BFenton	—	(John R Upson) *hld up in mid-div: fell 9th*	**25/1**
0604	**B**		**Francolino (FR)**[10] 1615 12-10-0 68 oh17 ow5	LStephens(5)	—	(Dr P Pritchard) *hld up towards rr: b.d 9th*	**40/1**
P/P-	**U**		**Bay Island (IRE)**[532] 46 9-11-9 86	(t) CLlewellyn	—	(M Pitman) *j.rt: led: blnd 5th: blnd and uns rdr 8th*	**15/2**[3]
-031	**U**		**Dark Thunder (IRE)**[141] 481 8-10-8 78	PJMcDonald(7)	—	(Ferdy Murphy) *bhd: bmpd 1st: rdn whn blnd and uns rdr 13th*	**10/1**
640-	**U**		**Jackie Boy (IRE)**[183] 4814 6-11-12 89	AntonyEvans	—	(N A Twiston-Davies) *mstkes: hdwy after 2nd: 4 l 4th whn blnd and uns rdr 11th*	**18/1**

6m 23.2s (-9.30) **Going Correction** -0.10s/f (Good) **14** Ran SP% **119.7**

Speed ratings: **101,98,97,95,93 90,86,84,—,— —,—,—,—** CSF £449.43 CT £7344.26 TOTE £28.30: £13.90, £9.30, £3.70; EX 1166.00.

Owner R E R Williams **Bred** Charles Keegan **Trained** Cowbridge, Vale Of Glamorgan

FOCUS

A decent sized field for this low-grade handicap and plenty of indifferent jumping. The winner has been rated value for twice the winning margin with the third rated to recent form.

NOTEBOOK

Mill Bank(IRE) raced prominently throughout and, avoiding the fallers in behind, won as he pleased. Formerly trained in Ireland, he was making his debut for his new stable and, while his best form in the past has been on quick ground, he handled the step up to three miles and these easier conditions well.

Cool Song has clearly had his training problems judging by how few starts he has had, but this was a promising return to action. He could never get to grips with the winner but stayed on well.

Runaway Bishop(USA), who is still on a mark 3lb higher than when last successful, showed the benefit of his recent reappearance and was plugging on at the death. *(op 16-1)*

Alabaster, a lightly-raced ten-year-old, ran one of her best races to date.

Ashgreen won on his reappearance on fast ground and he had a chance early in the straight under his 7lb penalty, but the winner was too strong and he lost three places from the second last. Perhaps the race came too soon. *(tchd 7-2)*

Waynesworld(IRE), a drifter in the market beforehand on account of the easing of the ground, made an early mistake and was never going thereafter. This was his third outing in 11 days and perhaps he needs a break. *(op 9-4 tchd 11-4 and 3-1 in places)*

Bay Island(IRE) was the subject of some market support for this return from a lengthy absence on his debut for his new stable. He tended to jump out to his right slightly and made a bad mistake at the fence where he unseated, but should be kept in mind for a similar contest as he is clearly thought capable of winning off his current mark. *(op 8-1)*

1714 EUROPEAN BREEDERS FUND "NATIONAL HUNT" NOVICES' HURDLE (QUALIFIER) (10 hdls) 2m

3:50 (3:52) (Class 4) 4-6-Y-0 **£3,304** (£944; £472)

Form	Pos	Btn	Horse	Jockey	RPR	Trainer / comment	SP
44-1	**1**		**Refinement (IRE)**[168] 70 6-10-7	APMcCoy	87+	(Jonjo O'Neill) *nt fluent: t.k.h in mid-div: hdwy 7th: led 2 out: drvn out*	**2/9**[1]
0-	**2**	*¾*	**Sir Pandy (IRE)**[228] 4069 5-11-0	AThornton	89	(R H Alner) *hld up in mid-div: hdwy after 7th: outpcd 3 out: rdn and rallied appr last: swtchd rt flat: r.o wl*	**33/1**
/04-	**3**	*1 ½*	**Flying Fuselier**[457] 938 6-11-0	RJohnson	88	(P J Hobbs) *a ldr: led appr 3 out to 2 out: nt qckn flat*	**20/1**
0-0	**4**	*7*	**Over The Blues (IRE)**[10] 1611 5-10-7	MrAJBerry(7)	81	(Jonjo O'Neill) *a.p: one pce fr 3 out*	**25/1**
0PP-	**5**	*9*	**Kirby's Vic (IRE)**[222] 4158 5-11-0	CLlewellyn	72	(N A Twiston-Davies) *hld up towards rr: mstke last: nvr nrr*	**50/1**
0-1	**6**	*1 ¾*	**Bannister Lane**[158] 210 5-11-1 107	StephenJCraine(5)	78+	(D McCain) *led: rdn and hdd appr 3 out: wkng whn mstke 2 out*	**12/1**[2]
0-0P	**7**	*6*	**Oui Exit (FR)**[143] 457 4-11-0	TScudamore	64	(M Scudamore) *hld up and bhd: short-lived effrt appr 3 out*	**100/1**
400-	**8**	*2 ½*	**Astral Dancer (IRE)**[243] 3785 5-11-0	PMoloney	62	(J Mackie) *hld up and bhd: short-lived effrt after 7th*	**80/1**
00-0	**9**	*5*	**Burnside Place**[157] 242 5-10-7	JPMcNamara	50	(C C Bealby) *hld up in mid-div: wknd after 7th*	**66/1**
030-	**10**	*8*	**Siyaran (IRE)**[228] 4062 4-11-0 97	JTizzard	49	(D R Gandolfo) *hld up in tch: rdn after 7th: sn wknd*	**40/1**
05F-	**U**		**Mongino (GER)**[206] 4479 4-10-7	(t) CPoste(7)	—	(M F Harris) *stmbld and uns rdr 1st*	**100/1**
03-	**P**		**Barton Park**[236] 3928 5-11-0	NFehily	—	(D P Keane) *t.k.h in rr: blnd 7th: t.o whn p.u bef 3 out*	**16/1**[3]

4m 1.10s (0.70) **Going Correction** +0.125s/f (Yiel)

WFA 4 from 5yo+ 13lb **12** Ran SP% **116.1**

Speed ratings: **103,102,101,98,93 93,90,88,86,82 —,—** CSF £16.27 TOTE £1.30: £1.10, £4.40, £2.60; EX 14.70.

Owner M Tabor **Bred** M Tabor **Trained** Cheltenham, Gloucs

FOCUS

Another interesting novice hurdle, featuring high-class bumper performer Refinement. She did not impress in victory, though, and her performance on this hurdling debut has been rated as three stone off the best of her bumper form with the placed horses running to their bumper marks.

NOTEBOOK

Refinement(IRE), a high-class performer in bumpers, sweated up badly beforehand, did not jump fluently, and made very hard work of landing the odds. Her half-brother Manners, who won his two starts in bumpers, was beaten at odds-on on his hurdling debut, and had the jockeys on the first two home been switched the same fate may have befallen her. She lacks size and will have to step up considerably on this in her next few starts. *(tchd 1-4 and 2-7 in places)*

Sir Pandy(IRE) ◆ did not run badly on his only start in a Kempton bumper last season, and he always looked the type to do better when sent hurdling. He is a half-brother to three winning staying jumpers and will need further than this in time, but a more positive ride here might have seen a different result.

Flying Fuselier, who is bred to make a chaser, had every chance over the final three flights but was just done for speed on the run-in.

Over The Blues(IRE) is a half-brother to Native Emperor and is another who will do better when sent over fences. *(op 66-1 tchd 20-1)*

Bannister Lane won a fairly weak affair at Hexham last time and had quite a task on his hands under his penalty. *(op 11-1 tchd 10-1)*

1715 BETFRED POKER H'CAP HURDLE (SERIES QUALIFIER) (14 hdls) 3m

4:25 (4:25) (Class 3) (0-120,120) 4-Y-0+ **£5,070** (£1,560; £780; £390)

Form — RPR

-01P **1** **Irishkawa Bellevue (FR)**[24] 1479 7-11-2 **110**........................(b) DCrosse 118+
(Jean-Rene Auvray) *a.p: led 10th: rdn after 11th: clr appr 2 out: 8 l ahd last: eased flat* **9/1**

2015 **2** *3 ½* **Little Task**[8] 1606 7-9-10 **97**........................ MrGTumelty(7) 95
(J S Wainwright) *hld up in mid-div: hit 3rd: hdwy after 8th: wnt 2nd appr 3 out: no ch w wnr* **5/1**[1]

65-P **3** *9* **Notanotherdonkey (IRE)**[165] 121 5-10-4 **98**........................ TScudamore 88+
(M Scudamore) *hdwy appr 4th: wknd after 3 out* **12/1**

3-3P **4** *6* **Navado (USA)**[10] 1617 6-11-0 **108**........................ APMcCoy 91
(Jonjo O'Neill) *j.lft: hld up and bhd: hdwy after 9th: rdn and sltly outpcd 10th: rallied appr 3 out: wknd appr 2 out* **7/1**[3]

PP-3 **5** *nk* **Alvaro (IRE)**[149] 385 8-10-3 **97**........................(b) RJohnson 80
(B J Llewellyn) *prom: pushed along 7th: wknd appr 10th* **8/1**

5P-5 **6** *1 ¾* **Keepers Mead (IRE)**[162] 168 7-11-2 **110**........................ RWalford 91
(R H Alner) *j.lft: w ldr: led 9th to 10th: wknd 3 out* **11/2**[2]

/P2- **7** *11* **Valerun (IRE)**[483] 764 9-10-5 **102**........................(b[1]) LMcGrath(3) 72
(R C Guest) *a bhd* **7/1**[3]

6150 **P** **Angie's Double**[35] 1436 5-9-7 **94** oh1........................ RSpate(7) —
(Mrs K Waldron) *a bhd: t.o whn p.u after 10th* **12/1**

0-34 **P** **Mondial Jack (FR)**[112] 814 6-11-12 **120**........................ RThornton —
(Mrs K Waldron) *hld up in tch: lost pl after 5th: t.o whn p.u bef 3 out* **7/1**[3]

54-P **P** **Look To The Future (IRE)**[166] 95 11-10-0 **99**....... StephenJCraine(5) —
(M J M Evans) *led to 9th: wknd qckly: t.o whn p.u bef 3 out* **25/1**

030- **P** **Sadler's Pride (IRE)**[214] 4329 5-10-11 **105**........................(t) NFehily —
(A J Deakin) *hld up in tch: lost pl 5th: short-lived effrt appr 10th: p.u and dismntd after 11th* **16/1**

6m 5.20s (0.20) **Going Correction** +0.125s/f (Yiel) 11 Ran SP% **115.8**

Speed ratings: **104,102,99,97,97 97,93,—,—,— —** CSF £53.52 CT £547.27 TOTE £11.90: £3.20, £1.90, £3.60; EX 82.60.

Owner The Magpie Partnership **Bred** G Leveque **Trained** Upper Lambourn, Berks

FOCUS

They went a fair pace in this modest staying handicap and it proved a proper test at the trip. Irishkawa Bellevue remains on the upgrade and was value for a ten-length victory with the runner-up setting the level.

NOTEBOOK

Irishkawa Bellevue(FR) has not set the world alight over fences but he continues on the upgrade over hurdles and defied a career-high mark, 10lb higher than when last successful. He likes this sort of ground, came home an easy winner and it would not be a surprise were he to defy another hike in the ratings. *(op 8-1)*

Little Task would have been pleased about the overnight rain easing the ground, and he stayed on well for a clear second. He is currently on a 7lb higher mark than when last successful so will probably have to find a bit more improvement to return to the winner's enclosure. *(op 6-1)*

Notanotherdonkey(IRE), having his first run since April, ran one of his better races. He is still a maiden over hurdles, though.

Navado(USA), trying this distance for the first time, jumped out to his left. He briefly threatened to get involved three out but failed to see the trip out as well as one or two of his rivals. *(op 6-1)*

Alvaro(IRE) began to lose touch with the principals leaving the back straight, but he plugged on.

Keepers Mead(IRE) was another who tended to jump left, and he weakened badly from the turn into the straight. *(op 7-1 tchd 5-1)*

Sadler's Pride(IRE) *Official explanation: jockey said gelding pulled up lame*

1716 BANK OF SCOTLAND H'CAP CHASE (12 fncs) 2m

5:00 (5:00) (Class 4) (0-110,110) 5-Y-0+ **£4,745** (£1,460; £730; £365)

Form — RPR

1114 **1** **Polished**[31] 1458 6-10-7 **91**........................(b) RJohnson 110+
(V R A Dartnall) *a.p: led 8th: clr fr 4 out: comf* **9/4**[1]

30-2 **2** *6* **Va Vavoom (IRE)**[104] 870 7-11-12 **110**........................ CLlewellyn 119+
(N A Twiston-Davies) *led 1st to 6th: rdn and ev ch appr 4 out: one pce* **5/2**[2]

3-33 **3** *3* **Lubinas (IRE)**[151] 354 6-10-11 **95**........................ LAspell 100
(F Jordan) *hld up in tch: outpcd 4 out: rallied and j.lft 2 out: no imp* **7/1**

-233 **4** *7* **Cansalrun (IRE)**[11] 1596 6-11-2 **100**........................ AThornton 98
(R H Alner) *led to 1st: chsd ldr: led 6th to 8th: wknd 2 out* **12/1**

P012 **5** *1 ¾* **College City (IRE)**[4] 1682 6-11-4 **105** 7ex........................(p) LMcGrath(3) 103+
(R C Guest) *hld up and bhd: hdwy appr 8th: wknd 2 out* **5/1**[3]

PU/ **6** *6* **Get Smart (IRE)**[155] 292 8-10-0 **87**........................ KJMercer(3) 77
(Ferdy Murphy) *a bhd* **10/1**

3P0- **7** *6* **Flower Of Pitcur**[212] 4363 8-10-3 **97**........................ WMcCarthy(10) 81
(T R George) *hld up: mstke 8th: hdwy appr 4 out: wknd after 3 out* **22/1**

2406 **U** **Dead Mans Dante (IRE)**[15] 1566 7-11-4 **109**........................ TJDreaper(7) —
(Ferdy Murphy) *bhd tl blnd and uns rdr 6th* **25/1**

4m 5.40s (0.40) **Going Correction** +0.10s/f (Yiel) 8 Ran SP% **113.5**

Speed ratings: **103,100,98,95,94 91,88,—** CSF £8.59 CT £31.64 TOTE £3.10: £1.50, £1.80, £2.10; EX 8.90.

Owner Cape Codders **Bred** Ewar Stud Farms **Trained** Brayford, Devon

FOCUS

An ordinary handicap run in driving rain. The winner was well-in on his hurdling form and has been rated value for a ten-length victory.

NOTEBOOK

Polished has shown improved form over hurdles in recent months and was returning to fences off a 17lb lower mark than his hurdles rating. Going clear from the fourth last to score in ready style, he looks capable of winning again over fences even after being reassessed. *(op 5-2 tchd 11-4 in places)*

Va Vavoom(IRE) jumped well enough on this chasing bow but lacked the pace to go with the winner from the home turn. He stuck on for second and a step up in trip should see him off the mark over fences. *(op 10-3 tchd 7-2)*

Lubinas(IRE), who does most of his racing over further, made a satisfactory return to action after a summer break. He is well handicapped and should be kept in mind when reverting to further. *(op 8-1)*

Cansalrun(IRE) ran plenty of good races over hurdles without managing to get her head in front. She ran respectably on this chasing bow but could have done without the rain. *(op 16-1)*

College City(IRE), making a quick reappearance, was well held under his penalty, which does not augur well for his prospects as he is due to race off a mark 5lb higher than this in future. *(op 7-2)*

1717 CREDIT SHIELD H'CAP HURDLE (10 hdls) 2m

5:35 (5:35) (Class 4) (0-100,99) 4-Y-0+ **£3,087** (£882; £441)

Form — RPR

2141 **1** **Sunnyland**[19] 1541 6-11-9 **96**........................ RJohnson 108+
(P J Hobbs) *hld up in mid-div: hdwy after 4th: rdn to ld appr 2 out: drvn out* **11/2**[2]

0-03 **2** *2* **Dont Ask Me (IRE)**[19] 1541 4-10-2 **85**........................(t) AGlassonbury(10) 94
(M C Pipe) *hld up in mid-div: hit 4th: rdn and hdwy appr 3 out: chsd wnr and mstke 2 out: kpt on same pce flat* **9/2**[1]

2504 **3** *17* **Jimmy Byrne (IRE)**[18] 1553 5-11-5 **95**........................ LMcGrath(3) 89+
(R C Guest) *a.p: led appr 5th: rdn and hdd appr 2 out: wknd appr last* **6/1**[3]

336- **4** *1* **Di's Dilemma**[199] 4587 7-11-3 **90**........................ NFehily 81
(C C Bealby) *w ldr: led 3rd tl appr 5th: wknd appr 2 out* **7/1**

/65- **5** *8* **Park City**[451] 1004 6-10-13 **93**........................ SWalsh(7) 76
(J Joseph) *prom to 5th* **25/1**

P05- **6** *8* **Eastern Dagger**[414] 1277 5-10-0 **73** oh1........................ AO'Keeffe 48
(Miss L V Davis) *plld hrd: led to 3rd: wknd 6th* **33/1**

0-00 **7** *3 ½* **John Jorrocks (FR)**[149] 389 6-10-0 **73** oh4........................ JMogford 45
(J C Tuck) *a bhd* **40/1**

0P-P **8** *½* **Heatherlea Squire (NZ)**[122] 724 7-9-12 **78**........................ RCummings(7) 49
(D J Wintle) *mstke 6th: a bhd* **25/1**

0402 **9** *nk* **Saorsie**[42] 1381 7-11-12 **99**........................ TScudamore 70
(J C Fox) *bhd fr 6th* **8/1**

0-P3 **10** *dist* **A Monk Swimming (IRE)**[99] 901 4-10-9 **82**........................ JGoldstein —
(Miss J S Davis) *hld up in tch: hit 4th: rdn and wknd after 7th: t.o* **25/1**

05-P **P** **In Good Faith (USA)**[66] 58 4-11-4 **91**........................ MFoley —
(N J Henderson) *a bhd: t.o whn p.u bef 2 out* **14/1**

00-0 **F** **Earl Of Spectrum (GER)**[44] 513 4-11-3 **90**........................ AntonyEvans —
(J L Spearing) *plld hrd in rr: stdy hdwy appr 5th: 6 l 5th whn fell 2 out* **14/1**

355- **U** **Businessmoney Jake**[200] 4565 4-11-8 **95**........................ ATinkler —
(V R A Dartnall) *hld up in mid-div: sme hdwy and 12 l 4th whn blnd and uns rdr 7th* **9/2**[1]

4m 8.10s (7.70) **Going Correction** +0.525s/f (Soft)

WFA 4 from 5yo+ 13lb 13 Ran SP% **119.9**

Speed ratings: **101,100,91,91,87 83,81,81,80,— —,—,—** CSF £29.21 CT £156.98 TOTE £5.60: £2.20, £2.40, £3.00; EX 13.90 Place 6 £102.29, Place 5 £91.99.

Owner D H Smith **Bred** C D Harrison **Trained** Withycombe, Somerset

FOCUS

A modest handicap run at a decent pace and the race could rate higher.

NOTEBOOK

Sunnyland was weak in the market as plenty of people had concerns regarding her ability to handle this rain-softened ground, but she proved the doubters wrong and coped admirably. Clearly progressing well, she could defy the Handicapper again. *(op 7-2)*

Dont Ask Me(IRE) showed the benefit of having a tongue tie fitted last time and confirmed his improvement in form with another good effort in defeat. He stayed on well from off the pace but the winner always just had his measure.

Jimmy Byrne(IRE), once in front, made it a proper test. He had most of his rivals in trouble rounding the turn into the straight but could not shake off the favourite and in the end cried enough heading towards the second last. *(op 7-1)*

Di's Dilemma, a consistent performer last season, is entitled to come on for this seasonal bow, but she will have to find improvement from somewhere to defy her current mark and lose her maiden tag. *(op 8-1)*

Park City was last seen on a racecourse in July 2004 so he was entitled to get a little tired in the ground.

In Good Faith(USA), who had a couple of spins on the Flat in the summer, ran no sort of race on her return to hurdling. *(op 9-1)*

Businessmoney Jake was not out of contention, at least for the places, when unseating his rider, and he should be kept in mind for a similar race with this seasonal reappearance under his belt. *(op 9-1)*

T/Plt: £170.10 to a £1 stake. Pool: £44,664.15. 191.60 winning tickets. T/Qpdt: £124.60 to a £1 stake. Pool: £2,543.10. 15.10 winning tickets. KH

520 WETHERBY (L-H)

Wednesday, October 12

OFFICIAL GOING: Good to firm (good in places)

2.8m. gallons of water had been put on the track over the previous two months and after 2mm overnight rain the ground was reckoned 'good, bit loose'

Wind: Light; half behind Weather: Fine.

1718 NORTHERN JUMP JOCKEYS SUPPORTING SPINAL RESEARCH JUVENILE NOVICES' HURDLE (9 hdls) 2m

2:30 (2:30) (Class 4) 3-Y-O **£3,612** (£1,032; £516)

Form — RPR

1 **The Pen**[37] 3-9-12........................ PMerrigan(7) 103+
(P C Haslam) *mid-div: hdwy 4th: chsd wnr 3 out: hit next: led appr last: styd on* **10/1**

1 **2** *1 ¾* **Toss The Caber (IRE)**[24] 1478 3-11-5........................ JimCrowley 113
(K G Reveley) *chsd ldrs: kpt on fr 3 out: nt qckn run-in* **11/2**[3]

2 **3** *2* **Finland (UAE)**[18] 1551 3-10-9........................ KJMercer(3) 104
(Mrs A Duffield) *wnt prom 4th: styd on same pce fr 2 out* **7/2**[1]

F **4** *¾* **Ellerslie Tom**[18] 1551 3-10-12........................ JMMaguire 105+
(T P Tate) *led: hit 6th: mstke 2 out: hdd appr last: wknd towards fin* **5/1**[2]

6 **5** *1 ½* **Dock Tower (IRE)**[18] 1551 3-10-12........................ DO'Meara 102
(M E Sowersby) *mid-div: hdwy 6th: styd on fr 2 out* **125/1**

6 *8* **Circumspect (IRE)**[25] 3-10-12........................ FKeniry 94
(P C Haslam) *hdwy 4th: one pce fr 3 out* **40/1**

0 **7** *4* **Bold Pursuit (IRE)**[17] [1563] 3-10-9 PAspell(3) 91+
(Mrs A Duffield) *chsd ldrs: 6th and wkng whn mstke 2 out* **100/1**

11 **8** *10* **Aviation**[21] [1512] 3-11-7 DCCostello(5) 97+
(G M Moore) *chsd ldrs 4th: rdn after 6th: wknd fr 3 out* **15/2**

9 *8* **Coleorton Dane**[42] 3-10-12 GLee 72
(K A Ryan) *in rr: sme hdwy 6th: wknd next* **9/1**

6S **10** *1* **Bellalou**[21] [1512] 3-10-5 MBradburne 64
(Mrs S A Watt) *chsd ldrs: wknd 3 out* **100/1**

11 *2 ½* **Ivana Illyich (IRE)**[21] 3-10-5 ARoss 61
(J S Wainwright) *bhd fr 6th* **100/1**

12 *2 ½* **Viable**[44] 3-10-12 WMarston 66
(Mrs P Sly) *j. bdly a bhd* **14/1**

42 **13** *1 ¾* **Sound And Vision (IRE)**[19] [1441] 3-10-12 BHarding 64
(M Dods) *chsd ldrs: wkng whn blnd 3 out* **20/1**

6 **14** *16* **Casalese**[21] [1512] 3-10-12 NPMulholland 48
(M D Hammond) *in tch to 6th: sn lost pl* **125/1**

P **Keyalzao (IRE)**[30] 3-9-12 CDSharkey(7) —
(A Crook) *bhd 6th: p.u bef next* **125/1**

P **Nakatani (IRE)**[142] 3-10-5 TBailey(7) —
(Mrs A V Roberts) *bhd 6th: p.u bef next* **150/1**

F **Another Misk**[121] 3-10-9 PBuchanan(3) —
(M E Sowersby) *bhd whn fell 2 out* **125/1**

P **Zagreus (GER)**[78] 3-10-9 MrTGreenall(3) —
(M W Easterby) *bhd whn p.u bef 3 out* **50/1**

P **El Rey Royale**[20] 3-10-12 ADobbin —
(M D Hammond) *mid-div: bhd fr 6th: p.u bef 2 out* **16/1**

P **Wayward Shot (IRE)**[30] 3-10-12 ADempsey —
(M W Easterby) *t.k.h in rr: bhd whn p.u bef 3 out* **33/1**

5 **P** **Eborarry (IRE)**[22] [1339] 3-10-12 RGarritty —
(T D Easterby) *in rr: mstke 4th: bhd whn p.u bef last* **33/1**

56 **P** **Emerald Destiny (IRE)**[10] [1601] 3-10-12 PJBrennan —
(D Carroll) *chsd ldrs to 4th: bhd whn p.u bef 6th* **33/1**

3m 45.0s (-14.40) **Going Correction** -0.725s/f (Firm) **22** Ran SP% **122.5**
Speed ratings: **107,106,105,104,104 100,98,93,89,88 87,86,85,77,— —,—,—,—,— —,—**
CSF £59.50 TOTE £9.60: £3.20, £2.60, £1.90; EX 69.50.
Owner M T Buckley **Bred** Mrs R D Peacock **Trained** Middleham, N Yorks

FOCUS
A fair time for a race like this. The winner was only modest on the Flat and was receiving lots of weight from her main rivals, so it remains to see how solid the form is, but the third sets a reasonable standard.

NOTEBOOK
The Pen, receiving lots of weight from the second, showed a nice attitude on her hurdling debut to land the spoils. She was only modest on the Flat, so it remains to be seen how good the race will turn out to be, and how she progresses. *(op 12-1)*
Toss The Caber(IRE), from the stable who won the race last year, probably found the concession of weight too much, but kept on nicely up the straight for pressure. He should get further in time. *(op 5-1 tchd 9-2)*
Finland(UAE) never managed to get his head in front on the Flat and could become equally frustrating over timber. He did not find a great deal after travelling nicely into the straight, and may benefit from further in time as he did keep on after coming under pressure. *(tchd 10-3)*
Ellerslie Tom was going quite nicely when tipping over on his hurdling debut, but showed no ill-effects of that spill, setting a fair pace in front. He failed to get home and weakened quickly after jumping the last. A sharp track will probably suit him. *(op 9-2 tchd 6-1)*
Dock Tower(IRE) ◆ got going too late but finished closer to Finland than he had done last time. He is going the right way and will be suited by a stiffer track or further. *(op 100-1)*
Circumspect(IRE) showed just about enough on his first attempt over hurdles to suggest he can win a race of some nature during the winter.
Bold Pursuit(IRE) looked seriously one paced all the way up the straight, and hurdling does not look his thing on his first two efforts.
Aviation, under a double penalty, never figured and ran well below his best. This was probably not his true form. *(op 6-1 tchd 8-1)*
Coleorton Dane was never tried at further than a mile on the Flat and was being pushed along in the back straight for a while. He did get around but did not give any clear indication he will get the trip over hurdles. *(op 14-1)*
Viable pulled very hard early and jumped poorly as a result. *(op 16-1 tchd 18-1)*
Emerald Destiny(IRE) *Official explanation: jockey said gelding lost its action*

1719 ROCOM NEC BEGINNERS' CHASE (18 fncs) 2m 7f 110y
3:05 (3:06) (Class 4) 5-Y-0+ **£3,120** (£960; £480; £240)

Form RPR

00-4 **1** **Model Son (IRE)**[146] [422] 7-10-7 PMerrigan(7) 119+
(Mrs H Dalton) *trckd ldrs: led 6th: pckd 3 out: j.lft next: smoothly* **6/5**[1]

56/- **2** *1 ½* **Premium First (IRE)**[548] [4783] 6-11-0 GLee 99
(Mrs H Dalton) *chsd ldrs: chsd wnr fr 14th: styd on fr 3 out: no imp* **5/1**[2]

2624 **3** *21* **Starbuck**[4] [1686] 11-10-9 80 DMcGann(5) 79+
(A M Crow) *chsd ldrs: outpcd whn mstke 14th: one pce fr next* **8/1**

P0P/ **4** *2 ½* **Dear Boy**[200] 6-11-0 ADobbin 76
(F P Murtagh) *led to 6th: one pce fr 4 out* **16/1**

53/5 **5** *2* **Rolling River (IRE)**[46] [1334] 8-10-11 PAspell(3) 74
(J Wade) *sn outpcd and in era: kpt on fr 4 out: nvr on terms* **14/1**

316U **6** *11* **Pikestaff (USA)**[10] [1603] 7-10-11 100 (t) PWhelan(3) 63
(M A Barnes) *chsd ldrs: drvn along 9th: lost pl 11th: sn bhd* **10/1**

P05F **7** *7* **Lambrini Mist**[17] [1560] 7-10-9 65 DLaverty(5) 59+
(Mrs L Williamson) *chsd ldrs: reminders after 9th: 5th and wkng whn blnd 3 out* **80/1**

650- **8** *17* **Frosty's Cousin (IRE)**[221] [4191] 6-11-0 88 TDoyle 39
(P R Webber) *chsd ldrs: lost pl 13th: sn bhd* **13/2**[3]

0P-4 **P** **Moss Campian**[8] [1634] 7-10-7 64 TBailey(7) —
(Mrs A V Roberts) *sn bhd: t.o 8th: p.u bef 12th* **150/1**

640/ **P** **Sweet Bird (FR)**[548] [4790] 8-10-11 (t) ONelmes(3) —
(Miss J R Gibney) *in tch: wknd 14th: bhd whn p.u bef last* **40/1**

5m 48.7s (-9.80) **Going Correction** -0.725s/f (Firm) **10** Ran SP% **112.5**
Speed ratings: **87,86,79,78,78 74,72,66,—,—** CSF £7.29 TOTE £1.80: £1.10, £2.20, £2.00; EX 7.70.
Owner P J Hughes Developments Ltd **Bred** Andrew Murphy **Trained** Norton, Shropshire

FOCUS
A very moderate time for the grade. Using the third as a fairly solid yardstick, the winner can already be rated as a fair type and is value for far more than the official margin.

NOTEBOOK
Model Son(IRE) ◆, who apparently boiled over last time when some jets flew over the course, made no mistake on his chasing debut for the Dalton stable - he had tried chasing in the past when trained in Ireland - and completely outclassed his rivals. Apart from a mistake at the third last, he was foot-perfect and is sure to win more races. *(op 11-8 tchd 11-10)*
Premium First(IRE), not seen for 548 days, was a winning pointer in Ireland in the past and showed enough on his chasing debut to suggest he can win a race of a similar nature in the future. However, he was returning after a long break and some caution should be taken before backing him next time in case this effort took a lot out of him. *(tchd 11-2)*
Starbuck, supported in the market before the race and making a quick reappearance, held every chance coming into the straight but never got close enough to trouble any of the leaders. *(op 12-1)*
Dear Boy, runner-up on his previous three outings between the flags, showed up in the early stages but faded all the way up the home straight. *(op 12-1)*
Rolling River(IRE) did well to finish after being under extreme pressure very early. He will need a lot further given this effort. *(tchd 16-1)*
Frosty's Cousin(IRE) looks every inch a chaser but folded very tamely under pressure in the back straight after receiving reminders passing the stands for the first time. *(op 5-1 tchd 7-1 and 8-1 in a place)*
Sweet Bird(FR) ran well for a long way and should benefit for the run after a long lay-off. *(op 33-1)*

1720 WETHERBY RACECOURSE "YOUR CONFERENCE VENUE FOR LEEDS" H'CAP HURDLE (9 hdls) 2m
3:40 (3:43) (Class 2) (0-140,132) 4-Y-0+ **£8,872** (£2,730; £1,365; £682)

Form RPR

6-11 **1** **Crathorne (IRE)**[12] [1591] 5-10-2 108 ADobbin 121+
(M Todhunter) *trckd ldr: led after 6th: styd on gamely fr 2 out* **11/2**[3]

0-11 **2** *½* **Mexican Pete**[8] [1633] 5-10-11 117 7ex TJMurphy 130+
(A W Carroll) *hld up: smooth hdwy appr 3 out: upsides next: no ex nr fin* **15/8**[1]

4411 **3** *15* **Snow's Ride**[15] [1569] 5-10-4 110 GLee 108
(M D Hammond) *chsd ldrs: outpcd 3 out: styd on between last 2: tk 3rd nr line* **10/1**

145/ **4** *nk* **Kentucky Blue (IRE)**[25] [4190] 5-11-3 123 RGarritty 120
(T D Easterby) *trckd ldrs: upsides 2 out: wknd appr last* **20/1**

0015 **5** *nk* **Overstrand (IRE)**[18] [1548] 6-10-9 118 (b) ONelmes(3) 115
(Robert Gray) *hld up: outpcd 6th: styd on fr 2 out: kpt on wl run-in* **16/1**

10F- **6** *1 ¾* **Town Crier (IRE)**[188] [4751] 10-10-8 114 DElsworth 111+
(Mrs S J Smith) *chsd ldrs: mstke 3rd: wknd 2 out* **10/3**[2]

0343 **7** *2* **Flame Phoenix (USA)**[4] [1668] 6-10-12 118 (t) JMMaguire 111
(D McCain) *chsd ldrs: drvn along 6th: outpcd approachinh next* **40/1**

0/3- **8** *½* **St Pirran (IRE)**[347] [1908] 10-11-5 125 HOliver 118
(R C Guest) *hld up: hdwy 4th: wl outpcd 6th: n.d after* **16/1**

0-31 **9** *16* **Nawamees (IRE)**[12] [1249] 7-11-12 132 (b) JEMoore 123+
(G L Moore) *chsd ldrs: rdn 6th: wknd next: eased run-in* **8/1**

-6U0 **10** *dist* **Migration**[24] [1487] 9-10-11 120 (p) LVickers(3) —
(Mrs S Lamyman) *j.rt: led tl after 6th: sn lost pl: t.o 2 out* **100/1**

F1-0 **P** **Classic Event (IRE)**[87] [61] 4-10-7 113 DO'Meara —
(T D Easterby) *hld up in last: bhdfr 6th: t.o whn p.u bef last* **66/1**

3m 42.9s (-16.50) **Going Correction** -0.725s/f (Firm)
WFA 4 from 5yo+ 13lb **11** Ran SP% **114.9**
Speed ratings: **112,111,104,104,103 103,102,101,93,—** — CSF £15.92 CT £100.27 TOTE £7.20: £2.10, £1.50, £2.00; EX 21.00 Trifecta £35.80 Pool: £595.70 - 11.80 winning units..
Owner FF Racing Services Partnership XVII **Bred** Shirley Blue Syndicate **Trained** Orton, Cumbria

FOCUS
A very competitive race with quite a few in form horses taking their chance. The form is rated through the third and should prove solid.

NOTEBOOK
Crathorne(IRE), taking a step up in class, was in exactly the right pace throughout the race and gained first run on most of his field. This should not detract from the performance as he battled back bravely after being headed, after looking likely to be swallowed up with ease. He is progressing nicely now he has found his form. *(op 5-1)*
Mexican Pete, 14lb higher than his opening victory of the season, was checked over by the vet prior to the race, but allowed to take his chance. He moved up stylishly towards the leaders up the straight and momentarily got in front after jumping the last. However, he succumbed to the winner's renewed effort and was just denied close to the line. *(op 9-4 tchd 5-2 in a place)*
Snow's Ride came into the race in great form but was readily outpaced three from home. He picked up again when straightened out which suggested he will be suited by further in the future. *(op 9-1)*
Kentucky Blue(IRE) showed more than enough on his return to hurdling to suggest he will be winning races this winter, especially when the ground eases. *(tchd 16-1)*
Overstrand(IRE) continues to run well for his new stable and is fairly handicapped on his best form. A return to a stiffer track in this sort of company would be ideal. *(op 25-1)*
Town Crier(IRE), a very decent novice chaser last season who goes well fresh, showed up well until tiring between the third and second last. He remains to be seen whether connections try and make use of his fair mark over hurdles or go back over fences, but the effort was not without promise for the future. *(op 7-2 tchd 11-4)*
St Pirran(IRE) ◆, a previous Cheltenham Festival winner over fences who was bought for 10,000gns by present connections, was restrained in rear and gave the impression he had more to give. He is nicely handicapped over both hurdles and fences and looks a sure-fire winner in the near future. *(op 12-1)*
Nawamees(IRE), winner of the race last season off a 2lb lower mark, ran a fine race on the Flat recently at huge odds but was noticeably weak in the market before the race and ran disappointingly. *(op 7-1 tchd 10-1)*

1721 SKYBET.COM SUPPORTING SPINAL RESEARCH BOBBY RENTON H'CAP CHASE (15 fncs) 2m 4f 110y
4:15 (4:15) (Class 2) (0-145,135) 5-Y-0+
£9,280 (£3,520; £1,760; £800; £400; £240)

Form RPR

F1-F **1** **Full House (IRE)**[18] [1550] 6-11-6 129 TDoyle 144+
(P R Webber) *trckd ldrs: smooth hdwy to ld 2 out: readily* **7/2**[1]

P5-0 **2** *4* **Vandas Choice (IRE)**[153] [318] 7-11-8 134 PBuchanan(3) 141
(Miss Lucinda V Russell) *chsd ldrs: pushed along 6th: rallied and wnt 2nd 2 out: no imp* **16/1**

4P0- **3** *9* **Glenelly Gale (IRE)**[173] [4972] 11-11-4 130 MrTGreenall(3) 128
(M W Easterby) *hld up: wnt prominnt 11th: outpcd fr 2 out* **16/1**

P-0P **4** *½* **Tacolino (FR)**[151] [360] 11-10-0 109 oh4 JEMoore 107
(O Brennan) *w ldr: led 5th: wandered and hdd 2 out: wknd run-in: fin tired* **50/1**

F60- **5** *¾* **St Matthew (USA)**[209] [4407] 7-11-8 131 DElsworth 130+
(Mrs S J Smith) *mstkes: led to 5th: outpcd whn hit 3 out: kpt on run-in* **7/2**[1]

004- **6** *1 ¼* **Turgeonev (FR)**[179] [4863] 10-11-12 135 DO'Meara 131
(T D Easterby) *trckd ldrs: wknd 2 out* **4/1**[2]

2P0- **7** *3 ½* **Just In Debt (IRE)**[186] [4772] 9-11-11 134 (p) ADobbin 126
(M Todhunter) *in tch: rdn and outpcd 11th: lost pl next* **9/1**[3]

0B0- **8** *1 ¾* **Europa**[186] [4772] 9-11-9 132 JMMaguire 122
(Ferdy Murphy) *in tch: outpcd 11th: n.d after* **7/2**[1]

5m 1.70s (-19.00) **Going Correction** -0.725s/f (Firm) **8** Ran SP% **110.4**
Speed ratings: **107,105,102,101,101 101,99,99** CSF £48.06 CT £739.30 TOTE £3.00: £1.80, £3.20, £3.40; EX 48.10.

Owner The Chamberlain Addiscott Partnership **Bred** Schwindibode Ag **Trained** Mollington, Oxon

FOCUS
The pace did not look that strong but the race time was not bad. Full House is making up into a nice handicapper and appreciated the quick ground. The race is rated through the runner-up but the fourth casts a slight doubt over the form.

NOTEBOOK
Full House(IRE) made amends for his fall last time, when looking to hold every chance, with a very smooth success. He is likely to make up into a nice handicapper as long as his jumping holds out, and will be better suited by a quicker pace. He is now likely to head to Windsor on November 19th for the Blue Square Chase. *(op 5-2 tchd 9-4)*
Vandas Choice(IRE) did well to finish so close as he was keen early and was being pushed along for much of the far straight. He shaped nicely and gives the impression he will get further than two-and-a-half miles. *(tchd 14-1)*
Glenelly Gale(IRE) moved well for most of the race but became slightly outpaced at the top of the home straight. A mistake two from home stopped his progress but he kept on nicely and suggested he can win a race this season from his current mark. *(tchd 20-1)*
Tacolino(FR) showed up for a long way amd ran well above expectations. It would be dangerous to take this effort at face value. *(op 40-1)*
St Matthew(USA) made a couple of costly errors during the race and had his chance ended with a blunder two from home. He is not obviously well handicapped at the moment. *(op 9-2)*
Turgeonev(FR) often runs well at the course and did enough to suggest he can make use of his favourable mark in the near future. *(tchd 7-2 and 9-2)*
Just In Debt(IRE) showed very little on his seasonal debut and this was almost certainly a warm-up for the Becher Chase. He goes really well at Aintree and will be of obvious interest if improving for the run. *(op 14-1)*
Europa was always towards the rear and never figured at any stage. *(tchd 4-1)*

1722 JIMMY & JANE FITZGERALD MEMORIAL NOVICES' HURDLE (10 hdls) 2m 4f 110y
4:50 (4:50) (Class 3) 4-Y-0+ **£5,151** (£1,585; £792; £396)

Form RPR
51 **1** **Flotta**[11] 1596 6-11-4 .... TJMurphy 121+
(B G Powell) *mde all: drvn out run-in* **4/7**[1]
232- **2** 1 ½ **Love That Benny (USA)**[204] 4507 5-10-9 105 .... PAspell(3) 112
(J Wade) *chsd wnr fr 3rd: rdn between last 2: styd on run-in: no real imp* **9/2**[2]
-114 **3** *dist* **Common Girl (IRE)**[139] 521 7-11-3 110 .... JEMoore 87
(O Brennan) *chsd ldrs: drvn along 6th: sn lft bhd by 1st 2: 33 l bhd* **8/1**[3]
244- **4** 2 ½ **Ambition Royal (FR)**[173] 4965 5-10-9 97 .... PBuchanan(3) 77
(Miss Lucinda V Russell) *chsd ldrs: pushed along 4th: outpcd fr 7th* **10/1**
0020 **5** ¾ **Lazy Lena (IRE)**[108] 839 6-10-5 75 .... TSiddall 69
(Miss L C Siddall) *in tch to 6th: sn outpcd and bhd* **50/1**
0P-0 **P** **Zeydnaa (IRE)**[8] 415 5-10-12 .... GLee —
(C R Wilson) *in tch: wknd qckly 7th: sn t.o and p.u* **25/1**
P **Wotabroad** 7-10-5 .... RMcGrath —
(K G Reveley) *bhd and drvn along 4th: hoplessly t.o whn p.u after 7th* **100/1**
0-60 **P** **Soviet Committee**[56] 1237 5-10-9 .... (t) PWhelan(3) —
(T J Fitzgerald) *in tch: reminders 6th: sn lost pl: t.o whn p.u bef 2 out* **50/1**

4m 53.1s (-15.80) **Going Correction** -0.725s/f (Firm) **8** Ran SP% **110.8**
Speed ratings: **101,100**,—,—,— —,—,— CSF £3.19 TOTE £1.40: £1.10, £1.20, £1.50; EX 3.20.
Owner G Hatchard,R Gunn,L Gilbert & R Williams **Bred** W G R Wightman **Trained** Morestead, Hants

FOCUS
A very un-Timmy Murphy like ride, making all at a modest pace. The first two were miles clear but the form probably means very little.

NOTEBOOK
Flotta did the job well enough after making all of the running. He almost certainly got bored in front, which made him look less-than-impressive, and he could improve again in a strong race. That said, he will probably need to go handicapping now as he would probably struggle under a double penalty in novice company. *(op 8-13 tchd 8-11)*
Love That Benny(USA) was the only horse to give the winner any serious competition throughout the final stages. He moved well for much of the race, albeit a bit keenly, and just could not get to the leader. An ordinary novice is well within his grasp. *(op 6-1)*
Common Girl(IRE) was dropped in the back straight and plugged on slowly to grab a place. The third next to her name but the form means very little. *(op 7-1 tchd 13-2)*
Ambition Royal(FR) was beaten a long way from home, and his second to Faasel last season is a distant memory. *(tchd 9-1 and 12-1)*
Lazy Lena(IRE) only gets credit for completing the course. *(tchd 40-1)*
Zeydnaa(IRE), a recent winner on the Flat in banded company, ran very poorly and continues to show nothing over timber. *Official explanation: jockey said gelding had a breathing problem (op 16-1)*

1723 SPINAL RESEARCH DAY NOVICES' H'CAP HURDLE (12 hdls) 3m 1f
5:25 (5:25) (Class 4) (0-90,90) 3-Y-0+ **£2,712** (£775; £387)

Form RPR
/00- **1** **Stoneravinmad**[311] 2655 7-10-0 **64** .... BHarding 68+
(Mrs E Slack) *wnt prom 5th: stmbld bnd after 9th: led 2 out: styd on wl run-in* **16/1**
440- **2** 1 **Pinnacle Ridge**[184] 4812 5-11-11 **89** .... RMcGrath 90
(Mrs K Walton) *hld up: hdwy to join ldrs 8th: led after next: hdd 2 out: styd on same pce* **5/1**[3]
P-41 **3** 1 ¼ **Mags Two**[17] 1564 8-10-9 **80** .... PMerrigan(7) 82+
(I McMath) *mid-div: wnt promient 8th: kpt on same pce between last 2* **7/2**[1]
P00- **4** 8 **Seveneightsix (IRE)**[176] 4920 5-10-2 **66** .... (b) WMarston 59+
(D J Wintle) *hld up: hdwy 8th: chsng ldrs next: wknd 2 out* **11/1**
3345 **5** 3 **True Temper (IRE)**[10] 1608 8-10-11 **80** .... DMcGann(5) 69
(A M Crow) *trckd ldrs: led 9th: hdd next: wknd bef 2 out* **14/1**
5PF- **6** *dist* **Place Above (IRE)**[185] 4800 9-10-13 **77** .... PJBrennan —
(E A Elliott) *w ldrs: drvn along 6th: wknd 8th: sn bhd: t.o: btn 46 l* **9/2**[2]
P601 **7** 10 **Super Boston**[52] 1279 5-11-1 **79** .... (b) TSiddall —
(Miss L C Siddall) *in tch: drvn along 8th: sn lost pl and bhd: t.o* **15/2**
3P6- **8** 27 **Celtic Flow**[264] 3462 7-10-5 **72** .... PAspell(3) —
(C R Wilson) *prom: lost pl 9th: struggling 7th: bhd fr 9th: sn t.o* **40/1**
U-44 **B** **Alpha Juliet (IRE)**[15] 1566 4-11-6 **85** .... FKeniry —
(G M Moore) *hld up: stdy hdwy 8th: prom whn b.d bnd after next* **10/1**
25/0 **P** **Some Trainer (IRE)**[4] 1686 9-11-1 **79** .... (t) ADobbin —
(J G Cromwell, Ire) *in tch to 8th: sn lost pl: bhd whn p.u bef 3 out* **12/1**
P-0P **P** **Mid Summer Lark (IRE)**[4] 1686 9-11-5 **90** .... MrDJewett(7) —
(I McMath) *chsd ldrs: reminders 3rd: lost pl 6th: sn t.o: p.u bef next* **66/1**
-0UP **P** **Crown Agent (IRE)**[10] 1608 5-9-9 **64** .... (p) DCCostello(5) —
(M E Sowersby) *led 3rd: hdd 7th: blnd next: wknd qckly after 9th: bhd whn p.u bef next* **40/1**
430P **F** **Ladies From Leeds**[10] 1619 6-11-2 **80** .... (v[1]) JamesDavies —
(A Crook) *led to 3rd: led 7th to 9th: struggling whn hmpd and b.d on bnd sn after* **20/1**

6m 3.50s (-11.00) **Going Correction** -0.725s/f (Firm)
WFA 4 from 5yo+ 15lb **13** Ran SP% **117.6**
Speed ratings: **88,87,87,84,83** —,—,—,— —,—,— CSF £91.66 CT £352.01 TOTE £23.50: £5.70, £2.20, £1.70; EX 451.40 Place 6 £10.84, Place 5 £6.52.
Owner Mrs Evelyn Slack **Bred** D Malcolm Drury **Trained** Hilton, Cumbria
■ Stewards' Enquiry : W Marston two-day ban: careless riding (Oct 23,25)

FOCUS
A moderate winning time for a race like this that took little winning. The race is rated through the third but will probably be of little relevance for the future.

NOTEBOOK
Stoneravinmad had been beaten a minimum of 31 lengths in every completed start prior to the race, and had shown nothing to suggest he would place let alone win. It is difficult to envisage him carrying a penalty to success next time unless the race is very ordinary. However, connections have done wonders getting him to win as he reportedly staked himself in the chest after falling at Cartmel two years ago. *(op 28-1)*
Pinnacle Ridge was beaten by a horse rated 25lb his inferior but appeared suited by the step up in trip. *(tchd 11-2)*
Mags Two never really got going under his 8lb higher mark until too late. He is clearly of limited ability but probably needs a stiffer test of stamina at this level. *(op 11-4)*
Seveneightsix(IRE) at least consented to start off on terms this time, but showed very little again. *(op 25-1 tchd 10-1)*
True Temper(IRE) was been running respectably at her level recently but was well beaten. *(tchd 12-1)*
Place Above(IRE) won three low-grade chases last season but showed absolutely nothing over hurdles from a very favourable mark. *(op 5-1 tchd 11-2)*
Alpha Juliet(IRE) was still going well enough when brought down. *(op 8-1)*
T/Jkpt: £246,238.59 to a £1 stake. Pool: £520,222.50. 1.50 winning tickets. T/Plt: £11.90 to a £1 stake. Pool: £73,633.50. 4,479.60 winning tickets. T/Qpdt: £6.70 to a £1 stake. Pool: £2,947.80. 325.00 winning tickets. WG

310 LUDLOW (R-H)
Thursday, October 13

OFFICIAL GOING: Good to firm
Wind: Moderate, half against Weather: Fine

1724 WELCOME BACK TO LUDLOW (S) HURDLE (9 hdls) 2m
2:10 (2:11) (Class 5) 4-7-Y-0 **£2,437** (£750; £375; £187)

Form RPR
0-12 **1** **Harry Potter (GER)**[49] 1319 6-11-3 109 .... (tp) ChristianWilliams 103+
(Evan Williams) *hld up in mid-div: hdwy appr 6th: lft in ld 2 out: r.o* **8/13**[1]
5302 **2** ½ **Let's Celebrate**[25] 1483 5-10-10 83 .... LAspell 96
(F Jordan) *hld up and bhd: hdwy 6th: rdn and ev ch last: kpt on* **14/1**
3 16 **Glenview Lass (IRE)**[27] 1477 6-10-0 .... (p) DFO'Regan(3) 75+
(T G McCourt, Ire) *led to 2nd: w ldr: rdn appr 3 out: btn whn hmpd 2 out* **25/1**
0064 **4** *shd* **Wardash (GER)**[8] 1640 5-11-3 88 .... (vt) TJMurphy 90+
(M C Pipe) *prom: rdn after 6th: btn whn hmpd 2 out* **8/1**[2]
PP-0 **5** 3 ½ **Jug Of Punch (IRE)**[8] 1643 6-10-5 86 .... MNicolls(5) 77+
(S T Lewis) *hld up in mid-div: hdwy appr 6th: rdn and wknd appr 3 out* **33/1**
0/P- **6** 17 **Down To The Woods (USA)**[504] 526 7-10-5 .... StephenJCraine(5) 59
(D McCain) *hld up in mid-div: hdwy appr 5th: wknd appr 3 out* **40/1**
P455 **7** 1 ½ **Blue Leader (IRE)**[39] 1409 6-11-10 95 .... RJohnson 71
(M B Shears) *hld up in tch: rdn and wknd appr 3 out* **16/1**
6P-P **8** 5 **Stokesies Boy**[20] 1541 5-10-10 81 .... OMcPhail 52
(C Roberts) *mstke 5th: a towards rr* **100/1**
5650 **F** **Royaltea**[7] 1654 4-9-12 79 .... LTreadwell(5) 79
(J T Stimpson) *led 2nd tl fell 2 out* **16/1**
565- **B** **Border Artist**[26] 2370 6-10-10 84 .... GLee —
(B G Powell) *hld up and bhd: b.d 4th* **17/2**[3]
F **This Is It (IRE)**[27] 1475 4-10-3 .... TDoyle —
(T G McCourt, Ire) *hld up: in tch whn fell 4th* **40/1**
P0-P **P** **Dinofelis**[127] 681 7-10-10 69 .... (vt) JPByrne —
(C W Moore) *a bhd: t.o whn p.u bef 6th* **100/1**
00 **F** **Urban Dream (IRE)**[36] 1432 4-10-3 .... (v[1]) MrTJO'Brien(7) —
(R A Farrant) *prom: mstke 3rd: fell 4th* **50/1**
0-0P **F** **Sean Nos (IRE)**[36] 1432 4-10-3 .... KHClarke(7) —
(W K Goldsworthy) *hld up and bhd: mstke 1st: hdwy 6th: wkng whn fell 3 out* **66/1**
6-60 **U** **Canadian Storm**[2] 1541 4-10-10 90 .... (p) AO'Keeffe 79+
(A G Juckes) *t.k.h in mid-div: hdwy 6th: hit 3 out: cl up whn hmpd and uns rdr 2 out* **33/1**

3m 42.7s (-9.60) **Going Correction** -0.60s/f (Firm)
WFA 4 from 5yo+ 13lb **15** Ran SP% **122.0**
Speed ratings: **100,99,91,91,89 81,80,78**,—,— —,—,—,—,— CSF £9.93 TOTE £1.70: £1.10, £2.90, £6.60; EX 10.40.The winner was bought in for 7,750gns.
Owner F Jeffers **Bred** Wilh Jackson **Trained** Cowbridge, Vale Of Glamorgan

FOCUS
The ground was riding as per the official description according to jockeys in action in this event. This was a routine selling hurdle, but there was no shortage of incident as half a dozen ended up on the deck, and despite that the form looks sound enough.

NOTEBOOK
Harry Potter(GER), back in the lowest grade, had just thrown down his challenge when he was left in front at the second last and he was always holding the runner-up thereafter. Useful in this grade, he sustained fractures to his legs when colliding with a car in the spring and has done well to win twice since returning to action. He may go novice chasing now. *(op 4-6 tchd 8-11 in places)*
Let's Celebrate travelled well and was produced to have every chance, but could not match the winner on the run-in. He is performing well at present and can find a race in similar company. *(tchd 16-1)*
Glenview Lass(IRE), a tall mare, had failed to trouble the judge in her home country but she showed more on this first foray into selling company. After racing prominently, she was held when obliged to sidestep a fallen jockey two from home.
Wardash(GER) was successful on his two previous ventures into this grade but he had no real excuses, although he might have been third had he not been caught up in the trouble at the second last. *(op 9-1 tchd 11-1)*
Jug Of Punch(IRE), having his second run back after a break, faded out of contention on the home turn. *(op 28-1)*
Blue Leader(IRE). who was doubly penalised, went without his usual headgear combination on this debut for the yard and was back-tracking on the home turn. *Official explanation: jockey said gelding finished lame*
Canadian Storm was still on the premises when he was unable to avoid the fallen Royaltea and unshipped his rider. How much he would have found is open to question. *(op 20-1)*

Royaltea was still just about in front when she stepped into the penultimate flight and came down, but they were queueing up to challenge her at the time and she would most likely have finished third had she stayed on her feet. She has had plenty of chances but this effort will have encouraged connections. *(op 20-1)*

1725 MANDY HORTON 50TH BIRTHDAY NOVICES' HURDLE (11 hdls) 2m 5f
2:45 (2:47) (Class 4) 4-Y-O+ **£3,419** (£1,052; £526; £263)

Form RPR

-F34 **1** **Redspin (IRE)**[25] 1482 5-10-12 102 DCrosse 98
(J S Moore) *hld up in mid-div: hdwy appr 8th: wnt 2nd 3 out: sn hrd rdn: swtchd rt appr last: led and edgd lft flat: styd on* **13/8**[1]

2022 **2** ½ **Murphy's Nails (IRE)**[8] 1645 8-10-12 95 (p) JPMcNamara 97
(K C Bailey) *chsd ldr: led after 8th: hrd rdn and hdd flat: styd on* **7/4**[2]

00-0 **3** 20 **Westcraft (IRE)**[12] 1596 5-10-12 ChristianWilliams 77
(A Ennis) *prom: reminder after 3rd: hit 7th: rdn appr 3 out: wknd appr 2 out* **40/1**

00- **4** 1 **West End Pearl**[255] 3626 4-10-5 MBradburne 69
(C G Cox) *prom: nt fluent 5th: rdn appr 3 out: wknd appr 2 out* **22/1**

0-4 **5** shd **Danbury (FR)**[154] 316 5-10-12 LAspell 77+
(O Sherwood) *hld up in mid-div: hdwy appr 7th: wkng whn nt fluent 3 out* **12/1**

6 24 **Chestall**[66] 4-10-2 AHawkins(10) 64+
(R Hollinshead) *hld up and bhd: sltly hmpd 6th: hdwy after 8th: sn rdn: wkng whn j.rt 3 out* **33/1**

4-1 **7** 6 **None-So-Pretty**[156] 277 4-10-5 BJCrowley 47+
(Miss E C Lavelle) *bhd: j. slowly 1st: mstke 6th: hdwy after 7th: rdn and wknd after 8th* **8/1**[3]

40 **8** 13 **Dark Rum**[32] 1454 9-10-12 TScudamore 33
(M Scudamore) *a bhd* **22/1**

-56P **9** 25 **La Folichonne (FR)**[111] 822 6-10-5 70 JMogford 1
(T Wall) *t.k.h: led: clr 4th: hdd after 8th: sn wknd: t.o* **100/1**

0-0 **10** 3 **Oasis Blue (IRE)**[8] 1640 4-10-12 TJMurphy 5
(M C Pipe) *a bhd: t.o* **20/1**

P **11** dist **Baden Vugie (IRE)**[95] 948 8-10-7 64 MNicolls(5) —
(S T Lewis) *hld up in mid-div: mstke 2nd: rdn after 5th: sn bhd: t.o fr 7th* **150/1**

5m 3.20s (-15.10) **Going Correction** -0.60s/f (Firm)
WFA 4 from 5yo+ 14lb 11 Ran SP% **113.8**
Speed ratings: **104,103,96,95,95 86,84,79,69,68** — CSF £4.24 TOTE £2.40: £1.10, £1.20, £4.10; EX 5.20.
Owner Mrs Fitri Hay **Bred** R Ergnst And Castletown Stud **Trained** Lambourn, Berks

FOCUS
A weak novice event in which the first two pulled well clear and ran close to their marks.

NOTEBOOK
Redspin(IRE), the pick on official figures, was hard at work turning for home but he ground down the leader on the flat and scored a shade comfortably in the end. This trip is the bare minimum for him and he is capable of better over further, but he is likely to prove vulnerable under a penalty. *(op 9-4 tchd 6-4)*
Murphy's Nails(IRE), stepping back up in trip, went for home three out but could not repel the winner on the flat. He has finished second on four of his last five starts now but his attitude could not be faulted here. *(tchd 2-1 tchd 85-40 in places)*
Westcraft(IRE) plugged on to claim third place on the run-in and this was certainly an improvement on his hurdles debut. He does need fast ground though so may not get his conditions too often in the weeks to come. *(op 28-1)*
West End Pearl made a satisfactory hurdling debut but will need to show considerable improvement if she is to win in this grade. *(op 25-1 tchd 18-1)*
Danbury(FR), who showed a little ability in bumpers, was ultimately well beaten on this hurdles debut. *(op 10-1)*
Chestall looked likely to be involved turning out of the back straight on this initial try over hurdles but his stamina soon gave way. *(op 40-1)*
None-So-Pretty, a bumper winner on her last start back in May, was a little novicey on this hurdling debut and should be capable of better with the experience behind her. *(op 6-1)*
Oasis Blue(IRE) was always at the back of the field over this longer trip. He might do a bit better when eligible for handicaps after one more run. *(op 16-1)*

1726 SUBSCRIBE TO RACING UK BEGINNERS' CHASE (13 fncs) 2m
3:20 (3:21) (Class 4) 4-Y-O+
£3,891 (£1,476; £738; £335; £167; £100)

Form RPR

50-5 **1** **Rooster's Reunion (IRE)**[34] 1444 6-11-6 TDoyle 116+
(D R Gandolfo) *t.k.h in rr: hit 9th: swtchd lft and hdwy appr 2 out: led last: readily* **5/1**[2]

1-30 **2** 1½ **Conroy**[145] 450 6-11-6 LAspell 108
(F Jordan) *hld up and bhd: hdwy appr 3 out: led appr 2 out: sn hung rt: hdd last: nt qckn* **14/1**

B242 **3** hd **The Glen**[25] 1487 7-11-6 115 RThornton 108
(R Lee) *a.p: ev ch 3 out: kpt on flat* **2/1**[1]

110- **4** ½ **Goblin**[153] 3728 4-10-7 PMoloney 94
(D E Cantillon) *hld up and bhd: hdwy on ins appr 4th: swtchd lft appr 2 out: r.o flat* **13/2**[3]

P13 **5** 3 **Monticelli (GER)**[22] 1509 5-11-6 RJohnson 104
(P J Hobbs) *hld up: rdn and hdwy appr 4 out: one pce fr 3 out* **2/1**[1]

-040 **6** shd **Milligan (FR)**[25] 1481 10-11-6 111 RGreene 104
(Dr P Pritchard) *led to 7th: led after 9th to 3 out: wknd appr last* **50/1**

7 1 **Robber Red**[152] 9-11-3 (t) CBolger(3) 104+
(Miss Suzy Smith) *chsd ldr: mstke 1st: led 7th tl after 9th: mstke 4 out: led briefly 3 out: wkng whn mstke last* **66/1**

2-00 **8** 10 **Moorlaw (IRE)**[148] 415 4-10-7 JMMaguire 84+
(D McCain) *t.k.h in tch: wknd after 3 out* **33/1**

3m 58.7s (-5.40) **Going Correction** -0.60s/f (Firm)
WFA 4 from 5yo+ 13lb 8 Ran SP% **109.7**
Speed ratings: **89,88,88,87,86 86,85,80** CSF £56.98 TOTE £6.10: £1.60, £1.90, £1.10; EX 78.30.
Owner Terry Warner **Bred** Miss E A Gandolfo **Trained** Wantage, Oxon

FOCUS
A steadily-run race which produced a moderate time for the class. The whole field was still in with a shout as they faced up to the fourth last and they finished in a heap. The form is held down by the seventh and may not prove too solid, but the winner is rated value for further.

NOTEBOOK
Rooster's Reunion(IRE) made a pleasing debut over fences. Given a hold-up ride, he weaved his way through to jump to the front at the final fence and won with something to spare in the end. He has had plenty of physical problems but ought to be able to build on this if remaining sound. *(op 11-2 tchd 6-1)*
Conroy, a chasing debutant, bided his time at the rear of the field in company with the eventual winner before improving once in line for home. After showing ahead going to the second last, he hung towards the rail and was soon collared, but he held on for second. His turn should come in ordinary company. *(op 20-1)*
The Glen, a hurdles winner at this track, boasted the most solid chasing form on offer and he ran his race with no apparent excuses. He is better over further. *(tchd 15-8)*
Goblin, a dual winner over hurdles last term, shaped with considerable promise on this chase debut and ought to improve for the experience. He has the scope for fences and, with the four-year-olds' allowance sure to come in handy, he should not be long in getting off the mark. *(op 9-2)*
Monticelli(GER) was the first to come under pressure, after the last in the back straight and, although not dropping away, he lacked the pace to land a serious blow. A step up in trip should suit him but he has questions to answer now. *(op 9-4 tchd 15-8)*
Milligan(FR) is nothing like as good now as he was in his hurdling heyday but this was a more encouraging effort. *(op 33-1)*
Robber Red, a former point-to-pointer, ran well for a long way on his debut over regulation fences and this sort of trip obviously suits him. *(op 50-1)*

1727 SHROPSHIRE H'CAP HURDLE (12 hdls) 3m
3:55 (3:55) (Class 3) (0-125,125) 4-Y-O+ **£4,634** (£1,426; £713; £356)

Form RPR

5266 **1** **Alikat (IRE)**[19] 1548 4-11-11 125 TJMurphy 132+
(M C Pipe) *hld up: hdwy 8th: led appr 2 out: clr last: styd on wl* **15/8**[2]

5424 **2** 9 **September Moon**[9] 1630 7-10-2 101 RJohnson 101+
(Mrs A M Thorpe) *led: j.lft 3 out: sn hdd: one pce* **5/2**[3]

4PP- **3** 18 **Lalagune (FR)**[176] 4932 6-11-0 113 MFoley 88
(Miss E C Lavelle) *bhd: lost tch 5th: styd on to take 3rd cl home* **28/1**

24-1 **4** ½ **Miss Shakira (IRE)**[21] 1528 7-10-0 99 oh2 CLlewellyn 75+
(N A Twiston-Davies) *prom tl wknd appr 3 out: eased and lost 3rd cl home* **7/4**[1]

1FF2 **5** 4 **Good Man Again (IRE)**[11] 1616 7-9-9 99 (b[1]) WKennedy(5) 70
(A Sadik) *prom: jnd ldr 7th: rdn and wknd appr 3 out* **12/1**

5m 38.2s (-16.40) **Going Correction** -0.60s/f (Firm)
WFA 4 from 6yo+ 15lb 5 Ran SP% **110.9**
Speed ratings: **103,100,94,93,92** CSF £7.19 TOTE £2.10: £1.30, £1.70; EX 5.80.
Owner D A Johnson **Bred** Sir A J F O'Reilly **Trained** Nicholashayne, Devon

FOCUS
They went a fair pace despite the small field. A personal best from the winner with the race rated through the winner to his mark.

NOTEBOOK
Alikat(IRE) is fully exposed, but she was able to gain reward for some consistent efforts in more competitive events. The step back up to this more suitable trip suited her admirably and she stayed on well after getting to the leader two out. *(op 5-2)*
September Moon, responsible for setting the decent gallop, was put in her place from the penultimate flight. She was 6lb above her previous winning mark and the Handicapper is unlikely to cut her any slack after this sound effort. *(op 10-3)*
Lalagune(FR), returning from a summer break, during which she has left the Alan King yard, was soon detached from the others and she still looked sure to finish last going to the final flight, but she found her feet on the flat and passed two labouring rivals. She ought to be capable of a good deal better with this run under her belt. *Official explanation: trainer said, regarding the running and riding, her orders were for mare to be settled in the early stages to give her a chance to get home, adding that mare was outpaced before being asked for an effort at the end of the back straight and staying on past weakening horses in the home straight (op 22-1)*
Miss Shakira(IRE), who went up 11lb after winning at Perth, was outpaced by the leading pair in the back straight but rallied to look a threat on the long home turn. After running wide into the straight she soon dropped right away and she was caught for third near the line. She is a dual winner over three miles in Irish points but does not look to stay the trip over hurdles, and easier ground probably suits her too. *Official explanation: jockey said mare was unsuited by the good to firm ground and 3m trip (op 11-8 tchd 2-1)*
Good Man Again(IRE) was claimed from Evan Williams' yard after finishing runner-up in a seller last time. Without the customary tongue tie, and with first-time blinkers replacing a visor, he was a spent force on the long run round to the home turn. *(op 10-1)*

1728 NEW SEASON H'CAP CHASE (19 fncs) 3m
4:30 (4:30) (Class 3) (0-115,113) 5-Y-O+
£4,750 (£1,801; £900; £409; £204; £122)

Form RPR

-321 **1** **Harry's Dream**[7] 1657 8-11-12 113 RJohnson 127+
(P J Hobbs) *hld up in tch: chalng whn blnd bdly 3 out: rallied to ld flat: all out* **4/1**[1]

0-12 **2** shd **Galtee View (IRE)**[8] 1639 7-10-8 95 7ex (p) PMoloney 104+
(Evan Williams) *hld up: hdwy 14th: led after 3 out: hrd rdn and hdd flat: r.o* **9/2**[2]

2611 **3** nk **Tudor King (IRE)**[7] 1652 11-10-4 91 GLee 100+
(Andrew Turnell) *a.p: rdn 4 out: ev ch fr 3 out: r.o flat* **6/1**

4554 **4** 4 **Judaic Ways**[34] 1446 11-9-9 87 oh7 TGreenway(5) 92+
(H D Daly) *hld up and bhd: hdwy after 15th: sn rdn: swtchd rt after 3 out: no ex flat* **16/1**

5 10 **Casadei (IRE)**[15] 1574 6-10-3 93 (t) DFO'Regan(3) 87
(T G McCourt, Ire) *bhd: rdn after 15th: nvr trbld ldrs* **16/1**

4123 **6** 2½ **Tommy Spar**[39] 1412 5-10-13 102 APMcCoy 100+
(P Bowen) *hld up in mid-div: hdwy 14th: rdn appr 4 out: hmpd 2 out: btn whn mstke last* **8/1**

6-65 **7** dist **Tribal Dancer (IRE)**[154] 311 11-10-4 91 SThomas —
(Miss Venetia Williams) *prom: hit 12th: bdly hmpd 13th: nt rcvr: sn t.o* **7/1**

6300 **8** 7 **Montreal (FR)**[19] 1550 8-11-10 111 (p) TJMurphy —
(M C Pipe) *a bhd: lost tch fr 15th: t.o* **20/1**

20-P **F** **Free Gift**[25] 1489 7-11-8 109 AThornton 112+
(R H Alner) *led tl after 3 out: 3rd whn fell 2 out* **5/1**[3]

UP60 **F** **Excellent Vibes (IRE)**[22] 1511 7-10-10 97 (b) CLlewellyn —
(N A Twiston-Davies) *chsd ldr tl rdn 12th: prom whn fell 13th* **33/1**

5m 53.9s (-18.20) **Going Correction** -0.60s/f (Firm)
WFA 5 from 6yo+ 2lb 10 Ran SP% **112.2**
Speed ratings: **106,105,105,104,101 100,—,—,—,—** CSF £22.10 CT £104.33 TOTE £4.50: £1.80, £2.00, £1.90; EX 16.70.
Owner Peter Partridge **Bred** P Partridge And R M Kellow **Trained** Withycombe, Somerset

FOCUS
An ordinary handicap which produced a cracking finish. The winner has been rated as value for 5l and the placed horses ran pretty much to their marks.

NOTEBOOK
Harry's Dream ◆, back over fences after landing the odds in a novices' hurdle last time, did remarkably well to win after surviving a diabolical blunder when challenging three from home. He was only third over the final fence but rallied gamely under a fine ride to edge ahead on the run-in. Stamina is his forte and he is probably capable of better still, although he will be put away when the ground turns against him. *(op 7-2 tchd 10-3)*
Galtee View(IRE) was 3lb well-in under his penalty and ran a third good race in the space of ten days. He should certainly remain competitive when his new mark kicks in. *(op 4-1 tchd 5-1 in places)*
Tudor King(IRE) was able to race off the same mark as when gaining the second of back-to-back wins last week and he went down fighting. Remarkably at his age, he appears to be better than ever, but he is due to go up 2lb to a career-high mark now. *(op 5-1)*

Judaic Ways has struggled for form of late, but he reserves his best for this track and he ran a better race from 7lb out of the weights. *(tchd 14-1)*
Casadei(IRE), a raider from Ireland, could never quite get into the action.
Tommy Spar was held when hampered by a faller at the second last and was allowed to finish in his own time. *(tchd 17-2)*
Excellent Vibes(IRE) unfortunately sustained an injury when falling. *(op 25-1)*
Free Gift made a good deal of the running but he had been headed prior to coming down at the second last. This prolific winning pointer has yet to find his feet under Rules but probably deserves another chance. *(op 25-1)*

1729 LUDLOW RACING PARTNERSHIP JUVENILE MAIDEN HURDLE (9 hdls) 2m

5:05 (5:07) (Class 4) 3-Y-O £3,451 (£1,062; £531; £265)

Form RPR
1 **Kristinor (FR)**[17] 3-11-0 .... PHide 89+
(G L Moore) *hld up in mid-div: hdwy appr 3 out: led and hit last: pushed out* **11/1**
2 *1 ½* **Paparaazi (IRE)**[26] 3-11-0 .... RJohnson 85+
(R A Fahey) *hld up: mstke 1st: hdwy appr 5th: led and j.rt 3 out: swvd lft 2 out: hdd last: hrd rdn: nt qckn* **7/4**[1]
34 3 *shd* **Dramatic Review (IRE)**[22] 1512 3-11-0 .... (t) APMcCoy 85+
(P C Haslam) *chsd ldr: led briefly 4th: rdn and ev ch last: nt qckn* **5/2**[2]
0 4 *5* **Lorna Dune**[5] 1679 3-10-4 .... ONelmes(3) 72
(J G M O'Shea) *hld up: hdwy after 6th: one pce fr 2 out* **40/1**
R054 5 *2 ½* **Josear**[12] 1594 3-11-0 .... MBradburne 77
(C J Down) *hld up and bhd: blnd 4th: hdwy appr 3 out: no further prog fr 2 out* **12/1**
40 6 *6* **Piran (IRE)**[12] 1594 3-11-0 .... (b) AThornton 72+
(R H Alner) *prom tl wknd 2 out* **15/2**[3]
P0 7 *1 ½* **Lara's Girl**[18] 1563 3-10-0 .... WPKavanagh(7) 62
(K G Wingrove) *nvr nr ldrs* **200/1**
8 *½* **Colonel Bilko (IRE)**[27] 3-11-0 .... (t) NFehily 69
(Miss S J Wilton) *t.k.h in rr: hdwy appr 3 out: wknd approachng 2 out* **10/1**
0 9 *2* **Jamaaron**[12] 1594 3-11-0 .... PJBrennan 67
(W G M Turner) *hld up in tch: wknd appr 2 out* **16/1**
U0 10 *9* **Bainoona**[12] 1594 3-10-2 .... (v[1]) LStephens(5) 51
(Evan Williams) *led: hit 3rd: hdd 4th: sn lost pl* **40/1**
P0 11 *½* **Keepasharplookout (IRE)**[34] 1441 3-11-0 .... JPByrne 57
(C W Moore) *racd wd: hdwy 4th: led appr 6th: hdd and wkng whn mstke 3 out* **100/1**
12 *5* **Look At The Stars (IRE)**[82] 3-11-0 .... DRDennis 52
(R Hollinshead) *mid-div: j. slowly 5th: bhd fr 6th* **20/1**
P 13 *dist* **Weet N Measures**[65] 1190 3-11-0 .... RGreene —
(T Wall) *plld hrd in rr: t.o whn mstke last* **66/1**
00 P **Ardasnails (IRE)**[18] 1563 3-11-0 .... (b) SCurran —
(K G Wingrove) *a bhd: t.o whn p.u bef 3 out* **150/1**
30 P **Optimum (IRE)**[47] 1339 3-11-0 .... RThornton —
(J T Stimpson) *t.k.h: prom to 6th: t.o whn p.u bef 3 out* **50/1**
0 P **Gogetter Girl**[18] 1563 3-10-7 .... (b) OMcPhail —
(J Gallagher) *hld up in tch: led after 4th tl appr 6th: sn wknd: t.o whn p.u bef 3 out* **66/1**

3m 45.8s (-6.50) **Going Correction** -0.60s/f (Firm) 16 Ran SP% **124.4**
Speed ratings: **92,91,91,88,87 84,83,83,82,77 77,75,—,—,— —** CSF £31.12 TOTE £8.70: £3.60, £1.40, £1.30; EX 38.90.
Owner A Grinter **Bred** S Richmond-Watson **Trained** Woodingdean, E Sussex

FOCUS
A modest time, even for a race like this. This looked a pretty moderate event of its type and most of these will struggle to make their mark over hurdles.

NOTEBOOK
Kristinor(FR), an inconsistent maiden on the Flat, latterly in headgear, always travelled well on this hurdling debut and won cosily under a confident ride. He might be up to defying a penalty before the better juveniles appear. *(op 9-1)*
Paparaazi(IRE), rated 72 on the Flat, showed ability on this hurdling debut but, after showing ahead, he jinked markedly going to the penultimate flight and was no match for the winner from the last. *(op 15-8 tchd 2-1)*
Dramatic Review(IRE) ran another sound race and looks the best guide to the form. He was slightly inconvenienced when the runner-up altered course going to the second last but that cannot be put down as an excuse. *(op 3-1)*
Lorna Dune, soundly beaten in a better race on her recent hurdles debut, was keeping on in the latter stages to finish best of the rest. *(op 66-1)*
Josearprobably ran to a similar level as when fourth at Fontwell earlier in the month. *(op 14-1)*
Colonel Bilko(IRE) showed a modicum of promise on his hurdling debut, but this two-year-old winner failed to get home. *(op 20-1)*

1730 LUDLOWRACECOURSE.CO.UK INTERMEDIATE OPEN NATIONAL HUNT FLAT RACE 2m

5:40 (5:40) (Class 6) 4-6-Y-O £2,385 (£734; £367; £183)

Form RPR
1 **Tell Henry (IRE)**[199] 4630 5-11-4 .... ChristianWilliams 94+
(Evan Williams) *plld hrd in rr: hdwy to ld after 2f: clr after 4f: r.o* **6/5**[1]
4 2 *7* **Sweep Home**[84] 1048 5-11-4 .... APMcCoy 86+
(P Bowen) *chsd wnr after 2f: rdn whn hung lft bnd 4f out: no imp* **13/2**[3]
05-2 3 *1 ¾* **Chunky Lad**[9] 1635 5-11-4 .... PJBrennan 82
(W G M Turner) *hld up and bhd: hdwy over 4f out: edgd lft ins fnl f: one pce* **20/1**
4 *shd* **Azure Wings (IRE)** 5-10-4 .... SCrawford(7) 75
(K C Bailey) *chsd ldrs: rdn and outpcd over 5f out: no real prog fnl 3f* **20/1**
5 *3 ½* **Goodleigh Buster** 5-11-4 .... TScudamore 79
(W S Kittow) *led 2f: outpcd 5f out: n.d after* **50/1**
6 *1 ½* **Strange Days (IRE)**[221] 5-10-11 .... RSpate(7) 77
(Mrs K Waldron) *prom tl wknd over 4f out* **14/1**
0 7 *11* **Fairlight Express (IRE)**[19] 1554 5-10-13 .... PCO'Neill(5) 66
(P L Gilligan) *hung lft bnd 3f out: a bhd* **10/1**
8 *dist* **Valleyofthekings (IRE)** 4-11-4 .... LAspell —
(O Sherwood) *a bhd: t.o fnl 4f* **11/4**[2]
00 9 *22* **Jane's Rug Rat**[32] 1459 6-10-11 .... (b[1]) TMessenger(7) —
(C L Popham) *a bhd: t.o fnl 6f* **100/1**

3m 45.0s (-7.20) **Going Correction** -0.60s/f (Firm)
WFA 4 from 5yo+ 13lb 9 Ran SP% **113.7**
Speed ratings: **94,90,89,89,87 87,81,—,—** CSF £9.04 TOTE £2.30: £1.40, £1.70, £2.20; EX 10.30 Place 6 £7.30, Place 5 £5.21.
Owner F Jeffers **Bred** Bill Ronayne **Trained** Cowbridge, Vale Of Glamorgan

FOCUS
A weak and uncompetitive bumper, rated around the first two. The field stood still for seven seconds after the tape went up.

NOTEBOOK
Tell Henry(IRE), placed twice from three attempts in Ireland, made a successful debut for this yard. Pulling his way into the lead after a couple of furlongs, he settled better once in front and stayed on much too well for his only real challenger. He has shown that he handles easy ground and has the size to make a hurdler, although he is clearly not a straightforward ride. *(op 6-4)*
Sweep Home, fourth on his debut back in the summer in a race which has not worked out, lost touch with the winner when running a little wide into the straight but plugged on to claim the runner-up spot. *Official explanation: jockey said gelding finished lame (op 6-1 tchd 11-2)*
Chunky Lad, beaten a similar distance in another weak race last week, took a remote third place entering the home straight. *(op 18-1 tchd 22-1)*
Azure Wings(IRE) is out of an unraced half-sister to smart chaser Observe and high-class hurdler Minorettes Girl (dam of Shotgun Willy and Mini Sensation). Sold cheaply last year, she showed only a modicum of promise on this debut. *(op 12-1)*
Goodleigh Buster is out of a winning pointer. *(op 33-1)*
Strange Days(IRE) landed a two and a half-mile maiden point in March on his only run between the flags. *(op 9-1)*
Valleyofthekings(IRE), who cost 21,000gns, is out of a mare who showed little on this track but is a half-sister to smart two-mile chaser Sound Reveille. He was sent off second favourite for this debut but showed nothing. *(op 3-1 tchd 10-3)*
T/Plt: £14.30 to a £1 stake. Pool: £38,817.60. 1,974.30 winning tickets. T/Qpdt: £7.60 to a £1 stake. Pool: £2,460.80. 237.30 winning tickets. KH

1731 - 1734a (Foreign Racing) - See Raceform Interactive

1630 HUNTINGDON (R-H)

Saturday, October 15

OFFICIAL GOING: Hurdle course - good to firm (good in places); chase course - good (good to firm in places)
After a dry spell 16mm water was put on the track over the previous two days resulting in 'lovely jumping ground, just on the fast side of good'.
Wind: Almost nil. Weather: Fine, sunny and warm

1735 WILLIAMHILLPOKER.COM H'CAP CHASE (19 fncs) 3m

2:20 (2:22) (Class 2) (0-145,136) 5-Y-0+£13,436 (£4,134; £2,067; £1,033)

Form RPR
231- 1 **Run For Paddy**[224] 4167 9-11-7 131 .... NFehily 138
(M Pitman) *hld up in rr: hdwy 3 out: styd on to ld after last: r.o* **6/1**[3]
1FP- 2 *2* **Backbeat (IRE)**[213] 4395 8-11-12 136 .... GLee 143+
(J Howard Johnson) *w ldrs: led 7th: hit 9th: blnd 14th: hdd next: disp ld appr 2 out: styd on same pce fnl 150yds* **14/1**
1UPP 3 *hd* **Mr Fluffy**[55] 1270 8-10-13 123 .... WHutchinson 128
(A W Carroll) *jnd ldrs 9th: led 15th: hdaded after last: no ex* **66/1**
-063 4 *5* **Cameron Bridge (IRE)**[20] 1561 9-11-4 128 .... RJohnson 129+
(P J Hobbs) *chsd ldrs: weakenening whn hit last* **20/1**
610- 5 *½* **Inca Trail (IRE)**[175] 4984 9-11-11 135 .... (b) RWalsh 136+
(P F Nicholls) *hld up: stdy hdwy 13th: upsides whn hit last: rdn and fnd v little* **9/2**[2]
3101 6 *17* **Little Big Horse (IRE)**[21] 1550 9-11-7 131 .... DElsworth 117+
(Mrs S J Smith) *led to 3rd: chsd ldrs: wknd 3 out* **9/2**[2]
5313 7 *6* **Swansea Bay**[49] 1342 9-10-12 122 .... AThornton 101+
(P Bowen) *in rr: hdwy whn blnd 12th and next: sn lost pl* **14/1**
P-PP 8 *½* **The Bandit (IRE)**[7] 1676 8-11-1 125 .... (t) BFenton 101
(Miss E C Lavelle) *prom: lost pl 3rd: bhd fr 13th* **9/1**
2-2F 9 *dist* **Harrycone Lewis**[146] 468 7-11-1 125 .... (b) WMarston —
(Mrs P Sly) *blnd 1st: led 3rd to 7th: mstke 10th: sn lost pl: t.o 14th* **12/1**
1F11 F **Celtic Boy (IRE)**[23] 1531 7-11-6 130 .... APMcCoy —
(P Bowen) *sn chsng ldrs: cl 4th whn fell 10th* **10/3**[1]

6m 2.60s (-9.70) **Going Correction** -0.10s/f (Good) 10 Ran SP% **111.0**
Speed ratings: **112,111,111,109,109 103,101,101,—,—** CSF £78.24 CT £4739.88 TOTE £6.10: £2.20, £4.10, £14.30; EX 62.50.
Owner B Perkins **Bred** D E S Smith **Trained** Upper Lambourn, Berks

FOCUS
A fair handicap run at a strong pace and five were in a line going to the final fence. The race has been rated through the winner with the placed horses stepping up on what they have previously achieved over fences.

NOTEBOOK
Run For Paddy, who has a history of breaking blood-vessels, has gone well when fresh in the past. Given a patient ride, he stuck to his guns and in the end ran out a decisive winner. *(op 11-2 tchd 9-2)*
Backbeat(IRE), who looked very fit, is not the most natural of jumpers but in the end he was just outpaced by the winner. Softer ground will slow the pace and offset his poor jumping technique. *(op 12-1 tchd 16-1)*
Mr Fluffy, pulled up over hurdles on his two most recent starts, has changed stables. Lacking any real experience over fences, after going on five out he was only found out on the run-in. *(op 40-1)*
Cameron Bridge(IRE), back on a winning mark, was stepping up in trip and his stamina looked at a very low ebb when he clouted the final fence. *(op 18-1)*
Inca Trail(IRE) looked fit and as usual travelled well, but he had already spat out the dummy when he hit the last. *(tchd 5-1)*
Little Big Horse(IRE), 8lb higher, does not seem the same force away from his beloved Market Rasen. *(tchd 4-1)*
The Bandit(IRE), pulled up on his last three starts, was declared with a tongue strap for the first time. It took a deal of fitting and had to be refitted at the start. He soon dropped out and it was reported that he did not finish the race with the strap in place. *(tchd 17-2)*
Harrycone Lewis *Official explanation: trainer said gelding bled from nose (op 14-1 tchd 16-1)*
Celtic Boy(IRE) was on the deck with over a circuit to go. *(op 7-2 tchd 3-1)*

1736 WILLIAMHILLGAMES.COM BEGINNERS' CHASE (16 fncs) 2m 4f 110y

3:00 (3:00) (Class 3) 4-Y-0+ £5,626 (£1,828; £984)

Form RPR
031- 1 **Napolitain (FR)**[177] 4943 4-10-7 .... RWalsh 111+
(P F Nicholls) *chsd ldr fr 3rd: hit 7th: led on bit 2 out: clr last: v easily* **8/13**[1]
2- 2 *26* **Rare Society (IRE)**[287] 3143 7-11-7 .... DElsworth 110+
(Mrs S J Smith) *led: hit 13th: hedaded 2 out: no ch w wnr whn j.lft last* **33/1**[3]
POOP 3 *dist* **Foreign Field (FR)**[22] 1540 6-11-7 64 .... (b) HOliver —
(Mrs Tracey Barfoot-Saunt) *tubed: dropped rr 8th: t.o 11th: btn 95 l* **66/1**
/12- F **Steppes Of Gold (IRE)**[302] 2869 8-11-7 .... APMcCoy 98
(Jonjo O'Neill) *hit 7th: jnd wnr 10th: mstke 12th: hung rt: hrd rdn after 3 out: sn wknd: 8 l 3rd whn tk heavy fall 2 out* **13/8**[2]

5m 9.60s (3.50) **Going Correction** -0.10s/f (Good)
WFA 4 from 6yo+ 14lb 4 Ran SP% **104.4**
Speed ratings: **89,79,—,—** CSF £10.53 TOTE £1.50; EX 6.60.

The Form Book, Raceform Ltd, Compton, RG20 6NL

Owner The Stewart Family **Bred** Francois Cottin **Trained** Ditcheat, Somerset

FOCUS
With Steppes Of Gold a major disappointment this was nothing more than a rewarding school round for the promising Napolitain which is reflected by the moderate time.

NOTEBOOK
Napolitain(FR) ◆, rated 129 over hurdles, jumped well on the whole and made this look very simple indeed. He looks a useful recruit. *(op 4-6 tchd 8-11 in places)*
Rare Society(IRE) led on sufferance and totally outclassed by the winner, his rider's sole objective at the last was to get him over safely. *(op 22-1)*
Foreign Field(FR), poor in points and novices' hurdle races, was pulled up on his debut over regulation fences. Now tubed, this may well prove to be the big pay-day of his career. *(op 80-1 tchd 100-1)*
Steppes Of Gold(IRE), runner-up on his chasing debut in December, has changed stables. He would not have a cut at his fences and hanging badly left under severe pressure, was well beaten off when he took a heavy fall two out. After this he has a lot to prove. *(op 6-4)*

1737 LEARN TO PLAY POKER AT WILLIAMHILLPOKER.COM JUVENILE MAIDEN HURDLE (8 hdls) 2m 110y
3:35 (3:35) (Class 3) 3-Y-O
£4,466 (£1,694; £847; £385; £192; £115)

Form	Pos	Dist	Horse	Jockey	RPR
0	1		**Voir Dire**[42] [1397] 3-10-9	RYoung(3)	90+
			(Mrs P N Dutfield) *trckd ldrs: led 5th: hung bdly lft run-in: kpt on*	**8/1**	
630	2	3	**Royal Wedding**[14] [1594] 3-10-12	RWalsh	86+
			(N J Gifford) *led to 5th: rdn and wl outpcd next: wnt mod 3rd 2 out: tk 2nd after last: styd on wl: nt rch wnr*	**7/2**[1]	
2	3	2 ½	**Looking Great (USA)**[14] [1594] 3-10-12	APMcCoy	84
			(R F Johnson Houghton) *sn trcking ldrs: wnt 2nd 3 out: no ex run-in*	**9/2**[2]	
	4	8	**Corker**[42] 3-10-12	JamesDavies	76
			(D B Feek) *sn bhd: hdwy 3 out: styd on between last 2*	**9/1**	
	5	½	**Able Charlie (GER)**[26] 3-10-12	HOliver	75
			(Mrs Tracey Barfoot-Saunt) *rr-div: hdwy 4th: hit 3 out: kpt on: nvr rchd ldrs*	**14/1**	
4	6	5	**Inchcape Rock**[7] [1679] 3-10-12	VSlattery	70
			(J G M O'Shea) *rr-div: sme hdwy 3 out: nvr a factor*	**9/1**	
	7	nk	**Accomplish**[14] 3-10-5	GLee	63
			(W J Haggas) *in tch: effrt 3 out: nvr nr ldrs*	**13/2**[3]	
	8	nk	**Flower Haven**[12] 3-10-5	SCurran	62
			(M J Gingell) *chsd ldrs: wknd appr 2 out*	**66/1**	
	9	1 ¼	**Wozani Dancer (IRE)**[48] 3-10-12	PMoloney	68
			(G A Huffer) *towards rr: sme hdwy appr 2 out: no ch whn hit last*	**22/1**	
	10	1	**Briannie (IRE)**[21] 3-9-12	(p) RLucey-Butler(7)	60
			(P Butler) *a in rr: nvr a factor*	**50/1**	
	11	4	**Ballycroy Girl (IRE)**[30] 3-10-0 ow2	BWharfe(7)	58
			(A Bailey) *sn bhd*	**28/1**	
	12	19	**Vettorious**[35] 3-10-12	WMarston	44
			(Mrs P Sly) *led: mstke 4th: hdd next: wknd after 3 out*	**12/1**	
F0	13	3	**Obstreperous Way**[14] [1594] 3-10-12	JAMcCarthy	41
			(P R Chamings) *in tch to 5th: sn lost pl*	**40/1**	
0	14	13	**Galaxy Dancer (IRE)**[20] [1563] 3-10-12	LAspell	28
			(Mrs L Wadham) *hld up towards rr: hdwy 4th: effrt 3f out: sn rdn and wknd*	**12/1**	
	P		**Kristikhab (IRE)**[75] 3-10-12	NPMulholland	—
			(A Berry) *prom: blnd 2nd: lost pl 4th: sn bhd: t.o whn p.u bef 2 out*	**100/1**	

3m 56.8s (1.10) **Going Correction** -0.10s/f (Good) 15 Ran SP% **121.6**
Speed ratings: **93,91,90,86,86 84,83,83,83,82 80,71,70,64,—** CSF £35.33 TOTE £6.80: £2.60, £2.00, £1.60; EX 56.60.
Owner Mrs Nerys Dutfield **Bred** Mrs Nerys Dutfield **Trained** Axmouth, Devon
■ Stewards' Enquiry : B Wharfe seven-day ban: failed to take all reasonable and permissible measures to obtain best possible placing (Oct 26-Nov 1)

FOCUS
A modest juvenile hurdle run at a very steady pace with the winner attempting to throw it away and the runner-up needing a stiffer test. The runner-up and the third set the standard.

NOTEBOOK
Voir Dire, one of the few in the line-up with any real substance, was a different proposition this time but did his best to throw it away hanging badly left on the run-in. *(op 11-1)*
Royal Wedding, without the tongue tie this time, set off infront but found himself serious tapped for toe on the final turn. To his credit he stuck to his task but the errant winner had flown. *(op 4-1)*
Looking Great(USA) travelled nicely and went in pursuit of the winner but was never going to get in a serious blow. *(op 5-1)*
Corker soon struggled and was out of contention until staying on late in the day. *(op 8-1)*
Able Charlie(GER) was trying to close when he flattened the third last. A winner over seven furlongs on the level, stamina did not seem to be a real issue. *(op 12-1)*
Flower Haven, one of the few in the line up with any substance, was a different proposition this time.

1738 PLAY BLACKJACK AT WILLIAMHILLCASINO.COM HURDLE (8 hdls) 2m 110y
4:10 (4:11) (Class 2) 4-Y-O+ **£8,801** (£2,708; £1,354; £677)

Form	Pos	Dist	Horse	Jockey	RPR
51-4	1		**Rooster Booster**[161] [208] 11-11-8 160	RJohnson	150+
			(P J Hobbs) *trecked ldr: led on bit 2 out: pushed clr run-in*	**7/4**[1]	
11-6	2	5	**Genghis (IRE)**[35] [208] 6-11-8 145	GLee	145
			(P Bowen) *led: t.k.h eraly: hit 2nd: hdd 2 out: 2 l down whn hit last: sn wl outpcd by wnr*	**7/4**[1]	
13-4	3	28	**Hasty Prince**[13] [1621] 7-11-8 157	APMcCoy	135+
			(Jonjo O'Neill) *wnt mod 3rd 4th: hit next: blnd next: nvr on terms*	**2/1**[2]	
0-00	4	29	**My Sharp Grey**[10] [1645] 6-10-7 93	RThornton	95+
			(J Gallagher) *ib last fr 4th: sn detached*	**100/1**[3]	

3m 47.5s (-8.20) **Going Correction** -0.10s/f (Good) 4 Ran SP% **107.1**
Speed ratings: **115,112,99,85** CSF £5.19 TOTE £2.20; EX 5.30.
Owner Terry Warner **Bred** Mrs E Mitchell **Trained** Withycombe, Somerset

FOCUS
Although not needing to run to his best, Rooster Booster's flame still burns bright and he soon put careless jumper Genghis in his place.

NOTEBOOK
Rooster Booster, who looked on very good terms with himself, thoroughly enjoyed this and, once in front, never looked like stopping. His best days are clearly behind him now but he will continue to thrill his many followers, and he was given a hero's reception afterwards. *(op 11-8 tchd 9-4)*
Genghis(IRE), after an outing on the level, looked fighting fit. He fought his rider early on then when allowed to stride on his jumping was anything but fault free. In the end the winner, rated a stone higher, simply toyed with him. *(op 2-1 tchd 13-8)*
Hasty Prince looked very fit indeed yet was already struggling badly when he ploughed through the third last. He lacks the substance to make a serious impact over fences. *(op 5-2 tchd 15-8)*
My Sharp Grey, totally outclassed, just had to complete to pick up fourth place prizemoney. *(op 66-1)*

1739 WILLIAM HILL POKER GRAND PRIX H'CAP CHASE (12 fncs) 2m 110y
4:45 (4:45) (Class 2) (0-140,135) 5-Y-O+ **£10,023** (£3,084; £1,542; £771)

Form	Pos	Dist	Horse	Jockey	RPR
2U2	1		**Bill's Echo**[8] [1666] 6-9-13 113	WKennedy(5)	130+
			(R C Guest) *hld up in last: stdy hdwy appr 2 out: led between last 2: sn clr: drvn out*	**7/2**[2]	
3101	2	7	**Wet Lips (AUS)**[8] [1666] 7-10-9 125	(bt) PMerrigan(7)	137+
			(R C Guest) *chsd ldrs: bmpd 3rd: hmpd 2 out: styd on to go 2nd after last: no ch w wnr*	**5/1**[3]	
062-	3	4	**Cobbet (CZE)**[293] [2976] 9-11-1 124	JMMaguire	131+
			(T R George) *chsd ldrs: 4th and one pce whn hit last*	**9/1**	
10-5	4	¾	**Palua**[147] [452] 8-11-11 134	BFenton	139
			(Miss E C Lavelle) *w ldr: led 7th tl between last 2: one pce*	**20/1**	
10-4	5	3	**Multeen River (IRE)**[22] [1542] 9-11-1 124	APMcCoy	129+
			(Jonjo O'Neill) *hld up towards rr: sme hdwy whn hit 3 out: kpt on fr next: nvr trbld ldrs*	**5/1**[3]	
U401	6	2	**Magic Sky (FR)**[22] [1542] 5-10-12 128	LHeard(7)	131+
			(P F Nicholls) *bmpd 1st: in rr whn j.lft 8th: one pce whn hmpd 2 out: hung rt and nvr a threat*	**5/2**[1]	
1PP-	F		**Tanikos (FR)**[181] [4880] 6-11-2 125	MFoley	130+
			(N J Henderson) *led to 7th: w ldr whn fell 2 out*	**8/1**	
4F-5	P		**Bonus Bridge (IRE)**[161] [219] 10-11-12 135	RThornton	—
			(H D Daly) *j.lft: chsd ldrs: drvn along 8th: sn wknd: t.o whn p.u bef 2 out*	**16/1**	

4m 4.70s (-4.60) **Going Correction** -0.10s/f (Good) 8 Ran SP% **115.9**
Speed ratings: **106,102,100,100,99 98,—,—** CSF £22.04 CT £144.92 TOTE £4.20: £1.10, £1.90, £2.30; EX 13.60.
Owner Burns Partnership **Bred** Miss Frances Baker **Trained** Brancepeth, Co Durham

FOCUS
A fair handicap chase, although just ordinary form, but a career best over fences from the winner with the third and fourth setting the standard.

NOTEBOOK
Bill's Echo, meeting his stablemate on 6lb better terms, found this much easier track much more in his favour and he had this won before he knew it. He has never lacked ability but needs everything to fall into place, just as it did here. *(op 13-2)*

Wet Lips(AUS), 6lb higher, was off the bridle when hampered two out and the winner left him for dead in a matter of strides. *(op 13-2)*

Cobbet(CZE), absent since Boxing Day, has run well when fresh in the past and is not sure to improve for the outing. *(op 13-2)*

Palua, absent since May, had the visor discarded and with the ground to suit ran a respectable race but perhaps he is better going the other way round. *(op 12-1)*

Multeen River(IRE), fighting fit, would not really have a cut at his fences and was never really in the argument. *(op 11-2)*

Magic Sky(FR), 6lb higher, never looked that happy and never looked like responding to his rider's urgings. He may be better going right-handed. *(op 3-1)*

Bonus Bridge(IRE) *Official explanation: jockey said the gelding ran flat (op 15-2)*

Tanikos(FR), who has gone well when fresh in the past cut out the running to halfway and was still bang in contention when crashing out. He would have finished third at best. *(op 15-2)*

1740 PLAY ROULETTE AT WILLIAMHILLCASINO.COM NOVICES' HURDLE (LISTED RACE) (8 hdls) 2m 110y
5:20 (5:20) (Class 1) 4-Y-O+ **£11,106** (£4,257; £2,128; £1,018)

Form	Pos	Dist	Horse	Jockey	RPR
1234	1		**Darrias (GER)**[7] [1677] 4-11-8 132	(t) RWalsh	129+
			(P F Nicholls) *trckd ldng pair: led 2 out: hit last: styd on wl*	**5/4**[1]	
	2	5	**Masafi (IRE)**[42] 4-11-0	GLee	118+
			(J Howard Johnson) *trckd ldr: hit 6th: sn led: hdd and stmbld 2 out: kpt on same pce*	**5/4**[1]	
5-	3	9	**Kylebeg Dancer (IRE)**[6] [1699] 4-10-13	(t) KHadnett	105
			(T Hogan, Ire) *led: hit 5th and next: hdd after 3 out: one pce*	**9/1**[2]	
6-	4	18	**Aoninch**[17] [1975] 5-10-7	RGreene	81
			(Mrs P N Dutfield) *hld up off pce: kpt on fr 3 out: nvr on terms*	**66/1**	
400-	5	1 ¾	**Simonovski (USA)**[196] [4691] 4-11-0 110	JAMcCarthy	86
			(S C Burrough) *bhd and pushed along 4th: nvr on terms*	**40/1**	
6-	6	½	**Sir Haydn**[22] [1811] 5-11-0	(v) LAspell	86
			(J R Jenkins) *in tch: rdn and lost pl after 5th*	**100/1**	
5522	P		**Convent Girl (IRE)**[96] [959] 5-10-7 98	RYoung	—
			(Mrs P N Dutfield) *in rr: mod 5th whn p.u bef 2 out*	**20/1**[3]	

3m 51.3s (-4.40) **Going Correction** -0.10s/f (Good) 7 Ran SP% **108.6**
Speed ratings: **106,103,99,90,90 89,—** CSF £2.70 TOTE £2.10: £1.30, £1.30; EX 4.50 Place 6 £114.90, Place 5 £11.54.
Owner Peter Hart **Bred** Gestut Rottgen **Trained** Ditcheat, Somerset

FOCUS
A sub-standard Listed novices' hurdle but it was run at a sound pace and the exposed winner is useful and the best guide to the form, while the second will progress.

NOTEBOOK
Darrias(GER), who keeps his form well, was quite happy to give the leading pair some rope. Landing in front two out, his rider left nothing at all to chance. *(op 6-4 tchd 7-4, 15-8 in places)*

Masafi(IRE) ◆, a winner of eight races on the Flat and rated 100, looked very fit but carried no bloom at all. He took quite a grip in second place and, after showing ahead for a few strides, was getting easily the worst of the argument when he stumbled on landing two out. The outing will have done him a power of good and he looks sure to make his mark, but how far he climbs remains to be seen. *(op 6-5 tchd Evens)*

Kylebeg Dancer(IRE), a dual winner on the Flat this summer and in good form over hurdles in Ireland, was ridden by a conditional unable to claim his allowance. He set a swinging pace but in the end was totally outclassed. *(op 7-1 tchd 6-1)*

Aoninch, rated 66 on the Flat, was far too keen on her only previous try over hurdles and here she seemed to be ridden with the idea of teaching her to settle. *(op 33-1)*

Simonovski(USA), 13th in last season's Triumph Hurdle, seems to be going backwards. *(op 25-1)*

T/Plt: £137.90 to a £1 stake. Pool: £40,463.40. 214.15 winning tickets. T/Qpdt: £14.40 to a £1 stake. Pool: £2,324.85. 118.85 winning tickets. WG

[1454] STRATFORD (L-H)
Saturday, October 15

OFFICIAL GOING: Chase course - good; hurdle course - good to firm (good in places)

The first fence in the home straight was omitted because of false ground.
Wind: Almost nil. Weather: Hazy sunshine.

1741 TOTEPLACEPOT BEGINNERS' CHASE (FOR THE ANTHONY ROBINSON MEMORIAL TROPHY) (15 fncs 3 omitted) 3m
2:15 (2:15) (Class 3) 5-Y-0+ **£5,434** (£1,672; £836; £418)

Form				RPR
1/P-	1		**Iceberge (IRE)**[398] [1418] 9-11-0 105 ... DRDennis 3/1[2] (Ian Williams) *a.p: led 3 out: hung lft appr last: drvn out*	111+
05-F	2	1 1/4	**Jiver (IRE)**[7] [1678] 6-11-0 110 ... TScudamore 2/1[1] (M Scudamore) *chsd ldr: led 8th: rdn and hdd 3 out: ev ch last: nt qckn*	110+
	3	14	**Captain Mac (IRE)**[25] [1504] 6-10-7 96 ... BCByrnes(7) 4/1[3] (E McNamara, Ire) *hld up: reminders after 5th: hdwy 8th: rdn 3 out: wkng whn hung lft sn after last*	99+
	4	11	**Mister Bean (FR)**[972] 8-10-7 ... MrSWaley-Cohen(7) 3/1[2] (R Waley-Cohen) *hld up: hdwy 8th: rdn 3 out: wknd after 2 out*	91+
/6P-	5	dist	**Joey Dunlop (IRE)**[14] 11-10-9 ow2 ... MrSClements(7) 20/1 (J Clements, Ire) *wl bhd most of way: reminders after 5th: t.o fr 10th*	—
0-00	P		**Will Tell**[53] [1297] 7-10-11 ... (t) LVickers(3) 50/1 (S R Bowring) *led: sn clr: hdd 8th: wknd 9th: t.o 10th: p.u bef 3 out*	—

5m 53.6s (-8.60) **Going Correction** -0.20s/f (Good) 6 Ran SP% **110.1**
Speed ratings: **106,105,100,97,—** — CSF £9.44 TOTE £3.20: £1.70, £2.00; EX 7.70.
Owner Mcmahon (contractors Services) Ltd **Bred** Mrs M B Murphy **Trained** Portway, Worcs

FOCUS
There was little previous chase form to go on, but the race is rated through the third and the runner-up to his hurdles mark.

NOTEBOOK
Iceberge(IRE), who fractured a knee on his only start for Jonjo O'Neill, is now back with Ian Williams. Making a successful switch to fences, his trainer thinks he will be better for the race and his hurdling form suggests he will stay further. *(op 2-1)*
Jiver(IRE), another who stayed well over hurdles, had got no further than the fourth on his chasing debut at Chepstow a week earlier. He did not go down without a fight and this should have done his confidence a power of good. *(op 5-2)*
Captain Mac(IRE), who had hardly been setting the world alight over fences in Ireland, had yet to prove he stays three miles. *(op 7-2)*
Mister Bean(FR), ex-French-trained, had returned after a long lay-off to score impressively in a maiden open at Larkhill in January and finished second at Tweseldown the following month. he *was well beaten on this debut under Rules in Britain. Official explanation: vet said gelding finished lame (op 5-1)*

1742 TOTEPOOL AWAYBET (S) HURDLE (8 hdls 1 omitted) 2m 110y
2:50 (2:50) (Class 5) 4-7-Y-0 **£3,010** (£860; £430)

Form				RPR
1100	1		**Miss Lehman**[55] [1272] 7-10-8 94 ... MissSGaisford(7) 12/1 (J D Frost) *hld up and bhd: hdwy after 6th: swtchd rt and led flat: r.o wl*	92+
4613	2	2	**Honan (IRE)**[10] [1645] 6-10-7 96 ... (v) AGlassonbury(10) 9/4[1] (M C Pipe) *a.p: wnt 2nd 5th: led after 6th: sn clr: hrd rdn and faltering whn j. slowly last: hdd and no ex flat*	94+
00F	3	nk	**Urban Dream (IRE)**[2] [1724] 4-10-5 ... MrTJO'Brien(7) 66/1 (R A Farrant) *hld up and bhd: stdy hdwy 6th: sn rdn: kpt on flat*	86+
354/	4	3 1/2	**Four Eagles (USA)**[64] [1199] 7-10-12 ... RWalford 11/1 (D R C Elsworth) *hld up in mid-div: hdwy 4th: rdn after 6th: wknd flat*	81
04	5	10	**Head Boy**[12] [1565] 4-10-12 ... JEMoore 6/1[3] (S Dow) *hld up towards rr: hdwy 6th: sn rdn: wknd appr 2 out*	71
5-00	6	1 3/4	**Holly Walk**[7] [1235] 4-10-5 85 ... (v) ATinkler 14/1 (A G Juckes) *t.k.h: prom: chsd ldr 3rd to 5th: wkng whn mstke 2 out*	62
000P	7	1/2	**Simiola**[87] [1037] 6-10-0 75 ... MNicolls(5) 50/1 (S T Lewis) *hld up towards rr: sme hdwy after 4th: nvr bttr than mid-div*	62
00P-	8	3 1/2	**Dmitri**[37] [4639] 5-10-7 59 ... CHonour(5) 66/1 (J D Frost) *led: rdn and hdd after 6th: wknd appr 2 out*	65
3646	9	9	**Lucky Arthur (IRE)**[23] [1520] 4-9-12 78 ow3 ... CDThompson(10) 20/1 (Mrs L Williamson) *mstke 2nd: a bhd*	52
P1P/	10	2 1/2	**Itcanbedone Again (IRE)**[35] [908] 6-10-2 ... DJBoland(10) 7/1 (Ian Williams) *hld up in tch: rdn after 5th: wknd after 6th*	54
000-	11	1 1/4	**Imtihan (IRE)**[247] [3777] 6-11-8 105 ... DCrosse 16/1 (J G M O'Shea) *chsd ldr to 3rd: wknd 5th*	63
106	12	nk	**Jack Durrance (IRE)**[9] [1653] 5-10-5 83 ... EDehdashti(7) 10/1 (G A Ham) *hld up in tch: rdn after 5th: sn wknd*	52
4	13	14	**Fine Palette**[54] [1077] 5-10-12 ... (p) TJMurphy 5/1[2] (B J Llewellyn) *mstke 1st: a bhd*	38
0	14	dist	**Grey Admiral (USA)**[59] [1235] 4-10-9 ... CBolger(3) 50/1 (B R Johnson) *hld up in tch: lost pl 4th: t.o after 6th*	—

3m 53.4s (-5.00) **Going Correction** -0.45s/f (Good)
WFA 4 from 5yo+ 13lb 14 Ran SP% **123.6**
Speed ratings: **93,92,91,90,85 84,84,82,78,77 76,76,70,—** CSF £40.18 TOTE £12.50: £5.00, £1.60, £24.70; EX 22.50.The winner was bought in for 8,000gns.
Owner P A Tylor **Bred** Mrs M C Reveley **Trained** Scorriton, Devon
■ Stewards' Enquiry : A Glassonbury two-day ban: used whip in the incorrect place and with excessive frequency (Oct 26-27)

FOCUS
A modest seller rated through the winner on previous winning form.

NOTEBOOK
Miss Lehman, freshened up by a two-month break, likes to come from well off the pace and surged through to collar the faint-hearted second.
Honan(IRE) looked in control turning for home but he began to put the brakes on under strong pressure nearing the final flight and was brushed aside after losing a lot of impetus. *(op 5-2)*
Urban Dream(IRE), who had been tried in a visor when falling at Ludlow two days earlier, stayed on up the short run-in after looking held at the second last. *(op 50-1)*
Four Eagles(USA) is an Irish import who is better known for his exploits over fences with his only victory coming in the Stewards' Room when he was awarded a two-mile beginners' chase at Tramore in April 2003. *(op 9-1)*
Itcanbedone Again(IRE) *Official explanation: jockey said gelding had been struck into (op 6-1)*

1743 TOTEQUADPOT H'CAP HURDLE (10 hdls) 2m 3f
3:25 (3:25) (Class 3) (0-135,129) 4-Y-0+
£12,342 (£4,681; £2,340; £1,064; £532; £319)

Form				RPR
1332	1		**Croix De Guerre (IRE)**[42] [1400] 5-11-11 128 ... (b) PJBrennan 9/2[2] (P J Hobbs) *a.p: mstke 3 out: rdn and chal appr 2 out: lft in ld nr fin*	130
00-1	2	1 3/4	**Just In Time**[53] [1296] 10-10-10 120 ... MrSClements(7) 10/1 (J Clements, Ire) *hld up in tch: led 7th: rdn appr 2 out: hdd appr last: no ex flat*	121+
653-	3	1 1/4	**Cool Roxy**[232] [4049] 8-11-6 128 ... (p) CHonour(5) 33/1 (A G Blackmore) *hld up in mid-div: hdwy after 5th: mstke 7th: rdn after 3 out: styd on flat*	127
-003	4	1 1/4	**Ingres**[23] [1525] 5-9-7 103 oh4 ... CMStudd(7) 16/1 (B G Powell) *hld up and bhd: hdwy appr 2 out: nvr nr to chal*	101
2112	5	1 1/4	**Screenplay**[14] [1598] 4-10-12 115 ... JGoldstein 11/2[3] (Miss Sheena West) *hld up and bhd: hdwy appr 7th: rdn appr 3 out: one pce fr 2 out*	113+
4336	6	5	**Kombinacja (POL)**[11] [1631] 7-11-3 120 ... (b[1]) CLlewellyn 14/1 (T R George) *prom: led after 6th to 7th: rdn and wknd appr 2 out*	113+
1002	7	9	**Herne Bay (IRE)**[53] [1300] 5-10-12 115 ... JPMcNamara 8/1 (R S Brookhouse) *hld up in mid-div: hdwy appr 6th: rdn and wknd appr 2 out*	98
0-66	8	3/4	**Brooklyn's Gold (USA)**[10] [570] 10-9-13 112 ... DJBoland(10) 12/1 (Ian Williams) *hld up in tch: rdn appr 7th: sn wknd*	94
0-02	9	18	**Grave Doubts**[21] [1548] 9-11-11 128 ... (t) RGreene 13/2 (K Bishop) *a bhd*	98+
46-P	10	26	**Fundamental**[14] [1598] 6-11-10 127 ... TJMurphy 20/1 (W K Goldsworthy) *j.rt: led: clr 2nd: hdd after 6th: wknd 3 out: t.o*	65
0354	P		**Castle River (USA)**[9] [1651] 6-10-0 103 oh10 ... MBatchelor 50/1 (O O'Neill) *bhd tl p.u lame bef 4th*	—
111-	U		**Valley Ride (IRE)**[215] [4362] 5-11-9 126 ... TDoyle 10/3[1] (C Tinkler) *hld up and bhd: hdwy appr 7th: rdn appr 2 out: led and hung rt appr last: 1l ahd whn swvd bdly rt nr fin and uns rdr*	130+

4m 23.1s (-12.20) **Going Correction** -0.45s/f (Good)
WFA 4 from 5yo+ 13lb 12 Ran SP% **120.1**
Speed ratings: **107,106,105,105,104 102,98,98,90,79 —,—** CSF £48.70 CT £1340.98 TOTE £4.80: £2.20, £3.90, £7.20; EX 73.50.
Owner Jack Joseph **Bred** T Wada **Trained** Withycombe, Somerset

FOCUS
A dramatic conclusion to a competitive handicap run at a decent pace. Despite the antics of Valley Ride, the form looks solid with runner-up, third and fifth close to their marks.

NOTEBOOK
Croix De Guerre(IRE), raised 5lb, was producing another sound effort against a less-exposed rival when handed the race in the shadow of the post. *(op 5-1 tchd 11-2)*
Just In Time could not overcome a 6lb hike in the ratings for making a successful debut for his current stable at Perth in August.
Cool Roxy, tried in cheekpieces, made a highly satisfactory reappearance and this should put an edge on him.
Ingres, 4lb out of the handicap, again gave the impression that he is capable of better things. His *rider reported that he got outpaced early and that he was unsuited by the good to firm ground. Official explanation: jockey said, regarding the running and riding, gelding was outpaced in the early stages and was not suited by the good to firm ground, adding that when asked for an effort in the back straight gelding passed a few horses and ran on in the home straight (op 20-1)*
Screenplay, 8lb higher than the second of his back-to-back wins, is going to find things tougher now. *(op 13-2)*
Kombinacja(POL) was blinkered for the first time on this return to hurdles.
Grave Doubts *Official explanation: jockey said gelding had a breathing problem*
Valley Ride(IRE), trying a longer trip on this switch to handicaps, threw the race away when unshipping his rider as he appeared to head for the paddock exit near the line. *(op 4-1)*

1744 TOTESPORT.COM H'CAP CHASE (FOR THE JOHN H. KENNY MEMORIAL CUP) (14 fncs 2 omitted) 2m 5f 110y
4:00 (4:00) (Class 3) (0-135,132) 5-Y-0+
£12,354 (£4,686; £2,343; £1,065; £532; £319)

Form				RPR
B115	1		**Tamango (FR)**[21] [1550] 8-11-9 129 ... PJBrennan 8/1[3] (P J Hobbs) *hld up: hdwy on ins to ld 11th: pckd last: all out*	141+
13/1	2	nk	**Black De Bessy (FR)**[42] [1400] 7-10-4 110 ... RWalford 11/4[2] (D R C Elsworth) *t.k.h in tch: hit 6th: hdwy appr 11th: ev ch last: hrd rdn and nt qckn flat*	123+
21-3	3	shd	**Ladalko (FR)**[21] [1550] 6-11-0 120 ... ChristianWilliams 7/4[1] (P F Nicholls) *chsd ldr: led after 10th to 11th: rdn and sltly outpcd appr last: swtchd lft and rallied flat*	132+
-100	4	2	**East Tycoon (IRE)**[21] [1550] 6-11-11 131 ... JEMoore 11/1 (Jonjo O'Neill) *hld up in tch: jnd ldrs 11th: rdn 2 out: styd on same pce*	141+
F110	5	18	**Fontanesi (IRE)**[56] [1265] 5-11-12 132 ... TJMurphy 14/1 (M C Pipe) *hld up: short-lived effrt and rdn appr 11th*	127+
0P-3	6	dist	**Majestic (IRE)**[59] [1234] 10-10-12 118 ... (bt) DRDennis 33/1 (Ian Williams) *led: sn clr: hdd after 10th: wknd 11th: t.o*	—
0014	F		**Xellance (IRE)**[21] [1548] 8-10-2 115 ... MrTJO'Brien(7) 8/1[3] (P J Hobbs) *prom: rdn 11th: wknd 3 out: 5th whn fell last*	118
F40-	P		**Three Days Reign (IRE)**[257] [3632] 11-10-2 108 ... ATinkler 12/1 (P D Cundell) *a in rr: rdn appr 9th: t.o whn p.u bef 11th*	—
211P	P		**Nephite (NZ)**[90] 11-10-4 110 ... SThomas 40/1 (Miss Venetia Williams) *prom: lost pl after 4th: dropped rr and mstke 7th: t.o whn p.u bef 11th*	—

5m 7.00s (-7.40) **Going Correction** -0.20s/f (Good) 9 Ran SP% **113.3**
Speed ratings: **105,104,104,104,97 —,—,—,—** CSF £30.87 CT £55.80 TOTE £7.10: £1.90, £1.90, £1.20; EX 25.80.
Owner The Brushmakers **Bred** Mme Dominique Le Drans **Trained** Withycombe, Somerset

FOCUS
Despite the relatively small field, this was a well-contested handicap for a decent prize. The form looks solid, rated through the second, while the winner could rate higher.

NOTEBOOK
Tamango(FR), whose trainer thought the ground was over-watered at Market Rasen last time, bounced back to form off a career-high mark. *(op 13-2)*
Black De Bessy(FR) was off the same rating as when beating the previous winner on the day Croix *De Guerre in a two-mile hurdle here last month. He could have settled better and lost little in* defeat. *(op 3-1)*
Ladalko(FR) had finished eight lengths ahead of Tamango on identical terms on ground that did not favour his rival at Market Rasen last month. *(op 13-8 tchd 15-8)*
East Tycoon(IRE), dropped 2lb, had trailed in behind both Tamango and Ladalko at Market Rasen. *(op 10-1)*
Three Days Reign(IRE) *Official explanation: jockey said gelding never travelled (op 20-1)*

1745 TOTEEXACTA MAIDEN HURDLE (9 hdls) 2m 110y
4:30 (4:30) (Class 3) 4-Y-0+ £6,896 (£2,549; £1,274; £579; £289)

Form RPR
0-21 **1** **Magical Legend**[14] [1600] 4-10-0 MrTJO'Brien(7) 106+
(L Corcoran) *hld up in tch: led appr 2 out: edgd lft flat: drvn out* **17/2**
44 **2** 3 ½ **Carte Sauvage (USA)**[10] [1642] 4-11-0 (v) PJBrennan 107+
(M F Harris) *a.p: rdn 6th: led after 3 out tl appr 2 out: one pce* **17/2**
103/ **3** shd **Green Iceni**[638] [3350] 6-11-0 ATinkler 109+
(N J Henderson) *hld up in mid-div: mstke 1st: hdwy and hit 3 out: ev ch whn blnd 2 out: nt rcvr* **7/1**[3]
0/5- **4** 6 **Alph**[420] [358] 8-10-11 CBolger(3) 100
(B R Johnson) *t.k.h in mid-div: styd on one pce fr 3 out* **50/1**
45-S **5** 4 **Cutthroat**[7] [1668] 5-10-9 107 RStephens(5) 96
(P J Hobbs) *hld up in mid-div: hdwy 3 out: sn wknd* **5/2**[1]
0-0 **6** 3 **Theatre Tinka (IRE)**[13] [1614] 6-10-4 AHawkins(10) 93
(R Hollinshead) *hld up and bhd: hdwy 5th: wknd 3 out* **33/1**
2 **7** 4 **Sunday City (JPN)**[20] [1562] 4-11-0 JEMoore 90+
(R A Fahey) *plld hrd: led to 2nd: led 4th tl after 3 out: sn wknd* **3/1**[2]
8 8 **Bythehokey (IRE)**[53] [1305] 4-11-0 TJMurphy 81
(B P J Baugh) *hld up and bhd: hdwy 5th: wknd after 3 out* **14/1**
9 13 **Bluegrass Boy**[23] 5-11-0 MBradburne 71+
(J A Geake) *hld up in mid-div: hdwy after 5th: j.rt and mstke 3 out: sn wknd* **20/1**
65F/ **10** 10 **Mr Lehman**[168] 8-10-9 CHonour(5) 58
(J D Frost) *a bhd* **40/1**
P- **11** nk **Sharp Rally (IRE)**[318] [2288] 4-11-0 (t) AThornton 58
(A J Wilson) *j.rt 5th: a bhd* **50/1**
03 **12** 17 **Dubai Dreams**[53] [1302] 5-10-11 (b) LVickers(3) 41
(S R Bowring) *led 2nd: sn clr: hdd 4th: wknd 6th* **20/1**
5F-U **13** 26 **Mongino (GER)**[3] [1714] 4-11-0 (t) BHitchcott 15
(M F Harris) *a bhd: t.o* **66/1**
P **Chasing The Dream (IRE)**[56] 4-10-7 TDoyle —
(P R Webber) *a bhd: t.o whn p.u bef 2 out* **14/1**
0 **P** **Court Alliance**[101] [911] 6-11-0 AO'Keeffe —
(R J Price) *a bhd: t.o whn p.u bef 2 out* **33/1**

3m 49.3s (-9.10) **Going Correction** -0.45s/f (Good) **15** Ran SP% **123.7**
Speed ratings: **103,101,101,98,96 95,93,89,83,78 78,70,58,—,—** CSF £74.13 TOTE £13.10: £3.20, £2.80, £3.10; EX 113.10.
Owner R H Kerswell **Bred** R H And Mrs Kerswell **Trained** Kingsbridge, Devon

FOCUS
No hanging about here with few getting into the contest. The time was reasonable and the winner is rated value for further.

NOTEBOOK
Magical Legend, a springer in the market, transferred his recent bumper form to hurdles. She took advantage of getting a stone from her two closest rivals with the help of O'Brien's allowance. *(op 14-1)*
Carte Sauvage(USA) showed improvement for the fitting of a visor for the first time over hurdles. *(op 8-1)*
Green Iceni ◆, previously trained by John Best, was let down by his jumping on this first start since the beginning of 2004. A similar event is there for the taking providing he can brush up his hurdling. *(op 15-2 tchd 8-1)*
Alph, last seen on the sand at Lingfield in August 2004, had been beaten a long way in his two previous outings over hurdles. *(op 33-1)*
Cutthroat, apparently none the worse for slipping up at Bangor last week, could only manage a short-lived effort. *(op 11-4)*
Sunday City(JPN) was ridden totally differently this time and ran much too freely. *(op 7-2)*
Court Alliance *Official explanation: vet said gelding was lame on its left fore*

1746 TOTESPORT 0800 221 221 H'CAP CHASE (11 fncs 2 omitted) 2m 1f 110y
5:00 (5:01) (Class 4) (0-105,106) 5-Y-0+ £5,577 (£1,716; £858; £429)

Form RPR
1-33 **1** **L'Oiseau (FR)**[154] [345] 6-11-5 **98** JTizzard 111+
(J G Portman) *hld up: hdwy on ins 6th: hit 3 out: rdn to ld sn after last: drvn out* **4/1**[2]
U001 **2** 2 **Nick The Jewel**[9] [1659] 10-11-13 **106** PJBrennan 115
(Andrew Turnell) *chsd ldr: hit 3rd: led after 7th: rdn and hdd sn after last: nt qckn* **11/4**[1]
P43P **3** 6 **Take The Oath (IRE)**[67] [1191] 8-10-0 **79** oh2 (b[1]) TDoyle 83+
(D R Gandolfo) *hld up towards rr: rdn 7th: hdwy appr 3 out: one pce fr 2 out* **10/1**
2541 **4** 13 **Power Unit**[7] [1673] 10-11-10 **103** BHitchcott 96+
(Mrs D A Hamer) *prom tl rdn and wknd appr last* **13/2**[3]
P1F5 **5** 10 **Knight's Emperor (IRE)**[7] [1673] 8-11-4 **97** JEMoore 82+
(J L Spearing) *hld up: mstke 5th: blnd 7th: sn rdn: bhd fr 8th* **9/1**
4P32 **6** 1 ½ **Lightin' Jack (IRE)**[11] [1631] 7-11-12 **105** BJCrowley 84
(Miss E C Lavelle) *hld up in tch: nt fluent 2nd: wknd 3 out* **4/1**[2]
P0-4 **7** dist **Ceresfield (NZ)**[135] [615] 9-11-0 **96** (p) LMcGrath(3) —
(R C Guest) *hld up in tch: rdn and wknd appr 3 out: t.o* **8/1**
-14F **8** 7 **Calon Lan (IRE)**[13] [1620] 14-11-0 **93** TJMurphy —
(B J Llewellyn) *sn bhd: rdn appr 5th: t.o fr 7th* **14/1**
-P04 **P** **Kaikovra (IRE)**[14] [1595] 9-11-1 **94** TScudamore —
(M F Harris) *led tl after 7th: wknd 8th: t.o whn p.u bef last* **33/1**

4m 10.0s (-2.50) **Going Correction** -0.20s/f (Good) **9** Ran SP% **119.8**
Speed ratings: **97,96,93,87,83 82,—,—,—** CSF £16.76 CT £104.86 TOTE £6.10: £2.00, £1.30, £3.80; EX 20.00.
Owner Milady Partnership **Bred** Jacques Cypres And Thierry Cypres **Trained** Compton, Berks

FOCUS
This did not turn out to be as competitive as the betting suggested, with the winner value for twice the winning margin and the placed horses running to their marks.

NOTEBOOK
L'Oiseau(FR), bought out of Len Lungo's yard for 21,000 gns in May, is equally at home over hurdles. Justifying market support, he travelled well through the race on this return to fences. *(op 15-2)*
Nick The Jewel could not cope with the winner having gone up 5lb for his win at Worcester. *(op 3-1)*
Take The Oath(IRE), 2lb 'wrong', was blinkered for the first time on this return to a shorter trip. *(op 11-1 tchd 14-1)*
Power Unit could not overcome a 7lb hike in the weights for his win at Bangor a week earlier. *(tchd 7-1)*
Knight's Emperor(IRE) was let down by his jumping. *(op 8-1 tchd 10-1)*
Calon Lan(IRE) *Official explanation: jockey said gelding never travelled (op 16-1)*

1747 TOTESPORTCASINO.COM LADY RIDERS' H'CAP HURDLE (9 hdls) 2m 110y
5:35 (5:35) (Class 4) (0-100,97) 4-Y-0+ £4,182 (£1,287; £643; £321)

Form RPR
1 **Tushna (IRE)**[21] [1557] 8-10-7 **85** MissEALalor(7) 90+
(E McNamara, Ire) *prom: led 3rd: clr whn hit 2 out: r.o wl* **9/1**[3]
50P/ **2** 7 **Zeloso**[9] [4540] 7-9-11 **75** (v) MissCarolineHurley(7) 73
(M F Harris) *led 2nd to 3rd: chsd wnr: no imp fr 2 out* **16/1**
561 **3** shd **Nesnaas (USA)**[9] [1653] 4-11-5 **93** MissNCarberry(3) 91
(M G Rimell) *hld up: hdwy after 3 out: sn rdn: one pce fr 2 out* **8/13**[1]
0-32 **4** 1 ¾ **Secret's Out**[7] [1668] 9-11-2 **94** MissHGrissell(7) 90
(F Lloyd) *hld up and bhd: rdn and outpcd after 3 out: styd on fr 2 out* **14/1**
01 **5** 3 **Uncle John**[21] [1553] 4-10-6 **84** (v) MissCDyson(7) 77
(Ian Williams) *led to 2nd: prom tl wknd appr 2 out* **8/1**[2]
210 **6** 3 ½ **Sharaab (USA)**[20] [1562] 4-11-3 **95** (t) MissLGardner(7) 85
(D E Cantillon) *plld hrd in tch: rdn and wknd appr 2 out* **12/1**
1336 **7** 2 ½ **Brochrua (IRE)**[62] [1218] 5-11-3 **95** MissSGaisford(7) 82
(J D Frost) *a bhd* **25/1**
2PPP **8** 5 **Dancinginthestreet**[97] [949] 5-11-5 **97** MissCTizzard(7) 79
(J L Flint) *hld up: reminders 5th: hdwy 6th: wknd after 3 out* **50/1**
5534 **9** 3 **Faddad (USA)**[9] [1659] 9-10-12 **90** (t) MrsLucyRowsell(7) 69
(Mrs A M Thorpe) *prom: lost pl 5th: rdn 6th: sn bhd* **16/1**

3m 54.4s (-4.00) **Going Correction** -0.45s/f (Good) **9** Ran SP% **115.0**
Speed ratings: **91,87,87,86,85 83,82,80,78** CSF £132.15 CT £215.99 TOTE £12.70: £2.50, £3.60, £1.10; EX 176.40 Place 6 £88.55, Place 5 £54.71 .
Owner S Braddish **Bred** Redmondstown Stud **Trained** Rathkeale, Co. Limerick
■ Stewards' Enquiry : Miss E A Lalor caution: careless riding

FOCUS
This low-grade affair was run at a muddling pace, with the fourth and sixth setting the level for the form.

NOTEBOOK
Tushna(IRE) kicked for home leaving the back straight in a race run at a modest gallop. He had it sewn up when rapping the penultimate hurdle. *(op 15-2)*
Zeloso, last seen over hurdles in April 2003, has had some success in low-grade staying events on the All-Weather. He really wants further on a course as sharp as this and would not have been suited by the way things panned out. *(op 12-1)*
Nesnaas(USA), raised 8lb, presumably started as such a hot favourite because of the Nina Carberry factor. *(op 8-11)*
Secret's Out got tapped for speed when the tempo eventually quickened. *(op 20-1)*
Uncle John had gone up 3lb after scraping home at Market Rasen. *(op 11-1 tchd 15-2)*
Sharaab(USA) proved a real handful to settle because of the lack of a gallop. *(op 9-1)*
T/Plt: £175.30 to a £1 stake. Pool: £43,487.50. 181.00 winning tickets. T/Qpdt: £32.80 to a £1 stake. Pool: £3,187.10. 71.70 winning tickets. KH

[742] HEREFORD (R-H)
Sunday, October 16

OFFICIAL GOING: Good to firm (firm in places)
Wind: Nil Weather: Fine

1749 DOROTHY GOODBODY'S NOVICES' CHASE (12 fncs) 2m
2:10 (2:10) (Class 4) 4-Y-0+ £4,754 (£1,463; £731; £365)

Form RPR
033- **1** **Avas Delight (IRE)**[184] [4857] 7-11-6 101 RWalford 95+
(R H Alner) *mde all: clr after 2nd to 8th: drew clr again fr 2 out: comf* **9/4**[2]
-06P **2** 5 **Let's Rock**[147] [459] 7-10-13 67 MrRHodges(7) 83
(Mrs A Price) *chsd wnr tl after 3rd: wnt 2nd again 8th: sn rdn: no imp fr 2 out* **33/1**
4-26 **3** 5 **Alexander Musical (IRE)**[159] [271] 7-11-1 62 MNicolls(5) 78
(S T Lewis) *hld up: bmpd 4th: hdwy 4 out: sn rdn: wknd after 2 out* **16/1**
-55F **4** 4 **True Mariner (FR)**[11] [1644] 5-11-6 105 JAMcCarthy 78+
(B I Case) *chsd wnr after 3rd tl blnd and lost pl 8th: n.d after* **7/2**[3]
53-5 **5** 11 **Kildee Lass**[153] [387] 6-10-13 100 JTizzard 59+
(J D Frost) *hld up: j.rt 4th: hdwy 4 out: wknd appr 2 out* **5/4**[1]
P0/0 **6** dist **Only For Gold**[10] [1654] 10-11-6 69 RGreene —
(Dr P Pritchard) *t.k.h in rr: nt fluent 1st: sn wl bhd: t.o* **50/1**

4m 1.80s (-0.70) **Going Correction** -0.40s/f (Good) **6** Ran SP% **108.2**
Speed ratings: **85,82,80,78,72** — CSF £41.35 TOTE £2.90: £1.90, £3.90; EX 85.20.
Owner P M De Wilde **Bred** Mrs Josephine Canavan **Trained** Droop, Dorset

FOCUS
A moderate time for a race like this and questionable form. The winner has been rated value for 12 lengths, but was still below his hurdles mark. The second and third both could be well treated on their current marks.

NOTEBOOK
Avas Delight(IRE) made a successful chasing debut. He was somewhat keen in the early stages, but settled better as the race progressed. Given a breather turning out of the back straight, allowing his pursuers to close, he drew clear again and was value for a greater margin of victory. *(op 15-8 tchd 7-4)*
Let's Rock has had no shortage of opportunities, but he had a stiffish task here and this was his best run to date. *(op 50-1)*
Alexander Musical(IRE), without the visor for this return to action, was being ridden along early on the final circuit and it to his credit that he did not drop away. He stays further and is well handicapped. *(tchd 18-1)*
True Mariner(FR) took a heavy fall last time and, following a blunder, he was allowed to complete in his own time and restore some confidence. *(op 4-1)*
Kildee Lass, an able hurdler, was rather disappointing on this chasing debut. Having her first run since May, she closed with four to jump but then appeared to blow up. *(op 11-8 tchd 6-4)*

1750 BET365 CALL 08000 322 365 NOVICES' HURDLE (8 hdls) 2m 1f
2:40 (2:41) (Class 4) 4-Y-0+ £3,919 (£1,206; £603; £301)

Form RPR
00 **1** **Davy's Luck**[8] [1680] 5-10-5 WMarston 81+
(J M Bradley) *hld up: hdwy 4th: rdn appr 2 out: led and mstke last: r.o* **9/1**
040 **2** 1 ¾ **Heisse**[129] [696] 5-10-12 (t) DRDennis 83
(Ian Williams) *a.p: rdn appr 2 out: r.o flat* **10/1**
3 1 ¼ **Absolutelythebest (IRE)**[20] 4-10-9 ONelmes(3) 82
(J G M O'Shea) *hld up and bhd: hdwy appr 5th: rdn appr 2 out: r.o flat* **7/2**[2]
20-2 **4** ½ **Coming Again (IRE)**[47] [1377] 4-10-7 104 (t) StephenJCraine(5) 84+
(D McCain) *hld up in tch: blnd 3rd: rdn to ld 2 out: sn hdd: kpt on same pce flat* **11/8**[1]
0P2 **5** nk **Brown Fox (FR)**[11] [1640] 4-10-5 MBradburne 74
(C J Down) *hld up in mid-div: hdwy 5th: ev ch 2 out: sn rdn: one pce* **8/1**[3]

6 4 **Devious Ayers (IRE)**[13] 4-10-12 .... WHutchinson 77
(J M Bradley) *hld up in mid-div: hdwy appr 5th: rdn appr 2 out: wknd last* **33/1**

0-0P 7 6 **Daisy Dale**[81] [1077] 7-10-5 75 .... RGreene 64
(S C Burrough) *hld up and bhd: hdwy appr 5th: wknd after 3 out: hmpd 2 out* **66/1**

P- 8 4 **Bonjour Bond (IRE)**[59] [4852] 4-10-12 .... VSlattery 67
(J G M O'Shea) *a bhd: no ch whn hmpd 2 out* **80/1**

P 9 7 **Pips Assertive Way**[35] [1454] 4-9-9 .... RichardGordon(10) 53
(A W Carroll) *t.k.h in tch: lost pl 3rd: bhd fr 4th* **20/1**

000- 10 dist **Billy Coleman (IRE)**[279] [3303] 7-10-12 .... TScudamore —
(D Brace) *chsd ldr to 3rd: wknd 4th: t.o* **50/1**

00/ 11 ½ **Top Stoppa**[752] [1436] 7-10-9 .... RYoung(3) —
(A J Whiting) *led: clr 2nd: hdd after 5th: wknd 6th: t.o* **66/1**

P 12 14 **Limogos (GER)**[8] [1680] 5-10-5 .... MissLGardner(7) —
(Mrs S Gardner) *prom: lost pl 3rd: rdn after 4th: sn bhd: t.o* **66/1**

F **Milk And Sultana**[13] 5-9-12 .... EDehdashti(7) —
(G A Ham) *prom: wkng whn fell 2 out* **10/1**

605/ P **Exhibit (IRE)**[812] [970] 7-10-5 65 .... KBurke(7) —
(N J Hawke) *a bhd: mstke 3rd: t.o whn p.u bef 5th* **66/1**

00-0 U **Pauls Plain**[14] [1614] 4-10-12 .... SCurran 85
(P W Hiatt) *j.lft: prom: led after 4th to 2 out: sn led again: hdd and 2nd whn blnd and uns rdr last* **100/1**

3m 56.3s (-6.80) **Going Correction** -0.675s/f (Firm) **15** Ran SP% **121.5**
Speed ratings: **89,88,87,87,87 85,82,80,77,— —,—,—,—,—** CSF £89.55 TOTE £9.40: £2.20, £3.00, £1.70; EX 72.40.
Owner D Smith (saul) **Bred** D And H J Smith **Trained** Sedbury, Gloucs

FOCUS
A moderate winning time, even for such a weak event, and the form is suspect. It has been rated through the fifth, with the first two improvers and the last-flight casualty assessed as having finished second.

NOTEBOOK
Davy's Luck showed little in a better race recently, but she was able to land a gamble in this lesser company. *She is likely to struggle under a penalty but a step up in trip might help.Official explanation: jockey said, regarding the improved form shown, mare had been very green on her first run at Huntingdon, but jumped better at Chepstow and ran on well in the home straight, adding that the Chepstow race seemed to be of a higher quality than today's (op 25-1 tchd 8-1)*
Heisse, the tongue tie applied for the first time over hurdles for this first run since June, was ridden more prominently. He was held in fourth place jumping the final flight but ran on up the short run-in. *(op 8-1)*
Absolutelythebest(IRE), a ten-furlong winner on Polytrack, stayed on for pressure over the last couple of flights on this hurdling debut and looks to need further. *(tchd 4-1)*
Coming Again(IRE), who survived an early blunder when he was unsighted going into the flight, *showed narrowly in front at the second last but was unable to fend off his challengers.Official explanation: trainer said gelding was unsuited by the good to firm (firm in places) ground (op 6-4 tchd 13-8)*
Brown Fox(FR) confirmed that she possesses a little ability but she appeared not to get home. *(tchd 15-2)*
Devious Ayers(IRE), a stablemate of the winner, was a banded-class performer on the level who regularly wore headgear.
Exhibit(IRE) *Official explanation: jockey said gelding had a breathing problem (tchd 80-1)*
Pauls Plain had shown nothing previously. Always in the front rank, he had just been headed and *looked set to finish in second spot when he stepped into the final flight and ejected his rider. (tchd 80-1)*

1751 WYE VALLEY BREWERY H'CAP HURDLE (13 hdls) 3m 2f
3:10 (3:10) (Class 4) (0-105,108) 4-Y-0+ **£4,075** (£1,254; £627; £313)

Form RPR

0- 1 **Harbour View (IRE)**[49] [1353] 6-10-1 87 .... BCByrnes(7) 93+
(E McNamara, Ire) *towards rr: reminders after 3rd: hdwy 7th: hrd rdn after 3 out: sltly outpcd 2 out: rallied to ld appr last: styd on wl* **5/2**[2]

11 2 4 **Habitual (IRE)**[8] [1685] 4-11-7 108 .... MrRQuinn(7) 109+
(John A Quinn, Ire) *hld up: hdwy 8th: led 3 out: rdn 2 out: hdd appr last: no ex* **9/4**[1]

3U-0 3 2½ **Prayerful**[10] [1658] 6-10-5 87 .... ONelmes(3) 87+
(J G M O'Shea) *hld up and bhd: stdy hdwy 6th: hit 8th: rdn and ev ch after 2 out: one pce* **40/1**

0U44 4 1¼ **Caper**[10] [1648] 5-9-10 85 ....(p) AHawkins(10) 83
(R Hollinshead) *hld up and bhd: hdwy 9th: one pce fr 2 out* **11/1**

P332 5 2½ **Sundawn Lady**[21] [1564] 7-9-8 80 ....(b) MrGTumelty(7) 76
(C P Morlock) *hld up: hdwy 5th: led after 7th: hit 8th: hdd 3 out: sn rdn: btn 2 out* **4/1**[3]

613- P **Hoh Nelson**[224] [4213] 4-11-11 105 .... JGoldstein —
(Mrs A Price) *sn bhd: t.o whn p.u bef 2 out* **16/1**

12F- P **Afeef (USA)**[271] [3402] 6-10-11 90 ....(t) SCurran —
(J A Danahar) *prom: lost pl after 5th: bhd fr 7th: p.u bef 8th* **14/1**

0-00 P **Welsh Doll (IRE)**[28] [1480] 6-10-0 79 oh11 .... TScudamore —
(D Brace) *hld up in tch: wknd appr 3 out: t.o whn p.u bef 2 out* **66/1**

010- P **Litzinsky**[73] [4105] 7-10-12 91 .... OMcPhail —
(J G M O'Shea) *prom: nt fluent 9th: sn rdn and wknd t.o whn p.u bef 2 out* **25/1**

-004 P **Noble Colours**[11] [1644] 12-10-3 82 .... BHitchcott —
(Mrs C J Ikin) *led after 1st tl after 7th: wknd 8th: t.o whn p.u bef last* **100/1**

-P03 P **Happy Hussar (IRE)**[56] [1279] 12-10-6 90 .... DrPPritchard(5) —
(Dr P Pritchard) *led tl after 1st: lost pl after 5th: bhd whn p.u bef 8th* **22/1**

402- P **Shannon Quest (IRE)**[176] 9-9-13 85 ....(p) TMessenger(7) —
(C L Popham) *hld up in mid-div: rdn after 7th: sn bhd: t.o whn p.u bef 2 out* **16/1**

0PP- P **Charlie's Cross (IRE)**[222] [4241] 7-10-0 79 oh15 ....(v[1]) ATinkler —
(J G Portman) *nt fluent: prom: rdn 6th: wknd appr 8th: t.o whn p.u bef 10th* **66/1**

6m 9.20s (-18.80) **Going Correction** -0.675s/f (Firm) **13** Ran SP% **120.7**
Speed ratings: **101,99,99,98,97 —,—,—,—,— —,—,—** CSF £8.46 CT £180.89 TOTE £4.10: £1.90, £2.30, £8.00; EX 10.90.
Owner Sean Greaney **Bred** Mrs Nora Johnston **Trained** Rathkeale, Co. Limerick

FOCUS
A fair handicap in which only five completed. The winner was well treated on his Irish form and the second improved again and can probably rate higher still.

NOTEBOOK
Harbour View(IRE) had done the vast majority of his racing in Ireland in soft conditions but had no problem with this ground. He was last of the five contenders and being ridden vigorously turning out of the back straight, and was still only third rounding the home turn, but stayed on to win going away in the end. *(op 7-2)*
Habitual(IRE) was bidding for a quick hat-trick off a 9lb higher mark. He did nothing wrong over this longer trip but could not hold off his compatriot going to the final flight. *(tchd 5-2, 11-4 in places)*
Prayerful, fitter for her recent return to action after six months out, has previously shown a preference for easy ground but this was a decent effort. She looks capable of winning off her current mark. *(op 33-1)*
Caper, tackling his longest trip to date, ran his race but is the sort who needs everything to fall right. *(op 9-1 tchd 12-1)*
Sundawn Lady continues to run well in defeat and her chance should come one day. *(op 9-2)*
Happy Hussar(IRE) *Official explanation: trainer said gelding never travelled (op 50-1)*
Welsh Doll(IRE), racing from 11lb out of the handicap, was one of a group of six to pull a long way clear of the others, but she weakened with three to jump and was pulled up. She is lightly raced and may be capable of a bit better. *(op 50-1)*

1752 BULMERS H'CAP CHASE (19 fncs) 3m 1f 110y
3:40 (3:40) (Class 4) (0-110,101) 5-Y-0+ **£4,813** (£1,481; £740; £370)

Form RPR

-4PU 1 **Hehasalife (IRE)**[56] [1276] 8-10-4 84 ....(b) PCO'Neill(5) 101+
(Mrs H Dalton) *sn chsng ldr: nt fluent 3rd and 7th: led 15th: clr whn mstke last: readily* **3/1**[2]

4- 2 8 **Peach Of A Citizen (IRE)**[27] [1502] 6-10-3 78 .... AO'Keeffe 83+
(Eugene M O'Sullivan, Ire) *hld up: hdwy whn mstke 11th: rdn to chse wnr after 4 out: no imp fr 2 out* **13/2**

3 15 **Smell The Coffee (IRE)**[28] [1492] 7-9-8 76 ....(p) BCByrnes(7) 66+
(E McNamara, Ire) *hld up in tch: reminders after 4th: lost pl 14th: n.d after* **5/1**[3]

-421 4 4 **Southerndown (IRE)**[46] [1385] 12-10-9 84 .... RThornton 67
(R Lee) *hld up and bhd: hdwy 10th: rdn after 13th: wknd 15th* **5/1**[3]

-213 5 7 **Sir Cumference**[14] [1615] 9-11-7 96 ....(b) SThomas 72
(Miss Venetia Williams) *led: hit 5th: hdd 15th: hit 4 out: wknd 3 out* **5/2**[1]

-200 6 dist **Alfred The Grey**[131] [673] 8-10-0 75 oh3 .... VSlattery —
(P A Blockley) *prom tl blnd and lost pl 10th: t.o fr 13th* **14/1**

-43P P **Maybeseven**[144] [503] 11-9-7 75 oh5 .... JPritchard(7) —
(R Dickin) *bhd fr 4th: rdn 8th: t.o whn p.u bef 14th* **22/1**

6m 19.9s (-14.30) **Going Correction** -0.40s/f (Good) **7** Ran SP% **111.3**
Speed ratings: **106,103,98,97,95 —,—** CSF £21.11 CT £89.63 TOTE £4.20: £3.10, £2.10; EX 19.40.
Owner Norton House Racing **Bred** Eddie J Kelly **Trained** Norton, Shropshire

FOCUS
The well handicapped winner was value for further. Low-grade Irish chasers seem less well treated than their hurdling counterparts and the race has been rated through the second, who ran to his mark.

NOTEBOOK
Hehasalife(IRE) ◆ has become very well handicapped and he cashed in with a comfortable success. He generally jumped well but lost concentration going to the last and walked through the fence. He has undergone two wind-related operations in the past year and, with his problems behind him, he can certainly win again, though fast ground is a must. *(op 9-2)*
Peach Of A Citizen(IRE) is a winning pointer in Ireland but has yet to score under Rules. She stays well and kept trying, but was no match for the winner. *(op 7-1 tchd 15-2)*
Smell The Coffee(IRE), a maiden under Rules who looked hard work for his rider, ran his best race since May. *(op 11-2 tchd 4-1)*
Southerndown(IRE) was running off his highest chase mark for a long time following his Newton Abbot victory and could never get into the argument. *(op 7-2)*
Sir Cumference made the running until the winner eased past at the fifth last and was then soon on the retreat. *(tchd 3-1)*

1753 RACING ADVERTISER LTD CONDITIONAL JOCKEYS' NOVICES' H'CAP HURDLE (10 hdls) 2m 3f 110y
4:10 (4:10) (Class 4) (0-95,95) 3-Y-0+ **£3,437** (£982; £491)

Form RPR

PP-3 1 **Penric**[161] [238] 5-11-3 86 .... RStephens 95+
(J K Price) *a.p: rdn to ld appr last: r.o* **14/1**

6P42 2 2 **Qualitair Pleasure**[9] [1663] 5-11-11 94 .... KJMercer 99
(J Hetherton) *hld up and bhd: hdwy 3 out: rdn 2 out: r.o one pce flat* **15/2**[3]

3P-3 3 2½ **Welsh Dane**[162] [218] 5-10-13 82 ....(p) ONelmes 85
(M Sheppard) *a.p: rdn and one pce fr 2 out* **11/1**

4-06 4 1¼ **He's The Gaffer (IRE)**[15] [1596] 5-10-3 82 ....(b[1]) PDavey(10) 83
(R H Buckler) *led: rdn and hdd appr last: wknd flat* **25/1**

6 5 1½ **Hi Laurie (IRE)**[11] [1645] 10-10-7 84 .... JKington(8) 84
(M Scudamore) *hld up in mid-div: hdwy appr 3 out: one pce fr 2 out* **9/2**[2]

0/P6 6 12 **Buz Kiri (USA)**[28] [1490] 7-10-8 85 .... RichardGordon(8) 73
(A W Carroll) *t.k.h towards rr: nt fluent 5th: nvr nr ldrs* **22/1**

1541 7 8 **Roman Candle (IRE)**[24] [1523] 9-11-2 88 .... SWalsh(3) 68
(Lucinda Featherstone) *a bhd* **17/2**

0P4- 8 3 **Magnetic Pole**[212] [4439] 4-11-12 95 ....(t) MNicolls 74+
(B I Case) *hld up in mid-div: rdn and hdwy appr 7th: wknd 2 out* **22/1**

0-01 9 9 **Banningham Blaze**[11] [1643] 5-11-3 86 ....(v) StephenJCraine 54
(A W Carroll) *hld up in mid-div: rdn appr 7th: bhd fr 3 out* **14/1**

00P0 P **Shaaban (IRE)**[10] [1655] 4-10-0 69 oh4 ....(v) TJMalone —
(R J Price) *nt j.w: a in rr: t.o whn p.u bef 5th* **25/1**

U-60 F **Mr Fisher (IRE)**[23] [1539] 8-9-10 70 ....(v) AngharadFrieze(5) —
(D Burchell) *bhd tl 6th and styng on whn fell last* **25/1**

040- P **Memories Of Gold (IRE)**[186] [4820] 5-10-12 86 .... RSpate(5) —
(J A Danahar) *hld up in tch: wknd 6th: bhd whn p.u bef 2 out* **40/1**

2113 P **Marathea (FR)**[37] [1443] 4-11-1 87 .... PCO'Neill(3) —
(Miss Venetia Williams) *hld up in mid-div: hdwy after 6th: in tch whn p.u lame bef 2 out* **10/3**[1]

P **Dorneys Well (IRE)**[210] [4489] 5-10-13 90 .... BCByrnes(8) —
(E McNamara, Ire) *hld up in mid-div: hdwy appr 5th: mstke 6th: wknd after 3 out: p.u bef 2 out* **9/2**[2]

4m 33.2s (-14.70) **Going Correction** -0.675s/f (Firm) **14** Ran SP% **126.1**
Speed ratings: **102,101,100,99,99 94,91,89,86,— —,—,—,—** CSF £110.47 CT £1229.68 TOTE £18.40: £5.70, £3.40, £3.30; EX 88.80.
Owner J K Price **Bred** Shadwell Estate Company Limited **Trained** Ebbw Vale, Blaenau Gwent

FOCUS
A low-level handicap, but a sound enough race of its type, rated around the first three, who were all close to their marks.

NOTEBOOK
Penric, formerly trained by Victoria Scott, was back up in trip for this first run since May. He will get a bit further and could win again now that he has got his head in front.
Qualitair Pleasure, raised 4lb for her short-head defeat at Carlisle, stayed on well from the rear of the field but was unable to get to the winner. She is in good form at present but looks a little high in the weights. *(op 9-1)*
Welsh Dane ran another decent race, and the combination of fast ground and cheekpieces seems to have made a difference. *(op 9-1 tchd 12-1)*
He's The Gaffer(IRE) enjoyed himself out in front in the first-time blinkers and only gave best going to the final flight. This was a much improved performance on his handicap debut and his bumper form suggests he could rate higher still. *(op 40-1)*

Hi Laurie(IRE), upped in trip, ran a bit better on this second start in this country but was still below the best of her form in Ireland. *(op 4-1)*
Buz Kiri(USA) passed beaten rivals in the latter stages. *(op 25-1)*
Magnetic Pole, upped in trip for this handicap debut, ran well for a long way but did not get home. *(op 18-1)*
Marathea(FR) was in touch when suddenly pulled up and dismounted after the third last. *Official explanation: jockey said filly pulled up lame (op 4-1)*

1754 COME RACING ON 6TH NOVEMBER H'CAP CHASE (14 fncs) 2m 3f
4:40 (4:40) (Class 4) (0-110,104) 5-Y-0+ **£4,901** (£1,508; £754; £377)

Form RPR
-U40 **1** **Welsh Main**[102] [914] 8-10-11 **89**................ RThornton 108+
(Miss Tor Sturgis) *hld up in tch: chal 3 out: led appr last: rdn out* **11/4**[1]
3642 **2** 2 ½ **Romany Dream**[11] [1647] 7-10-12 **90**................(b) BHitchcott 104
(R Dickin) *a.p: led after 4 out tl appr last: no ex* **7/2**[3]
P3P0 **3** 14 **Mantilla**[63] [1218] 8-10-6 **84**................(b) DRDennis 84
(Ian Williams) *prom tl wknd appr 2 out* **7/1**
-0P3 **4** 1 ¼ **Bearaway (IRE)**[10] [1659] 8-11-7 **104**................(t) PCO'Neill[(5)] 103
(Mrs H Dalton) *hld up and bhd: hdwy appr 3 out: no further prog fr 2 out* **3/1**[2]
404P **5** hd **Flahive's First**[28] [1489] 11-11-2 **101**................ LHeard[(7)] 100
(D Burchell) *hld up: lost pl 10th: styd on flat: n.d* **9/1**
434 **6** 16 **Young Owen**[14] [1620] 7-11-4 **96**................(p) JMogford 79
(A G Juckes) *set stdy pce: mstke 4 out: sn hdd: wknd 3 out: sn eased* **6/1**
F5-P **7** 7 **Special Agenda (IRE)**[8] [1673] 11-9-13 **82**................(t) StephenJCraine[(5)] 58
(M J M Evans) *mstkes: a bhd* **20/1**
-3P5 **8** 13 **Welsh Gold**[152] [398] 6-9-12 **81** oh19 ow3................ MNicolls[(5)] 44
(S T Lewis) *hld up: rdn after 8th: wknd 4 out* **33/1**

4m 42.8s (-3.80) **Going Correction** -0.40s/f (Good) **8** Ran SP% **118.4**
Speed ratings: **92,90,85,84,84 77,74,69** CSF £13.89 CT £61.38 TOTE £3.50: £1.40, £1.50, £2.10; EX 14.50.
Owner Miss Tor Sturgis **Bred** Juddmonte Farms **Trained** Kingston Lisle, Oxon
■ A winner with her first runner for Tor Sturgis.
■ Stewards' Enquiry : B Hitchcott 11-day ban: used whip with excessive force and frequency, and in an incorrect place in front of the stifle (Oct 28-Nov 7)

FOCUS
A weak event. The winning time was modest, even for a race of its type. The first two were both well treated over fences.

NOTEBOOK
Welsh Main, formerly trained by Georgina Browne, whose yard has been taken over by Sturgis, had shown little previously over fences but had become very well handicapped compared with his hurdles mark. He won this ordinary event decisively and there may be a bit more to come. *(op 4-1)*
Romany Dream, back over fences, nipped through the inside to lead on the bend turning out of the back straight but was collared on the run to the last. She has become well handicapped over fences. *(op 4-1 tchd 9-2)*
Mantilla, reverting to fences with blinkers on instead of a visor, faded out of contention from the second last. *(op 9-1)*
Bearaway(IRE) travelled well under a hold-up ride but did not find much when let down with three to jump and was not persevered with. *(tchd 4-1)*
Flahive's First, dropped 3lb, was doing his best work when it was all over. *(op 13-2)*
Young Owen, back down in trip and with cheekpieces on for the first time, reverted to front-running tactics but faded quite tamely once headed. *Official explanation: jockey said gelding never travelled and was unsuited by the track (op 7-1 tchd 11-2)*

1755 BBC HEREFORD AND WORCESTER STANDARD OPEN NATIONAL HUNT FLAT RACE 2m 1f
5:10 (5:13) (Class 6) 4-6-Y-0 **£2,079** (£594; £297)

Form RPR
0-06 **1** **Surfboard (IRE)**[155] [361] 4-10-8................ AngharadFrieze[(10)] 85
(P A Blockley) *a.p: led 6f out tl over 4f out: led over 3f out: r.o* **14/1**
2 ¾ **Dateldoo (IRE)** 6-10-4................ MrRhysHughes[(7)] 78+
(P D Williams) *hld up: hdwy after 6f: hrd rdn over 2f out: rn v wd ent st: rallied fnl f: r.o* **25/1**
3 2 ½ **Debris (IRE)**[525] 6-11-4................ BFenton 82
(Miss E C Lavelle) *hld up and bhd: hdwy 8f out: ev ch 2f out: sn rdn: one pce fnl f* **4/7**[1]
0 **4** 12 **Brave Jo (FR)**[8] [1681] 4-10-11................ KBurke[(7)] 70
(N J Hawke) *prom: led 8f out tl over 4f out: rdn over 3f out: wknd wl over 1f out* **33/1**
5 5 **Oakfield Legend** 4-11-4................ OMcPhail 65
(P S Payne) *hld up and bhd: hdwy 9f out: led over 4f out tl over 3f out: wknd wl over 1f out* **28/1**
6 18 **Chesnut Annie (IRE)** 4-10-11................ ChristianWilliams 40
(Miss H E Roberts) *hld up and bhd: hdwy on ins 8f out: wknd over 5f out* **20/1**
7 dist **Highworth Lady**[190] 5-10-4................ MrDGreenway[(7)] —
(H J Manners) *prom: rdn 7f out: wknd over 5f out: t.o* **50/1**
8 dist **Nature's Magic** 4-10-11................ AO'Keeffe —
(R J Price) *a bhd: t.o* **8/1**[3]
9 1 ¼ **Penny Strong** 5-10-8................ RYoung[(3)] —
(A J Whiting) *hld up: hdwy after 6f: rdn 8f out: wknd 7f out: t.o* **16/1**
10 hd **Inissam Storm** 4-11-4................ TScudamore —
(D Brace) *hld up in tch: wknd 9f out: t.o* **20/1**
11 15 **Sheknowsyouknow** 4-10-4................ MrJAJenkins[(7)] —
(H J Manners) *bhd after 6f: t.o* **13/2**[2]
0 **R** **Double Grace (IRE)**[35] [1459] 5-10-4................ MissLGardner[(7)] —
(Mrs S Gardner) *led: hung bdly lft after 5f: hdd after 6f: 2nd whn rn out and uns rdr bnd 8f out* **66/1**

3m 55.3s (-5.80) **Going Correction** -0.675s/f (Firm) **12** Ran SP% **123.9**
Speed ratings: **86,85,84,78,76 68,—,—,—,— —,—** CSF £320.72 TOTE £13.50: £3.10, £6.50, £1.02; EX 219.20 Place 6 £265.08, Place 5 £101.34.
Owner Bigwigs Bloodstock III **Bred** Airlie Stud **Trained** Coedkernew, Newport

FOCUS
One of the worst bumpers we can recall, and run in a slow time. It has been giving a token rating to the level of the winner's sixth of eight last time.

NOTEBOOK
Surfboard(IRE) was well held in three previous tries, the most recent in May. Steering a wide course throughout, he scored more easily than the margin suggests but this was a dire event. *(op 12-1)*
Dateldoo(IRE), a half-sister to a couple of Irish bumper winners, looked to have lost her chance when running very wide on the home turn but she rallied to good effect once straightened up. She had a relatively hard race on this debut. *(op 8-1)*
Debris(IRE), who created a good impression when winning his sole Irish point in May of last year, is a half-brother to successful staying chaser The Bud Club. He was rather disappointing on this debut under Rules, but is going to need further and remains the best long-term prospect in this poor field. *(op 4-5)*
Brave Jo(FR), a half-brother to winning hurdler Eau Pure who was well beaten on his recent debut, still looked green and was administered some reminders with a circuit to run. In all probability he is a very modest performer. *(op 22-1)*
Oakfield Legend, a half-brother to Pams Oak, a winning chaser for this yard, showed a hint of ability on this debut. *(op 20-1)*
Sheknowsyouknow, a half-sister to the Manners yard's winning hurdler Jonanaud, was the subject of on-course support but showed not a shred of ability. *(op 20-1)*
T/Plt: £786.30 to a £1 stake. Pool: £46,805.40. 43.45 winning tickets. T/Qpdt: £67.60 to a £1 stake. Pool: £4,003.90. 43.80 winning tickets. KH

1607 MARKET RASEN (R-H)
Sunday, October 16

OFFICIAL GOING: Good
The ground was described as 'mainly good but with some firm patches' which resulted in casualties.
Wind: Light, half behind Weather: Fine, sunny and warm

1756 RACING UK (S) H'CAP HURDLE (8 hdls) 2m 1f 110y
2:20 (2:20) (Class 5) (0-95,94) 4-Y-0+ **£2,331** (£666; £333)

Form RPR
3163 **1** **Sheer Guts (IRE)**[11] [1643] 6-11-9 **91**................(vt) AThornton 96+
(Robert Gray) *rr-div: pushed along and hdwy 4th: jnd ldr 2 out: styd on to ld nr fin* **8/1**
0-1P **2** ½ **Aleemdar (IRE)**[24] [1520] 8-10-4 **77**................(p) DLaverty[(5)] 81
(A E Jones) *hld up in mid-div: stdy hdwy 4th: led appr 2 out: hdd and no ex nr fin* **6/1**[1]
2-1P **3** 10 **Irish Blessing (USA)**[161] [237] 8-11-3 **85**................(tp) LAspell 80+
(F Jordan) *chsd ldrs: one pce fr 2 out* **7/1**[2]
-006 **4** 3 **Irish Prince (IRE)**[19] [1567] 9-10-4 **72**................(b) GLee 63
(Robert Gray) *led tl appr 2 out: grad weakaned* **9/1**
5506 **5** shd **Lone Soldier (FR)**[14] [1607] 9-11-0 **89**................ CDSharkey[(7)] 79
(S B Clark) *in rr: hdwy 3 out: kpt on same pce fr next* **15/2**[3]
2-P6 **6** 7 **Alpine Hideaway (IRE)**[14] [1610] 12-11-9 **94**................(p) MrTGreenall[(3)] 78+
(J S Wainwright) *in rr: hdwy 3 out: nvr nr ldrs* **12/1**
30P **7** 6 **Scippit**[22] [1553] 6-10-12 **80**................ DO'Meara 57
(Miss Tracy Waggott) *in rr and drvn along 3rd: sme hdwy 3 out: nvr on terms* **28/1**
0P66 **8** ¾ **Brother Ted**[52] [1322] 8-10-8 **76**................(t) NFehily 55+
(J K Cresswell) *chsd ldrs: hit 6th: wknd 2 out: j.lft last* **33/1**
60-6 **9** ½ **Noble Pursuit**[19] [1569] 8-10-5 **80**................ PKinsella[(7)] 56
(R E Barr) *hdwy 4th: chsng ldrs 3 out: wknd appr next* **14/1**
050 **10** ¾ **Longstone Lass**[69] [1180] 5-10-8 **83**................ MissCMetcalfe[(7)] 60+
(Miss Tracy Waggott) *swvd lft s: hdwy to chse ldrs 3rd: lost pl after 3 out* **9/1**
-520 **11** 18 **Protocol (IRE)**[50] [1344] 11-11-5 **90**................(tp) LVickers[(3)] 47
(Mrs S Lamyman) *a in rr* **16/1**
-650 **12** 1 ¼ **L'Etang Bleu (FR)**[42] [1409] 7-10-1 **76**................(tp) RLucey-Butler[(7)] 32
(P Butler) *a bhd* **33/1**
650F **13** 6 **Royaltea**[3] [1724] 4-10-6 **79**................ LTreadwell[(5)] 29
(J T Stimpson) *w ldrs: drvn along 4th: wknd qckly appr 2 out: sn bhd* **10/1**
-006 **P** **Luminoso**[11] [1636] 13-11-4 **91**................(p) WKennedy[(5)] —
(J D J Davies) *bhd fr 4th: p.u bef 2 out* **22/1**
0F-0 **P** **Chiqitita (IRE)**[5] [1565] 4-10-1 **69**................ JamesDavies —
(Miss M E Rowland) *sn bhd and drvn along: p.u bef 2 out* **66/1**
6UU2 **P** **Known Maneuver (USA)**[48] [1357] 7-9-7 **68**................ CMStudd[(7)] —
(M C Chapman) *in rr whn j.lft 3rd: t.o 4th: p.u bef next* **14/1**
50-P **P** **Awwal Marra (USA)**[19] [1566] 5-10-11 **79**................(b[1]) BHarding —
(E W Tuer) *chsd ldrs: lost pl 5th: bhd whn p.u bef 2 out* **25/1**

4m 19.6s (3.20) **Going Correction** +0.325s/f (Yiel)
WFA 4 from 5yo+ 13lb **17** Ran SP% **124.7**
Speed ratings: **105,104,100,99,98 95,93,92,92,92 84,83,81,—,— —,—** CSF £52.96 CT £364.99 TOTE £7.50: £2.20, £1.90, £2.30, £2.60; EX 76.60.The winner was bought in for 7,000gns.
Owner Naughty Diesel Ltd **Bred** E Tynan **Trained** Malton, N Yorks

FOCUS
Fairly solid form at a low level rated through the third.

NOTEBOOK
Sheer Guts(IRE), having his second outing for his new yard, took some rousting along. He stuck to his guns and, living up to his name, put his head in front where it matters most.
Aleemdar(IRE), pulled up last time, travelled strongly but after going on narrowly missed out at the line.
Irish Blessing(USA), absent since April, looked in top trim but this trip is too short for him now. *(op 9-1)*
Irish Prince(IRE), out of form, took them along and set the race up for his stablemate. *(op 10-1 tchd 11-1)*
Lone Soldier(FR) ran a shade better and may be worth another try over further. *(op 7-1 tchd 8-1)*
Alpine Hideaway(IRE), runner-up last year, was making his fourth attempt to carry off this prize but anno Domini seems to have caught up with him. *(op 8-1)*
Known Maneuver(USA) *Official explanation: jockey said gelding lost its action (op 16-1)*

1757 OCTOBER MAIDEN HURDLE (10 hdls) 2m 3f 110y
2:50 (2:52) (Class 4) 4-Y-0+ **£3,444** (£984; £492)

Form RPR
1 **Nicolas Mon Ami (FR)**[124] 4-11-2................ GLee 112+
(J Howard Johnson) *trckd ldrs: led on bit 2 out: sn clr: v easily: fin lame* **1/1**[1]
650 **2** 6 **The Boobi (IRE)**[22] [1554] 4-10-10 ow1................ JPMcNamara 76
(Miss M E Rowland) *mid-div: hdwy 3 out: styd on fr next: tk 2nd nr fin* **150/1**
36- **3** ¾ **Zouave (IRE)**[358] [1810] 4-11-2................ NFehily 81
(C J Mann) *trckd ldrs: led 7th: hdd appr 2 out: one pce* **5/2**[2]
0 **4** 11 **Lytham (IRE)**[139] [596] 4-10-11................ DCCostello[(5)] 70
(J J Quinn) *rr-div: hdwy 6th: one pce fr 3 out* **16/1**
00 **5** 4 **Land Sun's Legacy (IRE)**[14] [1614] 4-10-13................(p) ACCoyle[(3)] 66
(J S Wainwright) *mid-div: mstke 7th: nvr a factor* **200/1**
6/ **6** 3 **Europrime Games**[31] [1399] 7-10-9................ TJDreaper[(7)] 63
(M E Sowersby) *led to 2nd: chsd ldrs: wknd appr 2 out* **200/1**
335- **7** 3 ½ **Zealand**[288] [2364] 5-10-13................ PWhelan[(3)] 60
(R A Fahey) *mid-div: hdwy to chse ldrs 3 out: wknd appr next* **10/1**[3]
05-5 **8** 10 **Shulmin**[53] [1307] 5-10-6................ PAspell[(3)] 43
(J Wade) *in rr: sme hdwy 7th: sn wknd* **20/1**
003- **9** 11 **Myoss (IRE)**[251] [3744] 6-11-2................ MFoley 39
(Mrs V J Makin) *bhd: sme hdwy 7th: nvr a factor* **40/1**

5-0 **10** *5* **New Wish (IRE)**[9] 1661 5-10-9 .... CDSharkey(7) 34
(S B Clark) *hld up in rr: stdy hdwy 6th: lost pl 3 out* **33/1**

0 **11** *1* **Southern Bazaar (USA)**[95] 892 4-11-2 .... RMcGrath 33
(M E Sowersby) *in rr: sme hdwy 6th: lost pl 3 out* **150/1**

PP **12** *dist* **Thorny Issue**[14] 1619 6-10-12 ow3........(v[1]) MrMatthewSmith(7) —
(M J Gingell) *led 2nd: hdd 7th: wknd qckly: sn bhd: t.o* **200/1**

P- **P** **Back De Bay (IRE)**[336] 2230 5-10-9 .... APogson(7) —
(J R Cornwall) *bhd: t.o whn p.u bef 2 out* **200/1**

66- **P** **Actual**[202] 4625 5-11-2 .... BHarding —
(P D Niven) *bhd and reminders 5th: t.o whn p.u bef 2 out* **40/1**

0- **P** **The Rainbow Man**[275] 3346 5-11-2 .... LAspell —
(J Ryan) *t.k.h: w ldrs: lost pl 3rd: bhd whn p.u bef next* **20/1**

0-0 **P** **Miss Ocean Monarch**[17] 780 5-10-9 .... HOliver —
(Miss Tracy Waggott) *chsd ldrs to 5th: sn lost pl: bhd whn p.u bef 2 out* **125/1**

4m 58.6s (8.60) **Going Correction** +0.325s/f (Yiel) **16** Ran SP% **115.0**
Speed ratings: **95,92,92,87,86 85,83,79,75,73 72,—,—,—,— —** CSF £265.26 TOTE £1.80: £1.10, £12.80, £1.70; EX 110.30.
Owner Andrea & Graham Wylie **Bred** Guy De Villette **Trained** Billy Row, Co Durham

FOCUS
A modest time, even for a maiden hurdle, although the winner is value for considerably more than the official margin.

NOTEBOOK
Nicolas Mon Ami(FR), showed form on the Flat and over hurdles in his native France, is a grand type. He made this look very easy but was very lame pulling up and he faces a lengthy spell on the sidelines. *(tchd 6-5 and 5-4 in a place)*
The Boobi(IRE), who showed little in three starts in bumpers, is an exciteable type. She kept on to snatch second spot near the line but what she actually achieved is open to doubt.
Zouave(IRE), who has had throat surgery, went on but it was soon clear that he was no match for the winner and in the end he just missed out on second spot. *(tchd 9-4)*
Lytham(IRE) has yet to conclusively prove that he stays the trip over hurdles.
Land Sun's Legacy(IRE), beaten a long way in two previous outings, showed his first glimmer of form.
The Rainbow Man *Official explanation: jockey said gelding lost its action (op 16-1)*

1758 VICTOR LUCAS MEMORIAL NOVICES' CHASE (12 fncs) 2m 1f 110y
3:20 (3:27) (Class 3) 4-Y-0+ **£7,605** (£2,340; £1,170; £585)

Form RPR

1 **Hoo La Baloo (FR)**[198] 4-10-5 .... RWalsh 130+
(P F Nicholls) *j. boldly: mde all: lft virtually alone 2 out* **11/8**[1]

/14- **2** *dist* **The Rising Moon (IRE)**[338] 2166 6-11-4 .... APMcCoy 98
(Jonjo O'Neill) *in tch: mstke 4th: outpcd and lost pl 4 out: lft poor 2nd 2 out: btn 48l* **4/1**[3]

5P-1 **3** *dist* **Cyborg De Sou (FR)**[25] 1509 7-11-5 .... WKennedy(5) 81
(G A Harker) *stdd s: hld up in last: sme hdwat 8th: lft distant 3rd 2 out: btn 31 l* **28/1**

P **4** *dist* **Sandy Gold (IRE)**[9] 1662 7-11-4 .... PMoloney —
(Miss J E Foster) *in tch: reminders 6th: lost pl next: blnd 4 out: t.o whn lft 4th 2 out: btn 55 l* **400/1**

0R00 **L** **Dabus**[14] 1610 10-11-4 99 .... SStronge —
(M C Chapman) *whipped rnd and uns rdr s: tk no part* **150/1**

20-1 **F** **Tighe Caster**[42] 1411 6-11-10 .... TDoyle 128+
(P R Webber) *chsd ldrs: lft 2nd 3 out: 6l 2nd and wl btn whn fell 2 out* **6/1**

12-1 **F** **Coat Of Honour (USA)**[120] 208 5-11-4 .... GLee 123
(J Howard Johnson) *chsd wnr: rdn after 4 out: 4 l 2nd and styng on whn fell 3 out* **11/4**[2]

4m 25.2s (-5.90) **Going Correction** +0.225s/f (Yiel)
WFA 4 from 5yo+ 13lb **7** Ran SP% **107.4**
Speed ratings: **107,—,—,—,— —,—** CSF £6.51 TOTE £2.70: £1.80, £2.10; EX 9.90.
Owner The Stewart Family **Bred** N P Bloodstock **Trained** Ditcheat, Somerset

FOCUS
A decent novice chase for the track with the winner impressive despite the horses chasing him departing in the straight. The time was decent and the winner is rated value for 20 lengths over the fallers.

NOTEBOOK
Hoo La Baloo(FR) ◆, unbeaten in three starts over hurdles at Bordeaux after the turn of the year, was sent to post early and in the delay sweated profusely. He raced with zest and jumped soundly and already looked in total control when his main challenger departed. Left clear at the next he looks an exciting recruit. *(op 5-4 tchd 6-4 in places)*
The Rising Moon(IRE), a winner of his only point in Ireland, stopped to nothing four out but was eventually handed a remote second spot. The form of his trainer's runners at present must be a cause for concern. *(op 7-2 tchd 9-2)*
Cyborg De Sou(FR), faced with a very stiff task, was dropped in at the start and never got *competitive. He was reported to have finished distressed.Official explanation: trainer said gelding finished distressed (op 33-1 tchd 25-1)*
Sandy Gold(IRE), a winner and placed in Irish points, is a big type but he has shown next to nothing in two starts here now. *(op 200-1)*
Coat Of Honour(USA), winner of four of his five starts over hurdles and rated 143, stuck to his guns but was in vain pursuit of the winner when crashing out. None the worse, he should soon make his mark. *(tchd 3-1)*
Tighe Caster was booked for third spot three out and forfeited the runner-up spot when crashing out at the next. *(tchd 3-1)*

1759 MARKET RASEN H'CAP CHASE (17 fncs) 3m 1f
3:50 (3:57) (Class 3) (0-130,130) 5-Y-0+ **£7,475** (£2,300; £1,150; £575)

Form RPR

3141 **1** **Bushido (IRE)**[19] 1568 6-11-2 120 .... DElsworth 130
(Mrs S J Smith) *chsd ldrs: wnt cl 2nd and reminders 4 out: led last: r.o wl* **8/1**

264- **2** *1* **Lou Du Moulin Mas (FR)**[183] 4864 6-11-7 125 ....(t) RWalsh 135+
(P F Nicholls) *disp ld: def advantage 12th: hdd last: no ex last 100yds* **9/4**[1]

P14/ **3** *19* **Alvino**[541] 4955 8-11-0 118 .... TJMurphy 108
(Miss H C Knight) *trckd ldrs: one pce appr 3 out: tk mod 3rd run-in* **14/1**

606- **4** *1* **Limerick Leader (IRE)**[211] 4449 7-11-0 118 ....(b) RJohnson 110+
(P J Hobbs) *chsd ldrs: drvn along 7th: reminders 10th: outpcd appr 3 out: mod 3rd whn blnd 2 out* **7/2**[2]

F0U- **5** *30* **Bold Investor**[214] 4398 8-11-5 126 .... TJPhelan(3) 85
(Jonjo O'Neill) *j.rt: nvr in tch: in rr fr 11th* **28/1**

20P- **6** *18* **Boy's Hurrah (IRE)**[176] 4984 9-10-10 114 .... GLee 55
(J Howard Johnson) *disp ld to 12th: wknd 4 out: sn bhd* **6/1**[3]

-242 **P** **Dark Room (IRE)**[91] 1025 8-10-8 112 .... APMcCoy —
(Jonjo O'Neill) *in tch: lost pl and p.u lame after 11th* **7/2**[2]

U0P- **P** **Moss Harvey**[234] 4024 10-11-12 130 .... DCrosse —
(J G M O'Shea) *reminders 6th: lost tch 8th: bhd whn p.u bef 11th* **33/1**

6m 21.2s (-16.20) **Going Correction** +0.225s/f (Yiel) **8** Ran SP% **113.7**
Speed ratings: **107,106,100,100,90 84,—,—** CSF £27.19 CT £249.80 TOTE £6.40: £1.90, £1.40, £2.90; EX 25.50.
Owner Mrs B Ramsden **Bred** Mrs George Robinson **Trained** High Eldwick, W Yorks

FOCUS
A fair handicap run at a sound gallop and rated through the runner-up.

NOTEBOOK
Bushido(IRE), 6lb higher, is not that big but he is a sound jumper and sticking to the stands'-side rail, was right on top at the line even though the margin was narrow. *(op 7-1)*
Lou Du Moulin Mas(FR) did absolutely nothing wrong but he has now finished runner-up nine times balanced against just one success. *(op 7-2)*
Alvino, absent for a year and a half, had the right-handed track he needs but he was easily left *behind over the last three fences and was afterwards reported to have a breathing problem.Official explanation: jockey said gelding had a breathing problem (op 9-1)*
Limerick Leader(IRE) lacked confidence at his fences and was soon in trouble. He just stays but needs to get his jumping sorted out.
Bold Investor continues in the doldrums. *(op 16-1)*
Boy's Hurrah(IRE) stopped to nothing starting the final turn and was lame afterwards. *Official explanation: jockey said gelding finished lame (op 15-2 tchd 8-1)*
Dark Room(IRE) was pulled up early on the final circuit and came back in the horse ambulance. *Official explanation: trainer said gelding finished lame (op 4-1)*

1760 WEST LINDSEY DISTRICT COUNCIL EASTER CUP H'CAP HURDLE (10 hdls) 2m 6f
4:20 (4:25) (Class 3) (0-125,122) 4-Y-0+ **£4,862** (£1,496; £748; £374)

Form RPR

130- **1** **Jorobaden (FR)**[190] 4770 5-11-5 122 .... PMerrigan(7) 136+
(Mrs H Dalton) *trckd ldrs: led 4th: styd on strly between last 2* **4/1**[2]

02-3 **2** *10* **Nathos (GER)**[15] 1598 8-11-8 118 .... NFehily 122+
(C J Mann) *hld u in rr: stdy hdwy 5th: wnt 2nd 3 out: 2 l down and hld whn hit last: sn wknd* **17/2**

P112 **3** *14* **Wise Tale**[14] 1606 6-10-2 98 ....(v) GLee 80
(P D Niven) *w ldrs: led 3rd to next: reminders 5th: outpcd 3 out: lft mod 3rd next* **10/3**[1]

0152 **4** *1 ¾* **Little Task**[4] 1715 7-9-12 97 .... PAspell(3) 77
(J S Wainwright) *in rr: hdwy 7th: nvr nr ldrs* **12/1**

244- **5** *16* **Canni Thinkaar (IRE)**[181] 4914 4-9-7 96 oh4........(p) RLucey-Butler(7) 60
(P Butler) *chsd ldrs: drvn along 6th: lost pl next* **25/1**

5-0P **6** *¾* **Fantastic Champion (IRE)**[22] 1549 6-11-1 118 .... APogson(7) 82
(J R Cornwall) *reminders 1st: in rr fr 6th* **50/1**

4-2P **P** **Hestherelad (IRE)**[24] 1528 6-9-7 96 oh6 .... MrTCollier(7) —
(R Johnson) *sn bhd: t.o 7th: p.u bef 2 out* **66/1**

0P00 **P** **Ramblees Holly**[19] 1571 7-10-7 103 .... MFoley —
(R S Wood) *sn bhd: t.o 7th: p.u bef 2 out* **33/1**

400- **P** **Sharp Belline (IRE)**[197] 4687 8-11-6 116 .... DElsworth —
(Mrs S J Smith) *led to 3rd: lost pl 5th: t.o whn p.u bef 7th* **17/2**

P-0P **P** **Friedhelmo (GER)**[6] 1111 9-10-2 105 ....(t) CDSharkey(7) —
(D W Chapman) *chsd ldrs: wknd rapidly 3 out: bhd whn p.u bef next* **25/1**

1-02 **P** **Hopbine**[130] 689 9-10-8 104 ....(p) PJBrennan —
(J L Spearing) *chsd ldrs: rdn and wknd 6th: sn bhd: t.o whn p.u bef 2 out* **9/2**[3]

21-2 **U** **Cottam Grange**[57] 372 5-11-2 115 .... MrTGreenall(3) 109
(M W Easterby) *hld up in rr: stdy hdwy 6th: rdn 3 out: 4 l 3rd and hld whn blnd and uns rdr 2 out* **15/2**

5m 31.7s (3.40) **Going Correction** +0.325s/f (Yiel)
WFA 4 from 5yo+ 14lb **12** Ran SP% **115.9**
Speed ratings: **106,102,97,96,90 90,—,—,—,— —,—** CSF £34.92 CT £125.38 TOTE £4.60: £2.00, £3.10, £1.70; EX 38.80.
Owner P J Hughes Developments Ltd **Bred** R Le Poder **Trained** Norton, Shropshire

FOCUS
A modest handicap but the principals are rated better than the bare form and the winner is worth keeping on the right side.

NOTEBOOK
Jorobaden(FR) ◆, absent since Aintree in April and making his handicap bow, travelled strongly in front and, given his head going to the last, had this won in a matter of strides. He must be kept on the right side. *(op 9-2)*
Nathos(GER) went in pursuit of the winner but his stamina looked at a very low ebb when he crashed through the last. *(op 8-1)*
Wise Tale, struggling with a circuit to go, was handed a modest third two out. *(op 11-4)*
Little Task found this company too tough and his busy spell may be catching up on him.
Canni Thinkaar(IRE) was having his first outing for six months and is a doubtful stayer.
Hopbine, absent since June, ran poorly and was eventually pulled up. *(op 6-1)*
Cottam Grange, fit from the Flat, was booked for a modest third place when giving his rider no chance. He is still 17lb higher than his last success. *(op 6-1)*

1761 DR GRAHAM PARRY APPRECIATION NOVICES' H'CAP CHASE (14 fncs) 2m 6f 110y
4:50 (4:53) (Class 3) (0-115,112) 5-Y-0+ **£5,492** (£1,690; £845; £422)

Form RPR

6/32 **1** **Darina's Boy**[14] 1618 9-10-11 100 .... PWhelan(3) 110+
(Mrs S J Smith) *trckd ldrs: led 10th: clr after next: styd on wl: eased last 100yds* **3/1**[1]

2206 **2** *3* **Iris's Prince**[19] 1568 6-11-2 109 .... TJDreaper(7) 112+
(A Crook) *prom: hit 2nd: outpcd 8th: styd on to take mod 2nd last: no ch w wnr* **28/1**

1326 **3** *5* **Beat The Heat (IRE)**[28] 1489 7-11-12 112 ....(b) BHarding 109
(Jedd O'Keeffe) *chsd ldrs: outpcd 9th: styd on to go 2nd appr 3 out: kpt on same pce* **17/2**

3F-U **4** *3* **Balladeer (IRE)**[15] 1595 7-11-10 110 .... TJMurphy 104
(Miss H C Knight) *wnt prom 5th: outpcd 9th: kpt on same pce fr 3 out* **7/1**

F24- **5** *30* **Full On**[275] 3345 8-11-0 100 .... RJohnson 74+
(A M Hales) *led: hit 4th: hdd 10th: wknd appr 3 out: 5th and wl btn whn blnd 2 out: eased* **7/2**[2]

P-PP **F** **Monti Flyer**[14] 1609 7-9-13 92 .... CDSharkey(7) —
(S B Clark) *mstke 1st: hdwy and prom whn fell 7th* **40/1**

121P **P** **Lake Merced (IRE)**[22] 1552 5-11-5 107 .... APMcCoy —
(Jonjo O'Neill) *prom: outpcd and lost pl 7th: sn bhd: p.u bef 3 out* **6/1**[3]

32-1 **P** **Mandica (IRE)**[169] 132 7-11-4 104 .... JMMaguire —
(T R George) *w ldrs: blnd and lost pl 4th: wnt prom 7th: lost pl 9th: bhd whn p.u bef 3 out* **7/2**[2]

5m 55.1s (8.70) **Going Correction** +0.225s/f (Yiel) **8** Ran SP% **112.6**
Speed ratings: **93,91,90,89,78 —,—,—** CSF £63.24 CT £639.37 TOTE £4.10: £1.50, £4.60, £2.10; EX 86.70.
Owner Mrs C Steel **Bred** D O Walsh **Trained** High Eldwick, W Yorks

FOCUS
An ordinary contest and a modest winning time for the grade. The form is rated through the runner-up but does not look strong.

The Form Book, Raceform Ltd, Compton, RG20 6NL

NOTEBOOK

Darina's Boy took a decisive lead and was kept up to his work until able to ease off near the line. This will have done his confidence a power of good. *(op 7-2)*

Iris's Prince, having just his second start over fences, ran a lot better sticking to his guns but in the end the margin of defeat greatly flatters him. *(op 22-1)*

Beat The Heat(IRE) probably ran somewhere near his best even though he is marginally better going left-handed. *(op 8-1)*

Balladeer(IRE), having his second outing in two weeks after a year off, was struggling early on the final circuit. *(op 6-1)*

Full On was out on his feet when he almost went two out, and that first win over fences is proving elusive to say the very least. *(op 9-2)*

Mandica(IRE) was struggling to re-enter the argument after an early blunder. *(op 5-1)*

Lake Merced(IRE) was another from this stable to run badly. *(op 5-1)*

1762 OERLEMANS MAIDEN OPEN NATIONAL HUNT FLAT RACE 2m 1f 110y
5:20 (5:22) (Class 6) 4-6-Y-0 **£1,974** (£564; £282)

Form RPR

0- **1** **Not For Diamonds (IRE)**[239] 3960 5-10-9 .... PMerrigan(7) 106+
(Mrs H Dalton) *hld up in mid-field: hdwy to ld over 7f out: sddle sn slipped: qcknd over 2f out: 8l clr 1f out: rdr sat stl: jst hld on* **11/2**[3]

00- **2** ¾ **Our Joycey**[196] 4720 4-10-2 .... CDSharkey(7) 85
(Mrs K Walton) *chsd ldrs: drvn along and lost pl 7f out: hdwy 3f out: styd on to take 2nd nr fin: jst failed* **25/1**

30- **3** 1¼ **Geraldine**[307] 2817 4-10-6 .... LVickers(3) 83
(Mrs S Lamyman) *hld up in mid-field: hdwy 6f out: styd on same pce fnl 2f* **28/1**

02- **4** 1¾ **It's Bertie**[254] 3682 5-11-2 .... DElsworth 89
(Mrs S J Smith) *chsd ldrs: wnt 2nd 2f out: kpt on one pce* **7/4**[1]

2-3 **5** 2½ **Crafty Lady (IRE)**[157] 316 6-10-2 .... RLucey-Butler(7) 80+
(Miss Suzy Smith) *chsd ldrs: one pce fnl 2f* **4/1**[2]

4 **6** 2 **Stoneferry**[16] 1593 5-10-9 ....(t) MrTCollier(7) 84
(R Johnson) *hld up in rr: hdwy 4f out: edgd rt and one pce fnl 2f* **22/1**

4 **7** 1½ **Seymour Weld**[116] 817 5-10-9 .... APogson(7) 86+
(C T Pogson) *handful beforehand: led: rn wd bnd after 7f: hdd over 7f out: fdd fnl 2f* **16/1**

8 5 **Penny King** 4-11-2 .... LAspell 78
(F Jordan) *mid-div: dropped rr 7f out: hdwy 4f out: nvr a factor* **16/1**

9 1¾ **Branodunum** 4-11-2 .... ADempsey 76
(M W Easterby) *bhd: reminders and hdwy on outer 6f out: nvr on terms* **14/1**

/ **10** ½ **Watercress** 5-10-10 ow1 .... JPMcNamara 69
(Miss M E Rowland) *hld up in rr: hdwy to chse ldrs over 4f out: wknd fnl 2f* **8/1**

6 **11** 18 **Cottam Phantom**[14] 1613 4-10-13 .... MrTGreenall(3) 57
(M W Easterby) *hld up in rr: bhd fnl 5f* **14/1**

0 **12** 1¾ **Barneys Joy**[14] 1613 6-10-9 .... MrDAFitzsimmons(7) 56
(O Brennan) *chsd ldrs: lost pl 6f out: sn bhd* **50/1**

4m 23.9s (7.40) **Going Correction** +0.325s/f (Yiel) **12** Ran SP% **121.6**
Speed ratings: **96,95,95,94,93 92,91,89,88,88 80,79** CSF £143.52 TOTE £7.00: £2.40, £6.30, £6.60; EX 91.50 Place 6 £21.70, Place 5 £9.48.
Owner M J & J M Scott **Bred** Countess Doenhoff **Trained** Norton, Shropshire

FOCUS
A weak bumper but the winner is rated value for much more than the official margin, while the fourth and sixth set the level for the form.

NOTEBOOK

Not For Diamonds(IRE), who showed ability on his debut in February, was in trouble when his saddle slipped well forward leaving the back straight. Encouraged to draw clear, his rider performed miracles to keep the partnership intact late on. He was value for at least ten lengths. *(op 7-1)*

Our Joycey, who showed some ability in two starts in the spring, stuck to her guns and in the end was just denied. She looks to have more stamina than speed.

Geraldine, absent since disappointing on her second start in December, stuck on in her own time but like the remainder is greatly flattered by her proximity to the stricken winner. *(op 25-1)*

It's Bertie, absent since February, stuck on in his own time and should be better suited by hurdling. *(op 2-1)*

Crafty Lady(IRE), absent since May, is willing but looks to lack at least a couple of gears. *(op 3-1)*

Stoneferry sat off the pace and, though sticking on, he never looked like entering the argument. *(op 20-1 tchd 25-1)*

T/Plt: £26.10 to a £1 stake. Pool: £48,700.10. 1,360.10 winning tickets. T/Qpdt: £12.70 to a £1 stake. Pool: £2,999.00. 173.70 winning tickets. WG

1763 - 1771a (Foreign Racing) - See Raceform Interactive

[1478] PLUMPTON (L-H)
Monday, October 17

OFFICIAL GOING: Good
Wind: Almost nil Weather: Fine

1772 KEN MANLEY MOORCROFT CHARITY MAIDEN HURDLE (9 hdls) 2m
2:10 (2:11) (Class 4) 4-Y-0+ **£2,723** (£778; £389)

Form RPR

130- **1** **Dusky Lord**[191] 4774 6-11-2 .... LAspell 114+
(N J Gifford) *prom: trckd ldr 6th: led 3 out: j.lft 2 out: jnd flat: battled on gamely* **7/2**[2]

P-22 **2** nk **Turbo (IRE)**[11] 1654 6-11-2 109........................(p) TDoyle 111+
(T G Mills) *t.k.h: hld up in rr: gd prog fr 3 out: chal last: w wnr flat: nt qckn nr fin* **5/4**[1]

3 3 **Selective**[83] 6-11-2 ....(t) JimCrowley 109+
(K G Reveley) *prom: trckd ldr 4th to 6th: 2nd again 3 out: cl up and sltly hmpd 2 out: one pce flat* **14/1**

4 7 **Dream Merchant (IRE)**[42] 5-11-2 .... RJohnson 101
(P J Hobbs) *settled in rr: sme prog fr 6th: drvn and nt pce to rch ldrs after 3 out: kpt on* **6/1**[3]

5 hd **Kings Signal (USA)**[1244] 7-11-2 .... PHide 104+
(M J Hogan) *nt fluent: plld hrd: hld up wl in rr: stdy prog gng wl 3 out: wnt 4th 2 out: wl hld whn blnd last: eased: improve* **100/1**

44 **6** 10 **Coronado's Gold (USA)**[11] 1654 4-11-2 .... PMoloney 93+
(V Smith) *t.k.h: hld up in tch: prog to join ldrs whn blnd bdly 6th: fdd bef 2 out* **33/1**

4-0 **7** 1¼ **Man Ray (USA)**[9] 1680 4-11-2 .... APMcCoy 90
(Jonjo O'Neill) *reluctant to leave paddock: in tch: mstke 5th: effrt next: drvn to chse ldrs 3 out: wknd next* **25/1**

-510 **8** 5 **It's My Party**[16] 1596 4-10-9 .... RLucey-Butler(7) 85
(W G M Turner) *chsd ldr to 2nd: styd handy tl rdn and wknd after 3 out* **66/1**

9 ½ **Prime Powered (IRE)**[16] 4-11-2 .... JEMoore 84
(G L Moore) *hld up in rr: effrt 6th: chsd ldrs 3 out: sn wknd* **10/1**

064- **10** 1½ **Jades Double**[182] 4916 4-10-9 .... JGoldstein 76
(M Madgwick) *j. slowly 1st: in touh towards rr tl wknd bef 3 out* **100/1**

P- **11** 1¼ **Hiawatha (IRE)**[14] 3635 6-10-11 .... WKennedy(5) 82
(A M Hales) *hld up in rr: stdy prog fr 5th: effrt to dispute 2nd after 3 out: wknd rapidly and hit next* **100/1**

12 1¾ **Serious Man (IRE)**[87] 1052 7-11-2 .... MBatchelor 80
(Mrs P Townsley) *nt jump wl: t.k.h: hld up in rr: blnd 2nd: wknd bef 3 out* **80/1**

/6P5 **13** 3 **Rome (IRE)**[13] 1632 6-11-2 94........................(b) RThornton 77
(G P Enright) *led: mstke 5th: hdd & wknd 3 out* **16/1**

00- **14** 2 **No Way Back (IRE)**[193] 4760 5-11-2 .... BFenton 75
(Miss E C Lavelle) *s.s: t.k.h and hld up in detached last: bhd fr 6th* **40/1**

P **Queenstown (IRE)**[17] 4-10-11 .... DLaverty(5) —
(B A Pearce) *chsd ldr 2nd to 4th: wknd rapidly: p.u bef 6th: sddle slipped* **100/1**

50/ **P** **Meilleur (NZ)**[960] 3930 7-11-2 ....(t) JamesDavies —
(A J Whitehead) *t.k.h: hld up in tch: mstke 2nd: wknd u.p after 5th: t.o whn p.u bef 2 out* **100/1**

3m 49.5s (-11.70) **Going Correction** -0.80s/f (Firm)
WFA 4 from 5yo+ 13lb **16** Ran SP% **119.5**
Speed ratings: **97,96,95,91,91 86,86,83,83,82 82,81,79,78,— —** CSF £7.96 TOTE £6.00: £1.50, £1.10, £3.90; EX 11.00.
Owner The American Dream **Bred** J K M Oliver **Trained** Findon, W Sussex

FOCUS
An ordinary winning time despite being more than two seconds quicker than the later novices' handicap, but the front three pulled clear so the form is probably reliable. This was a decent novice event for the track and the winner was value for further.

NOTEBOOK

Dusky Lord gave another boost to the form of the Aintree Bumper won by The Cool Guy. Always there or thereabouts, he did give his supporters cause for concern with an alarming jump to his left two out, but when it came to a battle on the run-in he looked far more convincing than the runner-up. The form may not be that great, but he can only improve for this. *(tchd 9-2)*

Turbo(IRE) seemed to have timed his challenge just right, but when asked to go and win his race on the flat he was inclined to carry his head at a funny angle and was outbattled. He has now finished runner-up in his last three starts over hurdles, beaten less than a length each time, and his attitude on the run-in here suggests it is not a coincidence. *(op 6-4 tchd 11-10 and 13-8 in places)*

Selective, tongue-tied for this hurdling debut, ran with credit, but even though he was slightly hampered by the winner diving across him at the second last, it made no difference to the result. He should come on for this, but being a miler on the Flat he will probably always need a sharp track like this and a decent surface in order to see out the trip. *(op 9-1)*

Dream Merchant(IRE), rated around a stone inferior to the second and third on the level, was not disgraced on this hurdling debut, but having been placed over two miles on the Flat, probably found this too sharp. *(op 7-1 tchd 11-2)*

Kings Signal(USA), not seen since running on the Flat three and a half years ago, ran a most encouraging race on this hurdles debut and would probably have finished fourth had he not walked through the final flight. The problem is that he is a prime candidate to bounce if turned out again too soon, but his best form on the level came on a sound surface so the ground might turn against him whilst he is given time to get over this.

Coronado's Gold(USA) finished much further behind Turbo than he had done at Worcester last time, though he was down on his nose at the fourth last which would not have helped his chances at all. *(op 25-1)*

No Way Back(IRE) *Official explanation: jockey said gelding had a breathing problem*

Meilleur(NZ) *Official explanation: jockey said gelding had a breathing problem*

Queenstown(IRE) *Official explanation: jockey said saddle slipped*

1773 TOTEPOOL H'CAP HURDLE (14 hdls) 3m 1f 110y
2:40 (2:41) (Class 3) (0-120,117) 4-Y-0+ **£4,676** (£1,439; £719; £359)

Form RPR

46-5 **1** **Touch Of Fate**[161] 261 6-10-4 95........................ BJCrowley 96
(R Rowe) *led to after 2nd: styd handy: nt fluent 7th: drvn after 11th: effrt to ld 2 out: kpt on wl flat* **11/1**

5UP- **2** ¾ **Glacial Evening (IRE)**[250] 3759 9-11-7 117........................ WKennedy(5) 117
(R H Buckler) *hld up in tch: effrt 3 out: drvn to cl on ldrs fr 2 out: wnt 2nd flat: nt rch wnr* **9/1**

1543 **3** ¾ **Brigadier Benson (IRE)**[12] 1647 5-10-8 99........................ AThornton 98
(R H Alner) *prom: mde most fr 6th to 2 out: no ex flat* **7/2**[2]

P222 **4** 12 **Mylo**[16] 1595 7-11-9 114........................ APMcCoy 101
(Jonjo O'Neill) *racd wd: hld up: in tch 11th: sn rdn and fnd nil: n.d after 3 out* **7/1**[3]

5420 **5** 9 **Sound Skin (IRE)**[15] 1607 7-10-1 95........................(v[1]) CBolger(3) 77+
(A Ennis) *wl in tch: effrt to chal 3 out: wkng whn mstke 2 out: mstke last* **33/1**

P-31 **6** 12 **Glacial Delight (IRE)**[12] 1637 6-10-10 101........................ BFenton 73+
(Miss E C Lavelle) *plld way up to ld after 2nd: hdd 6th: w ldr after tl nt fluent 3 out: wknd rapidly: eased* **11/10**[1]

4-P5 **7** dist **Rollo (IRE)**[12] 1638 7-9-13 97........................(v) CPoste(7) —
(M F Harris) *prom tl wknd 9th: sn wl t.o* **33/1**

0PP/ **P** **Meticulous (USA)**[339] 2180 7-9-7 91 oh5........................ PMerrigan(7) —
(K J Burke) *in tch tl wknd after 11th: t.o whn p.u bef 2 out* **33/1**

6m 18.8s (-17.10) **Going Correction** -0.80s/f (Firm) **8** Ran SP% **109.5**
Speed ratings: **94,93,93,89,87 83,—,—** CSF £90.26 CT £387.63 TOTE £9.60: £2.70, £2.30, £1.40; EX 108.90.
Owner Richard Rowe Racing Partnership **Bred** Mrs T D Pilkington **Trained** Storrington, W Sussex

FOCUS
A modest pace for much of the way and the tempo did not increase until the last circuit. As a result the winning time was modest for the class. The riders took differing views as to where the best ground was with several taken wide at various stages. Sound form.

NOTEBOOK

Touch Of Fate, running for the first time since May, was never far away and found enough over the last couple of flights to keep his main rivals at bay. The way the race was run did not prove his stamina totally, but he did win a point over three miles and is still by no means exposed. *(op 9-1 tchd 8-1)*

Glacial Evening(IRE), racing for the first time in eight months and back over hurdles after a couple of unfortunate experiences over fences when last seen, is already a winner over this sort of trip and although he ran well he may have done even better in a more strongly-run race. *(op 8-1)*

Brigadier Benson(IRE), always up with the pace, was suited by the modest tempo as it helped conserve his stamina for this longer trip and it was not until the run-in that he was beaten. He did have the advantage of race fitness over the pair in front of him though. *(op 11-2)*

Mylo, back over hurdles for the first time since the spring having finished second in five of his six starts over fences in the meantime, travelled comfortably in the same old way and found nothing under pressure in the same old way. *(op 8-1 tchd 9-1)*

Sound Skin(IRE), visored for the first time, was trying beyond two and a half miles for the first time but did not appear to see it out despite the modest gallop.

Glacial Delight(IRE), raised a whopping 11lb for his Exeter victory, raced much more prominently this time, but not necessarily because his rider wanted it that way. Close enough until dropping *away tamely over the last half mile, either his recent win flattered him or this race came too soon.* *(op 4-5 tchd 5-4 in a place)*

1774 BETFAIR.COM NOVICES' H'CAP HURDLE (9 hdls) 2m
3:10 (3:12) (Class 4) (0-100,99) 3-Y-O+ **£3,346** (£956; £478)

Form RPR

400- **1** **Madison De Vonnas (FR)**[185] [4857] 5-11-12 **99**......................(t) BFenton 106+
(Miss E C Lavelle) *clr ldr tl stdd and hdd after 2nd: led again 4th: clr 6th: nt fluent 3 out and next: hrd pressed flat: hld on* **10/1**

2332 **2** ¾ **The Castilian (FR)**[11] [1649] 3-10-7 **97**......................(v) TJMurphy 85
(M C Pipe) *hld up wl in rr: stdy prog after 6th: chsd wnr after 3 out: clsd to chal after last: fnd little u.p flat* **9/2²**

5064 **3** 6 **Mariday**[25] [1525] 4-11-3 **90**.. LAspell 90+
(L Wells) *prom: chsd wnr 6th tl after 3 out: one pce* **20/1**

54-0 **4** 2½ **The Rip**[30] [306] 4-10-5 **85**.. SWalsh(7) 82+
(R M Stronge) *t.k.h: hld up wl in rr: stdy prog 3 out: wd bnd after and lost grnd: shkn up flat: nvr nrr: do bttr* **17/2**

6P1 **5** 8 **Dishdasha (IRE)**[22] [1563] 3-10-5 **95**.. NFehily 69+
(C R Dore) *hld up in rr: mstke 5th: effrt bef 3 out: no imp bef next* **7/1³**

02-0 **6** 21 **Lovely Lulu**[170] [134] 7-10-0 **73** oh6.. JMogford 41
(J C Tuck) *sweating: lost pl after 2nd: mstke 4th: rdn after next: lost tch w ldrs bef 3 out: eased 2 out* **25/1**

4045 **7** 2 **Alekhine (IRE)**[11] [1653] 4-10-9 **82**..(b¹) RJohnson 48
(P J Hobbs) *sweating: hld up: v awkward 2nd and nrly fell: mstke next: wknd bef 3 out: no ch whn blnd 2 out* **7/2¹**

00-0 **P** **Ace Coming**[175] [21] 4-10-9 **82**.. JamesDavies —
(D B Feek) *prom: mstke 3rd: wknd 6th: t.o whn p.u bef 2 out* **33/1**

0-60 **R** **Indigo Sky (IRE)**[22] [1562] 4-9-7 **73** oh9.. CMStudd(7) —
(B G Powell) *a in rr: wknd 6th: t.o in last trio whn ref 2 out* **40/1**

5/F- **P** **Spike Jones (NZ)**[288] [3176] 7-11-8 **95**.. RThornton —
(Mrs A M Thorpe) *t.k.h: led after 2nd to 4th: wknd 6th: t.o whn p.u bef 2 out* **10/1**

14-3 **F** **Tignasse (FR)**[11] [1651] 4-11-4 **98**.. MrTJO'Brien(7) 89
(G L Moore) *hld up in rr: effrt bef 6th: no imp on ldrs after 3 out: 6th and wl btn whn fell 2 out* **9/2²**

3m 51.6s (-9.60) **Going Correction** -0.80s/f (Firm)
WFA 3 from 4yo 17lb 4 from 5yo+ 13lb **11 Ran SP% 113.8**
Speed ratings: **92,91,88,87,83 72,71,—,—,—,—** CSF £51.35 CT £885.58 TOTE £12.50: £3.10, £2.00, £4.30; EX 54.10.
Owner N Mustoe **Bred** J Lamberet, & Mme Jaques Lamberet **Trained** Wildhern, Hants

FOCUS
An unsatisfactory contest in many ways, with the winning time over two seconds slower than the earlier maiden hurdle and the eventual winner gifted a sizeable advantage at the start. The form looks sound enough, however.

NOTEBOOK
Madison De Vonnas(FR), racing for the first time since April, was back over his best trip. Full marks must go to his rider who took a good six lengths out of his rivals at the start and that enabled him to keep enough in reserve for the business end in order to see off an unconvincing rival. This form has several question marks over it and the fact that he was already considered the best of these on BHB figures speaks volumes about his opponents. *(op 8-1)*
The Castilian(FR), on the face of it, appeared to run a decent race against his elders, but this was his fifth placing in as many starts over hurdles and he did not appear to battle as hard as the winner on the run-in when in with every chance. *(op 4-1 tchd 6-1)*
Mariday had every chance, but lacked pace in the closing stages and probably needs further than this.
The Rip, fit from the Flat, travelled well but was not asked for an effort until the last two flights and even then the response was limited. He did hint at some ability in four outings over hurdles for Tim *Easterby and does give the impression there is a bit more to come from him for his new yard.* *Official explanation: jockey said gelding failed to get the trip (op 8-1 tchd 9-1)*
Dishdasha(IRE) never offered a threat and this effort does rather show how bad the race was he won at Huntingdon. *(op 8-1 tchd 13-2)*
Alekhine(IRE), blinkered for the first time and completely awash with sweat, screwed badly at the second flight, landed at a strange angle and was very fortunate to keep his feet. He never looked happy after that and has plenty of questions to answer now. *(op 4-1 tchd 3-1)*
Tignasse(FR) ran her race, but would only have finished fourth at best had she not tumbled over at the second last. *(op 4-1)*

1775 COMMERCIAL FIRST MORTGAGES NOVICES' HURDLE (12 hdls) 2m 5f
3:40 (3:41) (Class 4) 4-Y-O+ **£3,360** (£960; £480)

Form RPR

062- **1** **Stern (IRE)**[180] [4933] 6-10-12.. BFenton 108+
(Miss E C Lavelle) *racd wd: hld up: prog to press ldr 9th: narrow ld fr 2 out tl drvn clr flat* **4/1²**

435- **2** 2½ **Helm (IRE)**[8] [4691] 4-10-12 103.. JimCrowley 103+
(R Rowe) *mstke 2nd: led 4th: narrowly hdd 2 out: w wnr last: one pce flat* **25/1**

12 **3** 6 **Almizan (IRE)**[16] [1596] 5-11-5.. JEMoore 103
(G L Moore) *hld up in tch: prog 9th: chsd ldng trio 3 out: no imp next: kpt on* **8/1**

11U2 **4** 1¼ **Itsmyboy (IRE)**[15] [1617] 5-11-12 122..(p) TJMurphy 111+
(M C Pipe) *hld up in tch: bdly outpcd 9th and drvn: plugged on again after 3 out: nvr rchd ldrs* **11/8¹**

12 **5** 3½ **Anticipating**[12] [1642] 5-11-5.. PHide 99
(G L Moore) *hld up in rr: stdy prog 9th: chsd ldng pair 3 out and gng wl enough: wknd after 2 out* **13/2³**

-031 **6** ½ **Miss Merenda**[25] [1522] 4-10-12 94.. APMcCoy 91
(J F Panvert) *led to 4th: styd prom: drvn to chal 9th: outpcd fr 3 out* **16/1**

5-32 **7** nk **L'Eau Du Nil (FR)**[26] [1508] 4-10-12 105.. RJohnson 92+
(P J Hobbs) *wl in tch: mstke 3rd: rdn whn mstke 3 out: wknd* **7/1**

40P- **8** dist **English Jim (IRE)**[204] [4576] 4-10-12.. MBatchelor —
(Miss A M Newton-Smith) *in touh to 9th: wknd rapidly: t.o* **100/1**

00/ **9** 3½ **It's Official (IRE)**[294] [3037] 6-10-12 79.. JPMcNamara —
(Miss A M Newton-Smith) *in tch to 9th: wknd rapidly: t.o* **100/1**

005- **10** 7 **Dundridge Native**[228] [4141] 7-9-12 85.. RLucey-Butler(7) —
(M Madgwick) *prom: chsd ldr briefly bef 9th: sn wknd: t.o* **100/1**

U **Bon Accord** 5-10-12.. BJCrowley —
(Miss E C Lavelle) *hld up in last: j.big 1st and 2nd: awkward jump 3rd and uns rdr* **33/1**

P **The Hardy Boy**[176] 5-10-9.. CBolger(3) —
(Miss A M Newton-Smith) *prom tl wknd rapidly after 8th: sn wl t.o: p.u bef last* **50/1**

5m 6.50s (-18.30) **Going Correction** -0.80s/f (Firm)
WFA 4 from 5yo+ 14lb **12 Ran SP% 116.7**
Speed ratings: **102,101,98,98,96 96,96,—,—,— —,—** CSF £95.23 TOTE £5.70: £1.60, £3.40, £2.80; EX 82.40.
Owner Adams, Payne, O'Connor, Gilchrist **Bred** Seamus Murphy **Trained** Wildhern, Hants

FOCUS
The pace seemed sound enough on this occasion but this does not look an easy race to rate. The third to fifth were probably below their best and the proximity of the sixth is a worry, but the race could have been rated higher.

NOTEBOOK
Stern(IRE) ♦, who had shown plenty of ability in two outings over hurdles when last seen back in April, maintained the progress on this reappearance and saw the trip out really well. He shapes as though he will get even further. *(tchd 7-2 and 5-1)*
Helm(IRE), given a spin on the Flat the previous week, was given a positive ride and was the only one able to live with the winner. He might be better off back in novices' handicaps on an easier surface.
Almizan(IRE) saw the trip out a bit better this time, but his penalty continues to do him few favours against progressive sorts like the winner. *(tchd 10-1)*
Itsmyboy(IRE) faced a stiff task under his double penalty, but tended to race in snatches and may need an even stiffer test and a return to handicaps. *(op 13-8 tchd 7-4)*
Anticipating was another facing a stiff task under a penalty, but lack of stamina was a bigger problem in this. *(op 6-1)*
Miss Merenda appears to need a much stiffer test of stamina than this and would be better off back in mares-only novice hurdles over further. *(op 14-1)*

1776 STERLING INSURANCE GROUP NOVICES' H'CAP CHASE (14 fncs) 2m 4f
4:10 (4:10) (Class 4) (0-95,87) 4-Y-O+
£3,723 (£1,412; £706; £321; £160; £96)

Form RPR

326- **1** **Mystical Star (FR)**[300] [2933] 8-11-0 **75**.. LAspell 95+
(M J Hogan) *t.k.h: trckd ldrs: wnt 2nd after 9th: led and j.lft 3 out: sn clr: mstke 2 out: kpt on* **5/1³**

234- **2** 7 **Five Alley (IRE)**[178] [4959] 8-11-12 **87**.. BHitchcott 97
(R H Buckler) *nvr gng that wl in rr: effrt 9th: chsd ldng pair 4 out: wnt 2nd 2 out: no real imp on wnr* **11/4¹**

5P-P **3** 5 **Charliemoore**[13] [1631] 9-11-10 **85**..(b¹) JEMoore 93+
(G L Moore) *led: mstke 9th and drvn: hdd and bmpd 3 out: no ch w wnr after: lost 2nd 2 out* **16/1**

060- **4** 12 **Moscow Gold (IRE)**[437] [1132] 8-10-3 **64**.. MBradburne 57
(A E Price) *mstke 1st: a in rr: lost tch fr 9th: wl bhd after* **16/1**

066- **5** nk **Miss Doublet**[223] [4241] 4-10-7 **82**.. AThornton 61
(J W Mullins) *mstkes: in tch in rr to 9th: sn struggling and bhd* **9/1**

0065 **6** 18 **Stopwatch (IRE)**[16] [1595] 10-10-5 **66**..(p) PHide 41
(Mrs L C Jewell) *prom: wnt 2nd briefly after 8th: blnd 9th: wknd 4 out: t.o* **13/2**

4F24 **F** **Gold Quest (IRE)**[22] [1560] 8-11-6 **81**.. DRDennis —
(Ian Williams) *chsd ldrs: drvn after 8th: sn btn: last and wl bhd whn crashing fall 3 out* **3/1²**

FPP **P** **Castle Oliver (IRE)**[13] [1631] 7-10-9 **70**.. SCurran —
(A J Chamberlain) *pressed ldr: nt fluent 8th: sn rdn and no rspnse: t.o in last whn p.u bef 10th* **12/1**

FU0/ **F** **New Leader (IRE)**[589] [4209] 8-10-8 **69**.. MBatchelor —
(Mrs L Richards) *hld up: mstkes 7th and 8th: effrt after next: disputing 4th and jst in tch whn fell 10th* **25/1**

5m 10.4s (-8.05) **Going Correction** -0.40s/f (Good)
WFA 4 from 7yo+ 14lb **9 Ran SP% 115.0**
Speed ratings: **100,97,95,90,90 83,—,—,—** CSF £19.84 CT £203.65 TOTE £7.40: £2.40, £1.80, £3.10; EX 25.10.
Owner Mrs Barbara Hogan **Bred** Satwa Farm **Trained** North End, W Sussex

FOCUS
A very poor event of its type and they finished well strung out, but at least the pace was sound. Selling-class form, rated through the runner-up.

NOTEBOOK
Mystical Star(FR), racing for the first time in ten months, made a successful chasing debut and basically had the race won when jumping past the long-time leader at the third last. He already looks likely to make a better chaser than he was a hurdler, but will need to find a similarly weak race if he is to win again. *(op 7-1)*
Five Alley(IRE), off since April, took an age to get going and, as befits a horse that has been running over further in his latest starts, was plodding on when the race was over. He is very moderate. *(op 7-2)*
Charliemoore, blinkered for the first time, made the running but looked to have run his race when colliding with the eventual winner in mid-air after jumping the third last. He at least completed this time, which about says it all. *(op 12-1)*
Moscow Gold(IRE) achieved nothing in finishing a remote fourth.
Gold Quest(IRE), who has run with such promise over hurdles and fences recently, ran a shocker and was a long way behind when failing to take off at the third last. *(op 7-2 tchd 11-4)*
New Leader(IRE) still had a small chance of making the frame when crashing out at the first fence in the back straight on the final circuit. He has now failed to complete in five of his seven starts over fences. *(op 7-2 tchd 11-4)*

1777 CENKOS SECURITIES MAIDEN OPEN NATIONAL HUNT FLAT RACE 2m 2f
4:40 (4:47) (Class 6) 4-6-Y-O **£1,925** (£550; £275)

Form RPR

33 **1** **Mr Ex (ARG)**[16] [1600] 4-11-4..(p) JEMoore 100
(G L Moore) *prom: trckd ldr 6f out: rdn to ld over 2f out: sn hrd pressed: kpt on: all out* **16/1**

2 hd **Malt Sunflower (IRE)**[148] 4-11-4.. NFehily 100
(C J Mann) *t.k.h: wl in tch: effrt 5f out: rdn to chse ldrs 3f out: str chal over 1f out: jst hld* **14/1**

34- **3** 1¼ **Nocturnally**[190] [4801] 5-11-4.. ATinkler 99
(V R A Dartnall) *t.k.h: hld up last: rapid prog 6f out: pressed ldrs over 2f out: chal over 1f out: nt qckn* **2/1¹**

/3-5 **4** 4 **The Baillie (IRE)**[9] [1681] 6-11-4.. APMcCoy 95
(C R Egerton) *w ldr: led after 6f: rdn 3f out: hdd over 2f out: nt qckn u.p* **9/2³**

5- **5** 5 **Geordie Peacock (IRE)**[181] [4922] 6-11-4.. SThomas 90
(Miss Venetia Williams) *led for 6f: trckd ldr to 6f out: drvn over 3f out: fdd* **11/2**

6 ½ **Summer Liric** 4-11-1.. RYoung(3) 90
(J W Mullins) *trckd ldrs: in tch over 3f out: grad wknd* **66/1**

7 2½ **Forensic Investor (IRE)** 5-11-4.. TDoyle 87
(P R Webber) *t.k.h: hld up in rr: effrt 1/2-way: pushed along and outpcd over 5f out: plugged on* **3/1²**

8 15 **Knocker Jock (FR)** 5-11-4.. BFenton 72
(R Rowe) *t.k.h: in tch: outpcd fr 6f out: no ch after* **33/1**

9 19 **Lord West** 4-11-4.. AThornton 53
(R H Alner) *hld up in last trio: wknd over 5f out: sn bhd* **25/1**

/0-3 **10** ½ **Jeepers Creepers**[13] [1635] 5-11-4.. RJohnson 53
(Mrs A M Thorpe) *trckd ldrs tl wknd 6f out* **25/1**

The Form Book, Raceform Ltd, Compton, RG20 6NL

11 *dist* **Charlie Chestnut** 5-11-1 .... CBolger(3) —
(Mrs P Townsley) *in tch to over 6f out: wknd rapidly: t.o* **50/1**

F **Corporal Pete** 4-10-11 .... MrJNewbold(7) —
(Lady Connell) *in tch to 6f out: sn wknd: 10th whn fell 2f out: dead* **80/1**

4m 14.7s (-10.05) **Going Correction** -0.80s/f (Firm)
WFA 4 from 5yo+ 13lb **12** Ran SP% **119.8**
Speed ratings: **90,89,89,87,85 85,84,77,68,68** —,— CSF £205.96 TOTE £17.00: £3.20, £3.50, £1.70; EX 99.00.
Owner N J Jones **Bred** Firmamento **Trained** Woodingdean, E Sussex

FOCUS
A modest bumper in which the early pace was modest and it developed into a sprint from the home turn. The jockeys seemed keen to race towards the outside of the track on the bends in search of better ground. The winner's Fontwell run is working out, and the fourth and fifth ran to their marks.

NOTEBOOK
Mr Ex(ARG), already placed in a couple of bumpers, just managed to prevail in the three-way battle up the home straight. The first-time cheekpieces may have had an effect, but in all probability he only needed to reproduce his previous efforts to win this. He will find things harder under a penalty and it may be wise to put him over hurdles now. *(op 12-1)*
Malt Sunflower(IRE), winner of an Irish point on his last start back in May, very nearly got up to win with the stands' rail to help him and looks as though he will need a test of stamina to show his best. *(op 11-1 tchd 10-1)*
Nocturnally, off since April, made a swift move from the back of the field down the back straight on the final circuit and had every chance up the straight, but was done for foot when it mattered. He will not find many greater tests of stamina than this in bumpers, so may be better off in staying novice hurdles. *(op 9-4)*
The Baillie(IRE) was not disgraced, but neither is he progressing in bumpers and is another that looks to need a switch to staying novice hurdles. *(op 7-2 tchd 11-2)*
Geordie Peacock(IRE), off since his debut in April, was given a positive ride but did not get home and he might just have needed it. *(op 5-1 tchd 6-1)*
Forensic Investor(IRE), whose dam was placed in an Irish bumper, was well backed to make a winning debut but never really held out much hope. *(op 9-2 tchd 5-1)*

1778 SIMON GIBSON H'CAP CHASE (18 fncs) 3m 2f
5:10 (5:15) (Class 3) (0-120,117) 5-Y-0+
£4,790 (£1,817; £908; £413; £206; £123)

Form RPR

2302 **1** **Tommy Carson**[29] [1484] 10-10-0 **94** .... CBolger(3) 104
(Jamie Poulton) *led: rdn and hdd 4 out: dropped to 3rd and looked btn 2 out: rallied last: drvn to ld nr fin* **5/2**[2]

3P-P **2** *½* **Midnight Gunner**[167] [176] 11-10-5 **96** .... MBradburne 106+
(A E Price) *w wnr: mstke 9th: led 4 out: hrd pressed 2 out: hdd nr fin* **16/1**

4453 **3** *1* **Keltic Lord**[12] [1637] 9-11-6 **111** .... RThornton 119
(P W Hiatt) *hld up in tch: prog 14th: rdn to chse ldr bef 2 out and sn chalng: upsides last: no ex flat* **11/2**

1F-4 **4** *11* **Radcliffe (IRE)**[9] [1670] 8-10-11 **102** .... SThomas 104+
(Miss Venetia Williams) *trckd ldrs: hit 2nd: mstke 12th: 3rd and in tch whn blnd 4 out: btn after* **9/4**[1]

141C **5** *5* **Charango Star**[9] [1678] 7-11-5 **110** .... TJMurphy 104+
(W K Goldsworthy) *hld up: prog on outer 12th: wl in tch 14th: sn rdn: wknd after 4 out* **5/1**[3]

1-6P **6** *dist* **Twisted Logic (IRE)**[16] [1599] 12-11-12 **117** .... RWalford —
(R H Alner) *chsd ldrs tl dropped to last 10th: lost tch 13th: sn bhd: t.o* **25/1**

P-03 **P** **Prokofiev (USA)**[16] [1599] 9-11-9 **114** ....(b) APMcCoy —
(Jonjo O'Neill) *chsd ldng pair: urged along fr 4th and nt keen: dropped away after 12th: t.o whn p.u bef 4 out* **7/1**

6m 55.1s (1.10) **Going Correction** -0.40s/f (Good) **7** Ran SP% **113.6**
Speed ratings: **82,81,81,78,76** —,— CSF £35.33 TOTE £3.10: £1.80, £6.90; EX 51.00 Place 6 £184.54, Place 5 £139.44.
Owner J Logan **Bred** W H F Carson **Trained** Telscombe, E Sussex
■ Colin Bolger's first winner since a gallops injury in March.

FOCUS
A race run at a very modest tempo and as a result the winning time was extremely slow. Not a race to get carried away with, and the winner has been rated to a similar level as when runner-up over course and distance recently.

NOTEBOOK
Tommy Carson, who has such a great record here, set only a moderate pace. He looked more likely to finish third than win starting up the home straight, but the early modest tempo meant that he had managed to keep a bit in reserve and, with the front pair not finding much, he rallied to snatch the race back in the dying strides. *(tchd 9-4)*
Midnight Gunner, off since May, helped set the modest tempo alongside the eventual winner until going for home at the middle fence in the back straight on the final circuit. However, he was never able to establish a significant advantage over his two nearest rivals and was unable to withstand the winner's rally. He has not managed a victory in two and a half years.
Keltic Lord was sent in pursuit of the leader rounding the home turn, but could not quite get to him whereas the winner's late rally nailed them both. He has been kept very busy since reappearing in the spring and looks ready for a break, especially with the ground now starting to turn against him. *(op 8-1)*
Radcliffe(IRE) may have found this coming a bit too soon after his recent reappearance, but some shoddy jumping was his main downfall. *(op 4-1)*
Charango Star took a walk in the market and performed accordingly. *(op 9-4)*
Prokofiev(USA) seems to have completely fallen out of love with the game. *(op 9-1)*
T/Plt: £245.30 to a £1 stake. Pool: £48,637.75. 144.70 winning tickets. T/Qpdt: £58.80 to a £1 stake. Pool: £3,949.70. 49.70 winning tickets. JN

[1636]EXETER (R-H)
Tuesday, October 18

OFFICIAL GOING: Good to soft
Wind: Nil Weather: Light rain; overcast

1779 RACING WELFARE AMATEUR RIDERS' NOVICES' HURDLE (11 hdls) 2m 6f 110y
2:10 (2:12) (Class 4) 4-Y-0+ **£3,510** (£1,080; £540; £270)

Form RPR

000/ **1** **Frosty Jak**[589] [4232] 7-11-1 .... MissSGaisford(3) 77
(J D Frost) *hld up: hdwy after 5th: lost pl 7th: rdn appr 3 out: rallied 2 out: hung rt flat: styd on to ld last strides* **33/1**

0025 **2** *nk* **Gray Knight (IRE)**[17] [1597] 8-10-13 75 ....(b) MrJETudor(5) 77
(Mrs T J Hill) *j.rt: led: clr whn rdn appr 3 out: ct last strides* **12/1**

05- **3** *3* **Star Double (ITY)**[285] [3238] 5-10-11 .... MrGTumelty(7) 76+
(N A Twiston-Davies) *t.k.h: a.p: mstke 1st: hit 7th: rdn to chse ldr 3 out: styd on same pce fr 2 out* **10/3**[2]

4 *25* **Bilton's Nap**[150] 6-10-11 .... MrlChanin(7) 49
(R H Alner) *hld up: lost pl and bhd 4th: hdwy appr 6th: rdn and wknd 8th* **11/10**[1]

6P0- **5** *2* **Cloneybrien Boy (IRE)**[209] [4526] 5-10-13 .... MrsLucyRowsell(5) 47
(Mrs A M Thorpe) *j.rt: t.k.h: prom: chsd ldr after 6th to 3 out: wknd 2 out* **100/1**

0-00 **F** **Oasis Blue (IRE)**[5] [1725] 4-10-10 .... MrRQuinn(7) —
(M C Pipe) *hld up in rr: hdwy and 6th whn fell 8th* **33/1**

F4/P **P** **Whispering John (IRE)**[16] [1615] 9-11-1 100 .... MrJSnowden(3) —
(W G M Turner) *bhd fr 6th: t.o whn p.u bef 3 out* **7/1**[3]

6 **P** **Pitton Prince**[37] [1459] 6-10-11 .... MrDavidTurner(7) —
(N R Mitchell) *hld up in tch: rdn 6th: sn wknd: no ch whn mstke 2 out: p.u bef last* **50/1**

F065 **P** **Regulated (IRE)**[13] [1643] 4-10-12 85 ....(b) MissFayeBramley(5) —
(P A Blockley) *j. and hung lft: prom tl wknd appr 6th: t.o whn p.u bef 3 out* **12/1**

0-05 **P** **Barum Belle**[13] [1640] 5-10-6 ....(t) MrSWaley-Cohen(5) —
(R A Farrant) *hld up and bhd: hdwy 5th: rdn appr 8th: wknd appr 3 out: bhd whn p.u bef last* **16/1**

5m 41.6s (2.30) **Going Correction** -0.05s/f (Good)
WFA 4 from 5yo+ 14lb **10** Ran SP% **113.3**
Speed ratings: **94,93,92,84,83** —,—,—,—,— CSF £354.12 TOTE £31.40: £6.20, £3.60, £1.10; EX 221.80.
Owner Commander L G Turner **Bred** J Joseph Bloodstock **Trained** Scorriton, Devon

FOCUS
A dire novice event, confined to amateur riders, and the first three came well clear. It has been rated through the runner-up.

NOTEBOOK
Frosty Jak , making his return from a 589-day layoff, looked to still have plenty of ground to make up turning into the home straight, but stuck to his task under pressure and just did enough to collar the long-time leader close home and score. He had shown very little in five previous outings at up to three miles, but he has clearly improved since last seen in 2004, and is entitled to come on again for this experience. *(op 40-1)*
Gray Knight(IRE) , beaten in selling handicaps on his previous three outings, looked at one point like finally getting his head back in front once more, but he was legless in the final 100 yards and proved powerless against the winner's late challenge. He would have found the easing ground against him and, when reverting to a faster surface and a shorter trip, may well be capable of finding compensation. *(op 9-1)*
Star Double(ITY) , well backed for this hurdling bow, lacked a change of gear and was disappointingly put in his place approaching the final flight. He has a fair bit to prove now. *(op 9-2 tchd 3-1)*
Bilton's Nap , winner of his last two outings between the flags, faded most disappointingly after moving into contention after halfway. While he may well leave this form behind when reverting to the larger obstacles, this effort leaves him with plenty to prove in the future. *(op 5-4 tchd 11-8)*

1780 HOMEOAK TRADING H'CAP CHASE (17 fncs) 2m 7f 110y
2:40 (2:41) (Class 4) (0-105,105) 5-Y-0+ **£4,784** (£1,472; £736; £368)

Form RPR

/P-U **1** **Bay Island (IRE)**[6] [1713] 9-10-7 **86** ....(t) NFehily 105+
(M Pitman) *hld up: hdwy after 13th: led 3 out: rdn and hung lft after 2 out: hdd last: rallied and hung lft flat: led cl home* **11/2**[2]

1-P **2** *¾* **Lord Anner (IRE)**[151] [440] 6-10-13 **92** .... RWalsh 110+
(P F Nicholls) *hld up in rr: hit 6th and 12th: hdwy 13th: rdn to ld last: hdd cl home* **6/5**[1]

114- **3** *19* **Surefast**[231] [4114] 10-11-5 **98** .... PJBrennan 98+
(K Bishop) *hld up in tch: led 4 out to 3 out: wknd after 2 out* **8/1**[3]

1405 **4** *nk* **It's Definite (IRE)**[10] [1678] 6-11-12 **105** ....(p) RJohnson 106+
(P Bowen) *bhd: mstkes 2nd and 7th (water): styd on fr 3 out: n.d* **16/1**

-060 **5** *1½* **Jumpty Dumpty (FR)**[119] [805] 8-10-0 **79** oh10 .... JMogford 77+
(J C Tuck) *hld up: hdwy 11th: cl up whn blnd 4 out: wknd 2 out* **33/1**

2053 **6** *6* **River Quoile**[13] [1639] 9-10-0 **79** oh2 .... RWalford 73+
(R H Alner) *prom: led 5th to 10th: mstke 13th: wknd 3 out* **14/1**

3P0- **7** *¾* **Dante's Back (IRE)**[200] [4680] 7-11-12 **105** .... CLlewellyn 98+
(N A Twiston-Davies) *hld up: hdwy after 10th: rdn appr 4 out: wkng whn blnd 3 out* **14/1**

PPP- **8** *1¼* **Hiers De Brouage (FR)**[208] [4537] 10-11-10 **103** ....(tp) TJMurphy 92
(J G Portman) *led to 5th: led 10th to 4 out: wknd 3 out* **28/1**

200- **9** *11* **Zimbabwe (FR)**[210] [4502] 5-11-5 **100** ....(p) AThornton 76
(N J Hawke) *prom tl wknd appr 3 out* **20/1**

F04- **P** **Leith Hill Star**[242] [3931] 9-10-10 **89** .... BFenton —
(R Rowe) *w ldr to 4th: lost pl 7th: bhd fr 11th: t.o whn p.u bef 3 out* **9/1**

5m 49.2s (-9.40) **Going Correction** -0.05s/f (Good) **10** Ran SP% **112.3**
Speed ratings: **113,112,106,106,105 103,103,103,99**,— CSF £12.31 CT £50.90 TOTE £7.90: £2.00, £1.10, £2.00; EX 24.60.
Owner B Perkins **Bred** Mrs J D Newman **Trained** Upper Lambourn, Berks

FOCUS
A decent winning time for a race like this and the form looks solid enough with the first two coming well clear.

NOTEBOOK
Bay Island(IRE) , who had unseated on his seasonal return six days previously when well backed, was again the subject of decent support in the betting and this time made amends with a dogged success. He looked at one stage like he may have to play second fiddle to the eventual runner-up, but dug deep when asked for maximum effort and actually looked to have a bit up his sleeve at the finish. It is possible he can improve again for a stiffer test. *(op 7-1 tchd 5-1)*
Lord Anner(IRE), who won over the course and distance on his debut under Rules last season, was produced to have every chance two out and looked like going on to score jumping the final fence, but he was ultimately worried out of it by the winner on the run-in. This imposing six-year-old did not totally convince over his fences in the main and, while he was well clear of the rest at the finish, it has to be deemed disappointing that he failed to capitalise on what looked a very lenient official mark for this handicap debut. *(op 5-4 tchd 6-4)*
Surefast , winner of this event last term off a 15lb lower mark, ran as though this seasonal bow was needed and can do better with the run under his belt. *(op 11-2)*
It's Definite(IRE) failed to jump with any real fluency and was still last jumping two out, but he picked up strongly for pressure and ultimately only just missed out on third place. On this evidence, he will no doubt be seen in a better light once again when reverting to a stiffer test.

1781 3663 DUCHY OF CORNWALL CHALLENGE CUP BEGINNERS' CHASE (17 fncs) 2m 7f 110y
3:10 (3:10) (Class 3) 5-Y-0+ **£5,395** (£1,660; £830; £415)

Form RPR

13P- **1** **Dancer Life (POL)**[420] [1275] 6-11-0 .... ChristianWilliams 125+
(Evan Williams) *hld up: hdwy appr 4 out: rdn to ld last: r.o wl* **20/1**[3]

111- **2** *6* **Blue Business**[187] [4835] 7-11-0 .... RWalsh 120+
(P F Nicholls) *a.p: led briefly appr 4 out: j.rt 4 out: hld whn lft 2nd last* **1/2**[1]

320- **3** *24* **It's Rumoured**[223] [4269] 5-10-12 93 .... JamesDavies 93
(Jean-Rene Auvray) *led tl j. slowly 2nd: prom tl wknd after 3 out* **20/1**[3]

4 2 **Harrihawkan**143 7-11-0 .... RThornton 93
(Mrs T J Hill) *led 2nd to 6th: led 12th tl appr 4 out: wknd 3 out* **20/1**3

0F0/ 5 dist **Senor Gigo**597 [4073] 7-11-0 .... PMoloney —
(Evan Williams) *t.k.h: hdwy to ld 6th: hdd 12th: wknd appr 4 out: t.o* **100/1**

6 8 **Wynford Eagle**212 6-11-0 .... RWalford —
(R H Alner) *t.k.h in tch: rdn and wknd appr 4 out: t.o* **50/1**

PP03 F **Floranz**25 [1540] 9-10-7 .... SCurran —
(Mrs M Evans) *hld up: last tl fell 8th* **100/1**

1P-1 F **Bowleaze (IRE)**165 [201] 6-11-0 .... AThornton 122+
(R H Alner) *hld up in tch: led on bit 4 out: rdn and hdd whn fell last* **3/1**2

5m 58.0s (-0.60) **Going Correction** -0.05s/f (Good) **8** Ran SP% **109.9**
Speed ratings: **99,97,89,88,— —,—,—** CSF £30.97 TOTE £15.10: £2.60, £1.10, £2.70; EX 41.60.
Owner Terry Reffell **Bred** Marian Pokrywka **Trained** Cowbridge, Vale Of Glamorgan

FOCUS
A fair novice chase, but the race turned into something of a dash approaching four out and the overall form has to rate as dubious.

NOTEBOOK
Dancer Life(POL) ran out a surprise winner on this chase debut for his new connections. He had previously failed to live up to expectations for Jonjo O'Neil after switching from the Flat in Poland in 2003, but his new trainer is becoming most adept at transforming other stables' cast offs, and the way the race was run played right into this former Polish Derby winner's strengths. While he is flattered by his winning margin, he could do no more than win as he did, and he looks a decent purchase at just 5,000gns. *(op 16-1)*
Blue Business , who progressed rapidly towards the end of last season and won his last four outings, jumped well enough in the main on this chasing bow. He was unsuited by the sedate early gallop, though, and proved no match for the winner's turn of foot when it mattered. As a half-brother to top-class See More Business, he can be expected to reach greater heights in this sphere and, while this was a disappointing start to his chasing career, he could well be the type to take higher order as the season progresses. *(tchd 8-15)*
It's Rumoured rather ran in snatches throughout and is clearly flattered by his finishing position. *(op 28-1)*
Harrihawkan , a 45,000gns purchase for connections having won a point in May, jumped neatly and showed up well until lacking the pace to remain competitive when the race got serious. He is one to keep an eye on for his up-and-coming yard. *(op 16-1)*
Bowleaze(IRE) , rated 120 over hurdles, has to be considered unlucky on this fencing debut. He would not have been suited by the ordinary gallop, but was still full of running approaching the final flight, before getting in too close and agonisingly coming to grief. It is fair to expect him to go on to better things in this sphere, but connections will no doubt be praying his confidence has not been too badly dented by this experience. *(op 10-3 tchd 7-2 and 11-4)*

1782 GERRARD NOVICES' HURDLE (8 hdls) 2m 1f
3:40 (3:40) (Class 4) 4-Y-0+ **£4,264** (£1,312; £656; £328)

Form RPR

1 1 **Boychuk (IRE)**13 [1640] 4-11-5 .... RJohnson 118+
(P J Hobbs) *a.p: rdn to ld after 2 out: r.o* **11/10**1

43/ 2 2 **French Envoy (FR)**545 [4920] 6-10-12 .... RThornton 109
(Ian Williams) *a.p: led 3 out: rdn and hdd after 2 out: mstke last: one pce* **25/1**

223- 3 1 ½ **Saltango (GER)**32 [3123] 6-10-12 114.......... APMcCoy 109+
(A M Hales) *t.k.h in rr: stdy hdwy 4th: rdn and ev ch 2 out: nt fluent last: one pce* **6/5**2

04- 4 8 **In Deep**31 [2558] 4-10-2 .... RYoung(3) 92
(Mrs P N Dutfield) *hld up in mid-div: hdwy after 5th: rdn and wknd 2 out* **50/1**

14-P 5 19 **Billyandi (IRE)**14 [1632] 5-10-12 .... CLlewellyn 80
(N A Twiston-Davies) *led to 3 out: wknd 2 out* **25/1**

60 6 5 **Glide**10 [1680] 4-10-12 .... WHutchinson 75
(J A B Old) *prom tl wknd appr 3 out* **100/1**

300- 7 1 ½ **Rude Health**229 [4143] 5-10-5 .... PJBrennan 67
(N J Hawke) *chsd ldr tl rdn appr 3 out: sn wknd* **66/1**

0- 8 14 **Stark Raven**234 [4069] 5-10-12 .... BFenton 60
(Miss E C Lavelle) *a bhd* **16/1**3

P 9 12 **Norman's Glories**78 [1123] 7-10-12 .... VSlattery 48
(R J Baker) *hld up in mid-div: rdn 4th: bhd fr 5th* **150/1**

-0P0 10 11 **Daisy Dale**2 [1750] 7-10-5 75.......... RGreene 30
(S C Burrough) *a bhd* **150/1**

0/PP 11 dist **Spud's Fancy**6 [1711] 6-10-5 .... ChristianWilliams —
(D A Rees) *a bhd: lost tch fr 5th: t.o* **200/1**

4m 7.70s (-1.50) **Going Correction** -0.05s/f (Good) **11** Ran SP% **112.9**
Speed ratings: **101,100,99,95,86 84,83,77,71,66** — CSF £28.02 TOTE £2.60: £1.02, £3.70, £1.20; EX 24.50.
Owner Mrs D L Whateley **Bred** Robert Donaldson **Trained** Withycombe, Somerset

FOCUS
This novice hurdle lacked any real strength in depth and the pace was moderate until the halfway stage, but the first three came nicely clear and the form looks sound.

NOTEBOOK
Boychuk(IRE) , off the mark on his hurdling debut for connections over course and distance 13 days previously, duly followed up with a workmanlike performance under his penalty and enhanced his yard's already impressive record in this event. He had not run on ground as soft as this before but he handled it without fuss and clearly has the potential to make up into a useful novice this season. *(op 5-4 tchd 6-4)*
French Envoy(FR) ◆ , who showed ability in both his previous bumper outings, made a very pleasing return from a 545-day layoff and made the winner work all the way to the line. His next outing will reveal more, but this was a promising start to his hurdling career and he looks nailed on to go one better before too long. *(op 40-1)*
Saltango(GER) , fit from a recent spin on the Flat, had his chance on this return to hurdling yet never really looked like hitting the front at any stage. This was still a respectable effort, however, and he does deserve to find a race over timber. *(op 5-4 tchd evens)*
In Deep , another fit from a recent outing on the level, was found wanting when it mattered but was not disgraced all the same. Considering her sole success on the Flat came over 14 furlongs, she ought to be happier when faced with a stiffer test over hurdles, and now qualifies for handicaps. *(op 40-1)*
Billyandi(IRE) again proved hard to settle and paid for his early exertions when push came to shove. He is clearly tricky, but appeals as the type who may improve over further as he gains more experience over hurdles. *(op 33-1)*

1783 TOTAL PUMPS BEGINNERS' CHASE (12 fncs) 2m 1f 110y
4:10 (4:10) (Class 3) 4-Y-0+ **£5,395** (£1,660; £830; £415)

Form RPR

36P- 1 **Chilling Place (IRE)**194 [4752] 6-11-6 .... RJohnson 141+
(P J Hobbs) *mde all: mstke 7th: rdn appr last: drvn out* **4/6**1

141- 2 ½ **Cornish Sett (IRE)**186 [4845] 6-11-6 .... RWalsh 141+
(P F Nicholls) *hld up: wnt 2nd after 8th: mstke 4 out: rdn after 3 out: ev ch whn cocked jaw and tried to run out briefly last: rallied flat* **11/8**2

2353 3 dist **Peeyoutwo**45 [1396] 10-11-6 113.......... BHitchcott 111
(Mrs D A Hamer) *chsd wnr tl after 8th: sn wknd* **25/1**3

0063 4 21 **Simon's Seat (USA)**13 [1636] 6-10-13 ....(p) JamesWhite(7) —
(S C Burrough) *chsd ldrs: reminders 2nd and after 4th: lost tch fr 5th: t.o* **66/1**

4m 12.9s (-4.00) **Going Correction** -0.05s/f (Good) **4** Ran SP% **107.4**
Speed ratings: **106,105,—,—** CSF £1.98 TOTE £1.30; EX 1.90.
Owner M J Tuckey **Bred** Wickfield Farm Partnership **Trained** Withycombe, Somerset

FOCUS
An intriguing beginners' chase featuring the eagerly anticipated chasing bows of two very useful novice hurdlers from last season in Chilling Place and Cornish Sett, who interestingly both possess the same official hurdle rating and totally vindicated the Handicapper by finishing almost upsides. Both can rate higher in this sphere.

NOTEBOOK
Chilling Place(IRE) , very useful as a novice over timber last season and rated 137, made all in dogged fashion on this eagerly anitcipated chasing bow, despite not looking totally foot-perfect at his fences. The recent easing of the ground would not have played to his strengths and he is entitled to improve a deal for the experience, but this was not quite the performance that could have been expected beforehand. No doubt he has the engine to reach great heights as a chaser, however, and as a former winning pointer it may well be that he needs a stiffer test in this sphere to be seen at best. *(op 8-11 tchd 4-5)*
Cornish Sett(IRE) , who won three of his five outings over hurdles last term and boasts an identical hurdle rating to the winner, made his first mistake when trying to challenge the winner four out and then looked to try and run out approaching the penultimate fence, so the fact that he finished as close as he did is testament to his ability. Like the winner, he may also just want a stiffer test in time over fences, but this was still a promising start to his chasing career and he lost very little in defeat. *(op 5-4)*
Peeyoutwo ran as well as could have been expected in defeat this time, and gives the form a decent look, as he is consistent and not flattered by his rating of 113. *(op 20-1)*

1784 AUDREY CHUDLEIGH MEMORIAL PERPETUAL H'CAP HURDLE (10 hdls) 2m 3f
4:40 (4:40) (Class 3) (0-115,110) 4-Y-0+ **£4,810** (£1,480; £740; £370)

Form RPR

-032 1 **Dont Ask Me (IRE)**6 [1717] 4-10-1 85..........(t) TScudamore 94+
(M C Pipe) *hld up towards rr: hdwy appr 5th: led 2 out: r.o wl* **11/4**1

3-B2 2 nk **Nippy Des Mottes (FR)**142 [563] 4-11-8 106..........(t) RWalsh 114+
(P F Nicholls) *hld up towards rr: stdy hdwy appr 3 out: swtchd lft after 2 out: hrd rdn and ev ch flat: nt qckn* **11/4**1

3P34 3 7 **Hard N Sharp**14 [1632] 5-10-10 94.......... RThornton 96+
(Mrs A M Thorpe) *a.p: led and hit 3 out: hdd 2 out: hit last: sn wknd* **11/1**3

405- 4 23 **The Gene Genie**269 [3492] 10-10-3 94.......... JamesWhite(7) 72
(R J Hodges) *hld up in tch: rdn and wknd appr 3 out* **16/1**

P1-P 5 ½ **Gan Eagla (IRE)**17 [1598] 6-11-10 108..........(b) SThomas 85
(Miss Venetia Williams) *prom: led 5th to 3 out: sn wknd* **20/1**

044- 6 5 **Freedom Now (IRE)**191 [4791] 7-11-12 110.......... RWalford 82
(R H Alner) *hld up in mid-div: short-lived effrt appr 3 out* **16/1**

/1-6 7 4 **Noble Calling (FR)**13 [1641] 8-11-9 107.......... RJohnson 75
(R J Hodges) *bhd: rdn and sme hdwy appr 6th: wknd appr 3 out* **16/1**

162- 8 8 **Bekstar**347 [2014] 10-10-5 89.......... JMogford 49
(J C Tuck) *bhd: rdn 6th: short-lived effrt appr 3 out* **33/1**

14P- 9 2 **Come Bye (IRE)**212 [4482] 9-11-12 110..........(bt) MBatchelor 68
(Miss A M Newton-Smith) *prom tl wknd appr 3 out* **33/1**

P36 10 6 **Mrs Philip**12 [1656] 6-10-13 97.......... PJBrennan 49
(P J Hobbs) *hld up in tch: rdn and wknd appr 3 out* **12/1**

3004 11 2 **Red Canyon (IRE)**13 [1641] 8-10-8 92..........(v) JTizzard 42
(C L Tizzard) *led to 5th: hit 6th: sn wknd* **14/1**

P6- 12 20 **Tiger Island (USA)**202 [4659] 5-10-1 85.......... ChristianWilliams 15
(A E Jones) *a bhd: t.o* **100/1**

020- P **Scarlet Mix (FR)**184 [4883] 4-11-6 104.......... TJMurphy —
(B G Powell) *a bhd: j.lft 6th: t.o whn p.u bef 3 out* **9/1**2

0226 P **Native Chancer (IRE)**26 [1525] 5-11-7 105.......... APMcCoy —
(Jonjo O'Neill) *a bhd: nt fluent 3rd: t.o whn p.u bef 3 out* **20/1**

4m 35.4s (-5.50) **Going Correction** -0.05s/f (Good)
WFA 4 from 5yo+ 13lb **14** Ran SP% **120.1**
Speed ratings: **109,108,105,96,96 93,92,88,88,85 84,76,—,—** CSF £9.62 CT £72.95 TOTE £3.70: £2.20, £1.30, £3.10; EX 11.40 Trifecta £70.30 Pool: £574.90 - 5.8 winning units.
Owner Jim Ennis **Bred** William J White **Trained** Nicholashayne, Devon

FOCUS
A modest handicap, but it was run at a solid pace and the first three came well clear. The form looks sound.

NOTEBOOK
Dont Ask Me(IRE) ◆ , runner-up at Uttoxeter six days previously, duly went one better with a dogged display and lost his maiden tag over timber at the seventh attempt. He has really improved since the recent application of a tongue tie, would have appreciated this rain-softened ground and proved suited by a more positive ride this time. No doubt he will go up in the weights a fair bit after this, but he appeared to have a touch up his sleeve at the finish and further improvement cannot be ruled out. *(op 3-1 tchd 9-4)*
Nippy Des Mottes(FR) , returning from a 142-day break, was given a patient ride and had yet to be asked a serious question approaching the penultimate flight, but ultimately found little when push came to shove and was outbattled on the run-in. Granted, he was giving plenty of weight away to the improving winner, but he has yet to find a race over hurdles and has questions to answer regarding his attitude after this. He was well clear of the rest, however, and is still only four years old, so is not one to write off just yet. *(op 3-1 tchd 7-2 and 4-1 in a place)*
Hard N Sharp was put in his place on the run-in but still turned in a solid effort in defeat and is a fair benchmark for this form. He can find easier opportunities in order to find a race. *(tchd 12-1)*
The Gene Genie kept on at the same pace and should come on a fair bit for this seasonal return.
Gan Eagla(IRE) was made to look one-paced when it mattered and, while this was more encouraging than his recent return at Ludlow, he does appear too high in the weights at present. It would come as little surprise to see him over fences before long.

1785 DAVE ACKLAND 50TH BIRTHDAY 'JUNIOR' STANDARD OPEN NATIONAL HUNT FLAT RACE 1m 5f
5:10 (5:10) (Class 6) 3-Y-0 **£2,978** (£851; £425)

Form RPR

1 **Sword Of Damascus (IRE)** 3-10-7 .... StephenJCraine(5) 90+
(D McCain) *a.p: rdn 4f out: led ins fnl f: all out* **7/1**3

2 1 **Brinkmanship (USA)** 3-10-5 .... PMerrigan(7) 89+
(Mrs H Dalton) *hld up towards rr: hmpd and rn wd bnd over 3f out: hdwy over 2f out: hrd rdn over 1f out: edgd rt ins fnl f: kpt on* **15/2**

3 2 ½ **Themanfromfraam** 3-10-12 .... RJohnson 85
(Mrs S M Johnson) *led: rdn over 1f out: hdd and no ex ins fnl f* **25/1**

4 2 ½ **Ausone** 3-10-2 .... ONelmes(3) 75
(Miss J R Gibney) *carried lft s: hdwy after 5f: rdn over 4f out: no ex fnl f* **20/1**

The Form Book, Raceform Ltd, Compton, RG20 6NL

5	5	**Devonia Plains (IRE)** 3-10-9 ... RYoung(3) (Mrs P N Dutfield) *t.k.h in rr: hdwy over 4f out: wknd over 1f out* **33/1**	76
6	nk	**Mahogany Blaze (FR)** 3-10-12 ... AntonyEvans (N A Twiston-Davies) *hld up and bhd: rdn whn hmpd 4f out: nvr nrr* **9/2**[2]	75
7	1	**Jabo (FR)** 3-10-12 ... CLlewellyn (N A Twiston-Davies) *chsd ldr: rdn over 3f out: wknd over 2f out* **7/1**[3]	74
8	9	**Garth Engineer** 3-10-5 ... JamesWhite(7) (R J Hodges) *plld hrd in mid-div: hdwy after 5f: wknd 3f out* **40/1**	62
9	3/4	**Camerons Future (IRE)** 3-10-12 ... BHitchcott (J A Geake) *s.i.s: a bhd* **12/1**	61
10	6	**Celtic Realm (IRE)** 3-10-12 ... APMcCoy (K G Reveley) *hld up in mid-div: hdwy 7f out: rdn 5f out: sn wknd* **6/4**[1]	54
11	15	**Magnate (IRE)** 3-10-7 ... LStephens(5) (Mrs S M Johnson) *prom: rdn over 3f out: sn wknd* **40/1**	34
12	2	**Funny Fellow** 3-10-12 ... BFenton (R Rowe) *wnt lft and s.s: a bhd* **33/1**	31
S		**Scots Brook Terror** 3-9-12 ... MrPCallaghan(7) (Mrs N S Evans) *hld up in tch: slipped up bnd 4f out* **66/1**	—

3m 12.9s **13** Ran SP% **123.5**
CSF £56.70 TOTE £9.40: £2.80, £4.40, £4.60; EX 88.10 Place 6 £9.16, Place 5 £2.16.
Owner Jon Glews **Bred** Sir E J Loder **Trained** Cholmondeley, Cheshire
■ Stewards' Enquiry : P MerriganM four-day ban: used whip with excessive force and frequency (Oct 29-31, Nov 1)
Stephen J CraineM three-day ban: used whip with excessive force and frequency (Oct 29-31)

FOCUS
The first junior bumper of the current season and, with no previous form amongst the field, the strength is not easy to assess. It was run at just an average pace and the field finished well strung out.

NOTEBOOK
Sword Of Damascus(IRE), who originally made 180,000gns as a yearling, was unraced for Sheikh Mohammed, but he got his career off a perfect start with a hard-fought success and provided his yard with a rare debut winner in this sphere. He responded well for pressure from two out, looked happy on the easing ground and looks a fair prospect for novice hurdles in due course. *(op 13-2 tchd 5-1)*
Brinkmanship(USA), who like the winner never made the track when owned by Sheikh Mohammed, ran distinctly green throughout and was doing all of his best work at the finish. He should improve plenty for this. *(op 9-2 tchd 8-1)*
Themanfromfraam was only picked off late on and made a pleasing enough debut. He may be better off with a more patient ride in the future. *(op 20-1)*
Ausone stayed on without posing a threat to the principals and, as a half-sister to last season's Supreme Novices' hero Arcalis, could well turn out to be the best of these in time. *(tchd 22-1)*
Devonia Plains(IRE) looked a threat to all approaching two out, but ultimately found little off the bridle and was well beaten. *(tchd 40-1)*
Mahogany Blaze(FR), half-brother to 12-furlong winner Red Lion, showed up well enough until finding little when it really mattered. *(tchd 4-1)*
Celtic Realm(IRE), well backed, never looked happy at any stage and was beaten a long way out. He has questions to answer now, but is clearly thought capable of a lot better. *(op 11-4 tchd 3-1)*
T/Jkpt: Not won. T/Plt: £26.20 to a £1 stake. Pool: £55,817.20. 1,552.40 winning tickets. T/Qpdt: £3.90 to a £1 stake. Pool: £3,313.10. 617.75 winning tickets. KH

1786 - (Foreign Racing) - See Raceform Interactive

617 PUNCHESTOWN (R-H)
Wednesday, October 19
OFFICIAL GOING: Good to yielding (good in places)

1787a DIFFUSION EVENT MANAGEMENT HURDLE (LISTED RACE) 2m 2f
3:15 (3:16) 5-Y-0+ **£14,774** (£4,334; £2,065; £703)

			RPR
1		**Rooftop Protest (IRE)**[10] 1548 8-11-5 130 ...(tp) DFFlannery(7) (T Hogan, Ire) *led: hdd 3rd: regained ld appr 4 out: drew clr after 2 out: eased after last* **5/2**[2]	134+
2	12	**Master Albert (IRE)**[325] 2521 7-11-6 123 ... MrJPMagnier(3) (David Wachman, Ire) *led fr 3rd: hdd appr 4 out: cl 3rd and pushed along next: mod 2nd and kpt on fr last* **7/1**	119
3	4	**Rocket Ship (IRE)**[3] 1767 5-11-6 135 ... PCarberry (Noel Meade, Ire) *hld up in rr: hit 2nd: prog 4 out: cl 2nd 3 out: rdn and outpcd after 2 out: no ex fr last* **4/5**[1]	112
4	20	**Oulart**[174] 92 6-11-5 128 ... NJO'Shea(7) (D T Hughes, Ire) *settled 3rd: dropped to rr 4 out: sn lost tch and wknd* **5/1**[3]	98

4m 27.3s **5** Ran SP% **113.3**
CSF £16.31 TOTE £3.30; DF 28.70.
Owner M G Byrne **Bred** J Costelloe **Trained** Nenagh, Co. Tipperary

NOTEBOOK
Rooftop Protest(IRE) proved himself a bit better than a handicapper, sauntering home to win unchallenged *(op 5/2 tchd 11/4)*
Master Albert(IRE), absent for almost a year, made a pleasing-enough reappearance. His hurdling was not foot perfect but he will have derived a lot of benefit from this. *(op 5/1)*
Rocket Ship(IRE), an odds-on flop at Cork the previous weekend, was the stand-in here for stable companion Wild Passion (withdrawn because overnight rain didn't materialise). He travelled well to two out but the white flag went up in a matter of strides. *(op 11/10)*

1790a TOTAL EVENTS RENTAL NOVICE CHASE (LISTED RACE) 2m 2f
4:45 (4:47) 5-Y-0+ **£14,774** (£4,334; £2,065; £703)

			RPR
1		**Justified (IRE)**[204] 4647 6-11-2 ... JRBarry (E Sheehy, Ire) *mde all: j.w: qcknd clr after 3 out: eased after last: impressive* **11/10**[1]	143+
2	9	**Doctor Linton (IRE)**[10] 1703 6-11-6 ... RWalsh (M J P O'Brien, Ire) *trckd ldrs: 3rd bef 1/2-way: impr into 2nd 5 out: no imp after 3 out: kpt on: nt trouble wnr* **2/1**[2]	135
3	20	**Django (IRE)**[173] 116 6-11-2 ... RMPower (Mrs John Harrington, Ire) *hld up in 5th: prog into 4th 5 out: mod 3rd and no imp fr bef 2 out* **25/1**	111
4	6	**Ursumman (IRE)**[45] 1421 6-11-9 124 ... NPMadden (Niall Madden, Ire) *trckd ldrs: 4th 1/2-way: impr into 2nd briefly 6 out: 3rd and pushed along after 4 out: sn lost tch* **6/1**[3]	112
5	25	**Carlesimo (IRE)**[25] 1555 7-11-9 ... PCarberry (Noel Meade, Ire) *trckd ldr in 2nd: slt mstke 5th: 5th and pushed along 5 out: wknd fr next* **8/1**	87
6	20	**Murrayfield (USA)**[25] 1555 8-10-13 ... AndrewJMcNamara(3) (C Byrnes, Ire) *a bhd: lost tch 1/2-way: trailing bef 4 out* **25/1**	60
R		**Cash And Carry (IRE)**[16] 1626 7-11-6 117 ... BJGeraghty (E J O'Grady, Ire) *ref to r* **12/1**	—

4m 40.4s **7** Ran SP% **121.7**
CSF £4.28 TOTE £2.20: £1.80, £1.80; DF 4.30.
Owner Braybrook Syndicate **Bred** Miss Maura McGuinness **Trained** Graiguenamanagh, Kilkenny

NOTEBOOK
Justified(IRE) put in an exciting display on his chase debut, quick, clean and unchallenged from from three out. Even at this stage he looks a serious Cheltenham Arkle contender. *(op 1/1 tchd 11/8)*
Doctor Linton(IRE), all of 22lb inferior to the winner on hurdle ratings, but with the benefit of a first time win over fences at Limerick ten days earlier, ran well but was left behind from the third last. *(op 5/2 tchd 2/1)*
Django(IRE) ran a bit better than might have been expected. *(op 20/1)*
Ursumman(IRE), runner-up in the Galway Plate, could not make his experience work here.
Carlesimo(IRE) was left behind from four out. *(op 7/1)*

1791 - 1792a (Foreign Racing) - See Raceform Interactive

207 HAYDOCK (L-H)
Thursday, October 20
OFFICIAL GOING: Good (good to firm in places on chase course)
Wind: Fresh, half-against Weather: Sunny intervals

1793 RACING POST "HANDS AND HEELS" JUMPS SERIES H'CAP HURDLE (CONDITIONAL JOCKEYS/AMATEURS) (8 hdls) 2m
2:00 (2:00) (Class 4) (0-105,105) 4-Y-0+ **£3,678** (£1,051; £525)

Form				RPR
3P-2	1		**Incursion**[26] 1206 4-11-2 98 ... MrGTumelty(3) (A King) *a.p: led 2 out: drew clr after last: eased cl home* **4/1**[1]	102+
0-P4	2	6	**Time To Roam (IRE)**[13] 1665 5-11-2 98 ...(b) NWalker(3) (Miss Lucinda V Russell) *trckd ldrs: rdn and outpcd appr last: kpt on to take 2nd cl home: no ch w wnr* **8/1**[3]	94
0-PP	3	shd	**Honest Endeavour**[23] 1568 6-11-7 105 ...(p) MrOWilliams(5) (J M Jefferson) *racd keenly: led: hdd 2 out: no ex run-in* **33/1**	101
4160	4	1 3/4	**Margarets Wish**[46] 1413 5-10-0 84 ... MrLEdwards(5) (T Wall) *sddled sn slipped: midfield: rdr lost iron 2 out: kpt on run-in* **33/1**	80+
0-05	5	1 1/4	**Mr Twins (ARG)**[20] 1591 4-10-4 86 ... AGlassonbury(3) (M A Barnes) *in tch: rdn appr 3 out: one pce fr 2 out* **14/1**	79
0443	6	6	**Beaver (AUS)**[12] 1687 6-10-11 95 ...(tp) JPFlavin(5) (R C Guest) *cl up: rdn appr 2 out: wkng whn mstke last* **11/2**[2]	83+
0-5P	7	3	**Noble Pasao (IRE)**[154] 428 8-11-7 100 ... MissRDavidson (N G Richards) *s.s: racd keenly: j.rt: bhd: sme hdwy appr 3 out: no imp on ldrs* **4/1**[1]	84+
451-	8	3/4	**Hail The King (USA)**[186] 4890 5-11-8 104 ... JKington(3) (R M Carson) *hld up: hdwy 4 out: rdn appr 2 out: wknd last* **8/1**[3]	87
52U2	9	12	**End Of An Error**[52] 1367 6-10-6 90 ... MrsEJSmith(5) (A W Carroll) *s.s: a bhd* **12/1**	61
0-50	10	1 1/2	**Reflex Blue**[15] 1645 8-9-13 83 ...(v) MrMPrice(5) (R J Price) *j. slowly 2nd: a bhd* **9/1**	53
P/50	11	hd	**Sarn**[12] 1671 6-10-1 83 ... TMessenger(3) (M Mullineaux) *struggling 3rd: a bhd* **20/1**	53

3m 49.0s (-10.10) **Going Correction** -0.625s/f (Firm)
WFA 4 from 5yo+ 13lb **11** Ran SP% **112.6**
Speed ratings: **100,97,96,96,95 92,90,90,84,83 83** CSF £33.64 CT £904.48 TOTE £4.90: £2.20, £1.80, £9.70; EX 21.40.
Owner Nigel Bunter **Bred** K J Mercer **Trained** Barbury Castle, Wilts

FOCUS
A moderate handicap but an easy enough winner and with the placed horses and fifth close to recent marks the form appears reliable.

NOTEBOOK
Incursion, who had shown enough in four previous starts over timber to suggest that he could win a race off this sort of mark, saw the trip out strongly and won eased down. He looks as though he will not mind a return to two and a half miles. *(op 10-3)*
Time To Roam(IRE), who has his headgear changed on a regular basis, had blinkers on this time. A winner off a mark of 110 back in March, he looks to be returning to form and should be capable of scoring off his current rating.
Honest Endeavour, who cut no ice on his chase debut last time, ran much better back over the smaller obstacles and with cheekpieces fitted for the first time. He seemed happier out in front. *(tchd 28-1)*
Margarets Wish, whose rider struggled with a slipped saddle from early on in the race, ran very well all things considered. A return to selling company could see her back in the winner's enclosure. *Official explanation: jockey said saddle slipped*
Mr Twins(ARG) had the tongue tie left off this time and reversed recent Hexham form with Beaver on 9lb better terms. *(op 20-1)*
Beaver(AUS) was worse off at the weights with Mr Twins compared with Hexham, and was unable to confirm that form. *(tchd 5-1)*
Noble Pasao(IRE), making his debut for his new stable, did not settle in rear and failed to make an impact. *Official explanation: jockey said gelding finished lame (tchd 9-2 in a place)*

1794 TONY LAWTON NOVICES' HURDLE (8 hdls) 2m
2:30 (2:30) (Class 3) 4-Y-0+ **£5,148** (£1,584; £792; £396)

Form				RPR
3	1		**Spring Breeze**[23] 1569 4-10-12 ...(v) BHarding (M Dods) *a.p: chsd ldr 5th: lft in ld after 2 out: clr last: styd on wl* **14/1**[3]	114+
3-2	2	10	**Barton Flower**[18] 1614 4-10-5 ... NFehily (D P Keane) *chsd ldr to 5th: rdn 3 out: wnt 2nd appr last: no ex flat* **11/2**[2]	96
1	3	hd	**Crow Wood**[18] 1614 6-11-4 ... RGarritty (J J Quinn) *led: clr 2nd: 4l ahd and gng wl whn blnd 2 out: sn hdd and nt rcvr* **4/9**[1]	118+
	4	13	**Step Perfect (USA)**[65] 4-10-12 ... FKeniry (G M Moore) *prom: rdn 3 out: wknd after next* **100/1**	90
3-03	5	12	**You Do The Math (IRE)**[166] 212 5-10-9 ... GBerridge(3) (L Lungo) *hld up: blnd 5th: nvr nr to chal* **25/1**	78
	6	5	**Mr Albanello (ARG)**[244] 6-10-9 ... KJMercer(3) (Ferdy Murphy) *hld up: nvr nr to chal* **100/1**	73
	7	1 3/4	**Backgammon**[24] 4-10-12 ... RMcGrath (K G Reveley) *hld up: mstke 3rd: hit 5th: nvr nr to chal* **25/1**	71
	8	3/4	**Carnt Spell**[142] 4-10-12 ... AThornton (J T Stimpson) *prom tl wknd after 5th* **100/1**	71
/100	9	2	**Acushnet**[27] 1543 6-10-12 ... GLee (J M Jefferson) *hld up: nvr nrr* **33/1**	69
	10	6	**Oulan Bator (FR)**[24] 5-10-12 ... PWhelan (R A Fahey) *prom: hit 2nd: rdn and wknd 3 out* **16/1**	63
0-	11	hd	**Lake Imperial (IRE)**[278] 3354 4-10-5 ... PMerrigan(7) (Mrs H Dalton) *hld up: hmpd 2nd: sme hdwy after 2 out: sn wknd* **50/1**	62

12 *13* **Pop Play Again**[26] 4-10-12 .... JimCrowley 49
(G A Swinbank) *hld up: hit 1st: mstke 3rd: a in rr* **100/1**
P/ **13** *14* **Miss Wizz**[52] 2136 5-10-5 ....(p) NPMulholland 28
(W Storey) *hld up: mstke 3rd: a in rr* **100/1**
0 **14** *5* **Shem Dylan (NZ)**[12] 1671 6-10-12 .... HOliver 30
(R C Guest) *hld up: hmpd 2nd: mstke next: a in rr* **100/1**
15 *7* **Yorker (USA)**[35] 7-10-9 .... CBolger(3) 23
(Ms Deborah J Evans) *hld up: a in rr* **100/1**
P **16** *13* **Kaysglory**[123] 780 6-10-9 .... PAspell(3) 10
(F P Murtagh) *chsd ldrs: hit 5th: sn wknd* **100/1**
F **Classic Lease**[23] 4-10-12 .... ADempsey —
(J Mackie) *fell 2nd* **100/1**
U **Young Mr Grace (IRE)**[34] 5-10-12 .... DO'Meara —
(T D Easterby) *hld up: hmpd and uns rdr 2nd* **25/1**
P **Tough Tales (IRE)**[186] 4891 6-10-12 .... PMoloney —
(J Mackie) *hld up: no ch whn p.u after 2 out* **100/1**

3m 45.6s (-13.50) **Going Correction** -0.625s/f (Firm)
WFA 4 from 5yo+ 13lb **19** Ran SP% **123.5**
Speed ratings: **108,103,102,96,90 87,87,86,85,82 82,76,69,66,63 56,—,—,—** CSF £85.04 TOTE £13.10: £1.90, £2.10, £1.10; EX 82.60.
Owner J N Blackburn **Bred** W P Churchward, D J Bloodstock And C Hue-Will **Trained** Denton, Co Durham

FOCUS
Not a terribly competitive novice hurdle, and the favourite looked an unlucky loser. The time was decent and the form should work out.

NOTEBOOK
Spring Breeze may have been a fortunate winner as Crow Wood was going well in front when making a bad blunder at the second last. However, this was still a decent performance by this three-time staying winner on the Flat. He needs a decent surface so be seen at his best. *(tchd 16-1)*
Barton Flower, runner-up to Crow Wood at Uttoxeter last time, got the better of him on this *occasion, although that was entirely due to the bad mistake made by his rival at the second last. (op 5-1 tchd 6-1)*
Crow Wood may have been an unlucky loser as he was going easily in front when making a terrible blunder at the second last from which he struggled to recover. He can certainly win again in similar company soon as long as the mistake did not cause him injury. *(tchd 2-5 and 1-2 in a place)*
Step Perfect(USA), lightly raced on the Flat, has clearly had his problems, but this was not a bad debut over hurdles. He might appreciate a sharper track.
You Do The Math(IRE), who showed last time over three miles that stamina is his strength, was not suited by the drop back in trip. He is now eligible for a handicap mark.
Backgammon *Official explanation: jockey said gelding was unnerved by fallers at 2nd hurdle (op 28-1)*

1795 MANSON INSURANCE GROUP H'CAP CHASE (15 fncs) 2m 4f
3:00 (3:00) (Class 4) (0-110,110) 5-Y-0+ **£4,212** (£1,296; £648; £324)

Form RPR
P5-P **1** **Melford (IRE)**[174] 103 7-11-9 **107** .... NFehily 120
(C J Mann) *in tch: hdwy appr 3 out: rdn bef last: led fnl 200 yds: styd on gamely* **16/1**
P-01 **2** *¾* **Pass Me By**[13] 1662 6-11-12 **110** ....(e) HOliver 123+
(R C Guest) *a.p: bmpd 8th and 9th: rdn between last 2: led after last: sn hdd narrowly: nt qckn towards fin* **11/2**[3]
1141 **3** *9* **Polished**[8] 1716 6-11-0 **98** 7ex ....(b) RJohnson 104+
(V R A Dartnall) *midfield: hdwy 6th: j.lft 8th and 9th: led 2 out: sn rdn: hdd after last: wknd run-in* **13/8**[1]
/24- **4** *7* **Ballyrobert (IRE)**[336] 2292 8-11-12 **110** .... ATinkler 108+
(C R Egerton) *led: nt fluent 5th: rdn and hdd 2 out: wkng whn nt fluent last* **9/2**[2]
32P- **5** *23* **Gangsters R Us (IRE)**[192] 4808 9-11-1 **99** .... ADempsey 72
(A Parker) *hld up: pushed along appr 2 out: nvr on terms* **22/1**
00U0 **6** *3* **Macgyver (NZ)**[15] 1645 9-9-7 **84** oh2 .... CaptLHorner(7) 54
(D L Williams) *midfield: lost pl 9th: n.d after* **33/1**
22-4 **7** *3½* **Glenfarclas Boy (IRE)**[162] 305 9-10-6 **93** ....(p) PBuchanan(3) 60
(Miss Lucinda V Russell) *a bhd* **10/1**
614P **P** **Helvetius**[109] 896 9-10-13 **97** .... AThornton —
(W T Reed) *prom to 2nd: sn bhd: t.o whn p.u bef 9th* **20/1**
166- **P** **Garde Bien**[265] 3570 8-11-6 **104** .... RGarritty —
(T D Easterby) *midfield tl wknd 11th: t.o whn p.u bef 3 out* **8/1**
1265 **P** **Ceannairceach (IRE)**[13] 1666 12-11-8 **106** .... GLee —
(J M Jefferson) *trckd ldrs tl wknd 4 out: t.o whn p.u bef 3 out* **20/1**

5m 9.60s (-14.60) **Going Correction** -0.625s/f (Firm) **10** Ran SP% **114.6**
Speed ratings: **104,103,100,97,88 86,85,—,—,—** CSF £94.65 CT £223.95 TOTE £21.70: £5.00, £1.50, £1.50; EX 122.30.
Owner Mrs J M Mayo **Bred** Mrs Nuala Delaney **Trained** Upper Lambourn, Berks

FOCUS
Ordinary chase form, but the front two were clear of the third and Melford recorded an improved effort on this first start since leaving the Knight yard. The form is rated through the well-handicapped runner-up.

NOTEBOOK
Melford(IRE) ◆, who did not fulfill his potential for Henrietta Knight, has clearly benefited from a change of stable and, having been given a well-judged, quiet ride by Fehily, he edged ahead on the long run-in. Good ground is the key to this son of Presenting and, with the run entitled to bring him on further, he is likely to take a bit of beating if heading to Aintree next month.
Pass Me By has got his act together in the eyeshield since being returned to fences and time may show this was a decent effort trying to concede 3lb to the winner. Being only six, he remains open to further improvement. *(tchd 6-1 and 5-1 in a place)*
Polished, although a winner over fences at Uttoxeter last time, lacks a bit of scope and he failed to see out this trip under his 7lb penalty. Future opportunities over the larger obstacles may be limited. *(op 15-8 tchd 2-1)*
Ballyrobert(IRE) is a useful sort on his day, but he has not won for almost two years now - although admittedly he has not had many runs - and as he usually goes well fresh it is debatable how much he can improve on this. *(tchd 5-1 in places)*
Gangsters R Us(IRE) is slipping back down to a winning mark now and, although ultimately well *beaten, he travelled well for most of the way and a win may not be too far around the corner. (tchd 20-1)*

1796 JMC.IT H'CAP HURDLE (12 hdls) 2m 7f 110y
3:35 (3:35) (Class 3) (0-115,115) 4-Y-0+ **£4,862** (£1,496; £748; £374)

Form RPR
3-11 **1** **Drumbeater (IRE)**[29] 1513 5-10-11 **100** .... RJohnson 118+
(P J Hobbs) *hld up: hdwy after 6th: chsd ldr 4 out: led next: clr last: eased flat* **3/1**[1]
-040 **2** *4* **Caesar's Palace (GER)**[126] 768 8-10-3 **95** ....(p) PBuchanan(3) 98
(Miss Lucinda V Russell) *led to 5th: rdn after 8th: wnt 2nd last: no ch w wnr* **20/1**
1221 **3** *14* **Brooklyn Brownie (IRE)**[102] 938 6-11-5 **108** .... GLee 97
(J M Jefferson) *hld up: hdwy 6th: chsd wnr 2 out: wknd last* **11/2**[2]
101- **4** *½* **Turaath (IRE)**[231] 4136 9-11-12 **115** .... JMMaguire 104
(A J Deakin) *hld up: hdwy appr 3 out: rdn and hung lft after next: sn wknd* **20/1**
0/3 **5** *2* **Good Potential (IRE)**[39] 1456 9-10-3 **92** ....(t) RThornton 79
(D J Wintle) *hld up: rdn 6th: nvr nrr* **14/1**
55-3 **6** *6* **Monsieur Georges (FR)**[175] 73 5-10-8 **97** .... LAspell 78
(F Jordan) *chsd ldrs: mstke 5th: wknd 7th* **33/1**
20P- **7** *5* **Flying Fortune (IRE)**[193] 4790 9-11-2 **105** .... CLlewellyn 84+
(Miss Tor Sturgis) *hld up: hdwy 4 out: ev ch next: sn rdn and wknd* **6/1**[3]
-511 **8** *9* **Lutin Du Moulin (FR)**[149] 483 6-10-8 **100** ....(b) GBerridge(3) 67
(L Lungo) *hld up: drvn along after 6th: wknd 4 out* **6/1**[3]
320- **9** *9* **Oysterhaven (IRE)**[223] 4314 7-11-2 **105** ....(b) NFehily 63
(D P Keane) *chsd ldr tl led 5th: clr after next: hdd & wknd 3 out* **14/1**
312/ **10** *dist* **Activist**[10] 1498 7-10-1 **95** .... JFLevins(5) —
(D Carroll) *hld up: a bhd* **33/1**
/4F- **P** **Le Royal (FR)**[313] 2765 6-11-11 **114** .... RMcGrath —
(K G Reveley) *chsd ldrs: hit 4 out: sn wknd: t.o whn p.u bef last* **20/1**
500/ **P** **Ingenu (FR)**[890] 247 9-10-7 **96** .... SCurran —
(P Wegmann) *prom: rdn and lost pl after 6th: bhd fr next: t.o whn p.u bef 3 out* **100/1**
0F1- **P** **Union Deux (FR)**[214] 4473 6-10-11 **100** .... RGarritty —
(T D Easterby) *hld up in tch: chsd ldr 7th: mstke and wknd next: t.o whn p.u bef last* **13/2**

5m 54.5s (-9.70) **Going Correction** -0.625s/f (Firm) **13** Ran SP% **116.8**
Speed ratings: **91,89,85,84,84 82,80,77,74,— —,—,—** CSF £67.31 CT £319.39 TOTE £3.40: £1.90, £5.20, £2.20; EX 102.20 Trifecta £460.00 Pool: £648 - 1 winning ticket.
Owner D Allen **Bred** Paul McDonnell **Trained** Withycombe, Somerset

FOCUS
A modest event and a moderate winning time, but the winner is rated value for 15l and should score again.

NOTEBOOK
Drumbeater(IRE) drew clear approaching the final flight and ran out an easy winner. He was value for a good ten lengths and is clearly a very progressive five-year-old. Connections will be keen to get him out again quickly under a penalty as the Handicapper is likely to punish him severely for this success. *(op 11-4)*
Caesar's Palace(GER), 9lb lower than when successful at Aintree this time last year, ran well on his return from a four-month break, and can be expected to come on for the run. *(tchd 25-1)*
Brooklyn Brownie(IRE), running for the first time since successful at Perth in July, appears to need a sound surface to show his best, so he may struggle when the ground changes. *(op 7-1)*
Turaath(IRE), 5lb higher for his most recent success, has done all his winning over timber on right-handed tracks.
Good Potential(IRE), having his second run back after a long absence, may need easier ground these days to be seen at his best. *(op 10-1)*
Flying Fortune(IRE) ran well enough for much of the way and this should have teed him up nicely for a return to chasing. *(op 10-1)*
Oysterhaven(IRE) also ran well for a long way but tired as though needing this seasonal return. He should last longer next time. *(op 12-1)*

1797 BANK OF IRELAND JUVENILE NOVICES' HURDLE (8 hdls) 2m
4:05 (4:07) (Class 3) 3-Y-0 **£4,836** (£1,488; £744; £372)

Form RPR
23 **1** **Finland (UAE)**[8] 1718 3-10-12 .... JTizzard 99+
(Mrs A Duffield) *led 1st: mstke 4th: hdd after 4 out: regained ld 2 out: edgd lft run-in: drvn out* **9/4**[1]
64P **2** *1¼* **First Fought (IRE)**[54] 1338 3-10-7 ....(t) StephenJCraine(5) 97
(D McCain) *midfield: hdwy after 4 out: ev ch last: swtchd rt run-in: styd on but a hld* **33/1**
6 **3** *3½* **Circumspect (IRE)**[8] 1718 3-10-12 .... FKeniry 94+
(P C Haslam) *midfield: hdwy 4 out: rdn appr 2 out: styd on run-in: nt trble front pair* **9/2**[2]
4 *¾* **Lodgician (IRE)**[22] 3-10-12 .... RGarritty 92
(J J Quinn) *a.p: led after 4 out: hdd 2 out: styd on same pce run-in* **5/1**[3]
00 **5** *1¾* **Madge**[18] 1601 3-10-5 ....(v) KRenwick 84
(W Storey) *midfield: hdwy after 4 out: kpt on u.p run-in* **100/1**
6 *1* **Ramsgill (USA)**[28] 3-10-12 .... PMoloney 90
(N P Littmoden) *midfield: hdwy appr 3 out: kpt on u.p run-in* **7/1**
0 **7** *13* **Ivana Illyich (IRE)**[8] 1718 3-10-5 .... ARoss 71+
(J S Wainwright) *midfield: outpcd 3 out: no imp whn mstke last* **100/1**
8 *6* **No Commission (IRE)**[39] 3-10-12 .... RMcGrath 75+
(R F Fisher) *hld up: hdwy appr 3 out: nvr trbld ldrs* **33/1**
9 *3½* **Esquillon**[33] 3-10-5 .... ADempsey 60
(J A Glover) *midfield: rdn and wknd after 4 out* **66/1**
00 **10** *nk* **Countrywide Sun**[18] 1601 3-10-12 .... JimCrowley 67
(A C Whillans) *hld up: no imp whn blnd last* **100/1**
3 **11** *1¼* **Maunby Reveller**[16] 1201 3-10-5 .... PMerrigan(7) 69+
(P C Haslam) *led tl j. slowly 1st: remained handy: mstke 4 out: wknd next* **16/1**
3 **12** *2½* **Desert Buzz (IRE)**[18] 1601 3-10-9 .... PAspell(3) 63
(J Hetherton) *hld up: rdn after 4 out: nvr on terms* **25/1**
13 *½* **Singhalongtasveer**[75] 3-10-12 ....(t) NPMulholland 62
(W Storey) *mstke 3rd: a bhd* **66/1**
14 *5* **Calfraz**[92] 3-10-12 .... GLee 57
(M D Hammond) *midfield: wknd 3 out* **33/1**
15 *7* **Port D'Argent (IRE)**[82] 3-9-12 .... AGlassonbury(7) 43
(Mrs H O Graham) *prom: mstke 3rd: mstke 4 out: sn wknd* **66/1**
16 *22* **Kalawoun (FR)**[163] 3-10-9 .... KJMercer(3) 28
(Ferdy Murphy) *a bhd* **5/1**[3]
0 **P** **Hamburg Springer (IRE)**[15] 1551 3-10-12 ....(b) RThornton —
(M J Polglase) *prom: mstke 4 out: sn wknd: t.o whn p.u bef 2 out* **100/1**

3m 49.5s (-9.60) **Going Correction** -0.625s/f (Firm) **17** Ran SP% **121.8**
Speed ratings: **99,98,96,96,95 94,88,85,83,83 82,81,81,78,75 64,—** CSF £87.60 TOTE £3.10: £1.80, £10.10, £2.90; EX 105.40.
Owner S Adamson **Bred** Darley **Trained** Constable Burton, N Yorks

FOCUS
An ordinary juvenile hurdle run at only a modest early gallop. The third sets the standard although the form could be rated slightly high.

NOTEBOOK
Finland(UAE), who sweated up beforehand, rallied gamely after being headed to get off the mark *over hurdles at the third time of asking. He might not be a star but he clearly has the right attitude. (op 5-2 tchd 11-4)*
First Fought(IRE), tongue tied for the first time, improved on his previous efforts and had his chance, but the winner proved the stronger.
Circumspect(IRE) probably did not improve on his performance when sixth at Wetherby, a view backed up by RPRs. *(tchd 5-1)*
Lodgician(IRE), a moderate middle-distance maiden on the Flat, looked the one to beat three out but he did not see the trip out as well as some of his rivals. He ran one of his best races on the Flat when held up in rear so maybe a change of tactics will benefit him. *(tchd 11-2)*

Madge, wearing headgear for the first time over hurdles, briefly looked a threat going to two out, but she never really got close enough. This was still a step up on her previous efforts, though.
Ramsgill(USA), in fair form recently on the Flat for his new stable, was not disgraced on his hurdling debut, but perhaps he will enjoy more success on the All-Weather this winter. *(op 10-1 tchd 11-1)*
Kalawoun(FR) *Official explanation: trainer said gelding was unsighted at first hurdle and never jumped thereafter (op 7-2)*

1798 BETDAQ.CO.UK H'CAP CHASE (18 fncs) 3m
4:40 (4:42) (Class 3) (0-120,120) 5-Y-O+ **£5,508** (£1,695; £847; £423)

Form RPR
-321 **1** **Catch The Perk (IRE)**[20] 1587 8-11-3 **114**.....................(p) PBuchanan(3) 127
(Miss Lucinda V Russell) *chsd ldr: pckd 4th: led 9th: mstke 15th: rdn appr 2 out : styd on wl* **5/1**
2P1- **2** *5* **Manbow (IRE)**[212] 4509 7-11-2 **110**.............................. GLee 118
(M D Hammond) *hld up: hdwy 4 out: chsd wnr next: rdn and no ex flat* **4/1**[2]
16P2 **3** *1 1/2* **Iverain (FR)**[13] 1664 9-10-9 **103**.............................. RMcGrath 110
(Sir John Barlow Bt) *prom: rdn appr 3 out: no ex flat* **9/2**[3]
P5-6 **4** *4* **Jungle Jinks (IRE)**[179] 12 10-11-9 **117**.............................. FKeniry 120
(G M Moore) *pckd 1st: prom: chsd wnr 11th to 3 out: wknd last* **7/2**[1]
04-3 **5** *17* **Shannon's Pride (IRE)**[173] 119 9-11-1 **112**.................... LMcGrath(3) 98
(R C Guest) *hld up: mstke 11th: hdwy next: wknd 3 out* **8/1**
223/ **6** *12* **Silver Knight**[551] 4865 7-11-12 **120**.............................. RGarritty 94
(T D Easterby) *hld up: mstke 11th: wknd appr 3 out* **8/1**
455- **P** **Spinofski**[191] 4815 10-11-3 **111**.............................. TDoyle —
(D R Stoddart) *led and mstke 1st: hdd 9th: wknd 11th: t.o whn p.u bef 3 out* **15/2**

6m 17.3s (-11.00) **Going Correction** -0.625s/f (Firm) **7** Ran SP% **111.1**
Speed ratings: **93,91,90,89,83 79,**— CSF £24.07 TOTE £4.50: £2.40, £2.90; EX 12.80.
Owner A A Bissett **Bred** Miss Yvonne McClintock And Mrs Jean O'Brien **Trained** Milnathort, Perth & Kinross

FOCUS
Despite the small field this was a fairly competitive affair and there were still four in with a chance at the last. The winning time was modest, but the first three were close to their marks and the form appears fairly solid.

NOTEBOOK
Catch The Perk(IRE) has been in good form over hurdles recently and followed up his Hexham success with a win back over the larger obstacles. Versatile with regard to ground preference, he had the edge in fitness over one or two of these and will find life tougher in future. *(op 9-2 tchd 4-1)*
Manbow(IRE), making his seasonal reappearance off a career-high mark, ran a super race in defeat, only finding the race-fit winner too strong on the run-in. With this outing under his belt he looks capable of improving on his impressive strike-rate over fences. *(tchd 9-2)*
Iverain(FR), another with the benefit of race-fitness, had every chance. He remains on a mark 1lb higher than when all out to win at Aintree in May.
Jungle Jinks(IRE), like the runner-up, was conceding race fitness to the winner and third, although that did not inconvenience him when he won this race last year off the same mark. Probably happier on easier ground, he is worth bearing in mind when the rains arrive. *(tchd 4-1)*
Shannon's Pride(IRE), another making his seasonal reappearance, has yet to prove he stays this far. *(op 7-1 tchd 17-2 in a place)*

1799 ALDER MAIDEN OPEN NATIONAL HUNT FLAT RACE 2m
5:10 (5:11) (Class 6) 4-6-Y-O **£2,037** (£582; £291)

Form RPR
1 **The Big Canadian (IRE)** 4-11-4.............................. RThornton 101+
(A King) *midfield: hdwy 1/2-way: led ins fnl f: r.o* **5/1**[3]
0- **2** *2* **Divex (IRE)**[222] 4323 4-11-4.............................. GLee 99
(M D Hammond) *hld up: hdwy over 5f out: styd on wl to take 2nd cl home: nt rch wnr* **25/1**
20- **3** *1/2* **Promise To Be Good**[194] 4774 4-11-4.............................. ATinkler 99
(N J Henderson) *midfield: hdwy 1/2-way: led over 5f out: rdn over 2f out: hdd ins fnl f: no ex* **11/2**
4 *1 3/4* **Templer (IRE)** 4-11-4.............................. RJohnson 97
(P J Hobbs) *hld up: hdwy over 6f out: rdn over 2f out: kpt on u.p fnl f* **7/2**[1]
5 *2 1/2* **Nevertika (FR)** 4-11-4.............................. RMcGrath 95
(Mrs K Walton) *midfield: hdwy over 4f out: one pce fr over 1f out* **100/1**
0- **6** *5* **Red Granite**[201] 4697 5-11-4.............................. JPMcNamara 90
(K C Bailey) *trckd ldrs: rdn over 2f out: wknd over 1f out* **16/1**
7 *3/4* **Silent Bay** 6-11-1.............................. PAspell(3) 89
(J Wade) *led: hdd after 2f: remained prom: regained ld over 7f out: hdd over 5f out: wknd over 2f out* **50/1**
3 **8** *1 3/4* **Topwell**[20] 1593 4-10-13.............................. PCO'Neill(5) 87
(R C Guest) *in tch: hdwy 1/2-way: rdn to chse ldrs over 2f out: wknd over 1f out* **25/1**
9 *1 1/4* **Buffers Lane (IRE)**[264] 6-11-4.............................. CLlewellyn 86
(N A Twiston-Davies) *cl up tl rdn and wknd 2f out* **9/2**[2]
10 *10* **Dark Rosalina** 4-10-11.............................. BJCrowley 69
(C W Moore) *bhd: rdn along after 4f: hdwy over 3f out: nvr trbld ldrs* **100/1**
11 *nk* **Secured (IRE)** 5-11-4.............................. PMoloney 75
(Ian Williams) *midfield: hdwy over 5f out: wknd over 2f out* **14/1**
0 **12** *1 1/2* **Aaron's Run**[56] 1323 5-11-4.............................. SCurran 74
(M R Bosley) *hld up: rdn over 4f out: nvr on terms* **100/1**
B **13** *9* **Desperate Dex (IRE)**[151] 470 5-11-4.............................. JMogford 65
(G J Smith) *midfield: rdn and outpcd 4f out: n.d after* **100/1**
00- **14** *1 1/2* **Create A Storm (IRE)**[222] 4333 5-10-11.............................. JTizzard 56
(J G Portman) *midfield: hdwy 6f out: rdn and wknd over 3f out* **33/1**
15 *8* **Harwood Dale**[206] 5-11-4.............................. RWalford 55
(T D Walford) *hld up: pushed along 1/2-way: n.d* **100/1**
16 *22* **It's No Easy (IRE)** 4-11-4.............................. BHarding 33
(N G Richards) *pushed along over 7f out: a bhd* **7/1**
17 *30* **Millestore** 5-11-1.............................. ACCoyle(3) 3
(M Mullineaux) *midfield tl wknd over 7f out* **100/1**
6 **18** *6* **Tongariro Crossing (IRE)**[154] 424 5-11-1.................... PBuchanan(3) —
(W T Reed) *racd keenly: trckd ldrs tl wknd over 6f out* **100/1**
00- **19** *dist* **Ben The Brave (IRE)**[269] 3520 6-11-4.............................. TDoyle —
(Mrs A M Thorpe) *midfield: lost pl after 6f: bhd after: t.o* **100/1**
20 *10* **Baltracy Cross (IRE)**[177] 46 4-11-4.............................. NFehily —
(C J Mann) *plld hrd: led after 2f: hdd over 7f out: wknd qckly: t.o* **100/1**

3m 46.4s (-10.00) **Going Correction** -0.625s/f (Firm) **20** Ran SP% **119.0**
Speed ratings: **100,99,98,97,96 94,93,92,92,87 87,86,81,81,77 66,51,48,**—,— CSF £131.14 TOTE £6.70: £2.40, £7.10, £2.10; EX 150.00 Place 6 £25.54, Place 5 £9.21.
Owner J Sigler,Knightsbridge B C & A King **Bred** John Kidd **Trained** Barbury Castle, Wilts

FOCUS
A fair bumper that should produce winners. It was run at a fairly steady early pace.

NOTEBOOK
The Big Canadian(IRE) ◆, a half-brother to bumper winner and promising novice hurdler Il Duce, had been flagged up by his trainer in the Racing Post stable tour two days earlier. Travelling well for much of the race, he ran green when asked to go on but, when finally realising what was required, picked up well. He has plenty of size and scope and looks the type to go on to better things. *(op 9-2 tchd 5-1)*
Divex(IRE), who stayed on well from off the pace for a pleasing second on this reappearance, should make his mark when sent hurdling.
Promise To Be Good, who ran in two good bumpers last term, is probably a good guide to the level of the form. He looks sure to pay his way over timber. *(op 6-1)*
Templer(IRE), who is a half-brother to very smart hurdler In Contrast and Irish bumper winner Maid of Clonmore, should do better with this experience under his belt, but he is not that big. *(op 5-2)*
Nevertika(FR), a French-bred, did not run at all badly on his debut for a stable not noted for its bumper winners.
Red Granite ran to a similar level as on his debut in a modest Newbury bumper in April. *(op 20-1)*
Silent Bay, a half-brother to three maiden jumpers, was left behind when the race began to get serious.
Buffers Lane(IRE), a half-brother to Irish two-and-a-half-mile hurdle winner Carramore Lass, is a winner of an Irish point-to-point. He could not cope with the injection of pace in the straight and will be better suited by a sterner test of stamina. *(op 4-1)*
It's No Easy(IRE), who is quite stoutly bred, came in for some market support but is likely to be seen to better effect when faced with a greater test of stamina. *(op 11-1 tchd 12-1)*
T/Jkpt: Not won. T/Plt: £8.80 to a £1 stake. Pool: £46,741.30. 3,856.15 winning tickets. T/Qpdt: £5.60 to a £1 stake. Pool: £2,723.90. 358.05 winning tickets. DO

1724 LUDLOW (R-H)
Thursday, October 20

OFFICIAL GOING: Good to firm (good in places)
Wind: Nil Weather: Fine

1800 RACING WELFARE WEEK (S) HURDLE (12 hdls) 3m
2:10 (2:11) (Class 5) 4-Y-O+ **£2,583** (£738; £369)

Form RPR
1 **Ballito (IRE)**[22] 1573 6-10-7.............................. (p) WKennedy(5) 90+
(John G Carr, Ire) *hld up in rr: hdwy 8th: led 2 out: hit last: styd on wl* **16/1**
05-3 **2** *1 3/4* **Knight Of Silver**[167] 206 8-10-12 83.............................. RGreene 86
(S C Burrough) *a.p: led appr 8th: clr after 9th: rdn and hdd 2 out: nt qckn flat* **7/1**[3]
3-P1 **3** *26* **Quizzical**[22] 1574 7-11-5 87.............................. (p) JamesDavies 67
(John G Carr, Ire) *hld up: hdwy appr 7th: one pce fr 9th* **11/2**[2]
P043 **4** *1/2* **Greencard Golf**[8] 1712 4-11-4 87.............................. AO'Keeffe 66
(Jennie Candlish) *hld up and bhd: hdwy 8th: no real prog fr 9th* **14/1**
PP-P **5** *26* **Dat My Horse (IRE)**[12] 1675 11-10-12 101.............................. RHobson 34
(Tim Vaughan) *nvr nr ldrs* **20/1**
4432 **6** *1/2* **Dante's Battle (IRE)**[58] 1299 13-10-12 96.............................. RSpate(7) 40
(Mrs K Waldron) *hld up and bhd: hdwy 8th: wknd after 9th* **12/1**
P-35 **7** *3 1/2* **Alvaro (IRE)**[8] 1715 8-11-5 97.............................. (b) LHeard(7) 44
(B J Llewellyn) *led to 3rd: rdn appr 7th: wkng whn mstke 8th* **15/2**
00 **8** *14* **Impatient Lady**[15] 1640 8-10-1 ow1.............................. CHonour(5) 9
(J D Frost) *unruly bef s: rel to r: a bhd* **25/1**
PP5F **9** *30* **Jivaty (FR)**[19] 1595 8-10-12 110.............................. SWalsh(7) —
(Mrs A J Hamilton-Fairley) *prom tl wknd appr 8th: t.o* **14/1**
F/P **10** *10* **Amanpuri (GER)**[20] 1587 7-10-2.............................. AngharadFrieze(10) —
(P A Blockley) *t.k.h: led 3rd: pckd 6th: hdd appr 7th: wknd 8th* **40/1**
0/P5 **P** **Roscam**[28] 1523 8-10-12 73.............................. PJBrennan —
(G A Ham) *bhd fr 7th: t.o whn p.u bef 2 out* **14/1**
6045 **P** **Port Sodrick**[52] 1367 4-10-4 82.............................. KBurke(7) —
(R H Alner) *prom: rdn 6th: wknd appr 8th: bhd whn p.u bef 3 out* **9/2**[1]
P3UU **P** **Audiostreetdotcom**[14] 1655 8-10-12 89.............................. (b) DJacob(7) —
(R A Harris) *mid-div: dropped rr and j. slowly 6th: p.u after 7th* **7/1**[3]

5m 47.0s (-7.60) **Going Correction** -0.50s/f (Good)
WFA 4 from 6yo+ 15lb **13** Ran SP% **115.0**
Speed ratings: **92,91,82,82,73 73,72,67,57,54** —,—,— CSF £117.77 TOTE £29.70: £9.70, £2.10, £1.80; EX 317.50.There was no bid for the winner.
Owner George Stanley **Bred** George Stanley **Trained** Maynooth, Co. Kildare

FOCUS
Riders involved in this were of the opinion that the ground was good. This very modest event concerned just the two from a long way out with the runner-up setting the level for the form.

NOTEBOOK
Ballito(IRE), previously trained by his owner George Stanley, has joined John Carr since falling on his recent chase debut. Moving into second place at the start of the long turn out of the back straight, he steadily reeled in the leader and the race was over once he struck the front at the second last. He has been running over shorter and the return to this longer trip helped. *(tchd 18-1)*
Knight Of Silver had compiled a handy lead by the fourth last but it soon became apparent that the eventual winner had him covered. The final quarter-mile was uncharted territory for him but he did not appear to be beaten through lack of stamina. This was a satisfactory return after his summer break.
Quizzical, a stablemate of the winner, has been well beaten in a couple of runs at Downpatrick since scrambling home at Sedgefield. He was a spent force with four to jump but held on to a detached third. *(op 13-2)*
Greencard Golf never got into the race, but did put in a sustained, and ultimately fruitless, challenge for a distant third place. *(tchd 16-1)*
Port Sodrick was on the retreat when pulled up and dismounted on the long home turn. *(op 5-1)*

1801 HAZLIN DOORS BEGINNERS' CHASE (17 fncs) 2m 4f
2:40 (2:44) (Class 4) 5-Y-O+ **£3,953** (£1,541; £804; £402)

Form RPR
/20- **1** **Valance (IRE)**[69] 2126 5-11-0.............................. APMcCoy 114+
(C R Egerton) *led to 2nd: chsd ldr: led and hit 4 out: hdd 3 out: btn whn lft clr last* **6/4**[1]
32-5 **2** *14* **Forever Dream**[19] 1598 7-11-0 119.............................. PJBrennan 98
(P J Hobbs) *hld up: hdwy 9th: rdn 4 out: one pce* **5/1**[3]
6-46 **3** *1/2* **She's My Girl (IRE)**[22] 1573 10-10-7.............................. JamesDavies 92+
(John G Carr, Ire) *a.p: rdn appr 4 out: blnd 3 out: one pce* **28/1**
0 **4** *29* **Robber Red**[7] 1726 9-10-7.............................. (t) RLucey-Butler(7) 69
(Miss Suzy Smith) *a bhd: t.o fr 9th* **25/1**
P **Dans Blarney (IRE)**[208] 8-10-9.............................. LStephens(5) —
(V J Hughes) *a bhd: t.o whn p.u bef 4 out* **50/1**
1/6- **P** **Jaskini**[130] 9-10-9.............................. HEphgrave(5) —
(L Corcoran) *plld hrd in rr: t.o fr 9th: p.u bef 13th* **20/1**
P0-6 **P** **Diamond Merchant**[163] 275 6-11-0.............................. WHutchinson —
(Ian Williams) *prom tl wknd 10th: t.o whn p.u bef 4 out* **17/2**

60P6 **P** **Pat Malone**[14] 891 5-10-7 .... RSpate(7) —
(Lucinda Featherstone) *a bhd: mstke 2nd: t.o whn j.lft 11th: p.u bef 4 out* **100/1**

0320 **P** **Lost In The Snow (IRE)**[14] 1659 7-11-0 80........ SThomas —
(M Sheppard) *a bhd: mstke 4th: j.lft 6th: sn t.o: p.u bef 4 out* **25/1**

5153 **F** **Chase The Sunset (IRE)**[52] 1365 7-11-0 105........ TJMurphy 118+
(Miss H C Knight) *led 2nd to 4 out: led 3 out: 4l clr whn fell last* **11/4**[2]

5m 0.70s (-10.00) **Going Correction** -0.35s/f (Good) **10** Ran SP% **112.7**
Speed ratings: **106,100,100,88,—** —,—,—,—,— CSF £8.29 TOTE £2.00: £1.50, £1.80, £6.50; EX 11.50.
Owner M Haynes, A & J Allison, J Weatherby **Bred** B H Bloodstock **Trained** Chaddleworth, Berks

FOCUS
Quite an interesting beginners' chase rated through the runner-up. With a fortunate winner the form looks nothing special.

NOTEBOOK
Valance(IRE) gained a debut victory over fences in fortuitous circumstances. A useful hurdler who was in winning form on the Flat in the summer, he moved to the front at the first in the home straight but an error there handed the initiative back to market rival Chase The Sunset, and he was booked for second when fate intervened at the last. Suited by fast ground, he generally jumped well and a drop back to two miles may be beneficial. *(tchd 7-4)*
Forever Dream, reverting to fences, looked a potential threat on the home turn but was soon left behind by the two leaders. He was fortunate to inherit second, a position with which he became familiar over hurdles. *(op 9-2)*
She's My Girl(IRE), an Irish mare who is not very big, ran her best race to date over the larger obstacles. *(op 25-1)*
Robber Red ran a better race over two miles here last week, although that was a slowly-run affair. *Official explanation: jockey said gelding hung left throughout (op 22-1)*
Chase The Sunset(IRE) was unfortunate not to get off the mark on this sixth attempt over fences. He was in command when overjumping at the last but had not really put a foot wrong before disaster struck. *(op 5-2 tchd 9-4)*
Diamond Merchant, who has left Alan King since his last run in May, did not shape with any great *promise on this chasing debut. Official explanation: jockey said gelding was struck into (op 5-2 tchd 9-4)*

1802 ALFA AGGREGATES JUVENILE NOVICES' HURDLE (9 hdls) 2m
3:15 (3:15) (Class 4) 3-Y-O **£4,043** (£1,244; £622; £311)

Form RPR

031 **1** **Palace Walk (FR)**[14] 1649 3-11-5 102........ TJMurphy 94+
(B G Powell) *mde all: j.rt: hit last: r.o wl* **11/4**[2]

2 *4* **Madam Caversfield**[10] 3-10-5 .... AntonyEvans 75+
(P D Evans) *hld up in mid-div: hdwy 5th: chsd wnr 3 out: hung lft 2 out: no imp* **6/1**[3]

BP52 **3** *5* **Time For You**[25] 1563 3-10-5 85........ WMarston 70+
(J M Bradley) *chsd wnr tl after 6th: mstke 3 out: lft 3rd 2 out: one pce* **10/1**

P00 **4** *7* **Keepasharplookout (IRE)**[7] 1729 3-10-12 .... JPByrne 69
(C W Moore) *plld hrd in rr: sme hdwy after 6th: nvr trbld ldrs* **100/1**

P00 **5** *4* **Lara's Girl**[7] 1729 3-9-12 .... WPKavanagh(7) 58
(K G Wingrove) *hld up in mid-div: hdwy 6th: rdn and wknd appr 3 out* **40/1**

1 **6** *5* **Kristinor (FR)**[7] 1729 3-11-5 .... PHide 77+
(G L Moore) *hld up: hdwy 6th: hit 3 out: 3rd whn blnd bdly 2 out: nt rcvr* **6/5**[1]

0 **7** *8* **Look At The Stars (IRE)**[7] 1729 3-10-2 .... AHawkins(10) 52
(R Hollinshead) *nvr nr ldrs* **33/1**

P **8** *nk* **Cloonavery (IRE)**[12] 1679 3-10-12 .... ChristianWilliams 52
(B Llewellyn) *nvr nr ldrs* **25/1**

00P **9** *7* **Ardasnails (IRE)**[7] 1729 3-10-5 .... MrDGreenway(7) 45
(K G Wingrove) *t.k.h in tch: j.rt 2nd: wknd after 6th* **150/1**

65 **10** *½* **Top Pursuit**[14] 1649 3-10-12 .... PJBrennan 44
(J L Spearing) *bhd: short-lived effrt 6th* **40/1**

11 *dist* **Inagh**[82] 3-9-12 .... CPoste(7) —
(R C Harper) *a bhd: t.o* **100/1**

P **F** **Harry's Simmie (IRE)**[12] 1679 3-10-0 .... MNicolls(5) —
(R C Harper) *prom: wkng whn fell 6th* **100/1**

4 **P** **Darko Karim**[50] 1380 3-10-5 .... JamesWhite(7) —
(R J Hodges) *nt fluent: prom to 4th: in rr whn hmpd 6th: t.o whn p.u bef 3 out* **25/1**

3m 47.5s (-4.80) **Going Correction** -0.50s/f (Good) **13** Ran SP% **114.6**
Speed ratings: **92,90,87,84,82 79,75,75,71,71** —,—,— CSF £17.45 TOTE £4.20: £1.80, £1.30, £2.00; EX 19.60.
Owner Winterbeck Manor Stud **Bred** Elevage Haras De Bourgeauville **Trained** Morestead, Hants

FOCUS
Not a strong juvenile event and the time was more than six seconds slower than the later handicap over the same trip. The winner may do better, but the form behind is very ordinary.

NOTEBOOK
Palace Walk(FR) is going the right way over hurdles and he defied the penalty for his win at Wincanton. Given a canny ride by Murphy, who kicked again on the approach to the home straight, he soon had matters under control but he will not always be able to dictate things as he did here. His hurdling has room for improvement too. *(tchd 5-2)*
Madam Caversfield was a fair filly on the Flat, successful twice in sellers recently. She made a satisfactory hurdling bow but was held when looking for a moment as if she wanted to run out at the second last. *(op 9-1)*
Time For You, the most experienced member of the field, ran her race again but does not look up to winning one of these at present. *(tchd 11-1)*
Keepasharplookout(IRE) settled better this time and does have a little ability.
Lara's Girl probably needs a stiffer test. *(op 33-1)*
Kristinor(FR)finished well ahead of today's fourth and fifth when successful here last week, but was a disappointment under the penalty. Ridden patiently again, he promised to be involved in the finish as he closed leaving the back straight but was already on the retreat when crashing through the second last. *(op Evens tchd 10-11)*

1803 AMATEUR JOCKEYS' ASSOCIATION H'CAP CHASE (FOR THE COURT OF HILL CHALLENGE CUP) (22 fncs) 3m 1f 110y
3:45 (3:45) (Class 4) (0-100,99) 5-Y-O+
£2,963 (£1,124; £562; £255; £127; £76)

Form RPR

003 **1** **Regal Vision (IRE)**[27] 1539 8-9-9 75 ow2........ MissCDyson(7) 92
(Miss C Dyson) *w ldr: led 7th tl after 9th: led 18th: j.lft fr 3 out: styd on* **13/2**

P2 **2** *5* **Oh My Lord (IRE)**[82] 1104 7-11-4 98........(t) MrJWFarrelly(7) 113+
(A J Martin, Ire) *hld up: nt fluent 15th: hdwy 18th: rdn appr 4 out: chsd wnr appr 2 out: slipped sn after last: one pce* **13/8**[1]

P065 **3** *1 ½* **Sunday Habits (IRE)**[15] 1639 11-9-10 76 oh8 ow3..... MrDavidTurner(7) 88+
(Dr P Pritchard) *a.p: rdn appr 15th: ev ch 4 out: one pce fr 3 out* **16/1**

333 **4** *25* **Pangeran (USA)**[15] 1646 13-10-3 76 ow3........ MissPGundry 62
(N B King) *w ldrs tl hit 10th: wknd appr 15th* **9/2**[3]

004P **5** *13* **Noble Colours**[4] 1751 12-9-9 73 oh12........ MissFayeBramley(5) 46
(Mrs C J Ikin) *led to 7th: led after 9th to 18th: wknd appr 4 out* **40/1**

0414 **6** *19* **Coppermalt (USA)**[25] 1564 7-9-11 73 oh15........ LNewnes(3) 27
(R Curtis) *a in rr: j. slowly 6th: t.o fr 12th* **7/2**[2]

FF25 **P** **Good Man Again (IRE)**[7] 1727 7-11-7 99........(t) MrJETudor(5) —
(A Sadik) *bhd tl p.u bef 10th* **10/1**

6m 38.8s (3.60) **Going Correction** -0.35s/f (Good) **7** Ran SP% **109.2**
Speed ratings: **80,78,78,70,66 60,—** CSF £16.74 TOTE £10.00: £4.10, £2.20; EX 36.10.
Owner Miss C Dyson **Bred** B Freiha **Trained** Lower Bentley, Worcs

FOCUS
A very weak affair, run in a pedestrian time, in which three of the field were out of the handicap. The form is very moderate.

NOTEBOOK
Regal Vision(IRE), who had run a decent race over hurdles last time, was always at the sharp end and he stayed on well enough under his owner/trainer. His wins come around infrequently and it could be some time before his turn arrives again. *(op 6-1 tchd 15-2)*
Oh My Lord(IRE), an Irish challenger, sat off the pace and allowed the leaders to do their own thing. Steadily improving, he briefly threatened to catch the leader but was held when losing his footing, and a bit of momentum, a stride or two after the last. He has now been a beaten favourite on each of his last five starts and it is not difficult to see why as he does not look to do anything quickly. *(op 7-4)*
Sunday Habits(IRE), a very modest performer, ran as well as expected given he was wrong at the weights.
Pangeran(USA) was below-par but plugged on to claim a distant fourth. *(op 11-4)*
Noble Colours disputed things with the eventual winner before fading on the home turn. *(op 33-1)*
Coppermalt(USA) was the subject of on-course support on this return to fences but trailed throughout. *(op 6-1)*

1804 OCTOBER H'CAP HURDLE (9 hdls) 2m
4:20 (4:20) (Class 3) (0-120,117) 4-Y-O+ **£4,634** (£1,426; £713; £356)

Form RPR

-112 **1** **Phar Out Phavorite (IRE)**[151] 460 6-11-10 115........(v) BFenton 120+
(Miss E C Lavelle) *chsd ldrs: led after 5th: rdn and r.o flat* **5/2**[1]

30-6 **2** *1* **Hatch A Plan (IRE)**[22] 911 4-10-6 97........ PHide 99
(Mrs A J Hamilton-Fairley) *hld up: hdwy 5th: chsd wnr 2 out: sn rdn: hit last: r.o* **10/1**

3243 **3** *¾* **Kentucky King (USA)**[14] 1653 5-10-7 98........(t) ChristianWilliams 99
(Mrs D A Hamer) *hld up and bhd: hdwy after 6th: kpt on u.p flat* **11/2**[2]

-022 **4** *7* **Critical Stage (IRE)**[61] 1263 6-11-0 110........ CHonour(5) 105+
(J D Frost) *hld up: hdwy 6th: rdn and ev ch 3 out: wknd last* **13/2**[3]

3220 **5** *½* **Artane Boys**[12] 1675 8-11-4 109........ TSiddall 103
(Jonjo O'Neill) *hld up and bhd: rdn and hdwy appr 3 out: wknd after 2 out* **15/2**

-P0S **6** *11* **Private Benjamin**[19] 1598 5-10-7 98........ MBatchelor 84+
(Jamie Poulton) *hld up and bhd: mstke 3rd: rdn and hdwy appr 3 out: wknd appr 2 out* **20/1**

1440 **7** *6* **Kims Pearl (IRE)**[12] 1668 7-10-13 104........ RGreene 84+
(S Lycett) *led to 4th: wknd 3 out* **33/1**

165- **8** *17* **Caspian Dusk**[194] 4780 4-10-13 104........ PJBrennan 64
(W G M Turner) *mstke 5th: a bhd* **16/1**

50FU **P** **A Bit Of Fun**[12] 1668 4-10-12 108........ LTreadwell(5) —
(J T Stimpson) *a bhd: t.o whn p.u bef 3 out* **12/1**

6-03 **P** **Cashel Dancer**[151] 460 6-10-8 99........ JPByrne —
(S A Brookshaw) *a bhd: t.o whn p.u bef 3 out* **10/1**

P60- **U** **Dream Falcon**[257] 3701 5-11-5 117........ JamesWhite(7) —
(R J Hodges) *w ldr: led 4th tl after 5th: 3rd whn blnd and uns rdr 6th* **14/1**

3m 41.2s (-11.10) **Going Correction** -0.50s/f (Good)
WFA 4 from 5yo+ 13lb **11** Ran SP% **115.2**
Speed ratings: **107,106,106,102,102 96,93,85,—,—** — CSF £27.52 CT £126.59 TOTE £2.90: £1.80, £3.90, £2.00; EX 43.40.
Owner Favourites Racing V **Bred** Mrs J Wilkinson **Trained** Wildhern, Hants

FOCUS
A reasonably well-contested handicap, run at a sound pace and the form appears solid.

NOTEBOOK
Phar Out Phavorite(IRE) eased to the front with four to jump and had most of his rivals in trouble turning for home. Fenton only went for him on the run-in and he found sufficient to hold on. Slightly below-par on his most recent run in May, which could be attributed to the easy ground, he is likely to turn his sights to fences before long. *(op 9-4 tchd 11-4)*
Hatch A Plan(IRE) ran with credit on his handicap debut and stayed on to cut into the winner's advantage after rapping the final flight. This was only his fourth run over hurdles and a small race could be within his reach. *(op 9-1 tchd 12-1)*
Kentucky King(USA) is proving fairly consistently at present and this was another creditable run. *The leaders got away from him after the third last but he was staying on again up the run-in. (op 15-2)*
Critical Stage(IRE), who faded going to the final flight, was raised 2lb in defeat last time and does not look particularly well treated at present. *(tchd 6-1)*
Artane Boys failed to improve for this return to two miles. *(op 13-2)*
Private Benjamin, who survived an early error, was close enough turning into the home straight but could make no further progress. *(op 18-1)*
Kims Pearl(IRE) paid for going off too quickly.
A Bit Of Fun *Official explanation: jockey said gelding lost its action (op 14-1 tchd 11-1)*

1805 REG LOMAS LIFETIME IN RACING H'CAP CHASE (13 fncs) 2m
4:50 (4:50) (Class 4) (0-100,97) 5-Y-O+**£3,288** (£1,257; £637; £298; £157)

Form RPR

U401 **1** **Welsh Main**[4] 1754 8-11-11 96 7ex........ APMcCoy 114+
(Miss Tor Sturgis) *hld up: hdwy 7th: led 3 out: clr fr 2 out: easily* **5/2**[2]

5256 **2** *7* **Karakum**[14] 1659 6-10-13 91........ MrJAJenkins(7) 99+
(A J Chamberlain) *led: mstke 8th: hdd 3 out: btn whn hit last* **33/1**

1F55 **3** *2* **Knight's Emperor (IRE)**[5] 1746 8-11-12 97........ AntonyEvans 103+
(J L Spearing) *bhd: blnd bdly 3rd: hdwy 4 out: styd on flat: nvr nrr* **14/1**

523P **4** *4* **Gipsy Cricketer**[18] 1612 9-10-7 78........ TScudamore 79+
(M Scudamore) *w ldr: ev ch 4 out: wknd appr 2 out* **11/1**

P-40 **5** *23* **Manolo (FR)**[127] 762 5-11-10 95........ SThomas 72
(Ian Williams) *blnd 4th: a bhd* **7/1**[3]

-402 **P** **My Galliano (IRE)**[25] 1559 9-11-3 88........ TJMurphy —
(B G Powell) *bhd: j.rt 2nd: p.u lame bef 6th: dead* **9/4**[1]

0-0 **U** **Kinkeel (IRE)**[15] 1645 6-11-2 87........ WHutchinson —
(A W Carroll) *hld up: hdwy and 4th whn blnd and uns rdr 7th* **28/1**

0000 **F** **Wages**[60] 1278 5-10-12 83........ ChristianWilliams —
(Evan Williams) *hld up: hdwy 7th: 4l 5th whn fell 8th* **7/1**[3]

-244 **P** **Meltonian**[18] 1612 8-10-11 89........ SWalsh(7) —
(K F Clutterbuck) *chsd clr ldrs: wknd appr 9th: 5th whn p.u lame bef 3 out* **12/1**

3m 59.6s (-4.50) **Going Correction** -0.35s/f (Good) **9** Ran SP% **113.4**
Speed ratings: **97,93,92,90,79** —,—,—,— CSF £64.98 CT £960.86 TOTE £3.20: £1.10, £3.00, £4.00; EX 58.20.
Owner Miss Tor Sturgis **Bred** Juddmonte Farms **Trained** Kingston Lisle, Oxon

FOCUS
Not too many managed to get involved in this modest handicap. The winner is value for more than the official margin and the placed horses set the standard.

NOTEBOOK
Welsh Main, successful at Hereford four days earlier, had no problem following up despite the three-furlong shorter trip. Value for further as he was eased down on the run-in with his race won, he was still 16lb lower than his current hurdles mark despite his penalty. *(op 2-1)*
Karakum, dropped 3lb, is a long-standing maiden but, while no match for the favourite, he deserves some credit for holding on to second after setting a decent gallop. His main problem is that he only just gets two miles. *(op 25-1)*
Knight's Emperor(IRE) survived a major blunder early on, Evans making a fine recovery, and stayed on from the back of the field for an unlikely third place.
Gipsy Cricketer, another doubtful stayer, kept the eventual runner-up company until fading from the third last. *(tchd 12-1)*
My Galliano(IRE) sadly injured a hind-leg early on the final circuit. *(op 25-1)*
Meltonian *Official explanation: jockey said gelding returned lame (op 25-1)*
Wages, a frustrating sort over hurdles, was without the cheekpieces for this chasing bow. He was just creeping into contention when crashing out. *(op 25-1)*
Kinkeel(IRE), on his chasing debut, was not out of it when parting company. *(op 25-1)*

1806 CHRISTMAS AT LUDLOW NOVICES' H'CAP HURDLE (11 hdls) 2m 5f
5:20 (5:21) (Class 4) (0-105,95) 3-Y-0+ **£3,393** (£1,044; £522; £261)

Form RPR
45-0 **1** **Astyanax (IRE)**[179] [5] 5-11-12 **95** MFoley 101+
(N J Henderson) *mde all: rdn and r.o flat* **3/1**[2]
B20- **2** ¾ **Teorban (POL)**[24] [3639] 6-11-12 **95** MBradburne 98
(D J S Ffrench Davis) *hld up and bhd: hdwy after 8th: chsd wnr fr 3 out: hrd rdn appr last: nt qckn flat* **9/1**
P-33 **3** *15* **Welsh Dane**[4] [1753] 5-10-10 **82** (p) ONelmes[(3)] 70
(M Sheppard) *chsd ldr: hit 3rd: lost 2nd 5th: lft 2nd after 8th: wknd appr 2 out* **5/1**[3]
0321 **4** *11* **Dont Ask Me (IRE)**[2] [1784] 4-11-9 **92** 7ex (t) TScudamore 70+
(M C Pipe) *hld up: hdwy 7th: rdn appr 3 out: wknd appr 2 out* **7/4**[1]
0411 **5** *nk* **Possible Gale (IRE)**[20] [1588] 7-11-7 **95** (tp) WKennedy[(5)] 74+
(John G Carr, Ire) *hld up and bhd: blnd 6th: short-lived effrt appr 3 out* **8/1**
303P **6** *27* **Mistified (IRE)**[85] [1079] 4-11-4 **94** WPKavanagh[(7)] 44
(J W Mullins) *hld up and bhd: short-lived effrt after 8th: t.o* **20/1**
4046 **7** *nk* **Tyup Pompey (IRE)**[15] [1637] 4-10-12 **81** JamesDavies 30
(Miss J S Davis) *hld up and bhd: stdy hdwy 3rd: wknd after 8th: t.o* **40/1**
065P **P** **Regulated (IRE)**[2] [1779] 4-10-6 **85** (p) AngharadFrieze[(10)] —
(P A Blockley) *a bhd: lost tch fr 7th: t.o whn p.u bef 3 out* **40/1**
P003 **P** **Raneen Nashwan**[15] [1640] 9-10-12 **81** (p) VSlattery —
(R J Baker) *prom: chsd wnr 5th: 2nd whn p.u lame after 8th* **33/1**
0 **P** **Bakhtyar**[64] [1242] 4-11-6 **89** APMcCoy —
(A J Martin, Ire) *hld up: hdwy appr 7th: wknd after 8th: t.o whn p.u bef 3 out* **16/1**

5m 8.40s (-9.90) **Going Correction** -0.50s/f (Good)
WFA 4 from 5yo+ 14lb **10** Ran SP% **117.6**
Speed ratings: **98,97,92,87,87 77,77**,—,—,— CSF £28.72 CT £130.74 TOTE £4.30: £2.00, £2.80, £2.20; EX 50.20 Place 6 £70.75, Place 5 £25.89.
Owner A Taylor **Bred** P D Player **Trained** Upper Lambourn, Berks

FOCUS
Just an ordinary handicap and with the time modest the form does not look strong.

NOTEBOOK
Astyanax(IRE), a one-time useful stayer on the Flat for Sir Mark Prescott, proved a disappointment in his first season as a hurdler but this was much more encouraging. Making every yard, he battled well to see off the runner-up and this looks to be his trip. *(op 11-2)*
Teorban(POL), who was fit from the Flat, delivered a sustained challenge but had to give best in the last 25 yards. He remains a maiden over hurdles and the Handicapper is not likely to drop him after this. *(op 12-1)*
Welsh Dane made a satisfactory return to action at the weekend and this was another decent effort. The way he was keeping on suggests he might benefit from a step up in trip. *(op 7-1 tchd 15-2)*
Dont Ask Me(IRE) was ultimately found wanting under his penalty. A combination of factors brought about this defeat, including the longer trip and faster ground, while this might well have come too soon after his exertions two days earlier. *(op 6-4 tchd 5-4)*
Possible Gale(IRE), bidding for a hat-trick after two wins in sellers, was in last place when surviving a blunder at the sixth. He stayed on in the latter stages over this longer trip but could never get into the hunt. *(op 7-1)*
Bakhtyar was beaten a long way in four previous tries over hurdles in Ireland and this marked step up in trip failed to bring out any change in fortune. *(op 8-1)*
T/Plt: £232.60 to a £1 stake. Pool: £34,096.50. 107.00 winning tickets. T/Qpdt: £32.10 to a £1 stake. Pool: £2,807.50. 64.70 winning tickets. KH

1807 - 1809a (Foreign Racing) - See Raceform Interactive

[1786]PUNCHESTOWN (R-H)
Thursday, October 20

OFFICIAL GOING: Hurdle course - good to yielding (good in places); chase course - good (good to yielding in places)

1810a DAILY STAR CHASE (LISTED RACE) 2m 6f
4:15 (4:16) 5-Y-0+ **£15,236** (£4,470; £2,129; £725)

RPR
1 **War Of Attrition (IRE)**[175] [89] 6-11-12 146 CO'Dwyer 164+
(M F Morris, Ire) *hld up in tch: tk clsr order 5 out: 3rd and drvn along after 3 out: rdn to ld next: edgd clr bef last: styd on wl* **7/1**[3]
2 *3* **Kicking King (IRE)**[176] [68] 7-11-12 175 BJGeraghty 159+
(T J Taaffe, Ire) *settled 3rd: impr 7th: j. into ld 6 out: hdd briefly 4 out: strly pressed after 3 out: hdd next: outpcd bef last: kpt on u.* **30/100**[1]
3 *shd* **Pizarro (IRE)**[176] [68] 8-11-12 149 RWalsh 159
(E J O'Grady, Ire) *trckd ldr in 2nd: cl 3rd 1/2-way: rdn to ld briefly 4 out: cl 2nd and chal after next: j. bdly rt 2 out: kpt on u.p* **11/2**[2]
4 *25* **Strong Project (IRE)**[12] [1692] 9-11-12 137 DJCasey 140+
(C F Swan, Ire) *led: pckd sltly and hdd 6 out: 4th and in tch 4 out: sn wknd* **14/1**
5 *25* **Splendour (IRE)**[56] [1325] 10-11-12 125 JLCullen 109
(Miss S Cox, Ire) *hld up in tch: hit 1st: rdn and wknd fr 5 out: t.o* **50/1**

5m 44.1s **6** Ran SP% **36.5**
CSF £10.72 TOTE £8.60: £3.00, £1.10; DF 10.40.
Owner Gigginstown House Stud **Bred** Miss B A Murphy **Trained** Fethard, Co Tipperary

NOTEBOOK
War Of Attrition(IRE) looked well but in need of plenty of tightening up. Nudged along from four out, he was not travelling any better than the other pair before the next but, widest into the straight, had come to land in front over the second last. He had over two lengths to spare at the final fence and stayed on well. Improvement is guaranteed and he has a favoured alternative at the meeting to the Gold Cup next March. He goes to Down Royal next on November 5th with a choice of engagements between the 3m James Nicholson Champion Chase or the 2m4f semi-novice Killultagh Properties Chase. *(op 4/1)*
Kicking King(IRE) was burly but enjoyed himself when at the head of affairs. Briefly outjumped four out, he was still travelling well between horses turning for home but was headed at the second last and appeared to blow up. Well held at the last, he still ran on again to snatch second place on the line. Plenty of improvement is anticipated with Haydock and the Betfair Bonus very much on target. *(op 1/3 tchd 2/7)*
Pizarro(IRE) was well held by Kicking King last season and did not impress with his attitude on a couple of occasions but he ran to his best, only flinching when going to the right at the second last but keeping on well once straightened. This could well prove his optimum trip, three miles seeming to stretch him. *(op 5/1 tchd 7/1)*
Strong Project(IRE) was totally outclassed from four out. *(op 10/1)*

1811 - 1813a (Foreign Racing) - See Raceform Interactive

[363]FAKENHAM (L-H)
Friday, October 21

OFFICIAL GOING: Good
Wind: Almost nil

1814 EASTERN DAILY PRESS CONDITIONAL JOCKEYS' (S) H'CAP HURDLE (8 hdls 1 omitted) 2m
2:10 (2:10) (Class 5) (0-90,90) 4-Y-0+ **£2,597** (£742; £371)

Form RPR
0644 **1** **Wardash (GER)**[8] [1724] 5-11-6 **87** (tp) TJMalone[(3)] 83+
(M C Pipe) *chsd ldr after 1st: led 7th: sn rdn: jst hld on* **10/3**[1]
-2U5 **2** ½ **Cadeaux Rouge (IRE)**[21] [1590] 4-10-11 **78** (t) PMerrigan[(3)] 74+
(D W Thompson) *w.w in mid-div: hdwy 5th: chal and hmpd bnd after 7th: styd on appr by-passed last: jst failed* **5/1**[3]
4000 **3** ¾ **Nutley Queen (IRE)**[100] [973] 6-9-10 **65** oh5 ow1 (t) RSpate[(5)] 58
(M Appleby) *t.k.h: mid-div: hdwy 7th: ev ch next: nt qckn last 100yds* **50/1**
U-35 **4** *shd* **Chariot (IRE)**[29] [1520] 4-10-12 **79** MrJAJenkins[(3)] 72
(M R Bosley) *hld up in rr: hdwy 5th: rdn to chal 2 out: one pce last last 100yds* **14/1**
0U50 **5** *12* **Hidden Smile (USA)**[20] [1597] 8-10-2 **69** (p) JDiment[(3)] 50
(F Jordan) *trckd ldrs: rdn and wknd after 7th* **11/1**
P-P2 **6** *2 ½* **Countback (FR)**[9] [1712] 6-11-0 **83** (b) TMessenger[(5)] 62
(C C Bealby) *in tch: rdn 4th: lost pl after next: no ch after* **4/1**[2]
5200 **7** *6* **Protocol (IRE)**[5] [1756] 11-11-12 **90** (t) CBolger 63
(Mrs S Lamyman) *led tl after 1st: lost pl and rdn 4th: wl bhd fr 6th* **11/2**
6-0R **8** *11* **Cicatrice**[15] [274] 4-10-11 **75** SCurling 37
(D R Gandolfo) *led after 1st: hdd 7th: wknd qckly next* **16/1**
0U66 **9** *6* **Tiger Talk**[150] [480] 9-11-4 **90** (b) JMoorman[(8)] 46
(R C Guest) *mid-div: mstke 5th: sn wl bhd* **10/1**
0050 **10** *7* **Bally Hall (IRE)**[33] [1483] 5-10-12 **76** (t) ONelmes 25
(M J Gingell) *stdd s: hdwy and in tch 5th: wknd qckly 7th* **20/1**
P-5P **P** **Past Heritage**[16] [1636] 6-10-4 **68** (p) DLaverty —
(A E Jones) *stdd s: bhd: mstke 4th: t.o whn p.u bef 2 out* **25/1**

4m 9.80s (0.90) **Going Correction** +0.10s/f (Yiel)
WFA 4 from 5yo+ 13lb **11** Ran SP% **115.7**
Speed ratings: **101,100,100,100,94 93,90,84,81,78** — CSF £19.88 CT £694.95 TOTE £4.20: £1.70, £2.10, £14.90; EX 20.90.The winner was sold to M. C. Chapman for 4,800gns.
Owner D A Johnson **Bred** Gestut Rottgen **Trained** Nicholashayne, Devon
■ Stewards' Enquiry : T J Malone two-day ban: careless riding (Nov 1-2)

FOCUS
A weak seller and the presence of the third holds the form down. The race is best rated through those in the frame behind the winner. The final flight was bypassed.

NOTEBOOK
Wardash(GER) has a decent strike rate in this grade on good ground and he enhanced that record with an all-out success. His jockey received a two-day ban for a back-straight manoeuvre that shut the door on the eventual runner-up and, in the circumstances, he was a shade fortunate to score. *(op 3-1 tchd 4-1)*
Cadeaux Rouge(IRE), well supported pre-race, did not enjoy the run of the race and was arguably unlucky not to land the gamble. She enjoyed the drop in class and can win a similar race. *(op 10-1)*
Nutley Queen(IRE), a maiden after six starts and beaten 67 lengths last time, is already exposed as modest and her proximity in a close third ensures the form has a weak look. *(op 40-1)*
Chariot(IRE) held every chance as the field bypassed the final flight and probably ran up to his best form. *(op 12-1)*
Hidden Smile(USA), nibbled at in the market, struggles to get home even over the minimum trip and the overnight rain did her no favours. *(op 14-1)*
Countback(FR) had the blinkers back on instead of the cheekpieces, but it appeared to make no difference even at a track where he has been placed on four previous occasions. *(op 5-1)*

1815 REX CARTER MEMORIAL H'CAP CHASE (18 fncs) 3m 110y
2:40 (2:41) (Class 4) (0-110,110) 5-Y-0+ **£6,906** (£2,244; £1,208)

Form RPR
-302 **1** **Strong Magic (IRE)**[19] [1620] 13-10-3 **92** MNicolls[(5)] 101+
(J R Cornwall) *mde all: clr fr 9th: in n.d fr 14th* **3/1**[2]
P22- **2** *dist* **Galapiat Du Mesnil (FR)**[183] [4947] 11-11-5 **110** RLucey-Butler[(7)] 67
(R Gurney) *chsd wnr: mstke 6th: rdn and wknd after 14th: btn 56l* **4/1**[3]
3-32 **3** *dist* **Hey Boy (IRE)**[139] [631] 6-11-4 **102** MFoley —
(Mrs S J Humphrey) *a wl bhd: lft poor 3rd 13th: reluctant bnd bef next: completed hopelessly t.o: btn 116l* **9/2**
5P35 **F** **Diamond Joshua (IRE)**[15] [1655] 7-11-2 **103** (v) ONelmes[(3)] —
(N B King) *fell 1st* **20/1**
-0P4 **U** **Tacolino (FR)**[9] [1721] 11-11-7 **105** JEMoore —
(O Brennan) *blnd and uns rdr 1st* **13/2**
0P03 **P** **Renvyle (IRE)**[13] [1684] 7-11-2 **103** (p) LMcGrath[(3)] —
(R C Guest) *nt fluent and j.lft: hld up: sme hdwy 7th: rdn and lost tch 11th: t.o 3rd whn p.u after 13th* **9/4**[1]

6m 44.6s (7.00) **Going Correction** +0.10s/f (Yiel) **6** Ran SP% **112.0**
Speed ratings: **92**,—,—,—,— — CSF £15.36 CT £51.13 TOTE £4.50: £2.20, £3.30; EX 14.70.
Owner J R Cornwall **Bred** Thomas Walsh **Trained** Long Clawson, Leics

FOCUS
A dreadful contest with two of the field falling at the first and two more reluctant to race after a circuit. That said, the winner showed some zest and can find another race providing the assessor does not over react.

NOTEBOOK
Strong Magic(IRE), from a yard among the winners, is in the veteran stage of his career, but what he lacks in youth he makes up for in resolution. This was a first career win at the track at the eighth attempt, however he took full advantage of a weak event with a fluent exhibition of jumping. *(op 9-2)*

Galapiat Du Mesnil(FR) was entitled to need the run after a six-month absence. However, he is clearly not the force he once was and was readily left behind by the winner. *(op 7-2)*
Hey Boy(IRE) was well backed but his temperament looks in question and he is no betting proposition. *(op 7-1)*
Tacolino(FR) was another to exit early. *(tchd 5-2)*
Diamond Joshua(IRE) got as far as the first fence. *(tchd 5-2)*
Renvyle(IRE) shaped as though a win at this level was within his compass last time at Hexham, *but was ponderous at his fences and looked less than enthusiastic, so remains one to avoid. (tchd 5-2)*

1816 RON AND JEAN GOLDEN WEDDING ANNIVERSARY H'CAP HURDLE (9 hdls) 2m
3:15 (3:16) (Class 4) (0-105,105) 4-Y-0+ **£5,835** (£1,795; £897; £448)

Form				RPR
5422	1		**Un Autre Espere**[19] 1612 6-9-7 **79** oh3 ... TMessenger(7) (C C Bealby) *lft in ld 1st: hdd 4th: led again 6th: hdd between last 2: lft in ld last: sn hdd again: rallied to ld post* **10/1**	75
-601	2	*shd*	**Teme Valley**[24] 1567 11-11-7 **105** ... (p) PCO'Neill(5) (R C Guest) *w.w in rr: hdwy after 3 out: led between last 2: hit and hdd last: rallied nr fin: jst failed* **16/1**	103+
24-6	3	*hd*	**Brigadier Du Bois (FR)**[174] 126 6-10-3 **82** ... LAspell (Mrs L Wadham) *chsd ldrs: ev ch and rdn 2 out: led after last: hdd and no ex nr fin* **7/2**[1]	78
06B4	4	*10*	**Siegfrieds Night (IRE)**[19] 1610 4-11-4 **100** ... (t) KJMercer(3) (M C Chapman) *w.w in mid-div: rdn and sme hdwy 5th: sn outpcd: kpt on fr 2 out* **13/2**[3]	86
1220	5	*2 ½*	**Keep On Movin' (IRE)**[53] 1366 4-11-8 **101** ... APMcCoy (N A Callaghan) *w.w in mid-div: stdy prog to chal after 3 out: rdn and wknd bef last* **9/2**[2]	84
-06F	6	*3*	**All Bleevable**[15] 1001 8-11-4 **100** ... (p) LVickers(3) (Mrs S Lamyman) *cl up: mstke 3rd: wknd 3 out* **16/1**	80
P0F-	7	*16*	**In The Hat (IRE)**[239] 4035 9-9-13 **85** ... RLucey-Butler(7) (J R Jenkins) *hld up in last: j.rt 3rd: n.d* **50/1**	49
00-F	8	*nk*	**La Muette (IRE)**[138] 651 5-9-13 **81** ... RYoung(3) (M Appleby) *hld up in rr: lost tch after 5th* **25/1**	45
010-	9	*1 ½*	**Honey's Gift**[215] 4482 6-11-12 **105** ... JamesDavies (G G Margarson) *rr: rdn after 5th: sn lost tch 5th* **20/1**	68
5043	10	*2*	**Jimmy Byrne (IRE)**[9] 1717 5-10-13 **95** ... (p) LMcGrath(3) (R C Guest) *mid-div whn mstke 2nd: trckd ldrs next: chal after 6th: rdn and wknd qckly bef 2 out: eased whn no ch* **7/2**[1]	59+
	11	*25*	**Padre Nostro (IRE)**[34] 2179 6-10-0 **86** ow2 ... APogson(7) (J R Holt) *led tl mstke and hdd 1st: led 4th to 6th: sn rdn and weakned: t.o* **10/1**	22
624-	P		**Iloveturtle (IRE)**[317] 2702 5-10-13 **97** ... TGreenway(5) (M C Chapman) *mid-div: rdn and wknd qckly 5th: bhd whn p.u bef next* **14/1**	—
R00L	P		**Dabus**[5] 1758 10-11-0 **100** ... AnnStokell(7) (M C Chapman) *whipped rnd: reluctant and uns rdr s: rmntd and continued hopelessly t.o: p.u 6th* **66/1**	—

4m 8.90s **Going Correction** +0.10s/f (Yiel)
WFA 4 from 5yo+ 13lb **13** Ran SP% **124.6**
Speed ratings: **104,103,103,98,97 96,88,87,87,86 73,—,—** CSF £155.48 CT £684.34 TOTE £12.70: £2.60, £5.20, £2.10; EX 149.80.
Owner Ricochet Management Limited **Bred** Backfield Ltd **Trained** Barrowby, Lincs

FOCUS
A strong gallop from the offset, but the time was only a second quicker than that of the seller. The winner is gradually improving and this was a creditable effort as he was prominent throughout and did best of the pacesetters. The form is rated around the principals.

NOTEBOOK
Un Autre Espere is a versatile sort and was not disgraced on his chasing debut at Market Rasen last time. He returned to hurdles and posted a thoroughly genuine effort, finding extra reserves when he appeared beaten after the last. *(op 13-2)*
Teme Valley is a Sedgefield specialist having won there 11 times, but he stepped up on his recent claiming form in the first-time cheekpieces. He may well have made it a winning debut for his new connections but for meeting the last wrong. *(op 11-1)*
Brigadier Du Bois(FR), backed from 7/1, is better known as a frustrating sort over fences, however he has a hurdle in him on this evidence even if the market support suggested there may not be too much improvement to come. *(op 7-1)*
Siegfrieds Night(IRE) has now finished strongly on his last two starts looking as though a step up in trip would suit. He has found his form of late in the tongue tie. *(op 8-1 tchd 17-2)*
Keep On Movin'(IRE) has plenty of pace as she proved when successful during the summer on fast ground. She did not find as much as expected when let down, though the easier ground may have found her out.
Jimmy Byrne(IRE) attracted plenty of market support but folded tamely and was eased when his chance had gone. *(op 5-1)*
Padre Nostro(IRE) *Official explanation: jockey said gelding had a breathing problem (op 9-1)*

1817 GEOFF HUBBARD MEMORIAL NOVICES' CHASE (16 fncs) 2m 5f 110y
3:50 (3:50) (Class 3) 5-Y-0+ **£10,006** (£3,079; £1,539; £769)

Form				RPR
603-	1		**The Dark Lord (IRE)**[196] 4767 8-10-12 ... LAspell (Mrs L Wadham) *racd wd: cl up: swtchd ins and led after 2 out: in command whn j.rt last: readily* **5/6**[1]	123+
2201	2	*2 ½*	**Tonic Du Charmil (FR)**[33] 1487 5-11-8 120 ... (t) TScudamore (M C Pipe) *led tl mstke and hdd 7th: lft in ld 10th: hdd sn after 2 out: no ch w wnr* **7/1**	127+
406U	3	*3*	**Dead Mans Dante (IRE)**[9] 1716 7-10-5 109 ... TJDreaper(7) (Ferdy Murphy) *hld up in last: wnt 4th after 11th: styd on appr last: nvr nrr* **33/1**	115+
1122	4	*2 ½*	**In The Frame (IRE)**[42] 1442 6-11-8 117 ... ChristianWilliams (Evan Williams) *cl up: mstke 2nd: lft in ld 7th: mstke and hdd 10th: mstke 13th: 3 l 3rd and btn whn blnd last* **9/2**[3]	125+
P5-1	5	*½*	**Hot Weld**[162] 317 6-10-9 ... KJMercer(3) (Ferdy Murphy) *w.w: struggling whn j. slowly 9th: rdn and outpcd 11th: styd on appr last: nvr nrr* **4/1**[2]	110

5m 48.3s (3.80) **Going Correction** +0.10s/f (Yiel) **5** Ran SP% **108.2**
Speed ratings: **97,96,95,94,93** CSF £6.76 TOTE £1.60: £1.20, £1.70; EX 6.10.
Owner A E Pakenham **Bred** Thomas Barry **Trained** Newmarket, Suffolk

FOCUS
A decent novice chase for the track but the winning time was 6.4 seconds slower than the later 73-99 handicap over the same trip. Despite that the form makes sense on paper with those in the frame behind the winner all close to form.

NOTEBOOK
The Dark Lord(IRE) was rated in the 130s over hurdles and made a pleasing start to life over fences. He was a little exuberant on occasions, but is sure to have learned a lot from this outing and is an exciting recruit to chasing. *(op Evens)*
Tonic Du Charmil(FR) is a reasonable yardstick with which to rate the form and emerges with credit after a solid effort under a penalty. He will not always face such a talented opponent and is versatile trip and ground wise. *(op 13-2)*
Dead Mans Dante(IRE) possesses rather unconvincing form figures but stayed on into third even if he was flattered to finish so close. He has ability but it takes some harnessing and he is remains a risky betting proposition. *(op 20-1)*
In The Frame(IRE) has been well placed by his connections this summer and is yet to convince over this trip. He may also prefer faster ground. *(op 7-2)*
Hot Weld attracted support in the market but a couple of slow jumps saw him become detached and he was never travelling with any fluency. *(op 5-1)*

1818 TRAFALGAR WEEKEND NOVICES' HURDLE (11 hdls) 2m 4f
4:20 (4:20) (Class 3) 4-Y-0+ **£4,810** (£1,480; £740; £370)

Form				RPR
1	1		**Cruzspiel**[17] 1632 5-11-4 ... APMcCoy (J R Fanshawe) *led to 5th: led and mstke 7th: drvn clr next: heavily eased run-in* **4/7**[1]	120+
160-	2	*11*	**Wee Robbie**[219] 4399 5-10-12 ... LAspell (N J Gifford) *w.w in tch: chsd wnr after 7th: rdn 2 out: 12l down and wl hld whn blnd last* **5/2**[2]	102+
0-	3	*21*	**Be Telling (IRE)**[268] 3533 6-10-12 ... PMoloney (B J Curley) *w.w in tch: outpcd 8th: mod 3rd whn mstke 3 out* **33/1**	69
2/	4	*nk*	**Loup Bleu (USA)**[1028] 2777 7-10-12 ... JMogford (Mrs A V Roberts) *t.k.h: chsd wnr: led 5th: hdd 7th: wknd qckly next* **50/1**	69
00	5	*dist*	**Busy Man (IRE)**[26] 1565 6-10-5 ... RLucey-Butler(7) (J R Jenkins) *stdd s: a detached in last: t.o 8th: btn 36l* **100/1**	—
2405	P		**Cash Return**[19] 1607 6-10-2 80 ... (tp) LVickers(3) (Mrs S Lamyman) *w.w in tch: lost pl 5th: p.u and dismntd bef next* **66/1**	—
14	P		**Thedublinpublican (IRE)**[19] 1611 5-11-4 ... NFehily (C C Bealby) *t.k.h: chsd wnr tl j.rt 4th: wknd after 7th: t.o whn p.u appr last* **15/2**[3]	—

5m 12.6s (0.40) **Going Correction** +0.10s/f (Yiel)
WFA 4 from 5yo+ 14lb **7** Ran SP% **111.4**
Speed ratings: **103,98,90,90,— —,—** CSF £2.19 TOTE £1.70: £1.10, £1.70; EX 2.40.
Owner P Garvey **Bred** Old Mill Stud **Trained** Newmarket, Suffolk

FOCUS
A workmanlike performance by the winner who is a classy recruit to hurdles. He is not the type to do anything quickly or indeed impressively, but he is progressing along the right lines.

NOTEBOOK
Cruzspiel is far from a natural at his new vocation, but he gets the job done and ran out an ultimately comprehensive winner as his odds suggested he would. A more galloping track will play to his strengths and it will be interesting to see how he copes with a step up in class. *(op 4-9)*
Wee Robbie has tons of scope and was another not suited by the contours of the track. It was no surprise that he was left behind when the winner moved up a gear and he was highly tried in bumpers last term, so is clearly quite highly regarded. A more orthodox venue should see him shed his maiden tag over hurdles. *(op 10-3)*
Be Telling(IRE), a winner of a three-mile point-to-point, shaped with some promise and could be interesting when handicapped.
Cash Return *Official explanation: vet said mare pulled up lame (op 10-1)*
Thedublinpublican(IRE) landed a gamble at Uttoxeter on his first start in this country, but has failed to reproduce that form since. *(op 10-1)*

1819 ROSALIE MONBIOT 70TH BIRTHDAY CELEBRATION H'CAP CHASE (16 fncs) 2m 5f 110y
4:55 (4:55) (Class 4) (0-100,99) 5-Y-0+ **£4,114** (£1,266; £633; £316)

Form				RPR
5343	1		**Reverse Swing**[19] 1612 8-10-3 **76** ... (t) JMogford (Mrs H Dalton) *prom: led 4th: mde rest: rdn 3 out: styd on run-in* **6/1**[2]	90+
5F/-	2	*1 ¼*	**Ashwell (IRE)**[578] 4511 6-11-3 **90** ... NFehily (C C Bealby) *hld in in mid-div: hdwy to trck wnr 13th: rdn appr last: unable qckn* **10/1**	104+
34PP	3	*13*	**Step In Line (IRE)**[13] 1686 13-9-7 **73** oh16 ... CDSharkey(7) (D W Thompson) *a.p: 4th and outpcd 3 out: rdr lost irons after next: kpt on to take mod 3rd last* **66/1**	73+
0-65	4	*1 ½*	**Caribbean Cove (IRE)**[13] 1670 7-11-7 **99** ... (b) PCO'Neill(5) (R C Guest) *hld up in mid-div: hdwy 11th: 3rd and rdn 3 out: sn outpcd* **9/4**[1]	98+
2-0U	5	*8*	**Walcot Lad (IRE)**[149] 505 9-10-12 **88** ... (p) CBolger(3) (A Ennis) *trckd ldrs: chal 12th: mstke next: sn rdn and outpcd* **11/1**	78
-2P0	6	*2*	**Tirley Storm**[19] 1620 10-10-1 **74** ... PMoloney (J S Smith) *hld up in rr: mstkes 4th and 9th: come hdwy whn mstke 12th: sn rdn and btn* **8/1**	62
2P2-	7	*dist*	**Ah Yeah (IRE)**[287] 3260 8-10-4 **80** ... ONelmes(3) (N B King) *led 2nd to 4th: chsd ldrs tl wknd qckly 12th: t.o: btn 57l* **13/2**[3]	—
-126	8	*11*	**Gale Star (IRE)**[19] 1609 12-11-0 **87** ... (t) JEMoore (O Brennan) *nt fluent 1st: hld up in rr: hdwy and in tch 11th: wl outpcd after next: t.o* **15/2**	—
050P	R		**Idlewild (IRE)**[19] 1607 10-10-0 **80** ... APogson(7) (C T Pogson) *bhd: mstke 3rd: last whn ref 6th* **25/1**	—
2000	P		**Balla D'Aire (IRE)**[59] 1299 10-9-9 **75** oh16 ow2 ... SWalsh(7) (K F Clutterbuck) *led to 2nd: steadily lost pl: last and rdn 11th: sn lost tch: t.o whn p.u bef 13th* **25/1**	—
2356	P		**Kercabellec (FR)**[19] 1612 7-10-7 **85** ... MNicolls(5) (J R Cornwall) *wnt to post early: trckd ldrs: rdn after 12th: sn outpcd: wl btn whn mstke 2 out: p.u bef last* **16/1**	—

5m 41.9s (-2.60) **Going Correction** +0.10s/f (Yiel) **11** Ran SP% **113.8**
Speed ratings: **108,107,102,102,99 98,—,—,—,— —** CSF £60.38 CT £3527.89 TOTE £7.60: £2.80, £3.20, £15.10; EX 61.40.
Owner The Herons Partnership **Bred** Mrs P Sly **Trained** Norton, Shropshire

FOCUS
A modest event won by a former selling plater. That said, there was a good margin back to the third and the winner was third in a race at Market Rasen which is working out well.

NOTEBOOK
Reverse Swing hails from a stable in a rich vein of form and battled on resolutely to score for the first time over fences. She saw the trip out well enough and could be placed to score again as she jumped tidily. *(op 5-1)*
Ashwell(IRE), off the track for 578 days, posted an eye-catching debut over fences as he travelled well and jumped fluently virtually throughout. He is well handicapped on the evidence of this display providing he does not 'bounce' next time. *(op 8-1)*
Step In Line(IRE), 16lb out of the handicap and pulled up on his previous two starts, posted a remarkable effort as his rider lost his irons after the third last, yet his mount stayed on remarkably strongly. He is in good heart, but it would be a danger to take this run literally as he is in the twilight of his career. *(op 50-1)*
Caribbean Cove(IRE) looked to have conditions in his favour but was a shade disappointing and may need some respite from the Handicapper. *(op 5-2 tchd 11-4)*
Walcot Lad(IRE) has won at the track, but prefers Fontwell where three of his four career wins have been recorded. A bad mistake when the pace quickened to not aid his cause. *(op 9-1 tchd 12-1)*

The Form Book, Raceform Ltd, Compton, RG20 6NL

Tirley Storm has won twice at the track, but does not look in great form at the moment and was below par again. *(tchd 17-2)*

1820 ALAN NORRIS LIFETIME IN RACING STANDARD OPEN NATIONAL HUNT FLAT RACE 2m

5:25 (5:25) (Class 6) 4-6-Y-0 **£2,906** (£830; £415)

Form			Horse	Jockey	RPR
/1-	1		**Roll Along (IRE)**[374] 1694 5-11-11	TJMurphy	124+
			(M Pitman) *hld up: prog 7f out: led on bit 2f out: sn clr: v easily*	**2/1**[1]	
21	2	9	**Bonchester Bridge**[13] 1674 4-11-4	ATinkler	97
			(N J Henderson) *led: stdd pce 1/2-way: qcknd 5f out: hdd 2f out: no ch w wnr*	**85/40**[2]	
2-4	3	1 1/4	**Could Be Alright (IRE)**[13] 1681 6-11-4	TDoyle	96
			(Noel T Chance) *swvd rt s: sn rcvrd: pressed ldr rdn 5f out: one pce fnl 2f*	**5/2**[3]	
5	4	10	**Stroom Bank (IRE)**[27] 1554 5-11-4	NFehily	86
			(C C Bealby) *t.k.h: in tch: 4th and rdn 4f out: sn wknd*	**12/1**	
63	5	15	**Goldsmeadow**[15] 1660 6-10-13	MNicolls(5)	71
			(O Brennan) *chsd ldng pair: rdn 5f out: sn outpcd*	**33/1**	
4	6	22	**Viennchee Run**[17] 1635 4-10-11	SWalsh(7)	49
			(K F Clutterbuck) *t.k.h: in tch: rdn and wknd 5f out: bhd whn hung rt bnd 3f out*	**33/1**	
	7	13	**Wheel Tapper (IRE)** 4-11-4	PJBrennan	36
			(P W Hiatt) *in tch: hdwy 1/2-way: rdn and wknd 5f out*	**25/1**	

4m 5.20s (-5.00) **Going Correction** +0.10s/f (Yiel)
WFA 4 from 5yo+ 13lb **7** Ran SP% **111.3**
Speed ratings: **107,102,101,96,89 78,71** CSF £6.16 TOTE £2.30: £2.40, £1.20; EX 6.30 Place 6 £68.96, Place 5 £38.70.
Owner B R H Burrough **Bred** Mrs M Brennan **Trained** Upper Lambourn, Berks

FOCUS
A decent bumper featuring some promising individuals. The winner is value for more than double the official margin and should make a good recruit to hurdles, but the form is rated through the runner-up and fourth.

NOTEBOOK
Roll Along(IRE), related to the useful Nahthen Lad, made light of his penalty picked up last season when turning over the talented Yes Sir. He should be an exciting prospect when he tackles hurdles. *(op 5-2)*
Bonchester Bridge, a comfortable winner at Bangor last time, could find no answer to the change of gear displayed by the winner. She had the run of the race from the front but was not disgraced. *(op 2-1)*
Could Be Alright(IRE) was solid in the market and his jockey was keen to sit on the heels of the pacesetter. He looks to have the scope for hurdles and is marking time in bumpers. *(tchd 11-4)*
Stroom Bank(IRE), from a stable in form, found the stop-start gallop against him as he was keen early. He only tired three furlongs from home. *(op 9-1)*
T/Plt: £128.40 to a £1 stake. Pool: £52,105.80. 296.10 winning tickets. T/Qpdt: £25.90 to a £1 stake. Pool: £4,641.70. 132.20 winning tickets. SP

764 AINTREE (L-H)

Saturday, October 22

OFFICIAL GOING: Good to soft (good in places)
The ground was described as 'almost soft, tiring and hard work'.
Wind: Almost nil Weather: Fine.

1821 INTERCASINO.COM INTRODUCTORY JUVENILE NOVICES' HURDLE (8 hdls 1 omitted) 2m 110y

1:10 (1:20) (Class 3) 3-Y-0 **£8,073** (£2,484; £1,242; £621)

Form			Horse	Jockey	RPR
	1		**Pace Shot (IRE)**[55] 3-11-0	JEMoore	111+
			(G L Moore) *trckd ldrs: disp ld 2 out: hung rt run-in: overall ldr nr line*	**10/1**[3]	
1	2	nk	**Federstar (GER)**[97] 1023 3-11-5	PJBrennan	115+
			(M F Harris) *trckd ldrs: led after 6th: edgd lft run-in: hdd nr fin*	**11/2**[2]	
	3	dist	**Mr Maxim**[23] 3-10-11	ACCoyle(3)	65
			(R M Whitaker) *in rr: outpcd 5th: kpt on fr 2 out: tk remote 3rd nr fin: btn 45l*	**66/1**	
1	4	1/2	**Vale De Lobo**[14] 1679 3-10-12 108	(t) RWalsh	65
			(P F Nicholls) *chsd ldrs: drvn along after 6th: sn wknd*	**8/11**[1]	
	5	3 1/2	**Gitche Manito (IRE)**[29] 3-11-0	RThornton	63
			(A King) *trckd ldr: led 4th tl after 6th: sn wknd*	**11/2**[2]	
5	6	25	**Jenkins Lane (IRE)**[31] 1512 3-10-9	PCO'Neill(5)	38
			(J J Lambe, Ire) *hld up in tch: pushed along 6th: sn lost pl: virtually p.u*	**50/1**	
	U		**Before Time**[133] 3-10-9	DLaverty(5)	—
			(Mrs A M Thorpe) *last whn mstke and uns rdr 1st*	**40/1**	
1	P		**Etoile Russe (IRE)**[32] 1440 3-10-12	(t) PMerrigan(7)	—
			(P C Haslam) *led: sn clr: stdd 3rd: hdd next: sn lost pl: bhd whn p.u bef 5th*	**14/1**	

4m 9.50s (4.90) **Going Correction** +0.50s/f (Soft) **8** Ran SP% **110.3**
Speed ratings: **108,107,—,—,— —,—,—** CSF £58.36 TOTE £11.80: £2.50, £1.30, £8.50; EX 69.80.
Owner R A Green **Bred** Joe Rogers **Trained** Woodingdean, E Sussex

FOCUS
The first two finished a long way clear marking this down as one of the stronger juvenile hurdles run so far. The second under his penalty takes the honours if not the gold medal. The third-last flight was bypassed.

NOTEBOOK
Pace Shot(IRE), a maiden rated 72 on the Flat, was on his toes beforehand. Throwing down the gauntlet two out, he hung towards the stands'-side rail on the run-in and did just enough. *(tchd 12-1)*
Federstar(GER), gelded since Stratford, delayed the start while a new bridle was fitted. He went on and stepped up the gallop but, edging away from the whip on the run-in, was in the end just denied. Under a penalty, this makes him one of the better juveniles seen out so far. *(op 7-2)*
Mr Maxim, a 50-rated maiden on the level, was soon struggling but in the end did just enough to secure a remote third spot.
Vale De Lobo, who looked very fit indeed, came off the bridle rounding the final turn and her response was limited to say the very least. *This was simply too bad to be true. Official explanation: vet said filly finished distressed (op 5-6 tchd evens and 10-11 in places)*
Gitche Manito(IRE), a 69-rated maiden on the Flat, went on and stepped up the pace but found little and stopped quickly rounding the home bend. *(op 8-1 tchd 9-1)*
Etoile Russe(IRE), as narrow as a kipper, stopped to nothing when headed and was found to have bled from the nose. *Official explanation: jockey said gelding bled from the nose (op 11-1)*

1822 INTERCASINO.COM MOLYNEUX NOVICES' CHASE (LISTED RACE) (12 fncs) 2m (Mildmay)

1:40 (1:49) (Class 1) 4-Y-0+ **£15,004** (£6,076; £3,348)

Form			Horse	Jockey	RPR
212-	1		**Baby Run (FR)**[273] 3474 5-11-4	AntonyEvans	140+
			(N A Twiston-Davies) *led: hung rt bnd after 4th: hdd 8th: led 3 out: styd on run-in*	**3/1**[2]	
1F-1	2	2	**Andreas (FR)**[165] 286 5-11-11 144	(t) RWalsh	145+
			(P F Nicholls) *trckd ldr: led 8th to 3 out: rdn between last 2: wknd last*	**5/6**[1]	
003-	3	1/2	**Exotic Dancer (FR)**[196] 4771 5-11-4	GLee	139+
			(Jonjo O'Neill) *lft handy 3rd 2nd: mstke 6th: effrt 9th: styd on fr 2 out: nvr a threat*	**9/2**[3]	
-111	F		**Feel The Pride (IRE)**[24] 217 7-11-1 128	TSiddall	—
			(Jonjo O'Neill) *3rd whn fell heavily 2nd*	**9/1**	
P006	B		**Northern Echo**[14] 1686 8-11-4 57	(p) FKeniry	—
			(K S Thomas) *kicked s: last whn bdly hmpd and uns rdr 2nd*	**150/1**	

4m 2.40s (1.40) **Going Correction** +0.40s/f (Soft) **5** Ran SP% **108.4**
Speed ratings: **112,111,110,—,—** CSF £6.07 TOTE £4.40: £1.90, £1.20; EX 6.80.
Owner Mr & Mrs Peter Orton **Bred** Haras De Preaux **Trained** Naunton, Gloucs

FOCUS
A decent novices' chase in which Baby Run hung badly on the paddock bend but eventually proved too strong for Andreas, who seemed to blow up but sets the level of the form, which couldbe rated higher and should work out. Exotic Dancer stuck to his guns and will have no trouble making his mark over further.

NOTEBOOK
Baby Run(FR), who looks every inch a chaser, hung badly on the bend away from the stands. He came back and had it won at the last only to idle in the closing stages. The raw ability is there and racing will improve his mind set. *(tchd 7-2 and 10-3 in places)*
Andreas(FR), who scraped into this novice chase, looked big and well and appeared in command when going through on the leader's inner to take the advantage. He suddenly came under serious pressure going to the last and, after jumping it level, was beaten in a matter of strides. He presumably needed thi and is the type to shine in strongly-run handicaps. *(op Evens tchd 6-5 and 11-10 in places)*
Exotic Dancer(FR) ◆, a big, strong-type, always seemed to be struggling to keep in touch. He stuck to his guns and closing the gap at the line, is sure to make his mark when stepped up in trip. *(op 4-1 tchd 5-1 in a place)*
Feel The Pride(IRE), typical of her trainer's fortunes at present, crashed out at an early stage. It was a crushing fall but hopefully she will be none the worse. *(op 7-1)*

1823 INTERCASINO.COM H'CAP HURDLE (9 hdls) 2m 110y

2:10 (2:17) (Class 3) (0-130,123) 4-Y-0+ **£8,287** (£2,550; £1,275; £637)

Form			Horse	Jockey	RPR
341-	1		**Brooklyn Breeze (IRE)**[190] 4848 8-11-6 120	GBerridge(3)	126+
			(L Lungo) *hld up: hdwy 3 out: styd on wl to ld last 100yds*	**13/2**[3]	
0F-6	2	2	**Town Crier (IRE)**[10] 1720 10-11-3 114	DElsworth	118
			(Mrs S J Smith) *trckd ldrs: led after 6th: clr next: hdd and no ex run-in*	**11/2**[2]	
152/	3	nk	**Pepe Galvez (SWE)**[710] 2097 8-11-9 120	MFoley	126+
			(Mrs L C Taylor) *chsd ldrs: outpcd 6th: hdwy whn hmpd 2 out: styd on wl run-in*	**9/1**	
-111	4	3/4	**Crathorne (IRE)**[10] 1720 5-11-7 118	GLee	121
			(M Todhunter) *chsd ldrs: pushed along 5th: styd on same pce fr 2 out*	**13/2**[3]	
613-	5	nk	**Nycteos (FR)**[183] 4954 4-11-9 120	RWalsh	123
			(P F Nicholls) *w ldrs: kpt on same pce fr 2 out*	**5/1**[1]	
45/4	6	7	**Kentucky Blue (IRE)**[10] 1720 5-11-12 123	RGarritty	120+
			(T D Easterby) *in rr: hdwy 3 out: nvr rchd ldrs*	**12/1**	
-12P	7	9	**Maclean**[21] 1598 4-10-13 110	(b) PHide	102+
			(G L Moore) *hld up in rr: stdy hdwy 3 out: rdn next: eased whn wl btn run-in*	**33/1**	
1-02	8	4	**Compton Eagle**[25] 1567 5-10-8 105 ow1	JPMcNamara	93+
			(J J Lambe, Ire) *trckd ldrs: 4th and one pce whn hit last: eased: fin lame*	**66/1**	
6432	9	6	**Castleshane (IRE)**[75] 1179 8-11-8 119	RThornton	99+
			(S Gollings) *led tl after 6th: hung bdly lft and lost pl 2 out*	**14/1**	
1-31	10	4	**Prairie Sun (GER)**[14] 1668 4-11-6 117	JTizzard	90
			(Mrs A Duffield) *prom: pushed along 6th: sn lost pl*	**5/1**[1]	
321-	P		**Basinet**[32] 1308 7-10-5 105	KJMercer(3)	—
			(J J Quinn) *bhd fr 3 out: p.u bef last*	**16/1**	
4400	P		**Why The Long Face (NZ)**[14] 1668 8-10-7 107	(p) LMcGrath(3)	—
			(R C Guest) *in rr: reminders 6th: sn bhd: p.u bef last*	**50/1**	
1-	F		**Predicament**[325] 2570 6-11-2 113	JEMoore	105+
			(Jonjo O'Neill) *t.k.h towards rr: hdwy 6th: 5th: rdn and hld whn fell 2 out*	**20/1**	

4m 7.50s (2.90) **Going Correction** +0.50s/f (Soft)
WFA 4 from 5yo+ 13lb **13** Ran SP% **116.8**
Speed ratings: **113,112,111,111,111 108,103,102,99,97 —,—,—** CSF £40.46 CT £325.23 TOTE £5.80: £2.60, £3.70, £3.90; EX 78.30 Trifecta £361.50 Pool: £1,018.52 - 2.00 winning tickets..
Owner Ashleybank Investments Limited **Bred** Patrick McGarrigle **Trained** Carruthterstown, D'fries & G'way

FOCUS
They went a good gallop resulting in a decent winning time for a race of its class. The winner now reverts to fences without any risk of his chase handicap mark being increased. The second and third should continue to give a good account of themselves and overall the form has a rock solid look.

NOTEBOOK
Brooklyn Breeze(IRE), who has undergone a wind operation, seemed out of it until picking up ground three out. Only seventh jumping the last, in the end he won going away. This will set him up nicely for the Paddy Power Chase over two and a half miles at Cheltenham next month. *(op 8-1 tchd 6-1)*
Town Crier(IRE), much fitter this time, looked nailed on when surging four lengths clear three out but in the end the winner ground him down. He thoroughly deserves to go one better but is a much better chaser. *(op 6-1)*
Pepe Galvez(SWE) ◆, absent for almost two years, looked in really good condition. Forced to take evasive action two out, he stayed on in fine style on the run-in. He should not be long making up for lost time. *(tchd 10-1 12-1 in a place)*
Crathorne(IRE), banged up a harsh 10lb after his Wetherby success, was being pushed along some way from home but to his credit kept battling on all the way to the line. *(op 11-2 tchd 7-1 in a place)*
Nycteos(FR), still on the weak side, looked to have plenty on at the weights on his handicap bow from his new quarters. He will make an even better chaser in time. *(op 7-1)*
Kentucky Blue(IRE), meeting Crathorne on 10lb better terms, never got competive.

Compton Eagle, runner-up in a claimer last time, was running out his skin and was hanging on to third spot when a mistake at the final flight resulted in him going lame on his off hind.*Official explanation: vet said gelding returned lame (op 50-1)*

Prairie Sun(GER), hoisted a ridiculous 17lb after her nearest pursuers fell by the wayside at Bangor, was struggling three quarters of a mile from home. Connections will be hoping the Handicapper has a radical rethink. *Official explanation: trainer had no explanation for the poor form shown (op 7-2)*

Predicament, winner of a novices' hurdle at Plumpton in December, did not look obviously well treated on his handicap bow. He would not settle and looked safely held when crashing out. *(op 18-1)*

1824 PLAY BLACKJACK AT INTERCASINO.COM MAIDEN HURDLE (9 hdls) 2m 110y

2:45 (2:49) (Class 3) 4-Y-O+ **£7,007** (£2,156; £1,078; £539)

Form				RPR
	1		**New Alco (FR)**[162] 4-10-13 ... KJMercer(3) *(Ferdy Murphy) trckd ldrs: led 3 out: clr whn hit last: v easily* **11/4**[2]	114+
	2	18	**Strident (USA)**[49] 4-11-2 ... JPMcNamara *(J J Lambe, Ire) in rr: hdwy to chse ldrs 6th: styd on fr 2 out: no ch w wnr* **14/1**	89
	3	1 1/2	**Showtime Annie**[12] 4-10-9 ... GLee *(A Bailey) hld up in rr: hdwy 6th: kpt on fr 2 out* **12/1**	81
	4	1/2	**Herakles (GER)**[370] 4-11-2 ... MFoley *(N J Henderson) nt fluent: hld up: hdwy to chse ldrs 6th: effrt and hit next: one pce* **7/4**[1]	89+
44-4	5	6	**Mr Lewin**[181] [3] 4-10-11 106 ... StephenJCraine(5) *(D McCain) chsd ldrs: led 5th to 3 out: wknd last* **13/2**[3]	82+
P605	6	14	**Starbright**[20] [1605] 4-11-2 67 ... RWalsh *(W G Young) chsd ldrs: rdn and lost pl 6th: hit 2 out* **16/1**	67
P	7	1 1/4	**Dictator (IRE)**[20] [1614] 4-11-2 ... (t) JTizzard *(D R Gandolfo) trckd ldrs: rdn and lost pl 6th* **14/1**	66
P0	8	1 1/4	**Daggy Boy (NZ)**[14] [1671] 5-10-11 ... PCO'Neill(5) *(R C Guest) in rr: drvn along 6th: nvr a factor* **66/1**	65
3	9	1/2	**Network Oscar (IRE)**[28] [1554] 4-11-2 ... DO'Meara *(M W Easterby) stdd s: a in rr* **14/1**	64
06/	10	29	**Galadhrim (IRE)**[238] 8-10-13 ... LMcGrath(3) *(J J Lambe, Ire) led to 5th: lost pl next: sn bhd and eased* **66/1**	35
5/	P		**Neophyte (IRE)**[866] [606] 6-11-2 ... PJBrennan *(B De Haan) trckd ldrs: lost pl 5th: wl bhd whn p.u after next* **18/1**	—

4m 12.4s (7.80) **Going Correction** +0.50s/f (Soft) **11** Ran SP% **118.2**

Speed ratings: **101,92,91,91,88 82,81,81,80,67** — CSF £41.11 TOTE £4.10: £1.50, £3.70, £2.30; EX 100.90.

Owner D McGowan and S Murphy **Bred** Vicomte Roger De Soultrait **Trained** West Witton, N Yorks

FOCUS

A weak novices' hurdle but a highly impressive winner who has already been placed over fences in France and is value for more than the official margin. The 67-rated sixth could be the best guide to the overall value of the contest.

NOTEBOOK

New Alco(FR) ◆, a tall French import, has been placed over both hurdles and fences there. He travelled supremely well and despite his rider having a tight grip of his head on the run-in he powered further and further away. It was a weak event but he could hardly have won more easily. *(op 5-1)*

Strident(USA), unplaced in five starts on the level, stayed on to come out second best but only with a distant view of the winner. *(op 12-1)*

Showtime Annie, who has gone backward on the Flat, seemed to be ridden with an eye on conserving her stamina and exactly what she achieved on her hurdling bow is open to doubt. *(op 11-1 tchd 10-1)*

Herakles(GER), a rangy German import, has been absent since winning over a mile and a half at Cologne 13 months ago, his fourth success on the level. Dropped in, his jumping let him down and he was struggling to make any impact after clouting the third last. He is surely capable of much better. *(op 6-4 tchd 2-1 and 15-8 in places)*

Mr Lewin, absent since April, looked to be carrying condition and ran as if in need of the outing. *(op 6-1 tchd 7-1)*

Network Oscar(IRE) *Official explanation: trainer said gelding finished stiff and returned home with a temperature (tchd 12-1)*

1825 £600 A YEAR FROM INTERCASINO.COM H'CAP CHSE (16 fncs) 2m 4f (Mildmay)

3:15 (3:15) (Class 3) (0-120,119) 5-Y-O+ **£10,273** (£3,161; £1,580; £790)

Form				RPR
331/	1		**Fair Prospect**[683] [2654] 9-11-12 119 ... RWalsh *(P F Nicholls) hld up: stdy hdwy 10th: hit next: effrt 3 out: led after 2 out: blnd last: rdn out* **7/2**[2]	130+
6P-0	2	7	**Soeur Fontenail (FR)**[167] [234] 8-10-8 101 ... JTizzard *(N J Hawke) chsd ldrs: lft in ld after 8th: pckd 2 out: sn hdd: kpt on run-in* **20/1**	104+
/0-U	3	1/2	**Cill Churnain (IRE)**[14] [1670] 12-11-5 112 ... DElsworth *(Mrs S J Smith) chsd ldrs: blnd 2nd: one pce fr 2 out* **14/1**	114
2-24	4	6	**Jallastep (FR)**[30] [1529] 8-10-6 99 ... GLee *(J S Goldie) in rr: hdwy 12th: one pce fr 2 out* **10/1**	97+
6-24	5	3 1/2	**King's Bounty**[156] [430] 9-10-12 105 ... DO'Meara *(T D Easterby) in rr: outpcd 11th: kpt on fr 3 out: nvr on terms* **8/1**	97
6P-3	6	shd	**The Nomad**[170] [195] 9-11-8 115 ... JEMoore *(M W Easterby) led: blnd bdly 7th: reluctant and hdd after next: rdn 4 out: wknd next* **11/1**	107
430-	7	27	**Deliceo (IRE)**[183] [4955] 12-10-13 106 ... RThornton *(M Sheppard) a in rr: lost tch 11th: t.o last* **16/1**	71
-435	U		**Fiori**[69] [1221] 9-10-8 108 ... PMerrigan(7) *(P C Haslam) blnd bdly and uns rdr 2nd* **15/2**[3]	—
24-4	F		**Roschal (IRE)**[20] [1609] 7-10-13 106 ... PJBrennan *(P J Hobbs) chsd ldrs: 4th whn fell 9th* **11/4**[1]	—
0/6	U		**Blitzy Boy (IRE)**[34] [1497] 11-10-0 93 oh1 ... NPMadden *(G T Lynch, Ire) last whn blnd and uns rdr 1st* **16/1**	—

5m 15.0s (6.10) **Going Correction** +0.40s/f (Soft) **10** Ran SP% **112.4**

Speed ratings: **103,100,100,97,96 96,85,—,—,—** CSF £63.14 CT £861.22 TOTE £3.70: £2.60, £4.60, £3.30; EX 71.30.

Owner Fourstar Partners **Bred** S Snelling **Trained** Ditcheat, Somerset

FOCUS

Plenty of carnage in what turned out to be a fairly weak handicap run at just a modest pace. The form may not amount to much but the winner can go on from here.

NOTEBOOK

Fair Prospect, absent since winning a novice chase at Fontwell in December 2003 on his only previous start over fences, looked fit. His jumping was sound on the whole and, travelling easily best when sent on, he survived a blunder at the last to forge clear. The experience and the outing will have done him a power of good and he should be capable of climbing another few rungs up the ladder after a short break to eliminate the bounce factor. *(op 10-3 tchd 3-1)*

Soeur Fontenail(FR), absent since May, found herself in front. She looked legless between the last two yet in the end still passed the post in second spot. *(op 16-1)*

Cill Churnain(IRE), having his second outing in two weeks after a lengthy absence, kept on in his own time but he hardly shaped like a horse likely to make an imminent return to winning form. *(op 16-1)*

Jallastep(FR) moved up onto the heels of the leading quartet going to the third last threatening to enter the argument, but his effort soon flattened out.

King's Bounty, absent since May, ran without his usual blinkers and the outing will not be lost on him. *(op 9-1)*

The Nomad did his best to demolish the second ditch and, reluctant to go out on to the second circuit, finally called it a day on the turn for home.

Roschal(IRE) was on the heels of the leaders when crashing out at what was the first fence on the second circuit. *(op 3-1)*

1826 CASINO FUN FROM INTERCASINO.COM NOVICES' H'CAP HURDLE (13 hdls) 3m 110y

3:50 (3:52) (Class 3) (0-110,110) 4-Y-O+ **£6,929** (£2,132; £1,066; £533)

Form				RPR
P-1P	1		**Nite Fox (IRE)**[149] [509] 6-10-8 99 ... (p) PMerrigan(7) *(Mrs H Dalton) trckd ldrs: wnt 2nd 3 out: styd on to ld nr fin* **7/1**[3]	101+
14-3	2	3/4	**Baikaline (FR)**[128] [767] 6-10-2 96 ... DJBoland(10) *(Ian Williams) trckd ldrs: led 3 out: hdd and no ex nr fin* **7/1**[3]	96
4-03	3	14	**Lord Rosskit (IRE)**[15] [1663] 5-10-7 91 ... FKeniry *(G M Moore) chsd ldrs: one pce fr 3 out* **5/1**[1]	77
442-	4	3/4	**Blue Rising**[249] [3865] 4-10-7 95 ... KJMercer(3) *(Ferdy Murphy) hld up in rr: drvn along 8th: hdwy to chse ldrs appr 3 out: one pce* **7/1**[3]	79
30-F	5	27	**Rowan Castle**[147] [548] 9-10-6 95 ... StephenJCraine(5) *(Sir John Barlow Bt) chsd ldrs: lost pl after 10th* **14/1**	53
0431	6	22	**Esters Boy**[18] [1630] 7-11-1 104 ... PCO'Neill(5) *(P G Murphy) chsd ldrs: wknd after 10th: sn bhd* **11/2**[2]	55+
00-1	P		**Front Rank (IRE)**[154] [456] 5-11-9 107 ... JPMcNamara *(K C Bailey) led: qcknd 8th: hdd appr 3 out: wknd qckly and last whn p.u bef last* **5/1**[1]	—
212-	P		**Son Of Greek Myth (USA)**[24] [4691] 4-11-4 103 ... (b) JEMoore *(G L Moore) in rr: outpcd and lost pl after 8th: last and out of tch whn blnd 3 out: t.o whn p.u after next* **5/1**[1]	—

6m 34.1s (17.70) **Going Correction** +0.50s/f (Soft)

WFA 4 from 5yo+ 15lb **8** Ran SP% **109.6**

Speed ratings: **91,90,86,86,77 70,—,—** CSF £49.77 CT £245.50 TOTE £8.30: £2.20, £1.70, £1.70; EX 65.20 Place 6 £249.93, Place 5 £60.03.

Owner Mrs A Beard Miss M Knapper & J Dalton **Bred** John Smiddy **Trained** Norton, Shropshire

FOCUS

Just a steady gallop in this staying novice resulting in a moderate winning time. The first two finished clear, both seeing out the trip, but overall it was a weak novices' handicap.

NOTEBOOK

Nite Fox(IRE), never travelling when pulled up at Huntingdon in May, made hard work of it a long way out but stuck to her guns in willing fashion to show ahead near the line. She had a tough race. *(op 11-2)*

Baikaline(FR), absent since June, has a maiden chase to her name. She went on travelling best but in the end was just worn down.

Lord Rosskit(IRE), in the thick of the action throughout, was made to look painfully one paced but the tiring ground may not have been entirely in his favour. *(tchd 9-2)*

Blue Rising, absent since February, looks more a long-term chasing prospect and he certainly has far more stamina than speed. *(op 8-1)*

Rowan Castle, having his first outing since May, has the look of a chaser. *(op 12-1)*

Esters Boy was on the retreat starting the home turn and may not appreciate ground as slow as this. *(op 7-1)*

Front Rank(IRE), having his first outing since May, took them along. Quickening up the gallop setting out onto the final circuit, he dropped away in a matter of strides and in the end his stamina seemed to give out completely. *Official explanation: jockey said horse had a breathing problem (op 11-2)*

Son Of Greek Myth(USA) would not have a cut and seemed to sulk before dropping himself out. After a wholesale blunder three out when detached in last, his rider wisely threw in the towel altogether. He is one to have severe reservations about now. *(op 11-2)*

T/Jkpt: Not won. T/Plt: £2,068.30 to a £1 stake. Pool: £54,825.20. 19.35 winning tickets. T/Qpdt: £212.90 to a £1 stake. Pool: £3,396.40. 11.80 winning tickets. WG

1675 CHEPSTOW (L-H)

Saturday, October 22

OFFICIAL GOING: Soft

Wind: Nil Weather: Fine

1827 ROYAL BRITISH LEGION POPPY APPEAL PERSIAN WAR NOVICES' HURDLE GRADE 2 (11 hdls) 2m 4f

1:25 (1:25) (Class 1) 4-Y-O+

£17,400 (£6,600; £3,300; £1,500; £750; £450)

Form				RPR
10-1	1		**Rimsky (IRE)**[14] [1680] 4-11-0 ... CLlewellyn *(N A Twiston-Davies) hld up: hdwy after 5th: chsd ldr 6th to 4 out: sn rdn and outpcd: rallied appr 2 out: led sn after last: drvn out* **5/2**[2]	130+
	2	1	**Massini's Maguire (IRE)**[173] [166] 4-11-0 ... RJohnson *(P J Hobbs) hld up: hdwy 6th: led 3 out: rdn appr last: hdd sn after last: styd on* **7/4**[1]	129+
	3	13	**Gungadu**[244] 5-11-0 ... ChristianWilliams *(P F Nicholls) led: rdn and hung lft whn hdd 3 out: wknd appr last* **7/2**[3]	116+
32-	4	12	**Patrixprial**[19] [2774] 4-11-0 ... LAspell *(M H Tompkins) hld up: hdwy appr 7th: rdn and wknd appr 3 out: hit last* **11/2**	109+
540-	5	30	**Biscar Two (IRE)**[218] [4433] 4-11-0 128 ... (b) TDoyle *(B J Llewellyn) chsd ldrs tl wknd 7th: t.o* **14/1**	73
4-45	6	18	**Letsplay (IRE)**[139] [654] 5-11-0 ... (b[1]) RGreene *(K J Burke) hld up in rr: short-lived effrt after 7th: t.o* **100/1**	55
235-	7	1/2	**Mokum (FR)**[247] [3899] 4-11-0 109 ... WHutchinson *(A W Carroll) w ldr to 5th: wknd after 7th: t.o* **50/1**	55

5m 9.30s (6.60) **Going Correction** +0.575s/f (Soft) **7** Ran SP% **112.2**

Speed ratings: **89,88,83,78,66 59,59** CSF £7.24 TOTE £3.20: £1.50, £2.30; EX 6.20.

Owner D J & S A Goodman **Bred** J Duggan **Trained** Naunton, Gloucs

FOCUS

A very slow time indeed for a race of its stature, 12.7 seconds slower than the Silver Trophy. It could be rated considerably higher but as a result of the time has been rated conservatively.

NOTEBOOK

Rimsky(IRE) ◆ looked in trouble when caught flat-footed early in the home straight but, with stamina coming into play, he managed to pull the race out of the fire. Well regarded, he should stay three miles and seems set to contest the major staying novice events this season. *(op 3-1)*

Massini's Maguire(IRE) ♦, the winner of a soft-ground Limerick bumper in May, seemed set to *score when striking the front. He did not go down without a fight and will be hard to beat next* time. *(op 6-4 tchd 2-1)*
Gungadu, who won three of his four points in Ireland, was proven on soft ground. He continually hung left once taken on and this problem will need to be ironed out. *(op 11-2)*
Patrixprial, given a recent pipe-opener on the Flat, had some decent form to his name last year. He should not have minded the longer trip but was up in grade. *(op 9-2)*

1828 LADBROKES.COM SILVER TROPHY H'CAP HURDLE (LISTED RACE) (11 hdls) 2m 4f
1:55 (2:00) (Class 1) 4-Y-0+
£26,100 (£9,900; £4,950; £2,250; £1,125; £675)

Form				RPR
224-	**1**		**Lacdoudal (FR)**[197] 4761 6-10-6 **133** ... RJohnson *(P J Hobbs) hld up in tch: led sn after 3 out: all out* **9/2**[2]	138+
330-	**2**	*nk*	**Howle Hill (IRE)**[66] 3807 5-10-8 **135** ... WHutchinson *(A King) hld up in mid-div: hdwy appr 7th: hrd rdn and r.o flat* **16/1**	139
104-	**3**	*½*	**Spring Pursuit**[12] 4553 9-10-1 **128** ... TDoyle *(E G Bevan) hld up and bhd: hdwy after 7th: swtchd lft after 3 out: rdn appr 2 out: nt qckn flat* **13/2**[3]	131
0-10	**4**	*hd*	**Mr Cool**[28] 1548 11-10-4 **141** ... AGlassonbury(10) *(M C Pipe) chsd ldr to 3rd: wnt 2nd again 7th: led appr 4 out: rdn and hdd sn after 3 out: nt qckn flat* **20/1**	144
406-	**5**	*15*	**Give Me Love (FR)**[189] 4862 5-9-10 **130** oh8 ow3 ... (t) LHeard(7) *(P F Nicholls) hld up in mid-div: hdwy 6th: rdn and wknd appr 2 out* **50/1**	118
0F0-	**6**	*2*	**Sharp Rigging (IRE)**[196] 4770 5-10-3 **130** ... JAMcCarthy *(A M Hales) hld up and bhd: hdwy on ins appr 6th: wknd appr 2 out* **20/1**	116
240-	**7**	*7*	**Attorney General (IRE)**[219] 4412 6-10-5 **132** ... CLlewellyn *(J A B Old) nvr nr ldrs* **25/1**	111
3111	**8**	*2 ½*	**Yes Sir (IRE)**[70] 1204 6-11-12 **153** ... WMarston *(P Bowen) led tl appr 4 out: wknd appr 3 out* **13/2**[3]	129
0U-S	**9**	*11*	**Forager**[28] 1548 6-10-5 **132** ... LAspell *(J Ryan) pckd 6th: a bhd* **33/1**	97
302-	**10**	*1 ¾*	**Salut Saint Cloud**[13] 4585 4-10-3 **130** ... BJCrowley *(G L Moore) hld up towards rr: no ch fr 4 out* **11/1**	94
330-	**11**	*¾*	**Le Duc (FR)**[182] 4983 6-10-10 **137** ... ChristianWilliams *(P F Nicholls) rdn appr 4 out: a bhd* **25/1**	100
112-	**12**	*4*	**Inch Pride (IRE)**[184] 4945 6-10-2 **129** ... TJMurphy *(M C Pipe) t.k.h: chsd ldr 3rd to 7th: wknd qckly appr 3 out* **5/2**[1]	103+
140-	**13**	*21*	**Mr Dinglawi (IRE)**[183] 4986 4-10-0 **127** oh2 ... JamesDavies *(D B Feek) hld up in tch: rdn and wknd after 7th: t.o* **50/1**	65
RR36	**L**		**Kalambari (IRE)**[14] 1675 6-9-7 **127** oh8 ... SWalsh(7) *(J D Frost) ref to r: tk no part* **100/1**	—
120-	**P**		**Yankeedoodledandy (IRE)**[29] 4433 4-10-10 **137** ... SThomas *(B G Powell) prom tl wknd after 7th: t.o whn p.u bef 2 out* **16/1**	—

4m 56.6s (-6.10) **Going Correction** +0.575s/f (Soft)
WFA 4 from 5yo+ 14lb **15** Ran SP% **118.6**
Speed ratings: **115,114,114,114,108 107,105,104,99,98 98,97,88,—,—** CSF £63.11 CT £472.34 TOTE £6.20: £2.10, £4.90, £2.00; EX 93.30 TRIFECTA Not won..
Owner Mrs R J Skan **Bred** Scea Terres Noires **Trained** Withycombe, Somerset

FOCUS
Traditionally a good early-season handicap and a fair winning time, even for such a competitive contest, 12.7 seconds quicker than the 'Persian War'. The form looks rock solid with those in the frame behind the winner close to their marks.

NOTEBOOK
Lacdoudal(FR) held on gamely to make a successful reappearance over hurdles off a mark around a stone lower than his current chase rating. The intention was always to use this as a stepping-stone to the Paddy Power Gold Cup at Cheltenham next month. *(op 11-2)*
Howle Hill(IRE), dropped 3lb, got the longer distance well and appeared to find something of a second wind on the short run-in. There must be a danger that the Handicapper will put him back up for this. *(op 20-1)*
Spring Pursuit loves soft ground and had shown his wellbeing when winning in the mud on the flat at Ayr recently. He did not do a lot wrong after his rider decided to switch him off the stands' rail into the centre of the course. *(op 8-1)*
Mr Cool, 6lb higher than when scoring at Haydock in May, had the help of his rider's 10lb allowance and showed that he is still useful on his day.
Give Me Love(FR), 8lb out of the handicap, has yet to prove he can be effective at this sort of trip in this country.
Sharp Rigging(IRE) may have been going well when falling at the second last in the Coral Cup at the Festival in March but he is another who has still to prove he gets this distance.
Inch Pride(IRE) was found to have a nasal discharge on routine post-race examination by the *Veterinary Officer. Official explanation: vet said mare had a nasal discharge (op 9-4 tchd 11-4 in places)*

1829 LEXUS BEGINNERS' CHASE (18 fncs) 3m
2:25 (2:31) (Class 3) 5-Y-0+ **£5,785** (£1,780; £890; £445)

Form				RPR
104-	**1**		**Red Georgie (IRE)**[184] 4945 7-11-0 ... CLlewellyn *(N A Twiston-Davies) mde all: clr whn pckd 2 out: r.o* **3/1**[2]	130+
212-	**2**	*10*	**Reflected Glory (IRE)**[253] 3787 6-11-0 ... ChristianWilliams *(P F Nicholls) t.k.h: prom: chsd wnr fr 4th: j.rt fr 11th: ev ch whn blnd and nrly uns rdr 4 out* **9/4**[1]	123+
2	**3**	*25*	**Jolejoker**[165] 271 7-11-0 ... RJohnson *(R Lee) hld up: hdwy 9th: no imp fr 12th* **16/1**	93
2224	**4**	*29*	**Windy Spirit (IRE)**[56] 1334 10-11-0 110 ... PMoloney *(Evan Williams) hld up and bhd: short-lived effrt 12th* **11/1**	64
	P		**Rosses Point (IRE)**[300] 2980 6-11-0 ... AThornton *(Evan Williams) bhd fr 12th: t.o whn p.u bef 5 out* **16/1**	—
F550	**P**		**Queen Excalibur**[29] 1541 6-10-7 ... OMcPhail *(C Roberts) a in rr: j. slowly 8th: p.u bef 9th* **66/1**	—
223/	**P**		**Howrwenow (IRE)**[548] 4939 7-11-0 115 ... TJMurphy *(Miss H C Knight) a bhd: hit 6th: t.o whn p.u bef 5 out* **6/1**	—
215/	**P**		**Kopeck (IRE)**[1008] 3187 7-11-0 ... LAspell *(Mrs L Wadham) j.rt: chsd wnr to 4th: wknd 11th: t.o whn p.u bef 5 out* **9/2**[3]	—

6m 29.3s (14.40) **Going Correction** +0.725s/f (Soft) **8** Ran SP% **109.8**
Speed ratings: **105,101,93,83,— —,—,—** CSF £9.77 TOTE £3.50: £1.70, £1.50, £2.50; EX 11.50.
Owner M P Wareing **Bred** W Sheldon **Trained** Naunton, Gloucs

FOCUS
An uncompetitive novice chase that had developed into a match fully a mile from home. The first two are rated close to their best hurdling form.

NOTEBOOK
Red Georgie(IRE) made his only blemish on his chasing debut at the downhill fence two out but the runner-up had already effectively beaten himself by then. He stays well and handles testing ground. *(op 4-1)*
Reflected Glory(IRE), making his chasing debut, started shooting himself in the foot when jumping *right-handed halfway down the back straight. A bad error at the final ditch put all doubts to rest. (op 2-1)*
Jolejoker had more to do than when second in a 19-furlong maiden chase at Hereford in May. *(tchd 20-1)*

1830 PERTEMPS H'CAP HURDLE (QUALIFIER) (12 hdls) 3m
3:00 (3:04) (Class 2) 4-Y-0+
£11,147 (£4,228; £2,114; £961; £480; £288)

Form				RPR
11-1	**1**		**Standin Obligation (IRE)**[175] 128 6-10-7 **129** ... TJMurphy *(M C Pipe) hld up in tch: led appr 4 out: readily* **11/2**	143+
4211	**2**	*3*	**Yourman (IRE)**[17] 1641 5-10-0 **122** oh1 ... RGreene *(M C Pipe) hld up and sn bhd: hdwy on ins appr 4 out: ev ch appr last: no ex flat* **14/1**	126
2661	**3**	*5*	**Alikat (IRE)**[9] 1727 4-10-8 **134** ... TJMalone(3) *(M C Pipe) hld up and sn bhd: hdwy after 8th: ev ch 4 out: wknd appr last* **11/1**	132
311-	**4**	*16*	**Mount Clerigo (IRE)**[280] 3370 7-10-7 **129** ... AThornton *(V R A Dartnall) hld up: hdwy 8th: ev ch 4 out: wknd appr 2 out* **9/4**[1]	114+
/32-	**5**	*5*	**Keen Leader (IRE)**[221] 4384 9-11-5 **148** ... MrAJBerry(7) *(Jonjo O'Neill) a.p: wnt 2nd 7th: ev ch appr 4 out: wknd 3 out* **4/1**[2]	126
440-	**6**	*28*	**L'Aventure (FR)**[196] 4772 6-10-2 **131** ... (bt) LHeard(7) *(P F Nicholls) chsd ldr to 7th: sn rdn and wknd: t.o* **5/1**[3]	81
11P-	**7**	*½*	**He's The Guv'Nor (IRE)**[252] 3809 6-10-0 **122** oh12 ... BHitchcott *(R H Buckler) hld up: hdwy appr 4 out: wknd appr 3 out: t.o* **33/1**	72
005-	**8**	*dist*	**Victory Gunner (IRE)**[197] 4767 7-10-0 **122** oh4 ... ChristianWilliams *(C Roberts) prom tl wknd appr 4 out: t.o* **12/1**	—
25-2	**P**		**Moorlands Again**[10] 1711 10-9-7 **122** oh8 ... SWalsh(7) *(M Sheppard) led: rdn appr 7th: hdd appr 4 out: wkng whn blnd 3 out: p.u bef 2 out* **22/1**	—

6m 13.2s (-3.60) **Going Correction** +0.575s/f (Soft)
WFA 4 from 5yo+ 15lb **9** Ran SP% **112.8**
Speed ratings: **109,108,106,101,99 90,89,—,—** CSF £73.52 CT £810.19 TOTE £3.80: £1.70, £3.40, £2.30; EX 24.40.
Owner D A Johnson **Bred** Mrs S Flood **Trained** Nicholashayne, Devon

FOCUS
Martin Pipe and David Johnson runners filled the first three places in what was a small field for one of these qualifiers. The winner is rated value for three times the winning margin with the third setting the level for the form.

NOTEBOOK
Standin Obligation(IRE), who completed a hat-trick in novice events back in April, scored with something in hand and remains unbeaten over hurdles. *(tchd 5-1 and 6-1)*
Yourman(IRE), just out of the handicap proper, delivered his challenge between the last two flights but the winner was rather toying with him.
Alikat(IRE), raised 9lb, was running off a career-high mark and may not have quite got home in ground that was on the slow side for her. *(op 12-1)*
Mount Clerigo(IRE) was stepping up to three miles on this switch to handicaps with ground conditions in his favour. Apparently well fancied by connections, one can only assume he blew up because stamina should not have been a problem. *(op 5-2 tchd 11-4, 3-1 in a place)*
Keen Leader(IRE) had not run over hurdles since falling two out when leading in the 2002 *Royal&SunAlliance at Cheltenham. This should have sharpened him up for a return to fences. (op 7-2 tchd 3-1)*

1831 JOHN AND IRIS WATTS REMEMBRANCE DAY H'CAP CHASE (12 fncs) 2m 110y
3:35 (3:39) (Class 3) (0-120,115) 5-Y-0+ **£5,700** (£1,754; £877; £438)

Form				RPR
0-22	**1**		**Va Vavoom (IRE)**[10] 1716 7-11-7 **110** ... CLlewellyn *(N A Twiston-Davies) mde all: clr tl appr 5 out: rdn appr last: r.o wl* **9/4**[1]	126+
F4-1	**2**	*6*	**Cosmocrat**[181] 4 7-11-12 **115** ... RJohnson *(R Lee) hld up: hdwy after 7th: ev ch 4 out: j.lft 2 out: one pce* **7/1**	121
P254	**3**	*3 ½*	**Just Muckin Around (IRE)**[34] 1489 9-10-3 **92** ... BHitchcott *(R H Buckler) a.p: ev ch 4 out: swtchd rt sn after 2 out: one pce* **8/1**	96+
F-1	**4**	*6*	**Dangerousdanmagru (IRE)**[172] 170 9-11-4 **107** ... AThornton *(A E Jones) sn chsng wnr: ev ch 5 out: wknd 3 out* **4/1**[3]	106+
00-0	**5**	*29*	**Euro Bleu (FR)**[154] 451 7-11-0 **103** ... PMoloney *(M Sheppard) wnt prom and j. slowly 2nd: wknd appr 5 out* **22/1**	71
361-	**6**	*½*	**Imaginaire (USA)**[231] 4175 10-11-9 **112** ... SThomas *(Miss Venetia Williams) hld up: rdn and short-lived effrt appr 5 out* **12/1**	79
244-	**F**		**East Lawyer (FR)**[184] 4944 6-11-6 **114** ... MrCJSweeney(5) *(P F Nicholls) hld up: fell 3rd* **5/2**[2]	—

4m 21.2s (-1.70) **Going Correction** +0.725s/f (Soft) **7** Ran SP% **115.0**
Speed ratings: **105,102,100,97,84 83,—** CSF £18.36 TOTE £2.50: £1.90, £3.30; EX 16.80.
Owner H R Mould **Bred** Owen Dermody **Trained** Naunton, Gloucs
■ Stewards' Enquiry : A Thornton one-day ban: anticipating the start (Nov 2)
S Thomas one-day ban: anticipating the start (Nov 2)
R Johnson one-day ban: anticipating the start (Nov 2)
B Hitchcott one-day ban: anticipating the start (Nov 9)
P Moloney one-day ban: anticipating the start (Nov 2)
Mr C J Sweeney one-day ban: anticipating the start (Nov 2)
C Llewellyn one-day ban: anticipating the start (Nov 2)

FOCUS
This modest contest took even less winning after the second favourite departed at the first ditch. The runner-up sets the standard.

NOTEBOOK
Va Vavoom(IRE), having only his second start over fences in this handicap, made sure the emphasis would be on stamina in the soft ground and found more than enough from the penultimate fence. *(op 11-4)*
Cosmocrat, 9lb higher than when winning over an extra half a mile at Ludlow in May, was just beginning to feel the pinch when jumping left-handed at the penultimate fence. *(op 13-2 tchd 15-2)*
Just Muckin Around(IRE), dropping back to two miles, had nothing more to offer after the runner-up took his ground at the second last.
Dangerousdanmagru(IRE) was 6lb higher than when scoring on heavy ground at Exeter when last seen in May. *(op 11-2)*

1832 RHYS HOWELLS MEMORIAL H'CAP CHASE (18 fncs) 3m
4:10 (4:11) (Class 4) (0-95,95) 5-Y-0+ **£3,835** (£1,180; £590; £295)

Form				RPR
03-3	**1**		**Anflora**[16] 1655 8-10-0 **69** ... TDoyle *(B J Llewellyn) hld up in mid-div: hdwy 12th: chal 4 out: led flat: drvn out* **16/1**	78+
41PP	**2**	*1 ¼*	**Billy Ballbreaker (IRE)**[104] 948 9-11-6 **92** ... (t) RYoung(3) *(C L Tizzard) hld up: sn in tch: lft in ld 4 out: hit 3 out: hdd flat: nt qckn* **14/1**	99

4444 **3** *dist* **Make It Easy (IRE)**[17] 1646 9-9-7 **69** oh3....................(p) CaptLHorner[(7)] 41
(D L Williams) *hld up and bhd: hdwy appr 8th: rdn 5 out: sn wknd* **20/1**

134- **4** *6* **Grumpy Stumpy**[187] 4912 10-11-11 **94**.................................. CLlewellyn 60
(N A Twiston-Davies) *led: mstke 2nd: hdd 3rd: led 8th tl after 13th: wkng whn hmpd 4 out* **3/1**[1]

332- **5** *1* **Apple Joe**[293] 3178 9-10-11 **80**.. JamesDavies 45
(A J Whiting) *prom tl wknd 12th* **13/2**[3]

3/0- **6** *8* **Dunbrody Millar (IRE)**[173] 155 7-11-12 **95**........................ RJohnson 56
(P Bowen) *w ldr: led 3rd: hdd 8th: wknd appr 5 out: bdly hmpd 4 out* **10/3**[2]

-006 **P** **Rufius (IRE)**[17] 1646 12-10-0 **69** oh21.................................. RGreene —
(P Kelsall) *a bhd: t.o whn p.u bef 5 out* **66/1**

PP-0 **P** **Master Brew**[18] 1631 7-10-0 **69** oh4...................................... DCrosse —
(J R Best) *a bhd: rdn 7th: t.o whn p.u bef 11th* **33/1**

P **Aisjem (IRE)**[318] 2712 6-10-11 **80**............................... ChristianWilliams —
(Evan Williams) *a bhd: t.o whn p.u bef 5 out* **8/1**

4/34 **P** **Alabaster**[10] 1713 10-9-7 **69** oh11.. KBurke[(7)] —
(N J Hawke) *hld up in mid-div: dropped rr and p.u bef 8th* **33/1**

1-2P **P** **Solve It Sober (IRE)**[136] 684 11-10-7 **81**........................ RStephens[(5)] —
(S G Griffiths) *a bhd: mstke 9th: t.o whn p.u bef 11th* **16/1**

42-P **P** **General O'Keeffe**[172] 169 8-11-5 **88**.................................. AThornton —
(R H Alner) *prom tl lost pl after 7th: t.o whn p.u bef 5 out* **12/1**

FP1- **P** **St Kilda**[222] 4365 8-9-11 **73**..........................(p) MissLucyBridges[(7)] —
(Miss Lucy Bridges) *prom: hit 12th: sn wknd: t.o whn p.u bef 4 out* **25/1**

220/ **F** **Freteval (FR)**[573] 4606 8-10-0 **74** ow2................................ JDiment[(5)] —
(S J Gilmore) *hld up in mid-div: hdwy 11th: led after 13th: slt ld whn fell 4 out* **33/1**

P5P6 **P** **Lost Treasure (IRE)**[48] 1412 8-10-1 **70**.................................... SCurran —
(Evan Williams) *prom: mstke 6th: rdn 10th: wkng whn blnd 13th: t.o whn p.u bef 5 out* **22/1**

60-3 **P** **Penalty Clause (IRE)**[20] 1609 5-11-0 **85**................................... LAspell —
(Lucinda Featherstone) *hld up and bhd: hdwy after 13th: wknd 5 out: t.o whn p.u bef 2 out* **16/1**

6m 32.5s (17.60) **Going Correction** +0.725s/f (Soft)
WFA 5 from 6yo+ 2lb **16** Ran SP% **127.8**
Speed ratings: **99,98,**—,—,—,—,—,—,—,—,—,—,—,—,—,— — CSF £211.76 CT £4492.56 TOTE £28.40: £3.50, £2.70, £5.30, £1.40; EX 296.30.

Owner Maenllwyd Racing Club **Bred** R H Philips **Trained** Fochriw, Caerphilly

FOCUS
The soft ground took its toll on this big field in a low-grade affair. The form is rated through the runner-up.

NOTEBOOK
Anflora, a modest winning pointer, had been let down by her jumping on her two previous starts over fences. She never put a foot wrong on this return to the major obstacles. *(tchd 20-1)*

Billy Ballbreaker(IRE), freshened up by a three-month break, likes this sort of ground and lost no caste in defeat.

Make It Easy(IRE), 3lb out of the handicap, is much more at home on a sounder surface. *(tchd 18-1)*

Grumpy Stumpy was already in trouble on his seasonal debut when hampered by a faller. *(op 9-2)*

Freteval(FR), off course since March last year, was being challenged on both sides when crashing out at the final ditch. He has yet to prove he stays this trip. *(op 25-1)*

1833 WESTCOUNTRYRACING.COM AFFORDABLE RACING SYNDICATES MAIDEN HURDLE (12 hdls) 3m
4:45 (4:48) (Class 4) 4-Y-0+ **£3,031** (£866; £433)

Form RPR

1 **Dunbell Boy (IRE)**[191] 4844 7-11-2 .... NFehily 97+
(C J Mann) *hld up: hdwy after 5th: led on bit appr 3 out: rdn appr last: jst hld on* **3/1**[2]

545- **2** *shd* **Gritti Palace (IRE)**[207] 4644 5-10-11 .... MNicolls[(5)] 97
(John R Upson) *bhd: pushed along fr 3rd: plenty to do whn styd on fr 2 out: hrd rdn and fin wl: jst failed* **50/1**

3 *5* **Micky Cole (IRE)**[272] 5-11-2 .... ChristianWilliams 92
(P F Nicholls) *a.p: rdn and ev ch 2 out: wknd towards fin* **2/1**[1]

4 *3 ½* **Mac Dargin (IRE)**[321] 6-11-2 .... CLlewellyn 89+
(N A Twiston-Davies) *sn chsng ldr: led appr 4 out: rdn and hdd appr 3 out: wknd flat* **7/2**[3]

0 **5** *25* **Little Word**[14] 1681 6-10-2 .... MrRhysHughes[(7)] 56
(P D Williams) *hld up and bhd: short-lived effrt appr 4 out* **50/1**

0PO- **P** **Knight Of The Road (IRE)**[195] 4797 6-11-2 68.......................... LAspell —
(P G Murphy) *a bhd: t.o whn p.u bef 4 out* **50/1**

20-6 **P** **Midnight Gold**[10] 1711 5-11-2 103.. SThomas —
(L P Grassick) *led: hdd & wknd appr 4 out: bhd whn p.u bef last* **13/2**

260- **P** **Zipalong Lad (IRE)**[195] 4801 5-11-2 .... RJohnson —
(P Bowen) *hld up and bhd: stdy hdwy 6th: lost action 7th: p.u bef 8th* **7/1**

4-34 **P** **Denarius Secundus**[165] 287 8-11-2 76............................ TScudamore —
(N R Mitchell) *chsd ldr tl after 1st: wknd 6th: t.o whn p.u bef 4 out* **25/1**

6m 29.7s (12.90) **Going Correction** +0.575s/f (Soft) **9** Ran SP% **116.1**
Speed ratings: **81,80,79,78,69** —,—,—,— CSF £126.80 TOTE £4.30: £1.30, £9.00, £1.60; EX 185.70 Place 6 £144.21, Place 5 £102.93.

Owner The Safest Syndicate **Bred** Mrs A Connolly **Trained** Upper Lambourn, Berks

FOCUS
A very moderate time even allowing for the conditions, 16.5 seconds slower than the Pertemps Qualifier and rated through the winner.

NOTEBOOK
Dunbell Boy(IRE), a winning pointer, had also been placed in a couple of heavy-ground Irish bumpers. He looks set to justify good market support in style when moving smoothly to the front but, in the end, the post arrived not a moment too soon. *(op 13-2)*

Gritti Palace(IRE), who showed a modicum of ability in bumpers, was being nudged along from quite early on. His rider deserves full marks for his perseverance and, shaping like an out-and-out stayer, he very nearly caused a big shock. *(op 40-1)*

Micky Cole(IRE), a narrow winner on heavy ground of his only Irish point, finally ran out of steam at the death. *(op 11-8)*

Mac Dargin(IRE), another who landed an Irish point in the soft, was eventually forced to give best on the short run-in. *(op 4-1)*

T/Plt: £58.80 to a £1 stake. Pool: £46,550.60. 577.75 winning tickets. T/Qpdt: £9.00 to a £1 stake. Pool: £2,617.10. 213.30 winning tickets. KH

[1601] KELSO (L-H)
Saturday, October 22

OFFICIAL GOING: Good to soft
Wind: Almost nil

1834 PREMIER TRAFFIC MANAGEMENT "NATIONAL HUNT" NOVICES' HURDLE (8 hdls) 2m 110y
2:30 (2:30) (Class 4) 4-Y-0+ **£3,627** (£1,116; £558; £279)

Form RPR

131- **1** **Rasharrow (IRE)**[189] 4865 6-10-12 .... BGibson 110+
(L Lungo) *keen: hld up: hdwy 3rd: led 3 out: shkn up last: r.o strly* **1/4**[1]

0P5- **2** *3 ½* **Polly Whitefoot**[285] 3293 6-10-5 .... PWhelan 92+
(R A Fahey) *prom: efffort and chsd wnr after 2 out: kpt on: no imp* **20/1**

0-24 **3** *9* **Aces Four (IRE)**[14] 1672 6-10-12 .... RMcGrath 90
(W McKeown) *trckd ldrs: effrt 2 out: kpt on same pce run in* **10/1**[2]

-334 **4** *6* **Chief Dan George (IRE)**[30] 1532 5-10-9 .... PAspell[(3)] 84
(D R MacLeod) *hld up: hdwy bef 3 out: kpt on but no imp fr next* **33/1**

42- **5** *2* **Kirkside Pleasure (IRE)**[183] 4971 4-10-12 .... MBradburne 82
(Mrs S C Bradburne) *nt fluent: towards rr: effrt u.p after 3 out: no imp fr next* **12/1**[3]

630- **6** *5* **Endless Power (IRE)**[183] 4971 5-10-12 .... BHarding 77
(J Barclay) *chsd ldrs: effrt 3 out: outpcd after next* **28/1**

50-0 **7** *¾* **Another Taipan (IRE)**[177] 82 5-10-5 .... EWhillans[(7)] 76
(A C Whillans) *bhd tl sme late hdwy: nvr on terms* **50/1**

-000 **8** *¾* **Bromley Abbey**[157] 406 7-10-2 73...................................... MrCStorey[(3)] 68
(Miss S E Forster) *midfield on outside tl wknd bef 2 out* **100/1**

0 **9** *4* **Yankee Holiday (IRE)**[30] 1532 5-10-12 .... KRenwick 71
(Mrs S C Bradburne) *bhd: pushed along bef 2 out: n.d* **100/1**

P00- **10** *¾* **Brora Sutherland (IRE)**[210] 4547 6-10-9 88..................... PBuchanan[(3)] 70
(Miss Lucinda V Russell) *towards rr: rdn bef 3 out: n.d* **40/1**

00-0 **11** *½* **Crystal Runner**[163] 323 5-9-12 .... CDSharkey[(7)] 63
(E J Jamieson) *towards rr: effrt bef 3 out: nvr on terms* **100/1**

0-64 **12** *22* **Batties Den (IRE)**[156] 431 5-10-12 .... JimCrowley 48
(P D Niven) *n.d* **100/1**

0P-0 **13** *11* **Hot Air (IRE)**[168] 210 7-10-9 .... MichalKohl[(3)] 37
(J I A Charlton) *keen: prom tl wknd bef 3 out* **100/1**

234- **14** *19* **Dunsemore**[394] 1483 5-10-0 .... DCCostello[(5)] 11
(Mrs A F Tullie) *keen: led 1st to 3 out: sn btn* **20/1**

P-P5 **15** *19* **Derainey (IRE)**[168] 212 6-10-12 .... KJohnson —
(R Johnson) *led to 1st: cl up tl lost pl bef 4th: t.o* **66/1**

0000 **16** *27* **Terimons Daughter**[14] 1683 6-10-5 .... NPMulholland —
(E W Tuer) *plld hrd: in tch: lost pl bef 4th: t.o* **100/1**

4m 1.50s (-2.20) **Going Correction** -0.05s/f (Good)
WFA 4 from 5yo+ 13lb **16** Ran SP% **124.5**
Speed ratings: **103,101,97,94,93 91,90,90,88,88 87,77,72,63,54 41** CSF £10.75 TOTE £1.30: £1.10, £2.70, £2.10; EX 8.40.

Owner Ashleybank Investments Limited **Bred** Mrs Elizabeth English **Trained** Carrutherstown, D'fries & G'way

FOCUS
Ordinary form behind the easy winner, who looks the sort to hold his own in stronger company in due course. The time was fair and the form appears reasonably solid.

NOTEBOOK
Rasharrow(IRE) ◆, one of the best bumper horses of last year, created a favourable impression on this hurdles debut and, although the opposition was modest and he did not really settle, he looks the sort to hold his own in stronger company. *(op 2-7 tchd 1-3 in places)*

Polly Whitefoot turned in her best effort over hurdles on this first run since January and, although flattered by her proximity to the easy winner, will be of more interest in ordinary handicaps in the near future. *(op 25-1)*

Aces Four(IRE) again ran creditably over hurdles and is probably the best guide to the worth of this form. However he is likely to remain vulnerable to the better novices in this type of event. *(tchd 8-1)*

Chief Dan George(IRE), who had shown ability in bumpers, was not disgraced on this hurdle debut but left the impression that ordinary handicaps and the step up to two and a half miles would see him in a better light. *(op 40-1)*

Kirkside Pleasure(IRE) had shown ability in bumpers but, although not totally disgraced on this hurdles debut, has room for improvement in the jumping department and is going to need a stiffer test than this to get off the mark. *(tchd 14-1)*

Endless Power(IRE) ran as though the race was needed on this hurdling debut and first run for his new stable. *He is another that is going to continue to look vulnerable in this type of race, though. (op 25-1 tchd 20-1)*

Dunsemore *Official explanation: trainer said mare finished lame*

1835 ROYAL CALEDONIAN HUNT BEGINNERS' CHASE (12 fncs) 2m 1f
3:05 (3:05) (Class 3) 4-Y-0+ **£5,421** (£1,668; £834; £417)

Form RPR

6-04 **1** **South Bronx (IRE)**[15] 1662 6-11-6 ....(t) MBradburne 110+
(Mrs S C Bradburne) *prom: led bef last: kpt on strly* **9/2**[3]

436/ **2** *10* **Albertino Lad**[547] 4946 8-11-3 .... PBuchanan[(3)] 100
(Miss Lucinda V Russell) *keen: cl up: led 2 out to bef last: kpt on same pce* **16/1**

302- **3** *14* **Fairy Skin Maker (IRE)**[221] 4387 7-11-6 .... RMcGrath 90+
(G A Harker) *hld up: hmpd 2nd: mstke next: nt fluent after: rdn 4 out: no imp fr 2 out* **9/4**[2]

012- **4** *1 ¾* **Kimbambo (FR)**[259] 3708 7-11-6 .... BGibson 85+
(J P L Ewart) *chsd ldrs: outpcd bef 3 out: btn next* **7/4**[1]

0020 **5** *shd* **Lion Guest (IRE)**[20] 1606 8-11-6 .... KRenwick 89+
(Mrs S C Bradburne) *led: jnd whn blnd bdly 2 out: nt rcvr* **25/1**

P/ **6** *dist* **Little Blackie**[913] 4750 8-10-6 .... MJMcAlister[(7)] —
(S J Marshall) *bhd: lost tch fr 1/2-way* **40/1**

P **U** **Winds Supreme (IRE)**[20] 1606 6-11-6 ....(t) PWhelan —
(M A Barnes) *blnd and uns rdr 2nd* **40/1**

P00- **F** **Ciacole**[210] 4547 4-9-9 .... DCCostello[(5)] —
(Mrs B K Thomson) *in tch whn fell 5th* **66/1**

44-5 **F** **Northern Minster**[15] 1662 6-11-6 .... BHarding —
(F P Murtagh) *cl up whn fell 3rd* **6/1**

635- **F** **Hollow Flight (IRE)**[225] 4300 7-11-3 78.............................. PAspell[(3)] —
(J N R Billinge) *mstkes in rr: sixth and wl btn whn fell last* **28/1**

4m 23.9s (0.70) **Going Correction** +0.15s/f (Yiel)
WFA 4 from 6yo+ 13lb **10** Ran SP% **119.1**
Speed ratings: **104,99,92,91,91** —,—,—,—,— CSF £60.21 TOTE £7.80: £1.50, £3.50, £1.30; EX 133.00.

Owner Mrs S Irwin **Bred** Mrs D M Pollock **Trained** Cunnoquhie, Fife

FOCUS
With the two market leaders disappointing this race did not take as much winning as seemed likely. The pace was fair and the form is rated through the runner-up to his best bumper form.

NOTEBOOK

South Bronx(IRE) bettered the form of his chasing debut and, although there are holes to be picked in this form with the market leaders disappointing, he jumped soundly, will stay further and may be able to defy a penalty in modest company. *(op 6-1 tchd 13-2)*

Albertino Lad ◆, having his first run for Lucinda Russell and making his chasing debut, showed *more than enough on this first start since April of last year to suggest a similar race can be found. (op 11-1)*

Fairy Skin Maker(IRE) looked to have decent claims on this chase debut if the pick of his hurdles form could be reproduced but he failed to have a proper cut at his fences after being hampered *early on. He will be suited by the return to further though and is not one to write off yet. (op 2-1 tchd 5-2)*

Kimbambo(FR), who has gone well fresh in the past and has a good record at Kelso, should have been suited by the overnight rain on this chase debut but was disappointing given he looks the type to win races over fences. He is worth another chance. *(op 9-4)*

Lion Guest(IRE) was in the process of running creditably on this chase debut when ploughing through the penultimate fence. It was too far out to say with any certainty where he would have finished and he is not the most consistent, but he looks capable of winning a small race over fences.

Little Blackie, having her first run since April 2003, offered no promise on this chase debut. *(op 33-1)*

1836 PETER DOYLE H'CAP HURDLE (8 hdls) 2m 110y

3:40 (3:40) (Class 3) (0-115,115) 4-Y-O+ **£4,901** (£1,508; £754; £377)

Form				RPR
0002	1		**Rising Generation (FR)**[30] [1530] 8-11-9 **112** BHarding (N G Richards) *mde virtually all: drew clr fr 2 out* **4/1**[2]	128+
433	2	19	**Big Wheel**[20] [1604] 10-9-13 **98** FDavis(10) (N G Richards) *keen: prom: effrt and chsd wnr after 2 out: no imp* **10/1**	94
2035	3	3/4	**Magico (NZ)**[20] [1620] 7-10-8 **97** HOliver (R C Guest) *cl up: effrt bef 2 out: one pce bef last* **9/1**[3]	92
303-	4	1 3/4	**Euro American (GER)**[248] [3889] 5-11-2 **105** BGibson (E W Tuer) *nt fluent: hld up: effrt bef 2 out: no imp fr last* **10/1**	98
040/	5	6	**Uptown Lad (IRE)**[560] [4729] 6-11-1 **104** (t) KJohnson (R Johnson) *hld up: rdn after 3 out: nvr rchd ldrs* **25/1**	92+
40-P	6	1 1/4	**Hollows Mill**[177] [84] 9-9-13 **95** EWhillans(7) (F P Murtagh) *keen in midfield: rdn after 3 out: wknd next* **33/1**	81
25-P	7	nk	**Culcabock (IRE)**[31] [1513] 5-11-5 **111** PBuchanan(3) (Miss Lucinda V Russell) *keen: hld up: effrt bef 3 out: wknd bef next* **25/1**	97
3-PF	8	6	**Minivet**[31] [1510] 10-11-4 **110** PAspell(3) (R Allan) *cl up tl wknd after 4 out* **25/1**	90
2642	9	22	**Bargain Hunt (IRE)**[15] [1665] 4-10-0 **89** KRenwick (W Storey) *bhd: drvn 4 out: nvr on terms* **12/1**	47
3-P1	B		**Top Style (IRE)**[30] [1530] 7-10-10 **104** WKennedy(5) (G A Harker) *hld up: b.d 4 out* **4/1**[2]	—
214-	F		**Rehearsal**[35] [4858] 4-11-2 **115** JPEnnis(10) (L Lungo) *keen in midfield: fell 4 out* **11/4**[1]	—
2102	P		**Talarive (USA)**[31] [1510] 9-10-11 **100** (tp) JimCrowley (P D Niven) *chsng ldrs whn p.u bef 4 out* **12/1**	—
0310	F		**Virtus**[60] [1297] 5-9-9 **89** oh4 DCCostello(5) (Mrs B K Thomson) *prom: effrt bef 2 out: 5th and outpcd whn fell last* **25/1**	70

4m 0.50s (-3.20) **Going Correction** -0.05s/f (Good)
WFA 4 from 5yo+ 13lb 13 Ran SP% **128.6**
Speed ratings: **105,96,95,94,92 91,91,88,78,— —,—,—** CSF £44.00 CT £358.76 TOTE £6.20: £1.80, £4.20, £3.60; EX 39.90.
Owner Rising Generation Partnership **Bred** N Pharaon **Trained** Greystoke, Cumbria
■ Stewards' Enquiry : H Oliver one-day ban: used whip with excessive frequency (Nov 2)

FOCUS

An ordinary handicap weakened by the departure of the two market leaders at the fourth last flight. The pace seemed sound but the form does not appear that solid.

NOTEBOOK

Rising Generation(FR), who hinted at a return to form at Perth last month, benefited by the departure of the two market leaders around halfway and won with a good deal in hand. Life will be tougher after reassessment, though. *(op 8-1)*

Big Wheel, who has not raced much since his last win (in this race) two years ago, was not disgraced given he failed to settle. Quicker ground will be more to his liking and he may be capable of winning again away from progressive or well handicapped sorts. *(op 8-1)*

Magico(NZ), back over hurdles, was not totally disgraced but, although he again shaped as though further would suit, he has struggled when upped in distance in the past and he does not look one to place maximum faith in. *(op 10-1)*

Euro American(GER) may be a bit better than the bare form given that he fared the best of those that attempted to make ground from off the pace. He is worth another try over two and a half miles and may be best on a sound surface. *(op 8-1)*

Uptown Lad(IRE) was not totally disgraced on this first start since April of last year but, although this run should have done him good, he may need to drop further in the weights before regaining the winning thread.

Hollows Mill did not shape with any conspicuous promise back over hurdles on this first start since April. *(op 25-1)*

Talarive(USA) *Official explanation: jockey said gelding lost its action (tchd 14-1)*

Top Style(IRE) did not get a chance to show what he was capable of from this 9lb higher mark but he is almost certainly well worth another chance in a similar event in the near future. *(tchd 14-1)*

Rehearsal, who progressed steadily over hurdles last year, had failed to settle but was still tanking along when coming to grief. Although it remains to be seen if this has affected his confidence, he is well worth another chance in this type of event. *(tchd 14-1)*

1837 MAYFIELD RESTAURANT H'CAP CHASE (FOR THE MARSHALL TROPHY) (19 fncs) 3m 1f

4:15 (4:15) (Class 4) (0-105,105) 5-Y-O+ **£4,875** (£1,500; £750; £375)

Form				RPR
P-42	1		**Primitive Way**[20] [1603] 13-10-8 **87** (v) BHarding (Miss S E Forster) *chsd ldrs: effrt 2 out: led run in: styd on wl* **5/1**[2]	98+
4234	2	1	**Pessimistic Dick**[20] [1603] 12-9-13 **83** DCCostello(5) (Mrs J C McGregor) *mde most to run in: kpt on towards fin* **14/1**	92
22P-	3	8	**Miss Mattie Ross**[251] [3826] 9-10-10 **96** MJMcAlister(7) (S J Marshall) *a cl up: hit 11th: ev ch tl outpcd bef last* **8/1**	99+
/10-	4	6	**D J Flippance (IRE)**[210] [4548] 10-11-2 **95** RMcGrath (A Parker) *pckd 1st: hld up: effrt u.p 15th: no imp fr 3 out* **5/1**[2]	90
5333	5	1	**Ideal Du Bois Beury (FR)**[14] [1686] 9-9-12 **80** PAspell(3) (P Monteith) *mstke 1st: bhd: rdn 15th: nvr on terms* **5/1**[2]	74
10/P	6	dist	**Minsgill Glen**[14] [1686] 9-9-11 **79** oh17 PBuchanan(3) (Mrs J K M Oliver) *in tch tl wknd fr 14th* **50/1**	—
00/4	7	1 1/4	**One Day (NZ)**[14] [1678] 7-11-7 **100** HOliver (R C Guest) *in tch: hit 5th: lost pl whn mstke 12th: sn btn* **6/1**[3]	—
P/4-	8	16	**Almire Du Lia (FR)**[521] [417] 7-11-12 **105** MBradburne (Mrs S C Bradburne) *chsd ldrs: reminders 10th: wknd bef 14th* **14/1**	—
430-	F		**Behavingbadly (IRE)**[183] [4970] 10-11-8 **101** ADempsey (A Parker) *fell heavily 1st* **7/1**	—
P0-5	F		**Contract Scotland (IRE)**[177] [80] 10-11-2 **95** BGibson (L Lungo) *in tch whn fell 14th* **4/1**[1]	—

6m 30.8s (1.20) **Going Correction** +0.15s/f (Yiel) 10 Ran SP% **123.2**
Speed ratings: **104,103,101,99,98 —,—,—,—,—** CSF £73.08 CT £566.32 TOTE £4.60: £2.10, £2.90, £3.00; EX 20.30.
Owner The Hon Gerald Maitland-Carew **Bred** D G Atkinson **Trained** Kirk Yetholm, Borders

FOCUS

A moderate handicap run at a fair gallop in the rain-softened ground and stamina was tested fully in the closing stages. The principals ran to their marks so the form looks reasonable.

NOTEBOOK

Primitive Way got the decent test of stamina he requires and showed the right attitude to break a losing run of over two years. He is only ordinary but should continue to give a good account in this sort of company, even after reassessment. *(op 13-2)*

Pessimistic Dick proved suited by the test of stamina that this race became and got closer on these better terms to the winner than he had done over this course and distance last time. He looks capable of winning a similar race from this mark. *(op 9-1)*

Miss Mattie Ross has a good record over fences at this course and, despite getting tired against two rivals that had the benefit of a previous run, showed enough on this first run for over eight months to suggest she can win another race. *(tchd 7-1)*

D J Flippance(IRE), very lightly raced in recent times, is not the most consistent but shaped as though an even stiffer test of stamina would have been in his favour. He would not be one to lump on next time, though. *(op 11-2)*

Ideal Du Bois Beury(FR) is an error-prone chaser who again never got competitive after an early mistake. He needs things to fall just right and remains one to tread carefully with. *(op 7-1)*

Minsgill Glen faced a very stiff task from so far out of the handicap and was again well beaten. *(op 25-1)*

Behavingbadly(IRE)was again let down badly by his jumping and he may not forget this experience in a while. *(tchd 8-1)*

Contract Scotland(IRE) was still travelling well within himself when coming to grief and, although too far out to say with certainty where he would have finished, he will remain of interest in similar company on goodish ground from this mark. *(tchd 8-1)*

1838 CLIFFORD FIRTH MEMORIAL H'CAP HURDLE (11 hdls) 2m 6f 110y

4:50 (4:50) (Class 4) (0-100,100) 4-Y-O+ **£3,679** (£1,132; £566; £283)

Form				RPR
5-55	1		**Tobesure (IRE)**[157] [410] 11-11-4 **95** MichalKohl(3) (J I A Charlton) *hld up: hdwy 4 out: led after 2 out: edgd rt run in: kpt on wl* **15/2**	101+
111-	2	6	**Nolife (IRE)**[288] [3258] 9-11-5 **96** PBuchanan(3) (Miss Lucinda V Russell) *led to after 2 out: kpt on same pce: bttr for r* **9/4**[1]	95
3455	3	2 1/2	**True Temper (IRE)**[10] [1723] 8-10-0 **79** DMcGann(5) (A M Crow) *cl up: ev ch tl outpcd fr 2 out* **20/1**	76
4-P0	4	14	**General Duroc (IRE)**[150] [501] 9-11-3 **98** MJMcAlister(7) (B Storey) *in tch: lost pl 1/2-way: kpt on fr 2 out: no imp* **16/1**	81
P-52	5	8	**Minster Abbi**[150] [496] 5-10-1 **75** (p) KRenwick (W Storey) *hld up towards rr: outpcd bef 4 out: kpt on fr 2 out: n.d* **14/1**	50
0103	6	8	**Green 'N' Gold**[14] [1685] 5-11-1 **89** NPMulholland (M D Hammond) *hld up: hdwy 4 out: rdn and no imp fr next* **6/1**[3]	56
60-0	7	6	**Welsh Dream**[163] [319] 8-11-3 **94** MrCStorey(3) (Miss S E Forster) *midfield: hdwy 1/2-way: rdn and wknd bef 3 out* **12/1**	55
6P5-	8	23	**Ballynure (IRE)**[202] [4713] 7-10-11 **90** DFlavin(5) (Mrs L B Normile) *a bhd: struggling fr 1/2-way* **20/1**	28
0050	9	5	**Silver Dagger**[34] [1486] 7-10-3 **80** (v) PAspell(3) (J C Haynes) *in tch tl wknd bef 4 out* **33/1**	13
-114	10	1 1/2	**Arctic Lagoon (IRE)**[125] [783] 6-11-2 **90** (t) MBradburne (Mrs S C Bradburne) *prom tl wknd fr 5 out* **8/1**	21
2113	11	1 1/4	**Wally Wonder (IRE)**[25] [1571] 7-11-12 **100** (v[1]) JimCrowley (R Bastiman) *midfield: wknd fr 7th* **10/1**	30
052-	P		**Political Cruise**[216] [4475] 7-10-1 **82** GThomas(7) (R Nixon) *a bhd: mstke 4th: sn btn: p.u after 6th* **14/1**	—
505-	P		**Washington Pink (IRE)**[348] [2101] 6-9-9 **76** (p) PKinsella(7) (C Grant) *cl up tl wknd bef 3 out: p.u bef next* **20/1**	—
P-05	P		**Word Gets Around (IRE)**[163] [320] 7-11-8 **96** BGibson (L Lungo) *hld up: hdwy and in tch bef 3 out: wknd qckly and p.u bef next* **5/1**[2]	—

5m 45.5s (7.80) **Going Correction** +0.375s/f (Yiel) 14 Ran SP% **137.8**
Speed ratings: **101,98,98,93,90 87,85,77,75,75 74,—,—,—** CSF £27.74 CT £366.25 TOTE £15.50: £3.90, £2.00, £5.30; EX 28.60.
Owner Richard Nixon **Bred** E Tierney **Trained** Stocksfield, Northumberland
■ The first winner in Britain for Czech-born Michal Kohl.

FOCUS

An ordinary event but a decent gallop and this form, rated through the first three, should stand up at a similar level.

NOTEBOOK

Tobesure(IRE) had the race run to suit and took advantage of a slipping mark to notch his first win over hurdles (has since won over fences) in over three years. He goes well here but his record suggests he would not be one to lump on at shortish odds next time. *(op 7-1 tchd 8-1)*

Nolife(IRE) ◆, a progressive performer last season, showed more than enough on this first start since January to suggest he can win races for his current stable for his stable that is back among the winners. *(op 7-2)*

True Temper(IRE) ran creditably on easier ground than she had encountered at Wetherby but, given her inconsistency and the fact she has yet to win in 20 starts, will be of only limited interest in similar company next time.

General Duroc(IRE) showed he retains ability on this first run since May and first run for his new stable. Softer ground may help and he is capable of winning from this mark, but he did not look an easy ride and still looks one to tread carefully with. *(op 10-1)*

Minster Abbi, who showed her first worthwile form at Cartmel last time, failed to build on that run on her handicap debut but she did shape as though the step up to three miles on a more galloping course would suit. *(op 20-1)*

Green 'N' Gold was again below the form of her Cartmel win in August and she remains one to have reservations about. *(op 15-2 tchd 8-1)*

Word Gets Around(IRE) has been disappointing and dropped out quickly, but this trip on rain-softened ground probably did not play to his strengths and he is worth another chance back on a sound surface from this mark. *(op 11-2 tchd 6-1)*

1839 EDINBURGH CITY F.C. CONDITIONAL JOCKEYS' NOVICES' HURDLE (11 hdls) 2m 6f 110y

5:20 (5:20) (Class 4) 4-Y-O+ **£3,653** (£1,124; £562; £281)

Form				RPR
322-	1		**King Of Confusion (IRE)**[249] [3859] 6-10-6 109 TJDreaper(6) (Ferdy Murphy) *hld up: smooth hdwy bef 7th: led on bit run in: shkn up and sn clr* **1/1**[1]	115+

-114 **2** *22* **Tandava (IRE)**[104] 938 7-11-12 112 ONelmes 104+
(Mrs S C Bradburne) *hld up: hdwy to ld after 3 out: hdd run in: no ch w wnr* **7/2**[2]

-640 **3** *5* **The Miner**[20] 1605 7-10-7 90 TMessenger(5) 82
(Miss S E Forster) *keen: chsd ldrs: ev ch 3 out: wknd run in* **9/1**

00PP **4** *8* **Hapthor**[125] 785 6-10-0 PJMcDonald(5) 67
(F Jestin) *keen: bhd: hdwy bef 2 out: kpt on: n.d* **66/1**

P **5** *1* **Master Farrier**[14] 1687 5-10-12 TGreenway 73
(Miss Lucinda V Russell) *led to 2nd: lost pl bef 7th: n.d after* **50/1**

6 *2* **Let's Be Subtle (IRE)**[139] 6-10-5 (t) DMcGann 64
(W Amos) *prom tl rdn and wknd after 3 out* **14/1**

P2P- **7** *16* **Cool Dessa Blues**[295] 3114 6-10-0 EWhillans(5) 48
(W Amos) *led 2nd: j.rt next: hdd after 3 out: sn btn* **33/1**

50-5 **8** *dist* **Now Then Auntie (IRE)**[22] 1593 4-10-4 PAspell —
(Mrs S A Watt) *a bhd* **33/1**

23-0 **9** *16* **Named At Dinner**[29] 320 4-10-6 89 ow3 (p) NWalker(8) —
(Miss Lucinda V Russell) *prom to 4 out: sn rdn and btn* **20/1**

0262 **10** *dist* **One Of Them**[48] 1410 6-10-12 92 DFlavin —
(M A Barnes) *chsd ldrs: hit 7th: wknd bef 3 out* **14/1**

3- **P** **Sportula**[420] 1303 4-9-13 PKinsella(5) —
(C Grant) *in tch to 1/2-way: sn lost pl* **16/1**

6 **P** **Solway Cloud**[22] 1590 5-9-13 MJMcAlister(6) —
(B Storey) *hld up: wknd and p.u bef 4 out* **66/1**

0- **P** **Master Speaker**[327] 2549 7-10-12 WKennedy —
(G A Harker) *a bhd: t.o whn p.u bef 2 out* **33/1**

P **Thuringe (FR)**[354] 4-9-10 FDavis(8) —
(N G Richards) *hld up: rdn 5 out: btn after next: p.u bef 2 out* **11/2**[3]

5m 50.6s (12.90) **Going Correction** +0.65s/f (Soft)
WFA 4 from 5yo+ 14lb **14** Ran SP% **135.4**
Speed ratings: **103,95,93,90,90 89,84,—,—,—,—,—,—,—** CSF £5.04 TOTE £2.00: £1.50, £1.90, £3.30; EX 5.60 Place 6 £66.21, Place 5 £59.16.
Owner J Taqvi **Bred** Jack Butler **Trained** West Witton, N Yorks
■ Tom Dreaper's first winner since turning professional.

FOCUS
Little strength in depth but a fair pace on ground nearer soft by this time and the winner was value for even further than the winning margin. The form could be rated higher.

NOTEBOOK
King Of Confusion(IRE) ◆ turned in an improved effort on this first start since February and looks value for even more than the winning margin. Given the way he powered through this race, he appeals as the sort to hold his own in stronger company. *(op 6-4 tchd 13-8 in places)*
Tandava(IRE) is likely to continue to look vulnerable in this grade under a double penalty but he is a fairly reliable yardstick on easy ground and seemed to give it his best shot. He should continue to give a good account. *(op 4-1)*
The Miner ran creditably in the face of a stiffish task against a couple of fair rivals and will be seen to better effect back over shorter and in ordinary handicap company. *(op 8-1)*
Hapthor showed his first worthwhile form and may be suited by handicaps and three miles but his proximity does hold this bare form down.
Master Farrier fared better than on his hurdle debut on this easier surface but is another whose proximity confirms this bare form is modest.
Let's Be Subtle(IRE), making her hurdling debut, is likely to continue to look vulnerable in novice events. *(op 16-1 tchd 12-1)*
One Of Them *Official explanation: jockey said gelding finished lame (tchd 16-1)*
T/Plt: £52.70 to a £1 stake. Pool: £35,594.80. 492.60 winning tickets. T/Qpdt: £15.80 to a £1 stake. Pool: £2,027.70. 94.40 winning tickets. RY

1840 - 1843a (Foreign Racing) - See Raceform Interactive

1821
AINTREE (L-H)
Sunday, October 23

OFFICIAL GOING: Hurdles course - soft; chase course - soft (good to soft in places)
After 14mm rain the ground was described as 'genuine soft'. The rail on the hurdle track on the home turn had been moved out by 12 yards.
Wind: Almost nil Weather: Fine

1844 DIGITAL PRINTS FROM BONUSPRINT.COM H'CAP HURDLE (13 hdls) 3m 110y
2:15 (2:15) (Class 3) (0-130,129) 4-Y-0+ **£9,568** (£2,944; £1,472; £736)

Form RPR
30-1 **1** **Jorobaden (FR)**[7] 1760 5-11-9 129 7ex PMerrigan(7) 139+
(Mrs H Dalton) *trckd ldrs: smooth hdwy to ld 2 out: smoothly* **3/1**[2]

0-11 **2** *3* **Midnight Creek**[12] 1616 7-11-3 116 JimCrowley 116+
(A Sadik) *trckd ldrs: led and hit 10th: hdd 2 out: styd on run-in: no imp* **14/1**

4112 **3** *6* **Michaels Dream (IRE)**[12] 1488 6-10-11 110 (b) KRenwick 103
(N Wilson) *jnd ldrs 8th: one pce fr 2 out* **14/1**

213- **4** *¾* **Darjeeling (IRE)**[246] 3958 6-10-10 109 RWalsh 101
(P F Nicholls) *hld up: smooth hdwy 10th: rdn to chse ldrs next: wknd last* **2/1**[1]

P4P- **5** *11* **Lord Jack (IRE)**[190] 4861 9-11-2 115 BHarding 97+
(N G Richards) *led: racd wd: qcknd 7th: hdd 10th: wknd next* **11/2**[3]

1524 **6** *13* **Little Task**[7] 1760 7-9-11 99 oh1 PAspell(3) 67
(J S Wainwright) *in rr: hit 3rd: hdwy 8th: wknd appr 3 out* **25/1**

140- **7** *27* **Lazy But Lively (IRE)**[246] 3934 9-11-6 122 KJMercer(3) 63
(R F Fisher) *in rr: reminders 9th: lost pl after next: sn bhd* **8/1**

06-0 **P** **No Picnic (IRE)**[156] 441 7-10-8 110 ONelmes(3) —
(Mrs S C Bradburne) *chsd ldrs: reminders 7th: lost pl 10th: bhd whn p.u bef next* **14/1**

05-P **P** **Majed (FR)**[174] 150 9-11-7 125 DFlavin(5) —
(Mrs L B Normile) *w ldrs: reminders and dropped bk 7th: sn bk on level terms: lost pl 10th: sn t.o: p.u bef 2 out* **50/1**

6m 40.6s (24.20) **Going Correction** +1.175s/f (Heav) **9** Ran SP% **110.6**
Speed ratings: **108,107,105,104,101 97,88,—,—** CSF £39.99 CT £478.46 TOTE £3.40: £1.60, £3.20, £2.30; EX 40.20 Trifecta £135.60 Pool: £420.20 - 2.20 winning units.
Owner P J Hughes Developments Ltd **Bred** R Le Poder **Trained** Norton, Shropshire

FOCUS
A fair handicap in which stamina and fitness was at a premium and the penalised winner was value for at least three times the official margin.

NOTEBOOK
Jorobaden(FR), under his penalty, was stepping up in trip and got warm beforehand. Despite pulling in the early stages, he took it up hard on the steel two out and scored with any amount in hand. He will still be competitive even from his revised mark. *(op 9-4)*
Midnight Creek, who looked ungenuine when runner-up in banded company at Southwell two weeks earlier, seems happier over hurdles and finished clear second best. However, he is not one to have total faith in. *(tchd 12-1)*
Michaels Dream(IRE), who lacks size and scope, has been beaten in banded company on the level since Uttoxeter. *The ground had rather turned against him and he is not a certain stayer.* *(op 10-1)*
Darjeeling(IRE), a grand type of mare, travelled strongly on her first outing for her new stable but she became leg-weary late on. She will have another outing over hurdles in a mares-only race at Wincanton before she switches to fences. *(op 9-4)*
Lord Jack(IRE), a stone and a half below his chase mark, made the running, kept wide. He dropped out at the third last and will no doubt soon be seen back over fences. *(op 6-1)*

1845 BONUSPRINT.COM NOVICES' CHASE (16 fncs) 2m 4f (Mildmay)
2:45 (2:45) (Class 3) 4-Y-0+ **£10,114** (£3,112; £1,556; £778)

Form RPR
133- **1** **Star De Mohaison (FR)**[193] 4826 4-10-5 RWalsh 132+
(P F Nicholls) *trckd ldrs: led 10th: qcknd and wnt 8l clr last: styd on strly: v comf* **11/4**[2]

110- **2** *13* **Supreme Serenade (IRE)**[221] 4397 6-10-12 RJohnson 128+
(P J Hobbs) *stdd s: trckd ldrs 7th: hit 10th: wnt handy 2nd whn mstke 13th: wknd between last 2* **15/8**[1]

441- **3** *6* **Ardaghey (IRE)**[263] 3647 6-11-5 CLlewellyn 129+
(N A Twiston-Davies) *chsd ldr: led 4th: hung rt bnd after 8th: hdd 10th: one pce fr 2 out* **3/1**[3]

3- **4** *14* **Show Me The River**[174] 160 6-11-5 BHarding 115+
(Ferdy Murphy) *hld up: mstke 3rd: wnt prom 9th: outpcd 13th: wknd next* **25/1**

P **Nykel (FR)**[154] 4-10-13 RThornton —
(A King) *led to 4th: hit next: lost pl 12th: bhd whn p.u bef 3 out* **7/1**

0112 **P** **Mocharamor (IRE)**[32] 1511 7-11-10 110 GLee —
(J J Lambe, Ire) *in tch: outpcd 11th: bhd whn p.u bef 3 out* **16/1**

5m 18.3s (9.40) **Going Correction** +0.725s/f (Soft)
WFA 4 from 6yo+ 14lb **6** Ran SP% **108.7**
Speed ratings: **110,104,102,96,— —** CSF £8.13 TOTE £3.60: £1.70, £1.60; EX 9.10.
Owner Sir Robert Ogden **Bred** J Veau **Trained** Ditcheat, Somerset

FOCUS
A good-class novices' chase run in a slightly slower time than Impek's handicap half an hour later. The winner looks a very useful prospect, while the runner-up and third will both improve and make their mark.

NOTEBOOK
Star De Mohaison(FR) ◆, who looks every inch an old fashioned three-mile chaser, shot clear going to the final fence and scored in most impressive fashion. He looks a smart recruit and his four-year-old allowance should help him win more decent races. *(op 5-2 tchd 9-4 and 11-4 in places)*
Supreme Serenade(IRE), rated 9lb better than the winner over hurdles, went in pursuit of that rival but was left for dead between the last two. Suited by a flat track although the majority of her wins have been going right-handed, she has her quirks but her class alone will surely enable her to make her mark. *(op 7-4 tchd 9-4)*
Ardaghey(IRE), a winning pointer, looked very fit. He was totally outpaced over the last two but, *better suited by three miles, will surely make his mark against lesser opponents.* *(op 7-2 tchd 4-1 in a place)*
Show Me The River, faced with a stiff task on his chasing debut, looks basically a stayer and he should make his mark in an ordinary three-mile novice chases. *(op 20-1)*
Nykel(FR), a dual winner over fences in France, had two handlers in the paddock and looks an exciteable type. He tended to jump right in the early stages and, dropping right out at the last down the back, this was hardly an auspicious start to his career here. *(tchd 8-1)*

1846 BONUSPRINT.COM OLD ROAN CHASE (A LIMITED H'CAP) GRADE 2 (16 fncs) 2m 4f (Mildmay)
3:20 (3:20) (Class 1) 5-Y-0+
£29,000 (£11,000; £5,500; £2,500; £1,250; £750)

Form RPR
2-22 **1** **Impek (FR)**[29] 1550 9-10-7 140 TJMurphy 152+
(Miss H C Knight) *mde all: wnt clr between last 2: styd on strly: eased nr fin* **4/1**[3]

521- **2** *2 ½* **My Will (FR)**[186] 4925 5-11-1 148 RWalsh 157+
(P F Nicholls) *trckd ldrs: mstke 10th: drvn along 13th: styd on to go 2nd appr last: no imp* **5/2**[1]

51F- **3** *11* **Supreme Prince (IRE)**[220] 4410 8-10-13 146 RJohnson 147+
(P J Hobbs) *w wnr: chal 3 out: wknd appr last* **10/3**[2]

220- **4** *7* **Supreme Developer (IRE)**[222] 4382 8-10-1 137 oh8 KJMercer(3) 127
(Ferdy Murphy) *in rr: sme hdwy 13th: styd on fr last* **12/1**

225- **5** *5* **Le Roi Miguel (FR)**[183] 4983 7-11-10 157 RThornton 145+
(P F Nicholls) *in tch: hit 9th: rdn and wknd 13th* **8/1**

254- **6** *22* **Alam (USA)**[13] 4453 6-10-4 137 oh12 KRenwick 100
(P Monteith) *in rr: bhd whn hit 11th: t.o 3 out* **100/1**

B0-0 **P** **Europa**[11] 1721 9-10-4 137 oh6 JMMaguire —
(Ferdy Murphy) *in rr: t.o whn p.u bef 3 out* **25/1**

PP4- **U** **Seebald (GER)**[183] 4983 10-11-3 150 TScudamore —
(M C Pipe) *chsd ldrs: disputing 3rd whn blnd bdly and uns rdr 12th* **17/2**

/6P- **P** **Valley Henry (IRE)**[220] 4408 10-9-13 139 RLucey-Butler(7) —
(R Gurney) *prom to 5th: lost pl 8th: t.o 11th: p.u after 13th* **25/1**

5m 15.6s (6.70) **Going Correction** +0.725s/f (Soft) **9** Ran SP% **109.7**
Speed ratings: **115,114,109,106,104 96,—,—,—** CSF £13.71 CT £32.42 TOTE £4.80: £1.30, £1.60, £1.50; EX 14.50 Trifecta £40.10 Pool: £779.68 - 13.80 winning units.
Owner Jim Lewis **Bred** Marc Trinquet & Bernard Trinquet **Trained** West Lockinge, Oxon

FOCUS
A decent limited handicap run in the sort of winning time one would expect for a race of its stature. The first three should continue to give a good account of themselves at this level.

NOTEBOOK
Impek(FR), hitherto regarded as best going right-handed, was given a peach of a ride. Attacking his fences and enjoying the new tactics, he went away between the last two to record his first handicap success over fences. *(tchd 9-2)*
My Will(FR), a second-season novice, went in pursuit of the winner but was never going to finish *anything but second best. In time he will be even better suited by three miles.* *(op 9-4 tchd 11-4 in places)*
Supreme Prince(IRE), at his best on flat tracks, looked a real threat when moving upsides three out but he seemed to blow up between the last two. He will improve for the outing but is now 4lb better than his last handicap success. *(op 4-1 tchd 3-1)*
Supreme Developer(IRE), 8lb out of the handicap, appreciates flat tracks and deserves credit for *the way he knuckled down late in the day. He will surely find easier opportunities.* *(op 14-1 tchd 16-1)*
Le Roi Miguel(FR), who faced a stiff task under his big weight, found the ground had turned *against him and his chance had gone at the cross fence. He will do better before much longer.* *(op 6-1)*
Alam(USA), considered badly handicapped, was racing from 12lb out of the handicap and was never on terms. *(op 66-1)*
Seebald(GER), who appeared very fit indeed, looked to be just starting to struggle on ground *plenty testing enough for him when he gave his rider no chance at the last in the back straight.* *(op 8-1 tchd 9-1)*

1847 BONUSPRINT EUROPEAN BREEDERS FUND "NATIONAL HUNT" NOVICES' HURDLE (11 hdls) 2m 4f

3:55 (3:56) (Class 3) 4-6-Y-0 **£6,825** (£2,100; £1,050; £525)

Form RPR

11 **1** **Jeremy Cuddle Duck (IRE)**[15] [1672] 4-11-4 .... CLlewellyn 125+
(N A Twiston-Davies) *trckd ldrs: rdn to ld appr 3 out: narrowly hdd 2 out: styd on grimly to ld towards fin* **11/4**[2]

11U- **2** *hd* **Karanja**[221] [4399] 6-10-12 .... AThornton 120+
(V R A Dartnall) *led in s: trckd ldrs: led and hit 2 out: j.lft last: hdd towards fin* **6/5**[1]

3-34 **3** *dist* **Double Gem (IRE)**[157] [418] 6-10-12 104 .... GLee 84
(J I A Charlton) *trckd ldrs: led 5th tl appr 3 out: wknd 2 out: btn 36l* **11/1**

31- **4** *5* **Regal Heights (IRE)**[187] [4922] 4-10-12 .... JMMaguire 79
(D McCain) *chsd ldrs: drvn along 8th: lost pl appr next: sn bhd* **20/1**

-4 **5** *12* **Highland Chief (IRE)**[182] [7] 5-10-12 .... TJMurphy 67
(Miss H C Knight) *led to 5th: wknd 3 out: sn bhd* **20/1**

-00F **P** **Lady Spur (IRE)**[21] [1619] 6-10-5 .... ARoss —
(J S Wainwright) *last: detached fr 7th: t.o whn p.u bef 3 out* **200/1**

213- **F** **Ain't That A Shame (IRE)**[246] [3960] 5-10-12 .... RWalsh 115+
(P F Nicholls) *t.k.h: in tch: smooth hdwy to trck 1st 2 3 out: swtchd lft between last 2: 2l 3rd and btn whn fell last* **9/2**[3]

5m 24.4s (20.70) **Going Correction** +1.175s/f (Heav) **7** Ran SP% **108.7**
Speed ratings: **105,104,—,—,—** —,— CSF £5.96 TOTE £3.30: £1.80, £1.40; EX 7.00.
Owner Trevor Hemmings **Bred** C Kenneally **Trained** Naunton, Gloucs
■ Stewards' Enquiry : A Thornton caution: used whip with excessive force

FOCUS
Just a steady pace and in effect a sprint over the final three flights, but the first two and the faller look decent prospects.

NOTEBOOK
Jeremy Cuddle Duck(IRE), under his penalty, proved very game and dug deep to put his head in front where it really matters. He looks basically a stayer. *(tchd 3-1 and 10-3 in places)*
Karanja, out of luck when losing his unbeaten bumper record in the Festival bumper at Cheltenham, was brought into the paddock very early and became very edgy and warm. Very fit, he was led in at the start and, after fluffing the last two flights, in the end despite a forceful ride he just missed out. A much stronger pace will see him in a different light, but he has yet to prove he will be as good over hurdles. *(op 5-4)*
Double Gem(IRE), asbent since May, looked in need of the outing and he tired badly over the last two flights. He needs his sights setting a lot lower.
Regal Heights(IRE), winner of a bumper at Towcester in April, was thrown in at the deep end on his hurdling debut and he was simply not up to the task. *(op 16-1)*
Highland Chief(IRE), fourth in an Irish point, looks much more of a long-term chasing prospect. *(op 16-1)*
Ain't That A Shame(IRE), a very narrow individual, showed decent form in three bumpers. He raced with the choke out but, after looking a real threat, he was held when taking a soft fall at the last. The potential is there but he will need to drop his bit. *(tchd 5-1)*

1848 DOUBLEPRINT H'CAP CHASE (FOR THE JOHN PARRETT MEMORIAL TROPHY) (19 fncs) 3m 1f (Mildmay)

4:30 (4:31) (Class 4) (0-110,105) 5-Y-0+ **£6,293** (£2,045; £1,101)

Form RPR

/F-2 **1** **Chabrimal Minster**[163] [333] 8-11-9 **102** .... GLee 121+
(R Ford) *trckd ldrs: lft 2nd 5th: blnd 15th: 13l clr whn blnd and lft virtually alone 2 out: heavily eased run-in: won by 40l* **6/4**[1]

PP2- **2** *dist* **Jardin De Beaulieu (FR)**[196] [4800] 8-11-12 **105** .... RJohnson 89
(Ian Williams) *hled up in tch: hit 11th: outpcd and hit 15th: 12l 3rd whn lft remote 2nd 2 out* **4/1**[2]

P/P- **3** *dist* **The Tall Guy (IRE)**[528] [320] 9-11-9 **102** .... CLlewellyn —
(N A Twiston-Davies) *led to 11th: wknd14th: poor 4th whn p.u after 16th: eventually wnt on to complete in distant 3rd* **9/2**[3]

144- **F** **Briar's Mist (IRE)**[191] [4850] 8-11-1 **94** .... RMcGrath —
(C Grant) *chsd ldrs: 2nd whn fell 5th* **11/2**

-650 **B** **Tribal Dancer (IRE)**[10] [1728] 11-10-12 **91** .... AO'Keeffe —
(Miss Venetia Williams) *prom: 3rd whn b.d 5th* **7/1**

F25P **F** **Good Man Again (IRE)**[3] [1803] 7-11-6 **99** .... (b) JMMaguire 96
(A Sadik) *nt fluent: in tch: mstke and wnt 2nd 14th: 13l 2nd whn fell 2 out* **25/1**

7m 5.30s (34.90) **Going Correction** +0.725s/f (Soft) **6** Ran SP% **109.9**
Speed ratings: **73,—,—,—,—** — CSF £7.80 TOTE £2.20: £1.30, £2.50; EX 6.00.
Owner B Mills, C Roberts, M & M Burrows **Bred** A Eubank **Trained** Cotebrook, Cheshire

FOCUS
A very pedestrian winning time, even in these conditions. Plenty of carnage but a wide-margin well-treated winner who has the potential to go on to better things.

NOTEBOOK
Chabrimal Minster, potentially well treated on his handicap debut, made more than one serious jumping error but was in third gear when left virtually alone two out. Even from his revised mark he will still be of interest. *(op 13-8 tchd 7-4)*
Jardin De Beaulieu(FR), possibly best when able to dominate in small fields, was out with the washing when handed second spot. *(tchd 5-1)*
The Tall Guy(IRE), who is well named, stopped in a matter of strides on his first outing for a year and a half. With third place going begging, he was eventually asked to complete. *(tchd 4-1)*
Good Man Again(IRE), with the blinkers on, was having his second outing in three days and was booked for a distant second when crashing out. *(op 20-1)*

1849 BONUSPRINT.COM STANDARD OPEN NATIONAL HUNT FLAT RACE 2m 1f

5:05 (5:07) (Class 6) 4-6-Y-0 **£3,546** (£1,091; £545; £272)

Form RPR

1 **Spartacus Bay (IRE)** 4-10-13 .... LTreadwell[(5)] 114+
(Miss Venetia Williams) *prom: hdwy to ld 4f out: styd on wl fnl f* **14/1**

2 *6* **Rothbury** 5-11-1 .... MichalKohl[(3)] 108
(J I A Charlton) *hld up in mid-div: hdwy 7f out: styd on to chse wnr 3f out: no imp* **50/1**

3 *1 ¼* **Aztec Warrior (IRE)** 4-11-4 .... TJMurphy 106+
(Miss H C Knight) *hdwy to chse ldrs 7f out: edgd lft and one pce over 1f out* **7/1**

4 *6* **Sobers (IRE)** 4-11-4 .... HOliver 100
(R C Guest) *hld up in rr: hdwy on outer to chse ldrs 7f out: outpcd over 3f out: styd on fnl 2f* **20/1**

1 **5** *1 ¼* **Balamory Dan (IRE)**[31] [1532] 4-11-6 .... WKennedy[(5)] 106
(G A Harker) *hld up towards rr: outpcd and drvn along over 5f out: styd on fnl 2f* **9/2**[1]

3 **6** *15* **Persian Prince (IRE)**[31] [1532] 5-11-1 .... PAspell[(3)] 84
(J Wade) *led: sn 30l clr: hdd 4f out: wknd over 2f out* **33/1**

7 *4* **Gunship (IRE)** 4-11-4 .... RJohnson 80
(P J Hobbs) *trckd ldrs: outpcd over 3f out: sn wknd* **5/1**[2]

8 *7* **Royal Attraction** 4-11-4 .... ATinkler 73
(W M Brisbourne) *hld up towards rr: hdwy 6f out: rdn and outpcd 4f out: sn wknd* **66/1**

10-P **9** *6* **Dreams Jewel**[168] [235] 5-11-11 .... AThornton 74
(C Roberts) *racd wd: hdwy to chse ldrs 7f out: wknd 4f out* **50/1**

10 *3* **Finsbury Fred (IRE)** 4-11-4 .... CLlewellyn 64
(N A Twiston-Davies) *chsd clr ldrs: lost pl over 3f out* **6/1**[3]

0- **11** *2* **Nile Moon (IRE)**[204] [4697] 4-11-4 .... GLee 62
(J Howard Johnson) *trckd ldrs: rdn over 3f out: sn btn* **7/1**

12 *8* **Dream On Maggie** 5-10-11 .... RThornton 47
(P Bowen) *mid-div: rdn and lost pl 5f out* **20/1**

4 **13** *2 ½* **Constantius**[59] [1323] 4-11-4 .... TScudamore 52
(K C Bailey) *hld up in rr: bhd fnl 4f* **13/2**

14 *½* **Young Rocky (IRE)** 4-11-4 .... RMcGrath 51
(C Grant) *rr-div: n.m.r and lost pl bnd after 6f: t.o 6f out* **33/1**

15 *dist* **The Knockinocker** 4-10-11 .... PMerrigan[(7)] —
(W M Brisbourne) *trckd ldrs: hmpd and lost bnd after 6f: sn bhd: t.o fnl 6f: btn 37l* **33/1**

4m 29.6s (12.00)
WFA 4 from 5yo 13lb **15** Ran SP% **117.9**
CSF £589.31 TOTE £17.30: £4.40, £15.10, £2.90; EX 831.80 Place 6 £56.53, Place 5 £15.17.
Owner You Can Be Sure **Bred** M Doran **Trained** Kings Caple, H'fords
■ Stewards' Enquiry : C Llewellyn one-day ban: careless riding (Nov 3)

FOCUS
A decent bumper and a promising winner in the four-year-old Spartacus Bay. The first four were newcomers and there was a healthy gap to the sixth.

NOTEBOOK
Spartacus Bay(IRE), who stands over plenty of ground, kept up the gallop in relentless fashion and looks a fair prospect. *(op 12-1)*
Rothbury, from the family of Idas Delight who did this stable proud, kept on to secure second spot and should improve and go one better. *(op 33-1)*
Aztec Warrior(IRE), one of the better types in the paddock, ran a pleasing first race but he basically looks a long-term chasing prospect. *(tchd 8-1)*
Sobers(IRE), a bit wild in the paddock, unseated his rider and charged about. Settled off the pace, he stuck on in his own time and this will hopefully have put him on the right path.
Balamory Dan(IRE), under his penalty, was very edgy in the paddock. He kept on after being outpaced and will need careful handling. *(op 4-1)*
Persian Prince(IRE) poached a long lead but was readily cut down to size.
Finsbury Fred(IRE), a danger to all in the paddock, looked very much on the backward side but this first outing will hopefully not be lost on him. *(tchd 11-2)*
T/Jkpt: £10,926.10 to a £1 stake. Pool: £30,778.00. 2.00 winning tickets. T/Plt: £148.90 to a £1 stake. Pool: £69,502.05. 340.70 winning tickets. T/Qpdt: £35.70 to a £1 stake. Pool: £3,479.70. 72.00 winning tickets. WG

[1642] TOWCESTER (R-H)

Sunday, October 23

OFFICIAL GOING: Good
Wind: Moderate, half-against

1850 LADBROKESPOKER.COM MARES' ONLY NOVICES' HURDLE (DIV I) (8 hdls) 2m

2:05 (2:05) (Class 3) 4-Y-0+ **£4,459** (£1,372; £686; £343)

Form RPR

4-11 **1** **Refinement (IRE)**[11] [1714] 6-11-4 .... APMcCoy 117+
(Jonjo O'Neill) *led 2nd: mde most after drew clr bef hit 2 out: eased run-in* **8/11**[1]

223- **2** *10* **Sweet Oona (FR)**[210] [4583] 6-10-12 98 .... SThomas 93+
(Miss Venetia Williams) *mid-div: hdwy appr 4th: wnt 2nd appr 2 out: kpt on but no ch w wnr* **3/1**[2]

440- **3** *2* **Bonnet's Pieces**[221] [4403] 6-10-12 89 .... AntonyEvans 90+
(Mrs P Sly) *led to 2nd: led again briefly 4th: rdn and wknd appr 2 out* **16/1**

232- **4** *6* **Retro's Girl (IRE)**[209] [4608] 4-10-2 .... (t) JKington[(10)] 86+
(M Scudamore) *trckd ldrs tl mstke 5th: nvr on terms after* **14/1**[3]

252- **5** *3* **Purple Patch**[229] [4238] 7-10-5 88 .... CMStudd[(7)] 81+
(C L Popham) *trckd ldrs tl wknd after 5th* **20/1**

31P- **6** *9* **Hot Lips Page (FR)**[189] [4883] 4-11-4 100 .... PMoloney 77
(Ian Williams) *mid-div tl wknd 5th* **16/1**

560- **7** *5* **Varuni (IRE)**[12] [4364] 4-10-5 69 ow3 .... TBurrows[(10)] 69
(P L Clinton) *mid-div: bhd after 4th* **125/1**

8 *26* **Secret Jewel (FR)**[345] 5-10-9 .... ACCoyle[(3)] 40
(Miss C J E Caroe) *a bhd* **100/1**

0/ **9** *17* **Ellie Moss**[960] [4060] 7-10-7 .... StephenJCraine[(5)] 23
(A W Carroll) *mid-div: tl wknd appr 5th* **66/1**

F **Tanmeya**[487] 4-10-9 .... LMcGrath[(3)] —
(R C Guest) *t.k.h: wl bhd whn fell 5th* **50/1**

00- **P** **Izzy Gets Busy (IRE)**[224] [4349] 5-10-12 .... (b[1]) JGoldstein —
(G F Bridgwater) *sn bhd: t.o whn p.u bef 5th* **100/1**

3m 53.9s (-17.50) **Going Correction** -1.025s/f (Hard)
WFA 4 from 5yo+ 13lb **11** Ran SP% **112.3**
Speed ratings: **102,97,96,93,91 87,84,71,63,—** — CSF £2.68 TOTE £1.50: £1.02, £1.80, £3.70; EX 2.90.
Owner M Tabor **Bred** M Tabor **Trained** Cheltenham, Gloucs

FOCUS
The stronger of the two divisions and a markedly faster winning time. The winner can be rated value for further and looks sure to rate much higher in this division.

NOTEBOOK
Refinement(IRE) ◆, who sweated profusely when only narrowly landing the odds on her recent hurdling debut at Uttoxeter, showed her true colours and followed up with a facile success under her penalty. She looked better suited to racing on the pace this time, put in a much more accomplished round of jumping and can be rated value for even further. Given that her useful dam won over three miles, it is little surprise that she looked more at home on this stiffer track, and it is likely that she now needs further to be seen at her best. A bold bid for the hat-trick can now be expected. *(op 8-13 tchd 4-5 in places)*
Sweet Oona(FR), well backed to trouble the favourite, emerged as the clear danger to that rival on the turn for home, but ultimately failed to sustain her effort and was firmly put in her place. She should improve for this comeback effort and certainly has a similar race within her compass this term. *(op 4-1)*
Bonnet's Pieces paid for trying to go with the winner when that rival asserted approaching the final bend, but kept to her task under pressure and ran close to her mark in defeat. She is another who can improve for the outing and clearly likes this venue. *(op 18-1)*

1851 LADBROKESPOKER.COM MARES' ONLY NOVICES' HURDLE (DIV II) (8 hdls) 2m

2:35 (2:35) (Class 3) 4-Y-0+ £4,459 (£1,372; £686; £343)

Form RPR

55-2 1 **Emmasflora**[21] [1611] 7-10-5 107 APogson(7) 103+
(C T Pogson) *mde all: rdn fr 3 out: pushed out run-in* **3/1**[2]

032 2 4 **Martovic (IRE)**[15] [1671] 6-10-12 JPMcNamara 98
(K C Bailey) *a in tch: strly rdn fr 3 out: styd on to go 2nd appr last: no imp on wnr run-in* **5/2**[1]

3 3 1/2 **Elegant Eskimo**[155] 6-10-12 TDoyle 95
(S E H Sherwood) *trckd wnr: rdn fr 3 out: no ex and lost 2nd appr last* **6/1**

P0 4 1 3/4 **Pips Assertive Way**[7] [1750] 4-10-7 StephenJCraine(5) 95+
(A W Carroll) *t.k.h: trckd ldrs: rdn 3 out: one pce after* **20/1**

21U- 5 6 **Gordon Highlander**[189] [4884] 6-11-4 100 (t) JAMcCarthy 93
(Mrs P Robeson) *in tch: rdn appr 5th: no hdwy after* **9/2**[3]

6-5 6 9 **Lets Get Busy (IRE)**[152] [487] 5-10-9 RYoung(3) 78
(J W Mullins) *mid-div: wknd after 5th* **9/1**

0-40 7 9 **Moorlands Milly**[15] [1680] 4-10-5 AScholes(7) 69
(D Burchell) *bhd whn mstke 3rd: no ch whn mstke last* **25/1**

8 11 **Silverpro**[311] 4-10-5 RCummings(7) 58
(D J Wintle) *a wl bhd* **50/1**

0- 9 8 **Just Filly (IRE)**[399] [1437] 4-10-9 ACCoyle(3) 50
(Miss C J E Caroe) *a bhd* **66/1**

0 10 3 **Orions Eclipse**[20] [655] 4-10-6 ow1 MrMatthewSmith(7) 48
(M J Gingell) *bhd tl sme hadway appr 4th: sn btn* **100/1**

3m 56.2s (-15.20) **Going Correction** -1.025s/f (Hard)
WFA 4 from 5yo+ 13lb **10** Ran SP% **109.1**
Speed ratings: **97,95,93,92,89 84,80,74,70,69** CSF £9.91 TOTE £2.80: £1.20, £1.30, £1.80; EX 7.10.

Owner C T Pogson **Bred** Mrs J D Goodfellow **Trained** Farnsfield, Notts

FOCUS
This was weaker than the first divsion, and the form is modest, but the winner did the job nicely.

NOTEBOOK
Emmasflora confirmed the promise of her recent debut for her current yard and made all in gutsy fashion to get off the mark at the fifth attempt. She clearly appreciated the stiff test over this trip, indeed she did more than enough to suggest she can improve again over further, and the good ground looked in her favour. Further success appears likely in this division and she may reportedly even go chasing before the season is out. *(op 11-4)*
Martovic(IRE) lacked a change of pace when it mattered and always looked like playing second fiddle to the winner. She is a decent yardstick for this form, was nicely clear of the rest in second, but the drop in trip clearly proved against her. *(op 2-1)*
Elegant Eskimo , a clear-cut winner of a point in May, turned in a respectable hurdling debut yet was found out by the stiff finish. She is entitled to improve for the experience and will no doubt be going chasing in due course. *(op 11-2 tchd 13-2, 7-1 in places)*
Pips Assertive Way paid for running too freely through the early parts, as she had done on her previous outing, but still turned in an improved effort all the same. She now qualifies for handicaps, and her shrewd stable may be able to place her to advantage in the future, providing she learns how to settle better. *(op 16-1)*
Gordon Highlander was popular in the betting ring on this return from a 189-day break, but ran as though the race was very much needed and never threatened. *(op 13-2 tchd 7-1)*

1852 LADBROKESPOKER.COM NOVICES' H'CAP CHASE (12 fncs) 2m 110y

3:10 (3:10) (Class 4) (0-105,96) 4-Y-0+ £4,153 (£1,278; £639; £319)

Form RPR

6603 1 **Donovan (NZ)**[15] [1673] 6-11-1 88 (p) LMcGrath(3) 99+
(R C Guest) *hld up: hdwy to trck ldr 6th: rdn appr 3 out: led last: drvn out run-in* **9/4**[1]

000- 2 1 1/4 **Lord On The Run (IRE)**[285] [3312] 6-11-9 96 RYoung(3) 109+
(J W Mullins) *set gd pce: rdn whn blnd 2 out: hdd last: no ex run-in* **6/1**

3511 3 6 **Pure Brief (IRE)**[76] [1176] 8-11-6 90 (p) PMoloney 93
(J Mackie) *in tch fr 4th: rdn appr 2 out: one pce appr last* **7/2**[2]

-P00 4 5 **Avadi (IRE)**[21] [1620] 7-10-12 82 TDoyle 81+
(P T Dalton) *prom tl wknd after 8th* **10/1**

0P-6 5 28 **Cusp**[176] [122] 5-11-7 91 JPMcNamara 81+
(Mrs A M Thorpe) *bhd tl hdwy 8th: sn rdn: wknd 3 out* **10/1**

-P5F P **Tumbleweed Glen (IRE)**[18] [1644] 9-9-12 71 oh13 ow1 (b) LVickers(3) —
(P Kelsall) *a bhd: t.o whn p.u bef 2 out* **33/1**

5PU1 P **Erins Lass (IRE)**[57] [1343] 8-11-4 88 SThomas —
(R Dickin) *mstke 3rd: lost tch after next: t.o whn p.u bef 2 out* **11/2**[3]

536- U **Tianyi (IRE)**[473] [900] 9-10-4 77 (v) TJMalone(3) —
(M Scudamore) *trcke leder to 6th: wkng whn blnd and uns rdr 3 out* **11/1**

4m 13.5s (-5.80) **Going Correction** -0.825s/f (Firm) **8** Ran SP% **112.1**
Speed ratings: **80,79,76,74,61** —,—,— CSF £15.80 CT £44.43 TOTE £3.70: £1.40, £1.90, £1.70; EX 23.20.

Owner Concertina Racing Too **Bred** B C Morton **Trained** Brancepeth, Co Durham

FOCUS
A very slow winning time and the field finished strung out. The form should be treated with a degree of caution.

NOTEBOOK
Donovan(NZ) , well backed, opened his account over fences at the third attempt yet has to rate a fortunate winner, as the runner-up would have probably scored but for making a hash of the penultimate fence. He could well build on this now, however, as he is rated much higher over hurdles than he is over fences and should still appear fairly treated in this sphere despite a future weight rise. *(op 3-1 tchd 2-1)*
Lord On The Run(IRE) ◆ , making his chasing debut for new connections after a 285-day break, looked set to make all prior to a crucial error two out and has to rate as unlucky. The recent change of stable looks to have had a positive effect, he did well to concede 8lb to the eventual winner prior to his blunder two out and, on this evidence, chasing looks set to be the making of him. *(op 8-1 tchd 9-1)*
Pure Brief(IRE) , bidding for a hat-trick on this return from a 76-day break, was found wanting from two out and finished very tired. The combination of this stiff track and a 7lb higher mark ultimately found him out, but he may well do better with this race under his belt back on a sharper track. *(tchd 4-1)*
Avadi(IRE) was firmly put in his place and merely kept on at the same pace in the straight. This was more encouraging than his recent efforts, however. *(op 12-1)*
Erins Lass(IRE) ran as though something was amiss on this first outing since winning in August from a 9lb lower mark and is capable of better than this when on song. *(op 4-1)*

1853 LADBROKES.COM H'CAP CHASE (16 fncs) 2m 6f

3:40 (3:40) (Class 3) (0-120,120) 5-Y-0+ £5,512 (£1,696; £848; £424)

Form RPR

F1P- 1 **Naunton Brook**[345] [2174] 6-11-8 116 AntonyEvans 130+
(N A Twiston-Davies) *mde all: clr 6th: unchal* **4/1**[2]

612- 2 5 **Early Start**[204] [4694] 7-11-4 115 RYoung(3) 122
(J W Mullins) *in tch: hdwy 9th: rdn to go 2nd appr 2 out: tired and jst hld on for 2nd run-in* **7/2**[1]

210- 3 nk **Kelantan**[229] [4239] 8-10-13 107 JPMcNamara 114
(K C Bailey) *trckd wnr tl rdn and lost 2nd appr 2 out: rallied run-in* **9/1**

U2-3 4 dist **Blunham Hill (IRE)**[182] [12] 7-10-2 96 JGoldstein —
(John R Upson) *in tch to 9th: wl bhd whn j. bdly lft 3 out: t.o* **4/1**[2]

251- F **Charlies Future**[210] [4586] 7-11-4 112 APMcCoy —
(S C Burrough) *mstke 1st: hld up: fell 8th* **5/1**[3]

1606 R **Green Prospect (FR)**[19] [1630] 5-11-5 120 SWalsh(7) —
(M J McGrath) *in rr whn rn out and uns rdr appr 4th* **50/1**

/F1- U **Latimer's Place**[342] [2245] 9-11-12 120 MBradburne 119+
(J A Geake) *trckd ldrs: mstke 9th: hit 11th: hld in 4th whn blnd and uns rdr 2 out* **4/1**[2]

5m 40.8s (-25.20) **Going Correction** -0.825s/f (Firm) **7** Ran SP% **110.8**
Speed ratings: **112,110,110,—,—** —,— CSF £17.64 CT £110.65 TOTE £3.90: £2.90, £2.00; EX 21.80.

Owner David Langdon **Bred** C W And Mrs Moore **Trained** Naunton, Gloucs

FOCUS
A decent winning time for a race of its class and the first three came well clear. The form looks solid.

NOTEBOOK
Naunton Brook ◆ , last seen pulling up lame at Newcastle 345 days previously, was given fine ride from the front by Evans and comfortably made all to resume winning ways. He will get further and it is most unlikely that we have seen the best of him over fences so far. *(op 11-4)*
Early Start ◆ , a fine second in the EBF Mares' Final at Newbury when last seen 204 days previously, shaped well enough on this chase bow and looked in need of the outing. It is interesting that she started life over the bigger obstacles in handicap company, but she will no doubt improve for this, and is one to keep on the right side of when racing against her own sex once again. *(op 3-1)*
Kelantan , progressive over fences last year, gave his all in defeat on this seasonal return and did more than enough to suggest he can find another race when reverting to further in due course. *(op 10-1)*
Blunham Hill(IRE) , a previous course-and-distance winner, never seriously threatened yet should do better as he gets more races under his belt this season. *(op 6-1)*
Latimer's Place was treading water prior to unshipping Bradburne two out. This was the second consecutive year he has failed to complete on his seasonal bow.

1854 LADBROKESCASINO.COM NOVICES' HURDLE (12 hdls) 3m

4:15 (4:15) (Class 4) 4-Y-0+ £3,493 (£1,075; £537; £268)

Form RPR

1 **Ballyfitz**[546] 5-10-12 AntonyEvans 110
(N A Twiston-Davies) *mid-div: hdwy 6th: led 9th: styd on wl fr 2 out* **11/1**

1321 2 2 1/2 **Mr Mischief**[26] [1571] 5-11-10 118 APMcCoy 119
(P C Haslam) *t.k.h: hld up: hdwy to trck ldr appr 8th: ev ch 2 out: no imp on resolute wnr after* **8/11**[1]

565- 3 26 **Strolling Vagabond (IRE)**[210] [4582] 6-10-12 68 JGoldstein 81
(John R Upson) *in tch: rdn appr 8th: kpt on past btn horses after* **25/1**

5/2- 4 1 **Albert House (IRE)**[383] [1598] 7-10-12 JPMcNamara 80
(R H Alner) *in tch: hit 6th: wnt 3rd 9th: wknd after 3 out* **9/1**[3]

00-0 5 17 **Hidden Storm (IRE)**[21] [1611] 6-10-5 DCrosse 56
(Mrs S J Humphrey) *trckd ldr tl appr 8th: sn wknd* **66/1**

0-5 6 29 **Chapel Bay**[17] [1660] 5-10-2 TJMalone(3) 27
(Mrs H Dalton) *a bhd: lost tch 7th* **14/1**

5 7 hd **Aitchjayem**[19] [1635] 5-10-5 MrJAJenkins(7) 34
(H J Manners) *trckd ldrs: wknd appr 7th* **50/1**

PP0 F **Thorny Issue**[7] [1757] 6-10-6 ow1 MrMatthewSmith(7) —
(M J Gingell) *bhd whn fell 8th* **100/1**

U20/ P **Montemoss (IRE)**[585] [4398] 8-10-5 SWalsh(7) —
(B N Pollock) *bahind whn bdly hmpd 8th: p.u bef next* **16/1**

0225 P **Explosive Fox (IRE)**[31] [1522] 4-11-3 105 (b) TDoyle —
(C P Morlock) *led: clr 2nd: hit 6th: wkng whn hdd 8th: t.o whn p.u bef 3 out* **7/1**[2]

6m 4.10s (-26.90) **Going Correction** -1.025s/f (Hard)
WFA 4 from 5yo+ 15lb **10** Ran SP% **109.6**
Speed ratings: **103,102,93,93,87 77,77,—,—,—** CSF £18.61 TOTE £10.20: £2.20, £1.10, £4.60; EX 23.00.

Owner F J Mills & W Mills **Bred** Helshaw Grange Farms Ltd **Trained** Naunton, Gloucs

FOCUS
No stength in depth to this novice event and the first two came well clear.

NOTEBOOK
Ballyfitz , who failed to make much of an impact in two Irish points previously, advertised his stable's excellent current form and got off the mark at the first time of asking for new connections. As a half-brother to winning staying hurdler Cresswell Gold, he could have been expected to relish a test of stamina, and so it proved, as he looked better the further he went on this stiffest of tracks. He should improve for the experience and, while his future clearly lies back over fences, further progression as a hurdler cannot be ruled out. *(tchd 10-1)*
Mr Mischief , reverting to novice company after resuming winning ways in a handicap last time, spoilt his chances of seeing out this first attempt at three miles by pulling too hard through the early stages. This proved his vulnerablility under a double penalty in this division now the season has kicked into top gear, but he really is a likeable sort, and has yet to finish out of the frame in eight outings over hurdles. He is worth another chance over this trip. *(tchd 4-6, 4-5 in places)*
Strolling Vagabond(IRE) , returning from a 210-day break, was ridden from halfway and merely kept on at the same pace throughout.
Albert House(IRE) , third on his chasing bow when last seen 383 days previously, looked much in need of the outing on this return to hurdling. He will most likely improve for the run, however, and it should not be that long before he tackles the larger obstacles once again.

1855 LADBROKESCASINO.COM H'CAP CHASE (14 fncs) 2m 3f 110y

4:50 (4:51) (Class 4) (0-105,105) 5-Y-0+ £3,809 (£1,172; £586; £293)

Form RPR

U-53 1 **Runaway Bishop (USA)**[11] [1713] 10-10-1 87 APogson(7) 100+
(J R Cornwall) *a in tch: chal 2 out: swtchd lft u.p run-in: styd on to ld gng away* **7/2**[1]

0/6U 2 3 **Blitzy Boy (IRE)**[1] [1825] 11-10-13 92 TDoyle 100
(G T Lynch, Ire) *hld up: hdwy 8th: j.lft and led 2 out: hrd ridden and j.lft again last: no ex and hdd run-in* **11/1**

54-4 3 10 **Bob The Builder**[19] [1631] 6-11-8 101 AntonyEvans 101+
(N A Twiston-Davies) *bhd tl hdwy to go 2nd 7th: ev ch 2 out: wknd appr last* **4/1**[2]

15-6 4 8 **Kappelhoff (IRE)**[151] [503] 8-10-0 79 oh8 (v) MBatchelor 69
(Mrs L Richards) *mid-div whn bdly hmpd 7th: styd on past btn horses fr 2 out* **25/1**

06PP 5 1 1/2 **Auditor**[18] [1646] 6-9-12 82 ow3 (b) MNicolls(5) 73+
(S T Lewis) *trckd ldrs: led 3rd: rdn and tiring whn hmpd and hdd 2 out: wknd* **50/1**

35P/ **6** *10* **Prairie Minstrel (USA)**[553] 4889 11-10-12 **91** SThomas 70
(R Dickin) *trckd ldr to 7th: wknd 10th* **25/1**

0-P3 **F** **Barton Hill**[21] 1620 8-11-3 **103** (b) DJacob[(7)] —
(D P Keane) *mid-div whn fell 7th* **9/2**[3]

0-66 **P** **Ready To Rumble (NZ)**[15] 1673 8-10-3 **85** (p) TJMalone[(3)] —
(R C Guest) *a bhd: p.u bef 9th* **12/1**

004- **P** **Lucky Luk (FR)**[217] 4483 6-10-3 **82** JAMcCarthy —
(K C Bailey) *mstke 3rd: p.u bef next* **12/1**

04P5 **U** **Flahive's First**[7] 1754 11-11-1 **101** MrRhysHughes[(7)] —
(D Burchell) *hmpd and uns rdr 7th* **20/1**

5560 **F** **Greenacres Boy**[11] 1713 10-9-9 **79** oh24 (b) StephenJCraine[(5)] —
(M Mullineaux) *bhd whn fell 6th* **66/1**

5004 **P** **Oulton Broad**[49] 1405 9-11-7 **105** (p) JDiment[(5)] —
(F Jordan) *trckd ldrs: blnd 8th: wknd appr 2 out: p.u bef last* **16/1**

2P6- **P** **Jongleur Collonges (FR)**[226] 4312 8-11-6 **99** JPMcNamara —
(R H Alner) *led to 3rd: styd prom tl wknd appr 3 out: p.u bef next* **9/2**[3]

5m 17.2s (-1.00) **Going Correction** -0.825s/f (Firm) **13** Ran SP% **124.1**
Speed ratings: **69,67,63,60,60 56,—,—,—,— —,—,—** CSF £40.58 CT £166.97 TOTE £4.50: £2.00, £3.40, £2.30; EX 78.50.
Owner J R Cornwall **Bred** Live Oak Stud **Trained** Long Clawson, Leics

FOCUS
A pedestrian winning time and the first two came clear on the run-in. The form is moderate.

NOTEBOOK
Runaway Bishop(USA) put his best foot forward approaching two out before staying on dourly to collar the runner-up on the flat to win this going away. He was well-backed for this, it was his third success from six outings at this venue over fences and, while he has struggled off higher marks in the past, should go close if found a suitable opportunity under a penalty. *(op 9-2)*

Blitzy Boy(IRE), who unseated at the first fence at Aintree just 24 hours previously, crept into contention to lead two from home and looked likely to score on jumping the final fence, but could offer no more when challenged by the eventual winner up the stiff finish. He is not easy to win with, but has to rate as slightly unfortunate, as he gave his all in defeat and was well clear of the rest. *(op 12-1)*

Bob The Builder, who jumped markedly left on his recent chasing bow at Huntingdon, jumped neatly this time and proved he does not necessarily need to go the other way around. However, after looking the most likely winner approaching the turn for home, he found nothing when asked for his effort and was ultimately well beaten. He may need further, but is becoming a little frustrating to follow now. *(tchd 9-2 in places)*

Kappelhoff(IRE), 8lb out of the handicap, was doing his best work when the race was all but finished and was not totally disgraced on this return from a 151-day break.

Auditor predictably paid for his exertions at the head of affairs from two out, but still ran one of his better races in defeat and at least completed this time. *(op 40-1)*

Barton Hill *(op 6-1)*

1856 LADBROKES.COM AMATEUR RIDERS' H'CAP HURDLE (8 hdls) 2m

5:20 (5:20) (Class 4) (0-100,97) 4-Y-0+ **£3,477** (£1,070; £535; £267)

Form RPR

545- **1** **The Hairy Lemon**[210] 4587 5-10-13 **91** MrGTumelty[(7)] 104+
(A King) *trckd ldrs: led appr 2 out: drew clr run-in* **7/4**[1]

440- **2** *7* **Deo Gratias (POL)**[399] 1444 5-10-9 **85** MrJETudor[(5)] 86
(M Pitman) *a in tch: wnt 2nd 2 out: nt pce of wnr run-in* **11/2**[2]

2U20 **3** *1 ½* **End Of An Error**[3] 1793 6-10-12 **90** MrsEJSmith[(7)] 90+
(A W Carroll) *slowly away and wl in rr tl styd on wl fr 3 out: nvr nrr* **20/1**

23-4 **4** *nk* **Rojabaa**[17] 1653 6-10-11 **85** MrJSnowden[(3)] 85+
(W G M Turner) *trckd ldrs: rdn 3 out: kpt on one pce after* **16/1**

2255 **5** *1 ¼* **Fiddles Music**[17] 1658 4-11-1 **93** MrRhysHughes[(7)] 91
(D Burchell) *mid-div: rapid hdwy on outside appr 2 out: one pce after* **16/1**

55-U **6** *nk* **Businessmoney Jake**[11] 1717 4-11-10 **95** MrNHarris 93
(V R A Dartnall) *mstke 1st: prom tl wknd 3 out* **10/1**

-500 **7** *3* **Reflex Blue**[3] 1793 8-10-5 **83** (v) MrMPrice[(7)] 78
(R J Price) *bhd tl mde sme late hdwy* **33/1**

/43- **8** *2 ½* **Road King (IRE)**[497] 731 11-10-7 **85** MrRBirkett[(7)] 77
(Miss J Feilden) *in tch tl outpcd 5th* **66/1**

4020 **9** *1 ¼* **Saorsie**[11] 1717 7-11-12 **97** MrDHDunsdon 89+
(J C Fox) *mid-div: rdn 5th: no hdwy after* **10/1**

302 **10** *1 ½* **Golly (IRE)**[56] 1372 9-11-6 **96** CaptLHorner[(5)] 85
(D L Williams) *in tch tl rdn and wknd 3 out* **25/1**

431 **11** *1 ¼* **Young Tot (IRE)**[18] 1645 7-10-13 **91** MrLRPayter[(7)] 79
(M Sheppard) *w ldr: led 4th: rdn and hdd appr 2 out: wknd rapidly* **6/1**[3]

-42U **12** *¾* **Upright Ima**[157] 429 6-10-2 **80** MissLAllan[(7)] 67
(Mrs P Sly) *hdwy appr 4th: wknd 3 out* **16/1**

/500 **13** *2 ½* **Sarn**[3] 1793 6-10-5 **83** MissMMullineaux[(7)] 68
(M Mullineaux) *a bhd* **33/1**

PP/P **14** *¾* **Meticulous (USA)**[6] 1773 7-10-8 **86** RCummings[(7)] 70
(K J Burke) *virtually ref to r: a bhd* **66/1**

4400 **15** *2* **Hylia**[31] 1525 6-10-10 **88** (tp) MrSPJones[(7)] 70
(Mrs P Robeson) *led to 4th: rdn and wknd 3 out* **20/1**

336- **16** *3 ½* **Foxmeade Dancer**[184] 4962 7-10-8 **86** MrRQuinn[(7)] 65
(P C Ritchens) *mid-div tl wknd 5th* **20/1**

U00/ **P** **Lunardi (IRE)**[590] 4306 7-10-11 **89** MissZoeLilly[(7)] —
(D L Williams) *a bhd: t.o whn p.u bef last* **50/1**

4P45 **P** **Hermitage Court (USA)**[49] 1408 4-11-6 **96** MrSWaley-Cohen[(5)] —
(M J McGrath) *prom tl wknd 5th: t.o whn p.u bef last* **50/1**

3m 54.9s (-16.50) **Going Correction** -1.025s/f (Hard) **18** Ran SP% **132.8**
WFA 4 from 5yo+ 13lb
Speed ratings: **100,96,95,95,94 94,93,92,91,90 90,89,88,88,87 85,—,—** CSF £11.05 CT £164.33 TOTE £2.80: £1.20, £1.90, £5.70, £2.80; EX 34.30 Place 6 £5.70, Place 5 £5.05.
Owner The Hairy Lemon Partnership **Bred** Houston Mill Stud **Trained** Barbury Castle, Wilts

FOCUS
A moderate handicap for amateur riders', run at a sound pace and the form looks fair. The winner could rate higher.

NOTEBOOK
The Hairy Lemon, returning from a 210-day break and making his debut for new connections, ran out a most decisive winner and landed a gamble in the process. He was given a straightforward ride by his capable amateur rider and, considering his only previous success came over further, it was little surprise that he relished the stiff track over this distance. Although a hike in the weights is now inevitable, he is still only five and could have more to offer this season. *(op 9-4 after early 5-2 in places and 11-4 in a place)*

Deo Gratias(POL), although not holding any chance with the winner, was doing all of his best work at the finish and ran his best race to date over timber on this handicap bow. He is entitled to improve for this first outing for 399 days and, while his stable remains in decent form, could build on this now and go one better from this mark. *(op 9-2)*

End Of An Error was not at all helped by losing ground at the start and then having to come wide with her challenge in the home straight, so deserves credit for getting as close as she did at the finish. She ideally needs further, and is on a fair mark at present, but is on a long losing run and has never been one to trust. *(op 33-1)*

Rojabaa ran close to his mark in defeat and can get closer in this grade when reverting to a sharper track. *(op 14-1)*

Businessmoney Jake, who unseated when well supported on his handicap bow last time, at least completed this time and probably needs further to be seen at his best.

Young Tot(IRE), raised 6lb for winning over course and distance 18 days previously, dropped out quickly from two out and disappointed. *(op 5-1)*

T/Plt: £4.60 to a £1 stake. Pool: £42,540.15. 6,709.40 winning tickets. T/Qpdt: £3.90 to a £1 stake. Pool: £2,280.60. 430.50 winning tickets. JS

1648 WINCANTON (R-H)

Sunday, October 23

OFFICIAL GOING: Good
Wind: Virtually nil.

1857 FIREWORKS HERE 5TH NOVEMBER "NATIONAL HUNT" NOVICES' HURDLE (8 hdls) 2m

1:50 (1:52) (Class 3) 4-Y-0+ **£4,777** (£1,470; £735; £367)

Form RPR

1 **Russian Around (IRE)** 4-10-12 LAspell 104+
(N J Gifford) *hld up in tch: rdn to chal appr last: hmpd sn after last: swtchd lft: r.o strly to ld cl home* **12/1**[3]

2 *nk* **Missyl (FR)**[231] 5-10-12 RWalford 100
(R H Alner) *trckd ldrs: rdn appr 2 out: led sn after last: no ex whn ct cl home* **40/1**

16- **3** *1 ¼* **Noland**[197] 4774 4-10-12 ChristianWilliams 99+
(P F Nicholls) *j.lft thrght: hld up: shkn up and hdwy to chse ldrs appr 2 out: rdn and j.lft last: kpt on same pce* **1/1**[1]

15-2 **4** *½* **Pak Jack (FR)**[173] 175 5-10-12 PJBrennan 99+
(P J Hobbs) *hld up: hit 5th: hdwy next to trck ldr: rdn appr 2 out: ev ch last: no ex* **11/8**[2]

056- **5** *hd* **Dearson (IRE)**[226] 4316 4-10-12 NFehily 99+
(C J Mann) *led: rdn appr last: drifted lft and hdd sn after last: kpt on same pce* **33/1**

6 **6** *dist* **Come To The Bar (IRE)**[168] 236 6-10-12 JTizzard —
(W W Dennis) *w ldr: j.lft 3rd and 4th: grad lost tch* **25/1**

056 **7** *1* **Its A Classic**[17] 1660 4-10-12 JMogford —
(Mrs N S Evans) *in tch tl wknd after 3 out* **200/1**

0-P0 **8** *1 ½* **Wizzical Lad**[28] 1565 5-10-5 (p) TMessenger[(7)] —
(B N Pollock) *chsd ldrs: rdn appr 2 out: sn wknd* **200/1**

3m 46.6s (-2.50) **Going Correction** -0.35s/f (Good) **8** Ran SP% **110.0**
Speed ratings: **92,91,91,90,90 —,—,—** CSF £248.39 TOTE £14.30: £2.30, £4.00, £1.10; EX 142.30.
Owner R F Eliot **Bred** Paul Marsh **Trained** Findon, W Sussex
■ Stewards' Enquiry : N Fehily three-day ban: dropped hands and lost fourth place (Nov 3-5)

FOCUS
A muddling novice hurdle given the pace was steady for much of the way, and the form is suspect. However, there were some nice types among them and this race should produce winners.

NOTEBOOK
Russian Around(IRE) ◆, the second foal of a maiden Irish pointer, created a very good impression on his racecourse debut. He still had it all to do jumping the last, and was nearly brought down when hampered on landing, but he recovered well and showed a decent turf of foot when switched to the inside on the run-in. With the first five home so close tougher, it is hard to know what to make of the form, but he is highly regarded by connections and could develop into a very useful sort. *(op 13-2)*

Missyl(FR), pulled up in two three-mile point-to-points, ran surprisingly well on his debut under Rules and was just denied. Although the bare form cannot be taken too literally, this was a good effort considering he is probably likely to do better with both time and distance. *(op 25-1)*

Noland, an impressive winner in a course bumper on his debut before running sixth in a good race at Aintree, ran nowhere near that level of form off the back of a 197-day break on his first run over obstacles. He tended to jump quite big and will need to improve in that department if he is to fulfill his potential over hurdles. *(op 8-11 tchd 5-4)*

Pak Jack(FR), a promising second on his return to hurdling at Ludlow when last seen 231 days previously, ran below that level of form and did not appear suited by the way the race was run. This was disappointing, but he can be given another chance. *(op 9-4 tchd 5-4)*

Dearson(IRE), having just his second start over hurdles off the back of a 226-day break, ran a big race under a positive ride and this was a much-improved performance, even if he was allowed to dictate a steady pace for much of the way. *(op 25-1)*

1858 STAN JAMES NOVICES' H'CAP CHASE (21 fncs) 3m 1f 110y

2:20 (2:21) (Class 3) (0-110,110) 5-Y-0+ **£5,434** (£1,672; £836; £418)

Form RPR

1-P2 **1** **Lord Anner (IRE)**[5] 1780 6-10-8 **92** ChristianWilliams 109+
(P F Nicholls) *chsd ldrs: mstke 4th (water): jnd ldr 14th: led appr 3 out: blnd next: hdd last: led sn after: drvn out* **5/4**[1]

3131 **2** *½* **Ultimate Limit**[28] 1560 5-10-8 **94** LAspell 107+
(A Ennis) *hld up in tch: trckd ldng pair 14th: pressed wnr fr 3 out: rdn to ld last: hdd sn after: kpt on* **10/3**[2]

FP03 **3** *13* **He's The Biz (FR)**[15] 1678 6-11-3 **101** JTizzard 102
(Nick Williams) *hld up bhd: styd on fr 4 out: wnt 3rd appr 2 out: nvr trbld ldrs* **12/1**

2-61 **4** *8* **Castlemore (IRE)**[18] 1638 7-11-12 **110** PJBrennan 106+
(P J Hobbs) *chsd ldr: mstke 2nd: led 11th: rdn and hdd appr 3 out: grad wknd* **7/1**[3]

P55- **5** *14* **Alfa Sunrise**[234] 4142 8-10-7 **91** BHitchcott 70
(R H Buckler) *hld up in tch: hit 1st: rdn appr 15th: wknd 4 out* **14/1**

34-2 **P** **Five Alley (IRE)**[6] 1776 8-10-3 **87** (b) RGreene —
(R H Buckler) *j.big and slow: sn t.o: p.u bef 10th* **8/1**

P/30 **P** **Prince On The Ter**[15] 1678 10-10-0 **87** oh22 ow3 CBolger[(3)] —
(B Scriven) *led tl 11th: grad lost tch: t.o and p.u bef 3 out* **66/1**

6m 23.6s (-16.30) **Going Correction** -0.50s/f (Good) **7** Ran SP% **107.0**
WFA 5 from 6yo+ 2lb
Speed ratings: **105,104,100,98,94 —,—** CSF £5.27 TOTE £2.10: £1.40, £2.20; EX 6.20.
Owner The Stewart Family **Bred** Miss Josephine Fox **Trained** Ditcheat, Somerset
■ Stewards' Enquiry : Christian Williams caution: used whip in an incorrect place

FOCUS
Probably not a bad novices' handicap chase for the grade. The winner can rate higher and the third and fourth set the level for the form.

NOTEBOOK
Lord Anner(IRE) ◆ has the potential to be a lot better than his current mark suggests, so he could have been considered a touch disappointing not to have won on his handicap debut at Exeter, and he made hard enough work of this. However, he is unlikely to go up too much as a result and really should progress. *(op Evens)*

Ultimate Limit, 8lb higher than when winning at Huntingdon on his previous start, continued his progression with a fine effort in defeat behind a winner who is a potentially a fair bit better than his current mark suggests. *(op 9-2 tchd 3-1)*

He's The Biz(FR), just as at Chepstow on his previous start, stayed on all too late and never really threatened. *(op 16-1 tchd 11-1)*
Castlemore(IRE) showed up well for a long way but weakened quite tamely and was below the form he showed to win a beginners' chase at Exeter on his previous start. *(op 9-2)*
Alfa Sunrise did not offer a great deal off the back of a 234-day break. *(op 16-1)*

1859 VIXEN HORSEFEEDS NOVICES' HURDLE (11 hdls) 2m 6f

2:55 (2:57) (Class 4) 4-Y-O+ **£3,435** (£1,057; £528; £264)

Form RPR

1 **Denman (IRE)**[217] 5-10-11 ChristianWilliams 117+
(P F Nicholls) *t.k.h in tch: trckd ldrs 7th: led appr 2 out: hung lft run-in: styd on wl to assert cl home: rdn out* **5/6**[1]

0 2 1 ¼ **Lyes Green**[22] 1596 4-10-11 LAspell 112+
(O Sherwood) *hld up: hdwy to trck ldrs 7th: pressed wnr appr last: rdn and ev ch run-in: no ex fnl 75yds* **16/1**

3 14 **Alphabetical (IRE)**[189] 6-10-11 NFehily 98
(C J Mann) *hld up bhd: gd hdwy appr 7th: led on bit after 8th: hdd 2 out: sn rdn: wknd last* **4/1**[2]

0316 4 13 **Miss Merenda**[6] 1775 4-10-11 94 PJBrennan 86+
(J F Panvert) *trckd ldrs: jnd ldr 4th tl 8th: sn rdn: one pced fr 3 out* **11/2**[3]

06-0 5 23 **Gaining Ground (IRE)**[15] 1671 5-10-11 WHutchinson 62
(John R Upson) *in tch tl 3 out* **100/1**

6 6 ½ **Offalevel**[112] 893 7-10-4 JamesWhite(7) 62
(R J Hodges) *towards rr: hdwy 8th: rdn after 3 out: sn wknd* **33/1**

352 7 29 **Mister Zaffaran (IRE)**[17] 1657 6-10-11 (t) JMogford 33
(Mrs N S Evans) *chsd ldrs tl wknd after 8th* **12/1**

U P **Bon Accord**[6] 1775 5-10-11 BJCrowley —
(Miss E C Lavelle) *led tl 3rd: led 4th tl after 8th: rn wd on bnd after 3 out and sn p.u* **40/1**

4/PP P **Whispering John (IRE)**[5] 1779 9-10-1 100 (p) SHaddon(10) —
(W G M Turner) *prom: led 4th tl next: j. slowly 7th: sn lost tch: p.u bef 3 out* **25/1**

5m 12.8s (-12.30) **Going Correction** -0.35s/f (Good)
WFA 4 from 5yo+ 14lb **9** Ran SP% **113.7**
Speed ratings: **108,107,102,97,89 89,78,—,—** CSF £15.27 TOTE £1.70: £1.20, £2.50, £1.30; EX 18.20.
Owner Paul K Barber & Mrs M Findlay **Bred** Colman O'Flynn **Trained** Ditcheat, Somerset

FOCUS
Just an ordinary novice hurdle and not that much strength in depth. The fourth sets the standard and, with the placed horses looking capable of scoring in this grade, the winner can rate higher.

NOTEBOOK
Denman(IRE), successful in a three-mile point-to-point in Ireland 217 days previously, made a winning debut under Rules but did have to work quite hard having raced keenly for the most of the way. He was far from impressive, but really ought to have learnt a lot from this. *(op 8-11 tchd Evens)*
Lyes Green, not without promise on his hurdling debut at Fontwell, ensured the favourite and a proper race and pulled well clear of the remainder in the process. He clearly has the potential to make a fair hurdler. *(op 12-1)*
Alphabetical(IRE), successful in a three-mile point on heavy ground in Ireland 189 days previously, travelled noticeably well for much of the way on his debut under Rules (his rider had quite a few looks round to see where the favourite was), but did not find that much under pressure and gave the impression he needed this. *(op 11-2 tchd 6-1)*
Miss Merenda would be better off in handicap company. *(op 4-1)*
Mister Zaffaran(IRE) *Official explanation: jockey said gelding hung left-handed (op 16-1)*
Bon Accord *Official explanation: jockey said gelding hung badly left-handed (op 33-1 tchd 50-1)*

1860 ROBERT ALNER OWNERS AND FRIENDS H'CAP CHASE (13 fncs) 2m

3:30 (3:32) (Class 4) (0-110,110) 5-Y-O+ **£4,728** (£1,455; £727; £363)

Form RPR

-331 1 **L'Oiseau (FR)**[8] 1746 6-11-7 105 JTizzard 121+
(J G Portman) *j.w: in tch: trckd ldrs and travelling wl 4 out: led after 3 out: r.o wl: comf* **5/2**[1]

12-5 2 4 **Green Gamble**[168] 246 5-10-10 94 JamesDavies 101
(D B Feek) *w ldr: led after 4 out: sn rdn: hdd after 3 out: kpt on but a hld by wnr* **9/2**[3]

0/ 3 1 **Gorthnacurra (IRE)**[15] 1695 9-11-2 100 BFenton 106
(Patrick Morris, Ire) *trckd ldrs: led 5th tl after 4 out: sn rdn: kpt on same pce* **5/1**

3445 4 4 **Runner Bean**[59] 1320 11-11-3 101 PJBrennan 105+
(R Lee) *hld up but in tch: wnt 4th appr 4 out: sn rdn: no further imp fr 3 out* **3/1**[2]

3241 5 3 ½ **The Mighty Sparrow (IRE)**[104] 958 12-10-11 95 (p) MFoley 95+
(A E Jones) *led tl 5th: w ldr tl wknd appr 4 out* **9/1**

13-P 6 18 **Game On (IRE)**[29] 1553 9-11-5 110 TMessenger(7) 91
(B N Pollock) *chsd ldrs: mstke 2nd and 9th: sn wknd* **10/1**

0/06 7 dist **Just Different (IRE)**[35] 1479 8-10-11 95 LAspell —
(P G Murphy) *in tch tl 9th: sn t.o* **25/1**

3m 52.6s (-9.30) **Going Correction** -0.50s/f (Good) **7** Ran SP% **111.4**
Speed ratings: **103,101,100,98,96 87,—** CSF £13.65 CT £48.96 TOTE £2.60: £2.30, £2.90; EX 9.40.
Owner Milady Partnership **Bred** Jacques Cypres And Thierry Cypres **Trained** Compton, Berks

FOCUS
Not a bad race for the graden that should work out and L'Oiseau looks one to keep on the right side of.

NOTEBOOK
L'Oiseau(FR) ♦ has a decent record over fences and made it three wins from six starts over the larger obstacles with another smooth display, supplementing last week's Stratford win. Always well placed, he jumped fluently throughout and often made ground at his fences. There seems certain to be more to come and a hat-trick looks a distinct possibility. *(op 2-1)*
Green Gamble was entitled to need this first outing since May and he ran a good race considering, beating all bar the progressive winner. Still only five, he is open to further improvement and it would be no surprise to see him go in next time. *(op 8-1 tchd 17-2)*
Gorthnacurra(IRE), an Irish raider, was of obvious interest having won earlier in the month at Gowran Park, but he was unable to match the unexposed front pair. He will find easier opportunities. *(op 4-1)*
Runner Bean is slipping back down to a reasonable mark and a win may not be far off. *(op 7-2 tchd 4-1)*
The Mighty Sparrow(IRE), up 10lb for his Newton Abbot romp, had every chance but was simply unable to cope with the rise against some progressive types. *(op 15-2)*

1861 FIELDSPRING DESERT ORCHID SILVER CUP (A H'CAP CHASE) 3m 4f

4:05 (4:07) (Class 2) (0-140,140) 5-Y-O+
£18,374 (£6,969; £3,484; £1,584; £792; £475)

Form RPR

12-1 1 **I Hear Thunder (IRE)**[15] 1676 7-10-7 121 BHitchcott 128+
(R H Buckler) *hld up: tk clsr order 9th: trckd ldrs 12th: wnt 2nd after 17th: rdn to ld after 2 out: hrd pressed run-in: all out* **6/1**

0F0- 2 hd **Merchants Friend (IRE)**[183] 4984 10-11-1 129 (p) NFehily 137+
(C J Mann) *hld up: stdy prog fr 18th: wnt 4th appr 3 out: styd on u.p to chal last: ev ch run-in: kpt on* **15/2**

1F-5 3 2 ½ **Le Jaguar (FR)**[15] 1676 5-9-11 120 oh3 ow4 (t) LHeard(7) 124+
(P F Nicholls) *in tch: hdwy to chse ldrs 17th: pckd 4 out: sn rdn: cl 3rd whn hit 2 out: kpt on same pce* **9/1**

510- 4 5 **Gunther McBride (IRE)**[239] 4066 10-11-7 135 PJBrennan 138+
(P J Hobbs) *led: rdn after 3 out: hit next: sn hdd: kpt on same pce* **4/1**[2]

1-F2 5 24 **Tom Sayers (IRE)**[22] 1599 7-10-0 119 RStephens(5) 99+
(P J Hobbs) *chsd ldrs tl mstke 16th: wknd after 18th* **7/2**[1]

540- 6 1 ½ **Willie John Daly (IRE)**[220] 4411 8-11-2 130 LAspell 104
(P J Hobbs) *chsd ldrs tl wknd appr 4 out* **11/2**[3]

14P- 7 4 **Auburn Spirit**[203] 4710 10-10-0 114 WHutchinson 84
(M D I Usher) *w ldr tl 14th: bhd fr 17th* **40/1**

115- 8 6 **Patches (IRE)**[301] 2941 6-11-12 140 ChristianWilliams 110+
(P F Nicholls) *hld up: nt fluent 12th: mstke 18th and rdr lost iron briefly: sn wknd* **8/1**

050- P **Bounce Back (USA)**[301] 2977 9-10-9 123 RGreene —
(M C Pipe) *sn drvn along in rr: mstke 18th: sn lost tch: p.u bef last* **14/1**

6m 45.8s
WFA 5 from 6yo+ 2lb **9** Ran SP% **113.9**
CSF £49.27 CT £400.69 TOTE £5.40: £1.70, £2.50, £3.40; EX 54.90.
Owner Nick Elliott **Bred** D H Lalor **Trained** Melplash, Dorset

FOCUS
A good staying handicap chase that is likely to produce winners with the runner-up setting the standard.

NOTEBOOK
I Hear Thunder(IRE) has returned in cracking form this season and supplemented his Chepstow win with a gritty display. Evidently a progressive young stayer, he looks capable of defying another rise and connections have the Rehearsal Chase followed by the Welsh National as an intended route, should all go well in the former event. *(op 15-2 tchd 11-2)*
Merchants Friend(IRE) is proven as a useful stayer and he gives the form a solid look in finishing second. He came with a strong late challenge having been in rear early, but the winner was too determined and he could not get past. He has a similar race in him off this sort of mark. *(op 10-1)*
Le Jaguar(FR) ♦, who shaped as though the run was needed on his seasonal return at Chepstow, was again partnered by his impressive young pilot and he ran a smashing race for a five-year-old. He hugged the rail for most of the way and was still in with every chance as they turned for home, but after hitting the second last his fate was sealed. He looks to have a fair amount of improvement in him and can land a decent prize this season. *(op 10-1 tchd 11-1)*
Gunther McBride(IRE), whose sole outing last season came when finishing down the field in the Racing Post Chase, has clearly had his problems over the last year or so, but there was plenty of promise to be taken from this and it was only in the final quarter mile that he lack of race-fitness began to tell. He will no doubt benefit from this outing and could once again develop into a contender for some of the leading staying chases. *(op 6-1)*
Tom Sayers(IRE) went down fighting on his reappearance at Fontwell, but he performed well below that level and never really threatened to stake a claim. He is better than this, but now has a bit to prove. *(op 11-4)*
Willie John Daly(IRE) shaped as though this first outing of the season was needed and it is safe to assume improvement will be forthcoming. *(op 6-1 tchd 13-2)*
Auburn Spirit was out of his league. *(op 33-1)*
Patches(IRE) had not been seen since finishing down the field in the Feltham Novices' Chase at Kempton on Boxing Day and, although boasting an excellent record at this venue, he was always likely to need the run. He should be eased a little in the weights following this and has to be respected in future when getting his favoured sound surface. *(op 11-2)*
Bounce Back(USA), another appearing for the first time in 2005, did not look interested and made Greene work for his riding fee. *Official explanation: vet said gelding was found to have sustained a cut (op 12-1 tchd 16-1)*

1862 R M PENNY PLANT HIRE / DEMOLITION H'CAP HURDLE (8 hdls) 2m

4:40 (4:43) (Class 4) (0-110,110) 4-Y-O+ **£3,532** (£1,087; £543; £271)

Form RPR

16-3 1 **Nanga Parbat (FR)**[15] 1677 4-11-5 110 (t) LHeard(7) 118+
(P F Nicholls) *hld up towards rr: smooth hdwy after 3 out to trck ldrs: hung rt after 2 out: led last: r.o wl: readily* **5/1**[3]

-0U2 2 2 ½ **Pirandello (IRE)**[19] 1633 7-11-10 108 LAspell 111
(K C Bailey) *led: rdn and hdd 2 out: ev ch last: kpt on but nt pce of wnr* **4/1**[1]

5613 3 1 ½ **Nesnaas (USA)**[8] 1747 4-10-11 95 JEMoore 97
(M G Rimell) *trckd ldr: led 2 out: sn rdn: hdd last: no ex* **9/2**[2]

1F2 4 1 ¼ **Gold Guest**[17] 1653 6-10-11 95 (t) NFehily 97+
(P D Evans) *hmpd 1st: bhd: styd on fr 2 out u.p: wnt 4th cl home: nrst fin* **7/1**

0231 5 nk **Looks The Business (IRE)**[17] 1651 4-11-0 103 PCO'Neill(5) 103
(W G M Turner) *trckd ldr: jnd ldr 2 out: sn rdn: kpt on same pce* **9/1**

3223 6 1 **Sir Walter (IRE)**[57] 1335 12-10-9 98 LStephens(5) 97
(D Burchell) *hld up bhd: hmpd by loose horse after 2nd: rdn and hdwy 2 out : styd on: nvr trbld ldrs* **33/1**

05-4 7 shd **The Gene Genie**[5] 1784 10-10-3 94 JamesWhite(7) 93
(R J Hodges) *in tch: chsd ldrs appr 2 out: one pced after* **25/1**

1152 8 hd **Outside Investor (IRE)**[17] 1651 5-10-12 103 (p) KBurke(7) 102
(P R Rodford) *mid div: hdwy 5th: ev ch appr 2 out: sn rdn: one pced after* **33/1**

5-12 9 6 **Sunnyarjun**[149] 536 7-10-9 93 JMogford 86
(J C Tuck) *mid div: rdn and effrt after 3 out: wknd next* **25/1**

2-34 10 ½ **Buffalo Bill (IRE)**[15] 1668 9-11-7 105 BFenton 98
(A M Hales) *trckd ldrs: short lived effrt 2 out: sn btn* **20/1**

6P5- 11 2 **Maximinus**[189] 4885 5-10-13 97 ChristianWilliams 88
(M Madgwick) *mid div tl 3 out* **50/1**

3423 12 10 **Olimpo (FR)**[55] 1366 4-10-0 84 PJBrennan 70+
(P J Hobbs) *mid div tl wknd appr 2 out* **7/1**

34F3 13 9 **Samandara (FR)**[136] 693 5-11-2 100 WHutchinson 72
(A King) *mid div: dropped rr after 4th: wknd appr 2 out* **20/1**

10- F **Fame**[13] 2731 5-11-7 110 RStephens(5) —
(P J Hobbs) *fell 1st* **16/1**

3m 42.7s (-6.40) **Going Correction** -0.35s/f (Good)
WFA 4 from 5yo+ 13lb **14** Ran SP% **120.8**
Speed ratings: **102,100,100,99,99 98,98,98,95,95 94,89,84,—** CSF £23.54 CT £99.02 TOTE £5.00: £1.90, £2.60, £1.90; EX 31.40 Place 6 £17.66, Place 5 £10.20.
Owner Mrs Kathy Stuart **Bred** P Landois And Classic Breeding Sarl **Trained** Ditcheat, Somerset

FOCUS
An ordinary handicap hurdle, but Nanga Parbat did it well and looks capable of plying his trade at a higher level. Those immediately behind the first two were close to their marks and the form looks solid.

NOTEBOOK

Nanga Parbat(FR), as with many of his stable's runners this season, shaped as though the run was needed when third on his reappearance at Chepstow, but he was able to step up on that and, despite hanging away to the right under pressure, he won with quite a bit to spare. He is viewed as a good handicap hurdle prospect for this season and looks sure to make his mark at a higher level in time. *(op 4-1)*

Pirandello(IRE) has never been the most consistent, but he managed to confirm the promise of his Huntingdon second from earlier in the month. Time may show he faced a stiff task trying to give the winner 5lb and he will find easier opportunities, but he is never one you would feel comfortable taking a shaort price about. *(op 9-2)*

Nesnaas(USA), unable to defy an 8lb rise when only third at Stratford last week, was up another 2lb and he ran as well as could have been expected. He struggled to see out even two miles and will need to be kept to speed tracks like this and Huntingdon. *(op 5-1 tchd 11-2 and 4-1)*

Gold Guest could be called a little unlucky as he was soon trailing having been hampered at the first and by the time he found top stride the contest was all over. He is one to take from the race and it will be interesting to see how he gets on next time.

Looks The Business(IRE) had his chance and was unable to build on his course win from earlier in the month. *(op 16-1)*

Olimpo(FR) continues to frustrate and he never really threatened to play a part. *(op 8-1 tchd 9-1)*
T/Plt: £33.60 to a £1 stake. Pool: £37,929.95. 822.15 winning tickets. T/Qpdt: £16.40 to a £1 stake. Pool: £2,762.20. 124.10 winning tickets. TM

1863 - 1869a (Foreign Racing) - See Raceform Interactive

47 CHELTENHAM (Old Course) (L-H)

Tuesday, October 25

OFFICIAL GOING: Good (good to soft in places)

Wind: Strong ahead

1870 WATERLAW PROPERTY DEVELOPERS NOVICES' HURDLE (13 hdls) 3m 1f 110y

2:10 (2:12) (Class 3) 4-Y-0+

£5,080 (£1,927; £963; £438; £219; £131)

Form				RPR
-111	**1**		**Ostfanni (IRE)**[17] [1590] 5-10-13 114 GLee (M Todhunter) *mid-div and in tch: hit 7th: hdwy 4 out: chsd ldr 3 out: rdn next: chal last: sn led: drvn out* **5/1**[3]	117+
1	**2**	*2 1/2*	**Darasim (IRE)**[18] [1661] 7-11-3 (v) APMcCoy (Jonjo O'Neill) *lw: ld after 1st: kpt narrow advantage and drvn along after 7th: nt fluent last and sn hdd: no ex u.p* **7/2**[1]	119+
3213	**3**	*4*	**Killonemoonlight (IRE)**[13] [1711] 6-10-10 110 TDoyle (D R Stoddart) *in tch: hdwy to chse ldrs 4 out: rdn 3 out: styd on same pce fr next* **9/2**[2]	107
2	**4**	*4*	**Restart (IRE)**[23] [1608] 4-10-11 JPMcNamara (Lucinda Featherstone) *rr but in tch fr 6th: chsd ldrs 4 out: rdn out: one pce fr next: no ch w ldrs whn blnd last* **7/1**	107+
	5	*dist*	**Hardybuck (IRE)**[177] 4-10-11 CLlewellyn (N A Twiston-Davies) *w'like: str: bit bkwd: rr but in tch fr 6th: hit 7th: chal next: rdn and wknd after 4 out: t.o* **9/2**[2]	—
122-	**6**	*15*	**Pardini (USA)**[343] [2254] 6-10-12 PJBrennan (M F Harris) *chsd ldrs: hit 6th: rdn 8th and sn wknd: t.o* **33/1**	—
2	**P**		**Thyne Spirit (IRE)**[151] [532] 6-10-7 MNicolls[(5)] (S T Lewis) *chsd ldrs: wknd 5th: t.o whn p.u bef 4 out* **80/1**	—
1143	**P**		**Common Girl (IRE)**[13] [1722] 7-10-13 107 JEMoore (O Brennan) *rr but in touxh fr 6th: blnd 8th and p.u bef next* **14/1**	—
	P		**Another Ticket (IRE)**[55] [1388] 5-10-12 88 RThornton (Eoin Griffin, Ire) *chsd ldrs: hit 8th and sn wknd: p.u bef next* **40/1**	—
2-P1	**P**		**Swifts Hill (IRE)**[152] [509] 7-11-3 103 RJohnson (T R George) *lw: led tl after 1st: styd pressing ldr tl blnd 4 out: wknd and p.u bef next* **8/1**	—

6m 24.9s (-0.30) **Going Correction** +0.15s/f (Yiel)
WFA 4 from 5yo+ 15lb **10** Ran SP% **112.1**
Speed ratings: **106,105,104,102,— —,—,—,—,—** CSF £22.18 TOTE £5.60: £2.00, £1.90, £1.60; EX 16.40.
Owner Ian Hall Racing **Bred** Mrs Brigitte Schlueter **Trained** Orton, Cumbria

FOCUS

A tricky contest that was wide open, run at a fair pace with the third and fourth the best guides to the form, which appears solid enough.

NOTEBOOK

Ostfanni(IRE) has improved dramatically in recent months and, having won three races at minor tracks, she raised her game with a gallant victory over high-class Flat stayer Darasim. Having tracked him into the straight, it was clear she had him covered as they jumped the last and in the end she won a shade comfortably. It is clear this is her trip, but she will have to raise her game again when the better staying hurdlers start to appear. *(op 4-1)*

Darasim(IRE) made hard work of winning on his hurdling debut over an inadequate trip at Carlisle, but this distance was expected to suit a good deal better and McCoy was allowed to dominate. He dictated the pace and looked the likely winner rounding for home, but he began to idle a little under a pressure and the final hill proved too much for him. At this stage it will be most surprising if he manages to make up into a contender for either of the major staying novice hurdles at the Festival, but he can win more races and is likely to improve as he gains further experience. *(op 3-1 tchd 9-2)*

Killonemoonlight(IRE), behind the potentially smart The Cool Guy at Uttoxeter last time, was nibbled at in the market beforehand and ran with credit, staying on right the way to the line. Stamina is her strong suit and she should remain capable of winning a similar race. *(tchd 5-1)*

Restart(IRE), a moderate sort on the Flat, shaped with promise when second on his hurdling debut at Market Rasen and stepped up on that with a fine fourth. He will find easier oportunities and can win races. *(op 13-2)*

Hardybuck(IRE), runner-up in an Irish point over two and a half miles, came into this with his stable on fire and looked to have major claims, but having travelled strongly and made smooth headway to come through and challenge around a mile out, he stopped quickly and was allowed to coast home in his own time. Reportedly a bit backward in the paddock, it is possible he did not stay and it would not surprise to see him dropped to two and a half miles next time. He is worth another chance. *(op 5-1 tchd 4-1)*

Swifts Hill(IRE) seems to have developed a habit of pulling up every other start and he can simply not be relied up on. *Official explanation: jockey said gelding pulled up lame (op 10-1)*

1871 CHELTENHAM.CO.UK NOVICES' CHASE (12 fncs) 2m

2:45 (2:47) (Class 3) 4-Y-0+ **£7,660** (£2,930; £1,484; £696; £367)

Form				RPR
2212	**1**		**Flying Spirit (IRE)**[47] [650] 6-11-10 124 (b) JEMoore (G L Moore) *mde all: rdn 2 out: styd on gamely run-in* **14/1**	137
2P-2	**2**	*1 1/2*	**Bold Bishop (IRE)**[81] [1155] 8-11-4 APMcCoy (Jonjo O'Neill) *lw: trckd ldrs: wnt 2nd 3 out to next: sn chsng wnr again: chal last and gng wl: fnd no ex and nt go by run-in* **11/4**[2]	129
	3	*5*	**Le Volfoni (FR)**[123] [837] 4-10-5 ChristianWilliams (P F Nicholls) *neat: lw: blnd 1st:hld up rr: hit 2nd: hdwy 4 out: chsd wnr 3 out tl blnd next: rdn and sn no ch w ldrs* **1/1**[1]	114+
3-12	**4**	*5*	**One Cornetto (IRE)**[100] [1024] 6-11-10 132 LAspell (L Wells) *hld up in rr: hdwy 4 out: chsd ldrs next: wknd fr 2 out* **15/2**[3]	125
0U5-	**5**	*28*	**In Contrast (IRE)**[520] [480] 9-11-4 RJohnson (P J Hobbs) *hit 2nd: chsd ldrs: hit 7th and lost pl: hdwy 3 out: wknd next* **9/1**	104+
0406	**F**		**Milligan (FR)**[12] [1726] 10-11-1 111 TJPhelan[(3)] (Dr P Pritchard) *w wnr to 3 out: cl 4th but hld whn fell 2 out* **100/1**	106+
-245	**P**		**Kings Brook**[32] [1542] 5-11-4 110 PJBrennan (Nick Williams) *rr: nt fluent 3rd: hdwy and hit 8th: sn wknd: taild off whn p.u bef 3 out* **40/1**	—

4m 7.00s (7.70) **Going Correction** +0.25s/f (Yiel)
WFA 4 from 5yo+ 13lb **7** Ran SP% **108.5**
Speed ratings: **90,89,86,84,70 —,—** CSF £48.64 TOTE £10.00: £3.10, £1.60; EX 31.70.
Owner Richard Green (fine Paintings) **Bred** Sean Madigan **Trained** Woodingdean, E Sussex

FOCUS

A weak race for the grade and the time was moderate. The race is rated through the fourth but could be slightly too high.

NOTEBOOK

Flying Spirit(IRE) looked a most unlikely winner, having to give weight to all bar one, but he jumped well at the head of affairs and simply stayed on too determinely for the principals. Inferior to many of these over hurdles, he has yet to finish out the first two in five starts over fences and is the type to do well in handicaps. *(op 12-1 tchd 16-1)*

Bold Bishop(IRE) has never looked the heartiest of characters and, having come through to throw down a challenge to Flying Spirit with a fine jump at the last, he seemed to back out of the battle. He has plenty of ability and can win races over fences, but it is always worth bearing in mind that he does not relish a battle. *(tchd 5-2 and 3-1 in a place)*

Le Volfoni(FR), tried at the top level over fences in France, was rightly made favourite, getting all the allowances, but he made too many mistakes and was left trailing by the front two after a blundering at the tricky second last. He should really have done better as he was receiving so much weight from the front two, but is only four so may yet have more to offer. *(op 6-5 tchd 10-11 and 5-4 in a place)*

One Cornetto(IRE) has not really built on an impressive chase debut win in two subsequent starts and he was always struggling in rear. The penalty he picked up for winning was too much for him to handle and a drop in class may help. *(op 8-1 tchd 9-1)*

In Contrast(IRE) has not taken to fences and is a shadow of the horse that was third in the Supreme Novices' back in 2002. He made several jumping errors and it would not surprise to see him once again return to hurdles. *(op 7-1)*

1872 THWAITES SMOOTH BEER HURDLE (H'CAP) (10 hdls) 2m 5f

3:20 (3:20) (Class 2) (0-140,138) 4-Y-0+

£9,952 (£3,775; £1,887; £858; £429; £257)

Form				RPR
121-	**1**		**The Market Man (NZ)**[270] [3569] 5-10-13 **125** MFoley (N J Henderson) *hld up mid-div: stdy hdwy: nt fluent and bmpd 3 out: trckd ldr next: led sn after: pushed out run-in: readily* **9/2**[1]	137+
0-1P	**2**	*1 1/4*	**Fire Dragon (IRE)**[17] [1677] 4-11-0 **126** APMcCoy (Jonjo O'Neill) *lw: hld up in rr: stdy hdwy 3 out: drvn on to go 2nd sn after last: gng on cl home but no imp on wnr* **14/1**	133
1-10	**3**	*3*	**Goblet Of Fire (USA)**[31] [1548] 6-11-6 **132** (b) ChristianWilliams (P F Nicholls) *chsd ldrs: rdn 2 out: one pce appr last* **16/1**	136
-004	**4**	*1 1/2*	**Keepthedreamalive**[24] [1598] 7-10-10 **122** BHitchcott (R H Buckler) *chsd ldrs tl slt ld 4 out: hdd after 2 out: wknd run-in* **33/1**	125
43-2	**5**	*2 1/2*	**Shalako (USA)**[17] [1675] 7-10-11 **123** RJohnson (P J Hobbs) *lw: hdwy 4 out: styng on whn hit 3 out: kpt on run-in but nvr gng pce to rch ldrs* **9/2**[1]	124+
140-	**6**	*1*	**Mirjan (IRE)**[10] [439] 9-11-6 **135** (v) GBerridge[(3)] (L Lungo) *mid-div: hdwy 3 out: hung lft fr 2 out: brough to stands side run-in and kpt on but nvr rchd ldrs* **9/1**[3]	135+
45U1	**7**	*3 1/2*	**Mcbain (USA)**[23] [1617] 6-10-11 **128** RStephens[(5)] (P J Hobbs) *bhd: hdwy 3 out: styd on fr 2 out but nvr gng pce to rch ldrs* **16/1**	124
-020	**8**	*1 1/2*	**Penny Pictures (IRE)**[10] [1270] 6-11-2 **138** AGlassonbury[(10)] (M C Pipe) *bhd: hdwy and hit 3 out: styd on fr next but nvr gng pce to rch ldrs* **20/1**	132
241-	**9**	*1/2*	**Flying Enterprise (IRE)**[198] [4793] 5-11-2 **128** SThomas (Miss Venetia Williams) *lw: chsd ldrs: rdn 2 out: sn wknd* **10/1**	122
P32	**10**	*1 1/4*	**Phar From Frosty (IRE)**[44] [1455] 8-10-13 **125** RThornton (C R Egerton) *chsd ldrs: rdn 3 out: wknd next* **33/1**	117
5000	**11**	*1 1/2*	**Anatar (IRE)**[17] [1675] 7-10-5 **117** TScudamore (M C Pipe) *bhd: rdn and kpt on fr 2 out: n.d* **25/1**	108
6P23	**12**	*6*	**Openide**[97] [1036] 4-10-6 **118** (v[1]) PJBrennan (B W Duke) *bit bkwd: led: hrd drvn fr 6th: narrowly hdd 4 out: wknd fr next* **33/1**	104+
-020	**13**	*3*	**Spectrometer**[31] [1548] 8-11-7 **138** PCO'Neill[(5)] (Ian Williams) *chsd ldrs: rdn 3 out: wknd next* **33/1**	120
P/P-	**14**	*10*	**Chicuelo (FR)**[485] [828] 9-11-4 **130** ATinkler (N J Henderson) *lw: bhd: effrt 6th: sn wknd* **50/1**	102
/3P-	**15**	*4*	**Tacin (IRE)**[195] [4823] 8-10-2 **114** TJMurphy (B G Powell) *chsd ldrs: wnt 2nd and mstke 3 out: sn wknd* **7/1**[2]	84+
136-	**16**	*6*	**Aldiruos (IRE)**[228] [4314] 5-10-0 **112** oh5 WHutchinson (A W Carroll) *bit bkwd: bhd fr 3rd* **33/1**	74
FFF-	**P**		**Kadoun (FR)**[338] [2363] 6-10-3 **115** (t) MBradburne (H D Daly) *chsd ldrs to 5th: wknd 6th: t.o whn p.u bef 4 out* **12/1**	—

5m 12.0s (-1.60) **Going Correction** +0.15s/f (Yiel)
WFA 4 from 5yo+ 14lb **17** Ran SP% **119.4**
Speed ratings: **109,108,107,106,105 105,104,103,103,102 102,100,98,95,93 91,—** CSF £58.37 CT £937.43 TOTE £5.30: £2.20, £2.40, £2.90, £5.70; EX 89.40 Trifecta £671.80 Pool: £1,135.50 - 1.20 winning units.
Owner Sir Robert Ogden **Bred** Monovale Holdings Ltd **Trained** Upper Lambourn, Berks

FOCUS

As expected, this was a competitive handicap hurdle and The Market Man impressed immensely with his winning performance. The time was reasonable and the form looks solid rated through those just outside the placings.

NOTEBOOK

The Market Man(NZ) ◆, who looked fit enough despite the layoff, shaped like a potentially smart sort last season and this reappearance win was quite impressive. Always travelling strongly, his rider knew he had it in the bag as they turned for home and he was value for around double the winning margin. He looks to have bright future and is one to keep on the right side of. *(tchd 4-1)*

Fire Dragon(IRE) was able to leave behind his effort at Chepstow when slipping up and, having travelled strongly throughout, he pulled away from the third for a clear second. He is at his best on a genuinely fast surface and should remain a threat in similar races. *(op 12-1)*

Goblet Of Fire(USA) ran well back in third, but he often struggles when upped in grade and was once again found out by the hill. He is not the easiest to place and needs to improve to score off this sort of mark. *(op 14-1)*

Keepthedreamalive is not the most consistent, but he ran well for a long way and it was only in the final furlong and half that he cried enough. It will be interesting to see if he is now put over fences.
Shalako(USA) has performed quite well since reverting to hurdles and followed his Chepstow second with a keeping on fifth. He may well have been closer had he not given the third last a smack and he will remain of interest off this sort of mark. *(op 6-1)*
Mirjan(IRE) is a strong stayer on the Flat and he made a pleasing return to hurdles. Three miles will help, but he could probably do with a little help from the Handicapper. *(op 6-1)*
Mcbain(USA), 5lb higher than when winning at Uttoxeter, never got into the race having been held up and may have benefited from a more positive ride.
Anatar(IRE) is slipping back down the weights and is worth keeping an eye on in the coming weeks.
Tacin(IRE) has not been seen on the racecourse much due to being a fragile sort, but he has plenty of ability and was understandably fancied in the betting. However, he failed to run up to expectations and trailed in some way adrift. His stable's horses have not been running particularly well of late, so maybe he can be given another chance, but overall he does not have the profile of a horse worth following. *(op 8-1)*
Kadoun(FR) *Official explanation: trainer had no explanation for the poor form shown (op 11-1)*

1873 SCARVAGH HOUSE STUD PTA JUVENILE NOVICES' HURDLE (8 hdls) 2m 110y
3:55 (3:58) (Class 3) 3-Y-O

£5,057 (£1,918; £959; £436; £218; £130)

Form RPR

5 **1** **Barnbrook Empire (IRE)**[17] [1679] 3-10-5 OMcPhail 85
(B J Llewellyn) *hld up in rr: nt fluent 3 out: hdwy next: styd on appr last to ld last half f: drvn out* **33/1**

46 **2** 1½ **Inchcape Rock**[10] [1737] 3-10-12 VSlattery 91
(J G M O'Shea) *bhd: stl plenty to do 2 out: hdwy and hung lft appr last: continued to hang: kpt on run-in to take 2nd last stride: nt rch* **14/1**

3 *shd* **Legally Fast (USA)**[14] 3-10-12 RGreene 91
(S C Burrough) *lw: unf: bhd: hdwy fr 3 out: slt ld and hrd drvn last: hdd last half f: ct for 2nd last stride* **16/1**

212 **4** 1½ **Moonfleet (IRE)**[37] [1478] 3-10-13 (v) RJohnson 90
(M F Harris) *chsd ldrs early dropped rr 4th but in tch: rdn 2 out: styd on run-in: gng on cl home* **11/2**[3]

P01 **5** 1¾ **Kerry's Blade (IRE)**[23] [1601] 3-11-2 (p) APMcCoy 92+
(P C Haslam) *trckd ldrs: led gng wl 2 out: rdn sn after: narrowly hdd last: wknd nr fin* **6/1**

11 **6** 1¼ **Wembury Point (IRE)**[51] [1404] 3-11-6 GLee 94
(B G Powell) *led to 3rd: styd pressing ldrs: ev ch 2 out: wknd run-in* **9/2**[1]

F42 **7** 2 **Strathtay**[55] [1380] 3-10-5 (v) TJMurphy 80+
(M C Pipe) *w ldr 2nd: slt ld 3rd: rdn 3 out: hdd next: wknd run-in* **10/1**

30 **8** 7 **Maunby Reveller**[5] [1797] 3-10-12 FKeniry 77
(P C Haslam) *rdn after 4 out: nvr nr ldrs* **28/1**

2410 **9** 17 **Shingle Street (IRE)**[30] [1563] 3-11-2 102 (t) AO'Keeffe 64
(Miss Venetia Williams) *chsd ldrs: rdn 4 out: wknd 3 out: no ch whn hmpd 2 out* **8/1**

U **Ghabesh (USA)**[134] 3-10-12 ChristianWilliams —
(Evan Williams) *scope: mstke and uns rdr 1st* **16/1**

431 **S** **Trigger Guard**[24] [1594] 3-11-2 103 (b) PHide —
(G L Moore) *lw: chsng ldrs whn slipped up after 2nd* **5/1**[2]

2 **F** **Madam Caversfield**[5] [1802] 3-10-5 AntonyEvans 79+
(P D Evans) *lw: in tch: hdwy hdwy 3 out: half l down: disputing 2nd and gng wl whn fell 2 out* **10/1**

4m 9.20s (10.00) **Going Correction** +0.15s/f (Yiel) **12** Ran SP% **118.6**
Speed ratings: **82,81,81,80,79 79,78,74,66,— —,—** CSF £430.65 TOTE £37.60: £5.60, £4.90, £4.50; EX 653.00.
Owner Harry Barnbrook **Bred** S Connolly **Trained** Fochriw, Caerphilly

FOCUS
This looked a poor contest for Cheltenham, with the first two rated just 45 on the Flat, and a very modest early gallop resulted in a pedestrian winning time for the type of race, although the majority of the first six ran close to their marks. The slippery ground seemed to take its toll and was almost certainly responsible for the exits of Madam Caversfield and Trigger Guard.

NOTEBOOK
Barnbrook Empire(IRE), who showed limited promise on her hurdling debut, gained a dour and surprising victory after hitting the front up the hill, but she was rated just 45 on the Flat which rather demonstrates how poor this form is. Things will be very tough for her under a penalty. *(op 25-1)*
Inchcape Rock, who had shown a small amount of ability in two previous outings over hurdles, like the winner is rated just 45 on the level. He stayed on from well off the pace to snatch the runner-up spot but probably did not improve on his previous form over timber and will do very well to win an ordinary novice hurdle. *(op 20-1 tchd 25-1)*
Legally Fast(USA), minus the headgear he successfully wore on his last start on the Flat, had every chance on this hurdling debut but was found wanting for pace up the hill. Considering he was successful at up to 14 furlongs on the level and was rated a stone superior to the front pair, this race was probably not run to suit and, though the form is poor, he might turn out to be the best of these. *(op 25-1)*
Moonfleet(IRE), wearing a visor for the first time over hurdles though she was successful with it on the Flat, seemed to run in snatches due to the modest early pace and though her stamina came into play and she was not beaten far at the end, the form probably does not add up to much. Truly-run races back on the minor tracks are where her future lies. *(op 4-1 tchd 6-1)*
Kerry's Blade(IRE), a winner at Kelso last time, came there cruising at the second last but could not get clear of his field and had nothing left up the hill. He did not prove that he stayed any further than a mile on the level, so will probably always need a sharp track in order to see out this trip over hurdles. *(op 11-2)*
Wembury Point(IRE) took a keen hold early and raced up with the pace until after the last. Even in a race as moderate as this, his double-penalty proved too much of a burden. *(op 5-1 tchd 11-2)*
Madam Caversfield was one of several battling for the lead when losing her footing after jumping the second last. Winner of two sellers on the Flat this year, that level of ability suggests she would have gone very close in this had she stood up. *(tchd 9-2 and 11-2)*
Trigger Guard, with the blinkers retained following his Fontwell victory, seemed to jump the second flight perfectly well but lost his footing a few strides later and crashed to the ground. *(tchd 9-2 and 11-2)*

1874 WINNING POST AT CHELTENHAM H'CAP CHASE (FOR AMATEUR RIDERS) (19 fncs) 3m 110y
4:30 (4:31) (Class 4) (0-125,118) 5-Y-O+

£5,127 (£1,944; £972; £442; £221; £132)

Form RPR

6- **1** **Darby Wall (IRE)**[34] [1517] 7-11-12 118 MrJTMcNamara 125
(E Bolger, Ire) *hld up in rr: hit 9th: stdy hdwy 4 out: drvn to ld last: hdd cl home: rallied to ld again last strides* **7/1**

-230 **2** *nk* **Penthouse Minstrel**[132] [761] 11-10-10 105 (v) MrJSnowden[(3)] 112
(R J Hodges) *trckd ldrs: chal fr 13th tl led 15th: narrowly hdd last: rallied gamely to ld again cl home: ct last strides* **25/1**

2453 **3** 1½ **Luneray (FR)**[17] [1670] 6-11-5 111 (bt) MrCJSweeney 120+
(P F Nicholls) *lw: hld up in tch: hdwy to trck ldrs 4 out: disp cl 2nd and gng wl whn stmbld bdly 2 out: kpt on again run-in but nt rcvr* **4/1**[2]

1200 **4** 2 **Totheroadyouvgone**[34] [1515] 11-11-1 112 (p) MrSWaley-Cohen[(5)] 117+
(A E Jones) *hld up in rr: hit 8th: hdwy 4 out: chsng ldrs whn bmpd 3 out: styd on same pce after next* **12/1**

P03P **5** 1¾ **Happy Hussar (IRE)**[9] [1751] 12-10-0 92 DrPPritchard 96+
(Dr P Pritchard) *led 2nd 4th: styd pressing ldr tl dropped rr 4 out: plenty to do 2 out: rallied and r.o strly again run-in* **33/1**

F5-P **6** 4 **Scotch Corner (IRE)**[152] [516] 7-10-2 101 MrGTumelty[(7)] 100+
(N A Twiston-Davies) *bit bkwd: led to 2nd: led again 11th to 15th: drvn to chal 2 out: wknd sn after* **3/1**[1]

3012 **7** 9 **Koumba (FR)**[17] [1678] 7-11-3 109 MrNWilliams 98
(Evan Williams) *chsd ldrs hit 6th: rdn to chal 2 out: wknd after next* **6/1**[3]

614- **8** 12 **Hazeljack**[225] [4370] 10-10-0 99 MrDGreenway[(7)] 76
(A J Whiting) *led 4th to 11th: wknd 15th* **12/1**

2-11 **P** **Mr Splodge**[37] [1484] 11-11-1 112 MrJETudor[(5)] —
(Mrs T J Hill) *lw: bhd: hdwy 8th: chal 10th: wknd 14th: t.o whn p.u bef 3 out* **4/1**[2]

6m 24.6s (1.70) **Going Correction** +0.25s/f (Yiel) **9** Ran SP% **114.0**
Speed ratings: **107,106,106,105,105 103,101,97,—** CSF £137.27 CT £790.67 TOTE £8.60: £2.60, £3.00, £1.80; EX 148.40.
Owner Matthew Cahill **Bred** M Cahill **Trained** Bruree, Co Limerick

FOCUS
An ordinary contest run at just a fair pace, but an exciting finish with the lead changing hands a couple of times on the run-in. The form looks solid enough with the placed horses running to their marks.

NOTEBOOK
Darby Wall(IRE), who looked very fit, was given a peach of a ride by his pilot who has such a good record at this track. Held up for most of the way, he was delivered with perfect timing at the last but had to show battling qualities to get the better of the rallying runner-up. He may return here for a similar contest next month where he is sure to run a big race, especially if the partnership is maintained. *(tchd 8-1)*
Penthouse Minstrel, who has a good record here, had the visor back on for the first time this year. Always up with the pace, he managed to force his head back in front up the hill after being headed at the last, but could not withstand his younger rival for a second time. He is still 9lb above his highest winning chase mark and his only victory beyond two miles five under Rules came in a walkover.
Luneray(FR) was right in the thick of the action when ploughing the turf with her nose after jumping the second last. She did keep going afterwards though and did not appear to be beaten through lack of stamina on this occasion. *(op 11-2)*
Totheroadyouvgone, well beaten in the Galway Plate and Kerry National since his last outing in this country, could never quite land an effective blow despite not being beaten far. He might prefer an even greater test of stamina than this now, but is not getting any younger.
Happy Hussar(IRE), returning to fences after three outings over hurdles needs a greater test of stamina and after losing his place, was finishing in decent style. He seems to retain some ability, but his age is not in his favour.
Scotch Corner(IRE), up there for much of the way, dropped away over the last couple of furlongs and probably just needed it. *(op 11-4 tchd 7-2)*
Hazeljack looked fit despite the break. *(op 14-1)*
Mr Splodge showed up prominently for the first circuit, but after jumping the water for the second time he gradually dropped out. This was disappointing in view of his promising Plumpton effort and he is better than this. *Official explanation: vet said gelding finished lame (op 3-1)*

1875 CHELTENHAM BUSINESS CLUB MAIDEN HURDLE (8 hdls) 2m 110y
5:05 (5:07) (Class 3) 4-Y-0+

£5,289 (£2,006; £1,003; £456; £228; £136)

Form RPR

3 **1** **Motorway (IRE)**[33] [1527] 4-11-2 RJohnson 113+
(P J Hobbs) *chsd ldrs: rdn and one pce 2 out: str run appr last and r.o wl run-in to ld fnl 100yds: drvn out* **9/2**[2]

2 **2** ½ **Desert Quest (IRE)**[17] [1680] 5-11-2 ChristianWilliams 113+
(P F Nicholls) *hld up rr but in tch: hdwy fr 4 out: hung bdly lft appr last and mstke:drvn to ld sn after: hdd and one pce fnl 100yds* **8/11**[1]

2224 **3** 3½ **Don And Gerry (IRE)**[32] [1541] 4-10-9 94 AntonyEvans 102
(P D Evans) *chsd ldrs: chal 2 out: sn ld: hdd after last: sn outpcd* **16/1**

4 15 **Chocolate Boy (IRE)**[13] 6-11-2 JEMoore 94
(G L Moore) *hld up in rr: hdwy and nt fluent 4 out: chsng ldrs whn stmbld 2 out: sn wknd* **33/1**

5 2½ **Grand Bay (USA)**[142] 4-11-2 APMcCoy 92
(Jonjo O'Neill) *w'like: keen hold early: hld up in rr: hday to chse ldrs 2 out: sn wknd* **11/2**[3]

300- **6** 6 **Lord Oscar (IRE)**[207] [4680] 6-10-13 TJMalone[(3)] 86
(M C Pipe) *scope: hit 1st: bhd: pushed along and mod prog form 2 out* **28/1**

0- **7** ½ **Black Shan (IRE)**[206] [4697] 5-11-2 PJBrennan 85
(A Ennis) *chsd ldrs: led after 4th: rdn 3 out: hdd sn after next and wknd qckly* **50/1**

P-05 **8** 1½ **Jug Of Punch (IRE)**[12] [1724] 6-10-9 79 PCStringer[(7)] 84
(S T Lewis) *chsd ldrs tl drvn and lost pl 4 out: mod hdwy again run-in* **200/1**

PP0- **9** 3½ **Lanos (POL)**[278] [3441] 7-11-2 83 WHutchinson 80
(W Davies) *ken hold: led after 1st tl after 4th: wknd 2 out* **200/1**

10 **10** 2½ **Flying Spur (IRE)**[32] [1543] 4-11-2 TJMurphy 78
(M C Pipe) *lw: t.k.h: chsd ldrs to 4 out: wknd next* **16/1**

P **11** 5 **Tashkandi (IRE)**[33] [1527] 5-11-2 CLlewellyn 81+
(P Bowen) *bit bkwd: led and hit 1st: sn hdd: styd chsng ldrs: chal fr 3 out to next: sn wknd* **28/1**

4m 7.20s (8.00) **Going Correction** +0.15s/f (Yiel) **11** Ran SP% **116.0**
Speed ratings: **87,86,85,78,76 74,73,73,71,70 67** CSF £8.10 TOTE £5.90: £1.60, £1.10, £2.50; EX 10.30 Place 6 £938.73, Place 5 £576.48.
Owner D Allen **Bred** Epona Bloodstock Ltd **Trained** Withycombe, Somerset
■ Stewards' Enquiry : Christian Williams one-day ban: careless riding (Nov 5)

FOCUS
Another race run at an early crawl and a poor winning time for the grade. The race developed into a sprint and despite the slow early gallop those that came from off the pace were favoured. The form is weak for the track and is rated through the third.

NOTEBOOK
Motorway(IRE), who offered promise on his Perth hurdling debut, was under pressure and looking more likely to finish third between the last two flights, but he found stamina coming to his aid up the hill and he snatched the race out of the fire. The form is suspect given the way the race was run, but he may be capable of a bit more given a truer pace. *(op 7-2)*
Desert Quest(IRE), well backed to gain compensation for his narrow Chepstow defeat, had hung left on the run-in that day but on this occasion he did it coming to the final flight just as he was getting on top of the leader, resulting in an awkward jump. It certainly did him few favours and gave the winner a chance to nail him. He has the ability to win over hurdles, but cannot be backed with any great confidence on the evidence so far. *(op 11-10)*

Don And Gerry(IRE), more experienced over hurdles than most in this field, shot to the front at the second last and appeared to have it won after establishing a significant advantage. However, the move was not decisive and her two nearest rivals found more finishing speed than her after the last. She has nothing in the way of scope, over this trip at least, and she may need a return to a longer distance.

Chocolate Boy(IRE), a 59-rated gelding on the Flat, was trying hurdling for the first time fairly late in life and probably achieved little in finishing a remote fourth. *(op 25-1)*

Grand Bay(USA), a dual winner on the Flat for John Hammond during the summer, looked like getting involved at the second-last flight but his effort came to nothing. He may have just needed it, but will need to improve a good deal to make his mark over timber. *(op 4-1 tchd 13-2)*

Lord Oscar(IRE) looks every inch a chaser and this trip would probably have been too sharp especially given the moderate pace, but he is still to convince at this game. *(op 25-1 tchd 33-1)*

Lanos(POL), returning from a layoff, nonetheless looked fit.

T/Jkpt: Not won. T/Plt: £1,253.30 to a £1 stake. Pool: £94,691.15. 55.15 winning tickets. T/Qpdt: £227.80 to a £1 stake. Pool: £5,666.50. 18.40 winning tickets. ST

1870 CHELTENHAM (Old Course) (L-H)

Wednesday, October 26

OFFICIAL GOING: Good (good to soft in places)

Wind: Half across

1876 JIM & MURIEL WARD 35TH ANNIVERSARY NOVICES' HURDLE (10 hdls) 2m 5f

2:00 (2:00) (Class 3) 4-Y-0+

£5,080 (£1,927; £963; £438; £219; £131)

Form			Horse	Jockey	RPR
2341	**1**		**Darrias (GER)**[11] 1740 4-11-6 132 (t) ChristianWilliams		122+
			(P F Nicholls) *rr:hit 5th: hdwy 4 out:chsd ldr hit 2 out: led bef last: 1l up: blnd bdly: lost a length and almost u.r: rallied to ld nr fin*	**10/11**[1]	
2-06	**2**	1 1/2	**Double Dizzy**[18] 1677 4-10-7 103	WKennedy[(5)]	106+
			(R H Buckler) *lw: led after 1st: hdd bef last: hld whn hmpd and lft w 1l ld sn after: hdd and outpcd nr fin*	**13/2**[3]	
P156	**3**	20	**Lago D'Oro**[24] 1614 5-10-7	TJPhelan[(3)]	83
			(Dr P Pritchard) *led tl after 1st: chsd ldr tl appr 3 out: sn btn*	**33/1**	
4-	**4**	14	**Classic Approach (IRE)**[10] 1765 5-11-6	TJMurphy	79
			(John Queally, Ire) *w'like: lw: chsd ldrs tl wknd after 4 out*	**2/1**[2]	
6	**5**	14	**Boytjie (IRE)**[176] 175 5-10-12	JTizzard	57
			(Miss H C Knight) *lengthy: rr but in tch tl wknd after 6th*	**33/1**	
PP/5	**6**	21	**Chocolate Bombe (IRE)**[24] 1619 8-10-12	RGreene	36
			(S Lycett) *w'like: always bhd: j. slowly 5th: t.o fr next*	**100/1**	

5m 15.0s (1.40) **Going Correction** +0.15s/f (Yiel) **6** Ran SP% **105.9**

Speed ratings: **103,102,94,89,84 76** CSF £6.42 TOTE £1.80: £1.30, £2.00; EX 6.20.

Owner Peter Hart **Bred** Gestut Rottgen **Trained** Ditcheat, Somerset

FOCUS

An uncompetitive race, but Darrias, with a little help from Christian Williams, managed to record his sixth win over hurdles. He is rated value for seven lengths and could rate higher.

NOTEBOOK

Darrias(GER) came into this off the back of a Listed success at Huntingdon (weak race for the grade), and he was able to record his sixth success over hurdles. He owes an awful lot to Williams however, as he managed to cling on to him as the pair nearly parted company at the last after the gelding slipped coming into the hurdle and jumped it sideways. Fortunately for him, the runner-up was tired at the time and was unable to take much of an advantage, and in the end he won a shade comfortably. A really progressive sort, he saw this longer trip out as connections would have hoped and he can now either go chasing where he would receive all the allowances being a four-year-old, or return to handicaps. *(op 4-5 tchd 8-11, 4-6 in places)*

Double Dizzy was tackling this sort of distance for the first time and he recorded an improved effort. Soon sent to the front, his rider was intent on making it a true stamina test at the distance and he momentarily looked to have been handed it when Darrias fluffed the last, but he did not have the legs to get up the hill and the Nicholls gelding reclaimed him close home. *(op 11-2)*

Lago D'Oro has as of yet been unable to build on her Market Rasen win back in July, but she was always going to struggle here and she was left trailing when the pace really quickened. *(op 25-1)*

Classic Approach(IRE) is nothing special and the fact he was a clear second favourite underlined the strength of the race. He failed to run a race and connections will no doubt have been disappointed at how quickly he was beaten. *(op 5-2 tchd 15-8)*

Boytjie(IRE) comes from a stable that has been struggling for winners for a while now and he did not look ready. He needs more time and will no doubt do better once handicapping. *(op 25-1)*

1877 ARKLE BOOKSHOP NOVICES' H'CAP CHASE (15 fncs) 2m 4f 110y

2:35 (2:35) (Class 3) (0-110,110) 5-Y-0+

£7,795 (£2,956; £1,478; £672; £336; £201)

Form			Horse	Jockey	RPR
4352	**1**		**Nazimabad (IRE)**[20] 1659 6-10-4 88	(t) ChristianWilliams	110+
			(Evan Williams) *mde all: clr fr 4th: unchal*	**10/1**	
5-P3	**2**	12	**Notanotherdonkey (IRE)**[14] 1715 5-11-0 98	TScudamore	110+
			(M Scudamore) *disp 2nd to 9th and mstke:but nvr nr unchal wnr: styd on to take 2nd cl home*	**20/1**	
-431	**3**	3/4	**Baloo**[66] 1271 9-10-12 101	CHonour[(5)]	110+
			(J D Frost) *disp 2nd but nvr nr unchal wnr fr 4th: clr 2nd 9th: mstke 2 out: wknd and lost n.d 2nd cl home*	**10/1**	
034-	**4**	11	**Darnayson (IRE)**[232] 4241 5-11-1 99	CLlewellyn	98+
			(N A Twiston-Davies) *lw: bhd: hdway to join chsng gp but nvr nr unchal wnr: weakend 4 out: no ch whn blnd 3 out*	**8/1**	
P-P2	**5**	1 1/4	**Rookery Lad**[21] 1644 7-11-2 100	DCrosse	98+
			(C N Kellett) *bhd: sme hdwy 7th: nver in contention: blnd and dropped rr 4 out: styd on again fr 2 out*	**25/1**	
006-	**6**	1	**Syncopated Rhythm (IRE)**[208] 4683 5-10-1 85	AntonyEvans	80
			(N A Twiston-Davies) *nt fluent: bhd: styd on fr 2 out: nvr in contention*	**14/1**	
-333	**7**	13	**Lubinas (IRE)**[14] 1716 6-10-10 94	APMcCoy	84+
			(F Jordan) *hmpd 2nd: j. poorly after and a wl bhd*	**11/2**[1]	
-213	**8**	14	**Muttley Maguire (IRE)**[153] 524 6-11-0 98	TJMurphy	76+
			(B G Powell) *chsd ldrs: blnd 6th: wknd fr next*	**6/1**[2]	
1-UF	**9**	2 1/2	**Stanway**[22] 1634 6-11-12 110	WMarston	75
			(Mrs Mary Hambro) *a in rr*	**33/1**	
245-	**U**		**Mon Mome (FR)**[191] 4911 5-11-7 105	SThomas	—
			(Miss Venetia Williams) *bhd whn uns rdr 3rd*	**14/1**	
F5P-	**U**		**Baton Charge (IRE)**[308] 2935 7-10-0 84 oh5	PJBrennan	—
			(T R George) *mstke and uns rdr 1st*	**16/1**	
P-46	**F**		**Tuesday's Child**[143] 654 6-10-5 89	JTizzard	—
			(Miss H C Knight) *lw: bhd whn fell 2nd*	**12/1**	
0-12	**P**		**Special Conquest**[168] 296 7-11-11 109	AThornton	—
			(J W Mullins) *bkwd: a in rr: t.o 8th: p.u bef 4 out*	**10/1**	
-263	**P**		**Alexander Musical (IRE)**[10] 1749 7-9-11 86 oh22 ow2	MNicolls[(5)]	—
			(S T Lewis) *in tch early: lost tch and t.o 9th: p.u bef 4 out*	**100/1**	
3-13	**F**		**Party Games (IRE)**[159] 436 8-11-12 110	PHide	113
			(G L Moore) *mid-div:hdwy to join chsng gp 8th but nvr nr unchal wnr: 4th and no ch whn fell 2 out*	**15/2**[3]	

5m 8.90s (-1.20) **Going Correction** +0.15s/f (Yiel) **15** Ran SP% **119.3**

Speed ratings: **108,103,103,98,98 98,93,87,86,— —,—,—,—,—** CSF £191.12 CT £2054.15 TOTE £14.00: £3.20, £5.20, £3.90; EX 330.70.

Owner Fox And Hounds Racing **Bred** His Highness The Aga Khan's Studs S C **Trained** Cowbridge, Vale Of Glamorgan

FOCUS

An ordinary race for the track, but another fine advertisment of the riding skills of Christian Williams, this time giving Nazimabad a quality front-running ride. The third sets a reasonable standard and the race should produce a fair amount of winners at a modest level.

NOTEBOOK

Nazimabad(IRE) ◆ was clearly expected to stay judging by the way he was sent into a clear early lead and Williams once again excelled. Taking the race by the scruff of the neck, he dominated throughout on a day where it seemed to help to race prominently, and jumping fluently, the pair always had things under control. He remains open to further improvement at this sort of distance and is one to keep on the right side of. *(op 9-1)*

Notanotherdonkey(IRE) seemed to enjoy his own private battle with Baloo for second, the pair disputing that position for most of the way, and he outstayed the nine-year-old on the rise to the line. A modest sort over hurdles, he is in the right hands to do well over fences and any improvement on this will see him winning. *(op 25-1 tchd 33-1)*

Baloo would not have appreciated the rain the course saw as he is at his best on a genuinely sound surface, but he ran well nonetheless and only lost out on second on the final climb to the line. *(op 8-1)*

Darnayson(IRE) ◆, whose stable won this last year with Gazump, was no great shakes over hurdles, but his stable excels with its chasers and this big, rangy type was always likely to improve for a switch to fences. However, he never landed a serious blow having been held up and stayed on under a considerate ride for a well-beaten fourth. One can expect to see considerable improvement with the run under his belt, and it will be surprising if he is not winning before Christmas.

Rookery Lad, although yet to win over fences, has run several good races in defeat and he kept on well enough considering he made an error at the fourth last.

Syncopated Rhythm(IRE) ◆, making his seasonal debut like stable companion Darnayson, had a very similar profile and he ran almost an identical race, the one difference being his rather slack jumping. Soon last, he gave ground away at his fences, 'ballooning' many of them, but he came home well and, as with Darnayson, was hardly punished. Three miles is likely to help and he too is worth keeping an eye out for next time. *(op 16-1)*

Lubinas(IRE) seemed to have his confidence knocked after being hampered early and as a result he was never jumping with any fluency. He has never been a frequent winner, but he is better than *this and deserves another chance. Official explanation: jockey said gelding lost a shoe and slipped on the home turn (op 5-1 tchd 6-1)*

Muttley Maguire(IRE) is the sort of horse his trainer does really well with, but Powell's runners are not at their peak yet and a blunder at the sixth seemed to take a fair bit out of him. He was looked *after by Murphy once beaten and much better can be expected of him next time.Official explanation: jockey said gelding lost a shoe, slipped at several fences and lost its confidence (op 9-2)*

Party Games(IRE) had run a fair race, but was well held when coming down at the dreaded second last. This was only his fourth start over fences and, as long as his confidence is not affected by this, he remains open to further progress. *(op 8-1)*

1878 CLUB 16-24 CONDITIONAL JOCKEYS' H'CAP HURDLE (8 hdls) 2m 110y

3:10 (3:13) (Class 4) (0-135,133) 4-Y-0+

£5,173 (£1,962; £981; £446; £223; £133)

Form			Horse	Jockey	RPR
1163	**1**		**Cantgeton (IRE)**[18] 1675 5-10-7 117	TJMalone[(3)]	126+
			(M C Pipe) *mde virtually all: drvn fr 2 out: swtchd rt to stands rail last: r.o strly*	**7/2**[1]	
413/	**2**	2 1/2	**Reiziger (FR)**[587] 4426 9-10-2 112	RStephens[(3)]	116
			(P J Hobbs) *b.bkwd: chsd ldrs: wnt def 2nd 2 out: kpt on run in but no imression on wnr*	**4/1**[2]	
055-	**3**	5	**Chockdee (FR)**[186] 4978 5-10-5 120	LHeard[(8)]	121+
			(P F Nicholls) *lw: hld up in rr: stdy hdwy 4 out: trckd ldrs gng wl after 2 out: propped last: sn rdn and btn*	**4/1**[2]	
-323	**4**	6	**Borora**[102] 1010 6-11-12 133	WKennedy	127+
			(R Lee) *bhd: hdwy fr 4 out: styd on fr 2 out but nvr gng pce to rch ldrs*	**10/1**	
000-	**5**	1 3/4	**Calatagan (IRE)**[22] 4860 6-11-7 128	GBerridge	120+
			(J M Jefferson) *sn chsing wnr: rdn 2 out: sn wknd*	**8/1**	
14-0	**6**	shd	**Transit**[22] 45 6-10-7 114	(p) KJMercer	105
			(B Ellison) *bhd: rdn 3 out: styd on and modearet prog fr 2 out*	**14/1**	
3430	**7**	11	**Flame Phoenix (USA)**[14] 1720 6-10-7 117	(t) StephenJCraine[(3)]	97
			(D McCain) *chsd ldrs: rdn 4 out: sn wknd*	**25/1**	
511F	**8**	7	**Space Cowboy (IRE)**[25] 1598 5-10-6 113	(b) CBolger	91+
			(G L Moore) *lw: in tch: hdwy 4 out: wknd 2 out*	**6/1**[3]	
4144	**9**	1 1/4	**Leopold (SLO)**[31] 1559 4-9-8 107 oh6	CPoste[(6)]	79
			(M F Harris) *rdn 4 out: a in rr*	**33/1**	
-000	**10**	1/2	**Constantine**[158] 450 5-10-2 115	EDehdashti[(6)]	86
			(G L Moore) *nt fluent 2nd and 4th: a in rr*	**20/1**	
4-30	**11**	1 1/4	**My Last Bean (IRE)**[96] 387 8-10-7 117	MrJAJenkins[(3)]	87
			(M R Bosley) *plld hrd early in tch: rdn 4 out: sn wknd*	**50/1**	

3m 59.2s **Going Correction** +0.15s/f (Yiel)

WFA 4 from 5yo+ 13lb **11** Ran SP% **116.9**

Speed ratings: **106,104,102,99,98 98,93,90,89,89 88** CSF £17.35 CT £58.19 TOTE £4.10: £1.50, £2.20, £1.90; EX 18.80.

Owner D A Johnson **Bred** John Murphy **Trained** Nicholashayne, Devon

FOCUS

A decent handicap hurdle for the grade rated through the third and the race is likely to produce winners.

NOTEBOOK

Cantgeton(IRE) was no doubt the first of many winners at Cheltenham this season for the Johnson/Pipe team, receiving a fine ride and staying on determinely to fend off the persistent Reiziger. He has the makings of a typically improving Pipe two-mile hurdler and should be up to defying a higher mark. *(op 10-3 tchd 3-1, 4-1 in places)*

Reiziger(FR), last seen finishing third in the 2004 Grand Annual, was returning to hurdles off a significantly lower mark and his prominent position in the market suggested he was ready to run a big race. He did just that, rallying bravely to challenge again after the last, but he was unable to reel in the winner. There is definitely a decent race in him if he stays sound, over hurdles or fences, and something like the Lanzarote could be a possible target. *(op 11-2)*

Chockdee(FR) would not be the most gutsy horse in training and that was again evident here as, having travelled well, he emptied out before the last. On the plus side, he is only a five-year-old and there may yet to a little improvement to come from him, so it will be interesting to see if he is put over fences. *(tchd 9-2)*

Borora was racing off a career-high mark over hurdles here, but as his third in last season's County Hurdle showed, he is very talented. He faced a stiff task, conceding so much weight, but he was putting in some good late work and a little further improvement should allow him to remain competitive in some of the better handicap hurdles.*Official explanation: trainer said gelding's poor performance was due to its being harshly treated by the handicapper (op 12-1)*

Calatagan(IRE), who has been running well in defeat on the Flat, has faced some stiff tasks on his last few starts over hurdles, but this was more realistic and he ran better. That said, he could probably do with a little help from the Handicapper. *(tchd 9-1 in a place)*

Transit enjoyed a pipe-opener on the Flat the other day, but he was at a disadvantage in being help up here and he could never get into it. *(op 16-1 tchd 20-1)*

1879 IAN WILLIAMS OWNERS NOVICES' CHASE (19 fncs) 3m 110y

3:45 (3:47) (Class 2) 5-Y-0+ **£9,791** (£4,012; £2,247)

Form RPR

5-11 **1** **Iris's Gift**[18] [1669] 8-11-8 .... APMcCoy 155+
(Jonjo O'Neill) *hit 3rd and 5th: disp ld tl slt advantage 6th: hit next and hdd: styd chalng: led 11th: c clr fr 4 out: v easily* **1/1**[1]

1122 **2** *17* **Sweet Diversion (IRE)**[32] [1549] 6-11-8 130..........(t) ChristianWilliams 130
(P F Nicholls) *lw: chsd ldrs but nvr in contention: styng on to chse wnr whn lft mod 2nd 4 out* **13/2**[3]

3 *dist* **Murphy's Magic (IRE)**[165] 7-11-0 .... RThornton —
(Mrs T J Hill) *w'like: unf: bhd fr 7th and sn t.o* **66/1**

1 **P** **Nick Junior (IRE)**[103] [998] 6-11-5 .... PMoloney —
(Evan Williams) *w'like: chsd ldrs to 9th: t.o whn p.u bef 15th* **16/1**

220- **P** **Zeta's River (IRE)**[186] [4984] 7-11-8 134.......... TJMurphy —
(M C Pipe) *lw: hld up in rr: rdn and hdwy to take 3rd 12th: wknd next: t.o whn p.u bef 4 out* **9/4**[2]

0P-1 **U** **You Owe Me (IRE)**[171] [239] 8-11-5 119.......... CLlewellyn —
(N A Twiston-Davies) *gd sort: lw: disp ld tl slt advantage 3rd tl hdd 6th: led again next: styd disputing ld tl 11th: tired and losing 2nd whn u* **12/1**

6m 18.3s (-4.60) **Going Correction** +0.15s/f (Yiel) **6** Ran SP% **109.2**
Speed ratings: **113,107**,—,—,— — CSF £7.69 TOTE £1.90: £1.30, £2.30; EX 5.80.
Owner Robert Lester **Bred** Mrs R Crank **Trained** Cheltenham, Gloucs

FOCUS

The best performance yet over fences from Iris's Gift, but given this was his fourth outing over the larger obstacles, his jumping left a lot to be desired. He is rated value for further but we learned little new about him and it would have been much more interesting had Zeta's River run his race.

NOTEBOOK

Iris's Gift, a top-class staying hurdler who was seen only once on the racecourse last season due to injury, had pleased with his two wins against vastly inferior opposition this season, but his most recent win at Bangor was workmanlike to say the least and he would have been pushed harder that day had the runner up had a proper crack at him. This step back up in distance was always going to suit the grey, but in Zeta's River he was facing a solid novice who had contested some good handicaps last season and the tricky fences here were also expected to prove much more of a test. However, with Zeta's River running a shocker and being beaten at half way, he was left with only the reopposing Sweet Diversion to beat and in the end it was the fences that proved his biggest danger. Although he never looked as though he was going to fall, his jumping left a lot to be desired, hitting several fences and having particular problems at the ditches, and it was only when You Owe Me, who had hassled him for much of the way, had been burned off that he started to leap more fluently. Undoubtedly a potentially top-class chaser, his trainer seems to favour a novice campaign, but his ambitious owner will no doubt have realised he is soon to be nine and it would not surprise to see him take on the 'big boys' this time around. He will always be hard to beat if jumping well, no matter where he goes this season, but it is worth bearing in mind how he jumped when taken on as he will not always be able to have a solo up front in the top races. *(op 11-10)*

Sweet Diversion(IRE), who ran respectably when second to the winner at Market Rasen in September, was better off at the weights, but he was slammed by the grey and came home in his own time for second. It is debatable whether he ran his race however as he needs a genuinely good/fast surface to be at his best, and he will find life easier back in handicaps now. *(op 8-1 tchd 6-1)*

Murphy's Magic(IRE), a decent pointer, could have been given an easier introduction to Rules racing and, although finishing third, he was never at the races. We will see an accurate gauge of his ability against more sensible opposition. *(op 50-1)*

You Owe Me(IRE), although winning his chase debut at Uttoxeter back in May, had a bit to prove against the likes of Iris's Gift and Zeta's River, but his stable is in good form and he showed up well for a long way, causing Iris's Gift to make several bad mistakes. However, he was unable to stick with him once McCoy turned the screw and he was going backwards when unseating Llewellyn four from the finish. He will find life easier back down in grade and is the type his trainer will waste little time with in sending him handicapping. *(tchd 2-1 and 5-2)*

Zeta's River(IRE) quickly made up into a useful handicapper last season and ended up being sent off only 7/1 for the Attheraces Gold Cup as a novice. The fact connections were taking Iris's Gift on suggested they think he could prove to be better than a handicapper in time, but he showed very little on this reappearance and was unable to provide the winner with any kind of a test. He is better than this, but now has a bit to prove. *Official explanation: jockey said gelding was never travelling (tchd 2-1 and 5-2)*

Nick Junior(IRE) was quite an impressive winner on his British debut at Southwell in July, but this was too big a step too soon and he began to struggle as soon as he was asked to improve his position. *(tchd 2-1 and 5-2)*

1880 JEWSON H'CAP HURDLE FINAL (8 hdls) 2m 110y

4:20 (4:23) (Class 2) 4-Y-0+

£11,327 (£4,296; £2,148; £976; £488; £292)

Form RPR

1U24 **1** **Itsmyboy (IRE)**[9] [1775] 5-11-7 122..........(p) TJMurphy 133+
(M C Pipe) *trckd ldrs: led 4 out: hit 2 out: rdn hung lft and narrowly hdd last: rallied and sn led again: drvn out* **12/1**

-135 **2** *1* **Theocritus (GER)**[18] [1680] 4-10-0 101 oh8.......... RJohnson 109
(Nick Williams) *hld up in rr: gd hday to trck ldrs 4th: chal 2 out: slt ld and rdn last: hdd sn after and no ex u.p* **20/1**

2-13 **3** *8* **Fandani (GER)**[159] [438] 5-11-7 122.......... NFehily 123+
(C J Mann) *hld up in rr: hday 3 out: chsd ldrs next: sn rdn and one pce* **5/1**[2]

1-12 **4** *3* **Portavadie**[159] [438] 6-11-9 127.......... GBerridge(3) 124
(J M Jefferson) *swtg: chsd ldrs: rdn 3 out: wknd after next* **14/1**

3252 **5** *2* **Reem Two**[26] [1590] 4-9-9 101 oh1.......... StephenJCraine(5) 96
(D McCain) *bhd: hdwy 3 out: sn rdn and nvr gng pce to trble ldrs* **50/1**

125 **6** *2* **Anticipating**[9] [1775] 5-10-7 108.......... PHide 103+
(G L Moore) *lw: mid-div: hdwy to chse ldrs 4 out: sn rdn: wknd fr next* **14/1**

3121 **7** *8* **Smart Boy Prince (IRE)**[21] [1642] 4-10-9 110.......... WHutchinson 95
(C Smith) *chsd ldrs: rdn 4 out: sn wknd: no ch whn blnd 2 out* **9/1**

1F24 **8** *6* **Tom Bell (IRE)**[18] [1680] 5-10-6 107.......... DCrosse 86
(J G M O'Shea) *mid-div whn hit 4th: sn bhd* **8/1**[3]

442 **9** *12* **Carte Sauvage (USA)**[11] [1745] 4-10-0 101 oh2..........(v) PJBrennan 72+
(M F Harris) *chsd ldr: hit 3rd: hrd drvn whn mstke 4 out: wknd sn after* **14/1**

2-FF **P** **Mister Mustard (IRE)**[21] [1642] 8-11-3 118.......... PMoloney —
(Ian Williams) *mstke 2nd: a bhd: t.o whn p.u bef 3 out* **20/1**

123 **P** **Almizan (IRE)**[9] [1775] 5-10-9 110.......... JEMoore —
(G L Moore) *bhd: hday 4th: wknd after 4 out: t.o whn p.u bef last* **10/1**

31-2 **P** **Earth Man (IRE)**[173] [203] 6-11-5 120.......... APMcCoy —
(P F Nicholls) *lw: chsd ldsrs to 3rd: rdn 4th: sn wknd: t.o whn p.u bef 2 out* **5/2**[1]

0110 **P** **Supply And Fix (IRE)**[29] [1569] 7-9-11 103.......... WKennedy(5) —
(J J Lambe, Ire) *led tl hdd and mstke 4 out: sn wknd: t.o whn p.u bef last* **50/1**

3m 58.9s (-0.30) **Going Correction** +0.15s/f (Yiel)
WFA 4 from 5yo+ 13lb **13** Ran SP% **116.6**
Speed ratings: **106,105,101,100,99 98,94,91,86**,— —,—,— CSF £223.66 CT £1354.14 TOTE £13.10: £3.50, £5.70, £2.30; EX 270.90 Trifecta £618.40 Pool: £1,568.00 - 1.80 winning units.
Owner D A Johnson **Bred** Padraig Moroney **Trained** Nicholashayne, Devon
■ Stewards' Enquiry : T J Murphy one-day ban: used whip in the incorrect place (Nov 6)

FOCUS

A fair handicap but not a great event for a final and the favourite running poorly did little to help the contest. The third and fourth set the standard with the time fair, and the form looks solid enough.

NOTEBOOK

Itsmyboy(IRE), who ran a lacklustre race when favourite in the first-time cheekpieces at Plumpton last time, looked to face a much stiffer task back in handicap company, but the headgear had more of an affect this time around and, despite conceding 21lb to the winner, he proved too strong on the climb to the line. His assured stamina was a great help and it will be interesting to see if he can improve further.

Theocritus(GER) is steadily improving and this was his best effort thus far. He would have fancied his chances jumping the last, being in receipt of so much weight, but the winner was too strong. He will go up again for this, but remains open to further improvement.

Fandani(GER) has plenty of speed and the rain the course saw would only have hampered his chance, but he ran a good race nonetheless and it was only in the final quarter mile that he waved the white flag. Speed tracks like Huntingdon and Wincanton suit him better and he remains an interesting prospect. *(op 4-1 tchd 7-2)*

Portavadie is a fine specimen of a horse and he came into this overpriced at 14/1, having finished ahead of Fandani last time. He was never far off the gallop and kept on the best he could, but in the end his big weight told. Fences will be the making of him and he remains a promising sort.

Reem Two ran well from out of the weights and stayed through tiring rivals for a never-nearer fifth. She will be more at home back down in grade.

Mister Mustard(IRE) *Official explanation: jockey said gelding was lame (tchd 11-4, 3-1 in places)*

Earth Man(IRE) should have been put spot-on for this when winning a charity race at Wincanton at the weekend, but like Fandani two miles is the absolute maximum for him and he too was unsuited by the rain. Despite this, he should still have done better and it would not surprise to learn that something was amiss with him. *Official explanation: trainer said gelding had a breathing problem (tchd 11-4, 3-1 in places)*

1881 STUDD CHALLENGE CUP H'CAP CHASE (13 fncs 2 omitted) 2m 4f 110y

4:55 (4:55) (Class 3) (0-135,134) 5-Y-0+

£9,526 (£3,613; £1,806; £821; £410; £246)

Form RPR

3112 **1** **Whispered Secret (GER)**[31] [1561] 6-11-12 134.......... RGreene 145
(M C Pipe) *swtg: blnd 1st: bhd: rdn into mid-div fr 7th: and continually pushed along: chsd ldr after 2 out: chal last: led last strid* **12/1**

5/4- **2** *hd* **Halexy (FR)**[332] [2517] 10-11-0 122.......... APMcCoy 133
(Jonjo O'Neill) *lw: hld up in tch: hdwy 9th: led appr 2 out: hrd rdn and kpt on whn strly chal run-in: ct last stride* **12/1**

1151 **3** *17* **Tamango (FR)**[11] [1744] 8-11-12 134.......... RJohnson 128
(P J Hobbs) *hit 3rd: bhd: rdn fr 9th: styd on fr 2 out but nvr nr ldrs* **6/1**[3]

1046 **4** *2 ½* **Bronzesmith**[31] [1561] 9-11-6 128.......... JTizzard 120
(B J M Ryall) *chsd ldrs: wknd 4 out: no ch whn mstke next* **12/1**

22U2 **5** *2 ½* **Deep King (IRE)**[33] [1542] 10-10-1 112.......... RYoung(3) 103+
(J W Mullins) *led: hit 3 out: hdd appr next and sn wknd* **20/1**

2041 **6** *dist* **Ball O Malt (IRE)**[49] [1435] 9-11-3 125.......... JEMoore 106
(R A Fahey) *lw: bhd tl blnd 3 out: t.o* **14/1**

315- **P** **You're Special (USA)**[313] [2877] 8-11-0 125.......... KJMercer(3) —
(Ferdy Murphy) *bkwd: rdn 6th: a bhd: t.o whn p.u bef 3 out* **6/1**[3]

612- **P** **Wrags To Riches (IRE)**[187] [4961] 8-11-0 127.......... CHonour(5) —
(J D Frost) *chsd ldr: hit 4th: wknd 9th: t.o whn p.u bef 2 out* **25/1**

12F- **F** **Big Rob (IRE)**[223] [4407] 6-10-13 121.......... TJMurphy 118
(B G Powell) *hld up: stdy hdwy fr 4 out: disputing 6l 4th and styng on whn fell 2 out* **11/4**[1]

412- **P** **Indien Royal (FR)**[187] [4974] 6-11-2 124..........(t) ChristianWilliams —
(P F Nicholls) *lw: in tch: rdn 9th: wknd 4 out: p.u after 2 out: dismntd* **9/2**[2]

5m 11.0s (0.90) **Going Correction** +0.15s/f (Yiel) **10** Ran SP% **111.8**
Speed ratings: **104,103,97,96,95** —,—,—,—,— CSF £136.29 CT £940.50 TOTE £12.80: £2.70, £3.10, £2.10; EX 205.00.
Owner David Manasseh Daniel Evans Dan Levine **Bred** G Baron Von Ullmann **Trained** Nicholashayne, Devon
■ Stewards' Enquiry : R Greene four-day ban: excessive use of the whip (Nov 6-9)

FOCUS

This is usually a decent race, but with virtually all the fancied runners disappointing it is debatable how good a renewal this was with the time modest. The third and fourth fences were omitted.

NOTEBOOK

Whispered Secret(GER), who got a little warm beforehand, has yet to do anything wrong over the larger obstacles and this was his third win in six attempts. Niggled along some way out by Greene, he kept responding and drew clear with Halexy as they turned for home, just proving too strong on the run to the line. He jumped well in the main after an early blunder and could be a possible for the Paddy Power Gold Cup, although connections are likely to have one or two stronger contenders. *(op 14-1)*

Halexy(FR) made a highly pleasing return to the action and made the winner pull out all the stops, both horse and jockey giving their all. He was a mile clear of the third and, as long as he goes the right way from this, can win a similar race.

Tamango(FR) has improved of late and he ran another good race here, but the front two were far too strong. He probably needs to improve to win off this sort of mark. *(op 11-2, 13-2 in a place)*

Bronzesmith has struggled since winning two in a row at Worcester in June and he needs some help from the handicapper.

Deep King(IRE) was receiving plenty of weight from all his rivals and he ran a fair race, but the slight ease in the ground was no good for him. *(op 16-1)*

You're Special(USA), making his debut for connections, was yet another to disappoint, but he did not look ready in the paddock beforehand and the run was clearly needed. *(op 11-2 tchd 4-1)*

Wrags To Riches(IRE) *Official explanation: jockey said gelding was never travelling (op 11-2 tchd 4-1)*

Indien Royal(FR) looked to hold strong claims on some decent pieces of form from last season, but he was struggling fully a mile from home and was dismounted having been pulled up. There was evidently something amiss and he remains an interesting prospect if it was nothing too serious. *Official explanation: jockey said gelding was lame (op 11-2 tchd 4-1)*

Big Rob(IRE), rated highly by connections, looked to be starting the season on a very attractive mark and, although falling when last seen at the Festival (staying on fourth at the time in the Jewson Novices' Handicap Chase), his jumping on the whole is usually good. Held up in rear early, he was not overpushed when the leaders looked to be getting away and unfortunately he suffered from a classic fall at the second last. This will not have done his confidence much good, and any *chance of him getting into the Paddy Power has now gone, so it is back to the drawing board. (op 11-2 tchd 4-1)*

1882 WEATHERBYS BANK STANDARD OPEN NATIONAL HUNT FLAT RACE 2m 110y

5:30 (5:34) (Class 6) 4-6-Y-O **£3,672** (£1,130; £565; £282)

Form RPR

1 **1** **Tokala**[165] 361 4-11-0 CMStudd(7) 101
(B G Powell) *b.bkwd: led 4f: racd wd and styd w ldr tl led again 1/2-way: rdn 2f out: styd on gamely run-in* **16/1**

4- **2** *nk* **Dream Alliance**[350] 2129 4-11-0 RJohnson 94
(P J Hobbs) *lw: in tch: chsd ldrs: rdn and kpt on fr 2f out: str chal last half f: no ex cl home* **5/2**[1]

3 *shd* **Mr Nick (IRE)** 5-11-0 JamesDavies 94
(N J Gifford) *lw: w'like: bhd: hdwy 7f out: chsd ldrs 2f out: r.o fnl f and str chal ins last: no ex cl home* **8/1**

4 *3 1/2* **Kevkat (IRE)**[139] 700 4-11-7 APMcCoy 97
(Eoin Griffin, Ire) *lw: in tch: chsd ldrs 1/2-way: wnt 2nd over 4f out:drvn to chal 1f out: wknd last half f* **9/2**[2]

5 *2* **El Bandindos (IRE)** 4-11-0 TJMurphy 88
(M C Pipe) *cmpt: b.bkwd: chsd ldrs: rdn 3f out: styd on same pce fnl 2f* **10/1**

6 *1 1/2* **Le Burf (FR)** 4-10-7 MrLRPayter(7) 87
(G R I Smyly) *b.bkwd: chsd ldrs: lost pl 1/2-way: styd on again fr over 2f out: fin wl* **66/1**

7 *1/2* **Butsadtohavetogo (IRE)**[171] 5-11-0 MFoley 86
(A E Jones) *w'like: bhd: hdwy 7f out: chsd ldrs over 4f out: wknd fr 2f out* **50/1**

8 *2* **Night Safe (IRE)** 4-10-7 MGoldstein(7) 84
(N A Twiston-Davies) *scope: str: b.bkwd: chsd ldrs: n.m.r and lost position 5f out: styd on fr over 1f out: gng on cl home* **20/1**

9 *3/4* **Royal Hilarity (IRE)** 5-11-0 RThornton 83
(Ian Williams) *unf: in tch: hdwy 1/2-way: pushed along 4f out: styd on same pce fnl 2f* **22/1**

10 *13* **Carrickerry (IRE)**[185] 5-10-11 AndrewJMcNamara(3) 70
(Michael Hourigan, Ire) *lw: chsd ldrs: rdn 6f out: wknd 4f out* **7/1**[3]

11 *10* **Kitebrook** 4-10-7 WMarston 53
(Mrs Mary Hambro) *w'like: b.bkwd: bhd: hdwy 1/2-way: chsd ldrs and rdn 4f out: sn wknd* **25/1**

0- **12** *7* **Muir Cottage**[277] 3487 4-10-11 TJMalone(3) 53
(L P Grassick) *w'like: b.bkwd: chsd ldrs: wknd 7f out* **100/1**

13 *nk* **Made In Bruere (FR)** 5-10-11 KJMercer(3) 53
(Ferdy Murphy) *str: b.bkwd: bhd most of way* **33/1**

14 *7* **Dopey Bob** 4-11-0 CLlewellyn 46
(N A Twiston-Davies) *gd sort: led after 4f: hdd 1/2-way: wknd 6f out* **8/1**

15 *3 1/2* **Double The Trouble** 4-11-0 BHitchcott 43
(R H Buckler) *w'like: chsd ldrs 11f* **50/1**

0-1 **16** *5* **Castlemainevillage (IRE)**[170] 266 5-11-7 SCurran 45
(M R Bosley) *str: chsd ldrs: rdn 6f out: wknd 5f out* **33/1**

17 *10* **Tom'n Ed** 4-11-0 TDoyle 28
(D R Gandolfo) *w'like: b.bkwd: bhd most of way* **50/1**

4m 3.60s (6.40) **Going Correction** +0.15s/f (Yiel) **17** Ran SP% **123.7**
Speed ratings: **90,89,89,88,87 86,86,85,84,78 74,70,70,67,65 63,58** CSF £51.90 TOTE £17.70: £4.80, £1.70, £2.70; EX 80.90 Place 6 £225.28, Place 5 £157.94.
Owner J Daniels **Bred** Greenfield Stud S A **Trained** Morestead, Hants

FOCUS
An ordinary bumper rated through the fourth, but there were one or two promising performances and the race should produce the odd winner.

NOTEBOOK
Tokala, a workmanlike winner on his debut at Worcester back in May, had his penalty offset by his rider's claim, but looked a bit short of peak fitness in the paddock and it was no surprise to see him dismissed in the betting. However, he has clearly improved over the summer and, although this was no vintage Cheltenham bumper, the victory represented a significant step up. Both he and jockey did well to fend off the favourite on the climb to the line and he is clearly a useful sort for hurdles. *(op 12-1 tchd 20-1)*
Dream Alliance, fourth on his debut in a juvenile bumper at Newbury last season, was clearly well fancied to make a winning reappearance and he came late with a strong challenge, but the winner had already done enough. *(op 4-1 tchd 9-2)*
Mr Nick(IRE), whose stable introduced a newcomer to win over hurdles at the weekend, was nibbled at in the market prior to the race and he did not let each-way supporters down, battling on best he could up the hill. The experience will have done him the world of good and he looks a ready-made bumper winner. *(op 12-1)*
Kevkat(IRE), a winner on his debut at Tipperary, was unable to follow up back there last time and he again looked vulnerable. He may improve for a switch to hurdles. *(op 5-1 tchd 11-2)*
El Bandindos(IRE), unusually for a Pipe horse, looked as though the run would do him and he stayed on nicely under considerate handling. He can win a bumper before going hurdling. *(op 5-1)*
Le Burf(FR) will no doubt have delighted connections with this debut effort and he is sure to appreciate further once sent hurdling. *(op 50-1 tchd 80-1)*
Night Safe(IRE) is a nice, scopey type and he was putting in some good late work. Staying hurdles, and eventually fences are going to be the making of him.
T/Jkpt: Part won. £13,775.40 to a £1 stake. Pool: £19,402.00. 0.50 winning tickets. T/Plt: £329.40 to a £1 stake. Pool: £94,400.90. 209.20 winning tickets. T/Qpdt: £45.10 to a £1 stake. Pool: £7,867.40. 129.00 winning tickets. ST

1566 SEDGEFIELD (L-H)

Wednesday, October 26

OFFICIAL GOING: Good to soft
Very unusually for the modern era, there were two sellers on the card.
Wind: Virtually nil.

1883 JOHN WADE FOR EQUINE FIBRE AND RUBBER (S) H'CAP HURDLE (QUALIFIER) (8 hdls) 2m 1f

1:45 (1:45) (Class 5) (0-90,86) 3-Y-O+ **£2,282** (£652; £326)

Form RPR

4FP **1** **Ball Games**[26] 1588 7-11-1 **85** MMcAvoy(10) 92+
(James Moffatt) *chsd ldrs: pushed along 4th: hdwy 3 ouyt: led and hit next: clr last: kpt on* **12/1**

0005 **2** *1 1/2* **Maunby Rocker**[57] 1375 5-11-4 **83** (p) PMerrigan(5) 89+
(P C Haslam) *trckd ldrs: bdly hmpd and lost pl 2nd: bhd tl hdwy 3 out: rdn to chse ldrs next: styd on u.p fr last* **5/1**[1]

-PP3 **3** *1* **Samson Des Galas (FR)**[58] 1357 7-10-3 **63** ADempsey 66
(R Ford) *hld up and bhd: stdy hdwy 1/2-way: chsd ldrs 3 out: rdn along next: kpt on* **14/1**

5406 **4** *8* **Two Steps To Go (USA)**[26] 1588 6-11-4 **78** (t) PWhelan 74+
(M A Barnes) *chsd ldrs: rdn along 3 out: drvn next and kpt on same pce appr last* **14/1**

0064 **5** *2 1/2* **Irish Prince (IRE)**[10] 1756 9-10-12 **72** (b) GLee 65
(Robert Gray) *led 2nd: rdn along and hdd after 3 out: grad wknd* **6/1**[3]

-154 **6** *1 3/4* **Diamond Jack (IRE)**[18] 1687 7-11-11 **85** (p) JPMcNamara 76
(J J Lambe, Ire) *trckd ldrs: hdwy to ld after 3 out: rdn along and hdd bef next: sn drvn and wknd* **5/1**[1]

013/ **7** *7* **Balakar (IRE)**[118] 878 9-11-9 **86** (t) LMcGrath(3) 70
(J J Lambe, Ire) *racd wd: hld up and bhd: hdwy 1/2-way: rdn along 3 out and nvr nr ldrs* **17/2**

400 **8** *3 1/2* **Azahara**[7] 1601 3-10-6 **83** RMcGrath 46
(K G Reveley) *hld up in rr: stdy hdwy 3 out: rdn bef next and sn btn* **11/2**[2]

/P-6 **9** *dist* **Ro Eridani**[18] 1683 5-10-5 **68** MrCStorey(3) —
(Miss S E Forster) *keen: prom: rdn along after 4th and sn wknd* **14/1**

P **P** **Port Natal (IRE)**[19] 1662 7-11-9 **86** PAspell(3) —
(J Wade) *bhd fr 1/2-way: p.u bef last* **66/1**

405F **P** **Coachman (IRE)**[29] 1566 7-10-1 **61** DO'Meara —
(A J Lockwood) *midfield: rdn along and wknd 5th: bhd whn p.u bef 2 out* **33/1**

0500 **P** **Bally Hall (IRE)**[5] 1814 5-10-9 **76** (v[1]) MrMatthewSmith(7) —
(M J Gingell) *prom: rdn along 5th: sn wknd and bhd whn p.u bef 2 out* **66/1**

65P0 **P** **Zahunda (IRE)**[64] 1297 6-10-4 **74** CareyWilliamson(10) —
(M J Gingell) *midfield: rdn along and wknd 5th: bhd whn p.u bef 2 out* **50/1**

6P5U **P** **Dottie Digger (IRE)**[26] 1592 6-10-10 **73** (v) PBuchanan(3) —
(Miss Lucinda V Russell) *led tl j. bdly rt and hdd 2nd: sn lost pl and bhd: p.u bef 3 out* **18/1**

4m 13.1s (6.60) **Going Correction** +0.20s/f (Yiel)
WFA 3 from 5yo+ 17lb **14** Ran SP% **114.4**
Speed ratings: **92,91,90,87,85 85,81,80,—,— —,—,—,—** CSF £67.54 CT £852.01 TOTE £13.40: £3.60, £2.20, £4.30; EX 89.60.There was no bid for the winner.
Owner Jennie Moffatt, Evan Munro **Bred** Cartmel Bloodstock **Trained** Cartmel, Cumbria
■ Michael McAvoy's first winner.

FOCUS
A dire event, run at a sound pace and the first three came clear.

NOTEBOOK
Ball Games , who had failed to complete on his previous two outings, showed his true colours and ran out a ready winner. This was just his second career success, and his highest winning mark to date, so whether he can follow-up off a higher future mark has to be considered a doubt.
Maunby Rocker ◆ was done no favours at the second flight and, having used up a fair amount of energy in making up his ground from off the pace, did well to finish as he did. The recent application of cheekpieces has brought about improvement and he can be placed to go one better in this grade while his yard remains in good form. *(tchd 11-2)*
Samson Des Galas(FR) turned in another improved effort and readily reversed his Cartmel form with the sixth horse on this easier ground. He never seriously threatened to get to the front, however.
Two Steps To Go(USA) was found wanting from two out, but still turned in a more encouraging effort in defeat. *(tchd 16-1)*
Irish Prince(IRE) *(op 11-2)*
Diamond Jack(IRE) had his chance and ran below par on this return to plating company. He may just need top of the ground to be at his best.
Azahara failed to make an impact from off the pace and looks very limited. *(op 5-1)*
Coachman(IRE) *Official explanation: jockey said gelding bled from the nose (op 28-1)*

1884 JOHN SMITH'S EXTRA SMOOTH AMATEUR RIDERS' H'CAP HURDLE (13 hdls) 3m 3f 110y

2:15 (2:15) (Class 4) (0-100,91) 4-Y-O+ **£2,919** (£834; £417)

Form RPR

0500 **1** **Longstone Lass**[10] 1756 5-10-13 **83** MissCMetcalfe(5) 87+
(Miss Tracy Waggott) *led 2nd: rdn along 2 out: edgd lft and styd on gamely flat* **25/1**

300- **2** *2* **Canavan (IRE)**[277] 3479 6-11-1 **85** MrMSeston(5) 86
(Ferdy Murphy) *in tch: hit 3rd: hdwy to chse wnr 3 out: rdn along next: drvn and ev ch appr last: no ex flat* **5/2**[1]

U203 **3** *26* **End Of An Error**[3] 1856 6-11-4 **90** MrsEJSmith(7) 65+
(A W Carroll) *hld up and sn wl bhd: hdwy 3 out: styd on appr last: tk 3rd nr line: too much to do* **4/1**[2]

P35F **4** *1 1/4* **Diamond Joshua (IRE)**[5] 1815 7-11-0 **86** (b) MrNPearce(7) 60
(N B King) *chsd ldrs: hit 3rd: rdn along 3 out: drvn and hit next: sn wknd* **20/1**

PP-0 **5** *6* **Minster Brig**[19] 1663 6-9-7 **65** oh5 (p) MrHHaynes(7) 33
(A Parker) *hld up towards rr: hdwy 10th: rdn along 3 out and nvr nr ldrs* **50/1**

525P **6** *10* **Greenfort Brave (IRE)**[18] 1685 7-10-12 **84** MrJPMcKeown(7) 42
(J J Lambe, Ire) *chsd ldrs: rdn along 9th: outpcd bef 3 out* **10/1**

4640 **7** *3* **Nobodysgonanotice (IRE)**[18] 1685 7-11-8 **87** MrCJSweeney 42
(J J Lambe, Ire) *led to 2nd: styd prom: rdn along 3 out and grad wknd appr next* **8/1**

4P46 **8** *3 1/2* **Uneven Line**[119] 854 9-10-7 **79** (p) MissCarlyFrater(7) 30
(Miss S E Forster) *hit 1st: prom tl rdn along 5th: sn lost pl and bhd fr 1/2-way* **14/1**

000- **P** **Colmcille (IRE)**[186] 4977 5-11-5 **91** MrMBriggs(7) —
(C C Bealby) *hld up: hdwy to chse ldrs 5th: rdn along 9th and sn outpcd* **10/1**

33P- **P** **The River Joker (IRE)**[230] 4278 9-11-1 **87** MrGTumelty(7) —
(John R Upson) *midfield: rdn along 1/2-way: sn bhd and p.u bef 3 out* **13/2**[3]

P-05 **P** **Lantern Leader (IRE)**[20] 1648 10-10-13 **85** (v) MrMatthewSmith(7) —
(M J Gingell) *chsd ldrs: pushed along and lost pl 7th: sn bhd and p.u bef 3 out* **40/1**

7m 0.30s (-3.60) **Going Correction** +0.20s/f (Yiel) **11** Ran SP% **110.9**
Speed ratings: **100,99,92,91,89 87,86,85,—,— —** CSF £82.25 CT £301.23 TOTE £28.40: £9.10, £1.40, £1.20; EX 128.10.
Owner Miss C Metcalfe **Bred** Miss Kerry Lane **Trained** Spennymoor, Co Durham
■ Stewards' Enquiry : Mrs E J Smith seven-day ban: asked for an effort too late (Nov 9-11, 17,21,24,25)

FOCUS
A weak handicap, confined to amateur riders, which saw the first two come well clear.

NOTEBOOK

Longstone Lass was on her best behaviour this time and duly got back to winning ways with a game display from the front. She has always been happiest with some cut, so this softer ground played right into her hands, and she saw out all of this much longer trip. It is interesting that both her previous victories were back-to-back and, providing that she can maintain this current mood, *she may be hard to pass at this level if turned out under a penalty.Official explanation: trainer said, regarding the improved form shown, mare was better suited by today's longer trip*

Canavan(IRE) , making his handicap debut after a 277-day break, had every chance yet tired on the run-in and was ultimately well held by the winner. He was miles clear of the rest, however, and with this outing under his belt, could soon be placed to open his account in this class. *(op 11-4 tchd 9-4)*

End Of An Error , third at Towcester three days previously, failed to improve for the step-up to this suitably longer trip and was given an awful lot to do from off the pace by her rider. While this ground may have been softer than ideal, she would have surely been a lot closer granted more *positive tactics. Official explanation: jockey said, regarding the running and riding, mare was unsuited by the ground which she considered to be soft as opposed to the official good to soft, adding that mare had to be ridden from behind in order to jump well and be able to pass horses (op 7-2)*

Diamond Joshua(IRE) , with blinkers replacing the visor for this return to hurdling, failed to see out the longer trip, but at least finished this time and his confidence should now be restored for a possible to return to chasing. *(op 16-1)*

1885 EUROPEAN BREEDERS FUND "NATIONAL HUNT" NOVICES' HURDLE (QUALIFIER) (8 hdls) 2m 1f

2:50 (2:50) (Class 4) 4-6-Y-O **£3,679** (£1,132; £566; £283)

Form RPR

1 **Echo Point (IRE)**[249] [3967] 5-11-0 BHarding 123+
(N G Richards) *led and sn clr: hit 3 out: styd on strly: unchal* **2/1**[1]

44- 2 *24* **Extra Smooth**[253] [3864] 4-11-0 JPMcNamara 93
(C C Bealby) *trckd ldrs: hdwy 3 out: rdn to chse wnr next: sn drvn and kpt on: no ch w wnr* **28/1**

021- 3 *3* **Bougoure (IRE)**[239] [4111] 6-11-0 DElsworth 90
(Mrs S J Smith) *a.p: rdn along to chse wnr fr 3rd: drvn and hit 2 out: sn one pce* **2/1**[1]

444- 4 *11* **Scotmail (IRE)**[187] [4971] 4-11-0 GLee 80+
(J Howard Johnson) *nt fluent 1st: trckd ldrs: effrt and rdn along appr 3 out: sn one pce* **6/1**[3]

50U 5 *17* **Thorn Of The Rose (IRE)**[18] [1688] 4-10-2 DCCostello(5) 55
(James Moffatt) *hld up in reaer: a bhd* **100/1**

00/ 6 *shd* **Rectory (IRE)**[641] [3482] 6-10-7 NCarter(7) 62
(Mrs S J Smith) *in tch: rdn along 1/2-way: wknd bef 3 out* **80/1**

03-0 7 *2* **Myoss (IRE)**[10] [1757] 6-11-0 TSiddall 60
(Mrs V J Makin) *hld up: hdwy 3 out: sn rdn and j. bdly lft 2 out: wknd* **80/1**

0- 8 *13* **Top Dawn (IRE)**[198] [4807] 5-11-0 BGibson 47
(L Lungo) *a bhd* **33/1**

0- 9 *11* **Victor One (IRE)**[390] [1554] 5-10-11 PAspell(3) 36
(J Wade) *mstke 2nd: a bhd* **100/1**

/00- 10 *12* **Fencote Gold**[249] [3953] 5-11-0 RGarritty 24
(P Beaumont) *keen: chsd wnr to 3rd: prom tl rdn along appr 3 out and sn wknd* **50/1**

P **Whatcanyasay** 4-10-4 SGagan(10) —
(Mrs E Slack) *a bhd: t.o 1/2-way: p.u after 2 out* **100/1**

42-3 P **Monsieur Delage**[24] [1611] 5-11-0 ATinkler —
(S Gollings) *prom: rdn along after 4th: lost pl next and bhd whn p.u bef 2 out* **5/1**[2]

/3-P P **Rosslare (FR)**[18] [1687] 6-11-0 PWhelan —
(R A Fahey) *hld up in midfield: mstke 4th and 5th: sn rdn and wknd: bhd whn p.u bef 2 out* **20/1**

4m 8.30s (1.80) **Going Correction** +0.20s/f (Yiel)
WFA 4 from 5yo+ 13lb **13** Ran SP% **116.2**
Speed ratings: **103,91,90,85,77 77,76,70,64,59** —,—,— CSF £60.90 TOTE £2.30: £3.90, £4.50, £1.10; EX 48.00.
Owner The Border Reivers **Bred** Mrs C M Hurley **Trained** Greystoke, Cumbria

FOCUS
A fair novice event which saw the field left trailing by the impressive winner.

NOTEBOOK

Echo Point(IRE) ◆ , an impressive winner of a Fairyhouse bumper when making all on his only previous start in February, translated that form to hurdles in no uncertain fashion with another impressive display of front-running on this debut for his new connections. He jumped neatly bar an error three out, it is fair to say he had the race in the bag at the halfway stage, and clearly enjoys himself out in front. His breeding suggests he ought to stay further, this ground was to his liking and he could take much higher order as a novice before the season's end. *(op 7-4)*

Extra Smooth , who showed a fair level of form in two bumpers last season, stayed on best of the rest on this hurdling bow and looked to enjoy the easy ground. He appeals as the type to fare better when eligible for handicaps over timber and can improve for the outing. *(op 25-1)*

Bougoure(IRE) , last seen winning a bumper at the fourth time of asking back in March, proved popular in the betting ring ahead of this hurdling bow yet his fate was apparent a long way from home. He should improve for the experience fitness-wise, is bred to do well over jumps at around *this trip, and could do better in time.Official explanation: jockey said, regarding the running and riding, his orders were to lie handy and go down the inside for better ground, adding that gelding was unable to lie up with the leader and became tired after jumping the third-last, after which point he rode hand and heels to keep the gelding balanced (op 5-2)*

Scotmail(IRE) , who ran to a similar level in three bumpers last season, failed to make an impact on his hurdling bow and was made to look very one paced. *(op 12-1)*

Monsieur Delage disappointingly failed to build on the promise of his recent hurdling bow at Market Rasen, but looked uneasy on the ground and should be given another chance to atone *when reverting to a faster surface. Official explanation: jockey said gelding was unsuited by the good to soft ground (op 7-2)*

1886 JOHN WADE FOR EQUINE FIBRE AND RUBBER (S) H'CAP CHASE (21 fncs) 3m 3f

3:25 (3:25) (Class 5) (0-90,85) 5-Y-0+ **£3,255** (£930; £465)

Form RPR

P6-0 1 **Celtic Flow**[14] [1723] 7-9-11 **59** oh1 PAspell(3) 75+
(C R Wilson) *trckd ldr: effrt to ld appr 4 out: rdn clr after next: drvn along appr last and kpt on* **13/2**

42P- 2 *4* **Chris And Ryan (IRE)**[192] [4873] 7-10-8 **67** NPMulholland 78+
(Mrs L B Normile) *led: rdn along 5 out: hdd appr next and blnd: sn drvn along: kpt on u.p* **10/1**

53P 3 *16* **Chancers Dante (IRE)**[152] [535] 9-10-1 **67** (b) TJDreaper(7) 66+
(Ferdy Murphy) *hld up towards rr: stdy hdwy 1/2-way: chsd ldng pair 4 out: drvn along next: plugged on same pce* **6/1**[3]

-P60 4 *30* **Bang And Blame (IRE)**[47] [1446] 9-10-6 **65** ADempsey 28
(M W Easterby) *trckd ldrs: hdwy to chse ldng pair 7th: rdn along 5 out and sn wknd* **7/1**

243 5 *3* **Starbuck**[14] [1719] 11-11-2 **80** DMcGann(5) 40
(A M Crow) *trckd ldrs: rdn along and lost pl 10th: drvn along and styd on to chse ldrs after 13th: wknd 15th: bhd whn blnd 3 out* **7/2**[1]

6P-5 6 *dist* **Joey Dunlop (IRE)**[11] [1741] 11-10-11 **77** ow1 MrSClements(7) —
(J Clements, Ire) *in rr whn blnd 3rd: sn bhd: t.o fr 7th* **25/1**

0340 P **Top Pack (IRE)**[19] [1663] 6-11-2 **75** (v) BHarding —
(N G Richards) *in tch: reminders 7th: rdn along nnext: sn wknd and bhd whn p.u after 14th* **4/1**[2]

-0PP P **Mid Summer Lark (IRE)**[14] [1723] 9-10-12 **78** (v) MrMSeston(7) —
(I McMath) *mstkes: chsd ldrs: rdn along fr 4th: lost pl 6th: bhd whn p.u after 8th* **16/1**

6345 P **Corries Wood (IRE)**[18] [1686] 6-11-12 **85** JPMcNamara —
(J J Lambe, Ire) *hld up: hdwy to chse ldrs 8th: rdn along and wknd after 12th bhd whn p.u after 15th* **7/1**

7m 4.10s (-2.70) **Going Correction** +0.20s/f (Yiel) **9** Ran SP% **113.7**
Speed ratings: **99,97,93,84,83** —,—,—,— CSF £66.18 CT £408.54 TOTE £6.30: £1.80, £3.00, £2.50; EX 71.90.The winner was bought in for 4,400gns.
Owner Exors of the late W R Wilson **Bred** W R Wilson **Trained** Manfield, N Yorks

FOCUS
A very poor event and the field finished strung out behind the ready winner.

NOTEBOOK

Celtic Flow showed the benefit of her recent comeback over timber eight days previously and lost her maiden tag at the 19th time of asking. The manner in which she travelled and jumped this time suggests that, despite being just moderate, she could be an improving sort this season and she clearly stays very well. *Official explanation: vet said mare bled from the nose (op 10-1)*

Chris And Ryan(IRE) had his chance from the front and, while he was readily brushed aside by the lightly-weighted winner, still finished a long way ahead of the remainder of his rivals. This was a pleasing return to action and he is clearly better suited by a longer trip. *(tchd 11-1)*

Chancers Dante(IRE) was hard ridden before four out and merely plugged on at the same pace thereafter on this return from a 152-day break. *(op 11-2)*

Bang And Blame(IRE) failed to really improve for this drop in class and remains one to avoid. *(op 8-1)*

Starbuck looked to be hating this softer ground and was well beaten. He should prove a totally *different proposition when reverting to a faster surface.Official explanation: jockey said gelding was unsuited by the good to soft ground (op 11-4 tchd 4-1)*

Mid Summer Lark(IRE) *Official explanation: jockey said gelding lost its action (tchd 7-2)*

Top Pack(IRE) , with the visor re-applied, ran no sort of race on this chasing bow and looks one to avoid at all costs. *(tchd 7-2)*

1887 BETFRED POKER H'CAP HURDLE (SERIES QUALIFIER) (10 hdls) 2m 5f 110y

4:00 (4:00) (Class 4) (0-105,103) 4-Y-O+ **£4,396** (£1,352; £676; £338)

Form RPR

-U62 1 **Nick The Silver**[21] [1643] 4-11-6 **97** (p) GLee 101+
(Robert Gray) *trckd ldrs: swtchd rt and hdwy to chal 2 out: rdn and sn led: drvn flat and styd on* **10/1**

3-33 2 *2* **Russian Sky**[24] [1606] 6-11-3 **101** TMessenger(7) 101
(Mrs H O Graham) *a.p: hit 5th: chal 3 out: rdn and slt ld next: sn hdd and drvn: kpt on* **2/1**[1]

402- 3 *12* **Red Man (IRE)**[228] [4321] 8-10-13 **100** SGagan(10) 90+
(Mrs E Slack) *keen: led and set decent pce: hit 2nd: rdn along and mstke 7th: drvn and hdd 2 out: wknd appr last* **11/2**[3]

220P 4 *7* **Cody**[103] [1002] 6-9-12 **78** (bt[1]) PAspell(3) 59
(James Moffatt) *in tch: hdwy to chse ldrs 6th: rdn along appr 3 out: sn wknd* **20/1**

3300 5 *1 ¼* **Hugo De Perro (FR)**[24] [1606] 10-11-9 **103** (v[1]) PBuchanan(3) 83
(Miss Lucinda V Russell) *chsd ldrs: outpcd and lost pl 7th: sn bhd* **20/1**

326- 6 *8* **Sands Rising**[187] [4966] 8-11-9 **100** (t) KJohnson 72
(R Johnson) *racd wd: in tch: rdn along appr 3 out and sn wknd* **12/1**

122- 7 *dist* **Flake**[225] [4391] 5-10-13 **100** ARAdams(10) —
(Mrs S J Smith) *plld hrd and cl up: blnd 1st: cl up tl lost pl 1/2-way: sn bhd* **4/1**[2]

0-00 P **Quay Walloper**[161] [414] 4-9-8 **78** oh13 ow1 (v) MrSFMagee(7) —
(J R Norton) *a rr: wl bhd fr 4th* **100/1**

PP-3 P **Classic Lash (IRE)**[177] [152] 9-9-9 **79** CDSharkey(7) —
(P Needham) *in tch: rdn along 7th: sn outpcd and bhd whn p.u bef 2 out* **9/1**

P **An Dun Ri (IRE)**[172] [225] 6-10-9 **86** JPMcNamara —
(J J Lambe, Ire) *hld up in rr: rdn along whn blnd 4th: sn bhd and p.u bef 2 out* **10/1**

5m 28.3s (12.60) **Going Correction** +0.20s/f (Yiel)
WFA 4 from 5yo+ 14lb **10** Ran SP% **115.1**
Speed ratings: **85,84,79,77,76 74**,—,—,—,— CSF £30.26 CT £124.70 TOTE £7.40: £1.90, £1.50, £1.80; EX 33.40.
Owner Naughty Diesel Ltd **Bred** Dr J M Leigh **Trained** Malton, N Yorks

FOCUS
A moderate handicap, run at a fair gallop in the conditions, and the form looks sound for the class.

NOTEBOOK

Nick The Silver , claimed out of Martin Pipe's yard after his second at Towcester last time, made a winning debut for new connections in this better class and showed a decent attitude in doing so. He had no trouble with the slower ground, looked better the further he went, and could have more to offer when returning to an even longer trip in the future. *(op 9-1 tchd 8-1)*

Russian Sky , whose last success was in this event last year off a 12lb lower mark, had every chance, but again found one too good despite giving his all under pressure. This was yet another sound effort and, while he is a decent benchmark for this form, clearly holds no secrets from the Handicapper. *(tchd 5-2)*

Red Man(IRE) paid for running too freely through the early parts at the head of affairs and his goose was cooked after the penultimate flight. He is entitled to improve for the outing. *(tchd 9-2 and 6-1)*

Flake proved way too keen on this return to action and eventually paid the price. He is capable of much better. *(tchd 9-2)*

1888 ST JAMES SECURITY NOVICES' CHASE (16 fncs) 2m 5f

4:35 (4:35) (Class 4) 4-Y-O+ **£4,856** (£1,578; £849)

Form RPR

4-30 1 **Celtic Blaze (IRE)**[20] [1341] 6-10-12 100 (t) ARoss 100+
(B S Rothwell) *hld up: hdwy 10th: rdn to ld 2 out: sn hdd and drvn: led last: kpt on gamely flat* **16/1**

4-P3 2 *1 ½* **Deja Vu (IRE)**[29] [1568] 6-11-5 105 GLee 108+
(J Howard Johnson) *trckd ldrs: chal 10th and ev ch tl rdn and outpcd 3 out: swtchd and rallied next: sn led: wandered and hdd last: kpt on* **11/8**[1]

-305 3 *½* **Nocatee (IRE)**[29] [1571] 4-10-5 102 FKeniry 89
(P C Haslam) *trckd ldrs: rdn along and outpcd appr 3 out: drvn next: styd on* **4/1**[3]

31-0 U **Underwriter (USA)**[180] [117] 5-10-12 105 TJDreaper(7) —
(Ferdy Murphy) *hld up in tch: blnd and uns rdr 8th* **11/4**[2]

The Form Book, Raceform Ltd, Compton, RG20 6NL

P-F0 **P** **Pottsy's Joy**^{172} [211] 8-11-5 89 DElsworth —
(Mrs S J Smith) *a rr: rdn along and hit 9th: sn bhd and blnd bdly 3 out: p.u after* **16/1**

PPF- **P** **Mad Max Too**^{230} [4271] 6-11-5 79 KRenwick —
(N Wilson) *led: mstke 3rd: hdd next: chsd ldrsm hit 7th: rdn along and blnd 10trh: sn bhd and p.u bef 2 out* **66/1**

05 **U** **Tornado Alley (IRE)**^{18} [1682] 6-11-5 92 JPMcNamara 96+
(J J Lambe, Ire) *cl up: led 4th: jnd 10th: rdn along 4 out: drvn and hdd whn blnd bdly and uns rdr 2 out* **14/1**

5m 32.5s (9.10) **Going Correction** +0.20s/f (Yiel)
WFA 4 from 5yo+ 14lb 7 Ran SP% **108.7**
Speed ratings: **90,89,89,—,— —,—** CSF £36.72 TOTE £22.30: £6.40, £1.10; EX 47.40.
Owner Michael Saunders **Bred** Edward Sexton **Trained** Nawton, N Yorks

FOCUS
A moderate novice chase, which saw just three complete, and the form is worth treating with caution.

NOTEBOOK
Celtic Blaze(IRE) , beaten in a banded event on the Flat last time, got her chasing career off to a perfect start with a brave success on ground she clearly enjoys. She was given a well-judged ride by Ross, her jumping was fluent in the main, and she may well prove better in this sphere. However, she will look much better off in handicaps in the future, rather than under a penalty in this division. *(tchd 18-1)*
Deja Vu(IRE) , third in a much better event over course and distance on his chase debut last time, failed to build on that effort despite having every chance and proved a tricky ride. He is proven on soft ground, so that does not look a viable excuse and, while he can find a race over fences in time, this must rate as a missed opportunity. *(op 5-4 tchd 6-5)*
Nocatee(IRE) , making his chase debut, was hard ridden from a fair way out and, despite finishing his race well, never really threatened to hit the front at any stage. However, this was still a fair effort and he could prove a different proposition back on faster ground. *(op 9-2)*
Underwriter(USA) , having his first outing over fences and returning from a 180-day break, gave his rider little chance of maintaining their partnership when blundering at the eighth fence. He had jumped well enough to that point, however. *(op 5-2 tchd 3-1)*

1889 GG.COM MAIDEN NATIONAL HUNT FLAT RACE (CONDITIONAL JOCKEYS' AND AMATEUR RIDERS' RACE) 2m 1f
5:10 (5:11) (Class 6) 4-6-Y-O **£1,918** (£548; £274)

Form RPR

3- **1** **According To Pete**^{221} [4451] 4-10-13 PMerrigan$^{(5)}$ 111+
(J M Jefferson) *hld up in rr: stdy hdwy 6f out: trckd ldrs 4f out: rdn to ld wl over 1f out: kpt on* **10/3**^{1}

2- **2** *1 ½* **Oscatello (USA)**^{340} [2351] 5-10-8 DJBoland$^{(10)}$ 107
(Ian Williams) *trckd ldrs: hdwy to ld 1/2-way: rdn and hdd wl over 1f out: kpt on u.p ins last* **10/3**^{1}

3 *9* **Mister Frog (FR)** 4-10-13 DCCostello$^{(5)}$ 98
(G A Swinbank) *hld up in rr: hdwy 1/2-way: chsd ldrs 3f out: rdn 2f out and kpt on same pce appr last* **4/1**^{2}

4 *2* **Stagecoach Opal** 4-10-11 NCarter$^{(7)}$ 96
(Mrs S J Smith) *trckd ldrs on inner: hdwy and cl up 1/2-way: rdn 3f out and ev ch tl drvn and wknd over 2f out* **11/1**

560- **5** *28* **Flemingstone (IRE)**^{199} [4788] 5-10-4 MrSFMagee$^{(7)}$ 61
(J R Norton) *in tch: hdwy to chse ldrs 6f out: rdn along 4f out and sn wknd* **25/1**

40 **6** *24* **Seymour Weld**^{10} [1762] 5-10-11 APogson$^{(7)}$ 44
(C T Pogson) *prom: rdn along over 4f out and sn wknd* **20/1**

54- **7** *1 ½* **Silver Dollars (FR)**^{218} [4513] 4-10-11 BSHughes$^{(7)}$ 43
(J Howard Johnson) *racd wd: prom tl rdn along over 4f out and sn wknd* **7/1**^{3}

8 *24* **Solway Raki** 4-10-11 MJMcAlister$^{(7)}$ 19
(B Storey) *chsd ldrs: rdn along 1/2-way: sn lost pl and bhd* **40/1**

0 **9** *5* **Dark Rebel (IRE)**^{34} [1532] 5-11-1 PAspell$^{(3)}$ 14
(J Wade) *a bhd* **66/1**

10 *dist* **What A Blaze (IRE)** 5-10-4 MrRTierney$^{(7)}$ —
(Robert Gray) *chsd ldr: led after 4f: rdn alonga nd hdd 1/2-way: sn lost pl and bhd* **10/1**

11 *1* **Barney (IRE)** 4-10-8 SGagan$^{(10)}$ —
(Mrs E Slack) *keen: led: rn wd bnd after 3f: hdd after 4f: rdn along 1/2-way and sn wknd* **10/1**

P0-0 **P** **Bodfari Sauvage**^{18} [1688] 5-10-11 (t) MrGO'Sullivan$^{(7)}$ —
(J J Lambe, Ire) *towards rr: rdn along and bhd fr 1/2-way: t.o whn p.u over 4f out* **100/1**

0 **P** **Whitsun**^{26} [1593] 5-10-11 EWhillans$^{(7)}$ —
(Miss Kate Milligan) *staretd slowly: hdwy on outer and in tch after 4f: rdn along after 6f: sn lost pl and bhd: t.o whn p.u over 4f out* **50/1**

4m 9.00s (2.10) **Going Correction** +0.20s/f (Yiel)
WFA 4 from 5yo+ 13lb **13** Ran SP% **120.7**
Speed ratings: **103,102,98,97,83 72,71,60,58,— —,—,—** CSF £13.53 TOTE £3.70: £1.70, £1.70, £2.40; EX 21.90 Place 6 £46.78, Place 5 £14.44.
Owner P Nelson **Bred** Peter Nelson **Trained** Norton, N Yorks

FOCUS
A potentially above average bumper for the track, run at an average pace, and the first two could both rate higher.

NOTEBOOK
According To Pete ◆ , third to the potentially smart novice Rimsky on his only previous outing 221 days previously, confirmed the promise of that effort and duly got off the mark in determined fashion. Considering his dam stayed three miles, he will most likely need further when sent over hurdles and, being a son of Accordion, may ideally prefer a quicker surface in the future. He could be useful. *(op 7-2 tchd 4-1 and 3-1)*
Oscatello(USA) ◆ , runner-up to subsequent Listed bumper winner Oscar Park on his sole outing last term, had every chance on this return from a 340-day absence but got outstayed by the winner. Time will most likely tell that there was little disgrace in this defeat, he was nicely clear in second, and he too looks a fair prospect for novice hurdles in due course. *(op 7-2 tchd 3-1)*
Mister Frog(FR) , a half-brother to a winning chaser in France, hails from a yard that does particularly well in this sphere and he did enough to suggest he can be found an opening with this debut experience under his belt. *(op 3-1)*
Stagecoach Opal , half-brother to winning chaser Colliers Court, had every chance on this debut until eventually lacking the pace to go with the principals. He is open to plenty of improvement and was in turn a long way clear of the remainder. *(op 9-1)*
Silver Dollars(FR) , who showed clear ability on the second of his two bumper starts last season, raced wide presumably in search of the better ground yet dropped out rather tamely when push came to shove. He is starting to look very expensive now. *(op 8-1)*
Barney(IRE) *Official explanation: jockey said gelding hung right-handed throughout and had a breathing problem (op 33-1 tchd 8-1)*
T/Plt: £81.00 to a £1 stake. Pool: £46,715.80. 420.60 winning tickets. T/Qpdt: £15.30 to a £1 stake. Pool: £4,515.90. 218.10 winning tickets. JR

1741 STRATFORD (L-H)
Thursday, October 27

OFFICIAL GOING: Chase course - soft (good to soft in places); hurdle course - good to soft (soft in places)
First fence in home straight omitted in all chases.
Wind: Light, across Weather: Fine and sunny

1890 BURCHELL EDWARDS FOUNDERS (S) HURDLE (9 hdls) 2m 110y
2:30 (2:30) (Class 5) 4-7-Y-O **£2,717** (£836; £418; £209)

Form RPR

6132 **1** **Honan (IRE)**^{12} [1742] 6-11-3 96 (v) APMcCoy 92+
(M C Pipe) *a.p: chsd clr ldr after 5th: led appr 2 out: sn rdn clr: eased nr fin* **4/5**^{1}

00F3 **2** *2 ½* **Urban Dream (IRE)**^{12} [1742] 4-10-12 88 RJohnson 81
(R A Farrant) *hld up: hdwy 6th: sn rdn: wnt 2nd appr last: no ch w wnr* **11/2**^{2}

00-0 **3** *4* **Imtihan (IRE)**^{12} [1742] 6-11-8 102 (v^{1}) DCrosse 87
(J G M O'Shea) *hld up: rdn 5th: styd on u.p fr 2 out: nt rch ldrs* **20/1**

/P66 **4** *hd* **Buz Kiri (USA)**^{11} [1753] 7-10-12 85 WHutchinson 77
(A W Carroll) *hld up: rdn 5th: styd on appr last: nrst fin* **11/2**^{2}

00P0 **5** *¾* **Simiola**^{12} [1742] 6-10-0 75 MNicolls$^{(5)}$ 71+
(S T Lewis) *chsd ldrs: mstke 6th: sn rdn: chsd wnr 2 out: wknd last* **33/1**

0 **6** *16* **Shergael (IRE)**^{7} [1614] 4-10-7 WKennedy$^{(5)}$ 62+
(J L Spearing) *led after 2nd: sn clr: rdn: hdd and wkng whn blnd 2 out* **10/1**^{3}

56P0 **7** *shd* **La Folichonne (FR)**^{14} [1725] 6-10-5 67 WMarston 53
(T Wall) *led: hdd after 2nd: chsd clr ldr tl after 5th: wknd next* **50/1**

0-P **8** *3 ½* **Sunny Daze**^{19} [1672] 5-10-12 GLee 57
(D McCain) *hld up: rdn and wknd after 5th* **33/1**

9 *26* **Fair Options**^{24} 4-10-12 (t) JGoldstein 31
(A P Jones) *hld up: mstkes 1st and 2nd: bhd fr 4th* **50/1**

0 **P** **Yorker (USA)**^{7} [1794] 7-10-12 AntonyEvans —
(Ms Deborah J Evans) *plld hrd and prom: wknd after 5th: t.o whn p.u bef 7th* **25/1**

4m 8.80s (10.40) **Going Correction** +0.575s/f (Soft)
WFA 4 from 5yo+ 13lb **10** Ran SP% **113.8**
Speed ratings: **98,96,94,94,94 86,86,85,73,—** CSF £4.76 TOTE £1.60: £1.10, £1.70, £3.20; EX 4.80.The winner was bought in for 6,500gns.
Owner Eminence Grise Partnership **Bred** Miss Ashling O'Connell **Trained** Nicholashayne, Devon
■ Stewards' Enquiry : D Crosse two-day ban: used whip with excessive frequency (Nov 7-8)

FOCUS
A very weak affair, run at a fair gallop and the winner can be rated value for further. The form makes sense with the first six close to form.

NOTEBOOK
Honan(IRE) , who would have most likely scored in this grade under a more patient ride last time, gained compensation with a facile success and can be rated value for at least double his winning margin. Four of his five career wins have now come under McCoy, and while this is very much his grade, he is clearly in great heart at present. *(op 10-11 tchd Evens)*
Urban Dream(IRE) finished his race well enough, but failed to rate a threat to the winner and is flattered by his proximity to that rival at the finish. On the evidence of his last two outings, he really does need a stiffer test to be seen at his best. *(tchd 5-1)*
Imtihan(IRE) , in the first-time visor, showed his best form for some time yet never threatened the front pair. It will be interesting to see whether he can build on this improved effort. *(op 16-1)*
Buz Kiri(USA) failed to improve for the drop into this class and was staying on all too late. He is happier on a faster surface, but remains one to avoid in the main. *(op 6-1 tchd 5-1)*

1891 KNIGHT FRANK BEGINNERS' CHASE (13 fncs 2 omitted) 2m 4f
3:00 (3:02) (Class 3) 5-Y-O+ **£5,460** (£1,680; £840; £420)

Form RPR

1/1 **1** **Spirit Of New York (IRE)**^{25} [1613] 6-11-0 APMcCoy 136+
(Jonjo O'Neill) *hld up: hdwy 7th: chsd ldr after 3 out: pckd last: rdn to ld nr fin* **11/2**^{3}

22-2 **2** *1 ¼* **Montgermont (FR)**^{19} [1669] 5-11-0 AThornton 134+
(Mrs L C Taylor) *chsd ldr 2nd: hit next: blnd 9th: led 3 out: mstke next: rdn flat: hdd nr fin* **7/4**^{1}

51P- **3** *25* **Classic Capers**^{229} [4330] 6-11-0 GLee 108
(J M Jefferson) *chsd ldrs to 10th* **14/1**

413- **4** *1* **Briery Fox (IRE)**^{222} [4463] 7-11-0 MBradburne 108+
(H D Daly) *chsd ldrs: mstke 3rd: hmpd 7th: wknd appr 2 out* **9/1**

00-0 **5** *27* **Its Crucial (IRE)**^{19} [1668] 5-11-0 AntonyEvans 80
(N A Twiston-Davies) *led: hdd & wknd 3 out* **16/1**

34- **6** *shd* **Cruising River (IRE)**^{209} [4679] 6-11-0 SThomas 80
(Miss H C Knight) *hld up: rdn 9th: wknd bef next* **8/1**

0/ **P** **Stars'N'Stripes (IRE)**^{200} 7-11-0 JAMcCarthy —
(W W Dennis) *blnd 1st: a bhd: t.o whn p.u bef 3 out* **25/1**

11P/ **P** **Tragic Ohio**^{600} [4190] 6-11-0 ChristianWilliams —
(P F Nicholls) *hld up: bhd whn p.u after 7th* **9/2**^{2}

5-3U **P** **Vingis Park (IRE)**^{26} [1595] 7-11-0 (tp) RThornton —
(V R A Dartnall) *chsd ldr to 2nd: mstke and wknd 9th: bhd whn p.u bef next* **28/1**

4m 58.1s (-1.90) **Going Correction** +0.575s/f (Soft) **9** Ran SP% **110.9**
Speed ratings: **105,104,94,94,83 83,—,—,—** CSF £15.29 TOTE £4.60: £1.40, £1.10, £3.80; EX 9.50.
Owner John P McManus **Bred** D Mitchell **Trained** Cheltenham, Gloucs

FOCUS
A decent novice event for the track, run at a sound pace and the first two had it to themselves a fair way out. Both look potentially smart prospects and the form could rate higher.

NOTEBOOK
Spirit Of New York(IRE) ◆, interestingly sent straight over fences after winning both his previous bumper outings, looked held on the final end, but stuck to his task and deserves credit for recovering from a pecking on landing over the final fence to get on top close home. He jumped well in the main, handled the softer ground without fuss and, as could be expected of half-brother to 2003 National Hunt Chase winner Native Emperor, relished the longer trip. Indeed, he should be seen to even better effect on a stiffer track in the future, and could prove smart before the season's end. *(op 5-1)*
Montgermont(FR), who made Iris's Gift pull out all the stops on his recent chasing bow at Bangor last time, looked all over the winner turning for home, but he lost momentum two out and may have been better served going for home earlier this time. That said, time may well tell there was little disgrace in this defeat, and he could be considered unfortunate to have bumped into two such rivals over fences thus far. He should soon be placed to make his mark in this sphere. *(op 2-1)*
Classic Capers, a dual winner over timber last term and rated 117 in that sphere, jumped well enough on this chasing bow and can certainly find easier opportunities in the future. *(op 16-1)*

Briery Fox(IRE), previously successful in a point, bumper and novice hurdle and rated 119 in the latter sphere, did enough to suggest he ought to improve for the outing/experience. He will also prefer the return to a faster surface in the future. *(tchd 10-1)*
Tragic Ohio *Official explanation: jockey said gelding was never travelling (tchd 4-1)*

1892 MIKE HARRISON 60TH BIRTHDAY MAIDEN HURDLE (12 hdls) 2m 6f 110y
3:30 (3:30) (Class 3) 4-Y-0+ **£5,616** (£1,728; £864; £432)

Form RPR
1 **Day Of Claies (FR)**[187] 4-11-1 .... CLlewellyn 105+
(N A Twiston-Davies) *a.p: led after 3 out: hdd bef next: 3l down and hld whn lft in ld last: rdn out* **9/2**[2]
6/04 2 1 ¾ **Scarlet Dawn (IRE)**[63] 1317 7-10-9 .... TScudamore 95
(D A Rees) *hld up: hdwy 9th: rdn appr 2 out: btn whn lft 2nd last: styd on* **66/1**
-124 3 11 **Youlbesolucky (IRE)**[19] 1671 6-11-2 .... APMcCoy 91
(Jonjo O'Neill) *chsd ldr to 2nd: remained handy: jnd ldr 8th: rdn and wknd appr 2 out* **13/2**
0- 4 3 **Malko De Beaumont (FR)**[245] 4026 5-11-2 .... JPMcNamara 88
(K C Bailey) *hld up: hdwy appr 8th: rdn and wknd after 3 out* **28/1**
5 1 ½ **Joe Brown**[193] 5-10-11 .... PMerrigan(5) 87
(Mrs H Dalton) *hld up: hmpd 2nd: styd on fr 2 out: nvr nr to chal* **12/1**
3 6 9 **Livingonaknifedge (IRE)**[133] 769 6-11-2 .... WHutchinson 79+
(Ian Williams) *prom to 3 out* **20/1**
05-5 7 10 **Royal Cliche**[180] 128 6-11-2 .... RJohnson 71+
(R T Phillips) *hld up: hdwy 6th: wknd after 8th* **33/1**
133- 8 4 **Crashtown Leader (IRE)**[297] 3198 6-11-2 .... TDoyle 76+
(C Tinkler) *chsd ldr 2nd tl led 4th: hdd and wkng whn hmpd after 3 out* **2/1**[1]
05- 9 dist **Longhope Boy**[236] 4179 6-11-2 .... AThornton —
(W J Musson) *hld up: wknd appr 8th* **66/1**
10 shd **Love Of Classics**[178] 5-10-13 .... ONelmes(3) —
(O Sherwood) *hld up: rdn 4th: a bhd* **66/1**
4- U **Taurus Oats**[201] 6-10-9 .... (t) ChristianWilliams —
(P F Nicholls) *mstke and uns rdr 2nd* **14/1**
P **Flying Spud**[21] 4-11-1 .... SCurran —
(A J Chamberlain) *led to 4th: wknd appr 8th: t.o whn p.u bef next* **100/1**
0- P **No Turning Back (IRE)**[286] 3346 6-11-1 ow4 .... MrNHarris(5) —
(C L Popham) *chsd ldr tl wknd after 7th: t.o whn p.u bef 9th* **66/1**
0-0 P **Pleased To Receive (IRE)**[156] 490 5-10-11 .... WKennedy(5) —
(A M Hales) *hld up: mstke 5th: a in rr: t.o whn p.u bef 3 out* **100/1**
6- P **Greenmoor House (IRE)**[198] 4814 7-11-2 .... RThornton —
(V R A Dartnall) *hld up: rdn and wknd appr 8th: t.o whn p.u bef next* **10/1**
F **Killaghy Castle (IRE)**[221] 5-11-2 .... LAspell 110+
(N J Gifford) *mid-div: hdwy after 5th: led appr 2 out: 3l clr whn fell last* **6/1**[3]

5m 38.9s (9.20) **Going Correction** +0.575s/f (Soft)
WFA 4 from 5yo+ 14lb **16** Ran SP% **121.7**
Speed ratings: **107,106,102,101,101 97,94,93,—,— —,—,—,—,— —** CSF £281.97 TOTE £6.30: £2.30, £10.20, £2.50; EX 303.00.
Owner Million In Mind Partnership **Bred** J P Chauvet And Mme Jean-Paul Chauvet **Trained** Naunton, Gloucs

FOCUS
A fair novice event, run at a sound pace with the faller rated a five-length winner, but the form should be treated with a degree of caution.

NOTEBOOK
Day Of Claies(FR) , the first runner from the Million In Mind partnership to represent this yard, was held by the winner prior to that rival falling at the final flight and has to rate a fortunate winner. However, he did little wrong throughout the race, looked suited by the trip/ground and this four-year-old clearly has a future for his new connections. *(tchd 5-1)*
Scarlet Dawn(IRE) turned in a personal best in defeat and relished the return to this longer trip. She is going the right way and, while her proximity at the finish has to raise a doubt as to the overall strength of this form, the suspicion is that this much-improved effort was no fluke. She now also qualifies for handicaps. *(op 50-1)*
Youlbesolucky(IRE) was made to look one paced approaching the final bend and again ran below expectations. He has yet to build on the promise of his summer bumper form, but he has yet to encounter fast ground in this sphere, and is not one to write off just yet. *(op 6-1)*
Malko De Beaumont(FR) , a dual winner on the Flat in France prior to his disappointing hurdling debut last season, shaped better this time and did enough to suggest he can improve for the outing now his yard appear to be emerging from its spell in the doldrums. *(op 25-1 tchd 33-1)*
Joe Brown , winner of his last point in April, was doing his best work at the finish on this hurdling bow. He should improve as he becomes more experienced in this sphere and will enjoy the return to further on this evidence.
Crashtown Leader(IRE) , a bumper winner on his debut last term and far from disgraced in two subsequent outings over timber, dropped out disappointingly after racing handily and was well beaten prior to being hampered three out. He now has the option of handicapping, and is entitled to improve for the outing, but this leaves him with a fair bit to prove now all the same. *(op 9-4 tchd 5-2)*
Taurus Oats , having her first outing for Paul Nicholls, fell too early to tell how she would have fared on this hurdling bow. *(op 7-1)*
Killaghy Castle(IRE) ◆, who showed definite promise when finishing runner-up in two Irish points earlier this year, had the race in the bag before agonisingly coming to grief at the final flight and must rate an unlucky loser. The manner in which he went about his business suggests he has a bright future and, on the evidence thus far this term, his stable currently looks to house some decent young talent. *(op 7-1)*
Greenmoor House(IRE) *Official explanation: vet said gelding pulled up lame (op 7-1)*

1893 REAL ESTATE PROPERTIES LTD H'CAP CHASE (FOR THE J.H. ROWE CHALLENGE TROPHY) (18 fncs 3 omitted) 3m 4f
4:00 (4:00) (Class 3) (0-120,115) 5-Y-0**£6,271** (£2,318; £1,159; £527; £263)

Form RPR
2-12 1 **Bob Ar Aghaidh (IRE)**[23] 1634 9-11-12 **115** .... TDoyle 128+
(C Tinkler) *led to 3rd: led 6th to 10th: led appr 13th: drvn out* **9/2**[1]
5-F2 2 2 ½ **Jiver (IRE)**[12] 1741 6-11-7 **110** .... TScudamore 120+
(M Scudamore) *a.p: chsd wnr 3 out: sn rdn: styd on same pce flat* **9/1**
204 3 5 **Waterberg (IRE)**[67] 1276 10-10-12 **101** .... (b) MBradburne 109+
(H D Daly) *hld up: hdwy 5th: rdn whn hit 2 out: no ex last* **16/1**
/4B- 4 18 **Infrasonique (FR)**[533] 304 9-11-0 **103** .... AThornton 101+
(Mrs L C Taylor) *led 3rd to 6th: led 10th to appr 13th: blnd and wknd 3 out* **6/1**[2]
6P-5 5 3 **Buzybakson (IRE)**[25] 1615 8-9-12 **92** .... MNicolls(5) 75
(J R Cornwall) *hld up: rdn 12th: lost tch next* **13/2**[3]
03-0 6 6 **Spanish Main (IRE)**[152] 547 11-11-4 **107** .... CLlewellyn 84
(N A Twiston-Davies) *prom: lost pl after 5th: drvn along 8th: hmpd 12th: sn wknd* **7/1**
10-6 7 15 **Follow The Flow (IRE)**[183] 55 9-11-1 **107** .... ONelmes(3) 69
(P A Pritchard) *hld up: hdwy 7th: hit 14th: sn wknd* **20/1**
-610 P **The Sister**[19] 1670 8-11-12 **115** .... (v) APMcCoy —
(Jonjo O'Neill) *hld up: blnd 11th: sn p.u* **9/1**
41C5 F **Charango Star**[10] 1778 7-11-7 **110** .... RJohnson —
(W K Goldsworthy) *chsd ldrs: mstke 7th: cl 3rd whn fell 12th* **6/1**[2]
1244 U **Uncle Mick (IRE)**[22] 1639 10-11-2 **105** .... (p) JTizzard —
(C L Tizzard) *hld up: rdn and hit 10th: in rr whn hmpd and uns rdr 12th* **8/1**

7m 22.9s (11.60) **Going Correction** +0.575s/f (Soft) **10** Ran SP% **114.3**
Speed ratings: **106,105,103,98,97 96,91,—,—,—** CSF £43.52 CT £591.11 TOTE £5.90: £2.80, £2.20, £5.80; EX 21.30.
Owner George Ward **Bred** George Ward **Trained** Compton, Berks

FOCUS
A fair handicap that proved a real war of attrition and the form looks sound with the third setting the level. The first two improved markedly for the longer trip.

NOTEBOOK
Bob Ar Aghaidh(IRE) , making his handicap debut over fences, dourly defied top weight on this marked step up in trip and was not stopping at the finish. He is a consistent performer, this was by far his best display to date, and he is clearly versatile as regards underfoot conditions. He is capable of defying an even higher mark in future over this sort of distance. *(op 5-1)*
Jiver(IRE) tried in vain to get to the winner from three out, but still turned in another improved effort and proved suited by the longer trip. He was clear in second, handled the softer ground and looks sure to be placed to advantage now connections can be confident he stays this far. *(tchd 10-1 in places)*
Waterberg(IRE) , with the blinkers back on, turned in a much more encouraging effort and only gave sway after an error at the penultimate fence. He is hard to predict, but has won off a mark of 112 in the past and is worth persevering with over this sort of trip.
Infrasonique(FR) showed up well enough until a tired error three out put paid to his chances on this return from a 533-day break. He was well backed for this belated return and is certainly entitled to improve a deal for the outing. *(tchd 13-2)*
Charango Star , whose best effort in the pointing arena came over 4m 2f at Kingston Blount in April, was still going well enough prior to departing. It is unlikely we have seen the best of him to date, and is one to bear in mind when facing this sort of distance in the future, as he gains further experience. *(op 13-2 tchd 11-2)*

1894 PRAGNELLS JEWELLERS H'CAP CHASE (11 fncs 2 omitted) 2m 1f 110y
4:30 (4:31) (Class 3) (0-120,116) 5-Y-0+ **£5,343** (£1,644; £822; £411)

Form RPR
/011 1 **Hakim (NZ)**[63] 1320 11-11-7 **111** .... APMcCoy 117+
(J L Spearing) *mde all: sn clr: hrd rdn flat: all out* **5/2**[2]
31/1 2 1 ¼ **Thalys (GER)**[35] 1524 7-10-12 **102** .... TDoyle 107
(P R Webber) *prom: mstke 5th: chsd wnr 3 out: rdn appr last: styd on u.p* **9/4**[1]
-463 3 19 **Log On Intersky (IRE)**[20] 1666 9-11-7 **116** .... MNicolls(5) 106+
(J R Cornwall) *chsd clr ldr to 3 out: wknd next* **7/1**
2543 4 18 **Just Muckin Around (IRE)**[5] 1831 9-10-2 **92** .... BHitchcott 67+
(R H Buckler) *chsd ldrs: hit 6th: rdn whn hit 8th: sn wknd* **7/2**[3]
0/3- 5 1 ¾ **Sargon**[33] 1555 6-10-13 **103** .... (b) AThornton 69
(Robert Gray) *nt fluent: a bhd* **7/1**

4m 20.2s (7.70) **Going Correction** +0.575s/f (Soft) **5** Ran SP% **106.6**
Speed ratings: **105,104,96,88,87** CSF £8.17 TOTE £2.40: £1.50, £1.30; EX 4.90.
Owner T N Siviter **Bred** Mrs B C Hennessy **Trained** Kinnersley, Worcs

FOCUS
A modest event for the class, but the pace was sound and the first two came well clear.

NOTEBOOK
Hakim(NZ) dug deep in the home straight to hold off the runner-up and make all to complete the hat-trick. This must rate a personal-best display, the softer ground was not enough to stop him, and he has returned from his layoff this season in superb form. Further improvement cannot be ruled out at this stage. *(op 9-4 tchd 15-8)*
Thalys(GER) , who made a winning return to action at Fontwell last time, made his move after four out and looked to be going the best approaching the home turn, but could not get past the determined winner try as he might. While the drop in trip was not totally against him, it was a more likely factor for his defeat than a recent 7lb hike in the weights, and this ground would have been plenty soft for his liking. He was a long way clear of the rest and should resume winning ways in due course. *(op 11-4 tchd 3-1 and 10-3 in a place)*
Log On Intersky(IRE) , claimed out of Howard Johnson's yard for 9,000gns after his latest effort, was firmly put in his place by the front pair from three out yet in turn finished clear in third. He has regressed, and still looks held by the Handicapper at present, but is not one to write off all the same. *(tchd 13-2 and 15-2)*
Just Muckin Around(IRE) dropped out tamely when the chips were down and ran below-par. However, she most likely found this coming too soon after her previous exertions at Chepstow five days previously and can do better. *(op 4-1 tchd 9-2)*
Sargon failed to jump with any fluency and was never a factor on this unsuitably soft surface. *Official explanation: vet said gelding had a cut pastern (op 9-2)*

1895 EUROPEAN BREEDERS FUND "NATIONAL HUNT" NOVICES' HURDLE RACE (QUALIFIER) (9 hdls) 2m 110y
5:00 (5:00) (Class 3) 4-6-Y-0
£5,040 (£1,911; £955; £434; £217; £130)

Form RPR
1 **College Ace (IRE)**[221] 4-10-12 .... RJohnson 114+
(P J Hobbs) *chsd ldr tl led 6th: drvn out* **7/1**
2 ½ **Fier Normand (FR)**[316] 2845 6-10-12 .... APMcCoy 113+
(Jonjo O'Neill) *hld up: hdwy 6th: rdn and ev ch fr after 3 out: unable qckn nr fin* **9/4**[2]
1 3 13 **Fourty Acers (IRE)**[46] 1459 5-10-12 .... RGreene 105+
(M C Pipe) *prom: mstkes 3rd and 5th: wkng whn blnd 2 out* **6/4**[1]
2-4 4 2 **Delightful Cliche**[166] 355 4-10-12 .... WMarston 98
(Mrs P Sly) *plld hrd and prom: wknd appr 2 out* **33/1**
044- 5 5 **High Altitude (IRE)**[231] 4284 4-10-12 .... RThornton 93
(A King) *chsd ldrs: rdn 6th: wknd after next* **3/1**[3]
200 6 17 **Granite Man (IRE)**[19] 1672 5-10-12 .... TSiddall 76
(Jonjo O'Neill) *j.rt: led to 6th: wknd after 3 out* **100/1**
00-P 7 4 **Kokopelli Mana (IRE)**[19] 1683 5-10-5 .... GLee 65
(J M Jefferson) *hld up: wkng whn mstke 3 out* **100/1**
00- 8 ½ **Talikos (FR)**[217] 4540 4-10-12 .... SThomas 72
(Miss H C Knight) *hld up: plld hrd: hdwy 6th: wkng whn mstke next* **100/1**

4m 8.90s (10.50) **Going Correction** +0.575s/f (Soft)
WFA 4 from 5yo+ 13lb **8** Ran SP% **114.2**
Speed ratings: **98,97,91,90,88 80,78,78** CSF £23.61 TOTE £8.10: £1.90, £1.50, £1.10; EX 26.00 Place 6 £22.26, Place 5 £17.17.
Owner Mrs Peter Prowting **Bred** Ailish Cunningham **Trained** Withycombe, Somerset

FOCUS
A modest winning time for the class and only fractionally faster than the seller, making the form appear suspect. However, the first two pulled clear and with the third could rate higher.

NOTEBOOK

College Ace(IRE) ◆, winner of a 2m 4f Irish point in March, maintained his yard's decent early season form and made a winning debut over timber in dogged fashion. He raced on the pace throughout, jumped like a natural, and showed a willing attitude to hold off the runner-up on the run-in. The return to further in due course will suit, he ought to be hard to beat under a penalty next time and could rate higher in due course. *(op 10-1)*

Fier Normand(FR) ◆, well-related and a winner of a Downpatrick bumper on his only previous outing 316 days previously, jumped the final flight in tandem with the winner yet could not quicken when it mattered on the run-in. He did nothing wrong in defeat, should improve for the outing and looks a sure-fire winner of the similar event before too long. *(op 15-8 tchd 5-2 and 11-4 in a place)*

Fourty Acers(IRE), a wide-margin bumper winner over course and distance on debut 46 days previously, did not jump all that fluently on this hurdling bow and was firmly put in his place by the first two. He will need to improve his jumping to progress in this sphere, but is entitled to do so at this stage. *(op 7-4 tchd 15-8)*

Delightful Cliche ran very freely through the early parts on this return from a 166-day break and did well to finish as close as she did. This was a fairly encouraging start to her hurdling career, and she will no doubt find easier opportunities in the future, but her proximity at the finish does hold down the form slightly.

High Altitude(IRE), who despite being well-touted failed to get his head in front in bumpers and novice hurdles last term, was found wanting when push came to shove and must rate *disappointing. He may come on for the run, but has become frustrating to follow nevertheless. (op 10-3 tchd 7-2 in a place)*

T/Plt: £11.80 to a £1 stake. Pool: £48,272.65. 2,965.55 winning tickets. T/Qpdt: £11.50 to a £1 stake. Pool: £3,246.40. 207.70 winning tickets. CR

TAUNTON (R-H)

Thursday, October 27

OFFICIAL GOING: Firm (good to firm in places)

The track had missed the recent rain but times did not back up the official going description; a strong cross-wind may have had an effect.

Wind: Strong, across

1896 FIRST OF THE SEASON "NATIONAL HUNT" NOVICES' HURDLE (9 hdls) 2m 1f

2:10 (2:10) (Class 3) 4-Y-0+ **£5,096** (£1,568; £784; £392)

Form				RPR
34-6	**1**		**Cappanrush (IRE)**[172] [230] 5-10-9 .... CBolger(3) (A Ennis) *j.lft virtually thrght: mde all: drew clr after 3 out: unchal* **10/11**[1]	83+
04P0	**2**	*12*	**So Cloudy**[30] [1569] 4-10-0 .... StephenJCraine(5) (D McCain) *t.k.h: trckd ldng pair: wnt 2nd after 4th: chsd wnr in vain after 3 out: hit 2 out and last* **20/1**	56
-00F	**3**	*6*	**Oasis Blue (IRE)**[9] [1779] 4-10-12 .... TJMurphy (M C Pipe) *trckd wnr tl after 4th: chsd ldrs: rdn after 3 out: sn btn* **5/2**[2]	57
050-	**4**	*11*	**Oscars Law**[235] [4207] 4-10-5 .... PJBrennan (J L Spearing) *in tch: hit 3rd: wknd 6th* **7/2**[3]	39
4P0-	**5**	*dist*	**Golden Tina**[232] [4252] 7-10-0 .... RStephens(5) (Mrs S M Johnson) *lost tch 5th: sn hung lft: t.o* **40/1**	—

4m 9.60s (0.80) **Going Correction** -0.25s/f (Good) **5** Ran SP% **110.4**

Speed ratings: **88,82,79,74,**— CSF £16.51 TOTE £1.70: £1.10, £4.30; EX 11.80.

Owner P W Middleton **Bred** Miss Anne Brooks And Jocelyn Targett **Trained** Beare Green, Surrey

FOCUS

This race had looked quite competitive at the original entry stage, but it cut up pretty badly and eventually took little winning and the winner is value for more than the official margin. The winning time was moderate, 6.6 seconds slower than the later handicap hurdle.

NOTEBOOK

Cappanrush(IRE), a dual winner in charity races lately, won easily on this second start over hurdles. This success told us very little about his true ability and he remains a horse of potential, despite his tendency to jump out to the left at his hurdles. However, it will be no easy task to follow up under a penalty in a stronger race. *(op Evens tchd 6-5)*

So Cloudy had been sent a long way by her owner/trainer, and rewarded him with second-place money. After showing very little to date, she was very keen for much of the early part of the race and clouted the last two hurdles, further strengthening the belief that this was a poor race. *(op 25-1)*

Oasis Blue(IRE) had shown only a modicum of ability to date, and was reunited with Murphy on this big drop in trip. He tracked the pace early but the jockey seemed to accept things entering the home straight, and he was well beaten. *(op 11-4)*

Oscars Law, who had shown some ability in a couple of 'junior' bumpers, was the disappointment of the race. She did not jump with any fluency and was already beaten jumping the first in the back straight on the final circuit. *(tchd 3-1)*

Golden Tina, making her debut for the stable, had been beaten 58 lengths on her last visit to the track, and did as well as could have been expected given the level of her form.

1897 SOUTH WEST RACING EXPERIENCE (S) H'CAP CHASE (14 fncs) 2m 3f

2:40 (2:42) (Class 5) (0-95,95) 5-Y-0+ **£2,702** (£772; £386)

Form				RPR
P-P3	**1**		**Charliemoore**[10] [1776] 9-11-2 **85** .... (b) JEMoore (G L Moore) *trckd ldrs: led 9th: clr after 4 out: eased run-in* **8/1**	99+
PU35	**2**	*6*	**Pristeen Spy**[21] [1656] 8-9-10 **70** .... StephenJCraine(5) (R Ford) *chsd ldrs: rdn and lost tch 9th: styd on to go 2nd after 2 out: no ch w wnr* **11/2**[2]	70
2050	**3**	*1 3/4*	**Mollycarrsbrekfast**[22] [1637] 10-9-11 **69** oh2.......... TJMalone(3) (K Bishop) *j.lft thrght: sn wl bhd: styd on fr 3 out: wnt 3rd run-in: nvr trbld ldrs* **9/2**[1]	67
-P30	**4**	*3 1/2*	**Master Henry (GER)**[21] [1659] 11-11-4 **87** .... PMoloney (Ian Williams) *led tl 9th: chsd wnr: wknd appr 2 out* **9/1**	83+
223-	**5**	*dist*	**Killy Beach**[263] 7-10-1 **75** .... CHonour(5) (J D Frost) *j.lft 1st tl 4th: in tch: tk clsr order 7th: wknd 4 out: blnd next* **7/1**[3]	51
33-	**P**		**Sammagefromtenesse (IRE)**[213] [4617] 8-10-3 **72** .... (p) MFoley (A E Jones) *sn t.o: p.u after 7th* **9/1**	—
-P06	**P**		**Just Midas**[53] [1411] 7-9-12 **70** .... TJPhelan(3) (N M Babbage) *a bhd: blnd 2nd: p.u bef 4 out* **33/1**	—
0634	**P**		**Simon's Seat (USA)**[9] [1783] 6-10-4 **80** .... (p) JamesWhite(7) (S C Burrough) *a bhd: t.o and p.u bef 4 out* **16/1**	—
5340	**P**		**Faddad (USA)**[12] [1747] 9-11-3 **86** .... (t) NFehily (Mrs A M Thorpe) *a towards rr: t.o and p.u bef 4 out* **9/1**	—
F553	**F**		**Knight's Emperor (IRE)**[7] [1805] 8-11-12 **95** .... PJBrennan (J L Spearing) *in tch: hit 7th: fell next* **9/2**[1]	—
66U	**U**		**Tellem Noting (IRE)**[22] [1644] 8-10-7 **76** .... (t) JamesDavies (B G Powell) *disp ld tl 4th: chsd ldrs: rdn in 3rd whn j.rt and uns rdr 4 out* **33/1**	—

4m 55.2s (2.40) **Going Correction** +0.125s/f (Yiel) **11** Ran SP% **117.1**

Speed ratings: **99,96,95,94,**— —,—,—,—,— — CSF £52.44 CT £222.87 TOTE £8.20: £2.30, £2.30, £2.20; EX 72.80.There was no bid for the winner.

Owner Bryan Pennick **Bred** K Higson **Trained** Woodingdean, E Sussex

■ Stewards' Enquiry : N Fehily one-day ban: anticipating the start (Nov 7)

T J Malone one-day ban: anticipating the start (Nov 7)

P Moloney one-day ban: anticipating the start (Nov 7)

P J Brennan one-day ban: anticipating the start (Nov 7)

M Foley one-day ban: anticipating the start (Nov 7)

C Honour one-day ban: anticipating the start (Nov 7)

Stephen J Craine one-day ban: anticipating the start (Nov 7)

J E Moore one-day ban: anticipating the start (Nov 7)

James White one-day ban: anticipating the start (Nov 7)

James Davies and N Fehily one-day ban: anticipating the start (Nov 7)

FOCUS

This seller did not take a great deal of winning, and most of those in behind the leaders will do well to land any kind of event in the near future. They went quickly early on, so much so that there was the best part of 30 lengths between first and last jumping the third. All of the jockeys except for Tom Phelan received a one-day ban for being 'unruly' at the start, breaking the tape on two occasions.

NOTEBOOK

Charliemoore has evidently had his problems, as this was only his 11th run at the age of nine. Without a win since his bumper success at Plumpton in April 2002. One of the six who sped off in front, he pulled out enough despite looking less than enthusiastic when left on his own coming down the home straight, and unsurprisingly there was no bid at the auction afterwards. *(tchd 9-1)*

Pristeen Spy came into the race with a couple of pieces of form that gave him a chance, but a drop in trip did not seem an obvious plus, and so it proved as he was outpaced in the back straight, before staying on again past very tired horses. *(op 5-1)*

Mollycarrsbrekfast, who usually races up with the pace, has not really gone on since his debut for the yard back in May, but never had the slightest chance after being well behind early. *(op 6-1)*

Master Henry(GER), after going off very quickly, was unsurprisingly very tired in the final stages and lost out to those running on from behind. *(tchd 8-1)*

Knight's Emperor(IRE) absolutely loves to bounce off a quick surface and was just behind the pace before coming down seven from home. He has his problems in the jumping department and remains a risky proposition. *(tchd 5-1)*

Tellem Noting(IRE) was up with the pace from the start and still in contention when he had a *difference of opinion with his rider jumping the last ditch, resulting in a spectacular departure. (tchd 5-1)*

1898 PITMINSTER NOVICES' HURDLE (10 hdls) 2m 3f 110y

3:10 (3:10) (Class 3) 4-Y-0+ **£5,492** (£1,690; £845; £422)

Form				RPR
22	**1**		**Desert Quest (IRE)**[2] [1875] 5-10-12 .... (b) PJBrennan (P F Nicholls) *hld up mid div: tk clsr order 7th: led and hit 2 out: sn qcknd clr: readily* **8/11**[1]	121+
	2	*14*	**Prideoftheyankees (IRE)**[179] 4-10-12 .... TJMurphy (W J Burke, Ire) *mid div: tk clsr order 7th: ev ch 2 out: sn rdn: nt pce of wnr: hit last* **8/1**	91+
5100	**3**	*nk*	**It's My Party**[10] [1772] 4-10-5 .... (p) RLucey-Butler(7) (W G M Turner) *in tch: led after 3 out: rdn and narrowly hdd next: kpt on same pce* **50/1**	90
36-3	**4**	*3*	**Zouave (IRE)**[11] [1757] 4-10-12 .... (b) NFehily (C J Mann) *mid div: hdwy to trck ldrs 7th: ev ch 2 out: one pced* **9/1**	87
66	**5**	*4*	**Offalevel**[4] [1859] 7-10-5 .... JamesWhite(7) (R J Hodges) *led tl after 3 out: sn rdn: wknd after 2 out* **100/1**	83
13-F	**6**	*nk*	**Boberelle (IRE)**[19] [1683] 5-10-5 .... JMMaguire (C Tinkler) *hld up bhd: hdwy after 3 out to chse ldrs: rdn and wknd after next* **15/2**[3]	76
5	**7**	*15*	**Xila Fontenailles (FR)**[39] [1491] 4-9-12 .... KBurke(7) (N J Hawke) *chsd ldr: rdn after 3 out: sn wknd* **80/1**	61
P0	**8**	*1*	**Norman's Glories**[9] [1782] 7-10-12 .... VSlattery (R J Baker) *chsd ldrs: rdn after 3 out: sn wknd* **250/1**	67
00-4	**9**	*10*	**West End Pearl**[14] [1725] 4-10-5 .... JEMoore (C G Cox) *chsd ldrs: hit 7th: sn wknd* **40/1**	50
	10	*dist*	**Dubious Deal**[508] 8-10-7 .... LStephens(5) (R J Hodges) *hmpd 2nd: a bhd: t.o fr 6th* **150/1**	—
P-0	**11**	*12*	**Bonjour Bond (IRE)**[11] [1750] 4-10-9 .... TJMalone(3) (J G M O'Shea) *j.lft thrght: a t.o* **150/1**	—
2433	**F**		**Kentucky King (USA)**[7] [1804] 5-10-7 98.......... (t) PCO'Neill(5) (Mrs D A Hamer) *dwlt: a bhd: fell last* **11/2**[2]	—

4m 39.5s (-6.50) **Going Correction** -0.25s/f (Good) **12** Ran SP% **114.5**

Speed ratings: **103,97,97,96,94 94,88,87,83,**— —,— CSF £7.13 TOTE £1.90: £1.10, £2.10, £10.30; EX 8.10.

Owner Mrs M Findlay **Bred** Ballygallon Stud **Trained** Ditcheat, Somerset

FOCUS

A moderate race but the winner responded to the application of blinkers and ran away from his rivals when given his head. He is value for twice the winning margin with the third and fourth to their marks.

NOTEBOOK

Desert Quest(IRE), who put up a slightly dubious-looking effort under pressure at Cheltenham earlier in the week, responded well to the application of blinkers for the first time over hurdles. Under a very quiet ride, he bounded clear between the last two flights and won with tons in hand, looking as good as his Flat rating suggested he might be. He may not be that well handicapped when he is assessed after getting close to a couple of decent types already over hurdles, and connections are leaning towards an attempt at the Grade Two novice hurdle at Cheltenham on the first day of the Paddy Power meeting. *(op 5-6 tchd 10-11)*

Prideoftheyankees(IRE) ◆, a point winner in Ireland on much softer ground, moved into the race nicely but made errors at the last two hurdles, and never threatened the winner. That said, he stayed on well enough to deny the more experienced third, and is likely to find a race when conditions are more testing. *(op 10-1)*

It's My Party, who also had no answer to the winner's turn of foot after travelling nicely into the lead off the home turn. *(tchd 66-1)*

Zouave(IRE) was not quite as good as Desert Quest on the Flat, and has yet to get his act together over hurdles. He had a throat operation before his last run, but was held up this time rather than forcing the pace, and was readily left behind as the tempo increased. He could be interesting if tried in handicap company next time and ridden positively. *(op 8-1 tchd 10-1)*

Offalevel, dropped in trip and ridden from the front, ran much better and only faded late on after setting a sedate early pace. *(op 66-1)*

Boberelle(IRE) never quite got to the leaders after jumping carefully throughout. She is worth a chance against her own sex, but her small stature might always count against her. *(op 6-1)*

West End Pearl *Official explanation: jockey said filly hung right-handed (op 33-1 tchd 50-1)*

Kentucky King(USA) again showed signs of stubbornness at the start and was well behind when falling at the last. *(tchd 6-1)*

1899 GET BEST PRICES WITH GG-ODDS.COM BEGINNERS' CHASE (17 fncs) 2m 7f 110y
3:40 (3:41) (Class 3) 5-Y-0+ **£5,411** (£1,665; £832)

Form				RPR
2-52	**1**		**Forever Dream**[7] [1801] 7-11-0 119 ......(b[1]) PJBrennan (P J Hobbs) *hld up bhd ldng pair: mstke 3rd: wnt 2nd appr 11th: hit 13th: led appr 3 out: shkn up after 2 out: idled run-in* **4/5**[1]	110+
3533	**2**	*2 ½*	**Peeyoutwo**[9] [1783] 10-10-9 113......(p) PCO'Neill[(5)] (Mrs D A Hamer) *trckd ldr: led 6th: nt fluent 12th: rdn and hdd appr 3 out: kpt on but a hld by wnr* **5/4**[2]	105
0PPF	**3**	*dist*	**Lescer's Lad**[22] [1638] 8-10-7 76...... CMStudd[(7)] (C L Popham) *led: nt fluent 4th: hdd 6th: lost tch after 11th: t.o* **20/1**[3]	—

6m 16.2s (16.20) **Going Correction** +0.125s/f (Yiel) **3** Ran SP% **104.8**
Speed ratings: **86,85,**— CSF £2.12 TOTE £1.50; EX 1.70.
Owner W McKibbin & A Stevens **Bred** C D Harrison **Trained** Withycombe, Somerset

FOCUS
A disappointing turnout and only two of the three runners held any chance from halfway down the back straight. The winning time was very moderate, 12.6 seconds slower than the later handicap and the form amounts to little.

NOTEBOOK
Forever Dream probably did not need the help of first-time blinkers to dispose of his only serious rival over the final three fences, but this will have boosted his confidence. If the headgear continues to work, he should be able to follow this up, but he did string a few too many seconds together over hurdles to be that confident of a win next time. *(tchd 5-6)*
Peeyoutwo took them along at a sedate pace after taking up the lead in the early stages but was feeling the pinch when a jumping error at the third last sealed his fate. He was well behind the winner's very classy stablemate Chilling Place last time and is probably high enough in the weights, with handicaps in mind, at this stage of his career. *(tchd 11-8)*
Lescer's Lad deserves credit for turning out so quickly after a horrific-looking fall last time at Exeter, and collected a reasonable cheque for getting around in his own time. *(op 14-1 tchd 25-1)*

1900 RACING POST "HANDS AND HEELS" JUMPS SERIES H'CAP HURDLE (CONDITIONAL JOCKEYS/AMATEURS) (10 hdls) 2m 3f 110y
4:10 (4:12) (Class 4) (0-100,99) 4-Y-0+ **£3,059** (£874; £437)

Form				RPR
45P-	**1**		**Devito (FR)**[194] [4871] 4-11-8 95...... MrDEdwards (G F Edwards) *mid div: hdwy to go prom after 5th: led 3 out: clr next: eased cl home* **28/1**	108+
-064	**2**	*2*	**He's The Gaffer (IRE)**[11] [1753] 5-10-9 82......(b) LHeard (R H Buckler) *mid div: hdwy after 5th: rdn to chse wnr after 3 out: kpt on same pce* **5/1**[3]	88
0P-1	**3**	*12*	**New Time (IRE)**[22] [1647] 6-11-5 92...... MrAJBerry (Jonjo O'Neill) *mid div: tk clsr order 6th: rdn to go 3rd after 3 out: no further imp fr next* **5/2**[1]	86
00-P	**4**	*nk*	**Oasis Banus (IRE)**[22] [1637] 4-9-9 73 oh4...... MrCHughes[(5)] (M C Pipe) *hld up bhd: styd on fr 3 out to go 4th appr 2 out: nvr trbld ldrs* **16/1**	67
-004	**5**	*2 ½*	**Tizi Ouzou (IRE)**[22] [1636] 4-11-0 92...... MrDPick[(5)] (M C Pipe) *hld up towards rr: styd on fr 3 out: n.d* **16/1**	83
P501	**6**	*14*	**Island Warrior (IRE)**[22] [1636] 10-10-3 79......(tp) JKington[(3)] (B P J Baugh) *prom: led appr 6th: hdd 3 out: sn rdn: wknd next* **20/1**	56
0005	**7**	*1*	**Better Moment (IRE)**[57] [1381] 8-11-5 95......(v) MrRQuinn[(3)] (M C Pipe) *chsd ldrs tl 3 out* **25/1**	71
35/3	**8**	*2*	**Quintus (USA)**[22] [1641] 10-11-9 99...... MrGTumelty[(3)] (A King) *in tch tl wknd appr 6th* **7/2**[2]	73
P360	**9**	*4*	**Mrs Philip**[9] [1784] 6-11-5 97...... MissRBooth[(5)] (P J Hobbs) *led tl 4th: led after 5th tl next: sn wknd: mstke 2 out* **9/1**	67
/5P0	**10**	*1 ¾*	**Golders Green**[32] [1562] 8-11-4 91 ow4...... MrAndrewMartin (P W Hiatt) *a bhd* **33/1**	59
PP/0	**11**	*14*	**Alpha Romana (IRE)**[88] [1109] 11-10-8 84...... DPO'Dwyer[(3)] (Mrs S E Busby) *a towards rr* **66/1**	38
P-PP	**R**		**Kadlass (FR)**[164] [385] 10-9-13 75...... RCummings[(3)] (Mrs D Thomas) *ref to r: tk no part* **100/1**	—
P002	**P**		**Suchwot (IRE)**[22] [1636] 4-9-13 77......(vt) MrCWallis[(5)] (M C Pipe) *p.u sn after 1st: dismntd* **12/1**	—
0-P0	**P**		**Perfect Venue (IRE)**[59] [1367] 12-10-4 80......(t) WMcCarthy[(3)] (A J Wilson) *a towards rr: p.u bef last: lame* **100/1**	—
0056	**F**		**Twentytwosilver (IRE)**[49] [1381] 5-10-10 86...... KBurke[(3)] (N J Hawke) *in tch: chsd ldrs after 5th: mstke next: wkng whn fell 2 out* **16/1**	—
05/P	**P**		**Exhibit (IRE)**[11] [1750] 7-9-13 77 oh8 ow4...... MrDBurton[(5)] (N J Hawke) *prom: led and mstke 4th: hdd after next: wknd qckly and p.u bef 6th* **100/1**	—

4m 37.8s (-8.20) **Going Correction** -0.25s/f (Good)
WFA 4 from 5yo+ 13lb **16** Ran SP% **122.3**
Speed ratings: **106,105,100,100,99 93,93,92,90,90 84,—,—,—,— —** CSF £160.35 CT £491.75 TOTE £59.40: £6.60, £1.30, £1.30, £3.00; EX 290.90.
Owner G F Edwards **Bred** Patrick Chedeville **Trained** Luckwell Bridge, Somerset
■ Stewards' Enquiry : Mr R Quinn caution: careless riding

FOCUS
A big field for this moderate contest, the latest round of the 'hands and heels' series, open to both conditionals and amateurs. The time was decent for the grade and the surprise winner scored with a fair amount in hand, the race could be rated higher and should work out.

NOTEBOOK
Devito(FR) ◆, making his first appearance since pulling up at Bangor at the end of last season in the hands of his regular pilot, moved into the lead effortlessly in the back straight, and won with plenty in hand. His previous best form over hurdles was on heavy ground, but he is worth following if turned out quickly given the ease of his victory.
He's The Gaffer(IRE), who the course commentator incorrectly suggested had got no further than the first, could never quite get to the easy winner, but his form is progressing since the application of blinkers and he can win a small race. *(op 6-1)*
New Time(IRE) had won in a very slow time at Towcester on his last run, seems to appreciate a sound surface. He was being niggled along quite a long way out and may need a stiffer test/track, despite winning at Stratford in the past. *(op 3-1 tchd 10-3)*
Oasis Banus(IRE) ran a much better race than last time, finishing quite nicely from well off the pace. His jockey gave him a really tidy ride, but he will be of more serious interest if ridden by the owner's retained jockey *(op 14-1)*
Tizi Ouzou(IRE), the stable companion of the fourth, seems to be running better since the headgear was left off and seems well suited by a sharp, right-handed track. *(tchd 20-1)*
Quintus(USA) was never likely to find this sharp track to his liking after staying on really well at Exeter last time. *(op 4-1)*
Mrs Philip gave her young jockey some excitement on her first ride before dropping right out of contention. *(tchd 11-1)*
Twentytwosilver(IRE) travelled well for a lot of the race but was back-pedalling under pressure when departing. He is very hard to win with. *(op 14-1)*

1901 BICKENHALL H'CAP CHASE (17 fncs) 2m 7f 110y
4:40 (4:40) (Class 4) (0-105,104) 5-Y-0+ **£4,410** (£1,357; £678; £339)

Form				RPR
4PU1	**1**		**Hehasalife (IRE)**[11] [1752] 8-10-8 91 7ex......(b) PCO'Neill[(5)] (Mrs H Dalton) *hld up: hit 2nd: stdy hdwy fom 8th to join ldr after 10th: led after 11th: styd on: pushed out* **13/8**[1]	101+
P035	**2**	*¾*	**Just Reuben (IRE)**[21] [1650] 10-9-11 78 oh3...... RYoung[(3)] (C L Tizzard) *led tl 4th: prom: led after 8th tl after 11th: chsd wnr: mstke 13th: sn rdn: rallied appr last: no ex run-in* **12/1**	85+
0-	**3**	*2*	**Icy Belle (IRE)**[14] [1731] 8-10-3 81...... TJMurphy (W J Burke, Ire) *hld up: hdwy to go 3rd appr 4 out: sn rdn: kpt on same pce* **3/1**[2]	85
-0P6	**4**	*9*	**Illineylad (IRE)**[21] [1655] 11-10-0 78 oh11...... JMogford (Mrs N S Evans) *hld up in tch: rdn after 12th: sme hdwy appr 3 out: wknd after 2 out* **40/1**	75+
6556	**5**	*10*	**Search And Destroy (USA)**[106] [975] 7-11-12 104......(b) JMMaguire (T R George) *prom: led after 7th tl next: rdn after 12th: wknd after 4 out* **6/1**	95+
0536	**6**	*27*	**River Quoile**[9] [1780] 9-10-0 78 oh1...... RWalford (R H Alner) *trckd ldrs: led 4th: hit next and 7th: reminders and sn hdd: grad fdd fr 11th: t.o* **4/1**[3]	36
/6P-	**P**		**Roymillon (GER)**[463] [1026] 11-10-0 78 oh9......(p) VSlattery (R J Baker) *sn struggling: a towards rr: t.o and p.u bef 4 out* **50/1**	—

6m 3.60s (3.60) **Going Correction** +0.125s/f (Yiel) **7** Ran SP% **109.5**
Speed ratings: **107,106,106,103,99 90,**— CSF £18.34 CT £48.34 TOTE £2.40: £1.40, £3.50; EX 24.50.
Owner Norton House Racing **Bred** Eddie J Kelly **Trained** Norton, Shropshire

FOCUS
A moderate handicap but run at a sound pace with the first three drawing clear. The winner is value for further and the third and fourth were close to their marks.

NOTEBOOK
Hehasalife(IRE), under a penalty for his win at Hereford, sailed into the lead in the back straight but was made to work hard for success by the runner-up. To be fair, he probably won a shade easier than the final winning distance suggested, as he appeared to do very little in front. From a very in-form stable, he has overcome his jumping problems and is in cracking form at present after a couple of wind operations. *(op 11-8 tchd 5-4)*
Just Reuben(IRE) finished well beaten last time but worried the winner all the way to the line. This was much his best effort for some time, and his overall form suggests he will be interesting if sent to one of the Sussex tracks, particularly Fontwell where he has a good record, next time. *(tchd 14-1)*
Icy Belle(IRE) was making a fairly quick reappearance after previously being off the track for 11 months. With Murphy replacing a 7lb claimer, she crept into the race nicely but could never quite bridge the gap to the leaders. A similar race is well within her compass. *(op 4-1)*
Illineylad(IRE) ran well above himself from so far out of the handicap on his return to chasing, but did not suggest he was about to win. *(op 28-1)*
Search And Destroy(USA) just managed to sneak into the race after the Handicapper had dropped him to a rating of 104 following some poor recent efforts. On his best form he was absolutely thrown in, but he again disappointed badly and is a shadow of his former self. *(tchd 13-2)*
River Quoile has been kept busy recently but continues to disappoint. Back on ground that suits him, heagain ran terribly and is becoming most regressive. *(op 5-1)*

1902 STAPLEMEAD H'CAP HURDLE (9 hdls) 2m 1f
5:10 (5:11) (Class 4) (0-100,99) 4-Y-0+ **£3,094** (£884; £442)

Form				RPR
-030	**1**		**Idle Journey (IRE)**[25] [1607] 4-10-7 90......(t) JKington[(10)] (M Scudamore) *trckd ldrs: led 4th: wnt lft and mstke 6th: drew clr after 3 out: r.o: rdn out* **10/1**	99+
3022	**2**	*6*	**Let's Celebrate**[14] [1724] 5-10-13 86...... NFehily (F Jordan) *hld up bhd: hdwy appr 2 out: styd on to go 2nd appr last: no ch w wnr: fin lame* **9/2**[2]	88+
3-44	**3**	*¾*	**Rojabaa**[4] [1856] 6-10-5 85...... RLucey-Butler[(7)] (W G M Turner) *led until 4th: chsd ldrs: sltly outpcd after 3 out: styd on again appr last* **10/1**	86
	4	*3*	**Major Jon (IRE)**[42] [1471] 5-11-3 90...... TJMurphy (W J Burke, Ire) *chsd ldrs: rdn after 3 out: kpt on same pce* **12/1**	89+
/60-	**5**	*1 ½*	**Top Trees**[18] [1635] 7-11-0 87...... JamesDavies (W S Kittow) *hld up towards rr: rdn and no imp after 3 out: styd on run -in* **8/1**[3]	84
-004	**6**	*1 ¾*	**My Sharp Grey**[12] [1738] 6-11-6 93...... JEMoore (J Gallagher) *mid div: hdwy appr 6th: rdn to chse wnr after 3 out: one pced fr next* **33/1**	88
U-50	**7**	*3 ½*	**Gallant Hero**[32] [1565] 6-11-12 99......(b[1]) PJBrennan (P J Hobbs) *hld up towar rr: hdwy to chse ldrs after 6th: rdn after 3 out: one pced after* **9/1**	92+
-000	**8**	*2*	**Bebe Factual (GER)**[22] [1636] 4-10-1 79...... CHonour[(5)] (J D Frost) *t.k.h bhd ldrs: rdn appr 3 out: sn wknd* **50/1**	68
0-62	**9**	*4*	**Hatch A Plan (IRE)**[7] [1804] 4-11-3 97...... SWalsh[(7)] (Mrs A J Hamilton-Fairley) *chsd ldrs: led 4th tl 6th: wknd appr 2 out* **7/2**[1]	82
	10	*1 ¾*	**Valley Ger (IRE)**[107] [967] 6-11-4 96...... MrCJSweeney[(5)] (Rodger Sweeney, Ire) *mid div: in tch whn hmpd 6th: wknd after 3 out* **16/1**	83+
4230	**P**		**Olimpo (FR)**[4] [1862] 4-10-6 84...... RStephens[(5)] (P J Hobbs) *a towards rr: wknd qckly 3 out: p.u bef next* **7/2**[1]	—

4m 3.00s (-5.80) **Going Correction** -0.25s/f (Good)
WFA 4 from 5yo+ 13lb **11** Ran SP% **120.4**
Speed ratings: **103,100,99,98,97 96,95,94,92,91** — CSF £56.86 CT £474.93 TOTE £13.10: £3.20, £1.40, £2.60; EX 79.70 Place 6 £14.18, Place 5 £8.32.
Owner Mrs N M Watkins **Bred** Eddie Kavanagh **Trained** Bromsash, Herefordshire

FOCUS
There did not appear to be a great deal of early pace in this moderate event but the overall time was reasonable. The form looks reasonabll sound with the third and fourth to their marks but is basically weak, with the runner-up having been beaten in selling company recently.

NOTEBOOK
Idle Journey(IRE)was allowed to get away from his rivals with an injection of speed on the far side of the track after a modest early gallop. He had previously failed to convince that he even stays the bare minimum over hurdles, so it was a very astute piece of riding by his young jockey, who *claimed 10lb, but he is very much one to oppose next time under a penalty.Official explanation: trainer said, regarding the improved form shown, gelding was better suited by today's good to firm ground (op 12-1)*
Let's Celebrate, gives credence to the weakness of the race, as he has been running well recently in selling company without winning. His jockey looked to have slightly overdone the waiting tactics on him in a slowly-run race, but reported that the gelding finished lame. *(op 4-1)*
Rojabaa was outpaced as the winner went for home, but kept on in good style after jumping the last in fifth. He would not have troubled the easy winner, but could have finished a bit closer with a clearer passage. *(tchd 11-1)*

The Form Book, Raceform Ltd, Compton, RG20 6NL

Major Jon(IRE), an Irish raider making his handicap debut having not shown a great deal in Ireland, went well for a long way before jumping the last two hurdles poorly, and ending any chance of snatching a place. *(op 11-1)*
Top Trees ◆ was the eyecatcher of the race. He never managed to reach a challenging position, but was not given a hard time in the final stages. It might be that the horse does not like the whip, but he definitely shaped better than his final position suggests. *(tchd 7-1)*
My Sharp Grey, who picked up some decent prizemoney for turning out against Rooster Booster at Huntingdon last time, appreciated the sharp track and fast ground, but will be better off back in sellers. *(op 28-1)*
Gallant Hero, in first-time headgear, fell when in second behind subsequent Arkle winner Contraband on his last run over timber. Virtually all of his Flat form entitled him to win by a country mile, but for whatever reason he has not translated all of that ability to timber, and again failed to get home. *(op 8-1 tchd 7-1)*
Hatch A Plan(IRE) is an inconsistent sort and proved very disappointing after a fair effort last time. *(tchd 4-1)*
Olimpo(FR), a stable companion of the top weight, was not too far behind the improving Mexican Pete a couple of runs ago, but really disappointed in a better race last time. He was well supported in the market before the race, but again let his supporters down. His jockey reported that he hung right-handed during the race. *Official explanation: jockey said gelding hung right-handed (op 6-1)*
T/Plt: £22.60 to a £1 stake. Pool: £38,583.50. 1,242.30 winning tickets. T/Qpdt: £4.40 to a £1 stake. Pool: £2,602.30. 436.60 winning tickets. TM

1711 UTTOXETER (L-H)
Friday, October 28

OFFICIAL GOING: Hurdle course - good to soft (good in places); chase course - soft (good to soft in places)
After 2" rain over the previous six days the ground was described as 'soft and hard work'. The running rail on the hurdle track had been removed.
Wind: Moderate, across Weather: Frequent showers, some very heavy.

1903 SCOTTISH EQUITABLE "NATIONAL HUNT" NOVICES' HURDLE (12 hdls) 2m 4f 110y
1:45 (1:45) (Class 4) 4-Y-0+ **£3,797** (£1,085; £542)

Form					RPR
11-	1		**Oscar Park (IRE)**[286] [3367] 6-10-12 *(C Tinkler) trckd ldrs: led on bit 2 out: clr last: smoothly*	TDoyle **13/8**[1]	126+
P-42	2	6	**Smart Mover**[26] [1619] 6-10-12 104 *(Miss H C Knight) mid-div: styd on fr 3 out: tk 2nd nr line*	TJMurphy **7/1**	107+
/20-	3	nk	**Terivic**[238] [4158] 5-10-12 *(K C Bailey) led tl hdd and mstke 2 out: kpt on same pce*	JPMcNamara **20/1**	107+
23B-	4	¾	**In Accord**[215] [4583] 6-10-12 115 *(H D Daly) hld up in mid-div: hdwy 9th: kpt on one pce fr 2 out*	MBradburne **4/1**[2]	105
P-21	5	½	**Good Samaritan (IRE)**[20] [1671] 6-11-5 *(M Pitman) chsd ldrs: rdn 9th: one pce fr 3 out*	ATinkler **6/1**[3]	112+
60/	6	3½	**Cornish Jester**[555] [4920] 6-10-9 *(C J Down) sn trcking ldrs: fdd 2 out*	ONelmes(3) **66/1**	101
05-	7	3	**Ellandshe (IRE)**[201] [4801] 5-10-7 *(P R Webber) hdwy to chse ldrs 9th: sn rdn: wknd 2 out*	MNicolls(5) **33/1**	98
4P0-	8	21	**Laharna**[209] [4696] 5-10-12 *(Miss E C Lavelle) hld up in rr: sme hdwy 9th: nvr on terms*	BFenton **10/1**	77
0	9	5	**Kyno (IRE)**[155] [529] 4-10-12 *(M G Quinlan) mid-div: mstke 8th: sn lost pl*	WMarston **66/1**	72
4	10	3½	**Nycos Des Ormeaux (FR)**[169] [323] 4-10-9 *(Ferdy Murphy) mid-div: drvn along and sme hdwy 9th: lost pl appr next*	KJMercer(3) **20/1**	68
	11	1½	**Joe McHugh (IRE)**[215] 6-10-12 *(C J Mann) a in rr*	NFehily **20/1**	67
PP/0	12	18	**Youpeeveecee (IRE)**[16] [1711] 9-10-5 85 *(Miss L V Davis) a in rr*	JPritchard(7) **100/1**	49
645-	13	23	**Classic Ruby**[260] [3771] 5-10-5 *(M R Bosley) bhd fr 6th*	SCurran **66/1**	19
4	14	hd	**Weldiva**[22] [1657] 5-9-12 *(B N Pollock) trckd ldrs: wknd after 7th: sn bhd*	TMessenger(7) **66/1**	19
00-0	15	dist	**Astral Dancer (IRE)**[16] [1714] 5-10-12 *(J Mackie) in rr: hdwy after 7th: lost pl after 9th: sn bhd: virtually p.u: t.o*	PMoloney **100/1**	—
0-00	P		**Times Up Barney**[40] [1485] 5-10-12 *(C W Moore) chsd ldrs: lost pl after 7th: wl bhd whn p.u bef 2 out*	JPByrne **100/1**	—

5m 1.20s (-10.90) **Going Correction** -0.425s/f (Good) 16 Ran SP% **120.1**
WFA 4 from 5yo+ 14lb
Speed ratings: **103,100,100,100,100 98,97,89,87,86 85,78,70,70,— —** CSF £11.99 TOTE £2.80: £2.10, £1.60, £4.10; EX 19.20.
Owner George Ward **Bred** Mrs B Byrne **Trained** Compton, Berks

FOCUS
A novices' hurdle confined to horses that have not run on the Flat proper and an easy unbeaten winner of some potential who was value for 20 lengths. The second, third and fifth ran to their marks and the race should produce future winners.

NOTEBOOK
Oscar Park(IRE) ◆, unbeaten in two bumpers, is not that big but well put together. His jumping was very novicey but running away when taking charge, he made an impressive hurdling bow. He will take it one step at a time. *(op 7-4 tchd 15-8)*
Smart Mover, left short of room leaving the back straight, stayed on in gutsy fashion to snatch second spot near the line. He looks to have a lot more stamina than speed.
Terivic set the pace but the winner left him for dead. Stamina was not a problem. *(op 16-1)*
In Accord, absent since March, cut in from the outside leaving the back straight and never looked like raising his game sufficiently. He looks to just stay. *(op 9-2)*
Good Samaritan(IRE), who looks every inch a potential chaser, was undone by his penalty and he could only keep on in his own time. *(op 11-2)*
Cornish Jester, who showed a glimmer of ability in two starts in bumpers, has changed stables and was far from disgraced on his hurdling bow.

1904 BET365 CALL 08000 322365 JUVENILE NOVICES' HURDLE (10 hdls) 2m
2:15 (2:17) (Class 4) 3-Y-O **£3,402** (£972; £486)

Form					RPR
	1		**Patman Du Charmil (FR)**[203] 3-10-12 *(N A Twiston-Davies) trckd ldrs: led 6th: 10 l clr whn hit last: eased towards fin*	CLlewellyn **2/1**[1]	113+
	2	6	**Gardasee (GER)**[118] 3-10-12 *(T P Tate) mde most to 6th: wl hld whn hit 3 out: eased run-in*	JMMaguire **8/1**[3]	99+
3	3	8	**Dusty Dane (IRE)**[20] [1679] 3-10-12 *(W G M Turner) chsd ldrs: rdn 7th: 3rd and wl hld whn mstke 2 out*	PJBrennan **3/1**[2]	89+
0P	4	3½	**Hamburg Springer (IRE)**[8] [1797] 3-10-12 *(M J Polglase) chsd ldrs: one pce fr 7th*	RGreene **100/1**	85
00	5	2½	**Bold Pursuit (IRE)**[16] [1718] 3-10-9 *(Mrs A Duffield) a wl in tch: rdn 7th: one pce*	KJMercer(3) **14/1**	82
33	6	10	**Verstone (IRE)**[41] [1440] 3-10-5 *(R F Fisher) in tch: mstke 3rd: rdn 7th: sn wknd*	JEMoore **11/1**	65
04	7	18	**Lorna Dune**[15] [1729] 3-10-2 *(J G M O'Shea) mid-div: hmpd by loose horse 4th: hdwy 6th: wknd after next*	ONelmes(3) **18/1**	47
	8	29	**Be Lucky Lady (GER)**[32] 3-10-0 *(N B King) bhd: sme hdwy 5th: sn lost pl*	CHonour(5) **80/1**	18
	9	dist	**Dizzy Future**[10] 3-10-12 *(B J Llewellyn) a detached in last: t.o: btn 31l*	OMcPhail **33/1**	—
	F		**Taj India (USA)**[417] 3-10-7 *(N J Hawke) in rr whn fell 1st*	JHarris(5) **20/1**	—
	U		**Lankawi**[29] 3-10-12 *(Jedd O'Keeffe) mid-div: mstke and uns rdr 2nd*	FKeniry **16/1**	—
	P		**Mount Ephram (IRE)**[260] 3-10-12 *(R F Fisher) bhd fr 5th: t.o whn p.u bef 2 out*	MFoley **50/1**	—
	P		**Glowette (IRE)**[13] 3-10-5 *(I W McInnes) mid-div: lost pl 6th: t.o whn p.u bef 3 out*	PWhelan **100/1**	—
	P		**Hannah's Tribe (IRE)**[183] 3-10-5 *(C W Moore) in rr whn mstke 5th: bhd whn p.u bef next*	JPByrne **100/1**	—
30	C		**Fu Manchu**[20] [1679] 3-10-12 *(Jonjo O'Neill) chsd ldrs: nt fluent ande lost pl 7th: bhd whn carried out by loose horse 2 out*	TSiddall **9/1**	—

3m 53.2s (-7.20) **Going Correction** -0.425s/f (Good) 15 Ran SP% **119.5**
Speed ratings: **101,98,94,92,91 86,77,62,—,— —,—,—,—,—** CSF £17.89 TOTE £3.00: £1.60, £2.20, £1.90; EX 22.20.
Owner H R Mould **Bred** Mme Guilhaine Le Borgne **Trained** Naunton, Gloucs

FOCUS
A modest juvenile hurdle but the experienced winner, rated value for much further, seems likely to go on to better things, and with the placed horses running to expectations the form should work out.

NOTEBOOK
Patman Du Charmil(FR) ◆, fourth in two starts over hurdles in the spring, is a rangy type who will make a chaser in time. He made this look very simple, value at least double the official margin, and he looks useful at least. *(op 15-8 tchd 9-4 in places and 7-4 in place)*
Gardasee(GER), rated just 51 on the Flat, is a big type. He was a bit novicey in front and in the end no match for the winner, was allowed to complete in his own time. He should go one better in a similar event. *(op 10-1)*
Dusty Dane(IRE), rated 65 on the level, is not that big and lacks any scope. *(tchd 11-4)*
Hamburg Springer(IRE), rated just 40 on the level, had been pulled up on his previous start.
Bold Pursuit(IRE), having his third start, looks essentially a non-stayer. *(op 16-1)*

1905 FIVE ARROWS COMMERCIAL FINANCE NOVICES' H'CAP CHASE (14 fncs 4 omitted) 3m
2:50 (2:50) (Class 4) (0-90,87) 5-Y-0+ **£4,016** (£1,305; £702)

Form					RPR
65	1		**Hi Laurie (IRE)**[12] [1753] 10-11-9 84 *(M Scudamore) prom: jnd ldr 10th: led next: 10l clr last: styd on strly*	TScudamore **7/1**[3]	100+
3-36	2	26	**New Perk (IRE)**[166] [365] 7-10-0 66 *(M J Gingell) w ldrs: led 9th to 4 out: wknd 2 out: fin tired*	CHonour(5) **5/1**[2]	66+
05P-	3	dist	**Bobby Brown (IRE)**[229] [4344] 5-10-0 68 *(Mrs H Dalton) in rr: lost pl 9th: sn bhd: lft distant 3rd after 4 out: btn 77l*	PMerrigan(5) **8/1**	—
-224	F		**Another Club Royal**[153] [546] 6-10-10 76 *(D McCain) chsd ldrs: cl 3rd whn fell 10th*	StephenJCraine(5) **9/2**[1]	—
3365	P		**Mikasa (IRE)**[26] [1612] 5-10-7 73 *(R F Fisher) hld up in rr: reminders 9th: sn wknd: bhd whn p.u bef next*	KJMercer(3) **11/1**	—
22P-	F		**Trenance**[189] [4970] 7-11-7 82 *(T R George) trckd ldrs: led 8th: hdd next: weakaned 10th: poor 3rd whn fell next*	JMMaguire **5/1**[2]	—
0502	P		**Swallow Magic (IRE)**[20] [1686] 7-11-5 87 *(Ferdy Murphy) t.k.h in front: led: mstke 7th: hdd next: rdn and wknd 9th: bhd whn p.u bef next*	(v) TJDreaper(7) **10/1**	—
P0-5	P		**Jolly Boy (FR)**[20] [1672] 6-10-8 69 *(Miss Venetia Williams) chsd ldrs: 6th and wkng whn blnd 9th: lft distant 3rd and mstke 4 out: p.u bef next*	AO'Keeffe **9/2**[1]	—

6m 15.3s (-17.20) **Going Correction** -0.50s/f (Good) 8 Ran SP% **110.7**
WFA 5 from 6yo+ 2lb
Speed ratings: **108,99,—,—,— —,—,—** CSF £39.50 CT £272.55 TOTE £8.60: £1.70, £1.50, £3.10; EX 40.40.
Owner Mrs N M Watkins **Bred** J J O'Neill **Trained** Bromsash, Herefordshire

FOCUS
A low-grade handicap but a wide margin winner who was making her chasing bow and she saw out the trip really well in the testing conditions and could rate higher. The first two fences in the back straight were omitted.

NOTEBOOK
Hi Laurie(IRE), bred to stay all day, had this won going to the last and drew further and further away on the run-in. She could hardly have made a better start to her chasing career and is already a better chaser than she was a hurdler. *(op 9-1)*
New Perk(IRE), a maiden after 26 starts over fences, went on but had nothing in reserve when tackled by the winner and in the end struggled to reach the finishing line. *(op 4-1)*
Bobby Brown(IRE), who showed little over hurdles, showed even less on his first try over fences. *(op 9-1)*
Trenance was a distant third and out on his feet when crashing out four from home. *(op 5-1 tchd 4-1)*
Another Club Royal was bang in the firing line but unproven on soft ground, the suspicion was that he was just starting to struggle when crashing out five from home. *(op 5-1 tchd 4-1)*
Jolly Boy(FR), having just his second start over fences and making his chase debut, was on the retreat when blundering five out. Left a poor third when making a mess of the fourth last, he soon called it a day. *(op 5-1 tchd 4-1)*

1906 WEATHERBYS BANK MARES' ONLY H'CAP HURDLE (14 hdls) 3m
3:25 (3:26) (Class 4) (0-110,109) 4-Y-0+ **£4,075** (£1,254; £627; £313)

Form					RPR
231-	1		**Marjina**[280] [3454] 6-11-12 109 *(Miss E C Lavelle) mde all: shkn up gng to 2 out: styd on strly: eased towards fin*	BFenton **11/4**[1]	115+
U-03	2	2½	**Prayerful**[12] [1751] 6-10-1 87 *(J G M O'Shea) in rr: hdwy 9th: sn drvn along: styd on to go 2nd last: no imp*	ONelmes(3) **8/1**	87

3 1 1/4 **Broken Gale (IRE)**[40] [1495] 5-10-5 **88** .... MDGrant 88+
(P Budds, Ire) *trckd ldrs: effrt appr 3 out: styd on same pce between last 2* **9/1**

212- **4** 9 **Princesse Grec (FR)**[386] [1627] 7-11-0 **97** .... TScudamore 89+
(M Scudamore) *chsd ldrs: wknd between last 2* **7/1**[3]

000P **5** 5 **Esterelle (USA)**[24] [1630] 10-9-13 **89** ow4 .... MrJAJenkins(7) 74
(H J Manners) *in rr: reminders 5th: bhd fr 7th: sme hdwy 3 out: styd on run-in* **25/1**

P-44 **6** 1/2 **Calomeria**[22] [1658] 4-11-4 **107** .... StephenJCraine(5) 91
(D McCain) *trckd ldrs: rdn 3 out: wknd between last 2* **12/1**

412- **7** 11 **Bdellium**[191] [4929] 7-9-12 **86** .... MNicolls(5) 63+
(B I Case) *rr-div: drvn along and sme hdwy 9th: lost pl 11th* **13/2**[2]

422- **8** 23 **Ede'Iff**[204] [4757] 8-10-12 **95** .... PJBrennan 46
(W G M Turner) *in rr: wl bhd fr 10th* **10/1**

030- **9** 23 **Starry Mary**[235] [4233] 7-10-0 **83** oh2 .... AO'Keeffe 11
(R J Price) *in rr: drvn along and lost tch 9th* **9/1**

625- **10** 15 **Nobodys Perfect (IRE)**[191] [4924] 5-10-9 **95** .... KJMercer(3) 8
(Ferdy Murphy) *a in rr: bhd and lost tch 9th* **10/1**

630/ **P** **Bedford Leader**[617] [3904] 7-10-0 **83** oh2 .... JGoldstein —
(A P Jones) *chsd ldrs: lost pl 9th: sn bhd: t.o last whn p.u bef 2 out* **50/1**

5m 54.9s (-10.10) **Going Correction** -0.30s/f (Good)
WFA 4 from 5yo+ 15lb **11 Ran SP% 115.3**
Speed ratings: **104,103,102,99,98 97,94,86,78,73** — CSF £24.87 CT £174.32 TOTE £3.60: £1.50, £2.40, £3.10; EX 30.00.
Owner Paul G Jacobs **Bred** P G Jacobs **Trained** Wildhern, Hants

FOCUS
A moderate handicap but the progressive winner, who was value for double the official margin, will make a better chaser. The second and third ran to their previous marks and the form looks sound.

NOTEBOOK
Marjina, making her handicap debut, is a big type who does not really respect the hurdles. She *enjoyed herself in front and scored with a fair bit in hand. She should make an even better chaser. (op 10-3)*
Prayerful, already tried over fences, likes soft ground and stuck on in grim fashion to snatch second spot near the line. All she seems to to do is stay. *(op 6-1)*
Broken Gale(IRE), an Irish point winner, looks to possess a lot more stamina than speed. *(op 12-1 tchd 8-1)*
Princesse Grec(FR), absent for a year, raced in the thick of things but became very leg weary between the last two and has yet to prove herself on soft ground. *(op 11-2)*
Esterelle(USA), 6lb higher than when runner-up in this race a year ago, looks to just stay.
Calomeria, a four-year-old taking on her elders, looked to run out of stamina late in the day. *(tchd 14-1 in a place)*

1907 SCOTTISH EQUITABLE/JOCKEYS ASSOCIATION H'CAP CHASE 2m 5f
(12 fncs 4 omitted)
4:00 (4:00) (Class 4) (0-110,108) 5-Y-0+ **£5,128** (£1,578; £789; £394)

Form RPR

PP-P **1** **Yassar (IRE)**[80] [1191] 10-10-2 **84** .... WMarston 94
(D J Wintle) *chsd ldrs: led 8th to 2 out: led last: styd on* **66/1**

01P- **2** 2 1/2 **Meggie's Beau (IRE)**[223] [4462] 9-11-3 **104** .... LStephens(5) 112+
(Miss Venetia Williams) *wnt prom 6th: led 2 out to last: no ex* **8/1**

12-0 **3** 1 **Tresor Preziniere (FR)**[20] [1675] 7-10-13 **95** .... RJohnson 103+
(P J Hobbs) *in tch: reminders 6th: outpcd and reminders 8th: hdwy appr 4 out: 2l 3rd and styng on whn blnd last* **2/1**[1]

22-3 **4** 3 **Thyne Man (IRE)**[182] [107] 7-11-7 **103** .... PMoloney 108+
(J Mackie) *hld up: wnt prom 7th: handy 3rd whn blnd 3 out: hung lft and one pce run-in* **9/1**

PU/6 **5** 2 1/2 **Get Smart (IRE)**[16] [1716] 8-9-12 **83** .... KJMercer(3) 84
(Ferdy Murphy) *hld up: wnt prom 6th: wknd after 3 out* **12/1**

6 3/4 **Mick Divine (IRE)**[211] [4675] 7-11-1 **97** .... NFehily 97
(C J Mann) *hld up: wnt prom 7th: wknd after 3 out* **11/2**[2]

F51- **7** 6 **Cetti's Warbler**[223] [4459] 7-11-12 **108** .... JAMcCarthy 103+
(Mrs P Robeson) *chsd ldrs: wknd 4 out* **7/1**[3]

P-3 **8** 7 **Armageddon**[181] [132] 8-10-3 **85** .... LAspell 78+
(O Sherwood) *hld up: hit 5th: hdwy and in tch 8th: wknd 4 out: 7th whn blnd last* **8/1**

P3P- **9** dist **Celtic Pride (IRE)**[189] [4970] 10-11-11 **107** .... (v) AO'Keeffe —
(Jennie Candlish) *sn in rr: t.o 8th: btn 44l* **25/1**

6/P- **P** **All Sonsilver (FR)**[440] [1179] 8-11-10 **106** .... RGreene —
(P Kelsall) *in tch: drvn along 4th: lost pl 6th: t.o whn p.u bef 8th* **25/1**

30P/ **P** **Ela La Senza (IRE)**[573] [4656] 8-11-4 **100** .... CLlewellyn —
(N A Twiston-Davies) *led to 8th: lost pl and in rr whn hit 4 out: p.u bef next* **14/1**

5m 20.6s (-6.90) **Going Correction** -0.30s/f (Good) **11 Ran SP% 117.0**
Speed ratings: **101,100,99,98,97 97,95,92,—,—** — CSF £524.89 CT £1584.54 TOTE £92.50: £15.40, £3.00, £1.60; EX 1047.00.
Owner Lavender Hill Stud L L C **Bred** Francis Small **Trained** Naunton, Gloucs

FOCUS
A decisive winner who has been bang out of form but it was no fluke and with the second, fourth and six running to their marks the form has a sound look. The first two fences in the back straight were omitted.

NOTEBOOK
Yassar(IRE), who looked to have lost the plot, had been pulled up on his three most recent start, He regain the lead at the last and there was certainly no fluke about this.
Meggie's Beau(IRE), hard to predict, had been absent since pulling when last seen out in March. He went on but in the end the winner proved much too strong. *(op 7-1)*
Tresor Preziniere(FR), returning to fences from a 21lb lower mark, only took a hand because of his rider's determination. Indeed but for fluffing his lines at the last, he might well have carried the day. *(op 15-8 tchd 5-2)*
Thyne Man(IRE), a threat when blundering three out, not for the first time hung left under pressure and is anything but hearty. *(op 12-1)*
Get Smart(IRE), having just his second outing here, looks a weak finisher. *(op 11-1)*
Mick Divine(IRE), bought for 15,000gns in May, overall has a regressive profile. *(op 6-1)*

1908 SIGNS 2000 FREE YOUR IMAGINATION 01785 220561 MAIDEN HURDLE (10 hdls) 2m
4:35 (4:35) (Class 4) 4-Y-0+ **£2,765** (£790; £395)

Form RPR

5 **1** **Mikado**[26] [1614] 4-11-0 .... JEMoore 116+
(Jonjo O'Neill) *hld up: hdwy 7th: chal 2 out: styd on to ld towards fin* **9/1**

2 nk **New Team (FR)**[345] 4-11-0 .... AThornton 115+
(R H Alner) *hld up towards rr: hd 7th: chsng ldrs next: led appr last: hdd and no ex towards fin* **33/1**

41-5 **3** 7 **Call Oscar (IRE)**[181] [131] 6-11-0 .... TDoyle 108+
(C Tinkler) *led 2nd: hdd appr last: kpt on same pce* **16/1**

4 1 3/4 **Eleazar (GER)**[145] 4-11-0 .... LAspell 105
(Mrs L Wadham) *rr-div: hdwy 5th: chsng ldrs 7th: wknd 2 out* **6/1**[3]

5 10 **Napoleon (IRE)**[382] 4-11-0 .... RJohnson 95
(P J Hobbs) *hld up: hdwy 6th: effrt appr 3 out: sn wknd* **11/4**[2]

46- **6** 6 **Sunisa (IRE)**[146] [3678] 4-10-7 .... (t) PJBrennan 82
(J Mackie) *hld up in mid-div: hdwy to chse ldrs 6th: wnt 2nd appr 3 out: sn wknd* **50/1**

7 9 **Prairie Law (GER)**[53] 5-10-7 .... TMessenger(7) 80
(B N Pollock) *led to 2nd: chsd ldrs: lost pl appr 3 out* **80/1**

03-0 **8** 6 **Danebank (IRE)**[60] [1364] 5-11-0 100 .... PMoloney 74
(J Mackie) *wnt prom 6th: lost pl appr 3 out* **16/1**

13 **9** 12 **Twelve Paces**[20] [1680] 4-11-0 .... TJMurphy 62
(M C Pipe) *hit 1st: hdwy to chse ldrs 4th: reminders next: sn lost pl* **5/4**[1]

10 1 1/4 **Sidcup's Gold (IRE)**[229] 5-11-0 .... MBradburne 61
(M Sheppard) *prom: rdn and lost pl after 4th: bhd fr 6th* **100/1**

11 1 **Hunting Lodge (IRE)**[75] 4-10-7 .... MrJAJenkins(7) 60
(H J Manners) *t.o last whn blnd 6th* **40/1**

3-P **12** 1/2 **Barton Park**[16] [1714] 5-11-0 .... NFehily 60
(D P Keane) *t.k.h in rr: bhd fr 7th* **33/1**

2/0- **P** **Mostakbel (USA)**[28] [3633] 6-11-0 .... WHutchinson —
(M D I Usher) *in tch: wknd 5th: t.o whn p.u bef 3 out* **66/1**

P **Two Of A Kind (IRE)**[235] 5-11-0 .... AO'Keeffe —
(Miss L V Davis) *j. bdly detached in rr: t.o whn p.u after 5th* **80/1**

06 **S** **Teutonic (IRE)**[60] [1360] 4-10-4 .... KJMercer(3) —
(R F Fisher) *chsd ldrs: 6th and wkng whn slipped up bnd after 7th* **100/1**

4m 0.20s (-0.20) **Going Correction** +0.025s/f (Yiel) **15 Ran SP% 123.4**
Speed ratings: **101,100,97,96,91 88,83,80,74,74 73,73,—,—,—** CSF £258.87 TOTE £9.50: £3.10, £8.00, £3.40; EX 122.10.
Owner John P McManus **Bred** Gerald W Leigh **Trained** Cheltenham, Gloucs

FOCUS
A slowly-run race. The first two have the potential but the race has been tentively rated through the bumper form of the third.

NOTEBOOK
Mikado, who lacks size and scope, stuck to his guns and finally mastered the runner-up near the line. How much he progresses remains to be seen. *(op 6-1)*
New Team(FR) ◆, a winner in maiden company on the flat in the French Provinces, is a rangy type who will make a chaser in time. He travelled strongly but after showing ahead missed out near the line. He will soon go one better.
Call Oscar(IRE), a big type, was a winner in three start in bumpers. He was soon taking them along but in the end the first two proved much too good. He can find an opening in lesser company.
Eleazar(GER), who has form to his credit in his native Germany, was having his first outing since April and will strip fitter next time. *(op 8-1)*
Napoleon(IRE), winner of a maiden at Rosscommon a year ago for Aidan O'Brien, tried to get on terms coming off the final turn but he was soon flat out and going nowhere. Whether he has the right attitude remains to be seen. *(tchd 3-1 in a place)*
Twelve Paces, struggling to keep up with a circuit to go, was soon beating a retreat. This was *simply too bad to be true. Official explanation: trainer's representative had no explanation for the poor form shown (op 6-4 tchd 6-5)*

1909 MOORLANDS RACING SYNDICATE STANDARD NH FLAT RACE (CONDITIONAL JOCKEYS AND AMATEUR RIDERS) 2m
5:10 (5:10) (Class 6) 4-6-Y-O **£1,981** (£566; £283)

Form RPR

1 **Hennessy (IRE)** 4-10-13 .... WKennedy(5) 108+
(M Pitman) *hld up: effrt over 4f out: wnt 2nd 3f out: led over 1f out: drvn clr* **5/2**[2]

1- **2** 7 **Inaro (IRE)**[352] [2129] 4-11-4 .... MrAJBerry(7) 105+
(Jonjo O'Neill) *sn trcking ldr: led over 3f out: sn rdn: hdd over 1f out: sn btn* **85/40**[1]

3 4 **So Long**[265] 5-10-4 .... TMessenger(7) 86
(C L Popham) *chsd ldrs: rdn and outpcd 4f out: styd on fnl 2f* **12/1**

4 6 **Nanard (FR)** 4-10-8 .... AGlassonbury(10) 87
(M C Pipe) *trckd ldrs: outpcd over 3f out: wknd over 2f out* **7/2**[3]

0- **5** 3 1/2 **Eluvaparty**[223] [4465] 5-10-11 .... DJacob(7) 83
(D P Keane) *led: qcknd 6f out: hdd over 3f out: wknd over 2f out* **10/1**

0 **6** 7 **Gold Vic (IRE)**[20] [1681] 5-10-11 .... LHeard(7) 76
(P Bowen) *hld up: drvn along over 5f out: sn lost pl* **20/1**

6 **7** 14 **Trizzy**[24] [1635] 5-10-4 .... MrJAJenkins(7) 55
(H J Manners) *hld up: hdwy over 5f out: lost pl 4f out* **66/1**

0 **8** 17 **Wheel Tapper (IRE)**[7] [1820] 4-10-13 .... MNicolls(5) 45
(P W Hiatt) *trckd ldrs: rdn 5f out: sn lost pl: virtually p.u fnl f* **33/1**

9 dist **Le Milliardaire (FR)** 6-11-1 .... ONelmes(3) —
(C J Down) *hld up in last: drvn along over 5f out: sn bhd: t.o 3f out: virtually p.u: btn 65l* **33/1**

4m 1.40s (1.60) **Going Correction** +0.025s/f (Yiel) **9 Ran SP% 111.7**
Speed ratings: **97,93,91,88,86 83,76,67,—** CSF £7.57 TOTE £3.40: £1.20, £1.30, £1.80; EX 6.30 Place 6 £205.21, Place 5 £120.51.
Owner Malcolm C Denmark **Bred** Mrs M Brophy **Trained** Upper Lambourn, Berks

FOCUS
Just a steady gallop until the final six furlongs. The winner looks a useful prospect with the fifth the best guide to the level.

NOTEBOOK
Hennessy(IRE), who stands over plenty of ground, looked fit and well on his racecourse debut. He went in pursuit of the winner and in the end came right away. He looks a decent prospect. *(op 3-1)*
Inaro(IRE), who took a mile and a half bumper at Newbury a year ago when trained in Ireland, went on travelling comfortably but his rider made the mistake of coming wide away from the better ground and in the end his mount was comprehensively outstayed. *(op 2-1)*
So Long, who is well named, had finished runner-up in a maiden point in February. She stuck on after being hopelessly outpaced and clearly has a lot more stamina than speed. *(op 20-1)*
Nanard(FR), a medium sized individual, is rather long in the back. He was struggling turning for home and soon dropped out. *(op 9-4)*
Eluvaparty, a big, rangy type, took them along. He set sail for home leaving the back straight but when challenged soon fell in a heap. *(op 12-1 tchd 9-1)*

T/Plt: £111.80 to a £1 stake. Pool: £47,459.25. 309.65 winning tickets. T/Qpdt: £43.40 to a £1 stake. Pool: £3,699.10. 63.00 winning tickets. WG

The Form Book, Raceform Ltd, Compton, RG20 6NL

[1718] WETHERBY (L-H)

Friday, October 28

OFFICIAL GOING: Soft

Wind: Nil

1910 BET365 CONDITIONAL JOCKEYS' NOVICES' H'CAP HURDLE (12 hdls) 2m 7f

1:55 (1:55) (Class 4) (0-105,100) 3-Y-O+ **£3,370** (£963; £481)

Form RPR

F25 **1** **Red Perk (IRE)**[153] [546] 8-11-0 **88**.....(p) RStephens 91+
(R C Guest) *chsd ldng pair: hdwy 4 out: cl up next: rdn to ld bef 2 out: drvn last: kpt on gamely flat* **4/1**[1]

041 **2** *shd* **Potts Of Magic**[35] [1539] 6-11-0 **88**..... WKennedy 90
(R Lee) *hld up and bhd: hdwy 7th: rdn along briefly next: hdwy 4 out: rdn to chal 2 out: drvn last: no ex nr fin* **4/1**[1]

PP-P **3** *30* **Quainton Hills**[155] [509] 11-10-5 **79**.....(t) TGreenway 51
(D R Stoddart) *led: rdn along 4 out: drvn next: sn hdd and plugged on same pce* **10/1**

-44B **4** *nk* **Alpha Juliet (IRE)**[16] [1723] 4-10-10 **85**..... DCCostello 56
(G M Moore) *hld up and bhd: stdy hdwy 1/2-way: cl up 4 out: rdn along next: sn drvn and plugged on same pce* **9/2**[2]

PP-5 **5** *7* **Kirby's Vic (IRE)**[16] [1714] 5-10-13 **93**..... MGoldstein[(6)] 58
(N A Twiston-Davies) *chsd ldr: cl up 4 out: rdn along next: sn drvn and wknd fr 2 out* **13/2**

524- **F** **Roman Rebel**[255] [3867] 6-11-6 **100**..... CDSharkey[(6)] —
(Mrs K Walton) *hld up towards rr whn fell 2nd* **5/1**[3]

24-P **P** **Iloveturtle (IRE)**[7] [1816] 5-11-4 **97**..... AGlassonbury[(5)] —
(M C Chapman) *a rr: bhd fr 1/2-way: t.o whn p.u bef 3 out* **11/1**

F-U0 **P** **Mongino (GER)**[13] [1745] 4-9-13 **80** ow1.....(t) CPoste[(6)] —
(M F Harris) *nt fluent in rr: hdwy to chse ldrs 6th: rdn along and mstke next: sn wknd and bhd fr 4 out: p.u bef last* **33/1**

5m 55.5s (-1.20) **Going Correction** +0.175s/f (Yiel)
WFA 4 from 5yo+ 14lb **8** Ran SP% **108.5**
Speed ratings: **109,108,98,98,95** —,—,— CSF £18.56 CT £128.91 TOTE £5.60: £1.90, £1.30, £2.30; EX 15.00.
Owner B Chorzelewski,P Davies & P Hodgkinson **Bred** Alex Heskin **Trained** Brancepeth, Co Durham

FOCUS
Ordinary stuff and the front two finished 30 lengths clear of the remainder and set the standard.

NOTEBOOK
Red Perk(IRE) continued the fine recent run of form of the Guest stable and just edged out Potts Of Magic in a thrilling finish. Evidently fit enough to win on this reappearance, he had little trouble with reverting to hurdles and looks the sort who has more to offer. *(op 9-2 tchd 5-1)*
Potts Of Magic has been running well and came into this off the back of a win at Worcester in September. He engaged in battle with the winner from quarter of a mile out and gave his all, but lost lost out in a tight finish. He was 30 lengths clear of the third and, although likely to go up again for this, he should remain capable of winning. *(tchd 10-3)*
Quainton Hills, pulled up in six of his last eight outings coming into this, ran a slightly better race in the tongue tie and at least he completed. He is getting no better at he age of 11, but this was at least a step back in the right direction. *(op 16-1)*
Alpha Juliet(IRE) came off worse in her own private battle with Quainton Hills for third and finished very tired. She has still to win a race, and needs to find some improvement from somewhere. *(op 4-1)*
Kirby's Vic(IRE) was perhaps the most interesting runner on show, this being his handicap debut and representing an in-form yard, but having chased the early leader and travelled well enough into the straight, he soon began to struggle and weakened disappointingly in the final quarter mile. Stamina should be his strong suit, but as he is only five he deserves another chance, and it is likely the best of him will not be seen until he tackles fences. *(op 5-1 tchd 9-2)*
Iloveturtle(IRE) *Official explanation: jockey said gelding had a breathing problem (op 10-1 tchd 9-1)*
Roman Rebel fell too early to determine how he would have fared. *(op 10-1 tchd 9-1)*

1911 BET365 BEGINNERS' CHASE (12 fncs) 2m

2:25 (2:27) (Class 4) 4-Y-O+ **£3,948** (£1,215; £607; £303)

Form RPR

/42- **1** **Albuhera (IRE)**[335] [2480] 7-11-6.....(t) JTizzard 139+
(P F Nicholls) *trckd ldrs: smooth hdwy and cl up 5 out: led 3 out: clr appr last* **11/4**[2]

13F- **2** *4* **Rebel Rhythm**[203] [4765] 6-11-6..... DElsworth 134+
(Mrs S J Smith) *led: qcknd appr 4 out: rdn: j.rt and hdd 3 out: drvn and one pce appr last* **4/6**[1]

11-0 **3** *20* **Rhapsody Rose**[184] [66] 4-10-0..... JamesDavies 94+
(P R Webber) *cl up: rdn along 4 out: wkng whn mstke 2 out: wl hld in 3rd whn hit last* **12/1**[3]

00LP **4** *10* **Dabus**[7] [1816] 10-11-6 99.....(b[1]) KJohnson 102
(M C Chapman) *chsd ldrs: rdn along after 5 out and sn outpcd* **100/1**

4-5F **5** *2* **Northern Minster**[6] [1835] 6-11-6..... BHarding 100
(F P Murtagh) *a rr: bhd fr 5 out* **33/1**

/65- **6** *12* **Konker**[367] [1847] 10-10-13..... APogson[(7)] 92+
(J R Cornwall) *in tch: rdn along after 5 out and sn wknd* **20/1**

P-U0- **U** **Government (IRE)**[162] [428] 4-10-0..... AScholes[(7)] —
(M C Chapman) *rr whn blnd and uns rdr 2nd* **200/1**

226- **F** **Beamish Prince**[25] [4978] 6-11-1..... DCCostello[(5)] —
(G M Moore) *keen: chsd ldrs tl fell 5th* **12/1**[3]

4m 8.80s (2.20) **Going Correction** +0.175s/f (Yiel)
WFA 4 from 6yo+ 13lb **8** Ran SP% **111.2**
Speed ratings: **101,99,89,84,83** **77**,—,— CSF £4.92 TOTE £3.20: £1.20, £1.10, £1.80; EX 5.50.

Owner D J & F A Jackson **Bred** K And Mrs Cullen **Trained** Ditcheat, Somerset

FOCUS
A good race with two smart hurdlers pulling clear as expected. Both already look useful and, despite being rated below their best hurdle marks, are sure to go on to better things.

NOTEBOOK
Albuhera(IRE), a smart hurdler of similar ability to favourite Rebel Rhythm, was widely expected to be outdone by the Smith-trained runner, this soft surface looking all against him, but he handled it surprisingly well and having travelled strongly/jumped fluently throughout, he steadily drew clear down the straight. This was impressive and he will no doubt be one of many potential Nicholls Arkle horses this term. It would not surprise to see him take his chance at the Paddy Power meeting next month. *(tchd 5-2 and 10-3)*
Rebel Rhythm, although running over a trip short of his best, was expected to make it a good test from the front in the ground, but having tried to make all he was simply done for speed by the winner. Clear of the third, he jumped well throughout and there were many positives to be taken from the run, so it will be surprising if he is not winning before long, probably over further. *(op 4-5 tchd 8-13)*
Rhapsody Rose, a fair hurdler on limited evidence, was simply outclassed by two potentially smart chasers and will find easier opportunities in her own sex group. *(op 8-1)*
Dabus has been running on and off in novice chases for around three years now and was always going to struggle here. *(op 66-1)*

1912 ROCOM SIEMENS H'CAP HURDLE (9 hdls) 2m

3:00 (3:00) (Class 3) (0-135,123) 4-Y-O+ **£6,789** (£2,089; £1,044; £522)

Form RPR

1-5 **1** **Ursis (FR)**[20] [1677] 4-11-6 **117**..... APMcCoy 121+
(Jonjo O'Neill) *mde all: rdn appr 3 out: j.rt and hit 2 out: drvn and mstke last: styd on* **6/4**[1]

5/46 **2** *5* **Kentucky Blue (IRE)**[6] [1823] 5-11-12 **123**..... RGarritty 121+
(T D Easterby) *chsd wnr: rdn along bef 3 out: drvn next and styng on whn mstke last: no ex flat* **11/2**[3]

416 **3** *8* **Karathaena (IRE)**[20] [1668] 5-11-2 **113**..... ADobbin 101
(M E Sowersby) *chsd ldrs: rdn along 3 out and kpt on same pce* **11/1**

312- **4** *18* **Pay Attention**[228] [4367] 4-11-11 **122**..... DO'Meara 92
(T D Easterby) *hld up in tch: hdwy 4 out: rdn along and outpcd fr next* **13/2**

6U00 **P** **Migration**[16] [1720] 9-11-1 **115**.....(p) LVickers[(3)] —
(Mrs S Lamyman) *a rr: rdn along 1/2-way: bhd whn p.u bef 3 out* **40/1**

11-2 **U** **Andre Chenier (IRE)**[9] [82] 4-11-4 **115**..... KRenwick 110
(P Monteith) *trckd ldrs: hdwy after 4 out: chsd wnr next: rdn: blnd and uns rdr 2 out* **5/2**[2]

3m 57.6s (-1.80) **Going Correction** +0.175s/f (Yiel)
WFA 4 from 5yo+ 13lb **6** Ran SP% **108.1**
Speed ratings: **111,108,104,95**,— — CSF £9.37 TOTE £2.20: £1.50, £2.10; EX 9.30.
Owner C H McGhie **Bred** Serge Bernereau Sarl **Trained** Cheltenham, Gloucs

FOCUS
An uncompetitive handicap hurdle won in good style by the potentially very useful Ursis with the runner-up setting the level of the form.

NOTEBOOK
Ursis(FR), who made a highly pleasing return to the action at Chepstow earlier in the month, was rightly made a short price favourite and, although lacking in experience, he led throughout and won tidily. Clearly a very useful handicapper, he remains open to tons of improvement and it would not surprise to see him land a decent prize this season. *(op 7-4 tchd 2-1)*
Kentucky Blue(IRE) has now had three quick runs in October and he seems to be taking them well, this being his best effort of the lot. He will find easier opportunities and time may show he faced a very stiff task trying to give the winner 6lb. *(op 6-1 tchd 5-1)*
Karathaena(IRE) was always likely to struggle and realistically her best chance was if all the fancied runners disappointed. Unfortunately for her they did not and third was as good as she could manage. *(tchd 9-1)*
Pay Attention, a stablemate of the runner-up, ran a rare poor race, but this was her first outing of the season and this tough mare deserves a chance to improve. *(op 4-1)*
Migration *Official explanation: trainer said gelding was subsequently found to have a low grade infection in its lungs (op 11-4)*
Andre Chenier(IRE) enjoyed a nice pipe-opener on the Flat the other day and he was in the process of running a decent race, albeit he looked held, when unshipping his pilot at the second last. Despite this mishap, he remains one to be interested in in future as he remains on a fair looking mark. *(op 11-4)*

1913 BET365 WHITE ROSE H'CAP CHASE (12 fncs) 2m

3:35 (3:35) (Class 3) (0-135,133) 5-Y-O+ **£7,410** (£2,280; £1,140; £570)

Form RPR

12F- **1** **Provocative (FR)**[275] [3543] 7-11-9 **130**..... GLee 142+
(M Todhunter) *a rpominent: led 4th: rdn along 3 out: drvn last: styd on gamely flat* **8/1**

02-4 **2** *1* **Almaydan**[174] [219] 7-11-12 **133**..... RThornton 142
(R Lee) *trckd ldrs on inner: hdwy 4 out: rdn along next: styd on to chal last: drvn and ev ch tl no ex towards fin* **5/1**[2]

0-45 **3** *5* **Multeen River (IRE)**[13] [1739] 9-11-0 **121**..... APMcCoy 127+
(Jonjo O'Neill) *hld up in tch: hdwy 5 out: rdn along 3 out: drvn appr last: styd on same pce flat* **11/2**[3]

55-6 **4** *½* **Sir Storm (IRE)**[176] [195] 9-10-10 **117**..... ARoss 123+
(G M Moore) *trckd ldrs: hdwy 6th: cl up 5 out tl hmpd next: sn rdn: styd on and ch appr last: sn drvn and wkndflat* **16/1**

223- **5** *5* **Super Nomad**[190] [4944] 10-11-3 **124**..... ADempsey 125+
(M W Easterby) *hld up in rr: hmpd 3rd: hdwy 5 out: chsd ldrs fr next: rdn along 2 out: wknd appr last* **7/1**

6/F- **F** **Flame Creek (IRE)**[321] [2762] 9-10-13 **120**..... ADobbin —
(Noel T Chance) *in tch whn blnd 1st and 2nd: fell 3rd* **9/2**[1]

5312 **P** **Gone Too Far**[26] [1604] 7-11-0 **121**.....(v) KRenwick —
(P Monteith) *chsd ldrs tl lost pl qckly and p.u bef 4th* **7/1**

1FP- **P** **Stormy Lord (IRE)**[196] [4846] 9-11-6 **127**..... BHarding —
(J Wade) *led to 4th: rdn along 6th: sn lost pl and bhd fr 5 out: p.u bef last* **16/1**

500- **P** **Jericho III (FR)**[216] [4555] 8-10-7 **119**.....(be) PCO'Neill[(5)] —
(R C Guest) *plld hrd: cl up and mstke 1st: sddle slipped and p.u after next* **14/1**

-112 **B** **Tribal Dispute**[145] [646] 8-11-6 **127**..... RGarritty —
(T D Easterby) *trckd ldrs: hdwy whn blnd bdly 5 out: chsd ldrs whn b.d by loose horse next* **12/1**

4m 5.70s (-0.90) **Going Correction** +0.175s/f (Yiel) **10** Ran SP% **112.5**
Speed ratings: **109,108,106,105,103** —,—,—,—,— CSF £47.01 CT £238.00 TOTE £7.50: £2.70, £2.10, £2.50; EX 59.80.
Owner Sir Robert Ogden **Bred** Marcel Poirier **Trained** Orton, Cumbria

FOCUS
A decent handicap run in a good time. The winner can rate higher and the race looks sure to produce future winners.

NOTEBOOK
Provocative(FR) has a mixed record over fences, but he has yet to finish out of the front two when completing and he recorded a fine effort in foiling classy handicapper Almaydan. The runner-up did not really have conditions to suit, but nothing should be taken away from him and he should be capable of building on this reappearance effort with the run under his belt. *(op 7-1)*
Almaydan made up into a very useful novice last season and this was a cracking reappearance effort on ground that would have been anything but ideal. Travelling well throughout, there was simply too much emphasis on stamina for him, but he beat the remainder well enough and looks certain to win off this sort of mark once granted more favourable conditions. *(tchd 11-2)*
Multeen River(IRE), dropped 3lb by the Handicapper, ran a bit better on this third start of the season, but was no match for the front two. He may need to drop a few further pounds before he is winning again. *(op 6-1 tchd 5-1)*
Sir Storm(IRE) has been in steady decline over the last year or so, but as a result he has dropped to a decent mark and this was a much-improved run. He goes well at this course and may soon be ready to win again.
Super Nomad was not disgraced and is entitled to come on for the first run since April. *(op 12-1)*
Gone Too Far *Official explanation: vet said gelding returned in a distressed state (tchd 16-1)*
Jericho III(FR) *Official explanation: jockey said saddle slipped (tchd 16-1)*

Flame Creek(IRE), who spent last season contesting graded hurdles, was without doubt the most interesting runner in the line-up, coming into this unbeaten in three starts over fences, but he got no further than the third. He had made mistakes at both the first two fences as well and Wetherby is not a course whose fences are to be messed with. It remains to be seen how this affects his confidence. *(tchd 16-1)*

Tribal Dispute had no luck at all. He was beginning to creep into it when hitting the fifth from home and then having got himself back together, was brought down by a loose horse when still in with a chance. *(tchd 16-1)*

1914 BET365 NOVICES' H'CAP CHASE (18 fncs) 3m 1f

4:10 (4:10) (Class 4) (0-105,98) 4-Y-0+ **£3,833** (£1,245; £670)

Form RPR

P54- **1** **Blame The Ref (IRE)**^{298} [3209] 8-11-9 **98** .... LVickers$^{(3)}$ 109+
(C C Bealby) *led to 3rd: cl up tl led again appr 4 out: sn rdn and styd on* **7/2**^{3}

323- **2** *13* **Bright Steel (IRE)**^{341} [2359] 8-10-7 **79** .... GLee 77
(M Todhunter) *hld up in tch: pushed along 6 out: hdwy to chse wnr 4 out: drvn 2 out and no imp* **6/4**^{1}

05F0 **3** *dist* **Lambrini Mist**^{16} [1719] 7-10-0 **72** oh7 .... (b^{1}) DCrosse 45
(Mrs L Williamson) *cl up tl rdn along and wknd fr 13th* **8/1**

0P-U **F** **Randolph O'Brien (IRE)**^{26} [1615] 5-11-10 **98** .... AntonyEvans —
(N A Twiston-Davies) *cl up: led 3rd: rdn along 5 out: sn hdd and wkng whn fell 4 out* **85/40**^{2}

6m 49.0s (9.00) **Going Correction** +0.175s/f (Yiel) **4** Ran SP% **105.3**
Speed ratings: **92,87,—,—** CSF £8.90 TOTE £4.00; EX 8.20.
Owner Michael Hill **Bred** Seamus Murphy **Trained** Barrowby, Lincs

FOCUS
An awful race in truth and a moderate time to boot. The winner is the best guide to the level of the form.

NOTEBOOK
Blame The Ref(IRE) has taken his time to get off the mark over fences, but he was found an excellent opportunity and powered clear to win easily. The form is worth little, but this will no doubt give his confidence a boost and there may be more to come. *(op 11-4 tchd 4-1)*
Bright Steel(IRE) was entitled to respect on his hurdles form, but he was no match for the winner on this fencing debut, despite the weight concession. There may be a small race in him at a similar lowly level. *(op 13-8 tchd 5-4, 7-4 in a place)*
Lambrini Mist showed little in the first-time blinkers and looks set to continue to struggle. *(op 9-1 tchd 7-1)*
Randolph O'Brien(IRE) was the potential fly in the ointment with his stable being in such good form and this being only his second start over fences. However, having travelled and jumped well early, he soon ran out of puff as they turned for home and he was well held when taking a nasty fall at the fourth last. It remains to be seen how this has affected his confidence. *(op 15-8 tchd 9-4)*

1915 BET365 "NATIONAL HUNT" NOVICES' HURDLE (10 hdls) 2m 4f 110y

4:45 (4:45) (Class 4) 4-Y-0+ **£3,752** (£1,072; £536)

Form RPR

3 **1** **Nor'Nor'East (IRE)**^{20} [1672] 7-10-12 .... APMcCoy 118+
(Jonjo O'Neill) *hld up and bhd: stdy hdwy 1/2-way: trckd ldrs 4 out: rdn to chse ldr 2 out: led appr last and styd on* **11/8**^{1}

2 *5* **Hockenheim (FR)**^{408} 4-10-12 .... GLee 110+
(J Howard Johnson) *a.p: hdwy to ld 3 out: rdn next: drvn and hdd appr last: kpt on same pce* **13/2**^{3}

6 **3** *11* **Laertes**^{28} [1593] 4-10-12 .... ADempsey 99+
(C Grant) *hld up and bhd: hdwy 4 out: styd on fr next: nrst fin* **66/1**

3 **4** *8* **Cirrus (FR)**^{47} [1454] 6-10-12 .... JimCrowley 90
(K G Reveley) *in tch: rdn along and outpcd after 4 out: styd on fr 2 out* **7/1**

23-3 **5** *2* **Oso Magic**^{167} [346] 7-10-12 .... DElsworth 88
(Mrs S J Smith) *led and sn wl clr: rdn along and hdd 3 out and sn wknd* **4/1**^{2}

503- **6** *½* **Cloudless Dawn**^{188} [4981] 5-10-5 .... ARoss 81
(P Beaumont) *chsd ldrs: rdn along after 4 out and sn wknd* **33/1**

7 *3* **Cedar Rapids (IRE)**^{558} 5-10-12 .... DO'Meara 85
(H P Hogarth) *in tch: hdwy to chse ldrs 4 out: sn rdn along and wknd next* **25/1**

400- **8** *½* **Jethro Tull (IRE)**^{305} [2996] 6-10-12 .... BHarding 84
(G A Harker) *racd wd: in tch: hdwy to chse ldrs 4 out: sn rdn along and wknd next* **16/1**

00-P **9** *12* **Morgan Be**^{72} [1231] 5-10-12 .... RMcGrath 72
(Mrs K Walton) *a rr: bhd fr 1/2-way* **100/1**

10 *dist* **Zaffiera (IRE)**^{180} 4-10-12 .... NPMulholland —
(M D Hammond) *a rr: bhd fr 1/2-way* **50/1**

11 *hd* **Dans Edge (IRE)** 5-10-5 .... PJMcDonald$^{(7)}$ —
(Ferdy Murphy) *a bhd* **12/1**

00-0 **P** **Culbann (IRE)**^{37} [1508] 6-10-5 **81** .... KRenwick —
(C Rae) *midfield: lost pl and bhd fr 1/2-way: bhd whn p.u bef 3 out* **100/1**

0 **P** **Harwood Dale**^{8} [1799] 5-10-7 .... DCCostello$^{(5)}$ —
(T D Walford) *prom: rdn along and lost pl 1/2-way: bhd whn p.u bef 3 out* **66/1**

104- **P** **Vital Spark**^{326} [2681] 6-10-9 .... GBerridge$^{(3)}$ —
(J M Jefferson) *prom: rdn along 1/2-way: wknd appr 4 out and p.u bef next* **20/1**

0-P **P** **Bhaydalko (FR)**^{175} [201] 5-10-12 .... RThornton —
(M Todhunter) *in tch on inner: pushed along 1/2-way: sn lost pl and bhd whn p.u bef 4 out* **25/1**

5m 13.5s (4.60) **Going Correction** +0.175s/f (Yiel) **15** Ran SP% **123.8**
Speed ratings: **98,96,91,88,88 87,86,86,82,— —,—,—,—,—** CSF £10.11 TOTE £2.40: £1.10, £3.00, £11.30; EX 13.90 Place 6 £54.16, Place 5 £28.45.
Owner John P McManus **Bred** Mrs C A Moore **Trained** Cheltenham, Gloucs

FOCUS
A modest novice hurdle likely to produce only the odd winner.

NOTEBOOK
Nor'Nor'East(IRE), who did not shape without promise on his debut at Bangor, appeared to face a relatively simple task against some modest sorts and he made no mistake. Soon to turn eight, it would not surprise to see connections waste little time in sending him chasing. *(op 2-1)*
Hockenheim(FR) was an interesting contender on this first start for top connections and he was able to step up on his sole start in France, staying on nicely into second without ever threatening to beat the favourite. He should have little trouble finding a race. *(op 15-2 tchd 9-1)*
Laertes made a highly pleasing hurdling debut and ran way above market expectations. He is going to appreciate three miles in time and can be found a small race.
Cirrus(FR) was unable to build on his debut third, but it was not a bad effort and he too shapes as though three miles will help. *(op 8-1 tchd 17-2)*
Oso Magic was always going to be vulnerable to something less exposed, but this should have set him straight for a return to fences. *(op 9-2 tchd 11-2 and 7-2)*
T/Plt: £56.00 to a £1 stake. Pool: £42,947.00. 559.55 winning tickets. T/Qpdt: £26.60 to a £1 stake. Pool: £2,505.50. 69.70 winning tickets. JR

LINGFIELD (L-H)

Saturday, October 29

OFFICIAL GOING: Chase course - good; hurdle course - soft; all-weather - standard
Wind: Mild, behind

1916 ROR SECOND CAREER FOR RACEHORSES NOVICES' HURDLE (8 hdls) 2m 110y

1:40 (1:40) (Class 4) 4-Y-0+ **£3,601** (£1,108; £554; £277)

Form RPR

4P0- **1** **Mikado Melody (IRE)**^{260} [3785] 6-10-12 .... WHutchinson 109+
(A King) *in tch: hdwy to ld 2 out: sn rdn: kpt on wl: rdn out* **9/1**

030- **2** *1¾* **Idris (GER)**^{239} [4159] 4-10-12 **110** .... JEMoore 107
(G L Moore) *in tch: rdn to press wnr appr 2 out: ev ch last: no ex* **9/2**^{3}

4-1 **3** *5* **Dr Cerullo**^{34} [1562] 4-11-5 .... TDoyle 109
(C Tinkler) *trckd ldrs: led after 5th: rdn and hdd 2 out: kpt on same pce: lft 3rd last* **2/1**^{1}

360- **4** *8* **Quarrymount**^{273} [3591] 4-10-12 **98** .... TJMurphy 94
(J A B Old) *prom: led briefly 5th: rdn appr 2 out: wknd next: lft 4th last* **7/2**^{2}

6 **5** *2* **Devious Ayers (IRE)**^{13} [1750] 4-10-12 .... WMarston 92
(J M Bradley) *mid div: hdwy after 5th: rdn appr 2 out: one pced after* **33/1**

4 **6** *8* **Millicent Cross (IRE)**^{135} [764] 7-10-12 .... JMMaguire 84
(R Ford) *hld up towards rr: hdwy after 5th: rdn appr 2 out: no imp after* **14/1**

00-0 **7** *1¾* **No Way Back (IRE)**^{12} [1772] 5-10-12 .... BFenton 82
(Miss E C Lavelle) *hld up and a towards rr* **33/1**

8 *¾* **Secret Divin (FR)**^{321} 5-10-12 .... DCrosse 82
(Jean-Rene Auvray) *mid div tl wknd 5th* **33/1**

PFP- **9** *11* **Elle Roseador**^{195} [4887] 6-10-5 .... JGoldstein 64
(M Madgwick) *chsd ldrs tl wknd after 5th* **66/1**

10 *2* **Ninah**^{11} 4-10-0 .... LStephens$^{(5)}$ 62
(J M Bradley) *keen and a towards rr* **50/1**

11 *dist* **Fools Entire**^{120} 4-10-5 .... MrMatthewSmith$^{(7)}$ —
(Miss J Feilden) *chsd ldrs tl wknd after 5th* **40/1**

12 *6* **Harbour House**^{26} 6-10-12 .... RGreene —
(J J Bridger) *t.k.h in mid div: wknd after 3 out* **66/1**

00- **F** **Nobel Bleu De Kerpaul (FR)**^{210} [4697] 4-10-12 .... PHide —
(P Winkworth) *fell 1st* **33/1**

0-P **P** **The Rainbow Man**^{13} [1757] 5-10-9 .... CBolger$^{(3)}$ —
(J Ryan) *led tl 5th: wknd qckly: p.u bef 2 out* **50/1**

P **African Star**^{35} 4-10-12 .... JamesDavies —
(J M Bradley) *mid div tl 5th: wknd qckly and p.u bef 2 out* **50/1**

5 **F** **Kings Signal (USA)**^{12} [1772] 7-10-12 .... LAspell 106
(M J Hogan) *mid div: hdwy after 3 out to chse ldrs: disputing cl 2nd whn fell last* **9/1**

4m 0.10s (-6.00) **Going Correction** -0.20s/f (Good) **16** Ran SP% **123.5**
Speed ratings: **106,105,102,99,98 94,93,93,88,87 —,—,—,—,—,—** CSF £47.73 TOTE £9.50: £3.00, £2.10, £1.40; EX 78.20.
Owner Mrs M C Sweeney **Bred** Mrs Joerg Vasicek **Trained** Barbury Castle, Wilts

FOCUS
A fair novice hurdle, rated through the third and fourth and the last-flight faller. A big step up in form from the winner.

NOTEBOOK
Mikado Melody(IRE) was quite a big disappointment last season, but he has clearly improved over the summer and stayed on too strongly for his rivals in the final quarter mile. This was only an average event and he will be doing well to defy a penalty, but handicaps are another option and he remains open to a little improvement. *(op 7-1)*
Idris(GER) always held a good position and threw down his challenge to the winner from two out, but he was always being held in the final furlong and had to make do with second. He is another who may find life easier in handicaps. *(op 11-2)*
Dr Cerullo did it nicely on his most recent start at Huntingdon back in September, but the combination of a slower surface and his 7lb penalty were enough to get him beaten. He is worthy of another chance on a faster surface. *(tchd 9-4 and 5-2 in a place)*
Quarrymount has been most disappointing since going hurdling and this reappearance effort, although better, was still some way below the level of form he could be expected to show. *(op 4-1)*
Devious Ayers(IRE) stepped up on his debut effort, but is unlikely to be winning until contesting handicap hurdles.
Millicent Cross(IRE) *Official explanation: jockey said, regarding the apparent tender ride, his orders were to drop in and get gelding settled as it had run too freely at Aintree last time, adding that gelding moved into the race coming down the hill then became tired approaching the last and had nothing more to give on the run-in (op 16-1)*
No Way Back(IRE) *Official explanation: jockey said, regarding the running and riding, his orders were to drop in and get gelding settled before riding a race, adding that gelding stayed on at one pace and would be better suited by better ground a longer trip in the future; trainer added that gelding is highly strung and had been difficult to settle in its races in the past*
Kings Signal(USA) was in the process of running a huge race when coming down at the last and, although he would not have won, he would not have been far away. *(op 7-1)*
African Star *Official explanation: jockey said gelding had a breathing problem (op 7-1)*

1917 GREATWOOD RESCUE AND REHABILITATION BEGINNERS' CHASE (14 fncs) 2m 4f 110y

2:15 (2:18) (Class 4) 4-Y-0+ **£4,290** (£1,320; £660; £330)

Form RPR

4B3- **1** **Copsale Lad**^{203} [4773] 8-11-7 **127** .... MFoley 141+
(N J Henderson) *j.w: trckd ldrs: led 7th: clr 2 out: r.o wl: easily* **10/3**^{2}

11P- **2** *13* **Back Nine (IRE)**^{198} [4835] 8-11-7 .... AThornton 129+
(R H Alner) *in tch: tk clsr order 4 out: j.rt fr 3 out: chsd wnr and hit 2 out: kpt on but no ch w wnr* **9/1**

053- **3** *3½* **Zabenz (NZ)**^{198} [4835] 8-11-7 .... RJohnson 127+
(P J Hobbs) *led tl 3rd: chsd ldrs: rdn after 4 out: hit 3 out: kpt on same pce* **13/2**

362- **4** *3* **Alderburn**^{199} [4820] 6-11-7 .... MBradburne 122+
(H D Daly) *chsd ldrs: rdn to chse wnr appr 3 out: kpt on same pce fr 2 out* **10/1**

114- **5** *12* **Bob Bob Bobbin**^{225} [4434] 6-11-7 .... JTizzard 113+
(C L Tizzard) *prom: led 3rd tl 7th: w wnr tl 4 out: wknd next* **11/4**^{1}

12- **6** *13* **Monte Vista (IRE)**^{349} [2212] 8-11-7 .... TJMurphy 103+
(Jonjo O'Neill) *hld up towards rr: lost tch fr 4 out* **6/1**^{3}

2-56 **7** *dist* **Unusual Suspect**^{162} [441] 6-11-7 .... JEMoore —
(G L Moore) *hld up towards rr: pckd bdly 9th: sn lost tch* **50/1**

0 **8** *9* **Serious Man (IRE)**[12] 1772 7-11-4 .... CBolger[(3)] —
(Mrs P Townsley) *a bhd* **100/1**

3-16 **9** *1/2* **Wayward Melody**[153] 566 5-11-0 .... PHide —
(G L Moore) *mid div tl 5th: sn wl bhd* **66/1**

40-0 **F** **Salt Cellar (IRE)**[182] 136 6-11-7 .... TDoyle —
(P R Webber) *mid div whn fell 8th* **66/1**

P **P** **Rosses Point (IRE)**[7] 1829 6-11-7 .... PMoloney —
(Evan Williams) *a towards rr: hmpd 8th: p.u bef 2 out* **100/1**

503- **P** **Quid Pro Quo (FR)**[200] 4817 6-11-7 .... ChristianWilliams —
(P F Nicholls) *in tch: rdn after 9th: wknd after 4 out: bhd and p.u bef 3 out* **12/1**

P **U** **Irish Raptor (IRE)**[21] 1669 6-11-7 .... AntonyEvans —
(N A Twiston-Davies) *hld up towards rr: sme hdwy fr 6th: wknd 9th: blnd and uns rdr 4 out* **20/1**

5m 4.00s (-15.00) **Going Correction** -0.45s/f (Good) course record **13** Ran SP% **115.8**
Speed ratings: **110,105,103,102,98 93,—,—,—,— —,—,—** CSF £30.95 TOTE £4.00: £1.70, £2.60, £2.10; EX 47.60.
Owner Swallow Partnership **Bred** G G A Gregson **Trained** Upper Lambourn, Berks

FOCUS
A decent beginners' chase won in great style by the very useful Copsale Lad and the time was decent for the grade too. The first six should all win races and the form ought to work out.

NOTEBOOK
Copsale Lad ran some smashing races as a novice last season, but for one reason or another he failed to win and as a result he was able to contest this beginners' chase. Still going well when brought down at the Festival last season, he made short work of this reasonable field and had the race won a long way from home. His jumping was near to perfect and with the run entitled to bring him forward, he should be a force in some of the better two and a half mile handicap chases this season. *(op 7-2 tchd 3-1 and 4-1 in a place)*

Back Nine(IRE), who quickly developed into a useful handicap hurdler last season, comes from a chase-orientated stable and he duly made a promising fencing debut. Given a nice introduction, he stayed on well down the straight for second and it will be surprising if he is not winning a similar race before Christmas. *(op 7-1 tchd 10-1)*

Zabenz(NZ), successful in Grade One company over fences in America, did little over hurdles last season, but this return to the larger obstacles brought about an improved effort and he kept on dourly for third. This form entitled him to win an average novice and he is in the right hands. *(op 8-1 tchd 11-2)*

Alderburn, a useful hurdler, ran well for a long way before his lack of peak fitness began to tell and connections can take plenty of positives from the outing. His trainer is beginning to come into a bit of form and natural progression should see him winning a small contest. *(tchd 12-1)*

Bob Bob Bobbin was the disappointment of the race. A really honest, progressive hurdler last season, he had not been seen since finishing fourth in the Spa Novices' Hurdle at the Festival and was rightfully made favourite, but having raced prominently early, he dropped away early in the straight. He is obviously better than this and it is hoped that he simply needed the run. *(tchd 7-2)*

Monte Vista(IRE) never got into it on this chasing debut and trailed in well beaten. He was a fair sort over hurdles, so maybe he is worth another chance. *(op 11-2 tchd 5-1)*

1918 LINGFIELD PARK H'CAP CHASE (LISTED RACE) (12 fncs) 2m

2:45 (2:48) (Class 1) (0-150,148) 5-Y-0+
£17,400 (£6,600; £3,300; £1,500; £750; £450)

Form RPR

036- **1** **Armaturk (FR)**[189] 4983 8-11-12 **148** .... ChristianWilliams 160+
(P F Nicholls) *chsd ldrs: shkn up after 4 out: led and pckd 3 out: kpt on gamely : rdn out* **3/1**[1]

002- **2** *2* **Bleu Superbe (FR)**[196] 4863 10-10-8 **130** .... AO'Keeffe 140
(Miss Venetia Williams) *led: hit 7th: hdd 3 out: sn rdn: kpt on* **7/1**[3]

5-24 **3** *2* **Pak Jack (FR)**[6] 1857 5-10-3 **125** .... RJohnson 133
(P J Hobbs) *hld up: hdwy fr 4th to join ldr 8th: rdn appr 3 out: kpt on same pce* **12/1**

1004 **4** *6* **East Tycoon (IRE)**[14] 1744 6-10-9 **131** .... JEMoore 137+
(Jonjo O'Neill) *hld up: mstke 5th: hmpd 7th: styd on to go 4th appr 3 out: kpt on same pce fr next: hit 2 out and last* **7/2**[2]

62-3 **5** *10* **Cobbet (CZE)**[14] 1739 9-10-0 **122** .... TJMurphy 114
(T R George) *in tch: hmpd 7th: sn wknd* **8/1**

2031 **6** *9* **Duke Of Buckingham (IRE)**[34] 1561 9-11-4 **140** .... JamesDavies 123
(P R Webber) *hld up: rdn and wknd after 4 out* **7/1**[3]

0-54 **7** *12* **Palua**[14] 1739 8-10-10 **132** .... BFenton 103
(Miss E C Lavelle) *chsd ldrs: hit 4th: nt fluent next: grad fdd* **20/1**

F4-3 **U** **Another Joker**[36] 1542 10-9-11 **122** .... TJPhelan[(3)] —
(J L Needham) *stmbld and uns rdr 1st* **14/1**

3321 **P** **Croix De Guerre (IRE)**[14] 1743 5-10-10 **137** ....(b) RStephens[(5)] —
(P J Hobbs) *chsd ldrs: wnt lft 7th: sn wknd: bhd and p.u bef 3 out* **16/1**

1024 **P** **Danish Decorum (IRE)**[52] 1435 6-10-0 **122** .... PMoloney —
(Evan Williams) *in tch: mstkes 2nd and 3rd: p.u bef next: broke leg: dead* **14/1**

3m 55.6s (-12.30) **Going Correction** -0.45s/f (Good) **10** Ran SP% **115.0**
Speed ratings: **112,111,110,107,102 97,91,—,—,—** CSF £24.44 CT £219.24 TOTE £4.80: £1.70, £2.60, £2.30; EX 31.40.
Owner Trevor Hemmings **Bred** Rene Collet And Mme Catherine Auniac **Trained** Ditcheat, Somerset

FOCUS
A repeat of last season's result with Armaturk leading home Bleu Superbe. Both horses were well handicapped on that form and just about reproduced their figures. Armaturk seems as good as ever and will no doubt have delighted new owner Trevor Hemmings with this reappearance win.

NOTEBOOK
Armaturk(FR), who returned in great form last season, seems to have been around for ever, but he is still only eight and he turned in another smart effort, making it two wins in a row in this event. This was a good weight-carrying performance on his first start in the Hemmings silks and he is likely to head to the Paddy Power meeting to again contest a race he was successful in last year. *(op 7-2)*

Bleu Superbe(FR) has never been consistent, but he is very useful on his day and he really served it up to the winner. However, he had to give best to the Armaturk for a second year in a row in this contest and he was unable to take advantage of the considerable weight concession. This effort would entitle him win a similar race, but he cannot be relied up on to repeat the effort. *(op 13-2)*

Pak Jack(FR), who ran below market expectation on his reappearance over hurdles at Wincanton last weekend, made some appeal on this return to fences and he shaped much better, coming through to challenge early in the straight before being outpaced. Still only five, he has further improvement in him and looks well worth a try at two and a half miles. *(op 11-1)*

East Tycoon(IRE) has not really gone on from his reappearance win at Stratford in August and this drop back to two miles did not really help him. He ran better, but probably remains a bit too high in the handicap. *(op 9-2)*

Cobbet(CZE), although receiving plenty of weight, was running out of his grade and he struggled to keep tabs. *(tchd 7-1)*

Duke Of Buckingham(IRE) finally got back to winning ways at Huntingdon last time, but he is not as good as he used to be and was always going to struggle giving weight to some useful types. *(op 6-1 tchd 11-2)*

1919 OWNERS SUPPORT RETRAINING OF RACEHORSES H'CAP HURDLE (8 hdls) 2m 110y

3:20 (3:20) (Class 3) (0-135,135) 4-Y-0+ **£10,192** (£3,136; £1,568; £784)

Form RPR

3P-0 **1** **Caracciola (GER)**[161] 450 8-11-9 **132** .... MFoley 139+
(N J Henderson) *hld up bhd ldrs: smooth hdwy after 3 out: led sn after 2 out: r.o: rdn out* **5/1**[2]

5/1- **2** *1 1/4* **Guru**[364] 1907 7-10-7 **116** .... PHide 121
(G L Moore) *trckd ldrs: chal appr 2 out: rdn and ev ch last : kpt on but no ex run-in* **11/4**[1]

61-1 **3** *1* **Fait Le Jojo (FR)**[28] 1598 8-11-7 **135** .... HEphgrave[(5)] 139
(L Corcoran) *led: hdd after 5th: led and nt fluent 2 out: sn hdd: kpt on* **12/1**

06-5 **4** *7* **Give Me Love (FR)**[7] 1828 5-10-3 **119** ....(t) LHeard[(7)] 118+
(P F Nicholls) *trckd ldrs: led after 5th: narrowly hdd 2 out: sn rdn: wknd last* **11/4**[1]

-121 **5** *8* **Harry Potter (GER)**[16] 1724 6-10-1 **110** ow1 ....(vt) ChristianWilliams 99
(Evan Williams) *hld up bhd ldrs: rdn and short lived effrt after 3 out: one pced fr next* **7/1**

405- **6** *24* **Master Rex**[205] 4751 10-10-13 **122** .... BFenton 87
(B De Haan) *trckd ldr tl 5th: rdn after 3 out: sn wknd* **11/2**[3]

R36L **R** **Kalambari (IRE)**[7] 1828 6-10-3 **119** .... SWalsh[(7)] —
(J D Frost) *ref to r: tk no part* **28/1**

3m 58.7s (-7.40) **Going Correction** -0.20s/f (Good) **7** Ran SP% **109.0**
Speed ratings: **109,108,107,104,100 89,—** CSF £17.73 TOTE £4.50: £2.90, £2.20; EX 19.60.
Owner P J D Pottinger **Bred** Frau I U A Brunotte **Trained** Upper Lambourn, Berks

FOCUS
Only a fair handicap hurdle but it was good to see Caracciola return to form. Like the runner-up, he looked well in.

NOTEBOOK
Caracciola(GER) is reasonably handicapped over hurdles compared with fences, but he ran a shocker under similar conditions when last seen in May and could not be confidently backed. However, with his stable's runners having made a bright start to the season, he was back to form and stayed on best of all to win a shade cosily. *(tchd 9-2)*

Guru, although lightly-raced over the past two years, was returning in a race he had taken last year off a 9lb lower mark and his ability to go well fresh stood him in good stead. He ran well, but the winner was always too strong for him and it is just hoped that he can stay sound and try and build on this. *(op 9-4 tchd 3-1 in a place)*

Fait Le Jojo(FR), who returned from Jersey in good form to win at Fontwell last time, found the 8lb rise asking too much of him, but he still ran well and kept on well enough having been headed. *(op 8-1)*

Give Me Love(FR), who ran well for a long way on his reappearance from out of the handicap at Chepstow, looked to face a much easier task but, having come through to lead at around half way, he faded disappointingly as the race began in earnest. *(op 10-3 tchd 7-2 and 4-1 in places)*

Harry Potter(GER) has been in good form this autumn, winning at both Southwell and Ludlow, but he faced a much stiffer task and the combination of having the visor back on and softer going contributed to his modest showing. *(tchd 15-2)*

Master Rex, who ran well just out of the places at both the Cheltenham and Aintree Festivals last season, was expected to need this reappearance outing back over hurdles and he got very tired in the straight. He was beaten a long way, but it is hoped he can return to form back over fences on a faster surface. *(op 7-1 tchd 5-1)*

1920 MOORCROFT RACEHORSE WELFARE CENTRE H'CAP CHASE (18 fncs) 3m

3:55 (3:55) (Class 3) (0-120,120) 5-Y-0+ **£6,929** (£2,132; £1,066; £533)

Form RPR

3-0P **1** **Stormy Skye (IRE)**[172] 288 9-10-2 **96** ....(b) PHide 106
(G L Moore) *trckd ldrs: pckd 2nd: led 5th tl 11th: pressed ldrs: rdn appr 3 out: styd on: led cl home* **18/1**

52-5 **2** *1 1/4* **Bee An Bee (IRE)**[182] 130 8-11-12 **120** ....(b) JMMaguire 130+
(T R George) *hld up in tch: trckd ldng pair appr 4 out: led 3 out: sn rdn: narrow advantage last: hung lft run-in: hdd cl home* **6/1**

/6-1 **3** *1 1/2* **Snowy Ford (IRE)**[28] 1599 8-11-11 **119** .... LAspell 131+
(N J Gifford) *j.rt thrght: hld up:mstke 10th: rapid prog to ld after 4 out tl next: ev ch last: rallying whn n.m.r cl home* **7/2**[1]

3021 **4** *11* **Tommy Carson**[12] 1778 10-10-1 **98** .... CBolger[(3)] 94
(Jamie Poulton) *prom: drvn along fr 9th: lost pl after 1th: styd on same pce fr 4 out* **9/2**[3]

5/-P **5** *1* **Magic Of Sydney (IRE)**[182] 132 9-10-4 **98** .... PMoloney 93
(R Rowe) *led: hit 1st: hdd 5th: chsd ldrs: led 11th tl next: rdn and one pced fr 4 out* **9/1**

22-6 **6** *8* **Pardini (USA)**[4] 1870 6-10-2 **96** .... TScudamore 83
(M F Harris) *hld up in tch: wnt prom 13th: rdn after 4 out: wknd next* **14/1**

63-P **7** *27* **Jones's Road (IRE)**[169] 330 7-11-5 **113** .... JEMoore 73
(Jonjo O'Neill) *in tch: pckd 12th: prog to trck ldrs after 4 out: j.rt 3 out: wknd* **8/1**

2-2F **P** **Jaoka Du Gord (FR)**[163] 430 8-10-12 **106** .... JamesDavies —
(P R Webber) *hld up: hdwy to ld 12th tl after 4 out: sn wknd: p.u bef last* **4/1**[2]

6m 16.9s (-6.80) **Going Correction** -0.45s/f (Good) **8** Ran SP% **107.7**
Speed ratings: **93,92,92,88,88 85,76,—** CSF £107.43 CT £414.12 TOTE £22.80: £3.60, £2.00, £1.80; EX 226.80.
Owner Jayne Moore, T Pollock, J Driscoll **Bred** Normanby Stud Ltd **Trained** Woodingdean, E Sussex
■ Stewards' Enquiry : J M Maguire five-day ban: careless riding (Nov 9-13)

FOCUS
A moderate winning time for the class of contest. This is probably not strong form.

NOTEBOOK
Stormy Skye(IRE), disappointing off this mark when last seen back in May, appreciated this slightly easier surface and received a good ride from Hide to come with a well-timed challenge and win going away. He is getting no better and is soon to be ten, but as he showed here he can still win races off the right sort of mark. *(tchd 20-1)*

Bee An Bee(IRE), who had to give the winner plenty of weight, found that really began to tell in the final furlong and he hung left under pressure as he got tired. This was a decent effort, but his progression seems to have stopped and he will remain vulnerable carrying such big weights. *(op 5-1 tchd 13-2)*

Snowy Ford(IRE), up 5lb for his Fontwell win, continually lost ground by tending to jump out to his right at fences, but he really picked up the bit as they turned into the straight and he stuck on well for pressure, looking unlucky not to finish a little closer after Bee An Bee hung into him. He should continue to go the right way. *(op 9-4)*

Tommy Carson is a dour stayer and, although in receipt of plenty of weight, he simply lacked the necessary pace. *(op 4-1)*

Magic Of Sydney(IRE) has dropped to a very decent mark, but he does not stand much racing and is not as good as he used to be. He may have a small race in him off this sort of mark, but he is hardly a horse to follow. *(op 16-1)*

Jaoka Du Gord(FR) stopped very quickly under pressure and, although this was his first outing of the season, one would have liked to see him last for longer. *(op 9-2)*

1921 BETFREDCASINO.COM NOVICES' H'CAP HURDLE (10 hdls) 2m 3f 110y

4:30 (4:30) (Class 4) (0-105,100) 3-Y-0+ **£3,562** (£1,096; £548; £274)

Form | | | | RPR
430- **1** **Magot De Grugy (FR)**[216] 4587 5-11-3 **90** .... AThornton 107+
(R H Alner) *trckd ldrs: led 3 out: hit next: styd on wl run-in: rdn out* **5/1**[2]
002- **2** *6* **Down's Folly (IRE)**[195] 4884 5-11-8 **95** .... RJohnson 107+
(H D Daly) *mid div: hdwy 6th: trckd wnr after 3 out: pckd 2 out: rdn to chal appr last: no ex run-in* **4/1**[1]
3322 **3** *9* **The Castilian (FR)**[12] 1774 3-10-9 **100** ....(v) TJMurphy 83+
(M C Pipe) *hld up bhd: mstke 1st: stdy hdwy fr 6th: chsd ldng pair after 3 out: sn rdn: one pced fr next* **5/1**[2]
P/-6 **4** *½* **Buster (IRE)**[34] 1565 6-10-5 **78** .... WHutchinson 77
(J Ryan) *bhd: drvn along fr 4th: styd on past btn horses fr 2 out* **16/1**
050- **5** *shd* **Flying Patriarch**[190] 4958 4-11-5 **99** ....(b) EDehdashti[(7)] 98
(G L Moore) *led tl 5th: chsd ldrs: rdn after 3 out: one pced* **12/1**
-035 **6** *2* **Corrib Drift (USA)**[28] 1596 5-10-12 **88** .... CBolger[(3)] 85
(Jamie Poulton) *hld up towards rr: hdwy after 6th: rdn after 3 out: no further imp* **25/1**
050- **7** *1¼* **Smeathe's Ridge**[374] 1778 7-10-12 **85** .... MBradburne 81
(J A B Old) *hld up towards rr: hdwy after 6th: rdn after 3 out: no further imp* **66/1**
423- **8** *8* **Longstone Lady (IRE)**[190] 4964 8-11-0 **92** .... CHonour[(5)] 80
(J D Frost) *a mid div* **25/1**
P-23 **9** *¾* **Rhetorical**[23] 1648 4-9-12 **78** .... RLucey-Butler[(7)] 65
(P Butler) *in tch tl 3 out* **16/1**
50-5 **10** *1* **Coralbrook**[177] 194 5-11-7 **94** .... JAMcCarthy 80
(Mrs P Robeson) *mid div tl 6th: sn bhd* **20/1**
03F- **11** *11* **Buckland Gold (IRE)**[213] 4664 5-11-7 **94** .... JamesDavies 69
(D B Feek) *trckd ldrs: led 5th tl 3 out: sn wknd* **20/1**
2-F0 **12** *23* **Wenger (FR)**[153] 568 5-11-9 **96** .... PHide 48
(P Winkworth) *hld up towards rr: hdwy after 6th: rdn after 3 out: sn wknd* **16/1**
P3/0 **P** **Before The Mast (IRE)**[21] 1680 8-10-6 **79** .... TScudamore —
(M F Harris) *a towards rr: t.o and p.u bef 2 out* **20/1**
001 **P** **Davy's Luck**[13] 1750 5-10-13 **86** .... WMarston —
(J M Bradley) *mid div tl 6th: sn bhd: t.o and p.u after 3 out* **12/1**
1-P2 **P** **Orinocovsky (IRE)**[25] 1632 6-11-10 **97** .... PMoloney —
(N P Littmoden) *trckd ldrs: led briefly 4th: wknd appr 3 out: p.u bef 2 out* **8/1**[3]

4m 57.0s (-5.70) **Going Correction** -0.20s/f (Good)
WFA 3 from 4yo 17lb 4 from 5yo+ 13lb **15** Ran SP% **120.9**
Speed ratings: **103,100,97,96,96 95,95,92,91,91 87,77,—,—,—** CSF £23.00 CT £108.11 TOTE £6.10: £1.70, £2.40, £1.80; EX 31.80.
Owner P M De Wilde **Bred** Earl La Grugerie **Trained** Droop, Dorset

FOCUS
Average form, but Magot De Grugy stepped up on last season's form and looks a nice chasing prospect. The form looks sound enough.

NOTEBOOK
Magot De Grugy(FR) became very frustrating in similar races last season, but he has clearly progressed over the summer and ran out a pretty emphatic winner. A scopey type who looks open to further improvement, he is one to keep on the right side and is now likely to head straight over fences. *(op 9-1)*
Down's Folly(IRE) raised his game for this handicap debut, staying on to finish clear of the third, *but the winner was simply too good. There should be a small race in him off this sort of mark. (op 10-3 tchd 9-2)*
The Castilian(FR) has yet to win over hurdles, but he has run many sound races in defeat and this was a fair effort for a three-year-old. *(op 4-1)*
Buster(IRE) was starting out handicap life off a measly mark and he duly stepped up on prevous efforts, running on well to snatch fourth. He would make obvious appeal in a similar contest, but possibly over further. *(tchd 20-1)*
Flying Patriarch was struggling from three out and he needs further assistance from the Handicapper. *(op 14-1)*
Orinocovsky(IRE) *Official explanation: jockey said gelding hung left (op 9-1)*

1922 BETFREDPOKER.COM STANDARD OPEN NATIONAL HUNT FLAT RACE 2m

5:00 (5:03) (Class 6) 4-6-Y-0 **£1,876** (£536; £268)

Form | | | | RPR
3 **1** **Schumann**[27] 1613 4-11-4 .... ATinkler 97+
(M Pitman) *chsd ldng pair: led 3f out: sn rdn: kpt on wl whn chal 1f out: rdn out* **11/8**[1]
2 *¾* **Yufo (IRE)** 5-11-4 .... LAspell 96+
(N J Gifford) *hld up towards rr: smooth hdwy fr 6f out to trck ldrs 4f out: ev ch 1f out: sn rdn: no ex* **6/1**[3]
P **3** *6* **Accumulus**[182] 131 5-11-4 .... WHutchinson 90
(Noel T Chance) *mid div: hdwy to trck ldrs over 6f out: ev ch over 2f out: kpt on same pce fnl 2f* **9/1**
4 **4** *3½* **Phriapatius**[23] 1660 4-10-11 .... WPKavanagh[(7)] 86
(Dr J R J Naylor) *towards rr: wl bhd 4f out: styd on fr over 2f out: wnt 4th 1f out: nvr trbld ldrs* **22/1**
2-35 **5** *9* **Crafty Lady (IRE)**[13] 1762 6-10-11 .... RJohnson 70
(Miss Suzy Smith) *led: rdn and hdd 3f out: sn wknd* **9/2**[2]
6 *9* **Delightful Touch (FR)** 4-11-4 .... JAMcCarthy 68
(C P Morlock) *a mid div* **33/1**
7 *1¼* **Romangod (IRE)**[20] 5-11-4 ....(t) GSupple 67
(J A Supple) *towards rr: sme late hdwy: nvr a danger* **66/1**
8 *4* **My Rosie Ribbons (IRE)** 6-10-4 .... MrMWall[(7)] 56
(B W Duke) *w ldr tl 4f out* **28/1**
9 *5* **Eudyptes** 6-11-4 .... MBatchelor 58
(N E Berry) *in tch: hdwy 8f out: wknd over 3f out* **66/1**
5 **10** *2* **Moonshine Gap**[17] 1688 5-11-4 .... TJMurphy 56
(R Ford) *in tch tl 4f out* **20/1**
11 *12* **Supreme Copper (IRE)** 5-11-4 .... BFenton 44
(Miss E C Lavelle) *keen early: trckd ldrs: wknd 6f out* **10/1**
12 *6* **Beauty Ballistic** 5-10-6 ow2 .... MrMLurcock[(7)] 33
(Miss J Feilden) *in tch tl 6f out: t.o* **50/1**
5 **13** *15* **Oakfield Legend**[13] 1755 4-11-4 .... OMcPhail 23
(P S Payne) *a bhd: t.o fnl 3f* **33/1**
14 *dist* **Mustang Jack** 5-10-11 ....(t) SWalsh[(7)] —
(M Wigham) *a bhd: t.o fnl 3f* **20/1**

3m 34.2s **14** Ran SP% **121.8**
CSF £8.37 TOTE £1.90: £1.50, £1.90, £2.50; EX 13.10 Place 6 £33.63, Place 5 £21.90.
Owner Something In The City Partnership **Bred** Cheveley Park Stud Ltd **Trained** Upper Lambourn, Berks

FOCUS
Ordinary bumper form, but Schumann and Yufo were clear of the third and the pair look worth following.

NOTEBOOK
Schumann, who is thought quite highly of at home, built on his recent debut third, but he was only workmanlike in winning and shaped as though more of a test would suit. He did get a decent pace however and he looks a fair prospect for hurdling, with further improvement for his in-form stable anticipated. *(tchd 6-4)*
Yufo(IRE), whose stable have made a positive start to the season, made the winner work hard enough for his win and was clear of the third. He handled the surface, but gave the impression he would be capable of better in bumpers on turf. *(op 8-1)*
Accumulus, pulled up on his bumper debut at Uttoxeter back in April appreciated this faster surface and kept on nicely for third without ever threatening to win. His stable do well in this sphere, but he gives the impression it may take a switch to hurdles for him to win. *(op 7-1)*
Phriapatius has twice shaped well in bumpers and he is another worthy of close inspection once sent hurdling. *(op 20-1)*
Crafty Lady(IRE) looked set to run her race after several decent efforts in similar races on turf, but she was always going to be vulnerable making the running and she faded disappointingly once the sprint for home began. *(tchd 5-1)*
Supreme Copper(IRE) *Official explanation: jockey said he was unable to steer gelding (op 8-1)*
Mustang Jack *Official explanation: jockey said gelding had a breathing problem*
T/Plt: £38.60 to a £1 stake. Pool: £44,740.70. 844.90 winning tickets. T/Qpdt: £12.40 to a £1 stake. Pool: £2,591.80. 153.65 winning tickets. TM

1910 WETHERBY (L-H)

Saturday, October 29

OFFICIAL GOING: Soft (good to soft in places)
Wind: Virtually nil.

1923 CONSTANT SECURITY WENSLEYDALE JUVENILE NOVICES' HURDLE (LISTED RACE) (9 hdls) 2m

1:45 (1:47) (Class 1) 3-Y-0
£11,327 (£4,296; £2,148; £976; £488; £292)

Form | | | | RPR
110 **1** **Aviation**[17] 1718 3-11-2 .... FKeniry 108+
(G M Moore) *hld up towards rr: stdy hdwy 4 out: chsd ldrs next: rdn to ld last: drvn out* **28/1**
65 **2** *1* **Dock Tower (IRE)**[17] 1718 3-10-12 .... PBuchanan 102
(M E Sowersby) *hld up towards rr: hdwy 1/2-way: cl up 3 out: led next: rdn and hdd last: drvn: carried hd high and edgd lft flat: kpt on* **40/1**
231 **3** *2½* **Finland (UAE)**[9] 1797 3-11-4 .... KJMercer 105
(Mrs A Duffield) *led: rdn along and hdd appr 3 out: drvn next and kpt fr 2 out* **12/1**
4 *12* **One More Time (FR)**[75] 3-10-5 .... GLee 82+
(J Howard Johnson) *tracked ldng pair: hdwy 5th: led after 4 out: rdn along 3 out: hdd next: sn drvn and wknd* **8/1**
12 **5** *2* **Toss The Caber (IRE)**[17] 1718 3-11-4 115 .... RMcGrath 93+
(K G Reveley) *trckd ldrs on inner: rdn along after 4 out: outpcd fr next* **17/2**
6 *16* **Twist Magic (FR)**[148] 3-11-6 .... PJBrennan 87+
(P F Nicholls) *trckd ldrs: hdwy 4 out: rdn along and blnd next: sn wknd* **11/10**[1]
1 **7** *1½* **The Pen**[17] 1718 3-10-9 .... APMcCoy 65
(P C Haslam) *hld up towards rr: hdwy 5th: rdn along & in tch whn mstke next: sn drvn and btn* **5/1**[2]
2P **8** *dist* **Negas (IRE)**[21] 1679 3-10-12 ....(t) BSHughes —
(J Howard Johnson) *cl up: led appr 4 out: sn rdn and hdd: wknd fr next* **100/1**
F **Le Corvee (IRE)**[20] 3-10-12 .... RThornton —
(A King) *hld up: fell 2nd* **13/2**[3]
P **Poirot**[92] 3-10-12 .... ADempsey —
(J Howard Johnson) *a rr: mstke 4th and sn bhd: p.u bef 3 out* **100/1**

4m 1.30s (1.90) **Going Correction** +0.30s/f (Yiel) **10** Ran SP% **114.8**
Speed ratings: **107,106,105,99,98 90,89,—,—,—** CSF £636.13 TOTE £42.40: £5.90, £6.80, £2.30; EX 1069.90.
Owner G R Orchard **Bred** D J And Mrs Deer **Trained** Middleham, N Yorks
■ Stewards' Enquiry : K J Mercer three-day ban: used whip with excessive frequency (Nov 9-11)

FOCUS
A low-grade renewal of what is usually an informative event, rated around the second and third, who ran to their recent course and distance marks. The conditions took their toll and the whole field appeared to finish tired.

NOTEBOOK
Aviation finished behind four of these opponents when losing his unbeaten record here last time, but that was not his running. The easier ground made a difference and he ran out a game winner, *but this was a weak Listed race. Official explanation: trainer had no explanation for the improved form shown*
Dock Tower(IRE), three places ahead of today's winner over course and distance last time, looked set to spring a surprise when showing ahead but he was soon tackled and rather hung in behind his rival on the run-in. He is obviously able but his resolution could be questioned. *(op 33-1)*
Finland(UAE) looked set to drop away when headed on the home turn, but to his credit he fought back to finish third, if no further threat to the first two.
One More Time(FR) won two non-thoroughbred Flat races at Vichy in France in August, both in soft ground. She showed plenty of ability but failed to get home, having been rather free in the first part of the race. *(tchd 7-1)*
Toss The Caber(IRE), runner-up over course and distance on his latest start, again shaped as if he will benefit from a longer trip. *(op 8-1)*
Twist Magic(FR) has had three runs at Auteuil, winning in very soft ground on the latest of them in June. Well regarded, he looked a real threat straightening up for home but had just come under pressure when blundering at the third last and was immediately beaten. He looks to need more time. *(op 5-4 tchd 11-8)*
The Pen beat no fewer than four of these rivals, including the winner, when making a successful hurdles debut at this track last month. Under a penalty, and on very different ground, she never looked like following up. *(op 11-2)*
Le Corvee(IRE) got no further than the second but is a useful middle-distance handicapper on the *Flat, with an official rating of 87, and is in the right hands to make his mark over hurdles. (op 11-2 tchd 7-1)*

1924 WEATHERBYS BANK H'CAP CHASE (LISTED RACE) (15 fncs) 2m 4f 110y
2:20 (2:20) (Class 1) (0-150,143) 5-Y-0+
£14,500 (£5,500; £2,750; £1,250; £625; £375)

Form | RPR
60-5 **1** **St Matthew (USA)**[17] 1721 7-10-12 **129** .... DElsworth 140+
(Mrs S J Smith) *cl up: led 3rd: rdn along and hdd 4 out: outpcd next: hit 2 out: styd on appr last: drvn flat to ld nr fin* **9/2**[3]
5-02 **2** ½ **Vandas Choice (IRE)**[17] 1721 7-11-1 **135** .... PBuchanan(3) 144
(Miss Lucinda V Russell) *hld up in tch: pushed along and outpcd 4 out: rdn and hdwy next: drvn to chal last: led flat: hdd and no ex nr fin* **4/1**[2]
325- **3** 1½ **Banker Count**[210] 4692 13-11-3 **134** .... SThomas 141
(Miss Venetia Williams) *trckd ldres: hit 7th: hdwy 10th: led 4 out: rdn 2 out: drvn last: hdd and one pce flat* **8/1**
553- **4** 2½ **Le Passing (FR)**[190] 4961 6-11-12 **143** .... PJBrennan 149+
(P F Nicholls) *trckd ldrs: mstke 9th: hdwy 5 out: chsd ldr after next: sn rdn and one pce appr last* **11/2**
00-P **5** 23 **Amberleigh House (IRE)**[21] 1676 13-11-4 **135** .... GLee 117
(D McCain) *led to 3rd: cl up tl rdn along and wknd appr 4 out* **33/1**
01-2 **6** dist **Quazar (IRE)**[186] 42 7-11-12 **143** .... (t) APMcCoy 115
(Jonjo O'Neill) *a rr: reminders 6th: rdn along 8th: hdwy and in tch 4 out: sn drvn and btn* **5/2**[1]
04-6 **P** **Turgeonev (FR)**[17] 1721 10-11-2 **133** .... DO'Meara —
(T D Easterby) *chsd ldrs: rdn along appr 5 out: sn wknd and bhd whn p.u bef next* **11/2**

5m 15.4s (-5.30) **Going Correction** -0.10s/f (Good) **7** Ran SP% **111.6**
Speed ratings: **106,105,105,104,95** —,— CSF £21.97 TOTE £5.60: £3.20, £3.20; EX 28.70.
Owner Keith Nicholson **Bred** Mrs J G Jones Sr **Trained** High Eldwick, W Yorks
■ Stewards' Enquiry : D Elsworth two-day ban: used whip with excessive force (Nov 9-10)

FOCUS
A rousing finish to this event, which had Listed status for the first time. This looks a solid piece of form, rated through those in the frame behind the well handicapped winner.

NOTEBOOK
St Matthew(USA) lost the lead on the home turn and was only fourth on the run to the final fence, but he rallied strongly to forge ahead on the run-in. Equally at home over three miles, he has become well handicapped and can rate a bit higher over fences. The Hennessy was mentioned as a possible target. *(tchd 5-1)*
Vandas Choice(IRE) came under pressure in the back straight, but found a second wind once in line for home. He stayed on to strike the front on the run-in but could not hold off the winner. *(op 5-1)*
Banker Count looked beaten turning out of the back straight but he rallied to jump ahead at the fourth from home. He was only worn down after the last, and this was a fine start to the season. *(op 10-1)*
Le Passing(FR) ran well on this return to action but appeared to blow up over the last two fences. He should improve for the run, but does look a couple of pounds too high at present. *(op 9-2)*
Amberleigh House(IRE) showed prominently until getting left behind on the approach to the fourth last. He seemed to enjoy himself and will now be ready for another crack at Aintree's Becher Chase.
Quazar(IRE) was always at the back of the field, and although he closed on the home turn it *required plenty of driving from McCoy for him to do so and he was soon left trailing again.Official explanation: jockey said gelding was unsuited by sticky ground (tchd 11-4)*

1925 JOHN SMITH'S HURDLE (REGISTERED AS THE WEST YORKSHIRE HURDLE) GRADE 2 (12 hdls) 3m 1f
2:50 (2:50) (Class 1) 4-Y-0+
£23,200 (£8,800; £4,400; £2,000; £1,000; £600)

Form | RPR
112- **1** **Inglis Drever**[203] 4771 6-11-8 163 .... GLee 160+
(J Howard Johnson) *trckd ldrs on inner: smooth hdwy after 4 out: led 2 out: rdn last: styd on wl* **2/1**[1]
000- **2** 3 **Redemption**[226] 4410 10-11-0 .... CLlewellyn 149+
(N A Twiston-Davies) *hld up: hdwy and hit 6th: in tch 4 out: effrt to chse wnr after 2 out: rdn to chal last: drvn and no ex flat* **33/1**
131/ **3** 9 **Tees Components**[21] 162 10-11-0 .... (t) JimCrowley 139
(K G Reveley) *a.p: hdwy to ld 8th: rdn 3 out: hdd next and kpt on same pce* **15/2**
1P3- **4** 1¾ **Crystal D'Ainay (FR)**[205] 4748 6-11-8 159 .... RThornton 145
(A King) *trckd ldrs: effrt appr 3 out: sn rdn and btn bef next* **13/2**[3]
232- **5** 6 **Brewster (IRE)**[204] 4765 8-11-4 150 .... APMcCoy 135
(Ian Williams) *chsd clr ldr: rdn along 4 out: drvn and btn after next* **7/2**[2]
040- **6** 6 **Rambling Minster**[226] 4412 7-11-0 132 .... RMcGrath 125
(K G Reveley) *midfield: hdwy on outer 4 out: rdn along bef next and sn outpcd* **33/1**
26-P **7** 15 **Yogi (IRE)**[184] 90 9-11-0 .... SThomas 110
(Thomas Foley, Ire) *led and sn clr: hit 4th: mstke 7th: hdd next: drvn 4 out and sn wknd* **25/1**
0F4- **8** hd **Tribal Venture (FR)**[192] 4925 7-11-0 .... TJDreaper 110
(Ferdy Murphy) *a rr* **66/1**
50-1 **P** **Carlys Quest**[184] 90 11-11-8 147 .... KJMercer —
(Ferdy Murphy) *a rr: bhd and rdn along 1/2-way: t.o whn p.u bef last* **18/1**
/5P- **P** **Sh Boom**[226] 4409 7-11-0 152 .... NFehily —
(S A Brookshaw) *in tch: rdn along after 8th: sn wknd and bhd whn p.u bef 3 out* **11/1**
405- **P** **Telemoss (IRE)**[196] 4862 11-11-8 143 .... ADobbin —
(N G Richards) *in tch: hdwy 1/2-way: chsd ldrs 4 out: sn rdn and wknd: bhd whn p.u bef last* **14/1**

6m 14.0s (-0.50) **Going Correction** +0.30s/f (Yiel) **11** Ran SP% **112.1**
Speed ratings: **112,111,108,107,105 103,98,98,**—,— — CSF £75.82 TOTE £2.50: £1.40, £5.90, £1.90; EX 98.50.
Owner Andrea & Graham Wylie **Bred** R J McAlpine And D O Pickering **Trained** Billy Row, Co Durham

FOCUS
A creditable winning time for a race like this. This was a decent renewal and Inglis Drever has been rated to within 7lb of his World Hurdle mark.

NOTEBOOK
Inglis Drever, last season's top staying hurdler and inaugural winner of the BHB's Order of Merit, made an impressive return to action, easing his trainer's fears about the well-being of his string. Saving ground as he was kept on the inside, he struck the front going well and kept on much too strongly for the runner-up. His World Hurdle price was trimmed after this and he looks the one to beat again at this stage. *(tchd 85-40 in a place)*
Redemption ran a cracker on this first run over hurdles for a year, coming there with every chance and losing nothing in defeat. He is still very well in over fences but his jumping is always liable to let him down.
Tees Components, fit from a Flat campaign, ran a fine race on his first run over jumps since May 2003. Despite his age, this was only his sixth run over hurdles and there could still be a decent prize in him. *(tchd 8-1)*
Crystal D'Ainay(FR) was close enough at the third from home but soon came under pressure and did not find much. He may go back over fences now - he held an alternative entry in the Charlie Hall on this card - and it would not be a surprise to see him fitted with some headgear again. *(op 6-1)*
Brewster(IRE) went well for a long way but could not go with the principals in the home straight. He is eight years old and now might be the time to switch him to fences. *(op 4-1)*
Rambling Minster, progressive last term, shaped with promise on this return and was not not given a hard time when he could not go with the principals from the third last. *(op 28-1)*
Yogi(IRE) quickly established a clear lead but it was no surprise that his exertions ultimately took their toll.
Carlys Quest was always at the back of the field on this first start for six months. His penalty for landing a weak Grade One at Punchestown is going to make life hard for him this season. *(op 12-1)*
Telemoss(IRE), who beat Crystal D'Ainay in a lesser renewal of this a year ago, might have needed this to put him right at his age. *(op 12-1)*
Sh Boom, who made just two appearances last season, showed little on this first run since leaving Jonjo O'Neill's yard. *(op 12-1)*

1926 BET365 CHARLIE HALL CHASE GRADE 2 (18 fncs) 3m 1f
3:25 (3:26) (Class 1) 5-Y-0+ **£45,750** (£18,750; £10,500)

Form | RPR
U12- **1** **Ollie Magern**[252] 3942 7-11-5 152 .... CLlewellyn 165+
(N A Twiston-Davies) *mde all: set sound pce: rdn 3 out: drvn last: styd on wl* **11/4**[1]
/2-4 **2** 1¼ **Kingscliff (IRE)**[185] 68 8-11-0 162 .... RWalford 160+
(R H Alner) *trckd ldrs: hit 12th: rdn along 3 out: hit next: drvn to chse wnr appr last: kpt on wl u.p flat* **10/3**[2]
UP-5 **3** 1½ **Take The Stand (IRE)**[52] 1434 9-11-0 163 .... ADobbin 159+
(P Bowen) *nt fluent: trckd ldrs: hdwy 5 out: rdn along appr 3 out: drvn and one pce fr next* **12/1**
32-5 **F** **Keen Leader (IRE)**[7] 1830 9-11-0 160 .... APMcCoy —
(Jonjo O'Neill) *in tch whn fell 4th* **9/2**
P40- **P** **Chives (IRE)**[196] 4861 10-11-10 148 .... DElsworth —
(Mrs S J Smith) *hld up: blnd 5th: sn bhd: mstke 9th and p.u after* **20/1**
FP-2 **U** **Colourful Life (IRE)**[21] 1676 9-11-6 140 .... PJBrennan —
(P F Nicholls) *chsd ldrs: rdn along and lost pl 10th: blnd and uns rdr next* **25/1**
151- **P** **Grey Abbey (IRE)**[205] 4748 11-11-10 169 .... GLee —
(J Howard Johnson) *chsd wnr: rdn along 5 out: wknd appr next and bhd whn p.u bef 2 out* **7/2**[3]
11-2 **U** **Joes Edge (IRE)**[183] 115 8-11-6 144 .... KJMercer —
(Ferdy Murphy) *hld up and bhd: sme hdwy 1/2-way: rdn along and outpcd fr 5 out: blnd and uns rdr next* **20/1**

6m 25.5s (-14.50) **Going Correction** -0.10s/f (Good) **8** Ran SP% **111.2**
Speed ratings: **119,118,118,**—,— —,—,— CSF £11.76 TOTE £3.80: £1.70, £1.60, £2.70; EX 15.30.
Owner Roger Nicholls **Bred** R Nicholls And T Smith **Trained** Naunton, Gloucs

FOCUS
The winner set a strong gallop, which sorted this field out, and resulted in a fair winning time, even for a Grade Two chase. This was an excellent renewal on paper but not an easy race to rate.

NOTEBOOK
Ollie Magern ◆, making his return, having had his novice season curtailed by injury, was very fresh and keen in the early stages. Nevertheless, he jumped well throughout and found plenty to score in impressive fashion, especially considering he had a tough task on official ratings. The race is not easy to rate, but this looks a significant step up on previous form for last season's top staying novice, and though he still has some catching up to do, he at least has Kicking King in his sights. He will have been reassessed by the time the Hennessy weights are published and is more likely to go for the Betfair Lancashire Chase at Haydock, the first leg of the chasing 'triple crown'. *(op 7-2)*
Kingscliff(IRE), with a new jockey on board, was effectively making his seasonal debut. Going well on the home turn, he was a little outpaced by the winner after the third last and got the next wrong, but was staying on well at the end. This was a thoroughly satisfactory return. *(tchd 7-2)*
Take The Stand(IRE) did not jump particularly fluently on this return to fences but only gave best from the second last. While he does handle soft ground, all his wins have been gained when the word 'good' has appeared in the official description, and he is obviously well capable of landing a big prize when conditions are right. *(tchd 11-1)*
Grey Abbey(IRE) won this event a year ago, but this time the writing was on the wall when he lost the lead to Ollie Magern before the first fence. He faded on the final turn and was a tired fourth *when pulled up two from home, but he should come on for the run.Official explanation: jockey said gelding ran flat (op 3-1 tchd 4-1)*
Colourful Life(IRE), who faced a very stiff task on these terms, lost touch at the first fence on the final circuit and was well out of it when departing at the next. *(op 3-1 tchd 4-1)*
Chives(IRE) was struggling from an early stage and his rider called it a day passing the stands with a circuit to run. *(op 3-1 tchd 4-1)*
Keen Leader(IRE) did not get far on this return to fences. *(op 3-1 tchd 4-1)*
Joes Edge(IRE), who had a good deal to find at the weights, just about kept tabs on the leading bunch until the fifth last but was well adrift when falling foul of the final ditch. *(op 3-1 tchd 4-1)*

1927 BET365 NOVICES' HURDLE (9 hdls) 2m
4:00 (4:04) (Class 3) 4-Y-0+ **£7,052** (£2,170; £1,085; £542)

Form | RPR
1 **Two Miles West (IRE)**[406] 4-11-0 .... APMcCoy 118+
(Jonjo O'Neill) *trckd ldrs: hit 4th: smooth hdwy 4 out: led next and sn qcknd clr: shkn up after 2 out: rdn and pckd last: drvn flat: kpt o* **5/2**[2]
2 hd **Circassian (IRE)**[59] 4-11-0 .... GLee 118+
(J Howard Johnson) *trckd ldrs: hit 4th: smooth hdwy 4 out: led briefly appr next: sn rdn: styd on appr last: drvn flat and jst hld* **13/8**[1]
0 **3** 13 **Iffy**[10] 729 4-11-0 .... RThornton 103
(R Lee) *midfield: stdy hdwy appr 4 out: chsd ldng pair next: sn rdn and kpt on same pce* **22/1**
0-5 **4** 4 **Water Taxi**[22] 1661 4-10-11 .... KJMercer(3) 99
(Ferdy Murphy) *towards rr: pushed along 1/2-way: gd hdwy after 4 out: rdn to chse ldrs next: kpt on same pce fr 2 out* **20/1**
0 **5** 11 **Backgammon**[9] 1794 4-11-0 .... RMcGrath 89+
(K G Reveley) *in tch: hdwy to chse ldrs 4 out: rdn next and grad wknd* **12/1**
14- **6** ¾ **Troll (FR)**[315] 2886 4-11-0 .... ADobbin 87
(L Lungo) *rr and mstke 1st: stdy hdwy appr 4 out: chsd ldrs appr next: sn rdn and grad wknd* **7/2**[3]
03-3 **7** 14 **Duke Orsino (IRE)**[175] 210 5-10-11 96 .... PBuchanan(3) 75+
(Miss Lucinda V Russell) *cl up: mstke 3rd: blnd 5th: rdn along 4 out and wknd bef next* **16/1**
8 8 **Shinko Femme (IRE)**[18] 4-10-2 .... DCCostello(5) 58
(M E Sowersby) *n.d* **100/1**
35-0 **9** 3½ **Zealand**[13] 1757 5-11-0 .... ARoss 64+
(R A Fahey) *midfield: stdy hdwy on outer to join ldrs whn blnd 4 out: sn rdn and wknd bef next* **40/1**

0-60 **10** *1 ¾* **Noble Pursuit**[13] [1756] 8-10-7 79.. MrMSeston(7) 60
(R E Barr) *chsd ldrs: rdn along 4 out and sn wknd* **66/1**

000- **11** *2 ½* **Nabir (FR)**[200] [4813] 5-11-0 82.. JimCrowley 58
(P D Niven) *a rr* **66/1**

6/6 **12** *¾* **Europrime Games**[13] [1757] 7-11-0 .... BHarding 57
(M E Sowersby) *led: rdn along 4 out: sn hdd & wknd* **200/1**

13 *6* **Novack Du Beury (FR)**[188] 4-10-7 .... TJDreaper(7) 51
(Ferdy Murphy) *a bhd* **33/1**

P5 **14** *12* **Dextrous**[18] [1567] 8-10-11 .... ACCoyle(3) 39
(P T Midgley) *a bhd* **80/1**

3m 59.5s (0.10) **Going Correction** +0.30s/f (Yiel) **14** Ran SP% **122.7**
Speed ratings: **111,110,104,102,96 96,89,85,83,82 81,81,78,72** CSF £6.87 TOTE £3.50: £1.70, £1.30, £2.50; EX 8.90.
Owner John P McManus **Bred** Tower Bloodstock **Trained** Cheltenham, Gloucs

FOCUS
This looked a fair race and it could have been rated even higher. The first two look decent prospects.

NOTEBOOK
Two Miles West(IRE) ◆, classically-bred, was a smart performer for Aidan O'Brien, sixth in the 2004 Irish St Leger when last seen on the Flat. Cutting down his market rival to lead at the third last, he soon pulled clear, but that rival was coming back at him on the run-in and he just held on. He jumped fluently, although he was a little awkward at the last, and can go on to better things after this very promising start to his hurdles career. *(tchd 11-4)*
Circassian(IRE) ◆, winner of a Listed race on the Flat in France two months ago, has since been sold out of Sir Mark Prescott's yard. Taking up the running on the home turn, he soon had all his rivals in trouble bar the eventual winner, who went past him at the first in the straight. He rallied well between the last two flights and threw down a strong challenge on the flat which only just failed. *A stiffer track will suit and he looks a potentially smart prospect. (op 6-4 tchd 15-8 tchd 2-1 in places)*
Iffy ◆, formerly with Peter Cundell, has won twice on the Flat since finishing well beaten on his hurdling debut in July. He closed travelling well on the home turn but was unable to go with the first two as they quickened away. *That was no disgrace and he can win an ordinary novice event. (op 33-1)*
Water Taxi again showed ability, closing from off the pace to latch on to the leading bunch, although in common with the rest of the field he was left standing when the first two pulled away from the third last.
Backgammon, a fair middle-distance handicapper on the Flat, has run two reasonable races over hurdles now. He could need further. *(op 9-1 tchd 17-2)*
Troll(FR) confirmed the impression he made in his bumpers in that he appeared to find two miles, even on a flat track such as this, an insufficient test of stamina. *(op 8-1)*
Shinko Femme(IRE) *Official explanation: jockey said filly had breathing problem*

1928 ARTHUR STEPHENSON NOVICES' H'CAP CHASE (15 fncs) 2m 4f 110y
4:35 (4:36) (Class 3) (0-115,110) 4-Y-0+ **£5,616** (£1,728; £864; £432)

Form RPR

44-6 **1** **Spring Gamble (IRE)**[22] [1662] 6-10-13 97.. FKeniry 110+
(G M Moore) *disp ld tl led 10th: rdn clr after 4 out: styd on wl* **12/1**

U31- **2** *8* **Jballingall**[195] [4872] 6-10-0 84 oh3.. KRenwick 87
(N Wilson) *disp ld to 10th: rdn along 4 out: drvn and kpt on same pce fr 2 out* **13/2**[3]

0353 **3** *3* **Magico (NZ)**[7] [1836] 7-10-7 96.. PCO'Neill(5) 97+
(R C Guest) *hld up in tch: hdwy 5 out: rdn along to chse ldrs next: kpt on same pce u.p fr 2 out* **7/1**

2PP/ **4** *shd* **Valleymore (IRE)**[268] [3673] 9-11-4 102..(t) NFehily 102
(S A Brookshaw) *chsd ldrs: rdn along 4 out: kpt on same pce* **9/1**

/321 **5** *hd* **Darina's Boy**[13] [1761] 9-11-12 110.. PWhelan 114+
(Mrs S J Smith) *chsd ldng pair: hdwy and cl up whn blnd 5 out: sn rdn along and wknd fr next* **5/1**[2]

6PP- **6** *dist* **One Five Eight**[287] [3370] 6-11-5 103.. ADempsey —
(M W Easterby) *a rr: blnd bdly 5th: bhd after* **33/1**

330- **P** **Jonny's Kick**[285] [3393] 5-10-13 97.. RGarritty —
(T D Easterby) *keen: mstkes: bhd fr 1/2-way: p.u bef 4 out* **9/1**

-542 **P** **Lothian Falcon**[163] [426] 6-11-2 103.. GCarenza(3) —
(P Maddison) *hld up in rr: hdwy and midfield whn blnd 9th: sn bhd and p.u bef 3 out* **20/1**

1- **P** **Good Judgement (IRE)**[320] [2811] 7-11-7 105.. APMcCoy —
(Jonjo O'Neill) *keen: hld up towards rr: hdwy whn blnd 7th: 8th and 9th: sn bhd and p.u bef 4 out* **2/1**[1]

5m 28.8s (8.10) **Going Correction** -0.10s/f (Good) **9** Ran SP% **111.2**
Speed ratings: **80,76,75,75,75** —,—,—,— CSF £83.14 CT £575.44 TOTE £15.10: £3.00, £2.00, £1.90; EX 66.90.
Owner J B Wallwin **Bred** Miss Catherine O'Byrne **Trained** Middleham, N Yorks

FOCUS
Not many got into this and the form is probably suspect, as the time was no less than 13.4 seconds slower than the earlier Listed handicap chase. However, this was a big step up from the winner, and the second and third ran close to their marks.

NOTEBOOK
Spring Gamble(IRE), sharper for his recent return to action, was always in the first two and drew clear over the last four fences for a decisive win. He jumped soundly and looks to be on the upgrade. *(op 11-1)*
Jballingall was without the headgear he wore when successful on his latest start back in April. After sharing the lead with the eventual winner, he was put in his place from the fourth last but kept going to hold second spot. *(op 6-1 tchd 7-1)*
Magico(NZ) ran his race on this return to fences without convincing that he really needs this far. *(op 15-2 tchd 8-1)*
Valleymore(IRE) has rejoined his former trainer after a fruitless spell with Paul Gilligan in Ireland. Without the blinkers for this first run since February, he was never near enough to trouble the leaders but was staying on at the end. *(op 8-1)*
Darina's Boy, raised 10lb for his Market Rasen win, had been seen off by the first two with four to jump but would have been much closer but for his blunder at the previous fence. *(op 4-1)*
Good Judgement(IRE) was successful in a novice hurdle last December on his only previous start. He closed on the leaders with a circuit to run, but made a trio of jumping errors in the back straight and, lappearing to lose his confidence, was soon left behind. *(tchd 7-4)*

1929 LEEDS RUGBY DAY SATURDAY 12TH NOVEMBER H'CAP HURDLE (10 hdls) 2m 4f 110y
5:10 (5:11) (Class 3) (0-125,123) 4-Y-0+ **£5,232** (£1,610; £805; £402)

Form RPR

0-23 **1** **Mister Arjay (USA)**[25] [1633] 5-11-2 113.. ADobbin 121
(B Ellison) *trckd ldng pair: hdwy 3 out: led next: sn rdn and hung lft appr last: drvn flat and styd on* **8/1**[3]

P12- **2** *1 ¾* **Haut De Gamme (FR)**[204] [4764] 10-11-6 120.. KJMercer(3) 127+
(Ferdy Murphy) *hld up and bhd: stdy hdwy after 4 out: chsd wnr after 2 out: rdn to chal and n.m.r last: drvn and no ex flat* **11/1**

450- **3** *12* **Better Days (IRE)**[204] [4764] 9-11-2 113.. DElsworth 109+
(Mrs S J Smith) *a cl up: effrt appr 3 out and ev ch tl rdn and one pce next: hit last* **9/1**

313- **4** *5* **Habitual Dancer**[19] [4184] 4-11-9 120.. BHarding 110+
(Jedd O'Keeffe) *led: rdn along 3 out: hdd appr next: sn drvn and wknd* **8/1**[3]

156- **5** *4* **Sherkin Island (IRE)**[322] [2758] 7-10-7 104.. APMcCoy 89
(Jonjo O'Neill) *hld up towards rr: stdy hdwy 1/2-way: rdn along to chse ldrs 3 out: sn btn* **5/2**[1]

041- **6** *2 ½* **Hidden Bounty (IRE)**[209] [4708] 9-11-12 123.. RMcGrath 106
(K G Reveley) *hld up in rr: stdy hdwy 4 out: in tch next: sn rdn and no imp* **16/1**

404- **7** *3 ½* **Vicars Destiny**[12] [4169] 7-11-2 120..(p) CDSharkey(7) 99
(Mrs S Lamyman) *in tch: rdn along bef 4 out and sn wknd* **12/1**

32-2 **8** *7* **Roobihoo (IRE)**[185] [64] 6-10-13 110.. GLee 84+
(C Grant) *chsd ldrs: rdn along 4 out: wknd bef next* **5/1**[2]

4F-P **9** *¾* **Le Royal (FR)**[9] [1796] 6-11-3 114..(t) JimCrowley 86
(K G Reveley) *hld up: hdwy and in tch on inner 4 out: sn rdn and wknd* **20/1**

12-P **P** **Powder Creek (IRE)**[163] [427] 8-10-8 115.. PKinsella(10) —
(K G Reveley) *chsd ldrs: rdn along 4 out appr 4 out and sn wknd* **20/1**

351- **U** **Huka Lodge (IRE)**[195] [4876] 8-10-7 104.. BGibson —
(L Lungo) *midfield: gd hdwy on inner to trck ldrs 5th: in contention whn blnd and uns rdr 4 out* **9/1**

5m 11.6s (2.70) **Going Correction** +0.30s/f (Yiel)
WFA 4 from 5yo+ 14lb **11** Ran SP% **118.9**
Speed ratings: **106,105,100,98,97 96,95,92,92**,— — CSF £92.69 CT £806.01 TOTE £7.80: £2.60, £3.50, £2.40; EX 118.90 Place 6 £1,022.70, Place 5 £38.49.
Owner Keith Middleton **Bred** Barbara Hunter **Trained** Norton, N Yorks

FOCUS
A fair handicap that could be rated a few pounds higher but seems about right based on the time. The gallop was only a modest one and not too many of these were able to get involved.

NOTEBOOK
Mister Arjay(USA), unlike the majority of his rivals, had a recent run under his belt. He was being ridden in third place rounding the home turn, but his stamina then kicked in over this longer trip and he forged ahead at the second last, staying on too strongly for the runner-up. He has done most of his racing on better ground but seemed to relish these conditions. *(op 13-2)*
Haut De Gamme(FR) was last seen when runner-up in the Topham Trophy over the big Aintree fences in April. The only one able to get involved from off the pace, he covered Mister Arjay's move at the second last but was unable to get past that opponent, who carried him over to the rail between the last two flights. *(op 9-1)*
Better Days(IRE) was appearing for the first time since finishing seven places behind today's runner-up in the Topham Trophy in April. Currently rated 13lb lower over hurdles, he ran a sound race and should come on fitness-wise for this reappearance. *(op 8-1 tchd 10-1)*
Habitual Dancer, fit from a couple of runs on the Flat, made the running but could not counter when headed by the winner at the second last. *(op 15-2 tchd 13-2)*
Sherkin Island(IRE), making his seasonal debut over hurdles, looked set to be involved leaving the back straight but came under pressure once in line for home and soon faded. *(op 4-1 tchd 9-4)*
Hidden Bounty(IRE), a versatile sort, shaped with promise over an inadequate trip on this seasonal reappearance. *(op 18-1)*
Huka Lodge(IRE) was by no means out of it when he lost his rider at the last flight down the far side. *(op 12-1)*
T/Plt: £3,299.40 to a £1 stake. Pool: £72,993.75. 16.15 winning tickets. T/Qpdt: £24.10 to a £1 stake. Pool: £5,458.90. 167.05 winning tickets. JR

1930 - 1936a (Foreign Racing) - See Raceform Interactive

1661 CARLISLE (R-H)
Sunday, October 30

OFFICIAL GOING: Heavy
After 8" rain since Oct 11 & nearly 9mm in the morning the ground was 'very' testing' and few managed to complete. Two flights and a fence omitted.
Wind: Light, 1/2 against Weather: Heavy rain during the morning but becoming dry for racing and mild.

1937 RACING UK CHANNEL 432 NOVICES' HURDLE (DIV I) (7 hdls 4 omitted) 2m 4f
12:45 (12:45) (Class 4) 4-Y-0+ **£3,017** (£862; £431)

Form RPR

1 **Best Profile (IRE)**[189] 5-10-12 .... CLlewellyn 103+
(N A Twiston-Davies) *trckd ldr: led 4th: sn hdd: led appr 2 out: drvn out* **6/5**[1]

2-36 **2** *1 ¾* **Nevada Red**[22] [1672] 4-10-12 .... JMMaguire 99
(D McCain) *chsd ldrs: chal 2 out: kpt on same pce run-in* **8/1**

3 *2* **Nine De Sivola (FR)**[170] 4-10-5 .... TJDreaper(7) 97
(Ferdy Murphy) *hld up in tch: hdwy to join ldrs 2 out: fdd run-in* **11/2**[2]

3 **4** *14* **Lord Baskerville**[23] [1661] 4-10-5 .... PJMcDonald(7) 85+
(W Storey) *led after 1st: j.lft: hdd 4th: sn led again: hdd appr 2 out: 4th and wkng whn hit last* **12/1**

6/6 **5** *dist* **Loner**[30] [1591] 7-10-12 .... DO'Meara —
(W S Coltherd) *in tch towards rr: hdwy 5th: wknd appr next: btn 90l* **25/1**

4410 **6** *11* **Cheery Martyr**[112] [941] 7-10-12 89.. FKeniry —
(P Needham) *prom: rdn 4th: lost pl appr 2 out* **7/1**[3]

6 **7** *3 ½* **Mr Albanello (ARG)**[10] [1794] 6-10-9 .... KJMercer(3) —
(Ferdy Murphy) *chsd ldrs: rdn 5th: lost pl appr next* **9/1**

500/ **8** *12* **Kicking Bear (IRE)**[176] 7-10-5 .... SGagan(7) —
(J K Hunter) *in tch: lost pl 5th: sn bhd* **50/1**

P00- **P** **Kempski**[193] [4923] 5-10-5 90.. GThomas(7) —
(R Nixon) *led tl after 1st: j.rt: rdn and wknd 4th: t.o next: p.u bef 2 out* **20/1**

5m 27.3s (10.20) **Going Correction** +0.625s/f (Soft)
WFA 4 from 5yo+ 14lb **9** Ran SP% **112.7**
Speed ratings: **104,103,102,96**,— —,—,—,— CSF £10.84 TOTE £2.10: £1.02, £3.00, £2.30; EX 11.40.
Owner H R Mould **Bred** Tom Fitzgerald **Trained** Naunton, Gloucs

FOCUS
A modest affair although the winner has some potential, stamina was at a premium and the third was below the form he showed in France. The fourth sets the standard.

NOTEBOOK
Best Profile(IRE), winner of an Irish point in April on his only previous outing, stands over plenty of ground and looks a potential chaser. Dictating things from the front, he was always doing enough and looks just a stayer. *(op Evens tchd 5-4 in a place)*
Nevada Red, a rangy, chasing-type, did much better this time but the winner always looked to have his measure. *(op 10-1)*

Nine De Sivola(FR), a tall, lightly-made individual, finished runner-up on his debut over hurdles in France but was below par on his next two starts. He travelled at least as well as the winner but, after looking a real danger, he became very leg weary on the run-in. *(op 5-1 tchd 9-2 and 6-1)*
Lord Baskerville, very moderate at up to a mile on the Flat, went to post early. Quite keen, he seemed to run out of stamina altogether and was out on his feet when flattening the last. Two and a half miles on bad ground certainly does not play to what strengths he has. *(op 11-1 tchd 14-1)*

1938 RACING UK CHANNEL 432 NOVICES' HURDLE (DIV II) (7 hdls 4 omitted) 2m 4f

1:20 (1:20) (Class 4) 4-Y-0+ **£3,010** (£860; £430)

Form				RPR
2-6	1		**Money Line (IRE)**[29] [1600] 6-10-12 .... APMcCoy (Jonjo O'Neill) *trckd ldrs: shkn up and wnt 2nd appr 2 out: led between last 2: styd on* **5/1**[3]	104+
4-	2	2	**No Guarantees**[367] [1871] 5-10-12 .... CLlewellyn (N A Twiston-Davies) *led: hit 2 out: sn hdd: one pce* **7/4**[1]	101+
62-0	3	5	**Rathowen (IRE)**[171] [323] 6-10-9 .... MichalKohl[(3)] (J I A Charlton) *chsd ldrs: outpcd appr 2 out: styd on run-in* **5/1**[3]	95
	4	12	**Clemax (IRE)**[217] 4-10-9 .... KJMercer[(3)] (Ferdy Murphy) *hld up: wnt prom 5th: sn chsng wnr: rdn appr 2 out: wknd between last 2* **7/2**[2]	88+
/P0-	5	dist	**Jofi (IRE)**[293] [3293] 6-10-9 .... PBuchanan[(3)] (Miss Lucinda V Russell) *chsd ldrs: wknd 2 out: v tired whn j. slowly last: eventually completed t.o: btn 79l* **100/1**	—
00-	P		**Paperchaser**[354] [2116] 5-10-12 .... ADobbin (F P Murtagh) *t.o 4th: p.u bef next* **40/1**	—
00	P		**Shem Dylan (NZ)**[10] [1794] 6-10-12 .... HOliver (R C Guest) *prom: lost pl after 4th: t.o whn p.u bef 2 out* **33/1**	—
0-0P	P		**Inmate (IRE)**[33] [1569] 4-10-12 .... BHarding (Mrs E Slack) *hld up in tch: wknd after 4th: t.o whn p.u bef 2 out* **100/1**	—
0-16	P		**Bannister Lane**[18] [1714] 5-11-5 107........ JMMaguire (D McCain) *chsd ldrs: wknd rapidly and distant 6th whn p.u bef 2 out* **10/1**	—
	P		**Moyne Pleasure (IRE)**[19] 7-10-12 .... KJohnson (R Johnson) *hld up in rr: mstke 4th: bhd whn hit next: t.o whn p.u bef 2 out* **50/1**	—
05P/	P		**Moonzie Laird (IRE)**[659] [3280] 7-10-7 .... DCCostello[(5)] (J N R Billinge) *hld up in rr: lost pl 4th: bhd whn mstke 5th: sn p.u* **20/1**	—

5m 31.4s (14.30) **Going Correction** +0.625s/f (Soft)
WFA 4 from 5yo+ 14lb **11** Ran SP% **115.1**
Speed ratings: **96,95,93,88,— —,—,—,—,— —** CSF £13.74 TOTE £6.40: £1.90, £1.50, £1.50; EX 14.50.
Owner John P McManus **Bred** Patrick Mulcahy **Trained** Cheltenham, Gloucs

FOCUS
A modest winning time for the grade and 4.1 seconds slower than the first division. However they stood still for four seconds when the tape went up. Again stamina was at a premium and the winner and third set the level for the form.

NOTEBOOK
Money Line(IRE), who ran badly on his return in a bumper a month earlier, was put about his business to go in pursuit of the leader but he looked second best and was matched at 25 on the exchanges. However, he stayed on much the better and looks to just stay. *(op 3-1)*
No Guarantees, doing plenty in front, looked in total charge and was matched at 1.16 on the exchanges. He clouted the second last and in the end the winner saw it out the better. He looked tired on the run-in. *(op 9-4)*
Rathowen(IRE), absent since May, looks basically slow and will not be seen to best effect until he tackles fences. *(op 8-1)*
Clemax(IRE), successful in a chase at Auteuil in March when last seen in action, stands over *plenty of ground. He went in pursuit of the leader but tired badly between the last two flights. (op 4-1 tchd 10-3)*

1939 SPARKY GAYLE NOVICES' CHASE (16 fncs 2 omitted) 3m 110y

1:55 (1:55) (Class 3) 5-Y-0+ **£7,166** (£2,205; £1,102; £551)

Form				RPR
0-41	1		**Model Son (IRE)**[18] [1719] 7-11-1 .... PCO'Neill[(5)] (Mrs H Dalton) *mde virtually all: clr 2 out: easily* **5/2**[1]	135+
16-	2	19	**See You There (IRE)**[192] [4945] 6-10-11 .... PBuchanan[(3)] (Miss Lucinda V Russell) *wnt mod 3rd 10th: j. bdly lft 4 out: kpt on to take mod 2nd last* **9/2**[3]	109
142-	3	17	**Kitski (FR)**[264] [3747] 7-10-11 .... KJMercer[(3)] (Ferdy Murphy) *chsd ldrs: wnt 2nd 8th: wknd 2 out: fin tired* **11/1**	102+
-43P	4	dist	**Kidithou (FR)**[28] [1606] 7-11-6 110........ BHarding (W T Reed) *chsd ldrs: wknd 11th: t.o 4 out: btn 56l* **25/1**	—
3/55	P		**Rolling River (IRE)**[18] [1719] 8-10-11 .... PAspell[(3)] (J Wade) *in rr fr 9th: bhd whn p.u bef 11th* **25/1**	—
133-	P		**Mickey Croke**[365] [1899] 8-11-0 .... ADobbin (M Todhunter) *prom: lost pl 9th: bhd whn p.u bef 11th* **8/1**	—
2031	P		**Boobee (IRE)**[57] [1396] 9-11-6 110........ AThornton (Robert Gray) *chsd ldrs: lost pl 9th: bhd whn p.u bef 11th* **10/1**	—
P/6	P		**Little Blackie**[8] [1835] 8-10-0 .... MJMcAlister[(7)] (S J Marshall) *mstkes: last: detached whn p.u after 8th* **100/1**	—
2062	R		**Iris's Prince**[14] [1761] 6-10-7 109........ TJDreaper[(7)] (A Crook) *nt fluent: prom: lost pl 11th: t.o 5th whn ref and uns rdr last* **14/1**	—
114-	P		**Baron Monty (IRE)**[218] [4554] 7-11-0 .... RMcGrath (C Grant) *hdwy to chse ldrs 9th: sn lost pl: losing tch whn p.u after 12th* **10/3**[2]	—

6m 48.0s **10** Ran SP% **113.7**
CSF £13.74 TOTE £3.60: £1.10, £1.60, £3.30; EX 17.50.
Owner P J Hughes Developments Ltd **Bred** Andrew Murphy **Trained** Norton, Shropshire

FOCUS
Model Son enjoyed himself in front and had no difficulty supplementing his Wetherby success. The form is not easy to rate but could be a little higher.

NOTEBOOK
Model Son(IRE), keen to get on with it, enjoyed himself out in front and in the end simply out-galloped the opposition. The plan is one more outing at this level before the Feltham at Christmas. *(tchd 11-4)*
See You There(IRE), an Irish point winner, was making his debut over fences on his first outing since April. He stayed on in his own time up the hill to secure a remote second spot at the last. This was a long way below the form he showed over hurdles but at least it should have taught him something. *(op 7-1)*
Kitski(FR), who has changed stable since he last ran in February, went in pursuit of the winner but in the end he struggled to reach the finishing line. He does not appreciate conditions as testing as this. *(op 8-1)*
Kidithou(FR), back over fences, stopped to nothing a mile from home. He will have a more realsitic chance in handicap company rather than competing in novice chases under his penalty.
Baron Monty(IRE), absent since March, shown some aptitude on his chasing debut but he stopped to nothing in a matter of strides. He will soon put this behind him. *(tchd 7-2)*
Boobee(IRE) *Official explanation: jockey said gelding pulled up lame (tchd 7-2)*

1940 MITCHELL & HEAP H'CAP HURDLE (6 hdls 3 omitted) 2m 1f

2:30 (2:33) (Class 3) (0-115,112) 4-Y-0+ **£7,166** (£2,205; £1,102; £551)

Form				RPR
03-6	1		**Wild Is The Wind (FR)**[183] [136] 4-11-10 110........ APMcCoy (Jonjo O'Neill) *hld up in mid-field: stdy hdwy 4th: led appr 2 out: clr last: eased towards fin* **10/1**[3]	130+
400P	2	12	**Why The Long Face (NZ)**[8] [1823] 8-11-1 104........(p) LMcGrath[(3)] (R C Guest) *hld up in rr: hdwy 4th: sn drvn along: chal 2 out: nt qckn between last 2* **40/1**	109+
-221	3	4	**Pebble Bay**[153] [593] 10-11-8 108........ DElsworth (Mrs S J Smith) *w ldrs: one pce fr 2 out* **9/2**[2]	108
/32-	4	16	**Bob The Piler**[328] [2671] 9-11-10 110........ ADobbin (N G Richards) *hld up in mid-div: hdwy 4th: effrt appr 2 out: 4th and wl hld whn hit last* **5/2**[1]	94
615-	5	1	**Emperor's Monarch**[208] [4735] 6-10-13 102........ PAspell[(3)] (J Wade) *chsd ldrs: wl outpcd appr 2 out: kpt on between last 2* **25/1**	85
350-	6	½	**Shares (IRE)**[11] [3658] 5-10-8 104........ DDaSilva[(10)] (P Monteith) *stdd s: hdwy to ld after 2nd: hdd appr 2 out: wknd between last 2* **22/1**	87
03U-	7	2½	**Nerone (GER)**[11] [4303] 4-11-5 105........ KRenwick (P Monteith) *hld up in rr: hdwy 4th: sn drvn along: chsng ldrs appr 2 out: sn wknd* **28/1**	87+
-055	8	3½	**Mr Twins (ARG)**[10] [1793] 4-10-0 86 oh1........ PWhelan (M A Barnes) *chsd ldrs: drvn along 4th: lost pl appr 2 out* **16/1**	63
-F1P	9	hd	**Isellido (IRE)**[175] [239] 6-11-12 112........ HOliver (R C Guest) *t.k.h in mid field: lost pl after 4th* **20/1**	88
4/F-	10	2	**Lucky Judge**[65] [1994] 8-11-0 100........ JimCrowley (G A Swinbank) *bhd fr 4th: t.o appr 2 out: kpt on between last 2* **14/1**	74
602/	11	hd	**Colway Ritz**[107] [2140] 11-10-0 86 oh8........ NPMulholland (W Storey) *chsd ldrs: lost pl appr 2 out* **50/1**	60
-P42	12	16	**Time To Roam (IRE)**[10] [1793] 5-10-9 98........(v) PBuchanan[(3)] (Miss Lucinda V Russell) *t.k.h: trckd ldrs: lost pl appr 2 out* **10/1**[3]	56
1631	13	dist	**Sheer Guts (IRE)**[14] [1756] 6-10-11 97........(vt) AThornton (Robert Gray) *chsd ldrs: wknd appr 2 out: t.o: btn 45l* **12/1**	—
52-4	14	nk	**Gospel Song**[189] [9] 13-10-4 97........ EWhillans[(7)] (A C Whillans) *led tl after 2nd: lost pl after next: t.o 2 out* **16/1**	—
0P-0	15	4	**Shady Man**[153] [592] 7-10-0 93 oh1 ow7........ GThomas[(7)] (J K Hunter) *stdd s:in rr whn hmpd 3rd: t.o 2 out* **66/1**	—
633	B		**Hugs Destiny (IRE)**[37] [1538] 4-10-4 90........ GLee (M A Barnes) *trckd ldrs: b.d 3rd* **12/1**	—
/0-F	F		**Robert The Bruce**[155] [544] 10-11-2 102........ BGibson (L Lungo) *prom tl fell 3rd* **20/1**	—

4m 33.8s (8.10) **Going Correction** +0.625s/f (Soft)
WFA 4 from 5yo+ 13lb **17** Ran SP% **125.8**
Speed ratings: **105,99,97,89,89 89,88,86,86,85 85,77,—,—,— —,—** CSF £369.91 CT £2069.57 TOTE £10.60: £2.80, £9.10, £1.30, £1.30; EX 448.50.
Owner T Mohan **Bred** N Pharaon **Trained** Cheltenham, Gloucs

FOCUS
Wild Is The Wind came good with a wide-margin success, finally fulfilling the potential he had shown on the level. The third sets the standard, and he was some way clear of the others.

NOTEBOOK
Wild Is The Wind(FR), fit on his first outing since April, was in no hurry to join issue. Sent on, he stayed on in fine style and in the end was value for at least 15 lengths.
Why The Long Face(NZ), who has slipped to a lenient mark, took some rousting along. He jumped two out upsides but it was soon very clear that he was booked for second spot. *(op 25-1)*
Pebble Bay, no spring chicken, enjoys his racing but he is now two stone higher than for the first of his four victories for this stable last season. *(tchd 5-1)*
Bob The Piler, back over hurdles on his first run since December, was out on his feet when flattening the last. He was reported to have returned with an overreach. *(op 10-3)*
Emperor's Monarch, who finished distressed when last seen in action in April, was making his handicap bow and looked paceless. It will not be long before he is seen over fences.
Shares(IRE), given a recent run on the Flat, was repeating the pattern of a year ago when he finished well beaten in this event. Dropped in at the start, he was soon taking them along but he *became very leg weary late on. Conditions as testing as this surely count against him. (op 20-1 tchd 25-1)*

1941 £1 MILLION TOTETENTOFOLLOW CUMBERLAND H'CAP CHASE (17 fncs 3 omitted) 3m 2f

3:05 (3:05) (Class 3) (0-135,135) 5-Y-0+**£27,352** (£8,416; £4,208; £2,104)

Form				RPR
2141	1		**Ross Comm**[23] [1664] 9-10-13 122........ DElsworth (Mrs S J Smith) *chsd ldrs: led 10th: clr 4 out: 28l clr last: fin tired* **11/1**	145+
4-35	2	23	**Shannon's Pride (IRE)**[10] [1798] 9-9-12 110........ LMcGrath[(3)] (R C Guest) *chsd ldrs: wnt 2nd 11th: one pced fr 5 out: hit 2 out: kpt on to retain 2nd* **25/1**	101
-012	3	nk	**Pass Me By**[10] [1795] 6-10-6 115........(e) HOliver (R C Guest) *chsd ldrs: outpcd 10th: styd on fr 3 out* **20/1**	106
23-1	4	7	**Ebony Light (IRE)**[22] [1670] 9-10-11 120........(p) GLee (D McCain) *led to 10th: outpcd next: plodded on fr 4 out* **5/1**[2]	104
000-	5	dist	**Whereareyounow (IRE)**[205] [4764] 8-11-7 130........ CLlewellyn (N A Twiston-Davies) *j.lft: hld up in rr: hdwy whn blnd 11th: no ch after: btn 31l* **9/1**	—
12-0	6	8	**Ossmoses (IRE)**[185] [91] 8-10-8 117........ RMcGrath (D M Forster) *in tch: outpcd 10th: sn no ch* **9/2**[1]	—
4F-4	7	20	**Harlov (FR)**[155] [547] 10-10-1 110........(p) KRenwick (A Parker) *in rr: bhd fr 9th: eventually completed* **50/1**	—
453-	P		**Hugo De Grez (FR)**[329] [2654] 10-10-4 113........ ADempsey (A Parker) *bhd: p.u bef 12th* **14/1**	—
3U3-	P		**Granit D'Estruval (FR)**[267] [3702] 11-11-1 127........ KJMercer[(3)] (Ferdy Murphy) *bhd fr 9th: p.u bef 12th* **25/1**	—
13/-	P		**Robbo**[13] [4951] 11-10-13 122........ JimCrowley (K G Reveley) *prom to 4th: bhd fr 10th: p.u bef 12th* **14/1**	—
0U-5	P		**Bold Investor**[14] [1759] 8-10-13 122........ AThornton (Jonjo O'Neill) *in rr: mstke 6th: bhd whn p.u bef 11th* **33/1**	—
U60-	P		**Your A Gassman (IRE)**[227] [4411] 7-11-8 131........ BHarding (Ferdy Murphy) *in rr: last and detached whn p.u after 9th* **14/1**	—
321/	P		**Over The Storm (IRE)**[666] [3186] 8-11-1 124........ DO'Meara (H P Hogarth) *mid-div: lost pl 10th: bhd whn p.u bef 12th* **25/1**	—
P0-0	P		**Just In Debt (IRE)**[18] [1721] 9-11-10 133........(p) ADobbin (M Todhunter) *prom: lost pl after 9th: bhd whn p.u bef next* **20/1**	—
061-	P		**Mini Sensation (IRE)**[331] [2606] 12-10-12 121........ APMcCoy (Jonjo O'Neill) *mid-div: outpcd whn blnd 9th: bhd whn p.u bef 12th* **10/1**	—

220- **P** **Strong Resolve (IRE)**[204] 4772 9-11-9 **135**...................... PBuchanan(3) —
(Miss Lucinda V Russell) *chsd ldrs to 9th: wknd next: bhd whn p.u bef 13th* **8/1**[3]

110- **P** **Supreme Breeze (IRE)**[218] 4548 10-10-6 **115**...................... PWhelan —
(Mrs S J Smith) *chsd ldrs: drvn along 8th: lost pl after next: bhd whn p.u bef 12th* **20/1**

7m 16.6s (8.40) **Going Correction** +0.55s/f (Soft) **17** Ran SP% **124.1**
Speed ratings: **109,101,101,99,**— —,—,—,—,— —,—,—,—,— —,— CSF £260.41 CT £5354.12 TOTE £12.00: £3.60, £5.30, £4.40, £1.30; EX 323.90.
Owner Kevin G Treanor **Bred** A Dawson **Trained** High Eldwick, W Yorks
■ Stewards' Enquiry : H Oliver one-day ban: used whip with excessive frequency (Nov 10)

FOCUS
A big field for this decent prize but in the conditions it was a war of attrition and from four out just a one-horse race. The winner is value for more than the official margin, but the form is not easy to rate.

NOTEBOOK
Ross Comm, up 9lb this time and 32lb since returning in June, galloped them into the ground and faces yet another big hike in the ratings. The very testing conditions if anything played to his strengths. *(op 10-1)*
Shannon's Pride(IRE) went in pursuit of the winner but, never a real threat, in the end managed to cling on to second spot. *(op 16-1)*
Pass Me By stuck on grimly up the hill and, with everything thrown at him on the run-in, he just failed to edge his stablemate out of second money. He looks to just stay.
Ebony Light(IRE), with Grand National pretensions, jumped off in front but was struggling a long way from home. In the end he completed in his own time. *(op 11-2)*
Whereareyounow(IRE), hard to predict, was closing when he blundered. That finished him completely. *(op 8-1)*
Ossmoses(IRE), absent since April, ran as if badly in need of the run mentally. *(op 11-2)*
Strong Resolve(IRE) stopped in a matter of strides but this will have put him spot on for the Becher Chase at Aintree. *(tchd 10-1 in a places)*

1942 HARRISON & HETHERINGTON NOVICES' H'CAP CHASE (11 fncs 1 omitted) 2m
3:40 (3:41) (Class 4) (0-105,105) 4-Y-0+ **£4,104** (£1,263; £631; £315)

Form RPR

131F **1** **Parisienne Gale (IRE)**[22] 1682 6-11-4 **97**...................... GLee 115+
(R Ford) *j.lft: w ldr: led after 3rd: hdd next: led 2 out: c clr run-in: comf* **3/1**[2]

4-14 **2** *11* **Miss Shakira (IRE)**[17] 1727 7-11-4 **97**...................... CLlewellyn 105+
(N A Twiston-Davies) *chsd ldrs: 3rd and rdn whn hit 3 out: styd on to take 2nd run-in: no ch w wnr* **5/2**[1]

-66P **3** *5* **Ready To Rumble (NZ)**[7] 1855 8-10-1 **85**......................(p) PCO'Neill(5) 86
(R C Guest) *trckd ldrs: reminders after 3rd: led next: hit 6th: hdd 2 out: wknd run-in* **14/1**

145- **4** *12* **Master Sebastian**[202] 4807 6-11-9 **105**...................... PBuchanan(3) 96+
(Miss Lucinda V Russell) *trckd ldrs: outpcd after 7th: wknd 2 out* **11/2**

-2B **5** *dist* **Assumetheposition (FR)**[150] 612 5-11-0 **96**...................... LMcGrath(3) —
(R C Guest) *stdd s: nt fluent: reminders 5th: bhd fr 7th: t.o 4 out: btn 32l* **7/2**[3]

2-10 **P** **Little Flora**[172] 305 9-10-10 **96**...................... MJMcAlister(7) —
(S J Marshall) *led tl after 3rd: lost pl 5th: t.o 4 out: p.u bef next* **8/1**

4m 25.3s (8.20) **Going Correction** +0.55s/f (Soft) **6** Ran SP% **109.0**
Speed ratings: **101,95,93,87,**— — CSF £10.61 CT £75.71 TOTE £3.80: £1.50, £2.20; EX 6.50.
Owner S J Manning **Bred** Edmond And Richard Kent **Trained** Cotebrook, Cheshire

FOCUS
Parisienne Gale, despite a tendency to jump left-handed, came clear on the run-in and was the only winner all day to finish full of running and could rate higher. Hurdle winner Miss Shakira probably ran to her mark on her chasing debut.

NOTEBOOK
Parisienne Gale(IRE), 12lb higher than Cartmel, made this look simple and was the one winner all day to finish like a fresh horse. She is probably even better going the other way round. *(op 5-2)*
Miss Shakira(IRE), a winner of two Irish points, was making her debut over regulation fences. Digging deep when hitting three out, she deserves credit for the way she stuck to her task. She can surely find an opening. *(tchd 11-4)*
Ready To Rumble(NZ), pulled up a week earlier, has yet to make any real impact over either hurdles or fences. *(op 12-1)*
Master Sebastian, under top weight on his chasing debut, was having his first outing since April and surely easier opportunities can be found for him. *(op 5-1 tchd 9-2)*
Assumetheposition(FR), dropped in at the start, jumped in very hesitant fashion and was out of contention early on the final circuit. This was his first outing since June over an inadequate trip and the usual cheekpieces were left off. *(op 5-1)*

1943 PERFORMANCE HOUSE AMATEUR RIDERS' NOVICES' H'CAP HURDLE (8 hdls 4 omitted) 3m 1f
4:10 (4:10) (Class 4) (0-90,87) 3-Y-0+ **£2,926** (£836; £418)

Form RPR

P/ **1** **Twotiming Gent (IRE)**[189] 12-10-1 **69**...................... MissLHaagensen(7) 75+
(P D Niven) *led early: chsd ldr: outpcd after 6th: styd on appr next: led appr last: kpt on* **25/1**

525 **2** *5* **Minster Abbi**[8] 1838 5-11-0 **75**......................(p) MissPRobson 74
(W Storey) *trckd ldrs: led after 6th: hdd 2 out: 2nd and one pce whn hit last* **10/3**[3]

00-1 **3** *7* **Stoneravinmad**[18] 1723 7-10-1 **69**...................... MrDAFitzsimmons(7) 64+
(Mrs E Slack) *trckd ldrs: led and blnd 2 out: hdd appr last: sn wknd* **3/1**[2]

P2P- **4** *12* **To The Future (IRE)**[218] 4556 9-11-5 **85**...................... MrMSeston(5) 65
(A Parker) *in tch: drvn along and outpcd 6th: sn btn* **11/4**[1]

0645 **5** *26* **Irish Prince (IRE)**[4] 1883 9-10-7 **75** ow3......................(b) MrMLurcock(7) 29
(Robert Gray) *sn led and clr to 4th: hdd after 6th: sn wknd* **6/1**

-P6P **P** **Rincoola (IRE)**[165] 417 6-10-12 **80**...................... MissWGibson(7) —
(J S Wainwright) *detached in last: t.o 5th: p.u bef next* **12/1**

-450 **P** **That's Racing**[112] 941 5-10-9 **73**...................... MissADeniel(3) —
(J Hetherton) *wnt prom 4th: wknd 6th: t.o whn p.u bef 2 out* **7/1**

7m 2.60s **7** Ran SP% **113.1**
CSF £105.00 CT £331.34 TOTE £33.00: £5.10, £2.10; EX 238.10 Place 6 £20.78, Place 5 £15.57..
Owner Miss L Haagensen **Bred** M Nolan **Trained** Barton-le-Street, N Yorks
■ A first winner for 23-year-old Laura Haagensen on her first ride over hurdles.
■ Stewards' Enquiry : Mr M Lurcock one-day ban: used whip when out of contention (Nov 10)
Mr D A Fitzsimmons one-day ban: used whip with excessive force (Nov 10)

FOCUS
A dire contest 10lb below the race ceiling and in the end the winner's stamina carried the day. The runner-up sets the standard for the form, which is very poor.

NOTEBOOK
Twotiming Gent(IRE), winner of an Irish bumper in the dim and distant past, had been pulled up on his last six starts in points. Matched at 200 on the exchanges when struggling to keep up, in the end he simply kept on in his own good time and that was sufficient to carry the day.
Minster Abbi, improved by the fitting of cheekpieces, had a top amateur but was booked for second spot when very tired, she flattened the last. *(op 3-1)*
Stoneravinmad, 5lb higher, went on travelling strongly but he had no more to give on the run-in despite his rider's use of the stick. *(op 11-4 tchd 7-2 in a place)*
To The Future(IRE), absent since March, was very ring rusty and this big type is surely better suited by fences. *(op 9-2)*
Irish Prince(IRE), keen to get on with it, soon showed in a clear lead but, legless going to two out, his rider seemed determined to extract the very last drop of blood. *(op 11-2)*
T/Plt: £8.50 to a £1 stake. Pool: £46,971.80. 4,010.40 winning tickets. T/Qpdt: £7.40 to a £1 stake. Pool: £4,280.00. 426.70 winning tickets. WG

1425 GALWAY (R-H)
Sunday, October 30
OFFICIAL GOING: Soft (heavy in places)

1944a TOTE EXACTA BALLYBRIT NOVICE CHASE (GRADE 3) (12 fncs) 2m 1f
3:05 (3:05) 5-Y-0+ **£25,244** (£6,095)

RPR

1 **Arteea (IRE)**[21] 1702 6-11-1 .... AndrewJMcNamara 137+
(Michael Hourigan, Ire) *lft in clr ld fr 1st: j.w: styd on wl fr last: easily* **11/8**[1]

2 *15* **Top Strategy (IRE)**[27] 1626 5-10-11 .... GTHutchinson 115
(T M Walsh, Ire) *mod 2nd: rdn and no imp fr last* **10/1**

F **Kahuna (IRE)**[27] 1626 8-11-1 133...................... JRBarry —
(E Sheehy, Ire) *ldng whn fell 1st* **15/8**[2]

F **Calorando (IRE)**[14] 1764 6-11-1 .... MPWatts —
(Anthony Mullins, Ire) *hld up in 3rd: pckd 5 out: rdn after slt mstke 3 out: no imp whn fell next* **7/2**[3]

4m 50.8s **4** Ran SP% **108.2**
CSF £11.42 TOTE £2.30; DF 12.50.
Owner Michael O'Flaherty **Bred** P O'Connell **Trained** Patrickswell, Co Limerick

NOTEBOOK
Arteea(IRE) had a virtual solo. He did not seem to appreciate being left in front but his jumping was solid and he won unchallenged. *(op 5/4 tchd 6/4)*
Top Strategy(IRE) ran second throughout without holding out any prospects. *(op 8/1)*
Calorando(IRE) was making no impression when falling two out. *Official explanation: trainer's representative said gelding scoped abnormally post race (op 9/4 tchd 7/4)*
Kahuna(IRE) was in front when exiting at the first. *(op 9/4 tchd 7/4)*

1945 - 1947a (Foreign Racing) - See Raceform Interactive

1772 PLUMPTON (L-H)
Monday, October 31
OFFICIAL GOING: Good to soft (soft in places on hurdle course)
Wind: Almost nil Weather: Overcast becoming fine

1948 TOTEPLACEPOT JUVENILE NOVICES' HURDLE (9 hdls) 2m
1:10 (1:11) (Class 3) 3-Y-O **£5,473** (£1,684; £842; £421)

Form RPR

1 **Flaming Weapon**[121] 3-10-12 .... JEMoore 99+
(G L Moore) *plld hrd: hld up in tch: smooth prog 3 out: led bef next: sn clr: easily* **14/1**

2 *8* **Pocketwood**[9] 3-10-12 .... DCrosse 87+
(Jean-Rene Auvray) *blnd 1st: nt jump wl after: rr and reminders 4th: prog u.p to ld 3 out: hdd bef next: no ch w wnr* **15/8**[1]

3 *5* **Cave Of The Giant (IRE)**[384] 3-10-12 .... JamesDavies 78
(T D McCarthy) *trckd ldrs: outpcd after 3 out: plugged on one pce* **33/1**

0 **4** *6* **Briannie (IRE)**[16] 1737 3-9-12 ....(p) RLucey-Butler(7) 65
(P Butler) *hld up and last tl 5th: stdy prog bef 3 out: rdn and no imp ldrs 2 out: fin tired* **66/1**

FP **5** *4* **Arno River**[23] 1679 3-10-9 .... RYoung(3) 68
(D Brace) *chsd ldrs: pushed along 5th: outpcd bef 3 out: n.d after* **100/1**

6 *5* **Sir Monty (USA)**[22] 3-10-12 .... JimCrowley 64+
(Mrs A J Perrett) *trckd ldrs: nt fluent 5th: effrt to chal after next: losing pl whn mstke 3 out: wknd* **2/1**[2]

7 *25* **Krasivi's Boy (USA)**[22] 3-10-12 .... PHide 38
(G L Moore) *nt a fluent: hld up: in tch 6th: sn outpcd: wknd bef 2 out* **10/1**

P **One Dream (FR)**[183] 3-10-5 .... AThornton —
(R H Alner) *in tch tl wknd rapidly 5th: sn p.u* **14/1**

P **Crystal Ka (FR)**[112] 3-10-12 .... MBatchelor —
(M R Hoad) *in tch: mstke 3rd: wknd 5th: t.o whn p.u bef next* **50/1**

P **P** **Goose Chase**[30] 1594 3-10-12 .... NFehily —
(C J Mann) *nt fluent: mde most tl after 6th: wknd rapidly: t.o whn p.u bef 2 out* **22/1**

23 **P** **Looking Great (USA)**[16] 1737 3-10-12 .... ATinkler —
(R F Johnson Houghton) *pressed ldr: mstke 3rd: led briefly after 6th: sn wknd: wl bhd whn p.u bef 2 out* **7/1**[3]

4m 2.30s (1.10) **Going Correction** +0.225s/f (Yiel) **11** Ran SP% **114.8**
Speed ratings: **106,102,99,96,94 92,79,**—,—,— — CSF £39.88 TOTE £11.60: £2.30, £1.90, £4.60; EX 60.00.
Owner B T M Racing **Bred** Cheveley Park Stud Ltd **Trained** Woodingdean, E Sussex

FOCUS
An ordinary event, but an impressive winner in Flaming Weapon and he looks worthy of his place in a higher grade.

NOTEBOOK
Flaming Weapon ◆, who cut little ice in seven starts for John Hills on the Flat, has joined a yard who do extrmely well with their juvenile hurdlers and he made a most impressive debut, always travelling and jumping well, and he cleared away with ease from the home turn. Enjoying the cut in the ground, he deserves a rise in grade on this evidence and it could be worth taking a chance on him if he turns out in the Grade Two juvenile novices' hurdle at the Paddy Power meeting.
Pocketwood, the best of these on the Flat, seemed to get unnerved after a blunder at the first and he was never jumping well thereafter, but he dug deep in typically game fashion and came through to take a narrow lead jumping the third last. However, the winner had barely broken sweat as they approached the second last and readily cleared away from him. If connections can get him jumping he will have little trouble winning a similar race and, in the long-run, he will stay beyond two miles. *(op 9-4)*
Cave Of The Giant(IRE) did not fulfil early potential on the level, so it is hoped he can build on this pleasing start to his hurdling career. Never far off the leaders, he lacked the principals pace in the end, but can win races on this evidence, possibly on a faster surface. *(op 25-1)*
Briannie(IRE) stepped up on her initial effort over hurdles, but she was very tired towards the finish and may be better on a faster surface at a tighter track. *(tchd 80-1)*
Arno River stayed on past a few tiring rivals and needs a drop in grade before he is winning.

Sir Monty(USA), not that far behind Pocketwood on the level, ran a poor race on this switch to hurdles and looked a non-stayer. He may be worthy of another chance on a better surface, but cannot be backed with any confidence. *(op 15-8 tchd 9-4)*
Krasivi's Boy(USA), the supposed Moore first string according to the market, looked the sort who may do well over hurdles, but he offered little and never jumped with any fluency. *(op 8-1)*
Looking Great(USA) had shaped well on both his previous hurdling experiences, but this was a *lesser effort and there was presumably something amiss. Official explanation: jockey said gelding was unsuited by the good to soft (soft in places) ground (op 9-1)*
Goose Chase, as his debut run suggested, is a blatant non-stayer and he will most likely soon be returning to the Flat. *(op 9-1)*

1949 IRISH POST CONDITIONAL JOCKEYS' H'CAP HURDLE (12 hdls) 2m 5f
1:40 (1:41) (Class 4) (0-90,90) 4-Y-0+ **£2,681** (£766; £383)

Form				RPR
22-2	**1**		**Saucy Night**[25] [1648] 9-10-1 **70** ... LHeard(5)	83+
			(Simon Earle) *j.rt: mde all: clr 9th: drvn and pressed briefly bef 2 out: sn clr again: kpt on* **11/10**[1]	
30-2	**2**	*11*	**Coustou (IRE)**[9] [105] 5-11-6 **90** ... (p) SWalsh(6)	91
			(R M Stronge) *hld up: prog and reminder 7th: chsd wnr after 9th: drvn and clsd bef 2 out: sn btn* **11/1**	
0-45	**3**	*5*	**Manque Neuf**[159] [501] 6-10-9 **76** ... (p) EDehdashti(3)	72
			(Mrs L Richards) *t.k.h: mostly chsd wnr tl after 9th: 4th and u.p after 3 out: plugged on* **14/1**	
/16-	**4**	*5*	**Otahuna**[222] [4520] 9-10-11 **83** ... WPKavanagh(8)	74
			(J W Mullins) *t.k.h: prom: rdn 9th: wnt 3rd after 3 out: no imp next: wknd last* **11/1**	
P34-	**5**	*8*	**Mrs Pickles**[222] [4522] 10-11-5 **89** ... LNewnes(6)	72
			(M D I Usher) *str reminder 2nd: sn wl in rr: wl t.o in last pair after 8th: styd on fr 3 out: nvr nrr* **20/1**	
0P/2	**6**	*1 1/4*	**Zeloso**[16] [1747] 7-10-7 **77** ... (v) CPoste(6)	59
			(M F Harris) *hld up in tch: effrt 8th: 6th and jst in tch whn blnd 9th: wknd* **10/1**[3]	
6P06	**7**	*8*	**Mr Dip**[13] [1040] 5-11-3 **81** ... CBolger	55
			(L A Dace) *t.k.h: hld up in last: lost tch w ldng gp 8th: stdy prog next: nvr on terms: wknd after 2 out* **20/1**	
00P-	**8**	*15*	**Geography (IRE)**[217] [4618] 5-11-4 **88** ... (p) RLucey-Butler(6)	47
			(P Butler) *hld up in last pair: wl bhd fr 8th: t.o next: no prog* **16/1**	
-00P	**9**	*1*	**Welsh Doll (IRE)**[15] [1751] 6-9-13 **68** ... JKington(5)	26
			(D Brace) *t.k.h: prom: chsd wnr briefly after 6th: wknd next: t.o* **50/1**	
5566	**10**	*13*	**Dawn Frolics**[39] [1523] 4-9-9 **64** ... TMessenger(5)	9
			(M J Gingell) *chsd ldrs tl wknd 7th: t.o after 9th* **33/1**	
P50-	**11**	*dist*	**Haikal**[511] [672] 8-10-2 **76** ... PDavey(10)	—
			(R H Buckler) *a in rr: toiling bef 8th: sn wl t.o* **12/1**	
P65-	**P**		**Bewleys Guest (IRE)**[197] [4884] 6-9-12 **65** ... LTreadwell(3)	—
			(Miss Venetia Williams) *t.k.h: prom tl wknd rapidly 8th: sn t.o: p.u bef 2 out* **11/2**[2]	

5m 28.0s (3.20) **Going Correction** +0.225s/f (Yiel) **12** Ran SP% **123.4**
Speed ratings: **102,97,95,94,90 90,87,81,81,76** —,— CSF £14.53 CT £126.87 TOTE £2.20: £1.10, £2.90, £4.60; EX 14.60.
Owner Equine Health Centre Ltd **Bred** Roland Hope **Trained** Sutton Veny, Wilts

FOCUS
A very weak event, run at a fair pace and the winner comfortably capitalised on his signicantly lower mark over hurdles.

NOTEBOOK
Saucy Night showed the benefit his recent comeback at Wincanton and, rather belatedly, took full advantage of his lenient rating in this sphere. Despite showing a tendency to jump right, he was fluent in the main and dug deep at the top of the straight to come clear of his rivals, having just started to idle approaching the home turn. The softer ground was more to his liking and, while the Handicapper will no doubt react now, he is a likeable performer and may have further improvement in him this season over both hurdles and fences. *(op 5-4 tchd 11-8)*
Coustou(IRE) looked the chief threat to the eventual winner as that rival started to idle turning out of the back straight, but ultimately the burden of top weight told and he was well held at the finish. He will not always bump into such well-handicapped rivals as the winner in this grade. *(tchd 10-1)*
Manque Neuf refused to settle early on and paid for that when the race got serious, but still improved a touch on his recent efforts all the same. *(op 25-1)*
Otahuna ran freely through the early parts on this return from a 222-day break and had no more to offer from the penultimate flight. He is at least entitled to improve for the outing. *(op 10-1)*
Bewleys Guest(IRE), making his handicap bow after a 197-day break and well backed, spoilt any chance of getting home by pulling too hard through the first half of the contest. This former winning pointer really has been very disappointing since joining current connections. *(op 8-1)*

1950 PLUMPTON RACECOURSE 'NATIONAL HUNT' NOVICES' HURDLE (12 hdls) 2m 5f
2:10 (2:10) (Class 4) 4-Y-0+ **£3,276** (£936; £468)

Form				RPR
3/	**1**		**Ask The Gatherer (IRE)**[692] [2652] 7-11-0 ... TJMurphy	104+
			(M Pitman) *prom: led 6th: hit 8th: drew clr after 3 out: shkn up after 2 out: styd on wl* **7/2**[2]	
	2	*3 1/2*	**Just For Now (IRE)**[205] 6-11-0 ... JMMaguire	97
			(T R George) *wl in tch: effrt 9th: chsd ldrs next: drvn to chse wnr 2 out: kpt on but no imp* **12/1**[3]	
312-	**3**	*10*	**Dancing Rock**[213] [4679] 7-11-7 122 ... RJohnson	97+
			(P J Hobbs) *cl up: chsd wnr 9th: sn pushed along: hit 3 out: lost 2nd u.p 2 out: wknd flat* **8/13**[1]	
00-	**4**	*2*	**Walter (IRE)**[289] [3367] 6-11-0 ... PHide	85
			(P Winkworth) *t.k.h: nt fluent early: pressed ldr to 6th: chsd wnr 8th to 9th: outpcd 2 out: kpt on again flat* **33/1**	
350-	**5**	*24*	**Alderbrook Girl (IRE)**[212] [4697] 5-10-4 ... CBolger(3)	54
			(R Curtis) *hld up: mstke 2nd: effrt and in tch after 9th: wknd 3 out* **50/1**	
0P-0	**6**	*3*	**English Jim (IRE)**[14] [1775] 4-11-0 ... MBatchelor	58
			(Miss A M Newton-Smith) *mde most to 6th: hit 8th: sn wknd* **66/1**	
/00-	**7**	*2 1/2*	**Great Benefit (IRE)**[328] [2686] 6-11-0 ... DCrosse	56
			(Miss H C Knight) *in tch to 8th: wl bhd after next* **40/1**	
	P		**Ballybean (IRE)**[576] 5-11-0 ... JPMcNamara	—
			(K C Bailey) *in tch tl wknd u.p 8th: sn bhd: p.u bef 2 out* **16/1**	
	P		**Ballykiln (IRE)**[232] 4-11-0 ... SThomas	—
			(Miss H C Knight) *hld up in tch: outpcd after 8th: wknd 3 out: wl bhd whn p.u bef 2 out* **14/1**	

5m 30.6s (5.80) **Going Correction** +0.225s/f (Yiel)
WFA 4 from 5yo+ 14lb **9** Ran SP% **113.2**
Speed ratings: **97,95,91,91,81 80,79**,—,— CSF £39.41 TOTE £5.70: £1.50, £1.30, £1.10; EX 36.90.
Owner Mrs Toni S Tipper **Bred** C Kenneally **Trained** Upper Lambourn, Berks

FOCUS
A modest winning time, 2.6 seconds slower than the preceding 64-90 handicap over the same trip, and the form looks worth treating with a degree of caution with the favourite failing to run his race.

NOTEBOOK
Ask The Gatherer(IRE), a former Irish bumper winner and third on his sole start for Paul Nicholls when last seen 692 days previously, had won a schooling hurdle at Cheltenham in the spring and connections clearly believed he retained all his ability, as he proved popular in the betting. That support proved justified, as he made a winning return to action in pleasing style under a positive ride from Murphy. His next outing will reveal more, but this half-bother to this season's promising novice Jeremy Cuddle Duck certainly remains open to further improvement this term. *(tchd 10-3)*
Just For Now(IRE), winner of a point when last seen in April, turned in a very respectable debut effort and looks sure to find a similar race in due course at around this trip. *(op 14-1)*
Dancing Rock , whose previous efforts fully entitled him to start a short price for this, ran well below expectations on this seasonal bow and his fate was clear some way out. While he is entitled to come on for this outing, he will have to improve plenty to justify a mark of 122 in handicaps now, as this was his last opportunity to race as a novice over timber. *(op 4-6 tchd 8-11 in places)*
Walter(IRE), who hinted at promise in two bumpers last season, ran far too freely through the early parts and lacked any real fluency in his jumping. He was keeping on at the finish, however, and will no doubt learn plenty from the experience. *(op 28-1)*

1951 £1 MILLION TOTETENTOFOLLOW NOVICES' H'CAP CHASE (18 fncs) 3m 2f
2:40 (2:42) (Class 4) (0-90,83) 5-Y-0+ **£3,681** (£1,408; £713; £334; £176)

Form				RPR
4-2P	**1**		**Five Alley (IRE)**[8] [1858] 8-11-12 **83** ... SThomas	101+
			(R H Buckler) *settled in rr: prog to chse ldng trio 11th: hit 13th: wnt 2nd bef 4 out: effrt to ld last: pushed clr* **7/2**[1]	
6P05	**2**	*5*	**Hill Forts Henry**[26] [1637] 7-10-12 **69** ... (p) AThornton	77
			(J W Mullins) *led to 4th: chsd ldng pair: rdn and effrt after 13th: led after next: hdd last: easily outpcd flat* **7/2**[1]	
P1-P	**3**	*30*	**St Kilda**[9] [1832] 8-10-4 **68** ... (p) MissLucyBridges(7)	51+
			(Miss Lucy Bridges) *pressed ldrs: led 7th: urged along after 13th: hdd after next: wknd bef 2 out: hit last* **6/1**[3]	
4443	**4**	*27*	**Make It Easy (IRE)**[9] [1832] 9-10-1 **65** ... (p) CaptLHorner(7)	16
			(D L Williams) *chsd ldrs: lost pl after 10th: nvr on terms or gng wl after: wl t.o fr 14th* **9/2**[2]	
5F03	**5**	*12*	**Lambrini Mist**[3] [1914] 7-10-3 **65** ... (b) DLaverty(5)	4
			(Mrs L Williamson) *u.p in midfield fr 6th: wknd 13th: wl t.o fr next: blnd 4 out* **9/1**	
400	**P**		**Dark Rum**[18] [1725] 9-10-10 **77** ... JKington(10)	—
			(M Scudamore) *j. ponderously and sn wl in rr: detached in last pair 5th: t.o whn p.u bef 12th* **12/1**	
U0/F	**P**		**New Leader (IRE)**[14] [1776] 8-10-8 **65** ... MBatchelor	—
			(Mrs L Richards) *hld up: prog 8th: blnd next: mstke 11th and wknd: mstke next: p.u bef 13th* **16/1**	
00-0	**P**		**Billy Coleman (IRE)**[15] [1750] 7-10-4 **64** ... RYoung(3)	—
			(D Brace) *w ldr: led 4th to 7th: styd pressing ldr tl mstke 13th and wknd v rapidly: t.o whn p.u bef next* **33/1**	
/34P	**U**		**Alabaster**[9] [1832] 10-9-7 **57** oh1 ... RLucey-Butler(7)	—
			(N J Hawke) *sn detached in last pair: tried to cl on main gp 10th: outpcd 12th: wnt poor 4th whn mstke and uns rdr 13th* **9/1**	

6m 54.2s (0.20) **Going Correction** -0.05s/f (Good) **9** Ran SP% **113.4**
Speed ratings: **97,95,86,77,74** —,—,—,— CSF £16.46 CT £69.31 TOTE £4.60: £1.20, £2.30, £2.60; EX 18.10.
Owner K C B Mackenzie **Bred** Navan Stables **Trained** Melplash, Dorset

FOCUS
A very weak handicap, which saw the field finish well strung out behind the comfortable winner who could have scored by further, and the form amongst the principals is fair.

NOTEBOOK
Five Alley(IRE) ◆, runner-up over course and distance on his penultimate outing, had disappointed subsequently when having blinkers re-applied at Wincanton, yet showed his true colours this time and belatedly opened his account under Rules in ready fashion. He was given a patient and well-judged ride by Thomas, looked better the further he went, and clearly appreciated the softer ground. While this race took little winning, he did to defy top weight and is certainly at *the right end of the handicap to progress further this term.Official explanation: trainer's representative said, regarding the improved form shown, gelding may have resented wearing blinkers last time out (op 11-4 tchd 4-1)*
Hill Forts Henry turned in a sound effort under a positive ride, but had no answer to the winner's challenge and was readily held. He was a long way clear of the remainder, however, and looks up to going one better off this mark if found a similar event in the coming weeks. *(op 4-1)*
St Kilda was a spent force prior to blundering at the final fence, yet still turned in a more encouraging display than on her comeback nine days previously. She is hard to predict, but could build on this and may prefer a slightly faster surface. *(op 11-2)*
Make It Easy(IRE) ran in snatches and failed to rate a threat at any stage. He probably requires faster ground. *(op 7-1)*

1952 PLUMPTON RACECOURSE NOVICES' CLAIMING HURDLE (9 hdls) 2m
3:10 (3:15) (Class 4) 4-Y-0+ **£2,576** (£736; £368)

Form				RPR
0	**1**		**Barking Mad (USA)**[6] [1235] 7-11-4 ... PHide	105+
			(J R Boyle) *nt j.w: mde all and sn clr: in n.d after 3 out* **15/2**[2]	
	2	*26*	**Somewhere My Love**[9] 4-9-8 ... RLucey-Butler(7)	62
			(P Butler) *hld up: outpcd 5th: wl bhd next: prog 3 out: wnt 2nd bef 2 out: no ch w wnr: hit last* **66/1**	
F005	**3**	*11*	**Waziya**[19] [1712] 6-10-1 70 ... (p) DCrosse	51
			(Mrs L Williamson) *chsd ldrs: outpcd 5th: t.o next: plugged on past wkng rivals fr 2 out* **40/1**	
F	**4**	*12*	**Milk And Sultana**[15] [1750] 5-10-4 ... EDehdashti(7)	49
			(G A Ham) *t.k.h: hld up: prog to chse wnr 6th: no imp: wknd 3 out* **16/1**	
	5	*3*	**Buthaina (IRE)**[18] 5-9-8 ... TMessenger(7)	36
			(Mrs L Williamson) *plld hrd: hld up in rr: prog after 5th: chsd wnr and blnd 3 out: wknd bef next: nrly uns rdr last: v tired* **66/1**	
0F-	**P**		**Paddy Boy (IRE)**[258] [3859] 4-10-5 ... (p) CBolger(3)	—
			(J R Boyle) *plld hrd: trckd ldrs tl wknd 4th: t.o whn p.u bef 6th* **25/1**	
P	**P**		**Queenstown (IRE)**[14] [1772] 4-11-3 ... (p) DLaverty(5)	—
			(B A Pearce) *nt j.w: sn struggling in rr: t.o after 4th: p.u after 6th* **40/1**	
P424	**P**		**Kristoffersen**[30] [1596] 5-11-4 109 ... (p) RJohnson	—
			(Ian Williams) *trckd ldrs: rdn after 4th: rel to r and sn t.o: p.u bef 6th* **2/5**[1]	
3/40	**P**		**Autumn Fantasy (USA)**[57] [1406] 6-10-8 88 ... (bt1) MBatchelor	—
			(M R Hoad) *mostly chsd wnr to 6th: wknd rapidly: t.o whn p.u bef 2 out* **14/1**[3]	

4m 11.7s (10.50) **Going Correction** +0.225s/f (Yiel)
WFA 4 from 5yo+ 13lb **9** Ran SP% **107.5**
Speed ratings: **82,69,63,57,56** —,—,—,— CSF £318.26 TOTE £7.20: £1.40, £9.40, £5.70; EX 210.20.The winner was claimed by Mr C. R. Dore for £10,000.
Owner M Khan X2 **Bred** Andrade Farm **Trained** Epsom, Surrey

FOCUS
A very slow winning time, 9.4 seconds slower than the opener, and the form is most dubious with the favourite running no sort of race.

NOTEBOOK
Barking Mad(USA) , unplaced on the Flat six days previously, failed to jump with any real fluency, but still ran out a most decisive winner and opened his account over timber at the second attempt. He did well to last home in this testing ground, and could do no more than score as he did, but his task was made simple as Kristoffersen ran no sort of race. *(op 7-1)*
Somewhere My Love , out of form on the Flat this year and rated just 40 in that sphere, ran on to finish a clear second and is entitled to improve for the experience. However, she has clearly already found her level over timber. *(op 40-1)*
Waziya , beaten in selling company the last twice, merely kept on at the same pace throughout and continues to run well below her rating. *(op 33-1)*
Milk And Sultana *(op 14-1)*
Kristoffersen , who had an obvious chance on official figures, ran a lifeless race in first-time cheekpieces and must rate bitterly disappointing. He needs a faster surface, but is clearly one to avoid at present on this evidence. *Official explanation: trainer's representative had no explanation for the poor form shown (tchd 4-11, 4-9 in places)*

1953 GUINNESS H'CAP CHASE (14 fncs) 2m 4f
3:40 (3:42) (Class 4) (0-110,110) 5-Y-0+ **£3,788** (£1,552; £869)

Form			Horse	Jockey	RPR
12-2	**1**		**Master D'Or (FR)**[187] [54] 5-10-11 **95** (P J Hobbs) *nt fluent early: hld up last: lft in 3rd and sltly hmpd 10th: wnt 2nd 2 out: led last: pushed clr* **5/4**[1]	RJohnson	114+
1/0-	**2**	*9*	**Manawanui**[542] [209] 7-11-5 **103** (R H Alner) *mde most: mstke 3 out: hdd last: easily outpcd flat* **7/1**	AThornton	112+
123-	**3**	*8*	**Myson (IRE)**[200] [4836] 6-11-6 **104** (D B Feek) *trckd ldrs: sltly hmpd and lft 2nd 10th: rdn and wknd 2 out* **7/2**[2]	JamesDavies	102
F1P-	**B**		**Haafel (USA)**[222] [4517] 8-11-12 **110** (G L Moore) *w ldr tl after 9th: cl 3rd whn b.d 10th* **14/1**	PHide	—
F-2	**F**		**Harry Collins**[180] [183] 7-11-7 **110** (B I Case) *wl in tch: effrt to chse ldr whn fell 10th* **8/1**	MNicolls[(5)]	—
03P-	**U**		**Royale Acadou (FR)**[22] [4405] 7-10-13 **100** (Mrs L J Mongan) *chsd ldrs: wl in tch whn bdly hmpd and uns rdr 10th* **50/1**	CBolger[(3)]	—
2P-3	**P**		**Lucky Sinna (IRE)**[27] [1631] 9-11-0 **98** (B G Powell) *racd wd: settled in last pair: in tch whn sltly hmpd 10th: wknd rapidly: p.u bef next* **13/2**[3]	TJMurphy	—

5m 14.4s (-4.05) **Going Correction** -0.05s/f (Good) **7** Ran SP% **112.2**
Speed ratings: **106,102,99,—,— —,—** CSF £10.32 TOTE £1.90: £1.80, £2.80; EX 17.80.
Owner Terry Warner **Bred** And Mrs M Vaultier **Trained** Withycombe, Somerset

FOCUS
A moderate handicap, run at a sound pace and the winner did the job nicely. The overall form should be treated with a degree of caution, however.

NOTEBOOK
Master D'Or(FR) ◆, whose sole success over hurdles came at this track in April, made a winning return to action and broke his duck over fences at the second attempt. He failed to impress with his early jumping, but got better as the race progressed, and should be rated value for further than his already wide winning margin. While this race ultimately took little winning, he should still look well-treated in relation to his hurdling form despite a future weight rise, and further success in this division looks assured. *(op 7-4)*
Manawanui showed up well at the head of affairs until his jumping fell apart from three out and he had no answer to the winner's challenge over the final fence. This must still rate an encouraging return from a 542-day break and he will not always bump into such well-treated rivals as the winner in this class. *(op 13-2)*
Myson(IRE) ran as though this seasonal return was needed, and is slightly flattered by his finishing position, but should improve for the experience. *(op 4-1 tchd 10-3)*
Haafel(USA) was still going well enough when being brought down and would have likely bagged a place but for that incident. *(op 12-1)*
Lucky Sinna(IRE) ran well below his best and has a fair deal to prove after this. *(op 12-1)*

1954 LEOPARDSTOWN RACECOURSE MAIDEN OPEN NATIONAL HUNT FLAT RACE 2m 2f
4:10 (4:12) (Class 6) 4-6-Y-0 **£1,890** (£540; £270)

Form			Horse	Jockey	RPR
2-	**1**		**Mars Rock (FR)**[226] [4465] 5-11-2 (Miss Venetia Williams) *cl up: trckd ldr 1/2-way: led over 2f out: drvn and kpt on wl fr over 1f out* **5/4**[1]	SThomas	97+
	2	*2*	**River Ripples (IRE)**[253] 6-11-2 (T R George) *cl up: wnt 3rd 1/2-way: effrt to chal over 2f out: chsd wnr after: kpt on wl but a hld* **2/1**[2]	JMMaguire	95
0-	**3**	*7*	**Boardroom Fiddle (IRE)**[548] [130] 6-11-2 (Miss E C Lavelle) *racd freely early: led at fair pce: hdd and bmpd over 2f out: fdd over 1f out* **9/1**	BFenton	91+
	4	*2 ½*	**Break The Ice** 4-10-9 (L A Dace) *hld up: prog on outer 1/2-way to chse ldng trio: rdn and nt on terms 4f out: kpt on fnl 2f but no imp* **22/1**	TJMurphy	79
00-	**5**	*dist*	**Just Ask**[204] [4801] 5-10-9 (N R Mitchell) *in tch: pushed along over 6f out: wknd over 5f out: sn bhd: btn 43 l* **40/1**	JEMoore	—
6	**6**	*dist*	**Summer Liric**[14] [1777] 4-10-13 (J W Mullins) *mostly chsd ldr to 1/2-way: sn lost pl: wknd 6f out: t.o: btn 98 l* **8/1**[3]	RYoung[(3)]	—
	7	*23*	**Lord Musgrave (IRE)**[163] 6-10-9 (L Wells) *prom to 1/2-way: sn wknd and t.o: btn 121 l* **14/1**	MrJMorgan[(7)]	—
0-	**8**	*18*	**Ray Mond**[280] [3520] 4-10-9 (M J Gingell) *in tch to 1/2-way: sn wknd and t.o: btn 139 l* **66/1**	MrMatthewSmith[(7)]	—
	P		**Shikoku Lass (IRE)** 5-10-4 (Mrs S Wall) *fractious s: a last: rdn after 6f: t.o whn p.u 8f out* **50/1**	MNicolls[(5)]	—

4m 26.7s (1.95) **Going Correction** +0.225s/f (Yiel)
WFA 4 from 5yo+ 13lb **9** Ran SP% **115.8**
Speed ratings: **104,103,100,98,— —,—,—,—** CSF £3.74 TOTE £2.30: £1.10, £1.10, £2.60; EX 5.20 Place 6 £55.45, Place 5 £22.62.
Owner John Nicholls (Trading) Ltd **Bred** S C E A Haras De Mirande **Trained** Kings Caple, H'fords

FOCUS
A potentially fair bumper, run at a sound gallop, and the form makes sense.

NOTEBOOK
Mars Rock(FR) , runner-up on his sole outing last term at Uttoxeter, went for home two out - a move that proved decisive - and he stayed on well thereafter to open his account in dogged fashion. He is bred to be useful over jumps and left the impression he will stay further, so looks a fair prospect for novice hurdling this season. *(op 2-1 tchd 9-4, 5-2 in a place)*
River Ripples(IRE), a former winning Irish-pointer, was not surprisingly caught flat-footed when the winner asserted two from home yet stuck to his task and was closing on that rival at the finish. He is going to relish the return to further in due course and, while his future lies over fences, is another who rates an interesting prospect for novice hurdling this term. *(tchd 7-4)*
Boardroom Fiddle(IRE) , who failed to make an impression on his debut 548 days previously, ran freely at the head of affairs and ultimately paid for those exertions when the race got serious at the top of the home straight. This was a much more encouraging effort, however, and he should be seen to better effect when faced with a stiffer test in due course. *(op 6-1)*
Break The Ice , out of a winning pointer, ran green and was doing all of her best work at the finish. She needs a stiffer test and, like many of her yard's newcomers, will no doubt improve plenty for this debut experience. *(op 16-1)*
T/Plt: £122.20 to a £1 stake. Pool: £36,828.05. 219.95 winning tickets. T/Qpdt: £46.20 to a £1 stake. Pool: £2,699.00. 43.20 winning tickets. JN

[216]WARWICK (L-H)
Monday, October 31

OFFICIAL GOING: Good
Wind: Nil Weather: Fine

1955 BURGIS & BULLOCK'S CORPORATE FINANCE "HIGH FLYERS" JUVENILE NOVICES' HURDLE (8 hdls) 2m
1:20 (1:21) (Class 4) 3-Y-O **£3,412** (£975; £487)

Form			Horse	Jockey	RPR
F	**1**		**Le Corvee (IRE)**[2] [1923] 3-10-12 (A King) *hld up: hdwy 3 out: led last: pushed out* **10/11**[1]	RThornton	105+
	2	*½*	**Bayard (USA)**[17] 3-10-12 (J R Fanshawe) *a.p: led 3 out to 2 out: hrd rdn: r.o* **9/2**[2]	APMcCoy	98+
	3	*5*	**Rawaabet (IRE)**[28] 3-10-12 (P W Hiatt) *hld up in rr: mstke 1st: hdwy after 3 out: ev ch whn hit last: wknd* **12/1**	MFoley	94+
6	**4**	*23*	**Theflyingscottie**[23] [1679] 3-10-7 (J D Frost) *hld up and bhd: rdn 5th: sme hdwy fr 3 out: n.d* **16/1**	CHonour[(5)]	70
	5	*1 ½*	**Mickey Pearce (IRE)**[27] 3-10-9 (J G M O'Shea) *plld hrd and bhd: hdwy whn mstke 3 out: sn wknd* **50/1**	ONelmes[(3)]	69
P0	**6**	*hd*	**Cloonavery (IRE)**[11] [1802] 3-10-12 (B Llewellyn) *prom tl wknd after 3 out* **28/1**	ChristianWilliams	68
	7	*4*	**Garhoud**[196] 3-10-12 (Miss K M George) *hld up in mid-div: rdn after 4th: bhd fr 3 out* **11/1**	GLee	64
	8	*dist*	**Halcyon Express (IRE)**[95] 3-10-5 (Mary Meek) *hld up in mid-div: mstke 3 out: sn struggling: t.o* **50/1**	(t) CMStudd[(7)]	—
PF	**9**	*7*	**Harry's Simmie (IRE)**[11] [1802] 3-10-5 (R C Harper) *a bhd: t.o* **100/1**	RGreene	—
0	**P**		**Inagh**[11] [1802] 3-9-12 (R C Harper) *prom: wknd qckly and nt fluent 4th: t.o whn p.u bef 2 out* **100/1**	JPritchard[(7)]	—
5	**F**		**Able Charlie (GER)**[16] [1737] 3-10-12 (Mrs Tracey Barfoot-Saunt) *t.k.h: led to 3 out: 4th and wkng whn fell 2 out* **9/1**[3]	HOliver	82
	P		**Brazen Hooker (IRE)**[43] 3-10-5 (Ms Joanna Morgan, Ire) *plld hrd: sn prom: chsd ldr after 2nd: wkng whn mstke 3 out: t.o whn p.u bef 2 out* **33/1**	PMoloney	—

3m 48.1s (-10.20) **Going Correction** -0.675s/f (Firm) **12** Ran SP% **114.8**
Speed ratings: **98,97,95,83,83 82,80,—,—,— —,—** CSF £4.55 TOTE £1.80: £1.10, £2.00, £2.60; EX 6.70.
Owner David Mason **Bred** Forenaghts Stud And David O'Reilly **Trained** Barbury Castle, Wilts

FOCUS
An average juvenile hurdle. The form is suspect but the front three were clear of the remainder and are probably worth following at a sensible level.

NOTEBOOK
Le Corvee(IRE), who only got as far as the second hurdle on his debut at Wetherby at the weekend, was making a quick reappearance and was clearly none the worse for his experience. Although by a sprinter, he stayed ten furlongs on the Flat and is viewed by King as one of his nicer juvenile prospects. Given a confident ride by Thornton, he made hard enough work of winning, but this will do great things for his confidence and it would not surprise to see him step up on this next time. *(op 11-10 tchd 6-5)*
Bayard(USA), a modest sort on limited evidence on the Flat, is evidently going to make a better hurdler and he made the favourite work for his win. He was clear of the third at the line and it will be surprising if he can not find a similar race before Christmas. *(op 4-1)*
Rawaabet(IRE) was not bad at all on the level at trips of around a mile, and he made a highly satisfactory hurdling debut. Having travelled strongly, he held every chance in the straight, but a mistake at the last ended any chance he had and he weakened on the run-in. There are races to be won with him over hurdles. *(tchd 14-1)*
Theflyingscottie finished well adrift of the front three and will find things easier in a lower grade. *(op 12-1)*
Mickey Pearce(IRE) did not get home having pulled hard and is going to have to learn to settle better. *(op 40-1)*
Able Charlie(GER) was in the process of running a really good race, but was beaten, when falling at the second last. He can win a small race as long as this does not affect his confidence too much. *(tchd 8-1)*

1956 BURGIS & BULLOCK'S FINANCIAL PLANNING "TAX SLASHERS" H'CAP CHASE (12 fncs) 2m 110y
1:50 (1:50) (Class 4) (0-105,101) 5-Y-O+ **£3,744** (£1,152; £576; £288)

Form			Horse	Jockey	RPR
6422	**1**		**Romany Dream**[15] [1754] 7-11-3 **92** (R Dickin) *sn chsng ldr: led 7th tl mstke 3 out: sn led again: rdn clr appr last: r.o wl* **5/2**[2]	(b) WHutchinson	101+
P04P	**2**	*3*	**Kaikovra (IRE)**[16] [1746] 9-10-11 **86** (M F Harris) *led to 7th: sn rdn: led briefly 3 out: one pce fr 2 out* **33/1**	PJBrennan	88+
-23P	**3**	*5*	**Wild Power (GER)**[75] [1236] 7-11-5 **97** (Mrs H R J Nelmes) *prom: hit 4th: lost pl 8th: rallied appr 2 out: swtchd lft flat: eased whn btn towards fin* **6/1**[3]	ONelmes[(3)]	95+
0P34	**4**	*1 ¾*	**Bearaway (IRE)**[15] [1754] 8-11-7 **101** (Mrs H Dalton) *hld up: hit 2nd: stdy hdwy 4th: one pce fr 3 out* **9/4**[1]	(t) PCO'Neill[(5)]	95
0200	**5**	*5*	**Saorsie**[8] [1856] 7-11-8 **97** (J C Fox) *hld up: hdwy 6th: rdn 4 out: wknd after 3 out* **20/1**	SCurran	86
0-0U	**6**	*2 ½*	**Kinkeel (IRE)**[11] [1805] 6-10-12 **87** (A W Carroll) *hld up: hdwy 7th: ev ch appr 2 out: sn rdn and wknd* **14/1**	AntonyEvans	74
4346	**L**		**Young Owen**[15] [1754] 7-11-4 **93** (A G Juckes) *ref to r: tk no part* **9/1**	JMogford	—
2415	**P**		**The Mighty Sparrow (IRE)**[8] [1860] 12-11-6 **95** (A E Jones) *prom: blnd and lost pl 4th: hit 5th and 6th: t.o whn p.u bef 7th* **7/1**	(p) MFoley	—

4m 0.50s (-2.10) **Going Correction** -0.675s/f (Firm) **8** Ran SP% **110.5**
Speed ratings: **77,75,73,72,70 68,—,—** CSF £57.66 CT £423.34 TOTE £3.80: £1.40, £6.40, £1.60; EX 130.20.

Owner The Snoozy Partnership **Bred** Mrs P Nicholson **Trained** Atherstone on Stour, Warwicks

FOCUS

A very slow winning time. This was fair form for the grade though and could be rated higher as Romany Dream was value for further.

NOTEBOOK

Romany Dream was 2lb higher than when runner-up at Hereford to Welsh Main, who has since franked the form. She jumped soundly, bar an error three from home which briefly lost her the lead, and came away for a decisive win. She was value for further. *(op 11-4 tchd 3-1)*

Kaikovra(IRE) ran his best race since returning from over a year on the sidelines. Although keen in the early stages, as is often the case, he was staying on at the end and it could be that a stiffer track is required. *(tchd 40-1)*

Wild Power(GER), who failed to stay two and a half miles last time, was 5lb lower and minus cheekpieces here. After losing his pitch in the back straight, he rallied on the home turn but was on the retreat again before the last. *(op 13-2 tchd 7-1 and 11-2)*

Bearaway(IRE), successful in this last year when 4lb higher, was behind today's winner at Hereford and a 5lb pull was not enough to turn things around. He is not firing this term but probably needs a truly-run race. *(op 2-1)*

Saorsie, making his chasing debut in a handicap, was no threat over the last four fences. *(op 16-1)*

Kinkeel(IRE) was right there on the final turn, but did not seem to get home and could have stamina limitations. *(op 12-1)*

The Mighty Sparrow(IRE) lost his place and his confidence after consecutive jumping errors and was pulled up. *Official explanation: trainer said gelding had bled from the nose (tchd 6-1)*

Young Owen planted himself as the runners were called in, but the starter still let them go as the front rank approached ready to jump off. *(tchd 6-1)*

1957 BURGIS & BULLOCK'S "GO FOR GROWTH" H'CAP HURDLE (8 hdls) 2m

2:20 (2:21) (Class 4) (0-110,106) 4-Y-0+ **£3,433** (£981; £490)

Form RPR

33U0 **1** **Lord Lington (FR)**[29] 1610 6-11-12 **106** WMarston 116+
(D J Wintle) *hld up and bhd: hdwy 5th: led appr 2 out: r.o wl* **20/1**

500- **2** *3 ½* **Lerubis (FR)**[304] 3123 6-10-7 **87** LAspell 92+
(F Jordan) *hld up and bhd: hdwy appr 3 out: swtchd rt appr last: r.o flat: nt trble wnr* **40/1**

260- **3** *2* **Just Superb**[280] 3519 6-11-4 **103** TGreenway(5) 105
(P A Pritchard) *hld up in tch: hdwy appr 5th: kpt on same pce flat* **10/1**

10-0 **4** *nk* **Honey's Gift**[10] 1816 6-11-9 **103** APMcCoy 104
(G G Margarson) *hld up: rdn and hdwy on ins appr 2 out: kpt on one pce flat* **8/1**

41 **5** *nk* **Sir Night (IRE)**[29] 1604 5-11-7 **101** BHarding 102
(Jedd O'Keeffe) *hld up in tch: hdwy 4th: rdn appr 2 out: no ex flat* **9/2**[1]

35-5 **6** *3* **Fortune Point (IRE)**[23] 1668 7-11-4 **98** WHutchinson 98+
(A W Carroll) *chsd ldr: led appr 5th to 3 out: wknd flat* **33/1**

FP-0 **7** *½* **Rocket Bleu (FR)**[186] 75 5-10-4 **89** LStephens(5) 88+
(D Burchell) *hld up: hdwy 3rd: led 3 out tl appr 2 out: wknd flat* **20/1**

643/ **8** *5* **Pawn Broker**[39] 2914 8-11-8 **102** (b) MFoley 95
(Miss J R Tooth) *hld up and bhd: hit 4th: short-lived effrt after 3 out* **10/1**

00P- **9** *2 ½* **Haditovski**[194] 4926 9-11-11 **105** (v) GLee 95
(J Mackie) *prom tl wknd 3 out* **7/1**[3]

000- **10** *2 ½* **Birchall (IRE)**[232] 4343 6-10-8 **88** CLlewellyn 76
(Ian Williams) *sn bhd* **7/1**[3]

410- **11** *1 ¼* **Killing Me Softly**[194] 4926 4-11-6 **100** (v) ChristianWilliams 86
(J Gallagher) *prom tl wknd 5th* **25/1**

2106 **12** *½* **Sharaab (USA)**[16] 1747 4-10-13 **93** (t) PMoloney 79
(D E Cantillon) *hld up in mid-div: hdwy 4th: wknd 3 out* **20/1**

304- **P** **Mcqueen (IRE)**[9] 4164 5-10-13 **98** PCO'Neill(5) —
(Mrs H Dalton) *prom: rdn 5th: sn wknd: bhd whn p.u bef 2 out* **11/2**[2]

535- **P** **Greenawn (IRE)**[317] 2880 6-11-3 **97** PJBrennan —
(M Sheppard) *led: hit 4th: sn hdd: wknd 3 out: bhd whn p.u bef 2 out* **14/1**

3m 44.4s (-13.90) **Going Correction** -0.675s/f (Firm)
WFA 4 from 5yo+ 13lb 14 Ran SP% **118.0**
Speed ratings: **107,105,104,104,103 102,102,99,98,97 96,96,—,—** CSF £598.97 CT £8179.32 TOTE £29.50: £8.60, £20.20, £3.60; EX 2484.00.

Owner Ocean Trailers Ltd **Bred** G Cherel **Trained** Naunton, Gloucs

FOCUS

The pace was sound and hold-up horses were favoured. The winner has been rated as value for around 6l and the form should work out well enough.

NOTEBOOK

Lord Lington(FR), held up in last place for the first part of the race before making rapid headway, came widest in the home straight to strike the front and scored comfortably. He was value for further and this was an improvement on his recent form. *Official explanation: trainer said, regarding the improved form shown, gelding was suited by the stronger pace of today's race (op 16-1)*

Lerubis(FR), whose most recent run was on New Year's Eve, ran his best race since his debut in this country. Making eye-catching progress from the back of the field, he was switched past toiling rivals on the run to the last and kept on steadily without promising to reach the winner. If he can reproduce this form he should be up to winning a little race. *(op 33-1)*

Just Superb ran a sound race on this first run since January and has now been placed on his last five visits to Warwick. He is capable of winning off this mark. *(op 9-1)*

Honey's Gift, sharper for her recent reappearance, was being strongly ridden on the home turn and kept plugging away. Both her wins have been at Fontwell. *(op 10-1 tchd 11-1)*

Sir Night(IRE) ran his race but the 7lb rise for his Kelso win eventually told. He needs decent ground so is unlikely to have his conditions too often in the coming weeks. *(op 6-1)*

Fortune Point(IRE) had not shown much over hurdles for some time but this was a more encouraging effort.

Rocket Bleu(FR), beaten favourite in a seller on his latest run in April, made a satisfactory return to action. *(tchd 25-1)*

Mcqueen(IRE) *Official explanation: jockey said gelding never travelled (op 7-2)*

1958 SYSTIMAX SOLUTIONS BUSINESSPARTNER NOVICES' CHASE (12 fncs) 2m 110y

2:50 (2:50) (Class 3) 4-Y-0+ **£7,101** (£2,185; £1,092; £546)

Form RPR

140- **1** **Cerium (FR)**[207] 4749 4-10-5 PJBrennan 121+
(P F Nicholls) *a.p: mstke 4th: wnt 2nd 6th: led 2 out: drvn out* **11/10**[1]

251/ **2** *1* **Garde Champetre (FR)**[578] 4629 6-11-4 APMcCoy 133+
(Jonjo O'Neill) *hld up: hdwy 6th: hit 7th: rdn appr 2 out: kpt on flat* **6/4**[2]

125- **3** *9* **Neltina**[192] 4974 9-11-3 110 LAspell 124+
(Mrs J E Scrase) *led to 2 out: wknd flat* **9/1**[3]

10-4 **4** *17* **Goblin**[18] 1726 4-10-5 PMoloney 93
(D E Cantillon) *hmpd s: hld up: no hdwy fr 8th* **22/1**

-066 **5** *4* **Wilfred (IRE)**[57] 1413 4-10-5 RThornton 89
(Jonjo O'Neill) *hld up: mstke 6th: n.d after* **25/1**

0LP4 **6** *21* **Dabus**[3] 1911 10-11-4 99 (b) KJohnson 81
(M C Chapman) *rel to r: a in rr* **100/1**

-35P **7** *11* **Nuit Sombre (IRE)**[23] 1675 5-11-1 ONelmes(3) 70
(J G M O'Shea) *chsd ldr: lost 2nd and j.slowly 6th: wknd 7th* **40/1**

3m 55.5s (-7.10) **Going Correction** -0.675s/f (Firm)
WFA 4 from 5yo+ 13lb 7 Ran SP% **109.2**
Speed ratings: **89,88,84,76,74 64,59** CSF £2.83 TOTE £2.20: £1.40, £1.60; EX 3.70.

Owner B Fulton, T Hayward, S Fisher, L Brady **Bred** Sarl Haras De Saint-Faust And Andre-Paul Larrieu **Trained** Ditcheat, Somerset

FOCUS

This was a decent novice event but it was a very slow winning time for a race of its class. The first two were both around a stone off their best hurdles form.

NOTEBOOK

Cerium(FR) ◆, one of last season's leading juvenile hurdlers, made a bright start to his chasing career. Jumping well, bar an error at the first ditch which was attributed to the sun getting in his eyes, he showed in front at the second last and saw off the late challenge of his market rival. Easier ground will suit him and the Arkle is a viable target for the season. *(op 8-11 tchd 6-5 in places)*

Garde Champetre(FR) ◆, winner of a Grade Two novices' hurdle at Aintree in April 2004 on his last appearance, was sold out of Paul Nicholls' yard for a cool 530,000gns at Doncaster shortly afterwards. He did not jump as fluently as the winner, to whom he was conceding 13lb, and was a bit outpaced by the leading pair on the turn out of the back straight, but he rallied to good effect and was running on strongly at the finish. He looks a smart recruit to chasing and will benefit greatly from a return to two and a half miles. *(op 5-2)*

Neltina jumped soundly in front and was only seen off from the second last. She stays further and could win a handicap if her current mark is left unchanged. *(tchd 8-1 and 10-1)*

Goblin was never within hailing distance of the principals, but he faced a stiff task and ran to the form of his recent chasing debut. *(op 20-1 tchd 16-1)*

Wilfred(IRE), O'Neill's second string, went without the blinkers on this chasing debut. He was never in the hunt but the experience will not be lost on him.

Nuit Sombre(IRE), making his chase debut, raced in second place until a slow jump at the sixth saw him drop rapidly back through the field. *(op 33-1)*

1959 B&B'S "MAKE IT AND KEEP IT" "NATIONAL HUNT" NOVICES' HURDLE (12 hdls) 3m 1f

3:20 (3:20) (Class 4) 4-Y-0+ **£3,412** (£975; £487)

Form RPR

02-1 **1** **Jackson (FR)**[186] 73 8-11-4 125 RThornton 109+
(A King) *hld up in tch: reminders 5th: hit 3 out: sn rdn: led appr 2 out: all out* **9/4**[2]

12-1 **2** *hd* **Harry Blade**[40] 1508 6-11-4 CLlewellyn 109+
(N A Twiston-Davies) *a.p: rdn and ev ch whn mstke 2 out: rallied flat: styd on* **9/2**[3]

161- **3** *3* **Sunset Light (IRE)**[232] 4344 7-11-4 TDoyle 106+
(C Tinkler) *led: mstke 6th: hit 9th: rdn and hdd appr 2 out: no ex flat* **15/8**[1]

000- **4** *14* **Running Lord (IRE)**[237] 4241 7-10-12 TScudamore 84
(D A Rees) *hld up in tch: w ldr whn hit 6th: rdn after 7th: wknd appr 8th* **150/1**

50 **5** *18* **Aitchjayem**[8] 1854 5-10-5 MrJAJenkins(7) 66
(H J Manners) *bhd fr 4th* **150/1**

0-P **6** *shd* **Runshan (IRE)**[29] 1608 5-10-12 PMoloney 66
(D G Bridgwater) *hld up and bhd: hdwy 8th: wknd 3 out* **100/1**

00/0 **7** *17* **It's Official (IRE)**[14] 1775 6-10-12 79 RGreene 49
(Miss A M Newton-Smith) *nt j.w: a bhd* **100/1**

P **Mr Bently**[163] 6-10-7 CHonour(5) —
(J D Frost) *a bhd: t.o whn p.u bef 8th* **50/1**

260- **P** **Lin D'Estruval (FR)**[319] 2853 6-10-12 JAMcCarthy —
(C P Morlock) *hld up: stmbld path after 6th: hdwy appr 8th: wknd appr 9th: bhd whn p.u bef 2 out* **14/1**

324- **P** **Grande Creole (FR)**[198] 4866 6-10-12 109 ChristianWilliams —
(P F Nicholls) *hld up and bhd: hdwy appr 7th: rdn appr 8th: sn wknd: bhd whn p.u bef 2 out* **5/1**

6m 8.20s (-22.10) **Going Correction** -0.675s/f (Firm) 10 Ran SP% **112.3**
Speed ratings: **108,107,106,102,96 96,91,—,—,—** CSF £12.50 TOTE £3.70: £1.70, £1.30, £1.10; EX 13.30.

Owner C B Brookes **Bred** Mme Yves Priouzeau **Trained** Barbury Castle, Wilts

FOCUS

The three penalised winners finished clear of the remainder. The race could have been rated a stone higher using the first and third.

NOTEBOOK

Jackson(FR) nipped through on the inside turning for home to show ahead and looked likely to win by a couple of lengths over the final flight, but his lead was being reduced on the run-in. He is a winning pointer and has previous experience over fences, so a return to chasing looks likely. *(tchd 11-4)*

Harry Blade, a close third when making an error at the penultimate flight, rallied to good effect and almost pulled the race out of the fire. He certainly stayed this longer trip. *(op 7-2)*

Sunset Light(IRE), successful on easier ground over course and distance in March, ran a decent race on this return to action. He set a sound pace until headed on the home turn and finished well clear of the remainder. *(op 9-4)*

Running Lord(IRE) was merely best of the rest but did show slightly more than he had on his hurdling debut. *(op 125-1 tchd 100-1)*

Aitchjayem *Official explanation: jockey said gelding finished lame (op 100-1)*

Runshan(IRE), placed in an Irish point, showed a glimmer of ability on this second run over hurdles. *(op 80-1)*

Grande Creole(FR) disappointed on his final run of last season and it was a similar story here. *(tchd 11-2)*

1960 B&B'S "TEAM MEMBER OF THE YEAR" H'CAP CHASE (20 fncs) 3m 2f

3:50 (3:50) (Class 4) (0-100,97) 5-Y-0+ **£3,486** (£996; £498)

Form RPR

P-P2 **1** **Midnight Gunner**[14] 1778 11-11-12 **97** APMcCoy 120+
(A E Price) *mde most to 7th: led 12th: drew clr fr 15th: eased considerably flat: unchal* **15/2**

-55P **2** *14* **Channahrlie (IRE)**[144] 694 11-10-10 **81** (p) WHutchinson 79
(R Dickin) *a.p: led 7th to 9th: one pce fr 15th* **12/1**

PP22 **3** *¾* **Lost In Normandy (IRE)**[29] 1615 8-10-0 **71** (b) TScudamore 68
(Mrs L Williamson) *a.p: led 9th to 12th: mstke 15th: one pce* **7/1**[3]

05-2 **4** *½* **Cool Song**[19] 1713 9-9-9 **71** oh3 WKennedy(5) 68
(Miss Suzy Smith) *hld up: stdy hdwy 4th: rdn 12th: outpcd appr 14th: styd on fr 2 out* **5/1**[1]

40-P **5** *19* **Noel's Pride**[34] 1568 9-11-1 **86** PJBrennan 71+
(C C Bealby) *prom: rdn appr 6th: wknd 14th* **14/1**

006P **6** *7* **Rufius (IRE)**[9] 1832 12-10-0 **71** oh23 (t) CLlewellyn 42
(P Kelsall) *mstke 6th: a bhd* **66/1**

40-U **7** *1 ¾* **Jackie Boy (IRE)**[19] 1713 6-11-4 **89** AntonyEvans 65+
(N A Twiston-Davies) *hld up: hdwy appr 14th: mstke 4 out: 4th and no ch w wnr whn blnd 3 out* **14/1**

/001 **8** *25* **Corkan (IRE)**[91] [1122] 11-9-11 **71** oh2.............................(p) TJMalone(3) 15
(A M Hales) *prom tl wknd 13th* **12/1**

P32P **P** **Vandante (IRE)**[29] [1615] 9-10-13 **84**.. RThornton —
(R Lee) *a bhd: t.o whn p.u bef 2 out* **12/1**

3P-3 **P** **House Warmer (IRE)**[25] [1656] 6-10-8 **79**..................................(t) LAspell —
(A Ennis) *a bhd: mstke 8th: t.o whn p.u after 13th* **11/1**

6113 **S** **Tudor King (IRE)**[18] [1728] 11-11-8 **93**.. GLee —
(Andrew Turnell) *bhd: nt fluent 10th: slipped up bnd appr 11th* **6/1**[2]

20/P **P** **Montemoss (IRE)**[8] [1854] 8-11-12 **97**.. RGreene —
(B N Pollock) *sn rdn along: bhd whn mstke 5th: lost tch 11th: t.o whn p.u bef 3 out* **33/1**

32-5 **P** **Apple Joe**[9] [1832] 9-10-9 **80**.. ChristianWilliams —
(A J Whiting) *prom: led briefly whn j.slowly 4th: j.slowly 5th: wknd 13th: t.o whn p.u bef 14th* **8/1**

6m 39.9s (-24.10) **Going Correction** -0.675s/f (Firm) **13** Ran SP% **115.5**
Speed ratings: **110,105,105,105,99 97,96,89,—,— —,—,—** CSF £90.56 CT £658.40 TOTE £5.70: £2.90, £4.70, £2.00; EX 51.70.

Owner M G Racing **Bred** Miss S Bather **Trained** Leominster, H'fords

FOCUS
A decent winning time for a race of its type. An ordinary race formwise though, and the easy winner has been rated value for 25l.

NOTEBOOK
Midnight Gunner bounced back to form to gain his first win since April 2003. Jumping well, he drew right away in the back straight and was never seriously challenged. He is set for a hefty rise back up the handicap now and will not always have things his own way like he did here. *(op 6-1)*

Channahrlie(IRE) finished a respectful distance behind the winner but this was still a reasonable effort on his first start since January. He has become well handicapped.

Lost In Normandy(IRE), dropped 3lb after his two recent seconds, could not live with the eventual winner after a mistake at the second fence in the back straight. *(op 9-1)*

Cool Song was no threat over the last six fences but was staying on at the end. *(op 11-2 tchd 6-1)*

Jackie Boy(IRE) made some horrendous errors in the latter stages and Evans did well to get him round. *(op 12-1)*

1961 EBF/DONCASTER BLOODSTOCK SALES MARES' ONLY STANDARD OPEN NATIONAL HUNT FLAT RACE (QUALIFIER) 2m

4:20 (4:22) (Class 6) 4-6-Y-O **£1,939** (£554; £277)

Form RPR

1 **Sovietica (FR)** 4-11-0 .... RThornton 95
(S Pike) *carried lft s: hld up and bhd: stdy hdwy 9f out: rdn to ld wl over 1f out: r.o* **16/1**

2 *½* **Dillay Brook (IRE)** 5-11-0 .... APMcCoy 95
(T R George) *hld up in tch: rdn over 3f out: ev ch wl over 1f out: kpt on ins fnl f* **4/1**[2]

3 *3½* **Treaty Flyer (IRE)**[176] 4-11-0 .... LAspell 91
(P G Murphy) *hld up towards rr: hdwy over 7f out: rdn over 3f out: ev ch wl over 1f out: one pce fnl f* **7/1**

4 *8* **Solent Sunbeam** 5-11-0 .... TScudamore 83
(K C Bailey) *mid-div: styd on fnl 3f: nvr trbld ldrs* **14/1**

5 *3½* **Flirty Jill**[204] 4-11-0 .... TDoyle 82+
(P R Webber) *a.p: led 5f out: rdn and hdd wl over 1f out: wknd fnl f* **7/4**[1]

6 *7* **Miss Morfire** 5-10-7 .... MissLGardner(7) 73
(Mrs S Gardner) *hld up and bhd: hdwy over 6f out: wknd 4f out* **50/1**

60- **7** *8* **Bamby (IRE)**[255] [3925] 5-11-0 .... WMarston 65
(D J Wintle) *carried lft s: t.k.h towards rr: hdwy 8f out: rdn and wknd 3f out* **5/1**[3]

40-6 **8** *4* **Call Me Bobbi**[170] [349] 6-10-9 .... LStephens(5) 61
(Mrs S M Johnson) *chsd ldr: led over 6f out to 5f out: wknd over 3f out* **16/1**

00 **9** *6* **Double Grace (IRE)**[15] [1755] 5-11-0 .... AntonyEvans 55
(Mrs S Gardner) *led: hdd over 6f out: wknd over 4f out* **50/1**

10 *23* **Overjoyed** 4-10-9 .... WKennedy(5) 32
(Miss Suzy Smith) *wnt lft s: hld up and bhd: hdwy over 7f out: wknd 5f out* **20/1**

34- **11** *5* **Devon Blue (IRE)**[425] [1348] 6-10-7 .... CMStudd(7) 27
(Mrs J G Retter) *hld up in tch: wknd 8f out* **12/1**

12 *dist* **Spring Chick** 5-11-0 .... ChristianWilliams —
(A J Whiting) *mid-div: rdn after 7f: bhd fnl 9f: t.o* **66/1**

3m 45.0s (-13.80) **Going Correction** -0.675s/f (Firm)
WFA 4 from 5yo+ 13lb **12** Ran SP% **121.8**
Speed ratings: **107,106,105,101,99 95,91,89,86,75 72,—** CSF £79.69 TOTE £20.80: £3.60, £1.90, £2.20; EX 84.50 Place 6 £120.32, Place 5 £97.15.

Owner Stewart Pike **Bred** Stewart Pike **Trained** Sidbury, Devon

FOCUS
A good time for a bumper, though there is not much form to go on and it was probably a weakish race.

NOTEBOOK
Sovietica(FR), related to a couple of winners in France, was led out unsold at 6,000gns at Doncaster in August. After taking the shortest route into the home straight she knuckled down well in the drive to the line. *(tchd 18-1)*

Dillay Brook(IRE) is a half-sister to a winning hurdler out of a winning pointer who was placed in bumpers and over hurdles. She went down narrowly and will benefit from a greater test of stamina. *(op 3-1)*

Treaty Flyer(IRE) was successful on her debut in an Irish point-to-point in May. She ran well on her British debut, if still green, and will appreciate a longer trip when she goes over hurdles. *(op 8-1 tchd 6-1)*

Solent Sunbeam, out of a half-sister to useful staying chaser Rightsaidfred, was never a factor but passed beaten horses in the latter stages. *(op 20-1)*

Flirty Jill was bought for 40,000gns after landing an Irish point in April. She looked set to go on and win twice a couple of lengths to the good rounding the home turn, but was soon cut down. *(op 2-1 tchd 9-4)*

Bamby(IRE) has ability but needs to settle better if she is going to get home. *(op 7-1)*

T/Plt: £135.30 to a £1 stake. Pool: £32,579.00. 175.75 winning tickets. T/Qpdt: £57.50 to a £1 stake. Pool: £2,339.80. 30.10 winning tickets. KH

1962 - 1967a (Foreign Racing) - See Raceform Interactive

1779 EXETER (R-H)

Tuesday, November 1

OFFICIAL GOING: Chase course - good to soft (good in places); hurdle course - good to soft (soft in places)
Wind: Moderate; half behind Weather: Fine

1968 WILLIAMHILL.CO.UK "NATIONAL HUNT" NOVICES' HURDLE (8 hdls) 2m 1f

1:40 (1:42) (Class 3) 4-Y-0+ **£5,926** (£1,740; £870; £434)

Form RPR

32- **1** **Black Hills**[223] [4519] 6-10-12 ....(t) JAMcCarthy 115+
(J A Geake) *hld up and bhd: led 2 out: sn clr: rdn out* **8/1**[3]

2 **2** *12* **Private Be**[24] [1672] 6-10-12 .... RJohnson 109+
(P J Hobbs) *hung lft thrght: led tl appr 3 out: rdn and ev ch 2 out: eased whn btn flat* **10/11**[1]

22- **3** *7* **Autumn Red (IRE)**[227] [4451] 5-10-12 .... TDoyle 95
(P R Webber) *prom: reminders after 3rd: wknd 3 out* **9/2**[2]

5-3 **4** *1¾* **Sabreur**[177] [249] 4-10-12 .... RThornton 93
(Ian Williams) *hld up in mid-div: hdwy and mstke 5th: wknd appr 2 out* **25/1**

2- **5** *2½* **Love Supreme (IRE)**[236] [4297] 5-10-5 .... DJCasey 84
(C F Swan, Ire) *hld up and bhd: hdwy 5th: sn rdn: no real prog fr 3 out* **16/1**

130- **6** *9* **There Is No Doubt (FR)**[230] [4399] 4-10-5 .... MissLucyBridges(7) 82
(Miss Lucy Bridges) *mid-div: hdwy after 5th: wknd 3 out* **20/1**

001- **7** *3* **Hi Humpfree**[213] [4697] 5-10-7 .... PCO'Neill(5) 79
(Mrs H Dalton) *hld up in tch: hit 5th: sn rdn: wknd 3 out* **12/1**

0-P0 **8** *¾* **Bollitree Bob**[24] [1672] 4-10-12 .... BJCrowley 78
(M Scudamore) *hld up and bhd: short-lived effrt 5th* **100/1**

0 **9** *29* **Cornish Jack**[24] [1681] 5-10-7 .... CHonour(5) 49
(J D Frost) *a bhd* **100/1**

-230 **10** *2½* **Abragante (IRE)**[138] [764] 4-10-12 100.. TJMurphy 47
(M C Pipe) *a bhd* **20/1**

00-0 **11** *dist* **Waterloo Son (IRE)**[171] [343] 5-10-12 .... DElsworth —
(H D Daly) *hld up towards rr: short-lived effrt 5th: t.o* **100/1**

0 **P** **Lord West**[15] [1777] 4-10-12 .... RWalford —
(R H Alner) *bhd fr 4th: t.o whn p.u bef 3 out* **100/1**

6F0- **P** **Cockatoo Ridge**[520] [571] 8-10-9 .... RYoung(3) —
(N R Mitchell) *prom: rdn 3rd: wknd 4th: t.o whn p.u bef 3 out* **80/1**

00-0 **P** **Ben The Brave (IRE)**[12] [1799] 6-10-5 .... MrsLucyRowsell(7) —
(Mrs A M Thorpe) *a bhd: j.rt 3rd: t.o whn p.u bef 3 out* **200/1**

4- **P** **Tarzan Du Mesnil (FR)**[240] [4207] 4-10-12 .... PJBrennan —
(N J Hawke) *prom: rdn after 4th: wknd 5th: bhd whn p.u bef 3 out* **50/1**

100- **U** **Nice Horse (FR)**[206] [4774] 4-10-12 .... TScudamore 110+
(M C Pipe) *hld up in tch: wnt 2nd 4th: led appr 3 out: hdd whn blnd and uns rdr 2 out* **8/1**[3]

4m 12.0s (2.80) **Going Correction** +0.25s/f (Yiel)
WFA 4 from 5yo+ 12lb **16** Ran SP% **127.4**
Speed ratings: **103,97,94,93,92 87,86,86,72,71 —,—,—,—,— —** CSF £16.11 TOTE £9.50: £3.00, £1.10, £2.00; EX 26.60.

Owner The Kingfisher Partnership **Bred** Dr J M Leigh **Trained** Kimpton, Hants

FOCUS
A fair novice hurdle, won by a decent sort, that is likely to produce winners.

NOTEBOOK
Black Hills ◆, a strong, imposing type, is built for jumping and connections had toyed with the idea of sending him straight over fences. He was just about in charge when Nice Horse unseated Scudamore at the second last, but still impressed with the way he galloped clear. He has speed, as one would expect for a son of a Coventry Stakes winner, but he is going to appreciate further in time and looks up to defying a penalty before taking a step up in class. *(op 16-1)*

Private Be, a good second to subsequent winner Jeremy Cuddle Duck on his debut at Bangor, was soon sent into the lead by Johnson, but he made life hard for himself in continually wanting to hang left and in the end he was well beaten. It is clear he needs to go left-handed and should enjoy more luck going that way around. *(tchd 4-5, 11-10 and 6-5 in a place)*

Autumn Red(IRE) showed some decent form in two bumper starts last term and he made a reasonable start to his hurdling career. He needed to be given a couple of liveners at a fairly early stage of the race and is entitled to come on for this. *(op 6-1 tchd 7-1)*

Sabreur, who was not totally discredited in a couple of bumpers, loomed up menacingly turning into the straight, but he was left behind as soon as the principals quickened. He is likely to improve a good deal on this initial outing over hurdles once given an extra half a mile. *(op 20-1)*

Love Supreme(IRE), an interesting Irish raider, enjoyed plenty of experience in bumpers last season and she made a little late headway having been held up well in rear early. She is another for whom a rise in distance is going to help and she should find success in races restricted to her own sex. *(tchd 20-1)*

There Is No Doubt(FR), a winner here on his debut last season, went well for a long way before getting tired and is likely to leave this behind with the run under his belt *(op 14-1)*

Nice Horse(FR), who found himself a bit outclassed in both the Cheltenham and Aintree Festival Championship bumpers last season, found this a more realistic assignment for his hurdling debut and he was in the process of running a cracker when unshipping Scudamore. He would have finished second and should not be long in gaining compensation for top connections. *(op 12-1 tchd 14-1)*

1969 WILLIAM HILL 0800 44 40 40 NOVICES' HURDLE (10 hdls) 2m 3f

2:10 (2:11) (Class 3) 4-Y-0+ **£5,731** (£1,682; £841; £420)

Form RPR

-B22 **1** **Nippy Des Mottes (FR)**[14] [1784] 4-10-12 111..(t) RWalsh 115+
(P F Nicholls) *hld up and bhd: hdwy appr 5th: led on bit 2 out: clr whn hit last: v easily* **4/5**[1]

2 *15* **Galteemountain Boy (IRE)**[40] [1535] 5-10-12 ....(p) DJCasey 100
(C F Swan, Ire) *hld up in tch: led after 7th: rdn and hdd whn hit 2 out: no ch w wnr* **28/1**

04-3 **3** *25* **Flying Fuselier**[20] [1714] 6-10-12 .... RJohnson 80+
(P J Hobbs) *led tl after 3rd: prom tl wknd 3 out* **5/1**[3]

0-4 **4** *26* **Spring Junior (FR)**[161] [490] 4-10-12 .... PJBrennan 49
(P J Hobbs) *w ldr: rdn and ev ch appr 3 out: sn wknd* **25/1**

FP- **5** *shd* **Stoop To Conquer**[173] [3764] 5-10-12 .... RThornton 49
(A W Carroll) *t.k.h: mstkes: prom: led after 3rd tl after 7th: sn wknd* **11/4**[2]

0P0- **6** *27* **Russian Lord (IRE)**[274] [3627] 6-10-12 .... VSlattery 22
(V R A Dartnall) *hld up in tch: wknd 4th: t.o* **66/1**

56P/ **7** *¾* **Baron Blitzkrieg**[687] [2770] 7-10-12 .... TJMurphy 21
(D J Wintle) *t.k.h: a bhd: t.o* **40/1**

0/ **8** *11* **Phazar**[638] [3649] 5-10-12 .... JAMcCarthy 10
(N J Hawke) *a bhd: t.o* **50/1**

6 **P** **Life Estates**^{27} [1640] 5-10-7 .... CHonour(5) —
(J D Frost) *a bhd: t.o* **100/1**
F **Lady Percy**^{802} 5-10-5 .... JEMoore —
(V R A Dartnall) *fell 1st: dead* **66/1**
510- **U** **Wishin And Hopin**^{123} [4774] 4-10-12 .... BJCrowley —
(A G Newcombe) *nt j.w: in rr: hmpd 1st: j. bdly lft and uns rdr 3rd* **20/1**
4m 42.7s (1.80) **Going Correction** +0.25s/f (Yiel) **11** Ran SP% **119.3**
Speed ratings: **106,99,89,78,78 66,66,61,—,—** — CSF £31.57 TOTE £1.70: £1.10, £9.10, £1.50; EX 32.10.
Owner Paul Green **Bred** Mme J Poirier **Trained** Ditcheat, Somerset

FOCUS
A weak race for the course and Nippy Des Mottes had little trouble finally getting off the mark.

NOTEBOOK
Nippy Des Mottes(FR), in need of the outing when not finding as much as once looked likely on his reappearance at the course, was much straighter today and, having stalked the leaders, was allowed to stride on after the second last and put the race to bed in a matter of strides. He has already been schooled over fences and looks sure to improve once tackling them, but he can be placed to win again over hurdles first. *(op Evens)*
Galteemountain Boy(IRE), an Irish raider, was a sitting duck for the winner in the straight and was quickly picked off. He can find a small race, but is not one to go overboard about. *(op 25-1)*
Flying Fuselier ran well to a point, but was unable to improve on his reappearance third at Uttoxeter and ultimately disappointed with the way he dropped away. Handicaps are likely to provide a better winning opportunity for the son of Gunner B. *(tchd 9-2 and 11-2)*
Spring Junior(FR) was up there from the off, but he began to drop away as they approached the straight and is another for whom handicaps will help. *(op 20-1)*
Stoop To Conquer again failed to jump fluently and has yet to convince as a hurdler. *Official explanation: jockey said gelding was never jumping (tchd 5-2)*

1970 WILLIAM HILL HALDON GOLD CUP CHASE (LIMITED H'CAP) GRADE 2 (12 fncs) 2m 1f 110y
2:40 (2:43) (Class 1) 5-Y-0+
£37,063 (£13,903; £6,961; £3,471; £1,742; £871)

Form RPR
213- **1** **Monkerhostin (FR)**^{304} [3149] 8-10-5 **145** .... RJohnson 163+
(P J Hobbs) *hld up and bhd: mstke 2nd (water): hdwy 6th: led 4 out: rdn clr appr last: r.o wl* **10/1**
112- **2** *4* **Kauto Star (FR)**^{274} [3623] 5-10-9 **149** ....(t) RWalsh 159+
(P F Nicholls) *hld up in tch: wnt 2nd 5th: ev ch 4 out: rdn after 2 out: one pce* **3/1**^{2}
421- **3** *9* **Ashley Brook (IRE)**^{206} [4769] 7-11-4 **158** .... PJBrennan 165+
(K Bishop) *led: clr 7th: blnd 8th: wknd 3 out* **7/4**^{1}
532- **4** *22* **See You Sometime**^{207} [4761] 10-10-6 **146** .... BFenton 125
(J W Mullins) *prom: lost pl 5th: styd on fr 3 out: j.rt last: n.d* **50/1**
103- **5** *2* **Contraband**^{192} [4983] 7-10-13 **153** .... TJMurphy 135+
(M C Pipe) *hld up and bhd: blnd bdly 4th: sme hdwy 8th: n.d* **11/1**
24F- **6** *shd* **Mister McGoldrick**^{207} [4763] 8-11-4 **158** .... DElsworth 135
(Mrs S J Smith) *prom: lost pl 5th: n.d after* **25/1**
1U2- **7** *7* **Kadount (FR)**^{208} [4751] 7-10-4 **144** oh1 .... RThornton 114
(A King) *hld up: hdwy 5th: wknd 8th* **8/1**^{3}
00P- **8** *5* **Hot Shots (FR)**^{193} [4972] 10-10-4 **144** oh4 .... PMoloney 109
(M Pitman) *a bhd* **50/1**
46-3 **9** *5* **Kadarann (IRE)**^{178} [219] 8-10-6 **146** .... ChristianWilliams 106
(P F Nicholls) *nt fluent 2nd (water): hit 6th: a bhd* **25/1**
F1-4 **10** *24* **Ground Ball (IRE)**^{20} [41] 8-10-12 **152** .... APMcCoy 88
(C F Swan, Ire) *hld up: hdwy appr 5th: wknd after 8th* **9/1**
/12- **P** **Best Mate (IRE)**^{308} [3063] 10-11-10 **164** .... PCarberry —
(Miss H C Knight) *chsd ldr to 5th: wknd 7th: p.u bef 3 out: dead* **12/1**
4m 13.2s (-3.70) **Going Correction** +0.175s/f (Yiel) **11** Ran SP% **119.2**
Speed ratings: **115,113,109,99,98 98,95,93,90,80** — CSF £41.03 CT £79.15 TOTE £14.60: £3.10, £2.10, £1.70; EX 68.20 Trifecta £379.60 Pool: £1,764.62 - 3.30 winning units.
Owner M G St Quinton **Bred** Mme Dominique Steverlynck **Trained** Withycombe, Somerset

FOCUS
A race that is traditionally one of the first real highlights of the National Hunt season and it looked a cracking renewal with last season's top two-mile novice chaser Ashley Brook meeting opposition from a horse who would have pushed him for that title had injury not curtailed his season, Kauto Star, and his somewhat 'forgotten' Arkle conqueror Contraband. However, the race will always be remembered for the tragic death of Triple Gold Cup winner Best Mate, who suffered a suspected heart attack. The winning time was as you would expect for a race like this and there was no place to hide with Ashley Brook setting a searching pace. The front three pulled well clear and look sure to win some good prizes between them this season.

NOTEBOOK
Monkerhostin(FR), whose last outing over fences saw him destroy a good field in the 2004 Bonusprint Gold Cup, was running away with Johnson for most of the way and some quick, fluent jumping down the back straight propelled him into a threatening position as they turned for home. Fitness began to tell over the final few fences as Kauto Star began to tire and he ultimately cleared away for an impressive victory. His record over fences since joining the Hobbs yard reads particularly well, his only defeat in four outings coming in the 2004 Paddy Power Gold Cup, and he has that as a likely target again, but in the long-run one would have to think he has major claims in something like the Ryanair Chase having beaten last year's winner Thisthatandtother pointless in the Bonusprint.
Kauto Star(FR) looks set to represent team Nicholls in all the top two-mile events this term with Azertyuiop out for the season and he will no doubt have delighted connections with this reappearance effort. Last seen finishing a controversial second in a novice chase here in January when Walsh remounted the gelding after he had capsized at the second-last (an incident that caused his injury), he was believed to be in need of this and so it was no surprise to see him get weary in the final quarter-mile having cantered into the straight. The extremely high regard in which connections hold him has to be respected and he remains an exciting prospect. *(tchd 10-3)*
Ashley Brook(IRE), last season's leading two-mile novice chaser, was ridden early to take a decisive lead. However, his rider's suspicion that he requires further proved founded as he seemed to be outpaced from the turn into the straight. A bad blunder at the eighth took a bit more out of him than had looked likely and as a result he deserves another chance. There is no doubting he has a huge engine and it is now likely that he will step up in distance. *(op 9-4 tchd 5-2 in places)*
See You Sometime was someway adrift of the front three, but he ran as well as could have been expected. Rising 11, the gelding has faced some stiff tasks in his time over fences and spent virtually all of last season racing exclusively in graded company, but he was rarely disgraced and this was a fine reappearance effort. He will remain hard to place however.
Contraband, last year's Arkle winner, is somewhat a forgotten horse and this looked a good opportunity for him to put his name back on the map, but his race was over after an horrendous error at the fourth that resulted in the fence being dolled off for the remainder off the afternoon. He did well to finish where he did considering and he could be an interesting contender for the Paddy Power if seeing out the trip. *(tchd 10-1)*
Mister McGoldrick earned a very high rating after some smashing efforts last season, but he was always likely to struggle here giving weight to some talented performers. It is safe to assume the run will bring him on and better can be expected next time. *(op 16-1)*
Kadount(FR) progressed into a smart novice chaser last season and rounded off the campaign with a gallant second to Fota Island at Aintree. It was reasonable therefore to expect a good show off of a feather-weight, but he was struggling from well over half a mile out and ultimately dropped away. This was not an easy race to make a seasonal reappearance in however, and it would not surprise to see him step up on this. *(op 7-1)*
Ground Ball(IRE) was the only runner to have had a recent outing (on the Flat 20 days ago) but it made little difference and he was beaten too far for this to be his true running. *(tchd 8-1)*
Best Mate(IRE), the Triple Gold Cup winner who has done wonderful things for racing, tragically collapsed near the final fence having suffered a suspected heart attack. A horse who has set the standard for staying chasers over the past four seasons, he will be sorely missed, but always remembered. Rarely has a horse caught the public's imagination as much as Best Mate and it can be said that he died a racing great.

1971 WILLIAMHILLCASINO.COM NOVICES' CHASE (11 fncs 1 omitted) 2m 1f 110y
3:10 (3:12) (Class 3) 5-Y-0+ **£9,524** (£2,796; £1,398; £698)

Form RPR
312- **1** **Racing Demon (IRE)**^{230} [4394] 5-10-12 .... TJMurphy 147+
(Miss H C Knight) *hld up: hdwy 6th: rdn to ld last: hung lft flat: drvn out* **9/4**^{1}
6P-1 **2** *1 1/2* **Chilling Place (IRE)**^{14} [1783] 6-11-4 .... RJohnson 148
(P J Hobbs) *led after 1st: rdn appr 2 out: hdd last: nt qckn* **9/4**^{1}
406- **3** *15* **Shuhood (USA)**^{207} [4765] 5-10-12 .... TDoyle 130+
(P R Webber) *led tl after 1st: prom: rdn appr 4 out: pckd bdly 3 out: sn wknd* **16/1**
000- **4** *7* **Green Tango**^{206} [4768] 6-10-12 .... ChristianWilliams 120
(H D Daly) *hld up: short-lived effrt appr 4 out* **33/1**
14-1 **5** *9* **Nyrche (FR)**^{188} [56] 5-11-4 .... RThornton 121+
(A King) *hld up in tch: wknd appr 4 out* **7/2**^{2}
1110 **6** *29* **Yes Sir (IRE)**^{10} [1828] 6-10-12 .... APMcCoy 102+
(P Bowen) *prom: mstke 1st: blnd bdly 4th: nt rcvr: t.o* **5/1**^{3}
5 **7** *25* **Honor And Glory**^{30} [1618] 5-10-12 .... PJBrennan 57
(Nick Williams) *a bhd: lost tch fr 4th: t.o* **100/1**
514- **P** **Wizard Of Edge**^{391} [1611] 5-10-5 .... JamesWhite(7) —
(R J Hodges) *plld hrd: p.u after 3rd: sddle slipped* **100/1**
4m 16.8s (-0.10) **Going Correction** +0.175s/f (Yiel) **8** Ran SP% **111.2**
Speed ratings: **107,106,99,96,92 79,68,—** CSF £7.43 TOTE £2.70: £1.10, £1.10, £2.60; EX 8.60.
Owner Mrs T P Radford **Bred** Con O'Keeffe **Trained** West Lockinge, Oxon

FOCUS
Probably the best novice chase of the season so far with Royal & SunAlliance Hurdle runner-up Racing Demon making a good start to his chasing career and providing the Knight camp with something to smile about. The open ditch past the stands was omitted.

NOTEBOOK
Racing Demon(IRE), not seen since finishing a slightly unlucky second to No Refuge in the Royal & SunAlliance Novices' Hurdle, was always going to flourish as a chaser and he displayed here that he has the necessary speed to develop into an Arkle contender. Recent course scorer Chilling Place set a good standard, he himself being a smart novice hurdler, but one always got the impression Murphy thought he had him covered and he found an extra gear after the last to win a shade comfortably. He was conceding race fitness and there is no doubting he is the most promising two-miler we have seen so far this term. *(op 2-1 tchd 5-2 in a place)*
Chilling Place(IRE) posted an excellent effort, leading from the outset and battling on well, but he was just lacking the winner's touch of class at the business end. This was a step up on his initial effort and he may yet be capable of further improvement on a genuinely sound surface. *(op 2-1)*
Shuhood(USA) struggled in two Grade One events at the major Festivals last season, but he made a satisfactory start to his chasing career. He was beginning to tire when pecking badly on landing at the third last and it is safe to assume he is a fair bit better than the bare result. He will find easier opportunities. *(op 20-1)*
Green Tango was inferior to most of these over hurdles and he was outclassed on this chasing debut. He is with a decent yard and will find more realistic opportunities.
Nyrche(FR) created a favourable impression when bolting up in a course-and-distance chase in heavy ground back in April, but as was the case last season, he was not so effective here in a better race. He is better than this, but now has a bit to prove. *(op 5-1)*
Yes Sir(IRE), officially rated the best of these over hurdles, never got a chance to show his true ability on this chase debut after a bad mistake at the fourth. He is worth another chance. *(op 4-1)*
Wizard Of Edge *Official explanation: jockey said saddle slipped (op 50-1)*

1972 WILLIAM HILL EDREDON BLEU H'CAP CHASE (16 fncs 1 omitted) 2m 7f 110y
3:40 (3:40) (Class 3) (0-125,123) 5-Y-0+ **£7,032** (£2,064; £1,032; £515)

Form RPR
P-01 **1** **Saffron Sun**^{27} [1639] 10-10-9 **106** .... ChristianWilliams 119+
(J D Frost) *a.p: led 3 out: sn rdn: j.rt 2 out: styd on wl* **15/2**
P3-5 **2** *5* **The Kew Tour (IRE)**^{191} [12] 9-11-6 **117** .... DElsworth 123+
(Mrs S J Smith) *led: rdn and hdd 3 out: one pce fr 2 out* **7/1**^{3}
51-F **3** *3/4* **Charlies Future**^{9} [1853] 7-11-1 **112** .... TDoyle 116
(S C Burrough) *hld up: hdwy 10th: outpcd appr 4 out: rallied 2 out: styd on* **14/1**
-6P6 **4** *3* **Twisted Logic (IRE)**^{15} [1778] 12-11-4 **115** .... RWalford 116
(R H Alner) *prom: hit 4 out: wknd 2 out* **20/1**
44F- **5** *7* **Lets Go Dutch**^{193} [4959] 9-10-3 **100** .... RGreene 94
(K Bishop) *bhd: hit 2nd: rdn and hdwy appr 4 out: sn no imp* **20/1**
33P- **6** *5* **Lucky Leader (IRE)**^{212} [4726] 10-9-11 **97** oh4 ....(b) RYoung(3) 88+
(N R Mitchell) *hld up in mid-div: hdwy 9th: ev ch 4 out: rdn and wknd appr 2 out* **25/1**
U0P- **7** *1 1/4* **Hawk's Landing (IRE)**^{318} [2902] 8-11-8 **119** .... APMcCoy 109+
(Jonjo O'Neill) *hld up: hdwy 12th: j.rt 3 out: sn wknd* **7/1**^{3}
212- **8** *25* **Beau Supreme (IRE)**^{227} [4462] 8-11-12 **123** .... JamesDavies 86
(C J Down) *mid-div: dropped rr and hmpd 7th (water): pckd 8th: t.o* **9/1**
10-3 **9** *12* **Even More (IRE)**^{179} [205] 10-11-1 **112** .... TJMurphy 63
(R H Alner) *prom to 9th: t.o* **14/1**
F-1F **U** **Moscow Whisper (IRE)**^{24} [1678] 8-11-4 **115** .... RJohnson —
(P J Hobbs) *n.m.r whn uns rdr 1st* **11/4**^{1}
122- **F** **Noble Baron**^{291} [3345] 9-11-0 **111** ....(t) JEMoore —
(C G Cox) *hld up in tch: nt fluent 7th (water): cl 4th whn fell 12th* **9/2**^{2}
6m 5.60s (7.00) **Going Correction** +0.175s/f (Yiel) **11** Ran SP% **118.3**
Speed ratings: **95,93,93,92,89 88,87,79,75,—** — CSF £58.12 CT £727.87 TOTE £8.40: £2.40, £3.10, £3.70; EX 47.40.
Owner Mrs J F Bury **Bred** G Blight **Trained** Scorriton, Devon

FOCUS
A routine handicap, won by a horse with a good record here, and a modest winning time for a race of its class. The open ditch past the stands was omitted.

NOTEBOOK
Saffron Sun, who has a particularly good record here, gained his sixth course win on very different ground to the surface he encountered when scoring here last month. Always close up, he battled on gamely once hitting the front and was always holding The Kew Tour. *(op 7-1)*
The Kew Tour(IRE), a raider from the North, set the pace and managed to shake off all bar the winner early in the straight, having to make do with second. Like Saffron Sun he has done most of his winning on a sound surface, so it was a good effort in the circumstances. *(tchd 8-1)*

Charlies Future, none the worse for his fall at Towcester last week, was allowed to creep into contention after the last ditch, but could never land a serious blow. *(op 9-1)*
Twisted Logic(IRE), another who loves this place, was just beginning to get tired when hitting the first in the straight and that put paid to his chance. *(op 16-1)*
Lets Go Dutch was not disgraced, but will find life easier back down in grade. *(op 14-1)*
Hawk's Landing(IRE) is proving a disappointing sort as he crept onto the heels of the leaders before the turn only to drop away tamely. He may have blown up on this first run for ten months but still has something to prove.
Noble Baron was not out of things when coming down and it would not have surprised to see him go close on a course he goes well at. *(op 5-1 tchd 11-2)*

1973 WILLIAMHILLPOKER.COM H'CAP HURDLE (13 hdls) 3m 110y
4:10 (4:10) (Class 4) (0-110,110) 4-Y-0+ **£4,840** (£1,421; £710; £354)

Form RPR
212- **1** **Toulouse-Lautrec (IRE)**[227] 4461 9-11-0 **98**.......................... APMcCoy 106+
(T R George) *racd wd: a.p: led appr 8th: rdn clr appr last: eased cl home* **10/11**[1]
5-32 **2** *4* **Knight Of Silver**[12] 1800 8-10-4 **88**.......................... RGreene 86
(S C Burrough) *hld up: rdn after 6th: hdwy 8th: styd on same pce fr 2 out* **50/1**
135- **3** *hd* **Rosetown (IRE)**[206] 4781 7-10-2 **96**..........................(b) WMcCarthy[(10)] 94
(T R George) *hld up: hdwy 4th: chsd wnr appr 3 out: sn rdn: no imp: lost 2nd last strides* **7/1**[2]
00/1 **4** *dist* **Frosty Jak**[14] 1779 7-10-0 **84** oh1.......................... RJohnson 62
(J D Frost) *hld up: rdn and hdwy 9th: wknd 2 out: eased whn btn* **7/1**[2]
030- **5** *dist* **Try Catch Paddy (IRE)**[193] 4967 7-11-12 **110**.......................... TJMurphy —
(M C Pipe) *hld up in rr: rdn appr 8th: no rspnse: t.o fr 10th* **10/1**
P-56 **P** **Keepers Mead (IRE)**[20] 1715 7-11-10 **108**.......................... RWalford —
(R H Alner) *prom to 8th: t.o whn p.u bef last* **8/1**[3]
034/ **P** **Master Billyboy (IRE)**[591] 4449 7-11-5 **110**.......................... MrDEdwards[(7)] —
(Mrs S D Williams) *prom to 9th: t.o whn p.u bef 2 out* **14/1**
563- **P** **Silkwood Top (IRE)**[224] 4502 6-10-7 **91**..........................(p) JEMoore —
(V R A Dartnall) *prom tl rdn and wknd appr 3 out: t.o whn p.u bef last* **20/1**
044/ **P** **Chateau Rose (IRE)**[588] 4519 9-10-7 **91**.......................... BFenton —
(Miss E C Lavelle) *j.lft: led tl appr 8th: sn lost pl: bhd whn p.u bef 2 out* **12/1**

6m 17.5s (4.20) **Going Correction** +0.25s/f (Yiel) **9** Ran SP% **118.7**
Speed ratings: **103,101,101,—,—— —,—,—,—** CSF £42.07 CT £235.70 TOTE £1.80: £1.10, £5.20, £1.70; EX 33.60 Place 6 £11.85, Place 5 £9.62.
Owner John French **Bred** Edwin Carlisle **Trained** Slad, Gloucs

FOCUS
A poor race to end with the winner probably value for further.

NOTEBOOK
Toulouse-Lautrec(IRE), favourably weighted over hurdles compared with fences, was always travelling well, but began to idle in front and looked to be allowing Knight Of Silver and Rosetown in for one last challenge. However a few sharp reminders from McCoy got his mind concentrated again and he galloped on resolutely to win comfortably. There is no reason why he cannot win again over hurdles before returning to the larger obstacles. *(op 11-8 tchd 6-4 in a place)*
Knight Of Silver deserves a good deal of credit for his persistent effort and the hard work Greene put in paid off as he just got up for second. Ridden from an early stage, neither he nor his rider knew when to give in and, although not the quickest, he deserves to win again. *(op 33-1)*
Rosetown(IRE), a stablemate of the winner, provided Tom George with a strong grasp on the race and he made a highly pleasing reappearance. Entitled to come on for the outing, he knows how to win and it will be interesting to see if he is switched to fences this term. *(op 8-1 tchd 9-1)*
Frosty Jak, a surprise winner here at the last meeting, was unable to consolidate that effort and ended up being beaten an awful long way. *(op 13-2)*
Try Catch Paddy(IRE) was never travelling and may need some further assistance from the Handicapper. *(op 12-1)*
T/Jkpt: £23,015.60 to a £1 stake. Pool: £129,665.50. 4.00 winning tickets. T/Plt: £13.40 to a £1 stake. Pool: £74,760.75. 4,057.60 winning tickets. T/Qpdt: £8.40 to a £1 stake. Pool: £4,007.30. 350.20 winning tickets. KH

1654 WORCESTER (L-H)
Tuesday, November 1

OFFICIAL GOING: Good

1974 BETFREDPOKER.COM MARES' ONLY NOVICES' HURDLE (8 hdls) 2m
1:50 (1:53) (Class 4) 4-Y-0+ **£4,215** (£1,237; £618; £309)

Form RPR
2- **1** **Novacella (FR)**[287] 3403 4-10-10.......................... AThornton 95+
(R H Alner) *chsd ldrs: chal 3 out: sn led: drvn out run-in* **13/8**[1]
345- **2** *2 ½* **Very Special One (IRE)**[250] 4029 5-10-10.......................... JPMcNamara 92
(K C Bailey) *w ldr: led 2nd: hdd 4th: styd chalng and ev ch 3 out: one pce next: rallied u.p run-in: no imp on wnr* **12/1**
26/ **3** *6* **Labelthou (FR)**[661] 3265 6-10-10.......................... JTizzard 86
(Mrs L Wadham) *led to 2nd: styd w ldr tl led again 4th: hdd after 3 out: one pce fr next* **9/2**[3]
60-0 **4** *1* **Hilarious (IRE)**[22] 185 5-10-10 83.......................... JGoldstein 85
(Dr J R J Naylor) *chsd ldrs: rdn 3 out: kpt on same pce* **25/1**
551- **5** *2 ½* **Makeabreak (IRE)**[218] 4608 6-10-10.......................... NFehily 83
(C J Mann) *chsd ldrs: rdn 3 out: wknd next: no ch w ldrs whn hit last* **4/1**[2]
00-0 **6** *15* **Ilongue (FR)**[178] 216 4-10-10 70.......................... WHutchinson 68
(R Dickin) *bhd: hdwy 4 out: chsd ldrs next: sn wknd* **100/1**
7 *2* **Theatre Belle**[161] 4-10-10.......................... AntonyEvans 66
(Ms Deborah J Evans) *bhd: sme hdwy 4 out: wknd qckly next* **100/1**
00- **8** *5* **Saddlers Express**[201] 4841 4-10-10.......................... MBradburne 61
(H D Daly) *nt fluent 1st: bhd: hit 4th: hday after next and in tch 3 out: sn wknd* **14/1**
5P6 **9** *6* **Daihannah (IRE)**[39] 1538 5-10-10.......................... JPByrne 55
(Miss H E Roberts) *j.slowly 3rd: a bhd* **100/1**
PF0- **10** *nk* **Smokin Grey**[62] 2973 5-10-5.......................... DLaverty[(5)] 54
(L Wells) *mid-div whn hit 3rd: wkng whn blnd 4 out* **66/1**
00- **11** *22* **Biscay Wind (IRE)**[327] 2721 5-10-10.......................... JMMaguire 32
(T R George) *chsd ldrs to 4 out* **50/1**
0P25 **F** **Brown Fox (FR)**[16] 1750 4-10-7.......................... ONelmes[(3)] —
(C J Down) *bhd: hday and mstke 4th: styng on to dispute 4th whn fell 3 out* **16/1**
2 **P** **Bella Bonkers**[24] 1674 5-10-10.......................... CLlewellyn —
(N A Twiston-Davies) *chsd ldrs: wknd qckly 4th: t.o whn blnd and p.u 4 out* **9/1**

3m 59.6s (11.20) **Going Correction** +0.825s/f (Soft) **13** Ran SP% **116.8**
Speed ratings: **105,103,100,100,99 91,90,88,85,84 73,—,—** CSF £22.53 TOTE £2.10: £1.10, £2.30, £2.10; EX 28.30.
Owner Mrs Norma Kelly **Bred** F Cottin And Mme Gilberte Chaignon **Trained** Droop, Dorset

FOCUS
A modest mares' novice hurdle, but the form amongst the principals should work out and the winner can rate higher.

NOTEBOOK
Novacella(FR), runner-up on her sole start last season after switching from France, was handy throughout and ultimately broke her duck over hurdles with a straightforward display. Having previously been placed in Listed company over timber in France on testing ground, she was obviously well at home on the easy surface, and her jumping was neat throughout. She will jump a fence in due course, but can rate higher in this division before the season's end. *(op 9-4)*
Very Special One(IRE), twice a beaten favourite over timber last term, ran as though the race would certainly bring her on fitness-wise and left the impression she would be better suited to a stiffer test. This was her best effort over hurdles to date and she can be found a winning opportunity in this division before long. *(op 9-1)*
Labelthou(FR), returning from a 661-day layoff, was strong in the market ahead of this return to action and pretty much justified that support with a sound effort in defeat. She may have benefitted from a slightly more patient ride after such a lengthy absence, as she tired markedly from two out, but this will have no doubt have pleased her connections and, providing she is given sufficient time to recover from these exertions, she ought to be winning before too long. *(tchd 4-1 and 11-2)*
Hilarious(IRE), fit from a recent spin on the Flat, turned in an improved effort in defeat. She would certainly look better off back in a handicap off her current mark. *(op 20-1)*
Makeabreak(IRE), making her debut for new connections having landed a bumper on her final outing last season for Richard Fahey, failed to find much when push came to shove and merely kept on at the same pace from three out. She is at least entitled to improve for the outing. *(op 7-2)*
Brown Fox(FR) *(op 33-1)*
Bella Bonkers *Official explanation: vet said mare finished distressed (op 33-1)*

1975 STEVE, CATH AND SNOWY DOYLE'S NOVICES' HURDLE (10 hdls) 2m 4f
2:20 (2:21) (Class 4) 4-Y-0+ **£3,513** (£1,031; £515; £257)

Form RPR
23-3 **1** **Saltango (GER)**[14] 1782 6-10-7 113.......................... WKennedy[(5)] 109+
(A M Hales) *trckd ldrs: wnt 2nd 4 out: led appr next: c clr 2 out: v easily* **5/4**[1]
2 *10* **Taking My Cut** 5-10-12.......................... RMcGrath 97+
(Jonjo O'Neill) *in tch: hdwy 6th: chsd ldrs fr 4 out: rdn and one pce 2 out: styd on run-in to take 2nd cl home: no ch w wnr* **18/1**
4-5 **3** *½* **Eight Fifty Five (IRE)**[152] 616 5-10-12.......................... WMarston 96
(R T Phillips) *chsd ldrs and n.m.r bnd appr 5th: rdn 3 out: chsd wnr last and sn no ch: lost 2nd cl home* **22/1**
4 *10* **Call Me Edward (IRE)**[219] 4-10-12.......................... CLlewellyn 88+
(N A Twiston-Davies) *chsd ldr 4th: nt fluent 6th: lost 2nd after 4 out: wknd fr 2 out* **5/1**[3]
0-0U **5** *4* **Pauls Plain**[16] 1750 4-10-12.......................... SCurran 82
(P W Hiatt) *t.k.h: hold: led tl hdd after 4 out: wknd qckly 2 out* **66/1**
P **6** *28* **Mount Benger**[24] 1680 5-10-12..........................(p) PHide 54
(Mrs A J Hamilton-Fairley) *bhd: sme hdwy 4 out: sn chsng ldrs: wknd and mstke next* **100/1**
6 **7** *1 ¾* **Almutasader**[150] 172 5-10-12.......................... WHutchinson 52
(J A B Old) *in tch: hit 6th: sn bhd* **33/1**
3210 **8** *¾* **West End Wonder (IRE)**[24] 1680 6-10-12 110.......................... AScholes[(7)] 59
(D Burchell) *in tch tl wknd 4 out* **13/2**
9 *dist* **Rifle Ryde (IRE)** 5-10-12.......................... JPMcNamara —
(K C Bailey) *a in rr* **50/1**
04- **P** **Noble Mind**[99] 4910 4-10-12.......................... LAspell —
(P G Murphy) *in tch to 6th: wknd 4 out: t.o whn p.u run-in* **100/1**
P/P5 **P** **Brandeston Ron (IRE)**[27] 1642 6-10-12..........................(t) ATinkler —
(M Pitman) *chsd ldrs to 4th: wknd rapidly next: t.o whn p.u bef 4 out* **40/1**
0-2 **P** **Sir Pandy (IRE)**[20] 1714 5-10-12.......................... AThornton —
(R H Alner) *rr but in tch: hdwy 5th: nt fluent and wknd next: t.o whn p.u bef 3 out* **7/2**[2]

5m 1.90s (13.90) **Going Correction** +0.825s/f (Soft)
WFA 4 from 5yo+ 13lb **12** Ran SP% **117.1**
Speed ratings: **105,101,100,96,95 84,83,83,—,— —,—** CSF £26.12 TOTE £2.10: £1.20, £3.70, £3.10; EX 35.90.
Owner CohenClearyKaplanMinnsPayneWatsonWilson **Bred** Gestut Wittekindshof **Trained** Quainton, Bucks
■ Stewards' Enquiry : W Marston caution: careless riding

FOCUS
A moderate novice event, run at a fair gallop and the winner can be rated for double his winning margin.

NOTEBOOK
Saltango(GER), up in trip, deservedly lost his maiden tag over hurdles at the fifth time of asking and came home pretty much as he pleased. He did not have to be at his best to score, but can be rated value for further, and it will be interesting to see whether he can progress further now his confidence should have been significantly boosted. *(op 6-4 tchd 7-4)*
Taking My Cut, whose dam was a dual bumper winner, emerged full of running with four to jump, but did not find as much as looked likely when it mattered and was well held at the finish. However, he still did more than enough to suggest he will improve a deal for the experience and when faced with a stiffer test. *(op 12-1)*
Eight Fifty Five(IRE), who had shown just modest form in two bumpers previously, could only muster the same pace when it mattered and did not obviously improve on this hurdling bow. That said, he could do better with this experience under his belt and may need further. *(op 25-1 tchd 20-1)*
Call Me Edward(IRE), runner-up on his sole start in the Irish point-to-point arena 219 days previously, not surprisingly got outpaced when the race became serious four out and would have probably been better served by making the running on this hurdling bow. He is not one to write off on the back of this display. *(op 11-2)*
Pauls Plain spoilt his chances of getting home over this longer trip by runing too freely at the head of affairs through the early parts. He now qualifies for handicaps.
West End Wonder(IRE), who broke his duck over course and distance in July, ran well below-par for the second consecutive occasion and has plenty to prove now. *(op 7-1)*
Sir Pandy(IRE), who ran the smart mare Refinement close on his recent hurdling bow at Uttoxeter, *proved most disappointing on this step-up in trip and something may well have been amiss. Official explanation: jockey said gelding was never travelling (op 10-3 tchd 3-1 and 4-1 in places)*

1976 FRED RIMELL MEMORIAL BEGINNERS' CHASE (18 fncs) 2m 7f 110y
2:50 (2:50) (Class 3) 5-Y-0+ **£5,608** (£1,646; £823; £411)

Form RPR
41P- **1** **Idle Talk (IRE)**[207] 4765 6-11-0.......................... JMMaguire 132+
(T R George) *led 2nd to 5th: styd pressing ldrs: led 9th to 12th: led 3 out: styd on wl u.p fr next* **7/2**[1]
22P- **2** *6* **Lord Killeshanra (IRE)**[198] 4887 6-11-0.......................... JTizzard 129+
(C L Tizzard) *blnd 1st: bhd: hdwy 14th: styd on to chse ldrs appr 4 out: one pce fr next: no imp on wnr whn mstke last* **12/1**
14-5 **3** *4* **Mel In Blue (FR)**[24] 1675 7-10-7.......................... MrSWaley-Cohen[(7)] 126+
(R Waley-Cohen) *chsd ldrs: led and nt fluent 12th: rdn and mstke 4 out: hdd next: one pce whn blnd last* **9/2**[3]

11-4 **4** 28 **Olney Lad**[24] 1669 6-11-0 RGarritty 94
(Mrs P Robeson) *chsd ldrs: hit 3rd: led 6th: hdd 9th: wknd appr 14th* **4/1**[2]

1P5- **5** 21 **Ferimon**[194] 4945 6-11-0 MBradburne 73
(H D Daly) *in tch: hdwy 10th: mstkes 13th and 14th: sn wknd* **12/1**

6 **P** **Wynford Eagle**[14] 1781 6-11-0 AThornton —
(R H Alner) *p.u bef 4th* **100/1**

P3PF **P** **Rich Song (IRE)**[30] 1615 7-10-7 83 NCarter(7) —
(Mrs S J Smith) *a bhd: t.o whn p.u bef 14th* **50/1**

P **Rockvale (IRE)**[171] 6-11-0 LAspell —
(Mrs J A Saunders) *j.slowly 3rd: a bhd: t.o whn p.u bef 14th* **40/1**

35-4 **P** **Millenaire (FR)**[30] 1608 6-11-0 RMcGrath —
(Jonjo O'Neill) *bhd: blnd 5th: t.o whn p.u bef 4 out* **7/1**

P **Ultramoderne (FR)** 8-10-11 LVickers(3) —
(C C Bealby) *in tch: chsd ldrs 9th: sn wknd: t.o whn p.u bef 4 out* **100/1**

306/ **P** **John Foley (IRE)**[183] 7-10-7 APogson(7) —
(J R Holt) *led to 2nd: led again 5th: hdd next: wknd and p.u bef 10th* **100/1**

42- **P** **Bengo (IRE)**[193] 4954 5-10-13 NFehily —
(B De Haan) *chsd ldrs: blnd 13th and next: sn wknd: t.o whn p.u bef last* **11/2**

0- **P** **Grasia (IRE)**[307] 3085 6-11-0 JPMcNamara —
(K C Bailey) *chsd ldrs: mstke 1st: blnd 5th: wknd 12th: t.o whn p.u bef 15th* **50/1**

P **Young Murf (IRE)**[562] 6-11-0 CLlewellyn —
(N A Twiston-Davies) *chsd ldrs: chal 7th to 8th: wknd 10th: t.o whn p.u bef 13th* **16/1**

6m 6.80s (11.90) **Going Correction** +0.825s/f (Soft) **14** Ran SP% **118.9**
Speed ratings: **113,111,109,100,93** —,—,—,—,— —,—,—,— CSF £44.29 TOTE £5.30: £1.40, £4.20, £1.60; EX 76.40.
Owner Mrs M J George **Bred** Roland Rothwell **Trained** Slad, Gloucs

FOCUS
A decent winning time for a race of its type and, despite only five completed, it still looks to be decent novice form.

NOTEBOOK
Idle Talk(IRE) ◆, who showed clear promise over timber as a novice prior to pulling-up in the Grade One Sefton Novices' Hurdle at Aintree when last seen in April, justified favouritism in great style and got his chase career off to a perfect start. He enjoyed the ground, jumped with aplomb throughout and clearly stays very well. It can confidently be expected that he will rate much higher in this sphere. *(op 10-3 tchd 4-1 in places)*
Lord Killeshanra(IRE), who developed a habit of finding one too good over hurdles last term, was given a patient ride and, having spent energy making up his ground down the back straight, kept on dourly from three out to fill a familiar position. He has always promised to reach greater heights as a chaser, and this was probably his best effort to date, so he should really be able to pick up a similar event in due course.
Mel In Blue(FR), winner of a bumper, a point and two handicap hurdles to date, lost out through jumping errors on this chase debut yet was far from disgraced in defeat. He will need to improve his jumping, but is entitled to, and is in the right hands to progress further over fences. *(op 11-2)*
Olney Lad failed to build on the promise of his recent chasing bow at Bangor behind Iris's Gift and *was beaten too far out for the longer trip to be an issue. Something may well have been amiss. (op 7-2)*
Ferimon, a dual winner as a novice hurdler last term and rated 123 in that sphere, ran very much as though this race was needed and his fortunes will no doubt improve when his stable hit form in due course.
John Foley(IRE) *Official explanation: jockey said gelding had a breathing problem (op 7-1)*
Wynford Eagle *Official explanation: jockey said gelding jumped out to the right and he felt it prudent to pull up before jumping the fourth fence (op 7-1)*
Bengo(IRE), well backed, travelled and jumped nicely until an error coming out of the back straight and was then disappointingly pulled up. He is another who has promised to do better as a chaser and he should leave this form behind as he gains further experience. *(op 7-1)*

1977 BETFREDCASINO.COM H'CAP HURDLE (10 hdls) 2m 4f
3:20 (3:20) (Class 4) (0-105,101) 4-Y-0+ **£3,467** (£1,018; £509; £254)

Form RPR

-260 **1** **Pardon What**[28] 1630 9-11-0 92 (b) KJMercer(3) 99+
(S Lycett) *trckd ldrs: lost position after 4 out: styd on strly fr 2 out to ld run-in: readily* **28/1**

0/0- **2** 5 **Eljutan (IRE)**[256] 3926 7-10-13 95 SWalsh(7) 94+
(J Joseph) *bhd: steady hdwy appr 3 out: styd on u.p fr 2 out to chal last: led sn after: edgd rt: styd on one pce* **66/1**

P343 **3** 5 **Hard N Sharp**[14] 1784 5-11-0 94 WKennedy(5) 89+
(Mrs A M Thorpe) *in tch: chsd ldrs 5th: slt ld fr next: rdn 2 out: hdd & wknd sn after last* **6/1**[2]

65-0 **4** 1 ¾ **Caspian Dusk**[12] 1804 4-11-5 101 (p) RLucey-Butler(7) 93
(W G M Turner) *bhd: hdwy 7th: chsd ldrs 4 out: rdn next: wknd after 2 out* **40/1**

604B **5** 1 ¾ **Francolino (FR)**[20] 1713 12-9-7 75 oh11 JPritchard(7) 65
(Dr P Pritchard) *led to 6th: rdn and outpcd appr 3 out: stayed on again appr last: gng on cl home* **100/1**

335- **6** 9 **Shaamit The Vaamit (IRE)**[205] 4793 5-11-4 93 NFehily 77+
(M Scudamore) *bhd: hdwy 5th: drvn to chse ldrs 3 out: wknd after next* **11/1**

5-14 **7** 1 ½ **Ask The Umpire (IRE)**[169] 385 10-11-3 92 (p) HOliver 72
(N E Berry) *chsd ldrs: rdn after 4 out: wknd 2 out* **20/1**

0/00 **8** 4 **Donie Dooley (IRE)**[24] 1675 7-11-8 97 AThornton 73
(P T Dalton) *chsd ldrs tl wknd appr 4 out* **50/1**

0314 **9** 5 **Doris Souter (IRE)**[72] 1272 5-10-9 84 WMarston 55
(D J Wintle) *pressed ldrs: wnt 2nd 3 out: sn rdn: wknd qckly fr next* **10/1**

2F-P **10** 13 **Afeef (USA)**[16] 1751 6-11-1 90 (tp) SCurran 48
(J A Danahar) *chsd ldrs 5th: wknd next* **40/1**

5U32 **11** 6 **Great Compton**[133] 801 5-10-3 78 OMcPhail 30
(B J Llewellyn) *bhd: sme hdwy 6th: wknd sn after: no ch whn blnd 2 out* **7/1**

POP- **12** 10 **Theprideofeireann (IRE)**[347] 2321 6-10-5 80 RMcGrath 22
(Jonjo O'Neill) *chsd ldrs: chal fr 6th to 4 out: wknd qckly u.p bef next* **3/1**[1]

044- **13** 10 **Muntasir**[365] 1948 5-10-13 88 LAspell 20
(P G Murphy) *bhd most of way* **25/1**

56-4 **14** 9 **Treasure Trail**[27] 1645 6-11-3 92 WHutchinson 15
(Ian Williams) *chsd ldrs tl wknd qckly sn after 3 out* **13/2**[3]

0P4- **15** 22 **Business Traveller (IRE)**[295] 3304 5-11-6 95 AO'Keeffe —
(R J Price) *bhd: sme hdwy 5th: sn wknd* **28/1**

53-4 **P** **Combe Florey**[163] 462 6-10-13 88 JPByrne —
(H D Daly) *trckd ldrs: stl wl there whn p.u bef 3 out: lame* **11/1**

2555 **P** **Fiddles Music**[9] 1856 4-10-13 93 LStephens(5) —
(D Burchell) *bhd: sme hdwy 5th: wknd qckly and p.u after 4 out: lame* **10/1**

5m 8.80s (20.80) **Going Correction** +0.825s/f (Soft)
WFA 4 from 5yo+ 13lb **17** Ran SP% **124.8**
Speed ratings: **91,89,87,86,85 82,81,79,77,72 70,66,62,58,49** —,— CSF £1198.92 CT £11903.52 TOTE £39.40: £6.00, £13.40, £2.40, £8.50; EX 1203.50.
Owner N E Powell **Bred** Mrs J Stuart Evans **Trained** Naunton, Gloucs

FOCUS
A moderate winning time for a race like this, almost seven seconds slower than the earlier novice hurdle, and the field finished fairly stung out. The form is weak.

NOTEBOOK
Pardon What finally consented to put his best foot forward, and the fact he scored so readily suggests the re-application of blinkers had the desired effect. He has looked positively mulish this year, but it is very interesting that his decent bumper form in 2002 was at this venue and this softer ground was clearly to his liking. It will be fascinating to see whether he can now build on this and his next run will reveal more.
Eljutan(IRE) , returning from a 256-day layoff, made an encouraging return to action on ground he would have found plenty soft enough. If he connections can keep him sound, he can be placed to advantage at this level during the season.
Hard N Sharp again filled a place, but this was still below the form of his recent efforts in defeat. He is a game sort and is happier on a faster surface. *(tchd 13-2)*
Caspian Dusk, with cheekpieces applied for the first time over hurdles, was not disgraced off top weight and should come on again fitness-wise for the outing. He left the impression he can get closer when reverting to shorter.
Francolino(FR), reverting to hurdles, ran a fair race from out of the handicap and his confidence should have been restored now. He blatantly wants further these days, however.
Theprideofeireann(IRE) , subject of a massive gamble on this first outing for 347 days, ran a shocker and his backers would have known their fate a fair way out. He is evidently thought capable of much better, but remains a maiden, and is clearly not one to trust. *(op 6-1 tchd 13-2)*
Treasure Trail ran a lifeless race with no apparent excuses. *(op 6-1)*

1978 RICHARD DAVIS MEMORIAL H'CAP CHASE (15 fncs) 2m 4f 110y
3:50 (3:51) (Class 3) (0-125,117) 5-Y-0+ **£6,847** (£2,010; £1,005; £502)

Form RPR

1P-4 **1** **Major Euro (IRE)**[178] 217 8-11-4 109 MFoley 120+
(S J Gilmore) *nt fluent 3rd:sn chsng ldr: led after 6th: drvn 3 out: styd on gamely run-in: all out* **11/2**[3]

45-U **2** nk **Mon Mome (FR)**[6] 1877 5-11-0 105 SThomas 115
(Miss Venetia Williams) *rr but in tch: hdwy 6th: rdn to chse wnr 2 out and edgd rt: chal last: kpt on but no ex u.p cl home* **5/1**[2]

50-P **3** 20 **Bunkum**[171] 353 7-10-13 109 WKennedy(5) 109+
(R Lee) *rr but in tch: hdwy 6th: chsd wnr 9th: rdn 4 out: wknd after 2 out* **6/1**

21F- **4** 3 ½ **Kosmos Bleu (FR)**[205] 4792 7-11-5 110 AThornton 97
(R H Alner) *chsd ldr to 5th: stdd next: mstke 10th: styd chsng ldrs tl wknd 4 out* **11/8**[1]

4P5U **5** 10 **Flahive's First**[9] 1855 11-10-4 100 LStephens(5) 77
(D Burchell) *in tch: hday 8th: wknd and blnd 10th* **14/1**

UP3- **P** **L'Orphelin**[205] 4792 10-11-10 115 (p) JTizzard —
(C L Tizzard) *led tl after 6th: wknd and blnd 10th: p.u bef next* **9/1**

13- **P** **Chantoue Royale (FR)**[511] 686 6-11-9 117 CBolger(3) —
(Mrs L J Mongan) *in tch: rdn 10th and sn wknd: t.o whn p.u bef 3 out* **16/1**

5m 25.1s (17.60) **Going Correction** +0.825s/f (Soft) **7** Ran SP% **111.0**
Speed ratings: **99,98,91,89,86** —,— CSF £30.86 TOTE £6.30: £1.80, £5.80; EX 25.60.
Owner Miss Jumbo Frost **Bred** John Staples **Trained** Sulgrave, Northants

FOCUS
A modest handicap, run at an ordinary pace and the first two came well clear.

NOTEBOOK
Major Euro(IRE) proved game under a positive ride from Foley and made a winning return from a 178-day break. This was his highest winning mark to date and therefore a personal-best display, and he again proved he is versatile with regards to underfoot conditions. The Handicapper should not be too harsh on him for this and, on this evidence, he may be able to progress further this season. *(tchd 6-1 in places)*
Mon Mome(FR) , who unseated on his chasing bow at Cheltenham six days previously, jumped fluently and went down all guns blazing. Although a maiden over timber, he looks well up to winning races over fences at this sort of level and his yard are in good form at present. *(tchd 6-1)*
Bunkum was firmly put in his place from two out, but he is fully entitled to improve for the outing and connections will no doubt have been encouraged by this return to action. *(op 8-1)*
Kosmos Bleu(FR) looked to blow up from four out, but while he should come on for the outing this *still rates a disappointing comeback effort. Official explanation: jockey said gelding finished very tired (op 15-8)*
L'Orphelin *Official explanation: trainer's representative said gelding pulled up lame (op 6-1)*

1979 BETFREDPOKER.COM STANDARD NATIONAL HUNT FLAT RACE (CONDITIONAL JOCKEYS/AMATEUR RIDERS) 2m
4:20 (4:20) (Class 6) 4-6-Y-O **£1,870** (£545; £272)

Form RPR

1 **Au Courant (IRE)** 5-10-13 SCurling(5) 101+
(N J Henderson) *trckd ldrs: wnt 2nd 5f out: drvn to ld appr fnl f: kpt on wl* **11/10**[1]

3 **2** 1 ½ **Busy Henry**[39] 1543 5-10-11 LHeard(7) 99
(Mrs K M Sanderson) *led: rdn over 2f out: hdd appr fnl furlong: no ex ins last* **7/1**[3]

3- **3** 11 **Different Class (IRE)**[319] 2871 6-10-11 MrAJBerry(7) 89+
(Jonjo O'Neill) *chsd ldrs: rdn 4f out: wknd over 2f out* **7/4**[2]

4 27 **Supreme Cara** 5-10-8 ONelmes(3) 54
(C J Down) *green early: rdn after 6f: sn wl bhd* **16/1**

5 dist **Larry The Tiger (IRE)** 5-10-11 NCarter(7) —
(Mrs S J Smith) *chsd ldrs to 5f out: sn rdn and wknd* **16/1**

4m 1.60s (13.80) **Going Correction** +0.825s/f (Soft) **5** Ran SP% **108.2**
Speed ratings: **98,97,91,78,**— CSF £8.91 TOTE £1.80: £1.10, £1.90; EX 6.00 Place 6 £118.52, Place 5 £79.03.
Owner Michael Buckley **Bred** Miss Hilary Gibson **Trained** Upper Lambourn, Berks

FOCUS
A modest little bumper, run at a steady early gallop and the first two came clear. The form looks fairly ordinary.

NOTEBOOK
Au Courant(IRE) was very well backed to make a winning debut and, despite taking time to master the runner-up in the straight, duly got off the mark at the first time of asking. He would probably have been seen to better effect with a stronger gallop and he is bred to jump a fence and stay further in due course. He should improve physically for this outing. *(op Evens tchd 10-11 and 5-4)*
Busy Henry , third on debut at this track on faster ground 39 days previously, made the winner pull out all the stops and ran an improved race in defeat. His previous experience told this time, but he *has done little wrong in both his starts now and is clearly up to going one better in this sphere. (op 8-1 tchd 6-1)*

Different Class(IRE), third on his only previous outing last season, dropped out tamely when the tempo increased entering the straight and ran well below the level of his debut form. He is entitled to improve for the outing, however, and will probably fare better when faced with hurdles in due course. *(op 13-8 tchd 2-1)*
Supreme Cara, whose unraced dam is related to National Hunt winners, looked much in need of the experience and never threatened. *(op 25-1)*
T/Plt: £233.70 to a £1 stake. Pool: £38,474.95. 120.15 winning tickets. T/Qpdt: £68.70 to a £1 stake. Pool: £2,797.20. 30.10 winning tickets. ST

[1827] CHEPSTOW (L-H)

Wednesday, November 2

OFFICIAL GOING: Heavy (soft in places)
A half an inch of rain overnight made the ground even softer than expected.
Wind: Light against Weather: Showers

1980 DERRY NICKLIN RETIREMENT NOVICES' HURDLE (11 hdls) 2m 4f
1:00 (1:00) (Class 4) 4-Y-O+ **£3,506** (£1,029; £514; £257)

Form RPR
1 **Neptune Collonges (FR)**[214] [4706] 4-10-12 .... RWalsh 132+
(P F Nicholls) *mde all: clr fr 2 out: easily* **1/3**[1]
410- 2 *7* **Mister Quasimodo**[231] [4399] 5-10-12 .... JTizzard 112
(C L Tizzard) *hld up: mstke 2nd: hdwy 7th: chsd wnr appr 2 out: sn rdn: no imp* **7/1**[2]
616- 3 *5* **Royal Coburg (IRE)**[194] [4971] 5-10-12 .... TScudamore 107
(N A Twiston-Davies) *a.p: chsd wnr after 7th: ev ch appr 3 out: rdn after 2 out: wknd flat* **14/1**[3]
530- 4 *14* **Kildonnan**[237] [4283] 6-10-12 .... WHutchinson 97+
(J A B Old) *chsd wnr tl after 7th: wknd appr 3 out: hit 2 out* **80/1**
4 5 *27* **Bilton's Nap**[15] [1779] 6-10-12 .... RWalford 66
(R H Alner) *bhd fr 7th* **25/1**
41- 6 *26* **Barton Legend**[228] [4465] 5-10-12 .... TJMurphy 40
(D P Keane) *hld up: stdy hdwy appr 4th: wknd after 7th: t.o* **16/1**
30P- P **A Pound Down (IRE)**[328] [2735] 8-10-12 .... DCrosse —
(N G Ayliffe) *hld up: hdwy after 4th: dropped rr and mstke 7th: sn t.o: p.u bef 2 out* **200/1**

5m 16.5s (13.80) **Going Correction** +0.725s/f (Soft) **7** Ran SP% **105.6**
Speed ratings: **101,98,96,90,79 69**,— CSF £2.48 TOTE £1.30: £1.10, £2.40; EX 2.80.
Owner J Hales **Bred** Gaec Delorme Freres **Trained** Ditcheat, Somerset

FOCUS
An uncompetitive event but won in good style by the favourite, who was value for much further, and rated through the third and fourth to their bumper marks.

NOTEBOOK
Neptune Collonges(FR) ◆ was unbeaten in all his completed starts over fences in France including a Group Three at Auteuil in April. He may not have had a great deal to beat but confirmed his preference for testing ground and won as he liked. He looks one to keep on the right side and will now be stepped up in class. *(op 2-7)*
Mister Quasimodo, the winner of a couple of soft-ground bumpers including one here, was making his hurdling debut. He found that the winner was on another planet but will not always come up against one so smart. *(op 15-2)*
Royal Coburg(IRE) had a similar profile to the second in that he won a bumper on heavy ground here and was graduating to timber. *(tchd 16-1)*

1981 KELLANDS (S) H'CAP CHASE (16 fncs) 2m 3f 110y
1:35 (1:35) (Class 5) (0-90,82) 5-Y-O+ **£2,514** (£732; £366)

Form RPR
0653 1 **Sunday Habits (IRE)**[13] [1803] 11-10-11 **74** .... MrDavidTurner(7) 83
(Dr P Pritchard) *hld up: hdwy 6th: led sn after 5 out: rdn appr 3 out: hdd 2 out: rallied to ld cl home* **7/1**
4-PP 2 *nk* **Look To The Future (IRE)**[21] [1715] 11-11-4 **79** .... LStephens(5) 88
(M J M Evans) *chsd ldr to 11th: wnt 2nd again appr 4 out: rdn to ld 2 out: hdd cl home* **5/1**[2]
-445 3 *dist* **Taksina**[28] [1646] 6-10-0 **61** .... RStephens(5) —
(R H Buckler) *hld up: short-lived effrt after 11th: tk poor 3rd flat* **5/2**[1]
P2-P 4 *4* **Adalie**[119] [916] 11-11-5 **82** .... (b[1]) SWalsh(7) —
(J D Frost) *t.k.h: hdwy 11th: sn rdn: wknd after 3 out* **6/1**[3]
1060 5 *23* **Ashgan (IRE)**[45] [1483] 12-12-12 **68** .... JMogford —
(Dr P Pritchard) *a bhd: lost tch fr 7th: t.o* **8/1**
04P5 P **Noble Colours**[13] [1803] 12-10-5 **61** .... RGreene —
(Mrs C J Ikin) *prom tl rdn and wknd 6th: t.o whn p.u bef 4 out* **14/1**
/30P P **Prince On The Ter**[10] [1858] 10-10-3 **62** .... CBolger(3) —
(B Scriven) *led to 11th: rdn and wknd appr 5 out: bhd whn p.u bef 3 out* **8/1**
02-P P **Shannon Quest (IRE)**[17] [1751] 9-11-5 **82** .... (b) CMStudd(7) —
(C L Popham) *hld up in tch: jnd ldr 9th: led 11th tl sn after 5 out: sn wknd: 4th whn p.u bef 3 out* **12/1**

5m 31.1s (19.80) **Going Correction** +0.80s/f (Soft) **8** Ran SP% **108.6**
Speed ratings: **92,91**,—,—,— —,—,— CSF £38.01 CT £99.12 TOTE £7.20: £1.70, £1.80, £1.80; EX 35.30.There was no bid for the winner
Owner The It's My Job Partnership **Bred** John J Hanlon **Trained** Purton, Gloucs

FOCUS
The decent gallop in the conditions took its toll on these platers and the slow time was down to the ground. The form is rated through the runner-up.

NOTEBOOK
Sunday Habits(IRE), dropped into selling company, had not run on ground anything like this since coming over from Ireland. He stays much further and the combination of the conditions and the way things panned out helped him gain the day. *(op 8-1)*
Look To The Future(IRE) was another who had proved he stays further when winning a selling hurdle over three and a quarter miles at Southwell. He seemed set to score when touching down ahead at the penultimate fence but the winner proved just too strong. *(op 6-1)*
Taksina did not give favourite backers much of a run for their money on this drop in grade. *(tchd 2-1)*
Prince On The Ter *Official explanation: trainer said gelding had mucus on lungs (op 9-1)*
Shannon Quest(IRE) *Official explanation: jockey said gelding had a breathing problem (op 9-1)*

1982 FOOD PARTNERS NOVICES' HURDLE (8 hdls) 2m 110y
2:10 (2:11) (Class 4) 4-Y-O+ **£3,396** (£997; £498; £248)

Form RPR
4 1 **Random Quest**[21] [1711] 7-10-12 .... OMcPhail 100+
(B J Llewellyn) *w ldr: led 2nd: clr appr 3 out: hit 2 out: sn rdn: jst hld on* **10/3**[2]
06- 2 *shd* **Fleurette**[239] [4238] 5-10-5 .... TDoyle 92+
(D R Gandolfo) *hld up in tch: outpcd appr 3 out: rdn appr last: r.o wl flat: jst failed* **12/1**
050- 3 *15* **Just A Splash (IRE)**[214] [4696] 5-10-12 .... ATinkler 85+
(N J Gifford) *hld up: hdwy 4 out: wknd appr last* **11/1**
-220 4 *4* **Argent Ou Or (FR)**[129] [838] 4-10-12 **99** .... TJMurphy 80
(M C Pipe) *bhd tl styd on fr 2 out: n.d* **11/2**
0 5 *½* **Tytheknot**[31] [1614] 4-10-12 .... RWalsh 82+
(O Sherwood) *hld up in tch: hit 2 out: wkng whn hit last* **5/1**[3]
6 *2* **Future Legend**[518] 4-10-12 .... WHutchinson 78
(J A B Old) *prom: hit 4 out: wnt 2nd 3 out: hit 2 out: sn wknd* **10/1**
0-5 7 *2* **Lord Hopeful (IRE)**[178] [249] 4-10-12 .... JAMcCarthy 77+
(C P Morlock) *hld up in tch: rdn appr 4 out: btn whn mstke 4 out* **50/1**
06-0 8 *13* **Classic Clover**[180] [201] 5-10-12 .... JTizzard 63
(C L Tizzard) *mstke 2nd: pckd 3rd: a bhd* **33/1**
9 *dist* **Sistema**[543] 4-10-12 .... (b[1]) MBradburne —
(A E Price) *t.k.h: mde most tl mstke 2nd: chsd wnr tl wknd appr 3 out: t.o* **40/1**
F240 F **Tom Bell (IRE)**[7] [1880] 5-11-5 **107** .... (v) DCrosse 84
(J G M O'Shea) *t.k.h: hdwy appr 4th: wknd 3 out: fell last* **3/1**[1]

4m 24.5s (14.10) **Going Correction** +0.725s/f (Soft)
WFA 4 from 5yo+ 12lb **10** Ran SP% **112.6**
Speed ratings: **95,94,87,86,85 84,83,77**,—,— CSF £39.71 TOTE £4.70: £1.40, £4.80, £3.00; EX 53.80.
Owner Terry Warner **Bred** Bottisham Heath Stud **Trained** Fochriw, Caerphilly

FOCUS
A modest event with a slow winning time for a race of its class and it is difficult to be confident about the form.

NOTEBOOK
Random Quest had the testing ground to put the emphasis on stamina on this big drop back in distance. He appeared to have it sewn up early in the long home straight but he only scraped home in the end. *(op 3-1 tchd 5-2)*
Fleurette ◆ appears to be going the right way and would surely have prevailed had her rider got busier sooner.
Just A Splash(IRE) probably had less to do than on his hurdling debut at Newbury back in April after a couple of outings in soft-ground bumpers. *(op 14-1)*
Argent Ou Or(FR), bred to act in this sort of ground, shaped like one that wants further. *(op 9-2 tchd 13-2)*
Tytheknot, a ten-furlong winner on soft ground at Newcastle, found his jumping suffering as his stamina gave out. *(op 7-1)*
Future Legend, a 37,000 guineas purchase, had not been seen since winning in the soft at Longchamp in June last year. *(op 8-1 tchd 15-2 and 12-1)*
Tom Bell(IRE), on ground on the soft side for him, may have seen too much daylight on the outside on the back straight. *(tchd 7-2)*

1983 COCA COLA NOVICES' H'CAP CHASE (18 fncs) 3m
2:45 (2:45) (Class 4) (0-105,101) 5-Y-O+ **£4,059** (£1,191; £595; £297)

Form RPR
534- 1 **Up The Pub (IRE)**[270] [3696] 7-10-5 **80** .... RWalford 90+
(R H Alner) *hld up in tch: hdwy appr 3 out: led last: drvn out* **3/1**[1]
3-31 2 *1* **Anflora**[11] [1832] 8-10-1 **76** .... TDoyle 83
(B J Llewellyn) *hld up: hdwy 10th: styd on flat* **7/2**[2]
PPP- 3 *hd* **Supreme Sir (IRE)**[306] [3122] 7-9-13 **77** oh11 ow2 .... CBolger(3) 85+
(P G Murphy) *a.p: led 12th to 5 out: lft in ld 2 out: hdd last: nt qckn* **50/1**
2-1P 4 *7* **Mandica (IRE)**[17] [1761] 7-11-12 **101** .... TJMurphy 102+
(T R George) *led to 3rd: w ldr: hung lft fr 4 out: wknd appr last* **6/1**[3]
20-3 5 *5* **It's Rumoured**[15] [1781] 5-11-3 **93** .... JamesDavies 93+
(Jean-Rene Auvray) *w ldr: led 3rd to 12th: led 5 out tl blnd 2 out: wknd last* **16/1**
1PP2 6 *6* **Billy Ballbreaker (IRE)**[11] [1832] 9-11-6 **95** .... (t) JTizzard 88+
(C L Tizzard) *t.k.h: nt fluent 5th and 6th: short-lived effrt after 13th* **7/2**[2]
5-42 7 *nk* **Moorland Monarch**[28] [1637] 7-10-0 **80** ow5 .... CHonour(5) 69
(J D Frost) *hld up: hdwy 8th: hit 4 out: wknd 3 out* **15/2**
POP- P **Mr Crawford**[299] [3263] 6-9-6 **75** oh11 .... StephenJCraine(5) —
(Nick Williams) *hld up in tch: hit 10th: wknd appr 5 out: bhd whn p.u bef 2 out* **66/1**
0-05 P **Euro Bleu (FR)**[11] [1831] 7-11-1 **95** .... (p) LStephens(5) —
(M Sheppard) *hld up: hdwy 5th: j. slowly and lost pl 8th: bhd fr 13th: p.u bef 2 out* **28/1**

6m 45.7s (30.80) **Going Correction** +0.80s/f (Soft)
WFA 5 from 6yo+ 1lb **9** Ran SP% **108.3**
Speed ratings: **80,79,79,77,75 73,73**,—,— CSF £12.77 CT £359.37 TOTE £3.60: £1.40, £1.80, £8.00; EX 20.20.
Owner P Cox, G Keirle, J Dunevein **Bred** Mrs Olive Lambert **Trained** Droop, Dorset

FOCUS
A slow winning time, even in these conditions, for this moderate novice handicap. The winner did not need to run to last season's form to score and the form looks weak.

NOTEBOOK
Up The Pub(IRE) was not disgraced when last seen over course and distance in February. He took advantage of a return to novice company with quite a hard-fought win. *(op 7-2 tchd 11-4)*
Anflora ran another sound race despite having gone up 7lb for her course and distance victory. *(op 10-3 tchd 4-1)*
Supreme Sir(IRE), 11lb out of the handicap, was a modest performer between the flags. Pulled up on his three chases in 2004, this was obviously a tremendous improvement. *(tchd 66-1)*
Mandica(IRE) was 6lb higher than when scoring at Uttoxeter in April. He has yet to prove he is effective at this trip and turned out to be a difficult ride. *(op 9-2)*
It's Rumoured held a narrow advantage when effectively blundering away his chance at the penultimate fence. *(op 11-1)*
Billy Ballbreaker(IRE) was disappointing after his good second behind the runner-up here last time. *(op 3-1)*

1984 BETFRED POKER H'CAP HURDLE (SERIES QUALIFIER) (11 hdls) 2m 4f
3:20 (3:20) (Class 3) (0-125,121) 4-Y-O+ **£4,788** (£1,405; £702; £351)

Form RPR
PU5- 1 **By Degree (IRE)**[206] [4791] 9-10-13 **115** .... JamesWhite(7) 123+
(R J Hodges) *hld up in tch: jnd ldrs 6th: led appr 2 out: rdn appr last: drvn out* **11/1**
5-01 2 *¾* **Mouseski**[25] [1675] 11-11-3 **112** .... RWalsh 119+
(P F Nicholls) *led to 7th: led 4 out: hdd and rdn appr 2 out: rallied and ev ch last: nt qckn towards fin* **4/5**[1]
041- 3 *25* **Pass Me A Dime**[249] [4060] 6-11-3 **112** .... JTizzard 94
(C L Tizzard) *plld hrd early in rr: sme hdwy whn hit 4 out: nvr nr ldrs* **8/1**[2]
4-20 4 *8* **Just Beth**[166] [441] 9-10-13 **113** .... DLaverty(5) 87
(G Fierro) *hld up in tch: sn wknd whn hit 4 out* **12/1**
116- 5 *5* **Laudamus**[203] [4825] 7-10-5 **100** .... RWalford 69
(R H Alner) *t.k.h: prom tl wknd 7th* **12/1**
-122 6 *23* **Latin Queen (IRE)**[108] [1021] 5-11-0 **114** .... CHonour(5) 71+
(J D Frost) *a.p: led 7th to 4 out: 3rd and wkng whn blnd 3 out* **16/1**

3P6- **7** *16* **Miss Fahrenheit (IRE)**[224] 4518 6-11-4 **113**............ ChristianWilliams 43
(C Roberts) *prom tl wknd appr 4 out* **9/1**[3]
100- **P** **Musimaro (FR)**[472] 1002 7-10-8 **103**............(p) WHutchinson —
(R J Price) *bhd fr 6th: p.u bef 4 out* **40/1**
PPP0 **P** **Dancinginthestreet**[18] 1747 5-9-9 **95**............ RStephens(5) —
(J L Flint) *a bhd: t.o whn p.u bef 2 out* **100/1**
60-U **P** **Dream Falcon**[13] 1804 5-11-8 **117**............ JamesDavies —
(R J Hodges) *plld hrd early: a bhd: t.o whn p.u after 5th* **33/1**
-300 **P** **Turkama (FR)**[39] 1548 8-11-6 **115**............ TJMurphy —
(L A Dace) *hld up in mid-div: short-lived effrt after 7th: no ch whn hit 4 out: p.u bef 3 out* **20/1**

5m 12.8s (10.10) **Going Correction** +0.725s/f (Soft) 11 Ran SP% **117.4**
Speed ratings: **108,107,97,94,92 83,76,—,—,—** — CSF £20.41 CT £82.30 TOTE £9.30: £1.90, £1.30, £1.90; EX 32.60.
Owner Fieldspring Racing **Bred** F Fennelly **Trained** Charlton Adam, Somerset

FOCUS
The first two pulled clear in this uncompetitive handicap and the pair could rate higher.

NOTEBOOK
By Degree(IRE), who stays further, was a springer in the market on his first start since April. His young rider deserves full marks for the way he competed in a driving finish against one of the best jockeys in the business. *(op 20-1 tchd 22-1)*
Mouseski, twice a winner in soft ground over fences, had been raised 10lb for his course and distance victory. He looked like pulling it out of the fire at the final flight but the winning partnership had other ideas. *(op 10-11 tchd Evens)*
Pass Me A Dime had not been seen since winning a maiden over course and distance back in February.
Dream Falcon *Official explanation: jockey said gelding was unsuited by the heavy (soft in places) ground (op 25-1)*

1985 LETHEBY & CHRISTOPHER INTERMEDIATE OPEN NATIONAL HUNT FLAT RACE 2m 110y
3:55 (3:56) (Class 6) 4-6-Y-O £1,891 (£551; £275)

Form RPR
2 **1** **Asudo (IRE)**[25] 1681 4-10-11 .... SCrawford(7) 107+
(N A Twiston-Davies) *mde all: clr over 1f out: comf* **6/4**[1]
2 *3 ½* **Leading Authority (IRE)** 4-11-4 .... JTizzard 103+
(C L Tizzard) *chsd wnr: rdn 3f out: one pce fnl 2f* **8/1**
3 *24* **Joseph Beuys (IRE)** 6-10-11 .... DJacob(7) 79
(D P Keane) *hld up: hdwy over 6f out: rdn over 4f out: wknd over 3f out* **12/1**
4 *1 ¼* **Lemon Tree** 5-10-4 .... SWalsh(7) 70
(N M Babbage) *hld up towards rr: hdwy on ins over 4f out: wknd and hung lft over 3f out* **40/1**
5 *1 ¼* **Grand Slam Hero (IRE)** 4-11-4 .... ChristianWilliams 76
(P Bowen) *prom tl wknd and hung lft over 2f out* **7/1**[3]
22 **6** *4* **I'm Lovin It (IRE)**[133] 816 5-11-4 .... RWalsh 74+
(P F Nicholls) *hld up: hdwy 7f out: wknd and hung lft over 2f out* **3/1**[2]
7 *dist* **Dryliner** 5-11-4 .... MBradburne —
(A E Price) *plld hrd in rr: short-lived effrt over 5f out: t.o* **40/1**
8 *14* **Ourcarl** 5-11-4 .... JEMoore —
(G Brown) *hld up in mid-div: hdwy over 7f out: rdn 6f out: sn wknd: t.o* **50/1**
9 *19* **Young Guns (IRE)**[234] 4-11-4 .... DCrosse —
(J G M O'Shea) *hld up in mid-div: hdwy over 7f out: rdn over 4f out: sn wknd: t.o* **20/1**
0 **10** *dist* **Nature's Magic**[17] 1755 4-10-11 .... AO'Keeffe —
(R J Price) *hld up in tch: wknd qckly 8f out: t.o* **66/1**
11 *dist* **At Loggerheads** 4-10-11 .... JamesDavies —
(C A Leafe) *a bhd: rdn 10f out: sn lost tch: t.o* **33/1**

4m 22.7s (12.50) **Going Correction** +0.725s/f (Soft)
WFA 4 from 5yo+ 12lb 11 Ran SP% **112.3**
Speed ratings: **99,97,86,85,84 83,—,—,—,—** — CSF £12.51 TOTE £2.60: £1.30, £1.80, £2.70; EX 12.20.
Owner D J & S A Goodman **Bred** J P Murphy **Trained** Naunton, Gloucs

FOCUS
The testing ground took its toll in what may not have been a great bumper. The winner is the best guide to the level of the form.

NOTEBOOK
Asudo(IRE) built on the promise of his second here last month. He may run at Cheltenham's Open meeting prior to switching to hurdles. *(op 11-8 tchd 5-4)*
Leading Authority(IRE) is a 23,000 guineas first foal of an unraced half-sister to Gold Cup winner Davy Lad. Although a shade flattered by his proximity to the winner, this was a decent start to his career. *(op 12-1)*
Joseph Beuys(IRE) is a half-brother to the winner of an Irish point. *(op 14-1 tchd 16-1)*
Lemon Tree *Official explanation: jockey said mare hung left on run-in (op 33-1)*
Grand Slam Hero(IRE), the first foal of a bumper and hurdles winner, got quite tired and hung in the closing stages. *(op 5-1)*
I'm Lovin It(IRE), having been runner-up in two bumpers on a sound surface in the early summer, found these conditions against him on this return to action. *(op 10-3 tchd 7-2 and 11-4)*

1986 LETHEBY & CHRISTOPHER H'CAP CHASE (12 fncs) 2m 110y
4:25 (4:25) (Class 3) (0-125,124) 5-Y-O+ **£5,292** (£1,553; £776; £388)

Form RPR
F-14 **1** **Dangerousdanmagru (IRE)**[11] 1831 9-10-9 **107**............ MFoley 123+
(A E Jones) *hld up: hdwy 7th: led on bit appr 5 out: clr 4 out: easily* **9/4**[2]
6P- **2** *4* **Macmar (FR)**[294] 3320 5-11-1 **113**............ RWalford 114
(R H Alner) *hld up: mstke 2nd: hdwy 6th: rdn appr 5 out: wnt 2nd 3 out: no ch w wnr* **14/1**
44-F **3** *5* **East Lawyer (FR)**[11] 1831 6-11-2 **114**............ RWalsh 113+
(P F Nicholls) *hld up: hit 1st and 3rd: wl bhd 5th: hdwy 4 out: one pce fr 2 out* **11/8**[1]
1256 **4** *6* **Sardagna (FR)**[27] 1658 5-11-12 **124**............ TJMurphy 114
(M C Pipe) *chsd ldr: ev ch 5 out: sn hung lft: wknd 3 out* **11/2**[3]
PP0- **5** *4* **Jaybejay (NZ)**[329] 2700 10-9-13 **107**............ WMcCarthy(10) 93
(T R George) *j.rt: led: clr after 1st: hdd appr 5 out: sn wknd* **8/1**

4m 32.4s (9.50) **Going Correction** +0.80s/f (Soft) 5 Ran SP% **106.0**
Speed ratings: **109,107,104,101,100** CSF £22.75 TOTE £3.30: £1.20, £4.80; EX 23.90 Place 6 £12.57, Place 5 £11.82.
Owner N F Glynn **Bred** Kashmir Breeding **Trained** Newchapel, Surrey

FOCUS
A typically small field for this two-mile handicap chase. The winner is value for further with the

NOTEBOOK
Dangerousdanmagru(IRE) loves the mud and could hardly have known he had been in a race. He can defy a penalty. *(op 5-2 tchd 2-1)*
Macmar(FR), blinkered for his only win over fences in the French Provinces, is greatly flattered by his proximity to the winner. *(op 9-1 tchd 16-1)*
East Lawyer(FR) gave the impression he remembered his heavy fall here last time and it took quite a while for his jumping to warm up. *(tchd 6-4)*
Sardagna(FR), reverting to fences, does appear to have gone off the boil. *(op 5-1 tchd 9-2)*
Jaybejay(NZ), dropping back in distance, tried to put the emphasis on stamina but jumping right-handed soon put a stop to that. *(tchd 15-2 and 9-1)*
T/Plt: £25.70 to a £1 stake. Pool: £39,508.45. 1,119.40 winning tickets. T/Qpdt: £14.70 to a £1 stake. Pool: £4,069.90. 203.80 winning tickets. KH

1735 HUNTINGDON (R-H)
Wednesday, November 2

OFFICIAL GOING: Hurdle course - good changing to good (good to soft in places) after race 2 (1.45); chase course - good (good to soft in places) changing to good to soft (good in places) after race 2 (1.45)
Light, across Overcast

1987 RACING UK CONDITIONAL JOCKEYS' H'CAP HURDLE (8 hdls) 2m 110y
1:10 (1:11) (Class 4) (0-110,108) 4-Y-0+ **£3,313** (£965; £483)

Form RPR
13P **1** **Irish Wolf (FR)**[25] 1671 5-11-12 **108**............ TGreenway 116+
(P Bowen) *mid-div: hdwy 4th: jnd ldr after 3 out: hit next: rdn to ld flat: styd on* **25/1**
36-4 **2** *1* **Di's Dilemma**[21] 1717 7-10-1 **88**............ TMessenger(5) 94
(C C Bealby) *chsd ldrs: hmpd 1st: led appr 3 out: rdn and hdd flat : styd on* **13/2**[1]
2412 **3** *3 ½* **Festive Chimes (IRE)**[41] 1522 4-11-7 **103**............ ONelmes 106
(N B King) *hld up: hdwy 4th: rdn 2 out: styd on same pce last* **10/1**
65-5 **4** *1 ¼* **Park City**[21] 1717 6-10-3 **90**............ LHeard(5) 91
(J Joseph) *hld up: hdwy 3 out: rdn appr last: styd on same pce* **16/1**
3422 **5** *½* **Resplendent Star (IRE)**[65] 1365 8-11-2 **108**............(v) MRoe(10) 110+
(Mrs L Wadham) *hld up: hdwy 3 out: hit next: rdn appr last: styd on same pce* **8/1**[3]
2205 **6** *3 ½* **Artane Boys**[13] 1804 8-11-3 **107**............ WJones(8) 104
(Jonjo O'Neill) *hld up: hdwy 5th: styd on same pce fr 2 out* **8/1**[3]
015 **7** *11* **Uncle John**[18] 1747 4-9-7 **83**............(v) DJBoland(8) 69
(Ian Williams) *chsd ldrs: led appr 4th: hdd bef 3 out: sn rdn and wknd* **8/1**[3]
15-3 **8** *shd* **Iberus (GER)**[31] 1610 7-11-9 **105**............(p) WKennedy 91
(S Gollings) *hld up: hdwy u.p appr 3 out: wknd bef next* **7/1**[2]
65-0 **9** *6* **The Footballresult**[141] 749 4-9-9 **82** oh10............(b) WPKavanagh(5) 62
(P R Johnson) *hld up: rdn after 4th: sn wknd* **66/1**
-PP3 **10** *4* **Honest Endeavour**[13] 1793 6-11-9 **105**............(p) PMerrigan 88+
(J M Jefferson) *led and j.rt 1st: hdd 3rd: slipped bnd after 4th: hit next: sn wknd* **10/1**
0301 **11** *9* **Idle Journey (IRE)**[6] 1902 4-10-7 **97** 7ex............ JKington(8) 69+
(M Scudamore) *chsd ldrs: led 3rd: hdd bef next: wknd appr 3 out* **7/1**[2]
-405 **12** *20* **Manolo (FR)**[13] 1805 5-10-13 **95**............ PCO'Neill 42
(Ian Williams) *chsd ldrs: hmpd 1st: lost pl appr 4th: bhd fr next* **14/1**
/0P- **13** *20* **Moon Emperor**[21] 2806 8-11-6 **105**............ RLucey-Butler(3) 32
(J R Jenkins) *hld up: a bhd* **14/1**
4-3F **P** **Tignasse (FR)**[16] 1774 4-10-9 **97**............ EDehdashti(6) —
(G L Moore) *hld up: hdwy 4th: wknd next: t.o whn p.u bef 2 out* **14/1**

4m 0.10s (4.40) **Going Correction** +0.425s/f (Soft)
WFA 4 from 5yo+ 12lb 14 Ran SP% **121.1**
Speed ratings: **106,105,103,103,103 101,96,96,93,91 87,77,68,—** CSF £183.33 CT £1767.23 TOTE £24.50: £5.90, £2.90, £2.80; EX 528.30.
Owner The Hacking Partnership **Bred** Mrs Magalen Bryant **Trained** Little Newcastle, Pembrokes

FOCUS
This was a competitive low-grade affair. The winner returned to form and the race looks solid enough, best rated through the placed horses.

NOTEBOOK
Irish Wolf(FR) proved disappointing on his last outing - in which he reportedly lost a front shoe - but with the cheekpieces removed, he travelled ominously well into the home straight and, despite making a mistake at the second last, found enough off the bridle to hang on. The return to two miles appeared to do the trick, and he can win again.
Di's Dilemma is a fair performer in her grade, but cannot get her head in front no matter how hard she tries. Connections are thinking of trying her over fences soon, and she is capable of getting that elusive victory. *(tchd 7-1)*
Festive Chimes(IRE) has been in consistent form since March, and proved a good money-spinner for her owner, as she has form at a variety of distances. Half a mile further is arguably her best trip, and she kept on plugging away after the last. Another race can be found for her, especially over slightly further. *(op 11-1)*
Park City, having his second run after a huge layoff, moved nicely throughout the race, and kept on in determined fashion under pressure. A seller can be won with him at the very least
Resplendent Star(IRE) showed plenty of promise on his chase debut when last seen on this *course, and shaped well on his return before going over the bigger obstacles again. (op 17-2 tchd 9-1)*
Iberus(GER) was in trouble starting the sweep into the final bend and is not particularly well handicapped on his winning form. *(tchd 8-1)*
Honest Endeavour was not jumping with any zest before he appeared to lose his footing after the fourth flight. His chance effectively ended at that point. *(op 8-1)*
Idle Journey(IRE) was probably outdone by his penalty. Despite his win last time, he still has to fully convince he stays two miles properly, as he probably snatched victory last time. *(op 6-1)*

1988 DEREK SLY NOVICES' H'CAP CHASE (19 fncs) 3m
1:45 (1:45) (Class 3) (0-110,110) 5-Y-0+ **£5,478** (£1,608; £804; £401)

Form RPR
F50- **1** **King Of Gothland (IRE)**[258] 3904 6-10-8 **92**............ JPMcNamara 105+
(K C Bailey) *hld up: hdwy 3 out: chsd ldr bef next: hmpd last: styd on u.p to ld towards fin* **16/1**
/5P- **2** *2* **Pedina (IRE)**[146] 699 7-11-4 **102**............ NFehily 112
(C J Mann) *hld up: hdwy 4 out: led after next: j.lft last: rdn and hdd towards fin* **5/1**[3]
00-0 **3** *21* **Ardashir (FR)**[179] 207 6-11-5 **103**............ BJCrowley 92
(Mrs S J Humphrey) *prom: j. slowly and lost pl 6th: hdwy 11th: outpcd 15th: styd on flat* **12/1**
452- **4** *nk* **Roman Court (IRE)**[199] 4889 7-10-8 **92**............ PJBrennan 81
(R H Alner) *led and hit 1st: sn hdd: chsd ldrs: led 9th: hdd after 3 out: wknd next* **10/3**[1]
P0-0 **5** *2 ½* **Dante's Back (IRE)**[15] 1780 7-11-3 **101**............ AntonyEvans 87
(N A Twiston-Davies) *hld up: hdwy and mstke 8th: rdn and wknd appr 2 out* **12/1**

525- **6** *8* **Fullards**[229] 4440 7-11-12 **110** WMarston 91+
(Mrs P Sly) *led after 1st: hdd 9th: rdn 14th: wknd 3 out* **6/1**

U3-3 **7** *dist* **The Holy Bee (IRE)**[31] 1618 6-11-6 **104** MBatchelor 70
(Miss H C Knight) *chsd ldrs: mstke 5th (water): hit 8th: rdn 10th: wknd 3 out* **12/1**

40-P **F** **Memories Of Gold (IRE)**[17] 1753 5-10-0 **85** oh2 SCurran —
(J A Danahar) *fell 1st* **66/1**

6-11 **P** **Stack The Pack (IRE)**[153] 612 8-11-5 **103** JMMaguire —
(T R George) *prom: hit 15th: wkng whn blnd 3 out: p.u bef next* **4/1**[2]

4054 **P** **It's Definite (IRE)**[15] 1780 6-11-3 **101** (p) ADobbin —
(P Bowen) *prom: lost pl 5th: in rr whn blnd 11th: bhd whn mstke next: sn p.u* **7/1**

6m 24.2s (11.90) **Going Correction** +0.60s/f (Soft)
WFA 5 from 6yo+ 1lb **10** Ran SP% **117.0**
Speed ratings: **104,103,96,96,95 92,—,—,—,—** CSF £96.14 CT £1012.12 TOTE £21.30: £4.00, £2.40, £5.30; EX 124.50.
Owner The Norfolk Neighbours **Bred** Mrs Ann Fortune **Trained** Preston Capes, Northants

FOCUS
This was a low-grade event, with a few in the field making their chasing debuts in handicap company, and could be rated higher. The winner looks sure to improve.

NOTEBOOK
King Of Gothland(IRE), a half-brother to the useful Dr Bones, moved easily through the field on the final circuit before getting to the leader jumping the last. The jockey had to keep him straight down the home straight, as he had a tendency to hang to the right, but the further he went, the further he stretched clear. More improvement can be expected, especially over further.
Pedina(IRE), making his English debut, did not seem too badly treated on his first attempt in handicap company over fences, given his best form over hurdles, and went for home going easily after the third last. He was unproven at the distance and probably did not get home quite as well as the winner, but he did not suggest that three miles will be beyond him. The jockey reported after the race that his mount had finished lame. *(op 13-2)*
Ardashir(FR), having his first run since leaving the Nigel Twiston-Davie's stable, never figured with any serious chance, but kept on really well after the last to snatch third. *(op 11-1)*
Roman Court(IRE), another making his chase debut in handicap company, jumped enthusiastically for much of the race, but weakened quickly after jumping the third last. He can be given another chance at slightly shorter. *(op 9-2)*
Dante's Back(IRE) never managed to get into a challenging position. He has been regressive since a good start to his hurdling career. *(op 10-1)*
Fullards, returning after a 229-day break, is very much a hit-and-miss performer and ran well for a long time before weakening. He should progress for the race. *(op 7-1 tchd 8-1)*
The Holy Bee(IRE) weakened right out of contention after momentarily getting into the race on the back straight. He is proving to be slightly disappointing. *(op 9-1 tchd 14-1)*
Stack The Pack(IRE), who was racing off a 13lb higher mark than the first of his two chase successes, may have been a most fortunate winner last time after his closest pursuers departed just behind him. He returned with a nasty cut that day, and had his interest ended when hitting the third last pretty hard. *Official explanation: trainer had no explanation for the poor form shown (op 13-2 tchd 6-1)*
It's Definite(IRE) was being pushed along passing the stands for the first time, and was pulled up early. *Official explanation: trainer said gelding finished lame (op 13-2 tchd 6-1)*

1989 HUNTINGDON-RACECOURSE.CO.UK H'CAP CHASE (19 fncs) 3m
2:20 (2:20) (Class 3) (0-120,113) 5-Y-0+ **£5,452** (£1,600; £800; £399)

Form RPR

2F-4 **1** **Mini Dare**[162] 488 8-10-0 **87** LAspell 103+
(O Sherwood) *hld up: hdwy 10th: chsd ldr 15th: led appr 2 out: hit last: styd on wl* **7/1**

4F2/ **2** *13* **Umbrella Man (IRE)**[945] 4448 9-11-1 **102** BFenton 106+
(Miss E C Lavelle) *hld up: hdwy 12th: hmpd 2 out: sn chsng wnr: mstke and no ex last* **13/2**[3]

0-PF **3** *6* **Free Gift**[20] 1728 7-11-8 **109** ADobbin 108+
(R H Alner) *led: hdd appr 2 out: wkng whn mstke last* **6/1**[2]

-226 **4** *11* **Master Tern (USA)**[25] 1670 10-11-6 **107** RMcGrath 93
(Jonjo O'Neill) *hld up: dropped rr 6th: hdwy 12th: wknd 14th* **7/1**

3021 **5** *dist* **Strong Magic (IRE)**[12] 1815 13-10-5 **97** MNicolls(5) —
(J R Cornwall) *hld up: hdwy 9th: wknd after 12th* **8/1**

-526 **P** **World Vision (IRE)**[26] 1664 8-11-5 **113** (p) TJDreaper(7) —
(Ferdy Murphy) *hld up: blnd 3rd and 8th: t.o whn p.u bef 13th* **14/1**

4533 **P** **Keltic Lord**[16] 1778 9-11-10 **111** JPMcNamara —
(P W Hiatt) *hld up: hdwy 11th: wknd 16th: t.o whn p.u bef 2 out* **9/1**

31-P **P** **The Extra Man (IRE)**[172] 346 11-11-7 **108** (b) RThornton —
(A King) *chsd ldrs: lost pl 8th: bhd fr next: t.o whn p.u bef 11th* **9/2**[1]

55-P **P** **Spinofski**[13] 1798 10-11-8 **109** (b[1]) NFehily —
(D R Stoddart) *hmpd 1st: chsd ldr to 9th: wknd next: t.o whn p.u bef 13th* **16/1**

200- **P** **Fin Bec (FR)**[298] 3278 12-11-8 **109** (b) JGoldstein —
(A P Jones) *j.rt 1st: chsd ldrs: hit 10th: wknd next: t.o whn p.u bef 13th* **25/1**

435- **P** **Tom Costalot (IRE)**[237] 4287 10-10-13 **100** PJBrennan —
(Mrs Susan Nock) *prom: chsd ldr 9th to 15th: wknd next: t.o whn p.u bef 2 out* **14/1**

6m 22.9s (10.60) **Going Correction** +0.60s/f (Soft) **11** Ran SP% **115.0**
Speed ratings: **106,101,99,96,— —,—,—,—,— —** CSF £51.56 CT £289.91 TOTE £13.90: £2.60, £3.00, £2.50; EX 55.10 Trifecta £410.90 Pool: £578.80 - 1 winning unit.
Owner Furrows Ltd,A Douglas & Mrs S Bridge **Bred** Shade Oak Stud **Trained** Upper Lambourn, Berks

FOCUS
This modest handicap was run at a good tempo which probably resulted in only five finishers and a fair time. The winner made full use of his weight allowance to win nicely.

NOTEBOOK
Mini Dare, one of the least experienced over fences in the field, reportedly had confidence problems when he was last tried over fences but, under a quiet ride, he worked his way to the front and won nicely. His favourable handicap mark is sure to suffer for this, and he will need to be turned out fairly quickly to make use of it. *(op 8-1)*
Umbrella Man(IRE), off for 945 days, almost credited his handler with one of the training feats of the year, as he loomed large behind the leaders in the back straight. It was a fine effort after a break but the concern will be the effect the race will have on him as he was tired in the closing stages. *(op 11-2)*
Free Gift set a really good pace in front and ran a much better race than his other most recent efforts. He will probably not quite scale the heights forecast for him before the season started, but this was a solid effort. *(op 11-2)*
Master Tern(USA) never got on terms with the leaders, and was well adrift of the third. *(op 15-2 tchd 8-1)*
Strong Magic(IRE) kept going in his own time and at least gets credit for finishing. *(op 9-1 tchd 10-1)*
Fin Bec(FR), making his seasonal debut, made too many mistakes to get competitive. *(op 5-1)*
The Extra Man(IRE) has yet to prove he stays three miles and reportedly sulked when he could not get to the head of the field. *Official explanation: jockey said gelding was unable to dominate and sulked (op 5-1)*
Spinofski, who had the blinkers fitted for the first time, could never dominate and weakened very early. *(op 5-1)*
Keltic Lord probably requires much quicker ground to be at his best. *(op 5-1)*
World Vision(IRE) made some really bad errors at the fences and stood no chance from an early stage. *(op 5-1)*

1990 H2ONATIONWIDE "NATIONAL HUNT" NOVICES' HURDLE (10 hdls) 2m 5f 110y
2:55 (2:55) (Class 3) 4-Y-0+ **£5,087** (£1,493; £746; £373)

Form RPR

24-3 **1** **Ungaro (FR)**[181] 194 6-10-10 108 JimCrowley 125+
(K G Reveley) *hld up: hdwy 5th: led appr 2 out: clr last: eased flat* **5/2**[2]

0 **2** *11* **Love Of Classics**[6] 1892 5-10-10 (p) LAspell 110+
(O Sherwood) *hld up: hdwy 6th: styd on same pce fr 2 out* **100/1**

5-1 **3** *6* **Etched In Stone (IRE)**[174] 323 6-10-10 ADobbin 112+
(N G Richards) *chsd ldr 2nd: led after 7th: hdd and hit 2 out: wknd last* **11/8**[1]

4 *dist* **Ballyowen (IRE)**[185] 6-10-10 WMarston —
(Mrs P Sly) *led: hdd after 7th: wknd next* **16/1**

000- **5** *10* **Irish Grouse (IRE)**[275] 3620 6-10-10 MBatchelor —
(Miss H C Knight) *hld up: a in rr* **80/1**

0-0 **6** *2* **Stark Raven**[15] 1782 5-10-10 NFehily —
(Miss E C Lavelle) *hld up: a in rr* **33/1**

520- **7** *16* **Oscardeal (IRE)**[231] 4399 6-10-3 APogson(7) —
(C T Pogson) *chsd ldr to 2nd: wknd after 6th* **8/1**[3]

UPP- **8** *dist* **Bright Present (IRE)**[229] 4440 7-10-3 TMessenger(7) —
(B N Pollock) *stmbld sn after s: mid-div: pushed along after 5th: wknd next* **66/1**

032- **B** **Knighton Lad (IRE)**[219] 4615 5-10-10 RThornton —
(A King) *hld up: b.d 2nd* **8/1**[3]

6 **F** **Supremely Smart (IRE)**[25] 1681 5-10-10 AntonyEvans —
(N A Twiston-Davies) *fell 2nd* **14/1**

0-0 **P** **Black Shan (IRE)**[8] 1875 5-10-10 PJBrennan —
(A Ennis) *chsd ldrs to 6th: t.o whn p.u bef 3 out* **25/1**

P0-P **P** **Great Expense**[31] 1616 6-10-10 JGoldstein —
(G R Pewter) *bhd fr 3rd: t.o whn p.u after 5th* **100/1**

0- **P** **Pocket Sevens (IRE)**[299] 3261 5-10-10 BFenton —
(Miss E C Lavelle) *hld up: blnd 4th: bhd whn p.u after 7th* **28/1**

5m 17.2s (6.40) **Going Correction** +0.425s/f (Soft) **13** Ran SP% **120.4**
Speed ratings: **105,101,98,—,— —,—,—,—,— —,—,—** CSF £240.59 TOTE £4.70: £1.40, £11.30, £1.30; EX 203.80.
Owner Sir Robert Ogden **Bred** Neustrian Associates **Trained** Lingdale, N Yorks

FOCUS
This looked an ordinary novice hurdle, weakened further by two early departures. The winner won impressively and is value for more than the official margin, while the favourite had excuses for his weak finish.

NOTEBOOK
Ungaro(FR), given an official rating of 108 after five runs over hurdles, set a reasonable standard and cruised to victory after being anchored towards the middle of the field early. The impressive nature of his win makes him one to keep on the right side of and the stable rate him quite highly. *(op 11-4 tchd 10-3)*
Love Of Classics seemed to show much-improved form for the application of cheekpieces but, in a race where very few got competitive, he is one to take on next time.
Etched In Stone(IRE) was just starting to get the worst of the argument with the winner when making a really bad mistake two from home. He did really well to stay on his feet when slipping on the bend starting his final circuit - not unlike Honest Endeavour in the first - and looked fairly sore after jumping the last. *(op 6-4 tchd 6-5)*
Ballyowen(IRE), who had winning form between the flags, led the field for a long way but was absolutely legless in the final stages. *(op 14-1)*
Knighton Lad(IRE) had no chance when brought down by a faller at the second. *(op 12-1 tchd 10-1)*
Supremely Smart(IRE) came down too steeply after jumping the second and never gave his jockey a chance of staying on. *(op 12-1 tchd 10-1)*

1991 BRAMPTON NOVICES' HURDLE (8 hdls) 2m 110y
3:30 (3:30) (Class 3) 4-Y-0+ **£5,009** (£1,470; £735; £367)

Form RPR

20 **1** **Sunday City (JPN)**[18] 1745 4-10-7 TGreenway(5) 104+
(P Bowen) *hld up: hdwy 5th: jnd ldrs 2 out: led flat: drvn out* **10/1**

006P **2** *1 1/4* **Meadow Hawk (USA)**[115] 949 5-10-12 86 ADobbin 103+
(A W Carroll) *chsd ldrs: led appr last: rdn and hdd flat: styd on* **20/1**

365- **3** *8* **Finely Tuned (IRE)**[227] 4479 6-10-12 105 NFehily 97+
(M Pitman) *chsd ldr tl led appr 3 out: rdn and hdd whe j.rt last: wknd flat* **5/2**[1]

U2-2 **4** *6* **Tingshaw Ring (IRE)**[25] 1683 5-10-12 PCO'Neill(5) 94
(Eoin Doyle, Ire) *chsd ldrs tl wknd 2 out* **6/1**

6 **5** *5* **Sgt Pepper (IRE)**[27] 1654 4-10-12 LAspell 84
(O Sherwood) *hld up: hdwy after 5th: swtchd outside bef next: wknd appr 2 out* **11/1**

6 **6** *5* **Archduke Ferdinand (FR)**[25] 1680 7-10-12 RThornton 80+
(A King) *hld up: racd keenly: hdwy 5th: wknd appr 2 out* **4/1**[2]

0-0 **7** *5* **Lake Imperial (IRE)**[13] 1794 4-10-7 PMerrigan(5) 74
(Mrs H Dalton) *hld up: nt fluent 2nd: nvr nrr* **50/1**

6 **8** *1 1/2* **Ring Of Destiny**[35] 1245 6-10-12 (t) JPMcNamara 72
(J Jay) *chsd ldrs tl wknd after 3 out* **20/1**

0 **9** *9* **Padre Nostro (IRE)**[12] 1816 6-10-5 81 APogson(7) 63
(J R Holt) *hld up: a in rr* **50/1**

P-0 **10** *1* **Sharp Rally (IRE)**[18] 1745 4-10-12 (t) WMarston 62
(A J Wilson) *hld up: a in rr* **66/1**

005 **11** *9* **Busy Man (IRE)**[12] 1818 6-10-5 RLucey-Butler(7) 53
(J R Jenkins) *hld up: hit 2nd: a in rr* **100/1**

4 **12** *2* **Dream Merchant (IRE)**[16] 1772 5-10-12 PJBrennan 51
(P J Hobbs) *mid-div: rdn and wknd appr 5th* **9/2**[3]

P34- **13** *4* **Mac's Elan**[154] 4362 5-10-9 97 ow4 MrNPearce(7) 52+
(A B Coogan) *led: hdd & wknd appr 3 out* **33/1**

0 **14** *dist* **Knocker Jock (FR)**[16] 1777 5-10-12 BFenton —
(R Rowe) *hld up: a in rr* **80/1**

660/ **P** **Captain Smoothy**[29] 3139 5-10-12 SCurran —
(M J Gingell) *chsd ldrs tl wknd after 4th: t.o whn p.u bef 3 out* **66/1**

4m 0.80s (5.10) **Going Correction** +0.425s/f (Soft) **15** Ran SP% **120.1**
Speed ratings: **105,104,100,97,95 93,90,90,85,85 81,80,78,—,—** CSF £185.47 TOTE £12.90: £3.50, £6.50, £1.50; EX 298.20.
Owner R Greenway **Bred** Shiraoi Farm **Trained** Little Newcastle, Pembrokes

FOCUS
This looked a fair race on paper, is rated around the fourth and fifth and should work out, although the proximity of the second casts doubts over the value of the form.

NOTEBOOK

Sunday City(JPN) moved into contention entering the home straight and kept on really well when asked to put his head down and battle, doing more than enough to win. This was his first start for the stable and his first success all told so, with his confidence boosted, a follow-up under a penalty is not beyond him. *(tchd 12-1)*

Meadow Hawk(USA) was supported in the market before the race at long odds, and looked like landing the gamble as he jumped the second last in contention. Clearly connections must believe they have found the key to him, and he appeared to run well above his recent efforts, including a defeat in claiming company three runs previously. His shrewd trainer will no doubt coax a win out of him. *(op 40-1)*

Finely Tuned(IRE) was going better than anything three from home, but was quickly caught and proved disappointing over the final two flights after travelling so well. He is worth another chance over slightly further and on better ground. *(op 2-1 tchd 11-4 and 3-1 in places)*

Tingshaw Ring(IRE) ran as well as she could have been expected under a double penalty. *(op 11-2)*

Sgt Pepper(IRE) was a smart two-year-old who managed to win in Listed company. His three-year-old career never got going in the same vein, and it is still not completely certain he stays the minimum trip over hurdles, especially on this ground. *(op 16-1)*

Archduke Ferdinand(FR) bumped into some decent opposition on his hurdling debut, but was again too keen for his own good over timber, and never got into a challenging position. He is the type who will be of more interest when handicapped and tried over much further given his form on the Flat. *(op 7-2)*

Dream Merchant(IRE) never jumped with much fluency and was most disappointing. *(op 4-1)*

1992 SPONSOR AT HUNTINGDON H'CAP HURDLE (12 hdls) 3m 2f

4:05 (4:06) (Class 3) (0-125,125) 4-Y-0+ **£4,775** (£1,401; £700; £350)

Form | RPR

1F-1 **1** **Tomina**[35] [109] 5-11-12 **125** .... BFenton 138+
(Miss E C Lavelle) *led 2nd: styd on strly* **5/2**[1]

320 **2** *12* **Phar From Frosty (IRE)**[8] [1872] 8-11-12 **125** .... RThornton 121+
(C R Egerton) *led to 2nd: chsd wnr: rdn and ev ch 2 out: mstke and no ex last* **11/1**

3 *12* **Burren Moonshine (IRE)**[45] [1495] 6-10-3 **102** .... GLee 84
(P Bowen) *chsd ldrs tl wknd appr 2 out* **5/1**

212- **4** *3 1/2* **Heir To Be**[319] [2895] 6-10-11 **110** .... LAspell 89
(Mrs L Wadham) *hld up: hdwy 8th: wknd appr 2 out* **4/1**[3]

0-55 **5** *3 1/2* **Diletia**[29] [1630] 8-10-3 **102** .... PJBrennan 77
(R H Alner) *prom: rdn after 7th: wknd after 3 out* **10/1**

4-12 **6** *dist* **Marlborough Sound**[42] [1513] 6-11-2 **115** .... ADobbin —
(N G Richards) *hld up: hdwy 8th: mstke and wknd 3 out* **3/1**[2]

6P-P **P** **Valley Henry (IRE)**[10] [1846] 10-11-5 **125** .... RLucey-Butler(7) —
(R Gurney) *prom to 9th: t.o whn p.u bef 2 out* **28/1**

6060 **P** **Green Prospect (FR)**[10] [1853] 5-10-6 **105** .... NFehily —
(M J McGrath) *chsd ldrs tl wknd after 8th: t.o whn p.u bef 2 out* **40/1**

6m 34.1s (11.70) **Going Correction** +0.425s/f (Soft) **8** Ran SP% **113.5**

Speed ratings: **99,95,91,90,89** —,—,— CSF £28.72 CT £127.25 TOTE £2.70: £1.10, £3.10, £2.20; EX 26.50 Place 6 £206.95, Place 5 £47.92.

Owner Paul G Jacobs **Bred** P G Jacobs **Trained** Wildhern, Hants

FOCUS

This was a most impressive performance by a fast-improving hurdler. He is rated value for further and the race could rate higher.

NOTEBOOK

Tomina ◆, returning from a short break after a fair effort of the Flat, routed his opposition in style. His jockey was keen to get on with things in front after the early pace looked sedate, and he gradually wound it up from the front to win going away. Plans for a chasing career have been firmly put on hold, and he could well develop into a smart staying hurdler. *(op 9-4 tchd 11-4)*

Phar From Frosty(IRE) kept tabs on the easy winner for the final part of the race, but had no answer to his turn of foot, and time will almost certainly tell he had little chance at the weights. *(op 10-1 tchd 12-1)*

Burren Moonshine(IRE) fared reasonably well on her first start for the now in-form Bowen stable. All of her best efforts had come on much quicker ground, but she kept on nicely and won the race for the also-rans. *(op 6-1 tchd 13-2)*

Heir To Be ◆ ran well on his first run after a long break, and travelled nicely for much of the race. There is every chance he will be suited by a drop in trip, given his form last season, and he possibly does not truly stay three miles, let alone this distance. *(op 13-2)*

Diletia was under pressure from an early stage and did not look an easy ride. *(op 9-1 tchd 8-1)*

Marlborough Sound ran very moderately after looking to be most progressive. Connections could not offer any explanation, but the ground may have gone against him and he is definitely worth another chance. *(op 5-2)*

Valley Henry(IRE) is becoming a sad sight on the racecourse. Good enough to finish fourth in a Gold Cup and start odds-on for the 2003 Charlie Hall Chase, he was back-pedalling from an early stage, and is clearly nothing like the horse who looked like going to the very top early in his career. *(op 20-1)*

T/Jkpt: Not won. T/Plt: £389.50 to a £1 stake. Pool: £46,527.15. 87.20 winning tickets. T/Qpdt: £18.10 to a £1 stake. Pool: £4,211.20. 171.60 winning tickets. CR

1996 - 2000a (Foreign Racing) - See Raceform Interactive

1793 HAYDOCK (L-H)

Thursday, November 3

OFFICIAL GOING: Soft

Persistent rain changed the going to soft after the first race and by mid-afternoon the jockeys reported it was riding' definitely heavy'.

Wind: Fresh across Weather: Persistent rain

2001 BET365 JUVENILE NOVICES' HURDLE (8 hdls) 2m

1:10 (1:10) (Class 3) 3-Y-0 **£4,814** (£1,413; £706; £352)

Form | RPR

5 **1** **Vocative (GER)**[55] [1441] 3-10-0 .... PMerrigan(5) 94+
(P C Haslam) *prom: gd hdwy after 3 out: led appr last: hung lef and swished tail: drvn clr* **12/1**

005 **2** *5* **Madge**[14] [1797] 3-10-5 .... (v) GLee 86
(W Storey) *mid-div: hdwy to chse ldrs whn mstke 4 out: styd on to take 2nd after last: no imp* **9/1**[3]

U **3** *1/2* **Lankawi**[6] [1904] 3-10-12 .... BHarding 93
(Jedd O'Keeffe) *chsd ldrs: led 2 out: hdd appr last: kpt on same pce* **20/1**

4 **4** *8* **Truckle**[68] [1338] 3-10-7 .... DCCostello(5) 85
(C W Fairhurst) *led: hit 3rd and 4th: hdd 2 out: wknd last* **20/1**

5 *3/4* **Rossin Gold (IRE)**[35] 3-10-12 .... KRenwick 84
(P Monteith) *mid-div: kpt on fr 3 out: nvr a threat* **20/1**

6 *5* **Zando**[63] 3-10-12 .... FKeniry 79
(P C Haslam) *mid-div: kpt on fr 3 out: nvr on terms* **50/1**

6S0 **7** *8* **Bellalou**[22] [1718] 3-10-2 .... (t) PBuchanan(3) 64
(Mrs S A Watt) *chsd ldrs: lost pl after 3 out* **28/1**

04 **8** *shd* **Swallow Falls (IRE)**[55] [1440] 3-10-5 .... JMMaguire 64
(D McCain) *in rr: nvr on terms* **50/1**

2- **9** *6* **Orki Des Aigles (FR)**[174] 3-10-9 .... KJMercer(3) 65
(Ferdy Murphy) *rr-div: drvn along 5th: nvr a factor* **7/2**[2]

10 *14* **Shaanbar (IRE)**[66] 3-10-2 .... PAspell(3) 44
(J Hetherton) *hld up in rr: sme hdwy 5th: wknd next: bhd whn blnd 2 out* **40/1**

63 **11** *20* **Circumspect (IRE)**[14] [1797] 3-10-12 .... APMcCoy 31
(P C Haslam) *chsd ldrs: wknd 3 out: bhd whn eased run-in* **2/1**[1]

12 *14* **Queen Nefitari**[75] 3-10-5 ow3 .... MrTGreenall(3) 13
(M W Easterby) *nt jump wl: a bhd: t.o 3 out* **33/1**

U **13** *14* **Ghabesh (USA)**[9] [1873] 3-10-12 .... ChristianWilliams —
(Evan Williams) *j. poorly: hmpd 2nd: a in rr: t.o 3 out* **22/1**

P **Woodford Consult**[16] 3-10-5 .... RMcGrath —
(M W Easterby) *j. poorly: in rr: bhd fr 4th: t.o whn p.u bef 3 out* **11/1**

U **Dante's Diamond (IRE)**[19] 3-10-12 .... JimCrowley —
(G A Swinbank) *in rr: j.lft 2nd: bhd whn swvd lft and uns rdr 3rd* **16/1**

4m 0.80s (1.70) **Going Correction** +0.225s/f (Yiel) **15** Ran SP% **118.8**

Speed ratings: **104,101,101,97,96 94,90,90,87,80 70,63,56,**—,— CSF £97.91 TOTE £20.00: £4.20, £2.60, £8.40; EX 173.10.

Owner Middleham Park Racing XXX **Bred** Stiftung Gestut Fahrhof **Trained** Middleham, N Yorks

FOCUS

Yet another weak juvenile hurdle run at a sensible pace on the best of the ground. The runner-up improved 5lb on her debut effort and the seventh ran to her mark.

NOTEBOOK

Vocative(GER), well beaten on her hurdling bow in at Bangor in September, came there strongly but once in front seemed to do her best to give it away. She is not one to have much trust in. *(op 16-1)*

Madge, with the visor on again, made a hash of the last down the back. She went in pursuit of the winner but was never going to find anything like sufficient to worry her out of it. *(op 12-1)*

Lankawi, a strongly-made type, jumped much better, but after showing ahead he was soon comprehensively outpaced. *(op 16-1)*

Truckle, given his own way in front, flattened a couple of flights. On his first outing since August, he became leg-weary on the run-in. *(op 16-1)*

Rossin Gold(IRE), rated just 48 on the level, kept on in his own time but never threatened to enter the argument.

Circumspect(IRE), who looked really well, stopped to nothing and looked all at sea on the soft ground. *Official explanation: jockey said gelding was unsuited by soft ground (op 9-4 tchd 5-2)*

2002 WILLIAMHILLPOKER.COM H'CAP HURDLE (8 hdls) 2m

1:40 (1:41) (Class 3) (0-120,109) 4-Y-0+ **£4,751** (£1,395; £697; £348)

Form | RPR

1352 **1** **Theocritus (GER)**[8] [1880] 4-10-10 **93** .... GLee 101+
(Nick Williams) *racd wd: trckd ldrs: styd on fr 3 out: led appr last: drvn rt out* **5/6**[1]

-P1B **2** *5* **Top Style (IRE)**[12] [1836] 7-11-2 **104** .... (p) WKennedy(5) 107+
(G A Harker) *trckd ldrs: led aand qcknd after 5th: hdd appr last: no ex* **11/4**[2]

41-2 **3** *9* **Bonny Grey**[189] [77] 7-11-5 **109** .... MrNPearce(7) 102
(D Burchell) *trckd ldrs: outpcd 3 out: n.d after* **13/2**[3]

56-6 **4** *5* **Dance Party (IRE)**[182] [197] 5-11-3 **103** .... MrTGreenall(3) 92+
(M W Easterby) *j.rt: led tl after 5th: wknd between last 2* **8/1**

5 *dist* **Alchimiste (FR)**[149] 4-11-4 **108** .... MrRLangley(7) —
(Mrs E Langley) *racd wd in last: lost tch after 5th: sn t.o: btn 50 l* **40/1**

4m 21.4s (22.30) **Going Correction** +0.575s/f (Soft)

WFA 4 from 5yo+ 12lb **5** Ran SP% **108.1**

Speed ratings: **67,64,60,57,**— CSF £3.50 TOTE £1.70: £1.20, £1.90; EX 3.70.

Owner Gale Force Three **Bred** Gestut Berg Eberstein **Trained** George Nympton, Devon

FOCUS

They stood still for over ten seconds when the tape went up and they ambled round to the halfway mark. The winner did not have to reproduce his Cheltenham effort and the race has been rated through the runner-up.

NOTEBOOK

Theocritus(GER), banged up a stone after Cheltenham, is a tall, weak-looking type. He was kept wide and, taking time to gain the upper hand, was right on top on the run-in. He will make a chaser in time. *(op 10-11 tchd Evens and 11-10 in places)*

Top Style(IRE), 9lb higher than Perth, went on and stepped up the pace but was eventually worn down and put in his place by the winner. *(op 5-2)*

Bonny Grey, absent since April, has changed stables and was comfortably left trailing once in line for home. *(tchd 6-1 and 7-1)*

Dance Party(IRE), absent since May, found herself in front. Jumping right-handed, she became very leg-weary on the run to the last. *(op 9-1)*

2003 HARVEY JONES H'CAP CHASE (15 fncs) 2m 4f

2:10 (2:10) (Class 3) (0-125,125) 5-Y-0+ **£5,399** (£1,585; £792; £395)

Form | RPR

F54- **1** **Il'Athou (FR)**[236] [4328] 9-11-9 **122** .... JTizzard 138
(S E H Sherwood) *mde all: j. boldly: kpt on gamely run-in: all out* **8/1**

145- **2** *1/2* **Aristoxene (FR)**[201] [4864] 5-11-12 **125** .... MFoley 141
(N J Henderson) *j.lft: hld up in tch: wnt 2nd after 3 out: upisdes last 150yds: no ex nr fin* **9/4**[1]

/4-2 **3** *28* **Halexy (FR)**[8] [1881] 10-11-9 **122** .... APMcCoy 115+
(Jonjo O'Neill) *prom: blnd 9th: hmpd 4 out: outpcd appr next: styd on to go mod 3rd last* **3/1**[2]

1-50 **4** *1 1/4* **Benrajah (IRE)**[110] [1013] 8-11-5 **118** .... GLee 104
(M Todhunter) *promient: outpcd 10th: lost pl appr 3 out: sn bhd: kpt on run-in* **11/1**

P-1P **5** *1 1/2* **Itsuptoharry (IRE)**[173] [344] 6-11-1 **114** .... JMMaguire 99
(D McCain) *trckd ldrs travelling strly: wknd appr 3 out* **33/1**

435U **6** *2* **Fiori**[12] [1825] 9-10-9 **108** .... FKeniry 91
(P C Haslam) *prom: lost pl 7th: bhd fr 3 out* **8/1**

-P33 **7** *3 1/2* **Cassia Heights**[140] [765] 10-10-10 **109** .... (t) ADobbin 88
(S A Brookshaw) *chsd ldrs: rdn 3 out: wknd next* **10/1**

54-6 **8** *19* **Alam (USA)**[11] [1846] 6-11-12 **125** .... KRenwick 85
(P Monteith) *prom: effrt u.p appr 3 out: sn wknd: eased whn no ch* **25/1**

0-U3 **U** **Cill Churnain (IRE)**[12] [1825] 12-10-13 **112** .... DElsworth —
(Mrs S J Smith) *chsd ldrs: 2nd whn blnd and uns rdr 4 out* **13/2**[3]

5m 23.9s (-0.30) **Going Correction** +0.15s/f (Yiel) **9** Ran SP% **115.5**

Speed ratings: **106,105,94,94,93 92,91,83,**— CSF £27.53 CT £67.40 TOTE £9.50: £1.80, £2.10, £1.40; EX 36.50.

Owner Lady Thompson **Bred** Mme Robert Jeannin **Trained** Bredenbury, H'fords

FOCUS

A sensible pace in the conditions and in the end the winner, a stone and a half higher at his peak, had to dig deep, the pair a long way clear.

NOTEBOOK

Il'Athou(FR), whose last win was from a 12lb higher mark, gave an exhibition round of jumping in front and deservedly held on. Best when given his own way in front, this is as far as he wants to go especially in this type of ground. *(op 9-1)*

Aristoxene(FR), who took well to fences last term, has youth on his side. Despite a tendency to jump left-handed, he seemed likely to prevail halfway up the long run-in but in the end was just denied. It was a tough return but he deserves to go one better. *(op 11-4 tchd 3-1)*
Halexy(FR), making a quickish return, made a bad blunder then was knocked out of his stride four out. *(op 5-2 tchd 7-2)*
Benrajah(IRE), in trouble down the back, was out of contention until getting his second wind on the run-in. He does not appreciate conditions as testing as they had become by now, although the official ground remained only soft. *(op 10-1)*
Itsuptoharry(IRE), pulled up when last seen in May, wouldn't settle and this trip looked way too far for him. *(tchd 40-1)*
Fiori was struggling with a full circuit to go. *(tchd 9-1)*
Cill Churnain(IRE) kept tabs on the winner and was by no means done with when giving his rider no chance four out. *(op 11-2)*

2004 BETDIRECT.CO.UK H'CAP HURDLE (10 hdls) 2m 4f
2:45 (2:46) (Class 4) (0-110,107) 4-Y-0+ **£3,477** (£1,020; £510; £254)

Form				RPR
3-43	**1**		**Vicario**[27] [1665] 4-11-12 **107** ... GLee (D McCain) *trckd ldrs: led appr 3 out: drvn clr after last: eased towards fin* **10/1**	120+
414-	**2**	*9*	**Marsh Run**[238] [4272] 6-11-7 **105** ... MrTGreenall(3) (M W Easterby) *j.rt: led tl appr 3 out: one pce appr last* **11/2**	108+
01-2	**3**	*9*	**Brandy Wine (IRE)**[189] [83] 7-10-4 **95** ... JPEnnis(10) (L Lungo) *chsd ldrs: rdn and outpcd 7th: wknd after next* **4/1**[3]	86
13-3	**4**	*4*	**Zaffaran Express (IRE)**[176] [302] 6-11-9 **104** ... ADobbin (N G Richards) *hld up towards rr: nt fluent: effrt appr 3 out: wnt mod 3rd 2 out: nvr a threat* **15/8**[1]	92+
0543	**5**	*6*	**Day Du Roy (FR)**[148] [689] 7-11-6 **101** ... TSiddall (Miss L C Siddall) *wnt prom 5th: mod 3rd whn hit 3 out: sn btn* **12/1**	82
0P-0	**6**	*3/4*	**Flying Fortune (IRE)**[14] [1796] 9-11-10 **105** ... APMcCoy (Miss Tor Sturgis) *hld up in last but wl in tch: drvn along 5th: hung lft and lost pl afert 7th* **7/2**[2]	85
00/P	**7**	*dist*	**Ingenu (FR)**[14] [1796] 9-11-1 **96** ... SCurran (P Wegmann) *hld up in tch: rdn and wknd 7th: sn bhd: t.o: btn 36 l* **50/1**	—

5m 17.1s (7.90) **Going Correction** +0.575s/f (Soft) 7 Ran SP% **111.1**
Speed ratings: **107,103,99,98,95 95,—** CSF £59.06 TOTE £9.90: £3.00, £3.20; EX 40.40.
Owner Jon Glews **Bred** Mrs A Yearley **Trained** Cholmondeley, Cheshire

FOCUS
The winner seemed to improve for the step up in trip but it was a relatively weak event and he might struggle from his revised mark.

NOTEBOOK
Vicario, suited by this stiffer test, galloped clear and was value for a dozen lengths. He will shoot up in the ratings though as a result of this. *(op 8-1)*
Marsh Run, who has yet to really fulfil the potential of her bumper days, continually gave away ground jumping to her right and in the end, on her first outing since March, she was left behind by the winner. *(op 9-2)*
Brandy Wine(IRE), last seen when runner-up over fences at Kelso in April, is basically just a galloper and he needs three miles at least. He looks the type who will keep going at the same pace all day. *(op 7-2)*
Zaffaran Express(IRE) was let down by her hurdling on her first outing since May and, very ring-rusty here, she will surely do much better next time. *(op 2-1)*
Day Du Roy(FR), absent since June, had little difficulty extending his losing run over hurdles to sixteen.
Flying Fortune(IRE), whose trainer stated that he would not run if there was too much rain, still ran even though the ground had changed from the forecast good to soft to heavy. *(op 11-2)*

2005 HERALD INNS & BARS NOVICES' CHASE (17 fncs) 2m 6f
3:20 (3:20) (Class 3) 4-Y-0+ **£5,383** (£1,580; £790; £394)

Form				RPR
-221	**1**		**Avitta (IRE)**[113] [972] 6-10-13 109 ... SThomas (Miss Venetia Williams) *led to 2nd: hmpd by loose horse and forced to jump rt 8th: led 2 out: smoothly: eased towards fin* **15/8**[1]	120+
F23-	**2**	*10*	**Onyourheadbeit (IRE)**[252] [4023] 7-11-6 107 ... JPMcNamara (K C Bailey) *led 2nd: blnd 4 out: hdd 2 out: eased whn wl hld last 100yds* **4/1**[3]	113+
-F25	**3**	*19*	**Lord Dundaniel (IRE)**[158] [570] 8-11-6 110 ... APMcCoy (B De Haan) *trckd ldrs: hmpd by loose horse 8th: mstke next (water): rdn and btn 3 out* **7/2**[2]	85
2244	**4**	*1 3/4*	**Windy Spirit (IRE)**[12] [1829] 10-11-6 110 ... ChristianWilliams (Evan Williams) *bmpd 1st: trckd ldrs: hmpd by loose horse 8th: outpcd 4 out: sn lost pl* **10/1**	83
1P-0	**U**		**He's The Guv'Nor (IRE)**[12] [1830] 6-11-1 110 ... WKennedy(5) (R H Buckler) *j.lft, bmpd and uns rdr 1st* **7/2**[2]	—

6m 5.40s (16.60) **Going Correction** +0.15s/f (Yiel) 5 Ran SP% **108.3**
Speed ratings: **75,71,64,63,—** CSF £9.31 TOTE £2.20: £1.30, £2.60; EX 7.70.
Owner P A Deal, A Hirschfeld & M Graham **Bred** Sheikh Mohammed Bin Rashid Al Maktoum **Trained** Kings Caple, H'fords

FOCUS
Everything fell right for Avitta who found this plain sailing, but it is not a race to have any confidence in. The winner has been rated value for 14 lengths.

NOTEBOOK
Avitta(IRE), absent since breaking her duck over fences at Uttoxeter in July, has won over hurdles round here and likes testing ground. She made this look very simple indeed. *(tchd 7-4 and 2-1)*
Onyourheadbeit(IRE), absent since February, survived a blunder four out but it was soon clear the winner was simply toying with him. *(op 9-2)*
Lord Dundaniel(IRE), who picked up four faults at the water, was on the retreat three out and may not appreciate conditions as testing as he encountered here. *(tchd 4-1)*
Windy Spirit(IRE), without a win under Rules for over five years, looked all at sea in the conditions. *(op 6-1)*
He's The Guv'Nor(IRE), out of the contest at the first, turned sideways across the field at the ditch in front of the stands and very nearly caused carnage. *(op 9-2)*

2006 RACING WELFARE NOVICES' HURDLE (8 hdls) 2m
3:50 (3:51) (Class 3) 4-Y-0+ **£4,783** (£1,404; £702; £350)

Form				RPR
420-	**1**		**L'Antartique (FR)**[238] [4293] 5-10-9 ... KJMercer(3) (Ferdy Murphy) *trckd ldrs: led on bith between last 2: v easily* **4/11**[1]	110+
	2	*5*	**Oddsmaker (IRE)**[36] 4-10-5 ... (t) BenOrde-Powlett(7) (M A Barnes) *hld up: hdwy to trck ldrs 3rd: led after 2 out: sn hdd: no ch w wnr* **33/1**	90+
0-P0	**3**	*3 1/2*	**Morgan Be**[6] [1915] 5-10-12 ... RMcGrath (Mrs K Walton) *hld up towards rr: stdy hdwy whn hit 3 out: 5th last: r.o to take 3rd* **100/1**	85+
0	**4**	*6*	**Carnt Spell**[14] [1794] 4-10-12 ... ChristianWilliams (J T Stimpson) *mde most: hdd after 2 out: wknd run-in* **66/1**	79
-064	**5**	*3/4*	**West Hill (IRE)**[41] [1322] 4-10-12 71 ... (t) GLee (D McCain) *hld up in rr: sme hdwy 5th: nvr on terms* **22/1**	78
P	**6**	*11*	**Gustavo**[26] [1671] 4-10-12 ... SThomas (Miss Venetia Williams) *hld up in rr: outpcd after 5tyh: nvr on terms* **14/1**[3]	67
	7	*3/4*	**Tiger King (GER)**[41] 4-10-12 ... KRenwick (P Monteith) *hld up in rr: nvr a factor* **22/1**	67
	8	*5*	**Robbie Will**[91] 4-10-12 ... JPMcNamara (F Jordan) *w ldr: lost pl appr 2 out* **100/1**	62
0/0-	**9**	*8*	**Supreme Destiny (IRE)**[355] [2203] 7-10-12 ... JimCrowley (G A Swinbank) *nt fluent: in rr and reminders 4th: bhd fr 3 out* **22/1**	54
3-	**10**	*10*	**Reap The Reward (IRE)**[195] [4971] 5-10-9 ... GBerridge(3) (L Lungo) *hld up: hdwy and in tch 5th: sn lost pl and bhd* **8/1**[2]	44

4m 9.30s (10.20) **Going Correction** +0.575s/f (Soft)
WFA 4 from 5yo+ 12lb 10 Ran SP% **110.5**
Speed ratings: **97,94,92,89,89 83,83,81,77,72** CSF £19.25 TOTE £1.30: £1.10, £4.60, £16.40; EX 18.20.
Owner Mrs A N Durkan **Bred** T Picard And Phillipe De Maeseneire **Trained** West Witton, N Yorks

FOCUS
A weak race but a highly impressive winner, value for 20l, who did not have to be anywhere near his very useful Irish form to account for this lot.

NOTEBOOK
L'Antartique(FR) ◆, an ordinary-looking individual, had chased home dual champion Hardy Eustace in a Grade 2 at Gowran Park in February. He travelled supremely well and there will not be an easier winner all season. The plan is another at this level before stepping up in class. *(op 1-3 tchd 2-5 and 4-9 in places)*
Oddsmaker(IRE), once rated 88 on the level, has lost his way of late, and after jumping ahead, he was easily brushed aside by the promising winner. *(op 25-1)*
Morgan Be, who had shown little in five previous starts, travelled strongly and stuck on under a very tender ride. He was reported to have a breathing problem.Official explanation: trainer said gelding had a breathing problem; trainer said gelding was found to have a dirty nose on returning home
Carnt Spell, well beaten on his debut, is a big type, and after making it at just a sensible pace he became very leg-weary on the run-in. *(tchd 100-1)*
West Hill(IRE) had finished well beaten in selling company on the Flat when fitted with blinkers on his previous outing. This was his eighth start over hurdles and he is rated just 71. *(op 20-1)*

2007 TOTESPORT NATIONAL HUNT SIRES INTERMEDIATE OPEN NATIONAL HUNT FLAT RACE 2m
4:20 (4:20) (Class 6) 4-6-Y-0 **£1,891** (£551; £275)

Form				RPR
	1		**Heraldry (IRE)** 5-11-4 ... FKeniry (P C Haslam) *hld up in mid-div: hdwy to chse ldrs over 4f out: wnt 2nd over 2f out: styd on to ld 1f out: forged clr* **4/1**[3]	103+
1-	**2**	*6*	**Oakapple Express**[339] [2549] 5-11-6 ... WKennedy(5) (G A Harker) *w ldr: led 6f out: hung rt bnd: clr over 2f out: hdd 1f out: no ex* **3/1**[1]	105+
0	**3**	*2*	**Silent Bay**[14] [1799] 6-11-1 ... PAspell(3) (J Wade) *led tl 6f out: kpt on same pce fnl 3f* **15/2**	95
	4	*1/2*	**Overamorous** 4-10-11 ... JMMaguire (J L Needham) *sn trcking ldrs: wnt 2nd over 3f out: sn rdn: one pce* **12/1**	88
2	**5**	*1 1/4*	**Super Revo**[130] [844] 4-11-4 ... RMcGrath (Mrs K Walton) *prom: rn green bnd after 3f: rdn over 3f out: one pce* **7/1**	93
3-0	**6**	*20*	**Clifford T Ward**[193] [7] 5-11-4 ... GLee (D McCain) *hld up in rr: hdwy to chse ldrs 6f out: wknd 3f out* **7/2**[2]	73
0-	**7**	*3*	**Just Libbi**[537] [359] 5-10-8 ... KJMercer(3) (Ferdy Murphy) *hld up: outpcd 6f out: sn bhd* **16/1**	63
0	**8**	*8*	**Tickhill Tom**[40] [1554] 5-10-13 ... DCCostello(5) (C W Fairhurst) *chsd ldrs: lost pl 6f out: sn bhd* **33/1**	62
	9	*19*	**Fly Tipper** 5-11-4 ... NPMulholland (W Storey) *sn trcking ldrs: lost pl over 5f out sn bhd* **22/1**	43
	10	*17*	**Stewarts Dream (IRE)** 4-11-4 ... ADobbin (B D Leavy) *in rr: drvn along 9f out: sn bhd: t.o 4f out* **22/1**	26

4m 11.9s (15.50) **Going Correction** +0.575s/f (Soft)
WFA 4 from 5yo+ 12lb 10 Ran SP% **116.7**
Speed ratings: **84,81,80,79,79 69,67,63,54,45** CSF £16.01 TOTE £5.80: £2.30, £1.60, £3.00; EX 25.60 Place 6 £153.90, Place 5 £20.81.
Owner Mrs Alurie O'Sullivan **Bred** Ben Sangster **Trained** Middleham, N Yorks

FOCUS
They stood still for five seconds when the tapes went up. Despite the lack of pace it turned out to be a test of stamina, rated through the third.

NOTEBOOK
Heraldry(IRE), classically-bred, stands over plenty of ground. He has a real soft-ground action and forged clear in the closing stages. *(op 5-1)*
Oakapple Express, followed home by two subsequent winners when winning first time at Newcastle a year ago, had trouble making the final turn. After looking to have it in the bag, in the end he was comprehensively outstayed by the winner. *(op 9-4 tchd 7-2)*
Silent Bay, bred exclusively for stamina, took them along and looks the type who will keep going all day in his own time. *(op 8-1)*
Overamorous, a springer in the market, is out of a winning chaser. She travelled strongly but, after being sent in pursuit of the leader, off the bit she could only stick on in her own time. *(op 25-1)*
Super Revo, who edged out and had to be driven along on the paddock bend, looks to have a lot more stamina than speed and should be capable of better over hurdles. *(op 8-1)*
Clifford T Ward, absent since April, again ran poorly on his second start after a sound debut effort. *(op 4-1 tchd 10-3 tchd 9-2 in places)*
T/Plt: £268.30 to a £1 stake. Pool: £41,302.05. 112.35 winning tickets. T/Qpdt: £13.20 to a £1 stake. Pool: £4,331.90. 241.05 winning tickets. WG

1850 TOWCESTER (R-H)
Thursday, November 3

OFFICIAL GOING: Soft
Conditions were not as testing as they might have been given the effects of a strong headwind coupled with rain-softened ground.
Wind: Strong, against Weather: Showers

2008 GG-ODDS.COM ODDS COMPARISON (S) HURDLE (8 hdls) 2m
12:50 (12:50) (Class 5) 4-Y-0+ **£2,884** (£840; £420)

Form				RPR
/34-	**1**		**Indian Star (GER)**[224] [4529] 7-10-12 84 ... (t) JMogford (J C Tuck) *hld up: hdwy 4th: chsd ldr next: led after 3 out: sn clr: comf* **7/1**	106+
1-60	**2**	*8*	**Noble Calling (FR)**[16] [1784] 8-11-8 104 ... RThornton (R J Hodges) *a.p: rdn and hit 2 out: styd on same pce* **7/2**[1]	101

150- **3** ½ **Ambersong**[224] 4533 7-11-8 91 WHutchinson 101
(A W Carroll) *hld up: hdwy 3 out: sn rdn: styd on same pce fr next* **11/1**

2460 **4** 1 ¾ **Gabor**[10] 1685 6-11-3 96 (b) RJohnson 95+
(D W Thompson) *chsd ldrs tl led 3rd: hdd after 3 out: sn rdn: styd on same pce* **5/1**[3]

004P **5** 6 **Oulton Broad**[11] 1855 9-11-8 103 (p) LAspell 96+
(F Jordan) *hld up: hdwy 3 out: wknd after 2 out* **9/2**[2]

-213 **6** *dist* **Mantles Prince**[149] 675 11-11-3 95 ATinkler —
(A G Juckes) *hld up in tch: lost pl whn blnd 4th: sn bhd* **7/2**[1]

P0-P **7** 6 **Blaise Wood (USA)**[113] 980 4-10-10 85 (t) TBurrows(7) —
(A L Forbes) *chsd ldr to 3rd: wknd after 3 out* **25/1**

0/0- **P** **Naked Flame**[337] 2570 6-10-7 (p) CHonour(5) —
(A G Blackmore) *chsd ldrs tl wknd appr 3 out: t.o whn p.u bef last* **66/1**

6440 **P** **Little Rort (IRE)**[115] 915 6-10-10 87 (t) PCStringer(7) —
(S T Lewis) *led to 3rd: hit 5th: wknd 3 out: t.o whn p.u bef last* **14/1**

4m 12.1s (0.70) **Going Correction** +0.15s/f (Yiel)
WFA 4 from 6yo+ 12lb **9** Ran SP% **112.1**
Speed ratings: **104,100,99,98,95** —,—,—,— CSF £31.17 TOTE £6.90: £1.60, £1.40, £3.70; EX 29.60.There was no bid for the winner.
Owner D J Neale **Bred** Gestut Schlenderhan **Trained** Oldbury on the Hill, Gloucs

FOCUS
A modest seller run at a fair pace in which the winner has been rated as value for 15 lengths.

NOTEBOOK
Indian Star(GER) ran out a ready winner. Having his first run since March, he already had the race in the bag when dragging his hind legs through the second last and came up the hill a fresh horse. His handicap mark will be hit after this and it may be that he is best when fresh, but he can win again while in this mood. *(op 9-1)*
Noble Calling(FR), whose best form is over further, was a little outpaced at the foot of the hill. After flattening the second last he was only fourth over the final flight but stayed on to get the best of the tussle for second. *(tchd 3-1)*
Ambersong ran respectably on this first appearance since March but his best form has been shown on flatter tracks. *(op 17-2)*
Gabor, who had a run for his new yard recently on the sand, could not go with the winner from the third last. The ground had gone against him. *(op 11-2 tchd 6-1)*
Oulton Broad, back over hurdles, was under pressure to improve on the home turn and he was a spent force between the last two flights. *(op 7-2)*
Naked Flame *(op 50-1)*

2009 GEOFFREY LEAVER SOLICITORS H'CAP CHASE (16 fncs) 2m 6f
1:20 (1:21) (Class 4) (0-105,94) 5-Y-0+ **£4,059** (£1,191; £595; £297)

Form RPR

P-P0 **1** **Never Awol (IRE)**[29] 1646 8-9-13 74 (p) TMessenger(7) 94+
(B N Pollock) *mde virtually all: 3 l clr whn tried to pull up run-in: r.o whn jnd by rival 50 yds fr line* **20/1**

P-U1 **2** 1 **Bay Island (IRE)**[16] 1780 9-11-12 94 (t) TJMurphy 111+
(M Pitman) *hld up: hdwy and hit 9th: chsd wnr next: ev ch fr 3 out: rdn whn nt fluent last: lft w ch on run-in whn wnr tried to pu: nt* **15/8**[1]

62-3 **3** 8 **Gola Supreme (IRE)**[184] 169 10-11-11 93 RJohnson 101+
(R Lee) *hld up: hdwy 12th: wkng whn j.rt last* **7/2**[2]

-531 **4** 8 **Runaway Bishop (USA)**[11] 1855 10-11-5 94 7ex APogson(7) 93
(J R Cornwall) *hld up in tch: mstke and wknd 12th* **6/1**

33P- **5** 7 **Dun Locha Castle (IRE)**[200] 4886 10-11-3 85 TScudamore 79+
(N R Mitchell) *prom: chsd wnr 8th to 10th: wknd 2 out* **14/1**

62P- **P** **Ballybrophy (IRE)**[199] 4912 10-10-13 81 BFenton —
(G Brown) *mstkes: bhd fr 4th: t.o whn p.u bef 7th* **14/1**

0605 **P** **Jumpty Dumpty (FR)**[16] 1780 8-10-1 69 JMogford —
(J C Tuck) *hld up: wknd 7th: bhd whn j. slowly next: sn p.u: bbv* **5/1**[3]

43PP **P** **Maybeseven**[18] 1752 11-10-2 70 (p) WHutchinson —
(R Dickin) *chsd wnr to 8th: wknd 10th: t.o whn p.u bef 2 out* **20/1**

6m 6.00s **Going Correction** +0.15s/f (Yiel) **8** Ran SP% **110.8**
Speed ratings: **106,105,102,99,97** —,—,— CSF £56.93 CT £161.91 TOTE £27.50: £6.60, £1.20, £1.70; EX 69.10.
Owner Charles and Rachel Wilson **Bred** R J McGlynn **Trained** Medbourne, Leics

FOCUS
A bizarre finish to this moderate handicap and a shock winner, who was well in on his previous course win and was value for further.

NOTEBOOK
Never Awol(IRE) had scored at 50-1 here a year ago but was coming into this off the back of six consecutive non-completions. After jumping soundly out in front, the game looked to be up when Bay Island eased past him after the fourth last, but he rallied to reclaim the lead soon afterwards. Shaking off the favourite, he found himself three lengths to the good on the flat but then almost pulled himself up to a walk, and it was only when the runner-up reached his quarters that he consented to run again. He is a character, but will be always be worth considering at this venue.
Bay Island(IRE) was 8lb higher than when scoring at Exeter but was still 2lb well in compared with future handicaps. He travelled well and looked sure to win when showing in front starting the home turn but, soon headed again, he found little for pressure and looked held after an error at the last. He was given another chance when the leader downed tools but it was snatched away from him *just as it looked as if he would claim victory. He is worth another chance on a conventional track.*
(tchd 2-1 and 85-40 in a place)
Gola Supreme(IRE) ran a fair race and is entitled to strip fitter for this first start since May. *(op 9-2)*
Runaway Bishop(USA), under his penalty, was disappointing as his previous record round here was good. *(op 9-2)*
Dun Locha Castle(IRE) is still 9lb above his last winning mark. *(tchd 16-1)*
Maybeseven, who won this last year from out of the handicap, has shown little since returning from his summer break. *(tchd 9-2)*
Jumpty Dumpty(FR) *Official explanation: vet said gelding bled from the nose (tchd 9-2)*

2010 LAMBERT SMITH HAMPTON H'CAP HURDLE (11 hdls) 2m 5f
1:50 (1:50) (Class 3) (0-125,120) 4-Y-0+ **£5,569** (£1,634; £817; £408)

Form RPR

500- **1** **After Eight (GER)**[194] 4982 5-11-7 120 PCO'Neill(5) 129+
(Miss Venetia Williams) *hld up: hdwy 4th: jnd ldr 7th: led 3 out: styd on wl* **9/4**[1]

UP-2 **2** 8 **Glacial Evening (IRE)**[17] 1773 9-11-7 120 RStephens(5) 117
(R H Buckler) *a.p: chsd wnr after 3 out: no imp fr next* **6/1**[3]

66-6 **3** 18 **Ireland's Eye (IRE)**[193] 13 10-9-8 95 MrSFMagee(7) 74
(J R Norton) *hld up: hdwy 6th: wknd after 3 out* **10/1**

5-36 **4** 23 **Monsieur Georges (FR)**[14] 1796 5-10-1 95 LAspell 51
(F Jordan) *chsd ldr to 5th: rdn and wkng whn mstke 3 out* **7/1**

0-P0 **P** **Jacdor (IRE)**[163] 489 11-11-5 113 (v) JEMoore —
(R Dickin) *hld up: wknd 7th: t.o whn p.u bef 2 out* **33/1**

103- **P** **Mnason (FR)**[238] 4279 5-11-1 109 RThornton —
(S J Gilmore) *hld up: wknd after 7th: t.o whn p.u bef 2 out* **7/1**

30R- **P** **Abzuson**[207] 4785 8-11-0 108 (v[1]) AThornton —
(J R Norton) *chsd ldrs: mstke and wknd 6th: t.o whn p.u bef next* **11/1**

/61- **P** **Szeroki Bor (POL)**[513] 685 6-10-8 102 TJMurphy —
(M Pitman) *led and j.lft: hdd & wknd 3 out: bhd whn p.u bef next* **9/2**[2]

5m 38.1s (-3.10) **Going Correction** +0.15s/f (Yiel)
WFA 4 from 5yo+ 13lb **8** Ran SP% **108.6**
Speed ratings: **111,107,101,92**,— —,—,— CSF £14.63 CT £95.65 TOTE £3.00: £1.20, £2.30, £2.30; EX 19.10.
Owner Let's Live Racing **Bred** Gestut Martinushof **Trained** Kings Caple, H'fords

FOCUS
A fair handicap run at a reasonable clip, which put the emphasis on stamina. The easy winner was value for 12 lengths.

NOTEBOOK
After Eight(GER), who ran creditably for little reward last term, seemed to appreciate the step down in grade on this seasonal debut. In command over the last three flights, he ran out a comfortable winner and this should have boosted his confidence ahead of a return to stronger company, although he will need to improve when reassessed. *(op 11-4)*
Glacial Evening(IRE), the only one to give the winner a race in the latter stages, stuck on valiantly *over a trip short of his best but was not helped by the 3lb rise for finishing second at Plumpton.*
(tchd 13-2)
Ireland's Eye(IRE), on what was effectively his seasonal debut, did not get home and filled only a remote third place. He is currently 4lb lower than when last getting his head in front 11 months ago. *(op 8-1 tchd 7-1)*
Monsieur Georges(FR) was well backed on course but failed to reward his supporters. This ground might have been too soft for him. *(op 12-1 tchd 14-1)*
Szeroki Bor(POL) made much of the running on this first start since June last year but was immediately beaten when headed. This ground was too soft for him. *(op 11-4)*

2011 LOCATION 3 PROPERTIES NOVICES' H'CAP CHASE (14 fncs) 2m 3f 110y
2:20 (2:20) (Class 4) (0-105,101) 5-Y-0+ **£4,049** (£1,188; £594; £296)

Form RPR

000- **1** **Harris Bay**[200] 4885 6-10-13 88 (t) TJMurphy 112+
(Miss H C Knight) *trckd ldrs: led appr last: eased flat* **9/2**[1]

P004 **2** 3 ½ **Avadi (IRE)**[11] 1852 7-10-7 82 TDoyle 94
(P T Dalton) *led: rdn after 3 out: hdd appr last: styd on same pce* **7/1**[3]

/2P- **3** 25 **Mandingo Chief (IRE)**[229] 4458 6-11-11 100 RJohnson 87
(R T Phillips) *hld up: hdwy 6th: wknd appraoching 2 out* **9/2**[1]

24-5 **4** 4 **Full On**[18] 1761 8-11-8 97 RThornton 80
(A M Hales) *hld up in tch: wknd after 3 out: mstke next* **5/1**[2]

26P- **5** 9 **Adelphie Lass**[199] 4914 5-10-12 87 JamesDavies 61
(D B Feek) *hld up: bhd fr 7th* **18/1**

P2-0 **U** **Ah Yeah (IRE)**[13] 1819 8-9-13 77 ONelmes(3) —
(N B King) *mstke and uns rdr 2nd* **10/1**

P4P- **P** **Riders Revenge (IRE)**[200] 4889 7-11-12 101 AO'Keeffe —
(Miss Venetia Williams) *hld up: wknd 7th: t.o whn p.u bef 2 out* **17/2**

-114 **P** **Terrible Tenant**[170] 395 6-10-11 89 RYoung(3) —
(J W Mullins) *w ldr: hit 10th: mstke and wknd 3 out: t.o whn p.u bef next* **7/1**[3]

4-43 **P** **Bob The Builder**[11] 1855 6-11-12 101 AntonyEvans —
(N A Twiston-Davies) *hld up: mstkes: hdwy after 4 out: hit next: sn rdn and wknd: t.o whn p.u bef 2 out* **9/1**

5m 32.1s (13.90) **Going Correction** +0.15s/f (Yiel) **9** Ran SP% **112.9**
Speed ratings: **78,76,66,65,61** —,—,—,— CSF £35.16 CT £147.79 TOTE £5.60: £2.20, £1.60, £2.10; EX 34.40.
Owner Mrs G M Sturges & H Stephen Smith **Bred** R J Spencer **Trained** West Lockinge, Oxon

FOCUS
The pace was only fair in this ordinary novices' handicap, in which the winner was value for a good deal further. Not an easy race to assess, it could have been rated higher.

NOTEBOOK
Harris Bay jumped nicely on his chasing debut and cruised past the leader between the last two fences for a facile success. He proved a disappointment over hurdles last term, but a wind operation and the application of a tongue tie have clearly made a big difference. *(op 6-1)*
Avadi(IRE) tried to kick clear on the home turn but the winner always had him covered. Due to race off 4lb lower in future handicaps, he was flattered by the margin of defeat in the end but this was something of a a return to form. *(op 12-1)*
Mandingo Chief(IRE) was one of half a dozen still in contention jumping the fourth last but faded into a distant third on this first run since March.
Full On had no apparent excuse and is beginning to run out of chances. *(op 4-1)*
Bob The Builder did not jump with any fluency and was beaten before the home turn. He is due to race off 3lb lower in future. *(op 11-2)*
Terrible Tenant showed prominently on this first run since the spring, but a couple of jumping errors eventually took their toll. His best form has come on quicker ground. *(op 11-2)*

2012 FREE TIPS @GG.COM MARES' ONLY "NATIONAL HUNT" NOVICES' HURDLE (8 hdls) 2m
2:55 (2:55) (Class 4) 4-Y-0+ **£4,118** (£1,209; £604; £301)

Form RPR

2/2- **1** **Viciana**[355] 2198 6-10-10 LAspell 100
(Mrs L Wadham) *mde all: hit 3 out: drvn out* **1/1**[1]

52-5 **2** 1 ½ **Purple Patch**[11] 1850 7-10-10 88 RWalford 98
(C L Popham) *w wnr tl nt fluent 2 out: sn rdn: styd on* **10/1**[3]

13- **3** 2 **Vertical Bloom**[325] 2817 4-10-10 WMarston 96
(Mrs P Sly) *chsd ldrs: rdn appr 2 out: styd on* **12/1**

050- **4** 9 **Bally Bolshoi (IRE)**[205] 4814 5-10-10 81 WHutchinson 87
(Mrs S D Williams) *prom: hit 2nd and 5th: wknd 2 out: hit last* **50/1**

430- **5** 1 **Harringay**[215] 4694 5-10-10 97 TJMurphy 86+
(Miss H C Knight) *hld up: nvr nr to chal* **9/4**[2]

2-22 **6** 14 **Amalfi Storm**[26] 1688 4-10-10 ADempsey 72
(M W Easterby) *hld up: bhd fr 4th* **12/1**

60-2 **7** *hd* **Kentford Lady**[177] 285 4-10-10 AThornton 72
(J W Mullins) *hld up: bhd fr 4th* **12/1**

4m 15.9s (4.50) **Going Correction** +0.15s/f (Yiel)
WFA 4 from 5yo+ 12lb **7** Ran SP% **114.9**
Speed ratings: **94,93,92,87,87 80,80** CSF £12.56 TOTE £2.00: £1.30, £3.10; EX 10.60.
Owner G W Paul **Bred** G W Paul **Trained** Newmarket, Suffolk

FOCUS
The order changed very little throughout this mares' event. The winner was 9lb off her best, while the runner-up showed improvement but was still below her best bumper figures.

NOTEBOOK
Viciana, formerly with Pip Payne and off the track for the best part of a year, had the form to win a race of this nature and made no mistake. Making just about all the running, she shook off the runner-up between the last two flights and, proven over further, stayed on well enough. *(op 6-4)*
Purple Patch ran a decent race considering she would have been 24lb better off with the winner in a handicap. After keeping that rival company, her fate was sealed with an untidy jump at the penultimate flight, but she kept on gamely for second. *(op 12-1)*
Vertical Bloom, on her hurdling debut, was in third place all the way. She was keeping on at the end and may get a bit further. *(op 8-1 tchd 7-1)*
Bally Bolshoi(IRE) did not impress with her jumping and was never close enough to get in a blow, but this was still an improvement on her efforts last season. *(op 40-1)*

Harringay, held up in fifth place, still looked to be travelling well at the foot of the hill as the race hotted up, but Murphy appeared to make no effort to go after the leaders and the mare was allowed to come home in her own time. Connections reported that she has a history of breathing problems and that she made a noise, but the Stewards took a dim view. However, the penalties were *quashed on appeal. Official explanation: jockey said mare made a noise and would probably have come to a stop if he had asked for an effort at an earlier stage of the race (op 5-2 tchd 11-4)*

Kentford Lady *Official explanation: jockey said filly was unsuited by the soft ground and the course (op 10-1)*

2013 EBF "JUNIOR" STANDARD OPEN NATIONAL HUNT FLAT RACE (DIV I) 1m 5f 110y

3:30 (3:32) (Class 6) 3-Y-O **£2,487** (£724; £362)

Form	Pos	Dist	Horse	Jockey	RPR
	1		**Saratogane (FR)** 3-10-5 (M C Pipe) *led: hdd over 10f out: led 1/2-way: rdn out* **11/8**[1]	TScudamore	94+
	2	2 ½	**Zhivago's Princess (IRE)** 3-10-5 (C G Cox) *hld up in tch: rdn to chse wnr over 1f out: styd on* **3/1**[2]	MBradburne	89+
	3	11	**Reveal (IRE)** 3-9-12 (H E Haynes) *chsd ldrs: rdn over 2f out: wknd over 1f out* **10/1**	LHeard(7)	78
	4	3	**Mohayer (IRE)** 3-10-7 (D McCain) *prom: rdn to chse wnr over 2f out: wknd over 1f out* **6/1**[3]	StephenJCraine(5)	82
	5	7	**Ballinger Venture** 3-10-5 (N M Babbage) *hld up: wknd over 3f out* **16/1**	BFenton	68
	6	10	**Bradders** 3-10-12 (J R Jenkins) *w wnr tl led over 10f out: hdd 1/2-way: rdn and wknd over 2f out* **14/1**	LAspell	65
	7	18	**The Whispering Oak (IRE)** 3-10-5 (P S Payne) *hld up: rdn 1/2-way: hung lft and wknd 4f out* **20/1**	OMcPhail	40
	8	25	**Midnight Fury** 3-10-2 (J G M O'Shea) *hld up: rdn over 5f out: wknd 4f out* **33/1**	ENolan(10)	22

3m 54.3s **8** Ran **SP% 110.7**
CSF £5.03 TOTE £2.00: £1.10, £1.30, £2.10; EX 6.60.

Owner Pipe Monkees **Bred** M R Portier **Trained** Nicholashayne, Devon

FOCUS
This turned into a three-furlong sprint as the field dawdled their way round, having been reluctant to break into a gallop at all for several seconds after the tape went back. While the form is somewhat dubious, the first two home both have decent pedigrees and could be capable of better.

NOTEBOOK
Saratogane(FR) found plenty in front when asked to quicken things up. She is a half-sister to connections' smart hurdler Lough Derg and obviously possesses a slice of his ability. *(op Evens tchd 6-4)*

Zhivago's Princess(IRE) made an encouraging debut despite showing signs of greenness. A half-sister to the ill-fated Decoupage, who won the Tote Gold Trophy and the Henry VIII Novices' Chase, she should pay her way over hurdles when she is likely to prove best over the minimum trip. *(op 4-1)*

Reveal(IRE) was sold very cheaply in July and this was a pleasing start to her career. *(op 14-1 tchd 16-1)*

Mohayer(IRE), whose stablemate Spirit Of Damascus landed the second division of this event, is related to decent winners in France and is not without ability. *(op 15-2)*

2014 EBF "JUNIOR" STANDARD OPEN NATIONAL HUNT FLAT RACE (DIV II) 1m 5f 110y

4:00 (4:00) (Class 6) 3-Y-O **£2,487** (£724; £362)

Form	Pos	Dist	Horse	Jockey	RPR
1	1		**Sword Of Damascus (IRE)**[16] [1785] 3-11-0 (D McCain) *hld up: outpcd over 4f out: hdwy over 3f out: rdn to ld over 1f out: edgd rt ins fnl f: all out* **7/2**[2]	StephenJCraine(5)	90
6	2	nk	**Mahogany Blaze (FR)**[16] [1785] 3-10-12 (N A Twiston-Davies) *led: hdd over 9f out: hung lft over 5f out: led over 3f out: rdn and hdd over 2f out: swtchd lft over 1f out: styd on u.p* **4/1**[3]	TScudamore	83
	3	1	**Inherent (IRE)** 3-10-5 (C G Cox) *a.p: led over 2f out: rdn and hdd over 1f out: no ex nr fin* **3/1**[1]	MBradburne	75
	4	8	**Cape Guard** 3-10-12 (F Jordan) *prom: rdn over 3f out: styd on same pce fnl 2f* **9/1**	LAspell	75+
	5	16	**Lansdowne Princess** 3-10-5 (G A Ham) *hld up: hdwy over 8f out: weaakened over 2f out* **20/1**	JAMcCarthy	51
	6	1 ½	**Whatsinitforme (IRE)** 3-10-12 (Mrs D A Hamer) *chsd ldrs tl wknd over 2f out* **7/1**	(t) RJohnson	56
	7	1 ¼	**Blazing Ember** 3-10-0 (J W Tudor) *chsd ldr: led over 9f out: hdd over 3f out: wknd over 2f out* **40/1**	RStephens(5)	48
	8	¾	**Lagan Gunsmoke** 3-10-12 (Dr J R J Naylor) *hld up: wknd 4f out* **16/1**	AThornton	54
	9	14	**It's A Hottie** 3-10-12 (P Winkworth) *hld up: wknd over 3f out* **28/1**	PHide	40
	10	4	**Ginger For Pluck** 3-10-2 (J G Given) *hld up: plld hrd: hdwy 8f out: rdn and ev ch 3f out: sn hung lft and wknd* **16/1**	LVickers(3)	29

3m 40.6s **10** Ran **SP% 112.1**
CSF £16.70 TOTE £3.20: £1.70, £1.40, £1.40; EX 12.40 Place 6 £11.13, Place 5 £4.51.

Owner Jon Glews **Bred** Sir E J Loder **Trained** Cholmondeley, Cheshire

FOCUS
This was much more truly-run than division one. It has been rated through the winner who ran to his Exeter mark.

NOTEBOOK
Sword Of Damascus(IRE), penalised for landing another of these on his debut at Exeter, followed up in gritty style to give a solid look to the form. Having seen off the third, he only just held on as Mahogany Blaze, who had been sixth in the Exeter race, finished strongly to divide the pair. He could well struggle under a double penalty but there seems no reason why he should not make his mark over hurdles. *(op 10-3)*

Mahogany Blaze(FR) was just over 11 lengths behind Sword Of Damascus on their respective debuts but was 7lb better off here. After becoming a little outpaced up the straight he was staying on strongly at the death and would have snatched the race with a bit further to go. *(op 11-4 tchd 9-2 in a place)*

Inherent(IRE), a half-sister to winning hurdler Serpentine Rock, shaped with plenty of promise and was only seen off in the last 50 yards. She is in good hands and her turn will come. *(op 7-2)*

Cape Guard made a pleasing start and is likely to improve over a longer trip. *(op 10-1 tchd 11-1)*

T/Plt: £16.30 to a £1 stake. Pool: £43,642.95. 1,951.65 winning tickets. T/Qpdt: £6.10 to a £1 stake. Pool: £3,752.30. 452.00 winning tickets. CR

1594 FONTWELL (L-H)

Friday, November 4

OFFICIAL GOING: Soft (good to soft in places)
Wind: Moderate, half-behind

2015 CHATSWORTH FORGE LTD CLASSIFIED HURDLE (9 hdls) 2m 2f 110y

1:10 (1:10) (Class 4) 4-Y-O+ **£2,542** (£740; £370)

Form	Pos	Dist	Horse	Jockey	RPR
460-	1		**Brave Spirit (FR)**[219] [4656] 7-11-0 87 (C L Tizzard) *prom: lost pl after 5th: rdn next: styd on fr 2 out to ld last strides* **3/1**[1]	(p) JTizzard	105
003-	2	shd	**Presenting Express (IRE)**[267] [3766] 6-11-0 85 (Miss E C Lavelle) *a in tch: led sn after 5th: mstke and hdd briefly 2 out: rdn and kpt on: hdd last strides* **4/1**[2]	BFenton	107+
504/	3	12	**Photographer (USA)**[679] [2952] 7-11-0 88 (S Lycett) *w.w: hdwy after 5th: led briefly 2 out: wknd and lost 2nd run-in* **10/1**	RGreene	94+
-443	4	7	**Rojabaa**[8] [1902] 6-10-7 85 (W G M Turner) *hld up in rr: hdwy to trck ldrs 6th: wknd after 3 out* **10/1**	RLucey-Butler(7)	86
060-	5	3 ½	**North Lodge (GER)**[302] [3239] 5-11-0 88 (A King) *in tch tl wknd appr 2 out* **3/1**[1]	RThornton	84+
0643	6	23	**Mariday**[18] [1774] 4-10-9 90 (L Wells) *in tch tl wknd appr 3 out* **13/2**[3]	(b[1]) DLaverty(5)	60
F50-	7	dist	**Alasil (USA)**[235] [4378] 5-10-7 85 (Mrs N Smith) *trckd ldrs tl rdn and wknd 6th: t.o* **16/1**	(p) LHeard(7)	—
P66-	8	26	**Gotta Get On**[197] [4936] 4-10-11 64 (R H Alner) *prom to 5th: sn bhd: t.o* **80/1**	RWalford	—
600-	P		**Puff At Midnight**[260] [3910] 5-10-11 75 (D P Keane) *led tl sn after 5th: wknd qckly: t.o whn p.u after 3 out* **33/1**	PJBrennan	—

4m 40.8s (4.80) **Going Correction** +0.275s/f (Yiel)
WFA 4 from 5yo+ 12lb **9** Ran **SP% 111.6**
Speed ratings: **100,99,94,91,90 80,—,—,—** CSF £14.57 TOTE £4.10: £1.80, £1.70, £2.50; EX 16.90.

Owner The Con Club **Bred** Ctsse Bertrand De Tarragon **Trained** Milborne Port, Dorset

FOCUS
Although this was confined to horses rated 90 or less there were several in the line-up with the potential to rate a fair bit better. The first three all look capable of winning over hurdles.

NOTEBOOK
Brave Spirit(FR), better known as a staying chaser, was outpaced as the tempo quickened, but his stamina came into play in the closing stages and he got his head in front in the last strides. He was very well treated here in this 0-90 hurdle, as he has an official mark of 123 over fences. He could go in again over timber off a higher mark if stepped up in trip, but apparently the plan is to come back here for a staying chase on 13 November. *(op 11-4 tchd 5-2)*

Presenting Express(IRE) hung left going to the final flight, did not jump it that well, and was outstayed on the run-in. He was out of sorts last season, like so many from his stable, but he looks the part and can be expected to come on for this first outing in 267 days. He will presumably be back over fences soon but looks well capable of winning a novice handicap over hurdles first. *(tchd 9-2)*

Photographer(USA) had been off the track since Boxing Day 2003 but was the subject of some interest in the market and ran well until understandably getting tired in the closing stages. He has shown better form than this in the past and hopefully he can build on it. *(op 12-1)*

Rojabaa, a winner of two races on the Flat on good to firm ground, has also shown his best form over hurdles on a quick surface. *(op 9-1)*

North Lodge(GER), who won a Listed race on the Flat in Germany as a three-year-old, did not show a lot in three starts in novice company last season, but this race looked far weaker and so it was disappointing that he did not make more of an impact. He was later reported to have finished *lame behind, so he can be given another chance. Official explanation: vet said gelding was lame behind (op 5-2)*

Mariday, blinkered for the first time, probably found the ground against him. *(op 8-1 tchd 9-1)*

2016 OFFSPEC KITCHENS H'CAP CHASE (13 fncs) 2m 2f

1:40 (1:41) (Class 3) (0-125,122) 5-Y-O+ **£5,403** (£1,586; £793; £396)

Form	Pos	Dist	Horse	Jockey	RPR
2012	1		**Tonic Du Charmil (FR)**[14] [1817] 5-11-12 122 (M C Pipe) *mde all: mstke 4 out: kpt up to work fr next: styd on wl run-in* **5/2**[2]	(t) TScudamore	130+
3010	2	6	**Master T (USA)**[43] [1524] 6-10-9 105 (G L Moore) *in tch: styd on wl to go 2nd appr last: no imp run-in* **9/1**	PHide	105+
3311	3	5	**L'Oiseau (FR)**[12] [1860] 6-11-2 112 7ex (J G Portman) *racd 3rd: hdwy to trck wnr 5th: hit 3 out: wknd next and lost 2nd appr last: no ex* **13/8**[1]	JTizzard	109+
5-00	4	11	**The Newsman (IRE)**[161] [534] 13-10-13 109 (G Wareham) *trckd wnr to 5th: lost pl 7th and sn wl bhd: styd on one pce fr 3 out* **16/1**	LAspell	92
0-51	5	¾	**Rooster's Reunion (IRE)**[22] [1726] 6-11-10 120 (D R Gandolfo) *hld up: effrt after 4 out: wknd bef next* **11/4**[3]	TDoyle	102

4m 47.2s (12.10) **Going Correction** +0.60s/f (Soft) **5** Ran **SP% 109.2**
Speed ratings: **97,94,92,87,86** CSF £20.46 TOTE £3.50: £1.50, £3.60; EX 23.10.

Owner Roger Stanley & Yvonne Reynolds **Bred** Mme Guilhaine Le Borgne **Trained** Nicholashayne, Devon

FOCUS
Most of these were unhappy in the ground so the form may not be reliable.

NOTEBOOK
Tonic Du Charmil(FR), who had the advantage of being fully effective in the ground, had to be ridden along from some way out but he kept responding to pressure. He is pretty tough and was drawing further clear at the line. *(op 7-2)*

Master T(USA), who has done all his winning over hurdles and fences on good ground or faster, closed up to briefly look a threat to Tonic Du Charmil going to the last but the winner pulled out more on the run-in. He will remain vulnerable in handicaps off this sort of mark. *(op 10-1 tchd 12-1)*

L'Oiseau(FR), 3lb well in at the weights under his penalty, travelled well in behind the leader and looked all set to take his measure going to the third last, but he made a mess of the obstacle and emptied quickly. The combination of the stiffer track and softer ground clearly did not suit. *(tchd 6-4 and 7-4 tchd 15-8 in places)*

The Newsman(IRE), having his first outing since May, is not dropping in the handicap fast enough to remain competitive. *(op 10-1)*

Rooster's Reunion(IRE), a winner on his chasing debut at Ludlow, had completely different ground conditions to deal with this time, and he failed to handle them. *(op 5-2 tchd 9-4 and 3-1)*

2017 BETFRED POKER H'CAP HURDLE (SERIES QUALIFIER) (10 hdls) 2m 4f

2:10 (2:10) (Class 4) (0-110,108) 4-Y-0+ **£3,396** (£997; £498; £248)

Form RPR

4P-0 **1** **Come Bye (IRE)**[17] [1784] 9-11-12 **108**................................(bt) MBatchelor 112+
(Miss A M Newton-Smith) *mde all: rdn appr 2 out: styd on and in command run-in* **5/2**[2]

/13- **2** *4* **Assoon**[400] [1541] 6-11-9 **105**.. JEMoore 106+
(G L Moore) *hld up in tch: wnt 2nd 3 out: rdn and 1l down whn hit last: no imp run-in* **6/4**[1]

03P6 **3** *10* **Mistified (IRE)**[15] [1806] 4-10-7 **92**... RYoung[(3)] 82
(J W Mullins) *a in tch: trckd wnr 5th tl mstke 3 out: rdn appr next: one pce after* **11/2**

44-5 **4** *dist* **Canni Thinkaar (IRE)**[19] [1760] 4-10-3 **92**..................(p) RLucey-Butler[(7)] —
(P Butler) *trckd wnr tl mstke 5th: rdn and hit next: wknd rapidly: t.o* **7/2**[3]

5m 7.20s (3.40) **Going Correction** +0.275s/f (Yiel)
WFA 4 from 6yo+ 13lb 4 Ran SP% **106.2**
Speed ratings: **104,102,98,**— CSF £6.56 TOTE £3.60; EX 5.50.
Owner Pps Racing **Bred** Timothy Coffey **Trained** Jevington, E Sussex

FOCUS
A none-too competitive handicap. The first two ran to their marks..

NOTEBOOK
Come Bye(IRE) was not badly handicapped on a mark 3lb higher than for his last win, he was race-fit, and he had the ground to suit on his return to a track where he had won twice before. Allowed his own way in front, he still made fairly hard work of it. *(op 2-1 tchd 11-4)*
Assoon, racing on the softest ground he has ever encountered, had every chance from the second last but made a bit of a mess of the final flight and the winner's race-fitness told on the run-in. He should benefit considerably from this first outing in 400 days, and will go close next time provided he does not 'bounce'. *(op 5-4)*
Mistified(IRE) finished third for the fifth time in his last nine starts. Still seeking his first win under either code, he remains opposable. *(tchd 13-2)*
Canni Thinkaar(IRE), whose jumping soon fell to pieces, dropped himself out of contention pretty quickly. *It was later reported that he had lost a shoe during the race.Official explanation: trainer said gelding lost a shoe (op 5-1)*

2018 FLAT JOCKEYS SUPPORTING CHRIS KINANE TRUST MARES' ONLY NOVICES' CHASE (15 fncs) 2m 4f

2:40 (2:40) (Class 4) 5-Y-0+ **£4,661** (£1,368; £684; £341)

Form RPR

330- **1** **Dedrunknmunky (IRE)**[208] [4799] 6-10-12 **93**.............................. MFoley 111+
(Miss Tor Sturgis) *led to 4 out: rallied to go 2nd 2 out: led sn after last: styd on wl* **8/1**

0F-1 **2** *2* **Reseda (GER)**[176] [314] 6-10-12 105....................................... APMcCoy 109+
(Ian Williams) *sn trckd ldrs: hit 7th: led 4 out: rdn and hdd sn after last: no ex* **1/1**[1]

4P5- **3** *18* **Easibrook Jane**[220] [4641] 7-10-12 104.. JTizzard 97+
(C L Tizzard) *hld up: hdwy to go 2nd 9th: ev ch 4 out: rdn and sn btn* **5/2**[2]

-PUP **4** *12* **Cool Carroll (IRE)**[38] [1570] 7-10-12 86.................................. OMcPhail 79
(Mrs Tracey Barfoot-Saunt) *hld up in tch: rdn appr 9th: sn btn* **25/1**

55-U **P** **Minnie The Moocher**[34] [1595] 5-10-9 76.................................. RYoung[(3)] —
(J W Mullins) *trckd wnr to 9th: sn bhd: p.u bef 11th* **33/1**

LRP- **P** **Starlight Express (FR)**[257] [3970] 5-10-12 96............................ BFenton —
(Miss E C Lavelle) *slowly away: trckd ldrs 3rd: hit 4th: sn bhd: p.u bef 6th* **6/1**[3]

5m 17.2s (9.30) **Going Correction** +0.60s/f (Soft) 6 Ran SP% **110.8**
Speed ratings: **105,104,97,92,**— — CSF £17.05 TOTE £8.40: £2.50, £1.50; EX 21.90.
Owner The Faith In The Ladies **Bred** John Byrne **Trained** Kingston Lisle, Oxon

FOCUS
A mares' only novice chase in which stamina ultimately won the day.

NOTEBOOK
Dedrunknmunky(IRE), who stayed three miles over hurdles and has won a point-to-point in Ireland, was never going to be found out for stamina, and while she looked beaten when left behind by Reseda after the fourth last, she rallied gamely and outstayed the favourite in the end. This was an encouraging chase debut under Rules and she should achieve even better form when stepped up to three miles. *(tchd 15-2 and 9-1)*
Reseda(GER), making her chasing debut, looked like going on to a comfortable success when pulling out a gap on her main rivals running to the third last, but she found this, the longest trip she has tackled to date, too much of a stamina test on this stiff track in the ground, and she was outstayed after landing just in front at the last. There was plenty to like about her performance, though, and she will be winning when speed is at more of a premium. *(op 11-8 tchd 6-4 in a place)*
Easibrook Jane had conditions to suit and had the benefit of previous chasing experience over the first two, but she did not make it count. *(op 2-1)*
Cool Carroll(IRE) had failed to complete on her last three starts over fences and this should have done her confidence some good. *(op 20-1)*

2019 NAPSCHALLENGE.COM AND SPORTSLIVE RADIO H'CAP CHASE (19 fncs) 3m 2f 110y

3:10 (3:10) (Class 4) (0-105,97) 5-Y-0+ **£4,815** (£1,494; £804)

Form RPR

133- **1** **Kausse De Thaix (FR)**[223] [4556] 7-11-12 **97**.............................. LAspell 110+
(O Sherwood) *hld up: hdwy to trck ldrs 5th: wnt 2nd 9th: lft clr 15th: unchal after: easily* **13/8**[1]

P13- **2** *20* **Commanche Jim (IRE)**[196] [4959] 9-11-11 **96**......................... AThornton 74
(R H Alner) *led to 3rd: 2nd 9th tl lost tch 11th: lft poor 2nd 15th: plugged on but no ch w wnr* **3/1**[3]

2006 **3** *dist* **Alfred The Grey**[19] [1752] 8-9-13 **73** ow1..............................(p) CBolger[(3)] —
(P A Blockley) *trckd ldr tl wknd qckly 7th: lft remote 3rd 15th: t.o* **14/1**

651 **F** **Hi Laurie (IRE)**[7] [1905] 10-11-5 **90** 7ex................................. TScudamore —
(M Scudamore) *led 3rd tl fell 15th* **7/4**[2]

7m 15.2s (14.10) **Going Correction** +0.60s/f (Soft) 4 Ran SP% **106.1**
Speed ratings: **103,97,**—,— CSF £6.47 TOTE £2.20; EX 5.20.
Owner Andrew L Cohen **Bred** Michel Bourgneuf **Trained** Upper Lambourn, Berks

FOCUS
Not a very competitive affair, but both Kausse De Thaix and Hi Laurie look capable of winning more races.

NOTEBOOK
Kausse De Thaix(FR) jumped well and was left clear to come home a very easy winner when his only real challenger Hi Laurie departed at the 15th. He looked value for at least 30 lengths and he stays particularly well, so he should be set for further success this season. *(op 7-4 tchd 15-8)*
Commanche Jim(IRE) begins the season on a fairly stiff mark and he was easily seen off by Hi Laurie and Kausse De Thaix on this reappearance. He inherited second place on the departure of the former, but will have to come on a lot for this run to be competitive off a rating in the mid 90s. *(tchd 10-3)*
Alfred The Grey has not won for over three years and needs faster ground than this. *(op 20-1 tchd 12-1)*
Hi Laurie(IRE), who impressed when winning on her chasing debut at Uttoxeter, jumped well in the main prior to her fall and it is to be hoped that this tumble does not affect her confidence. *(op 11-8)*

2020 HARDINGS BAR & CATERING SERVICES NOVICES' HURDLE (10 hdls) 2m 4f

3:40 (3:40) (Class 4) 4-Y-0+ **£3,247** (£946; £473)

Form RPR

0-3 **1** **Soleil Fix (FR)**[189] [100] 4-10-9 .... MrDHDunsdon[(3)] 107
(N J Gifford) *led tl hdd 3 out: rallied to ld again last: drvn out* **7/2**[2]

3-31 **2** *¾* **Saltango (GER)**[3] [1975] 6-11-0 113...................................... WKennedy[(5)] 113
(A M Hales) *hld up in rr: hdwy appr 7th: led 3 out: rdn and hdd last: no ex run-in* **4/7**[1]

331 **3** *20* **Mr Ex (ARG)**[18] [1777] 4-10-5 .... JEMoore 84+
(G L Moore) *hld up in tch: hit 3rd: 3rd whn rdn 3 out: no hdwy after* **8/1**[3]

23-4 **4** *13* **Hatteras (FR)**[180] [230] 6-10-5 107.................................. RLucey-Butler[(7)] 73
(Miss M P Bryant) *trckd ldrs: jnd wnr 5th: wknd fr 3 out* **14/1**

5 *5* **Gold Tariff (IRE)** 5-10-12 .... LAspell 68
(P Winkworth) *hld up in tch: mstke 3rd: wknd appr 3 out* **40/1**

0F0- **6** *dist* **Desertmore Chief (IRE)**[198] [4933] 6-10-12 .... BJCrowley —
(B De Haan) *trckd ldrs: wknd appr 7th: t.o* **66/1**

00- **7** *dist* **Fine Enough (IRE)**[216] [4697] 6-10-12.. BFenton —
(R Rowe) *hld up in tch: hit 3rd: 3rd tl rdn and wknd rapidly 3 out: t.o* **100/1**

5m 13.8s (10.00) **Going Correction** +0.275s/f (Yiel)
WFA 4 from 5yo+ 13lb 7 Ran SP% **108.6**
Speed ratings: **91,90,82,77,75** —,— CSF £5.49 TOTE £4.10: £1.60, £1.20; EX 7.00.
Owner David Dunsdon **Bred** F X Cordier And Andre Berty **Trained** Findon, W Sussex

FOCUS
Suspect form, as they went only a steady pace and then sprinted, but the first two could both be all right.

NOTEBOOK
Soleil Fix(FR), who finished third in a race that has worked out well on his hurdling debut last spring, built on that promise, getting the better of a decent novice who has plenty of solid form to his name in Saltango. The pair finished nicely clear and this well-regarded four-year-old looks sure to go on to better things, although his trainer said afterwards that he will not have too many races this season. *(op 4-1 tchd 3-1)*
Saltango(GER), making a quick reappearance after his Worcester stroll three days earlier, just found giving 7lb to the promising winner too much. He has plenty of solid form in the book and there is no reason to believe that he did not give his running. *(op 8-13 tchd 4-6 in places)*
Mr Ex(ARG), who was receiving a stone from the favourite on this hurdling debut, was done for speed by the first two, and will be seen to better effect in a more strongly-run race. *(op 7-1 tchd 17-2)*
Hatteras(FR), who ran well in a seller here last year, has an official rating which flatters him and had a tough task against a few of these on his reappearance, but he will not be without hope back in plating class company. *(op 12-1)*
Gold Tariff(IRE), a half-brother to a modest maiden hurdler/chaser, was soon left behind when the pace quickened on the run from the third last. *(op 33-1)*

2021 HBLB MARES' ONLY INTERMEDIATE OPEN NATIONAL HUNT FLAT RACE 2m 2f 110y

4:10 (4:10) (Class 6) 4-6-Y-0 **£1,713** (£499; £249)

Form RPR

1 **1** **Ben's Turn (IRE)**[180] [242] 4-11-5 .... RThornton 103+
(A King) *in tch: rdn to go 2nd over 4f out: led over 1f out: edged rt u.p fnl f: hld on* **6/5**[1]

3 **2** *2* **Twist The Facts (IRE)**[166] [463] 5-10-5 .... MrNMoore[(7)] 92+
(N P Littmoden) *trckd ldrs: led 6f out: rdn and hdd 6f out: rallying whn sltly impeded ins fnl f: kpt on* **12/1**

02-0 **3** *3½* **Karawa**[177] [300] 6-10-12 .... JTizzard 86
(C L Tizzard) *mid-div styd on wl to go 3rd fnl f* **10/1**

4 *5* **Saddlers Cloth (IRE)**[186] 5-10-12 .... MBradburne 82+
(J A Geake) *mid-div: hdwy 4f out: wnt 3rd over 2f out: wknd fnl f* **7/2**[2]

0 **5** *11* **My Rosie Ribbons (IRE)**[6] [1922] 6-10-5 .... MrMWall[(7)] 70
(B W Duke) *led to 10f out: prom tl wknd 3f out* **50/1**

/ **6** *9* **Madam Fleet (IRE)** 6-10-12 .... RGreene 61
(M J Coombe) *trckd ldr tl wknd 4f out* **100/1**

7 *11* **Drink Light (IRE)** 5-10-12 .... TDoyle 50
(P R Webber) *a rr: lost tch 3f out* **13/2**[3]

8 *3* **Homeleigh Sun** 6-10-12 .... LAspell 47
(N J Gifford) *hld up on outside: a bhd* **9/1**

9 *dist* **Journals Rosy (IRE)** 4-10-12 .... TScudamore —
(M Scudamore) *trckeed ldrs: led 10f out: hdd 6f out: weakend qckly: t.o* **50/1**

P **Tribal Dancing** 5-10-12 .... BFenton —
(D R Gandolfo) *mid-div to 7f out: sn wknd: t.o whn p.u 3f out* **50/1**

4m 45.49s (6.19) **Going Correction** +0.275s/f (Yiel) 10 Ran SP% **114.7**
Speed ratings: **97,96,94,92,87 84,79,78,**—,— CSF £17.44 TOTE £2.00: £1.10, £1.70, £2.20; EX 6.20 Place 6 £63.42, Place 5 £40.01.
Owner C B Brookes **Bred** Miss E Violet Sweeney **Trained** Barbury Castle, Wilts
■ Stewards' Enquiry : T Doyle two-day ban: careless riding (Nov 15, 16)

FOCUS
Mares' only bumpers rarely take much winning and this was only a fair race of its type. However, the winner was carrying a penalty and was value for further, and the runner-up improved on her debut effort.

NOTEBOOK
Ben's Turn(IRE) stays well and this extended distance suited her. She did not win without giving her supporters a fright, though, as she wandered about once in front and hampered the runner-up as that one attempted to rally next to the rail. She was the best horse in the race and is better than the bare form, but had the winning distance been less the stewards may have had to reverse the places. *(op 11-8 tchd 11-10)*
Twist The Facts(IRE) kicked for home rounding the final turn and looked to have the favourite in trouble for a moment, but she was reeled in up the straight. Her rival ran green and idled in front, though, and had there been more room next to the rail she might well have got back up to win. The stewards let the result stand, though, which was the correct decision. *(op 9-1)*
Karawa, who finished runner-up at Cheltenham the last time she ran in a bumper restricted to horses of her own sex, appreciated returning to this less competitive form of racing. She ran a solid race and should do all right when sent hurdling. *(op 11-1 tchd 12-1)*
Saddlers Cloth(IRE), a half-sister to modest novice hurdler Blank Canvas, was sent off favourite for each of her three starts in point-to-points, winning the third of them, and looks the type to do better when faced with obstacles. *(tchd 4-1)*
My Rosie Ribbons(IRE), who is a sister to staying hurdle winner The Grey Butler, showed up well for a fair way, as she had on her debut, but lacked the speed to remain competitive when the tempo increased.

T/Plt: £142.70 to a £1 stake. Pool: £42,921.55. 219.55 winning tickets. T/Qpdt: £15.30 to a £1 stake. Pool: £3,680.50. 177.50 winning tickets. JS

1682 HEXHAM (L-H)
Friday, November 4

OFFICIAL GOING: Soft
Wind: Gusty, against

2022 MENCAP CONDITIONAL JOCKEYS' H'CAP CHASE (15 fncs) 2m 4f 110y
12:50 (12:51) (Class 4) (0-105,102) 5-Y-0+ **£4,385** (£1,287; £643; £321)

Form				RPR
00	1		**Devondale (IRE)**[38] 1570 9-10-4 **83** KJMercer(3) *(Ferdy Murphy) trckd ldr: led 6th: rdn 3 out: clr next and styd on wl* **14/1**	102+
6403	2	12	**The Miner**[13] 1839 7-10-11 **92** TMessenger(5) *(Miss S E Forster) hld up in rr: stdy hdwy 8th: chsd wnr 11th: cl up whn hit 2 out: blnd bdly next: sn one pce* **9/2**[2]	99+
PP-1	3	26	**Alfy Rich**[27] 1684 9-11-12 **102** GBerridge *(M Todhunter) trckd ldrs: blnd 2nd: pushed along 10th: rdn along and outpcd 12th: plugged on fr 2 out* **7/2**[1]	81
3/6P	4	5	**Moss Bawn (IRE)**[27] 1686 9-10-0 **81** (b) PKinsella(5) *(B Storey) chsd ldrs: rdn along 12th: sn outpcd* **20/1**	55
302U	5	30	**Risky Way**[27] 1684 9-10-13 **92** TJDreaper(3) *(W S Coltherd) chsd ldrs: mstkes 3rd and 4th: nt fluent after: blnd bdly and lost pl 10th: hdwy whn blnd 2 out: sn wknd* **11/2**[3]	36
02P5	6	dist	**Pavey Ark (IRE)**[27] 1684 7-10-0 **76** oh1 DCCostello *(James Moffatt) in tch: rdn along 11th: sn outpcd and bhd* **8/1**	—
2B5	F		**Assumetheposition (FR)**[5] 1942 5-10-10 **96** (p) JPFlavin(10) *(R C Guest) in tch whn fell 4th* **11/2**[3]	—
616-	U		**Wilful Lord (IRE)**[201] 4872 8-9-12 **77** PAspell(3) *(J Wade) hld up in rr whn bdly hmpd and uns rdr 4th* **9/2**[2]	—
U10-	P		**Jumbo's Dream**[223] 4551 14-10-0 **76** oh1 (p) DMcGann *(J E Dixon) led to 5th: rdn along and lost pl 8th: bhd fr next and p.u bef 4 out* **28/1**	—

5m 23.8s (12.40) **Going Correction** +0.675s/f (Soft) **9** Ran SP% **115.3**
Speed ratings: **103,98,88,86,75** —,—,—,— CSF £77.20 CT £274.18 TOTE £19.60: £4.50, £1.70, £1.10; EX 77.70.
Owner Mrs A N Durkan & F Murphy **Bred** Larry Mulvany **Trained** West Witton, N Yorks

FOCUS
An ordinary event weakened by the below-par effort of the favourite. The pace was sound, though, and the form could be all right.

NOTEBOOK
Devondale(IRE) notched his first win since 2001 and his first over fences on only his third start for this stable. Although he may be flattered by the bare form, he will not mind the return to three miles *and appeals as the type to win again over fences. Official explanation: trainer said, regarding the improved form shown, gelding was better suited being ridden more positively on softer ground (op 12-1)*
The Miner, back over fences, would have gone much closer had his jumping not gone to pieces in the closing stages. He remains capable of winning a similar event away from progressive sorts but his inconsistency means he is not one to lump on. *(op 11-2)*
Alfy Rich, 8lb higher in the weights than when winning on fast ground over course and distance on his previous start, was easy to back and proved a disappointment after an early blunder. He has run well in soft but may be happiest on a sounder surface. *(op 11-4)*
Moss Bawn(IRE), who has slipped to a potentially favourable mark, did not show enough back over this trip to suggest a return to winning ways is imminent. *(op 25-1)*
Risky Way did not jump with any fluency and was well below his best on ground that was almost certainly softer than ideal. *(op 5-1)*
Pavey Ark(IRE) is a disappointing sort who was soundly beaten back in testing ground. *(op 9-1)*

2023 BARBOUR MAIDEN CHASE (19 fncs) 3m 1f
1:20 (1:21) (Class 4) 5-Y-0+ **£3,575** (£1,049; £524; £262)

Form				RPR
222-	1		**Capybara (IRE)**[239] 4272 7-11-0 DO'Meara *(H P Hogarth) cl up: led 8th to 10th: led again 5 out: rdn clr 2 out: styd on* **9/4**[2]	120+
2-2	2	10	**Rare Society (IRE)**[20] 1736 7-11-0 DElsworth *(Mrs S J Smith) led to 8th: led again 12th: pushed along and hdd 5 out: rdn to chse wnr fr next: one pce fr 2 out* **6/1**	109+
3/	3	6	**Lord Payne (IRE)**[571] 4783 7-11-0 KRenwick *(P Monteith) trckd ldng pair: pushed along 5 out: rdn after next: one pce fr 2 out* **11/2**[3]	102+
3-4	4	dist	**Show Me The River**[12] 1845 6-11-0 BHarding *(Ferdy Murphy) hld up in tch: hdwy to trck ldrs 13th:cl up whn hit 5 out: sn rdn: blnd 3 out and sn btn* **15/8**[1]	—
0P	P		**In Ainm De (IRE)**[75] 1279 9-10-0 CDSharkey(7) *(N Wilson) a rr: bhd fr 13th: p.u bef 15th* **50/1**	—
PP-0	P		**Lucken Howe**[181] 210 6-10-11 PBuchanan(3) *(Mrs J K M Oliver) a rr: bhd whn p.u bef 15th* **100/1**	—
6	P		**Let's Be Subtle (IRE)**[13] 1839 6-10-4 (t) GBerridge(3) *(W Amos) hld up: hdwy 1/2-way: rdn along and outpcd fr 13th: bhd whn p.u bef 3 out* **20/1**	—
62-3	P		**Wild About Harry**[190] 83 8-10-11 **70** KJMercer(3) *(A R Dicken) chsd ldrs: led 10th to 12th: rdn along next: sn wknd and bhd whn p.u bef 2 out* **8/1**	—

6m 47.6s (15.70) **Going Correction** +0.675s/f (Soft) **8** Ran SP% **114.0**
Speed ratings: **101,97,95**,—,— —,—,— CSF £15.95 TOTE £5.90: £2.00, £1.30, £5.60; EX 15.00.
Owner Hogarth Racing **Bred** Tom Fitzgerald **Trained** Stillington, N Yorks

FOCUS
An ordinary event but the winner was quite impressive and has been rated a stone higher than his best hurdling form.

NOTEBOOK
Capybara(IRE) ◆ turned in an improved effort on this first run since March. He stays well, goes on soft ground and appeals as the type to win again in this sphere. *(op 7-2)*
Rare Society(IRE), on his first run on soft ground over regulation fences, ran creditably and looks the type to win in ordinary handicap company around this trip. *(op 5-1)*
Lord Payne(IRE) ◆, having his first run over fences and first run for Peter Monteith, jumped soundly and showed more than enough on this first start since last April to suggest he can win a similar event in due course. *(op 7-2)*
Show Me The River, up in trip and back in more realistic company, was in the process of running creditably until his jumping let him down in the closing stages, and he will have to brush up in this department if he is to progress. *(op 13-8 tchd 2-1 in a place)*
Wild About Harry had something to find at the weights but proved disappointing. Consistency is not his strongest suit and he remains one to have reservations about. *(op 16-1)*

2024 WEATHERBYS BANK NOVICES' HURDLE (10 hdls) 2m 4f 110y
1:50 (1:53) (Class 4) 4-Y-0+ **£3,690** (£1,083; £541; £270)

Form				RPR
	1		**High Day**[442] 1154 5-10-9 KJMercer(3) *(Ferdy Murphy) hld up in tch: smooth hdwy after 2 out: led appr last: pushed out* **2/1**[1]	112+
2	2		**Unexplored (IRE)**[278] 5-10-12 GLee *(J Howard Johnson) trckd ldrs: hdwy to ld after 2 out: hdd approachoing last: rdn and kpt on flat* **4/1**[2]	102
3-50	3	12	**The Connor Fella**[43] 991 4-10-7 DCCostello(5) *(F P Murtagh) hld up and bhd: hdwy after 3 out: rdn after next: styd on fr last: nrst fin* **66/1**	90
0-0P	4	3/4	**Another Jameson (IRE)**[148] 693 5-10-5 DO'Meara *(J M Jefferson) led to 2nd: prominent tl rdn along and one pce between last 2* **66/1**	83
R-03	5	1/2	**August Rose (IRE)**[27] 1683 5-10-2 PBuchanan(3) *(Miss Lucinda V Russell) in tch: effrt 2 out: sn rdn along and kpt on same pce* **20/1**	82
3344	6	7	**Chief Dan George (IRE)**[13] 1834 5-10-9 PAspell(3) *(D R MacLeod) hld up towards rr: effrt and hdwy 2 out: sn rdn along and n.d* **12/1**	82
24-F	7	6	**Roman Rebel**[7] 1910 6-10-12 **100** RMcGrath *(Mrs K Walton) prom: rdn along after 3 out: wknd after next* **8/1**	76
5	8	15	**Nearly Never**[56] 1445 10-10-5 NCarter(7) *(Mrs S J Smith) in tch: rdn along bef 2 out: sn wknd* **100/1**	61
0-00	9	18	**Another Taipan (IRE)**[13] 1834 5-10-5 EWhillans(7) *(A C Whillans) a rr: bhd fr 1/2-way* **66/1**	43
	10	7	**Ring You Later** 4-10-12 ADempsey *(J Howard Johnson) a rr: bhd fr 1/2-way* **66/1**	36
2123	P		**Bluecoat (USA)**[28] 1667 5-10-9 MrTGreenall(3) *(M W Easterby) a rr: bhd whn p.u bef last* **10/1**	—
35-5	P		**Neidpath Castle**[190] 82 6-10-12 **101** BHarding *(A C Whillans) midfield: rdn along 3 out: sn wknd and bhd whn p.u bef last* **6/1**[3]	—
2-	P		**Neagh (FR)**[274] 3660 4-10-5 MissRDavidson(7) *(N G Richards) chsd ldrs: led 3rd: rdn along after 2 out: sn hdd & wknd qckly: p.u bef last* **6/1**[3]	—
00	P		**Yankee Holiday (IRE)**[13] 1834 5-10-12 KRenwick *(Mrs S C Bradburne) cl up: led 2nd to next: prom tl rdn along 2 out: wknd qckly and p.u bef last* **66/1**	—

5m 28.2s (18.60) **Going Correction** +0.775s/f (Soft) **14** Ran SP% **123.0**
Speed ratings: **95,94,89,89,89 86,84,78,71,69** —,—,—,— CSF £9.80 TOTE £2.60: £1.30, £1.90, £18.50; EX 31.20.
Owner Sean J Murphy **Bred** Meon Valley Stud **Trained** West Witton, N Yorks

FOCUS
Ordinary form on the face of it but the winner won with plenty in hand (value for ten lengths) and is the type to win more races.

NOTEBOOK
High Day ◆, a fair Flat performer who had shown plenty of promise, despite two falls over hurdles, turned in a pleasing effort on this first run for over a year and debut for Ferdy Murphy. He won with plenty in hand and, given the way he went through the race, looks sure to win a similar event at the very least. *(op 9-4 tchd 5-2)*
Unexplored(IRE) ◆, a point winner in Ireland in January, shaped well on this first start for Howard Johnson. He will stay three miles and is the type to win a similar event. *(tchd 7-2)*
The Connor Fella had shown little in bumpers or on the Flat, but seemed to show much improved form on only this second outing over obstacles. It remains to be seen whether this run flatters him but, on this evidence, he will be of more interest over three miles in ordinary handicaps. *(op 50-1)*
Another Jameson(IRE), having her first run since June and only her second over hurdles, is another whose proximity holds this form down. Nevertheless, this represented an improved effort and she too may be suited by three miles and modest handicaps.
August Rose(IRE) was not disgraced on this first start on a soft surface but is likely to continue to look vulnerable in this grade. The switch to modest handicaps around this trip will suit and she may be capable of winning a small event. *(op 18-1 tchd 16-1)*
Chief Dan George(IRE) was not totally disgraced but he is another that is going to continue to look vulnerable in this type of event and he will be suited by the step into handicap company. *(tchd 16-1)*

2025 CENTURY FM (S) H'CAP HURDLE (10 hdls) 2m 4f 110y
2:20 (2:22) (Class 5) (0-90,88) 4-Y-0+ **£2,350** (£684; £342)

Form				RPR
0052	1		**Maunby Rocker**[9] 1883 5-11-2 **83** (p) PMerrigan(5) *(P C Haslam) hld up: stdy hdwy 2 out: led appr last: sn rdn: drvn flat and jst hld on* **9/4**[1]	90+
PP33	2	hd	**Samson Des Galas (FR)**[9] 1883 7-10-1 **63** GLee *(R Ford) hld up and bhd: stdy hdwy 2 out: rdn to chse ldrs last: drvn and styd on wl flat: jst failed* **7/2**[2]	69+
3-04	3	nk	**Chivvy Charver (IRE)**[181] 215 8-10-8 **77** EWhillans(7) *(A C Whillans) in tch: hdwy 3 out: rdn to chse wnr and hit last: drvn flat and styd on wl* **7/1**[3]	82
0205	4	1 3/4	**Lazy Lena (IRE)**[23] 1722 6-10-13 **75** TSiddall *(Miss L C Siddall) hld up towards rr: hdwy 2 out: sn rdn to chse ldrs: drvn last: kpt on flat* **14/1**	78
4064	5	3 1/2	**Two Steps To Go (USA)**[9] 1883 6-10-9 **78** (p) BenOrde-Powlett(7) *(M A Barnes) a.p: led 3 out: rdn after next: hdd & wknd appr last* **16/1**	78+
U660	6	2	**Tiger Talk**[14] 1814 9-11-2 **88** (b) JMoorman(10) *(R C Guest) hld up and bhd: hdwy 3 out: rdn next and no imp appr last* **20/1**	85
0-5P	7	3 1/2	**Just Sal**[138] 781 9-10-4 **73** GThomas(7) *(R Nixon) in tch: hdwy to chse ldrs 4th: rdn along 2 out: grad wknd* **20/1**	68+
20P4	8	1/2	**Cody**[9] 1887 6-10-13 **78** (bt) PAspell(3) *(James Moffatt) in tch: rdn along 2 out: sn wknd* **12/1**	71
2345	9	15	**Star Trooper (IRE)**[113] 988 9-10-13 **78** (p) MrCStorey(3) *(Miss S E Forster) chsd ldrs: hdwy to ld 5th: rdn along and hdd next: wknd after 2 out* **7/1**[3]	56
3	10	dist	**Glenview Lass (IRE)**[22] 1724 6-10-12 **74** (p) JPMcNamara *(T G McCourt, Ire) led to after 2nd: chsd ldrs to 5th: sn outpcd and bhd fr next* **12/1**	—
-00P	P		**Quay Walloper**[9] 1887 4-9-9 **64** (p) CDSharkey(7) *(J R Norton) a rr: t.o fr 1/2-way: p.u bef last* **100/1**	—
PP	P		**Port Natal (IRE)**[9] 1883 7-11-10 **86** (b) ADempsey *(J Wade) plld hrd: hdwy to ld after 2nd: hdd 5th: wknd qckly and p.u next* **50/1**	—
PPP-	P		**Fifteen Reds**[364] 2021 10-10-11 **80** MJMcAlister(7) *(J C Haynes) prom: rdn along 3 out and sn wknd: bhd whn p.u bef last* **40/1**	—

5m 32.5s (22.90) **Going Correction** +0.775s/f (Soft)
WFA 4 from 5yo+ 13lb **13** Ran SP% **120.8**
Speed ratings: **87,86,86,86,84 84,82,82,76,— —,—,—** CSF £10.18 CT £48.96 TOTE £4.00: £1.10, £1.50, £3.10; EX 15.30.There was no bid for the winner. Samson des Galas was claimed by Naughty Diesel Ltd for £6,000.
Owner P A Hill-Walker **Bred** Bearstone Stud **Trained** Middleham, N Yorks

FOCUS
A modest event in which the pace was fair. The first two have been rated close to their Sedgefield marks.

NOTEBOOK
Maunby Rocker confirmed the bit of promise shown last time to win a weak event but he did not look the easiest of rides under pressure and would not be an obvious one to follow up in anything but the worst company next time. *(tchd 5-2)*
Samson Des Galas(FR), a consistent enough performer in this grade, was closely weighted with *Maunby Rocker on previous form and almost reversed Sedgefield form over this longer trip. (op 5-1)*
Chivvy Charver(IRE), who stays three miles, appreciated the drop in grade, and had he not hit the last flight the margin between himself and the winner may have been even narrower. *(op 9-1)*
Lazy Lena(IRE) seemed to run creditably in this ordinary event but, given her lack of consistency *and the fact that she has yet to win a race, she is not one to place too much faith in next time. (op 16-1)*
Two Steps To Go(USA), an inconsistent performer wearing cheekpieces for the first time, failed to get home over this longer trip in the ground, and will be suited by a return to two miles.
Tiger Talk was again below his best and does not look one to place too much faith in at present. *(op 16-1)*

2026 RON WOODMAN CELEBRATION NOVICES' H'CAP CHASE (12 fncs) 2m 110y
2:50 (2:50) (Class 4) (0-95,94) 4-Y-0+ **£3,614** (£1,061; £530; £264)

Form				RPR
13-3	**1**		**Corrib Lad (IRE)**[194] 9 7-11-12 **94** BGibson (L Lungo) *cl up: led 2nd: rdn along 3 out: styd on* **2/1**[1]	109+
3335	**2**	*1 ¾*	**Ideal Du Bois Beury (FR)**[13] 1837 9-10-6 **77** PAspell(3) (P Monteith) *hld up and bhd: hdwy 2 out: sn ridde: styd on strly fr last: nt rch wnr* **9/2**[2]	86
66P3	**3**	*2 ½*	**Ready To Rumble (NZ)**[5] 1942 8-10-12 **85** (p) PCO'Neill(5) (R C Guest) *a.p: rdn along and sltly outpcd bef 2 out: styd on u.p appr last* **8/1**	91
0205	**4**	*3*	**Lion Guest (IRE)**[13] 1835 8-10-11 **79** KRenwick (Mrs S C Bradburne) *led to 2nd: prom: ev ch 3 out: sn rdn and wknd last* **7/1**	84+
65-0	**5**	*10*	**Persian Point**[152] 643 9-10-12 **83** MrCStorey(3) (Miss S E Forster) *bhd: sme hdwy fr 2 out: nvr a factor* **10/1**	76
36/2	**6**	*10*	**Albertino Lad**[13] 1835 8-11-9 **94** PBuchanan(3) (Miss Lucinda V Russell) *in tch: hdwy to chse ldrs whn hit 7th: rdn along 3 out: mstke next and sn wknd* **8/1**	79+
0600	**P**		**Tin Healy's Pass**[67] 1360 5-10-9 **77** BHarding (I McMath) *a bhd: p.u bef 4 out* **40/1**	—
F-55	**F**		**Silver Sedge (IRE)**[28] 1665 6-10-10 **85** TJDreaper(7) (Mrs A Hamilton) *in tch whn fell 1st* **6/1**[3]	—
FPP/	**P**		**Gohh**[559] 4957 9-11-3 **88** (t) MrTGreenall(3) (M W Easterby) *chsd ldrs: rdn along and wknd8th: bhd whn p.u bef last* **20/1**	—

4m 25.2s (16.10) **Going Correction** +0.675s/f (Soft) **9** Ran SP% **116.8**
Speed ratings: **89,88,87,85,80 76,—,—,—** CSF £12.18 CT £59.31 TOTE £3.70: £2.70, £1.10, £1.70; EX 8.80.
Owner Liam Mulryan **Bred** E Cawley **Trained** Carrutherstown, D'fries & G'way
■ Stewards' Enquiry : K Renwick two day ban: used whip with excessive force and in the incorrect place (Nov 15, 16)

FOCUS
Little strength in depth and just a fair pace but it will be no surprise to see the winner, who has been rated for further, go in again.

NOTEBOOK
Corrib Lad(IRE) ◆, a strapping sort, jumped soundly and created a favourable impression on this chase debut and first run since April. Although the bare form is nothing special, he appeals strongly as the type to win more races. *(op 5-2)*
Ideal Du Bois Beury(FR), who has not won since 2002, ran a typical race returned to this trip and, although capable of winning an ordinary event if things drop right, is not one to place any great faith in. *(op 5-1)*
Ready To Rumble(NZ) ran his best race over fences with the cheekpieces on again and left the impression that he would be worth a try over a bit further.
Lion Guest(IRE) again ran creditably over fences and may do better away from progressive sorts returned to two and a half miles. *(op 11-2)*
Persian Point, an inconsistent maiden hurdler, did not show enough on this chasing debut to suggest he will be of much interest in the near future. *(op 12-1)*
Albertino Lad ran well for a long way but may have found this coming too soon after his recent reappearance run after a layoff, and he is not one to write off just yet. *(op 13-2)*

2027 MENCAP H'CAP HURDLE (8 hdls) 2m 110y
3:20 (3:21) (Class 4) (0-100,100) 4-Y-0+ **£3,110** (£906; £453)

Form				RPR
45P2	**1**		**The Names Bond**[166] 466 7-11-5 **100** MissRDavidson(7) (N G Richards) *in tch: stdy hdwy after 2 out: led appr last: rdn and kpt on flat* **11/2**	115+
P3-2	**2**	*3*	**Jolika (FR)**[188] 119 8-10-11 **95** JPEnnis(10) (L Lungo) *trckd ldrs: led 4th: rdn along qafter 2 out: hdd appr last: kpt on u.p flat* **4/1**[2]	103
046-	**3**	*6*	**Silver Seeker (USA)**[36] 4303 5-10-5 **82** KJMercer(3) (A R Dicken) *bhd: hdwy 2 out: rdn and styd on appr last: nrst fin* **12/1**	84
156-	**4**	*shd*	**Polar Gunner**[197] 4944 8-10-9 **86** FKing(3) (J M Jefferson) *trckd ldrs: smooth hdwy to chse ldr 5th: ev ch 2 out: sn rdn and wknd bef last* **3/1**[1]	88
520-	**5**	*9*	**Bramantino (IRE)**[20] 4810 5-10-10 **84** ADobbin (T A K Cuthbert) *chsd ldrs: rdn along and outpcd 2 out: styd on u.p appr last* **5/1**[3]	77
0P0-	**6**	*4*	**Upswing**[332] 2696 8-10-5 **79** KJohnson (R C Guest) *hld up towards rr: stdy hdwy 5th: chsd ldrs 2 out: rdn and and wknd bef last* **8/1**	68
0000	**7**	*14*	**Bromley Abbey**[13] 1834 7-9-12 **75** oh1 ow1 (p) MrCStorey(3) (Miss S E Forster) *in tch: hdwy to chse ldrs 5th: rdn along 2 out and wknd bef last* **25/1**	50
00-0	**8**	*1*	**Nabir (FR)**[6] 1927 5-10-8 **82** ARoss (P D Niven) *a rr* **16/1**	56
0F-P	**9**	*25*	**Grafton Truce (IRE)**[72] 1308 8-9-11 **74** oh4 PBuchanan(3) (Miss Lucinda V Russell) *led to 4th: cl up tl rdn alonga nd wknd appr 2 out* **66/1**	23
	P		**Komoto**[6] 1932 4-11-5 **98** PCO'Neill(5) (T G McCourt, Ire) *in tch: rdn along bef 3 out: sn wknd and bhd whn p.u bef last* **14/1**	—
/FP-	**P**		**Long Shot**[506] 764 8-11-10 **98** TSiddall (Miss L C Siddall) *chsd ldr: rdn alOong 1/2-way: sn lost pl and bhd whn p.u bef last* **28/1**	—

4m 24.7s (9.50) **Going Correction** +0.775s/f (Soft)
WFA 4 from 5yo+ 12lb **11** Ran SP% **117.2**
Speed ratings: **108,106,103,103,99 97,91,90,78,— —** CSF £27.78 CT £255.97 TOTE £5.10: £1.10, £2.00, £3.00; EX 21.90 Trifecta £259.40 Part won. Pool: £365.36 - 0.60 winning tickets..
Owner Mr & Mrs Duncan Davidson **Bred** D R Tucker **Trained** Greystoke, Cumbria

FOCUS
A run-of-the-mill handicap run at a fair pace and rated through the third.

NOTEBOOK
The Names Bond ◆ turned in an improved effort back over hurdles on his debut for Nicky Richards and on this first run since May. He travelled strongly and looks the sort to win again in ordinary company. *(tchd 6-1)*

Jolika(FR) shaped as though retaining all her ability on this first start since April. She stays a mile and a half, goes well on testing ground and looks sure to win a similar race this winter. *(op 5-1)*

Silver Seeker(USA), returned to hurdles, shaped as though worth a try over further but, given that *he has not won a race since 2002 (Flat), he would not be one to place too much faith in. (op 10-1 tchd 14-1)*

Polar Gunner, who is officially rated 26lb lower over hurdles than over fences, shaped as though *this first run since April was just needed and he is not one to write off just yet in this sphere. (tchd 7-2)*

Bramantino(IRE), who is on a potentially favourable mark over hurdles, was again below his best *for his current stable and will have to show more before he is a serious betting proposition. (op 11-2)*

Upswing, having his first run for Richard Guest, shaped better than the bare result suggests on this first run since December and is not one to be writing off just yet. *(op 7-1)*

Komoto *Official explanation: jockey said gelding never travelled (op 16-1 tchd 12-1)*

2028 MENCAP MARES' ONLY STANDARD OPEN NATIONAL HUNT FLAT RACE 2m 110y
3:50 (3:51) (Class 6) 4-6-Y-0 **£2,487** (£724; £362)

Form				RPR
30-	**1**		**Zaffie Parson (IRE)**[215] 4720 4-10-12 RMcGrath (G A Harker) *hld up in rr: hdwy 1/2-way: pushed along and outpcd 5f out: styd on fr 3f out: rdn ins last: led last 100 yds* **8/1**	94
	2	*¾*	**Political Pendant** 4-10-5 GThomas(7) (R Nixon) *hld up in rr: stdy hdwy 1/2-way: led 3f out and sn pushed clr: rdn 1f out: hdd and no ex last 100 yds* **50/1**	93
00-2	**3**	*9*	**Our Joycey**[19] 1762 4-10-5 CDSharkey(7) (Mrs K Walton) *hld up towards rr: hdwy 6f out: rdn to chse ldng pair 3f out: hung rt over 1f out and sn one pce* **5/1**[3]	85+
	4	*16*	**Witch Power** 4-10-7 DMcGann(5) (A M Crow) *keen: in tch: hdwy to chse ldrs 1/2-way: rdn along and outpcd 4f out: kpt on u.p fnl 2f* **16/1**	68
	5	*6*	**Filey Flyer** 5-10-12 GLee (J R Turner) *clsoe up: led 1/2-way: rdn along and hdd 3f out: sn wknd* **14/1**	62
24	**6**	*13*	**Bonnie Rock (IRE)**[28] 1667 5-10-9 MichalKohl(3) (J I A Charlton) *in tch on inner: hdwy to chse ldrs 1/2-way: rdn along over 4f and sn wknd* **4/1**[1]	49
0-0	**7**	*1 ¾*	**Brundeanlaws**[43] 1532 4-10-5 TMessenger(7) (Mrs H O Graham) *led: hdd 1/2-way: sn pushed along and bhd fnl 4f* **33/1**	47
0-	**8**	*19*	**New's Full (FR)**[211] 4753 4-10-9 KJMercer(3) (Ferdy Murphy) *chsd ldrs: rdn along 4f out: sn wknd* **9/2**[2]	28
	9	*dist*	**Claudia May** 4-10-9 PBuchanan(3) (Miss Lucinda V Russell) *hld up: hdwy to trck ldng pair 6f out: rdn along 4f out: wknd 3f out* **20/1**	—
	10	*19*	**Fae Taylor (IRE)** 5-10-5 PJMcDonald(7) (Ferdy Murphy) *a rr: wl bhd fnl 6f* **16/1**	—
	P		**Little Sioux (IRE)** 5-10-12 ADobbin (L Lungo) *in tch: hdwy to chse ldrs 6f out: rdn along 4f out: sn drvn and wknd over 2f out: p.u over 1f out* **4/1**[1]	—

4m 25.4s (12.70) **Going Correction** +0.775s/f (Soft) **11** Ran SP% **114.1**
Speed ratings: **101,100,96,88,86 79,79,70,—,— —** CSF £350.61 TOTE £12.80: £3.20, £11.40, £1.40; EX 381.50 Place 6 £31.30, Place 5 £16.04.

Owner David Adair **Bred** Miss B Sykes **Trained** Thirkleby, N Yorks

FOCUS
A modest event run at a fair pace and rated through the third.

NOTEBOOK
Zaffie Parson(IRE), from a stable that has done well in this type of event, turned in an improved effort to get off the mark after a break. Stamina is her strong suit and she will need at least two and a half miles over hurdles. *(tchd 9-1)*

Political Pendant, a half-sister to inconsistent staying hurdler Political Sox, was worn down late on having looked sure to win and showed more than enough on this racecourse debut to suggest that a similarly modest event can be found. *(op 25-1)*

Our Joycey was not disgraced on this first start on a soft surface and is likely to need a decent test of stamina when sent over obstacles. *(op 7-1)*

Witch Power, a half-sister to a two mile six furlong hurdle winner in Come Home Alone, was not disgraced on this racecourse debut but, although a good test of stamina should suit, she is likely to continue to look vulnerable in this grade. *(op 20-1)*

Filey Flyer, who is out of a winning hurdler, had the run of the race and showed a modest level of ability, but she is another that is likely to continue to look vulnerable in this type of event. *(op 16-1)*

Bonnie Rock(IRE) had shown ability in ordinary company on fast ground but was well below that level on her first start on a soft surface. *(op 11-2)*

T/Jkpt: Not won. T/Plt: £21.40 to a £1 stake. Pool: £43,231.90. 1,470.20 winning tickets. T/Qpdt: £7.70 to a £1 stake. Pool: £3,689.50. 350.80 winning tickets. JR

2029 - 2030a (Foreign Racing) - See Raceform Interactive

[1402]DOWN ROYAL (R-H)

Friday, November 4

OFFICIAL GOING: Hurdle course - soft to heavy; chase course - soft (heavy in places)

Saturday's card, due to feature the James Nicholson Wine Merchant Champion Chase, was abandoned after two races following a bomb scare.

2031a EUROPEAN BREEDERS FUND SCARVAGH HOUSE STUD MARES NOVICE HURDLE (GRADE 3) 2m

2:05 (2:18) 4-Y-0+ **£18,468** (£5,418; £2,581; £879)

RPR

1 **Laetitia (IRE)**[12] 1865 5-10-10 .... DNRussell 113+
(C Byrnes, Ire) *mid-div: hdwy to 3rd 4 out: led 3 out: rdn 2 out: kpt on wl* **7/4**[1]

2 *3* **High Priestess (IRE)**[15] 1808 6-11-0 111 .... RWalsh 114
(M J P O'Brien, Ire) *chsd ldrs: led after 4 out: rdn and hdd 3 out: kpt on* **2/1**[2]

3 *2* **No Sound (FR)**[12] 1865 4-10-5 100 .... PCarberry 103
(Noel Meade, Ire) *bhd: hdwy to 5th bef 3 out: impr to 3rd bef 2 out: kpt on* **10/1**

4 *10* **Kylebeg Dancer (IRE)**[20] 1740 4-10-5 106 ....(t) KHadnett 93
(T Hogan, Ire) *chsd ldr: 4th and rdn 4 out: sn btn: mod 7th 2 out: kpt on again* **6/1**[3]

5 *hd* **Sauterelle (IRE)**[15] 1808 5-10-10 99 ....(t) RMPower 98
(Thomas Mullins, Ire) *bhd: hdwy to 5th bef st: rdn 3 out: sn no ex* **16/1**

6 *6* **Name For Fame (USA)**[33] 1623 6-10-10 103 .... NPMadden 92
(R Donohoe, Ire) *mid-div: hdwy to cl 6th 4 out: 4th and rdn bef 3 out: sn no ex* **10/1**

7 *2* **Rays Venture (IRE)**[26] 1704 5-10-3 .... NJO'Shea(7) 90
(D M Leigh, Ire) *mid-div: rr and rdn 4 out: kpt on: nvr a threat* **20/1**

8 *1* **Marguerita (FR)**[12] 1864 4-10-5 95 .... AndrewJMcNamara 84
(A J McNamara, Ire) *rr of mid-div: hdwy to 6th bef st: rdn bef 3 out: no imp* **10/1**

9 *5* **Sue Sue**[32] 1628 5-10-10 99 ....(t) DJCasey 84
(Gerard Stack, Ire) *a bhd: nvr a danger* **12/1**

10 *7* **Rajayla (IRE)**[19] 1763 4-10-5 .... DFO'Regan 72
(T G McCourt, Ire) *chsd ldrs: rdn after 4 out: sn wknd* **12/1**

11 *12* **Lorna's Star (IRE)**[16] 1788 6-10-5 99 .... KTColeman(5) 65
(F Flood, Ire) *mid-div: dropped to rr bef 4 out: n.d* **14/1**

12 *2* **Freeze Frame (IRE)**[19] 1763 4-10-2 90 .... RCColgan(3) 58
(G A Kingston, Ire) *mid-div: rdn 4 out: sn btn* **16/1**

13 *20* **Rock Back (IRE)**[107] 1061 4-9-12 .... ADLeigh(7) 38
(Mrs John Harrington, Ire) *chsd ldrs: rdn 4 out: sn wknd: t.o* **25/1**

14 *hd* **Bella Liana (IRE)**[67] 1356 5-10-10 85 .... NPMulholland 43
(J Clements, Ire) *led: hdd after 4 out: sn wknd* **25/1**

4m 16.0s
WFA 4 from 5yo+ 12lb **14 Ran SP% 157.5**
CSF £7.54.

Owner Mrs Mary M Hayes **Bred** John McLoughlin **Trained** Ballingarry, Co Limerick

NOTEBOOK

Laetitia(IRE) continues to progress and was impressive on her second start over hurdles, despite running very green on the aproach to the second last. She showed a lot more determination than the runner-up and was in control again after the last. *(op 7/4 tchd 9/4)*

High Priestess(IRE) went on well before the straight but found little when headed by the winner. She had every chance to capitalise after two out but the resolution is not there. *(op 9/4 tchd 7/4)*

No Sound(FR) ran her best race to date but was never a threat to the first pair.

Kylebeg Dancer(IRE) is just not effective on this heavy ground. *(op 5/1)*

2032a ANGLO IRISH BANK HURDLE 2m

2:35 (2:44) 4-Y-0+ **£13,851** (£4,063; £1,936; £659)

RPR

1 **Feathard Lady (IRE)**[321] 2906 5-11-1 .... RWalsh 141+
(C A Murphy, Ire) *settled in 5th: impr to 3rd 3 out: rdn to ld last: styd on wl* **9/4**[1]

2 *4* **Sky's The Limit (FR)**[26] 1699 4-11-4 125 ....(b) BJGeraghty 140
(E J O'Grady, Ire) *chsd ldr: led after 3 out: rdn and hdd last: no ex* **9/4**[1]

3 *10* **Royal Paradise (FR)**[33] 1621 5-11-12 137 .... CO'Dwyer 138
(Thomas Foley, Ire) *led: hdd after 3 out: no ex bef next* **10/3**[2]

4 *8* **All Heart**[26] 1699 4-10-6 112 .... RMPower 110
(Thomas Mullins, Ire) *racd 4th: 3rd fr half-way: 5th and rdn 3 out: no ex and kpt on* **16/1**[3]

5 *7* **Rocket Ship (IRE)**[16] 1787 5-11-2 130 .... PCarberry 113
(Noel Meade, Ire) *settled in rr: hdwy to 4th bef st: rdn 3 out: sn wknd* **10/3**[2]

6 *dist* **Aspharasyousee (IRE)**[56] 1449 7-10-5 79 .... MrPJCosgrave(7) 87
(J G Cosgrave, Ire) *racd 3rd: 4th half-way: rr and rdn 4 out: sn wknd: completely t.o* **100/1**

4m 13.5s
WFA 4 from 5yo+ 12lb **6 Ran SP% 114.6**
CSF £8.07.

Owner Lord of the Ring Syndicate **Bred** J C Condon **Trained** Gorey, Co Wexford

NOTEBOOK

Feathard Lady(IRE) extended her unbeaten run to five despite not having raced for almost a year. She went into the race with a mark of 128, which looked plenty high enough, and emerged on 137. Her rider was suitably impressed and she remains an interesting prospect.

Sky's The Limit(FR) was no match for the winner when headed at the last. His BHB rating is 9lb above his Irish mark.

Royal Paradise(FR), full of mucus on his reappearance, is obviously not right yet. *(op 3/1)*

Rocket Ship(IRE) again disappointed, travelling well and finding absolutely nothing when asked. At the moment he is one to avoid. *(op 11/4)*

2033 - 2035a (Foreign Racing) - See Raceform Interactive

[1834]KELSO (L-H)

Saturday, November 5

OFFICIAL GOING: Good to soft

Wind: Almost nil

2036 PETER SCOTT SCOTTISH CASHMERE "NATIONAL HUNT" NOVICES' HURDLE (11 hdls) 2m 6f 110y

12:40 (12:41) (Class 4) 4-Y-0+ **£3,477** (£1,020; £510; £254)

Form RPR

22-1 1 **King Of Confusion (IRE)**[14] 1839 6-10-5 115 .... TJDreaper(7) 122+
(Ferdy Murphy) *hld up: stdy hdwy 4 out: led gng wl appr last: easily* **1/4**[1]

3-64 2 *17* **Bywell Beau (IRE)**[29] 1661 6-10-9 97 ....(t) MichalKohl(3) 102
(J I A Charlton) *keen: hld up: hdwy to ld after 6th: hdd appr last: no ch w wnr* **20/1**

-243 3 *27* **Aces Four (IRE)**[14] 1834 6-10-12 .... RMcGrath 75
(W McKeown) *chsd ldrs: outpcd 4 out: no imp fr next* **16/1**[3]

2 4 *11* **Auntie Kathleen**[180] 261 6-10-5 .... ADobbin 57
(J J Quinn) *led to after 6th: rdn and wknd bef 3 out* **15/2**[2]

/00- 5 *25* **Generals Laststand (IRE)**[297] 3321 7-10-7 .... DFlavin(5) 39
(Mrs L B Normile) *in tch: outpcd 5 out: sn btn* **100/1**

6P-0 6 *19* **Bodkin Boy (IRE)**[29] 1661 5-10-12 .... KRenwick 20
(Mrs S C Bradburne) *hld up: rdn 5 out: sn btn* **100/1**

5 P **Stoneriggs Merc (IRE)**[165] 484 4-10-7 .... DCCostello(5) —
(Mrs E Slack) *a bhd: t.o whn p.u bef 7th* **50/1**

0-0 P **Theatre Rights (IRE)**[177] 323 5-10-12 .... BGibson —
(J S Haldane) *sn wl bhd: t.o whn p.u bef 7th* **150/1**

0- P **Border Craic (IRE)**[238] 4323 5-10-12 .... NPMulholland —
(B Mactaggart) *j. slowly in rr: t.o whn p.u after 4th* **125/1**

P5 P **Master Farrier**[14] 1839 5-10-9 .... PBuchanan(3) —
(Miss Lucinda V Russell) *cl up tl wknd after 6th: p.u bef 3 out* **66/1**

60- P **Diamond Jim (IRE)**[199] 4923 5-10-5 .... MissRDavidson(7) —
(Mrs R L Elliot) *cl up: chal briefly 6th: wknd bef next: t.o whn p.u bef 3 out* **100/1**

5m 31.2s (-6.50) **Going Correction** -0.10s/f (Good)
WFA 4 from 5yo+ 13lb **11 Ran SP% 110.3**
Speed ratings: **107,101,91,87,79 72,—,—,—,—** — CSF £8.33 TOTE £1.30: £1.02, £2.60, £2.00; EX 5.90.

Owner J Taqvi **Bred** Jack Butler **Trained** West Witton, N Yorks

FOCUS

Ordinary form behind the easy winner, who remains one to keep on the right side and has been rated value for 20l. The second ran to his mark.

NOTEBOOK

King Of Confusion(IRE) ◆ did not have to improve to win a modest race with more in hand than the official margin suggests. He should prove equally effective over three miles and will be interesting in ordinary handicaps for his in-form stable. *(op 3-10)*

Bywell Beau(IRE) ran creditably in the first time tongue-tie against a fair sort on these unfavourable terms but, although capable of winning a modest event, is not the most consistent and the fact he has yet to win a race is a bit of a worry. *(op 16-1)*

Aces Four(IRE) was disappointing upped to this trip and, although the step into ordinary handicap company will be in his favour, he may not be one to place maximum faith in. *(op 12-1)*

Auntie Kathleen failed to build on the form of her hurdle debut but she may have needed this first start for six months and she may do better in ordinary handicaps in due course. *(op 7-1 tchd 8-1)*

Generals Laststand(IRE) again achieved nothing over hurdles.

Bodkin Boy(IRE) was again soundly beaten in the face of another stiff task.

2037 DAILY RECORD FIRST FOR RACING H'CAP CHASE (16 fncs 1 omitted) 2m 6f 110y

1:10 (1:11) (Class 3) (0-120,117) 5-Y-0+ **£5,562** (£1,633; £816; £407)

Form RPR

2P-3 1 **Miss Mattie Ross**[14] 1837 9-9-10 **94** .... MJMcAlister(7) 113+
(S J Marshall) *mde virtually all: rdn and styd on gamely fr 2 out* **6/1**[3]

24-3 2 *9* **Interdit (FR)**[34] 1603 9-11-5 **110** .... KRenwick 120
(Mrs B K Thomson) *in tch: hdwy and cl up 10th: outpcd after 2 out: kpt on fr last: no ch w wnr* **9/2**[1]

215- 3 *2* **Undeniable**[210] 4773 7-11-6 **111** .... DElsworth 119
(Mrs S J Smith) *chsd ldrs: chal 2 out: rdn and one pce bef last* **13/2**

-251 4 *18* **Snowy (IRE)**[34] 1602 7-11-0 **105** .... ADobbin 98+
(J I A Charlton) *hld up: hdwy 12th: outpcd 14th: n.d after* **5/1**[2]

113- 5 *3 ½* **Devil's Run (IRE)**[245] 4183 9-11-9 **117** .... PAspell(3) 104
(J Wade) *mstkes in rr: outpcd whn blnd 11th: nvr on terms* **16/1**

PF/P 6 *2* **Eyze (IRE)**[34] 1606 9-10-8 **99** .... NPMulholland 89+
(B Mactaggart) *cl up: hit 13th: mstke 2 out: sn wknd* **66/1**

20- 7 *7* **Green Finger**[48] 1497 7-11-4 **109** .... RMcGrath 87
(J J Quinn) *hld up: outpcd 1/2-way: nvr on terms* **16/1**

-245 8 *11* **King's Bounty**[14] 1825 9-10-13 **104** ....(b) RGarritty 71
(T D Easterby) *cl up tl wknd bef 12th* **6/1**[3]

/6-0 U **The Tinker**[29] 1666 10-10-5 **99** .... ONelmes(3) —
(Mrs S C Bradburne) *blnd and uns rdr 1st* **33/1**

0-43 U **Tipsy Mouse (IRE)**[76] 1276 9-11-2 **107** ....(p) HOliver —
(R C Guest) *in tch whn blnd and uns rdr 8th* **9/1**

330- P **Ulusaba**[234] 4398 9-11-9 **117** .... KJMercer(3) —
(Ferdy Murphy) *bhd and detached: t.o whn p.u bef 3 out* **10/1**

5m 46.9s (-9.70) **Going Correction** -0.10s/f (Good) **11 Ran SP% 112.0**
Speed ratings: **112,108,108,101,100 100,97,93,—,—** — CSF £32.40 CT £178.82 TOTE £9.40: £2.80, £2.20, £2.70; EX 45.70.

Owner S J Marshall **Bred** S J Marshall **Trained** Alnwick, Northumberland

FOCUS

An ordinary handicap in which the pace was sound and the bare form should prove reliable. The winner improved 10lb on her previous best. The second-last flight was bypassed.

NOTEBOOK

Miss Mattie Ross jumped soundly and notched her fourth win over fences at this course. She again showed the right attitude, will not mind the return to further and should continue to go well, but may find life tougher after reassessment. *(op 7-1)*

Interdit(FR) was ridden with a bit more patience than is usually the case in this truly-run race but ran creditably. He will not mind the return to three miles and looks capable of winning again away from progressive or well handicapped sorts. *(tchd 5-1)*

Undeniable, who stays three miles and handles fast ground, showed more than enough on this first run for seven months to suggest a similar race can be found with this run behind him. *(op 11-2)*

Snowy(IRE), who looked better than ever when winning on fast ground over this course and distance after a break last time, had the race run to suit but was disappointing and this ground may well have been softer than ideal. *(op 11-2 tchd 6-1)*

Devil's Run(IRE), an improved performer over fences earlier this year, failed to have a proper cut at his fences and was well below that level after a break. He will have to jump better if he is to win from his current mark. *(op 20-1)*

Eyze(IRE), who failed to get round on his previous four starts over hurdles and fences, shaped as *though better than the bare form but once again some shoddy jumping let him down.Official explanation: jockey said gelding right-handed throughout*
King's Bounty *Official explanation: trainer said gelding was found to have broken a blood vessel (op 11-2)*

2038 GRAHAM TODD HAULAGE AND FRIENDS H'CAP HURDLE (11 hdls) 2m 6f 110y
1:40 (1:40) (Class 3) (0-125,125) 4-Y-O+ **£4,840** (£1,421; £710; £354)

Form — RPR
42-4 **1** **Tynedale (IRE)**[45] [1513] 6-10-8 **114** TJDreaper(7) 119
(Mrs A Hamilton) *prom: rdn bef 2 out: led run in: hung lft: styd on wl* **15/2**
-332 **2** *1 ¾* **Russian Sky**[10] [1887] 6-9-12 **104** AGlassonbury(7) 108+
(Mrs H O Graham) *cl up: led 5 out: hdd appr last: ev ch run in: kpt on* **6/1**[3]
3 *3 ½* **Texas Holdem (IRE)**[176] [340] 6-10-6 **112** MJMcAlister(7) 112
(M Smith) *cl up: rdn and led appr last: hdd and no ex run in* **16/1**
302- **4** *5* **Totally Scottish**[193] [4711] 9-11-2 **115** RMcGrath 111+
(K G Reveley) *hld up: rdn bef 3 out: kpt on fr last: nrst fin* **6/1**[3]
432- **5** *6* **Harrovian**[216] [4708] 8-10-6 **105** ADobbin 95+
(Miss P Robson) *keen: hld up: effrt bef 3 out: no imp fr next* **3/1**[1]
F-41 **6** *½* **Thoutmosis (USA)**[178] [304] 6-10-9 **118** JPEnnis(10) 107+
(L Lungo) *hld up: hdwy and in tch 4 out: hung lft and outpcd fr 2 out* **4/1**[2]
40-0 **7** *1 ¾* **Lazy But Lively (IRE)**[13] [1844] 9-11-6 **122** KJMercer(3) 109
(R F Fisher) *hld up: shkn up bef 3 out: n.d* **16/1**
5-P0 **8** *5* **Culcabock (IRE)**[14] [1836] 5-10-6 **108** PBuchanan(3) 90
(Miss Lucinda V Russell) *hld up: hdwy 4 out: wknd 2 out* **20/1**
P2-0 **9** *dist* **Valerun (IRE)**[24] [1715] 9-9-11 **99** (p) LMcGrath(3) —
(R C Guest) *a bhd* **20/1**
2U20 **10** *4* **Bodfari Signet**[112] [1010] 9-10-10 **112** ONelmes(3) —
(Mrs S C Bradburne) *mstkes in rr: struggling fr 4 out* **25/1**
2650 **11** *½* **Political Sox**[129] [859] 11-10-1 **107** GThomas(7) —
(R Nixon) *in tch to 1/2-way: sn struggling* **33/1**
-PF0 **12** *3* **Minivet**[14] [1836] 10-10-3 **105** PAspell(3) —
(R Allan) *led to 5 out: wknd after next* **25/1**
5-PP **13** *25* **Majed (FR)**[13] [1844] 9-11-7 **125** DFlavin(5) —
(Mrs L B Normile) *in tch to 5th: sn lost pl* **66/1**

5m 33.0s (-4.70) **Going Correction** -0.10s/f (Good) **13** Ran SP% **118.8**
Speed ratings: **104,103,102,100,98 98,97,95,—,— —,—,—** CSF £47.38 CT £709.19 TOTE £9.10: £2.00, £2.00, £5.00; EX 68.80.
Owner Ian Hamilton **Bred** Miss Mary A and Mrs H T Murphy **Trained** Great Bavington, Northumbland

FOCUS
Mainly exposed handicappers and only a fair pace meant those racing prominently held the edge. Not a strong race.

NOTEBOOK
Tynedale(IRE), who ran creditably on his reappearance in September, reversed form with Russian Sky and notched his second win over hurdles. The return to three miles should suit and he should continue to give a good account. *(op 8-1)*
Russian Sky is a consistent sort who could not confirm recent Perth placings with the winner but again ran his race and looks the best guide to the worth of this form. He is edging up the weights but should continue to give a good account. *(op 7-1)*
Texas Holdem(IRE), having his first run for his new stable and his first outing since a good run in a race that worked out well in May, shaped as though retaining plenty of ability and may be capable of winning a similar event this winter. *(op 14-1)*
Totally Scottish ran a typical race on this first run since April to fare best of those held up, but he needs things to drop perfectly and the fact that he has not won a handicap for nearly three years means he is one to tread carefully with in this type of event. *(op 11-2)*
Harrovian attracted support on this first run since April and back over hurdles from this 14lb lower mark. Although a stronger gallop may have suited, he proved a bit of a disappointment but would not be one to write off just yet. *(op 7-2 tchd 4-1)*
Thoutmosis(USA), the winner of three of his five starts last year, may not be the easiest of rides (tends to hang), but shaped as though retaining plenty of ability on this reappearance run and he should be better for the outing.

2039 GAGA-JUJU NOVICES' H'CAP CHASE (17 fncs 2 omitted) 3m 1f
2:15 (2:15) (Class 4) (0-100,92) 5-Y-O+ **£4,059** (£1,191; £595; £297)

Form — RPR
00-P **1** **Sharp Belline (IRE)**[20] [1760] 8-11-11 **91** DElsworth 117+
(Mrs S J Smith) *cl up: lft in ld 11th: blnd and hdd 3 out: rallied and led after next: styd on to go clr run in* **5/1**[3]
3P3 **2** *10* **Chancers Dante (IRE)**[10] [1886] 9-9-7 **66** oh1 (b) PJMcDonald(7) 80+
(Ferdy Murphy) *rn in snatches: bhd: effrt after 3 out: kpt on to chse wnr run in: no imp* **7/1**
1140 **3** *8* **Arctic Lagoon (IRE)**[14] [1838] 6-10-11 **80** (t) ONelmes(3) 86+
(Mrs S C Bradburne) *prom: lft in ld 3 out: hdd after next: outpcd fr last* **6/1**
224F **4** *½* **Another Club Royal**[8] [1905] 6-10-5 **76** StephenJCraine(5) 83+
(D McCain) *prom: rdn whn hit 14th: rallied next: wknd 2 out* **4/1**[2]
1P4/ **5** *dist* **Algarve**[665] [3272] 8-11-9 **92** KJMercer(3) —
(Ferdy Murphy) *chsd ldrs tl wknd fr 2 out* **8/1**
P/1 **F** **Twotiming Gent (IRE)**[6] [1943] 12-10-3 **69** ARoss —
(P D Niven) *led tl fell 11th* **15/2**
23-2 **P** **Bright Steel (IRE)**[8] [1914] 8-10-13 **79** (p) ADobbin —
(M Todhunter) *hld up in tch: reminders 7th: sn struggling: p.u after 11th* **3/1**[1]

6m 31.2s (1.60) **Going Correction** -0.10s/f (Good) **7** Ran SP% **111.3**
Speed ratings: **93,89,87,87,— —,—** CSF £36.06 CT £206.93 TOTE £7.50: £3.00, £2.90; EX 71.50.
Owner Townville C C Racing Club **Bred** Pinfold Stud And Farms Ltd **Trained** High Eldwick, W Yorks

FOCUS
A modest event in which the pace was only fair. The winner, very well in on his hurdles form, was value for a 12l victory over the runner-up who ran to his mark. The open ditch before the straight was omitted.

NOTEBOOK
Sharp Belline(IRE), who is not very big, recovered well from a bad blunder to show improved form over fences from this 24lb lower chase mark. He will find life tougher in more competitive company after reassessment. *(op 4-1)*
Chancers Dante(IRE), an inconsistent performer over obstacles, looked less than an easy ride once again but, although not disgraced in terms of form in this ordinary event, would not be one to get heavily involved with next time. *(op 10-1 tchd 11-1 and 13-2)*
Arctic Lagoon(IRE), a winner over hurdles and fences in May, was not disgraced on only this *second start after a break and may be capable of winning from this mark over the coming months. (op 13-2)*
Another Club Royal, who has yet to win over fences, was not foot perfect and was again below his best. He will have to show more before he is worth a bet. *(op 5-1)*
Algarve, having his first run since January of last year, shaped as though better than the bare form on this chasing debut. He has the size and scope to progress over fences and is well worth another chance in this sphere. *(op 9-2 tchd 9-1)*
Twotiming Gent(IRE) jumped soundly until falling on this chase debut but, although it remains to be seen how his confidence is affected, he has the size and scope for this game and is worth another chance. *(op 4-1 tchd 11-4)*
Bright Steel(IRE), who hinted at ability on his chasing debut, proved a big disappointment tried in cheekpieces. This run may have come too soon or he may have resented the headgear but, either *way, he is not one to get heavily involved in. Official explanation: trainer's representative had no explanation for poor form shown (op 4-1 tchd 11-4)*

2040 HARROW HOTEL (DALKEITH) NOVICES' (S) HURDLE (8 hdls) 2m 110y
2:50 (2:50) (Class 5) 4-6-Y-O **£2,655** (£773; £387)

Form — RPR
0U **1** **Nuzzle**[28] [1683] 5-10-5 ADobbin 83+
(N G Richards) *hld up in tch: hdwy 5th: led bef last: rdn and r.o wl* **6/1**[3]
4-0 **2** *1 ¾* **Timbuktu**[36] [1591] 4-10-12 RMcGrath 88+
(B Storey) *prom: effrt and ev ch bef last: kpt on run in* **9/2**[2]
3-00 **3** *13* **Named At Dinner**[14] [1839] 4-10-9 89 (b) PBuchanan(3) 75+
(Miss Lucinda V Russell) *cl up: led briefly 2 out: outpcd last* **10/3**[1]
P-60 **4** *dist* **Ro Eridani**[10] [1883] 5-10-2 64 MrCStorey(3) —
(Miss S E Forster) *led: blnd 3rd: hdd 4th: wknd next* **11/1**
5 *dist* **Charlie George**[20] 4-10-2 DDaSilva(10) —
(P Monteith) *cl up: ev ch tl wknd 3 out* **20/1**
00 **6** *3* **Jordans Spark**[17] [1527] 4-10-12 KRenwick —
(P Monteith) *towards rr: wknd fr 1/2-way* **6/1**[3]
7 *2* **Roan Raider (USA)**[35] 5-10-9 (p) LMcGrath(3) —
(R C Guest) *bhd: lost tch fr 4th* **14/1**
P-P **8** *2* **Jarvo**[34] [1614] 4-10-9 ONelmes(3) —
(Mark Campion) *bhd: no ch fr 4th* **50/1**
P/0 **9** *29* **Miss Wizz**[16] [1794] 5-10-5 (p) NPMulholland —
(W Storey) *a bhd: struggling fr 4th* **25/1**
6056 **P** **Starbright**[14] [1824] 4-10-12 67 RGarritty —
(W G Young) *cl up: led 4th: mstke and hdd 2 out: p.u lame* **7/1**
6-PP **P** **Safe Shot**[20] [1508] 6-10-7 68 (p) DCCostello(5) —
(Mrs J C McGregor) *prom tl wknd bef 4th: t.o whn p.u bef 3 out* **20/1**

4m 2.60s (-1.10) **Going Correction** -0.10s/f (Good) **11** Ran SP% **112.7**
Speed ratings: **98,97,91,—,— —,—,—,—,— —** CSF £30.51 TOTE £5.30: £3.10, £1.60, £1.70; EX 20.80.The winner was bought in for 6,000gns.
Owner Brian Morton & Paul Montgomery **Bred** Side Hill Stud **Trained** Greystoke, Cumbria

FOCUS
A modest event in which the gallop was strong.

NOTEBOOK
Nuzzle, dropped in grade, and with Tony Dobbin replacing an inexperienced rider, showed improved form to get off the mark over hurdles at the third time of asking. She would not be an obvious one to follow up, though. *(op 11-2)*
Timbuktu, down in grade, ran creditably but, given his inconsistency and the fact he has yet to win a race, would not really be one to lump on next time. *(op 11-2 tchd 6-1)*
Named At Dinner ran a bit better dropped in grade but, given he is without a win in 25 career starts, remains one to have reservations about. *(op 3-1)*
Ro Eridani, a poor and inconsistent maiden on the Flat and over hurdles, went off too quickly and was again well beaten. She is not really one to be interested in. *(op 10-1)*
Charlie George, a poor Flat maiden, was soundly beaten on this hurdles debut and is of no interest in the near future. *(op 16-1)*
Jordans Spark, a winner at Newcastle on the Flat last time, showed nothing on this return to hurdles and remains one to tread carefully with. *(tchd 13-2)*
Starbright was in the process of running creditably when going lame but, given his record is one of inconsistency, would not be one to place too much faith in next time. *(op 15-2 tchd 8-1)*
Safe Shot *Official explanation: jockey said gelding lost its action and returned sound (op 15-2 tchd 8-1)*

2041 JOHN N. DUNN MARES' ONLY NOVICES' CHASE (10 fncs 2 omitted) 2m 1f
3:20 (3:20) (Class 4) 4-Y-O+ **£4,033** (£1,184; £592; £295)

Form — RPR
31F1 **1** **Parisienne Gale (IRE)**[6] [1942] 6-11-9 97 ADobbin 108+
(R Ford) *cl up: blnd bdly 2nd: led 3 out: drew clr fr next: eased nr fin* **1/1**[1]
P460 **2** *8* **Uneven Line**[10] [1884] 9-10-13 64 (p) MrCStorey(3) 83+
(Miss S E Forster) *bhd tl styd on fr 2 out: wnt 2nd run in: no ch w wnr* **33/1**
2233 **3** *6* **Valuable (IRE)**[39] [1567] 8-11-2 84 KJohnson 76
(R Johnson) *wl bhd tl kpt on fr 2 out: nvr on terms* **16/1**
2P2- **4** *1* **Clouding Over**[197] [4969] 5-11-2 104 RMcGrath 75
(K G Reveley) *wl bhd: hdwy 7th: wnt modest 2nd between last 2: wknd run in* **9/4**[2]
-10P **5** *29* **Little Flora**[6] [1942] 9-10-9 96 MJMcAlister(7) 46
(S J Marshall) *led: blnd 5th: hdd 3 out: wknd after next* **6/1**[3]
P5UP **6** *9* **Dottie Digger (IRE)**[10] [1883] 6-10-13 63 PBuchanan(3) 37
(Miss Lucinda V Russell) *chsd ldrs tl wknd fr 7th* **50/1**
P-2F **F** **Shakwaa**[187] [149] 6-10-9 89 CDSharkey(7) —
(E A Elliott) *chsd ldrs: hit 5th: wknd after next: no ch whn fell last* **16/1**

4m 26.7s (3.50) **Going Correction** -0.10s/f (Good) **7** Ran SP% **111.7**
Speed ratings: **87,83,80,79,66 62,—** CSF £27.27 TOTE £2.10: £1.40, £14.10; EX 32.70.
Owner S J Manning **Bred** Edmond And Richard Kent **Trained** Cotebrook, Cheshire

FOCUS
A modest event in which the pace was sound. The winner was value for 18l. Open ditch before the straight omitted.

NOTEBOOK
Parisienne Gale(IRE) recovered from an early blunder to win with more in hand than the official margin suggests. Although she will be up in the weights for this, she may still be of interest in ordinary company after reassessment. *(op 5-4 tchd 11-8)*
Uneven Line shaped as though the return to further would suit but, as she may be flattered given the way this race unfolded and given her inconsistency, would not be one to lump on at shortish odds next time.
Valuable(IRE), who has only won once from 33 career starts, is another that may be flattered by the way events unfolded here and, given her record, remains one to tread carefully with. *(op 14-1)*
Clouding Over, a winning hurdler in March, shaped as though a bit better than the bare form on this first start since April. She is in good hands and is not one to write off just yet. *(op 2-1)*
Little Flora almost certainly set too strong a pace for her own good and not surprisingly had little to offer when it mattered. However she will have to show more before she is worth a bet. *(op 13-2)*
Dottie Digger(IRE), a winning hurdler at this course, has yet to show any worthwhile form over fences.

2042 BELHAVEN BEST CONDITIONAL JOCKEYS' H'CAP HURDLE (6 hdls 4 omitted) 2m 2f

3:55 (3:55) (Class 4) (0-110,107) 4-Y-0+ £3,513 (£1,031; £515; £257)

Form RPR

02-3 **1** **Red Man (IRE)**[10] [1887] 8-10-9 **100**.......... SGagan(10) 108
(Mrs E Slack) *cl up: led last: rdn and hld on wl* **7/2**[2]

50-6 **2** *2 ½* **Shares (IRE)**[6] [1940] 5-11-6 **104**.......... TJDreaper(3) 109
(P Monteith) *hld up: smooth hdwy to press wnr run in: rdn 250yds out: edgd lft and one pce* **5/1**[3]

F104 **3** *1 ¼* **Prince Adjal (IRE)**[28] [1682] 5-10-0 **81**.......... DCCostello 85
(Miss S E Forster) *mde most to last: one pce last 250yds* **13/2**

105- **4** *2* **Silken Pearls**[197] [4966] 9-11-4 **102**.......... GBerridge(3) 104
(L Lungo) *chsd ldrs: outpcd 3 out: kpt on run in: no imp* **2/1**[1]

3301 **5** *30* **Lofty Leader (IRE)**[29] [1665] 6-11-7 **107**.......... AGlassonbury(5) 79
(Mrs H O Graham) *chsd ldrs tl wknd fr 2 out* **13/2**

006- **6** *17* **Major Royal (FR)**[197] [4965] 5-10-1 **82**.......... KJMercer 37
(A Parker) *blnd 1st: hld up: rdn and wknd fr 2 out* **16/1**

450- **7** *10* **Blue Morning**[216] [4713] 7-10-0 **81** oh5.......... (p) PAspell 26
(Mrs J C McGregor) *chsd ldrs to 2 out: wknd* **25/1**

310F **8** *dist* **Virtus**[14] [1836] 5-10-4 **85**.......... TGreenway —
(Mrs B K Thomson) *bhd: struggling 3 out: t.o* **14/1**

4m 30.4s (-9.50) **Going Correction** -0.10s/f (Good) **8 Ran SP% 115.3**
Speed ratings: **103,101,101,100,87 79,75,—** CSF £21.81 CT £108.29 TOTE £5.10: £1.40, £1.70, £1.80; EX 22.30 Place 6 £83.13, Place 5 £73.37.
Owner A Slack **Bred** Patrick Stamp **Trained** Hilton, Cumbria

FOCUS
A modest event in which the two flights in the home straight were omitted on each circuit due to the low trajectory of the sun.

NOTEBOOK
Red Man(IRE) is not the most consistent but notched his second win from only two starts at this course. He showed a more willing attitude than the runner-up but it remains to be seen whether this will be reproduced next time. *(tchd 4-1)*
Shares(IRE), whose sole win from 20 career starts has been at this course, travelled like the best horse in the race for much of the way. However he did not find as much as seemed likely and, although not disgraced in terms of form, is not one to place maximum faith in. *(op 4-1 tchd 11-2)*
Prince Adjal(IRE) returned to hurdles, had the run of the race and was not disgraced on this first start for his current stable but his record suggests he would not be certain to put it all in next time. *(tchd 7-1)*
Silken Pearls proved a disappointment and, although a stiffer test of stamina would have been in her favour, she has flattered to decieve in the past and and, while capable of winning again, remains one to be wary of at short odds. *(tchd 7-2 in a place)*
Lofty Leader(IRE), who notched his second win of the year at Carlisle last time, was well beaten from this 12lb higher mark. Consistency has never been his strong suit. *(op 6-1)*
Major Royal(FR) did not show enough on this handicap debut and first run since April to suggest he is of interest in similar company in the short term. *(op 14-1)*
T/Plt: £187.60 to a £1 stake. Pool: £35,310.35. 137.35 winning tickets. T/Qpdt: £95.20 to a £1 stake. Pool: £2,251.40. 17.50 winning tickets. RY

SANDOWN (R-H)

Saturday, November 5

OFFICIAL GOING: Chase course - good to soft (soft in places); hurdle course - heavy (soft in back straight)
Wind: Virtually nil

2043 BRITISHHORSERACING.COM CONDITIONAL JOCKEYS' H'CAP HURDLE (9 hdls) 2m 4f 110y

12:55 (12:56) (Class 4) (0-105,95) 4-Y-0+ £3,536 (£1,038; £519; £259)

Form RPR

052- **1** **Harley**[218] [4683] 7-11-2 **85**.......... GCarenza 95+
(Mrs P Sly) *mde all: 6l clr last: sn rdn: wknd fnl 100yds: hld on all out* **3/1**[1]

2 *1* **Danse Macabre (IRE)**[145] [739] 6-11-6 **94**.......... WMcCarthy(5) 100
(A W Carroll) *hld up in rr: hdwy 3 out: chsd wnr wl bef 2 out: 6l down last but styd on as wnr wknd fnl 100yds: hld cl home* **5/1**[3]

100- **3** *14* **Breezer**[184] [4813] 5-10-12 **89**.......... (p) SElliott(8) 81
(J A Geake) *in tch: hdwy 3 out: styd on appr 2 out but nvr nr ldrs* **11/1**

56-P **4** *4* **Land Rover Lad**[183] [202] 7-11-3 **89**.......... (b) SWalsh(3) 77
(C P Morlock) *a in rr: junmped slowly 3 out* **14/1**

/P3- **5** *16* **Coolbythepool**[33] [478] 5-11-2 **90**.......... RSpate(5) 62
(M J Gingell) *hld up in rr: stdy hdwy fr 4 out: chsd wnr after 3 out tl wknd wl bef 2 out* **20/1**

5401 **6** *5* **Penny's Crown**[24] [1712] 6-11-4 **90**.......... EDehdashti(3) 57
(G A Ham) *lw: chsd wnr tl after 3 out: sn wknd* **7/1**

P-00 **7** *11* **Greatest By Phar**[30] [1655] 4-11-6 **89**.......... PMerrigan 45
(J Akehurst) *a bhd* **10/1**

3/0P **8** *4* **Before The Mast (IRE)**[7] [1921] 8-10-1 **76**.......... CPoste(6) 28
(M F Harris) *chsd ldrs: hit 3 out: sn wknd* **22/1**

-P4P **P** **Peppershot**[143] [763] 5-11-12 **95**.......... (p) DLaverty —
(R Gurney) *lw: bhd fr 4th: t.o 5th: p.u bef last* **16/1**

4-63 **R** **Brigadier Du Bois (FR)**[15] [1816] 6-10-6 **85**.......... MRoe(10) —
(Mrs L Wadham) *disputing cl 2nd whn rn out 5th* **7/2**[2]

5m 18.7s (5.30) **Going Correction** +0.35s/f (Yiel)
WFA 4 from 5yo+ 13lb **10 Ran SP% 115.5**
Speed ratings: **103,102,97,95,89 87,83,82,—,—** CSF £18.63 CT £144.16 TOTE £3.80: £1.60, £2.00, £3.60; EX 20.00.
Owner Thorney Racing Club **Bred** Mrs P Sly **Trained** Thorney, Cambs

FOCUS
A moderate event and very few got into The first two finished well clear, and the winner looks value for further.

NOTEBOOK
Harley, whose second at Newbury in the spring looks all the better now, made every yard, but it got pretty desperate after the last as lack of peak fitness and the soft ground began to take their toll. He was crying out for the line in the closing stages but just had enough in hand. *(op 10-3 tchd 7-2 in places)*
Danse Macabre(IRE) was not given a hard ride on this first outing for his new stable. He looked held at the last but the eventual winner began to tread water soon after and he closed him right down at the line. He only won one race in 20 starts in Ireland but this was a promising effort. *(op 6-1)*
Breezer, who won off a mark 5lb lower mark in March, was wearing cheekpieces for the first time and did not run badly on his first outing since May. *(tchd 12-1)*
Land Rover Lad, returning from a six-month absence, seemed happier over these smaller obstacles. *(op 10-1)*
Coolbythepool had the benefit of being fit from the Flat, but it did not do him much good. He would be better employed on the All-Weather.
Penny's Crown was disappointing as she had conditions to suit and was coming here on the back of a win at Uttoxeter last time. She clearly found even this modest company too competitive. *(op 6-1)*

2044 RAY WARD & MERVIN COX BEGINNERS' CHASE (13 fncs) 2m

1:25 (1:27) (Class 3) 4-Y-0+ £5,465 (£1,604; £802; £400)

Form RPR

005- **1** **Without A Doubt**[206] [4820] 6-11-5.......... PMoloney 126+
(M Pitman) *lw: trckd ldrs: chal 3 out: slt ld fr next: rdn and r.o strly run-in* **6/1**[2]

445- **2** *½* **Lustral Du Seuil (FR)**[217] [4696] 6-11-5.......... MFoley 126+
(N J Henderson) *lw: hld up in rr: nt fluent 1st: hdwy and hit 9th: trckd wnr 2 out: chal last: styd on wl but no ex nr fin* **4/1**[1]

3 *16* **Offemont (FR)**[140] 4-10-7.......... TDoyle 98+
(Mrs L C Taylor) *tall: str: scope: rr: nt fluent 2nd: hdwy 6th: chsd ldrs fr 8th: rdn 3 out: wknd and hit 2 out* **8/1**

24-0 **4** *nk* **Cossack Dancer (IRE)**[181] [247] 7-11-5 114.......... (p) MBatchelor 110+
(M Bradstock) *led tl hdd and hit 4th: j. slowly 6th: led appr next: rdn 3 out: hdd next: sn wknd* **12/1**

16-1 **5** *7* **O'Toole (IRE)**[189] [136] 6-11-5.......... RJohnson 105+
(P J Hobbs) *blnd 1st: sn chsng ldrs: mstke 8th: chsd ldrs fr 4 out: wknd and blnd 2 out* **4/1**[1]

15/P **6** *2 ½* **Kopeck (IRE)**[14] [1829] 7-11-5.......... LAspell 100
(Mrs L Wadham) *hit 2nd: bhd: hdwy 7th: wknd 3 out* **15/2**

7 *¾* **Launde (IRE)**[188] 6-10-12.......... TMessenger(7) 100+
(B N Pollock) *w'like: chsd ldrs: hit 2nd and 5th: blnd 9th: bhd whn hit 3 out: styd on again run-in* **66/1**

2F4- **8** *5* **De Blanc (IRE)**[204] [4847] 5-10-12.......... SThomas 90+
(Miss Venetia Williams) *chsd ldrs: j. slowly and lost pl 3rd: hit 4th: hdwy 8th: wknd and hit 4 out* **7/1**[3]

2P- **9** *5* **Mighty Matters (IRE)**[242] [4241] 6-11-5.......... JMMaguire 89
(T R George) *chsd ldr: led 4th: hdd appr 7th: wknd after 4 out* **33/1**

222- **10** *2 ½* **I D Technology (IRE)**[476] [989] 9-11-5.......... PHide 86
(G L Moore) *j. slowly 4th: hdwy 8th: wknd 4 out* **25/1**

122- **U** **Charlton Kings (IRE)**[202] [4887] 7-10-12.......... JamesWhite(7) —
(R J Hodges) *mstke and uns rdr 1st* **8/1**

4m 3.80s (1.30) **Going Correction** +0.225s/f (Yiel)
WFA 4 from 5yo+ 12lb **11 Ran SP% 116.7**
Speed ratings: **105,104,96,96,93 91,91,88,86,85** — CSF £30.49 TOTE £8.60: £2.10, £2.00, £2.60; EX 23.70.
Owner Malcolm C Denmark **Bred** Shadwell Estate Company Limited **Trained** Upper Lambourn, Berks

FOCUS
This looked a decent beginners' chase, featuring a number of interesting prospects. The first two have been rated through their hurdles form, but there is a good chance their figures underestimate them.

NOTEBOOK
Without A Doubt ◆, from a stable which can do little wrong at present, made an impressive start to his chasing career, jumping well and drawing clear with the runner-up from the second last. He is clearly effective over two miles, but he was seventh in the Spa Novices' Hurdle over three miles at the Cheltenham Festival last season, and will not have any trouble getting two and a half over fences. *(op 13-2)*
Lustral Du Seuil(FR) ◆, whose stable won this race last year, was not rated quite so highly as the winner over hurdles but he too made a bright start to his chasing career. He made a couple of mistakes but had every chance from the second last and was simply not quite good enough on the day. He will not always run into such a useful opponent. *(op 7-2)*
Offemont(FR), a French-bred who has chasing experience in his native land, was making his debut in this country for his new stable and acquitted himself well. He shapes as though he will get further and his four-year-old allowance will remain a big help. *(op 10-1)*
Cossack Dancer(IRE), whose hurdling form left him with a bit to find with the likes of the first two, ran well for a long way and will be interesting on a sharper track against less demanding opposition.
O'Toole(IRE), who won a handicap hurdle off a mark of 108 on his last outing in the spring, showed a liking for fast ground that day so these conditions may not have been ideal on his chasing debut. *(tchd 9-2)*
Kopeck(IRE), who jumped right at Chepstow on his reappearance from a lengthy absence, appreciated going this way round and showed a bit more this time. *(op 8-1)*

2045 HAMPTONS INTERNATIONAL INTRODUCTORY JUVENILE NOVICES' HURDLE (8 hdls) 2m 110y

1:55 (1:58) (Class 3) 3-Y-0 £4,788 (£1,405; £702; £351)

Form RPR

1 **Alfred The Great (IRE)**[17] 3-10-12.......... FKeniry 100+
(P C Haslam) *lw: trckd ldrs: shkn up after 3 out: led bef 2 out: styd on gamely u.p whn chal run-in: all out* **5/6**[1]

2 *shd* **Kanpai (IRE)**[17] 3-10-12.......... TDoyle 100
(J G M O'Shea) *chsd ldrs: nt fluent 4 out: styd on fr 2 out: str chal run-in: no ex last strides* **14/1**

3 *3 ½* **Victorias Groom (GER)**[122] 3-10-12.......... LAspell 97+
(Mrs L Wadham) *tall: str: scope: bit bkwd: rr but in tch: hdwy to chse ldrs 3 out: drvn to chal 2 out: wknd run-in* **5/1**[3]

4 **4** *9* **Corker**[21] [1737] 3-10-12.......... RJohnson 87
(D B Feek) *hit 3rd: bhd: hdwy to chse ldrs 3 out: wknd 2 out* **9/2**[2]

5 *2* **Golden Square**[30] 3-10-12.......... WHutchinson 85
(A W Carroll) *chsd ldr after 2nd: led briefly wl bef 2 out: sn wknd* **25/1**

6 *14* **Wandering Act (IRE)**[22] 3-10-12.......... JMMaguire 71
(A W Carroll) *rr but in tch: hdwy 3 out: wknd and blnd 2 out* **50/1**

0 **7** *9* **Flower Haven**[21] [1737] 3-10-5.......... SCurran 55
(M J Gingell) *chsd ldrs: wandered and led 3 out: hdd wl bef 2 out and sn wknd* **33/1**

8 *dist* **Mujazaf**[70] 3-10-12.......... JGoldstein —
(Miss Sheena West) *led to 3 out: sn wknd t.o* **12/1**

4m 16.0s (7.10) **Going Correction** +0.35s/f (Yiel) **8 Ran SP% 112.5**
Speed ratings: **97,96,95,91,90 83,79,—** CSF £13.48 TOTE £1.80: £1.10, £2.80, £1.40; EX 14.40.
Owner Les Buckley **Bred** Mrs Rebecca Philipps **Trained** Middleham, N Yorks
■ Stewards' Enquiry : F Keniry one day ban: used whip with excessive frequency (Nov 17)
T Doyle one day ban: used whip with excessive frequency (Nov 17)

FOCUS
A weak looking juvenile event for Sandown, and probably modest form. It has provisionally been rated through the fourth.

NOTEBOOK

Alfred The Great(IRE), representing the stable which won this race last year, was the best of these on the Flat, having recently won at Newcastle. He asserted after the second last but did not find a lot in front and in the end he was pushed very close. Connections pointed out he was green and inexperienced, but he will clearly need to step up greatly on this if he is going to defy a penalty. *(op 4-5 tchd 8-11 and 10-11 and Evens in places)*

Kanpai(IRE), a stayer on the Flat rated 17lb lower than the winner, gave every indication that he is going to be better as a hurdler, pushing the hot favourite very close. A longer trip will suit him in time. *(op 12-1)*

Victorias Groom(GER), runner-up on both starts on the Flat when trained in Germany, looked a big threat when challenging two out but was just found wanting late on. Unlike the first two, who were both fit from the Flat, he had been off the track since July, so he is entitled to come on for the run. *(op 8-1)*

Corker could not make the benefit of previous hurdling experience tell in a race in which he was one of only two with that advantage. He might just need faster ground. *(op 7-2)*

Golden Square, a plating-class maiden on the Flat after 24 starts, did not get home in the ground on this hurdling debut. *(op 33-1)*

2046 AMLIN H'CAP CHASE (22 fncs) 3m 110y
2:30 (2:30) (Class 3) (0-130,125) 5-Y-0+ **£8,139** (£2,389; £1,194; £596)

Form				RPR
5P1-	**1**		**Native Ivy (IRE)**[246] [4153] 7-11-9 **122** ... TDoyle (C Tinkler) *lw: chsd ldr fr 4th: chal 10th to 16th: rdn after 4 out: rallied to chal 3 out: led sn after: hld on gamely u.p run-in* **7/2**[1]	130+
P/1-	**2**	*3/4*	**Ken'tucky (FR)**[401] [1542] 7-11-10 **123** ... WHutchinson (A King) *lw: chsd ldrs: hit 17th: lost pl: rallied 4 out: styng on to press ldrs whn n.m.r and swtchd rt run-in: no ex cl home* **9/1**	130+
10-3	**3**	*1*	**Kelantan**[13] [1853] 8-10-8 **107** ...(p) JPMcNamara (K C Bailey) *lw: led: rdn and hdd after 3 out: blnd next: rallied to chal last: styd on same pce u.p* **7/2**[1]	114+
/1P-	**4**	*17*	**Eurotrek (IRE)**[349] [2360] 9-11-12 **125** ...(t) JTizzard (P F Nicholls) *h.d.w: lw: rr but in tch: hdwy 11th: hit 13th and lost pl: rallied 17th: wknd after 4 out* **4/1**[2]	118+
211-	**5**	*8*	**Calvic (IRE)**[264] [3853] 7-11-7 **120** ... PMoloney (T R George) *hit 2nd: bhd: hdwy and j. slowly 14th: hdwy 17th: wknd after 4 out* **5/1**	100
06-4	**6**	*nk*	**Limerick Leader (IRE)**[20] [1759] 7-11-3 **116** ... RJohnson (P J Hobbs) *chsd ldrs: rdn 11th: no ch after* **9/2**[3]	96

6m 31.0s (-0.50) **Going Correction** +0.225s/f (Yiel) **6** Ran SP% **109.3**
Speed ratings: **109,108,108,103,100 100** CSF £29.25 TOTE £3.90: £2.00, £4.00; EX 41.00.
Owner George Ward **Bred** S G And W R Deacon **Trained** Compton, Berks

FOCUS

This looked an interesting handicap and it should produce winners. The first two are improvers, and the third looked back to his best level of 2003.

NOTEBOOK

Native Ivy(IRE) ◆ looked second best jumping the Pond Fence for the final time but he found reserves to see out the trip strongest of all. He has a good strike-rate and should be kept on side when conditions demand bottomless stamina.

Ken'tucky(FR) ◆, for whom testing conditions are not thought to be ideal, ran particularly well given that he had been off the track for 401 days. He lost touch with Native Ivy and Kelantan leaving the back straight, but as those two got tired running to the last he found himself getting back into contention, so much so that his momentum looked likely to carry him to success after jumping the final fence, where he had to be switched. Like the winner he was having just his second chase start, and there should be improvement to come. *(op 15-2)*

Kelantan, far more experienced than the first two over fences, also had the advantage of race-fitness over them. A consistent performer who had conditions to suit and the cheekpieces refitted, his performance suggests the form is solid. *(op 4-1)*

Eurotrek(IRE) has been lightly raced over the years and has clearly not been easy to train, but a mark of 125 did not look too harsh given that he was considered SunAlliance Chase material early last season. He guessed at the first down the back straight on the final circuit and was struggling to keep in touch with the principals thereafter, but he is entitled to improve for this reappearance outing. *(op 3-1)*

Calvic(IRE), who won three times as a novice chaser last season, had more to do off a mark of 120 in this handicap. He needed his seasonal reappearance last term and once again ran as though he would come on for his first run of the campaign. *(op 11-2)*

Limerick Leader(IRE) is well handicapped, but that is of no use at the moment as he is struggling for form. *(op 11-2)*

2047 RUDDY FIT-OUT H'CAP HURDLE (8 hdls) 2m 110y
3:05 (3:05) (Class 3) (0-125,125) 4-Y-0+ **£5,452** (£1,600; £800; £399)

Form				RPR
0F-0	**1**		**Verasi**[190] [100] 4-11-2 **115** ... PHide (G L Moore) *trckd ldrs: j. slowly 4th: qcknd to lead sn after 2 out: easily* **16/1**	126+
01-	**2**	*6*	**Kawagino (IRE)**[508] [755] 5-10-8 **110** ... RYoung(3) (J W Mullins) *t.k.h rr but in tch: hit 2nd: hdwy 4th: trckd ldr gng wl after 3 out: rdn after 2 out: kpt on wl but no ch w wnr* **22/1**	111+
341-	**3**	*3/4*	**Serpentine Rock**[309] [3123] 5-11-4 **117** ... RJohnson (P J Hobbs) *h.d.w: bit bkwd: disp 2nd to 3 out: rdn appr next: no ch w wnr whn hit last and one pce* **4/1**[3]	116
110-	**4**	*1 1/4*	**Redi (ITY)**[58] [4386] 4-11-0 **113** ...(t) MFoley (A M Balding) *hit 1st: hld up rr but in tch: hdwy 2 out: styd on one pce and nvr gng pce to trble ldrs* **8/1**	111+
100-	**5**	*7*	**Manorson (IRE)**[210] [4770] 6-11-12 **125** ... LAspell (O Sherwood) *t.k.h: led: hit 3rd: rdn 2 out: hdd sn after: wkng and no ch whn nt fluent last* **7/4**[1]	121+
11F0	**6**	*26*	**Space Cowboy (IRE)**[10] [1878] 5-10-5 **111** ...(b) EDehdashti(7) (G L Moore) *chsd ldrs to 4 out: sn wknd* **9/1**	76
210-	**7**	*21*	**Migwell (FR)**[210] [4770] 5-11-12 **125** ... JTizzard (Mrs L Wadham) *disp 2nd to 3 out: wknd bef next* **3/1**[2]	69

4m 12.7s (3.80) **Going Correction** +0.35s/f (Yiel)
WFA 4 from 5yo+ 12lb **7** Ran SP% **112.7**
Speed ratings: **105,102,101,101,97 85,75** CSF £242.41 TOTE £27.60: £7.70, £4.60; EX 254.10.

Owner F Ledger J Bateman **Bred** D J And Mrs Deer **Trained** Woodingdean, E Sussex

FOCUS

Ordinary handicap form. The winner has improved and has been rated value for ten lengths. The second was potentially well in and can rate higher.

NOTEBOOK

Verasi drew clear easily from the second last to record a very comfortable victory. The testing ground played to his strengths as he stays further than this, and he looks to have improved over the summer.

Kawagino(IRE) ◆, whose win in the summer came on fast ground, took quite a keen hold in rear on this handicap debut so it is to his credit that he kept on well enough to take second in these very different conditions. Third in the Coventry at two, he is the sort to appreciate an easier track and better ground, and also probably a more strongly-run race. *(op 20-1)*

Serpentine Rock had conditions to suit on his handicap debut, but he had not been out since New Year's Eve last year and looked in need of the run beforehand. He should come on quite a bit for the outing. *(tchd 9-2 in places)*

Redi(ITY) did not show a lot in two outings on the Flat in August and September, but he ran a better race back over timber. He does not look particularly well handicapped at the moment, though. *(op 7-1)*

Manorson(IRE) found this far too great a test of stamina on this stiff track in the ground, and he did not help himself by not settling in front. He will be of more interest when speed is more of a requirement. *(op 15-8 tchd 2-1)*

Space Cowboy(IRE) found the ground all against him. *Official explanation: jockey said horse was unsuited by the heavy (soft places) ground* *(op 8-1)*

2048 JOHNNO SPENCE CONSULTING H'CAP CHASE (17 fncs) 2m 4f 110y
3:40 (3:41) (Class 3) (0-135,134) 5-Y-0+ **£8,080** (£2,372; £1,186; £592)

Form				RPR
126-	**1**		**Schuh Shine (IRE)**[199] [4927] 8-10-10 **118** ... SThomas (Miss Venetia Williams) *lw: chsd ldrs: hit 5th: chal 8th: slt ld fr 10th: c clr 3 out: 10l ahd last: wknd bdly run-in: hld on all out* **10/3**[2]	129+
41P-	**2**	*1 3/4*	**Durlston Bay**[218] [4681] 8-10-0 **108** oh7 ... LAspell (S Dow) *bit bkwd: prom early: stdd rr 7th: eased whn apprntly no ch after 4 out: styd on after 2 out: clsd on wkng wnr run-in: nt g* **16/1**	112+
/P0-	**3**	*3/4*	**Be My Better Half (IRE)**[211] [4764] 10-11-2 **124** ... JTizzard (Jonjo O'Neill) *hit 2nd: bhd: hit 7th and 8th: plenty to do after 4 out: styd on fr 2 out to chse wkng wnr run-in: gng on cl home* **6/1**	128+
03-P	**4**	*17*	**Spring Grove (IRE)**[189] [130] 10-11-8 **130** ... JPMcNamara (R H Alner) *lw: chsd ldrs: rdn and wknd 4 out* **3/1**[1]	116
416-	**5**	*3*	**Uncle Wallace**[240] [4287] 9-10-6 **114** ... TDoyle (P R Webber) *lw: hld up rr but in tch: hit 7th: hdwy to trck ldrs fr 10th: wknd appr 3 out* **5/1**	97
4-3U	**6**	*dist*	**Another Joker**[7] [1918] 10-11-0 **122** ... JMMaguire (J L Needham) *led to 10th: styd pressing wnr to 4 out: sn wknd: t.o* **10/1**	95
102-	**7**	*hd*	**Kalca Mome (FR)**[217] [4686] 7-11-12 **134** ... RJohnson (P J Hobbs) *lw: t.k.h early: prom: chsd wnr after 4 out but sn no ch: wknd 2 out: j.v.slowly and stmbld over last: t.o* **9/2**[3]	105

5m 30.4s (9.60) **Going Correction** +0.225s/f (Yiel) **7** Ran SP% **112.2**
Speed ratings: **90,89,89,82,81** —,— CSF £44.55 TOTE £2.70: £2.10, £6.90; EX 73.00.
Owner Mrs Gill Harrison **Bred** Mrs Maria Mulcahy **Trained** Kings Caple, H'fords

FOCUS

They went a fair pace in the conditions and that took its toll in the closing stages. Schuh Shine had this won a long way out and the bare form underestimates him.

NOTEBOOK

Schuh Shine(IRE) ◆ did not look badly treated for his return and deserves rating a far better winner than the official margin suggests, as he was well clear over the last, only to tire very badly on the run-in. It is to his advantage that the Handicapper cannot take too harsh a view of this performance and he could be in for another good season. *(op 11-4)*

Durlston Bay ◆, who was racing from 7lb out of the handicap, had lost a good early position and looked well beaten going to the Pond Fence three out, when his rider appeared to accept the situation, but he found the rest stopping in front of him and suddenly began to make ground between the last two fences. As the leader got very weary on the run-in he whittled the deficit down so much that one has to think the result might have been different had his rider not more or less given up on his chance earlier on in the race. *(op 20-1)*

Be My Better Half(IRE) benefited from the way the race was run in a similar way to the runner-up in that he finished well past beaten horses, having looked well held turning into the straight. *(op 7-1)*

Spring Grove(IRE) has a good record fresh so the lack of a recent run was not of great concern, but he ran as though he needed it. *(tchd 10-3)*

Uncle Wallace, who has now run nine times out of 11 over fences on right-handed tracks, had conditions to suit but he begins the season on a mark 9lb higher than for his last win. *(op 8-1)*

Another Joker set a pace which proved unsustainable in the conditions. *(op 8-1 tchd 11-1)*

Kalca Mome(FR) weakened badly going to the last and, although he clambered over it in second place, he had nothing to give on the run-in. He ran a better race than his final position suggests but he had a hard race and might need a little time to recover from it. *(op 7-2)*

2049 BARRY DENNIS STANDARD OPEN NATIONAL HUNT FLAT RACE 2m 110y
4:10 (4:13) (Class 6) 4-6-Y-0 **£2,247** (£655; £327)

Form				RPR
321/	**1**		**Here's Johnny (IRE)**[598] [4407] 6-11-0 ... MrJJDoyle(7) (V R A Dartnall) *h.d.w: hld up rr but in tch: stdy hdwy 4 out: led 2f out: c clr over 1f out: v easily* **11/4**[1]	125+
	2	*12*	**Art Virginia (FR)**[221] 6-11-0 ... MFoley (N J Henderson) *gd sort: str: scope: bit bkwd: chsd ldrs: led 3 out: sn rdn: hdd 2f out: outpcd sn after: hld on all out for 2nd* **5/1**[3]	103
1-	**3**	*1/2*	**Clyffe Hanger (IRE)**[207] [4819] 5-11-7 ... JTizzard (R H Buckler) *rr but in tch: rdn and one pce over 3f out: styd on again fnl f to press for 2nd nr fin: no ch w wnr* **9/2**[2]	110
	4	*1*	**Stoney Drove (FR)** 5-11-0 ... SThomas (Miss H C Knight) *rangy: scope: lw: chsd ldrs: rdn 4f out: one pce fnl 3f* **17/2**	102
4-	**5**	*7*	**Whosethatfor (IRE)**[278] [3633] 5-11-0 ... WHutchinson (J A B Old) *lw: sn disputing ld tl led over 5f out: hdd 3f out: wknd 2f out* **12/1**	95
	6	*13*	**Wenlocks Wonder** 4-11-0 ... JPMcNamara (K C Bailey) *str: tall: scope: in tch: chsd ldrs 6f out: rdn and wknd 3f out* **25/1**	82
34-	**7**	*3/4*	**Double Law**[207] [4819] 5-11-0 ... TDoyle (P R Webber) *chsd ldrs: rdn 4f out: sn wknd* **8/1**	81
	8	*16*	**Joyryder** 4-11-0 ... PMoloney (M Pitman) *str: lw: disp ld tl dropped to 2nd over 5f out: wknd 4f out* **9/2**[2]	65

4m 10.3s (0.05) **Going Correction** +0.35s/f (Yiel)
WFA 4 from 5yo+ 12lb **8** Ran SP% **112.9**
Speed ratings: **97,91,91,90,87 81,80,73** CSF £16.13 TOTE £4.20: £1.50, £1.80, £1.80; EX 13.10 Place 6 £1,187.78, Place 5 £636.03.
Owner The Big Boys Toys Partnership **Bred** M And Mrs McNamara **Trained** Brayford, Devon
■ A first winner in Britain for Jack Doyle, sixteen-year-old son of Irish trainer Pat Doyle.

FOCUS

An interesting bumper won in impressive fashion by Here's Johnny, who has been rated value for 15 lengths and looks classy.

NOTEBOOK

Here's Johnny(IRE) ◆, whose stable won this race last year, is well regarded at home. He showed decent bumper form when last seen in the spring of 2004 but a leg injury had kept him off the track subsequently. This performance showed that he retains all his ability, though, as he travelled well throughout and came home an impressive winner. His hurdling debut is eagerly anticipated. *(op 3-1 tchd 7-2)*

Art Virginia(FR), a dual point-to-point winner in March, was having his first outing for his new stable and ran with plenty of promise. He should have a future when taking on a flight of obstacles.

Clyffe Hanger(IRE), who was a shock winner of an Exeter bumper on his only previous start, was not disgraced under his penalty and should pay his way over timber. *(op 11-2)*

Stoney Drove(FR) was not particularly strong in the market but he still did best of the newcomers. He looks sure to come on for this outing and is worth bearing in mind for a similar contest. *(op 6-1)*
Whosethatfor(IRE), who had finished fourth in a lesser event at Kempton on his only previous start, ran well enough for a long way, leading them into the straight before being put in his place. *(op 10-1 tchd 14-1)*
Joyryder, whose dam is a half-sister to smart Irish hurdler/chaser Well Ridden, weakened on the turn into the straight. Still weak at present, he needs time. *(tchd 5-1)*
T/Plt: £2,330.70 to a £1 stake. Pool: £41,825.95. 13.10 winning tickets. T/Qpdt: £239.60 to a £1 stake. Pool: £2,461.70. 7.60 winning tickets. ST

1857 WINCANTON (R-H)

Saturday, November 5

OFFICIAL GOING: Good (good to soft in places)
Wind: Moderate behind

2050 EBF TOTEPLACEPOT "NATIONAL HUNT" NOVICES' HURDLE (QUALIFIER) (8 hdls) 2m

1:05 (1:07) (Class 3) 4-6-Y-O **£6,915** (£2,030; £1,015; £507)

Form | | | | RPR
-111 **1** **Refinement (IRE)**[13] 1850 6-11-3 ... APMcCoy 133+
(Jonjo O'Neill) *mde all: shkn up appr last: r.o: pushed out* **4/9**[1]
43- **2** *1 ½* **Pirate Flagship (FR)**[202] 4887 6-11-0 ... RWalsh 124
(P F Nicholls) *bit bkwd: tall: trckd ldrs: rdn to chal and hit 2 out: ev ch last: kpt on but a hld run-in* **11/1**[3]
2 **3** *dist* **Missyl (FR)**[13] 1857 5-11-0 ... RWalford 89
(R H Alner) *hld up bhd ldrs: rdn after 3 out: sn outpcd: hit next: wnt 3rd sn after: no ch w ldng pair* **12/1**
2 **4** *13* **Paradise Bay (IRE)**[195] 7 4-11-0 ... DCrosse 81
(C J Mann) *trckd ldrs: hit 5th: rdn after 3 out: wknd next* **16/1**
00- **5** *dist* **Noviciate (IRE)**[277] 3640 5-11-0 ... WMarston —
(Simon Earle) *bit bkwd: a bhd* **150/1**
324- **F** **Sea The Light**[236] 4373 5-11-0 ... RThornton —
(A King) *lw: hld up bhd ldrs: trckd wnr fr 4th: gng wl enough whn fell 6th* **5/1**[2]

3m 44.1s (-5.00) **Going Correction** -0.10s/f (Good)
WFA 4 from 5yo+ 12lb **6** Ran SP% **108.5**
Speed ratings: **108,107,—,—,—,—** — CSF £5.88 TOTE £1.40: £1.10, £2.40; EX 5.10.
Owner M Tabor **Bred** M Tabor **Trained** Cheltenham, Gloucs

FOCUS
The winner was rated value for further and is approaching her best bumper figure now, while this was a big step up in forrm from the second.

NOTEBOOK
Refinement(IRE), who sweated up again in the preliminaries, made it three from three over hurdles. Although not overly impressive, she jumps much better now and she possessed too much speed for the runner-up on the flat with McCoy not needing to draw his stick. *(op 8-15)*
Pirate Flagship(FR), very much a chasing type, was stepping back in trip for this seasonal return. Closing the gap on the mare to challenge at the second last, which he clouted, he could not quite match his pacier rival on the run-in. He is well capable of winning an ordinary novice hurdle, but it would not surprise to see him switched to fences before long. *(op 12-1)*
Missyl(FR), who looks as though he will make a chaser, had been runner-up in a slowly-run event over course and distance and he was put in his place in this better grade. *(op 14-1 tchd 16-1)*
Paradise Bay(IRE), sold out of Nicky Henderson's yard for 50,000gns after a promising bumper debut in April, made more than one jumping error on this first try over hurdles and ended up well beaten. He was not knocked about when held, however, and is probably capable of better. *(op 14-1)*
Noviciate(IRE), who had a recent spin in a charity race here, trailed throughout, having been reluctant to line up. *(op 100-1)*
Sea The Light, who raced with his head low to the ground, had yet to be asked a question when coming down. He looks to have the ability to win races over hurdles and, from the family of Martin's Lamp and Hurricane Lamp, should make a chaser in a season or two. *(op 4-1)*

2051 TOTEPOOL AWAYBET H'CAP CHASE (17 fncs) 2m 5f

1:35 (1:35) (Class 3) (0-120,119) 5-Y-0+ **£7,029** (£2,063; £1,031; £515)

Form | | | | RPR
3/12 **1** **Black De Bessy (FR)**[21] 1744 7-11-5 **112** ... AThornton 129+
(D R C Elsworth) *a travelling wl: trckd ldrs: led appr 3 out: styd on wl: pushed out* **7/2**[1]
/23- **2** *2* **Ruby Gale (IRE)**[358] 2169 9-11-12 **119** ... RWalsh 130+
(P F Nicholls) *mid div: lost pl and dropped towards rr appr 4 out: gd hdwy on inner appr 3 out: styd on to go 2nd last* **9/1**
F1-U **3** *3* **Latimer's Place**[13] 1853 9-11-11 **118** ... JAMcCarthy 126+
(J A Geake) *hld up towards rr: mstke 5th: hdwy 10th: led 13th: rdn and hdd appr 3 out: kpt on* **20/1**
014F **4** *5* **Xellance (IRE)**[21] 1744 8-11-2 **114** ... RStephens(5) 116
(P J Hobbs) *in tch: hdwy 11th to trck ldrs: rdn and effrt appr 3 out: kpt on same pce* **20/1**
22-0 **5** *shd* **Ede'Iff**[8] 1906 8-10-5 **105** ... RLucey-Butler(7) 107
(W G M Turner) *hld up towards rr: rdn after 4 out: styd on fr next* **40/1**
2302 **6** *1* **Penthouse Minstrel**[11] 1874 11-10-8 **108** ... (v) MrJSnowden(7) 110+
(R J Hodges) *trckd ldrs: rdn and effrt after 4 out: kpt on same pce* **22/1**
/14- **7** *5* **Tribal King (IRE)**[287] 3489 10-11-9 **116** ... RThornton 115+
(A King) *trckd ldrs: led 4th tl 13th: rdn appr 3 out: wknd 2 out* **9/2**[2]
F12- **8** *1 ¾* **Kew Jumper (IRE)**[218] 4681 6-11-5 **112** ... GLee 106
(Andrew Turnell) *hld up towards rr: hdwy to mid div 8th: rdn and wknd appr 3 out* **5/1**[3]
0-31 **9** *5* **Toulouse (IRE)**[167] 466 8-11-10 **117** ... RWalford 107+
(R H Alner) *hld up and a towards rr* **20/1**
4-4F **10** *15* **Roschal (IRE)**[14] 1825 7-10-13 **106** ... PJBrennan 85+
(P J Hobbs) *mid div: hdwy 11th: chalng whn mstke 4 out: sn wknd* **13/2**
22-6 **11** *1 ½* **Roofing Spirit (IRE)**[192] 71 7-11-8 **115** ... TJMurphy 88
(D P Keane) *hld up and a towards rr* **12/1**
20F- **12** *8* **Joe Deane (IRE)**[314] 2978 9-11-1 **108** ... RGreene 73
(M J Coombe) *bit bkwd: led tl 4th: chsd ldrs: nt fluent 9th (water): mstke 11th: sn wknd* **33/1**
P-10 **U** **Sacrifice**[63] 1398 10-10-1 **97** ... CBolger(3) —
(K Bishop) *w ldr tl blnd and uns rdr 10th* **25/1**

5m 19.5s (-3.60) **Going Correction** -0.10s/f (Good) **13** Ran SP% **116.0**
Speed ratings: **102,101,100,98,98 97,95,95,93,87 87,83,—** CSF £29.71 CT £550.42 TOTE £4.60: £2.00, £2.80, £6.80; EX 41.40.
Owner Mrs Derek Fletcher **Bred** A D'Agnese **Trained** Newmarket, Suffolk

FOCUS
A fair handicap in which plenty still had chances jumping the cross fence, four from home. In the end the winner scored comfortably and was value for further. Solid form from all of the first six.

NOTEBOOK
Black De Bessy(FR) ◆ was put up a couple of pounds after his good run at Stratford. Travelling well behind the leaders, if a little keen, he showed ahead at the first in the home straight and ran out a ready winner. There is more to come from him. *(op 4-1)*
Ruby Gale(IRE), without the headgear for this first run in a year, ran well under topweight. He lost his pitch going to the cross fence but soon closed again, and although never getting to the winner he was keeping on to the line. Still to win over fences, he should put that right before long if in the mood. *(op 8-1)*
Latimer's Place, all the better for his recent reappearance, made good progress to take up the running down the back and did not drop away once headed by the winner early in the home straight.
Xellance(IRE), currently a stone lower over fences than hurdles, ran a sound race but could never quite get in a blow. *(op 16-1)*
Ede'Iff, who made her reappearance over hurdles, was staying on at the end and should be approaching peak fitness now. *(op 33-1)*
Penthouse Minstrel ran his race but remains 12lb higher than when scoring over course and distance in March. *(op 25-1)*
Tribal King(IRE), who reportedly suffered a stress fracture when last seen in January, was given a forcing ride on this return but lack of a recent outing eventually told. *(op 4-1)*
Roschal(IRE) was a close second when diving through the cross fence and quickly dropping away. His jumping is a concern. *Official explanation: vet said gelding lost near-fore shoe (op 6-1)*

2052 TOTESPORT 0800 221 221 RISING STARS NOVICES' CHASE GRADE 2 (17 fncs) 2m 5f

2:10 (2:10) (Class 1) 4-Y-0+
£19,957 (£7,486; £3,748; £1,869; £938; £469)

Form | | | | RPR
23P- **1** **Celtic Son (FR)**[203] 4862 6-11-6 ... (t) TJMurphy 152+
(M C Pipe) *lw: j.w: hld up bhd ldrs: j. into ld 10th: in command fr 13th: heavily eased run-in: impressive* **2/1**[1]
31-1 **2** *3* **Napolitain (FR)**[21] 1736 4-10-11 ... RWalsh 123+
(P F Nicholls) *hld up bhd ldrs: wnt 2nd 13th: rdn after 4 out: sn no ch w wnr: hit next* **9/4**[2]
P21 **3** *½* **Unleash (USA)**[92] 1155 6-11-6 ... PJBrennan 130+
(P J Hobbs) *hld up: hit 12th: rdn after 13th: styd on to go 3rd appr 3 out* **11/1**
20-1 **4** *23* **Stance**[163] 510 6-11-10 ... JEMoore 110
(G L Moore) *bit bkwd: trckd ldrs: rdn in cl 3rd appr 4 out: wknd appr 3 out* **12/1**
210- **5** *7* **Senor Sedona**[232] 4434 6-11-6 ... JamesDavies 99
(N J Gifford) *led tl 5th: prom: led 7th tl 10th: wknd after 12th* **9/1**
41-3 **6** *½* **Ardaghey (IRE)**[13] 1845 6-11-6 ... CLlewellyn 99
(N A Twiston-Davies) *lw: prom: led 5th tl mstke and hdd 7th: led briefly appr 10th: wknd after 12th* **8/1**[3]
F11F **P** **Celtic Boy (IRE)**[21] 1735 7-11-10 130 ... GLee —
(P Bowen) *hld up: mstke 5th: lost tch 8th: bhd and p.u bef 10th* **9/1**

5m 17.8s (-5.30) **Going Correction** -0.10s/f (Good)
WFA 4 from 6yo+ 13lb **7** Ran SP% **111.2**
Speed ratings: **106,104,104,95,93 93,—** CSF £6.75 TOTE £3.10: £2.10, £1.90; EX 8.90.
Owner D A Johnson **Bred** Gil M Protti **Trained** Nicholashayne, Devon

FOCUS
A high-quality novice event and a hugely impressive winner in Celtic Son, who was value for 20l and is potentially top-class. The runner-up improved to the level of his hurdles form and the third improved too, although he still ran a fair way off his hurdles form.\n\x\x .

NOTEBOOK
Celtic Son(FR) ◆ was a very useful hurdler, successful five times as a novice last season and ending the campaign rated 138, but he has the potential to go right to the top over fences. This looked a hot novice, yet he could hardly have been more impressive on this chasing debut, putting in a fault-free round and coasting home without breaking sweat. The Royal & SunAlliance looks the obvious long-term target and he may gain valuable experience of Cheltenham at the Open meeting. *(op 9-4 tchd 15-8)*
Napolitain(FR), successful in an ordinary race at Huntingdon, was no match at all for the classy winner and is greatly flattered to have got within three lengths of him, but he is a decent novice nevertheless and will win more races over fences. *(op 5-2 tchd 11-4)*
Unleash(USA) kept staying on over the last three fences and would have finished second with a bit further to go. He needs three miles and has been taken out of two races over that trip due to unsuitable ground since his win at Worcester. *(op 7-1)*
Stance appeared in need of this first run since his winning chase debut back in May but ran well until fading turning into the home straight. This may have been too far for him in such smart company, although he does stay marathon trips on the Flat, and he will do better. *(op 9-1)*
Senor Sedona, off the track since the Cheltenham Festival, was found out in this company on his chasing debut but should win races at a slightly lower level. *(op 16-1)*
Ardaghey(IRE) could not go with the rest in the back straight and looks in need of a step up to three miles. *(op 13-2)*
Celtic Boy(IRE) ran and jumped as if his confidence has taken a dent. *(op 11-1)*

2053 £1MILLION TOTETENTOFOLLOW MARES' ONLY H'CAP HURDLE (11 hdls) 2m 6f

2:40 (2:40) (Class 3) (0-130,120) 4-Y-0+
£7,941 (£2,345; £1,172; £587; £292; £147)

Form | | | | RPR
11-1 **1** **Penneyrose Bay**[30] 1658 6-11-12 **120** ... MBradburne 140+
(J A Geake) *lw: mde all: drew wl clr after 3 out: unchal* **11/4**[2]
230- **2** *14* **Almah (SAF)**[205] 4837 7-11-4 **117** ... PCO'Neill(5) 114
(Miss Venetia Williams) *trckd ldrs: chsd wnr after 5th: rdn after 3 out: sn no ch w wnr* **4/1**[3]
-321 **3** *18* **Tirikumba**[150] 679 9-10-4 **103** ... RStephens(5) 85+
(S G Griffiths) *hld up in tch: rdn after 3 out: remote 3rd whn j. bdly lft 2 out* **28/1**
13-4 **4** *7* **Darjeeling (IRE)**[13] 1844 6-11-1 **109** ... RWalsh 81
(P F Nicholls) *hld up: rdn after 3 out: wnt remote 4th appr next: nvr a danger* **7/4**[1]
2/5- **5** *15* **Burnt Out (IRE)**[222] 4635 6-11-1 **116** ... CMStudd(7) 78+
(B G Powell) *chsd wnr tl 5th: wknd appr 3 out* **33/1**
0F0- **6** *dist* **Calamintha**[21] 3151 5-11-12 **120** ... TJMurphy —
(M C Pipe) *slowly away: nvr fluent in rr: lost tch fr 7th: t.o* **20/1**
12-2 **P** **Early Start**[13] 1853 7-11-7 **115** ... AThornton —
(J W Mullins) *hld up: hdwy to go 3rd 7th: p.u after next: lame* **7/1**
122- **P** **Floreana (GER)**[241] 4267 4-11-9 **117** ... DCrosse —
(C J Mann) *hld up in tch: rdn after 7th: wknd after 3 out: p.u bef next* **16/1**

5m 21.6s (-3.50) **Going Correction** -0.10s/f (Good)
WFA 4 from 5yo+ 13lb **8** Ran SP% **112.6**
Speed ratings: **102,96,90,87,82 —,—,—** CSF £13.81 CT £242.73 TOTE £4.30: £1.50, £1.80, £4.70; EX 20.00.

Owner Sir Christopher Wates **Bred** Sir Christopher Stephen Wates **Trained** Kimpton, Hants

FOCUS

The improving winner set a good gallop which quickly had her rivals stretched. She has been rated value for 23l, and although one could make stamina or fitness excuses for the beaten horses she could just be very good.

NOTEBOOK

Penneyrose Bay made every yard at a good clip and ran her field ragged. She is improving fast and an 11lb rise for her win at Worcester was nowhere near enough to stop her. Value for more than 20 lengths, she can defy another hike in the handicap. *(op 3-1 tchd 10-3)*

Almah(SAF) ran respectably on this first outing since the spring but had only a distant view of the *winner over the last three flights. She has yet to convince that she really wants this far. (op 5-1 tchd 7-2)*

Tirikumba, who prefers genuine fast ground, made a satisfactory return after a five-month break. *(op 25-1)*

Darjeeling(IRE) ran a lacklustre race and her attentions are likely to be switched to fences now. *(op 2-1)*

Burnt Out(IRE) was formerly trained by Al O'Connell in Ireland, where she gained her two victories *with cut in the ground. She looks high enough in the weights at present.Official explanation: jockey said mare hung right-handed throughout (op 25-1)*

Calamintha was down the field in the Cesarewitch last month. Best when able to dominate, she would have struggled to reach the front with Penneyrose Bay in opposition and it became immaterial after she gave away lengths at the start. *(tchd 25-1)*

Early Start, reverting to hurdles, unfortunately appeared to go lame landing over the eighth flight. *(op 11-2)*

2054 BADGER ALES TROPHY (A H'CAP CHASE) (LISTED RACE) (21 fncs) 3m 1f 110y

3:15 (3:16) (Class 1) (0-150,143) 5-Y-0+

£39,914 (£14,973; £7,497; £3,738; £1,876; £938)

Form	Pos	Dist	Horse / Trainer / Comment	Jockey / SP	RPR
000-	1		**Iris Bleu (FR)**[196] [4984] 9-11-2 **133** (M C Pipe) *hld up towards rr: hit 1st and 7th: smooth hdwy on inner after 4 out: rdn to ld appr last: styd on wl to draw clr run-in*	TJMurphy **10/1**	150+
112-	2	3 ½	**Red Devil Robert (IRE)**[206] [4824] 7-11-2 **133** (P F Nicholls) *rangy: mid div: stdy prog fr 15th: gng wl and led 2 out: hdd last: sn rdn: no ex*	RWalsh **2/1**[1]	146+
/05-	3	12	**Windsor Boy (IRE)**[406] [1511] 8-10-4 **121** (M C Pipe) *hld up towards rr: hdwy 14th: wnt 2nd briefly after 17th: rdn to chal appr 3 out: kpt on same pce*	APMcCoy **5/1**[3]	122
4-26	4	hd	**Double Honour (FR)**[132] [842] 7-11-5 **136** (P J Hobbs) *prom: led 10th: rdn appr 3 out: mstke and hdd 2 out: wkng whn blnd last: lost 3rd fnl strides*	(b) PJBrennan **25/1**	140+
P00-	5	2	**Joly Bey (FR)**[196] [4984] 8-11-9 **143** (N J Gifford) *chsd ldrs tl dropped rr 17th: styd on again fr 3 out*	(t) MrDHDunsdon(3) **20/1**	142
10-5	6	2 ½	**Inca Trail (IRE)**[21] [1735] 9-10-10 **134** (P F Nicholls) *hld up towards rr: short lived effrt after 4 out: no further imp fr next*	(b) LHeard(7) **25/1**	131+
205-	7	¾	**Too Forward (IRE)**[211] [4761] 9-10-12 **129** (M Pitman) *mid div: nt fluent 4th (water): hmpd 8th: chsd ldrs 17th: rdn after 4 out: wknd after next*	GLee **16/1**	127+
13-4	F		**Duncliffe**[193] [42] 8-11-7 **138** (R H Alner) *lw: trcking ldrs whn fell 8th*	RThornton **33/1**	—
2P3-	U		**All In The Stars (IRE)**[245] [4189] 7-9-12 **122** (D P Keane) *bit bkwd: hld up towards rr: bdly hmpd and uns rdr 8th*	DJacob(7) **28/1**	—
P3-1	P		**Trust Fund (IRE)**[189] [130] 7-10-10 **127** (R H Alner) *mid div: blnd 6th: bhd 8th: lost tch 13th: t.o and p.u bef 17th*	RWalford **66/1**	—
1P-1	P		**Naunton Brook**[13] [1853] 6-10-8 **125** (N A Twiston-Davies) *led tl 10th: prom: mstke 14th: sn wknd: p.u bef 17th*	CLlewellyn **10/1**	—
211-	P		**Distant Thunder (IRE)**[259] [3941] 7-11-5 **136** (R H Alner) *hld up towards rr: tk clsr order 16th: rdn and short lived effrt appr 4 out: wknd appr 3 out: p.u bef 2 out*	AThornton **7/2**[2]	—

6m 26.3s (-13.60) **Going Correction** -0.10s/f (Good) **12** Ran SP% **116.6**

Speed ratings: **116,114,111,111,110 109,109,—,—,— —,—** CSF £28.89 CT £116.11 TOTE £13.90: £2.90, £1.60, £2.40; EX 32.60 Trifecta £170.10 Pool £958.60 - 4.00 winning tickets..

Owner D A Johnson **Bred** Fabrice Besnouin **Trained** Nicholashayne, Devon

FOCUS

A competitive renewal of this valuable event, rated through the third to seventh, who were all within a couple of pounds of their marks. The winner was thrown in on his old form and the runner-up is still progressing.

NOTEBOOK

Iris Bleu(FR) took advantage of a 7lb drop in the handicap which saw him on the same mark as when gaining his last win in the Agfa Diamond Chase at Sandown in February 2003. Given a patient ride, he was produced to lead at the last and stayed on too strongly for the favourite. He looks an obvious Hennessy contender, and will still be well in on his best form when he has been reassessed, although it should be remembered that he did not go on from a promising reappearance last season. *(op 16-1)*

Red Devil Robert(IRE), who looked plenty fit enough for this reappearance, was still travelling well when jumping to the front at the second last but could not repel the winner's challenge. Still progressing, his early-season target has always been the Hennessy and that remains the plan despite this defeat. *(op 11-4)*

Windsor Boy(IRE) ◆, a smart three-year-old for Paul Cole, was having his first run since September last year, when he was trained by Edward O'Grady in Ireland. He ran a good race but had never run over this far before and he did not quite see it out. A decent handicap over a bit shorter should come his way. *(op 7-2)*

Double Honour(FR) ran well on this first outing since June, only collared at the second last and edged out of third place close home. Aintree's Becher Chase, in which he was fourth last year, looks the obvious next step. *(op 28-1 tchd 33-1)*

Joly Bey(FR) made a pleasing reappearance, staying on again over the last three fences, having looked set at one stage to finish out the back.

Inca Trail(IRE) reportedly had an abscess under his jaw when beaten at Huntingdon. The Nicholls second string here, he never promised to get involved. *(op 20-1)*

Distant Thunder(IRE), a smart novice last term, was disappointing on this seasonal return but *much better should be seen from him with the run under his belt.Official explanation: trainer had no explanation for poor form shown (op 5-1)*

Naunton Brook, put up 9lb for winning at Towcester, made the running to past halfway but was soon in trouble after a mistake at the fourteenth. *(op 5-1)*

2055 TOTESPORT.COM ELITE HURDLE (A LIMITED H'CAP) GRADE 2 (8 hdls) 2m

3:50 (3:52) (Class 1) 4-Y-0+

£28,510 (£10,695; £5,355; £2,670; £1,340; £670)

Form	Pos	Dist	Horse / Trainer / Comment	Jockey / SP	RPR
2F-P	1		**Royal Shakespeare (FR)**[5] [208] 6-11-1 **150** (S Gollings) *trckd ldrs: rdn to ld appr last: kpt on wl: drvn out*	GLee **5/1**[2]	149+
460-	2	1 ½	**Intersky Falcon**[210] [4771] 8-11-10 **159** (Jonjo O'Neill) *w ldr: led 2nd tl next: prom: led 2 out: sn rdn: hdd last: kpt on*	(b) APMcCoy **6/1**[3]	156
3411	3	shd	**Darrias (GER)**[10] [1876] 4-9-11 **139** oh7 (P F Nicholls) *hld up: hdwy appr 3 out: rdn to chse ldrs appr 2 out: kpt on to take 3rd run-in*	(t) LHeard(7) **7/1**	136
/1F-	4	3 ½	**Sporazene (IRE)**[368] [1970] 6-11-5 **154** (P F Nicholls) *trckd ldrs tl mstke 4th: in tch: rdn after 3 out: kpt on same pce*	RWalsh **10/3**[1]	148+
-51P	5	4	**Perouse**[111] [1024] 7-11-1 **150** (P F Nicholls) *led tl 2nd: regained ld after 3rd: rdn and hdd 2 out: kpt on same pce*	(t) PJBrennan **8/1**	139
154-	6	14	**Hawadeth**[266] [3807] 10-10-5 **140** (V R A Dartnall) *bit bkwd: hld up: mstke 3rd: lost tch 3 out*	JimCrowley **16/1**	115
24-0	7	shd	**Berengario (IRE)**[30] [1651] 5-10-4 **139** oh33 (S C Burrough) *chsd ldrs: rdn appr 2 out: sn wknd*	JAMcCarthy **125/1**	114
44-6	8	2	**Freedom Now (IRE)**[18] [1784] 7-10-4 **139** oh32 (R H Alner) *in tch tl 3 out*	RWalford **100/1**	112
306-	9	hd	**Marcel (FR)**[211] [4762] 5-10-8 **143** (M C Pipe) *lw: hld up: sme hdwy after 3 out: wknd 2 out: n.d*	TJMurphy **10/3**[1]	116

3m 41.0s (-8.10) **Going Correction** -0.10s/f (Good)

WFA 4 from 5yo+ 12lb **9** Ran SP% **108.4**

Speed ratings: **116,115,115,113,111 104,104,103,103** CSF £31.59 CT £183.97 TOTE £6.40: £2.00, £2.10, £1.90; EX 38.30 Trifecta £74.60 Pool £536.20 - 5.10 winning tickets..

Owner J B Webb **Bred** London Thoroughbred Services & Mme A Rothschild **Trained** Scamblesby, Lincs

FOCUS

Though run at a decent gallop, this is a tricky race to rate. It could be rated 6lb higher using the first two, but that would not fit in with the time and the two rank outsiders were a bit close for comfort.

NOTEBOOK

Royal Shakespeare(FR) was fit from a recent spin on Polytrack. Travelling well in third place and jumping fluently throughout, he struck the front at the last and gained his first victory since the spring of 2004 in decisive fashion. *(op 11-2)*

Intersky Falcon has had plenty of problems and managed only three runs last season. Without the tongue-tie for this return to action, he showed plenty of zest and was in the first two throughout, but the winner had his measure on the flat. *(op 9-2)*

Darrias(GER) has been on the go since February but continues to run well and this was a cracking effort from 7lb out of the handicap. He would have been second had his rider got after him slightly earlier on the run-in and a return to further will suit him. *(op 6-1)*

Sporazene(IRE) suffered a setback on the gallops a year ago which ruled him out for the rest of his novice chase season. He made a pleasing return to the track and could remain over hurdles until the new year, when he has the Victor Chandler Chase as his target. *(op 11-2)*

Perouse, disappointing in a novice chase when last seen in July, was successful in this a year ago when 7lb lower. After sharing the lead with the eventual runner-up he had no answers when headed for a second time two from home. *(tchd 9-1)*

Hawadeth ran as if in need of this first outing since splitting a pastern in the spring. *(op 14-1)*

Berengario(IRE) goes well here and only dropped away going to the second last. This looks a good effort from no less than 33lb out of the handicap.

Marcel(FR) was below-par on his final three runs last season and it was a similar story here. He could well go chasing now. *(op 11-4)*

2056 JOHN HARVEY MEMORIAL INTERMEDIATE OPEN NATIONAL HUNT FLAT RACE 2m

4:20 (4:23) (Class 6) 4-6-Y-0 **£1,911** (£557; £278)

Form	Pos	Dist	Horse / Trainer / Comment	Jockey / SP	RPR
-	1		**Craven (IRE)** 5-11-4 (N J Henderson) *lw: hld up towards rr: stdy hdwy 4f out: rdn to chse ldr over 2f out: edgd lft ins fnl f: led fnl stride*	APMcCoy **8/11**[1]	100+
	2	shd	**Commander Kev (IRE)** 4-10-13 (Noel T Chance) *str: lw: scope: trck ldrs: led over 3f out: rdn and edgd lft 1f out: ct fnl stride*	WKennedy(5) **10/1**[3]	100+
	3	5	**Winter Sport (IRE)** 4-11-4 (P J Hobbs) *w'like: mid div: tk clsr order 5f out: rdn and effrt 3f out: kpt on same pce*	PJBrennan **4/1**[2]	95
40	4	½	**Thenford Lord (IRE)**[28] [1681] 4-11-4 (D J S Ffrench Davis) *scope: chsd ldr: rdn and effrt 3f out: kpt on same pce*	(b[1]) MBradburne **50/1**	94
2-	5	1 ¼	**Miller's Monarch**[401] [1547] 5-11-4 (Andrew Turnell) *bit bkwd: mid div: tk clsr order over 3f out: sn rdn: kpt on same pce*	GLee **12/1**	93
0P-	6	shd	**Earth Moving (IRE)**[221] [4644] 5-11-4 (P F Nicholls) *lw: scope: hld up towards rr: styd on fr over 2f out: nvr trbld ldrs*	RWalsh **12/1**	93+
P	7	9	**Willhebemyguy**[80] [1237] 6-11-4 (Mrs H R J Nelmes) *w'like: led: rdn and hdd over 3f out: wknd 2f out*	CLlewellyn **100/1**	86+
	8	½	**Rosewater Bay** 4-10-4 (P F Nicholls) *unf: hld up: sme hdwy over 3f out: no imp after*	LHeard(7) **10/1**[3]	76
	9	3 ½	**Loose Morals (IRE)** 4-10-11 (Miss E C Lavelle) *unf: scope: bit bkwd: hld up: short lived effrt over 3f out*	BFenton **20/1**	73
	10	3 ½	**That's My Charlie (NZ)** 4-10-11 (Jonjo O'Neill) *leggy: mid div: hdwy 6f out: rdn over 3f out: sn wknd*	MrAJBerry(7) **20/1**	76
	11	5	**So Wise So Young** 4-11-4 (R H Buckler) *str: bit bkwd: chsd ldrs: rdn over 3f out: sn wknd*	TJMurphy **25/1**	71
	12	dist	**Jazz Junior** 6-10-13 (M J Weeden) *str: bit bkwd: bhd fr 1/2-way*	RStephens(5) **100/1**	—

3m 48.0s (-3.70) **Going Correction** -0.10s/f (Good) **12** Ran SP% **128.8**

Speed ratings: **105,104,102,102,101 101,97,96,95,93 90,—** CSF £10.03 TOTE £1.70: £1.10, £2.40, £2.20; EX 9.90 Place 6 £29.36, Place 5 £22.98.

Owner Sir Robert Ogden **Bred** Mrs Ann Cunningham **Trained** Upper Lambourn, Berks

■ Something Crystal (9/2) was withdrawn (refused to be saddled). R4 applies, deduct 15p in the £.

FOCUS

Probably only a fair bumper for the track, rated through the fifth. The early pace was slow and they finished in something of a heap.

NOTEBOOK
Craven(IRE), whose dam was placed over hurdles and fences, is a half-brother to some modest winning jumpers. Only ninth straightening up for home, he made up ground quickly to throw down his challenge with around two furlongs to run but became locked in battle with the leader and only scrambled home in the end. A stiffer test of stamina will suit him. *(new market op 11-10)*
Commander Kev(IRE), who was sold for 36,000gns as a three-year-old, went on early in the home straight. Joined by the favourite with two furlongs to run, he wandered under pressure but looked likely to hold on until pipped on the line. *(new market op 11-1 tchd 16-1)*
Winter Sport(IRE), whose unraced dam is from the family of Thisthatandtother, made a pleasing debut and should make the grade when put over hurdles. *(new market op 6-1 tchd 13-2)*
Thenford Lord(IRE) showed improved form in the first-time headgear and looks the type to do even better over obstacles. *(new market op 100-1)*
Miller's Monarch, reappearing after an absence of over a year, looked as though he had done plenty of work but was still a bit backward in his coat. *(new market op 20-1)*
Earth Moving(IRE), who had excuses for two disappointing runs earlier in the year, stayed on *steadily from off the pace in the latter stages to confirm that he has ability. (new market op 16-1 tchd 20-1)*
T/Plt: £53.60 to a £1 stake. Pool: £59,857.05. 814.90 winning tickets. T/Qpdt: £27.10 to a £1 stake. Pool: £4,462.40. 121.50 winning tickets. TM

2057 - 2061a (Foreign Racing) - See Raceform Interactive

AYR (L-H)
Sunday, November 6
OFFICIAL GOING: Soft (good to soft in places)
Wind: breezy, half-against

2062 ALAN MACKAY INSURANCE INTRODUCTORY NOVICES' HURDLE (8 hdls 1 omitted) 2m
1:00 (1:01) (Class 3) 4-Y-O+ **£4,856** (£1,425; £712; £356)

Form RPR
31-1 **1** **Rasharrow (IRE)**[15] [1834] 6-11-5 .... ADobbin 120+
(L Lungo) *hld up: smooth hdwy 5th: led bef last: drvn and kpt on wl* **1/5**[1]
2 1 1/4 **First Look (FR)**[41] 5-11-0 .... KRenwick 112+
(P Monteith) *in tch: led bef 2 out to bef last: kpt on u.p* **100/1**
2 **3** 19 **Oddsmaker (IRE)**[3] [2006] 4-10-7 ....(t) BenOrde-Powlett[(7)] 98+
(M A Barnes) *prom: ev ch bef 2 out: outpcd after 2 out: hld in 4th whn lft 3rd last* **20/1**[3]
3 **4** 18 **Showtime Annie**[8] [1824] 4-10-4 .... ACCoyle[(3)] 68
(A Bailey) *chsd ldrs: outpcd 3 out: n.d after* **40/1**
5 11 **Boris The Spider**[27] 4-11-0 .... FKeniry 64
(M D Hammond) *cl up: led bef 5th to bef 2 out: sn btn* **100/1**
361- **6** 1/2 **Powerlove (FR)**[198] [4971] 4-10-7 .... MBradburne 56
(Mrs S C Bradburne) *prom to 3 out: sn wknd* **25/1**
30-6 **7** 3 1/2 **Endless Power (IRE)**[15] [1834] 5-11-0 .... BGibson 60
(J Barclay) *chsd ldrs: drvn 3 out: sn wknd* **66/1**
8 5 **Ballyhurry (USA)**[42] 8-11-0 .... RMcGrath 55
(J S Goldie) *midfield: outpcd 5th: n.d after* **66/1**
5-22 **9** 17 **Dalawan**[45] [1532] 6-10-11 .... PAspell[(3)] 38
(Mrs J C McGregor) *nt fluent: a bhd* **40/1**
P **10** 12 **Whatcanyasay**[11] [1885] 4-10-4 .... SGagan[(10)] 26
(Mrs E Slack) *sn bhd: no ch fr 1/2-way* **200/1**
11 11 **Glenisla Mist** 4-10-0 .... DDaSilva[(7)] —
(Mrs S C Bradburne) *cl up tl wknd fr 3 out* **200/1**
0 **12** 4 **Barney (IRE)**[11] [1889] 4-10-7 .... EWhillans[(7)] 11
(Mrs E Slack) *hmpd 1st: nvr on terms* **100/1**
13 1/2 **Moscow Ali (IRE)** 5-10-11 .... PBuchanan[(3)] —
(Miss Lucinda V Russell) *nt jump wl in rr: struggling fr 4th* **100/1**
534/ **F** **Datbandito (IRE)**[603] [4316] 6-10-4 .... JPEnnis[(10)] —
(L Lungo) *fell 1st* **100/1**
P **Golden Remedy**[55] 4-10-7 .... DO'Meara —
(A R Dicken) *a bhd: t.o whn p.u bef 3 out* **200/1**
/00- **P** **Moffied (IRE)**[296] [3348] 5-10-11 .... GBerridge[(3)] —
(J Barclay) *led and clr: blnd 2nd: hdd bef 5th: wknd qckly and p.u bef next* **200/1**
115- **F** **Funny Times**[213] [4753] 4-10-7 .... BHarding 98+
(N G Richards) *nt fluent: hld up: hdwy and in tch bef 2 out: sn pushed along: 6l down and one pce whn fell last* **9/1**[2]
3m 52.7s (-4.60) **Going Correction** -0.15s/f (Good)
WFA 4 from 5yo+ 12lb **17** Ran SP% **116.7**
Speed ratings: **105,104,94,85,80 80,78,75,67,61 55,53,53,—,— —,—** CSF £55.53 TOTE £1.20: £1.02, £16.80, £2.80; EX 62.40.
Owner Ashleybank Investments Limited **Bred** Mrs Elizabeth English **Trained** Carrutherstown, D'fries & G'way

FOCUS
Little strength in depth to this novice event, but the winning time was respectable and the form should work out. The second-last flight was bypassed.

NOTEBOOK
Rasharrow(IRE) , off the mark in a facile manner on his hurdling bow at Kelso 15 days previously, duly followed-up under his penalty yet had to work very hard in order to do so. Having cruised up to the head of the affairs in the home straight looking booked for a cosy success, he failed to quicken as looked likely when push came to shove on the run-in, and had to pull out the stops to shake off the runner-up. While that rival may prove above-average in time, and the ground may have been too soft for his liking, this effort leaves him with a little to prove when stepping up in class. *(op 1-4)*
First Look(FR) ◆ , who showed little on his debut for connections on the Flat in September, ran a race full of promise on this debut over timber, defying his odds of 100/1, and made the hot favourite pull out all the stops on the run-in. He jumped well througout, travelled nicely on the soft ground and finished a long way clear of the rest. He looks sure to go one better in a similar contest on this sort of surface before too long and clearly has a future as a hurdler.
Oddsmaker(IRE) , runner-up on his debut in this sphere at Haydock just three days previously, had every chance before eventually being put in his place from two out. He was in-turn clear of the remainder at the finish, and may have found this coming too soon, but his future in this sphere clearly lies with the Handicapper. *(op 14-1)*
Showtime Annie , third on debut at Aintree in October, ran below that form and still has to prove she truly stays this distance. She may fare better when handicapped. *(op 25-1)*
Moffied(IRE) *Official explanation: Vet said gelding bled from the nose (op 100-1)*
Funny Times , who showed very useful form in bumpers last term, failed to jump with any real fluency on this hurdling bow, yet was still booked for a place prior to falling at the final hurdle. She will have to improve her jumping if she is to progress in this sphere, but it is too early to be writing her off yet. *(op 100-1)*

2063 ROGER DYSON RECOVERY NOVICES' H'CAP CHASE (18 fncs) 2m 5f 110y
1:30 (1:30) (Class 4) (0-105,98) 5-Y-O+ **£4,212** (£1,307; £704)

Form RPR
P4-3 **1** **Silver Jack (IRE)**[29] [1682] 7-11-12 **98** .... ADobbin 115+
(M Todhunter) *mstke 2nd: chsd ldrs: led 11th: drew clr fr 5 out: easily* **2/1**[1]
/646 **2** 21 **Mounthooley**[130] [858] 9-10-10 **82** .... NPMulholland 61
(B Mactaggart) *mstkes and j.rt: prom: chsd wnr 12th: no ex fr 5 out* **10/3**[3]
523- **3** 1 1/2 **Fountain Brig**[266] [3825] 9-10-9 **84** .... PBuchanan[(3)] 62
(N W Alexander) *mde most to 11th: outpcd after next: n.d after* **11/4**[2]
365P **P** **Mikasa (IRE)**[9] [1905] 5-10-0 **72** oh1 ....(b) RMcGrath —
(R F Fisher) *cl up tl wknd after 10th: t.o whn p.u after 5 out* **5/1**
35-F **P** **Hollow Flight (IRE)**[15] [1835] 7-9-12 **73** .... PAspell[(3)] —
(J N R Billinge) *nt fluent in rr: reminders and wknd 10th: p.u bef 13th* **16/1**
5m 57.0s (3.30) **Going Correction** +0.20s/f (Yiel) **5** Ran SP% **105.6**
Speed ratings: **102,94,93,—,—** CSF £8.31 TOTE £2.10: £1.40, £1.90; EX 8.20.
Owner B Batey **Bred** Mrs Mary O'Doherty **Trained** Orton, Cumbria

FOCUS
This novices' handicap was notably weakened by the withdrawl of Arctic Lagoon and ultimately the favourite proved in a different league to his rivals, being value for much more than the official margin.

NOTEBOOK
Silver Jack(IRE) , third on his recent chasing bow over two miles at Hexham, showed the clear benefit of that experience and broke his duck over fences with a near-faultless display under top weight. The longer trip was to his advantage, as was the the much softer ground, and it is interesting that both his career victories have come at this venue. While it should be noted that this event took little winning - mainly due to the withdrawl of Artic Lagoon - the manner in which he jumped and travelled suggests he will prove much better in this sphere. Connections will be praying the Handicapper does not take this form too literally, however. *(op 7-4 tchd 9-4)*
Mounthooley , returning from a 130-day break, spoilt his chances with some sloppy jumping and was firmly put in his place by the winner. While on this evidence he should prove better suited by racing on a right-handed track, he remains a maiden and is one to have reservations about. *(op 7-2)*
Fountain Brig , runner-up in this event last season off this mark on his seasonal bow, ran well below that form and proved disappointing. He is yet to win a race of any description and has clearly had his problems. *(tchd 5-2 and 3-1)*
Mikasa(IRE) , tried in blinkers having been pulled up on his last outing nine days previously, threw *in the towel down the back straight and turned in another moody display. He is one to avoid. (tchd 11-2 and 6-1 in places)*

2064 FAMOUS GROUSE NOVICES' H'CAP HURDLE (11 hdls) 2m 4f
2:00 (2:02) (Class 4) (0-105,100) 3-Y-O+ **£3,428** (£1,006; £503; £251)

Form RPR
2P-5 **1** **Aston Lad**[27] [596] 4-11-12 **100** .... FKeniry 104+
(M D Hammond) *hld up: hdwy 4 out: effrt whn checked 2 out: kpt on wl fr last to ld towards fin* **8/1**[3]
3PP- **2** shd **Flaming Heck**[234] [4418] 8-10-11 **90** .... DFlavin[(5)] 94+
(Mrs L B Normile) *led: rdn bef 2 out: kpt on wl run in: hdd cl home* **33/1**
44-4 **3** 1 1/4 **Ambition Royal (FR)**[25] [1722] 5-11-6 **97** .... PBuchanan[(3)] 99
(Miss Lucinda V Russell) *chsd ldrs: effrt bef 3 out: kpt on u.p fr last* **5/1**[2]
3-12 **4** nk **Baawrah**[35] [1605] 4-10-5 **79** .... ADobbin 81
(M Todhunter) *a cl up: drvn bef 3 out: one pce last* **3/1**[1]
000 **5** 6 **Countrywide Sun**[17] [1797] 3-9-12 **96** oh3 ow5 .... EWhillans[(7)] 76+
(A C Whillans) *prom: effrt bef 3 out: outpcd after next* **10/1**
FP-6 **6** 11 **Allez Mousson**[29] [1671] 7-10-7 **84** ....(p) ACCoyle[(3)] 69
(A Bailey) *blnd 1st: cl up to 4 out: sn lost pl* **10/1**
/306 **7** 9 **Howards Dream (IRE)**[3] [936] 7-10-9 **83** ....(t) RMcGrath 59
(D A Nolan) *bhd: struggling 7th: nvr on terms* **50/1**
6201 **8** 22 **Good Investment**[35] [1605] 3-9-8 **92** ....(p) SWalsh[(7)] 29
(P C Haslam) *cl up tl lost pl after 4 out: btn after next* **3/1**[1]
42-3 **9** 9 **Fearless Foursome**[192] [80] 6-11-7 **95** .... KRenwick 40
(N W Alexander) *hld up: rdn bef 4 out: sn btn* **9/1**
5m 13.3s (0.60) **Going Correction** -0.15s/f (Good)
WFA 3 from 4yo+ 16lb **9** Ran SP% **110.9**
Speed ratings: **92,91,91,91,88 84,80,72,68** CSF £188.35 CT £1391.24 TOTE £7.50: £1.70, £4.10, £1.80; EX 202.70.
Owner S T Brankin **Bred** Micky Hammond Racing Ltd And S Branklin **Trained** Middleham, N Yorks

FOCUS
A moderate novices' handicap, and the form makes enough sense with the third, fourth and fifth to their marks, despite it being run at a steady gallop.

NOTEBOOK
Aston Lad , making his handicap debut in this sphere and fit from a recent spin on the Flat, most gamely defied top weight to break his duck over hurdles at the seventh attempt. He deserves extra credit for making up ground from off the steady pace, had no trouble with the deep ground, and can be rated a touch better than the bare form. *(op 7-1)*
Flaming Heck set the modest tempo from the start and was only denied in the dying strides. He had very much the run of the race in front, but this was an encouraging return to action, and it should tee him up nicely for a return to chasing in due course. *(op 25-1)*
Ambition Royal(FR) had his chance and improved on his recent comeback at Wetherby, appreciating the softer ground. He is a decent benchmark for this form, and this consistent *performer thoroughly deserves to finally find a race this term, but he is fully exposed. (op 11-2 tchd 9-2)*
Baawrah was caught flat-footed when the tempo increased approaching the turn for home and merely kept on at the same pace under pressure in the straight. He is probably happier on less testing ground and should be seen to better effect once more when getting a stronger pace over this trip. *(op 11-4)*
Countrywide Sun *(op 9-1)*
Good Investment , off the mark at Kelso last time when equipped with first-time cheekpieces, proved very disappointing. However, he was beaten by the much softer ground rather than his *recent 8lb weight rise and is not one to write off just yet. Official explanation: jockey said gelding was unsuited by the soft (good to soft places) ground (op 5-2 tchd 10-3)*

2065 FAMOUS GROUSE NOVICES' CHASE (12 fncs) 2m
2:30 (2:30) (Class 3) 4-Y-O+ **£7,603** (£2,360; £1,270)

Form RPR
521- **1** **Monet's Garden (IRE)**[213] [4747] 7-11-3 .... ADobbin 150+
(N G Richards) *j.w: sn chsng ldr: led 5th: drew clr fr 5 out: readily* **2/5**[1]
10-1 **2** 9 **Darkness**[35] [1618] 6-11-9 136 .... BFenton 141+
(C R Egerton) *led to 5th: chsd wnr: hit 7th: no imp fr 5 out: 11l down whn mstke 2 out* **11/4**[2]
5/3- **3** 25 **Kharak (FR)**[394] [1637] 6-11-3 .... MBradburne 115+
(Mrs S C Bradburne) *mstkes: chsd ldrs to 7th: sn wknd* **20/1**[3]
0P/ **F** **Jerom De Vindecy (FR)**[634] [3767] 8-11-0 .... PBuchanan[(3)] —
(Miss Lucinda V Russell) *last but in tch: rdn and effrt after 7th: 5l down and keeping on whn fell next* **66/1**
4m 2.80s (-1.70) **Going Correction** +0.20s/f (Yiel) **4** Ran SP% **104.3**
Speed ratings: **112,107,95,—** CSF £1.75 TOTE £1.20; EX 1.40.

Owner David Wesley Yates **Bred** William Delahunty **Trained** Greystoke, Cumbria

FOCUS

An interesting little novice event, which saw a smart debut performance from the exciting Monet's Garden, who was value for 15 lengths and should rate highly in due course. The runner-up was very close to the form of his debut win and sets the standard of the form.

NOTEBOOK

Monet's Garden(IRE) , rated 157 over hurdles and making his eagerly-awaited chase debut, was foot-perfect throughout and simply came home as he pleased. With the ground to suit, he could hardly have disposed of the useful Darkness any easier, and should be rated value for at least double his winning margin. The only surprise was that connections opted to start him off over the minimum trip, as he stayed very well over timber, and will surely be at more home when upped to a longer trip over fences in the future. It will be fascinating to see where he is pitched in next and he clearly possesses all the right attributes to reach the top as a chaser. *(op 4-11)*

Darkness , off the mark on his chasing bow at Uttoxeter over further last time, was firmly put in his place by the winner and was not that convincing with his jumping this time. However, there was no disgrace in this defeat and he too remains a useful prospect for novice chasing, with the return to a longer trip sure to be of benefit in the future. *(tchd 5-2)*

Kharak(FR) , returning from a 394-day layoff, failed to jump with any fluency and was predictably outclassed. He should come on for this outing, and will find his level in due course, but has yet to really convince he is a natural chaser. *(op 16-1)*

2066 IVECO H'CAP HURDLE (12 hdls) 3m 110y

3:00 (3:00) (Class 4) (0-110,103) 4-Y-0+ **£3,370** (£989; £494; £247)

Form RPR

5001 **1** **Longstone Lass**[11] 1884 5-10-6 **90** ... MissCMetcalfe[(7)] 100+
(Miss Tracy Waggott) *hld up: hdwy to ld 6th: styd on strly fr 3 out* **12/1**

20-P **2** *4* **Strong Resolve (IRE)**[7] 1941 9-11-3 **97** ... PBuchanan[(3)] 99+
(Miss Lucinda V Russell) *a cl up: effrt bef 3 out: one pce after next* **11/4**[1]

-P04 **3** *11* **General Duroc (IRE)**[15] 1838 9-11-0 **98** ...(p) MJMcAlister[(7)] 88
(B Storey) *cl up: rdn fr 8th: outpcd bef 2 out* **14/1**

0402 **4** *½* **Caesar's Palace (GER)**[17] 1796 8-11-4 **95** ...(p) KRenwick 85
(Miss Lucinda V Russell) *cl up: dropped rr 1/2-way: rallied 3 out: no ch w front three* **5/1**[2]

3064 **5** *4* **Speed Kris (FR)**[35] 1606 6-11-12 **103** ...(v) MBradburne 92+
(Mrs S C Bradburne) *hld up: hdwy u.p after 4 out: no imp fr next* **9/1**

0566 **6** *dist* **Old Nosey (IRE)**[35] 1606 9-10-3 **87** ... EWhillans[(7)] —
(B Mactaggart) *in tch: outpcd bef 4 outt: n.d after* **25/1**

0550 **7** *½* **Mr Twins (ARG)**[7] 1940 4-10-1 **85** ...(t) BenOrde-Powlett[(7)] —
(M A Barnes) *midfield: hdwy and cl up 1/2-way: wknd fr 4 out* **33/1**

2P-0 **P** **Cool Dessa Blues**[15] 1839 6-10-1 **81** ow1 ... GBerridge[(3)] —
(W Amos) *a bhd: t.o whn p.u bef 7th* **50/1**

0/P- **P** **Mystic Lord (IRE)**[209] 4808 8-11-8 **102** ... PAspell[(3)] —
(J N R Billinge) *a bhd: t.o whn p.u bef 4 out* **66/1**

P-40 **P** **You'Re The Man (IRE)**[183] 215 8-10-7 **84** ...(p) BHarding —
(Mrs E Slack) *cl up tl wknd 8th: t.o whn p.u bef 3 out* **10/1**

22-2 **P** **Gimme Shelter (IRE)**[192] 80 11-10-2 **79** ... DO'Meara —
(S J Marshall) *led to 6th: lost pl after next: t.o whn p.u bef 4 out* **7/1**

3-31 **P** **Topanberry (IRE)**[150] 693 6-11-11 **102** ... ADobbin —
(N G Richards) *hld up: hdwy and prom 8th: wknd next: t.o whn p.u bef 3 out* **11/2**[3]

6m 20.6s (-11.20) **Going Correction** -0.15s/f (Good) **12** Ran SP% **114.9**
WFA 4 from 5yo+ 14lb
Speed ratings: **111,109,106,106,104** —,—,—,—,— —,— CSF £43.73 CT £477.44 TOTE £14.50: £4.30, £1.80, £3.40; EX 113.40 Trifecta £314.10 Part won. Pool £422.50 - 0.20 winning units..

Owner Miss C Metcalfe **Bred** Miss Kerry Lane **Trained** Spennymoor, Co Durham

FOCUS

A moderate staying handicap, run at a fair pace, and the winner can be rated value for double her winning margin.

NOTEBOOK

Longstone Lass , raised 7lb after resuming winning ways at Sedgefield 11 days previously, maintained her recent progression and ran out a decisive winner. She has been much-improved since joining her current connections and stepping up to this sort of trip, clearly loves soft ground, and should be rated value for double her winning margin. In this mood, she ought to be hard to peg back in her quest for the hat-trick.

Strong Resolve(IRE) , pulled up on his seasonal debut at Carlisle a week previously and well backed for this return to hurdling, never looked like reeling in the winner yet still finished clear of the remainder of his rivals. This was more encouraging and, while he will no doubt have future targets over the larger obstacles, is clearly capable of taking advantage of his much lower rating in this sphere. *(op 7-2 tchd 4-1 in places)*

General Duroc(IRE) posted an improved display on this step back up to a more suitable trip, but continues to perform well below his official rating. He should do better as the season unfolds, and may be worth trying over an even longer trip, as he really is a dour stayer. *(op 12-1)*

Caesar's Palace(GER) , fourth in this event last term off an 11lb higher mark, ran in snatches from halfway and merely plugged on for an identical placing this time around. He clearly has his quirks, but is capable of a fair deal better on his day. *(op 9-2)*

Topanberry(IRE) , last seen winning against her own sex back in June on fast ground, had previous form on this softer ground yet disappointingly failed to make any sort of impression. She was entitled to need this run, but still has a fair bit to prove now all the same. *(op 9-2)*

2067 AYRSHIRE EXTRA H'CAP CHASE (12 fncs) 2m

3:30 (3:33) (Class 3) (0-120,119) 5-Y-0+ **£5,407** (£1,587; £793; £396)

Form RPR

21-2 **1** **Encore Cadoudal (FR)**[185] 193 7-11-6 **113** ... DO'Meara 121+
(H P Hogarth) *in tch: hdwy to ld after 7th: jnd whn lft 4l clr 3 out: j.rt last two: kpt on* **9/4**[1]

-0U0 **2** *1½* **Polyphon (FR)**[30] 1665 7-10-11 **104** ... KRenwick 106
(P Monteith) *hld up: hdwy bef 4 out: lft 4l 2nd next: kpt on fr last* **15/2**

0-P6 **3** *1* **Hollows Mill**[15] 1836 9-10-6 **102** ... GBerridge[(3)] 103
(F P Murtagh) *hld up: hdwy u.p bef 4 out: kpt on run in* **16/1**

00-P **4** *13* **Jericho III (FR)**[9] 1913 8-11-7 **119** ...(e[1]) PCO'Neill[(5)] 117+
(R C Guest) *led: mstke and rdr lost irons 6th: hdd after next: rallied bef 4 out: wknd fr next* **11/1**

-624 **5** *10* **Jefertiti (FR)**[30] 1666 8-10-0 **96** ... PBuchanan[(3)] 79+
(Miss Lucinda V Russell) *chsd ldrs tl rdn and wknd bef 4 out* **11/4**[2]

145- **F** **Do L'Enfant D'Eau (FR)**[218] 4693 6-11-8 **115** ... BHarding —
(B Storey) *in tch: hdwy and ev ch whn fell 3 out* **16/1**

-244 **P** **Jallastep (FR)**[15] 1825 8-10-5 **98** ... ADobbin —
(J S Goldie) *hld up in tch: wknd 7th: t.o whn p.u bef 4 out* **9/2**[3]

4m 5.40s (0.90) **Going Correction** +0.20s/f (Yiel) **7** Ran SP% **107.5**
Speed ratings: **105,104,103,97,92** —,— CSF £16.69 TOTE £2.30: £1.40, £3.30; EX 22.20.

Owner Hogarth Racing **Bred** Pascal Deshayes And Jean-Paul Deshayes **Trained** Stillington, N Yorks

FOCUS

A modest handicap. The winner is value for further then his winning margin and, with the placed horses close to their marks, the form looks sound for the grade.

NOTEBOOK

Encore Cadoudal(FR) ◆ made a triumphant return from a 185-day break, and should be rated value for further, as he looked to be idling when in front late on. Soft ground clearly suits, as does this trip, and he is not yet totally exposed as a chaser, so could well strike again in the coming weeks while his yard remains in decent form. *(op 11-4 tchd 3-1 and 2-1)*

Polyphon(FR) posted a much-improved effort on this return to chasing and was another to enjoy the softer ground. He is on a fair mark at present, but has never been the easiest to predict. *(op 6-1 tchd 8-1)*

Hollows Mill ran his best race for some time on this return to the larger obstacles and was doing all of his best work at the finish. He is back on a reasonable mark at present and, given that three of his previous four career wins have been at Carlisle, will be entitled to respect when returning to that venue in due course. *(tchd 20-1)*

Jericho III(FR), tried in a first-time eye-shield, would have finished a fair deal closer but for his rider losing his irons at a crucial stage. He is better than the bare form and can build on this. *(op 9-1 tchd 12-1)*

Do L'Enfant D'Eau(FR) , who regressed for Phillip Hobbs after breaking his duck over fences at Exeter in January, was still in with every chance prior to departing three from home. This was a very encouraging debut for his new connections, and this former useful hurdler could be fairly treated at present in this sphere, providing his confidence has not been too badly dented by this experience. *(op 12-1 tchd 20-1)*

2068 KERR AND SMITH EBF "JUNIOR" STANDARD OPEN NATIONAL HUNT FLAT RACE 1m 6f

4:00 (4:00) (Class 6) 3-Y-0 **£1,829** (£533; £266)

Form RPR

1 **Programme Girl (IRE)** 3-10-5 ... ADobbin 85+
(G A Swinbank) *prom: led over 2f out: rdn and edgd lft over 1f out: kpt on wl* **3/1**[2]

2 *1¾* **Modicum (USA)** 3-10-5 ... MissRDavidson[(7)] 90+
(N G Richards) *hld up: smooth hdwy and ev ch over 1f out: rdn ent last: kpt on same pce* **6/5**[1]

3 *2½* **Burnt Oak (UAE)** 3-10-12 ... FKeniry 87
(C W Fairhurst) *keen in tch: effrt over 2f out: one pce over 1f out* **14/1**

4 *6* **Asrar** 3-10-2 ... PBuchanan[(3)] 73
(Miss Lucinda V Russell) *chsd ldrs: outpcd over 2f out: n.d after* **20/1**

5 *3½* **Hardknott (IRE)** 3-10-12 ... RMcGrath 76
(R F Fisher) *in tch: outpcd over 2f out: n.d after* **20/1**

6 *nk* **Classy Chav (IRE)** 3-10-12 ... KRenwick 75
(P Monteith) *cl up: led over 3f to over 2f out: sn btn* **7/1**[3]

7 *10* **Lily Tara** 3-10-0 ... DMcGann[(5)] 56
(A M Crow) *set slow pce: hdd over 3f out: wknd over 2f out* **20/1**

8 *11* **Master Pip** 3-10-12 ... BHarding 50
(R F Fisher) *hld up in tch: rdn and wknd fr 3f out* **25/1**

3m 37.4s **Going Correction** 0.0s/f (Good) **8** Ran SP% **107.8**
CSF £5.96 TOTE £3.40: £1.40, £1.10, £3.80; EX 5.60 Place 6 £31.80, Place 5 £28.34..

Owner David C Young **Bred** Patrick Cummins **Trained** Melsonby, N Yorks

FOCUS

Probably just an average junior bumper and the form is very hard to assess. The field finished strung out.

NOTEBOOK

Programme Girl(IRE) , a 7,000euros half-sister to a dual mile winner in Italy, got her career off to a perfect start with a fairly decisive performance. She handled the ground, shaped as though she will get further and has a future. Her next outing should reveal more, however. *(op 11-4 tchd 10-3)*

Modicum(USA) , a 35,000gns purchase whose dam was champion turf mare in the US at five, looked to be going best of all approaching the final furlong, yet failed to find the necessary change of gear when it mattered and was well held by the winner at the finish. He is entitled to improve for the experience, however, and may well turn out to be the best of these in time. *(op 5-4 tchd 11-10)*

Burnt Oak(UAE) , whose dam was a ten-furlong winner on her only outing, rather spoilt his chances of getting home in the soft ground by refusing to settle through the early parts. This was still a fair debut effort, however, and he should improve plenty for this experience. *(op 10-1)*

Asrar , a sister to winning hurdler Critical Stage, lacked the pace to go with the principals when it really mattered and already looks to be in need of two miles. *(tchd 25-1)*

T/Jkpt: £2,797.90 to a £1 stake. Pool: £37,437.50. 9.50 winning tickets. T/Plt: £102.50 to a £1 stake. Pool: £40,050.20. 285.10 winning tickets. T/Qpdt: £58.10 to a £1 stake. Pool: £2,105.00. 26.80 winning tickets. RY

[1749] HEREFORD (R-H)

Sunday, November 6

OFFICIAL GOING: Good to soft

Wind: nil Weather: fine

2069 G G INDUSTRIES LTD JUVENILE NOVICES' HURDLE (8 hdls) 2m 1f

1:10 (1:11) (Class 4) 3-Y-0 **£3,747** (£1,100; £550; £274)

Form RPR

64P2 **1** **First Fought (IRE)**[17] 1797 3-10-7 ...(t) StephenJCraine[(5)] 102+
(D McCain) *hld up: hdwy appr 5th: led appr last: sn clr: r.o wl* **7/2**[2]

2 **2** *7* **Double Spectre (IRE)**[29] 1679 3-10-12 ... DCrosse 90+
(Jean-Rene Auvray) *w ldr: led 2nd: rdn and hdd appr last: sn btn* **7/4**[1]

0545 **3** *1* **Josear**[24] 1729 3-10-12 **95** ... PHide 88
(C J Down) *a.p: ev ch 2 out: sn rdn: one pce* **15/2**

P523 **4** *5* **Time For You**[17] 1802 3-10-5 **85** ... WMarston 76
(J M Bradley) *t.k.h: prom: hit 3rd: wknd appr 2 out* **9/1**

04 **5** *1* **Ghaill Force**[31] 1649 3-10-5 ...(t) RLucey-Butler[(7)] 82
(P Butler) *hld up and bhd: hdwy appr 5th: rdn and wknd after 2 out* **33/1**

6 *3½* **Come What Augustus**[154] 3-10-12 ... JPMcNamara 79
(R M Stronge) *bhd: j.rt 1st: sme hdwy 3 out: nvr trbld ldrs* **25/1**

7 *9* **Cava Bien**[36] 3-10-12 ... ChristianWilliams 70
(B J Llewellyn) *prom tl wknd appr 5th* **7/1**[3]

0 **8** *8* **Winter Coral (FR)**[100] 1095 3-10-5 ...(p) JMogford 55
(Mrs N S Evans) *led to 2nd: chsd ldr to 3 out: sn wknd* **100/1**

9 *9* **Arthurs Dream (IRE)**[23] 3-10-9 ... ONelmes[(3)] 53
(J G M O'Shea) *bhd fr 5th* **16/1**

10 *dist* **Emma Lilley (USA)**[29] 3-10-2 ... TJMalone[(3)] —
(J G M O'Shea) *hit 4th: sn bhd: t.o* **20/1**

11 *nk* **Miss Defying**[189] 3-10-5 ... MFoley —
(R Curtis) *bhd fr 4th: t.o* **100/1**

P **Rockys Girl**[8] 3-10-0 ... RStephens[(5)] —
(R Flint) *a bhd: hit 3rd: sn t.o: p.u bef 2 out* **16/1**

P004 **P** **Keepasharplookout (IRE)**[17] 1802 3-10-12 **85** ... JPByrne —
(C W Moore) *bhd fr 5th: mstke 3 out: t.o whn p.u bef 2 out* **33/1**

4m 11.9s (8.80) **Going Correction** +0.575s/f (Soft) **13** Ran SP% **121.1**
Speed ratings: **102,98,98,95,95 93,89,85,81,**— —,—,— CSF £9.85 TOTE £5.10: £1.10, £1.10, £2.40; EX 13.60.

Owner G & P Barker Ltd/globe Engineering **Bred** Malih Lahij Al Basti **Trained** Cholmondeley, Cheshire

FOCUS

A moderate and uncompetitive juvenile hurdle with the winner rated value for double the winning margin and the fourth and fifth close to their marks.

NOTEBOOK

First Fought(IRE), who showed improved form in a first-time tongue-tie when second at 33/1 in a similar event at Haydock last time, found this slightly easier and got off the mark with plenty in hand. Things will be tougher under a penalty, but he is progressing well. *(op 10-3)*

Double Spectre(IRE), a 67-rated maiden on the Flat, did not really build on the promise he showed when second on his hurdling debut at Chepstow. It remains to be seen which way he will go in the long run. *(op 9-4)*

Josear ran a creditable race in third and seems to be going the right way. He could well pick up a seller, or a race at a similar level. *(op 7-1 tchd 8-1)*

Time For You again fell just short of what was required and is another who may do better in selling company.

Ghaill Force finished up well held but may do better now he is qualified for a handicap mark. *(op 25-1)*

Keepasharplookout(IRE) *Official explanation: trainer said gelding lost a front shoe and did not feel right (op 25-1)*

2070 Q INTERNATIONAL MAIDEN HURDLE (8 hdls) 2m 1f

1:40 (1:42) (Class 4) 4-Y-0+ **£3,864** (£1,134; £567; £283)

Form RPR

1 **Miss Pebbles (IRE)**[20] 5-10-9 .... WHutchinson 111+
(R Dickin) *hld up: hdwy appr 5th: led on bit appr last: comf* **6/1**

33- 2 *5* **Tessanoora**[223] [4608] 4-10-9 .... ATinkler 101
(N J Henderson) *hld up in tch: led after 3 out: rdn and hdd appr last: hit last: one pce* **9/2**[1]

3 *11* **Bauhaus (IRE)**[388] 4-11-2 .... WMarston 97
(R T Phillips) *hld up and bhd: hdwy after 4th: ev ch 2 out: wkng whn hit last* **11/2**[3]

4 *11* **Blue Hills**[19] 4-11-2 .... JAMcCarthy 86
(P W Hiatt) *mid-div: sme hdwy fr 2 out: n.d* **66/1**

5 *3* **Wychbury (USA)**[29] 4-10-11 .... PMerrigan(5) 83
(Mrs H Dalton) *hld up: hdwy after 3 out: wknd after 2 out* **5/1**[2]

3 6 *1* **Absolutelythebest (IRE)**[21] [1750] 4-10-13 .... ONelmes(3) 82
(J G M O'Shea) *hld up in tch: hit 3 out: sn wknd* **5/1**[2]

6502 7 *1 1/4* **The Boobi (IRE)**[21] [1757] 4-10-9 .... JPMcNamara 74
(Miss M E Rowland) *a towards rr* **12/1**

/ 8 *1 3/4* **Orrezzo (GER)**[51] 5-10-9 .... MrRQuinn(7) 79
(G E Jones) *prom to 3 out* **66/1**

3-0 9 *26* **Kayceecee (IRE)**[190] [131] 4-10-11 .... TGreenway(5) 73+
(H D Daly) *t.k.h: hung lft thrght: led: clr 3rd: hdd and rn v wd bnd 3 out: sn lost pl: t.o* **14/1**

10 10 *4* **Ericas Charm**[77] [1274] 5-10-9 .... ChristianWilliams 42
(P Bowen) *a bhd: t.o* **11/1**

11 *17* **Island Light (USA)**[521] 5-11-2 .... SCurran 32
(P Wegmann) *plld hrd: prom tl wknd qckly 4th: t.o* **50/1**

P **Miniperse (FR)**[196] 5-11-2 .... TSiddall —
(G R I Smyly) *a bhd: t.o whn p.u 3 out* **50/1**

0-P0 F **Dreams Jewel**[14] [1849] 5-11-2 .... BJCrowley —
(C Roberts) *bhd whn fell 2nd* **40/1**

P **Our Sion**[204] 5-10-11 .... (t) DLaverty(5) —
(Mrs A M Thorpe) *plld hrd: a bhd: t.o whn p.u bef last* **100/1**

P **Seven Shirt**[32] 4-11-2 .... JMMaguire —
(E G Bevan) *a bhd: nt fluent 1st: t.o whn p.u bef 4th* **100/1**

0 P **Dream On Maggie**[14] [1849] 5-10-9 .... TScudamore —
(P Bowen) *chsd ldr to 3 out: wknd qckly: t.o whn p.u bef 2 out* **33/1**

4m 10.0s (6.90) **Going Correction** +0.575s/f (Soft)
WFA 4 from 5yo 12lb **16** Ran SP% **118.1**
Speed ratings: **106,103,98,93,91 91,90,90,77,75 67,—,—,—,—** — CSF £31.58 TOTE £9.30: £6.70, £1.10, £2.70; EX 49.60.

Owner The Alscot Blue Group **Bred** A Lyons Bloodstock **Trained** Atherstone on Stour, Warwicks

FOCUS

Modest hurdle form, but Miss Pebbles ran out an easy winner, being value for double the official margin, and looks the type to win again.

NOTEBOOK

Miss Pebbles(IRE), a winner up to ten furlongs on the Flat, could not have made a more impressive transition to hurdles and gave a modest field a good thrashing. Always jumping and, as a result, travelling well, she eased clear under a confident Hutchinson and looks sure to take a deal of beating under a penalty. *(tchd 7-1)*

Tessanoora, who shaped well in both her bumpers last season, made a pleasing start to her hurdling career and, although no match for the winner, there was a fair gap back to the third. Her stable is sure to get a win out of her and she will be suited by competing exclusively against her own sex. *(op 7-2)*

Bauhaus(IRE), a fair sort on the Flat in Ireland, had not been seen since winning at Tramore in October 2004 so it is safe to assume this is going to bring him forward fitness wise. He was tired when blundering at the last and is the sort his trainer will do well with. *(op 7-1 tchd 15-2)*

Blue Hills, a regressive sort on the level, is likely to need farther than this in time and he plugged on to claim a remote fourth. He is likely to be capable of better.

Wychbury(USA) progressed well on the Flat this season, but he failed to make an impact on this hurdling debut and stopped as though he might be a non-stayer.

Absolutelythebest(IRE) has always been a quirky individual incapable of performing to a consistent level and this was a step in the wrong direction having made an encouraging hurdling debut at the course last month. *(op 6-1 tchd 13-2)*

2071 JAMES NICHOLAS CONDITIONAL JOCKEYS' (S) HURDLE (10 hdls) 2m 3f 110y

2:10 (2:10) (Class 5) 4-Y-0+ **£2,220** (£647; £323)

Form RPR

PP0P 1 **Dancinginthestreet**[4] [1984] 5-10-12 95.......... RStephens 96+
(J L Flint) *mde all: rdn whn mstke 2 out: drvn out* **16/1**

4363 2 *1 1/2* **Rifleman (IRE)**[45] [1528] 5-10-12 98.......... (t) TGreenway 94
(P Bowen) *hld up in tch: hit 3 out: sn rdn: ev ch last: nt qckn* **15/8**[1]

4604 3 *1 1/2* **Gabor**[3] [2008] 6-11-5 96.......... (b) PMerrigan 99
(D W Thompson) *hld up in mid-div: hdwy appr 3 out: rdn appr last: nt qckn* **7/1**[3]

-602 4 *1* **Noble Calling (FR)**[3] [2008] 8-11-6 104.......... JamesWhite(6) 105
(R J Hodges) *a.p: rdn and one pce fr 2 out* **11/4**[2]

06-P 5 *20* **Peggy's Prince**[123] [913] 7-10-7 82.......... (p) TMessenger(5) 71
(J D Frost) *hld up in tch: rdn and wknd appr last* **20/1**

0-03 6 *26* **Imtihan (IRE)**[10] [1890] 6-12-5 99.......... (v) ONelmes 66
(J G M O'Shea) *hld up: reminders after 4th: bhd fr 7th* **12/1**

2P6/ 7 *dist* **Eastwood Drifter (USA)**[183] 8-10-12 .... (t) TJMalone —
(Miss L Day) *a bhd: t.o fr 7th* **22/1**

2-60 8 *16* **Cybele Eria (FR)**[84] [1218] 8-10-5 90.......... MNicolls —
(John Allen) *prom tl: wknd 7th: t.o* **8/1**

/F-P 9 *19* **Spike Jones (NZ)**[20] [1774] 7-10-12 92.......... DLaverty —
(Mrs A M Thorpe) *s.s: plld hrd in rr: hdwy appr 7th: wknd 3 out: t.o* **12/1**

50P- 10 *1 1/2* **Son Of Man (IRE)**[286] [3518] 6-10-7 80.......... LHeard(5) —
(B D Leavy) *a bhd: t.o fr 7th* **50/1**

5m 1.30s (13.40) **Going Correction** +0.575s/f (Soft) **10** Ran SP% **117.4**
Speed ratings: **96,95,94,94,86 76,—,—,—,—** CSF £47.17 TOTE £8.50: £4.90, £1.02, £2.20; EX 78.80.There was no bid for the winner. Rifleman (no.9) was claimed by Naughty Diesel Ltd for £6,000.

Owner J L Flint **Bred** Palm Tree Thoroughbreds **Trained** Kenfig Hill, Bridgend

FOCUS

A run-of -the-mill seller and a race full of horses who find winning hard. The form looks reasonably sound for the grade rated through those in the frame behind the winner.

NOTEBOOK

Dancinginthestreet, whose recent form over hurdles has been shocking to say the least, was subject to a change of tactics and it brought about a vastly-improved effort. Soon in the lead, he kept finding under pressure and held Rifleman comfortably. He can win again if holding this level of form, but that is a big 'if'. *Official explanation: trainer said, regarding the improved form shown, gelding benefited from being ridden prominently and from the right-handed track*

Rifleman(IRE) has now gone 15 starts over hurdles without a win and he once again found less than had looked likely under pressure. He is bound to find a race one day, but following him until he does could prove expensive. *(op 9-4 tchd 5-2)*

Gabor was able to reverse recent Towcester form with Noble Calling and a slightly more positive ride may have seen him involved in the finish. *(op 13-2 tchd 6-1)*

Noble Calling(FR) was unable to confirm Towcester form with Gabor over this extra distance, but it was not through lack of stamina that he fell short. *(op 3-1 tchd 10-3)*

Peggy's Prince was well adrift of the front three and did not improve for the cheekpieces. *(op 25-1)*

2072 BETFRED.COM NOVICES' CHASE (19 fncs) 3m 1f 110y

2:40 (2:41) (Class 4) 5-Y-0+ **£4,720** (£1,385; £692; £346)

Form RPR

1-0U 1 **Underwriter (USA)**[11] [1888] 5-10-8 105.......... KJMercer(3) 124+
(Ferdy Murphy) *a.p: led 11th: clr fr 15th: unchal* **11/4**[1]

33-5 2 *12* **Superrollercoaster**[182] [236] 5-10-8 105.......... ONelmes(3) 102
(O Sherwood) *led to 8th: lost pl 9th: wnt 2nd appr 3 out: no ch w wnr* **9/2**[3]

0034 3 *30* **Ingres**[22] [1743] 5-10-11 103.......... JPMcNamara 72
(B G Powell) *bhd: mstke 12th: no ch after* **9/2**[3]

04-4 4 *1 3/4* **Jacarado (IRE)**[192] [73] 7-10-12 65.......... (v[1]) WHutchinson 71
(R Dickin) *w ldr: led 8th to 11th: wknd 14th* **33/1**

4313 5 *3 1/2* **Baloo**[11] [1877] 9-10-7 101.......... CHonour(5) 68
(J D Frost) *prom: hit 11th: wknd 13th* **3/1**[2]

3033 P **Combat Drinker (IRE)**[30] [1662] 7-10-12 97.......... (t) JMMaguire —
(D McCain) *hld up: hdwy 11th: chsd wnr 12th tl wknd and p.u bef 3 out* **9/2**[3]

6m 49.2s (15.00) **Going Correction** +0.575s/f (Soft)
WFA 5 from 7yo+ 1lb **6** Ran SP% **109.2**
Speed ratings: **99,95,86,85,84** — CSF £14.53 TOTE £2.00: £1.10, £2.80; EX 19.30.

Owner Mrs Diane O'Rourke **Bred** Derry Meeting Farm & London Thbd Services Ltd **Trained** West Witton, N Yorks

FOCUS

A very uncompetitive novice chase although the winner was value for nearly double the official margin and could rate higher.

NOTEBOOK

Underwriter(USA), a maiden hurdle winner here towards the end of last season, unseated on his chasing debut at Sedgefield but, upped to his furthest trip to date, got round this time and took a moderate event in comfortable fashion. This was an uncompetitive race and he is likely to find things harder under a penalty, but there is always the option of going handicapping. *(tchd 3-1)*

Superrollercoaster, a 105-rated maiden over hurdles, never posted a serious threat on his chasing debut, despite finishing second, and did probably not achieve a great deal. Still, the experience could bring him on. *(op 4-1 tchd 5-1)*

Ingres, a 103-rated hurdler, ran well below that level on his chasing debut. *(op 11-2 tchd 4-1)*

Jacarado(IRE), given another chance over fences in a first-time visor, was well beaten. *(op 28-1)*

Baloo ran no sort of race and his record suggests he needs fast ground to be seen at his best. *(op 9-4)*

Combat Drinker(IRE) did not shape badly on his chasing debut over two and a half miles on fast ground at Carlisle, but he could not build on that faced with conditions he should not have minded, and perhaps something was amiss. *(op 13-2)*

2073 SKYWAYS WORLDWIDE H'CAP HURDLE (13 hdls) 3m 2f

3:10 (3:10) (Class 4) (0-85,90) 4-Y-0+ **£3,461** (£1,016; £508; £253)

Form RPR

-142 1 **Temper Lad (USA)**[102] [1079] 10-10-10 **76**.......... MissSGaisford(7) 82+
(J D Frost) *hld up in mid-div: stdy hdwy 9th: led after 2 out: sn clr* **8/1**[3]

3325 2 *11* **Sundawn Lady**[21] [1751] 7-11-0 **80**.......... (b) MrGTumelty(7) 74
(C P Morlock) *a.p: led 7th to 10th: led 2 out: sn hdd: one pce* **11/1**

P 3 *12* **Kiss The Girls (IRE)**[29] [1671] 6-11-4 **77**.......... AO'Keeffe 63+
(Jennie Candlish) *hld up and bhd: nt fluent 1st: hdwy 7th: nt fluent 8th: led 10th to 3 out: wknd after 2 out* **25/1**

P/26 4 *11* **Zeloso**[6] [1949] 7-11-4 **77**.......... (v) PJBrennan 48
(M F Harris) *bhd tl hdwy 9th: wknd 2 out* **14/1**

00-2 5 *4* **Canavan (IRE)**[11] [1884] 6-11-10 **90**.......... (p) TJDreaper(7) 61+
(Ferdy Murphy) *hld up: mstke 3rd: hdwy 7th: led briefly appr 10th: led 3 out to 2 out: sn wknd* **7/2**[1]

65-3 6 *6* **Strolling Vagabond (IRE)**[14] [1854] 6-11-4 **77**.......... JGoldstein 38
(John R Upson) *hld up and bhd: hdwy appr 8th: wknd appr 10th* **12/1**

PP6- 7 *16* **Star Time (IRE)**[230] [4494] 6-11-6 **79**.......... (v) TScudamore 24
(M Scudamore) *hld up in mid-div: hdwy 5th: wknd 10th* **12/1**

000- 8 *13* **Radnor Lad**[239] [4324] 5-10-10 **74**.......... LStephens(5) 6
(Mrs S M Johnson) *hld up: sn mid-div: lost pl 7th: bhd fr 9th* **33/1**

6-00 9 *11* **Kaid (IRE)**[49] [1486] 10-10-9 **75**.......... MrTCollier(7) —
(R Lee) *mid-div: hmpd 8th: sn bhd* **25/1**

53-P P **Jesnic (IRE)**[163] [532] 5-11-1 **74**.......... WHutchinson —
(R Dickin) *a bhd: t.o whn p.u bef 2 out* **16/1**

00P- P **Baudolino**[32] [3539] 8-11-2 **80**.......... MNicolls(5) —
(R J Price) *prom to 8th: t.o whn p.u bef 2 out* **66/1**

-P40 B **Beyond Borders (USA)**[145] [749] 7-10-13 **79** ow2.....(v) MrDEdwards(7) —
(G F Edwards) *mid-div: rdn whn b.d 8th* **20/1**

24-6 F **Algymo**[187] [167] 5-11-0 **80**.......... (b) WPKavanagh(7) —
(S C Burrough) *hld up in tch: rdn after 7th: fell 8th* **25/1**

-230 P **Rhetorical**[8] [1921] 4-10-12 **78**.......... RLucey-Butler(7) —
(P Butler) *mid-div: lost pl 6th: bhd whn p.u after 9th* **22/1**

/1 P **Mill Bank (IRE)**[25] [1713] 10-11-3 **76**.......... PMoloney —
(Evan Williams) *led to 6th: wknd appr 8th: t.o whn p.u bef 10th* **4/1**[2]

P/00 **P** **Youpeeveecee (IRE)**[9] 1903 9-11-5 **85** JPritchard(7) —
(Miss L V Davis) *hld up: hdwy 7th: hit 8th: wknd appr 10th: p.u after 3 out* **50/1**

122- **P** **Monks Error (IRE)**[495] 834 12-11-12 **85** ChristianWilliams —
(B J Llewellyn) *prom: led 6th to 7th: wknd appr 10th: t.o whn p.u bef 2 out* **10/1**

6m 50.7s (22.70) **Going Correction** +0.575s/f (Soft)
WFA 4 from 5yo+ 14lb **17** Ran SP% **125.7**
Speed ratings: **88,84,80,77,76 74,69,65,62,—** —,—,—,—,— —,— CSF £85.76 CT £2140.26 TOTE £19.70: £1.80, £5.50, £20.40, £7.70; EX 103.60.
Owner Jack Joseph **Bred** Juddmonte Farms **Trained** Scorriton, Devon

FOCUS
A moderate handicap hurdle and a real stamina test, so it is difficult to know what the form is worth.

NOTEBOOK
Temper Lad(USA), returning from a 102-day break off a mark just 3lb higher than when last successful, ran out a clear-cut winner under a well-timed ride. He has rediscovered his form since being stepped up to this sort of trip and should continue to go well. *(op 10-1)*
Sundawn Lady is still a maiden but this represented yet another decent effort, especially considering the winner was probably not too badly handicapped. *(op 10-1)*
Kiss The Girls(IRE), pulled up on his British debut at Bangor, stepped up significantly on that effort and offered plenty of promise in third. This was also an improvement on his Irish form, so there could well be a small race in him.
Zeloso ran creditably upped to his furthest trip to date but failed to truly prove his stamina.
Canavan(IRE), in first-time cheekpieces, failed to run up to the level of form he showed when second at Sedgefield on his reappearance and has to be considered disappointing. *(op 9-2)*
Mill Bank(IRE), 2lb higher than when winning over fences at Uttoxeter on his previous start, ran no *sort of race returned to the smaller obstacles and is yet to prove as effective over hurdles.Official explanation: jockey said gelding hung badly left after 2nd hurdle (op 3-1)*

2074 WEATHERBYS INSURANCE H'CAP CHASE (12 fncs) 2m
3:40 (3:42) (Class 4) (0-100,100) 5-Y-O+ **£4,450** (£1,306; £653; £326)

Form RPR
/U0- **1** **Lindsay (FR)**[230] 4500 6-11-2 **95** TGreenway(5) 116+
(H D Daly) *a.p: led after 4 out: r.o wl fr 2 out* **5/1**[1]

000F **2** *6* **Wages**[17] 1805 5-10-9 **83** ChristianWilliams 96
(Evan Williams) *hld up and bhd: hdwy after 4 out: ev ch 2 out: one pce* **13/2**[3]

5344 **3** *6* **Jupon Vert (FR)**[145] 744 8-11-5 **93** TScudamore 100
(R J Hodges) *hld up: hdwy 4 out: one pce fr 3 out* **11/2**[2]

6PP5 **4** *4* **Auditor**[14] 1855 6-9-13 **78** ow1 MNicolls(5) 81
(S T Lewis) *mid-div: hdwy 8th: rdn after 4 out: no imp* **16/1**

5020 **5** *13* **Pollensa Bay**[25] 1713 6-10-0 **74** oh3 (b) MFoley 74+
(S A Brookshaw) *chsd ldr tl mstke 7th: wknd after 4 out* **14/1**

04P2 **6** *12* **Kaikovra (IRE)**[6] 1956 9-10-12 **86** (v[1]) PJBrennan 64
(M F Harris) *led tl after 4 out: sn wknd: no ch whn mstke last* **5/1**[1]

340P **7** *2 1/2* **Faddad (USA)**[10] 1897 9-10-3 **84** (t) MrsLucyRowsell(7) 60
(Mrs A M Thorpe) *dropped rr and hmpd bnd after 6th: sn lost tch* **25/1**

11P/ **8** *21* **Sam Adamson**[763] 1521 10-11-5 **93** (t) AThornton 48
(J W Mullins) *hld up in tch: short-lived effrt 4 out: t.o* **12/1**

-P25 **F** **Rookery Lad**[11] 1877 7-11-10 **98** DCrosse —
(C N Kellett) *bhd tl fell 5th* **12/1**

F0/5 **P** **Senor Gigo**[19] 1781 7-10-6 **80** PMoloney —
(Evan Williams) *bhd tl p.u bef 4th* **25/1**

4P0- **P** **Kadito**[211] 4780 9-11-4 **92** (v) WHutchinson —
(R Dickin) *bhd fr 8th: blnd 3 out: p.u bef 2 out* **12/1**

23P4 **S** **Gipsy Cricketer**[17] 1805 9-9-5 **75** (t) JKington(10) —
(M Scudamore) *bhd: mstke 5th: slipped up bnd after 6th* **8/1**

UP4- **P** **Moyliscar**[228] 4520 6-10-3 **77** JMMaguire —
(Capt J A George) *hld up in tch: wknd 4 out: bhd whn p.u bef 2 out* **20/1**

4m 10.5s (8.00) **Going Correction** +0.575s/f (Soft) **13** Ran SP% **121.2**
Speed ratings: **103,100,97,95,88 82,81,70,—,—** —,—,— CSF £37.85 CT £186.71 TOTE £6.50: £3.20, £6.20, £1.60; EX 88.50.
Owner John R Wilson **Bred** Rene Ricous And Mrs Ricous **Trained** Stanton Lacy, Shropshire

FOCUS
Moderate handicap form rated through the runner-up, but a race that is unlikely to prove a frequent source of winners.

NOTEBOOK
Lindsay(FR) ◆, who disappointed badly in a course and distance hunter chase when last seen back in March, looked to be starting out handicap life off a reasonable mark and made no mistake, staying on strongly in the final quarter mile to win cosily. His stable is be beginning to get going now, having had a winner earlier in the day at Market Rasen, and this unexposed sort should be capable of winning again. *(op 11-2 tchd 6-1)*
Wages has yet to win in 17 starts over either hurdles or fences, but it is not for the want of trying *that he has yet to get his head in front and on this evidence will find a race eventually. (op 11-2 tchd 7-1)*
Jupon Vert(FR) is a consistent sort, but he is another who finds winning harder than most and he *was forced to settle for a place. He will remain vulnerable to anything less exposed than himself. (op 5-1)*
Auditor has never been the most consistent, but he is still capable of the odd fair effort and he is the type to pop up at a decent price one day. *(op 12-1)*
Pollensa Bay remains winless after 25 attempts and makes little future appeal. *(op 12-1 tchd 20-1)*
Kaikovra(IRE) failed to improve for the first-time visor and this unreliable sort was beaten with half a mile to run. *(op 7-1)*
Senor Gigo *Official explanation: jockey said gelding was knocked into by rival at 2nd fence and he felt something was wrong*

2075 BETFRED.COM STANDARD OPEN NATIONAL HUNT FLAT RACE 2m 1f
4:10 (4:11) (Class 6) 4-6-Y-O **£1,932** (£563; £281)

Form RPR
1- **1** **Rosita Bay**[217] 4720 4-11-1 ONelmes(3) 100+
(O Sherwood) *hld up: smooth hdwy over 6f out: led over 4f out: clr 2f out: comf* **3/1**[2]

0- **2** *12* **Cardinal Sinn (UAE)**[235] 4406 4-11-4 CLlewellyn 88+
(M Pitman) *hld up in tch: wnt 2nd over 2f out: no ch w wnr* **7/1**[3]

3 *4* **Whatcanisay**[190] 6-10-11 MissSGaisford(7) 82
(J D Frost) *hld up in tch: led over 6f out tl over 4f out: one pce fnl 2f* **50/1**

4 *3/4* **Butler Services (IRE)** 5-10-11 MrAJBerry(7) 81
(Jonjo O'Neill) *mid-div: outpcd 5f out: styd on fnl 3f* **9/1**

5 *6* **Khadija** 4-10-4 JPritchard(7) 68
(R Dickin) *led: hdd 9f out: wknd over 3f out* **33/1**

30- **6** *1* **Bright Spirit**[213] 4760 4-11-4 ATinkler 77+
(N J Henderson) *hld up in tch: rdn over 4f out: wknd over 1f out* **11/10**[1]

7 *dist* **Another Flint (IRE)** 5-10-11 MrJETudor(7) —
(R Flint) *w ldr: led 9f out tl over 6f out: wknd 4f out: t.o* **20/1**

0/ **8** *19* **Barfleur (IRE)**[570] 4846 5-10-11 ChristianWilliams —
(P Bowen) *prom tl wknd over 7f out: t.o* **14/1**

9 *3* **Mo Chailin** 6-10-11 TScudamore —
(P Bowen) *a bhd: t.o* **25/1**

0 **10** *9* **Dark Rosalina**[17] 1799 4-10-11 JPByrne —
(C W Moore) *bhd fnl 5f: t.o* **50/1**

11 *27* **Desertmore King (IRE)**[189] 5-10-11 RSpate(7) —
(J A Danahar) *a bhd: t.o* **100/1**

00/ **12** *shd* **Valderrama**[575] 4739 5-11-4 PHide —
(C J Down) *plld hrd early: a bhd: t.o* **66/1**

4m 10.3s (9.20) **Going Correction** +0.575s/f (Soft) **12** Ran SP% **119.7**
Speed ratings: **101,95,93,93,90 89,—,—,—,—** —,— CSF £23.18 TOTE £5.60: £2.00, £3.20, £12.70; EX 34.00 Place 6 £54.98, Place 5 £41.17..
Owner R Waters **Bred** G R Waters **Trained** Upper Lambourn, Berks

FOCUS
Ordinary bumper form, but an impressive performance by Rosita Bay and the race should still produce the odd winner.

NOTEBOOK
Rosita Bay, successful on her debut at Market Rasen back in April, has clearly progressed in the interim and impressed with the style in which she cleared away to win here. With hot favourite Bright Spirit disappointing it is debatable what the form is worth, but she is going to stay further over hurdles and should rack up a sequence in mares-only company. *(op 7-2 tchd 4-1)*
Cardinal Sinn(UAE), whose stable have started the season at a high tempo, made smooth headway to chase the leader before the turn-in, but he was left trailing as she sprinted clear and *was simply outclassed. This represented a step up and he can probably find a race in this sphere. (op 7-2)*
Whatcanisay, who enjoyed little success in two point-to-point outings, plugged on for a *well-beaten third and will not be winning until contesting two and a half miles over hurdles. (op 25-1)*
Butler Services(IRE), whose stable has started the season positively, kept on into fourth without being given an overly hard time and could have finished closer had his pilot got a bit more serious. He will stay further over hurdles, but can probably win in this sphere. *(op 8-1)*
Khadija took them along early, but was struggling as the pace quickened and she is unlikely to be winning until contesting low-grade hurdles. *(op 40-1)*
Bright Spirit, beaten favourite on both his outings last term, was again short in the betting for this reappearance and once again he failed to deliver. He was toiling with half a mile to run and looks one to avoid. *(op 13-8 tchd Evens)*
T/Plt: £72.50 to a £1 stake. Pool: £46,983.50. 472.45 winning tickets. T/Qpdt: £33.60 to a £1 stake. Pool: £2,803.80. 61.60 winning tickets. KH

1756 MARKET RASEN (R-H)
Sunday, November 6

OFFICIAL GOING: Heavy
After 12mm of rain over the previous five days, 5mm before racing turned the ground heavy. Hurdles had been moved inside, third-last fence omitted all chases.
Wind: moderate, half-against Weather: Heavy rain for the first race but drying up though breezy and on the cold side.

2076 BOOK ONLINE @MARKETRASENRACES.CO.UK JUVENILE NOVICES' HURDLE (8 hdls) 2m 1f 110y
12:50 (12:53) (Class 4) 3-Y-O **£3,575** (£1,049; £524; £262)

Form RPR
00 **1** **Ivana Illyich (IRE)**[17] 1797 3-10-5 ARoss 81
(J S Wainwright) *chsd ldrs: 4th whn hit 3 out: wnt 2nd appr next: styd on to ld last 50yds* **12/1**

P **2** *1 1/4* **Crimson Bow (GER)**[43] 1551 3-10-2 (b[1]) LVickers(3) 91+
(J G Given) *led: 2l up whn hit last: hdd towards fin* **50/1**

3 *2* **Lane Marshal**[19] 3-10-5 PJMcDonald(7) 85
(M E Sowersby) *sn in rr: hdwy 3 out: 5th next: styd on wl run-in: nt rch 1st 2* **80/1**

5P **4** *3* **Eborarry (IRE)**[25] 1718 3-10-12 RGarritty 82
(T D Easterby) *hdwy to chse ldrs 4th: rdn appr 2 out: kpt on same pce* **14/1**

0 **5** *5* **Esquillon**[17] 1797 3-10-5 NFehily 74+
(J A Glover) *chsd ldr: reminders 5th: 4th and wkng whn hit last: eased* **10/1**

0P4 **6** *18* **Hamburg Springer (IRE)**[9] 1904 3-10-12 (t) SThomas 59
(M J Polglase) *chsd ldrs: mstke and lost pl 4th: no ch after* **9/1**

7 *2* **Rockpiler**[61] 3-10-5 BSHughes(7) 57
(J Howard Johnson) *trckd ldrs: wknd qckly and eased appr 2 out* **20/1**

0 **8** *1 1/2* **Queen Nefitari**[3] 2001 3-10-3 ow1 MrTGreenall(3) 49
(M W Easterby) *in rr: bhd fr 5th* **40/1**

9 *shd* **Lobengula (IRE)**[120] 3-10-12 PWhelan 55
(I W McInnes) *chsd ldrs: lost pl appr 2 out* **10/1**

10 *dist* **Double Ells** 3-10-5 GLee —
(J M Jefferson) *in raer: t.o 2 out: btn 34l* **11/2**[3]

30C **P** **Fu Manchu**[9] 1904 3-10-12 APMcCoy —
(Jonjo O'Neill) *mid-div: rdn and no rspnse 5th: t.o whn p.u bef 2 out* **5/1**[2]

P **Wolf Hammer (USA)**[100] 3-10-12 (b[1]) ADempsey —
(J Howard Johnson) *stdd s: bhd and reminders 5th: t.o whn p.u bef 2 out* **20/1**

U **Purple Dancer (FR)**[52] 3-10-7 DCCostello(5) —
(G A Swinbank) *hld up: sme hdwy 5th: rdn and lost pl after next: bhd whn hit 2 out and uns rdr* **5/2**[1]

4m 32.9s (16.50) **Going Correction** +1.10s/f (Heav) **13** Ran SP% **118.3**
Speed ratings: **107,106,105,104,102 94,93,92,92,—** —,—,— CSF £501.71 TOTE £19.70: £3.50, £20.40, £20.50; EX 1267.30.
Owner Hurn Racing Club **Bred** Gerald Morrin **Trained** Kennythorpe, N Yorks
■ Stewards' Enquiry : L Vickers one-day ban: anticipating start (Nov 17)
B S Hughes one-day ban: anticipating start (Nov 17)

FOCUS
Yet another weak juvenile hurdle which is unlikely to throw up too many future winners outside selling or claiming company.

NOTEBOOK
Ivana Illyich(IRE), a maiden after 22 starts on the Flat, stepped up on her two previous efforts over hurdles but the form probably amounts to very little. *(op 11-1)*
Crimson Bow(GER), who showed little in five outings on the Flat, wore blinkers on her second start over hurdles having being pulled up first time. Holding the upper hand when clouting the last, she could not quite last home.
Lane Marshal, unplaced in 14 starts over various distances on the level, has changed stables. He stuck on really strongly and was closing the first two down at the line. *(op 66-1)*
Eborarry(IRE), who at least broke his duck on the Flat, was having his third start over hurdles and may be capable of a bit better on less testing ground. *(op 20-1)*

Esquillon tried to take on the leader but would not have a cut at her hurdles and she was out on her feet when flattening the final flight. *(op 14-1)*
Fu Manchu found nothing when rousted along and was afterwards reported to have a breathing problem. *Official explanation: jockey said gelding had a breathing problem (op 4-1)*
Purple Dancer(FR), edgy beforehand, was given a patient ride but he emptied in a matter of strides and was well in arrears when losing his rider, the video will definitely not feature in his rider's video library! *(op 4-1)*

2077 BRUCE AND JOE CARR MEMORIAL TROPHY H'CAP CHASE (14 fncs 3 omitted) 3m 1f
1:20 (1:23) (Class 4) (0-110,109) 5-Y-0+ **£3,705** (£1,087; £543; £271)

Form				RPR
66-2	**1**		**Moustique De L'Isle (FR)**[35] [1609] 5-11-2 **100** NFehily (C C Bealby) *chsd ldrs: reminders and lost pl 10th: rallied 2 out: 4th last: styd on wl to ld towards fin* **5/2**[1]	104
650B	**2**	½	**Tribal Dancer (IRE)**[14] [1848] 11-10-8 **91** SThomas (Miss Venetia Williams) *led: hdd nr fin* **7/2**[3]	96
212-	**3**	3½	**Tom Fruit**[203] [4876] 8-11-12 **109** RGarritty (T D Easterby) *hld up: wnt prom 8th: chalng whn hit last: kpt on same pce* **3/1**[2]	112+
1-P	**4**	½	**Good Judgement (IRE)**[8] [1928] 7-11-8 **105** APMcCoy (Jonjo O'Neill) *nt fluent: wnt prom 8th: hrd drvn 3 out: one pce between last 2* **17/2**	107+
P/4-	**5**	3½	**Major Benefit (IRE)**[378] [1826] 8-11-12 **109** ARoss (Mrs K Waldron) *chsd ldr: hrd drvn 3 out: one pce* **7/1**	107+
3020	**P**		**Golly (IRE)**[14] [1856] 9-11-4 **101** GLee (D L Williams) *wnt prom 8th: wknd 3 out: bhd whn p.u bef next* **11/1**	—
303P	**P**		**John Rich**[98] [1110] 9-9-7 **83** oh13 (tp) PJMcDonald[(7)] (M E Sowersby) *wnt prom 8th: wknd 3 out: bhd whn p.u bef next* **16/1**	—

6m 57.3s (19.90) **Going Correction** +1.10s/f (Heav)
WFA 5 from 7yo+ 1lb **7 Ran SP% 113.0**
Speed ratings: **112,111,110,110,109** —,— CSF £11.80 CT £25.92 TOTE £3.00: £1.70, £2.50; EX 16.30.
Owner Michael Hill **Bred** Philippe Sayet **Trained** Barrowby, Lincs

FOCUS
The complexion of the race changed dramatically late on and the winner was matched at 999-1 when looking a lost cause on the turn for home. The form is rated through the winner but looks dubious.

NOTEBOOK
Moustique De L'Isle(FR) looked in trouble when under pressure early on the final circuit. His stamina eventually came into play and, from what looked a hopeless position, he put his head in front where it really matters. Only five, he should make a nice staying chaser in time. *(op 2-1)*
Tribal Dancer(IRE), overdue a change of luck, looked to have it in the bag when jumping the last much better than his challenger only to miss out near the line. *(op 11-2)*
Tom Fruit, a big fellow, likes soft ground but, after looking a serious threat, he was just getting the worst of the argument when missing out the final fence. This should have put him spot on. *(op 4-1)*
Good Judgement(IRE) jumped better than on his chasing debut at Wetherby but he still does not look a natural. He worked hard to enter the argument but was going up and down on the spot between the last two fences. *(op 4-1)*
Major Benefit(IRE), having just his second outing in a year and a half and absent for 12 months, was far from disgraced but clearly has his problems. *(op 10-1 tchd 12-1 and 16-1 in places)*

2078 RACING UK ON CHANNEL 432 NOVICES' CHASE (12 fncs 2 omitted) 2m 4f
1:50 (1:55) (Class 3) 4-Y-0+ **£5,838** (£1,812; £975)

Form				RPR
221-	**1**		**Von Origny (FR)**[218] [4685] 4-10-7 118 RJohnson (H D Daly) *trckd ldrs: led 4th: j.lft last 2: shkn up and r.o strly run-in: readily* **11/10**[1]	121+
544-	**2**	3	**Nadover (FR)**[223] [4616] 4-10-7 113 NFehily (C J Mann) *trckd ldrs: wnt 2nd after 3 out: chal next: no ex run-in* **3/1**[3]	114
30-P	**3**	dist	**Jonny's Kick**[8] [1928] 5-11-6 97 RGarritty (T D Easterby) *chsd ldrs: drvn along 9th: lost pl and lft mod 3rd appr 2 out: bhd whn eased run-in: t.o: btn 54l* **20/1**	—
F31-	**P**		**Blairgowrie (IRE)**[215] [4735] 6-11-6 120 GLee (J Howard Johnson) *led: hit 2nd: hdd 4th: mstke 8th: rdn: lost pl and p.u bef 2 out* **5/2**[2]	—

5m 22.1s (19.40) **Going Correction** +1.10s/f (Heav)
WFA 4 from 5yo+ 13lb **4 Ran SP% 106.0**
Speed ratings: **105,103**,—,— CSF £4.58 TOTE £1.80; EX 5.50.
Owner E R Hanbury **Bred** Bruno Matt **Trained** Stanton Lacy, Shropshire

FOCUS
A pleasing debut over fences for Von Origny, who has the make and shape of a chaser, and a sound first try over the major obstacles by the runner-up. The race could be rated a fair bit higher.

NOTEBOOK
Von Origny(FR) ◆, a rugged type, jumped soundly and was clever putting himself right over the *final two fences. He scored with real authority and should climb several rungs up the chase ladder. (op 6-5 tchd Evens)*
Nadover(FR), rated 5lb inferior to the winner over hurdles, travelled almost as well and looked a *real threat but in the end was very much second best. He thoroughly deserves to go one better. (tchd 10-3)*
Jonny's Kick, pulled up on his chasing debut a week earlier, tired badly going to two out and eventually completed in his own time. He ought to be capable of better. *(op 12-1)*
Blairgowrie(IRE), quite a big-type, is rated 2lb ahead of the winner over hurdles. He hit the first ditch in the back straight on each circuit and, stopping to nothing in a matter of strides, was wisely not asked to jump two out. He cantered back none the worse and can surely put this reverse behind him. *(tchd 9-4 in places)*

2079 MARKET RASEN TATTERSALLS & RAILS BOOKMAKERS H'CAP HURDLE (10 hdls) 2m 3f 110y
2:20 (2:23) (Class 3) (0-125,124) 4-Y-0+ **£4,892** (£1,436; £718; £358)

Form				RPR
2-32	**1**		**Nathos (GER)**[21] [1760] 8-11-6 **118** NFehily (C J Mann) *trckd ldrs: led 7th: 5 l up 2 out: j.lft last: styd on strly: eased nr fin* **11/4**[2]	125+
3-61	**2**	6	**Wild Is The Wind (FR)**[7] [1940] 4-11-5 **117** 7ex APMcCoy (Jonjo O'Neill) *hld up wl in tch: wnt 2nd after 3 out: effrt appr 2 out: no imp* **1/1**[1]	117+
1-2U	**3**	5	**Cottam Grange**[21] [1760] 5-11-0 **115** MrTGreenall[(3)] (M W Easterby) *trckd ldrs: wnt 3rd 2 out: kpt on same pce* **11/1**	109
4163	**4**	½	**Karathaena (IRE)**[9] [1912] 5-10-9 **112** DCCostello[(5)] (M E Sowersby) *hld up in tch: effrt 7th: one pce fr next* **14/1**	106
21-0	**5**	5	**Arrayou (FR)**[29] [1677] 4-11-12 **124** (b) LAspell (O Sherwood) *trckd ldrs: hrd drvn 3 out: one pce* **8/1**[3]	114+
6B44	**6**	5	**Siegfrieds Night (IRE)**[16] [1816] 4-10-0 **98** (t) KJohnson (M C Chapman) *led to 1st: drvn along and outpcd 3 out: no threat after* **18/1**	82
-0PP	**7**	dist	**Friedhelmo (GER)**[21] [1760] 9-9-9 **100** (t) BSHughes[(7)] (S B Clark) *led 1st: t.k.h: hdd 7th: sn lost pl: t.o 2 out* **33/1**	—

5m 11.6s (21.60) **Going Correction** +1.10s/f (Heav) **7 Ran SP% 111.0**
Speed ratings: **100,97,95,95,93 91**,— CSF £5.71 CT £20.57 TOTE £4.30: £1.90, £1.40; EX 5.70.
Owner J Davies, A Merritt & J Sunley **Bred** H -P Kremer And S Rustler **Trained** Upper Lambourn, Berks

FOCUS
They stood still for five seconds when the tapes went up resulting in a moderate time. The runner-up was not the same horse seen at Carlisle but the winner deserves full marks.

NOTEBOOK
Nathos(GER), suited by going right-handed, stuck on strongly and had this won two out. He was *value for ten lengths and now may be the time for him to go back over fences. (op 5-1 tchd 11-2 in a place)*
Wild Is The Wind(FR) went in pursuit of the winner but in truth was never going to prove a match. This may have come too soon for him after Carlisle. *(op 11-10 tchd 10-11, 6-5 in a place)*
Cottam Grange is still 17lb higher than for his sole hurdle-race success. *(op 10-1)*
Karathaena(IRE), who likes it round this track, was 8lb higher than for her win here and she does not appreciate conditions as testing as this. *(op 10-1)*
Arrayou(FR) ran better than on his return but he still looks plenty high enough in the weights. *(op 5-1)*

2080 RON WALL MEMORIAL H'CAP CHASE (12 fncs 2 omitted) 2m 4f
2:50 (2:52) (Class 4) (0-100,98) 4-Y-0+ **£3,172** (£924; £462)

Form				RPR
0042	**1**		**Avadi (IRE)**[3] [2011] 7-10-6 **78** TDoyle (P T Dalton) *chsd ldrs: wnt 3rd after 3 out: led next: drvn clr run-in* **7/4**[1]	91
U6P-	**2**	6	**Extra Cache (NZ)**[197] [4977] 12-10-0 **72** oh4 JEMoore (O Brennan) *trckd ldrs: led after 9th: hdd 2 out: nt qckn run-in* **5/1**[3]	80+
1310	**3**	13	**Lanmire Tower (IRE)**[35] [1615] 11-10-11 **88** (p) WKennedy[(5)] (S Gollings) *in tch: outpcd 7th: wnt 2nd after 9th: wknd appr 2 out: j.rt last* **8/1**	86+
4U3-	**4**	22	**Polish Pilot (IRE)**[238] [4343] 10-10-0 **79** ow1 APogson[(7)] (J R Cornwall) *prom: outpcd 3 out: sn bhd* **17/2**	51
0P50	**5**	12	**Cromwell (IRE)**[42] [1564] 10-10-0 **72** oh13 (b) KJohnson (M C Chapman) *led: qcknd 7th: hdd after 9th: sn lost pl: t.o 2 out* **14/1**	32
4PP3	**P**		**Step In Line (IRE)**[16] [1819] 13-9-9 **72** oh6 DCCostello[(5)] (D W Thompson) *chsd ldrs: lost pl after 9th: sn t.o: p.u bef 2 out* **16/1**	—
0450	**P**		**Barneys Reflection**[90] [1176] 5-10-2 **74** (v) GLee (A Crook) *prom: outpcd whn stmbld landing 8th: lost pl after next: t.o 3 out: p.u bef next* **4/1**[2]	—

5m 30.8s (28.10) **Going Correction** +1.10s/f (Heav) **7 Ran SP% 107.2**
Speed ratings: **87,84,79,70,65** —,— CSF £9.72 CT £43.51 TOTE £2.30: £1.40, £2.40; EX 11.30.
Owner Mrs Julie Martin **Bred** E J O'Grady **Trained** Bretby, Derbys

FOCUS
The winner's stamina eventually carried the day but in truth this did not take that much winning.

NOTEBOOK
Avadi(IRE), running from a 4lb lower mark, made very hard work of it but in the end his stamina carried the day.
Extra Cache(NZ), 4lb out of the handicap, has slid to a lenient mark and came in for support. He went on travelling marginally easier but in the end the winner saw it out much the better. At least this proves he is no back number. *(op 11-2 tchd 6-1)*
Lanmire Tower(IRE) likes it here but the ground had turned against him. *(op 5-1)*
Polish Pilot(IRE), absent since March, is unproven over this trip and the conditions were too testing for him. The outing though will not be lost on him. *(op 11-1)*
Barneys Reflection, 16lb lower than his last success, was struggling when tripping on landing at the first ditch down the back. He looks basically out of sorts. *(tchd 7-2)*

2081 CIRCUS SUNDAY NOVICES' HURDLE (DIV I) (10 hdls) 2m 3f 110y
3:20 (3:22) (Class 4) 4-Y-0+ **£3,142** (£922; £461; £230)

Form				RPR
02	**1**		**Lyes Green**[14] [1859] 4-10-12 LAspell (O Sherwood) *trckd ldrs: styd on appr 2 out: wnt 2nd sn after last: led last 150yds: sn clr* **13/8**[1]	99+
0-5F	**2**	6	**Imperial Royale (IRE)**[29] [1671] 4-10-2 84 TBurrows[(10)] (P L Clinton) *led: qcknd 6th: 5l clr last: hdd and no ex run-in* **33/1**	92
302-	**3**	3	**Coach Lane**[283] [3554] 4-10-12 110 SThomas (Miss Venetia Williams) *trckd ldrs: wnt clr 2nd after 3 out: rdn appr next: kpt on same pce* **2/1**[2]	89
000-	**4**	13	**Perfect Balance (IRE)**[27] [2679] 4-10-7 DCCostello[(5)] (D W Thompson) *chsd ldrs: outpcd 3 out: n.d after* **14/1**	77+
6PP4	**5**	10	**Maria Bonita (IRE)**[49] [1491] 4-10-5 JamesDavies (C N Kellett) *hld up: hdwy to chse ldrs 7th: wknd appr 2 out* **33/1**	59
4-PP	**6**	5	**Iloveturtle (IRE)**[9] [1910] 5-10-12 95 (t) KJohnson (M C Chapman) *hld up detached in last: sme hdwy appr 2 out: nvr a factor* **16/1**	61
0	**7**	1½	**Secret Jewel (FR)**[14] [1850] 5-10-5 PWhelan (Miss C J E Caroe) *in tch: lost pl after 3 out* **66/1**	53
	8	9	**Vrisaki (IRE)**[36] 4-10-12 ADempsey (M E Sowersby) *in rr: bhd fr 7th* **66/1**	51
	9	8	**True To Yourself (USA)**[26] 4-10-9 LVickers[(3)] (J G Given) *nt fluent: chsd ldrs: lost pl after 3 out* **11/1**	43
P-P	**10**	10	**Back De Bay (IRE)**[21] [1757] 5-10-5 APogson[(7)] (J R Cornwall) *bhd fr 6th* **100/1**	33
6	**11**	7	**Majorca**[45] [1527] 4-10-12 GLee (J Howard Johnson) *trckd ldrs: lost pl after 3 out* **9/1**[3]	26
00	**12**	19	**Southern Bazaar (USA)**[21] [1757] 4-10-9 MrTGreenall[(3)] (M E Sowersby) *hld up in rr: hdwy 6th: lost pl after next: sn bhd* **100/1**	—

5m 15.7s (25.70) **Going Correction** +1.10s/f (Heav)
WFA 4 from 5yo 12lb **12 Ran SP% 113.2**
Speed ratings: **92,89,88,83,79 77,76,73,69,65 63,55** CSF £60.92 TOTE £2.40: £1.10, £7.20, £1.10; EX 62.00.
Owner Absolute Solvents Ltd **Bred** P K Gardner **Trained** Upper Lambourn, Berks

FOCUS
A very steady gallop, much the slower division. The form looks dubious rated through the fourth.

NOTEBOOK
Lyes Green, who is not that big, seemed to be held together on the final turn and as a result was matched at 44. Set alight on the run-in, in the end he won going right away and it seems the further he goes the better he is. *(op 6-4 tchd 7-4)*
Imperial Royale(IRE), whose win on the level came in banded company, tried to steal it from the front but, after looking to have done so, he was mowed down by the strong-finishing winner late on the run-in.

The Form Book, Raceform Ltd, Compton, RG20 6NL

Coach Lane, who looked very fit, is proving very expensive to follow over hurdles and certainly did not improve for the step up in trip. *(op 9-4 tchd 15-8)*
Perfect Balance(IRE), in better form of late on the Flat, ran better but he still came up a long way short. *(op 16-1)*

2082 CIRCUS SUNDAY NOVICES' HURDLE (DIV II) (10 hdls) 2m 3f 110y
3:50 (3:52) (Class 4) 4-Y-0+ **£3,142** (£922; £461; £230)

Form	Pos	Dist	Horse	Jockey	RPR
023/	1		**Hoh Viss**[626] 3894 5-10-12	NFehily	116+
			(C J Mann) *hld up in rr: stdy hdwy 6th: jnd ldrs 3 out: led appr next: sn hdd: led last: edgd lft and drvn clr* **8/1**		
210-	2	5	**Lennon (IRE)**[235] 4399 5-10-12	GLee	111+
			(J Howard Johnson) *trckd ldrs: t.k.h: slt ld appr 2 out: hdd last and no ex* **10/11**[1]		
1243	3	15	**Youlbesolucky (IRE)**[10] 1892 6-10-12	RJohnson	96
			(Jonjo O'Neill) *t.k.h in tch: jnd ldrs 3 out: wl outpcd appr next* **13/2**[3]		
	4	18	**Key In**[141] 4-10-2	(t) LVickers(3)	71
			(I W McInnes) *w ldrs: led after 7th: hdd & wknd appr 2 out* **66/1**		
6/60	5	dist	**Europrime Games**[8] 1927 7-10-12	ADempsey	—
			(M E Sowersby) *led to 3rd: rdn and lost pl 3 out: t.o: btn 44l* **50/1**		
5-00	6	dist	**New Wish (IRE)**[21] 1757 5-10-5	BSHughes(7)	—
			(S B Clark) *tk fierce hold in rr: bhd fr 7th: t.o: btn 44l* **100/1**		
0	7	3	**Shinko Femme (IRE)**[8] 1927 4-10-0	DCCostello(5)	—
			(M E Sowersby) *prom: lost pl after 7th: sn bhd: t.o* **66/1**		
0-0	P		**Just Filly (IRE)**[14] 1851 4-10-5	PWhelan	—
			(Miss C J E Caroe) *in rr: bhd fr 6th: t.o whn p.u bef 3 out* **150/1**		
-U0U	P		**Government (IRE)**[9] 1911 4-10-12 69	KJohnson	—
			(M C Chapman) *in rr: reminders 5th: sn bhd: t.o whn p.u bef 3 out* **200/1**		
005	P		**Land Sun's Legacy (IRE)**[21] 1757 4-10-12 79	(p) ARoss	—
			(J S Wainwright) *prom: rdn and lost pl 7th: t.o whn p.u bef 2 out* **66/1**		
00-0	P		**Create A Storm (IRE)**[17] 1799 5-10-5	JTizzard	—
			(J G Portman) *w ldrs: led 3rd tl after 7th: sn lost pl: t.o whn p.u bef 2 out* **33/1**		
/0-P	P		**Getaway Girl**[71] 1340 7-10-5	JEMoore	—
			(O Brennan) *chsd ldrs: reminders and lost pl 5th: sn bhd: t.o whn p.u after 3 out* **100/1**		
	P		**High Charter**[27] 4-10-12	APMcCoy	—
			(J R Fanshawe) *trckd ldrs: chal 3 out: wknd rapidly appr next: poor 5th whn p.u between last 2* **10/3**[2]		

5m 7.50s (17.50) **Going Correction** +1.10s/f (Heav) **45** Ran SP% **112.4**
WFA 4 from 5yo+ 12lb
Speed ratings: **109,107,101,93,**— —,—,—,—,— —,—,— CSF £15.31 TOTE £9.40: £1.80, £1.10, £1.70; EX 23.60 Place 6 £96.47, Place 5 £3.74..
Owner D F Allport **Bred** D F Allport **Trained** Upper Lambourn, Berks

FOCUS
Much the faster division and both the first two may be capable of building on this.

NOTEBOOK
Hoh Viss, absent for a year and a half, dug deep and in the end won going away. He should be able to build on this.
Lennon(IRE), a useful bumper horse, really took the eye in the paddock. He edged head travelling the better but in the end the winner saw the trip out much the better. His trainer's jumpers are still not exactly firing and he will leave this behind in due course. *(op Evens tchd 11-10 in places)*
Youlbesolucky(IRE), a tall-type, has yet to reproduce his bumper form over hurdles. The testing conditions may not have played to his strengths. *(op 5-1)*
Key In, who has changed stables, is a longstanding maiden on the level. *(op 50-1)*
Just Filly(IRE) *Official explanation: jockey said filly was unsuited by the heavy ground (op 80-1)*
High Charter looked exceptionally well and travelled strongly but he stopped to nothing on the turn *for home and was well in arrears when calling it a day. The ground was much too testing for him. Official explanation: jockey said gelding was unsuited by the heavy ground (op 80-1)*
T/Plt: £132.90 to a £1 stake. Pool: £39,712.05. 218.10 winning tickets. T/Qpdt: £2.70 to a £1 stake. Pool: £4,187.20. 1,111.90 winning tickets. WG

2084 - (Foreign Racing) - See Raceform Interactive

2059 AUTEUIL (L-H)
Sunday, November 6

OFFICIAL GOING: Very soft

2085a PRIX CAMBACERES (GRANDE COURSE DE HAIES DES 3ANS) (HURDLE) (GROUP 1) 2m 2f
2:20 (2:25) 3-Y-O
£79,787 (£39,007; £23,050; £15,957; £8,865; £6,206)

Pos	Dist	Horse	Jockey	RPR
1		**Tidal Fury (IRE)**[28] 1705 3-10-3	DGallagher	123
		(J Jay) *made all, comfortably (6/5F)* **6/5**[1]		
2	6	**Card'Son (FR)**[39] 3-10-3	CPieux	117
		(B Secly, France)		
3	2 ½	**Chiaro (FR)**[28] 1705 3-10-3	(b) FEstrampes	114
		(J-L Pelletan, France) **29/1**[2]		
4	2 ½	**Hairball**[28] 3-10-3	RegisSchmidlin	112
		(B Secly, France)		
5	½	**Etoile Des Iles (FR)**[28] 1705 3-9-13	LGerard	107
		(M Nigge, France)		
6	1 ½	**Gold Heart (FR)**[28] 1705 3-10-3	JacquesRicou	110
		(G Macaire, France)		
7	10	**Turange (FR)**[15] 3-10-3	TMajorcryk	100
		(J-P Gallorini, France)		
8	6	**Sastar (FR)**[32] 3-10-3	CGombeau	94
		(B Barbier, France)		
9	dist	**Santarco (FR)**[22] 3-10-3	DJolibert	—
		(P Demercastel, France)		
P		**Orest (FR)**[52] 3-10-3	SBeaumard	—
		(F-M Cottin, France)		

4m 21.0s **10** Ran SP% **48.8**
PARI-MUTUEL: WIN 2.20; PL 1.30, 2.00, 3.20; DF 10.00.
Owner Twelfth Night **Bred** Robert De Vere Hunt **Trained** Newmarket, Suffolk

NOTEBOOK
Tidal Fury(IRE) never saw another horse and his easy victory completed one of the fairytales of 2005. Sent to France, where three-year-olds can begin hurdling so much earlier, only because an aversion to starting stalls meant that he was banned from running on the Flat, he has now won almost £186,000 in five Auteuil starts. The track clearly suits him and, given that he was most disappointing on his only British start over timber, it is no surprise that he will now be given a break before contesting the top Auteuil races in the spring.

1937 CARLISLE (R-H)
Monday, November 7
2087 Meeting Abandoned - Waterlogged

1890 STRATFORD (L-H)
Monday, November 7
2093 Meeting Abandoned - Waterlogged

1987 HUNTINGDON (R-H)
Tuesday, November 8

OFFICIAL GOING: Chase course - good to soft; hurdle course - good to soft (good in places)
Wind: Strong, across Weather: Sunny spells

2099 BETFREDPOKER NOVICES' HURDLE (8 hdls) 2m 110y
1:00 (1:01) (Class 4) 4-Y-O+ **£3,515** (£1,024; £512)

Form	Pos	Dist	Horse	Jockey	RPR
5-	1		**Gallant Approach (IRE)**[264] 3902 6-10-12	ATinkler	110+
			(C R Egerton) *chsd ldr: led 3 out: rdn out* **11/2**[2]		
51	2	½	**Mikado**[11] 1908 4-11-5	APMcCoy	116+
			(Jonjo O'Neill) *a.p: rdn to chse wnr last: r.o* **7/2**[1]		
4-13	3	17	**Dr Cerullo**[10] 1916 4-11-5	TDoyle	98
			(C Tinkler) *led to 3 out: wknd bef next* **7/2**[1]		
	4	1	**Xamborough (FR)**[139] 4-10-12	TJMurphy	95+
			(B G Powell) *chsd ldrs: rdn appr 2 out: wkng whn blnd last* **8/1**[3]		
32	5	3	**Kilty Storm (IRE)**[156] 643 6-10-12	TScudamore	87
			(M C Pipe) *hld up: hdwy after 5th: rdn next: hung lft and wknd bef 2 out* **8/1**[3]		
	6	½	**Nobelmann (GER)**[26] 6-10-12	WHutchinson	86
			(A W Carroll) *hld up: hdwy 3 out: wkng whn j.rt last* **50/1**		
34-0	7	1 ½	**Mac's Elan**[6] 1991 5-10-5 97	MrMatthewSmith(7)	85
			(A B Coogan) *hld up: hdwy appr 3 out: wkng whn j.rt 2 out* **66/1**		
P0	8	2	**Dictator (IRE)**[17] 1824 4-10-12	(t) JTizzard	84+
			(D R Gandolfo) *chsd ldrs: mstke 5th: wkng whn hmpd 2 out* **50/1**		
FP-6	9	1 ¾	**Yes Ses Les**[51] 1485 6-10-7	DLaverty(5)	81
			(G Fierro) *a bhd* **200/1**		
100	10	2 ½	**Flying Spur (IRE)**[14] 1875 4-10-9	TJMalone(3)	78
			(M C Pipe) *hld up: nvr nr to chal* **40/1**		
	11	dist	**Cryfield**[20] 8-10-12	RJohnson	—
			(N Tinkler) *hld up: a in rr* **28/1**		
12P0	12	¾	**Maclean**[17] 1823 4-11-5 108	(b) JEMoore	—
			(G L Moore) *hld up: hdwy after 5th: wknd appr 2 out* **9/1**		
P-	13	16	**Polish Rhapsody (IRE)**[232] 4495 4-10-5	GSupple	—
			(J A Supple) *hld up: a in rr* **200/1**		
	14	1 ¼	**Blake Hall Lad (IRE)**[4] 4-10-12	JAMcCarthy	—
			(P S McEntee) *hld up: hit 5th: a in rr* **150/1**		
UOUP	15	15	**Government (IRE)**[2] 2082 4-10-12 69	JGoldstein	—
			(M C Chapman) *hld up: wknd 4th* **200/1**		
056-	P		**Terminology**[287] 3521 7-10-12	(t) JPMcNamara	—
			(K C Bailey) *hld up: mstkes: bhd whn blnd 3 out: sn p.u* **10/1**		
0	P		**Made In Bruere (FR)**[13] 1882 5-10-5	TJDreaper(7)	—
			(Ferdy Murphy) *hld up: hit 2nd and 5th: a bhd: t.o whn p.u bef 3 out* **80/1**		

4m 2.10s (6.40) **Going Correction** +0.55s/f (Soft) **17** Ran SP% **115.8**
Speed ratings: **106,105,97,97,95 95,94,94,93,92** —,—,—,—,— —,— CSF £23.46 TOTE £6.20: £2.40, £2.00, £1.60; EX 20.90.
Owner Byrne Bros (Formwork) Limited **Bred** N J Connors **Trained** Chaddleworth, Berks

FOCUS
A solid-looking novice event, with the front two nicely clear of the third. The pace looked to be sound - at least half of the field never figured with any chance - and winners should come out of the race.

NOTEBOOK
Gallant Approach(IRE), who made his hurdling debut in very decent company at Sandown last time, was always kept close to the pace, and always looked like holding on after taking the lead. He will make a lovely chaser in the future, and a step up in trip could see him follow up under a penalty in novice company, as he should certainly appreciate some extra distance. *(op 9-2)*
Mikado, another to race prominently, could never quite get to the winner despite giving his all under a strong ride. It was, however, a fine effort under his penalty, and further than two miles should certainly help him in the future. *(op 3-1)*
Dr Cerullo, a winner over the course and distance, was left well behind when the front two quickened past him down the side of the course. He almost certainly bumped into a couple of decent prospects, and will have his chance again in lesser novice company, although handicaps are now open to him as well. *(op 5-1)*
Xamborough(FR) shaped with plenty of promise under a good ride. With normal improvement, he can go very close next time.
Kilty Storm(IRE), dropped down in trip, never got to the leaders and looked very one paced against some potentially decent types. A step back up in trip looks sure to suit him in the future. *(op 6-1)*
Nobelmann(GER) ◆ definitely showed enough promise to suggest he can win races over hurdles. Held up well off the pace, he made ground during the final circuit but never got to the leaders. It was an eyecatching performance and races can be won with him. *(op 66-1)*
Dictator(IRE) did not run too badly and is now qualified for handicaps. However, he did not look the most enthusiastic when under pressure.
Made In Bruere(FR) *Official explanation: jockey said gelding bled from the nose (op 66-1)*

2100 BETFREDCASINO NOVICES' CHASE (16 fncs) 2m 4f 110y
1:30 (1:30) (Class 3) 5-Y-O+ **£5,452** (£1,600; £800; £399)

Form	Pos	Dist	Horse	Jockey	RPR
12-	1		**Wicked Nice Fella (IRE)**[401] 1572 7-10-12 109	NFehily	126+
			(C C Bealby) *prom: jnd ldr 5th: led 8th: clr last* **11/2**[3]		
-13F	2	7	**Party Games (IRE)**[13] 1877 8-10-12 108	PHide	116+
			(G L Moore) *led to 8th: styd on same pce fr 2 out* **9/4**[1]		
42/P	3	7	**Bell Lane Lad (IRE)**[193] 106 8-10-12 91	WHutchinson	106
			(A King) *hld up: reminders 8th: outpcd 12th: styd on flat* **20/1**		
F-P0	4	3	**Le Royal (FR)**[10] 1929 6-10-12 110	(t) RMcGrath	104+
			(K G Reveley) *hld up: hdwy 13th: wkng whn mstke last* **11/1**		

63P- **5** *9* **King Georges (FR)**[200] 4960 7-10-12 110 .... JMogford 98+
(J C Tuck) *chsd ldr to 5th: outpcd 11th: rallied 13th: wknd after 3 out* **18/1**

44-P **F** **Misty Dancer**[131] 332 6-10-12 109 .... SThomas —
(Miss Venetia Williams) *fell 3rd* **9/1**

160- **U** **Direct Flight (IRE)**[311] 3159 7-10-12 110 .... TDoyle —
(Noel T Chance) *chsd ldr tl uns rdr 5th* **7/2**[2]

100- **P** **Wenceslas (IRE)**[209] 4820 5-10-12 101 .... TJMurphy —
(Miss H C Knight) *hld up: hdwy 9th: wknd 4 out: t.o whn p.u after 3 out* **13/2**

5m 22.4s (16.30) **Going Correction** +0.775s/f (Soft) **8** Ran SP% **110.1**
Speed ratings: **99,96,93,92,89 —,—,—** CSF £17.65 TOTE £5.80: £1.70, £1.10, £3.80; EX 12.60.
Owner Mrs Joan Martin **Bred** James G Kehoe **Trained** Barrowby, Lincs

FOCUS
A very impressive success by the winner, who has a long-term target of the Jewson Novices' Handicap Chase. Those in behind were outclassed and that form is best rated through the second.

NOTEBOOK
Wicked Nice Fella(IRE) produced a very taking performance on his debut under Rules. Always jumping nicely, he sauntered clear of his rivals up the straight and won with plenty in hand. His background in point-to-points stood him in good stead, and he already looks a likely candidate for the Jewson Novices' Handicap Chase at Cheltenham next March. A penalty is unlikely to stop him next time if kept to a sensible grade, and a left-handed track may improve him even more, as he jumped slightly left the fences. The trainer reported after the race that the horse would not have wanted the ground any softer. *(op 5-1)*
Party Games(IRE) almost certainly bumped into a very progressive winner and had no chance off level weights - he escaped a penalty because his win over fences had been much earlier in the year. More races can be won with him over the big obstacles, but will find his lack of fluency at his fences a hindrance. *(op 5-2)*
Bell Lane Lad(IRE) stayed on resolutely from well off the pace to close on the second after jumping the last. A step up in trip looks needed, and he would be interesting if tried over three miles next time. *(tchd 25-1)*
Le Royal(FR) did not get home and continues to disappoint. *(op 10-1 tchd 12-1)*
King Georges(FR) did not run without promise, and can be expected to improve for the outing. *(op 14-1)*
Misty Dancer did not get very far and will have to get further before his aptitude for chasing can be judged. *(tchd 4-1)*
Direct Flight(IRE) was in the process of running a fair race before unseating. *(tchd 4-1)*
Wenceslas(IRE) shaped well in the early part of the race, but he weakened quickly under pressure, giving the impression something may not have been quite right with him. *(tchd 4-1)*

2101 WEATHERBYS BANK JUVENILE NOVICES' HURDLE (8 hdls) 2m 110y
2:00 (2:01) (Class 3) 3-Y-O **£4,840** (£1,421; £710; £354)

Form RPR
1 **Reaching Out (IRE)**[34] 3-10-12 .... MFoley 99+
(N J Henderson) *hld up: hdwy 3 out: led last: r.o wl* **1/1**[1]
2 *4* **Equilibria (USA)**[19] 3-10-12 .... JEMoore 89+
(G L Moore) *hld up: plld hrd: hdwy appr 3 out: ev ch next: nt fluent last: sn outpcd* **7/2**[2]
3 *2 1/2* **Proprioception (IRE)**[19] 3-10-5 .... WHutchinson 80
(A King) *hld up: hdwy 4th: led appr 2 out: hdd and no ex last* **7/1**[3]
4 *3 1/2* **David's Symphony (IRE)**[24] 3-10-12 .... NFehily 83
(A W Carroll) *hld up in tch: rdn after 3 out: sn wknd* **40/1**
0 **5** *5* **Halcyon Express (IRE)**[8] 1955 3-10-5 ....(t) CMStudd(7) 78
(Mary Meek) *plld hrd and sn prom: led 3rd: hdd & wknd after 3 out* **100/1**
6 *2 1/2* **Lojo**[30] 3-10-5 .... JGoldstein 69
(Miss Sheena West) *chsd ldrs: led after 3 out: sn hdd & wknd* **40/1**
45 **7** *1 1/2* **Just Beware**[38] 1594 3-9-12 ....(p) RLucey-Butler(7) 67
(Miss Z C Davison) *led: hdd after 1st: wknd after 5th* **11/1**
0 **8** *1/2* **Jabo (FR)**[21] 1785 3-10-12 .... TScudamore 74
(N A Twiston-Davies) *trckd ldrs tl rdn and wknd appr 3 out* **8/1**
9 *3* **Trackattack**[112] 3-10-12 .... ATinkler 71
(P Howling) *plld hrd: led after 1st: ev ch appr 3 out: sn wknd* **33/1**

4m 14.7s (19.00) **Going Correction** +0.55s/f (Soft) **9** Ran SP% **113.0**
Speed ratings: **77,75,73,72,69 68,68,67,66** CSF £4.45 TOTE £2.10: £1.10, £1.30, £2.50; EX 5.30.
Owner Peter Webb **Bred** Roundhill Stud And Gleadhill House Stud Ltd **Trained** Upper Lambourn, Berks

FOCUS
Probably not a strong race, given most of the runners' ability on the Flat. The winner is value for more than the official margin and could turn out to be alright, but those in behind will need to improve.

NOTEBOOK
Reaching Out(IRE) did the job very nicely after tracking the pace throughout. The race as a whole was probably not the strongest event ever run, but he won it in good style and should hold his own under a penalty. *(op 11-8 tchd 6-4 in places)*
Equilibria(USA), from the stable who won the race the previous season with the useful Diego Cao, ran with a lot of promise and should find a race over timber, having not won on the level. *(op 3-1)*
Proprioception(IRE), who did not show a great deal on the Flat, ran with enough promise on her hurdling debut to suggest she can win a race of some description over timber. *(op 13-2 tchd 8-1)*
David's Symphony(IRE) did not appear to get home and is sure to have stamina doubts given his form on the Flat. *(op 33-1)*
Halcyon Express(IRE) did not get home after racing with plenty of zest early. *(op 66-1)*
Jabo(FR) disappointed for the second time in a row, and may need more time to develop. Clearly connections believe he has ability given his starting price on both runs to date. *(op 7-1 tchd 6-1)*

2102 BETFRED MACER GIFFORD MEMORIAL H'CAP CHASE (16 fncs) 2m 4f 110y
2:30 (2:30) (Class 3) (0-130,129) 5-Y-0+ **£7,221** (£2,120; £1,060; £529)

Form RPR
0P-P **1** **Dark'n Sharp (GER)**[194] 91 10-11-12 129 .... RJohnson 146+
(R T Phillips) *hld up in tch: ev ch whn lft in ld 3 out: j.lft last: styd on wl* **14/1**
-4P5 **2** *3* **Marked Man (IRE)**[115] 1013 9-11-4 121 .... TDoyle 133+
(R Lee) *hld up: hdwy 10th: blnd 3 out: rdn to chse wnr last: no ex flat* **7/1**[3]
15-P **3** *8* **You're Special (USA)**[13] 1881 8-11-1 125 .... TJDreaper(7) 127
(Ferdy Murphy) *chsd ldrs: rdn and lost pl 7th: styd on flat* **33/1**
221/ **4** *1 1/2* **Pietro Vannucci (IRE)**[640] 3726 9-10-11 114 .... APMcCoy 115
(Jonjo O'Neill) *hld up: hdwy 10th: mstke 4 out: styd on flat: nvr trbld ldrs* **11/2**[2]
13-F **5** *5* **Key Phil (FR)**[193] 97 7-11-4 121 .... NFehily 119+
(D J Wintle) *prom: ev ch 3 out: wkng whn blnd last* **16/1**
1256 **6** *21* **Figaro Du Rocher (FR)**[46] 1542 5-11-7 124 ....(t) TScudamore 105+
(M C Pipe) *led to 4 out: wknd appr 2 out* **12/1**
310 **7** *21* **Nawamees (IRE)**[9] 1720 7-11-10 127 .... PHide 81
(G L Moore) *hld up: mstke and wknd 10th* **25/1**
2F-F **U** **Big Rob (IRE)**[13] 1881 6-11-4 121 .... TJMurphy —
(B G Powell) *prom: chsd ldr 8th: led 4 out: blnd and uns rdr next* **13/8**[1]
2-PP **P** **Powder Creek (IRE)**[10] 1929 8-10-13 116 .... RMcGrath —
(K G Reveley) *hld up: rdn and wknd 11th: bhd whn p.u bef last* **22/1**
4P-1 **P** **Icy Prospect (IRE)**[37] 1620 7-10-9 112 .... TSiddall —
(N A Twiston-Davies) *chsd ldr to 8th: wknd after next: t.o whn p.u bef 2 out* **11/2**[2]

5m 15.7s (9.60) **Going Correction** +0.775s/f (Soft) **10** Ran SP% **112.7**
Speed ratings: **112,110,107,107,105 97,89,—,—,—** CSF £102.11 CT £3140.78 TOTE £13.90: £2.90, £2.50, £4.60; EX 106.40 Trifecta £336.00 Part won. Pool: £473.30 - 0.10 winning tickets..
Owner Ascot Five Plus One **Bred** Gestut Wiesengrund **Trained** Adlestrop, Gloucs

FOCUS
A strong renewal of a well-established race. The winner had a sound chance at the weights, while Big Rob departed late in the day when travelling smoothly. The form looks sound and should work out.

NOTEBOOK
Dark'n Sharp(GER), who has had a tendon injury, returned to form off a very favourable handicap mark. His cause was aided by the departure of the favourite late in the day, but it was a welcome return to form for this once classy individual and, with his confidence restored, he could win again in similar company if not penalised too heavily. A sound surface also seems needed after a disappointing effort at Punchestown in April. *(op 20-1)*
Marked Man(IRE) was starting to become nicely handicapped after a tough last season, but will find his solid effort pushing him up the weights again. He gave chase to the winner all the way up the straight but was never getting to him quickly enough to cause him any problems. A step up in trip may suit him in his current form. *(op 8-1)*
You're Special(USA) is a consistent type over fences and ran well again, after needing the run last time. Staying on really well after being well behind at one point of the race, he should pick up races throughout the season in a slightly lower grade, and possibly over slightly further. *(op 25-1)*
Pietro Vannucci(IRE) shaped with plenty of encouragement after a huge break, and should go close next time given normal improvement. *(op 6-1 tchd 7-1)*
Key Phil(FR) ◆ ran with plenty of promise after his break. Less-exacting company will probably suit him much better, and is one to keep an eye on next time on softer ground. *(op 14-1)*
Figaro Du Rocher(FR) is not well handicapped on his winning form over fences, and will need to come down the weights to have a clear winning chance. However, he ran a sound race and could be interesting for one of the handicaps at Cheltenham next March if coming down the weights enough. *(tchd 14-1)*
Big Rob(IRE) was in the process of running a big race until failing to complete for the third time in a row. He obviously has a lot of talent, and was going really well in front, but it would be no surprise to see connections return him to hurdles for some confidence-boosting runs before going chasing again. If he can get his jumping together, he will be a more than useful type. *(op 15-8)*
Icy Prospect(IRE) reportedly broke a blood-vessel during the race. *Official explanation: vet said gelding bled from the nose (op 15-8)*

2103 BETFRED 540 SHOPS NATIONWIDE H'CAP HURDLE (8 hdls) 2m 110y
3:00 (3:01) (Class 3) (0-115,112) 4-Y-0+ **£4,879** (£1,432; £716; £357)

Form RPR
/31- **1** **Into The Shadows**[11] 2764 5-10-13 99 .... RMcGrath 120+
(K G Reveley) *hld up: hdwy 4th: mstke 3 out: led appr next: clr whn j.rt last: eased flat* **13/8**[1]
0U22 **2** *5* **Pirandello (IRE)**[16] 1862 7-11-10 110 .... JPMcNamara 111+
(K C Bailey) *chsd ldr to appr 4th: outpcd after 3 out: wnt 2nd last: no ch w wnr* **4/1**[2]
3P-6 **3** *2 1/2* **Gaelic Flight (IRE)**[31] 1682 7-10-12 103 .... WKennedy(5) 102+
(Noel T Chance) *hld up: hdwy 4th: led after 3 out: sn hdd: wknd appr last* **16/1**
10-F **4** *1/2* **Fame**[16] 1862 5-11-10 110 .... RJohnson 107
(P J Hobbs) *hld up: hdwy appr 3 out: wknd after next* **10/1**
00-1 **5** *3* **Madison De Vonnas (FR)**[22] 1774 5-11-4 104 ....(t) BFenton 98
(Miss E C Lavelle) *chsd ldrs tl wknd appr 2 out* **10/1**
00-0 **6** *8* **Ndola**[21] 764 6-10-6 92 .... PMoloney 78
(B J Curley) *hld up in tch: lost pl 4th: wknd appr 3 out* **20/1**
004- **7** *3 1/2* **Silk Trader**[252] 4107 10-11-12 112 .... PJBrennan 97+
(J Mackie) *chsd ldrs tl wknd appr 3 out* **50/1**
030- **8** *9* **Captain Miller**[143] 4926 9-11-7 107 .... ATinkler 90+
(N J Henderson) *led: hdd & wknd after 3 out* **15/2**[3]
0-0U **9** *17* **Domenico (IRE)**[24] 1481 7-10-9 95 .... TJMurphy 52
(J R Jenkins) *hld up: n.m.r bnd after 3rd: rdn 5th: wknd bef next* **8/1**

4m 2.80s (7.10) **Going Correction** +0.55s/f (Soft) **9** Ran SP% **111.8**
Speed ratings: **105,102,101,101,99 96,94,90,82** CSF £8.46 CT £70.15 TOTE £2.40: £1.10, £1.70, £3.90; EX 6.90.
Owner R C Mayall **Bred** Mrs Linda Corbett And Mrs Mary Mayall **Trained** Lingdale, N Yorks

FOCUS
A moderate-looking hurdle won in decisive fashion and the winner is value for four times the official margin. The runner-up and fourth set the level for the form.

NOTEBOOK
Into The Shadows ◆ won in good style and is clearly on a very favourable handicap mark. She can be followed if turned out fairly quickly, as she will get a hefty rise in the weights for this success. *(tchd 7-4)*
Pirandello(IRE) has not won since 2003 and hardly gets any respite from the Handicapper, given his fairly consistent profile. This was a solid effort at a course he has run well at before, and a try over further looks required again after he finished strongly from well off the pace. *(op 5-1)*
Gaelic Flight(IRE) came with a promising effort into the straight, which petered out very quickly after looking to hold every chance on entering the straight. He is a consistent sort but is without a win outside novice company. *(op 14-1)*
Fame was held up off the pace and never got to the leaders. A stronger pace and better ground might suit him in the future. *(op 12-1)*
Madison De Vonnas(FR) moved into the lead going easily, but back-pedalled very quickly when joined and was a bit disappointing. The 5lb rise in the weights since his success appears to be anchoring him. *Official explanation: trainer said gelding had a breathing problem (op 8-1)*
Ndola did not show a great deal on his handicapping debut, and will need to improve a lot to be competitive off his relatively low-rating. *(op 10-1)*
Captain Miller weakened very quickly after making the early pace. *Official explanation: vet said gelding was in a distressed state (op 8-1 tchd 17-2)*

2104 H2O NATIONWIDE H'CAP CHASE (19 fncs) 3m
3:30 (3:30) (Class 4) (0-105,103) 5-Y-0+ **£3,895** (£1,209; £651)

Form RPR
40/P **1** **Sweet Bird (FR)**[27] 1719 8-10-13 93 ....(t) ONelmes(3) 107+
(Miss J R Gibney) *hld up in tch: led appr 2 out: styd on wl* **25/1**
-504 **2** *8* **Sitting Duck**[154] 671 6-10-3 80 .... JamesDavies 89+
(B G Powell) *chsd ldr tl led 4th: clr 7th: hdd appr 2 out: blnd and wknd last* **15/2**[3]
0-03 **3** *17* **Ardashir (FR)**[6] 1988 6-11-12 103 .... MFoley 92
(Mrs S J Humphrey) *chsd ldrs to 4 out: lft remote 3rd 3 out* **10/1**
113S **P** **Tudor King (IRE)**[8] 1960 11-10-11 93 .... JDiment(5) —
(Andrew Turnell) *led to 4th: blnd 13th: sn p.u* **12/1**

The Form Book, Raceform Ltd, Compton, RG20 6NL

P11- **P** **Gray's Eulogy**[263] 3931 7-11-5 96 (b) TDoyle —
(D R Gandolfo) *chsd ldrs: lost pl 10th: wknd 14th: bhd whn p.u bef 4 out* **4/1**[2]

F-41 **F** **Mini Dare**[6] 1989 8-11-3 94 7ex LAspell —
(O Sherwood) *hld up: hdwy 9th: chsd ldr and mstke 12th: disputing cl 2nd whn fell 3 out* **4/5**[1]

6m 31.4s (19.10) **Going Correction** +0.775s/f (Soft) **6** Ran SP% **107.9**
Speed ratings: **103,100,94,—,—** — CSF £164.80 TOTE £31.90: £6.40, £3.00; EX 156.30.

Owner Andrew L Cohen **Bred** Mme Veuve Ginette Gayet **Trained** Shenley, Herts
■ First winner as a trainer for Rachael Gibney.

FOCUS
A competitive low-grade chase, which had some interesting contenders. The form, rated through the third, should be reliable at a low level.

NOTEBOOK
Sweet Bird(FR), a first winner for his trainer since taking her licence out in July, showed the benefit of a pipe-opener at Wetherby last time after a long absence, to grind out success after hitting the front close to the home straight. He jumps fairly well and can follow up in a similar grade, even after being reassessed, and looks an ideal type for staying chases at a modest level. *(op 33-1)*

Sitting Duck was too keen for his own good on his chasing debut to fully see out the trip, and nearly came down at the last when looking pretty tired. However, he looks like emulating his half-brother, Colonel Frank, by being a better horse over fences than hurdles. *(tchd 13-2)*

Ardashir(FR) kept on in his own time and was well beaten. *(op 12-1)*

Tudor King(IRE) led the field until the eventual second took command. A mistake down the back straight ended his chances. Official explanation: trainer said gelding was unsuited by the good to soft ground *(op 15-2 tchd 14-1)*

Mini Dare was in the process of closing on the leader when he came down. He has reportedly had problems with his confidence over fences before, and it remains to be seen how the fall will affect him in the short-term whilst being so well handicapped. *(op 15-2 tchd 14-1)*

Gray's Eulogy, returning from a break, showed very little and did not give any immediate promise for the future. Official explanation: jockey said gelding never travelled *(op 15-2 tchd 14-1)*

2105 EBF "JUNIOR" STANDARD OPEN NATIONAL HUNT FLAT RACE 1m 6f
4:00 (4:02) (Class 6) 3-Y-O **£1,898** (£553; £276)

Form					RPR
	1		**Jass** 3-10-12 RMcGrath (K G Reveley) *hld up: hdwy 1/2-way: led over 1f out: rdn out* **13/8**[1]		95+
	2	*1*	**Milan Deux Mille (FR)** 3-10-12 GSupple (M C Pipe) *a.p: chsd ldr 4f out: led over 2f out: rdn and hdd over 1f out: styd on* **7/2**[2]		94+
	3	*5*	**Rourke Star** 3-10-9 LVickers[(3)] (S R Bowring) *hld up: plld hrd: hdwy over 3f out: nt rch ldrs* **66/1**		89
	4	*6*	**Beau Largesse** 3-10-5 MrDavidTurner[(7)] (A J Chamberlain) *led: clr 1/2-way: hdd over 2f out: wknd over 1f out* **66/1**		83
	5	*2*	**Ember Dancer** 3-10-12 DNolan (Ian Williams) *hld up: hdwy over 4f out: rdn and wknd over 1f out* **25/1**		81
5	**6**	*10*	**Devonia Plains (IRE)**[21] 1785 3-10-9 RYoung[(3)] (Mrs P N Dutfield) *prom: chsd ldr 1/2-way: rdn and wknd over 2f out* **12/1**		73+
6	**7**	*7*	**Bradders**[5] 2013 3-10-5 RLucey-Butler[(7)] (J R Jenkins) *hld up: n.d* **33/1**		64
	8	*3*	**Naemi (GER)** 3-10-5 TJMurphy (S L Keightley) *hld up: nvr nrr* **16/1**		54
	9	*1 3/4*	**Chateau (IRE)** 3-10-12 (t) JPMcNamara (G A Swinbank) *hld up: n.d* **4/1**[3]		59
	10	*26*	**Grunzig** 3-10-12 LAspell (Mrs C A Dunnett) *hld up: n.d* **28/1**		33
	11	*2 1/2*	**Scarlet Romance** 3-10-2 MrTGreenall[(3)] (M W Easterby) *plld hrd and prom: wknd over 4f out* **18/1**		24
	12	*dist*	**Superior Dream** 3-10-12 PJBrennan (J F Panvert) *hld up in tch: rdn and wknd over 5f out* **33/1**		—
	13	*3/4*	**Precious Pride** 3-9-12 RSpate[(7)] (M J Gingell) *plld hrd: trckd ldr: lost pl 8f out: sn wknd* **100/1**		—

3m 28.7s **Going Correction** 0.0s/f (Good) **13** Ran SP% **116.3**
CSF £6.28 TOTE £2.30: £1.40, £1.90, £11.00; EX 9.50 Place 6 £333.48, Place 5 £248.06.

Owner The Scarth Racing Partnership **Bred** Mrs Jennie M Raymond **Trained** Lingdale, N Yorks

FOCUS
This looked a fair bumper before the race. The winner took his time to get going but won going away, while the second shaped well and the pair could be above average. The sixth and seventh set the standard.

NOTEBOOK
Jass took a while to get going but eventually won going away. It looked a strong bumper on paper, so he may be capable of defying a penalty, something that is not very easy to do. *(op 9-4)*

Milan Deux Mille(FR) travelled powerfully for much of the race and was just outpaced by the winner in the closing stages. A similar race should be won with him before he goes hurdling. *(op 4-1 tchd 10-3)*

Rourke Star ran an amazing race for a horse so far off the pace. He made relentless headway under pressure to finish on the heels of the front two. If this effort can be believed, he looks sure to win a bumper, especially one over two miles when allowed to contest one. Official explanation: jockey said gelding hung left

Beau Largesse ran a fair race after setting a decent early pace. Having cost very little at the sales, one has to be a tiny bit dubious of the effort, but on the face of it he ran a very promising race. *(tchd 100-1)*

Ember Dancer was given a nice introductory ride and will no doubt improve for the experience. *(op 20-1)*

Chateau(IRE), who is related to some very decent types on the Flat and, once owned by Sheikh Mohammed, showed very little on his debut, and does not seem in the same league as the stable's other formerly Arab-owned cast-offs. *(op 7-2 tchd 9-2)*

Superior Dream Official explanation: jockey said gelding hung left

Precious Pride Official explanation: jockey said filly lost its action *(op 66-1)*

T/Jkpt: Not won. T/Plt: £260.40 to a £1 stake. Pool: £43,116.30. 120.85 winning tickets. T/Qpdt: £163.20 to a £1 stake. Pool: £2,625.80. 11.90 winning tickets. CR

1883 SEDGEFIELD (L-H)
Tuesday, November 8

OFFICIAL GOING: Soft (good to soft in places) changing to soft after race 5 (2.40)
Wind: Strong, half-across

2106 JOHN SMITH'S EXTRA SMOOTH NOVICES' HURDLE (DIV I) (8 hdls) 2m 1f
12:40 (12:40) (Class 4) 4-Y-O+ **£3,070** (£901; £450; £225)

Form				RPR
3-11	**1**		**Chef De Cour (FR)**[156] 645 4-11-12 113 ADobbin (L Lungo) *hld up in midfield: hit 2nd: hdwy to trck ldrs 4th: led appr 2 out: rdn clr and hit last: kpt on* **10/11**[1]	121+
	2	*6*	**Canada Street (IRE)**[275] 4-10-12 GLee (J Howard Johnson) *midfield: pushed along 4th: hdwy to trck ldrs 3 out: rdn to chse wnr next: sn drvn and hit last: kpt on same pce* **7/2**[2]	95+
055-	**3**	*16*	**Springaway**[342] 2569 6-10-12 NPMulholland (Miss Kate Milligan) *midfield: hdwy to trck ldrs 5th: rdn along after 3 out: kpt on same pce: wl hld in 3rd whn hit last* **33/1**	79
-330	**4**	*5*	**Pearson Glen (IRE)**[30] 1591 6-10-7 97 (t) DCCostello[(5)] (James Moffatt) *led and sn clr: hit 5th and next: rdn along and jnd 3 out: hdd bef 2 out and sn wknd: tired whn hit last* **13/2**[3]	75+
F	**5**	*1 1/4*	**Tanmeya**[16] 1850 4-10-2 LMcGrath[(3)] (R C Guest) *hld up and bhd: stdy hdwy appr 3 out: rdn to chse ldrs bef next: sn drvn and wknd: tired whn hit last* **66/1**	66
664-	**6**	*19*	**Top Tenor (IRE)**[291] 3464 5-10-9 77 ow2 MrMThompson[(5)] (V Thompson) *prom: chsd ldr fr 3rd tl rdn along: hit 3 out and sn wknd* **50/1**	56
P	**7**	*15*	**Remus Lupin**[48] 1508 4-10-12 BHarding (F P Murtagh) *a rr: bhd fr 1/2-way* **150/1**	39
	P		**Red Wharf** 4-10-9 PAspell[(3)] (J Wade) *a rr: mstke 4th and sn bhd: t.o whn p.u bef 2 out* **80/1**	—
00-	**P**		**Northern News (IRE)**[327] 2852 5-10-12 JimCrowley (G A Swinbank) *a rr: bhd fr 1/2-way: t.o whn p.u bef 2 out* **25/1**	—
	P		**Chanteuse**[185] 5-9-12 PKinsella[(7)] (Mrs Marjorie Fife) *chsd ldrs tl lost pl qckly 4th: bhd whn p.u bef 3 out* **28/1**	—
	F		**Ile Maurice (FR)**[849] 5-10-2 KJMercer[(3)] (Ferdy Murphy) *hld up and bhd: hdwy 3 out: rdn along and keeping on whn fell last* **22/1**	56
	U		**Nowa Huta (FR)**[576] 4-9-12 BenOrde-Powlett[(7)] (Jedd O'Keeffe) *chsd ldrs: rdn along 3 out: disputing 3rd whn blnd and uns rdr next* **66/1**	72
0P-U	**P**		**Torkin Wind**[185] 214 4-10-5 64 MissAngelaBarnes[(7)] (M A Barnes) *plld hrd: chsd ldrs tl jinked bdly 3rd: sn lost pl and bhd whn p.u after 5th* **200/1**	—

4m 18.5s (12.00) **Going Correction** +0.825s/f (Soft) **13** Ran SP% **109.9**
Speed ratings: **104,101,93,91,90 81,74,—,—,— —,—,—** CSF £3.21 TOTE £1.80: £1.10, £1.30, £9.00; EX 3.90.

Owner Ashleybank Investments Limited **Bred** Andre Blee **Trained** Carrutherstown, D'fries & G'way

FOCUS
No stength in depth to this novice event, but the pace was fair and the winner, who was value for double the official margin, can rate higher in due course.

NOTEBOOK
Chef De Cour(FR) settled better than had been the case when winning at Perth last time and duly bagged the hat-trick with a most decisive success under his double penalty. While he may not have beaten a great deal, he is clearly improving with each outing and deserves a crack at a higher level now. *(op Evens tchd 5-6)*

Canada Street(IRE), who fell on his only start in the point arena, has joined top connections and was bidding to enhance their decent record in this event. However, he only got the hang of things from halfway and, while he was ultimately outclassed by the winner, shaped as though he would improve a great deal with this experience under his belt. He is also bred to appreciate further in time. *(tchd 4-1)*

Springaway, returning from a 342-day absence, plugged on to bag a place without ever posing a threat. He may prefer a faster surface, however, and now qualifies for handicaps. *(op 28-1)*

Pearson Glen(IRE), well backed, looked to set off too fast for his own good and finished legless. He could be better off in handicaps off his current rating. *(op 7-1 tchd 11-2)*

Ile Maurice(FR), who showed little in two outings on the Flat in France, was doing all of his best work at the finish on this debut for new connections and was a little unlucky not to have finished. He should strip a lot fitter for this outing and is in the right hands to progress over timber this season. *(op 14-1)*

Nowa Huta(FR), last of four on her sole outing on the Flat in France, was running a big race on this hurdling bow for new connections prior to unseating and would most likely have bagged a place. She can build on this and enjoyed the easy ground. *(op 14-1)*

2107 JOHN WADE FOR EQUINE FIBRE & RUBBER (S) HURDLE (QUALIFIER) (10 hdls) 2m 5f 110y
1:10 (1:12) (Class 5) 4-6-Y-O **£2,124** (£619; £309)

Form				RPR
6310	**1**		**Sheer Guts (IRE)**[9] 1940 6-11-12 97 (vt) AThornton (Robert Gray) *led: reminders after 6th: rdn along after 3 out: drvn and hdd after 2 out: rallied u.p last to ld last 100 yds* **5/1**[3]	96
44B4	**2**	*2 1/2*	**Alpha Juliet (IRE)**[11] 1910 4-10-0 83 DCCostello[(5)] (G M Moore) *hld up: hdwy 1/2-way: trckd ldrs 3 out: cl up next: sn rdn to ld and 1 1/2l up whn hit last: hdd and no ex last 100 yds* **6/4**[1]	75+
6F1-	**3**	*7*	**North Landing (IRE)**[451] 1181 5-11-2 LMcGrath[(3)] (R C Guest) *trckd ldrs: hit 3rd: mstke 6th: rdn along 3 out and plugged on one pce fr next* **4/1**[2]	80
-550	**4**	*10*	**Sylvie D'Orthe (FR)**[44] 1564 4-10-0 70 DMcGann[(5)] (Cooper Wilson) *chsd ldr: rdn along 7th: outpcd after 3 out* **11/2**	56
05-P	**P**		**Washington Pink (IRE)**[17] 1838 6-10-12 76 (p) ADobbin (C Grant) *chsd ldr: rdn along 7th: wknd 3 out and bhd whn p.u bef next* **17/2**	—
	P		**Giveasummerdance (IRE)**[104] 1081 6-10-0 PMerrigan[(5)] (Barry Potts, Ire) *plld hrd: trckd ldrs: rdn along and outpcd fr next: bhd whn p.u bef 3 out* **14/1**	—

5m 41.0s (25.30) **Going Correction** +0.825s/f (Soft)
WFA 4 from 5yo+ 13lb **6** Ran SP% **109.2**
Speed ratings: **87,86,83,79,—** — CSF £12.68 TOTE £4.30: £2.90, £1.50; EX 11.60.There was no bid for the winner. Alpha Juliet was claimed by Mr C. Teague for £5,000.

Owner Naughty Diesel Ltd **Bred** E Tynan **Trained** Malton, N Yorks

FOCUS

A dire event, run at a steady early gallop and the first two came clear. The winner is the best guide to the form.

NOTEBOOK

Sheer Guts(IRE) relished the drop back to a more suitable grade and, very much living up to his name, ground down the runner-up after the final flight to regain the lead and resume winning ways. He is clearly versatile as regards underfoot conditions, this is very much his level, and he can be seen to even better effect when getting a stronger pace over this trip. *(tchd 4-1)*

Alpha Juliet(IRE), well backed for this first outing in such lowly company, looked all over the winner approaching the final flight, but she met it wrong and was ultimately outbattled by the winner thereafter. This could be deemed a missed opportunity, and she is yet to win a race of any description, but she still finished clear of the rest and is worth perservering with in this class. *(op 15-8 tchd 2-1)*

North Landing(IRE), last seen taking a selling handicap at Bangor 451 days previously, was not totally disgraced on this return to action and should be seen to better effect in this grade on faster ground in the future. *(op 10-3)*

Sylvie D'Orthe(FR) was put in her place from the fourth last and, on this evidence, will benefit for the return to faster ground and a longer trip. *(op 7-1 tchd 8-1 in a place)*

2108 JOHN SMITH'S EXTRA SMOOTH NOVICES' HURDLE (DIV II) (8 hdls) 2m 1f

1:40 (1:41) (Class 4) 4-Y-0+ **£3,064** (£899; £449; £224)

Form				RPR
4-	1		**Charlie Tango (IRE)**25 [2567] 4-10-12 ... GLee (D W Thompson) *trckd ldrs: hdwy to ld after 4th: rdn clr after 2 out: hit last and kpt on* **7/2**[2]	96+
4	2	*8*	**Step Perfect (USA)**19 [1794] 4-10-12 ... FKeniry (G M Moore) *a.p: effrt to chse wnr 3 out: rdn next: drvn and kpt on same pce appr last* **11/4**[1]	88+
	3	*10*	**Third Empire**137 4-10-12 ... ADobbin (C Grant) *hld up in midfield: stdy hdwy 1/2-way: chsd ldrs 3 out: rdn bef next and kpt on same pce* **5/1**[3]	80+
	4	*7*	**Bohemian Brook (IRE)** 4-10-12 ... ADempsey (J Howard Johnson) *in tch: pushed along and outpcd 1/2-way: kpt on u.p fr 3 out* **12/1**	70
00-	5	*7*	**El Andaluz (FR)**295 [3393] 5-10-12 ... JimCrowley (M Todhunter) *racd wd: led tl after 4th: rdn along 3 out and sn wknd* **50/1**	63
	6	*nk*	**Montara (IRE)**52 6-10-7 ... PMerrigan(5) (Barry Potts, Ire) *hld up towards rr: hdwy 5th: rdn 3 out: drvn to chse ldrs bef next: sn btn* **7/2**[2]	62
50U5	7	*nk*	**Thorn Of The Rose (IRE)**13 [1885] 4-10-0 ... DCCostello(5) (James Moffatt) *bhd tl styd on appr 2 out: nvr nr ldrs* **40/1**	55
00-0	8	*hd*	**Rosedale Gardens**39 [1593] 5-10-12 ... KRenwick (M W Easterby) *bhd: sme hdwy 6th: styd on fr next: n.d* **100/1**	62
	9	*18*	**Acca Larentia (IRE)**127 4-10-5 ... PWhelan (R M Whitaker) *chsd ldrs: rdn along 5th: wknd fr 3 out* **66/1**	37
	10	*1 3/4*	**Shamwari Fire (IRE)**17 5-10-5 ... PJMcDonald(7) (I W McInnes) *chsd ldrs: rdn along 1/2-way: sn outpcd and bhd* **16/1**	42
0-0	11	*6*	**Top Dawn (IRE)**13 [1885] 5-10-12 ... BGibson (L Lungo) *hld up: a rr* **33/1**	36
	12	*1 1/4*	**Red Bluff (IRE)**189 5-10-12 ... JPByrne (H Alexander) *midfield: rdn along 5th: sn lost pl and bhd* **50/1**	35
	P		**Matthew My Son (IRE)**40 5-10-9 ... GBerridge(3) (F P Murtagh) *in tch: rdn along and lost pl 4th: sn bhd and p.u bef 2 out* **50/1**	—

4m 23.6s (17.10) **Going Correction** +0.825s/f (Soft) **13** Ran SP% **115.1**

Speed ratings: **92,88,83,80,76 76,76,76,68,67 64,63,—** CSF £12.88 TOTE £4.20: £1.90, £2.50, £1.70; EX 9.30.

Owner South View Winning Ways Partnership **Bred** Newtown Stud And T J Pabst **Trained** Bolam, Co Durham

FOCUS

A moderate novice event, rated through the runner-up, and the field finished strung out behind the comfortable winner.

NOTEBOOK

Charlie Tango(IRE), out of luck on the level this year and fourth on his only previous outing over hurdles in 2004, ran out a comfortable winner on this debut for new connections. He handled the easy ground without fuss, jumped neatly in the main, and the manner of this success would suggest he ought to go close in similar company under a penalty next time. *(op 3-1 tchd 11-4)*

Step Perfect(USA) was put in his place by the winner and failed to really improve on his recent debut at Haydock. However, he was still a clear second-best, and should fare better when eligible for handicaps after his next outing. *(tchd 3-1)*

Third Empire, rated 62 on the Flat, just got found out with two to jump, but ran well to that point and made a satisfactory hurdling bow for his new connections. He is entitled to improve for the outing. *(op 13-2)*

Bohemian Brook(IRE), whose dam is related to minor jump winners, proved easy to back and shaped as though he is going to appreciate further in the future. *(op 8-1)*

Montara(IRE), rated 55 on the Flat and well backed ahead of this hurdling debut, failed to make much of an impression and his fate was sealed a long way from home. His best form on the level was on much faster ground, however, and he could do better than this when reverting to a less-testing surface. *(op 11-2)*

2109 SIS MAIDEN CHASE (FOR THE ARTHUR STEPHENSON MEMORIAL TROPHY) (16 fncs) 2m 5f

2:10 (2:10) (Class 4) 4-Y-0+ **£4,433** (£1,301; £650; £325)

Form				RPR
O6U3	1		**Dead Mans Dante (IRE)**18 [1817] 7-11-3 109 ... KJMercer(3) (Ferdy Murphy) *hld up in rr: stdy hdwy 1/2-way: trckd ldrs 5 out: hdwy to chse ldr next: led appr 2 out: styd on wl* **3/1**[2]	115+
P30-	2	*14*	**Roaringwater (IRE)**202 [4923] 6-11-6 ... WMarston (R T Phillips) *cl up: led after 1st: hit 9th: pushed along 4 out: rdn and hdd bef 2 out: sn drvn and kpt on same pce* **13/8**[1]	98+
34	3	*3 1/2*	**Cirrus (FR)**11 [1915] 6-11-6 ... JimCrowley (K G Reveley) *hld up in rr and hmpd after 1st: hdwy 4 out: rdn to chse ldng pair next: sn drvn and kpt on same pce* **9/2**[3]	92
460-	4	*27*	**Profowens (IRE)**338 [2650] 7-11-6 ... RGarritty (P Beaumont) *in tch j. slowly 3rd: rdn along 5 out and sn wknd* **8/1**	65
56-P	F		**Missoudun (FR)**185 [212] 5-11-6 ... BHarding (A Crook) *in tch tl fell 8th* **100/1**	—
5530	S		**Nomadic Blaze**162 [593] 8-11-6 ... MBradburne (P G Atkinson) *trckd ldrs whn slipped up bnd after 1st* **16/1**	—
/55P	P		**Rolling River (IRE)**9 [1939] 8-11-3 ... PAspell(3) (J Wade) *chsd ldrs: rdn along and outpcd whn blnd 9th: sn bhd and p.u bef 3 out* **28/1**	—
33P-	R		**Jimmys Duky (IRE)**272 [3752] 7-11-6 72 ... KJohnson (D M Forster) *chsd ldrs: rdn along bef 4 out: grad wknd and hld in 4th whn ref 2 out* **33/1**	—
	P		**Deltic Arrow**185 7-11-6 ... AThornton (D L Williams) *led and mstke 1st: sn hdd and cl up tl hit 10th: sn rdn along and wknd appr 4 out: bhd whn p.u bef 2 out* **12/1**	—

5m 40.5s (17.10) **Going Correction** +0.65s/f (Soft) **9** Ran SP% **113.3**

Speed ratings: **93,87,86,76,— —,—,—,—** CSF £8.42 TOTE £4.50: £1.40, £1.30, £1.90; EX 9.70.

Owner S Hubbard Rodwell **Bred** P O'Connell **Trained** West Witton, N Yorks

FOCUS

A modest maiden chase, run at a fair pace and the field finished strung out on the deep surface. The form makes sense and the winner is value for a little further.

NOTEBOOK

Dead Mans Dante(IRE), who improved significantly when third to The Dark Lord at Fakenham last time, confirmed that effort and came home pretty much as he pleased to finally break his duck at the 16th attempt. He was given a patient ride by his ever-improving conditional jockey, put in by far his best round of jumping, and looked right at home on the easy ground. He is obviously in good heart now, and while connections will be hoping the Handicapper does not take this form too literally, he may have more to offer over stiffer test. *(op 11-4 tchd 5-2)*

Roaringwater(IRE), who failed to build on his debut bumper win on heavy ground last season, shaped nicely enough at the head of affairs until his lack of fitness told and he was a sitting duck for the winner from four out. As a former pointer, he has always appealed as the type to do better as a chaser, and would have claims of reversing form with the winner in the future with this outing under his belt. *(tchd 6-4 tchd 7-4 in a place)*

Cirrus(FR), popular in the betting ring for this chasing bow, was making only his third career start. After being hampered early on, he took time to find his feet, and was always playing catch-up. He could be rated slightly better than the bare form and now qualifies for a handicap mark. *(op 7-1)*

Profowens(IRE), another who has promised to improve as a chaser, ran a touch freely and never figured on this return from a 338-day break. *(tchd 9-1)*

2110 BETFRED POKER H'CAP HURDLE (SERIES QUALIFIER) (10 hdls) 2m 5f 110y

2:40 (2:41) (Class 3) (0-125,117) 4-Y-0+ **£4,807** (£1,411; £705; £352)

Form				RPR
4-31	1		**Ungaro (FR)**6 [1990] 6-11-10 115 7ex ... JimCrowley (K G Reveley) *hld up towards rr: smooth hdwy 1/2-way: trckd ldng pair 3 out: led on bit next: easily* **13/8**[1]	133+
5/5-	2	*8*	**San Peire (FR)**556 [114] 8-10-1 92 ... GLee (J Howard Johnson) *hld up in tpouch: hdwy after 3 out: rdn to chse wnr appr last: sn drvn and kpt on flat* **7/1**[2]	90
3/-P	3	*2 1/2*	**Robbo**9 [1941] 11-11-9 117 ... (b) FKing(3) (K G Reveley) *chsd ldr: led 6th: rdn along after 3 out: hdd next: sn drvn and wknd appr last* **20/1**	113
6012	4	*5*	**Teme Valley**18 [1816] 11-10-13 109 ... (p) PCO'Neill(5) (R C Guest) *hld up towards rr racing wd: hdwy 4 out: rdn bef 2 out: styd on u.p fr 2 out: nvr nr ldrs* **14/1**	100
0-00	5	*2*	**Corlande (IRE)**192 [127] 5-11-10 115 ... DElsworth (Mrs S J Smith) *in tch on inner: rdn along 3 out and sn one pce* **12/1**	104
423P	6	*6*	**Dream Castle (IRE)**31 [1668] 11-11-2 112 ... PMerrigan(5) (Barry Potts, Ire) *led to 6th: cl up tl rdn along bef 2 out and grad wknd* **20/1**	95
40/5	7	*dist*	**Uptown Lad (IRE)**17 [1836] 6-10-11 102 ... (t) KJohnson (R Johnson) *hld up and bhd: sme hdwy 6th: rdn along next: sn outpcd and bhd fr 3 out* **20/1**	—
U621	8	*3 1/2*	**Nick The Silver**13 [1887] 4-10-11 102 ... (p) AThornton (Robert Gray) *chsd ldrs: rdn along 7th: wknd 3 out* **15/2**[3]	—
P0OP	9	*19*	**Ramblees Holly**23 [1760] 7-10-11 102 ... KRenwick (R S Wood) *midfield: pushed along and outpcd fr 7th: sn bhd* **100/1**	—
02-3	10	*17*	**Fairy Skin Maker (IRE)**17 [1835] 7-11-5 110 ... BHarding (G A Harker) *midfield: rdn along 7th: sn outpcd and bhd* **8/1**	—
5/	P		**Louisville (IRE)**114 [557] 6-11-2 107 ... ADobbin (C A McBratney, Ire) *bhd whn p.u 7th* **12/1**	—
05-6	P		**Simlet**134 [468] 10-11-0 112 ... PKinsella(7) (E W Tuer) *midfield: pushed along and outpcd 6th: bhd whn p.u bef 2 out* **28/1**	—
4-23	P		**Dark Ben (FR)**166 [525] 5-11-4 112 ... PBuchanan(3) (Miss Kate Milligan) *in tch: rdn along 6th: sn outpcd and bhd whn p.u bef 2 out* **12/1**	—

5m 31.5s (15.80) **Going Correction** +0.825s/f (Soft)

WFA 4 from 5yo+ 13lb **13** Ran SP% **121.9**

Speed ratings: **104,101,100,98,97 95,—,—,—,— —,—,—** CSF £12.88 CT £177.31 TOTE £2.20: £1.70, £2.10, £4.40; EX 16.10.

Owner Sir Robert Ogden **Bred** Neustrian Associates **Trained** Lingdale, N Yorks

FOCUS

A fair and competitive handicap for the class, which was made to look very one-sided by the progressive winner, who can be rated value for plenty further, in a race that could rate higher.

NOTEBOOK

Ungaro(FR), a facile winner over this trip at Huntingdon in novice company six days previously, translated that form to the handicap sphere and followed-up in a similarly facile manner under his penalty. The softer ground proved no problems and, while he will no doubt take a hike in the ratings now, he is clearly a fast-improving hurdler. *(op 7-4 tchd 15-8 and 6-4)*

San Peire(FR), subject of strong support on this return from a 556-day break, tried in vain to reel in the winner from off the pace and may have been better served by a more prominent ride over this shorter trip. This still rates a sound comeback effort, however, and while he will go up in the weights after this, he will be happier when reverting to a longer trip. *(op 12-1)*

Robbo, with the blinkers re-applied, posted a sound effort under top weight on this return to hurdling and is a fair benchmark for the form.

Teme Valley, a real course specialist, was doing all of his best work at the finish and left the impression he still has a race or two in him on this track when reverting to faster ground. *(op 10-1)*

Nick The Silver, off the mark for new connections over course and distance 13 days previously, faded in the straight and looked to be found out by his 5lb higher mark. *(op 6-1 tchd 8-1)*

Fairy Skin Maker(IRE) ran well below her best on this return to the smaller obstacles with no apparent excuses.

2111 BETFRED.COM H'CAP CHASE (13 fncs) 2m 110y

3:10 (3:10) (Class 4) (0-110,108) 5-Y-0+ **£4,824** (£1,416; £708; £353)

Form				RPR
5150	1		**Loulou Nivernais (FR)**39 [1592] 6-10-3 85 ... ADempsey (M Todhunter) *mde all: rdn 3 out: clr whn hit last: styd on wl* **5/1**[3]	101+
22-0	2	*6*	**Flake**13 [1887] 5-11-8 104 ... DElsworth (Mrs S J Smith) *a chsng wnr: rdn along 3 out: drvn next: kpt on same pce* **9/2**[2]	112
26-6	3	*5*	**Sands Rising**13 [1887] 8-11-9 105 ... (t) KJohnson (R Johnson) *r wd: hld up: hdwy 5 out: rdn 3 out: drvn last: styd on u.p flat* **6/1**	108

33-5 **4** 2 **Mexican (USA)**[3] 84 6-10-3 **85**....(v) KRenwick 86
(M D Hammond) *hld up in rr: stdy hdwy 3 out: rdn appr last: drvn and one pce flat* **9/1**

-3P0 **5** 5 **Bernardon (GER)**[177] 370 9-11-2 **103**.... PMerrigan(5) 99
(Barry Potts, Ire) *a rr* **14/1**

143- **6** 5 **King Of The Arctic (IRE)**[225] 4626 7-11-9 **108**.... PAspell(3) 101+
(J Wade) *chsd ldrs: rdn along and mistke 3 out: drvn next and sn wknd* **4/1**[1]

611- **7** 12 **Green Ideal**[225] 4626 7-11-7 **106**....(b) KJMercer(3) 89+
(Ferdy Murphy) *chsd ldrs: rdn along 3 out: grad wknd* **4/1**[1]

66-P **8** 12 **Garde Bien**[19] 1795 8-11-5 **101**.... RGarritty 74+
(T D Easterby) *chsd ldrs: rdn along 7th: wknd bef 3 out: sn bhd* **12/1**

4m 20.1s (5.90) **Going Correction** +0.65s/f (Soft) 8 Ran SP% **113.5**
Speed ratings: **112,109,106,105,103 101,95,89** CSF £27.77 CT £136.50 TOTE £8.10: £2.20, £1.30, £2.10; EX 56.30.
Owner F G Steel **Bred** J Dufour **Trained** Orton, Cumbria

FOCUS
A modest handicap which was run at a decent clip. The winner won nicely and the form looks fair and the form could rate higher.

NOTEBOOK
Loulou Nivernais(FR) clearly relished the switch to front-running tactics as he bounced right back to his best with a clear-cut success off his light weight. He acted on the soft ground, jumped with aplomb prior to the final fence, and showed no strong signs of temperament this time. While his overall profile suggests he is unlikely to follow-up, he should still be feasibly treated despite a future weight rise on his former hurdle form in Ireland, and may have more to offer as connections *look to have finally found the key to him. Official explanation: trainer said, regarding the improved form shown, gelding was better suited by a return to front-running tactics (op 11-2 tchd 9-2)*
Flake, disappointing on his comeback over course and distance 13 days previously, showed his true colours on this return to chasing and had clearly improved for that outing. He likes this venue and, while he is hard to win with, is a fair benchmark for the form. *(op 6-1)*
Sands Rising, with the ground in his favour, showed the benefit of his recent seasonal bow over timber and was doing his best work at the finish. He is clearly worth trying again over further in this sphere. *(op 15-2)*
Mexican(USA), unplaced at Southwell three days previously, looked booked for a place at the top *of the straight but, not for the first time, he lacked conviction at the business end of the race. (op 17-2)*
King Of The Arctic(IRE), progressive as a novice last season, dropped out tamely after an error three from home and could be deemed disappointing. He is entitled to improve a deal for the outing, however. *(op 9-2)*
Green Ideal ran well below expectations on this seasonal bow, but his yard's chasers have invariably been improving for their first outing this term, so it would be unwise to write him off just yet. *(op 5-2 tchd 5-1 in places)*

2112 BETFRED 0800 7311210 STANDARD OPEN NATIONAL HUNT FLAT RACE 2m 1f
3:40 (3:40) (Class 6) 4-6-Y-0 **£1,856** (£541; £270)

Form RPR

35- **1** **Custom Design**[295] 3395 4-11-4 .... BHarding 108
(G A Harker) *mde most: rdn along ovrr 3f out: drvn wl over 1f out: styd on gamely* **12/1**

33/ **2** 1 ½ **Sabreflight**[605] 4328 5-10-11 .... GLee 99
(J Howard Johnson) *hld up: stdy hdwy 6f out: effrt to chse wnr 2f out: rdn to chal over 1f out: ev ch tl drvn and no ex ins last* **5/2**[2]

3 6 **Character Building (IRE)** 5-11-4 .... RGarritty 100
(J J Quinn) *trckd ldrs: hdwy and cl up 1/2-way: effrt over 3f out and ev ch tl rdn 2f out and grad wknd* **15/8**[1]

23- **4** 10 **Tous Chez (IRE)**[299] 3332 6-11-4 .... DElsworth 92+
(Mrs S J Smith) *trckd ldrs: effrt 4f out and ev ch tl rdn over 2f out and grad wknd* **4/1**[3]

3 **5** dist **Overnight**[31] 1688 5-10-11 .... EWhillans(7) —
(Mrs A C Hamilton) *chsd ldrs: rdn along 4f out: drvn 3f out and sn wknd* **66/1**

43 **6** 2 ½ **Mulligan's Pride (IRE)**[150] 719 4-11-4 .... JimCrowley —
(G A Swinbank) *a rr* **8/1**

30 **7** 5 **Topwell**[19] 1799 4-10-8 .... JPFlavin(10) —
(R C Guest) *chsd ldrs: rdn along 5f out: drvn and wknd over 3f out* **14/1**

8 4 **Forty Shakes (IRE)**[178] 6-11-1 .... PAspell(3) —
(J Wade) *chsd ldrs: rdn along over 4f out: sn wknd* **50/1**

44 **9** 22 **Redditzio**[31] 1688 4-10-6 .... DCCostello(5) —
(C W Thornton) *in tch on inner: rdn along over 6f out and sn wknd* **33/1**

46 **10** 29 **Stoneferry**[23] 1762 5-11-4 .... KJohnson —
(R Johnson) *prom tl lost pl 1/2-way and sn bhd: t.o fnl 4f* **33/1**

0 **11** 2 **Branodunum**[23] 1762 4-11-4 .... ADempsey —
(M W Easterby) *a rr: wl bhd fnl 4f* **100/1**

4m 16.4s (9.50) **Going Correction** +0.825s/f (Soft)
WFA 4 from 5yo+ 12lb 11 Ran SP% **119.1**
Speed ratings: **97,96,93,88,— —,—,—,—,— —** CSF £42.13 TOTE £18.90: £3.30, £1.60, £1.10; EX 53.20 Place 6 £7.72, Place 5 £6.34.
Owner A S Ward & A Cooper **Bred** D A Taylor And Mrs A B Collins **Trained** Thirkleby, N Yorks

FOCUS
A modest bumper, run at no more than an ordinary gallop and the first two came clear. The form looks fair, rated through the runner-up.

NOTEBOOK
Custom Design, who showed ability in two outings last season, put that previous experience to good effect and gamely lost his maiden tag on this return to action. The ground was up his street, he will clearly stay further in time and clearly possesses a willing atttitude. *(op 10-1 tchd 9-1)*
Sabreflight ♦, third on both her previous outings for Richard Fahey, was only held in the final 50 yards having made a strong challenge from off the pace in the straight. She has joined a top yard, is entitled to improve plenty for this first run for 605 days, and is well up to going one better in due course. *(op 11-4)*
Character Building(IRE) ♦, whose stable produced a similar type to win first-time up at Hexham recently, was backed on course as if defeat was out of the question. However, after racing handily throughout, he never really looked like landing the gamble when race got serious turning for home. This was still a respectable debut, however, and he can reward his supporters in a similar race - perhaps on faster ground - in due course. *(op 9-2)*
Tous Chez(IRE), placed on both his bumper starts last term, had every chance two out, yet lacked the pace to stay with the principals and was eventually well beaten. He may need a faster surface to be seen at his best and can improve with this outing under his belt. *(op 3-1 tchd 5-1)*
T/Plt: £25.00 to a £1 stake. Pool: £35,067.30. 1,022.15 winning tickets. T/Qpdt: £20.40 to a £1 stake. Pool: £2,861.20. 103.40 winning tickets. JR

2116 - 2118a (Foreign Racing) - See Raceform Interactive

1668 BANGOR-ON-DEE (L-H)
Wednesday, November 9

2119 Meeting Abandoned - Waterlogged

1916 LINGFIELD (L-H)
Wednesday, November 9

OFFICIAL GOING: Chase course - soft (heavy in places); hurdle course - heavy (soft in places); all-weather - standard
Wind: Nil Weather: fine

2125 SUPPORT RETRAINING OF RACEHORSES MARES' ONLY NOVICES' HURDLE (12 hdls) 2m 7f
1:00 (1:00) (Class 4) 4-Y-0+ **£3,379** (£992; £496; £247)

Form RPR

23-F **1** **Heltornic (IRE)**[38] 1619 5-10-12 .... TScudamore 112+
(M Scudamore) *mde all: hit 3 out: clr bef next: nt fluent last: shkn up flat: kpt on* **4/9**[1]

2PP- **2** 1 ¾ **Amber Starlight**[221] 4694 7-10-12 97.... JimCrowley 105
(R Rowe) *hld up: prog 7th: chsd wnr 9th: rdn and no imp after 3 out: tried to cl last: kpt on flat but a hld* **4/1**[2]

6-56 **3** dist **Lets Get Busy (IRE)**[17] 1851 5-10-9 .... RYoung(3) 69
(J W Mullins) *t.k.h early: tended to jump lft: in tch to 8th: sn bhd: plugged on to take 3rd after last: btn 38l* **16/1**

000 **4** 1 **Logies Lass**[32] 1674 6-10-12 .... WMarston 68
(J S Smith) *t.k.h: hld up in last: lost tch 7th: sn t.o: styd on fr 2 out: tk 4th flat: btn 39l* **66/1**

3164 **5** 2 **Miss Merenda**[17] 1859 4-11-5 95.... PJBrennan 73
(J F Panvert) *chsd wnr to 9th: sn btn u.p: wknd 2 out: lost 2nd pls flat: btn 41l* **17/2**[3]

00-P **P** **Izzy Gets Busy (IRE)**[17] 1850 5-10-5 .... EDehdashti(7) —
(G F Bridgwater) *in tch: mstke 5th: sn wknd: t.o whn p.u bef 7th* **100/1**

6m 0.40s (-6.60) **Going Correction** -0.05s/f (Good) 6 Ran SP% **108.1**
Speed ratings: **109,108,—,—,— —** CSF £2.40 TOTE £1.50: £1.10, £1.70; EX 2.30.
Owner Stephen W Molloy **Bred** A W Buller **Trained** Bromsash, Herefordshire

FOCUS
The winner looks potentially useful and is value for more than the official margin, but those in behind are no more than moderate, and the form may not be totally reliable.

NOTEBOOK
Heltornic(IRE) secured victory with a strong front-running performance, as is her trait. The race took little winning and the ground may not have been entirely suitable, but she reaffirmed that she *has plenty of ability, and will be a major force against her own sex over hurdles. (tchd 8-15 tchd 4-7 in places)*
Amber Starlight did really well to get so close the winner, as she looked well beaten turning for home. She started the season off brightly last year, but her form tailed off badly afterwards, and it remains to be seen whether she will follow the same path this time. *(tchd 7-2)*
Lets Get Busy(IRE) shaped with a modicum of promise after looking well beaten at one stage of the race. She does not, however, appeal as a likely winner next time in similar company. *(tchd 20-1)*
Logies Lass did not significantly improve for the step up in trip.
Miss Merenda failed to produce her best on ground she was unproven on. *(op 7-1)*

2126 OXTED VETERINARY CLINIC NOVICES' H'CAP CHASE (18 fncs) 3m
1:30 (1:31) (Class 4) (0-90,90) 5-Y-0+ **£4,176** (£1,226; £613; £306)

Form RPR

655/ **1** **Precious Bane (IRE)**[191] 7-10-7 **71**.... AThornton 108+
(M Sheppard) *mde all: hit 8th: clr fr 1/2-way: in n.d fr 4 out: 25l ahd whn nt fluent 3 out: eased flat* **9/2**[3]

/0-6 **2** 16 **Dunbrody Millar (IRE)**[18] 1832 7-11-12 **90**.... RJohnson 103+
(P Bowen) *chsd wnr: blnd 10th: lost 2nd at 13th: lft 2nd again bef 3 out: no imp* **10/1**

-2P1 **3** 1 ½ **Five Alley (IRE)**[9] 1951 8-11-12 **90** 7ex.... SThomas 101
(R H Buckler) *in tch in chsng gp: dropped to rr 1/2-way and nt gng wl: effrt 14th: plugged on fr 3 out: no ch* **3/1**[2]

34-1 **4** 15 **Up The Pub (IRE)**[7] 1983 7-11-9 **87** 7ex.... RWalford 88+
(R H Alner) *prom in chsng gp: chsd wnr 13th: no ch whn hmpd by loose horse bnd bef 3 out: nt rcvr* **11/4**[1]

-P42 **5** 6 **Valley Warrior**[34] 1656 8-10-13 **77**.... WMarston 67
(J S Smith) *nt fluent in rr: effrt 10th: struggling and no prog fr 14th* **16/1**

06-6 **6** 1 ¾ **Syncopated Rhythm (IRE)**[14] 1877 5-11-3 **82**.... TScudamore 69
(N A Twiston-Davies) *nt jump wl: reminders after 5th: effrt and prom in chsng gp 10th: lost pl 13th: sn btn* **15/2**

000- **U** **Banaluso (IRE)**[211] 4814 5-11-0 **79**.... JPMcNamara —
(B G Powell) *in tch in chsng gp: hmpd and uns rdr 10th* **33/1**

-P50 **P** **Rollo (IRE)**[23] 1773 7-11-11 **89**....(v) PJBrennan —
(M F Harris) *nt jump wl: dropped to last after 5th: t.o whn p.u bef 7th* **33/1**

6P3- **P** **Pip Moss**[206] 4875 10-10-6 **70**.... BFenton —
(J A B Old) *prom in chsng gp: blnd 12th: sn btn: tailing off whn blnd 2 out: p.u bef last* **12/1**

5P0- **P** **Croghan Loch (IRE)**[287] 3535 8-10-8 **72**.... LAspell —
(P G Murphy) *hld up in last pair: brief effrt 10th: sn wknd: t.o in last whn p.u bef 2 out* **40/1**

6m 33.8s (10.10) **Going Correction** +0.70s/f (Soft)
WFA 5 from 7yo+ 1lb 10 Ran SP% **112.6**
Speed ratings: **111,105,105,100,98 97,—,—,—,—** CSF £45.18 CT £153.70 TOTE £3.50: £1.80, £3.00, £1.70; EX 53.00.
Owner M W & A N Harris **Bred** Rowanstown Stud **Trained** Eastnor, H'fords

FOCUS
The winner was incredibly well handicapped after a couple of wins between the flags, and won with a ton in hand. The form is probably sound at a low level.

NOTEBOOK
Precious Bane(IRE) made a complete mockery of his handicap mark on his return to racing under Rules. A dual winner in soft ground between the flags, he had the race won a long way from home and was value for much more than the official winning distance. He should win again if turned out before the Handicapper has a chance to reassess him. *(op 4-1 tchd 7-2)*
Dunbrody Millar(IRE) had absolutely no chance with the winner, but kept on nicely to beat the rest. His jumping remains a slight concern over fences, but an opportunity should be found for him soon in similar company. *(op 6-1)*
Five Alley(IRE), who looked far from co-operative at the rear of the field early in the race, kept on for maximum pressure and does not look a completely straightforward ride. He possibly did not enjoy going the quick pace set by the eventual winner. *(tchd 10-3 tchd 7-2 in a place)*

Up The Pub(IRE) was already well beaten when a loose horse took him very wide on the home turn. He should have handled underfoot conditions without a problem, so the race may have come too quickly for him after his success at Chepstow last time. *(op 10-3 tchd 7-2 in a place)*
Valley Warrior did not jump particularly well behind the strong pace, on only his second outing over fences. He can be given another chance. *(op 14-1)*
Syncopated Rhythm(IRE) was another in the race to not jump with any fluency, and never featured with a serious winning chance. *(op 10-1)*

2127 EBF "NATIONAL HUNT" NOVICES' HURDLE (QUALIFIER) (10 hdls) 2m 3f 110y
2:00 (2:06) (Class 3) 4-6-Y-0 **£5,126** (£1,505; £752; £375)

Form RPR
06-2 **1** **Fleurette**[7] 1982 5-10-7 .... TDoyle 103+
(D R Gandolfo) *trckd ldrs: effrt 2 out: rdn to ld last: styd on wl flat: jst hld on* **7/2**[2]
100- **2** *shd* **It's In The Stars**[203] 4935 5-11-0 .... RJohnson 109+
(H D Daly) *mde most at stdy pce: rdn and hdd last: rallied strly nr fin: jst failed* **6/1**
1/4- **3** *17* **Cruising Clyde**[385] 1776 6-11-0 .... NFehily 92
(C J Mann) *prom: cl up 2 out: wknd and mstke last* **4/1**[3]
0 **4** *1 3/4* **Finsbury Fred (IRE)**[17] 1849 4-11-0 .... TScudamore 90
(N A Twiston-Davies) *mostly trckd ldr fr 2nd: hit 3 out: wknd after 2 out* **33/1**
2-61 **5** *4* **Money Line (IRE)**[10] 1938 6-11-7 .... APMcCoy 93
(Jonjo O'Neill) *hld up in tch: effrt 7th: rdn 3 out: wknd after 2 out* **5/2**[1]
353- **6** *16* **Follow Your Heart (IRE)**[211] 4819 5-11-0 .... LAspell 70
(N J Gifford) *wl in tch: stl chsng ldrs bef 2 out: wknd tamely* **11/2**
0-3 **7** *29* **Be Telling (IRE)**[19] 1818 6-11-0 .... PMoloney 41
(B J Curley) *racd wd: in tch: swtchd to inner after 3 out: wknd and mstke 2 out: eased flat* **33/1**
400- **F** **Captain Aubrey (IRE)**[204] 4922 6-11-0 .... PJBrennan —
(J A B Old) *chsd ldrs tl fell 5th* **33/1**
24 **P** **Silverio (GER)**[146] 769 4-11-0 .... JEMoore —
(G L Moore) *in tch in rr to 6th: sn wknd: t.o whn p.u after 3 out* **40/1**
030- **P** **Ellas Recovery (IRE)**[203] 4933 5-11-0 .... JamesDavies —
(D B Feek) *a in rr: rdn and wknd 6th: t.o whn p.u after 3 out* **100/1**
511 **P** **Hill Forts Timmy**[154] 685 5-11-0 .... AThornton —
(J W Mullins) *chsd ldrs tl wknd rapidly 7th: t.o whn p.u after 3 out* **20/1**
F **Ben Tally Ho** 4-11-0 .... WHutchinson —
(Ian Williams) *hld up in rr: prog 5th: wl in tch after 3 out: 6th and wkng whn fell last: winded* **33/1**

5m 9.20s (6.50) **Going Correction** -0.05s/f (Good)
WFA 4 from 5yo+ 12lb **12 Ran SP% 120.4**
Speed ratings: **85,84,78,77,75 69,57,—,—,— —,—** CSF £23.73 TOTE £4.60: £1.20, £2.60, £2.80; EX 27.50.
Owner Starlight Racing **Bred** A W F Clapperton **Trained** Wantage, Oxon

FOCUS
This was probably a fair novice event. The first two look to be above average, while a few in behind ran with promise for the future. The form is rated through the third and the race should produce winners.

NOTEBOOK
Fleurette ◆ looked slightly unlucky not to have won last time, but made amends in good style, showing a good turn of foot in very sticky ground. She looks sure to get further and looks a very promising prospect. *(op 11-4)*
It's In The Stars ◆ showed more than enough on his first run of the season to suggest he will win a race of a similar nature. Having won a bumper in heavy ground, he may need the mud to be flying to be at his very best. *(op 13-2 tchd 5-1)*
Cruising Clyde moved stylishly for most of the race before not quickening in the home straight. He can be given another chance on less-demanding ground. *(op 5-1)*
Finsbury Fred(IRE) was always close to the lead, but could only keep on at one pace as the race became competitive. To his credit, he stayed on really resolutely up the straight, and appeals as the sort likely to improve for a step up in trip.
Money Line(IRE) was being pushed along from an early stage, and it cannot be certain that it was just his penalty that stopped him from being involved in the finish. He looked a hard ride at Carlisle when winning last time, and almost certainly requires a stiffer track to be most effective. *(op 11-4)*
Follow Your Heart(IRE) ◆ appeared to be going nicely coming into the straight, but found little under pressure and almost certainly got tired in the ground. He is entitled to progress for the race and definitely has ability. *(op 9-1)*
Ben Tally Ho shaped nicely on this debut before falling and reportedly winding himself. It must be hoped that it does not affect his confidence. *(op 14-1)*
Hill Forts Timmy came into the race on the back of two consecutive wins in bumper company. However, on vastly different ground, he never got competitive and will surely be better suited by a sounder surface. *(op 14-1)*

2128 GREATWOOD RESCUE AND REHABILITATION H'CAP CHASE (11 fncs 1 omitted) 2m
2:30 (2:30) (Class 3) (0-130,125) 5-Y-0+ **£8,264** (£2,565; £1,381)

Form RPR
1P-B **1** **Haafel (USA)**[9] 1953 8-10-11 **110** .... PHide 119+
(G L Moore) *pressed ldr: led 8th: rdn bef last: kpt on wl flat* **7/2**[3]
PP-F **2** *1 1/2* **Tanikos (FR)**[25] 1739 6-11-12 **125** .... MFoley 133+
(N J Henderson) *led to 8th: pressed wnr after: chal after last: no ex nr fin* **13/8**[1]
61-6 **3** *3* **Imaginaire (USA)**[18] 1831 10-10-13 **112** .... SThomas 116
(Miss Venetia Williams) *hld up in 3rd: effrt 3 out: rdn and one pce fr 2 out* **5/2**[2]
25U3 **F** **Vigoureux (FR)**[138] 825 6-9-9 **99** oh4 .... (p) WKennedy[(5)] —
(S Gollings) *hld up in last: effrt to dispute cl 3rd whn fell 3 out* **9/2**

4m 16.0s (8.10) **Going Correction** +0.70s/f (Soft) **4 Ran SP% 107.1**
Speed ratings: **107,106,104,—** CSF £9.56 TOTE £3.20; EX 8.00.
Owner D R Hunnisett **Bred** Shadwell Farm Inc **Trained** Woodingdean, E Sussex

FOCUS
A trappy event despite the lack of runners and it would have been even tighter had Vigoureux not come down three out. The form is rated through the winner and third.

NOTEBOOK
Haafel(USA), still going well when brought down on his reappearance at Plumpton, comes from a yard that is firing in the winners at present and he stayed on too strongly for Tanikos in the final quarter mile. This was his second win over fences and he looks capable of adding further successes on ground he seems to handle well. *(op 10-3)*
Tanikos(FR), a horse who has had problems with his jumping in the past, took up his customary position at the head of affairs and jump soundly on his occasion, but he was simply not good enough for the winner and was always being held. A little leniency from the Handicapper may see him back winning. *(tchd 6-4)*
Imaginaire(USA) stepped up on his reappearance effort, but was left behind from the second last and could only plug on. He is another who may need a little further help from the Handicapper before he is winning. *(op 3-1)*
Vigoureux(FR) was bang there and would have been involved in the finish in some way had he not come down at the third last. He has yet to win over fences, but his turn will not be far off if this does not affect his confidence too badly. *(op 4-1)*

2129 OWNERS SUPPORT RETRAINING OF RACEHORSES AMATEUR RIDERS' H'CAP CHASE (13 fncs 1 omitted) 2m 4f 110y
3:00 (3:01) (Class 4) (0-90,88) 5-Y-0+ **£3,959** (£1,228; £613; £306)

Form RPR
3103 **1** **Lanmire Tower (IRE)**[3] 2080 11-11-5 **88** .... (p) MrTFWoodside[(7)] 95+
(S Gollings) *racd freely: mde most fr 2nd to 7th: led again next: j.rt 3 out: clr last: pushed along and hld on flat* **11/1**
-140 **2** *1/2* **Ask The Umpire (IRE)**[8] 1977 10-11-4 **80** .... (p) MrTGreenall 86
(N E Berry) *hld up in last: prog to trck wnr 4 out: rdn and nt qckn 2 out: kpt on flat and gaining at fin* **9/4**[1]
343- **3** *13* **Regal River (IRE)**[266] 3884 8-10-0 **69** .... MrGTumelty[(7)] 62
(John R Upson) *settled in 4th: outpcd fr 9th: wnt modest 3rd bef 3 out: no imp ldng pair tl styd on flat* **3/1**[2]
PP3- **4** *13* **Tallow Bay (IRE)**[205] 4912 10-10-1 **66** .... MrJMorgan[(3)] 46
(Mrs S Wall) *led to 2nd: led and nt fluent 7th: hdd next: j.rt next 2 and wknd* **7/1**[3]
20/F **U** **Freteval (FR)**[18] 1832 8-10-9 **74** ow2 .... MrPCowley[(3)] —
(S J Gilmore) *led briefly 5th: cl 3rd whn blnd and uns rdr 8th* **9/4**[1]

5m 35.3s (16.30) **Going Correction** +0.70s/f (Soft) **5 Ran SP% 107.4**
Speed ratings: **96,95,90,85,—** CSF £34.48 TOTE £10.50: £2.70, £1.40; EX 22.10.
Owner Mrs D Dukes **Bred** Miss Emer Carty **Trained** Scamblesby, Lincs

FOCUS
The front pair drew well clear in what was a moderate handicap chase. The winner and second are the best guides to the form. First fence on far side omitted. Trevor Woodside's first winner.

NOTEBOOK
Lanmire Tower(IRE) was on the pace throughout and saw his race out remarkably well considering he was a bit keen early on. It developed into a dual from some way out and, although looking set to come off second-best for most of the straight, the second did not pick up immediately and he was always holding him. He more than pays his way and will continue to win in his turn. *(op 7-1 tchd 12-1)*
Ask The Umpire(IRE) ran a shocker off this mark when last seen over fences, but he was in much better form this time and left behind a poor recent effort over hurdles. He finished well, but was always being held and his inability to run two races alike means he is one to continue to tread carefully with. *(op 2-1)*
Regal River(IRE) ◆ hails from a yard whose horses often need a run and this fellow looked another case in point. It will be disappointing if he cannot win at least once off his lowly mark this season. *(op 7-2)*
Tallow Bay(IRE) showed up briefly, but he was soon toiling after a couple of mistakes and remains winless in almost three years. *(op 8-1)*
Freteval(FR), narrowly ahead when falling on his reappearance, was again going well when unseating and, whilst he looks a winner waiting to happen, he clearly has a few problems in the jumping department.

2130 ROR SECOND CAREER FOR RACEHORSES H'CAP HURDLE (12 hdls) 2m 7f
3:30 (3:30) (Class 3) (0-115,113) 4-Y-0+ **£4,781** (£1,403; £701; £350)

Form RPR
24P- **1** **Miko De Beauchene (FR)**[210] 4825 5-11-8 **109** .... AThornton 117+
(R H Alner) *hld up in rr: cl up fr 1/2-way: mstke 3 out: prog to ld bef 2 out: j.lft last 2: styd on wl* **5/1**[3]
F51- **2** *7* **Jaloux D'Estruval (FR)**[296] 3401 8-11-12 **113** .... MFoley 114
(Mrs L C Taylor) *hld up in last: cl up fr 1/2-way: prog to chse wnr 2 out: rdn and no imp bef last* **5/2**[2]
0/35 **3** *11* **Good Potential (IRE)**[20] 1796 9-10-3 **90** .... (t) WMarston 83+
(D J Wintle) *in tch: rdn and struggling 3 out: mstke 2 out: kpt on after: tk 3rd and hit last* **14/1**
141- **4** *8* **Barrys Ark (IRE)**[227] 4583 7-11-7 **108** .... WHutchinson 90
(J A B Old) *trckd ldrs: effrt to ld after 3 out: hdd & wknd bef next* **10/1**
/0P- **5** *3* **Celtic Major (IRE)**[327] 2875 7-10-12 **99** .... RJohnson 78
(P Bowen) *mstkes: prom: led 7th: blnd 9th: hdd after 3 out: wknd and eased bef next: pushed along again flat* **6/1**
0P-0 **6** *2 1/2* **Geography (IRE)**[9] 1949 5-9-8 **88** .... (p) RLucey-Butler[(7)] 65
(P Butler) *chsd ldr to 7th: rdn and wknd after 3 out* **33/1**
1 **P** **Dunbell Boy (IRE)**[18] 1833 7-11-4 **105** .... NFehily —
(C J Mann) *settled towards rr: cl up 1/2-way: rdn 9th: no rspnse and sn wknd: p.u bef 2 out* **2/1**[1]
PP-3 **P** **Lalagune (FR)**[27] 1727 6-11-12 **113** .... BFenton —
(Miss E C Lavelle) *led at decent pce: stdd after 6th: hdd next: lost pl: reminders 8th: sn last: p.u after 3 out* **20/1**

6m 2.80s (-4.20) **Going Correction** -0.05s/f (Good) **8 Ran SP% 116.3**
Speed ratings: **105,102,98,95,94 94,—,—** CSF £18.78 CT £164.82 TOTE £5.90: £1.40, £1.70, £2.60; EX 20.30.
Owner Andrew Wiles **Bred** Raymond Bellanger **Trained** Droop, Dorset

FOCUS
A modest contest, but the runners finished well strung out and Miko De Beauchene ran out a tidy winner with the runner-up close to his best and setting the standard.

NOTEBOOK
Miko De Beauchene(FR) failed to win last season, but he ran many good races in defeat, including when putting together a run comprising of four seconds. Rising six, he looks to have strengthened over the summer and romped away with this, staying on strongly right the way to the line. A chaser in the making, there are more races in him over hurdles first and he looks deserving of a rise in grade. *(op 11-2)*
Jaloux D'Estruval(FR) has improved since being fitted with a hood and he made a pleasing reappearance, keeping on to finish clear of the third. He is more of a chaser, despite having failed to complete in seven of his 12 outings over fences, and is worth risking again over the larger obstacles. *(op 11-4 tchd 3-1)*
Good Potential(IRE) is back on a decent mark, but he did not offer a great deal and needs to do better. His jumping could have been slicker. *(op 16-1)*
Barrys Ark(IRE) looks a nice chasing prospect and this run was always likely to be needed. He *showed up well for a long way before getting tired and can be expected to improve considerably. (op 8-1)*
Celtic Major(IRE) was the disappointment of the race and he does not look to be progressing. Several early mistakes did him no favours and he was left trailing in the straight. He may do better over fences, but needs to. *(op 8-1)*
Lalagune(FR) *Official explanation: jockey said mare hung right (tchd 9-4)*
Dunbell Boy(IRE), an ex-Irish horse who made a winning hurdling debut at Chepstow last month, was unable to build on that and the way he stopped suggested there may have been something *amiss. He is better than this and deserves another chance. Official explanation: trainer had no explanation for the poor form shown (tchd 9-4)*

The Form Book, Raceform Ltd, Compton, RG20 6NL

2131 MOORCROFT RACEHORSE WELFARE CENTRE INTERMEDIATE OPEN NATIONAL HUNT FLAT RACE 2m

4:00 (4:01) (Class 6) 4-6-Y-O **£1,808** (£527; £263)

Form RPR
1 **Swaythe (USA)** 4-10-11 .... TDoyle 95+
(P R Webber) *trckd ldrs: prog to ld over 2f out: clr over 1f out: r.o wl* **5/1**[2]
0-6 **2** *6* **Flyingwithoutwings**[179] [355] 6-11-4 .... WHutchinson 92
(A King) *t.k.h: hld up towards rr: prog over 3f out: rdn to chse wnr wl over 1f out: no imp* **8/1**
0- **3** *1 ½* **Katy Jones**[270] [3810] 5-10-11 .... (t) BJCrowley 84
(Noel T Chance) *t.k.h: hld up in last pair: gd prog over 2f out: shkn up and one pce fr over 1f out* **16/1**
4 *2 ½* **Top Brass (IRE)** 4-11-4 .... APMcCoy 88
(K G Reveley) *trckd ldrs: pushed along over 3f out: outpcd fr 2f out: n.d after* **1/1**[1]
5 *1 ½* **She's The Lady** 5-10-6 .... MNicolls[(5)] 80
(R S Brookhouse) *hld up towards rr: prog 7f out: trckd ldrs gng easily over 2f out: shkn up and wknd over 1f out* **22/1**
0-50 **6** *nk* **Daramoon (IRE)**[32] [1674] 4-10-11 .... MBradburne 79
(D J S Ffrench Davis) *towards rr: rdn over 3f out: sme prog over 2f out: nt clr run and swtchd rt over 1f out: plugged on* **66/1**
0-2 **7** *1 ¼* **Thenameescapesme**[179] [355] 5-11-4 .... NFehily 85
(T R George) *sn trckd ldrs: rdn and wl in tch over 2f out: wknd over 1f out* **10/1**
0 **8** *1 ¾* **Romangod (IRE)**[11] [1922] 5-10-11 .... (t) MrRQuinn[(7)] 83
(J A Supple) *settled midfield: outpcd 3f out: plugged on fnl 2f* **100/1**
336/ **9** *5* **Stoneyford Ben (IRE)**[597] [4517] 6-11-4 .... RJohnson 78
(S Gollings) *t.k.h: led 10f out: kicked on over 3f out: hdd & wknd over 2f out* **7/1**[3]
4 **10** *1 ¼* **Azure Wings (IRE)**[27] [1730] 5-10-4 .... SCrawford[(7)] 70
(K C Bailey) *led to 10f out: lost pl over 5f out: sn struggling in rr* **25/1**
440 **11** *nk* **Allez Melina**[39] [1600] 4-10-11 .... (t) ATinkler 70
(Mrs A J Hamilton-Fairley) *hld up in last pair: outpcd 4f out: bhd after* **50/1**
0 **12** *3* **Eudyptes**[11] [1922] 6-11-4 .... MBatchelor 74
(N E Berry) *prom: chsd ldr over 7f out to 4f out: wknd* **100/1**

3m 40.8s
WFA 4 from 5yo+ 12lb **12** Ran SP% **118.9**
CSF £42.53 TOTE £7.10: £2.40, £2.50, £3.70; EX 60.60 Place 6 £81.16, Place 5 £74.88.
Owner The Syndicators **Bred** Juddmonte Farms Inc **Trained** Mollington, Oxon

FOCUS
As is the norm with Polytrack bumpers it turned into something of a sprint and the form is a bit suspect, albeit the winner would have scored regardless of how the race was run. The runner-up sets the level for the present.

NOTEBOOK
Swaythe(USA), a well-bred filly hailing from a stable that enjoys its share of success in this sphere, was always likely to be well-equipped for this sort of test, being by Swain and a relation of smart staying hurdler Stromness, and she showed a decent change of gear to go clear from the turn-in. She will face an altogether different test on a slower surface on turf, but she could not have made a more pleasing debut. *(tchd 6-1)*
Flyingwithoutwings may have got a bit closer had he been better placed in the race, but he would not have beaten the winner anyhow. He did not see out his two previous races, but should stay a bit further over hurdles and this was at least a step in the right direction. *(op 6-1)*
Katy Jones, highly tried on her only previous attempt, was travelling too well for her own good early and she came from a long way back to claim a never-nearer third. There are races to be won with her and she can score in this sphere. *Official explanation: jockey said mare hung right throughout (op 14-1)*
Top Brass(IRE), whose stable won a bumper with a newcomer the previous day, was solid in the market and was clearly expected to make a winning debut, but he lacked the pace of the winner and was run out of the places in the straight. He will stay further in time, but can win a bumper on turf. *(op 11-10 tchd 10-11, after 11-8 and 5-4 in places)*
She's The Lady shaped most promisingly and will no doubt have delighted connections with how strongly she travelled. The run will bring her forward and she may find a mares-only race. *(op 20-1)*
Stoneyford Ben(IRE) was subject to a positive ride, but he was readily brushed aside at the business end and was ultimately well beaten. *(tchd 9-1)*
T/Plt: £40.60 to a £1 stake. Pool: £51,329.15. 922.85 winning tickets. T/Qpdt: £14.80 to a £1 stake. Pool: £3,568.40. 178.20 winning tickets. JN

2132 - 2138a (Foreign Racing) - See Raceform Interactive

1800 LUDLOW (R-H)

Thursday, November 10

OFFICIAL GOING: Good (good to soft in places)
Wind: Almost nil Weather: Some light rain

2139 TEME CONDITIONAL JOCKEYS' (S) HURDLE (9 hdls) 2m

1:00 (1:00) (Class 5) 4-Y-O+ **£2,439** (£716; £358; £178)

Form RPR
0/0- **1** **Auetaler (GER)**[49] [1536] 11-10-4 .... (p) BCByrnes[(6)] 100+
(E McNamara, Ire) *hld up in tch: led on bit appr 3 out: rdn appr 2 out: drvn out* **7/1**
0046 **2** *2* **My Sharp Grey**[14] [1902] 6-10-3 91 .... RStephens 91
(J Gallagher) *hld up: hdwy appr 5th: rdn to chse wnr 3 out: nt qckn fr 2 out* **9/1**
50-3 **3** *5* **Ambersong**[7] [2008] 7-10-10 91 .... GCarenza 94+
(A W Carroll) *hld up in mid-div: lost pl after 4th: rdn and hdwy appr 3 out: no imp whn hit last* **5/1**[3]
4FP1 **4** *3 ½* **Ball Games**[15] [1883] 7-10-8 90 .... MMcAvoy[(8)] 96
(James Moffatt) *hld up and bhd: hdwy after 6th: one pce fr 2 out* **14/1**
1 **5** *¾* **Ballito (IRE)**[21] [1800] 6-11-2 90 .... (p) WKennedy 95
(John G Carr, Ire) *hld up in mid-div: rdn 6th: styd on fr 3 out: nt trble ldrs* **12/1**
1230 **6** *1 ¾* **Nowator (POL)**[88] [1221] 8-10-2 104 .... WMcCarthy[(8)] 87
(T R George) *led to 3rd: led 4th: rdn and hdd appr 3 out: wkng whn hit 2 out* **5/2**[1]
5-40 **7** *2 ½* **The Gene Genie**[18] [1862] 10-10-4 92 .... JamesWhite[(6)] 86+
(R J Hodges) *hld up in mid-div: hit 2nd: no real prog fr 3 out* **9/2**[2]
8 *¾* **Trianger (IRE)**[19] [1195] 6-10-10 .... TJMalone 84
(P J Rothwell, Ire) *hld up and bhd: hdwy appr 3 out: hung rt and wknd fr 2 out* **20/1**
9 *9* **Weet Watchers**[45] 5-10-7 .... MGoldstein[(3)] 77+
(T Wall) *hld up: hdwy after 6th: wknd 2 out: hit last* **100/1**
0P05 **10** *3 ½* **Simiola**[14] [1890] 6-10-3 75 .... MNicolls 68+
(S T Lewis) *hld up: hdwy after 5th: rdn after 6th: sn wknd* **100/1**
0-56 **11** *1 ½* **Forbearing (IRE)**[67] [1405] 8-10-7 95 .... (p) JDiment[(3)] 70
(F Jordan) *hld up in mid-div: rdn 4th: hit 6th: sn bhd* **33/1**
12 *1* **Red Rocky**[33] 4-9-9 .... AHawkins[(8)] 62
(R Hollinshead) *t.k.h: a in rr* **100/1**
3P4S **13** *30* **Gipsy Cricketer**[4] [2074] 9-10-2 69 .... JKington[(8)] 39
(M Scudamore) *w ldr: led 1st to 4th: wknd appr 3 out: t.o* **50/1**
P0-0 **14** *6* **Lanos (POL)**[16] [1875] 7-10-10 83 .... TGreenway 33
(W Davies) *chsd ldrs tl wknd 6th: t.o* **66/1**

3m 47.6s (-4.70) **Going Correction** -0.10s/f (Good)
WFA 4 from 5yo+ 12lb **14** Ran SP% **114.4**
Speed ratings: **107,106,103,101,101 100,99,98,94,92 91,91,76,73** CSF £62.52 TOTE £10.40: £2.60, £4.00, £1.90.There was no bid for the winner. Nowator was claimed by Naughty Diesel Ltd for £6,000.
Owner James McNamara **Bred** Dr G Briel **Trained** Rathkeale, Co. Limerick

FOCUS
Not a bad race for the grade with formerly smart hurdler Auetaler turning back the years to win his first race since 2001. The winner and third set a reasonable standard for the form which should work out.

NOTEBOOK
Auetaler(GER), a really smart performer with Martin Pipe a few years back, showed he can still do it at the lowest level with a workmanlike win. His last win was in a novice chase back in 2001, but he was always likely to go well in such a bad race and he may be capable of scoring again at a similar level. *(op 9-2)*
My Sharp Grey scored back-to-back wins at this course back in the winter of 2003, but she has been unable to get her head in front since and it required a drop in grade for her to show some form again. She was far enough clear of the third to suggest she can pick up a similar race. *(op 10-1 tchd 12-1)*
Ambersong moved into a challenging position as they turned for home, but he had already began to flatten out when hitting the last and it did not affect his finishing position. A similar effort should see him go close in this type of race. *(op 11-2)*
Ball Games kept on all too late and a more positive ride in future may help.
Ballito(IRE), a surprise winner here last month over three miles, was always likely to find this test against him and it was no surprise to see him running on too late in the day. A return to further should allow him to win again *(op 10-1)*
Nowator(POL) took them along for much of the way, but he was readily brushed aside on the approach to the third last and this has to go down as a disappointing effort. *(op 3-1 tchd 9-4)*
Lanos(POL) *Official explanation: jockey said gelding had a breathing problem (op 50-1)*

2140 SPONSOR AT LUDLOW H'CAP HURDLE (11 hdls) 2m 5f

1:30 (1:31) (Class 4) (0-85,85) 4-Y-O+ **£3,532** (£1,037; £518; £259)

Form RPR
-050 **1** **Jug Of Punch (IRE)**[16] [1875] 6-10-13 79 .... PCStringer[(7)] 86+
(S T Lewis) *hld up: hdwy appr 8th: chalng whn jinked lft 3 out: led sn after last: rdn out* **50/1**
2 *2 ½* **Moscow Summit (IRE)**[131] [889] 7-11-3 83 .... BCByrnes[(7)] 87
(E McNamara, Ire) *t.k.h in mid-div: hdwy 7th: led on bit appr 3 out: rdn whn hung lft appr 2 out: hdd sn after last: nt qkn* **20/1**
00-4 **3** *4* **Seveneightsix (IRE)**[29] [1723] 5-10-7 66 .... (b) WMarston 67+
(D J Wintle) *hld up: hdwy 3rd: rdn appr 3 out: mstke 2 out: one pce* **7/1**[2]
2-21 **4** *6* **Saucy Night**[10] [1949] 9-10-4 70 .... LHeard[(7)] 67+
(Simon Earle) *prom: jnd ldr 4th: led appr 6th: rdn and hdd appr 3 out: wknd appr last* **8/13**[1]
30-0 **5** *17* **Deliceo (IRE)**[19] [1825] 12-11-12 85 .... MBradburne 62
(M Sheppard) *mid-div: mstke 5th: rdn after 7th: no real prog fr 3 out* **22/1**
36-U **6** *2 ½* **Tianyi (IRE)**[18] [1852] 9-11-12 85 .... (v) TScudamore 59
(M Scudamore) *hld up in tch: wknd 8th* **40/1**
002- **7** *2 ½* **Mounts Bay**[304] [3300] 6-11-0 80 .... JamesWhite[(7)] 52
(R J Hodges) *hld up towards rr: hdwy appr 7th: rdn appr 8th: wknd appr 3 out* **16/1**
00-0 **8** *9* **Fair Touch (IRE)**[180] [357] 6-11-7 80 .... (t) JAMcCarthy 43
(C P Morlock) *reminders after 5th: a bhd* **40/1**
6/ **9** *28* **Constant Husband**[214] 12-9-12 64 .... MGoldstein[(7)] —
(R N Bevis) *plld hrd: led after 2nd tl appr 6th: wknd appr 8th: t.o* **66/1**
F35- **10** *dist* **Miss Rideamight**[268] [3858] 6-10-11 75 .... MNicolls[(5)] —
(G Brown) *a bhd: t.o* **20/1**
0022 **B** **Think Quick (IRE)**[79] [1297] 5-11-1 84 .... AHawkins[(10)] —
(R Hollinshead) *hld up in rr: b.d 6th* **10/1**[3]
-PP0 **U** **Firstflor**[79] [1297] 6-10-9 68 .... JPMcNamara —
(F Jordan) *hld up and bhd: hit 3rd: stdy hdwy whn hmpd and uns rdr 7th* **66/1**
P5FP **P** **Tumbleweed Glen (IRE)**[18] [1852] 9-10-6 68 .... (b) LVickers[(3)] —
(P Kelsall) *prom tl lost pl appr 6th: t.o whn p.u bef 2 out* **100/1**
U00/ **F** **Could It Be Legal**[616] [4145] 8-9-13 63 .... LStephens[(5)] —
(Evan Williams) *plld hrd: led tl after 2nd: wkng whn fell 7th* **25/1**
PFP- **F** **Does It Matter**[281] [3644] 8-10-0 59 oh3 .... JPByrne —
(Evan Williams) *plld hrd: hdwy 2nd: lost pl 4th: bhd whn stmbld and fell 6th* **66/1**

5m 17.0s (-1.30) **Going Correction** -0.10s/f (Good) **15** Ran SP% **119.4**
Speed ratings: **98,97,95,93,86 85,84,81,70,—** —,—,—,—,— CSF £760.42 CT £7648.15 TOTE £64.20: £8.50, £6.50, £1.20; EX 434.30.
Owner Simon T Lewis **Bred** T J Monaghan **Trained** Longdon, Worcs

FOCUS
A race little better than the opening seller and Jug Of Punch caused quite a shock. The form looks unreliable.

NOTEBOOK
Jug Of Punch(IRE) left behind a few disappointing efforts and was finally able to get off the mark over hurdles, causing quite a shock in the process. He cleared away on the run-in to ultimately win with a bit to spare and it will be interesting to see if this lowly-rated gelding can go on and win again.
Moscow Summit(IRE), an Irish-raider, travelled strongly for much of the way and looked the likely winner when cruising into the lead three out, but he had no answer to the winner's late burst and will have to wait another day before finally getting his head in front.
Seveneightsix(IRE) has looked a slightly improved mare of late since sporting the blinkers and this was a sound effort. She has yet to win, but there is a race in her at a lowly level. *(op 11-1 tchd 13-2)*
Saucy Night had not finished outside the front two in any of his seven most recent starts (hurdles & fences) and as a result was rightly made a short-price favourite. However, having raced prominently and led them into the straight, he began to struggle and was soon left toiling, eventually being run out of the places. This was an uncharacteristic run and there appeared to be no obvious excuse.
Deliceo(IRE), reverting to hurdles off a favourable mark compared with his chase rating, lacked the pace of the leading quintet and is unlikely to be winning over hurdles at this stage of his career. *(op 20-1)*

2141 ARROW NOVICES' H'CAP CHASE (13 fncs) 2m
2:00 (2:03) (Class 4) (0-105,105) 4-Y-0+
£3,901 (£1,152; £576; £288; £143; £72)

Form RPR
-46F 1 **Tuesday's Child**[15] [1877] 6-10-10 **89** TJMurphy 108+
(Miss H C Knight) *hld up in tch: led 3 out: shkn up after 2 out: lft clr last* **7/1**[3]
P0-0 2 4 **Flower Of Pitcur**[29] [1716] 8-10-13 **92** JPMcNamara 100+
(T R George) *hld up in tch: lost pl 5th: hit 9th: hdwy appr 4 out: r.o flat: nt trble wnr* **14/1**
-660 3 1 **Brooklyn's Gold (USA)**[26] [1743] 10-11-12 **105** RJohnson 111
(Ian Williams) *hld up and bhd: hdwy 4 out: rdn 3 out: kpt on flat* **8/1**
-463 4 5 **She's My Girl (IRE)**[21] [1801] 10-11-3 **96** (p) JamesDavies 98+
(John G Carr, Ire) *hld up in tch: rdn after 4 out: lft 2nd briefly and hit last: wknd* **20/1**
5113 5 nk **Pure Brief (IRE)**[18] [1852] 8-10-11 **90** (p) PMoloney 93+
(J Mackie) *hld up in mid-div: rdn after 8th: hdwy appr 4 out: btn whn j.lft 3 out* **9/2**[2]
5/ 6 23 **It Was'Nt Me (IRE)**[19] [1840] 8-11-11 **104** MBradburne 82
(M Sheppard) *a bhd* **33/1**
2006 7 dist **Granite Man (IRE)**[14] [1895] 5-10-2 **81** RMcGrath —
(Jonjo O'Neill) *sn bhd: t.o fr 6th* **14/1**
263P P **Alexander Musical (IRE)**[15] [1877] 7-9-11 **81** oh17 ow2 MNicolls(5) —
(S T Lewis) *a bhd: t.o whn p.u bef 6th* **66/1**
6P33 P **Ready To Rumble (NZ)**[6] [2026] 8-9-13 **83** (b[1]) PCO'Neill(5) —
(R C Guest) *chsd ldrs tl rdn and wknd after 9th: bhd whn p.u after 3 out* **4/1**[1]
00-2 P **Lord On The Run (IRE)**[18] [1852] 6-11-6 **102** RYoung(3) —
(J W Mullins) *j. bdly lft: led tl after 8th: wkng whn eased and p.u bef 4 out* **4/1**[1]
F **Nayodabayo (IRE)**[466] [1094] 5-11-7 **105** (p) MrNWilliams(5) 120+
(Evan Williams) *prom: led after 8th: hit 4 out: rdn and hdd 3 out: ev ch whn fell last* **10/1**

4m 1.30s (-2.80) **Going Correction** 0.0s/f (Good) **11** Ran SP% **113.4**
Speed ratings: **107,105,104,102,101 90,—,—,—,—** — CSF £90.76 CT £795.92 TOTE £7.50: £2.90, £4.40, £2.20; EX 131.90.
Owner Jim Lewis **Bred** Mrs Valerie J Curl And Miss Catherine Cunningham **Trained** West Lockinge, Oxon

FOCUS
Moderate form rated through the second, but Tuesday's Child did it well in the end having been left clear at the last and looks the sort to progress further.

NOTEBOOK
Tuesday's Child ◆, an early faller on his fencing debut at Cheltenham, showed little sign of a dent in confidence and jumped neatly throughout. Sent on approaching the third last, he still had to dispose of Nayodabayo when that one fell at the last, leaving him clear. A lightly-raced sort open to further improvement, he is one to keep on the right side of and may well win again with his stable beginning to hit top stride. *(op 10-1)*
Flower Of Pitcur has yet to win in six starts over fences, but this was his best effort thus far and he capitalised on Nayodabayo's fall to claim second. Good, fast ground is important to him and he can win a small race when encountering such conditions. *(tchd 16-1)*
Brooklyn's Gold(USA) is lightly raced over fences and this was a fair effort, but he is not getting any better and needs a little further assistance from the Handicapper. *(op 9-1)*
She's My Girl(IRE) was not disgraced with the cheekpieces refitted, but she achieved little in finishing fourth and makes little appeal with the future in mind. *(op 14-1)*
Pure Brief(IRE) made a little late headway, but again gave the impression he is not going to be able to win off of this sort of mark. *(tchd 5-1)*
Nayodabayo(IRE), making his English debut with the cheekpieces applied, was in the process of running a cracker and came through to virtually join the winner at the last, but he could not get the landing gear down quickly enough and came to grief. He will soon be gaining compensation if this has not affected his confidence too badly. *(op 3-1 tchd 9-2)*
Lord On The Run(IRE) continually forfeited ground by jumping out to the left and had nothing left to *offer when wisely being pulled up with half a mile to run. Official explanation: trainer's representative had no explanation for the poor form shown (op 3-1 tchd 9-2)*
Ready To Rumble(NZ) has never been the most consistent and the first-time blinkers did little for *him. He remains a risky betting proposition. Official explanation: jockey said gelding was never travelling (op 3-1 tchd 9-2)*

2142 EUROPEAN BREEDERS FUND "NATIONAL HUNT" NOVICES' HURDLE (QUALIFIER) (9 hdls) 2m
2:30 (2:30) (Class 4) 4-6-Y-0 **£4,372** (£1,283; £641; £320)

Form RPR
4- 1 **Menchikov (FR)**[222] [4697] 5-11-0 MFoley 103+
(N J Henderson) *a.p: hit 3rd: chalng whn hit 3 out: hrd rdn to ld cl home* **1/1**[1]
4-P5 2 1 **Billyandi (IRE)**[23] [1782] 5-10-7 MGoldstein(7) 99
(N A Twiston-Davies) *led: hrd rdn and hdd cl home* **20/1**
30-P 3 11 **Charming Fellow (IRE)**[33] [1672] 5-11-0 TJMurphy 89+
(Miss H C Knight) *hld up in tch: ev ch appr 3 out: swtchd rt appr 2 out: sn wknd* **10/1**[3]
-P00 4 5 **Bollitree Bob**[9] [1968] 4-11-0 BJCrowley 83
(M Scudamore) *plld hrd in rr: hdwy appr 3 out: no real prog fr 2 out* **50/1**
545- 5 1 ¼ **Britesand (IRE)**[246] [4267] 5-11-0 JamesDavies 82
(J S Moore) *prom: hit 2nd: wkng whn hit 2 out* **100/1**
36-0 6 10 **Ice Bucket (IRE)**[194] [131] 5-11-0 SThomas 77+
(Miss H C Knight) *t.k.h: short-lived effrt appr 3 out: btn whn blnd 2 out* **66/1**
43- 7 5 **One Of The Boys (IRE)**[228] [4589] 4-11-0 TDoyle 67
(P R Webber) *prom tl wknd appr 3 out* **12/1**
03- 8 2 ½ **Manque Pas D'Air (FR)**[229] [4560] 5-10-7 JPMcNamara 57
(T R George) *bhd fr 6th* **6/1**[2]
5-5 9 dist **Sandmartin (IRE)**[33] [1671] 5-11-0 RJohnson —
(P J Hobbs) *a bhd: j. slowly 3rd: t.o whn reluctant 3 out* **6/1**[2]
-0P0 P **Oui Exit (FR)**[29] [1714] 4-11-0 TScudamore —
(M Scudamore) *a bhd: t.o whn p.u bef 3 out* **66/1**
54- P **Alright Now M'Lad (IRE)**[250] [4174] 5-11-0 RMcGrath —
(Jonjo O'Neill) *hld up in mid-div: hdwy 6th: wknd and p.u bef 3 out* **16/1**

3m 48.7s (-3.60) **Going Correction** -0.10s/f (Good)
WFA 4 from 5yo 12lb **11** Ran SP% **111.9**
Speed ratings: **105,104,99,96,95 90,88,87,—,—** — CSF £24.95 TOTE £1.80: £1.10, £3.90, £2.80; EX 33.80.
Owner Sir Robert Ogden **Bred** S Boucheron **Trained** Upper Lambourn, Berks

FOCUS
An uncompetitive novices' hurdle and the front two drew clear of the third. The form looks ordinary rated through the second, but makes sense.

NOTEBOOK
Menchikov(FR), a promising fourth on his bumper debut at Newbury back in April, made hard work of landing the odds, but he was well on top at the line and gave the impression he will improve a good deal for an extra half mile. His stable have made a bright start to the season and, *although the form is nothing special, he is entitled to go well under a penalty. (op 11-10 tchd 5-4 and 11-8 in places)*
Billyandi(IRE), a bumper winner, looks to be getting the hang of hurdles and he ran his best race to date, pushing the winner all the way from the front. He failed to get home having raced keenly on his only previous try at two and a half, but he looks to be settling better now and is well worth another try at it.
Charming Fellow(IRE) has not built on his initial promise in bumpers and could not have made a worse start to his hurdling career when pulling up at Bangor last month. Given a confident ride here by Murphy, he looked to have a chance turning in, but soon became outpaced and was not given an overly hard time in defeat. He has the ability to win a race, but looks delicate and is unlikely to be seen at his best until sent chasing. *(op 12-1)*
Bollitree Bob made a little late headway and ideally wants further, but he continues to have trouble *in settling and he will not be winning races until he does so. Official explanation: jockey said, regarding the running and riding, his orders were to get gelding to relax in order to finish its race as it tends to be very keen early, adding that gelding would not settle in early stages and only dropped the bridle at the end of the back straight; having got its second wind it stayed on without finding much when asked for an effort (tchd 66-1)*
Britesand(IRE) failed to get home on his hurdling debut over 2m6f, but this drop to two miles was also against him and he was readily outpaced in the straight having showed up well early. He may be in need of more time.
Manque Pas D'Air(FR) ran below expectations and is unlikely to be winning until contesting low-grade handicap hurdles. *(op 11-2 tchd 13-2 in places)*
Sandmartin(IRE) put in a mulish display and was always languishing in rear. He has shown he has ability, but on this evidence he is not one to trust. *(op 5-1)*
Oui Exit(FR) *Official explanation: jockey said gelding lost its action but returned sound (op 50-1)*
Alright Now M'Lad(IRE) *Official explanation: jockey said gelding lost its action (op 50-1)*

2143 CORVE H'CAP CHASE (19 fncs) 3m
3:00 (3:00) (Class 3) (0-120,115) 5-Y-0+
£6,413 (£1,894; £947; £474; £236; £118)

Form RPR
4533 1 **Luneray (FR)**[16] [1874] 6-11-10 **113** (bt) ChristianWilliams 122+
(P F Nicholls) *hld up: hit 6th: hdwy appr 4 out: rdn whn lft in ld last: hung lft flat: jst hld on* **9/4**[1]
23/P 2 shd **Russian Gigolo (IRE)**[33] [1670] 8-11-8 **111** TScudamore 120+
(N A Twiston-Davies) *a.p: lft in ld 11th: rdn appr 2 out: blnd and hdd last: rallied towards fin: jst failed: unlucky* **12/1**
3F1- 3 5 **Dickens (USA)**[222] [4688] 5-11-1 **105** SThomas 105
(Miss Venetia Williams) *hld up: rdn after 15th: hdwy 4 out: one pce fr 2 out* **9/2**[2]
43U 4 5 **Tipsy Mouse (IRE)**[5] [2037] 9-10-13 **107** (p) PCO'Neill(5) 103
(R C Guest) *prom: rdn appr 4 out: wknd appr last* **6/1**[3]
526P 5 5 **World Vision (IRE)**[8] [1989] 8-11-10 **113** (p) BHarding 104
(Ferdy Murphy) *hld up: hdwy 4 out: wknd 2 out* **10/1**
6- 6 3 ½ **Boyackasha (IRE)**[60] [1464] 7-10-9 **98** TJMurphy 86+
(E McNamara, Ire) *hld up: stdy hdwy on ins 11th: wknd appr 2 out* **8/1**
61-0 7 16 **Mounsey Castle**[170] [489] 8-11-6 **109** RJohnson 87+
(P J Hobbs) *prom: rdn appr 4 out: hit 3 out: sn wknd* **9/2**[2]
3P-0 8 14 **Celtic Pride (IRE)**[13] [1907] 10-11-4 **107** (v) JPByrne 64
(Jennie Candlish) *led tl blnd and lost pl 11th (water): lost tch 15th* **40/1**
610P F **The Sister**[14] [1893] 8-11-12 **115** (v) RMcGrath —
(Jonjo O'Neill) *fell 1st* **22/1**

6m 11.9s (-0.20) **Going Correction** 0.0s/f (Good)
WFA 5 from 6yo+ 1lb **9** Ran SP% **116.1**
Speed ratings: **100,99,98,96,94 93,88,83,—** CSF £28.98 CT £114.17 TOTE £3.30: £1.20, £2.90, £2.40; EX 38.70 Trifecta £157.70 Pool: £555.52 - 2.50 winning units.
Owner Sandicroft Stud **Bred** Mrs Emile Ouvry **Trained** Ditcheat, Somerset

FOCUS
A race that revolved around the hard-luck of runner-up Russian Gigolo, and although the first two are rated better than the bare result, the form is not strong.

NOTEBOOK
Luneray(FR), 8lb higher than when last winning at Worcester in May, got lucky and only just held on from the renewed challenge of Russian Gigolo. It will be surprising if she can defy a rise, but she is still only six and may yet be open to further improvement. *(tchd 2-1)*
Russian Gigolo(IRE), who got tired before being pulled up on his reappearance at Bangor, was ridden much more positively and had them all in trouble as they turned for home. However, luck was against him on this occasion and a blunder at the last caused him to lose his footing on touching down and handed the race to Luneray. He would have won cosily otherwise and it was to his credit that he rallied bravely and very nearly got back up. He should soon gain compensation, but his cover is now blown. *(op 10-1)*
Dickens(USA) ◆, who showed improved form in a visor in the spring, had it left off for this reappearance and as a result deserves some credit for his effort. It is safe to assume he will come on for this and he will not be long in winning. *(op 6-1)*
Tipsy Mouse(IRE) was a useful staying handicapper a couple of seasons back, but he continues to go the wrong way and this was another average effort. *(op 7-1 tchd 15-2)*
World Vision(IRE) has largely struggled off this sort of mark since winning at Musselburgh in January and he looks in need of some help from the Handicapper. *(op 8-1)*
Boyackasha(IRE), a lowly-weighted Irish-raider, moved into a challenging position turning in, but he was soon beaten and stopped quickly under pressure. *(op 11-1 tchd 12-1)*

2144 SEVERN MAIDEN HURDLE (11 hdls) 2m 5f
3:30 (3:32) (Class 4) 4-Y-0+ **£3,454** (£1,014; £507; £253)

Form RPR
0422 1 **Air Guitar (IRE)**[46] [1565] 5-11-2 103 PMoloney 106+
(M G Quinlan) *a.p: led 5th: clr fr 3 out: easily* **15/2**[3]
4 2 10 **Mac Dargin (IRE)**[19] [1833] 6-10-6 BWharfe(10) 89
(N A Twiston-Davies) *j. slowly and lost pl 1st: hdwy 5th: rdn and outpcd appr 7th: rallied 3 out: styd on flat: no ch w wnr* **17/2**
516- 3 1 ½ **Oscar Foxbow (IRE)**[274] [3760] 6-11-2 TScudamore 88
(C Tinkler) *hld up in tch: chsd wnr fr 7th: rdn appr 2 out: no imp* **16/1**
6F0- 4 4 **Portavo (IRE)**[311] [3189] 5-11-2 SThomas 85+
(Miss H C Knight) *hld up and bhd: hdwy 7th: wknd 3 out* **66/1**
5 4 **Penny Park (IRE)**[165] 6-11-2 RJohnson 80
(P J Hobbs) *hld up towards rr: hdwy 7th: wknd 3 out* **6/5**[1]
0-03 6 5 **Star Fever (IRE)**[167] [531] 4-11-2 TJMurphy 75
(Miss H C Knight) *bhd: nt fluent 6th: nvr nr ldrs* **40/1**
364- 7 3 ½ **Banchory Two (IRE)**[212] [4814] 5-11-2 113 ChristianWilliams 75+
(P F Nicholls) *hld up in tch: hung lft bnd appr 3 out: sn wknd* **11/4**[2]
46-P 8 10 **Point**[194] [137] 8-11-2 100 WMarston 61
(W Jenks) *a bhd* **22/1**
53- 9 26 **Freeline Fury**[224] [4673] 5-11-2 TDoyle 35
(P R Webber) *prom tl wknd 7th: t.o* **33/1**

The Form Book, Raceform Ltd, Compton, RG20 6NL

0 **10** *1* **Dans Edge (IRE)**[13] 1915 5-10-9 .... PJMcDonald(7) 34
(Ferdy Murphy) *hmpd 1st: a bhd: t.o* **100/1**
50 **P** **Oakfield Legend**[12] 1922 4-11-2 .... OMcPhail —
(P S Payne) *prom tl lost pl 4th: t.o whn p.u bef 7th* **200/1**
0-P **P** **Pocket Sevens (IRE)**[8] 1990 5-11-2 .... MFoley —
(Miss E C Lavelle) *led to 5th: wknd 8th: t.o whn p.u bef 3 out* **50/1**

5m 17.8s (-0.50) **Going Correction** -0.10s/f (Good) **12** Ran SP% **115.0**
Speed ratings: **96,92,91,90,88 86,85,81,71,71** —,— CSF £63.41 TOTE £7.50: £1.50, £2.40, £3.50; EX 40.30.
Owner Liam Mulryan **Bred** Noel Finegan **Trained** Newmarket, Suffolk

FOCUS
Modest hurdle form with the well-touted hot favourite disappointing, although the winner is value for more than the official margin. The second sets the standard and the form could rate higher, but is held down by the moderate time.

NOTEBOOK
Air Guitar(IRE) has shown a consistent level of form this season and was always likely to be thereabouts, but with the hot favourite failing to live up to expectations the door was left ajar and he grabbed the opportunity with both hands, clearing away down the straight to win easily. Equally effective at shorter, he is going to stay three miles and looks sure to continue to pay his way, with the possibility of further improvement in handicaps. *(op 13-2 tchd 6-1)*
Mac Dargin(IRE), who did not quite see out the three miles in heavy ground when fourth on his Rules debut, seemed quite well suited to this sounder surface and he ran a promising race, staying on well down the straight for second. He will stay three miles on this sort of ground and this point winner looks sure to be winning sooner rather than later. *(op 12-1)*
Oscar Foxbow(IRE), a bumper winner here last season, was able to improve for this step up in trip and it was only in the final quarter mile that he got tired. His stable is starting to find their form and this fellow can win races over hurdles.
Portavo(IRE) ran his best race yet under Rules, but is unlikely to be winning until tackling fences, having won a point in Ireland last year. His stable is starting to find its form and he is going to stay further.
Penny Park(IRE), unlucky not to be two from two in Irish points, came into this with a bit of a reputation but, having made headway to track the leaders, he soon began to struggle and was beaten with fully half a mile to run. He is surely better than this and deserves to be given another chance, but does have a bit to prove. *(tchd 11-10, 5-4 in places)*
Star Fever(IRE), as with stablemate Portavo, he looks in need of more time and will not be seen at his best until tackling fences. *(tchd 50-1)*
Banchory Two(IRE) has clearly made no improvement over the summer and not for the first time he found little under pressure. Fences may make a man of him, but something needs to. *(tchd 10-3)*

2145 VYRNWY INTERMEDIATE NATIONAL HUNT FLAT RACE (CONDITIONAL JOCKEYS' AND AMATEUR RIDERS') 2m
4:00 (4:00) (Class 6) 4-6-Y-O **£2,387** (£700; £350; £175)

Form RPR
1 **The Hollow Bottom** 4-10-8 .... BWharfe(10) 104
(N A Twiston-Davies) *chsd ldr: rdn to ld 1f out: drvn out* **16/1**
- **2** *1 1/4* **Gold Beach (IRE)** 5-11-1 .... MrMRimell(3) 103
(M G Rimell) *led: rdn and hdd 1f out: nt qckn* **10/1**
3 *1 1/2* **It Would Appear (IRE)** 6-10-11 .... MrAJBerry(7) 101
(Jonjo O'Neill) *hld up in tch: ev ch whn hung lft bnd over 3f out: sn rdn: r.o one pce fnl 2f* **9/2**[3]
1 **4** *9* **Unjust Law (IRE)**[191] 179 4-11-8 .... MrTGreenall(3) 102+
(N J Henderson) *hld up: hdwy 5f out: hung lft bnd over 3f out: wknd over 1f out* **15/8**[2]
5 *2 1/2* **Roadmaker (IRE)**[18] 1869 5-10-13 .... WKennedy(5) 90
(John G Carr, Ire) *bhd: pushed along 8f out: n.d after* **7/4**[1]
6 *dist* **Cleverality (IRE)**[235] 5-10-13 .... MrNWilliams(5) —
(Evan Williams) *plld hrd: prom tl wknd over 5f out: t.o* **25/1**
7 *2* **Harder Steel (IRE)** 4-10-13 .... MNicolls(5) —
(K C Bailey) *hld up: pushed along over 6f out: sn struggling: t.o* **25/1**

3m 51.2s (-1.00) **Going Correction** -0.10s/f (Good) **7** Ran SP% **112.0**
Speed ratings: **98,97,96,92,90** —,— CSF £151.16 TOTE £15.60: £3.80, £4.50; EX 59.10 Place 6 £770.10, Place 5 £284.49.
Owner The Hollow Partnership **Bred** Mrs Susan Corbett **Trained** Naunton, Gloucs

FOCUS
Modest bumper form that could be a few pounds out either way.

NOTEBOOK
The Hollow Bottom, friendless in the market beforehand, comes from a stable that traditionally does well in these events and he battled on too strongly for long-time leader Gold Beach. A staying type, he will benefit from a switch to hurdles and in the long run should make a chaser, but it is debatable whether he can defy a penalty in this sphere. *(op 9-1)*
Gold Beach(IRE) took them along for virtually all the journey, but he could not repel the winner's sustained run and had to settle for second. He can find a similar race on this evidence, but will be vulnerable to anything with a change of gear. *(op 12-1 tchd 14-1)*
It Would Appear(IRE) was given a nice introductory ride and still showed signs of greenness, hanging off the final bend. He clearly has the ability to win a bumper and is the one to take from the race. *(tchd 6-1)*
Unjust Law(IRE), a winner on his debut at the course back in May, was badly exposed under a penalty and quite simply did not look up to it. He is one of his stable's lesser lights, but will no doubt be placed to pick up a moderate race or two over hurdles. *(op 11-8 tchd 5-4)*
Roadmaker(IRE) came into this with plenty of experience having run well in each of his three bumpers in Ireland, and was rightly made favourite. However, he was under pressure from halfway and never got involved, running very flat. He is better than this, but now has a little bit to prove. *(op 5-2)*

T/Jkpt: Not won. T/Plt: £3,331.10 to a £1 stake. Pool: £38,787.00. 8.50 winning tickets. T/Qpdt: £82.30 to a £1 stake. Pool: £4,227.10. 38.00 winning tickets. KH

1896 TAUNTON (R-H)
Thursday, November 10

OFFICIAL GOING: Good to firm
Wind: Virtually nil Weather: Fine

2146 SOUTH WEST RACING EXPERIENCE (S) H'CAP HURDLE (9 hdls) 2m 1f
1:10 (1:10) (Class 5) (0-90,90) 4-7-Y-O **£2,365** (£689; £344)

Form RPR
-5PP **1** **Past Heritage**[20] 1814 6-9-12 **67** ow1 .... DLaverty(5) 72
(A E Jones) *mid div: hdwy appr 5th: jnd ldr after 3 out: led appr last: rdn out* **33/1**
6-53 **2** *1 3/4* **Handa Island (USA)**[39] 1607 6-11-9 **87** .... GLee 91+
(M W Easterby) *trckd ldrs: led on bit after 3 out: rdn and hdd whn blnd last: no ex* **2/1**[1]
052- **3** *12* **Pedler's Profiles**[443] 1272 5-10-9 **73** .... BHitchcott 64
(Miss K M George) *mid div: rdn appr 3 out: styd on fr 2 out: tk 3rd fnl strides* **14/1**
-60U **4** *shd* **Canadian Storm**[28] 1724 4-11-9 **87** ....(p) AO'Keeffe 78
(A G Juckes) *hld up towards rr: hdwy after 5th: wnt 3rd after 3 out: kpt on same pce* **20/1**
-010 **5** *1 1/4* **Banningham Blaze**[25] 1753 5-11-7 **85** ....(v) WHutchinson 75
(A W Carroll) *hld up towards rr: rdn and styd on fr 2 out: nvr trbld ldrs* **12/1**
0000 **6** *3 1/2* **Bebe Factual (GER)**[14] 1902 4-10-5 **74** .... CHonour(5) 61+
(J D Frost) *chsd ldrs: rdn and one pced fr 3 out* **50/1**
0045 **7** *2 1/2* **Tizi Ouzou (IRE)**[14] 1900 4-11-5 **90** .... MrRQuinn(7) 75+
(M C Pipe) *led tl after 3 out: sn rdn: one pced* **13/2**[3]
P/P- **8** *shd* **Pop Gun**[536] 478 6-11-0 **85** .... RSpate(7) 69
(Mrs K Waldron) *chsd ldrs: rdn after 3 out: sn one pced* **50/1**
0003 **9** *1 1/2* **Nutley Queen (IRE)**[20] 1814 6-10-2 **66** ....(t) RGreene 48
(M Appleby) *a towards rr* **20/1**
-0PF **10** *9* **Sean Nos (IRE)**[28] 1724 4-9-7 **64** .... KHClarke(7) 37
(W K Goldsworthy) *mid div: hdwy after 5th: rdn to press ldrs after 3 out: sn wknd* **100/1**
6460 **11** *5* **Lucky Arthur (IRE)**[26] 1742 4-10-0 **74** ....(p) CDThompson(10) 42
(Mrs L Williamson) *a towards rr* **28/1**
/05- **12** *25* **Shogoon (FR)**[344] 2573 6-10-5 **69** .... MBatchelor 12
(N E Berry) *a bhd* **20/1**
P/64 **U** **Raheel (IRE)**[123] 943 5-10-6 **70** ....(tp) ADobbin —
(Evan Williams) *bdly hmpd and uns rdr 1st* **3/1**[2]
-53P **P** **Twist N Turn**[158] 651 5-9-9 **64** oh1 .... StephenJCraine(5) —
(D McCain) *in tch tl sddle slipped and p.u after 3rd* **33/1**
00-4 **P** **Isleofhopeantears (IRE)**[142] 806 6-10-3 **67** ....(p) ATinkler —
(A E Jones) *a towards rr: lost tch 3 out: p.u bef next* **22/1**
0053 **P** **Waziya**[10] 1952 6-10-6 **70** ....(p) DCrosse —
(Mrs L Williamson) *w ldr: rdn and wknd appr 3 out: bhd and p.u bef 2 out* **50/1**

4m 9.20s (0.40) **Going Correction** -0.025s/f (Good) **16** Ran SP% **120.9**
Speed ratings: **98,97,91,91,90 89,88,88,87,83 80,68**,—,—,— — CSF £91.28 CT £1040.51 TOTE £75.60: £11.90, £1.10, £2.80, £3.20; EX 643.70.There was no bid for the winner.
Owner Mrs J Frost **Bred** G Brown **Trained** Newchapel, Surrey

FOCUS
A moderate selling handicap that was run at a fair gallop and the first two pulled well clear in the home straight.

NOTEBOOK
Past Heritage, who had shown virtually nothing in six outings since winning a firm-ground bumper at this venue last year, bounced back to form and ran out a ready winner. Given a patient ride, he found plenty when asked to win his race in the straight and ultimately sealed the matter with tidy jumps over the final two flights. This is clearly his level and, if able to maintain this current mood, *he may be able to win again in this company given similar ground in the future.Official explanation: trainer said, regarding the improved form shown, gelding appeared to be a bad traveller (op 50-1)*
Handa Island(USA), well backed for this drop in grade, travelled up to the leaders going best of all at the top of the straight, but he failed to find all that much when push come to shove and lost the race with two messy leaps over the last two hurdles. He was a long way ahead of the rest in second, and is up to getting off the mark in this class, but this has to rate a missed opportunity. *(op 5-2 tchd 15-8)*
Pedler's Profiles, returning from a 443-day layoff, ran very much as though this race would bring him on fitness wise and he should be capable of getting closer at this level next time.
Canadian Storm never looked a serious threat, but kept on well enough under pressure and improved on his recent efforts. *(op 11-1 tchd 10-1)*
Raheel(IRE), well backed ahead of this first run for his new connections and sporting a new combination of headgear, gave his rider no chance of staying aboard at the first flight. *(op 9-2)*

2147 BLUESTONE SOUTH WEST NOVICES' HURDLE (12 hdls) 3m 110y
1:40 (1:41) (Class 3) 4-Y-O+ **£5,465** (£1,604; £802; £400)

Form RPR
63-2 **1** **Present Glory (IRE)**[200] 8 6-10-11 .... AThornton 112+
(C Tinkler) *hld up bhd ldrs: led after 2nd: mde rest: clr 3 out: easily* **8/11**[1]
2 *29* **Moonshine Surprise (IRE)**[222] 5-10-11 .... RGreene 77+
(M C Pipe) *chsd ldrs: drvn to go 2nd after 8th: no ch w wnr fr 3 out* **11/4**[2]
6-00 **3** *7* **Classic Clover**[8] 1982 5-10-11 .... JTizzard 69
(C L Tizzard) *prom tl lost tch appr 8th: styd on again to go 3rd after 2 out* **33/1**
04B5 **4** *3 1/2* **Francolino (FR)**[9] 1977 12-10-4 64 .... JPritchard(7) 65
(Dr P Pritchard) *led tl after 2nd: chsd ldrs tl 5th: sn dropped rr: nvr a danger after* **100/1**
4420 **5** *14* **Carte Sauvage (USA)**[15] 1880 4-10-11 99 ....(v) PJBrennan 58+
(M F Harris) *trckd ldrs: wnt 2nd after 7th tl after next: sn rdn: wknd after 3 out* **7/1**[3]
6-34 **P** **Zouave (IRE)**[14] 1898 4-10-11 94 ....(b) NFehily —
(C J Mann) *hld up: hit 5th: hdwy after 7th: rdn after next: wknd qckly: t.o and p.u bef 2 out* **16/1**

6m 2.10s (-6.50) **Going Correction** -0.025s/f (Good)
WFA 4 from 5yo+ 14lb **6** Ran SP% **106.9**
Speed ratings: **109,99,97,96,91** — CSF £2.68 TOTE £1.40: £1.10, £1.90; EX 4.20.
Owner George Ward **Bred** Frank Fagan **Trained** Compton, Berks

FOCUS
A modest staying novices' hurdle in which the pace was fairly steady until halfway and the field came home well and truly strung out. The winner is value for more than the official margin but the form is rated through the fourth.

NOTEBOOK
Present Glory(IRE) had the perfect opportunity to open his account over timber, which he duly did, with a bloodless success. His rider's decision to kick on as they entered the final circuit paid dividends and, as expected, he saw out the longer trip without fuss. He is very much a future chasing type, should improve again for this outing, and is in the right hands to progress over timber this term before going over fences in the future. *(op 10-11)*
Moonshine Surprise(IRE), winner of two of his four outings between the flags, tended to run in snatches on this debut for his powerful stable and was always playing second fiddle to the winner. He is entitled to come on for this experience, and is another who will fare better when reverting to the bigger obstacles in due course, but is clearly far from one of his trainer's leading lights. *(op 5-2)*
Classic Clover, unplaced over two miles on heavy ground at Chepstow eight days previously, improved a touch for this longer trip - as his pedigree strongly suggested - yet failed to rate a serious threat at any stage. His future lies as a chaser and, while he is only modest, he may fare better when qualified for handicaps after his next outing. *(tchd 40-1)*
Francolino(FR) turned in another moody effort, but was keeping on again at the finish after getting detached down the back straight. *(op 66-1)*
Carte Sauvage(USA) dropped out late on and ran below expectations for the second consecutive occasion. He is clearly regressing, but will find life easier when reverting to shorter in the future. *(op 6-1 tchd 11-2)*

2148 CHILDRENS HOSPICE SOUTH WEST MAIDEN HURDLE (9 hdls) 2m 1f
2:10 (2:10) (Class 4) 4-Y-O+ **£4,073** (£1,195; £597; £298)

Form RPR

6- **1** **Silver City**[217] 4756 5-11-2 .... PJBrennan 87+
(P J Hobbs) *trckd ldrs: led 3 out: clr next: blnd last: kpt on: rdn out* **5/1**[2]

2 *1¼* **Tech Eagle (IRE)**[81] 5-11-2 .... DCrosse 84
(R Curtis) *mid div: stdy hdwy after 3 out to go 3rd whn hmpd next: kpt on* **16/1**[3]

4/ **3** *nk* **Landescent (IRE)**[33] 4854 5-11-2 .... BHitchcott 83
(Miss K M George) *chsd ldrs: rdn to chse wnr after 3 out: kpt on same pce fr next* **22/1**

5-23 **4** *1½* **Chunky Lad**[28] 1730 5-10-9 .... RLucey-Butler(7) 82
(W G M Turner) *hld up bhd: hdwy after 3 out: rdn and styd on fr next* **25/1**

65 **5** *½* **Sgt Pepper (IRE)**[8] 1991 4-11-2 .... LAspell 81+
(O Sherwood) *hld up towards rr: styd on fr 2 out: hit last: nrst fin* **5/1**[2]

P6 **6** *1* **Mount Benger**[9] 1975 5-11-2 .... (p) PHide 81+
(Mrs A J Hamilton-Fairley) *in tch: rdn after 3 out: kpt on same pce* **66/1**

7 *1¼* **Smoothly Does It**[134] 4-11-2 .... ATinkler 80+
(Mrs A J Bowlby) *hld up towards rr: hdwy fr 5th to chse ldrs after 3 out: sn rdn: wknd run-in* **50/1**

8 *hd* **Torinmoor (USA)**[32] 4-11-2 .... JimCrowley 81+
(Mrs A J Perrett) *mid div: hdwy after 3 out to go 2nd briefly appr next: sn rdn: wknd last* **4/5**[1]

0 **9** *9* **Ninah**[12] 1916 4-10-9 .... GLee 63
(J M Bradley) *led tl 3 out: wknd next* **50/1**

356- **10** *1¼* **Harrival**[270] 3837 5-10-9 .... MrGTumelty(7) 69
(Miss M Bragg) *in tch tl wknd 3 out* **100/1**

11 *dist* **Zilla (FR)**[179] 4-10-2 .... MissLucyBridges(7) —
(Miss Lucy Bridges) *t.k.h in rr: nvr fluent: lost tch appr 3 out* **40/1**

5/ **P** **King Darshaan**[117] 2008 5-11-2 .... VSlattery —
(N I M Rossiter) *sn bhd: t.o and p.u bef 5th* **33/1**

P **P** **African Star**[12] 1916 4-11-2 .... WHutchinson —
(J M Bradley) *mid div tl wknd 3 out: bhd and p.u bef 2 out* **200/1**

5 **P** **Buthaina (IRE)**[10] 1952 5-10-2 .... TMessenger(7) —
(Mrs L Williamson) *t.k.h trcking ldrs: mstke 3rd: wknd after 5th: t.o and p.u bef 2 out* **200/1**

4m 10.8s (2.00) **Going Correction** -0.025s/f (Good)
WFA 4 from 5yo 12lb **14** Ran SP% **115.7**
Speed ratings: **94,93,93,92,92 91,91,91,86,86** —,—,—,— CSF £67.74 TOTE £8.10: £1.60, £2.90, £4.50; EX 154.80.
Owner Mrs Kathy Stuart And Mrs Susie Chown **Bred** Bloomsbury Stud **Trained** Withycombe, Somerset
■ Stewards' Enquiry : L Aspell seven-day ban: failed to take all reasonable and permissible measures to gain best possible placing (Nov 21-27)

FOCUS
This was probably just a weak maiden hurdle, and although the early pace was sound the overall time was slower than the seller. The winner and third set the level for the form.

NOTEBOOK
Silver City, whose stable landed this race last term with the useful McBain, was all out to hold on at the finish. Given that he stayed 12 furlongs well on the Flat, it was no surprise to see him ridden handily over this sharp track, and the fact his rider elected to kick for home at the top of the straight ultimately won the day. He still has room for improvement in the jumping department, but he is fully entitled to improve again for this outing, and he could prove useful in this sphere when facing a stiffer test in the future. *(op 8-1)*
Tech Eagle(IRE) ◆, a five-time winner on the Flat in Germany, was really motoring at the finish and may well have made a winning debut for new connections had he not run into the back of the weakening Torinmoor at the penultimate flight. Considering this ground may have been plenty fast enough for him, this has to rate a promising start to his hurdles career and he looks nailed on to go one better in this company before too long. *(op 17-2)*
Landescent(IRE), last seen winning in banded company in October and having just his second outing in this sphere, was another to finish his race well and posted a very pleasing effort in defeat. He will be eligible for handicaps after his next outing, is clearly suited by a sharp track, and looks more than capable of tasting success as a hurdler in the future. *(op 20-1 tchd 25-1)*
Chunky Ladtook time to get going on this hurdling bow, but was keeping on well enough in the final stages and turned in a respectable effort. This looks to be his trip and he enjoys a decent surface. *(op 33-1)*
Sgt Pepper(IRE)got going far too late and would have been much better served by a more positive ride. He is now eligible for handicaps, this effort suggests he could be worth trying over a stiffer track, and he is capable of better than this. His rider was subsequently banned by the Stewards for seven days for failing to obtain the best possible placing. *(op 4-1 tchd 11-2)*
Torinmoor(USA), rated 93 on the Flat, who found nothing when push came to shove in the straight and was well beaten. He did not really convince with his hurdling and, while he is entitled to improve with the experience under his belt, this effort leaves him a lot to prove now. *(tchd 8-11 and 5-6)*

2149 BLUESTONE SOUTH WEST NOVICES' H'CAP CHASE (14 fncs) 2m 3f
2:40 (2:40) (Class 4) (0-105,104) 4-Y-O+ **£4,928** (£1,446; £723; £361)

Form RPR

P-U **1** **Supreme Tadgh (IRE)**[188] 202 8-10-10 **95** .... SElliott(7) 112+
(J A Geake) *chsd ldrs: shkn up appr 4 out: chal fr 3 out: rdn to ld appr last: styd on wl* **9/2**[3]

6P6- **2** *2½* **River Trapper (IRE)**[257] 4062 6-11-8 **100** .... PJBrennan 112+
(Miss H C Knight) *chsd ldrs: hit 4 out: sn led: narrow advantage whn pckd 3 out: sn rdn: hdd appr last: no ex* **10/3**[2]

020- **3** *½* **Lizzie Bathwick (IRE)**[221] 4725 6-10-12 **90** .... NFehily 101
(D P Keane) *mid div: hdwy to chse ldng pair out: sn rdn: styd on run-in* **14/1**

P25F **4** *9* **Rookery Lad**[4] 2074 7-11-6 **98** .... DCrosse 102+
(C N Kellett) *chsd ldrs: mstke 5th: rdn after 4 out: 4th and hld whn hit 2 out* **11/1**

0P0/ **5** *2* **Wild Oats**[571] 4897 7-11-3 **95** .... JTizzard 95
(B J M Ryall) *hld up: sltly outpcd appr 4 out: styd on again fr 3 out* **16/1**

3-44 **6** *1½* **Hi Fi**[176] 413 7-11-12 **104** .... WHutchinson 102
(Ian Williams) *in tch: rdn and sme hdwy after 4 out: no further imp fr 2 out* **14/1**

3521 **7** *3* **Nazimabad (IRE)**[15] 1877 6-11-9 **101** .... (t) LAspell 97+
(Evan Williams) *led tl after 4 out: grad wknd* **9/4**[1]

5-50 **8** *dist* **Kellys Fable**[172] 469 5-10-5 **83** .... AThornton —
(J W Mullins) *hld up: lost tch appr 4 out: t.o* **10/1**

PPF3 **P** **Lescer's Lad**[14] 1899 8-9-7 **78** oh9 .... CMStudd(7) —
(C L Popham) *hit 4th: 8th and 9th: a in rr: p.u bef 10th* **66/1**

4m 52.9s (0.10) **Going Correction** +0.15s/f (Yiel) **9** Ran SP% **110.2**
Speed ratings: **105,103,103,99,99 98,97**,—,— CSF £19.08 CT £177.55 TOTE £6.00: £2.00, £1.20, £3.60; EX 23.70.
Owner Dr & Mrs Peter Leftley **Bred** John Byrne **Trained** Kimpton, Hants

FOCUS
An interesting novices' handicap, run at a sound gallop thanks to the habitual front-runner Nazimabad, and the form could prove fair for the grade and should work out.

NOTEBOOK
Supreme Tadgh(IRE) ◆, who unseated when in with place prospects in a similar race on his previous outing 188 days previously, put in a fine round of jumping this time and duly landed his first event under Rules on this second start for his current yard. He was given a fine ride, had no trouble with the quick surface, and did more than enough to suggest he is finally ready to fulfill his potential this season. *(tchd 11-2)*
River Trapper(IRE), making his chase and handicap debut, did not help his cause with some messy jumps late on, but was always looking held by the winner in the straight. There is little doubt he has begun handicap life on a fair mark, should improve fitness-wise for the outing, and can find compensation in this division before too long. *(op 3-1 tchd 4-1)*
Lizzie Bathwick(IRE), who failed to build on her maiden hurdle success last season, ran a race full of promise on this chasing bow and should improve a deal for the experience. She was never a serious threat to the first two, but on a stiffer track and softer ground she would have claims of reversing this form. *(op 12-1)*
Rookery Lad, who fell at Hereford four days previously, put in an improved display and probably ran close to his best in defeat. *(tchd 10-1)*
Wild Oats found this an insufficient test and will be seen to better effect when reverting to a stiffer track in the future. *(tchd 18-1)*
Hi Fi ran very much as though this return from a break was needed and never really threatened. He is hard to predict, but is capable of better. *(op 8-1)*
Nazimabad(IRE)recorded a personal best when making all decisively at Cheltenham last time, but that was a weak event for the track, and he looks to have been anchored by a 13lb hike in the weights for that display. *(op 5-2 tchd 15-8)*

2150 OPENING MEETS AMATEUR RIDERS' H'CAP HURDLE (10 hdls) 2m 3f 110y
3:10 (3:10) (Class 4) (0-110,110) 4-Y-O+ **£3,868** (£1,199; £599; £299)

Form RPR

06P2 **1** **Meadow Hawk (USA)**[8] 1991 5-9-9 **86** .... MrGTumelty(7) 99+
(A W Carroll) *in tch: rdn to chse ldr after 3 out: led and hit next: styd on wl* **5/2**[1]

P-33 **2** *3* **Lord Nellsson**[24] 509 9-10-6 **97** .... MrDGreenway(7) 103+
(Andrew Turnell) *chsd ldrs tl 7th: sn towards rr: styd on wl fr 2 out: wnt 2nd run-in* **9/1**

1321 **3** *3½* **Red Dahlia**[53] 1482 8-10-4 **91** .... MrJSnowden(3) 91
(M Pitman) *in tch: rdn to go 4th after 3 out: kpt on same pce* **17/2**

3360 **4** *½* **Brochrua (IRE)**[26] 1747 5-10-2 **93** .... MrBMoorcroft(7) 93
(J D Frost) *towards rr: rdn after 7th: hdwy 2 out: r.o wl to go 4th run-in: nrst fin* **66/1**

3214 **5** *¾* **Dont Ask Me (IRE)**[21] 1806 4-10-0 **91** .... (t) MrCHughes(7) 90+
(M C Pipe) *hld up towards rr: gd hdwy after 6th: led 3 out: rdn and hdd next: one pced after* **6/1**[2]

4-60 **6** *3½* **Freedom Now (IRE)**[5] 2055 7-11-2 **107** .... MrAnthonyKnott(7) 103+
(R H Alner) *hld up towards rr: hdwy 7th into mid div: no further imp* **25/1**

5P-1 **7** *3* **Devito (FR)**[14] 1900 4-11-4 **107** .... MrDEdwards(5) 103+
(G F Edwards) *chsd ldrs: rdn to chse ldr after 3 out: wknd after next* **12/1**

0050 **8** *5* **Better Moment (IRE)**[14] 1900 8-10-2 **93** .... (v) MrCWallis(7) 80
(M C Pipe) *prom tl 7th* **33/1**

2/1- **9** *2½* **Doctor Wood**[231] 4536 10-10-6 **97** .... MissVStephens(7) 82
(Miss V A Stephens) *hld up bhd:sme hdwy after 3 out* **20/1**

5332 **10** *1¼* **Peeyoutwo**[14] 1899 10-10-5 **96** .... MrRhysHughes(7) 80
(Mrs D A Hamer) *a towards rr* **33/1**

60-5 **11** *¾* **Top Trees**[14] 1902 7-9-11 **86** .... MrDavidTurner(5) 69
(W S Kittow) *mid div: hdwy to chse ldrs 3 out: wknd 2 out* **14/1**

4016 **12** *1½* **Penny's Crown**[5] 2043 6-10-6 **90** .... MissEJJones 71
(G A Ham) *a towards rr* **50/1**

U222 **13** *2½* **Pirandello (IRE)**[2] 2103 7-11-7 **110** .... MrSWaley-Cohen(5) 89
(K C Bailey) *chsd ldrs: mstke 7th: sn wknd* **8/1**[3]

4310 **14** *12* **Young Tot (IRE)**[18] 1856 7-9-13 **90** .... (p) MrLRPayter(7) 57
(M Sheppard) *led tl appr 3 out: sn wknd* **20/1**

5-04 **15** *4* **Caspian Dusk**[9] 1977 4-10-10 **101** .... (p) MrJBarnes(7) 64
(W G M Turner) *mid div tl 6th* **50/1**

1001 **P** **Miss Lehman**[26] 1742 7-10-10 **97** .... MissSGaisford(3) —
(J D Frost) *a towards rr: p.u run-in* **16/1**

4m 46.0s **Going Correction** -0.025s/f (Good)
WFA 4 from 5yo+ 12lb **16** Ran SP% **119.4**
Speed ratings: **99,97,96,96,95 94,93,91,90,89 89,88,87,83,81** — CSF £22.04 CT £171.13 TOTE £3.30: £1.10, £2.90, £1.70, £9.20; EX 33.10.
Owner Mrs Susan Keable **Bred** Golden Gate Farm And Henri Mastey **Trained** Cropthorne, Worcs
■ Stewards' Enquiry : Mr G Tumelty one-day ban: careless riding (Nov 21)

FOCUS
A moderate handicap for amateur riders, run at just an average gallop, and the field came home fairly strung out. The winner is value for more than double the official margin with the third and fourth close to form.

NOTEBOOK
Meadow Hawk(USA), who improved markedly on his debut for current connections when runner-up at Huntingdon eight days previously, confirmed the promise of that effort and duly went one better in ready fashion. He saw out the longer trip well, had no trouble with the faster ground and was given a decent ride by his capable amateur. However, considering he was already due to race off a 14lb higher mark in the future, he was entitled to score as he did at the weights, and will need to keep progressing in order to defy a higher rating in the future. *(op 11-4 tchd 3-1)*
Lord Nellsson, despite getting squeezed out going away from the stands, displayed his quirks by running in snatches throughout the first half of the contest on this return to hurdling and was staying on all too late in the day. He remains a maiden over jumps, and is very hard to catch right, but is clearly weighted to find a race, and will benefit plenty for the return to a suitably stiffer test in the future. *(tchd 17-2 and 10-1)*
Red Dahlia, raised 5lb for winning at Plumpton last time, stuck to her task under pressure but could only keep on at the same pace in the straight. She looks held by the Handicapper now. *(tchd 9-1 in a place)*
Brochrua(IRE) took an age to find her stride, but was motoring at the finish and turned in her best effort for some time. She likes this venue and can get closer off this mark under a more positive ride. *(op 100-1)*
Dont Ask Me(IRE) looked to go for home plenty soon enough and was readily held at the finish. He can do better off this mark. *(tchd 7-1)*
Pirandello(IRE) ran well below his recent level and clearly found this coming too soon. *(op 13-2)*

2151 ROYAL WELSH REGIMENT H'CAP CHASE (17 fncs) 2m 7f 110y
3:40 (3:40) (Class 4) (0-105,105) 5-Y-O+ **£4,840** (£1,421; £710; £354)

Form RPR

316 **1** **Glacial Delight (IRE)**[24] 1773 6-11-8 **101** .... BFenton 117+
(Miss E C Lavelle) *stdd s: hld up bhd: smooth hdwy after 11th: blnd 13th: led on bit next: styd on wl: comf* **8/1**

-23S **2** *3 1/2* **Sissinghurst Storm (IRE)**[36] [1646] 7-10-0 **79** oh11.......... WHutchinson 86
(R Dickin) *hld up: hit 10th: hdwy appr 4 out: rdn appr 3 out: styd on wl run-in to go 2nd cl home* **20/1**

6 **3** *1* **Mick Divine (IRE)**[13] [1907] 7-11-3 **96**.. NFehily 102
(C J Mann) *mid div: hdwy to trck ldrs after 4 out: rdn after 3 out: kpt on same pce* **11/1**

P2-2 **4** *9* **Jardin De Beaulieu (FR)**[18] [1848] 8-11-6 **99**................................ GLee 96
(Ian Williams) *trckd ldrs: jnd ldrs 12th: hit next: rdn appr 3 out: kpt on same pce* **7/1**[3]

-122 **5** *2 1/2* **Galtee View (IRE)**[28] [1728] 7-11-5 **98**.......................................(p) LAspell 95+
(Evan Williams) *hld up: hit 4 out: sn rdn and short lived effrt appr 3 out: no further imp* **3/1**[2]

0352 **6** *21* **Just Reuben (IRE)**[14] [1901] 10-10-0 **79** oh1.............................. RGreene 62+
(C L Tizzard) *led tl 4 out: sn one pced* **14/1**

PPF- **7** *14* **Cillamon**[294] [3434] 8-10-11 **93**.. ONelmes(3) 53
(K Bishop) *a towards rr: lost tch fr 12th* **33/1**

-10U **8** *nk* **Sacrifice**[5] [2051] 10-11-1 **97**.. CBolger(3) 56
(K Bishop) *in tch: tk clsr order 10th: rdn 13th: sn wknd* **22/1**

PU11 **P** **Hehasalife (IRE)**[14] [1901] 8-10-12 **96**...............................(b) PMerrigan(5) —
(Mrs H Dalton) *chsd ldrs tl 4 out: sn wknd qckly and p.u bef 3 out* **11/4**[1]

-614 **F** **Castlemore (IRE)**[18] [1858] 7-11-12 **105**...................................... PJBrennan 107
(P J Hobbs) *w ldr tl 4 out: sn rdn to chse wnr: 3rd and hld whn fell last* **7/1**[3]

6m 8.70s (3.60) **Going Correction** +0.15s/f (Yiel) **10** Ran SP% **114.8**
Speed ratings: **100,98,98,95,94 87,83,82,—,—** CSF £140.17 CT £1751.36 TOTE £10.20: £2.30, £3.80, £2.80; EX 157.30.
Owner The Friday Night Racing Club **Bred** Patrick Tarrant **Trained** Wildhern, Hants

FOCUS
This was a moderate, but fairly competitive handicap for the class, run at a fair gallop. The first three came clear and the winner is value for more than double the winning distance, with the placed horses close to their marks.

NOTEBOOK
Glacial Delight(IRE) ◆ ran out an impressive winner and made amends for a rather disappointing effort over hurdles last time. Having bided his time out the back through the first half of the contest, he scythed through the pack to take up the running four out and never really appeared in danger thereafter. His jumping was particularly impressive considering he was taking on handicappers for this introduction to fencing and, while he won his point on an easy surface last year, clearly this quick ground is right up his street. Unexposed over this sort of trip, he is in good hands and appeals as the type to rate higher in this sphere before the season is out. *(op 7-1 tchd 9-1)*
Sissinghurst Storm(IRE), 11lb out of the handicap, was expectedly doing all of his best work at the finish on this drop back in trip. He still turned in a much-improved effort, however, and should be of interest back over further on a similar surface in the coming weeks, providing he does not go up too much for this. *(op 16-1)*
Mick Divine(IRE) showed the benefit of his recent pipe-opener at Uttoxeter and duly improved for the step-up to this longer trip. He can improve again for this outing and, while he is not obviously well handicapped on his previous hurdles form in Ireland, may have more to offer over this sort of distance. *(op 10-1)*
Jardin De Beaulieu(FR) was handy throughout, but could only muster the same pace when it mattered. His rider later reported his mount had suffered a breathing problem. *(op 10-1)*
Galtee View(IRE) failed to make much of an impression from off the pace on this drop back in distance. He is capable of better. *(op 7-2)*
Just Reuben(IRE) failed to run up to the level of this recent effort over course and distance. He never seems to run two races alike. *(op 16-1)*
Hehasalife(IRE), bidding for the hat-trick, dropped out very quickly when push came top shove and ran as though something was amiss. *(op 13-2 tchd 6-1)*
Castlemore(IRE) was still very much in contention for a place prior to departing at the final flight *and, while he has been prone to mistakes in the past, he had jumped well up to that point. (op 13-2 tchd 6-1)*

2152 BACK AND LAY ON GGBET.COM MAIDEN OPEN NATIONAL HUNT FLAT RACE 2m 1f

4:10 (4:10) (Class 6) 4-6-Y-O **£1,877** (£547; £273)

Form RPR

5- **1** **Gentleman Jimmy**[264] [3960] 5-11-4 .... JimCrowley 101+
(H Morrison) *trckd ldrs: pressed ldr fr 5f out: edgd rt over 1f out: r.o to ld ins fnl f: pushed out* **5/1**

2-32 **2** *3/4* **Miss Midnight**[183] [300] 4-10-11 .... JEMoore 90
(R J Hodges) *prom: led 5f out: rdn and hrd pressed fr 3f out: no ex whn hdd ins fnl f* **4/1**[3]

3 *1 3/4* **Bring Me Sunshine (IRE)** 4-11-4 .... JTizzard 95
(C L Tizzard) *hld up in tch: tk clsr order 5f out: sn rdn: styd on ins fnl f: tk 3rd cl home* **7/2**[2]

6/ **4** *nk* **Mister Knight (IRE)**[208] 6-11-4 .... GLee 95
(P F Nicholls) *hld up in tch: tk clsr order 5f out: rdn and effrt 3f out: kpt on same pce* **20/1**

3 **5** *1 3/4* **So Long**[13] [1909] 5-10-4 .... CMStudd(7) 86
(C L Popham) *prom: rdn over 3f out: kpt on but wandered u.p fr over 1f out* **25/1**

2 **6** *7* **Silver Sister**[122] [963] 4-10-6 .... CHonour(5) 80+
(J D Frost) *hld up bhd: hdwy over 4f out: sn rdn: no further imp* **20/1**

2-2 **7** *4* **Earl Of Forestry (GER)**[180] [361] 4-11-4 ....(t) PJBrennan 84+
(P F Nicholls) *hld up in tch: tk clsr order 5f out: rdn and effrt 3f out: wknd over 1f out* **11/8**[1]

0- **8** *12* **Daliadot**[217] [4760] 5-11-4 .... WHutchinson 70
(Miss M Bragg) *chsd ldrs tl 5f out* **100/1**

04 **9** *shd* **Brave Jo (FR)**[25] [1755] 4-10-11 .... KBurke(7) 70
(N J Hawke) *led tl 5f out: sn wknd* **66/1**

P **Jasper** 6-11-4 .... LAspell —
(Evan Williams) *hld up in tch: wknd rapidly 1/2-way and sn p.u* **25/1**

4m 8.00s (-0.60) **Going Correction** -0.025s/f (Good)
WFA 4 from 5yo+ 12lb **10** Ran SP% **120.7**
Speed ratings: **100,99,98,98,97 94,92,87,86,—** CSF £24.08 TOTE £8.30: £2.30, £1.70, £1.50; EX 26.70 Place 6 £269.36, Place 5 £132.37.
Owner Burridge,Burridge,Pilkington & Rutland **Bred** J G St Paul Burridge **Trained** East Ilsley, Berks

FOCUS
This could prove to be a fair bumper as the season progresses, despite being run at just an ordinary pace until halfway, and the front pair had it to themselves from two out. The fifth sets the level for the form.

NOTEBOOK
Gentleman Jimmy, who hails from a stable that does well in this sphere, dug deep to hold off the runner-up in the straight and got off the mark at the second time of asking with a little up his sleeve. He has scope, is versatile as regards underfoot conditions and is bred to be useful over jumps, so rates a nice prospect for novice hurdling. *(op 15-2)*
Miss Midnight, placed in her three previous outings in this sphere, again managed to find one too good yet did little wrong in defeat. She deserves to find an opening and, while she may be ready to tackle hurdles and a bit further now, she is a decent benchmark for this form. *(op 5-1 tchd 11-2)*
Bring Me Sunshine(IRE), half-brother to several jump winners, most notably the smart handicapper Super Tactics, was doing his best work at the finish having been outpaced at the top of the straight. He was well backed for this, should come on plenty for the run and will be seen too much better effect when facing a stiffer test in due course. *(op 8-1)*
Mister Knight(IRE), who failed to make an impression in three outings between the flags earlier in the year, was not at all disgraced on this debut for his top stable and was staying on at the finish. He is an imposing sort who needs a stiffer test and his future clearly lies back over fences in due course. *Official explanation: jockey said gelding had been lame (op 9-1)*
So Long turned in another creditable effort and again left the impression she is in need of further. *(op 12-1)*
Earl Of Forestry(GER) proved disappointing on this return to action and dropped out tamely when the tempo quickened. He is entitled to have needed this run, but has it all to prove now all the same. *(tchd Evens and 6-4)*
T/Plt: £617.00 to a £1 stake. Pool: £40,824.35. 48.30 winning tickets. T/Qpdt: £182.00 to a £1 stake. Pool: £3,395.60. 13.80 winning tickets. TM

2158 - 2160a (Foreign Racing) - See Raceform Interactive

[1876]CHELTENHAM (L-H)
Friday, November 11

OFFICIAL GOING: Chase & hurdle courses - good to soft (good in places) changing to good to soft after race 3 (2.25); cross-country course - good (good to soft in places run on the Old Course.
slight, ahead

2161 ANGLO IRISH BANK NOVICES' HURDLE (REGISTERED AS THE SHARP NOVICES' HURDLE) GRADE 2 (8 hdls) 2m 110y

1:15 (1:18) (Class 1) 4-Y-O+
£17,106 (£6,417; £3,213; £1,602; £804; £402)

Form RPR

11 **1** **Boychuk (IRE)**[24] [1782] 4-11-0 126.. RJohnson 133+
(P J Hobbs) *in tch: chsd ldrs 4 out: outpcd and pushed along next: hrd rdn and r.o appr last: qcknd to ld fnl 100yds: readily* **8/1**

1111 **2** *2* **Buena Vista (IRE)**[118] [1010] 4-11-7 135.................................. TJMurphy 137
(M C Pipe) *lw: led: rdn after 2 out: kpt on wl run-in: hdd and no ex fnl 100yds* **9/4**[1]

1 **3** *2 1/2* **Two Miles West (IRE)**[13] [1927] 4-11-7 .... APMcCoy 137+
(Jonjo O'Neill) *lw: chsd ldrs: pushed along fr 3 out: styng on u.p whn hmpd on landing last: kpt on same pce* **7/2**[2]

13 **4** *1 1/4* **Crow Wood**[22] [1794] 6-11-0 .... RGarritty 127
(J J Quinn) *lw: chsd ldrs: wnt 2nd after 3 out: rdn to chal after next: wknd run-in* **7/1**[3]

11 **5** *3* **Natal (FR)**[175] [438] 4-11-7 ....(t) RWalsh 132+
(P F Nicholls) *blnd 1st: bhd: hdwy after 4 out: chsd ldrs and pushed along appr 2 out: wknd appr last* **12/1**

05-1 **6** *18* **French Accordion (IRE)**[40] [1623] 5-11-7 .... BJGeraghty 115+
(Paul Nolan, Ire) *str: lw: chsd ldrs tl after 3 out: wknd sn after next* **8/1**

7 *10* **Danehill Diamond (IRE)**[158] 6-10-7 .... MrJPO'Farrell 88
(Michael Joseph Fitzgerald, Ire) *cmpt: b.bkwd: sn in tch: chsd ldrs 4 out: rdn next: sn btn* **100/1**

1563 **8** *1 1/4* **Lago D'Oro**[16] [1876] 5-10-11 94.. TJPhelan 91
(Dr P Pritchard) *chsd ldrs early: wl bhd fr 4 out* **250/1**

1 **9** *hd* **Off Spin**[195] [131] 5-11-0 .... TDoyle 94
(P R Webber) *mstke 2nd: j. slowly 3rd: sn wl bhd* **40/1**

0-11 **10** *8* **Rimsky (IRE)**[20] [1827] 4-11-7 .... CLlewellyn 93
(N A Twiston-Davies) *nt fluent 2nd: bhd: j. slowly 3rd: nt fluent next and lost tch* **9/1**

4m 2.00s (2.80) **Going Correction** +0.40s/f (Soft) **10** Ran SP% **109.2**
Speed ratings: **109,108,106,106,104 96,91,91,91,87** CSF £24.74 TOTE £8.30: £2.40, £1.70, £1.50; EX 20.70 Trifecta £59.50 Pool: £1,401.60 - 16.70 winning units..
Owner Mrs D L Whateley **Bred** Robert Donaldson **Trained** Withycombe, Somerset

FOCUS
The best novice event run over the distance so far this season. The pace was generous and the form, rated through Buena Vista's Market Rasen win, looks solid. The winner and third were much improved and the fourth and fifth both lookcapable of better.

NOTEBOOK
Boychuk(IRE), unpenalised for his previous two wins since switching to Britain, maintained his unbeaten record over hurdles with a dogged display. Having taken time to hit full stride as the race became serious, he relished the rising ground from two out and showed a great attitude under pressure to mow down his rivals up the run-in. While his lack of penalties was a big advantage, there was an awful lot to like about the manner of his success, and he clearly likes a stiff test over this trip. His stable have made a decent start to the season, and while the Spring Festivals are still *some way off, it would come as little surprise to see him line up in the Supreme Novice in March. (op 13-2)*
Buena Vista(IRE) ◆ had won his last four over timber and who came into this with a very similar profile to his stable's two previous winners, Marcel and Kailash. He set out to make all in this search for the five-timer and was only run down up the run-in. This has to rate a very solid effort under his double penalty and it is unlikely that we have seen the best of him just yet. He would have obvious claims of getting revenge on the winner at level weights in the future. *(op 5-2)*
Two Miles West(IRE) ◆ created a decent impression when holding off Circassion at Wetherby on his recent debut and confirmed it with a sound effort under his penalty. He would have been closer but for being hampered at the final flight when contesting the lead with Buena Vista and he remains open to further improvement, but he left the impression that he may just need further to be seen at best, an opinion his form on the Flat would back up. *(tchd 10-3 and 4-1 in a place)*
Crow Wood, who would have made it two wins from as many starts in this sphere but for a shocking late error at Haydock last time, looked a big player as he loomed up to Buena Vista turning for home, but he ultimately failed to see out the race as well as the principals. This effort still bodes well for his future in this division, however, and it could be that he will be more at home on a flat track in the future. *(tchd 13-2)*
Natal(FR) ◆, winner of his both his previous hurdle outings, was by no means disgraced on this step-up in class. He still looked in need of the experience, and got detached from the principals after his mistake at the first. Having closed on them down the hill he may not have totally enjoyed *the stiff finish, so it will be surprising if he is not capable of better as he becomes more streetwise. (op 10-1)*
French Accordion(IRE), full-bother to his stable's leading Arkle hope Accordion Etoile, came into this in search of a hat-trick, having landed a Grade Three at Tipperary last time out. Having raced handily, he was found wanting approaching four from home and came home a very tired up the rising finish. He may not be easy to place now, but could benefit for the return to a sharper track in the future. *(op 10-1)*
Rimsky(IRE), who made it two wins from as many starts over timber when gamely taking the Grade Two Persian War at Chepstow last time, failed to go the early pace on this drop back in trip and never figured. This was disappointing, but he will surely leave the form behind back over further. *(op 8-1)*

2162 PADDYPOWER.COM AMATEUR RIDERS' H'CAP CHASE (19 fncs) 3m 110y

1:50 (1:50) (Class 4) (0-135,129) 5-Y-0+

£10,533 (£3,290; £1,644; £823; £410; £207)

Form RPR

2211 **1** **Getoutwhenyoucan (IRE)**[82] 1269 5-10-11 **122**............... MrRQuinn(7) 144+
(M C Pipe) *lw: mde all: clr fr 4 out: nt fluent last: idled run-in: unchal* **5/2**[1]

2-52 **2** *9* **Bee An Bee (IRE)**[13] 1920 8-10-10 **120**.....................(b) MrRMcCarthy(7) 132+
(T R George) *chsd ldrs: mstke 4 out: hit next: styd on to chse wnr last: kpt on but no ch* **5/1**[3]

40-6 **3** *5* **Willie John Daly (IRE)**[19] 1861 8-11-11 **128**...................... MrTGreenall 133+
(P J Hobbs) *bhd 6th: hit 8th: pushed along fr 10th: styng on whn hit 3 out: tk 3rd run-in* **8/1**

P-1U **4** *2* **You Owe Me (IRE)**[16] 1879 8-10-9 **119**........................... MrGTumelty(7) 122+
(N A Twiston-Davies) *chsd wnr: nt fluent 12th: no ch fr 4 out: wknd and lost 2nd last* **6/1**

/50- **5** *12* **Fasgo (IRE)**[355] 2362 10-11-5 **122**...................................... MrCJSweeney 112
(P F Nicholls) *hdwy 7th: lost position 11th: hdwy 13th: wknd fr 15th* **14/1**

-F22 **6** *5* **Jiver (IRE)**[15] 1893 6-10-10 **113**...................................... MissNCarberry 98
(M Scudamore) *chsd ldrs: j. slowly 6th: nt fluent 9th: rdn 11th: wknd 14th* **9/2**[2]

3- **7** *dist* **Dix Villez (FR)**[79] 1313 6-10-12 **115**................................ MrAFitzgerald —
(Paul Nolan, Ire) *w'like: swtg: a in rr and nt jump wl: no ch whn blnd 14th: t.o* **14/1**

026- **P** **Lord Who (IRE)**[13] 1934 8-11-12 **129**.........................(b[1]) MrJTMcNamara —
(P M J Doyle, Ire) *tall: str: lw: a bhd: no ch whn hit 12th: t.o whn p.u bef 14th* **20/1**

1P- **P** **Mamideos (IRE)**[209] 4869 8-10-7 **113**..........................(t) MrJSnowden(3) —
(T R George) *chsd ldrs: nt fluent 6th: blnd 14th: hit next: sn wknd: t.o whn p.u bef last* **20/1**

6m 24.9s (2.00) **Going Correction** +0.20s/f (Yiel)
WFA 5 from 6yo+ 1lb **9** Ran SP% **111.7**
Speed ratings: **104,101,99,98,95 93,—,—,—** CSF £15.16 CT £82.92 TOTE £2.90: £1.60, £1.80, £2.40; EX 15.00 Trifecta £83.20 Pool: £1,371.88 - 11.70 winning units..
Owner D A Johnson **Bred** M J Halligan **Trained** Nicholashayne, Devon

FOCUS
A fair handicap, run at a decent gallop and the winner did the job impressively, showing massively improved form and confirming himself a smart novice. The form looks sound.

NOTEBOOK
Getoutwhenyoucan(IRE) ◆ made all in emphatic style to win his third straight race, and his second over regulation fences to date. His jumping was most accomplished for a novice against hardened handicappers, he clearly stays all day long, and he should be rated value for further as he was idling up the long run-in. While the Handicapper will have his say now, this scopey grey is clearly a smart young novice and he remains open to plenty of further improvement. One day he could well turn out a National prospect. *(op 9-4 tchd 11-4 in places)*
Bee An Bee(IRE), a fast-finishing fifth in the National Hunt Chase at the Festival in March, turned in another sound effort and finished clear of the rest. He is consistent but will continue to be vulnerable to anything progressive off this sort of mark. *(tchd 11-2)*
Willie John Daly(IRE), runner-up in this event last season off a 3lb lower mark, was plugging on at the finish and posted much his best effort for some time. This was more encouraging, but he continues to make mistakes and is a hard horse to predict these days. *(op 7-1)*
You Owe Me(IRE) ◆, who took a tired fall on his seasonal bow over course and distance last time, looked the clear danger to the eventual winner down the back straight, but ultimately failed to get home. He looks to have begun handicap life over fences on a fair mark and will be much happier when dropping back in trip, so he is well worth another chance. *(op 11-2)*
Fasgo(IRE), returning from a 355-day layoff, was not given too hard a time of things and should come on a deal of the outing. However, he does appear regressive. *(op 12-1)*
Jiver(IRE), who proved his stamina when posting a personal best at Stratford last time, ran well below par and his fate was sealed a long way out. *(op 6-1 tchd 13-2)*

2163 BEARDS JEWELLERS CUP (A H'CAP CHASE) (12 fncs) 2m

2:25 (2:25) (Class 2) 5-Y-0+

£17,021 (£5,027; £2,513; £1,258; £627; £315)

Form RPR

P-22 **1** **Bold Bishop (IRE)**[17] 1871 8-10-0 **129**..................................... BHarding 142+
(Jonjo O'Neill) *bhd: rdn 4 out: stl plenty to do after next: styd on strly appr last: led last half f: kpt on wl* **8/1**

60-2 **2** *2 ½* **Tiger Cry (IRE)**[20] 1840 7-10-2 **131**... DJCasey 142
(A L T Moore, Ire) *chsd ldr: rdn and nt fluent 2 out: slt ld last: hdd and no ex last half f* **6/1**[3]

046- **3** *¾* **Made In Japan (JPN)**[209] 4859 5-10-10 **139**.......................(b) RJohnson 149
(P J Hobbs) *led: rdn 2 out: narrowly hdd last: one pce run-in* **14/1**

234- **4** *1* **Tysou (FR)**[238] 4437 8-10-7 **136**... MFoley 145
(N J Henderson) *hld up in rr: hdwy 2out: rdn and kpt on appr last: one pce run-in* **11/2**[2]

36-1 **5** *4* **Armaturk (FR)**[13] 1918 8-11-12 **155**............................ ChristianWilliams 160
(P F Nicholls) *lw: chsd ldrs: rdn 3 out: one pce u.p fr next* **13/2**

F-12 **6** *6* **Andreas (FR)**[20] 1822 5-11-1 **144**..(t) RWalsh 145+
(P F Nicholls) *hld up in rr: hdwy 4 out: disp 2nd 3 out: wknd u.p after next* **7/2**[1]

23-1 **7** *2* **Bambi De L'Orme (FR)**[188] 219 6-10-9 **138**........................ APMcCoy 135
(Ian Williams) *lw: mid-div: hit 2nd and 7th: hdwy 4 out: chsd ldrs and hrd drvn 2 out: wknd appr last* **11/2**[2]

-124 **8** *¾* **One Cornetto (IRE)**[17] 1871 6-10-1 **130**...................................... LAspell 127+
(L Wells) *chsd ldrs: hit 7th: wknd after 4 out* **50/1**

P4-U **9** *8* **Seebald (GER)**[19] 1846 10-11-7 **150**................................ TScudamore 138
(M C Pipe) *lw: prom early: bhd fr 8th* **20/1**

41-0 **10** *1 ¼* **Full Irish (IRE)**[174] 450 9-10-11 **140**.................................... JimCrowley 129+
(L Lungo) *bhd: hit 5th: nt fluent after and nvr in contention* **12/1**

3m 58.6s (-0.70) **Going Correction** +0.20s/f (Yiel) **10** Ran SP% **112.8**
Speed ratings: **109,107,107,106,104 101,100,100,96,95** CSF £54.27 CT £658.36 TOTE £9.20: £2.70, £2.20, £2.90; EX 76.20 Trifecta £333.40 Pool: £1,643.78 - 3.50 winning units..
Owner Mrs Gay Smith **Bred** Miss C Cunningham-Hogg **Trained** Cheltenham, Gloucs

FOCUS
A decent handicap, run at a solid gallop, and the form appears rock-solid, with the first two unexposed novices, the third potentially well in on hurdles form, and the next three all reasonably close to their marks.

NOTEBOOK
Bold Bishop(IRE) ◆ looked a bit reluctant when runner-up in a novice event over course and distance last time and took an age to find his stride from off the gallop, but once the penny dropped he really flew up the hill and eventually won going away after a fine leap at the last. He is clearly tricky, but also very talented and will always rate a danger in this type of event when the pace is strong.
Tiger Cry(IRE) ◆, who took a beginners' chase at Fairyhouse 20 days previously, ran a blinder on this handicap bow over fences and only gave way up the run-in. Having been handy from the start, he jumped like a seasoned pro, and dug deep to lead at the final fence before proving unable to resist the winner's late challenge. Given that he fared best of those to race up the early pace, he could be rated a touch better than the bare form and remains open to plenty of further improvement in this sphere. Long-term, he looks a live contender for the Grand Annual over this course and distance at the Festival in March, a race his trainer won with Fadoudal Du Cochet in 2002.
Made In Japan(JPN), the Triumph Hurdle winner in 2004, had failed to build on an impressive chase debut last season but set about making all at a decent clip and only gave way approaching the final fence. This was arguably his best effort to date over fences and it will be fascinating to see whether he can progress this season, as he still has time on his side.
Tysou(FR) was making his third appearance in this event, racing off the same mark as when fourth in the Grand Annual on his latest outing in March. Given a patient ride, he turned in another solid effort, but could only find the one pace when it really mattered in the straight. He is a likeable performer, and entitled to improve for the outing, but he has not won since he was a novice and remains unlikely to get much respite from the Handicapper. *(op 5-1 tchd 6-1)*
Armaturk(FR) took this race off a 1lb higher mark last year, having previously made a winning return at Lingfield - a feat which he repeated this term. He ran close to his mark, but was in trouble three out and is not going to be easy to place now. *(tchd 7-1)*
Andreas(FR), who had scored on his only previous outing at the track, was produced full of running to join the leaders four out, yet he failed to find anything when push came to shove turning for home and was ultimately left behind. He is probably happier on a faster surface, and has age on his side. *(op 4-1)*
Bambi De L'Orme(FR), who ended on a high note last season when beating River City at Warwick, did not jump all that fluently on this return to action and dropped out tamely having still held a chance approaching the final fence. He still has to prove he is up to this career-high mark, but his stable have yet to hit top form and he could do better with the run under his belt. *(tchd 6-1)*

2164 SPORTING INDEX CHASE (A CROSS COUNTRY CHASE) (32 fncs) 3m 7f

3:00 (3:01) (Class 2) 5-Y-0+

£18,789 (£5,550; £2,775; £1,389; £693; £348)

Form RPR

110- **1** **Spot Thedifference (IRE)**[19] 1866 12-11-8 .... MrJTMcNamara 137+
(E Bolger, Ire) *lw: travelled wl in tch: trckd ldrs 25th: hit 27th: rdn to ld appr last: styd on wl: rdn out* **13/8**[1]

4P-5 **2** *2 ½* **Lord Jack (IRE)**[19] 1844 9-11-8 125.. BHarding 133+
(N G Richards) *travelled wl: trckd ldrs: gd jump to ld 21st: rdn and hdd appr last: kpt on gamely but no ex run-in* **13/2**[3]

P22 **3** *2* **Oh My Lord (IRE)**[22] 1803 7-11-2 ....(t) DFO'Regan 123
(A J Martin, Ire) *hld up towards rr: hdwy into midfield 11th: trckd ldrs 25th: rdn and outpcd after 3 out: styd on wl to go 3rd appr last* **16/1**

40-6 **4** *½* **L'Aventure (FR)**[20] 1830 6-10-12 131..............................(t) PJBrennan 120+
(P F Nicholls) *mid div: tk clsr order 18th: wnt 2nd 27th: ev ch 4 out: sn outpcd: styd on again to go 4th appr last* **11/2**[2]

0/0- **5** *11* **Il De Boitron (FR)**[199] 39 7-11-8 .... DNRussell 120+
(Thomas Gerard O'Leary, Ire) *trckd ldrs: rdn in cl 4th after 3 out: 3rd and hung rt appr last: wknd* **33/1**

-F6R **6** *3* **Luzcadou (FR)**[33] 1710 12-11-8 115.....................................(b) AO'Keeffe 116+
(Ferdy Murphy) *hld up towards rr: hmpd 10th: hdwy next into midfield: chsd ldrs 27th: 3rd and rdn after 3 out: wknd appr last* **12/1**

03P5 **7** *15* **Happy Hussar (IRE)**[17] 1874 12-11-2 91........................... DrPPritchard 102+
(Dr P Pritchard) *led: clr 4th: 10 l clr whn nrly tk wrong crse and lost advantage: hit 17th: hdd 21st: hit 24th: grad fdd* **100/1**

P325 **8** *5* **Wildfield Rufo (IRE)**[40] 1603 10-11-5 110.......................(p) JimCrowley 92
(Mrs K Walton) *mid div: hmpd 18th: lost tch fr 25th* **25/1**

0PP- **9** *nk* **Historg (FR)**[265] 3952 10-10-10 111.. TJDreaper 82
(Ferdy Murphy) *a bhd: t.o fr 23rd* **16/1**

FP/ **10** *11* **Native Ray (IRE)**[11] 11-11-5 .... DJCasey 80
(Miss Noreen Hayes, Ire) *neat: mid divison: j.rt 10th: sn dropped rr: bhd whn slow jump 20th: t.o* **50/1**

5-66 **11** *dist* **Multi Talented (IRE)**[166] 567 9-11-2 101............................ MrJMorgan —
(L Wells) *a towards rr: rdr lost irons 13th: hmpd 18th: sn wl bhd* **66/1**

2-66 **12** *12* **Pardini (USA)**[13] 1920 6-11-2 95..................................... SStronge —
(M F Harris) *mid div: hdwy to chse ldrs 10th: jnd ldrs 25th: mstke 27th: sn wknd: t.o* **100/1**

34-4 **F** **Grumpy Stumpy**[20] 1832 10-11-5 91..................................... CLlewellyn —
(N A Twiston-Davies) *in tch: lost position 15th: fell 18th* **20/1**

1 **P** **Good Step (IRE)**[11] 1963 7-11-8 107.. CO'Dwyer —
(E Bolger, Ire) *str: lw: mid div tl lost pl fr 15th: wl bhd fr 20th: t.o and p.u bef 28th* **7/1**

8m 38.1s (-5.20) **Going Correction** +0.075s/f (Yiel) **14** Ran SP% **115.8**
Speed ratings: **109,108,107,107,104 104,100,98,98,96 —,—,—,—** CSF £11.01 TOTE £2.70: £1.40, £2.60, £2.60; EX 15.70 Trifecta £91.80 Pool: £1,888.12 - 14.60 winning units..
Owner John P McManus **Bred** Fenlon Bros **Trained** Bruree, Co Limerick

FOCUS
A good renewal of this unique test which saw six come clear on the turn for home. The winner is in a different league in this sphere and did not have to be at his best to score as he was much favoured by the weights. The placed horses ought to have real claims of reversing form on handicap terms in December.

NOTEBOOK
Spot Thedifference(IRE) ◆, unbeaten in three previous starts on this unique course, including when winning at the Festival in March, confirmed his supremacy in this sphere and won this readily for the second consecutive year. Fit from a recent spin over timber, he was ridden more positively than has often been the case. While he was entitled to score as he did at the weights, he is clearly in a different league to his rivals in such events and will no doubt continue to be hard to beat here. *(op 15-8 tchd 2-1 and 6-4 in a place)*
Lord Jack(IRE) ◆, fit from a spin over hurdles in Ocotber, ran a cracker in defeat and looked well suited by the nature of this test. Given that he had a lot to find with the winner at these weights, he emerges with real credit, and it will be interesting to see whether he can now build on this improved display. The next event over this course in December is a handicap, and he ought to have decent claims of reversing form. *(tchd 7-1)*
Oh My Lord(IRE) ◆, a beaten favourite on his last five outings over fences, was still sixth turning for home and had a lot to do, but he relished the rising finish and was staying on with real effect on the run-in. He appeared to enjoy the switch to these unique fences, got the trip without fuss, and looks the sort to do much better if kept to this division. It should be noted that his trainer won this twice from three attempts in the last ten years, with Linden's Lotto, and clearly knows the type of horse required for the job.
L'Aventure(FR), who had a real chance at the weights according to official figures, was in with every chance four out, yet she struggled to sustain her effort before staying on again all too late at the finish. She jumped well enough, but again looked quirky and really is very hard to predict. *(op 5-1 tchd 6-1)*
Il De Boitron(FR) was handy throughout and only gave way turning for home.This must rate his best effort for some time, but this trip clearly stretched his stamina.
Luzcadou(FR), who refused in the Pardubicke last time for the second consecutive year, ran well enough yet failed to see out the race as well as the principals.

Good Step(IRE), a stablemate of the winner, had won the La Touche Cup at Punchestown in April and was also fit from a recent spin over hurdles. However, he ran no sort of race on this return to chasing and was later reported to have lost his action. It is unlikely we have still to see the best of *him just yet. Official explanation: jockey said gelding made a mistake and lost its confidence (op 13-2)*

2165 STEEL PLATE AND SECTIONS NOVICES' CHASE (19 fncs) 3m 110y
3:35 (3:35) (Class 2) 5-Y-0+ **£10,572** (£3,224; £1,684; £915)

Form | | | | RPR
6-1 **1** **Church Island (IRE)**[19] [1868] 6-11-8 ..... DFO'Regan 146+
(Michael Hourigan, Ire) *cmpt: chsd ldrs: chal 14th to next: led appr 3 out: hrd rdn last and styd on strly* **12/1**
3P-1 **2** *8* **Celtic Son (FR)**[6] [2052] 6-11-8 ..... (t) TJMurphy 140+
(M C Pipe) *lw: hld up in tch: nt fluent 7th: hdwy 12th: hit 3 out: styng on whn whn lft 2nd and sltly hmpd 2 out: rdn and fnd no ex run-in* **8/13**[1]
04-1 **3** *dist* **Red Georgie (IRE)**[20] [1829] 7-11-5 ..... CLlewellyn 116
(N A Twiston-Davies) *w ldr: led 3rd to 6th: styd chalng: slt ld 9th to 12th: dropped to 3rd 15th: wknd after 4 out: no ch whn hmpd 2 out* **10/1**[3]
4P/ **4** *dist* **Fisherman Jack**[600] 10-11-0 ..... JMogford —
(G J Smith) *led to 3rd: styd pressing ldrs and rdn 12th: wknd qckly 4 out: t.o* **125/1**
0/ **P** **Battling Buster (IRE)**[1343] [4158] 8-11-0 ..... BHitchcott —
(R H Buckler) *hit 1st: 3rd and 5th: t.o 8th: p.u after 12th* **200/1**
14-5 **U** **Bob Bob Bobbin**[13] [1917] 6-11-0 ..... JTizzard —
(C L Tizzard) *trckd ldrs: blnd 9th: disputing cl 5th and gng wl whn blnd and uns rdr 14th* **11/2**[2]
11-2 **F** **Blue Business**[24] [1781] 7-11-0 ..... (b) RWalsh 132+
(P F Nicholls) *lw: w ldrs: chal 5th: led next: hdd 9th: led again 12th: hdd appr 3 out: length 2nd and rdn whn fell 2 out* **11/2**[2]

6m 41.8s (18.90) **Going Correction** +0.20s/f (Yiel) **7** Ran SP% **110.8**
Speed ratings: **77,74,—,—,— —,—** CSF £19.96 TOTE £9.00: £2.50, £1.30; EX 21.00.
Owner B J Craig **Bred** J S Bolger **Trained** Patrickswell, Co Limerick

FOCUS
This was run at a sedate early gallop, hence the slow winning time, yet the field came home well strung out. The overall form must be treated with caution, but the winner still looks to have improved considerably.

NOTEBOOK
Church Island(IRE) ◆ has progressed rapidly over fences this autumn, winning his last three races, including a Grade Three on his penultimate run. Handy throughout, he hardly put a foot wrong and, responding kindly for pressure up the rising finish, completed his four-timer with a smart display, looking full value for his winning margin. He has improved since being upped in trip and while the lack of early pace must cast a doubt as to the strength of the overall form, he could do no more than win as he did. He is quite rightly due to be aimed at the SunAlliance Chase at the Festival in March. *(op 14-1)*
Celtic Son(FR), so impressive when landing a Grade Two at Wincanton on his chase debut six days previously, compromised his chance of getting home over this longer trip by refusing to settle behind the sedate early pace. He also lacked the same fluency over his fences as he displayed at Wincanton, and though he still emerged to have his chance turning for home, he was always playing second fiddle to the winner and was very tired at the finish. Although this leaves him with something to prove, it is far too early to be dismissing his SunAlliance prospects, for his hurdles form suggests he should stay the trip and he may simply have found this coming too soon. Equally he could simply have met a superior rival in Church Island. *(op 4-7 tchd 4-6 in places and 1-2 in a place)*
Red Georgie(IRE), who decisively made all on his recent chasing bow, was outclassed and made to look very one paced when it really mattered. That said, he remains open to improvement as a chaser and can find easier assignments in the future.
Blue Business, unsuited by the lack of pace when beaten at odds-on at Exeter on his chase debut, had blinkers back on but was again not helped by the lack of pace. He was under pressure and looked held by the winner when departing two out, but he will no doubt be seen to better effect when getting the decent pace he clearly needs. *(tchd 5-1)*
Bob Bob Bobbin, who shaped well until appearing to blow-up on his chase debut at Lingfield previously, was given a more patient ride over this longer trip and was still very much a player prior to unseating down the back straight, having survived an earlier blunder. He has always appealed as the type to reach greater heights over fences, but he clearly needs more practice before he can fulfil his potential. *(tchd 5-1)*

2166 ABACUS GLOBAL CONDITIONAL JOCKEYS' H'CAP HURDLE (10 hdls) 2m 5f
4:10 (4:10) (Class 4) (0-115,115) 4-Y-0+
£9,582 (£2,830; £1,415; £708; £353; £177)

Form | | | | RPR
-14F **1** **Water King (USA)**[34] [1675] 6-10-12 **107** ..... SWalsh[(6)] 120
(R M Stronge) *bhd: hdwy 4 out: chsd ldr after 3 out: styd on u.p appr last: kpt on wl run-in to ld cl home* **50/1**
2 *½* **Mouftari (USA)**[19] [1864] 4-10-2 **94** ..... (b) MJFerris[(3)] 106+
(C Byrnes, Ire) *small: hld up in rr: stdy hdwy 6th: led appr 3 out: drvn 10l clr after 2 out: hdd and no ex cl home* **14/1**
/0F- **3** *13* **Newtown Dancer (IRE)**[33] [1698] 6-11-1 **110** ..... (tp) DFFlannery[(6)] 110+
(T Hogan, Ire) *w'like: chsd ldrs: rdn and styd on same pce fr 3 out* **66/1**
-012 **4** *1 ½* **Mouseski**[9] [1984] 11-11-1 **112** ..... LHeard[(8)] 110
(P F Nicholls) *in tch: pushed along 4 out: styd on fr 2 out but nvr gng pce to rch ldrs* **4/1**[1]
5-01 **5** *8* **Astyanax (IRE)**[22] [1806] 5-10-10 **102** ..... SCurling[(3)] 94+
(N J Henderson) *chsd ldrs: slt ld 5th: hdd 4 out: wknd after 3 out* **12/1**
2601 **6** *1 ¼* **Pardon What**[10] [1977] 9-10-10 **99** 7ex ..... (b) TJPhelan 87
(S Lycett) *chsd ldrs: rdn 4 out: one pce fr 3 out* **50/1**
35-2 **7** *¾* **Helm (IRE)**[25] [1775] 4-11-2 **105** ..... PAspell 93
(R Rowe) *bhd: rdn fr 4 out: styd on appr last but nvr in contention* **25/1**
0000 **8** *4* **Anatar (IRE)**[17] [1872] 7-11-4 **115** ..... AGlassonbury[(8)] 99
(M C Pipe) *mid-div: rdn 4 out: kpt on fr 2 out but nvr a danger* **25/1**
2204 **9** *3 ½* **Argent Ou Or (FR)**[9] [1982] 4-10-7 **99** ..... TJMalone[(3)] 79
(M C Pipe) *chsd ldrs to 4 out: sn rdn and wknd* **8/1**
10 *¾* **Good Thyne Jack (IRE)**[53] [1501] 7-10-0 **95** ..... BCByrnes[(6)] 74
(E McNamara, Ire) *str: lw: bhd: hrd drvn 4 out: styd on fr 2 out: n.d* **12/1**
1123 **11** *5* **Michaels Dream (IRE)**[19] [1844] 6-11-4 **110** ..... (b) TJDreaper[(3)] 84
(N Wilson) *bhd: stl plenty to do 2 out: kpt on appr last: nvr a danger* **25/1**
0/4 **12** *3 ½* **Nassaro (IRE)**[34] [1691] 5-11-9 **112** ..... (t) TGMRyan 83
(M Halford, Ire) *cmpt: in tch: hdwy to chse ldrs 5th: wknd fr 3 out* **20/1**
333/ **13** *½* **Better Think Again (IRE)**[26] [1767] 11-11-6 **109** ..... WJLee 79
(Miss Susan A Finn, Ire) *nvr bttr than mid-div* **80/1**
/5-F **14** *3 ½* **Montevideo**[69] [1399] 5-11-5 **108** ..... MPWalsh 75
(Jonjo O'Neill) *prom early: bhd fr 6th* **6/1**[3]
-062 **15** *2 ½* **Double Dizzy**[16] [1876] 4-11-5 **108** ..... WKennedy 72
(R H Buckler) *chsd ldrs: rdn 4 out: wknd qckly fr next* **33/1**
16 *dist* **Oxybau (FR)**[22] [1809] 6-11-2 **108** ..... SMMcGovern[(3)] —
(T J Taaffe, Ire) *neat: chsd ldrs to 6th: t.o* **16/1**
2/0- **17** *1 ½* **Allstar Leader (IRE)**[40] [1624] 8-11-3 **106** ..... DFO'Regan —
(Michael Joseph Fitzgerald, Ire) *mid-div: rdn 6th: sn wknd: t.o* **66/1**
2236 **18** *dist* **Sir Walter (IRE)**[19] [1862] 12-10-5 **97** ..... APogson[(3)] —
(D Burchell) *a bhd: t.o* **100/1**
514- **P** **Kilgowan (IRE)**[224] [4683] 6-11-9 **112** ..... ONelmes —
(Ian Williams) *bhd: fr 1/2-way: t.o whn p.u bef last* **20/1**
1-P5 **P** **Gan Eagla (IRE)**[24] [1784] 6-11-1 **107** ..... (b) LTreadwell[(3)] —
(Miss Venetia Williams) *chsd ldrs to 6th: t.o whn p.u bef 3 out* **100/1**
322 **P** **Martovic (IRE)**[19] [1851] 6-10-11 **100** ..... MNicolls —
(K C Bailey) *chsd ldrs: rdn and n.m.r 4 out: wknd after next: t.o whn p.u bef last* **20/1**
-012 **F** **Miss Skippy**[36] [1658] 6-10-12 **101** ..... PMerrigan 89
(A G Newcombe) *bhd: hdwy 4 out: 7th and styng on but plenty to do whn fell 2 out* **33/1**
PP5/ **P** **Take A Drop (IRE)**[104] [1105] 10-10-7 **99** ..... SGMcDermott[(3)] —
(Seamus O'Farrell, Ire) *w'like: in tch: rdn 5th: wknd nxt: t.o whn p.u after 4 out* **100/1**
111- **P** **Lord Of Illusion (IRE)**[314] [3148] 8-11-5 **108** ..... PCO'Neill —
(T R George) *led to 5th: led again 4 out: hdd appr next and sn wknd: t.o whn p.u bef last* **11/2**[2]

5m 17.4s (3.80) **Going Correction** +0.40s/f (Soft)
WFA 4 from 5yo+ 13lb **24** Ran SP% **131.5**
Speed ratings: 108,107,102,102,99 98,98,96,95,95 93,92,91,90,89 —,—,—,— —,—,—,— CSF £603.12 CT £36771.27 TOTE £69.10: £10.20, £3.30, £6.30, £2.10; EX 1902.60 TRIFECTA Not won. Place 6 £57.83, Place 5 £46.28..
Owner Hellyer, Clark, St Quinton **Bred** Skymarc Farm Inc & Castlemartin Stud **Trained** Beedon, Berks
■ Stewards' Enquiry : S Walsh two-day ban: used whip in the incorrect place and without giving gelding time to respond (Nov 22-23)

FOCUS
Acompetitive conditional riders' handicap which saw the first two pull well clear at the finish. The winner has threatened to be this good before, and with the second an improver and the third to his Irish mark the form of the principals looks decent.

NOTEBOOK
Water King(USA) looked held by the winner turning for home, but stuck to his task under pressure and, as that rival started to tread water up the rising finish, just did enough to get on top near the line. Although he won in selling company last term, he has improved since then and, on the overall balance of his form, he really was a huge price for this. *(op 40-1)*
Mouftari(USA), a late springer in the betting ring, shot clear approaching the climb for home and looked all over the winner, but his stride shortened after the final flight and he was agonisingly reeled in close home. While it may appear that he went for home plenty soon enough, it was more the case that he was left in front too soon as the leaders folded three out, and he has to rate a little unlucky. However, he has never been the easiest to win with and, as a weight rise in now inevitable, he will be hard to place now. *(op 20-1 tchd 25-1 in a place)*
Newtown Dancer(IRE) was put in her place when the leader asserted turning for home, yet stuck gamely to her task up the rising finish and ran very close to her mark. She is probably at her best over a shorter trip, however.
Mouseski, just denied off this mark at Chepstow last time, was doing all of his best work from two out and got going too late. This still rates another solid effort, however, considering his veteran status. *(op 9-2 tchd 5-1 in places)*
Astyanax(IRE), raised 7lb for getting off the mark on fast ground last time, was made to look one paced when the race got serious. He kept on under pressure, however, and could do better off this mark back on quicker ground. *(op 11-1)*
Pardon What, back to winning ways at Worcester, was found out by a 7lb higher mark yet was not disgraced in defeat. *(op 40-1)*
Argent Ou Or(FR) failed to find anything when asked for his effort with four to run and failed to improve as expected over the longer trip. *(op 7-1)*
Montevideo met support in the betting ring, yet turned in a moody effort and never looked a threat. *(op 13-2 tchd 8-1 in a place and 7-1 in places)*
Lord Of Illusion(IRE) , rated 2 stone higher over fences and having his first outing since winning at this venue on New Year's Day, ran well until hitting a brick wall approaching the climb for home and was rather disappointingly pulled up. He is entitled to improve a deal for the outing, and will no *doubt be back over fences before long, but this effort leaves him with a little to prove again. (op 5-1 tchd 6-1)*
T/Jkpt: Not won. T/Plt: £83.70 to a £1 stake. Pool: £145,098.85. 1,265.35 winning tickets. T/Qpdt: £39.10 to a £1 stake. Pool: £6,233.60. 117.80 winning tickets. ST

NEWCASTLE (L-H)
Friday, November 11

OFFICIAL GOING: Good to soft (good in the last 3f)
Wind: strong, half-against

2167 IBM & LENOVO JUVENILE NOVICES' HURDLE (9 hdls) 2m
1:00 (1:01) (Class 4) 3-Y-0 **£3,487** (£1,016; £508)

Form | | | | RPR
3 **1** **Patxaran (IRE)**[48] [1551] 3-10-0 ..... (t) RStephens[(5)] 99+
(P C Haslam) *prom: hdwy and ev ch 3 out: rdn whn hit last: styd on wl to ld towards fin* **2/1**[1]
125 **2** *nk* **Toss The Caber (IRE)**[13] [1923] 3-10-9 113 ..... PKinsella[(10)] 113+
(K G Reveley) *chsd clr ldr: led bef 3 out: sn hrd pressed: kpt on fr last: hdd towards fin* **3/1**[2]
44 **3** *13* **Truckle**[8] [2001] 3-10-7 ..... DCCostello[(5)] 96+
(C W Fairhurst) *cl up: ev ch 3 out: rdn and wknd fr next* **14/1**
4 **4** *19* **Lodgician (IRE)**[22] [1797] 3-10-12 ..... RMcGrath 76+
(J J Quinn) *in tch tl rdn and wknd qckly fr 3 out* **7/2**[3]
0 **5** *7* **Kalawoun (FR)**[22] [1797] 3-10-12 ..... AThornton 67
(Ferdy Murphy) *in tch tl rdn and wknd bef 3 out* **9/1**
3P **6** *5* **Dennick**[63] [1441] 3-10-12 ..... FKeniry 62
(P C Haslam) *keen: led after 2nd: sn clr: hdd & wknd bef 3 out* **25/1**
0 **7** *½* **Shaanbar (IRE)**[8] [2001] 3-10-5 ..... MBradburne 55
(J Hetherton) *hld up: rdn 5th: sn btn* **100/1**
P **Tarkar (IRE)** 3-10-7 ..... DMcGann[(5)] —
(J Howard Johnson) *bhd: struggling 1/2-way: t.o whn p.u bef 3 out* **20/1**
P **With Honours**[29] 3-10-5 ..... PWhelan —
(T J Fitzgerald) *towards rr: wknd 4th: t.o whn p.u bef 3 out* **100/1**
60 **P** **Casalese**[6] [1718] 3-10-12 ..... KRenwick —
(M D Hammond) *mstkes in rr: no ch fr 1/2-way: p.u bef 3 out* **100/1**
0 **P** **Coleorton Dane**[30] [1718] 3-10-12 ..... GLee —
(K A Ryan) *hld up midfield: outpcd bef 4 out: no ch whn p.u bef next* **20/1**
P **Compton Classic**[8] 3-10-12 ..... ADempsey —
(J S Goldie) *bhd: reminders after 3rd: sn btn: t.o whn p.u bef 3 out* **100/1**
0 **P** **Port D'Argent (IRE)**[22] [1797] 3-9-12 ..... TMessenger[(7)] —
(Mrs H O Graham) *midfield: struggling fr 4th: t.o whn p.u bef 3 out* **100/1**

0 **P** **Singhalongtasveer**[22] [1797] 3-10-12 ....(t) NPMulholland —
(W Storey) *towards rr: mstke 3rd: sn btn: t.o whn p.u bef 3 out* **100/1**

4m 0.40s (-5.90) **Going Correction** -0.50s/f (Good) **14** Ran SP% **116.5**
Speed ratings: **94,93,87,77,74 71,71,—,—,— —,—,—,—** CSF £7.27 TOTE £3.00: £1.60, £1.80, £2.90; EX 10.40.
Owner David H Morgan **Bred** Eddie O'Leary **Trained** Middleham, N Yorks

FOCUS
Little strength in depth but the pace was fair and the first two pulled clear over the last two flights. The form is rated through the runner-up to his previous mark.

NOTEBOOK
Patxaran(IRE) confirmed the bit of promise shown on her debut to score with the first-time tongue-tie applied. She should stay two and a half miles and may be capable of better in this sphere. *(op 9-4 tchd 7-4)*
Toss The Caber(IRE), below his best at Wetherby on soft last time, returned to something like his best in this less-testing ground but, although he should continue to go well, may be vulnerable to more progressive sorts in this type of event. *(tchd 7-2)*
Truckle, who is now qualified for a handicap mark in this sphere, was not totally disgraced but did leave the impression that less of a test of stamina would have suited. *(op 11-1)*
Lodgician(IRE), who has yet to win in 16 career starts, failed to build on the promise of his hurdles debut and, although capable of winning a modest event in this sphere, may not be one to place too much faith in. *(op 9-2 tchd 5-1)*
Kalawoun(FR), a winner on the Flat in France, showed a bit more than on his hurdling debut but was again well beaten and appeals as the type that may do better in modest handicaps in due course. *(op 8-1)*
Dennick did not give himself much chance of lasting home given he failed to settle and, although modest handicaps will offer his best chance of succcess, he will have to become more amenable to restraint if he is to progress.

2168 IBM TOTALSTORAGE BEGINNERS' CHASE (16 fncs) 2m 4f
1:35 (1:35) (Class 4) 4-Y-0+ **£3,988** (£1,170; £585; £292)

Form RPR
141- **1** **Wild Cane Ridge (IRE)**[222] [4707] 6-11-6 .... GLee 124+
(L Lungo) *mde all: rdn and styd on strly fr 3 out* **4/6**[1]
115- **2** *8* **Eskimo Pie (IRE)**[265] [3933] 6-11-6 .... NFehily 109+
(C C Bealby) *cl up: pushed along 6 out: effrt and chsd wnr 4 out: kpt on same pce bef 2 out* **11/4**[2]
/24- **3** *12* **Moonlit Harbour**[376] [1938] 6-11-6 .... RMcGrath 99+
(Ferdy Murphy) *prom: chsd wnr 5 out to next: wknd bef 2 out* **11/2**[3]
FP2- **4** *14* **Do Keep Up**[269] [3869] 8-11-1 73.................... DCCostello(5) 83
(J R Weymes) *in tch tl wknd fr 5 out* **50/1**
2 **5** *2 ½* **Wee William**[35] [1662] 5-11-6 .... RWalford 81
(T D Walford) *chsd wnr tl wknd fr 11th* **20/1**
PP-P **6** *dist* **Fifteen Reds**[7] [2025] 10-10-13 .... MJMcAlister(7) —
(J C Haynes) *bhd: hit and wknd 9th* **100/1**
P **The Associate (IRE)** 8-11-3 .... PBuchanan(3) —
(Miss Lucinda V Russell) *a bhd: t.o whn p.u bef 4 out* **66/1**

5m 16.3s (-12.40) **Going Correction** -0.50s/f (Good) **7** Ran SP% **111.2**
Speed ratings: **104,100,96,90,89 —,—** CSF £2.75 TOTE £1.80: £1.40, £1.70; EX 3.10.
Owner Ashleybank Investments Limited **Bred** Greenville House Stud And M Morgan **Trained** Carrutherstown, D'fries & G'way

FOCUS
Another race lacking strength but a pleasing chase debut from Wild Cane Ridge, who appeals as the type to win again over fences.

NOTEBOOK
Wild Cane Ridge(IRE) ◆, a 130-rated hurdler, had the run of the race but jumped soundly and created a favourable impression for this chase debut. The step up to three miles will suit and he appeals as the type to win more races over fences. *(op 4-5 tchd 10-11 in a place)*
Eskimo Pie(IRE), a 120-rated hurdler whose wins came in testing ground, showed more than enough on this chase debut and first run since February on ground that may have been quick enough to suggest he can win a race over fences. *(op 10-3 tchd 7-2)*
Moonlit Harbour, having his second start for his in-form stable, travelled strongly and shaped as though in need of this first run for over a year. He will be of more interest in a truly-run race back over two miles in ordinary handicap company. *(op 7-2)*
Do Keep Up was well beaten in the face of a stiff task and is likely to remain vulnerable in this type of event.
Wee William, a point winner who showed ability in a race that worked out well on his debut over regulation fences last time, failed to build on that effort and is another who may do better in modest handicaps. *(op 12-1)*
Fifteen Reds was predictably outclassed on these terms.

2169 I.T.P.S. 5TH BIRTHDAY NOVICES' HURDLE (11 hdls) 2m 4f
2:10 (2:10) (Class 4) 4-Y-0+ **£3,446** (£1,004; £502)

Form RPR
1 **1** **Ballyfitz**[19] [1854] 5-10-11 .... MGoldstein(7) 123+
(N A Twiston-Davies) *led to 3 out: rallied to ld bef last: styd on strly* **13/2**[3]
1 **2** *1* **New Alco (FR)**[20] [1824] 4-11-4 .... AThornton 120
(Ferdy Murphy) *cl up: led gng wl 3 out: hdd bef last: kpt on run in* **6/4**[1]
21-1 **3** *22* **Brave Rebellion**[38] [1635] 6-10-11 .... RMcGrath 91+
(K G Reveley) *hld up: hdwy and prom after 4 out: rdn and outpcd fr next* **12/1**
00/6 **4** *1 ¼* **Rectory (IRE)**[16] [1885] 6-10-11 .... DElsworth 90
(Mrs S J Smith) *chsd ldrs: rdn 4 out: outpcd bef next* **100/1**
423 **5** *3 ½* **Toni Alcala**[40] [1608] 6-10-11 104....................(p) JAMcCarthy 87+
(R F Fisher) *hld up: nt fluent 5th: rdn after 4 out: wknd bef next* **16/1**
2 **6** *2* **Hockenheim (FR)**[14] [1915] 4-10-11 .... GLee 84
(J Howard Johnson) *prom: rdn bef 3 out: sn btn* **9/4**[2]
F25- **7** *10* **Em's Royalty**[215] [4785] 8-10-11 105.................... ADempsey 74
(A Parker) *chsd ldrs tl wknd bef 3 out* **28/1**
8 *24* **Doris's Gift** 4-10-4 .... LBerridge(7) 50
(J Howard Johnson) *bhd: rdn 7th: nvr on terms* **40/1**
0F6/ **9** *nk* **Caymans Gift**[43] [4908] 5-10-4 .... EWhillans(7) 50
(A C Whillans) *midfield: rdn and wknd fr 4 out* **100/1**
00-0 **10** *½* **Jethro Tull (IRE)**[14] [1915] 6-10-11 .... BGibson 49
(G A Harker) *hld up: pushed along 7th: sn btn* **33/1**
-320 **11** *17* **King's Protector**[156] [691] 5-10-11 102.................... NPMulholland 32
(M D Hammond) *towards rr: drvn 7th: sn btn* **28/1**
00P **12** *dist* **Shem Dylan (NZ)**[12] [1938] 6-10-1 .... JPFlavin(10) —
(R C Guest) *hld up: sme hdwy bef 7th: struggling next* **200/1**
0- **P** **Lade Braes (IRE)**[203] [4971] 4-10-4 .... BSHughes(7) —
(J Howard Johnson) *a bhd: t.o whn p.u bef 3 out* **200/1**
P- **P** **Thorsgill**[399] [1636] 7-10-8 .... GBerridge(3) —
(M Todhunter) *cl up tl wknd 4 out: t.o whn p.u bef next* **100/1**
55- **P** **Primitive Rebel**[363] [2196] 6-10-11 .... DO'Meara —
(H P Hogarth) *in tch tl wknd 6th: t.o whn p.u bef 3 out* **40/1**
5P/P **P** **Moonzie Laird (IRE)**[12] [1938] 7-10-8 .... FKing(3) —
(J N R Billinge) *in tch to 1/2-way: sn lost pl: t.o whn p.u bef 3 out* **200/1**
05-P **P** **Gaelic Jig**[188] [212] 6-10-8 ....(t) MichalKohl(3) —
(J I A Charlton) *plld hrd: hdwy and cl up after 4th: wknd bef 4 out: t.o whn p.u bef next* **200/1**

5m 4.10s (-11.70) **Going Correction** -0.50s/f (Good) **17** Ran SP% **117.4**
Speed ratings: **103,102,93,93,91 91,87,77,77,77 70,—,—,—,— —,—** CSF £15.71 TOTE £6.30: £2.40, £1.30, £2.90; EX 19.90.
Owner F J Mills & W Mills **Bred** Helshaw Grange Farms Ltd **Trained** Naunton, Gloucs

FOCUS
A good novice for the track, featuring a couple of promising sorts who did well to pull well clear of the remainder in the straight. The race could be rated higher and both appeal as type to win again over obstacles.

NOTEBOOK
Ballyfitz ◆, who beat a previous winner on his hurdle debut, set a fair pace and showed the right attitude in the closing stages to follow up over this shorter trip. The return to three miles will suit and he is sure to win another race.
New Alco(FR) ◆, who created a favourable impression on his hurdling debut, travelled like the best horse for much of the way but was worn down by an equally promising sort in the closing stages. However, he lost little in defeat and is the type to win more races. *(op 15-8 tchd 2-1 in a place)*
Brave Rebellion, who showed a fair level in bumpers on a sound surface, ran creditably against a couple of potentially useful sorts on this hurdle debut and is sure to be placed to best advantage by shrewd connections. *Official explanation: jockey said gelding ran too freely early (tchd 14-1)*
Rectory(IRE) fared better than on his hurdle debut and looks the sort that may do better in ordinary handicap company over this trip and beyond in due course.
Toni Alcala is now qualified for a handicap mark in this sphere but, although the switch into handicaps may be in his favour, his record under both codes this year means he is not one for maximum faith.
Hockenheim(FR), from a stable that has struggled to find its feet in the last few months, failed to build on a fair hurdle debut but would not be one to write off yet. *(op 15-8 tchd 5-2)*

2170 CELLULAR SOLUTIONS H'CAP CHASE (18 fncs) 3m
2:45 (2:45) (Class 4) (0-110,110) 5-Y-0+ **£4,059** (£1,191; £595; £297)

Form RPR
001 **1** **Devondale (IRE)**[7] [2022] 9-9-7 **84** oh1.................... PJMcDonald(7) 100+
(Ferdy Murphy) *prom: led 4 out: styd on strly* **5/2**[1]
251 **2** *1 ¼* **Red Perk (IRE)**[14] [1910] 8-10-1 **85**....................(p) KJohnson 97
(R C Guest) *prom: effrt and chsd wnr after 3 out: nt fluent next: kpt on fr last* **3/1**[2]
5110 **3** *12* **Lutin Du Moulin (FR)**[22] [1796] 6-11-5 **103**....................(b) KRenwick 105+
(L Lungo) *chsd ldrs: led 5 out to next: outpcd fr 2 out* **10/1**
414- **4** *17* **Has Scored (IRE)**[245] [4302] 7-11-12 **110**.................... RMcGrath 93
(Ferdy Murphy) *bhd: outpcd 11th: sme late hdwy: nvr on terms* **10/1**
P3P/ **5** *1* **Kung Hei Fat Choi (IRE)**[686] [2904] 10-10-7 **91**.................... GLee 73
(J S Goldie) *hld up in tch: rdn after 5 out: wknd next* **16/1**
30-F **6** *6* **Behavingbadly (IRE)**[20] [1837] 10-11-3 **101**.................... ADempsey 77
(A Parker) *nt fluent in rr: outpcd 1/2-way: nvr on terms* **25/1**
/4-0 **7** *4* **Almire Du Lia (FR)**[20] [1837] 7-11-4 **102**....................(v) MBradburne 74
(Mrs S C Bradburne) *cl up tl lost pl 5th to 5 out: wkng whn hit next* **12/1**
5-P6 **8** *27* **Scotch Corner (IRE)**[17] [1874] 7-10-8 **99**.................... MGoldstein(7) 44
(N A Twiston-Davies) *cl up tl outpcd after 5 out: wkng whn hit next* **5/1**[3]
5/1F **P** **Infini (FR)**[40] [1609] 9-11-3 **101**.................... DElsworth —
(Mrs S J Smith) *led: hit 1st: nt fluent and hdd 5th: p.u bef 8th* **11/1**

6m 9.90s (-14.90) **Going Correction** -0.50s/f (Good) **9** Ran SP% **114.2**
Speed ratings: **104,103,99,93,93 91,90,81,—** CSF £10.79 CT £61.28 TOTE £2.80: £1.30, £1.40, £2.60; EX 9.70.
Owner Mrs A N Durkan & F Murphy **Bred** Larry Mulvany **Trained** West Witton, N Yorks

FOCUS
An ordinary event in which the pace was only fair but the winner is a progressive sort and the form looks reasonably solid with the placed horses running to form.

NOTEBOOK
Devondale(IRE) ◆, escaping a penalty for last week's Hexham win, duly proved well suited by the return to three miles and turned in an improved effort to win this stronger event. Life will be tougher from tomorrow as he is due to race from a 10lb higher mark but he is the type to win more races over fences. *(op 15-8)*
Red Perk(IRE) is not always the most reliable but seemed to run up to his best returned to fences. He is capable of winning from this mark over the larger obstacles but his record suggests he would be no certainty to put it all in next time. *(op 9-2)*
Lutin Du Moulin(FR), well beaten after a break last time, shaped a fair bit better this time back over the larger obstacles. His jumping was sound in the main and he is sure to be placed to best advantage in due course. *(tchd 9-1)*
Has Scored(IRE) was well beaten on this first start since March but, given his stable is in good form and he is only relatively lightly raced, he is not one to be writing off just yet. *(op 11-1 tchd 12-1)*
Kung Hei Fat Choi(IRE) should be all the better for this first start in nearly two years but will have to show more before he is worth a bet. *(op 22-1)*
Behavingbadly(IRE), an inconsistent chaser who has had problems with his jumping, got round safely after a heavy fall last time but is not the best betting proposition around. *(op 20-1)*

2171 O2 H'CAP HURDLE (11 hdls) 2m 4f
3:20 (3:20) (Class 4) (0-90,90) 4-Y-0+ **£3,021** (£880; £440)

Form RPR
024- **1** **Piraeus (NZ)**[255] [4105] 6-11-7 **85**.................... KJohnson 101+
(R Johnson) *in tch: chsd ldr after 4 out: ev ch whn nt fluent 2 out and last: led run in: kpt on wl* **12/1**
-55F **2** *4* **Silver Sedge (IRE)**[7] [2026] 6-11-2 **85**.................... DCCostello(5) 91
(Mrs A Hamilton) *in tch: hdwy to ld 4 out: rdn after next: hdd run in: kpt on same pce* **9/1**
P5-0 **3** *8* **Ballynure (IRE)**[20] [1838] 7-11-7 **90**.................... DFlavin(5) 88
(Mrs L B Normile) *prom: effrt bef 3 out: kpt on same pce* **33/1**
0-05 **4** *nk* **Villago (GER)**[25] [509] 5-11-6 **87**.................... FKing(3) 85
(E W Tuer) *hld up: hdwy and in tch 1/2-way: effrt bef 3 out: one pce* **7/1**[3]
3-PP **5** *12* **Kyber**[10] [1337] 4-11-7 **85**.................... JAMcCarthy 71
(R F Fisher) *hld up: pushed along bef 4 out: no imp bef next* **40/1**
640- **6** *3* **Caesarean Hunter (USA)**[213] [4813] 6-11-2 **80**....................(tp) WMarston 63
(R T Phillips) *in tch: drvn fr 5th: outpcd bef 3 out* **6/1**[2]
6P0- **7** *5* **Our Jasper**[223] [4685] 5-11-10 **88**.................... RMcGrath 66
(K G Reveley) *hld up: hdwy and prom bef 7th: rdn and wknd bef 3 out* **33/1**
252 **8** *7* **Minster Abbi**[12] [1943] 5-10-11 **75**....................(p) NPMulholland 46
(W Storey) *midfield: outpcd bef 7th: n.d after* **9/1**
64-0 **9** *1 ¾* **Terramarique (IRE)**[188] [215] 6-10-11 **78**.................... GBerridge(3) 47
(L Lungo) *prom tl outpcd 6th: n.d after* **4/1**[1]
5000 **10** *2 ½* **Nifty Roy**[35] [1663] 5-11-4 **82**.................... FKeniry 49
(K W Hogg) *cl up to 4 out: sn rdn and btn* **25/1**
2-2P **11** *3 ½* **Gimme Shelter (IRE)**[5] [2066] 11-10-8 **79**.................... MJMcAlister(7) 42
(S J Marshall) *cl up tl lost pl 5th: sn btn* **14/1**
0P42 **12** *½* **Hello Baby**[34] [1685] 5-11-0 **85**.................... EWhillans(7) 48
(A C Whillans) *chsd ldrs to 1/2-way: sn lost pl* **7/1**[3]

P **13** 1 3/4 **Leonia's Rose (IRE)**[35] 1663 6-10-10 **77** PBuchanan(3) 38
(Miss Lucinda V Russell) *midfield: outpcd after 5th: sn n.d* **66/1**
0PP4 **14** 1 **Hapthor**[20] 1839 6-10-5 **76** PJMcDonald(7) 36
(F Jestin) *nt fluent: a bhd* **25/1**
6606 **15** 5 **Tiger Talk**[7] 2025 9-11-0 **88** (b) JMoorman(10) 43
(R C Guest) *keen in midfield: wknd bef 6th* **28/1**
0-06 **16** 14 **Ballinruane (IRE)**[176] 425 6-10-10 **74** ARoss 15
(B S Rothwell) *led to 4 out: sn btn* **40/1**
000/ **P** **First Grey**[601] 4459 6-10-9 **80** PKinsella(7) —
(E W Tuer) *a bhd: t.o whn p.u bef 3 out* **100/1**
P0P- **P** **Captain's Leap (IRE)**[237] 4452 9-11-10 **88** BGibson —
(L Lungo) *sn bhd: lost tch and p.u after 5th* **50/1**
454P **P** **Kyle Of Lochalsh**[27] 1528 5-11-4 **82** GLee —
(J S Goldie) *hld up: outpcd whn blnd 6th: p.u bef 4 out* **11/1**
00P- **P** **Iowa (IRE)**[253] 4134 5-10-13 **84** BenOrde-Powlett(7) —
(Jedd O'Keeffe) *bhd: lost tch 1/2-way: t.o whn p.u bef 3 out* **40/1**

5m 11.6s (-4.20) **Going Correction** -0.50s/f (Good)
WFA 4 from 5yo+ 13lb **20** Ran SP% **130.8**
Speed ratings: **88,86,83,83,78 77,75,72,71,70 69,68,68,67,65 60,—,—,—,—** CSF £111.59 CT £3527.26 TOTE £16.60: £2.30, £2.60, £22.00, £1.60; EX 192.10.
Owner Jimmy Rogers **Bred** Est Late N J Taylor & Mrs A A Taylor **Trained** Newburn, Tyne & Wear
■ Stewards' Enquiry : J Moorman one-day ban: used whip when out of contention (Nov 22)

FOCUS
An ordinary event that suited those racing close to the pace. Those in the frame behind the winner were close to their marks although the form is not strong.

NOTEBOOK
Piraeus(NZ) turned in an improved effort on this reappearance run and will be worth a try over a bit further. There is still room for improvement in the jumping department and he looks the type to win again over hurdles. *(tchd 14-1)*
Silver Sedge(IRE), a faller on his chase debut last time, had the run of the race back over hurdles and performed right up to his best. His record suggests this is not certain to be reproduced next time, though. *(tchd 10-1)*
Ballynure(IRE) fared better than on his reappearance and left the impression he would be worth another try over further. He has not proved the most consistent so far but may be capable of picking up a small event. *(op 28-1)*
Villago(GER), returned to hurdles, fared best of those to come from just off the pace and, given he stays well on the Flat, he is worth a try over a bit further over obstacles. *(op 8-1)*
Kyber was not knocked about back over hurdles in a race that suited those racing prominently, but his record suggests he would not be one for much faith next time. *(op 33-1)*
Caesarean Hunter(USA), with the cheekpieces added to the tongue-tie this time, did not look the easiest of rides on this first run since April and will have to fare a good deal better to open his account over hurdles.
Terramarique(IRE) was disappointing in this ordinary event, even considering his lack of a recent run and, although not one to write off just yet, is not one for maximum faith, either.
Captain's Leap(IRE) *Official explanation: jockey said gelding had a breathing problem*

2172 NOKIA "CONNECTING PEOPLE" H'CAP CHASE (13 fncs) 2m 110y
3:55 (3:56) (Class 4) (0-105,101) 5-Y-O+ **£3,919** (£1,150; £575; £287)

Form RPR
3-35 **1** **Oso Magic**[14] 1915 7-11-12 **101** DElsworth 125+
(Mrs S J Smith) *cl up: led after 4 out: clr bef 2 out: easily* **6/4**[1]
0314 **2** 12 **Karo De Vindecy (FR)**[45] 1570 7-11-0 **89** GLee 101+
(M D Hammond) *cl up: led 5th to after 4 out: one pce fr 2 out* **3/1**[2]
2-40 **3** 8 **Glenfarclas Boy (IRE)**[22] 1795 9-10-13 **91** PBuchanan(3) 91
(Miss Lucinda V Russell) *prom: pushed along fr 1/2-way: outpcd 5 out: plugged on fr 2 out: no imp* **10/1**
2-53 **4** 6 **Bob's Buster**[42] 1592 9-11-5 **94** (p) KJohnson 92+
(R Johnson) *hld up in tch: effrt and cl up 5 out: outpcd next: btn whn mstke 2 out* **9/2**[3]
00-P **5** dist **Superior Weapon (IRE)**[34] 1673 11-10-3 **78** (t) ADempsey —
(A Robson) *led to 5th: ev ch 5 out: wknd next* **11/1**
4535 **P** **Apadi (USA)**[40] 1604 9-10-10 **88** LMcGrath(3) —
(R C Guest) *rel to r and lost 25l s: p.u after 3rd* **7/1**

4m 13.2s (-10.00) **Going Correction** -0.50s/f (Good) **6** Ran SP% **113.1**
Speed ratings: **103,97,93,90,— —** CSF £6.85 TOTE £2.40: £1.70, £1.90; EX 9.90 Place 6 £11.02, Place 5 £7.32..
Owner Michael Thompson **Bred** M H Ings **Trained** High Eldwick, W Yorks

FOCUS
An ordinary event in which the pace was just fair with the runner-up the best guide to the level. The form should work out well enough.

NOTEBOOK
Oso Magic, who had a spin over hurdles after a break last month, turned in an improved effort back over fences to rout some ordinary rivals but he will find things tougher after reassessment. *(op 7-4)*
Karo De Vindecy(FR) had the run of the race back over this shorter trip but was readily brushed aside by the easy winner. The return to further will be in his favour. *(op 10-3 tchd 7-2)*
Glenfarclas Boy(IRE) showed why he is not the best betting proposition around with another laboured display and, although not totally disgraced, remains one to tread carefully with. *(op 6-1)*
Bob's Buster would have preferred a much stronger overall gallop and is a bit better than the bare form but his inconsistency and his losing run are becoming a worry. *(op 5-1)*
Superior Weapon(IRE), who won over this course and distance last November, was again well beaten and is best watched for now. *(op 14-1 tchd 16-1)*
Apadi(USA), back over fences, turned in a temperamental display and is not one to place much faith in. *(tchd 13-2)*
T/Plt: £27.90 to a £1 stake. Pool: £37,871.70. 989.50 winning tickets. T/Qpdt: £31.40 to a £1 stake. Pool: £2,824.70. 66.50 winning tickets. RY

2161 CHELTENHAM (L-H)
Saturday, November 12

OFFICIAL GOING: Good to soft
Races run on the Old Course. The ground appeared somewhat tacky, as the ground dried following rain.
Weather: fine Wind: Nil

2173 RACING UK NOVICES' H'CAP HURDLE (8 hdls) 2m 110y
1:05 (1:07) (Class 3) (0-110,110) 3-Y-O+
£11,320 (£3,343; £1,671; £836; £417; £209)

Form RPR
040- **1** **Not Left Yet (IRE)**[288] 3568 4-11-10 **108** TJMurphy 128+
(M C Pipe) *h.d.w: lw: hld up rr: stdy hdwy 4th: led 2 out: pushed out run-in: comf* **15/8**[1]
03/3 **2** 3 1/2 **Green Iceni**[28] 1745 6-11-1 **99** ATinkler 109+
(N J Henderson) *lw: hld up mid-div: hdwy 4 out: chsd ldrs next: rdn to chse wnr after 2 out: kpt on u.p but no ch* **8/1**[3]
2300 **3** 1 1/4 **Abragante (IRE)**[11] 1968 4-10-11 **98** (p) TJMalone(3) 106
(M C Pipe) *in tch: hdwy to prss ldrs fr 4th: stl disputing 2nd 2 out: styd on same pce appr last* **25/1**
2243 **4** 4 **Don And Gerry (IRE)**[18] 1875 4-11-0 **98** GLee 102
(P D Evans) *chsd ldrs: hit 3 out: stl wl there next: wknd last* **20/1**
5 1 1/2 **Dare To Dance**[54] 1501 7-10-12 **96** RMPower 99
(R Donohoe, Ire) *w'like: lw: bhd: hdwy after 4 out: chsd ldrs and rdn 2 out: styd on same pce tl kpt on again u.p run-in* **66/1**
34-5 **6** 6 **Bollin Thomas**[9] 59 7-10-13 **100** PAspell(3) 97
(R Allan) *bhd: hdwy 4 out: chsd ldrs 3 out: wknd after next* **40/1**
7 shd **Havetoavit (USA)**[81] 1305 4-11-12 **110** BJGeraghty 106
(Thomas Cooper, Ire) *leggy: hld up in ready stdy hdwy 3 out: chsd ldrs next: rdn and wknd sn after* **16/1**
1 **8** 5 **Star Member (IRE)**[62] 1454 6-11-7 **105** PMoloney 96
(Ian Williams) *led tl hdd 2 out: sn wknd* **5/1**[2]
311 **9** 3 **Lucky Do (IRE)**[103] 1121 8-11-8 **106** MFoley 94
(A E Jones) *bhd: hdwy 3 out: styd on one pce fr next* **33/1**
10 3/4 **Danticat (USA)**[31] 1628 4-11-7 **105** (bt) RWalsh 93
(John J Coleman, Ire) *nest: str: chsd ldrs: disp 2nd 4 out to 3 out: wknd fr 2 out* **33/1**
11 **11** 15 **United Spirit (IRE)**[35] 1683 4-11-2 **100** BHarding 73
(Jedd O'Keeffe) *hit 1st: t.k.h and bhd: kpt on fr 3 out but nvr nr ldrs* **20/1**
12 2 **Alternative Route (IRE)**[44] 1586 6-11-0 **98** DNRussell 69
(T Doyle, Ire) *cmpt: bhd: sme hdwy 4th: wknd fr 3 out* **16/1**
00-5 **13** 2 1/2 **Simonovski (USA)**[28] 1740 4-11-4 **107** RStephens(5) 75
(S C Burrough) *in tch to 4th* **66/1**
5-34 **14** 3 1/2 **Kylebeg Dancer (IRE)**[8] 2031 4-11-9 **110** (t) KHadnett(3) 75
(T Hogan, Ire) *mid-div: sme hdwy 4th: sn wknd* **18/1**
5-21 **15** 8 **Emmasflora**[20] 1851 7-11-2 **107** APogson(7) 64
(C T Pogson) *chsd ldrs early: bhd fr 4th* **20/1**
35-0 **16** 11 **Mokum (FR)**[21] 1827 4-11-11 **109** CLlewellyn 55
(A W Carroll) *a bhd* **40/1**
50-5 **P** **Flying Patriarch**[14] 1921 4-11-0 **98** (b) JEMoore —
(G L Moore) *chsd ldrs to 4th: sn wknd: t.o whn p.u 2 out* **25/1**
0222 **F** **Murphy's Nails (IRE)**[30] 1725 8-11-0 **98** (p) TScudamore 80
(K C Bailey) *chsd ldrs: disp 2nd and rdn 3 out: sn wknd: fell next* **33/1**
41 **F** **Random Quest**[10] 1982 7-11-7 **105** RJohnson —
(B J Llewellyn) *chsd ldrs 4th: sn drvn along: disputing 6l 8th whn fell 4 out* **9/1**

4m 2.90s (3.70) **Going Correction** +0.375s/f (Yiel) **19** Ran SP% **128.3**
Speed ratings: **106,104,103,101,101 98,98,95,94,94 87,86,85,83,79 74,—,—,—** CSF £14.48 CT £311.04 TOTE £2.80: £1.40, £2.40, £6.70, £4.10; EX 20.90 Trifecta £859.50 Pool: £1,452.80 - 1.20 winning tickets.
Owner D A Johnson **Bred** T Cox **Trained** Nicholashayne, Devon
■ A fifth successive win in this event for Martin Pipe if one allows for the later upgrading of 2002 second Bongo Fury .

FOCUS
An ordinary novices' handicap for the prizemoney but an easy winner, who was value for a lot more than the official margin and has provisionally been rated as having improved a massive 36lb on his previous best. The form looks solid and there was no fluke about his success.

NOTEBOOK
Not Left Yet(IRE) ◆, who showed promise in one of his three outings last season but was beaten out of sight in the other two, was all the rage and won like the good thing that support suggested, showing vastly improved form. He had reportedly done well over the summer and after going on at the bottom of the hill, always had matters in control. He will go up a fair amount but starts from a modest mark and the Handicapper may have some catching up to do. *(op 9-4 tchd 7-4 and 5-2 in places)*
Green Iceni ◆, who showed promise despite not jumping fluently on his return from a 21-month absence last month, settled off the pace and went in pursuit of the winner off the home turn but was always being held. He looks more than capable of winning races off his current mark. *(tchd 9-1)*
Abragante(IRE), a stable companion of the winner, was in the front rank from the start and stuck on really well up the hill. The cheekpieces seemed to help him concentrate and he should be winning if they have the same effect next time.
Don And Gerry(IRE) has been running consistently on a sound surface throughout the summer without winning. She travelled well on this easier surface but when asked for an effort could only keep on at one pace. Lack of a turn of foot is her problem, but the application of some sort of headgear may help her. *(op 25-1)*
Dare To Dance, an Irish raider with form on a sound surface, ran on from the rear but never reached a challenging position. He may need a return to further.
Bollin Thomas, who has had a decent spell on the Flat this summer, has yet to get off the mark over hurdles but will find easier opportunities in the north off his current mark.
Havetoavit(USA), 18lb higher than when winning a maiden hurdle at Tralee back in August, came on the scene on the downhill run looking a potential danger, but his effort fizzled out soon after jumping the second last and may have found the ground against him. *(op 20-1)*
Star Member(IRE) set the pace but was brushed aside and soon beaten once the winner made his move. *(op 13-2 tchd 7-1)*

2174 JIM BROWN MEMORIAL NOVICES' CHASE (15 fncs) 2m 4f 110y
1:35 (1:38) (Class 2) 5-Y-O+
£10,427 (£3,080; £1,540; £770; £384; £193)

Form RPR
1 **Crozan (FR)**[244] 5-10-13 MFoley 147+
(N J Henderson) *tall: str: scope: a.p: chsd ldr 2 out: led appr last: rdn out* **6/1**[3]
601- **2** 7 **Lough Derg (FR)**[213] 4823 5-10-13 TScudamore 140+
(M C Pipe) *h.d.w: lw: chsd ldr to 3rd: remained handy: rdn appr last: styd on* **7/2**[1]
03-3 **3** 1 1/4 **Exotic Dancer (FR)**[21] 1822 5-10-13 GLee 142+
(Jonjo O'Neill) *lw: chsd ldr 3rd: j.lft 7th: mstke 10th: led 3 out: rdn and hdd whn blnd last: no ex* **11/2**[2]
51/2 **4** 5 **Garde Champetre (FR)**[12] 1958 6-10-13 APMcCoy 137+
(Jonjo O'Neill) *hld up: hit 8th: rdn appr 3 out: hdwy next: wknd last* **7/2**[1]
0-02 **5** 10 **Doctor Linton (IRE)**[24] 1790 6-11-7 RWalsh 131
(M J P O'Brien, Ire) *w'like: lw: hld up: hdwy 2 out: wknd bef last* **12/1**
2121 **6** 13 **Flying Spirit (IRE)**[18] 1871 6-11-7 136 (b) JEMoore 119+
(G L Moore) *led: bmpd 7th: mstke 9th (water): hdd 3 out: wknd after next* **16/1**
233- **7** 11 **Tumbling Dice (IRE)**[27] 1764 6-11-7 BJGeraghty 119+
(T J Taaffe, Ire) *chsd ldrs: rdn after 3 out: slipped on landing and wknd next* **7/2**[1]

101/ **P** **Yardbird (IRE)**[578] 4819 6-10-13 **113**........ RThornton —
(A King) *hld up: a in rr: t.o whn p.u bef last* **66/1**

P5/P **P** **Take A Drop (IRE)**[1] 2166 10-10-13 .... MrJPO'Farrell —
(Seamus O'Farrell, Ire) *hld up: mstke 4th: lost tch 8th: t.o whn p.u bef 12th* **200/1**

5m 12.5s (2.40) **Going Correction** +0.375s/f (Yiel) **9** Ran SP% **111.9**
Speed ratings: **110,107,106,104,101 96,92,—,—** CSF £27.01 TOTE £8.00: £1.90, £2.10, £1.80; EX 41.70 Trifecta £217.50 Pool: £1,960.60 - 6.40 winning tickets.
Owner Trevor Hemmings **Bred** H Carion **Trained** Upper Lambourn, Berks

FOCUS
A decent and competitive-looking novices' chase, run at a sound pace. The winner looks a good novice and will do better, while the second did well to get within around 10lb of his hurdles mark on his chasing debut.

NOTEBOOK
Crozan(FR) ◆, a French import with quite a bit of experience over the tricky Auteuil fences, took well to the British obstacles and, always travelling well, asserted off the home turn for an emphatic victory. He beat some potentially useful sorts with a fair amount in hand and looks a likely sort for races like the Fulke Walwyn Chase and the Feltham Chase and, if all goes well, the Royal and SunAlliance Chase back here in the spring. *(op 11-2 tchd 7-1 in a place)*
Lough Derg(FR), a three-time winner over hurdles here, was making his debut and ran quite well without looking totally happy at his fences. His record suggests he may be better suited by a sounder surface. *(tchd 4-1 and 9-2 in places)*
Exotic Dancer(FR) has been quite lightly raced and built on his chasing debut despite a couple of jumping errors. Having run a bit keen, he tried to stretch the field on the downhill run but was ultimately no match for the winner. He looked second best until tiring up the run-in after a blunder at the last. *(tchd 6-1)*
Garde Champetre(FR), who ran well on his chasing debut 12 days previously after a long absence, made a mistake at the downhill fence going away from the stands and never quite got back into contention. It may be that he 'bounced', and he should be given a chance to prove he is better than this. *(op 10-3)*
Doctor Linton(IRE), runner-up to the useful Justified giving that rival weight last time, was given what appeared to be an over-confident ride in rear and never got into contention. However, ratings suggest he ran to his previous mark. *(op 20-1)*
Flying Spirit(IRE), who beat the previous day's handicap winner Bold Bishop here last month, made the odd mistake and may have found this sticky ground against him. *(op 20-1)*
Tumbling Dice(IRE), third in the Coral Cup last March, had won well on his chasing debut at Cork and was well supported beforehand. However, he was never travelling that well and was struggling when a slip at the penultimate fence ended his chance. *(op 10-3)*

2175 LOMBARD PROPERTIES H'CAP HURDLE (LISTED RACE) (13 hdls) 3m 1f 110y

2:10 (2:12) (Class 1) 4-Y-O+

£25,659 (£9,625; £4,819; £2,403; £1,206; £603)

Form RPR

1-11 **1** **Standin Obligation (IRE)**[21] 1830 6-11-2 **137**........ TJMurphy 146+
(M C Pipe) *lw: in tch: hdwy 8th: trcking ldrs whn nt fluent 4 out: chal next: sn led: hrd drvn and kpt on wl run-in* **7/4**[1]

/4-4 **2** *1 1/2* **Oodachee**[27] 1770 6-9-10 **122**........ JFLevins(5) 127
(C F Swan, Ire) *str: lw: hld up in tch: hdwy 8th: trckd ldrs gng wl 2 out: swtchd lft and qcknd last: chsd wnr sn after but no imp* **16/1**

120- **3** *1 1/4* **Olaso (GER)**[241] 4394 6-10-4 **125**........ APMcCoy 129
(Jonjo O'Neill) *bhd: hdwy 6th: chsd ldrs fr 4 out: drvn to chal appr last: one pce and lost 2nd run-in* **9/1**

40-6 **4** *6* **Rambling Minster**[14] 1925 7-10-11 **132**........ RMcGrath 131+
(K G Reveley) *hld up in rr: hdwy 9th: chsd ldrs and rdn fr 3 out: one pce next: wknd last* **7/1**[2]

2-11 **5** *1 1/2* **Jackson (FR)**[12] 1959 8-10-4 **125**........ RThornton 121
(A King) *lw: chsd ldrs: lft 2nd after 7th tl rdn appr 3 out: wknd appr last* **8/1**[3]

5PU- **6** *8* **Native Emperor**[217] 4772 9-10-9 **130**........ NFehily 118
(Jonjo O'Neill) *bhd: j. slowly 3rd: hdwy 4 out: chsd ldrs next: wknd after 2 out* **33/1**

5-11 **7** *2 1/2* **Rooftop Protest (IRE)**[9] 1787 8-10-2 **130**........(tp) DFFlannery(7) 116
(T Hogan, Ire) *racd wd: chsd ldr tl lft in ld after 7th: hit 8th: rdn whn chal 3 out: hdd sn after: wknd 2 out* **7/1**[2]

000- **8** *4* **Zibeline (IRE)**[217] 4770 8-10-8 **129**........(p) GLee 113+
(B Ellison) *bhd: hdwy 4 out: chsd ldrs next: wknd 2 out* **50/1**

/0U- **9** *3* **World Wide Web (IRE)**[252] 4189 9-10-5 **126**........ BHarding 105
(Jonjo O'Neill) *bhd tl drvn and styd on fr 3 out: nvr a danger* **50/1**

/P-0 **10** *1/2* **Chicuelo (FR)**[18] 1872 9-10-9 **130**........ MFoley 108
(N J Henderson) *bhd: mod hdwy fr 2 out* **50/1**

202 **11** *5* **Phar From Frosty (IRE)**[10] 1992 8-10-4 **125**........ ATinkler 98
(C R Egerton) *in tch: rdn to chse ldrs 4 out: wknd next* **33/1**

6-46 **12** *22* **Limerick Leader (IRE)**[7] 2046 7-11-0 **135**........(b) PJBrennan 86
(P J Hobbs) *chsd ldrs: rdn 4 out: sn wknd* **50/1**

-46F **13** *17* **Grey Report (IRE)**[160] 650 8-11-11 **146**........ RJohnson 80
(P J Hobbs) *led tl ref to r after 7th and dropped wl bhd* **25/1**

P-22 **14** *1/2* **Glacial Evening (IRE)**[9] 2010 9-9-9 **121** oh1........ RStephens(5) 55
(R H Buckler) *mid-div: sme hdwy 8th: sn wknd* **25/1**

0-1P **15** *hd* **Carlys Quest**[14] 1925 11-11-5 **147**........ TJDreaper(7) 80
(Ferdy Murphy) *a in rr* **33/1**

F341 **P** **Redspin (IRE)**[30] 1725 5-10-0 **121** oh19........ JamesDavies —
(J S Moore) *nvr bttr than mid-div: bhd fr 8th: t.o whn p.u bef last* **100/1**

11-0 **P** **Holland Park (IRE)**[189] 207 8-11-5 **140**........ JTizzard —
(Mrs S D Williams) *chsd ldrs tl wknd rapidly 4 out: t.o whn p.u bef last* **20/1**

6m 26.1s (0.90) **Going Correction** +0.375s/f (Yiel) **17** Ran SP% **118.5**
Speed ratings: **113,112,112,110,109 107,106,105,104,104 102,96,90,90,90** —,— CSF £25.47 CT £208.32 TOTE £2.60: £1.50, £2.90, £1.80, £1.90; EX 44.80 Trifecta £244.60 Pool: £2,240.00 - 6.50 winning tickets.
Owner D A Johnson **Bred** Mrs S Flood **Trained** Nicholashayne, Devon

FOCUS
A decent staying handicap, but it featured only three from the turn in. The winner continues to progress and held off the challenges in good style to retain his unbeaten record. There were personal bests from both the second and third too.

NOTEBOOK
Standin Obligation(IRE) ◆, representing the same connections as the first winner and also heavily backed, duly maintained his unbeaten record. He was ridden positively and although he had a number of rivals close on his heels at the bottom of the hill he responded to every challenge in determined fashion and in the end won decisively. He has a good attitude and can win more good races over hurdles, but he will be even more interesting when switched to fences. *(tchd 15-8 and 2-1 in places)*
Oodachee ◆, stepping up in trip, stalked the winner throughout and looked to be going marginally the better on the home turn. However, the winner had plenty in reserve and he could not get past. He looks reasonably weighted, is effective on a sound surface and is one to bear in mind if returning here for the Coral Cup in the spring. *(tchd 20-1)*
Olaso(GER) did not really go on from his debut over hurdles last season and was another stepping up in trip. He travelled well and looked a big danger to the winner going to the final flight, but his effort petered out up the hill. He appeared not to stay but he may be seen to better effect back on a flat track.
Rambling Minster was racing off a mark 13lb higher than when completing a hat-trick last December but was nevertheless well fancied. He settled off the pace but never got close enough to land a real blow at the leader. He could do with being dropped a few pounds. *(op 13-2 tchd 15-2)*
Jackson(FR), who stays well but is possibly best on a sound surface, was in with every chance on the downhill run but faded up the hill. He does not look particularly well treated over hurdles and the time may be right for a return to novice chasing. *(op 9-1 tchd 7-1 in places)*
Native Emperor, better known as a staying chaser, ran well for a long way on this return from nine months off. It should have helped his confidence and blown the cobwebs away, and he looks a likely Welsh National contender. *(op 25-1)*
Rooftop Protest(IRE) has been in terrific form both on the Flat and over hurdles this autumn, especially since fitted with cheekpieces. Stepping up in trip, he raced up with the pace but was left behind from the bottom of the hill, and appeared not to stay. *(op 13-2)*
Phar From Frosty(IRE)looked set to figure when going in pursuit of the leaders on the downhill run but dropped away before the turn. He is better off on a sounder surface. *(op 25-1)*
Holland Park(IRE) reportedly strained a tendon and is likely to be out of action for some time. *Official explanation: jockey said gelding returned lame*

2176 SERVO COMPUTER SERVICES TROPHY H'CAP CHASE GRADE 3 (21 fncs) 3m 3f 110y

2:45 (2:48) (Class 1) 5-Y-O+

£31,361 (£11,764; £5,890; £2,937; £1,474; £737)

Form RPR

210- **1** **Innox (FR)**[14] 9-10-6 **135**........(b) APMcCoy 149
(F Doumen, France) *lw: prom: outpcd 5 out: hdwy after 3 out: led flat: styd on wl* **9/1**

64-2 **2** *7* **Lou Du Moulin Mas (FR)**[27] 1759 6-10-1 **130**........(t) PJBrennan 138+
(P F Nicholls) *chsd ldr 3rd: led 3 out: rdn appr last: hdd and no ex flat* **20/1**

3PP- **3** *3* **Control Man (IRE)**[210] 4861 7-10-6 **135**........(v) TJMurphy 142+
(M C Pipe) *lw: hld up: hdwy appr 3 out: nt rch ldrs* **5/1**[1]

121- **4** *1* **King Harald (IRE)**[240] 4407 7-10-5 **134**........ MBatchelor 143+
(M Bradstock) *led to 3 out: rdn and ev ch whn blnd last: no ex* **6/1**[2]

/P-0 **5** *4* **Montayral (FR)**[34] 1700 8-10-4 **133**........ TDoyle 132
(P Hughes, Ire) *hld up: nvr nrr* **40/1**

F0-2 **6** *1* **Merchants Friend (IRE)**[20] 1861 10-10-3 **132**........(p) NFehily 130
(C J Mann) *hld up: hit 10th: nvr nrr* **16/1**

/14- **7** *4* **A Glass In Thyne (IRE)**[336] 2773 7-9-8 **130**........ TMessenger(7) 124
(B N Pollock) *prom: mstke 15th (water): wknd 3 out* **33/1**

11P- **8** *3/4* **Captain Corelli**[240] 4407 8-10-1 **130**........ RJohnson 125+
(P J Hobbs) *hld up: mstkes: hdwy 4 out: wknd appr last* **9/1**

421- **9** *10* **Jack High (IRE)**[14] 1934 10-10-9 **138**........ GCotter 124+
(T M Walsh, Ire) *lw: hld up: blnd 2nd: sme hdwy appr 3 out: sn wknd* **13/2**[3]

2-11 **10** *21* **I Hear Thunder (IRE)**[20] 1861 7-10-0 **129** oh3........ BHitchcott 91
(R H Buckler) *lw: hld up: hdwy 11th: hit 5 out: wknd next* **14/1**

0PP- **P** **Stormez (FR)**[203] 4984 8-11-0 **143**........(t) BJGeraghty —
(M C Pipe) *a in rr: bhd whn blnd 4 out: p.u bef next* **14/1**

43P- **P** **Sir Rembrandt (IRE)**[219] 4748 9-11-12 **155**........ AThornton —
(R H Alner) *lw: prom to 15th: t.o whn p.u bef 3 out* **11/1**

U1P- **P** **Whitford Don (IRE)**[218] 4761 7-10-5 **134**........(b) RWalsh —
(P F Nicholls) *hld up in tch: wknd 3 out: bhd whn p.u bef next* **14/1**

11P- **P** **Grattan Lodge (IRE)**[301] 3366 8-10-8 **137**........ GLee —
(J Howard Johnson) *bkwd: hld up: a in rr: t.o whn p.u bef 12th* **25/1**

F4-0 **P** **Tribal Venture (FR)**[14] 1925 7-10-0 **136**........ TJDreaper(7) —
(Ferdy Murphy) *j.big 1st and rdr lost irons: p.u after next* **16/1**

P2-5 **P** **First Gold (FR)**[199] 68 12-11-4 **147**........ RThornton —
(F Doumen, France) *chsd ldrs: lost pl 5th: wknd after 11th: t.o whn p.u bef 4 out* **33/1**

7m 12.8s **Going Correction** +0.375s/f (Yiel) **16** Ran SP% **121.3**
Speed ratings: **108,106,105,104,103 103,102,102,99,93** —,—,—,—,— — CSF £179.39 CT £1010.84 TOTE £11.00: £2.70, £5.10, £2.10, £2.10; EX 251.50 TRIFECTA Not won..
Owner John P McManus **Bred** Bernard Trinquet And Marc Trinquet **Trained** Bouce, France

FOCUS
This was run at a sound gallop and stamina won the day for Innox after King Harald and Lou du Moulin Mas had taken each other on. This wasn't the strongest renewal of a race that tends to have limited bearing on the Hennessy, but the first two ran to their marks and the third can win when he jumps better.

NOTEBOOK
Innox(FR), a proven stayer who had previously saved his best efforts in this country for Sandown, showed the benefit of his recent warm-up race at Enghien and, having shown up well most of the way, reeled in the two clear leaders from the home turn to win going away. He will have to carry a penalty if he goes for the Hennessy, but that may come a little too soon in any case. *Official explanation: trainer said, regarding the improved form shown, gelding was unsuited by track at Enghien last time out (op 10-1)*
Lou Du Moulin Mas(FR), who met the winner on the same terms as when beaten nine lengths at Sandown last season, looked as if he was going to gain a long overdue win when collaring the long-time leader at the bottom of the hill. However, he began to tread water on the climb to the last and it was soon clear he was going to be overhauled. He does little wrong and really deserves to pick up a decent prize, but he is not one for win-only betting.
Control Man(IRE) was a decent novice at this time last year before losing his way in the spring. However, with his yard in such fine form and looking very fit in the paddock, he was backed down to favourite. He hit the first ditch and was not totally fluent, but gradually ran on, although the leaders had too much rope. *(op 13-2 tchd 7-1 in places)*
King Harald(IRE), winner of the novices' handicap chase over two miles five at the Festival, had form in excess of three miles prior to that. He went off in front and jumped in his usual flamboyant fashion, but was taken on by the eventual runner-up, who wore him down at the bottom of the hill. Despite rallying, he was legless when a mistake at the last almost brought him to a standstill. He had a harder race than ideal so close to the Hennessy, but connections reported he came out of it well. *Official explanation: vet said gelding finished distressed (op 9-2 tchd 13-2 in a place)*
Montayral(FR) , who was third in this in 2003, has not won for two years but was absent for 16 months during that time. He was never competitive and merely stayed on past tired horses, but this represented a step in the right direction on just his third run back. *(op 33-1)*
Merchants Friend(IRE), who disappointed in this last year, could never get into the race having been held up and his recent wins have been when the ground has been very testing. *(op 14-1)*
A Glass In Thyne(IRE), lightly raced and having his first outing for 11 months, showed up well for a long way against more experienced handicappers and will be all the better with this outing under his belt.
Captain Corelli looked a potentially useful novice last season until making mistakes and disappointing behind King Harald at the Festival on ground too quick for him. He has since changed stables but again made mistakes and perhaps this track does not suit him. *(tchd 10-1 in places)*

Jack High(IRE), winner of last season's Betfred Gold Cup and runner-up in the Irish National, looked ideally suited to this test and had had a warm-up over hurdles. However, he was never going that well after an early error and an effort running to three out proved short-lived. *(op 6-1 tchd 7-1)*
Stormez(FR), twice a previous winner of this race, was always struggling and found jumping even more difficult in this sticky ground. *(op 16-1)*
Sir Rembrandt(IRE), giving weight all round, showed up for a long way but was well behind when his rider drew stumps. This should bring him on though. *(op 16-1)*
Tribal Venture(FR) *Official explanation: jockey said buckle broke on stirrup leather (op 16-1)*

2177 PADDY POWER GOLD CUP CHASE (A H'CAP) GRADE 3 (15 fncs) 2m 4f 110y
3:20 (3:35) (Class 1) 5-Y-0+

£62,722 (£23,529; £11,781; £5,874; £2,948; £1,474)

Form — RPR

FPP- **1** **Our Vic (IRE)**[219] 4748 7-11-7 **149** TJMurphy 166+
(M C Pipe) *lw: pressed ldrs: led 8th to 9th: led again appr 3 out: hrd drvn and styd on wl run-in* **9/2**[1]
13-1 **2** *2 ½* **Monkerhostin (FR)**[11] 1970 8-11-9 **151** 6ex RJohnson 166+
(P J Hobbs) *lw: nt fluent 2nd: blnd 5th: hdwy appr 3 out: blnd next: styd on u.p to chse wnr run-in but a hld* **5/1**[2]
132- **3** *1 ½* **Kandjar D'Allier (FR)**[287] 3590 7-10-7 **135** RThornton 146
(A King) *hit 1st: bhd: hdwy 4 out: chsd ldrs 2 out: chsd wnr sn after: one pce last: lost 2nd run-in* **14/1**
02P- **4** *4* **Fondmort (FR)**[217] 4772 9-11-12 **154** MFoley 161
(N J Henderson) *lw: in tch: rdn fr 3 out: styd on fr 2 out but nvr gng pce to rch ldrs* **25/1**
F3P- **5** *3 ½* **Lord Sam (IRE)**[321] 2943 9-11-5 **147** NFehily 153+
(V R A Dartnall) *led to 4th: led again 5th to 6th: led 7th to 8th: j. slowly 11th: styd on same pce fr 2 out* **14/1**
24-1 **6** *2* **Lacdoudal (FR)**[21] 1828 6-11-4 **146** PJBrennan 148
(P J Hobbs) *in tch: hdwy to chse ldrs 8th: rdn 4 out: wknd 2 out* **8/1**[3]
410- **7** *shd* **Liberthine (FR)**[218] 4764 6-10-3 **138** MrSWaley-Cohen(7) 140+
(N J Henderson) *lw: bhd: rdn 4 out: styd on fr 2 out but nvr gng pce to rch ldrs* **33/1**
6-F3 **8** *2* **Mariah Rollins (IRE)**[34] 1700 7-10-9 **137** GLee 138+
(P A Fahy, Ire) *chsd ldrs: blnd 10th: styd prom tl wknd and hmpd 2 out* **9/1**
21-2 **9** *1 ½* **My Will (FR)**[20] 1846 5-11-7 **149** RWalsh 147
(P F Nicholls) *chsd ldrs: rdn 3 out: wknd fr next* **12/1**
500- **10** *7* **Royaleety (FR)**[217] 4770 6-10-3 **131** PMoloney 122
(Ian Williams) *b.bkwd: lw: hdwy 6th: hrd rdn 4 out: no ch fr next* **66/1**
12-1 **11** *1 ¼* **Forget The Past**[200] 42 7-11-11 **153** BJGeraghty 147+
(M J P O'Brien, Ire) *gd sort: str: bkwd: w ldrs: slt ld fr 9th tl hdd appr 3 out: wknd sn after* **14/1**
41-1 **12** *6* **Brooklyn Breeze (IRE)**[21] 1823 8-11-1 **143** ADobbin 135+
(L Lungo) *blnd 6th: a bhd: no ch whn bdly hmpd 2 out* **14/1**
330- **13** *11* **Therealbandit (IRE)**[203] 4984 8-11-10 **152** APMcCoy 125
(M C Pipe) *mid-div whn blnd 10th: sn no ch* **12/1**
25-3 **14** *27* **Banker Count**[14] 1924 13-10-6 **134** SThomas 80
(Miss Venetia Williams) *led 4th to 5th: led again 6t to 7th: styd prom: wknd qckly 4 out* **66/1**
1-F1 **P** **Full House (IRE)**[31] 1721 6-10-10 **138** TDoyle —
(P R Webber) *a bhd: t.o whn p.u bef 3 out* **33/1**
0044 **F** **East Tycoon (IRE)**[14] 1918 6-10-2 **130** (p) BHarding 128
(Jonjo O'Neill) *bhd: hdwy 8th: rdn 4 out: wknd next: fell 2 out* **66/1**
00-2 **F** **Redemption**[14] 1925 10-10-8 **136** CLlewellyn 153
(N A Twiston-Davies) *bhd: stdy hdwy appr 4 out: styng on wl and length 2nd whn fell 2 out* **12/1**
4-6P **U** **Turgeonev (FR)**[14] 1924 10-10-2 **130** (b[1]) RMcGrath 100
(T D Easterby) *chsd ldrs: stl in tch whn blnd 4 out: no ch whn hmpd 2 out: blnd and uns rdr last* **100/1**

5m 9.70s (-0.40) **Going Correction** +0.375s/f (Yiel) **18** Ran SP% **120.9**
Speed ratings: **115,114,113,111,110 109,109,109,108,105 105,103,98,88,— —,—,—** CSF £26.19 CT £298.98 TOTE £5.40: £2.60, £2.10, £3.60, £4.70; EX 18.60 Trifecta £855.60 Pool: £23,138.58 - 19.20 winning tickets.
Owner D A Johnson **Bred** Col W B Mullins **Trained** Nicholashayne, Devon
■ An eighth winner of this race for trainer Martin Pipe, six of them being for owner David Johnson.

FOCUS
A good renewal of this hot handicap chase, run at a decent gallop. Our Vic and faller Redemption stood out at the weights and have been rated as having dead heated. Monkerhostin improved yet again, despite his mistakes, and like Our Vic, is now on the fringe of championship class.The start was delayed due to concerns over the low sun, but no fences were omitted.

NOTEBOOK
Our Vic(IRE), who lost his way last season after falling when in the lead in the Bonusprint Gold Cup here and presenting the race to Monkerhostin, was 17lb better off with that rival and, well backed, made the pull count. Given a positive ride, he had to work hard to prevail but deserved this. He could go for the Hennessy under a 6lb penalty, but he had a hard race and is not guaranteed to stay that trip, so he may be better off coming back here next month for the race now named in honour of Robin Cook. *(op 4-1 tchd 5-1 in places and 11-2 in a place)*
Monkerhostin(FR), whose last outing over fences saw him destroy a good field in the 2004 Bonusprint Gold Cup, was running away with Johnson for most of the way and some quick, fluent jumping down the back straight propelled him into a threatening position as they turned for home. Fitness began to tell over the final few fences as Kauto Star began to tire and he ultimately cleared away for an impressive victory. His record over fences since joining the Hobbs yard reads particularly well, his only defeat in four outings coming in the 2004 Paddy Power Gold Cup, and he has that as a likely target again, but in the long-run one would have to think he has major claims in something like the Ryanair Chase having beaten last year's winner Thisthatandtother pointless in the Bonusprint. *(op 9-2 tchd 11-2 in a place)*
Kandjar D'Allier(FR), who made up into a useful handicapper in a relatively light campaign last season, was supported at long odds and overcame an early error to run well before tiring up the hill. He has been placed in his last three runs in good handicaps at this track, and looks likely to return for the Robin Cook Memorial next month. *(op 16-1)*
Fondmort(FR), a previous winner of this race, has not won since that victory two years ago but put up an encouraging effort. He could do with a little help from the Handicapper as he is still 4lb above that winning mark.
Lord Sam(IRE) ◆, who had his problems last season, has been treated for sinus and back problems and looked much more like his old self. He raced up with the pace and did not drop away when headed, despite this being his first run for ten months. He could now go for the Hennessy, in which the extra distance should be in his favour. *(op 20-1 tchd 25-1 in a place)*
Lacdoudal(FR) is a genuine sort and was in the mix from the start. He hit a flat spot at the top of the hill but was running on again at the finish. He is in the Hennessy, but the Windsor Castle Gold Cup may offer a more suitable opportunity. *(tchd 9-1 in places)*
Liberthine(FR), winner of the Mildmay Of Flete last season, is 10lb higher and never got into contention.
Mariah Rollins(IRE), dropping back in trip, ran well for a long way but may need the ground softer than this. *(op 10-1)*
My Will(FR), who ran well in a similar contest at Aintree last month, was disappointing on this occasion and may need softer ground, although he does not have the best record on this track.
Forget The Past was made plenty of use of and dropped away from the third last. *(op 16-1)*
Redemption, who had never won over fences on this track in eight previous attempts, settled at the back and had moved up smoothly to join the leader when coming down at the trappy second-last fence. He deserves to win a decent prize and a trip up to Wetherby, where he has a good record, may give him the opportunity.

2178 CONCORD AT JET.COM JUVENILE NOVICES' HURDLE GRADE 2 (8 hdls) 2m 110y
3:55 (4:08) (Class 1) 3-Y-0

£17,106 (£6,417; £3,213; £1,602; £804; £402)

Form — RPR

U11 **1** **Fair Along (GER)**[91] 1201 3-10-12 RJohnson 125+
(P J Hobbs) *mde all: clr 2nd: mstke 2 out: drvn out* **11/2**[3]
2 *3* **Afsoun (FR)**[120] 3-10-12 MFoley 120
(N J Henderson) *tall: str: prom: chsd wnr after 5th: rdn appr last: styd on* **3/1**[1]
3 **3** *8* **Kasbah Bliss (FR)**[34] 1705 3-11-6 ADuchene 121+
(F Doumen, France) *tall: scope: lw: mid-div: hdwy after 5th: rdn appr last: nt trble ldrs* **4/1**[2]
F1 **4** *4* **Le Corvee (IRE)**[12] 1955 3-10-12 RThornton 109+
(A King) *lw: hld up: hdwy after 5th: mstke 2 out: sn rdn and no imp* **8/1**
116 **5** *shd* **Wembury Point (IRE)**[18] 1873 3-10-12 (b) RWalsh 110+
(B G Powell) *hld up: hdwy appr 2 out: blnd last: nvr trbld ldrs* **25/1**
1 **6** *11* **Patman Du Charmil (FR)**[15] 1904 3-10-12 CLlewellyn 97
(N A Twiston-Davies) *leggy: chsd clr ldr tl after 5th: wknd 2 out* **4/1**[2]
0311 **7** *3* **Palace Walk (FR)**[23] 1802 3-10-12 109 TJMurphy 94
(B G Powell) *chsd ldrs tl wknd after 3 out* **25/1**
431S **8** *8* **Trigger Guard**[18] 1873 3-10-12 103 (b) PHide 88+
(G L Moore) *hld up: rdn 3 out: no ch whn hit next* **40/1**
5F **9** *7* **Able Charlie (GER)**[12] 1955 3-10-12 HOliver 79
(Mrs Tracey Barfoot-Saunt) *hld up: a bhd* **100/1**
2F **10** *1 ¼* **Madam Caversfield**[18] 1873 3-10-5 PJBrennan 71
(P D Evans) *hld up: a bhd* **50/1**
462 **11** *1 ¾* **Inchcape Rock**[18] 1873 3-10-12 VSlattery 76
(J G M O'Shea) *hld up: a bhd* **66/1**
12 *21* **Battledress (IRE)**[54] 1500 3-11-2 (p) BJGeraghty 59
(K J Condon, Ire) *str: lw: hld up: plld hrd: wknd 3 out* **33/1**
4 **P** **One More Time (FR)**[14] 1923 3-10-5 GLee —
(J Howard Johnson) *hld up: effrt after 5th: sn wknd: bhd whn p.u bef last* **18/1**

4m 2.10s (2.90) **Going Correction** +0.375s/f (Yiel) **13** Ran SP% **114.3**
Speed ratings: **108,106,102,100,100 95,94,90,87,86 85,75,—** CSF £20.67 TOTE £7.20: £2.40, £2.30, £2.00; EX 30.50 Trifecta £103.90 Pool: £1,288.10 - 8.80 winning tickets. Place 6 £22.71, Place 5 £11.19.
Owner Alan Peterson **Bred** Gestut Harzburg **Trained** Withycombe, Somerset

FOCUS
This looked a decent race, but several fancied runners were unable to land a blow and there were only ever two possible winners. Fair Along is still a stone off the mark of a serious Triumph Hurdle candidate, but his earlier form could rate higher. The runner-up looks promising.

NOTEBOOK
Fair Along(GER) has taken to hurdling in great style and, making his debut for new connections, went off like a scalded cat. Having raced well clear from an early stage, he got the second last wrong just as the favourite was closing, but then as soon as that rival got to within challenging distance he picked up again and won well. Whether he can sustain this sort of front-running style remains to be seen, and the Triumph Hurdle is a long way off, but at present he is arguably the best juvenile we have seen. *(op 6-1)*
Afsoun(FR) ◆, a half-brother to Afrad from a successful Aga Khan family and a good stayer in France, was made favourite despite his lack of experience. He was forced to commit in pursuit of the leader at the top of the hill as there were no others capable of doing so, and the effort ultimately told on the climb to the line. This was a decent effort though and he should win his share of races this season. *(op 11-4 tchd 10-3 in a place)*
Kasbah Bliss(FR), winner of a Listed Hurdle and placed in Graded company in France, had a stiff penalty to overcome and could never land a blow. His form suggests he needs softer ground than he encountered here. *(op 9-2)*
Le Corvee(IRE) improved a shade on his Warwick win, despite being unable to get near the front two and tiring up the hill after a mistake two out. He is improving with experience. *(op 10-1)*
Wembury Point(IRE), a dual winner in the late summer, seemed to improve for the fitting of blinkers and was running on well despite a blunder at the final flight, but for which he would have finished fourth. He will be suited by an even stiffer test of stamina. *(tchd 33-1)*
Patman Du Charmil(FR), an easy winner on his British debut, could not go with the early leader and dropped away rather tamely. He had looked better than this on his debut and can be given another chance. *(op 3-1)*
T/Jkpt: Part won. £47,248.70 to a £1 stake. Pool: £66,547.50. 0.50 winning tickets. T/Plt: £57.10 to a £1 stake. Pool: £187,215.59. 2,390.90 winning tickets. T/Qpdt: £9.90 to a £1 stake. Pool: £10,797.20. 806.65 winning tickets. ST

[1903] UTTOXETER (L-H)
Saturday, November 12

OFFICIAL GOING: Heavy
The final hurdle in the back straight was omitted and the slow times reflected the state of the ground.
Wind: Almost nil Weather: Sunny

2179 PAUL FLEURY 50TH BIRTHDAY NOVICES' HURDLE (9 hdls 1 omitted) 2m
12:45 (12:49) (Class 4) 4-Y-0+ **£3,504** (£1,021; £510)

Form — RPR

1 **1** **High Day**[8] 2024 5-11-2 KJMercer(3) 122+
(Ferdy Murphy) *a gng wl: led on bit 3 out: clr appr last: v easily* **1/1**[1]
4-0 **2** *12* **Haunted House**[196] 131 5-10-12 MBradburne 95
(H D Daly) *hld up mid-div: mstke 2nd: hdwy after 6th: ev ch 3 out: btn whn hit last* **28/1**
46-6 **3** *¾* **Sunisa (IRE)**[15] 1908 4-10-5 (t) TSiddall 87
(J Mackie) *hld up and bhd: hdwy appr 3 out: rdn appr 2 out: one pce* **25/1**
4 *5* **What'Sonyourmind (IRE)**[297] 3432 5-10-12 BFenton 92+
(Jonjo O'Neill) *wnt lft s: hld up in mid-div: hdwy after 5th: rdn after 6th: wkng whn hit 2 out* **9/2**[3]
20-3 **5** *4* **Terivic**[15] 1903 5-10-12 110 JPMcNamara 85
(K C Bailey) *led to 3 out: wknd after 2 out* **4/1**[2]

2 **6** *hd* **George Stubbs (USA)**[46] [1569] 7-10-12 ADempsey 85
(B Ellison) *t.k.h in mid-div: hdwy appr 3 out: wknd appr 2 out* **8/1**
04 **7** *9* **Carnt Spell**[9] [2006] 4-10-12 BJCrowley 79+
(J T Stimpson) *prom: rdn after 3 out: sn wknd* **50/1**
8 *5* **Chigorin**[29] 4-10-12 JAMcCarthy 71
(Miss S J Wilton) *sn w ldr: ev ch appr 3 out: sn rdn and wknd* **100/1**
9 *18* **Twist Bookie (IRE)**[100] 5-10-12 DCrosse 53
(J S Moore) *t.k.h: bhd most of way* **100/1**
46 **10** *½* **Millicent Cross (IRE)**[14] [1916] 7-10-7 StephenJCraine[(5)] 53
(R Ford) *mstke 1st: a bhd* **28/1**
0/P- **11** *8* **Star Wonder**[285] [3620] 5-9-12 60 RLucey-Butler[(7)] 38
(G R I Smyly) *t.k.h: a bhd* **200/1**
5/P **P** **Neophyte (IRE)**[21] [1824] 6-10-7 (t) WKennedy[(5)] —
(B De Haan) *a bhd: t.o whn p.u bef 3 out* **100/1**
0/0 **P** **Ellie Moss**[20] [1850] 7-10-5 WMarston —
(A W Carroll) *a bhd: t.o whn p.u bef 3 out* **100/1**
P **Phantom Footsteps**[1966] 8-10-12 JPByrne —
(C N Kellett) *a bhd: t.o whn p.u bef 6th* **150/1**
00P- **P** **Fortanis**[205] [4936] 6-10-5 AO'Keeffe —
(P C Ritchens) *a bhd: mstke 6th: t.o whn p.u bef 3 out* **200/1**
510- **P** **Pinkerton Mill**[212] [4841] 5-10-0 LTreadwell[(5)] —
(J T Stimpson) *hld up in tch: wknd after 6th: t.o whn p.u bef 3 out* **40/1**
P0P/ **P** **Jeanie's Last**[251] 6-10-5 SCurran —
(G J Smith) *hld up in tch: hit 5th: sn rdn and wknd: t.o whn p.u bef 3 out* **150/1**

4m 8.40s (8.00) **Going Correction** +0.575s/f (Soft)
WFA 4 from 5yo+ 12lb **17** Ran SP% **120.7**
Speed ratings: **103,97,96,94,92 92,87,85,76,75 71,—,—,—,— —,—** CSF £38.15 TOTE £1.80: £1.10, £4.50, £6.00; EX 41.80.
Owner Sean J Murphy **Bred** Meon Valley Stud **Trained** West Witton, N Yorks

FOCUS
They went 25/1 bar four in this ordinary novice hurdle. The winner is value for 20 lengths and the race could rate higher, but the placed horses tend to limit confidence.

NOTEBOOK
High Day was brought back to two miles after it was considered he was a bit free at Hexham. Scoring in the style of a promising sort, a hat-trick could well be on the cards. *(op 5-4)*
Haunted House, graduating from bumpers, does need to brush up his jumping. He held on well for second but was never going to give the winner a fright. *(tchd 25-1)*
Sunisa(IRE), a stretch mile winner at Wolverhampton, could not get past the runner-up but seemed to prove she stays.
What'Sonyourmind(IRE) won a heavy-ground bumper at Navan back in January on his only previous start but was quite easy to back. *(op 3-1)*
Terivic, reverting back to two miles, paid the penalty for setting quite a strong pace for the conditions. *(op 5-1)*
George Stubbs(USA) was another who failed to get home in the heavy ground. *(op 14-1)*

2180 MATT HANSON "30TH" BIRTHDAY NOVICES' CHASE (18 fncs) 3m
1:20 (1:20) (Class 4) 5-Y-0+ **£3,765** (£1,168; £629)

Form RPR
5-U2 **1** **Mon Mome (FR)**[11] [1978] 5-11-2 110 AO'Keeffe 120
(Miss Venetia Williams) *hld up: hdwy whn hit 13th: wnt 2nd 14th: rdn 3 out: led 2 out: drvn out* **11/2**[3]
F-21 **2** *4* **Chabrimal Minster**[20] [1848] 8-10-7 105 StephenJCraine[(5)] 112
(R Ford) *led 2nd: blnd 9th: rdn 3 out: hdd and mstke 2 out: no ex flat* **5/4**[1]
PP/4 **3** *23* **Valleymore (IRE)**[14] [1928] 9-10-12 101 (t) TSiddall 97+
(S A Brookshaw) *hld up: jnd ldrs 7th: pushed along appr 13th: lft 8l 3rd and wkng whn bdly hmpd 4 out* **10/1**
4P/3 **F** **Toon Trooper (IRE)**[188] [244] 8-10-7 103 WKennedy[(5)] —
(R Lee) *prom: hit 9th: wknd 14th: poor 4th whn fell 3 out* **12/1**
-0U1 **F** **Underwriter (USA)**[6] [2072] 5-11-1 105 KJMercer[(3)] —
(Ferdy Murphy) *hld up in rr: hdwy after 14th: 5l 3rd whn fell 4 out* **5/2**[2]
23P/ **P** **Oscar Performance (IRE)**[995] [3732] 10-10-12 105 BFenton —
(R H Buckler) *led to 2nd: lost pl 6th: last whn mstke 11th: sn p.u* **25/1**

6m 43.0s (10.50) **Going Correction** +0.525s/f (Soft) **6** Ran SP% **109.0**
Speed ratings: **103,101,94,—,— —** CSF £12.76 TOTE £5.50: £2.30, £1.60; EX 17.90.
Owner Mrs Vida Bingham **Bred** A Deschere **Trained** Kings Caple, H'fords

FOCUS
A slowly-run affair in the testing conditions which suited the winner. The race could rate higher.

NOTEBOOK
Mon Mome(FR) built on the promise of his narrow defeat at Worcester and jumped better than the runner-up. *(op 7-1)*
Chabrimal Minster, unpenalised for his Aintree win, was considered a "penalty kick" by his trainer. However, his jumping again showed definite room for improvement. *(tchd 11-8)*
Valleymore(IRE) only finished third because of the demise of Underwriter. *(op 13-2)*
Underwriter(USA), patiently ridden in this much softer ground, had yet to be asked a question when coming to grief. *(tchd 9-4)*

2181 CENTRAL CIVIL SUPPLIES NOVICES' H'CAP HURDLE (12 hdls 2 omitted) 3m
1:55 (2:00) (Class 4) (0-90,83) 3-Y-0+ **£2,946** (£858; £429)

Form RPR
/-64 **1** **Buster (IRE)**[14] [1921] 6-11-7 78 BFenton 83
(J Ryan) *hld up: rdn after 7th: hdwy to chse clr ldr 9th: styd on to ld last: sn clr* **4/1**[2]
651F **2** *8* **Hi Laurie (IRE)**[8] [2019] 10-11-2 83 JKington[(10)] 81+
(M Scudamore) *led 2nd: sn clr: rdn and hdd last: sn btn* **6/4**[1]
600- **3** *29* **Rosadare (IRE)**[250] [4233] 7-11-0 78 RSpate[(7)] 46
(Mrs K Waldron) *bhd tl hdwy 9th: wnt poor 3rd appr 3 out* **12/1**
P40B **4** *dist* **Beyond Borders (USA)**[6] [2073] 7-10-13 77 MrDEdwards[(7)] —
(G F Edwards) *bhd: short-lived effrt 9th: t.o* **12/1**
0-05 **5** *10* **Hidden Storm (IRE)**[20] [1854] 6-11-2 73 DCrosse —
(Mrs S J Humphrey) *led to 2nd: chsd ldr tl 4th: rdn after 7th: wknd after 9th: t.o* **20/1**
0P0- **R** **Avanti Tiger (IRE)**[270] [3858] 6-10-11 68 WMarston —
(C C Bealby) *hld up: rdn whn lost pl and p.u bef 8th* **8/1**
0PP- **P** **Cleymor House (IRE)**[207] [4917] 7-10-10 74 MrGTumelty[(7)] —
(John R Upson) *prom to 8th: t.o whn p.u bef 3 out* **20/1**
346 **P** **Safe To Blush**[150] [763] 7-11-4 80 TGreenway[(5)] —
(P A Pritchard) *prom: wnt 2nd briefly appr 9th: wknd after 10th: p.u bef 3 out* **5/1**[3]
PFP- **P** **Framlingham**[208] [4913] 10-9-9 59 CMStudd[(7)] —
(R Curtis) *hld up: hdwy to chse clr ldr 4th: wknd qckly appr 8th: t.o whn p.u bef 3 out* **50/1**

6m 28.8s (23.80) **Going Correction** +1.025s/f (Soft) **9** Ran SP% **114.6**
Speed ratings: **101,98,88,—,— —,—,—,—** CSF £10.41 CT £63.93 TOTE £4.90: £1.40, £1.20, £3.20; EX 10.80.
Owner Extraman Ltd, Duncan Sykes, Gary Waller **Bred** Miss Helena Gaskin **Trained** Newmarket, Suffolk

FOCUS
Three miles in heavy going took its toll on these novices in a weak contest.

NOTEBOOK
Buster(IRE) found the combination of a longer trip in demanding ground enabling him to outstay the runner-up after he had looked held early in the home straight. This was the first winner for his trainer since he took over the licence from his father. *(op 7-2 tchd 10-3)*
Hi Laurie(IRE), reverting back to hurdles off a 7lb lower mark, looked in control at the third last but having had plenty of use made of her eventually took its toll. *(op 10-11)*
Rosadare(IRE), who won a bumper in this sort of ground at Tramore early last year, was never really in the hunt. *(op 16-1)*
Safe To Blush *Official explanation: trainer said mare lost its action but returned sound (op 14-1)*

2182 CLIFF BAILEY IS "70" TOMORROW H'CAP HURDLE (10 hdls 2 omitted) 2m 4f 110y
2:30 (2:30) (Class 4) (0-100,98) 4-Y-0+ **£2,891** (£842; £421)

Form RPR
P2U- **1** **Young Lorcan**[256] [4114] 9-10-6 85 RSpate[(7)] 90+
(Mrs K Waldron) *hld up: hdwy appr 7th: led last: rdn out* **3/1**[1]
62-2 **2** *¾* **Lochiedubs**[198] [81] 10-10-8 85 (p) DFlavin[(5)] 86
(Mrs L B Normile) *j.lft: chsd ldr: led 6th: rdn after 3 out: hung lft after 2 out: hdd last: nt qckn* **7/2**[2]
F-P0 **3** *2* **Spike Jones (NZ)**[6] [2071] 7-11-1 92 DLaverty[(5)] 91
(Mrs A M Thorpe) *hld up: mstkes 1st and 6th: hdwy whn nt fluent 3 out: outpcd 2 out: styd on flat* **14/1**
42U0 **4** *1* **Upright Ima**[20] [1856] 6-10-6 78 WMarston 77+
(Mrs P Sly) *hld up in tch: ev ch whn hit 2 out: sn rdn: no ex flat* **4/1**[3]
36-0 **5** *3* **Foxmeade Dancer**[20] [1856] 7-10-12 84 AO'Keeffe 81+
(P C Ritchens) *prom: lost pl appr 3 out: rallied 2 out: 2l 4th whn mstke last: wknd* **4/1**[3]
5/ **6** *dist* **Carthago (IRE)**[558] 8-11-12 98 OMcPhail —
(Miss T McCurrich) *led to 6th: wknd appr 3 out: t.o* **6/1**

5m 46.0s (33.90) **Going Correction** +1.20s/f (Heav) **6** Ran SP% **108.2**
Speed ratings: **83,82,81,81,80** — CSF £12.95 TOTE £3.00: £1.50, £1.90; EX 6.00.
Owner Nick Shutts **Bred** Mrs Norma Dyer **Trained** Stoke Bliss, Worcs

FOCUS
This modest affair turned out to be pretty competitive, probably helped by the slow gallop. The winner is well in on his chase form and could score again.

NOTEBOOK
Young Lorcan, already a heavy ground winner over fences here, had also shown in the past that he could win when fresh. *(op 7-2)*
Lochiedubs, better known over fences these days, could not cope with the winner after jumping and eventually hanging left. *(op 4-1 tchd 10-3)*
Spike Jones(NZ), tailed off in a Hereford seller last weekend, ran as if he would have preferred a stronger gallop in this much softer ground.
Upright Ima, appeared to handle the ground, travelling as well as any until she rapped the penultimate hurdle.
Foxmeade Dancer was probably held when missing out at the final flight. *(op 7-2)*

2183 MASON JAMES FINANCIAL SERVICES H'CAP CHASE (12 fncs) 2m
3:00 (3:00) (Class 3) (0-120,119) 4-Y-0+ **£6,701** (£1,967; £983; £491)

Form RPR
-141 **1** **Dangerousdanmagru (IRE)**[10] [1986] 9-11-3 117 (p) LHeard[(7)] 128+
(A E Jones) *hld up: hdwy appr 4 out: led and hit 3 out: clr 2 out: pushed out* **1/1**[1]
0-P4 **2** *12* **Jericho III (FR)**[6] [2067] 8-11-7 119 (e) PCO'Neill[(5)] 121+
(R C Guest) *j.rt: led: mstke 2nd: hdd 3 out: sn btn* **5/2**[2]
24P- **3** *12* **Advance East**[256] [4116] 13-9-9 93 oh16 LStephens[(5)] 82+
(M J M Evans) *hld up: hdwy 4 out: wknd 3 out* **16/1**
11PP **4** *11* **Nephite (NZ)**[28] [1744] 11-11-3 110 AO'Keeffe 86
(Miss Venetia Williams) *prom tl wknd 4 out* **8/1**
340- **5** *¾* **Mistral De La Cour (FR)**[224] [4696] 5-11-5 117 StephenJCraine[(5)] 92
(R Ford) *prom: rdn appr 4 out: wknd appr 3 out* **6/1**[3]

4m 15.7s (10.70) **Going Correction** +0.65s/f (Soft) **5** Ran SP% **109.9**
Speed ratings: **99,93,87,81,81** CSF £4.08 TOTE £1.80: £1.10, £1.70; EX 3.20.
Owner N F Glynn **Bred** Kashmir Breeding **Trained** Newchapel, Surrey

FOCUS
Yet again a small field for a two-mile handicap chase. The race could rate much higher but conditions temper confidence.

NOTEBOOK
Dangerousdanmagru(IRE) again scored in pretty emphatic fashion with his promising young rider off-setting most of his 10lb hike in the weights. He is also a force to be reckoned with when the mud is flying. *(op 11-10 tchd 5-4 and 6-5 in places)*
Jericho III(FR) did not help his cause by jumping right-handed and found that the walls were tumbling around him when taken on by the winner. *(tchd 11-4)*
Advance East, on his first outing since March, could only manage a short-lived effort albeit from 16lb out of the handicap. *(op 12-1)*

2184 BETFRED POKER H'CAP HURDLE (SERIES QUALIFIER) (12 hdls 2 omitted) 3m
3:35 (3:35) (Class 3) (0-125,125) 4-Y-0+ **£5,790** (£1,699; £849; £424)

Form RPR
411- **1** **Overserved**[231] [4549] 6-10-10 109 ADempsey 113+
(A Parker) *hld up in tch: rdn after 2 out: led flat: drvn out* **4/1**[2]
0-06 **2** *2* **Mythical King (IRE)**[75] [207] 8-11-7 125 PMerrigan[(5)] 125
(R Lee) *hld up in rr: hdwy after 9th: led 2 out: sn rdn: hdd flat: nt qckn* **15/2**
132- **3** *4* **Woodlands Genpower (IRE)**[244] [4344] 7-11-5 118 MBradburne 116+
(P A Pritchard) *led 2nd to 7th: led 8th to 3 out: sn rdn: wknd last* **10/3**[1]
3-33 **4** *4* **The Flyer (IRE)**[174] [468] 8-10-11 110 (t) JAMcCarthy 102
(Miss S J Wilton) *hld up in tch: rdn appr 3 out: wknd appr last* **16/1**
141- **5** *3½* **Irish Legend (IRE)**[7] [4671] 5-10-13 117 WKennedy[(5)] 106
(C Roberts) *hld up: hdwy appr 3 out: sn rdn: wknd 2 out* **13/2**
P00- **6** *¾* **Standing Bloom**[223] [4717] 9-10-0 99 oh1 WMarston 88+
(Mrs P Sly) *led to 2nd: chsd ldr: hit 5th: led 7th to 8th: led 3 out to 2 out: wknd last* **13/2**
111- **7** *6* **Always Waining (IRE)**[43] [3947] 4-11-7 120 SStronge 102
(P L Clinton) *hld up in rr: struggling whn mstke 3 out* **5/1**[3]
5-16 **8** *24* **Monger Lane**[193] [168] 9-11-2 115 RGreene 73
(K Bishop) *hld up in rr: rdn after 9th: wkng whn nt fluent 3 out* **14/1**

6m 30.8s (25.80) **Going Correction** +1.20s/f (Heav) **8** Ran SP% **110.7**
Speed ratings: **105,104,103,101,100 100,98,90** CSF £31.34 CT £103.94 TOTE £5.90: £1.50, £2.60, £1.70; EX 72.70.

Owner Mr & Mrs Raymond Anderson Green **Bred** D G Ford **Trained** Lockerbie, D'fries & G'way

FOCUS

All of these lacked a recent run over hurdles, but the winner is on the upgrade and is value for more than the official margin with the second close to his mark.

NOTEBOOK

Overserved completed a hat-trick on this step up to three miles having not been out since February. Considered a chaser in the making, he will remain over hurdles this season. *(op 3-1)*

Mythical King(IRE) had ground conditions in his favour and his form on the Flat suggests he should get this trip. *(op 7-1 tchd 8-1)*

Woodlands Genpower(IRE) found his usual front-running tactics setting things up for others on his first start for six months. *(tchd 3-1)*

The Flyer(IRE) was another having his first run since May. *(op 20-1)*

Irish Legend(IRE), 6lb higher than when successful at Ludlow at the end of March, had the benefit of a recent pipe-opener at Wolverhampton. *(op 9-1)*

Standing Bloom was just out of the handicap for her first start since April. *(tchd 6-1 and 15-2)*

2185 HARP STANDARD OPEN NATIONAL HUNT FLAT RACE — 2m

4:05 (4:06) (Class 6) 4-6-Y-O **£1,856** (£541; £270)

Form / RPR

2- **1** **What A Vintage (IRE)**[244] 4349 5-10-11 .... WMarston 93+
(R T Phillips) *hld up: hdwy 6f out: led over 2f out: drvn out* **7/4**[1]

4 **2** *1 ¾* **Sobers (IRE)**[20] 1849 4-10-13 .... PCO'Neill(5) 98+
(R C Guest) *hld up and bhd: hdwy over 3f out: chsd wnr over 1f out: nt qckn ins fnl f* **15/8**[2]

3 *10* **Triple Mint (IRE)** 4-10-13 .... StephenJCraine(5) 88
(D McCain) *prom: rdn 4f out: wknd over 1f out* **6/1**[3]

66 **4** *2 ½* **Must Be Keen**[50] 1543 6-10-11 .... AGlassonbury(7) 86
(Ernst Oertel) *led: rdn and hdd over 2f out: wknd over 1f out* **14/1**

6 **5** *nk* **Strange Days (IRE)**[30] 1730 5-10-13 .... CHonour(5) 85
(Mrs K Waldron) *hld up: lost pl 6f out: n.d after* **20/1**

26-0 **6** *18* **A Few Kind Words (IRE)**[202] 7 4-10-11 .... RSpate(7) 67
(Mrs K Waldron) *hld up: hdwy over 5f out: rdn and hung lft over 3f out: wknd over 2f out* **8/1**

7 *7* **Tuckers Bay** 4-10-6 .... LTreadwell(5) 53
(J R Holt) *prom: pushed along 7f out: wknd over 4f out* **25/1**

6P **8** *nk* **Walton Way**[143] 816 5-11-4 .... JPMcNamara 60
(P W Hiatt) *a bhd* **33/1**

4m 17.5s (17.70) **Going Correction** +1.20s/f (Heav) **8** Ran SP% **114.8**

WFA 4 from 5yo+ 12lb

Speed ratings: **103,102,97,95,95 86,83,83** CSF £5.16 TOTE £2.20: £1.10, £1.10, £1.90; EX 3.60 Place 6 £6.51, Place 5 £3.59.

Owner The Someday's Here Racing Partnership **Bred** John Costello **Trained** Adlestrop, Gloucs

FOCUS

A poor bumper with the form horses having matters to themselves.

NOTEBOOK

What A Vintage(IRE) had less to do and built on the promise of her second in a big field at Warwick last March. *(op 6-4)*

Sobers(IRE) did not do much wrong but it is unlikely that he is going to prove to be as good as his namesake. *(op 7-4 tchd 13-8)*

Triple Mint(IRE) is a half-brother to the mud-loving staying hurdler Beyond Control. *(op 10-1 tchd 11-1)*

Must Be Keen had far different ground to contend with this time.

Strange Days(IRE) probably wants a much sounder surface.

T/Plt: £6.60 to a £1 stake. Pool: £35,972.35. 3,970.95 winning tickets. T/Qpdt: £3.50 to a £1 stake. Pool: £2,077.10. 430.60 winning tickets. KH

1923 WETHERBY (L-H)

Saturday, November 12

OFFICIAL GOING: Soft

Wind: Slight, across

2186 "LEEDS RUGBY DAY" MAIDEN HURDLE (10 hdls) — 2m 4f 110y

12:40 (12:40) (Class 4) 4-Y-O+ **£3,727** (£1,086; £543)

Form / RPR

3 **1** **Nine De Sivola (FR)**[13] 1937 4-10-9 .... PJMcDonald(7) 112+
(Ferdy Murphy) *midfield: stdy hdwy 1/2-way: trckd ldrs 4 out: led 2 out: pushed clr appr last: kpt on* **4/1**[2]

63 **2** *6* **Laertes**[15] 1915 4-10-13 .... MrTGreenall(3) 102
(C Grant) *hld up towards rr: hdwy whn hit 6th: pushed along to chse ldrs after 3 out: rdn next: styd on to chse wnr last: kpt on same* **7/1**

5 **3** *6* **Joe Brown**[16] 1892 5-10-11 .... PMerrigan(5) 97+
(Mrs H Dalton) *hld up in midfield: hdwy whn mstke 4 out: hit next and sn rdn along styd on fr 2 out: hld in 3rd whn mstke last* **6/1**[3]

00- **4** *½* **Spectested (IRE)**[12] 1914 4-11-2 .... WHutchinson 96
(A W Carroll) *hld up and bhd: stdy hdwy appr 3 out: rdn along next and kpt on same pce* **25/1**

3-P **5** *13* **Sportula**[21] 1839 4-10-2 .... PKinsella(7) 76
(C Grant) *trckd ldrs: rdn along: lost pl and bhd 4 out: styd on u.p fr 2 out* **40/1**

02-4 **6** *¾* **It's Bertie**[27] 1762 5-11-2 .... DElsworth 82
(Mrs S J Smith) *racd wd: cl up tl rdn along 3 out: wkng whn hit next* **6/1**[3]

100 **7** *1 ½* **Ericas Charm**[6] 2070 5-10-9 .... ChristianWilliams 74+
(P Bowen) *trckd ldrs: hdwy to ld appr 3 out: rdn and hdd next: sn drvn and wknd* **25/1**

150- **8** *½* **Seymar Lad (IRE)**[210] 4865 5-11-2 .... RGarritty 80
(P Beaumont) *led: hit 3rd: rdn along 4 out: hdd bef next and grad wknd* **20/1**

2-03 **9** *1 ¾* **Rathowen (IRE)**[13] 1938 6-10-13 .... MichalKohl(3) 78
(J I A Charlton) *in tch: hit 5th: rdn along after next and sn wknd* **8/1**

F5 **10** *13* **Tanmeya**[4] 2106 4-10-6 .... LMcGrath(3) 58
(R C Guest) *keen: hld up and bhd: stdy hdwy whn blnd 4 out: nt rcvr* **66/1**

P5-2 **11** *11* **Polly Whitefoot**[21] 1834 6-10-9 94 .... PWhelan 47
(R A Fahey) *trckd ldrs: hdwy 4 out: rdn along appr next and sn wknd: bhd whn blnd bdly 2 out* **7/2**[1]

0 **12** *26* **Zaffiera (IRE)**[15] 1915 4-11-2 .... NPMulholland 28
(M D Hammond) *in tch: rdn along 6th: sn lost pl and bhd* **100/1**

P **Balasari (IRE)**[120] 1003 5-10-13 .... PBuchanan(3) —
(Miss Kariana Key) *midfield: hit 4th: rdn along and lost pl after 6th: bhd whn p.u bef 3 out* **33/1**

5m 23.3s (14.40) **Going Correction** +0.30s/f (Yiel) **13** Ran SP% **114.7**

Speed ratings: **84,81,79,79,74 74,73,73,72,67 63,53,**— CSF £28.59 TOTE £4.10: £2.00, £2.80, £2.00; EX 35.10.

Owner The DPRP Sivola Partnership **Bred** G Trapenard **Trained** West Witton, N Yorks

FOCUS

A weak maiden hurdle, run at an average gallop, and the field finished strung out in the testing conditions. The winner could rate higher with the second to his mark.

NOTEBOOK

Nine De Sivola(FR) , given a patient ride, ran out a comfortable winner and got off the mark over timber at the fifth attempt. She jumped well throughout, saw out the trip without fuss and is clearly suited by a deep surface. *(op 7-2)*

Laertes turned in another improved effort and was again doing all of his best work in the finish. He is entitled to improve again for the experience, shapes as though he needs a stiffer test, and is eligible for handicaps after his next outing. *(op 13-2)*

Joe Brown was not fluent over his hurdles and lacked a change of gears over this shorter trip. He should do better in this sphere as he gains further experience, but this former pointer will only come into his own when tackling the bigger obstacles again in the future. *(op 13-2)*

Spectested(IRE), who stays this trip on the Flat, was not given a hard time on this return to hurdles. He needed this in order to qualify for a handicap mark and can be expected to improve when switched to that sphere in due course. *(tchd 33-1)*

Tanmeya *Official explanation: jockey said filly had a breathing problem and hung right in straight*

Polly Whitefoot, who posted a personal-best when runner-up to the promising Rasharrow last time, ran a tame race and never looked like justifying market support. She dropped out quickly *when push came to shove and something may well have been amiss. Official explanation: trainer was unable to explain the poor form shown (op 4-1)*

2187 INTEGRATED TECHNICAL SYSTEMS - BARRIE MCDERMOTT TESTIMONIAL NOVICES' H'CAP CHASE (15 fncs) — 2m 4f 110y

1:15 (1:15) (Class 4) (0-105,102) 4-Y-O+ **£3,854** (£1,131; £565; £282)

Form / RPR

1 **Dun Doire (IRE)**[14] 1933 6-10-3 79 .... JimCrowley 90+
(A J Martin, Ire) *hld up in rr: hdwy 4 out: rdn after next: styd on last: drvn flat to ld nr fin* **1/2**[1]

004/ **2** *½* **Jimmy Bond**[574] 4873 6-10-6 82 .... NPMulholland 90+
(M D Hammond) *trckd ldrs: hdwy to chse ldr 1/2-way: cl up 4 out: rdn to ld appr 2 out: drvn flat: hdd and no ex towards fin* **12/1**

0-P3 **3** *5* **Jonny's Kick**[6] 2078 5-11-7 97 .... RGarritty 101+
(T D Easterby) *led: rdn along 4 out: hdd and blundereed 2 out: sn drvn and kpt on same pce* **15/2**[3]

2B5F **4** *dist* **Assumetheposition (FR)**[8] 2022 5-11-3 96 .... (p) LMcGrath(3) —
(R C Guest) *hld up: hit 6th: hdwy 10th: cl up 5 out: rdn along appr next and sn wknd* **6/1**[2]

PP-6 **F** **One Five Eight**[14] 1928 6-11-9 102 .... MrTGreenall(3) 86
(M W Easterby) *chsd ldr to 1/2-way: in tch: rdn along 5 out: wknd after next and hld in 4th whn fell 2 out* **16/1**

5m 36.7s (16.00) **Going Correction** +0.40s/f (Soft) **5** Ran SP% **106.3**

Speed ratings: **85,84,82,**—,— CSF £6.22 TOTE £1.40: £1.20, £3.60; EX 8.00.

Owner Dunderry Racing Syndicate **Bred** Mrs Sarah Martin **Trained** Kildalkey, Co Meath

FOCUS

A moderate handicap, notably weakened by the withdrawl of Corrib Lad, and the first two came clear on the run-in. The placed horses suggest the form is solid enough.

NOTEBOOK

Dun Doire(IRE) ◆ showed the benefit of his recent comeback at Naas and, under a most patient ride, ground down the runner-up after the final fence and scored with a fair amount up his sleeve. The return to a longer trip was much to his liking, he remains relatively unexposed and should still look fairly treated despite a future weight rise. *(op 2-5)*

Jimmy Bond, making his chase debut after a 574-day layoff, posted a very pleasing effort and did nothing wrong in defeat. This looks as far as he wants to go, but he was clear of the rest and is clearly capable of finding a race in this sphere.

Jonny's Kick, well beaten on his comeback in novice company six days previously, has just started to tire when losing all chance with an error at the penultimate fence. This must rate a much more encouraging effort, he has some fair bumper form in early 2004, and should be placed to advantage at this level as he gains further experience. *(op 8-1)*

Assumetheposition(FR), a faller at Hexham eight days previously, looked careful throughout and threw in the towel approaching four out. He has a fair amount to prove now and it would be no surprise to see him back over hurdles before long. *(op 8-1)*

2188 "LEEDS TYKES" (S) H'CAP HURDLE (12 hdls) — 2m 7f

1:50 (1:50) (Class 5) (0-95,88) 4-Y-O+ **£2,302** (£670; £335)

Form / RPR

PP-P **1** **The Pecker Dunn (IRE)**[193] 169 11-11-12 88 .... JMogford 90+
(Mrs N S Evans) *trckd ldr: led 8th: j.rt fr 4 out: rdn after 2 out: kpt on* **6/1**[3]

P460 **2** *2* **Northern Rambler (IRE)**[41] 1602 8-10-0 72 .... (p) JReveley(10) 71
(K G Reveley) *led: reminders 5th: hdd 8th: rdn along 2 out: drvn last: no imp* **13/8**[1]

0500 **3** *28* **Silver Dagger**[21] 1838 7-11-0 76 .... (p) FKeniry 47
(J C Haynes) *hld up: hdwy whn mstke 8th: cl up 4 out: rdn along next and sn outpcd* **3/1**[2]

0P-0 **4** *dist* **Son Of Man (IRE)**[6] 2071 6-10-11 80 .... TBurrows(7) —
(B D Leavy) *trckd ldrs: pushed along 8th: blnd bdly 4 out and bhd after* **12/1**

43-0 **U** **Casas (IRE)**[202] 11 8-10-5 74 .... (t) MrSFMagee(7) —
(J R Norton) *hld up in tch tl blnd and uns rdr 7th* **3/1**[2]

6m 18.0s (21.30) **Going Correction** +0.30s/f (Yiel) **5** Ran SP% **110.1**

Speed ratings: **74,73,63,**—,— CSF £16.62 TOTE £7.80: £2.20, £1.50; EX 13.90.There was no bid for the winner.

Owner The Illiney Group **Bred** Kevin Dwan **Trained** Pandy, Gwent

FOCUS

A dire event for the track, run at a modest gallop and the first two came clear. The second sets a very moderate standard.

NOTEBOOK

The Pecker Dunn(IRE), pulled up on his previous four outings, bounced back to form and, despite making hard work of it from three out, did enough to register just his second success over hurdles. Despite shouldering top weight, he was entitled to win according to official figures, and is far from certain to follow up. *(op 7-1)*

Northern Rambler(IRE), dropped in class for this return to hurdling, was up on the pace throughout, but was always being held by the winner and looked very one paced. He remains a maiden, but was a long way clear of the rest at the finish and is not without hope in this class. *(op 9-4)*

Silver Dagger never rated a threat from off the pace and is a better horse on faster ground. *(op 7-2)*

Casas(IRE), having his first outing in this grade and returning from a 202-day break, was going well enough prior to unseating. *(op 2-1)*

2189 TOTESPORT.COM H'CAP CHASE (18 fncs) — 3m 1f

2:25 (2:25) (Class 3) (0-130,126) 5-Y-O+ **£10,734** (£3,151; £1,575; £787)

Form / RPR

-122 **1** **Mckelvey (IRE)**[35] 1670 6-11-12 126 .... ChristianWilliams 146+
(P Bowen) *j.w: cl up: led after 4 out: rdn clr after 2 out: styd on strly* **10/3**[2]

5-64 **2** *11* **Jungle Jinks (IRE)**[23] [1798] 10-11-2 **116** .... FKeniry 122
(G M Moore) *a cl up: rdn along after 5 out: ev ch 3 out: sn drvn and one pce fr next* **3/1**[1]

23/6 **3** *1 1/2* **Silver Knight**[23] [1798] 7-11-2 **116** .... RGarritty 121
(T D Easterby) *hld up in rr: stdy hdwy to trck ldrs 5 out: rdn along after next: hit 2 out and sn one pce* **10/1**

POP- **4** *1 3/4* **Artic Jack (FR)**[218] [4766] 9-11-8 **122** .... DElsworth 125
(Mrs S J Smith) *mde most tl hdd after 5 out: rdn along after next: drvn 2 out and sn one pce* **5/1**

431- **P** **Imperial Dream (IRE)**[210] [4864] 7-11-3 **117** .... DO'Meara —
(H P Hogarth) *trckd ldrs: mstke 9th: pushed along 12th: rdn 4 out and grad wknd: bhd whn p.u bef last* **9/2**[3]

3211 **P** **Catch The Perk (IRE)**[23] [1798] 8-11-3 **120** ....(p) PBuchanan[(3)] —
(Miss Lucinda V Russell) *trckd ldrs: nt fluent 6th: pushed along 12th: grad wknd and bhd whn p.u bef 4 out* **6/1**

6m 44.7s (4.70) **Going Correction** +0.40s/f (Soft) **6** Ran SP% **106.3**
Speed ratings: **108,104,104,103,—** — CSF £12.52 TOTE £3.20: £2.30, £2.00; EX 14.30.
Owner N Elliott **Bred** John Quane **Trained** Little Newcastle, Pembrokes

FOCUS
A fair staying handicap, run at an average pace and the winner looks progressive and is value for further.

NOTEBOOK
Mckelvey(IRE) ◆ confirmed himself an improving stayer with a convincing success under top weight. He jumped neatly throughout, loved the deep surface and looked better the further he went. Considering he is still a novice, this must rate a decent effort and, if he continues to progress, it would come as little surprise to see his ambitious trainer aim him at the one of the Nationals this season. *(op 11-4)*

Jungle Jinks(IRE) had every chance, but was unable to stay with the winner when it mattered and was well held. He is in fair form at present and can find easier assignments off this current mark.

Silver Knight showed the benefit of his recent comeback at Haydock and, despite never looking a *real threat, posted an improved effort. He should do better as he gains more races this term. (tchd 11-1)*

Artic Jack(FR) , making his seasonal bow, shaped well from the front until finding his lack of fitness an issue approaching the penultimate fence. He should be a lot sharper next time. *(op 6-1)*

Catch The Perk(IRE) , raised 6lb for his latest success, was unable to dictate as he prefers, but *still performed well below his recent efforts all the same. He could be in need of a break.Official explanation: jockey said gelding was unsuited by the soft ground (tchd 4-1)*

Imperial Dream(IRE) was none to convincing over his fences, and tended to run in snatches, before his rider finally conceded defeat approaching the final fence. It will come as no surprise to see the blinkers back on for his next outing and he is capable of better than this. *(tchd 4-1)*

2190 TOTESCOOP6 H'CAP HURDLE (9 hdls) 2m

2:55 (2:57) (Class 3) (0-130,129) 4-Y-0+ **£7,351** (£2,158; £1,079; £539)

Form RPR

03-P **1** **Jake Black (IRE)**[36] [1010] 5-10-6 **112** .... FKing[(3)] 129+
(J J Quinn) *a.p: led after 4 out: clr 2 out: easily* **5/1**[2]

/00- **2** *9* **Adopted Hero (IRE)**[252] [2879] 5-11-2 **126** .... BSHughes[(7)] 131+
(J Howard Johnson) *hld up in rr: gd hdwy whn hmpd home turn: in tch next: effrt to chse wnr appr last: sn no imp* **20/1**

26-P **3** *4* **Fenix (GER)**[199] [67] 6-11-12 **129** ....(b) LAspell 129
(Mrs L Wadham) *in tch: hdwy appr 3 out: rdn along to chse wnr next: sn drvn and one pce* **15/2**

2-31 **4** *1* **Red Man (IRE)**[7] [2042] 8-9-13 **105** .... ONelmes[(3)] 105+
(Mrs E Slack) *chsd ldr: pushed along after 4 out: rdn next: hit 2 out and grad wknd* **7/1**[3]

230- **5** *3* **Argento**[252] [4170] 8-10-9 **112** .... FKeniry 108
(G M Moore) *midfield: hdwy and in tch on outer 4 out: rdn along next and sn one pce* **25/1**

02B- **6** *2* **Welcome To Unos**[252] [4177] 8-9-10 **109** .... PKinsella[(10)] 103
(K G Reveley) *hld up in rr: pushed along 4 out: styd on fr next: nt rch ldrs* **20/1**

4-06 **7** *11* **Transit**[17] [1878] 6-10-6 **112** ....(p) GBerridge[(3)] 95
(B Ellison) *hld up towards rr: hdwy appr 4 out: rdn along next and sn no imp* **8/1**

4530 **8** *11* **Merryvale Man**[133] [784] 8-9-9 **103** oh1 .... DMcGann[(5)] 75
(Miss Kariana Key) *chsd ldrs to 1/2-way: sn lost pl and bhd* **33/1**

26-F **9** *2 1/2* **Beamish Prince**[15] [1911] 6-10-9 **117** .... DCCostello[(5)] 87
(G M Moore) *midfield: hdwy to chse ldrs appr 4 out: rdn along next and sn wknd* **16/1**

11P- **10** *19* **Torkinking (IRE)**[223] [4711] 6-10-10 **113** .... JimCrowley 64
(M A Barnes) *led: rdn along and hit 4 out: sn hdd & wknd qckly* **7/1**[3]

011- **11** *1 1/2* **Fair Spin**[14] [4547] 5-10-12 **115** ....(v) KRenwick 64
(M D Hammond) *chsd ldrs on outer: rdn along appr 4 out and sn wknd* **14/1**

04/ **12** *17* **Ticket To Ride (FR)**[181] 7-11-0 **117** ....(tp) RWalford 49
(A J Wilson) *a rr: bhd fr 1/2-way* **12/1**

/462 **P** **Kentucky Blue (IRE)**[15] [1912] 5-11-6 **123** ....(p) RGarritty —
(T D Easterby) *trckd ldrs: hdwy 5th: chsd ldrs next: rdn along 3 out: sn wknd and p.u bef last* **4/1**[1]

4m 0.70s (1.30) **Going Correction** +0.30s/f (Yiel) **13** Ran SP% **121.1**
Speed ratings: **108,103,101,101,99 98,93,87,86,76 76,67,—** CSF £104.56 CT £757.63 TOTE £6.30: £2.50, £5.40, £3.50; EX 204.50.
Owner G A Lucas **Bred** Yeomanstown Stud **Trained** Settrington, N Yorks

FOCUS
A modest handicap, run at a fair pace and the field came home strung out behind the easy winner. The winner is value for more than the official margin, the time was decent, the third and fourth were close to their marks and the race should work out.

NOTEBOOK
Jake Black(IRE), handy throughout, shot clear when asked to win his race before three out and came home an easy winner on this return to hurdling. This was by far his best effort to date in this sphere, the ground was much in his favour and, on this evidence, could be the type to defy an inevitably higher mark in the future.\n\x\x , handy throughout, shot clear when asked to win his race before three out and came home an easy winner on this return to hurdling. This was by far his best effort to date in this sphere, the ground was much in his favour and, on this evidence, could be the type to defy an inevitably higher mark in the future.\n\x\x , handy throughout, shot clear when asked to win his race before three out and came home an easy winner on this return to hurdling. This was by far his best effort to date in this sphere, the ground was much in his favour and, on this evidence, could be the type to defy an inevitably higher mark in the future.\n\x\x handy throughout, shot clear when asked to win his race before three out and came home an easy winner on this return to hurdling. This was by far his best effort to date in this sphere, the ground was much in his favour and, on this evidence, could be the type to defy an inevitably higher mark in the future.

Adopted Hero(IRE), making his debut for Howard Johnson, made a very pleasing return to action and would have finished closer with a clear passage at the top of the straight. While he appears high enough in the weights at present, his form as a novice was of a decent level, and he could *have more to offer this season if his current handler can rekindle his enthusiasm.Official explanation: jockey said, regarding the running and riding, his orders were to take his time and not use his whip as gelding tends to stop when hit, adding he suffered interference on bottom bend; trainer's representative concurred and said gelding was sour in work at home (op 22-1)*

Fenix(GER), last seen pulling up at Punchestown 199 days previously, produced a sound effort under top weight on ground he loves. He should strip fitter for this experience and should continue to pay his way in competitive handicaps this term from his current mark. *(op 8-1)*

Red Man(IRE), raised 5lb for winning at Kelso a week previously, was just starting to go backwards prior to making an error two and looked to find this ground plenty soft enough. He remains in good form, but while he may be happier on a less taxing surface in the future, still has to prove he is up to this higher mark.\n\x\x , raised 5lb for winning at Kelso a week previously, was just starting to go backwards prior to making an error two and looked to find this ground plenty soft enough. He remains in good form, but while he may be happier on a less taxing surface in the future, still has to prove he is up to this higher mark.\n\x\x , raised 5lb for winning at Kelso a week previously, was just starting to go backwards prior to making an error two and looked to find this ground plenty soft enough. He remains in good form, but while he may be happier on a less taxing surface in the future, still has to prove he is up to this higher mark.\n\x\x , raised 5lb for winning at Kelso a week previously, was just starting to go backwards prior to making an error two and looked to find this ground plenty soft enough. He remains in good form, but while he may *be happier on a less taxing surface in the future, still has to prove he is up to this higher mark. (op 10-1)*

Kentucky Blue(IRE) ran well below expectations and was disappointingly pulled up before the final *flight after finding nothing for pressure in the straight. He has plenty to prove now.Official explanation: jockey said gelding never travelled (tchd 5-1)*

2191 "LEEDS RHINOS" NOVICES' H'CAP HURDLE (9 hdls) 2m

3:30 (3:30) (Class 4) (0-105,103) 3-Y-0+ **£3,521** (£1,026; £513)

Form RPR

5646 **1** **Celtic Legend (FR)**[157] [690] 6-10-3 **90** .... JReveley[(10)] 93+
(K G Reveley) *midfield: hdwy on outer to trck ldrs 1/2-way: hdwy 3 out: led next: rdn last: edgd rt flat: jst hld on* **8/1**

2 *hd* **Amazing Valour (IRE)**[35] [1689] 3-10-7 **100** ....(v[1]) JimCrowley 88+
(P Hughes, Ire) *rn in snatches: chsd ldrs: rdn along 5th: bdly hmpd next: rdn and hdwy on outer 2 out: drvn last: styd on flat: jst failed* **7/2**[1]

3U-0 **3** *1 1/2* **Nerone (GER)**[13] [1940] 4-11-12 **103** .... KRenwick 102
(P Monteith) *hld up towards rr: stdy hdwy appr 3 out: rdn to chse wnr and swtchd lft last: drvn and one pce flat* **10/1**

030 **4** *9* **Dubai Dreams**[28] [1745] 5-10-9 **89** ....(b) LVickers[(3)] 81+
(S R Bowring) *led: rdn along 4 out: hdd next: sn drvn and one pce* **25/1**

P6P- **5** *1 1/4* **Bobsourown (IRE)**[229] [4625] 6-9-13 **79** .... PBuchanan[(3)] 68
(D McCain) *trckd ldrs: hdwy and cl up 5th: led 3 out: sn rdn and hdd next: drvn and wknd appr last* **12/1**

02/0 **6** *hd* **Colway Ritz**[13] [1940] 11-10-1 **78** .... NPMulholland 67
(W Storey) *hld up towards rr: hmpd 4 out: styd on fr 2 out: nvr nr ldrs* **16/1**

4-00 **7** *3 1/2* **Mac's Elan**[4] [2099] 5-10-10 **94** .... MrMatthewSmith[(7)] 79
(A B Coogan) *trckd ldrs: hdwy 4 out: ev ch next: sn rdn and wknd after next* **12/1**

2P-6 **8** *5* **Miss Pross**[202] [9] 5-11-5 **96** .... RWalford 76
(T D Walford) *in tch on outer: rdn along appr 3 out and sn outpcd* **6/1**[2]

6/65 **9** *1 1/2* **Loner**[13] [1937] 7-10-6 **83** .... DO'Meara 62
(W S Coltherd) *a rr* **14/1**

-033 **10** *22* **Lord Rosskit (IRE)**[21] [1826] 5-11-0 **91** .... FKeniry 48
(G M Moore) *cl up: rdn along 5th: wknd 4 out: sn bhd* **7/1**[3]

-64P **11** *23* **Macchiato**[41] [1607] 4-10-6 **83** .... ARoss 17
(I W McInnes) *chsd ldrs: rdn along 5th: wkng and towards rr whn hmpd 4 out: bhd after* **25/1**

0120 **F** **Dubonai (IRE)**[36] [1661] 5-11-4 **100** ....(t) DCCostello[(5)] —
(G M Moore) *midfield: hdwy 5th: cl up whn fell 4 out* **6/1**[2]

4m 9.40s (10.00) **Going Correction** +0.30s/f (Yiel)
WFA 3 from 4yo+ 15lb **12** Ran SP% **119.1**
Speed ratings: **87,86,86,81,81 80,79,76,75,64 53,—** CSF £37.01 CT £285.86 TOTE £9.30: £2.60, £2.10, £2.90; EX 46.20.
Owner Jemm Partnership Limited **Bred** Peter Savill **Trained** Lingdale, N Yorks

FOCUS
A moderate handicap, run at an ordinary gallop, and the first three came clear. The form is very modest but the third to sixth were close to their marks. James Reveley's first winner as a conditional

NOTEBOOK
Celtic Legend(FR), returning from a 157-day break, ran out a game winner under a fine ride by his inexperienced jockey. This proved his effectiveness on an easy surface, he has clearly benefited from a recent wind operation, and will be high on confidence now for an impending return to fences. *(op 10-1)*

Amazing Valour(IRE) ◆, an Irish-raider making his handicap debut in a first-time visor, raced lazily and did not help his rider throughout the first half of the contest. However, he found his stride before being hampered four out by a faller, and the manner in which he stormed home suggests he would have got up with a clear run. He remains a maiden and, while he is clearly a tricky ride, is well up to going one better off his current mark this term.

Nerone(GER) settled better than had been the case on his recent seasonal bow at Carlisle and posted his best effort for some time. He can build on this, and looks feasibly handicapped at present, but may just want a longer trip in the future.

Dubai Dreams, making his handicap debut, turned in a fair effort from the front and stuck to his task once headed three from home. He is worth persevering with off this sort of mark.

Miss Pross, well backed, failed to quicken when it mattered and ran as though this outing was needed. *(op 15-2)*

Macchiato *Official explanation: jockey said filly hung left-handed (tchd 33-1)*

Dubonai(IRE) was still in contention prior to falling four from home. *(op 5-1)*

2192 WETHERBY RACES NEXT WEDNESDAY 23RD NOVEMBER INTERMEDIATE OPEN NATIONAL HUNT FLAT RACE 2m

4:00 (4:03) (Class 6) 4-6-Y-0 **£1,959** (£571; £285)

Form RPR

2/0- **1** **Supreme's Legacy (IRE)**[348] [2549] 6-11-4 .... JimCrowley 106+
(K G Reveley) *cl up: led over 3f out: shkn up ent last and kpt on wl* **5/2**[1]

2 *1 3/4* **Kealshore Lad** 4-10-13 .... DCCostello[(5)] 97
(G M Moore) *towards rr: pushed along 5f out: gd hdwy over 3f out: rdn to chse wnr over 1f out: kpt on wl fnl f* **20/1**

0- **3** *7* **Chateau Rouge (IRE)**[231] [4552] 4-11-4 .... FKeniry 90
(M D Hammond) *towards rr: hdwy and pushed along 5f out: rdn to chse ldrs 3f out: drvn and kpt on same pce fnl 2f* **33/1**

5-3 **4** *5* **Trafalgar Man (IRE)**[177] [431] 4-11-4 .... NPMulholland 86+
(M D Hammond) *in tch: hdwy to chse ldrs 4f out: rdn wl over 2f out and sn one pce* **9/1**

5 5 **Boulders Beach (IRE)** 5-10-11 NCarter(7) 80
(Mrs S J Smith) *trckd ldrs: hdwy 4f out and ev ch tl rdn and outpcd wl over 2f out* **25/1**

5- **6** *shd* **Cash King (IRE)**[259] 4069 5-11-4 DElsworth 80
(Mrs S J Smith) *cl up: led 7f out: rdn along and hdd 3f out: drvn and wknd 2f out* **11/4**[2]

7 *9* **Lookafterme (IRE)**[237] 5-11-4 WHutchinson 71
(A W Carroll) *hld up in midfield: hdwy to chse ldrs 4f out: rdn along wl over 2f out and sn one pce* **8/1**

8 *27* **Overfields** 5-11-1 LVickers(3) 44
(S R Bowring) *bhd: sme hdwy on inner 4f out: sn rdn and nvr a factor* **66/1**

9 *3* **The Ringer** 5-11-1 MichalKohl(3) 41
(J I A Charlton) *prom: rdn along over 5f out: wknd 4f out* **16/1**

10 *2* **Trawbreaga Bay** 5-11-4 ARoss 39
(P Beaumont) *chsd ldrs: rdn along 5f out: sn wknd* **33/1**

11 *2 ½* **Northern Quest (IRE)** 4-11-4 DO'Meara 36
(H P Hogarth) *in tch: hdwy to chse ldrs over 5f out: rdn over 4f out and sn wknd* **18/1**

12 *3* **Darcy Wells** 4-11-4 RGarritty 33
(T D Easterby) *trckd ldrs: rdn along 6f out: sn wknd* **11/2**[3]

13 *22* **Vincere** 6-11-1 ACCoyle(3) 11
(L R James) *a rr* **66/1**

60 **14** *2* **Cottam Phantom**[27] 1762 4-11-1 MrTGreenall(3) 9
(M W Easterby) *led: rdn along 1/2-way: hdd over 7f out and sn wknd* **66/1**

4m 2.00s (-2.40) **Going Correction** +0.30s/f (Yiel)
WFA 4 from 5yo+ 12lb **14** Ran SP% **121.8**
Speed ratings: **92,91,87,85,82 82,78,64,63,62 60,59,48,47** CSF £60.08 TOTE £3.60: £1.70, £6.10, £5.40; EX 95.40 Place 6 £59.97, Place 5 £19.44.
Owner The Supreme Alliance **Bred** J Mernagh **Trained** Lingdale, N Yorks

FOCUS
A modest bumper, run at a fair gallop and the first two came nicely clear. The winner is value for much more than the winning margin and, rated through the fourth, the form looks above average.

NOTEBOOK
Supreme's Legacy(IRE) ◆ responded kindly to his rider's urgings from three out and ran out a ready winner on this return from 348-day layoff. He has clearly had his problems, but this confirms the real impression he made on his Aintree debut in 2003, and that he is versatile as regards underfoot conditions. Providing connections manage to keep him sound, they look to have a nice prospect for novice hurdling, and he should get further in time. *(op 9-4 tchd 11-4)*
Kealshore Lad, a half-brother to a nine-furlong winner on the All-Weather, emerged to finish a clear second-best and posted a promising debut effort. He looks sure to benefit for the experience, enjoyed the soft ground and looks up to going one better in this sphere. *(op 33-1)*
Chateau Rouge(IRE), who showed little on her debut last season, posted a much more encouraging effort and looks to have improved for her break. She may just want faster ground in the future.
Trafalgar Man(IRE), who showed ability in two similar events last season, appeared to blow up from three out and his effort proved short-lived. He should do better with this outing under his belt. *(tchd 17-2)*
Boulders Beach(IRE), out of an unraced half-sister to Elena's River, showed ability before being left behind in the closing stages. *(op 20-1)*
Cash King(IRE), who showed promise on his debut at Kempton last term when with Paul Webber, ran as through this race was badly needed and should not be written off yet. *(op 5-2)*
T/Plt: £61.40 to a £1 stake. Pool: £37,894.35. 450.10 winning tickets. T/Qpdt: £44.50 to a £1 stake. Pool: £2,371.80. 39.40 winning tickets. JR

2193 - 2194a (Foreign Racing) - See Raceform Interactive

[1930]NAAS (L-H)
Saturday, November 12

OFFICIAL GOING: Heavy

2195a WOODLANDS PARK 100 POPLAR SQUARE CHASE (GRADE 3) 2m
1:45 (1:45) 5-Y-O+ £16,159 (£4,741; £2,258; £769)

RPR

1 **Watson Lake (IRE)**[34] 1702 7-11-12 146 PCarberry 155+
(Noel Meade, Ire) *2nd and disp: led 5 out: drew clr after 2 out: nt extended easily* **8/15**[1]

2 *2 ½* **Green Belt Flyer (IRE)**[14] 1931 7-11-8 127 TPTreacy 143
(Mrs John Harrington, Ire) *hld up in tch: 5th 3 out: prog into 3rd next: 2nd and rdn bef last: kpt on wout troubling wnr* **12/1**

3 *1 ½* **Euro Leader (IRE)**[34] 1700 7-11-8 141 DJCondon 142
(W P Mullins, Ire) *hld up in tch: prog into 4th bef 1/2-way: impr into 3rd 2 out: sn rdn: 3rd and no imp fr last* **8/1**[3]

4 *9* **Strong Project (IRE)**[23] 1810 9-11-8 137 DJCasey 133
(C F Swan, Ire) *trckd ldrs in 3rd: cl up fr 5 out: 2nd and rdn to chal after 3 out: no ex fr next* **12/1**

5 *shd* **Ned Kelly (IRE)**[229] 4636 9-11-1 134 CO'Dwyer 125
(E J O'Grady, Ire) *hld up in rr: drvn along and outpcd 3 out: styd on fr bef last* **8/1**[3]

6 *dist* **Kahuna (IRE)**[13] 1944 8-10-11 133 JRBarry —
(E Sheehy, Ire) *led and disp: hdd and slt mstke 5 out: slt mstke 3 out: wknd next* **6/1**[2]

4m 19.6s **Going Correction** +0.15s/f (Yiel) **6** Ran SP% **117.1**
Speed ratings: **115,113,113,108,108** — CSF £8.65 TOTE £1.40: £1.10, £3.70; DF 8.90.
Owner John Corr **Bred** Thomas F O'Brien **Trained** Castletown, Co Meath

NOTEBOOK
Watson Lake(IRE) made it two out of two for the season, defying top weight, and put up a very solid performance. His jumping was unblemished, and he won very easily, but the jury is still out as to what his optimum may be. Still open to further improvement, he is one to have on your side when the ground is soft. *(op 4/6)*
Green Belt Flyer(IRE) won a handicap here off 119 two weeks previously and this was a major step up. He never looked like getting to the winner, but kept on nicely and is clearly progressing. *(op 10/1)*
Euro Leader(IRE), who swerved the Paddy Power for this, did not enjoy the ground and needs much further. There was little disgrace in this defeat.
Strong Project(IRE) went with the winner from five out but was spent before the straight. He still looked to run very near to his mark, however, and helps set the level of this form. *(op 10/1)*
Ned Kelly(IRE) was struggling before three out and left the impression he may prefer a stiffer test now. He is entitled to improve a deal for the outing. *(op 7/1)*
Kahuna(IRE) again disappointed after leading until a mistake five out. He can find easier assignments in the future, however. *(op 5/1)*

2196 - 2199a (Foreign Racing) - See Raceform Interactive

[1937]CARLISLE (R-H)
Sunday, November 13
2200 Meeting Abandoned - Waterlogged

[2173]CHELTENHAM (L-H)
Sunday, November 13

OFFICIAL GOING: Good to soft
Races run on the Old Course.
Wind: Nil

2206 GIDEON KASLER NOVICES' HURDLE (10 hdls) 2m 5f
1:05 (1:06) (Class 2) 4-Y-O+ £10,897 (£3,219; £1,609; £805; £401; £201)

Form RPR

11-1 **1** **Black Jack Ketchum (IRE)**[42] 1619 6-11-5 APMcCoy 143+
(Jonjo O'Neill) *lw: a.p: led 2 out: clr whn slipped on landing last: rdn out* **13/2**

2 *2 ½* **Powerstation (IRE)**[15] 1935 5-11-0 DNRussell 133
(C Byrnes, Ire) *small: hld up: hdwy 3 out: rdn to chse wnr last: styd on* **11/1**

2 **3** *3* **Massini's Maguire (IRE)**[22] 1827 4-11-0 RJohnson 131+
(P J Hobbs) *chsd ldrs: ev ch 3 out: rdn appr last: styd on same pce* **4/1**[2]

1 **4** *9* **Neptune Collonges (FR)**[11] 1980 4-11-5 RWalsh 127+
(P F Nicholls) *chsd ldrs: led 5th: hdd & wknd 2 out* **11/4**[1]

0 **5** *6* **The Spoonplayer (IRE)**[15] 1935 6-11-8 TDoyle 123
(H De Bromhead, Ire) *str: chsd ldrs: rdn after 7th: wknd appr 2 out* **100/1**

2 **6** *¾* **Circassian (IRE)**[15] 1927 4-11-0 GLee 114
(J Howard Johnson) *hld up: hdwy after 6th: rdn and wknd 2 out* **11/2**[3]

7 *3 ½* **Naples**[45] 1586 6-11-8 PCarberry 120+
(Noel Meade, Ire) *tall: str: lw: racd keenly: trckd ldrs: rdn and wknd appr 2 out* **25/1**

8 *11* **The Squatter (IRE)**[59] 1472 6-11-0 PJBrennan 100
(V Clifford, Ire) *cmpt: str: lw: hld up: hdwy 5th: wknd 3 out* **100/1**

60 **9** *2* **Almutasader**[12] 1975 5-11-0 WHutchinson 98
(J A B Old) *hld up: nvr nr to chal* **200/1**

10 *½* **Robert (IRE)**[108] 1092 6-11-8 DJCasey 105
(D T Hughes, Ire) *str: led to 5th: rdn and wknd after 3 out* **14/1**

3 **11** *12* **Alphabetical (IRE)**[21] 1859 6-11-0 NFehily 85
(C J Mann) *hld up: a in rr* **66/1**

04-6 **12** *16* **Too Posh To Share**[158] 680 7-10-7 73 JMogford 62
(D J Wintle) *racd keenly: prom to 7th* **200/1**

5- **13** *1 ¼* **Seomra Hocht (IRE)**[108] 1090 8-11-0 104 JLCullen 68
(William Coleman O'Brien, Ire) *neat: mstke 3rd: a in rr* **100/1**

14 *7* **Flash Cummins (IRE)**[219] 5-11-0 TJMurphy 63+
(M C Pipe) *cmpt: hld up: mstke 2nd: wknd after 6th* **16/1**

0 **15** *1 ¾* **Sidcup's Gold (IRE)**[16] 1908 5-11-0 MBradburne 59
(M Sheppard) *hld up: a in rr* **200/1**

0 **16** *nk* **Joe McHugh (IRE)**[16] 1903 6-11-0 KGTobin 59
(C J Mann) *hld up: a in rr* **200/1**

-PP6 **17** *dist* **Iloveturtle (IRE)**[7] 2081 5-11-0 95 (t) KJohnson —
(M C Chapman) *hld up: a in rr* **300/1**

111 **P** **Jeremy Cuddle Duck (IRE)**[21] 1847 4-11-8 CLlewellyn —
(N A Twiston-Davies) *mid-div: rdn and wknd after 4th: t.o whn p.u bef 6th* **10/1**

5m 13.8s (0.20) **Going Correction** +0.175s/f (Yiel) **18** Ran SP% **116.0**
Speed ratings: **106,105,103,100,98 97,96,92,91,91 86,80,80,77,76 76,—,—** CSF £71.19 TOTE £7.00: £2.40, £3.40, £2.30; EX 101.50 Trifecta £733.70 Part won. Pool: £1,033.40 - 0.50 winning tickets..
Owner Mrs Gay Smith **Bred** E Morrissey **Trained** Cheltenham, Gloucs

FOCUS
A decent contest, which should certainly throw up future winners. The form, rated through the third, suggests the winner is potentially high class. He and the second were both much improved.

NOTEBOOK
Black Jack Ketchum(IRE) ◆ travelled well throughout and powered up the hill in fine style. He stumbled after jumping the last, which caused him to lose a little momentum, but he quickly recovered and saw the trip out really strongly, retaining his unbeaten record in the process. He looks potentially high class and the Royal & SunAlliance Hurdle is the obvious long-term target. *(op 6-1 tchd 11-2 in places)*
Powerstation(IRE), having his fourth start over hurdles, has yet to win a race but he has now finished runner-up on the last three occasions. He saw the trip out well, recording a career-best effort in the process, and it should not be long before he puts the record straight and gets off the mark over timber. *(op 14-1 tchd 10-1 in places)*
Massini's Maguire(IRE) ◆ had run well in the Persian War at Chepstow on his reappearance and this performance has been rated equal to that effort. He clearly possesses a decent amount of ability and should soon be winning over timber, but, longer term, he has the look of a chaser in the making.
Neptune Collonges(FR), highly regarded and a winner in desperate ground at Chepstow on his British debut, led at the second last, albeit under pressure, but he was unable to hold off his challengers. He might need softer ground than this to be seen at his best. *(op 5-2 tchd 3-1 and 9-4 in places)*
The Spoonplayer(IRE) was 2lb worse off with Powerstation having been beaten four lengths by him when they both ran at Naas last time, so it was not a great surprise that the form was confirmed.
Circassian(IRE) was expected to appreciate the step up in trip, as he was a winning stayer on the Flat, and the form of his Wetherby run had been held up by the solid performance of Two Miles West on the first day of this meeting, but he was a shade disappointing. He might do better granted a quicker surface, as his wins on the Flat came on good or faster. *(op 5-1)*
Naples ran well for a long way but he has done all his winning on good to firm or firm ground so these conditions may not have been ideal. *(op 33-1)*
Almutasader was out of his depth in this company but this was his third run over timber and connections now have the option of going handicapping with him.
Robert(IRE), who enjoyed a successful summer, winning three times on fast ground, found conditions more testing on this reappearance under his big penalty. *(op 12-1)*
Jeremy Cuddle Duck(IRE) *Official explanation: vet said gelding had bled from the nose (op 12-1)*

2207 PADDYPOWERPOKER.COM HURDLE (INTERMEDIATE H'CAP HURDLE) (10 hdls) 2m 5f

1:35 (1:40) (Class 3) (0-135,135) 4-Y-0+

£19,493 (£5,758; £2,879; £1,441; £718; £361)

Form			Horse	RPR
1P-0	1		**Hordago (IRE)**[50] 1556 5-10-1 **117**.......................(p) BCByrnes(7) (E McNamara, Ire) *hdwy to chse ldrs 4th: rdn 4 out: chal fr 3 out and styd upsides tl drvn to ld sn after last: all out* **12/1**	128
1P1-	2	hd	**Il Duce (IRE)**[205] 4954 5-11-7 **130**....................... RThornton (A King) *h.d.w: lw: sn trcking ldrs: chal fr 3 out tl led wl bef last: nt fluent: hdd sn after:rallied and gng on cl home: nt quite get up* **12/1**	143+
125-	3	8	**Dom D'Orgeval (FR)**[244] 4371 5-10-10 **119**....................... PJBrennan (Nick Williams) *bhd: hdwy fr 4 out: chal and rdn 2 out: stl upsides appr last: outpcd run-in* **25/1**	122
613-	4	1 ½	**Manx Royal (FR)**[204] 4978 6-11-9 **132**....................... TScudamore (M C Pipe) *bhd: hdwy 5th: chsd ldrs 4 out: slt ld next: sn rdn: hdd wl bef last: wknd run-in* **33/1**	134
32-0	5	2 ½	**Cherub (GER)**[190] 208 5-11-7 **130**....................... ADobbin (Jonjo O'Neill) *in tch: chsd ldrs 4 out: chal fr 3 out to next: wknd appr last* **16/1**	129+
1631	6	¾	**Cantgeton (IRE)**[18] 1878 5-11-4 **127**....................... TJMurphy (M C Pipe) *chsd ldrs: rdn to chal 3 out to next: wknd appr last* **9/1**[2]	126
1	7	¾	**Millanymare (IRE)**[25] 1789 6-10-5 **114**....................... DNRussell (A J Martin, Ire) *w'like: bhd: hdwy 6th: chsd ldrs and n.m.r 3 out: styd on same pce after next* **10/1**[3]	113+
1125	8	¾	**Screenplay**[29] 1743 4-10-6 **115**....................... JGoldstein (Miss Sheena West) *in tch: lost position after 6th: rdn 3 out: styd on appr last: nt rch ldrs* **50/1**	112
1-11	9	hd	**Penneyrose Bay**[8] 2053 6-11-7 **135**....................... PCO'Neill(5) (J A Geake) *lw: mde most tl narrowly hdd 3 out: wknd fr next* **11/2**[1]	132
0	10	1 ¼	**Rights Of Man (IRE)**[28] 1765 6-10-9 **118**....................... JLCullen (D E Fitzgerald, Ire) *w'like: bhd: hdwy 4 out: chsd ldrs and hit 3 out: sn one pce* **33/1**	115+
02-0	11	1	**Salut Saint Cloud**[22] 1828 4-11-6 **129**....................... BJCrowley (G L Moore) *lw: bhd: hdwy 6th: shkn up and in tch whn hmpd 2 out: kpt on again run-in* **50/1**	126+
2-20	12	¾	**Jockser (IRE)**[25] 1675 4-10-2 **114**....................... RYoung(3) (J W Mullins) *in tch: rdn 2 out: kpt on again run-in* **25/1**	109+
3	13	2 ½	**Rory Sunset (IRE)**[15] 1934 7-10-4 **113**....................... DJCasey (C F Swan, Ire) *neat: bhd: hdwy 5th: rdn 3 out: wknd after next* **50/1**	104
13-4	14	7	**Habitual Dancer**[15] 1929 4-10-11 **120**....................... BHarding (Jedd O'Keeffe) *trckd winner and chal fr 4th: stl upsides 3 out: wknd next* **66/1**	104
211-	15	3	**Alagon (IRE)**[185] 4878 5-10-7 **116**.......................(v) GLee (Ian Williams) *sn chsng ldrs: wknd after 3 out* **50/1**	97
321P	16	3	**Croix De Guerre (IRE)**[15] 1918 5-11-11 **134**.......................(b) RJohnson (P J Hobbs) *chsd ldrs to 3 out: sn wknd* **33/1**	112
00-0	17	2	**Urban (IRE)**[15] 1934 4-10-11 **120**....................... APMcCoy (Joseph Crowley, Ire) *cmpt: str: bhd: hit 6th: hdwy and pushed wd after 4 out: chsng ldrs whn n.m.r and mstke next: sn wknd* **14/1**	96
11-U	18	4	**Valley Ride (IRE)**[29] 1743 5-11-9 **132**....................... TDoyle (C Tinkler) *sn chsng ldrs: rdn 4 out: sn wknd* **11/1**	104
513-	19	14	**Waltzing Beau**[262] 4032 4-10-13 **127**....................... JFLevins(5) (B G Powell) *chsd ldrs tl wknd 6th: no ch whn bdly hmpd 2 out* **33/1**	85
110-	20	3 ½	**Pretty Star (GER)**[239] 4460 5-11-3 **126**....................... WHutchinson (A King) *chsd ldrs to 4 out* **33/1**	81
210-	P		**Diego Cao (IRE)**[22] 4433 4-11-6 **129**....................... SThomas (G L Moore) *blnd 1st: a bhd: t.o whn p.u bef 4 out* **22/1**	—
B221	F		**Nippy Des Mottes (FR)**[12] 1969 4-10-2 **111**.......................(t) RWalsh (P F Nicholls) *bhd: hdwy 5th: disputing cl 4th and gng wl whn fell 2 out* **11/2**[1]	117+
	P		**Owennacurra Bobby (IRE)**[15] 1934 5-10-13 **122**.......................(p) PCarberry (Thomas Cooper, Ire) *chsd ldrs to 4 out: t.o whn j.v.slowly last and p.u run-in* **50/1**	—

5m 13.4s (-0.20) **Going Correction** +0.175s/f (Yiel)
WFA 4 from 5yo+ 13lb **23** Ran **SP% 124.2**
Speed ratings: 107,106,103,103,102 102,101,101,101,100 100,100,99,96,95 94,93,92,86,85 —,—,— CSF £126.48 CT £3543.95 TOTE £15.20: £3.60, £2.90, £9.30, £7.10; EX 271.10 TRIFECTA Not won..
Owner S Braddish **Bred** Airlie Stud **Trained** Rathkeale, Co. Limerick

FOCUS
They went a decent pace here and the form looks rock solid for the grade. The first two are big improvers, and the third and fourth are still progressive. The race should work out.

NOTEBOOK
Hordago(IRE) was an unconsidered 33-1 shot when successful at this meeting last year but he was afforded a little more respect this time. Wearing cheekpieces for the first time, he showed the right attitude up the hill and connections are now planning a return visit in March for the Coral Cup.
Il Duce(IRE) ◆ made a mistake at the last which probably cost him the momentum to win the race, but this was still a good effort off a mark of 130, and he clearly has the ability to win a nice handicap over timber. However, he is a chaser in the making and the sooner he is sent over the bigger obstacles the better. *(op 14-1)*
Dom D'Orgeval(FR) won his first handicap in July 2004 off a mark of 81, so he has improved quite a bit in the last 16 months. Although he was seen off by the first two running to the last, he kept the rest at bay well enough to suggest that a mark in the low 120s will not be insurmountable this term.
Manx Royal(FR) ◆ appeared to have a stiff task at the weights but he ran a great race on his reappearance. He just did not get home, so maybe a sharper track or quicker ground will help. *(op 50-1)*
Cherub(GER) ◆ made a solid start to the season over a longer trip than he had ever raced over before. He is well handicapped on his two-mile form from this time last year and, with his stable now back in top form, will be of interest when returning to shorter.
Cantgeton(IRE), raised 10lb for winning over an extended two miles here last month, was not disgraced in this stronger event. *(tchd 8-1 in places)*
Millanymare(IRE), who attracted market support, was given a patient ride. Squeezed up jumping the third last, she kept on well afterwards without getting close enough to land a blow. She ran well given that her wins have come on quicker ground. *(tchd 11-1 and 12-1 in places)*
Screenplay, who did best of the four-year-olds, is worth persevering with over this longer trip.
Penneyrose Bay, 15lb higher than when successful at Wincanton eight days earlier, set a decent pace in front and paid for her effort in the closing stages. *(op 7-2)*
Rights Of Man(IRE), knocked about jumping the third last, could not stay in touch from the turn in but did not disgrace himself. He will be of more interest if returned to two miles.
Salut Saint Cloud was hampered by the fall of Nippy Des Mottes at the second last so he did not shape too badly in the circumstances.
Nippy Des Mottes(FR) ◆ would surely have been involved in the finish as he was probably travelling best of all when crashing out at the second last. It is to be hoped that his confidence is not shattered by this heavy fall. *(op 6-1)*

2208 INDEPENDENT NEWSPAPER NOVICES' CHASE (REGISTERED AS THE NOVEMBER NOVICES' CHASE) GRADE 2 (12 fncs) 2m

2:05 (2:11) (Class 1) 4-Y-0+

£22,808 (£8,556; £4,284; £2,136; £1,072; £536)

Form			Horse	RPR
-162	1		**Accordion Etoile (IRE)**[35] 1702 6-11-5....................... JLCullen (Paul Nolan, Ire) *hld up in tch: chsd ldr and mstke 2 out: sn rdn: styd on u.p to ld post* **5/2**[1]	152+
024-	2	shd	**Tamarinbleu (FR)**[205] 4973 5-11-5....................... APMcCoy (M C Pipe) *lw:hld up: mstke 2nd: hdwy 5th: hit 7th: chsd ldr 9th: led 3 out: hrd rdn flat: hdd post* **3/1**[2]	149+
42-1	3	6	**Albuhera (IRE)**[16] 1911 7-11-5.......................(t) RWalsh (P F Nicholls) *lw: hld up: hdwy 9th: styd on same pce fr 2 out* **9/2**[3]	143+
10/0	4	7	**Davenport Democrat (IRE)**[28] 1766 7-11-11....................... PCarberry (W P Mullins, Ire) *lft in ld 1st: hdd 3 out: wknd next* **25/1**	141
P-12	5	½	**Chilling Place (IRE)**[12] 1971 6-11-9....................... RJohnson (P J Hobbs) *chsd ldr to 9th: wknd appr 2 out* **3/1**[2]	139
3-01	6	26	**Master Ofthe Chase (IRE)**[41] 1626 7-11-11....................... DJCasey (C F Swan, Ire) *str: lw: hld up: wknd 8th* **20/1**	121+
-221	7	4	**Va Vavoom (IRE)**[22] 1831 7-11-9 120....................... CLlewellyn (N A Twiston-Davies) *prom: lost pl 5th: sn bhd* **16/1**	109
0/06	8	dist	**Only For Gold**[28] 1749 10-11-5 69....................... JMogford (Dr P Pritchard) *bhd fr 3rd* **300/1**	—
0-2	U		**Mattys Joy (IRE)**[50] 1555 6-10-12 102.......................(p) DNRussell (Daniel Mark Loughnane, Ire) *led: blnd and unseated rdr 1st* **66/1**	—
LP46	P		**Dabus**[13] 1958 10-11-5 99.......................(b) KJohnson (M C Chapman) *lw: chsd ldrs: mstke 7th: sn wknd: t.o whn p.u bef 2 out* **300/1**	—

3m 58.0s (-1.30) **Going Correction** +0.175s/f (Yiel) **10** Ran **SP% 113.4**
Speed ratings: **110,109,106,103,103 90,88,—,—,—** CSF £10.06 TOTE £3.40: £1.70, £1.70, £1.90; EX 13.40 Trifecta £75.90 Pool: £1,251.08 - 11.70 winning units.
Owner Banjo Syndicate **Bred** John McKeever **Trained** Enniscorthy, Co. Wexford

FOCUS
A classy renewal run at a decent pace and no doubt a strong pointer to the Arkle in March. The winner is a high-class novice but is still some way off his best hurdles form. The second and third have both been assessed as having run to their hurdles level.

NOTEBOOK
Accordion Etoile(IRE), the best of these over hurdles, let the eventual runner-up get away from him slightly running down the hill, but he engaged top gear in the straight and finished very strongly to win well, albeit by the shortest distance. He consolidated his position at the head of the Arkle market and it is difficult to argue with quotes of around 6-1, as the likely quicker ground conditions in March will be even more in his favour. *(tchd 3-1)*
Tamarinbleu(FR) has always gone well fresh and so it was no surprise to see him well backed for this debut over fences. Jumping well running down the hill, he looked to have the favourite in trouble rounding the turn into the straight, but, although he jumped the last in front, he could not hold off the strong run of the winner on the run-in. He ran a blinder in defeat but one would caution against backing him at short odds if he makes a quick return to the track, as he has been beaten in such circumstances in the past. Given time between his races he will surely win a decent prize this term as he clearly has plenty of ability on his day. *(tchd 10-3)*
Albuhera(IRE), officially rated 6lb lower than the runner-up over hurdles, was patiently ridden and jumped well. He did not do a lot wrong for a stable which is not firing on all cylinders at present and, while he looks a little short of Arkle class on this evidence, he could yet be back here in March for a race like the Grand Annual. *(op 4-1)*
Davenport Democrat(IRE), chasing a four-timer, tried to put his experience to good use and set a decent pace. He had a stiff ask in this better grade and this was an improved effort giving 6lb to the first three.
Chilling Place(IRE) gave Racing Demon 6lb and was only beaten a length and a half at Exeter last time, and while he probably would not want the ground any softer than this, one would not have thought that it was bad enough to stop him running to his best. However, he has been rated as running 10lb off his Exeter effort. *(tchd 11-4)*
Master Ofthe Chase(IRE), a winner of his two previous starts over fences, carried the maximum penalty and found the step up to this grade all too much. *(op 25-1)*
Va Vavoom(IRE) was out of his depth in this company, but he will be suited by a greater test of stamina and will win more races. *(op 22-1)*

2209 GREATWOOD H'CAP HURDLE GRADE 3 (8 hdls) 2m 110y

2:40 (2:44) (Class 1) 4-Y-0+

£28,510 (£10,695; £5,355; £2,670; £1,340; £670)

Form			Horse	RPR
121/	1		**Lingo (IRE)**[680] 3184 6-10-6 **140**....................... APMcCoy (Jonjo O'Neill) *b.bkwd: hld up in rr: stdy hdwy fr 4th: trckd ldrs 3 out: led gng wl after 2 out: c clr last: easily* **5/1**[2]	152+
521/	2	3 ½	**Tramantano**[715] 2455 6-10-0 **134**....................... CLlewellyn (N A Twiston-Davies) *b.bkwd: bhd: hdwy 4 out: shkn up and outpcd after 3 out: drvn and styd on strly appr last: chsd wnr run-in but no ch* **50/1**	140+
252-	3	1 ¼	**Phar Bleu (FR)**[220] 4749 4-10-2 **136**....................... RWalsh (P F Nicholls) *in tchm trckd ldrs fr 4th: slt ld 3 out: narrowly hdd but upside next: rdn sn after: kpt on same pce* **8/1**	141
/P4-	4	½	**Adamant Approach (IRE)**[25] 1789 11-10-0 **134** oh2....................... DJCasey (W P Mullins, Ire) *bhd: hdwy 3f out: sn rdn styd on u.p appr last: fin wl but nt rch ldrs* **25/1**	139
30-2	5	nk	**Howle Hill (IRE)**[22] 1828 5-10-5 **139**....................... RThornton (A King) *in tch: hdwy 4th: chal fr 3 out to next: stl upsides sn after: one pce appr last* **12/1**	143
15-0	6	3	**Handy Money**[197] 127 8-10-0 **134** oh5....................... WHutchinson (A King) *b.bkwd: chsd ldrs: rdn 3 out: kpt on fr 2 out: one pce run-in* **150/1**	135
03-4	7	1 ½	**Dalaram (IRE)**[53] 1509 5-10-4 **138**....................... GLee (J Howard Johnson) *lw: chsd ldrs: pushed along and one pce 3 out: kpt on again run-in* **50/1**	138
1-13	8	½	**Fait Le Jojo (FR)**[15] 1919 8-10-1 **135** ow5....................... HEphgrave(5) (L Corcoran) *led appr 2nd: hdd appr 4 out: styd pressing ldrs to next: outpcd 2 out: kpt on again run-in* **50/1**	139
111-	9	2	**Mighty Man (FR)**[219] 4762 5-10-5 **139**....................... SThomas (H D Daly) *b.bkwd: mid-div: hdwy 4th: chsd ldrs 4 out: rdn and one pce after 3 out: kpt on again run-in* **10/1**	136
4R-4	10	2	**Westender (FR)**[190] 207 9-11-9 **157**.......................(b) TScudamore (M C Pipe) *chsd ldrs: rdn 3 out: wknd after next* **33/1**	152
2-	11	1 ½	**Don't Be Shy (FR)**[189] 258 4-10-6 **140**....................... TJMurphy (M C Pipe) *gd sort: rangy: scope: b.bkwd: sn chsng ldrs: chal 3 out: slt ld next: hdd sn after: wknd bef last* **6/1**[3]	134
102-	12	hd	**Self Defense**[22] 4973 8-11-5 **153**....................... FKeniry (Miss E C Lavelle) *chsd ldrs: rdn 3 out: wknd next* **10/1**	147

3234 **13** *shd* **Borora**[18] [1878] 6-10-0 **134** oh2 .... TDoyle 127
(R Lee) *in tch: rdn 3 out: sn wknd* **66/1**

1-41 **14** *20* **Rooster Booster**[29] [1738] 11-11-12 **160** .... RJohnson 148+
(P J Hobbs) *b.bkwd: hld up in rr: hdwy 4 out: chsd ldrs next: sn wknd* **14/1**

/05- **15** *4* **Power Elite (IRE)**[13] [3807] 5-10-6 **140** .... PCarberry 128+
(Noel Meade, Ire) *lw: t.k.h: hld up in rr: hdwy on ins after 4 out: shkn up and carried hd high bef next: fnd no ex and sn btn* **7/2**[1]

4113 **16** *2* **Darrias (GER)**[8] [2055] 4-9-10 **137** oh2 ow3 .... (t) LHeard[(7)] 104
(P F Nicholls) *hit 4th: a bhd* **16/1**

1105 **17** *5* **Fontanesi (IRE)**[29] [1744] 5-9-13 **136** .... TJMalone[(3)] 98
(M C Pipe) *chsd ldr: chal 4th: led appr 4 out: hdd & wknd 3 out* **66/1**

1106 **18** *½* **Yes Sir (IRE)**[12] [1971] 6-11-5 **153** .... WMarston 115
(P Bowen) *t.k.h: led and nt fluent 1st: hdd appr next: wknd 4 out* **66/1**

00-4 **19** *11* **Eye Candy (IRE)**[178] [432] 4-9-7 **134** oh9 .... PKinsella[(7)] 85
(Mrs Sandra McCarthy, Ire) *bhd fr 4th* **66/1**

3m 55.8s (-3.40) **Going Correction** +0.175s/f (Yiel)
WFA 4 from 5yo+ 12lb **19** Ran SP% **122.0**
Speed ratings: **115,113,112,112,112 110,110,110,109,108 107,107,107,97,96 95,92,92,87**
CSF £242.08 CT £1996.23 TOTE £6.80: £2.20, £10.90, £2.50, £4.70; EX 414.80 Trifecta £2083.10 Part won. Pool of £2,934.00 - 0.20 winning units..
Owner John P McManus **Bred** Francis Montauban **Trained** Cheltenham, Gloucs

FOCUS
A competitive renewal of this high-class handicap run at a decent pace. The form can be questioned on the back of disappointing efforts from those at the top of the weights, but the winner did it well and gave early notice of Champion Hurdle pretensions.

NOTEBOOK
Lingo(IRE) ♦, who missed the whole of last season because of the virus which hit his trainer's yard, had not been seen on a racecourse for 680 days, but he was well backed on this comeback run and won in the manner of a horse going places. He travelled particularly well off a decent pace, quickened up in the straight and ran out a decisive winner. The Handicapper is likely to put him up to a mark around 150 now which will leave him with a stone to find to be a proper Champion Hurdle contender, but this was only his fourth start over hurdles so there should be room for plenty of improvement. Quotes of around 10-1 look fair enough at this stage. *(op 8-1)*
Tramantano ♦ was another returning from a lengthy absence, in his case 715 days. Last seen when beating Sporazene in the Gerry Fielden, he stayed on strongly from off the pace, relishing the uphill finish. He clearly retains all his ability and will be of great interest when stepped up in trip.
Phar Bleu(FR) did by far the best of the four-year-olds. Traditionally those who run well in the Triumph Hurdle tend to struggle the following season over hurdles, but this effort suggests he might buck that trend. *(op 9-1)*
Adamant Approach(IRE), who fell at the last when looking the winner of the Supreme Novices' in 2002, is now an 11-year-old, but he retains plenty of ability, as his fourth place in the Pierse Hurdle in January suggests. He had the benefit of a previous run this season here and ran well, but the Handicapper looks to have his measure at the moment. *(tchd 28-1)*
Howle Hill(IRE), who ran well on his reappearance behind Lacdoudal at Chepstow, lost three places on the run-in but this was still a good effort. He gets two and a half miles well these days so perhaps his future lies over the longer trip.
Handy Money followed his stablemate home. Running from 5lb out of the handicap, he ran a great race at the weights but his last win came off a mark of 123, so he looks likely to remain in the grip of the Handicapper after being reassessed. *(op 100-1)*
Dalaram(IRE), who hails from a stable which is not in top form at present, was missing the tongue strap he wore when last seen over hurdles in the Scottish Champion Hurdle.
Fait Le Jojo(FR) ran well considering he was up with the pace throughout in what was a strongly-run affair.
Mighty Man(FR), winner of the big two-mile novice hurdle at Aintree last season and unbeaten in four previous starts coming into this, was found out off a mark of 139 on this handicap debut. *(op 9-1)*
Westender(FR), who was second in this race last year off a 3lb higher mark, usually runs well here but this was a disappointing effort.
Don't Be Shy(FR), a highly-regarded four-year-old who won three times over hurdles when trained in France, including in graded company, jumped the second last just in front but was outpaced in the straight. He might need softer ground, or a longer trip to be seen at his best. *(op 5-1 tchd 13-2)*
Self Defense, last seen finishing runner-up in a Group Three at Newbury on the Flat, does not win very often but this was too bad to be true. *(op 9-1)*
Rooster Booster, who had the race run to suit, was bang there three out and looked poised to get into contention, but the veteran failed to deliver under top weight. *(op 12-1)*
Power Elite(IRE) was a popular favourite on his return to hurdling following a short, successful spell on the Flat this autumn. Under pressure turning out of the back straight, though, he put his head in the air and looked far from co-operative. He has questions to answer now. Official explanation: vet said gelding returned lame *(op 10-3)*

2210 JERSEY H'CAP CHASE (11 fncs 4 omitted) 2m 4f 110y
3:15 (3:18) (Class 3) (0-125,123) 5-Y-0+

£10,803 (£3,191; £1,595; £798; £398; £200)

Form RPR

306- **1** **Bannow Strand (IRE)**[205] [4958] 5-10-6 **103** .... TJMurphy 140+
(M C Pipe) *h.d.w: chsd ldrs: led 6th: nt extended* **11/8**[1]

3-25 **2** *8* **Shalako (USA)**[19] [1872] 7-11-3 **114** .... RJohnson 126
(P J Hobbs) *hld up: hdwy and mstke 2 out: styd on: no ch w wnr* **7/1**[2]

6-34 **3** *6* **Mark Equal**[173] [489] 9-11-3 **114** .... (t) TScudamore 120
(M C Pipe) *hld up: hdwy 7th: styd on same pce fr last* **20/1**

3/4 **4** *3* **Dantes Reef (IRE)**[15] [1931] 9-11-12 **123** .... APMcCoy 126
(A J Martin, Ire) *w'like: hld up: sme hdwy appr 2 out: n.d* **14/1**

2P0- **5** *1 ¼* **The Villager (IRE)**[241] [4410] 9-11-6 **117** .... SThomas 119
(T R George) *chsd ldrs: mstke 6th: wknd appr last* **16/1**

4-12 **6** *½* **Cosmocrat**[22] [1831] 7-11-4 **115** .... TDoyle 116
(R Lee) *hld up: hdwy and mstke 9th: wknd last* **25/1**

1P-2 **7** *6* **Meggie's Beau (IRE)**[16] [1907] 9-10-3 **105** .... LStephens[(5)] 102+
(Miss Venetia Williams) *hld up: hdwy after 3 out: wknd last* **16/1**

5-2P **8** *3 ½* **Moorlands Again**[22] [1830] 10-11-1 **112** .... (t) MBradburne 104
(M Sheppard) *prom to 9th* **50/1**

51-0 **9** *1 ¼* **Cetti's Warbler**[16] [1907] 7-10-11 **108** .... (t) JAMcCarthy 99
(Mrs P Robeson) *lw:chsd ldrs: rdn 7th: wknd 9th* **33/1**

-003 **10** *hd* **Prince Of Pleasure (IRE)**[41] [1627] 11-11-3 **119** .... RJMolloy[(5)] 109
(D Broad, Ire) *lw: chsd ldr: led 4th: hdd 6th: wknd 2 out* **40/1**

160- **11** *4* **Christopher**[241] [4410] 8-11-12 **123** .... PJBrennan 109
(P J Hobbs) *prom: chsd wnr 8th: wknd after 2 out* **12/1**

6/5- **12** *28* **Charging (IRE)**[24] [1812] 9-10-8 **105** .... PCarberry 63
(John Joseph Murphy, Ire) *w'like: hld up: mstkes: a in rr* **11/1**

4U3- **13** *11* **Acertack (IRE)**[209] [4915] 8-9-11 **101** oh1 ow4 .... BCByrnes[(7)] 48
(R Rowe) *hld up: effrt appr 4 out: sn wknd* **50/1**

/P-P **P** **All Sonsilver (FR)**[16] [1907] 8-10-8 **105** .... (tp) VSlattery —
(P Kelsall) *a in rr: t.o whn p.u bef 9th* **100/1**

0/ **P** **Newratking (IRE)**[24] [1812] 9-10-0 **97** .... (tp) AO'Keeffe —
(C Byrnes, Ire) *lengthy: a in rr: t.o whn p.u bef 9th* **14/1**

61-5 **P** **Gazump (FR)**[53] [1513] 7-11-9 **120** .... CLlewellyn —
(N A Twiston-Davies) *led to 4th: mstke and wknd 8th: t.o whn p.u bef 2 out* **9/1**[3]

5m 6.50s (-3.60) **Going Correction** +0.175s/f (Yiel) **16** Ran SP% **124.6**
Speed ratings: **113,109,107,106,106 105,103,102,101,101 100,89,85,—,—** — CSF £11.67 CT £148.37 TOTE £2.50: £1.20, £2.00, £4.10, £3.10; EX 16.20 Trifecta £166.20 Pool: £1,264.40 - 5.40 winning units.
Owner D A Johnson **Bred** W E McCluskey **Trained** Nicholashayne, Devon
■ Stewards' Enquiry : R J Molloy one-day ban: anticipating start (Nov 24)

FOCUS
The three fences in the home straight (four in total) were omitted due to the low sun, making this less of a test of jumping than it should have been. The result was never in doubt as Bannow Strand took the race to pieces and is value for 25 lengths with the placed horses running to their marks.

NOTEBOOK
Bannow Strand(IRE) ♦ made a mockery of his handicap mark of 103 on this chase debut. To be fair to the Handicapper he could hardly have given him a higher rating based on his efforts over hurdles, but this is a horse that has always been waiting for fences. A huge tank of a horse, he treated these obstacles with more respect than he did hurdles, and won embarrassingly easily. His rider could do little to conceal the ease of the win and the Handicapper is sure to take his revenge, but he will still look well handicapped off a probable revised rating in the mid-120s. *(op 13-8 tchd 7-4 and 5-4 in places)*
Shalako(USA) ran on well on the flat after jumping the last some way out, and won the separate race for second well enough. The absence of four of the fences that would normally have been jumped helped him out as he is a better hurdler than he is a chaser. *(tchd 15-2)*
Mark Equal, stablemate of the winner, is a fairly consistent sort although hard to win with. He ran a decent race again despite being 3lb above his last winning mark. *(op 16-1)*
Dantes Reef(IRE) did not run at all badly under top weight, although he does not appear to have anything in hand of the Handicapper at present. *(op 12-1)*
The Villager(IRE), having his first start since finishing in midfield in the Mildmay of Flete at the Festival in March, has changed stables in the interim. He is not badly handicapped on his best form and is entitled to come on for this run. *(op 18-1 tchd 20-1)*
Cosmocrat did not run badly off a mark which looks high enough for what he has achieved. *(tchd 33-1)*

2211 FESTIVAL OF FOOD BUMPER (A STANDARD OPEN NATIONAL HUNT FLAT RACE) (LISTED RACE) 2m 110y
3:50 (3:53) (Class 1) 4-6-Y-0

£9,793 (£3,673; £1,839; £917; £460; £230)

Form RPR

1 **1** **Leading Contender (IRE)**[36] [1681] 4-11-4 .... RJohnson 123+
(P J Hobbs) *hld up rr: stdy hdwy fr 7f out: chsd wnr ins fnl 2f: hrd drvn to ld ins last: all out* **15/8**[1]

11 **2** *1 ¼* **Tokala**[18] [1882] 4-11-0 .... CMStudd[(7)] 125+
(B G Powell) *lw: led: rdn and kpt on gamely fr 2f out: hdd and nt qckn ins last* **20/1**

3 *4* **Midnight Gift (IRE)**[13] [1967] 5-10-11 .... MrAFitzgerald 111
(T Hogan, Ire) *w'like: chsd ldrs: rdn fr 3f out: styd on fnl 2f but nvr gng pce to chal* **50/1**

4 *¾* **Go Silver Bullet (FR)**[62] [1470] 4-11-4 .... DJCasey 117
(C F Swan, Ire) *str: scope: chsd ldrs: wnt 2nd 7f out: rdn over 3f out: lost 2nd ins fnl 2f: wknd fnl f* **11/1**

5 *7* **Molostiep (FR)**[210] 5-11-0 .... WMarston 107+
(Mrs Susan Nock) *lw: rangy: str: scope: mid-div: hdwy 1/2-way: rdn over 3f out:styd on u.p fnl 2f but nvr gng pce of ldrs* **100/1**

1 **6** *1 ¼* **Briscoe Place (IRE)**[51] [1543] 5-11-4 .... APMcCoy 109
(Jonjo O'Neill) *sn in tch: hdwy 7f out: chsd ldrs and rdn 3f out: wknd over 2f out* **13/2**[3]

6- **7** *2* **Kaldouas (FR)**[225] [4697] 4-11-0 .... PJBrennan 103
(P F Nicholls) *bhd: hdwy 7f out: rdn and effrt over 3f out: nvr nr ldrs and wknd over 2f out* **6/1**[2]

6-1 **8** *1 ½* **Slick (FR)**[189] [249] 4-11-4 .... ATinkler 105
(N J Henderson) *hld up in rr: rdn and sme hdwy over 3f out: sn no imp* **12/1**

61-1 **9** *nk* **Malt De Vergy (FR)**[178] [424] 5-11-4 .... GBerridge[(3)] 108
(L Lungo) *mid-div: rdn to chse ldrs 4f out: wknd qckly 2f out* **33/1**

46- **10** *1 ¼* **Reach For The Top (IRE)**[232] [4559] 4-11-0 .... CLlewellyn 100
(Miss H C Knight) *stdd rr: kpt on fnl 2f: nvr a danger* **50/1**

2 **11** *3 ½* **Rothbury**[21] [1849] 5-10-11 .... MichalKohl[(3)] 96
(J I A Charlton) *bhd: sme hdwy fnl 3f* **28/1**

0 **12** *4* **Limestream (IRE)**[199] [93] 5-10-7 .... PACarberry 85
(John G Carr, Ire) *cmpt: str: chsd ldrs: rdn 6f out: wknd fr 3f out* **25/1**

13 *nk* **Go Commercial (IRE)** 4-11-0 .... TJMurphy 94+
(M C Pipe) *b.bkwd: hld up in rr: sme hdwy 1/2-way: wknd 4f out* **13/2**[3]

21 **14** *10* **Asudo (IRE)**[11] [1985] 4-10-11 .... SCrawford[(7)] 86
(N A Twiston-Davies) *chsd ldr: rdn 1/2-way: wknd 6f out* **20/1**

1 **15** *5* **Star Shot (IRE)**[164] [616] 4-11-4 .... TDoyle 81
(P R Webber) *bhd most of way* **16/1**

60-0 **16** *8* **Bamby (IRE)**[13] [1961] 5-10-7 .... JMogford 62
(D J Wintle) *a in rr* **100/1**

17 *¾* **Crossing**[9] [2035] 4-10-7 .... JPSullivan[(7)] 68
(William J Fitzpatrick, Ire) *neat: chsd ldrs tl rdn and wknd 6f out* **66/1**

0 **18** *1 ¼* **Butsadtohavetogo (IRE)**[18] [1882] 5-11-0 .... MFoley 67
(A E Jones) *chsd ldrs to 1/2-way* **100/1**

2-1 **19** *25* **Mars Rock (FR)**[13] [1954] 5-11-4 .... SThomas 46
(Miss Venetia Williams) *chsd ldrs to 1/2-way* **33/1**

3m 56.2s (-1.00) **Going Correction** +0.175s/f (Yiel) **19** Ran SP% **128.7**
Speed ratings: **109,108,106,106,102 102,101,100,100,99 98,96,96,91,89 85,85,84,72** CSF £49.26 TOTE £3.00: £1.50, £5.50, £11.50; EX 41.90 TRIFECTA Not won. Place 6 £449.74, Place 5 £159.75.
Owner Mrs Joanna Peppiatt **Bred** Noel Walsh **Trained** Withycombe, Somerset

FOCUS
Unusually for a race of this type the pace was decent and provided a proper test. The form looks good and should work out.

NOTEBOOK
Leading Contender(IRE) had had the form of his debut success boosted by the subsequent victory of Asudo, who finished nine lengths behind him that day (and re-opposed here) and he was a well-supported favourite. He wore down the eventual runner-up on the uphill run to the line, showing himself well suited to this stiff finish, and he has been pencilled in for a return visit in March for the Champion Bumper, following an outing at Chepstow over Christmas. *(op 2-1 tchd 9-4 and 7-4 in places)*
Tokala, a narrow victor here last month, ran well in defeat as he had to give 3lb to the winner. Making most of the running, he coped well with the easier ground and is clearly improving with racing. *(op 16-1)*
Midnight Gift(IRE), an Irish raider, stepped up on her recent effort at Galway and had every chance. She was staying on well at the finish and might prefer slower ground than this.
Go Silver Bullet(FR), another from across the Irish Sea, had won easily on his previous start at Roscommon, but found the competition tougher in this company. *(tchd 12-1 and 10-1 in places)*

Molostiep(FR) ◆, one of only two in the line-up who had not previously had a start under Rules, ran with considerable promise. A maiden point-to-point winner and half-brother to several winners in France, he might find a bumper at a lesser track before being sent over obstacles. *(op 66-1)*
Briscoe Place(IRE) was travelling well and looked a danger to all running down the hill, but he did not find as much as his main rivals on the uphill run from the turn into the straight. He might be seen to better effect on quicker ground and/or a sharper track. *(op 7-1 tchd 6-1)*
Kaldouas(FR) lacked the pace to get seriously involved. Representing a stable which is not at the top of its game at present, he shapes as though he will be suited by further when sent over hurdles. *(op 8-1 tchd 9-1 in places)*
Slick(FR), who won a minor event at Worcester in May, had a lot more to do in this company and found it just a bit too hot.
Malt De Vergy(FR) looked to have plenty on his plate under his big penalty following two easy wins in modest contests in the north. He had every chance running down the hill, but was seen off from the turn in.
Go Commercial(IRE), a brother to Irish bumper winner and useful two-mile hurdler Master Albert, did not attract the market support which other Pipe-trained horses had come in for over the course of the three-day meeting, and that lack of confidence on this racecourse debut was justified. He never really got close enough to throw down a challenge, but he should benefit from the experience and do better in time. *(op 11-2)*
T/Jkpt: Not won. T/Plt: £491.10 to a £1 stake. Pool: £139,279.70. 207.00 winning tickets. T/Qpdt: £35.50 to a £1 stake. Pool: £10,816.10. 225.20 winning tickets. ST

2015 FONTWELL (L-H)
Sunday, November 13

OFFICIAL GOING: Good to soft (good in places)
Wind: Fresh against

2212 STROKE ASSOCIATION MAIDEN HURDLE (9 hdls 1 omitted) 2m 4f
12:40 (12:40) (Class 4) 4-Y-O+ **£3,545** (£1,040; £520; £259)

Form / RPR

1 **Kipsigis (IRE)**[41] 4-11-2 ... AThornton 106+
(Lady Herries) *mid-div: gd hdwy to go 2nd after 2 out: styd on to ld sn after last: kpt on* **25/1**

24- 2 3 ½ **Hibernian (IRE)**[207] [4935] 5-11-2 ... LAspell 102+
(O Sherwood) *trckd ldrs: led appr 2 out: rdn and hdd sn after last: kpt on one pce* **5/1**[2]

64-0 3 12 **Jades Double**[27] [1772] 4-10-2 ... RLucey-Butler(7) 83
(M Madgwick) *bhd tl styd on fr 2 out: nvr nrr* **66/1**

2- 4 nk **Rotheram (USA)**[327] [2927] 5-11-2 ... DCrosse 90
(C J Mann) *trckd ldrs: rdn appr 2 out: one pce after* **7/1**[3]

2P-4 5 6 **Ballyhoo (IRE)**[43] [1600] 5-10-2 ... WPKavanagh(7) 77
(J W Mullins) *bhd: mde som hdwy fr 2 out: nvr nr to chal* **66/1**

3- 6 ½ **Mooresini (IRE)**[272] [3857] 5-11-2 ... PHide 83
(N J Gifford) *nvr bttr than mid-div* **8/1**

43/2 7 12 **French Envoy (FR)**[26] [1782] 6-11-2 ... JimCrowley 71
(Ian Williams) *trckd ldrs: rdn appr 2 out: sn wknd* **13/8**[1]

543- 8 10 **Mistress Nell**[229] [4644] 5-10-4 ... WKennedy(5) 54
(A J Lidderdale) *trckd ldrs: racd wd: rdn and wknd 2 out* **33/1**

643- 9 3 **Lunch Was My Idea (IRE)**[206] [4941] 5-11-2 ... ChristianWilliams 58
(P F Nicholls) *trckd ldrs to 7th: rdn and sn wknd* **11/1**

4 10 18 **Chocolate Boy (IRE)**[19] [1875] 6-11-2 ... JEMoore 40
(G L Moore) *mid-div: effrt after 7th: wknd after 2 out* **12/1**

P- 11 17 **Cambo (FR)**[188] [2032] 4-10-9 ... MGoldstein(7) 23
(Miss Sheena West) *trckd ldr: led sn after 6th: rdn and hdd appr 2 out: wknd qckly* **66/1**

00 12 22 **Cornish Jack**[12] [1968] 5-10-11 ... CHonour(5) —
(J D Frost) *mid-div tl wknd after 7th* **100/1**

/0P- 13 12 **Mother Says**[286] [3628] 9-11-2 ... MBatchelor —
(B W Duke) *led tl after 6th: rdn and wknd qckly* **66/1**

P **Malibu (IRE)**[180] 4-11-2 ... JTizzard —
(S Dow) *a bhd: t.o whn p.u bef last* **40/1**

0 P **Penny Strong**[28] [1755] 5-10-9 ... JamesDavies —
(A J Whiting) *a in rr: t.o whn p.u after 6th* **100/1**

3-3 P **Different Class (IRE)**[12] [1979] 6-11-2 ... BFenton —
(Jonjo O'Neill) *hld up in rr: rdn 6th and sn lost tch: p.u after next* **11/1**

4m 56.3s (-8.60) **Going Correction** +0.25s/f (Yiel)
WFA 4 from 5yo+ 13lb **16** Ran SP% **119.9**
Speed ratings: **103,101,96,96,94 94,89,85,84,76 70,61,56,—,— —** CSF £143.01 TOTE £38.30: £9.00, £2.60, £12.20; EX 498.50.
Owner Lady Sarah Clutton **Bred** Angmering Park Stud **Trained** Patching, W Sussex

FOCUS
A modest novice hurdle, run at a sound enough pace, and the first two came clear. The form should be treated with a little caution, as the favourite failed to run his race. Last flight bypassed.

NOTEBOOK
Kipsigis(IRE), a modest maiden on the Flat, got his hurdling career off to a perfect start and did the job in good style. He jumped neatly for a debutant, looked suited by the soft ground and got the trip without fuss. On this evidence, he looks like proving better over timber than he was on the level, and it will be interesting to see how he fares under a penalty next time. *(op 33-1)*
Hibernian(IRE), who shaped with promise in two bumpers last term, ran a solid race in defeat on this hurdle debut and was only outpaced by the Flat-bred winner on the run-in. He is entitled to improve for the outing, finished clear of the rest and is clearly up to winning a similar race. His future lies over fences, however. *(op 7-2)*
Jades Double, who showed little on her seasonal and hurdling debut last time, saw out the longer trip well and posted her best effort to date. She looked better the further she went and, considering her dam is half-sister to 1995 Gold Cup winner Master Oats, it is possible this late-maturing filly could be an improver over this sort of trip. However, her proximity at the finish still holds down this form.
Rotheram(USA), last seen finishing second over further on this hurdling debut at this track 327 days previously, just lacked the pace to stay with the principals from two out and shaped as though the race was needed. He still did more than enough to suggest he ought to win as a novice over hurdles and should be seen to better effect when reverting to a stiffer test in the future. *(op 8-1)*
Ballyhoo(IRE), fourth in a moderate bumper at the track last time, took time to get going and was always staying on too late. She can build on this, however, and may be better off against her own sex in the future.
French Envoy(FR) disappointingly dropped out when push came to shove and failed to see out the longer trip. Considering his debut conqueror, Boychuk, subsequently won in graded company at Cheltenham, this has to be considered a missed opportunity. However, he may have bounced this time and is not one to write off just yet.
Lunch Was My Idea(IRE), who ran respectably without winning in four bumpers last season, including when third at this track, failed to make an impression on this hurdling bow and looks slow. *(op 10-1)*

2213 BETFREDCASINO BEGINNERS' CHASE (13 fncs) 2m 2f
1:15 (1:15) (Class 4) 4-Y-O+ **£4,814** (£1,413; £706; £352)

Form / RPR

000- 1 **Royal Hector (GER)**[242] [4397] 6-11-5 ... BFenton 120+
(Jonjo O'Neill) *hld up in tch: trckd ldrs 4 out: led 2 out: r.o wl* **5/1**[3]

2 5 **Ballez (FR)**[235] 4-10-7 ... ChristianWilliams 101+
(P F Nicholls) *a.p: wnt 4 out: chal and led next: j. bdly rt and hdd 2 out: one pce after* **2/1**[1]

351- 3 3 ½ **Carthys Cross (IRE)**[224] [4721] 6-11-5 ... AThornton 109+
(T R George) *trckd ldr: led 4 out to 3 out: ev ch next: one pce after* **9/1**

0044 4 1 ¾ **Keepthedreamalive**[19] [1872] 7-11-5 ... BHitchcott 109+
(R H Buckler) *led tl blnd and hdd 4 out: styd on fr 2 out but n.d after* **9/4**[2]

22-3 5 ¾ **Alrafid (IRE)**[132] [450] 6-11-5 ... PHide 109+
(G L Moore) *hld up in tch: hmpd 7th: cl up whn hmpd 2 out: swtchd lft appr last: one pce after* **10/1**

52-0 6 14 **Jonanaud**[36] [1675] 6-10-12 117 ... MrJAJenkins(7) 92
(H J Manners) *hld up: brief effrt after 4 out: sn btn* **33/1**

0343 7 dist **Ingres**[7] [2072] 5-11-5 103 ... JPMcNamara —
(B G Powell) *in rr: wl bhd fr 7th: t.o* **16/1**

F **Sett Aside**[211] 7-11-5 ... LAspell —
(Mrs L C Jewell) *trckd ldrs tl fell 7th* **66/1**

50 P **Honor And Glory**[12] [1971] 5-11-5 ... JTizzard —
(Nick Williams) *in tch to 6th: blnd bdly 8th: p.u bef next* **40/1**

4m 42.3s (7.20) **Going Correction** +0.45s/f (Soft)
WFA 4 from 5yo+ 12lb **9** Ran SP% **112.6**
Speed ratings: **102,99,98,97,97 90,—,—,—** CSF £15.58 TOTE £5.50: £1.70, £1.40, £2.50; EX 19.70.
Owner Three Counties Racing 2 **Bred** Gestut Katharinenhof **Trained** Cheltenham, Gloucs
■ Stewards' Enquiry : Christian Williams three-day ban: used whip with excessive force (Nov 24-26)

FOCUS
A decent novice chase for the track. The winner is value for a bit further with the third to his hurdles form. The pace was fair and it should throw up future winners in this sphere.

NOTEBOOK
Royal Hector(GER), who enjoyed a purple patch in handicap hurdles at this time last year after joining Martin Pipe, lost his way towards the latter part of last season, when the Handicapper had his measure, and had subsequently joined Jonjo O'Neill at the start of this month. Having been given time to find his feet early on, he responded positively when asked to join the leaders, and ultimately ran out a ready winner on this chase debut. He is entitled to improve for this experience, is the type to hold his form well, and could well be set for a decent season in this sphere. *(tchd 11-2)*
Ballez(FR), who had managed just the one win from nine outings over hurdles in France previously, proved easy in the betting prior to this chase debut, despite being well-touted by his new connections and having the benefit of his four-year-old weight allowance. He failed to give his rider much help during the race, running lazily and not convincing over his fences, and was ultimately well held by the winner. While he should find a race or two this season, and time may tell there was no disgrace in this defeat, he does not appear to be one of his yard's leading lights. *(op 6-4 tchd 9-4 in a place)*
Carthys Cross(IRE) ◆, winner of a bumper and a novice hurdle previously, had every chance approaching the penultimate fence yet was ulitmately found out up the rising finish. He has always appealed as the type to improve as a chaser, still has few miles on the clock and may also prefer less-testing ground in the future. *(op 10-1)*
Keepthedreamalive, fourth in a competitive handicap hurdle at Cheltenham last time and well backed for this chase debut, shaped well until losing his chance with a serious error four out. He was staying on again up straight, and should be all the wiser for this experience, so is worth another chance to atone. *(op 7-2)*
Alrafid(IRE), rated 117 over timber and making his chase debut after a 132-day break, ran better than his finishing position suggests and would have been closer but for being slightly hampered at the penultimate fence. This has to rate a promising effort, especially given that all his best previous form is on much faster ground, and he clearly has a future over fences. *(op 8-1 tchd 15-2)*
Jonanaud, another to be having his first run over fences, jumped well enough and will find easier opportunities in the future.

2214 HARDINGS BAR & CATERING SERVICES NOVICES' H'CAP HURDLE (11 hdls) 2m 6f 110y
1:45 (1:45) (Class 4) (0-95,92) 4-Y-O+ **£3,428** (£1,006; £503; £251)

Form / RPR

P-06 1 **English Jim (IRE)**[13] [1950] 4-10-8 **74** ... MBatchelor 77
(Miss A M Newton-Smith) *hdwy 4th: 2nd 3 out: rdn to ld appr last: styd on u.p run-in* **50/1**

006/ 2 2 **Justino**[588] [4676] 7-11-2 **82** ... BHitchcott 83
(J A Geake) *led 4th: often j.rt: hdd appr last: rallied gamely run-in: no ex fnl 50yds* **4/1**[2]

4116 3 4 **Waynesworld (IRE)**[32] [1713] 7-10-11 **87** ... JKington(10) 84
(M Scudamore) *bhd tl styd on fr 3 out: nvr nrr* **3/1**[1]

0-22 4 8 **Coustou (IRE)**[13] [1949] 5-11-10 **90** ... (p) SStronge 83+
(R M Stronge) *mid-div: hdwy after 7th: cloe 3rd 3 out: wknd after 2 out* **4/1**[2]

4146 5 29 **Coppermalt (USA)**[24] [1803] 7-10-12 **78** ... DCrosse 38
(R Curtis) *bhd: rdn after 6th: sme hdwy 8th: wknd after 3 out* **9/1**

FP-0 6 2 **Elle Roseador**[15] [1916] 6-10-10 **76** ... LAspell 34
(M Madgwick) *hld up in tch: chsd ldrs 3 out: wknd sn after next* **20/1**

P060 7 hd **Mr Dip**[13] [1949] 5-10-12 **81** ... CBolger(3) 39
(L A Dace) *a bhd* **25/1**

U320 8 29 **Great Compton**[12] [1977] 5-10-12 **78** ... ChristianWilliams 7
(B J Llewellyn) *in tch to 7th: sn t.o* **5/1**[3]

-45P P **Rutland (IRE)**[171] [518] 6-10-12 **85** ... TMessenger(7) —
(C J Drewe) *trckd ldrs: in tch whn p.u appr 8th* **50/1**

P4PP U **Peppershot**[8] [2043] 5-11-5 **92** ... (bt[1]) RLucey-Butler(7) —
(R Gurney) *led tl after 1st: cloe up whn mstke and uns rdr 3rd* **25/1**

P6/0 P **Eastwood Drifter (USA)**[7] [2071] 8-10-5 **76** ... RStephens(5) —
(Miss L Day) *trckd ldrs to 7th: sn wknd: t.o whn p.u bef last* **33/1**

P0-5 P **Cloneybrien Boy (IRE)**[26] [1779] 5-10-0 **73** oh2 ow7 MrsLucyRowsell(7) —
(Mrs A M Thorpe) *led after 1st: continually j.rt: hdd 4th: rdn and wknd appr 3 out: t.o whn p.u bef last* **20/1**

5m 48.1s (3.30) **Going Correction** +0.25s/f (Yiel)
WFA 4 from 5yo+ 13lb **12** Ran SP% **115.7**
Speed ratings: **104,103,101,99,89 88,88,78,—,— —,—** CSF £226.75 CT £806.77 TOTE £27.20: £6.80, £2.00, £1.90; EX 297.80.
Owner Peter Hempenstall **Bred** John J M Power **Trained** Jevington, E Sussex

FOCUS
A moderate novices' handicap, run at a sound gallop, and the field finished well strung out. The two handicap debutants duly fought out the finish, with the runner-up the best guide to the level.

NOTEBOOK

English Jim(IRE), who had shown just weak form in bumpers and three novice hurdles previously, dug deep to lead over the last flight and fought off the runner-up on the run-in to score on his handicap debut. This was a vast improvement, but he has clearly begun handicap life on a decent mark, and appreciated every yard of the longer trip. While his next outing should reveal more, he is bred to make his mark over jumps, and has plenty of time on his side.

Justino ◆, very well backed to maintain his stable'e excellent run of recent form, appeared the most likely winner approaching the climb for home, yet found his lack of fitness an issue from two out and was always being held by the winner on the run-in. This must rate a pleasing effort after his 558-day layoff, he showed a decent attitude under pressure and, like the winner, has clearly begun handicap life on a decent mark. *(op 9-2)*

Waynesworld(IRE), a dual handicap winner over fences in October, stayed on too late in the day after racing lazily until the home turn. He is now rated 9lb higher over fences and should get closer in this sphere under a more prominent ride at this trip. *(op 11-4 tchd 4-1)*

Coustou(IRE) had still to be asked for maximum effort turning for home, but he found the rising finish against him and was woefully one paced from the penultimate flight. He is a frustrating sort, but is capable of getting closer when reverting to a sharper track in the future. *(op 7-2)*

Great Compton turned in another tame effort and never figured. *(op 9-2 tchd 11-2)*

Rutland(IRE) *Official explanation: jockey said gelding lost its action*

2215 BETFREDPOKER H'CAP CHASE (21 fncs) 3m 4f
2:20 (2:20) (Class 3) (0-125,123) 5-Y-0+ **£10,006** (£2,937; £1,468; £733)

Form				RPR
P3-U	1		**All In The Stars (IRE)**[8] [2054] 7-11-4 **122** DJacob(7) (D P Keane) *hld up in rr: hdwy fr 13th to trck ldrs 15th: chal appr 3 out: led bef next: styd on strly* **8/1**[3]	139+
15P-	2	8	**Classic Native (IRE)**[241] [4411] 7-11-8 **119** BFenton (Jonjo O'Neill) *in tch: hit 10th: hdwy 13th: ev ch fr 4 out tl rdn and one pce fr 2 out* **11/4**[1]	130+
14-0	3	6	**Hazeljack**[19] [1874] 10-10-0 **97** JamesDavies (A J Whiting) *j.w: led 4th and mde most tl rdn and hdd appr 2 out: wknd bef last* **25/1**	100
60-1	4	nk	**Brave Spirit (FR)**[9] [2015] 7-11-12 **123** (p) JTizzard (C L Tizzard) *in cl tch tl outpcd 15th: styd on fr 3 out* **11/4**[1]	126
P033	5	10	**He's The Biz (FR)**[21] [1858] 6-10-2 **99** ChristianWilliams (Nick Williams) *hld up: hdwy 10th: rdn after 16th: one pce after* **8/1**[3]	95+
4P-0	6	18	**Auburn Spirit**[21] [1861] 10-11-1 **112** JEMoore (M D I Usher) *a in tch: ev ch 4 out but rdn and sn wknd* **16/1**	87
6P64	7	dist	**Twisted Logic (IRE)**[12] [1972] 12-11-3 **114** RWalford (R H Alner) *a bhd: lost tch 1/2-way: t.o* **14/1**	—
22-P	P		**Monks Error (IRE)**[7] [2073] 12-10-1 **98** OMcPhail (B J Llewellyn) *mid-div tl dropped rr and p.u after 15th* **25/1**	—
1C5F	P		**Charango Star**[17] [1893] 7-10-6 **108** PMerrigan(5) (W K Goldsworthy) *bhd after blnd 10th: t.o whn p.u after 4 out* **6/1**[2]	—
22-2	F		**Galapiat Du Mesnil (FR)**[23] [1815] 11-10-2 **106** RLucey-Butler(7) (R Gurney) *prom tl wknd appr 5th: t.o whn fell 2 out* **20/1**	—
126/	P		**Mr Cospector**[596] [4572] 8-11-9 **120** AThornton (D L Williams) *led to 4th: wkng whn hit 15th: p.u bef next: dismntd* **20/1**	—

7m 30.3s (-2.50) **Going Correction** +0.45s/f (Soft) 11 Ran SP% **119.6**
Speed ratings: **105,102,101,100,98 92,—,—,—,—** — CSF £30.33 CT £533.34 TOTE £9.70: £2.50, £1.70, £4.90; EX 46.20.
Owner Mrs H R Cross **Bred** Denis Paul Cremin **Trained** North End, Dorset

FOCUS

A fair handicap with decent prizemoney, which proved a real test of stamina, and the field came home strung out. The form looks sound with the first two close to form and those immediately behind close to their marks.

NOTEBOOK

All In The Stars(IRE) ◆, who unseated when hampered on his recent comeback at Wincanton, resumed winning ways under a well-judged ride and is full value for his winning margin. His jumping was sound, he saw out the trip really well and had no trouble with this softer ground. Considering he boasted some decent form last season before injury struck, he can be expected to keep progressing - providing the Handicapper is none too harsh - and could make up into a National horse in the future. *(op 11-2)*

Classic Native(IRE), who won on his handicap and seasonal bow last year, had been the subject of decent support for the National Hunt Chase when last seen 241 days previously and was again well backed ahead of this comeback. He jumped fluently in the main, and had every chance, but just failed to see out the trip as well as the winner. While he is capable of winning from this mark, and is probably happier on a less-testing surface, the suspicion is that he may be best caught fresh. *(op 3-1 tchd 10-3)*

Hazeljack, who crept in at the bottom of the handicap, showed the benefit of his recent comeback at Cheltenham and turned in a decent effort on ground that clearly suits. However, he may have benefited from a more patient ride as this trip clearly stretches his stamina, plus a likely weight rise will make life even tougher for him now.

Brave Spirit(FR), previously unbeaten on this track, turned in his usual game effort on this return to chasing yet was unable to raise his game under top weight. He has to prove the Handicapper has not got his measure in this sphere, but he may have found this coming too soon after his recent hurdling success at this venue, and should not be written off. *(op 9-4)*

Mr Cospector *Official explanation: jockey said gelding was lame (op 16-1)*

Charango Star, who fell at Stratford on his handicap bow last time, looked positively mulish throughout the first half of the contest and not surprisingly his rider finally threw in the towel before four out. He has it all to prove now. *Official explanation: jockey said gelding never travelled (op 16-1)*

2216 BETFRED 540 SHOPS NATIONWIDE CLAIMING HURDLE (9 hdls) 2m 2f 110y
2:55 (2:55) (Class 4) 4-Y-0+ **£2,535** (£738; £369)

Form				RPR
0224	1		**Critical Stage (IRE)**[24] [1804] 6-11-3 109 CHonour(5) (J D Frost) *in tch: wnt 2nd 5th: led 3 out: rdn clr: hit last: fin tired* **9/4**[1]	110+
-066	2	5	**Shaman**[154] [726] 8-11-0 99 JEMoore (G L Moore) *hld up: hdwy 5th: cl 3rd 3 out: styd on same pce* **7/1**	94
04P5	3	1/2	**Oulton Broad**[10] [2008] 9-10-10 103 (p) LAspell (F Jordan) *in rr tl styd on after 3 out: nvr nrr* **6/1**	89
20-P	4	11	**Scarlet Mix (FR)**[14] [1784] 4-10-10 101 (b1) JPMcNamara (B G Powell) *trckd ldr: led 4th: hdd 3 out: wknd qckly* **5/1**[3]	83+
424P	5	5	**Kristoffersen**[13] [1952] 5-11-2 109 HOliver (Ian Williams) *in tch: trckd ldrs 4th: wknd after 6th* **7/2**[2]	79
0F-P	6	6	**Paddy Boy (IRE)**[13] [1952] 4-10-8 PHide (J R Boyle) *prom tl wknd 6th* **50/1**	65
3P-U	7	10	**Royale Acadou (FR)**[13] [1953] 7-10-8 102 CBolger(3) (Mrs L J Mongan) *prom to 5th: sn bhd* **16/1**	58
005-	P		**Purr**[253] [4173] 4-10-3 77 MrSRees(7) (M Wigham) *bhd: lost tch 4th: t.o whn p.u after 5th* **50/1**	—
2	P		**Somewhere My Love**[13] [1952] 4-9-8 RLucey-Butler(7) (P Butler) *a bhd: lost tch 4th: t.o whn p.u after 3 out* **20/1**	—
0	P		**Harbour House**[15] [1916] 6-10-12 RGreene (J J Bridger) *led to 4th: dropped out qckly: t.o whn p.u bef 6th* **66/1**	—
0	P		**Hunting Lodge (IRE)**[16] [1908] 4-11-5 MrJAJenkins(7) (H J Manners) *bhd tl hdwy 4th: wknd appr 3 out: t.o whn p.u bef last* **50/1**	—

4m 40.1s (4.10) **Going Correction** +0.25s/f (Yiel) 11 Ran SP% **114.5**
Speed ratings: **101,98,98,94,91 89,85,—,—,—** — CSF £17.46 TOTE £2.70: £1.50, £1.70, £2.50; EX 16.90.
Owner Le Rochjobi Partnership **Bred** Park Place International Ltd **Trained** Scorriton, Devon

FOCUS

A basically weak event that saw the field finish strung out behind the easy winner, who is rated value for further.

NOTEBOOK

Critical Stage(IRE), having his first run at this lowly level, relished the drop in grade and ultimately ran out an easy winner. He had the race in the bag prior to a tired error at the final flight and, while he was entitled to win according to official figures, this should have boosted his confidence for an impending return to handicaps. *(op 5-2 tchd 2-1)*

Shaman, dropping back in class and returning from a 154-day break, posted a fair effort in defeat and should strip fitter for the outing. This is clearly now his level. *(op 6-1)*

Oulton Broad would have been closer with a more prominent ride and was doing his best work at the finish over this slighlty longer trip. That said, he continues to run well below his current official rating, and is very hard to predict these days. *Official explanation: jockey said gelding was never travelling (op 5-1)*

Scarlet Mix(FR), equipped with first-time blinkers on this return to hurdling, dropped out tamely when push came to shove and again disappointed. He is one to avoid. *(op 11-2)*

Kristoffersen, with the cheekpieces left off, turned in another moody effort and appears to have lost the plot. *Official explanation: jockey said gelding had been lame (op 4-1 tchd 9-2)*

Purr *Official explanation: jockey said gelding was unsuited by the good to soft ground*

2217 HARBENS EQUINE CARE CENTRE H'CAP CHASE (13 fncs) 2m 2f
3:30 (3:30) (Class 4) (0-100,100) 5-Y-0+ **£3,389** (£995; £497; £248)

Form				RPR
102-	1		**Julies Boy (IRE)**[244] [4361] 8-9-8 **78** (t) WMcCarthy(10) (T R George) *trckd ldr tl lft in ld 3rd: mde rest: r.o on strly to go clr run-in* **5/1**[3]	99+
26-1	2	6	**Mystical Star (FR)**[27] [1776] 8-10-11 **85** LAspell (M J Hogan) *hld up: hdwy 7th: wnt 2nd appr 4 out: ev ch tl rdn and nt pce of wnr run-in* **11/4**[1]	101+
23P3	3	20	**Wild Power (GER)**[13] [1956] 7-11-4 **95** (p) ONelmes(3) (Mrs H R J Nelmes) *prom tl rdn and wknd 3 out* **16/1**	90
4221	4	hd	**Romany Dream**[13] [1956] 7-11-1 **99** (b) JStevenson(10) (R Dickin) *trckd wnr 3rd tl appr 4 out: wknd bef next* **8/1**	94
2005	5	13	**Saorsie**[13] [1956] 7-11-7 **95** SCurran (J C Fox) *hld up towards rr: sme hdwy 8th: wknd appr 4 out* **33/1**	80+
5434	6	17	**Just Muckin Around (IRE)**[17] [1894] 9-11-1 **89** BHitchcott (R H Buckler) *chsd ldrs to 7th: j. slowly next: sn wl bhd* **8/1**	54
/23-	F		**Barton Gate**[354] [2419] 7-11-5 **100** (v) DJacob(7) (D P Keane) *led tl fell 3rd* **25/1**	—
2/5-	P		**Glenogue (IRE)**[382] [1853] 7-11-10 **98** JPMcNamara (K C Bailey) *mstkes and bhd: p.u bef 7th* **9/2**[2]	—
-0U5	P		**Walcot Lad (IRE)**[23] [1819] 9-10-9 **86** (p) CBolger(3) (A Ennis) *chsd ldrs to 5th: bhd whn p.u bef 8th* **10/1**	—
-P31	P		**Charliemoore**[17] [1897] 9-11-5 **93** (b) JEMoore (G L Moore) *mid-div tl rdn 9th: wl bhd whn p.u bef 3 out* **7/1**	—
0P-P	R		**Mr Crawford**[11] [1983] 6-9-7 **74** oh10 RLucey-Butler(7) (Nick Williams) *mstke 2nd: a bhd: ref and uns rdr 3 out* **50/1**	—

4m 42.0s (6.90) **Going Correction** +0.45s/f (Soft) 11 Ran SP% **120.0**
Speed ratings: **102,99,90,90,84 77,—,—,—,—** — CSF £20.05 CT £210.23 TOTE £6.00: £2.50, £1.90, £3.30; EX 34.80.
Owner R P Foden **Bred** Patrick Slattery **Trained** Slad, Gloucs

FOCUS

A moderate affair, but the pace was fair, and the form looks sound for the class with the first two coming well clear and the runner-up setting the standard.

NOTEBOOK

Julies Boy(IRE), well backed for this seasonal bow, duly landed the gamble under a positive ride by his inexperienced jockey. He proved game when pressed by the runner-up in the staight, jumped with accuracy, and was well on top at the finish. He will take a hike in the weights for this, but is a likeable performer, and probably has more to offer this season. *(op 7-1)*

Mystical Star(FR) ◆, off the mark over fences at Plumpton last time on this return from a break, confirmed himself an improving chaser with a solid effort in defeat off a 10lb higher mark. He was a long way clear of the rest at the finish, will benefit for a return to further, and should strike again in this grade. *(op 10-3 tchd 7-2)*

Wild Power(GER), with the cheekpieces re-applied, was found wanting when push came to shove, yet still managed to marginally reverse Warwick form with Romany Dream on these better terms. He is more at home on a faster surface, but is never one for win-only betting. *(op 12-1)*

Romany Dream, who deservedly ended her losing run at Warwick 13 days previously, ran well below par and just failed to confirm that form with Wild Power. She ideally needs faster ground, but has a fair amount to prove after this. *(op 11-2)*

Glenogue(IRE) jumped poorly on this return to action and it came as little surprise when his rider elected to call it a day. He has clearly had his problems and is one to avoid until showing signs of renewed enthusiasm. *Official explanation: jockey said mare lost its action (tchd 5-1)*

2218 BETFRED H'CAP HURDLE (9 hdls) 2m 2f 110y
4:00 (4:00) (Class 4) (0-110,112) 4-Y-0+ **£3,463** (£1,016; £508; £253)

Form				RPR
4123	1		**Festive Chimes (IRE)**[11] [1987] 4-11-3 **104** ONelmes(3) (N B King) *a.p: wnt 2nd 3 out: led next: hit last: tired and wandered run-in: hld on* **5/1**	110+
1-P0	2	3/4	**Jayed (IRE)**[145] [806] 7-9-13 **90** PCStringer(7) (M Bradstock) *led: sn clr: hdd and hit 2 out: rallied run-in* **25/1**	93
-F00	3	8	**Wenger (FR)**[15] [1921] 5-10-12 **96** (b) PHide (P Winkworth) *hld up in rr: hdwy 6th: chsd first 2 fr 3 out: one pce* **16/1**	91
55F4	4	4	**True Mariner (FR)**[28] [1749] 5-11-2 **100** LAspell (B I Case) *bhd tl styd on after 6th: nvr nr to chal* **14/1**	91
P-01	5	7	**Come Bye (IRE)**[9] [2017] 9-12-0 **112** (bt) MBatchelor (Miss A M Newton-Smith) *sn trckd ldr: rdn appr 6th and lost 2nd 3 out: wkng whn mstke 2 out* **4/1**[2]	96
0/2-	6	2 1/2	**Shirazi**[499] [864] 7-11-7 **105** BFenton (D R Gandolfo) *chsd ldrs tl hit 6th: sn wknd* **20/1**	87
0-04	7	7	**Honey's Gift**[13] [1957] 6-11-5 **103** JamesDavies (G G Margarson) *hld up: a in rr* **7/2**[1]	78
0-1P	8	dist	**Front Rank (IRE)**[22] [1826] 5-11-7 **105** (bt) JPMcNamara (K C Bailey) *hld up: a bhd: t.o* **9/2**[3]	—
12-P	9	20	**Son Of Greek Myth (USA)**[22] [1826] 4-11-5 **103** (b) JEMoore (G L Moore) *chsd ldrs tl wknd 5th: t.o* **13/2**	—

23P/ P **Carly Bay**[622] 4102 7-10-10 **104** .... JPemberton(10) —
(G P Enright) *a bhd: t.o whn p.u run-in* **33/1**

4m 39.43s (3.43) **Going Correction** +0.25s/f (Yiel)
WFA 4 from 5yo+ 12lb **10** Ran SP% **114.5**
Speed ratings: **102,101,98,96,93 92,89,—,—,—** CSF £115.04 CT £1844.92 TOTE £5.70: £1.90, £5.70, £4.00; EX 120.90 Place 6 £72.40, Place 5 £11.81 .
Owner Nolan Catterwell & W Persse **Bred** Burton Agnes Stud Co Ltd **Trained** Newmarket, Suffolk

FOCUS
A modest handicap, run at a decent pace, and another event on the card which saw the first two pulled clear of their rivals.

NOTEBOOK
Festive Chimes(IRE) did just enough to hold off the renewed challenge of the runner-up and score a deserved success. This proved her effectiveness on easy ground, although she is at best on a quick surface, and she has yet to really run a bad race over hurdles to date.
Jayed(IRE), last seen running poorly on fast ground in June, bravely attempted to make all and ran by far his best race for some time. Having looked set to fold when headed by the winner at the penultimate flight, he responded positively for maximum pressure and was coming right back at that rival on the run-in. He is capable on his day, but hard to predict all the same, and his next outing should reveal more.
Wenger(FR), with the blinkers re-applied, once again travelled smoothly off the pace before making hard work of things when asked for maximum effort. He is somewhat of an enigma and, despite the fact he prefers a quicker surface, looks to be going the wrong way.
True Mariner(FR) turned in his best effort for some time on this return to hurdling and ran better than his finishing position suggests. He was a four-time winner in France over timber prior to joining current connections and is one to note in this sphere when the market speaks in his favour.
Come Bye(IRE) was unable to dictate this time and failed to see out his race as a result. This was not such a bad effort under his big weight, however.
Shirazi *Official explanation: jockey said, regarding the running and riding, his orders were to ride up with the pace to the first flight, then slot back in and ride a race, adding that on top bend of final circuit he kept squeezing gelding but it had become very leg weary and he pulled up within 3 strides; trainer concurred and added that he wanted the rider to take better ground on outside*
Honey's Gift, whose only two previous wins have come over course and distance, never looked like justifying favouritism at any stage and was disappointing. *Official explanation: jockey said mare was unsuited by the good to soft ground*
Front Rank(IRE), pulled up over three miles on his recent comeback, failed to improve for the drop back in trip and the re-application of blinkers. This effort leaves him with plenty to prove.
T/Plt: £181.70 to a £1 stake. Pool: £42,283.70. 169.85 winning tickets. T/Qpdt: £25.60 to a £1 stake. Pool: £4,967.90. 143.40 winning tickets. JS

2219 - 2226a (Foreign Racing) - See Raceform Interactive

701 NAVAN (L-H)
Sunday, November 13

OFFICIAL GOING: Soft (soft to yielding in places)

2227a PHILIPS ELECTRONICS LISMULLEN HURDLE (GRADE 2) 2m 4f
1:30 (1:30) 4-Y-0+ **£23,085** (£6,773; £3,226; £1,099)

RPR

1 **Solerina (IRE)**[7] 1621 8-11-7 158 .... GTHutchinson 157+
(James Bowe, Ire) *mde all: rdn clr after 2 out: styd on wl: comf* **4/6**[1]
2 4 **Back In Front (IRE)**[243] 4383 8-11-12 161 .... BJGeraghty 152+
(E J O'Grady, Ire) *trckd ldrs: 3rd fr 3rd: impr into 2nd after 4 out: sn rdn: no imp after slt mstke 2 out: kpt on* **9/4**[2]
3 7 **Prince Of Tara (IRE)**[379] 1923 8-11-5 .... MrKBBowens 138
(S J Mahon, Ire) *cl 2nd: 3rd and rdn after 4 out: no imp fr next: kpt on same pce* **25/1**
4 4 ½ **Emotional Moment (IRE)**[199] 90 8-11-10 150 .... DFO'Regan 139+
(T J Taaffe, Ire) *in tch: 4th 4 out: rdn and no imp fr next* **9/1**[3]
5 6 **Yogi (IRE)**[15] 1925 9-11-8 136 .... NPMadden 131
(Thomas Foley, Ire) *chsd ldrs: 6th and drvn along after 5 out: no imp fr 3 out* **33/1**
6 13 **Ray Boy (IRE)**[188] 267 6-11-2 133 .... CO'Dwyer 112
(P C O'Connor, Ire) *hld up towards rr: prog into 5th after 5 out: no imp whn mstke 3 out: wknd next* **12/1**
7 hd **Holy Orders (IRE)**[7] 80 8-11-12 ....(b) DJCondon 121
(W P Mullins, Ire) *hld up towards rr: slt mstke 4th: trailing fr 4 out* **16/1**
P **Splendour (IRE)**[24] 1810 10-11-8 111 .... JRBarry —
(Miss S Cox, Ire) *3rd early: lost pl whn mstke 5th: bhd whn p.u bef 3 out* **50/1**

5m 3.40s **Going Correction** +0.425s/f (Soft) **9** Ran SP% **123.1**
Speed ratings: **113,111,108,106,104 99,99,—** CSF £2.74 TOTE £1.50: £1.10, £1.60, £3.20; DF 3.20.
Owner John P Bowe **Bred** Michael J Bowe **Trained** Thurles, Co. Tipperary

NOTEBOOK
Solerina(IRE) took this for the second year, and while there was nothing flamboyant about this front-running success, she still did the job comfortably. She will follow her usual pattern with the Hatton's Grace Hurdle at Fairyhouse next and it should be noted that she had a major fitness edge over these. *(op 4/5)*
Back In Front(IRE) carried a fair bit of condition for this seasonal bow but was the only one to offer any opposition to the mare. He was under pressure before the third last and a slight mistake at the next made no difference to the outcome. He will be more interesting next time and will have claims of reversing form with the winner in the future. *(op 2/1 tchd 5/2)*
Prince Of Tara(IRE), having his first outing for over a year, arguably put up a personal best. He blew up early in the straight but kept on well once he got his second wind. *(op 20/1)*
Emotional Moment(IRE) was not going to be a factor after the fourth last, but should improve a deal for the outing and left the impression he may be back on an upward curve. *(op 8/1)*
Yogi(IRE) was outclassed before the straight but still probably ran above himself in defeat. *(op 20/1)*
Ray Boy(IRE), a fair novice last term, was taking a big step up in class and ran as though the race was badly needed. *(op 10/1)*

2228a BANK OF IRELAND "FOR AUCTION" NOVICE HURDLE (GRADE 3) 2m
2:00 (2:02) 4-Y-0+ **£16,159** (£4,741; £2,258; £769)

RPR

1 **O'Muircheartaigh (IRE)**[28] 1769 5-11-1 .... BJGeraghty 129+
(E J O'Grady, Ire) *in tch: cl 3rd 4 out: led next: rdn and kpt on wl fr last: easily* **4/5**[1]
2 4 **Alpha Royale (IRE)**[13] 1963 5-11-1 ....(b) AndrewJMcNamara 122
(C Byrnes, Ire) *hld up in rr: cl 5th 4 out: prog next: 2nd 2 out: sn rdn: slt mstke last: no ex* **10/3**[2]
3 3 ½ **Up Above (IRE)**[13] 1962 5-10-10 .... AELynch(5) 118
(S Donohoe, Ire) *led: strly pressed 4 out: hdd next: no ex fr 2 out* **8/1**
4 6 **Ballintra Boy (IRE)**[13] 1963 6-11-1 110 .... DFO'Regan 112
(Noel Meade, Ire) *2nd early: 4th 4 out: 5th and no ex after 3 out: lft 4th fr next* **14/1**
U **Ballyagran (IRE)**[15] 1935 5-11-1 .... NPMadden —
(Noel Meade, Ire) *prom: 2nd fr 5th: chal 4 out: rdn next: 3rd and no imp whn mstke and uns rdr 2 out* **7/2**[3]

4m 1.20s **Going Correction** +0.425s/f (Soft) **5** Ran SP% **118.6**
Speed ratings: **113,111,109,106,—** CSF £4.47 TOTE £1.70: £1.10, £2.00; DF 3.30.
Owner Mrs W T O'Grady **Bred** John P Kiely **Trained** Ballynonty, Co Tipperary

NOTEBOOK
O'Muircheartaigh(IRE) boosted his already lofty reputation with a facile success on his first start over hurdles. A 13-length winner of a Cork bumper, he led three out and had the race sewn up before the last. He was subsequently promoted to favouritism in many ante-post lists for the Supreme Novices', and he is one to follow. *(op 4/5 tchd 8/11)*
Alpha Royale(IRE) went after the winner from two out, but was making no impression when fluffing the last. He looks tricky under pressure. *(op 7/2)*
Up Above(IRE) ran in front to the third last, but had no more to offer thereafter. He remains progressive. *(op 7/1)*
Ballintra Boy(IRE) was done with after the third last yet was not disgraced this time. *(op 12/1)*
Ballyagran(IRE) was in third place and struggling when unseating at the second last. *(op 3/1)*

2230a FORTRIA CHASE (GRADE 2) 2m
3:00 (3:01) 5-Y-0+ **£20,776** (£6,095; £2,904; £989)

RPR

1 **Central House**[13] 1965 8-11-12 152 ....(t) RLoughran 163+
(D T Hughes, Ire) *disp ld: slt advantage appr 3 out: rdn and narrowly hdd 2 out: regained ld after last: styd on wl* **8/1**[3]
2 3 ½ **Moscow Flyer (IRE)**[201] 41 11-11-12 180 .... BJGeraghty 159+
(Mrs John Harrington, Ire) *sn disp ld: narrowly hdd appr 3 out: led 2 out: sn rdn: hdd after last: no ex whn eased nr fin* **4/11**[1]
3 2 ½ **Hi Cloy (IRE)**[13] 1965 8-11-12 150 .... AndrewJMcNamara 157
(Michael Hourigan, Ire) *hld up: impr into 3rd 5 out: 4th travelling wl after 3 out: 3rd whn slt mstke last: no ex* **5/1**[2]
4 1 ½ **Native Upmanship (IRE)**[32] 41 12-11-12 154 .... CO'Dwyer 155
(A L T Moore, Ire) *settled 3rd: dropped to rr and outpcd 4 out: 3rd again after 3 out: 4th and no imp fr 2 out* **12/1**
5 5 **Always**[36] 1692 6-11-7 138 ....(b) DFO'Regan 145
(Noel Meade, Ire) *hld up in tch: 4th 4 out: last and no ex after 3 out* **20/1**

4m 10.6s **Going Correction** +0.45s/f (Soft) **5** Ran SP% **113.5**
Speed ratings: **117,115,114,113,110** CSF £12.78 TOTE £12.30: £3.10, £1.10; DF 21.70.
Owner John F Kenny **Bred** A J Ilsley **Trained** Osborne Lodge, Co. Kildare

NOTEBOOK
Central House was well held in a Galway handicap a fortnight earlier but made his fitness edge tell to advantage here. Always in the first pair and outjumping the favourite at some fences, he stumbled slightly turning for home but forfeited no ground. He lost his advantage after the third last but travelled the better downhill, led after the last and very quickly asserted to go clear. *(op 7/1)*
Moscow Flyer(IRE) only impresses in apperance in the spring and looked burly enough. He was never able to dominate and was outjumped on more than a couple of occasions. Beginning to feel the pinch after four out, he took a slight bump on the home turn, but he was in front after the third last and over the next. Leg weary on the approach to the last, he had nothing left to give early on the flat. The Tingle Creek remains on the agenda, and while it would be folly to write him off at this stage, he still has a fair amount to prove all the same. *(op 1/3)*
Hi Cloy(IRE) went round behind, but improved a bit to go third after five out. He kept on nicely from between the last two but was never on terms to challenge. He is on the way back and will appreciate a return to further in due course. *(op 9/2)*
Native Upmanship(IRE), now into veteran status, dropped away before four out, but came back to flatter briefly after the next. He was well held before two out, but should improve plenty for the outing, and a stiffer test in the future. *(op 10/1)*

2235 - (Foreign Racing) - See Raceform Interactive

400 FOLKESTONE (R-H)
Monday, November 14

OFFICIAL GOING: Chase course - good to firm; hurdle course - good to soft (soft in places)
Wind: Almost nil Weather: Sunny

2236 PARKER STEEL JUVENILE MAIDEN HURDLE (9 hdls) 2m 1f 110y
12:40 (12:40) (Class 4) 3-Y-O **£4,118** (£1,209; £604; £301)

Form RPR

1 **Sasso**[46] 3-11-0 .... APMcCoy 103+
(Jonjo O'Neill) *t.k.h: mostly trckd ldr: led after 2 out: drew clr bef last: comf* **8/11**[1]
44 2 5 **Corker**[9] 2045 3-11-0 .... JamesDavies 91+
(D B Feek) *hld up midfield: prog after 3 out: rdn to chse wnr between last 2: no imp* **12/1**
3 10 **Sole Agent (IRE)**[26] 3-11-0 .... JEMoore 80
(G L Moore) *prom: mstke 4th: hit 3 out: drvn to dispute 2nd between last 2: sn btn* **7/1**[3]
4 2 **He's A Star**[25] 3-11-0 .... JTizzard 78
(Miss Gay Kelleway) *hld up in rr: rdn and lost tch bef 2 out: kpt on after: n.d* **12/1**
33 5 1 ½ **Dusty Dane (IRE)**[17] 1904 3-10-7 .... RLucey-Butler(7) 77
(W G M Turner) *hld up in rr: effrt 2 out: drvn and no imp ldrs after: one pce* **11/2**[2]
6 10 **Isitloveyourafter (IRE)**[27] 3-10-7 .... PHide 60
(G L Moore) *hld up wl in rr: outpcd and btn 2 out: plugged on* **33/1**
7 1 ¾ **Lord Of Adventure (IRE)**[12] 3-11-0 .... BHitchcott 65
(Mrs L C Jewell) *hld up wl in rr: j. slowly 4th: rdn and lost tch bef 2 out : styd on fr last* **50/1**
8 ½ **Sugitani (USA)**[118] 3-10-11 .... ONelmes(3) 64
(N B King) *prom: j. slowly 5th: rdn and wknd 2 out: mstke last* **25/1**
9 ¾ **Femme D'Avril (FR)**[155] 3-10-0 .... MissLucyBridges(7) 57
(Miss Lucy Bridges) *plld hrd: ldng trio to 2 out: wknd* **25/1**
10 dist **Karrnak**[48] 3-10-7 .... MrMatthewSmith(7) —
(Miss J Feilden) *led: j. slowly 5th: hit 3 out: hdd & wknd after 2 out: eased: t.o* **50/1**
11 27 **King After**[56] 3-11-0 .... DCrosse —
(J R Best) *j. bdly: a in rr but in tch to 2 out: wknd rapidly and t.o* **16/1**
F **A Qui Le Tour**[209] 3-11-0 .... LAspell —
(M R Hoad) *mstke 3rd: hld up midfield: wl in tch whn fell 3 out* **50/1**
P **Rathcannon Beauty**[390] 3-10-0 .... MGoldstein(7) —
(Mrs L P Baker) *sddle slipped sn after s: p.u bef 3rd: dismntd* **66/1**

4m 33.5s (4.20) **Going Correction** +0.15s/f (Yiel) **13** Ran SP% **125.1**
Speed ratings: **96,93,89,88,87 83,82,82,82,— —,—,—** CSF £11.30 TOTE £1.70: £1.30, £2.60, £1.60; EX 16.00.

Owner John P McManus **Bred** G Reed **Trained** Cheltenham, Gloucs

FOCUS

A modest juvenile hurdle, but Sasso could not have done it any easier and looks a useful prospect. He has been rated as having won by 12 lengths.

NOTEBOOK

Sasso, whose stable is really beginning to hit top form now, did not fulfil his potential on the Flat but he did manage to win on his final outing at Ayr and he made a highly pleasing hurdling debut. Always well positioned under McCoy, he came clear with the minimum of fuss and should not be too hard pushed to defy a penalty. *(op 5-6 tchd 10-11 and evens in places)*

Corker had shown only average form in two previous attempts, but his experience counted for a lot and he kept on best of the rest for second. He will find easier opportunities *(op 10-1)*

Sole Agent(IRE), a modest sort on the Flat, comes from a stable who do extremely well with their juvenile hurdlers and a big run could have been expected. However, he weakened in the final furlong or so having raced prominently and had to settle for third. A more restrained ride may help in future. *(op 8-1 tchd 9-1)*

He's A Star had quite a bit to find with these on Flat form, but he made a little late headway from the rear and a more positive ride in future may see an improved effort.

Dusty Dane(IRE) had shaped quite well on his two previous attempts at hurdling, but this was not such a good effort and he was unable to quicken sufficiently to make ground into a challenging position. *(op 5-1)*

A Qui Le Tour, a poor sort on the level, was still going well enough when falling three out on this hurdling debut and deserves another chance, although it remains to be seen how this affects his confidence.

Rathcannon Beauty *Official explanation: jockey said saddle slipped*

2237 COLOUR DECOR NOVICES' H'CAP CHASE (18 fncs) 3m 1f

1:10 (1:10) (Class 4) (0-95,91) 5-Y-0+ **£4,059** (£1,191; £595; £297)

Form RPR

0/FP **1** **New Leader (IRE)**[14] [1951] 8-10-0 **64** oh12 MBatchelor 78+
(Mrs L Richards) *hld up: clsd on ldrs 11th: led 15th: drew clr bef 2 out: easily* **20/1**

04-P **2** *7* **Ebony Jack (IRE)**[195] [169] 8-10-3 **67** (t) JTizzard 71
(C L Tizzard) *chsd ldr to 7th: mstke 11th: rdn and struggling 13th: kpt on to take 2nd 2 out: no ch w wnr* **7/2**[3]

-160 **3** *9* **Wayward Melody**[16] [1917] 5-11-12 **91** PHide 85
(G L Moore) *j.lft: nvr gng wl: u.p and lost tch after 12th: plugged on fr 2 out* **6/1**

P0-P **4** *1 3/4* **Croghan Loch (IRE)**[5] [2126] 8-10-8 **72** LAspell 65
(P G Murphy) *j.rt 1st: trckd ldr 7th: mstke 12th: upsides 15th: chsd wnr after: mstke next (3 out) and rdn: wknd rapidly 2 out* **20/1**

P32 **U** **Chancers Dante (IRE)**[9] [2039] 9-9-12 **65** (b) KJMercer[(3)] —
(Ferdy Murphy) *bmpd and uns rdr 1st* **9/4**[2]

P052 **R** **Hill Forts Henry**[14] [1951] 7-10-4 **71** (p) RYoung[(3)] 59
(J W Mullins) *j. ponderously: mde most to 15th: immediately btn: last and wl bhd whn ref last* **15/8**[1]

6m 21.3s (-12.10) **Going Correction** -0.80s/f (Firm) **6** Ran SP% **111.6**
Speed ratings: **87,84,81,81,—** — CSF £86.50 TOTE £25.70: £7.00, £2.40; EX 101.50.

Owner M E Thompsett **Bred** W Austin **Trained** Funtington, W Sussex

FOCUS

A poor contest that saw New Leader finally get off the mark over fences. The time was modest.

NOTEBOOK

New Leader(IRE) had completed in only two of his previous six outings over fences and as a result was understandably dismissed in the betting, but he made light work of his field and coasted clear to win tidily. Scoring here off a mark of just 64, this should do his confidence the world of good and he can defy a penalty. *(op 14-1)*

Ebony Jack(IRE), sporting a tongue tie for this reappearance, plodded on again to claim second having lost his place. He achieved very little but is relatively lightly raced and may yet improve. *(tchd 4-1)*

Wayward Melody stepped up on her initial effort over fences, but she was never travelling fluently and continually lost momentum by jumping out to the left. She will need to step up significantly on this if she is to be winning. *(op 13-2 tchd 7-1 and 11-2)*

Croghan Loch(IRE) obtained his best finishing position to date over fences, but the way he stopped quickly suggested he may have a problem. *(op 16-1)*

Chancers Dante(IRE), whose stable are firing in the winners at present, got no further than the first and was unable to add his name to the ever-growing list of winners. *(tchd 5-2 in places and 2-1 in places)*

Hill Forts Henry had run his race when deciding enough was enough and refusing to jump the last. *Official explanation: jockey said gelding never travelled (tchd 5-2 in places and 2-1 in places)*

2238 E B F NASONS OF CANTERBURY "NATIONAL HUNT" NOVICES' HURDLE (QUALIFIER) (9 hdls) 2m 1f 110y

1:40 (1:40) (Class 4) 4-6-Y-0 **£3,506** (£1,029; £514; £257)

Form RPR

F **1** **Killaghy Castle (IRE)**[18] [1892] 5-11-0 LAspell 120+
(N J Gifford) *prom: mstke 3rd: trckd ldr 2 out: effrt to ld bef last: rdn clr* **7/2**[2]

220- **2** *5* **Snakebite (IRE)**[243] [4399] 5-11-0 CLlewellyn 113+
(M Pitman) *led: hdd and hit 2nd: led again bef next: rdn and hdd bef last: kpt on but no ch w wnr flat* **3/1**[1]

10- **3** *2* **Glasker Mill (IRE)**[219] [4774] 5-11-0 SThomas 110+
(Miss H C Knight) *hld up in rr: mstke 3rd: prog to chse ldrs 5th: lost pl 2 out: shkn up and kpt on same pce* **5/1**[3]

/2-1 **4** *nk* **Viciana**[11] [2012] 6-11-0 112 JAMcCarthy 110
(Mrs L Wadham) *led 2nd tl bef next: chsd ldr to 5th: stl cl up after 2 out: rdn and kpt on same pce* **7/1**

1-2 **5** *nk* **Inaro (IRE)**[17] [1909] 4-11-0 APMcCoy 110
(Jonjo O'Neill) *hld up towards rr: clsd fr 3 out: trckd ldrs and looked to be gng wl enough after 2 out: shkn up and nt qckn bef last* **7/1**

30-2 **6** *11* **Idris (GER)**[16] [1916] 4-11-0 110 JEMoore 104+
(G L Moore) *hld up towards rr: in tch but mstkes fr 1/2-way including bad blunder 3 out: chsd ldrs after 2 out: wknd bef last* **6/1**

30-6 **7** *7* **There Is No Doubt (FR)**[13] [1968] 4-10-7 MissLucyBridges[(7)] 92
(Miss Lucy Bridges) *prom: chsd ldr 5th: mstke next: lost pl 2 out: sn wknd : mstke last* **33/1**

25- **8** *18* **Lannigans Lock**[207] [4941] 4-11-0 BJCrowley 80+
(R Rowe) *hld up midfield: wl in tch 2 out: wknd rapidly between fnl 2: mstke last* **66/1**

00-4 **9** *23* **Walter (IRE)**[14] [1950] 6-11-0 PHide 51
(P Winkworth) *trckd ldrs: lost pl 5th: wknd next: wl t.o 2 out* **66/1**

0-0P **10** *9* **Black Shan (IRE)**[12] [1990] 5-10-11 CBolger[(3)] 42
(A Ennis) *hld up in rr: blnd 3rd: lost tch after 5th: sn t.o* **66/1**

0 **11** *1/2* **Rifle Ryde (IRE)**[13] [1975] 5-11-0 TScudamore 41
(K C Bailey) *in tch tl wknd after 5th: wl t.o 2 out* **66/1**

46- **P** **Alpha Gamble (IRE)**[332] [2873] 5-11-0 BFenton —
(R Rowe) *hld up in rr: outpcd 3 out: sn wknd: t.o in last whn p.u bef last* **40/1**

4m 28.3s (-1.00) **Going Correction** +0.15s/f (Yiel)
WFA 4 from 5yo+ 12lb **12** Ran SP% **114.5**
Speed ratings: **108,105,104,104,104 99,96,88,78,74 74,—** CSF £13.83 TOTE £4.00: £1.50, £1.50, £2.00; EX 17.30.

Owner Mrs S N J Embiricos **Bred** Gabriel White **Trained** Findon, W Sussex

FOCUS

A decent novice, with the winner rated a seven-length winner. A fair winning time for the grade, over five seconds quicker than the opener.

NOTEBOOK

Killaghy Castle(IRE) ◆, who had the race at his mercy when falling at the last on his hurdling debut at Stratford, was clearly none the worse for that experience and cleared away stylishly on the run-in. His stable often dig up a smart sort and he looks capable of defying a penalty before taking a rise in grade. *(op 11-4)*

Snakebite(IRE) found this course against him when turned over at odds of 4/11 on his third start in bumpers and he once again was not seen at his best despite Llewellyn making plenty of use of him. Highly thought of by connections, he had not been seen since finishing down the field in the Festival bumper and it is safe to assume that he will improve a good deal once tackling two and a half miles plus. *(op 7-2)*

Glasker Mill(IRE) comes from a stable which is beginning to find the winners and he made a pleasing debut over what would have been an inadequate trip. He was not mentally ready for the Aintree Championship Bumper last season, but still ran well to a point and, like Snakebite, considerable improvement can be expected when he steps up in trip. *(op 4-1)*

Viciana was unable to defy her penalty for winning at Towcester, but this was a significantly better race and she ran as well as could have been expected. She can find further success in mares-only company. *(tchd 8-1)*

Inaro(IRE), a fair bumper performer, was unable to add to his stable's fine recent run of success, being readily outpaced over the final couple of flights. Still only four, he looks open to improvement and can do well at a similar level, probably over further. *Official explanation: jockey said gelding made a noise (op 15-2 tchd 13-2)*

Idris(GER) was always likely to struggle against several decent, unexposed sorts, and a series of bad jumps ended any chance he had. *(op 8-1)*

2239 PENTINS BUSINESS SOLUTIONS H'CAP CHASE (12 fncs) 2m

2:10 (2:10) (Class 3) (0-115,115) 4-Y-0+ **£6,782** (£1,991; £995; £497)

Form RPR

P60- **1** **Lorient Express (FR)**[256] [4140] 6-10-7 **96** SThomas 113+
(Miss Venetia Williams) *t.k.h: hld up: mstke 8th: smooth prog next: led bef 2 out: sn in command: pushed out* **7/2**[1]

5-31 **2** *2 1/2* **Winsley**[40] [1644] 7-11-12 **115** LAspell 124
(O Sherwood) *chsd ldrs: cl up 3 out: rdn bef next: kpt on to take 2nd last: no ch w wnr* **7/2**[1]

2-52 **3** *2* **Green Gamble**[22] [1860] 5-10-5 **94** JamesDavies 101
(D B Feek) *chsd ldr to 4th and fr 6th: led 9th: rdn and hdd bef 2 out: lost 2nd last* **5/1**[2]

3443 **4** *5* **Jupon Vert (FR)**[8] [2074] 8-10-4 **93** TScudamore 96+
(R J Hodges) *settled midfield: pushed along 9th: wl in tch after 3 out: sn rdn and nt qckn* **8/1**[3]

24-4 **5** *1 1/2* **Ballyrobert (IRE)**[25] [1795] 8-11-6 **109** APMcCoy 113+
(C R Egerton) *led: mstke 3rd: j.lft fr 6th: hdd 9th: in tch after 3 out: sn btn* **7/2**[1]

0102 **6** *13* **Master T (USA)**[10] [2016] 6-11-2 **105** PHide 93
(G L Moore) *hld up in last pair: lost tch w ldng gp fr 9th: no ch after* **10/1**

22-0 **7** *24* **I D Technology (IRE)**[9] [2044] 9-11-2 **105** JEMoore 69
(G L Moore) *prom: chsd ldr 4th to 6th: losing pl whn mstke 9th: wknd rapidly* **20/1**

10-P **P** **Fantasmic**[199] [108] 9-11-0 **106** ONelmes[(3)] —
(Miss J R Gibney) *nt jump wl: lost tch bef 6th: t.o whn p.u bef 8th* **25/1**

3m 52.2s (-14.60) **Going Correction** -0.80s/f (Firm) **8** Ran SP% **112.1**
Speed ratings: **104,102,101,99,98 92,80,—** CSF £16.05 CT £58.80 TOTE £5.00: £1.90, £1.30, £1.70; EX 24.30.

Owner Let's Live Racing **Bred** D Laupretre **Trained** Kings Caple, H'fords

FOCUS

Fair form and the race should produce the odd winner.

NOTEBOOK

Lorient Express(FR) lost his way towards the end of last season but was resuming off a reasonable mark and, with his stable going well, he was able to make a winning reappearance. Receiving plenty of weight from the runner-up, he got first run and had it in the bag from before the last. He may be up to defying a penalty, but may need to improve a little. *(op 4-1)*

Winsley missed an engagement the other week because of heavy ground and was much better suited to this faster surface, running on well to claim second on this handicap debut. The weight did look to anchor him, however, and a return to novice company looks the best option now. *(op 5-2)*

Green Gamble has been running well off this sort of mark and he again lost little in defeat, but he remains vulnerable to something less exposed. *(op 11-2)*

Jupon Vert(FR) continues to be unable to take advantage of his ever-declining mark, and this was another average effort. *(op 7-1)*

Ballyrobert(IRE) dropped away disappointingly in the straight and remains a bit below his best *Official explanation: jockey said gelding jumped left throughout (op 9-2)*

2240 HARTMAN MARINE SERVICES LTD MARES' ONLY H'CAP HURDLE (10 hdls) 2m 4f 110y

2:40 (2:40) (Class 3) (0-125,117) 4-Y-0+ **£5,061** (£1,485; £742; £371)

Form RPR

/14- **1** **Lady Of Fortune (IRE)**[250] [4252] 6-11-0 **105** MFoley 115+
(N J Henderson) *hld up in tch: prog to ld 2 out: drew clr bef last: comf* **2/1**[2]

150- **2** *7* **Elfkirk (IRE)**[226] [4694] 6-10-9 **100** BHitchcott 100+
(R H Buckler) *trckd ldrs: mstkes 7th and 3 out: prog to join wnr after 2 out: btn bef last* **25/1**

22-P **3** *7* **Floreana (GER)**[9] [2053] 4-11-12 **117** NFehily 107
(C J Mann) *hld up: rdn 6th: lost tch w ldrs after 3 out: plugged on to take modest 3rd last* **8/1**[3]

31-1 **4** *1* **Marjina**[17] [1906] 6-11-11 **116** BFenton 107+
(Miss E C Lavelle) *nt fluent: prom: chsd ldr 6th: led briefly bef 2 out: u.p and btn sn after 2 out* **1/1**[1]

/5-5 **5** *5* **Burnt Out (IRE)**[9] [2053] 6-11-4 **116** CMStudd[(7)] 102+
(B G Powell) *led at decent pce: stdd 5th: hanging rt and hdd after 3 out: sn btn and eased: j. bdly rt last: kpt on* **25/1**

04-P **6** *6* **Leith Hill Star**[27] [1780] 9-10-11 **102** LAspell 80
(R Rowe) *chsd ldr to 6th: lost pl 3 out: sn rdn and btn* **12/1**

25-0 **7** 9 **Nobodys Perfect (IRE)**[17] 1906 5-10-1 95........................ KJMercer(3) 64
(Ferdy Murphy) *hld up in last: rdn and struggling fr 5th: lost tch next: no ch after* **16/1**

5m 35.8s (3.00) **Going Correction** +0.15s/f (Yiel) **7** Ran SP% **115.7**
Speed ratings: **100,97,94,94,92 90,86** CSF £42.02 TOTE £3.80: £1.50, £4.30; EX 44.90.
Owner Gary Stewart **Bred** Paul Murphy **Trained** Upper Lambourn, Berks

FOCUS
A fair mares'-only handicap hurdle, won in impressive style by the fairly unexposed Lady Of Fortune.

NOTEBOOK
Lady Of Fortune(IRE) comes from a stable which has made a really positive start to the season and she was able to add her name to the ever growing list of winners, coming clear after the second last to win easily. With the favourite disappointing it is debatable what the form is worth, but she looks a useful mare capable of recording further success at the right level. *(tchd 9-4)*
Elfkirk(IRE), last seen finishing down the field in the Mares' Finale at Newbury, made a pleasing reappearance and ran better than her odds suggested she would. She lacked the winner's change of pace at the business end, but she looks a fair chasing prospect and remains open to further improvement. *(op 20-1)*
Floreana(GER), disappointingly pulled up on her reappearance at Wincanton in a competitive race, showed that running to be all wrong and ran as well as could have been expected under such a big weight. *This was a step in the right direction and she is another likely to do well over fences. (op 10-1 tchd 12-1)*
Marjina, an easy winner on her reappearance at Uttoxeter, found the combination of a drop in trip and 7lb rise contributing to a below-par performance. Never jumping with any real fluency, she came through with a chance before turning in, but dropped away disappointingly in the straight. *She is better than this and a switch to fences is likely to see her in a better light. (tchd 10-11 and 11-10)*
Burnt Out(IRE) has not shown a great deal in two starts since arriving from Ireland, but she is in the right hands and a little help from the Handicapper may see her winning.

2241 HSBC NOVICES' CHASE (13 fncs 2 omitted) 2m 5f
3:10 (3:10) (Class 3) 5-Y-0+ **£6,749** (£1,981; £990; £494)

Form RPR
5-4P **1** **Millenaire (FR)**[13] 1976 6-10-12 115........................ APMcCoy 128+
(Jonjo O'Neill) *hld up in tch: effrt to ld 3 out: in command whn mstke 2 out: sn rdn clr: eased flat* **9/2**[2]
2211 **2** 5 **Avitta (IRE)**[11] 2005 6-10-5 115........................ SThomas 114+
(Miss Venetia Williams) *hld up in tch: mstke 2nd: effrt to chal 4 out: n.m.r next: drvn to chse wnr bef 2 out: nt qckn and sn hld* **4/6**[1]
41-3 **3** 3 ½ **Pass Me A Dime**[12] 1984 6-10-12 112........................ JTizzard 115+
(C L Tizzard) *w ldr: led 7th to 8th: led again next: hdd and blnd 3 out: sn btn: plugged on* **11/2**[3]
-340 **4** 5 **Buffalo Bill (IRE)**[22] 1862 9-10-12 103........................ JAMcCarthy 109
(A M Hales) *hld up in last: lost tch w ldrs 9th: effrt 3 out: disp 3rd bef 2 out: sn wknd* **12/1**
/0-2 **5** 5 **Adelphi Theatre (USA)**[33] 566 8-10-12 105........................ BFenton 104
(R Rowe) *led to 7th: led 8th to 9th: wknd 3 out: wl bhd whn blnd last* **8/1**

5m 12.4s (-12.00) **Going Correction** -0.80s/f (Firm) **5** Ran SP% **112.4**
Speed ratings: **90,88,86,84,82** CSF £8.68 TOTE £5.00: £2.80, £1.10; EX 10.70.
Owner The Risky Partnership **Bred** Pierre J Delage **Trained** Cheltenham, Gloucs

FOCUS
This developed into a bit of a sprint and the time was moderate for the class of contest.

NOTEBOOK
Millenaire(FR), who showed very little when pulled up on his chase debut at Worcester earlier in the month, was much more on his game today and put in a fluent round of jumping to give hot favourite Avitta a good beating. A fair hurdler, he is evidently going to make a useful chaser and he looks the type to land a decent handicap, with further improvement expected. *(op 5-1)*
Avitta(IRE) created an excellent impression in winning her last two races at Uttoxeter and Haydock, but a change in tactics led to a slightly disappointing effort and she was comfortably held by the winner. She remains a useful sort, especially in mares'-only company, and a return to more aggressive tactics is likely to see her return to winning ways. *(op 1-2 tchd 8-11)*
Pass Me A Dime was tackling this ground for the first time and did not shape without promise, keeping on well having been headed after a mistake at the third last. He is entitled to improve on this initial outing over fences and is in good hands. *(op 6-1)*
Buffalo Bill(IRE), a modest hurdler, is starting out over fences rather late in life and did not shape with a great amount of promise on this fencing debut. He was always likely to struggle against some useful types, however, and is going to find easier oportunities. *(op 14-1)*
Adelphi Theatre(USA) showed up well to a point, but he was readily brushed aside and needs to improve. *(tchd 9-1)*

2242 SANDOM ROBINSON STANDARD OPEN NATIONAL HUNT FLAT RACE 2m 1f 110y
3:40 (3:40) (Class 6) 4-6-Y-0 **£1,870** (£545; £272)

Form RPR
5- **1** **Major Miller**[206] 4971 4-11-4........................ ATinkler 113+
(N J Henderson) *hld up: prog 7f out: led wl over 3f out: hrd pressed fr over 1f out: hld on wl* **9/2**[2]
2 1 ¼ **Bradley Boy (IRE)** 4-11-4........................ CLlewellyn 110+
(M Pitman) *hld up in last pair: prog to join ldrs 1/2-way: effrt to chal 4f out: rdn 2f out: pressed wnr fnl f: jst hld* **10/1**
3 **3** 9 **Kobai (IRE)**[198] 131 6-11-4........................ WHutchinson 101
(A King) *hld up: effrt 5f out: drvn to chse ldng pair fnl 3f: kpt on one pce: nvr able to chal* **11/4**[1]
4 8 **Hambaphambili**[260] 5-11-4........................ LAspell 93
(O Sherwood) *hld up wl in rr: prog to trck ldrs 1/2-way: outpcd over 4f out: no imp after* **9/1**
5 nk **Riffles** 5-10-4........................ SWalsh(7) 86
(Mrs A J Bowlby) *lost pl and in rr 12f out: prog 7f out: outpcd over 4f out: n.d after* **50/1**
6 1 ¼ **Lone Rider (IRE)** 4-11-4........................ APMcCoy 91
(Jonjo O'Neill) *hld up in rr: prog 7f out: rdn and outpcd over 4f out: no ch after* **9/2**[2]
7 7 **Ilringuback (IRE)** 5-10-13........................ MrMJO'Connor(5) 84
(A J Chamberlain) *led at fair pce: hdd and hrd rdn wl over 3f out: wknd* **7/1**
8 10 **Triggernometry** 4-11-4........................ JTizzard 74
(C L Tizzard) *prom: rdn over 5f out: steadily wknd* **6/1**[3]
5/5- **9** 23 **Top Dog (IRE)**[410] 1547 6-10-11........................ MrJMorgan(7) 51
(L Wells) *t.k.h: prom to 5f out: wkng whn rn wd over 3f out* **50/1**
10 nk **Latin Player (IRE)** 6-10-8........................ JBunsell(10) 51
(B G Powell) *t.k.h: hld up wl in rr: rn wd bnd over 9f out: prog to trck ldrs 7f out: wknd over 4f out* **33/1**
0- **11** 3 **Golden Crew**[254] 4193 5-11-1........................ CBolger(3) 48
(Miss Suzy Smith) *in tch to 1/2-way: bhd fnl 6f* **50/1**
12 dist **Light Tackle (IRE)** 4-10-13........................ DLaverty(5) —
(A Ennis) *prom to 1/2-way: sn wknd: t.o* **40/1**
P- **13** 6 **Adam's Belle (IRE)**[416] 1500 5-10-8........................ ONelmes(3) —
(N B King) *prom to 1/2-way: sn wknd: t.o whn virtually p.u fnl f* **50/1**

4m 27.2s (-6.90) **Going Correction** +0.15s/f (Yiel) **13** Ran SP% **122.1**
Speed ratings: **97,96,92,88,88 88,85,80,70,70 68,—,—** CSF £47.95 TOTE £7.10: £1.90, £3.90, £1.50; EX 44.40 Place 6 £39.61, Place 5 £30.38.
Owner W H Ponsonby **Bred** M J Coombe **Trained** Upper Lambourn, Berks

FOCUS
Unusually there was a fair pace on for this bumper and Major Miller and Bradley Boy pulled clear in the straight, suggesting that they could be above average.

NOTEBOOK
Major Miller hardly shaped with immense potential when only fifth on his debut at Perth in April, but he has clearly done well since, and came through under a confident Tinkler to take it up before they turned for home. He had to battle to hold off debutant Bradley Boy, but was always holding him and he looks the sort to pay his way in novice hurdles. *(op 7-2 tchd 5-1)*
Bradley Boy(IRE), whose stable has started the season brightly, travelled well throughout and threw down a challenge to the winner, but he was always being held and had to settle for second. Clear of the third, the experience should serve him well and it will be both disappointing and surprising if he fails to win a bumper before going hurdling.
Kobai(IRE) was unable to step up on his debut third, but the likelihood is that he bumped into a couple of decent sorts. He will be helped by further once sent hurdling. *(op 7-2 tchd 4-1)*
Hambaphambili, a winner in points in Ireland, found this too much of a speed test and was unable to keep tabs on the principals as the pace quickened. There was a deal of promise to be taken from this and he looks a fair hurdling prospect. *(op 7-1)*
Riffles, withdrawn on her debut because of fast ground, made some late headway having dropped back through the field and will find life easier in mares'-only company.
Lone Rider(IRE) lacked the knowhow to get involved and it is safe to assume that he is going to be capable of much better in time. *(op 11-2)*
Ilringuback(IRE) knew his job and took them along at a decent pace, but he paid for it in the end and faded out of it in the final quarter mile. He showed enough to suggest that he can win at a moderate level when sent hurdling. *(op 15-2 tchd 13-2)*
Triggernometry comes from a stable which is capable of readying one for a bumper, but he weakened disappointingly having held a prominent early position. Likely to be capable of better, he will not be seen at his best until tackling obstacles. *(op 11-2)*
T/Plt: £57.60 to a £1 stake. Pool: £30,319.10. 383.90 winning tickets. T/Qpdt: £10.20 to a £1 stake. Pool: £3,538.30. 255.30 winning tickets. JN

LEICESTER (R-H)
Monday, November 14

OFFICIAL GOING: Chase course - good to firm (good in places; good to soft on hurdle crossing); hurdle course - good to soft (soft in places)
Wind: Light, half-behind Weather: Sunny spells

2243 LADBROKES.COM H'CAP CHASE (18 fncs) 2m 7f 110y
12:50 (12:50) (Class 4) (0-105,105) 5-Y-0+ **£4,866** (£1,428; £714; £356)

Form RPR
55P2 **1** **Channahrlie (IRE)**[14] 1960 11-9-12 79........................(p) TJMalone(3) 93+
(R Dickin) *led to 2nd: led after 5th: rdn appr 2 out: styd on* **5/1**[3]
2135 **2** 2 ½ **Sir Cumference**[29] 1752 9-11-2 94........................(b) AO'Keeffe 100
(Miss Venetia Williams) *a.p: chsd wnr 10th: rdn appr 2 out: styd on* **6/1**
40F0 **3** 20 **Jazz Du Forez (FR)**[72] 1395 8-9-7 78 oh9........................ AScholes(7) 66+
(John Allen) *prom: hit 5th: wknd 14th: hit next* **80/1**
5314 **4** 7 **Runaway Bishop (USA)**[11] 2009 10-10-9 94........................ APogson(7) 73
(J R Cornwall) *hld up: bhd 9th: styd on flat* **20/1**
F2/2 **5** nk **Umbrella Man (IRE)**[12] 1989 9-11-10 102........................ JimCrowley 81
(Miss E C Lavelle) *hld up: j.rt: hdwy 10th: lft 3rd 4 out: wknd next* **9/2**[2]
130- **6** 5 **Forest Dante (IRE)**[285] 3654 12-11-3 95........................(p) KJohnson 74+
(F Kirby) *led 2nd: slipped 5th: sn hdd: wknd 14th: bhd whn blnd last* **33/1**
1312 **7** dist **Ultimate Limit**[22] 1858 5-11-6 99........................ PJBrennan —
(A Ennis) *hld up: pushed along 10th: nt running on whn hit 4 out* **11/4**[1]
100- **F** **Geton (IRE)**[282] 3703 5-11-12 105........................ TJMurphy —
(M C Pipe) *hld up: hdwy 12th: cl 3rd whn fell 4 out* **6/1**
4-32 **P** **Baikaline (FR)**[23] 1826 6-11-0 92........................ RThornton —
(Ian Williams) *prom to 13th: t.o whn p.u bef 4 out* **9/1**

5m 52.6s (-12.80) **Going Correction** -0.60s/f (Firm) **9** Ran SP% **109.0**
Speed ratings: **97,96,89,87,87 85,—,—,—** CSF £31.63 CT £1889.75 TOTE £6.20: £2.00, £2.30, £18.20; EX 38.20.
Owner J C Clemmow **Bred** Mrs Laura Drumm **Trained** Atherstone on Stour, Warwicks

FOCUS
A modest handicap, run at an average gallop, which saw the first two come well clear. The winner can be rated value for further.

NOTEBOOK
Channahrlie(IRE) ◆ took the race by the scruff of the neck from an early stage and ran out a most ready winner, being value for further as he was idling in front from the penultimate fence. Having slipped to a decent mark, he could well build on this, despite being an eleven-year-old, as he tends to hold his form well and there was plenty to like about this display. *(op 9-2)*
Sir Cumference, whose trainer's two other previous runners in this event were both successful, was the only runner to pose a threat to the winner in the home straight and turned in an improved effort in defeat. He finished well clear of the rest but, while he is capable of finding another race from this mark, he remains vulnerable to an improver. *(op 7-1)*
Jazz Du Forez(FR), 9lb out of the weights, did not jump all that well on this return from a break and never threatened. However, the way he plugged on to finish a clear third suggests he could get closer if dropped in class in the coming weeks. *(op 66-1)*
Runaway Bishop(USA) was allowed to plug on at his own pace and ran well below his mark. *(tchd 25-1)*
Umbrella Man(IRE), runner-up on his return from a 945-day layoff at Huntingdon 12 days previously, tended to jump right over his fences and his fate was sealed a long way out. He probably found this coming too soon, however, and is capable of better. *(tchd 5-1)*
Ultimate Limit, raised 5lb for finishing second at Wincanton last time, ran a lifeless race and something may well have been amiss.
Geton(IRE), making his chase and handicap debut after a 282-day break, had yet to be asked a serious question prior to departing and can be rated value for a place at the least. He has to be considered unfortunate, has clearly started handicap life on a fair mark and, providing his confidence is not too badly dented by this, he looks like proving better over fences that he was over timber. *(tchd 5-1)*

2244 GEORGE MICALLEF 60TH BIRTHDAY MARES' ONLY NOVICES' H'CAP HURDLE (12 hdls) 2m 4f 110y
1:20 (1:21) (Class 4) (0-100,96) 3-Y-0+ **£4,147** (£1,217; £608; £304)

Form RPR
0-43 **1** **Seveneightsix (IRE)**[4] 2140 5-9-7 70 oh4....................(p) RCummings(7) 80+
(D J Wintle) *chsd ldrs: led 3rd: drvn out* **11/2**[2]

The Form Book, Raceform Ltd, Compton, RG20 6NL

00-0 **2** *6* **Rude Health**[27] [1782] 5-10-6 **76** PJBrennan 80
(N J Hawke) *hld up: hdwy appr 3 out: ev ch next: rdn appr last: fnd nil* **16/1**

330- **3** *12* **Ishka Baha (IRE)**[226] [4694] 6-11-4 **88** JMMaguire 80
(T R George) *hld up: hdwy 6th: wknd appr 2 out* **7/1**[3]

23-2 **4** *7* **Sweet Oona (FR)**[22] [1850] 6-11-7 **96** PCO'Neill[(5)] 83+
(Miss Venetia Williams) *hld up in tch: hit 3rd: chsd ldr 6th: ev ch whn nt fluent 3 out: wknd bef next* **11/4**[1]

0300 **5** *½* **Nice Baby (FR)**[40] [1637] 4-11-2 **86** (vt) GSupple 71
(M C Pipe) *hld up: hdwy 7th: rdn and wknd appr 2 out* **25/1**

433- **6** *3* **Esplendidos (IRE)**[294] [3511] 6-11-6 **90** TJMurphy 72
(D P Keane) *hld up: mstke 6th: hdwy appr 3 out: sn rdn and wknd* **11/4**[1]

0-04 **7** *15* **Hilarious (IRE)**[13] [1974] 5-10-13 **83** JGoldstein 50
(Dr J R J Naylor) *chsd ldrs: hit 3rd: rdn and wknd appr 3 out* **8/1**

8 *hd* **Hazel Bank Lass (IRE)**[683] [3148] 9-10-12 **85** GCarenza[(3)] 51
(Andrew Turnell) *hld up: hdwy 4th: wknd after 3 out* **25/1**

-42P **9** *dist* **The Wife's Sister**[168] [591] 4-10-12 **87** StephenJCraine[(5)] —
(D McCain) *prom to 7th* **20/1**

45F/ **P** **Sovereign Gale (IRE)**[548] 11-10-7 **77** OMcPhail —
(Miss T McCurrich) *led to 3rd: wknd appr 7th: t.o whn p.u bef 2 out* **33/1**

P04 **P** **Pips Assertive Way**[22] [1851] 4-11-3 **94** MrGTumelty[(7)] —
(A W Carroll) *racd keenly: chsd ldr to 3rd: wknd 7th: t.o whn p.u bef last* **20/1**

5m 12.8s (-22.00) **Going Correction** -0.90s/f (Hard)
WFA 4 from 5yo+ 13lb **11** Ran SP% **118.4**
Speed ratings: **105,102,98,95,95 94,88,88,—,— —** CSF £75.59 CT £629.24 TOTE £6.00: £1.80, £6.70, £2.40; EX 91.50.
Owner Mrs R K Choudhury **Bred** Mrs Anne Macdermott **Trained** Naunton, Gloucs

FOCUS
A moderate mares' handicap, run at a decent pace, and the field came home fairly strung out.

NOTEBOOK
Seveneightsix(IRE), who improved again to finish third at Ludlow four days previously, jumped well throughout and responded to all of her rider's urgings to record a decisive success. Despite the fact that she was 4lb out of the handicap, her rider's claim helped offset that, and the switch from blinkers to cheekpieces clearly had a positive effect. She could have more to offer in this division now that she has finally got her head in front, and her yard is in good form at present. *(op 7-1)*
Rude Health, making her handicap bow, showed the benefit of her seasonal return at Exeter 27 days previously and, despite being put in her place by the winner, turned in her best effort to date for her current yard. She will benefit from a drop in trip and looks weighted to go one better.
Ishka Baha(IRE), making her return from a 226-day break, had her chance yet failed to find much when it really mattered. She is entitled to improve for this, but looks fairly high in the weights on this evidence and remains a maiden after eight outings. *(op 8-1)*
Sweet Oona(FR), put in her place behind Refinement on her comeback at Towcester 22 days previously, turned for home going as well as any, but once again she failed to find anything when push came to shove and was well held. She has yet to win a race of any description and is clearly tricky. *(op 3-1 tchd 10-3)*
Nice Baby(FR) was another who failed to find anything for maximum pressure, having looked a brief threat at the top of the straight, and continues to frustrate. *(tchd 28-1)*
Esplendidos(IRE) failed to rate a serious threat from off the gallop and proved disappointing. However, in keeping with the majority of her stable's runners this term, she could improve a deal with this seasonal debut under her belt. *(op 5-2 tchd 9-4)*

2245 LADBROKES.COM (S) HURDLE (9 hdls) 2m
1:50 (1:53) (Class 5) 3-5-Y-0 **£2,857** (£832; £416)

Form RPR

6 **1** **Zando**[11] [2001] 3-10-0 PMerrigan[(5)] 79
(P C Haslam) *a.p: bmpd appr 3 out: led last: rdn out* **7/2**[3]

F420 **2** *1¼* **Strathtay**[20] [1873] 3-10-0 93 (v) TJMurphy 73
(M C Pipe) *hld up in tch: rdn whn nt fluent 2 out: r.o u.p flat* **7/4**[1]

5234 **3** *hd* **Time For You**[8] [2069] 3-10-0 85 WMarston 73
(J M Bradley) *chsd ldrs: led 3 out: hdd next: sn rdn: styd on* **9/1**

0- **4** *1* **Blue Mariner**[151] [3534] 5-11-7 (t) JPMcNamara 93
(J Jay) *hld up: hmpd 1st: hdwy appr 3 out: ev ch next: sn rdn: styd on* **22/1**

3632 **5** *hd* **Rifleman (IRE)**[8] [2071] 5-11-7 98 (t) AThornton 93
(Robert Gray) *hld up: hdwy appr 3 out: led next: rdn and hdd last: no ex flat* **3/1**[2]

4P **6** *6* **Darko Karim**[7] [1802] 3-10-5 (v) ChristianWilliams 71
(R J Hodges) *hld up: pushed along 3rd: hdwy and j. slowly next: ev ch 3 out: wknd after next* **9/1**

60-0 **7** *14* **Varuni (IRE)**[22] [1850] 4-10-4 69 TBurrows[(10)] 66
(P L Clinton) *trckd ldrs: ev ch 3 out: rdn and wknd bef next* **100/1**

0 **8** *8* **Roan Raider (USA)**[9] [2040] 5-11-2 (p) PCO'Neill[(5)] 65
(R C Guest) *hld up: rdn and wknd 3 out* **80/1**

000- **9** *20* **Zabadou**[339] [2753] 4-11-7 81 KJohnson 45
(F Kirby) *chsd ldrs tl wknd after 3 out* **100/1**

U **Jenna Stannis**[40] 3-10-0 TDoyle —
(R M Beckett) *j. slowly 1st: bhd whn swvd lft and uns rdr next* **25/1**

0- **P** **St Barchan (IRE)**[56] [1794] 4-11-7 OMcPhail —
(A G Juckes) *hld up: mstke 3rd: wknd 5th: t.o whn p.u bef 2 out* **66/1**

040 **P** **Lorna Dune**[17] [1904] 3-9-11 (p) TJMalone[(3)] —
(J G M O'Shea) *led: hit 4th: hdd and hmpd 3 out: sn wknd: t.o whn p.u bef next* **25/1**

3m 57.1s (-10.50) **Going Correction** -0.90s/f (Hard)
WFA 3 from 4yo+ 15lb **12** Ran SP% **120.3**
Speed ratings: **90,89,89,88,88 85,78,74,64,— —,—** CSF £10.08 TOTE £4.40: £1.40, £1.80, £3.20; EX 13.80.The winner was sold to Mr E. G. Bevan for 5,500gns.
Owner Blue Lion Racing VI **Bred** Mrs P A Reditt And M J Reditt **Trained** Middleham, N Yorks

FOCUS
A slowly-run race and modest winning time, even for a seller, and the form is weak.

NOTEBOOK
Zando, dropped in class, duly got off the mark on his second attempt over timber in ready fashion and justified strong support in the betting ring. While he remains open to improvement in this sphere, however, this does look to be his sort of level. *(op 5-1)*
Strathtay, another dropped in grade, took an age to hit full stride and was staying on all too late on the run-in. She is clearly tricky, but has a similar race within her compass. *(op 15-8 tchd 2-1, 85-40 in place)*
Time For You turned in another fair effort in defeat and had every chance, but she failed to improve for the drop down to this class. She is moderate, but is at least consistent enough, and helps set the standard for the form. *(op 15-2)*
Blue Mariner, equipped with a tongue tie for this return to hurdling, came to have every chance before failing to quicken after the penultimate flight. He looks the one to take from the race, as he should improve for the run, and will certainly have claims of getting closer when switched to a sharper track in the future. *(op 20-1 tchd 25-1)*

Rifleman(IRE), making his debut for new connections, once again flattered off the bridle and threw in the towel when maximum pressure was applied. He really is one of the most frustrating hurdlers in training, and is one to avoid at all costs, but is a fair benchmark nevertheless. *(tchd 11-4)*

2246 LADBROKES.COM NOVICES' CHASE (12 fncs) 2m
2:20 (2:20) (Class 3) 4-Y-0+ **£5,439** (£1,596; £798; £398)

Form RPR

3U01 **1** **Lord Lington (FR)**[14] [1957] 6-11-5 113 WMarston 116+
(D J Wintle) *hld up and bhd: j.big 2nd: hdwy 4 out: chsd ldr after next: led appr last: rdn clr* **7/1**[3]

22-1 **2** *6* **Allumee**[39] [1654] 6-11-5 114 RJohnson 108
(P J Hobbs) *trckd ldr: racd keenly: led and pckd 5th: mstke 3 out: rdn and hdd appr last: wknd flat* **5/6**[1]

1-03 **3** *1¾* **Rhapsody Rose**[17] [1911] 4-10-0 107 TDoyle 88+
(P R Webber) *led and hit 1st: hdd 5th: rdn whn hmpd 3 out: styd on same pce fr next* **7/4**[2]

0-P0 **4** *2½* **Blaise Wood (USA)**[11] [2008] 4-10-0 82 (t) TBurrows[(7)] 92
(A L Forbes) *hld up: mstke 3rd (water): rdn appr last: nvr trbld ldrs* **66/1**

-000 **F** **Moorlaw (IRE)**[32] [1726] 4-10-2 107 StephenJCraine[(5)] —
(D McCain) *chsd ldrss: hit 4th: rdn 6th: mstke next: disputing cl 3rd whn fell 3 out* **33/1**

4m 3.10s (-4.50) **Going Correction** -0.60s/f (Firm)
WFA 4 from 6yo+ 12lb **5** Ran SP% **107.9**
Speed ratings: **87,84,83,81,—** CSF £13.63 TOTE £8.20: £1.60, £1.20; EX 22.00.
Owner Ocean Trailers Ltd **Bred** G Cherel **Trained** Naunton, Gloucs

FOCUS
A moderate winning time for the grade, but the winner did the job nicely and could rate higher.

NOTEBOOK
Lord Lington(FR) ◆, back to winning ways over timber at Warwick two weeks previously, translated that form to the bigger obstacles and followed up in emphatic style. Considering this was his first experience of fences, his jumping was particularly accurate, and he did enough to suggest that he may even get a touch further in this sphere. He looks to be finally coming good and, considering he was well regarded when with Paul Nicholls, he could rate higher before the season is out. *(op 11-2)*
Allumee, finally off the mark over hurdles last time, had his chance but was a sitting duck for the winner at the top of the straight and was ultimately well beaten. While this may be considered disappointing, he is entitled to improve for the experience and probably still ran close to his recent hurdle form in defeat. *(op 10-11 tchd Evens)*
Rhapsody Rose, third in a better race on her recent chasing bow at Wetherby, failed to improve with that experience under her belt and again made mistakes when under pressure. She may prefer easier ground than this, but will need to improve her jumping if she is to progress as a chaser. *(op 15-8 tchd 13-8, 2-1 in places)*
Blaise Wood(USA) was not disgraced at the weights on this chase debut, despite failing to threaten, and could be of interest when his sights are lowered in due course.

2247 LADBROKES.COM H'CAP HURDLE (9 hdls) 2m
2:50 (2:50) (Class 3) (0-120,120) 4-Y-0+
£7,872 (£2,325; £1,162; £581; £290; £145)

Form RPR

220- **1** **Daryal (IRE)**[244] [4386] 4-11-10 **118** RThornton 131+
(A King) *hld up: hit 4th: hdwy appr 3 out: rdn to ld and hit last: styd on* **2/1**[1]

-344 **2** *4* **Papillon De Iena (FR)**[146] [803] 5-11-6 **117** TJMalone[(3)] 125
(M C Pipe) *chsd ldrs: led appr 3 out: rdn and hdd last: no ex* **18/1**

0P-0 **3** *4* **Haditovski**[14] [1957] 9-10-5 **102** (v) FKing[(3)] 106
(J Mackie) *hld up: hdwy appoaching 3 out: sn rdn: styd on same pce appr last* **14/1**

60-3 **4** *6* **Just Superb**[14] [1957] 6-10-4 **103** TGreenway[(5)] 101
(P A Pritchard) *chsd ldrs: outpcd 5th: hmpd next: styd on flat* **10/1**

10-0 **5** *10* **Killing Me Softly**[14] [1957] 4-10-4 **98** (v) ChristianWilliams 86
(J Gallagher) *led: hdd appr 3rd: wknd appr 3 out* **22/1**

30-1 **6** *½* **Ghadames (FR)**[177] [452] 11-10-4 **103** (p) PCO'Neill[(5)] 96+
(R C Guest) *chsd ldr tl led appr 3rd: hdd bef 3 out: wknd bef next* **10/3**[2]

P-21 **7** *3* **Harrycat (IRE)**[75] [1222] 4-11-1 **109** (p) PMoloney 94
(V Smith) *prom tl rdn and wknd 3 out* **9/1**[3]

60P- **8** *26* **Mobasher (IRE)**[236] [4518] 6-11-12 **120** AO'Keeffe 79
(Miss Venetia Williams) *hld up: hdwy 4th: blnd and rdr lost nr side iron 5th: sn wknd* **20/1**

102/ **U** **Zimbabwe**[579] [4839] 5-11-5 **120** EDehdashti[(7)] —
(G L Moore) *hld up: hit 2nd: 7th and rdn whn blnd and uns 3 out* **9/1**[3]

22-U **F** **Charlton Kings (IRE)**[9] [2044] 7-11-7 **115** RJohnson 113
(R J Hodges) *hld up in tch: rdn appr 2 out: 4th and wkng whn fell last* **11/1**

3m 48.8s (-18.80) **Going Correction** -0.90s/f (Hard)
WFA 4 from 5yo+ 12lb **10** Ran SP% **114.9**
Speed ratings: **111,109,107,104,99 98,97,84,—,—** CSF £36.61 CT £402.42 TOTE £3.40: £2.10, £4.00, £2.50; EX 90.70 Trifecta £293.30 Part won. Pool: £413.20 - 0.20 winning tickets..
Owner Let's Live Racing **Bred** His Highness The Aga Khan's Studs S C **Trained** Barbury Castle, Wilts
■ Stewards' Enquiry : T J Malone one-day ban: used whip with excessive frequency (Nov 25)

FOCUS
A fair winning time for the class and the quickest of the three races over the trip at the meeting. The form looks very solid for the class and it should produce future winners.

NOTEBOOK
Daryal(IRE) ◆, who showed useful form as a juvenile last season, made a winning return to action in ready fashion under a well-judged ride from Thornton. While he has clearly started this term on a decent mark, there was plenty to like about this, his best display to date over timber, and he is certainly capable of progressing to a higher level before the season's end. He may also get a bit further on this evidence. *(op 5-2 tchd 11-4 in places, tchd 10-3 in a place)*
Papillon De Iena(FR) ◆, returning from a 146-day break, paid late on for chasing the strong early gallop and was no match for the progressive winner. However, this still has to rate a pleasing return to hurdling, and it is arguably his best effort to date. He can be placed to go one better before long and may appreciate the return to slightly further in the future. *(op 20-1)*
Haditovski failed to quicken when it really mattered but turned in an improved effort nevertheless, and showed the benefit of his recent comeback at Warwick. While he scored over fences in 2004, he is on a long losing run over timber and is clearly tricky, but he can certainly find easier oppotunitites off this sort of mark in the future. *(tchd 16-1)*
Just Superb, third on his comeback at Warwick two weeks previously, failed to confirm that form with Haditovski and was made to look one-paced on this easier ground. *(op 11-1)*
Killing Me Softly *(op 33-1 tchd 40-1)*
Ghadames(FR), last seen winning from a 16lb higher mark over fences in May, paid for chasing the strong pace on this return to hurdling and was well beaten. He is entitled to improve for this outing and is undeniably well handicapped in this sphere, but at the age of 11 he may continue to find things happening all too quickly over hurdles. *(op 11-4)*

Harrycat(IRE), raised 4lb for winning on his last outing over hurdles back in August, was another who paid for helping to set the generous pace on this handicap bow. He looks worth another chance off this mark. *(tchd 10-1)*

Charlton Kings(IRE), who unseated on his recent seasonal and chase debut, looked to be running *close to his mark prior to departing at the last. His confidence will need restoring after this. (tchd 12-1)*

2248 PRIMA FLOOR H'CAP CHASE (15 fncs) 2m 4f 110y

3:20 (3:20) (Class 4) (0-100,100) 4-Y-0+ **£4,215** (£1,237; £618; £309)

Form			Horse	Jockey	RPR
2424	1		**Eau Pure (FR)**[44] [1599] 8-11-2 **90**	RJohnson	100+
			(G L Moore) *hld up: hdwy 9th: led appr 2 out: rdn clr flat: eased nr fin*	**6/1**[2]	
540-	2	3	**First De La Brunie (FR)**[237] [4506] 4-10-7 **94**	RThornton	86
			(A King) *a.p: mstke 4 out: chsd wnr 2 out: styd on same pce last*	**7/1**[3]	
0/P-	3	12	**Tacita**[327] [2935] 10-9-7 **74** oh16	MrMWall(7)	67
			(M D McMillan) *hld up in tch: racd keenly: hit 5th: wknd 2 out*	**100/1**	
-P0P	4	3 ½	**Jacdor (IRE)**[11] [2010] 11-11-5 **96**	(v) TJMalone(3)	86
			(R Dickin) *chsd ldr 3rd: hit 5th: led next: hdd 7th: led after 4 out: hdd appr 2 out: wkng whn lft poor 3rd last*	**50/1**	
3533	5	2	**Magico (NZ)**[16] [1928] 7-11-2 **95**	PCO'Neill(5)	83
			(R C Guest) *hld up: rdn appr 3 out: sn wknd*	**20/1**	
PP-0	6	2 ½	**Hiers De Brouage (FR)**[27] [1780] 10-11-10 **98**	(tp) TJMurphy	83
			(J G Portman) *chsd ldr to 3rd: remained handy tl wknd 3 out*	**12/1**	
400-	7	hd	**Captains Table**[214] [4838] 12-11-12 **100**	TDoyle	85
			(F Jordan) *led to 6th: led next: hdd after 4 out: wknd appr 2 out*	**20/1**	
2P06	8	dist	**Tirley Storm**[24] [1819] 10-10-0 **74** oh3	WMarston	—
			(J S Smith) *hld up: a bhd*	**66/1**	
U/65	U		**Get Smart (IRE)**[17] [1907] 8-10-0 **81**	PJMcDonald(7)	—
			(Ferdy Murphy) *hld up: mstke 6th (water): bhd whn uns rdr 10th*	**7/1**[3]	
0-	U		**Prince Roscoe**[12] [1999] 9-10-8 **82**	DNRussell	81+
			(D E Fitzgerald, Ire) *hld up: hdwy and hmpd 4 out: mstke 2 out: 3rd and wkng whn blnd and uns rdr last*	**5/6**[1]	

5m 9.70s (-13.90) **Going Correction** -0.60s/f (Firm)
WFA 4 from 7yo+ 13lb **10** Ran SP% **115.5**
Speed ratings: **102,100,96,94,94 93,93,—,—,—** CSF £43.31 CT £3744.33 TOTE £6.40: £1.40, £2.90, £20.90; EX 46.70.
Owner Trevor Painting **Bred** Ste Elevage Des Chartreux **Trained** Woodingdean, E Sussex

FOCUS
A moderate handicap, run at a fair gallop, and the first two came clear. The form is worth treating with a degree of caution, though, considering the proximity of the 100-1 third.

NOTEBOOK
Eau Pure(FR), with the cheekpices left off, was the subject of decent support in the betting and duly obliged under a patient ride from Johnson. She jumped neatly throughout, enjoyed the drop in trip and, on this evidence, will surley go close if turned out under a penalty. *(op 7-1)*
First De La Brunie(FR), who failed to really find his feet over timber last term after switching from France, ran an improved race on this return to chasing and shaped as though he will benefit from the outing. The jury remains out regarding his best trip, but he may just prefer reverting to a sharper test in the future. He still has time on his side. *(op 8-1)*
Tacita, absent for 327 days, showed greatly-improved form on this return to action and belied her odds of 100-1. However, considering that she was 12lb out of the handicap and stayed on despite racing freely early on, her proximity at the finish must raise a doubt as to the overall strength of this form.
Jacdor(IRE), who seems to have two styles of running, turned in one of his better efforts yet still ran below his official mark.
Prince Roscoe, who looked very well treated on his exploits over hurdles in Ireland, had turned in a solid effort off a 4lb lower mark on his return to fences at Punchestown 12 days previously and was understandably well backed for this. However, he falied to really convince with his jumping, and was beaten when eventually unshipping Russell at the final fence. *(op 11-10)*

2249 LADBROKES.COM NOVICES' HURDLE (9 hdls) 2m

3:50 (3:50) (Class 3) 4-Y-0+ **£5,022** (£1,474; £737; £368)

Form			Horse	Jockey	RPR
	1		**Nous Voila (FR)**[411] 4-10-12	TJMurphy	113+
			(M C Pipe) *chsd ldr 3rd: led appr 3 out: rdn out*	**5/4**[1]	
4P2-	2	2 ½	**Dhehdaah**[23] [3899] 4-10-12 105	WMarston	108+
			(Mrs P Sly) *a.p: chsd wnr 2 out: sn rdn: styd on*	**10/1**	
	3	1 ¼	**Sangiovese**[59] 6-10-12	JimCrowley	106
			(H Morrison) *hld up: hdwy 5th: rdn appr last: styd on same pce flat*	**7/1**[3]	
5-	4	16	**Winapenny (IRE)**[375] [1997] 6-10-12	RMcGrath	90
			(Ferdy Murphy) *hld up: hdwy 4th: wknd 2 out*	**25/1**	
420-	5	4	**Amarula Ridge (IRE)**[244] [4386] 4-10-12 118	RJohnson	90+
			(P J Hobbs) *hld up: hdwy 4th: chsd wnr 3 out: wknd next*	**2/1**[2]	
0	6	1 ½	**Ol' Man River (IRE)**[174] [490] 5-10-12	MBradburne	84
			(H D Daly) *prom tl wknd appr 3 out*	**100/1**	
	7	1 ¼	**Muntami (IRE)**[12] 4-10-12	ChristianWilliams	83
			(John A Harris) *hld up: hdwy 5th: wknd after next*	**33/1**	
05-	8	hd	**Mayyas**[388] [1802] 5-10-12	JPMcNamara	83
			(C C Bealby) *prom tl wknd appr 2 out*	**200/1**	
0	9	4	**Prairie Law (GER)**[17] [1908] 5-10-5	TMessenger(7)	79
			(B N Pollock) *hld up: effrt 5th: wknd 3 out*	**100/1**	
P	10	shd	**Miniperse (FR)**[8] [2070] 5-10-9	GCarenza(3)	79
			(G R I Smyly) *led: clr 3rd: hdd & wknd appr 3 out*	**200/1**	
	11	nk	**Najca De Thaix (FR)**[185] 4-10-12	AThornton	78
			(Mrs L Wadham) *hld up: nvr nr to chal*	**40/1**	
6	12	nk	**Future Legend**[12] [1982] 4-10-12	TDoyle	78
			(J A B Old) *hld up: hdwy 5th: wknd next*	**33/1**	
	13	24	**Castle Frome (IRE)**[27] 6-10-7	PMerrigan(5)	54
			(A E Price) *chsd ldr to 3rd: mstke and wknd 3 out*	**66/1**	
P6	14	10	**Gustavo**[11] [2006] 4-10-12	AO'Keeffe	44
			(Miss Venetia Williams) *hld up: rdn and wknd after 5th*	**80/1**	
05-	15	1 ¼	**Homelife (IRE)**[294] [3517] 7-10-12	OMcPhail	43
			(Mrs J A Saunders) *hld up: rdn and wknd after 5th*	**100/1**	
F	16	3 ½	**Classic Lease**[25] [1794] 4-10-9	FKing(3)	39
			(J Mackie) *rel to r: a bhd*	**125/1**	
50-	17	shd	**Tuesday Club (IRE)**[303] [3367] 6-10-12	JMMaguire	39
			(J A B Old) *hld up: a in rr*	**100/1**	
	18	dist	**Desiree (IRE)**[129] 4-10-5	VSlattery	—
			(John Berry) *hld up: a in rr*	**100/1**	
P	19	9	**Seven Shirt**[8] [2070] 4-10-12	PMoloney	—
			(E G Bevan) *hld up: plld hrd: mstke 3rd: a in rr*	**200/1**	
65	P		**Burning Moon**[52] 4-10-12	PJBrennan	—
			(K A Morgan) *hld up: plld hrd: a in rr: t.o whn p.u bef 2 out*	**100/1**	
	P		**Devious Ayers (IRE)**[16] [1916] 4-10-7	StephenJCraine(5)	—
			(J M Bradley) *prom: sddle slipped after 2nd: wknd after 4th: p.u bef next*	**66/1**	

3m 50.9s (-16.70) **Going Correction** -0.90s/f (Hard)
WFA 4 from 5yo+ 12lb **21** Ran SP% **124.0**
Speed ratings: **105,103,103,95,93 92,91,91,89,89 89,89,77,72,71 69,69,—,—,— —** CSF £14.82 TOTE £2.70: £1.10, £3.60, £2.70; EX 34.20 Place 6 £208.42, Place 5 £57.57.
Owner D A Johnson **Bred** Haras De Saint-Voir **Trained** Nicholashayne, Devon

FOCUS
Little strength in depth, but this was still a fair novice event for the track, and the form looks sound. The winner can rate higher.

NOTEBOOK
Nous Voila(FR) ◆, very well supported to maintain his stable's excellent run of recent form, duly landed the gamble with a convincing display on this hurdling debut. Having won and finished runner-up in his two outings on the Flat in France, he clearly possesses plenty of ability, and he had no trouble translating that talent to hurdling and should be rated value for further. The ground was to his liking, he shaped as though he will get further, and he will no doubt be hard to stop under a penalty next time. *(op 11-8 tchd 6-4 in places)*
Dhehdaah, fit from two recent spins on the Flat, proved no match for the winner on this return to jumping but still ran a personal best in defeat. He will look better off in handicaps from his current rating and is well worth another try over further. *(tchd 12-1)*
Sangiovese, a fair middle-distance handicapper on the level, was doing his best work at the finish and posted an encouraging hurdling debut. He should be seen to better effect when eligible for handicaps and ought to appreciate further in this sphere. *(op 8-1)*
Winapenny(IRE), fifth on his debut under Rules 375 days previously, ran as though the race was needed and was not disgraced. He is another who will probably fare better when handicapped and upped to a suitably longer distance.
Amarula Ridge(IRE), who had some decent placed form last term, failed to make a serious impression on this return from a break and again disappointed. He has yet to convince that he gets home, even over the minimum trip, and clearly a sharper track will help in that regard. *(op 7-4)*
Future Legend *Official explanation: jockey said gelding had a breathing problem*
Desiree(IRE) *Official explanation: trainer said that after returning home filly was found to have pulled muscles in her hindquarters (op 200-1)*
Devious Ayers(IRE) *Official explanation: jockey said saddle slipped (op 50-1)*
T/Jkpt: £74,147.90 to a £1 stake. Pool: £104,433.75. 1.00 winning ticket. T/Plt: £629.70 to a £1 stake. Pool: £40,159.65. 46.55 winning tickets. T/Qpdt: £22.10 to a £1 stake. Pool: £4,527.20. 151.10 winning tickets. CR

2253 - 2255a (Foreign Racing) - See Raceform Interactive

1814 FAKENHAM (L-H)

Tuesday, November 15

OFFICIAL GOING: Good
Wind: Light, across Weather: Overcast

2256 MACMILLAN CANCER RELIEF (S) H'CAP HURDLE (11 hdls) 2m 4f

1:00 (1:01) (Class 5) (0-95,92) 4-Y-0+ **£2,507** (£730; £365)

Form			Horse	Jockey	RPR
5-26	1		**Chickapeakray**[187] [310] 4-9-12 **69**	StephenJCraine(5)	86+
			(D McCain) *w ldr tl led 4 out: clr next: eased flat*	**28/1**	
2FF6	2	13	**Approaching Land (IRE)**[58] [1486] 10-11-3 **86**	MrTGreenall(3)	86+
			(M W Easterby) *prom: chsd wnr appr 2 out: no imp: blnd last*	**8/1**	
410P	3	5	**Macreater**[121] [1028] 7-10-9 **75**	(p) PJBrennan	68
			(K A Morgan) *led to 4 out: wknd appr 2 out*	**25/1**	
P664	4	¾	**Buz Kiri (USA)**[19] [1890] 7-11-3 **83**	WHutchinson	75
			(A W Carroll) *hld up: mstke 5th: styd on appr last: nvr nrr*	**11/2**[3]	
P064	5	5	**Phase Eight Girl**[38] [1685] 9-10-4 **70**	RJohnson	57
			(J Hetherton) *prom: lost pl 6th: n.d after*	**13/2**	
P-43	6	3 ½	**Tioga Gold (IRE)**[49] [1566] 6-11-0 **80**	PHide	64
			(L R James) *chsd ldrs tl wknd after 4 out*	**8/1**	
3-40	7	2 ½	**Double Royal (IRE)**[41] [1645] 6-11-6 **86**	RThornton	67
			(Mrs T J Hill) *hld up: effrt after 4 out: sn wknd*	**5/1**[2]	
-1P3	8	13	**Irish Blessing (USA)**[30] [1756] 8-11-5 **85**	(tp) LAspell	53
			(F Jordan) *chsd ldrs: rdn 7th: wknd next*	**9/2**[1]	
5P0P	9	5	**Zahunda (IRE)**[20] [1883] 6-9-8 **70**	(v[1]) CareyWilliamson(10)	33
			(M J Gingell) *hld up: hdwy 5th: wknd after 4 out*	**33/1**	
600-	10	10	**Darialann (IRE)**[341] [2717] 10-11-9 **92**	LVickers(3)	45
			(O Brennan) *hld up: rdn 6th: a in rr*	**20/1**	
U0-1	11	2	**Clydeoneeyed**[184] [363] 6-9-11 **70**	SWalsh(7)	21
			(K F Clutterbuck) *prom: lost pl 4th: bhd fr 7th*	**11/1**	
40P-	P		**Gamma-Delta (IRE)**[206] [4977] 10-11-4 **91**	APogson(7)	—
			(C T Pogson) *hld up: rdn 5th: t.o whn p.u bef 8th*	**20/1**	

5m 19.0s (6.80) **Going Correction** +0.125s/f (Yiel)
WFA 4 from 6yo+ 13lb **12** Ran SP% **113.9**
Speed ratings: **91,85,83,83,81 80,79,73,71,67 67,—** CSF £215.96 CT £5586.17 TOTE £27.20: £6.50, £4.20, £7.00; EX 525.40.The winner was bought in for 5,600gns.
Owner Ray Pattison **Bred** J Singleton **Trained** Cholmondeley, Cheshire

FOCUS
This looked a very weak seller, but it was won in very easy style by the winnner. The winning time was modest, even for a seller, and apart from the winner, the form looks limted and unlikely to be reliable.

NOTEBOOK
Chickapeakray was going so well that she could be called the winner with almost a circuit to go. Travelling with plenty of enthusiasm from the outset, she was never in any serious danger and won with any amount in hand, forging well clear of her rivals from the third-last. She looks one to follow *at a similarly sharp course, but would probably struggle to get home on a more conventional track. (op 25-1)*
Approaching Land(IRE) steadily became outpaced with a circuit to go after being kept close to the pace by his jockey in the early stages. To his credit, he kept on well for strong pressure throughout the final lap, and is a tricky ride at three miles in this grade. A switch to fences will also make him of interest at a low level. *(op 6-1)*
Macreater helped force the modest early pace but did not appear to get home over the trip. Her best form has been at Towcester over two miles.
Buz Kiri(USA) did stay on reasonably well in the final stages despite never posing a serious threat. A much stiffer track may help him in the future. *(tchd 5-1)*
Phase Eight Girl, who was niggled along at an early stage, gave the impression at one stage that she was about be pulled up by her jockey down the back straight on the final circuit, before flying home after jumping the second last. A step up in trip will help, but she does not look a straightforward ride. *(op 9-1)*
Tioga Gold(IRE), who was covered up in midfield, never looked like getting involved at any stage and proved very disappointing. *(tchd 17-2)*
Irish Blessing(USA) was beaten a long way from home and ran as though something was amiss. *Official explanation: vet said gelding returned moving stiffly (op 4-1)*

2257 WEATHERBYS BANK H'CAP CHASE (12 fncs) 2m 110y
1:30 (1:30) (Class 4) (0-95,93) 5-Y-0+ **£4,124** (£1,210; £605; £302)

Form				RPR
2343	**1**		**Amadeus (AUS)**^{106} [1126] 8-11-5 **86** .... TScudamore (M Scudamore) *hld up: hdwy 6th: led appr 3 out: sn clr* **9/2**^{3}	105+
-630	**2**	*20*	**Brigadier Du Bois (FR)**^{10} [2043] 6-10-12 **79** .... LAspell (Mrs L Wadham) *hld up: hdwy 5th: wknd appr 2 out* **3/1**^{2}	78
0-5P	**3**	*14*	**Jolly Boy (FR)**^{18} [1905] 6-10-0 **67** .... (b^{1}) AO'Keeffe (Miss Venetia Williams) *nt jump wl: chsd ldrs: hit 3rd: led 8th: hdd appr 3 out: wkng whn blnd 2 out and last* **7/1**	66+
0PP-	**4**	*2 ½*	**Interstice**^{422} [1449] 8-10-3 **75** .... CHonour$^{(5)}$ (M J Gingell) *hld up: hdwy 5th: wknd appr 2 out* **100/1**	58
356P	**5**	*½*	**Kercabellec (FR)**^{25} [1819] 7-10-11 **85** .... APogson$^{(7)}$ (J R Cornwall) *led 2nd: sn hdd: lft in ld after 4th: hdd and blnd 8th: sn wknd* **14/1**	77+
PP3P	**6**	*8*	**Step In Line (IRE)**^{9} [2080] 13-9-7 **67** oh1 .... TMessenger$^{(7)}$ (D W Thompson) *chsd ldrs: lost pl 4th: n.d after* **25/1**	41
0U06	**7**	*3 ½*	**Macgyver (NZ)**^{26} [1795] 9-10-1 **75** .... MissLHorner$^{(7)}$ (D L Williams) *prom to 6th* **14/1**	46
13-P	**8**	*29*	**Cool Chilli**^{199} [135] 7-11-2 **86** .... (t) LVickers$^{(3)}$ (N J Pomfret) *hld up: effrt appr 4 out: sn wknd* **20/1**	28
0-40	**9**	*17*	**Ceresfield (NZ)**^{31} [1746] 9-11-9 **93** .... (vt^{1}) LMcGrath$^{(3)}$ (R C Guest) *chsd ldrs: lost pl 6th: in rr whn hit next: sn bhd* **14/1**	18
4221	**U**		**Un Autre Espere**^{25} [1816] 6-10-12 **79** .... NFehily (C C Bealby) *led to 2nd: sn led again: tried to run out and uns rdr after 4th* **11/4**^{1}	—

4m 19.9s (-0.70) **Going Correction** +0.125s/f (Yiel) **10** Ran SP% **111.9**
Speed ratings: **106,96,90,88,88 84,83,69,61,**— CSF £17.93 CT £90.40 TOTE £4.80: £1.10, £2.20, £2.60; EX 17.50.
Owner Hereford Journal Racing Club **Bred** Woodlands Stud Syndicate Nsw **Trained** Bromsash, Herefordshire

FOCUS
Another easy winner on the day, almost certainly due to the very quick early pace and horses weakening.

NOTEBOOK
Amadeus(AUS), who was held up behind the quick pace, made his way past horses on the final circuit and eventually came well clear of his rivals after the second last. He was on a fair handicap mark coming into the race, but will probably struggle after being reassessed as he may have been slightly flattered by the winning distance due to the strong early pace. *(op 5-1)*
Brigadier Du Bois(FR), another in the race who sat well off the early pace, steadily moved into contention as the front-runners weakened, but could never bridge the gap to the winner, and gave the impression that a step up in trip will help. *(tchd 11-4 and 10-3)*
Jolly Boy(FR) did really well to complete, let alone get competitive, after some shocking leaps. Given some stiff reminders early in the race, he does not look an easy ride. *(op 9-1)*
Interstice shaped reasonably well after a really long break and ran better than his final position suggested. A bit further over fences may help his cause. *(tchd 80-1)*
Kercabellec(FR), who helped to set a really quick early pace, was on the retreat when making a really bad error at the first fence on the final circuit. He did surprisingly well considering that mistake as he lost all impetus and almost unshipped his jockey, who had to cling around his neck for a few strides. *(op 16-1)*
Un Autre Espere was going along nicely in front when he attempted to run out on a bend, causing his jockey to unseat. He clearly has his quirks and cannot be trusted. *(op 9-4)*

2258 NGK SPARK PLUGS JUVENILE NOVICES' HURDLE (9 hdls) 2m
2:00 (2:00) (Class 3) 3-Y-0 **£4,853** (£1,424; £712; £355)

Form				RPR
2	**1**		**Bayard (USA)**^{15} [1955] 3-10-12 .... APMcCoy (J R Fanshawe) *w ldr: hmpd 1st: led 5th: pushed clr and nt fluent last: eased nr fin* **4/9**^{1}	89+
	2	*3*	**Knock Bridge (IRE)**^{18} 3-10-5 .... RThornton (P D Evans) *a.p: chsd wnr and hit 3 out: sn rdn: styd on same pce appr last* **7/2**^{2}	77+
00	**3**	*5*	**Flower Haven**^{10} [2045] 3-10-0 .... CHonour$^{(5)}$ (M J Gingell) *hld up: hdwy 4th: mstke 2 out: styd on same pce* **66/1**	70+
0	**4**	*5*	**Lobengula (IRE)**^{9} [2076] 3-10-9 .... LVickers$^{(3)}$ (I W McInnes) *chsd ldrs tl wknd appr 2 out* **33/1**	71
	5	*1 ½*	**Best Game**^{32} 3-10-7 .... DCCostello$^{(5)}$ (D W Thompson) *hld up: hdwy 6th: wknd aproaching 2 out* **28/1**	70
	6	*2 ½*	**Ngauruhoe (IRE)**^{38} 3-10-2 ow4 .... MrMatthewSmith$^{(7)}$ (John Berry) *hld up: hdwy 3 out: wknd bef next* **50/1**	64
	7	*21*	**Mister Aziz (IRE)**^{24} 3-10-12 .... JMogford (J R Jenkins) *hld up: rdn 3 out: n.d* **66/1**	46
0	**8**	*6*	**Trackattack**^{7} [2101] 3-10-12 .... ATinkler (P Howling) *chsd ldrs tl wknd appr 3 out* **40/1**	40
0	**9**	*25*	**Vettorious**^{31} [1737] 3-10-12 .... WMarston (Mrs P Sly) *led and j.rt 1st: hdd 5th: wknd appr 3 out* **18/1**^{3}	15
FP	**10**	*5*	**Champagne Rossini (IRE)**^{80} [1338] 3-10-12 .... KJohnson (M C Chapman) *hld up: plld hrd: pckd 3rd: a bhd* **80/1**	10
	P		**Golden Squaw**^{426} 3-9-12 .... TMessenger$^{(7)}$ (Miss C J E Caroe) *bhd whn j.rt 2nd: t.o whn p.u bef 2 out* **100/1**	—

4m 11.2s (2.30) **Going Correction** +0.125s/f (Yiel) **11** Ran SP% **112.7**
Speed ratings: **99,97,95,92,91 90,80,77,64,62** — CSF £1.90 TOTE £1.50: £1.10, £1.30, £5.30; EX 2.60.
Owner Mr & Mrs G Middlebrook/Mr & Mrs P Brain **Bred** And Mrs G Middlebrook & Brain International Lt **Trained** Newmarket, Suffolk

FOCUS
A very average juvenile hurdle that took little winning.

NOTEBOOK
Bayard(USA) won like an odds-on shot, taking a clear lead from the fourth-last and rarely looking in any danger after. He was no great shakes on the Flat, so is opposable under a penalty next time, despite winning nicely. *(tchd 1-2 tchd 8-15 in a place)*
Knock Bridge(IRE) ran with plenty of promise despite hitting the third-last very hard. Her stamina is not guaranteed over hurdles, given her Flat form, but a race at a course that does not test her staying power too much can be won with her, as she beat the rest clearly. *(op 4-1)*
Flower Haven appeared to run well above her previous form, and she will win a similar race in the future if this effort can be believed. *(op 50-1)*
Lobengula(IRE) was very keen in the early stages and failed to get home. He has winning form on the Flat and could be one to watch when handicapped. *(op 20-1)*
Best Game, under pressure from an early stage, did well to finish as close as he did. He is far from certain to stay two miles over hurdles as he has winning form below a mile on the Flat, but he ran respectably. *(op 25-1 tchd 33-1)*
Ngauruhoe(IRE) did not show a great deal on the Flat and was well behind before staying on in the latter stages on this hurdling debut. She did not totally disgrace herself and might win a race at some stage over hurdles. *(tchd 66-1)*

2259 JEWSON H'CAP CHASE (16 fncs) 2m 5f 110y
2:30 (2:30) (Class 4) (0-105,105) 5-Y-0+ **£5,074** (£1,489; £744; £372)

Form				RPR
-362	**1**		**New Perk (IRE)**^{18} [1905] 7-9-12 **82** oh13 ow3 .... CHonour$^{(5)}$ (M J Gingell) *a.p: chsd ldr and mstke 4 out: outpcd appr 2 out: rallied bef last: led flat: rdn out* **18/1**	90+
1U1-	**2**	*1 ¼*	**Alcopop**^{229} [4670] 6-11-12 **105** .... SThomas (Miss Venetia Williams) *led to 2nd: led 12th: clr 3 out: rdn and mstke last: hdd and no ex flat* **3/1**^{2}	116+
0U5P	**3**	*1 ¾*	**Walcot Lad (IRE)**^{2} [2217] 9-10-4 **86** .... (p) CBolger$^{(3)}$ (A Ennis) *led 2nd to 12th: outpcd appr 2 out: rallied last: no ex flat* **20/1**	92+
542P	**4**	*10*	**Lothian Falcon**^{17} [1928] 6-11-7 **103** .... GCarenza$^{(3)}$ (P Maddison) *hld up: hdwy 12th: wknd 2 out* **20/1**	97
2-03	**5**	*18*	**Tresor Preziniere (FR)**^{18} [1907] 7-11-4 **97** .... RJohnson (P J Hobbs) *hld up: hdwy 6th: hit 11th: wknd after next* **11/4**^{1}	73
P43-	**6**	*¾*	**Moscow Leader (IRE)**^{442} [1322] 7-11-2 **98** .... (p) LMcGrath$^{(3)}$ (R C Guest) *prom: mstke 3rd: wknd 12th* **25/1**	73
4-42	**F**		**Rainbow Tree**^{44} [1607] 5-11-2 **95** .... LAspell (C C Bealby) *hld up: fell 9th* **4/1**^{3}	—
2-34	**P**		**Thyne Man (IRE)**^{18} [1907] 7-11-9 **102** .... PMoloney (J Mackie) *prom: mstke and lost pl 3rd: bhd whn p.u bef 6th* **11/2**	—
-323	**P**		**Hey Boy (IRE)**^{25} [1815] 6-11-4 **97** .... MFoley (Mrs S J Humphrey) *hld up in tch: lost pl 7th: bhd fr next: t.o whn p.u bef 3 out* **33/1**	—

5m 41.8s (-2.70) **Going Correction** +0.125s/f (Yiel) **9** Ran SP% **108.6**
Speed ratings: **109,108,107,104,97 97,—,—,—** CSF £65.93 CT £995.83 TOTE £20.60: £3.30, £1.80, £3.00; EX 56.00.
Owner A White **Bred** Tim Mulhare **Trained** North Runcton, Norfolk

FOCUS
A fair winning time for the grade. New Perk finally got his head in front when Alcopop stopped very quickly in the straight. The form is probably best rated through the third.

NOTEBOOK
New Perk(IRE), racing from 13lb out of the handicap and carrying 3lb overweight, finally managed to break his duck when clear leader Alcopop stopped quickly in the home straight. Given a second chance after looking held exiting the back straight, he put his head down and made full use of the weight concession to get in front. He had always threatened to win a race and deserved his first success, but he is far from guaranteed to follow up. *(op 25-1)*
Alcopop, returning after a long layoff, managed to snatch defeat from certain-looking victory after jumping the last. Having been clear and apparently travelling well leaving the back straight, he still held a decent advantage coming to the last, where a combination of a slight error, a hefty weight concession and time off the track caught up with him, and he was passed close to the line. He can be considered slightly unlucky not to have held on. *(op 7-2)*
Walcot Lad(IRE), making a very quick reappearance after a disappointing effort, is nicely handicapped again and should go close next time if not raised by the Handicapper too much for the effort. *(op 16-1)*
Lothian Falcon ◆ ran a bit better than his final position suggested, having been with the chasing bunch until the second-last. A step back up in trip will suit him. *(op 22-1 tchd 16-1)*
Tresor Preziniere(FR) was a huge disappointment, never travelling particularly well at any stage. He is possibly better suited by a stiffer track, but not many other excuses can be made for his effort. *(op 7-4)*
Thyne Man(IRE) lost his place after a mid-air collision over the third fence, and never recovered his position. *Official explanation: jockey said gelding lost its action (op 13-2 tchd 5-1)*
Rainbow Tree was still going well enough until meeting the ninth fence all wrong and coming to grief. *(op 13-2 tchd 5-1)*

2260 MACMILLAN CANCER RELIEF NOVICES' CHASE (18 fncs) 3m 110y
3:00 (3:00) (Class 3) 5-Y-0+ **£7,468** (£2,192; £1,096; £547)

Form				RPR
-103	**1**		**Goblet Of Fire (USA)**^{21} [1872] 6-11-0 .... (b) ChristianWilliams (P F Nicholls) *hld up: hdwy 6th: jnd ldr 9th: led 13th: pckd 2 out: drvn out* **2/1**^{2}	122+
213	**2**	*1 ¾*	**Unleash (USA)**^{10} [2052] 6-11-6 .... RJohnson (P J Hobbs) *hld up: hdwy 11th: chsd wnr appr 3 out: rdn after next: styd on same pce last* **4/5**^{1}	125+
0604	**3**	*22*	**Sunny South East (IRE)**^{44} [1618] 5-10-1 .... WKennedy$^{(5)}$ (S Gollings) *prom: chsd ldr 5th: led 7th to next: wknd 14th* **50/1**	89
2133	**4**	*3 ½*	**Killonemoonlight (IRE)**^{21} [1870] 6-10-2 110 .... MNicolls$^{(5)}$ (D R Stoddart) *chsd ldr to 5th: rdn after 13th: mstke and wknd 4 out* **13/2**^{3}	89+
P	**5**	*16*	**Deltic Arrow**^{7} [2109] 7-11-0 .... AThornton (D L Williams) *led to 7th: led next to 13th: mstke 4 out: wknd next* **50/1**	86+
P-P0	**6**	*21*	**Back De Bay (IRE)**^{9} [2081] 5-10-6 .... APogson$^{(7)}$ (J R Cornwall) *chsd ldrs: lost pl 12th: bhd whn blnd next* **150/1**	56
00/P	**P**		**Lunardi (IRE)**^{23} [1856] 7-10-7 70 .... MissLHorner$^{(7)}$ (D L Williams) *hld up: wknd 12th: t.o whn p.u bef 2 out* **150/1**	—

6m 50.8s (13.20) **Going Correction** +0.125s/f (Yiel)
WFA 5 from 6yo+ 1lb **7** Ran SP% **107.5**
Speed ratings: **83,82,75,74,69 62,**— CSF £3.66 TOTE £3.30: £1.70, £1.10; EX 4.30.
Owner Mrs Angela Tincknell **Bred** Compagnia Generale **Trained** Ditcheat, Somerset

FOCUS
The race only concerned two from some way from home. The winner was always well positioned and used that advantage to secure victory. The pace was steady and the winning time very slow.

NOTEBOOK
Goblet Of Fire(USA), the only runner for his stable on the card, was always in exactly the right position throughout the race to make a successful chasing debut. With favourite Unleash always behind, he kept finding a bit more for his jockey's urgings, and never allowed the second to get past him. He will face much stiffer tasks in future, and his fluency over fences will need to improve, but he did the job nicely enough and is sure to win more races. *(op 15-8 tchd 9-4)*
Unleash(USA) had his chance but could never get past the eventual winner. His 6lb penalty may have just anchored him, but Goblet Of Fire was full value for his win. *(tchd 8-11 and 5-6 in places)*
Sunny South East(IRE) travelled nicely when the pace was sedate, but was readily outpaced as the leaders went for home and did well to secure third place after struggling down the back straight. With some scope for improvement, she can be placed to win a race in time. *(op 100-1)*
Killonemoonlight(IRE) proved disappointing given her fair form over hurdles. She never looked like she was enjoying it from an early stage and must convince next time that fences are what she requires. *(op 15-2 tchd 8-1)*
Deltic Arrow ◆ showed up nicely for much of the race and can definitely win a low-grade affair over fences.

2261 LAY BACK AND BET AT GG.COM NOVICES' H'CAP HURDLE (9 hdls) 2m
3:30 (3:30) (Class 4) (0-105,110) 3-Y-0+ **£3,487** (£1,023; £511; £255)

Form				RPR
/5-4	**1**		**Alph**^{31} [1745] 8-11-1 **93** .... MBatchelor (B R Johnson) *hld up: hdwy 5th: led after 3 out: clr appr last: eased nr fin* **11/2**^{3}	111+

222/ **2** 1 ½ **Rebel Raider (IRE)**[17] [889] 6-11-1 **93** .... AThornton 103
(B N Pollock) *chsd ldrs: led 3 out: sn hdd: rdn appr last: styd on* **12/1**
4221 **3** 11 **Air Guitar (IRE)**[5] [2144] 5-12-4 **110** 7ex .... PMoloney 110+
(M G Quinlan) *hld up: hdwy after 5th: wknd appr 2 out* **5/1**[2]
5 **4** 8 **Dare To Dance**[3] [2173] 7-11-4 **96** .... APMcCoy 89+
(R Donohoe, Ire) *hld up: hdwy after 5th: ev ch whn hit 3 out: wkng whn nt fluent next* **11/4**[1]
0-04 **5** 6 **Pick Of The Crop**[51] [1562] 4-10-10 **88** .... JMogford 73
(J R Jenkins) *chsd ldrs tl wknd after 6th* **66/1**
0-25 **6** 7 **Dargaville (NZ)**[171] [544] 6-11-1 **98** .... (tp) PCO'Neill(5) 76
(R C Guest) *chsd ldrs: rdn after 5th: sn wknd* **12/1**
4-61 **7** 20 **Cappanrush (IRE)**[19] [1896] 5-11-1 **96** .... CBolger(3) 54
(A Ennis) *hld up: bhd fr 5th* **16/1**
446 **8** 1 ¾ **Coronado's Gold (USA)**[29] [1772] 4-11-4 **96** .... (v[1]) PHide 52
(V Smith) *led: clr 4th: hdd & wknd 3 out* **11/1**
01 **9** 6 **Barking Mad (USA)**[15] [1952] 7-11-10 **102** .... TScudamore 52
(C R Dore) *chsd ldr to 5th: wknd after next* **12/1**
0-16 **10** 4 **Bayadere (GER)**[184] [367] 5-10-9 **94** .... SWalsh(7) 40
(K F Clutterbuck) *hld up: bhd fr 5th* **40/1**
6441 **11** 5 **Wardash (GER)**[25] [1814] 5-10-7 **92** .... AGlassonbury(7) 33
(M C Chapman) *hld up: bhd fr 5th* **25/1**
P3-5 **12** 3 ½ **Coolbythepool**[10] [2043] 5-10-6 **89** .... CHonour(5) 27
(M J Gingell) *hld up:: bhd fr 5th* **25/1**
0-24 **13** 11 **Coming Again (IRE)**[30] [1750] 4-11-7 **104** .... (t) StephenJCraine(5) 31
(D McCain) *hld up in tch: rdn and wknd after 5th* **16/1**
P/P- **P** **Nautical**[55] [1560] 7-10-12 **90** .... WHutchinson —
(A W Carroll) *hld up: bhd fr 5th: t.o whn p.u bef 2 out* **25/1**

4m 7.10s (-1.80) **Going Correction** +0.125s/f (Yiel)
WFA 4 from 5yo+ 12lb **14** Ran SP% **117.4**
Speed ratings: **109,108,102,98,95 92,82,81,78,76 73,72,66,—** CSF £63.53 CT £353.43 TOTE £7.70: £2.80, £2.30, £2.70; EX 79.70 Place 6 £138.57, Place 5 £12.86.
Owner Andy Chard Boris Thompson Alan Jackson **Bred** G A And Mrs Antill **Trained** Ashtead, Surrey

FOCUS
A decent early pace resulted in a fair winning time for the class. The form is probably best rated through the third and the winner looked value for further.

NOTEBOOK
Alph ◆ was suited by the quick early pace and came home an easy winner. He does not appear to stand much racing but is clearly decent when making the track, and is very much one to keep on the right side of in the near future. Connections suggested he will go chasing now, but it would not be a surprise to see him run one more race over hurdles, as he looks well handicapped. *(tchd 6-1)*
Rebel Raider(IRE), not seen over hurdles since 2003, did not appear to quite get home after leading down the back straight. A banded performer on the Flat, it was a reasonable effort back over timber and he should win a similar race in due course. A run of seconds should also not be construed as a sign of being ungenuine, as he did not appear to give up at any stage.
Air Guitar(IRE), dropping down in trip, became outpaced under his welter burden when the pace increased, and did well to finish third after looking fourth-best exiting the back straight. *(op 9-2 tchd 4-1)*
Dare To Dance looked to have a good chance after his effort at Cheltenham the previous weekend but, much like that effort, he could never quite get on terms and looks sure to appreciate further in time. *Official explanation: jockey said horse finished lame (op 3-1)*
Pick Of The Crop never got involved but stayed on respectably after being settled off the pace. He might be suited by a step up in trip and a drop to the basement grade.
Coronado's Gold(USA), wearing a first-time visor, went off far too quickly and had no chance of getting home. He will need handling with more restraint to be competitive in the future. *(op 12-1)*
Barking Mad(USA) got involved in a speed duel early in the race and never had a chance of getting home. He will be seen to better effect when granted an uncontested lead.
Nautical *Official explanation: jockey said gelding had a breathing problem (op 22-1)*
T/Plt: £129.50 to a £1 stake. Pool: £52,228.20. 294.40 winning tickets. T/Qpdt: £7.80 to a £1 stake. Pool: £4,921.00. 464.90 winning tickets. CR

[2022] HEXHAM (L-H)
Wednesday, November 16
OFFICIAL GOING: Good to soft (soft in places)
Wind: Light, half-against. Last flight in back straight omitted

2262 EBF FREE ARCHIVE VIDEO FORM ON ATTHERACES.COM "NATIONAL HUNT" NOVICES' HURDLE (QUALIFIER) (6 hdls 2 omitted) 2m 110y
12:20 (12:21) (Class 3) 4-6-Y-0 **£4,739** (£1,391; £695; £347)

Form RPR
44-4 **1** **Scotmail (IRE)**[21] [1885] 4-11-0 .... GLee 107+
(J Howard Johnson) *chsd ldrs: rdn after 2 out: led last: styd on wl* **11/1**
51-0 **2** 5 **Arumun (IRE)**[39] [1681] 4-11-0 .... TScudamore 101
(M Scudamore) *led tl hdd last: kpt on same pce* **10/1**
3- **3** 5 **Windy Hills**[249] [4323] 5-11-0 .... ADobbin 98+
(N G Richards) *a cl up: effrt and ev ch bef last: lft 3rd last: no ex* **4/1**[2]
0-41 **4** 9 **Jontys'Lass**[181] [431] 4-10-4 .... KJMercer(3) 80
(A Crook) *chsd ldrs: outpcd after 3 out: rallied appr last: nvr rchd ldrs* **40/1**
00- **5** 2 **Scotmail Too (IRE)**[214] [4865] 4-10-7 .... BSHughes(7) 85
(J Howard Johnson) *bhd tl kpt on bef last: n.d* **100/1**
4043 **6** 1 **Oscar's Lady (IRE)**[47] [1590] 4-10-2 .... DCCostello(5) 77
(G A Swinbank) *bhd tl hdwy between last two: nvr nrr* **20/1**
-615 **7** 3 **Money Line (IRE)**[7] [2127] 6-11-7 .... APMcCoy 88
(Jonjo O'Neill) *chsd ldrs tl wknd fr 2 out* **5/1**[3]
3-30 **8** dist **Duke Orsino (IRE)**[18] [1927] 5-10-11 96 .... PBuchanan(3) —
(Miss Lucinda V Russell) *in tch tl wknd after 2 out* **28/1**
0-00 **9** 6 **Rosedale Gardens**[8] [2108] 5-11-0 .... ADempsey —
(M W Easterby) *hld up: reminders 1/2-way: struggling fr 3 out* **100/1**
000- **10** 20 **Papawaldo (IRE)**[227] [4713] 6-10-11 .... LMcGrath(3) —
(R C Guest) *a bhd* **100/1**
1-2 **F** **Dancing Partner (USA)**[45] [1613] 4-10-11 .... MrTGreenall(3) —
(M W Easterby) *hld up: fell 4th* **8/1**
2-16 **P** **Notaproblem (IRE)**[195] [194] 6-11-7 100 .... RMcGrath —
(G A Harker) *in tch to 3 out: sn wknd: t.o whn p.u bef last* **7/2**[1]
21 **F** **Cloudy Lane**[178] [470] 5-11-0 .... JMMaguire 107+
(D McCain) *hld up midfield: effrt 2 out: rallied and chalng whn fell heavily last* **4/1**[2]

4m 26.2s (11.00) **Going Correction** +0.425s/f (Soft)
WFA 4 from 5yo+ 12lb **13** Ran SP% **121.0**
Speed ratings: **91,88,86,82,81 80,79,—,—,— —,—,—** CSF £110.29 TOTE £13.10: £3.20, £5.60, £1.90; EX 65.70.
Owner Gordon Brown/bert Watson **Bred** Paul Smyth **Trained** Billy Row, Co Durham

FOCUS
An ordinary event in which the pace was fair. The form looks reasonable, but a slow time tempers confidence somewhat.

NOTEBOOK
Scotmail(IRE) proved well suited by this much stiffer course and, although his task was simplified by a faller at the last, he showed the right attitude. Two and a half miles will suit and he appeals as the type to progress again. *(op 14-1)*
Arumun(IRE), a good-ground bumper winner, had the run of the race but showed ability on this hurdles debut and, although he may do better in handicaps over two and a half miles, he is entitled to come on for this experience. *(op 9-1 tchd 12-1)*
Windy Hills, who ran creditably on his debut in an Ayr bumper when last seen in March, shaped as though the race was needed on this hurdling debut and he is likely to be placed to best advantage in due course. *(op 5-1)*
Jontys'Lass, a fast-ground bumper winner at Wetherby when last seen in May, left the impression on this hurdling debut that the step up to two and a half miles on a galloping course will see her in a better light. *(op 33-1)*
Scotmail Too(IRE), well beaten on both starts in bumpers, only hinted at ability on this hurdling debut, but he appeals as the type to do better over further and with a much stiffer test of stamina.
Oscar's Lady(IRE) ◆, easy to back, has now qualified for a handicap mark and once again left the strong impression that a much stiffer test of stamina will suit over hurdles. She is one to keep an eye on in modest company. *(op 50-1)*
Cloudy Lane, a bumper winner at Southwell on his previous start in May, was in the process of running creditably when falling heavily on this hurdling debut. He looks sure to win a race over two and a half miles plus when getting over this experience. *(op 5-1)*

2263 AT THE RACES RED BUTTON BETTING JUVENILE MAIDEN HURDLE (6 hdls 2 omitted) 2m 110y
12:50 (12:52) (Class 4) 3-Y-O **£3,131** (£912; £456)

Form RPR
2 **1** **Gardasee (GER)**[19] [1904] 3-11-0 .... JMMaguire 125+
(T P Tate) *mde all: clr fr 3rd: unchal* **1/1**[1]
2 30 **Orang Outan (FR)** 3-10-11 .... (t) GBerridge(3) 91+
(J P L Ewart) *in tch: drvn 3 out: chsd wnr between last two: no imp* **33/1**
0005 **3** 14 **Countrywide Sun**[10] [2064] 3-10-7 88 .... EWhillans(7) 76
(A C Whillans) *in tch: drvn fr 3 out: no imp after next* **20/1**
4 hd **Ophistrolie (IRE)**[39] 3-10-9 .... DCCostello(5) 76
(J R Weymes) *bhd: sme hdwy after 2 out: nvr on terms* **40/1**
3 **5** 6 **Lane Marshal**[10] [2076] 3-10-7 .... PJMcDonald(7) 70
(M E Sowersby) *nvr on terms* **20/1**
2-0 **6** 24 **Orki Des Aigles (FR)**[13] [2001] 3-10-11 .... KJMercer(3) 46
(Ferdy Murphy) *in tch: outpcd 1/2-way: n.d after* **8/1**
P **Mercari**[48] 3-10-7 .... BHarding —
(A R Dicken) *bhd whn blnd bdly 2nd: sn p.u* **100/1**
P **Mist Opportunity (IRE)**[446] 3-10-9 .... PMerrigan(5) —
(P C Haslam) *a bhd: t.o whn p.u bef last* **40/1**
P **Cadogen Square**[23] 3-10-0 .... PKinsella(7) —
(Mrs Marjorie Fife) *a bhds: no ch whn p.u bef last* **100/1**
0 **P** **Diatonic**[36] [1563] 3-10-9 .... (b) JFLevins(5) —
(D Carroll) *prom tl wknd bef 3 out: t.o whn p.u bef last* **100/1**
56P **P** **Emerald Destiny (IRE)**[35] [1718] 3-11-0 .... ADempsey —
(D Carroll) *in tch tl wknd 1/2-way: t.o whn p.u bef last* **66/1**
343 **P** **Dramatic Review (IRE)**[18] [1729] 3-11-0 97 .... (t) APMcCoy —
(P C Haslam) *chsd ldrs tl wknd between last two: p.u bef last* **11/2**[3]
P **Bronze Dancer (IRE)**[15] 3-11-0 .... ADobbin —
(G A Swinbank) *nt fluent 1st: midfield: hdwy 1/2-way: chsd wnr briefly 2 out: wknd and p.u bef last* **4/1**[2]

4m 17.4s (2.20) **Going Correction** +0.425s/f (Soft) **13** Ran SP% **118.3**
Speed ratings: **111,96,90,90,87 76,—,—,—,— —,—,—** CSF £47.99 TOTE £2.00: £1.30, £3.50, £3.70; EX 52.30.
Owner A S Helaissi **Bred** Gestut Romerhof **Trained** Tadcaster, N Yorks

FOCUS
There was a decent gallop on and the winning time was very smart for the grade, almost nine seconds quicker than the opener, but there was little of note behind the easy winner, who should score again over hurdles. The race has been rated through the third.

NOTEBOOK
Gardasee(GER), a grand sort, won an uncompetitive event with plenty in hand. He is open to plenty of improvement and appeals strongly as the type to win more races over obstacles. *(op 6-4)*
Orang Outan(FR), a brother to a bumper winner, was far from disgraced on this racecourse debut but left the impression that a stiffer test of stamina in modest handicap company will suit in due course. *(op 28-1)*
Countrywide Sun, who ran his best race over hurdles on his handicap debut last time, had his limitations exposed back in this grade. The return to modest handicaps and to a longer trip should provide his best chance of success. *(op 25-1)*
Ophistrolie(IRE), who did not show much on the Flat, was well beaten on this hurdling debut and is likely to remain vulnerable in this grade. *(op 50-1 tchd 33-1)*
Lane Marshal, who was not disgraced in a bad race on his hurdling debut, had his limitations exposed and is likely to continue to look vulnerable in this grade. *(op 11-1)*
Orki Des Aigles(FR), who showed ability over hurdles in France, was again a big disappointment for his in-form stable, and he looks one to tread carefully with at present. *(op 6-1)*
Mist Opportunity(IRE) *Official explanation: jockey said gelding hung left (op 20-1)*
Bronze Dancer(IRE), out of sorts when last seen on the Flat, showed ability before tiring on this hurdling debut, but he left the impression that less of a test of stamina would have been in his favour. *(op 20-1)*

2264 AT THE RACES 3G H'CAP HURDLE (8 hdls 2 omitted) 2m 4f 110y
1:20 (1:21) (Class 3) (0-120,119) 4-Y-O+ **£6,818** (£2,001; £750; £750)

Form RPR
3 **1** **Texas Holdem (IRE)**[11] [2038] 6-10-12 **112** .... MJMcAlister(7) 116
(M Smith) *chsd ldrs: effrt between last two: led run in: hld on wl* **9/1**
161- **2** shd **Vic The Piler (IRE)**[227] [4713] 6-11-5 **112** .... ADobbin 116
(N G Richards) *hld up midfield: hdwy bef 3 out: ev ch between last two: sn outpcd: kpt on wl fr last: jst hld* **6/4**[1]
313- **3** ½ **Posh Stick**[208] [4966] 8-9-11 **97** oh16 ow4 .... BenOrde-Powlett(7) 100
(J B Walton) *lft in ld 3rd: hdd 5th: led next to run in: kpt on: hld nr fin* **28/1**
14-2 **3** dht **Marsh Run**[13] [2004] 6-10-9 **105** .... MrTGreenall(3) 108
(M W Easterby) *hld up: hdwy and pushed along 2 out: kpt on wl fr last* **8/1**[3]
2-41 **5** 3 ½ **Tynedale (IRE)**[11] [2038] 6-11-5 **119** .... TJDreaper(7) 119
(Mrs A Hamilton) *chsd ldrs: drvn and outpcd after 2 out: rallied bef last: no imp* **17/2**
6-63 **6** 21 **Ireland's Eye (IRE)**[13] [2010] 10-9-9 **95** .... MrSFMagee(7) 74
(J R Norton) *in tch: drvn bef 3 out: rallied next: sn wknd* **20/1**
14-P **7** 3 ½ **Progressive (IRE)**[54] [1542] 7-10-11 **104** .... APMcCoy 79
(Jonjo O'Neill) *hld up: hdwy and ev ch between last two: sn wknd* **7/2**[2]

123- **8** 1 **Sara Monica (IRE)**[241] 4475 8-10-2 **105** .... JPEnnis(10) 79
(L Lungo) *bhd: struggling 3 out: nvr on terms* **16/1**
F1P0 **9** 17 **Isellido (IRE)**[17] 1940 6-10-7 **110** ....(e1) JPFlavin(10) 67
(R C Guest) *cl up: led 4 out to next. hit 2 out: sn wknd* **33/1**
00P0 **10** 1 3/4 **Ramblees Holly**[8] 2110 7-10-4 **102** .... DMcGann(5) 58
(R S Wood) *keen: in tch tl hit and wknd 3 out* **66/1**
2-40 **U** **Gospel Song**[17] 1940 13-9-10 **96** ow1 .... EWhillans(7) —
(A C Whillans) *led tl blnd and uns rdr 3rd* **66/1**
441- **P** **Aberdare**[210] 4924 6-10-8 **104** .... GBerridge(3) —
(J R Bewley) *prom tl wknd 3 out: t.o whn p.u bef last* **40/1**
332- **P** **County Classic**[255] 4210 6-10-12 **105** .... RGarritty —
(T D Easterby) *hld up: rdn 3 out: btn after next: t.o whn p.u bef last* **20/1**

5m 16.4s (6.80) **Going Correction** +0.425s/f (Soft) **13** Ran SP% **121.1**
Speed ratings: **104,103,103,103,102 94,93,92,86,85** —,—,—PL: Texas Holdem £2.40, Vic The Piler £1.20, Marsh Run £1.00, Posh Stick £3.50. TRIC: TH/VTP/MR £59.97, TH/VTP/PS £193.05. CSF £22.46 TOTE £10.40; EX 53.50.
Owner Michael Smith **Bred** Burren Racing Syndicate **Trained** Kirkheaton, Northumberland

FOCUS
An ordinary handicap in which the pace was only fair in the first half of the contest. The winner has been rated as back to the pick of his Irish form.

NOTEBOOK
Texas Holdem(IRE) fully confirmed the bit of promise shown after a break on his previous start and showed the right attitude in the closing stages. He should not go up too much for this win and is likely to continue to give a good account. *(op 8-1 tchd 10-1)*
Vic The Piler(IRE) ◆, having his first start since April, was well supported and turned in an improved effort on this handicap debut. He shaped as though a better end-to-end gallop would have suited and, with this run behind him, is one to keep on the right side in similar company. *(op 2-1)*
Posh Stick, returned to hurdles on this first start since April, had the run of the race but ran a blinder carrying 20lb more than her allotted mark. The handicapper is unlikely to do her many favours but she remains capable of winning a race in this sphere. *(op 7-1 tchd 13-2 and 9-1)*
Marsh Run fully confirmed reappearance promise and fared best of those that came from the back of the field. A stiffer test over this trip would have suited and he remains capable of better this season. *(op 7-1 tchd 13-2 and 9-1)*
Tynedale(IRE), 5lb higher than when successful at Kelso last time, could not confirm placings with Texas Holdem but was not disgraced. Although vulnerable to progressive sorts off this mark, he should be suited by a return to three miles. *(op 12-1)*
Ireland's Eye(IRE), an inconsistent performer, was again below his best on this second run back after a break of over six months. He has slipped back to a fair mark but remains one to tread very carefully with. *(op 16-1)*
Progressive(IRE), who jumped badly on his chase debut last time, was disappointing for this return to hurdles and, although lightly raced enough to be open to further improvement, looks one to tread carefully with at present. *(tchd 4-1)*

2265 PETER FLETCHER ASSOCIATES NORTHUMBERLAND NATIONAL H'CAP CHASE (25 fncs) 4m
1:50 (1:50) (Class 3) (0-130,130) 5-Y-0+
£13,127 (£3,877; £1,938; £970; £484; £243)

Form RPR
10-P **1** **Supreme Breeze (IRE)**[17] 1941 10-10-8 **112** .... DElsworth 120
(Mrs S J Smith) *in tch: pushed along bef 3 out: rallied to ld run in: styd on wl* **14/1**
61-P **2** 3/4 **Mini Sensation (IRE)**[17] 1941 12-11-1 **119** ....(v1) APMcCoy 127+
(Jonjo O'Neill) *cl up: led 20th: sn rdn: hdd 3 out: rallied to ld bef last: hdd run in: kpt on* **9/1**
22-1 **3** 2 **Capybara (IRE)**[12] 2023 7-10-11 **115** .... DO'Meara 120
(H P Hogarth) *prom: hit 16th: outpcd bef 3 out: rallied bef last: kpt on wl run in* **11/2**[1]
F-40 **4** 1/2 **Harlov (FR)**[17] 1941 10-10-3 **107** ....(p) ADempsey 113+
(A Parker) *hld up: hdwy 19th: rdn after 4 out: rallied bef last: kpt on run in* **7/1**[3]
0123 **5** 5 **Pass Me By**[17] 1941 6-10-6 **115** ....(e) PCO'Neill(5) 117+
(R C Guest) *cl up: led 3 out to bef last: wknd run in* **10/1**
U44- **6** 26 **Falchion**[227] 4710 10-10-1 **108** ow1 ....(t) GBerridge(3) 82
(J R Bewley) *nt fluent in rr: effrt u.p 4 out: nvr rchd ldrs* **28/1**
3-06 **7** 8 **Spanish Main (IRE)**[20] 1893 11-10-3 **107** .... CLlewellyn 73
(N A Twiston-Davies) *midfield: lost pl 1/2-way: n.d after* **8/1**
-2P0 **8** 1/2 **Gimme Shelter (IRE)**[5] 2171 11-9-7 **104** oh13 .... MJMcAlister(7) 69
(S J Marshall) *mde most to 20th: wknd after 4 out* **16/1**
60-P **9** dist **Your A Gassman (IRE)**[17] 1941 7-11-12 **130** ....(b1) BHarding —
(Ferdy Murphy) *hld up: hdwy 1/2-way: hit and wknd 20th* **20/1**
U40- **10** 3 **Harry Hooly**[220] 4787 10-9-7 **104** oh1 .... MissRDavidson(7) —
(Mrs H O Graham) *a bhd: lost tch fr 1/2-way* **28/1**
51-U **R** **Huka Lodge (IRE)**[18] 1929 8-10-13 **117** .... BGibson —
(L Lungo) *bhd: blnd 9th: ref next* **11/2**[1]
4-32 **P** **Interdit (FR)**[11] 2037 9-10-1 **110** .... TGreenway(5) —
(Mrs B K Thomson) *prom tl wknd fr 5 out: t.o whn p.u bef last* **6/1**[2]
43P4 **U** **Kidithou (FR)**[17] 1939 7-9-11 **104** .... PBuchanan(3) —
(W T Reed) *midfield: hit 11th: outpcd whn blnd bdly and uns rdr 19th* **40/1**

8m 46.5s **13** Ran SP% **114.4**
CSF £123.20 CT £781.89 TOTE £17.70: £4.50, £5.00, £2.20; EX 97.00.
Owner The Supreme Three **Bred** Mrs Maureen Ring **Trained** High Eldwick, W Yorks

FOCUS
A fair handicap in which the pace was sound throughout. The form has been rated through the first and third and looks solid.

NOTEBOOK
Supreme Breeze(IRE), who is well suited by a decent test of stamina, left his reappearance form a long way behind and showed the right attitude in the closing stages. He should continue to give a good account when the emphasis is on stamina. *(op 12-1)*
Mini Sensation(IRE) is not the most predictable and has not always been the easiest of rides but travelled much more sweetly this this time and ran right up to his best over a trip that is ideal. Whether this will be reproduced next time remains to be seen, though. *(op 8-1)*
Capybara(IRE) ◆, having only his third run over fences, turned in his best effort yet and, given there is room for improvement in the jumping department, appeals strongly as the type to win a similar race when the emphasis is on stamina. *(op 4-1)*
Harlov(FR), soundly beaten after a five-month break on bad ground at Carlisle last time, ran right up to his recent best. A good test of stamina suits him ideally but he is rarely one to place maximum faith in. *(op 10-1 tchd 11-1)*
Pass Me By, having only his fifth race over fences, looks a bit better than the bare form as it was only in the closing stages that he got tired having helped to set a decent gallop, and he looks sure to win another race in this sphere. *(tchd 12-1)*
Falchion, who is not the most accomplished of jumpers, was again well beaten and does not look the best betting proposition around at present.
Interdit(FR) *Official explanation: trainer said gelding scoped dirty post-race (tchd 11-2)*

2266 HEXHAM NOVICES' H'CAP CHASE (19 fncs) 3m 1f
2:25 (2:25) (Class 4) (0-105,100) 5-Y-0+ **£4,079** (£1,197; £598; £299)

Form RPR
55/1 **1** **Precious Bane (IRE)**[7] 2126 7-10-4 **78** 7ex .... AThornton 95+
(M Sheppard) *mde all: sn clr: pushed along 2 out: kpt on wl* **1/1**[1]
P4/5 **2** 1 1/2 **Algarve**[11] 2039 8-10-10 **87** .... KJMercer(3) 100
(Ferdy Murphy) *chsd wnr: effrt bef 3 out: kpt on fr last* **8/1**[3]
1403 **3** 10 **Arctic Lagoon (IRE)**[11] 2039 6-10-0 **77** ....(t) ONelmes(3) 82+
(Mrs S C Bradburne) *prom: drvn after 4 out: rallied: outpcd between last two* **7/2**[2]
25-1 **4** 7 **Getinbybutonlyjust**[181] 429 6-11-7 **95** .... BHarding 91
(Mrs Dianne Sayer) *towards rr: hit 4th: pushed along fr 13th: no imp* **9/1**
03PP **5** 5 **John Rich**[10] 2077 9-9-7 **74** oh4 ....(tp) PJMcDonald(7) 65
(M E Sowersby) *nt fluent: a bhd* **66/1**
2-3P **F** **Wild About Harry**[12] 2023 8-9-11 **74** oh4 .... PAspell(3) —
(A R Dicken) *chsng ldrs whn fell 13th* **25/1**
P **Trovaio (IRE)**[283] 8-10-13 **90** .... PBuchanan(3) —
(Miss Lucinda V Russell) *chsd ldrs tl outpcd 11th: t.o whn p.u bef 14th* **20/1**
4-F0 **P** **Roman Rebel**[12] 2024 6-11-12 **100** .... RMcGrath —
(Mrs K Walton) *hld up: hdwy 4 out: 5th and no imp whn blnd next: sn p.u* **25/1**
40-5 **P** **Magnificent Seven (IRE)**[197] 174 6-11-7 **95** .... GLee —
(J Howard Johnson) *towards rr: outpcd whn hmpd 13th: sn btn: p.u after next* **20/1**

6m 39.7s (7.80) **Going Correction** +0.60s/f (Soft) **9** Ran SP% **112.0**
Speed ratings: **111,110,107,105,103** —,—,—,— CSF £8.12 CT £20.39 TOTE £2.00: £1.20, £2.60, £1.10; EX 7.40.
Owner M W & A N Harris **Bred** Rowanstown Stud **Trained** Eastnor, H'fords

FOCUS
A decent winning time for a race like this, but the winner did not have to be at his best.

NOTEBOOK
Precious Bane(IRE) followed up last week's Lingfield success under his penalty and was value for more than the winning margin suggested. Life will be tougher from the weekend, when he is due to go up a further 12lb, but he may well be capable of better in this sphere when allowed his own way in front. *(op 4-6 tchd 11-10)*
Algarve ◆, confirmed the bit of promise shown on his chasing debut after a lengthy break last time and lost nothing in defeat against an in-form and well-treated rival. He looks sure to win a race in this sphere. *(tchd 9-1)*
Arctic Lagoon(IRE) has yet to show his best this term but was almost certainly not disgraced against a well-treated winner and an unexposed runner-up. He will be of more interest on a sounder surface away from progressive sorts. *(op 7-1)*
Getinbybutonlyjust, failed to match the pick of his hurdling form on this chase debut and first start since May. However, he is built to jump a fence and is not one to write off just yet. *(op 8-1 tchd 12-1)*
John Rich, a modest and inconsistent maiden chaser, again showed nothing.
Roman Rebel, making his chase debut, was in the process of running just a fair race when a bad blunder at a crucial stage ended any chance he had. He has not always proved reliable, though, and may be best watched next time. *(op 50-1)*

2267 AT THE RACES "TIP TOP" MARES' ONLY H'CAP CHASE (15 fncs) 2m 4f 110y
3:00 (3:00) (Class 4) (0-105,101) 4-Y-0+ **£6,610** (£1,940; £970; £484)

Form RPR
-F3F **1** **Ornella Speed (FR)**[150] 783 5-9-8 **76** ....(t) PJMcDonald(7) 93+
(A Crook) *hld up and bhd: smooth hdwy 2 out: led run in: rdn clr* **16/1**
4602 **2** 10 **Uneven Line**[11] 2041 9-9-12 **76** ....(p) MrCStorey(3) 83
(Miss S E Forster) *bhd: hdwy after 4 out: led bef last: hdd run in: no ch w wnr* **3/1**[2]
12-4 **3** 1 1/4 **Princesse Grec (FR)**[19] 1906 7-11-3 **92** .... TScudamore 98
(M Scudamore) *cl up: led 6th: rdn and hdd bef last: sn btn* **13/8**[1]
-301 **4** 7 **Celtic Blaze (IRE)**[21] 1888 6-11-12 **101** ....(t) ARoss 100
(B S Rothwell) *in tch: hdwy 1/2-way: effrt after 2 outt: wknd bef last* **8/1**[3]
P10- **5** 25 **Moon Mist**[249] 4318 7-10-10 **88** .... PBuchanan(3) 62
(N W Alexander) *chsd ldrs: outpcd 9th: n.d after* **8/1**[3]
10P5 **6** 12 **Little Flora**[11] 2041 9-10-10 **92** .... MJMcAlister(7) 54
(S J Marshall) *led to 6th: nt fluent 10th and 12th: sn btn* **14/1**
1036 **7** 11 **Green 'N' Gold**[25] 1838 5-10-13 **88** .... NPMulholland 39
(M D Hammond) *towards rr: reminders 1/2-way: struggling fr 10th* **8/1**[3]

5m 26.6s (15.20) **Going Correction** +0.60s/f (Soft) **7** Ran SP% **109.0**
Speed ratings: **95,91,90,88,78 73,69** CSF £59.21 TOTE £23.90: £8.10, £1.70; EX 88.20.
Owner Paul T Murphy **Bred** Mme Simone Mousset **Trained** Harmby, N Yorks

FOCUS
An uncompetitive event but the pace was sound and the leaders did not get home. The form has been rated through the runner-up's recent level.

NOTEBOOK
Ornella Speed(FR), who had fallen in three of her previous five starts over fences, jumped soundly on this first start for her new stable and first run since June. Although she may be a shade flattered given the way this race unfolded, this represented a much improved effort and she may be capable of winning again in this sphere. *(tchd 22-1)*
Uneven Line ran creditably but, although unfortunate to bump into a rival who was showing much improved form, remains a maiden under rules (has won a point) after 18 starts and is not one to place too much faith in. *(op 11-2)*
Princesse Grec(FR) looks a bit better than the bare form as she set a decent gallop in ground that was almost certainly too testing for her, and she will be of more interest back on a sound surface. *(tchd 11-8)*
Celtic Blaze(IRE), off the mark at the first time of asking over fences last time, was found out on her handicap debut in this sphere. Consistency is not her strong suit and she remains one to tread carefully with. *(op 5-1)*
Moon Mist, who stays further and handles testing ground, shaped as though this first start for just over eight months was needed, but she will have to show more before she is worth a bet. *(op 9-1 tchd 10-1)*
Little Flora, an inconsistent chaser, did not jump with much fluency and was well beaten back over this longer trip. *(op 8-1)*

2268 AT THE RACES INTERMEDIATE OPEN NATIONAL HUNT FLAT RACE 2m 110y
3:35 (3:36) (Class 6) 4-6-Y-0 **£1,987** (£579; £289)

Form RPR
1 **Red Poker** 5-11-4 .... RMcGrath 108+
(G A Harker) *set stdy pce: mde all: rdn over 2f out: kpt on wl* **3/1**[2]
2- **2** 1 3/4 **My Final Bid (IRE)**[214] 4865 6-11-1 .... PBuchanan(3) 101
(Mrs A C Hamilton) *keen: prom: chsd wnr over 4f out: effrt over 2f out: kpt on fnl f* **12/1**[3]
3 7 **Mister Nelson (IRE)** 4-11-4 .... ADobbin 95+
(N G Richards) *hld up in tch: hdwy over 4f out: effrt over 2f out: sn one pce* **2/1**[1]

	4	11	**Mr Ironman** 4-11-1 ... LMcGrath[(3)] (R C Guest) *hld up: effrt outer over 5f out: wknd over 3f out* **100/1**	83
0-	5	1	**Sticky End**[333] [2886] 4-10-11 ... BenOrde-Powlett[(7)] (J B Walton) *keen: hld up: outpcd over 3f out: rallied 2f out: no imp* **200/1**	82
51-	6	6	**Allegedly So (IRE)**[220] [4788] 4-11-4 ... EWhillans[(7)] (D W Whillans) *hld up midfield: outpcd over 5f out: n.d after* **14/1**	83
	7	3/4	**Kenny** 5-10-8 ... MSO'Connell[(10)] (Mrs S J Smith) *cl up tl rdn and wknd over 3f out* **80/1**	75
	8	15	**Scout Leader** 6-11-4 ... DElsworth (C Grant) *chsd ldrs tl wknd over 3f out* **20/1**	60
	9	16	**Bishop's Brig** 5-11-1 ... PAspell[(3)] (N W Alexander) *a bhd* **100/1**	44
0	10	12	**Redeswire Ruby**[39] [1688] 4-10-8 ... ONelmes[(3)] (Mrs H O Graham) *cl up tl wknd over 4f out* **200/1**	25
	F		**Panthers Run**[404] [1649] 5-11-11 ... APMcCoy (Jonjo O'Neill) *in tch: drvn and outpcd whn fell over 4f out* **2/1**[1]	—

4m 26.8s (14.10) **Going Correction** +0.425s/f (Soft)
WFA 4 from 5yo+ 12lb **11 Ran SP% 115.0**
Speed ratings: **75,74,70,65,65 62,62,55,47,41** — CSF £35.89 TOTE £2.80: £1.20, £3.20, £1.40; EX 39.10 Place 6 £92.19, Place 5 £19.86.
Owner R Brewis **Bred** R Brewis **Trained** Thirkleby, N Yorks

FOCUS
An ordinary event in which the winner was given a well-judged ride from the front. The time was slow and this bare form may not prove reliable, but Red Poker has been rated as value for a bit further.

NOTEBOOK
Red Poker, a half-brother to a winning pointer, is from a stable that does well in this sphere and turned in a pleasing debut effort. Although he enjoyed the run of the race this time, he appeals as the sort to win again over obstacles. *(op 11-4 tchd 9-4 and 10-3)*
My Final Bid(IRE), having his first start since April, again shaped well in a race that was not really run to suit, and he will be of more interest granted a stiffer test when sent over obstacles. *(op 11-1 tchd 10-1)*
Mister Nelson(IRE), the first foal of a sister to two-mile hurdle and three-mile chase winner Copper Coin, is in very good hands and showed more than enough to suggest a similar event can be found with this experience behind him. *(op 7-4 tchd 9-4)*
Mr Ironman, out of a poor novice hurdler, hinted at ability on this racecourse debut and may be the type to do better once handicapped over obstacles. *(op 50-1)*
Sticky End was soundly beaten on his debut last December and his proximity on this only subsequent start holds the form down. *(op 100-1)*
Allegedly So(IRE), who won an ordinary event over this course and distance when last seen in April, had his limitations exposed under a penalty in this better event. *(op 20-1 tchd 22-1)*
Panthers Run, a bumper winner at Gowran Park in October last year, was already under strong pressure when stumbling and coming to grief. He may do better over obstacles granted a stiffer test if none-the-worse for this experience. *(op 11-4 tchd 3-1)*
T/Plt: £171.40 to a £1 stake. Pool: £38,609.50. 164.40 winning tickets. T/Qpdt: £36.30 to a £1 stake. Pool: £3,733.10. 75.90 winning tickets. RY

2050 WINCANTON (R-H)
Wednesday, November 16

OFFICIAL GOING: Good
Wind: Slight, behind

2269 EBF BETFREDCASINO.COM "NATIONAL HUNT" NOVICES' HURDLE (QUALIFIER) (8 hdls) 2m
1:10 (1:11) (Class 3) 4-6-Y-0 **£5,074** (£1,489; £744; £372)

Form				RPR
3-P0	1		**Barton Park**[19] [1908] 5-11-0 ... NFehily (D P Keane) *bhd: hdwy 4 out: pressed ldrs fr 2 out: disp ld after 2 out: chalng and gng ok whn lft clr last: easily* **100/1**	102+
004-	2	11	**Foxtrot Yankee (IRE)**[240] [4499] 6-10-9 ... JDiment[(5)] (Andrew Turnell) *hmpd 1st: bhd: j. slowly 2nd: blnd 4th: hdwy and hit 4 out: chal 2 out: wknd appr last* **200/1**	89+
34-3	3	nk	**Nocturnally**[30] [1777] 5-11-0 ... JEMoore (V R A Dartnall) *hmpd 1st: sn in tch: chsd ldrs fr 4th: slt ld 2 out: hdd sn after and wknd appr last* **20/1**	88
00-0	4	3	**Talikos (FR)**[20] [1895] 4-11-0 ... SThomas (Miss H C Knight) *bdly hmpd 1st: in tch: hdwy to chse ldrs 4th: rdn appr 2 out: wknd sn after* **200/1**	87+
511/	5	3	**Toemac**[594] [4636] 6-11-0 ... MBatchelor (M Bradstock) *led and j. bdly rt 1st and 2nd: hdd sn after: j. slowly 4th: drvn to chal 2 out: sn wknd* **14/1**[3]	83+
6P	6	3	**Pitton Prince**[29] [1779] 6-10-7 ... MrDavidTurner[(7)] (N R Mitchell) *hmpd 1st: chsd ldrs: drvn to chal 2 out: sn wknd* **200/1**	79
0	7	10	**Gunship (IRE)**[24] [1849] 4-11-0 ... RJohnson (P J Hobbs) *bhd: hit 4th and 4 out: rdn 3 out: nvr gng pce to rch ldrs* **50/1**	69
/0-0	8	3 1/2	**Bob's Temptation**[189] [300] 6-11-0 ... (t) WMarston (A J Wilson) *nt jump wl: a in rr* **200/1**	65
500-	9	8	**She's No Muppet**[216] [4841] 5-10-7 ... JAMcCarthy (N R Mitchell) *bhd: sme hdwy after 3 out: sn wknd* **100/1**	50
00-	10	7	**Star Galaxy (IRE)**[223] [4760] 5-11-0 ... PJBrennan (Andrew Turnell) *bdly hmpd 1st: chsd ldrs to 3 out: wknd bef next* **150/1**	50
	11	9	**Castletown Lad**[605] 5-11-0 ... TJMurphy (M C Pipe) *mstke 3rd: a in rr* **50/1**	41
13-F	B		**Ain't That A Shame (IRE)**[24] [1847] 5-11-0 ... RWalsh (P F Nicholls) *bdly hmpd and b.d 1st: dead* **2/1**[2]	—
34-0	F		**Double Law**[11] [2049] 5-11-0 ... JamesDavies (P R Webber) *bdly hmpd 1st: led after 2nd: hdd and wkng whn fell 2 out* **66/1**	65
121-	U		**Senorita Rumbalita**[223] [4753] 4-10-7 ... RThornton (A King) *hmpd 1st: in tch: hdwy 4th: trckd ldrs next: chal 2 out: upside and gng wl whn sddle slipped and uns rdr last* **4/6**[1]	102+

3m 49.1s **Going Correction** +0.075s/f (Yiel) **14 Ran SP% 114.8**
Speed ratings: **103,97,97,95,94 92,87,86,82,78 74,—,—,—** CSF £3683.48 TOTE £88.60: £12.50, £18.30, £2.50; EX 1244.90.
Owner Lady Clarke **Bred** P Easterby **Trained** North End, Dorset

FOCUS
An eventful opening contest and unsatisfactory result with both hot favourite Senorita Rumbalita and Ain't That A Shame failing to complete. Despite that the form is believable and makes sense on time.

NOTEBOOK
Barton Park, who had excuses for his two previous disappointments over hurdles, was still in with a chance when the favourite departed at the last, but the likelihood is that he would have come off second best, albeit that would have been a fair effort in its own right. The return to a sound surface was a help and he gives the impression that there may be more to come granted similar conditions.
Foxtrot Yankee(IRE) showed only moderate form in bumpers last season and so finishing second was quite a shock. Like the winner, he made good headway around runners to hold every chance jumping two out, but soon found himself outpaced. He is a good-looking gelding and will improve for a step up to two and a half miles. *(op 100-1)*
Nocturnally failed to progress in bumpers and it was rather disappointing he could manage only third on this hurdles debut. An increase in distance may help, but he is unlikely to be winning until handicapped. *(op 22-1)*
Talikos(FR) ran his best race to date and did well to finish so close up having been badly hampered at the first. He still looks in need of more time and will not be seen at his best until tackling fences. *(op 100-1)*
Toemac, a dual bumper winner last year, was returning from a lengthy layoff and could always be expected to need this. His jumping improved as the contest went on and there were enough positives to be taken from this to suggest he can win a similar event. *(op 12-1)*
Gunship(IRE) looks in need of more time and will be more at home in handicaps. *(op 25-1)*
Castletown Lad, a faller on his only start in points, was never jumping fluently in rear, and at this stage he looks one of his stable's lesser lights. He is another likely to be capable of better in time, though. *(op 25-1)*
Ain't That A Shame(IRE), a faller on his reappearance at Aintree, was tossing his head around and not fully concentrating on the first flight when impeded in mid-air, and he was unable to get the landing gear down in time. He suffered fatal injuries and was sadly put down. *(op 5-2)*
Senorita Rumbalita, who rounded off a fine first season with victory in a Listed mares' bumper at Aintree, was fully expected to make a winning hurdling debut and she looked set to do so when the saddle slipped and she unseated Robert Thornton at the last. This was hardly an ideal start to the season, but it was a mere blip and she remains a smart prospect. *(op 5-2)*

2270 BETFRED "THE BONUS KING" NOVICES' CHASE (13 fncs) 2m
1:40 (1:40) (Class 3) 4-Y-0+ **£8,371** (£2,598; £1,399)

Form				RPR
4-15	1		**Nyrche (FR)**[15] [1971] 5-11-9 ... RThornton (A King) *mde all: styng on wl and 1l up whn lft clr last* **5/4**[1]	136+
0-1F	2	10	**Tighe Caster**[31] [1758] 6-11-9 ... JPMcNamara (P R Webber) *chsd ldrs tl dropped rr and hit 7th: hdwy to chse ldrs 4 out:wknd next: no ch whn hit 2 out: lft mod 2nd last* **9/2**[3]	128+
4-00	3	18	**Berengario (IRE)**[11] [2055] 5-11-3 ... RGreene (S C Burrough) *chsd wnr: blnd 2nd: wknd appr 3 out: lft poor 3rd last* **50/1**	103+
51P5	F		**Perouse**[11] [2055] 7-11-9 ... (t) RWalsh (P F Nicholls) *hld up in tch: trckd ldrs fr 8th: wnt 2nd after 4 out: chal next: 1l down, drvn but styng on whn fell last* **15/8**[2]	130+
U5-5	P		**In Contrast (IRE)**[22] [1871] 9-11-3 ... RJohnson (P J Hobbs) *bhd: j. slowly 3rd: hdwy to chse ldrs after 5th: wknd and hit 4 out: no ch whn tried to refuse next: p.u sn after* **14/1**	—

3m 59.3s (-2.60) **Going Correction** +0.075s/f (Yiel) **5 Ran SP% 106.0**
Speed ratings: **109,104,95,—,—** CSF £6.70 TOTE £2.40: £2.80, £1.70; EX 8.00.
Owner Tony Fisher & Mrs Jeni Fisher **Bred** M Dolic **Trained** Barbury Castle, Wilts

FOCUS
A disappointing turnout for the prize, but Nyrche put in a good round of jumping and looks a good handicap prospect. The time was decent and the first two ran to their marks.

NOTEBOOK
Nyrche(FR), a disappointment on his reappearance in a hot race at Exeter, was soon in a nice lead, jumping fluently, and he looked to have Perouse held when that one came down at the last. The less competitive nature of this race suited him well and it will be interesting to see what sort of handicap mark he gets, as that is now surely the wisest route for him. *(op 11-8 tchd 11-10, 6-4 in a place)*
Tighe Caster, in the process of recording a decent effort behind Hoo La Baloo when falling two out at Market Rasen back in October, was careful at his fences and never really threatened the winner, but connections will no doubt have been pleased to see him get his confidence back. Handicaps will be more his bag and he looks the type that connections will do well with. *(op 7-2)*
Berengario(IRE) had a lot to find with these on hurdles ratings and was well beaten.
In Contrast(IRE) is a shadow of the horse that finished third in the 2002 Supreme Novices' and he continues to disappoint. *(op 12-1)*
Perouse, a smart hurdler on his day, lacks the size and scope to make a real go at it over fences, but he was in the process of running a satisfactory race when getting the last all wrong. He will find a small race or two when the emphasis is on speed, as long as this has not jolted his confidence. *(op 12-1)*

2271 BETFREDPOKER.COM H'CAP HURDLE (11 hdls) 2m 6f
2:15 (2:15) (Class 3) (0-120,113) 4-Y-0+ **£5,513** (£1,618; £809; £404)

Form				RPR
111-	1		**He's A Leader (IRE)**[352] [2540] 6-11-3 104 ... TJMurphy (M C Pipe) *hld up in rr: hdwy and hit 7th: trckd ldr appr 2 out: drvn to ld last: styd on strly* **5/4**[1]	113+
21P0	2	5	**Middleham Park (IRE)**[140] [864] 5-10-13 107 ... WPKavanagh[(7)] (J W Mullins) *trckd ldrs: chal 3 out: led sn after: rdn 2 out: hdd and hit last: sn one pce* **25/1**	107+
415F	3	4	**Arm And A Leg (IRE)**[42] [1641] 10-11-2 108 ... LStephens[(5)] (Mrs D A Hamer) *chsd ldrs: wnt 2nd after 3 out: rdn 2 out: sn btn* **40/1**	103
20-2	4	8	**Teorban (POL)**[27] [1806] 6-10-13 100 ... MBradburne (D J S Ffrench Davis) *hit 2nd: bhd: hrd drvn fr 3 out: styd on u.p appr 2 out but nvr gng pce to rch ldrs* **15/2**[3]	89+
3	5	5	**Burren Moonshine (IRE)**[14] [1992] 6-11-1 102 ... RJohnson (P Bowen) *chsd ldr: slt ld fr 7th tl hdd sn after 3 out: wknd bef next* **11/4**[2]	84
300P	6	3	**Turkama (FR)**[14] [1984] 8-11-2 110 ... CMStudd[(7)] (L A Dace) *chsd ldrs to 3 out: sn wknd* **66/1**	89
454-	P		**Apollo Theatre**[218] [4817] 7-11-8 109 ... BFenton (R Rowe) *bhd: sme hdwy 7th: wknd qckly 3 out: t.o whn p.u bef 2 out* **8/1**	—
454-	P		**Bak To Bill**[237] [4528] 10-11-5 113 ... MissLGardner[(7)] (Mrs S Gardner) *in tch early: bhd fr 6th: t.o whn p.u bef 2 out* **33/1**	—
1U-5	P		**Gordon Highlander**[24] [1851] 6-10-13 100 ... (t) JAMcCarthy (Mrs P Robeson) *led tl narrowly hdd 7th: styd chalng to 3 out: sn wknd: t.o whn p.u bef 2 out* **10/1**	—

5m 27.4s (2.30) **Going Correction** +0.075s/f (Yiel) **9 Ran SP% 113.8**
Speed ratings: **98,96,94,91,90 88,—,—,—** CSF £33.79 CT £839.21 TOTE £2.20: £1.50, £5.40, £3.40; EX 37.70.
Owner M Archer & The Late Jean Broadhurst **Bred** Eamonn Walsh **Trained** Nicholashayne, Devon

FOCUS
An ordinary event and, as was to be expected, He's A Leader proved too strong for this largely exposed field. he is value for nearly double the official margin.

NOTEBOOK
He's A Leader(IRE) was always likely to take a good deal of beating if returning in good shape (been off with shoulder problems) and, although needing plenty of help from the saddle, he was well on top at the line. Winning here off a mark of 104, this was his fourth victory in succession and one gets the impression that the sequence may not stop here. Viewed as a future chaser, he is one to keep on the right side as he could improve again for a step up to three miles. *(op 11-8)*
Middleham Park(IRE) had not been seen at his best in his two most recent starts since going handicapping, but he was fresh for this and really served it up to the winner. He finished a comfortable second and there is probably a similar race in him if going the right way. *(op 22-1)*

Arm And A Leg(IRE) ran above market expectations and was at least able to leave behind the memories of his fall at Exeter last month. Rising 11, he will continue to be vulnerable off this sort of mark. *(op 33-1)*

Teorban(POL), up 5lb for his pleasing reappearance second at Ludlow, plugged on at his own pace and shaped as though he will be worth another try at three miles. *(op 13-2 tchd 9-1)*

Burren Moonshine(IRE) was expected to give the winner most to think about, but she was not certain to be suited by this drop in trip and found herself backpeddling soon after being headed. *(op 10-3)*

Turkama(FR) *Official explanation: vet said gelding finished lame (op 50-1)*

Apollo Theatre *Official explanation: trainer said gelding scoped dirty following the race (tchd 9-1)*

2272 BETFRED.COM H'CAP CHASE (17 fncs) 2m 5f

2:50 (2:50) (Class 3) (0-135,129) 5-Y-0+

£9,738 (£2,876; £1,438; £719; £359; £180)

Form				RPR
55-0	**1**		**Scots Grey**[181] 422 10-11-12 **129** MFoley (N J Henderson) *led to 11th: styd pressing ldr tl led after 13th: styd on to go clr 2 out: comf* **3/1**[1]	148+
06-0	**2**	14	**Atum Re (IRE)**[140] 864 8-11-5 **122** RWalsh (P F Nicholls) *in tch: nt fluent 1st: 2nd and 5th: lost pl 10th: styd on to chse ldrs fr 4 out: wnt 2nd and rdn 3 out: sn no imp and btn* **7/2**[3]	131+
1-U3	**3**	6	**Latimer's Place**[11] 2051 9-11-1 **118** JAMcCarthy (J A Geake) *bhd: hit 3rd: hday 9th: chsd ldrs and rdn 4 out: wknd qckly next* **10/3**[2]	117
0634	**4**	5	**Cameron Bridge (IRE)**[32] 1735 9-11-10 **127** RJohnson (P J Hobbs) *chsd wnr 4th tl led 11th:hdd after 13th: wknd qckly after 4 out* **9/2**	125+
12-5	**5**	4	**Spring Lover (FR)**[201] 97 6-11-6 **123** SThomas (Miss Venetia Williams) *chsd wnr to 4th: hit 7th: rdn 12th: wknd 4 out* **7/1**	113
111/	**6**	dist	**Biliverdin (IRE)**[572] 4955 11-11-10 **127** MBradburne (J A Geake) *j. poorly in rr thrght: t.o fr 9th* **11/1**	—

5m 17.2s (-5.90) **Going Correction** +0.075s/f (Yiel) **6 Ran SP% 109.3**

Speed ratings: **114,108,106,104,102** — CSF £13.32 TOTE £3.60: £2.00, £2.60; EX 16.80.

Owner W H Ponsonby **Bred** W H F Carson **Trained** Upper Lambourn, Berks

FOCUS

A fair time for a contest like this and the race could rate higher judged on the efforts of the third and fourth.

NOTEBOOK

Scots Grey, who was below his best last season, had gone without a win since scoring at Kempton in December 2003, but he had slipped to a fair mark as a result (4lb lower than when finishing fifth in the Mildmay Of Flete at last season's Festival) and, with his stable in such good form, he was always likely to take a good deal of beating. Jumping fluently throughout, he came right away in the the final quarter mile and connections now have the two and a half mile handicap chase at Newbury on Hennessy Day in mind. *(op 9-4 tchd 2-1)*

Atum Re(IRE), subject to a soft-palate operation in the summer in a bid to get his career back on track, was never jumping with any real fluency and, despite getting back into a challenging position as they approached the second-last, the winner soon put the result beyond doubt. There is undoubtedly a race in him off this sort of mark, but he has little in the way of scope and needs to brush up his fencing. *(op 4-1)*

Latimer's Place came in for support in the market beforehand and looked to hold solid claims having run well to finish third in a race at the course earlier in the month, but he stopped rather sharply in the straight and it would not be a surprise to learn that there was a problem. *(op 4-1 tchd 3-1)*

Cameron Bridge(IRE) was another unable to go through with his effort and he looks in need of some help from the Handicapper. *(op 6-1 tchd 13-2)*

Spring Lover(FR) had not been seen since disappointing at Bangor in April and he failed to shape with much promise for the immediate future. *(op 11-2 tchd 8-1)*

Biliverdin(IRE) has never had much luck with injuries and it was sad to see him have to miss the whole of last season having run up a hat-trick of wins early in 2004. The market suggested there was little confidence behind him making a winning return, however, and he was soon in rear making mistakes. He can be expected to step up on this in future and it is to be hoped that he can stay sound. *(op 10-1)*

2273 WIN AN IPOD AT BETFREDPOKER.COM H'CAP CHASE (21 fncs) 3m 1f 110y

3:25 (3:25) (Class 3) (0-115,115) 5-Y-0+ **£5,481** (£1,609; £804; £401)

Form				RPR
-P21	**1**		**Lord Anner (IRE)**[24] 1858 6-10-11 **100** (b[1]) RWalsh (P F Nicholls) *trckd ldr 6th:slt ld next: hit 10th: c clr after 4 out: hit 2 out: comf* **5/4**[1]	117+
22-F	**2**	9	**Noble Baron**[15] 1972 9-11-8 **111** (t) MBradburne (C G Cox) *in tch: hit 5th: j. slowly next: hit 10th: chsd ldrs and j. slowly 4 out: chsd wnr fr next but no ch* **11/2**[2]	120+
2-05	**3**	4	**Ede'Iff**[11] 2051 8-10-7 **103** RLucey-Butler[(7)] (W G M Turner) *hld up in rr: hit 10th: hdwy 13th: hit 15th: chsd ldrs next: wknd fr 3 out* **20/1**	106+
14-P	**4**	1 3/4	**Dante Citizen (IRE)**[198] 150 7-11-4 **107** NFehily (T R George) *led to 7th: styd chalng to 11th: remained 2nd tl wknd after 4 out* **6/1**[3]	108+
3P-6	**5**	16	**Lucky Leader (IRE)**[15] 1972 10-10-1 **93** (b) RYoung[(3)] (N R Mitchell) *bhd: hit 10th: rdn 11th: hit 16th: mod prog fr 3 out* **20/1**	77
P-3P	**6**	7	**Lucky Sinna (IRE)**[16] 1953 9-10-5 **94** TJMurphy (B G Powell) *bhd: sme hdwy fr 16th: nvr rchd ldrs: wknd 4 out* **14/1**	71
0-30	**7**	6	**Even More (IRE)**[15] 1972 10-11-6 **109** RWalford (R H Alner) *chsd ldrs: pushed along fr 8th: wknd 15th* **11/1**	80
610-	**8**	2	**Earl's Kitchen**[244] 4411 8-11-12 **115** JTizzard (C L Tizzard) *j. slowly 5th:chsd ldr to 6th: styd prom tl j. slowly 14th: wknd next* **14/1**	84
-UF0	**P**		**Stanway**[21] 1877 6-11-5 **108** WMarston (Mrs Mary Hambro) *chsd ldrs: rdn fr 11th: wknd 13th: t.o whn p.u bef 15th* **50/1**	—
3026	**P**		**Penthouse Minstrel**[11] 2051 11-10-11 **107** (v) MrJSnowden[(7)] (R J Hodges) *chsd ldrs: wknd 15th: t.o whn p.u bef 2 out* **14/1**	—

6m 37.9s (-2.00) **Going Correction** +0.075s/f (Yiel) **10 Ran SP% 113.9**

Speed ratings: **106,103,102,101,96 94,92,91,—,—** CSF £8.55 CT £88.93 TOTE £2.00: £1.20, £1.90, £6.10; EX 9.50.

Owner The Stewart Family **Bred** Miss Josephine Fox **Trained** Ditcheat, Somerset

FOCUS

Modest handicap form but the third sets the standard and the winner can rate higher.

NOTEBOOK

Lord Anner(IRE), racing enthusiastically throughout in the first-time blinkers, jumped cleanly throughout and had them all in trouble rounding the turn for home. Once Noble Baron began to close he was able to go on again and, as he was winning here off a mark of just 100, it will be surprising if he cannot complete the hat-trick. *(op 11-10)*

Noble Baron was still in contention when falling on his reappearance at his beloved Exeter and his jumping today was not as fluent as a result. He kept on as best as he could for second, but found the concession of 11lb to the favourite too much. He can find a race off this mark and will appreciate a return to Devon. *(op 13-2 tchd 7-1)*

Ede'Iff does not find winning easy and she is always vulnerable to something a bit less exposed. This was a fair effort by her standards and a return to shorter will help. *(op 16-1)*

Dante Citizen(IRE) ran well for a long way, but his lack of race fitness began to tell as they turned for home and it is safe to assume that he can step up on this. *(op 9-1)*

Lucky Leader(IRE) is back on a winning mark, but he did nothing more here than plod on through beaten rivals, and he needs to raise his game. *(tchd 25-1)*

Lucky Sinna(IRE) *Official explanation: jockey said gelding had a breathing problem (op 16-1)*

Earl's Kitchen, an interesting staying handicap prospect for this season, showed up well to a point, but his jumping fell apart as the pace quickened and he dropped away disappointingly. He is beter than this and probably deserves a chance to show it. *(op 12-1)*

2274 WIN A TRIP TO VEGAS AT BETFREDPOKER.COM JUVENILE NOVICES' HURDLE (8 hdls) 2m

3:55 (3:56) (Class 4) 3-Y-0 **£3,487** (£1,023; £511; £255)

Form				RPR
	1		**Tritonville Lodge (IRE)**[28] 3-10-12 BFenton (Miss E C Lavelle) *bhd: hdwy 4th: chsd ldrs 4 out: chal fr next tl slt ld last: r.o gamely whn strly chal run-in* **10/3**[1]	107+
	2	nk	**Rosecliff**[28] 3-10-12 RThornton (A M Balding) *chsd ldrs: rdn appr 2 out: chal last: disp ld u.p sn after: no ex nr fin* **9/2**[2]	105+
	3	6	**Spidam (FR)**[157] 3-11-5 RWalsh (P F Nicholls) *chsd ldrs: chal 4th: slt ld fr 4 out: narrowly hdd u.p whn mstke last: sn btn* **10/3**[1]	107+
	4	12	**Joli Classical (IRE)**[128] 3-9-12 JamesWhite[(7)] (R J Hodges) *t.k.h: bhd: hdwy to chse ldrs 3 out: shkn up and outpcd sn after: one pce fr next* **66/1**	80
	5	5	**Patronage**[46] 3-10-12 NFehily (Jonjo O'Neill) *chsd ldrs: blnd 4th: sn rcvrd: chal 3 out: wknd appr next* **8/1**[3]	86+
	6	7	**Bay Hawk**[63] 3-10-12 TJMurphy (B G Powell) *nt fluent 1st and 2nd: sme hdwy after 3 out: nvr gng pce to rch ldrs: wknd bef next* **16/1**	75
	7	1 3/4	**Rashida**[96] 3-9-12 RSpate[(7)] (M Appleby) *chsd ldrs to 3 out: sn wknd* **66/1**	67
	8	1/2	**Desert Moonbeam (IRE)**[25] 3-10-0 JHarris[(5)] (R J Hodges) *mstke 4th: a bhd* **100/1**	66
422	**9**	6	**Compton Quay**[73] 1404 3-10-12 **95** (p) JPMcNamara (Miss K M George) *bhd most of way* **11/1**	67
0	**10**	3	**Garhoud**[16] 1955 3-10-12 (p) BHitchcott (Miss K M George) *led to 4 out: stl ev ch next: sn wknd* **66/1**	64
	11	dist	**Numidas (POL)**[353] 3-10-12 RJohnson (P J Hobbs) *chsd ldrs: hit 3rd: chal 4 out: wknd qckly after next: t.o* **9/2**[2]	—

3m 50.0s (0.90) **Going Correction** +0.075s/f (Yiel) **11 Ran SP% 113.3**

Speed ratings: **100,99,96,90,88 84,83,83,80,79** — CSF £17.87 TOTE £4.10: £1.10, £2.20, £2.00; EX 15.70 Place 6 £220.20, Place 5 £6.07.

Owner P McKiernan **Bred** Grangemore Stud **Trained** Wildhern, Hants

FOCUS

An interesting contest that looks sure to produce winners. The front three were clear of the remainder and look useful sorts.

NOTEBOOK

Tritonville Lodge(IRE) ◆ finished narrowly ahead of Rosecliff on their most recent outing on the Flat at Bath back in October and the pair set down to do battle here after the last. He had always looked the type likely to do well over hurdles and, despite handing the advantage to Rosecliff with a slight mistake at the last, he quickened up well to regain the lead close home. As this was probably a decent juvenile event it is entirely possible he could defy a penalty, with the likelihood of more to come. *(op 9-2 tchd 5-1)*

Rosecliff ◆, whose sire Montjeu has already thrown up a juvenile hurdle winner this season, raced freely for much of the way and tracked the leaders into the straight before quickening up to take a slight lead at the last. However, the winner was soon upsides again and in the end he just lacked that finishing kick. It will be disappointing if he does not win next time and it is to be hoped that he can learn to settle better. *(op 11-4)*

Spidam(FR) ◆, successful on his only start in France for Guillaume Macaire, is a tall, attractive gelding and he was simply done for speed after the last by a couple of ex-Flat racers. This was a highly promising effort and softer ground will help in future, but it would not pay to over-race this future chaser this season as he looks more of a long-term prospect. *(op 4-1 tchd 9-2)*

Joli Classical(IRE), someway inferior to these on the Flat, stayed on best of the rest and will find easier opportunities.

Patronage ran a little better than his finishing position suggests as a bad blunder at the fourth would have done him no favours. He still came there travelling before the turn in, but he got tired in the straight and either needed the run or failed to stay. *(op 9-1 tchd 10-1)*

Bay Hawk *Official explanation: jockey said colt had a breathing problem (tchd 14-1)*

Numidas(POL), a Polish import who had done his winning over five furlongs, was representing top connections but he looked a blatant non-stayer and quickly went backwards from half a mile out. *(op 4-1 tchd 7-2)*

T/Plt: £830.90 to a £1 stake. Pool: £45,017.70. 39.55 winning tickets. T/Qpdt: £10.00 to a £1 stake. Pool: £5,980.30. 440.50 winning tickets. ST

2275 - 2281a (Foreign Racing) - See Raceform Interactive

2069 HEREFORD (R-H)

Thursday, November 17

OFFICIAL GOING: Good

Wind: Virtually nil Weather: Sunny

2282 HAVE YOUR XMAS PARTY AT THE RACECOURSE AMATEUR RIDERS' H'CAP CHASE (19 fncs) 3m 1f 110y

12:50 (12:50) (Class 4) (0-100,98) 5-Y-0+ **£3,538** (£1,097; £548; £274)

Form				RPR
6-15	**1**		**Ashgreen**[36] 1713 8-11-0 **92** MrWBiddick[(7)] (Miss Venetia Williams) *led tl appr 7th: led 12th: clr fr 2 out: easily* **4/1**	112+
-30	**2**	20	**Armageddon**[20] 1907 8-10-5 **83** MrDGreenway[(7)] (O Sherwood) *w ldr tl j.lft 2nd: lost pl 6th: hit 8th: rallied after 13th: wnt 2nd 15th: mstke 4 out: no ch w wnr fr 2 out* **17/2**	85+
-312	**3**	1 1/2	**Anflora**[15] 1983 8-10-5 **76** MrSWalker (B J Llewellyn) *hld up in tch: hit 15th: one pce fr 3 out* **3/1**[1]	77+
2P-P	**4**	dist	**Ballybrophy (IRE)**[14] 2009 10-10-0 **76** (p) MissLHorner[(5)] (G Brown) *w ldr: led appr 7th to 8th: lft in ld 11th: hdd 12th: wknd after 13th* **20/1**	—
-344	**5**	1 1/4	**Paddy The Optimist (IRE)**[156] 746 9-11-0 **92** MrRMcCarthy[(7)] (D Burchell) *a bhd: mstke 7th: rdn after 11th: lost tch fr 14th* **7/2**[3]	—

40P0 **6** *9* **Faddad (USA)**[11] 2074 9-10-8 84..............................(t) MrsLucyRowsell(5) —
(Mrs A M Thorpe) *bhd: mstke 9th: short-lived effrt appr 14th* **33/1**

34-4 **R** **Darnayson (IRE)**[22] 1877 5-11-7 98.................................. MrGTumelty(5) —
(N A Twiston-Davies) *j.lft: sn w ldr: led 8th tl hung lft and rn out 11th* **10/3**[2]

6m 38.0s (3.80) **Going Correction** +0.30s/f (Yiel) **7 Ran SP% 108.5**
Speed ratings: **106,99,99,—,—,— —,—** CSF £31.93 TOTE £5.60: £3.30, £4.00; EX 30.70.
Owner C J Green **Bred** C J And T L Green **Trained** Kings Caple, H'fords

FOCUS
Just a moderate handicap chase in which Ashgreen's task was made easier when Darnayson ran out. The form looks weak with the runner-up the best guide. Will Biddick's first winner under Rules.

NOTEBOOK
Ashgreen, having won well on his reappearance at Towcester, proved a touch disappointing under a penalty at Uttoxeter on his next outing, but that may well have come too soon and, given plenty of time to recover, he returned to form with an easy victory under a good ride from his 7lb amateur. Given he will go up significantly for this, he would effectively be well-in if turned out under a penalty, but that may not be ideal given he seems best with time between his races and things will be tougher from now on. *(op 5-1 tchd 11-2)*

Armageddon looked likely to pose a threat at one stage on this step back up in trip, but his jumping was not always fluent under pressure and he finished up well held in second. *(op 8-1)*

Anflora has been in good form recently but, like the second, she did not always jump fluently when she needed to and probably would have preferred softer ground. *(op 9-4)*

Ballybrophy(IRE), with the cheekpieces back on, again failed to see out his race. *(op 16-1)*

Paddy The Optimist(IRE), a dual course-and-distance winner, was not at his best off the back of a 156-day break. *(tchd 4-1)*

Darnayson(IRE) was still going well when running out at the 11th fence. *(op 4-1 tchd 3-1)*

2283 SIDNEY PHILLIPS AUCTIONEERS (S) HURDLE (8 hdls) 2m 1f
1:20 (1:20) (Class 5) 4-6-Y-0 **£2,178** (£635; £317)

Form RPR

P0P1 **1** **Dancinginthestreet**[11] 2071 5-11-0 90.............................. TScudamore 89
(J L Flint) *led to 3rd: remained prom: rdn appr 3 out: rallied to ld flat: r.o* **11/8**[1]

0-0F **2** *1* **Earl Of Spectrum (GER)**[28] 1717 4-11-0 90.......................... PJBrennan 88
(J L Spearing) *hld up: hdwy 4th: led after 3 out: rdn after 2 out: hdd and hung rt flat: nt qckn* **3/1**[2]

53PP **3** *20* **Twist N Turn**[7] 2146 5-10-2 63...................................... StephenJCraine(5) 61
(D McCain) *prom: rdn after 5th: wknd appr 2 out* **14/1**

-354 **4** *3* **Chariot (IRE)**[27] 1814 4-11-0 80... SCurran 65
(M R Bosley) *hld up in mid-div: hdwy appr 4th: led 5th tl after 3 out: sn wknd* **7/1**[3]

0-F0 **5** *5* **La Muette (IRE)**[27] 1816 5-10-0 78... RSpate(7) 53
(M Appleby) *prom: led 3rd to 5th: rdn and wknd after 3 out* **14/1**

-5F5 **6** *11* **Hunter Pudding**[129] 961 5-10-0 79..................................... CMStudd(7) 42
(C L Popham) *hld up and bhd: short-lived effrt after 4th* **20/1**

-006 **7** *5* **Holly Walk**[33] 1742 4-10-7 79..(p) JMogford 37
(A G Juckes) *sn bhd* **12/1**

5000 **8** *dist* **Sarn**[25] 1856 6-10-11 80... ACCoyle(3) —
(M Mullineaux) *bhd fr 3rd: t.o* **20/1**

P **9** *shd* **Our Sion**[11] 2070 5-11-0 .... PHide —
(Mrs A M Thorpe) *a bhd: blnd 3 out: sn t.o* **100/1**

6F0 **P** **Olympian Time**[60] 1485 5-10-2 64......................................(p) MNicolls(5) —
(Miss J E Foster) *prom tl wknd 3rd: t.o whn p.u bef 2 out* **40/1**

P **P** **Flying Spud**[21] 1892 4-11-0 .... VSlattery —
(A J Chamberlain) *prom tl wknd appr 5th: t.o whn p.u bef last* **40/1**

60P- **P** **Dame Beezil**[290] 3621 6-10-7 ....(t) WHutchinson —
(K Bishop) *j.lft: hld up in tch: lost pl 3rd: no ch whn hit 3 out: t.o whn p.u bef 2 out* **66/1**

4m 7.70s (4.60) **Going Correction** +0.30s/f (Yiel) **12 Ran SP% 117.5**
Speed ratings: **101,100,91,89,87 82,79,—,—,— —,—** CSF £4.93 TOTE £3.30: £1.30, £1.50, £3.30; EX 5.80.There was no bid for the winner. Earl of Spectrum (GER) was the subject of a friendly claim.
Owner J L Flint **Bred** Palm Tree Thoroughbreds **Trained** Kenfig Hill, Bridgend

FOCUS
As is to be expected with sellers, a very moderate event but the form looks reasonably sound rated through the placed horses to their marks.

NOTEBOOK
Dancinginthestreet, successful in a similar event over two-miles-three furlongs here on his previous start, looked to find this trip a touch on the short side and had a bit to do on turning in, but he showed the right attitude and eventually wore down the leader. A return to further should suit, but this is very much his level. *(op 7-4 tchd 15-8 in places)*

Earl Of Spectrum(GER) had shown very limited ability on his previous five starts over hurdles, and was beaten off a mark of 46 on the Flat on his latest outing, but he was the second best off at the weights on this drop in grade on his return to obstacles, and was just held. Well clear of the remainder, he showed enough to suggest he can find a similar race. *(op 4-1 tchd 11-4)*

Twist N Turn had been pulled up in her last two starts in similar company, but her yard are in good form and this was a lot better, especially considering she had so much to find at the weights. No match for the front two, she looked very one paced under pressure and may be worth another try over further. *(op 11-1)*

Chariot(IRE) did not find very much under pressure in the closing stages and remains a maiden. *(op 6-1)*

La Muette(IRE) finished up well held and is another who remains winless over hurdles. *(op 12-1)*

2284 GET YOUR ANNUAL BADGE NOW NOVICES' H'CAP CHASE (12 fncs) 2m
1:50 (1:50) (Class 4) (0-105,98) 4-Y-0+ **£4,394** (£1,290; £645; £322)

Form RPR

-142 **1** **Miss Shakira (IRE)**[18] 1942 7-11-12 97.............................. TScudamore 117+
(N A Twiston-Davies) *a.p: reminder after 4th: rdn to ld 3 out: clr appr last: eased towards fin* **9/4**[1]

32-F **2** *6* **Call Me Jack (IRE)**[181] 437 9-10-1 77............................(t) LStephens(5) 87
(M J M Evans) *led 2nd to 8th: ev ch whn n.m.r 3 out: rdn and one pce fr 2 out* **10/1**

3 *3 1/2* **Arctic Cherry (IRE)**[214] 7-10-11 82.. PJBrennan 89
(R Ford) *led to 2nd: j.lft 4th and 5th: hdd 8th: rdn and hdd 3 out: one pce fr 2 out* **10/3**[2]

6-42 **4** *4* **Sailor A'Hoy**[186] 371 9-10-10 84... ACCoyle(3) 90+
(M Mullineaux) *hld up: hdwy appr 7th: wknd 2 out* **4/1**[3]

63PP **5** *5* **Alexander Musical (IRE)**[7] 2141 7-9-13 75 oh9 ow4.......(b) MNicolls(5) 74+
(S T Lewis) *hld up and bhd: hit 2nd: hdwy 7th: mstke 4 out: wknd 3 out* **25/1**

1P-6 **6** *27* **Hot Lips Page (FR)**[25] 1850 4-11-1 98...................................... PMoloney 57
(Ian Williams) *hld up: hdwy 5th: wknd after 3 out* **10/1**

06P2 **P** **Let's Rock**[32] 1749 7-10-0 78 oh4 ow7.................................... MrRHodges(7) —
(Mrs A Price) *a bhd: rdn after 4th: lost tch 6th: t.o whn p.u bef 4 out* **4/1**[3]

4m 5.90s (3.40) **Going Correction** +0.30s/f (Yiel)
WFA 4 from 7yo+ 12lb **7 Ran SP% 115.9**
Speed ratings: **103,100,98,96,93 80,—** CSF £24.17 TOTE £3.00: £1.50, £3.80; EX 12.40.
Owner F J Mills & W Mills **Bred** Tom Fitzgerald **Trained** Naunton, Gloucs

FOCUS
A moderate handicap chase for novices but a decent enough performance from the winner, who is value for ten lengths and can win again.

NOTEBOOK
Miss Shakira(IRE) ◆ had run well to be second over this trip in a similar event on her chasing debut at Carlisle but, twice a winner over three miles in point-to-points, she just took a little while to get going early. However, given a good and persistent ride, she eventually outclassed her rivals and looked to win with something in hand. There are plenty more races to be won with her and she ought to prove just as effective, if not better, back over further. *(op 5-2 tchd 3-1)*

Call Me Jack(IRE) found only the potentially well-handicapped winner too good off the back of a 181-day break and offered plenty of promise on his debut for a new trainer. He is better known as *a point-to-pointer these days, but showed enough to suggest he could find a similar event. (op 12-1)*

Arctic Cherry(IRE), successful in a point-to-point earlier in the year, ran respectably off the back of a 181-day break over a trip that is probably short enough. Given this was his first run under Rules since 2003, better can be expected in future. *(op 5-1)*

Sailor A'Hoy was well held in fourth and did not appear ideally suited by this significant drop back in trip. *(op 7-2 tchd 10-3)*

Alexander Musical(IRE) was well held from 13lb out of the handicap including his rider's overweight, but did at least manage to complete this time.

Hot Lips Page(FR) ran nowhere near the level of form she is capable of over hurdles on her chasing debut and has something to prove now. *(op 8-1)*

Let's Rock failed to build on his recent course second from effectively 11lb out of the handicap *including his rider's overweight. Official explanation: jockey said gelding was unsuited by the ground - found it too soft*

2285 WEATHERBYS INSURANCE NOVICES' H'CAP HURDLE (10 hdls) 2m 3f 110y
2:20 (2:20) (Class 4) (0-100,100) 3-Y-0+ **£3,838** (£1,126; £563; £281)

Form RPR

-154 **1** **Little Brave**[158] 724 10-10-8 87.. LStephens(5) 93+
(C Roberts) *prom: lost pl after 3rd: sltly hmpd 5th: hdwy after 3 out: led after 2 out: sn clr: r.o wl* **12/1**

545- **2** *6* **Abraham Smith**[215] 4866 5-11-7 100....................................... MNicolls(5) 99
(B J Eckley) *hld up in tch: rdn and ev ch after 2 out: one pce* **16/1**

46P- **3** *1* **Indian Solitaire (IRE)**[7] 2201 6-10-13 90.........................(p) TJPhelan(3) 88
(B P J Baugh) *hld up and bhd: hdwy 7th: rdn 3 out: one pce fr 2 out* **25/1**

-P03 **4** *3* **Spike Jones (NZ)**[5] 2182 7-11-4 92.. PHide 88+
(Mrs A M Thorpe) *hld up: hdwy 5th: ev ch after 2 out: wknd flat* **8/1**

0-06 **5** *1 1/4* **Ilongue (FR)**[16] 1974 4-10-0 74 oh4...................................... WHutchinson 68
(R Dickin) *hld up in mid-div: rdn 3 out: hdwy appr last: nvr trbld ldrs* **25/1**

F/P0 **6** *1 1/2* **Amanpuri (GER)**[28] 1800 7-10-6 90.......................... AngharadFrieze(10) 83+
(P A Blockley) *led 1st tl after 2 out: wknd flat* **50/1**

P-31 **7** *5* **Penric**[32] 1753 5-11-1 94.. WKennedy(5) 81
(J K Price) *hld up in mid-div: blnd 5th: hdwy 3 out: wknd after 2 out* **5/1**[2]

02-2 **8** *1* **Down's Folly (IRE)**[19] 1921 5-11-7 100.......................... TGreenway(5) 86
(H D Daly) *prom tl wknd after 2 out* **5/4**[1]

-5F2 **9** *6* **Imperial Royale (IRE)**[11] 2081 4-10-0 84.......................... TBurrows(10) 64
(P L Clinton) *hld up in mid-div: hdwy 5th: wknd 2 out* **13/2**[3]

5-53 **10** *20* **Blackthorn**[86] 1293 6-10-9 90.. RSpate(7) 50
(M Appleby) *hit 2nd: a bhd* **20/1**

-214 **P** **Dalida**[51] 1567 4-11-12 100... JMogford —
(Miss M E Rowland) *prom tl wknd 7th: t.o whn p.u bef last* **20/1**

P/56 **P** **Chocolate Bombe (IRE)**[22] 1876 8-9-8 75 oh10 ow1.......(b[1]) SWalsh(7) —
(S Lycett) *led to 1st: chsd ldr to 5th: wknd 6th: t.o whn p.u bef 7th* **33/1**

4m 53.8s (5.90) **Going Correction** +0.30s/f (Yiel) **12 Ran SP% 121.2**
Speed ratings: **100,97,97,96,95 94,92,92,90,82 —,—** CSF £159.39 CT £4663.27 TOTE £11.90: £4.20, £6.70, £9.10; EX 180.30.
Owner James Hearne **Bred** C H Bothway **Trained** Newport, Newport

FOCUS
An ordinary handicap hurdle for novices and the form is not worth as much as it might have been with the front two in the betting both running well below form.

NOTEBOOK
Little Brave's only previous success over hurdles came in a seller but, returning from a 158-day break, he found this a good opportunity and won most decisively. Surprisingly for his age, he seems quite progressive at this lowly level and, given he should be sharper next time, could find further opportunities. *(tchd 14-1)*

Abraham Smith made a promising return from a 215-day break and could do even better back over a little further.

Indian Solitaire(IRE), racing over hurdles for the first time in just over a year but fit from three recent runs on the Flat, offered some encouragement on his return to obstacles.

Spike Jones(NZ) again seemed to lack a change of pace when it mattered and may do better returned to two miles, where a likely stronger gallop ought to suit. *(op 12-1)*

Ilongue(FR) ◆, from 4lb out of the handicap, was not without promise and hinted at better to come. *(tchd 28-1)*

Amanpuri(GER) ◆ ran well for a long way and could yet do better.

Penric failed to reproduce the form of his recent course-and-distance success, even allowing for an 8lb higher mark, but he did not really get the run of things in behind a wall of horses and it may be worth forgiving him this. *(op 4-1)*

Down's Folly(IRE) had shaped well when second on his reappearance at Lingfield, but failed to *confirm that promise and has to be considered pretty disappointing.Official explanation: trainer said gelding lost a front and a hind shoe (op 7-4)*

Imperial Royale(IRE) was 13lb lower than in future handicaps following his recent second in a novice hurdle at Market Rasen, but he ran no sort of race and could struggle from his revised mark in the short term. *(op 5-1)*

2286 JOIN THE BUSINESS CLUB JUVENILE MAIDEN HURDLE (8 hdls) 2m 1f
2:50 (2:50) (Class 4) 3-Y-0 **£3,832** (£1,124; £562; £280)

Form RPR

1 **Baie Des Flamands (USA)**[31] 3-10-12 .... HOliver 96
(Miss S J Wilton) *a.p: led 5th: rdn after 2 out: hung lft flat: drvn out* **9/1**

2 *1/2* **Hawridge King**[38] 3-10-12 .... PJBrennan 96+
(W S Kittow) *hld up and bhd: hdwy appr 5th: chsd wnr appr 2 out: rdn and swtchd rt flat: r.o* **8/1**

3 *1 3/4* **Take A Mile (IRE)**[27] 3-10-7 .... JFLevins(5) 94
(B G Powell) *hld up and bhd: hdwy appr 3 out: nt qckn flat* **28/1**

0 **4** *shd* **Cava Bien**[11] 2069 3-10-12 .... PMoloney 94
(B J Llewellyn) *hld up: hdwy 3rd: outpcd after 3 out: rallied appr last: styd on flat* **33/1**

3 **5** *7* **Proprioception (IRE)**[9] 2101 3-10-5 .... WHutchinson 80
(A King) *hld up towards rr: hdwy appr 5th: wknd 2 out* **6/1**[3]

6 16 **Oh Mister Pinceau (FR)**[123] 3-10-12 TScudamore 71
(H D Daly) *hld up: hdwy 3rd: led 4th to 5th: wknd 2 out* **3/1**[2]

4 **7** 3 ½ **David's Symphony (IRE)**[9] [2101] 3-10-12 WMarston 67
(A W Carroll) *lft in ld 1st: sn hdd and hmpd by loose horse: wknd appr 5th* **20/1**

P **8** shd **Leprechaun's Maite**[40] [1679] 3-10-12 VSlattery 67
(P A Blockley) *bhd: short-lived effrt appr 5th* **100/1**

5 **9** 12 **Mickey Pearce (IRE)**[17] [1955] 3-10-9 ONelmes(3) 55
(J G M O'Shea) *hld up in mid-div: hdwy appr 5th: wknd 3 out* **50/1**

10 1 ¾ **Nepal (IRE)**[147] 3-10-2 ACCoyle(3) 46
(M Mullineaux) *a bhd* **66/1**

11 14 **Picot De Say**[65] 3-10-12 OMcPhail 39
(C Roberts) *led after 1st: j.rt 3rd: hdd 4th: wknd qckly* **20/1**

0 **P** **Magnate (IRE)**[30] [1785] 3-10-7 LStephens(5) —
(Mrs S M Johnson) *sn t.o: p.u bef 2 out* **100/1**

U **Prime Contender**[18] 3-10-12 MFoley —
(B W Hills) *led tl j.rt and uns rdr 1st* **7/4**[1]

U **Beaumont Girl (IRE)**[38] 3-10-5 JMogford —
(Miss M E Rowland) *prom whn j.rt and uns rdr 1st* **50/1**

P **Branston Lily**[26] 3-9-12 MrJAJenkins(7) —
(D Brace) *prom tl rdn and wknd appr 5th: t.o whn p.u bef 2 out* **66/1**

30 **P** **Desert Buzz (IRE)**[28] [1797] 3-10-12 PWhelan —
(J Hetherton) *hld up in tch: wknd 3 out: bhd whn p.u bef 2 out* **22/1**

4m 11.0s (7.90) **Going Correction** +0.30s/f (Yiel) **16** Ran SP% **125.9**
Speed ratings: **93,92,91,91,88 81,79,79,73,72 66,—,—,—,—** — CSF £73.74 TOTE £14.60: £3.40, £3.30, £6.30; EX 58.10.
Owner John Pointon And Sons **Bred** Pacelco S A **Trained** Wetley Abbey, Staffs

FOCUS
Probably not a bad race of its type for the time of year, but the winning time was 3.3 seconds slower than the seller. The form could be rated higher but has been treated negatively as the time was slower than the seller.

NOTEBOOK
Baie Des Flamands(USA), a Ripon maiden winner over just short of ten furlongs and rated 76 on the Flat, took well to hurdling at the first attempt and showed the right attitude under pressure. Things will be harder under a penalty, but his jockey was very bullish afterwards and there could be better to come when he is stepped up to two and a half miles. *(tchd 10-1)*
Hawridge King performed with credit for these connections over middle-distances throughout the Flat season, but always found one or two too good and is still a maiden. Making his debut over hurdles, he had every chance when it mattered despite having raced keenly early on, but was again content to settle for a place. He does not look ungenuine, but lacks the will to win and also gave the impression he needed this first experience of hurdling. *(op 15-2)*
Take A Mile(IRE), a 60-rated ten-furlong winner on the Flat, made a pleasing debut over hurdles and looks up to making the grade.
Cava Bien, unlike many of his rivals, had the benefit of previous hurdling experience and stepped up on what he showed on his debut over this course and distance with a fast-finishing fourth.
Proprioception(IRE) failed to progress as one might have hoped from her promising debut at Huntingdon, but this may have been a slightly more competitive affair and she was of limited ability on the Flat in any case. *(op 7-1)*
Oh Mister Pinceau(FR) looked a nice type for juvenile hurdles judged on his Flat form in France *which included a win over a mile and a half, but he finished up well held and will need to improve. (tchd 7-2)*
Picot De Say stopped quickly and something may well have been amiss.
Desert Buzz(IRE) *Official explanation: jockey said gelding pulled up lame (tchd 25-1)*
Prime Contender, successful on his last two starts on the Flat, the latter over ten furlongs off a mark of 68, got rid of his rider at the first on his hurdling debut. *(tchd 25-1)*

2287 FEDERAL EXPRESS H'CAP CHASE (14 fncs) 2m 3f
3:20 (3:21) (Class 4) (0-110,110) 5-Y-0+ **£4,443** (£1,304; £652; £325)

Form RPR

60-U **1** **Direct Flight (IRE)**[9] [2100] 7-11-7 **110** WKennedy(5) 130+
(Noel T Chance) *hld up: smooth hdwy 10th: led on bit 3 out: clr 2 out: hit last: comf* **7/2**[2]

-05P **2** 6 **Euro Bleu (FR)**[15] [1983] 7-9-9 **84** (tp) LStephens(5) 92+
(M Sheppard) *hld up: hdwy 10th: outpcd 4 out: rallying whn mstke last: styd on: no ch w wnr* **11/1**

1-3P **3** 1 ½ **Woodenbridge Dream (IRE)**[137] [896] 8-10-2 **86** WMarston 91
(R Lee) *led: rdn and hdd 3 out: one pce fr 2 out* **4/1**[3]

1236 **4** ½ **Tommy Spar**[35] [1728] 5-11-3 **101** PJBrennan 106
(P Bowen) *chsd ldr tl after 4 out: sn rdn: one pce fr 2 out* **5/1**

1/12 **5** 10 **Thalys (GER)**[21] [1894] 7-11-6 **104** JamesDavies 101+
(P R Webber) *hld up in tch: rdn 4 out: wknd appr 2 out* **11/8**[1]

4m 50.1s (3.50) **Going Correction** +0.30s/f (Yiel) **5** Ran SP% **109.3**
Speed ratings: **104,101,100,100,96** CSF £30.97 TOTE £3.90: £3.40, £2.50; EX 34.60.
Owner Top Flight Racing **Bred** Tom McCartan **Trained** Upper Lambourn, Berks

FOCUS
With Thalys running below form, Direct Flight's task was made much easier and he totally outclassed his other three rivals. He is value for double the official margin and the form might work out with the third and fourth close to their marks.

NOTEBOOK
Direct Flight(IRE), in the process of running a fair race on his chasing debut at Huntingdon before unseating a little way out, put in a clear round this time and got off the mark over the larger obstacles in comfortable fashion. Even though his main rival was not at his best and the remainder finished in a bunch, the Handicapper could hit him hard for this and that would make things a lot tougher, but he looks capable of fulfilling his potential and had to be respected regardless of the rise. *(op 4-1 tchd 9-2)*
Euro Bleu(FR) got the best of the battle for second and looked to post his best effort to date over fences, but he was still readily left behind by the winner and may need to step up again to find a similar event. *(op 16-1)*
Woodenbridge Dream(IRE) ran creditably enough in third off the back of a 137-day break and could be better for the run. *(op 5-1)*
Tommy Spar was not quite at his best and has to be considered a touch disappointing. *(op 7-2)*
Thalys(GER) looked to have conditions to suit, and had been in good form since returning to *Rules, but this was a disappointing effort. Official explanation: trainer said gelding was found to have ripped a muscle in its back (op 5-4 tchd 6-4 in places)*

2288 FUTURE STARS MAIDEN NATIONAL HUNT FLAT RACE (CONDITIONAL JOCKEYS/AMATEUR RIDERS) 2m 1f
3:50 (3:50) (Class 6) 4-6-Y-0 **£1,918** (£559; £279)

Form RPR

1 **Legal Glory (IRE)** 5-10-11 MrSPJones(7) 90+
(B G Powell) *hld up towards rr: hdwy over 4f out: led wl over 1f out: sn edgd rt: r.o* **12/1**

00-4 **2** 2 **Jimmy Bedney (IRE)**[193] [249] 4-11-1 MrMRimell(3) 87+
(M G Rimell) *t.k.h: led after 2f: hung lft over 2f out: hdd wl over 1f out: nt qckn ins fnl f* **10/1**

4 **3** 1 ½ **Northern Endeavour**[201] [138] 6-10-13 WKennedy(5) 84
(Simon Earle) *led 2f: a.p: rdn and nt qckn fnl 2f* **10/1**

4 nk **Lord Ryeford (IRE)** 5-10-11 MrRMcCarthy(7) 84
(T R George) *hld up in mid-div: hdwy over 6f out: rdn and r.o one pce fnl 2f* **20/1**

4 **5** 3 ½ **Butler Services (IRE)**[11] [2075] 5-10-11 MrAJBerry(7) 80
(Jonjo O'Neill) *hld up in tch: rdn 8f out: wknd over 1f out* **5/1**[3]

6 5 **Coleraine (IRE)** 5-11-1 ONelmes(3) 75
(O Sherwood) *hld up: hdwy 9f out: wknd over 1f out* **4/1**[2]

00 **7** 1 ¼ **Aaron's Run**[28] [1799] 5-10-13 JDiment(5) 74
(M R Bosley) *t.k.h: prom: hung lft over 4f out: wknd 2f out* **50/1**

50- **8** 7 **Pearly Star**[238] [4540] 4-10-11 MrGTumelty(7) 67
(A King) *hld up in tch: wknd 4f out* **8/1**

0-0 **9** 4 **Bitta Dash**[201] [138] 5-10-11 WMcCarthy(7) 63
(A J Wilson) *nvr nr ldrs* **66/1**

10 3 **Four For A Laugh (IRE)** 6-11-1 GCarenza(3) 60
(A King) *mid-div: lost pl after 4f: n.d after* **3/1**[1]

11 4 **Hatton House (IRE)** 5-10-13 StephenJCraine(5) 56
(D McCain) *hld up and bhd: hdwy on ins 9f out: rdn 6f out: wknd 5f out* **12/1**

0 **12** 21 **Ourcarl**[15] [1985] 5-10-13 MNicolls(5) 35
(G Brown) *mid-div: rdn 9f out: sn bhd* **66/1**

13 4 **Oscar Royal (IRE)** 4-10-11 SWQuinlan(7) 31
(Mrs S E Busby) *hld up in mid-div: rdn 6f out: bhd fnl 5f* **50/1**

R **Im A Tanner** 4-10-11 MissCDyson(7) —
(Miss C Dyson) *a bhd: t.o whn hung lft and rn out bnd 4f out* **80/1**

4m 7.10s (6.00) **Going Correction** +0.30s/f (Yiel)
WFA 4 from 5yo+ 12lb **14** Ran SP% **119.2**
Speed ratings: **97,96,95,95,93 91,90,87,85,84 82,72,70,—** CSF £120.79 TOTE £8.40: £4.90, £2.50, £3.30; EX 124.90 Place 6 £6,246.60, Place 5 £1,005.37.
Owner J W Mursell **Bred** Mrs Sheila O'Ryan **Trained** Morestead, Hants

FOCUS
The bare form of this bumper is just ordinary, but there were a few interesting types on show. The fifth and seventh set a weak standard. Sam Jones's first winner under Rules.

NOTEBOOK
Legal Glory(IRE) ◆, a full-brother to the yard's talented but luckless staying chaser Big Rob, was always going well and, produced with a well-timed effort, found plenty when asked despite looking as though he will improve a fair bit just for the experience alone. He should progress and could be decent when faced with obstacles. *(op 11-1)*
Jimmy Bedney(IRE), making his debut for a new yard off the back of a 193-day break, got the run of the race in front and seemed to step up on his previous efforts in second. *(op 14-1)*
Northern Endeavour, a promising fourth on his debut at Worcester 201 days previously, again offered promise and should do even better when faced with obstacles. *(op 8-1)*
Lord Ryeford(IRE), a 10,000gns full-brother to two-and-a-half mile hurdle-winner Lord Dundaniel, made a pleasing debut and is another who can do better over obstacles.
Butler Services(IRE) was not beaten that far, but failed to really improve on the form he showed over course and distance on his debut. *(op 7-2)*
Coleraine(IRE), a 40,000euros purchase out of a mare who was placed in Irish points, was in trouble a fair way out and never really looked like posing a serious threat. *(op 10-3 tchd 3-1)*
Pearly Star did not offer a great deal off the back of a 238-day break. *(op 9-1)*
Four For A Laugh(IRE), a 24,000euros half-brother to a winner over a mile and ten furlongs as well as a bumper scorer, ran below market expectations on his racecourse debut. *(op 11-2)*
Hatton House(IRE) ◆, a 130,000euros half-brother to the 2004 Grand National winner Amberleigh House, finished up beaten a long way but there was definite promise and he can do a lot better in time.
T/Plt: £7,502.70 to a £1 stake. Pool: £36,485.85. 3.55 winning tickets. T/Qpdt: £581.70 to a £1 stake. Pool: £3,380.60. 4.30 winning tickets. KH

2076 MARKET RASEN (R-H)
Thursday, November 17

OFFICIAL GOING: Hurdle course - good to soft (good in places); chase course - good to soft (soft in places)
The hurdles were again bang on the inside. The ground was described as 'very tacky, hard work'.
Wind: Virtually nil Weather: Fine and sunny

2289 RACING UK LADY RIDERS' H'CAP HURDLE (8 hdls) 2m 1f 110y
12:40 (12:40) (Class 4) (0-100,100) 4-Y-0+ **£3,268** (£952; £476)

Form RPR

1F11 **1** **Parisienne Gale (IRE)**[12] [2041] 6-10-9 **90** MissCarolineHurley(7) 105+
(R Ford) *mde all: styd on strly fr 2 out: readily* **5/6**[1]

P0-6 **2** 2 ½ **Upswing**[13] [2027] 8-9-11 **78** ow1 MissCMetcalfe(7) 85
(R C Guest) *hdwy to chse ldrs 4th: wnt 2nd 2 out: kpt on: no real imp* **11/2**[2]

U-65 **3** 13 **Nobel (FR)**[190] [301] 4-11-5 **100** MissRDavidson(7) 95+
(N G Richards) *trckd ldrs: wnt 2nd after 3 out: 3rd and wl btn whn hit last* **11/2**[2]

6325 **4** ½ **Rifleman (IRE)**[3] [2245] 5-11-3 **98** (t) MissAArmitage(7) 94+
(Robert Gray) *prom: outpcd 3 out: kpt on between last 2* **11/1**[3]

B446 **5** ½ **Siegfrieds Night (IRE)**[11] [2079] 4-11-3 **98** (t) MissADeniel(7) 91
(M C Chapman) *chsd wnr: wl outpcd and hrd rdn 3 out: kpt on between last 2* **12/1**

-45P **6** 10 **Pornic (FR)**[177] [481] 11-11-3 **94** MissEJJones(3) 77
(A Crook) *chsd ldrs: lost pl after 5th* **33/1**

405- **7** 3 **Commemoration Day (IRE)**[221] [4782] 4-10-9 **90** (b) AnnStokell(7) 70
(M E Sowersby) *prom: rdn and lost pl after 5th* **25/1**

-P66 **8** 1 ½ **Alpine Hideaway (IRE)**[32] [1756] 12-10-12 **93** (p) MissSBrotherton(7) 72
(J S Wainwright) *in rr: pushed along 3rd: bhd fr 5th* **25/1**

0PP0 **9** dist **Friedhelmo (GER)**[11] [2079] 9-11-5 **100** (t) MissRachelClark(7) —
(S B Clark) *stdd s: a last: t.o 2 out: btn 33l* **66/1**

4m 22.5s (6.10) **Going Correction** +0.575s/f (Soft) **9** Ran SP% **113.5**
Speed ratings: **109,107,102,101,101 97,95,95,—** CSF £5.73 CT £15.43 TOTE £1.70: £1.10, £1.40, £1.70; EX 7.60.
Owner S J Manning **Bred** Edmond And Richard Kent **Trained** Cotebrook, Cheshire
■ Stewards' Enquiry : Miss S Brotherton caution: used whip when out of contention

FOCUS
An end-to-end gallop resulted in a decent time for a race like this and a most convincing winner - the first two were clear and the form looks solid with the third running to his mark.

NOTEBOOK
Parisienne Gale(IRE), returning to hurdling from a lower mark, made this a true test and kept up *the gallop in relentless fashion. She has done nothing but improve and is a credit to her trainer. (op Evens)*

Upswing, having his second outing for his new yard, kept on in grim pursuit of the winner. Yet to win a race of any description, he has the build more of a chaser than a hurdler and will surely break his duck this time. *(op 13-2 tchd 7-1)*
Nobel(FR), making his handicap debut on his first outing since May, went in pursuit of the winner but was well beaten when hitting the last. In the end he only just held on to third spot. *(op 9-2)*
Rifleman(IRE), making a quick return, seemed to drop the baton starting the final turn. He was staying on when it was all over but seems to have a mind of his own nowadays. *(op 10-1)*
Siegfrieds Night(IRE), left for dead starting the final turn, kept on under what is best described as a vigorous ride. *(op 14-1 tchd 16-1)*
Pornic(FR), absent since May, looked to be carrying plenty of condition and time is not on his side now. *(op 25-1)*

2290 BUY YOUR TICKETS ONLINE@MARKETRASENRACES.CO.UK (S) H'CAP HURDLE (10 hdls) 2m 6f
1:10 (1:10) (Class 5) (0-90,90) 4-Y-O+ **£2,172** (£633; £316)

Form RPR
2054 **1** **Lazy Lena (IRE)**[13] 2025 6-10-12 76........ TSiddall 84+
(Miss L C Siddall) *hld up: hdwy to trck ldrs 3rd: led and j.lft 2 out: edgd lft and styd on wl run-in* **5/1**[3]
P332 **2** *3 ½* **Samson Des Galas (FR)**[13] 2025 7-10-2 66........ (p) GLee 69
(Robert Gray) *sn trcking ldrs: rdn appr 2 out: almost upsides last: swtchd rt and no ex run-in* **2/1**[1]
P0-0 **3** *nk* **Avanti Tiger (IRE)**[5] 2181 6-10-4 68........ (b[1]) NFehily 71
(C C Bealby) *trckd ldr: led 6th: hdd appr 2 out: 3rd and hit last: styd on towards fin* **15/2**
52P- **4** *24* **Flemming (USA)**[247] 4390 8-10-8 72........ ATinkler 51
(I A Brown) *in rr: outpcd and bhd fr 7th* **14/1**
-P60 **5** *¾* **Sea Maize**[173] 545 7-9-11 64........ (p) PAspell[(3)] 42
(C R Wilson) *chsd ldrs: wknd after 7th: sn bhd* **20/1**
P505 **6** *dist* **Cromwell (IRE)**[11] 2080 10-11-2 80........ (b) KJohnson —
(M C Chapman) *j. slowly: led: hdd 6th: sn lost pl: t.o 2 out: btn 60l* **16/1**
3 **U** **Astronaut**[85] 1310 8-11-5 88........ (p) PCO'Neill[(5)] —
(R C Guest) *hld up towards rr: mstke and uns rdr 5th* **3/1**[2]
-P3P **P** **Comfortable Call**[151] 781 7-11-12 90........ (t) JPByrne —
(H Alexander) *in rr: bhd fr 7th: p.u bef next* **16/1**
30P/ **P** **Ilton**[970] 4352 6-10-7 76........ DCCostello[(5)] —
(M E Sowersby) *mstke: in tch: mstke and lost pl 6th: bhd whn p.u bef 2 out* **33/1**

5m 41.1s (12.80) **Going Correction** +0.575s/f (Soft) **9** Ran SP% **112.9**
Speed ratings: **99,97,97,88,88** —,—,—,— CSF £15.47 CT £72.64 TOTE £6.20: £1.60, £1.30, £2.30; EX 15.10.The winner was bought in for 3,600gns
Owner Mrs Theresa O'Toole **Bred** J Neville **Trained** Colton, N Yorks
■ A first winner for Tom Siddall since he broke his pelvis at Fontwell in March.

FOCUS
A low-grade seller run at a sound pace. The winner and third look to have improved slightly, the runner-up is the key.

NOTEBOOK
Lazy Lena(IRE), who is only small, travelled strongly. Distracted by a loose horse in the home straight, in the end she was kept right up to her work to get off the mark at the 15th attempt. *(op 11-2)*
Samson Des Galas(FR), ahead of the winner at Hexham, has changed stables since and had the cheekpieces fitted. He worked hard to land almost level at the final flight but was then put firmly in his place. *(op 9-4 tchd 15-8)*
Avanti Tiger(IRE), in first-time blinkers, did not lack market support. After going on he looked well cooked when clouting the last but found reserves and would have taken second spot in a few more strides. He looks to have a little more ability than he is prepared to show. *(op 11-1)*
Flemming(USA), absent since March, does not handle conditions as testing as he encountered here. *(op 10-1)*
Cromwell(IRE) *Official explanation: jockey said gelding had a breathing problem (op 14-1)*
Astronaut, absent since finishing lame at Perth in August, was happy to sit off the pace but a slight error at the last flight with a circuit to go was enough to dislodge his rider. After that he was quite happy to make a nuisance of himself. *(op 5-2 tchd 10-3)*

2291 A J NEARY MEMORIAL BEGINNERS' CHASE (14 fncs) 2m 6f 110y
1:40 (1:41) (Class 4) 5-Y-O+ **£3,879** (£1,204; £648)

Form RPR
111- **1** **Julius Caesar**[250] 4330 5-10-13........ GLee 130+
(J Howard Johnson) *hld up: hdwy to trck ldrs 5th: jnd ldr 4 out: trav easily best whn lft clr last: easily* **9/2**[3]
1P-3 **2** *19* **Classic Capers**[21] 1891 6-10-11 117........ FKing[(3)] 116+
(J M Jefferson) *jnd ldrs 3rd: outpcd appr 3 out: lft 12l 2nd last* **12/1**
12-2 **3** *28* **Martha's Kinsman (IRE)**[201] 128 6-11-0........ MBradburne 96+
(H D Daly) *chsd ldrs: wkng whn sltly hmpd 4 out: sn bhd: eased whn j.rt 2 out* **3/1**[1]
-P06 **P** **Seraph**[46] 1608 5-10-13........ NFehily —
(O Brennan) *in rr: bhd fr 8th: mstke next: sn p.u* **100/1**
2PP- **F** **Muhtenbar**[250] 4330 5-10-13........ TJMurphy —
(Miss H C Knight) *t.k.h: led: j.rt: hdd and wkng whn fell 4 out* **12/1**
61-1 **P** **Bellaney Jewel (IRE)**[201] 124 6-10-7........ ADobbin —
(J J Quinn) *nt fluent: lost tch 8th: t.o 4 out: p.u bef next* **10/1**
00-5 **P** **El Andaluz (FR)**[9] 2108 5-10-13........ ADempsey —
(M Todhunter) *t.k.h: w ldr: sddle sn slipped: p.u bef 2nd: continued to fin crse* **66/1**
250- **F** **King Killone (IRE)**[223] 4765 5-10-13 118........ DO'Meara 126+
(H P Hogarth) *trckd ldrs: led 4 out: narrowly hdd whn slipped bdly landing last and fell* **4/1**[2]
14-2 **P** **The Rising Moon (IRE)**[32] 1758 6-11-0........ APMcCoy —
(Jonjo O'Neill) *mstkes: chsd ldrs: stmbld 10th: wkng whn sltly hmpd next: bhd whn p.u bef 3 out* **3/1**[1]

5m 56.4s (10.00) **Going Correction** +0.575s/f (Soft) **9** Ran SP% **115.1**
Speed ratings: **105,98,88**,—,— —,—,—,— CSF £54.36 TOTE £4.00: £1.70, £3.00, £1.70; EX 62.70.
Owner Jack Coupe and John Thompson **Bred** Juddmonte Farms **Trained** Billy Row, Co Durham

FOCUS
A good-class novices' chase and the winner has the potential to go far. The runner-up sets the standard and the faller King Killone is sure to make his mark.

NOTEBOOK
Julius Caesar ◆, who progressed into a 124-rated hurdler last term, looked in tip-top trim. He travelled smoothly and, held together, was still on the steel not having been asked any sort of question when he was left clear at the final fence. He looks capable of going a long way but, under the present system, opportunities in the north will be limited. *(op 4-1)*
Classic Capers, having just his second outing over fences, was left for dead over the final three fences before being handed second spot at the last. With his sights set lower he can surely make his mark though he will struggle in handicap company from a mark of 117. *(tchd 14-1)*
Martha's Kinsman(IRE), runner-up to Standin Obligation when last seen out at Uttoxeter in April, looks every inch a chaser but was most disappointing on his first try over fences. He can surely do a lot better than this. *(op 10-3 tchd 4-1)*
The Rising Moon(IRE), stepping up in trip, lacked any confidence at his fences and was on the retreat when having to sidestep a faller four out. *This Irish point winner now has plenty to prove. Official explanation: trainer's representative had no explanation for the poor form shown (op 9-2 tchd 5-1)*
King Killone(IRE) ◆, a big, strapping type, is closely related to Wayward Lad and has an Irish point win to his credit. Now trained by his owner, he took to fences like a duck to water and was only a neck down but booked for second spot when he unluckily fell at the last. He should have a bright future. *(op 9-2 tchd 5-1)*
Muhtenbar, pulled up behind the winner at Sandown in March, was keen in front even with Murphy in the saddle and looked to be running on empty when hitting the deck four out. He will need to settle much better. *(op 9-2 tchd 5-1)*
El Andaluz(FR), unplaced in three starts over hurdles, has the make and shape of a chaser but he pulled very hard and his saddle soon slipped forward. His rider was unable to pull him up and *finished the course running much of the way on the hurdle track. At least this showed he is very fit. Official explanation: jockey said saddle slipped (op 9-2 tchd 5-1)*

2292 PERTEMPS H'CAP HURDLE (SERIES QUALIFIER) (10 hdls) 2m 6f
2:10 (2:12) (Class 2) 4-Y-O+ **£12,288** (£3,607; £1,803; £900)

Form RPR
-321 **1** **Nathos (GER)**[11] 2079 8-11-0 **125** 7ex........ NFehily 130+
(C J Mann) *hld up: hdwy 7th: led 2 out: styd on strly run-in* **10/1**[3]
40-1 **2** *1 ¾* **Not Left Yet (IRE)**[5] 2173 4-10-4 **115** 7ex........ TJMurphy 120+
(M C Pipe) *hld up in rr: hdwy on outer 7th: chal 2 out: nt qckn run-in* **4/7**[1]
0416 **3** *3* **Ball O Malt (IRE)**[22] 1881 9-10-4 **115**........ ARoss 116
(R A Fahey) *hld up: stdy hdwy 7th: effrt appr 2 out: styd on wl run-in: fin best* **40/1**
214- **4** *nk* **Campaign Trail (IRE)**[265] 4052 7-11-5 **130**........ APMcCoy 130
(Jonjo O'Neill) *hld up towards rr: hdwy on outer 7th: effrt appr 2 out: styd on same pce appr last* **25/1**
12-4 **5** *1 ¼* **Heir To Be**[15] 1992 6-10-0 **111** oh1........ LAspell 111+
(Mrs L Wadham) *chsd ldrs: rdn along 7th: styd on same pce between last 2* **8/1**[2]
-312 **6** *1 ¾* **Saltango (GER)**[13] 2020 6-10-2 **113**........ JEMoore 111
(A M Hales) *trckd ldrs: led 7th to 2 out: one pce appr last* **12/1**
-231 **7** *6* **Mister Arjay (USA)**[19] 1929 5-10-9 **120**........ RGarritty 113+
(B Ellison) *led to 7th: wknd appr last* **18/1**
-204 **8** *1 ½* **Just Beth**[15] 1984 9-9-11 **113**........ DLaverty[(5)] 103
(G Fierro) *chsd ldrs: drvn along 6th: outpcd fr 2 out* **33/1**
04-0 **9** *3 ½* **Vicars Destiny**[19] 1929 7-10-9 **120**........ (p) ADempsey 106
(Mrs S Lamyman) *hld up in rr: sme hdwy 3 out: nvr a factor* **40/1**
-2U3 **10** *4* **Cottam Grange**[11] 2079 5-10-4 **118** ow3........ MrTGreenall[(3)] 100
(M W Easterby) *towards rr: hdwy 6th: fdd appr 2 out* **33/1**
1411 **11** *9* **Bushido (IRE)**[32] 1759 6-11-0 **125**........ DElsworth 98
(Mrs S J Smith) *chsd ldrs: lost pl bef 2 out* **16/1**
51F- **12** *3* **Freetown (IRE)**[257] 4183 9-11-12 **137**........ ADobbin 107
(L Lungo) *mid-div: drvn and lost pl 6th: bhd fr 3 out* **40/1**
40P- **13** *¾* **Jack Martin (IRE)**[221] 4787 8-10-4 **115**........ RMcGrath 85
(S Gollings) *chsd ldrs: lost pl appr 2 out* **50/1**
PP60 **14** *13* **Iloveturtle (IRE)**[4] 2206 5-10-0 **111** oh16........ (t) KJohnson 68
(M C Chapman) *a in rr: last whn mstke 6th: bhd fr next* **150/1**
-431 **P** **Vicario**[14] 2004 4-10-4 **115**........ GLee —
(D McCain) *prom: rdn and hit 7th: lost pl next: bhd whn p.u bef 2 out* **20/1**

5m 36.5s (8.20) **Going Correction** +0.575s/f (Soft)
WFA 4 from 5yo+ 13lb **15** Ran SP% **127.1**
Speed ratings: **108,107,106,106,105 105,102,102,101,99 96,95,94,90**,— CSF £16.27 CT £281.31 TOTE £12.80: £2.60, £1.10, £14.40; EX 28.70 Trifecta £434.30 Part won. Pool: £611.70 - 0.10 winning units..
Owner J Davies, A Merritt & J Sunley **Bred** H -P Kremer And S Rustler **Trained** Upper Lambourn, Berks

FOCUS
A well-contested qualifier with all but half a dozen still in with a shout going to two out. The form has a rock solid look and should work out, and there should be plenty of future winners out of the race.

NOTEBOOK
Nathos(GER), under his 7lb penalty, was in no hurry to join issue. After striking for home he always looked to have the upper hand. He is clearly right at the top of his game and this extended trip seemed to play to his strengths. *(op 14-1)*
Not Left Yet(IRE), 7lb well-in under the penalty he picked up for winning at Cheltenham on his previous start, was quite excitable beforehand. Taken wide, he always looked like finishing second best on the run-in despite battling hard all the way to the line. He should bounce back after a short break. *(op 4-6 tchd 8-15)*
Ball O Malt(IRE), returning to hurdling from a lower mark, took quite a grip. Caught flat-footed going to two out, he stayed on in fine style on the run-in to snatch third spot. He can surely find an opening to get off the mark over hurdles. *(op 33-1)*
Campaign Trail(IRE), who is not that big, was returning to hurdles for his first outing since February. Taken wide, he was not over-punished and just kept on in his own time over the last two. This should have boosted his confidence with a return to fences a likely option. *(op 20-1)*
Heir To Be, dropping back in trip, mixed it from the off and deserves credit for this. *(op 11-1 tchd 12-1)*
Saltango(GER), on his handicap bow, was quite keen to get on with it and deserves credit for the way he stuck on all the way to the line. *(op 11-1)*
Mister Arjay(USA), 7lb higher, was stepping up in distance but in the end found this step up in class beyond him. He is possibly better suited going the other way round. *(op 16-1)*

2293 SYMES BAINS BROOMER H'CAP CHASE (19 fncs) 3m 4f 110y
2:40 (2:43) (Class 3) (0-120,114) 5-Y-O+ **£5,725** (£1,680; £840; £419)

Form RPR
226- **1** **Garryvoe (IRE)**[245] 4411 7-11-10 **112**........ JMMaguire 125+
(T R George) *hld up: mstke 7th: wnt prom 9th: led 4 out: styd on wl* **11/4**[1]
2-P5 **2** *2 ½* **Heidi III (FR)**[41] 1664 10-11-8 **110**........ (p) GLee 119
(M D Hammond) *chsd ldrs: wnt 2nd appr 3 out: styd on same pce* **8/1**
53P- **3** *2* **Villair (IRE)**[249] 4346 10-10-12 **100**........ NFehily 107
(C J Mann) *in rr: drvn along and hdwy 4 out: styd on same pce fr next* **4/1**[2]
25P- **4** *5* **Bob's The Business (IRE)**[257] 4183 11-11-3 **105**........ ADobbin 108+
(Ian Williams) *chsd ldrs: rdn 4 out: one pce* **8/1**
00-P **5** *dist* **Fin Bec (FR)**[15] 1989 12-11-2 **104**........ (b) LAspell 87
(A P Jones) *led: blnd and hdd 4 out: wknd appr next: eased whn t.o last: btn 37l* **16/1**
0P-0 **6** *15* **Hawk's Landing (IRE)**[16] 1972 8-11-12 **114**........ APMcCoy 97
(Jonjo O'Neill) *in tch: lost pl appr 3 out: sn bhd: eased whn t.o run-in* **5/1**

0-60 **P** **Follow The Flow (IRE)**[21] 1893 9-10-12 **107**...................... TJDreaper(7) —
(P A Pritchard) *prom: lost pl 12th: bhd whn p.u bef 15th* **12/1**

P-55 **P** **Buzybakson (IRE)**[21] 1893 8-10-2 **90**.. JEMoore —
(J R Cornwall) *sn in rr and pushed along: reminders 7th: t.o 13th: p.u bef 15th* **9/2**[3]

7m 54.5s (16.50) **Going Correction** +0.575s/f (Soft) **8** Ran SP% **117.3**
Speed ratings: **100,99,98,97,**— —,—,— CSF £25.44 CT £88.38 TOTE £3.70: £1.50, £2.20, £1.90; EX 29.20.
Owner Lady Clarke **Bred** Mrs M McGearty **Trained** Slad, Gloucs

FOCUS
A modest handicap chase that could rate higher but the form is not strong.

NOTEBOOK
Garryvoe(IRE), sixth in the four mile National Hunt Chase at Cheltenham in March, just stays and after taking charge he was never going to be overhauled. The further he goes the better. *(op 7-2 tchd 4-1)*
Heidi III(FR), suited by the give underfoot, went in pursuit of the winner but in truth was never going to finish anything but second best.
Villair(IRE), who has run well when fresh in the past, was happy to lob round in the rear. He kept on over the last three but is not one to have great faith in. *(op 5-1 tchd 11-2)*
Bob's The Business(IRE), absent since bursting at Kelso in March, will be better for the outing.
Hawk's Landing(IRE) dropped out in a matter of strides on the turn for home and he has yet to prove his stamina for this sort of distance. *(op 7-2 tchd 11-2)*
Buzybakson(IRE), who won from an 8lb higher mark here in December 2004, was a major mover on the betting front but he never went a yard. *(op 7-1)*
Follow The Flow(IRE) *Official explanation: jockey said gelding lost a front shoe (op 7-1)*

2294 BOOK FOR BOXING DAY H'CAP CHASE (14 fncs) 2m 4f
3:10 (3:14) (Class 3) (0-115,113) 5-Y-0+ **£5,426** (£1,592; £796; £397)

Form RPR

25U4 **1** **Fiery Peace**[40] 1673 8-11-3 **107**.. MrTGreenall(3) 121+
(C Grant) *j.rt: hld up in rr: hdwy and prom 8th: chalng whn lft in ld 3 out: hit next: 4l clr last: rdn rt out* **9/1**

66P- **2** *3* **Deep Water (USA)**[211] 4927 11-11-8 **109**.................................. ADobbin 119+
(M D Hammond) *chsd ldrs: pushed along 8th: chalng whn lft clr 2nd 3 out: kpt on wl run-in* **8/1**

3263 **3** *15* **Beat The Heat (IRE)**[32] 1761 7-11-9 **110**..............................(p) BHarding 104
(Jedd O'Keeffe) *chsd ldrs: rdn 4 out: wl outpcd appr next* **5/1**[2]

215 **4** *shd* **Bergerac (NZ)**[171] 593 7-11-1 **107**.. PCO'Neill(5) 101
(R C Guest) *prom: effrt 4 out: wl outpcd appr next* **11/2**[3]

0P4U **5** *17* **Tacolino (FR)**[27] 1815 11-11-4 **105**... NFehily 92+
(O Brennan) *led to 2nd: led 8th: hdd next: lost pl appr 3 out: bhd whn eased run-in* **9/1**

P0-5 **P** **Jaybejay (NZ)**[15] 1986 10-11-3 **104**.. JMMaguire —
(T R George) *led 2nd to 9th: lost pl next: bhd whn p.u bef 3 out* **10/1**

42-3 **F** **Kitski (FR)**[18] 1939 7-11-9 **113**.. KJMercer(3) 109+
(Ferdy Murphy) *chsd ldrs: slt mstkes: led 9th: strly chal whn fell heavily 3 out* **10/3**[1]

3-P0 **P** **Jones's Road (IRE)**[19] 1920 7-11-11 **112**.................................. APMcCoy —
(Jonjo O'Neill) *prom: drvn along 8th: lost pl next: bhd whn p.u bef 3 out* **5/1**[2]

5m 19.3s (16.60) **Going Correction** +0.575s/f (Soft) **8** Ran SP% **112.0**
Speed ratings: **89,87,81,81,74** —,—,— CSF £72.83 CT £398.46 TOTE £9.50: £2.40, £2.10, £1.80; EX 91.70.
Owner Panther Racing Ltd **Bred** Mrs Sarah Watson **Trained** Newton Bewley, Co Durham

FOCUS
A moderate winning time for a race of this grade. The winner is reckoned more of a stayer by his new trainer, Kitski looked on a harsh mark but might well have given him plenty to do.

NOTEBOOK
Fiery Peace, without a win for 16 months, has changed stables. Suited by going right-handed, he was handed the advantage three out and from that point on was always doing more than enough. The trip if anything looked in his favour. *(op 10-1 tchd 8-1)*
Deep Water(USA), 11lb lower than when last successful in February 2004, went down fighting but time is no longer on his side. *(tchd 9-1)*
Beat The Heat(IRE), better going left-handed, wore cheekpieces rather than the usual blinkers. *(op 9-2 tchd 6-1)*
Bergerac(NZ), having just his second start over fences, was having his first race since May and seemed to need it to blow away the cobwebs. *(op 15-2)*
Kitski(FR), having just his second outing over fences, was hesitant at some of his fences. He was being challenged on both sides when crashing out three from home. He definitely has the ability to open his account over fences even from this sort of mark. *(op 3-1)*

2295 MIDLANDS RACING - 10 GREAT VENUES "NATIONAL HUNT" NOVICES' HURDLE (10 hdls) 2m 3f 110y
3:40 (3:42) (Class 4) 4-Y-0+ **£3,405** (£992; £496)

Form RPR

14- **1** **Mr Pointment (IRE)**[278] 3810 6-10-12 .... ATinkler 114+
(C R Egerton) *trckd ldrs: wnt 2nd 5th: led appr 2 out: styd on wl run-in* **11/8**[1]

31 **2** *1 ¾* **Nor'Nor'East (IRE)**[20] 1915 7-11-5 .... APMcCoy 118
(Jonjo O'Neill) *trckd ldrs: wnt 2nd 2 out: upsides sn after last: no ex* **13/8**[2]

4-2 **3** *4* **No Guarantees**[18] 1938 5-10-12 .... CLlewellyn 107
(N A Twiston-Davies) *led tl appr 2 out: kpt on same pce appr last* **6/1**[3]

602/ **4** *4* **Elvis Returns**[620] 4216 7-10-9 .... FKing(3) 103
(J M Jefferson) *mid-div: hdwy to chse ldrs 6th: outpcd whn hit 2 out: kpt on run-in* **25/1**

0- **5** *9* **Kilmackilloge**[209] 4971 6-10-12 .... GLee 95+
(M Todhunter) *hld up towards rr: hdwy 7th: nvr nr ldrs* **50/1**

44-2 **6** *3 ½* **Extra Smooth**[22] 1885 4-10-12 .... NFehily 91
(C C Bealby) *mid-div: hdwy 7th: outpcd appr 2 out* **12/1**

7 *4* **Nagam (FR)** 4-10-12 .... LAspell 87+
(A Ennis) *in rr: sme hdwy 7th: nvr a factor* **50/1**

01-0 **8** *10* **Hi Humpfree**[16] 1968 5-10-7 .... PMerrigan(5) 79+
(Mrs H Dalton) *mid-div: hit 4th: sme hdwy 7th: lost pl appr 2 out* **12/1**

0 **9** *21* **Cedar Rapids (IRE)**[20] 1915 5-10-12 .... DO'Meara 65+
(H P Hogarth) *prom: lost pl after 7th* **50/1**

/P0- **10** *5* **Griffens Brook**[272] 3921 5-10-12 .... TJMurphy 51
(Mrs P Sly) *chsd ldrs: lost pl appr 3 out* **50/1**

66-P **11** *19* **Actual**[32] 1757 5-10-12 .... FKeniry 32
(P D Niven) *a in rr: bhd fr 7th* **200/1**

50 **12** *1* **Nearly Never**[13] 2024 10-10-5 .... NCarter(7) 31
(Mrs S J Smith) *in rr fr 6th: t.o 3 out* **100/1**

2-0 **F** **Thievery**[201] 131 4-10-12 .... MBradburne —
(H D Daly) *chsd ldrs: slipped landing 6th and fell* **40/1**

04P- **P** **Howsham Lad**[208] 4981 6-10-12 .... RMcGrath —
(G P Kelly) *sn detached in rr: t.o 3rd: p.u after 5th* **200/1**

P **P** **Max 'n Limbo (IRE)**[199] 147 5-10-9 .... MrTGreenall(3) —
(M W Easterby) *in rr: bhd fr 6th: t.o whn p.u after 3 out* **150/1**

50- **P** **Turnnocard (IRE)**[211] 4933 6-10-5 .... ADobbin —
(Ian Williams) *chsd ldrs: wknd rapidly after 5th: detached in rr whn p.u after next* **100/1**

4m 59.5s (9.50) **Going Correction** +0.575s/f (Soft)
WFA 4 from 5yo+ 12lb **16** Ran SP% **127.6**
Speed ratings: **104,103,101,100,96 95,93,89,81,79 71,71,**—,—,— — CSF £3.99 TOTE £2.50: £1.10, £1.40, £1.60; EX 7.40 Place 6 £15.80, Place 5 £14.15.
Owner Stockton Heath Racing **Bred** Miss A Gibson Fleming and Mrs E Cooper **Trained** Chaddleworth, Berks

FOCUS
A decent novices' hurdle which went to a useful bumper horse. The runner-up sets the standard with several of those close up near their marks, and the winner can rate higher.

NOTEBOOK
Mr Pointment(IRE), a useful bumper performer, is a potential chaser in the making. He went on and was always doing enough to keep his challenger at bay. He should go on from here. *(tchd 7-4)*
Nor'Nor'East(IRE) worked hard to get upsides but the winner always looked like containing his challenge. A stiffer test of stamina will be in his favour. *(op 9-4 tchd 5-2 in a place)*
No Guarantees, a free-going sort, took them along and kept on surprisingly well. He should make a better chaser than hurdler. *(op 9-2 tchd 4-1)*
Elvis Returns, absent since finishing runner-up in March 2004, will improve for the outing. *(op 33-1)*
Kilmackilloge, making his debut over hurdles, looks much more of a chaser. *(op 33-1)*
Extra Smooth sumply found this company too tough. *(op 16-1)*
T/Jkpt: Not won. T/Plt: £18.40 to a £1 stake. Pool: £37,135.95. 1,470.65 winning tickets. T/Qpdt: £8.60 to a £1 stake. Pool: £2,414.10. 207.60 winning tickets. WG

[2269]WINCANTON (R-H)
Thursday, November 17

OFFICIAL GOING: Good
Wind: Nil Weather: Fine & dry

2296 SOUTH WEST RACING CLUB H'CAP HURDLE (11 hdls) 2m 6f
1:30 (1:30) (Class 4) (0-105,105) 4-Y-0+ **£3,525** (£1,027; £513)

Form RPR

-332 **1** **Lord Nellsson**[7] 2150 9-11-4 **97**.. RJohnson 103+
(Andrew Turnell) *prom: led after 5th: drvn along fr 7th: rdn appr 2 out: styd on: rdn out* **5/2**[2]

F-FU **2** *5* **Big Rob (IRE)**[9] 2102 6-11-1 **94**.. JPMcNamara 94
(B G Powell) *prom: led 3rd tl after 5th: w wnr: rdn and ev ch appr 2 out: kpt on same pce: lft 2nd last* **15/8**[1]

P5-0 **3** *2* **Maximinus**[25] 1862 5-11-4 **97**.. ChristianWilliams 95
(M Madgwick) *towards rr: rdn and styd on steadily fr 3 out: wnt 4th after 2 out: lft 3rd last* **40/1**

5/30 **4** *4* **Quintus (USA)**[21] 1900 10-11-4 **97**..............................(v[1]) RThornton 91
(A King) *mid div: stdy prog fr 3 out: rdn appr 2 out: kpt on same pce: lft 4th last* **16/1**

P/0- **5** *8* **Protagonist**[9] 1357 7-11-2 **102**.. TMessenger(7) 88
(B N Pollock) *hld up mid div: taking clsr order whn mstke 3 out: no imp after* **40/1**

021/ **6** *1 ½* **Euradream (IRE)**[585] 4762 7-11-12 **105**.. DCrosse 90
(Jean-Rene Auvray) *hld up bhd: styd on fr 3 out: nvr a danger* **22/1**

-355 **7** *8* **Kadam (IRE)**[148] 812 5-11-5 **105**..(b) LHeard(7) 82
(P F Nicholls) *trckd ldrs: rdn and ev ch after 3 out: wknd next* **8/1**

-322 **8** *27* **Knight Of Silver**[16] 1973 8-10-9 **88**.. RGreene 38
(S C Burrough) *j. slowly 1st: bhd fr 6th* **20/1**

FP-P **9** *22* **Cloudy Blues (IRE)**[195] 202 7-10-2 **81**.. BHitchcott 9
(R H Buckler) *led tl 3rd: sn bhd* **66/1**

0P0- **10** *8* **Skye Blue (IRE)**[322] 3108 8-9-11 **79** oh4..............................(p) RYoung(3) —
(M J Weeden) *chsd ldrs tl 8th: wknd next* **100/1**

50-3 **11** *28* **Ideal Jack (FR)**[195] 202 9-9-10 **82**..............................(t) EDehdashti(7) —
(G A Ham) *mid div tl 8th: sn wknd* **40/1**

16-5 **P** **Laudamus**[15] 1984 7-11-7 **100**.. AThornton —
(R H Alner) *mid div tl 8th: bhd and p.u bef 2 out (dismntd)* **5/1**[3]

00-4 **F** **Courant D'Air (IRE)**[3] 275 4-11-6 **104**.. RStephens(5) 106+
(Lucinda Featherstone) *mid div: tk clsr order 5th to trck ldrs: sltly outpcd after 3 out: styd on fr next: clsng in 2nd whn fell last* **33/1**

5m 25.3s (0.20) **Going Correction** +0.05s/f (Yiel)
WFA 4 from 5yo+ 13lb **13** Ran SP% **118.9**
Speed ratings: **101,99,98,97,94 93,90,80,72,69 59,**—,— CSF £7.13 CT £146.30 TOTE £3.60: £1.90, £1.70, £8.00; EX 9.60.
Owner Dajam Ltd **Bred** Miss Diana Rockingham Gill **Trained** Broad Hinton, Wilts

FOCUS
A modest handicap and, although several were close to their marks, it is unlikely to be a source of many future winners.

NOTEBOOK
Lord Nellsson appreciated the longer distance and got off the mark over jumps at the 25th time of asking. He might have had a fight on his hands had Courant D'Air not fallen at the last, but he ended up being left with a handy lead, and hopefully this consistent type can now build on this. *(op 3-1)*
Big Rob(IRE), who is rated 27lb lower over hurdles than he is over fences, was being given a confidence booster having tipped up or unseated on his last three starts over the larger obstacles. Many thought he would be difficult to beat off this lowly rating but he failed to improve on his previous efforts over hurdles. Hopefully this will have done his confidence some good, though. *(op 6-4 tchd 2-1)*
Maximinus, ridden to get the trip, stayed on from off the pace and inherited third place when Courant D'Air fell at the last. He still looks a shade high in the weights at the moment. *(op 33-1 tchd 50-1)*
Quintus(USA), visored for the first time, is well handicapped on the best of his Irish form, but time seems to be catching up with him. *(op 20-1)*
Protagonist, who showed nothing in an All-Weather banded contest on the Flat last time, ran alright on his return to hurdling, but he needs help from the Handicapper. *(tchd 33-1 and 50-1)*
Kadam(IRE), having his first outing since June, looked a threat jumping the third last but he dropped out of contention in the manner of a horse who needed this run. *(op 9-1 tchd 10-1)*
Courant D'Air(IRE) looked likely to throw down the biggest challenge to the winner as they approached the final hurdle, and although he jumped the obstacle well enough, he lost his footing on landing. He got the longer trip well and should be kept in mind for a similar contest. *(op 28-1)*
Laudamus *Official explanation: trainer said gelding had been struck into (op 28-1)*

2297 EUROPEAN BREEDERS FUND/TATTERSALLS (IRELAND) MARES' ONLY NOVICES' CHASE (QUALIFIER) (17 fncs) 2m 5f

2:00 (2:00) (Class 3) 4-Y-0+ **£5,497** (£1,613; £806; £403)

Form				RPR
3U2-	1		**Motcombe (IRE)**[233] [4641] 7-11-4 95 ....(v) AThornton (R H Alner) *lft in ld 1st: hdd 7th: led 10th tl 4 out: sltly outpcd next: rallied after 2 out: led sn after last: styd on wl* **18/1**	103+
10-2	2	1 ½	**Supreme Serenade (IRE)**[25] [1845] 6-11-4 .... RJohnson (P J Hobbs) *hld up: hdwy 8th: jnd ldrs and mstke 11th: led on bit 4 out: wnt lft 2 out: sn rdn: hdd sn after last: no ex* **8/13**[1]	103+
F4-0	3	6	**De Blanc (IRE)**[12] [2044] 5-11-4 .... SThomas (Miss Venetia Williams) *in tch: jnd ldrs 13th: rdn to press ldr appr 3 out: n.m.r and swtchd lft appr last: kpt on same pce* **16/1**	97+
2334	4	7	**Cansalrun (IRE)**[36] [1716] 6-11-4 97.... RWalford (R H Alner) *chsd ldrs: led 7th tl 10th: outpcd after 13th: styd on again fr 3 out* **20/1**	89
P4-P	5	½	**Moyliscar**[11] [2074] 6-10-11 77.... MrJSnowden[(7)] (Capt J A George) *chsd ldrs tl 13th: sn outpcd: styd on again fr 3 out* **100/1**	89+
42P-	6	1 ¼	**Priscilla**[229] [4694] 7-11-4 96.... JPMcNamara (K Bishop) *trckd ldrs: jnd ldr 11th: mstke 13th: wknd fr next* **25/1**	88+
2F0-	7	18	**Kingsbay**[244] [4434] 6-11-4 .... JimCrowley (H Morrison) *mstke 4th: a towards rr: lost tch fr 12th* **12/1**[3]	69
P5-3	8	13	**Easibrook Jane**[13] [2018] 7-11-4 101.... (t) JTizzard (C L Tizzard) *hld up and a towards rr: lost tch fr 12th* **28/1**	56
3-44	F		**Darjeeling (IRE)**[12] [2053] 6-11-4 .... ChristianWilliams (P F Nicholls) *fell 1st* **11/2**[2]	—
104-	F		**Caballe (USA)**[212] [4919] 8-10-8 83.... (v[1]) JKington[(10)] (M Scudamore) *hld up bhd: fell 8th* **66/1**	—
130-	U		**Sword Lady**[217] [4837] 7-11-4 .... (b) RGreene (Mrs S D Williams) *led tl stmbld bdly and uns rdr 1st* **16/1**	—

5m 21.0s (-2.10) **Going Correction** +0.05s/f (Yiel) 11 Ran SP% **116.6**
Speed ratings: **106,105,103,100,100 99,92,88,—,— —** CSF £30.16 TOTE £12.20: £2.60, £1.10, £3.40; EX 32.00.
Owner Lady Cobham **Bred** Lady Cobham **Trained** Droop, Dorset

FOCUS
A fair mares' novice chase but the favourite ran well below her hurdles mark. The form is suspect despite a decent time.

NOTEBOOK
Motcombe(IRE), who failed to get off the mark in her first season over fences last term, stays well and, while she looked beaten turning into the home straight, her stamina, coupled with the favourite's lack of resolution in front, ensured that she finally got off the mark over obstacles. She *is entitled to come on for this seasonal reappearance and will be suited by a step up in trip. (op 16-1 tchd 20-1)*
Supreme Serenade(IRE), by far the best of these over hurdles and fit following her reappearance at Aintree, looked to be going well turning into the straight but, once required to work for her win after jumping the second last, she found little. While she is clearly talented, she has always been a bit tricky, and all her wins have come in races of 14 runners or more where she has generally been *held up and been brought with a late run. She is not a mare to back at short prices. (op 4-6 tchd 8-11)*
De Blanc(IRE), stepping up in trip, did not see it out as strongly as the winner but this was still a big step up on her debut over fences. *(op 20-1)*
Cansalrun(IRE) is a consistent type and ran another fair race in defeat. She will remain vulnerable in this type of event and will be better off when allowed to take her chance in handicaps. *(op 25-1)*
Moyliscar is fairly well exposed and is over moderate ability.

2298 RACING POST "HANDS AND HEELS" JUMPS SERIES NOVICES' HCAP HURDLE (CONDITIONAL/AMATEUR RIDERS) (8 hdls) 2m

2:30 (2:32) (Class 4) 3-Y-0+ **£3,399** (£997; £498; £249)

Form				RPR
	1		**Albarino (IRE)**[59] [1501] 6-11-9 **99**.... JKington[(3)] (M Scudamore) *hld up bhd: smooth hdwy on bit after 3 out: wnt 2nd appr last: shkn up to ld run-in: r.o: readily* **13/2**	117+
53-4	2	1 ¼	**Nagano (FR)**[193] [248] 7-10-11 **87**.... DJBoland[(3)] (Ian Williams) *in tch: jnd ldrs 3 out: led and j.rt 2 out: sn drvn: no ex whn hdd run-in* **6/4**[1]	101+
5453	3	3 ½	**Josear**[11] [2069] 3-10-4 **95**.... AGlassonbury[(3)] (C J Down) *led: hdd appr 2 out: kpt on same pce* **11/2**[3]	90
4-04	4	11	**The Rip**[31] [1774] 4-10-12 **85**.... LHeard (R M Stronge) *hld up: drvn and hdwy after 3 out: short lived effrt next: wknd* **3/1**[2]	84
/300	5	15	**Sunset King (USA)**[42] [1653] 5-10-7 **80**.... JamesWhite (R J Hodges) *mid div: hdwy after 3 out to chse ldng pair: wknd after 2 out* **12/1**	64
60P-	6	½	**La Professoressa (IRE)**[15] [4560] 4-11-2 **92**.... DPO'Dwyer[(3)] (Mrs P N Dutfield) *hld up: hdwy after 3 out: rdn next: wknd appr last* **25/1**	76
-U03	7	2 ½	**Glowing Ember**[53] [1562] 5-10-10 **86**.... JPemberton[(3)] (J F Panvert) *chsd ldr tl rdr lost iron after 3rd: grad fdd* **12/1**	67
-P00	8	30	**Wizzical Lad**[25] [1857] 5-11-0 **87**.... (tp) TMessenger (B N Pollock) *in tch: hdwy to join ldrs 4th: hit 3 out: sn wknd* **50/1**	38
P-PR	P		**Mr Rhubarb (IRE)**[191] [279] 7-11-0 **90**.... KBurke[(3)] (C J Drewe) *chsd ldrs tl 5th: wknd next: t.o and p.u bef 2 out* **40/1**	—

3m 47.2s (-1.90) **Going Correction** +0.05s/f (Yiel)
WFA 3 from 4yo 15lb 4 from 5yo+ 12lb 9 Ran SP% **117.3**
Speed ratings: **106,105,103,98,90 90,89,74,—** CSF £17.35 CT £58.92 TOTE £8.20: £2.30, £1.40, £1.50; EX 21.20.
Owner Mrs N M Watkins **Bred** Michael And Fiona O'Connor **Trained** Bromsash, Herefordshire

FOCUS
A weak contest featuring plating-class performers, but the form could rate a bit higher and should work out.

NOTEBOOK
Albarino(IRE), having his first start in this country for his new stable, did not look to have been done many favours by the Handicapper, but he came in for a bit of market support and travelled easily into contention entering the straight. He broke his duck with more in hand than the margin suggests and could well be capable of going in again after re-assessment. *(op 8-1)*
Nagano(FR) is rated much lower over hurdles than he is over fences and he ran a solid race in defeat, just being unable to cope with the well-treated winner. He should be capable of winning a similar race off this sort of mark. *(op 11-4 tchd 3-1)*
Josear, the only three-year-old in the field, could not hold off the first two over the final couple of flights but this was still a fair effort on his handicap debut against his elders. *(tchd 9-2)*
The Rip was a bit of an eyecatcher at Plumpton last time but he proved disappointing, finding little under pressure. *(op 11-4 tchd 9-4 and 7-2)*
Sunset King(USA), who is still a maiden under both codes, ran about as well as he did at this track last time out.

2299 HAMILTON LITESTAT H'CAP CHASE 3m 4f

3:00 (3:01) (Class 3) (0-135,135) 5-Y-0+ **£10,149** (£2,979; £1,489; £744)

Form				RPR
0-56	1		**Inca Trail (IRE)**[12] [2054] 9-11-2 **132**.... (b) MissCTizzard[(7)] (P F Nicholls) *patiently rdn: hld up in tch: tk clsr order 17th: wnt 2nd 3 out: w.w bhd ldr: str run after last to ld fnl 100yds* **11/1**	143+
0-20	2	2	**Koquelicot (FR)**[40] [1670] 7-10-9 **118**.... (b[1]) RJohnson (P J Hobbs) *led: clr 15th: nt fluent next: rdn appr 3 out: hdd fnl 100yds: kpt on but nt pce of wnr* **9/2**[2]	124
-F25	3	8	**Tom Sayers (IRE)**[25] [1861] 7-10-10 **119**.... JTizzard (P J Hobbs) *chsd ldr: rdn after 4 out: lost 2nd next: kpt on same pce* **9/2**[2]	117
F-53	4	¾	**Le Jaguar (FR)**[25] [1861] 5-10-3 **120**.... (t) LHeard[(7)] (P F Nicholls) *chsd ldrs: sltly outpcd after 18th: styd on again fr 3 out* **3/1**[1]	117+
-011	5	22	**Saffron Sun**[16] [1972] 10-10-5 **114**.... ChristianWilliams (J D Frost) *chsd ldrs: rdn after 18th: wknd after 4 out* **10/1**	89
20P-	6	1 ½	**Zaffamore (IRE)**[210] [4946] 9-11-0 **123**.... SThomas (Miss H C Knight) *hld up: hdwy to chse ldrs after 18th: sn rdn: wknd after 4 out* **14/1**	97
23P-	P		**Fox In The Box**[299] [3491] 8-11-0 **123**.... AThornton (R H Alner) *lost tch qckly after slow jump 5th and immediately p.u* **6/1**[3]	—
114-	P		**Whitenzo (FR)**[208] [4984] 9-11-5 **135**.... (t) MrJSnowden[(7)] (P F Nicholls) *hld up in tch: hit 9th: reminders after 13th: wknd after 15th: bhd and p.u after 18th* **8/1**	—

7m 5.00s (-15.00)
WFA 5 from 7yo+ 1lb 8 Ran SP% **110.9**
CSF £56.93 CT £247.43 TOTE £15.10: £3.10, £1.90, £2.00; EX 66.60.
Owner Mrs Susie Chown & Mrs Kathy Stuart **Bred** Ballysheehan Stud **Trained** Ditcheat, Somerset

FOCUS
A fair staying handicap noteworthy for the ride given by Charlotte Tizzard to the tricky Inca Trail, who is rated value for five lengths.

NOTEBOOK
Inca Trail(IRE), down in grade, is the type who likes to do things on the bridle and he was given a splendidly patient ride by Charlotte Tizzard, who only asked the nine-year-old to pick up the leader after jumping the last. He quickly made up the two-length deficit and won with a lot more in hand *than the winning margin suggests, improving his already smart course figures to read 12161. (op 8-1)*
Koquelicot(FR) is back on a fair mark now and ran a very creditable race in first-time blinkers. He was done for a turn of foot after the last but showed he can win races off this sort of rating. *(op 6-1)*
Tom Sayers(IRE) continues to pay for a successful spring when he won three races on the *bounce. He did not do a lot wrong but the Handicapper has his measure for the time being. (op 5-1 tchd 11-2)*
Le Jaguar(FR), who ran well over the course and distance last time out, was a bit disappointing in this lesser contest but he could probably have done with a stronger all-round pace. *(op 4-1)*
Saffron Sun, chasing a hat-trick, appears to reserve his best for Exeter. *(op 8-1 tchd 7-1)*
Whitenzo(FR) *Official explanation: jockey said gelding had a breathing problem (op 11-2 tchd 9-1)*
Fox In The Box *Official explanation: jockey said gelding was never jumping or travelling (op 11-2 tchd 9-1)*

2300 TOTESPORT.COM H'CAP CHASE (13 fncs) 2m

3:30 (3:34) (Class 3) (0-115,115) 5-Y-0+ **£5,448** (£1,599; £799; £399)

Form				RPR
2-60	1		**Roofing Spirit (IRE)**[12] [2051] 7-11-1 **111**.... DJacob[(7)] (D P Keane) *hld up: nt fluent 6th: tk clsr order after 9th: jnd ldrs after 4 out: led and blnd 2 out: kpt on: drvn out* **15/2**	122+
4454	2	¾	**Runner Bean**[25] [1860] 11-10-10 **99**.... RThornton (R Lee) *trckd ldrs: n.m.r briefly on bnd after 9th: rdn after 4 out: hung rt fr 3 out: styd on to go 2nd run-in* **4/1**[3]	110+
25-3	3	½	**Neltina**[17] [1958] 9-11-11 **114**.... JimCrowley (Mrs J E Scrase) *led tl mstke and hdd 8th: led again next: rdn and hdd 2 out: ev ch last: no ex* **10/3**[2]	124
0012	4	4	**Nick The Jewel**[33] [1746] 10-11-6 **109**.... RJohnson (Andrew Turnell) *trckd ldrs: rdn and ev ch appr 3 out: kpt on same pce fr 2 out* **13/8**[1]	115
3113	P		**L'Oiseau (FR)**[13] [2016] 6-11-12 **115**.... JTizzard (J G Portman) *hld up: lost tch fr 8th: p.u bef 4 out* **13/2**	—

4m 2.10s (0.20) **Going Correction** +0.05s/f (Yiel) 5 Ran SP% **106.3**
Speed ratings: **101,100,100,98,—** CSF £32.86 TOTE £8.40: £2.70, £1.80; EX 32.70.
Owner F J Matthews **Bred** Mrs Sheila Fortune **Trained** North End, Dorset
■ Stewards' Enquiry : D Jacob caution: careless riding

FOCUS
An ordinary handicap run at a decent clip with the third and fourth close to their marks.

NOTEBOOK
Roofing Spirit(IRE), who is at his best in a race run at a decent pace, found things panning out perfectly, as Crowley on Neltina, who ideally needs further, was keen to make it a test. He blundered at the second last but still held a narrow advantage at the final fence and kept on gamely on the run-in. *(op 5-1 tchd 8-1)*
Runner Bean, successful in two of his previous three starts over the course and distance, including in this race last year, is certainly on a winning mark at present. However, he only threatened briefly on the run-in when the race was all but over and needs to find some improvement from somewhere. *(op 3-1)*
Neltina, who finished third behind Cerium on her seasonal reappearance, did not do a lot for that form. She stays further than this so her rider tried to stretch the field, but she never got clear, and, although she had every chance on the run-in, she was unable to quicken. *(op 7-2 tchd 3-1)*
Nick The Jewel was a disappointing favourite, perhaps paying for trying to keep tabs with the decent pace set by Neltina. *(op 2-1 tchd 9-4 and 6-4)*

2301 HAMILTON LITESTAT NOVICES' HURDLE (10 hdls 1 omitted) 2m 6f

4:00 (4:01) (Class 3) 4-Y-0+ **£5,009** (£1,470; £735; £367)

Form				RPR
1	1		**Denman (IRE)**[25] [1859] 5-11-4 .... ChristianWilliams (P F Nicholls) *mde all: shkn up appr 2 out: sn drew clr: styd on strly: eased cl home* **2/1**[2]	124+
1U-2	2	16	**Karanja**[25] [1847] 6-10-12 .... AThornton (V R A Dartnall) *trckd ldrs: hit 4th and 3 out: sn jnd wnr: rdn appr 2 out: kpt on but no ch w wnr fr next* **8/11**[1]	99+
	3	2 ½	**Surface To Air**[133] 4-10-9 .... RYoung[(3)] (Mrs P N Dutfield) *mid div: hdwy after 3 out: rdn next: styd on to go 3rd run-in* **100/1**	96
263-	4	4	**Spartan Place**[275] [3859] 5-10-12 111.... JAMcCarthy (J A Geake) *trckd wnr: rdn and effrt appr 2 out: kpt on same pce* **9/1**[3]	92
-45	5	1 ½	**Highland Chief (IRE)**[25] [1847] 5-10-12 .... SThomas (Miss H C Knight) *mid div: hdwy after 3 out: sn rdn: kpt on same pce* **50/1**	90
P0-0	6	17	**Laharna**[20] [1903] 5-10-12 .... BFenton (Miss E C Lavelle) *w wnr tl 4th: in tch: hdwy to join ldrs after 3 out: sn rdn: wknd qckly next* **50/1**	73

7 ½ **Candlelight Valley (IRE)** 6-10-12 .... RJohnson 81+
(P J Hobbs) *hld up towards rr: hdwy after 3 out: sn rdn: wknd next: stmbld appr last and blnd bdly* **25/1**

1003 8 5 **It's My Party**[21] [1898] 4-10-5 97..(p) RLucey-Butler(7) 68
(W G M Turner) *mid div: rdn after 7th: wknd appr 2 out* **66/1**

506- 9 dist **Ballistigo (IRE)**[218] [4820] 6-10-12 .... RThornton —
(A King) *mid div tl wknd after 3 out* **16/1**

0 10 10 **Secret Divin (FR)**[19] [1916] 5-10-12 .... DCrosse —
(Jean-Rene Auvray) *mid div tl wknd 3 out* **100/1**

11 29 **Barney Blue (IRE)** 5-10-12 .... JimCrowley —
(Ian Williams) *reminders after 3rd: t.o fr 5th* **200/1**

0/P 12 dist **Battling Buster (IRE)**[6] [2165] 8-10-12 .... BHitchcott —
(R H Buckler) *chsd ldrs tl 4th: sn bhd: t.o* **100/1**

5m 23.9s (-1.20) **Going Correction** +0.05s/f (Yiel)
WFA 4 from 5yo+ 13lb **12** Ran SP% **119.8**
Speed ratings: **104,98,97,95,95 89,88,87,—,— —,—** CSF £3.90 TOTE £3.00: £1.20, £1.30, £16.80; EX 5.60 Place 6 £45.10, Place 5 £30.85.
Owner Paul K Barber & Mrs M Findlay **Bred** Colman O'Flynn **Trained** Ditcheat, Somerset

FOCUS
A fair novice hurdle and a smart performance from the winner, who should take higher rank. The time was reasonable and the fifth and sixth give the form a fairly sound appearance.

NOTEBOOK
Denman(IRE) followed up his workmanlike success on his debut over hurdles with a more polished display under a 6lb penalty. He drew clear in the straight and he had the race in very safe keeping when slipping slightly on landing at the last. He is clearly progressing nicely and deserves to step up in grade now. *(op 9-4 tchd 5-2)*
Karanja was a smart bumper performer but this was his second defeat at short odds over hurdles, and he did not beat Highland Chief anywhere near as far as he had at Aintree. So far he does not look like matching his ability on the level over timber, but his next outing will qualify him for handicaps. *(op 10-11)*
Surface To Air, a moderate staying handicapper on the Flat, posted a surprising performance on his debut over timber, staying on well for third place. He is entitled to come on for the experience, should get three miles and looks to have a future at this game. *(tchd 125-1)*
Spartan Place, having his first run since February, did not shape too badly but he would be better employed in handicap company. *(op 7-1 tchd 10-1)*
Highland Chief(IRE), beaten a long way behind Karanja at Aintree on his hurdling debut, got a lot closer to that rival this time. *(tchd 66-1)*
Laharna ran better than his finishing position suggests as he was with the principals to the turn into the straight but then weakened. A winner of an Irish point-to-point, he will be seen to better effect when sent over the larger obstacles. *(op 25-1 tchd 66-1)*
T/Plt: £32.90 to a £1 stake. Pool: £51,419.90. 1,138.00 winning tickets. T/Qpdt: £11.50 to a £1 stake. Pool: £2,926.60. 187.10 winning tickets. TM

2302 - 2303a (Foreign Racing) - See Raceform Interactive

1863 CLONMEL (R-H)
Thursday, November 17
OFFICIAL GOING: Hurdle course - soft; chase course - yielding to soft

2304a CLONMEL OIL CHASE (GRADE 2) 2m 4f
2:05 (2:06) 5-Y-0+ **£27,702** (£8,127; £3,872; £1,319)

RPR

1 **War Of Attrition (IRE)**[28] [1810] 6-11-8 157.. CO'Dwyer 158+
(M F Morris, Ire) *hld up in rr: 4th 5 out: 3rd after 3 out: 2nd bef next: sn rdn to chal: slt advantage appr last: kpt on wl run-in* **1/2**[1]

2 ½ **Rathgar Beau (IRE)**[205] [41] 9-11-12 157.. JRBarry 158+
(E Sheehy, Ire) *hld up in tch: 4th after 3 out: 3rd next: lft 2nd last: chal run-in: kpt on wl* **2/1**[2]

3 20 **Alcapone (IRE)**[39] [1700] 11-11-12 132.. BJGeraghty 136
(M F Morris, Ire) *led after 1st: hdd 5th: 2nd and rdn bef 3 out: wknd bef next: lft remote 3rd fr last* **33/1**

4 6 **Well Presented (IRE)**[202] [115] 7-11-6 133.. RMPower 124
(Mrs John Harrington, Ire) *chsd ldrs in 3rd: rdn and wknd bef 3 out* **20/1**

U **Strong Project (IRE)**[5] [2195] 9-11-4 137.. DJCasey 146
(C F Swan, Ire) *settled 2nd: led fr 5th: rdn after 3 out: strly pressed fr next: narrowly hdd whn stmbld and uns rdr last* **16/1**[3]

5m 13.0s **5** Ran SP% **113.6**
CSF £2.10 TOTE £1.50: £1.10, £1.70; DF 2.00.
Owner Gigginstown House Stud **Bred** Miss B A Murphy **Trained** Fethard, Co Tipperary

NOTEBOOK
War Of Attrition(IRE) took over on the run to the last and was comfortably in command on the flat. Not ridden for stamina even though a stronger-run race would have suited better, he showed a nice turn of foot and didn't have a hard race. His jumping was sound and Punchestown's John Durkan Memorial is next on the agenda. *(op 1/2 tchd 8/15)*
Rathgar Beau(IRE), successful in the race last season, was switched left at a crucial stage going to the last and certainly gave away more distance than he was eventually beaten by. He quickened up well on the flat but the winner had gained first run. An encouraging reappearance. *(op 2/1 tchd 5/2)*
Alcapone(IRE) had dropped right out before the second last. *(op 25/1)*
Strong Project(IRE), a long way behind the winner at Punchestown last month, had just relinquished the lead when stumbling and unseating after the last. He would have finished a close third at worst and that fact renders the form somewhat questionable. *(op 12/1)*

2305 - 2308a (Foreign Racing) - See Raceform Interactive

1968 EXETER (R-H)
Friday, November 18
OFFICIAL GOING: Good to soft (good in places)
Wind: Light, across Weather: Sunny. Open ditch after stands omitted.

2309 EXETER RACECOURSE CONFERENCE CENTRE NOVICES' HURDLE (8 hdls) 2m 1f
12:40 (12:41) (Class 3) 4-Y-0+ **£5,156** (£1,513; £756; £378)

Form RPR

24-F 1 **Sea The Light**[13] [2050] 5-10-12 .... RThornton 113+
(A King) *hld up in mid-div: hdwy appr 5th: rdn appr 3 out: led appr 2 out: drvn out* **9/4**[1]

13 2 nk **Fourty Acers (IRE)**[22] [1895] 5-10-12 .... RGreene 112
(M C Pipe) *a.p: led after 5th: rdn appr 3 out: hdd appr 2 out: ev ch last: r.o* **6/1**

440- 3 1½ **Good Citizen (IRE)**[251] [4330] 5-10-12 112.. JMMaguire 111
(T R George) *hld up towards rr: hdwy 3rd: rdn after 5th: kpt on fr 2 out* **3/1**[2]

4 6 **The Luder (IRE)**[229] 4-10-12 .... ChristianWilliams 105
(P F Nicholls) *hld up in tch: hdwy appr 5th: ev ch 3 out: sn rdn: wknd appr last* **14/1**

50 5 shd **Xila Fontenailles (FR)**[22] [1898] 4-9-12 .... KBurke(7) 97
(N J Hawke) *prom: lost pl appr 5th: rallied appr 3 out: styd on same pce fr 2 out* **100/1**

5 6 ¾ **Napoleon (IRE)**[21] [1908] 4-10-12 .... RJohnson 104
(P J Hobbs) *prom: led 3rd to 4th: rdn after 3 out: wknd after 2 out* **9/2**[3]

-P0F 7 19 **Dreams Jewel**[12] [2070] 5-10-12 .... BJCrowley 87+
(C Roberts) *bhd tl hdwy appr 3 out: no imp whn hit 2 out* **100/1**

005/ 8 1¼ **Plantaganet (FR)**[624] [4145] 7-10-12 .... JimCrowley 85+
(Ian Williams) *hld up and bhd: hdwy after 4th: wkng whn hit 2 out* **50/1**

9 15 **Nero West (FR)**[130] 4-10-5 .... DJacob(7) 68
(Miss Lucy Bridges) *prom tl wknd 5th* **50/1**

5-50 10 2½ **Sandmartin (IRE)**[8] [2142] 5-10-12 .... PJBrennan 66
(P J Hobbs) *bhd fr 4th* **40/1**

23 11 nk **Missyl (FR)**[13] [2050] 5-10-12 .... AThornton 66
(R H Alner) *sltly hmpd 3rd: a bhd* **10/1**

6-4 12 9 **Aoninch**[34] [1740] 5-10-2 .... RYoung(3) 50
(Mrs P N Dutfield) *led to 3rd: led 4th tl after 5th: wknd appr 3 out* **25/1**

000 13 3 **Cornish Jack**[5] [2212] 5-10-5 .... MissSGaisford(7) 54
(J D Frost) *hld up towards rr: sme hdwy 4th: wknd after 5th* **100/1**

6P 14 5 **Life Estates**[17] [1969] 5-10-7 .... CHonour(5) 49
(J D Frost) *hld up and bhd: hdwy 4th: wknd appr 3 out* **150/1**

00- 15 6 **Eveon (IRE)**[249] [4373] 5-10-5 .... TJMurphy 36
(Ian Williams) *a bhd* **66/1**

P **Tom Tobacco**[174] 8-10-12 .... JAMcCarthy —
(A S T Holdsworth) *a in rr: t.o fr 2nd: p.u bef 3 out* **100/1**

P- U **Red Jester**[290] [3635] 4-10-7 .... DLaverty(5) —
(A E Jones) *hld up in tch: hit 2nd: lost pl and uns rdr 3rd* **150/1**

4m 10.5s (1.30) **Going Correction** +0.25s/f (Yiel)
WFA 4 from 5yo+ 12lb **17** Ran SP% **121.0**
Speed ratings: **106,105,105,102,102 101,92,92,85,84 84,79,78,76,73 —,—** CSF £15.73 TOTE £4.10: £1.90, £2.00, £1.90; EX 19.70.
Owner Mr & Mrs F C Welch **Bred** Mrs S C Welch **Trained** Barbury Castle, Wilts

FOCUS
With Racing Demon and Ashley Brook winning the last two renewals of the race, Sea The Light has a bit to live up to. The pace looked fair and the race should produce winners.

NOTEBOOK
Sea The Light, a faller last time, needed every yard of the trip to get on top of his rivals. Making relentless headway down the middle of the course up home straight, and jumping sightly to his left over the hurdles, he battled on well for pressure and should be suited by further in time. *(tchd 11-4)*
Fourty Acers(IRE) travelled well in the early stages but kept over-jumping the hurdles. He battled on well for strong pressure, and a stiffer test of stamina is likely to suit him in the future
Good Citizen(IRE) came from a long way off the pace to finish just behind the front two. A step up in trip is definitely required, as he never threatened to take a hand in the finish until the race was effectively over. It would be no surprise to see him over fences soon. *(op 7-2 tchd 11-4)*
The Luder(IRE), making his debut under Rules, moved ominously into the lead entering the home straight, but found very little as soon as the pressure was applied after jumping the third-last. A winning Irish pointer, he should improve for the run and will be straighter next time. *(op 9-1)*
Xila Fontenailles(FR) appeared to run well above what she had previously shown on the track and would be very interesting if tried in handicap company, given her proximity to some decent types.
Napoleon(IRE) was always to the fore but weakened disappointingly as the race took shape. He cost a lot of money from the Coolmore team, but is not one to be interested in until he gets involved in a finish. *(tchd 11-2)*

2310 HOMEOAK TRADING LTD NOVICES' H'CAP HURDLE (11 hdls) 2m 6f 110y
1:10 (1:11) (Class 4) (0-105,105) 3-Y-0+ **£3,822** (£1,122; £561; £280)

Form RPR

30-1 1 **Magot De Grugy (FR)**[20] [1921] 5-11-7 100.. AThornton 112+
(R H Alner) *hld up in tch: led on bit 3 out: rdn appr last: drvn out* **11/4**[2]

-434 2 ¾ **The Gangerman (IRE)**[44] [1647] 5-10-6 92.. MGoldstein(7) 99
(N A Twiston-Davies) *led to 2nd: prom: rdn and outpcd appr 3 out: rallied and chsd wnr appr last: r.o flat* **5/1**

12-P 3 19 **Wrags To Riches (IRE)**[23] [1881] 8-11-7 105.. CHonour(5) 93
(J D Frost) *sn w ldr: led 2nd to 8th: sn led again: rdn and hdd 3 out: wknd after 2 out* **13/2**

6-P4 4 19 **Land Rover Lad**[13] [2043] 7-10-10 89..(b) JAMcCarthy 58
(C P Morlock) *prom: nt fluent and lost pl whn reminders 5th: sn rdn: bhd fr 8th* **25/1**

455- 5 27 **M'Lord**[296] [3533] 7-11-9 102.. RJohnson 44
(J A Geake) *hld up in rr: hmpd 2nd: hdwy 6th: led briefly 8th: wknd appr 3 out* **5/2**[1]

PPPP 6 22 **Gordy's Joy**[92] [1155] 5-9-11 79 oh14.. RYoung(3) —
(G A Ham) *hld up: struggling in rr whn hit 6th: t.o* **100/1**

3433 F **Hard N Sharp**[17] [1977] 5-11-0 93.. RThornton —
(Mrs A M Thorpe) *fell 2nd* **4/1**[3]

5m 52.5s (13.20) **Going Correction** +0.25s/f (Yiel) **7** Ran SP% **110.1**
Speed ratings: **87,86,80,73,64 56,—** CSF £15.65 TOTE £3.10: £1.80, £3.20; EX 13.20.
Owner P M De Wilde **Bred** Earl La Grugerie **Trained** Droop, Dorset

FOCUS
A very moderate staying hurdle, run at a pedestrian early pace resulting in a moderate time. The form looks very ordinary.

NOTEBOOK
Magot De Grugy(FR) moved nicely throughout the race and took up the running after jumping the second-last. He may not have quite got home despite winning, and it would be no surprise to see him dropped backed in trip by a couple of furlongs next time. He is, however, in good form and has an option to go chasing, as he has reportedly schooled well at home. *(op 5-2)*
The Gangerman(IRE) finished with a real flourish and would not have been suited by the slow early gallop. The course suited him, so a stronger pace or a little further would be ideal. *(op 11-2 tchd 6-1 in places)*
Wrags To Riches(IRE), who helped set the sedate pace, regained the lead entering the home straight - after being passed my M'Lord jumping the fourth-last - but had no answer to the winner as he cruised upsides in the straight. *(op 8-1)*
Land Rover Lad was under pressure at various stages of the race and was ultimately well beaten. *(op 20-1)*
M'Lord ran a bizarre race. After being held up at the rear of the field and racing with the choke out, he jumped into the lead at the fourth-last - going easily - only to find nothing when asked. He can *be given another chance next time in case he needed the outing after a layoff.Official explanation: jockey said gelding failed to stay the trip (op 9-4 tchd 3-1)*
Gordy's Joy, running from a stone out of the handicap, managed to stop a run of letters in her form by completing the course.
Hard N Sharp clipped the top of the second flight and slipped over on the other side. *(op 9-2 tchd 5-1)*

2311 SOUTH-WEST RACING EXPERIENCE NOVICES' CHASE (16 fncs 1 omitted) 2m 7f 110y

1:40 (1:42) (Class 3) 5-Y-0+ **£7,468** (£2,192; £1,096; £547)

Form					RPR
2P-2	1		**Lord Killeshanra (IRE)**[17] 1976 6-10-12 ... JTizzard (C L Tizzard) *hld up: sn in tch: led appr 4 out: rdn appr 2 out: drvn out* **7/1**		139+
0-03	2	2 ½	**Very Optimistic (IRE)**[195] 207 7-10-12 ... NFehily (Jonjo O'Neill) *hld up in mid-div: hdwy appr 9th: pckd 13th: jnd wnr 4 out: rdn appr last: nt qckn flat* **13/2**		138+
12-2	3	12	**Reflected Glory (IRE)**[27] 1829 6-10-12 ... PJBrennan (P F Nicholls) *hld up in tch: ev ch appr 4 out: sn rdn: hit 3 out: wknd 2 out* **6/1**[3]		126+
53-3	4	¾	**Zabenz (NZ)**[20] 1917 8-10-12 ...(b) RJohnson (P J Hobbs) *prom: led after 8th: rdn and hdd appr 4 out: sn btn* **4/1**[2]		124+
11P-	5	25	**Loup Charter (FR)**[224] 4765 6-10-12 ... TJMurphy (Miss H C Knight) *hld up and bhd: short-lived effrt appr 9th* **4/1**[2]		98
	6	28	**Squires Lane (IRE)**[187] 6-10-9 ... GCarenza(3) (Andrew Turnell) *a bhd: mstke 3rd: t.o fr 9th* **150/1**		70
	F		**Euro Two (IRE)** 8-10-9 ... RYoung(3) (N R Mitchell) *fell 2nd* **200/1**		—
05-0	F		**Victory Gunner (IRE)**[27] 1830 7-10-12 ... ChristianWilliams (C Roberts) *prom: 5th whn fell 8th* **20/1**		—
235-	U		**Double Header (IRE)**[220] 4814 6-10-12 ... RGreene (Mrs S D Williams) *hit 1st: blnd and uns rdr 2nd* **33/1**		—
220-	P		**Dare Too Dream**[220] 4819 6-10-12 ... OMcPhail (K Bishop) *bhd: hmpd 2nd: t.o whn j.lft 8th: p.u bef 9th* **50/1**		—
-411	P		**Model Son (IRE)**[19] 1939 7-11-3 133 ... PMerrigan(5) (Mrs H Dalton) *led tl after 8th: wknd qckly and p.u bef 9th* **3/1**[1]		—
	P		**Mighty Moose (IRE)**[222] 5-10-11 ... JMMaguire (Nick Williams) *hld up in tch: lost pl after 8th: t.o whn p.u bef 4 out* **100/1**		—
0/	U		**Kewlake Lane**[230] 7-10-5 ... AThornton (R H Alner) *towards rr: lost tch fr 8th: t.o whn blkd by loose horse and uns rdr 13th* **50/1**		—

5m 47.8s (-10.80) **Going Correction** -0.15s/f (Good) **13** Ran SP% **118.9**
Speed ratings: **112,111,107,106,98 89,—,—,—,— —,—,—** CSF £50.44 TOTE £9.60: £2.50, £2.60, £2.30; EX 67.60.
Owner G F Gingell **Bred** Mrs B Eggo **Trained** Milborne Port, Dorset

FOCUS
This was a decent novice chase run at a true gallop in a good time. Despite the favourite running disappointingly, the form should prove sound and the race ought to produce winners.

NOTEBOOK
Lord Killeshanra(IRE), a big, imposing type, moved into the lead smoothly exiting the home turn, after being nicely settled behind the early pace. He was, however, joined up the straight by Very Optimistic, and had to work hard for victory. Staying distances are sure to suit, and he could make up into a Welsh National type next season. The valuable novice chase at Lingfield, won last year by L'Ami, could be the ideal race for him next. *(op 8-1)*
Very Optimistic(IRE), the top-rated hurdler coming into the race, was another who tracked the strong gallop and moved into the race quietly. A slow jump five out looked to have cost him his chance, but he was pulled together and jumped upsides Lord Killeshandra at the next. The eventual winner kept on just the better, but little was lost in defeat on his chasing debut, and he looks a dour stayer. *(op 5-1)*
Reflected Glory(IRE) did not do a lot wrong on only his second run over fences, but never really looked like winning at any stage. He should win his fair share of staying chases in time, especially on softer ground, and the four miler at the Cheltenham Festival should be right up his street. *(op 9-2)*
Zabenz(NZ), with blinkers refitted, came in for some support before the race and helped set a decent gallop. He was, however, closed down by pursuers coming into the straight, and weakened as his earlier exertions took their toll. A drop in trip will probably help him, or a less-demanding track *(op 6-1)*
Loup Charter(FR) never reached a challenging position but, with the experience of fences now under his belt, a much better showing can be expected next time. *(op 7-2)*
Model Son(IRE), carrying a double penalty after a couple of impressive performances in the north, almost certainly went off too quickly in front and was pulled before halfway. He is worth another chance to show his previous form. *Official explanation: trainer had no explanation for the poor form shown (op 4-1)*
Dare Too Dream jumped badly from the outset. *(op 4-1)*

2312 SOUTH-WEST RACING CLUB H'CAP CHASE (11 fncs 1 omitted) 2m 1f 110y

2:15 (2:15) (Class 3) (0-125,124) 5-Y-0+ **£6,893** (£2,023; £1,011; £505)

Form				RPR
41-3	1		**Serpentine Rock**[13] 2047 5-11-5 **117** ... RJohnson (P J Hobbs) *a.p: led 3 out: hrd rdn appr last: drvn out* **5/2**[1]	123+
224-	2	6	**Jacks Craic (IRE)**[257] 4201 6-11-5 **117** ... PJBrennan (J L Spearing) *t.k.h: hit 1st: hdwy after 7th: led 4 out to 3 out: sn rdn: one pce fr 2 out* **4/1**[2]	117+
0200	3	5	**Spectrometer**[24] 1872 8-11-5 **117** ... NFehily (Ian Williams) *led to 5th: rdn appr 4 out: 3rd and btn whn blnd last* **6/1**	117+
6P-2	4	11	**Macmar (FR)**[16] 1986 5-11-1 **113** ... AThornton (R H Alner) *hld up in tch: hit 6th: ev ch appr 4 out: sn rdn and wknd* **7/1**	97
4-F3	5	1 ¾	**East Lawyer (FR)**[16] 1986 6-11-1 **113** ... ChristianWilliams (P F Nicholls) *hld up: in rr whn mstke 2nd (water): mstke 5th: sn struggling* **4/1**[2]	99+
404-	F		**Visibility (FR)**[234] 4643 6-11-12 **124** ...(p) TJMurphy (M C Pipe) *prom: reminders after 3rd: hrd rdn after 7th: sn wknd: 5th whn fell 4 out* **5/1**[3]	—

4m 19.0s (2.10) **Going Correction** -0.15s/f (Good) **6** Ran SP% **112.0**
Speed ratings: **89,86,84,79,78** — CSF £12.96 TOTE £2.70: £1.50, £2.70; EX 16.10.
Owner C de P Berry, C Moore, P Rowe **Bred** Burns Farm Stud **Trained** Withycombe, Somerset

FOCUS
This was a modest novice event, in which the steady pace resulted in a moderate time, although the form could rate higher. The finish was fought out between the only two horses without any chasing experience, who should win more races between them.

NOTEBOOK
Serpentine Rock, making his chasing debut, jumped like an old handicapper and won in good style. Not over-raced for his age, he looks sure to win again and has plenty of scope for improvement. *(op 11-4 tchd 3-1)*
Jacks Craic(IRE), the other horse in the field making its chasing debut, did not get home after racing too freely during the race. With normal progression, and a stronger pace, he will pick up a similar race. *(op 5-1)*
Spectrometer was staying on fairly well when making a bad mistake at the last. He does not seem the same horse that was once capable of finishing third in the Coral Cup at the Cheltenham Festival *(op 5-1 tchd 13-2)*
Macmar(FR) held every chance entering the home straight before finding little for pressure. He wore blinkers for his only success in France, and it would be no surprise to see them reintroduced next time he runs. *(op 13-2 tchd 6-1)*
East Lawyer(FR) lost all chance with a couple of early mistakes, one at the water jump. *(op 7-2)*
Visibility(FR), wearing first-time cheekpieces, ran in snatches and was in the process of going backwards when falling at the fourth-last. He does not look one to trust. *(op 6-1 tchd 7-1)*

2313 SOUTH-WEST RACING EXPERIENCE NOVICES' H'CAP CHASE (14 fncs 1 omitted) 2m 3f 110y

2:50 (2:51) (Class 4) (0-105,105) 4-Y-0+ **£4,879** (£1,432; £716; £357)

Form				RPR
000-	1		**King Coal (IRE)**[259] 4164 6-11-2 **95** ... BJCrowley (R Rowe) *j.w: mde all: lft clr 2 out: 12l ahd last: eased considerably flat* **20/1**	113+
-420	2	5	**Moorland Monarch**[16] 1983 7-9-12 **82** oh4 ow3 ... CHonour(5) (J D Frost) *hld up in tch: btn whn lft 2nd 2 out: kpt on same pce* **7/1**	87+
330-	3	hd	**Toomebridge (IRE)**[231] 4680 7-11-12 **105** ... PJBrennan (Andrew Turnell) *a.p: hung lft and one pce fr 3 out* **8/1**	108
04P-	4	2 ½	**Opportunity Knocks**[253] 4289 5-9-8 **80** ... KBurke(7) (N J Hawke) *hld up in tch: no hdwy fr 4 out* **33/1**	80
540-	5	4	**Drat**[274] 3904 6-11-0 **93** ... JMMaguire (R Mathew) *hld up in tch: hit 7th: no real prog fr 10th* **80/1**	90+
2-21	6	5	**Master D'Or (FR)**[18] 1953 5-11-12 **105** ... RJohnson (P J Hobbs) *hld up and bhd: hdwy 9th: wknd after 4 out* **11/4**[1]	98+
2/P3	7	14	**Bell Lane Lad (IRE)**[10] 2100 8-10-12 **91** ... RThornton (A King) *hld up in mid-div: mstke 5th (water): j.lft and bmpd 7th: rdn 9th: bhd fr 4 out* **7/2**[2]	71+
00-0	8	15	**Great Benefit (IRE)**[18] 1950 6-10-9 **88** ... TJMurphy (Miss H C Knight) *hld up and bhd: stdy hdwy whn mstke 8th: wknd 4 out* **12/1**	50
P-PR	9	4	**Mr Crawford**[5] 2217 6-9-7 **79** oh15 ... MGoldstein(7) (Nick Williams) *hld up in mid-div: hmpd 7th: bhd fr 8th* **66/1**	37
/43-	U		**Lucky Penny**[494] 936 9-10-0 **79** oh3 ... RGreene (K Bishop) *bhd tl p.u bef 8th* **33/1**	—
6P-5	P		**Uncle Ada (IRE)**[194] 244 10-10-0 **79** oh6 ... VSlattery (D J Minty) *a bhd: t.o 7th: p.u bef 4 out* **200/1**	—
20-0	P		**Oysterhaven (IRE)**[29] 1796 7-11-12 **105** ...(b) NFehily (D P Keane) *hld up: mstkes 6th and 7th: bhd whn p.u bef 8th* **8/1**	—
P-U1	F		**Supreme Tadgh (IRE)**[8] 2149 8-11-2 **102** 7ex ... SElliott(7) (J A Geake) *a.p: ev ch 4 out: mstke 3 out: 3l 2nd whn fell 2 out* **13/2**[3]	112+
3-	P		**Minat Boy**[240] 4523 9-10-0 **79** oh6 ... OMcPhail (Mrs Tracey Barfoot-Saunt) *prom: wkng whn hit 8th: t.o whn p.u bef 4 out* **66/1**	—

4m 52.8s (-1.10) **Going Correction** -0.15s/f (Good) **14** Ran SP% **120.0**
Speed ratings: **96,94,93,92,91 89,83,77,76,— —,—,—,—** CSF £151.34 CT £1236.09 TOTE £27.00: £7.10, £3.00, £2.40; EX 352.40.
Owner Anthony D Kerman **Bred** J R Weston **Trained** Storrington, W Sussex

FOCUS
This was a competitive low-grade chase, won in imposing style by King Coal, who showed very little over hurdles. The winner is value for much more and looks capable of being a bit better than his current mark, while the rest probably ran up to their previous form.

NOTEBOOK
King Coal(IRE), a big, strong sort - measured at 18 hands - making his chasing debut in handicap company, jumped superbly out in front and never gave his rivals a chance of getting involved. If kept to a sensible level, he can win again. *(tchd 22-1)*
Moorland Monarch, who was nicely supported before the race, never got to the easy winner and was ultimately well beaten. The stable often do well at the course, so he could be interesting if returned to the track for a race over further. *(op 14-1)*
Toomebridge(IRE), running for a stable bang in form, never really got competitive under his big weight, and needs a drop in the handicap given this effort. *(tchd 7-1 and 9-1)*
Opportunity Knocks shaped quite nicely on his seasonal debut, albeit well beaten. He is probably going to make a better chaser than he was a hurdler.
Drat holds some respectable form and has the ability to win a minor race in due course. *(op 100-1)*
Master D'Or(FR) weakened tamely after making his way towards the leaders down the side of the course. The 10lb rise in the weights for his win last time appeared too much for him. *(tchd 10-3, 7-2 in a place)*
Bell Lane Lad(IRE) made too many costly jumping errors to be judged on this effort. Clearly, his jumping will need to improve for him to have a chance next time. *(op 4-1)*
Great Benefit(IRE), who shaped nicely for much of the race, never got to the leaders after a mistake. He is capable of better. *(op 11-1)*
Minat Boy *Official explanation: trainer said gelding had lost a front shoe during the race (op 6-1)*
Supreme Tadgh(IRE) was beaten in second place when coming down two from home. This was the second time he has lost his jockey in the final stages of a race. *(op 6-1)*

2314 GG.COM H'CAP HURDLE (8 hdls) 2m 1f

3:25 (3:25) (Class 4) (0-105,105) 4-Y-0+ **£4,046** (£1,188; £594; £296)

Form				RPR
-120	1		**Sunnyarjun**[26] 1862 7-10-12 **91** ... JMogford (J C Tuck) *hld up: hdwy 5th: rdn appr last: led flat: r.o* **7/2**[1]	97+
4-00	2	nk	**Man Ray (USA)**[32] 1772 4-11-2 **95** ... NFehily (Jonjo O'Neill) *hld up: hdwy 4th: led on bit 2 out: hdd flat: rdn and r.o* **16/1**	102+
-320	3	8	**L'Eau Du Nil (FR)**[32] 1775 4-11-11 **104** ... RJohnson (P J Hobbs) *led: mstke 3 out: rdn and hdd 2 out: wknd flat* **9/2**[2]	103+
00-3	4	7	**Breezer**[13] 2043 5-10-3 **89** ...(p) SElliott(7) (J A Geake) *hld up: reminders after 3rd: hdwy appr 3 out: no real prog fr 2 out* **9/2**[2]	80
-446	5	3 ½	**Calomeria**[21] 1906 4-11-7 **105** ... StephenJCraine(5) (D McCain) *chsd ldr: rdn after 5th: wknd appr 2 out* **11/2**[3]	93
/05-	6	10	**Westernmost**[503] 549 7-11-2 **95** ... RGreene (K Bishop) *hld up in tch: rdn and wknd appr 3 out* **20/1**	73
0/0-	7	15	**Galant Eye (IRE)**[509] 830 6-11-1 **94** ... VSlattery (R J Baker) *bhd fr 4th* **25/1**	57
P25F	8	hd	**Brown Fox (FR)**[17] 1974 4-10-0 **79** ... JAMcCarthy (C J Down) *hld up and bhd: hdwy 5th: wknd appr 3 out* **9/1**	41
-1P2	9	dist	**Aleemdar (IRE)**[33] 1756 8-9-11 **81** ...(p) DLaverty(5) (A E Jones) *prom to 5th: t.o* **8/1**	—
/6-P	P		**Jaskini**[29] 1801 9-10-2 **86** oh9 ow7 ... HEphgrave(5) (L Corcoran) *a bhd: t.o whn p.u bef last* **16/1**	—

4m 16.7s (7.50) **Going Correction** +0.25s/f (Yiel) **10** Ran SP% **115.5**
Speed ratings: **92,91,88,84,83 78,71,71,—,—** CSF £55.75 CT £256.83 TOTE £4.80: £1.70, £2.90, £1.60; EX 76.40 Place 6 £215.57, Place 5 £155.46.
Owner The Sunny Five **Bred** J C Tuck **Trained** Oldbury on the Hill, Gloucs

FOCUS
A very weak race with the third the best guide to the level. The winner landed a small gamble, but the form looks unreliable.

NOTEBOOK
Sunnyarjun took all of the two-mile trip to get on top of his rivals, and land a small gamble. He clearly likes a stiff track and could follow this up, as he should no be penalised too much given the winning distance. *(op 5-1)*

Man Ray(USA), making his handicap debut, looked like winning easily before finding a lot less off the bridle than looked likely. He has displayed some temperament problems in the past, and may not be a straightforward character. *(op 15-2)*
L'Eau Du Nil(FR), making his handicap debut, did not run too badly but, despite showing plenty of promise in the past, he finds in difficult to win. *(op 5-1)*
Breezer only has one win to his name, a seller, and ran up to his best. A drop back to the basement grade would suit. *(op 7-1)*
Calomeria, from a stable that has been in fine form, is clearly not the filly who was capable of winning a Listed hurdle last year. The big drop down in trip did not produce any improvement. *(op 7-2)*
Brown Fox(FR) failed to reproduce her promising effort last time - was closing in on the leaders when falling three from home - and is one to treat with caution. She is, however, handicapped to win a race off her current mark. *(op 10-1)*
T/Plt: £141.30 to a £1 stake. Pool: £51,721.85. 267.20 winning tickets. T/Qpdt: £77.00 to a £1 stake. Pool: £4,340.00. 41.70 winning tickets. KH

2036 KELSO (L-H)
Friday, November 18
2315 Meeting Abandoned - Frost

WINDSOR (R-H)
Friday, November 18

OFFICIAL GOING: Good
Wind: Nil Weather: Sunny and cold. Open dtch past stands omitted.

2322 AT THE RACES NOVICES' HURDLE (10 hdls) 2m 4f
1:00 (1:02) (Class 4) 4-Y-O+ **£3,662** (£1,075; £537; £268)

Form				RPR
11-1	1		**Oscar Park (IRE)**[21] [1903] 6-11-5 .... TDoyle (C Tinkler) *led 2nd: mde most after: clr fr 6th: nt fluent next: unchal and easily* **2/7**[1]	126+
56-5	2	14	**Dearson (IRE)**[26] [1857] 4-10-12 .... DCrosse (C J Mann) *hld up: prog 5th: chsd wnr 3 out: no imp whn mstkes 2 out and last* **20/1**	99+
55P0	3	4	**Men Of Destiny (IRE)**[135] [912] 4-10-5 .... CMStudd(7) (B G Powell) *in tch: pushed along in rr fr 4th: bhd fr 6th: plugged on fr 3 out: drvn flat to snatch 3rd nr fin* **100/1**	89
32-B	4	½	**Knighton Lad (IRE)**[16] [1990] 5-10-12 .... WHutchinson (A King) *in tch: outpcd whn mstke 7th: sn bhd and rdn: plugged on fr 3 out: styd on flat* **10/1**[2]	89
0/	5	1	**Mountain Mayhem (IRE)**[726] [2328] 7-10-12 .... GLee (M G Rimell) *t.k.h: prom: chsd wnr 6th to 3 out: btn after: wknd flat and lost 2 pls nr fin* **25/1**	88
0-	6	2 ½	**Well Actually (IRE)**[279] [3810] 5-10-12 .... JPMcNamara (B G Powell) *cl up: rdn and struggling bef 3 out: plugged on fr next* **20/1**	85
	7	24	**Vengeance**[481] 5-10-12 .... LAspell (S Dow) *nt a fluent: hld up in rr: prog 6th: wl in tch after next: wknd rapidly bef 3 out: t.o* **14/1**[3]	61
000-	8	28	**Optimo (GER)**[230] [4696] 4-10-12 .... PHide (G L Moore) *led to 2nd: lost pl after 4th: last and struggling 6th: t.o* **66/1**	33
00-	P		**Duncanbil (IRE)**[303] [1476] 4-10-5 .... MBatchelor (J J Bridger) *t.k.h: w wnr fr 3rd to 5th: sn wknd: t.o whn p.u bef 2 out* **80/1**	—

5m 8.50s (6.80) **Going Correction** +0.50s/f (Soft)
WFA 4 from 5yo+ 13lb 9 Ran SP% **110.6**
Speed ratings: **106,100,98,98,98 97,87,76,—** CSF £10.04 TOTE £1.30: £1.10, £2.40, £8.10; EX 5.80.
Owner George Ward **Bred** Mrs B Byrne **Trained** Compton, Berks

FOCUS
A race that was at the mercy of Oscar Park barring a mishap and he once again impressed and is value for more than the winning distance.

NOTEBOOK
Oscar Park(IRE) ◆, a very useful bumper performer, is quickly developing into a smart novice hurdler and, although he had little to beat, he could hardly have done it any easier. The true test will come when he is upped in grade, but being a Listed winner in bumpers there is no reason why he should not be up to the task and races like the Winter Novices' Hurdle at Sandown and Challow Hurdle at Newbury look realistic targets. *(op 1-3 tchd 1-4 in a place)*
Dearson(IRE) shaped as though a rise in distance would help when fifth on his reappearance at Wincanton last month, and he was the only one who ever looked like getting near the winner. Ultimately well held, he will face easier opportunities in future and looks a likely type for handicaps. *(op 16-1)*
Men Of Destiny(IRE) kept on best of the rest for a modest third and recorded easily his best effort to date over hurdles. He has gone the wrong way since running out on his bumper debut at Taunton last season (race at his mercy), but it is hoped he can go the right way from this and he would make some appeal in handicaps. *(op 50-1)*
Knighton Lad(IRE) had a disasterous start to the season when brought down early at Huntingdon earlier in the month and in all honesty this was a bit disappointing. He may have needed a confidence boost however and as a result deserves another chance. *(op 9-1 tchd 8-1)*
Mountain Mayhem(IRE) made a pleasing return and may be capable of a little improvement upped to three miles. *(op 20-1)*
Well Actually(IRE), a stablemate of third-placed Men Of Destiny, showed up well for a long way before getting tired and he was not given a hard time once his chance had gone. Thrown in at the deep end behind Karanja in a graded bumper at Newbury on his only previous outing, he is clearly well regarded and improvement can be expected next time.

2323 SUMMERFRUIT COMPANY H'CAP CHASE (11 fncs 1 omitted) 2m
1:30 (1:31) (Class 4) (0-100,100) 5-Y-O+ **£3,379** (£992; £496; £247)

Form				RPR
02-1	1		**Julies Boy (IRE)**[5] [2217] 8-10-4 85 7ex .... (t) WMcCarthy(7) (T R George) *led to 2nd: trckd ldr to 4 out: effrt to ld bef 2 out: sn in command: pushed out* **11/10**[1]	99+
2P56	2	5	**Pavey Ark (IRE)**[14] [2022] 7-10-0 74 oh1 .... (v[1]) GLee (James Moffatt) *wl in tch: mstke 5th: prog 7th: trckd ldr 4 out: upsides next: outpcd by wnr fr 2 out* **13/2**[3]	82
60P	3	7	**Manoram (GER)**[56] [1542] 6-11-12 100 .... (v) PMoloney (Ian Williams) *led and j.lft 2nd: blnd 3 out: sn hdd: 3rd and wl btn whn j.lft last* **10/1**	105+
P31P	4	17	**Charliemoore**[5] [2217] 9-11-5 93 .... (b) JEMoore (G L Moore) *in tch: pushed along fr 4th: mstke 6th: u.p fr 8th: blnd 4 out and lost all ch* **8/1**	79+
0/4-	5	3 ½	**Another Native (IRE)**[319] [3194] 7-11-10 98 .... DCrosse (C J Mann) *numerous mstkes in last: brief effrt and in tch 8th: btn fr next: eased 2 out* **4/1**[2]	79
0656	6	nk	**Stopwatch (IRE)**[32] [1776] 10-10-0 74 oh17 .... (p) BHitchcott (Mrs L C Jewell) *trckd ldrs tl wknd 4 out* **33/1**	54
65-6	7	dist	**Konker**[21] [1911] 10-10-9 90 .... APogson(7) (J R Cornwall) *in tch: mstkes 4th and 6th: wknd 8th: t.o* **16/1**	—

4m 9.10s (4.00) **Going Correction** +0.30s/f (Yiel) 7 Ran SP% **110.0**
Speed ratings: **102,99,96,87,85 85,—** CSF £8.29 CT £41.46 TOTE £2.00: £1.20, £3.00; EX 7.30.
Owner R P Foden **Bred** Patrick Slattery **Trained** Slad, Gloucs

FOCUS
Moderate stuff but solid enough rated through the winner and a fair time for the grade.

NOTEBOOK
Julies Boy(IRE), a comfortable winner on his reappearance at Fontwell, stayed on strongly down the straight to win going away and ultimately had no trouble defying the penalty. He has clearly returned an improved gelding and seems suited by this sort of trip, but he does stay further which opens up more opportunities for him in his search for a hat-trick. *(op Evens tchd 10-11)*
Pavey Ark(IRE) has been on the go since May and came into this off the back off several moderate efforts, but the first-time visor seemed to spark him back into life and he made the winner work hard enough. He may find a small race off this sort of mark if the headgear has the same effect in future. *(op 8-1)*
Manoram(GER) has hit a bad patch since winning at Worcester in May, but he showed much more life and ran a reasonable race under top weight.
Charliemoore was never going after an error at the fourth last and deserves another chance. *(op 7-1 tchd 9-1 in a place)*
Another Native(IRE), who shaped with a fair amount of promise on his debut in this country when fourth at Exeter in January, was always likely to find this trip on the sharp side and he never got into a rhythm, making several blunders. He is better than this and deserves another chance back up in trip. *(op 9-2 tchd 5-1 in a place)*

2324 BLUE SQUARE 0800 5870200 H'CAP HURDLE (8 hdls) 2m
2:05 (2:06) (Class 3) (0-120,120) 4-Y-O+ **£6,935** (£2,036; £1,018; £508)

Form				RPR
301-	1		**Priors Dale**[305] [3396] 5-11-12 120 .... BFenton (Miss E C Lavelle) *mstke 1st: mde all: jnd 2 out and sn rdn: kpt on gamely fr last* **10/1**	130+
/0-6	2	2	**Silver Prophet (IRE)**[27] [1263] 6-10-11 105 .... SCurran (M R Bosley) *trckd ldrs: rdn and effrt 3 out: chsd wnr last: kpt on but a hld* **20/1**	111
226-	3	5	**The Local**[223] [4777] 5-11-4 112 .... ATinkler (C R Egerton) *mstke 1st: chsd wnr: rdn to chal and upsides 2 out: btn last: wknd flat* **5/1**[2]	113
0000	4	1 ¼	**Constantine**[23] [1878] 5-11-5 113 .... (b) JEMoore (G L Moore) *trckd ldrs: nt qckn and outpcd 3 out: kpt on again after 2 out: one pce and looked reluctant after last* **14/1**	113
0P0	5	8	**Border Tale**[28] [947] 5-11-1 109 .... (t) GLee (James Moffatt) *hld up in rr: outpcd bef 3 out: rdn and kpt on bef 2 out: no ch* **16/1**	101
16-	6	5	**Foodbroker Founder**[32] [4201] 5-11-7 115 .... RWalford (D R C Elsworth) *trckd ldrs: lost pl after 5th: rdn and struggling bef 3 out* **3/1**[1]	102
2-40	7	½	**Cunning Pursuit**[119] [571] 4-11-2 110 .... MFoley (N J Henderson) *settled in midfield: outpcd and rdn bef 3 out: n.d after* **8/1**[3]	96
-620	8	3 ½	**Hatch A Plan (IRE)**[22] [1902] 4-10-5 99 .... PHide (Mrs A J Hamilton-Fairley) *hld up in rr: mstke 3rd: gng wl enough but plenty to do whn blnd 3 out: no ch after* **14/1**	82
0-0	9	29	**Twist 'n Shout**[41] [1668] 8-10-13 107 .... APMcCoy (Jonjo O'Neill) *hld up towards rr: mstke 5th: sn rdn and btn: t.o* **12/1**	61
/41-	10	3	**First Boy (GER)**[541] [500] 6-10-8 102 .... WMarston (D J Wintle) *hld up in last pair: prog 5th and in tch bef next: sn wknd: 9th and no ch whn terrible blunder and nrly uns rdr 2 out* **5/1**[2]	68+
5-54	11	18	**Park City**[16] [1987] 6-9-8 95 oh4 ow1 .... SWalsh(7) (J Joseph) *a in rr: lost tch 4th: sn t.o* **20/1**	28

3m 56.4s (-2.80) **Going Correction** +0.50s/f (Soft)
WFA 4 from 5yo+ 12lb 11 Ran SP% **115.0**
Speed ratings: **105,104,101,100,96 94,94,92,77,76 67** CSF £179.40 CT £1110.93 TOTE £6.90: £2.90, £6.00, £2.70; EX 250.50 Trifecta £571.20 Pool: £804.52 - 1.00 winning tickets..
Owner Mrs L Alexander **Bred** John Davis **Trained** Wildhern, Hants

FOCUS
Not a bad little handicap hurdle run at a sound gallop and, rated through the third, it is likely to produce winners.

NOTEBOOK
Priors Dale showed some fair form in a short spell hurdling last season, but shouldering top weight on this first start since January was going to take some doing, so he will no doubt have delighted connections with his all-the-way win. He momentarily looked vulnerable down the straight as he began to get weary, but he responded gamely and won with a bit to spare. There should be more to come from the progressive gelding and he is worthy of consideration in future. *(op 6-1)*
Silver Prophet(IRE), like the winner, is lightly raced over hurdles, but he is evidently a fair sort on his day and made the winner work hard for his victory. His sole win over obstacles came at Huntingdon in March 2004 but he should be up to supplementing that this season. *(op 25-1)*
The Local was bang there with every chance taking the second last, but he became tired soon after and faded on the run-in. He has largely struggled to win off this sort of mark and may need a little further help from the Handicapper. *(tchd 9-2)*
Constantine made some appeal with Moore back in the saddle, but he simply lacked the pace to throw down a challenge and he looked none too keen under pressure. A step up in distance is likely to help, but he is not one to rely on. *(op 16-1)*
Border Tale has a pip-opener on the Flat last month and ran respectably without ever getting involved, keeping on late past beaten rivals. He is likely to be capable of better with more positive tactics used.
Foodbroker Founder ran well here on the Flat last month and it was easy to understand why he was fancied for this return to hurdles, but he failed to live up to expectations and was beaten virtually half a mile from home. He now has a bit to prove. *(op 11-4 tchd 5-2)*
Twist 'n Shout *Official explanation: jockey said gelding pulled up lame*

2325 BLUE SQUARE H'CAP CHASE (16 fncs 2 omitted) 3m
2:40 (2:40) (Class 3) (0-115,112) 5-Y-O+ **£7,111** (£2,087; £1,043; £521)

Form				RPR
33-1	1		**Kausse De Thaix (FR)**[14] [2019] 7-11-1 101 .... LAspell (O Sherwood) *led 2nd: mde rest: jnd 3 out: rdn and styd on wl fr 2 out* **5/2**[1]	121+
62P-	2	11	**Rudolf Rassendyll (IRE)**[249] [4370] 10-11-7 107 .... SThomas (Miss Venetia Williams) *settled in midfield: prog fr 10th: rdn to join wnr 3 out: btn next: fdd* **16/1**	117+

23-3 **3** *15* **Myson (IRE)**[18] [1953] 6-11-1 **101** .... JamesDavies 95
(D B Feek) *hld up: prog 1/2-way: chsd wnr 12th tl bef 3 out: wknd* **7/1**[2]

-2FP **4** *hd* **Jaoka Du Gord (FR)**[20] [1920] 8-11-5 **105** .... TDoyle 99
(P R Webber) *blnd 1st: j. wildly 3rd: hld up in last trio: prog 1/2-way: chsd wnr 11th to 12th: wknd 3 out* **7/1**[2]

043 **5** *hd* **Waterberg (IRE)**[22] [1893] 10-11-1 **101** .... (b) MBradburne 95
(H D Daly) *hld up in last trio: sme prog 10th: outpcd fr 12th and lost tch : styd on fr 3 out: nrly snatched 3rd: hopeless task* **10/1**

00-6 **6** *12* **Florida Dream (IRE)**[41] [1678] 6-11-12 **112** .... CLlewellyn 94
(N A Twiston-Davies) *hmpd after 2nd and j. slowly 3rd: nt fluent after: mostly chsd wnr to 11th: u.p and wknd bef 4 out* **8/1**[3]

1-F3 **7** *3* **Charlies Future**[17] [1972] 7-11-12 **112** .... APMcCoy 91
(S C Burrough) *blnd 3rd: nt jump wl after: styd in tch tl wknd u.p after 12th* **9/1**

0215 **8** *4* **Strong Magic (IRE)**[16] [1989] 13-10-0 **93** .... APogson(7) 68
(J R Cornwall) *chsd ldrs to 12th: sn struggling and bhd* **33/1**

0-35 **9** *14* **It's Rumoured**[16] [1983] 5-10-6 **93** .... DCrosse 53
(Jean-Rene Auvray) *prom tl wknd after 11th: t.o bef 4 out* **16/1**

F-2F **U** **Harry Collins**[18] [1953] 7-11-5 **110** .... MNicolls(5) —
(B I Case) *blnd and uns rdr 1st* **14/1**

-560 **F** **Unusual Suspect**[20] [1917] 6-11-1 **101** .... (b) JEMoore —
(G L Moore) *towards rr tl fell heavily 6th* **33/1**

0-P3 **U** **Bunkum**[17] [1978] 7-11-1 **106** .... WKennedy(5) —
(R Lee) *mstke and hmpd 1st: settled in midfield: disputing 7th and in tch whn uns rdr 12th* **16/1**

20U- **P** **Kittenkat**[210] [4959] 11-11-5 **105** .... TScudamore —
(N R Mitchell) *led to 2nd: hmpd bef next: wknd and mstke 9th: sn t.o and jumping rt: p.u bef 4 out* **25/1**

6m 16.7s (4.40) **Going Correction** +0.30s/f (Yiel)
WFA 5 from 6yo+ 1lb **13** Ran SP% **117.8**
Speed ratings: **104,100,95,95,95 91,90,88,84,— —,—,—** CSF £40.46 CT £250.14 TOTE £3.40: £1.60, £5.20, £2.50; EX 56.00 Trifecta £382.50 Pool: £808.10 - 1.50 winning tickets..
Owner Andrew L Cohen **Bred** Michel Bourgneuf **Trained** Upper Lambourn, Berks

FOCUS
A modest staying handicap won in great style by the progressive Kausse De Thaix, who should rate higher. The runner-up sets the level for the form.

NOTEBOOK
Kausse De Thaix(FR) is a fine physical specimen who has clearly improved again over the summer and he made it two wins from two this season with another resolute galloping performance. Having led for most of the journey, he was joined with three to jump, but he soon saw off Rudolf Rassendyll and won with plenty in hand. He has gone up a total of 24lb since winning at Towcester six starts back and will need to improve again to defy what is likely to be a hefty rise, but he has the scope to do so and he remains one to keep on the right side. *(op 11-4 tchd 3-1)*
Rudolf Rassendyll(IRE) has not won since April of last year, but he offered plenty of hope for the future with a good second to a younger, progressive rival and the fact he was 15 lengths clear of the third also augurs well. He can surely be placed to score off what is still a reasonable mark.
Myson(IRE) looked to find two and a half miles an inadequate test on his return at Plumpton and was well worth a try at this distance, but he did not see his race out as strongly as one may have hoped and it is likely the three-mile trip was too far. *(tchd 13-2)*
Jaoka Du Gord(FR) was in need of the outing when pulling up on his return at Lingfield and he fared a little better here, but was beaten a longish way and may need a little help from the Handicapper. *(op 13-2 tchd 6-1)*
Waterberg(IRE) got going all too late and just missed out on a place, but he is at least beginning to run into form now and may be able to find a small race off his ever-declining mark. *(op 11-1)*
Florida Dream(IRE) was expected to take to fencing like a duck to water being a brother to Florida Pearl, but he has yet to convince in two attempts and his jumping was again far from foot perfect. He is with a good stable however and will no doubt get his act together eventually, by which time he may have dropped to an attractive mark. *(op 7-1 tchd 9-1)*

2326 BLUE SQUARE SPEED DIAL 64555 HURDLE (REGISTERED AS THE ASCOT HURDLE) GRADE 2 (10 hdls) 2m 4f
3:10 (3:11) (Class 1) 4-Y-0+ **£22,915** (£8,663; £4,391; £2,243; £1,179)

Form RPR

211- **1** **No Refuge (IRE)**[247] [4394] 5-11-4 148 .... GLee 151+
(J Howard Johnson) *nt jump wl: trckd ldrs: rdn after 3 out: chsd ldr bef next but looked hld: rallied to ld sn after last: styd on wl* **7/4**[1]

110- **2** *2 ½* **Blue Canyon (FR)**[17] [4771] 7-11-8 .... APMcCoy 150
(F Doumen, France) *hld up in last pair: smooth prog 7th: led after 3 out: rdn next: hdd and one pce after last* **11/4**[2]

F-P1 **3** *6* **Royal Shakespeare (FR)**[13] [2055] 6-11-4 154 .... TScudamore 142+
(S Gollings) *trckd ldr: mstke 6th: lost 2nd after next: mstke 3 out and rdn: sn outpcd: plugged on fr last* **7/2**[3]

-104 **4** *3 ½* **Mr Cool**[27] [1828] 11-11-0 144 .... JEMoore 133
(M C Pipe) *led tl after 3 out: wknd last* **13/2**

5P-P **5** *26* **Sh Boom**[20] [1925] 7-11-0 150 .... TSiddall 107
(S A Brookshaw) *hld up in last pair: rdn after 7th: wknd next: t.o* **25/1**

511/ **P** **Accipiter**[595] [4641] 6-11-0 .... BHitchcott —
(J A Geake) *trckd ldrs tl broke down and p.u after 7th: dead* **10/1**

5m 5.30s (48.60) **Going Correction** +0.50s/f (Soft) **6** Ran SP% **111.5**
Speed ratings: **112,111,108,107,96** — CSF £6.90 TOTE £2.30: £1.70, £1.80; EX 6.40.
Owner Andrea & Graham Wylie **Bred** Cathal M Ryan **Trained** Billy Row, Co Durham

FOCUS
A smashing event and it was great to see the Royal & SunAlliance winner No Refuge make a winning return with the runner-up the best guide although the form could rate higher. The winning time was nothing more than acceptable for the class of contest though.

NOTEBOOK
No Refuge(IRE) ◆, who took the Royal & SunAlliance Hurdle on his final start last term, is from a yard that has hardly made a bright start to the season. Although he had to work very hard to win, he was well on top at the line, having responded extremely well to Lee's urgings. He can be expected to some on appreciably for this and will be a major force in all the two and a half to three-mile hurdles this season, and it may be he who gives reigning World Hurdle champ Inglis Drever most to do at Cheltenham come March. *(op 9-4)*
Blue Canyon(FR), a stand-in for Baracouda, developed into a smart two and a half miler last season. Given a nice prep for this when winning on the Flat in his homeland earlier in the month, he held a fitness advantage over the winner which made up for the 4lb concession and ran a cracking race. Travelling best as they began to straighten for home, looked to have No Refuge's measure as they took the second last, but the winner's superior stamina and class won him the day. He is likely to embark on a chasing career sooner rather than later and is likely to make an impact in some of the better races for novices. *(op 3-1)*
Royal Shakespeare(FR), who scored a deserved success on his reappearance at Wincanton, had won over this trip in his novice season, but that was against inferior opposition and he was not as effective at this distance. All his best form is at two miles and he will continue to be a contender for all the graded hurdles at around that distance. *(op 11-4)*
Mr Cool is a grand old campaigner who went agonisingly close to claiming the scalp of Baracouda in this race at Ascot back in 2002. He went about his business from the front and towed them along until the race for home began, at which point he was found wanting. He will continue to find winning hard, but always has the option of a return to chasing as in the one season he won three of his five outings. *(tchd 6-1 and 7-1)*
Sh Boom was a high-class staying hurdler a couple of seasons back, but he has not been the same horse since falling in the 2004 Stayers' Hurdle and a change of scenery has failed to do anything for him.
Accipiter, a real gutsy novice who scored at the top level at Aintree when last seen back in April 2004, was making his return from injury and was perhaps the most interesting runner on show, but he broke down badly at past halfway and had to be put down.

2327 CLOSE PROPERTY FINANCE NOVICES' HURDLE (12 hdls) 3m 110y
3:45 (3:45) (Class 4) 4-Y-0+ **£3,526** (£1,035; £517; £258)

Form RPR

1 **Super Lord (IRE)**[222] 7-10-12 .... WHutchinson 119+
(J A B Old) *trckd ldrs: led after 3 out: sn clr: easily* **14/1**

02 **2** *7* **Love Of Classics**[16] [1990] 5-10-12 .... (p) LAspell 107
(O Sherwood) *hld up: pushed along after 7th: effrt bef 3 out: chsd wnr 2 out: kpt on but no imp* **16/1**

1 **3** *7* **Day Of Claies (FR)**[22] [1892] 4-11-4 .... CLlewellyn 110+
(N A Twiston-Davies) *trckd ldrs: nt fluent 6th and 7th: sn pushed along: drvn to chse ldng pair after 9th: one pce and btn whn mstke 2 out* **7/4**[1]

2 **4** *6* **Just For Now (IRE)**[18] [1950] 6-10-12 .... JPMcNamara 96+
(T R George) *led: rdn and hdd after 3 out: sn wknd: mstke last* **11/4**[2]

- **5** *10* **Good Call (IRE)** 6-10-12 .... APMcCoy 84
(Jonjo O'Neill) *hld up: nt fluent 8th and pushed along: effrt after next: wknd bef 2 out* **8/1**

23- **6** *11* **Definite Approach (IRE)**[255] [4241] 7-10-12 .... WMarston 73
(R T Phillips) *settled in rr: shkn up and wknd after 9th: bhd fr next* **11/2**[3]

P **Mister Apple's (FR)**[205] 5-10-12 .... GLee —
(Ian Williams) *mostly chsd ldr to 9th: wknd rapidly: t.o whn p.u bef next* **17/2**

6m 20.3s **7** Ran SP% **112.6**
CSF £176.04 TOTE £15.50: £4.00, £4.70; EX 166.00 Place 6 £396.07, Place 5 £320.75.
Owner W E Sturt **Bred** Gerard Kennedy **Trained** Barbury Castle, Wilts

FOCUS
An ordinary novice hurdle, but an impressive performance by dual point winner Super Lord, who came right away to win easily and is value for nearly double the official margin with the third and fourth close to their marks.

NOTEBOOK
Super Lord(IRE), a dual winner in points, provided connections with a welcome winner and made quite an impressive rules debut. Always travelling strongly, he came clear with the minimum of fuss and, although those he beat were nothing out of the ordinary, the manner of his victory suggested he may be up to defying a penalty before a possible rise in class. *(op 12-1)*
Love Of Classics ◆ turned around 77 lengths with favourite Day Of Claies on their recent Stratford running and, while it is highly likely the favourite failed to run his race, he does seem to have improved for the fitting of cheekpieces. He will not always bump into one as today's winner and is a likely future scorer. *(op 10-1)*
Day Of Claies(FR) had a hard enough race when winning on his debut, but he should still have fared a bit better here and he appeared to run flat. He deserves another chance, but is clearly no star. *(op 2-1)*
Just For Now(IRE) failed to build on his recent Plumpton second and found disappointingly little having been headed. It is likely he will not be at his best until tackling fences, but handicap hurdles may provide him with a better opportunity of winning. *(op 10-3)*
Good Call(IRE), a Roselier half-brother to No Shenanigans, did not offer a great deal on this hurdles debut and is likely to need more time. *(op 11-2)*
Definite Approach(IRE) had some reasonable form last season, but signed off on a low note and this reappearance was not much better. *(op 6-1 tchd 5-1)*
Mister Apple's(FR), a chase winner in France, stopped most quickly and there may well have been something amiss on this British debut. As a result he deserves another chance. *(op 9-1)*
T/Jkpt: £1,451.70 to a £1 stake. Pool: £22,491.50. 11.00 winning tickets. T/Plt: £201.20 to a £1 stake. Pool: £67,071.10. 243.25 winning tickets. T/Qpdt: £100.60 to a £1 stake. Pool: £5,877.60. 43.20 winning tickets. JN

2328 - 2333a (Foreign Racing) - See Raceform Interactive

2001 HAYDOCK (L-H)
Saturday, November 19

OFFICIAL GOING: Good to soft (soft in places)
The ground was described as 'very sticky due to the frost'. The last two fences in the back straight were omitted due to the frost.
Wind: Almost nil Weather: Fine and sunny but cold

2334 DRINK J.W. LEES BITTER JUMP V FLAT JOCKEYS H'CAP HURDLE (8 hdls) 2m
12:45 (12:45) (Class 3) (0-130,128) 4-Y-0+
£12,920 (£3,816; £1,908; £955; £476; £239)

Form RPR

41-0 **1** **Flying Enterprise (IRE)**[25] [1872] 5-11-12 **128** .... NFehily 140+
(Miss Venetia Williams) *trckd ldrs: led 5th: wnt clr appr last: styd on wl* **12/1**

00-5 **2** *7* **Calatagan (IRE)**[24] [1878] 6-11-9 **125** .... KDarley 129+
(J M Jefferson) *trckd ldrs: lost pl appr 3 out: mod 5th last: shkn up and fin wl: tk 2nd nr fin* **12/1**

0021 **3** *1 ¾* **Rising Generation (FR)**[28] [1836] 8-11-9 **125** .... ADobbin 128+
(N G Richards) *chsd ldrs: chal 3 out: no ex appr last* **13/2**[3]

15-1 **4** *1 ¼* **Hernando's Boy**[18] [85] 4-11-4 **120** .... TJMurphy 121
(K G Reveley) *hld up towards rr: hdwy 5th: prom next: one pce fr 2 out* **3/1**[1]

/3-0 **5** *1 ¼* **St Pirran (IRE)**[38] [1720] 10-11-7 **123** .... DeanMcKeown 125+
(R C Guest) *trckd ldrs: effrt appr 2 out: wknd run-in* **22/1**

314/ **6** *30* **Salhood**[623] [4194] 6-11-5 **121** .... CLlewellyn 91
(S Gollings) *led: hdd 5th: hit next and lost pl: in rr whn blnd 2 out* **16/1**

06-6 **7** *13* **Proud To Be Irish (IRE)**[112] [1081] 6-10-11 **113** .... PCarberry 70
(Seamus O'Farrell, Ire) *t.k.h in last: stdy hdwy 5th: lost pl appr next* **9/1**

-306 **8** *17* **Nick's Choice**[168] [633] 9-10-12 **114** .... NCallan 54
(D Burchell) *in rr whn sltly hmpd 2nd: t.o 5th* **33/1**

10- **9** *22* **Gift Voucher (IRE)**[266] [4067] 4-10-10 **112** .... EAhern 30
(P R Webber) *chsd ldrs: hrd drvn 5th: lost pl appr next: sn bhd and eased* **8/1**

0/ **F** **Almier (IRE)**[52] [1573] 7-11-3 **119** .... JPSpencer —
(Michael Hourigan, Ire) *w ldr whn fell 2nd* **8/1**

036- **P** **Marrel**[252] 4329 7-11-2 **118** .... (v) ACulhane —
(D Burchell) *in rr: losing tch whn p.u bef 5th* **66/1**

F-F **U** **Emotional Article (IRE)**[20] 1945 5-11-0 **116** .... BJGeraghty —
(T J Taaffe, Ire) *mid-div: bdly hmpd and uns rdr 2nd* **6/1**[2]

3m 51.2s (-7.90) **Going Correction** -0.20s/f (Good)
WFA 4 from 5yo+ 12lb **12** Ran SP% **114.9**
Speed ratings: **111,107,106,106,105 90,83,75,64,—** —,— CSF £139.05 CT £1019.77 TOTE £14.80: £3.20, £3.90, £2.20; EX 109.90.
Owner Malcolm Edwards **Bred** Gainsborough Stud Management Ltd **Trained** Kings Caple, H'fords

FOCUS
A novelty race, featuring some leading Flat jockeys. It was the fastest of the three hurdle races run over the trip on the card. A much improved effort from the winner, a seemingly eye-catching run from the second , and the third setting the standard.

NOTEBOOK
Flying Enterprise(IRE), dropping back in trip, had the advantage of a jump jockey and he showed vastly improved form, looking the likely winner a long way out and coming right away before the final flight. He will continue to be of real interest, even from his revised mark. *(op 10-1)*
Calatagan(IRE), former champion Flat jockey Kevin Darley's first ride over hurdles, settled much better than on some occasions in the past. Having dropped out on the final turn, he sprouted wings on the run-in to snatch second spot. *(op 16-1 tchd 11-1)*
Rising Generation(FR), 13lb higher, had the benefit of his regular rider Tony Dobbin and he probably ran right up to his best. *(op 9-2)*
Hernando's Boy moved up looking a possible threat, but when asked a serious question he could only keep on in his own time. *(op 4-1)*
St Pirran(IRE), much more highly rated over fences, gave Dean McKeown a good first ride over hurdles and this will put him right for a return to fences. *(op 20-1)*

2335 GORDON PLANT MEMORIAL NEWTON NOVICES' HURDLE (LISTED RACE) (8 hdls) 2m
1:20 (1:20) (Class 1) 4-Y-0+ **£15,264** (£5,714; £2,854; £1,426)

Form RPR

1 **Wanango (GER)**[21] 1930 4-11-6 .... WJLee 135+
(T Stack, Ire) *trckd ldrs 3rd: wnt 2nd last: rdn and hung lft: styd on to ld last 150yds* **7/1**[3]

1 **2** *7* **Echo Point (IRE)**[24] 1885 5-11-4 .... ADobbin 127+
(N G Richards) *led and sn clr: hit last: wknd and hdd last 150yds: eased towards fin* **6/4**[2]

2 **3** *8* **First Look (FR)**[13] 2062 5-11-0 .... KRenwick 112
(P Monteith) *chsd ldrs: wnt 2nd 3 out: fdd last* **9/1**

11 **4** *1 ¾* **High Day**[7] 2179 5-11-4 .... KJMercer 114
(Ferdy Murphy) *chsd ldr to 3 out: one pace* **11/8**[1]

5 *21* **Trust Rule**[42] 5-11-0 .... MrTGreenall 89
(M W Easterby) *hld up: hdwy and prom 5th: sn wknd: t.o whn hit last* **33/1**

6 *dist* **Pont Neuf (IRE)**[35] 5-10-7 .... (t) TJDreaper —
(A Crook) *sn bhd: mstkes: t.o 4th: btn 62 l* **100/1**

2- **7** *12* **Clearly Oscar (IRE)**[160] 737 6-11-0 .... (t) MrJPO'Farrell —
(Michael Joseph Fitzgerald, Ire) *outpcd and lost pl 4th: t.o 3 out* **100/1**

5P **8** *dist* **Buthaina (IRE)**[9] 2148 5-10-7 .... DLaverty —
(Mrs L Williamson) *stdd s: t.k.h: mstkes: t.o 4th: btn 56 l* **400/1**

3m 53.5s (-5.60) **Going Correction** -0.20s/f (Good) **8** Ran SP% **109.8**
Speed ratings: **106,102,98,97,87** —,—,— CSF £17.16 TOTE £7.10: £1.80, £1.10, £1.40; EX 14.20.
Owner P Piller **Bred** Stiftung Gestut Fahrhof **Trained** Golden, Co Tipperary

FOCUS
The winner was the pick of the paddock and the fast pace set by the runner-up played to his strengths. The third and fourth ran to their pre-race marks and the form looks sound.

NOTEBOOK
Wanango(GER), quite a tall individual, stayed on to chase the leader jumping the last and his stamina carried him clear in the closing stages. This was much improved form and he will be entitled to take his place in the better novices' next spring. *(op 13-2 tchd 6-1)*
Echo Point(IRE) did too much in front and was just starting to tie up when he missed out the last, and once overtaken the situation was quickly accepted. He is better than the bare form and other opportunities will surely be found for him. *(tchd 7-4)*
First Look(FR) found this an even tougher test. He likes soft ground and will surely find an opening when his sights are set lower. *(op 8-1)*
High Day didn't travel nearly as well this time and he was struggling fully three flights from home. This was not his true running. *(op 6-4 tchd 6-5 and 13-8 in places)*
Trust Rule, thrown in at the deep end, picked up £250 appearance money and this school round will have done him no harm at all.

2336 BETFAIRPOKER.COM H'CAP HURDLE (12 hdls) 2m 7f 110y
1:50 (1:51) (Class 2) 4-Y-0+ **£43,841** (£12,950; £6,475; £3,241; £1,617; £812)

Form RPR

0-51 **1** **St Matthew (USA)**[21] 1924 7-11-4 **137** .... PWhelan 145+
(Mrs S J Smith) *chsd ldr: racd wd in bk st: led after 9th: 3 l clr whn hit last: jst hld on* **25/1**

102- **2** *nk* **My Way De Solzen (FR)**[226] 4752 5-11-9 **142** .... RThornton 148+
(A King) *hld up: hdwy and prom 8th: wnt 2nd 1f out: styd on wl: jst failed* **4/1**[2]

31/3 **3** *9* **Tees Components**[21] 1925 10-11-5 **138** .... (t) JimCrowley 135
(K G Reveley) *chsd ldrs: wnt 2nd after 3 out: one pce run-in* **15/2**

0/4- **4** *2 ½* **Inching Closer**[385] 1916 8-10-9 **135** .... BSHughes[(7)] 129
(J Howard Johnson) *hld up: hdwy and prom 9th: one pce fr 2 out* **66/1**

0-64 **5** *nk* **Rambling Minster**[7] 2175 7-10-13 **132** .... RMcGrath 126
(K G Reveley) *trckd ldrs: effrt appr 2 out: one pce* **10/1**

6613 **6** *½* **Alikat (IRE)**[28] 1830 4-11-1 **134** .... RGreene 127
(M C Pipe) *in rr and drvn 6th: hdwy and prom 8th: one pce fr 3 out* **25/1**

4-1P **7** *3 ½* **Nonantais (FR)**[48] 1617 8-10-4 **123** .... MBatchelor 113
(M Bradstock) *led: hdd after 9th: wknd 2 out* **50/1**

04-3 **8** *15* **Spring Pursuit**[18] 1828 9-10-12 **131** .... BJGeraghty 111+
(E G Bevan) *hld up in rr: hdwy and prom 9th: sn rdn: wknd next* **18/1**

1/2- **9** *1 ½* **True Lover (GER)**[35] 110 8-10-7 **126** .... PCarberry 107+
(J W Mullins) *chsd ldrs: rdn and lost pl after 9th* **13/2**[3]

0-11 **P** **Jorobaden (FR)**[27] 1844 5-11-1 **139** .... PMerrigan[(5)] —
(Mrs H Dalton) *chsd ldrs: p.u bef 6th* **10/1**

0-00 **P** **Lazy But Lively (IRE)**[14] 2038 9-9-12 **120** .... KJMercer[(3)] —
(R F Fisher) *in rr: t.o 8th: p.u bef 3 out* **66/1**

U5-1 **P** **By Degree (IRE)**[17] 1984 9-9-12 **124** .... JamesWhite[(7)] —
(R J Hodges) *prom: 7th and outpcd whn p.u after 3 out* **20/1**

-111 **P** **Standin Obligation (IRE)**[7] 2175 6-11-12 **145** .... TJMurphy —
(M C Pipe) *trckd ldrs: rdn and wknd after 9th: bhd whn p.u bef 2 out* **2/1**[1]

001- **P** **The Bajan Bandit (IRE)**[273] 3934 10-11-12 **145** .... (b[1]) ADobbin —
(L Lungo) *chsd ldrs: hit 6th: sn lost pl and bhd: t.o 8th: p.u bef 3 out* **33/1**

6m 5.80s (1.60) **Going Correction** -0.20s/f (Good)
WFA 4 from 5yo+ 13lb **14** Ran SP% **122.2**
Speed ratings: **89,88,85,85,84 84,83,78,78,—** —,—,—,— CSF £121.62 CT £855.36 TOTE £31.50: £5.20, £2.40, £2.30; EX 258.80 Trifecta £998.60 Pool: 1,406.60 - 1.00 winning unit..
Owner Keith Nicholson **Bred** Mrs J G Jones Sr **Trained** High Eldwick, W Yorks

FOCUS
A moderate winning time for a race of this class, slower than the Betfair Chase run over half a furlong further, but the form has a very solid look about it.

NOTEBOOK
St Matthew(USA) was running from an 8lb higher mark than when winning a decent chase last time, but he was still well in over hurdles on last season's Graded form at Wetherby. Kept wide in the back straight both times, he looked to have it in the bag when he clouted the last, and in the end it was a close run thing.
My Way De Solzen(FR) ◆, absent since finishing runner-up in a Grade 2 at Aintree in April, benefited from a patient ride. He stuck on really strongly in pursuit of the winner on the run-in and in the end was only just held at bay. He deserves to go one better overhurdles, but it may not be long before he is seen over fences. *(op 9-2 tchd 5-1)*
Tees Components went in pursuit of the winner but was never going to land a blow. With him it is a case of the softer the ground the better. *(op 17-2 tchd 9-1)*
Inching Closer, winner of the Pertemps Final in 2003, was having his first outing for over a year and it looked as though it would do him a power of good.
Rambling Minster travelled perhaps a shade too strongly and after looking a real danger he could only keep on in his own time. *(op 8-1)*
Alikat(IRE), hard at work with a full circuit to go, did well to keep going sufficiently to finish as close as she did. She looks weighted to the very limit at present.
Standin Obligation(IRE), 8lb higher than at Cheltenham, suddenly came under pressure after the *fourth last and the response was very limited. This almost certainly came too soon. Official explanation: jockey said run may have come too soon (tchd 5-2)*

2337 BETFAIR CHASE (REGISTERED AS THE LANCASHIRE CHASE) GRADE 1 (14 fncs 4 omitted) 3m
2:20 (2:24) (Class 1) 5-Y-0+
£85,530 (£32,085; £16,065; £8,010; £4,020; £2,010)

Form RPR

2-42 **1** **Kingscliff (IRE)**[21] 1926 8-11-8 162 .... RWalford 170+
(R H Alner) *j.w: chsd ldr: led 7th to 9th: led appr 3 out: styd on gamely run-in* **8/1**[3]

12P- **2** *1 ¼* **Beef Or Salmon (IRE)**[41] 4435 9-11-8 .... PCarberry 169+
(Michael Hourigan, Ire) *hld up in tch: effrt 3f out: styd on to chse wnr after last: no imp last 150yds* **8/1**[3]

1-12 **3** *9* **Kicking King (IRE)**[30] 1810 7-11-8 .... BJGeraghty 162+
(T J Taaffe, Ire) *trckd ldrs on outer: hdwy to chal 2 out: wknd fnl f: eased towards fin* **4/5**[1]

2-5F **4** *10* **Keen Leader (IRE)**[21] 1926 9-11-8 160 .... NFehily 151+
(Jonjo O'Neill) *trckd ldrs: led 10th tl appr 3 out: 3rd and one pce whn mstke 2 out: sn wknd* **14/1**

42F- **5** *½* **Royal Auclair (FR)**[210] 4984 8-11-8 155 .... (t) ChristianWilliams 152+
(P F Nicholls) *prom: hit 5th: drvn along 9th: lost pl 11th* **40/1**

P-53 **6** *hd* **Take The Stand (IRE)**[21] 1926 9-11-8 161 .... ADobbin 151+
(P Bowen) *chsd ldrs: effrt 11th: 5th and hld whn hit 2 out: sn wknd* **25/1**

12-1 **7** *dist* **Ollie Magern**[21] 1926 7-11-8 163 .... CLlewellyn 131
(N A Twiston-Davies) *led to 7th: led 9th to next: lost pl bef 3 out: bhd and eased last: btn 38 l* **4/1**[2]

6m 5.40s (-22.90) **Going Correction** -0.475s/f (Good) **7** Ran SP% **110.7**
Speed ratings: **119,118,115,112,112 112,**— CSF £61.41 TOTE £9.90: £3.20, £2.20; EX 45.80.
Owner A J Sendell **Bred** Ian Gault **Trained** Droop, Dorset

■ The first running of this valuable chase. The winner picks up a £1 million bonus if adding the King George and Gold Cup.

■ Stewards' Enquiry : R Walford two-day ban: used whip with excessive frequency (Nov 30-Dec 1)

FOCUS
The sort of winning time you would expect for a race of its status. The winner turned in a personal best, but Kicking King turned out to have had a valid excuse. The next three home dropped out tamely over the last two fences and were well below their best.

NOTEBOOK
Kingscliff(IRE) made these big fences look small and, having been in the thick of the things throughout, dug really deep. He was a deserving winner, and while the bonus will take a deal of winning, running the King George at Sandown rather than Kempton ought to be to his advantage, and he has won on both of his previous visits to Cheltenham. *(op 9-1 tchd 10-1)*
Beef Or Salmon(IRE) still does not look a natural jumper of fences. He proved very game and made the winner dig really deep in the end. He looked as though the outing would bring him on but the fences are his problem.
Kicking King(IRE), still carrying condition, settled better. He landed upsides with a clumsy jump two out but weakened noticeably in the closing stages and afterwards was found to have twisted a shoe and punctured the wall of a back hoof. This was around a stone off his best form, but he will hopefully be right again in time for the King George and he still sets the standard they all have to beat at Cheltenham in March. *(op 10-11 tchd Evens in places)*
Keen Leader(IRE) seemed to travel well withim himself, but his chance was slipping when he met the second last all wrong. He has promised much over the years but in truth has seldom delivered, certainly not at this level.
Royal Auclair(FR), runner-up in the Grand National, has gone well when fresh in the past but he was in trouble here with over a circuit to go. He has been a big money earner over the years and no doubt Aintree next April is again in his trainer's mind.
Take The Stand(IRE), happier on better ground, did not run as well as Wetherby and his chance had gone out of the window when he hit two out.
Ollie Magern, who lacks the size and scope of most of these, did not have things his own way in front this time and, having seemingly lost all interest turning in, in the end completed in his own *time. The sticky ground was not in his favour but that could hardly have been the full story. Official explanation: trainer had no explanation for the poor form shown (op 10-3)*

2338 CASINO 36 CLASSIC NERAK HURDLE (A LIMITED H'CAP) (7 hdls 1 omitted) 2m
2:50 (2:52) (Class 2) 4-Y-0 **£16,895** (£5,244; £2,823)

Form RPR

1-1 **1** **Admiral (IRE)**[42] 1677 4-11-10 **145** .... TJMurphy 148+
(R C Guest) *led: qcknd 3 out: hdd 1f out: crowded and rallied to ld last strides* **10/3**[3]

221- **2** *shd* **Faasel (IRE)**[226] 4749 4-11-9 **144** .... ADobbin 147+
(N G Richards) *hld up in tch: effrt 3 out: wnt 2nd last: led and edgd lft 1f out: hdd nr fin* **5/4**[1]

111- **3** *8* **Penzance**[246] 4433 4-11-10 **145** .... RThornton 142+
(A King) *trckd ldrs: wnt 2nd 4th: hit 3 out: rdn between last 2: wknd run-in* **7/4**[2]

P230 **D** 9 **Openide**[25] 1872 4-9-11 **125** oh10 (b[1]) MrMWall(7) 110
(B W Duke) *chsd wnr to 4th: sn rdn: outpcd and lft bhd fr 3 out: fin 4th: disq* **25/1**

3m 54.7s (-4.40) **Going Correction** -0.20s/f (Good) **4** Ran SP% **107.7**
Speed ratings: **103,102,98,94** CSF £8.07 TOTE £4.20; EX 7.50.
Owner Willie McKay **Bred** R Lee **Trained** Brancepeth, Co Durham
■ Stewards' Enquiry : Mr M Wall 13-day ban: taking the wrong course (10 days) and failing to pull up (three days) (Nov 30, Dec 4,7-8,10,13,15,18, Jan 2,10,12,18)

FOCUS
A tactical race and on the day it seemed to be lost by Faasel, rather than won by Admiral. The first three all ran close to their marks. Last flight in back straight omitted.

NOTEBOOK
Admiral(IRE), happy to be gifted the lead, set sail for home and really flew the second last. After the runner-up left him very short of room on the run-in, he put his head in front where it matters most. His trainer has bags of confidence in him, but in the shorter term he may struggle for winning opportunities. *(op 4-1)*
Faasel(IRE), beaten a head by Penzance in the Triumph, had the visor left off. He really took the eye in the paddock, but after going a neck up he seemed to hang fire and was just edged out. His trainer is unlikely to waste any time before refitting the headgear. *(op 11-10)*
Penzance looks to have done himself well during the break. He came under pressure between the last two and was leg weary on the run-in. Although he had beaten the first two in the Trioumh Hurdle, they had both shown improved form afterwards. Like the other juveniles, he has an awful lot to find to trouble Hardy Eustace and company next March. *(tchd 15-8 in a place)*
Openide, out of his depth and 10lb out of the handicap, wore blinkers for the first time. He crashed through a protruding doll after three out, his rider failing to look where he was going, and as a resut he forfeited fourth place prize money. *(op 33-1)*

2339 EDWARD HANMER MEMORIAL H'CAP CHASE (10 fncs 2 omitted) 2m
3:25 (3:26) (Class 3) (0-130,130) 5-Y-0+ **£13,363** (£3,923; £1,961; £979)

Form / RPR

5P2- **1** **Island Faith (IRE)**[212] 4944 8-11-6 **124** ADobbin 140+
(J Howard Johnson) *hld up in tch: hdwy to chse 1st two 3 out: styd on to ld last: hrd rdn and forged clr: eased nr fin* **15/2**[3]

06-1 **2** *7* **Bannow Strand (IRE)**[6] 2210 5-10-6 **110** 7ex TJMurphy 120+
(M C Pipe) *trckd ldrs: upsides 7th: led 3 out to last: no ex* **4/7**[1]

02-2 **3** *2 1/2* **Bleu Superbe (FR)**[21] 1918 10-11-12 **130** AO'Keeffe 139+
(Miss Venetia Williams) *chsd ldrs: stmbld 7th: sn led: hdd 3 out: nt qckn run-in* **13/2**[2]

5-64 **4** *1 3/4* **Sir Storm (IRE)**[22] 1913 9-10-12 **116** ARoss 119
(G M Moore) *in tch: wnt prom 7th: one pce fr 3 out* **18/1**

-666 **5** *nk* **Kids Inheritance (IRE)**[58] 1529 7-10-7 **111** JimCrowley 113
(J M Jefferson) *hld up in last but in tch: effrt 3 out: kpt on: nvr rchd ldrs* **33/1**

4P-2 **6** *11* **New Bird (GER)**[42] 1673 10-10-6 **110** RThornton 104+
(Ian Williams) *chsd ldrs: rdn 7th: lost pl appr 3 out* **20/1**

112B **7** *8* **Tribal Dispute**[22] 1913 8-11-9 **127** RGarritty 121+
(T D Easterby) *in tch: 4th: prom and clsng whn blnd 3 out: sn btn* **12/1**

-P42 **8** *10* **Jericho III (FR)**[7] 2183 8-10-8 **117** (be) PMerrigan(5) 90
(R C Guest) *led tl after 7th: hung lft and sn lost pl* **20/1**

4m 1.40s (-5.60) **Going Correction** -0.475s/f (Good) **8** Ran SP% **114.2**
Speed ratings: **95,91,90,89,89 83,79,74** CSF £12.72 CT £30.50 TOTE £8.10: £1.80, £1.10, £1.60; EX 15.70.
Owner K Lee **Bred** M J Cassidy **Trained** Billy Row, Co Durham
■ A new-look Edward Hanmer Chase, the old version over three miles having been replaced by the Betfair Lancashire Chase.

FOCUS
A modest time for the class, but solid handicap form nevertheless.

NOTEBOOK
Island Faith(IRE) has won three times first time out. He had to dig deep to get the better of the favourite, but was able to ease off in the end. This was a career best effort but whether he can build on it remains to be seen. *(op 8-1)*
Bannow Strand(IRE), a very big horse, looked very well in under his penalty, but he still looks on the weak side and this may well have come too soon after Cheltenham. He travelled strongly, but in the end did not see it out anywhere near as well as the winner. He is likely to be off a stiffer mark *when he has been reassessed for Cheltenham, but this defeat will not hurt in that respect. (op 1-2 tchd 4-6)*
Bleu Superbe(FR), who hasn't won for over two years, keeps running well but as a result receives little relief. *(op 7-1)*
Sir Storm(IRE) ran better without ever really threatening. *(op 16-1 tchd 14-1)*
Kids Inheritance(IRE) is still 1lb higher than his last win and never got competitive.

2340 BERT STAFFORD MEMORIAL STANDARD OPEN NATIONAL HUNT FLAT RACE 2m
3:55 (3:55) (Class 6) 4-6-Y-0 **£1,932** (£563; £281)

Form / RPR

1 **Albertas Run (IRE)** 4-11-4 NFehily 103
(Jonjo O'Neill) *in tch: hdwy to ld over 2f out: hrd rdn and styd on: hld on wl* **5/1**[3]

2 *1* **Marshalls Run (IRE)** 5-11-4 RThornton 102
(A King) *stdd s: hdwy 6f out: sn trcking ldrs: upsides over 1f out: no ex ins last* **4/1**[2]

3 *3/4* **Bedlam Boy (IRE)** 4-11-4 ADobbin 101
(N G Richards) *in tch: hdwy to chal 3f out: nt qckn ins last* **7/1**

5 **4** *1 1/4* **Nevertika (FR)**[30] 1799 4-11-1 KJMercer(3) 100
(Mrs K Walton) *in rr: hdwy 3f out: kpt on wl fnl f* **25/1**

5 *3* **Le Briar Soul (IRE)** 5-10-11 MrJJDoyle(7) 98+
(V R A Dartnall) *mid-div: hdwy to chse ldrs 3f out: wknd appr fnl f* **5/1**[3]

5- **6** *3/4* **Major Oak (IRE)**[252] 4323 4-11-4 FKeniry 96
(G M Moore) *chsd ldrs: rdn and lost pl over 5f out: styd on wl fnl 2f* **33/1**

/0-1 **7** *5* **Supreme's Legacy (IRE)**[7] 2192 6-11-11 JimCrowley 98
(K G Reveley) *w ldrs: led after 6f tl 5f out: wknd over 1f out* **5/2**[1]

8 *3/4* **Prince Ickarus (IRE)** 5-10-8 ARAdams(10) 91
(Mrs S J Smith) *w ldrs: led 5f out tl over 2f out: sn wknd* **40/1**

9 *shd* **Stormy Bay (IRE)** 4-10-8 JPFlavin(10) 90
(R C Guest) *sn in rr: styd on fnl 3f: nvr nr ldrs* **100/1**

10 *3* **Sparkling Taff** 6-11-4 PWhelan 87
(Mrs S J Smith) *trckd ldrs: stmbld bnd over 3f out: lost pl over 1f out* **25/1**

6R- **11** *5* **Ring The Boss (IRE)**[242] 4513 4-11-4 RMcGrath 82
(K G Reveley) *hld up in rr: hdwy 6f out: sn chsng ldrs: lost pl 2f out* **16/1**

12 *6* **Scarlet Cloak (USA)** 4-10-13 DFlavin(5) 76
(Mrs L B Normile) *in rr: hdwy 6f out: prom 3f out: wknd 2f out* **50/1**

B0 **13** *19* **Desperate Dex (IRE)**[30] 1799 5-11-4 DVerco 57
(G J Smith) *chsd ldrs: lost pl over 5f out: t.o 3f out* **100/1**

0- **14** *18* **Dusky Dawn (IRE)**[336] 2886 4-11-1 FKing(3) 39
(J M Jefferson) *mid-div: lost pl 5f out: t.o 2f out* **50/1**

P- **15** *21* **Luscat (IRE)**[308] 3374 5-10-11 TJDreaper(7) 18
(A Crook) *stdd s: a in rr: bhd fnl 6f: t.o 4f out* **100/1**

3- **16** *24* **Midnight Star**[243] 4499 4-11-1 ACCoyle(3) —
(M Mullineaux) *led 6f: lost pl 7f: hoplessly t.o 4f out* **66/1**

4m 2.40s (6.00) **Going Correction** -0.20s/f (Good)
WFA 4 from 5yo+ 12lb **16** Ran SP% **121.7**
Speed ratings: **69,68,68,67,66 65,63,62,62,61 58,55,46,37,26 14** CSF £23.76 TOTE £6.80: £2.30, £1.80, £2.20; EX 15.70 Place 6 £699.92, Place 5 £176.26.
Owner Trevor Hemmings **Bred** Oliver And Salome Brennan **Trained** Cheltenham, Gloucs

FOCUS
No gallop to the halfway mark, resulting in a pedestrian winning time, even for a bumper. There were some nice big types in the paddock and the first three should go on from here, but overall the form is slightly dubious.

NOTEBOOK
Albertas Run(IRE), who stands over plenty of ground, is bred to stay all day. His stamina was decisive in the end. *(op 10-1)*
Marshalls Run(IRE), a very big boy, cost 50,000euros. He came there travelling strongly but in the end just missed out. The outing and the experience should not be lost on him. *(op 9-2)*
Bedlam Boy(IRE), from the family of Cab On Target, cost 38,000euros. He was just found wanting inside the last furlong, but he has plenty of size and scope and should improve enough to find an opening. *(op 12-1 tchd 13-2)*
Nevertika(FR) improved on his debut run and stamina looks his strong suit.
Le Briar Soul(IRE), a very tall type, was bang in contention until tiring coming to the final furlong. He looks as though he may need more time yet. *(op 9-2 tchd 11-2 and 4-1 in places)*
Major Oak(IRE), who made his debut in March, stayed on after getting left behind and he may need a trip over timber. *(op 25-1)*
Supreme's Legacy(IRE) went on and stepped up the pace but was not up to defying his penalty. *(op 15-8 tchd 11-4)*

T/Jkpt: Not won. T/Plt: £504.10 to a £1 stake. Pool: £72,407.45. 104.85 winning tickets. T/Qpdt: £73.40 to a £1 stake. Pool: £3,959.10. 39.90 winning tickets. WG

2099 HUNTINGDON (R-H)
Saturday, November 19

OFFICIAL GOING: Good (good to firm in places on hurdle course)
The jockeys described the going as dead despite the official description.
Wind: Nil Weather: Sunny

2341 TOTEPLACEPOT H'CAP HURDLE (12 hdls) 3m 2f
12:25 (12:26) (Class 4) (0-105,103)
4-Y-0+ **£4,798** (£1,408; £704; £351)

Form / RPR

0F-0 **1** **In The Hat (IRE)**[29] 1816 9-10-5 **82** JMogford 82
(J R Jenkins) *hld up: rdn and hdwy 3 out: wnt 2nd and j.rt 2 out: led flat: styd on* **16/1**

-032 **2** *1 1/4* **Prayerful**[22] 1906 6-10-10 **90** ONelmes(3) 90+
(J G M O'Shea) *hld up: hdwy 9th: led appr 2 out: rdn whn hit last: hdd flat: nt qckn* **9/2**[2]

/2-4 **3** *5* **Albert House (IRE)**[27] 1854 7-11-11 **102** JPMcNamara 97+
(R H Alner) *chsd ldrs: hit 7th: wnt 2nd appr 9th: led appr 3 out tl appr 2 out: no ex flat* **15/2**

34-5 **4** *1* **Mrs Pickles**[19] 1949 10-10-5 **89** LNewnes(7) 82
(M D I Usher) *chsd ldrs: j. slowly 3rd: one pce fr 3 out* **16/1**

465- **5** *13* **Porthilly Bay**[213] 4929 5-10-13 **90** RJohnson 73+
(H D Daly) *hld up: hit 6th: hdwy 9th: sn rdn: wknd after 3 out* **5/1**[3]

00-P **6** *1* **Colmcille (IRE)**[24] 1884 5-10-11 **91** (b) LVickers(3) 70
(C C Bealby) *w ldr: led appr 6th tl appr 3 out: wknd appr 2 out* **25/1**

PUP6 **7** *nk* **Jack Weighell**[177] 523 6-10-0 **77** oh2 GLee 56
(J M Jefferson) *hld up in mid-div: bhd 6th: short-lived effrt appr 3 out* **14/1**

40F- **8** *2 1/2* **Emphatic (IRE)**[243] 4494 10-11-7 **103** (b) StephenJCraine(5) 79
(J G Portman) *led tl appr 6th: rdn 9th: wknd appr 3 out* **18/1**

46-1 **9** *9* **Southerncrosspatch**[44] 1655 14-10-3 **80** BHitchcott 47
(Mrs Barbara Waring) *a bhd* **12/1**

P **Peter Elkra (IRE)**[6] 2221 7-9-11 **81** (t) DFFlannery(7) —
(T Hogan, Ire) *iron broke sn after s: p.u after 2nd* **9/1**

2033 **P** **End Of An Error**[24] 1884 6-10-13 **90** JMMaguire —
(A W Carroll) *a bhd: rdn 8th: t.o whn p.u bef 2 out: lame* **4/1**[1]

6m 30.9s (8.50) **Going Correction** +0.225s/f (Yiel) **11** Ran SP% **111.8**
Speed ratings: **95,94,93,92,88 88,88,87,84,— —** CSF £83.84 CT £587.21 TOTE £21.90: £6.20, £2.00, £2.20; EX 126.90.
Owner N Trevithick **Bred** Mrs Valerie Dalgetty **Trained** Royston, Herts

FOCUS
A weak staying handicap hurdle, rated through the second and third. In The Hat did not need to run to the level of his old Irish form to win.

NOTEBOOK
In The Hat(IRE), who won a three mile hurdle at Listowel way back in April 2002, was not seen for two and a half years prior to reappearing over here in January. He looked much more at home back over this sort of trip and appears to have rediscovered some form. *(op 20-1)*
Prayerful confirmed how well she stays but could not quite overcome a 3lb rise for finishing second at Uttoxeter. *(op 5-1)*
Albert House(IRE) was all the better for his recent comeback run following a year off after he had twisted a fetlock on his chasing debut. He found his big weight anchoring him from the final flight.
Mrs Pickles ran well for one who loves the mud, but whether she will be effective over this sort of distance in those conditions remains to be seen. *(op 14-1)*
Porthilly Bay still has his stamina to prove over this sort of trip.
Jack Weighell *Official explanation: jockey said gelding had a breathing problem*
End Of An Error, whose rider was found to have ridden an ill-judged race in an ameteurs' handicap *on her previous start, ran no sort of race this time and was later reported to be lame.Official explanation: vet said mare pulled up lame (op 7-2)*

2342 TOTESPORT 0800 221 221 H'CAP CHASE (16 fncs) 2m 4f 110y
12:55 (12:56) (Class 3) (0-115,111)
5-Y-0+ **£5,569** (£1,634; £817; £408)

Form / RPR

15-3 **1** **Undeniable**[14] 2037 7-11-12 **111** DElsworth 128+
(Mrs S J Smith) *chsd ldr to 10th: rdn appr 2 out: led sn after last: r.o* **9/4**[1]

-PF3 **2** *1/2* **Free Gift**[17] 1989 7-11-2 **108** DJacob(7) 123
(R H Alner) *led: rdn appr 2 out: hdd sn after last: r.o* **5/2**[2]

22-U **3** *16* **Brown Teddy**[192] 305 8-11-9 **108** GLee 108+
(R Ford) *hld up: hit 6th: hdwy 8th: wnt 2nd 10th: ev ch 2 out: sn rdn: wknd qckly last* **11/4**[3]

40-P **4** *20* **Three Days Reign (IRE)**[35] 1744 11-11-4 **103** LAspell 82
(P D Cundell) *a bhd: lost tch fr 12th* **11/2**

3-P6 **5** *17* **Game On (IRE)**[27] 1860 9-11-3 **109** TMessenger(7) 71
(B N Pollock) *nt jump wl: bhd fr 11th: t.o* **20/1**

5m 5.60s (-0.50) **Going Correction** +0.225s/f (Yiel) **5** Ran SP% **106.2**
Speed ratings: **109,108,102,95,88** CSF £7.83 TOTE £2.60: £1.70, £1.70; EX 7.70.

The Form Book, Raceform Ltd, Compton, RG20 6NL

Owner Keith Nicholson **Bred** Ahmed Al Shafar **Trained** High Eldwick, W Yorks

FOCUS

This was quite competitive despite the small field and teh form has been viewed positively. The first two both appeared to improve by around 10lb.

NOTEBOOK

Undeniable lived up to his name and confirmed just how versatile he is with regard to distance. *(tchd 2-1 in places)*

Free Gift does like to make the running and lost nothing in defeat on this drop back from three miles. *(op 9-4)*

Brown Teddy jumped well enough on this occasion. He may have blown up jumping the final fence on his first start since May but this trip is probably as far as he wants to go. *(op 3-1)*

Three Days Reign(IRE) disappointed again and never looked likely to repeat last year's win in this event off a pound higher mark. *(tchd 7-1)*

2343 TOTEEXACTA NOVICES' HURDLE (10 hdls) 2m 4f 110y

1:25 (1:25) (Class 3) 4-Y-0+ **£5,243** (£1,539; £769; £384)

Form				RPR
125-	1		**Be Be King (IRE)**[245] 4463 6-10-12 RWalsh (P F Nicholls) *a.p: chall whn hit 2 out: led last: drvn out* **8/11**[1]	111+
60-2	2	2 ½	**Wee Robbie**[29] 1818 5-10-12 LAspell (N J Gifford) *hld up: hdwy after 3rd: led 6th tl last: nt qckn* **5/2**[2]	105+
2-44	3	7	**Delightful Cliche**[23] 1895 4-10-12 PMoloney (Mrs P Sly) *hld up: hdwy 6th: rdn appr 2 out: wknd appr last* **12/1**[3]	98
4	4	7	**Blue Hills**[13] 2070 4-10-12 (p) JPMcNamara (P W Hiatt) *led to 6th: ev ch 3 out: sn rdn: wknd 2 out* **25/1**	94+
	5	16	**Alexander Sapphire (IRE)**[12] 4-10-2 ONelmes[(3)] (N B King) *nt fluent: nvr nr ldrs* **50/1**	68
0	6	14	**Novack Du Beury (FR)**[21] 1927 4-10-5 PJMcDonald[(7)] (Ferdy Murphy) *a bhd* **66/1**	61
P0	7	11	**Tashkandi (IRE)**[25] 1875 5-10-7 TGreenway[(5)] (P Bowen) *prom: nt fluent 1st and 2nd: rdn and wknd after 7th* **16/1**	50
/0-P	8	15	**Mostakbel (USA)**[22] 1908 6-10-5 (b[1]) LNewnes[(7)] (M D I Usher) *sn prom: rdn and wknd after 7th* **50/1**	35
0PF/	P		**Breuddwyd Lyn**[979] 4191 7-10-7 LStephens[(5)] (Mrs D A Hamer) *plld hrd in rr: lost tch fr 6th: t.o whn p.u bef 2 out* **100/1**	—
000-	P		**Lady Radmore**[223] 4795 6-9-12 SCrawford[(7)] (J G M O'Shea) *mid-div: nt jump wl: reluctant 3rd: bhd fr 6th: t.o whn p.u bef 3 out* **100/1**	—

5m 1.20s (5.90) **Going Correction** +0.225s/f (Yiel) **10** Ran SP% **111.3**

Speed ratings: **97,96,93,90,84 79,75,69,—,—** CSF £2.42 TOTE £1.80: £1.10, £1.20, £1.80; EX 2.10.

Owner C G Roach **Bred** P E Atkinson **Trained** Ditcheat, Somerset

FOCUS

They went no pace in this moderate affair in which the forecast second favourite was one of several withdrawals. The race has been rated through the third, and the first two have yet to match their bumper form.

NOTEBOOK

Be Be King(IRE), whose future is likely to lie over fences, is a bit hit and miss at his hurdles at the moment and flattened the second last. He was a long way off his bumper level here and needed keeping right up to his work, but he is open to plenty of improvement still and is expected to do better on a a stiffer more galloping course. *(tchd 4-5)*

Wee Robbie ◆ seems to be going the right way and a similar event is within his compass. *(op 11-4)*

Delightful Cliche settled better this time and should not have been inconvenienced by the extra half a mile. *(op 10-1)*

Blue Hills was fitted with the cheekpieces he had worn once on the Flat. He duly improved on his debut effort at Hereford, despite failing to convince as a stayer *(op 16-1)*

Mostakbel(USA) *Official explanation: jockey said gelding had a breathing problem (op 33-1)*

2344 TOTESPORT.COM NOVICES' CHASE (16 fncs) 2m 4f 110y

1:55 (1:55) (Class 3) 4-Y-0+ **£7,498** (£2,201; £1,100; £549)

Form				RPR
124-	1		**Billyvoddan (IRE)**[224] 4770 6-11-4 RJohnson (H D Daly) *chsd ldrs: wnt 2nd 11th: rdn to ld last: drvn out* **11/4**[1]	135+
31P-	2	¾	**Kasthari (IRE)**[72] 4397 6-11-4 GLee (J Howard Johnson) *j.lft: led 3rd: mstke 11th (water): rdn and hdd last: nt qckn* **7/1**[3]	135+
0-44	3	dist	**Goblin**[19] 1958 4-10-5 PMoloney (D E Cantillon) *hld up and bhd: hmpd 4th: sme hdwy 11th: tk poor 3rd fr 4 out* **33/1**	94
103-	4	9	**Murphy's Quest**[252] 4334 9-11-4 119 TScudamore (Lady Herries) *mstke 9th: a bhd* **18/1**	97
6/	5	dist	**Livret Bleu (FR)**[675] 3328 6-10-13 StephenJCraine[(5)] (A E Jessop) *t.k.h: hit 12th: a bhd: t.o* **250/1**	—
40-3	6	shd	**Bonnet's Pieces**[27] 1850 6-10-8 GCarenza[(3)] (Mrs P Sly) *prom: chsd ldr 4th: hit 7th: wkng whn mstke 4 out: t.o* **100/1**	—
124-	F		**Go For Bust**[220] 4825 6-11-4 ATinkler (N J Henderson) *fell 4th* **14/1**	—
5/P6	B		**Kopeck (IRE)**[14] 2044 7-11-4 LAspell (Mrs L Wadham) *bhd tl b.d 7th* **28/1**	—
1-12	F		**Napolitain (FR)**[14] 2052 4-10-11 RWalsh (P F Nicholls) *hld up in tch: fell 5th* **11/4**[1]	—
/4-1	F		**Splash Out Again**[94] 1232 7-11-10 BJCrowley (P Bowen) *led tl hit 3rd: 3rd whn fell 5th* **50/1**	—
3F-2	F		**Rebel Rhythm**[22] 1911 6-11-4 DElsworth (Mrs S J Smith) *prom tl nt fluent and lost pl 2nd (water): towards rr whn fell 7th* **3/1**[2]	—

5m 4.60s (-1.50) **Going Correction** +0.225s/f (Yiel)

WFA 4 from 6yo+ 13lb **11** Ran SP% **112.5**

Speed ratings: **111,110,—,—,— —,—,—,—,— —** CSF £20.97 TOTE £3.90: £1.50, £2.50, £4.60; EX 35.60.

Owner Trevor Hemmings **Bred** D P O'Brien **Trained** Stanton Lacy, Shropshire

FOCUS

There were some potentially decent novice chasers in the line up, but the fences took their toll and the field was much reduced with a circuit still to go. Nevertheless, the two principals both look promising young chasers.

NOTEBOOK

Billyvoddan(IRE) ◆, progressive over hurdles at this trip, made a successful switch to fences despite the track being on the sharp side for him and the going too dead. He looked held going to the penultimate fence but came through to take advantage of the runner-up jumping left and looks a useful recruit to the ranks of novice chasers. *(op 3-1 tchd 10-3 in places)*

Kasthari(IRE) ◆, who dead-heated for last year's Doncaster Cup, was making his first appearance since finishing third in the same event in September. He made a highly satisfactory chasing debut and appeared to enjoy hiself in the lead, but he but compromised his chance by continually jumping out to the left. It will be interesting to see if he races the other way next time, for the ability is obviously there. *(op 15-2)*

Goblin faced a stiff task and was allowed to come home in his own time once the first two were clear. He will do better with his sights lowered back at the minimum distance.

Bonnet's Pieces *Official explanation: vet said mare bled from the nose*

2345 TOTEPOOL INTRODUCTORY JUVENILE NOVICES' HURDLE (8 hdls) 2m 110y

2:30 (2:30) (Class 2) 3-Y-0 **£13,480** (£3,957; £1,978; £988)

Form				RPR
	1		**Kalmini (USA)**[142] 3-10-7 JGoldstein (Miss Sheena West) *a.p: rdn to ld appr 2 out: qcknd and clr flat: eased cl home* **28/1**	94+
2	2	6	**Kanpai (IRE)**[14] 2045 3-11-0 RWalsh (J G M O'Shea) *a.p: rdn whn sltly hmpd 2 out: kpt on flat: no ch w wnr* **7/1**[3]	97+
1	3	1 ½	**Pace Shot (IRE)**[28] 1821 3-11-5 JEMoore (G L Moore) *plld hrd: sddle sn slipped: ld 2nd to 5th: ev ch 2 out: mstke last: one pce* **6/4**[1]	103+
	4	nk	**Desert Secrets (IRE)**[126] 3-10-7 GLee (J G Portman) *led to 2nd: remained prom: led 5th tl appr 2 out: one pce* **18/1**	85
1	5	¾	**Reaching Out (IRE)**[11] 2101 3-11-5 MFoley (N J Henderson) *hld up: blnd 3rd: hdwy after 3 out: kpt on same pce fr 2 out* **7/4**[2]	99+
	6	13	**Satin Rose**[60] 3-10-7 GCarenza (K J Burke) *hld up: hdwy 5th: wknd 3 out* **66/1**	71
	7	1 ¼	**Misters Sister**[164] 3-10-7 MBradburne (C A Dwyer) *hld up: nt fluent 4th: hdwy after 5th: wknd after 3 out* **100/1**	70
	8	1	**Brendan's Surprise**[14] 3-11-0 RCummings (K J Burke) *a bhd* **80/1**	76
	9	4	**Trappeto (IRE)**[32] 3-11-0 LAspell (C Smith) *t.k.h: hit 5th: a bhd* **50/1**	72
	F		**Leo's Lucky Star (USA)**[56] 3-11-0 TSiddall (R S Brookhouse) *t.k.h: hdwy after 5th: ev ch whn fell 2 out* **10/1**	97+

4m 1.80s (6.10) **Going Correction** +0.225s/f (Yiel) **10** Ran SP% **112.3**

Speed ratings: **94,91,90,90,89 83,83,82,80,—** CSF £199.48 TOTE £36.60: £4.20, £1.50, £1.10; EX 152.40.

Owner Gerald West **Bred** Darley **Trained** Lewes, E Sussex

FOCUS

A modest pace meant that this interesting juvenile event was still wide open turning for home. It is difficult to work up much enthusiasm for the form, which has been assessed through the second and fifth.

NOTEBOOK

Kalmini(USA) ◆, a seven-furlong two-year-old winner for Mick Channon, stayed a mile and a quarter. Giving an instant return on her 14,000 gns purchase price, there was a lot to like about this performance. Whether she lives up to her long-term target of the Triumph Hurdle remains to be seen but she could be useful on this evidence. *(tchd 25-1 and 33-1)*

Kanpai(IRE) ◆ found this a totally different kettle of fish to Sandown in heavy ground. He needs a *stiffer test of stamina and looks sure to turn out to be better over hurdles than he was on the Flat. (op 8-1)*

Pace Shot(IRE) refused to accept restraint and his saddle soon slipped as a consequence. Given that he also missed out at the last, this was not a bad effort under a penalty. *(op 5-4)*

Desert Secrets(IRE), no great shakes on the level for John Hills, made a satisfactory start to her hurdling career. *(tchd 16-1 and 20-1)*

Reaching Out(IRE) could never quite make his presence felt after he was fortunate to survive a bad error at the third. *(op 2-1 tchd 85-40 in places)*

Leo's Lucky Star(USA) lost his way badly on the Flat after a respectable start to the year. Despite racing keenly, he was bang in contention and had yet to be asked a question when coming down two out. *(tchd 11-1)*

2346 TOTESPORT PETERBOROUGH CHASE GRADE 2 (16 fncs) 2m 4f 110y

3:00 (3:00) (Class 1) 5-Y-0+

£42,194 (£15,828; £7,925; £3,951; £1,983; £991)

Form				RPR
-221	1		**Impek (FR)**[27] 1846 9-11-6 145 APMcCoy (Miss H C Knight) *led tl after 2nd: remained prom: led 4 out: clr appr last: easily* **5/1**[3]	166+
3-12	2	5	**Monkerhostin (FR)**[7] 2177 8-11-6 154 RJohnson (P J Hobbs) *hld up and bhd: hdwy on ins 12th: rdn appr 2 out: one pce* **5/2**[1]	160+
214-	3	3 ½	**Thisthatandtother (IRE)**[226] 4748 9-11-10 159 RWalsh (P F Nicholls) *hld up: rdn and hdwy after 3 out: kpt on flat* **3/1**[2]	158
543-	4	3 ½	**Hand Inn Hand**[225] 4766 9-11-0 154 MBradburne (H D Daly) *led after 2nd to 4 out: rdn appr 2 out: wknd flat* **8/1**	145+
4F-6	5	¾	**Mister McGoldrick**[18] 1970 8-11-10 155 DElsworth (Mrs S J Smith) *hld up in mid-div: hdwy 8th: no real prog fr 2 out* **25/1**	153
1P2/	6	24	**Iris Royal (FR)**[611] 4427 9-11-0 142 MFoley (N J Henderson) *hld up and bhd: short-lived effrt 3 out* **16/1**	119
25-5	7	3	**Le Roi Miguel (FR)**[27] 1846 7-11-10 156 PJBrennan (P F Nicholls) *hld up in mid-div: nt fluent 8th: mstke 9th: bhd fr 4 out* **14/1**	129+
60-0	8	5	**Colca Canyon (IRE)**[34] 1766 8-11-6 (p) PACarberry (David P Myerscough, Ire) *prom: mstkes at 3rd and 7th: wknd 4 out* **66/1**	117
0P-0	P		**Hot Shots (FR)**[18] 1970 10-11-0 138 PMoloney (M Pitman) *mstkes: a in rr: t.o whn p.u bef 2 out* **100/1**	—
4-U0	P		**Seebald (GER)**[8] 2163 10-11-0 150 (b[1]) TScudamore (M C Pipe) *prom tl wknd 4 out: bhd whn p.u bef last* **40/1**	—
F21-	P		**El Vaquero (IRE)**[287] 3700 7-11-5 149 GLee (J Howard Johnson) *hld up: hdwy 8th: rdn and wknd after 3 out: p.u bef 2 out* **6/1**	—

5m 0.60s (-5.50) **Going Correction** +0.225s/f (Yiel) **11** Ran SP% **117.0**

Speed ratings: **119,117,115,114,114 105,103,101,—,— —** CSF £18.24 TOTE £7.20: £2.00, £1.50, £1.70; EX 16.70 Trifecta £132.80 Pool: £22,753.77 - 121.60 winning units..

Owner Jim Lewis **Bred** Marc Trinquet & Bernard Trinquet **Trained** West Lockinge, Oxon

■ A sixth win in eight runnings for Henrietta Knight and Jim Lewis, following wins with Edredon Bleu (four) and Best Mate.

FOCUS

An impressive performance from Impek against what looked a strong line-up He has provisionally been assessed as having shown career best form, although there are reservations.

NOTEBOOK

Impek(FR) has really got his act together again, having apparently overcome his nervous problem. The manner of his victory could not be faulted and this looks a new personal best, although it is conceivable that the runner-up had the edge taken off him by Cheltenham and that the third and fourth needed the race. He has been given what his trainer described as a 'sly entry' for the King George and may well take his chance. *(op 8-1)*

Monkerhostin(FR) proved no match for the winner, but this was his third run in top-class company in less than three weeks and he was entitled to have had the edge taken off him by his earlier exertions. *(op 2-1)*

Thisthatandtother(IRE) was not disgraced on this reappearance and may well take his chance in the King George. He shaped as if well worth trying over further again, but whether he stays three miles up the hill at Sandown remains to be seen. *(op 11-4)*
Hand Inn Hand was 12lb better off than when just over six lengths behind Thisthatandtother at Cheltenham in March. He went well for a long way but ultimately shaped as if he needed this.
Mister McGoldrick has yet to score going right-handed. *(op 28-1)*
Iris Royal(FR) had been off the track since his second in the 2004 Cathcart and was beaten quickly starting the home turn. *(op 20-1)*
Le Roi Miguel(FR) won the corresponding race in 2004 but did not jump well enough this tme and was in trouble down the far side. *(op 16-1)*
El Vaquero(IRE) was making his debut for new connections. He should improve for the race.
Official explanation: jockey said gelding lost its action (tchd 7-1)

2347 TOTESCOOP6 H'CAP HURDLE (10 hdls) 2m 4f 110y
3:30 (3:32) (Class 3) (0-120,118) 4-Y-O+**£13,812** (£4,054; £2,027; £1,012)

Form				RPR
6-42	**1**		**All Star (GER)**[105] [420] 5-11-7 **118** SCurling(5) (N J Henderson) *hld up gng wl in mid-div: hdwy 6th: led appr 2 out: sn clr: easily* **5/1**[1]	140+
201	**2**	15	**Sunday City (JPN)**[17] [1991] 4-10-6 **103** TGreenway(5) (P Bowen) *hld up and bhd: hdwy fr 7th: hit 3 out: kpt on same pce fr 2 out* **6/1**[2]	104+
3430	**3**	½	**Ingres**[6] [2213] 5-10-4 **103** CMStudd(7) (B G Powell) *hld up towards rr whn carried lft 6th: rdn and hdwy after 3 out: r.o flat* **16/1**	102
1-60	**4**	hd	**Prince Of Persia**[179] [488] 5-11-7 **113** (p) JPMcNamara (R S Brookhouse) *hld up and bhd: hdwy 7th: hit 3 out: 2nd and btn whn blnd last* **50/1**	114+
1210	**5**	hd	**Smart Boy Prince (IRE)**[24] [1880] 4-11-4 **110** LAspell (C Smith) *a.p: one pce fr 2 out* **33/1**	110+
214	**6**	½	**Dubai Ace (USA)**[143] [861] 4-11-4 **110** JGoldstein (Miss Sheena West) *hld up in tch: ev ch 3 out: sn rdn: one pce fr 2 out* **33/1**	108
2-P0	**7**	nk	**Son Of Greek Myth (USA)**[6] [2218] 4-10-11 **103** (b) RWalsh (G L Moore) *hld up in mid-div: hdwy fr 2 out: nvr nrr* **33/1**	101
0F-3	**8**	¾	**Newtown Dancer (IRE)**[8] [2166] 6-10-11 **110** (tp) DFFlannery(7) (T Hogan, Ire) *chsd ldr: led 7th tl after 3 out: no ex fr 2 out* **12/1**	107
0P1-	**9**	1½	**Fortune Island (IRE)**[22] [4235] 6-11-9 **115** (vt) TScudamore (M C Pipe) *hld up: gd hdwy appr 7th: led briefly after 3 out: wknd appr last* **5/1**[1]	111
P422	**10**	¾	**Qualitair Pleasure**[34] [1753] 5-10-6 **98** ADempsey (J Hetherton) *hld up in mid-div: j.lft and rdn 6th: styd on fr 2 out: n.d* **25/1**	93
-005	**11**	12	**Corlande (IRE)**[11] [2110] 5-11-7 **113** DElsworth (Mrs S J Smith) *prom: rdn appr 7th: sn wknd* **20/1**	96
30-2	**12**	4	**Almah (SAF)**[14] [2053] 7-11-11 **117** SThomas (Miss Venetia Williams) *hld up in mid-div: mstke 6th: sn struggling* **9/1**	96
01-P	**13**	1¼	**Barney McAll (IRE)**[99] [117] 5-11-3 **109** (t) RJohnson (R T Phillips) *led to 7th: wknd qckly after 3 out* **25/1**	87
164-	**14**	3	**Dere Lyn**[233] [4671] 7-10-8 **105** LStephens(5) (Mrs D A Hamer) *hld up in tch: wknd 6th* **50/1**	80
13-2	**15**	9	**Assoon**[15] [2017] 6-10-13 **105** JEMoore (G L Moore) *keen early: in tch tl lost pl after 7th* **11/1**	71
213	**16**	6	**Brooklyn Brownie (IRE)**[30] [1796] 6-11-2 **108** GLee (J M Jefferson) *hld up in mid-div: bhd fr 3 out* **7/1**[3]	68
01-4	**17**	1	**Turaath (IRE)**[30] [1796] 9-11-4 **115** StephenJCraine(5) (A J Deakin) *blnd bdly 3rd: sn bhd* **40/1**	74
1231	**18**	23	**Festive Chimes (IRE)**[6] [2218] 4-11-2 **111** 7ex ONelmes(3) (N B King) *a bhd: t.o* **22/1**	47
36-0	**P**		**Aldiruos (IRE)**[25] [1872] 5-11-1 **107** JMMaguire (A W Carroll) *a bhd: t.o whn p.u bef 2 out* **25/1**	—

4m 52.0s (-3.30) **Going Correction** +0.225s/f (Yiel)
WFA 4 from 5yo+ 13lb **19** Ran SP% **127.9**
Speed ratings: **115,109,109,109,108 108,108,108,107,107 102,101,100,99,96 94,93,84,—**
CSF £30.88 CT £466.21 TOTE £5.70: £1.80, £2.40, £2.60, £8.80; EX 53.40 Place 6 £15.97, Place 5 £4.10.
Owner Lynn Wilson, Nick Wilson, Martin Landau **Bred** G Schiergen **Trained** Upper Lambourn, Berks
■ Stewards' Enquiry : D F Flannery two-day ban: used whip with excessive frequency and without giving mare time to respond (Nov 30, Dec 1)

FOCUS
This competitive-looking handicap turned out to be a one-horse race, with All Star rated value for at least 20 lengths and improving by around a stone. The third to the seventh were all close to their marks, and the winning time was decent for the grade.

NOTEBOOK
All Star(GER) ◆ had run well in staying handicaps on the Flat in the summer and appreciated the step up in trip, for he absolutely annihilated this big field under top weight. The Handicapper is likely to take a dim view of this and connections may be well advised to run him under a penalty. *(op 4-1)*
Sunday City(JPN) was not inconvenienced by the extra half-mile. However, all he could do was hold on in a tight finish in the separate race for the runner-up spot. *(op 15-2)*
Ingres looked much more at home back over timber and did his best work in the home straight. Softer ground should help.
Prince Of Persia, like the rest, was completely outclassed by the winner, but a mistake at the last probably cost him second place. *(op 40-1)*
Smart Boy Prince(IRE) likes to dominate but that was never going to be easy in a race like this.
Dubai Ace(USA), without the tongue tie, made a satisfactory reappearance after a five-month absence.
Son Of Greek Myth(USA) ◆ was noted staying on in the later stages to give notice of a possible return to form. He looks worth another try over further.
T/Plt: £23.70 to a £1 stake. Pool: £43,566.45. 1,339.30 winning tickets. T/Qpdt: £5.30 to a £1 stake. Pool: £3,069.20. 425.60 winning tickets. KH

[2322]WINDSOR (R-H)
Saturday, November 19
2348 Meeting Abandoned - frost

2354 - 2363a (Foreign Racing) - See Raceform Interactive

[1993]PUNCHESTOWN (R-H)
Saturday, November 19
OFFICIAL GOING: Hurdle course - soft, chase course - soft to heavy

2364a IRISH FIELD NOVICE CHASE (GRADE 3) 2m 6f
2:45 (2:45) 5-Y-O+ **£17,775** (£5,215; £2,484; £846)

				RPR
	1		**Slim Pickings (IRE)**[19] [1966] 6-11-2 DJCasey (Robert Tyner, Ire) *trckd ldrs in 3rd: slt mstke 6 out: led appr 4 out: slt mstke and rdn 3 out: strly pressed next: kpt on wl u.p fr last* **11/8**[1]	126
	2	hd	**Kerryhead Windfarm (IRE)**[9] [2155] 7-11-2 AndrewJMcNamara (Michael Hourigan, Ire) *trckd ldrs: mstke 5th: impr into 3rd whn mstke 4 out: 2nd and chal 2 out: ev ch last: kpt on u.p* **7/4**[2]	126
	3	13	**Mamouna Gale (IRE)**[6] [2223] 7-11-3 117 JLCullen (E J O'Grady, Ire) *cl up: slow 2nd: led bef 4th: hdd appr 4 out: rallied to chal 2 out: no ex bef last* **4/1**[3]	114
	4	6	**Van Ness (IRE)**[3] [2156] 6-11-2 104 NPMadden (Michael John Phillips, Ire) *led: hdd bef 4th: 2nd whn mstke 10th: rdn and outpcd 4 out: sn no ex* **16/1**	107
	5	4½	**Safe Route (USA)**[9] [2155] 7-10-11 GCotter (W J Austin, Ire) *hld up in tch: dropped to rr 7 out: wknd fr 5 out* **14/1**	97

6m 0.60s **5** Ran SP% **111.0**
CSF £4.41 TOTE £2.70: £1.80, £1.30; DF 10.40.
Owner Doubtful Five Syndicate **Bred** T A O'Donnell **Trained** Kinsale, Co Cork

NOTEBOOK
Slim Pickings(IRE) led four out and just managed to hold on. His jumping wasn't fluent and he appeared to idle in front. As a former pointer he will certainly appreciate further. *(op 5/4 tchd 6/4)*
Kerryhead Windfarm(IRE) has more experience han the winner but wasn't footperfect. He had every chance from two out and would also appreciate further.
Mamouna Gale(IRE) is a handicapper and was struggling after four out. *(op 3/1)*
Van Ness(IRE) was out of his depth.

2365 - 2366a (Foreign Racing) - See Raceform Interactive

[1844]AINTREE (L-H)
Sunday, November 20
OFFICIAL GOING: Good to soft
The meeting was in doubt due to frost until mid-day. The going was described as 'dead and tacky', because of the frost coming out of the ground.
Wind: Nil Weather: Fine but cold

2367 WEATHERBYS BANK JUVENILE NOVICES' HURDLE (9 hdls) 2m 110y
1:05 (1:05) (Class 2) 3-Y-O **£10,146** (£2,978; £1,489; £743)

Form				RPR
U111	**1**		**Fair Along (GER)**[8] [2178] 3-11-6 131 RJohnson (P J Hobbs) *racd keenly: mde all: clr to 5th and again 2 out: nt fluent last: rdn briefly after: eased towards fin* **4/7**[1]	135+
	2	21	**Ortolan Bleu (FR)**[57] 3-10-12 GLee (J Howard Johnson) *chsd clr ldr: clsd 5th: nt fluent 3 out: sn rdn and btn: eased whn no ch run-in* **10/1**	112+
1101	**3**	dist	**Aviation**[22] [1923] 3-11-6 FKeniry (G M Moore) *towards rr: reminders after 3rd: wnt poor 3rd appr 3 out: nvr on terms* **9/1**[3]	86
1	**4**	14	**Flaming Weapon**[20] [1948] 3-11-2 ADobbin (G L Moore) *chsd ldrs tl mstke and wknd 5th* **11/2**[2]	70
21	**5**	19	**Royal Master**[62] [1339] 3-11-2 RThornton (P C Haslam) *hld up: wknd appr 3 out: t.o* **16/1**	51
4P21	**6**	6	**First Fought (IRE)**[14] [2069] 3-11-2 (t) StephenJCraine (D McCain) *a bhd: blnd 1st: n.d whn mstke 3 out: t.o* **20/1**	45

4m 9.30s (4.70) **Going Correction** +0.30s/f (Yiel) **6** Ran SP% **108.8**
Speed ratings: **100,90,—,—,—,—** — CSF £6.61 TOTE £1.60: £1.20, £2.70; EX 7.60.
Owner Alan Peterson **Bred** Gestut Harzburg **Trained** Withycombe, Somerset

FOCUS
Another step up in form from the winner who looks a very useful juvenile. A tricky race to assess, though, with the third to sixth beaten so far.

NOTEBOOK
Fair Along(GER) completed the four-timer in a similar manner to his three previous victories, scoring in impressive style. He is clearly a very smart juvenile and a real Triumph Hurdle candidate even at this stage, although front runners do not have a good record in that event. *(op 1-2)*
Ortolan Bleu(FR) ◆ won over an extended thirteen furlongs on the Flat in the French provinces and his dam was a winning jumper. The only one to get anywhere near the winner on this hurdling debut, having closed to within four lengths at one stage, he was well held in the end but looks certain to win races over hurdles. *(op 11-1 tchd 12-1)*
Aviation, under a penalty for winning a weak listed event at Wetherby, was well below par and was beaten 59 lengths by the winner.
Flaming Weapon was an impressive winner at Plumpton but was found out in this better company and is going to need to jump better. *(op 7-1 tchd 15-2)*
Royal Master, runner-up on the Flat since his hurdles win, closed into a moderate third down the back straight but that was as near as he got. *Official explanation: jockey said gelding made a mistake at third-last and finished very tired (op 14-1)*
First Fought(IRE), who won a moderate event at Hereford, was always trailing after a first-flight blunder in this much better race.

2368 TOTEPOOL GRAND SEFTON H'CAP CHASE (18 fncs) 2m 5f 110y
1:40 (1:42) (Class 3) (0-130,130) 5-Y-O+
£37,578 (£11,100; £5,550; £2,778; £1,386; £696)

Form				RPR
0111	**1**		**Hakim (NZ)**[24] [1894] 11-10-12 **116** PJBrennan (J L Spearing) *mde all: j.w: styd on wl fr 2 out: gamely* **18/1**	130+
35U6	**2**	2½	**Fiori**[17] [2003] 9-10-3 **107** FKeniry (P C Haslam) *chsd ldrs: outpcd 3 out: rallied next: wnt 2nd last: hung lft and no ex last 150yds* **100/1**	118

-352 **3** *4* **Shannon's Pride (IRE)**[21] [1941] 9-10-3 **110**......................... LMcGrath(3) 118+
(R C Guest) *chsd ldrs: wnt 2nd 4 out: kpt on same pce between last 2* **20/1**

506- **4** *5* **Tanterari (IRE)**[220] [4836] 7-10-9 **113**... TJMurphy 121+
(M C Pipe) *hld up in rr: blnd 4th (water): gd hdwy 11th (Foinavon): sn chsng ldrs: swtchd rt elbow: wknd fnl 150yds* **9/1**[1]

P330 **5** *½* **Cassia Heights**[17] [2003] 10-10-2 **106**.......................................(t) ADobbin 108
(S A Brookshaw) *prom: jnd ldrs 13th (Valentine's): sn drvn along: wknd appr last* **11/1**[3]

3P0- **6** *¾* **Wain Mountain**[226] [4764] 9-11-8 **126**.................................... WHutchinson 127
(J A B Old) *in rr: drvn along and hdwy 14th: styd on fr 2 out: nt rch ldrs* **20/1**

50-3 **7** *4* **Better Days (IRE)**[22] [1929] 9-11-8 **126**..................................... DElsworth 124+
(Mrs S J Smith) *chsd ldrs: wknd between last 2* **10/1**[2]

5-P1 **8** *10* **Melford (IRE)**[31] [1795] 7-10-11 **115**.. NFehily 105+
(C J Mann) *in rr: sme hdwy 4 out: nvr a factor* **14/1**

3-14 **9** *1* **Ebony Light (IRE)**[21] [1941] 9-10-10 **119**...................(p) StephenJCraine(5) 115+
(D McCain) *many mstkes: mid-div whn blnd 8th: bhd whn blnd 14th: nvr on terms* **25/1**

14-0 **10** *2½* **Tribal King (IRE)**[15] [2051] 10-10-9 **113**.................................... RThornton 96
(A King) *hld up in rr: bhd whn mstke 12th (Canal Turn): nvr a factor* **14/1**

6P23 **11** *3* **Iverain (FR)**[31] [1798] 9-10-0 **104** oh1... RMcGrath 84
(Sir John Barlow Bt) *bhd: blnd 5th: t.o 3 out* **33/1**

00-5 **12** *3* **Whereareyounow (IRE)**[21] [1941] 8-11-10 **128**....................... CLlewellyn 105
(N A Twiston-Davies) *bhd: j. bdly lft 13th (Valentine's)* **9/1**[1]

43U4 **13** *28* **Tipsy Mouse (IRE)**[10] [2143] 9-9-11 **106**............................(p) PMerrigan(5) 55
(R C Guest) *j. slowly: sn bhd: t.o fr 13th (Valentine's)* **28/1**

504 **14** *17* **Benrajah (IRE)**[17] [2003] 8-10-12 **116**... GLee 48
(M Todhunter) *mid-div: blnd 7th: t.o fr 4 out* **22/1**

2-35 **F** **Cobbet (CZE)**[22] [1918] 9-11-3 **121**... JMMaguire —
(T R George) *rr-div whn fell 9th* **66/1**

P-02 **F** **Soeur Fontenail (FR)**[29] [1825] 8-9-7 **104** oh3........................... KBurke(7) —
(N J Hawke) *w ldrs: fell 5th* **50/1**

-4F0 **F** **Roschal (IRE)**[15] [2051] 7-10-2 **106**... RJohnson —
(P J Hobbs) *bhd whn fell 3rd (Chair)* **22/1**

54-1 **F** **Il'Athou (FR)**[17] [2003] 9-11-10 **128**.. JTizzard —
(S E H Sherwood) *w ldrs: fell 11th (Foinavon)* **11/1**[3]

30-P **U** **Ulusaba**[15] [2037] 9-10-6 **113**..(p) KJMercer(3) —
(Ferdy Murphy) *rr-div whn hmpd and uns rdr 3rd (Chair)* **20/1**

P0-3 **F** **Be My Better Half (IRE)**[15] [2048] 10-11-5 **123**......................... BHarding —
(Jonjo O'Neill) *rr-divsion: hdwy and prom whn fell 10th (Becher's)* **16/1**

5-1 **F** **Rocking Ship (IRE)**[72] [1451] 7-10-8 **112**................................... DNRussell —
(Ms Joanna Morgan, Ire) *chsd ldrs blnd 2nd: wkng and in mid-field whn fell 14th* **33/1**

161- **F** **Almost Broke**[214] [4927] 8-11-12 **130**............................. ChristianWilliams —
(P F Nicholls) *chsd ldrs: mstke 10th (Becher's): fell 13th (Valentine's)* **12/1**

4-23 **F** **Halexy (FR)**[17] [2003] 10-11-10 **128**.. MFoley 133+
(Jonjo O'Neill) *hld up: stdy hdwy 10th (Becher's): disputing 3rd and travelling strly whn fell 2 out* **25/1**

5m 37.2s (-1.30) **Going Correction** +0.125s/f (Yiel) **23** Ran SP% **122.4**
Speed ratings: **107,106,104,102,102 102,100,97,96,96 94,93,83,77,—** —,—,—,—,—,—,— CSF £1190.00 CT £30400.59 TOTE £20.50: £4.50, £28.70, £4.90, £3.30; EX 3238.80 TRIFECTA Not won..

Owner T N Siviter **Bred** Mrs B C Hennessy **Trained** Kinnersley, Worcs

FOCUS

A competitive handicap in which all-the-way winner Hakim improved by the best part of a stone. The runner-up ran to his mark.

NOTEBOOK

Hakim(NZ), who is most progressive, shrugged off a 5lb rise to complete the four-timer. Jumping superbly on what was only his sixth run over fences, he stayed on gamely over this longer trip. There could still be more improvement in him and a return visit for the Topham in April looks on the cards. *(op 16-1 tchd 20-1)*

Fiori, who is rated 18lb lower over fences compared with hurdles, ran a much better race. Rallying *from the second last, he was closing on the winner up the run-in and stayed this longer trip well. (op 66-1)*

Shannon's Pride(IRE), who failed to stay three and a quarter miles last time, put in a good round of jumping and was only caught for second place on the flat. This was a return to something like his best. *(op 22-1)*

Tanterari(IRE) did very well to get into contention after sprawling on landing over the water jump and dropping into last place. Coming under pressure after hitting the second last, he was still in with a chance at the elbow but tired in the final 150 yards. *(op 7-1)*

Cassia Heights ran a solid race over a track he likes, but is still winless since landing the Topham Trophy over course and distance in the spring of last year. *(op 12-1)*

Wain Mountain, who also jumped round here in the Topham last spring, was 4lb lower and minus the tongue tie on this first run since.

Better Days(IRE) again showed an aptitude for these fences but, like in last season's Topham, he did not get home. *(op 8-1)*

Melford(IRE), 8lb higher than at Haydock, ran as if in need of a step up in trip. *(op 16-1)*

Ebony Light(IRE) was fortunate to get round and looks unlikely to make up into another National horse for his trainer.

Whereareyounow(IRE) got round for the third time in four visits to the track but that was the only positive. *(op 11-1)*

Halexy(FR) had gradually eased his way into contention before coming down at the second last. He would have been in the shake-up and, still lightly raced, there should be a race for him before long.

Almost Broke, down on his nose at Becher's, was rather wide at the Canal Turn but was still in contention when falling foul of Valentine's.

2369 WILLIAM HILL/STANLEYBET CHILDREN IN NEED H'CAP HURDLE (11 hdls) 2m 4f

2:15 (2:15) (Class 2) (0-140,136) 4-Y-0+

£16,927 (£5,000; £2,500; £1,251; £624; £313)

Form RPR

054- **1** **Covent Garden**[249] [4397] 7-11-3 **127**.. GLee 136+
(J Howard Johnson) *j.rt: in tch: pushed along and lost pl after 5th: clsd after 4 out: led appr next: r.o wl after last* **5/1**[1]

0200 **2** *4* **Penny Pictures (IRE)**[26] [1872] 6-11-2 **136**.................. AGlassonbury(10) 139
(M C Pipe) *hld up: hdwy 4 out: lft 2nd last: nt qckn run-in* **16/1**

2213 **3** *2½* **Pebble Bay**[21] [1940] 10-10-0 **110** oh2.. DElsworth 111
(Mrs S J Smith) *led: hdd after 2nd: remained cl up: outpcd appr 3 out: rallied bef last: styd on run-in: nt rch ldng pair* **11/2**[2]

2040 **4** *2½* **Just Beth**[3] [2292] 9-9-12 **113**.. DLaverty(5) 111
(G Fierro) *midfield: rdn approching 7th: outpcd after 4 out: styd on bef last: nt rch ldrs* **33/1**

4300 **5** *2½* **Flame Phoenix (USA)**[25] [1878] 6-9-13 **114**...............(t) StephenJCraine(5) 110
(D McCain) *hld up: rdn after 4 out: hdwy appr next: one pce fr 2 out* **66/1**

23-6 **6** *3* **Paddy The Piper (IRE)**[185] [422] 8-11-11 **135**.......................... ADobbin 128
(L Lungo) *hld up: hit 7th: effrt appr 3 out: no ex run-in* **15/2**[3]

41-0 **7** *3* **The Persuader (IRE)**[197] [207] 5-10-11 **121**..............(t) ChristianWilliams 112+
(P F Nicholls) *bhd: hdwy after 5th: hung lft run-in: nvr on terms* **14/1**

32-0 **8** *20* **Monolith**[183] [127] 7-11-8 **135**.. GBerridge(3) 105
(L Lungo) *a bhd* **33/1**

12-0 **F** **Inch Pride (IRE)**[29] [1828] 6-11-5 **129**....................................... TJMurphy 125+
(M C Pipe) *in tch: rdn and hld in 5th whn fell last* **5/1**[1]

1114 **B** **Crathorne (IRE)**[29] [1823] 5-10-8 **118**... ADempsey 109
(M Todhunter) *prom: wknd appr 3 out: btn whn b.d last* **11/1**

0UF- **P** **Cloudy Grey (IRE)**[288] [3708] 8-11-11 **135**.................................. BFenton —
(Miss E C Lavelle) *led after 2nd: hdd appr 3 out: sn wknd: t.o whn p.u bef last* **10/1**

211- **F** **Halcon Genelardais (FR)**[246] [4463] 5-11-6 **130**..................... RThornton 136+
(A King) *midfield: hdwy 4 out: chsd wnr appr 2 out: jst over 2l down and rdn whn fell last* **5/1**[1]

5m 2.60s (-1.10) **Going Correction** +0.30s/f (Yiel) **12** Ran SP% **114.5**
Speed ratings: **114,112,111,110,109 108,107,99,—,—** —,— CSF £76.60 CT £454.14 TOTE £6.40: £2.00, £5.20, £2.20; EX 107.60 Trifecta £350.80 Part won. Pool: £494.10 - 0.10 winning tickets..

Owner Ada Partnership **Bred** Side Hill Stud And Orpendale **Trained** Billy Row, Co Durham

FOCUS

A decent handicap run at a good gallop and a fair winning time for the class. This looks pretty solid form with the placed horses to their marks and a personal best from the winner.

NOTEBOOK

Covent Garden was a pound lower than when fourth in the Coral Cup on his last start but no less than 25lb higher than when winning this event two years ago. He needed a reminder early on the final circuit to wake him up, but showed ahead turning into the straight and stayed on strongly after his nearest pursuer fell at the last. Three miles may suit and there could be a bit more improvement in him back on a right-handed track. *(op 9-2)*

Penny Pictures(IRE) ran a decent race and ran to his mark, but may continue to prove vulnerable until he has been dropped a few pounds. *(op 20-1)*

Pebble Bay, a consistent sort, ran well from 2lb out of the handicap and rallied after being unable to go with the leaders on the home turn. *(op 9-2)*

Just Beth had only one behind her over the third last but stayed on from the next, although her finishing position flatters her as three in front of her fell at the last. The return to three miles will suit. *(op 40-1)*

Flame Phoenix(USA) tried to get involved on the home turn but, over this longer trip, could only find the same pace from the second last.

Paddy The Piper(IRE), currently rated 10lb higher over hurdles than fences, ran as if just in need of this first outing since sustaining a hock injury. *(op 9-1)*

Crathorne(IRE) has twice been held from this mark and this longer trip found him out too. Beaten when brought down by the fall of Halcon Genelardais at the last, he stayed down for some time before getting to his feet. *(op 8-1)*

Cloudy Grey(IRE) seemed to enjoy himself out in front and was not given a hard time when headed on the home turn, eventually being pulled up. A hard horse to get fit, he should derive plenty of improvement for this first run since February. *(op 8-1)*

Inch Pride(IRE), who had an excuse on her seasonal debut, ran a a better race but was held when falling heavily at the final flight. *(op 8-1)*

Halcon Genelardais(FR) ◆ ran well on his first appearance of the season but just looked held in second when coming down at the final flight, the winner having jumped across him. A progressive sort, he looks sure to win more races if none the worse for this fall, after which he lay winded for some time. *(op 8-1)*

2370 TOTESPORT BECHER H'CAP CHASE (LISTED RACE) (22 fncs) (3m 3f Gd Nat)

2:50 (2:51) (Class 1) 5-Y-0+

£57,020 (£21,390; £10,710; £5,340; £2,680; £1,340)

Form RPR

-065 **1** **Garvivonnian (IRE)**[42] [1700] 10-10-4 **130**.................................... GCotter 139
(Edward P Mitchell, Ire) *chsd ldrs: led 14th (Becher's): rdn and hdd briefly bef elbow: styd on gamely* **33/1**

30-0 **2** *¾* **Le Duc (FR)**[29] [1828] 6-10-10 **136**.. JTizzard 144
(P F Nicholls) *hld up: hdwy 17th (Valentine's): rdn and ev ch last: nt qckn appr elbow: styd on cl home* **25/1**

0-0P **3** *nk* **Just In Debt (IRE)**[21] [1941] 9-10-5 **131**.................................... ADempsey 139
(M Todhunter) *in tch: hdwy 13th: ev ch last: led briefly bef elbow: nt qckn cl home* **25/1**

042- **4** *½* **It Takes Time (IRE)**[213] [4946] 11-11-12 **152**............................ RJohnson 161+
(M C Pipe) *hld up: mstke 5th: stdy hdwy fr 17th (Valentine's): hit 2 out: rdn and ev ch last: kpt on u.p: hld cl home* **9/1**

12-2 **5** *1* **Haut De Gamme (FR)**[22] [1929] 10-10-8 **137**......................... KJMercer(3) 144+
(Ferdy Murphy) *hld up: hdwy appr 2 out: kpt on run-in: hld whn n.m.r cl home* **16/1**

1P0- **6** *7* **Heros Collonges (FR)**[225] [4772] 10-10-13 **139**........... ChristianWilliams 139+
(P F Nicholls) *midfield: hdwy 8th (water): rdn and ev ch last: no ex fnl 100 yds* **18/1**

0-P5 **7** *1¼* **Amberleigh House (IRE)**[22] [1924] 13-10-9 **135**............................... GLee 133
(D McCain) *hld up: hdwy 14th (Becher's): rdn and ev ch last: one pce bef elbow* **25/1**

560- **8** *22* **Bindaree (IRE)**[225] [4772] 11-11-5 **145**...................................... CLlewellyn 121
(N A Twiston-Davies) *prom: led after 4th: hdd 11th: blnd 15th (Foinavon): wkng whn hit 16th (Canal Turn)* **40/1**

416- **9** *25* **Nil Desperandum (IRE)**[20] [1964] 8-11-0 **140**........................... BHarding 91
(Ms F M Crowley, Ire) *a bhd* **11/1**

/0-3 **10** *18* **What Odds (IRE)**[206] [91] 9-10-0 **126**.................................... RGeraghty 59
(T K Geraghty, Ire) *nt jump wl: a bhd: bdly hmpd 1st (Valentine's) and 2nd: rdr lost iron briefly after 3 out: n.d* **20/1**

41-0 **11** *16* **Cregg House (IRE)**[208] [45] 10-10-6 **132**................................. DNRussell 49
(S Donohoe, Ire) *midfield: hdwy 8th (water): wknd appr 3 out: virtually p.u run-in* **28/1**

102- **F** **Juveigneur (FR)**[211] [4984] 8-10-13 **139**.. MFoley —
(N J Henderson) *fell 1st (Valentine's)* **8/1**[3]

/14- **F** **Direct Access (IRE)**[276] [3900] 10-10-0 **126**................................ ADobbin —
(N G Richards) *fell 1st (Valentine's)* **7/1**[2]

10-0 **F** **Philson Run (IRE)**[43] [1676] 9-10-2 **128**.................................... DElsworth —
(Nick Williams) *fell 1st (Valentine's)* **25/1**

115- **U** **Forest Gunner**[225] [4772] 11-10-13 **142**......................... MissNCarberry(3) —
(R Ford) *led tl blnd and uns rdr 3rd* **11/2**[1]

0-P2 **F** **Strong Resolve (IRE)**[14] [2066] 9-10-5 **134**.......................... PBuchanan(3) —
(Miss Lucinda V Russell) *prom whn fell 2nd* **10/1**

0/0- **U** **Exit Swinger (FR)**[515] [810] 10-10-3 **134**.............................. PMerrigan(5) —
(P F Nicholls) *blnd and uns rdr 1st (Valentine's)* **66/1**

-264 **F** **Double Honour (FR)**[15] 2054 7-10-9 **135**..........(b) PJBrennan —
(P J Hobbs) *prom: lft in ld 3rd: j.rt next: sn hdd: stl in tch whn fell 14th (Becher's)* **9/1**

-031 **P** **Rheindross (IRE)**[147] 842 10-10-3 **129**.......... NFehily —
(C J Mann) *cl up: pckd 2nd: led 11th: hdd 14th (Becher's): wknd 18th: t.o whn p.u bef 2 out* **16/1**

7m 11.3s **19** Ran SP% **123.9**
CSF £671.76 CT £18934.75 TOTE £46.50: £7.70, £5.50, £7.00, £2.40; EX 1405.20 TRIFECTA Not won..
Owner Mrs A Long **Bred** John Long **Trained** Kilmallock, Co Limerick
■ A first winner in Britain for Limerick trainer Ned Mitchell.
■ Stewards' Enquiry : J Tizzard two-day ban: used whip with excessive frequency (Dec 1-2)

FOCUS
A steadily-run event in which there were seven in with a chance over the last, and the form is slightly suspect.

NOTEBOOK
Garvivonnian(IRE) was without a win since landing the Cork Grand National a year ago, but these big fences brought out the best in him. Showing ahead at Becher's, he had six horses snapping at his heels over the final fence but he battled on bravely up the run-in. He will return here for the Grand National.
Le Duc(FR), third in the Topham last season, jumped really well back over these fences. He was slightly outpaced by those around him early on the flat but stayed on strongly to snatch second close home. The National is the aim. *(op 22-1)*
Just In Debt(IRE), without the cheekpieces, ran his best race since finishing second in this event a year ago. He jumped and travelled well and momentarily nosed ahead on the run-in before the winner battled back to the front.
It Takes Time(IRE) made an excellent seasonal debut and, after clouting the second last, only admitted defeat in the final 75 yards. He was fourth in the Grand National last season and the big race is likely to be on his schedule again. *(tchd 10-1 in places)*
Haut De Gamme(FR), who ran well over hurdles on his reappearance, improved to chase the leaders after the third last. Keeping on over this longer trip, he was held when slightly short of room near the finish. *(op 14-1)*
Heros Collonges(FR) ran well on his seasonal reappearance and was right in the mix at the final fence before tiring up the run-in. He was eighth in last year's Grand National and will return for another crack this season, but while he should jump round stamina could prove a problem again.
Amberleigh House(IRE) had no problem laying up with the pace and challenged at the final fence before others had his measure up the long run-in. He has an outstanding record over this track, as since being brought down in a pile-up in the 2001 National he has completed the course on all nine attempts, including a win in this event four years ago and the 2004 National. *(tchd 22-1)*
Bindaree(IRE), who has a mixed record here since his 2002 Grand National victory, ran well for a long way, despite putting in a few rather careful jumps, and his retirement has been postponed.
Cregg House(IRE), winner of the Topham last term, did not stay this longer trip on his first run since April. *(op 25-1)*
Forest Gunner, 17lb higher than when landing this race in fine style a year ago, took off too soon at the third and unshipped Carberry, who was having her first ride over these fences. *(op 9-1)*
Double Honour(FR), fourth a year ago, was just behind the leaders when coming down at Becher's Brook. *(op 9-1)*
Rheindross(IRE), having his first run since landing the Summer National at Uttoxeter in June, showed prominently until fading from the fifth last. Pulled up with two to jump, he reportedly broke down and has been retired. *(op 9-1)*
Juveigneur(FR), runner-up in the Betfred Gold Cup when last seen, was one of four casualties at the first - one of the biggest fences on the course - and rider Marcus Foley sustained a broken wrist. *(op 9-1)*

2371 INTERSKY NOVICES' CHASE (12 fncs) 2m (Mildmay)
3:20 (3:26) (Class 2) 4-Y-O+ **£10,450** (£3,244; £1,746)

Form RPR

40-1 **1** **Cerium (FR)**[20] 1958 4-11-0 .... PJBrennan 128+
(P F Nicholls) *chsd ldr: effrt 3 out: looked hld whn lft in ld next: rdn out* **11/8**[1]

0-14 **2** *5* **Stance**[15] 2052 6-11-9 ....(p) RJohnson 132
(G L Moore) *nt fluent: prom: mstke 4th: kpt on to go 2nd appr 2 out: no imp* **11/2**

111F **3** *5* **Feel The Pride (IRE)**[29] 1822 7-11-5 128.......... NFehily 124+
(Jonjo O'Neill) *trckd ldrs: t.k.h: rdn 3 out: sn wknd* **10/1**

100- **U** **Roman Ark**[249] 4394 7-11-4 .... FKing —
(J M Jefferson) *j.rt: hld up in tch: outpcd 9th: sn lost pl: bhd whn blnd and uns rdr 2 out* **9/2**[3]

-151 **P** **Nyrche (FR)**[4] 2270 5-11-12 .... WHutchinson 140+
(A King) *led: qcknd 8th: mstke next: 2 l up and travelling strly whn rdr tk him out to the lft of the 2nd last fence* **7/2**[2]

4m 12.6s (11.60) **Going Correction** +0.95s/f (Soft)
WFA 4 from 5yo+ 12lb **5** Ran SP% **107.0**
Speed ratings: **109,106,104,—,—** CSF £8.51 TOTE £2.20: £1.60, £2.70; EX 8.80.
Owner B Fulton, T Hayward, S Fisher, L Brady **Bred** Sarl Haras De Saint-Faust And Andre-Paul Larrieu **Trained** Ditcheat, Somerset
■ Stewards' Enquiry : W Hutchinson 14-day ban: took wrong course (Dec 1-10, 12-15)

FOCUS
Nyrche would probably have won but for Hutchinson's brainstorm, but he has been rated as having dead-heated with Cerium, who improved on his debut win without looking Arkle material.

NOTEBOOK
Cerium(FR) maintained his unbeaten start to his chasing career but fortune was on his side as he appeared held in second when Nyrche presented him with the lead at the second last. He stayed on well once in front and his trainer observed that if the ground were to come up fast at the Festival then two miles would be too short for him. *(op 6-5)*
Stance was down in trip for this third run over fences and had cheekpieces fitted for the first time. He ran a better race than at Wincanton, but did not jump with much fluency and probably still needs more experience. *(op 6-1)*
Feel The Pride(IRE), who took a heavy fall here a month ago, ran a fair race but was somewhat keen and did not find much from the second last. *(tchd 8-1)*
Roman Ark, making his chasing debut on this first run since the Cheltenham Festival, was a little novicey. He dropped back to last with a mistake at the cross fence and was well held when unseating at the second last, but he is worth another chance in easier company. *(op 4-1)*
Nyrche(FR) ◆ jumped boldly out in front and was still going well, looking the likely winner, when he was suddenly steered around the second last fence. Hutchinson, banned for two weeks for taking the wrong course, reported that he had heard shouts from behind him, which he thought were warning him that he was going the wrong way. The gelding is a promising novice who should not be long in gaining compensation. *(op 4-1)*

2372 JIM ENNIS CONSTRUCTION LTD NOVICES' H'CAP HURDLE (11 hdls) 2m 4f
3:50 (3:51) (Class 3) (0-115,109) 3-Y-O+ **£6,847** (£2,010; £1,005; £502)

Form RPR

-3UP **1** **Vingis Park (IRE)**[24] 1891 7-11-5 **105**..........(b[1]) MrJJDoyle(7) 116+
(V R A Dartnall) *trckd ldr: led 4th: rdn wl clr after 2 out* **16/1**

6-P2 **2** *11* **Sergio Coimbra (IRE)**[43] 1687 6-11-6 **99**.......... ADobbin 99
(N G Richards) *in tch: drvn along and outpcd after 8th: styd on fr next: tk 2nd nr line* **7/2**[1]

565/ **3** *1* **Zoltano (GER)**[575] 4459 7-10-13 **92**.......... GLee 92+
(M Todhunter) *trckd ldrs: wnt 2nd 3 out: kpt on same pce: lost 2nd nr line* **6/1**[2]

2525 **4** *9* **Reem Two**[25] 1880 4-11-2 **100**.......... StephenJCraine(5) 90
(D McCain) *chsd ldrs: drvn along and outpcd 6th: one pce fr 3 out* **10/1**

P015 **5** *14* **Kerry's Blade (IRE)**[26] 1873 3-10-7 **107**..........(b) PMerrigan(5) 67
(P C Haslam) *hld up detached in last: sme hdwy 8th: wknd bef next* **8/1**[3]

3110 **6** *6* **Palace Walk (FR)**[8] 2178 3-11-0 **109**.......... RJohnson 63
(B G Powell) *prom: outpcd 6th: hdwy 8th: sn lost pl* **6/1**[2]

60-4 **7** *4* **Quarrymount**[22] 1916 4-11-5 **98**.......... WHutchinson 64
(J A B Old) *t.k.h: trckd ldrs: wknd after 3 out* **7/2**[1]

8 *dist* **Flying Jody (IRE)**[84] 1353 6-11-6 **99**.......... RMcGrath —
(Sir John Barlow Bt) *t.k.h: trckd ldrs to 5th: lost pl after 8th: sn bhd: t.o: btn 38 l* **16/1**

PP-2 **9** *2* **Flaming Heck**[14] 2064 8-10-8 **92**.......... DFlavin(5) —
(Mrs L B Normile) *mstkes: led to 4th: wknd rapidly 8th: sn bhd: t.o fr next* **11/1**

5m 7.10s (3.40) **Going Correction** +0.30s/f (Yiel)
WFA 3 from 4yo 16lb 4 from 5yo+ 13lb **9** Ran SP% **113.3**
Speed ratings: **105,100,100,96,91 88,87,—,—** CSF £71.47 CT £381.27 TOTE £20.30: £5.70, £1.90, £2.70; EX 159.80 Place 6 £277.24, Place 5 £210.26.
Owner Nick Viney **Bred** Victor Robinson **Trained** Brayford, Devon

FOCUS
The race has been rated around the second running to the level of his recent Hexham run, but it could have been rated around 6lb higher using the third and the fourth.

NOTEBOOK
Vingis Park(IRE), reverting to hurdles after two non-completions over fences, wore blinkers for the first time but was without the tongue tie. He came clear between the last two flights for a comprehensive victory, finally returning to the form he showed on his bumper debut in April 2003, *but it remains to be seen whether the blinkers will work again.Official explanation: trainer said, regarding the improved form shown, gelding was suited by the return to hurdling - having been running in chases - and by the application of first-time blinkers (op 14-1)*
Sergio Coimbra(IRE), on his handicap debut, looked in trouble leaving the back straight but stayed on over the last three flights. He promises to get three miles. *(op 4-1)*
Zoltano(GER) had not been seen since the spring of 2004 so this was a pleasing return to action. *(tchd 7-1)*
Reem Two, back over a more suitable trip, was being ridden along quite vigorously early on the final circuit and could never get into the action from that point.
Kerry's Blade(IRE), with blinkers replacing cheekpieces, failed to see out the trip having been ridden as if lack of stamina was going to prove a problem. *(op 13-2)*
Palace Walk(FR), whose wins came on fast ground, was ridden differently here on this step up in trip and was in trouble turning into the straight. *(op 11-2 tchd 13-2)*
Quarrymount was keen in the early part of the race and, after racing prominently, he began to weaken once into the home straight. *(tchd 10-3)*
T/Jkpt: Not won. T/Plt: £1,963.40 to a £1 stake. Pool: £87,950.00. 32.70 winning tickets. T/Qpdt: £73.30 to a £1 stake. Pool: £7,883.10. 79.50 winning tickets. DO

1948 PLUMPTON (L-H)
Sunday, November 20

OFFICIAL GOING: Good to soft
Wind: Nil Weather: Sunny, crisp and cold

2373 ALEXANDER CATERING (EVENTS) JUVENILE MAIDEN HURDLE (9 hdls) 2m
12:25 (12:26) (Class 3) 3-Y-O **£5,608** (£1,646; £823; £411)

Form RPR

2 **1** **Equilibria (USA)**[12] 2101 3-10-12 .... JEMoore 87+
(G L Moore) *t.k.h: hld up midfield: mstke 2nd: prog to press ldrs and mstke 3 out: led 2 out: drvn out* **4/1**[3]

2 *¾* **Tora Bora (GER)**[140] 3-10-12 .... JPMcNamara 87+
(B G Powell) *w ldrs: j. slowly 3rd and lost pl: prog 6th: led after 3 out to 2 out: kpt on flat: a jst hld* **15/8**[1]

3 *½* **Laconicos (IRE)**[39] 3-10-9 .... GCarenza(3) 84+
(W B Stone) *wl plcd: chal 3 out: cl 3rd 2 out: one pce after* **25/1**

045 **4** *1* **Ghaill Force**[14] 2069 3-10-5 92..........(t) RLucey-Butler(7) 82
(P Butler) *hld up wl in rr: nt on terms after 6th: stdy prog gng wl fr 3 out: wnt 4th next: rdn bef last: kpt on* **20/1**

5 *3* **Dance Hall Diva**[41] 3-9-12 .... LNewnes(7) 72
(M D I Usher) *taken down early: w ldrs: hmpd 3rd and lost pl: nt on terms after 6th: hrd rdn and prog after 3 out: one pce fr next* **50/1**

6 **6** *4* **Come What Augustus**[14] 2069 3-10-12 .... JimCrowley 76+
(R M Stronge) *t.k.h: nrly uns rdr 1st: prog to ld after 3rd: hdd after 3 out: wknd 2 out: blnd last* **20/1**

6 **7** *23* **Lojo**[12] 2101 3-10-5 .... JGoldstein 45
(Miss Sheena West) *hld up midfield: nt on terms after 6th: wknd 3 out* **20/1**

8 *1* **Keresforth**[15] 3-10-12 .... BHitchcott 51
(Mrs L C Jewell) *hld up in rr: blnd 5th and lost tch: no ch after* **50/1**

0 **9** *9* **King After**[6] 2236 3-10-12 .... DCrosse 42
(J R Best) *t.k.h: hld up wl in rr: effrt and in tch 6th: wknd 3 out* **25/1**

10 *3* **Emile Zola**[81] 3-10-12 .... AO'Keeffe 39
(Miss Venetia Williams) *trckd ldrs: cl up 3 out: wknd rapidly sn after* **5/2**[2]

P **Stunning Spark**[10] 3-10-5 .... TDoyle —
(S Dow) *pressed ldrs: mstke 5th and lost pl: wknd 3 out: wl bhd whn p.u bef next* **50/1**

U **Another Mistress**[10] 3-10-5 .... MBatchelor —
(R M Flower) *plld hrd: mstke 1st: mde most tl tried to run out and uns rdr 3rd* **66/1**

P **F** **Rathcannon Beauty**[6] 2236 3-9-12 .... MGoldstein(7) —
(Mrs L P Baker) *set off in detached last: rapid prog 3rd: cl 3rd whn fell 6th* **66/1**

4m 6.40s (5.20) **Going Correction** +0.175s/f (Yiel) **13** Ran SP% **114.2**
Speed ratings: **94,93,91,91,89 87,76,75,71,69 —,—,—** CSF £10.28 TOTE £4.80: £1.40, £1.70, £4.70; EX 11.50.
Owner Dr C A Barnett **Bred** Calumet Farm **Trained** Woodingdean, E Sussex

FOCUS
Just a modest juvenile maiden hurdle, run at an ordinary pace and best rated through fourth and sixth.

NOTEBOOK
Equilibria(USA) confirmed the promise he showed when second on his hurdling debut at Huntingdon to run out a decisive enough winner. He did not have that much in hand, but should remain competitive under a penalty.

Tora Bora(GER) ◆, a winner over a mile and placed in Listed company over a mile and a half on the Flat in Germany, was just held on his hurdling debut off the back of a 140-day break. This was a promising introduction and he should be hard to beat in similar company next time. *(op 2-1 tchd 7-4 and 9-4 in a place)*

Laconicos(IRE), a 68-rated maiden on the Flat, made a pleasing debut over hurdles behind a couple of reasonable enough types for time of year. He gave the impression he would improve for the experience and should step up on this.

Ghaill Force was noted finishing quite well but never really threatened and may be better off in handicap company.

Dance Hall Diva, very moderate in two runs on the Flat, ran better switched to hurdles, especially considering she lost her place early on after getting hampered, and this looks more her game. *(op 66-1)*

Come What Augustus was keen and after recovering from an early error showed up until fading from the home turn. *(op 16-1)*

King After *Official explanation: jockey said gelding made a noise (op 33-1)*

Emile Zola, successful over a mile and placed over a mile and a half on the Flat (rated 71), showed up well for a lot of the way on his hurdling debut, but stopped quickly and something may have been amiss. *(op 2-1)*

2374 SOUTHERN FM NOVICES' HURDLE (9 hdls) 2m

12:55 (12:56) (Class 3) 4-Y-0+ **£5,048** (£1,482; £741; £370)

Form				RPR
	1		**Cold Turkey**[21] 5-10-12 ... JEMoore (G L Moore) *t.k.h: hld up in rr: prog bef 3 out and stl keen: chsd ldr 2 out: drvn and r.o flat to ld last strides* **7/4**[1]	111+
5F	**2**	*hd*	**Kings Signal (USA)**[22] 1916 7-10-12 ... PHide (M J Hogan) *t.k.h: hld up midfield: prog 6th: led gng easily bef 2 out where wandered: rdn flat: r.o: hdd last strides* **7/1**[2]	111+
34-3	**3**	*5*	**Armariver (FR)**[43] 1671 5-10-5 ... LHeard(7) (P F Nicholls) *trckd ldrs: mstke 5th: cl up 3 out: rdn and nt qckn bef next: mstke 2 out: styd on same pce* **7/4**[1]	106
3-44	**4**	*6*	**Hatteras (FR)**[16] 2020 6-10-5 105 ... RLucey-Butler(7) (Miss M P Bryant) *mde most to bef 2 out: fdd* **50/1**	100
	5	*4*	**Warningcamp (GER)**[459] 4-10-12 ... TDoyle (Lady Herries) *t.k.h: hld up in rr: stdy prog 3 out: chsd ldrs bef next: nudged along and no imp after* **16/1**[3]	96
511P	**6**	*7*	**Hill Forts Timmy**[11] 2127 5-10-12 ... AO'Keeffe (J W Mullins) *prom: effrt to chse ldr 3 out: wknd rapidly bef next* **25/1**	89
30P/	**7**	*8*	**Herecomestanley**[266] 6-10-12 ... BHitchcott (M F Harris) *plld hrd: hld up in rr: in tch 3 out: wknd bef next* **100/1**	81
3313	**8**	*2½*	**Mr Ex (ARG)**[16] 2020 4-10-5 ... EDehdashti(7) (G L Moore) *w ldr to 5th: sn pushed along: wknd 3 out* **16/1**[3]	79
0-50	**9**	*4*	**Lord Hopeful (IRE)**[18] 1982 4-10-12 ... JAMcCarthy (C P Morlock) *hld up in rr: lost tch bef 6th: wl bhd after: kpt on* **66/1**	75
	10	*25*	**Turtle Patriarch (IRE)**[30] 4-10-12 ... JimCrowley (Mrs A J Perrett) *nt jump wl: prom tl wknd rapidly after 3 out* **20/1**	50
0-0	**P**		**Ray Mond**[20] 1954 4-10-5 ... MrMatthewSmith(7) (M J Gingell) *set off wl bhd: j. bdly: in tch 5th: wknd next: t.o whn p.u bef 2 out* **100/1**	—

4m 2.60s (1.40) **Going Correction** +0.175s/f (Yiel)
WFA 4 from 5yo+ 12lb **11** Ran SP% **111.0**
Speed ratings: **103,102,100,97,95 91,87,86,84,72** — CSF £13.74 TOTE £2.60: £1.70, £1.80, £1.10; EX 17.90.
Owner A Grinter **Bred** Worksop Manor Stud **Trained** Woodingdean, E Sussex

FOCUS
A modest novice hurdle, but Cold Turkey probably did well to win having raced keenly throughout and looks capable of rating much higher. The third and fourth ran to their marks suggesting the form should work out.

NOTEBOOK
Cold Turkey ◆, a very useful middle-distance/stayer on the Flat, only scraped home on his hurdling debut, but is much better than the bare form would suggest as he was very keen almost throughout off a pace that was nowhere near as strong as he would have liked. A promising recruit, he can leave the bare form of this success behind in better company. *(tchd 13-8)*

Kings Signal(USA), who showed promise on his hurdling debut here last month, and was in the process of running a big race before falling at Lingfield on his latest start, got round this time and ran very well behind the potentially useful winner. While time may show he was flattered to get so close to Cold Turkey, he looks like making a fair hurdler. *(op 13-2 tchd 15-2)*

Armariver(FR), who shaped as though this drop in trip would suit when a beaten favourite over two and a half miles at Bangor on his previous start, again proved a little disappointing. He made some mistakes and is not yet the finished article. *(op 13-8 tchd 15-8 in places)*

Hatteras(FR) got the run of the race in front and posted a very creditable effort. He may do even better in handicap company, although his official mark looks high enough. *(op 40-1)*

Warningcamp(GER) ◆, rated 80 on the Flat when last seen 459 days ago, offered some promise on his debut over hurdles and looks capable of leaving the bare form of this effort behind in time. *(op 20-1)*

Ray Mond *Official explanation: jockey said gelding lost its action coming down hill*

2375 IBETX ELLIE MAY CHALLIS NOVICES' CHASE (18 fncs) 3m 2f

1:30 (1:31) (Class 3) 5-Y-0+ **£6,524** (£1,990; £1,039; £564)

Form				RPR
-411	**1**		**State Of Play**[43] 1678 5-10-13 120 ... PMoloney (Evan Williams) *cl up: led 13th: clr and in command fr 3 out: comf* **9/4**[1]	131+
23/P	**2**	*9*	**Howrwenow (IRE)**[29] 1829 7-11-0 115 ... MBatchelor (Miss H C Knight) *led to after 2nd: styd cl up: chsd wnr briefly 14th: sn rdn: wnt 2nd again after 2 out: no ch* **7/2**[3]	119+
22-1	**3**	*½*	**Admiral Peary (IRE)**[201] 168 9-11-0 118 ... ATinkler (C R Egerton) *t.k.h: led after 2nd: blnd 12th: hdd: j.rt next: wnt 2nd 15th tl mstke 2 out: kpt on* **3/1**[2]	120+
0/P1	**4**	*dist*	**Sweet Bird (FR)**[12] 2104 8-11-0 101 ... (t) PHide (Miss J R Gibney) *hld up: in tch to 14th: btn bef next: bhd whn mstke 2 out and eased: btn 62l* **7/1**	80
P-06	**U**		**Geography (IRE)**[11] 2130 5-10-6 86 ... RLucey-Butler(7) (P Butler) *a last: struggling fr 7th: bhd whn blnd and uns rdr 10th* **33/1**	—
42F/	**U**		**Stavordale Lad (IRE)**[670] 3419 7-10-7 110 ... LHeard(7) (P F Nicholls) *racd on outer: wl in tch: cl 4th whn blnd and uns rdr 14th* **5/1**	—

6m 45.8s (-8.20) **Going Correction** -0.10s/f (Good)
WFA 5 from 7yo+ 1lb **6** Ran SP% **110.1**
Speed ratings: **108,105,105,—,—** — CSF £10.29 TOTE £2.90: £1.90, £1.70; EX 12.20.
Owner William Rucker **Bred** Roland Lerner **Trained** Cowbridge, Vale Of Glamorgan

FOCUS
Not a bad-looking novice chase, but State Of Play totally outclassed his rivals, is value for more than the official margin, and looks a very useful prospect.

NOTEBOOK
State Of Play ◆, off the mark on his chasing debut over three miles at Chepstow, followed up over this slightly longer trip in most impressive fashion. He never looked in any danger and is quickly developing into a very useful novice. *(op 2-1 tchd 11-4)*

Howrwenow(IRE) had shown some useful form over form over both hurdles and fences a couple of seasons back, but was pulled up back over fences on his return from an absence at Chepstow. With the benefit of that run, this was better, but he proved no match whatsoever for the easy winner and was below the pick of his form. *(op 5-1)*

Admiral Peary(IRE), making his chasing debut off the back of a 201-day break, did not really jump well enough and ran below the pick of his hurdles form. *(op 9-4 tchd 2-1)*

Sweet Bird(FR) would have found this tougher than the Huntingdon handicap he won off a mark of 93 on his previous start, but ran no sort of race in any case. *(op 9-1)*

Stavordale Lad(IRE) unseated his rider a fair way out on his return from a 670-day absence, so this did not tell us a great deal. *(op 11-2 tchd 13-2)*

2376 IBETX YOU DO IBETX YOU DON'T "NATIONAL HUNT" NOVICES' HURDLE (12 hdls) 2m 5f

2:05 (2:05) (Class 4) 4-Y-0+ **£3,532** (£1,037; £518; £259)

Form				RPR
50-3	**1**		**Just A Splash (IRE)**[18] 1982 5-10-12 ... ATinkler (N J Gifford) *hld up in rr: effrt and prog after 9th: led after 3 out: rdn clr fr next: hit last* **3/1**[2]	96+
1	**2**	*7*	**Pan The Man (IRE)**[193] 300 4-10-12 ... AThornton (J W Mullins) *hld up: nt fluent 8th: prog next: w wnr after 3 out to 2 out: one pce u.p* **5/1**[3]	87
2	**3**	*15*	**River Ripples (IRE)**[20] 1954 6-10-12 ... JPMcNamara (T R George) *trckd ldrs: chal 9th: bdly outpcd and struggling after 3 out: plugged on again bef last* **5/4**[1]	72
0P-	**4**	*5*	**Tenko**[300] 3511 6-10-5 ... BHitchcott (M D McMillan) *hld up: prog 5th: led 9th to after 3 out: wknd next* **100/1**	60
00	**5**	*17*	**Joe McHugh (IRE)**[7] 2206 6-10-12 ... DCrosse (C J Mann) *led to 9th: sn rdn: wknd 3 out* **10/1**	55+
0-	**6**	*5*	**Northern Link (IRE)**[509] 838 6-10-12 ... MBatchelor (Miss Tor Sturgis) *nt fluent: in tch to 9th: sn wknd and bhd* **25/1**	45
24P	**7**	*10*	**Silverio (GER)**[11] 2127 4-10-12 ... JEMoore (G L Moore) *v hesitant at several hurdles: w ldr: led 8th tl veered bef next: wknd 3 out* **10/1**	35
F	**P**		**Sett Aside**[7] 2213 7-10-12 ... TDoyle (Mrs L C Jewell) *prom to 5th: struggling fr 8th: t.o whn p.u bef 2 out* **25/1**	—
00	**P**		**Rose Amber**[179] 507 4-10-5 ... RGreene (J J Bridger) *hld up: last whn blnd 5th: wkng whn blnd 7th and p.u* **100/1**	—

5m 22.8s (-2.00) **Going Correction** +0.175s/f (Yiel) **9** Ran SP% **114.0**
Speed ratings: **110,107,101,99,93 91,87,—,—** CSF £17.77 TOTE £3.90: £1.10, £1.80, £1.50; EX 10.50.
Owner Mrs T Brown **Bred** A W Buller **Trained** Findon, W Sussex

FOCUS
Just an ordinary novice hurdle, but won by a nice long-term prospect in Just A Splash. The winning time was fair for a race of its type and the runner-up looks the best guide to the level of the form.

NOTEBOOK
Just A Splash(IRE) ◆, a promising third over two miles at Chepstow on his reappearance, improved for the step up in trip and ran out a convincing winner - he did not appear to do much once in front and looked value for even further. A nice prospect, he should continue to go the right way and can make a decent staying chaser in time. *(op 10-3)*

Pan The Man(IRE), successful in an Exeter bumper on his only previous start 193 days ago, made a pleasing reappearance behind the promising winner. He ought to come a fair bit for both the run and experience, and looks well up to making his mark in this sphere. *(op 6-1)*

River Ripples(IRE), a winner pointer over three miles in Ireland, he offered plenty of promise on his debut under Rules when second in a course bumper, but failed to confirm that switched to hurdles for the first time and was most disappointing. Surely he is better than this. *(tchd 11-8 and 6-4 in places)*

Tenko had not shown a great deal in one run in a bumper and one run over hurdles but, returned from a 300 days off, this was better and offered some hope. *(op 66-1)*

Joe McHugh(IRE), faced with a more realistic task, finished up well held. He is now qualified for a handicap mark. *(op 14-1)*

Silverio(GER) *Official explanation: jockey said gelding ran green (op 8-1)*

2377 FARMERS MARKET BEGINNERS' CHASE (12 fncs) 2m 1f

2:40 (2:42) (Class 3) 4-Y-0+ **£5,429** (£1,739; £966)

Form				RPR
220-	**1**		**Big Moment**[51] 3972 7-11-5 ... JimCrowley (Mrs A J Perrett) *trckd ldng pair: lft 2nd at 4th: shkn up to ld 2 out: styd on wl* **1/1**[1]	130+
34-6	**2**	*5*	**Cruising River (IRE)**[24] 1891 6-11-5 ... SThomas (Miss H C Knight) *pressed ldr: lft in ld 4th: hdd and mstke 2 out: one pce* **7/2**[3]	117+
32-F	**3**	*30*	**Lewis Island (IRE)**[151] 452 6-11-5 115 ... JEMoore (G L Moore) *t.k.h: hld up: trckd ldng pair fr 5th: stl pulling after 8th: wknd tamely after 4 out* **8/1**	97+
10-F	**F**		**Golano**[27] 127 5-11-5 ... TDoyle (P R Webber) *mde most tl ploughed st into 4th* **3/1**[2]	—
/F0-	**P**		**Mr Micky (IRE)**[224] 4791 7-10-12 ... MrRWoollacott(7) (M B Shears) *hld up: mstke 5th: wknd next: p.u after 7th* **33/1**	—

4m 21.4s (-2.70) **Going Correction** -0.10s/f (Good) **5** Ran SP% **111.3**
Speed ratings: **102,99,85,—,—** CSF £5.16 TOTE £2.10: £1.20, £2.30; EX 6.70.
Owner R Doel,A Black,Dr J Howells,R & P Scott **Bred** Juddmonte Farms **Trained** Pulborough, W Sussex

FOCUS
Just the five runners and, with Golano falling early on, Big Moment's task was made easier and he proved good enough to make a winning debut over fences. The winner is value for more than the official margin and the runner-up sets the standard.

NOTEBOOK
Big Moment, a smart hurdler, was making his chasing debut off the back of a Flat campaign where he ended the season rated 89. His task was made a little easier with Golano falling early on, and he won in decent enough style. He has a little way to go yet before he can match his hurdles form, but this was a good start and he should go on from this. *(op 6-4)*

Cruising River(IRE), dropped three furlongs in trip, stepped up significantly on the form he showed on his chasing debut at Stratford with a solid effort behind the decent winner. He showed reasonable form over hurdles and, an Irish point winner, he has the potential to progress over fences this season. *(tchd 3-1)*

Lewis Island(IRE), who unseated and fell on his only two previous starts over fences, managed to complete on his return to the larger obstacles, but raced too keenly early on and finished up well beaten. *(op 15-2 tchd 7-1 and 9-1)*

Golano, three times a winner on the Flat and twice successful over hurdles, had a bad experience on his chasing debut. He seemed to completely misjudge the fourth and almost landed on top of it. It has to be hoped this does not leave its mark. *(op 9-4)*

2378 PLUMPTON RACECOURSE NOVICES' H'CAP HURDLE (14 hdls) 3m 1f 110y
3:10 (3:10) (Class 4) (0-90,85) 4-Y-0+ **£2,494** (£726; £363)

Form RPR
-453 **1** **Manque Neuf**[20] 1949 6-11-3 **76**....................(p) JPMcNamara 82+
(Mrs L Richards) *prom: led 7th: mde rest: abt 4l clr fr 10th: kpt on fr 2 out* **6/1**[3]
-055 **2** *3* **Hidden Storm (IRE)**[8] 2181 6-10-11 **70**....................(b[1]) DCrosse 68
(Mrs S J Humphrey) *hld up in last pair: prog to chse ldng pair 10th: rdn 3 out: kpt on to take 2nd last: no imp on wnr* **33/1**
00-5 **3** *4* **Irish Grouse (IRE)**[18] 1990 6-10-10 **69**.................... MBatchelor 64+
(Miss H C Knight) *hld up: prog to chse wnr 10th: rdn and no real imp fr 3 out: lost 2nd last* **10/1**
052R **4** *13* **Hill Forts Henry**[6] 2237 7-11-3 **76**.................... AThornton 57
(J W Mullins) *hld up in last pair: rdn and outpcd after 10th: plugged on fr 3 out : n.d* **7/1**
0-P4 **5** *5* **Oasis Banus (IRE)**[24] 1900 4-10-10 **69**.................... RGreene 45
(M C Pipe) *trckd ldrs: cl up 10th: rdn to chse ldng trio next: sn struggling: wl btn 3 out* **6/4**[1]
3252 **6** *13* **Sundawn Lady**[14] 2073 7-11-0 **80**....................(b) MrGTumelty[(7)] 43
(C P Morlock) *t.k.h: prom to 9th: sn wknd: t.o* **7/2**[2]
05-0 **7** *dist* **Dundridge Native**[34] 1775 7-11-5 **85**.................... MGoldstein[(7)] —
(M Madgwick) *settled in rr: rdn 8th: sn btn: wl bhd fr 11th: t.o* **20/1**
30-P **P** **Ellas Recovery (IRE)**[11] 2127 5-11-8 **81**.................... JamesDavies —
(D B Feek) *led 3rd to 7th: wknd rapidly after 9th: p.u bef 11th* **25/1**
230P **P** **Rhetorical**[14] 2073 4-10-10 **76**....................(p) RLucey-Butler[(7)] —
(P Butler) *led to 3rd: in tch tl wknd 10th: sn t.o: poor 6th whn p.u bef 2 out* **20/1**

6m 38.0s (2.10) **Going Correction** +0.175s/f (Yiel)
WFA 4 from 5yo+ 14lb **9** Ran SP% **114.4**
Speed ratings: **103,102,100,96,95 91,—,—,—** CSF £171.29 CT £1929.59 TOTE £6.50: £1.50, £11.40, £2.30; EX 182.10.
Owner B Seal **Bred** Burton Agnes Stud Co Ltd **Trained** Funtington, W Sussex
■ Stewards' Enquiry : D Crosse caution: used whip without giving mare time to respond

FOCUS
A very moderate handicap hurdle for novices although the winner seemed improved for the longer trip.

NOTEBOOK
Manque Neuf proved well suited by the step back up in trip and got off the mark over hurdles at the 13th attempt with a game success. He should not go up too much for this and ought to remain competitive. *(op 7-1 tchd 15-2)*
Hidden Storm(IRE) had shown a very moderate level of form on her previous starts over hurdles but, fitted with blinkers or the first time, she produced her best performance yet. Given she managed to win an Irish point-to-point, this effort is not a total shock and she is clearly not without hope. *(op 25-1)*
Irish Grouse(IRE), upped to his furthest trip to date and switched to handicaps for the first time, ran a creditable enough race. He is clearly very moderate, but could eventually find a minor race. *(op 9-1 tchd 12-1)*
Hill Forts Henry, returned to hurdles having refused at the last over fences at Folkestone on his previous start, and without the cheekpieces, was well beaten and remains a maiden. *(op 8-1)*
Oasis Banus(IRE), upped significantly in trip, failed to build on the form he showed to be fourth at Taunton on his previous start and was a major disappointment. He has plenty to prove now. *(op 11-8 tchd 11-10)*
Sundawn Lady had been running well in defeat recently, but raced keenly this time and was well below her best. *(op 9-2)*

2379 PLUMPTON RACECOURSE H'CAP HURDLE (9 hdls) 2m
3:40 (3:42) (Class 4) (0-110,109) 4-Y-0+ **£4,827** (£1,417; £708; £353)

Form RPR
301- **1** **Dolzago**[10] 1440 5-11-3 **100**....................(b) PHide 100+
(G L Moore) *settled in tch: effrt after 3 out: chsd ldr after 2 out: rdn to ld sn after last: styd on wl* **7/1**
-000 **2** *1 ¼* **Silistra**[140] 895 6-10-0 **83**....................(p) BHitchcott 81
(Mrs L C Jewell) *prom: led after 3 out and kicked on: hdd sn after last: kpt on* **20/1**
POP2 **3** *2 ½* **Isam Top (FR)**[50] 1597 9-9-9 **83** oh6.................... RStephens[(5)] 78
(M J Hogan) *led to 2nd: styd prom: chal and upsides bef 2 out: sn nt qckn: eased whn hld nr fin* **20/1**
51-0 **4** *¾* **Hail The King (USA)**[31] 1793 5-10-13 **103**.................... RLucey-Butler[(7)] 97
(R M Carson) *hld up in last trio: blnd 6th and lost tch: shuffled along and stdy prog fr 3 out: rdn and styd on flat: nvr nr ldrs* **8/1**
POS6 **5** *2* **Private Benjamin**[31] 1804 5-10-13 **96**.................... MBatchelor 89+
(M R Hoad) *nt fluent: hld up in last trio: prog 3 out: sn chsd ldrs: mstke 2 out: no ex after* **12/1**
P-0F **6** *shd* **Sunley Future (IRE)**[43] 1672 6-11-2 **99**.................... JPMcNamara 91
(M F Harris) *set off last: plld way through to ld 2nd: hdd after 3 out: one pce* **16/1**
20-P **7** *18* **Amnesty**[192] 312 6-10-12 **95**.................... JEMoore 83+
(G L Moore) *settled midfield: effrt 3 out: rdn to chal and n.m.r bnd bef 2 out: sn wknd and eased* **3/1**[1]
-0U0 **8** *1 ½* **Domenico (IRE)**[12] 2103 7-10-7 **90**.................... JMogford 63
(J R Jenkins) *settled midfield: rdn 3 out: sn wknd* **7/1**
1-23 **9** *shd* **Bonny Grey**[17] 2002 7-11-5 **109**.................... MrNPearce[(7)] 82
(D Burchell) *t.k.h: prom: lost pl 5th: wl in rr after next: wknd* **9/2**[2]
130- **10** *17* **Batswing**[247] 4437 10-11-4 **108**.................... EDehdashti[(7)] 64
(G L Moore) *settled in last trio: last and losing tch 6th: sn t.o* **13/2**[3]

4m 3.40s (2.20) **Going Correction** +0.175s/f (Yiel) **10** Ran SP% **115.7**
Speed ratings: **101,100,99,98,97 97,88,87,87,79** CSF £127.02 CT £2644.35 TOTE £5.10: £2.60, £4.00, £5.00; EX 240.90 Place 6 £15.70, Place 5 £9.42.
Owner R Kiernan, Paul Chapman **Bred** Cheveley Park Stud Ltd **Trained** Woodingdean, E Sussex

FOCUS
A moderate handicap hurdle and not a race to be positive about. The third and fifth are the best guides to the level of the form.

NOTEBOOK
Dolzago was well beaten in two runs on the Flat recently, but they clearly put him spot on for his return to hurdling and, just 1lb higher than when winning over course and distance on last start over obstacles 427 days previously, proved good enough to follow up. He should not go up too much for this and could well complete the hat-trick. *(op 6-1)*
Silistra is still a maiden but this was a decent enough effort off the back of a 140-day break, and he could surely find a similar race off his current mark. *(tchd 22-1)*
Isam Top(FR) has an awful wins-to-runs record and this was just another respectable effort in defeat. *(op 16-1)*
Hail The King(USA) was given plenty to do but still seemed to run close to his best. *(tchd 9-1)*
Private Benjamin's only previous hurdles success came over course and distance, and this was a reasonable effort.
Amnesty, pulled up at Ludlow when last seen 192 days previously, was in the process of running a good race when he was hampered on the bend before the second last. Better than he showed as a result, he can be given another chance. *(op 7-2 tchd 4-1)*
Bonny Grey did not shape too badly on her reappearance, but this was disappointing. *(op 5-1 tchd 7-2)*
T/Plt: £19.80 to a £1 stake. Pool: £41,264.55. 1,519.90 winning tickets. T/Qpdt: £12.20 to a £1 stake. Pool: £3,404.80. 205.60 winning tickets. JN

2008 TOWCESTER (R-H)
Sunday, November 20
2380 Meeting Abandoned - Frost

2387 - 2394a (Foreign Racing) - See Raceform Interactive

2360 PUNCHESTOWN (R-H)
Sunday, November 20

OFFICIAL GOING: Soft

2395a VOLKSWAGON JETTA CRADDOCKSTOWN NOVICE CHASE (GRADE 2) 2m
1:15 (1:15) 4-Y-0+ **£27,702** (£8,127; £3,872; £1,319)

RPR
1 **Justified (IRE)**[32] 1790 6-11-4.................... JRBarry 146+
(E Sheehy, Ire) *mde all: nt fluent 4 out: drew clr after 3 out: styd on strly: impressive* **1/1**[1]
2 *14* **Wild Passion (GER)**[18] 1998 5-11-1.................... PCarberry 124
(Noel Meade, Ire) *cl 2nd: slt mstke 4 out: rdn and outpcd after 3 out: no ex fr next* **13/8**[2]
3 *7* **Top Strategy (IRE)**[21] 1944 5-11-1.................... RWalsh 115
(T M Walsh, Ire) *hld up in rr: lost tch bef 5 out: styd on fr 3 out* **25/1**
4 *25* **Arteea (IRE)**[21] 1944 6-11-7.................... AndrewJMcNamara 96
(Michael Hourigan, Ire) *chsd ldrs in 3rd: rdn and outpcd bef 4 out: no ex fr next* **6/1**[3]
5 *1* **Lissbonney Project (IRE)**[10] 2156 7-11-4.................... BJGeraghty 92
(Philip Fenton, Ire) *hld up: slt mstke 6 out: trailing fr next* **25/1**

4m 15.5s **Going Correction** +0.20s/f (Yiel) **5** Ran SP% **110.1**
Speed ratings: **113,106,102,90,89** CSF £3.13 TOTE £2.20: £1.10, £1.60; DF 3.70.
Owner Braybrook Syndicate **Bred** Miss Maura McGuinness **Trained** Graiguenamanagh, Kilkenny

NOTEBOOK
Justified(IRE), not fluent four out, was clear and going on from the next. A slight mistake two out didn't break his stride and he won very easily. He looks a genuine Arkle prospect and his temperament seems to have settled down. *(op 5/4)*
Wild Passion(GER), very much the weaker in the market, ran second throughout. Not clever at the fourth last, he couldn't go with the winner from the next and was very tired when drifting left at the last fence. *(op 6/4)*
Top Strategy(IRE) was never placed to play any role.
Arteea(IRE) ran a fair third until weakening four out. *(op 9/2)*
Lissbonney Project(IRE) jumped a fence on the way to the start but never play a role in the race itself.

2397a MAPLEWOOD DEVELOPMENTS MORGIANA HURDLE (GRADE 2) 2m
2:15 (2:18) 4-Y-0+ **£32,319** (£9,482; £4,517; £1,539)

RPR
1 **Brave Inca (IRE)**[205] 114 7-11-12 **166**.................... APMcCoy 161+
(C A Murphy, Ire) *led: rdn and strly pressed 3 out: hdd appr last: rallied to regain ld early run-in: styd on wl u.p* **11/4**[3]
2 *½* **Essex (IRE)**[35] 4383 5-11-7 **152**.................... RWalsh 156
(M J P O'Brien, Ire) *a.p: 2nd and chal after 2 out: slt advantage appr last: hdd early run-in: styd on wl u.p* **9/4**[2]
3 *4* **Harchibald (FR)**[49] 1621 6-11-12 **166**.................... PCarberry 160+
(Noel Meade, Ire) *hld up in 4th: hdwy after 2 out: cl 3rd on inner whn bdly hmpd early st: sn swtchd: no imp fr bef last* **7/4**[1]
4 *1 ½* **Newmill (IRE)**[206] 89 7-11-12 **140**.................... AndrewJMcNamara 155
(John Joseph Murphy, Ire) *hld up in rr: kpt on wout threatening fr 2 out* **50/1**
5 *½* **Macs Joy (IRE)**[205] 114 6-11-12 **164**.................... BJGeraghty 155
(Mrs John Harrington, Ire) *prom: 2nd 3 out: 3rd after slt mstke 2 out: no ex st* **11/2**

4m 14.7s **Going Correction** +0.575s/f (Soft) **5** Ran SP% **111.1**
Speed ratings: **98,97,95,95,94** CSF £9.62 TOTE £4.10: £1.80, £1.50; DF 8.60.
Owner Novices Syndicate **Bred** D W Macauley **Trained** Gorey, Co Wexford
■ Stewards' Enquiry : P Carberry two-day ban (reduced from three on appeal): careless riding (Dec 7,8)

NOTEBOOK
Brave Inca(IRE) was turned out in immaculate style but still carried a fair bit of condition. He made virtually all in a steadily run race. McCoy wouldn't let Carberry through on his inner on the long run to the last and then had to peg back Essex's narrow advantage early on the flat. But on both occasions the response was instant and willing, although he had a hard enough race for his reappearance. The decision to postpone going over fences for another year looks a correct one at this stage. *(op 5/2)*
Essex(IRE) went with the winner from two out and gained a slight initiative after the last but had to surrender to the winner's determination. He too had a hard race. *(op 3/1)*
Harchibald(FR), last year's winner, travelled well on the inner from two out and was always holding his position. In full flight early in the straight, Carberry seized an opportunity to go between Brave Inca and the rails but came out of the encounter with a three-day ban. The horse collided with the rails and then switched out. Even had he got through that tight gap, there would have been more than a possibility that Harchibald would have seen too much daylight. He remains unlucky, but the trouble is of his own making. *(op 6/4)*
Newmill(IRE) was right behind them in the straight and his proximity raises a question mark but it was a slowly run contest.
Macs Joy(IRE), second over the third last, was a spent force in the straight and looked in need of this. *(op 5/1)*

2396 - 2404a (Foreign Racing) - See Raceform Interactive

2139 LUDLOW (R-H)

Monday, November 21

2405 Meeting Abandoned - Frost

2106 SEDGEFIELD (L-H)

Tuesday, November 22

OFFICIAL GOING: Good (good to soft in places) changing to good to soft after race 2 (1.00) (meeting abandoned after race 6 (3.00) due to fog)

The last race was abandoned due to fog.

Wind: Nil

2412 GROSSICKRACING.CO.UK MARES' ONLY MAIDEN HURDLE (DIV I) (8 hdls) 2m 1f

12:30 (12:35) (Class 4) 4-Y-O+ **£2,719** (£798; £399; £199)

Form RPR

43-5 **1** **Air Of Affection**[211] 27 4-11-0 GLee 92
(J R Turner) *led after 1st: rdn appr last: styd on wl flat* **14/1**

6-1 **2** ¾ **Camden Bella**[192] 349 5-11-0 ADobbin 91
(N G Richards) *trckd ldrs: nt fluent and reminders 3rd: hdwy 3 out: rdn to chse wnr next: styd on u.p flat* **11/8**[1]

6-63 **3** 9 **Sunisa (IRE)**[10] 2179 4-11-0 92 (t) ADempsey 82
(J Mackie) *trckd ldrs: hdwy to chse wnr 3 out: rdn along bef next and kpt on same pce* **10/3**[2]

61-6 **4** nk **Powerlove (FR)**[16] 2062 4-10-11 KJMercer(3) 82
(Mrs S C Bradburne) *hld up in tch: pushed along 3 out: rdn along to chse ldrs appr next: kpt on flat* **11/2**[3]

34 **5** 3½ **Showtime Annie**[8] 2062 4-10-11 ACCoyle(3) 78
(A Bailey) *in tch: hdwy to chse ldrs 5th: rdn along after 3 out and sn wknd* **14/1**

U **6** 1½ **Nowa Huta (FR)**[14] 2106 4-10-7 BenOrde-Powlett(7) 77
(Jedd O'Keeffe) *chsd ldrs: rdn along 3 out: sn wknd* **25/1**

0U50 **7** 6 **Thorn Of The Rose (IRE)**[14] 2108 4-10-9 DCCostello(5) 71
(James Moffatt) *hit 3rd: a rr* **100/1**

340 **8** 5 **Silver Bow**[45] 1674 4-11-0 DO'Meara 66
(J M Jefferson) *keen: led tl after 1st: prom tl rdn along appr 3 out and sn wknd* **33/1**

5-0 **9** 1¼ **Penney Lane**[191] 375 4-10-11 PBuchanan(3) 64
(Miss Kate Milligan) *keen: chsd ldrs: rdn along 1/2-way: sn wknd* **100/1**

05- **10** 3 **Connaught Lady (IRE)**[509] 858 6-10-7 TJDreaper(7) 61
(Ferdy Murphy) *a rr* **20/1**

4m 20.0s (13.50) **Going Correction** +0.375s/f (Yiel)
WFA 4 from 5yo+ 12lb **10** Ran SP% **107.4**
Speed ratings: **83,82,78,78,76 75,73,70,70,68** CSF £30.85 TOTE £11.10: £3.60, £1.10, £1.10; EX 23.90.

Owner Miss S J Turner **Bred** Mrs Celia Miller **Trained** Norton-le-Clay, N Yorks

FOCUS
A race run at a modest pace and a very moderate winning time, over eight seconds slower than the second division. The third is the best guide to the level of the form.

NOTEBOOK
Air Of Affection, who showed some ability in four bumpers, was left alone to set a modest gallop on this hurdling debut. Her rider cannily injected a bit of pace rounding the home turn and that probably made the difference between victory and defeat. The way the race was run and the slow time does make the form suspect, however. *(op 16-1 tchd 18-1)*
Camden Bella, another making her hurdling debut, was almost certainly undone by the way the race was run as she could never quite summon the speed to get to the shrewdly-ridden winner. She should go one better in a more truly-run race or when faced with a stiffer test. *(op Evens)*
Sunisa(IRE), who had the edge in hurdling experience over the front pair, had every chance but proved one-paced over the last couple of flights and is beginning to look exposed. She may be better off in a novices' handicap. *(op 7-2 tchd 3-1)*
Powerlove(FR) did not really progress from her hurdling debut, but was another probably undone by the lack of pace and is worth another chance. *(op 8-1)*
Showtime Annie did not seem to see out the trip even in a race run at such a moderate pace. *(op 18-1)*

2413 BETFRED 0800 7311210 H'CAP CHASE (21 fncs) 3m 3f

1:00 (1:01) (Class 4) (0-95,95) 5-Y-O+ **£3,583** (£1,044; £522)

Form RPR

P604 **1** **Bang And Blame (IRE)**[27] 1886 9-9-9 69 oh9 MJMcAlister(5) 86+
(M W Easterby) *cl up: led 6th: rdn along 3 out: lft wl clr next: styd on* **33/1**

2P-4 **2** 14 **To The Future (IRE)**[23] 1943 9-11-2 85 ADempsey 83
(A Parker) *chsd ldrs: rdn along 5 out: outpcd next: hit 3 out and sn drvn: lft poor 2nd 2 out* **14/1**

6-01 **3** 11 **Celtic Flow**[27] 1886 7-9-11 69 oh3 PAspell(3) 61+
(C R Wilson) *led to 5th: cl up: hit 11th: rdn along and outpcd fr 4 out: tired whn hit next: plugged on* **7/1**[3]

-F0P **4** 16 **Pottsy's Joy**[27] 1888 8-11-1 84 PWhelan 55
(Mrs S J Smith) *midfield: hdwy to chse ldrs 11th: rdn along and lost pl 16th: sn bhd* **25/1**

-140 **5** 13 **Ta Ta For Now**[53] 1589 8-11-3 89 PBuchanan(3) 47
(Mrs S C Bradburne) *a rr: t.o fr 1/2-way* **18/1**

P26- **6** 14 **Sylviesbuck (IRE)**[219] 4875 8-11-1 84 FKeniry 28
(G M Moore) *a bhd: t.o fr 1/2-way* **10/1**

P-05 **P** **Minster Brig**[27] 1884 6-10-0 69 oh9 (p) BHarding —
(A Parker) *a bhd: p.u after 14th* **50/1**

211 **P** **Tee-Jay (IRE)**[45] 1686 9-11-10 93 NPMulholland —
(M D Hammond) *prom: lost pl 8th: bhd whn p.u bef 11th* **8/1**

32U **P** **Chancers Dante (IRE)**[8] 2237 9-9-11 69 oh4 (b) KJMercer(3) —
(Ferdy Murphy) *in tch: rdn along and wknd 15th: bhd whn p.u bef 3 out* **9/1**

44-F **P** **Briar's Mist (IRE)**[30] 1848 8-11-11 94 (b) RMcGrath —
(C Grant) *towards rr: hit 11th: sn rdn along and mstke 14th: p.u after* **14/1**

P340 **P** **Benefit**[167] 690 11-11-0 83 TSiddall —
(Miss L C Siddall) *midfield: pushed along and lost pl 1/2-way: bhd whn puleld up bef 16th* **28/1**

0-5F **P** **Contract Scotland (IRE)**[31] 1837 10-11-12 95 (p) ADobbin —
(L Lungo) *chsd ldrs: hit 7th: rdn along and wknd 11th: bhd whn p.u after 14th* **17/2**

343 **P** **Cirrus (FR)**[14] 2109 6-11-12 95 JimCrowley —
(K G Reveley) *midfield: pushed along 1/2-way: rdn along and lost pl 13th: bhd whn p.u bef 17th* **11/2**[1]

3-2P **P** **Bright Steel (IRE)**[17] 2039 8-10-10 79 (b[1]) GLee —
(M Todhunter) *cl up: led 5th tl mstke and hdd next: hit 8th and sn rdn along: sn wknd and bhd whn puleld up bef 15th* **14/1**

031U **U** **Dark Thunder (IRE)**[41] 1713 8-10-2 78 (b) PJMcDonald(7) 90
(Ferdy Murphy) *hld up: stdy hdwy 1/2-way: chsd ldrs 6 out: chal 4 out: rdn next: 2 l down whn blnd and uns rdr 2 out* **13/2**[2]

6m 59.9s (-6.90) **Going Correction** +0.375s/f (Yiel) **15** Ran SP% **119.4**
Speed ratings: **100,95,92,87,84 79,—,—,—,— —,—,—,—,—** CSF £420.72 CT £3595.29 TOTE £75.80: £21.20, £10.00, £1.90; EX 1189.10.

Owner Edward C Wilkin **Bred** Miss Sandra Hunter **Trained** Sheriff Hutton, N Yorks

FOCUS
An ordinary race of its type, but it still proved a stiff task for many with only six of the 15 runners completing. The winner is rated through previous marks, but the form is not worth a great deal.

NOTEBOOK
Bang And Blame(IRE), 9lb out of the handicap and well beaten in all four of his starts this season, was given a very positive ride. He had a lead of about a length and was being strongly pressed when his only danger departed two from home, leaving him to come home clear and register his *first victory under Rules. The form does not look anything special though. Official explanation: trainer's representative said, regarding the improved form shown, gelding was better suited by making the running*
To The Future(IRE) had every chance and ran his race, but the ground was probably not soft enough for him.
Celtic Flow, still 3lb out of the handicap despite going up 7lb for her course-and-distance victory last month, was still in with a shout when a blunder five from home signalled the beginning of the end.
Pottsy's Joy has become well handicapped on the best of his hurdles form and should have liked this ground, but performed only adequately without looking a winner waiting to happen.
Ta Ta For Now ran moderately and seemed to have gone off the boil.
Contract Scotland(IRE) *Official explanation: jockey said gelding never travelled (op 9-1)*
Tee-Jay(IRE) *Official explanation: jockey said gelding was unsuited by the good (good to soft places) ground (op 9-1)*
Cirrus(FR), stepping up six furlongs from his promising chasing debut on this first try in a *handicap, ran poorly and now has something to prove. Official explanation: jockey said gelding never travelled (op 9-1)*
Dark Thunder(IRE), a winner over course and distance on his last visit, had every chance and was about a length down when he hit the top of the second last and sent his rider over his head. *(op 9-1)*

2414 GROSSICKRACING.CO.UK MARES' ONLY MAIDEN HURDLE (DIV II) (8 hdls) 2m 1f

1:30 (1:32) (Class 4) 4-Y-O+ **£2,719** (£798; £399; £199)

Form RPR

1 **Charlotte Vale**[21] 4-11-0 ADobbin 106+
(M D Hammond) *in tch: hdwy 1/2-way: led 2 out: rdn last: styd on wl flat* **7/2**[2]

33/2 **2** 5 **Sabreflight**[14] 2112 5-11-0 GLee 99
(J Howard Johnson) *trckd ldrs on inner: hdwy to ld 5th: rdn along and hdd 2 out: drvn and rallied appr last: one pce flat* **15/8**[1]

F **3** 4 **Ile Maurice (FR)**[14] 2106 5-10-11 KJMercer(3) 95+
(Ferdy Murphy) *hld up: hdwy 1/2-way: chsd ldrs 3 out: rdn and kpt on same pce fr next* **25/1**

152- **4** 3½ **Diklers Rose (IRE)**[233] 4707 6-11-0 RMcGrath 94+
(K G Reveley) *hld up and bhd: stdy hdwy 5th: chsd ldrs whn mstke 2 out: sn rdn and btn* **15/8**[1]

0-50 **5** 14 **Now Then Auntie (IRE)**[31] 1839 4-10-11 PBuchanan(3) 78
(Mrs S A Watt) *prom: rdn along 5th: wknd 3 out* **66/1**

514 **6** 5 **Rising Tempest**[45] 1674 4-11-0 DElsworth 73
(Mrs S J Smith) *prom: rdn along and hit 3 out: sn wknd* **14/1**[3]

/24- **7** 8 **Leap Year Lass**[531] 699 5-10-11 MrTGreenall(3) 65
(C Grant) *midfield: hdwy to join ldrs 3rd: cl up tl rdn and wknd 3 out* **33/1**

4 **8** ¾ **Key In**[16] 2082 4-11-0 (t) PWhelan 64
(I W McInnes) *led to 5th: sn rdn along and wknd appr 3 out* **25/1**

4 **9** 17 **Entre Amis**[53] 1590 5-11-0 FKeniry 47
(G M Moore) *bhd fr 1/2-way* **50/1**

0P- **10** 3½ **Team Resdev (IRE)**[286] 3753 5-10-11 GBerridge(3) 43
(F P Murtagh) *chsd ldrs to 4th: sn lost pl and bhd* **100/1**

0 **P** **Glenisla Mist**[16] 2062 4-10-7 DDaSilva(7) —
(Mrs S C Bradburne) *chsd ldrs to 4th: sn lost pl and bhd: p.u bef last* **100/1**

4m 11.9s (5.40) **Going Correction** +0.375s/f (Yiel)
WFA 4 from 5yo+ 12lb **11** Ran SP% **114.5**
Speed ratings: **102,99,97,96,89 87,83,83,75,73** — CSF £10.07 TOTE £5.60: £1.20, £1.40, £3.50; EX 10.60.

Owner Peter J Davies **Bred** Snailwell Stud Co Ltd **Trained** Middleham, N Yorks

FOCUS
As in the first division, the early tempo was steady but the pace picked up much earlier and the winning time was more than eight seconds faster, if still only creditable for the type of race. The second sets the standard and the form should work out.

NOTEBOOK
Charlotte Vale, a triple 12-furlong winner on the level, took well to this game at the first time of asking and was able to utilise her Flat speed to maximum effect from the final flight. This stiff track seemed to suit her and she should be able to build on this. *(op 4-1 tchd 9-2 in a place)*
Sabreflight was entitled to 'bounce' having only recently returned from a 20-month layoff in a bumper on this track, but she ran with plenty of credit on this hurdling debut having been up with the pace from the off. She could not match the winner's Flat speed from the final flight and shapes as though a stiffer test will bring out the best in her. *(op 7-4)*
Ile Maurice(FR) managed to complete this time, but she lacked a turn of foot over the last couple of flights and will benefit from an extra half-mile at least. *(op 16-1)*
Diklers Rose(IRE) has already shown form over further and found this an inadequate test on her first run since April, but it should at least bring her on. *(op 9-4)*
Now Then Auntie(IRE) probably did not achieve a great deal. *(op 50-1)*
Rising Tempest, a bumper winner making her hurdling debut, should have lacked nothing in fitness but she made a mistake three from home just when she did not need it and she gradually dropped away from that point. *(tchd 12-1)*

2415 JOHN HELLENS MAIDEN CHASE (16 fncs) 2m 5f

2:00 (2:01) (Class 4) 4-Y-O+ **£4,128** (£1,211; £605; £302)

Form RPR

06- **1** **Theatre Knight (IRE)**[375] 2173 7-11-6 GLee 109+
(J Howard Johnson) *in tch: hdwy 9th: pushed along 4 out: j. slowly and outpcd 3 out rdn and styd on flat to ld on lin* **6/1**[3]

2-22 **2** shd **Rare Society (IRE)**[18] 2023 7-11-6 104 DElsworth 110+
(Mrs S J Smith) *a.p: effrt 4 out: sn led: rdn appr last: drvn flat: hdd on line* **3/1**[1]

-P33 **3** *8* **Jonny's Kick**[10] 2187 5-11-6 92 RGarritty 101+
(T D Easterby) *cl up: led 12th: rdn along next: sn hdd: drvn 2 out and wknd appr last* **12/1**

4 *14* **King Barry (FR)**[589] 6-11-6 RMcGrath 86+
(Miss P Robson) *prom: led 10th: pushed along and hdd 12th: rdn 4 out and grad wknd* **4/1**[2]

-34P **5** *¾* **Thyne Man (IRE)**[7] 2259 7-11-6 102 ADempsey 85
(J Mackie) *chsd ldrs: mstke 7th: hdwy 5 out: drvn along after next and btn after 3 out* **10/1**

00 **6** *dist* **Zaffiera (IRE)**[10] 2186 4-10-7 NPMulholland —
(M D Hammond) *mstke 1st: a rr* **100/1**

7 *3½* **Dannymolone (IRE)**[205] 6-11-6 FKeniry —
(M D Hammond) *midfield: hdwy 1/2-way: in tch whn hmpd 11th: sn rdn along and wknd bef 4 out* **16/1**

0-25 **8** *29* **Canavan (IRE)**[16] 2073 6-11-3 KJMercer(3) —
(Ferdy Murphy) *rr whn blnd 6th: a b ehind* **7/1**

4-04 **9** *10* **I'm Your Man**[167] 687 6-11-6 BHarding —
(Mrs Dianne Sayer) *a bhd* **33/1**

04-P **F** **Vital Spark**[25] 1915 6-11-6 DO'Meara —
(J M Jefferson) *midfield: hdwy and in tch whn hit 10th: fell next* **20/1**

530S **P** **Nomadic Blaze**[14] 2109 8-11-3 92 LMcGrath(3) —
(P G Atkinson) *led to 10th: grad wknd and bhd whn p.u bef 2 out* **20/1**

P-0P **P** **Lucken Howe**[18] 2023 6-11-3 GBerridge(3) —
(Mrs J K M Oliver) *mstkes: midfield tl lost pl 1/2-way: bhd whn p.u bef 10th* **100/1**

-6PP **P** **Loch Torridon**[131] 990 6-11-3 64 (t) PBuchanan(3) —
(James Moffatt) *midfield: rdn along and outpcd 1/2-way: bhd whn p.u bef 12th* **100/1**

5- **P** **Perfect Punch**[34] 2888 6-11-6 ADobbin —
(K G Reveley) *hld up: hdwy and in toyuch qwhn hit 8th: rdn along 12th: sn outpcd and bhd whn p.u bef 2 out* **12/1**

5m 27.1s (3.70) **Going Correction** +0.375s/f (Yiel)
WFA 4 from 5yo+ 13lb **14** Ran SP% **117.6**
Speed ratings: **107,106,103,98,98** —,—,—,—, —,—,—,— CSF £23.32 TOTE £6.00: £2.00, £1.60, £4.30; EX 18.80.

Owner Andrea & Graham Wylie **Bred** Miss Penny Downes **Trained** Billy Row, Co Durham

FOCUS
They went a decent pace in this maiden chase and, though it did not look a great contest on paper, the front pair may be worth noting, with the runner-up setting the level.

NOTEBOOK
Theatre Knight(IRE) ◆, a winning pointer in Ireland making his debut over regulation fences following a year off, looked a beaten fifth rounding the home turn but his rider never gave up and the combination eventually ground out victory in the final stride. He will probably need plenty of time to get over this, but looks to have a future. *(op 13-2)*
Rare Society(IRE) ◆ was probably unlucky not to break his duck this time. Up there from the off, he was in front from the home turn and was not helped by having to be steadied coming to the final fence and losing impetus as a result, but perhaps even more significant was that after giving his mount total assistance on the run-in, his rider eased off a stride before the line and the combination were mugged. There was no doubting his resolution judging by this effort and he will surely put matters right soon. *(op 11-4)*
Jonny's Kick ran well for a long way, but this was the eighth time he has finished third in his 12 career starts including in bumpers and over hurdles, which does suggest he lacks a killer punch. He may also be better off back in novices' handicaps. *(tchd 11-1)*
King Barry(FR), unbeaten in two points in the spring of 2004 and not seen since, showed up for a long way before understandably tiring. If given a bit of time to get over this, he should make his mark at this game. *(op 6-1)*
Thyne Man(IRE) was firmly put in his place from the home turn and has nothing at all in the way of scope. *(op 9-1)*
Lucken Howe *Official explanation: jockey said gelding bled from the nose*
Vital Spark, pulled up over hurdles on his return from a ten-month absence last month, was making his chasing debut and was still in with every chance when departing six from home.

2416 BETDIRECT.CO.UK NOVICES' H'CAP HURDLE (10 hdls) 2m 5f 110y
2:30 (2:30) (Class 4) (0-100,96) 3-Y-0+ **£3,142** (£922; £461; £230)

Form RPR

-054 **1** **Villago (GER)**[11] 2171 5-11-2 86 ADempsey 95+
(E W Tuer) *hld up: stdy hdwy 1/2-way: chsd ldrs 3 out: rdn to chal next: led appr last: drvn and styd on strly flat* **10/1**[3]

00-4 **2** *8* **Perfect Balance (IRE)**[16] 2081 4-10-11 84 KJMercer(3) 86+
(D W Thompson) *chsd ldrs: hdwy appr 3 out: rdn to chal next: ev ch tl drvn last and one pce flat* **25/1**

3-22 **3** *1½* **Bohemian Spirit (IRE)**[178] 555 7-11-5 96 MissRDavidson(7) 95
(N G Richards) *keen: led and sn clr: pushed along after 3 out: rdn next: hdd & wknd appr last* **7/1**[2]

5444 **4** *nk* **Sconced (USA)**[175] 603 10-10-9 82 (b) LMcGrath(3) 81
(R C Guest) *in tch: rdn along and outpcd after 4 out: styd on fr 2 out: nrst fin* **20/1**

24-1 **5** *3* **Piraeus (NZ)**[11] 2171 6-11-8 92 KJohnson 89+
(R Johnson) *racd wd: chsd ldrs tl rdn along and outpcd fr 3 out* **3/1**[1]

-035 **6** *15* **You Do The Math (IRE)**[33] 1794 5-11-5 89 ADobbin 77+
(L Lungo) *hld up: stdy hdwy to trck ldrs 6th: ev ch 3 out: sn rdn and wknd appr next* **3/1**[1]

5500 **7** *12* **Mr Twins (ARG)**[16] 2066 4-10-6 83 BenOrde-Powlett(7) 52
(M A Barnes) *bhd: mstke 4th: nvr a factor* **40/1**

4-02 **8** *2* **Timbuktu**[17] 2040 4-11-6 90 RMcGrath 57
(B Storey) *midfield: hdwy 1/2-way: rdn along and outpcd bef 3 out* **25/1**

0330 **9** *dist* **Lord Rosskit (IRE)**[10] 2191 5-11-6 90 FKeniry —
(G M Moore) *chsd ldr: rdn along 6th: sn lost pl and bhd fr 3 out* **25/1**

42-4 **10** *4* **Blue Rising**[31] 1826 4-11-4 95 TJDreaper(7) —
(Ferdy Murphy) *a rr* **14/1**

4B42 **11** *dist* **Alpha Juliet (IRE)**[14] 2107 4-10-7 82 DCCostello(5) —
(C J Teague) *a rr: mstke 7th and bhd after* **33/1**

300 **F** **Maunby Reveller**[28] 1873 3-9-11 93 GBartley(10) 65+
(P C Haslam) *rr and hit 1st: stdy hdwy 3 out: rdn along and in tch whn fell 2 out* **16/1**

-PP0 **P** **Wee Sean (IRE)**[56] 1566 5-10-6 79 PBuchanan(3) —
(Miss Lucinda V Russell) *chsd ldrs: rdn along and lost pl 6th: b ehind whn p.u bef 2 out* **50/1**

00-1 **P** **Melmount Star (IRE)**[87] 1337 7-11-6 90 GLee —
(J Howard Johnson) *hld up: hdwy to chse ldrs 1/2-way: rdn along and wknd 3 out: p.u bef next* **7/1**[2]

5m 21.4s (5.70) **Going Correction** +0.375s/f (Yiel)
WFA 3 from 4yo 16lb 4 from 5yo+ 13lb **14** Ran SP% **120.3**
Speed ratings: **104,101,100,100,99 93,89,88**,—,— —,—,—,— CSF £231.62 CT £1870.84 TOTE £8.80: £2.30, £9.10, £3.10; EX 360.90.

Owner E Tuer **Bred** Gestut Hof Ittlingen **Trained** Great Smeaton, N Yorks

FOCUS
A solid pace to this novices' handicap and the form should work out with the winner capable of winning again.

NOTEBOOK
Villago(GER) duly relished this longer trip and the further they went the better he was going. He did not stay when tried over longer trips than this last season, but is in much better form now and looks well worth another try. *(op 16-1)*
Perfect Balance(IRE) ran his race and seemed to get the trip well enough, but ran into a rival that was far too good for him. He may have preferred the ground even softer than this. *(tchd 33-1)*
Bohemian Spirit(IRE) has tried just about every other discipline before this - Flat turf, sand, pointing and hunter chasing - but this was his first try over hurdles on his 29th career start under Rules or otherwise. Enthusiastic out in front from the start, he did very well to hang on for as long as he did and looks worth another try. *(op 8-1)*
Sconced(USA), off since May, ran as though he needs an even greater test of stamina these days but he is always going to be vulnerable to younger horses in races like this. *(op 16-1)*
Piraeus(NZ), 8lb worse off with Villago having had him over twelve lengths behind when winning on his reappearance at Newcastle, could not confirm the form over this longer trip but may not have been at his best and still has a bit of scope. *(op 10-3)*
You Do The Math(IRE), making his handicap debut, should have had no problem with the trip or ground so this was a little disappointing. *(op 7-2)*
Maunby Reveller was in seventh place and well held when crumpling on landing two out. *(op 10-1)*
Melmount Star(IRE) *Official explanation: jockey said gelding lost its action (op 10-1)*

2417 BETFRED POKER H'CAP HURDLE (SERIES QUALIFIER) (13 hdls) 3m 3f 110y
3:00 (3:00) (Class 3) (0-115,115) 4-Y-0+ **£4,759** (£1,397; £698; £348)

Form RPR

0-00 **1** **Jethro Tull (IRE)**[11] 2169 6-9-12 92 WKennedy(5) 98
(G A Harker) *hld up in tch: hdwy 3 out: led after 2 out: sn rdn and styd on wl* **7/2**[1]

3322 **2** *2* **Russian Sky**[17] 2038 6-10-11 107 TMessenger(7) 111
(Mrs H O Graham) *trckd ldrs: effrt 3 out: rdn to chse wnr after next: drvn and kpt on flat* **6/1**[3]

0P4- **3** *3* **Forever Eyesofblue**[214] 4967 8-10-11 100 ADempsey 101
(A Parker) *a.p: led 3 out: sn rdn and hdd between last 2: kpt on same pce* **18/1**

0645 **4** *10* **Speed Kris (FR)**[16] 2066 6-10-7 103 (v) DDaSilva(7) 94
(Mrs S C Bradburne) *a.p: rdn along 3 out and grad wknd* **12/1**

02-4 **5** *1* **Totally Scottish**[17] 2038 9-11-2 115 JReveley(10) 105
(K G Reveley) *in tch: one pce fr 3 out* **10/1**

4024 **6** *26* **Caesar's Palace (GER)**[16] 2066 8-10-3 95 (p) PBuchanan(3) 59
(Miss Lucinda V Russell) *led to 3rd: rdn along and lost pl 5th: bhd fr 9th* **10/1**

011/ **7** *nk* **Corbie Lynn**[604] 4601 8-11-4 107 DO'Meara 71
(W S Coltherd) *a bhd* **33/1**

0P00 **8** *28* **Ramblees Holly**[6] 2264 7-10-11 100 PWhelan 36
(R S Wood) *bhd fr 1/2-way* **33/1**

0011 **9** *5* **Longstone Lass**[16] 2066 5-10-3 99 MissCMetcalfe(7) 30
(Miss Tracy Waggott) *prom: led 3rd tl hdd & wknd bef 3 out: sn bhd* **4/1**[2]

5-6P **P** **Simlet**[14] 2110 10-11-9 112 (tp) BHarding —
(E W Tuer) *bhd fr 1/2-way: p.u bef 2 out* **25/1**

31 **P** **Nine De Sivola (FR)**[10] 2186 4-11-4 110 KJMercer(3) —
(Ferdy Murphy) *a rr: mstke 8th: bhd whn p.u bef 2 out* **7/1**

4141 **P** **Relix (FR)**[167] 687 5-10-11 105 (t) DMcGann(5) —
(A M Crow) *chsd ldrs: rdn along 9th: sn wknd and bhd whn p.u bef 2 out* **16/1**

6m 53.2s (-10.70) **Going Correction** +0.375s/f (Yiel)
WFA 4 from 5yo+ 14lb **12** Ran SP% **115.8**
Speed ratings: **105,104,103,100,100 93,92,84,83**,— —,— CSF £23.99 CT £324.70 TOTE £4.10: £2.10, £2.90, £4.60; EX 39.80 Trifecta £280.30 Part won. Pool: £394.90 - 0.60 winning tickets. Place 6 £178.40, Place 5 £136.36.

Owner John J Maguire **Bred** Ian Hannon **Trained** Thirkleby, N Yorks

FOCUS
The visibility was particularly poor during this race. A fair contest in which the front three pulled well clear of the others and can all win races.

NOTEBOOK
Jethro Tull(IRE), making his handicap debut, relished this longer trip and always appeared to be travelling well just behind the leaders. He found plenty when asked for his effort and in the end won with a degree of comfort, so there is probably a bit more to come from him in these types of contests. *(op 4-1 tchd 10-3 and 3-1 in a place)*
Russian Sky ran with plenty of credit over this extended trip though he may be a little flattered to finish so close to the winner. He makes the frame regularly, but has only managed one victory in his career yet is creeping up the handicap despite not winning. *(tchd 13-2)*
Forever Eyesofblue, already a winner over this course and distance, ran another solid race having been given a positive ride and is entitled to come on for this first start in seven months. *(op 20-1)*
Speed Kris(FR) showed up for a long way, but did not appear to see out this extended trip and is still looking for his first win since arriving in this country.
Totally Scottish, trying a longer trip, ran his usual unconvincing race. *(op 8-1)*
Longstone Lass, bidding for a hat-trick, may have been racing off a 9lb higher mark but the way she dropped away suggests there may have been other reasons for this poor effort.
Relix(FR) *Official explanation: trainer said gelding had been unsuited by the good to soft ground (op 20-1)*
Nine De Sivola(FR) *Official explanation: jockey said gelding lost its action (op 20-1)*

2418 JOHN SMITH'S EXTRA SMOOTH H'CAP CHASE (13 fncs) 2m 110y
() (Class 4) (0-105,) 5-Y-0+ £

T/Plt: £396.00 to a £1 stake. Pool: £31,822.70. 58.65 winning tickets. T/Qpdt: £58.40 to a £1 stake. Pool: £3,632.50. 46.00 winning tickets. JR

1955 WARWICK (L-H)
Tuesday, November 22

OFFICIAL GOING: Good (good to soft in places)
Wind: Nil Weather: Overcast

2419 2006 ANNUAL MEMBERSHIP H'CAP HURDLE (8 hdls 1 omitted) 2m 3f
12:50 (12:50) (Class 4) (0-100,100) 4-Y-0+ **£2,706** (£788; £394)

Form RPR

056- **1** **Petwick (IRE)**[340] 2874 6-11-8 96 WHutchinson 110+
(A King) *hld up towards rr: hdwy 6th: slipped and rdr lost iron briefly bnd appr 2 out: led after 2 out: nt fluent last: r.o wl* **9/4**[1]

/P-0 **2** *7* **Pop Gun**[12] 2146 6-10-1 82 RSpate(7) 84
(Mrs K Waldron) *hld up in tch: led after 6th tl appr 2 out: no ex flat* **66/1**

3-00 **3** *2* **Danebank (IRE)**^{25} [1908] 5-11-5 **98**.. SCurling$^{(5)}$ 99+
(J Mackie) *a.p: led appr 2 out tl appr last: one pce* **14/1**
6-05 **4** *hd* **Foxmeade Dancer**^{10} [2182] 7-10-9 **83**.................................. AThornton 83
(P C Ritchens) *t.k.h: hdwy after 3rd: kpt on flat* **16/1**
50-0 **5** *2½* **Killer Cat (FR)**^{185} [451] 4-11-8 **96**..(t) APMcCoy 97+
(M C Pipe) *hld up: hdwy appr 5th: 4th and hld whn mstke last* **8/1**
/6P- **6** *1½* **Classic Rock**^{535} [648] 6-10-2 **76**.. CLlewellyn 72
(J W Unett) *w ldrs tl appr 4th: lost pl appr 5th: n.d after* **40/1**
450- **7** *2½* **Royal Niece (IRE)**^{233} [4725] 6-10-11 **85**................................ WMarston 79
(D J Wintle) *bhd tl sme hdwy appr 2 out: n.d* **10/1**
314- **8** *1¼* **Parish Oak**^{214} [4956] 10-10-4 **78**.. PMoloney 70
(Ian Williams) *hld up in mid-div: hdwy whn mstke 5th: n.d after* **6/1**^{3}
6-1 **9** *shd* **Silver City**^{12} [2148] 5-11-9 **97**... RJohnson 89
(P J Hobbs) *hld up and bhd: hdwy 6th: sn rdn and wknd* **10/3**^{2}
5016 **10** *10* **Island Warrior (IRE)**^{26} [1900] 10-10-1 **78**.........................(tp) TJPhelan$^{(3)}$ 63+
(B P J Baugh) *prom tl wknd 6th* **40/1**
-040 **11** *5* **Caspian Dusk**^{12} [2150] 4-11-1 **99**.......................................(p) SHaddon$^{(10)}$ 76
(W G M Turner) *bhd fr 4th* **33/1**
P0-P **12** *16* **Kadito**^{16} [2074] 9-10-8 **92**...(v) JStevenson$^{(10)}$ 53
(R Dickin) *prom: led 4th tl after 6th: wknd qckly* **50/1**
0304 **13** *½* **Dubai Dreams**^{10} [2191] 5-10-11 **88**..(b) LVickers$^{(3)}$ 49
(S R Bowring) *mde most to 4th: wknd after 6th* **25/1**
P-0P **14** *¾* **Master Brew**^{31} [1832] 7-10-5 **79**.. DCrosse 39
(J R Best) *towards rr: reminders after 3rd: pushed along after 4th: sn struggling* **33/1**
5 **15** *26* **Alchimiste (FR)**^{19} [2002] 4-11-5 **100**.................................. MrRLangley$^{(7)}$ 34
(Mrs E Langley) *a bhd: t.o* **100/1**

4m 35.0s (-9.00) **Going Correction** -0.425s/f (Good)
WFA 4 from 5yo+ 12lb **15** Ran SP% **119.9**
Speed ratings: **101,98,97,97,96 95,94,93,93,89 87,80,80,80,69** CSF £168.65 CT £1762.41 TOTE £3.60: £1.70, £10.50, £4.60; EX 245.10.
Owner Gilco **Bred** Patrick Kennedy **Trained** Barbury Castle, Wilts

FOCUS
A pretty moderate handicap hurdle, but Petwick looked to win with a bit in hand on his debut for Alan King. He is value for nearly double the official margin with the third and fourth running to their marks.

NOTEBOOK
Petwick(IRE), making his handicap debut on his first start for Alan King, stepped up on the form he showed when last seen 340 days previously and ran out a ready winner. He could easily have lost his chance when stumbling badly on the turn for home, but he recovered well and clearly had plenty left in reserve. This was a moderate race, but he ought to remain competitive off much higher marks. *(op 3-1 tchd 7-2)*
Pop Gun, well held in a seller on his return from a break at Taunton, stepped up significantly on that effort and seemed to run his best race to date in second. This effort was something of a surprise, but he did show promise in maiden hurdles back in 2003 and could confirm this. *(op 80-1)*
Danebank(IRE) had appeared to lose his way recently but this effort confirmed earlier promise, and he is clearly not without hope. *(op 9-1)*
Foxmeade Dancer ran a solid race in fourth, but his two previous wins came in selling company.
Killer Cat(FR), fitted with a tongue-tie for the first time off the back of a six-month break, never posed a serious threat but was not without promise. *(op 9-1 tchd 7-1)*
Silver City ran well below the form he showed to win a novice hurdle at Taunton on his previous start, and gave the impression a return to more forcing tactics would suit. *(op 7-2 tchd 3-1)*

2420 RACING UK H'CAP CHASE (12 fncs) 2m 110y
1:20 (1:21) (Class 4) (0-110,107) 5-Y-0+ **£3,744** (£1,099; £549; £274)

Form RPR
2214 **1** **Romany Dream**^{9} [2217] 7-11-4 **99**.......................................(b) WHutchinson 110+
(R Dickin) *a.p: rdn to ld last: edgd lft flat: r.o wl* **10/1**
4434 **2** *3½* **Jupon Vert (FR)**^{8} [2239] 8-10-12 **93**.................................. TScudamore 101
(R J Hodges) *a.p: led 6th: rdn appr 2 out: hdd last: one pce* **9/2**^{2}
011 **3** *1¼* **Welsh Main**^{33} [1805] 8-11-10 **105**.. APMcCoy 113+
(Miss Tor Sturgis) *hld up: lost pl after 6th: reminder after 5th: hdwy whn nt fluent 6th: rdn and rallied after 3 out: no ex flat* **9/4**^{1}
U0-1 **4** *shd* **Lindsay (FR)**^{16} [2074] 6-11-12 **107**.. RJohnson 116+
(H D Daly) *led and mstke 2nd: ev ch 3 out: sn rdn: one pce fr 2 out* **9/4**^{1}
-P3F **5** *7* **Barton Hill**^{30} [1855] 8-11-1 **103**..(b) DJacob$^{(7)}$ 104+
(D P Keane) *hld up: hdwy 6th: hit 7th: n.d after* **15/2**^{3}
0055 **6** *8* **Saorsie**^{9} [2217] 7-11-0 **95**... SCurran 86
(J C Fox) *a bhd* **33/1**
4P26 **7** *1* **Kaikovra (IRE)**^{16} [2074] 9-10-4 **85**.. PJBrennan 75
(M F Harris) *led to 2nd: hit 3rd: wknd 8th* **14/1**

4m 0.10s (-2.50) **Going Correction** -0.10s/f (Good) **7** Ran SP% **110.2**
Speed ratings: **102,100,99,99,96 92,92** CSF £50.34 TOTE £9.50: £3.00, £3.00; EX 58.00.
Owner The Snoozy Partnership **Bred** Mrs P Nicholson **Trained** Atherstone on Stour, Warwicks

FOCUS
A moderate handicap chase but competitive enough and the third and fourth set a reasonable standard.

NOTEBOOK
Romany Dream was slightly disappointing at Fontwell on her last start having won over this course and distance the time before, but Wayne Hutchinson, who won on her that day, replaced a 10lb claimer, and she returned to form with a determined victory. This is the highest mark she has ever won off, and things will be tougher in future. *(op 9-1 tchd 11-1 in a place)*
Jupon Vert(FR), winless since taking this race last year from a 6lb higher mark, ran a creditable race in second and can surely end his losing run whilst in this sort of form *(tchd 5-1)*
Welsh Main, chasing the hat-trick off a mark 9lb higher than when scoring at Ludlow last time, and a 16lb higher mark than when gaining the first of those two wins, was in trouble a fair way out and it was only really Tony McCoy's strength that saw him finish as close as he did. *(op 2-1)*
Lindsay(FR) could not defy a 12lb rise for his recent Hereford success. *(tchd 2-1)*
Barton Hill never posed a serious threat and still looks high enough in the weights. *(op 9-1)*

2421 WEATHERBYS INSURANCE NOVICES' HURDLE (11 hdls) 2m 5f
1:50 (1:51) (Class 4) 4-Y-0+ **£3,515** (£1,024; £512)

Form RPR
3/1 **1** **Ask The Gatherer (IRE)**^{22} [1950] 7-11-5 .... PMoloney 116+
(M Pitman) *hld up in tch: rdn to ld appr 2 out: drew clr flat: readily* **6/1**^{3}
66 **2** *3½* **Archduke Ferdinand (FR)**^{20} [1991] 7-10-12 .... WHutchinson 101
(A King) *plld hrd in rr: hdwy after 5th: ev ch 2 out: no ex flat* **20/1**
22-3 **3** *6* **Autumn Red (IRE)**^{21} [1968] 5-10-12 .... TDoyle 95
(P R Webber) *a.p: ev ch 3 out: one pce fr 2 out* **4/1**^{2}
10- **4** *1½* **Yaboya (IRE)**^{251} [4399] 6-10-12 .... APMcCoy 94
(P J Hobbs) *hld up and bhd: hdwy appr 7th: styd on same pce fr 2 out* **1/1**^{1}
0 **5** *½* **Buffers Lane (IRE)**^{33} [1799] 6-10-12 .... CLlewellyn 94+
(N A Twiston-Davies) *led to 3rd: led after 5th: hit 6th: rdn and hdd appr 2 out: one pce* **28/1**
4-33 **6** *5* **Flying Fuselier**^{21} [1969] 6-10-12 .... RJohnson 90+
(P J Hobbs) *hld up in tch: rdn after 8th: eased whn btn appr 2 out* **14/1**
0- **7** *1¾* **Confluence (IRE)**^{361} [2454] 4-10-12 .... NFehily 87+
(Jonjo O'Neill) *bhd tl sme hdwy appr 7th: no real prog fr 2 out* **33/1**
5 **8** *1½* **Penny Park (IRE)**^{12} [2144] 6-10-12 .... PJBrennan 85
(P J Hobbs) *hld up in tch: rdn and ev ch appr 2 out: wknd qckly flat: fin tired* **22/1**
0-P6 **9** *nk* **Runshan (IRE)**^{22} [1959] 5-10-12 .... TScudamore 84
(D G Bridgwater) *prom to 8th* **100/1**
0 **10** *21* **Royal Hilarity (IRE)**^{27} [1882] 5-10-12 .... ChristianWilliams 63
(Ian Williams) *hld up and bhd: hdwy whn nt fluent 7th: n.d after: mstke 3 out* **66/1**
2-03 **11** *dist* **Karawa**^{18} [2021] 6-10-5 .... AThornton —
(C L Tizzard) *sn bhd: rdn 5th: t.o* **25/1**
05-0 **12** *6* **Ellandshe (IRE)**^{25} [1903] 5-10-7 .... MNicolls$^{(5)}$ —
(P R Webber) *hld up in tch: wknd 7th: t.o* **18/1**
4 **13** *dist* **Ballyowen (IRE)**^{20} [1990] 6-10-12 .... WMarston —
(Mrs P Sly) *t.k.h: w ldr: led 3rd tl after 5th: wknd after 6th: t.o* **66/1**
P-0 **14** *7* **Cambo (FR)**^{9} [2212] 4-10-5 .... MGoldstein$^{(7)}$ —
(Miss Sheena West) *mid-div: nt fluent 5th: bhd: fr 8th: t.o* **100/1**
P **A One (IRE)**^{96} 6-10-5 .... MrJAJenkins$^{(7)}$ —
(H J Manners) *t.k.h in rr: t.o whn p.u bef 7th* **100/1**
P **Tequinha**^{192} 5-10-12 .... JAMcCarthy —
(C P Morlock) *bhd fr 7th: t.o whn p.u bef 3 out* **100/1**
U **Mere Conquest** 7-10-12 .... JMMaguire —
(R M Beckett) *towards rr whn blnd and uns rdr 6th* **100/1**
P **First Tee (IRE)** 6-10-12 .... BFenton —
(Jonjo O'Neill) *j. slowly 1st: a bhd: t.o whn p.u bef 3 out* **50/1**

5m 12.3s (-3.80) **Going Correction** -0.425s/f (Good)
WFA 4 from 5yo+ 13lb **18** Ran SP% **125.5**
Speed ratings: **90,88,86,85,85 83,83,82,82,74** —,—,—,— —,—,— CSF £117.78 TOTE £7.10: £2.00, £6.20, £1.80; EX 122.40.
Owner Mrs Toni S Tipper **Bred** C Kenneally **Trained** Upper Lambourn, Berks

FOCUS
Just an ordinary novice hurdle, and the time was moderate, but Ask The Gatherer defied his penalty in good style, is value for further and is progressing well. The race should produce future winners.

NOTEBOOK
Ask The Gatherer(IRE), the winner of a similar event over this trip at Plumpton on his return from a long absence, has clearly gone the right way since and defied his penalty with what was ultimately quite a comfortable success. Although there were plenty of runners, it remains to be seen how strong this form is, and things may have been tougher had the eventual runner-up jumped better, *but he is quickly developing into a useful sort and deserves to take his chance in better company. (op 9-2 tchd 13-2)*
Archduke Ferdinand(FR), the 2001 Northumberland Plate winner, improved on the form of his two previous efforts over hurdles on this step up from two miles but, keen for a lot of the way, he did not jump that fluently under pressure and gave the impression he would progress again for the experience. He looks up to winning a similar event, but also has the option of going handicapping (even if this effort has somewhat ruined his rating) and should soon make his mark. *(op 14-1)*
Autumn Red(IRE), up four furlongs in trip, confirmed both the promise he showed in bumpers and on his hurdling debut at Exeter, but he again just found a couple too good. He clearly has the ability to find a similar race, but is clearly also vulnerable to anything above average. *(op 9-2)*
Yaboya(IRE) looked of some potential when winning at Wincanton on his debut last season, but was well beaten in the Champion Bumper next time. Upped in trip for his hurdling debut, and reappearing after a 251-day break, he was in trouble a long way out never really looked winning. He has a fair bit to prove now. *(op 11-8)*
Buffers Lane(IRE), a winning pointer, stepped up on the form he showed on his debut under Rules in a Haydock bumper, and should continue to progress. *(op 25-1)*
Ballyowen(IRE) *Official explanation: trainer said gelding finished distressed*
Cambo(FR) *Official explanation: trainer said gelding bled from the nose*
A One(IRE) *Official explanation: jockey said, regarding the running and riding, his orders were to hold gelding up - as it was a runaway on flat, having run over 1m2f - to relax it and get it jumping, adding that due to a fast early pace he was unable to settle it, and gelding pulled hard down back straight; having been given a chance to get its second wind down the hill he felt it had no more to give 5 out, and as yard's horses had been held back in their work by frost, he felt it prudent to pull up (tchd 66-1)*
First Tee(IRE) *Official explanation: jockey said gelding hung right-handed (tchd 66-1)*

2422 HIGHFLYER BLOODSTOCK FOUR YEARS OLD NOVICES' CHASE (12 fncs) 2m 110y
2:20 (2:21) (Class 3) 4-Y-0 **£6,993** (£2,053; £1,026; £512)

Form RPR
633- **1** **Voy Por Ustedes (FR)**^{220} [4858] 4-10-10 .... APMcCoy 137+
(A King) *t.k.h in rr: hdwy 6th: hit 4 out: rdn to ld appr last: r.o wl* **6/5**^{1}
3 **2** *3½* **Le Volfoni (FR)**^{28} [1871] 4-10-10 .... RWalsh 129+
(P F Nicholls) *hld up in tch: led 6th to 7th: led 8th: rdn and hdd appr last: no ex* **7/4**^{2}
41-0 **3** *10* **Norma Hill**^{185} [450] 4-10-3 .... PMoloney 116+
(R Hollinshead) *led to 6th: led 7th to 8th: wknd last* **9/1**^{3}
4 *10* **No Full (FR)**^{168} 4-11-4 .... MAFitzgerald 120+
(P R Webber) *hld up in tch: chsd ldr 4th tl appr 6th: wknd 4 out* **10/1**
6- **P** **Oh Golly Gosh**^{386} [1958] 4-10-10 ....(p) JMMaguire —
(N P Littmoden) *chsd ldr to 4th: wknd 5th: t.o whn p.u bef 4 out* **66/1**
0665 **P** **Wilfred (IRE)**^{22} [1958] 4-10-10 **105**.. NFehily —
(Jonjo O'Neill) *hld up in tch: wknd appr 6th: bhd whn p.u bef 7th* **33/1**

3m 58.1s (-4.50) **Going Correction** -0.10s/f (Good) **6** Ran SP% **105.3**
Speed ratings: **107,105,100,95,**— — CSF £3.26 TOTE £2.00: £1.40, £1.20; EX 3.00.
Owner Sir Robert Ogden **Bred** Ecurie Macaire Guillaume, And Francis Picoulet **Trained** Barbury Castle, Wilts

FOCUS
Only four of the six completed, but this was still a decent novice chase and two potentially useful chasers in Voy Por Ustedes and Le Volfoni finished clear. The form should work out.

NOTEBOOK
Voy Por Ustedes(FR), a 130-rated hurdler, looked as though he could be even better over fences. Having raced keenly for much of the way, he appeared to have a fair bit to do on the turn for home when his main market rival had a clear advantage in front, but he responded well to pressure - certainly better than some might have expected given the way he pulled - and eventually ran out a ready winner. He can go on from this and deserves the chance to prove himself in better company, where a likely stronger pace should ensure he settles better. *(op 5-4 tchd 11-10)*
Le Volfoni(FR) ◆ was disappointing when a beaten favourite on his British debut at Cheltenham given the level of form he showed in his native France, but this was quite a bit better. He may have finished even closer had Ruby Walsh kicked for home when the eventual winner momentarily looked in trouble at the top of the straight, as he could only keep on at the one pace when that one recovered to challenge, but this was still a decent effort. Going the right way, he should soon be winning. *(op 13-8)*
Norma Hill was rated 126 over hurdles, but she still had no easy task behind two useful novices and finished well held in third. Still, this was a creditable performance and, open to plenty of improvement, she is likely to find plenty of easier opportunities. *(tchd 10-1)*

No Full(FR), the winner of a two and a half-mile chase at Auteuil when last seen in June, had no easy task on his British debut and was last of the four to complete. *(op 9-1 tchd 12-1)*

2423 WARWICK NOVICES' HURDLE (8 hdls) 2m
2:50 (2:51) (Class 4) 4-Y-0+ **£3,545** (£1,033; £516)

Form RPR

1 **Siberian Highness (FR)**[123] 4-10-5 WHutchinson 108+
(A King) *hld up: hdwy appr 4th: led last: shkn up and qcknd clr flat: comf* **85/40[2]**

3 2 5 **Bauhaus (IRE)**[16] 2070 4-10-12 WMarston 104+
(R T Phillips) *t.k.h: a.p: rdn to ld 2 out: hdd last: one pce* **14/1**

4 3 1 1/2 **Xamborough (FR)**[14] 2099 4-10-12 RWalsh 101
(B G Powell) *hld up in tch: lost pl 5th: styd on fr 2 out* **12/1**

4 4 1 1/2 **Eleazar (GER)**[25] 1908 4-10-12 JAMcCarthy 101+
(Mrs L Wadham) *hld up in tch: led 3 out: rdn and hdd 2 out: hit last: wknd flat* **8/1[3]**

P 5 2 1/2 **Zonic Boom (FR)**[85] 1364 5-10-7 PMerrigan(5) 98+
(Mrs H Dalton) *t.k.h: led tl appr 4th: one pce fr 2 out* **66/1**

6 6 11 **Nobelmann (GER)**[14] 2099 6-10-12 CLlewellyn 86
(A W Carroll) *hld up and bhd: hdwy 4th: no real prog fr 3 out* **100/1**

00-U 7 1 3/4 **Nice Horse (FR)**[21] 1968 4-10-12 APMcCoy 84
(M C Pipe) *prom: led appr 4th: rdn and hdd 3 out: wknd appr 2 out* **2/1[1]**

3 8 2 1/2 **Selective**[36] 1772 6-10-12 NFehily 84+
(A W Carroll) *hld up in tch: wknd appr 2 out* **8/1[3]**

9 1/2 **First Centurion**[393] 4-10-12 PMoloney 81
(Ian Williams) *bhd: blnd last: nvr nr ldrs* **66/1**

0 10 nk **Robbie Will**[19] 2006 4-10-12 JPMcNamara 81
(F Jordan) *nvr nr ldrs* **100/1**

40 11 2 **Dream Merchant (IRE)**[20] 1991 5-10-12 RJohnson 79
(P J Hobbs) *hld up and bhd: mstke 3rd: short-lived effrt 4th* **25/1**

12 1/2 **Knotty Ash Girl (IRE)**[42] 6-10-5 HOliver 71
(D J Wintle) *a bhd* **100/1**

5 13 1/2 **Khadija**[16] 2075 4-9-12 JPritchard(7) 71
(R Dickin) *hld up in tch: wknd 4th* **66/1**

64-4 14 dist **Negus De Beaumont (FR)**[206] 131 4-10-12 TDoyle —
(F Jordan) *led 2nd tl appr 4th: wknd appr 5th: t.o* **66/1**

15 1/2 **Moondancer (GER)**[10] 6-10-7 JFLevins(5) —
(B G Powell) *a bhd: t.o* **66/1**

P/ 16 dist **Stylish Prince**[653] 1007 5-10-12 (t) AO'Keeffe —
(R Lee) *a bhd: t.o* **100/1**

0P P **Hunting Lodge (IRE)**[9] 2216 4-10-5 MrJAJenkins(7) —
(H J Manners) *hld up in mid-div: hdwy 3rd: wknd 5th: p.u bef 2 out* **100/1**

3m 51.6s (-6.70) **Going Correction** -0.425s/f (Good)
WFA 4 from 5yo+ 12lb 17 Ran SP% **118.2**
Speed ratings: **99,96,95,95,93 88,87,86,85,85 84,84,84,—,— —,—** CSF £29.40 TOTE £2.90: £1.60, £3.30, £3.30; EX 28.00.
Owner Million In Mind Partnership **Bred** Haras De Manneville Et Al **Trained** Barbury Castle, Wilts
■ A first treble for jockey Wayne Hutchinson and a treble for the trainer Alan King.

FOCUS
Siberian Highness created a good impression and is value for more than double the winning margin, but this was a pretty ordinary novice hurdle with the sixth the best guide to the form.

NOTEBOOK
Siberian Highness(FR), a dual ten-furlong winner on the Flat in her native France, travelled strongly throughout on her hurdling debut and found enough in the straight to run out a comfortable winner. This was the ideal start to her new career, and she is open to plenty of improvement, but the form in behind is pretty limited so it would be unwise to get too carried away until she proves herself in better company. *(op 11-8 tchd 9-4 and 5-2 in a place)*
Bauhaus(IRE), a promising third in a modest maiden hurdle at Hereford on his debut over obstacles, has clearly gone the right way since then and ran creditably in second. He probably just bumped into a nice prospect in the winner, and looks up to finding a similar race. *(op 18-1 tchd 20-1)*
Xamborough(FR) looked to step up on the form he showed when fourth on his hurdling debut at Huntingdon. He just seemed to get outpaced at a crucial point, and could benefit from a longer distance in time. *(op 16-1)*
Eleazar(GER) confirmed the ability he showed when fourth on his hurdling debut at Uttoxeter, but again found a few too good. He seems to be going the right way, but is likely to find things easier when handicapped. *(op 10-1)*
Zonic Boom(FR), pulled up on his hurdling debut 85 days previously, was noted going quite well down the back straight and was able to see his race out this time. He should continue to progress. *(op 50-1)*
Nobelmann(GER) ◆, who caught the eye on his hurdling debut, again gave the impression he will be able to show improved form in due course. Perhaps he will be one to watch when handicapped.
Nice Horse(FR), who would have gone close had he not unseated in a decent event on his hurdling debut, failed to build on that and proved disappointing. He failed to progress after winning on his debut last season - albeit he was highly tried - and, after this dismal effort, he has to prove that he is not just effective when fresh. *(op 3-1)*
Hunting Lodge(IRE) *Official explanation: jockey said gelding lost its action but returned sound*

2424 SIMPSON STRONG-TIE H'CAP CHASE (20 fncs) 3m 2f
3:20 (3:20) (Class 4) (0-95,94) 5-Y-0+ **£3,381** (£985; £493)

Form RPR

5-24 1 **Cool Song**[22] 1960 9-9-12 **69** ow1 CBolger(3) 81+
(Miss Suzy Smith) *led 2nd to 3rd: remained prom: rdn 14th: led 4 out to 2 out: led flat: drvn out* **5/1[2]**

0-62 2 nk **Dunbrody Millar (IRE)**[13] 2126 7-11-8 **90** (p) RJohnson 103+
(P Bowen) *led 3rd: mstke 14th: rdn and hdd 4 out: led 2 out to flat: styd on* **11/2[3]**

23S2 3 3 **Sissinghurst Storm (IRE)**[12] 2151 7-10-7 **75** WHutchinson 85+
(R Dickin) *hld up and bhd: hdwy 11th: rdn appr 14th: one pce fr 2 out* **9/2[1]**

1352 4 3 **Sir Cumference**[8] 2243 9-11-12 **94** (b) SThomas 100+
(Miss Venetia Williams) *hld up: hdwy 7th: pckd 14th: rdn after 15th: wknd flat* **6/1**

4-P2 5 2 1/2 **Ebony Jack (IRE)**[8] 2237 8-10-0 **68** oh1 (t) TScudamore 71
(C L Tizzard) *led to 2nd: remained prom: rdn 3 out: wknd last* **9/1**

4214 6 17 **Southerndown (IRE)**[37] 1752 12-11-2 **84** TDoyle 70
(R Lee) *bhd: sme hdwy appr 14th: wknd 15th* **16/1**

P223 7 12 **Lost In Normandy (IRE)**[22] 1960 8-10-0 **68** (b) DCrosse 42
(Mrs L Williamson) *prom: rdn appr 14th: hit 15th: sn wknd* **7/1**

4-44 8 16 **Jacarado (IRE)**[16] 2072 7-9-11 **68** oh3 (v) TJMalone(3) 26
(R Dickin) *hld up and bhd: hdwy whn pckd 14th: hit 15th: sn wknd* **16/1**

P-3P 9 dist **House Warmer (IRE)**[22] 1960 6-10-4 **72** (p) ChristianWilliams —
(A Ennis) *a bhd: t.o* **16/1**

0P-P P **Baudolino**[16] 2073 8-10-2 **75** MNicolls(5) —
(R J Price) *bhd fr 8th: sn rdn: t.o 10th: p.u bef 13th* **66/1**

1-P3 P **St Kilda**[22] 1951 8-9-7 **68** oh3 (p) MissLucyBridges(7) —
(Miss Lucy Bridges) *hld up in mid-div: lost pl 7th: t.o 10th: p.u bef 14th* **16/1**

6m 41.1s (-22.90) **Going Correction** -0.10s/f (Good) 11 Ran SP% **112.0**
Speed ratings: **101,100,99,99,98 93,89,84,—,— —** CSF £31.74 CT £130.31 TOTE £6.50: £2.30, £2.90, £2.10; EX 43.60.
Owner M J Weaver **Bred** Ronald A Giles **Trained** Lews, E Sussex

FOCUS
A pretty moderate handicap chase but solid enough form with those immediately behind the first two running to their marks.

NOTEBOOK
Cool Song, winless since taking a beginners' chase in November 2003, had dropped to a career-low mark and took advantage in determined fashion. He is at the right end of the handicap, but his overall record suggests he is not one to take a short price about following up. *(op 11-2 tchd 6-1)*
Dunbrody Millar(IRE) had the cheekpieces re-fitted, but again just found one too good. Given this was just his third start for Peter Bowen, he could yet do better. *(op 4-1)*
Sissinghurst Storm(IRE), back up in trip following her second over just short of three miles at Taunton, was not that far off her best form in third, but is not the easiest to win with. *(op 5-1 tchd 11-2 in a place)*
Sir Cumference rarely runs a bad race but looks high enough in the weights. *(op 4-1)*
Ebony Jack(IRE) did not run badly but looked to be found out in this slightly better company. *(op 11-1)*

2425 EBF "JUNIOR" STANDARD OPEN NATIONAL HUNT FLAT RACE 1m 6f
3:50 (3:50) (Class 6) 3-Y-0 **£2,274** (£663; £331)

Form RPR

1 **Belita** 3-10-5 JGoldstein 95+
(Miss Sheena West) *hld up in tch: rdn over 1f out: led ins fnl f: r.o* **25/1**

1 2 1 1/2 **Saratogane (FR)**[19] 2013 3-10-12 TScudamore 101+
(M C Pipe) *prom: led over 5f out: rdn over 2f out: edgd rt and hdd ins fnl f: nt qckn* **7/2[2]**

3 9 **Zuzu Summit (IRE)** 3-9-12 JKington(7) 85
(M Scudamore) *prom: lost pl over 5f out: rdn over 3f out: styd on fnl 2f* **40/1**

2 4 1/2 **Zhivago's Princess (IRE)**[19] 2013 3-10-5 MBradburne 85+
(C G Cox) *a.p: rdn over 1f out: sn wknd* **9/2[3]**

3 5 6 **Rourke Star**[14] 2105 3-10-9 LVickers(3) 85
(S R Bowring) *hld up in rr: gd hdwy 6f out: no imp fnl 3f* **16/1**

6 2 1/2 **Aubigny (FR)** 3-10-12 WHutchinson 83
(A King) *bhd tl hdwy over 2f out: nvr trbld ldrs* **9/1**

7 2 1/2 **Lilian Alexander** 3-10-0 ow2 APogson(7) 75
(J R Holt) *hld up towards rr: hdwy 3f out: nvr nr ldrs* **66/1**

8 2 **Ihuru** 3-10-12 ATinkler 78
(J G Portman) *bhd tl sme hdwy fnl 2f: n.d* **66/1**

9 7 **Lets Cast Again** 3-10-12 TDoyle 73+
(P R Webber) *hld up in mid-div: hdwy 7f out: wknd over 3f out* **11/4[1]**

4 10 2 **Ausone**[35] 1785 3-10-2 ONelmes(3) 62
(Miss J R Gibney) *hld up in tch: wknd over 3f out* **12/1**

11 4 **Becky's Hill** 3-10-5 VSlattery 58
(Mrs Mary Hambro) *hld up in tch: rdn over 6f out: sn wknd* **40/1**

4 12 1 1/4 **Cape Guard**[19] 2014 3-10-12 APMcCoy 64
(F Jordan) *pushed along after 4f: a bhd* **16/1**

13 1/2 **Just Smudge** 3-10-12 SThomas 63
(A E Price) *chsd ldr: led 8f out tl over 5f out: rdn and wknd 4f out* **40/1**

14 3 **Blackbury** 3-10-5 WMarston 53
(J W Unett) *bhd: short-lived effrt over 8f out* **20/1**

15 24 **Incalotte** 3-10-5 JAMcCarthy 29
(J A Supple) *a bhd: t.o* **66/1**

16 nk **Brackenorah** 3-10-5 RGreene 29
(S C Burrough) *hld up in tch: rdn over 7f out: sn wknd: t.o* **50/1**

17 7 **Wizard Roc** 3-10-12 HOliver 29
(N E Berry) *a bhd: t.o* **66/1**

3m 19.1s 17 Ran SP% **120.4**
CSF £104.28 TOTE £46.20: £5.50, £2.00, £13.50; EX 289.60 Place 6 £120.51, Place 5 £47.52.
Owner Paul Hancock **Bred** Crandon Park Stud **Trained** Lewes, E Sussex

FOCUS
A modest bumper at best rated around the fourth and fifth.

NOTEBOOK
Belita, a 13,000gns half-sister to several winners, including fair hurdler Barneys Lyric, as well as bumper winner Alaskan Fizz, out of a middle-distance scorer on the Flat, did well to get the better of the more-experienced Pipe runner and make a winning debut. Things would be harder under a penalty in this sphere, but she ought to make a hurdler. *(op 33-1)*
Saratogane(FR) ran well under the penalty she picked up for winning at Towcester on her debut and did not look to have any major excuses. A half-sister to Lough Derg, she should make the grade over obstacles. *(op 11-4)*
Zuzu Summit(IRE), a half-sister to Summit Up, who was placed in bumpers, was noted travelling well down the back straight and stayed on after appearing to get a little outpaced.
Zhivago's Princess(IRE) was beaten only two and a half lengths by today's runner-up at Towcester on her debut, but she raced too keenly this time and was below form. *(tchd 4-1)*
Rourke Star ran creditably enough without proving his debut effort did not flatter him. *(op 20-1)*
Lets Cast Again, a half-brother to mile and a half sand winner Queen's Fantasy, was popular in the betting but looked in trouble some way out. *(op 3-1)*
T/Plt: £154.50 to a £1 stake. Pool: £40,407.35. 190.85 winning tickets. T/Qpdt: £12.10 to a £1 stake. Pool: £4,029.60. 245.60 winning tickets. KH

1980 CHEPSTOW (L-H)
Wednesday, November 23

OFFICIAL GOING: Good to soft
Wind: Nil Weather: Misty with spells of fog

2426 WEATHERBYS MESSAGING SERVICE "NATIONAL HUNT" NOVICES' HURDLE (DIV I) (11 hdls) 2m 4f
12:30 (12:34) (Class 4) 4-Y-0+ **£3,109** (£912; £456; £228)

Form RPR

10-2 1 **Mister Quasimodo**[21] 1980 5-10-12 JTizzard 114+
(C L Tizzard) *hld up: stdy hdwy 7th: rdn to ld after 3 out: r.o wl* **6/4[1]**

30-4 2 2 **Kildonnan**[21] 1980 6-10-12 WHutchinson 110
(J A B Old) *chsd ldr: rdn and kpt on same pce fr 2 out* **20/1**

10-3 3 3 1/2 **Glasker Mill (IRE)**[9] 2238 5-10-12 SThomas 107+
(Miss H C Knight) *hld up in tch: rdn whn hit 2 out: one pce* **2/1[2]**

1- **4** *7* **Calusa Charlie (IRE)**^{241} [4589] 6-10-12 .... TDoyle 99
(B G Powell) *hld up in mid-div: hdwy approaching 3 out: hit 2 out: nvr trbld ldrs* **16/1**

3 **5** *4* **Micky Cole (IRE)**^{32} [1833] 5-10-12 .... (b^{1}) RWalsh 95
(P F Nicholls) *prom tl wknd appr 3 out* **8/1**^{3}

5-50 **6** *shd* **Royal Cliche**^{27} [1892] 6-10-12 .... RJohnson 95
(R T Phillips) *hld up in tch: wknd appr 3 out* **50/1**

-061 **7** *2* **Surfboard (IRE)**^{38} [1755] 4-10-12 .... PJBrennan 98+
(P A Blockley) *led tl after 3 out: wknd after 2 out: tired whn mstke last* **40/1**

4 **8** *5* **Call Me Edward (IRE)**^{22} [1975] 4-10-12 .... CLlewellyn 88
(N A Twiston-Davies) *prom tl wknd 3 out* **25/1**

130 **9** *12* **Twelve Paces**^{26} [1908] 4-10-9 .... TJMalone$^{(3)}$ 76
(M C Pipe) *a in rr* **14/1**

3 **10** *3 ½* **Joseph Beuys (IRE)**^{21} [1985] 6-10-12 .... NFehily 72
(D P Keane) *a bhd* **66/1**

0/ **11** *dist* **The Gerry Man (IRE)**^{616} [4407] 6-10-12 .... WMarston —
(D J Wintle) *bhd: mstke 5th: nt fluent 6th: sn lost tch: t.o* **100/1**

course record
WFA 4 from 5yo+ 13lb **11** Ran SP% **112.5**
CSF £35.20 TOTE £2.40: £1.10, £3.90, £1.20; EX 55.90.
Owner J M Dare, T Hamlin, J W Snook **Bred** H T Cole **Trained** Milborne Port, Dorset

FOCUS
The visibility was poor for this contest and with no official time returned it is impossible to compare this race with the second division. The winner and third set the level and the form look fair for the grade.

NOTEBOOK
Mister Quasimodo confirmed the promise of his hurdling debut here earlier this month and had no Neptune Collonges to worry about this time. He won this with a degree of comfort and can probably win again under similar conditions, but it will be over fences that the best of him will be seen. *(op 2-1)*
Kildonnan ◆, always up with the pace, stuck in there and finished much closer to Mister Quasimodo than he did here last time. He should soon find a race over hurdles.
Glasker Mill(IRE) failed to really build on his Folkestone hurdling debut and even over this longer trip he always seemed to be struggling for pace. It may be he needs an even greater test. *(op 15-8)*
Calusa Charlie(IRE) ◆, racing for the first time since winning a bumper on his debut in the spring, showed enough to suggest he has a future at this game with this effort under his belt. *(tchd 20-1)*
Micky Cole(IRE), blinkered for the first time, was dropping half a mile in trip and was never able to match the principals for pace up the home straight. *(op 7-1)*
Surfboard(IRE), winner of a poor bumper at Hereford last month, made the majority of the running but did not appear to see out the trip. There looks to be a modest novice hurdle in him when the emphasis is less on stamina.

2427 WEATHERBYS MESSAGING SERVICE "NATIONAL HUNT" NOVICES' HURDLE (DIV II) (11 hdls) 2m 4f
1:05 (1:05) (Class 4) 4-Y-0+ **£3,103** (£911; £455; £227)

Form RPR

3 **1** **Gungadu**^{32} [1827] 5-10-12 .... RWalsh 122+
(P F Nicholls) *a gng wl: led after 7th: clr fr 2 out: easily* **1/5**^{1}

224- **2** *21* **Wellpict One (IRE)**^{277} [3953] 5-10-12 .... CLlewellyn 97+
(N A Twiston-Davies) *prom: led after 3rd: faltered paddock exit after 4th: hdd after 7th: no ch w wnr fr 2 out* **12/1**^{2}

3 *10* **Caveman**^{206} 5-10-12 .... TDoyle 82
(P R Webber) *hld up in tch: rdn appr 3 out: sn wknd* **25/1**

0-56 **4** *17* **Redlynch Spirit (IRE)**^{147} [866] 5-10-12 .... JTizzard 65
(C L Tizzard) *plld hrd early in rr: mstke 5th: poor 4th whn hit 2 out* **100/1**

020/ **5** *11* **Pin High (IRE)**^{589} [4819] 6-10-12 .... SThomas 54
(Miss H C Knight) *plld hrd early: hdwy after 7th: wknd 4 out* **33/1**

05 **6** *3 ½* **Little Word**^{32} [1833] 6-9-12 .... MrRhysHughes$^{(7)}$ 44
(P D Williams) *led: pckd 1st: hdd after 3rd: wkng whn mstke 7th* **66/1**

7 *6* **Oddington (IRE)**^{220} 5-10-12 .... PJBrennan 45
(Mrs Susan Nock) *hld up: hdwy 7th: wknd appr 4 out* **16/1**^{3}

8 *1 ½* **They Grabbed Me (IRE)**^{45} [1699] 4-9-12 .... MrCHughes$^{(7)}$ 36
(M C Pipe) *t.k.h early in rr: wl bhd fr 5th* **25/1**

404- **9** *14* **Montrolin**^{239} [4644] 5-10-12 .... RGreene 29
(S C Burrough) *hld up in tch: rdn 5th: nt fluent 7th: sn wknd* **66/1**

5m 1.80s (-0.90) **Going Correction** +0.025s/f (Yiel)
WFA 4 from 5yo+ 13lb **9** Ran SP% **111.5**
Speed ratings: **102,93,89,82,78 77,74,74,68** CSF £2.60 TOTE £1.20: £1.02, £1.90, £3.40; EX 3.40.
Owner Paul K Barber & Mrs M Findlay **Bred** Mrs Hugh Maitland-Jones **Trained** Ditcheat, Somerset

FOCUS
A one-horse race according to the market and so it proved. The winner looks a very nice prospect and is value for more than the official margin, with the runner-up and fourth to their bumper marks.

NOTEBOOK
Gungadu ◆, third in a slowly-run Grade Two on his hurdling debut here earlier this month, found this a whole lot easier and won just as his prohibitive odds suggested he should. He is likely to go back up in grade now and should make his presence felt in a few of the top staying novice hurdles. *(tchd 1-4)*
Wellpict One(IRE), placed in a couple of bumpers and racing for the first time since February, did not do much wrong apart from being awkward at the crossing on the bottom bend just past the stands and stuck with the short-priced favourite for as long as he could. He was very much second-best in this contest and will not always bump into one so smart. *(op 14-1 tchd 16-1)*
Caveman, racing for the first time since finishing runner-up in a point in May, did hint at some ability but the best of him may not be seen until he goes over regulation fences.
Redlynch Spirit(IRE), making his hurdling debut after finishing unplaced in three bumpers, may be capable of a bit better if he ever consents to settle.
Pin High(IRE) ended up well beaten, but was entitled to blow up on this return from a 19-month break.

2428 CHEPSTOW BOOKMAKERS SUPPORT INJURED JOCKEYS FUND (S) HURDLE (8 hdls) 2m 110y
1:35 (1:35) (Class 5) 4-7-Y-0 **£2,144** (£625; £312)

Form RPR

5/4- **1** **Beyondtherealm**^{555} [398] 7-10-7 .... CHonour$^{(5)}$ 90+
(J D Frost) *hld up in tch: wnt 2nd appr 4 out: led sn after last: r.o* **5/1**^{3}

/P06 **2** *2 ½* **Amanpuri (GER)**^{6} [2285] 7-10-12 90 .... CLlewellyn 89+
(P A Blockley) *led: hit 2 out: stmbld last: sn hdd: no ex* **4/1**^{2}

4434 **3** *11* **Rojabaa**^{19} [2015] 6-10-12 85 .... PJBrennan 76
(W G M Turner) *plld hrd early: hdwy 4th: wknd appr 3 out* **7/2**^{1}

0F32 **4** *1 ¼* **Urban Dream (IRE)**^{27} [1890] 4-10-12 88 .... RJohnson 74
(R A Farrant) *hld up in rr: rdn appr 3 out: styd on fr 2 out: nvr nrr* **7/2**^{1}

0450 **5** *2 ½* **Tizi Ouzou (IRE)**^{13} [2146] 4-10-5 88 .... (v) MrCHughes$^{(7)}$ 73+
(M C Pipe) *chsd ldr tl rdn and wknd appr 4 out* **11/2**

42P0 **6** *12* **The Wife's Sister**^{9} [2244] 4-10-0 87 .... StephenJCraine$^{(5)}$ 53
(D McCain) *hld up and bhd: rdn and short-lived effrt after 4th* **11/1**

40B4 **7** *9* **Beyond Borders (USA)**^{11} [2181] 7-10-12 74 .... (v) RGreene 51
(G F Edwards) *chsd ldrs: sn pushed along: rdn and wknd appr 4 out* **25/1**

00 **8** *dist* **Eudyptes**^{14} [2131] 6-10-12 .... HOliver —
(N E Berry) *sn bhd: t.o fr 4th* **50/1**

P0 **9** *dist* **Our Sion**^{6} [2283] 5-10-7 .... DLaverty$^{(5)}$ —
(Mrs A M Thorpe) *t.k.h: prom to 3rd: t.o* **66/1**

4m 10.6s (0.20) **Going Correction** +0.025s/f (Yiel)
WFA 4 from 5yo+ 12lb **9** Ran SP% **112.1**
Speed ratings: **100,98,93,93,91 86,82,—,—** CSF £24.63 TOTE £5.60: £1.50, £2.00, £1.50; EX 22.00.There was no bid for the winner. Amanpuri was claimed by Mrs A. M. Thorpe for £6,000.
Owner J D Frost **Bred** R G Frost **Trained** Scorriton, Devon

FOCUS
A routine seller which only concerned the front pair from a long way out. The form is solid enough with the winner to his mark.

NOTEBOOK
Beyondtherealm, reappearing after an 18-month layoff and dropping in grade, had only the eventual runner-up to worry about from a long way out and jumping the final flight much better than his rival made all the difference. Provided he remains sound, he may be able to find another modest race as he is still relatively lightly raced. *(op 7-2)*
Amanpuri(GER), dropping in trip, tried to make stamina count and made a bold bid to lead the whole way. He needed a good jump at the last with the eventual winner almost alongside, but instead he landed in a heap and that helped decide the outcome. *(op 6-1)*
Rojabaa never looked like getting on terms with the front two and may have found the ground softer than ideal. *(op 4-1)*
Urban Dream(IRE), even on this stiffer track, was always struggling to lay up and merely passed beaten horses up the home straight. A longer trip is required. *(tchd 4-1)*
Tizi Ouzou(IRE) did not improve for the reapplication of the visor and has become very untrustworthy. *(op 9-2 tchd 6-1)*

2429 KPMG NOVICES' H'CAP CHASE (12 fncs) 2m 110y
2:10 (2:11) (Class 4) (0-100,100) 4-Y-0+ **£4,001** (£1,174; £587; £293)

Form RPR

25F4 **1** **Rookery Lad**^{13} [2149] 7-11-6 94 .... DCrosse 103+
(C N Kellett) *chsd ldr fr 2nd: led 5 out: rdn appr 2 out: r.o wl* **5/1**^{3}

641/ **2** *2* **Afro Man**^{749} [1946] 7-11-12 100 .... NFehily 110+
(C J Mann) *t.k.h: hld up in tch: hit 1st: blnd 2nd: mstke 4 out: chsd wnr fr 3 out: r.o one pce* **9/4**^{1}

5000 **3** *1 ¾* **Reflex Blue**^{31} [1856] 8-10-6 80 .... (v) AO'Keeffe 86+
(R J Price) *hld up and bhd: hdwy appr 5 out: j.lft last: one pce* **14/1**

403- **4** *8* **Uncle Max (IRE)**^{441} [1394] 5-11-7 95 .... CLlewellyn 96+
(N A Twiston-Davies) *hdwy 3rd: ev ch 4 out: nt fluent 3 out: sn rdn: wknd flat* **10/3**^{2}

-PP2 **5** *10* **Look To The Future (IRE)**^{21} [1981] 11-10-6 85 .... LStephens$^{(5)}$ 71
(M J M Evans) *chsd ldr to 2nd: sn lost pl and bhd* **7/1**

0/5P **6** *2* **Senor Gigo**^{17} [2074] 7-10-2 76 .... (p) ChristianWilliams 60
(Evan Williams) *led: clr appr 2nd: hdd 5 out: wknd 4 out* **12/1**

23-5 **P** **Killy Beach**^{27} [1897] 7-10-0 79 oh1 ow5 .... CHonour$^{(5)}$ —
(J D Frost) *bhd tl p.u bef 2 out* **13/2**

4m 20.3s (-2.60) **Going Correction** +0.025s/f (Yiel) **7** Ran SP% **110.7**
Speed ratings: **107,106,105,101,96 95,—** CSF £16.24 TOTE £6.20: £1.90, £1.70; EX 18.90.
Owner S Kitching & Mrs K Taylor **Bred** B R Cambidge **Trained** Woodlane, Staffs

FOCUS
A modest contest of its type, but thanks to Senor Gigo at least the pace was decent. The form is solid enough with the third and fourth close to their hurdle marks.

NOTEBOOK
Rookery Lad, well handicapped on the pick of his hurdles form after sliding down the weights in recent months, would probably have preferred a quicker surface but got it right nonetheless and won his first chase at the tenth attempt. It would probably be wise to keep him in races like this rather than run him in non-handicap novice chases with a penalty. *(op 6-1 tchd 9-2)*
Afro Man, making his chasing debut after two years off, was well supported in the market and, despite some iffy jumping, he still appeared to be travelling best of the leading quartet over the last few fences, but he did not find as much off the bridle as had looked likely. He is entitled to come on for this, but will need to brush up his fencing technique. *(op 11-4)*
Reflex Blue, making a fairly belated debut over fences, had every chance up the home straight but could never land an effective blow. This effort did not really convince whether he has a future at this game, but he has become very hard to win with over hurdles so he may as well persevere or go back onto sand on which he has enjoyed a fair degree of success in the last couple of years.
Uncle Max(IRE), another making his chasing debut, was close enough if good enough starting up the home straight, but a slow jump three out soon saw him struggling. *(tchd 4-1)*
Look To The Future(IRE) ideally needs further, but age is not on his side in contests like this. *(op 11-2)*
Senor Gigo probably went off too fast in the cheekpieces and had run himself into the ground soon after turning for home. *(op 9-1)*

2430 GG RACING H'CAP HURDLE (12 hdls) 3m
2:45 (2:45) (Class 3) (0-125,120) 4-Y-0+ **£5,016** (£1,472; £736; £367)

Form RPR

143- **1** **On Y Va (FR)**^{221} [4866] 7-11-6 114 .... (t) RJohnson 114+
(R T Phillips) *hld up in rr: hdwy 4 out: sn rdn: sltly outpcd 2 out: styd on u.p to ld cl home* **9/2**^{2}

01P1 **2** *nk* **Irishkawa Bellevue (FR)**^{42} [1715] 7-11-12 120 .... (b) DCrosse 120+
(Jean-Rene Auvray) *w ldr: rdn after 8th: ev ch 3 out: pckd last: styd on* **5/1**^{3}

-56P **3** *½* **Keepers Mead (IRE)**^{22} [1973] 7-10-11 105 .... RWalford 103
(R H Alner) *led to 3 out: sn rdn and hung lft: styd on flat* **7/1**

/40- **4** *½* **Shamawan (IRE)**^{228} [4772] 10-10-13 107 .... NFehily 108+
(Jonjo O'Neill) *hld up: hdwy after 8th: led 3 out: in command whn hit 2 out: sn rdn: hdd and no ex cl home* **11/4**^{1}

5B-F **5** *20* **Field Roller (IRE)**^{115} [1110] 5-11-1 112 .... TJMalone$^{(3)}$ 95+
(M C Pipe) *hld up: hdwy 4 out: sn rdn: wknd 3 out* **11/1**

3213 **6** *7* **Tirikumba**^{18} [2053] 9-10-4 103 .... RStephens$^{(5)}$ 82+
(S G Griffiths) *prom: jnd ldrs after 8th: wknd after 4 out* **11/2**

P6-0 **7** *dist* **Miss Fahrenheit (IRE)**^{21} [1984] 6-11-5 113 .... ChristianWilliams —
(C Roberts) *prom: lost pl 4th: lost tch fr 7th: t.o* **6/1**

6m 17.0s (0.20) **Going Correction** +0.025s/f (Yiel) **7** Ran SP% **112.0**
Speed ratings: **100,99,99,99,92 90,—** CSF £25.91 CT £152.28 TOTE £5.90: £2.50, £3.30; EX 26.40.
Owner ROA Red Alligator Partnership **Bred** M Van De Kerchove And Herve Bezobry **Trained** Adlestrop, Gloucs

FOCUS
A fair staying handicap run at an even pace with fortunes changing quickly on the run-in. The first two are the best guides to the level.

NOTEBOOK
On Y Va(FR), who has been very lightly raced since his first encounter with fast ground in June last year, was settled off the pace and showed he stays this trip by keeping on to grab the advantage on the flat. He should not go up much for this and there may be more to come. *(tchd 4-1)*

Irishkawa Bellevue(FR) has shown this autumn that he is happier over hurdles rather than fences and ran a race full of credit despite having gone up 20lb for his two wins. After being up with the pace from the start, he rallied well under pressure in the straight and lost out only narrowly. His opportunities may be limited now as his form suggests this is is ground and he would not want it any more testing. *(op 4-1)*

Keepers Mead(IRE) has been out of form for a while but but had dropped back to a winning mark and both his previous wins were gained in November, so it is clearly his time of year. He set the pace and, after looking beaten halfway up the straight, came again with the runner-up after the last. He does not tend to hold his form for long, but if able to repeat this effort next time, could add to his score. *(op 8-1)*

Shamawan(IRE) ◆, whose previous appearance was when last home in the Grand National, appreciated the return to hurdles and travelled well. He looked all over the winner when hitting the front, but his stamina appeared to give out after the last and he was run out of it. He has never won beyond two miles but still qualifies for novice hurdles, and two and threequarter miles on a right-handed track may be up his street, with the Pertemps Qualifier at Wincanton over Christmas appealing as a suitable target. *(op 9-2)*

Field Roller(IRE), an early faller on his chasing debut last time, was quite keen early on and dropped out from ther home turn. He has yet to prove he stays this far. *(op 7-1)*

Tirikumba tracked the leaders for much of the way but succumbed quickly after a brief effort to get to the front on the home turn. She disappointed on her only previous run here and may prefer going the other way around. *(op 13-2)*

2431 WEATHERBYS BANK H'CAP CHASE (16 fncs) 2m 3f 110y

3:20 (3:21) (Class 4) (0-110,106) 5-Y-0+ **£5,321** (£1,562; £781; £390)

Form				RPR
P-06	1		**Hiers De Brouage (FR)**[9] 2248 10-10-13 **98**.........(tp) StephenJCraine(5) (J G Portman) *chsd ldr: led 8th: rdn appr 4 out: clr appr 3 out: drvn out* **9/1**	109+
1-PP	2	1 ½	**The Extra Man (IRE)**[21] 1989 11-11-12 **106**..................(b) WHutchinson (A King) *led to 8th: chsd wnr: rdn appr 4 out: kpt on flat* **6/1**	113
653-	3	3 ½	**Tradingup (IRE)**[239] 4641 6-10-12 **92**.................................... PJBrennan (Andrew Turnell) *a.p: hit 10th: rdn appr 4 out: nt fluent 3 out: one pce fr 2 out* **4/1**[2]	98+
F0P-	4	7	**Semi Precious (IRE)**[300] 3557 7-10-13 **93**.................................... NFehily (D P Keane) *hld up and bhd: stdy hdwy whn j.rt and bmpd 5 out: no real prog fr 3 out* **9/2**[3]	94+
U1-2	5	4	**Alcopop**[8] 2259 6-11-11 **105**.. SThomas (Miss Venetia Williams) *hld up in tch: rdn appr 4 out: wknd appr 2 out* **11/4**[1]	98
053-	P		**Alakdar (CAN)**[478] 1101 11-10-0 **80** oh6.................................. VSlattery (Jane Southcombe) *a bhd: t.o whn p.u bef 5 out* **33/1**	—
F2P-	P		**Boundary House**[215] 4955 7-10-5 **85**.....................................(t) CLlewellyn (J A B Old) *a bhd: nt fluent 5th: t.o 9th: p.u bef 5 out* **8/1**	—
301-	U		**Jour De Mee (FR)**[245] 4525 8-10-9 **94**.................................. PCO'Neill(5) (Mrs H Dalton) *hld up: rdn and struggling whn hmpd and uns rdr 5 out* **14/1**	—

5m 14.7s (3.40) **Going Correction** +0.025s/f (Yiel) **8** Ran SP% **109.9**

Speed ratings: **94,93,92,89,87** —,—,— CSF £56.77 CT £233.65 TOTE £11.00: £2.40, £2.20, £2.10; EX 45.20.

Owner Seddon - Brown Partnership **Bred** Alain Bretel **Trained** Compton, Berks

FOCUS

A moderate handicap run at a steady gallop and a modest time for the grade. The first three held those positions throughout and the runner-up sets the level.

NOTEBOOK

Hiers De Brouage(FR), winner of this race last year, has not won since and had failed to finish on four of his six subsequent appearances. However, he travelled well up with the pace until going on around halfway, and stuck to his guns really well up the straight. He clearly likes this track and is now three from four over course and distance.

The Extra Man(IRE), another who has failed to finish in two outings since scoring over course and distance in the spring, set the pace and responded well to pressure after being headed around halfway, chasing the winner all the way to the line. He seems suited by the track and is one to bear in mind if returning here. *(op 5-1 tchd 9-2)*

Tradingup(IRE), a former winning pointer who ran well over three miles here in the spring, was well supported. He had the principals in his sights from the start, but was unable to produce the pace to get past and a return to further is likely to be in his favour. *(tchd 9-2)*

Semi Precious(IRE), lightly raced over fences, goes well fresh and seemed to travel well enough off the pace. However, he failed to pick up in the straight and, as he has gained his two wins over *two miles on a right-handed track, it may be that he will do better when gets those conditions.* *(op 5-1)*

Alcopop, who usually makes the running, was settled off the pace on this occasion and did not run up to recent efforts. His best form has been on flatter tracks, so it is possible this undulating course did not suit him. *(tchd 3-1)*

Alakdar(CAN) *Official explanation: jockey said gelding was unsuited by the good to soft ground (op 28-1)*

Boundary House *Official explanation: trainer said gelding lost three shoes during race and may have resented tongue tie (op 28-1)*

2432 CHEPSTOW BOOKMAKERS SUPPORT INJURED JOCKEYS FUND STANDARD OPEN NATIONAL HUNT FLAT RACE 2m 110y

3:55 (3:55) (Class 6) 4-6-Y-0 **£1,850** (£539; £269)

Form				RPR
42-	1		**Zanzibar Boy**[247] 4499 6-11-4 .... TScudamore (H Morrison) *hld up: hdwy after 5f: led on bit over 3f out: shkn up over 1f out: r.o wl* **5/2**[2]	105+
0P-6	2	3 ½	**Earth Moving (IRE)**[18] 2056 5-11-4 .... RWalsh (P F Nicholls) *hld up in rr: plenty to do whn stdy hdwy over 4f out: chsd wnr over 1f out: sn rdn: one pce* **9/1**	102+
2	3	9	**Leading Authority (IRE)**[21] 1985 4-11-4 .... JTizzard (C L Tizzard) *a.p: rdn and ev ch over 3f out: wknd 2f out* **2/1**[1]	94+
	4	nk	**Great Memories** 6-10-11 .... MrAJBerry(7) (Jonjo O'Neill) *hld up in tch: rdn and ev ch over 3f out: wknd over 1f out* **9/1**	92
	5	shd	**Wee Anthony (IRE)** 6-11-4 .... RGreene (Jonjo O'Neill) *hld up in mid-div: hdwy over 5f out: one pce fnl 3f* **20/1**	92
	6	hd	**Forest Miller** 6-11-4 .... RJohnson (R T Phillips) *bhd: rdn 7f out: hdwy over 4f out: one pce fnl 3f* **8/1**[3]	92
	7	10	**Bartercard (USA)** 4-11-4 .... NFehily (C J Mann) *hld up: hdwy over 6f out: wknd over 3f out* **20/1**	84+
4	8	7	**Supreme Cara**[22] 1979 5-10-6 .... CHonour(5) (C J Down) *nvr nr ldrs* **100/1**	68
0	9	shd	**Ilringuback (IRE)**[9] 2242 5-11-4 .... SCurran (A J Chamberlain) *prom: led over 5f out tl over 3f out: wknd over 2f out* **20/1**	75
	10	9	**Jobsworth (IRE)** 5-11-4 .... ChristianWilliams (Evan Williams) *a bhd* **33/1**	66
0-	11	17	**Tanzanite Dawn**[245] 4519 4-10-11 .... PJBrennan (Andrew Turnell) *mid-div: hdwy over 6f out: wknd 5f out* **50/1**	42
0	12	29	**Dopey Bob**[28] 1882 4-11-4 .... CLlewellyn (N A Twiston-Davies) *sn led: hdd over 5f out: sn wknd: t.o* **12/1**	20
/00-	13	7	**Bonny Grove**[293] 3668 5-11-4 .... VSlattery (H J Evans) *prom 5f: t.o* **200/1**	—
/00-	14	dist	**Byland**[342] 2852 5-10-13 .... LStephens(5) (Miss L Day) *led early: prom tl wknd 5f out: t.o* **100/1**	—

4m 9.00s (-1.20) **Going Correction** +0.025s/f (Yiel)

WFA 4 from 5yo+ 12lb **14** Ran SP% **122.4**

Speed ratings: **103,101,97,96,96 96,92,88,88,84 76,62,59,**— CSF £23.82 TOTE £3.30: £1.80, £3.00, £1.10; EX 39.60 Place 6 £22.19, Place 5 £17.72.

Owner Lady Lewinton **Bred** J R Bosley And Mrs E Bosley **Trained** East Ilsley, Berks

FOCUS

A fair bumper run at a decent pace in which the front pair came well clear. The winner especially looks a nice prospect.

NOTEBOOK

Zanzibar Boy ◆, racing for the first time since finishing runner-up in a 14-furlong bumper in March, absolutely relished this stiffer track and was always cruising. The way he won this could *not have failed to impress and he looks a very nice prospect for when he goes hurdling. (op 7-2 tchd 4-1)*

Earth Moving(IRE) was switched right off at the back of the field in the early stages. He gradually crept closer on the bridle as the race progressed with his rider apparently reluctant to go for him until absolutely necessary. When it did become necessary, he unfortunately found that the winner was not stopping and he could make no further inroads. He obviously has ability, but may not be entirely straightforward. *(tchd 8-1)*

Leading Authority(IRE), runner-up in heavy ground on his debut here earlier this month, had every chance but was completely done for foot over the last couple of furlongs and almost certainly needs a stiffer test. *(op 7-2 tchd 4-1)*

Great Memories, a 47,000gns gelding out of a half-sister to Mucklemeg, was bang there with a chance halfway up the home straight before getting left behind by the front two. This was a fair debut. *(op 5-1)*

Wee Anthony(IRE) showed plenty of ability on this debut to finish alongside his stable companion and being a full-brother to a couple of winning staying hurdlers in Ireland, is likely to appreciate a test of stamina himself in time. *(tchd 16-1)*

Forest Miller, a half-brother to several winners on the Flat and over jumps including Silverdale Lad and Prince Nicholas, showed enough on this debut to suggest he will make his mark in due course. *(op 9-2)*

T/Plt: £52.40 to a £1 stake. Pool: £45,695.35. 635.70 winning tickets. T/Qpdt: £38.20 to a £1 stake. Pool: £3,831.50. 74.10 winning tickets. KH

2125 LINGFIELD (L-H)

Wednesday, November 23

2439 Meeting Abandoned - Frost

2186 WETHERBY (L-H)

Wednesday, November 23

OFFICIAL GOING: Good to soft

After the frost the ground was described as 'very holding and tacky. The last hurdle had been moved forward and the run-in was only about 175 yards.

Wind: Light, half-behind Weather: Fine and sunny but cold

2440 "WETHERBY TICKETS - AN IDEAL CHRISTMAS PRESENT!" CONDITIONAL JOCKEYS' H'CAP HURDLE (11 hdls 1 omitted) 2m 7f

12:25 (12:27) (Class 4) (0-100,100) 4-Y-0+ **£2,727** (£794; £397)

Form				RPR
1-23	1		**Brandy Wine (IRE)**[20] 2004 7-10-13 **95**...........................(p) JPEnnis(8) (L Lungo) *mde most: pushed clr 3 out: rdn next: hit last: drvn flat and jst hld on* **7/2**[1]	99
-16P	2	shd	**Notaproblem (IRE)**[7] 2262 6-11-12 **100**................................ WKennedy (G A Harker) *hld up and bhd: stdy hdwy approaching 3 out: trckd wnr next: chal last: sn rdn and kpt on: jst failed* **7/1**[3]	104
/F-0	3	12	**Lucky Judge**[24] 1940 8-11-9 **97**.. DCCostello (G A Swinbank) *hld up towards rr: hdwy 4 out: chsd ldrs next: sn rdn and one pce appr last* **10/1**	89
B5F4	4	7	**Assumetheposition (FR)**[11] 2187 5-10-12 **96**..................(p) JPFlavin(10) (R C Guest) *trckd ldrs: effrt to chse wnr 3 out: rdn and hit next: sn drvn and wknd* **14/1**	83+
-641	5	22	**Primitive Poppy**[179] 545 6-10-11 **85**.. PAspell (Mrs A Hamilton) *trckd ldrs: hdwy 4 out: rdn along bef next and sn btn* **5/1**[2]	48
-124	6	10	**Baawrah**[17] 2064 4-10-6 **80**.. GBerridge (M Todhunter) *hld up: hdwy on inner 1/2-way: rdn along bef 4 out and sn outpcd* **5/1**[2]	33
4602	7	1 ¾	**Northern Rambler (IRE)**[11] 2188 8-9-6 **74** oh2.................... JReveley(8) (K G Reveley) *hld up in rr: sme hdwy 5th: rdn along and bhd fr 7th* **10/1**	25
P600	8	2	**Iloveturtle (IRE)**[6] 2292 5-11-0 **95**................................(t) MSO'Connell(7) (M C Chapman) *chsd ldrs: rdn along after 4 out and sn wknd* **33/1**	44
605	9	11	**Europrime Games**[17] 2082 7-10-2 **76**..................................... KJMercer (M E Sowersby) *chsd ldrs: rdn along after 4 out: sn wknd* **18/1**	14
000P	F		**In Good Faith**[46] 1685 13-9-13 **78**.. PKinsella(5) (R E Barr) *hld up in rr: fell 3rd* **33/1**	—
P-P3	P		**Quainton Hills**[26] 1910 11-10-3 **77**.. JDiment (D R Stoddart) *cl up: rdn along 8th: sn wknd* **20/1**	—
5-30	P		**Happy Boy (IRE)**[202] 194 4-9-13 **79**......................... BenOrde-Powlett(6) (M A Barnes) *chsd ldrs to 1/2-way: sn wknd and bhd whn p.u bef 3 out* **12/1**	—

5m 52.8s (-3.90) **Going Correction** +0.025s/f (Yiel)

WFA 4 from 5yo+ 13lb **12** Ran SP% **116.5**

Speed ratings: **107,106,102,100,92 89,88,87,84,**— —,— CSF £27.33 CT £220.95 TOTE £3.70: £1.80, £2.60, £3.00; EX 26.00.

Owner Ashleybank Investments Limited **Bred** Joel McCleary **Trained** Carrutherstown, D'fries & G'way

FOCUS

A very moderate hurdle but the winner, who sets the standard, will stay further and should be a chaser in time. Fourth last flight bypassed. A first winner in Britain for John Ennis.

NOTEBOOK

Brandy Wine(IRE), wearing first-time cheekpieces, enjoyed the slight step up in trip to win all out after stealing an advantage at the top of the home straight. He looks every inch a resolute galloper, and should make a nice staying chaser when going back over fences. *(tchd 4-1)*

Notaproblem(IRE), making his handicap debut after a couple of disappointing efforts, returned to the form that saw him perform very consistently at the start of his career. Wetherby appears to suit him well, and he was only just denied in a close finish after travelling supremely well during the race. *(op 5-1)*
Lucky Judge, who was stepping up in trip, travelled nicely for most of the race, but never got home as well as the front two. *(op 11-1)*
Assumetheposition(FR), returning to hurdles after a spell over fences, found very little for pressure up the home straight, and was well beaten. *(op 20-1)*
Primitive Poppy, returning to the track after a 179-day absence, had every chance off the home turn but found nothing up the straight. She is, however, entitled to improve for the run. *(op 11-2)*
Baawrah never got involved after being held-up off the pace. His best form is over shorter, so he may have been ridden too conservatively in the circumstances. *(op 11-2)*
Quainton Hills *Official explanation: jockey said gelding had a breathing problem (op 20-1)*
Happy Boy(IRE) *Official explanation: jockey said gelding had a breathing problem (op 20-1)*

2441 HARRY ATKINSON MEMORIAL BEGINNERS' CHASE (18 fncs) 3m 1f

12:55 (12:55) (Class 4) 5-Y-O+ **£3,854** (£1,131; £565; £282)

Form				RPR
1FP-	**1**		**Bewleys Berry (IRE)**[229] [4765] 7-11-2 ... GLee (J Howard Johnson) *j.w: led 4th: clr fr 4 out: easily* **4/7**[1]	143+
13-4	**2**	*12*	**Briery Fox (IRE)**[27] [1891] 7-11-2 ... MBradburne (H D Daly) *trckd ldng pair: blnd 5th: chsd wnr fr 1/2-way: cl up whn mstke 5 out: rdn along and one pce fr next: blnd last* **13/2**[3]	123+
5-15	**3**	*8*	**Hot Weld**[33] [1817] 6-10-13 ... KJMercer[(3)] (Ferdy Murphy) *led 4th: cl up: mstke 9th: pushed along next: rdn along and hit 5 out: sn outpcd* **4/1**[2]	108
062R	**4**	*dist*	**Iris's Prince**[24] [1939] 6-10-9 109 ... TJDreaper[(7)] (A Crook) *in tch: pushed along 10th: rdn and outpcd whn hit 5 out: bhd whn blnd 4 out: plodded on* **25/1**	—
	F		**Hillary Harbour (IRE)**[297] 6-10-2 ... MrPJCosgrave[(7)] (J G Cosgrave, Ire) *fell 1st* **16/1**	—
0R-P	**U**		**Abzuson**[20] [2010] 8-11-2 ... FKeniry (J R Norton) *in tch tl blnd bdly and uns rdr 11th* **66/1**	—
4	**P**		**Dark Diva**[181] [523] 7-10-9 ... BHarding (W T Reed) *in tch: pushed along and outpcd whn mstke 5 out: sn wknd and p.u bef next* **50/1**	—

6m 38.2s (-1.80) **Going Correction** +0.025s/f (Yiel) **7** Ran SP% **110.2**
Speed ratings: **103,99,96,—,—** —,— CSF £4.58 TOTE £1.50: £1.10, £3.20; EX 5.20.
Owner Andrea & Graham Wylie **Bred** David Connors **Trained** Billy Row, Co Durham

FOCUS
This was an easy first chasing success under Rules for the potentially smart Bewleys Berry. The winner was value for further and has the potential to be competitive in a higher grade, while the rest were well beaten.

NOTEBOOK
Bewleys Berry(IRE) brushed aside his rivals with minimal fuss. His background in Irish points clearly stood him in good stead for a career over fences, and he will face much stiffer tests in the future. The most impressive feature of his performance was his very fluent jumping technique, and it would be no surprise to see him take in the Grade Two chase that Ollie Magern won last season over course and distance. *(op 8-13 tchd 4-6 in places)*
Briery Fox(IRE) did well to finish in second after making a couple of jumping errors on the way around, which included one very bad blunder early in the race, and then another at the last. He bumped into a potential top-class prospect, and will find much easier tasks. *(op 6-1 tchd 7-1)*
Hot Weld lost his place down the far side and came home in his own time. He is another in the field that will find much easier opportunities in the future, as he does have the talent to land a novice event. *(op 9-2)*
Iris's Prince was beaten some way from home. Jumping mistakes at the fences in the latter stages did not aid his cause. *(op 20-1)*
Hillary Harbour(IRE), a wide-margin winner of a mares' maiden point in Ireland, overpitched at the first and came down. *(op 20-1)*

2442 "BUY YOUR WETHERBY BOXING DAY TICKETS NOW!" JUVENILE NOVICES' HURDLE (9 hdls) 2m

1:25 (1:26) (Class 4) 3-Y-O **£3,439** (£1,002; £501)

Form				RPR
U3	**1**		**Lankawi**[20] [2001] 3-10-12 ... BHarding (Jedd O'Keeffe) *cl up: led after 3rd: rdn along and hit 3 out: drvn last: styd on gamely flat* **12/1**	101+
	2	*½*	**Dafarabad (IRE)**[121] 3-10-12 ... APMcCoy (Jonjo O'Neill) *hld up in tch: hit 4th: hdwy to chse ldng pair and hit 3 out: rdn next: drvn to chal last: edgd lft flat and kpt on* **15/8**[1]	101+
62	**3**	*4*	**Mahogany Blaze (FR)**[20] [2014] 3-10-12 ... TSiddall (N A Twiston-Davies) *a chsng ldng pair: rdn along to chse wnr after 4 out: hit next: drvn and hit 2 out: hld whn hit last* **16/1**	97+
51	**4**	*3½*	**Vocative (GER)**[20] [2001] 3-10-7 ... PMerrigan[(5)] (P C Haslam) *hld up towards rr: stdy hdwy 1/2-way: chsd ldrs fr 3 out: rdn next and kpt on: nrst fin* **4/1**[3]	92
P	**5**	*18*	**Woodford Consult**[20] [2001] 3-10-5 ... ADempsey (M W Easterby) *hld up in rr: hdwy 4 out: rdn along next: nvr rch ldrs* **20/1**	69+
P	**6**	*2½*	**Mist Opportunity (IRE)**[7] [2263] 3-10-2 ... GBartley[(10)] (P C Haslam) *hld up in rr: sme hdwy 4 out: sn rdn along and nvr a factor* **66/1**	72
P2	**7**	*dist*	**Crimson Bow (GER)**[17] [2076] 3-10-2 ...(b) LVickers[(3)] (J G Given) *led tl after 3rd: cl up tl rdn along: hit 4 out and sn wknd* **25/1**	—
	8	*3*	**Young Thomas (IRE)**[174] 3-10-12 ...(t) RMcGrath (James Moffatt) *a bhd* **100/1**	—
00	**9**	*14*	**Queen Nefitari**[17] [2076] 3-10-5 ow3 ... MrTGreenall[(3)] (M W Easterby) *a rr: bhd fr 1/2-way: blnd 3 out* **66/1**	—
F	**P**		**Another Misk**[42] [1718] 3-10-9 ... PBuchanan[(3)] (M E Sowersby) *hit 1st: a bhd: p.u bef 3 out* **100/1**	—
005	**P**		**Bold Pursuit (IRE)**[26] [1904] 3-10-12 93 ... ADobbin (S B Clark) *midfield: pushed along 4 out: sn wknd and p.u bef next* **25/1**	—
652	**P**		**Dock Tower (IRE)**[25] [1923] 3-10-12 ... GLee (M E Sowersby) *chsd ldrs: rdn along appr 3 out: hld in 5th whn hit 2 out 2 out and p.u bef last* **11/4**[2]	76
0	**P**		**Double Ells**[17] [2076] 3-10-5 ... DO'Meara (J M Jefferson) *in tch: pushed along and mstke 4th: rdn after next: lost pl after 4 out and bhd whn p.u bef 2 out* **100/1**	—

4m 0.30s (0.90) **Going Correction** +0.025s/f (Yiel) **13** Ran SP% **113.4**
Speed ratings: **98,97,95,94,85 83,—,—,—,— —,—,—** CSF £32.53 TOTE £14.40: £2.30, £1.40, £3.10; EX 53.50.
Owner Four Winds Racing **Bred** Wood Farm Stud (waresley) **Trained** Middleham Moor, N Yorks

FOCUS
Probably only a modest juvenile event rated through winner and fourth. Dafarabad shaped well on his debut, while Dock Tower ran way below form.

NOTEBOOK
Lankawi, who was no great shakes on the Flat, had been progressing with experience over hurdles and, like so many on the card, was never headed after taking the lead down the back straight. The form is probably not reliable, but at least he is going the right way.
Dafarabad(IRE), a useful performer on the Flat without being anything special, made a slightly disappointing hurdling debut. Noticeably weak in the market before the race, he did not jump that fluently and could never get on terms with Lankawi. He will no doubt be better for the experience. *(op 6-4 tchd 9-4)*
Mahogany Blaze(FR), who had taken an unusual route into juvenile hurdles via junior bumpers, stayed on really well for pressure and will be better suited by a stiffer track at a two-mile trip. He continues to go in the right direction and will win races. *(op 18-1)*
Vocative(GER), who had finished in front of Lankawi last time, tried to come off the pace and, like so many others on the day, never got to the leaders. The penalty she carried for her win last time out was probably enough to stop her. *(op 9-2)*
Woodford Consult, pulled up on her debut over hurdles, ran with much more promise, staying on from the back after being held-up. She will improve with experience. *(op 33-1)*
Mist Opportunity(IRE) kept plugging away up the straight, but looked very tired in the closing stages. *(op 80-1)*
Dock Tower(IRE) ran no sort of race, and is probably feeling the effects of a few tough races already this season. *Official explanation: jockey said gelding had a breathing problem; trainer said gelding was found to be distressed on returning to the yard (op 7-2)*

2443 "WETHERBY BOXING DAY - £99 VIP MARQUEE PACKAGE" H'CAP CHASE (12 fncs) 2m

2:00 (2:02) (Class 3) (0-125,123) 4-Y-O+ **£7,091** (£2,081; £1,040; £519)

Form				RPR
56-4	**1**		**Polar Gunner**[19] [2027] 8-11-1 112 ... ADobbin (J M Jefferson) *led: rdn along 4 out: drvn after 2 out: hdd flat: rallied to ld nr fin* **7/1**	123+
23-5	**2**	*nk*	**Super Nomad**[26] [1913] 10-11-9 123 ... MrTGreenall[(3)] (M W Easterby) *trckd ldrs: smooth hdwy 5 out: cl up next: rdn 2 out: led flat: sn drvn: hdd nr fin* **6/1**	133
30-5	**3**	*12*	**Argento**[11] [2190] 8-11-5 116 ... FKeniry (G M Moore) *hld up in midfield: hdwy to chse ldrs 5 out: rdn after next and kpt on same pce* **6/1**	114
-PPP	**4**	*7*	**Powder Creek (IRE)**[15] [2102] 8-11-2 113 ...(p) RMcGrath (K G Reveley) *hld up towards rr: hdwy and hit 5 out: rdn along next: sn no imp* **14/1**	105+
2-02	**5**	*3*	**Flake**[15] [2111] 5-10-8 105 ... DElsworth (Mrs S J Smith) *keen: disp ld: blnd 1st: cl up tl rdn along appr 5 out and grad wknd* **5/1**[2]	93
5435	**6**	*2*	**Day Du Roy (FR)**[20] [2004] 7-11-9 120 ... TSiddall (Miss L C Siddall) *chsd ldrs: pushed along and hit 5 out: sn rdn and outpcd fr next: hit 2 out* **25/1**	106
-P63	**7**	*7*	**Hollows Mill**[17] [2067] 9-10-2 102 ... GBerridge[(3)] (F P Murtagh) *hld up in rr: sme hdwy 5 out: blnd next and bhd after* **14/1**	85+
1-21	**8**	*6*	**Encore Cadoudal (FR)**[17] [2067] 7-11-10 121 ... DO'Meara (H P Hogarth) *in tch: hdwy to chse wnr 1/2-way: rdn along 5 out: wknd next* **4/1**[1]	100+
P46P	**9**	*14*	**Dabus**[10] [2208] 10-10-2 99 ...(b) KJohnson (M C Chapman) *cl up: hit 4th: sn lost pl and bhd fr 5 out* **50/1**	60+
/P1-	**P**		**The Laird's Entry (IRE)**[256] [4320] 10-11-1 112 ... GLee (J Howard Johnson) *midfield: hdwy to chse ldrs 6th: rdn and wknd 5 out: p.u bef next* **11/2**[3]	—

4m 3.20s (-3.40) **Going Correction** +0.025s/f (Yiel) **10** Ran SP% **112.3**
Speed ratings: **109,108,102,99,97 96,93,90,83,—** CSF £47.44 CT £264.99 TOTE £7.50: £2.90, £2.20, £2.30; EX 63.90 Trifecta £479.90 Part won. Pool: £675.92 - 0.70 winning tickets..
Owner Mrs M E Dixon **Bred** Mrs P Nicholson **Trained** Norton, N Yorks

FOCUS
A competitive race for the grade, where the pace looked sound throughout. However, most of the horses in the race find winning difficult, so the form is worth treating with caution.

NOTEBOOK
Polar Gunner made just about all, and found plenty for strong pressure to hold off the persistent challenge of Super Nomad. He is starting to creep up the ratings over fences which will make winning more difficult, so he would be interesting if tried over hurdles, where his handicap mark is very favourable in comparison. *(op 11-2)*
Super Nomad looked to be travelling the best of the front two coming down the home straight, but just failed to last out when the pressure was fully applied. He is without a win since 2002, and his consistent form never allows the Handicapper to drop him much in the weights. *(tchd 5-1)*
Argento moved into contention leaving the back straight but failed to land a blow on front two. He battled on in good fashion but was another in the field that had not won for some considerable time. *(op 7-1 tchd 15-2)*
Powder Creek(IRE), who was pulled up on all of his last three starts, kept on nicely down the straight for sympathetic handling. He does not look the most straightforward of characters, and probably needs riding in a quiet manner. *(op 16-1 tchd 12-1)*
Flake, who was keen in the early stage which caused him to blunder badly at the first, raced up with the leaders for much of the race, but was soon backpedalling turning out of the back straight. He would prefer further than two miles over fences. *(op 11-2 tchd 6-1)*
Day Du Roy(FR) moved well for much of the race, but found little under pressure. He has a breathing problem, so almost certainly finds things difficult as soon as pressure is applied. *(op 33-1)*
Encore Cadoudal(FR), raised 8lb for his win last time, was niggled along for much of the race and never looked like getting involved in the finish. *(op 10-3 tchd 9-2)*
The Laird's Entry(IRE) *Official explanation: jockey said gelding was lame behind (op 6-1)*

2444 ROCOM AND BT NETWORK FIRST NOVICES' HURDLE (9 hdls) 2m

2:35 (2:36) (Class 4) 4-Y-O+ **£3,741** (£1,090; £545)

Form				RPR
14	**1**		**Whispered Promises (USA)**[143] [892] 4-11-5 ... JPMcNamara (R S Brookhouse) *mde all: styd on strly fr 3 out: readily* **40/1**	128+
20-1	**2**	*6*	**L'Antartique (FR)**[20] [2006] 5-11-2 ... KJMercer[(3)] (Ferdy Murphy) *trckd ldrs: wnt 2nd 6th: nt qckn between last 2* **4/6**[1]	122+
110-	**3**	*3*	**The Duke's Speech (IRE)**[228] [4774] 4-10-12 ... JMMaguire (T P Tate) *chsd ldrs: 3rd and styng on same pce whn mstke last* **7/1**[3]	114+
U2-	**4**	*15*	**Harmony Brig (IRE)**[328] [3100] 6-10-12 ... ADobbin (N G Richards) *hmpd 2nd: wnt prom 4th: blnd next: outpcd fr 3 out* **5/1**[2]	100+
26	**5**	*nk*	**George Stubbs (USA)**[11] [2179] 7-10-12 ... BHarding (B Ellison) *sltly hmpd 2nd: hdwy 6th: kpt on fr next: nvr on terms* **33/1**	97
1R3/	**6**	*5*	**Dark Character**[721] [2530] 6-10-7 ... WKennedy[(5)] (G A Swinbank) *mid-div: hdwy 6th: wknd after next* **20/1**	92
1-13	**7**	*4*	**Brave Rebellion**[12] [2169] 6-10-12 ... RMcGrath (K G Reveley) *t.k.h in rr: stdy hdwy fr 3 out: hit next: nvr on terms* **20/1**	88
	8	*9*	**Penel (IRE)**[25] 4-10-12 ... DO'Meara (P T Midgley) *mid-div: hit 5th: nvr on terms* **100/1**	79
	9	*nk*	**Springvic (IRE)**[223] [4844] 5-10-12 ... FKeniry (G M Moore) *mid-div: outpcd fr 6th* **100/1**	79

Form	Pos	Dist	Horse	Jockey	SP	RPR
	10	*nk*	**Swahili Dancer (USA)**[228] 4-10-12 (M D Hammond) *mid-div: outpcd fr 6th*	NPMulholland	100/1	78
0	11	*1 ¾*	**Compton Dragon (USA)**[45] [1527] 6-10-12 (R Johnson) *t.k.h in rr: sme hdwy 3 out: nvr a factor*	KJohnson	100/1	77
0/	12	*2*	**Old Barns (IRE)**[179] [4050] 5-10-9 (G A Swinbank) *hld up in rr: sme hdwy 3 out: nvr on terms*	PAspell(3)	100/1	75
30	13	*6*	**Network Oscar (IRE)**[32] [1824] 4-10-12 (M W Easterby) *mid-div: reminders 5th: nvr on terms*	BGibson	100/1	69
	14	*shd*	**Gala Sunday (USA)**[58] 5-10-9 (M W Easterby) *a in rr*	(t) MrTGreenall(3)	100/1	69
	15	*5*	**Viking Star (IRE)**[18] 4-10-12 (A D Brown) *chsd ldrs to 5th: sn wknd*	MBradburne	100/1	64
	16	*8*	**Field Spark**[51] 5-10-9 (J G Given) *in rr fr 6th*	(p) LVickers(3)	100/1	56
	17	*8*	**Nigwell Forbees (IRE)** 4-10-5 (J Howard Johnson) *sn bhd and drvn along*	BSHughes(7)	100/1	48
-	18	*2*	**Carpe Momentum (USA)** 6-10-9 (R C Guest) *a in rr*	(t) LMcGrath(3)	100/1	46
	19	*dist*	**Makin Air** 4-10-12 (J Howard Johnson) *bhd whn blnd 6th: t.o*	ADempsey	100/1	—
F0	F		**Classic Lease**[9] [2249] 4-10-9 (J Mackie) *w ldrs: fell 2nd*	PBuchanan(3)	100/1	—
42	U		**Step Perfect (USA)**[15] [2108] 4-10-7 (G M Moore) *w ldrs whn mstke and uns rdr 2nd*	DCCostello(5)	50/1	—
-503	F		**The Connor Fella**[19] [2024] 4-10-9 (F P Murtagh) *chsd ldrs: lost pl and fell 3 out*	GBerridge(3)	66/1	—
	F		**Double Vodka (IRE)**[44] 4-10-12 (C Grant) *t.k.h towards rr: stdy hdwy 6th: clr 4th best whn fell last*	GLee	16/1	105+

3m 58.3s (-1.10) **Going Correction** +0.025s/f (Yiel) **23** Ran SP% **126.3**
Speed ratings: **103,100,98,91,90 88,86,81,81,81 80,79,76,76,74 70,66,65,—,— —,—,—**
CSF £67.72 TOTE £42.30: £11.70, £1.10, £2.80; EX 157.90.

Owner Mrs S J Brookhouse **Bred** Springwood Llc And Morgan's Ford Farm **Trained** Wixford, Warwicks

FOCUS
A fair novice event, possibly spoilt again by a bias to horses who led leaving the back straight. L'Antartique can be rated much better than the bare result, as he was given too much to do on ground that probably did not suit. There were some eyecatching performances in behind the front two, and the race should produce winners.

NOTEBOOK
Whispered Promises(USA) held a prominent position during the race and got first run on all his rivals. Despite his starting price, he had every chance on his previous form over hurdles, and looked to appreciate the return to two miles after getting outpaced over three furlongs further last time. He may have stolen victory from the front, but he is capable of more progression. *(op 33-1)*
L'Antartique(FR) was given too much to do on a day where horses were not stopping in front. He is much better than the bare result, and he can easily be given another chance, especially on much softer ground. He remains an exciting prospect over hurdles. *(op 8-11 tchd 4-5)*
The Duke's Speech(IRE), who made a really bad error at the last, ran with enough promise on his hurdling debut to suggest he will pick up a similar race. The Aintree bumper in which he finished ninth has worked out really well, and he will no doubt add to the tally of winners who have emerged from that race. *(op 10-1)*
Harmony Brig(IRE), sidelined with a minor injury since his last promising effort, shaped nicely behind the leaders and will be of interest next time if hurdling more fluently and stepped up in trip. *(op 9-2)*
George Stubbs(USA) never got into the thick of the action, but is now handicapped and will be very interesting in that sphere, especially over further.
Dark Character, who had some really good bumper form in the past, ran well on his comeback after a long absence, and should improve for the run.
Brave Rebellion was not ideally placed throughout the race and the effort is best ignored, as he is better than his final position suggests. *Official explanation: jockey said gelding ran too free early stages*
Compton Dragon(USA) *Official explanation: jockey said gelding hung left-handed (op 66-1)*
Gala Sunday(USA) *Official explanation: jockey said gelding had a breathing problem (op 66-1)*
Double Vodka(IRE), making his debut for a new stable, was in the process of making a sound debut when coming down at the last. He was quite a capable performer on the Flat and handled most ground, including soft, so plenty of opportunities should come his way

2445 WETHERBY RACES NEXT SATURDAY 3RD DECEMBER H'CAP CHASE (18 fncs) 2m 7f 110y

3:10 (3:11) (Class 3) (0-125,125) 5-Y-0+ **£5,595** (£1,642; £821; £410)

Form	Pos	Dist	Horse	Jockey	SP	RPR
0-P1	1		**Sharp Belline (IRE)**[18] [2039] 8-10-2 **101** (Mrs S J Smith) *set stdy pce: hit 11th: qcknd clr 4 out: rdn and hit 2 out: styd on strly flat*	DElsworth	5/1[2]	117+
P1-2	2	*8*	**Manbow (IRE)**[34] [1798] 7-10-13 **112** (M D Hammond) *hld up in tch: hdwy 5 out: chsd wnr fr 3 out and sn rdn: drvn appr last and no imp*	GLee	7/4[1]	118
1/6-	3	*1 ¼*	**King Bee (IRE)**[567] [174] 8-10-7 **106** (H D Daly) *cl up: hit 8th: rdn along 5 out: drvn and mstke 3 out: hld whn hit next and kpt on same pce*	MBradburne	12/1	112+
11-0	4	*shd*	**Green Ideal**[15] [2111] 7-10-4 **106** (Ferdy Murphy) *hld up and bhd: hdwy after 5 out: rdn along 3 out and kpt on: nrst fin*	KJMercer(3)	20/1	112+
015-	5	*21*	**Kerry Lads (IRE)**[221] [4861] 10-11-9 **125** (Miss Lucinda V Russell) *chsd ldrs: hit 11th: sn pushed along: rdn and outrpced fr 5 out*	(p) PBuchanan(3)	25/1	109
32-5	6	*1 ¾*	**Harrovian**[18] [2038] 8-11-4 **117** (Miss P Robson) *hld up towards rr: effrt: pushed along and in tch whn hmpd 5 out and bhd after*	RMcGrath	8/1[3]	106+
3P4U	F		**Kidithou (FR)**[7] [2265] 7-10-5 **104** (W T Reed) *fell 1st*	BHarding	50/1	—
12-3	B		**Tom Fruit**[17] [2077] 8-10-10 **109** (T D Easterby) *hld up in tch: hdwy whn b.d 5 out*	RGarritty	5/1[2]	—
31-P	F		**Imperial Dream (IRE)**[11] [2189] 7-11-4 **117** (H P Hogarth) *trckd ldng pair: hdwy and cl up whn blnd 10th: mstke 12th: ev ch whn fell 5 out*	(b) DO'Meara	8/1[3]	—

6m 4.60s (6.10) **Going Correction** +0.025s/f (Yiel) **9** Ran SP% **110.2**
Speed ratings: **90,87,86,86,79 79,—,—,—** CSF £13.70 CT £89.88 TOTE £6.10: £2.00, £1.30, £3.50; EX 16.00.

Owner Townville C C Racing Club **Bred** Pinfold Stud And Farms Ltd **Trained** High Eldwick, W Yorks

FOCUS
Sharp Belline won his second race in a row after a competent front-running ride. Runner-up Manbow is a shade high in the handicap, as is Green Ideal, so the form is questionable. It was a modest time for the class.

NOTEBOOK
Sharp Belline(IRE), apparently revitalised by fences again, won in good style after leading for almost the entire race. As he is on the small side, the Handicapper could soon get to grips with him over fences, and is one to take on next time if faced with some decent opposition. *(op 4-1)*
Manbow(IRE), who had shaped with promise on his seasonal debut, is performing like a horse that is 11lb higher in the weights than for his last win. After travelling nicely for much of the race, he failed to quicken when asked and merely kept on for pressure. *(op 2-1)*
King Bee(IRE) ran nicely on his return to the track after a 567-day absence, and will no doubt improve considerably for the run. *(op 14-1 tchd 16-1)*
Harrovian was starting to make some ground when hampered by the fall of Imperial Dream. He was not overly persevered with after that incident, and can be given another chance in similar company. *(op 7-1)*
Kidithou(FR) is having problems negotiating fences, and came down at the first. *(op 33-1)*
Tom Fruit was going well enough when brought down by a faller. *(op 33-1)*
Imperial Dream(IRE) was going fairly well when sprawling on the landing side of the fifth last and losing his jockey. Not only did he fall, but he brought down Tom Fruit and hampered Harrovian. *(op 33-1)*

2446 EBF/DONCASTER BLOODSTOCK SALES MARES' ONLY STANDARD OPEN NATIONAL HUNT FLAT RACE (QUALIFIER) 2m

3:40 (3:43) (Class 6) 4-6-Y-0 **£2,685** (£782; £391)

Form	Pos	Dist	Horse	Jockey	SP	RPR
5	1		**She's The Lady**[14] [2131] 5-11-0 (R S Brookhouse) *mde all: shkn up wnt wnt clr 1f out: eased towards fin*	JPMcNamara	25/1	105+
	2	*4*	**Blackbriery Thyne (IRE)**[193] 6-10-9 (H D Daly) *chsd ldrs: wnt 2nd over 3f out: kpt on same pce fnl f*	TGreenway(5)	25/1	100
2	3	*5*	**Dillay Brook (IRE)**[23] [1961] 5-11-0 (T R George) *hld up in rr: hdwy 6f out: chsng ldrs 4f out: kpt on one pce fnl 2f*	JMMaguire	11/2[3]	95
-	4	*¾*	**Little Venus (IRE)** 5-11-0 (H D Daly) *hdwy to chse ldrs after 6f: edgd lft and fdd over 2f out*	MBradburne	5/1[2]	94
	5	*2 ½*	**Mi Fa Sol Aulmes (FR)**[256] 5-11-0 (W T Reed) *bhd: hdwy to chse ldrs 4f out: one pce*	ADempsey	100/1	92
	6	*3*	**Lady Wilde (IRE)** 5-10-9 (Noel T Chance) *hld up in mid-div: hdwy to chse ldrs 6f out: rdn over 2f out: wknd over 1f out*	WKennedy(5)	7/4[1]	89
	7	*¾*	**Kahysera** 4-10-9 (Mrs H Dalton) *in rr: mid-div and drvn along 6f out: kpt on fnl 2f*	PMerrigan(5)	20/1	88
2	8	*1 ¼*	**Political Pendant**[19] [2028] 4-10-7 (R Nixon) *mid-div: hdwy 6f out: chsng ldrs 4f out: sn wknd*	GThomas(7)	20/1	87
30-1	9	*shd*	**Zaffie Parson (IRE)**[19] [2028] 4-11-7 (G A Harker) *trckd ldrs: rdn over 3f out: sn btn*	RMcGrath	20/1	94
	10	*1 ¾*	**Lindamarie (IRE)** 4-10-7 (C C Bealby) *chsd ldrs: drvn along 5f out: lost pl over 3f out*	TMessenger(7)	66/1	85
5	11	*shd*	**Filey Flyer**[19] [2028] 5-11-0 (J R Turner) *chsd ldrs: wknd over 3f out*	ADobbin	33/1	85
	12	*4*	**More Likely** 4-10-9 (Mrs A F Tullie) *mid-div: hdwy 6f out: lost pl 4f out*	DCCostello(5)	40/1	81
0	13	*¾*	**Kitebrook**[28] [1882] 4-11-0 (Mrs Mary Hambro) *in rr: hdwy 7f out: lost pl over 4f out*	APMcCoy	22/1	80
	14	*7*	**Celtic Flame** 6-10-11 (O Brennan) *prom: lost pl 6f out*	LVickers(3)	50/1	73
	15	*1 ¼*	**Follow My Leader (IRE)** 5-11-0 (R Ford) *hld up in rr: hdwy 6f out: sn lost pl*	GLee	11/1	72
0-0	16	*12*	**Just Libbi**[20] [2007] 5-10-11 (Ferdy Murphy) *in rr: bhd fnl 6f*	KJMercer(3)	100/1	60
	17	*8*	**Young Siouxsie** 5-10-7 (N A Twiston-Davies) *mid-div: lost pl 7f out: sn bhd*	SCrawford(7)	20/1	52
	18	*19*	**Cherry's Echo** 5-11-0 (H P Hogarth) *in rr: bhd fnl 6f*	DElsworth	66/1	33
0	19	*dist*	**What A Blaze (IRE)**[28] [1889] 5-10-11 (Robert Gray) *chsd ldrs: lost pl 7f out: sn bhd: wl t.o: virtually p.u*	PBuchanan(3)	100/1	—

3m 55.1s (-9.30) **Going Correction** +0.025s/f (Yiel) **19** Ran SP% **121.1**
Speed ratings: **97,95,92,92,90 89,89,88,88,87 87,85,85,81,80 74,70,61,—** CSF £520.02 TOTE £22.80: £4.30, £6.80, £2.10; EX 650.70 Place 6 £24.85, Place 5 £11.16.

Owner R S Brookhouse **Bred** Woodsway Stud And Chao Racing And Bloodstock Ltd **Trained** Wixford, Warwicks

FOCUS
This looked a fair event prior to the race, won in emphatic style by She's The Lady, who confirmed the promise on the debut. The third is the benchmark for the form.

NOTEBOOK
She's The Lady, a well-related sort, completed a long-priced double for the stable under a very similar ride to their previous winner on the card. She was signalled as having ability on her debut, and fully justified that promise under a positive ride. Another victory under a penalty in bumper company can be achieved if kept to a realistic level. *(op 16-1)*
Blackbriery Thyne(IRE), a half-sister to Briery Fox, already had some experience between the flags, and kept on in good style, but never got to the easy winner. She may need further or a stiffer track in the future.
Dillay Brook(IRE) was pushed along up the straight and gave the impression a stiffer test was required. *(op 8-1)*
Little Venus(IRE) was another just in behind that looked as though the experience would do her the world of good. *(op 6-1 tchd 9-2)*
Mi Fa Sol Aulmes(FR) moved nicely for much of the race but got a little tired in the closing stages. She looks a chaser in the making. *(op 50-1)*
Lady Wilde(IRE), a half-sister to the stable's useful pair Victom's Chance and Murphy's Cardinal, apparently came to the track with a good reputation and travelled like a nice horse during the race. Things did not fall into place for her on the day, but she is certainly worth another chance. *(op 2-1 tchd 5-2 in places)*
Kahysera, a half-sister to the useful hurdler Heart, did not shape without promise on her debut, and should derive plenty of improvement for the experience. *(tchd 25-1)*

T/Jkpt: Not won. T/Plt: £34.90 to a £1 stake. Pool: £45,678.45. 955.30 winning tickets. T/Qpdt: £31.50 to a £1 stake. Pool: £3,498.30. 82.00 winning tickets. JR

^{1937}CARLISLE (R-H)

Thursday, November 24

OFFICIAL GOING: Soft (heavy in places)

Wind: Fresh across.

2447 OG'S RACING CLUB NORTHERN TOUR NOVICES' HURDLE (DIV I) (6 hdls 3 omitted) 2m 1f

12:10 (12:11) (Class 4) 4-Y-0+ **£2,912** (£848; £424)

Form				RPR
	1		**Percussionist (IRE)**^{161} 4-10-12 GLee (J Howard Johnson) *j.rt 1st: cl up: led bef 2 out: styd on strly* **2/7**^{1}	112+
110-	**2**	*6*	**Witch Wind**^{229} [4774] 5-10-7 DMcGann$^{(5)}$ (A M Crow) *chsd ldrs: nt fluent 3rd: rdn and outpcd bef 2 out: kpt on to go 2nd towards fin: no imp* **12/1**^{2}	101+
0-F2	**3**	*½*	**Hollywood Critic (USA)**^{48} [1661] 4-10-2 110 DDaSilva$^{(10)}$ (P Monteith) *hld up midfield: hdwy after 3 out: wnt 2nd bef next: edgd rt and no ex run in* **16/1**^{3}	99
P	**4**	*dist*	**Moyne Pleasure (IRE)**^{25} [1938] 7-10-12 KJohnson (R Johnson) *hld up in tch: effrt 3 out: wknd bef next* **100/1**	69
0-0	**5**	*1 ¼*	**Stravonian**^{189} [418] 5-10-12 JimCrowley (G A Swinbank) *in tch tl rdn and wknd bef 2 out* **66/1**	68
	6	*19*	**Dolans Bay (IRE)** 4-10-12 FKeniry (G M Moore) *a bhd: lost tch 4th* **50/1**	49
34/F	**7**	*hd*	**Datbandito (IRE)**^{18} [2062] 6-10-12 BGibson (L Lungo) *nt fluent 1st: sn wl bhd* **40/1**	49
P0	**P**		**Kaysglory**^{35} [1794] 6-10-7 DCCostello$^{(5)}$ (F P Murtagh) *a bhd: t.o whn p.u bef 2 out* **200/1**	—
	P		**Silloth Spirit**^{145} 5-10-12 ARoss (Mrs A M Naughton) *a bhd: t.o whn p.u bef 2 out* **200/1**	—
03/	**P**		**Rainha**^{593} 8-10-5 BHarding (A C Whillans) *led to after 2nd: wknd 4th: t.o whn p.u bef 2 out* **40/1**	—
23	**F**		**Oddsmaker (IRE)**^{18} [2062] 4-10-5 (t) BenOrde-Powlett$^{(7)}$ (M A Barnes) *keen: led after 2nd tl bef 2 out: 5l down and outpcd whn fell 2 out* **12/1**^{2}	91
00-0	**P**		**Brora Sutherland (IRE)**^{33} [1834] 6-10-9 85 PBuchanan$^{(3)}$ (Miss Lucinda V Russell) *keen: chsd ldrs to 4th: sn wknd: t.o whn p.u bef 2 out* **80/1**	—

4m 29.8s (4.10) **Going Correction** +0.35s/f (Yiel) **12** Ran SP% **110.6**

Speed ratings: **104,101,100,—,— —,—,—,—,— —,—** CSF £3.70 TOTE £1.30: £1.10, £1.20, £2.40; EX 4.60.

Owner Andrea & Graham Wylie **Bred** Swettenham Stud **Trained** Billy Row, Co Durham

FOCUS

Little strength in depth and only ordinary form but a pleasing hurdle debut from one that should hold his own in stronger company. The third is the best guide to the level of the form.

NOTEBOOK

Percussionist(IRE) ◆, a very smart Flat stayer, did everything required of him after a sticky first jump on this hurdle debut and, although this bare form is only ordinary, he will stay further and appeals as the sort to hold his own in stronger company. *(op 3-10)*

Witch Wind, a fair sort in bumpers, ran creditably on this hurdle debut. Although flattered by his proximity to a potentially useful sort, he will appreciate two and a half miles and should do better in ordinary handicaps.

Hollywood Critic(USA) again ran creditably. Effective on a sound surface, he is another that is capable of winning an ordinary event in due course when his stable is in better form.

Moyne Pleasure(IRE), poor on the Flat nowadays, was not totally disgraced in the face of a stiff task. He may do better in handicaps when there is less of an emphasis on stamina. *(op 80-1)*

Stravonian shaped as though this first run in six months and first for his new yard was needed and, although he again achieved little over hurdles, is in good hands and is likely to do better in modest handicaps.

Oddsmaker(IRE), a three-time Flat winner, had run well until coming to grief and, although he really needs to settle better, he may be capable of winning a small handicap when there is less of an emphasis on stamina. *(op 10-1)*

2448 OG'S RACING CLUB NORTHERN TOUR NOVICES' HURDLE (DIV II) (6 hdls 3 omitted) 2m 1f

12:40 (12:40) (Class 4) 4-Y-0+ **£2,912** (£848; £424)

Form				RPR
0-	**1**		**Planters Punch (IRE)**^{21} [2679] 4-10-12 FKeniry (G M Moore) *chsd ldrs: effrt bef 2 out: led run in: styd on wl* **16/1**	109+
5-4	**2**	*nk*	**Winapenny (IRE)**^{10} [2249] 6-10-9 KJMercer$^{(3)}$ (Ferdy Murphy) *led to 1st: lft in ld after next: rdn 2 out: edgd rt and hdd run in: kpt on towards fin* **9/4**^{1}	109+
53-0	**3**	*16*	**Mr Tim (IRE)**^{197} [301] 7-10-9 GBerridge$^{(3)}$ (L Lungo) *keen: hdwy and cl up 3rd: rdn and wknd bef 2 out* **11/2**^{2}	95+
/F5-	**4**	*20*	**Random Native (IRE)**^{236} [4685] 7-10-12 BHarding (N G Richards) *hld up: rdn after 3 out: no imp next* **7/1**	78+
00P	**5**	*11*	**Yankee Holiday (IRE)**^{20} [2024] 5-10-12 RMcGrath (Mrs S C Bradburne) *cl up to 3 out: sn rdn and wknd* **100/1**	62
0	**6**	*3*	**Tiger King (GER)**^{21} [2006] 4-10-12 KRenwick (P Monteith) *hld up: effrt and hdwy after 3 out: wknd bef next* **14/1**	59
	7	*nk*	**Zandeed (IRE)**^{5} 7-10-5 EWhillans$^{(7)}$ (A C Whillans) *bhd: blnd 2nd: nvr on terms* **33/1**	59
4	**8**	*13*	**Bohemian Brook (IRE)**^{16} [2108] 4-10-12 GLee (J Howard Johnson) *prom tl rdn and wknd after 3 out* **13/2**^{3}	46
5	**9**	*6*	**Boris The Spider**^{18} [2062] 4-10-12 ADobbin (M D Hammond) *hld up: rdn after 3 out: btn bef next* **14/1**	40
302-	**L**		**Baffling Secret (FR)**^{318} [3298] 5-10-12 BGibson (L Lungo) *w.r.s: ref to r* **11/1**	—
34	**R**		**Lord Baskerville**^{25} [1937] 4-10-5 PJMcDonald$^{(7)}$ (W Storey) *keen: led 1st tl hung bdly lft and rn out after next* **10/1**	—

4m 27.6s (1.90) **Going Correction** +0.35s/f (Yiel)

WFA 4 from 5yo+ 12lb **11** Ran SP% **112.6**

Speed ratings: **109,108,101,91,86 85,85,79,76,— —** CSF £51.16 TOTE £23.50: £4.80, £1.40, £2.50; EX 72.80.

Owner D Neale **Bred** Miss Sarah Thompson **Trained** Middleham, N Yorks

■ Stewards' Enquiry : K J Mercer two-day ban: used whip with excessive frequency (Dec 5,12)

FOCUS

Another ordinary event in which the pace was decent and the first two did well to pull clear in the straight. The form could rate higher with the third the best guide.

NOTEBOOK

Planters Punch(IRE), who has a modest strike-rate on the Flat, jumped much better than on his hurdle debut and turned in an improved effort. On this evidence he will have no problems with two and a half miles and he should win another race. *(op 20-1)*

Winapenny(IRE) ◆, given his stiffest test of stamina to date, turned in an improved effort and he should have no problems staying two and a half miles. He looks sure to win a race in this sphere before he goes over the larger obstacles. *(tchd 5-2)*

Mr Tim(IRE), back in trip, was not totally disgraced on this first run for over six months and, although he again looked less than straightforward, may do better in ordinary handicap company in due course. *(tchd 6-1)*

Random Native(IRE), a dual bumper winner on a sound surface in 2003, will now be handicapped on his ordinary hurdle form on easy and soft ground this year and will be interesting over further when conditions are more to his liking. *(op 8-1 tchd 9-1)*

Yankee Holiday(IRE) was again well beaten over hurdles and is likely to continue to look vulnerable in this type of event. *(op 66-1)*

Tiger King(GER), a Flat winner in Germany, again finished well beaten, but hinted at ability and may do better in ordinary handicaps in time. *(op 16-1)*

2449 WINTERTHUR LIFE NOVICES' CHASE (16 fncs) 2m 4f

1:15 (1:16) (Class 3) 5-Y-0+ **£7,351** (£2,158; £1,079; £539)

Form				RPR
331-	**1**		**Turpin Green (IRE)**^{231} [4752] 6-11-0 ADobbin (N G Richards) *cl up: led bef 8th: hdd briefly 4 out: kpt on gamely u.p fr last* **1/1**^{1}	142+
F-2F	**2**	*2 ½*	**Rebel Rhythm**^{5} [2344] 6-11-0 DElsworth (Mrs S J Smith) *led to bef 8th: led briefly 4 out: outpcd appr 2 out: rallied last: no ex towards fin* **7/2**^{2}	137+
421-	**3**	*27*	**Leading Man (IRE)**^{218} [4923] 5-10-11 KJMercer$^{(3)}$ (Ferdy Murphy) *hld up and bhd: kpt on fr 4 out: no ch w first two* **12/1**	110+
201-	**4**	*2*	**Trisons Star (IRE)**^{217} [4945] 7-10-9 DFlavin$^{(5)}$ (Mrs L B Normile) *chsd ldrs to 9th: outpcd fr 5 out* **14/1**	108
16-0	**5**	*½*	**Italiano**^{210} [82] 6-11-0 108 RGarritty (P Beaumont) *prom: chsd clr ldrs but no imp fr 9th: lost 3rd run in* **66/1**	107
-5F5	**6**	*7*	**Northern Minster**^{27} [1911] 6-11-0 100 BHarding (F P Murtagh) *hld up: rdn 10th: sn btn* **100/1**	100
/3-3	**7**	*hd*	**Kharak (FR)**^{18} [2065] 6-11-0 RMcGrath (Mrs S C Bradburne) *prom in chsng gp tl outpcd fr 6 out* **20/1**	100
3/3	**8**	*17*	**Lord Payne (IRE)**^{20} [2023] 7-11-0 KRenwick (P Monteith) *in tch chsng gp tl wknd fr 10th* **33/1**	83
P-P6	**P**		**Fifteen Reds**^{13} [2168] 10-10-9 MJMcAlister$^{(5)}$ (J C Haynes) *a bhd: t.o whn p.u bef 11th* **200/1**	—
1P0-	**P**		**Skenfrith**^{216} [4967] 6-11-0 112 JimCrowley (Miss S E Forster) *sn bhd: t.o whn p.u bef 11th* **100/1**	—
151-	**P**		**Supreme Leisure (IRE)**^{241} [4625] 8-11-0 GLee (J Howard Johnson) *midfield: rdn and wknd 10th: t.o whn p.u bef 4 out* **7/1**^{3}	—
0P/F	**P**		**Jerom De Vindecy (FR)**^{18} [2065] 8-10-11 PBuchanan$^{(3)}$ (Miss Lucinda V Russell) *nt fluent in rr: t.o whn p.u bef 4 out* **50/1**	—

5m 23.6s (3.70) **Going Correction** +0.35s/f (Yiel) **12** Ran SP% **112.7**

Speed ratings: **106,105,94,93,93 90,90,83,—,— —,—** CSF £4.16 TOTE £1.90: £1.20, £1.60, £1.50; EX 4.80.

Owner Trevor Hemmings **Bred** Pat Leyden **Trained** Greystoke, Cumbria

FOCUS

A well above-average race for the track and the sound pace means this form should stand up with the placed horses plus the fifth and sixth close to their hurdles marks. The first two appeal as sorts to hold their own in better company over fences and this race should throw up a few winners from further down the field.

NOTEBOOK

Turpin Green(IRE) ◆, a very useful hurdler, created a very favourable impression on this chasing debut. His jumping was sound, he showed the right attitude and, although he had a hard race, he will appreciate three miles and appeals as the type to do better in stronger company. *(op 5-4 tchd 11-8 in a place)*

Rebel Rhythm ◆ ran his best race over fences against a potentially very smart sort. His jumping was sound, he should have no problems staying three miles and looks sure to win races over the larger obstacles. *(op 5-2)*

Leading Man(IRE) ◆, very much a chaser on looks, probably matched the pick of his hurdle form on his first run over the larger obstacles. While no match for two potentially smart sorts, he appeals as the type to win races in this sphere, especially when upped to three miles. *(op 14-1)*

Trisons Star(IRE) has the make and shape of a chaser and was anything but disgraced on this first run for nearly seven months. He should be all the better for this experience and is one to keep an eye on against lesser company. *(op 20-1)*

Italiano, an ordinary hurdler, shaped as though better than the bare form of this chasing debut on this first run for nearly seven months. He certainly showed more than enough to suggest he can pick up a race in this sphere.

Northern Minster was soundly beaten in the face of a stiff task and may do better in ordinary handicap company.

2450 EUROPEAN BREEDERS FUND "NATIONAL HUNT" NOVICES' HURDLE (QUALIFIER) (7 hdls 4 omitted) 2m 4f

1:50 (1:53) (Class 4) 4-6-Y-0 **£3,832** (£1,124; £562; £280)

Form				RPR
	1		**Numero Un De Solzen (FR)** 4-10-11 GBerridge$^{(3)}$ (J P L Ewart) *hld up: effrt and chsd ldr bef 2 out: 1l down and keeping on whn lft 13l clr last: pushed out* **40/1**	113+
16-3	**2**	*10*	**Royal Coburg (IRE)**^{22} [1980] 5-10-7 MGoldstein$^{(7)}$ (N A Twiston-Davies) *chsd ldrs: outpcd after 3 out: rallied and chsd wnr after last: no imp* **7/4**^{1}	101+
-362	**3**	*2 ½*	**Nevada Red**^{25} [1937] 4-10-9 StephenJCraine$^{(5)}$ (D McCain) *chsd ldrs: lost pl 4th: rallied 2 out: kpt on fr last: no imp* **9/1**^{3}	97
3-0	**4**	*2 ½*	**Reap The Reward (IRE)**^{21} [2006] 5-11-0 BGibson (L Lungo) *hld up: mstke 3 out: sn outpcd: kpt on fr last: no imp* **33/1**	97+
11-	**5**	*2 ½*	**Sotovik (IRE)**^{249} [4477] 4-11-0 JimCrowley (A C Whillans) *keen: cl up: effrt bef 2 out: sn outpcd: lft 13l 2nd last: sn btn* **6/1**^{2}	92
	6	*3 ½*	**Noir Et Vert (FR)**^{260} 4-10-11 KJMercer$^{(3)}$ (Ferdy Murphy) *cl up: led 3 out to bef next: sn btn* **16/1**	89
0	**P**		**Solway Raki**^{29} [1889] 4-10-9 MJMcAlister$^{(5)}$ (B Storey) *a bhd: t.o whn p.u bef 2 out* **200/1**	—
	F		**Ley Preacher (IRE)**^{194} 4-11-0 FKeniry (G M Moore) *a bhd: struggling 3 out: btn whn fell next* **66/1**	74
2	**F**		**Unexplored (IRE)**^{20} [2024] 5-11-0 GLee (J Howard Johnson) *chsd ldrs: led bef 2 out: 1l up and rdn whn fell last* **7/4**^{1}	111
P0-5	**P**		**Jofi (IRE)**^{25} [1938] 6-10-11 PBuchanan$^{(3)}$ (Miss Lucinda V Russell) *led to 4th: sn btn: t.o whn p.u bef 2 out* **200/1**	—

5m 22.3s (5.20) **Going Correction** +0.35s/f (Yiel) **10** Ran SP% **110.8**

Speed ratings: **103,99,98,97,96 94,—,—,—,—** CSF £108.28 TOTE £34.00: £5.70, £1.60, £1.60; EX 165.10.

Owner Maleissye,Ewart,Lockhart-Smith,Kesson **Bred** C Ricous-Guerin & Jacques Guerin **Trained** Craigcleuch, Dumfries & G'way

FOCUS
An ordinary event in which the winner was left clear at the final flight. The third sets the standard but it could be rated too high.

NOTEBOOK
Numero Un De Solzen(FR), a brother to a winning chaser, was in the process of running creditably and had every chance when left clear at the last on this hurdle debut. Whether he would have beaten the leader had that one stood up at the last is open to debate, but he should stay three miles and may do better in ordinary company over obstacles. *(op 50-1)*
Royal Coburg(IRE) again ran creditably on this second start over hurdles but left the strong impression that he would be suited by the step up to three miles. He looks capable of winning over obstacles when the emphasis is on stamina. *(op 15-8 tchd 13-8 and 2-1 in places)*
Nevada Red, who is now qualified for a handicap mark over hurdles, also shaped as though the step up to three miles and the switch into ordinary handicaps would be in his favour. *(op 10-1)*
Reap The Reward(IRE), very easy to back, hinted at ability on only this second run over obstacles and, given he is in very good hands, is another that should do better in ordinary handicaps when upped to three miles.
Sotovik(IRE), a dual bumper winner at this course, shaped as though a bit better than the bare form on this hurdle debut and first run since March. He is likely to improve, especially as he learns to settle. *(op 7-1)*
Noir Et Vert(FR), easy to back on this first run for new connections, was not disgraced on this first start since March and he may be capable of better in time. *(op 20-1)*
Unexplored(IRE), who shaped well behind a subsequent winner on his hurdle debut last time, was in the process of matching that effort when coming to grief. Although under pressure, he would have gone close had he stood up and is sure to win a similar event. *(op 6-4 tchd 2-1)*

2451 ASHLEYBANK INVESTMENTS H'CAP CHASE (18 fncs) 3m 110y
2:25 (2:25) (Class 3) (0-135,133) 5-Y-O+ **£8,116** (£2,382; £1,191; £595)

Form					RPR
3/63	**1**		**Silver Knight**[12] 2189 7-10-6 **113** (T D Easterby) *in tch: outpcd 5 out: rallied 3 out: led last: drvn out* **11/2**[3]	DO'Meara	128+
P-31	**2**	*1 ¼*	**Miss Mattie Ross**[19] 2037 9-9-9 **107** oh3 (S J Marshall) *mde most to last: kpt on u.p run in: hld towards fin* **10/1**	MJMcAlister(5)	120
4-31	**3**	*25*	**Silver Jack (IRE)**[18] 2063 7-10-0 **107** oh1 (M Todhunter) *trckd ldrs: hit 10th and 13th: ev ch 4 out: sn rdn: wknd bef 2 out* **9/2**[1]	FKeniry	98+
-U3U	**4**	*nk*	**Cill Churnain (IRE)**[21] 2003 12-10-5 **112** (Mrs S J Smith) *cl up: ev ch 4 out: rdn and wknd bef next* **6/1**	DElsworth	99
53-P	**5**	*21*	**Hugo De Grez (FR)**[25] 1941 10-10-3 **110** (A Parker) *chsd ldrs tl wknd fr 12th* **12/1**	ADempsey	76
5-P3	**6**	*14*	**You're Special (USA)**[16] 2102 8-10-12 **122** (t) (Ferdy Murphy) *in tch tl wknd fr 12th* **7/1**	KJMercer(3)	74
1F-0	**P**		**Freetown (IRE)**[7] 2292 9-11-6 **127** (L Lungo) *bhd: mstke 4th: sn struggling: t.o whn p.u after 9th* **7/1**	ADobbin	—
44-6	**P**		**Falchion**[8] 2265 10-10-0 **107** (t) (J R Bewley) *hld up: rdn 11th: sn wknd: t.o whn p.u bef 14th* **20/1**	KRenwick	—
1P-P	**P**		**Grattan Lodge (IRE)**[12] 2176 8-11-12 **133** (b[1]) (J Howard Johnson) *sn bhd: reminders 3rd: t.o whn p.u after 9th* **5/1**[2]	GLee	—

6m 36.8s **9** Ran SP% **111.1**
CSF £54.27 CT £257.33 TOTE £4.60: £1.90, £3.50, £1.40; EX 56.40 Trifecta £83.20 Pool: £598.20 - 5.10 winning units..

Owner C H Stevens **Bred** M H Easterby **Trained** Great Habton, N Yorks

FOCUS
An ordinary event in which several of the market leaders disappointed but one run at a decent gallop and placed the emphasis on stamina. The winner could rate higher on his old form.

NOTEBOOK
Silver Knight turned in his best effort since his long break and showed the right attitude in the closing stages. Stamina is his forte and this sound jumper can win again away from progressive sorts when he gets a decent test. *(op 9-2 tchd 6-1)*
Miss Mattie Ross, up in the weights and in grade (3lb out of the handicap), showed she was as effective at this much stiffer course as she is at Kelso. Her jumping was again sound, she showed the right attitude and she should continue to give a good account. *(op 11-1)*
Silver Jack(IRE), who had jumped well when winning an ordinary event at Ayr, made a couple of mistakes and had his limitations exposed over this longer trip in this testing ground. Two and a half miles may suit better and he is not one to write off yet. *(op 11-2)*
Cill Churnain(IRE) has won over three miles on soft ground over fences but, although jumping soundly, proved a bit of a disappointment. He has not had much racing since his last win in 2003 but may be one to tread carefully with. *(op 11-2 tchd 5-1)*
Hugo De Grez(FR) figures on a fair mark at present but did not really show enough under ideal conditions at his favourite course to suggest he is of much interest in the short term. *(op 14-1)*
Freetown(IRE) *Official explanation: jockey said gelding was never travelling. (op 6-1)*
Grattan Lodge(IRE), who showed the right attitude to win this last year, ran a stinker in the *first-time blinkers and remains one to tread carefully with at present.Official explanation: jockey said gelding would not face first-time blinkers (op 6-1)*

2452 C.F.M. H'CAP HURDLE (6 hdls 3 omitted) 2m 1f
3:00 (3:01) (Class 3) (0-125,120) 4-Y-O+ **£4,807** (£1,411; £705; £352)

Form					RPR
21P-	**1**		**Diamond Sal**[236] 4694 7-10-10 **104** (J Howard Johnson) *hld up: hdwy 1/2-way: gng wl bef 2 out: led last: rdn and r.o wl* **5/2**[1]	GLee	113+
12-4	**2**	*2 ½*	**Pay Attention**[27] 1912 4-11-12 **120** (T D Easterby) *in tch: hdwy to ld after 3 out: hdd bef next: styd upsides and ev ch last: kpt on same pce* **10/1**	RGarritty	124+
003/	**3**	*3 ½*	**Castle Richard (IRE)**[593] 4729 8-10-8 **102** (G M Moore) *midfield: hdwy to ld bef 2 out: hdd last: sn outpcd* **25/1**	FKeniry	102
-060	**4**	*6*	**Transit**[12] 2190 6-10-13 **110** (p) (B Ellison) *hld up: hdwy and ev ch bef 2 out: wknd bef last* **12/1**	KJMercer(3)	105+
0/50	**5**	*3*	**Uptown Lad (IRE)**[16] 2110 6-10-6 **100** (t) (R Johnson) *hld up: effrt u.p bef 2 out: nvr rchd ldrs* **7/1**[2]	KJohnson	91
31F/	**6**	*6*	**Thosewerethedays**[663] 3597 12-11-7 **115** (Miss P Robson) *trckd ldrs tl wknd appr 2 out* **10/1**	BHarding	100
1P00	**7**	*4*	**Isellido (IRE)**[8] 2264 6-10-6 **110** (e) (R C Guest) *hld up: rdn bef 2 out: n.d* **20/1**	JPFlavin(10)	91
P1B2	**8**	*8*	**Top Style (IRE)**[21] 2002 7-11-1 **109** (p) (G A Harker) *prom tl wknd bef 2 out* **9/1**	RMcGrath	82
2-64	**9**	*7*	**Crackleando**[45] 667 4-11-2 **110** (A R Dicken) *hld up: hdwy and disp ld after 3 out: wknd bef next* **25/1**	ADobbin	76
-40U	**10**	*4*	**Gospel Song**[8] 2264 13-9-9 **96** ow1 (A C Whillans) *cl up: led 3rd to after next: wknd bef 2 out* **50/1**	EWhillans(7)	58
-P00	**11**	*3 ½*	**Culcabock (IRE)**[19] 2038 5-10-8 **105** (Miss Lucinda V Russell) *hld up: rdn bef 2 out: sn btn* **16/1**	PBuchanan(3)	64
0-62	**12**	*¾*	**Shares (IRE)**[19] 2042 5-10-11 **105** (P Monteith) *hld up: effrt bef 2 out: sn btn* **15/2**[3]	KRenwick	63
0-00	**13**	*3 ½*	**Welsh Dream**[33] 1838 8-9-11 **94** (Miss S E Forster) *sn bhd: no ch fr 1/2-way* **20/1**	MrCStorey(3)	48
5300	**14**	*14*	**Merryvale Man**[12] 2190 8-10-1 **100** (Miss Kariana Key) *led to 3rd: wknd after next* **25/1**	DMcGann(5)	40

4m 30.5s (4.80) **Going Correction** +0.35s/f (Yiel) **14** Ran SP% **117.6**
Speed ratings: **102,100,99,96,94 92,90,86,83,81 79,79,77,71** CSF £23.91 CT £514.16 TOTE £3.30: £1.40, £2.60, £8.60; EX 18.30.

Owner Andrea & Graham Wylie **Bred** Goldford Stud **Trained** Billy Row, Co Durham

FOCUS
An ordinary event in which the gallop was fair but the winner appeals as the type to win more races. The time was ordinary but the third sets the standard and the form should work out.

NOTEBOOK
Diamond Sal ◆, back in trip for this reappearance run, travelled strongly and turned in an improved effort to win with more in hand than the official margin suggests. She stays two and a half miles and appeals as the type to win again this term. *(op 7-2)*
Pay Attention, all the better for a recent run at Wetherby, returned to something like her best and looks a good guide to the level of this form. She may be vulnerable to progressive sorts from this mark but should continue to give a good account. *(op 13-2)*
Castle Richard(IRE) caught the eye on this first run since April of last year. On this evidence he is sure to win another race but his record suggests he is not certain to reproduce this next time.
Transit, below his best at Wetherby last time, was not disgraced but left the impression that he would continue to look vulnerable from his current mark in the near future. *(op 14-1)*
Uptown Lad(IRE) is not very consistent but ran his best race for a while and left the impression that the return to further would be in his favour. However, whether he reproduces this next time remains to be seen.
Thosewerethedays, returned to hurdles on this first start since January last year, shaped as though retaining ability. He should be all the better for this run and, although nearing the veteran *stage, has not had much racing and is one to keep an eye on.Official explanation: jockey said, regarding the running and riding, his orders were to be handy and sit where gelding was comfortable, adding that since gelding had been off for almost two years with leg trouble he tried to pick the best ground, but gelding tired in home straight under hands and heels; trainer added that although gelding was entered in a more suitable race over further at Newcastle, she feared that meeting would be abanadoned (op 9-1)*
Shares(IRE) *Official explanation: jockey said gelding hung left-handed throughout (op 8-1)*

2453 D & C MITCHELL AMATEUR RIDERS' H'CAP HURDLE (7 hdls 4 omitted) 2m 4f
3:30 (3:30) (Class 4) (0-105,105) 4-Y-O+ **£3,210** (£987; £493)

Form					RPR
P043	**1**		**General Duroc (IRE)**[18] 2066 9-10-12 **96** (p) (B Storey) *cl up: effrt after 3 out: kpt on wl to ld cl home* **10/1**	MrMSeston(5)	109
10-4	**2**	*nk*	**D J Flippance (IRE)**[33] 1837 10-10-4 **90** (A Parker) *led: rdn 3 out: kpt on fr last: hdd cl home* **8/1**	MrSWByrne(7)	103
F1-3	**3**	*7*	**North Landing (IRE)**[16] 2107 5-10-5 **91** (R C Guest) *hld up: hdwy after 3 out: effrt next: kpt on same pce last* **16/1**	MrSFMagee(7)	97
3-22	**4**	*6*	**Jolika (FR)**[20] 2027 8-11-6 **99** (L Lungo) *hld up: hdwy bef 3 out: effrt and rdn next: wknd bef last* **7/2**[1]	MrTGreenall	101+
520	**5**	*8*	**Minster Abbi**[13] 2171 5-9-7 **79** oh4 (p) (W Storey) *prom tl rdn and wknd bef 2 out* **11/1**	MrHHaynes(7)	71
-314	**6**	*8*	**Red Man (IRE)**[12] 2190 8-11-5 **105** (Mrs E Slack) *keen: hld up: outpcd 4 out: n.d after* **6/1**[3]	MissJSayer(7)	92+
5504	**7**	*6*	**Sylvie D'Orthe (FR)**[16] 2107 4-9-7 **79** oh11 (p) (Cooper Wilson) *chsd ldrs to 4 out: sn rdn and btn* **33/1**	RCummings(7)	57
2-22	**8**	*2 ½*	**Lochiedubs**[12] 2182 10-10-2 **88** (p) (Mrs L B Normile) *midfield: outpcd bef 4 out: sn n.d* **14/1**	MrCJCallow(7)	64
-5P0	**9**	*24*	**Just Sal**[20] 2025 9-9-7 **79** oh6 (R Nixon) *bhd: no ch fr 4 out* **25/1**	MrMEllwood(7)	31
406-	**10**	*9*	**Needwood Spirit**[218] 4928 10-9-7 **79** oh4 (Mrs A M Naughton) *a wl bhd* **16/1**	MrRTierney(7)	22
55F2	**11**	*1 ½*	**Silver Sedge (IRE)**[13] 2171 6-10-9 **88** (Mrs A Hamilton) *in tch tl wknd bef 3 out* **9/2**[2]	MissPRobson	29
PU	**12**	*½*	**Winds Supreme (IRE)**[33] 1835 6-10-0 **86** (t) (M A Barnes) *cl up to 4 out: wknd fr next* **50/1**	MissAngelaBarnes(7)	27
3450	**13**	*dist*	**Star Trooper (IRE)**[20] 2025 9-9-7 **79** oh2 (p) (Miss S E Forster) *sn t.o: nvr on terms* **14/1**	MissCarlyFrater(7)	—
600/	**P**		**Tolcea (IRE)**[753] 1895 6-9-9 **79** oh17 (A C Whillans) *a bhd: t.o whn p.u bef 2 out* **40/1**	MissRDavidson(5)	—
F-P0	**P**		**Grafton Truce (IRE)**[20] 2027 8-10-0 **86** oh12 ow7 (Miss Lucinda V Russell) *prom tl wknd after 3rd: t.o whn p.u bef last* **50/1**	MrDOakden(5)	—

5m 22.9s (5.80) **Going Correction** +0.35s/f (Yiel)
WFA 4 from 5yo+ 13lb **15** Ran SP% **121.5**
Speed ratings: **102,101,99,96,93 90,87,86,77,73 73,72,—,—,—** CSF £85.09 CT £1284.37 TOTE £14.70: £4.10, £2.30, £5.20; EX 139.90 Place 6 £10.30, Place 5 £9.50.

Owner F S Storey **Bred** Frank Burke **Trained** Kirklinton, Cumbria

FOCUS
An ordinary event but a decent gallop and a thorough test of stamina. The first three were close to their marks.

NOTEBOOK
General Duroc(IRE) ran his best race for his current stable and showed the right attitude in the closing stages. The return to three miles will be in his favour and, on this evidence, he should win more races granted a suitable test.
D J Flippance(IRE), returned to hurdles, had conditions to suit over a trip that is a bare minimum and showed more than enough to suggest a similar event can be found in the near future. *(op 10-1)*
North Landing(IRE) turned out quickly on this second run after a long break, confirmed the promise shown last time and looks capable of winning another race for his astute handler. *(op 12-1)*
Jolika(FR) travelled well for a long way but was a shade disappointing on this second fairly quick run after a break. However, she goes on most ground and is not one to be writing off just yet. *(tchd 4-1)*
Minster Abbi, an inconsistent maiden, has run well over three miles on bad ground at this course but did not get home this time and remains one to tread carefully with. *(op 10-1)*
Red Man(IRE) failed to settle early on and was below his best in a race that placed the emphasis firmly on stamina. Better ground may help but he is not one to place maximum faith in. *(op 7-1)*
Silver Sedge(IRE), who stays this trip and has form in testing ground, ran poorly for no apparent reason and is one to tread carefully with. *(op 11-2)*

T/Plt: £12.30 to a £1 stake. Pool: £33,280.10. 1,959.55 winning tickets. T/Qpdt: £6.40 to a £1 stake. Pool: £2,572.00. 296.80 winning tickets. RY

[2146]TAUNTON (R-H)

Thursday, November 24

OFFICIAL GOING: Good to firm

Wind: Strong across

2454 HOARY MORNING JUVENILE NOVICES' (S) HURDLE (9 hdls) 2m 1f

12:30 (12:30) (Class 5) 3-Y-O **£2,329** (£678; £339)

Form				RPR
4202	1		**Strathtay**[10] [2245] 3-10-3 93 (v) TScudamore (M C Pipe) *chsd ldrs: led appr 5th: drvn clr after 3 out: edgd rt run-in: rdn out* **2/1**[1]	80+
00	2	7	**Jamaaron**[35] [1729] 3-10-3 RLucey-Butler(7) (W G M Turner) *hld up bhd: hdwy after 3 out to go 2nd appr next: edgd lft run-in: no ch w wnr* **12/1**	79
4220	3	2 ½	**Compton Quay**[8] [2274] 3-10-10 95 BHitchcott (Miss K M George) *chsd ldrs: carried wd on bnd after 4th: rdn after 5th: kpt on same pce* **11/2**[3]	79+
4620	4	2 ½	**Inchcape Rock**[12] [2178] 3-10-10 107 VSlattery (J G M O'Shea) *chsd ldr tl carried wd on bnd after 4th: chsd ldrs: rdn and one pced fr 3 out* **9/4**[2]	79+
4P6	5	3 ½	**Darko Karim**[10] [2245] 3-10-10 (b[1]) RGreene (R J Hodges) *rn in snatches: mid div: drvn along fr 4th: one pced fr 3 out* **10/1**	71
	6	4	**Smokey The Bear**[44] 3-10-10 JGoldstein (A P Jones) *mid div: hdwy to chse wnr after 6th: nt fluent next: sn rdn: wknd appr 2 out* **50/1**	67
FP5	7	½	**Arno River**[24] [1948] 3-10-3 MrJAJenkins(7) (D Brace) *towards rr: nt fluent 4th: hdwy next: rdn appr 6th: chsd wnr briefly after 3 out: wknd* **14/1**	66
0P	F		**Magnate (IRE)**[7] [2286] 3-10-3 MrRhysHughes(7) (Mrs S M Johnson) *towards rr: fell 3rd* **66/1**	—
	R		**Lightening Fire (IRE)**[54] 3-10-10 (p) OMcPhail (B J Llewellyn) *rel to r: ref & uns rdr 1st* **28/1**	—
0	U		**Miss Defying**[18] [2069] 3-10-3 TDoyle (R Curtis) *chsng ldrs whn wnt bdly lft and uns rdr 1st* **66/1**	—
	P		**King Marrakech (IRE)**[42] 3-10-10 DCrosse (M D I Usher) *j. slowly 1st: a bhd: t.o and p.u bef 6th* **33/1**	—
00	P		**Galaxy Dancer (IRE)**[19] [1737] 3-10-5 CHonour(5) (N B King) *led tl rn wd on bnd after 4th: chsd wnr tl wknd 3 out: p.u bef 2 out* **25/1**	—

4m 9.70s (0.90) **Going Correction** -0.125s/f (Good) **12** Ran SP% **118.1**

Speed ratings: **92,88,87,86,84 82,82,—,—,— —,—** CSF £24.90 TOTE £2.40: £1.10, £4.00, £2.30; EX 36.50.The winner was sold to D Tunnman for 8,000gns.

Owner E Nisbet **Bred** Broughton Bloodstock **Trained** Nicholashayne, Devon

FOCUS

The riders' opinion of the ground was that it was good. This was probably a reasonable event of its type rated through the winner, although as is often the case with juvenile sellers there was a certain amount of mayhem.

NOTEBOOK

Strathtay was left in front when the leader ran wide on the bend past the stands with a circuit to run. Responding well to a positive ride once in front, she was clear turning for home. She was not winning out of turn and could well pick up another of these for her new yard, although she is not a straightforward ride. *(op 9-4 tchd 5-2)*

Jamaaron, beaten in this grade on the Flat since his two hurdles runs, made progress from the rear to move into second place two from home but was never near the winner. He has a little ability, but lack of stamina could prove a problem. *(op 14-1)*

Compton Quay, without the cheekpieces and descending to this level, ran better than he did last time on this second start since leaving Alan King, but he is not progressing.

Inchcape Rock had today's winner behind when runner-up at Cheltenham two starts back but could not take advantage of this considerable drop in class. He probably needs easier ground and/or a stiffer test. *(op 5-2)*

Darko Karim looked less than keen to exert himself until it was all over, despite the different variety of headgear. *(op 9-1 tchd 11-1)*

Smokey The Bear, a poor plater on the Flat, travelled well for some way on this hurdling debut but just did not stay. *(op 40-1)*

2455 BEAUTY OF BATH MAIDEN HURDLE (9 hdls) 2m 1f

1:05 (1:05) (Class 3) 4-Y-0+ **£5,439** (£1,596; £798; £398)

Form				RPR
	1		**Acambo (GER)**[83] 4-11-2 RGreene (M C Pipe) *hld up mid div: shkn up and gd hdwy appr 2 out: wnt 2nd appr last: qcknd up wl to ld run-in: readily* **20/1**	118+
	2	2 ½	**Spanish Don**[54] 7-11-2 RWalford (D R C Elsworth) *led:1 l clr last: sn rdn and hdd: nt pce of wnr* **5/2**[1]	110
0-26	3	4	**Idris (GER)**[10] [2238] 4-11-2 110 JEMoore (G L Moore) *chsd ldrs: pckd 6th: ev ch 3 out: sn rdn: kpt on same pce* **4/1**[2]	107+
	4	hd	**Mick Jerome (IRE)**[61] 4-11-2 MBatchelor (Rune Haugen, Norway) *in tch: tk clsr order 3 out: sn rdn: kpt on same pce* **11/2**	106
	5	nk	**Topkat (IRE)**[41] 4-10-13 (t) TJMalone(3) (M C Pipe) *in tch: pressed ldr 6th: rdn and ev ch 2 out: nt qckn* **5/1**[3]	107+
03	6	10	**Iffy**[26] [1927] 4-11-2 TDoyle (R Lee) *mid div: tk clsr order 3 out: sn rdn: wknd after next* **6/1**	96
	7	2 ½	**Barathea Blue**[24] 4-11-2 TScudamore (M C Pipe) *hld up bhd: hdwy after 6th to chse ldrs: wknd appr 2 out* **11/1**	93
600-	8	½	**Salopian**[229] [4775] 5-11-2 MBradburne (H D Daly) *mid div: wkng whn rn wd on bnd after 3 out* **100/1**	93
	9	23	**Huckster (ZIM)**[187] 6-11-2 AO'Keeffe (Miss Venetia Williams) *mid div: wkng whn carried wd on bnd after 3 out* **25/1**	70
	10	30	**Anna Panna**[453] 4-10-2 SWalsh(7) (R H Alner) *nvr fluent in rr: t.o fr 5th* **50/1**	33
POFO	11	¾	**Dreams Jewel**[6] [2309] 5-11-2 OMcPhail (C Roberts) *chsd ldr tl 6th: sn wknd: t.o* **100/1**	39
45	12	¾	**Butler Services (IRE)**[7] [2288] 5-11-2 MAFitzgerald (Jonjo O'Neill) *bhd fr 5th: sn t.o* **40/1**	38
0	F		**Island Light (USA)**[18] [2070] 5-11-2 SCurran (P Wegmann) *hld up towards rr: fell 6th* **150/1**	—

4m 1.30s (-7.50) **Going Correction** -0.125s/f (Good)

WFA 4 from 5yo+ 12lb **13** Ran SP% **118.9**

Speed ratings: **112,110,108,108,108 104,102,102,91,77 77,76,—** CSF £69.80 TOTE £13.20: £7.40, £2.60, £1.50; EX 42.70.

Owner D A Johnson **Bred** A Groschler **Trained** Nicholashayne, Devon

FOCUS

An above-average maiden hurdle for Taunton, run no less than eight seconds faster than the seller despite a fairly sedate early pace, and it should produce its share of winners. The third and sixth ran to their marks and the form should work out.

NOTEBOOK

Acambo(GER) ◆, four times a winner on the Flat in Germany, was the longest-priced of Pipe's three runners on this hurdling debut. Wanting to go quicker in the early parts, he was in a bit of trouble turning out of the back straight as the leading pair threatened to get away and he found himself short of room behind toiling rivals, but he really found his feet from the second last and came with a strong run to cut down the leader on the flat and win going away. This was a nice performance and he looks a useful recruit. *(op 12-1 tchd 25-1)*

Spanish Don remains winless since landing the 2004 Cambridgeshire at 100/1, but he should not be long in getting off the mark over hurdles judged on this promising debut. Jumping pretty well and steadily winding up the pace from the front, he was only caught after the last by what is probably a decent novice. His trainer suggested a trip to Dubai could also be on the cards for him in the New Year. *(op 2-1 tchd 11-4 and 3-1 in a place)*

Idris(GER), one of the most experienced of these over hurdles, filled third place for much of the way but was outpaced when the leaders kicked entering the straight. He is exposed and pegs this form down a little, but looks capable of winning a novices' handicap. *(tchd 7-2)*

Mick Jerome(IRE) is a Classic winner - albeit it was last year's Norwegian Derby - and he shaped with promise in this warmish race on his hurdles debut, nearly snatching third. *(op 5-1)*

Topkat(IRE), the shortest-priced of the Pipe trio, was a dual mile and a half winner on the Flat who was making his hurdling bow having been sold out of David Elsworth's yard for 30,000gns. After challenging his former stablemate Spanish Don on the home turn, he clouted the second last and was soon on the retreat. He is probably capable of better. *(op 8-1)*

Iffy failed to live up to the promise he showed at Wetherby and is going to have to settle better, but has the ability to be granted another chance. *(op 7-1)*

Barathea Blue, previously with Walter Swinburn, was regressive on the Flat. He did not show a great deal on this hurdles debut but is obviously in the right hands to improve. *(op 25-1)*

Anna Panna *Official explanation: jockey said filly had breathing problem (op 40-1)*

2456 SOUTH-WEST RACING CLUB BEGINNERS' CHASE (12 fncs) 2m 110y

1:40 (1:40) (Class 3) 4-Y-0+ **£5,513** (£1,618; £809; £404)

Form				RPR
53-3	1		**Crossbow Creek**[201] [208] 7-11-5 JEMoore (M G Rimell) *j. fluently: t.k.h: hld up: hdwy to trck ldrs 7th: led after 3 out: a in command after: readily* **8/11**[1]	132+
245P	2	5	**Kings Brook**[30] [1871] 5-11-5 110 TDoyle (Nick Williams) *trckd ldrs: led after 6th: j.lft fr 3 out: hdd appr 2 out: sn no ch w wnr: pckd last* **20/1**	117
55-3	3	9	**Chockdee (FR)**[29] [1878] 5-11-5 JTizzard (P F Nicholls) *t.k.h: hld up in tch: hdwy to trck ldrs after 6th: j.lft fr 4 out: chalng whn nt fluent next: kpt on same pce* **10/3**[2]	113+
F	4	6	**Nayodabayo (IRE)**[14] [2141] 5-11-5 110 (p) PMoloney (Evan Williams) *led: blnd 5th: hdd after next: chsd ldr: rdn after 4 out: one pced after* **20/1**	108+
00-0	5	shd	**Zibeline (IRE)**[12] [2175] 8-11-5 WHutchinson (B Ellison) *hld up: hit 2nd: pckd 4th: hdwy to chse ldrs after 7th: rdn after 4 out: no imp* **8/1**[3]	102
0460	6	10	**Tyup Pompey (IRE)**[35] [1806] 4-10-7 JGoldstein (Miss J S Davis) *hld up and a towards rr* **125/1**	81+
0642	7	4	**He's The Gaffer (IRE)**[28] [1900] 5-11-5 85 (b) BHitchcott (R H Buckler) *trckd ldr tl 5th: sn bhd* **25/1**	88
6-PP	8	dist	**Jaskini**[6] [2314] 9-11-0 70 HEphgrave(5) (L Corcoran) *chsd ldrs tl 4 out: sn bhd: t.o* **66/1**	—

4m 6.70s (-8.80) **Going Correction** -0.425s/f (Good)

WFA 4 from 5yo+ 12lb **8** Ran SP% **107.7**

Speed ratings: **103,100,96,93,93 88,86,—** CSF £16.50 TOTE £1.80: £1.10, £2.60, £1.30; EX 18.90.

Owner Mrs M R T Rimell **Bred** Mrs M R T Rimell **Trained** Leafield, Oxon

FOCUS

Quite an interesting beginners' event, and the winner is value for further and looks a smart recruit.

NOTEBOOK

Crossbow Creek ◆ produced a taking performance on his chasing debut. A high-class handicapper over hurdles last term, rated 137 over the smaller obstacles, he travelled strongly, taking a hold as the gallop was not sufficiently strong for him, before easing to the front three for home and asserting for a ready success. He jumped accurately throughout and is likely to step up into Grade Two company in the Henry VIII Novices' Chase early next month provided the ground comes up good. *(op 10-11 tchd 4-6)*

Kings Brook seemed to appreciate being ridden more positively and this was an improvement on his previous chase form, although the winner was in a different class. He jumped pretty well and should find a little race, although he is not the sort to find much for pressure. *(op 16-1 tchd 25-1)*

Chockdee(FR), a quirky individual, was a little disappointing on this chasing bow even if he did have 17lb to find with Crossbow Creek on BHB hurdles ratings. He jumped out to his left when the heat was on but has the talent to win in ordinary novice company. *(op 4-1)*

Nayodabayo(IRE) jumped pretty well until crashing out at the last on his recent British debut at Ludlow, but he made a couple of errors here and was beaten with four to jump. Minor handicaps should be more his scene. *(op 15-2)*

Zibeline(IRE), the second highest rated of these over hurdles but not at his best for some time, did not look a natural over fences in two attempts last winter and confirmed that impression here. In his defence, he probably needs further these days. *(op 7-1 tchd 11-1)*

2457 LEATH JEWELLERS & VALUERS CHALLENGE TROPHY "NATIONAL HUNT" MARES' ONLY NOVICES' HURDLE (10 hdls) 2m 3f 110y

2:15 (2:15) (Class 3) 4-Y-0+ **£7,338** (£2,154; £1,077; £538)

Form				RPR
30P-	1		**Pearly Bay**[217] [4936] 7-10-12 JEMoore (M G Rimell) *hld up in tch: tk cl order after 7th: led after 3 out: styd on: rdn out* **9/2**[2]	95+
-322	2	7	**Miss Midnight**[14] [2152] 4-10-12 TScudamore (R J Hodges) *in tch: sltly outpcd after 6th: styd on u.p to go 2nd 2 out: hld whn wnt bdly rt last* **9/2**[2]	90+
F111	3	3	**Parisienne Gale (IRE)**[7] [2289] 6-11-5 90 TJMalone(3) (R Ford) *led: rdn and hdd after 3 out: kpt on same pce* **4/5**[1]	95
66-0	4	7	**Gotta Get On**[20] [2015] 4-10-12 64 RWalford (R H Alner) *chsd ldr: jnd ldr after 5th: rdn after 3 out: sn wknd* **80/1**	78
5	5	hd	**Missy Moscow (IRE)**[189] [426] 7-10-12 VSlattery (H J Evans) *towards rr: drvn along fr 6th: sme hdwy appr 3 out: no further imp* **33/1**	78
60-1	6	dist	**Ballymena**[208] [138] 4-10-7 LStephens(5) (C Roberts) *nt fluent 4th: a towards rr: lost tch fr 6th* **20/1**	—
5	7	1	**Classy Chick (IRE)**[194] [349] 4-10-12 MBradburne (H D Daly) *nt fluent 1st: a towards rr: wl bhd fr 7th* **16/1**[3]	—
0/0	8	1 ¼	**Barfleur (IRE)**[18] [2075] 5-10-12 TDoyle (P Bowen) *chsd ldr tl hit 6th: sn dropped rr: t.o* **40/1**	—

4400 **9** *22* **Allez Melina**[15] 2131 4-10-12 ....(t) PHide —
(Mrs A J Hamilton-Fairley) *a towards rr: t.o fr 7th* **66/1**

5041 **P** **Distant Romance**[54] 1597 8-10-5 77 .... RLucey-Butler(7) —
(Miss Z C Davison) *hld up: mstke 5th: bhd fr next: t.o and p.u after 3 out: b.b.v* **25/1**

4m 45.3s (-0.70) **Going Correction** -0.125s/f (Good)
WFA 4 from 5yo+ 12lb **10** Ran SP% **114.5**
Speed ratings: **96,93,92,89,89** —,—,—,—,— CSF £22.79 TOTE £6.00: £1.50, £1.60, £1.10; EX 25.50.
Owner Sandicroft Stud **Bred** Mrs R E Hambro **Trained** Leafield, Oxon

FOCUS
This was run at a good gallop and the form looks fairly solid for the grade with the first two close to their bumper marks.

NOTEBOOK
Pearly Bay sat a little off the pace before reeling in the leader on the home turn and pulling away for a decisive victory. A bumper winner for this yard, she rejoined Mark Rimell after losing her way for Paul Nicholls last term and, as this was only her second run over hurdles, she should have further improvement in her. *(op 5-1 tchd 6-1)*
Miss Midnight, runner-up in three of her four bumpers and third in the other, again found one too good, but this was a promising hurdles debut and her turn will come. Her attitude is not in question. *(op 5-1)*
Parisienne Gale(IRE) set a strong pace but could never get clear and the game was up when she was headed on the turn out of the back straight. The double penalty told this time but this versatile mare could yet enhance her admirable record back in handicap company. *(op evens)*
Gotta Get On shadowed the favourite for much of the way, and while she was well held in the end this was much her best run to date. She ought to be capable of more improvement as she gains experience. *(op 66-1 tchd 100-1)*
Missy Moscow(IRE), a former pointer, shaped with no particular promise on this first run since May and first outing since leaving Tom Tate. *(op 66-1)*
Ballymena, winner of a weak bumper on her latest start in April, was always trailing on this hurdles bow. *(op 11-1)*
Distant Romance *Official explanation: vet said mare bled from nose (op 20-1)*

2458 GOLDEN KNOB H'CAP CHASE (19 fncs) 3m 3f
2:50 (2:50) (Class 3) (0-115,114) 5-Y-0+ **£5,709** (£1,676; £838; £418)

Form RPR

0-55 **1** **Comanche War Paint (IRE)**[136] 960 8-11-12 114 .... JTizzard 130+
(P F Nicholls) *trckd ldrs: lft in 2nd after 9th: led 11th: hit 15th: in command fr 3 out: styd on wl: comf* **7/2**[2]

63 **2** *11* **Mick Divine (IRE)**[14] 2151 7-10-3 91 .... DCrosse 95+
(C J Mann) *hld up but in tch: tk clsr order next:hit 12th: rdn to chse wnr after 4 out: kpt on but no further imp fr next* **5/2**[1]

-300 **3** *6* **Even More (IRE)**[8] 2273 10-11-7 109 .... RWalford 104
(R H Alner) *led tl 11th: chsd wnr tl after 4 out: one pced after: mstke last* **10/1**

2U2- **4** *10* **Menphis Beury (FR)**[221] 4886 5-11-5 108 .... MBradburne 96+
(H D Daly) *hld up in tch: hit 8th: trckd ldrs after next: chalng for 3rd whn mstke 3 out: wknd* **7/2**[2]

30-5 **5** *16* **Try Catch Paddy (IRE)**[23] 1973 7-11-8 110 ....(p) RGreene 79
(M C Pipe) *hld up in tch: rdn after 14th: wknd 4 out* **12/1**

2444 **P** **Windy Spirit (IRE)**[21] 2005 10-11-8 110 ....(p) PMoloney —
(Evan Williams) *hld up bhd ldrs: lost tch after 13th: t.o 4 out: p.u bef 2 out* **12/1**

054P **P** **It's Definite (IRE)**[22] 1988 6-10-13 101 ....(p) TDoyle —
(P Bowen) *nvr fluent: slow jump 1st: chsd ldr: mstke 8th: blnd bdly 9th and broke bridle: immediately eased: p.u after next* **13/2**[3]

6m 58.8s (-16.60) **Going Correction** -0.425s/f (Good)
WFA 5 from 6yo+ 1lb **7** Ran SP% **110.8**
Speed ratings: **107,103,101,99,94** —,— CSF £12.36 TOTE £4.20: £2.60, £2.50; EX 15.80.
Owner Tony Fear & Tim Hawkins **Bred** Dr C G Lowry **Trained** Ditcheat, Somerset

FOCUS
This ordinary handicap was run at a solid pace and the form could rate higher.

NOTEBOOK
Comanche War Paint(IRE) took up the running with a circuit to go and steadily increased the pace. Showing no signs of rustiness on this first start since July, he stayed on strongly and has the cross-country race at Cheltenham next month as his target, having shown an aptitude for that unique course before. *(op 10-3 tchd 3-1)*
Mick Divine(IRE), lowered 5lb despite an encouraging second run for this yard last time, put in a shaky round but stayed this longer trip. Easier ground will suit him. *(op 10-3 tchd 7-2)*
Even More(IRE), who won this event last year from a 3lb lower mark, lost the lead to the eventual winner passing the stands with a circuit to run and never looked likely to regain it thereafter. He is due to be dropped a pound in future handicaps. *(op 8-1 tchd 7-1)*
Menphis Beury(FR) is entitled to improve with this first start since April behind him but he is still prone to the odd mistake. *(tchd 4-1)*
Try Catch Paddy(IRE) should have had the stamina for this trip on his chasing debut, but the cheekpieces told their own tale and he looked less than enthusiastic. *(op 16-1)*
Windy Spirit(IRE) had no excuses on account of the ground but looks in need of a drop in the weights. *(tchd 14-1)*
It's Definite(IRE) got away with a mistake at the eighth but a worse one at the next saw his bridle break and take the cheekpieces with it. *Official explanation: jockey said bridle broke (tchd 14-1)*

2459 SOPS IN WINE H'CAP HURDLE (9 hdls 1 omitted) 2m 3f 110y
3:20 (3:20) (Class 3) (0-120,119) 4-Y-0+ **£5,178** (£1,520; £760; £379)

Form RPR

P-10 **1** **Devito (FR)**[14] 2150 4-10-9 109 ow2 .... MrDEdwards(7) 116+
(G F Edwards) *hld up bhd: smooth hdwy fr 6th: led sn after 2 out: styd on wl: eased cl home* **14/1**

00-0 **2** *4* **Candarli (IRE)**[51] 1633 9-10-11 109 .... SCurling(5) 108
(D R Gandolfo) *chsd ldrs: rdn and ev ch after 2 out: 2nd and hld whn j.rt last* **25/1**

-606 **3** *18* **Freedom Now (IRE)**[14] 2150 7-10-13 106 .... RWalford 92+
(R H Alner) *in tch: jnd ldrs after 5th: rdn appr 7th: one pced fr 2 out* **4/1**[2]

0605 **4** *3 ½* **Ashgan (IRE)**[22] 1981 12-9-10 94 oh17 ow1 .... DrPPritchard(5) 72
(Dr P Pritchard) *j. slowly 1st: sn t.o: rdn and styd on after 2 out: tk 4th run-in: nvr a danger* **66/1**

0121 **5** *2* **Tonic Du Charmil (FR)**[20] 2016 5-11-12 119 ....(t) TScudamore 95
(M C Pipe) *prom tl 7th: sn rdn: wknd after 2 out* **7/2**[1]

6024 **6** *½* **Noble Calling (FR)**[18] 2071 8-10-2 102 .... JamesWhite(7) 77
(R J Hodges) *sn outpcd and bhd: styd on fr 2 out: n.d* **28/1**

0/- **7** *4* **Adecco (IRE)**[904] 99 6-10-1 94 .... JEMoore 65
(G L Moore) *racd freely: prom: led 3rd tl 3 out: wknd qckly* **5/1**[3]

1P02 **8** *21* **Middleham Park (IRE)**[8] 2271 5-10-7 107 .... WPKavanagh(7) 57
(J W Mullins) *mid div: rdn after 6th: wknd appr 2 out: t.o* **11/2**

12-0 **9** *½* **Damarisco (FR)**[192] 389 5-9-13 97 .... RStephens(5) 47
(P J Hobbs) *set str pce: led tl after 1st: prom tl hit 7th: sn wknd: t.o* **11/2**

-25F **P** **Titian Flame (IRE)**[137] 949 5-9-13 97 ....(p) LStephens(5) —
(D Burchell) *led after 1st and maintained str pce: hdd and sddle slipped 3rd: p.u bef next* **16/1**

4m 37.8s (-8.20) **Going Correction** -0.125s/f (Good)
WFA 4 from 5yo+ 12lb **10** Ran SP% **111.0**
Speed ratings: **111,109,102,100,100 99,98,89,89,**— CSF £274.81 CT £1604.54 TOTE £20.60: £4.30, £6.50, £1.80; EX 144.80 Place 6 £13.50, Place 5 £7.79.
Owner G F Edwards **Bred** Patrick Chedeville **Trained** Luckwell Bridge, Somerset

FOCUS
A moderate event which saw too many of these want a slice of the action up front, setting things up for the held-up winner. The winning time was 7.5 seconds faster than the earlier contest over the same trip and the second-last flight was bypassed on the final circuit.

NOTEBOOK
Devito(FR) came through from off the pace as the leaders went off too fast and ran out a comfortable winner. He was well beaten off this mark last time, having landed a 'hands and heels' contest off 12lb lower two runs back, but everything fell into place for him here. *(op 12-1)*
Candarli(IRE) did best of those to race up with the speed but could not go with the winner from the home turn. He has dropped to a fair mark and this was his best effort since gaining his latest win a year ago. *(tchd 28-1)*
Freedom Now(IRE) has become well handicapped, but he was already in trouble when diving at the penultimate flight, the last down the back as the first in the home straight was bypassed. He probably needs further these days. *(op 5-1 tchd 11-2)*
Ashgan(IRE), a long way out of the weights, could not go the early pace and his trainer/rider looked set to pull him up with a lap to go, but he stayed on past tired rivals from the home turn.
Tonic Du Charmil(FR), reverting to hurdles for the first time since finishing third in this race a year ago and currently 10lb lower than he is over fences, paid for contesting the lead. *(op 9-2)*
Adecco(IRE), previously with Richard Guest, was rather fresh on this first run for two and a half years and debut for this yard and did not get home. He has dropped to a fair mark and should step up on this next time. *(op 4-1)*
Titian Flame(IRE) *Official explanation: jockey said saddle slipped*
T/Jkpt: Not won. T/Plt: £27.30 to a £1 stake. Pool: £45,851.85. 1,222.25 winning tickets. T/Qpdt: £13.20 to a £1 stake. Pool: £3,689.40. 206.00 winning tickets. TM

2179 UTTOXETER (L-H)
Thursday, November 24

OFFICIAL GOING: Good to soft (soft in places) changing to soft after race 3 (1.25)
Wind: Fresh, against Weather: Squally showers

2460 WEATHERBYS INSURANCE NOVICES' HURDLE (DIV I) (10 hdls) 2m
12:20 (12:20) (Class 4) 4-Y-0+ **£2,987** (£870; £435)

Form RPR

31U- **1** **The Mick Weston**[253] 4399 6-10-12 .... RJohnson 111+
(R T Phillips) *hld up: plld hrd: tried to run out 6th: hdwy next: led appr 3 out: clr next* **4/11**[1]

05-0 **2** *10* **Mayyas**[10] 2249 5-10-12 .... NFehily 91
(C C Bealby) *hld up: hdwy to chse wnr 3 out: styng on same pce whn mstke next* **16/1**[3]

05 **3** *6* **Tytheknot**[22] 1982 4-10-9 .... ONelmes(3) 85
(O Sherwood) *chsd ldrs tl wknd after 3 out* **7/1**[2]

P00 **4** *11* **Dictator (IRE)**[16] 2099 4-10-12 ....(t) SThomas 74
(D R Gandolfo) *hld up: hdwy appr 3 out: sn wknd* **25/1**

0 **5** *6* **Chigorin**[12] 2179 4-10-12 .... JAMcCarthy 68
(Miss S J Wilton) *mid-div: hdwy after 5th: wknd appr 3 out* **16/1**[3]

66-0 **6** *23* **Courageous Dove**[31] 1654 4-10-9 .... ACCoyle(3) 45
(A Bailey) *j.rt 1st: prom: wknd appr 6th* **33/1**

-P00 **7** *dist* **Pridewood Dove**[162] 758 6-10-1 ow1 .... MNicolls(5) —
(R J Price) *chsd ldrs: wkng whn hmpd 6th* **50/1**

PP- **U** **Presenter (IRE)**[160] 3907 5-10-12 .... PJBrennan —
(M Sheppard) *hld up: mstke and uns rdr 6th* **50/1**

40-0 **P** **My Good Lord (IRE)**[203] 192 6-10-12 .... JamesDavies —
(B D Leavy) *hld up: hdwy 6th: wknd next: t.o whn p.u bef 3 out* **50/1**

05 **P** **Woolstone Boy (USA)**[31] 1562 4-10-12 ....(t) JPMcNamara —
(J Jay) *chsd ldr tl led 7th: hdd & wknd bef next: t.o whn p.u bef last* **16/1**[3]

10-P **P** **Pinkerton Mill**[12] 2179 5-10-0 .... LTreadwell(5) —
(J T Stimpson) *led to 7th: led again bef next: sn hdd & wknd: t.o whn p.u bef last* **40/1**

4m 12.5s (12.10) **Going Correction** +0.85s/f (Soft)
WFA 4 from 5yo+ 12lb **11** Ran SP% **118.6**
Speed ratings: **103,98,95,89,86 75,**—,—,—,— — CSF £7.32 TOTE £1.40: £1.10, £2.50, £1.40; EX 7.20.
Owner Mick Weston **Bred** C F C Jackson **Trained** Adlestrop, Gloucs

FOCUS
A very uncompetitive novice hurdle in which the winner is value for double the official margin and can rate higher, with hte third and fifth the best guides to the level.

NOTEBOOK
The Mick Weston ◆ made a winning debut over hurdles off the back of a 253-day break in what was ultimately quite comfortable fashion. Although he beat nothing of note, he has the potential to be very good, and was given a 25/1 quote for the Royal & SunAlliance Novices' Hurdle. That, though, is a long way off, and connections said they will probably just try and find a similar race in the coming weeks. *(op 2-5 tchd 4-9 in places)*
Mayyas, always going quite well, left his previous efforts behind with a good second. He is flattered by his proximity to the winner, but showed enough to suggest he can find his level over hurdles. *(op 14-1)*
Tytheknot ran creditably enough in third and should find easier opportunities now he is qualified for a handicap mark. *(op 15-2)*
Dictator(IRE) never posed a threat and should do better in low-grade handicaps. *(op 20-1)*

2461 EMPOWER TRAINING NOVICES' HURDLE (14 hdls) 3m
12:50 (12:51) (Class 4) 4-Y-0+ **£3,443** (£1,003; £502)

Form RPR

U-22 **1** **Karanja**[7] 2301 6-10-12 .... NFehily 120+
(V R A Dartnall) *a.p: chsd ldr 6th: led next: clr whn nt fluent 3 out: drvn out* **1/1**[1]

1 **2** *13* **Best Profile (IRE)**[25] 1937 5-11-4 .... CLlewellyn 111+
(N A Twiston-Davies) *led to 7th: rdn and wknd 3 out* **5/2**[2]

45-2 **3** *2 ½* **Gritti Palace (IRE)**[33] 1833 5-10-7 .... MNicolls(5) 97
(John R Upson) *hld up: mstke 9th: styd on fr 3 out: nvr nrr* **14/1**

5- **4** *hd* **Woodview (IRE)**[389] 1927 6-10-12 .... JPMcNamara 97
(K C Bailey) *prom: rdn 10th: wknd next* **16/1**

32-4 **5** *dist* **Retro's Girl (IRE)**[32] 1850 4-9-12 ....(t) JKington(7) —
(M Scudamore) *chsd ldr to 6th: hit next: wknd 10th* **22/1**

4-53 **6** *½* **Eight Fifty Five (IRE)**[23] 1975 5-10-12 .... RJohnson —
(R T Phillips) *hld up: hdwy 7th: wknd 10th* **9/1**[3]

4235 **7** *6* **Toni Alcala**[13] 2169 6-10-9 100 (p) PAspell(3) —
(R F Fisher) *chsd ldrs to 10th* **16/1**

4 **P** **Break The Ice**[24] 1954 4-9-12 CMStudd(7) —
(L A Dace) *prom to 4th: t.o whn p.u bef 9th* **50/1**

0- **P** **Drongo**[219] 4922 4-10-12 JAMcCarthy —
(Mrs P Robeson) *hld up: t.o whn p.u bef 9th* **50/1**

65 **P** **Strange Days (IRE)**[12] 2185 5-10-5 RSpate(7) —
(Mrs K Waldron) *bhd fr 4th: t.o whn p.u bef 10th* **50/1**

035/ **P** **Staroski**[724] 2504 8-10-5 WMarston —
(Simon Earle) *hld up: bhd whn hit 3rd and 4th: t.o whn p.u bef 3 out* **40/1**

P/P- **P** **Hell Of A Time (IRE)**[261] 4241 8-10-12 JMogford —
(Mrs N S Evans) *hld up: bhd and rdn 8th: t.o whn p.u bef 10th* **66/1**

6m 40.8s (35.80) **Going Correction** +1.10s/f (Heav)
WFA 4 from 5yo+ 14lb **12** Ran SP% **121.2**
Speed ratings: **84,79,78,78,**— —,—,—,—,— —,— CSF £3.45 TOTE £2.20: £1.20, £1.60, £2.50; EX 4.90.
Owner D G Staddon **Bred** Mrs Diane Brown **Trained** Brayford, Devon

FOCUS
Not much strength in depth in this novice hurdle and the time was slow, but still a pretty impressive performance from the winner, who with the third sets the level for the form.

NOTEBOOK
Karanja ◆, a very useful bumper performer, had run below expectations in two runs over hurdles this season but, upped to his furthest trip to date and with Fehily taking over, he ran out an impressive winner. On the evidence of this performance, he looks well up to at the very least matching the level of form he showed in bumpers, and is a novice to follow. *(op 11-10)*
Best Profile(IRE), an Irish Point winner who won well over two and a half miles at Carlisle on his debut under Rules, found Karanja far too good. He is clearly going to have his limitations over hurdles, but is a long-term chasing prospect. *(tchd 11-4)*
Gritti Palace(IRE), beaten just a short-head on his hurdling debut over this trip at Chepstow, found this tougher and is likely to do better when handicapped. *(op 12-1)*
Woodview(IRE), as on his hurdling debut at Carlisle, offered promise in defeat. He can probably do even better in time when handicapped.
Eight Fifty Five(IRE) failed to build on the promise he showed on his hurdling debut at Worcester, despite shaping as though this step up in trip would suit. *(op 10-1)*
Break The Ice *Official explanation: jockey said filly was unsuited by the soft ground*

2462 WEATHERBYS INSURANCE NOVICES' HURDLE (DIV II) (10 hdls) 2m
1:25 (1:26) (Class 4) 4-Y-0+ **£2,987** (£870; £435)

Form RPR

6-21 **1** **Rare Coincidence**[12] 1607 4-10-9 98 (p) PAspell(3) 100
(R F Fisher) *mde all: drvn out* **9/2**[3]

2 *1 ½* **Rustarix (FR)**[76] 4-10-12 RThornton 99
(A King) *hld up: hdwy 6th: chsd wnr 3 out: ev ch next: sn rdn: edgd lft and styd on same pce flat* **3/1**[2]

P/ **3** *9* **Buddhi (IRE)**[1096] 2117 7-10-12 ATinkler 91+
(M Pitman) *hld up in tch: rdn appr 2 out: styd on same pce* **5/1**

1 **4** *10* **Nocivo (FR)**[184] 490 4-10-12 RJohnson 88+
(H D Daly) *hld up: hdwy appr 3 out: wkng whn pckd next* **5/2**[1]

5 *3* **Smokey Mountain (IRE)**[83] 1393 4-10-5 APogson(7) 77
(J R Holt) *chsd ldr to 7th: wknd bef next* **20/1**

4-45 **6** *6* **Mr Lewin**[33] 1824 4-10-12 102 JMMaguire 71
(D McCain) *chsd ldrs tl wknd appr 3 out* **12/1**

040 **7** *9* **Carnt Spell**[12] 2179 4-10-12 AThornton 62
(J T Stimpson) *hld up: hit 7th: sn wknd* **33/1**

0- **8** *29* **Glen Thyne (IRE)**[301] 3558 5-10-12 JPMcNamara 33
(K C Bailey) *hld up: rdn and wknd after 7th* **33/1**

0-45 **P** **Danbury (FR)**[42] 1725 5-10-9 ONelmes(3) —
(O Sherwood) *in rr whn mstke 3rd: bhd fr 5th: t.o whn p.u bef 3 out* **16/1**

P **Dandygrey Russett (IRE)**[153] 4-10-5 JamesDavies —
(B D Leavy) *hld up: plld hrd: sddle slipped 1st: p.u bef next* **40/1**

4m 14.7s (14.30) **Going Correction** +1.10s/f (Heav) **10** Ran SP% **115.1**
Speed ratings: **108,107,102,97,96 93,88,74,**—,— CSF £17.87 TOTE £4.50: £1.60, £1.40, £2.10; EX 19.50.
Owner A Kerr **Bred** D R Tucker **Trained** Ulverston, Cumbria

FOCUS
A moderate novice hurdle, and not as good as the first division. The form could rate higher but is difficult to assess.

NOTEBOOK
Rare Coincidence, held in two runs on the Flat since winning over hurdles at Market Rasen, appreciated the return to obstacles and followed up off a 9lb higher mark. This was a game success and the hat-trick cannot be ruled out. *(op 4-1)*
Rustarix(FR), a maiden over hurdles and fences in France, made a pleasing British debut in second. His stable is having a good season, and he can add to the overall score. *(op 7-2)*
Buddhi(IRE), who was in the process of running a good race before pulling up in a decent Aintree bumper no less than 1096 days previously, made a pleasing return from his long absence. If he can go the right way from this, there are races to be won with him over hurdles. *(op 9-2)*
Nocivo(FR), successful in a Worcester bumper on his only previous start 184 days ago, ran a lacklustre race on his hurdling debut and was disappointing. *(tchd 9-4 and 3-1)*
Smokey Mountain(IRE), who showed promise in bumpers in Ireland, did not offer that much on his hurdling debut off the back of an 83-day break.
Dandygrey Russett(IRE) *Official explanation: jockey said saddle slipped approaching the second flight (op 33-1)*
Danbury(FR) *Official explanation: jockey said gelding was unsuited by the soft ground (op 33-1)*

2463 WORTHINGTON CREAMFLOW (S) H'CAP HURDLE (10 hdls) 2m
2:00 (2:00) (Class 5) (0-90,86) 4-Y-0+ **£2,213** (£645; £322)

Form RPR

/0P0 **1** **Before The Mast (IRE)**[19] 2043 8-10-12 72 SThomas 74+
(M F Harris) *a.p: chsd ldr and hit 3 out: led next: drvn out* **13/2**[3]

PP45 **2** *1 ¼* **Maria Bonita (IRE)**[18] 2081 4-10-4 69 TGreenway(5) 66
(C N Kellett) *hld up: hdwy after 7th: outpcd next: rallied appr last: styd on u.p* **9/1**

0/B- **3** *hd* **Lady Maranzi**[449] 1345 6-11-5 79 RJohnson 78+
(Mrs D A Hamer) *hld up: hdwy 7th: led bef next: hdd 2 out: sn rdn: hit last: styd on u.p* **8/1**

P4S0 **4** *13* **Gipsy Cricketer**[14] 2139 9-10-2 69 (t) JKington(7) 53
(M Scudamore) *chsd ldrs: led 7th: hdd bef next: wknd 2 out* **12/1**

2-06 **5** *nk* **Lovely Lulu**[38] 1774 7-10-7 67 JMogford 55+
(J C Tuck) *hld up: hdwy 7th: nt fluent next: wkng whn hit last* **7/1**

6060 **6** *6* **Tiger Talk**[13] 2171 9-11-2 86 (b) JMoorman(10) 63
(R C Guest) *chsd ldrs to 5th* **10/1**

-006 **7** *12* **New Wish (IRE)**[18] 2082 5-10-10 73 PAspell(3) 38
(S B Clark) *hld up: hit 6th: hdwy after next: wknd 2 out* **22/1**

/0-0 **8** *1 ¼* **Sofisio**[59] 760 8-11-1 75 (tp) JAMcCarthy 39
(Miss S J Wilton) *led to 3rd: wknd appr 7th* **20/1**

0-06 **P** **Baker Of Oz**[19] 681 4-10-10 70 (p) WMarston —
(D Burchell) *prom to 6th: t.o whn p.u bef 3 out* **6/1**[2]

P660 **P** **Brother Ted**[39] 1756 8-11-0 74 NFehily —
(J K Cresswell) *hld up: rdn after 4th: t.o whn p.u bef 6th* **25/1**

/64U **P** **Raheel (IRE)**[14] 2146 5-10-10 70 (tp) AThornton —
(Evan Williams) *hld up: plld hrd: hdwy 7th: wknd bef next: bhd whn p.u bef 2 out* **9/2**[1]

0-00 **P** **Varuni (IRE)**[10] 2245 4-9-13 69 TBurrows(10) —
(P L Clinton) *chsd ldr tl led 3rd: hit next: hdd 7th: wknd bef next: t.o whn p.u bef last* **12/1**

4m 25.2s (24.80) **Going Correction** +1.25s/f (Heav)
WFA 4 from 5yo+ 12lb **12** Ran SP% **116.8**
Speed ratings: **88,87,87,80,80 77,71,71,**—,— —,— CSF £61.03 CT £477.62 TOTE £7.30: £2.40, £2.50, £3.10; EX 105.10.There was no bid for the winner.
Owner Walk The Plank Partnership **Bred** John McGuinness **Trained** Edgcote, Northants

FOCUS
A modest time for what was a poor handicap hurdle, even by selling standards. The placed horses ran to their marks but the form is weak.

NOTEBOOK
Before The Mast(IRE) proved well suited by the drop in trip and, more crucially, the drop into selling company, and gained his first success since winning a bumper for Noel Chance in October 2003. He looks one to take on outside of this level. *(op 15-2)*
Maria Bonita(IRE) ran well dropped back in grade and trip, and was just held. This was a very moderate race, but she could eventually find a similar contest. *(op 8-1)*
Lady Maranzi, who was in the process of running a reasonable race before she was brought down in a novice hurdle at Newton Abbot when last seen 449 days previously, ran most creditably dropped in grade off the back of such a long absence. *(op 7-1)*
Gipsy Cricketer ran better with the tongue-tie re-fitted, but remains on a long-losing run.
Lovely Lulu would have appreciated the return to this level, but she was still well held and remains a maiden. *(op 8-1)*
Brother Ted *Official explanation: jockey said gelding was never travelling (op 4-1 tchd 5-1)*
Raheel(IRE) did not helping his chance by pulling and was beaten a long way out. *Official explanation: jockey said gelding was never travelling (op 4-1 tchd 5-1)*
Baker Of Oz offered little on his return to hurdles and remains winless over obstacles. *(op 4-1 tchd 5-1)*

2464 HOLLAND FINNEY & ASSOCIATES BEGINNERS' CHASE (16 fncs) 2m 6f 110y
2:35 (2:35) (Class 4) 5-Y-0+ **£4,313** (£1,266; £633; £316)

Form RPR

11-4 **1** **Mount Clerigo (IRE)**[33] 1830 7-11-0 AThornton 123+
(V R A Dartnall) *a.p: chsd ldr 8th: led 5 out: hit 2 out: drvn out* **11/4**[1]

111/ **2** *2* **Supreme Toss (IRE)**[1027] 3404 9-11-0 RJohnson 118
(R T Phillips) *hld up: hdwy appr 3 out: chsd wnr last: styd on* **9/2**[3]

15-2 **3** *1 ¼* **Eskimo Pie (IRE)**[13] 2168 6-11-0 NFehily 117
(C C Bealby) *a.p: chsd wnr 4 out: rdn next: styd on* **11/2**

20- **4** *dist* **Simon**[241] 4633 6-11-0 JPMcNamara 92
(J L Spearing) *chsd ldr tl led 4th: hit 6th: hdd next: led 8th to 5 out: wknd 3 out* **17/2**

111- **F** **Rowley Hill**[222] 4866 7-11-0 RThornton —
(A King) *hld up in tch: fell 2nd* **10/3**[2]

110/ **F** **Tighten Your Belt (IRE)**[617] 4394 8-11-0 SThomas —
(Miss Venetia Williams) *hld up: fell 6th* **7/1**

303- **P** **Alfie's Sun**[228] 4797 6-11-0 JAMcCarthy —
(D E Cantillon) *hld up: wknd 5 out: t.o whn p.u bef 3 out* **25/1**

465- **P** **Shoulton (IRE)**[342] 2870 8-10-11 LVickers(3) —
(G H Yardley) *led to 4th: blnd 6th: lost pl 8th: bhd fr next: t.o whn p.u bef 4 out* **100/1**

56P- **P** **Cleopatras Therapy (IRE)**[310] 3408 8-10-7 BWharfe(7) —
(T H Caldwell) *prom: hit 2nd: led 7th to next: sn lost pl: bhd whn hit 9th and next: sn p.u* **100/1**

6m 11.6s **9** Ran SP% **112.2**
CSF £15.19 TOTE £4.20: £1.80, £2.00, £1.40; EX 18.70.
Owner Stewart Andrew **Bred** Martin J Keane **Trained** Brayford, Devon

FOCUS
An intriguing beginners' chase and, although some of the interest was lost when both Rowley Hill and Tighten Your Belt fell, the form still looks strong and Mount Clerigo created a very good impression. The third sets the level based on his hurdle form.

NOTEBOOK
Mount Clerigo(IRE) ◆, a very useful bumper performer and hurdler, won well on his chasing debut and looks likely to fulfill his undoubted potential over fences. He was a little slow over the last two, which allowed his rivals to get a bit close for comfort, but he kept responding on the run-in, and looked better than the bare form might suggest. He could now go for a novices' chase at Lingfield on December 10th, a race his stable won with Lord Sam, and is very much one to have on your side. *(op 5-2 tchd 3-1 in places)*
Supreme Toss(IRE) was quickly developing into a very useful novice hurdler in the 2002/03 season, but fractured a pelvis and had not been seen since. Making his debut over fences off the back of a 1027-day break, he chased home a potentially smart sort and offered a great deal promise. If he can stand his racing and go the right way from this, he could easily make up for lost time. *(tchd 5-1)*
Eskimo Pie(IRE) ◆, a promising second on his chasing debut at Newcastle, ran a fine race in third behind two potentially very useful novices. On the evidence of this performance, he looks like making a fine chaser. *(op 7-1)*
Simon, an Irish-point winner who reached was rated 116 over hurdles in that country, proved a touch disappointing on what was both his first start in this country, and his first over fences. To be fair, he could hardly have started in a hotter race. *(op 14-1)*
Tighten Your Belt(IRE), a very useful novice hurdler who was seventh in a very good Royal & SunAlliance when last seen 617 days previously, took a spectacular fall on his chasing debut and it has to be hoped this does not leave its mark. *(op 13-2)*
Rowley Hill, a useful, progressive hurdler last season, fell early on his chasing debut off the back of a 222-day break. *(op 13-2)*

2465 NETWORK SECURITY FREEPHONE 0800 369 74 89 H'CAP CHASE (18 fncs) 3m
3:10 (3:20) (Class 4) (0-100,100) 5-Y-0+ **£3,532** (£1,037; £518; £259)

Form RPR

2U-1 **1** **Young Lorcan**[12] 2182 9-10-13 94 RSpate(7) 109+
(Mrs K Waldron) *hld up: hdwy 11th: led and blnd 5 out: rdn out* **4/1**[1]

213- **2** *5* **Finzi (IRE)**[354] 2661 7-10-10 91 JKington(7) 101+
(M Scudamore) *chsd ldrs: rdn appr 4 out: styd on same pce flat* **11/2**[3]

0/40 **3** *8* **One Day (NZ)**[33] 1837 7-11-7 100 (p) PCO'Neill(5) 106+
(R C Guest) *hld up: reminders 3rd: hdwy 11th: rdn appr 4 out: wkng blnd last* **10/1**

5P-0 **4** *dist* **Indian Laburnum (IRE)**[43] 1713 8-10-1 78 (b[1]) LVickers(3) —
(C C Bealby) *chsd ldrs tl rdn and wknd appr 4 out* **5/1**[2]

410- **P** **Lantern Lad (IRE)**[282] 3869 9-10-12 86 JMMaguire —
(R Ford) *hld up: rdn and wknd 5 out: p.u bef next* **11/1**

4P-3 **P** **Advance East**[12] [2183] 13-9-12 **77** WKennedy(5) —
(M J M Evans) *hld up: a in rr: t.o whn p.u bef 4 out* **16/1**

2-5P **P** **Apple Joe**[24] [1960] 9-10-0 **74** JamesDavies —
(A J Whiting) *prom: rdn 11th: wknd 13th: t.o whn p.u bef next* **9/1**

13P- **P** **Test Of Friendship**[279] [3922] 8-10-11 **90** PMerrigan(5) —
(Mrs H Dalton) *hld up in tch: mstke 6 out: wknd next: t.o whn p.u bef 4 out* **6/1**

P-P1 **P** **Yassar (IRE)**[27] [1907] 10-11-2 **90** WMarston —
(D J Wintle) *prom: jnd ldr 4th: led 6th: hdd 5 out: sn rdn: wknd 3 out: p.u bef next* **8/1**

51P- **P** **Red Alert Man (IRE)**[252] [4416] 9-9-9 **74** oh6 (b) DLaverty(5) —
(Mrs L Williamson) *led to 6th: rdn and wknd after 10th: t.o whn p.u bef 3 out* **20/1**

6m 48.7s (16.20) **Going Correction** +0.70s/f (Soft) **10 Ran SP% 115.5**
Speed ratings: **101,99,96,—,— —,—,—,—,—** CSF £26.65 CT £204.91 TOTE £3.10: £1.60, £1.80, £4.20; EX 9.90.
Owner Nick Shutts **Bred** Mrs Norma Dyer **Trained** Stoke Bliss, Worcs

FOCUS
Just a moderate handicap chase and over half the field pulled up. The first two were close to their marks.

NOTEBOOK
Young Lorcan, 9lb higher than when winning a two and a half mile hurdle here on his previous start, followed up under a confident ride from his 7lb claimer. He goes particularly well at this track, but is worthy of respect elsewhere whilst in this sort of form. *(op 10-3 tchd 5-1)*
Finzi(IRE), returning from a 354-day break, was always going quite well and kept on right the way to the line. This was a promising return. *(op 9-2 tchd 4-1)*
One Day(NZ), fitted with cheekpieces for the first time, was nursed into contention by O'Neill, but could not quite sustain his run long enough. *(op 18-1 tchd 20-1)*
Indian Laburnum(IRE) did not perform with the blinkers replacing cheekpieces. *(op 8-1)*
Test Of Friendship failed to see out his race, just as he did when last seen 279 days previously. *Official explanation: jockey said gelding had been unsuited by the soft ground*

2466 BET365 CALL 08000 322365 H'CAP HURDLE (12 hdls) 2m 6f 110y
3:40 (3:41) (Class 4) (0-110,108) 4-Y-0+ **£3,832** (£1,124; £562; £280)

Form RPR

15F3 **1** **Arm And A Leg (IRE)**[8] [2271] 10-11-12 **108** RJohnson 110
(Mrs D A Hamer) *hld up: hit 4th: hdwy 8th: rdn appr 3 out: styd on to ld fnl 50 yds* **6/1**[3]

51F2 **2** 2 ½ **Hi Laurie (IRE)**[12] [2181] 10-9-10 **85** JKington(7) 87+
(M Scudamore) *hld up: hdwy 7th: led appraoching 3 out: sn clr: wkng whn blnd last: hdd fnl 50 yds* **6/4**[1]

4303 **3** 1 ½ **Ingres**[5] [2347] 5-11-0 **103** CMStudd(7) 101
(B G Powell) *mid-div: hdwy 6th: rdn appr 3 out: styd on flat* **5/1**[2]

30-0 **4** 1 ¼ **Starry Mary**[27] [1906] 7-9-9 **82** oh1 PMerrigan(5) 80+
(R J Price) *hld up: rdn 6th: hdwy after 3 out: hung lft flat: styd on same pce* **16/1**

/000 **5** 24 **Donie Dooley (IRE)**[23] [1977] 7-10-13 **95** AThornton 68
(P T Dalton) *hld up: hdwy to join ldr 8th: led next: hdd bef 3 out: wknd last* **22/1**

P4-0 **6** 21 **Business Traveller (IRE)**[23] [1977] 5-10-8 **95** MNicolls(5) 47
(R J Price) *bhd fr 3rd* **20/1**

0/2- **P** **Icare D'Oudairies (FR)**[564] [249] 9-11-4 **100** (t) NFehily —
(A L Forbes) *chsd ldr 2nd: wknd 8th: t.o whn p.u bef 3 out* **14/1**

P **Koln Stars (IRE)**[46] [1698] 7-10-13 **100** LTreadwell(5) —
(Jennie Candlish) *led to 1st: lost pl 6th: sn bhd: t.o whn p.u bef 4 out* **25/1**

2FU **P** **Harry Collins**[6] [2325] 7-10-13 **95** CLlewellyn —
(B I Case) *chsd ldrs: led appr 8th: hdd and hit next: sn wknd: bhd whn p.u bef 2 out* **5/1**[2]

0 **P** **Open Range (IRE)**[116] [1116] 5-11-10 **106** JPByrne —
(Jennie Candlish) *s.s: plld hrd: hdwy to ld 1st: hit next: j.rt: hdd & wknd appr 8th: t.o and p.u bef 3 out* **25/1**

6m 11.6s (26.90) **Going Correction** +1.25s/f (Heav) **10 Ran SP% 117.0**
Speed ratings: **103,102,101,101,92 85,—,—,—,—** CSF £15.15 CT £47.71 TOTE £5.90: £1.90, £1.10, £1.80; EX 10.40 Place 6 £20.56, Place 5 £18.14.
Owner H L Davies **Bred** Martyn J McEnery **Trained** Nantycaws, Carmarthens

FOCUS
A moderate handicap hurdle in which the first four were close to their marks although the runner-up can rate higher.

NOTEBOOK
Arm And A Leg(IRE) looked high enough in the weights when only third at Wincanton on his previous start, but he responded well to a determined ride and got on top close home. Things will *be tougher off higher marks, but he could well get three miles on the evidence of this performance.* *(op 8-1)*
Hi Laurie(IRE), a beaten favourite over three miles here on her previous start, looked likely to gain compensation from some way out, but she made a mess of the last and weakened quickly on the run-in. There are races to be won with her over hurdles this season, but she may need producing later. *(op 13-8 tchd 7-4)*
Ingres ran a solid race in third and can have few excuses. His sole win came in a maiden hurdle in Ireland nearly a year ago. *(op 9-2)*
Starry Mary stepped up on the form she showed on her reappearance and could well progress again.
Donie Dooley(IRE) weakened tamely having looked a threat before the race got really serious. *(op 16-1)*
Harry Collins, returned to hurdles for the first time since May 2004, offered little. *(op 9-2 tchd 11-2)*
T/Plt: £13.70 to a £1 stake. Pool: £37,374.70. 1,978.30 winning tickets. T/Qpdt: £13.10 to a £1 stake. Pool: £2,647.60. 148.50 winning tickets. CR

2467 - 2473a (Foreign Racing) - See Raceform Interactive

MUSSELBURGH (R-H)
Friday, November 25

OFFICIAL GOING: Good to firm (firm in places)
Wind: Fresh, against

2474 RACING UK CHANNEL 432 CONDITIONAL JOCKEYS' H'CAP HURDLE 3m 110y
12:20 (12:20) (Class 4) (0-110,105) 4-Y-0+ **£4,069** (£1,194; £597; £298)

Form RPR

1 **Not Today Sir (IRE)**[12] [2221] 7-11-7 **100** AndrewJMcNamara 107+
(S Donohoe, Ire) *hld up in tch: smooth hdwy 4 out: rdn to ld and hit last: drvn out* **2/1**[1]

60-0 **2** 1 ¼ **Lorio Du Misselot (FR)**[59] [1569] 6-9-11 **79** KJMercer(3) 83
(Ferdy Murphy) *cl up: hit 4th: pushed along 4 out: rdn after next: drvn and ev ch last: kpt on wl flat* **10/1**

5666 **3** 1 ¾ **Old Nosey (IRE)**[19] [2066] 9-10-1 **85** PJMcDonald(5) 88+
(B Mactaggart) *mde most: rdn along 2 out: drvn: hdd and hit last: kpt on flat* **6/1**

2U-P **4** 2 ½ **The Weaver (FR)**[196] [334] 6-11-3 **99** GBerridge(3) 100+
(L Lungo) *hld up in tch: hdwy 4 out: ev ch next: n.m.r and pshd along whn hit 2 out: sn rdn and kpt on same pce* **7/2**[2]

45P6 **5** dist **Pornic (FR)**[8] [2289] 11-10-12 **94** TJDreaper(3) —
(A Crook) *chsd ldrs: hit 5th: rdn along 5 out and outpcd fr next* **40/1**

6500 **6** 20 **Political Sox**[20] [2038] 11-11-7 **105** SMarshall(5) —
(R Nixon) *a rr: rdn along 1/2-way: sn bhd* **12/1**

0-0P **7** 12 **Culbann (IRE)**[28] [1915] 6-9-11 **79** oh4 (t) MJMcAlister(3) —
(C Rae) *hld up in tch: hdwy to chse ldr whn hit 5 out: sn rdn along and wknd bef 3 out* **100/1**

PF00 **P** **Minivet**[20] [2038] 10-11-7 **100** (v[1]) PAspell —
(R Allan) *trckd ldrs tl sddle slipped and p.u bef 4th* **20/1**

P420 **U** **Hello Baby**[14] [2171] 5-10-1 **85** EWhillans(5) —
(A C Whillans) *blnd 1st and rdr lost iron: blnd and uns rdr 2nd* **9/2**[3]

6m 2.80s (1.00) **Going Correction** +0.125s/f (Yiel) **9 Ran SP% 113.0**
Speed ratings: **103,102,102,101,— —,—,—,—** CSF £21.16 CT £101.68 TOTE £3.10: £1.10, £2.80, £3.50; EX 29.70.
Owner Seamus Ross **Bred** John Bourke **Trained** Cootehill Road, Co. Cavan

FOCUS
A modest conditionals' handicap run at an even pace. The form looks solid enough with the runner-up and fourth close to their marks.

NOTEBOOK
Not Today Sir(IRE) ◆, better known in Ireland as a pointer/hunter chaser, has recent form over hurdles and justified favouritism under a good ride. He handled the ground well, won with a little in hand, handles most going and looks capable of defying a higher mark. *(op 15-8)*
Lorio Du Misselot(FR), an inexperienced novice, was taking a big step up in trip on this handicap debut. He was given a positive ride, being up with the pace throughout, and kept on all the way to the line. He looks capable of picking up a small race on this evidence. *(op 9-1)*
Old Nosey(IRE), back on his favoured fast ground, was suited by the return to positive tactics and was only run out of it on the flat. He may struggle to find a similar surface in the next couple of months though. *(op 13-2 tchd 7-1)*
The Weaver(FR) tracked the leading group travelling well, and looked a big threat when moving up entering the straight. However, he found much less than looked likely once asked for an effort. He *goes well at this track but may need some form of headgear to make him put his best foot* forward. *(op 4-1)*
Political Soxlast year's winner, was never travelling and seems to have lost his way. *(op 15-2)*
Minivet *Official explanation: jockey said saddle slipped (op 11-2 tchd 6-1)*
Hello Baby, supported in the market, did not last long in the race; a mistake at the first flight caused his jockey to lose an iron and he was unshipped at the second. *(op 11-2 tchd 6-1)*

2475 RACING UK SUBSCRIBE ON 08700 506954 MAIDEN HURDLE (12 hdls) 2m 4f
12:50 (12:50) (Class 4) 4-Y-0+ **£3,008** (£876; £438)

Form RPR

1 **How Art Thou (IRE)**[9] [2277] 4-10-13 AndrewJMcNamara(3) 99+
(S Donohoe, Ire) *hld up in tch: smooth hdwy after 4 out: rdn to ld last: styd on* **9/2**[2]

0-54 **2** 2 ½ **Water Taxi**[27] [1927] 4-10-13 108 KJMercer(3) 95+
(Ferdy Murphy) *cl up: led 4th: hit next: pushed along 3 out: rdn and hdd whn hit last: kpt on same pce* **7/2**[1]

05 **3** 1 ¼ **Backgammon**[27] [1927] 4-11-2 RMcGrath 92
(K G Reveley) *hld up in midfield: smooth hdwy 4 out: cl up next and ev ch tl rdn and one pce last* **5/1**[3]

P0-0 **4** 1 **Our Jasper**[14] [2171] 5-10-6 88 PKinsella(10) 91
(K G Reveley) *hld up in rr: hdwy after 4 out: rdn along to chse ldrs after 2 out: kpt on same pce fr last* **20/1**

3200 **5** 3 ½ **King's Protector**[14] [2169] 5-11-2 102 NPMulholland 90+
(M D Hammond) *trckd ldrs: hdwy 8th: effrt 3 out: sn rdn and hld in 4th whn hit last* **8/1**

0 **6** 5 **Ballyhurry (USA)**[19] [2062] 8-10-9 MrATDuff(7) 84+
(J S Goldie) *hld up in rr: stdy hdwy appr 4 out: chsd ldrs bef 2 out: sn rdn and one pce* **20/1**

-220 **7** 2 **Dalawan**[19] [2062] 6-10-9 TJDreaper(7) 81
(Mrs J C McGregor) *chsd ldrs: rdn along 3 out: one pce fr next* **16/1**

46-3 **8** 9 **Silver Seeker (USA)**[21] [2027] 5-11-2 82 BHarding 72
(A R Dicken) *hld up: hdwy after 4 out: chsd ldrs next: sn rdn and wknd 2 out* **14/1**

3446 **9** 7 **Chief Dan George (IRE)**[21] [2024] 5-10-13 PAspell(3) 65
(D R MacLeod) *hld up in rr: mstke 8th: a bhd* **16/1**

3252 **10** 20 **Summer Special**[138] [936] 5-11-2 104 KRenwick 45
(Mrs S C Bradburne) *in tch: hdwy on inner appr 3 out: rdn next and sn btn* **9/2**[2]

0- **11** 14 **Ebac (IRE)**[223] [4865] 4-11-2 (t) GLee 31
(J Howard Johnson) *prom: led 2nd to 4th: cl up: rdn along and wkng whn hit 3 out: sn lost pl and bhd* **14/1**

0/ **P** **Aljumbo**[1987] [638] 11-10-11 DCCostello(5) —
(Robert Gray) *rr whn mstke 7th and p.u after* **100/1**

0-0 **P** **Romanov Rambler (IRE)**[197] [323] 5-10-13 PBuchanan(3) —
(Mrs S C Bradburne) *a rr: mstke 6th:l sn bhd and p.u bef 3 out* **100/1**

0-P **P** **Sirroco Wind**[170] [687] 5-10-11 DFlavin(5) —
(Mrs L B Normile) *led to 2nd: prom tl rdn along and wkng whn mstke 8th: sn lost pl and bhd whn p.u bef 3 out* **66/1**

4m 56.4s (1.90) **Going Correction** +0.125s/f (Yiel) **14 Ran SP% 124.5**
Speed ratings: **101,100,99,99,97 95,94,91,88,80 74,—,—,—** CSF £21.04 TOTE £5.80: £1.70, £1.90, £2.50; EX 17.10.
Owner Mrs S Donohoe **Bred** Esker House **Trained** Cootehill Road, Co. Cavan

FOCUS
A moderate maiden hurdle run at a steady pace. The first two were close to their marks and the form appears solid enough.

NOTEBOOK
How Art Thou(IRE), who has been racing on much softer ground of late, was given a similar ride to that of his stable companion in the opening race. Settled off the pace, he came through to lead at the final flight and ran out a ready winner. *(op 5-1 tchd 4-1 in a place)*
Water Taxi, who has been progressing with experience, went on from halfway and stepped up the pace but had no answer to the winner's challenge. This was a creditable effort over this longer trip and, although he seemed to stay it, similar tactics over shorter may pay dividends. *(op 4-1)*
Backgammonfinished closer to the runner-up than he had at Wetherby, but seemed to lack pace in the straight and a return to softer ground over this trip may help. *(op 6-1)*
Our Jasper, a stable companion of the third, connections will find a return to handicaps may offer better opportunities.
King's Protector has had plenty of chances and does not seem to be progressing, although he may be better back at two miles. *(op 10-1)*
Ballyhurry(USA)better known as a Flat performer, moved up turning for home, but faded as if not getting the trip.

Chief Dan George(IRE) never got into a challenging position.
Summer Special, stepping up in trip, was settled off the pace and never landed a blow. *(tchd 4-1)*
Ebac(IRE), making his hurdling debut, ran and jumped pretty well until fading in the straight. He should benefit from the outing. *(op 12-1)*
Sirroco Wind *Official explanation: jockey said gelding had a breathing problem (tchd 100-1)*

2476 WATCH LIVE RACING ON RACING UK NOVICES' H'CAP CHASE (16 fncs) 2m 4f

1:20 (1:20) (Class 4) (0-105,104) 4-Y-0+ **£4,108** (£1,206; £603; £301)

Form RPR

1 **Lanaken (IRE)**[12] [2224] 5-11-0 **95**........................(b) AndrewJMcNamara(3) 102+
(S Donohoe, Ire) *mde all: sn clr: mstke 7th: pushed along and mstke 5 out: rdn along 3 out: hit 2 out: kpt on* **8/1**

-05P 2 3 **Word Gets Around (IRE)**[34] [1838] 7-11-3 **95**........................ ADobbin 98+
(L Lungo) *trckd ldng pair: hdwy to chse wnr 1/2-way: cl up 5 out: rdn along after next and hit 3 out: drvn and kpt on same pce* **11/2**[3]

0-5P 3 5 **El Andaluz (FR)**[8] [2291] 5-10-2 **80**........................ ADempsey 77+
(M Todhunter) *chsd wnr to 1/2-way: pushed along and outpcd 5 out: kpt on same pce fr next* **14/1**

P2-4 4 5 **Clouding Over**[20] [2041] 5-11-12 **104**........................ RMcGrath 95+
(K G Reveley) *hld up and bhd tl styd on fr 4 out: nvr nr ldrs* **14/1**

3352 5 1 **Ideal Du Bois Beury (FR)**[21] [2026] 9-9-11 **78** oh1................ PAspell(3) 68
(P Monteith) *towards rr: pushed along and sme hdwy whn hit 8th: nvr a factor* **9/2**[1]

4145 6 2 1/2 **Goodbadindiferent (IRE)**[54] [1602] 9-10-8 **86**........................ BHarding 74
(Mrs J C McGregor) *chsd ldrs: rdn along 10th: sn outpcd* **6/1**

5434 7 14 **Lascar De Ferbet (FR)**[56] [1592] 6-10-10 **88**........................ GLee 62
(R Ford) *a towards rr: bhd fr 1/2-way* **5/1**[2]

F3F1 U **Ornella Speed (FR)**[9] [2267] 5-9-12 **83** 7ex....................(t) PJMcDonald(7) —
(J R Weymes) *s.s: a wl bhd: blnd and uns rdr 4 out* **8/1**

2054 P **Lion Guest (IRE)**[21] [2026] 8-10-0 **78** oh2........................ KRenwick —
(Mrs S C Bradburne) *midfield: rdn along and blnd 5 out: bhd and p.u bef next* **10/1**

4m 54.8s (-4.60) **Going Correction** -0.275s/f (Good) **9** Ran SP% **109.2**
Speed ratings: **98,96,94,92,92 91,85,—,—** CSF £47.57 CT £551.51 TOTE £10.80: £2.20, £1.50, £3.50; EX 62.30.
Owner Strike It Lucky Syndicate **Bred** Gerry Dillon **Trained** Cootehill Road, Co. Cavan
■ Stewards' Enquiry : R McGrath seven-day ban: making insufficient effort (Dec 6-13)

FOCUS
A moderate novices' chase run at a good early pace; the field were soon strung out and very few got into the race although the time was modest. The form is difficult to rate and it is not a race to be confident about.

NOTEBOOK
Lanaken(IRE) had conditions to suit and, adopting the tactics he had previously used over hurdles, set off like a scalded cat. Jumping reasonably well, he soon had his rivals well strung out, and shook off his only challenger early in the straight. He looks capable of winning more chases given a sharp track and fast ground, but may struggle to get those conditions in his homeland in the near future. *(op 9-1)*
Word Gets Around(IRE), a three-time winner in 2004 who has struggled to get home on soft ground, was making his chasing debut. He was one of only three to get involved in the race. He close the gap on the winner turning for home, but when that rival kicked again he had nothing more to offer. *(tchd 6-1)*
El Andaluz(FR), whose saddle slipped on his chasing debut, was dropping back in trip. He chased the winner from the start, but gradually dropped further behind from halfway despite keeping on for the minor placing. *(op 16-1)*
Clouding Over, most of whose form has been with cut in the ground, was settled way off the pace - not the right tactics on this occasion. She was keeping on at the finish but never got into contention, and can do better than this. *(op 11-1 tchd 10-1)*
Ideal Du Bois Beury(FR) was held up off the pace but did not help his cause by making several errors. *(op 5-1)*
Ornella Speed(FR), racing for a third different trainer in her last three outings, stays further and seems best on softer ground, but was held up way off the pace, never got competitive and was well behind when departing. *Official explanation: trainer said mare was unsuited by the track (op 9-2)*

2477 RACING UK SUBSCRIBE ON 08700 506954 JUVENILE NOVICES' HURDLE (9 hdls) 2m

1:55 (1:55) (Class 4) 3-Y-0 **£3,363** (£987; £493; £246)

Form RPR

32 1 **Comical Errors (USA)**[17] [1601] 3-10-7 .... PMerrigan(5) 86+
(P C Haslam) *cl up: led 2nd: pushed clr flat: easily* **2/1**[2]

0052 2 3 1/2 **Madge**[22] [2001] 3-10-5 ....(v) GLee 69
(W Storey) *hld up in tch: hdwy on inner after 4 out: chal 2 out: rdn and ev ch last: nt qckn flat* **13/8**[1]

5 3 1 1/2 **Best Game**[10] [2258] 3-10-7 .... DCCostello(5) 75
(D W Thompson) *trckd ldrs: hdwy and cl up 4 out: rdn along after next: one pce* **11/2**[3]

P 4 1 3/4 **Lerida**[46] [1512] 3-10-9 .... PBuchanan(3) 73
(Miss Lucinda V Russell) *led to 2nd: cl up tl rdn along 3 out and one pce fr next: hit last* **100/1**

5 7 **Grandma's Girl**[27] 3-10-2 .... ONelmes(3) 61+
(Robert Gray) *in tch: hdwy to chse ldrs 3 out: rdn along next: wkng whn hit last* **12/1**

P 6 1 3/4 **Tarkar (IRE)**[14] [2167] 3-10-12 .... ADempsey 64
(J Howard Johnson) *hld up: hdwy 4 out: chsd ldrs next: sn rdn and wknd bef 2 out* **25/1**

0 7 1 1/4 **Ballycroy Girl (IRE)**[41] [1737] 3-10-5 .... BHarding 58+
(A Bailey) *prom: rdn along 3 out: wknd next: hit last* **10/1**

P 8 29 **Mercari**[9] [2263] 3-10-2 .... KJMercer(3) 27
(A R Dicken) *a bhd* **25/1**

9 3/4 **Sterling Supporter**[27] 3-10-2 .... PAspell(3) 26
(D W Thompson) *hld up in rr: hdwy and in tch after 4 out: rdn and wknd next* **66/1**

P 10 12 **Cadogen Square**[9] [2263] 3-9-12 .... PKinsella(7) 14
(Mrs Marjorie Fife) *chsd ldrs: mstke 4th: sn lost pl and bhd fr 4 out* **66/1**

3m 59.4s (8.20) **Going Correction** +0.125s/f (Yiel) **10** Ran SP% **115.3**
Speed ratings: **84,82,81,80,77 76,75,61,60,54** CSF £5.56 TOTE £3.00: £1.20, £1.10, £2.00; EX 4.90.
Owner Mrs C Barclay **Bred** M A Sullivan **Trained** Middleham, N Yorks

FOCUS
A modest juvenile hurdle in which the field stood still when the tapes went up as nobody wanted to make the running,. resulting in a very slow time. The winner is value for further but the form looks weak.

NOTEBOOK
Comical Errors(USA), a market drifter, is from a yard that does well in this sort of event and had beaten the favourite on similar ground at Kelso last month. He went on at the third and picked up the pace and, given a confident ride, always had the favourite's measure. This will have helped his confidence. *(op 13-8 tchd 5-2)*
Madge, a well-supported favourite, settled just behind the pace and delivered her challenge early in the straight, only to find the winner always holding her. She was clear second-best and can win a similar contest. *(op 7-4 tchd 2-1 and 6-4)*
Best Game, a sprinter/miler on the Flat, was quite keen but ran his race before tiring in the straight. He has yet to prove he truly gets the trip, but a sharp track and fast ground offers his best chance of doing so. *(op 7-1)*
Lerida, lightly raced on the Flat, ran better this time than he had on his hurdling debut behind today's winner at Perth in September.
Ballycroy Girl(IRE), whose jockey was banned for an injudicious ride on her debut, raced prominently but was quite keen and faded early in the straight. *(op 12-1)*

2478 MORTON FRASER H'CAP HURDLE (9 hdls) 2m

2:30 (2:30) (Class 3) (0-115,115) 4-Y-0+
£6,701 (£1,979; £989; £495; £247; £124)

Form RPR

5-6U 1 **Saif Sareea**[37] [973] 5-10-1 **90**........................ GLee 99+
(R A Fahey) *hld up in tch: hdwy and cl up whn mstke 3 out: led next: pushed clr flat* **2/1**[1]

-625 2 2 1/2 **Sovereign State (IRE)**[41] [1296] 8-11-5 **111**....................(p) ONelmes(3) 112
(D W Thompson) *a prom: hdwy 6th: led 3 out: rdn and hdd next: drvn and one pce flat* **50/1**

5U41 3 hd **Fiery Peace**[8] [2294] 8-10-4 **96**........................ MrTGreenall(3) 97
(C Grant) *hld up: hdwy 6th: rdn to chse ldrs 2 out: styd on one pce last* **12/1**

14-F 4 5 **Rehearsal**[34] [1836] 4-11-9 **115**........................ GBerridge(3) 112+
(L Lungo) *hld up: smooth hdwy 6th: wd st and cl up whn hit 3 out: swtchd rt 2 out: sn rdn and kpt on same pce* **9/4**[2]

15 5 1 **Sir Night (IRE)**[25] [1957] 5-10-12 **101**........................ BHarding 96
(Jedd O'Keeffe) *a.p: cl up and ev ch 3 out: sn rdn and hit next grad wknd* **12/1**

6 2 1/2 **Mango Catcher (IRE)**[48] [1690] 5-11-0 **110**........................ RMMoran(7) 103+
(Paul Nolan, Ire) *led: rdn along after 4 out: hdd next: sn drvn and wknd fr 2 out* **7/1**[3]

633B 7 1/2 **Hugs Destiny (IRE)**[26] [1940] 4-9-11 **93** ow3............ BenOrde-Powlett(7) 85
(M A Barnes) *hld up in rr: hdwy after 3 out: rdn along and kpt on fr 2 out: nrst fin* **50/1**

U200 8 3/4 **Bodfari Signet**[20] [2038] 9-11-0 **110**........................ TMessenger(7) 101
(Mrs S C Bradburne) *midfield: pushed along and outpcd after 4 out: styd on fr 2 out: n.d* **20/1**

4-56 9 hd **Bollin Thomas**[13] [2173] 7-10-7 **99**........................ PAspell(3) 90
(R Allan) *towards rr: rdn along appr 3 out: n.d* **14/1**

666 10 nk **Royal Glen (IRE)**[47] [1604] 7-10-5 **94**........................ RMcGrath 85
(W S Coltherd) *slowly away: a bhd* **50/1**

3304 11 13 **Pearson Glen (IRE)**[17] [2106] 6-9-12 **92**........................(t) DCCostello(5) 70
(James Moffatt) *trckd ldrs: pushed along 4 out: sn rdn and wknd next* **33/1**

P05 12 19 **Border Tale**[7] [2324] 5-11-6 **109**........................(t) ADobbin 68
(James Moffatt) *chsd ldrs tl rdn along 4 out and sn wknd* **14/1**

0P44 P **King's Envoy (USA)**[64] [1527] 6-9-11 **89** oh3........................ PBuchanan(3) —
(Mrs J C McGregor) *chsd ldrs: mstke 4th: wknd qckly and p.u bef next* **50/1**

3m 48.4s (-2.80) **Going Correction** +0.125s/f (Yiel) **13** Ran SP% **120.9**
Speed ratings: **112,110,110,108,107 106,106,105,105,105 99,89,—** CSF £116.99 CT £975.43 TOTE £3.20: £2.00, £12.20, £5.20; EX 149.90.
Owner The Ipso Facto Syndicate **Bred** Mrs M Beddis **Trained** Musley Bank, N Yorks

FOCUS
A modest handicap but an easy winner in a decent time for the grade. The runner-up sets the standard and the race could rate higher.

NOTEBOOK
Saif Sareea ◆ had improved considerably on the Flat during the summer and had winning form on fast ground over hurdles. He looked well treated on this return to jumping, was well supported and won accordingly. He will take a rise in the handicap for this but may be able to follow up. *(op 7-4 tchd 5-2)*
Sovereign State(IRE), another returning to jumping after a spell racing on the Flat, ran a good race despite having no chance with the winner, being up with the pace throughout. A sharp track and fast ground suits him and a drop of a couple of pounds should see him winning again given those conditions.
Fiery Peace ◆, who is better known as a chaser, ran quite well on this switch to the smaller obstacles, only being beaten for pace late on. He is rated 16lb lower over hurdles than over fences and could be capable of picking up a race in a slightly lower grade. *(tchd 14-1)*
Rehearsal, a course and distance winner last season, had been going well when falling on his seasonal return. He travelled well on this occasion and closed on the leaders looking a big threat, but his effort petered out after a mistake at the third last. *(op 5-2 tchd 11-4 in places)*
Sir Night(IRE), 7lb higher than for his win at Kelso, seemed to run his race but was left behind in the straight. His form suggests a track with a stiffer finish may suit him better. *(op 10-1)*
Mango Catcher(IRE), still a maiden over hurdles despite being runner-up six times, made the running but was brushed aside in the straight. The time was decent and he possibly went off too quickly for his own good. *(op 10-1)*
Border Tale *Official explanation: jockey said gelding had a breathing problem (op 16-1)*

2479 JOBS @ PERTEMPS H'CAP CHASE (12 fncs) 2m

3:00 (3:00) (Class 4) (0-110,105) 5-Y-0+
£6,500 (£1,920; £960; £480; £239; £120)

Form RPR

U42 1 **Kalou (GER)**[65] [1509] 7-11-7 103........................ MrTGreenall(3) 114+
(C Grant) *hld up in rr: stdy hdwy 5 out: chsd ldrs 3 out: rdn to ld last: styd on* **7/1**

1501 2 1 1/2 **Loulou Nivernais (FR)**[17] [2111] 6-11-1 94........................ ADempsey 104+
(M Todhunter) *a.p: led 5 out: rdn along and hit 2 out: drvn and hdd last: one pce flat* **9/2**[3]

0U02 3 3 **Polyphon (FR)**[19] [2067] 7-11-12 105........................ GLee 113+
(P Monteith) *trckd ldrs: smooth hdwy and cl up 5 out: effrt 3 out and ev ch tl rdn appr last and one pce flat* **9/4**[1]

22P4 4 11 **Super Dolphin**[94] [1299] 6-10-2 84........................ PBuchanan(3) 83+
(R Ford) *led: blnd 1st: hdd 4th: mstke 6th: rdn along appr 5 out and sn wknd* **7/2**[2]

/32- 5 19 **Waltzing Along (IRE)**[355] [2651] 7-10-1 80........................ BHarding 56
(L Lungo) *hld up towards rr: stdy hdwy appr 5 out: chsd ldrs next sn rdn and wknd* **5/1**

6 21 **Closed Orders (IRE)**[74] [1467] 8-10-6 88 ONelmes(3) 43
(Robert Gray) *cl up: led 4th: hdd 5 out and sn wknd* **16/1**
05P0 **P** **Ratty's Band**[56] [1592] 11-10-0 79 oh13 NPMulholland —
(Mrs L B Normile) *mstkes: a bhd: p.u bef 2 out* **25/1**
P5-P **F** **No Kidding**[202] [213] 11-10-1 83 MichalKohl(3) —
(J I A Charlton) *hld up: hdwy to chse ldrs 5 out: rdn along and wkng whn fell next* **25/1**
3m 50.7s (-7.50) **Going Correction** -0.275s/f (Good) **8** Ran SP% **113.9**
Speed ratings: **107,106,104,99,89 79,—,—** CSF £38.70 CT £92.22 TOTE £8.30: £1.80, £2.40, £1.90; EX 35.90.
Owner W Raw **Bred** Gestut Etzean **Trained** Newton Bewley, Co Durham

FOCUS
A moderate handicap chase but run at a sound gallop with the first two slight improvers and the third setting the standard.

NOTEBOOK
Kalou(GER) has had a few near-misses over fences but, despite racing off his highest chasing mark, was able to come through late on to record his first success over the bigger obstacles. The decent pace suited and he seemed to outstay his rivals. He may have a little more improvement in him. *(op 6-1)*
Loulou Nivernais(FR), who won on soft ground last time, was 9lb higher but had no problems with these conditions having won on them at Uttoxeter earlier in the autumn. He once again raced up with the pace and battled well to resist the effort of the third before finding the winner too strong. He is going the right way and is young enough to find more improvement. *(op 5-1)*
Polyphon(FR), last year's winner, looked to be running into form last time after a break, travelled well and looked likely to score early in the straight. However, not for the first time he found less than expected under pressure and was already being held by the runner-up when the winner came between the pair. *(op 11-4)*
Super Dolphin, returning from a break, set the pace but his jumping was not up to scratch and he was struggling from some way out. He is better treated over fences than over hurdles, but will need to jump better to give himself a chance. *(op 9-2 tchd 3-1)*
Waltzing Along(IRE), returning from nearly a year off, was settled at the back before moving up at the end of the back straight. His effort soon petered out and he may have needed this, but he was *not the first runner from the stable on the day whose finishing effort was lacklustre.Official explanation: jockey said gelding finished distressed (op 4-1)*

2480 SCOTTISH RACING YOUR BEST BET MAIDEN OPEN NATIONAL HUNT FLAT RACE 2m
3:35 (3:35) (Class 6) 4-6-Y-0 **£2,192** (£639; £319)

Form RPR
1 **Agent Lois (IRE)**[6] [2359] 4-10-6 AndrewJMcNamara(3) 89+
(S Donohoe, Ire) *hld up: smooth hdwy 5f out: rdn to ld wl over 1f out: kpt on* **11/4**[1]
246 **2** 2 **Bonnie Rock (IRE)**[21] [2028] 5-10-6 MichalKohl(3) 85
(J I A Charlton) *chsd clr ldr: hdwy and cl up 5f out: rdn to ld over 2f out: sn hdd: drvn and one pce fnl f* **8/1**
3 2 ½ **Tory Island (IRE)**[16] [2137] 4-10-9 MrATDuff(7) 90
(S Donohoe, Ire) *midfield: hdwy and in tch 6f out: effrt 3f out: sn rdn and ev ch tl drvn and one pce appr last* **9/2**[2]
4 ½ **Duke Of Stradone (IRE)**[193] [393] 5-10-11 (b[1]) PMerrigan(5) 89
(S Donohoe, Ire) *hld up and bhd: stdy hdwy 5f out: rdn to chse ldrs over 3f out: one pce fnl 2f* **16/1**
0- **5** ½ **Grand Daum (FR)**[274] [4027] 4-11-2 BHarding 89
(T P Tate) *led and sn clr: rdn along 4f out: drvn and hdd wl over 2f out: grad wknd* **12/1**
0 **6** 14 **Fly Tipper**[22] [2007] 5-11-2 NPMulholland 75
(W Storey) *in tch: hdwyu to chse ldrs over 5f out: rdn along over 3f out and sn wknd* **50/1**
0-0 **7** 1 ¼ **What's Ahead**[197] [323] 5-10-6 PAspell(3) 66
(Mrs J C McGregor) *chsd ldrs: rdn along 5f out: wknd over 3f out* **40/1**
8 ½ **Flamethrower (IRE)** 5-11-2 RMcGrath 73
(E A Elliott) *midfield: hdwy to chse ldrs 5f out: rdn along and wknd wl over 2f out* **20/1**
9 dist **Border Sovereign** 5-11-2 ADempsey —
(J S Haldane) *chsd ldrs 6f: sn lost pl and bhd fnl 4f* **33/1**
10 1 ½ **Crackpot (IRE)** 5-11-2 KRenwick —
(C Rae) *a rr* **40/1**
0- **11** 18 **Rab Cee**[331] [3078] 5-11-2 ow7 MrTDavidson(7) —
(W G Young) *a rr* **66/1**
12 5 **The Bay Bogle** 4-10-9 BenOrde-Powlett(7) —
(M A Barnes) *in tch: rdn along over 5f out: sn wknd* **28/1**
3- **13** 17 **My Best Secret**[364] [2466] 6-11-2 ADobbin —
(L Lungo) *hld up and bhd: sme hdwy on inner 6f out: rdn along over 4f out and sn wknd* **11/2**[3]
0-0 **14** dist **Boxclever**[64] [1532] 4-11-2 GLee —
(J M Jefferson) *chsd ldng pair: rdn along 6f out: sn wknd* **6/1**
3m 48.5s (-2.80) **Going Correction** +0.125s/f (Yiel)
WFA 4 from 5yo+ 12lb **14** Ran SP% **118.7**
Speed ratings: **97,96,94,94,94 87,86,86,—,— —,—,—,—** CSF £23.12 TOTE £4.00: £1.90, £3.20, £1.50; EX 21.80 Place 6 £26.45, Place 5 £14.38.
Owner Mrs S Donohoe **Bred** Gerard Mulcaire **Trained** Cootehill Road, Co. Cavan
■ A 566/1 four-timer for Irish trainer Shane Donohoe and jockey Andrew McNamara, with stablemates third and fourth.

FOCUS
An ordinary bumper dominated by the Irish challengers, but solid enough with the first two and fourth to their marks.

NOTEBOOK
Agent Lois(IRE), who had shown promise in two heavy-ground bumpers in her homeland, clearly appreciated these less-testing conditions and, well supported, completed a four-timer for trainer and jockey with little fuss. She should make her mark in mares' hurdle races if the ground is not too soft. *(tchd 5-2)*
Bonnie Rock(IRE), having her fourth run in bumpers, had only disappointed when encountering soft ground last time. She ran her race again and sets the standard, and will now switch to hurdles where she can make her mark against her own sex. *(op 10-1 tchd 11-1)*
Tory Island(IRE), a stable companion of the winner and backed against her having been just behind her on his debut, travelled well turning in but could not quicken from halfway up the straight. He may be suited by an easier surface. *(op 6-1)*
Duke Of Stradone(IRE), with more experience than his two stable companions having raced in point-to-points, ran well enough in the first-time blinkers but looks likely to do better faced with a longer trip and easier ground.
Grand Daum(FR), having only his second outing and first since February, led for a long way and kept going once headed. With a trainer who gives his horses plenty of time, he can be expected to improve from this. *(tchd 14-1 in a place)*
My Best Secret, returning from a year off following his debut, never figured at any stage. *(op 6-1 tchd 13-2, 7-1 in a place)*
T/Plt: £88.40 to a £1 stake. Pool: £32,593.80. 268.95 winning tickets. T/Qpdt: £27.90 to a £1 stake. Pool: £2,955.30. 78.30 winning tickets. JR

NEWBURY (L-H)
Friday, November 25

OFFICIAL GOING: Good
Wind: Virtually nil

2481 Q ASSOCIATES JUVENILE NOVICES' HURDLE (8 hdls) 2m 110y
1:00 (1:02) (Class 3) 3-Y-O **£7,156** (£2,101; £1,050; £524)

Form RPR
1 **Turko (FR)**[92] 3-11-4 RWalsh 132+
(P F Nicholls) *gd sort: tall: lengthy: trckd ldrs: nt fluent 4th: wnt 2nd appr 2 out:led sn after: drvn out run-in* **5/2**[1]
2 1 ¾ **My Immortal**[77] 3-10-12 TJMurphy 121
(M C Pipe) *lw: str: led tl appr 2nd: styd chsng ldr tl slt ld 3 out: hder after 2 out: rallied to chal last: one pce u.p* **3/1**[2]
3- **3** 11 **Restless D'Artaix (FR)**[180] [583] 3-11-4 MAFitzgerald 117+
(N J Henderson) *tall: rangy: in tch: hdwy to chse ldrs after 4 out: drvn to go 3rd 2 out: sn hrd rdn and one pce* **10/3**[3]
4 5 **Prize Fighter (IRE)**[27] 3-10-12 APMcCoy 105
(Jonjo O'Neill) *bhd: hdwy 4 out: clsd on ldrs appr 3 out: wknd sn after* **6/1**
5 8 **Garibaldi (GER)**[15] 3-10-12 RWalford 98+
(D R C Elsworth) *chsd ldrs: nt fluent 4th: rdn and wknd 3 out* **25/1**
6 3 ½ **Tanzanite (IRE)**[34] 3-10-5 JamesDavies 90+
(D W P Arbuthnot) *led appr 2nd: narrowly hdd and nt fluent 3 out: wknd and hit next: hit last* **12/1**
7 26 **Grasp**[37] 3-10-12 (t) JEMoore 68
(G L Moore) *a in rr* **33/1**
0 **8** 1 ¼ **Brendan's Surprise**[6] [2345] 3-10-5 RCummings(7) 67
(K J Burke) *chsd ldrs: nt fluent 4th: sn wknd* **100/1**
PP **9** dist **Goose Chase**[25] [1948] 3-10-12 NFehily —
(C J Mann) *nt fluent: a in rr: t.o* **100/1**
6 **10** 7 **Bay Hawk**[9] [2274] 3-10-12 JPMcNamara —
(B G Powell) *a bhd: t.o* **50/1**
61 **P** **Zando**[11] [2245] 3-10-13 TGreenway(5) —
(E G Bevan) *a in rr: no ch whn p.u and dismntd appr last* **66/1**
22 **P** **Double Spectre (IRE)**[19] [2069] 3-10-12 ATinkler —
(Jean-Rene Auvray) *lw: a bhd: t.o whn p.u after 4 out* **20/1**
3m 58.0s (-5.60) **Going Correction** -0.025s/f (Good) **12** Ran SP% **115.6**
Speed ratings: **112,111,106,103,99 98,86,85,—,— —,—** CSF £9.51 TOTE £3.20: £1.60, £1.40, £1.90; EX 12.80.
Owner The Stewart Family **Bred** B Forges **Trained** Ditcheat, Somerset

FOCUS
One of the better juvenile hurdles run so far this season, run at a solid pace and the time was decent as a result. The front pair look high-class hurdling prospects, whilst there was also promise from a few in behind. The form should work out and the race should produce winners.

NOTEBOOK
Turko(FR) ◆, a winner over hurdles in France in his last outing three months previously and penalised as a result, eventually managed to get the better of a protracted duel with the runner-up and this was probably a good effort to give him weight and a beating. His jumping was not perfect on occasions, but that should improve as he gets used to British hurdles and he would not mind more testing conditions than these. He looks yet another good import for the yard. *(op 11-4)*
My Immortal ◆, a useful handicapper on the Flat for John Gosden, was given a positive ride on this hurdling debut though he was unable to dictate on his own. Despite that, he fought bravely all the way to the line and just ran into a more experienced rival on the day. He is also a nice prospect for this game, but the fact that he won over just short of two miles on the level probably means that he will appreciate a greater test of stamina than this over timber. *(op 4-1)*
Restless D'Artaix(FR) ◆, like the winner already successful over hurdles in France and carrying a penalty as a result, had every chance but this was his first start since winning a Listed hurdle at Auteuil in May and he might just have needed it. Softer ground would not bother him either and he should certainly pay his way, though he strikes as a chasing type in the longer term. *(op 11-4 tchd 7-2)*
Prize Fighter(IRE), a useful handicapper on the Flat, made a decent hurdling debut and was by no means beaten up in the latter stages. There may be a stamina issue with him, however, as he barely seemed to stay ten furlongs on the level so may need a sharper track than this to help him get the trip. *(tchd 13-2)*
Garibaldi(GER), winner of a 12-furlong Polytrack maiden a fortnight earlier, showed up for a long way but was firmly put in his place down the home straight. He was rated a fair way behind a few of these on the level so may need his sights lowered a little over hurdles. *(op 33-1)*
Tanzanite(IRE), a useful handicapper at up to ten furlongs on the Flat, helped set the pace but once the runner-up had got her measure at the third last her jumping went to pieces as she began to tire. Softer ground and being ridden with a bit more restraint should help her. *(op 10-1)*
Bay Hawk *Official explanation: jockey said colt had a breathing problem*
Zando *Official explanation: jockey said gelding had made a mistake and felt sore, but subsequently returned sound (tchd 25-1)*
Double Spectre(IRE) *Official explanation: jockey said saddle slipped (tchd 25-1)*

2482 CANTORSPREADFAIR.COM BEGINNERS' CHASE (13 fncs) 2m 1f
1:35 (1:35) (Class 3) 4-Y-O+ **£7,059** (£2,072; £1,036; £517)

Form RPR
41-2 **1** **Cornish Sett (IRE)**[38] [1783] 6-11-5 (b[1]) RWalsh 138+
(P F Nicholls) *hld up in tch: hdwy 4 out: chsd ldrs next: hrd drvn and styd on appr last: led sn after: rdn out* **13/8**[1]
00-4 **2** 3 **Green Tango**[24] [1971] 6-11-5 RJohnson 133+
(H D Daly) *lw: chsd ldrs: wnt 2nd 7th: led after 9th: mstke 4 out: rdn next: hit last: hdd sn after: kpt on same pce* **11/2**
1121 **3** 1 ½ **Phar Out Phavorite (IRE)**[36] [1804] 6-11-5 BFenton 133+
(Miss E C Lavelle) *lw: led: j.rt: hdd after 9th: styd front rnk: rdn 2 out: ev ch and hit last: one pce* **14/1**
45-2 **4** nk **Lustral Du Seuil (FR)**[20] [2044] 6-11-5 MAFitzgerald 131+
(N J Henderson) *in tch: hit 4th: blnd 9th: chsd ldr 3 out: ev ch last: sn one pce* **9/2**[3]
1/24 **5** 1 ¼ **Garde Champetre (FR)**[13] [2174] 6-11-5 APMcCoy 131+
(Jonjo O'Neill) *chsd ldr tl blnd 6th: nt fluent 9th: styd chsng ldrs: hit 4 out: styd on one pce u.p fr 2 out* **10/3**[2]
0/0- **6** 24 **Tusk**[384] [2050] 5-11-5 DO'Meara 105
(H P Hogarth) *t.k.h: bhd but in tch: hit 9th: wknd and blnd 4 out* **20/1**
2P-0 **7** nk **Mighty Matters (IRE)**[20] [2044] 6-11-5 JMMaguire 107+
(T R George) *a bhd: wknd and mstke 4 out* **66/1**
3 **P** **Offemont (FR)**[20] [2044] 4-10-7 AThornton —
(Mrs L C Taylor) *chsd ldrs: hit 6th and 9th: wknd and mstke 4 out: blnd 3 out: p.u bef next* **33/1**
4m 7.70s (-1.70) **Going Correction** -0.025s/f (Good)
WFA 4 from 5yo+ 12lb **8** Ran SP% **110.6**
Speed ratings: **103,101,100,100,100 88,88,—** CSF £10.36 TOTE £2.40: £1.10, £2.00, £1.90; EX 14.40.

The Form Book, Raceform Ltd, Compton, RG20 6NL

Owner Peter Hart **Bred** J F C Maxwell **Trained** Ditcheat, Somerset

FOCUS
A decent race, but there was no great pace on early and there were still five in with a chance jumping the last. The second and fourth set the standard and the race should produce winners.

NOTEBOOK
Cornish Sett(IRE), blinkered for the first time following his Exeter antics, was given a waiting ride in a moderately-run race and was produced with precision timing to lead at the last and showed by far the best turn of foot on the run-in. Despite being successful, this race may not have been run to suit him so there is every possibility he will prove himself capable of even better in a truly-run race, or when faced with a stiffer test. *(tchd 6-4 and 7-4 in a place)*

Green Tango, fourth behind a couple of very smart prospects on his chasing debut at Exeter, confirmed the promise of that effort here having been up with the pace the whole way. Although he could not match the winner's turn of foot on the run-in, it is only a matter of time before he wins over the larger obstacles and should prove himself at least as good over fences as he was over hurdles. *(op 7-1)*

Phar Out Phavorite(IRE), a progressive sort over hurdles this year, had the visor left off for this chasing debut and did remarkably well to hang in there for so long as he jumped right-handed throughout, sometimes alarmingly so. It is obviously significant that all ten of his outings over hurdles, including three victories, were on right-handed tracks. *(tchd 16-1)*

Lustral Du Seuil(FR), as on his chasing debut, made one or two mistakes but still had every chance until done for foot from the final fence. Whether this was an improvement on his Sandown effort is debatable. *(op 11-2)*

Garde Champetre(FR) jumped moderately and never looked convincing, despite still being in with some sort of chance coming to the last. This trip would have been inadequate especially given the modest early pace, but he has not really set the world alight for his new yard over fences since returning from his lengthy absence. *(op 5-2 tchd 7-2)*

Offemont(FR) *Official explanation: trainer said gelding had been struck into (op 40-1)*

2483 PERTEMPS H'CAP HURDLE RACE (QUALIFIER) (13 hdls) 3m 110y

2:10 (2:10) (Class 2) (0-140,135) 4-Y-0+

£13,878 (£4,099; £2,049; £1,026; £511; £257)

Form				RPR
1-1	1		**The Market Man (NZ)**[31] [1872] 5-11-10 **133** .... MAFitzgerald (N J Henderson) *hld up rr but in tch: hdwy 7th: chal 2 out: sn ld:drvn and kpt on wl run-in* **15/8**[1]	142+
1211	2	3	**Amicelli (GER)**[54] [1608] 6-10-9 **118** .... RJohnson (P J Hobbs) *chsd ldrs: chal 7th: led next: rdn fr 3 out: hdd sn after next: rallied last: nt qckn run-in* **13/2**[3]	122+
41-6	3	1 ½	**Hidden Bounty (IRE)**[27] [1929] 9-11-0 **123** .... JimCrowley (K G Reveley) *bhd: hdwy 6th: chsd ldrs fr 4 out: rdn next: kpt on wl fr 2 out but nt qckn run-in* **25/1**	125
1111	4	2 ½	**Ostfanni (IRE)**[31] [1870] 5-10-11 **120** .... RWalsh (M Todhunter) *hld up in rr: hdwy fr 4 out: shkn up after 3 out: kpt on appr last and r.o run-in: nt pce to trble ldrs* **17/2**	119
0U-0	5	3 ½	**World Wide Web (IRE)**[13] [2175] 9-11-3 **126** .... APMcCoy (Jonjo O'Neill) *lw: bhd: rdn 3 out: styd on after 2 out: fin wl but nvr gng pce to rch ldrs* **25/1**	122
53-3	6	2 ½	**Cool Roxy**[41] [1743] 8-11-1 **129** .... CHonour[(5)] (A G Blackmore) *bhd: hdwy after 4 out: rdn 3 out: styd on u.p fr next but nvr trbld ldrs* **33/1**	123+
2020	7	4	**Phar From Frosty (IRE)**[13] [2175] 8-11-2 **125** .... ATinkler (C R Egerton) *chsd ldrs: led 5th: hdd 8th: wknd 3 out* **40/1**	115+
-062	8	8	**Mythical King (IRE)**[13] [2184] 8-10-13 **129** .... MrTCollier[(7)] (R Lee) *led tl after 1st: styd chsng ldrs tl wknd 3 out: no ch whn bdly hmpd last* **33/1**	115+
50-P	9	dist	**Bounce Back (USA)**[33] [1861] 9-11-12 **135** .... (v) TScudamore (M C Pipe) *in tch: hdwy and j. slowly 8th: rdn appr 3 out: sn wknd: t.o* **50/1**	—
-203	10	26	**Global Challenge (IRE)**[128] [1039] 6-11-2 **125** .... JEMoore (P G Murphy) *a bhd:t.o* **40/1**	—
PP0-	11	8	**Redde (IRE)**[272] [4059] 10-9-7 **109** oh4 .... CMStudd[(7)] (Mrs J G Retter) *led after 1st to 5th: wknd 4 out: t.o* **100/1**	—
40-3	B		**Versus (GER)**[212] [54] 5-9-5 **110** .... KGTobin[(10)] (C J Mann) *lw: chsd ldrs: rdn to go 2nd 3 out: sn wknd: no ch whn b.d last* **25/1**	99
P1-2	F		**Il Duce (IRE)**[12] [2207] 5-11-7 **130** .... RThornton (A King) *lw: sn chsng ldrs: wnt 2nd 7th to 3 out: wknd 2 out: disputing 5th and wkng whn fell last* **2/1**[2]	126+

5m 59.8s (-2.30) **Going Correction** -0.025s/f (Good) **13** Ran SP% **117.2**

Speed ratings: **102,101,100,99,98 97,96,94,—,— —,—,—** CSF £12.61 CT £232.27 TOTE £2.90: £1.40, £2.20, £4.10; EX 17.80 Trifecta £353.50 Pool: £1,145.28 - 2.30 winning units..

Owner Sir Robert Ogden **Bred** Monovale Holdings Ltd **Trained** Upper Lambourn, Berks

■ This was Mick Fitzgerald's first winner since returning from a broken neck sustained in July.

■ Stewards' Enquiry : R Thornton one-day ban: threw whip at an opposing jockey (Dec 6)

FOCUS
A competitive handicap, though the early pace did not look that strong. The winner is value for more than the official margin, and with those in the frame close to their marks the form looks solid.

NOTEBOOK
The Market Man(NZ) ◆, raised 8lb for his Cheltenham victory, proved well suited by this drying ground and travelled sweetly behind the leaders the whole way. Leading two from home, his rider was then looking round for dangers and he found plenty when finally put under pressure. He still has plenty of scope and his liking for good ground will be a big plus with the Cheltenham and Aintree Festivals in mind later in the season. *(op 2-1 tchd 9-4 in places)*

Amicelli(GER), who was beaten out of sight off a 9lb lower mark in his only previous try in a handicap in the spring of last year, has been in great form in novice hurdles since returning to the track in May of this year. Given a positive ride, he was the only one able to stay with the winner over the last couple of hurdles and this effort shows that he is perfectly capable off this mark. However, like the winner he may not want the ground to soften up too much. *(tchd 7-1)*

Hidden Bounty(IRE) ◆, a dual winner over fences last season, was all the better for his recent reappearance over hurdles at Wetherby and was one of only three with any sort of chance over the last couple of flights. This was a cracking effort in defeat and he can surely win another race over hurdles on this evidence, but if it does not work out there is always the option of going back over fences. *(op 20-1)*

Ostfanni(IRE), bidding for a nap-hand over hurdles after winning a maiden hurdle and three novice events, was given a typically patient ride by his jockey but, although she kept staying on over the last mile or so, she was never quite doing it quickly enough. A stronger pace would have suited her, but at least this performance shows that she can be competitive off this sort of mark. *(op 10-1)*

World Wide Web(IRE), whose last few outings have been well spread out, was struggling for pace a fair way out and it was his stamina that enabled him to plug on to finish where he did. Softer ground would suit him, but he does not look that well handicapped over hurdles these days and has obviously not been easy to train. *(op 33-1)*

Cool Roxy, with the cheekpieces left off this time, was not disgraced but looks high enough in the weights just now. *(op 25-1)*

Il Duce(IRE), pulled up in his only previous try over this trip, albeit in a Grade One novice hurdle at Aintree back in the spring, had every chance turning in but seemed to have reached the limit of his stamina and was on the retreat when coming down at the last. He was due to go up another 7lb the day after this, but may still be competitive off his new mark when returned to shorter. *(tchd 15-8)*

2484 UNICOIN HOMES NOVICES' CHASE (REGISTERED AS THE WORCESTER NOVICES' CHASE) GRADE 2 (18 fncs) 3m

2:40 (2:41) (Class 1) 5-Y-0+ **£18,332** (£6,930; £3,512; £1,794; £943)

Form				RPR
0-12	1		**Darkness**[19] [2065] 6-11-2 136 .... BFenton (C R Egerton) *chsd ldrs: hit 12th: hdwy 13th: slt ld 4 out: c clr fr 2 out: easily* **14/1**	154+
-111	2	13	**Iris's Gift**[30] [1879] 8-11-9 150 .... APMcCoy (Jonjo O'Neill) *lw: led: hit 4th and 7th:blnd 9th: hit 13th:hdd after next:ev ch ev4 out: lft chsng wnr 3 out: sn no ch: jst hld on for 2nd* **4/7**[1]	148+
132	3	shd	**Unleash (USA)**[10] [2260] 6-11-2 .... RJohnson (P J Hobbs) *in tch: hdwy 10th:nt fluent and lost pl 12th: sn bhd:kpt on again fr 2 out:fin wl:jst failed to take 2nd but no ch wnr* **16/1**	140+
1031	4	29	**Goblet Of Fire (USA)**[10] [2260] 6-11-9 .... (b) RWalsh (P F Nicholls) *a bhd: no ch whn nt fluent 12th* **20/1**	116
03-1	5	11	**The Dark Lord (IRE)**[35] [1817] 8-11-9 .... JAMcCarthy (Mrs L Wadham) *lw: bhd fr 6th and mstke: nt fluent: mstkes 9th and 11th and sn wl bhd* **12/1**[3]	105
10-5	U		**Senor Sedona**[20] [2052] 6-11-2 .... JamesDavies (N J Gifford) *hit 3rd: sn bhd: blnd 5th: t.o 10th: blnd and uns rdr 11th* **40/1**	—
01-2	F		**Lough Derg (FR)**[13] [2174] 5-11-1 .... TScudamore (M C Pipe) *chsd ldr: chal after 13th tl led after next: hdd 4 out: 2l 2nd: rdn and hld whn fell 3 out* **4/1**[2]	140+

5m 53.7s (-11.30) **Going Correction** -0.025s/f (Good)

WFA 5 from 6yo+ 1lb **7** Ran SP% **111.1**

Speed ratings: **117,112,112,102,99 —,—** CSF £22.79 TOTE £13.90: £3.60, £1.30; EX 35.60.

Owner Lady Lloyd-Webber **Bred** Heatherwold Stud **Trained** Chaddleworth, Berks

FOCUS
A decent line-up for this valuable novice chase and run at a solid pace thanks to Iris's Gift and Lough Derg, which resulted in a more than acceptable time. Although the result was not the one most people expected, nothing should be taken away from the winner. The form is reasonably solid.

NOTEBOOK
Darkness ◆, over a much more suitable trip after his defeat by Monet's Garden over two miles at Ayr last time, jumped much better than in his two previous chases. Racing in third for most of the way, he always seemed to have the two leaders in his sights and, when asked to pick them up turning for home, did so in most impressive style and eventually forged further and further clear. He understandably shortened for the Royal & SunAlliance after this, but Cheltenham is not the be all and end all and he should be capable of picking up other decent prizes in the meantime. *(op 12-1)*

Iris's Gift, bidding for a four-timer over fences, made the majority of the running though Lough Derg made sure he never had an easy time of it. He did not look happy from some way out and he would probably have finished third had Lough Derg stood up. Although his fencing was again unconvincing, he arguably jumped better than he did at Cheltenham and it now looks a case of back to the drawing board. *(op 1-2 tchd 8-13)*

Unleash(USA) managed to reverse Fakenham form with Goblet Of Fire, but never looked like winning and it was only when his stamina eventually kicked in that he stayed on and almost caught the flagging Iris's Gift for second. He will find easier opportunities than this. *(tchd 20-1)*

Goblet Of Fire(USA), given a very patient ride, never figured at all and the fact that he finished so far behind his Fakenham victim Unleash this time puts the effort into perspective. It may be that he found this trip on a much more demanding track too much for him. *(tchd 25-1)*

The Dark Lord(IRE) was very disappointing after the promise of his Fakenham victory and his jumping was moderate to say the least. *(op 14-1)*

Lough Derg(FR), runner-up to a potentially useful sort on his chasing debut at Cheltenham, had not proved his stamina for this trip but was ridden as though it was not going to be an issue. He kept Iris's Gift company for most of the way and looked to have taken his measure turning for home, only to find the winner arriving at the same time travelling better than both of them. He would probably have finished second had he not come down at the final ditch three from home. There are certainly races to be won with him over fences. *(tchd 7-2)*

2485 JOHN DAVIES OF BIGMORE ASSOCIATES CELEBRATION AMATEUR RIDERS' H'CAP CHASE (18 fncs) 3m

3:15 (3:15) (Class 4) (0-125,123) 5-Y-0+

£10,359 (£3,236; £1,617; £809; £403; £203)

Form				RPR
1-33	1		**Ladalko (FR)**[41] [1744] 6-11-11 **122** .... MrCJSweeney (P F Nicholls) *lw: bhd: hit 3rd and 6th: hdwy 13th: trckd ldr next: led 4 out: c clr fr 2 out: readily* **7/2**[2]	143+
-252	2	5	**Shalako (USA)**[12] [2210] 7-11-0 **114** .... MrTJO'Brien[(3)] (P J Hobbs) *chsd ldrs: pushed along 10th: rdn 4 out: chsd wnr and blnd next: kpt on same pce* **5/1**[3]	126+
35-P	3	1 ½	**Tom Costalot (IRE)**[23] [1989] 10-9-7 **97** oh3 .... MrSPJones[(7)] (Mrs Susan Nock) *bhd: pushed along fr 11th: hday 4 out: styd on fr 2 out and kpt on run-in: nt rch ldrs* **33/1**	106
12-0	4	3 ½	**Beau Supreme (IRE)**[24] [1972] 8-11-4 **122** .... MrRQuinn[(7)] (C J Down) *lw: chsd leders: rdn 12th: blnd and bhd 13th: styd on again fr 2 out: kpt on run-in but nvr a danger* **50/1**	127
-151	5	1	**Ashgreen**[8] [2282] 8-10-2 **99** 7ex .... MissNCarberry (Miss Venetia Williams) *hit 3rd: chsd ldr fr 4th tl hit 9th: on pce 4 out: rallied and styng on for 3rd whn blnd bdly last* **5/1**[3]	107+
3-11	6	½	**Kausse De Thaix (FR)**[7] [2325] 7-10-8 **108** 7ex .... MrJSnowden[(3)] (O Sherwood) *bmpd 1st: chsd ldrs: wnt 2nd 9th: led next: hit 12th and 13th: hdd and hit 4 out: one pce fr next* **3/1**[1]	115+
6-14	7	12	**Tom's Prize**[197] [311] 10-11-12 **123** .... MrNWilliams (J L Spearing) *led and bmpd 1st: hdd 10th: wknd fr 4 out* **20/1**	123+
13F2	8	12	**Party Games (IRE)**[17] [2100] 8-10-11 **108** .... MrSMorris (G L Moore) *hit 10th: bhd most of way* **25/1**	88
-522	9	dist	**Bee An Bee (IRE)**[14] [2162] 8-11-2 **120** .... (p) MrRMcCarthy[(7)] (T R George) *in tch whn blnd 7th: n.d after and sn bhd: t.o* **7/1**	—
212-	P		**Cinnamon Line**[241] [4645] 9-10-12 **109** .... MrDHDunsdon (R Lee) *a bhd: t.o 11th: p.u bef next* **33/1**	—
/P-3	P		**The Tall Guy (IRE)**[33] [1848] 9-9-11 **99** .... MrGTumelty[(5)] (N A Twiston-Davies) *chsd ldrs: wknd and mstke 12th: t.o whn p.u bef 4 out* **25/1**	—

6m 1.20s (-3.80) **Going Correction** -0.025s/f (Good) **11** Ran SP% **113.4**

Speed ratings: **105,103,102,101,101 101,97,93,—,— —** CSF £18.76 CT £483.99 TOTE £4.60: £1.80, £2.30, £9.90; EX 23.80.

Owner Paul K Barber & Mrs M Findlay **Bred** G Cherel **Trained** Ditcheat, Somerset

FOCUS

Quite a competitive event of its type, and run at a solid pace. Those in the frame behind the winner ran to their marks, indicating the form is sound, and the winner is rated value for nearly double the official margin.

NOTEBOOK

Ladalko(FR) ♦, trying three miles for the first time, seemed to relish it and was given a very proficient ride by his amateur, eventually winning with a deal in hand. He is very well handicapped on his hurdles form, and now that he has hit the target looks capable of going in again. *(op 3-1 tchd 4-1 in a place)*

Shalako(USA), like the winner trying this trip for the first time and rated lower over fences than he is over hurdles, had every chance when making a monumental blunder three from home which would not have done him any good, but it is doubtful it made much difference to the result. Despite consistently making the frame since his last win 15 months ago, there is no doubting his application. *(op 9-2)*

Tom Costalot(IRE), pulled up on his reappearance, performed much better this time though he never looked like winning and merely plugged on from the rear to snatch third. Despite being 3lb wrong here, he has become very well handicapped if the spark still exists.

Beau Supreme(IRE), still 7lb higher than for his last win, plugged on again after losing his place exiting the back straight and looking likely to finish out with the washing.

Ashgreen, carrying a 7lb penalty for his Hereford romp, was unable to dominate like he did there against these better rivals and was only playing for places when walking through the last. *(op 15-2 tchd 8-1)*

Kausse De Thaix(FR), bidding for a hat-trick under his 7lb penalty, was always up with the pace but was sending out distress signals starting up the home straight and he was soon on the retreat. His rider was of the opinion that this race might have come too soon. *(op 11-4 tchd 5-2)*

Cinnamon Line *Official explanation: vet said gelding was distressed*

2486 JOHN SMITH'S EBF MARES' ONLY "NATIONAL HUNT" NOVICES' HURDLE (QUALIFIER) (11 hdls) 2m 5f

3:45 (3:46) (Class 4) 4-Y-0+ **£5,100** (£1,497; £748; £373)

Form | | | | RPR

P-45 **1** **Ballyhoo (IRE)**[12] [2212] 5-10-5 WPKavanagh(7) 95+
(J W Mullins) *bhd: hdwway and hit 4 out: rdn and styd on fr 3 out: chsd ldr last: led fnl 75yds: drvn out* **28/1**

00P- **2** 1 1/4 **Forest Fauna**[229] [4789] 5-10-12 PHide 95+
(J W Mullins) *lw: chsd ldr: led 4 out: hit next: sn rdn: hdd and no ex fnl 75yds* **80/1**

212 **3** 3 **Bonchester Bridge**[35] [1820] 4-10-12 MAFitzgerald 92+
(N J Henderson) *w'like: chsd ldrs: rdn 3 out: one pce fr 2 out* **5/1**[2]

4-03 **4** 9 **Jades Double**[12] [2212] 4-10-12 JGoldstein 83+
(M Madgwick) *bhd: hdwy after 4 out: styd on one pce fr 2 out* **25/1**

-1P0 **5** 3/4 **Fallout (IRE)**[164] [753] 4-11-4 93 RWalsh 87
(J W Mullins) *bhd: pushed along 3 out: blnd 2 out: kpt on run-in but nvr a danger* **40/1**

236- **6** 1/2 **Ballybawn House**[258] [4333] 4-10-12 SCurran 81
(J C Fox) *chsd ldrs: hit 6th: wknd 2 out* **50/1**

0-20 **7** 3 1/2 **Kentford Lady**[22] [2012] 4-10-12 AThornton 77
(J W Mullins) *bhd: hdwy appr 3 out: shkn up 2 out: nvr gng pce to rch ldrs* **40/1**

0-0P **8** dist **Create A Storm (IRE)**[19] [2082] 5-10-12 JPMcNamara —
(J G Portman) *plld hrd in rr: a bhd: t.o* **100/1**

03-0 **9** 4 **Manque Pas D'Air (FR)**[15] [2142] 5-10-5 WMcCarthy(7) —
(T R George) *bhd: hdwy 5th: rdn to chse ldrs after 4 out: sn wknd: t.o* **25/1**

50-5 **10** 14 **Alderbrook Girl (IRE)**[25] [1950] 5-10-9 CBolger(3) —
(R Curtis) *a bhd:t.o* **66/1**

5 **11** 14 **Flirty Jill**[25] [1961] 4-10-12 TDoyle —
(P R Webber) *chsd ldrs tl wknd qckly 4 out: t.o* **16/1**

P **Two Hoots**[592] 7-10-12 NFehily —
(C J Mann) *leggy: chsd ldrs early: wknd 5th: t.o whn p.u bef 3 out* **18/1**

10- **U** **Grenfell (IRE)**[232] [4753] 6-10-12 RJohnson 81
(R T Phillips) *in tch to 4 out: no ch whn bdly hmpd and uns rdr 2 out* **15/2**[3]

3-F1 **F** **Heltornic (IRE)**[16] [2125] 5-11-4 TScudamore 93
(M Scudamore) *lw: led tl hdd 4 out: wknd 3 out: 7th and no ch whn fell 2 out* **8/11**[1]

5m 11.9s (-1.10) **Going Correction** -0.025s/f (Good)

WFA 4 from 5yo+ 13lb **14** Ran SP% **119.2**

Speed ratings: **101,100,99,95,95 94,94,—,—,— —,—,—,—** CSF £1272.31 TOTE £34.20: £5.30, £23.70, £1.70; EX 1300.00 Place 6 £60.81, Place 5 £44.82.

Owner Ian M McGready **Bred** Miss Annette McMahon **Trained** Wilsford-Cum-Lake, Wilts

FOCUS

A race run at a fair-enough pace, but a moderate contest for the track with the bookies betting 16/1 bar three. A big-priced one-two for trainer Seamus Mullins, but difficult to know what to make of the form with two of the three market leaders running stinkers, and best rated around the third and fourth.

NOTEBOOK

Ballyhoo(IRE), who hinted at some ability on her hurdling debut at Fontwell, came from well off the pace to eventually get the better of her flagging stable companion on the run-in and looks very much a stayer. This was an ordinary race for the track though and she will almost certainly need to improve in order to win again. *(op 25-1)*

Forest Fauna, not seen since running poorly over hurdles in the spring, was a different proposition this time. Racing closest to the favourite, she moved past that rival without too much fuss about a mile from home and soon set up what looked an unassailable lead. Starting to tire racing up the home straight, landing on all-fours at the second last did not help and she had nothing left when her stable companion collared her on the run-in. Despite this improved performance, her earlier moderate form does suggest this was not a great race. *(op 50-1)*

Bonchester Bridge, making her hurdling debut after showing plenty of ability in bumpers, had every chance down the home straight but lacked a change of gear where it mattered. On the face of it this looked a promising effort, but in reality it was disappointing that she ended up being beaten fair and square by modest-looking outsiders. *(op 4-1)*

Jades Double had finished over six lengths in front of Ballyhoo at Fontwell last time which suggests she did not achieve a great deal here. *(tchd 28-1)*

Fallout(IRE), off since June, never looked like taking a hand and her final placing was as close as she got. Her penalty for winning a dire contest in the spring will remain a problem. *(op 33-1)*

Grenfell(IRE), off since April and making her hurdling debut, was well beaten when running into the stricken favourite two from home and losing her rider. *(op 6-1)*

Heltornic(IRE), so impressive at Lingfield, ran a shocker. Once again making the running, she could do nothing to stop the eventual runner-up going past her a mile from home and was shot to pieces when coming down two out. The faster ground may have been one possible excuse, but she did win a bumper on good ground. *(op 6-1)*

T/Jkpt: £62,388.90 to a £1 stake. Pool: £175,743.50. 2.00 winning tickets. T/Plt: £45.10 to a £1 stake. Pool: £77,364.40. 1,251.40 winning tickets. T/Qpdt: £21.50 to a £1 stake. Pool: £4,561.90. 156.30 winning tickets. ST

2481 NEWBURY (L-H)

Saturday, November 26

OFFICIAL GOING: Good

Wind: Nil

2487 CANTORSPREADFAIR.COM NOVICES' HURDLE (8 hdls) 2m 110y

12:35 (12:35) (Class 3) 4-Y-0+ **£7,202** (£2,127; £1,063; £532; £265; £133)

Form | | | | RPR

115 **1** **Natal (FR)**[15] [2161] 4-11-8 128 (t) RWalsh 143+
(P F Nicholls) *lw: trckd ldrs in 3rd: qcknd to chal 3 out: sn led: c clr fr 2 out: shkn up run-in: easily* **5/2**[1]

-133 **2** 16 **Fandani (GER)**[31] [1880] 5-11-5 122 RJohnson 123+
(C J Mann) *hdwy fr 4th: clsd on ldrs after 4 out: chsd wnr after 2 out but no ch: hld on all out for 2nd* **5/1**

3 3/4 **Odiham**[42] 4-11-0 TDoyle 116
(H Morrison) *in tch tl nt fluent and dropped rr 4th: hdwy fr 3 out: styd on wl run-in to cl on 2nd cl home but no ch w wnr* **8/1**

4 **4** 9 **Herakles (GER)**[35] [1824] 4-11-0 MAFitzgerald 108+
(N J Henderson) *led and t.k.h: hdd after 3 out: wknd wl bef last* **20/1**

2- **5** 4 **Some Touch (IRE)**[231] [4774] 5-11-0 GLee 104+
(J Howard Johnson) *hld up in rr: hdwy fr 4 out: chsd ldrs 3 out: wkng whn hmpd next* **10/3**[2]

6 6 **Dance World**[38] 5-10-7 MrMatthewSmith(7) 99+
(Miss J Feilden) *in tch: rdn after 4 out: wknd fr next* **100/1**

04/3 **7** 5 **Photographer (USA)**[22] [2015] 7-11-0 88 RGreene 92
(S Lycett) *chsd ldr tl appr 3 out: sn wknd* **66/1**

8 2 1/2 **Tamreen (IRE)**[76] 4-11-0 JEMoore 90
(G L Moore) *tall: scope: bit bkwd: bhd: hdwy after 4 out and one pce whn mstke 3 out and sn wknd* **66/1**

51- **9** 16 **Royal Stardust**[280] [3946] 4-11-0 PHide 74
(G L Moore) *lw: hit 1st: sn in tch: rdn after 4 out: wknd bef next* **50/1**

00 **10** 9 **Gunship (IRE)**[10] [2269] 4-10-9 RStephens(5) 65
(P J Hobbs) *sn bhd and nvr in contention* **100/1**

5 **11** 1 1/2 **Street Life (IRE)**[22] [438] 7-11-0 AThornton 63
(W J Musson) *chsd ldrs after 4 out and sn wknd* **50/1**

50-2 **12** 22 **Celtic Jem (IRE)**[210] [138] 5-11-0 CLlewellyn 41
(P Bowen) *lw: a in rr* **33/1**

/0-0 **13** 6 **Amir Zaman**[10] [838] 7-11-0 96 PMoloney 35
(J R Jenkins) *chsd ldrs: hit 4 out: sn wknd* **150/1**

F **Able Baker Charlie (IRE)**[101] 6-11-0 APMcCoy 115+
(J R Fanshawe) *hld up in rr: hdwy 3 out: styng on to dispute 8l 4th whn fell 2 out* **4/1**[3]

3m 55.9s (-7.70) **Going Correction** -0.275s/f (Good) **14** Ran SP% **116.7**

Speed ratings: **107,99,99,94,93 90,87,86,79,74 74,63,61,—** CSF £14.30 TOTE £3.80: £1.90, £2.10, £2.60; EX 13.60.

Owner Mrs Monica Hackett **Bred** Yves D'Armaille **Trained** Ditcheat, Somerset

FOCUS

High-class novice form, rated through the winner. The race should work out.

NOTEBOOK

Natal(FR) bounced back from his defeat at Cheltenham, where he found himself with too much to do after a first-flight error. Ridden more prominently, he moved to the front after the third last and the race was effectively over from that point. He was eased down on the run-in and was value for even further. *(tchd 3-1)*

Fandani(GER) was 7lb better off with today's winner on their meeting at Stratford in May, but he was beaten over ten lengths further. This was still a solid run, however. *(op 11-2)*

Odiham was a useful stayer on the Flat, in a visor latterly, and this was a promising start to his hurdles career. He lost his pitch after an error in the back straight, but was staying on in the latter stages and would have been second with a bit further to run. A step up in trip should suit him. *(op 9-1 tchd 10-1)*

Herakles(GER), held up on his debut, this time made the running and his jumping was a lot better, but he had no answer when the winner cruised past him at the first in the straight. *(op 16-1)*

Some Touch(IRE) was a smart bumper performer, runner-up to The Cool Guy at Aintree on Grand National day on his latest start. He showed promise on this introduction to hurdling, if fading from the third last, and can do better with the experience behind him. *(op 7-2 tchd 3-1)*

Dance World, a fair middle-distance handicapper on the Flat, ran a respectable race in this warm company on his hurdling debut. He should be up to winning in lesser grade.

Able Baker Charlie(IRE), a useful handicapper on the Flat, gained his most recent win over ten furlongs at this track in July. He was the subject of encouraging reports prior to this debut over hurdles, but was held when coming down at the second last. He would probably have made the frame and is worth another chance, although he still has his stamina to prove. *(op 7-2)*

2488 SODEXHO PRESTIGE NOVICES' H'CAP CHASE (15 fncs) 2m 2f 110y

1:05 (1:06) (Class 3) (0-125,125) 4-Y-0+ **£11,223** (£3,315; £1,657; £829; £413; £207)

Form | | | | RPR

13- **1** **Taranis (FR)**[293] [3719] 4-10-9 121 RWalsh 130+
(P F Nicholls) *h.d.w: lw: hld up in tch: jnd ldr appr 11th: led after 3 out: sn clr: blnd last: comf* **7/2**[2]

2442 **2** 9 **Escompteur (FR)**[139] [946] 5-11-2 115 TJMurphy 123+
(M C Pipe) *lw: chsd ldrs: jnd ldr 7th: lft in ld 9th: rdn and hdd after 3 out: kpt on but no ch w wnr* **9/4**[1]

2-22 **3** 3 **Montgermont (FR)**[30] [1891] 5-11-12 125 AThornton 134+
(Mrs L C Taylor) *chsd ldrs: hit 2nd: led briefly and blnd 6th: hmpd 9th: hit 4 out: sn rdn: lft 4th 2 out: kpt on same pce* **5/1**[3]

01-2 **4** 1/2 **Kawagino (IRE)**[21] [2047] 5-10-11 110 PHide 120+
(J W Mullins) *nt a fluent: stmbld bdly 1st: hld up: hmpd 4th and 9th: hdwy after 10th: blnd 4 out: sn rdn: styd on fr 2 out* **20/1**

44-2 **5** 4 **Nadover (FR)**[20] [2078] 4-10-1 113 PMoloney 99
(C J Mann) *lw: mid div: tk clsr order appr 11th: rdn appr 4 out: one pced after* **6/1**

6-15 **6** 1 1/4 **O'Toole (IRE)**[21] [2044] 6-11-4 117 RJohnson 115+
(P J Hobbs) *hld up: hdwy to trck ldrs 10th: rdn after 4 out: lft 3rd 2 out: wknd last* **33/1**

4-PF **F** **Misty Dancer**[18] [2100] 6-10-10 109 SThomas —
(Miss Venetia Williams) *led tl fell 9th* **66/1**

14-P **P** **Wizard Of Edge**[25] [1971] 5-11-7 120 JamesDavies —
(R J Hodges) *a towards rr: lost tch fr 10th: t.o and p.u bef 3 out* **66/1**

-P60 **P** **Scotch Corner (IRE)**[15] [2170] 7-10-0 99 oh3 CLlewellyn —
(N A Twiston-Davies) *j.rt 4th: lost tch fr 8th: t.o and p.u bef 11th* **25/1**

P-63 **F** **Gaelic Flight (IRE)**[18] 2103 7-9-13 **103**.......... WKennedy(5) 106+
(Noel T Chance) *j.lft thrght: hld up: mstke 9th: hdwy after next: cl 3rd and rdn whn fell 2 out* **33/1**

/05- **P** **Royal Katidoki (FR)**[294] 3694 5-11-2 **115**.......... (t) MAFitzgerald —
(N J Henderson) *chsd ldrs: nt fluent 5th (water): rdn and wknd qckly 4 out: p.u bef next* **6/1**

4m 33.8s (-7.60) **Going Correction** -0.275s/f (Good) 11 Ran SP% **115.7**
WFA 4 from 5yo+ 12lb
Speed ratings: **105,101,99,99,98 97,—,—,—,—** — CSF £11.30 CT £37.88 TOTE £5.10: £2.10, £1.70, £2.10; EX 14.50.
Owner Foster Yeoman Limited **Bred** P De Maleissye Melun **Trained** Ditcheat, Somerset

FOCUS
Quite a competitive event, run at a decent pace, but it was littered with jumping errors.The winner has been rated as value for 15 lengths with the runner-up the best guide to the level.

NOTEBOOK
Taranis(FR) ◆ made an impressive chasing debut on this first start since February. Striking the front after the final ditch, he was already going clear when he walked through the last fence, but the blunder failed to stop his momentum and he coasted home with his ears pricked. This was a big step up on his hurdles form and there is better to come.
Escompteur(FR), absent since July, ran a solid race but could do nothing about it when the eventual winner headed him in the straight. He is currently rated 11lb better over hurdles and this was his best chase run to date, but he now has seven seconds to his name over fences and has yet to get his head in front. *(op 7-2)*
Montgermont(FR), down slightly in trip, made several jumping errors and had to settle for place money again. He needs softer ground. *(op 6-1 tchd 13-2)*
Kawagino(IRE) did well to complete on this chasing debut, as he had a nightmare round following a stumble at the first. He was keeping on steadily at the end over this longer trip and can win off this mark if the fences do not get in the way. *(op 25-1)*
Nadover(FR) was slightly disappointing on this second run over fences in this country. He became a little outpaced as the leaders quickened and could only keep on without landing a blow thereafter. *(op 7-1)*
O'Toole(IRE) ran a decent race on this second run over fences and was still in third spot when making a tired error at the last. This ground was slower than ideal for him.
Royal Katidoki(FR), lightly raced over hurdles, did not jump particularly well on this chase debut but was close enough until weakening quickly at the first in the home straight. It appears that his *breathing problem resurfaced, despite the use of a tongue tie.Official explanation: jockey said gelding had a breathing problem (tchd 40-1)*
Gaelic Flight(IRE), back over fences, jumped out to his left for most of the way and came down when doing so at the second last. He was in third place at the time and would probably have made the frame, although he was not going to trouble the easy winner. *(tchd 40-1)*

2489 UK HYGIENE H'CAP CHASE (FOR THE JIM JOEL MEMORIAL TROPHY) (13 fncs) 2m 1f
1:35 (1:37) (Class 2) (0-145,145) 5-Y-0+

£21,920 (£6,475; £3,237; £1,620; £808; £406)

Form RPR

F-62 **1** **Town Crier (IRE)**[35] 1823 10-11-4 **137**.......... DElsworth 154+
(Mrs S J Smith) *trckd ldrs: hit 5th and 4 out: chal 3 out: sn led: comf* **16/1**

46-3 **2** 2 ½ **Made In Japan (JPN)**[15] 2163 5-11-6 **139**.......... (b) RJohnson 151
(P J Hobbs) *lw: chsd ldrs: rdn fr 4 out: hit 2 out: styd on u.p but nvr gng pce to trble wnr* **5/1**[1]

1FP- **3** 1 ½ **Le Seychellois (FR)**[280] 3954 5-11-0 **133**.......... RWalsh 144+
(P F Nicholls) *lw: hld up in rr: hit 7th: hdwy 4 out: kpt on u.p fr 2 out and r.o run-in: nt rch ldrs* **8/1**

000- **4** 1 **Non So (FR)**[233] 4751 7-11-6 **139**.......... APMcCoy 149+
(N J Henderson) *hld up in rr: hit 6th: hdwy to trck ldrs whn blnd 9th: chsd ldrs fr 4 out: one pce fr 2 out* **15/2**

2-23 **5** hd **Bleu Superbe (FR)**[7] 2339 10-10-10 **129**.......... SThomas 139+
(Miss Venetia Williams) *led: hit 1st: sn hdd: chsd ldr: led again 9th: hit 4 out: hdd sn after next: kpt on same pce u.p* **11/1**

P-F2 **6** 11 **Tanikos (FR)**[17] 2128 6-10-6 **125**.......... ATinkler 123
(N J Henderson) *chsd ldrs: rdn 4 out: wknd next* **22/1**

-243 **7** 4 **Pak Jack (FR)**[28] 1918 5-10-4 **123**.......... TJMurphy 117
(P J Hobbs) *bhd: styd on fr 3 out but nvr in contention* **11/1**

05-6 **8** 7 **Master Rex**[28] 1919 10-11-2 **135**.......... BFenton 122
(B De Haan) *blnd 5th: hit 6th: wl bhd 8th: mod hdwy fr 3 out* **16/1**

P-01 **9** 2 ½ **Caracciola (GER)**[28] 1919 8-11-10 **143**.......... MAFitzgerald 131+
(N J Henderson) *hit 5th: sn in tch: hdwy to chse ldrs 9th: wknd after 4 out* **11/2**[2]

2-42 **10** 2 ½ **Almaydan**[29] 1913 7-11-2 **135**.......... TDoyle 119+
(R Lee) *hit 2nd: reminders: effrt 8th: sn wknd: no ch whn veered lft 3 out* **8/1**

0-00 **11** 24 **Colca Canyon (IRE)**[7] 2346 8-10-13 **137**.......... (p) SCurling(5) 95
(David P Myerscough, Ire) *a bhd* **40/1**

F-5P **P** **Bonus Bridge (IRE)**[42] 1739 10-10-12 **131**.......... AThornton —
(H D Daly) *lw: bhd: hit 4th: blnd 5th and sn p.u* **33/1**

1-5P **F** **Gazump (FR)**[13] 2210 7-10-1 **120**.......... (b[1]) CLlewellyn —
(N A Twiston-Davies) *ld after 1st: hdd 9th: wkng whn crossed and fell 3 out* **33/1**

U2-0 **P** **Kadount (FR)**[25] 1970 7-11-10 **143**.......... RThornton —
(A King) *lw: in tch: hdwy 7th: rdn and wknd fr 9th: no ch whn bdly hmpd and p.u 3 out* **7/1**[3]

4m 1.20s (-8.20) **Going Correction** -0.275s/f (Good) 14 Ran SP% **119.6**
Speed ratings: **108,106,106,105,105 100,98,95,94,92 81,—,—,—** CSF £92.82 CT £706.20 TOTE £12.60: £3.80, £2.00, £3.50; EX 38.40.
Owner Trevor Hemmings **Bred** Frank Tobin **Trained** High Eldwick, W Yorks

FOCUS
Rock-solid handicap form, in a race run at a good tempo. The winner is rated value for further with the fifth the best guide to the level and the form looks solid.

NOTEBOOK
Town Crier(IRE), back over fences, took the lead travelling well after the third last and only had to be nudged along from that point. Value for double the winning margin, he may be able to defy a higher mark.
Made In Japan(JPN) made Johnson earn his fee as he needed to come under pressure some way out, but he stayed on well after the last to get the best of the tussle for second. This was a good effort and he looks ready for another try over two and a half miles. *(op 6-1)*
Le Seychellois(FR) ◆, off the track since February, made a promising return although he did not pick up quite as well as he had promised when moving into contention. This was his best run so far over fences and he is capable of better yet.
Non So(FR) had a frustrating time of it last term, losing his way after a couple of luckless falls. He still looked to lack confidence in his jumping, but this was an encouraging return to action. Having said that, he does go well fresh. *(tchd 7-1)*
Bleu Superbe(FR), just a pound lower, ran his race again and was still in second place over the last before being run out of the frame. *(op 12-1)*
Tanikos(FR) usually goes off in front but had to chase the pace here. He ran respectably but faded from the third last. *(op 25-1)*
Pak Jack(FR) never got into the action and again shaped as if in need of further. *(op 12-1)*
Caracciola(GER), the shortest-priced of Henderson's three, was 11lb higher than when scoring over hurdles last time. He could not go with the leaders from the fourth last. *(op 6-1 tchd 13-2 in a place)*
Kadount(FR) *Official explanation: jockey said gelding never travelled (op 6-1)*

2490 BALLYMORE PROPERTIES LONG DISTANCE HURDLE GRADE 2 (13 hdls) 3m 110y
2:05 (2:06) (Class 1) 4-Y-0+

£22,808 (£8,556; £4,284; £2,136; £1,072; £536)

Form RPR

12-1 **1** **Inglis Drever**[28] 1925 6-11-8 163.......... GLee 162+
(J Howard Johnson) *lw: hld up bhd ldng pair: niggled along after 9th: jnd ldr after 3 out: led sn after next: wnt lft at last: styd on wl: pus* **8/13**[1]

112- **2** 1 ¼ **Baracouda (FR)**[254] 4409 10-11-8.......... APMcCoy 160+
(F Doumen, France) *lw: hld up bhd: stdy prog fr 9th: wnt 3rd after 3 out: 3l down last: rdn and effrt run-in: styd on but no ex fnl 75yds* **3/1**[2]

P3-4 **3** 3 **Crystal D'Ainay (FR)**[28] 1925 6-11-8 159.......... RThornton 157
(A King) *trckd ldr: led appr 3 out: hdd and rdn after 2 out: nt fluent last: kpt on same pce* **16/1**

256- **4** 24 **Korelo (FR)**[233] 4747 7-11-0 157.......... TJMurphy 125
(M C Pipe) *hld up in tch: nt fluent 8th: rdn after next: sn outpcd* **15/2**[3]

-1P0 **5** 8 **Carlys Quest**[14] 2175 11-11-8 144.......... KJMercer 125
(Ferdy Murphy) *hld up in tch: dropped rr 6th: nvr a danger after* **100/1**

1044 **6** 3 ½ **Mr Cool**[8] 2326 11-11-0 144.......... RGreene 114
(M C Pipe) *led tl 3 out: wknd* **50/1**

5m 49.3s (-12.80) **Going Correction** -0.275s/f (Good) 6 Ran SP% **107.5**
Speed ratings: **109,108,107,99,97 96** CSF £2.51 TOTE £1.70: £1.20, £1.50; EX 2.10.
Owner Andrea & Graham Wylie **Bred** R J McAlpine And D O Pickering **Trained** Billy Row, Co Durham

FOCUS
The winning time was merely acceptable for a race of its type given the sound surface. This was a high-class renewal, the third sets the standard and the first two can rate even higher this season.

NOTEBOOK
Inglis Drever raced in third place for much of the way and was still half a dozen lengths behind the leading pair turning into the home straight, where he briefly hit a flat spot. Soon back on the bridle and showing ahead after the third last, he edged to his right between the last two flights before veering left on the approach to the obstacle. Straightened up on the run-in, he found plenty to hold off his old rival. His World Hurdle crown is going to take some dislodging. *(tchd 4-7 and 4-6)*
Baracouda(FR), winner of this event for the last two years, was not sent off favourite for the first time since his British debut nearly five years ago. Set a lot to do as usual, he was only third over the last but closed the gap on Inglis Drever on the run-in and finished closer to him than he had at Cheltenham. His rival had race fitness on his side and this was a fine return to action, but it is hard to see him beating the younger horse in the World Hurdle. *(op 11-4)*
Crystal D'Ainay(FR) tracked the pacesetting Mr Cool before jumping ahead at the third last, but he was soon headed by the favourite. Still in second over the final flight, he ran up to his best and is set to stay over hurdles in the near future. There should be a nice prize for him this term if he can avoid the two who beat him here. *(op 18-1)*
Korelo(FR) was in receipt of 8lb from this principals on this seasonal bow but was still found wanting, although he was keeping on at the end. He could prove hard to place this season. *(op 7-1 tchd 8-1)*
Carlys Quest, who needs soft ground, is not up to tackling this sort of company. *(tchd 125-1 in a place)*
Mr Cool made the running at just a fair gallop, and got in too close to the fifth last as Greene tried to lift the tempo. He was soon on the retreat once headed and was relegated two places on the run-in.

2491 HENNESSY COGNAC GOLD CUP CHASE (H'CAP) GRADE 3 (21 fncs) 3m 2f 110y
2:40 (2:42) (Class 1) 5-Y-0+

£71,275 (£26,737; £13,387; £6,675; £3,350; £1,675)

Form RPR

221- **1** **Trabolgan (IRE)**[255] 4395 7-11-12 **151**.......... MAFitzgerald 168+
(N J Henderson) *lw: trckd ldrs: blnd 13th:hit 17th:chal fr 4 out tl slt ld 2 out: r.o strly whn chal run-in: forged clr cl home* **13/2**[2]

143- **2** 2 ½ **L'Ami (FR)**[20] 2086 6-11-5 **144**.......... DJCasey 155
(F Doumen, France) *lw: trckd ldrs: chal 4 out: slt ld next and gng wl: narrowly hdd 2 out: upsides last: swtchd rt run-in and nt qckn w wnr* **10/1**

332- **3** 1 ¾ **Cornish Rebel (IRE)**[224] 4861 8-11-11 **150**.......... RWalsh 162+
(P F Nicholls) *lw: hld up in rr: hit 10th: hdwy 13th: hmpd 15th: hit 17th: n.m.r and lost position after 17th:styd on wl fr 2 out:one pce* **11/2**[1]

2P6- **4** 1 ½ **Comply Or Die (IRE)**[217] 4984 6-11-7 **146**.......... TJMurphy 155+
(M C Pipe) *lw: mid-div: hdwy 13th: chsd ldrs fr 15th: chalng whn hit 4 out: styd on same pce fr 2 out* **12/1**

3-U1 **5** 1 ½ **All In The Stars (IRE)**[13] 2215 7-9-8 **126** oh3 ow1.......... DJacob(7) 136+
(D P Keane) *lw: bhd: hit 12th: hmpd 16th: blnd 17th: hdwy 4 out: blnd 3 out: kpt on wl fr 2 out: fin strly: nt rch ldrs* **14/1**

12-2 **6** 1 ½ **Red Devil Robert (IRE)**[21] 2054 7-10-12 **137**.......... JTizzard 143+
(P F Nicholls) *lw: chsd ldrs: hit 12th: rdn and mistake 17th: rdn 4 out: one pce fr 3 out* **10/1**

31-1 **7** ½ **Run For Paddy**[42] 1735 9-10-13 **138**.......... PMoloney 143
(M Pitman) *bhd: hmpd 16th: stl plenty to do 3 out: kpt on fr 2 out: fin wl but nt rch ldrs* **40/1**

0-2F **8** 4 **Redemption**[14] 2177 10-10-11 **136**.......... CLlewellyn 138+
(N A Twiston-Davies) *bhd: stdy hdwy fr 16th: chsd ldrs 4 out: sn rdn: wknd fr 2 out* **12/1**

-511 **9** dist **St Matthew (USA)**[7] 2336 7-10-9 **134**.......... PWhelan —
(Mrs S J Smith) *chsd ldrs: hit 12th and 14th: wknd fr 17th: t.o* **33/1**

-113 **10** 5 **Ballycassidy (IRE)**[133] 1013 9-11-6 **145**.......... RJohnson 138+
(P Bowen) *chsd ldrs: led 7th: hdd sn after 4 out: wknd qckly: t.o* **33/1**

1-2U **11** 1 ¾ **Joes Edge (IRE)**[28] 1926 8-11-2 **144**.......... KJMercer(3) —
(Ferdy Murphy) *bhd: hmpd 16th: no ch whn blnd 3 out: t.o* **50/1**

11-P **12** 4 **Lord Of Illusion (IRE)**[15] 2166 8-10-13 **138**.......... JMMaguire —
(T R George) *led: hit 9th: hdd 17th: sn wknd: t.o* **20/1**

P-2U **P** **Colourful Life (IRE)**[28] 1926 9-10-8 **140**.......... LHeard(7) —
(P F Nicholls) *a bhd: blnd 17th: t.o whn p.u bef 2 out* **100/1**

00-1 **P** **Iris Bleu (FR)**[21] 2054 9-11-3 **142**.......... APMcCoy —
(M C Pipe) *bhd: bmpd 7th: hit 9th and 12th: t.o whn p.u bef 16th* **14/1**

21-4 **U** **King Harald (IRE)**[14] 2176 7-10-9 **134**.......... MBatchelor —
(M Bradstock) *chsd ldr to 13th: 6th and one pce whn blnd and uns rdr 15th* **17/2**[3]

1411 **F** **Ross Comm**[27] 1941 9-10-10 **135**.......... DElsworth —
(Mrs S J Smith) *in tch: chsd ldrs and hit 13th: stl wl there whn blnd and fell 16th* **25/1**

32-3 **P** **Kandjar D'Allier (FR)**[14] [2177] 7-10-10 **135**.......................... RThornton —
(A King) *blnd 2nd: bhd: hdwy 11th: hit 14th: wknd 16th: t.o whn p.u bef 2 out* **9/1**

4-0P **P** **Tribal Venture (FR)**[14] [2176] 7-10-11 **136**.......................... GLee —
(Ferdy Murphy) *bhd: rdn and hdwy into mid-div after 11th: wknd 14th: t.o whn p.u after 17th* **66/1**

11-P **P** **Distant Thunder (IRE)**[21] [2054] 7-10-9 **134**.......................... AThornton —
(R H Alner) *bhd: hit 12th: hdwy 14th: chsd ldrs after 16th: wknd after next: t.o whn p.u last* **16/1**

6m 31.7s (-14.90) **Going Correction** -0.275s/f (Good) **19** Ran SP% **123.4**
Speed ratings: **111,110,109,109,108 108,108,107,—,— —,—,—,—,— —,—,—,—** CSF £65.09 CT £390.73 TOTE £7.20: £2.80, £3.40, £2.20, £3.50; EX 97.50 Trifecta £683.60 Pool: £16,466.35 - 17.10 winning tickets..
Owner Trevor Hemmings **Bred** Michael Lysaght **Trained** Upper Lambourn, Berks
■ A first Hennessy for both Nicky Henderson and Mick Fitzgerald, the latter back from a neck injury only days previously.

FOCUS
A fair winning time for a race of this class given the conditions. The weights were raised 9lb at the overnight stage following the defections of Celestial Gold, Our Vic and Forget The Past. The first four home were the first four in last season's Royal & SunAlliance Chase, albeit in a slightly revised order, and this is very solid form, although the overall level is the lowest in at least 11 years. Trabolgan improved on his Festival form by 8lb and was value for a bit further.

NOTEBOOK
Trabolgan(IRE) put up a fine weight-carrying performance, becoming the first topweight to win this event since Burrough Hill Lad in 1984. Always well placed, he loomed alongside L'Ami in the straight but Fitzgerald did not want to commit too soon and it was only after the last that he asserted, scoring with a bit to spare. Confirming the form of his Royal & SunAlliance victory, he *looks genuine Gold Cup material and we will know more after the King George at Sandown. (op 11-2)*
L'Ami(FR), fourth to Trabolgan at Cheltenham, has been third twice at Auteuil this autumn, most recently in the Grade 1 Prix La Haye Jousselin. After showing narrowly in front three from home, it quickly became apparent that the winner alongside him was going the better and he was forced to concede defeat on the run-in. This was a fine performance on ground that was faster than he would have liked. *(op 9-1)*
Cornish Rebel(IRE) was only a pound better off with Trabolgan for a six-length beating in the SunAlliance, but he stepped up on that form over a track he likes. Staying on well from the second last, he goes to the Welsh National with bright prospects now and in the long term looks the sort for the Grand National at Aintree. *(op 8-1)*
Comply Or Die(IRE), runner-up in the Royal & SunAlliance, was 5lb better off for three lengths with Trabolgan. Representing last year's winning connections, he ran a sound race on this seasonal bow but was not helped by a couple of jumping errors and could not quicken up over the last two fences. *(op 10-1)*
All In The Stars(IRE) went up 9lb for winning at Fontwell and, 3lb out of the handicap here, was effectively 5lb well in with the overweight taken into account. Racing in the last three, he got away with a couple of mistakes and was staying on very strongly from the second last, suggesting that a return to further will suit. *(op 16-1)*
Red Devil Robert(IRE), discarded by Ruby Walsh in favour of Cornish Rebel, travelled strongly as usual but just failed to see out the trip. Three miles will not be a problem and his trainer sees him as just the type for the Topham Trophy at Aintree over two miles five and a half furlongs.
Run For Paddy had ground conditions as he likes them and did best of the established handicappers, staying on from the rear without ever reaching the leaders.
Redemption put in a clear round of jumping and made up ground from the rear to look a danger at the Cross Fence, but he did not see out the trip. *(tchd 14-1)*
Ballycassidy(IRE) was still narrowly in front over the fourth last but finished well beaten in the end, in common with the others who forced the pace. *(tchd 40-1)*
Iris Bleu(FR), always trailing, was pulled up when out of contention with six to jump. *(op 9-1)*
Kandjar D'Allier(FR), off the same mark as when third in the Paddy Power, did not jump well and was in the rear division before being pulled up two out. This did not tell us whether or not he stayed this longer trip. *(op 9-1)*
King Harald(IRE), in second place for the first circuit, had lost that position but was still in touch when blundering away his rider seven out. *(op 9-1)*
Ross Comm, another 13lb higher, was still in the thick of things when departing. *(op 9-1)*
Distant Thunder(IRE) latched on to the leading bunch turning out of the back straight, still going well, but was outpaced with three to jump and behind when pulled up before the last. He has something to prove now. *(op 9-1)*

2492 LADBROKES.COM H'CAP CHASE (16 fncs) 2m 4f
3:15 (3:19) (Class 2) (0-145,145) 5-Y-0+
£31,315 (£9,250; £4,625; £2,315; £1,155; £580)

Form RPR

-221 **1** **Bold Bishop (IRE)**[15] [2163] 8-11-3 **136**.......................... APMcCoy 153+
(Jonjo O'Neill) *hld up towards rr: gd hdwy on inner appr 4 out: rdn to ld last: kpt on wl: rdn out* **7/1**

0-0P **2** *¾* **Europa**[34] [1846] 9-10-12 **131**.......................... JMMaguire 146+
(Ferdy Murphy) *hld up towards rr: hdwy after 12th to chse ldrs: led after 3 out: narrowly hdd last: kpt on but no ex cl home* **25/1**

/121 **3** *8* **Black De Bessy (FR)**[21] [2051] 7-10-3 **122**.......................... RWalford 129+
(D R C Elsworth) *mid div: lost pl and towards rr after 11th: styd on again u.p fr 3 out: wnt 3rd run-in* **3/1**[1]

53-4 **4** *¾* **Le Passing (FR)**[28] [1924] 6-11-9 **142**..........................(b[1]) RWalsh 147
(P F Nicholls) *in tch: hdwy to trck ldrs 12th: rdn after 4 out: kpt on same pce* **17/2**

323- **5** *½* **Kelrev (FR)**[273] [4068] 7-10-9 **128**.......................... SThomas 134+
(Miss Venetia Williams) *lw: in tch: trckd ldr 8th: led 4 out: rdn and hdd after 3 out: one pced fr next* **22/1**

13P- **6** *8* **Chauvinist (IRE)**[232] [4761] 10-11-4 **137**.......................... MAFitzgerald 139+
(N J Henderson) *lw: led: hit 9th: hdd and mstke 4 out: sn rdn: wknd after next* **10/1**

3-P4 **7** *7* **Spring Grove (IRE)**[21] [2048] 10-10-9 **128**.......................... AThornton 118
(R H Alner) *mid div tl dropped rr after 11th* **25/1**

240- **8** *2½* **Claymore (IRE)**[287] [3807] 9-11-3 **136**.......................... GLee 126+
(O Sherwood) *lw: mid div: hit 9th: hdwy 12th: chsng ldrs whn mstke 4 out and next: wknd* **13/2**[3]

61-2 **9** *9* **Mixsterthetrixster (USA)**[211] [97] 9-11-3 **136**.......................... JTizzard 114
(Mrs Tracey Barfoot-Saunt) *chsd ldrs tl after 12th: sn wknd* **40/1**

2210 **10** *1¾* **Va Vavoom (IRE)**[13] [2208] 7-10-1 **120**.......................... CLlewellyn 97
(N A Twiston-Davies) *a towards rr* **33/1**

1F-3 **11** *27* **Supreme Prince (IRE)**[34] [1846] 8-11-12 **145**.......................... RJohnson 95
(P J Hobbs) *lw: in tch: rdn and effrt appr 4 out: wknd appr 3 out* **11/2**[2]

20P- **P** **Tana River (IRE)**[241] [4657] 9-10-12 **131**.......................... BFenton —
(Miss E C Lavelle) *mstke 2nd: a bhd: t.o and p.u after 11th* **20/1**

P-P1 **P** **Dark'n Sharp (GER)**[18] [2102] 10-11-4 **137**.......................... RThornton —
(R T Phillips) *lw: a towards rr: t.o and p.u bef 12th* **12/1**

5P-0 **P** **Jakari (FR)**[133] [1013] 8-11-1 **134**.......................... JEMoore —
(H D Daly) *lw: chsd ldr tl 10th: grad fdd: bhd and p.u bef 4 out* **25/1**

2-5P **U** **First Gold (FR)**[14] [2176] 12-11-12 **145**..........................(b) DJCasey —
(F Doumen, France) *chsd ldrs tl 11th: bhd whn blnd and uns rdr 3 out* **33/1**

02-0 **F** **Kalca Mome (FR)**[21] [2048] 7-10-7 **133**.......................... MrTJO'Brien(7) —
(P J Hobbs) *towards rr: nt fluent 5th (water): sme hdwy after 12th: wkng whn fell 3 out* **66/1**

4m 56.2s (-10.20) **Going Correction** -0.275s/f (Good) **16** Ran SP% **124.0**
Speed ratings: **109,108,105,105,105 101,99,98,94,93 82,—,—,—,— —** CSF £170.65 CT £647.75 TOTE £5.40: £1.70, £5.70, £1.60, £2.10; EX 323.10 TRIFECTA Not won..
Owner Mrs Gay Smith **Bred** Miss C Cunningham-Hogg **Trained** Cheltenham, Gloucs

FOCUS
Solid handicap form, which has been rated through the runner-up and third, and plenty of winners should come out of it. It was run at a good pace and the principals came from the rear.

NOTEBOOK
Bold Bishop(IRE), raised 7lb after Cheltenham, was well suited by the strong pace of this race and made good progress up the inside to strike the front at the last. Staying on dourly back over this longer trip, he is on the upgrade now and entitled to be regarded as one of the season's top novices on this run. *(op 8-1)*
Europa looked like becoming his owner's third winner of the afternoon when striking the front but he was collared at the final fence. Well handicapped now, he liked this ground and this was his best run since his third in last season's bonusprint.com Gold Cup at Cheltenham.
Black De Bessy(FR), raised 10lb after Wincanton, stayed on well over the last three fences but in truth never promised to get to the leaders. This was slightly disappointing and he looks unlikely to take up his engagement in the King George at Sandown, although the step up to three miles should suit him on this evidence. *(op 11-2)*
Le Passing(FR), blinkered for the first time, ran a sound race on ground that was faster than ideal but will probably remain vulnerable from this sort of mark. *(op 8-1 tchd 9-1 in a place)*
Kelrev(FR) tried to slip the field when going to the front four from home but was soon cut down. *His strike rate is poor, but he is quite well handicapped at present and one day he will last home. (op 25-1)*
Chauvinist(IRE), who sweated up at the start, set a brisk pace and paid for it in the end, but this was a satisfactory seasonal reappearance. *(op 8-1)*
Claymore(IRE) had been runner-up in this event in the past two runnings, and this was his first run over fences since last season's race. He ran well enough on this seasonal debut but mistakes at the first two fences in the home straight did for his chance. *(op 6-1)*
Mixsterthetrixster(USA) ran a decent race on this seasonal return until fading turning out of the back straight. *(op 33-1)*
Supreme Prince(IRE), last year's winner, was only 3lb higher than when taking the Vodafone Gold Cup over course and distance in March. He was close enough straightening up for home but was soon left behind by the principals. *(tchd 6-1)*
Dark'n Sharp(GER) *Official explanation: jockey said gelding unable to go fast early pace and made mistakes (op 10-1)*
First Gold(FR) had the blinkers back on for this second run of the season but ran another lacklustre race. He is not the horse he was and retirement cannot be far away. *(op 10-1)*

2493 STAN JAMES INTERMEDIATE HURDLE (A LIMITED H'CAP) (LISTED RACE) (8 hdls) 2m 110y
3:50 (3:51) (Class 1) (0-145,145) 4-Y-0+
£17,106 (£6,417; £3,213; £1,602; £804; £402)

Form RPR

00-5 **1** **Manorson (IRE)**[21] [2047] 6-10-9 **125**.......................... GLee 133+
(O Sherwood) *lw: mde all: rdn and styd on strly whn chal fr 2 out* **7/1**

25-3 **2** *3* **Dom D'Orgeval (FR)**[13] [2207] 5-10-4 **120** oh1.......................... RJohnson 125
(Nick Williams) *bhd: rdn fr 3 out: kpt on wl appr last to take 2nd run-in: no imp on wnr* **14/1**

105- **3** *nk* **Only Vintage (USA)**[233] [4752] 5-11-3 **133**.......................... TJMurphy 139+
(Miss H C Knight) *chsd wnr to 3rd: one pce 3 out: nt fluent next: kpt on again run-in* **28/1**

52-3 **4** *2* **Phar Bleu (FR)**[13] [2209] 4-11-8 **138**.......................... RWalsh 141
(P F Nicholls) *lw: t.k.h: chsd ldrs: drvn to chal 3 out: rdn next: wknd run-in* **5/2**[1]

2-24 **5** *¾* **Afrad (FR)**[42] [450] 4-10-11 **127**.......................... MAFitzgerald 130+
(N J Henderson) *chsd wnr fr 3rd: chal fr 3 out: stl upsides next and sn rdn: wknd run-in* **6/1**[3]

1-01 **6** *7* **Flying Enterprise (IRE)**[7] [2334] 5-11-7 **137**.......................... SThomas 132
(Miss Venetia Williams) *lw: rr but in tch: hdwy to chse ldrs 3 out: wknd fr 2 out* **12/1**

2-05 **7** *shd* **Cherub (GER)**[13] [2207] 5-11-0 **130**.......................... APMcCoy 125
(Jonjo O'Neill) *hld up rr but in tch: sme hdwy 3 out: sn rdn: wknd 2 out* **7/1**

112- **8** *6* **It's Just Harry**[322] [3276] 8-11-10 **140**.......................... RThornton 132+
(C R Egerton) *lw: blnd 1st: sn in tch: chsd ldrs fr 4th: wknd 3 out* **7/1**

10-0 **9** *12* **Migwell (FR)**[21] [2047] 5-10-7 **123**.......................... AThornton 104+
(Mrs L Wadham) *chsd ldrs to 4th: wknd after 4 out* **50/1**

132- **10** *2* **Dusky Warbler**[232] [4762] 6-11-8 **138**.......................... JEMoore 125+
(G L Moore) *lw: t.k.h: hld up rr but in tch: hdwy appr 3 out: sn rdn and wknd* **5/1**[2]

3m 53.7s (-9.90) **Going Correction** -0.275s/f (Good)
WFA 4 from 5yo+ 12lb **10** Ran SP% **116.8**
Speed ratings: **112,110,110,109,109 105,105,102,97,96** CSF £96.93 CT £2566.18 TOTE £8.20: £2.50, £4.10, £5.40; EX 119.60 TRIFECTA Not won. Place 6 £15.55, Place 5 £8.01.
Owner Byrne Bros (Formwork) Limited **Bred** Jeremy Hill **Trained** Upper Lambourn, Berks

FOCUS
A creditable winning time for a Listed hurdle, and this was a good handicap with the fourth the best guide to the level.

NOTEBOOK
Manorson(IRE) has had valid excuses for his defeats since landing back-to-back novice hurdles last season and he bounced back to form. Making all the running, he looked vulnerable between the last two flights but pulled out plenty when challenged. This is his ground. *(op 6-1)*
Dom D'Orgeval(FR)maintained his quietly progressive profile, staying on to go second on the flat. The return to further will be in his favour. *(op 16-1)*
Only Vintage(USA) became a little outpaced at the first in the straight, and was far from fluent at the next, but stayed on well after the last. Declared to make his chasing debut at Windsor's recent abandoned meeting, he should make a nice novice chaser. *(op 25-1)*
Phar Bleu(FR), raised a couple of pounds after a good reappearance at Cheltenham, ran his race again but did not seem to be helping his jockey between the last two flights. Easier ground is ideal for him. *(op 3-1 tchd 10-3)*
Afrad(FR) has improved on the Flat since his last hurdles run back in May but was well beaten when a heavily-backed favourite in the Cesarewitch last time. He looked a threat to the winner jumping the second last, but failed to go through with his effort and showed a high head carriage, although he still jumped the last in second place before fading. He is able but looks one to be wary of. *(tchd 11-2, 13-2 in a place)*
Flying Enterprise(IRE) was a comfortable winner of a jockeys' challenge race at Haydock last *time, but the ease of that victory flattered him and he was found wanting off a 9lb higher mark. (op 10-1)*

The Form Book, Raceform Ltd, Compton, RG20 6NL

It's Just Harry had been off the track since January, having sustained a stress fracture of a cannonbone and pulled muscles in his back when runner-up in the Tolworth Hurdle at Sandown. After surviving an error at the first, he faded over the last three flights. He needs further and is entitled to come on for the run. *(op 9-1)*
Dusky Warbler failed to settle in the early stages, then hung when brought under pressure in the home straight. A smart novice last season, he is surely better than this. *(op 9-2 tchd 4-1)*
T/Jkpt: £1,290.90 to a £1 stake. Pool: £10,000.00. 5.50 winning tickets. T/Plt: £17.50 to a £1 stake. Pool: £112,533.65. 4,680.75 winning tickets. T/Qpdt: £8.80 to a £1 stake. Pool: £6,726.70. 563.40 winning tickets. ST

2167 NEWCASTLE (L-H)
Saturday, November 26

OFFICIAL GOING: Good to soft changing to soft after race 5 (2.25)
After 1/2" rain overnight the ground was described as 'easy side of good'. Rain over the last three turned it to soft in the end.
Wind: Light 1/2 behind Weather: Fine at first, rain last three.

2494 FREECLAIM I.D.C. JUVENILE NOVICES' HURDLE (9 hdls) 2m
12:15 (12:16) (Class 3) 3-Y-O **£4,892** (£1,436; £718; £358)

Form				RPR
	1		**Renada**[43] 3-9-12 ... BSHughes(7) *(J Howard Johnson) chsd ldrs: hit 2nd: effrt 3 out: led after last: rdn and r.o* **4/1**[2]	68+
3P6	2	1 1/4	**Dennick**[15] 2167 3-10-12 ... (t) FKeniry *(P C Haslam) led: rdn whn hit last: sn hdd: kpt on same pce* **7/1**[3]	75+
05	3	4	**Kalawoun (FR)**[15] 2167 3-10-5 ... TJDreaper(7) *(Ferdy Murphy) hld up: hdwy to chse ldrs bef 3 out: outpcd appr next: kpt on fr last: no imp* **12/1**	71+
0	4	1/2	**Calfraz**[37] 1797 3-10-12 ... NPMulholland *(M D Hammond) chsd ldrs: outpcd after 4 out: kpt on fr 2 out: no imp* **28/1**	70
0	5	dist	**No Commission (IRE)**[37] 1797 3-10-12 ... ADobbin *(R F Fisher) hld up in tch: outpcd after 4 out: sn btn* **11/1**	—
P	6	nk	**With Honours**[15] 2167 3-10-5 ... ADempsey *(T J Fitzgerald) hld up: outpcd 1/2-way: nvr on terms* **80/1**	—
5	7	dist	**Rossin Gold (IRE)**[23] 2001 3-10-12 ... KRenwick *(P Monteith) keen: chsd ldrs: outpcd after 4 out: btn next* **2/1**[1]	—
	P		**Firmount (IRE)**[21] 3-10-12 ... ARoss *(B S Rothwell) bhd: lost tch fr 3rd: t.o whn p.u bef 3 out* **50/1**	—
	P		**Swell Lad**[193] 3-10-12 ... TScudamore *(S Gollings) cl up tl wknd qckly 5th: t.o whn p.u bef 3 out* **15/2**	—
336	P		**Verstone (IRE)**[29] 1904 3-10-5 ... RMcGrath *(R F Fisher) bhd: hdwy u.p 4 out: wknd bef next: t.o whn p.u bef last* **7/1**[3]	—

4m 14.4s (8.10) **Going Correction** +0.025s/f (Yiel) **10** Ran SP% **112.8**
Speed ratings: **80,79,77,77,—** —,—,—,—,— CSF £30.73 TOTE £4.50: £3.00, £2.70, £2.50; EX 37.30.
Owner Andrea & Graham Wylie **Bred** The Thoroughbred Corporation **Trained** Billy Row, Co Durham
■ The first winner in Britain and over hurdles for Brian Hughes, who rode 19 on the Flat in Ireland.

FOCUS
A modest event and a steady gallop meant a very slow winning time, even for a race like this. the runner-up sets the standard.

NOTEBOOK
Renada, who had shown modest Flat form, showed the right attitude to win on this hurdle debut. Although this form is ordinary, she appeals as the type to improve, especially granted a stiffer test of stamina in ordinary handicaps. *(op 7-2)*
Dennick, fitted with the first time tongue-tie, settled better than he had done over course and distance last time and turned in an improved effort. He is likely to remain vulnerable in this grade against unexposed types but looks capable of winning a small event. *(op 6-1)*
Kalawoun(FR), who finished in front of the runner-up over course and distance last time, failed to confirm those placings but left the impression that the step up in trip and the switch to handicaps should suit. *(op 10-1)*
Calfraz bettered the form of his hurdle debut and left the impression a stiffer test of stamina would suit but he is likely to remain vulnerable to progressive or unexposed sorts in this type of event.
No Commission(IRE) failed by a long chalk to build on the form of his hurdle debut and, although he may do better on a sounder surface, is likely to remain vulnerable in this type of race.
Rossin Gold(IRE), who was not disgraced in a race that threw up winners on his hurdle debut, proved a big disappointment in this modest event. While he is likely to remain vulnerable in this grade, *his stable has yet to hit form and he is not one to write off yet.Official explanation: jockey said gelding finished distressed (op 5-2 tchd 15-8)*

2495 GOSFORTH DECORATING AND BUILDING SERVICES H'CAP CHASE (18 fncs) 3m
12:50 (12:50) (Class 4) (0-100,98) 5-Y-O+ **£3,604** (£1,058; £529; £264)

Form				RPR
4-00	1		**Almire Du Lia (FR)**[15] 2170 7-11-8 94 ... (v) KRenwick *(Mrs S C Bradburne) chsd ldrs: led 11th to 5 out: led bef 3 out: rdn and hung rt run in: all out* **25/1**	108
43-6	2	hd	**Moscow Leader (IRE)**[11] 2259 7-11-5 94 ... (p) LMcGrath(3) *(R C Guest) hld up outside: hdwy and prom 1/2-way: led 5 out: nt fluent next: hdd bef 3 out: kpt on wl fr last: jst hld* **8/1**	109+
2P-5	3	10	**Gangsters R Us (IRE)**[37] 1795 9-11-11 97 ... ADempsey *(A Parker) hld up: stdy hdwy fr 1/2-way: chsng ldrs bef 4 out: rdn next: one pce fnl 2* **15/2**[3]	101
3P/5	4	2 1/2	**Kung Hei Fat Choi (IRE)**[15] 2170 10-11-0 86 ... RMcGrath *(J S Goldie) hld up: hdwy and in tch bef 4 out: no imp fr next* **14/1**	87
3P-R	5	9	**Jimmys Duky (IRE)**[18] 2109 7-9-9 72 ... DCCostello(5) *(D M Forster) keen: in tch: effrt after 5 out: outpcd fr 3 out* **14/1**	64
/65U	6	2	**Get Smart (IRE)**[12] 2248 8-10-6 78 ... WHutchinson *(Ferdy Murphy) hld up: rdn after 5 out: nvr rchd ldrs* **7/1**[2]	68
403	7	15	**Glenfarclas Boy (IRE)**[15] 2172 9-11-1 90 ... (p) PBuchanan(3) *(Miss Lucinda V Russell) chsd ldrs: outpcd bef 11th: n.d after* **14/1**	65
0/P6	8	3 1/2	**Minsgill Glen**[35] 1837 9-9-9 72 oh13 ... MJMcAlister(5) *(Mrs J K M Oliver) mstkes: prom tl lost pl 7th: struggling fr 10th* **100/1**	44
14PP	9	dist	**Helvetius**[37] 1795 9-11-9 95 ... BHarding *(W T Reed) a bhd: struggling fnl circ* **20/1**	—
1405	P		**Ta Ta For Now**[4] 2413 8-11-3 89 ... DO'Meara *(Mrs S C Bradburne) outpcd and p.u bef 3rd* **20/1**	—
F/P6	P		**Eyze (IRE)**[21] 2037 9-11-0 86 ... NPMulholland *(B Mactaggart) led to 6th: p.u qckly bef 9th* **12/1**	—
0011	U		**Devondale (IRE)**[15] 2170 9-11-1 94 ... PJMcDonald(7) *(Ferdy Murphy) in tch whn stmbld and uns rdr 1st* **11/4**[1]	—
P-14	P		**Diamond Cottage (IRE)**[203] 211 10-11-0 86 ... ARoss *(S B Bell) midfield: outpcd 13th: sn btn: p.u bef 4 out* **9/1**	—
P605	P		**Sea Maize**[9] 2290 7-9-11 72 oh10 ... (b) PAspell(3) *(C R Wilson) cl up: led 6th tl hit and hdd 11th: wknd 5 out: t.o whn p.u bef last* **66/1**	—

6m 19.5s (-5.30) **Going Correction** -0.30s/f (Good) **14** Ran SP% **115.6**
Speed ratings: **96,95,92,91,88 88,83,81,—,—** —,—,—,— CSF £199.60 CT £1661.64 TOTE £46.50: £7.90, £2.50, £1.80; EX 374.20.
Owner Hardie, Cochrane, Paterson & Steel **Bred** Alain Trepeu, And Valerie Dasque **Trained** Cunnoquhie, Fife

FOCUS
A race comprising mainly disappointing sorts and the one in-form and progressive runner departed at the first fence. The pace was sound and the third and fourth are the best guides to the level of the form.

NOTEBOOK
Almire Du Lia(FR) ran easily his best race of the year and took his tally at this course to three wins from four starts over obstacles. Stamina is clearly his strong suit but his record suggests he is no *certainty to reproduce this next time.Official explanation: trainer said, regarding the improved form shown, she could offer no explanation other than gelding had taken first two runs of the season to get fit. (op 28-1)*
Moscow Leader(IRE), who showed he retained ability after a long break at Fakenham last time, duly bettered that effort. He pulled clear of the remainder and looks capable of winning a similar event this winter. *(op 10-1)*
Gangsters R Us(IRE) is on a fair mark at present and again travelled strongly for a long way back over this longer trip. He should be spot-on now and will be of interest on quicker ground returned to Musselburgh, the scene of his three chase wins, in the near future. *(op 9-1)*
Kung Hei Fat Choi(IRE) was anything but disgraced and should now be spot-on after two starts following a lengthy break. He is certainly on a fair mark and is one to consider in similar company next time. *(op 18-1)*
Jimmys Duky(IRE) has proved a bit of a disappointment since his first three starts over fences, got round this time but did not really show enough to suggest he would be of interest next time.
Get Smart(IRE), an inconsistent chaser who has not won for over two years, was again below his best and looks one to tread carefully with. *(op 8-1)*
Helvetius *Official explanation: jockey said gelding was unsuited by the good to soft ground (op 25-1)*
Devondale(IRE), the one progressive performer in the field, stumbled on landing at the first fence, giving his rider little chance of staying aboard. Although 10lb higher than for his last win, he is well worth another chance in similar company. *(op 6-1)*
Eyze(IRE) *Official explanation: jockey said gelding hung right-handed throughout (op 6-1)*
Ta Ta For Now *Official explanation: jockey said gelding felt wrong behind but returned sound (op 6-1)*

2496 MILLER HOMES NOVICES' CHASE (18 fncs) 3m
1:20 (1:20) (Class 3) 5-Y-O+ **£7,731** (£2,400; £1,292)

Form				RPR
50-F	1		**King Killone (IRE)**[9] 2291 5-10-13 120 ... DO'Meara *(H P Hogarth) cl up: led 12th: mde rest: rdn and hld on wl run in* **5/2**[2]	127+
41-1	2	shd	**Wild Cane Ridge (IRE)**[15] 2168 6-11-6 ... ADobbin *(L Lungo) led: hit 9th: blnd 11th: hdd next: cl up: rdn whn hit and outpcd 3 out: kpt on wl fr last: jst hld* **8/13**[1]	138+
00/	3	dist	**More Flair**[559] 8-10-0 ... BenOrde-Powlett(7) *(J B Walton) sn t.o* **66/1**	—
011-	P		**Galero**[283] 3885 6-11-0 ... ADempsey *(J Howard Johnson) chsd ldrs: reminders after 8th: wknd and p.u bef 10th* **13/2**[3]	—

6m 14.7s (-10.10) **Going Correction** -0.30s/f (Good)
WFA 5 from 6yo+ 1lb **4** Ran SP% **105.3**
Speed ratings: **104,103,—,—** CSF £4.47 TOTE £3.70; EX 5.40.
Owner Hogarth Racing **Bred** Sylvester Barrett **Trained** Stillington, N Yorks

FOCUS
Not a competitive event but a fair gallop and a couple of decent sorts, who both appeal as the type to win again over fences and are rated close to previous form.

NOTEBOOK
King Killone(IRE) ◆ showed himself none-the-worse for his Market Rasen fall and fully confirmed the promise of that chase debut - in the process showing the right attitude to edge out a rival whose jumping badly let him down. He jumped soundly, is in good hands and, given his physique, appeals as the type to win again over fences. *(op 11-4)*
Wild Cane Ridge(IRE) ◆ upped in trip and under a penalty for his recent easy course win, did not jump with anywhere near the same fluency this time and that proved his undoing against a progressive rival. He did really well to get so close given the mistakes he made on the final circuit and is sure to win more races when his jumping holds up. *(op 4-6 tchd 8-11 in a place)*
More Flair, a triple point winner, faced a very stiff task on this first run since May of last year and first run over regulation fences and was predictably outclassed. *(op 40-1)*
Galero, an Irish point winner who won two of his three starts over hurdles last season, proved a disappointment on this chase debut and was beaten before the race started in earnest but is not one to write off just yet. *Official explanation: jockey said gelding never travelled (op 9-2)*

2497 E B F PAGEBET "NATIONAL HUNT" NOVICES' HURDLE (QUALIFIER) (11 hdls) 2m 4f
1:50 (1:52) (Class 4) 4-6-Y-O **£4,274** (£1,254; £627; £313)

Form				RPR
2433	1		**Youlbesolucky (IRE)**[20] 2082 6-11-0 ... NFehily *(Jonjo O'Neill) chsd clr ldr: lft in ld bef 5th: hdd 3 out: sn rdn: rallied to ld run in: jst hld on* **13/2**[2]	116
311	2	shd	**Ungaro (FR)**[18] 2110 6-11-10 125 ... JimCrowley *(K G Reveley) keen in tch: led 3 out: hdd run in: rallied: jst failed* **8/15**[1]	128+
60-P	3	1 1/4	**Zipalong Lad (IRE)**[35] 1833 5-11-0 ... WHutchinson *(P Bowen) midfield: hdwy after 4 out: effrt and ev ch last: kpt on same pce* **28/1**	115
42-5	4	dist	**Kirkside Pleasure (IRE)**[35] 1834 4-11-0 ... KRenwick *(Mrs S C Bradburne) in tch: drvn 4 out: outpcd bef next* **33/1**	78
0	5	10	**Doris's Gift**[15] 2169 4-11-0 ... ADempsey *(J Howard Johnson) hld up: outpcd 6th: n.d after* **40/1**	68
0-2	6	2	**Divex (IRE)**[37] 1799 4-11-0 ... ADobbin *(M D Hammond) hld up: hdwy to chse ldrs bef 4 out: wknd bef next* **10/1**[3]	66
	7	7	**Run Junior (FR)** 4-10-11 ... GBerridge(3) *(J P L Ewart) hld up: hdwy and prom 7th: wknd bef 3 out: collapsed after r: dead* **16/1**	59
0-U0	8	24	**Cloudmor (IRE)**[186] 484 4-11-0 ... BGibson *(L Lungo) nt fluent: a bhd* **100/1**	—
4-43	9	3/4	**Ambition Royal (FR)**[20] 2064 5-10-11 98 ... PBuchanan(3) *(Miss Lucinda V Russell) prom tl rdn and wknd after 4 out* **14/1**	—
300-	10	dist	**Buffy**[218] 4971 5-10-7 ... NPMulholland *(B Mactaggart) prom to 7th: sn btn* **100/1**	—
00	R		**Cedar Rapids (IRE)**[9] 2295 5-11-0 ... DO'Meara *(H P Hogarth) keen: led and sn clr: rn out appr 5th* **66/1**	—

00- **U** **Intavac Flight**[252] [4465] 5-11-0 .... FKeniry —
(C W Thornton) *in tch: lost pl whn hit and uns rdr 5th* **150/1**

P **Harry Boy (IRE)** 5-11-0 .... BHarding —
(N G Richards) *mstkes: hld up: hdwy and prom whn blnd 4 out: broke leg bef next: dead* **25/1**

5m 13.7s (-2.10) **Going Correction** +0.025s/f (Yiel)
WFA 4 from 5yo+ 13lb **13** Ran SP% **117.0**
Speed ratings: **105,104,104,**—,— —,—,—,—,— —,—,— CSF £10.08 TOTE £5.80: £1.60, £1.10, £7.70; EX 17.10.

Owner Mrs Gay Smith **Bred** M W And Mrs M Doran **Trained** Cheltenham, Gloucs

FOCUS

An ordinary event in which the pace seemed fair and the first three pulled clear in the straight. The time was reasonable and the form should work out.

NOTEBOOK

Youlbesolucky(IRE), a fast-ground bumper winner, still looked far from the finished article under pressure but turned in his best effort to date over hurdles for his in-form stable. This showed him to be effective on easy ground and he may be capable of further improvement.

Ungaro(FR), under a double penalty for facile wins at Huntingdon and Sedgefield, was made to work much harder this time but did show the right attitude after racing a shade keenly. He will find things tougher back in handicaps from his 125 mark but may be capable of further improvement. *(op 4-6 tchd 8-11 in places)*

Zipalong Lad(IRE), who showed ability in bumpers, left the form of his hurdle debut a long way behind and he should stay three miles. On this evidence he looks capable of winning a small event in this sphere. *(op 25-1)*

Kirkside Pleasure(IRE), upped in trip, was again found out in this grade but looks the type to do better in ordinary handicaps around this trip in due course.

Doris's Gift was again well beaten and may do better over further in modest handicaps in due course. *(op 20-1)*

Divex(IRE), who ran well in a bumper at Haydock last time, hinted at ability before dropping out rather tamely for this hurdles debut, but he is not a bad sort and would not be one to write off just yet. *(op 8-1)*

Cedar Rapids(IRE) *Official explanation: jockey said gelding hung badly left-handed*

2498 INTERSKY H'CAP CHASE (16 fncs) 2m 4f

2:25 (2:25) (Class 3) (0-125,122) 5-Y-0+ **£5,556** (£1,631; £815; £407)

Form RPR

-351 **1** **Oso Magic**[15] [2172] 7-11-0 **110** .... DO'Meara 134+
(Mrs S J Smith) *cl up: led bef 5 out: clr fr next: unchal* **2/1**[1]

13-3 **2** *25* **Posh Stick**[10] [2264] 8-10-4 **107** .... BenOrde-Powlett[(7)] 109+
(J B Walton) *prom: effrt bef 4 out: kpt on: no ch w wnr* **8/1**[3]

6-0U **3** *4* **The Tinker**[21] [2037] 10-10-0 **99** .... PAspell[(3)] 92+
(Mrs S C Bradburne) *chsd ldrs: lost pl whn blnd 10th: styd on fr 2 out: nvr rchd ldrs* **33/1**

45-F **4** *nk* **Do L'Enfant D'Eau (FR)**[20] [2067] 6-11-5 **115** .... BHarding 107
(B Storey) *hld up midfield: hit and outpcd 9th: no imp fr 4 out* **9/1**

244P **5** *8* **Jallastep (FR)**[20] [2067] 8-10-0 **96** .... ADempsey 80
(J S Goldie) *bhd: outpcd after 10th: n.d after* **18/1**

356- **6** *12* **Sound Of Cheers**[225] [4848] 8-11-0 **110** .... (t) KJohnson 82
(F Kirby) *prom tl rdn and wknd bef 4 out* **14/1**

PPP4 **7** *shd* **Powder Creek (IRE)**[3] [2443] 8-11-3 **113** .... (p) RMcGrath 85
(K G Reveley) *mstkes: in tch tl wknd after 5 out* **11/1**

4-60 **P** **Alam (USA)**[23] [2003] 6-11-12 **122** .... KRenwick —
(P Monteith) *cl up tl wknd 8th: t.o whn p.u bef 4 out* **40/1**

21/4 **P** **Pietro Vannucci (IRE)**[18] [2102] 9-11-1 **111** .... NFehily —
(Jonjo O'Neill) *hld up: outpcd and p.u after 8th* **5/2**[2]

24-1 **P** **Gatorade (NZ)**[211] [97] 13-11-3 **118** .... (p) PCO'Neill[(5)] —
(R C Guest) *hld up: outpcd 11th: t.o whn p.u bef 2 out* **14/1**

2306 **P** **Nowator (POL)**[16] [2139] 8-11-7 **117** .... ADobbin —
(Robert Gray) *mde most to bef 5 out: wknd 3 out: p.u and dismntd 2 out* **33/1**

5m 20.5s (-8.20) **Going Correction** -0.30s/f (Good) **11** Ran SP% **118.3**
Speed ratings: **104,94,92,92,89 84,84,**—,—,— — CSF £18.82 CT £410.91 TOTE £3.20: £1.60, £1.70, £5.80; EX 17.00.

Owner Michael Thompson **Bred** M H Ings **Trained** High Eldwick, W Yorks

FOCUS

An ordinary handicap run at a sound pace and another improved effort from Oso Magic, with the runner-up setting the standard.

NOTEBOOK

Oso Magic, 9lb higher than when winning easily over two miles here last time, turned in a career-best effort back over this longer trip. He is a fair and progressive sort but can expect little respite from the Handicapper after this 25-length win. *(tchd 9-4 in places)*

Posh Stick, back over fences, had little chance with a rival who is clearly a fair way in front of the Handicapper but ran her race and she looks a reliable guide to the worth of this form. She should continue to give a good account.

The Tinker's tendency to make mistakes has cost him in the past and a bad blunder in the back straight on the final circuit arguably cost him second place. He is not the most consistent and remains one to tread carefully with. *(op 25-1)*

Do L'Enfant D'Eau(FR) got round this time but did not improve for the step up to this trip and was again not foot perfect. He is not one to write off yet but will have to brush up his jumping if he is to progress over fences.

Jallastep(FR), who is not the most consistent around, was again well beaten and is one to tread carefully with at present. *(op 20-1)*

Sound Of Cheers, who has won over hurdles and over fences (twice) at this course, shaped as though this reappearance run was needed. Although well beaten on his last three starts, he is on a fair mark and is not one to write off yet. *(op 20-1)*

Pietro Vannucci(IRE), who shaped well after a lengthy break on his first run for the yard less than three weeks ago, ran no sort of race this time but this race almost certainly came too quickly and he is worth another chance. *Official explanation: jockey said gelding never travelled (op 7-2)*

Nowator(POL) ran better than his form figure suggests, as he only dropped out of contention in the home straight on his first run over a trip further than ideal. The return to two miles should suit but he does look high enough in the weights. *Official explanation: jockey said gelding lost its action (op 7-2)*

2499 PAGEBET REHEARSAL CHASE (A H'CAP) (LISTED RACE) (18 fncs) 3m

3:00 (3:00) (Class 1) 5-Y-0+

£33,804 (£12,732; £6,372; £3,186; £1,596; £798)

Form RPR

14-F **1** **Direct Access (IRE)**[6] [2370] 10-10-0 **127** oh1 .... BHarding 142+
(N G Richards) *chsd ldrs: led 4 out: styd on strly* **8/1**[3]

U-P6 **2** *6* **Risk Accessor (IRE)**[49] [1676] 10-10-9 **136** .... NFehily 145
(Jonjo O'Neill) *cl up: led 12th to 4 out: kpt on same pce after 2 out* **25/1**

1016 **3** *16* **Little Big Horse (IRE)**[42] [1735] 9-10-2 **129** .... DO'Meara 122
(Mrs S J Smith) *hmpd 1st: chsd ldrs: drvn bef 4 out: sn no ex* **8/1**[3]

F-65 **4** *1 ½* **Mister McGoldrick**[7] [2346] 8-11-12 **153** .... JimCrowley 145
(Mrs S J Smith) *hld up: hdwy and chsd ldrs 5 out: rdn and wknd after next* **12/1**

-022 **5** *7* **Vandas Choice (IRE)**[28] [1924] 7-10-7 **137** .... PBuchanan[(3)] 122
(Miss Lucinda V Russell) *in tch: lost pl whn mstke 10th: rallied 13th: sn no imp* **10/1**

20-4 **6** *2 ½* **Supreme Developer (IRE)**[34] [1846] 8-9-9 **129** .... PJMcDonald[(7)] 121+
(Ferdy Murphy) *chsng ldrs whn nrly fell 1st: sn bhd and nt fluent: nvr on terms* **7/1**[2]

411/ **7** *hd* **Lord Maizey (IRE)**[700] [2982] 8-10-1 **128** .... TScudamore 110
(N A Twiston-Davies) *hmpd 1st: prom tl wknd after 5 out* **8/1**[3]

F25- **8** *¾* **Alexanderthegreat (IRE)**[287] [3804] 7-10-2 **129** .... WHutchinson 110
(Ferdy Murphy) *midfield: hdwy and prom bef 13th: wknd bef 4 out* **10/1**

/-P3 **9** *16* **Robbo**[18] [2110] 11-10-0 **127** oh10 .... (b) RMcGrath 92
(K G Reveley) *cl up tl lost pl 7th: n.d after* **22/1**

00-5 **P** **Joly Bey (FR)**[21] [2054] 8-10-11 **141** .... (t) MrDHDunsdon[(3)] —
(N J Gifford) *mde most to 12th: wknd bef 4 out: p.u bef next* **10/3**[1]

303- **P** **Sonevafushi (FR)**[227] [4824] 7-10-1 **128** .... FKeniry —
(Miss Venetia Williams) *in tch tl wknd fr 13th: t.o whn p.u bef 4 out* **8/1**[3]

2PR- **P** **Ballybough Rasher (IRE)**[231] [4772] 10-10-8 **135** .... ADempsey —
(J Howard Johnson) *bhd: struggling 1/2-way: t.o whn p.u bef 4 out* **25/1**

6m 13.0s (-11.80) **Going Correction** -0.30s/f (Good) **12** Ran SP% **117.9**
Speed ratings: **107,105,99,99,96 96,95,95,90,**— —,— CSF £183.20 CT £1639.77 TOTE £7.80: £2.50, £6.20, £2.30; EX 287.10 TRIFECTA Not won..

Owner The Direct Access Partnership **Bred** Geoffrey Thompson **Trained** Greystoke, Cumbria

■ This event was previously run at Chepstow.

FOCUS

Few progressive sorts but an ordinary gallop and an ordinary winning time for a race of its class, just 1.7 seconds quicker than the earlier four-runner novice chase. The race could rate a little higher.

NOTEBOOK

Direct Access(IRE), who has a history of going particularly well fresh, was effectively having his first run of the season having fallen at the first at Aintree the previous week. He is a very capable staying chaser on his day but his record over fences suggests he would not be one to lump on at short odds next time. *(tchd 9-1)*

Risk Accessor(IRE), again without the tongue tie, ran easily his best race on his third start for his current stable. He did nothing wrong on this occasion (has often found little) but a 136 mark may well hold him back against progressive or unexposed types in a more competitive event. *(tchd 28-1)*

Little Big Horse(IRE) jumped soundly and ran creditably but left the impression that he is going to remain vulnerable to progressive or unexposed sorts in the better handicaps in the short term. *(op 9-1)*

Mister McGoldrick, a very smart chaser at up to two and a half miles, travelled strongly for a long way but seemed to find this three-mile trip beyond him. He will have to be at his best to win from this mark returned to shorter, but will be of more interest from a lower hurdles mark if returned to the smaller obstacles. *(op 8-1)*

Vandas Choice(IRE), back to something like his best at Wetherby on his previous start, did not improve for the step up to this trip. The return to two and a half miles will suit but he is another that looks high enough in the weights at present. *(tchd 12-1)*

Supreme Developer(IRE) could not recover from a bad mistake at the first and is worth another chance.

Lord Maizey(IRE), who missed last year, ran well for a long way until lack of peak fitness told. He has won three of his six starts over the larger obstacles, has age on his side and may well add to his tally this season. *(op 9-1)*

Joly Bey(FR), who was well supported, failed by a long chalk to confirm reappearance promise and his form over fences since his Sandown win in February has been patchy to say the least. *Official explanation: jockey said gelding had a breathing problem (tchd 7-2)*

2500 PERTEMPS "FIGHTING FIFTH" HURDLE GRADE 1 (9 hdls) 2m

3:30 (3:36) (Class 1) 4-Y-0+

£45,072 (£16,976; £8,496; £4,248; £2,128; £1,064)

Form RPR

431- **1** **Arcalis**[256] [4381] 5-11-7 146 .... ADobbin 158+
(J Howard Johnson) *hld up in tch: smooth hdwy and ev ch whn mstke 3 out: led bef next: qcknd clr appr last: readily* **9/4**[1]

-P13 **2** *5* **Royal Shakespeare (FR)**[8] [2326] 6-11-7 154 .... TScudamore 150
(S Gollings) *racd wd: jnd ldrs 4th: led 4 out to bef 2 out: no ch w wnr* **8/1**

300- **3** *shd* **The French Furze (IRE)**[224] [4860] 11-11-7 140 .... BHarding 150
(N G Richards) *cl up: outpcd bef 3 out: rallied last: kpt on* **33/1**

02-0 **4** *4* **Self Defense**[13] [2209] 8-11-7 153 .... FKeniry 146
(Miss E C Lavelle) *hld up: drvn 4th: rallied and prom bef 3 out: outpcd next* **7/2**[3]

1-62 **5** *nk* **Genghis (IRE)**[42] [1738] 6-11-7 145 .... WHutchinson 147+
(P Bowen) *w ldrs: mstke 4 out: sn ev ch: no ex bef 2 out* **10/1**

3-43 **6** *5* **Hasty Prince**[42] [1738] 7-11-7 150 .... (b[1]) RMcGrath 142+
(Jonjo O'Neill) *cl up tl wknd appr 3 out* **25/1**

0155 **7** *26* **Overstrand (IRE)**[45] [1720] 6-11-7 117 .... (p) GBerridge 115
(Robert Gray) *in tch: outpcd bef 4th: lost tch fr 4 out* **200/1**

1-11 **8** *15* **Admiral (IRE)**[7] [2338] 4-11-7 145 .... PCO'Neill 100
(R C Guest) *set stdy pce to 4 out: wknd bef next* **8/1**

60-2 **P** **Intersky Falcon**[21] [2055] 8-11-7 160 .... (b) NFehily —
(Jonjo O'Neill) *chsd ldrs tl wknd after 4 out: p.u bef next* **3/1**[2]

4m 0.60s (-5.70) **Going Correction** +0.025s/f (Yiel) **9** Ran SP% **116.6**
Speed ratings: **115,112,112,110,110 107,94,87,**— CSF £21.18 TOTE £3.00: £1.50, £2.20, £4.70; EX 29.50 Trifecta £378.70 Pool: £906.98 - 1.70 winning tickets. Place 6 £318.08, Place 5 £132.33.

Owner Andrea & Graham Wylie **Bred** P E Clinton **Trained** Billy Row, Co Durham

FOCUS

A pedestrian gallop for much of the way in deteriorating ground surprisingly resulted in an acceptable winning time for a race of this prestige. The winner is value for more than the official margin and looks destined for better things.

NOTEBOOK

Arcalis ◆, having his first run since winning the Supreme Novices' Hurdle in March, turned in a taking display. Although the gallop was steady and the ground softer than ideal, he impressed with the way he powered through the race before quickening clear in a matter of strides. His jumping was sound in the main and, although the Champion Hurdle will be a very different test to this, he is a most progressive sort who has already proved himself in a strongly-run race over two miles at Cheltenham, and he is likely to be a leading player in what is shaping up to be a fascinating event. *(op 11-4)*

Royal Shakespeare(FR), third in this race last year behind Harchibald and Inglis Drever, had the run of the race and ran creditably on ground that was almost certainly softer than ideal. He falls short of what it takes to win at the top level but looks capable of winning a decent prize this term. *(op 9-1)*

The French Furze(IRE), a regular in this race, having won it in 2003 and been second three times, ran creditably in a muddling event. Although he left the impression that a stiffer test of stamina would have been in his favour, he is likely to continue to be vulnerable in this type of contest. *(op 40-1)*

Self Defense was not disgraced in a muddling event and, although a stronger gallop would have played more to his strengths, he did not travel through the race with much fluency and is not really one for short odds. *(op 5-1)*

Genghis(IRE), a most progressive performer in the first half of this year, was not disgraced in this stronger grade. He seems vulnerable in handicaps or in this type of event over two miles but is well worth another try over two and a half. *(op 8-1 tchd 11-1)*

Hasty Prince did not improve for the fitting of blinkers and is another that is not going to be easy to place successfully from his current mark. *(op 33-1)*

Admiral(IRE), turned out quickly after outbattling Faasel at Haydock the previous weekend, had the rub of this steadily-run race but proved a big disappointment and this may have come too quickly. He is worth another chance. *Official explanation: jockey said race came too soon (op 7-1 tchd 13-2)*

Intersky Falcon, who looked to retain much of his ability when second to Royal Shakespeare at Wincanton on his reappearance, ran as though something was amiss on this softer ground and it transpired he had a breathing problem. He is not one to write off yet but is also not one to place maximum faith in. *Official explanation: jockey said gelding had a breathing problem (op 11-4 tchd 7-2)*

T/Plt: £952.30 to a £1 stake. Pool: £47,032.70. 36.05 winning tickets. T/Qpdt: £77.30 to a £1 stake. Pool: £3,262.10. 31.20 winning tickets. RY

[2008] TOWCESTER (R-H)

Saturday, November 26

OFFICIAL GOING: Soft (good to soft in places)

The open ditch running down the hill was omitted in all chases.

Wind: Fresh, across Weather: Overcast

2501 FREE TIPS @ GG.COM MARES' ONLY NOVICES' HURDLE (8 hdls) 2m

12:25 (12:26) (Class 3) 3-Y-0+ **£5,191** (£1,524; £762; £380)

Form RPR

2-52 **1** **Purple Patch**[23] [2012] 7-11-5 92 .... RWalford 95
(C L Popham) *hld up: hdwy appr 4th: outpcd after next: rallied 2 out: styd on u.p to ld post* **11/2**[3]

13-3 **2** *nk* **Vertical Bloom**[23] [2012] 4-11-5 .... WMarston 97+
(Mrs P Sly) *hld up in tch: jnd ldrs 4th: mstke 3 out: led bef next: clr last: rdn and hdd post* **5/1**[2]

6 **3** *3* **Carraig (IRE)**[56] [1594] 3-9-13 .... LStephens(5) 78+
(Evan Williams) *hld up: hit 1st: hdwy after 3 out: rdn appr last: styd on same pce flat* **12/1**

-210 **4** *5* **Emmasflora**[14] [2173] 7-11-4 105 .... APogson(7) 93
(C T Pogson) *chsd ldrs: led 4th: rdn and hdd appr 2 out: wknd bef last* **9/2**[1]

6/0- **5** *16* **Black Collar**[398] [1823] 6-11-5 .... JPMcNamara 71
(K C Bailey) *led to 4th: wknd 3 out* **11/1**

6 *7* **Methodical**[172] 3-10-3 ow4 .... JFLevins(5) 53
(B G Powell) *bhd: sme hdwy appr 3 out: n.d* **66/1**

3 **7** *2 ½* **Treaty Flyer (IRE)**[26] [1961] 4-11-2 .... CBolger(3) 62
(P G Murphy) *chsd ldrs tl wknd appr 2 out* **15/2**

/P0- **8** *13* **Lunar Fox**[361] [2551] 6-11-5 .... JPByrne 49
(J L Needham) *a in rr* **100/1**

P04P **9** *1 ¾* **Pips Assertive Way**[12] [2244] 4-11-0 94 .... StephenJCraine(5) 47
(A W Carroll) *mid-div: hdwy after 3rd: wknd next* **22/1**

10 *hd* **Noun De La Thinte (FR)**[279] 4-11-5 .... AO'Keeffe 47
(Miss Venetia Williams) *chsd ldrs tl rdn and wknd appr 3 out* **6/1**

50-4 **11** *9* **Oscars Law**[30] [1896] 4-11-5 .... HOliver 38
(J L Spearing) *hld up: j. slowly 3rd: rdn and wknd next* **14/1**

6 **12** *8* **Isitloveyourafter (IRE)**[12] [2236] 3-9-11 .... EDehdashti(7) 15
(G L Moore) *prom to 5th* **33/1**

13 *6* **Galandora**[84] 5-11-5 .... JMogford 24
(Dr J R J Naylor) *hld up: a in rr* **40/1**

00 **14** *3* **Orions Eclipse**[34] [1851] 4-10-12 .... MrNPearce(7) 21
(M J Gingell) *hld up: a in rr* **150/1**

0S-0 **15** *24* **She's Our Daisy (IRE)**[213] [70] 5-11-5 .... BHitchcott —
(R H Buckler) *chsd ldr tl after 3rd: wknd appr 5th* **28/1**

4m 5.80s (-5.60) **Going Correction** +0.30s/f (Yiel)
WFA 3 from 4yo+ 15lb **15** Ran SP% **115.3**
Speed ratings: **105,104,103,100,92 89,88,81,80,80 76,72,69,67,55** CSF £30.37 TOTE £7.70: £1.50, £2.00, £5.70; EX 17.70.

Owner Mrs C C Scott **Bred** C Hitchings **Trained** West Bagborough, Somerset

FOCUS

A very moderate mares-only novices hurdle in which those with previous course experience came to the fore. The form looks solid enough.

NOTEBOOK

Purple Patch, who ran well here earlier in the month in a similar contest, confirmed form with today's runner-up but only just. She was held up this time, but picked up well up the hill and ran on strongly to get up near the line. She deserved this, will have no problems with a return to further and should not be too badly treated in handicaps. *(op 6-1)*

Vertical Bloom ◆ made a bold bid under a prominent ride and looked to have matters in hand once going on off the home turn. However, the stiff climb to the finish took its toll and she could not hold the late surge of the winner. This was still an improvement on her previous run here and, relatively inexperienced, looks capable of gaining compensation in a similar event *(tchd 11-2)*

Carraig(IRE), a miler on the Flat, was held up to get the trip as she had been on her debut. She picked up well climbing the hill without ever looking likely to reel in the leaders. Now she has proved she gets the trip, connections can adopt more positive tactics. *(tchd 14-1)*

Emmasflora, who made all when scoring over course and distance last month, adopted similar tactics. However, the ground was more testing on this occasion and that counted against her from the turn in. A return to a sounder surface will be in her favour. *(op 11-2)*

Black Collar, a dual point winner in 2004, has yet to look as effective in bumpers and over hurdles. She was ridden positively but dropped away on the run to the straight. She will be better off over longer trips on good ground. *(op 12-1)*

Treaty Flyer(IRE), another ex-pointer, looked to be travelling really well at the bottom of the hill on this hurdling debut, but a slight mistake at the third last effectively ended her chance. *(op 7-1)*

Noun De La Thinte(FR), a market drifter on this British debut and first outing for nine months, ran as the market suggested, fading on the climb to the straight. *(op 5-1)*

2502 COMPARE ODDS @ GG-ODDS.COM H'CAP CHASE (16 fncs) 2m 6f

12:55 (12:57) (Class 3) (0-120,107) 5-Y-0+ **£5,465** (£1,604; £802; £400)

Form RPR

2-34 **1** **Blunham Hill (IRE)**[34] [1853] 7-10-5 91 .... MNicolls(5) 103
(John R Upson) *prom: lost pl 7th: hdwy appr 3 out: styd on u.p to ld towards fin* **13/2**[2]

3144 **2** *1* **Runaway Bishop (USA)**[12] [2243] 10-10-3 91 .... APogson(7) 104+
(J R Cornwall) *a.p: chsd ldr 4th: rdn whn mstke last: led fnl 50 yds: hdd towards fin* **9/1**

0-P5 **3** *1 ¾* **Fin Bec (FR)**[9] [2293] 12-11-1 101 .... (b) DLaverty(5) 111+
(A P Jones) *led: rdn whn j.rt last: hdd fnl 50 yds* **16/1**

5U62 **4** *13* **Fiori**[6] [2368] 9-11-7 107 .... PMerrigan(5) 103
(P C Haslam) *chsd ldrs: rdn and wknd appr 2 out* **6/1**[1]

P24- **5** *4* **Dalus Park (IRE)**[252] [4458] 10-10-12 98 .... MrSMorris(5) 90
(C C Bealby) *hld up: hdwy 7th: wknd 10th* **7/1**[3]

21P- **6** *15* **Jack Fuller (IRE)**[231] [4778] 8-11-5 100 .... (p) WMarston 77
(P R Hedger) *hld up: hdwy 7th: wknd 11th* **16/1**

3P/P **7** *dist* **Oscar Performance (IRE)**[14] [2180] 10-11-5 100 .... BHitchcott —
(R H Buckler) *chsd ldrs: lost pl whn blnd 5th: sn bhd* **50/1**

14-3 **P** **Surefast**[39] [1780] 10-10-10 94 .... CBolger(3) —
(K Bishop) *sn pushed along in rr: t.o whn p.u after 7th* **6/1**[1]

P-20 **P** **Meggie's Beau (IRE)**[13] [2210] 9-11-10 105 .... AO'Keeffe —
(Miss Venetia Williams) *chsd ldrs to 9th: bhd whn p.u bef 11th* **13/2**[2]

23-2 **P** **Onyourheadbeit (IRE)**[23] [2005] 7-11-12 107 .... JPMcNamara —
(K C Bailey) *hld up: hdwy 5th: wknd 3 out: remote 6th whn p.u bef last* **8/1**

/4-5 **P** **Major Benefit (IRE)**[20] [2077] 8-11-5 107 .... RSpate(7) —
(Mrs K Waldron) *mid-div: pckd 3rd: sn lost pl: bhd 7th: t.o whn p.u bef 4 out* **12/1**

5m 50.9s (-15.10) **Going Correction** +0.10s/f (Yiel) **11** Ran SP% **110.3**
Speed ratings: **105,104,104,99,97 92,—,—,—,— —** CSF £59.70 CT £840.39 TOTE £8.50: £2.50, £3.00, £5.00; EX 82.10.

Owner The Reserved Judgment Partnership **Bred** Oliver McDonnell **Trained** Maidford, Northants

FOCUS

A moderate handicap in which fortunes changed late on. The form looks solid as the first four all have form on the track and will be relevant to races back here.

NOTEBOOK

Blunham Hill(IRE), who likes this track and gained his only previous win here, lost a good early position but plugged on steadily from the bottom of the hill as stamina came into play and, with the rail to help him after the last, galloped past the two in front of him near the finish. He is relatively inexperienced and, locally trained, will continue to be a force round here. *(op 15-2)*

Runaway Bishop(USA) ◆ is another that loves this course and extended his record to three wins and four places in seven appearances over fences here. He chased the leader for much of the way and eventually battled his way to the front on the flat, only to be collared by the winner near the line. He should remain reasonably treated and could gain compensation if returning here for the Boxing Day meeting. *(op 10-1)*

Fin Bec(FR) is a veteran nowadays and has not had much racing of late, but does like this track. He was touched off in this race last season and much the same thing happened this time, as he led until collared after the last. He is clearly still capable of winning modest races and is currently well treated, being a stone lower than for his first outing last season. *(op 12-1)*

Fiori, who had a hard race when runner-up in the Grand Sefton Chase the previous weekend, has yet to win over more than an extended two miles despite some decent efforts at around this trip. However, the stamina test and the effects of the Aintree race may have blunted his performance. *(op 9-2)*

Surefast was never going from an early stage and his rider drew stumps before the final circuit. *Official explanation: jockey said gelding lost its action (op 7-1)*

Meggie's Beau(IRE) showed up well before dropping away quickly and being pulled up in the back straight as if something was amiss. *Official explanation: jockey said gelding bled from the nose (op 7-1)*

2503 EUROPEAN BREEDERS FUND "NATIONAL HUNT" NOVICES' HURDLE (QUALIFIER) (11 hdls) 2m 5f

1:25 (1:27) (Class 3) 4-6-Y-0 **£5,842** (£1,715; £857; £428)

Form RPR

243- **1** **Jaunty Times**[220] [4933] 5-10-12 111 .... MBradburne 106+
(H D Daly) *chsd ldrs: led 3 out: sn clr: hit last: rdn out* **5/4**[1]

50- **2** *3 ½* **Optimistic Alfie**[266] [4193] 5-10-12 .... JPMcNamara 99
(B G Powell) *hld up: hdwy appr 3 out: chsd wnr last: styd on* **20/1**

1- **3** *1 ¼* **Cash And New (IRE)**[279] [3980] 6-10-5 .... WMarston 92+
(R T Phillips) *hld up: nt fluent: hdwy 6th: chsd wnr appr 2 out: sn rdn: styd on same pce last* **4/1**[2]

2-2 **4** *9* **Dan's Man**[202] [241] 4-10-5 .... BWharfe(7) 91+
(N A Twiston-Davies) *plld hrd and prom: wknd 2 out* **15/2**

-16P **5** *dist* **Bannister Lane**[27] [1938] 5-10-13 105 .... StephenJCraine(5) —
(D McCain) *chsd ldr tl led 6th: hit next: hdd & wknd 3 out* **33/1**

004- **6** *10* **Astral Affair (IRE)**[507] [898] 6-10-0 74 .... TGreenway(5) —
(P A Pritchard) *hld up: hdwy 8th: wknd after next* **40/1**

6-05 **7** *16* **Gaining Ground (IRE)**[34] [1859] 5-10-7 .... MNicolls(5) —
(John R Upson) *hld up: a in rr* **50/1**

BPP- **8** *15* **Kiwi Riverman**[286] [3835] 5-10-12 .... BHitchcott —
(D P Keane) *led to 6th: ev ch appr 3 out: sn wknd* **40/1**

/4-3 **P** **Cruising Clyde**[17] [2127] 6-10-12 .... DCrosse —
(C J Mann) *hld up: rdn after 7th: sn wknd: t.o whn p.u bef 2 out* **9/2**[3]

40 **P** **Weldiva**[29] [1903] 5-9-12 .... TMessenger(7) —
(B N Pollock) *plld hrd and prom: rdn 7th: sn wknd: t.o whn p.u bef 2 out* **100/1**

5m 40.6s (-0.60) **Going Correction** +0.60s/f (Soft)
WFA 4 from 5yo+ 13lb **10** Ran SP% **109.9**
Speed ratings: **99,97,97,93,— —,—,—,—,—** CSF £28.24 TOTE £2.40: £1.10, £3.30, £2.00; EX 70.20.

Owner J B Sumner **Bred** B J Eckley **Trained** Stanton Lacy, Shropshire

FOCUS

A moderate novice hurdle run at a steady early pace. The third and fourth set the level, but confidence is limited.

NOTEBOOK

Jaunty Times, who came up against some decent sorts in similar races last season, got off the mark in decisive style. Always close up, his rider went ahead at the flight before the home turn and soon opened up a clear advantage, which he never looked like relinquishing. Although he will eventually make a chaser, he looks capable of adding to this before making the switch to fences. *(op 6-4 tchd 6-5)*

Optimistic Alfie, making his hurdling debut having been well beaten in two bumpers in the spring, came from well back to chase home the winner without ever looking likely to catch him. This was a decent first effort and connections should be able to find a suitable opening for him. *(op 28-1)*

Cash And New(IRE), winner of a mares' bumper here on her only start back in February, could have jumped better but moved up to give chase to the winner off the turn, then failed to reduce the deficit. She may find an opportunity against her own sex, and her jumping should improve with experience. *(op 3-1)*

Dan's Man, another who was making his hurdling debut having run well in a couple of bumpers in the spring, was too keen for his own good and paid the penalty on the final climb. He will need to settle to make the necessary improvement, and may be better making the running. *(op 11-2 tchd 5-1)*

Astral Affair(IRE) was quite keen early on this return from a 16-month absence, and faded up the hill after briefly moving into contention.

Cruising Clyde, a bumper winner on good ground, has been beaten every time he has encountered softer conditions. He was quite keen under restraint, but dropped away disappointingly and may have had excuses. *(op 11-2)*

2504 BRYAN GORDON MEMORIAL NOVICES' CHASE (12 fncs) 2m 110y
1:55 (1:56) (Class 3) 5-Y-O+ **£5,399** (£1,585; £792; £395)

Form RPR

0-35 **1** **Terivic**[14] [2179] 5-11-0 107 JPMcNamara 121+
(K C Bailey) *mde all: mstke 4 out: hung lft appr 2 out: drvn out* **12/1**

-U21 **2** *1 ½* **Mon Mome (FR)**[14] [2180] 5-11-0 115 AO'Keeffe 120+
(Miss Venetia Williams) *a.p: chsd wnr 5th: rdn appr 2 out: styd on* **11/4**[1]

3P5P **3** *14* **Rash Moment (FR)**[69] [1485] 6-10-7 105 RSpate(7) 106+
(Mrs K Waldron) *hld up: lft 4th 6th: mstke next: styd on same pce fr 3 out* **33/1**

102- **4** *3* **Star Angler (IRE)**[223] [4878] 7-11-0 113 MBradburne 103+
(H D Daly) *prom: lft 3rd 6th: rdn 3 out: wknd next* **7/2**[3]

/13- **U** **Sharp Jack (IRE)**[331] [3100] 7-11-0 112 WMarston —
(R T Phillips) *hld up: last whn mstke and uns rdr 6th* **11/4**[1]

/12- **F** **Tiger Tips Lad (IRE)**[567] [232] 6-11-0 110 TSiddall —
(N A Twiston-Davies) *chsd wnr to 5th: disputing 2nd whn fell next* **3/1**[2]

4m 16.1s (-3.20) **Going Correction** +0.40s/f (Soft) **6** Ran SP% **111.2**
Speed ratings: **105,104,97,96,—** — CSF £44.77 TOTE £12.60: £3.40, £1.40; EX 47.60.
Owner G W Paul **Bred** G W Paul **Trained** Preston Capes, Northants
■ Stewards' Enquiry : A O'Keeffe one-day ban: used whip with arm above shoulder height (Dec 7)

FOCUS
A modest novices' chase but a tight contest judged on official ratings, and run at a sound pace. The second sets the standard with the winner an improver.

NOTEBOOK
Terivic, making his chasing debut, had previous course experience and stayed further over hurdles, and put that to good use. Making all the running, he stuck to his task up the hill and a better jump at the last settled it. He looks capable of further progress. *(tchd 14-1)*
Mon Mome(FR), a winner over three miles on testing ground last time, was ridden close to the pace but could not get past the all-the-way winner. Stamina was not an issue so lack of acceleration probably made the difference. *(op 5-2 tchd 3-1 in places)*
Rash Moment(FR), who was out of form in the summer on fast ground, was held up at the back and merely stayed on at one pace on this return from a break. His best efforts have been on flatter tracks
Star Angler(IRE), making his chasing debut on his first run since the spring, ran as if the outing was needed and should do better with this experience under his belt. *(op 9-2 tchd 5-1)*
Tiger Tips Lad(IRE), who gained his only hurdles win on this track, was up with the leaders when coming down and if none the worse can find opportunities. *(op 4-1)*
Sharp Jack(IRE), having his first run for 11 months and making his chasing debut, was in rear but had not been asked a question when departing. He is another who can do better in time. *(op 4-1)*

2505 READ MALCOLM HEYHOE @ GG.COM H'CAP HURDLE (12 hdls) 3m
2:30 (2:30) (Class 3) (0-115,113) 4-Y-O+ **£4,853** (£1,424; £712; £355)

Form RPR

35-3 **1** **Rosetown (IRE)**[25] [1973] 7-10-2 96 (b) WMcCarthy(7) 97+
(T R George) *chsd ldrs: led 3 out: rdn out* **7/4**[1]

0412 **2** *2* **Potts Of Magic**[29] [1910] 6-9-13 91 (b) PMerrigan(5) 90
(R Lee) *hld up: hdwy 9th: chsd wnr 2 out: sn rdn: styd on same pce flat* **11/4**[2]

50P- **3** *14* **Old Feathers (IRE)**[232] [4767] 8-11-12 113 (b) BHitchcott 100+
(Jonjo O'Neill) *chsd ldrs: ev ch 3 out: wknd last* **14/1**

00-6 **4** *3 ½* **Standing Bloom**[14] [2184] 9-10-11 98 WMarston 80
(Mrs P Sly) *led to 8th: led next to 3 out: wknd bef next* **13/2**

50-P **5** *10* **Scarlet Fantasy**[213] [54] 5-10-9 101 TGreenway(5) 73
(P A Pritchard) *hld up: hdwy 9th: wknd after 3 out* **20/1**

2F13 **6** *¾* **Bustisu**[53] [1630] 8-9-9 89 RCummings(7) 60
(D J Wintle) *hld up in tch: led 8th to next: wknd after 3 out* **5/1**[3]

30/P **7** *dist* **Bedford Leader**[29] [1906] 7-9-9 87 oh6 DLaverty(5) —
(A P Jones) *chsd ldrs to 9th* **40/1**

35-P **8** *19* **Ironside (IRE)**[216] [8] 6-10-13 100 MBradburne —
(H D Daly) *chsd ldr to 8th: sn rdn: wknd next* **14/1**

6m 35.6s (4.60) **Going Correction** +0.60s/f (Soft) **8** Ran SP% **113.6**
Speed ratings: **90,89,84,83,80 79,—,—** CSF £7.16 CT £46.79 TOTE £2.50: £1.40, £1.70, £2.60; EX 5.50.
Owner Timothy N Chick **Bred** Mrs F Harrington **Trained** Slad, Gloucs

FOCUS
A moderate stayers' hurdle run at a steady pace that did not pick up until the final mile. The race could rate higher but is limited by the time.

NOTEBOOK
Rosetown(IRE), well suited by a good test of stamina, showed the benefit of his encouraging reappearance at the beginning of the month and, once going on at the flight climbing towards the straight, always looked to have matters under control. He is still reasonably treated and should be capable of winning more races, and always has the option of returning to fences if the Handicapper catches up with him. *(tchd 15-8)*
Potts Of Magic, a winner on fast ground in September, but touched off on soft ground last month, was another 3lb higher but had the blinkers reapplied. He was settled off the pace and went in pursuit of the winner when that rival kicked for home, but never looked like reeling him in. His recent efforts suggest he is better suited by a flat, left-handed track. *(op 7-2)*
Old Feathers(IRE), returning from a near eight-month absence, put up a fair effort under top weight and should be better for the outing. *(op 8-1)*
Standing Bloom, whose half-sister was touched off in the opening race, made the running but was brushed aside up the hill. She likes soft ground but seems better suited by less-testing tracks. *(op 6-1)*
Bustisu seemed to have every chance but faded climbing the hill. She is another whose best form has been on faster ground and sharper tracks. *(op 7-1)*

2506 GG-POKER.COM CONDITIONAL JOCKEYS' H'CAP CHASE (18 fncs) 3m 110y
3:05 (3:07) (Class 4) (0-95,92) 5-Y-O+ **£3,594** (£1,055; £527; £263)

Form RPR

-P01 **1** **Never Awol (IRE)**[23] [2009] 8-10-6 80 (p) TMessenger(8) 95+
(B N Pollock) *chsd ldr tl led 3rd: rdn and hdd flat: rallied to ld last strides* **11/2**[3]

4B54 **2** *½* **Francolino (FR)**[16] [2147] 12-9-9 66 oh5 JPritchard(5) 76
(Dr P Pritchard) *a.p: chsd wnr 11th: rdn to ld flat: edgd rt and hdd last strides* **18/1**

3PPP **3** *18* **Maybeseven**[23] [2009] 11-9-6 66 oh3 (v[1]) JStevenson(8) 58
(R Dickin) *chsd ldrs to 9th: sn lost pl: n.d after* **12/1**

2-0U **4** *1 ½* **Ah Yeah (IRE)**[23] [2011] 8-10-11 77 ONelmes 68
(N B King) *hld up: hdwy 10th: wknd 2 out* **11/1**

0-1P **5** *10* **Our Jolly Swagman**[188] [464] 10-11-3 91 (v) WPKavanagh(8) 72
(J W Mullins) *hld up: hdwy 5th: wknd 2 out* **10/1**

PP-3 **P** **Supreme Sir (IRE)**[24] [1983] 7-10-11 77 CBolger —
(P G Murphy) *led to 3rd: chsd ldrs: rdn and wknd after 3 out: p.u bef next* **8/1**

0-4P **U** **Monster Mick (FR)**[193] [398] 7-9-12 72 BWharfe(8) —
(N A Twiston-Davies) *nt jump wl: mid-div: lost pl 7th: in rr whn bmpd and uns rdr 12th* **4/1**[1]

P02- **P** **Bayoss (IRE)**[248] [4523] 9-11-6 86 TGreenway —
(Mrs Tracey Barfoot-Saunt) *chsd ldrs: mstke 2nd: wknd after 9th: t.o whn p.u bef 4 out* **14/1**

-55P **U** **Buzybakson (IRE)**[9] [2293] 8-11-4 87 APogson(3) —
(J R Cornwall) *hld up: bhd 4th: rdn after 3 out: 6th and no ch whn mstke and uns rdr 2 out* **6/1**

2-33 **P** **Gola Supreme (IRE)**[23] [2009] 10-11-12 92 WKennedy —
(R Lee) *hld up: slipped 7th: sn rdn: hdwy whn j. slowly 10th: sn bhd: t.o whn p.u bef 2 out* **5/1**[2]

6m 40.5s (-6.10) **Going Correction** +0.40s/f (Soft)
WFA 5 from 7yo+ 1lb **10** Ran SP% **114.5**
Speed ratings: **107,106,101,100,97 —,—,—,—,—** CSF £90.29 CT £1133.58 TOTE £4.10: £1.50, £4.80, £6.20; EX 83.20.
Owner Charles and Rachel Wilson **Bred** R J McGlynn **Trained** Medbourne, Leics

FOCUS
A very moderate conditionals' handicap but run at a sound gallop. The runner-up sets the mark but the form is very moderate.

NOTEBOOK
Never Awol(IRE), is a quirky customer, but goes well at this track and his rider knows him well. Setting off in front, he looked in control until pulling himself up and waiting for the runner-up after jumping the last, as he did when winning here last time, and then picking up to regain the lead close home. He clearly has a fair amount of ability but is a 'character'. *(op 9-2)*
Francolino(FR), a veteran whose only win in this country was in October 2000, ran quite well from 5lb out of the handicap and briefly looked like ending that sequence when the winner appeared to down tools on the run-in, but that rival was only toying with him. *(op 25-1)*
Maybeseven, pulled up on his last three outings, has won here but does have a somewhat mixed record on the track. The visor seemed to help him complete, but he was well beaten. *(op 22-1)*
Ah Yeah(IRE), still a maiden under Rules, was stepping back up in trip and was given a waiting ride. He moved up looking a threat but seemed to not to get home on a track that places maximum emphasis on stamina. *(op 12-1)*
Gola Supreme(IRE) ran disappointingly over a track and on ground that he has previously shown an aptitude for, and an early slip may have affected his confidence. *(tchd 6-1)*
Monster Mick(FR) was well backed on this return to a softer surface, but for the second time in succession here, ran and jumped poorly. He clearly has some ability but this track does not appear to suit him. *(tchd 6-1)*

2507 GG.COM STANDARD OPEN NATIONAL HUNT FLAT RACE 2m
3:35 (3:35) (Class 6) 4-6-Y-O **£3,653** (£1,072; £536; £267)

Form RPR

1 **1** **Heraldry (IRE)**[23] [2007] 5-11-6 PMerrigan(5) 114+
(P C Haslam) *hld up: hdwy 1/2-way: led over 1f out: edgd lft ins fnl f: styd on* **7/2**[2]

2 *1 ½* **Deep Moon (IRE)** 5-11-4 SStronge 106
(Miss H C Knight) *hld up: hdwy over 4f out: rdn to chse wnr fnl f: styd on* **10/1**

12/ **3** *7* **The Sawyer (BEL)**[592] [4816] 5-11-11 BHitchcott 106
(R H Buckler) *chsd ldrs: rdn and ev ch over 2f out: wknd fnl f* **9/1**

10- **4** *3 ½* **Best Actor (IRE)**[332] [3085] 6-11-11 ATinkler 103+
(M Pitman) *trckd ldrs: led on bit 3f out: rdn and hdd over 1f out: sn wknd* **11/4**[1]

5 *2 ½* **Farmer Brent (IRE)** 5-11-4 JAMcCarthy 93
(C J Down) *hld up: hdwy 1/2-way: wknd 2f out* **28/1**

6 *½* **Bonnie Blue** 6-10-11 SCurran 85
(Mrs Norma Pook) *hld up: hdwy over 6f out: wknd wl over 1f out* **20/1**

4- **7** *3* **Lordington Lad**[255] [4406] 5-11-4 JPMcNamara 89
(B G Powell) *led: racd wd tl jnd main gp after 3f: rdn and hdd 3f out: wknd over 1f out* **9/2**[3]

- **8** *8* **Huron (FR)** 4-11-4 MBradburne 81
(H D Daly) *mid-div: rdn over 6f out: sn bhd* **9/1**

35 **9** *6* **So Long**[16] [2152] 5-10-4 TMessenger(7) 68
(C L Popham) *chsd ldrs: lost pl 1/2-way: wknd over 6f out* **20/1**

330- **10** *2* **Easby Mandarin**[259] [4323] 4-11-4 RGarritty 73
(C W Thornton) *chsd ldrs tl rdn and wknd 3f out* **20/1**

44 **11** *13* **Phriapatius**[28] [1922] 4-10-11 WPKavanagh(7) 60
(Dr J R J Naylor) *mid-div: rdn 1/2-way: sn wknd* **22/1**

P0- **12** *1 ¼* **Kossies Mate**[301] [3598] 6-10-11 HOliver 52
(P W Hiatt) *chsd ldrs over 12f* **50/1**

-P **13** *dist* **Beam Me Up**[202] [242] 5-11-4 JMogford —
(G J Smith) *chsd ldr 7f: wknd over 6f out* **40/1**

14 *21* **Wine River (IRE)** 6-10-13 MNicolls(5) —
(John R Upson) *hld up: bhd fr 1/2-way* **28/1**

15 *22* **The Money Pit** 4-10-13 WKennedy(5) —
(J R Turner) *hld up: a bhd* **50/1**

16 *2* **Winsome Wendy (IRE)** 5-10-6 TGreenway(5) —
(P A Pritchard) *hld up: a bhd* **50/1**

3m 59.9s (-12.00) **Going Correction** +0.60s/f (Soft)
WFA 4 from 5yo+ 12lb **16** Ran SP% **130.0**
Speed ratings: **106,105,101,100,98 98,97,93,90,89 82,81,—,—,—** — CSF £36.23 TOTE £5.60: £2.60, £2.70, £5.10; EX 30.90 Place 6 £196.25, Place 5 £80.51.
Owner Mrs Alurie O'Sullivan **Bred** Ben Sangster **Trained** Middleham, N Yorks

FOCUS
A decent race of its type for the track, run at a sound gallop, being 5.9sec faster than the opening novices' hurdle. The race could be rated higher and should produce winners.

NOTEBOOK
Heraldry(IRE), who is very much Flat-race bred, nevertheless is suited by soft ground and followed up his Haydock win with another decent performance under a penalty. He looks capable of making his mark over hurdles, and his shrewd trainer is likely to find suitable opportunities for him. *(op 4-1)*
Deep Moon(IRE) ◆, a half-brother to the chaser Lord North from a decent jumping family, was settled off the pace and really picked up well up the hill to give the winner a race. He looks sure to benefit from the experience and can win a similar contest en-route to a successful jumping career.
The Sawyer(BEL), who beat the winner of the earlier novice chase in a bumper here in March 2004, has not been seen since failing to defy a penalty the following month. He was up with the pace from the start and, although tiring up the hill, this should have put him straight for a switch to hurdles. *(op 10-1)*
Best Actor(IRE), who won on his debut, has not been seen since disappointing in a Grade Two contest 11 months ago. He again travelled well and looked the likely winner turning in, but once asked for an effort faded rather tamely. He should make a hurdler, but there may be a reason why he seems to fade tamely when let down. *(op 10-3)*
Farmer Brent(IRE), a debutant with a jumping pedigree, being related to the useful Belvederian, ran well on this debut and can be expected to improve from the experience. *(op 20-1)*
Bonnie Blue, who is more Flat-bred on her dam's side, was another to show ability on this racecourse debut.

Lordington Lad, a half-brother to Colonel Frank who made his debut in the spring on faster ground, set off to ensure a good gallop, but once the principals took him on had nothing more to offer. He may be better switched to hurdles now. *(op 4-1)*
T/Plt: £211.50 to a £1 stake. Pool: £33,796.55. 116.65 winning tickets. T/Qpdt: £13.20 to a £1 stake. Pool: £2,072.50. 116.00 winning tickets. CR

2508 - 2514a (Foreign Racing) - See Raceform Interactive

DONCASTER (L-H)

Sunday, November 27

OFFICIAL GOING: Good

After just 2mm of overnight and morning rain the ground was described as 'just on the easy side of good'.
Wind: Moderate, half-behind Weather: overcast and cold

2515 COUNTRY WEEK MARES' ONLY NOVICES' HURDLE (10 hdls) 2m 3f 110y
12:10 (12:12) (Class 3) 4-Y-0+ **£5,126** (£1,505; £752; £375)

Form RPR
03-6 **1** **Cloudless Dawn**[30] [1915] 5-10-12 .... RGarritty 109+
(P Beaumont) *trckd ldrs: led 7th: wnt clr between last 2: eased towards fin* **12/1**
52-4 **2** *10* **Diklers Rose (IRE)**[5] [2414] 6-10-12 .... RMcGrath 96
(K G Reveley) *trckd ldrs: chsd wnr 3 out: no imp* **5/2**[2]
3-22 **3** *12* **Barton Flower**[38] [1794] 4-10-5 98 .... DJacob[(7)] 87+
(D P Keane) *chsd ldrs: one pce fr 3 out* **7/4**[1]
0- **4** *7* **Big Bertha**[260] [2424] 7-10-12 .... GLee 78+
(M D Hammond) *trckd ldrs: 4th and outpcd whn hit 3 out* **15/2**[3]
-414 **5** *2* **Jontys'Lass**[11] [2262] 4-10-9 .... MrTGreenall[(3)] 75
(A Crook) *led to 1st: chsd ldrs: rdn appr 3 out: sn btn* **18/1**
0-0 **6** *7* **New's Full (FR)**[23] [2028] 4-10-9 .... KJMercer[(3)] 68
(Ferdy Murphy) *hld up: hdwy 6th: lost pl appr 3 out* **50/1**
0 **7** *4* **Theatre Belle**[26] [1974] 4-10-12 .... WHutchinson 64
(Ms Deborah J Evans) *chsd ldrs: wknd appr 3 out* **100/1**
2U52 **8** *1 ¼* **Cadeaux Rouge (IRE)**[37] [1814] 4-10-12 80 ....(t) TSiddall 63
(D W Thompson) *chsd ldrs: lost pl after 7th* **25/1**
1 **9** *18* **Granny Shona (IRE)**[216] [27] 4-10-12 .... TDoyle 45
(P R Webber) *led 1st: hdd 7th: wknd appr next* **11/1**
00 **10** *11* **Shinko Femme (IRE)**[21] [2082] 4-10-7 .... DCCostello[(5)] 34
(M E Sowersby) *bhd fr 7th* **100/1**
60-5 **11** *1* **Flemingstone (IRE)**[32] [1889] 5-10-5 .... MrSFMagee[(7)] 33
(J R Norton) *nt jump wl: rdn and lost pl after 6th* **80/1**
12 *6* **Fillameena**[43] 5-10-12 .... KJohnson 27
(P T Midgley) *hld up: hdwy 5th: lost pl after 7th* **40/1**
203- **13** *10* **Dormy Two (IRE)**[399] [1822] 5-10-9 .... PAspell[(3)] 17
(J S Wainwright) *bhd fr 6th* **25/1**
0-P0 **14** *11* **Kokopelli Mana (IRE)**[31] [1895] 5-10-12 .... DO'Meara 6
(J M Jefferson) *j. poorly: in rr: bhd fr 6th: t.o 3 out* **150/1**
60- **15** *dist* **Luscious (IRE)**[282] [3925] 5-10-12 .... AO'Keeffe —
(K C Bailey) *promient: lost pl 5th: sn bhd: t.o 3 out: btn 51l* **66/1**
P **Luchi**[194] 4-10-9 .... TJMalone[(3)] —
(M Scudamore) *t.k.h in rr: bhd fr 4th: sn t.o: p.u bef 3 out* **66/1**
0 **P** **Fae Taylor (IRE)**[23] [2028] 5-10-5 .... PJMcDonald[(7)] —
(Ferdy Murphy) *bhd whn mstke 6th: sn t.o: p.u bef 3 out* **100/1**

4m 44.9s (-8.70) **Going Correction** -0.30s/f (Good) **17** Ran SP% **117.9**
Speed ratings: **105,101,96,93,92 89,88,87,80,76 75,73,69,64,— —,—** CSF £39.85 TOTE £14.80: £3.10, £1.40, £1.30; EX 53.30.
Owner Us Lot **Bred** Mrs J D Goodfellow **Trained** Stearsby, N Yorks

FOCUS
A weak mares-only novices' hurdle but a winner of some potential, one of the few in the line-up with any size and scope. The runner-up sets the level for the form.

NOTEBOOK
Cloudless Dawn, who has plenty of size about her, did not go unbacked. She went on and skipped clear between the last two to score with plenty in hand. The opposition was weak but she should go on from here. *(op 18-1)*
Diklers Rose(IRE), a keen type, ran a lot better than Sedgefield just five days earlier. Suited by the step up in trip, she finished clear second best and three miles will be even more in her favour. She can surely find a similar event. *(op 10-3)*
Barton Flower was left behind by the first two over the final three flights and the step up in trip definitely did not improve her. *(op 2-1 tchd 9-4 in places)*
Big Bertha, well named, had two handlers in the paddock. She was struggling to keep up when clouting the third last but the experience, it was just her second start over hurdles, will not be lost on her. *(op 8-1 tchd 7-1)*
Jontys'Lass was in trouble turning in on just her second start over hurdles. Her bumper win was on fast ground.
Shinko Femme(IRE) *Official explanation: jockey said filly had a breathing problem*

2516 YORKSHIREPOSTTODAY.COM NOVICES' CHASE (A LIMITED H'CAP) (11 fncs 1 omitted) 2m 110y
12:40 (12:40) (Class 3) (0-130,128) 4-Y-0+ **£8,148** (£2,392; £1,196; £597)

Form RPR
11F3 **1** **Feel The Pride (IRE)**[7] [2371] 7-11-10 **128** .... BHarding 131+
(Jonjo O'Neill) *trckd ldrs: stdy hdwy 7th: led between last 2: rdn rt out* **11/4**[3]
51-3 **2** *¾* **Carthys Cross (IRE)**[14] [2213] 6-10-13 **117** .... JMMaguire 119
(T R George) *trckd ldrs: led 3 out: sn rdn: hdd appr last: kpt on wl: no ex last 75yds* **15/8**[1]
-515 **3** *10* **Rooster's Reunion (IRE)**[23] [2016] 6-11-2 **120** .... GLee 113+
(D R Gandolfo) *hld up in last: reminders 7th: kpt on to take mod 3rd run-in* **5/2**[2]
64-0 **4** *4* **Banchory Two (IRE)**[17] [2144] 5-10-9 **113** .... TDoyle 105+
(P F Nicholls) *led 1st: rdn after 7th: hdd 3 out: 3rd and btn whn hit 2 out: sn wknd* **9/2**
46P0 **5** *12* **Dabus**[4] [2443] 10-10-4 **108** oh9 ....(b) KJohnson 84
(M C Chapman) *t.k.h: led to 1st: lost pl appr 4 out: t.o last* **50/1**

4m 3.50s (-5.50) **Going Correction** -0.15s/f (Good) **5** Ran SP% **110.2**
Speed ratings: **106,105,100,99,93** CSF £8.64 TOTE £2.90: £1.10, £1.70; EX 4.90.
Owner Mrs M Liston **Bred** Thomas B Russell **Trained** Cheltenham, Gloucs

FOCUS
A fair novices' chase run at a reasonable pace and rated through the winner.

NOTEBOOK
Feel The Pride(IRE), who took a heavy fall two outings ago, still lacks confidence at her fences. She made hard work of getting her head in front but this will have done her at least some good. *(op 7-4 tchd 6-4 in places)*
Carthys Cross(IRE), having just his second start over fences and running from his hurdle-race mark, seemed to hang fire in front. He came back for more on the run-in and deserves to go one better. *(op 11-4 tchd 3-1 in a place)*
Rooster's Reunion(IRE), happy to sit off the pace, made very hard work of it and was never going to get anywhere near the first two. *(op 3-1)*
Banchory Two(IRE), making his debut over fences, was out on his feet when hitting the second last and, even though he needs further, he will struggle in handicap company from a mark of 113. *(op 11-2)*

2517 YORKSHIRE SPORT NOVICES' H'CAP HURDLE (11 hdls) 3m 110y
1:15 (1:15) (Class 4) (0-100,100) 4-Y-0+ **£4,319** (£1,268; £634; £316)

Form RPR
4220 **1** **Qualitair Pleasure**[8] [2347] 5-11-7 **98** .... KJMercer[(3)] 99
(J Hetherton) *hld up: hdwy 7th: sn chsng ldrs: led between last 2: hld on towards fin* **17/2**[3]
00 **2** *½* **Kyno (IRE)**[30] [1903] 4-11-2 **90** .... TDoyle 91
(M G Quinlan) *trckd ldrs: styd on to chse wnr run-in: no ex towards fin* **14/1**
-333 **3** *2 ½* **Welsh Dane**[38] [1806] 5-10-9 **83** ....(p) WHutchinson 82+
(M Sheppard) *led: hit 2 out: sn hdd: one pce run-in* **8/1**[2]
00-4 **4** *3 ½* **Running Lord (IRE)**[27] [1959] 7-11-12 **100** .... MBradburne 96+
(D A Rees) *w ldrs: one pce appr last* **16/1**
PP-P **5** *6* **Cleymor House (IRE)**[15] [2181] 7-10-0 **77** ow3 ....(b[1]) LVickers[(3)] 67+
(John R Upson) *chsd ldrs: one pce fr 3 out* **33/1**
5-36 **6** *13* **Strolling Vagabond (IRE)**[21] [2073] 6-10-1 **75** .... DO'Meara 51
(John R Upson) *chsd ldrs: drvn along 5th: wknd appr 3 out* **10/1**
150 **7** *1 ¾* **Uncle John**[25] [1987] 4-10-6 **83** ....(p) PBuchanan[(3)] 57
(M E Sowersby) *hld up: hdwy 7th: chsng ldrs next: wknd 3 out* **18/1**
4-14 **8** *1* **Tickateal**[185] [509] 5-11-7 **95** .... BHarding 68+
(R D E Woodhouse) *hdwy 7th: sn chsng ldrs: wkng whn stmbld 2 out* **8/1**[2]
6020 **9** *11* **Northern Rambler (IRE)**[4] [2440] 8-9-4 **74** oh2 .... JReveley[(10)] 36
(K G Reveley) *chsd ldrs: lost pl 7th: sn in rr* **16/1**
0UP0 **10** *dist* **Government (IRE)**[19] [2099] 4-10-0 **74** oh10 .... KJohnson —
(M C Chapman) *t.k.h in rr: bhd fr 7th: t.o 3 out* **100/1**
6000 **P** **Iloveturtle (IRE)**[4] [2440] 5-11-0 **95** ....(t) MrBKing[(7)] —
(M C Chapman) *mstkes: bhd fr 8th: p.u bef last* **33/1**
236- **P** **Kynance Cove**[523] [801] 6-9-7 **74** oh10 .... RSpate[(7)] —
(C P Morlock) *in rr: bhd fr 7th: t.o whn p.u bef 3 out* **33/1**
1163 **P** **Waynesworld (IRE)**[14] [2214] 7-10-10 **87** .... TJMalone[(3)] —
(M Scudamore) *in rr: lost tch after 7th: bhd whn p.u bef 3 out* **4/1**[1]
P3 **P** **Kiss The Girls (IRE)**[21] [2073] 6-10-2 **76** .... AO'Keeffe —
(Jennie Candlish) *hld up in rr: bhd fr 7th: t.o whn p.u bef 3 out* **18/1**
13 **P** **High Country (IRE)**[58] [1591] 5-11-12 **100** .... GLee —
(M D Hammond) *hdwy 7th: chsng ldrs next: wknd 3 out: 8th whn p.u bef 2 out* **4/1**[1]

6m 7.90s (-8.60) **Going Correction** -0.30s/f (Good)
WFA 4 from 5yo+ 14lb **15** Ran SP% **120.6**
Speed ratings: **101,100,100,98,97 92,92,91,88,— —,—,—,—,—** CSF £117.37 CT £999.08 TOTE £11.70: £3.30, £8.10, £2.70; EX 146.70.
Owner PSB Holdings Ltd **Bred** Qualitair Stud Ltd **Trained** Norton, N Yorks
■ Stewards' Enquiry : K J Mercer one-day ban: used whip in the incorrect place (Dec 8)

FOCUS
A moderate novices' handicap rated through third and fifth and the form is average.

NOTEBOOK
Qualitair Pleasure, a tough mare, likes decent ground and the step up in trip proved no problem. She had to dig deep but was always going to hold on. *(op 11-1 tchd 8-1)*
Kyno(IRE), having his second outing in a month after a five-month break, was a springer in the market on just his second outing here. He stayed on to go in pursuit of the winner and battled all the way to the line. *(op 20-1)*
Welsh Dane, better for the five-week break, set a good gallop and seemed to relish the step up to three miles. He was certainly not stopping on the run-in. *(op 15-2 tchd 17-2)*
Running Lord(IRE), making his handicap debut on just his fourth start, was far from disgraced but looks to have started life in handicaps from a stiffish mark. *(op 20-1 tchd 22-1)*
Cleymor House(IRE), tried in blinkers, showed a fraction more but it was after all his 15th career start.
High Country(IRE) dropped out in a matter of strides at the third last and it transpired that he had been struck into. *Official explanation: jockey said gelding had been struck into (op 6-1)*
Waynesworld(IRE) ran poorly for no apparent reason. *Official explanation: trainer had no explanation for the poor form shown (op 6-1)*

2518 YORKSHIRE POST H'CAP CHASE (18 fncs 1 omitted) 3m 2f
1:45 (1:46) (Class 3) (0-125,124) 5-Y-0+ **£10,432** (£3,062; £1,531; £764)

Form RPR
42P4 **1** **Lothian Falcon**[12] [2259] 6-10-0 **98** .... MBradburne 111+
(P Maddison) *in tch: hdwy 14th: wnt 2nd next: led 3 out: hld on wl run-in* **12/1**
3-52 **2** *1 ½* **The Kew Tour (IRE)**[26] [1972] 9-11-5 **117** .... DElsworth 127
(Mrs S J Smith) *led to 3 out: rallied last: no ex* **3/1**[2]
0-P6 **3** *1* **French Executive (IRE)**[139] [960] 10-11-2 **121** .... MissCTizzard[(7)] 130
(P F Nicholls) *t.k.h: trckd ldrs: effrt 4 out: kpt on same pce fr 2 out* **7/1**
24-P **4** *19* **Jimmy Tennis (FR)**[190] [454] 8-10-13 **111** .... AO'Keeffe 101
(Miss Venetia Williams) *w ldr: wknd 4 out* **9/1**
/1-2 **5** *3* **Ken'tucky (FR)**[22] [2046] 7-11-12 **124** .... WHutchinson 111
(A King) *trckd ldrs: outpcd appr 4 out: sn lost pl* **9/4**[1]
03-P **6** *dist* **Tyndarius (IRE)**[182] [572] 14-10-4 **105** .... PAspell[(3)] —
(A Crook) *sn last: outpcd and drvn along 9th: t.o 4 out: btn 40l* **25/1**
21/P **P** **Over The Storm (IRE)**[28] [1941] 8-11-7 **119** .... DO'Meara —
(H P Hogarth) *chsd ldrs: reminders 11th: rdn and lost pl 13th: bhd whn p.u bef 4 out* **4/1**[3]

6m 31.8s (-8.30) **Going Correction** -0.15s/f (Good) **7** Ran SP% **109.8**
Speed ratings: **106,105,105,99,98 —,—** CSF £45.29 CT £255.82 TOTE £12.30: £5.40, £1.70; EX 54.90.
Owner Peter Maddison **Bred** C J And Mrs Wilson, Mrs D Du Feu And Mrs O J **Trained** Skewsby, N Yorks

FOCUS
A fair handicap run in a fair time, and although the winner looked improved the form behind is sound enough.

NOTEBOOK
Lothian Falcon, having just his third start over fences, relished the step up in trip and showed a willing attitude to repel the runner-up's renewed effort on the run-in. This was a much improved effort. *(op 14-1)*
The Kew Tour(IRE) took them along at a sound gallop and went down fighting. He deserves a change of luck. *(op 10-3 tchd 7-2)*
French Executive(IRE), back on a winning mark, has won for this rider in the past. He tends to do his own thing and only seemed to be half putting it in. *(op 5-1)*

Jimmy Tennis(FR), absent since May and with the blinkers left off, took on the leaders but seemed to fold tamely. *(op 10-1)*
Ken'tucky(FR), having just his third start over fences, found himself tapped for toe on the run *round to four out and he soon called it a day. This was basically too bad to be true. Official explanation: trainer had no explanation for the poor form shown (op 2-1 tchd 15-8)*
Over The Storm(IRE), pulled up on his return a month ago, was racing on much better ground but he ran a tame sort of race and his response to pressure was limited to say the very least. *(op 11-2)*

2519 SPORTS MONDAY H'CAP HURDLE (10 hdls) 2m 3f 110y

2:20 (2:20) (Class 3) (0-135,135) 4-Y-0+ **£6,974** (£2,047; £1,023; £511)

Form RPR

54U- **1** **October Mist (IRE)**[177] 4812 11-9-5 **110**.................... JReveley(10) 111
(K G Reveley) *chsd ldrs: drvn along 7th: wnt 2nd next: styd on to ld last 75yds* **22/1**

5-14 **2** *hd* **Hernando's Boy**[8] 2334 4-10-11 **120**.................... RMcGrath 122+
(K G Reveley) *trckd ldrs: led 7th: hdd and no ex towards fin* **4/1**[2]

-130 **3** *3/4* **Fait Le Jojo (FR)**[14] 2209 8-11-7 **135**.................... HEphgrave(5) 135
(L Corcoran) *led 2nd to 7th: kpt on fr 3 out: no ex last 100yds* **4/1**[2]

11-0 **4** *6* **Always Waining (IRE)**[15] 2184 4-10-1 **120**.................... TBurrows(10) 115+
(P L Clinton) *chsd ldrs: 4th and one pce whn hit last* **14/1**

1634 **5** *4* **Karathaena (IRE)**[21] 2079 5-9-12 **110**.................... KJMercer(3) 100
(M E Sowersby) *in rr: outpcd 6th: hdwy 3 out: nvr trbld ldrs* **9/1**

21- **6** *9* **Credit (IRE)**[141] 3887 4-10-10 **119**.................... GLee 100
(J Howard Johnson) *hld up in rr: hdwy to chse ldrs 7th: drvn along appr 3 out: nvr a real threat: eased between last 2* **2/1**[1]

/3-5 **7** *10* **Sargon**[31] 1894 6-10-3 **112**.................... (b) MBradburne 83
(Robert Gray) *sn chsng ldrs: lost pl appr 3 out* **66/1**

4-11 **8** *4* **Swift Swallow**[185] 525 7-11-4 **127**.................... TDoyle 94
(O Brennan) *hld up in rr: effrt 7th: nvr a factor: in rr whn hit 2 out* **13/2**[3]

-533 **P** **Low Cloud**[53] 1644 5-9-10 **110**.................... DCCostello(5) —
(J J Quinn) *t.k.h: led to 2nd: mstke 5th: sn lost pl: t.o whn p.u bef 3 out* **33/1**

4m 42.3s (-11.30) **Going Correction** -0.30s/f (Good)
WFA 4 from 5yo+ 12lb **9** Ran SP% **112.1**
Speed ratings: **110,109,109,107,105 102,98,96,—** CSF £105.38 CT £432.04 TOTE £25.10: £5.10, £1.70, £1.70; EX 39.50.
Owner Mrs E A Murray **Bred** Michael Maye **Trained** Lingdale, N Yorks
■ Stewards' Enquiry : R McGrath caution: careless riding

FOCUS
A fair handicap in which the form looks solid and the first four were all close to their marks

NOTEBOOK
October Mist(IRE), without a win for over three years, stuck on in determined fashion and in the end his young rider's 10lb claim proved decisive. *(op 25-1 tchd 20-1)*
Hernando's Boy, back up in trip, went on and fought hard all the way to the line only to be foiled by his lesser fancied stablemate. *(tchd 7-2)*
Fait Le Jojo(FR), in good form for this yard, enjoyed himself in front and battled back all the way to the line. *(op 5-1)*
Always Waining(IRE) ran much better than on his two starts since his summer break. He will improve again for the outing. *(op 12-1)*
Karathaena(IRE) struggled to keep up and, on ground faster than she cares for, she simply stayed on in her own time up the home straight. *(op 12-1)*
Credit(IRE), who won on his second and final start over hurdles last term, looked feasibly weighted but he was in trouble before stamina became an issue on the final turn. He can surely do a fair bit better than this. *(tchd 9-4 and 15-8 in places)*

2520 E B F YELLER "JUNIOR" STANDARD OPEN NATIONAL HUNT FLAT RACE (DIV I) 1m 5f

2:50 (2:51) (Class 6) 3-Y-O **£1,850** (£539; £269)

Form RPR

1 **Wolds Way** 3-10-12.................... RGarritty 95+
(T D Easterby) *hld up: hdwy 6f out: led over 3f out: hung lft: kpt on wl ins t last* **8/1**

2 *1* **Tooting (IRE)** 3-10-12.................... GLee 94+
(J Nicol) *hld up: hdwy 6f out: chal 3f out: no ex ins last* **7/2**[2]

3 *9* **Graphex** 3-10-12.................... WHutchinson 82+
(A King) *in rr: drvn along 7f out: hdwy over 3f out: nvr nr 1st 2* **2/1**[1]

4 *1/2* **Of Course (FR)** 3-10-9.................... PBuchanan(3) 81
(Miss Kate Milligan) *hld up in rr: hdwy on outside to chse ldrs over 4f out: one pce fnl 3f* **66/1**

5 **5** *9* **Ballinger Venture**[24] 2013 3-10-2.................... TJPhelan(3) 63
(N M Babbage) *sn chsng ldrs: hung lft over 3f out: wknd over 2f out* **50/1**

6 *3 1/2* **Now Then Katie** 3-10-5.................... ADempsey 58
(C Grant) *chsd ldrs: wknd over 3f out* **12/1**

35 **7** *1 1/4* **Rourke Star**[5] 2425 3-10-9.................... (b[1]) LVickers(3) 63
(S R Bowring) *trckd ldrs: led over 6f out: hung lft and hdd over 3f out: sn lost pl* **17/2**

8 *5* **Amadores** 3-10-0.................... StephenJCraine(5) 50
(J Ryan) *mid-div: drvn along 9f out: lost pl over 3f out* **25/1**

9 *16* **Smart Street** 3-10-12.................... RMcGrath 36
(K G Reveley) *prom: drvn along 4f out: sn lost pl* **6/1**[3]

10 *3/4* **Rectangle Blue** 3-10-12.................... KRenwick 35
(M D Hammond) *mid-div: drvn along 6f out: sn lost pl* **66/1**

0 **11** *18* **Chateau (IRE)**[19] 2105 3-10-7.................... DCCostello(5) 12
(G A Swinbank) *chsd ldrs: lost pl 4f out: sn bhd* **16/1**

0 **12** *7* **Master Pip**[21] 2068 3-10-12.................... DNolan 3
(R F Fisher) *repeatedly bucked after s: led: hdd over 6f out: sn lost pl and bhd* **50/1**

3m 5.00s **12** Ran SP% **115.8**
CSF £34.38 TOTE £7.20: £2.10, £2.10, £1.60; EX 33.60.
Owner D B Lamplough **Bred** D B Lamplough **Trained** Great Habton, N Yorks

FOCUS
Although the form could rate higher, this was much the slower and almost certainly the weaker division.

NOTEBOOK
Wolds Way, a big, rangy type, has an exaggerated knee action. His inexperience was evident but he showed the right spirit to repel his sole challenger. *(op 13-2 tchd 5-1)*
Tooting(IRE), a lengthy son of Dr Devious, moved up travelling smoothly but in the end was definitely second best, though a long way clear of the remainder. *(op 10-3)*
Graphex, who stands over plenty of ground, was soon struggling and it was only his rider's persistance that enabled him to claim third spot in the end. *(op 3-1)*
Of Course(FR), a very big individual, moved up on the outer turning in but, soon flat out, was made to look very slow. He will need plenty of time. *(op 50-1)*
Ballinger Venture, a handful in the paddock, would not go forward in a straight line and looks a real madam.
Now Then Katie was very noisy in the paddock. *(op 14-1)*
Smart Street *Official explanation: jockey said gelding lost its action (op 9-2)*

2521 E B F YELLER "JUNIOR" STANDARD OPEN NATIONAL HUNT FLAT RACE (DIV II) 1m 5f

3:25 (3:25) (Class 6) 3-Y-O **£1,850** (£539; £269)

Form RPR

3 **1** **Burnt Oak (UAE)**[21] 2068 3-10-12.................... FKeniry 99+
(C W Fairhurst) *hld up: smooth hdwy over 4f out: led over 3f out: clr over 1f out: readily* **9/1**

2 *4* **Cheer Us On** 3-10-9.................... MrTGreenall(3) 91
(M W Easterby) *in tch: effrt over 3f out: sn chsng ldrs: styd on fnl f: tk 2nd nr fin* **4/1**[2]

3 *1/2* **Nodform William** 3-10-12.................... GLee 90
(Karen McLintock) *trckd ldrs: led 5f out tl over 3f out: kpt on same pce fnl 2f* **13/2**[3]

3 **4** *hd* **Inherent (IRE)**[24] 2014 3-10-5.................... MBradburne 83
(C G Cox) *hld up: hdwy 5f out: chsd wnr 3f out: kpt on same pce* **9/4**[1]

5 *3* **Sandysnowing (FR)** 3-10-5.................... BSHughes(7) 86
(J Howard Johnson) *chsd ldrs: edgd lft and one pce fnl 2f* **12/1**

6 *5* **Itsy Bitsy** 3-10-5.................... JMMaguire 72
(W J Musson) *rr-div: hdwy 5f out: sn prom: wknd fnl 2f* **33/1**

7 *8* **Taras Knight (IRE)** 3-10-12.................... RGarritty 69
(J J Quinn) *hld up towards rr: hdwy 5f out: chsng ldrs over 3f out: sn wknd* **14/1**

5 **8** *1 3/4* **Hardknott (IRE)**[21] 2068 3-10-9.................... PAspell(3) 67
(R F Fisher) *chsd ldrs: rdn and lost pl 3f out* **33/1**

9 *6* **Spring Ice** 3-10-2.................... TJMalone(3) 52
(M Scudamore) *swvd lft s: detached in rr: nvr on terms* **25/1**

10 *3* **City Of Manchester (IRE)** 3-10-12.................... ADempsey 55
(D Nicholls) *hld up towards rr: drvn along over 4f out: lost pl over 3f out* **20/1**

0 **11** *27* **Celtic Realm (IRE)**[40] 1785 3-10-12.................... RMcGrath 20
(K G Reveley) *led: hdd 5f out: sn lost pl and bhd* **7/1**

12 *15* **Cold Call** 3-10-12.................... NPMulholland —
(C W Thornton) *chsd ldrs: rdn over 5f out: sn lost pl and bhd* **33/1**

3m 2.70s **12** Ran SP% **118.4**
CSF £42.12 TOTE £12.60: £3.30, £2.40, £2.90; EX 57.20 Place 6 £64.56, Place 5 £50.23.
Owner Glasgow House Racing Syndicate **Bred** Darley **Trained** Middleham, N Yorks

FOCUS
Probably the better of the two divisions with much the nicer types in the paddock, a stronger pace and a faster time and the form could be reasonable.

NOTEBOOK
Burnt Oak(UAE), a decent type, came there on the bridle and made this look very simple. He should have a future. *(op 8-1)*
Cheer Us On, who stands over a fair amount of ground, was well fancied. He was making hard work of it once in line for home and it was his stamina that in the end saw him claim second spot. He will appreciate the full two miles. *(op 6-1 tchd 13-2 and 7-2 in places)*
Nodform William, who has a fair amount of size and scope, made a pleasing debut taking it up before the home turn and keeping on all the way to the line. *(op 6-1 tchd 7-1)*
Inherent(IRE), quite a tall type, tended to hang and, making hard work of it when sent in pursuit of the winner, was never a real threat. The ground was much less testing and this track and Towcester are totally different. *(tchd 2-1 and 5-2)*
Sandysnowing(FR), a medium-sized, quite well-made gelding, was in the thick of things from the off but his inexperience showed as he came off a straight line under pressure. *(op 9-1 tchd 16-1)*
Taras Knight(IRE) *Official explanation: jockey said gelding had a breathing problem (op 10-1)*
T/Plt: £78.10 to a £1 stake. Pool: £38,141.80. 356.40 winning tickets. T/Qpdt: £51.90 to a £1 stake. Pool: £2,500.70. 35.60 winning tickets. WG

[2243] LEICESTER (R-H)

Sunday, November 27

OFFICIAL GOING: Chase course - good to firm; hurdle course - good to soft (soft in places)
Wind: Almost nil Weather: Showers

2522 LADBROKES.COM CLASSIFIED CHASE (15 fncs) 2m 4f 110y

12:50 (12:51) (Class 4) 5-Y-O+ **£4,925** (£1,445; £722; £361)

Form RPR

502P **1** **Swallow Magic (IRE)**[30] 1905 7-10-7 87.................... (v) TJDreaper(7) 98+
(Ferdy Murphy) *led to 2nd: led 4th: rdn out* **11/2**[2]

U5P3 **2** *1/2* **Walcot Lad (IRE)**[12] 2259 9-10-11 86.................... (p) CBolger(3) 96
(A Ennis) *led 2nd to 4th: rdn appr 3 out: r.o* **12/1**

4241 **3** *3 1/2* **Eau Pure (FR)**[13] 2248 8-11-3 96.................... JEMoore 96
(G L Moore) *hld up: hdwy 7th: rdn appr 2 out: styd on same pce last* **7/4**[1]

4346 **4** *1 3/4* **Just Muckin Around (IRE)**[14] 2217 9-11-0 87.................... BHitchcott 91
(R H Buckler) *chsd ldrs: rdn 3 out: styd on same pce fr next* **10/1**

6/0 **5** *11* **Constant Husband**[17] 2140 12-10-7 65.................... MrGTumelty(7) 82+
(R N Bevis) *hld up: hdwy appr 3 out: nt trble ldrs* **66/1**

031 **6** *hd* **Regal Vision (IRE)**[38] 1803 8-10-7 82.................... MissCDyson(7) 80
(Miss C Dyson) *prom: rdn 8th: wknd after 3 out* **11/1**

5P/6 **7** *shd* **Prairie Minstrel (USA)**[35] 1855 11-10-7 90.................... (p) JPritchard(7) 84+
(R Dickin) *chsd ldrs: rdn 4 out: wknd last* **13/2**

06/P **8** *27* **John Foley (IRE)**[26] 1976 7-10-7 90.................... (t) APogson(7) 52
(J R Holt) *chsd ldrs: n.m.r and lost pl bnd after 5th: n.d after* **33/1**

/56P **9** *nk* **Chocolate Bombe (IRE)**[10] 2285 8-10-11 64.................... TJPhelan(3) 52
(S Lycett) *hld up: a bhd* **66/1**

P-65 **F** **Cusp**[35] 1852 5-10-6 90.................... DLaverty(5) 75
(Mrs A M Thorpe) *hld up: hdwy 5th: rdn 9th: wkng whn fell 2 out* **25/1**

-424 **U** **Sailor A'Hoy**[10] 2284 9-10-11 82.................... (p) ACCoyle(3) —
(M Mullineaux) *hld up: rdn 8th: in rr whn blnd and uns rdr 4 out* **6/1**[3]

0-3P **P** **Penalty Clause (IRE)**[36] 1832 5-10-7 85.................... SWalsh(7) —
(Lucinda Featherstone) *hld up: blnd 7th: hit 3 out: t.o whn p.u bef next* **20/1**

5m 11.3s (-12.30) **Going Correction** -0.50s/f (Good) **12** Ran SP% **119.0**
Speed ratings: **103,102,101,100,96 96,96,86,86,— —,—** CSF £63.42 TOTE £6.60: £1.70, £2.50, £1.60; EX 69.60.
Owner J D Gordon **Bred** Foreneish Racing **Trained** West Witton, N Yorks
■ Stewards' Enquiry : J Pritchard caution: allowed gelding to coast home without assistance

FOCUS
A moderate classified chase but the form looks pretty solid with the runner-up to mark.

NOTEBOOK
Swallow Magic(IRE), pulled up over three miles on soft ground at Uttoxeter on his previous start, proved well suited by this much faster surface and coped well enough with the drop in trip. It would appear he must have decent ground. *(op 5-1 tchd 9-2)*
Walcot Lad(IRE), as when third at Fakenham on his previous start, posted a good effort in defeat. He looks up to winning a similar race whilst in this sort of form. *(op 11-1)*

Eau Pure(FR), the best off at the weights, looked to have an obvious chance of following up her recent course and distance success, but she could only produce the one pace. *(op 9-4 tchd 5-2 in places)*
Just Muckin Around(IRE) has dropped to a mark 2lb lower than when last winning and offered some hope in fourth. *(op 8-1)*
Constant Husband, back over fences, was given too much to do.
Prairie Minstrel(USA) *Official explanation: jockey said gelding hung right (op 11-2)*
Sailor A'Hoy, back up in trip with the cheekpieces re-fitted, looked to have it all to do when unseating. *(op 8-1)*

2523 LADBROKES.COM (S) HURDLE (9 hdls) 2m
1:25 (1:25) (Class 5) 4-7-Y-0 **£3,536** (£1,038; £519; £259)

Form			Horse	RPR
3PU-	**1**		**Birdwatch**[148] 4298 7-11-0 94 ....(b[1]) JimCrowley *(K G Reveley) led to 2nd: chsd ldr: led 3 out: styd on* **9/2**[3]	93+
34-1	**2**	*2 ½*	**Indian Star (GER)**[24] 2008 7-11-10 99 ....(t) JMogford *(J C Tuck) hld up: hdwy after 5th: chsd wnr 2 out: rdn and hit last: styd on same pce flat* **6/4**[1]	100
POF/	**3**	*3 ½*	**He's A Rascal (IRE)**[85] 3921 7-11-0 ....(p) JAMcCarthy *(A J Lidderdale) hld up: hdwy appr 3 out: sn outpcd: styd on appr last: nt trble ldrs* **16/1**	87
0	**4**	*6*	**Weet Watchers**[17] 2139 5-10-7 .... MGoldstein[(7)] *(T Wall) chsd ldrs tl wknd appr last* **20/1**	81
P-45	**5**	*4*	**Makandy**[166] 743 6-10-7 .... MrRArmson[(7)] *(R J Armson) led 2nd: sn clr: hdd 3 out: wknd bef next* **50/1**	77
3254	**6**	*1 ½*	**Rifleman (IRE)**[10] 2289 5-10-11 96 ....(t) CBolger[(3)] *(Robert Gray) hld up in tch: mstke 3rd: rdn appr 2 out: wknd bef last* **5/2**[2]	77+
5F56	**7**	*28*	**Hunter Pudding**[10] 2283 5-10-0 74 .... TMessenger[(7)] *(C L Popham) bhd fr 4th* **33/1**	40
0-0P	**8**	*10*	**Just Filly (IRE)**[21] 2082 4-10-4 .... ACCoyle[(3)] *(Miss C J E Caroe) plld hrd and prom: wknd appr 3 out* **50/1**	30
0	**9**	*21*	**Fools Entire**[29] 1916 4-11-0 .... WMarston *(Miss J Feilden) plld hrd and prom: rdn and wknd appr 2 out* **16/1**	16
05-P	**10**	*4*	**Purr**[14] 2216 4-10-7 77 .... MrSRees[(7)] *(M Wigham) a bhd* **25/1**	12
0-0P	**F**		**Ray Mond**[7] 2374 4-10-10 ow3 .... MrMMackley[(7)] *(M J Gingell) fell 2nd* **50/1**	—
	P		**Grumpyintmorning**[11] 6-10-9 .... CHonour[(5)] *(M J Gingell) bhd fr 3rd: t.o whn p.u bef 2 out* **18/1**	—
	P		**Hallahoise Hydro (IRE)**[52] 4-11-0 .... ARoss *(B S Rothwell) mstke 2nd: bhd fr next: t.o whn p.u bef 3 out* **50/1**	—

3m 56.2s (-11.40) **Going Correction** -0.675s/f (Firm)
WFA 4 from 5yo+ 12lb **13** Ran SP% **123.2**
Speed ratings: **101,99,98,95,93 92,78,73,62,60** —,—,— CSF £11.71 TOTE £4.80: £2.10, £1.10, £8.50; EX 12.60.The winner was bought in for 10,000gns.
Owner Jeremy Mitchell And Janet Powney **Bred** W R Lewis **Trained** Lingdale, N Yorks

FOCUS
As is to be expected with selling hurdles, a moderate race, but the first two ran to their marks and the time was fair.

NOTEBOOK
Birdwatch, a 30-rated maiden on the Flat who was racing over three miles when last seen hurdling, took well to the fitting of blinkers on this significant drop in trip and gained his first success under any code at the 17th attempt. It remains to be seen if can repeat this next time. *(tchd 5-1)*
Indian Star(GER), successful in this grade at Towcester on his previous start, again ran well and just failed to follow up. *(op 15-8 tchd 2-1)*
He's A Rascal(IRE) has been very lightly raced in recent times, but he was not without promise in a couple of runs on the Flat this year and, returned to hurdles for the first time since 2002 with the cheekpieces re-fitted, he offered plenty of promise. He will almost certainly get a much longer trip, and looks up to gaining a deserved first success. *(op 20-1)*
Weet Watchers stepped up on the form he showed on his hurdling debut at Ludlow. *(op 25-1 tchd 18-1)*
Makandy was well held off the back of a 166-day break. *(op 40-1)*
Rifleman(IRE) was the best off at the weights on this return to selling company, but he ran well below his mark and surprisingly remains a maiden over hurdles. *Official explanation: jockey said, regarding appearing to prematurely ease mount on run-in, gelding hung approaching the line and appeared to have lost its action but subsequently pulled up sound (tchd 9-4, 11-4 and 3-1 in places)*

2524 LADBROKES.COM LEICESTERSHIRE H'CAP CHASE (18 fncs) 2m 7f 110y
1:55 (1:55) (Class 3) (0-120,105) 5-Y-0+ **£6,832** (£2,018; £1,009; £504; £252)

Form			Horse	RPR
2150	**1**		**Strong Magic (IRE)**[9] 2325 13-10-3 89 .... APogson[(7)] *(J R Cornwall) hld up: hdwy 11th: chsd ldr appr 3 out: led flat: styd on wl* **5/1**[3]	—
P0P4	**2**	*7*	**Jacdor (IRE)**[13] 2248 11-11-0 93 ....(v) JEMoore *(R Dickin) chsd ldr tl led 9th: hdd 12th: led 14th: rdn and edgd rt appr last: wknd and hdd flat* **5/1**[3]	—
0-05	**3**	*2*	**Deliceo (IRE)**[17] 2140 12-11-9 102 .... JAMcCarthy *(M Sheppard) hld up: hdwy 11th: styd on same pce fr 2 out* **8/1**	—
PF-6	**4**	*26*	**Place Above (IRE)**[46] 1723 9-10-12 98 .... TJDreaper[(7)] *(E A Elliott) chsd ldrs: hit 10th: sn lost pl: wknd 5 out* **8/1**	—
-660	**5**	*10*	**Pardini (USA)**[16] 2164 6-11-2 95 .... BHitchcott *(M F Harris) chsd ldrs: rdn 9th: wknd 5 out: bhd whn hit 3 out* **13/2**	—
-PPP	**6**	*15*	**Ankles Back (IRE)**[166] 746 8-11-7 105 .... TGreenway[(5)] *(H D Daly) racd keenly: led to 9th: led 12th to 14th: rdn and wknd after 4 out* **10/3**[1]	—
3P50	**U**		**Happy Hussar (IRE)**[16] 2164 12-10-7 91 .... DrPPritchard[(5)] *(Dr P Pritchard) prom tl blnd and uns rdr 5th* **9/2**[2]	—

5m 58.5s (-6.90) **Going Correction** -0.50s/f (Good) **7** Ran SP% **110.1**
Speed ratings: **91,88,88,79,76 71**,— CSF £27.74 TOTE £7.20: £2.70, £1.90; EX 25.70.
Owner J R Cornwall **Bred** Thomas Walsh **Trained** Long Clawson, Leics

FOCUS
A very moderate handicap chase and the winning time was very ordinary. Although the form is weak the first two ran to their marks.

NOTEBOOK
Strong Magic(IRE) had not been in much form since winning at Fakenham the previous month, but he was 3lb lower than when gaining that success as a result, and ran out a ready winner under a well-judged ride from his 7lb claimer. He will go back up in the weights for this, and that will make things tougher. *(tchd 9-2)*
Jacdor(IRE) ◆ had lost his way since winning two on the bounce at the beginning of last year, but he offered promise over two and a half miles here on his previous start, and this was even more encouraging. Now 9lb lower than when last winning, he is one to keep on the right side of. *(op 4-1 tchd 11-2)*
Deliceo(IRE) would have appreciated the return to chasing and ran respectably enough in third. *(op 13-2)*
Place Above(IRE), back over fences, was again well held. *(op 15-2)*
Pardini(USA) continues out of form. *(op 7-1)*
Ankles Back(IRE), returning from a 166-day break, managed to complete this time but was still beaten a mile. *Official explanation: trainer had no explanation for the poor form shown (op 4-1)*
Happy Hussar(IRE) got the fifth all wrong. *(op 5-1)*

2525 HEART 106 H'CAP HURDLE (9 hdls) 2m
2:30 (2:30) (Class 3) (0-120,113) 5-Y-0+ **£6,601** (£1,949; £974; £488; £243; £122)

Form			Horse	RPR
PP30	**1**		**Honest Endeavour**[25] 1987 6-10-11 105 ....(p) TJDreaper[(7)] *(J M Jefferson) led 2nd: rdn clr flat* **25/1**	—+
P-03	**2**	*7*	**Haditovski**[13] 2247 9-10-8 102 ....(v) MrGTumelty[(7)] *(J Mackie) hld up in tch: chsd wnr 5th: rdn appr 2 out: styd on same pce appr last* **9/2**[2]	—
P-60	**3**	*1*	**Miss Pross**[15] 2191 5-10-3 95 .... PCO'Neill[(5)] *(T D Walford) chsd ldrs: rdn whn mstke last: wknd flat* **9/2**[2]	95+
1-F	**4**	*2*	**Predicament**[36] 1823 6-11-12 113 .... JimCrowley *(Jonjo O'Neill) hld up: hdwy appr 3 out: rdn and wknd last* **5/1**[3]	—
0004	**5**	*2*	**Constantine**[9] 2324 5-11-11 112 ....(b) JEMoore *(G L Moore) chsd ldrs: ev ch 3 out: rdn and wknd after next* **8/1**	—
U011	**6**	*12*	**Lord Lington (FR)**[13] 2246 6-11-12 113 .... WMarston *(D J Wintle) hld up: hdwy appr 3 out: rdn and wknd bef next* **4/1**[1]	—
312-	**7**	*1*	**Simply Mystic**[310] 3460 5-11-7 108 .... JAMcCarthy *(P D Niven) hld up: wknd 5th* **9/1**	—
24/0	**8**	*1*	**Tory Boy**[196] 370 10-10-1 88 .... HOliver *(D T Turner) prom: j. slowly and lost pl 3rd: wknd 5th* **33/1**	—
102P	**9**	*3 ½*	**Talarive (USA)**[36] 1836 9-10-13 100 ....(tp) ARoss *(P D Niven) led to 2nd: chsd wnr to 5th: wknd appr 3 out* **20/1**	—
03-P	**10**	*2 ½*	**Mnason (FR)**[24] 2010 5-11-3 109 .... JDiment[(5)] *(S J Gilmore) hld up: rdn and wknd appr 3 out* **12/1**	—

3m 53.8s (-13.80) **Going Correction** -0.675s/f (Firm) **10** Ran SP% **113.4**
Speed ratings: **107,103,103,102,101 95,94,94,92,91** CSF £130.12 CT £610.83 TOTE £26.10: £7.30, £1.80, £2.50; EX 80.70.
Owner Warren Butterworth & Terry Pryke **Bred** J And Mrs S Cleeve **Trained** Norton, N Yorks

FOCUS
A modest handicap hurdle for the class rated through the third and the form appears solid.

NOTEBOOK
Honest Endeavour returned to form to gain his first success since winning a novice hurdle at Uttoxeter just over a year previously. In this form, he could well go in again and would have an obvious chance under a penalty. *Official explanation: trainer's representative had no explanation for the improved form shown (op 20-1)*
Haditovski, just as when third over course and distance on his previous start, ran a promising-enough race in defeat and could yet end a losing run over hurdles that stretches back to December 2001. *(op 7-2)*
Miss Pross may have been a little closer had she jumped the last better. She is still a maiden, but looks up to finding a minor race eventually. *(op 9-1)*
Predicament, held when falling at Aintree on his reappearance, got round this time but did not really find as much as had looked likely. *(op 9-2 tchd 7-2)*
Constantine looks to need more of a stamina test. *(op 7-1)*
Lord Lington(FR), winner of a similar race at Warwick two starts ago before taking a novice chase here on his last outing, had a 7lb higher mark to contend with on his return to hurdling but was not at his best in any case. *(tchd 9-2)*

2526 LADBROKES.COM MARES' ONLY NOVICES' CHASE (12 fncs) 2m
3:00 (3:00) (Class 4) 4-Y-0+ **£5,373** (£1,577; £788; £394)

Form			Horse	RPR
1421	**1**		**Miss Shakira (IRE)**[10] 2284 7-10-9 107 .... MGoldstein[(7)] *(N A Twiston-Davies) mde all: clr whn blnd 2 out: eased flat* **5/6**[1]	114+
3344	**2**	*9*	**Cansalrun (IRE)**[10] 2297 6-11-0 94 .... WMarston *(R H Alner) chsd wnr to 5th: wnt 2nd again 8th: rdn appr 2 out: sn btn* **5/2**[2]	98+
5630	**3**	*5*	**Lago D'Oro**[16] 2161 5-11-0 94 .... JMogford *(Dr P Pritchard) hld up: hit 2nd: styd on flat: nvr nr to chal* **12/1**	92
3014	**4**	*1 ¼*	**Celtic Blaze (IRE)**[11] 2267 6-11-0 101 ....(t) ARoss *(B S Rothwell) prom: chsd wnr 5th: blnd next: lost 2nd 8th: rdn and wknd 3 out* **13/2**[3]	93+
5660	**5**	*18*	**Dawn Frolics**[27] 1949 4-10-1 64 ow4 .... CHonour[(5)] *(M J Gingell) a bhd: hit 2 out* **33/1**	65
-2FF	**P**		**Shakwaa**[22] 2041 6-11-0 89 .... JAMcCarthy *(E A Elliott) hld up: hit 5th: t.o whn p.u bef 4 out* **33/1**	—

4m 7.30s (-0.30) **Going Correction** -0.50s/f (Good)
WFA 4 from 5yo+ 12lb **6** Ran SP% **110.0**
Speed ratings: **80,75,73,72,63** — CSF £3.26 TOTE £1.60: £1.10, £2.00; EX 3.80.
Owner F J Mills & W Mills **Bred** Tom Fitzgerald **Trained** Naunton, Gloucs

FOCUS
An uncompetitive mares-only novice chase in which Miss Shakira was value for more than the official margin. The winning time was slow for the class but the form looks reasonable.

NOTEBOOK
Miss Shakira(IRE) ◆ is possibly better suited by further, but she is unexposed over fences and was able to defy a 10lb higher mark than when winning over this trip at Hereford on her previous start. She remains one to have on your side, especially with improvement to come when she steps back up in distance. *(tchd 10-11)*
Cansalrun(IRE) probably ran about as well as could have been expected behind the unexposed winner, and could find easier opportunities in handicaps. *(tchd 3-1)*
Lago D'Oro, totally outclassed at Cheltenham last time, found this a much more suitable grade for her chasing debut and did not run too badly. *(op 10-1 tchd 14-1)*
Celtic Blaze(IRE) did not appear suited by this drop in trip, but may have been a fair bit closer with better jumping and is not one to write off. *(op 7-1 tchd 6-1)*

2527 LADBROKES.COM NOVICES' HURDLE (12 hdls) 2m 4f 110y
3:35 (3:36) (Class 3) 4-Y-0+ **£6,995** (£2,066; £1,033; £517; £258; £129)

Form			Horse	RPR
1-3	**1**		**Clyffe Hanger (IRE)**[22] 2049 5-11-0 .... BHitchcott *(R H Buckler) hld up: hdwy 3rd: lft 2nd 5th: rdn to ld appr 2 out: styd on wl* **9/2**[2]	98+
	2	*6*	**Ballyshan (IRE)**[594] 7-10-7 .... MGoldstein[(7)] *(N A Twiston-Davies) chsd ldr 2nd: lft in ld and pckd 5th: rdn and hdd appr 2 out: hung lft bef last: wknd flat* **11/2**[3]	93+
3	**3**	*nk*	**It Would Appear (IRE)**[17] 2145 6-10-4 .... WJones[(10)] *(Jonjo O'Neill) hld up: hdwy 3rd: rdn and ev ch appr 2 out: hung lft and wknd flat* **12/1**	92+
00	**4**	*26*	**Secret Jewel (FR)**[21] 2081 5-10-4 .... ACCoyle[(3)] *(Miss C J E Caroe) chsd ldrs: mstke 6th: rdn and wknd after 3 out* **66/1**	58
00	**5**	*23*	**Dans Edge (IRE)**[17] 2144 5-10-7 .... TJDreaper[(7)] *(Ferdy Murphy) hld up: wknd after 7th* **50/1**	42

0060 **6** ½ **Blazing Batman**[65] [1542] 12-10-9 77 DrPPritchard(5) 42
(Dr P Pritchard) *chsd ldr to 2nd: lost pl next: sn bhd* **25/1**

-510 **7** *dist* **Walsingham (IRE)**[144] [912] 7-11-0 90 JEMoore —
(R Lee) *hld up: plld hrd: hdwy 7th: wknd bef next* **16/1**

/F-0 **R** **Franco (IRE)**[201] [281] 7-10-7 95 MrRJBarrett(7) —
(Mrs A E Brooks) *led tl rn out and uns rdr 5th* **28/1**

23/1 **F** **Hoh Viss**[21] [2082] 5-11-5 120 NFehily —
(C J Mann) *hld up: hdwy 6th: disputing cl 2nd whn fell 3 out* **4/6**[1]

06 **P** **Novack Du Beury (FR)**[8] [2343] 4-11-0 JimCrowley —
(Ferdy Murphy) *hld up: wknd after 7th: t.o whn p.u bef last* **40/1**

5m 18.9s (-15.90) **Going Correction** -0.675s/f (Firm)
WFA 4 from 5yo+ 13lb **10** Ran SP% **120.3**
Speed ratings: **103,100,100,90,81 81,—,—,—,—** CSF £29.02 TOTE £5.20: £1.10, £2.90, £2.70; EX 35.70 Place 6 £44.91, Place 5 £28.13.
Owner Mrs William Hall **Bred** Rodney Deacon **Trained** Melplash, Dorset

FOCUS
A very ordinary novice hurdle for the grade, but there was plenty to like about Clyffe Hanger's performance. The race could rate higher but is not easy to pin down. The third is the best guide and the form looks suspect.

NOTEBOOK
Clyffe Hanger(IRE) ◆, who showed fair form in two runs in bumpers, including when third under a penalty at Sandown on his reappearance, took well to hurdling at the first attempt and ran out a convincing winner. While this may not have been the strongest of races for the grade, he should not be underestimated in future and could be reasonably priced given he does not hail from one of the major yards. *(op 5-1)*
Ballyshan(IRE), runner-up in an Irish Point 594 days previously, made a respectable debut under Rules behind a reasonable sort. Open to improvement, he should make his mark this season and ought to make a chaser in time. *(op 4-1 tchd 6-1)*
It Would Appear(IRE) confirmed the promise he showed when third in a Ludlow bumper on his debut, but he looked awkward under pressure in the straight, even allowing for this being just his second racecourse appearance, and could be one to have reservations about. *(op 17-2 tchd 8-1)*
Secret Jewel(FR) was a well-beaten fourth, but she is now qualified for a handicap mark and could find easier opportunities.
Hoh Viss, a recent Market Rasen winner, had every chance when falling. *(op 11-10)*
T/Plt: £85.00 to a £1 stake. Pool: £41,413.30. 355.45 winning tickets. T/Qpdt: £16.60 to a £1 stake. Pool: £3,087.70. 136.90 winning tickets. CR

2487 NEWBURY (L-H)
Sunday, November 27

OFFICIAL GOING: Good
Wind: Almost nil

2528 SPORTING INDEX "NATIONAL HUNT" MAIDEN HURDLE (8 hdls) 2m 110y
12:30 (12:30) (Class 3) 4-Y-0+ **£6,229** (£1,828; £914; £456)

Form RPR

43-2 **1** **Pirate Flagship (FR)**[22] [2050] 6-11-2 ChristianWilliams 106+
(P F Nicholls) *chsd ldrs: chal 3 out: led sn after: drvn appr last: kpt on strly run-in* **15/8**[1]

2- **2** 6 **Wogan**[221] [4935] 5-11-2 MAFitzgerald 98+
(N J Henderson) *h.d.w: lw: chsd ldrs: rdn 3 out: kpt on u.p to take 2nd sn after last but no ch w wnr* **11/4**[2]

0- **3** 2½ **Loita Hills (IRE)**[267] [4193] 5-11-2 RJohnson 95
(P J Hobbs) *bit bkwd: led: rdn 3 out: hdd sn after: kpt on u.p fr 2 out: sn no ch w wnr: lost 2nd sn after last* **33/1**

6-06 **4** 3½ **Ice Bucket (IRE)**[17] [2142] 5-11-2 SThomas 91
(Miss H C Knight) *lw: chsd ldrs: rdn and one pce after 3 out: kpt on again run-in but n.d* **50/1**

33- **5** *nk* **Original Thought (IRE)**[221] [4935] 5-11-2 DCrosse 92+
(B De Haan) *bit bkwd: chsd ldrs: wnt 2nd after 4 out: nt fluent next: hrd drvn fr 2 out: one pce* **20/1**

24 **6** ¾ **Paradise Bay (IRE)**[22] [2050] 4-11-2 NFehily 90
(C J Mann) *hld up in rr: stdy hdwy after 4 out: chsd ldrs next: sn rdn: wknd fr 2 out* **33/1**

10/ **7** 4 **Alf Lauren**[740] [2223] 7-11-2 RThornton 86
(A King) *lw: mid-div: hdwy to chse ldrs after 4 out: rdn: next: wknd 2 out* **33/1**

0-2P **8** 2½ **Lord On The Run (IRE)**[17] [2141] 6-11-2 96 AThornton 85+
(J W Mullins) *bhd: hit 4th: sme hdwy fr 3 out: styng on whn hit last: kpt on again cl home* **20/1**

45-5 **9** 1¾ **Britesand (IRE)**[17] [2142] 5-11-2 JamesDavies 82
(J S Moore) *prom early: sn bhd: rdn after 4 out: sme prog u.p fr 2 out* **100/1**

2-46 **10** 1¾ **It's Bertie**[15] [2186] 5-11-2 PWhelan 80
(Mrs S J Smith) *chsd ldrs: hit 3rd: wknd fr 3 out* **16/1**

11 3 **Nelson Du Ronceray (FR)** 4-11-2 TJMurphy 80+
(M C Pipe) *w'like: hld up in rr: hit 3rd: rapid hdwy after 4 out to chse ldrs next: wknd fr 2 out* **6/1**[3]

030- **12** 5 **Coltscroft**[239] [4697] 5-11-2 SCurran 72
(J C Fox) *bhd tl mod prog fr 2 out* **33/1**

0 **13** 13 **Another Flint (IRE)**[21] [2075] 5-10-11 LStephens(5) 59
(R Flint) *bhd most of way* **100/1**

0-20 **14** 20 **Ice Cream (FR)**[187] [490] 4-10-9 BJCrowley 32
(M E D Francis) *mid-div whn hit 3rd and 4 out: sn wknd* **80/1**

00P **15** *dist* **Rose Amber**[7] [2376] 4-10-9 RGreene —
(J J Bridger) *chsd ldr tl appr 4 out: wknd rapidly: t.o* **100/1**

0P/0 **16** *dist* **Herecomestanley**[7] [2374] 6-10-9 CPoste(7) —
(M F Harris) *a in rr: t.o* **100/1**

2-3 **U** **Scalini'S (IRE)**[50] [1681] 5-11-2 BFenton —
(Jonjo O'Neill) *lw: in tch: hdwy to chse ldrs after 4 out: shkn up and one pce whn blnd and uns rdr 3 out* **11/1**

4m 1.90s (-1.70) **Going Correction** -0.075s/f (Good) **17** Ran SP% **118.4**
Speed ratings: **101,98,97,95,95 94,92,91,90,90 88,86,80,70,— —,—** CSF £5.79 TOTE £2.60: £1.30, £1.80, £9.90; EX 7.20.
Owner Mr & Mrs Mark Woodhouse **Bred** Haras De Preaux **Trained** Ditcheat, Somerset
■ Stewards' Enquiry : Christian Williams one-day ban: careless riding (Dec 8)

FOCUS
This looked no more than a fair novice hurdle for the track and the form looks weaker than average.

NOTEBOOK
Pirate Flagship(FR), whose effort behind Refinement suggested that he would be the one to beat here, had the rail to help from between the last two flights and eventually drew clear to win fairly easily. Defying a penalty will be tougher, but a longer trip might help. Connections plan to send him chasing in the spring. *(op 6-4)*
Wogan, representing an in-form stable, ran a promising race on his hurdling debut and is entitled to come on for this seasonal reappearance. A similar race could be within his ability. *(tchd 3-1)*
Loita Hills(IRE) looked as though the run would bring him on and the market did not speak in his favour, so it was a promising effort to run so well on his hurdling debut. He should be sharper next time. *(op 28-1)*
Ice Bucket(IRE), a 66-1 shot when sixth on his hurdling debut at Ludlow, did a bit better this time, but his performance suggests the form is nothing out of the ordinary. *(op 66-1)*
Original Thought(IRE), placed in a couple of bumpers last spring, including when one place behind Wogan at Worcester, was another who looked in need of the outing. He can improve for the run. *(op 16-1)*
Paradise Bay(IRE) finished a long way behind Pirate Flagship on his hurdling debut but got closer to that rival with that experience under his belt.
Nelson Du Ronceray(FR), a half-brother to the yard's high-class but ill-fated chaser Gloria Victis, came in for market support but proved disappointing. Fences will no doubt see him in a better light in due course. *(op 9-1)*
Ice Cream(FR) *Official explanation: trainer said filly bled from the nose (tchd 100-1)*

2529 EUROPEAN BREEDERS FUND NOVICES' H'CAP CHASE (18 fncs) 3m
1:00 (1:01) (Class 3) (0-120,117) 5-Y-0+
£8,361 (£2,469; £1,234; £618; £308; £154)

Form RPR

0120 **1** **Koumba (FR)**[33] [1874] 7-11-3 108 ChristianWilliams 121+
(Evan Williams) *a.p: wnt 2nd 7th: led appr 9th: hdd next: led again 11th: styd on wl and drew clr fr 2 out* **25/1**

50-1 **2** 7 **King Of Gothland (IRE)**[25] [1988] 6-10-10 101 ow1 JPMcNamara 108+
(K C Bailey) *lw: hld up: hdwy 5 out: styd on to go 2nd appr 2 out but sn no ch w wnr* **8/1**[3]

F253 **3** 3½ **Lord Dundaniel (IRE)**[24] [2005] 8-11-2 107 PMoloney 109
(B De Haan) *lw: trckd ldrs: rdn 3 out: kpt on one pce after* **10/1**

3P-0 **4** 4 **Tacin (IRE)**[33] [1872] 8-11-9 114 TJMurphy 114+
(B G Powell) *a.p: chsd wnr after 5 out tl wknd 2 out* **8/1**[3]

6-21 **5** *shd* **Moustique De L'Isle (FR)**[21] [2077] 5-10-13 105 NFehily 101
(C C Bealby) *hld up in rr: lost tch 10th but mde sme late hdwy fr 2 out* **12/1**

U10/ **6** 6 **Master Trix (IRE)**[604] [4643] 8-11-10 115 RJohnson 108+
(P J Hobbs) *bit bkwd: led 2nd: hdd appr 9th: led again 10th to 11th: prom whn bmpd 5 out: wknd bef next* **9/2**[1]

3215 **7** 9 **Darina's Boy**[29] [1928] 9-11-4 109 PWhelan 91
(Mrs S J Smith) *mid-div: rdn after 8th: wknd appr 4 out* **8/1**[3]

U2-1 **8** 3½ **Motcombe (IRE)**[10] [2297] 7-10-9 100 AThornton 82+
(R H Alner) *lost pl 7th: bhd whn blnd 13th: nvr on terms after* **9/2**[1]

-220 **P** **Glacial Evening (IRE)**[15] [2175] 9-11-12 117 JTizzard —
(R H Buckler) *lw: blnd 2nd: t.o fr 10th: p.u bef 13th* **33/1**

-12P **P** **Special Conquest**[32] [1877] 7-11-4 109 PHide —
(J W Mullins) *led to 2nd: lost pl 11th: t.o whn p.u bef last* **25/1**

53P- **P** **Gulabill**[228] [4825] 6-10-4 95 CLlewellyn —
(N A Twiston-Davies) *hld up: hdwy after 8th: blnd 13th and no ch after: t.o whn p.u bef last* **14/1**

161 **P** **Glacial Delight (IRE)**[17] [2151] 6-11-8 113 BFenton —
(Miss E C Lavelle) *hld up in rr: gd hdwy fr 11th: cl 3rd whn blnd bdly 5 out: nt rcvr: p.u bef next* **11/2**[2]

6m 2.70s (-2.30) **Going Correction** -0.075s/f (Good)
WFA 5 from 6yo+ 1lb **12** Ran SP% **119.2**
Speed ratings: **100,97,96,95,95 93,90,88,—,— —,—** CSF £211.87 CT £2155.93 TOTE £26.50: £5.90, £1.80, £2.50; EX 217.70.
Owner Mr and Mrs Glynne Clay **Bred** Herve D'Armaille **Trained** Cowbridge, Vale Of Glamorgan

FOCUS
Modest chasing form for the track.

NOTEBOOK
Koumba(FR) did not run well at Cheltenham last time but, ridden more prominently here, defied what had looked a stiff enough mark. He seems at his best on decent ground so any softening of conditions in the coming weeks is likely to be against him.
King Of Gothland(IRE), who won at Huntingdon on his chasing debut, had been raised 9lb for that performance. This was a solid effort in defeat and he is clearly more at home jumping fences than he ever was over timber. *(op 7-1)*
Lord Dundaniel(IRE), who is still a maiden over fences, has dropped a fair way in the ratings but has so far failed to take advantage. *(op 9-1)*
Tacin(IRE), who last ran over fences in a Grade Two event at this meeting two years ago, again attracted some market support. He was up there for a long way but blundered through the first in the home straight and dropped out of contention. A little help from the Handicapper would not go amiss. *(op 10-1)*
Moustique De L'Isle(FR), a winner in heavy ground last time out, found these conditions too quick. *(op 10-1)*
Master Trix(IRE), making his chase debut, ran quite well for a long way on his return from a 604-day absence and his first start for his new stable. He should come on for the run and will not mind easier ground. *(op 11-2)*
Glacial Delight(IRE) ◆ was still going well in third when making a bad mistake at the cross fence (fifth last). His rider did well to stay on board but had no option but to pull him up soon afterwards. He looked likely to be involved at the finish so must be considered for a similar event off his current mark. *Official explanation: jockey said saddle slipped (op 9-2 tchd 6-1 in a place)*

2530 ANN AND RICHARD PLUMMER GOLDEN WEDDING NOVICES' H'CAP HURDLE (10 hdls 1 omitted) 2m 5f
1:35 (1:36) (Class 3) (0-120,120) 3-Y-0+ **£8,783** (£2,578; £1,289; £643)

Form RPR

1250 **1** **Screenplay**[14] [2207] 4-11-2 115 PMerrigan(5) 121+
(Miss Sheena West) *lw: chsd ldrs: led appr 2 out: drvn and hld on wl run-in* **25/1**

0-41 **2** ¾ **Shining Strand**[185] [521] 6-11-3 111 ATinkler 116+
(N J Henderson) *t.k.h: hld up in rr: nt fluent: hdwy appr bypassed 3rd last: rdn appr last: r.o u.p run-in: gng on fin* **10/1**

3126 **3** *nk* **Saltango (GER)**[10] [2292] 6-11-0 113 WKennedy(5) 117
(A M Hales) *in tch: hdwy 4th: chal and rdn 2 out: stl ev ch last: kpt on run-in: nt qckn nr fin* **33/1**

-015 **4** ½ **Astyanax (IRE)**[16] [2166] 5-10-1 100 SCurling(5) 105+
(N J Henderson) *lw: chsd ldr fr 3rd: rdn appr 2 out: chal and hit last: one pce u.p* **16/1**

2-1 **5** ½ **Novacella (FR)**[26] [1974] 4-10-0 94 RWalford 97
(R H Alner) *in tch: hdwy appr bypassed 3rd last: rdn next: kpt on u.p run-in but nt rch ldrs* **14/1**

3UP1 **6** *hd* **Vingis Park (IRE)**[7] [2372] 7-10-11 112 7ex (b) MrJJDoyle(7) 116+
(V R A Dartnall) *led: rdn and hdd appr 2 out: styd on u.p last: one pce run-in* **12/1**

221F **7** 3½ **Nippy Des Mottes (FR)**[14] [2207] 4-11-3 111 (t) ChristianWilliams 110
(P F Nicholls) *hld up in rr: hdwy appr bypassed 3rd last: chsd ldrs and hrd drvn next: wknd run-in* **4/1**[2]

021 **8** *1* **Lyes Green**[21] 2081 4-10-10 **107** ONelmes(3) 105
(O Sherwood) *hld up rr: hdwy fr 6th: shkn up appr bypassed 3rd last: sn one pce: wknd appr last* **6/1**[3]

-422 **9** *16* **Smart Mover**[30] 1903 6-10-10 **104** PMoloney 90+
(Miss H C Knight) *bhd most of way* **14/1**

0-31 **10** *10* **Soleil Fix (FR)**[23] 2020 4-10-11 **108** MrDHDunsdon(3) 80
(N J Gifford) *lw: in tch: hit 3rd: bhd fr 5th* **33/1**

2-55 **11** *17* **Spring Lover (FR)**[11] 2272 6-10-6 **100** SThomas 55
(Miss Venetia Williams) *lw: chsd ldrs: rdn after 4 out: sn wknd* **25/1**

P20/ **12** *7* **Thistlecraft (IRE)**[631] 4197 6-11-2 **110** JPMcNamara 58
(C C Bealby) *lw: hit 1st: hld up in rr: hdwy appr bypassed 3rd last: sn rdn: wknd next* **50/1**

204- **13** *1 ½* **Cousin Nicky**[251] 4496 4-11-4 **112** RJohnson 59
(P J Hobbs) *bit bkwd: chsd ldrs to 6th* **14/1**

F55- **P** **Swazi Prince**[241] 4669 6-10-5 **99** CLlewellyn —
(N A Twiston-Davies) **50/1**

3003 **P** **Abragante (IRE)**[15] 2173 4-10-8 **102** (p) TJMurphy —
(M C Pipe) *prom early: bhd fr 4th: t.o whn p.u after 3 out* **7/2**[1]

U0-P **P** **Avalanche (FR)**[211] 130 8-11-2 **110** RThornton —
(J R Best) *bit bkwd: blnd 1st: a bhd: t.o whn p.u bef 6th* **33/1**

5m 4.80s (-8.20) **Going Correction** -0.075s/f (Good)
WFA 4 from 5yo+ 13lb **16** Ran SP% **119.6**
Speed ratings: **112,111,111,111,111 111,109,109,103,99 93,90,89,—,— —** CSF £242.48 CT £8029.72 TOTE £37.20: £5.60, £2.20, £6.10, £3.90; EX 342.70.
Owner The Horse Players **Bred** Juddmonte Farms **Trained** Lewes, E Sussex
■ Stewards' Enquiry : R Walford one-day ban: used whip with excessive frequency (Dec 8)

FOCUS
A modest handicap but a decent winning time for the grade. The first six were only covered by about two lengths at the finish, though, so the form might not be the strongest.

NOTEBOOK
Screenplay ran quite well at Cheltenham last time and, while more exposed than a few of his rivals, he is a consistent animal who knows how to win. A decent surface sees him at his best and conditions were in his favour here.
Shining Strand, having his first outing since May, did not settle in the early stages so it was to his credit that he had enough in reserve to throw down a late challenge. He is another who seems happiest on a decent surface. *(op 9-1)*
Saltango(GER) did not look particularly well handicapped beforehand, hence his position in the market, but he found this class of opposition less demanding and ran a race which probably rates as a personal best. *(tchd 40-1)*
Astyanax(IRE), who ran well at Cheltenham last time, albeit in a lesser event, got to race off a 2lb lower mark here. This sort of ground suits him so rain in the near future would not be welcome.
Novacella(FR), a winner against her own sex at Worcester on her seasonal reappearance, got the longer trip well and finished to good effect next to the stands'-side rail. She is a half-sister to last season's high-class novice Marcel, and will make a chaser in time.
Vingis Park(IRE) may not have gained as much from the blinkers this time as he did when wearing them for the first time at Aintree a week earlier. He has, however, been rated as running to the same level as for that win. *(op 14-1)*
Nippy Des Mottes(FR) was understandably fancied in the market to make up for his unfortunate experience at Cheltenham, but he took a heavy fall that day and perhaps his confidence has been shaken a little. *(op 7-2)*
Avalanche(FR) *Official explanation: jockey said gelding had a breathing problem (op 11-4 tchd 4-1)*
Abragante(IRE), third behind stablemate Not Left Yet at the Paddy Power meeting at Cheltenham last time, was all the rage in the market beforehand on this step up in trip, but he ran poorly and this was clearly not his form. Connections clearly believe he is capable of winning a handicap off his current mark, and he should be kept in mind. *Official explanation: jockey said gelding never travelled (op 11-4 tchd 4-1)*

2531 DUBAI DUTY FREE FULKE WALWYN NOVICES' CHASE GRADE 2 (16 fncs) 2m 4f
2:05 (2:08) (Class 1) 5-Y-0+ **£18,460** (£7,059; £3,641; £1,923)

Form RPR

2-13 **1** **Albuhera (IRE)**[14] 2208 7-11-0 (t) JTizzard 149+
(P F Nicholls) *trckd ldr for most of r: chal 4 out: led next: pushed clr run-in* **9/4**[2]

B3-1 **2** *8* **Copsale Lad**[29] 1917 8-11-0 134 MAFitzgerald 142+
(N J Henderson) *lw: led tl rdn and hdd 3 out: no ch w wnr run-in* **6/5**[1]

05-1 **3** *15* **Without A Doubt**[22] 2044 6-11-4 PMoloney 129+
(M Pitman) *lw: hld up: mstke 8th: lost tch 11th: styd on to go poor 3rd sn after last* **9/1**

1121 **4** *½* **Whispered Secret (GER)**[32] 1881 6-11-7 142 RGreene 134+
(M C Pipe) *t.k.h: chsd wnr 4th to 6th: rdn fr next: 3rd and making no imp whn hit 5 out* **7/1**[3]

00-1 **P** **Royal Hector (GER)**[14] 2213 6-11-0 BFenton —
(Jonjo O'Neill) *hld up: mstke 8th: lost tch 11th: t.o whn p.u bef 3 out* **14/1**

4m 58.9s (-7.50) **Going Correction** -0.075s/f (Good) **5** Ran SP% **105.4**
Speed ratings: **112,108,102,102,—** CSF £3.28 TOTE £3.10: £1.80, £1.40; EX 5.30.
Owner D J & F A Jackson **Bred** K And Mrs Cullen **Trained** Ditcheat, Somerset

FOCUS
An acceptable, if unspectacular, winning time for a Grade Two event. Good novice chase form.

NOTEBOOK
Albuhera(IRE), third behind Accordion Etoile and Tamarinbleu at Cheltenham last time, gave that form a huge boost with a polished display of jumping, seeing this longer trip out in fine style. There are plenty of races open to him now, but connections are apparently keen on dropping back to the minimum distance next for the Castleford Chase at Wetherby on December 27. *(tchd 2-1)*
Copsale Lad, given the nod in the market over Albuhera on account of his proven stamina for the trip, ran well in defeat but had no excuses. He finished nicely clear of the rest and there is a good race to be won with him this winter. *(op 5-4)*
Without A Doubt impressed on his chasing debut but he did not beat anything of Albuhera's class that day. This was not a bad run at all and he should be kept in mind for a nice handicap this season. *(tchd 10-1)*
Whispered Secret(GER), a progressive sort over the summer and autumn, is now on a stiff mark for handicaps, and giving weight away in this type of contest is always going to prove difficult. He did not run to his best either and this fast-ground lover may just need a break now. *(tchd 9-1 in a place)*
Royal Hector(GER), who would ideally have preferred easier ground, is a decent performer but he was up against it in this class. *Official explanation: vet said gelding had lost a near-fore shoe*

2532 RACING UK H'CAP CHASE (17 fncs) 2m 6f 110y
2:40 (2:40) (Class 3) (0-130,130) 5-Y-0+
£12,626 (£3,729; £1,864; £933; £465; £233)

Form RPR

05-0 **1** **Too Forward (IRE)**[22] 2054 9-11-9 **127** CLlewellyn 147+
(M Pitman) *in tch: chsd ldrs fr 9th: led and hit 13th: drvn and styd on to go clr fr 2 out: comf* **10/1**

13U- **2** *5* **Graphic Approach (IRE)**[255] 4407 7-11-12 **130** BFenton 140+
(C R Egerton) *bit bkwd: t.k.h: hld up rr: hit 5th and 6th: blnd 9th: hdwy 11th: hit 13th: trckd ldrs 4 out: chsd wnr last: rdn and one pc* **6/1**[3]

-343 **3** *5* **Mark Equal**[14] 2210 9-10-10 **114** (t) TScudamore 116
(M C Pipe) *in tch: hday 7th: hit 13th: chal 4 out: stl ev ch next: wknd appr last* **9/1**

2564 **4** *½* **Sardagna (FR)**[25] 1986 5-11-2 **121** TJMurphy 122
(M C Pipe) *chsd ldrs: rdn 4 out: wknd and hit 2 out* **12/1**

45-2 **5** *1 ½* **Aristoxene (FR)**[24] 2003 5-11-11 **130** MAFitzgerald 130+
(N J Henderson) *lw: chsd ldrs: drvn along fr 12th: one pce whn mstke 4 out:btn next* **11/4**[1]

F3P- **6** *¾* **Dungarvans Choice (IRE)**[253] 4462 10-11-8 **126** ATinkler 125
(N J Henderson) *bit bkwd: hld up in rr: nt fluent 7 (water): blnd 10th: hdwy and nt fluent 13th: wknd after 4 out* **8/1**

635- **7** *dist* **Parsons Legacy (IRE)**[228] 4821 7-11-10 **128** RJohnson 102
(P J Hobbs) *led to 12th: wknd bef next: t.o* **11/2**[2]

131- **P** **Home James (IRE)**[290] 3767 8-11-12 **130** RThornton —
(A King) *lw: chsd ldrs: hit 6th: 8th and 9th: sn wknd: t.o whn p.u bef 4 out* **7/1**

61F/ **P** **Be My Destiny (IRE)**[631] 4195 8-11-4 **122** PMoloney —
(Miss H C Knight) *behiind: j.big 9th: hdwy to cl on ldrs 10th: wknd 13th: t.o whn p.u bef 3 out* **20/1**

P **Holy Joe (FR)**[378] 8-11-10 **128** SThomas —
(Miss Venetia Williams) *neat: bkwd: chsd ldrs: wnt 2nd 8th: led 12th: hdd 13th: rdn and disputing clsoe 3rd whn blnd 4 out and p.u* **25/1**

5m 44.1s (-3.60) **Going Correction** -0.075s/f (Good) **10** Ran SP% **115.3**
Speed ratings: **103,101,99,99,98 98,—,—,—,—** CSF £68.90 CT £564.24 TOTE £12.10: £3.30, £2.40, £2.40; EX 120.60 Trifecta £677.40 Part won. Pool: £954.10 - 0.30 winning tickets..
Owner T L Gibson & D Mathias **Bred** Patrick Kinsella **Trained** Upper Lambourn, Berks

FOCUS
A competitive handicap with only 16lb separating the top weight from the bottom weight. The winner is rated for double the official margin although the form is probably not the strongest

NOTEBOOK
Too Forward(IRE), who ran well for a long way at Wincanton on his reappearance, had clearly benefited from that outing and ran out an easy winner of what had looked a competitive handicap on paper. The drop in trip suited and, as he copes with softer ground than this, he could be set for further success this winter if the Handicapper does not punish him too much. *(tchd 11-1)*
Graphic Approach(IRE), not seen since unseating at the Festival last March, ran a very promising race on his reappearance, keeping on well for a clear second place behind the impressive winner. He looks sure to come on for the run and this relatively lightly raced seven-year-old appears fairly handicapped. *(op 5-1 tchd 13-2)*
Mark Equal, not for the first time, failed to find as much off the bridle as was promised. He is running to a consistent level at present but remains opposable. *(op 14-1)*
Sardagna(FR), who raced throughout the summer and autumn, did not run too badly although she looked to fail the stamina test. She will be happier when dropped back to trips around two miles.
Aristoxene(FR) was another who did not appear to see out the trip. Softer ground may also be a requirement for him. *(tchd 3-1 and 10-3 in a place)*
Dungarvans Choice(IRE) had never in 17 previous starts run on ground which did not have the word soft or heavy somewhere in the going description. *(tchd 7-1)*
Holy Joe(FR), a winner over hurdles and fences in France, was making his British debut for his new trainer. He was being niggled along but was still in the front rank when blundering badly at the fourth last, an error that failed to dislodge his rider but immediately ended his race. *(tchd 33-1)*

2533 LEXUS IS250 CONDITIONAL JOCKEYS' H'CAP HURDLE (8 hdls) 2m 110y
3:15 (3:15) (Class 4) (0-130,125) 4-Y-0+
£8,192 (£2,419; £1,209; £605; £302; £151)

Form RPR

31 **1** **Motorway (IRE)**[33] 1875 4-10-8 **110** RStephens(3) 123+
(P J Hobbs) *lw: mde all: rdn whn chal 2 out: pushed out run-in* **5/1**[3]

P52- **2** *2* **Prairie Moonlight (GER)**[226] 4847 5-10-6 **115** KGTobin(10) 127+
(C J Mann) *bit bkwd: hld up in rr: hdwy fr 5th to go 2nd and chal 2 out: rdn and no imp run-in* **20/1**

52/3 **3** *8* **Pepe Galvez (SWE)**[36] 1823 8-11-8 **121** WKennedy 125+
(Mrs L C Taylor) *trckd ldrs: rdn appr 2 out: one pce after* **5/1**[3]

6-31 **4** *3 ½* **Nanga Parbat (FR)**[35] 1862 4-10-11 **118** (t) LHeard(8) 120+
(P F Nicholls) *lw: hld up in tch: hdwy after 4th: wknd after 2 out* **3/1**[2]

31-1 **5** *4* **Into The Shadows**[19] 2103 5-10-5 **112** PKinsella(8) 109+
(K G Reveley) *lw: trckd wnr tl rdn 2 out: wknd sn after* **9/4**[1]

-020 **6** *6* **Grave Doubts**[43] 1743 9-11-12 **125** (t) ONelmes 115
(K Bishop) *hld up: effrt 4th: wknd appr 3 out* **33/1**

2P00 **7** *nk* **Maclean**[19] 2099 4-10-0 **105** (b) EDehdashti(6) 95+
(G L Moore) *hld up: hdwy 4th: rdn whn mstke 2 out* **66/1**

3521 **8** *8* **Theocritus (GER)**[24] 2002 4-10-8 **107** PMerrigan 88
(Nick Williams) *prom tl lost pl 3rd: rdn after 5th: sn wknd* **7/1**

1 **9** *13* **Albarino (IRE)**[10] 2298 6-10-1 **108** JKington(8) 79+
(M Scudamore) *hld up: in rr whn blnd 5th: nvr on terms* **20/1**

4m 0.90s (-2.70) **Going Correction** -0.075s/f (Good)
WFA 4 from 5yo+ 12lb **9** Ran SP% **115.6**
Speed ratings: **103,102,98,96,94 91,91,88,81** CSF £89.62 CT £525.92 TOTE £5.30: £1.90, £4.00, £2.00; EX 126.50.
Owner D Allen **Bred** Epona Bloodstock Ltd **Trained** Withycombe, Somerset

FOCUS
Quite a competitive affair and the winner looks progressive, but the form may not be that solid with the third and fourth the best guides to the level.

NOTEBOOK
Motorway(IRE), granted a clear lead by his rivals soon after the start, made full use of their generosity to lead from pillar to post. The pack was on his tail entering the straight but he kept finding more for pressure and probably won with a bit in hand. He looks progressive. *(op 9-2 tchd 11-2 in a place)*
Prairie Moonlight(GER), 6lb higher than when runner-up at Ayr on her last start back in the spring, ran a personal best on her seasonal reappearance. This gives hope that she can do even better now that she has a run under her belt. *(op 14-1)*
Pepe Galvez(SWE), having his second run back after an absence of almost two years, had been given over a month off to get over his Aintree effort, but failed to reproduce that level of form. Rising nine, he might just need a little help from the Handicapper. *(op 7-1)*
Nanga Parbat(FR), who won over this course and distance off a 13lb lower mark on his handicap debut in March, could not cope with an 8lb hike for his recent Wincanton victory. A speed horse, he seems at his very best on sharp tracks. *(op 10-3 tchd 7-2)*
Into The Shadows was the disappointment of the race. She held every chance going to the second last but dropped out tamely thereafter, her 13lb higher mark in a better race clearly finding her out. *(op 2-1 tchd 5-2 and 11-4 in places)*
Grave Doubts, more exposed than his main rivals, needs to drop a few pounds to get competitive.

2534 LONDON RACING CLUB STANDARD OPEN NATIONAL HUNT FLAT RACE 2m 110y

3:45 (3:45) (Class 6) 4-Y-O **£3,724** (£1,093; £546; £273)

Form RPR

1 **Wichita Lineman (IRE)** 4-10-13 .... MrJPMagnier(5) 122+
(Jonjo O'Neill) *neat: str: lw: hld up in rr: stready hdwy fr 5f out: qckn to chal ins 2f: led ins last: drvn and kpt on strly* **7/4**[1]

2 1 1/4 **Presentandcorrect (IRE)** 4-11-4 .... RJohnson 116
(P J Hobbs) *neat: hld up in rr: hdwy on ins over 5f out: trckd ldrs 3f out: led appr fnl 2f: hdd ins last: kpt on wl u.p* **16/1**

15 3 7 **Balamory Dan (IRE)**[35] [1849] 4-11-11 .... JPMcNamara 116
(G A Harker) *led tl hdd 10f out: led again over 4f out: hdd appr fnl 2f: outpcd over 1f out but kpt on wl for 3rd* **20/1**

3 4 3 **Aztec Warrior (IRE)**[35] [1849] 4-11-4 .... TJMurphy 106
(Miss H C Knight) *hld up in rr: hdwy fr 7f out: chsd ldrs 4f out: outpcd fr 2f out* **9/2**[2]

2 5 3 **Commander Kev (IRE)**[22] [2056] 4-10-13 .... WKennedy(5) 103
(Noel T Chance) *lw: in tch: pushed along 5f out: rdn over 3f out: wknd ins fnl 2f* **15/2**[3]

6 1 1/2 **Senora Snoopy (IRE)** 4-10-11 .... AThornton 95+
(Ferdy Murphy) *w'like: bit bkwd: n.m.r and hung lft over 3f out: rn green over 2f out: kpt on fr over 1f out: nt rch ldrs* **33/1**

7 2 1/2 **Kalamazoo (IRE)** 4-10-13 .... PMerrigan(5) 99
(Nick Williams) *w'like: prom early: dropped rr after 5f: hdwy over 3f out: kpt on wl fr over 1f out but n.d* **66/1**

0- 8 nk **Lady Bling Bling**[234] [4753] 4-10-8 .... GCarenza(3) 92
(P J Jones) *bit bkwd: chsd ldrs: rdn over 4f out: one pce over 3f out: wknd 2f out* **100/1**

9 1 3/4 **John Diamond (IRE)** 4-10-11 .... MrJJarrett(7) 97
(Miss H C Knight) *rangy: lw: bhd: hdwy 7f out: chsd ldrs 5f out: wknd 2f out* **100/1**

1-1 10 3 1/2 **Rosita Bay**[21] [2075] 4-11-4 .... ONelmes(3) 96
(O Sherwood) *swtg: hld up in rr: pushed along and hdwy fr 4f out: nvr gng pce to rch ldrs* **8/1**

6- 11 4 **Kline (IRE)**[225] [4865] 4-11-4 .... MAFitzgerald 89
(N J Henderson) *lw: chsd ldrs: rdn and outpcd over 5f out: kpt on again fnl 2f* **16/1**

404 12 1 **Thenford Lord (IRE)**[22] [2056] 4-11-4 .... (b) CLlewellyn 88
(D J S Ffrench Davis) *plld hrd: chsd ldr: led 10f out: hdd over 4f out: wknd 3f out* **66/1**

65- 13 hd **King Louis (FR)**[239] [4697] 4-11-4 .... BJCrowley 88
(R Rowe) *bkwd: mid-div: sme hdwy fnl 2f* **66/1**

1 14 nk **The Big Canadian (IRE)**[38] [1799] 4-11-11 .... RThornton 95
(A King) *t.k.h: chsd ldrs: rdn 4f out: wknd fr 3f out* **9/1**

15 1 **King's Silver (IRE)** 4-11-4 .... VSlattery 87
(N I M Rossiter) *w'like: bit bkwd: bhd: sme hdwy fnl 2f* **100/1**

0 16 1 **That's My Charlie (NZ)**[22] [2056] 4-10-11 .... MrAJBerry(7) 86
(Jonjo O'Neill) *keen hold in rr: sme hdwy and n.m.r over 3f out: nvr rchd ldrs* **50/1**

17 9 **Something Cristal (FR)** 4-11-4 .... MBatchelor 77
(M Bradstock) *w'like: bit bkwd: chsd ldrs: rdn 4f out: wknd 3f out* **9/1**

2 18 shd **Even Flo**[203] [249] 4-10-11 .... JamesDavies 70
(Jean-Rene Auvray) *bit bkwd: bhd most of way* **66/1**

19 3 **Native Forest (IRE)** 4-11-4 .... SThomas 74
(Miss H C Knight) *neat: bhd most of way* **50/1**

0- 20 dist **Barons Knight**[221] [4935] 4-10-13 .... MNicolls(5) —
(P R Webber) *lw: chsd ldrs over 11f: t.o* **66/1**

21 21 **Lifes A Beach (IRE)** 4-11-4 .... RGreene —
(J J Bridger) *cmpt: chsd ldrs 11f: t.o* **100/1**

4m 0.10s (-3.20) **Going Correction** -0.075s/f (Good) **21 Ran SP% 132.2**
Speed ratings: **104,103,100,98,97 96,95,95,94,92 90,90,90,90,89 89,85,84,83,— —** CSF £35.20 TOTE £2.90: £1.90, £4.50, £6.70; EX 51.30 Place 6 £958.49, Place 5 £675.19.

Owner Mrs John Magnier **Bred** Pat Tobin **Trained** Cheltenham, Gloucs

FOCUS
Probably a decent bumper run in a fair time, and there was plenty to like about the well-bred winner's performance as he was value for further. The fourth and fifth help to set the level for the form.

NOTEBOOK
Wichita Lineman(IRE) ◆, a half-brother to top-class Rhinestone Cowboy, was well backed for this debut and won in the manner of an exciting prospect. Having travelled well into the straight, he picked up when asked to make up ground from mid-division and in the end drew nicely clear with the runner-up. He won with a bit up his sleeve and looks an early candidate for the Cheltenham Festival Bumper shortlist. *(op 5-2 tchd 11-4)*

Presentandcorrect(IRE) ◆, a half-brother to a couple of Irish point-to-point winners, could not cope with the finish of the winner, but he still had a seven-length advantage over the third horse at the line. He should certainly be capable of winning a typical bumper.

Balamory Dan(IRE), as at Aintree, had a tough task under his penalty and did not fare badly in the circumstances.

Aztec Warrior(IRE) finished over seven lengths in front of Balamory Dan at Aintree on his debut *but was disappointingly unable to confirm that form on the same terms on this better ground. (op 11-2 tchd 6-1)*

Commander Kev(IRE) ran well enough without building substantially on the promise of his debut run. A sharper track might suit him best. *(tchd 8-1 in places)*

Senora Snoopy(IRE), a half-sister to several winners over obstacles, including winning pointer/useful hurdler Snoopy Loopy and fairly useful staying hurdler/chaser Royal Snoopy, will be suited by a sterner test of stamina when faced with a flight of hurdles. *(op 25-1)*

Kalamazoo(IRE), a half-brother to high-class chaser Farmer Jack, is another likely to do better in time and when there is a greater emphasis on stamina. *(tchd 100-1)*

Rosita Bay, trying to make it a hat-trick of wins in bumpers, had plenty on her plate in this hotter company under her big weight, and she never really got into a competitive position. *(op 6-1)*

The Big Canadian(IRE) *Official explanation: jockey said gelding ran too free (op 8-1)*

T/Jkpt: Not won. T/Plt: £757.20 to a £1 stake. Pool: £64,625.40. 62.30 winning tickets. T/Qpdt: £168.70 to a £1 stake. Pool: £4,719.70. 20.70 winning tickets. ST

2535 - (Foreign Racing) - See Raceform Interactive

2226 NAVAN (L-H)

Sunday, November 27

OFFICIAL GOING: Soft

2536a TOTE EXACTA "MONKSFIELD" NOVICE HURDLE (GRADE 3) 2m 4f

1:10 (1:10) 4-Y-O+ **£16,159** (£4,741; £2,258; £769)

RPR

1 **Powerstation (IRE)**[14] [2206] 5-11-2 .... DNRussell 138
(C Byrnes, Ire) *trckd ldrs: 5th 4 out: smooth hdwy next: cl 2nd travelling wl 2 out: disputing ld whn hit last: rallied u.p: led on line* **7/2**[3]

2 shd **Travino (IRE)**[15] [2193] 6-11-2 .... RWalsh 138
(Ms Margaret Mullins, Ire) *trckd ldr: impr to disp ld 6th: led bef 4 out: rdn and strly pressed bef 2 out: jnd briefly last: styd on wl u.p: hdd on li* **13/8**[1]

3 14 **Vic Venturi (IRE)**[27] [1963] 5-11-2 .... (t) BJGeraghty 124
(Philip Fenton, Ire) *trckd ldrs in 3rd: slt mstke 5th: 2nd whn mstke 3 out: sn outpcd* **10/1**

4 6 **Tardenois (FR)**[14] [2226] 6-10-11 .... AELynch(5) 118
(J T R Dreaper, Ire) *led: clr early: jnd 6th: slt mstke next: hdd 4 out: kpt on same pce fr next* **7/1**

5 9 **Hear The Echo (IRE)**[23] [2030] 4-10-11 .... CO'Dwyer 104
(David Wachman, Ire) *hld up early: impr into 3rd after 4 out: no ex fr next* **12/1**

6 dist **Maille Blu (FR)**[18] [2133] 5-11-2 .... APMcCoy —
(T M Walsh, Ire) *a in rr: lost tch fr 4 out: eased fr 2 out* **33/1**

F **Nicanor (FR)**[14] [2226] 4-10-11 .... PCarberry 127
(Noel Meade, Ire) *hld up: 6th whn slt mstke 4 out: hdwy next: cl 3rd and stl on bridle whn fell 2 out* **3/1**[2]

5m 1.70s
WFA 4 from 5yo+ 13lb **7 Ran SP% 117.5**
CSF £10.43 TOTE £7.20: £2.10, £1.90; DF 16.50.

Owner Fat Frog Syndicate **Bred** John Byrne **Trained** Ballingarry, Co Limerick

NOTEBOOK
Powerstation(IRE) was able to give a strong line between the merits of the leading novices here and in Britain after his Cheltenham second to Black Jack Ketchum. The fact remains that it took five runs over hurdles to break his duck, though, and it was strength and experience that clinched it for him here after a mistake at the last flight. His previous Irish form leaves him pretty well exposed.
Travino(IRE) went on after the fourth last and would probably have preferred to have been taken along at a stronger pace. He looked vulnerable before the second last and, although keeping on dourly, *there was not much sign of the pace that he displayed when winning three bumpers. (op 6/4 tchd 7/4)*
Vic Venturi(IRE) was not particularly fluent and a mistake three out put paid to his chance. *(op 8/1)*
Tardenois(FR) was untidy at some hurdles and was inclined to hang right. Headed four out, he was done with when hampered at the second last. *(op 12/1)*
Hear The Echo(IRE) faded out from the third last and was put in his place on this step-up in class. *(op 8/1)*
Nicanor(FR) was not fluent at some flights but was still travelling well in third place on the run to *the second last. He took a heavy fall there but would certainly have been concerned in the finish. (op 11/4 tchd 5/2)*

2539a WILLIAM HILL IN IRELAND TROYTOWN H'CAP CHASE (GRADE B) 3m

2:40 (2:41) (0-150,137) 4-Y-0+ **£39,244** (£11,514; £5,485; £1,868)

RPR

1 **Prince Of Tara (IRE)**[14] [2227] 8-10-4 118 ow2.................... BJGeraghty 129+
(S J Mahon, Ire) *sn trckd ldrs: 4th 1/2-way: led 7 out: bad mstke and strly pressed 3 out: kpt on wl u.p fr next* **11/2**[3]

2 1 **A New Story (IRE)**[7] [2390] 7-10-1 115.................... AndrewJMcNamara 125+
(Michael Hourigan, Ire) *hld up: 8th 4 out: 3rd 2 out: 2nd and kpt on wl fr last* **5/1**[2]

3 2 1/2 **Monterey Bay (IRE)**[67] [1515] 9-10-1 115.................... RWalsh 123
(Ms F M Crowley, Ire) *led: hdd 7 out: remained prom: 4th and rdn whn slt mstke 3 out: kpt on fr last* **7/2**[1]

4 3/4 **Adarma (IRE)**[27] [1965] 7-10-8 122.................... APMcCoy 129
(C Roche, Ire) *hld up in tch: 7th whn mstke 5 out: 6th and rdn after 3 out: kpt on fr last* **9/1**

5 shd **Star Clipper**[49] [1700] 8-10-12 126.................... DNRussell 133
(Noel Meade, Ire) *hld up: 9th 4 out: rdn and kpt on fr 2 out* **10/1**

6 1 1/2 **Pearly Jack**[7] [2388] 7-10-4 123.................... MrMJO'Connor(5) 128
(D E Fitzgerald, Ire) *trckd ldrs: 5th after 1/2-way: 4th 4 out: cl 2nd and chal next: ev ch: no ex fr last* **7/1**

7 4 **Ransboro (IRE)**[14] [2229] 6-9-10 110.................... DJCasey 111
(C F Swan, Ire) *prom: 2nd 1/2-way: 3rd and rdn 3 out: no ex fr bef last* **12/1**

8 7 **One Four Shannon (IRE)**[55] [1627] 8-9-9 112.................... TGMRyan(3) 106
(D J Ryan, Ire) *mid-div: mstke 6th: rdn 3 out: no ex fr next* **10/1**

9 2 **Point Barrow (IRE)**[8] [2365] 7-11-5 133.................... JPElliott 125
(P Hughes, Ire) *mid-div: 6th 6 out: 5th 4 out: wknd next* **12/1**

10 20 **Fatherofthebride (IRE)**[7] [2390] 9-10-2 116.................... (b) TPTreacy 88
(Joseph Crowley, Ire) *cl up: nt fluent 1st: slt mstke 5th: 5th 6 out: wknd fr 4 out* **12/1**

11 dist **Marcus Du Berlais (FR)**[232] [4772] 8-11-9 137.................... CO'Dwyer —
(A L T Moore, Ire) *a towards rr: slt mstke 8th: trailing after 4 out: t.o* **20/1**

12 5 **Well Presented (IRE)**[10] [2304] 7-11-4 132.................... RMPower —
(Mrs John Harrington, Ire) *4th whn mstke and lost pl 4th: nt fluent jumping after: t.o* **20/1**

P **G V A Ireland (IRE)**[212] [115] 7-10-5 124.................... KTColeman(5) —
(F Flood, Ire) *hld up towards rr: hdwy into 7th 4 out: wknd next: p.u bef 2 out* **20/1**

6m 23.1s **13 Ran SP% 132.3**
CSF £36.86 CT £113.40 TOTE £4.60: £1.80, £2.50, £1.80; DF 40.20.

Owner James J Swan **Bred** Oldtown Bloodstock Hedges Ltd **Trained** Stamullen, Co Meath

■ Stewards' Enquiry : D N Russell caution: used whip down the shoulder in the forehand position

NOTEBOOK
Prince Of Tara(IRE) is difficult to train and this was his first chase appearance in over a year and only his third start over fences. Third here behind Solerina over hurdles a fortnight ago, he exploited his handicap mark, and lack of experience, in some style, despite having to carry 2lb overweight and making a serious mistake at the third last. *(op 6/1)*
A New Story(IRE) has made a rapid climb in the handicap and was 24lb higher after two recent successes at Limerick and Cork. His sustained challenge from two out never quite looked like being successful.

2540 - 2551a (Foreign Racing) - See Raceform Interactive

[2236]FOLKESTONE (R-H)

Monday, November 28

OFFICIAL GOING: Chase course - good; hurdle course - good to soft (soft in places)

Wind: Almost nil Weather: Overcast

2552 DAILY MAIL CONDITIONAL JOCKEYS' NOVICES' H'CAP HURDLE (10 hdls) 2m 4f 110y

12:30 (12:30) (Class 4) (0-100,94) 3-Y-0+ **£3,247** (£946; £473)

Form				RPR
F-P6	1		**Paddy Boy (IRE)**[15] [2216] 4-10-4 **72** StephenCraine (J R Boyle) *nt fluent: cl up: led 6th: rdn clr after 2 out: 7 l ahd last: eased flat* **16/1**	83+
3P63	2	*3*	**Mistified (IRE)**[24] [2017] 4-11-0 **90** WayneKavanagh[(8)] (J W Mullins) *hld up in tch: effrt 7th: rdn to chse wnr after 2 out: no imp bef last* **8/1**[2]	92+
45-2	3	*1 ½*	**Very Special One (IRE)**[27] [1974] 5-11-8 **90** MarkNicolls (K C Bailey) *cl up: pressed ldr 5th to next: chsd wnr tl after 2 out: hrd rdn and kpt on same pce* **2/1**[1]	91+
62-0	4	*14*	**Barranco (IRE)**[214] [78] 4-10-13 **87** (b) EamonDehdashti[(6)] (G L Moore) *wl in tch: rdn after 7th: struggling next: no ch whn mstke 2 out: plugged on* **14/1**	73
F0-6	5	*dist*	**Desertmore Chief (IRE)**[24] [2020] 6-10-4 **80** (b[1]) TomasBosak[(8)] (B De Haan) *hld up: lost tch after 4th: sn t.o: kpt gng slowly fnl circ: btn 74 l* **40/1**	—
-32P	6	*3 ½*	**Nod's Star**[146] [905] 4-10-7 **85** (t) CraigMessenger[(10)] (Mrs L C Jewell) *trckd ldrs: wl in tch 3 out: rdn and wknd next: t.o: btn 78 l* **10/1**[3]	—
20-0	P		**Cosi Celeste (FR)**[192] [441] 8-11-11 **93** TomGreenway (John Allen) *in tch to 5th: wknd u.p bef next: p.u bef 3 out* **33/1**	—
-U0P	P		**Mongino (GER)**[31] [1910] 4-10-1 **75** (v[1]) CharliePoste[(6)] (M F Harris) *w ldr to 5th: sn wknd u.p: t.o 3 out: poor 9th whn p.u bef last* **66/1**	—
P63-	P		**Dancing Shirley**[379] [2219] 7-10-9 **77** ColinBolger (Miss A M Newton-Smith) *led to 6th: sn wknd: t.o 2 out: poor 7th whn p.u bef last* **20/1**	—
40-2	P		**Deo Gratias (POL)**[36] [1856] 5-11-5 **87** WilliamKennedy (M Pitman) *in tch: rdn 6th: sn struggling: no ch after 3 out: t.o in 8th whn p.u bef last* **2/1**[1]	—
-160	P		**Bayadere (GER)**[13] [2261] 5-11-9 **94** ShaneWalsh[(3)] (K F Clutterbuck) *hld up: nt fluent 5th: sn rdn and struggling: mstke 7th: t.o whn p.u bef 2 out* **20/1**	—

5m 41.7s (8.90) **Going Correction** +0.175s/f (Yiel)

WFA 4 from 5yo+ 13lb **11** Ran SP% **115.8**

Speed ratings: **90,88,88,82,— —,—,—,—,— —** CSF £125.42 CT £371.31 TOTE £18.30: £3.80, £2.90, £1.10; EX 258.60.

Owner Brian McAtavey **Bred** Brian McAtavey **Trained** Epsom, Surrey

■ Stewards' Enquiry : Tomas Bosak caution: used whip when out of contention

FOCUS

A very moderate handicap hurdle for novices in which Paddy Boy stepped up on his previous efforts to run out a convincing winner, being value for nine lengths. The winning time was moderate for the class.

NOTEBOOK

Paddy Boy(IRE), a very moderate maiden, was not looking much better over hurdles either but, stepped back up in trip and partnered by a very talented conditional, he responded well to a positive ride to run out a convincing winner. This must have been a pretty moderate race, but connections look to have found the key to him and he will avoid a penalty if turned out before being reassessed. *Official explanation: trainer said, regarding the improved form shown, gelding was suited by the right-handed track and benefited from the drop in class (op 25-1)*

Mistified(IRE) ran another creditable race in defeat but remains a long-standing maiden. *(op 10-1)*

Very Special One(IRE) failed to build on the promise she showed when second on her reappearance at Worcester, despite shaping as though this sort of trip would suit. *(op 7-4 tchd 9-4)*

Barranco(IRE) was well held in fourth and continues to underachieve. *(op 12-1)*

Deo Gratias(POL) could not reproduce the form he showed to be second off the back of a long break at Towcester and was in trouble a fair way out. *Official explanation: jockey said gelding made a noise (tchd 7-4)*

2553 DAILY MAIL MARES' ONLY BEGINNERS' CHASE (IN MEMORY OF LADY HARMSWORTH BLUNT) (18 fncs) 3m 1f

1:00 (1:00) (Class 4) 5-Y-0+ **£4,749** (£1,394; £697; £348)

Form				RPR
6043	1		**Sunny South East (IRE)**[13] [2260] 5-10-8 WilliamKennedy[(5)] (S Gollings) *trckd ldrs: effrt and rdn 14th: chsd ldr 3 out: 10 l down and no ch whn lft in ld last: drvn out* **8/1**	93+
/5-P	2	*3*	**Glenogue (IRE)**[15] [2217] 7-11-0 98 (b[1]) JohnMcNamara (K C Bailey) *hld up: prog 12th: chsd ldr next: rdn and lost 2nd 3 out: wl btn whn lft 2nd at last* **13/2**	91+
1603	3	*3 ½*	**Wayward Melody**[14] [2237] 5-10-13 86 (p) PhilipHide (G L Moore) *nt fluent: trckd ldr: led 5th to 13th: wl outpcd fr 15th: no ch after: styd on again fr 2 out: lft 3rd last* **10/1**	85
P5F-	4	*1 ½*	**Scratch The Dove**[226] [4868] 8-11-0 WayneHutchinson (A E Price) *hld up: in tch 12th: wl outpcd fr 15th: no ch after: styd on again fr 2 out: lft 4th last* **20/1**	85
	5	*11*	**Orbys Girl (IRE)**[61] [1575] 5-10-10 (t) GinoCarenza[(3)] (K J Burke) *hld up: j. slowly 5th and reminder: nt gng wl fr 11th: wl bhd fr 14th* **40/1**	73
30-U	6	*9*	**Sword Lady**[11] [2297] 7-11-0 (b) RichardJohnson (Mrs S D Williams) *mstke 2nd: nvr gng that wl after: last fr 5th: lost tch 13th: no ch after* **10/3**[2]	65
3366	P		**Kombinacja (POL)**[44] [1743] 7-11-0 98 (b) JasonMaguire (T R George) *t.k.h: prom tl p.u after 10th: broke down* **3/1**[1]	—
433	U		**Sarahs Quay (IRE)**[78] [1455] 6-10-7 ShaneWalsh[(7)] (K J Burke) *j. slowly and lft 1st: already out of tch whn j.lft 2nd and uns rdr* **33/1**	—
0/U	P		**Kewlake Lane**[10] [2311] 7-11-0 AndrewThornton (R H Alner) *hanging lft: led to 5th: trckd ldr to 11th: lost pl 13th: sn eased and bhd: last whn p.u bef last* **16/1**	—
50-2	R		**Elfkirk (IRE)**[14] [2240] 6-11-0 BenjaminHitchcott (R H Buckler) *cl up: wnt 2nd 11th: led and j.lft 13th: drew clr fr 3 out: j. bdly lft next: 10 l up whn tried to refuse and rn out last* **4/1**[3]	106+

6m 25.0s (-8.40) **Going Correction** -0.35s/f (Good)

WFA 5 from 6yo+ 1lb **10** Ran SP% **117.6**

Speed ratings: **99,98,96,96,92 90,—,—,—,—** CSF £58.57 TOTE £9.10: £2.30, £2.00, £3.50; EX 66.00.

Owner Gregg Stafford **Bred** Mrs Ann Fortune **Trained** Scamblesby, Lincs

FOCUS

Elfkirk would have won this mares'-only beginners' chase pretty convincingly had she not tried to refuse at the last but, with the likes of Sword Lady and Kombinacja below their best, the form is moderate.

NOTEBOOK

Sunny South East(IRE) would have been well held in second had Elfkirk not tried to refuse at the last. Things will be tougher under a penalty in novice company, and she is likely to be better off in handicaps from now on. *(op 11-1)*

Glenogue(IRE), pulled up over two miles two at Fontwell on her reappearance, ran better over this longer trip with blinkers on for the first time, but may need to improve again to find a similar event. *(op 8-1 tchd 9-1)*

Wayward Melody, with cheekpieces refitted, showed up well for much of the way but was ultimately held and ought to find things easier back in handicaps. *(op 11-1)*

Scratch The Dove, making her chasing debut off the back of a 226-day break, ought to improve for both the run and experience.

Sword Lady, who unseated on her chasing debut at Wincanton, managed to complete this time, but she never really recovered from a mistake at the second and was well below her hurdling mark of 119. *Official explanation: trainer had no explanation for the poor form shown (op 11-4)*

Kombinacja(POL), given another chance over fences, sadly pulled up injured. *(tchd 7-2)*

Elfkirk(IRE), a 100-rated hurdler who was stepping up to her furthest trip to date on her chasing debut, would have run out a convincing winner had she not tried to refuse at the last and crashed through the wing on the left-hand side of the fence. She is likely to be kept to left-handed tracks from now on and, providing that curbs her wayward tendencies, she should find a similar race. *(tchd 7-2)*

2554 E B F DAILY MAIL "NATIONAL HUNT" NOVICES' HURDLE (QUALIFIER) (9 hdls) 2m 1f 110y

1:30 (1:30) (Class 4) 4-6-Y-0 **£3,409** (£1,000; £500; £249)

Form				RPR
21-U	1		**Senorita Rumbalita**[12] [2269] 4-10-7 RobertThornton (A King) *cl up: trckd ldr 4th: led between last 2: cruised clr* **2/7**[1]	127+
41-	2	*14*	**Liathroidisneachta (IRE)**[268] [4179] 5-11-0 APMcCoy (Jonjo O'Neill) *trckd ldr to 4th: styd cl up: hit 2 out: chsd wnr between last 2: sn brushed aside* **12/1**[3]	110+
001-	3	*5*	**Sunley Shines**[235] [4760] 5-10-7 TimmyMurphy (B G Powell) *t.k.h: led: hanging lft and often j.lft: hdd between last 2: sn outpcd* **20/1**	98+
53-6	4	*8*	**Follow Your Heart (IRE)**[19] [2127] 5-11-0 MickFitzgerald (N J Gifford) *hld up: shkn up and outpcd bef 2 out: plugged on bef last* **9/1**[2]	95
16/	5	*13*	**Scaramouche**[697] [3139] 5-11-0 NoelFehily (B De Haan) *trckd ldrs: j. slowly 4th: effrt to chse ldng trio 2 out: sn shuffled along and outpcd: wknd bef last* **40/1**	82
	6	*5*	**Shaka's Pearl** 5-11-0 LeightonAspell (N J Gifford) *hld up in rr: outpcd fr 3 out: shuffled along and one pce after* **14/1**	77
53-6	7	*18*	**Orange Street**[188] [490] 5-10-11 ColinBolger[(3)] (Mrs L J Mongan) *mstke 2nd: in tch: rdn 3 out: wknd next* **66/1**	59
0/0	8	*8*	**Phazar**[27] [1969] 5-11-0 JimmyMcCarthy (N J Hawke) *t.k.h: hld up: in tch 3 out: sn wknd* **80/1**	51
/5-0	9	*6*	**Top Dog (IRE)**[14] [2242] 6-10-7 JustinMorgan[(7)] (L Wells) *hld up in rr: mstke 1st: lost tch 5th: t.o after* **50/1**	45
24P0	10	*5*	**Silverio (GER)**[8] [2376] 4-11-0 JamieMoore (G L Moore) *in tch tl wknd 5th: sn wl bhd: t.o* **40/1**	40

4m 29.7s (0.40) **Going Correction** +0.175s/f (Yiel)

WFA 4 from 5yo+ 12lb **10** Ran SP% **116.4**

Speed ratings: **106,99,97,94,88 86,78,74,71,69** CSF £4.35 TOTE £1.20: £1.02, £2.00, £3.20; EX 6.90.

Owner Let's Get Ready To Rumble Partnership **Bred** Wothersome Grange Stud **Trained** Barbury Castle, Wilts

FOCUS

The bare form of this novice hurdle looked just ordinary and provided Senorita Rumbalita with a straightforward opportunity to gain compensation for unseating on her debut over obstacles, but she was still pretty impressive and demands to be followed.

NOTEBOOK

Senorita Rumbalita ◆, a useful bumper performer last season, would probably have won on her hurdling debut at Wincanton had she not unseated at the last (saddle slipped). This looked like a straightforward enough race for her to gain compensation, but she was still pretty impressive, winning with any amount in hand. Connections will have the option of qualifying her for both the EBF Novices' Hurdle at Sandown and the valuable Mares' Final at Newbury in March, but by that time she could well be worth a place at Cheltenham. *(op 1-4)*

Liathroidisneachta(IRE), successful in a moderate bumper at Huntingdon when last seen 268 days previously, had no chance behind the very useful winner and ought to find easier opportunities in time.

Sunley Shines, a bumper winner at Taunton when last seen 235 days previously, showed a tendency to hang a little to her left and was ultimately well held in third. Open to some improvement, she could find easier opportunities in mares'-only company. *(op 25-1 tchd 16-1)*

Follow Your Heart(IRE) ran respectably enough in fourth, but she needs one more run for a mark and will probably find things easier once handicapped.

Scaramouche ◆, a promising enough bumper performer when last seen 697 days ago, ran with promise on his debut and can leave this form behind when he is race fit.

Silverio(GER) *Official explanation: trainer said gelding was found to be jarred up the following morning (op 33-1)*

2555 DAILY MAIL NOVICES' H'CAP CHASE (15 fncs) 2m 5f

2:00 (2:01) (Class 4) (0-95,94) 4-Y-0+ **£4,346** (£1,275; £637; £318)

Form				RPR
03-2	1		**Presenting Express (IRE)**[24] [2015] 6-11-0 **80** BarryFenton (Miss E C Lavelle) *racd wd: prom: mstke 6th: led 8th to 9th: led 10th: mstke next: hdd and mstke 2 out: rallied to ld last: rdn out* **5/2**[1]	97+
20-3	2	*1 ½*	**Lizzie Bathwick (IRE)**[18] [2149] 6-11-12 **92** NoelFehily (D P Keane) *hld up in rr: prog to trck ldrs 8th: rdn 4 out: effrt on inner to ld 2 out: hdd last: nt qckn* **8/1**[3]	103
500-	3	*2 ½*	**Bar Gayne (IRE)**[250] [4514] 6-11-10 **90** JasonMaguire (T R George) *settled midfield: effrt 11th: ddrvn to chse ldrs 3 out: kpt on same pce fr next* **25/1**	99

2- **4** *shd* **Gerrard (IRE)**^{264} [4253] 7-10-12 **78** (v) CarlLlewellyn 86
(Mrs A Barclay) *prom: led 9th to 10th: lost pl u.p 3 out: effrt again bef next: kpt on same pce* **10/1**

04-P **5** *5* **Lucky Luk (FR)**^{36} [1855] 6-11-2 **82** JohnMcNamara 87+
(K C Bailey) *hld up in rr: prog 10th: blnd next: chsd ldrs 3 out but nt on terms: no imp fr 2 out* **25/1**

40-2 **6** *5* **First De La Brunie (FR)**^{14} [2248] 4-11-1 **94** RobertThornton 83+
(A King) *trckd ldrs: gng wl 11th: wnt 3rd and rdn 3 out: wknd 2 out: j. slowly last* **4/1**^{2}

/FP1 **7** *10* **New Leader (IRE)**^{14} [2237] 8-10-3 **69** MatthewBatchelor 61+
(Mrs L Richards) *hld up wl in rr: stdy prog fr 9th: chsd wnr 12th tl wknd bef 2 out* **12/1**

4P-4 **8** *16* **Opportunity Knocks**^{10} [2313] 5-10-13 **79** PhilipHide 51
(N J Hawke) *settled in midfield: nt fluent 8th: lost tch w ldng gp fr 12th: n.d after* **16/1**

0-00 **9** *3 1/2* **Great Benefit (IRE)**^{10} [2313] 6-11-5 **85** SamThomas 54
(Miss H C Knight) *led to 2nd: rdn 11th: sn wknd* **20/1**

0-P4 **10** *7* **Croghan Loch (IRE)**^{14} [2237] 8-10-0 **66** HenryOliver 28
(P G Murphy) *chsd ldrs: blnd 6th: mstke 10th: sn rdn and nt look keen: bhd fr 12th* **66/1**

P0-0 **11** *dist* **Magic Red**^{64} [1564] 5-10-11 **80** ColinBolger$^{(3)}$ —
(J Ryan) *nt jump wl: toiling in rr fr 7th: t.o 10th: ploughed on* **50/1**

5042 **P** **Sitting Duck**^{20} [2104] 6-11-0 **80** TimmyMurphy —
(B G Powell) *led 2nd to 8th: wknd fr 10th: t.o whn p.u bef 3 out* **8/1**^{3}

52-4 **P** **I'm For Waiting**^{213} [107] 9-10-0 **71** MarkNicolls$^{(5)}$ —
(John Allen) *last and losing tch 8th: t.o whn p.u bef 11th* **25/1**

3PP/ **P** **Thorpeness (IRE)**^{696} [3170] 6-11-12 **92** AndrewTinkler —
(P D Cundell) *a wl in rr: lost tch 11th: wl bhd whn p.u bef last* **33/1**

-06U **P** **Geography (IRE)**^{8} [2375] 5-10-13 **86** (p) RobertLucey-Butler$^{(7)}$ —
(P Butler) *hels up in last pair: blnd 6th: tailing off whn p.u after next* **100/1**

0/00 **P** **It's Official (IRE)**^{28} [1959] 6-10-13 **79** (p) JamesDavies —
(Miss A M Newton-Smith) *screwed 1st: prom to 5th: sn lost pl: t.o fr 9th: p.u bef 11th* **40/1**

5m 13.15s (-11.25) **Going Correction** -0.35s/f (Good)
WFA 4 from 5yo+ 13lb **16** Ran SP% **119.6**
Speed ratings: **107,106,105,105,103 101,97,91,90,87** —,—,—,—,— CSF £20.07 CT £415.82 TOTE £2.90: £1.60, £2.20, £9.00, £2.80; EX 27.90 Trifecta £288.10 Pool: £487.00 - 1.20 winning tickets..

Owner N Mustoe **Bred** Patrick O'Dwyer **Trained** Wildhern, Hants

FOCUS
A pretty good novices' handicap chase for a 0-95, and it should produce a few winners at a similar level. The form looks solid and the time was fair.

NOTEBOOK
Presenting Express(IRE) ◆ did not totally convince with his jumping when last seen over fences in February, but he shaped with promise over hurdles on his reappearance, and built on that to gain his first success under Rules on his return to chasing, despite again making mistakes. There is room for improvement, especially when he steps back up in trip on a more galloping track, and he is likely to still be reasonably handicapped when reassessed. *(tchd 9-4)*
Lizzie Bathwick(IRE) ◆ confirmed the promise she showed when third on her chasing debut at Taunton. This was a good effort considering the winner is by no means badly handicapped, and she should not be too long in finding a similar race.
Bar Gayne(IRE), successful in a bumper on his debut but winless in three runs over hurdles, made a promising debut over fences. On the evidence of this performance he is on a very fair mark and looks up to winning a similar race or two.
Gerrard(IRE), returning from a 264-day break, confirmed the promise he showed in two runs over fences last season. *(op 12-1)*
Lucky Luk(FR), an encouraging fourth on his chasing debut at Fontwell before pulling up at Towcester, returned to some sort of form, especially considering he made quite a bad blunder, and confirmed that initial promise. *(tchd 33-1)*
First De La Brunie(FR), a promising second on his first run over fences in this country at Leicester last time, looked like confirming that promise when travelling well for much of the way, but he weakened out of contention most disappointingly. *(op 7-2)*
It's Official(IRE) *Official explanation: jockey said gelding hung badly left throughout*

2556 DAILY MAIL H'CAP HURDLE (11 hdls) 2m 6f 110y
2:30 (2:30) (Class 4) (0-105,101) 4-Y-O+ **£4,215** (£1,237; £618; £309)

Form RPR

6016 **1** **Pardon What**^{17} [2166] 9-11-9 **101** (b) KeithMercer$^{(3)}$ 106+
(S Lycett) *t.k.h: nt fluent: hld up in rr: outpcd fr 3 out: styd on after next: clsd last: rdn to ld flat* **9/1**

P4-P **2** *1 1/2* **Putup Or Shutup (IRE)**^{205} [215] 9-11-9 **98** JohnMcNamara 101+
(K C Bailey) *prom: chsd ldr 8th: rdn 2 out: led bef last: hdd and one pce flat* **9/2**^{1}

/353 **3** *3 1/2* **Good Potential (IRE)**^{19} [2130] 9-10-13 **88** (t) WarrenMarston 87
(D J Wintle) *w ldr: led 5th: drvn and looked wnr between last 2: hdd and one pce bef last* **11/2**^{3}

/0-5 **4** *1 1/4* **Protagonist**^{11} [2296] 7-11-4 **100** TomMessenger$^{(7)}$ 97
(B N Pollock) *prom: outpcd after 3 out: sn drvn: rallied u.p between last 2: styd on flat* **16/1**

530- **5** *8* **The Bo'sun**^{241} [4679] 8-11-2 **91** TomDoyle 82+
(A E Jessop) *hld up in rr: prog 3 out: outpcd and rdn 2 out: no hdwy bef last* **33/1**

/0-2 **6** *29* **Eljutan (IRE)**^{27} [1977] 7-11-2 **98** ShaneWalsh$^{(7)}$ 58
(J Joseph) *mstkes: struggling in last 6th: u.str.p and nt on terms 3 out: no ch* **16/1**

3F-0 **F** **Buckland Gold (IRE)**^{30} [1921] 5-11-2 **91** JamesDavies —
(D B Feek) *sn trckd ldrs: 8th and losing pl whn fell 8th* **16/1**

44/P **P** **Chateau Rose (IRE)**^{27} [1973] 9-11-2 **91** (p) BarryFenton —
(Miss E C Lavelle) *racd wd: prom: mstke 6th: wknd 3 out: t.o whn p.u bef last* **6/1**

0-30 **P** **Be Telling (IRE)**^{19} [2127] 6-11-4 **93** PaulMoloney —
(B J Curley) *plld hrd early: hld up: blnd 4th: wknd and mstke 8th: t.o whn p.u bef next* **10/1**

4-54 **P** **Canni Thinkaar (IRE)**^{24} [2017] 4-10-8 **90** (p) RobertLucey-Butler$^{(7)}$ —
(P Butler) *led to 5th: rdn whn mstke 8th: sn wknd: t.o in last after 2 out: p.u bef last* **20/1**

3213 **P** **Red Dahlia**^{18} [2150] 8-11-2 **91** AndrewTinkler —
(M Pitman) *hld up in rr: stdy prog 8th: chsd ldrs after 3 out: wknd and eased after 2 out: p.u bef last* **5/1**^{2}

46-P **P** **Alpha Gamble (IRE)**^{14} [2238] 5-11-8 **97** BrianCrowley —
(R Rowe) *t.k.h: hld up: smooth prog to trck ldng pair 3 out: wknd after next: eased: 6th whn p.u bef last: do bttr* **14/1**

6m 11.4s (2.30) **Going Correction** +0.175s/f (Yiel)
WFA 4 from 5yo+ 13lb **12** Ran SP% **115.6**
Speed ratings: **103,102,101,100,98 87**,—,—,—,— —,— CSF £48.81 CT £246.76 TOTE £9.90: £2.40, £2.40, £3.50; EX 64.00.

Owner N E Powell **Bred** Mrs J Stuart Evans **Trained** Naunton, Gloucs

FOCUS
A moderate handicap hurdle in which half the field failed to complete, and yet the form might work out alright.

NOTEBOOK
Pardon What came from a mile back to get up close home and defy a 9lb higher mark than when winning at Worcester two starts previously. Things will be harder when he is reassessed, but there may be more to come returned to a more galloping track and stepped back up in trip. *(op 8-1)*
Putup Or Shutup(IRE) had pulled up on three of his last four starts but, returning from a 205-day break, he was just denied. Given his inconsistent nature, it remains to be seen which way he will go. *(op 11-2)*
Good Potential(IRE) has dropped to a very fair mark and only gave way late on. *(op 6-1)*
Protagonist kept responding to pressure and could do even better back on softer ground.
The Bo'sun ◆ travelled very well for a lot of the way off the back of his 241-day break and could do better with the benefit of this run.
Chateau Rose(IRE), just as on his reappearance, failed to get home and the cheekpieces made no difference. *(op 8-1)*
Red Dahlia travelled well for a lot of the way, but stopped quite quickly and was said to have lost her action. *Official explanation: jockey said mare lost its action (op 8-1)*

2557 DAILY MAIL H'CAP CHASE (18 fncs) 3m 1f
3:00 (3:00) (Class 4) (0-110,103) 5-Y-O+ **£5,269** (£1,547; £773; £386)

Form RPR

2130 **1** **Muttley Maguire (IRE)**^{33} [1877] 6-11-7 **98** TimmyMurphy 112+
(B G Powell) *racd wd: mde most: mstke 15th: rdn 2 out: jnd flat: forged ahd again flat* **5/1**

/52- **2** *2 1/2* **Majestic Moonbeam (IRE)**^{390} [1986] 7-11-8 **99** APMcCoy 107
(Jonjo O'Neill) *hld up: prog 14th: chsd wnr after 3 out: rdn to chal 2 out: upsides last: nt qckn flat* **11/4**^{1}

4B-4 **3** *7* **Infrasonique (FR)**^{32} [1893] 9-11-12 **103** MarkBradburne 105+
(Mrs L C Taylor) *trckd ldrs: rdn 3 out: stl in tch 2 out: wknd last* **4/1**^{2}

P-U0 **4** *14* **Royale Acadou (FR)**^{15} [2216] 7-11-6 **100** ColinBolger$^{(3)}$ 93+
(Mrs L J Mongan) *w wnr to 3 out: wknd rapidly 2 out: eased flat* **50/1**

-660 **5** *1 1/4* **Multi Talented (IRE)**^{17} [2164] 9-11-3 **101** (b) JustinMorgan$^{(7)}$ 87
(L Wells) *a in rr: rdn 11th: lost tch next: wl bhd 14th: r.o flat* **20/1**

0-P4 **6** *nk* **Three Days Reign (IRE)**^{9} [2342] 11-11-7 **98** LeightonAspell 83
(P D Cundell) *mstke 2nd: settled in rr: lost tch 13th: pushed along next: no ch after: r.o flat* **14/1**

P1-3 **U** **Calcot Flyer**^{204} [240] 7-11-7 **98** RobertThornton —
(A King) *prom whn blnd and uns rdr 4th* **9/2**^{3}

-0P1 **F** **Stormy Skye (IRE)**^{30} [1920] 9-11-8 **99** (b) JamieMoore —
(G L Moore) *trckd ldng pair tl fell 7th* **11/2**

6m 23.1s (-10.30) **Going Correction** -0.35s/f (Good) **8** Ran SP% **110.3**
Speed ratings: **102,101,98,94,94 93**,—,— CSF £18.46 CT £55.35 TOTE £4.80: £1.90, £1.80, £1.60; EX 23.60.

Owner Mrs Jean R Bishop **Bred** A W Buller **Trained** Morestead, Hants

FOCUS
Just an ordinary handicap chase for the grade, but Muttley Maguire gave the impression that there could be more to come.

NOTEBOOK
Muttley Maguire(IRE) looked as though he would be much better for the run when only eighth at Cheltenham on his return from a break and duly improved enough to run out a game winner. He should not go up much for this and will have a big chance of following up in similar company. *(op 11-2)*
Majestic Moonbeam(IRE) ran a fine race in second off the back of a 390-day absence, but looked to get tired over the last couple of fences and should improve for the run. *(tchd 5-2)*
Infrasonique(FR) was comfortably held in third and did not seem to improve as much as one might have hoped from his reappearance. *(op 6-1)*
Royale Acadou(FR), back over hurdles, ran a lot better than when beaten in a claiming hurdle on her previous start. *(op 40-1)*
Multi Talented(IRE) ran a little better with the blinkers back on, but needed to be hard ridden and was still well beaten.
Stormy Skye(IRE) fell before the race got serious. *(op 4-1)*
Calcot Flyer, returning from a 204-break, fell too early to know how he might have got on. *(op 4-1)*

2558 DAILY MAIL MARES' ONLY INTERMEDIATE OPEN NATIONAL HUNT FLAT RACE 2m 1f 110y
3:30 (3:30) (Class 6) 4-6-Y-O **£1,891** (£551; £275)

Form RPR

11 **1** **Ben's Turn (IRE)**^{24} [2021] 4-11-10 RobertThornton 114
(A King) *settled midfield: pushed along briefly 7f out: prog to trck ldrs 5f out: rdn to chse ldr 2f out: led 1f out: hld on u.p* **9/4**^{1}

-5 **2** *hd* **Colline De Fleurs**^{190} [470] 5-11-0 MarkBradburne 104
(J A B Old) *hld up: smooth prog to trck ldrs 5f out: led 3f out: rdn 2f out: hdd 1f out: kpt on wl: jst hld* **10/1**

3 *5* **Miss Chippy (IRE)** 5-11-0 JasonMaguire 99
(T R George) *hld up: prog to trck ldrs 5f out: chal 3f out: cl up 2f out: one pce after* **14/1**

4 *1/2* **Quotable** 4-11-0 LeightonAspell 98
(O Sherwood) *hld up: prog to trck ldrs 5f out: chal 3f out: rdn and one pce fnl 2f* **5/1**^{2}

5 **5** *13* **Riffles**^{14} [2242] 5-10-7 ShaneWalsh$^{(7)}$ 86+
(Mrs A J Bowlby) *led to 10f out: styd chsng ldrs: effrt 4f out: outpcd whn c v wd bnd over 2f out: n.d after* **33/1**

32 **6** *10* **Twist The Facts (IRE)**^{24} [2021] 5-10-7 MrNMoore$^{(7)}$ 83+
(N P Littmoden) *trckd ldrs: effrt to ld briefly over 3f out: wknd over 2f out* **7/1**^{3}

0 **7** *17* **Overjoyed**^{28} [1961] 4-10-11 ColinBolger$^{(3)}$ 58
(Miss Suzy Smith) *trckd ldrs: hrd rdn 6f out: outpcd and btn wl over 4f out: wknd* **100/1**

0- **8** *3* **Attitude**^{239} [4720] 4-11-0 WayneHutchinson 55
(A King) *prom: led 4f out to over 3f out: wknd rapidly* **14/1**

0-3 **9** *5* **Katy Jones**^{19} [2131] 5-11-0 (t) BrianCrowley 50
(Noel T Chance) *stdd s: t.k.h and hld up in last trio: rapid prog to ld 9f out to 6f out: sn rdn and wknd* **8/1**

0- **10** *11* **Will She Spin**^{270} [4138] 4-10-9 MrJMead$^{(5)}$ 39
(J W Mullins) *racd wd: a in rr: lost tch 6f out: plugged on* **66/1**

33 **11** *3/4* **Milanshan (IRE)**^{51} [1674] 5-11-0 RJGreene 39
(J W Mullins) *t.k.h: pressed ldr: led 10f out to 9f out: rdn to ld 6f out to 5f out: wknd* **16/1**

0 **12** *7* **The Laying Hen (IRE)**^{212} [131] 5-11-0 NoelFehily 32
(D P Keane) *in tch to over 5f out: wknd* **33/1**

6 **13** *6* **Supreme Nova**^{176} [656] 5-10-9 MarkNicolls$^{(5)}$ 26
(John Allen) *cl up: led 5f out to 4f out: wknd v rapidly* **50/1**

P-0 **14** *4* **Adam's Belle (IRE)**^{14} [2242] 5-10-11 (b^{1}) OwynNelmes$^{(3)}$ 22
(N B King) *in tch in rr: drvn and wknd over 6f out* **66/1**

15 *dist* **Romney Marsh** 4-11-0 .... TomDoyle —
(R Curtis) *a in rr: rdn 9f out: wknd 6f out: t.o* **14/1**
16 *dist* **West Bay Mist** 4-11-0 .... CarlLlewellyn —
(Mrs H R J Nelmes) *lost tch after 7f: sn wl t.o* **100/1**

4m 33.1s (-1.00) **Going Correction** +0.175s/f (Yiel) **16** Ran SP% **118.8**
Speed ratings: **97,96,94,94,88 84,76,75,73,68 67,64,62,60,—** — CSF £23.95 TOTE £3.40: £1.40, £3.80, £4.10; EX 44.30 Place 6 £34.10, Place 5 £18.23.
Owner C B Brookes **Bred** Miss E Violet Sweeney **Trained** Barbury Castle, Wilts

FOCUS
As is to be expected with mares'-only bumpers, the form is limited, but the well-above average Ben's Turn gamely completed the hat-trick.

NOTEBOOK
Ben's Turn(IRE), successful on both her previous starts in similar company, defied her double *penalty to complete the hat-trick. This was a game effort and she could develop into a fair hurdler.* *(op 5-2 tchd 11-4 in places)*
Colline De Fleurs stepped up significantly on the form she showed on her debut at Southwell 190 days previously and was just held having travelled well throughout. Her long-term future is obviously going to be over obstacles, but she is clearly up to winning in this sort of company.
Miss Chippy(IRE), a half-sister to several winners both on the Flat and over Jumps, including a nine-furlong Listed winner and an Irish bumper scorer, made a promising debut in third. She should improve for the experience and could find a similar event.
Quotable, whose dam showed moderate form in bumpers, is out of a half-sister to Champion Hurdle winner Make A Stand. She travelled well for some of the way but could not really sustain her effort in the straight and gave the impression that she will improve for the run. *(op 9-2)*
Riffles was again comfortably held.
Twist The Facts(IRE) was very disappointing considering she was just two lengths behind the winner at Fontwell on her previous start. *(op 5-1)*
T/Jkpt: Not won. T/Plt: £90.50 to a £1 stake. Pool: £45,144.75. 363.75 winning tickets. T/Qpdt: £8.60 to a £1 stake. Pool: £4,201.90. 359.40 winning tickets. JN

[2282]HEREFORD (R-H)
Tuesday, November 29

OFFICIAL GOING: Good
Wind: Nil Weather: Sunny

2559 WEATHERBYS MESSAGING SERVICE NOVICES' HURDLE (10 hdls) 2m 3f 110y
12:40 (12:41) (Class 4) 4-Y-0+ **£3,910** (£1,147; £573; £286)

Form RPR
1 **Magnifico (FR)**[38] 4-11-5 .... APMcCoy 123+
(M C Pipe) *hld up in tch: led appr 7th: mstke 2 out: sn rdn: r.o* **6/4**[1]
600- **2** *1 ½* **Beau De Turgeon (FR)**[223] [4933] 4-10-12 .... NoelFehily 111
(Ian Williams) *hld up in tch: rdn appr 2 out: wnt 2nd last: kpt on* **100/1**
1 **3** *7* **Miss Pebbles (IRE)**[23] [2070] 5-10-12 114 .... WayneHutchinson 106+
(R Dickin) *hld up in mid-div: hdwy 6th: ev ch 2 out: sn rdn: wknd flat* **9/4**[2]
-310 **4** *13* **Penric**[12] [2285] 5-10-7 93 .... RobertStephens[(5)] 95+
(J K Price) *prom: rdn after 6th: 4th and wkng whn mstke 2 out* **25/1**
43-0 **5** *14* **Lunch Was My Idea (IRE)**[16] [2212] 5-10-12 .... JoeTizzard 82+
(P F Nicholls) *bhd tl sme hdwy appr 2 out: n.d* **33/1**
35 **6** *13* **Micky Cole (IRE)**[6] [2426] 5-10-12 .... ChristianWilliams 64
(P F Nicholls) *towards rr: sn pushed along: nvr nr ldrs* **15/2**[3]
5 **7** *7* **It's The Limit (USA)**[54] [1654] 6-10-12 .... JamieMoore 57
(W K Goldsworthy) *hld up in mid-div: hdwy 6th: rdn and wknd after 3 out* **10/1**
8 *3* **Fill The Bunker (IRE)**[276] 5-10-12 .... CarlLlewellyn 54
(N A Twiston-Davies) *prom tl wknd 3 out* **20/1**
3 **9** *1 ¼* **Elegant Eskimo**[37] [1851] 6-10-5 .... TomDoyle 46
(S E H Sherwood) *led tl appr 7th: wknd 3 out* **22/1**
/0 **10** *14* **Orrezzo (GER)**[23] [2070] 5-10-5 .... MrRQuinn[(7)] 39
(G E Jones) *prom tl wknd 7th* **150/1**
-036 **11** *28* **Star Fever (IRE)**[19] [2144] 4-10-12 .... TimmyMurphy 11
(Miss H C Knight) *bhd fr 4th: t.o* **33/1**
0P **12** *8* **Dream On Maggie**[23] [2070] 5-10-5 .... TomScudamore —
(P Bowen) *bhd fr 4th: t.o* **150/1**
460P **13** *dist* **Judy The Drinker**[52] [1681] 6-10-5 .... DaveCrosse —
(J G M O'Shea) *a bhd: rdn 5th: t.o* **150/1**
50-0 **P** **Pearly Star**[12] [2288] 4-10-12 .... RobertThornton —
(A King) *a bhd: t.o whn p.u bef 7th* **33/1**

4m 48.9s (1.00) **Going Correction** +0.15s/f (Yiel) **14** Ran SP% **116.4**
Speed ratings: **104,103,100,95,89 84,81,80,80,74 63,60,—,—** CSF £198.97 TOTE £2.70: £1.30, £29.00, £1.10; EX 141.70.
Owner Nick Shutts **Bred** J De Muynck **Trained** Nicholashayne, Devon

FOCUS
Ordinary form, but the winner looks fairly smart and the race should produce its share of winners.

NOTEBOOK
Magnifico(FR), runner up on his final start in France in October, travelled strongly for most of the way before coming through to take it up leaving the back straight. Although he was made to work hard by outsider Beau De Turgeon, it was a fair effort under a penalty. A strong galloper, softer ground is likely to help in future, as will a step up in distance, and he may be the type to do well in handicaps. *(op 13-8 tchd 7-4)*
Beau De Turgeon(FR) did not show a great deal in two bumpers and a novice hurdle last season, but he has clearly done well over the summer and this represented a vastly improved effort. He moved smoothly into contention before being outpaced as the winner and third upped the tempo, but he stayed on again to take second. He too is going to be suited by further in time, but the way he travelled suggests that he can win at this distance. *(op 80-1)*
Miss Pebbles(IRE), easy winner of a bad race here on her debut, faced a stiffer task this time but she fared well and this probably represented a step up on her debut win. A return to two miles may not go amiss judging by the way she travelled, and there are more races in her, possibly in mares-only company. *(op 2-1 tchd 5-2 in a place)*
Penric is not up to much, as his rating of 93 suggests, and he was well held back in fourth. He has struggled since winning here two starts back, but a return to handicaps will at least give him a chance. *(op 22-1)*
Lunch Was My Idea(IRE) is moderate and it is unlikely he will be seen at his best until tackling low-grade handicaps over fences. *(op 28-1 tchd 25-1)*
Micky Cole(IRE) took another step in the wrong direction and has a bit to prove at present. *(op 10-1 tchd 7-1)*
It's The Limit(USA), a formerly useful ex-Flat racer, again had his ground, but he was unable to step up on his debut effort, even over this more suitable trip. *(op 14-1)*
Fill The Bunker(IRE), whose trainer commented before the race that he believed him to be one of the stable's nicer novice hurdle prospects, went the wrong way in the market and, as was to be expected for a three-mile point winner, he found this an inadequate stamina test. He is likely to be better with the experience behind him and an improved effort can be expected once he tackles three miles. *(op 16-1)*

2560 GILLIAN GORDON ASSOCIATES (S) HURDLE (8 hdls) 2m 1f
1:10 (1:11) (Class 5) 4-7-Y-0 **£2,206** (£643; £321)

Form RPR
0-4 **1** **Blue Mariner**[15] [2245] 5-10-12 .... (t) LeightonAspell 98+
(J Jay) *hld up and bhd: hdwy appr 5th: led after 2 out: comf* **5/2**[2]
60U4 **2** *5* **Canadian Storm**[19] [2146] 4-10-12 87 .... (p) AlanO'Keeffe 86
(A G Juckes) *t.k.h in rr: hdwy whn hit 5th: led briefly after 2 out: one pce* **7/1**
5430 **3** *13* **Siena Star (IRE)**[51] [1297] 7-10-12 86 .... APMcCoy 73
(P Bowen) *hld up in mid-div: hdwy appr 5th: wknd after 2 out* **9/4**[1]
0-33 **4** *3* **Ambersong**[19] [2139] 7-10-12 95 .... NoelFehily 71+
(A W Carroll) *hld up and bhd: rdn appr 5th: hdwy appr 2 out: no further prog* **4/1**[3]
P-00 **5** *2 ½* **Bonjour Bond (IRE)**[33] [1898] 4-10-9 .... (v) OwynNelmes[(3)] 67
(J G M O'Shea) *prom: lost pl appr 3rd: no real prog fr 3 out* **66/1**
4P02 **6** *4* **So Cloudy**[33] [1896] 4-10-0 .... StephenCraine[(5)] 56
(D McCain) *t.k.h in mid-div: hdwy 3rd: led briefly 2 out: sn wknd* **16/1**
0-00 **7** *½* **Lanos (POL)**[19] [2139] 7-10-12 83 .... (t) TomScudamore 63
(W Davies) *led to 2 out: sn wknd* **25/1**
04 **8** *6* **Weet Watchers**[2] [2523] 5-10-5 .... MarcGoldstein[(7)] 57
(T Wall) *t.k.h: prom tl wknd appr 2 out* **16/1**
PPP6 **9** *27* **Gordy's Joy**[11] [2310] 5-9-12 65 .... (vt[1]) EamonDehdashti[(7)] 23
(G A Ham) *chsd ldr: disp ld 5th: rdn and wknd after 3 out* **66/1**
10 *dist* **Topple**[50] 4-10-5 .... JodieMogford —
(P W Hiatt) *bhd fr 4th: t.o* **50/1**
0 **P** **Tia Marnie**[67] [1538] 7-10-5 .... RJGreene —
(S Lycett) *prom: rdn after 2nd: wknd 4th: t.o whn p.u bef last* **50/1**
0- **P** **Master Moneyspider**[349] [2831] 6-10-12 .... WayneHutchinson —
(C J Price) *nt j.w in rr: t.o whn p.u bef 4th* **50/1**
P050 **P** **Simiola**[19] [2139] 6-9-12 75 .... PatrickCStringer[(7)] —
(S T Lewis) *hld up in tch: lost pl appr 3rd: t.o whn p.u bef 3 out* **33/1**

4m 6.30s (3.20) **Going Correction** +0.15s/f (Yiel)
WFA 4 from 5yo+ 12lb **13** Ran SP% **119.3**
Speed ratings: **98,95,89,88,86 85,84,82,69,—** —,—,— CSF £19.72 TOTE £3.40: £1.90, £1.80, £2.30; EX 24.90.The winner was bought in for 14,000gns.
Owner Graham & Lynn Knight **Bred** Mrs M F Taylor And James F Taylor **Trained** Newmarket, Suffolk

FOCUS
A race that took little winning, but Blue Mariner is unexposed over hurdles and probably a decent sort for the grade.

NOTEBOOK
Blue Mariner ◆, who was not disgraced on either of his two previous attempts over obstacles, raced clear of Canadian Storm from the turn in and the way he won suggested that there may be *more to come at a similar level. He is a decent sort for the grade and one to keep on the right side.* *(op 7-2 tchd 4-1)*
Canadian Storm has never been a strong finisher over hurdles and he once again ran out of puff having travelled strongly into contention. He can win a race at this level, but his inability to see out his races will continue to hinder him. *(op 10-1)*
Siena Star(IRE) again failed to deliver, this drop in grade failing to help. He continues to frustrate and remains one to avoid. *(op 5-2 tchd 3-1)*
Ambersong was once again doing his best work late and he continues to shape as though a step up to two and a half miles will help. *(op 5-2 tchd 2-1)*
Bonjour Bond(IRE) ran one of his better race with the visor on for the first time over hurdles.
So Cloudy travelled up well and looked set to play a hand at one stage, but she was soon in trouble after the second last and faded disappointingly. *(op 14-1)*
Simiola *Official explanation: jockey said mare was never travelling*
Master Moneyspider *Official explanation: jockey said gelding was very reluctant to race after the third hurdle*

2561 SAVAGE & WINTERMAN NOVICES' H'CAP CHASE (12 fncs) 2m
1:40 (1:42) (Class 4) (0-95,91) 4-Y-0+ **£3,773** (£1,107; £553; £276)

Form RPR
-5P3 **1** **Jolly Boy (FR)**[14] [2257] 6-10-1 **64** .... (b) AlanO'Keeffe 87+
(Miss Venetia Williams) *a.p: led 3 out: sn clr: hit last: easily* **9/1**
60-4 **2** *11* **Moscow Gold (IRE)**[43] [1776] 8-9-11 **63** oh3 .... OwynNelmes[(3)] 72
(A E Price) *hld up in mid-div: stdy hdwy 8th: wnt 2nd jst bef last: no ch w wnr* **66/1**
114P **3** *4* **Terrible Tenant**[26] [2011] 6-11-5 **89** .... WayneKavanagh[(7)] 94
(J W Mullins) *hld up: hdwy 8th: one pce fr 3 out* **17/2**
221U **4** *shd* **Un Autre Espere**[14] [2257] 6-10-9 **79** .... TomMessenger[(7)] 85+
(C C Bealby) *chsd ldr: led 4 out to 3 out: 2nd and btn whn hit 2 out* **7/1**[3]
0205 **5** *1 ½* **Pollensa Bay**[23] [2074] 6-10-8 **71** .... (b) TomSiddall 76+
(S A Brookshaw) *hld up in tch: hit 8th: btn whn hit 2 out* **12/1**
6-U6 **6** *8* **Tianyi (IRE)**[19] [2140] 9-10-6 **76** .... (v) JohnKington[(7)] 71
(M Scudamore) *nvr nr ldrs* **33/1**
4655 **7** *2 ½* **Spider Boy**[55] [1645] 8-10-0 **70** .... (p) RobertLucey-Butler[(7)] 63
(Miss Z C Davison) *a bhd* **22/1**
0003 **8** *19* **Reflex Blue**[6] [2429] 8-11-3 **80** .... (v) RichardJohnson 54
(R J Price) *hld up towards rr: hdwy 7th: mstke 3 out: sn wknd* **7/1**[3]
0-00 **P** **Astral Dancer (IRE)**[32] [1903] 5-11-6 **83** .... PaulMoloney —
(J Mackie) *bhd fr 7th: p.u bef 3 out* **28/1**
04-F **P** **Caballe (USA)**[12] [2297] 8-11-6 **83** .... TomScudamore —
(M Scudamore) *bhd: blnd 4th: p.u bef 5th* **16/1**
00F2 **U** **Wages**[23] [2074] 5-11-11 **88** .... ChristianWilliams —
(Evan Williams) *in rr tl hmpd and uns rdr 4th* **4/1**[1]
-0U6 **P** **Kinkeel (IRE)**[29] [1956] 6-11-7 **84** .... NoelFehily —
(A W Carroll) *bhd: short-lived effrt 7th: p.u bef 3 out* **14/1**
-P04 **P** **Blaise Wood (USA)**[15] [2246] 4-10-9 **91** .... (t) ThomasBurrows[(7)] —
(A L Forbes) *a bhd: rdn 5th: t.o whn p.u bef 3 out* **14/1**
0F-0 **P** **Salim**[54] [1653] 8-10-0 **63** oh1 .... JamesDavies —
(Miss J S Davis) *hld up in tch: mstke 7th: sn wknd: p.u bef 4 out* **66/1**
5P-U **P** **Baton Charge (IRE)**[34] [1877] 7-11-2 **79** .... JasonMaguire —
(T R George) *led: clr 3rd: hdd and mstke 4 out: wknd qckly: p.u bef 3 out* **6/1**[2]

4m 0.10s (-2.40) **Going Correction** 0.0s/f (Good)
WFA 4 from 5yo+ 12lb **15** Ran SP% **120.4**
Speed ratings: **106,100,98,98,97 93,92,82,—,—** —,—,—,—,— CSF £504.15 CT £5135.55 TOTE £7.10: £1.90, £24.30, £3.50; EX 429.20.
Owner Favourites Racing **Bred** Georges Lacombe **Trained** Kings Caple, H'fords

FOCUS
Jolly Boy put in an improved round of jumping and beat a bad field with any amount in hand. The form is poor but solid enough for the grade.

NOTEBOOK
Jolly Boy(FR), an unreliable sort who has had problems with his jumping in the past, spoiled his chance by racing too keenly in the first-time blinkers on his reappearance at Fakenham, but he settled much better here and an improved round of jumping enabled him to win easily. Racing off a lowly mark of 64, he sprinted away once given the go ahead but, although he looks an obvious candidate to follow up, he would never be one to take too short a price about. *(op 8-1 tchd 7-1)*
Moscow Gold(IRE) had done little in three starts over fences since falling on his chase debut and it was debatable whether this drop back in trip was going to suit, but he kept on well off his feather to claim second and there is surely a selling chase in him off a mark in the 60s.
Terrible Tenant just got up to deny the tired Un Autre Espere for third and was able to leave behind him a recent disappointment at Towcester. *(op 9-1 tchd 8-1)*
Un Autre Espere, who unseated when trying to run out at Fakenham last time, showed no such wayward tendencies here, but he had done his running as they began the turn into the straight and was just run out of the places. *(tchd 15-2)*
Pollensa Bay has yet to win in 26 starts and, although not beaten that far here, remains below a winning level. *(tchd 16-1)*
Salim *Official explanation: jockey said gelding had a breathing problem (op 20-1 tchd 22-1)*
Caballe(USA) *Official explanation: jockey said mare made a mistake and he lost his irons (op 20-1 tchd 22-1)*
Wages never had a chance to build on his recent course second, unseating his rider early having been hampered. He will remain of interest next time. *(op 20-1 tchd 22-1)*

2562 FAMOUS GROUSE H'CAP CHASE (14 fncs) 2m 3f
2:10 (2:10) (Class 4) (0-110,109) 5-Y-O+ **£4,482** (£1,315; £658; £328)

Form RPR
4542 **1** **Runner Bean**[12] 2300 11-11-2 **99** .... RobertThornton 112+
(R Lee) *hld up in tch: led on bit 3 out: rdn appr last: clr flat: eased towards fin* **13/2**[2]
5/6 **2** *5* **It Was'Nt Me (IRE)**[19] 2141 8-11-2 **99** .... MarkBradburne 104+
(M Sheppard) *hld up in tch: ev ch 2 out: sn rdn: one pce* **50/1**
3445 **3** *15* **Paddy The Optimist (IRE)**[12] 2282 9-9-13 **89** .... LiamHeard(7) 77
(D Burchell) *hld up: lost pl 6th: hdwy 9th: no real prog fr 3 out* **7/1**[3]
3431 **4** *1 ¾* **Reverse Swing**[39] 1819 8-10-1 **84** ....(t) JodieMogford 73+
(Mrs H Dalton) *w ldr: led 4th: mstke 10th: rdn after 4 out: hdd 3 out: wknd 2 out* **9/1**
P0/5 **5** *26* **Wild Oats**[19] 2149 7-10-12 **95** .... JoeTizzard 55
(B J M Ryall) *w ldrs tl wknd after 8th* **8/1**
0/P0 **6** *2 ½* **Ingenu (FR)**[26] 2004 9-10-5 **88** .... SeanCurran 46
(P Wegmann) *keen early: in tch: lost pl 4th: bhd fr 9th* **150/1**
32PP **P** **Vandante (IRE)**[29] 1960 9-10-0 **83** oh2 .... TomDoyle —
(R Lee) *led to 4th: wknd 8th: bhd whn p.u bef 3 out* **16/1**
00-P **P** **Musimaro (FR)**[27] 1984 7-11-6 **103** ....(p) AlanO'Keeffe —
(R J Price) *bhd: mstkes 2nd and 7th: t.o whn p.u bef 4 out* **33/1**
0-PP **F** **Fantasmic**[15] 2239 9-11-5 **102** .... LeightonAspell 79
(O Sherwood) *hld up: hdwy 6th: wknd appr 3 out: fell last* **28/1**
PP60 **P** **Half An Hour**[72] 1489 8-11-6 **103** .... ChristianWilliams —
(P Bowen) *hld up in tch: wknd appr 6th: t.o whn p.u after 8th* **12/1**
46F1 **P** **Tuesday's Child**[19] 2141 6-11-1 **98** .... TimmyMurphy —
(Miss H C Knight) *hld up: hdwy 4th: wknd qckly 3 out: p.u bef 2 out* **15/8**[1]
1-P0 **P** **Barney McAll (IRE)**[10] 2347 5-11-12 **109** ....(t) RichardJohnson —
(R T Phillips) *bhd: nt fluent 3rd: short-lived effrt appr 9th: t.o whn p.u bef 3 out* **9/1**

4m 50.6s (4.00) **Going Correction** 0.0s/f (Good) **12** Ran SP% **114.3**
Speed ratings: **91,88,82,81,70 69,—,—,—,— —,—** CSF £265.44 CT £2317.96 TOTE £7.30: £2.20, £8.10, £3.00; EX 132.10.
Owner H F P Foods Limited **Bred** Helshaw Grange Farms Ltd **Trained** Byton, H'fords

FOCUS
Only half of the 12 managed to complete and it was Runner Bean, who was well suited by this step back up in trip, that came away to win comfortably, being value for eight lengths. The winning time was modest for the grade though.

NOTEBOOK
Runner Bean, 4lb lower than when winning at Wincanton back in April, struck the front going well at the second last and had little trouble disposing of outsider It Wasn't Me. This step back up in trip suited the gelding, who had not had things go his way at Wincanton the last twice, and he will be entitled to respect if turned out under a penalty. *(op 5-1 tchd 7-1)*
It Was'Nt Me(IRE), who showed little on his recent British debut, was a multiple winner over hurdles in Ireland and had been dropped 5lb for that initial effort. He was no match for the winner, but pulled a long way clear of the third and can be expected to improve again on this.
Paddy The Optimist(IRE), a regular at this course, found this too much of a speed test and was no match for the front two. A return to further will help and he will no doubt continue to pay his way. *(op 12-1)*
Reverse Swing raced prominently throughout but was unable to hold off the challengers off this 8lb higher mark. *(op 8-1)*
Wild Oats was unable to build on his mildly pleasing reappearance/chasing debut, but he may still have been in need of the outing and is not one to give up on just yet. *(op 10-1)*
Tuesday's Child, 9lb higher than when scoring at Ludlow, looked a big threat turning out of the back straight, but he stopped worryingly quickly around three out and connections put it down to *the tacky ground. He may be worth another chance back on a sound surface. Official explanation: trainer's representative said gelding was unsuited by today's good ground (op 2-1 tchd 7-4)*
Fantasmic ran well for a long way before falling and, as long as the tumble has not affected his confidence, he can be placed to pick up a small race. *(op 2-1 tchd 7-4)*

2563 HAPPY CHRISTMAS ANN & DEREK GODFREY AMATEUR RIDERS' NOVICES' H'CAP HURDLE (8 hdls) 2m 1f
2:40 (2:43) (Class 4) (0-95,94) 3-Y-O+ **£3,039** (£934; £467)

Form RPR
60-5 **1** **North Lodge (GER)**[25] 2015 5-11-1 **88** .... MrGTumelty(5) 106+
(A King) *hld up in tch: hdwy 4th: wnt 2nd appr 2 out: rdn appr last: led flat: drvn out* **3/1**[1]
0-00 **2** *2 ½* **City Palace**[55] 1645 4-9-13 **70** .... MrTJO'Brien(3) 83
(Evan Williams) *led tl appr 3rd: led 3 out: hit last: rdn and hdd flat: no ex* **4/1**[2]
560- **3** *15* **Waziri (IRE)**[60] 3319 4-10-9 **84** .... MrLRPayter(7) 82
(M Sheppard) *hld up and bhd: hdwy appr 5th: wknd 2 out* **25/1**
0645 **4** *nk* **West Hill (IRE)**[26] 2006 4-10-4 **72** ow1 ....(t) MrTGreenall 70
(D McCain) *hld up: hdwy appr 5th: wknd 2 out* **10/1**
-000 **5** *nk* **Mac's Elan**[17] 2191 5-11-5 **94** .... MrNPearce(7) 92
(A B Coogan) *hld up and bhd: hdwy on ins after 3 out: wknd 2 out* **22/1**
/6F- **6** *3* **Red Lion (FR)**[385] 2115 8-11-4 **93** .... MrDAFitzsimmons(7) 88
(D McCain) *prom tl wknd appr 2 out* **40/1**
P000 **7** *2* **My Retreat (USA)**[167] 760 8-10-2 **77** .... RyanCummings(7) 70
(R Fielder) *hld up and bhd: short-lived effrt 5th: btn whn hit 2 out* **28/1**
-0F2 **8** *shd* **Earl Of Spectrum (GER)**[12] 2283 4-11-7 **94** .... MrSWaley-Cohen(5) 87
(J L Spearing) *plld hrd: sn prom: led appr 3rd to 3 out: wknd 2 out* **9/1**
0-50 **9** *15* **Coralbrook**[31] 1921 5-11-3 **92** .... MrSPJones(7) 70
(Mrs P Robeson) *prom: rdn after 4th: wknd 5th* **8/1**[3]
004P **10** *dist* **Keepasharplookout (IRE)**[23] 2069 3-9-9 **85** .... MrTCollier(7) —
(C W Moore) *swvd bdly lft and lost many l s: a t.o* **33/1**

4m 5.60s (2.50) **Going Correction** +0.15s/f (Yiel)
WFA 3 from 4yo+ 16lb **10** Ran SP% **92.2**
Speed ratings: **100,98,91,91,91 90,89,89,82,—** CSF £8.72 CT £99.17 TOTE £3.00: £1.30, £1.20, £12.20; EX 11.70.
Owner Prd Holdings Limited **Bred** Gestut Wittekindshof **Trained** Barbury Castle, Wilts

FOCUS
The withdrawal at the start of Don't Ask Me made life a lot easier for the others and North Lodge was able to get off the mark at the fifth attempt. The form has been rated around the third and fourth.

NOTEBOOK
North Lodge(GER), a formerly smart German Flat racer, contested some decent novice hurdles last year and finished lame when disappointing on his reappearance at Fontwell, so he came into this still fairly unexposed. He looked set to have to settle for second as they turned for home, but he saw the race out strongly and ultimately won with a bit to spare.\n\x\x Although not over big, he *may have some improvement in him at further. Official explanation: trainer said, regarding the improved form shown, gelding was a progressive sort (tchd 9-4 in a place)*
City Palace, who shaped reasonably well on his handicap debut at Towcester, was strongly supported here to step up again and he duly did. He looked to have them all beaten off leaving the back straight but North Lodge had narrowed the gap by the time they straightened for home and stayed on far too strongly for him. He is sure to go up a bit in the weights for this, but should not have too much trouble winning at a similarly moderate level. *(op 13-2 tchd 7-2)*
Waziri(IRE) made little impression in three hurdle races for Hughie Morrison last season and he again looked set to struggle after a series of early blunders, but his jumping warmed up as the contest went on and, although eventually well beaten by the front two, he battled on nicely to keep third. He is another who can find a race off this sort of mark. *(op 20-1 tchd 28-1)*
West Hill(IRE) appreciated the return to handicap company having finished behind a useful sort in L'Antartique at Haydock last time, and he may be capable of winning once granted a step up in distance. *(op 12-1)*
Mac's Elan ran his best race for a while and was doing some good work late on. He still needs to show more before being worth a bet, however. *(op 20-1)*

2564 BELL INN AT TILLINGTON REGULARS BEGINNERS' CHASE (19 fncs) 3m 1f 110y
3:10 (3:10) (Class 4) 5-Y-O+ **£4,560** (£1,338; £669; £334)

Form RPR
3-34 **1** **Zabenz (NZ)**[11] 2311 8-11-0 ....(b) RichardJohnson 143+
(P J Hobbs) *mde all: clr fr 12th: unchal* **4/1**
0FP- **2** *29* **Lord Olympia (IRE)**[262] 4330 6-11-0 .... SamThomas 113+
(Miss Venetia Williams) *chsd wnr: mstke 10th: no imp whn hit 15th* **12/1**
5-0F **3** *2* **Victory Gunner (IRE)**[11] 2311 7-10-9 .... LeeStephens(5) 102
(C Roberts) *hit 1st and 2nd: wl bhd 7th: styd on fr 2 out* **20/1**
000- **4** *¾* **Team Tassel (IRE)**[257] 4412 7-11-0 .... TimmyMurphy 101
(M C Pipe) *hld up: hdwy 11th: wkng whn mstke 15th* **11/4**[2]
-115 **5** *2 ½* **Jackson (FR)**[17] 2175 8-11-0 .... RobertThornton 99
(A King) *hld up in tch: mstke 2nd: wknd 12th: 4th and no ch whn mstke 4 out* **7/2**[3]
1-2F **6** *6* **Blue Business**[18] 2165 7-11-0 138 ....(b) ChristianWilliams 100+
(P F Nicholls) *prom: nt fluent 3rd: rdn after 10th: wknd 12th* **2/1**[1]
-F60 **7** *3* **Witness Time (IRE)**[160] 814 9-10-9 .... MarkNicolls(5) 90
(B J Eckley) *wl bhd fr 8th* **66/1**
PP **8** *29* **Rosses Point (IRE)**[31] 1917 6-11-0 .... PaulMoloney 61
(Evan Williams) *lost tch 7th: t.o* **100/1**

6m 31.8s (-2.40) **Going Correction** 0.0s/f (Good) **8** Ran SP% **117.2**
Speed ratings: **103,94,93,93,92 90,89,80** CSF £45.80 TOTE £5.20: £1.60, £3.40, £3.20; EX 42.50.
Owner Michael H Watt **Bred** Glenmorgan Farm Ltd **Trained** Withycombe, Somerset

FOCUS
An excellent turnout with a field that would not look out of place at one of the top tracks, but the end result was disappointing and the race ultimately took little winning with both Blue Business and Team Tassel disappointing, Jackson failing to jump fluently and Zabenz's only danger from a long way out, Lord Olympia, getting tired on this reappearance.

NOTEBOOK
Zabenz(NZ) went a decent gallop from the off and galloped them into submission, jumping well from the outset. Allowed to contest races such as this despite having already won a Grade One chase in America, he had looked a non-stayer when fading late on at Exeter last time, so had quite a bit to prove over the extra quarter mile, but the gallop was relentless and, as the old cliché goes, he could have gone round again. Similar tactics in future should see him defy a penalty and he may yet be capable of a bit better. *(op 5-1)*
Lord Olympia(IRE) developed into a useful hurdler last season but ended the term on a low note, failing to complete in each of his final two starts. Always viewed as a chaser by his trainer, he was expected to come on for this first outing of the season and, having showed up well for a long way, the winner's tireless gallop proved too much for him. He jumped well in the main and, if kept to a sensible level, should win his share this season. *(tchd 11-1)*
Victory Gunner(IRE) is a dour stayer who hardly had the ideal introduction to fences when falling at Exeter behind Zabenz last time, but this war of attrition was right up his alley and he stayed on from some way back to claim third. He may find a small novice race when the ground is testing, but the best of him will not be seen until tackling staying handicaps. *(op 33-1)*
Team Tassel(IRE) had won first time out for each of the two previous seasons he had raced and the support for him in the market beforehand was obviously a positive sign. However, he was on and off the bridle from past halfway and could only plod on for a disappointing fourth. The tacky ground may have played a part and he may be worth another chance, but he does now have quite a bit to prove. *(op 4-1)*
Jackson(FR), a multiple point winner last year, made up into a useful staying novice hurdler last season, but this rules debut over fences did not go to plan and he was struggling to jump fluently from an early stage. He undoubtedly has the ability to make a decent chaser, but will need to step up markedly on this. *(op 11-4 tchd 4-1)*
Blue Business, who was still in with every chance of maintaining his 100 per cent record in blinkers when falling at the second-last behind Church Island at Cheltenham last time, looked far from enthusiastic from a very early stage and appeared to completely lose interest. He is evidently one to tread carefully with and cannot be backed with any real confidence, with the only glimmer of *hope being that his four consecutive wins last season came after Christmas. Official explanation: jockey said gelding was never travelling (tchd 5-2)*

2565 EASIBED STANDARD OPEN NATIONAL HUNT FLAT RACE 2m 1f
3:40 (3:41) (Class 6) 4-6-Y-O **£2,048** (£597; £298)

Form RPR
1 **Wind Instrument (IRE)** 4-11-4 .... NoelFehily 110+
(T R George) *hld up: hdwy 9f out: chal over 2f out: rdn to ld ins fnl f: drvn out* **7/1**
2 *hd* **Hot 'N' Holy** 6-11-4 .... ChristianWilliams 110+
(P F Nicholls) *hld up and bhd: hdwy on outside over 5f out: led over 2f out: rdn and hdd ins fnl f: r.o* **4/1**[2]

3 *10* **Sky Mack (IRE)** 4-11-4 .... PaulMoloney 100
(Evan Williams) *hld up and bhd: hdwy on ins over 4f out: wknd 2f out* **33/1**

4 *2* **Old Benny** 4-11-4 .... RobertThornton 98
(A King) *hld up: rdn and hdwy 6f out: wknd 2f out* **14/1**

5 *1* **Black And Tan (IRE)** 5-11-4 .... RichardJohnson 98+
(P J Hobbs) *a.p: rdn to ld briefly over 2f out: wknd wl over 1f out* **11/4**[1]

6 *7* **Hue And Cry** 4-11-4 .... MickFitzgerald 91+
(N J Henderson) *hld up in tch: rdn 5f out: sn wknd* **9/2**[3]

7 *8* **Hold That Thought (IRE)** 5-11-4 .... TimmyMurphy 85+
(Miss H C Knight) *prom: led over 9f out tl over 2f out: sn wknd* **9/1**

0-2 8 *4* **Cardinal Sinn (UAE)**[23] 2075 4-11-4 .... CarlLlewellyn 78
(M Pitman) *prom tl wknd 4f out* **7/1**

4 9 *5* **Overamorous**[26] 2007 4-10-11 .... JasonMaguire 66
(J L Needham) *racd wd: prom tl wknd 5f out* **16/1**

10 *6* **Swete Deva** 5-10-13 .... RobertStephens(5) 67
(C Roberts) *led: hdd over 9f out: wknd over 4f out* **66/1**

11 *nk* **Kadanza** 4-11-4 .... APMcCoy 67
(P Bowen) *hld up in tch: rdn over 6f out: sn wknd* **25/1**

12 *dist* **Quiteb'Chance (IRE)** 4-10-11 .... JamesDavies —
(Miss J S Davis) *a bhd: lost tch 8f out: t.o* **100/1**

4m 2.50s (1.40) **Going Correction** +0.15s/f (Yiel) **12** Ran SP% **121.7**
Speed ratings: **102,101,97,96,95 92,88,86,84,81 81,**— CSF £35.45 TOTE £6.70: £2.30, £1.80, £16.10; EX 58.40 Place 6 £269.51, Place 5 £206.53.
Owner Ryder Racing Ltd **Bred** John P Kiely **Trained** Slad, Gloucs

FOCUS
A well-above average bumper for the course that is sure to produce its share of winners.

NOTEBOOK
Wind Instrument(IRE) had reportedly been pleasing connections at home and was bred for the job with his dam having won a bumper. Held up in rear early, he was locked in battle with Hot 'N' Holy leaving the back straight and just got the better of him in a bobbing finish. Clearly a potentially useful sort, it is likely that his trainer will have left a bit to work on and he may be up to defying a penalty. *(op 10-1)*

Hot 'N' Holy, a brother to high-class hurdler Marello making his debut rather late in life, was an expensive purchase as a four-year-old (150,000gns) and was entitled to plenty of respect with his stable in such good form. He may well have won had his rider been more organised in the finish, *but he should not be long in gaining compensation and will improve for a switch to obstacles. (op 11-2 tchd 7-2)*

Sky Mack(IRE) is bred to appreciate a much stiffer test, so connections will no doubt have been delighted with his third placing. He was unable to keep tabs on the leading pair as they quickened *away, but kept on well for third and may be capable of winning in this sphere at a stiffer track. (op 40-1)*

Old Benny ◆ looks a nice staying prospect and he put in some good late work. His stable are in decent form at present and he is another for whom a stiffer track will help. *(op 16-1)*

Black And Tan(IRE) comes from a stable with an admirable record in bumpers here over the years and was understandably made favourite, what with the yard housing several decent bumper horses this season. Always well positioned, he narrowly edged ahead around two out, but was soon brushed aside and in the end was rather disappointing. \n\x\x He may do better now he has this run under his belt and is likely to appreciate a stiffer test over hurdles. *(op 7-2)*

Hue And Cry, a well-bred gelding with both speed and stamina influences, was a drifter beforehand in the market and he never really got into it. This was a hot race for the grade and he will find easier opportunities. *(op 5-2 tchd 5-1)*

Hold That Thought(IRE) ◆, a tall, attractive gelding, was given a positive ride by Murphy and travelled strongly for a long way before getting tired. Not knocked about once his chance had gone, *he is definitely one for the future, but he showed enough to suggest he can win a bumper. (op 11-1 tchd 12-1)*

Cardinal Sinn(UAE), the only runner with previous experience, was unable to build on his recent course second and found the competition too hot. *(op 9-1 tchd 12-1)*

T/Plt: £185.20 to a £1 stake. Pool: £44,874.00. 176.80 winning tickets. T/Qpdt: £51.80 to a £1 stake. Pool: £4,072.80. 58.10 winning tickets. KH

CATTERICK (L-H)

Wednesday, November 30

OFFICIAL GOING: Good (good to firm in places)

Wind: Almost nil

2566 RICHMONDSHIRE CONDITIONAL JOCKEYS' H'CAP HURDLE (10 hdls) 2m 3f

12:30 (12:31) (Class 4) (0-110,109)
4-Y-0+ **£3,623** (£1,063; £531; £265)

Form RPR

2B-6 **1** **Welcome To Unos**[18] 2190 8-11-2 **107** .... PhilKinsella(8) 111
(K G Reveley) *midfield: hdwy 3 out: led after last: drvn out* **12/1**

-211 **2** *3* **Rare Coincidence**[6] 2462 4-11-8 **105** 7ex .... (p) KeithMercer 106
(R F Fisher) *led 2nd to 4 out: led bef 2 out to after last: one pce* **8/1**[2]

0124 **3** *7* **Teme Valley**[22] 2110 11-11-2 **109** .... (p) JohnFlavin(10) 103
(R C Guest) *hld up: hdwy 3 out: rdn bef next: kpt on: nt rch first two* **16/1**

4465 **4** *3* **Siegfrieds Night (IRE)**[13] 2289 4-10-3 **93** .... (t) ThomasBurrows(7) 84
(M C Chapman) *rn in snatches: midfield: kpt on fr 2 out: no imp* **16/1**

3146 **5** *1 ¼* **Red Man (IRE)**[6] 2453 8-11-0 **105** .... StevenGagan(8) 95
(Mrs E Slack) *mstkes: cl up: led 4 out to bef 2 out: sn outpcd* **10/1**

0521 **6** *1 ¾* **Maunby Rocker**[26] 2025 5-9-13 **90** .... GaryBartley(8) 78
(P C Haslam) *hld up: stdy hdwy 1/2-way: effrt 3 out: n.d* **5/1**[1]

01-1 **7** *1 ¼* **Muckle Flugga (IRE)**[201] 334 6-10-9 **100** .... EwanWhillans(8) 87
(N G Richards) *bhd: pushed along 1/2-way: sme late hdwy: nvr on terms* **11/1**

-142 **8** *1* **River Mist (IRE)**[190] 483 6-11-4 **101** .... TJPhelan 88+
(Karen McLintock) *led to 2nd: cl up: hit 6th: wknd appr 2 out* **17/2**[3]

1440 **9** *¾* **Leopold (SLO)**[35] 1878 4-10-12 **101** .... CharliePoste(6) 86
(M F Harris) *midfield: hdwy 4 out: wknd bef 2 out* **16/1**

1130 **10** *6* **Wally Wonder (IRE)**[39] 1838 7-10-8 **99** .... JamesReveley(8) 78
(K G Reveley) *prom tl wknd fr 4 out* **10/1**

51P- **11** *¾* **Top The Bill (IRE)**[309] 3530 5-11-5 **105** .... ThomasDreaper(3) 83
(Mrs S A Watt) *sn wl bhd: nvr on terms* **28/1**

05-0 **12** *nk* **Commemoration Day (IRE)**[13] 2289 4-9-11 **85** ..(v) PatrickMcDonald(5) 63
(M E Sowersby) *towards rr: drvn 1/2-way: nvr on terms* **40/1**

-025 **13** *2* **Flake**[7] 2443 5-10-7 **100** .... MichaelO'Connell(10) 76
(Mrs S J Smith) *cl up: blnd 3rd: wknd bef 3 out* **20/1**

0PP- **14** *4* **Kingfisher Sunset**[260] 4389 9-9-8 **85** .... AndrewAdams(8) 57
(Mrs S J Smith) *sn bhd: struggling fr 1/2-way* **33/1**

4332 **15** *1 ½* **Big Wheel**[39] 1836 10-10-7 **98** .... FearghalDavis(8) 68
(N G Richards) *bhd: rdn and struggling fr 1/2-way* **12/1**

045- **16** *dist* **Show No Fear**[223] 4943 4-11-5 **102** .... DougieCostello —
(G M Moore) *hld up midfield: smooth hdwy 4 out: rdn and wknd qckly after next* **14/1**

4m 38.9s (-11.60) **Going Correction** -0.35s/f (Good) **16** Ran SP% **118.1**
Speed ratings: **110,108,105,104,104 103,102,102,102,99 99,99,98,96,95** — CSF £98.22 CT £1552.09 TOTE £17.90: £4.30, £1.90, £4.80, £2.90; EX 160.30.
Owner J W Andrews **Bred** P D And Mrs Player **Trained** Lingdale, Redcar & Cleveland
■ Philip Kinsella's first winner after turning professional.

FOCUS
A fair winning time for a race like this. The form is not strong but should be reasonably sound for the grade with the third to form, despite a few horses preferring different conditions and others requiring a drop in the handicap to be at their very best.

NOTEBOOK
Welcome To Unos, landing his first success since December 2003, enjoyed the step back up in trip to win nicely after coming from well off the pace. He clearly needs at least this distance to be at his best. *(op 14-1)*

Rare Coincidence made a bold bid for victory up the home straight and only gave way to the winner inside the final furlong. He is in fine form at the moment and is worth considering next time in similar company. *(tchd 15-2)*

Teme Valley has been in good form recently but never managed to reach a challenging position this time. A similarly moderate affair back at Sedgefield would see him have every chance, as he is not badly handicapped on his winning form. *(tchd 14-1)*

Siegfrieds Night(IRE) did not run too badly but is unproven at the trip, and failed to convince that he got home, even on the prevailing quick ground. *(op 18-1)*

Red Man(IRE) shared the lead entering the home straight but slowly weakened out of contention *from that point. He needs to come down the handicap a bit more to have a clear winning chance. (op 12-1)*

Maunby Rocker, without the cheekpieces he wore when successful last time, was most disappointing as he never got competitive at any stage. It is possible that he requires a stiffer test of stamina. *(op 6-1)*

Show No Fear *Official explanation: jockey said gelding had a breathing problem (op 12-1)*

2567 SKEEBY (S) H'CAP HURDLE (8 hdls) 2m

1:00 (1:00) (Class 5) (0-95,95) 4-Y-0+ **£2,912** (£848; £424)

Form RPR

FP14 **1** **Ball Games**[20] 2139 7-11-2 **95** .... MichaelMcAvoy(10) 95
(James Moffatt) *hld up: pushed along bef 4th: hdwy after 3 out: led appr last: drvn out run in* **8/1**[2]

/650 **2** *½* **Loner**[18] 2191 7-10-11 **80** .... GrahamLee 79
(W S Coltherd) *hld up in tch: mstke 4 out: effrt bef 2 out: chsd wnr run in: r.o* **8/1**[2]

0030 **3** *1* **Nutley Queen (IRE)**[20] 2146 6-9-8 **69** oh4 ow1 .... (t) RichardSpate(7) 68
(M Appleby) *chsd ldrs: led 2 out to appr last: kpt on same pce* **20/1**

000 **4** *¾* **Southern Bazaar (USA)**[24] 2081 4-9-11 **69** oh4 .... (p) KeithMercer(3) 66
(M E Sowersby) *hld up midfield: outpcd 4 out: rallied and in tch bef 2 out: kpt on run* **25/1**

0-0P **5** *1 ¼* **Pucks Court**[207] 214 8-9-12 **74** .... PatrickMcDonald(7) 70
(I A Brown) *hld up: struggling 4 out: gd hdwy bef last: r.o: nt rch ldrs* **50/1**

3P0- **6** *1 ½* **Armentieres**[241] 4709 4-10-9 **88** .... StevenGagan(10) 83
(Mrs E Slack) *in tch: outpcd and drvn 3 out: rallied bef next: sn no imp* **16/1**

0P01 **7** *nk* **Before The Mast (IRE)**[6] 2463 8-10-3 **79** 7ex .... CharliePoste(7) 73
(M F Harris) *mstkes: chsd ldrs tl rdn and no ex fr 2 out* **7/1**[1]

P0-P **8** *1 ½* **Karyon (IRE)**[207] 213 5-9-9 **69** oh3 .... MichaelMcAlister(5) 62
(Miss Kate Milligan) *led to 3rd: cl up: led after 3 out tl hit and hdd next: sn btn* **50/1**

-600 **9** *2* **Noble Pursuit**[32] 1927 8-10-3 **79** .... (t) PhilKinsella(7) 70
(R E Barr) *hld up: sme hdwy after 3 out: no imp fr next* **20/1**

-003 **10** *4* **Named At Dinner**[25] 2040 4-11-0 **86** .... (v) PeterBuchanan(3) 74+
(Miss Lucinda V Russell) *chsd ldrs tl wknd bef 2 out* **10/1**

06-0 **11** *6* **Needwood Spirit**[6] 2453 10-10-6 **75** .... PadgeWhelan 56
(Mrs A M Naughton) *towards rr: drvn 1/2-way: nvr on terms* **14/1**

0060 **12** *12* **New Wish (IRE)**[6] 2463 5-10-1 **73** .... PaddyAspell(3) 42
(S B Clark) *bhd: hdwy and prom after 3 out: wknd bef next* **20/1**

00-0 **13** *3 ½* **Zabadou**[16] 2245 4-10-9 **78** .... (p) KennyJohnson 43
(F Kirby) *keen: cl up tl wknd fr 3 out* **40/1**

P-00 **14** *2 ½* **Shady Man**[31] 1940 7-10-9 **85** .... GarethThomas(7) 48
(J K Hunter) *a bhd* **66/1**

PP00 **P** **Friedhelmo (GER)**[13] 2289 9-11-3 **93** .... (t) MissRachelClark(7) —
(S B Clark) *nt fluent in rr: t.o whn p.u bef last* **20/1**

0/0- **P** **Senor Eduardo**[18] 2103 8-10-6 **80** .... WilliamKennedy(5) —
(S Gollings) *chsd ldrs tl wknd bef 3 out: t.o whn p.u bef next* **9/1**[3]

P50 **P** **Dextrous**[32] 1927 8-10-7 **79** .... AnthonyCoyle(3) —
(P T Midgley) *cl up: led 3rd to after 3 out: wknd qckly and p.u bef next* **20/1**

FF62 **P** **Approaching Land (IRE)**[15] 2256 10-10-13 **85** .... MrTGreenall(3) —
(M W Easterby) *hld up: reminders 1/2-way: sn btn: t.o whn p.u bef last* **8/1**[2]

3m 56.0s (-0.30) **Going Correction** -0.35s/f (Good)
WFA 4 from 5yo+ 12lb **18** Ran SP% **113.0**
Speed ratings: **86,85,85,84,84 83,83,82,81,79 76,70,68,67,**— —,—,— CSF £55.11 CT £1225.56 TOTE £6.70: £2.30, £1.90, £5.90, £8.80; EX 58.30.There was no bid for the winner.
Owner Jennie Moffatt, Evan Munro **Bred** Cartmel Bloodstock **Trained** Cartmel, Cumbria

FOCUS
A moderate winning time, even for a seller, 5.3 seconds slower than the later novice hurdle. The form looks very poor indeed, despite the first two being pretty much to their marks.

NOTEBOOK
Ball Games, who won this race 12 months earlier, did the job nicely but there is little doubt that the contest took little winning, and he is not one to rely on to reproduce his best next time. He was dismounted shortly after the winning post.

Loner, dropped into the basement grade for the first time, stayed on in good style after the last, and can win a similar race. *(op 15-2)*

Nutley Queen(IRE) had her chance approaching the last hurdle but could not resist the challenge of the first two home after that flight. She kept on in good style and can break her maiden tag given a similarly weak race.

Southern Bazaar(USA), wearing cheekpieces for the first time, stayed on stoutly after the last and did not disgrace himself in this grade. *(op 28-1)*

Pucks Court, returning from a break, stayed on in good style but it is worth remembering that he remains a maiden at the age of eight.

Before The Mast(IRE) did not feature under his penalty.

Shady Man *Official explanation: trainer said gelding finished distressed (op 50-1)*

2568 MAURICE YOUNG MEMORIAL H'CAP CHASE (19 fncs) 3m 1f 110y
1:30 (1:30) (Class 4) (0-110,101) 5-Y-O+ **£4,166** (£1,293; £696)

Form RPR

30-6 **1** **Forest Dante (IRE)**[16] [2243] 12-11-2 **91**........................(p) KennyJohnson 102+
(F Kirby) *cl up: led 14th: hld on run in* **5/2**[1]

-053 **2** 1/2 **Ede'Iff**[14] [2273] 8-11-5 **101**................................ RobertLucey-Butler(7) 108
(W G M Turner) *chsd ldrs: lft 2nd 14th: effrt bef 2 out: 2l down whn nt fluent last: kpt on towards fin* **5/2**[1]

P-53 **3** *dist* **Gangsters R Us (IRE)**[4] [2495] 9-11-8 **97**................ AlanDempsey 84
(A Parker) *chsd ldrs: shkn up whn slipped bnd bef 3 out: sn btn and eased* **5/2**[1]

3PP5 **R** **John Rich**[14] [2266] 9-9-7 **75** oh12..................(tp) PatrickMcDonald(7) —
(M E Sowersby) *bhd whn j. bdly rt and rn out 10th* **9/1**[3]

5F56 **U** **Northern Minster**[6] [2449] 6-11-11 **100**........................ BrianHarding —
(F P Murtagh) *chsd ldr: led bef 4th: hit 12th: blnd and uns rdr 14th* **7/1**[2]

6m 36.5s (-11.90) **Going Correction** -0.35s/f (Good) **5** Ran SP% **108.2**
Speed ratings: **104,103,—,—,—** CSF £9.00 TOTE £3.60: £2.10, £2.00; EX 6.50.
Owner Fred Kirby **Bred** Thomas Foy **Trained** Streetlam, N Yorks

FOCUS
A moderate event but Forest Dante always goes well at the course and did just enough to hold on, while the second is a fair benchmark for the form.

NOTEBOOK
Forest Dante(IRE) secured his fifth course victory on ground he relishes. He did appear to slightly down tools close to the line, but had enough in reserve to hang on. *(op 9-4)*
Ede'Iff, who has been in reasonable form recently, gave Forest Dante plenty to think about after jumping the last but, on the day, was clearly second best. She is probably better suited by more ease in the ground. *(op 7-2)*
Gangsters R Us(IRE), making a fairly quick reappearance, was just starting to get left behind when slipping on the home bend. He is without a win for well over a year, but is becoming nicely handicapped again. *(op 2-1)*
John Rich, running from 12lb out of the handicap, steered himself off the course after jumping badly out to the right at the tenth. *(op 15-2 tchd 8-1)*
Northern Minster, trying three miles for the first time, was still going well when blundering badly and losing his jockey on the far side of the course. *(op 15-2 tchd 8-1)*

2569 ELLERTON JUVENILE NOVICES' HURDLE (8 hdls) 2m
2:00 (2:00) (Class 3) 3-Y-O **£7,052** (£2,070; £1,035; £517)

Form RPR

2114 **1** **Goldstar Dancer (IRE)**[67] [1551] 3-11-5 106................ DougieCostello(5) 102
(J J Quinn) *trckd ldrs: effrt 2 out: nt fluent last: kpt on wl to ld last 50yds* **6/1**[3]

321 **2** 1 **Comical Errors (USA)**[5] [2477] 3-10-13 .... PaddyMerrigan(5) 95
(P C Haslam) *cl up: led 4th: hdd briefly bef 2 out: rdn between last 2: kpt on run in: hdd last 50yds* **2/1**[1]

003 **3** 2 1/2 **Flower Haven**[15] [2258] 3-10-0 .... ChrisHonour(5) 79
(M J Gingell) *trckd ldrs: effrt bef 2 out: kpt on same pce fr last* **20/1**

6 **4** 8 **Satin Rose**[11] [2345] 3-10-5 .... GrahamLee 71
(K J Burke) *chsd ldrs: led briefly bef 2 out: rdn and wknd between last 2* **14/1**

550 **5** 5 **Golden Feather**[95] [1338] 3-10-7 .... PaulO'Neill(5) 74+
(R C Guest) *hit 1st: cl up tl rdn and wknd bef 2 out* **8/1**

443 **6** 11 **Truckle**[19] [2167] 3-10-12 .... FinbarKeniry 62
(C W Fairhurst) *led to 4th: hit 3 out: rdn and wknd bef next* **3/1**[2]

7 3 **Obara D'Avril (FR)** 3-10-2 .... PeterBuchanan(3) 52
(Miss Kate Milligan) *bhd: sme hdwy 3 out: rdn and no imp bef next* **50/1**

05 **8** 3 1/2 **No Commission (IRE)**[4] [2494] 3-10-12 .... TonyDobbin 56
(R F Fisher) *towards rr: rdn bef 3 out: btn bef next* **16/1**

040 **9** 1 1/2 **Swallow Falls (IRE)**[27] [2001] 3-10-0 .... StephenCraine(5) 47
(D McCain) *racd wd in midfield: rdn and wknd fr 3 out* **40/1**

0 **10** 15 **Rashida**[14] [2274] 3-9-12 .... RichardSpate(7) 32
(M Appleby) *hld up: rdn 4 out: nvr on terms* **25/1**

11 *dist* **Balgarth (USA)**[134] 3-10-9 .... TJPhelan(3) —
(K J Burke) *nt fluent: a bhd* **66/1**

6 **P** **Ansells Legacy (IRE)**[73] [1338] 3-10-12 .... NeilMulholland —
(A Berry) *a bhd: t.o whn p.u bef last* **33/1**

P **Harrys House**[19] 3-10-12 .... RussGarritty —
(J J Quinn) *bhd: hdwy bef 3 out: wknd and p.u bef next* **25/1**

P **P** **Hunipot**[125] [1011] 3-9-12 .... PatrickMcDonald(7) —
(M E Sowersby) *plld hrd in rr: wknd 1/2-way: p.u bef 2 out* **200/1**

0 **P** **Asteem**[95] [1339] 3-10-12 .... AlanDempsey —
(M E Sowersby) *plld hrd in midfield: wknd 1/2-way: t.o whn p.u bef 2 out* **200/1**

0 **P** **Young Thomas (IRE)**[7] [2442] 3-10-12 .... RichardMcGrath —
(James Moffatt) *midfield: struggling after 4 out: t.o whn p.u bef 2 out* **100/1**

3m 50.7s (-5.60) **Going Correction** -0.35s/f (Good) **16** Ran SP% **119.6**
Speed ratings: **100,99,98,94,91 86,84,83,82,74** —,—,—,—,— — CSF £17.19 TOTE £5.00: £1.80, £1.40, £3.00; EX 16.80.
Owner Double Eight Syndicate **Bred** D Maher **Trained** Settrington, N Yorks

FOCUS
Not an easy race to assess with the first three stepping up on previous form, but treated positively through the fourth.

NOTEBOOK
Goldstar Dancer(IRE) secured his third victory of the season despite hitting the last very hard. He is a very tough customer but will probably have to ply his trade in handicap company soon, as a third penalty will be very hard to carry against better opposition. *(op 8-1)*
Comical Errors(USA), who looks very much on the small side, harassed Goldstar Dancer all the way to the line and lost little in defeat. Another small race can be won with him. *(op 9-4 tchd 5-2)*
Flower Haven ran right up to her best and pulled nicely clear of the fourth. She deserves to win a minor race soon. *(op 25-1)*
Satin Rose had every chance turning into the straight but became outpaced as the race took shape. Her Flat form suggests she will get further than two miles over hurdles, and she is one to keep a note of when handicapped.
Golden Feather is starting to prove very disappointing as a hurdler as he was an 83-rated horse on the Flat. There did not appear to be any excuses. *(op 9-1)*
Truckle did not appear to get home after leading for a lot of the race. He will probably be better off in handicap company in due course. *(op 5-2)*

2570 ASKRIGG H'CAP CHASE (12 fncs) 2m
2:30 (2:30) (Class 4) (0-105,105) 4-Y-O+ **£4,126** (£1,211; £605; £302)

Form RPR

154 **1** **Bergerac (NZ)**[13] [2294] 7-11-7 **105**.................................... PaulO'Neill(5) 117+
(R C Guest) *hld up: hdwy 7th: chsd wnr bef 2 out: effrt after 2 out: kpt on wl to ld towards fin* **11/2**[3]

6461 **2** 3/4 **Celtic Legend (FR)**[18] [2191] 6-10-13 **92**......................... RichardMcGrath 103+
(K G Reveley) *hld up in tch: hdwy to ld after 4 out: rdn last: edgd rt: hdd towards fin* **4/1**[2]

1135 **3** 9 **Pure Brief (IRE)**[20] [2141] 8-10-10 **89**................................(p) PaulMoloney 93+
(J Mackie) *chsd ldrs: drvn 4 out: rallied 2 out: nt rch first two* **15/2**

P562 **4** 5 **Pavey Ark (IRE)**[12] [2323] 7-9-11 **79** oh6....................(p) PeterBuchanan(3) 76
(James Moffatt) *prom: hit and outpcd 7th: rallied bef 2 out: no imp* **12/1**

265P **5** 2 1/2 **Ceannairceach (IRE)**[41] [1795] 12-11-1 **101**............... ThomasDreaper(7) 96
(J M Jefferson) *towards rr: drvn 4 out: n.d* **11/1**

PP/P **6** 1 1/2 **Gohh**[26] [2026] 9-10-4 **83**..(t) AlanDempsey 77+
(M W Easterby) *hld up: hdwy 8th: rdn and wknd 3 out* **33/1**

3142 **7** 2 1/2 **Karo De Vindecy (FR)**[19] [2172] 7-10-10 **89**......................... GrahamLee 83+
(M D Hammond) *cl up: led 5th to after 4 out: wknd next* **11/4**[1]

02U5 **8** *hd* **Risky Way**[26] [2022] 9-10-13 **92**.. DavidO'Meara 82
(W S Coltherd) *towards rr: outpcd 1/2-way: nvr on terms* **9/1**

P260 **9** 2 1/2 **Kaikovra (IRE)**[8] [2420] 9-9-12 **84**..................................... CharliePoste(7) 75+
(M F Harris) *keen: w ldrs tl wknd bef 3 out* **25/1**

6 **P** **Closed Orders (IRE)**[5] [2479] 8-10-9 **88**..............................(p) TonyDobbin —
(Robert Gray) *led to 5th: sn lost pl: t.o whn p.u bef 3 out* **25/1**

3m 55.2s (-7.80) **Going Correction** -0.35s/f (Good) **10** Ran SP% **110.5**
Speed ratings: **105,104,100,97,96 95,94,94,93,—** CSF £26.37 CT £155.03 TOTE £4.30: £1.10, £2.00, £2.50; EX 30.50.
Owner Paul Beck **Bred** J D O'Flaherty & Mrs M L O'Flaherty **Trained** Brancepeth, Co Durham

FOCUS
A fair race for the grade run in a good time and the form looks pretty solid.

NOTEBOOK
Bergerac(NZ), dropping down in trip, just got up despite hanging to his left and Celtic Legend hanging to the right after the last, making his passage to the front difficult. He is value for more than the winning distance and seems well suited by a good test at two miles. *(op 10-1)*
Celtic Legend(FR) only just got caught after holding a healthy advantage up the straight. He did not do a great deal wrong, despite slightly hanging to his right after the last, and it was also noticeable that his jockey never resorted to his whip until it was to late, which might mean that the horse resents being hit. *(tchd 7-2)*
Pure Brief(IRE) was under strong pressure coming into the straight and kept on well for his jockey's urgings. He has been in fine form at a low level this season, and is the benchmark for the form. *(op 11-2)*
Pavey Ark(IRE), trying cheekpieces for the first time and racing from 6lb out of the handicap, has been without a victory for over a year and was firmly put in his place again. *(op 14-1)*
Ceannairceach(IRE) was just about last of the remaining runners jumping the last, and did well to finish where he did. *(op 17-2)*
Karo De Vindecy(FR) was going really nicely exiting the back straight, but soon came under *pressure and found nothing. He is still well above his highest winning mark over fences.Official explanation: trainer said gelding was feeling effects of a long season (op 9-4)*
Closed Orders(IRE) *Official explanation: jockey said gelding had a breathing problem (op 20-1)*

2571 STREETLAM "NATIONAL HUNT" NOVICES' HURDLE (10 hdls) 2m 3f
3:00 (3:01) (Class 4) 4-Y-O+ **£3,555** (£1,043; £521; £260)

Form RPR

21-3 **1** **Bougoure (IRE)**[35] [1885] 6-10-10 .... DominicElsworth 113+
(Mrs S J Smith) *cl up: led after 3 out: jnd next: styd on strly fr last* **3/1**[2]

-130 **2** 2 **Brave Rebellion**[7] [2444] 6-10-10 .... RichardMcGrath 110+
(K G Reveley) *hld up midfield: hdwy 3 out: effrt and disp ld next: kpt on same pce run in* **13/2**[3]

4163 **3** 8 **Ball O Malt (IRE)**[13] [2292] 9-10-10 117............................... AnthonyRoss 102
(R A Fahey) *hld up: hdwy to chse ldrs after 3 out: rdn and outpcd fr next* **11/10**[1]

54-0 **4** 6 **Silver Dollars (FR)**[35] [1889] 4-10-10 .... GrahamLee 96+
(J Howard Johnson) *trckd ldrs: rdn and ev ch bef 2 out: sn outpcd* **20/1**

-443 **5** 19 **Delightful Cliche**[11] [2343] 4-10-10 .... WarrenMarston 77
(Mrs P Sly) *in tch: drvn 3 out: outpcd fr next* **9/1**

65- **6** 4 **Ballyhale (IRE)**[366] [2543] 7-10-10 .... TonyDobbin 73
(P D Niven) *midfield: drvn 4 out: sn outpcd* **25/1**

7 3/4 **The Frisky Friar**[270] 7-10-3 .... MrSFMagee(7) 72
(G A Harker) *bhd: rdn 1/2-way: n.d* **66/1**

-505 **8** 3 1/2 **Now Then Auntie (IRE)**[8] [2414] 4-10-0 .... KeithMercer(3) 62
(Mrs S A Watt) *bhd: effrt u.p bef 3 out: sn btn* **66/1**

00-0 **9** *hd* **Fencote Gold**[35] [1885] 5-10-10 .... TomSiddall 69
(P Beaumont) *led to after 3 out: sn btn* **50/1**

006- **10** 6 **Cragg Prince (IRE)**[265] [4272] 6-10-3 .... NickCarter(7) 63
(Mrs S J Smith) *towards rr: drvn 4 out: sn btn* **100/1**

0 **11** 4 **Scout Leader**[14] [2268] 6-10-10 .... AlanDempsey 59
(C Grant) *bhd: rdn 4 out: nvr on terms* **80/1**

6-0 **P** **Ontario Sunset**[61] [1591] 4-10-5 .... DougieCostello(5) —
(G M Moore) *a bhd: t.o whn p.u bef 2 out* **100/1**

PP **P** **Max 'n Limbo (IRE)**[13] [2295] 5-10-7 .... MrTGreenall(3) —
(M W Easterby) *cl up tl wknd after 4 out: p.u bef 2 out* **200/1**

00P- **P** **Viking Song**[310] [3517] 5-10-10 .... KennyJohnson —
(F Kirby) *in tch to 5th: sn btn: t.o whn p.u bef 2 out* **200/1**

3-12 **P** **Scotts Court**[192] [470] 5-10-10 .... RussGarritty —
(N Tinkler) *prom to 3 out: sn wknd: t.o whn p.u bef next* **25/1**

Going Correction 0.0s/f (Good) course record **15** Ran SP% **117.6**
CSF £20.74 TOTE £3.80: £1.50, £2.00, £1.30; EX 25.30.
Owner Trevor Hemmings **Bred** John Meagher **Trained** High Eldwick, W Yorks

FOCUS
Visibility was poor for the race, but it was a decent novice hurdle for the course, could be rated higher and should produce winners.

NOTEBOOK
Bougoure(IRE) entered the straight going well and stayed on strongly to the line. He is progressing nicely and will probably get further. *(op 9-2)*
Brave Rebellion ran far more encouragingly than last time, when he had excuses, and should be more than capable of adding to his two wins in bumpers. *(op 6-1 tchd 15-2)*
Ball O Malt(IRE), dropping down in trip after a good run in handicap company, never got on terms *with the front two after being ridden with restraint. He is worth another chance.* *(op 5-4 tchd Evens tchd 11-8 in places)*
Silver Dollars(FR) is getting better with experience and almost certainly bumped into three above-average hurdlers. He showed just enough to warrant interest next time, but his optimum trip is still unclear. *(op 14-1)*
Delightful Cliche was not beaten that far last time behind a fair type, but was well and truly left behind as the principals went for home. He will be of interest in handicap company and should get further. *(tchd 10-1)*
Scotts Court has some respectable bumper form but showed very little on his hurdling debut. No *reason was given for his poor showing, and he is worth another chance given his previous form. (op 28-1)*

2572 GO RACING AT WETHERBY THIS SATURDAY INTERMEDIATE OPEN NATIONAL HUNT FLAT RACE 2m

3:30 (3:31) (Class 6) 4-6-Y-O £1,911 (£557; £278)

Form RPR

3-1 **1** **According To Pete**[35] [1889] 4-11-6 .... PaddyMerrigan(5) 115+
(J M Jefferson) *midfield: hdwy over 3f out: wnt far side and led over 1f out: clr ins fnl f: easily* **13/2**

3 **2** *4* **Character Building (IRE)**[22] [2112] 5-11-4 .... RussGarritty 100
(J J Quinn) *cl up: led over 6f out to over 2f out: kpt on fnl f: no ch w wnr* **3/1**[1]

23-4 **3** *shd* **Tous Chez (IRE)**[22] [2112] 6-11-4 .... DominicElsworth 100
(Mrs S J Smith) *chsd ldrs: effrt and led over 2f out to over 1f out: one pce fnl f* **9/2**[3]

0-3 **4** *3* **Chateau Rouge (IRE)**[18] [2192] 4-11-4 .... GrahamLee 97
(M D Hammond) *hld up: hdwy over 3f out: kpt on fnl 2f: no imp* **22/1**

42 **5** *1 1/4* **Sobers (IRE)**[18] [2185] 4-10-13 .... PaulO'Neill(5) 96
(R C Guest) *chsd ldrs: drvn over 3f out: one pce fr 2f out* **4/1**[2]

20 **6** *2* **Rothbury**[17] [2211] 5-11-1 .... MichalKohl(3) 94
(J I A Charlton) *cl up tl rdn and outpcd fr 2f out* **15/2**

7 *11* **Stolen Moments (FR)** 4-11-4 .... TonyDobbin 83
(P D Niven) *towards rr: outpcd over 6f out: sme late hdwy: nvr on terms* **25/1**

4 **8** *1 3/4* **Stagecoach Opal**[35] [1889] 4-10-11 .... NickCarter(7) 81
(Mrs S J Smith) *chsd ldrs tl wknd over 3f out* **33/1**

9 *10* **Persian Native (IRE)** 5-11-1 .... LeeVickers(3) 71
(C C Bealby) *towards rr: drvn 1/2-way: nvr on terms* **12/1**

5 **10** *10* **Larry The Tiger (IRE)**[29] [1979] 5-10-8 .... AndrewAdams(10) 61
(Mrs S J Smith) *in tch to 1/2-way: sn btn* **100/1**

11 *11* **Kissinthepeach (IRE)** 4-10-11 .... RichardMcGrath 43
(Mrs K Walton) *sn bhd: no ch fr 1/2-way* **50/1**

0 **12** *2 1/2* **Northern Quest (IRE)**[18] [2192] 4-11-4 .... DavidO'Meara 48
(H P Hogarth) *midfield: rdn over 6f out: sn outpcd* **100/1**

6 **13** *1 3/4* **Alisons Treasure (IRE)**[53] [1688] 6-11-4 .... KennyJohnson 46
(R Johnson) *racd wd: hld up: struggling fr 1/2-way* **100/1**

14 *3 1/2* **Lady Victoria** 4-10-11 .... WilsonRenwick 35
(Karen McLintock) *sn bhd: no ch fr 1/2-way* **100/1**

0- **15** *dist* **Kiwijimbo (IRE)**[249] [4552] 5-11-4 .... BrianHarding —
(A C Whillans) *led to over 6f out: sn lost pl* **40/1**

16 *1 1/4* **Northern Matriarch** 4-10-4 .... PhilKinsella(7) —
(H P Hogarth) *a bhd* **100/1**

16 Ran SP% **116.5**

CSF £23.58 TOTE £5.80: £2.10, £2.10, £1.90; EX 24.50 Place 6 £66.37, Place 5 £18.96.

Owner P Nelson **Bred** Peter Nelson **Trained** Norton, N Yorks

FOCUS

Visibility was very poor, but all the right horses were involved in the finish, and the form looks sound for the track rated through the placed horses. Plenty of winners, some more than useful, should come out of the race.

NOTEBOOK

According To Pete ◆ looked a potentially smart sort as he quickened away from his rivals. Carrying penalties in bumpers is never easy, but he won with lots in hand and should hold his own in better company. He looks the type who could take in the Championship bumper at Aintree rather than the one at Cheltenham towards the end of the season, if connections do not send him hurdling. *(op 9-1 tchd 10-1)*

Character Building(IRE) is clearly well regarded as he has been made favourite for both of his outings. He almost certainly bumped into a decent recruit to the winter game here and will find far easier opportunities to get off the mark. *(op 7-2 tchd 11-4)*

Tous Chez(IRE) got much closer to Character Building than he had done last time, and is progressing well with racing. *(op 13-2)*

Chateau Rouge(IRE) again gave the impression that he will be better suited by further in time. *(op 25-1)*

Sobers(IRE), described by his trainer in a recent interview as "quite simply the best horse I have ever trained", again did not shape badly, but he gives the impression that further will suit him in time. *(op 3-1)*

Rothbury travelled nicely into the straight but became readily outpaced as the race took shape. *(op 13-2)*

Kissinthepeach(IRE) *Official explanation: jockey said filly ran too free early*

T/Plt: £48.70 to a £1 stake. Pool: £34,493.90. 517.05 winning tickets. T/Qpdt: £6.70 to a £1 stake. Pool: £2,669.30. 290.75 winning tickets. RY

2373 PLUMPTON (L-H)

Wednesday, November 30

OFFICIAL GOING: Good

Wind: Light, against Weather: Overcast

2573 CORTAFLEX FOR HORSES NOVICES' HURDLE (9 hdls) 2m

12:40 (12:41) (Class 3) 4-Y-0+ £5,009 (£1,470; £735; £367)

Form RPR

1256 **1** **Anticipating**[35] [1880] 5-11-5 107 .... PhilipHide 114+
(G L Moore) *racd wd: trckd ldrs: led 2 out: drew clr flat: comf* **7/1**[3]

2 *5* **Quartier Latin (USA)**[67] 4-10-12 .... APMcCoy 98
(C Von Der Recke, Germany) *trckd ldrs: hit 4th: led after 3 out: rdn and hdd next: one pce* **7/2**[2]

00-F **3** *9* **Nobel Bleu De Kerpaul (FR)**[32] [1916] 4-10-12 .... BrianCrowley 89
(P Winkworth) *t.k.h early: sn hld up in midfield: mstke 3 out: outpcd bef next: shuffled along and styd on: n.d to ldng pair* **66/1**

4 *1 3/4* **Lunar Sovereign (USA)**[494] 6-10-12 .... TimmyMurphy 87
(M C Pipe) *hld up in last trio: prog to trck ldrs 6th: rdn and outpcd bef 2 out: one pce* **10/1**

5 *1* **Fuss**[50] 4-10-5 .... RichardJohnson 79
(P J Hobbs) *pressed ldrs: outpcd bef 2 out: fdd last* **14/1**

6 *3/4* **Saraba (FR)**[115] 4-10-2 .... ColinBolger(3) 79
(Mrs L J Mongan) *mstkes in midfield: drvn and effrt after 3 out: kpt on but no ch* **50/1**

0 **7** *1/2* **Vengeance**[12] [2322] 5-10-12 .... LeightonAspell 85
(S Dow) *hld up wl in rr: stl at bk of main gp 3 out: prog next: kpt on flat: nvr nrr* **25/1**

2 **8** *1* **Haloo Baloo**[154] [866] 5-10-12 .... NoelFehily 84
(Jonjo O'Neill) *hld up in last trio: shkn up after 3 out: kpt on: n.d* **33/1**

9 *nk* **Our Glenard**[58] 6-10-12 .... MatthewBatchelor 84
(J E Long) *hld up in last trio: effrt bef 3 out: no imp ldrs bef next* **100/1**

0 **10** *2 1/2* **Spanish Tan (NZ)**[59] [1614] 5-10-5 .... MrAJBerry(7) 81
(Jonjo O'Neill) *settled in midfield: rdn after 6th: sn lost pl: n.d after 3 out* **100/1**

0 **11** *4* **Twist Bookie (IRE)**[18] [2179] 5-10-12 .... DaveCrosse 77
(J S Moore) *hld up in midfield: lost pl after 4th: wl in rr 6th: shuffled along and sme prog after 3 out: no ch* **100/1**

2 **12** *1/2* **Tech Eagle (IRE)**[20] [2148] 5-10-12 .... TomDoyle 78+
(R Curtis) *t.k.h: hld up in tch: grad wknd after 3 out* **14/1**

13 *1 1/2* **Smart (SLO)**[1501] 6-10-12 .... CarlLlewellyn 75
(M Pitman) *mde most to 2nd: steadily lost pl: wl in rr but stl gng wl 3 out: nudged along and no prog* **20/1**

3 **14** *2 1/2* **Sangiovese**[16] [2249] 6-10-12 .... JimCrowley 75+
(H Morrison) *led briefly 2nd: chsd ldr after: rdn after 6th: sn struggling: wknd and eased 3 out: lame* **11/8**[1]

P **Silver Reign**[109] 4-10-5 .... SimonElliott(7) —
(J A Geake) *in tch: mstke 5th: wknd bef next: t.o whn p.u bef 2 out* **100/1**

F **Little Gannet**[46] 4-10-5 .... JamesDavies —
(T D McCarthy) *t.k.h: led after 2nd tl sn after 3 out: 10th and wkng whn fell 2 out* **100/1**

3m 54.9s (-6.30) **Going Correction** -0.30s/f (Good)

WFA 4 from 5yo+ 12lb **16** Ran SP% **119.2**

Speed ratings: **103,100,96,95,94 94,94,93,93,92 90,89,89,87,—** — CSF £30.11 TOTE £8.90: £1.70, £2.00, £25.60; EX 42.30.

Owner D R Hunnisett **Bred** George Strawbridge **Trained** Woodingdean, E Sussex

FOCUS

An interesting novice hurdle run at a fair pace, but perhaps a little disappointing that it was won by the most exposed hurdler in the field, who was value for nearly twice the official margin.

NOTEBOOK

Anticipating, the most experienced over hurdles in this field but held since making a winning debut over the course and distance in September, was always close to the pace and, once hitting the front two out, had the race in safe keeping. Considering that he stayed 14 furlongs on the Flat, it is surprising how well suited he is by this sharp track, and the decent ground was obviously the key. Conditions like these are unlikely to persist for too much longer though, and as the penalties are mounting up connections may need to consider handicaps for him now. *(op 9-1 tchd 10-1)*

Quartier Latin(USA), a winner in Listed company on the Flat in his native Germany, was in front rounding the home turn but was done for foot by the winner over the last couple of flights. He showed enough to suggest that he can win races over timber, but he would probably prefer a stiffer track than this and will also not mind more testing ground. *(tchd 4-1 and 5-1 in a place and 9-2 in places)*

Nobel Bleu De Kerpaul(FR), who got no further than the first on his hurdling debut, was comfortably held by the front pair but was still best of the rest and did show signs of ability this time. His dam won over hurdles in France and this effort suggests he will follow suit at an ordinary level in due course.

Lunar Sovereign(USA) was a winner on the Flat as a juvenile for David Loder before going stateside and landing the 2003 Man O'War Stakes at Belmont Park, and then acted as a pacemaker for Godolphin last year. Making his hurdling debut following a 16-month break, he was close enough racing down the back straight on the final circuit but had nothing left over the last couple of flights. The yard's representatives are usually straight enough at the first time of asking, so he may not come on much for this and this may be as good as he is. *(op 11-2)*

Fuss, a banded-class stayer on the Flat making her hurdling debut, would probably not have been suited by this sharp two miles so the fact that she managed to finish where she did does not do a lot for the value of the form. *(op 25-1)*

Smart(SLO), a winner on the Flat in Slovakia, was racing for the first time in over four years. He looked to need this and may be capable of better with this experience under his belt and when he can get his toe in. *(op 16-1)*

Sangiovese, raced prominently until past halfway, but gradually lost his place racing down the far side on the final circuit to eventually come home last of the finishers. He was subsequently found to be lame. *Official explanation: vet said gelding finished lame (op 13-8 tchd 5-4 and 7-4 in places)*

2574 CORTAFLEX FOR PEOPLE BEGINNERS' CHASE (14 fncs) 2m 4f

1:10 (1:11) (Class 4) 5-Y-0+

£4,709 (£1,391; £695; £348; £173; £87)

Form RPR

1-33 **1** **Pass Me A Dime**[16] [2241] 6-11-0 112 .... JoeTizzard 123+
(C L Tizzard) *mde virtually all: pressed and mstke 2 out: shkn up and drew clr last: pushed out* **9/2**[2]

3 **2** *9* **Smart Cavalier**[211] [171] 6-11-0 ....(t) ChristianWilliams 113+
(P F Nicholls) *plld hrd: hld up in midfield: j.rt 3rd: mstke 9th: prog next: trckd wnr 4 out: rdn to chal 2 out: btn bef last* **6/1**[3]

63- **3** *7* **The Grocers Curate (IRE)**[252] [4514] 5-11-0 .... MickFitzgerald 104
(N J Henderson) *tended to jump rt: prom: trckd wnr 10th to 4 out: hrd rdn and btn after 3 out* **11/10**[1]

2-00 **4** *9* **I D Technology (IRE)**[16] [2239] 9-11-0 100 .... PhilipHide 95
(G L Moore) *settled in midfield: mstke 8th: rdn and lost tch w ldrs bef 4 out* **50/1**

3-30 **5** *nk* **The Holy Bee (IRE)**[28] [1988] 6-11-0 99 .... SamThomas 98+
(Miss H C Knight) *prom: wnt 2nd briefly bef 10th: rdn and wknd 4 out: mstke 2 out* **25/1**

P **6** *dist* **The Hardy Boy**[44] [1775] 5-11-0 .... MatthewBatchelor —
(Miss A M Newton-Smith) *chsd wnr bef 4th tl bef 10th: sn wknd: btn 64 l* **66/1**

22U- **7** *14* **General Grey (IRE)**[231] [4825] 5-11-0 104 .... TimmyMurphy —
(Miss H C Knight) *hld up in rr: sltly hmpd 4th: wknd 10th: sn t.o: stl nring last as wnr fin* **14/1**

640- **F** **Horcott Bay**[232] [4814] 5-10-7 95 .... JamieMoore —
(M G Rimell) *w wnr to 3rd: pushed along in 3rd whn fell next* **25/1**

2/4 **P** **Loup Bleu (USA)**[40] [1818] 7-11-0 .... JodieMogford —
(Mrs A V Roberts) *hld up in rr: mstke 8th: wknd rapidly next: p.u bef 10th* **50/1**

14- **F** **Prato (GER)**[29] 5-11-0 .... RichardJohnson —
(C Von Der Recke, Germany) *hld up: blnd 5th: 7th and losing tch whn fell heavily 10th* **8/1**

4 **P** **Harrihawkan**[43] [1781] 7-11-0 .... RobertThornton —
(Mrs T J Hill) *settled in midfield: mstke 7th and reminder: wknd rapidly 9th: p.u bef next* **20/1**

5m 1.55s (-16.90) **Going Correction** -0.625s/f (Firm) **11** Ran SP% **115.7**

Speed ratings: **108,104,101,98,97** —,—,—,—,— — CSF £28.54 TOTE £5.50: £1.60, £2.00, £1.10; EX 21.90.

Owner Cherry Bolberry Partnership **Bred** C Raymond **Trained** Milborne Port, Dorset

FOCUS

Probably a fair little race of its type that could rate higher. It was run at a decent pace and the winning time was over a second quicker than the later Class D handicap chase over the same trip.

NOTEBOOK

Pass Me A Dime ◆ confirmed the promise of his Folkestone chasing debut with a fine front-running display and impressed with the way he went clear again after looking to face a serious challenge two from home. He still has relatively few miles on the clock and can add to this. *(op 5-1)*

Smart Cavalier, a three-time winning pointer and third in his only try over regulation fences in a hunter chase back in May, was keen enough yet still ran a fine race until lack of a recent run took its toll from the second last. This sounder surface seemed to suit him much better and, provided he can learn to settle, he should find a race when those conditions prevail. *(op 9-2)*
The Grocers Curate(IRE), making his chasing debut and racing for the first time since March, was inclined to jump right and also ballooned a couple, which in one instance caused his rider to lose an iron. He still ran well for a long way, though, and a stiffer track and easier ground should bring out the best in him. *(op 6-5 tchd 5-4)*
I D Technology(IRE) did not seem suited by this longer trip, but he has still to really convince in three starts over fences since returning from his long layoff. *(op 66-1)*
Loup Bleu(USA) *Official explanation: vet said gelding returned with a sore leg (tchd 7-1)*
Harrihawkan *Official explanation: jockey said gelding was unsuited by the good ground (tchd 7-1)*
Prato(GER), a winner over hurdles in this country back in the spring and making his chasing debut, would probably have preferred softer ground. He was already on the retreat when taking a spectacular fall at the first downhill fence on the final circuit. *(tchd 7-1)*

2575 CORTAFLEX FOR CATS AND DOGS AMATEUR RIDERS' H'CAP CHASE (FOR "GALLEANO" CHALLENGE TROPHY) (18 fncs) 3m 2f

1:40 (1:42) (Class 4) (0-100,94) 5-Y-0+
£3,115 (£973; £486; £182; £182; £61)

Form				RPR
-P25	**1**		**Ebony Jack (IRE)**[8] 2424 8-9-11 **68** oh1....................(p) MissCTizzard[(3)] *(C L Tizzard) mde virtually all: jnd 14th: rdn and in command again 2 out: kpt on wl* **4/1**[2]	81+
2-PP	**2**	*10*	**Monks Error (IRE)**[17] 2215 12-11-2 **91**.............................. MrRQuinn[(7)] *(B J Llewellyn) settled in midfield: trckd ldng pair 12th: rdn 14th: chal and blnd 4 out: tired but tk 2nd last: no imp wnr* **20/1**	96+
411-	**3**	*2*	**Just Anvil (IRE)**[306] 3575 7-10-12 **83**............................. JustinMorgan[(3)] *(L Wells) cl up: trckd wnr 11th: chal fr 14th: btn 2 out: tired and lost 2nd last* **7/1**	85+
-3P6	**4**	*1 ¼*	**Lucky Sinna (IRE)**[14] 2273 9-11-3 **92**............................... MrSPJones[(7)] *(B G Powell) nt fluent: hld up in rr: effrt 13th: chsd clr ldng trio after 3 out: plugged on* **8/1**	92
2P13	**4**	*dht*	**Five Alley (IRE)**[21] 2126 8-11-4 **89**................................ MrJSnowden[(3)] *(R H Buckler) settled in midfield: rn in snatches fr 7th: u.p 14th: no imp tl kpt on fr 2 out* **11/4**[1]	89
3P-5	**6**	*24*	**Dun Locha Castle (IRE)**[27] 2009 10-10-13 **84**............... MrTJO'Brien[(3)] *(N R Mitchell) mstke 2nd: prog fr rr to chse ldng trio 14th: sn no imp: wknd 3 out* **9/2**[3]	60
5-64	**7**	*1*	**Kappelhoff (IRE)**[38] 1855 8-10-3 **71**....................................(v) MrSWalker *(Mrs L Richards) a in rr: pushed along 7th: mstke 11th: no imp on ldrs 4 out: wkng whn blnd 2 out* **9/1**	46
P-P4	**P**		**Ballybrophy (IRE)**[13] 2282 10-9-12 **71**.........................(p) MissLHorner[(5)] *(G Brown) w wnr: blnd 8th: wknd rapidly 11th: t.o 14th: p.u bef 3 out* **14/1**	—
-P3P	**P**		**St Kilda**[8] 2424 8-9-9 **68** oh3...(p) MissLucyBridges[(5)] *(Miss Lucy Bridges) chsd ldng pair to 9th: sn lost pl: last at 11th: poor 8th whn p.u bef 4 out* **14/1**	—

6m 46.4s (-7.60) **Going Correction** -0.625s/f (Firm) **9** Ran SP% **116.6**
Speed ratings: **86,82,82,81,81 74,74,—,—** CSF £71.84 CT £546.84 TOTE £3.70: £1.70, £7.80, £2.40; EX 122.90.
Owner K S B Bloodstock **Bred** Mrs Joerg Vasicek **Trained** Milborne Port, Dorset

FOCUS
A low-grade handicap chase and a moderate winning time, even for a race like this, with the third setting the standard.

NOTEBOOK
Ebony Jack(IRE), tried in cheekpieces rather than the tongue tie, was given his normal positive ride. Despite being given no peace by Ballybrophy, the pair establishing a clear lead over the rest, even after that rival had fallen away he still managed to retain enough energy to keep all his rivals at bay and run out a clear winner. The decent ground was almost certainly the crucial factor. *(tchd 7-2)*
Monks Error(IRE), pulled up in both outings since returning from a 17-month break, was close enough starting the final circuit but a mistake at the middle fence down the far side did him few favours and from that point the runner-up spot was the best he could hope for. At least he managed to complete this time and should be fully fit now, but he is not getting any younger.
Just Anvil(IRE), has gone well fresh in the past, but after holding every chance on the final circuit the way he faded did suggest this first run in ten months was needed. *(op 15-2)*
Lucky Sinna(IRE), who is gradually falling down the handicap, lacked the pace to get on terms with the leaders and has still to convince over this sort of trip. Despite numerous placings, he is still looking for his first win of any description. *(op 3-1 tchd 10-3 and 7-2 in places)*
Five Alley(IRE), a course-and-distance winner last month, was never travelling with any great enthusiasm at any point and only finished where he did because others had almost come to a standstill. He cannot be trusted. *(op 3-1 tchd 10-3 and 7-2 in places)*
Dun Locha Castle(IRE), winner of this race last year off a 12lb lower mark, seemed to travel well enough off the pace but found disappointingly little once off the bridle. *(op 4-1)*
Kappelhoff(IRE) *Official explanation: trainer said gelding returned with swelling under the girth (tchd 10-1)*
Ballybrophy(IRE) eventually paid for trying to match strides with the eventual winner and looks to have lost his way. *(op 18-1)*

2576 EQUINE AMERICA CLAIMING HURDLE (12 hdls) 2m 5f

2:10 (2:10) (Class 4) 4-Y-0+ **£2,487** (£724; £362)

Form				RPR
3-20	**1**		**Assoon**[11] 2347 6-11-8 105...(p) JamieMoore *(G L Moore) in tch: drvn fr 7th: chsd ldng pair 9th: u.str.p but clsd 2 out: led flat: all out* **3/1**[1]	103
62-0	**2**	*1 ¼*	**Bekstar**[43] 1784 10-10-7 87... JodieMogford *(J C Tuck) led 4th tl blnd 7th: pressed ldr after: drvn to ld bef 2 out: hdd 2 out: upsides last: nt qckn flat* **11/2**	87
0500	**3**	*¾*	**Better Moment (IRE)**[20] 2150 8-10-1 91.........................(v) MrCHughes[(7)] *(M C Pipe) prom: led 7th: rdn and hit 3 out: hdd bef 2 out: hrd drvn to ld 2 out: hdd and nt qckn flat* **11/1**	87
0160	**4**	*13*	**Penny's Crown**[20] 2150 6-10-0 88.............................. EamonDehdashti[(7)] *(G A Ham) trckd ldrs: rdn to chse ldng pair 8th to next: struggling fr 3 out* **14/1**	76+
4P53	**5**	*20*	**Oulton Broad**[17] 2216 9-10-10 100...........................(p) LeightonAspell *(F Jordan) hld up in rr: effrt and cl up 9th: wknd 3 out* **9/2**[2]	56
0030	**6**	*4*	**It's My Party**[13] 2301 4-10-11 97....................................(p) MrTJO'Brien[(7)] *(W G M Turner) in tch tl wknd u.p bef 9th: t.o* **9/1**	60
30-0	**7**	*dist*	**Batswing**[10] 2379 10-11-4 108.. PhilipHide *(G L Moore) led to 4th: sn lost pl: bhd fr 8th: ms bhd next: j. 2 out as wnr fin* **10/1**	
00/0	**P**		**Sussex Mist**[188] 513 6-10-3 .... MatthewBatchelor *(J E Long) nt jump wl: t.o 5th: p.u bef 8th* **66/1**	—
140/	**P**		**Rebel Son**[1446] 2689 11-10-8 .... ChristianWilliams *(B J Llewellyn) trckd ldrs: wknd suddenly 7th: p.u bef next* **5/1**[3]	—
3P/P	**P**		**Carly Bay**[17] 2218 7-10-9 102.......................................(p) JayPemberton[(10)] *(G P Enright) prom tl wknd u.p 8th: poor 6th whn p.u bef 2 out* **33/1**	—

5m 16.5s (-8.30) **Going Correction** -0.30s/f (Good)
WFA 4 from 6yo+ 13lb **10** Ran SP% **113.8**
Speed ratings: **103,102,102,97,89 88,—,—,—,—** CSF £19.19 TOTE £3.90: £1.80, £1.70, £5.50; EX 34.60.
Owner Bryan Pennick **Bred** B V And C J Pennick **Trained** Woodingdean, E Sussex

FOCUS
An ordinary claiming hurdle, but notable for a fine piece of riding by Jamie Moore. It is a difficult race to be positive about.

NOTEBOOK
Assoon, taking a big drop in class, had the ground in his favour but is obviously a lazy sort as he was being given slaps down the neck with the whip by his rider walking out of the paddock. It was even worse during the race, as he was off the bridle with over a circuit left and his prospects did not look great, but his jockey never gave up and his persistence paid off as the combination stayed on for a dour victory. Even though this was a poor race this ride should get the recognition it deserves. *(tchd 7-2)*
Bekstar stepped up from her recent reappearance following an 11-month layoff under a positive ride, but could not match the winner's speed from the final flight. She is getting on a bit now, but still has the ability to win a moderate handicap off her proper mark given a sound surface. *(op 7-1 tchd 15-2 in a place)*
Better Moment(IRE), a regular in low-grade contests like this, mixed it with the eventual runner-up for a long way but, like him, failed to match the winner on the run-in. *(op 10-1)*
Penny's Crown is not firing at present and even though she has form on a sound surface, she does seem to prefer it easier.
Oulton Broad was comfortably left behind over the last half-mile and this was another mediocre effort. *(op 4-1)*

2577 EQUINE AMERICA H'CAP CHASE (13 fncs 1 omitted) 2m 4f

2:40 (2:40) (Class 3) (0-125,122) 5-Y-0+
£6,623 (£1,956; £978; £489; £244; £122)

Form				RPR
-02F	**1**		**Soeur Fontenail (FR)**[10] 2368 8-10-5 **101**.................. AndrewThornton *(N J Hawke) trckd ldr 3rd: effrt to ld 10th: hrd pressed 2 out: hdd last: rallied u.p to ld fnl stride* **14/1**	111
U3-0	**2**	*shd*	**Acertack (IRE)**[17] 2210 8-10-0 **96**.................................. TimmyMurphy *(R Rowe) in tch: chsd ldng pair 7th: chsd wnr bypassing 4 out: rdn to ld last: hdd u.str.p fnl stride* **14/1**	106
3-33	**3**	*2*	**Myson (IRE)**[12] 2325 6-10-3 **99**.. JamesDavies *(D B Feek) hld up in rr: prog 7th: chsd ldng trio next: wnt 3rd 3 out: cl enough next: one pce flat* **11/4**[1]	107
-126	**4**	*27*	**Cosmocrat**[17] 2210 7-11-5 **115**.. TomDoyle *(R Lee) blnd 1st: in tch: effrt to chse ldrs and in tch 10th: wknd 3 out* **5/1**[2]	96
6-02	**5**	*7*	**Atum Re (IRE)**[14] 2272 8-11-12 **122**.........................(b[1]) ChristianWilliams *(P F Nicholls) led after 2nd and set decent pce: hdd 10th: wknd 3 out* **6/1**[3]	96
-004	**6**	*4*	**The Newsman (IRE)**[26] 2016 13-10-9 **105**...................... LeightonAspell *(G Wareham) settled in midfield: outpcd fr 9th: wl bhd after next* **40/1**	75
3-F5	**7**	*5*	**Key Phil (FR)**[22] 2102 7-11-8 **118**.. NoelFehily *(D J Wintle) prom to 5th: losing pl whn mstke 8th: bhd fr 10th* **8/1**	83
-521	**F**		**Forever Dream**[34] 1899 7-11-4 **114**...........................(b) RichardJohnson *(P J Hobbs) in tch whn fell 5th* **14/1**	—
10-F	**U**		**Farlington**[159] 823 8-11-12 **122**.................................... WayneHutchinson *(P Bowen) in tch whn bdly hmpd and uns rdr 5th* **20/1**	—
P-06	**P**		**Hawk's Landing (IRE)**[13] 2293 8-10-11 **107**........................ APMcCoy *(Jonjo O'Neill) mstkes and nvr gng wl: lost tch 8th: t.o whn p.u bef 3 out* **7/1**	—
P-B1	**P**		**Haafel (USA)**[21] 2128 8-11-3 **113**.. PhilipHide *(G L Moore) led tl after 2nd: lost tch w ldrs 9th: last and wl bhd whn p.u bef 2 out* **12/1**	—
13-P	**P**		**Chantoue Royale (FR)**[29] 1978 6-10-13 **112**.................... ColinBolger[(3)] *(Mrs L J Mongan) prom: mstkes 4th and 5th: sn lost pl: bhd fr 8th: t.o whn p.u bef 3 out* **66/1**	—

5m 2.70s (-15.75) **Going Correction** -0.625s/f (Firm) **12** Ran SP% **117.6**
Speed ratings: **106,105,105,94,91 89,87,—,—,—,—,—** CSF £184.02 CT £703.77 TOTE £14.70: £5.00, £3.40, £1.80; EX 100.80 Trifecta £304.70 Pool: £600.86 - 1.40 winning tickets..
Owner La Connection Francaise **Bred** S Dupuy **Trained** Hewish, Somerset
■ Stewards' Enquiry : Andrew Thornton caution: used whip in an incorrect place

FOCUS
A decent-looking handicap in which the early pace was strong, but the fact that the winning time was slower than the beginners' chase suggests they paid for it late on. The runner-up sets the level for the form. The fourth last fence was bypassed.

NOTEBOOK
Soeur Fontenail(FR), none the worse for her recent fall, was always close to the pace and, after taking it up around a mile from home, battled on in game style after looking likely to get swallowed up. She clearly likes this track as three of her four wins over fences have come here. *(op 12-1)*
Acertack(IRE), another with a decent record at this track, seemed to have timed his effort to perfection but the winner would just not go away and nailed him again right on the line. He remains 7lb above his last winning mark and that seems unlikely to change much.
Myson(IRE), whose last victory came over the course and distance off a 4lb lower mark, was well backed to repeat the feat and he looked a big danger rounding the home bend, but he was inclined to hang in behind the front pair between the last two fences and there was nothing more to come. *(op 7-2 tchd 5-2)*
Cosmocrat ran as though not seeing out the trip, but he has won over it in the past and it is more likely that he is simply finding life tough off a 9lb higher mark than for his last win. *(op 6-1)*
Atum Re(IRE) probably went off too quickly in the first-time blinkers and had run himself into the ground on reaching the first fence in the back straight on the final circuit. *(op 9-2)*
Hawk's Landing(IRE), dropping a mile in trip, was never travelling or jumping well and seems to have fallen out of love with the game. *(tchd 8-1)*

2578 CLINICALLY PROVEN CORTAFLEX NOVICES' H'CAP HURDLE (12 hdls) 2m 5f

3:10 (3:11) (Class 4) (0-105,105) 3-Y-0+ **£3,396** (£997; £498; £248)

Form				RPR
5-U6	**1**		**Businessmoney Jake**[38] 1856 4-11-9 **93**........................... JamieGoldstein *(V R A Dartnall) settled in tch: trckd ldng trio 9th: effrt to ld bef 2 out: sn rdn clr* **4/1**[3]	102+
442	**2**	*6*	**Corker**[16] 2236 3-11-4 **104**.. JamesDavies *(D B Feek) hld up in rr: prog 9th: effrt to press ldrs whn n.m.r sn after 3 out: nt qckn and outpcd: kpt on again flat* **8/1**	91+
4531	**3**	*½*	**Manque Neuf**[10] 2378 6-10-13 **83** 7ex..........................(p) JohnMcNamara *(Mrs L Richards) mstkes: pressed ldr: led 7th: hrd rdn and hdd bef 2 out: one pce* **10/3**[2]	86+

2 **4** 1 1/4 **Amazing Valour (IRE)**[18] 2191 3-11-5 105 APMcCoy 87
(P Bowen) *str reminders in rr 5th: prog 7th: jnd ldr u.p 3 out: btn bef next* **9/4**[1]
1541 **5** 24 **Little Brave**[13] 2285 10-11-7 96 LeeStephens(5) 70
(C Roberts) *prom: reminders 7th: wknd 3 out* **11/1**
0-5P **6** 5 **Flying Patriarch**[18] 2173 4-11-11 95 (b) JamieMoore 64
(G L Moore) *led to 7th: wknd rapidly after next: t.o* **14/1**
4-60 **7** 5 **Too Posh To Share**[17] 2206 7-10-3 73 JodieMogford 37
(D J Wintle) *hld up in tch: effrt 9th: wknd bef 3 out: t.o* **10/1**
05P- **P** **Marron Prince (FR)**[247] 4618 5-10-7 77 JimCrowley —
(R Rowe) *racd on inner: in tch to 8th: wknd rapidly: p.u bef next* **50/1**
-PRP **P** **Mr Rhubarb (IRE)**[13] 2298 7-11-3 87 BenjaminHitchcott —
(C J Drewe) *blnd 3rd: a bhd: wknd and mstke 8th: p.u bef next* **100/1**

5m 16.05s (-8.75) **Going Correction** -0.30s/f (Good)
WFA 3 from 4yo+ 17lb **9** Ran SP% **112.0**
Speed ratings: **104,101,101,101,91 90,88,—,—** CSF £34.32 CT £115.64 TOTE £4.80: £2.00, £3.90, £1.30; EX 43.30.
Owner Business Money Limited **Bred** Mrs I Lefroy **Trained** Brayford, Devon
■ Stewards' Enquiry : James Davies two-day ban: used whip in an incorrect place and with excessive force (Dec 12-13)
John McNamara one-day ban: careless riding (Dec 12)

FOCUS
A poor race, but a fair pace and the winning time was slightly faster than the earlier claiming hurdle won by the 105-rated Assoon. The first three are rated positively with the placed horses to their marks.

NOTEBOOK
Businessmoney Jake ◆, appreciated this longer trip and pulled clear for a cosy success. The form is nothing special but he is unexposed, especially over this sort of distance, and is probably capable of better. *(op 11-2)*
Corker ◆, stepping up in trip for this first start in a handicap, was in with every chance when running out of room exiting the back straight and it was not until after the last that he found his stride again. His best form on the Flat came on fast ground and, even though he has performed with credit on soft ground over hurdles before this, similar conditions to these are probably what he wants. *Official explanation: jockey said gelding hung right (op 6-1)*
Manque Neuf, carrying a 7lb penalty for his victory over more than half a mile further here last time, tried to make his stamina count from some way out, but he handicapped himself with some sloppy jumping and that eventually told. *(op 4-1 tchd 9-2 in a place)*
Amazing Valour(IRE) was stepping up five furlongs in trip with the headgear removed but, as on his British debut at Wetherby, he did not seem to want to exert himself at all early on and it needed all the Champion's strength and persistence to get him into the race at all. He looks one to avoid. *(op 15-8 tchd 5-2 in places)*
Little Brave, raised 9lb for his Hereford victory, was on the retreat fully half a mile from home. *(tchd 10-1)*

2579 CLINICALLY PROVEN CORTAFLEX HBLB INTERMEDIATE OPEN NATIONAL HUNT FLAT RACE 2m 2f
3:40 (3:42) (Class 6) 4-6-Y-O **£1,966** (£573; £286)

Form RPR
1 **Ice Tea (IRE)** 5-11-4 JamieMoore 113+
(M G Rimell) *prom: led 7f out: kicked on 3f out: rn green fnl 2f: unchal* **11/4**[1]
2 7 **Sydney Greenstreet (GER)** 4-11-4 APMcCoy 103
(C R Egerton) *prom: chsd wnr over 3f out: sn rdn: no imp fnl 2f* **7/2**[3]
2/ **3** 5 **Top Of The Agenda**[782] 1611 6-11-4 CarlLlewellyn 98
(M Pitman) *hld up towards rr: outpcd and nudged along over 3f out: shaken up and styd on fr over 1f out* **12/1**
3 **4** 3/4 **Bring Me Sunshine (IRE)**[20] 2152 4-11-4 JoeTizzard 97
(C L Tizzard) *prom: gng wl 4f out: rdn and outpcd over 3f out: one pce after* **4/1**
5 7 **Bally Rainey (IRE)**[207] 6-11-4 LeightonAspell 90
(Mrs L C Jewell) *led at v stdy pce: hdd 7f out: chsd wnr to over 3f out: fdd* **25/1**
6 1 **Dawn Wager** 4-10-11 JamesDavies 82
(D B Feek) *wl in tch: effrt 5f out: outpcd over 3f out: n.d after* **66/1**
3 **7** 1 **Winter Sport (IRE)**[25] 2056 4-11-4 RichardJohnson 88
(P J Hobbs) *wl in tch: pushed along over 5f out: outpcd over 3f out: no ch fnl 2f* **10/3**[2]
5-0 **8** 2 **Lord Leonardo (IRE)**[189] 507 5-10-11 JustinMorgan(7) 86
(L Wells) *hld up in tch: gng wl 5f out: reminders 4f out: no rspnse: one pce after* **25/1**
0 **9** 15 **So Wise So Young**[25] 2056 4-11-4 BenjaminHitchcott 71
(R H Buckler) *t.k.h: hld up towards rr: effrt 5f out: wknd 3f out* **100/1**
10 1/2 **Squeaker** 4-10-11 JohnMcNamara 64
(H E Haynes) *t.k.h: hld up in last trio: wknd over 3f out* **50/1**
664 **11** 18 **Must Be Keen**[18] 2185 6-11-1 ColinBolger(3) 53
(Ernst Oertel) *t.k.h: hld up in last trio: brief effrt 5f out: sn wknd* **25/1**
F **12** 9 **Charm Indeed**[206] 249 5-11-1 OwynNelmes(3) 44
(N B King) *plld hrd: hld up in last trio: wknd over 3f out* **100/1**

4m 29.4s (4.65) **Going Correction** -0.30s/f (Good) **37** Ran SP% **116.6**
Speed ratings: **77,73,71,71,68 67,67,66,59,59 51,47** CSF £11.61 TOTE £3.90: £1.40, £2.60, £3.70; EX 11.90 Place 6 £79.86, Place 5 £31.46.
Owner Sandicroft Stud **Bred** Eugene McDermott **Trained** Leafield, Oxon

FOCUS
A moderate pace for over a circuit and as a result a very slow winning time, even for a bumper. The winner scored nicely, though, and looks to have a future with the fourth setting the standard.

NOTEBOOK
Ice Tea(IRE) ◆, a half-brother to a couple of winners over jumps including Fiery Ring, was very well supported in the market to make a winning debut and did so in fine style. The slow winning time should not count against him as the market support suggested he was highly regarded in any case and he looks one to keep onside. *(op 5-1)*
Sydney Greenstreet(GER), a half-brother to Seebald, was never far away and, though he could not match the winner from the final bend, there was still plenty to like about this performance. He looks to have a future. *(op 5-2)*
Top Of The Agenda did have the advantage of a previous outing over the front pair, though that was more than two years ago. Looking more likely to finish out the back rather than in the money for a long way, he stayed on nicely up the home straight and should be all the better with this outing under his belt. *(op 16-1)*
Bring Me Sunshine(IRE), from a stable looking for a hat-trick on the day, looked sure to play a part racing down the far side on the final circuit but got caught out as the pace increased and there was no way back. He would not have been suited by the way the race was run and still looks to possess a fair degree of potential given a more truly-run contest. *(op 5-1)*
Bally Rainey(IRE), winner of an Irish point and racing for the first time since May, was allowed to set a very modest pace on the first circuit and stayed close to the action until not surprisingly getting done for toe from the home bend.
Winter Sport(IRE) travelled well enough for a long way but once the tempo increased he was found wanting. This was disappointing in view of his promising debut, but the way the race was run does give him a viable excuse. *(op 2-1)*

T/Jkpt: Not won. T/Plt: £211.00 to a £1 stake. Pool: £48,621.40. 168.20 winning tickets. T/Qpdt: £63.90 to a £1 stake. Pool: £5,022.60. 58.10 winning tickets. JN

2522 LEICESTER (R-H)
Thursday, December 1

OFFICIAL GOING: Hurdle course - soft (good to soft in places); chase course - good (good to firm in places)
Wind: fresh, across Weather: Overcast

2580 RIGHTON LTD. JUVENILE NOVICES' HURDLE (9 hdls) 2m
1:00 (1:00) (Class 3) 3-Y-O **£5,673** (£1,665; £832; £415)

Form RPR
1 **Caribou (FR)**[160] 3-10-12 LeightonAspell 98+
(O Sherwood) *hld up: hdwy 3 out: led next: sn rdn: eased nr fin* **7/1**
04 **2** 1 **Cava Bien**[14] 2286 3-10-12 TimmyMurphy 94
(B J Llewellyn) *hld up: pushed along 4th: hdwy after 3 out: r.o flat: nt rch wnr* **5/1**[3]
3 1 **Copper Bay (IRE)**[43] 3-10-12 WarrenMarston 93
(A King) *plld hrd and prom: led after 3 out: hdd next: no ex flat* **3/1**[1]
5 **4** 9 **Golden Square**[26] 2045 3-10-12 CarlLlewellyn 86+
(A W Carroll) *chsd ldrs: rdn appr 2 out: wkng whn mstke last* **11/1**
4 **5** 3 **He's A Star**[10] 2236 3-10-5 MrMatthewSmith(7) 81
(Miss Gay Kelleway) *hld up: hdwy 5th: ev ch next: rdn and wknd appr last* **8/1**
00 **6** 5 **Winter Coral (FR)**[25] 2069 3-10-5 (p) JodieMogford 69
(Mrs N S Evans) *led: hdd after 3 out: wknd next* **80/1**
7 15 **Next Lord (FR)**[30] 3-10-12 MickFitzgerald 66+
(C Von Der Recke, Germany) *mid-div: mstkes 3rd and next: hdwy 5th: rdn and wkng whn j.lft 2 out* **4/1**[2]
8 6 **Glowing Dawn (IRE)**[43] 3-10-5 JamieGoldstein 48
(Miss J S Davis) *chsd ldrs tl wknd 3 out* **66/1**
0 **9** 5 **Picot De Say**[14] 2286 3-10-12 OllieMcPhail 50
(C Roberts) *plld hrd: trckd ldr to 5th: wknd after 3 out* **33/1**
P0 **10** 3/4 **Leprechaun's Maite**[14] 2286 3-10-12 VinceSlattery 49
(P A Blockley) *prom tl wknd appr 3 out* **66/1**
11 5 **Innpursuit**[145] 3-10-12 JimmyMcCarthy 44
(J M P Eustace) *hld up: rdn appr 3 out: a in rr* **18/1**
0 **12** 14 **Tudor Oak (IRE)**[60] 1601 3-10-12 MarkBradburne 30
(Mark Campion) *hld up: hdwy 5th: wknd bef next* **80/1**
00 **13** dist **King After**[11] 2373 3-10-12 DaveCrosse —
(J R Best) *hld up: a in rr* **28/1**
P **The Iron Giant (IRE)**[170] 3-10-12 SamThomas —
(Miss H C Knight) *hld up: a in rr: bhd whn p.u bef 2 out* **14/1**

4m 0.90s (-6.70) **Going Correction** -0.275s/f (Good) **14** Ran SP% **117.4**
Speed ratings: **105,104,104,99,98 95,88,85,82,82 79,72,—,—** CSF £40.21 TOTE £9.70: £2.90, £1.90, £1.70; EX 66.10.
Owner It Wasn't Us **Bred** Haras De Nonant Le Pin **Trained** Upper Lambourn, Berks

FOCUS
Quite a test for these juveniles in the ground, and probably no more than modest form.

NOTEBOOK
Caribou(FR), who finished in mid-division in a fair race at Auteuil on his only previous start, won with a bit up his sleeve on this British debut. In what turned out to be quite a stamina test, this chasing sort saw it out well, and he looks the type to progress. *(op 9-1 tchd 10-1)*
Cava Bien, tackling the softest ground he has ever encountered, once again finished his race strongly, but the winner had gone beyond recall. He shapes as though he needs a stiffer test, which he will get to enjoy in the new year. *(op 9-2 tchd 11-2)*
Copper Bay(IRE), a fair maiden on the Flat, did not settle in the early stages so it is to his credit that he was involved in the finish. He is entitled to improve for this and a sharper track might suit him better. *(op 11-4 tchd 10-3)*
Golden Square again failed to see it out but he has a bit of ability and will be of interest in moderate handicap company in the new year after one more run. *(tchd 10-1)*
He's A Star was again far from disgraced. He is only moderate but his recent effort on Fibresand and his two starts over hurdles suggest that he should pay his way at both codes this winter. *(tchd 9-1)*
Winter Coral(FR) ran as though finding this stiff track rather taxing. *(op 66-1)*

2581 AGETUR (UK) LTD. MAIDEN CHASE (18 fncs) 2m 7f 110y
1:30 (1:30) (Class 4) 5-Y-O+ **£4,905** (£1,440; £720; £359)

Form RPR
-43P **1** **Bob The Builder**[28] 2011 6-11-2 98 CarlLlewellyn 118+
(N A Twiston-Davies) *trckd ldrs: j.lft: led appr 6th: hdd 11th: led and mstke 4 out: clr next: eased towards fin* **11/2**[2]
3-52 **2** 5 **Superrollercoaster**[25] 2072 5-11-2 105 (p) LeightonAspell 108
(O Sherwood) *led to 3rd: outpcd 12th: styd on to go 2nd 2 out: no ch w wnr* **7/2**[1]
2 **3** 29 **Moonshine Surprise (IRE)**[21] 2147 5-11-2 RJGreene 79
(M C Pipe) *led 3rd: hdd appr 6th: rdn 9th: hit 11th: mstke and wknd 4 out* **7/2**[1]
4P-P **4** 9 **Merry Storm (IRE)**[207] 236 6-10-9 RichardSpate(7) 70
(Mrs K Waldron) *hld up: hdwy 5th: led 11th to 4 out: wknd after next* **50/1**
P **Mr Bashir (IRE)**[214] 6-10-13 OwynNelmes(3) —
(N B King) *sn bhd: t.o whn p.u bef 3 out* **16/1**
60-P **P** **Lin D'Estruval (FR)**[31] 1959 6-11-2 104 JimmyMcCarthy —
(C P Morlock) *bhd fr 4th: hit next: t.o whn p.u bef 4 out* **10/1**
3 **P** **Murphy's Magic (IRE)**[36] 1879 7-10-9 (p) MrJETudor(7) —
(Mrs T J Hill) *prom: rdn and dropped rr after 5th: t.o whn p.u bef 6 out* **7/1**[3]
P **Blue Sovereign**[228] 5-11-2 WarrenMarston —
(J L Spearing) *hld up in tch: reminders after 6th: disputing cl 3rd whn blnd bdly 5 out: p.u bef next* **7/2**[1]

5m 59.8s (-5.60) **Going Correction** -0.275s/f (Good) **8** Ran SP% **111.5**
Speed ratings: **98,96,86,83,— —,—,—** CSF £24.48 TOTE £5.10: £2.20, £1.60, £1.20; EX 15.00.
Owner Mr & Mrs Peter Orton **Bred** Mrs Susan Orton **Trained** Naunton, Gloucs

FOCUS
A moderate maiden chase and weak form.

NOTEBOOK
Bob The Builder, not for the first time, tended to jump out to his left, but the step up in trip suited him well and he drew clear in the straight for an easy win. The form is not strong but he stays well and he might be worth trying the other way round next time. *(op 9-2)*
Superrollercoaster, who had the cheekpieces on for the first time over fences, again got outpaced before staying on all too late in the day. He looks a lay-to-back horse. *(tchd 4-1)*
Moonshine Surprise(IRE), tackling easier ground on his chase debut under Rules, did not look the most straightforward, coming on and off the bridle throughout. *(op 10-3 tchd 3-1)*

Merry Storm(IRE), having his first outing since May, ran well for a long way but he was seen off by the winner in the straight and lost second and third place from the third last. This was his first completion since finishing fourth over the course and distance on his Rules debut.

Blue Sovereign, a winner of a point-to-point on decent ground in the spring, was still in touch but under pressure when making a bad mistake at the fifth last. Pulled up soon afterwards, he can be given another chance on quicker ground. *(tchd 10-3)*

2582 MAWDSLEYS (S) H'CAP HURDLE (12 hdls) 2m 4f 110y

2:00 (2:00) (Class 5) (0-90,90) 4-Y-O+ **£2,966** (£864; £432)

Form RPR

4343 **1** **Rojabaa**[8] 2428 6-11-0 **85** .... RobertLucey-Butler(7) 92
(W G M Turner) *hld up: hdwy 5th: rdn to ld appr 2 out: styd on* **6/1**[3]

-400 **2** *8* **Double Royal (IRE)**[16] 2256 6-10-12 **83** .... MrJETudor(7) 82
(Mrs T J Hill) *chsd ldr tl led 7th: hdd appr 2 out: wknd flat* **5/1**[2]

6644 **3** *2* **Buz Kiri (USA)**[16] 2256 7-11-5 **83** .... TimmyMurphy 80
(A W Carroll) *hld up: styd on after 2 out: nt fluent last: nvr nrr* **5/1**[2]

P-P1 **4** *3/4* **The Pecker Dunn (IRE)**[19] 2188 11-11-12 **90** .... JodieMogford 86
(Mrs N S Evans) *prom: rdn and ev ch after 3 out: mstke and wknd last* **10/1**

0-34 **5** *8* **Breezer**[13] 2314 5-11-2 **87** ....(p) SimonElliott(7) 75
(J A Geake) *chsd ldrs: rdn appr 3 out: wknd bef next* **9/4**[1]

5-P0 **6** *dist* **Purr**[4] 2523 4-10-6 **77** .... MrSRees(7) —
(M Wigham) *chsd ldrs to 7th* **33/1**

3-0U **P** **Casas (IRE)**[19] 2188 8-10-3 **74** ....(t) MrGTumelty(7) —
(J R Norton) *hld up: hdwy 4th: wknd next: t.o whn p.u bef 2 out* **9/1**

FP-P **P** **Framlingham**[19] 2181 10-10-0 **64** oh5 .... DaveCrosse —
(R Curtis) *led to 7th: wknd bef next: t.o whn p.u bef 2 out* **33/1**

F-P0 **P** **Afeef (USA)**[30] 1977 6-11-0 **85** ....(tp) RichardSpate(7) —
(J A Danahar) *hld up: hdwy after 6th: wknd appr 3 out: t.o whn p.u bef next* **12/1**

5m 32.2s (-2.60) **Going Correction** -0.275s/f (Good)
WFA 4 from 5yo+ 11lb **9** Ran SP% **111.1**
Speed ratings: **93,89,89,88,85** —,—,—,— CSF £34.40 CT £154.33 TOTE £6.50: £1.70, £2.20, £1.70; EX 33.40.The winner was sold for 7,800gns to Barry Leavy.

Owner Rojabaa Partnership **Bred** The Lavington Stud **Trained** Sigwells, Somerset

FOCUS

A poor race run in a modest time, even for a seller.

NOTEBOOK

Rojabaa had looked to be going best for a while before finally taking up the running approaching the second last, and although he had to be kept up to his work he eventually won quite comfortably. The soft ground proved no barrier to him getting off the mark at the 13th attempt, but this was a poor heat. He was sold at the auction. *(op 5-1)*

Double Royal(IRE), who reversed recent Fakenham form with Buz Kiri on 3lb better terms, seemed happier racing prominently. *(op 11-2 tchd 6-1)*

Buz Kiri(USA) stayed on late but was never a threat. He would be better employed in banded races on the All-Weather. *Official explanation: jockey said gelding was never travelling (op 9-2)*

The Pecker Dunn(IRE), weak in the market despite being the only runner in the line-up with a recent win to his name, had his chance running to the second last but could not deliver. He is an inconsistent type. *(op 8-1)*

Breezer was disappointing back at this lowly level as his two previous efforts this term suggested he would have a leading chance in this company. *(op 11-4)*

2583 M & A DOOCEY CIVIL ENGINEERING H'CAP CHASE (15 fncs) 2m 4f 110y

2:30 (2:31) (Class 3) (0-115,107) 5-Y-O+ **£5,582** (£1,638; £819; £409)

Form RPR

3305 **1** **Cassia Heights**[11] 2368 10-11-11 **106** ....(t) TonyDobbin 115
(S A Brookshaw) *chsd ldrs: reminders after 5th: rdn appr last: led flat: styd on u.p* **7/2**[2]

/66- **2** *1* **Good Outlook (IRE)**[473] 1193 6-10-13 **97** .... LarryMcGrath(3) 107+
(R C Guest) *hld up: plld hrd: hdwy to ld 4th: mstke 9th: hit 4 out: hdd flat: styd on same pce* **5/1**[3]

0-25 **3** *3* **Adelphi Theatre (USA)**[17] 2241 8-11-10 **105** .... BarryFenton 111+
(R Rowe) *hld up: mstke 2nd: hdwy appr 3 out: sn rdn: styd on same pce flat* **6/1**

5P21 **4** *5* **Channahrlie (IRE)**[17] 2243 11-10-3 **87** ....(b) TomMalone(3) 88+
(R Dickin) *led to 4th: chsd ldr: rdn and ev ch fr 3 out tl wknd last* **9/4**[1]

00-0 **5** *15* **Captains Table**[17] 2248 12-11-1 **96** .... TomDoyle 81
(F Jordan) *chsd ldr to 3rd: reminders next: wknd appr 2 out* **15/2**

P5P3 **6** *5* **Rash Moment (FR)**[5] 2504 6-11-3 **105** .... RichardSpate(7) 85
(Mrs K Waldron) *hld up: hit 8th: rdn 10th: a in rr* **12/1**

1PP4 **P** **Nephite (NZ)**[19] 2183 11-11-12 **107** .... SamThomas —
(Miss Venetia Williams) *chsd ldrs: rdn after 5th: mstke next (water): wknd 9th: t.o whn p.u bef 3 out* **16/1**

5m 15.8s (-7.80) **Going Correction** -0.275s/f (Good) **7** Ran SP% **109.3**
Speed ratings: **103,102,101,99,93** **91**,— CSF £19.42 TOTE £6.00: £2.20, £3.30; EX 28.60.

Owner B Ridge & D Hewitt **Bred** Mrs S Birchall And R And Mrs Kent **Trained** Wollerton, Shropshire

■ Stewards' Enquiry : Tony Dobbin caution: used whip with excessive frequency

FOCUS

An ordinary handicap chase and a fair pace thanks to the hard-pulling Good Outlook. There were still four horses within a length or so of each other coming to the last.

NOTEBOOK

Cassia Heights has mostly been running over further since landing the 2004 Topham Trophy off a 9lb higher mark, but he needed every yard of the trip to get the better of the persistent runner-up, *and the combination of the favourable mark and good ground was the key to this performance. (op 9-2)*

Good Outlook(IRE) deserves an awful lot of credit for this performance. Not only was he returning from a 16-month absence, but he took a fierce grip early and eventually pulled his way to the front. He made two serious jumping errors on the final circuit too, yet still kept on finding more and it was not until the run-in following a protracted duel with the winner that he was forced to concede defeat. As with all horses that run such a massive race after a lengthy break, he will need time to get over this and is liable to bounce if turning out again too quickly. *(op 6-1)*

Adelphi Theatre(USA), having only his second start over fences and without a win in four years, though he was absent for two, was travelling better than anything turning for home but, although he was close enough coming to the last, he did not find as much off the bridle as had looked likely. He is not the horse he was and still has it to prove over the larger obstacles. *(tchd 5-1)*

Channahrlie(IRE), a three-time winner here, set the early pace before being forced to take a lead from the headstrong Good Outlook but stayed in there fighting until jumping the last. He seems to need further these days. *(op 15-8)*

Captains Table was receiving reminders very early and never really looked like winning. He has yet to show much since returning this season, despite a slipping handicap mark, and is not getting any younger. *(op 10-1)*

2584 LARKSHILL ENGINEERING NOVICES' HURDLE (9 hdls) 2m

3:00 (3:01) (Class 3) 4-Y-O+ **£6,011** (£1,764; £882; £440)

Form RPR

1 **1** **Nous Voila (FR)**[17] 2249 4-11-4 .... TimmyMurphy 110+
(M C Pipe) *mde all: clr 2 out: eased flat* **10/11**[1]

54- **2** *4* **Magnesium (USA)**[225] 4696 5-10-12 **109** .... JohnMcNamara 96+
(B G Powell) *hld up: hmpd 5th: hdwy to chse wnr 2 out: hit last: nvr nr to chal* **6/1**[2]

3 *3* **Schooner (GER)**[733] 5-10-12 .... LeightonAspell 90
(Lady Herries) *hld up: styd on fr 2 out: nrst fin* **10/1**

0 **4** *1 1/4* **Najca De Thaix (FR)**[17] 2249 4-10-12 .... TomDoyle 89
(Mrs L Wadham) *prom: chsd wnr 4th to 3 out: styd on same pce fr next* **40/1**

5 *1* **Arry Dash**[69] 5-10-12 .... BarryFenton 90+
(M J Wallace) *hld up: hdwy after 5th: chsd wnr after 3 out: mstke next: wknd last* **14/1**

3-00 **6** *5* **Kayceecee (IRE)**[25] 2070 4-10-12 .... MarkBradburne 84+
(H D Daly) *hld up: hdwy appr 3 out: sn rdn: wknd bef next* **66/1**

60/P **7** *1 1/4* **Captain Smoothy**[29] 1991 5-10-9 .... OwynNelmes(3) 82
(M J Gingell) *chsd ldrs tl wknd after 3 out* **150/1**

0PP **8** *1/2* **Hunting Lodge (IRE)**[9] 2423 4-10-5 .... MrJAJenkins(7) 81
(H J Manners) *chsd wnr to 4th: wknd after 3 out* **125/1**

66 **9** *1/2* **Nobelmann (GER)**[9] 2423 6-10-12 .... PaulMoloney 81
(A W Carroll) *hld up: hdwy 5th: chsd wnr 3 out: sn rdn: wknd appr last* **33/1**

P-00 **10** *7* **Sharp Rally (IRE)**[29] 1991 4-10-12 ....(t) WarrenMarston 74
(A J Wilson) *hld up: rdn appr 5th: n.d* **100/1**

301- **11** *4* **Sommelier**[253] 4519 5-10-12 .... CarlLlewellyn 75+
(N A Twiston-Davies) *nt jump wl: bhd fr 3rd* **9/1**[3]

P00 **12** *2* **Daggy Boy (NZ)**[40] 1824 5-10-7 .... PaulO'Neill(5) 68
(R C Guest) *prom tl wknd after 3 out* **100/1**

00 **13** *1 1/2* **Prairie Law (GER)**[17] 2249 5-10-5 .... TomMessenger(7) 66
(B N Pollock) *chsd ldrs tl wknd appr 3 out* **100/1**

P60 **14** *1* **Gustavo**[17] 2249 4-10-12 .... SamThomas 65
(Miss Venetia Williams) *a in rr* **66/1**

0U- **15** *3* **The Player**[52] 3907 6-10-12 .... TonyDobbin 62
(A M Balding) *hld up: sme hdwy appr 3 out: sn wknd* **33/1**

16 *11* **Sonnenglanz (GER)**[25] 6-10-12 .... MickFitzgerald 51
(C Von Der Recke, Germany) *mid-div: hdwy 4th: mstke next: rdn and wknd appr 3 out* **12/1**

0 **17** *2 1/2* **Cryfield**[23] 2099 8-10-12 .... JamieGoldstein 49
(N Tinkler) *hld up: a in rr* **40/1**

P **Musical Shares**[77] 4-10-12 ....(t) JimmyMcCarthy —
(J A Geake) *hld up: a in rr: t.o whn p.u bef 2 out* **66/1**

0-P0 **P** **Mostakbel (USA)**[12] 2343 6-10-5 ....(b) LeeNewnes(7) —
(M D I Usher) *mid-div: hmpd 1st: hdwy 3rd: mstke next: rdn and wknd 5th: t.o whn p.u bef 2 out* **100/1**

4m 0.20s (-7.40) **Going Correction** -0.275s/f (Good) **19** Ran SP% **120.8**
Speed ratings: **107,105,103,102,102 99,99,99,98,95 93,92,91,91,89 84,82**,—,— CSF £5.70 TOTE £1.80: £1.80, £1.60, £1.90; EX 9.00.

Owner D A Johnson **Bred** Haras De Saint-Voir **Trained** Nicholashayne, Devon

FOCUS

This was not as competitive as the size of the field might suggest and they bet 33-1 bar six. The winning time was the fastest of the three hurdles over the trip on the day, but not by a great margin.

NOTEBOOK

Nous Voila(FR) made it two out of two over hurdles, both over course and distance, and after setting the pace from the off he never looked in the remotest danger. He could have won by much further had his rider wanted and is beginning to look decidedly useful. *(tchd 4-5)*

Magnesium(USA), who showed signs of ability in two outings over hurdles last spring, was racing for the first time since April and was staying on nicely over the last couple of flights. He never had a prayer with the winner and a mistake at the last made no difference, but this was still an encouraging return and he should go one better before too long. *(tchd 13-2)*

Schooner(GER), not seen since running in three Polytrack maidens in the autumn of 2003, did not go off unbacked and was doing some pleasing late work. This race may have lacked strength in depth, but this effort still suggests he has a future at this game. *(op 14-1)*

Najca De Thaix(FR) narrowed the gap between himself and the winner from their first meeting by about 23 lengths and even though the favourite could have won by further, this does suggest he is moving in the right direction. He may be more the type for novice handicaps.

Arry Dash, an 80-rated handicapper on the Flat, tried to get on terms with the favourite starting up the home straight but was awkward at the second last and did not appear to get home. He may have just needed this after a short break and although he scored over ten furlongs on the level, he may need a sound surface to help him see out this trip over hurdles. *(op 12-1)*

Sommelier, winner of a bumper in soft ground when last seen in March, was in a complete mess at the first flight and things did not get much better after that. *(op 8-1)*

Prairie Law(GER) *Official explanation: jockey said gelding had a breathing problem*

2585 TONY GREEN ASSOCIATES H'CAP HURDLE (9 hdls) 2m

3:30 (3:31) (Class 4) (0-100,97) 4-Y-O+ **£4,245** (£1,246; £623; £311)

Form RPR

0-05 **1** **Killing Me Softly**[17] 2247 4-11-12 **97** ....(v) BarryFenton 102
(J Gallagher) *led: clr 3rd: hdd appr 3 out: sn rdn: led last: styd on u.p* **8/1**

-U00 **2** *1/2* **Bestam**[67] 1562 6-11-1 **86** .... JodieMogford 90
(Mrs A V Roberts) *hld up: hdwy appraoching 2 out: sn rdn: ev ch and mstke last: styd on* **33/1**

1321 **3** *5* **Honan (IRE)**[35] 1890 6-11-12 **97** ....(v) TimmyMurphy 96
(M C Pipe) *mid-div: rdn appr 5th: styd on fr 2 out: nt rch ldrs* **13/2**

-000 **4** *3/4* **Darkshape**[127] 1077 5-10-5 **76** .... SamThomas 76+
(Miss Venetia Williams) *hld up: hdwy 5th: led appr 3 out: sn clr: rdn and hdd last: wknd towards fin* **9/2**[3]

PP0U **5** *8* **Firstflor**[21] 2140 6-9-11 **71** oh3 .... OwynNelmes(3) 61
(F Jordan) *hld up: hdwy appr 3 out: rdn and wknd after next* **33/1**

-431 **6** *4* **Seveneightsix (IRE)**[17] 2244 5-10-4 **75** ....(p) WarrenMarston 61
(D J Wintle) *plld hrd and prom: lost pl 4th: sn bhd and drvn: t.o after next: styd on appr last* **3/1**[1]

0-62 **7** *3/4* **Upswing**[14] 2289 8-10-11 **82** .... KennyJohnson 68
(R C Guest) *chsd ldrs tl wknd appr 2 out* **4/1**[2]

0/ **8** *3 1/2* **Monroe Gold**[33] 2470 5-10-10 **81** .... AlanO'Keeffe 63
(Jennie Candlish) *hld up: hdwy 5th: rdn and wknd after next* **50/1**

40-0 **9** *3* **Speed Venture**[221] 9 8-11-2 **94** ....(t) MrGTumelty(7) 73
(J Mackie) *chsd ldrs: wkng whn mstke 3 out* **12/1**

633/ **10** *18* **Munadil**[213] 7-10-7 **81** .... TomMalone(3) 42
(A M Hales) *hld up: hdwy to join wnr 5th: rdn and wknd after next* **22/1**

The Form Book, Raceform Ltd, Compton, RG20 6NL

0-06 **11** *30* **Ndola**[23] 2103 6-11-5 **90**.. PaulMoloney 21
(B J Curley) *chsd ldrs tl wknd appr 3 out* **14/1**

4m 2.90s (-4.70) **Going Correction** -0.275s/f (Good) **11** Ran SP% **114.2**
Speed ratings: **100,99,97,96,92 90,90,88,87,78 63** CSF £229.29 CT £1802.48 TOTE £7.60: £3.30, £5.90, £2.00; EX 155.50 Place 6 £70.65, Place 5 £45.97..
Owner Stuart Prior **Bred** S R Prior **Trained** Chastleton, Oxon

FOCUS
The slowest of the three hurdle races run over the trip on the day, despite the decent early pace set by the eventual winner, but this looked a contest in which a few seemed reluctant to exert themselves.

NOTEBOOK
Killing Me Softly, a winner on his only previous visit here over hurdles, put up a remarkable performance. Soon in a clear lead, he looked to have run his race when the pack swamped him starting up the home straight, but the leader was doing little in front and he managed to find reserves from somewhere to rally and eventually grind out a dour victory. The form does not look great, but connections are toying with the idea of putting him over fences.
Bestam, yet to win over hurdles and beaten out of sight in two starts following a summer break, came from off the pace to hold every chance but could never quite reel the winner in. He should be able to win off this modest mark, but may need a little bit further.
Honan(IRE), patiently ridden, may have only reached his final position because others had given up. He probably needs a sharper track and better ground. *(op 4-1)*
Darkshape, unplaced in five previous outings over hurdles, pulling up in two, was in a handicap for the first time. The race looked to be his when he cruised past the long-time leader turning for home still on the bridle, but the distress signals started to appear coming to the second last and he had absolutely nothing left once collared. *(op 5-1)*
Firstflor, who has shown absolutely nothing over hurdles so far, is probably flattered by her finishing position given the way the race panned out. *(tchd 40-1)*
Seveneightsix(IRE), a winner over half a mile further here last time, ran a thoroughly moody race, dropping herself out at halfway and not deciding to run on until the contest was over. Even allowing *for this trip being too sharp, this effort makes her one to treat with great caution.Official explanation: jockey had no explanation for the poor form shown (tchd 11-4)*
T/Plt: £56.00 to a £1 stake. Pool: £39,456.85. 514.00 winning tickets. T/Qpdt: £23.90 to a £1 stake. Pool: £2,434.80. 75.30 winning tickets. CR

2289 MARKET RASEN (R-H)

Thursday, December 1

OFFICIAL GOING: Hurdle course - good to soft; chase course - soft (heavy in places)
After 3 1/2mm rain overnight the going was described as 'very tacky, hard work and more testing on the chase course'.
Wind: moderate, half-behind Weather: overcast and cold

2586 RACING POST "HANDS AND HEELS" JUMP SERIES (S) H'CAP HURDLE (COND JOCKS/AM RIDERS) (10 hdls) 2m 3f 110y
12:50 (12:50) (Class 5) (0-95,88) 4-Y-0+ **£2,192** (£639; £319)

Form RPR
/264 **1** **Zeloso**[25] 2073 7-10-10 **75**...(v) JohnKington[(3)] 78+
(M F Harris) *hld up in tch: wnt prom 6th: chal 2 out: led last: styd on* **7/2**[2]
05L5 **2** *1 1/2* **Joe Malone (IRE)**[54] 1685 6-11-1 **80**........................ FearghalDavis[(3)] 81
(N G Richards) *chsd ldrs: styd on to take 2nd run-in* **9/2**[3]
2P-4 **3** *1 1/4* **Flemming (USA)**[14] 2290 8-10-7 **72**................................ PhilKinsella[(3)] 72
(I A Brown) *wnt prom 4th: nt qckn between last 2* **7/1**
P06P **4** *1 1/2* **Seraph**[14] 2291 5-10-13 **78**.. DarrenO'Dwyer[(3)] 78+
(O Brennan) *led to 2 out: one pce run-in* **16/1**
43-0 **5** *3* **Road King (IRE)**[39] 1856 11-11-3 **84**.................................. MrRBirkett[(5)] 80
(Miss J Feilden) *wnt prom 4th: one pce fr 3 out* **14/1**
3322 **6** *dist* **Samson Des Galas (FR)**[14] 2290 7-10-1 **66**............ RyanCummings[(3)] —
(Robert Gray) *chsd ldrs: pushed along 5th: lost pl 3 out: sn bhd: t.o: btn 44 l* **3/1**[1]
0200 **7** *7* **Northern Rambler (IRE)**[4] 2517 8-10-7 **72**..............(p) JamesReveley[(3)] —
(K G Reveley) *chsd ldrs: lost pl after 7th: t.o 2 out* **6/1**
513- **P** **Dark Slaney (IRE)**[493] 1048 10-10-11 **76**........................ MrRTierney[(3)] —
(P D Niven) *racd in last: struggling whn blnd 5th: bhd whn p.u bef 3 out* **12/1**
P3PP **P** **Comfortable Call**[14] 2290 7-11-12 **88**.............................(t) EwanWhillans —
(H Alexander) *w ldrs: drvn along 5th: lost pl 7th: t.o whn p.u bef 2 out* **40/1**

4m 51.1s (1.10) **Going Correction** 0.0s/f (Good) **9** Ran SP% **114.9**
Speed ratings: **97,96,95,95,94** —,—,—,— CSF £19.93 CT £103.49 TOTE £3.60: £1.20, £1.80, £2.70; EX 26.50.The winner was bought in for 8,200gns.
Owner The Paxford Optimists **Bred** Coln Valley Stud **Trained** Edgcote, Northants

FOCUS
Standard selling-grade form.

NOTEBOOK
Zeloso, dropping back in trip, did just enough but connections had to dig deep to retain this banded Flat winner at the auction. *(op 4-1)*
Joe Malone(IRE), unplaced in six of his previous seven starts and refusing to race in the other, did nothing wrong but with under the rules of the race his rider was unable to give him a slap with the stick. That might have made all the difference. *(op 6-1)*
Flemming(USA), having his second start after a break, ran better and looks back to his best. *(op 9-1)*
Seraph, out of sorts over both hurdles and fences for this yard, ran better and after making the running he kept on all the way to the line. *(op 22-1 tchd 25-1)*
Road King(IRE), having his second outing in five weeks after a break of over a year, ran better but looks to have a lot more stamina than speed. *(op 9-1)*
Samson Des Galas(FR), with the cheekpieces left off, ran no race at all and was in trouble with a full circuit to go. *(op 11-4)*

2587 XMAS IS COMING JUVENILE NOVICES' HURDLE (8 hdls) 2m 1f 110y
1:20 (1:20) (Class 4) 3-Y-0 **£3,336** (£972; £486)

Form RPR
1 **Astronomical (IRE)**[65] 3-10-12 .... NoelFehily 99
(Miss S J Wilton) *in tch: wnt prom 5th: effrt appr 2 out: led last: kpt on wl towards fin* **15/2**[2]
2 *1* **Gidam Gidam (IRE)**[47] 3-10-12 ....(p) TomSiddall 98
(J Mackie) *led 2nd: hit 2 out: hdd last: no ex last 75yds* **20/1**
1 **3** *1 1/4* **Sasso**[17] 2236 3-11-5 .... APMcCoy 106+
(Jonjo O'Neill) *led to 2nd: w ldrs: upsides whn nt fluent last 2: nt qckn run-in* **1/3**[1]
5F0 **4** *11* **Able Charlie (GER)**[19] 2178 3-10-12 .... HenryOliver 86
(Mrs Tracey Barfoot-Saunt) *trckd ldrs: rdn and wknd appr 2 out* **25/1**
0 **5** *11* **Nepal (IRE)**[14] 2286 3-10-2 .... AnthonyCoyle[(3)] 68
(M Mullineaux) *hld up in rr: hdwy to chse ldrs 3 out: lost pl appr next* **100/1**
35 **6** *nk* **Lane Marshal**[15] 2263 3-10-5 .... PatrickMcDonald[(7)] 74
(M E Sowersby) *trckd ldrs: rdn and lost pl after 3 out* **33/1**
05 **7** *16* **Esquillon**[25] 2076 3-10-5 .... GrahamLee 51
(J A Glover) *w ldrs: drvn along 4th: sn lost pl* **14/1**[3]
000 **8** *3* **Queen Nefitari**[8] 2442 3-10-5 .... AlanDempsey 48
(M W Easterby) *hdwy and prom: 3rd: wknd 3 out: 7th whn blnd next* **80/1**
FP **9** *3/4* **Another Misk**[8] 2442 3-10-7 .... DougieCostello[(5)] 55
(M E Sowersby) *in rr: bhd fr 5th* **100/1**
10 *dist* **Aviemore**[57] 3-10-7 .... AdamPogson[(5)] —
(J R Cornwall) *j. bdly: in rr: bhd fr 4th: t.o 3 out* **25/1**

4m 14.6s (-1.80) **Going Correction** 0.0s/f (Good) **10** Ran SP% **112.1**
Speed ratings: **104,103,103,98,93 93,85,84,84,**— CSF £111.93 TOTE £6.50: £1.60, £5.80, £1.02; EX 161.30.
Owner John Pointon And Sons **Bred** Pollards Stables **Trained** Wetley Rocks, Staffs
■ Esquillon was trainer Jeremy Glover's last runner before retirement.

FOCUS
Average form as the favourite flopped and the runner-up is rated just 50 on the Flat.

NOTEBOOK
Astronomical(IRE), rated 78 on the Flat, showed a willing attitude and will be even better on less testing ground. *(op 9-2)*
Gidam Gidam(IRE), placed just once in 11 starts on the level, looks like making a much better hurdles and he battled back bravely when headed. *(tchd 25-1)*
Sasso was the reluctant early leader. He ran a shade freely but it was his clumsy jumps at the last two that were the final nails in the coffin. *(op 4-9 tchd 1-2 in places)*
Able Charlie(GER), a keen type, won a seven-furlong seller on the Flat. Back at a more realistic level, he fought his rider in the early stages and had no more to give in the final straight. *(op 16-1)*
Nepal(IRE), tailed off first time, showed a glimmer more but still has an awful lot to find before she can make any impact.
Lane Marshal seems likely to continue to struggle outside selling or claiming company. *(op 25-1)*

2588 BOOK FOR BOXING DAY H'CAP CHASE (14 fncs) 2m 6f 110y
1:50 (1:50) (Class 3) (0-120,113) 5-Y-0+ **£5,426** (£1,592; £796; £397)

Form RPR
0-5P **1** **Magnificent Seven (IRE)**[15] 2266 6-10-3 **90**....................... GrahamLee 104+
(J Howard Johnson) *in rr: reminders 7th: gd hdwy to go 3rd after 4 out: led appr next: clr between last 2: styd on* **4/1**[3]
1031 **2** *6* **Lanmire Tower (IRE)**[22] 2129 11-9-13 **91**..............(p) WilliamKennedy[(5)] 95
(S Gollings) *hit 4th: out of tch and drvn along 7th: hdwy 4 out: styd on to go 2nd after last: kpt on wl fin* **3/1**[2]
U-5P **3** *12* **Bold Investor**[32] 1941 8-11-10 **111**... APMcCoy 106+
(Jonjo O'Neill) *w ldr: led 7th: hdd appr 3 out: wknd last* **11/4**[1]
2450 **4** *5* **King's Bounty**[26] 2037 9-11-1 **102**....................................(b) RussGarritty 89
(T D Easterby) *mde most to 7th: cl up: wknd between last 2* **9/2**
P4U5 **P** **Tacolino (FR)**[14] 2294 11-11-1 **102**.. NoelFehily —
(O Brennan) *trckd ldrs pair: wknd 9th: bhd whn p.u after 4 out* **13/2**
4633 **P** **Log On Intersky (IRE)**[35] 1894 9-11-7 **113**................... AdamPogson[(5)] —
(J R Cornwall) *in last. lost tch 5th: sn t.o: p.u bef 3 out* **10/1**

6m 15.0s (28.60) **Going Correction** +0.825s/f (Soft) **6** Ran SP% **112.3**
Speed ratings: **94,91,87,86,**— — CSF £16.69 TOTE £6.40: £2.70, £1.90; EX 19.10.
Owner George Tobitt **Bred** Kilian Farm **Trained** Billy Row, Co Durham

FOCUS
They went off at a strong gallop in the ground and the first two both came from off the pace. It was a much improved effort from the winner but overall the form has a doubtful look.

NOTEBOOK
Magnificent Seven(IRE), pulled up two weeks earlier, did not go without support. He looked out of contention until suddenly making great strides starting the final turn. In front before the next, he galloped right away. The testing ground and the test of stamina were clearly right up his street. *(op 6-1)*
Lanmire Tower(IRE), who loves it round here, struggled on the ground but to his credit stayed on to chase home the winner and he was even closing the gap at the line. *(op 11-4 tchd 7-2)*
Bold Investor, rated two stone higher at his peak, took them along at a sound gallop but he was very leg weary between the last two. His glory days are well behind him now. *(op 7-2)*
King's Bounty, who broke a blood-vessel at Kelso, went head to head with Bold Investor but they both finished tired and he was the first to crack. *(op 4-1 tchd 7-2)*

2589 WILLINGHAM WOODS H'CAP CHASE (19 fncs) 3m 4f 110y
2:20 (2:21) (Class 4) (0-110,102) 5-Y-0+ **£5,426** (£1,592; £796; £397)

Form RPR
3P-3 **1** **Villair (IRE)**[14] 2293 10-11-10 **100**... NoelFehily 108
(C J Mann) *racd in last: detached 6th: hdwy 14th: gd hdwy to ld 3 out: clr between last 2* **3/1**[1]
2P00 **2** *12* **Gimme Shelter (IRE)**[15] 2265 11-10-10 **91**............. MichaelMcAlister[(5)] 87
(S J Marshall) *led: blnd 1st: hit 10th: lft clr next: jnd 13th: hdd and lft clr 2nd 3 out: wknd between last 2* **13/2**
0-F6 **3** *2 1/2* **Behavingbadly (IRE)**[20] 2170 10-11-6 **96**........................ AlanDempsey 97+
(A Parker) *hld up: wnt prom 13th: cl 4th whn blnd and lost pl 3 out* **9/2**[2]
1103 **4** *16* **Lutin Du Moulin (FR)**[20] 2170 6-11-12 **102**.................(b) WilsonRenwick 91+
(L Lungo) *wnt prom 13th: cl up and rdn 4 out: 5th and hld whn bdly hmpd next* **13/2**
6041 **F** **Bang And Blame (IRE)**[9] 2413 9-9-7 **76** 7ex oh2............ PhilKinsella[(7)] —
(M W Easterby) *w ldr: fell 11th* **3/1**[1]
26-6 **F** **Sylviesbuck (IRE)**[9] 2413 8-10-8 **84**...............................(p) FinbarKeniry —
(G M Moore) *hit 7th: blnd and lft 2nd 11th: cl 3rd whn fell 3 out* **6/1**[3]

7m 59.1s (21.10) **Going Correction** +0.825s/f (Soft) **6** Ran SP% **109.1**
Speed ratings: **103,99,99,94,**— — CSF £20.30 TOTE £3.10: £1.80, £3.80; EX 16.20.
Owner The Safest Syndicate **Bred** William Montgomery **Trained** Upper Lambourn, Berks

FOCUS
The two leaders went off very fast and the winner, detached at one stage, relished the stiff test of stamina. The complexion of the race changed at the third last fence and the form does not look at all reliable.

NOTEBOOK
Villair(IRE), shuffling round in the rear, stuck to the inner and made ground hand over fist on the final turn. He had it in the bag when he jumped very low at the last. A real character, his rider deserves the plaudits. *(op 7-2)*
Gimme Shelter(IRE), who just jumps and stays, took them along at a very strong pace. She looked to have little more to give with a full circuit to go yet retained her lead as far as the third last. *(tchd 6-1)*
Behavingbadly(IRE) travelled strongly and still looked to have something to give when blowing away his chances three out. *(op 6-1)*
Lutin Du Moulin(FR), stepping up beyond three miles for the first time, looked to have no more to give when knocked right out of his stride at the third last. *(op 5-1)*
Bang And Blame(IRE), again 9lb 'wrong', crashed out at the second last with over a full circuit to go. *(op 7-1)*

Sylviesbuck(IRE), a big mover on the morning line, wore cheekpieces for the first time. His jumping was hardly blemish free but he still looked a candidate for the runner-up spot when departing three out. *(op 7-1)*

2590 LEGSBY ROAD H'CAP HURDLE (10 hdls) 2m 3f 110y
2:50 (2:51) (Class 3) (0-120,120) 4-Y-0+ **£5,920** (£1,738; £869; £434)

Form RPR

2105 **1** **Smart Boy Prince (IRE)**[12] [2347] 4-11-2 **110**........................ APMcCoy 116+
(C Smith) *w ldr: led after 3 out: styd on strly: eased towards fin: v comf* **7/2**[1]

6-42 **2** *1 3/4* **Di's Dilemma**[29] [1987] 7-9-11 **94** oh2.............................. LeeVickers(3) 94+
(C C Bealby) *chsd ldrs: wnt 2nd appr 2 out: kpt on wl: no imp* **5/1**[2]

-416 **3** *3 1/2* **Thoutmosis (USA)**[26] [2038] 6-11-0 **118**.......................... JohnEnnis(10) 116+
(L Lungo) *chsd ldrs: drvn along 7th: wnt 2nd appr 2 out: one pce* **8/1**[3]

4-00 **4** *1 3/4* **Vicars Destiny**[14] [2292] 7-11-9 **117**..............................(p) AlanDempsey 111
(Mrs S Lamyman) *in tch: outpcd 6th: styd on fr 3 out: wnt 4th last* **8/1**[3]

4-23 **5** *9* **Marsh Run**[15] [2264] 6-10-12 **109**.................................... MrTGreenall(3) 97+
(M W Easterby) *chsd ldrs: lost pl appr 2 out* **7/2**[1]

21-P **6** *2* **Basinet**[40] [1823] 7-10-8 **102**.. GrahamLee 87+
(J J Quinn) *sn trcking ldrs: lost pl appr 2 out* **14/1**

-6PU **7** *5* **Turgeonev (FR)**[19] [2177] 10-11-10 **118**.......................(b) RichardMcGrath 96
(T D Easterby) *led tl after 3 out: lost pl appr next* **9/1**

3000 **8** *1/2* **Merryvale Man**[7] [2452] 8-10-1 **100**............................... DeclanMcGann(5) 77
(Miss Kariana Key) *mstkes: in tch: lost pl after 7th* **25/1**

32-P **9** *13* **County Classic**[15] [2264] 6-10-11 **105**................................. RussGarritty 69
(T D Easterby) *in tch: pushed along 5th: lost pl after 7th* **14/1**

/00- **10** *8* **Valeureux**[351] [2836] 7-11-9 **120**....................................... PaddyAspell(3) 76
(J Hetherton) *hld up in tch: hit 7th: sn bhd* **25/1**

4m 46.9s (-3.10) **Going Correction** 0.0s/f (Good)
WFA 4 from 6yo+ 10lb **10** Ran SP% **114.4**
Speed ratings: **106,105,103,103,99 98,96,96,91,88** CSF £21.31 CT £127.10 TOTE £4.00: £1.70, £2.60, £2.70; EX 26.30.
Owner Phil Martin **Bred** J Kennedy **Trained** Temple Bruer, Lincs

FOCUS
Reasonable handicap form in which the winner has been rated value for six lengths.

NOTEBOOK
Smart Boy Prince(IRE), hugging the inner, travelled best and scored with a fair bit in hand, the trip no problem whatsoever. *(op 9-2)*
Di's Dilemma, in effect racing from a 6lb higher mark, gave his all but the fact remains that he has yet to strike gold in 16 starts now. *(op 6-1 tchd 13-2)*
Thoutmosis(USA) often travels well but fails to deliver. This time he was making hard work of it some way out yet kept galloping in his own time all the way to the line. Now may be the time to try fences. *(op 13-2)*
Vicars Destiny, off the boil for some time now, may be worth another try over three miles. *(tchd 9-1)*
Marsh Run, struggling to make a real impact over hurdles, was on the retreat going to two out. *(tchd 4-1)*
Basinet, pulled up on his return, shaped a lot better but this trip looked to stretch to his stamina to breaking point. *(op 11-1)*

2591 RACING UK "NATIONAL HUNT" NOVICES' HURDLE (8 hdls) 2m 1f 110y
3:20 (3:22) (Class 3) 4-Y-0+ **£4,840** (£1,421; £532; £532)

Form RPR

10-2 **1** **Lennon (IRE)**[25] [2082] 5-10-12 .... GrahamLee 105+
(J Howard Johnson) *hld up wl in tch: wnt 3rd after 3 out: led on bit next: v easily* **1/5**[1]

30 **2** *1* **Alphabetical (IRE)**[18] [2206] 6-10-12 .... NoelFehily 95+
(C J Mann) *trckd ldr 2nd: led 3 out: hdd next: kpt on: no ch w wnr* **13/2**[2]

03/- **3** *4* **The Frosty Ferret (IRE)**[592] [4881] 7-10-12 .... DavidO'Meara 88
(J M Jefferson) *set modest pce: hdd 3 out: outpcd appr next: kpt on run-in* **25/1**[3]

00-6 **3** *dht* **Keen Warrior**[207] [241] 5-10-9 .... LeeVickers(3) 88
(Mrs S Lamyman) *nt fluent: chsd ldrs: one pce fr 2 out* **80/1**

300 **5** *2 1/2* **Network Oscar (IRE)**[8] [2444] 4-10-9 .... MrTGreenall(3) 86
(M W Easterby) *prom: outpcd appr 2 out* **40/1**

00 **6** *dist* **Branodunum**[23] [2112] 4-10-12 .... AlanDempsey —
(M W Easterby) *in rr fr 4th: bhd fr 3 out: t.o: btn 41 l* **50/1**

00-0 **P** **Crackington (FR)**[191] [484] 5-10-9 .... AnthonyCoyle(3) —
(H Alexander) *hld up in rr: hdwy to chse ldrs 3 out: sn lost pl: bhd whn blnd 2 out: sn p.u* **125/1**

4m 25.2s (8.80) **Going Correction** 0.0s/f (Good) **7** Ran SP% **106.9**
Speed ratings: **80,79,77,77,76** —,— CSF £1.45 TOTE £1.30: £1.10, £2.10; EX 1.80 Place 6 £17.11, Place 5 £6.28..
Owner Andrea & Graham Wylie **Bred** Henry Phipps **Trained** Billy Row, Co Durham

FOCUS
They crawled around in the early stages resulting in a slow time for the grade, 10.6 seconds slower than the earlier juvenile hurdle. As the betting suggested, it was a one-horse race.

NOTEBOOK
Lennon(IRE) was found a simple task and he completed it in exemplary fashion barely breaking sweat. At least it will have done his confidence a power of good. *(tchd 1-6 and 2-9)*
Alphabetical(IRE), a big type, is an Irish point winner. He went on but it was clear the winner was simply waiting to strike. He should make a better chaser than hurdler. *(tchd 6-1 and 7-1)*
The Frosty Ferret(IRE), who made his debut over hurdles a year and a half ago, has a bad case of stringhalt. He ambled round in front and will need a much stiffer test. *(op 20-1)*
Keen Warrior, who had two handlers in the paddock jumped in slip-shod fashion on his hurdling debut. *(op 20-1)*
Network Oscar(IRE), tailed off on his only two previous starts over hurdles, is at least now qualified for a handicap mark. *(tchd 50-1)*
T/Plt: £31.50 to a £1 stake. Pool: £31,023.70. 718.60 winning tickets. T/Qpdt: £14.10 to a £1 stake. Pool: £2,274.00. 119.00 winning tickets. WG

2296 WINCANTON (R-H)
Thursday, December 1

OFFICIAL GOING: Good to soft
Wind: strong, head-on

2592 JOHN MEADEN "NATIONAL HUNT" NOVICES' H'CAP HURDLE (11 hdls) 2m 6f
1:10 (1:10) (Class 4) (0-100,100) 3-Y-0+ **£3,569** (£1,040; £520)

Form RPR

656- **1** **Thedreamstillalive (IRE)**[298] [3719] 5-10-13 **87**............... JasonMaguire 91+
(J A B Old) *hld up bhd: mstke 6th: stdy hdwy fr next: led on bit soon after 2 out: kpt on wl: pushed out* **7/1**

6-51 **2** *7* **Touch Of Fate**[45] [1773] 6-11-11 **99**....................................... BrianCrowley 99+
(R Rowe) *in tch: led appr 2 out: hdd soon after: sn rdn: 2nd and hld whn blnd last* **6/1**[3]

5632 **3** *8* **Seeador**[155] [861] 6-11-5 **100**.................................... WayneKavanagh(7) 89
(J W Mullins) *mid div: drvn along after 5th: hdwy u.p to chse ldrs after 3 out: one pced fr next* **12/1**

5-00 **4** *4* **Dundridge Native**[11] [2378] 7-10-4 **85**........................... MarcGoldstein(7) 70
(M Madgwick) *towards rr: mstke 4th: hdwy appr 3 out to chse ldrs: sn rdn: one pced fr next* **50/1**

6P/0 **5** *3/4* **Baron Blitzkrieg**[30] [1969] 7-10-4 **78**................................ RobertThornton 62
(D J Wintle) *hld up mid div: tk clsr order after 8th: rdn after 3 out: one pced fr 2 out: veered lft cl home* **14/1**

-003 **6** *15* **Classic Clover**[21] [2147] 5-10-8 **82**....................................... TomScudamore 51
(C L Tizzard) *led tl 3rd: led 5th: rdn and hdd appr 2 out: wknd* **14/1**

P034 **7** *3 1/2* **Spike Jones (NZ)**[14] [2285] 7-11-0 **93**............................. DerekLaverty(5) 59
(Mrs A M Thorpe) *hld up towards rr: hdwy after 5th: trckd ldrs 7th: rdn after 3 out: sn wknd* **20/1**

543- **8** *25* **Boddidley (IRE)**[228] [4884] 7-11-4 **99**................................... LiamHeard(7) 40
(P F Nicholls) *mid div tl 3 out: sn t.o* **11/2**[2]

P-06 **9** *17* **Elle Roseador**[18] [2214] 6-9-7 **74** oh1........................... EamonDehdashti(7) —
(M Madgwick) *mid div: hdwy after 3 out: sn rdn: wknd qckly next* **50/1**

06/2 **10** *20* **Justino**[18] [2214] 7-10-11 **85**.. BenjaminHitchcott —
(J A Geake) *mid div: wnt 3rd after 5th: rdn after 8th: sn btn: t.o* **7/2**[1]

-533 **11** *dist* **One Wild Night**[205] [285] 5-11-2 **95**................................... JohnLevins(5) —
(J L Spearing) *chsd ldrs tl 6th: sn wl bhd: t.o* **25/1**

45-2 **12** *1/2* **Abraham Smith**[14] [2285] 5-11-7 **100**................................. MarkNicolls(5) —
(B J Eckley) *slow jump 1st and 2nd: a bhd* **8/1**

0-U0 **P** **Jackie Boy (IRE)**[31] [1960] 6-10-8 **89**........................... StevenCrawford(7) —
(N A Twiston-Davies) *mid div: bhd whn mstke 6th: t.o whn p.u bef 3 out* **14/1**

PF3P **P** **Lescer's Lad**[21] [2149] 8-9-7 **74** oh5.. CharlieStudd(7) —
(C L Popham) *chsd ldr: led 3rd tl 5th: wknd qckly 8th: t.o and p.u after 3 out* **100/1**

5m 35.2s (10.10) **Going Correction** +0.575s/f (Soft) **14** Ran SP% **116.7**
Speed ratings: **104,101,98,97,96 91,90,81,74,67** —,—,—,— CSF £45.61 CT £499.82 TOTE £7.30: £2.50, £1.90, £2.60; EX 48.70.
Owner W E Sturt **Bred** Frank O'Malley **Trained** Barbury Castle, Wilts

FOCUS
The rain had got in and riders in the first reported that the ground matched the official decription. A strong wind helped place the emphasis on stamina and not many got home in this routine novices' handicap. The form looks fair for the grade. Beaten distances from the tenth horse down are estimated.

NOTEBOOK
Thedreamstillalive(IRE) has had an operation to correct a breathing problem since his last appearance, an eyecatching run at Hereford in February, and he showed the benefit on this handicap debut. Travelling well before challenging two from home, he was going the better when left clear at the final flight for what was ultimately a comfortable win. This longer trip suited him *well and there should be more improvement to come.Official explanation: trainer said, regarding the improved form shown, gelding has had a breathing operation (op 6-1)*
Touch Of Fate, the only previous hurdles scorer in the field, ran well off a 4lb higher mark than when successful at Plumpton. Quickly tackled by the winner after showing ahead turning into the home straight, he was renewing his challenge but just looked held when a blunder at the last ended his chance. *(op 9-1)*
Seeador ran respectably under topweight on this first appearance for five months. A return to three miles will suit him, but he seems thoroughly exposed. *(op 11-1)*
Dundridge Native, who plugged on for fourth, is due to race off 5lb lower in future handicaps.
Baron Blitzkrieg showed a little more on this second run back after a long absence. *(tchd 16-1)*
Classic Clover was in and out of the lead until weakening once in the home straight. A half-brother to dual Gold Cup runner-up Go Ballistic, he is going to need three miles and fences. *(op 16-1)*
Justino appeared to be a victim of the 'bounce' and now seems likely to go chasing. *Official explanation: jockey said he thought gelding was lame; vet later found him to be sound (op 4-1)*
Lescer's Lad *Official explanation: jockey said gelding lost its action*

2593 GUINNESS BEGINNERS' CHASE (17 fncs) 2m 5f
1:40 (1:40) (Class 3) 5-Y-0+ **£5,709** (£1,676; £838; £418)

Form RPR

1 **Preacher Boy**[180] 6-11-0 .... JimCrowley 123+
(R J Hodges) *led tl 5th: w ldr: led 9th: drew clr fr 13th: unchal after: j.lft fr 4 out* **11/1**

-003 **2** *17* **Berengario (IRE)**[15] [2270] 5-10-9 106........................... PaddyMerrigan(5) 103
(S C Burrough) *hld up wl bhd: wnt distant 3rd 6th:chsd wnr in vain appr 3 out: nvr on terms* **3/1**[2]

-500 **3** *dist* **Kellys Fable**[21] [2149] 5-11-0 80.. AndrewThornton —
(J W Mullins) *chsd ldng pair in distant 3rd tl 6th: sn t.o* **20/1**

5PP/ **4** *7* **Toy Boy (IRE)**[593] [4868] 7-11-0 .... MatthewBatchelor —
(P W Hiatt) *a wl bhd: t.o* **33/1**

F0P- **F** **Galaxy Sam (USA)**[246] [4655] 6-11-0 98...........................(t) JamesDavies —
(N J Gifford) *fell 1st* **9/2**[3]

0- **P** **Made In Montot (FR)**[327] [3276] 5-11-0 .... ChristianWilliams —
(P F Nicholls) *w wnr: led 5th tl 9th: wknd qckly appr 13th: 25 l 2nd and tired whn p.u bef 3 out* **10/11**[1]

5m 34.2s (11.10) **Going Correction** +0.725s/f (Soft) **6** Ran SP% **111.6**
Speed ratings: **107,100**,—,—,— — CSF £43.75 TOTE £7.60: £2.10, £2.30; EX 23.30.
Owner Hunt & Co (bournemouth) Ltd **Bred** M H Ings **Trained** Charlton Adam, Somerset

FOCUS
Conditions were pretty testing by now. This beginners' chase was something of a farce, with the favourite pulled up with a problem and the second favourite given too much to do.

NOTEBOOK
Preacher Boy, a dual winning pointer, made a winning debut under Rules. Disputing the lead with the favourite, the pair a mile clear, he was back in front early on the final circuit and merely had to keep galloping to collect as Made In Montot dropped away. Not always fluent, he jumped out to his left over the last four fences and did not have much left in the tank at the end. He was nothing special between the flags and this form is pretty suspect, so he may well struggle to follow this up, although a step up to three miles will help. *(op 14-1)*
Berengario(IRE), held up at the rear of the field, presumably with his doubtful stamina in mind over this longer trip, was very quickly a long way adrift of the first two, not helped by being hampered at the first. He did move into a distant third place with well over a circuit to run but his rider did not seem too anxious to close the gap until it was too late and he was fortunate to inherit second place. He is better than this. *(op 4-1 tchd 5-2)*
Kellys Fable was soon struggling and outstayed Toy Boy for a distant third. He looks a very limited performer. *(op 25-1 tchd 16-1)*
Toy Boy(IRE), previously with Henrietta Knight, showed next to nothing on this chase debut and first run since April last year. *(op 40-1 tchd 50-1)*
Galaxy Sam(USA), reverting to fences with the tongue-strap retained, was in fourth place when overjumping at the first and landing steeply. *(op 5-1 tchd 13-2)*

Made In Montot(FR) had reportedly schooled well ahead of this chasing debut, but he surrendered the lead pretty tamely going out on the final circuit and was a remote second when his rider called it a day with three to jump. He broke a blood-vessel on his British debut in the Tolworth Hurdle back in January and is obviously not over his problems. *Official explanation: vet said gelding was distressed (op 5-1 tchd 13-2)*

2594 ANDREW HOPKINS CONCRETE CONDITIONAL JOCKEYS' H'CAP CHASE (17 fncs) 2m 5f

2:10 (2:10) (Class 4) (0-105,103) 5-Y-0+ **£2,625** (£2,625; £595; £297)

Form				RPR
4453	**1**		**Taksina**[29] 1981 6-9-4 **77** oh17 PaulDavey[(10)] *(R H Buckler) led: rdn whn chal 3 out: hdd appr last: rallied gamely run-in: jnd ldr fnl stride* **16/1**	86+
PP-4	**1**	*dht*	**Eggmount (IRE)**[212] 170 7-10-10 **95** WillieMcCarthy[(8)] *(T R George) in tch: mstke 6th: wnt 2nd after 13th: rdn to chal appr 3 out: led approachng last: jnd fnl stride* **9/4**[1]	106+
1402	**3**	*23*	**Ask The Umpire (IRE)**[22] 2129 10-10-2 **82** (p) ThomasDreaper[(3)] *(N E Berry) chsd ldrs tl lost position 6th: drvn along in tch fr 8th: kpt on same pce fr 4 out: wnt 3rd run-in* **9/2**[3]	67
P3F5	**4**	*5*	**Barton Hill**[9] 2420 8-11-6 **103** (b) DarylJacob[(6)] *(D P Keane) hld up: hdwy 11th: rdn after 4 out to chse ldrs: lft 3rd next: wknd 2 out* **7/2**[2]	83
0F-0	**5**	*29*	**Joe Deane (IRE)**[26] 2051 9-11-10 **101** (p) DerekLaverty *(M J Coombe) chsd ldrs tl 6th: in tch: rdn after 13th: wknd after next* **9/1**	52
6PP/	**P**		**Renaloo (IRE)**[638] 4119 10-10-0 **77** oh4 (b[1]) JohnLevins *(R Rowe) hld up: lost tch 10th: t.o and p.u bef 4 out* **20/1**	—
-446	**P**		**Hi Fi**[21] 2149 7-11-11 **102** RobertStephens *(Ian Williams) hld up: lost tch 11th: t.o and p.u bef 13th* **10/1**	—
1P/0	**F**		**Sam Adamson**[25] 2074 10-10-8 **93** (t) WayneKavanagh[(8)] *(J W Mullins) chsd ldrs: rdn after 13th: fading whn fell 3 out* **12/1**	—
-43P	**P**		**Quizzling (IRE)**[138] 1015 7-10-0 **77** oh1 MarkNicolls *(B J M Ryall) hld up: hdwy 13th: sn rdn: wnt 3rd after 4 out: slithered to a halt and p.u after next* **10/1**	—
P-1P	**P**		**Heartache**[201] 346 8-10-0 **77** oh10 (b) StephenCraine *(R Mathew) chsd ldrs: wnt 2nd at the 10th: mstke 13th: sn wknd: bhd whn bdly hmpd 3 out: p.u bef next* **16/1**	—

5m 41.6s (18.50) **Going Correction** +0.725s/f (Soft) **10** Ran SP% **123.6**
Speed ratings: **93,93,84,82,71** —,—,—,—,—WIN: Eggmount £1.70, Taksina £11.00; PL: E £1.10, T £4.10, ATU £1.70; EX: E/T £28.20, T/E £28.20; CSF: E/T £19.71, T/E £28.80; TC: E/T/A £80.22; T/E/A £101.71.
Owner Mrs Timothy Lewis **Bred** Mrs T Lewis And R H Buckler **Trained** Melplash, Dorset
■ Dead-heater Taksina was Paul Davey's first winner.
Owner R P Foden **Bred** Liam O'Donoghue **Trained** Slad, Gloucs
■ Dead-heater Taksina was Paul Davey's first winner.

FOCUS
A modest winning time for the grade, 7.4 seconds slower than the preceding beginners' chase. This low-grade handicap concerned only two from the home turn, and they were inseparable at the line.

NOTEBOOK
Taksina, a maiden who was beaten favourite in a seller last time, sweated up beforehand despite the conditions. Attempting to make all, she jumped well bar an error at the cross fence and managed to shake off all her rivals apart from Eggmount, who caught her at the final fence. She was weary and the game looked up, but she rallied bravely under her inexperienced rider to claim a dead-heat on the line. Racing from 17lb out of the handicap, although her rider's claim offset some of that, she escapes a penalty and may bid for a quick follow-up, but she had a hard race here. *Official explanation: trainer said, regarding the improved form shown, mare was better suited by jumping off in front today and handled the ground better than at Chepstow last time, where it was tacky. (op 11-4)*
Eggmount(IRE), having his first run since May, looked sure to win outright after wearing down the long-time leader at the last and going a length up, but he had to settle for a share of the spoils. He handles this sort of ground well and this longer trip suited him. *(op 11-4)*
Ask The Umpire(IRE) struggled on to collect a remote third prize, much of the credit going to his jockey who was hard at work from an early stage.
Barton Hill could never get to the leaders, but he is due to be dropped 3lb which will help his cause. *(op 4-1)*
Sam Adamson, having his second run back following injury, was beaten when taking a crunching fall at the third last. He needs better ground. *(tchd 22-1)*
Renaloo(IRE) was reportedly coming out of retirement for this first run since March 2004. The first-time blinkers did not have much effect and he was never seen with a chance. *(tchd 22-1)*
Quizzling(IRE), reappearing after his summer break, had moved into a remote third place and was staying on when all but coming down at the third last, horse and rider somehow defying gravity. *(tchd 22-1)*

2595 WEATHERBYS SUPPORT THE INJURED JOCKEYS FUND H'CAP HURDLE (8 hdls) 2m

2:40 (2:40) (Class 3) (0-120,120) 4-Y-0+ **£4,846** (£1,422; £711; £355)

Form				RPR
26-3	**1**		**The Local**[13] 2324 5-11-4 **112** AndrewTinkler *(C R Egerton) mde all: 15 l clr 2 out: drvn out* **6/1**[2]	120+
-411	**2**	*3*	**Bishop's Bridge (IRE)**[187] 553 7-11-4 **112** JasonMaguire *(Andrew Turnell) chsd ldrs: wnt 2nd after 3 out: sn rdn: styd on run-in: no ch w wnr* **20/1**	112
05-6	**3**	*¾*	**Westernmost**[13] 2314 7-9-9 **94** oh1 StephenCraine[(5)] *(K Bishop) hld up towards rr: hdwy after 3 out: styd on fr next: wnt 3rd run-in: nrst fin* **40/1**	93
1P6-	**4**	*2*	**L'Oudon (FR)**[229] 4858 4-11-5 **120** LiamHeard[(7)] *(P F Nicholls) hld up towards rr: hdwy after 3 out to chal for 2nd: sn rdn : kpt on same pce* **14/1**	117
1226	**5**	*6*	**Latin Queen (IRE)**[29] 1984 5-10-13 **114** ShaneWalsh[(7)] *(J D Frost) chsd ldrs: rdn after 3 out: kpt on same pce* **40/1**	105
2-UF	**6**	*hd*	**Charlton Kings (IRE)**[17] 2247 7-11-0 **115** JamesWhite[(7)] *(R J Hodges) chsd ldrs: rdn after 3 out: kpt on same pce* **18/1**	106
3-55	**7**	*4*	**Kildee Lass**[46] 1749 6-10-1 **100** ChrisHonour[(5)] *(J D Frost) hld up towards rr: sme hdwy appr 2 out: nvr a danger* **20/1**	87
0-F4	**8**	*5*	**Fame**[23] 2103 5-11-1 **109** RichardJohnson *(P J Hobbs) hld up towards rr: hdwy and short lived effrt after 3 out: wknd after next* **14/1**	91
6200	**9**	*26*	**Hatch A Plan (IRE)**[13] 2324 4-10-4 **98** PhilipHide *(Mrs A J Hamilton-Fairley) a towards rr* **40/1**	54
0662	**10**	*27*	**Shaman**[18] 2216 8-10-3 **97** JamieMoore *(G L Moore) chsd ldrs tl wknd 3 out* **16/1**	26
5-F0	**F**		**Montevideo**[20] 2166 5-10-5 **106** MrAJBerry[(7)] *(Jonjo O'Neill) in tch: losing position whn fell 3 out* **22/1**	—
221	**U**		**Desert Quest (IRE)**[35] 1898 5-11-6 **114** (b) ChristianWilliams *(P F Nicholls) in tch whn blnd and uns rdr 5th* **11/10**[1]	—
4/2-	**P**		**Ilabon (FR)**[582] 49 9-10-13 **107** (v) TomScudamore *(M C Pipe) chsd wnr tl bdly blkd by loose horse 3 out: sn bhd: p.u bef next* **9/1**[3]	—

3m 58.3s (9.20) **Going Correction** +0.575s/f (Soft)
WFA 4 from 5yo+ 10lb **13** Ran SP% **117.6**
Speed ratings: **100,98,98,97,94 94,92,89,76,63** —,—,— CSF £121.35 CT £4287.91 TOTE £6.10: £2.40, £3.10, £13.40; EX 66.60 Trifecta £296.80 Part won. Pool £418.09 - 0.10 winning units..
Owner Barry Marsden **Bred** Chippenham Lodge Stud And Rathbarry Stud **Trained** Chaddleworth, Berks

FOCUS
Quite a competitive handicap run at a strong pace, resulting in a slow-motion finish. The winner has been rated value for eight lengths.

NOTEBOOK
The Local made every yard, his cause helped by the departure of the favourite. Well suited by the rain-softened conditions, he had this sewn up rounding the home turn but only scored by three lengths in the end as he got tired on the run-in. He is hard to peg back when on song and should remain competitive even when reassessed, although he may go chasing now. *(op 13-2)*
Bishop's Bridge(IRE) deserves credit for the way he kept staying on to reduce the winner's advantage on this first start since May. He handled the softening ground and is likely to go chasing now.
Westernmost, proven over further, plugged on past beaten rivals on this second run since leaving Martin Todhunter, for whom he gained his most recent win off 4lb higher than he was here.
L'Oudon(FR) made a pleasing reappearance, closing to dispute second on the entrance to the home straight but unable to pick up from that point. He ought to be sharper for the run. *(op 10-1)*
Latin Queen(IRE) never got in a blow and remains beatable off this mark. *(op 33-1)*
Charlton Kings(IRE) ran a fair race and the clear round will have helped his confidence. *(op 16-1)*
Ilabon(FR), ridden prominently on this first run since April but unable to get to the front, was in second place but under pressure when a loose horse cannoned into him on landing over the the third last. Quickly dropping back through the field, he was pulled up before the next. *(op 8-1)*
Desert Quest(IRE), potentially well treated for this handicap bow over hurdles, was travelling well enough when unseating his rider. *(op 8-1)*

2596 WEATHERBYS BANK SILVER BUCK H'CAP CHASE (21 fncs) 3m 1f 110y

3:10 (3:10) (Class 3) (0-120,121) 5-Y-0+ **£8,275** (£2,429; £1,214; £606)

Form				RPR
-551	**1**		**Comanche War Paint (IRE)**[7] 2458 8-11-8 **121** 7ex LiamHeard[(7)] *(P F Nicholls) a.p: lft in ld at the 16th: rdn and hrd pressed fr 3 out: styd on wl u.p run-in: rdn out* **15/8**[1]	133+
4-P4	**2**	*5*	**Dante Citizen (IRE)**[15] 2273 7-11-0 **106** JasonMaguire *(T R George) prom: rdn to chal 3 out: ev ch appr last: no ex run-in* **4/1**[3]	113
0335	**3**	*28*	**He's The Biz (FR)**[18] 2215 6-10-4 **96** ChristianWilliams *(Nick Williams) hld up: sltly outpcd 15th: wnt 3rd appr 4 out: sn lost tch w ldng pair* **5/1**	75
0/1P	**4**	*dist*	**Bertiebanoo (IRE)**[143] 960 7-11-12 **118** (t) TomScudamore *(M C Pipe) chsd ldrs: rdn after 14th: lft 3rd at the 16th: sn wknd* **8/1**	—
F253	**F**		**Tom Sayers (IRE)**[14] 2299 7-11-7 **118** RobertStephens[(5)] *(P J Hobbs) led: travelling wl and narrow advantage whn fell 16th* **11/4**[2]	—

7m 3.00s (23.10) **Going Correction** +0.725s/f (Soft) **5** Ran SP% **109.2**
Speed ratings: **93,91,82**,—,— CSF £9.49 TOTE £2.20: £1.70, £2.20; EX 9.30.
Owner Tony Fear & Tim Hawkins **Bred** Dr C G Lowry **Trained** Ditcheat, Somerset

FOCUS
A moderate winning time for the class of contest. The race produced a good tussle from the home turn but the form is probably not the strongest.

NOTEBOOK
Comanche War Paint(IRE) was officially 4lb well in under the penalty he picked up at Taunton. Allaying his trainer's fears over the ground, he stayed on stronger than his challenger from the final fence to get the better of a lively duel. He will go to Cheltenham for a cross-country race next if coming out of this satisfactorily. *(op 11-8 tchd 2-1)*
Dante Citizen(IRE) was all the better for his recent return to action and he only conceded defeat on the run-in. He stays well and his turn should come, although he is curently 5lb higher than his last winning mark. *(op 5-1 tchd 7-2)*
He's The Biz(FR) is easing down the weights again but has not recaptured the form he was in back in the spring. *(op 8-1)*
Bertiebanoo(IRE) had a breathing problem when last in action in the summer and had a tongue tie on here. He was being pushed along from an early stage and eventually lost touch in the back straight. *(tchd 9-1)*
Tom Sayers(IRE), who really needs faster ground, was going well in front when coming down. He had jumped well prior to his fall, in which he appeared to pick up an injury to his off hind. *(op 5-2)*

2597 AJC CATERERS JUVENILE NOVICES' HURDLE (8 hdls) 2m

3:40 (3:41) (Class 4) 3-Y-0 **£3,590** (£1,046; £523)

Form				RPR
6	**1**		**Twist Magic (FR)**[33] 1923 3-11-5 ChristianWilliams *(P F Nicholls) trckd ldr: led appr 2 out: kpt on wl: comf* **10/3**[2]	115+
13	**2**	*9*	**Pace Shot (IRE)**[12] 2345 3-11-5 JamieMoore *(G L Moore) rn in snatches: mid div: hdwy 3 out: sn rdn: styd on to go 2nd after 2 out: mstke last: no ch w wnr* **7/4**[1]	105+
4533	**3**	*3*	**Josear**[14] 2298 3-10-5 97 ShaneWalsh[(7)] *(C J Down) led: rdn and hdd appr 2 out: kpt on same pce* **12/1**	93
	4	*4*	**Blue Bajan (IRE)**[35] 3-10-9 GinoCarenza[(3)] *(Andrew Turnell) hld up mid div: hit 3rd: stdy prog fr 3 out: rdn after 2 out: 4th and hld whn hit last* **9/2**[3]	90+
335	**5**	*10*	**Dusty Dane (IRE)**[17] 2236 3-10-5 (t) MrTJO'Brien[(7)] *(W G M Turner) chsd ldrs: blnd 3 out: sn rdn: one pced whn lft 5th 2 out* **8/1**	81+
U	**6**	*14*	**Before Time**[40] 1821 3-10-7 DerekLaverty[(5)] *(Mrs A M Thorpe) wnt rt 1st and 2nd: mid div: rdn after 3 out: wknd next* **100/1**	65
0	**7**	*1*	**Femme D'Avril (FR)**[17] 2236 3-9-12 MissLucyBridges[(7)] *(Miss Lucy Bridges) mid div: chsd ldrs 5th: wknd after 3 out* **66/1**	57
60	**8**	*7*	**Bay Hawk**[6] 2481 3-10-12 PhilipHide *(B G Powell) a towards rr* **25/1**	57
64	**9**	*4*	**Theflyingscottie**[31] 1955 3-10-7 ChrisHonour[(5)] *(J D Frost) mid div tl wknd after 3 out* **66/1**	53
	10	*18*	**Silver Dreamer (IRE)**[40] 3-10-0 StephenCraine[(5)] *(H S Howe) mid div: lost position on outer on appr 3rd and dropped rr: sn lost tch* **50/1**	28
30CP	**11**	*21*	**Fu Manchu**[25] 2076 3-10-5 MrAJBerry[(7)] *(Jonjo O'Neill) a towards rr: lost tch 3 out* **16/1**	14
0	**12**	*11*	**Numidas (POL)**[15] 2274 3-10-12 RichardJohnson *(P J Hobbs) chsd ldrs tl 3 out: wknd qckly* **16/1**	—
	U		**Inn For The Dancer**[145] 3-10-7 PaddyMerrigan[(5)] *(Mrs H Dalton) hld up towards rr: blnd and uns rdr 5th* **28/1**	—
6	**F**		**Methodical**[5] 2501 3-10-0 JohnLevins[(5)] *(B G Powell) chsd ldrs: rdn after 3 out: 5th and hld whn fell next* **33/1**	74

3m 57.3s (8.20) **Going Correction** +0.575s/f (Soft) **14** Ran SP% **124.4**
Speed ratings: **102,97,96,94,89 82,81,78,76,67 56,51,**—,— CSF £9.77 TOTE £4.20: £1.90, £1.50, £2.60; EX 13.90 Place 6 £201.67, Place 5 £64.10..
Owner Barry Fulton Tony Hayward Michael Lynch **Bred** Dr Georg Hastrich And Co **Trained** Ditcheat, Somerset

FOCUS
This was probably just a fair juvenile event.

NOTEBOOK
Twist Magic(FR) had flopped on his British debut at Wetherby and connections are in the dark as as to why, but he made amends somewhat on this drop in grade. He won well enough after collaring the long-time leader early in the straight, but the acid test will come when he takes on better company again. *(op 9-4 tchd 2-1 and 7-2)*
Pace Shot(IRE) had just moved into second when he rapped the final flight, but in truth he never looked like getting to the winner. He is not a straightforward ride and is probably going to remain vulnerable under his penalty. *(op 9-4)*
Josear set a reasonable pace and stuck on well enough for third once headed. He has had plenty of chances and pegs down the form, but is running respectably at present. *(op 14-1)*
Blue Bajan(IRE) won twice at 12 furlongs on the Flat for this yard in October, the latter on *Polytrack, and he showed ability on this hurdling debut without being given too hard a time. (tchd 7-1)*
Dusty Dane(IRE), who had his tongue tied for the first time, looks the type to do better in handicaps. *(op 16-1)*
Numidas(POL) again looked a non-stayer over hurdles. *(op 25-1)*
Methodical would probably have finished fifth had she not come down at the second last. *(op 28-1)*
T/Jkpt: Not won. T/Plt: £136.90 to a £1 stake. Pool: £45,989.25. 245.10 winning tickets. T/Qpdt: £12.10 to a £1 stake. Pool: £3,455.20. 211.00 winning tickets. TM

2598 - 2604a (Foreign Racing) - See Raceform Interactive

2309 EXETER (R-H)
Friday, December 2

OFFICIAL GOING: Soft (heavy in places)
With the combination of 18mm of rain the course had seen and the blustery conditions, runners finished out on their feet throughout the afternoon.
Wind: Moderate, across Weather: Heavy showers

2605 GG.COM CONDITIONAL JOCKEYS' NOVICES' H'CAP HURDLE (9 hdls 1 omitted) 2m 3f
12:40 (12:40) (Class 4) (0-95,88) 3-Y-O+ **£3,090** (£900; £450)

Form					RPR
40-6	**1**		**Caesarean Hunter (USA)**[21] 2171 6-10-10 **80** .... SeanQuinlan(8) (R T Phillips) *hld up in rr: hdwy 6th: rdn to ld 3 out: drvn clr appr last: r.o wl*	**8/1**	101+
50-4	**2**	*13*	**Bally Bolshoi (IRE)**[29] 2012 5-11-0 **81** .... LiamHeard(5) (Mrs S D Williams) *led to 2nd: w ldr: led 5th to 3 out: 8 l 2nd and btn whn mstke last*	**7/2**[1]	90+
-563	**3**	*12*	**Lets Get Busy (IRE)**[23] 2125 5-10-13 **83** .... WayneKavanagh(8) (J W Mullins) *hld up and bhd: styd on u.p fr 2 out: nvr nr ldrs*	**8/1**	78
34P	**4**	*1 ½*	**Denarius Secundus**[41] 1833 8-11-0 **76** .... OwynNelmes (N R Mitchell) *prom tl wknd appr 3 out*	**15/2**	70
00P/	**5**	*½*	**Stakeholder (IRE)**[695] 3226 7-10-1 **66** .... DarylJacob(3) (Mrs H E Rees) *w ldrs tl wknd 3 out*	**33/1**	59
00F3	**6**	*10*	**Oasis Blue (IRE)**[36] 1896 4-10-7 **72** .... TomMalone(3) (M C Pipe) *hld up and bhd: hdwy 5th: rdn and wknd 3 out*	**4/1**[2]	55
6-P5	**7**	*10*	**Peggy's Prince**[26] 2071 7-10-12 **79** ....(b1) TomMessenger(5) (J D Frost) *hld up in mid-div: hdwy appr 4th: sn shkn up: nt fluent 6th: sn wknd*	**14/1**	52
P062	**8**	*2 ½*	**Amanpuri (GER)**[9] 2428 7-11-12 **88** .... DerekLaverty (Mrs A M Thorpe) *prom tl wknd appr 3 out*	**13/2**[3]	59
/33-	**9**	*1 ½*	**Le Forezien (FR)**[506] 955 6-11-8 **87** .... RobertLucey-Butler(3) (C J Gray) *bhd fr 5th*	**16/1**	56
45PP	**P**		**Rutland (IRE)**[19] 2214 6-11-4 **85** .... JohnKington(5) (C J Drewe) *led 2nd to 5th: wknd 6th: bhd whn p.u bef 3 out*	**40/1**	—
3005	**P**		**Sunset King (USA)**[15] 2298 5-10-10 **78** .... JamesWhite(6) (R J Hodges) *hld up in tch: lost pl 5th: sn rdn and rallied: wknd after 6th: bhd whn p.u bef 3 out*	**14/1**	—

5m 2.10s (21.20) **Going Correction** +1.15s/f (Heav)
WFA 4 from 5yo+ 10lb **11** Ran SP% **114.1**
Speed ratings: **101,95,90,89,89 85,81,80,79,**— — CSF £35.75 CT £232.74 TOTE £10.90: £2.60, £1.90, £1.80; EX 50.30.
Owner A A Wickham **Bred** Lee R Oakford **Trained** Adlestrop, Gloucs
■ The first winner in Britain for Sean Quinlan.

FOCUS
As was the case throughout the afternoon, runners finished tired and came home at lengthy intervals. The form might well work out. Hurdle past the stands omitted.

NOTEBOOK
Caesarean Hunter(USA), whose trainer voiced his concerns over how well he would cope with the ground pre-race, won the day with his superior staying power and, if anything, the ground seemed to bring about an improved performance. Unplaced in all seven previous outings, he came right away once hitting the front and, with his stable now beginning to pick up the pace, he may well be able to defy a higher mark. *Official explanation: trainer said, regarding the improved form shown, gelding was better suited by being dropped in (op 13-2)*
Bally Bolshoi(IRE) had shaped well when fourth in a novice hurdle on her return at Towcester and looked to hold obvious claims on this handicap debut. She travelled strongly throughout on the outside of runners and went to the front taking four out, but the winner had reeled her in by the time they reached three from home and she ultimately finished very tired. There are races in her off this *sort of mark and the way in which she travelled suggests she will be as effective back over* shorter. *(tchd 4-1)*
Lets Get Busy(IRE) ran a strange race, staying on from a hopeless position to snatch third, having been driven along some way from the finish. She had recently been tried over virtually three miles at Lingfield and a return to that sort of distance is likely to help.
Denarius Secundus ran well here under similar conditions back in May and stepped up on his reappearance effort at Chepstow. He is not up to much, but there may be a race in him at selling level. *(tchd 7-1)*
Stakeholder(IRE) ran well for a long way on this first start since January of last year and is entitled to come on for the outing. *(op 40-1)*
Oasis Blue(IRE), who was well supported beforehand, looked to find the ground too soft and had *nothing left from half a mile out. He is not progressing as connections would have hoped. (op 5-1 tchd 11-2 and 7-2)*

2606 EUROPEAN BREEDERS FUND "NATIONAL HUNT" NOVICES' HURDLE (QUALIFIER) (7 hdls 1 omitted) 2m 1f
1:10 (1:12) (Class 4) 4-6-Y-O **£4,489** (£1,317; £658; £329)

Form					RPR
1-25	**1**		**Inaro (IRE)**[18] 2238 4-11-0 .... APMcCoy (Jonjo O'Neill) *hld up: stdy hdwy 2nd: led on bit 3 out: clr appr last: easily*	**5/1**[2]	116+
4-5	**2**	*5*	**Whosethatfor (IRE)**[27] 2049 5-11-0 .... JasonMaguire (J A B Old) *led: edgd lft and hdd 3 out: one pce fr 2 out*	**8/1**[3]	101
32-1	**3**	*shd*	**Black Hills**[31] 1968 6-11-7 ....(t) JimmyMcCarthy (J A Geake) *hld up: stdy hdwy 3rd: rdn whn mstke 3 out: one pce*	**6/5**[1]	111+
000-	**4**	*13*	**River Indus**[254] 4526 5-11-0 .... BenjaminHitchcott (R H Buckler) *hld up in mid-div: no real prog fr 3 out*	**100/1**	88
	5	*6*	**Happy Shopper (IRE)**[593] 5-11-0 .... TomScudamore (M C Pipe) *w ldr tl rdn and wknd 3 out*	**5/1**[2]	82
0-60	**6**	*2*	**There Is No Doubt (FR)**[18] 2238 4-10-7 .... MissLucyBridges(7) (Miss Lucy Bridges) *hld up in tch: lost pl 3rd: n.d after*	**16/1**	80
3	**7**	*24*	**Whatcanisay**[26] 2075 6-10-9 .... ChrisHonour(5) (J D Frost) *prom: n.m.r 2nd: wknd 3rd*	**50/1**	56
2-5	**8**	*5*	**Miller's Monarch**[27] 2056 5-11-0 .... NoelFehily (Andrew Turnell) *prom tl wknd 3rd*	**16/1**	51
P004	**9**	*10*	**Bollitree Bob**[22] 2142 4-10-7 .... JohnKington(7) (M Scudamore) *plld hrd in rr: hdwy appr 2nd: wknd appr 3 out*	**20/1**	41
0	**10**	*dist*	**Castletown Lad**[16] 2269 5-10-11 .... TomMalone(3) (M C Pipe) *lost tch appr 2nd: t.o*	**66/1**	—
0/2-	**11**	*5*	**Sativa Bay**[574] 204 6-11-0 .... AndrewThornton (J W Mullins) *lost tch 2nd: t.o*	**14/1**	—

4m 33.2s (24.00) **Going Correction** +1.50s/f (Heav)
WFA 4 from 5yo+ 10lb **11** Ran SP% **117.5**
Speed ratings: **103,100,100,94,91 90,79,77,72,**— — CSF £43.41 TOTE £6.40: £2.20, £2.50, £1.10; EX 48.40.

Owner John P McManus **Bred** P Kelly **Trained** Cheltenham, Gloucs

FOCUS
Hurdle past the stands omitted. A race that was always going to take little winning, with Black Hills being the only previous victor over hurdles in the line up and Inaro stepped up on his initial hurdling effort to win impressively, value for 15l.

NOTEBOOK
Inaro(IRE), a fair sort in bumpers, was suspected to have a breathing problem when disappointong on his hurdling debut at Folkestone and, although there had to be a worry as to how well this heavy going would suit, he travelled strongly and won with any amount in hand, pulling away on the bridle under a confident McCoy. It will be interesting to see how he gets on under heavy pressure in future, but there is no denying he is a potentially useful sort. *(op 4-1)*

Whosethatfor(IRE) appeared to get a little warm beforehand, but it did not affect his performance and he made a highly satisfactory hurdling debut. In the lead from the off, his jumping was fluent and with his stable beginning to run into a bit of form, he should be up to winning a similar race before Christmas.

Black Hills, who is held in quite high regard by connections, was expected to take a good deal of beating despite having to shoulder a 7lb penalty, but he did not seem as effective in the very soft ground and produced a rather laboured effort. He plugged on to just miss out on second close home and better can be expected back on a sounder surface. *(op 5-4 tchd 11-10)*

River Indus stepped up on his previous efforts and will no doubt have delighted connections with this reappearance effort. He can find a race once contesting handicaps.

Happy Shopper(IRE) was perhaps the most interesting runner in the field having not been seen since winning a Cork point-to-point back in April 2004. He tracked the early leader for most of the way, but appeared to get tired in the straight and will probably not be seen at his best until tackling fences. *(op 7-1)*

There Is No Doubt(FR) has hardly set the world alight since going hurdling, but he made a little late headway and is another who will do better once handicapping. *(tchd 20-1)*

Sativa Bay *Official explanation: jockey said gelding never jumped or travelled on the heavy ground (op 16-1)*

2607 HARRY DUTFIELD MEMORIAL NOVICES' CHASE (15 fncs) 2m 3f 110y
1:40 (1:41) (Class 2) 4-Y-O+ **£12,231** (£3,590; £1,795; £896)

Form					RPR
21S-	**1**		**The Listener (IRE)**[265] 4330 6-11-4 .... AndrewThornton (R H Alner) *j.w: led tl after 7th: led 3 out: v easily*	**6/1**	154+
33-1	**2**	*9*	**Star De Mohaison (FR)**[40] 1845 4-11-0 .... ChristianWilliams (P F Nicholls) *a.p: led after 7th to 3 out: no ch w wnr fr 2 out*	**9/4**[1]	135+
0444	**3**	*11*	**Keepthedreamalive**[19] 2213 7-11-4 123 .... BenjaminHitchcott (R H Buckler) *prom: lost pl 8th: rdn and rallied appr 4 out: wknd 3 out*	**12/1**	123
F0-6	**4**	*2*	**Sharp Rigging (IRE)**[41] 1828 5-11-4 .... JimmyMcCarthy (A M Hales) *hld up: hdwy after 7th: wknd 4 out*	**14/1**	121
1/11	**5**	*9*	**Spirit Of New York (IRE)**[36] 1891 6-11-9 .... APMcCoy (Jonjo O'Neill) *hld up in 2nd: nt fluent 5th (water): bhd fr 9th*	**4/1**[3]	120+
21-1	**6**	*dist*	**Von Origny (FR)**[26] 2078 4-10-11 120 .... MarkBradburne (H D Daly) *prom: lost pl appr 8th: j.lft 11th: bhd fr 4 out: t.o*	**3/1**[2]	—
6P	**7**	*dist*	**Wynford Eagle**[31] 1976 6-11-4 .... RobertWalford (R H Alner) *bhd fr 8th: t.o*	**150/1**	—
5PP-	**P**		**Peveril Pride**[395] 1972 7-11-4 .... HenryOliver (J A Geake) *plld hrd: a bhd: t.o whn p.u bef 4 out*	**100/1**	—
35-U	**P**		**Double Header (IRE)**[14] 2311 6-11-4 .... MatthewBatchelor (Mrs S D Williams) *a in rr: t.o whn p.u bef 4 out*	**50/1**	—
34/P	**P**		**Master Billyboy (IRE)**[31] 1973 7-11-4 .... JasonMaguire (Mrs S D Williams) *bhd fr 7th: t.o whn blnd 4 out: p.u bef 3 out*	**66/1**	—

5m 5.20s (11.30) **Going Correction** +0.80s/f (Soft)
WFA 4 from 5yo+ 10lb **10** Ran SP% **109.5**
Speed ratings: **109,105,101,100,96** —,—,—,—,— CSF £19.03 TOTE £8.70: £1.50, £1.30, £3.90; EX 15.90.

Owner Old Moss Farm **Bred** Daniel C And Patrick Keating **Trained** Droop, Dorset

FOCUS
A very good novices' chase with four potentially useful sorts on show, and The Listener won in the style of a potentially smart novice, value for 15l. The race looks sure to produce its share of winners.

The Form Book, Raceform Ltd, Compton, RG20 6NL

NOTEBOOK

The Listener(IRE) ◆, always viewed as an out-and-out chaser, really got his act together over hurdles last season and the bog-like ground conditions held no fears for the son of Roselier. Disputing the lead throughout, he was always travelling and put in an exhibition round of jumping without making a semblance of a mistake - if anything jumping too big at some. Given he is a strong galloper who is ideally suited by distances of around three miles, this has to go down as a top effort and, with plenty of improvement anticipated - Alner rarely has them wound up first time up - he is one to bear in mind for a good prize this season as he fully deserves a step up to graded company. It will be interesting to see if connections are tempted by a tilt at the Feltham Novices' Chase at Sandown on Boxing Day. *Official explanation: , always viewed as an out-and-out chaser, really got his act together over hurdles last season and the bog-like ground conditions held no fears for the son of Roselier. Disputing the lead throughout, he was always travelling and put in an exhibition round of jumping without making a semblance of a mistake - if anything jumping too big at some. Given he is a strong galloper who is ideally suited by distances of around three miles, this has to go down as a top effort and, with plenty of improvement anticipated - Alner rarely has them wound up first time up - he is one to bear in mind for a good prize this season as he fully deserves a step up to graded company. It will be interesting to see if connections are tempted by a tilt at the Feltham Novices' Chase at Sandown on Boxing Day.*

Star De Mohaison(FR) could hardly have been more impressive when making a winning debut over fences at Aintree back in October, but the form had not exactly worked out with the second, third and fourth all being beaten next time. Never far from the winner, he took over down the back, but the winner was simply too classy and romped clear of him down the straight. He is a useful sort, but nothing more and he will find easier opportunities in future. *(op 7-4)*

Keepthedreamalive found 2m 2f around Fontwell on the sharp side when only fourth on his chase debut and this proved a more suitable test. He was well held in third, but a place was realistically the best he could have hoped for against this calibre of opposition and he will find easier opportunities. *(op 14-1 tchd 16-1)*

Sharp Rigging(IRE), a useful is somewhat luckless hurdler, travelled strongly before the ground took its toll and he faded out of it in the straight. There was plenty of promise to be taken from this and a lesser race on better ground should see him off the mark over fences. *(op 11-1 tchd 16-1)*

Spirit Of New York(IRE) has returned from injury in top form and picked up from where he left off when maintaining his 100% record in bumpers at Market Rasen in early October. A bold decision by connections not to mess around with hurdles paid off when the sizeable gelding made a successful fencing debut at Stratford later that month, but he faced a vastly stiffer task here in trying concede upwards of 5lb to his rivals and a couple of mistakes were enough to see him off. *He is a winner in soft ground, but has to be given another chance back on a decent surface. (op 7-2)*

Von Origny(FR), an unexposed four-year-old getting upwards of 3lb from all his rivals, made the ideal start to his chasing career when running out a comfortable winner in similar ground at Market Rasen early last month, but he seemed to find the competition too hot and ultimately trailed in sixth. His three previous wins had come in similar ground, so that cannot be used as an excuse, but he too looks worthy of another chance as this effort was not in keeping with his previously progressive profile. *Official explanation: trainer had no explanation for the poor form shown (op 4-1)*

2608 AXMINSTER CARPETS DEVON MARATHON H'CAP CHASE 4m

2:15 (2:16) (Class 3) (0-125,125) 5-Y-0+ **£12,166** (£3,571; £1,785; £891)

Form				RPR
-141	**1**		**Dead-Eyed Dick (IRE)**[75] 1489 9-11-4 **117**................. ChristianWilliams (Nick Williams) *hld up and bhd: hdwy 15th: led on bit 4 out: clr 3 out: styd on* **16/1**	131+
12-1	**2**	*9*	**Toulouse-Lautrec (IRE)**[31] 1973 9-11-12 **125**................ JasonMaguire (T R George) *a.p: hit 1st: led 16th: rdn and hdd 4 out: sn btn* **4/1**[1]	125
3-1P	**3**	*15*	**Trust Fund (IRE)**[27] 2054 7-11-9 **122**................................ RobertWalford (R H Alner) *hld up and bhd: hdwy after 17th: 4 l 3rd whn slipped 4 out: nt rcvr* **8/1**	117+
0U-P	**4**	*9*	**Kittenkat**[14] 2325 11-10-5 **104**....................................... MatthewBatchelor (N R Mitchell) *sn w ldr: led 3rd tl after 10th: lft in ld 11th: hdd appr 15th: rdn 17th: sn wknd* **7/1**[3]	84+
F226	**P**		**Jiver (IRE)**[21] 2162 6-11-0 **113**... AntonyEvans (M Scudamore) *nt j.w: rdn after 6th: sn struggling: p.u bef 11th* **11/1**	—
-460	**P**		**Limerick Leader (IRE)**[20] 2175 7-10-5 **111**.................(b) MrTJO'Brien[(7)] (P J Hobbs) *prom: hit 10th: tk wrong crse 11th (water) & p.u* **14/1**	—
42-0	**P**		**Will Of The People (IRE)**[216] 127 10-11-10 **123**.....(v) TomScudamore (M C Pipe) *hld up in tch: mstke 9th: bhd fr 14th: t.o whn p.u bef 17th* **28/1**	—
P-06	**P**		**Auburn Spirit**[19] 2215 10-10-10 **109**...................................... DaveCrosse (M D I Usher) *led to 3rd: w ldr: led after 10th: tk wrong crse 11th (water) & p.u* **12/1**	—
31-1	**P**		**Sir Frosty**[188] 547 12-10-8 **107**.. APMcCoy (B J M Ryall) *hld up in tch: lost pl 3rd: rallied 11th: ev ch appr 4 out: sn rdn and wknd: p.u bef last* **4/1**[1]	—
5P-4	**P**		**Bob's The Business (IRE)**[15] 2293 11-10-4 **103**.................. NoelFehily (Ian Williams) *hld up: hdwy appr 3rd: lost pl 8th: rallied appr 14th: led appr 15th: hdd and nt fluent 16th: wknd appr 4 out* **9/2**[2]	—

9m 3.10s **10** Ran SP% **113.8**
CSF £79.36 CT £559.28 TOTE £13.50: £4.50, £1.70, £4.40; EX 38.90 Trifecta £473.00 Pool: £732.94 - 1.10 winning tickets..

Owner Mrs Jane Williams **Bred** Edward And Teresa Forde **Trained** George Nympton, Devon

■ Stewards' Enquiry : Dave Crosse 10-day ban: taking wrong course (Dec 13-22)
Mr T J O'Brien 10-day ban: taking wrong course (Dec 13,15,18 Jan 2,6,10,12,18,23,31)

FOCUS

A race recommended for only the most hardcore of stayers and it was no surprise to see less than half of the 10 runners manage to complete in what was truly a bitter slog. The winner has been rated value for 14l.

NOTEBOOK

Dead-Eyed Dick(IRE), whose previous best form had come on good, fast ground, handled the atrocious conditions surprisingly well and seemed to relish every moment of the four-mile grind. Now a winner of seven of his 18 starts over fences, he has been most progressive over the last couple of seasons and particularly impressed here with the way in which he quickly drew clear down the straight. He is evidently one to keep on the right side and with his effectiveness in such conditions now unquestionable, connections now have a few more options. *(op 10-1)*

Toulouse-Lautrec(IRE) is nothing if not game and bravely shouldered top weight into second. A winner over hurdles here on his reappearance, he was simply unable to stick with the winner as that one found another gear, but came home well clear of the third. He seems as good as ever and will continue to set the standard for races such as this, but it is worth noting he was racing here off a 12lb higher mark than when last winning over fences and his consistency is unlikely to see him dropped much by the Handicapper. *(op 7-2 tchd 9-2)*

Trust Fund(IRE) is prone to throwing in the odd bad run, but this was a much easier task than he faced on his reappearance in the Badger Beer at Wincanton and, having travelled well in rear for over three miles, he stuck on pluckily for third. This was only his eighth start under Rules and, being a seven-year-old, remains open to further improvement. *(tchd 15-2 and 9-1)*

Kittenkat often saves her best for this place and she negotiated the course safely to be last of the four finishers. She may need a little help from the Handicapper before winning again. *(op 10-1)*

Sir Frosty has run poorly on his seasonal reappearance for the past two seasons and once again failed to live up to expectations on this return. This test should have suited, but a better run can be expected next time. *(tchd 16-1)*

Bob's The Business(IRE) is relatively unexposed for an 11-year-old and he ran well for a long way here before getting tired. *(tchd 16-1)*

Auburn Spirit was still in with every chance when going the wrong side of the water jump second time around - omitted on the first circuit as it would have been the first fence - although it was too early to tell how he would have fared. *(tchd 16-1)*

Limerick Leader(IRE) followed Auburn Spirit the wrong way around the water, but again it was too early to tell how he would have got on. *(tchd 16-1)*

2609 SOUTH-WEST RACING CLUB H'CAP HURDLE (10 hdls 1 omitted) 2m 6f 110y

2:45 (2:51) (Class 3) (0-115,113) 4-Y-0+ **£5,465** (£1,604; £802; £400)

Form				RPR
56P3	**1**		**Keepers Mead (IRE)**[9] 2430 7-11-4 **105**.......................... RobertWalford (R H Alner) *led tl after 2nd: a.p: led 6th: rdn and hung lft appr last: hung lft flat: rdn out* **7/1**[2]	112+
P-0U	**2**	*2 ½*	**He's The Guv'Nor (IRE)**[29] 2005 6-11-9 **110**............ BenjaminHitchcott (R H Buckler) *hld up in tch: hrd rdn after 2 out: kpt on flat* **15/2**[3]	113
0246	**3**	*hd*	**Noble Calling (FR)**[8] 2459 8-11-1 **102**........................ TomScudamore (R J Hodges) *hld up in tch: rdn and ev ch 2 out: nt qckn flat* **16/1**	106+
64-0	**4**	*16*	**Dere Lyn**[13] 2347 7-10-13 **105**.. LeeStephens[(5)] (Mrs D A Hamer) *hld up in tch: lost pl and mstke 5th: rallied after 7th: wknd 3 out* **14/1**	92
/4C-	**5**	*nk*	**Clan Royal (FR)**[237] 4772 10-11-8 **109**.................................... APMcCoy (Jonjo O'Neill) *hld up in rr: stdy hdwy appr 5th: wknd after 3 out* **2/1**[1]	99+
6-00	**6**	*1 ½*	**Miss Fahrenheit (IRE)**[9] 2430 6-11-12 **113**................ ChristianWilliams (C Roberts) *led 2nd to 6th: ev ch 3 out: wknd appr last* **20/1**	98
/0-0	**7**	*dist*	**Galant Eye (IRE)**[14] 2314 6-10-4 **91**.................................. VinceSlattery (R J Baker) *a bhd: t.o* **40/1**	—
54-P	**8**	*9*	**Bak To Bill**[16] 2271 10-11-5 **113**....................................... MissLGardner[(7)] (Mrs S Gardner) *led after 1st to 2nd: prom tl wknd after 7th: t.o* **28/1**	—
P0-0	**9**	*3 ½*	**Redde (IRE)**[7] 2483 10-10-11 **105**.................................. CharlieStudd[(7)] (Mrs J G Retter) *prom tl wknd 5th: t.o* **66/1**	—
-400	**10**	*dist*	**The Gene Genie**[22] 2139 10-9-10 **90**.............................. JamesWhite[(7)] (R J Hodges) *bhd fr 6th: hit 7th: t.o* **14/1**	—
PPF-	**P**		**Chanticlier**[273] 4155 8-11-9 **110**.. JimmyMcCarthy (R T Phillips) *bhd tl p.u bef 3 out* **10/1**	—
0P5-	**P**		**Vanormix (FR)**[234] 4816 6-11-4 **112**..................... RobertLucey-Butler[(7)] (C J Gray) *bhd tl p.u after 3 out* **33/1**	—
30P-	**P**		**Kiwi Babe**[224] 4960 6-11-4 **112**.. DarylJacob[(7)] (D P Keane) *hld up in mid-div: wknd 6th: bhd whn p.u bef 2 out* **12/1**	—
4-54	**P**		**Mrs Pickles**[13] 2341 10-9-9 **89**... LeeNewnes[(7)] (M D I Usher) *mid-div: rdn 7th: sn struggling: bhd whn p.u bef last* **15/2**[3]	—

6m 16.0s (36.70) **Going Correction** +1.725s/f (Heav) **14** Ran SP% **120.4**
Speed ratings: **105,104,104,98,98 97,—,—,—,— —,—,—,—** CSF £56.13 CT £824.23 TOTE £7.90: £2.70, £3.40, £4.50; EX 40.10.

Owner J C Browne **Bred** James Hale **Trained** Droop, Dorset

FOCUS

Hurdle past the stands omitted. Keepers Mead was well in on last year's form and put up a dour staying performance to record his third career success.

NOTEBOOK

Keepers Mead(IRE), who travelled strongly in the lead for most of the way, battled on doggedly under pressure to record the third win of his career. His recent third at Chepstow was a step up on his first two efforts of the season and, with his stable starting to hit form, it was no surprise that he got his head in front. Consistency is hardly his strong point, but he is the type to do better once chasing and it will be interesting to see if connections wait until next season to send him over the larger obstacles. *(op 5-1 tchd 15-2)*

He's The Guv'Nor(IRE) had lost his form a bit since pulling up at Newbury on his final start of last season when he reportedly failed to stay three miles, but this was an improved effort and the way he finished to just get up for the second suggested he is well worth another try at further. He will make a nice staying chaser in time. *(op 8-1)*

Noble Calling(FR) has twice been beaten in sellers this season, but he shaped well in a better race at Taunton last time and ran a cracker here in ground that he was previously unproven on, just getting nailed for second. The extra distance clearly suited and on this evidence he should have little trouble winning back at a lowly level.

Dere Lyn stepped up on his reappearance effort, making some late headway into fourth, and will be of interest when the headgear he did so well in last year is reapplied.

Clan Royal(FR) was making his eagerly awaited reappearance and was well in for this return to hurdles. Detached in last place early, he travelled with his usual gusto and if anything was doing too much for McCoy's liking, but made good headway to sit in a threatening position behind the leaders at one stage, only to fade in the straight as those early exertions began to tell. The Stewards were not happy with McCoy's effort, but they took no further action and it will be *interesting to see if the ten-year-old is kept to hurdles in his build-up to Aintree once moreOfficial explanation: jockey said, regarding running and riding, his orders were to drop gelding in and settle him but on no account to hit him, adding that he ran too freely for first 2m, and found nothing off the bridle in closing stages (op 9-2)*

Miss Fahrenheit(IRE) showed signs of a return to form, running well for a long way under top weight, and looks to be on her way back to form. *(op 12-1)*

Chanticlier made some appeal on his first start for a new yard having lost his way last season. He raced towards the rear of the field for much of the way and made good headway into a threatening position at one stage, but he got tired in the end and was pulled up soon after they turned for home. *(tchd 11-1)*

2610 SERGEANT CECIL TRIPLE VICTORY NOVICES' H'CAP CHASE (17 fncs) 2m 7f 110y

3:20 (3:20) (Class 4) (0-105,104) 4-Y-0+ **£5,074** (£1,489; £744; £372)

Form				RPR
2P-F	**1**		**Trenance**[35] 1905 7-10-4 **82**... JasonMaguire (T R George) *led tl after 2nd: led after 12th to 13th: rallied u.p to ld cl home* **9/1**	92
0	**2**	*1 ¼*	**Hazel Bank Lass (IRE)**[18] 2244 9-10-7 **85**............................ NoelFehily (Andrew Turnell) *hld up in tch: led 13th: hrd rdn and hdd cl home* **25/1**	94
-41F	**3**	*5*	**Mini Dare**[24] 2104 8-11-5 **97**.. LeightonAspell (O Sherwood) *hld up and bhd: hdwy 12th: rdn appr last: wknd flat* **4/1**[2]	103+
4-14	**4**	*16*	**Up The Pub (IRE)**[23] 2126 7-10-5 **83**.............................. RobertWalford (R H Alner) *hld up in mid-div: lost pl 10th: hdwy after 13th: wknd after 3 out* **2/1**[1]	75+
P3P-	**5**	*20*	**Shuffling Pals (IRE)**[226] 4931 8-10-0 **78** oh5........................ HenryOliver (S E H Sherwood) *prom: mstke 1st: wknd 4 out* **28/1**	46
00-0	**6**	*dist*	**Zimbabwe (FR)**[45] 1780 5-11-3 **95**..............................(p) AndrewThornton (N J Hawke) *led after 2nd: slipped 12th: sn hdd: wknd after 13th: t.o* **16/1**	—
40-5	**P**		**Drat**[14] 2313 6-10-13 **91**... AntonyEvans (R Mathew) *bhd whn p.u bef 11th* **33/1**	—
4/P-	**P**		**Pen-Almozon**[333] 3192 9-10-0 **78** oh9............................(p) VinceSlattery (N J Hawke) *prom to 9th: bhd whn p.u bef 10th* **66/1**	—

PP26 **U** **Billy Ballbreaker (IRE)**[30] [1983] 9-11-3 **95**..............(tp) ChristianWilliams —
(C L Tizzard) *blnd and uns rdr 2nd* **13/2**[3]

2P-6 **P** **Priscilla**[15] [2297] 7-11-4 **96**.. JohnMcNamara —
(K Bishop) *hld up and bhd: hdwy 11th: wknd 3 out: p.u bef last* **7/1**

2P-1 **P** **Brisbane Road (IRE)**[208] [229] 8-11-3 **95**......................(tp) OllieMcPhail —
(B J Llewellyn) *nt j.w: lost tch 6th: t.o whn p.u bef 9th* **20/1**

650- **U** **Huw The News**[234] [4813] 6-10-7 **85**................................ MarkBradburne —
(S C Burrough) *hld up in mid-div: mstke 6th: blnd and uns rdr 13th* **40/1**

6m 33.3s (34.70) **Going Correction** +1.525s/f (Heav) **12** Ran SP% **114.0**
Speed ratings: **103,102,100,95,88** —,—,—,—,— —,— CSF £198.75 CT £1037.54 TOTE £8.60: £2.50, £6.80, £1.80; EX 368.40.

Owner Mr & Mrs D A Gamble **Bred** D A Gamble **Trained** Slad, Gloucs

FOCUS
Modest form, but Trenance should receive a good confidence boost from this win and may be capable of defying a penalty.

NOTEBOOK
Trenance, who had managed to complete in only three of his seven outings over fences, got it right this time and handled the swamp-like conditions admirably. This should do his confidence good and it is likely he can win again off what should still be a reasonable mark after being reassessed. *(op 8-1)*

Hazel Bank Lass(IRE) had shown very little in five previous attempts, four of which had been in Ireland, and she looked to have little chance in this switch to fences at the age of nine. However, she shocked many with a cracking effort, leading over the last and only being collared close home. If this was no fluke she can probably find a small race, but she could hardly be recommended as one to follow.

Mini Dare, a faller when still in with a chance at Huntingdon last time, travelled well for a long way, but was unable to pick up in the ground. *(tchd 5-1)*

Up The Pub(IRE), who had won in this ground earlier in the season at Chepstow, appeared to have no obvious excuse for the disappointing run, but he had previously looked progressive and may be worthy of another chance. *(op 3-1 tchd 15-8)*

Shuffling Pals(IRE) had failed to complete in two previous starts over fences, but it was no surprise to see the son of Roselier run better here. He got in quite low at a lot of his fences and will need to step up again if he is to be winning any time soon. *(op 25-1)*

Zimbabwe(FR) was the only other to complete but, having shown up well in front for a long way, he faded badly after making a mess of the last ditch. *(op 12-1)*

Priscilla came into this off the back of a fair chase debut effort at Wincanton last month and was nibbled at in the betting beforehand, but she was yet another who failed to get home in the conditions having travelled well, and ran better than her finishing position suggests. *(op 13-2 tchd 8-1)*

2611 E B F "JUNIOR" STANDARD OPEN NATIONAL HUNT FLAT RACE 1m 5f
3:50 (3:51) (Class 6) 3-Y-O **£2,977** (£867; £434)

Form RPR

2 **1** **Milan Deux Mille (FR)**[24] [2105] 3-10-12 .... GerrySupple 104+
(M C Pipe) *plld hrd: led after 2f: hung lft over 2f out: rdn and hung bdly lft ins fnl f: r.o* **9/4**[1]

2 *1 ½* **Over The Flow** 3-10-5 .... BenjaminHitchcott 96+
(R H Buckler) *led 2f: a.p: rdn and ev ch whn carried lft ins fnl f: swtchd rt cl home: r.o* **16/1**

3 *13* **Willy The Slip** 3-10-12 .... AndrewThornton 85
(R H Alner) *hld up and bhd: hdwy 7f out: rdn and one pce fnl 3f* **9/1**

3 **4** *nk* **Reveal (IRE)**[29] [2013] 3-9-12 .... LiamHeard[(7)] 78
(H E Haynes) *t.k.h: hdwy over 5f out: wknd over 1f out* **8/1**

3 **5** *2* **Themanfromfraam**[45] [1785] 3-10-5 .... MrTJO'Brien[(7)] 82
(Mrs S M Johnson) *prom tl wknd 2f out* **7/1**[3]

6 *5* **River Role** 3-10-0 .... RobertStephens[(5)] 69
(J W Tudor) *hld up and bhd: hdwy over 3f out: nvr trbld ldrs* **66/1**

7 *13* **Jomelamin** 3-10-0 .... JayHarris[(5)] 52
(R J Hodges) *t.k.h: sn prom: wknd over 3f out* **25/1**

8 *¾* **Paul Superstar (FR)** 3-10-5 .... KeiranBurke[(7)] 58
(N J Hawke) *hld up in tch: rdn and wknd over 4f out* **20/1**

9 *¾* **Greenacre Legend** 3-10-12 .... JamesDavies 57
(D B Feek) *a bhd* **25/1**

10 *27* **Marlowe (IRE)** 3-10-5 .... JamesWhite[(7)] 22
(R J Hodges) *bhd fnl 8f: t.o* **10/3**[2]

11 *13* **Equivocate** 3-10-5 .... JasonMaguire —
(R Mathew) *hld up in tch: rdn and wknd over 3f out: t.o* **33/1**

12 *shd* **Maenflora** 3-10-5 .... ChristianWilliams —
(B J Llewellyn) *a bhd: t.o* **25/1**

P **Wotabirthday** 3-10-12 .... MarkBradburne —
(S C Burrough) *a bhd: t.o whn p.u 5f out: b.b.v* **50/1**

3m 26.6s **13** Ran SP% **116.0**
CSF £36.24 TOTE £3.10: £1.10, £2.80, £3.40; EX 38.50 Place 6 £151.83, Place 5 £67.10.

Owner Neil J Edwards **Bred** Gaetan Gilles **Trained** Nicholashayne, Devon

FOCUS
A controversial finish to end the day with favourite Milan Deux Mille hanging badly across Over The Flow in the final furlong and possibly costing the latter the race.

NOTEBOOK
Milan Deux Mille(FR), runner-up to a fair sort on his debut at Huntingdon, handled the conditions better than most and saw his race out well considering he pulled in the early stages, although he did hang badly late on. On this evidence he will struggle to defy a penalty, but Pipe runners have a habit of improving and as a result he cannot be discounted. *(op 2-1 tchd 5-2)*

Over The Flow raced prominently throughout and pulled clear with the favourite. Hitchcott had yet to get serious with the filly when the interference began to take place and she finished well once switched around her rival, but it was not to be her day. A similar race will come her way on this evidence.

Willy The Slip, a product of Derby-winning sire Benny The Dip, kept on again into third and, although well held by the front two, he will be up to winning once tackling a stiffer test over hurdles. *(op 13-2)*

Reveal(IRE) had the benefit of previous experience, but did not see her race out in the ground. *(op 14-1)*

Themanfromfraam failed to build on his initial effort, but he is hardly bred to stay forever and this ground would not have helped. *(op 6-1)*

Marlowe(IRE), a supremely well-bred gelding who cost 300,000gns as a yearling, offered very little and, although bred to be effective in soft ground, this heavy surface may have proved too much for him. He probably deserves another chance. *(op 5-1 tchd 3-1)*

Wotabirthday *Official explanation: jockey said gelding bled from the nose (op 28-1)*

T/Jkpt: Not won. T/Plt: £54.50 to a £1 stake. Pool: £53,053.45. 710.60 winning tickets. T/Qpdt: £21.30 to a £1 stake. Pool: £4,091.60. 141.70 winning tickets. KH

[2043] SANDOWN (R-H)
Friday, December 2

OFFICIAL GOING: Chase course - soft; hurdle course - heavy (soft in places)
Wind: Slight, ahead

2612 CELIA BLAKER 80TH BIRTHDAY JUVENILE NOVICES' HURDLE (8 hdls) 2m 110y
1:00 (1:00) (Class 3) 3-Y-O **£5,621** (£1,650; £825; £412)

Form RPR

3 **1** **Spidam (FR)**[16] [2274] 3-11-4 .... BJGeraghty 118+
(P F Nicholls) *lw: trckd ldr 3rd: led 4 out: c clr appr 2 out: easily* **6/4**[1]

22 **2** *20* **Kanpai (IRE)**[13] [2345] 3-11-0 .... TomDoyle 97+
(J G M O'Shea) *chsd ldrs: chal and blnd 3 out: wknd and no ch w wnr appr 2 out* **3/1**[2]

3 **3** *6* **Cave Of The Giant (IRE)**[32] [1948] 3-11-0 .... JimCrowley 83+
(T D McCarthy) *hit 1st: rr but in tch: rdn after 3 out and nvr any ch w ldrs* **16/1**

4 *15* **Ameeq (USA)**[41] 3-11-0 .... JamieMoore 68
(G L Moore) *lw: scope: hdwy 3rd: chsd ldrs nd hit 3 out: wknd bef next and mstke: no ch whn blnd 2 out and last* **5/1**[3]

1165 **5** *16* **Wembury Point (IRE)**[20] [2178] 3-11-3 115....................(b) JohnLevins[(5)] 60
(B G Powell) *chsd ldr to 3rd: rdn next: wknd 3 out* **9/1**

PF **P** **Rathcannon Beauty**[12] [2373] 3-10-0 .... MarcGoldstein[(7)] —
(Mrs L P Baker) *a bhd: t.o whn p.u after 3 out* **66/1**

22P **P** **Double Spectre (IRE)**[7] [2481] 3-11-0 .... AndrewTinkler —
(Jean-Rene Auvray) *led tl hdd 4 out: blnd next and wknd: t.o whn p.u bef last* **20/1**

4 **P** **Desert Secrets (IRE)**[13] [2345] 3-10-7 .... GrahamLee —
(J G Portman) *hld up in rr: brief effrt after 4 out: wknd qckly after next and p.u bef 2 out* **14/1**

4m 19.6s (10.70) **Going Correction** +0.70s/f (Soft) **8** Ran SP% **110.5**
Speed ratings: **102,92,89,82,75** —,—,— CSF £5.71 TOTE £2.20: £1.10, £1.40, £3.40; EX 5.40.

Owner Terry Warner **Bred** P Bonnaudet And Daniel Bonnaudet **Trained** Ditcheat, Somerset

FOCUS
A real stamina test for three-year-olds, which saw the field finish strung out behind the easy winner, and the form looks straightforward.

NOTEBOOK
Spidam(FR), third on his recent British debut on good ground at Wincanton, relished the switch to this more testing surface and ultimately outclassed his rivals to score easily. The stiffer track was much in his favour and, considering he still looked in need of the experience, he can be expected to improve again a deal for this outing. He is very much a future chaser, and will not be too highly tried this term over timber, but still could bag a decent prize in this division when the ground is genuinely soft. *(op 7-4 tchd 5-4)*

Kanpai(IRE) again managed to find one too good, but would have been a touch closer to the winner but for an error three out, and was himself clear of the rest in second. This was another fair effort and he should find a race in due course. He now becomes eligible for handicaps. *(op 11-4 tchd 10-3)*

Cave Of The Giant(IRE) was not given too hard a time on ground that looked plenty soft enough for him and still improved a touch on his recent debut third at Plumpton. He should fare better when qualifying for handicaps. *(op 20-1)*

Ameeq(USA), a fair maiden on the Flat and rated 79 in that sphere, showed up well enough until tiring markedly on ground that would have most likely been against him. He has joined the right stable to win races in this sphere and should prove a different proposition when racing on a faster surface. *(tchd 6-1)*

Wembury Point(IRE), rated 115 and who set the standard on his previous efforts over timber, was *another who looked to hate this ground and is capable of better.Official explanation: jockey said gelding was unsuited by the heavy (soft in places) ground*

Double Spectre(IRE) *Official explanation: jockey said gelding was unsuited by the heavy (soft in places) ground (op 22-1)*

2613 WILLIAMHILLCASINO.COM NOVICES' H'CAP CHASE (17 fncs) 2m 4f 110y
1:30 (1:32) (Class 3) (0-120,108) 4-Y-0+ **£6,782** (£1,991; £995; £497)

Form RPR

00-1 **1** **Harris Bay**[29] [2011] 6-11-6 **102**.......................................(t) TimmyMurphy 116+
(Miss H C Knight) *hld up rr but in tch: hdwy 10th: trckd ldr next: chal 3 out: led next: stdd and j. slowly last: comf* **9/4**[1]

-U1F **2** *3* **Supreme Tadgh (IRE)**[14] [2313] 8-11-2 **105**.................... SimonElliott[(7)] 112
(J A Geake) *rr but in tch: pushed along and hdwy to chse ldrs 4 out: styd on to chse wnr appr last but no imp* **8/1**

00-1 **3** *19* **King Coal (IRE)**[14] [2313] 6-11-12 **108**............................... BrianCrowley 100+
(R Rowe) *lw: stdd s: blnd 1st: led next and t.k.h early: rdn 3 out: hdd next: wknd and blnd last* **5/2**[2]

-1P4 **4** *1 ½* **Mandica (IRE)**[30] [1983] 7-11-3 **99**................................. RobertThornton 90+
(T R George) *chsd ldrs: hit 9th: blnd 4 out: wknd next* **3/1**[3]

P6-2 **P** **River Trapper (IRE)**[22] [2149] 6-11-7 **103**........................... SamThomas —
(Miss H C Knight) *led tl hdd and hit 2nd: hit 7th: wknd 4 out: p.u bef 2 out* **11/2**

5m 34.1s (13.30) **Going Correction** +0.575s/f (Soft) **5** Ran SP% **110.8**
Speed ratings: **97,95,88,88,**— CSF £17.76 TOTE £2.80: £1.60, £3.10; EX 22.90.

Owner Mrs G M Sturges & H Stephen Smith **Bred** R J Spencer **Trained** West Lockinge, Oxon

FOCUS
A fair handicap which saw the first two come clear. It was modest winning time for the grade.

NOTEBOOK
Harris Bay, off the mark on his seasonal and chasing debut at Towcester, followed up with a gritty success off a 14lb higher mark and was well on top at the finish. He is clearly an improving horse, enjoys testing ground, and does jump well, so could still be ahead of the Handicapper after another rise in the weights. *(tchd 2-1)*

Supreme Tadgh(IRE) turned in a solid performance and was only found wanting from two out. This will have restored his confidence and, while he handles some cut, he is probably more at home on quicker ground. He helps set the standard for this form. *(op 7-1)*

King Coal(IRE) failed to build on his decisive success at Exeter last time and did not look happy on this deep surface. He is a huge individual and still looks in need of more experience, so should not be written off on the back of this display. *(op 9-4 tchd 11-4 and 3-1 in a place)*

Mandica(IRE), very well backed on course, never really threatened to take advantage of his recent drop in the weights and made two crucial mistakes. He is hard to predict. *(op 11-2)*

River Trapper(IRE), runner-up to Supreme Tadgh on his chase debut last time, simply hated this much softer ground and ran a tame race. *(op 4-1)*

2614 WILLIAM HILL WINTER NOVICES' HURDLE GRADE 2 (9 hdls) 2m 4f 110y
2:05 (2:05) (Class 1) 4-Y-0+ £16,464 (£6,487; £3,497)

Form RPR
14 1 **Neptune Collonges (FR)**[19] [2206] 4-11-0 BJGeraghty 145+
(P F Nicholls) *trckd ldr: led 4th: c wl clr bef 2 out: easily* **6/4**[1]
23 2 dist **Massini's Maguire (IRE)**[19] [2206] 4-11-0 RichardJohnson 105
(P J Hobbs) *in tch: hdwy to chse wnr 5th: nt fluent 3 out: wknd bef 2 out: t.o* **3/1**[3]
4-23 3 16 **No Guarantees**[15] [2295] 5-11-0 CarlLlewellyn 80
(N A Twiston-Davies) *led tl hdd and hit 4th: wknd and blnd 6th: lft distant 3rd out* **25/1**
1 P **Percussionist (IRE)**[8] [2447] 4-11-0 GrahamLee —
(J Howard Johnson) *in tch: wnt 3rd 6th: rdn and effrt after 3 out: sn no imp and wknd: poor 3rd whn p.u 2 out* **13/8**[2]

5m 19.0s (5.60) **Going Correction** +0.70s/f (Soft) 4 Ran SP% **106.9**
Speed ratings: **117,—,—,—** CSF £6.14 TOTE £2.60; EX 6.10.
Owner J Hales **Bred** Gaec Delorme Freres **Trained** Ditcheat, Somerset

FOCUS
A decent, if select, renewal of this Grade Two novice event, and the winner simply outclassed his rivals in the testing ground. It was a very respectable winning time for a race of its grade in the conditions.

NOTEBOOK
Neptune Collonges(FR) ◆ showed his true colours, relishing the return to a deep surface, and galloped his rivals into submission with a dour performance. He is clearly a smart performer, had little trouble in reversing Cheltenham form with the runner-up on this more testing ground, and will be high on confidence again now. While he is without doubt near the top of the tree in the staying novice division, he is not nearly so effective on quicker ground, so his chance of Grade One honours this term will be determined by the weather. In the longer term, he really does look a very exciting chase prospect. *(op 7-4 tchd 15-8)*
Massini's Maguire(IRE), in front of the winner at Cheltenham last time, was firmly put in his place after an error three out and failed to confirm the form on this much softer ground. He may prove better on quicker ground and is worth another chance to prove his worth at this level. *(op 5-2)*
No Guarantees was never a factor in this better class and jumped poorly throughout. His future lies with the Handicapper. *(op 33-1)*
Percussionist(IRE) drifted in the betting ahead of this step-up in class and turned in a most disappointing effort. He had not been so impressive when scoring against weak opposition at Carlisle last time, and while he could have found this coming a touch too soon, this effort leaves *him with it all to prove over hurdles now and he does look to have his share of temperament. Official explanation: jockey said gelding had a breathing problem (op 11-8)*

2615 JOHN SMITH'S FUTURE STARS CHASE (INTERMEDIATE RACE) (22 fncs) 3m 110y
2:35 (2:38) (Class 2) 5-Y-0+ £16,410 (£4,889; £2,475; £1,269; £663)

Form RPR
4-16 1 **Lacdoudal (FR)**[20] [2177] 6-11-4 143 RichardJohnson 153+
(P J Hobbs) *trckd ldrs: led 5th: shkn up 2 out: kpt on strly run-in* **3/1**[3]
1-20 2 6 **My Will (FR)**[20] [2177] 5-11-10 148 BJGeraghty 154+
(P F Nicholls) *lw: trckd wnr fr 6th: blnd 17th: hit 18th: rdn 3 out: lost 2nd 2 out: styd on again to chse wnr nr fin: but no ch* **11/4**[2]
21-P 3 ¾ **El Vaquero (IRE)**[13] [2346] 7-11-10 149 GrahamLee 154+
(J Howard Johnson) *hld up but in tch: hdwy 12th: chsd ldrs 14th: mstke 16th: wnt 2nd 2 out: effrt and mstke last sn btn: lost 2nd cl home* **8/1**
3P-1 4 18 **Dancer Life (POL)**[45] [1781] 6-10-8 124 PaulMoloney 121+
(Evan Williams) *a in rr* **33/1**
32-4 5 23 **See You Sometime**[31] [1970] 10-11-10 145 BarryFenton 117+
(J W Mullins) *chsd ldrs: blnd 12th: hit 16th: wknd 4 out* **9/1**
2111 P **Getoutwhenyoucan (IRE)**[21] [2162] 5-10-8 135 TimmyMurphy —
(M C Pipe) *lw: led to 5th: styd disputing 2nd: j. slowly 8th: rdn and dropped rr 16th: t.o whn p.u after 3 out* **15/8**[1]

6m 38.7s (7.20) **Going Correction** +0.575s/f (Soft) 6 Ran SP% **110.5**
Speed ratings: **111,109,108,103,95** — CSF £11.62 TOTE £4.30: £2.20, £2.00; EX 11.10.
Owner Mrs R J Skan **Bred** Scea Terres Noires **Trained** Withycombe, Somerset

FOCUS
A fair renewal of this decent chase, run at a solid pace. The winner was allowed to dictate and did not need to run to his Cheltenham Festival form, and the overall form is not too solid.

NOTEBOOK
Lacdoudal(FR), sixth on his return to chasing in the Paddy Power last time, was positively ridden on this step up in trip and ultimately ran out a convincing winner. He handled the softer ground without any fuss, again jumped neatly, and really is a most tough and consistent performer. This could be his year, and his versatility is a notable advantage, yet he will have to improve again to be able to figure in the Robin Cook Memorial at Cheltenham next week - his next intended target - as he now picks up a 6lb penalty for that. *(op 10-3 tchd 7-2)*
My Will(FR), ninth in the Paddy Power last time, enjoyed the step up to this longer trip and the return to softer ground, yet never looked a serious threat to the winner. He is a good benchmark for *this form, but is not going to be that easy to place successfully from his current rating this term. (tchd 3-1)*
El Vaquero(IRE), disappointingly pulled up on his recent debut for current connections, stepped up markedly on that effort and was only found wanting at the penultimate fence. He probably wants better ground, can improve again for the experience, and could be the type to bag a decent handicap before the season's end. However, he still has to conclusively prove he gets this trip and may just prove best back over two and a half miles. *(tchd 9-1 in a place)*
Dancer Life(POL), winner of a steadily-run affair on his chasing debut last time, looked to have a very stiff task according to official ratings, and so it proved. He needs his sights lowering and probably found this deep surface against him. *(op 25-1)*
See You Sometime, a remote fourth in the Haldon Gold Cup on his reappearance, ran well below that form and lacked fluency over his fences. He has a deal to prove now, but will be better off when reverting in distance. *(op 10-1)*
Getoutwhenyoucan(IRE), impressive when making all to land a hat-trick at the Open meeting at Cheltenham last time, looked well treated at the weights yet paid for jumping to his left throughout and his fate was sealed a long way out. This has to rate disappointing, but he may not have enjoyed this more testing ground, and could prove a different proposition when reverting to a left-handed track. It should also be noted that he is not the first of his yard's winners at the Open *Meeting to have subsequently run below expectations next time out.Official explanation: trainer had no explanation for the poor form shown (op 7-4 tchd 2-1)*

2616 CHRISTINE AND PETE HARRIS - FAMILY REMEMBERED H'CAP CHASE (22 fncs) 3m 110y
3:10 (3:11) (Class 3) (0-120,117) 5-Y-0+ £6,798 (£1,995; £997; £498)

Form RPR
-U33 1 **Latimer's Place**[16] [2272] 9-11-7 117 PaulO'Neill(5) 136+
(J A Geake) *hld up rr but in tch: hdwy 13th: chsd ldr 4 out: led next: c clr fr 2 out: comf* **10/3**[2]
11-P 2 10 **Gray's Eulogy**[24] [2104] 7-10-5 96 (b) TomDoyle 103
(D R Gandolfo) *in tch: hdwy and hit 12th: disp 2nd fr 18th: chsd wnr fr 2 out but no ch* **5/1**
1P-2 3 11 **Durlston Bay**[27] [2048] 8-11-3 108 MickFitzgerald 109+
(S Dow) *led 3rd: mitake 5th (water): hdd appr 12th: led again 14th: hit 7th: hdd 3 out: wknd next: no ch whn blnd last* **5/1**
2P-2 4 28 **Rudolf Rassendyll (IRE)**[14] [2325] 10-11-2 107 SamThomas 75
(Miss Venetia Williams) *lw: in tch:j. slowly 7th and 16th: sn rdn: wknd next* **3/1**[1]
0P-6 5 14 **Boy's Hurrah (IRE)**[47] [1759] 9-11-9 114 GrahamLee 68
(J Howard Johnson) *led to 3rd: chsd wnr tl led appr 12th: hdd and mstke 14th: j. slowly and wknd 18th: blnd 2 out* **4/1**[3]
0/5- 6 14 **Sea Drifting**[391] [2041] 8-10-13 104 WarrenMarston 44
(Miss M E Rowland) *b.bkwd: hit 1st and 2nd: bhd: rdn fr 9th: blnd 13th: wknd 15th* **14/1**

6m 42.4s (10.90) **Going Correction** +0.575s/f (Soft) 6 Ran SP% **108.1**
Speed ratings: **105,101,98,89,84 80** CSF £18.32 TOTE £4.30: £2.00, £2.30; EX 26.60.
Owner Sir Christopher Wates **Bred** Sir Christopher Stephen Wates **Trained** Kimpton, Hants

FOCUS
Not the most solid piece of form, and the field finished well and truly strung out, but the winner did the job easily nevertheless.

NOTEBOOK
Latimer's Place, who looked laboured when failing to justify market support at Wincanton last time, showed his true colours with a fine round of jumping and was not fully extended to score comfortably. The softer ground and stiffer track played to his strengths - it is well worth remembering that he was a convincing Grade Three winner over hurdles at this venue in 2002 - and this conclusively proves he gets three miles. A likely hike in the weights should ensure he gets *a run in the Agfa Chase over course and distance and he is fully entitled to take his chance there. (op 7-2 tchd 4-1)*
Gray's Eulogy, pulled up on his comeback in November, left that behind with a much more encouraging effort, despite never rating a threat to the winner. He likes this track and will find easier opportunities off this sort of mark in the future. *(op 7-1)*
Durlston Bay was found out by the longer trip, but would have finished closer with more fluent jumping under pressure. He looks in need of respite from the Handicapper, yet will probably be happier back over a shorter trip. *(tchd 9-2)*
Rudolf Rassendyll(IRE), second behind a progressive rival at Windsor on his seasonal return last time, ran below that form and was beaten a long way from home. It could be that he found this *coming a touch too soon, however, and he is not one to write off when dropping in trip. (op 5-2 tchd 100-30)*
Boy's Hurrah(IRE), who has a good record at the track and was the winner of this event in 2004 off a 10lb lower mark, faded tamely when push came to shove and disappointed. While he may not *have enjoyed this testing ground, he has now shown very little in two outings this term.Official explanation: jockey said gelding was unsuited by the soft ground (op 3-1)*

2617 FAUCETS FOR GROHE "NATIONAL HUNT" NOVICES' HURDLE (8 hdls) 2m 110y
3:40 (3:42) (Class 3) 4-Y-0+ £5,660 (£1,661; £830; £414)

Form RPR
31-1 1 **Its A Dream (IRE)**[220] [44] 5-11-0 MickFitzgerald 127+
(N J Henderson) *chsd ldrs: rdn to chal 2 out: sn led: clr and kpt on strly last* **11/8**[1]
2 15 **Pablo Du Charmil (FR)**[41] 4-11-8 RJGreene 120
(M C Pipe) *tall: leggy: trckd ldr: chal fr 3rd tl slt ld 3 out: rdn and hdd sn after 2 out: no ch w wnr after but clr 2nd* **7/4**[2]
0-06 3 dist **Laharna**[15] [2301] 5-11-0 BarryFenton 78
(Miss E C Lavelle) *bhd: hdwy fr 3 out: effrt appr next: n.d and sn wknd: t.o* **16/1**
4 2 **Nice Try (IRE)**[551] 6-11-0 SamThomas 76
(Miss Venetia Williams) *str: mid-div: j. slowly 4th: brief effrt after 3 out: sn wknd: t.o* **25/1**
46-0 5 4 **Reach For The Top (IRE)**[19] [2211] 4-11-0 TimmyMurphy 72
(Miss H C Knight) *bhd: hdwy and no fluent 3 out: nvr rchd ldrs and wknd bef 2 out: t.o* **8/1**[3]
-P52 6 dist **Billyandi (IRE)**[22] [2142] 5-11-0 CarlLlewellyn —
(N A Twiston-Davies) *led tl narrowly hdd 3 out: wknd qckly: t.o* **8/1**[3]
31 P **Schumann**[34] [1922] 4-11-0 AndrewTinkler —
(M Pitman) *a behund: t.o whn p.u bef 2 out* **16/1**

4m 18.5s (9.60) **Going Correction** +0.70s/f (Soft) 7 Ran SP% **116.3**
Speed ratings: **105,97,—,—,— —,—** CSF £4.34 TOTE £2.60: £1.40, £1.90; EX 4.60 Place 6 £46.76, Place 5 £33.16.
Owner Mrs R Murdoch & David Murdoch **Bred** Mrs Esther Power **Trained** Upper Lambourn, Berks

FOCUS
A decent novice event, run at a fair gallop, and the field came home well strung out in the testing ground. The winner is an exciting prospect and joins the list of top-class novices to have landed this race in recent years.

NOTEBOOK
Its A Dream(IRE) ◆, a smart bumper performer last season, got his hurdling career off to a perfect start with an authorititive success and looked better the further he went. He clearly enjoyed the deep surface and jumped fluently throughout. He can be rated value for further as he looked to idle up the run-in, and he is likely to prove even better when faced with a stiffer test. He is entitled to *come on for the outing, so it will be fascinating to see where connections pitch him in next. (op 5-4 tchd 13-8)*
Pablo Du Charmil(FR) ◆, previously unbeaten over hurdles in two outings at Auteuil in October and making his debut for Martin Pipe, hit the front full of running three from home, yet his stride started to shorten up the hill and he was eventually readily brushed aside by the winner. This was a still a decent performance under his double penalty and he has time on his side. He will not mind the return to further and could be very useful. *(op 5-2 tchd 13-8)*
Laharna plugged on at the same pace up the straight and never figured. He will be much better off in novice handicaps. *(op 14-1)*
Nice Try(IRE), last seen landing a point on good to firm in May 2004, ran as though the race was much needed and probably found this ground against him. As a half-brother to the smart Irish Chaser Jack High - winner of the Betfred Gold Cup last term - he can be expected to do much better in time.
Reach For The Top(IRE) failed to pick up from off the pace on this hurdling bow and proved *disappointing. He is well thought of by his connections, yet still looks far from the finished article. (tchd 7-1)*
Billyandi(IRE) faded tamely when push came to shove and failed to improve for the return to soft ground. He needs his sights lowered.
Schumann, last seen winning a Polytrack bumper, was found out by the testing ground on this *hurdling debut. Official explanation: jockey said gelding was unsuited by the heavy (soft in places) ground (op 10-1)*

T/Plt: £80.70 to a £1 stake. Pool: £61,799.90. 558.55 winning tickets. T/Qpdt: £25.40 to a £1 stake. Pool: £3,903.40. 113.60 winning tickets. ST

2426

CHEPSTOW (L-H)

Saturday, December 3

OFFICIAL GOING: Heavy

The ground was very testing after recent heavy rain and the third last hurdle was omitted.

Wind: Light, across Weather: Fine

2618 TOTESPORTCASINO.COM MAIDEN HURDLE (DIV I) (7 hdls 1 omitted) 2m 110y

12:35 (12:36) (Class 4) 4-Y-0+ **£3,155** (£926; £463; £231)

Form RPR

02-3 **1** **Coach Lane**[27] 2081 4-10-11 107 .... PaulO'Neill(5) 95+
(Miss Venetia Williams) *hld up: hdwy and wnt 2nd after 4th: rdn and* **chalng whn pckd 3 out: no ch w clr ldr whn lft 2nd last: r.o under pressur** **3/1**[2]

2 *½* **Noble Bily (FR)**[28] 4-11-2 .... TomScudamore 94+
(M C Pipe) *sn chsng clr ldr: led after 4th: rdn and hdd after 3 out: no ch w clr ldr whn lft in ld last: hdd nr fin* **7/1**[3]

PP-U **3** *7* **Presenter (IRE)**[9] 2460 5-10-9 .... MrLRPayter(7) 86
(M Sheppard) *bhd: pckd 3rd: styd on fr 2 out: nvr nrr* **100/1**

4 *16* **Nudge And Nurdle (IRE)** 4-10-9 .... BernieWharfe(7) 70
(N A Twiston-Davies) *hld up: hdwy after 4th: sn rdn: wknd appr 3 out* **25/1**

000 **5** *19* **Gunship (IRE)**[7] 2487 4-10-11 .... RobertStephens(5) 51
(P J Hobbs) *a bhd* **33/1**

0610 **6** *28* **Surfboard (IRE)**[10] 2426 4-11-2 .... LeightonAspell 23
(P A Blockley) *led: hdd and mstke 1st: wknd after 4th: t.o* **8/1**

P **Pure Magic (FR)**[168] 4-11-2 .... JamesDavies —
(Miss J S Davis) *a bhd: t.o whn p.u bef 3 out* **66/1**

00P- **P** **Kingtobee (IRE)**[249] 4640 7-11-2 .... MarkBradburne —
(J A B Old) *a bhd: t.o whn p.u bef 3 out* **33/1**

P **P** **A One (IRE)**[11] 2421 6-10-9 .... MrJAJenkins(7) —
(H J Manners) *plld hrd: led 1st: sn clr: hdd after 4th: sn wknd: t.o whn p.u bef last* **66/1**

255- **P** **Baranook (IRE)**[225] 4958 4-11-2 104 .... OllieMcPhail —
(B J Llewellyn) *mid-div: rdn after 3rd: sn struggling: t.o whn p.u bef 3 out* **8/1**

F **Blu Teen (FR)**[401] 5-11-2 .... JoeTizzard 115+
(P F Nicholls) *hld up: hdwy after 4th: led on bit after 3 out: 12 l clr and stl gng wl whn fell last* **6/4**[1]

4m 28.7s (18.30) **Going Correction** +1.075s/f (Soft) **11 Ran SP% 113.4**
Speed ratings: **99,98,95,87,79 65,—,—,—,— —** CSF £21.83 TOTE £4.00: £1.10, £1.90, £18.20; EX 19.20.
Owner B Moore & E C Stephens **Bred** Juddmonte Farms **Trained** Kings Caple, H'fords

FOCUS

A modest maiden hurdle in which Blu Teen, who fell at the last, has been rated value for a 20-length success.

NOTEBOOK

Coach Lane just managed to get the better of the runner-up in a driving finish, but he has to be considered a very fortunate winner after Blu Teen fell at the last. *(op 10-3 tchd 7-2 and 11-4)*

Noble Bily(FR) has shaped like a stayer in two outings over hurdles on this sort of ground at Auteuil. He could not quite make best use of a golden opportunity after the favourite departed at the final flight. *(op 5-1)*

Presenter(IRE), third in banded company over a mile at Leicester in May, was unproven over further but did stay on in the testing ground.

Kingtobee(IRE) *Official explanation: jockey said gelding had a breathing problem*

Blu Teen(FR) ◆ sustained a minor injury after finishing a promising second in the heavy at Auteuil just over a year ago. All set for an impressive victory when getting the final flight all wrong, he can be considered a winner without a penalty.

Pure Magic(FR) *Official explanation: jockey said gelding was unsuited by the heavy ground*

2619 TOTEPLACEPOT NOVICES' HURDLE (9 hdls 2 omitted) 2m 4f

1:05 (1:07) (Class 4) 4-Y-0+ **£3,662** (£1,075; £537; £268)

Form RPR

3B-4 **1** **In Accord**[36] 1903 6-10-12 110 .... MarkBradburne 115+
(H D Daly) *hld up in tch: led on bit after 3 out: clr last: pushed out* **5/2**[2]

0 **2** *9* **Nagam (FR)**[16] 2295 4-10-12 .... LeightonAspell 102+
(A Ennis) *hld up in mid-div: hdwy 4th: led 6th: rdn and hdd after 3 out: one pce fr 2 out* **20/1**

61-F **3** *11* **Almost Broke**[13] 2368 8-10-12 .... JoeTizzard 90+
(P F Nicholls) *plld hrd early towards rr: hdwy 5th: rdn appr 2 out: wknd appr last* **2/1**[1]

/23- **4** *6* **Le Rochelais (FR)**[373] 2453 6-10-12 .... RobertWalford 84
(R H Alner) *chsd ldrs tl wknd 2 out* **9/2**[3]

5 **5** *11* **Wee Anthony (IRE)**[10] 2432 6-10-12 .... NoelFehily 73
(Jonjo O'Neill) *hld up towards rr: hdwy after 6th: wknd 3 out* **16/1**

302- **6** *2* **Kings Rock**[252] 4557 4-10-2 100 .... AngharadFrieze(10) 71
(P A Blockley) *bhd fr 4th* **33/1**

00 **7** *2* **Sidcup's Gold (IRE)**[20] 2206 5-10-12 .... PaulMoloney 69
(M Sheppard) *hld up in mid-div: hdwy after 6th: wknd 3 out* **66/1**

042- **8** *3½* **Durante (IRE)**[289] 3904 7-10-7 100 .... PaulO'Neill(5) 66
(J A B Old) *hld up and bhd: hdwy on outside after 6th: wknd 3 out* **6/1**

06 **9** *25* **Ol' Man River (IRE)**[19] 2249 5-10-12 .... JimmyMcCarthy 41
(H D Daly) *hld up in mid-div: rdn 5th: hdwy 6th: wknd 3 out* **50/1**

0/P0 **10** *dist* **Battling Buster (IRE)**[16] 2301 8-10-2 .... PaulDavey(10) —
(R H Buckler) *led tl appr 4th: wknd qckly: t.o fr 6th* **100/1**

0 **P** **Zilla (FR)**[23] 2148 4-10-5 .... DaveCrosse —
(Miss Lucy Bridges) *plld hrd early: a bhd: rdn after 5th: t.o whn p.u bef 2 out* **100/1**

PF/P **P** **Breuddwyd Lyn**[14] 2343 7-10-7 .... LeeStephens(5) —
(Mrs D A Hamer) *chsd ldr: led appr 4th to 6th: wknd qckly 3 out: p.u bef 2 out* **100/1**

-564 **P** **Redlynch Spirit (IRE)**[10] 2427 5-10-12 .... TomScudamore —
(C L Tizzard) *hld up in mid-div: short-lived effrt 6th: t.o whn p.u bef 2 out* **66/1**

5m 20.4s (17.70) **Going Correction** +1.075s/f (Soft)
WFA 4 from 5yo+ 11lb **13 Ran SP% 115.9**
Speed ratings: **107,103,99,96,92 91,90,89,79,— —,—,—** CSF £50.48 TOTE £3.70: £1.40, £2.80, £1.70; EX 47.70.
Owner T F F Nixon **Bred** T F F Nixon **Trained** Stanton Lacy, Shropshire

FOCUS

Few could be fancied here and the bookmakers went 16-1 bar four. The easy winner has been rated value for 15 lengths.

NOTEBOOK

In Accord was already proven in this ground over further and turned out to be far too good for some modest opposition. *(op 9-4)*

Nagam(FR) stepped up on his recent hurdling debut on this softer surface but proved no match for the winner. *(op 14-1)*

Almost Broke was reverting to hurdles after his fall over the Grand National fences. He may have paid the price for refusing to settle early on. *(tchd 7-4)*

Le Rochelais(FR) may have have blown up following a year on the sidelines with a leg problem. *(op 7-1)*

Wee Anthony(IRE), who shaped quite promisingly in a bumper here last month, could only manage a short-lived effort in these more testing conditions.

2620 TOTEPOOL AWAYBET BEGINNERS' CHASE (12 fncs) 2m 110y

1:35 (1:38) (Class 3) 4-Y-0+ **£5,686** (£1,669; £834; £416)

Form RPR

32 **1** **Le Volfoni (FR)**[11] 2422 4-10-7 .... JoeTizzard 127+
(P F Nicholls) *chsd ldrs: wnt 2nd 6th: led after 7th: clr appr last: comf* **10/11**[1]

12-F **2** *6* **Steppes Of Gold (IRE)**[49] 1736 8-11-4 .... NoelFehily 132
(Jonjo O'Neill) *hld up and bhd: hdwy 7th: hung lft fr 5 out: wnt 2nd appr last: no ch w wnr* **5/1**[3]

6-54 **3** *9* **Give Me Love (FR)**[35] 1919 5-10-11 .... (t) LiamHeard(7) 124+
(P F Nicholls) *hld up in tch: ev ch 3 out: sn rdn: wknd last* **3/1**[2]

4 *dist* **Beaufort County (IRE)**[282] 4037 8-11-4 120 .... PaulMoloney —
(Evan Williams) *hld up and bhd: hdwy appr 5 out: wknd appr 4 out: 4th and no ch whn j.rt 2 out* **12/1**

35-P **5** *2½* **Greenawn (IRE)**[33] 1957 6-11-4 .... SamStronge —
(M Sheppard) *chsd ldr: led 3rd tl after 7th: wknd appr 5 out* **28/1**

P/0- **6** *13* **Goldseam (GER)**[415] 1709 6-11-4 .... MarkBradburne —
(S C Burrough) *led to 3rd: wknd appr 5 out* **50/1**

2-PP **7** *2* **Shannon Quest (IRE)**[31] 1981 9-10-11 82 .... (bt) CharlieStudd(7) —
(C L Popham) *a bhd* **66/1**

/060 **F** **Only For Gold**[20] 2208 10-10-11 69 .... JohnPritchard(7) —
(Dr P Pritchard) *a bhd: blnd 2nd: no ch whn fell 3 out* **150/1**

4m 26.2s (3.30) **Going Correction** +0.325s/f (Yiel)
WFA 4 from 5yo+ 10lb **8 Ran SP% 109.3**
Speed ratings: **105,102,97,—,— —,—,—** CSF £5.43 TOTE £1.90: £1.10, £1.10, £1.30; EX 5.80.
Owner Million In Mind Partnership **Bred** I Plessis And Bertrand Plessis **Trained** Ditcheat, Somerset

FOCUS

Good novice form and the race should work out. The first three in the betting had the race to themselves early in the long home straight.

NOTEBOOK

Le Volfoni(FR), twice a winner over hurdles on this sort of ground in France, relished the testing *conditions. He should be suited by another half a mile and is now likely to be kept to soft ground. (op 5-6 tchd evens in places)*

Steppes Of Gold(IRE) again showed a definite tendency to hang left, which he had done prior to falling at Huntingdon. *(tchd 9-2)*

Give Me Love(FR) was by no means disgraced on this switch to fences and looked more of a threat to his stable companion than the runner-up until he eventually got tired. *(tchd 7-2)*

2621 TOTESPORT 0800 221 221 H'CAP HURDLE (12 hdls) 3m

2:10 (2:11) (Class 3) (0-125,122) 4-Y-0+

£4,960 (£1,465; £732; £366; £182; £91)

Form RPR

4342 **1** **The Gangerman (IRE)**[15] 2310 5-9-7 96 .... StevenCrawford(7) 106+
(N A Twiston-Davies) *chsd ldr: rdn to ld 2 out: drvn out* **5/1**[2]

0404 **2** *2* **Just Beth**[13] 2369 9-10-10 111 .... DerekLaverty(5) 116
(G Fierro) *a.p: rdn after 3 out: ev ch appr last: nt qckn flat* **7/1**

0124 **3** *12* **Mouseski**[22] 2166 11-11-3 120 .... LiamHeard(7) 113
(P F Nicholls) *hld up in tch: rdn after 3 out: wkng whn hung lft appr last* **9/2**[1]

PP-2 **4** *2* **Amber Starlight**[24] 2125 7-10-7 103 ow4 .... BrianCrowley 98+
(R Rowe) *led: rdn and hdd whn hit 2 out: 3rd and wkng whn blnd last* **13/2**[3]

-334 **5** *10* **The Flyer (IRE)**[21] 2184 8-11-0 110 .... (t) JimmyMcCarthy 91
(Miss S J Wilton) *hld up in tch: wknd after 7th* **25/1**

51-2 **6** *23* **Jaloux D'Estruval (FR)**[24] 2130 8-11-5 115 .... MarkBradburne 73
(Mrs L C Taylor) *racd wd: hld up: hdwy appr 5th: wknd appr 3 out* **9/2**[1]

40-4 **7** *3½* **Shamawan (IRE)**[10] 2430 10-11-0 110 .... NoelFehily 65
(Jonjo O'Neill) *hld up and bhd: hdwy 7th: wknd 3 out* **9/2**[1]

04-F **8** *2* **Visibility (FR)**[15] 2312 6-11-5 122 .... (p) MrCHughes(7) 75
(M C Pipe) *a bhd* **50/1**

0-PP **9** *23* **Saint Par (FR)**[178] 689 7-11-2 117 .... RobertStephens(5) 47
(Tim Vaughan) *hld up in mid-div: hit and lost pl 4th: bhd fr 5th: t.o* **66/1**

36-P **10** *18* **Marrel**[14] 2334 7-11-0 117 .... MrRMcCarthy(7) 29
(D Burchell) *bhd fr 7th: t.o whn p.u bef 3 out* **50/1**

3060 **P** **Nick's Choice**[14] 2334 9-11-3 113 .... JoeTizzard —
(D Burchell) *a bhd: t.o whn p.u bef 3 out* **16/1**

3/F- **P** **Perfect Liaison**[410] 1772 8-11-10 120 .... RobertWalford —
(R H Alner) *hld up towards rr: hdwy 6th: wknd appr 3 out: t.o whn p.u bef last* **20/1**

6m 41.6s (24.80) **Going Correction** +1.175s/f (Heav) **2 Ran SP% 116.9**
Speed ratings: **105,104,100,99,96 88,87,86,79,73 —,—** CSF £37.50 CT £169.82 TOTE £5.30: £1.70, £2.50, £2.20; EX 56.70.
Owner Agetur (UK) Ltd **Bred** Jack Deacon **Trained** Naunton, Gloucs

FOCUS

This did not prove to be as competitive as expected with the testing conditions taking their toll. The race has been rated around the runner-up.

NOTEBOOK

The Gangerman(IRE) had shaped like a real stayer when runner-up over slightly shorter on better ground at Exeter last time. This slog in the mud suited him well. *(op 11-2 tchd 6-1 in a place)*

Just Beth is an out-and-out stayer but the weight concession to the winner proved too much. *(op 10-1 tchd 11-1)*

Mouseski fell at the first in a hunter chase on his only previous attempt at this trip. He may well have hung left simply through exhaustion. *(op 11-2)*

Amber Starlight was a shade disappointing after her second at Lingfield and it could be that she is best when fresh. *(op 5-1)*

Nick's Choice *Official explanation: trainer said gelding was found to have burst a blood vessel (op 20-1)*

2622 TOTESPORT.COM H'CAP CHASE (16 fncs) 2m 3f 110y

2:45 (2:46) (Class 3) (0-130,130) 5-Y-0+ **£7,861** (£2,397; £1,252; £680)

Form RPR

415- **1** **Noisetine (FR)**[232] 4848 7-11-7 130 .... PaulO'Neill(5) 140+
(Miss Venetia Williams) *mde virtually all: clr 2 out: r.o wl* **10/1**

2-P3 **2** *5* **Wrags To Riches (IRE)**[15] 2310 8-11-4 **127** ChrisHonour(5) 130
(J D Frost) *hld up: hdwy appr 6th: disp ld 7th to 9th: rdn appr 4 out: chsd wnr fr 3 out: no imp fr 2 out* **12/1**
444/ **3** *7* **No Visibility (IRE)**[625] 4426 10-11-0 **118** RobertWalford 114
(R H Alner) *hld up: hit 10th: sme hdwy whn nt fluent 5 out: styd on to take 3rd sn after last* **9/1**
1-31 **4** *9* **Serpentine Rock**[15] 2312 5-11-2 **125** RobertStephens(5) 115+
(P J Hobbs) *prom: jnd wnr 10th: rdn appr 3 out: wknd appr 2 out: fin tired* **11/4**[1]
P **Lulumar (FR)**[172] 6-11-12 **130** LeightonAspell —
(O Sherwood) *hld up in tch: wknd after 11th: t.o whn p.u bef 5 out* **15/2**
24-2 **P** **Jacks Craic (IRE)**[15] 2312 6-10-13 **117** TomScudamore —
(J L Spearing) *plld hrd: prom tl wknd 5 out: bhd whn p.u bef 2 out* **3/1**[2]
1411 **P** **Dangerousdanmagru (IRE)**[21] 2183 9-11-2 **127** LiamHeard(7) —
(A E Jones) *hld up in rr: short-lived effrt after 11th: bhd whn p.u bef 2 out* **4/1**[3]

5m 28.5s (17.20) **Going Correction** +1.05s/f (Soft) **7** Ran SP% **110.2**
Speed ratings: **107,105,102,98,— —,—** CSF £99.28 TOTE £10.90: £3.20, £4.90; EX 77.00.
Owner Mrs Jean F P Yeomans **Bred** Hubert Le Baron And Dominique Le Baron **Trained** Kings Caple, H'fords

FOCUS
The three in-form horses who headed the market all disappointed, but the winner looks progressive nevertheless.

NOTEBOOK
Noisetine(FR) put up a fine performance on her return from a six-month absence. She jumped well in the muddy ground according to her rider, who also added that she kept pulling out more when asked. *(op 9-1)*
Wrags To Riches(IRE), reverting to fences, had to be content to play second fiddle from the second last.
No Visibility(IRE) had been off the course since finishing fourth in the 2004 Grand Annual at the Cheltenham Festival. Racing off an 11lb lower mark, ground conditions were in his favour but he has never scored beyond an extended two miles. He looks well handicapped and the signs are that he has retained some ability. *(tchd 10-1)*
Serpentine Rock, raised 8lb, would not have minded the ground but appeared to get found out by the slightly longer trip. *(op 3-1)*
Dangerousdanmagru(IRE) had gone up another 10lb but he should not have been that inconvenienced by the longer trip and ran a stinker. *(op 9-2)*

2623 TOTEEXACTA H'CAP CHASE (18 fncs) 3m
3:15 (3:16) (Class 4) (0-110,110) 5-Y-0+ **£4,157** (£1,220; £610; £304)

Form RPR
P1P- **1** **Datito (IRE)**[227] 4931 10-10-13 **97** JimmyMcCarthy 113
(R T Phillips) *hld up towards rr: hdwy 8th: wnt 2nd 5 out: rdn appr 3 out: chal 2 out: styd on to ld cl home* **33/1**
5/11 **2** *hd* **Precious Bane (IRE)**[17] 2266 7-10-6 **90** MarkBradburne 107+
(M Sheppard) *led: mstke 10th: clr 4 out: rdn after 2 out: pckd last: hdd cl home* **4/1**[1]
-P32 **3** *dist* **Notanotherdonkey (IRE)**[38] 1877 5-11-0 **98** TomScudamore —
(M Scudamore) *hld up in mid-div: hdwy after 7th: wknd appr 4 out* **9/1**
4-03 **4** *11* **Hazeljack**[20] 2215 10-10-12 **96** JamesDavies —
(A J Whiting) *prom tl wknd after 13th* **6/1**[3]
13-2 **P** **Commanche Jim (IRE)**[29] 2019 9-10-10 **94** RobertWalford —
(R H Alner) *a bhd: t.o 8th: p.u bef 12th* **11/2**[2]
P-PP **P** **All Sonsilver (FR)**[20] 2210 8-10-11 **95** (b[1]) HenryOliver —
(P Kelsall) *bhd fr 7th: t.o 9th: p.u bef 12th* **66/1**
66-4 **P** **El Hombre Del Rio (IRE)**[207] 289 8-11-12 **110** AndrewTinkler —
(V G Greenway) *a bhd: t.o 9th: p.u bef 12th* **33/1**
P-65 **P** **Lucky Leader (IRE)**[17] 2273 10-10-0 **87** RichardYoung(3) —
(N R Mitchell) *bhd: hit 4th: t.o 9th: p.u bef 12th* **20/1**
P-3P **P** **Supreme Sir (IRE)**[7] 2506 7-10-2 **86** oh7 ow2 LeightonAspell —
(P G Murphy) *prom tl wknd 13th: t.o whn p.u bef 4 out* **25/1**
10-0 **P** **Earl's Kitchen**[17] 2273 8-11-12 **110** JoeTizzard —
(C L Tizzard) *prom: lost pl 5th: mstke 6th: sn bhd: t.o whn p.u bef 9th* **12/1**
4-4F **U** **Grumpy Stumpy**[22] 2164 10-10-0 **91** BernieWharfe(7) —
(N A Twiston-Davies) *hld up in tch: lost pl appr 3rd: blnd and uns rdr 6th* **7/1**
2P-3 **P** **Mandingo Chief (IRE)**[30] 2011 6-11-1 **99** (t) PaulMoloney —
(R T Phillips) *hld up and bhd: hdwy whn mstke 8th: wknd 12th: t.o whn p.u bef 5 out* **8/1**
1-P4 **P** **Good Judgement (IRE)**[27] 2077 7-11-6 **104** NoelFehily —
(Jonjo O'Neill) *hld up in mid-div: hdwy appr 5th: nt fluent 8th: wknd appr 5 out: 5th and no ch whn p.u bef 2 out* **11/1**

6m 43.1s (28.20) **Going Correction** +1.25s/f (Heav) **13** Ran SP% **115.3**
Speed ratings: **103,102,—,—,— —,—,—,—,— —,—,—** CSF £154.71 CT £1319.77 TOTE £27.40: £5.60, £2.50, £2.00; EX 195.20.
Owner G Lansbury **Bred** Dennis Deas Andrew **Trained** Adlestrop, Gloucs

FOCUS
Only four completed in what predictably proved to be a war of attrition.

NOTEBOOK
Datito(IRE) had previously landed a Haydock bumper and a two-horse novice chase at Newcastle, both on heavy ground. He sprang a surprise on his first outing since April from a stable that had been ravaged by the virus last term. *(tchd 28-1)*
Precious Bane(IRE) could not quite complete a hat-trick having gone up a total of 19lb in a race where it was something of a case of the last man standing. *(op 3-1)*
Notanotherdonkey(IRE), who had struggled to stay this trip over hurdles on much better ground, had his stamina limitations exposed. *(tchd 8-1)*
Hazeljack did not have the same excuses as the third on the grounds of stamina or going. *(op 7-1)*
Earl's Kitchen *Official explanation: jockey said gelding never travelled (op 7-1)*
Mandingo Chief(IRE) *Official explanation: jockey said gelding got very tired at end of back straight (op 7-1)*

2624 TOTESPORTCASINO.COM MAIDEN HURDLE (DIV II) (7 hdls 1 omitted) 2m 110y
3:50 (3:51) (Class 4) 4-Y-0+ **£3,148** (£924; £462; £230)

Form RPR
40-5 **1** **Biscar Two (IRE)**[42] 1827 4-11-2 128 (b) OllieMcPhail 99+
(B J Llewellyn) *hld up towards rr: rdn and struggling 3rd: 15 l adrift whn j.lft and hmpd 3 out: hdwy whn j.lft 2 out: led last:* **3/1**[2]
4 **2** *nk* **The Luder (IRE)**[15] 2309 4-11-2 JoeTizzard 96+
(P F Nicholls) *prom: led on bit 3 out: rdn after 2 out: hdd last: rallied towards fin* **9/4**[1]
3 *1* **Count Boris**[45] 4-11-2 JimmyMcCarthy 95
(J A Geake) *bhd: reminders 2nd: hdwy appr 3 out: rdn and ev ch appr last: nt qckn flat* **14/1**
0 **4** *15* **Nero West (FR)**[15] 2309 4-11-2 DaveCrosse 80
(Miss Lucy Bridges) *bhd: mstke 4th: hdwy appr 2 out: hrd rdn and wknd appr last* **66/1**
05 **5** *3* **Chigorin**[9] 2460 4-11-2 HenryOliver 77
(Miss S J Wilton) *prom: rdn and ev ch 3 out: wknd appr last* **33/1**
6 *3* **Mr Smithers Jones**[627] 5-11-2 JodieMogford 74
(Dr P Pritchard) *t.k.h in rr: hdwy appr 3rd: rdn appr 2 out: wknd appr last* **50/1**
0 **7** *dist* **Barathea Blue**[9] 2455 4-11-2 TomScudamore —
(M C Pipe) *w ldr: rdn and wknd after 3 out: t.o* **5/1**
600/ **P** **Mount Vernon (IRE)**[919] 487 9-11-2 SeanCurran —
(P Wegmann) *a bhd: t.o whn p.u bef 3 out* **100/1**
U **Guymur (FR)**[251] 5-10-11 RobertStephens(5) —
(P J Hobbs) *hld up in tch: wkng whn mstke and uns rdr 3 out* **9/2**[3]
23P- **P** **Shernatra (IRE)**[227] 4935 6-11-2 JasonMaguire —
(J A B Old) *led to 3 out: sn wknd: bhd whn p.u bef 2 out* **15/2**
00-0 **P** **Star Galaxy (IRE)**[17] 2269 5-11-2 NoelFehily —
(Andrew Turnell) *hld up and bhd: short-lived effrt appr 3 out: bhd whn p.u bef last* **66/1**

4m 42.2s (31.80) **Going Correction** +1.95s/f (Heav) **11** Ran SP% **117.9**
Speed ratings: **103,102,102,95,93 92,—,—,—,— —** CSF £10.39 TOTE £4.20: £1.30, £1.60, £4.70; EX 12.40 Place 6 £463.35, Place 5 £134.82.
Owner Maenllwyd Racing Club **Bred** Michael O'Dwyer **Trained** Fochriw, Caerphilly

FOCUS
This was significantly slower than the first division after the runners stood still at the start for five seconds.

NOTEBOOK
Biscar Two(IRE) had some useful juvenile form to his name and had stayed on strongly when second in the Finale Hurdle here on similar ground. This quirky individual appeared to draw stumps on the short run-in after coming from what appeared to be a pretty hopeless position. *(tchd 10-3)*
The Luder(IRE) looked set to score when leading early in the home straight and, with the winner idling, nearly pulled it out of the fire. He should do better when tackling further. *(tchd 5-2 in a place)*
Count Boris ◆ won an extended mile and a quarter handicap on good to soft at Warwick in March. *Making a highly satisfactory debut over hurdles, he seems capable of taking a similar event. (op 10-1 tchd 16-1)*
Nero West(FR), who showed some ability on the Flat in France, improved on his debut at Exeter where he finished no less than 36 lengths behind The Luder. *(op 50-1)*
Chigorin, who won an extended ten furlong Haydock seller for James Eustace in September, ran *better than in his two outings at Uttoxeter. A sounder surface should help him get the trip. (tchd 40-1)*
Mr Smithers Jones showed signs of ability having won a Fibresand maiden over 14 furlongs at the beginning of 2004 and had been off the course since March that year. *(tchd 66-1)*
Shernatra(IRE) *Official explanation: jockey said gelding lost its action (op 7-1 tchd 13-2 and 8-1)*
T/Plt: £228.80 to a £1 stake. Pool: £48,444.60. 154.50 winning tickets. T/Qpdt: £56.20 to a £1 stake. Pool: £3,403.60. 44.80 winning tickets. KH

2334 HAYDOCK (L-H)
Saturday, December 3

OFFICIAL GOING: Soft (good to soft in places)
Wind: Virtually nil Weather: Showers

2625 GARSTANG CONDITIONAL JOCKEYS' H'CAP HURDLE (8 hdls) 2m
12:20 (12:20) (Class 4) (0-110,103) 4-Y-0+ **£3,477** (£1,013; £506)

Form RPR
-633 **1** **Sunisa (IRE)**[11] 2412 4-11-1 **92** (t) WilliamKennedy 96+
(J Mackie) *hld up: hdwy after 4 out: led appr last: all out* **6/1**[3]
P420 **2** *2* **Time To Roam (IRE)**[34] 1940 5-10-13 **98** (b) NeilWalker(8) 98
(Miss Lucinda V Russell) *t.k.h: led 1st: hdd 4th: rdn and outpcd appr 3 out: styd on to take 2nd run-in: nt rch wnr* **8/1**
4465 **3** *8* **Calomeria**[15] 2314 4-11-9 **103** (b) StephenCraine(3) 95
(D McCain) *led to 1st: remained in tch: chsd ldr appr 3 out: rdn bef next: lost 2nd run-in: wknd fnl 100 yds* **6/1**[3]
6-64 **4** *3 ½* **Dance Party (IRE)**[30] 2002 5-11-9 **100** PaddyAspell 90+
(M W Easterby) *hld up: stdy hdwy fr 4th: rdn appr 2 out: mstke last: sn wknd* **9/2**[2]
0-16 **5** *hd* **Ghadames (FR)**[19] 2247 11-11-1 **102** (p) JohnFlavin(10) 90
(R C Guest) *t.k.h: prom: led 4th: clr after 4 out: hdd appr last: sn wknd* **7/2**[1]
-F05 **6** *2 ½* **La Muette (IRE)**[16] 2283 5-9-11 **77** oh2 RichardSpate(3) 63
(M Appleby) *hld up: hdwy appr 4 out: no real imp: wknd bef 2 out* **20/1**
0000 **7** *1 ¼* **Merryvale Man**[2] 2590 8-11-0 **98** MichaelO'Connell(7) 83
(Miss Kariana Key) *handy tl rdn and wknd after 4 out* **16/1**
2450 **8** *13* **Pilca (FR)**[87] 1434 5-10-13 **96** ShaneWalsh(6) 68
(R M Stronge) *in tch: rdn after 4 out: wknd next* **8/1**
64-P **9** *12* **Tunes Of Glory (IRE)**[167] 784 9-11-9 **100** TomMalone 60
(D McCain) *midfield: lost pl 4th: bhd after* **25/1**
P **P** **Koln Stars (IRE)**[9] 2466 7-11-7 **98** LiamTreadwell —
(Jennie Candlish) *a bhd: p.u bef last* **33/1**

4m 9.20s (10.10) **Going Correction** +0.325s/f (Yiel) **10** Ran SP% **108.6**
Speed ratings: **87,86,82,80,80 78,78,71,65,—** CSF £47.42 CT £267.51 TOTE £6.50: £1.90, £1.90, £2.30; EX 53.30.
Owner G A Greaves **Bred** H De Bromhead **Trained** Church Broughton , Derbys
■ Stewards' Enquiry : William Kennedy three-day ban: used whip with excessive frequency (Dec 14-16)

FOCUS
Modest stuff and a moderate time, more than four seconds slower than the later novice event. The filly Sunisa was finally able to get off the mark over hurdles.

NOTEBOOK
Sunisa(IRE), who looked as though she was beginning to head the right way with a couple of thirds last month, proved up to the task on this handicap debut and showed a willing attitude in winning. A fair Flat performer, she looks open to further improvement over hurdles as this was only her sixth start, and it is not hard to see her winning again. *(op 5-1)*
Time To Roam(IRE), sporting yet another different piece of headgear, stayed on again after the last to claim a clear second, but the winner had already gone beyond recall. His previous efforts over two and a half miles were poor, but on this evidence he is well worth another try. *(op 7-1)*
Calomeria, wearing blinkers for the first time over hurdles, was never far off the lead and looked *Sunisa's only danger from over two out, but she tired on the run-in and had to settle for third. (tchd 11-2)*
Dance Party(IRE) never really featured and remains below the form she showed last season. She continues to edge down the weights, but remains below a winning level. *(op 11-2)*
Ghadames(FR) went into a clear lead at one stage, but he paid for it in the closing stages and dropped away. He is favourably weighted over hurdles compared to fences and a more restrained ride in future may see him winning. *(op 3-1)*
Pilca(FR) *Official explanation: jockey said gelding was unsuited by the soft ground (op 9-1)*

2626 NEWTON POLICE H'CAP CHASE (12 fncs) 2m
12:50 (12:50) (Class 3) (0-125,120)
4-Y-0+ £5,390 (£1,582; £791; £395)

Form				RPR
306P	1		Nowator (POL)[7] 2498 8-11-9 117 TonyDobbin (Robert Gray) a.p: mstke 5th: pckd 7th: led 2 out: drvn out 8/1	124
40-5	2	3	Mistral De La Cour (FR)[21] 2183 5-11-3 114 (p) PeterBuchanan(3) (R Ford) a.p: led after 4 out: hdd 2 out: one pce towards fin 10/1	118
P420	3	4	Jericho III (FR)[14] 2339 8-11-7 115 (be) AndrewThornton (R C Guest) led: hdd after 4 out: kpt on same pce fr 3 out 9/2[3]	115
P-13	4	2 ½	Cyborg De Sou (FR)[48] 1758 7-10-9 108 WilliamKennedy(5) (G A Harker) hld up: hdwy 8th: hit 2 out whn chsd ldrs: wknd fnl 150 yds 11/4[2]	106
1-63	5	dist	Imaginaire (USA)[24] 2128 10-11-2 110 SamThomas (Miss Venetia Williams) hld up: mstke 8th: sn lost tch: t.o 5/2[1]	—
56-P	P		Made In France (FR)[196] 452 5-11-9 120 TomMalone(3) (M C Pipe) hld up: j. slowly 6th: lost tch after 8th: t.o whn p.u bef 3 out 11/2	—

4m 18.0s (11.00) **Going Correction** +0.45s/f (Soft) 6 Ran SP% **109.0**
Speed ratings: **90,88,86,85,—** — CSF £67.44 TOTE £11.80: £3.30, £2.60; EX 131.00.
Owner Naughty Diesel Ltd **Bred** Sk Moszna **Trained** Malton, N Yorks

FOCUS
Not the strongest of handicaps and it turned into quite a slog for a two-mile event. The time was moderate, and Nowator simply stayed on too well for the others.

NOTEBOOK
Nowator(POL), pulled up at Newcastle the previous weekend with his rider thinking he had broken down, had tended to be kept away from soft ground in the past, but handled it better than expected and was always just doing enough once edging ahead two out. He momentarily looked vulnerable on the long run-in, but won with a little bit up his sleeve and it will be interesting to see whether he is up to defying a rise. *(op 17-2 tchd 10-1)*
Mistral De La Cour(FR), who shaped as though the run was needed when weakening on his reappearance, gave a bold show for a long way and kept on pluckily on the run-in, but was always *being held by the winner. He continues to creep down the weights and is on a fair mark at present. (op 9-1)*
Jericho III(FR), who dropped away once headed after the fourth-last, found a second wind and stayed on doggedly to claim third. He is another who continues to come down in the weights, but is not the most reliable and could never be backed with any great confidence. *(op 4-1)*
Cyborg De Sou(FR), outclassed behind the smart Hoo La Baloo on his most recent outing at Market Rasen back in October, ran well for a long way on this handicap debut, but a mistake at the second-last ended any realistic chance he had and he faded on the run-in. There is definitely a race in him off this sort of mark. *(op 3-1 tchd 10-3)*
Imaginaire(USA) comes from a stable who are going well at present, but a mistake at the eighth *seemed enough to put the wind up him and he was soon struggling.Official explanation: jockey said he had no explanation for the poor form shown (op 10-3 tchd 7-2 in places)*
Made In France(FR) looked to face a very stiff task here in ground that would not have suited and he was struggling some way from the finish. The five-year-old is in need of some help from the Handicapper. *(op 7-2)*

2627 BETDIRECT.CO.UK NOVICES' HURDLE (8 hdls) 2m
1:20 (1:20) (Class 3) 4-Y-0+ £5,399 (£1,585; £792; £395)

Form				RPR
	1		Border Castle[148] 4-10-12 SamThomas (Miss Venetia Williams) a handy: led last: rdn out 10/1	114+
P2-2	2	2 ½	Dhehdaah[19] 2249 4-10-12 112 WarrenMarston (Mrs P Sly) midfield: hdwy 4th: led after 3 out: rdn and hdd last: no ex towards fin 5/2[1]	108
	3	2 ½	Akarem[28] 4-10-12 FinbarKeniry (K R Burke) in tch: ev ch fr 3 out tl one pce run-in 7/2[2]	106
F0	4	7	Millennium Hall[72] 1527 6-10-9 PeterBuchanan(3) (Miss Lucinda V Russell) midfield: hdwy appr 3 out: ev ch whn mstke 2 out: edgd lft and wknd after last 33/1	100+
30P-	5	6	Protective[28] 4749 4-10-12 JimCrowley (J G Given) hld up: hdwy 4th: chsd ldrs 3 out: rdn and wknd appr last 14/1	93
5	6	1 ½	Trust Rule[14] 2335 5-10-9 PaddyAspell(3) (M W Easterby) hld up: sme hdwy appr 2 out: n.d 20/1	91
	7	½	Futoo (IRE)[18] 4-10-12 AndrewThornton (G M Moore) prom: led 2nd: hdd appr 3rd: remained prom: led bef 3 out and nt fluent: hdd bef next: wknd appr last 33/1	92+
6-0	8	5	Willies Way[217] 138 5-10-12 RichardMcGrath (Mrs S J Smith) j.lft: midfield: lost pl 4th: hdwy appr 3 out: wknd bef last 40/1	86
	9	2	Total Turtle (IRE)[34] 6-10-12 DavidO'Meara (T D Easterby) hld up: hdwy after 4 out: chsd ldrs 3 out: wknd next 7/1[3]	86+
	10	¾	Calculaite[47] 4-10-12 TonyDobbin (M Todhunter) hld up: sme hdwy appr 3 out: wknd bef next 16/1	83
60-	11	5	Esteban[484] 1131 5-10-12 TomSiddall (J J Quinn) midfield: rdn and btn after 4 out 100/1	78
4/F0	12	15	Datbandito (IRE)[9] 2447 6-10-12 BruceGibson (L Lungo) rdn after 4 out: a bhd 100/1	63
0P	13	14	Galahad (FR)[186] 602 4-10-12 BrianHarding (B Storey) a bhd 100/1	49
	14	2 ½	Overdrawn (IRE)[65] 4-10-12 DominicElsworth (Mrs S J Smith) cl up: mstke 3 out: sn wknd 25/1	46
PP/	15	dist	Hurricane Coast[4] 1806 6-10-7 (b) JohnLevins(5) (K McAuliffe) midfield: rdn and wknd appr 2 out: virtually p.u run- in 33/1	—
5P0	F		Buthaina (IRE)[14] 2335 5-9-12 ThomasBurrows(7) (Mrs L Williamson) a bhd: rdn after 4 out: fell 2 out 200/1	—
0	P		Peggy Naylor[96] 1360 4-10-0 MarkNicolls(5) (Miss J E Foster) midfield: wknd after 4 out: t.o whn p.u bef last 150/1	—
	P		Barathea Blazer[813] 6-10-12 JohnMcNamara (K C Bailey) prom: led appr 3rd: hdd bef 3 out: wknd qckly: p.u bef 2 out 8/1	—
0645	P		Two Steps To Go (USA)[29] 2025 6-10-11 77 (tp) BenOrde-Powlett(7) (M A Barnes) sn led: hdd 2nd: remained handy tl wknd appr 3 out: t.o whn p.u bef last 100/1	—

4m 5.10s (6.00) **Going Correction** +0.325s/f (Yiel) 19 Ran SP% **121.0**
Speed ratings: **98,96,95,92,89 88,88,85,84,84 81,74,67,65,—** —,—,—,— CSF £32.60 TOTE £9.00: £2.70, £1.70, £3.20; EX 36.80.
Owner D E Harrison **Bred** The Queen **Trained** Kings Caple, H'fords

FOCUS
Not a bad contest and it is likely that the odd winner will emerge from it.

NOTEBOOK
Border Castle, a useful but inconsistent sort on the Flat, looks a decent recruit to hurdles and stayed on far too strongly for the honest Dhehdaah on this hurdling debut. To the fore throughout, he travelled sweetly and handled the very soft ground well, coming clear in good style. It is to be hoped that he goes the right way from this and he may well be up to defying a penalty.
Dhehdaah again gave his all in defeat but, unfortunately for him, had to make do with second for the fourth time over hurdles. The winner had a little too much class for him at the business end, but he will find a race eventually if continuing to perform so honestly. *(op 3-1 tchd 2-1)*
Akarem, a smart ex-Irish Flat performer, comes from a stable which is better known for its Flat success, but on this evidence they are going to have plenty of fun with the colt over hurdles and he kept on nicely late on to claim third. He is likely to stay further in time, but is probably best kept to this distance for now. *(op 2-1 tchd 4-1)*
Millennium Hall ran his best race to date over obstacles, being bang there with every chance taking two from home, but he failed to see his race out as well as the others and missed out on a place. This was a decent contest and he will find easier opportunities in future.
Protective has faced stiff tasks the last twice, over hurdles and on the Flat, but this was more realistic and he ran well. He can find a race or two once contesting handicaps. *(tchd 16-1)*
Trust Rule was putting in some good late work and is the type connections will do well with in handicaps. *Official explanation: jockey said gelding had a breathing problem*
Total Turtle(IRE), a very useful stayer on the Flat, did not offer a great deal on this hurdling debut and needs to step up next time. *(op 8-1)*
Two Steps To Go(USA) *Official explanation: jockey said gelding lost its action (op 12-1)*
Barathea Blazer, a formerly smart Flat performer with Peter Harris, had not been seen since September 2003 and was always going to need this hurdling debut. He travelled too well for his own good in the early stages and stopped quickly in the sraight, but deserves another chance with the outing under his belt. *(op 12-1)*

2628 TOMMY WHITTLE H'CAP CHASE (18 fncs) 3m
1:55 (1:56) (Class 2) 5-Y-0+
£19,477 (£5,753; £2,876; £1,439; £718; £360)

Form				RPR
1P-0	1		Captain Corelli[21] 2176 8-9-9 128 MrTJO'Brien(7) (P J Hobbs) hld up: hdwy 12th: led 3 out: clr last: styd on wl 13/2	149+
4F1-	2	20	Lord Transcend (IRE)[315] 3477 8-11-12 152 TonyDobbin (J Howard Johnson) led: mstke 9th and rdr lost iron briefly: hdd 3 out: wl btn fr last 2/1[1]	155+
21P-	3	5	Malek (IRE)[226] 4946 9-10-3 129 RichardMcGrath (K G Reveley) hld up: rdn and effrt appr 3 out: nvr on terms w ldrs 22/1	122
26-1	4	6	Schuh Shine (IRE)[28] 2048 8-10-1 127 oh1 ow1 SamThomas (Miss Venetia Williams) cl up: mstke 9th and 14th: wknd bef 2 out 9/2[2]	115+
-110	5	½	I Hear Thunder (IRE)[21] 2176 7-10-0 126 BenjaminHitchcott (R H Buckler) in tch: blnd 9th (water): lost pl 12th: struggling whn nt fluent 4 out and rdr lost irons: n.d after 12/1	117+
020-	6	11	Horus (IRE)[239] 4766 10-10-11 140 TomMalone(3) (M C Pipe) hld up: effrt appr 3 out: wknd bef 2 out 6/1[3]	124+
P-1P	7	2	Naunton Brook[28] 2054 6-10-0 126 oh2 CarlLlewellyn (N A Twiston-Davies) prom: lost pl 12th: n.d after 16/1	100
3P-P	P		Sir Rembrandt (IRE)[21] 2176 9-11-11 151 (v1) AndrewThornton (R H Alner) prom: mstke 13th: wknd after 4 out: p.u bef next: dismntd 7/1	—

6m 27.2s (-1.10) **Going Correction** +0.45s/f (Soft) 8 Ran SP% **109.6**
Speed ratings: **119,112,110,108,108 104,104,—** CSF £19.09 CT £244.03 TOTE £7.60: £1.90, £1.60, £3.10; EX 19.90.
Owner Patrick Bancroft **Bred** E G Fewtrell **Trained** Withycombe, Somerset
■ A new look for the Tommy Whittle Chase, previously a more valuable Grade 2 non-handicap.
■ Stewards' Enquiry : Mr T J O'Brien caution: used whip on a horse that was clearly winning

FOCUS
A good staying handicap, run in a decent time, with top and bottom weights Lord Transcend and Captain Corelli having the race between themselves from the turn in. Unsurprisingly, it was he one at the foot of the weights that prevailed and the eight-year-old looks one to keep on the right side.

NOTEBOOK
Captain Corelli developed into a useful chaser last season but found things happening all too quickly at Cheltenham on his final start, and that was again the case there on his reappearance when his jumping was sloppy. This, though, represented a much more suitable test and, with the ground riding deep, he had plenty of time at his fences and virtually no weight to carry with his good, young rider claiming 7lb. Always travelling strongly, he had latched on to the tail of top weight Lord Transcend rounding for home and the writing was on the wall for the gallant runner-up as he went on three out. A horse who must have soft ground, connections have their sights set on Aintree in April, but it is somewhat puzzling that he holds no Welsh National entry as that race would surely have suited him down to the ground. *(op 15-2)*
Lord Transcend(IRE) showed last season when fourth in the Hennessy that he goes well first time up and he ran a smashing race here off top weight. Soon in the lead, he jumped soundly barring a blunder at the ninth and it was between himself and the winner as they turned for home, but the huge weight difference was always going to tell and he was playing for second place only from over two out. He has an exciting season ahead of him if staying sound, with the Pillar looking his next obvious target, but the Gold Cup is the long-term aim and there would be worse outsiders if turning up in good form on the day. *(tchd 9-4)*
Malek(IRE) is a real old stayer, as he showed when scoring over four miles at Kelso last season, and it was no surprise to see him keeping on late past tiring rivals. Unlikely to have been fully wound up for this reappearance, he will be a force in all the major northern staying handicaps this season. *(op 25-1 tchd 20-1)*
Schuh Shine(IRE), a really progressive gelding who had won five of his last seven starts coming into this, had to be respected in receipt of so much weight, but he lacks the touch of class the winner has and faded out of it in the final quarter mile. There is no reason why he cannot win off this sort of mark back down in grade. *(tchd 5-1)*
I Hear Thunder(IRE), behind the winner at Cheltenham last time, was always likely to struggle in this testing ground and he dropped away after a mistake at the fourth last. His progression looks to *have levelled out for the time being, but he may be one for the spring when back on good ground. Official explanation: jockey said stirrup iron broke (op 10-1)*
Horus(IRE) has a good record fresh and took the Edward Hanmer first time up over course and distance last season. Ridden with restraint, he crept into contention turning in, but that was as far as he got and he dropped away down the straight. This was a bit disappointing and it may well be that he is too high in the weights. *(op 9-2)*
Naunton Brook, although probably unsuited by the ground, has gone the wrong way from an impressive reappearance win and was unable to leave behind a poor effort in the Badger Ales Trophy. *(tchd 11-1)*
Sir Rembrandt(IRE), placed in the last two Gold Cups, has now pulled up on each of his last three starts and the first-time visor failed to inject any life into him. The fact that he was dismounted *suggests there may have been something amiss, and he looks best left alone for the time being. Official explanation: jockey said gelding lost its action (op 15-2 tchd 8-1)*

2629 RECTANGLE GROUP H'CAP HURDLE (10 hdls) 2m 4f
2:30 (2:30) (Class 3) (0-125,124) 4-Y-0+ £4,886 (£1,434; £717; £358)

Form				RPR
431P	1		Vicario[16] 2292 4-10-12 115 StephenCraine(5) (D McCain) in tch: clsd 4 out: led 3 out: drvn out 18/1	120+

0-30 **2** ½ **Better Days (IRE)**[13] 2368 9-11-1 **113** DominicElsworth 118
(Mrs S J Smith) *a.p: led 4 out: hdd next: sn rdn and lost 2nd: wandered u.p fr bef last: styd on to take 2nd towards* **9/2**[2]
/3-1 **3** 5 **Ever Present (IRE)**[220] 64 7-11-4 **116** TonyDobbin 118+
(N G Richards) *hld up: hdwy 6th: wnt 2nd appr 2 out: nt fluent last: lost 2nd and no ex towards fin* **7/2**[1]
113/ **4** 20 **Jexel (FR)**[1112] 1987 8-10-2 **100** RichardMcGrath 80
(B Storey) *hld up: hdwy appr 3 out: n.d* **33/1**
F2P- **5** 1 **Cordilla (IRE)**[231] 4864 7-10-7 **112** ScottMarshall(7) 91
(N G Richards) *hld up: hdwy appr 4 out: wknd next* **14/1**
13-U **6** 9 **Sharp Jack (IRE)**[7] 2504 7-11-0 **112** WarrenMarston 82
(R T Phillips) *t.k.h: sn in tch: mstke 2nd: rdn appr 3 out: sn wknd* **7/1**
U- **7** 15 **Maletton (FR)**[271] 4230 5-11-12 **124** (b) SamThomas 79
(Miss Venetia Williams) *midfield: hdwy 6th: rdn 4 out: wknd next* **16/1**
124/ **8** 6 **Mirant**[849] 1060 6-10-9 **110** TomMalone(3) 59
(M C Pipe) *handy tl wknd after 4 out* **12/1**
3-40 **9** hd **Habitual Dancer**[20] 2207 4-11-6 **118** BrianHarding 66
(Jedd O'Keeffe) *prom: rdn after 4 out: sn wknd* **16/1**
016/ **10** 3½ **Corroboree (IRE)**[729] 2571 8-10-4 **102** CarlLlewellyn 47
(N A Twiston-Davies) *led: hdd 4 out: sn rdn: wknd next* **13/2**[3]
0/5- **11** 13 **Great As Gold (IRE)**[12] 110 6-11-11 **123** (p) FinbarKeniry 55
(B Ellison) *midfield: rdn appr 4 out: sn wknd* **33/1**
1B20 **P** **Top Style (IRE)**[9] 2452 7-10-5 **108** (p) WilliamKennedy(5) —
(G A Harker) *a bhd: t.o whn p.u bef 2 out* **16/1**
120- **P** **Bollin Annabel**[225] 4969 4-10-13 **111** DavidO'Meara —
(T D Easterby) *a bhd: t.o whn p.u bef 2 out* **25/1**

5m 10.0s (0.80) **Going Correction** +0.325s/f (Yiel)
WFA 4 from 5yo+ 11lb **13** Ran SP% **113.2**
Speed ratings: **111,110,108,100,100 96,90,88,88,86 81,—,—** CSF £92.20 CT £353.92 TOTE £20.90: £4.60, £1.60, £2.10; EX 103.00.
Owner Jon Glews **Bred** Mrs A Yearley **Trained** Cholmondeley, Cheshire
■ Stewards' Enquiry : Dominic Elsworth one-day ban: used whip with excessive frequency (Dec 14)
Stephen Craine one-day ban: used whip with excessive frequency and without giving gelding time to respond (Dec 14)

FOCUS
A decent handicap hurdle, run in a fair time, in which the front three pulled well clear, and the form looks pretty solid.

NOTEBOOK
Vicario, a winner here two runs back, appreciated the thorough stamina test and really dug deep on the run-in to hold the renewed challenge of Better Days. Still only four, this tough individual is well suited by a galloping track and, given the first three pulled well clear of the remainder, it is *quite possible he has further improvement in him.Official explanation: trainer said, regarding the improved form shown, gelding never travelled at Market Rasen last time out, and was better suited by today's track and less competitive race (tchd 20-1)*
Better Days(IRE), back over hurdles having run over the National fences at Aintree last time, travelled strongly on the pace and responded well to pressure, but could not get his way back to the front despite a gallant late challenge. This was his second good effort over hurdles this season and it is surely only a matter of time before he wins one. *(op 5-1 tchd 4-1)*
Ever Present(IRE) is quite lightly raced and evidently not the easiest to train, but he shaped promisingly on this return and kept on well in third. He was some distance ahead of the fourth and should find a race. *(tchd 4-1)*
Jexel(FR), returning from over three years off the track, was well held in fourth, but McGrath was not unduly hard on him and he made a little late headway. He still has plenty of time to fulfil his potential and has to be of interest next time.
Cordilla(IRE) would have used this to get him straight for a return to fences and he showed enough to suggest he can pick up a handicap or two this term.
Corroboree(IRE), another returning from a lengthy absence, was solid in the market beforehand but, having led for around two miles of the contest, he soon became very tired and faded out of things. His stable is sure to get the best out of him and he should make a chaser. *(op 6-1 tchd 7-1)*

2630 GARY YATES TESTIMONIAL NOVICES' H'CAP CHASE (14 fncs 1 omitted) 2m 4f
3:00 (3:00) (Class 3) (0-110,110) 4-Y-O+ **£5,556** (£1,631; £815; £407)

Form RPR
1 **1** **Dun Doire (IRE)**[21] 2187 6-10-1 **85** JimCrowley 96+
(A J Martin, Ire) *hld up: hdwy 7th (water): led last: r.o* **13/8**[1]
-P32 **2** 4 **Deja Vu (IRE)**[38] 1888 6-11-4 **105** PeterBuchanan(3) 108
(J Howard Johnson) *midfield: hmpd 6th: hdwy appr 3 out: led bef 2 out: rdn and hdd last: no ex towards fin* **9/1**
P/43 **3** 8 **Valleymore (IRE)**[21] 2180 9-11-1 **99** (t) TomSiddall 94+
(S A Brookshaw) *j.rt: prom: led after 2nd: hdd 4 out: wknd appr last* **10/1**
12P/ **4** 7 **Predestine (FR)**[658] 3825 5-11-7 **105** JohnMcNamara 93
(K C Bailey) *bhd: kpt on run-in: nvr on terms w ldrs* **20/1**
0421 **5** nk **Avadi (IRE)**[27] 2080 7-9-12 **85** TomMalone(3) 75+
(P T Dalton) *cl up: led 4 out: hit 3 out: hdd appr next: wknd bef last* **9/2**[2]
P333 **6** 17 **Jonny's Kick**[11] 2415 5-10-13 **97** DavidO'Meara 75
(T D Easterby) *prom tl rdn and wknd appr 3 out* **14/1**
-U45 **7** dist **Fencote (IRE)**[191] 521 8-11-4 **102** BrianHarding —
(P Beaumont) *a bhd: t.o* **33/1**
4-61 **8** 22 **Spring Gamble (IRE)**[35] 1928 6-11-7 **105** FinbarKeniry —
(G M Moore) *led: hdd after 2nd: remained cl up: wknd 4 out: t.o* **14/1**
122- **F** **Le Biassais (FR)**[244] 4713 6-11-12 **110** TonyDobbin —
(L Lungo) *fell 1st* **11/2**[3]
P/3F **U** **Toon Trooper (IRE)**[21] 2180 8-10-9 **98** WilliamKennedy(5) —
(R Lee) *midfield: blnd and uns rdr 6th* **33/1**
60-4 **P** **Profowens (IRE)**[25] 2109 7-11-3 **101** RichardMcGrath —
(P Beaumont) *hld up: blnd bdly 4 out: nt rcvr: sn p.u* **50/1**

5m 33.6s (9.40) **Going Correction** +0.45s/f (Soft) **11** Ran SP% **116.7**
Speed ratings: **99,97,94,91,91 84,—,—,—,— —** CSF £16.19 CT £114.29 TOTE £2.60: £1.60, £1.60, £3.10; EX 18.00.
Owner Dunderry Racing Syndicate **Bred** Mrs Sarah Martin **Trained** Summerhill, Co. Meath

FOCUS
A fair contest in which the front two looked well handicapped. The winner has been rated value for eight lengths. One fence bypassed second circuit.

NOTEBOOK
Dun Doire(IRE), who stayed on late to win a shade comfortably at Wetherby, got the job done with more authority on this occasion and won comfortably. Evidently well handicapped, he can *complete the hat-trick before taking a rise in class and looks one to keep on the right side. (op 2-1 tchd 9-4 in places)*
Deja Vu(IRE) is clearly a better chaser than hurdler and drew far enough clear of the third for this to go down as a decent effort. He is in good hands and can win off this mark. *(op 12-1)*
Valleymore(IRE) is bizarrely still a novice and continues to frustrate. His jumping is still sketchy *given that he has been chasing for some time and he remains below a winning level. (op 11-1 tchd 12-1)*
Predestine(FR) was not disgraced on this return from a layoff and the five-year-old looks open to a certain amount of improvement. *(op 14-1)*
Avadi(IRE), up 7lb for winning at Market Rssen, had his chance and was headed after a mistake at the third-last. *(tchd 5-1)*
Spring Gamble(IRE) *Official explanation: jockey said gelding never travelled (op 11-1)*
Profowens(IRE) *Official explanation: jockey said gelding blundered and lost its action (op 9-2 tchd 6-1 in places)*
Le Biassais(FR) is a huge specimen of a horse and there was little worry about him shouldering top weight, but he got the first all wrong and hit the deck on this chase debut. It is to be hoped that this will wake him up and he remains a useful prospect if none the worse. *(op 9-2 tchd 6-1 in places)*

2631 RED SQUARE VODKA "NATIONAL HUNT" NOVICES' HURDLE (10 hdls) 2m 4f
3:35 (3:35) (Class 3) 4-7-Y-O **£5,152** (£1,512; £756; £377)

Form RPR
1-21 **1** **The Cool Guy (IRE)**[52] 1711 5-11-5 CarlLlewellyn 135+
(N A Twiston-Davies) *a.p: mstke 3rd: hung lft fr after 3 out: led and pckd 2 out: styd on to draw clr run-in* **4/7**[1]
U2-4 **2** 7 **Harmony Brig (IRE)**[10] 2444 6-10-12 TonyDobbin 118+
(N G Richards) *led: hdd 2 out: sn rdn: no ex run-in* **13/2**[3]
24-2 **3** 5 **Hibernian (IRE)**[20] 2212 5-10-12 BrianHarding 113+
(O Sherwood) *midfield: hdwy 4 out: wknd appr 2 out* **6/1**[2]
-P03 **4** ¾ **Morgan Be**[30] 2006 5-10-9 PeterBuchanan(3) 111
(Mrs K Walton) *midfield: hdwy 6th: wknd appr 2 out* **50/1**
23- **5** dist **Master Of The Ward (IRE)**[245] 4690 5-10-7 StephenCraine(5) —
(D McCain) *midfield: blnd 5th: wknd 4 out* **100/1**
0-0 **6** 17 **Glen Thyne (IRE)**[9] 2462 5-10-7 MarkNicolls(5) —
(K C Bailey) *a bhd* **100/1**
53 **7** 1¼ **Joe Brown**[21] 2186 5-10-12 JimCrowley —
(Mrs H Dalton) *a bhd* **16/1**
-5 **8** 23 **Good Call (IRE)**[15] 2327 6-10-5 MrAJBerry(7) —
(Jonjo O'Neill) *in tch: mstke 6th: wknd 4 out* **33/1**
2-0F **9** 5 **Thievery**[16] 2295 4-10-12 AndrewThornton —
(H D Daly) *trckd ldrs tl wknd 4 out* **50/1**
50-0 **10** 8 **Seymar Lad (IRE)**[21] 2186 5-10-12 RichardMcGrath —
(P Beaumont) *midfield: wknd 4 out* **40/1**
00-U **P** **Intavac Flight**[7] 2497 5-10-12 FinbarKeniry —
(C W Thornton) *a bhd: t.o whn p.u bef 3 out* **100/1**
0-P **F** **Grasia (IRE)**[32] 1976 6-10-12 JohnMcNamara —
(K C Bailey) *hld up: sme hdwy after 4 out: n.d whn fell last* **100/1**
6PPP **P** **Loch Torridon**[11] 2415 6-10-2 64 (p) MichaelMcAvoy(10) —
(James Moffatt) *in tch: bhd after 4th: t.o whn p.u bef 3 out* **200/1**
5-6 **P** **Cash King (IRE)**[21] 2192 5-10-12 DominicElsworth —
(Mrs S J Smith) *midfield: hdwy appr 5th: wknd bef 3 out: t.o whn p.u bef last* **18/1**

5m 13.1s (3.90) **Going Correction** +0.325s/f (Yiel)
WFA 4 from 5yo+ 11lb **14** Ran SP% **116.2**
Speed ratings: **105,102,100,99,—** —,—,—,—,— —,—,—,— CSF £4.27 TOTE £1.50: £1.10, £2.00, £2.00; EX 4.90 Place 6 £ 341.90, Place 5 £101.07.
Owner Frosty's Four **Bred** Kieran Strain **Trained** Naunton, Gloucs

FOCUS
An uncompetitive race and The Cool Guy eventually ran out a comfortable winner.

NOTEBOOK
The Cool Guy(IRE), shock winner of last season's Championship Bumper at Aintree, did it easily on his hurdling debut at Uttoxeter and was always going to take a good deal of stopping under a penalty. He had to work hard enough to get to the lead, but it was plain sailing in the final furlong or so and he was ultimately an easy winner. There is no doubting he is a high-class prospect, but whether he would have the pace for a good ground Royal & SunAlliance Hurdle is open to question. *(op 8-11 tchd 4-5 in places)*
Harmony Brig(IRE) served it up to the winner and made him work hard enough, but he was comfortably held in the final quarter mile and in the end was no match. He will find easier opportunities and the way he travelled suggests two miles will not be a problem. *(op 4-1)*
Hibernian(IRE) got going late and came through to claim a place, but was no match for the front *two. Three miles is going to suit in time and he should improve further for a switch to hurdles. (op 13-2 tchd 7-1)*
Morgan Be proved his shock third here last month to be no fluke and just missed out on a place. He will find easier opportunities and should win his share in handicaps. *(op 40-1)*
Cash King(IRE) could have been expected to finish third or fourth, but he ran a stinker and offered little. *(op 20-1)*
T/Plt: £272.40 to a £1 stake. Pool: £40,941.40. 109.70 winning tickets. T/Qpdt: £6.60 to a £1 stake. Pool: £3,064.10. 342.30 winning tickets. DO

[2612] SANDOWN (R-H)
Saturday, December 3

OFFICIAL GOING: Chase course - soft (heavy in places); hurdle course - heavy
The plain fence in front of the stands was jumped in place of the open ditch
Wind: Almost nil Weather: Changeable, rain race 3

2632 FRANCIS AND JANE HUTCHINSON MEMORIAL NOVICES' H'CAP HURDLE (8 hdls) 2m 110y
12:55 (12:56) (Class 3) (0-110,110) 3-Y-O+ **£6,896** (£2,024; £1,012; £505)

Form RPR
3/32 **1** **Green Iceni**[21] 2173 6-11-6 **104** MickFitzgerald 114+
(N J Henderson) *lw: trckd ldrs: rdn and struggling bef 2 out: mstke 2 out: rallied last: drvn and styd on to ld fnl 75yds* **4/1**[1]
-002 **2** 1¾ **Man Ray (USA)**[15] 2314 4-11-2 **100** APMcCoy 108+
(Jonjo O'Neill) *mounted on crse: hld up in rr: stdy prog fr 5th: chal 2 out: lft in ld last: nt run on u.p: hdd fnl 75yds* **5/1**[2]
5-41 **3** nk **Alph**[18] 2261 8-11-5 **103** MatthewBatchelor 113+
(B R Johnson) *hld up in rr: prog 4th: chal and lft in ld 2 out: blnd bdly last and hdd: tried to rally flat: kpt on* **7/1**[3]
2040 **4** 10 **Argent Ou Or (FR)**[22] 2166 4-10-13 **97** TimmyMurphy 94
(M C Pipe) *mostly trckd ldr tl rdn and fdd bef 2 out* **7/1**[3]
-444 **5** 4 **Hatteras (FR)**[13] 2374 6-11-0 **105** RobertLucey-Butler(7) 98
(Miss M P Bryant) *prom tl wknd bef 2 out* **50/1**
2021 **6** dist **Strathtay**[9] 2454 3-9-11 **98** oh3 (v) OwynNelmes(3) —
(M Appleby) *a in rr: t.o 3 out: btn 47 l* **20/1**
33-6 **7** 6 **Esplendidos (IRE)**[19] 2244 6-9-13 **90** DarylJacob(7) —
(D P Keane) *in tch to 5th: wknd u.p sn after 3 out: t.o: btn 54 l* **10/1**
P2-4 **8** 3½ **Sargasso Sea**[214] 172 8-11-12 **110** JasonMaguire 83+
(J A B Old) *led: clr 3rd: pressed whn blnd and hdd 2 out: v tired and crawled over last: walked in: btn 57 l* **5/1**[2]
0-P0 **9** 6 **Amnesty**[13] 2379 6-10-10 **94** (b) JamieMoore —
(G L Moore) *in tch: mstke 5th: j.rt 3 out: sn wknd u.p: t.o: btn 63 l* **33/1**

16 **P** **Kristinor (FR)**[44] [1802] 3-10-2 **100** .... PhilipHide —
(G L Moore) *a in rr: wknd 3 out: t.o in 12th whn p.u bef 2 out* **22/1**

00-P **P** **Duncanbil (IRE)**[15] [2322] 4-10-0 **87** oh13 ow3 .... ColinBolger(3) —
(J J Bridger) *in tch to 4th: wknd and t.o 3 out: last whn p.u bef next* **100/1**

6P21 **P** **Meadow Hawk (USA)**[23] [2150] 5-11-2 **100** .... GrahamLee —
(A W Carroll) *swtg: in tch tl wknd sn after 3 out: t.o in 13th whn p.u bef 2 out* **14/1**

3223 **P** **The Castilian (FR)**[35] [1921] 3-10-2 **100** .... (v) RJGreene —
(M C Pipe) *wl in tch: chsd ldrs after 3 out: sn u.p: wknd and wl btn 7th 2 out: p.u bef last* **14/1**

0P2/ **P** **Instant Appeal**[1007] [3926] 8-10-6 **90** .... BarryFenton —
(P Winkworth) *set off last: rapid prog to trckd ldr 2nd: restrained and last by next: sn t.o: keeping on in poor 11th whn p.u bef 2 out* **100/1**

4m 20.7s (11.80) **Going Correction** +0.725s/f (Soft)
WFA 3 from 4yo 13lb 4 from 5yo+ 10lb **14** Ran SP% **116.7**
Speed ratings: **101,100,100,95,93** —,—,—,—,— —,—,—,— CSF £22.18 CT £135.59 TOTE £4.10: £1.70, £2.30, £3.00; EX 14.30.

Owner Paul Hudson **Bred** Mrs F S Williams **Trained** Upper Lambourn, Berks

FOCUS

A race run at a true gallop thanks to Sargasso Sea, and a quite remarkable performance from Green Iceni, who came from an unpromising position to win going away. The form looks solid enough and has been rated around the fourth.

NOTEBOOK

Green Iceni has returned from a spell on the sidelines in great form and followed placed efforts at Stratford and Cheltenham with a remarkable victory here, coming from what looked an impossible position to win going away. Probably disliking the ground, he was struggling before the turn in, but was still in touch taking two out despite making a mistake and flew home under the Fitzgerald drive. Still unexposed, a sounder surface suits him better and, although he had quite a hard race here, there is every chance he can win again. *(op 7-2)*

Man Ray(USA), who showed improved form when runner-up on his handicap debut at Exeter, was given a quiet ride by McCoy and had crept into a challenging position as they turned for home. A mistake from Alph at the last left him in the lead and appeared to present him the race on a plate, but he soon began to idle and was swamped late on. Still only four, it does look down to greenness rather than attitude that he lost the race, and this scopey individual will not be long in winning as he gains further experience. *(op 4-1)*

Alph is very lightly raced for one of his age and looked to hold obvious claims here despite being up 10lb for winning at Fakenham last month. He began to make headway having been restrained in rear early, and went on when front-runner Sargasso Sea blundered at the second-last, but a serious error at the final flight cost him ground and momentum. He did rally bravely, but it could not be said that he would definitely have won as he would have provided the idling Man Ray with something to race with. Either way, he remains a promising sort and connections will presumably waste little time in sending him chasing. *(tchd 15-2)*

Argent Ou Or(FR) has largely been disappointing since sent hurdling, and he again failed to live up to market expectations when down the field at the Paddy Power meeting. Although well held here, the front three are all progressive, unexposed sorts and it is likely that he will find life easier down a grade. *(tchd 13-2 and 15-2)*

Hatteras(FR) has yet to win in ten starts since coming to Britain, but he ran well to a point here and some further assistance from the Handicapper should enable him to find a small race.

Sargasso Sea comes from a stable which is beginning to hit top stride, and the strong support in the market beforehand suggested a big run was expected. Carrying top weight in this sort of ground is never easy so it was a bit surprising to see him sent into a clear lead. He still held a nice advantage as they turned for home, but his lead had been significantly reduced when he blundered two out and he just about managed to scramble over the last. He showed enough to suggest he can find a small race, but it would be a slight concern that he finished so tired here. *(op 7-1)*

2633 WILLIAMHILLPOKER.COM H'CAP HURDLE (11 hdls) 2m 6f

1:30 (1:33) (Class 3) (0-130,128) 4-Y-0+ **£10,533** (£3,092; £1,546; £772)

Form RPR

312 **1** **Nor'Nor'East (IRE)**[16] [2295] 7-11-0 **116** .... APMcCoy 120+
(Jonjo O'Neill) *hld up off the pce: nt fluent 4th: prog fr 8th: chsd clr ldr bef 2 out: drvn and clsd last: led fnl 100yds* **4/1**[2]

-1P0 **2** *1 ¼* **Nonantais (FR)**[14] [2336] 8-10-13 **122** .... PatrickCStringer(7) 125
(M Bradstock) *led at gd pce: clr fr 8th: 12 l ahd after 3 out: reeled in fr 2 out: hdd and no ex last 100yds* **16/1**

0000 **3** *12* **Anatar (IRE)**[22] [2166] 7-10-11 **113** .... (v[1]) TimmyMurphy 106+
(M C Pipe) *chsd clr ldng trio: effrt fr 3 out: chsd ldr briefly bef 2 out: 3rd and btn whn tired jump last* **12/1**

0/0- **4** *3* **Derivative (IRE)**[581] [110] 7-11-4 **120** .... AlanO'Keeffe 108
(Miss Venetia Williams) *chsd clr ldng pair: u.p 3 out: lost pl and btn bef next: plugged on again flat* **20/1**

2 **5** *shd* **Danse Macabre (IRE)**[28] [2043] 6-9-7 **102** oh2 .... WillieMcCarthy(7) 90
(A W Carroll) *hld up in last trio and wl off the pce: rdn 3 out: plugged on fr next: n.d* **7/1**[3]

-1FU **6** *9* **Moscow Whisper (IRE)**[32] [1972] 8-11-0 **116** .... RichardJohnson 95
(P J Hobbs) *t.k.h: trckd ldr tl wknd bef 2 out* **16/1**

0-00 **7** *5* **Migwell (FR)**[7] [2493] 5-11-0 **123** .... RobertLucey-Butler(7) 97
(Mrs L Wadham) *settled in last trio and wl off the pce: effrt 3 out: sn rdn: no real imp bef next* **7/1**[3]

4P-1 **8** *hd* **Miko De Beauchene (FR)**[24] [2130] 5-11-1 **117** .... RobertThornton 91
(R H Alner) *lw: hld up in midfield and wl off the pce: effrt to chse ldrs after 3 out: sn u.p: wknd and j.lft 2 out* **11/4**[1]

0620 **9** *dist* **Mythical King (IRE)**[8] [2483] 8-11-7 **128** .... PaddyMerrigan(5) —
(R Lee) *a in rr gp: rdn and wknd 8th: wl bhd 3 out: btn 75 l* **14/1**

2146 **10** *dist* **Dubai Ace (USA)**[14] [2347] 4-10-8 **110** .... JamieGoldstein —
(Miss Sheena West) *off the pce in midfield: wknd 3 out: t.o whn virtually p.u flat: btn 125 l* **25/1**

2-45 **P** **Totally Scottish**[11] [2417] 9-10-10 **112** .... GrahamLee —
(K G Reveley) *off the pce in midfield: wknd 3 out: poor 10th whn p.u bef 2 out* **14/1**

54-P **P** **Apollo Theatre**[17] [2271] 7-10-7 **109** .... (t) BarryFenton —
(R Rowe) *chsd clr ldrs to 5th: losing pl whn bmpd bnd bef next: sn last and t.o: p.u bef 2 out* **33/1**

5m 49.5s (11.60) **Going Correction** +0.725s/f (Soft)
WFA 4 from 5yo+ 11lb **12** Ran SP% **116.0**
Speed ratings: **107,106,102,101,101 97,95,95**,—,— —,— CSF £61.64 CT £708.38 TOTE £3.70: £1.90, £5.00, £3.60; EX 119.40.

Owner John P McManus **Bred** Mrs C A Moore **Trained** Cheltenham, Gloucs

FOCUS

A smart effort by both Nor'Nor'East and Nonantais, who were ridden very differently to each other, and who look capable of better still.

NOTEBOOK

Nor'Nor'East(IRE), making his handicap debut for top connections, ran most creditably in defeat last time when finding only the potentially useful Mr Pointment too good (gave7lb), and the good gallop set by Nonantais here seemed to suit him well. Held up in the main group, it was clear from half a mile out that if something was going to get to the clear leader it was going to be him, and fluent leaps at both the last two flights enabled him to come through and win going away. Considering that this was only his fourth start over hurdles, it is safe to assume that there is more to come, and this future chaser fully deserves his place at a higher level. *(op 3-1)*

Nonantais(FR), a very useful novice a couple of seasons back, stepped up on his reappearance effort when running well for a long way at Haydock, and this was another step towards a return to something like his best. Soon leading at a good gallop, he received a fine ride from his young pilot and had been kicked into around a 12-length lead taking the third-last, but he was unable to repel the late challenge of the winner and, heart-breakingly, had to make do with second. Clear of the third, he will go back up in the weights for this, but should still be up to winning a decent prize this term. *(tchd 18-1 in a place)*

Anatar(IRE) has dropped to a very reasonable mark and the first-time visor enabled him to run his best race for some time. He travelled strongly into the straight, but was unable to go with Nor'Nor'East and ultimately finished very tired.

Derivative(IRE), returning from a lengthy spell on the sidelines, had been due to run at Windsor the other week when it was abandoned, so had an extra couple of weeks to sharpen up. In ground he has won in, it was no surprise to see him run a big race on this return. He understandably got tired *but kept on to just grab fourth, and it will be interesting to see if connections send him chasing. (op 25-1)*

Danse Macabre(IRE) ran well here in a lesser race last month and it was not hard to see him go well off a feather weight. He kept on from a long way back to just miss out on fourth and was perhaps taken aback by the way the race was run. There is definitely a race in him off this sort of mark. *(op 10-1)*

Moscow Whisper(IRE), who has not really taken to fences, was a bit keen in the early stages and failed to get home. *(op 20-1 tchd 25-1)*

Migwell(FR) could have been expected to do better on this return to a more favourable distance, *but he never got into it having been held up and this has to go down as a disappointing run. (tchd 8-1)*

Miko De Beauchene(FR), up 8lb for his Lingfield win, should really have done better in ground he likes, and he clearly failed to run to form. *(tchd 3-1 in a place)*

Apollo Theatre *Official explanation: jockey said gelding had a breathing problem*

2634 SODEXHO PRESTIGE HENRY VIII NOVICES' CHASE GRADE 2 (13 fncs) 2m

2:05 (2:08) (Class 1) 4-Y-0+ **£18,332** (£6,930; £3,512; £1,794; £943)

Form RPR

12-1 **1** **Racing Demon (IRE)**[32] [1971] 5-11-10 .... TimmyMurphy 162+
(Miss H C Knight) *lw: tended to jump rt: hld up in last: reminder after 3rd: prog fr 7th: trckd ldr 3 out: led sn after 2 out: drvn and styd* **6/4**[1]

1 **2** *4* **Hoo La Baloo (FR)**[48] [1758] 4-10-13 .... MickFitzgerald 147+
(P F Nicholls) *racd keenly: led and sn clr: pressed 3 out: hdd sn after next: kpt on but readily hld by wnr flat* **6/1**

0-11 **3** *10* **Cerium (FR)**[13] [2371] 4-10-13 .... ChristianWilliams 139+
(P F Nicholls) *lw: trckd ldr fr 3rd to 3 out: rdn bef next: btn whn mstke last* **4/1**[2]

12U- **4** *24* **Iron Man (FR)**[226] [4948] 4-10-7 .... GrahamLee 107
(J Howard Johnson) *hld up in tch: cl enough 10th: wknd bef next: fin tired* **15/2**

151P **5** *1 ¼* **Nyrche (FR)**[13] [2371] 5-11-10 .... RobertThornton 123
(A King) *lw: chsd ldr to 3rd: lost pl: last fr 7th: struggling fr 10th* **15/2**

1240 **F** **One Cornetto (IRE)**[22] [2163] 6-11-8 127 .... PhilipHide —
(L Wells) *fell 1st* **66/1**

3-31 **B** **Crossbow Creek**[9] [2456] 7-11-8 .... JamieMoore —
(M G Rimell) *lw: b.d 1st* **11/2**[3]

4m 6.10s (3.60) **Going Correction** +0.725s/f (Soft)
WFA 4 from 5yo+ 10lb **7** Ran SP% **114.7**
Speed ratings: **120,118,113,101,100** —,— CSF £11.35 TOTE £2.40: £1.60, £2.30; EX 8.00.

Owner Mrs T P Radford **Bred** Con O'Keeffe **Trained** West Lockinge, Oxon

FOCUS

A cracking renewal and a smart winning time, 0.7sec quicker than the Tingle Creek. Admittedly, they did go a good gallop here, thanks to promising youngster Hoo La Baloo, and he probably set it up for Racing Demon, but the winner is potentially top-class as it was no mean feat giving the four-year-old 11lb. The pair look two of the more likely Arkle winners at this stage.

NOTEBOOK

Racing Demon(IRE) ◆, a comfortable winner on his fencing debut at Exeter and perhaps the most exciting two-mile novice around, enhanced his Arkle claims further with a smart effort in giving 11lb and a four-length beating to another potentially high-class sort in Hoo La Baloo. Concerns over how he would handle the ground were quashed by his trainer beforehand and, having travelled strongly under a typically cool Murphy ride, he jumped ahead taking two out and quickly settled the issue. Runner-up in last season's Royal & SunAlliance Hurdle, his ability to stay further will stand him in good stead when it comes to races like the Arkle and, at this stage, he sets the standard in the two-mile novice division. *(op 13-8 tchd 15-8)*

Hoo La Baloo(FR) ◆, who set many tongues wagging with an impressive round of jumping when destroying his field on his chase debut at Market Rasen, comes from a stable which often houses one of the leading Arkle candidates and, although beaten here, he looks a top prospect. Soon sent into the lead, he received an aggressive ride from Fitzgerald and again put in several spectacular leaps, but in going off in front he gave Racing Demon something to aim at and was unable to match him from two out. Privileged to receive the four-year-old weight-for-age allowance here, he will not get as much weight at the Festival, but he should appreciate the likely better ground there *and it would not come as a surprise at all to see him go close in March. (op 11-2 tchd 5-1 and 7-1 in a place)*

Cerium(FR), long billed as an Arkle prospect by connections, was only workmanlike in winning on his debut over fences at Warwick and looked held by Nyrche when that one took the wrong course at Aintree last time, leaving him clear. A real soft-ground lover, the testing conditions were expected to bring about an improved effort, and he did run with credit in third, but he was no match for the front pair and, on this evidence, is no Arkle contender. It will be interesting to see what sort of mark he gets for handicaps because at this stage his Festival target is more likely to be the Grand Annual, ground permitting. *(tchd 9-2)*

Iron Man(FR), a useful juvenile last season, could not have asked for a tougher introduction to fences and, although ultimately well beaten, he went well for a long way and jumped soundly in the main. His stable would not have introduced him in this type of race unless they thought he was at least useful, and a drop in grade should see him off the mark. *(op 11-1)*

Nyrche(FR) would probably have come into this with three wins from four over fences had he not taken the wrong course at Aintree last time, but he was always going to face a stiff task trying to concede weight to all his rivals bar one, and he turned in a tame effort. This was not his form, but he has developed a habit of throwing in the odd bad run, and the handicap route looks a more realistic option for him to take now. *(tchd 8-1)*

Crossbow Creek, a stylish winner on his fencing debut at Taunton, is at his best on a sound surface and was made a surprisingly short price here given the prevailing going. Unfortunately for *him he was in the wrong place at the wrong time and was brought down by outsider One Cornetto. (op 6-1 tchd 13-2)*

One Cornetto(IRE) was out of his league and it was a shame that he brought down a genuine contender after falling at the first. *(op 6-1 tchd 13-2)*

2635 WILLIAM HILL - TINGLE CREEK TROPHY CHASE GRADE 1 (13 fncs) 2m

2:35 (2:42) (Class 1) 5-Y-O+

£71,275 (£26,737; £13,387; £6,675; £3,350; £1,675)

Form				RPR
12-2	**1**		**Kauto Star (FR)**[32] 1970 5-11-7 150..............................(t) MickFitzgerald (P F Nicholls) *trckd ldr fr 5th: upsides fr 9th: led 3 out: in command next: 4 l ahd last: drvn out* **5/2**[1]	169+
21-3	**2**	*1 ½*	**Ashley Brook (IRE)**[32] 1970 7-11-7 158................................ APMcCoy (K Bishop) *lw: mde most: rdn and hdd 3 out: outpcd next: rallied flat: a hld* **5/2**[1]	166+
114-	**3**	*8*	**Oneway (IRE)**[262] 4396 8-11-7 157.. GrahamLee (M G Rimell) *hld up: prog to trck ldng pair 10th: rdn and no imp fr 3 out: one pce* **4/1**[2]	158+
-122	**4**	*¾*	**Monkerhostin (FR)**[14] 2346 8-11-7 154........................ RichardJohnson (P J Hobbs) *several slow jumps: hld up: last fr 5th: lost tch 8th: styd on fr 3 out: nvr able to chal* **9/2**[3]	158+
43-4	**5**	*20*	**Hand Inn Hand**[14] 2346 9-11-7 152................................ RobertThornton (H D Daly) *lw: trckd ldrs: shkn up after 10th: wknd fr 3 out* **14/1**	136
110-	**6**	*2*	**Locksmith**[224] 4983 5-11-7 148.. TimmyMurphy (M C Pipe) *racd freely: pressed ldr to 5th: wknd 10th* **40/1**	134
1F-4	**F**		**Sporazene (IRE)**[28] 2055 6-11-7 155........................... ChristianWilliams (P F Nicholls) *hld up: last whn fell 3rd* **20/1**	—

4m 6.80s (4.30) **Going Correction** +0.725s/f (Soft) **7** Ran SP% **109.2**
Speed ratings: **118,117,113,112,102 101,**— CSF £8.48 TOTE £3.30: £2.00, £2.10; EX 10.10.
Owner Clive D Smith **Bred** Mme H Aubert **Trained** Ditcheat, Somerset

FOCUS
With the three leading two-milers (Moscow Flyer, Well Chief and Azertyuiop) absent this has to go down as a below-par renewal, and while both Kauto Star and Ashley Brook are on the verge of championship class, the winner's improved form here still leaves him around a stone short of Moscow Flyer at his peak. Third-placed Oneway has been rated a touch below his Queen Mother form, and Monkerhostin was again below par in fourth. Despite being run in a slightly slower time than the previous novice chase, the winning time was still very acceptable for a race of its stature and, unlike in the novice event, there was no great pace on in the early stages.

NOTEBOOK
Kauto Star(FR), undoubtedly the most promising two-mile chaser around at present, made a highly satisfactory return from injury last month when second to the then very well handicapped Monkerhostin in the Haldon Gold Cup, but this was a different ball game altogether off level weights and, strictly on the ratings, he had a bit to find with Haldon third Ashley Brook. However, that run had brought him on significantly in terms of fitness and the fact that they went only a sensible gallop enabled him to outpace McCoy's mount after the Pond Fence. The runner-up was getting back at him on the climb to the line, but Fitzgerald always had things under control and he was value for a little more than the official winning margin. His jumping was sound and, in what looks an open year for the Queen Mother Champion Chase, he looks to have major claims, although whether he deserves his place ahead of reigning champion Moscow Flyer in many lists is open to question. He is now likely to have a break before returning for the Game Spirit Chase at Newbury in February. *(op 9-4 tchd 2-1 and 11-4 in places)*

Ashley Brook(IRE), last season's leading two mile novice chaser, was ridden early to take a decisive lead, but those who were looking for a performance of Champion Chase proportions from him will have been disappointed. Last season's efforts in both the Arkle and at Aintree suggested he could pose a threat to the likes of Moscow Flyer and the now injured Well Chief, but his rider's suspicions that he requires further proved founded as he seemed to be outpaced from the turn into the straight. He had made winning reappearances at this course for each of the previous two seasons, but a bad blunder at the eighth took a bit more out of him than had looked likely and as a result he deserves another chance. There is no doubting he has a huge engine and it is now likely that he will step up in distance. *(tchd 11-4)*

Oneway(IRE) was one of last season's big improvers, winning five on the bounce in handicap company before finishing a highly creditable fourth in the Champion Chase and shooting up from a mark of 107 to 157 in the space of six outings. Conceding race fitness to the front two, he has won with cut in the ground, but his best efforts have come on a sound surface, so this testing going would not have been to his liking. He ran a bold race nonetheless and, although unable to race on with the front two, he showed more than enough to suggest that he deserves his place in the Queen Mother again this year. He too looks likely to turn up next in the Castleford Chase, and better ground there should give him realistic chances of reversing form with Ashley Brook. *(op 9-2)*

Monkerhostin(FR) made a blistering start to the season in the Haldon Gold Cup and was a little unlucky when finishing second in the Paddy Power, but his form since then has taken a dip, and this fourth run at a high level in just over a month was always likely to bring about a 'flat' run. Failing to jump with any real zest, he plugged on up the straight, but was unable to get to Oneway and is now surely in line for a break. He would be a major player in the Ryanair Chase at the Festival if returning to peak form, and it would not be a surprise to see him have a spin over hurdles beforehand. *(op 5-1)*

Hand Inn Hand was the most popular outsider, with his ability to handle testing ground unquestionable, but his previous form over two miles was nothing to get excited about and it was no surprise to see him readily outpaced having travelled well to a point. He is not up to it at this distance, but could go well in something like the Ascot Chase at Lingfield in February over a more suitable trip.

Locksmith developed into a very useful novice last season but found things too hot to handle on his final start in the Celebration Chase at Sandown, and this reappearance was a big ask for the youngster. He is going to find life tough this season off his current sort of rating, but he is the sort his trainer could pick up a nice race with once back down to a decent mark.

Sporazene(IRE), a potentially smart novice back in 2004, had last season cut short through an injury acquired when falling at Exeter on his second start over fences and, as a result had to be thrown in at the deep end here as a consequence of his rating being so high. He had not shaped with a great amount of promise on his reappearance in the Elite Hurdle at Wincanton and made an early exit here, and while he clearly has masses of natural ability, he will continue to be very hard to place. *(op 16-1)*

2636 WILLIAM HILL H'CAP HURDLE (LISTED RACE) (8 hdls) 2m 110y

3:10 (3:14) (Class 1) (0-140,137) 4-Y-O+

£28,510 (£10,695; £5,355; £2,670; £1,340; £670)

Form				RPR
F-01	**1**		**Verasi**[28] 2047 4-10-13 124...(p) JamieMoore (G L Moore) *settled midfield: mstke 3 out and lost pl: 14th and rdn sn after: styd on strly again bef 2 out: led last 100yds: sn clr* **12/1**	134+
-050	**2**	*2 ½*	**Cherub (GER)**[7] 2493 5-11-4 129..(t) APMcCoy (Jonjo O'Neill) *hld up wl in rr: stdy prog on outer fr 5th: trckd ldrs 2 out: rdn to ld last: hdd and outpcd fnl 100yds* **16/1**	136
0-	**3**	*4*	**Victram (IRE)**[38] 4768 5-9-10 112... AELynch[(5)] (Adrian McGuinness, Ire) *lw: hld up in last pair early: smooth prog bef 3 out: led gng easily sn after 2 out: rdn and hdd last: wknd flat* **3/1**[1]	115+
UF-P	**4**	*2*	**Cloudy Grey (IRE)**[13] 2369 8-11-10 135............................ BarryFenton (Miss E C Lavelle) *led to sn after 2 out: stl cl up last: fdd flat* **33/1**	136
-421	**5**	*1 ¾*	**All Star (GER)**[14] 2347 5-11-5 130...................................... MickFitzgerald (N J Henderson) *hld up in midfield: effrt to chse ldrs 2 out: no imp u.p bef last: wknd flat* **15/2**[2]	129
20-1	**6**	*¾*	**Daryal (IRE)**[19] 2247 4-11-1 126...................................... RobertThornton (A King) *settled midfield: rdn and no prog bef 2 out: kpt on flat: nt rch ldrs* **10/1**	125
3442	**7**	*5*	**Papillon De Iena (FR)**[19] 2247 5-9-13 120.....(p) AndrewGlassonbury[(10)] (M C Pipe) *wl in tch: trckd ldrs gng easily after 3 out: rdn 2 out: sn wknd* **14/1**	114
6-P3	**8**	*½*	**Fenix (GER)**[21] 2190 6-11-4 129..................................(b) RichardJohnson (Mrs L Wadham) *prom: trckd ldr 5th: rdn to chal 2 out: wknd bef last* **11/1**	122
0604	**9**	*6*	**Transit**[9] 2452 6-9-11 111 oh1.......................................(p) OwynNelmes[(3)] (B Ellison) *hld up wl in rr: rdn and no prog bef 2 out: n.d* **50/1**	101+
/1-2	**10**	*9*	**Guru**[35] 1919 7-10-6 117.. PhilipHide (G L Moore) *trckd ldrs tl wknd u.p bef 2 out* **12/1**	101+
21/2	**11**	*¾*	**Tramantano**[20] 2209 6-11-5 137.................................... MarcGoldstein[(7)] (N A Twiston-Davies) *mstke 1st: hld up in midfield: in tch whn blnd 3 out: sn drvn: wknd bef 2 out* **14/1**	120+
30-2	**12**	*15*	**Frontier**[76] 1481 8-10-9 120..(t) ChristianWilliams (B J Llewellyn) *a in rr: drvn and wknd 3 out: t.o whn blnd last* **66/1**	82
P1-0	**13**	*15*	**Fortune Island (IRE)**[14] 2347 6-9-12 114...............(vt) PaddyMerrigan[(5)] (M C Pipe) *prom: chsd ldr 3rd to 5th: u.p and wknd rapidly bef 2 out: t.o* **16/1**	61
B00-	**P**		**New Entic (FR)**[260] 4433 4-10-11 125.................................. ColinBolger[(3)] (G L Moore) *chsd ldrs: wknd u.str.p after 3 out: p.u bef next* **100/1**	—
006-	**P**		**Polar Red**[226] 4946 8-11-7 132...(vt) RJGreene (M C Pipe) *drvn and nt keen after 2nd: t.o fr 4th: p.u bef 2 out* **50/1**	—
100-	**P**		**Medison (FR)**[225] 4973 5-11-8 133...................................... TimmyMurphy (M C Pipe) *hld up wl in rr: shkn up and no repsonse 3 out: sn t.o: p.u bef next* **8/1**[3]	—
1050	**P**		**Fontanesi (IRE)**[20] 2209 5-11-10 135.................................... GerrySupple (M C Pipe) *chsd ldr to 3rd: dropped rt out u.p and t.o fr 5th: p.u bef 2 out* **66/1**	—
P0P-	**P**		**Barton Nic**[271] 4234 12-10-6 124......................................(b) DarylJacob[(7)] (D P Keane) *t.k.h: trckd ldrs tl wknd u.p sn after 3 out: t.o whn p.u bef next* **100/1**	—
00-2	**P**		**Adopted Hero (IRE)**[21] 2190 5-11-4 129.............................. GrahamLee (J Howard Johnson) *hld up in midfield: mstke 3 out: wknd tamely: t.o whn p.u bef 2 out* **9/1**	—

4m 15.9s (7.00) **Going Correction** +0.725s/f (Soft)
WFA 4 from 5yo+ 10lb **19** Ran SP% **127.6**
Speed ratings: **112,110,108,108,107 106,104,104,101,97 96,89,82,—,— —,—,—,—** CSF £190.99 CT £738.87 TOTE £16.30: £2.90, £3.30, £1.90, £7.10; EX 248.00 Trifecta £2858.30 Pool £12,882.80. 3.20 winning units.
Owner F Ledger J Bateman **Bred** D J And Mrs Deer **Trained** Woodingdean, E Sussex

FOCUS
A top handicap that proved to be quite a slog and Verasi put up a remarkable performance in coming from nowhere to win going away. There were plenty of eyecatching performances in behind the winner and it is likely the race will prove a good source of future winners. Rock solid form.

NOTEBOOK
Verasi, a course and distance winner in heavy ground last month, was ideally equipped to handle the prevailing conditions and connections had opted to fit him with cheekpieces in an attempt to get him racing more enthusiastically. Never jumping that well, a mistake three out looked to have ended his chance as he dropped back through the field but, as with Green Iceni in the first, he came with a strong, sustained run in the final quarter mile and scampered up the hill in the style of a useful sort. Hitting a flat spot in his races will be a major problem for him in better races on a sounder surface, but he is most genuine and a longer distance may enable him to improve further. *(tchd 14-1)*

Cherub(GER), a Grade One winner at Punchestown as a novice, has struggled since then and often showed a fair amount of temperament, but there is no denying he has plenty of ability and he ran one of his best races here. He clearly has the ability to win a decent race, but could never be backed with confidence and it may take a switch to fences to get the best out of him.

Victram(IRE) ◆ failed to live up to expectations when down the field at Aintree last season, but he has been in decent form on the Flat since then and held obvious claims here with his lowly weight. Always travelling strongly, his rider was oozing confidence as they approached two out, but he fell in a hole once coming off the bridle and did not get up the hill. His Flat form suggests he ought to be capable of a fair bit better still, and he will be well worth another chance when the track and ground place more emphasis on speed. *(op 10-3 tchd 7-2)*

Cloudy Grey(IRE) ran a huge race under top weight and it was great to see this formerly smart bumper performer finally return to form. Always to the fore, he was still travelling strongly as they took two out, but the weight began to tell and he faded into fourth on the climb to the line. Although nearly nine, he is lightly raced and has the physique of a chaser, so it will be fascinating to see if connections opt to go over the larger obstacles.

All Star(GER), rightfully raised 12lb for his Huntingdon romp, was dropping five furlongs in trip and tackling vastly different ground conditions, but with his stable in such grand form it was hard to discount him. He moved into a challenging position turning in, but was never going quite well enough to get on terms with the leaders. He may improve for a return to further, but is going to need to if he is to defy this sort of mark. *(op 6-1 tchd 8-1)*

Daryal(IRE), raised 8lb for winning on his reappearance at Leicester, was unable make an impression, having been held up, and never really got involved. He was going on at the death and shapes as though he will stay a bit further. *(op 12-1)*

Papillon De Iena(FR) was weighted to reverse Leicester form with Daryal, but he lacks the scope of that one and failed to see out his race. He is not really up to this grade and will find easier opportunities.

Guru, a stablemate of the winner, probably found this a bit too hot and will be more home down a grade or two. *(op 14-1)*

Tramantano, who made a highly pleasing reappearance when a fast-finishing second to Lingo in the Greatwood, made a few jumping errors and was never really going that well. This was a tough ask for him on his second start back and he may well have 'bounced'. *(tchd 16-1)*

Adopted Hero(IRE) failed to build on his promising Wetherby second and stopped worryingly quickly. He is talented, but consistency would not be one of his strong points. *(op 11-1 tchd 12-1)*

Medison(FR) ended last season on a down note and has really struggled since being required to compete off this sort of mark. He travelled well to a point, but found little off the bridle and probably found this a bit too tough first time back. He is an interesting chasing prospect. *(op 11-1 tchd 12-1)*

2637 WILLIAMHILL.CO.UK MARATHON CHASE (H'CAP) (LISTED RACE) (24 fncs) 3m 5f 110y

3:40 (3:48) (Class 1) (0-145,139) 5-Y-O+ **£23,877** (£9,625; £5,353)

Form				RPR
0-63	**1**		**Willie John Daly (IRE)**[22] 2162 8-11-0 127.................. RichardJohnson (P J Hobbs) *disp ld fr 3rd: sustained duel w runner-up tl lft clr 2 out: idled bdly and jnd last: urged along and jst prevailed* **7/2**	137+
0-14	**2**	*shd*	**Brave Spirit (FR)**[20] 2215 7-10-8 121............................(p) MickFitzgerald (C L Tizzard) *lw: mstkes: led: jnd 3rd: duelled w wnr tl terrible blunder 2 out: rallied and upsides last: epic battle flat: jst failed* **10/3**[3]	131+

06-4 **3** *dist* **Tanterari (IRE)**[13] [2368] 7-10-0 **113**.................................. TimmyMurphy —
(M C Pipe) *lw: hld up: nt fluent 13th: chsd ldng pair 16th: wknd rapidly and p.u bef 2 out: resumed: btn 96 seconds* **3/1**[2]
14-4 **F** **Campaign Trail (IRE)**[16] [2292] 7-10-7 **120**.............................. APMcCoy —
(Jonjo O'Neill) *hld up: mstke 4th: in tch whn fell 14th* **11/4**[1]
1P-P **P** **Whitford Don (IRE)**[21] [2176] 7-11-4 **131**.....................(b) ChristianWilliams —
(P F Nicholls) *chsd ldng pair: jumping wnt to pieces fr 15th: sn t.o: p.u bef 3 out* **6/1**
8m 5.50s (42.10) **Going Correction** +0.725s/f (Soft) **5** Ran SP% **111.3**
Speed ratings: **72,71,—,—,—** CSF £15.41 TOTE £4.80: £2.10, £1.90; EX 13.60 Place 6 £105.68, Place 5 £56.57.
Owner D R Peppiatt **Bred** Daniel O'Connell Jnr **Trained** Withycombe, Somerset

FOCUS
A pedestrian winning time for a race of its class, but a thrilling finish, with the front two locked in battle up the run-in after the winner had threatened to refuse at the last.

NOTEBOOK
Willie John Daly(IRE) showed the benefit of his reappearance run when a staying-on third at Cheltenham last month and disputed the lead with Brave Spirit from an early stage. Inseperable throughout, he was handed the initiative as the runner up blundered two out, but not wanting to leave his pal behind, he started to stop to a walk and allowed Brave Spirit back in. Locked together on the climb to the line, it was a proper old head-bobber and he just did enough. A dour stayer, he clearly has a little quirk, but there was nothing wrong with the way in which he battled on and he now has the option of running in the Welsh National, in which he would carry a penalty. *(op 9-2 tchd 5-1 in places)*
Brave Spirit(FR) matched strides with Willie John Daly for a long way, and did well to recover from a shocking mistake at the second-last to challenge the winner again on the climb to the line. He only just missed out and deserves at least as much credit as the winner. A resolute galloper, he will continue to be a threat when stamina is at a premium. *(op 3-1 tchd 7-2)*
Tanterari(IRE), trying this sort of trip for the first time, travelled well under a patient Murphy ride, but he began to niggle along around half a mile out and it was soon clear he was not going to join in with the front two. He has won over three miles one, but this was just too far. *(op 5-2 tchd 9-4 and 10-3)*
Campaign Trail(IRE), given a pipe-opener over hurdles at Market Rasen, was still in touch, going well when coming down at around half way. He has a race or two in him off this sort of mark, if none the worse for the experience. *(op 3-1 tchd 5-2)*
Whitford Don(IRE) is a moody character and looked reluctant as soon as he was asked to close. *(op 3-1 tchd 5-2)*
T/Jkpt: £51,825.30 to a £1 stake. Pool: £72,993.50. 1.00 winning ticket. T/Plt: £85.70 to a £1 stake. Pool: £119,932.15. 1,020.95 winning tickets. T/Qpdt: £19.30 to a £1 stake. Pool: £7,633.90. 292.40 winning tickets. JN

2440 WETHERBY (L-H)
Saturday, December 3

OFFICIAL GOING: Heavy
Wind: Virtually nil

2638 WETHERBY CHRISTMAS RACES 26TH & 27TH DECEMBER NOVICES' HURDLE (12 hdls) 2m 7f
12:10 (12:10) (Class 3) 4-Y-0+ **£4,993** (£1,465; £732; £366)

Form RPR
31P **1** **Nine De Sivola (FR)**[11] [2417] 4-10-11 110................ PatrickMcDonald[(7)] 118+
(Ferdy Murphy) *trckd ldrs: smooth hdwy 4 out: led 2 out: clr whn hit last: kpt on* **6/1**[3]
02/4 **2** *7* **Elvis Returns**[16] [2295] 7-10-5 .... ThomasDreaper[(7)] 103+
(J M Jefferson) *trckd ldrs: hdwy and cl up 4 out: led appr next: rdn and hdd 2 out: kpt on same pce* **5/1**[2]
632 **3** *14* **Laertes**[21] [2186] 4-10-9 .... MrTGreenall[(3)] 88
(C Grant) *hld up: hdwy 5 out: rdn along to chse ldng pair after 3 out: drvn and no imp fr next* **6/1**[3]
42 **4** *8* **Mac Dargin (IRE)**[23] [2144] 6-10-12 .... AntonyEvans 80
(N A Twiston-Davies) *cl up: led 8th: rdn along and hdd appr 3 out: sn wknd* **8/1**
1142 **5** *27* **Tandava (IRE)**[42] [1839] 7-11-3 112.......................... TomMessenger[(7)] 65
(Mrs S C Bradburne) *chsd ldrs: rdn along 8th: sn outpcd and bhd fr next* **10/1**
06 **6** *dist* **Tiger King (GER)**[9] [2448] 4-10-12 .... WilsonRenwick —
(P Monteith) *a rr: wl bhd fr 1/2-way* **66/1**
P **Abbotsford (IRE)** 5-10-7 .... BrianHughes[(5)] —
(J Howard Johnson) *a rr: bhd fr 1/2-way: p.u bef 3 out* **40/1**
0/ **P** **Pride Of Finewood (IRE)**[637] [4179] 7-10-12 .... RussGarritty —
(E W Tuer) *a rr: bhd fr 1/2-way: p.u after 4 out* **50/1**
40 **P** **Ballyowen (IRE)**[11] [2421] 6-10-9 .... GinoCarenza[(3)] —
(Mrs P Sly) *in tch: rdn along 8th: sn wknd and bhd whn p.u bef 3 out* **80/1**
33-0 **P** **Crashtown Leader (IRE)**[37] [1892] 6-10-12 110.................. TomDoyle —
(C Tinkler) *led: pushed along and hdd 8th: rdn 4 out: sn drvn and wknd qckly: p.u bef 3 out* **7/2**[1]
P **Cooldine Lad (IRE)**[412] 5-10-12 .... AlanDempsey —
(J Howard Johnson) *prom: hit 3rd:miostake 8th and sn pushed along: rdn and lost pl 4 out: p.u bef next* **5/1**[2]
6m 15.1s (63.50) **Going Correction** +1.175s/f (Heav)
WFA 4 from 5yo+ 11lb **11** Ran SP% **111.5**
Speed ratings: **105,102,97,94,85** —,—,—,—,— — CSF £34.10 TOTE £6.40: £2.80, £1.80, £1.60; EX 45.30.
Owner The DPRP Sivola Partnership **Bred** G Trapenard **Trained** West Witton, N Yorks

FOCUS
A modest novice event, run at an ordinary pace, and the field finished weary in the tesing ground. The winner is progressive.

NOTEBOOK
Nine De Sivola(FR) got back to winning ways and had the race in safe keeping prior to an error at the final flight. This was his best effort to date, the trip proved to his liking, and he is clearly well at home on a deep surface. Still only four, he can defy a higher mark in this sphere, before ultimately jumping a fence in due course. *(op 9-2)*
Elvis Returns failed to see out the longer trip as well as the winner, but still finished a clear second-best and turned in another decent effort. He should soon be going one better in this division.
Laertes, behind the winner over shorter at this track last time, failed to really improve for the step up to this trip and again took too long to find his stride. He was clear in third, and will probably get closer over this trip on a less taxing surface, so should not be written off now that he qualifies for handicaps. *(op 15-2)*
Mac Dargin(IRE) failed to sustain his effort in the home straight and looked to be found out by the deep surface. He can do better, will appreciate better ground in the future, and now has the option of handicaps. *(op 10-1)*
Tandava(IRE) was well beaten and still has to convince over this sort of trip. While he is probably at best over shorter, he is not going to prove easy to place in this division under his penalty, or in handicaps from his current mark. *(op 8-1)*
Cooldine Lad(IRE), a winning Irish pointer in 2004 who has joined top connections, drifted in the betting and ran too bad to be true on this hurdling bow. He has it to prove now, but is surely capable of better than this. *(op 4-1 tchd 9-2 and 100-30 in a place)*
Crashtown Leader(IRE) stopped very quickly when push came to shove as though something may have been amiss. He has now shown very little in two outings since resuming this term. *Official explanation: jockey said gelding had a breathing problem (op 4-1 tchd 9-2 and 100-30 in a place)*

2639 KNAGGSIE BOY NOVICES' H'CAP HURDLE (10 hdls) 2m 4f 110y
12:40 (12:41) (Class 4) (0-105,104)
3-Y-0+ **£3,480** (£1,014; £507)

Form RPR
03-4 **1** **Euro American (GER)**[42] [1836] 5-11-12 **104**...................... AlanDempsey 114+
(E W Tuer) *hld up and bhd: stdy hdwy 4 out: rdn to ld last: styd on wl flat* **15/2**
P-51 **2** *1 ¼* **Aston Lad**[27] [2064] 4-11-7 **102**.. KeithMercer[(3)] 110+
(M D Hammond) *hld up and bhd: stdy hdwy 4 out: cl up fr next: ev ch last: rdn and kpt on flat* **4/1**[1]
06P- **3** *8* **Greek Star**[298] [3750] 4-11-3 **95**.. RussGarritty 92
(K A Morgan) *a.p: led 4 out: rdn along appr 2 out: drvn and hdd last: kpt on same pce* **12/1**
4553 **4** *29* **True Temper (IRE)**[42] [1838] 8-9-10 **79**......................... DeclanMcGann[(5)] 47
(A M Crow) *trckd ldrs: hdwy and cl up 5th: rdn along after 4 out: wknd fr next* **5/1**[3]
5-2P **5** *18* **Iron Warrior (IRE)**[134] [212] 5-10-8 **91**......................... DougieCostello[(5)] 41
(G M Moore) *a.p: rdn along on inner to chse ldr appr 3 out: drvn and wknd bef next* **8/1**
045/ **6** *2* **Batto**[649] [3976] 5-10-5 **83**... AnthonyRoss 31
(G M Moore) *hld up in rr: sme hdwy 1/2-way: sn rdn along and outpcd: bhd fr 4 out* **20/1**
0053 **P** **Countrywide Sun**[17] [2263] 3-9-9 **95** oh2 ow2.................. EwanWhillans[(7)] —
(A C Whillans) *chsd ldrs to 6th: sn lost pl and bhd whn p.u bef 3 out* **10/1**
64P0 **P** **Macchiato**[21] [2191] 4-10-5 **83**.. WilsonRenwick —
(I W McInnes) *chsd ldrs: rdn along after 4 out: drvn and wknd bef next: p.u bef 2 out* **22/1**
P04- **P** **Colwyn Jake (IRE)**[336] [3157] 6-10-2 **90**........................ DavidBoland[(10)] —
(Ian Williams) *hld up in midfield: effport 5th: rdn along and bhd appr 4 out p.u bef next* **16/1**
042P **P** **The Yellow Earl (IRE)**[101] [1310] 5-9-7 **78** oh8.................. PhilKinsella[(7)] —
(J M Jefferson) *keen: led after 1st: rdn along and hdd 4 out: wknd qckly and p.u bef next* **16/1**
6P-5 **P** **Bobsourown (IRE)**[21] [2191] 6-10-1 **79** oh1 ow1..................... TomDoyle —
(D McCain) *led to after 1st: trckd ldrs tl lost pl 4th: pushed along and mstke next: sn rdn along and bhd: p.u bef 3 out* **9/2**[2]
5m 33.8s (24.90) **Going Correction** +1.175s/f (Heav)
WFA 3 from 4yo 14lb 4 from 5yo+ 11lb **11** Ran SP% **115.4**
Speed ratings: **99,98,95,84,77 76**,—,—,—,— — CSF £37.54 CT £359.08 TOTE £9.00: £2.30, £2.40, £4.60; EX 20.30.
Owner Shore Property **Bred** Euro-American Bet Verm Gmbh **Trained** Great Smeaton, N Yorks

FOCUS
A moderate handicap run at a fair gallop, and the first three came clear. All three look capable of further improvement.

NOTEBOOK
Euro American(GER) ◆ finally opened his account over timber at the tenth time of asking with a dogged display over this longer trip. He was given a well-judged ride by Dempsey, jumped neatly throughout and, on this evidence, would be hard to stop under a penalty. *(op 8-1)*
Aston Lad, raised 2lb for winning a similar event at Ayr last time, came from a similar position as the winner and only gave way to that rival on the run-in. He is clearly in good heart at present, was clear of the rest at the finish, and can strike again from this mark. *(op 7-2)*
Greek Star, having his first outing since February, made an encouraging return to action on ground he would have found plenty soft enough. He remains a maiden over timber but is still only four and is very much entitled to improve for this experience. *(op 16-1)*
True Temper(IRE) ran below her recent level and did not appear overly suited by the drop in trip. She is one to have reservations about. *(tchd 11-2)*

2640 YORK MAILING H'CAP CHASE (15 fncs) 2m 4f 110y
1:10 (1:11) (Class 3) (0-125,118) 5-Y-0+ **£5,673** (£1,665; £832; £415)

Form RPR
542- **1** **Edmo Yewkay (IRE)**[225] [4966] 5-11-12 **118**...............(b) RussGarritty 140+
(T D Easterby) *j.w: cl up: led 3rd: rdn clr appr 3 out: styd on strly* **11/2**
1-04 **2** *23* **Green Ideal**[10] [2445] 7-10-11 **106**....................................(b) KeithMercer[(3)] 103
(Ferdy Murphy) *trckd wnr fr 3rd: rdn along 4 out: drvn appr next and kpt on same pce* **11/4**[1]
6P-2 **3** *17* **Deep Water (USA)**[16] [2294] 11-11-3 **109**......................... WilsonRenwick 89
(M D Hammond) *hld up in tch: hit 4th: hdwy to chse ldng pair after 5 out: rdn along next: one pce fr 3 out* **7/2**[2]
-644 **4** *11* **Sir Storm (IRE)**[14] [2339] 9-11-8 **114**.................................. AnthonyRoss 83
(G M Moore) *trckd ldrs: pushed along 6 out: rdn next and sn outpcd* **4/1**[3]
-PP0 **P** **Majed (FR)**[28] [2038] 9-10-13 **110**...................................(b) DesFlavin[(5)] —
(Mrs L B Normile) *led to 3rd: rdn along and lost pl after 6th: sn bhd and p.u bef 4 out* **20/1**
U3U4 **P** **Cill Churnain (IRE)**[9] [2451] 12-11-4 **110**............................ PadgeWhelan —
(Mrs S J Smith) *trckd ldrs: blnd 4th: mstke next: blnd bdly 6th: rdn along and outpcd fr 6 out: bhd whn p.u bef 4 out* **7/2**[2]
5m 41.2s (20.50) **Going Correction** +1.175s/f (Heav) **6** Ran SP% **111.3**
Speed ratings: **107,98,91,87**,— — CSF £21.01 TOTE £5.60: £3.00, £1.80; EX 22.80.
Owner Edmolift Uk Ltd **Bred** Mrs Sheila Morrissey **Trained** Great Habton, N Yorks

FOCUS
A modest handicap which saw the runners finish well and truly strung out behind the facile winner.

NOTEBOOK
Edmo Yewkay(IRE), returning from a 225-day break with the blinkers applied for the first time over fences, proved different class to his rivals - despite the burden of top weight - and simply came home as he pleased. This has to rate a very encouraging start to the current campaign, he is clearly suited by testing ground, and it is interesting that both his wins over fences have now come over course and distance. He can expect a hike in the weights, but he is still only five and could have more to offer this term. *(op 9-2 tchd 6-1)*
Green Ideal, with the blinkers re-applied, could not live with the winner and looked to perform below his current rating. He is a frustrating customer but will most likely be happier back over further in the future. *(op 10-3)*
Deep Water(USA), runner-up in this event last season off a 10lb higher mark, failed to find as much as looked likely off the bridle from the top of the straight and was disappointingly well beaten. He may have found this stiff test coming too soon after his recent comeback at Market Rasen, however, and is worth another chance to atone off his current rating. *Official explanation: jockey said gelding was lame (tchd 4-1)*

Sir Storm(IRE), whose previous best efforts have mostly come at this track, was in trouble a long way out and ran a tame race by his own standards.

Cill Churnain(IRE) made too many mistakes over his fences and it was no surprise when his rider finally conceded defeat. He seemingly has two ways of running. *(op 4-1)*

2641 ROCOM GUNS N ROSES H'CAP HURDLE (9 hdls) 2m

1:45 (1:45) (Class 3) (0-135,133) 4-Y-0+ **£6,571** (£1,929; £964; £481)

Form | | | | RPR
/5-0 **1** **Bob Justice (IRE)**[219] [91] 9-11-3 **129**.......... BrianHughes(5) 129+
(J Howard Johnson) *cl up: led 5th: rdn along and hdd 3 out: rallied u.p next: drvn last: led flat: styd on wl* **9/1**

462P **2** *1 ½* **Kentucky Blue (IRE)**[21] [2190] 5-11-2 **123**..........(p) RussGarritty 121
(T D Easterby) *hld up in tch: hdwy 4 out: led next: rdn and wandered 2 out: drvn last: sn hdd and one pce* **4/1**[3]

3-05 **3** *dist* **St Pirran (IRE)**[14] [2334] 10-10-12 **122**.......... LarryMcGrath(3) 87
(R C Guest) *hld up in rr: hdwy appr 4 out: rdn bef next and sn btn* **7/4**[1]

02-P **4** *11* **Ebinzayd (IRE)**[140] [1013] 9-11-9 **133**.......... GaryBerridge(3) 85
(L Lungo) *in tch: hit 4th: rdn along and outpcd after next: bhd fr 4 out* **12/1**

4113 **5** *8* **Snow's Ride**[52] [1720] 5-10-3 **110**.......... NeilMulholland 54
(M D Hammond) *in tch: rdn along after 5th: sn wknd and bhd* **7/2**[2]

244- **6** *4* **Through The Rye**[192] [4846] 9-11-9 **133**.......... KeithMercer(3) 73
(E W Tuer) *led to 5th: rdn along and wkng whn hit nedxt: sn lost pl and bhd* **5/1**

4m 14.1s (14.70) **Going Correction** +1.175s/f (Heav) **6** Ran SP% **112.9**

Speed ratings: **110,109,**—,—,— — CSF £44.40 TOTE £12.50: £4.30, £2.00; EX 61.40.

Owner Andrea & Graham Wylie **Bred** M J Foley **Trained** Billy Row, Co Durham

FOCUS

A fair handicap, run at a sound pace in the conditions, and the first two came clear. The form is worth treating with a degree of caution.

NOTEBOOK

Bob Justice(IRE) ◆, well backed for this return to hurdling, ground down the runner-up to lead over the final flight and make a winning debut for his new connections. Indeed this was his first success since 2002, and he had been far from certain to enjoy this shorter trip, considering that most of his recent form in Ireland has been over fences and a longer trip. However, enjoy the stiff test over this trip he certainly did, and the deep surface was also much to his liking. On this evidence he looks like proving a decent acquisition for his top connections, as he is currently rated 20lb lower over fences, and should really be placed to advantage on his return to that sphere. *(tchd 10-1)*

Kentucky Blue(IRE) had every chance, finished miles clear of the rest, and was only outstayed by the winner on the run-in. This was much more like his true form, but while he is capable of going one better from this sort of mark, still looks fairly tricky under pressure. *(op 9-2 tchd 5-1)*

St Pirran(IRE), who had hinted at improvment in two previous outings over timber this term, was found out by the deep surface and was beaten at the top of the straight. He is undeniably well-treated in this sphere in relation to his chase form, and will appreciate better ground in the future, but at the age of ten is always likely to prove vulnerable to a progressive rival over hurdles. Official explanation: jockey said gelding was unsuited by the heavy ground *(op 13-8 tchd 15-8 in a place)*

Ebinzayd(IRE), last seen pulling-up over fences at Market Rasen 140 days previously, shaped very much as though this was needed and never threatened. He is too high in the weights over hurdles at present and will find life easier when reverting to fences in due course. *(op 11-1)*

Snow's Ride ran well below expectations and looked all at sea on this much softer surface. *(tchd 4-1)*

Through The Rye eventually paid for his early exertions at the head of affiars and was another to disappoint. *(op 13-2)*

2642 EUROPEAN BREEDERS FUND "JUNIOR" STANDARD OPEN NATIONAL HUNT FLAT RACE 1m 6f

2:20 (2:20) (Class 6) 3-Y-O **£2,172** (£633; £316)

Form | | | | RPR
1 **Alfie Flits** 3-10-12.......... TomDoyle 106+
(G A Swinbank) *hld up in tch: smooth hdwy 5f out: led 3f out: rdn clr 2f out: kpt on* **5/2**[1]

2 *3 ½* **Astarador (FR)** 3-10-5.......... LiamBerridge(7) 101+
(J Howard Johnson) *trckd ldrs: hdwy 6f out: led over 4f out: rdn and hdd 3f out: kpt on u.p fnl 2f* **16/1**

3 *18* **Raider Of The East (IRE)** 3-10-9.......... KeithMercer(3) 79
(K A Morgan) *trckd ldrs: hdwy 1/2-way: cl up 5f out: rdn over 3f out and grad wknd* **16/1**

4 *8* **Tahaddi Turtle (IRE)** 3-10-12.......... RussGarritty 70
(T P Tate) *keen: hld up and bhd: hdwy on outer over 5f out: rdn along 3f out kpt on fnl 2f: nvr a factor* **11/2**[3]

5 *1* **Olmetta (FR)** 3-10-2.......... GaryBerridge(3) 61
(J P L Ewart) *hld up in midfield: hdwy over 5f out: rdn along 4f out and sn no imp* **9/1**

6 *11* **Golden Streak (IRE)** 3-10-9.......... MrTGreenall(3) 55
(C R Egerton) *chsd ldrs on inner: rdn along over 5f out and sn wknd* **7/2**[2]

7 *1 ¼* **Celtic Saloon (IRE)** 3-10-12.......... AlanDempsey 54
(K G Reveley) *in tch: pushed along over 5f out and grad wknd* **7/1**

8 *1* **Insurgent (IRE)** 3-10-9.......... LarryMcGrath(3) 53
(R C Guest) *in tch on outer: pushed along to chse ldrs 6f out: rdn over 4f out and sn wknd* **28/1**

0 **9** *18* **Lily Tara**[27] [2068] 3-10-0.......... DeclanMcGann(5) 24
(A M Crow) *cl up: rdn along 5f out: grad wknd* **40/1**

10 *28* **Hello Noddy** 3-10-12.......... NeilMulholland —
(B Mactaggart) *midfield: rdn along 5f out: wknd 4f out* **20/1**

11 *3* **Bora Shaamit (IRE)** 3-9-12.......... JohnKington(7) —
(M Scudamore) *led: rdn along 6f out: hdd & wknd over 4f out* **25/1**

0 **12** *dist* **Precious Pride**[25] [2105] 3-9-12.......... TomMessenger(7) —
(M J Gingell) *midfield: rdn along and lost pl after 6f: t.o fnl 6f* **100/1**

3m 41.0s **12** Ran SP% **115.9**

CSF £41.48 TOTE £2.90: £1.60, £6.00, £4.10; EX 43.30.

Owner Dom Flit **Bred** Shadwell Estate Company Limited **Trained** Melsonby, N Yorks

FOCUS

As if often the case in such events, the overall form is not easy to assess, but the first two came clear and both look above average.

NOTEBOOK

Alfie Flits ◆, a 15,000gns purchase whose dam won over ten furlongs on the Flat, got his career off to a perfect start with a ready success and justified his position at the top of the market. Despite being a son of Machiavellian, he had no trouble with the heavy ground, and clearly stays very well. His yard have a decent strike-rate in this sphere, and tend to excel with this type of horse, so it would be no surprise to see him develop into a useful dual-purpose performer in the future. *(op 3-1 tchd 10-3 and 9-4)*

Astarador(FR) ◆, whose dam won on the Flat and over hurdles and fences in France, was produced to win his race at the top of the straight but failed to cope with the winner's challenge around three out and was readily held at the finish. He still finished a long way in front of the remainder of his rivals, however, and should improve a deal for this experience. It is also most likely that he will come into his own when faced with a stiffer test. *(op 20-1)*

Raider Of The East(IRE), who originally cost 260,000gns as a yearling and falied to make the track when with Sir Michael Stoute, showed up well enough until tiring in the straight and should improve for the outing. *(op 12-1)*

Tahaddi Turtle(IRE), half-brother to Irish hurdle winners Game Ball Ali and No Where To Hyde, did little to help his rider by refusing to settle early on under restraint and did well to finish as he did in the circumstances. He acted well enough on the deep surface and, providing he learns to settle, does possess the scope to leave this form well behind in due course. *(op 9-2)*

Olmetta(FR) *(op 8-1 tchd 10-1)*

Golden Streak(IRE), a 50,000gns purchase and half-brother to most notably the Irish-trained dual-purpose winner Tribal Princess, failed to find anything for pressure when it mattered and proved disappointing. *(op 10-3)*

2643 ONE MAN NOVICES' CHASE (18 fncs) 3m 1f

2:50 (2:50) (Class 2) 5-Y-O+ **£11,192** (£4,208)

Form | | | | RPR
21-3 **1** **Leading Man (IRE)**[9] [2449] 5-11-0.......... KeithMercer 132+
(Ferdy Murphy) *j.w: a.p: chsd ldr fr 6 out: one l down whn lft clr 4 out: kpt on* **16/1**

11-1 **2** *12* **Julius Caesar**[16] [2291] 5-11-5.......... AlanDempsey 130+
(J Howard Johnson) *trckd ldrs: hit 3rd: blnd 8th and nt jump wl after: rdn along and outpcd 5 out: lft 2nd next: kpt on same pce* **2/1**[2]

1221 **U** **Mckelvey (IRE)**[21] [2189] 6-11-8 135.......... TomDoyle —
(P Bowen) *trckd ldrs: led 9th: one l up whn blnd and uns rdr 4 out* **1/1**[1]

4110 **P** **Bushido (IRE)**[16] [2292] 6-11-8 128.......... PadgeWhelan —
(Mrs S J Smith) *hit 2nd: cl up: hit 9th: sn rdn along and outpcd fr 6 out: p.u bef 4 out* **14/1**

4-13 **P** **Red Georgie (IRE)**[22] [2165] 7-11-5.......... AntonyEvans —
(N A Twiston-Davies) *j. deliberately and to the rt: led to 9th: sn rdn along and outpcd fr 6 out: p.u bef 4 out* **13/2**[3]

7m 6.00s (26.00) **Going Correction** +1.175s/f (Heav) **5** Ran SP% **109.2**

Speed ratings: **105,101,**—,—,— CSF £48.08 TOTE £14.50: £2.80, £1.30; EX 35.40.

Owner Mrs C McKeane **Bred** Mrs Catriona M McKeane **Trained** West Witton, N Yorks

FOCUS

A decent staying novices' chase, run at a sound pace, and the winner looks progressive despite being flattered by his winning margin.

NOTEBOOK

Leading Man(IRE) ◆, a distant third behind Turpin Green on his recent chase bow at Carlisle, showed the clear benefit of that experience and, despite having to rate a slightly fortunate winner, he relished the return to this longer trip. This is his ground, he has always appealed as the type to peak as a chaser, and clearly stays all day long, so further improvement this season looks assured. *(op 18-1 tchd 20-1)*

Julius Caesar, a clear-cut winner on his recent chasing bow at Market Rasen and bidding for a five-timer, lacked the same fluency over his fences and was always struggling to go the pace. It would be folly to write him off on the back of this display, however, as he remains open to further improvement in this sphere and most probably needs better ground. *(op 15-8)*

Bushido(IRE) *(tchd 11-10)*

Mckelvey(IRE), reverting to novice company having run out a clear-cut winner of a handicap over the course and distance 21 days previosuly, was still full of running prior to unseating at the top of the straight and has to rate as unlucky. He would have gone very close with a clear round and remains a progressive young stayer. *(tchd 11-10)*

Red Georgie(IRE), put in his place when upped to this grade at Cheltenham last time, spoilt his chance by jumping right throughout and was found out by the testing surface. He has a fair amount to prove now. *(tchd 11-10)*

2644 SKYBET PRESS RED TO BET ON CHANNEL 4 H'CAP CHASE (18 fncs) 3m 1f

3:25 (3:25) (Class 3) (0-130,129) 5-Y-0+ **£8,652** (£2,540; £1,270; £634)

Form | | | | RPR
/631 **1** **Silver Knight**[9] [2451] 7-11-9 **121**.......... RussGarritty 137+
(T D Easterby) *jmped wl: trckd ldrs: led 9th: rdn 3 out: hit next: rdn out* **3/1**[2]

-642 **2** *4* **Jungle Jinks (IRE)**[21] [2189] 10-10-11 **114**.......... DougieCostello(5) 122
(G M Moore) *cl up: rdn along 4 out: drvn 2 out: kpt on u.p* **5/2**[1]

2-56 **3** *4* **Harrovian**[10] [2445] 8-11-4 **116**.......... AlanDempsey 122+
(Miss P Robson) *hld up: pushed along 11th: hdwy and cl up 4 out: sn rdn and kpt on same pce appr last* **9/1**

3523 **4** *dist* **Shannon's Pride (IRE)**[13] [2368] 9-10-9 **110**.......... LarryMcGrath(3) —
(R C Guest) *trckd ldrs on outer: pushed along 6 out: rdn and outpcd next: bhd whn blnd 4 out* **9/2**[3]

-121 **F** **Bob Ar Aghaidh (IRE)**[37] [1893] 9-11-11 **123**.......... TomDoyle —
(C Tinkler) *led to 3rd: w ldrs whn fell 7th* **9/2**[3]

124- **F** **Gingerbread House (IRE)**[334] [3192] 7-11-12 **124**.......... AntonyEvans —
(R T Phillips) *cl up: led 3rd to 9th: blnd next: w ldrs whn fell 13th* **10/1**

7m 4.20s (24.20) **Going Correction** +1.175s/f (Heav) **6** Ran SP% **109.0**

Speed ratings: **108,106,105,**—,—,— CSF £10.62 CT £50.62 TOTE £3.20: £2.10, £1.80; EX 6.90 Place 6 £452.15, Place 5 £177.67.

Owner C H Stevens **Bred** M H Easterby **Trained** Great Habton, N Yorks

FOCUS

A fair handicap, run at a decent pace on the testing surface, and the form looks sound. The race has been rated through the runner-up, who has been given the same mark as he received when filling the same spot on his previous start over the course and distance.

NOTEBOOK

Silver Knight ◆, back to winning ways with a battling success at Carlise nine days previously, followed up with another dour success and defied an 8lb higher mark in the process. Clearly back in top form, he does love this sort of ground and should go close when bidding for the hat-trick, despite another inevitable rise in the weights. *(op 7-2)*

Jungle Jinks(IRE) could not cope with the in-form winner late on, but still posted another solid effort and looked to run very close to the level of his previous outing over the course and distance. He deserves to tatse success once again. *(op 11-4)*

Harrovian stepped up on the level of his previous effort, only tiring approaching the final flight. He is slowly going the right way again and will have better claims over this trip on less taxing ground. *(op 10-1 tchd 8-1)*

Shannon's Pride(IRE) failed to build on the promise of his recent improved efforts and probably found this too gruelling a test. *(op 5-1)*

Bob Ar Aghaidh(IRE), raised 8lb for winning over further at Stratford last time, had yet to be asked a serious question when falling. He can be given another chance. *(op 13-2)*

Gingerbread House(IRE), returning from a 334-day layoff, was just starting to tire prior to falling. He has few miles on the clock, but does still have to prove he is up to defying his current mark. *(op 13-2)*

T/Plt: £291.60 to a £1 stake. Pool: £38,718.05. 96.90 winning tickets. T/Qpdt: £29.10 to a £1 stake. Pool: £2,410.80. 61.10 winning tickets. JR

2132 FAIRYHOUSE (R-H)
Saturday, December 3

OFFICIAL GOING: Heavy

2645a WINTER FESTIVAL JUVENILE 3-Y-O HURDLE (GRADE 3) (9 hdls) 2m
12:15 (12:16) 3-Y-O £14,774 (£4,334; £2,065; £703)

RPR

1 **The Last Stand**[56] [1689] 3-10-6 .... MPWatts(7) 117
(Anthony Mullins, Ire) *led: rdn and hdd briefly appr 2 out: lft clr last: kpt on u.p: all out to hold on nr fin* **5/1**[2]

2 *hd* **Ballygally Bay**[14] [2360] 3-10-9 .... BJGeraghty 113
(S J Mahon, Ire) *mod 3rd: slt mstke 4th: 4th 3 out: no imp bef 2 out: styd on u.p fr last: jst failed* **3/1**[1]

3 *3 1/2* **Vox Populi (USA)**[6] [2535] 3-10-9 .... PCarberry 109
(S J Mahon, Ire) *settled 5th: impr into 3rd after 3 out: rdn bef next: 2nd and chalng whn bad mstke last: no ex run-in* **7/1**[3]

4 *6* **Packie Tam (IRE)**[6] [2535] 3-10-6 ....(t) MFMooney(3) 103
(Patrick O Brady, Ire) *trckd ldr in 2nd: rdn to chal after 3 out: led appr 2 out: bad mstke and hdd: 3rd whn mstke last: no ex* **12/1**

5 *4* **Astalanda (FR)**[38] 3-9-11 .... SGCarey(7) 94
(Garvan Donnelly, Ire) *mid-div: 7th bef 3 out: kpt on same pce fr next* **14/1**

6 *dist* **Timber Scorpion (UAE)**[34] [1946] 3-10-9 .... JPElliott —
(P Hughes, Ire) *trckd ldrs in mod 4th: impr into 3rd 5 out: slt mstke 3 out: sn rdn and wknd: virtually p.u fr last* **3/1**[1]

7 *hd* **Annie's Dream (IRE)**[9] [2469] 3-10-1 ....(tp) TGMRyan(3) —
(T Hogan, Ire) *bhd: j. poorly thrght: t.o 1/2-way: styd on fr 3 out* **50/1**

8 *25* **Battledress (IRE)**[21] [2178] 3-10-13 ....(p) DFO'Regan —
(K J Condon, Ire) *mid-div: 6th 4 out: wknd fr next: t.o* **12/1**

9 *dist* **Gallantian (IRE)**[63] 3-10-9 .... GTHutchinson —
(Alan Fleming, Ire) *nvr a factor: t.o* **16/1**

10 *13* **Deerpark (IRE)**[90] 3-10-9 .... CO'Dwyer —
(John F Gleeson, Ire) *a towards rr: t.o* **10/1**

11 *dist* **Miss Una (IRE)**[34] 3-10-4 .... JohnnyMurtagh —
(M Halford, Ire) *mid-div: 6th appr 1/2-way: no ex bef 3 out: t.o* **8/1**

4m 20.3s **11 Ran SP% 129.3**
CSF £23.15 TOTE £5.20: £1.70, £2.20, £1.80; DF 17.00.
Owner Cathal McCarthy **Bred** The Hon D K & Mrs J Oliver **Trained** Gowran, Co Kilkenny

NOTEBOOK
The Last Stand made virtually all on ground that does not really suit to gain his third success in four runs, but he was stopping towards the end and just held on. It is difficult to judge the merit of the juveniles so far but they do not look to be anything out of the ordinary. *(op 4/1)*
Ballygally Bay should have won. Not fluent and appearing to be eased before two out, he came along with a wet sail on the run-in and would have been in front in another couple of strides. It was an extraordinary display. *(op 5/2)*
Vox Populi(USA), a stable companion of the runner-up, is still a maiden. He had every chance when clouting the last. *(op 7/1 tchd 8/1)*
Packie Tam(IRE) flattered till making a mistake two out and was beaten when hitting the last. He is still a maiden after six attempts.
Timber Scorpion(UAE), in front of the winner at Listowel, burst a blood vessel. *Official explanation: vet said gelding broke a blood vessel (op 3/1 tchd 5/2)*

2650a LADBROKES.IE H'CAP HURDLE (GRADE C) (9 hdls) 2m
2:55 (2:56) 4-Y-O+ £18,468 (£5,418; £2,581; £879)

RPR

1 **Feathard Lady (IRE)**[29] [2032] 5-11-7 137 .... PCarberry 159+
(C A Murphy, Ire) *hld up towards rr: stdy hdwy 4 out: 4th next: 2nd 2 out: led appr last: styd on wl* **7/4**[1]

2 *2 1/2* **Don't Be Bitin (IRE)**[13] [2388] 4-10-7 123 .... BJGeraghty 139
(Eoin Griffin, Ire) *led: clr early: rdn and strly pressed 2 out: hdd appr last: kpt on u.p* **12/1**

3 *1 1/2* **No Where To Hyde (IRE)**[34] [1945] 5-9-11 116 .... MPWalsh(3) 131+
(C Roche, Ire) *towards rr: hdwy on outer after 3 out: 7th appr 2 out: styd on wl fr last* **20/1**

4 *4* **Escrea (IRE)**[209] [252] 6-9-10 112 .... GTHutchinson 129+
(Paul Nolan, Ire) *hld up: 9th and prog appr 3 out: 6th bef 2 out: kpt on* **16/1**

5 *7* **No Complications (IRE)**[230] [4891] 7-9-6 113 .... RJMolloy(5) 117
(Paul Nolan, Ire) *settled 2nd: rdn bef 3 out: 4th bef 2 out: sn no ex* **25/1**

6 *hd* **Steel Band**[247] [4674] 7-9-7 112 .... JMAllen(3) 115
(Paul A Roche, Ire) *mid-div: 9th 1/2-way: mstke 3 out: kpt on* **20/1**

7 *3* **French Accordion (IRE)**[22] [2161] 5-9-12 119 ....(t) RMMoran(5) 119
(Paul Nolan, Ire) *prom: impr into 2nd after 3 out: 3rd and rdn next: wknd bef last* **10/1**[3]

8 *shd* **Kadoun (IRE)**[35] [1934] 8-11-7 140 .... MrDWCullen(3) 140
(M J P O'Brien, Ire) *mid-div: dropped towards rr bef 3 out: styd on fr next* **20/1**

9 *nk* **Ross River**[14] [2361] 9-10-0 116 .... JohnnyMurtagh 116
(A J Martin, Ire) *towards rr: effrt after 3 out: kpt on same pce fr next* **8/1**[2]

10 *1* **Commonchero (IRE)**[13] [2398] 8-10-3 122 .... TGMRyan(3) 121
(M J P O'Brien, Ire) *rr of mid-div: no imp fr 3 out* **8/1**[2]

11 *1* **Demesne**[21] [2196] 5-9-4 113 ow1 .... DGHogan(7) 111
(P Hogan, Ire) *mod 3rd to 4 out: sn no ex* **50/1**

12 *2 1/2* **Kilbeggan Lad (IRE)**[34] [1945] 7-10-2 118 .... DFO'Regan 113
(Michael Hourigan, Ire) *mid-div: 10th appr 3 out: sn no ex* **12/1**

13 *4* **Baron De Feypo (IRE)**[27] [1934] 7-10-10 129 .... MFMooney(3) 120
(Patrick O Brady, Ire) *mid-div: prog into 6th bef 4 out: wknd fr next* **14/1**

14 *1* **Masrahi (IRE)**[31] [1993] 4-9-10 112 .... NPMadden 102
(Noel Meade, Ire) *hld up in rr: hdwy after 4 out: 7th bef 2 out: sn no ex and wknd* **14/1**

15 *2* **Ennistown Lady (IRE)**[21] [2196] 6-9-10 112 .... RGeraghty 100
(R P Burns, Ire) *trckd ldrs: 7th 1/2-way: 5th 3 out: wknd next* **20/1**

16 *25* **Joueur D'Estruval (FR)**[13] [2398] 8-10-6 122 .... AndrewJMcNamara 85
(W P Mullins, Ire) *rr of mid-div: rdn and no imp 3 out: virtually p.u after 2 out: t.o* **14/1**

17 *4* **Pom Flyer (FR)**[14] [2354] 5-10-0 121 .... KTColeman(5) 80
(F Flood, Ire) *hld up: 11th and effrt 3 out: sn no ex: eased bef last: t.o* **14/1**

18 *dist* **Native House (IRE)**[20] [2222] 7-9-7 112 .... WJLee(3) —
(Edward Cawley, Ire) *prom: 5th 1/2-way: wknd bef 3 out: t.o* **25/1**

P **Silk Screen (IRE)**[13] [2398] 5-10-11 127 .... DJCasey —
(W P Mullins, Ire) *settled 4th: wknd appr 3 out: p.u after 2 out* **8/1**[2]

4m 20.5s
WFA 4 from 5yo+ 10lb **19 Ran SP% 155.4**
CSF £29.19 CT £411.18 TOTE £2.10: £1.80, £2.30, £7.10, £4.40; DF 20.90.
Owner Lord of the Ring Syndicate **Bred** J C Condon **Trained** Gorey, Co Wexford

NOTEBOOK
Feathard Lady(IRE), unbeaten and running in her first handicap, didn not have a lot to beat in what ultimately was not a very competitive race. Taking over before the last, she had an easy time of it on the run-in. She goes up 11lb to 148 but there are question marks all over this win, as she beat nothing. This was probably her last handicap and she remains relatively unexposed and deserving of respect wherever she goes at Christmas, be it Leopardstown or Sandown. *(op 2/1)*
Silk Screen(IRE) *Official explanation: vet said horse was blowing hard and scoped badly post race (op 6/1)*

2646 - 2651a (Foreign Racing) - See Raceform Interactive

2036 KELSO (L-H)
Sunday, December 4

OFFICIAL GOING: Soft (good to soft in places)
Wind: Almost nil

2652 GG.COM MAIDEN HURDLE (DIV I) (8 hdls) 2m 110y
12:20 (12:20) (Class 4) 4-Y-O+ £3,316 (£966; £483)

Form RPR

1 **Serbelloni**[80] 5-11-2 .... TonyDobbin 107+
(M D Hammond) *hld up midfield: smooth hdwy 4 out: led after 2 out: drvn out* **7/1**[3]

04- 2 *3/4* **Edgehill (IRE)**[65] [1688] 4-11-2 .... RichardMcGrath 107+
(R Ford) *trckd ldrs: rdn bef 2 out: rallying whn stmbld last: rdn and hung lft run in: kpt on towards fin* **9/1**

11-5 3 *6* **Sotovik (IRE)**[10] [2450] 4-11-2 .... BrianHarding 101+
(A C Whillans) *trckd ldrs: hit 4 out and next: ev ch 2 out: hung lft and one pce run in* **9/2**[2]

4 *2* **Turnstile**[100] 4-11-2 .... GrahamLee 97+
(J Howard Johnson) *hld up in tch: smooth hdwy after 4 out: led briefly 2 out: rdn and outpcd run in* **5/4**[1]

60-0 5 *20* **Norminster**[176] [720] 4-10-9 .... GarethThomas(7) 77
(R Nixon) *towards rr: drvn after 3rd: kpt on fr 2 out: n.d* **100/1**

6 *1 1/4* **Auenmoon (GER)**[77] 4-11-2 .... WilsonRenwick 76
(P Monteith) *cl up: led 3rd to 2 out: sn btn* **11/1**

P4 7 *3 1/2* **Moyne Pleasure (IRE)**[10] [2447] 7-11-2 .... KennyJohnson 72
(R Johnson) *bhd: shaken up bef 2 out: nvr on terms* **50/1**

0 8 *26* **Swahili Dancer (USA)**[11] [2444] 4-11-2 .... FinbarKeniry 46
(M D Hammond) *towards rr: rdn whn nt fluent 4 out: nvr on terms* **33/1**

00-6 9 *13* **Daniel's Dream**[199] [431] 5-11-1 ow6 .... MrTDavidson(7) 39
(J E Dixon) *mstkes: cl up tl wknd fr 4 out* **100/1**

06 10 *13* **Fly Tipper**[9] [2480] 5-11-2 .... NeilMulholland 20
(W Storey) *a bhd* **100/1**

2-P 11 *1 1/2* **Neagh (FR)**[30] [2024] 4-10-9 .... MissRDavidson(7) 19
(N G Richards) *keen: chsd ldrs to 4 out: sn wknd* **9/1**

12 *2 1/2* **Logistical**[50] 5-10-13 .... KeithMercer(3) 16
(Ferdy Murphy) *hld up: rdn 4 out: nvr on terms* **33/1**

P 13 *8* **Golden Remedy**[28] [2062] 4-10-6 ....(p) LarryMcGrath(3) 1
(A R Dicken) *keen: cl up tl lost pl 3rd: sn n.d* **100/1**

0/ 14 *10* **Sea Otter (IRE)**[946] [109] 8-10-13 .... PaddyAspell(3) —
(N W Alexander) *led to 3rd: lost pl next: hit 4 out: wknd* **100/1**

0 P **Claudia May**[30] [2028] 4-10-6 .... PeterBuchanan(3) —
(Miss Lucinda V Russell) *a bhd: t.o whn p.u bef last* **100/1**

4m 6.20s (2.50) **Going Correction** +0.45s/f (Soft)
WFA 4 from 5yo+ 10lb **15 Ran SP% 117.2**
Speed ratings: **112,111,108,107,98 97,96,84,77,71 71,69,66,61,—** CSF £63.78 TOTE £10.80: £2.20, £2.50, £2.00; EX 86.90.
Owner D Tumman & R F Bloodstock **Bred** Pendley Farm **Trained** Middleham, N Yorks

FOCUS
A fair novice event in which the pace was sound and the winning time was 7.3 seconds faster than the second division. The first four could all be capbale of better.

NOTEBOOK
Serbelloni ♦, a triple All-Weather winner up to two miles last winter, created a favourable impression on this hurdle debut. Always travelling strongly, he showed the right attitude and should have no problems staying further. He is likely to win again.
Edgehill(IRE), a dual Flat middle-distance winner for Charlie Egerton this year, ran creditably back over hurdles on this first run for his new stable, especially as he nearly unshipped his rider at the final flight. He looks up to winning an ordinary event in this sphere. *(op 14-1)*
Sotovik(IRE), who shaped as though better than the bare form on his hurdle debut last month, ran creditably and should stay further. He may do better over obstacles when brushing up in the jumping department. *(op 4-1)*
Turnstile, an 86-rated triple Flat winner up to a mile and six for Richard Hannon, was well supported on this first run for his new yard and showed enough on ground softer than ideal to suggest he can be placed to best advantage. *(op 6-4 tchd 13-8 in places)*
Norminster, who showed nothing in bumpers in the first half of this year, fared better on this hurdle debut and, although likely to remain vulnerable in this grade, may do better in modest handicaps with more of an emphasis on stamina.
Auenmoon(GER), a multiple German Flat winner on good and softer ground up to a mile and a quarter, showed ability on this hurdle debut and first start for his new stable and will be more of interest when the yard is in better form. *(op 12-1 tchd 10-1)*

2653 ERIC GILLIE HORSE TRANSPORT 30TH ANNIVERSARY "NATIONAL HUNT" NOVICES' H'CAP HURDLE (11 hdls) 2m 6f 110y
12:50 (12:50) (Class 4) (0-105,101) 3-Y-O+ £3,477 (£1,013; £506)

Form RPR

4-15 1 **Piraeus (NZ)**[12] [2416] 6-11-3 92 .... KennyJohnson 101+
(R Johnson) *led to after 6th: rdn 3 out: rallied bef next: edgd lft and led run in: styd on wl* **7/2**[1]

-642 2 *1 3/4* **Bywell Beau (IRE)**[29] [2036] 6-11-5 97 ....(t) MichalKohl(3) 102
(J I A Charlton) *plld hrd: hdwy to chse ldrs 4th: led after 6th: rdn and hdd run in: kpt on* **11/2**[2]

-261 3 *11* **Chickapeakray**[19] [2256] 4-10-0 80 .... StephenCraine(5) 75+
(D McCain) *cl up: rdn and ev ch 3 out: one pce appr next* **10/1**

00-5 4 *1/2* **Generals Laststand (IRE)**[29] [2036] 7-10-0 75 oh2 .... GrahamLee 69
(Mrs L B Normile) *midfield: effrt bef 3 out: no imp fr next* **20/1**

PP40 5 *3* **Hapthor**[23] [2171] 6-9-8 76 .... PatrickMcDonald(7) 67
(F Jestin) *bhd tl hdwy bef 2 out: sn no imp* **33/1**

5205 **6** 3/4 **Minster Abbi**[10] 2453 5-10-0 **75**......(p) NeilMulholland 65
(W Storey) *in tch: lost pl 1/2-way: rallied bef 3 out: btn after next* **16/1**

2-13 **7** 8 **Prince Of Slane**[199] 421 6-10-5 **85**...... DougieCostello(5) 67
(G A Swinbank) *midfield: lost pl 4th: sme late hdwy: nvr on terms* **6/1**[3]

6415 **8** 12 **Primitive Poppy**[11] 2440 6-10-7 **85**...... PeterBuchanan(3) 55
(Mrs A Hamilton) *prom tl wknd after 4 out* **10/1**

P0P- **9** 1 1/4 **Celia's High (IRE)**[226] 4965 6-9-11 **75** oh4...... PaddyAspell(3) 44
(D McCain) *hld up: rdn 4 out: nvr on terms* **50/1**

000- **10** dist **Seeking Shelter (IRE)**[294] 3827 6-10-0 **75** oh8...... BrianHarding —
(N G Richards) *a bhd* **12/1**

5-03 **11** dist **Ballynure (IRE)**[23] 2171 7-10-9 **89**...... DesFlavin(5) —
(Mrs L B Normile) *in tch tl wknd bef 4 out* **9/1**

00-0 **12** 5 **Papawaldo (IRE)**[18] 2262 6-10-0 **78** oh1 ow3......(p) LarryMcGrath(3) —
(R C Guest) *bhd: struggling 1/2-way: t.o* **25/1**

2220 **P** **Bella Liana (IRE)**[18] 2278 5-10-7 **85**...... KeithMercer(3) —
(J Clements, Ire) *cl up tl wknd fr 4 out: t.o whn p.u bef last* **9/1**

5m 46.0s (8.30) **Going Correction** +0.45s/f (Soft)
WFA 4 from 5yo+ 11lb **13** Ran SP% **117.2**
Speed ratings: **103,102,98,98,97 97,94,90,89,— —,—,—** CSF £21.64 CT £176.92 TOTE £4.40: £2.10, £2.10, £3.30; EX 14.90.
Owner Jimmy Rogers **Bred** Est Late N J Taylor & Mrs A A Taylor **Trained** Newburn, Tyne & Wear

FOCUS
A run-of-the-mill handicap in which the pace was sound but once again those up with the pace held the edge. The form looks pretty solid with the first two running to their latest marks.

NOTEBOOK
Piraeus(NZ) ◆, a bit disappointing last time in view of his improved reappearance form when winning at Newcastle, returned to winning ways and showed the right attitude. He should stay three miles and is capable of further success at a modest level. *(op 5-1)*
Bywell Beau(IRE), making his handicap debut, ran as well as he ever has, especially as he failed to settle in the first half of the race. He looks capable of winning a race but he really does need to be more amenable to restraint. *(op 6-1 tchd 5-1)*
Chickapeakray, 11lb higher than when successful in a weak selling handicap last time, ran at least as well in this stronger race on this softer ground and over this longer trip. She will have to improve to win from this mark, though. *(op 9-1)*
Generals Laststand(IRE) a bumper winner on his debut in 2002, showed his first worthwhile form over hurdles to fare the best of those to come from off the pace. He left the impression that a stiffer test of stamina would have been in his favour.
Hapthor has run his best races over this course and distance but, while a stiffer test of stamina may help, he is an inconsistent maiden who will have to improve to get off the mark in similar company.
Minster Abbi, an inconsistent maiden over hurdles, again did not get home. She did not loook the easiest of rides and remains one to tread carefully with.
Prince Of Slane, returned to hurdles for this first start since May, was below his best and he may do better back on a sound surface.

2654 PARIS PIKE NOVICES' CHASE (17 fncs) 2m 6f 110y
1:20 (1:20) (Class 3) 5-Y-0+ **£7,507** (£2,204; £1,102; £550)

Form RPR

4-53 **1** **Mel In Blue (FR)**[33] 1976 7-10-7...... MrSWaley-Cohen(7) 126+
(R Waley-Cohen) *t.k.h: hld up bhd ldrs: hdwy 1/2-way: led bef 12th: blnd 2 out: rdn and styd on wl fr last* **5/1**[2]

-041 **2** 2 1/2 **South Bronx (IRE)**[43] 1835 6-11-6 109......(t) GrahamLee 126
(Mrs S C Bradburne) *cl up: led 7th to bef 12th: effrt 2 out: kpt on u.p run in* **12/1**

31-1 **3** 5 **Turpin Green (IRE)**[10] 2449 6-11-10...... TonyDobbin 127+
(N G Richards) *in tch: hit 6th: nt fluent 10th: effrt 2 out: edgd lft and one pce run in* **1/2**[1]

6-0P **4** 12 **No Picnic (IRE)**[42] 1844 7-10-11...... PaddyAspell(3) 103
(Mrs S C Bradburne) *chsd ldrs: lost pl 9th: n.d after* **50/1**

3/30 **5** 1/2 **Lord Payne (IRE)**[10] 2449 7-11-0...... WilsonRenwick 102
(P Monteith) *chsd ldrs tl lost pl 9th: no imp fnl circ* **66/1**

2133 **U** **Pebble Bay**[14] 2369 10-11-6 108...... DominicElsworth —
(Mrs S J Smith) *blnd and uns rdr 1st* **7/1**[3]

P0-P **F** **Skenfrith**[10] 2449 6-11-0 112...... BrianHarding —
(Miss S E Forster) *bhd whn fell heavily 7th* **100/1**

6462 **P** **Mounthooley**[28] 2063 9-11-0 77...... NeilMulholland —
(B Mactaggart) *led to 7th: blnd 10th: outpcd whn blnd 13th: t.o whn p.u bef 2 out* **100/1**

6m 2.90s (6.30) **Going Correction** +0.375s/f (Yiel) **8** Ran SP% **109.0**
Speed ratings: **104,103,101,97,97 —,—,—** CSF £47.12 TOTE £5.40: £1.40, £1.90, £1.10; EX 48.50.
Owner Robert Waley-Cohen **Bred** Murielle Legriffon **Trained** Ratley, Warweick

FOCUS
A decent event but, with the favourite performing below the form of his recent Carlisle win, this race did not take as much winning as seemed likely. Otherwise the form looks pretty solid.

NOTEBOOK
Mel In Blue(FR), who already looks like making up into a better chaser than a hurdler, took advantage of the below-par run of the favourite to get off the mark at the second attempt over fences. Apart from one error, his jumping was sound and he appeals as the type to win again in this sphere. *(op 11-2)*
South Bronx(IRE), off the mark over fences at this course last time, ran better still over this much longer trip and looks a good guide to the worth of this form. He should stay three miles and should continue to give a good account.
Turpin Green(IRE), who created a favourable impression, despite having a hard race, on his chase debut after a break at Carlisle recently, was a long way below that level under his penalty at this very different course. His jumping was not foot-perfect but it is far too early to write him off and he is well worth another chance to prove himself a smart chaser. *(tchd 8-15 in places)*
No Picnic(IRE), who has only won once from 25 starts, was not totally disgraced in terms of bare form on this chase debut but he is likely to continue to look vulnerable in this type of event. *(tchd 100-1)*
Lord Payne(IRE) was much closer to Turpin Green than at Carlisle but that rival was a long way below his best. His stable has yet to hit top form and he may be one to tread carefully with at present over fences. *(op 50-1)*
Pebble Bay, who ran as well as he has ever done over hurdles last time, gave his rider little chance of staying aboard back over the larger obstacles. He is worth another chance. *(op 6-1)*

2655 ERIC SCARTH MEMORIAL NOVICES' H'CAP CHASE (12 fncs) 2m 1f
1:50 (1:52) (Class 4) (0-100,99) 4-Y-0+ **£3,968** (£1,165; £582; £290)

Form RPR

P-6F **1** **One Five Eight**[22] 2187 6-11-7 **97**...... MrTGreenall(3) 93
(M W Easterby) *prom: outpcd 1/2-way: lft 4th 2 out: rallied to ld run-in: kpt on* **20/1**

3525 **2** 2 **Ideal Du Bois Beury (FR)**[9] 2476 9-10-4 **77**...... WilsonRenwick 74+
(P Monteith) *hld up in tch: outpcd 6th: lft modest 5th 2 out: rallied last: keeping on but no imp whn hmpd run-in: fin 3rd: plcd 2nd* **5/1**[3]

5-05 **3** 6 **Persian Point**[30] 2026 9-10-6 **82**...... MrCStorey(3) 81+
(Miss S E Forster) *prom: outpcd 1/2-way: no imp whn lft 2nd 2 out: led last: hdd run-in: edgd lft and no ex: fin 2nd: plcd 3rd* **25/1**

6031 **4** 2 **Donovan (NZ)**[42] 1852 6-11-6 **96**......(p) LarryMcGrath(3) 94+
(R C Guest) *cl up: rdn 4 out: 7l 3rd whn lft in ld 2 out: sn hdd: outpcd run-in* **11/4**[1]

563/ **5** 1/2 **Grand Slam (IRE)**[595] 4880 10-10-5 **85**...... EwanWhillans(7) 76
(A C Whillans) *hld up in tch: outpcd 1/2-way: no imp whn lft 3rd 2 out: sn led: hdd last: sn wknd* **33/1**

41P **U** **Longdale**[168] 780 7-11-12 **99**...... AlanDempsey —
(M Todhunter) *hld up: uns rdr 2nd* **20/1**

/2-4 **F** **What If (IRE)**[67] 1573 8-11-3 **93**...... PeterBuchanan(3) —
(I Buchanan, Ire) *hld up: fell 2nd* **8/1**

054P **P** **Lion Guest (IRE)**[9] 2476 8-10-2 **75**...... GrahamLee —
(Mrs S C Bradburne) *cl up tl wknd 1/2-way: t.o whn p.u bef 3 out* **13/2**

5012 **F** **Loulou Nivernais (FR)**[9] 2479 6-11-8 **95**...... TonyDobbin 106+
(Robert Gray) *led: 4l in front and gng wl whn fell heavily 2 out* **10/3**[2]

3PP3 **U** **Twist N Turn**[17] 2283 5-9-9 **73** oh6...... StephenCraine(5) 74
(D McCain) *hld up: hdwy to chse ldrs 7th: 4l down and rdn whn lft in ld, bdly hmpd and uns rdr 2 out* **28/1**

4m 32.3s (9.10) **Going Correction** +0.375s/f (Yiel) **10** Ran SP% **110.6**
Speed ratings: **93,89,90,88,88 —,—,—,—,—** CSF £105.98 CT £2409.94 TOTE £20.70: £5.50, £1.30, £4.60; EX 91.90.
Owner J W P Curtis **Bred** Nightingale Bloodstock **Trained** Sheriff Hutton, N Yorks
■ Stewards' Enquiry : Mr C Storey three-day ban: careless riding (Dec 15-17)
Wilson Renwick five-day ban: used whip with excessive frequency (Dec 15-19)

FOCUS
A very eventful race, run in a modest time, and the bare form of this contest is best treated with a large degree of caution. Loulou Nivernais has been rated as the 10-length winner with actual winner One Five Eight rated as five lengths third.

NOTEBOOK
One Five Eight, an inconsistent hurdler, had shown only modest form in two starts over fences but ran his best race to take a very eventful handicap. He will be suited by the return to further but, given the way things panned out, he would be no good thing to follow up from a higher mark next time. *(op 16-1)*
Ideal Du Bois Beury(FR) ran another typical race and, although promoted to second after being hampered in the closing stages, would not have won and remains one to have reservations about at present. *(op 6-1)*
Persian Point, an inconsistent sort, was looking held when left in a prominent position at the penultimate fence but, although not beaten that far, looks one to field against next time.
Donovan(NZ) was disappointing given his Towcester win and that the two in front of him came to grief at the penultimate fence. This course should not have been a problem (has won twice over hurdles here) and, although not one to write off yet, he is one to tread carefully with on this evidence. *(op 3-1)*
Grand Slam(IRE) shaped as though retaining ability on this first start since April of last year but although he should be better for this run, he is not the most consistent around. *(op 25-1 tchd 20-1 in places)*
Loulou Nivernais(FR), having his first run for his new stable, was in the process of showing improved form and looked the most likely winner before coming to grief. He is capable of winning from this mark but would not be one to lump on at short odds next time after this experience. *(op 11-4 tchd 5-2)*
Twist N Turn, a poor maiden hurdler, was in the process of running arguably her best race on this chase debut before being put out of the race at the penultimate fence. She may be able to win a small race in this sphere. *(op 11-4 tchd 5-2)*

2656 EASTWOOD BOOKMAKERS CHAMPION CHASE (A H'CAP CHASE) (19 fncs) 3m 1f
2:20 (2:22) (Class 2) (0-145,142) 5-Y-0+ **£11,220** (£3,343; £1,692; £867; £453)

Form RPR

2-06 **1** **Ossmoses (IRE)**[35] 1941 8-10-0 **116** oh1...... RichardMcGrath 135
(D M Forster) *led or disp ld: hdd 2 out: rallied to regain ld run in: all out* **11/2**[3]

5-31 **2** shd **Undeniable**[15] 2342 7-10-0 **116**...... DominicElsworth 135
(Mrs S J Smith) *trckd ldrs: led 2 out to run in: rallied: jst failed* **7/2**[2]

F51- **3** 22 **Rosie Redman (IRE)**[245] 4710 8-10-1 **117**...... GrahamLee 114
(J R Turner) *hld up in tch: stdy hdwy 1/2-way: outpcd bef 3 out: kpt on fr last: no ch w first two* **3/1**[1]

-312 **4** 6 **Miss Mattie Ross**[10] 2451 9-9-9 **116** oh6...... MichaelMcAlister(5) 107
(S J Marshall) *led or disp ld fr 3rd to 12th: ev ch 3 out: wknd after next* **13/2**

25-0 **5** 12 **Alexanderthegreat (IRE)**[8] 2499 7-10-8 **127**...... KeithMercer(3) 110+
(Ferdy Murphy) *sn bhd and detatched: no imp whn hit 3 out: nvr on terms* **11/2**[3]

15-U **P** **Forest Gunner**[14] 2370 11-11-9 **142**...... PeterBuchanan(3) —
(R Ford) *in tch: outpcd 7th: lost tch and p.u bef 13th* **9/1**

1235 **U** **Pass Me By**[18] 2265 6-9-9 **116** oh3......(e) DougieCostello(5) —
(R C Guest) *prom: mstke 2nd: outpcd 7th: blnd and uns rdr 10th* **9/1**

124- **P** **Flight Command**[232] 4859 7-10-12 **128**...... RussGarritty —
(P Beaumont) *hld up: hdwy and prom 9th: wknd bef 4 out: p.u bef next* **25/1**

6m 31.0s (1.40) **Going Correction** +0.375s/f (Yiel) **8** Ran SP% **115.2**
Speed ratings: **112,111,104,103,99 —,—,—** CSF £26.00 CT £68.26 TOTE £5.60: £1.60, £1.80, £1.90; EX 29.10 Trifecta £80.40 Pool: £532.28 - 4.70 winning tickets..
Owner D M Forster **Bred** Mrs Julia Foran **Trained** Redworth, Co Durham
■ Stewards' Enquiry : Dominic Elsworth one-day ban: used whip with excessive frequency (Dec 15)

FOCUS
A fair handicap for the course and the decent pace meant this was a decent test of stamina. The first two both ran to their marks but the third and fourth were both around 20lb off.

NOTEBOOK
Ossmoses(IRE) ◆, a progressive chaser with a decent strike-rate, showed that his reappearance run at Carlisle had not done him any justice. He jumped soundly, showed the right attitude and appeals as the type to win more races. *(op 8-1)*
Undeniable, back over this longer trip, ran as well has he ever has done from this 5lb higher mark. He saw out the trip really well and, although he will be up again in the weights, should continue to give a good account. *(op 4-1)*
Rosie Redman(IRE), who has a good strike-rate over fences, ran as though this first start since winning over three and a half miles at this course in early April was needed, and she looks capable of adding to her tally over the larger obstacles away from progressive sorts. *(tchd 10-3 and 7-2 in places)*
Miss Mattie Ross who ran her best race at Carlisle when second to a subsequent winner last time, was returned to a course where she goes particularly well but was found out from this 9lb higher mark (6lb out of the handicap) in this better race. She will be of more interest in lesser company from her proper mark. *(op 7-1)*
Alexanderthegreat(IRE) was again below his best on only this second start since February and this second start for his current stable and he will have to show more before he is worth a bet again. *(op 6-1)*

Forest Gunner, a casualty on his reappearance at Aintree last month, was easy to back and a long way below his best on what was effectively his reappearance. He is capable of a good deal better but things are not going to be easy from this mark this term. *(tchd 28-1)*
Flight Command has not always found as much as expected off the bridle but may well have needed this first run since April. However, he may well continue to struggle against unexposed or progressive sorts from his current mark. *(tchd 28-1)*

2657 URESHARE INVESTMENT CLUB AMATEUR RIDERS' H'CAP HURDLE (10 hdls) 2m 2f
2:50 (2:50) (Class 4) (0-90,90) 4-Y-0+ **£2,993** (£920; £460)

Form RPR
0356 **1** **You Do The Math (IRE)**[12] [2416] 5-11-4 **87** .... MrGTumelty(5) 106+
(L Lungo) *a.p: chsd wnr 4 out: led last: sn rdn and r.o strly* **4/1**[1]
450P **2** *9* **That's Racing**[35] [1943] 5-10-5 **72** .... MissADeniel(3) 81
(J Hetherton) *led 3rd: clr 4 out: hdd last: kpt on same pce* **25/1**
3 *13* **My Lucky Rose (IRE)**[7] [2537] 7-11-5 **88** .... (b) MrATDuff(5) 84
(S Donohoe, Ire) *led to 3rd: cl up: rdn and one pce fr 3 out* **9/1**[2]
6022 **4** *3* **Uneven Line**[18] [2267] 9-10-8 **79** .... (p) MissCarlyFrater(7) 72
(Miss S E Forster) *prom: outpcd 4 out: rallied 2 out: no imp* **16/1**
-010 **5** *3* **Acceleration (IRE)**[168] [784] 5-11-8 **86** .... MrTGreenall 76
(R Allan) *in tch: drvn 4 out: no imp fr next* **12/1**
5P00 **6** *nk* **Just Sal**[10] [2453] 9-10-2 **73** .... MrMEllwood(7) 63
(R Nixon) *chsd ldrs: outpcd 3 out: no imp whn hung lft run in* **33/1**
0125 **7** *¾* **College City (IRE)**[53] [1716] 6-11-9 **90** .... (p) MrCMulhall(3) 79
(R C Guest) *hld up bhd: shkn up bef 3 out: nvr nrr* **4/1**[1]
8 *hd* **Turn The Corner (IRE)**[25] [2135] 6-11-3 **88** .... MrSClements(7) 77
(J Clements, Ire) *bhd tl hdwy 3 out: nt fluent next: n.d* **11/1**[3]
2/06 **9** *½* **Colway Ritz**[22] [2191] 11-10-11 **75** .... MissPRobson 63
(W Storey) *hld up: hdwy after 3 out: rdn and btn next* **12/1**
50-0 **10** *10* **Blue Morning**[29] [2042] 7-10-5 **76** .... (b[1]) MrSWByrne(7) 54
(Mrs J C McGregor) *midfield: rdn bef 4 out: sn btn* **33/1**
5U0- **11** *4* **Browneyes Blue (IRE)**[328] [3295] 7-10-9 **76** .... (t) MrMSeston(3) 50
(D R MacLeod) *in tch to 1/2-way: sn lost pl: n.d after* **33/1**
20-5 **12** *3½* **Bramantino (IRE)**[30] [2027] 5-10-12 **83** .... MissHCuthbert(7) 54
(T A K Cuthbert) *midfield: effrt bef 3 out: btn after next* **11/1**[3]
5-PP **13** *2* **Washington Pink (IRE)**[26] [2107] 6-10-3 **74** .... MrBenHamilton(7) 43
(C Grant) *towards rr: hdwy and prom after 5th: wknd after next* **33/1**
4500 **14** *1¾* **Star Trooper (IRE)**[10] [2453] 9-10-13 **77** .... (p) MrCStorey 44
(Miss S E Forster) *chsd ldrs: outpcd whn hit 3 out: sn btn* **22/1**
330- **15** *1¼* **Fiddlers Creek (IRE)**[205] [4088] 6-11-5 **90** .... MrDAFitzsimmons(7) 56
(R Allan) *a bhd* **33/1**
64-6 **16** *3* **Top Tenor (IRE)**[26] [2106] 5-10-13 **77** .... MrMThompson 40
(V Thompson) *towards rr: drvn 1/2-way: nvr on terms* **33/1**
P-06 **17** *28* **Sandy Bay (IRE)**[63] [1605] 6-10-4 **75** .... (v) MissJRiding(7) —
(W G Harrison) *bhd: rdn 1/2-way: nvr on terms* **33/1**
5003 **18** *15* **Silver Dagger**[22] [2188] 7-10-2 **73** .... (p) MrSFMagee(7) —
(J C Haynes) *towards rr: blnd bdly 2nd: no ch fr 1/2-way* **50/1**

4m 40.7s (0.80) **Going Correction** +0.375s/f (Yiel) **18** Ran SP% **118.7**
Speed ratings: **101,97,91,89,88 88,88,88,87,83 81,80,79,78,77 76,64,57** CSF £106.18 CT £860.57 TOTE £5.00: £1.50, £8.40, £2.60, £2.20; EX 334.40.
Owner www.gardenshedracing.com **Bred** Mrs Christine Kelly **Trained** Carrutherstown, D'fries & G'way

FOCUS
Probably a weak race in which College City was disappointing from this much lower hurdle mark but an improved effort from the winner, who may be capable of better.

NOTEBOOK
You Do The Math(IRE) ◆, who was disappointing on his handicap debut last time, showed that form to be all wrong with a fluent success back in trip and, although this was not much of a race, the manner of the win suggested he may be able to win again after reassessment. *(tchd 9-2)*
That's Racing, an inconsistent maiden hurdler, had the run of the race and ran his best race to date dropped markedly in trip. He is capable of winning a small event but he would not be guaranteed to put it all in next time.
My Lucky Rose(IRE), an inconsistent sort over obstacles in Ireland, had the run of the race in a handicap that suited those racing close to the pace. On this evidence the return to further will suit but she may not be one for maximum faith. *(op 10-1)*
Uneven Line, back over hurdles and back in trip, shaped as though a much stiffer test of stamina would have suited but, given her record under Rules, remains one to tread carefully with. *(op 14-1)*
Acceleration(IRE), an inconsistent hurdler with a modest strike-rate, shaped as though a stiffer test would have suited but he is another in this field to tread carefully with.
Just Sal, who has not won for some time, was again below her best and did not look the easiest of rides. She remains one to have reservations about.
College City(IRE), who has been in good form over fences, looked interesting returned to hurdles from a 20lb lower mark but ran no sort of race in a handicap that suited those racing prominently. He is not one to write off yet in this sphere. *(op 5-1)*

2658 GG.COM MAIDEN HURDLE (DIV II) (8 hdls) 2m 110y
3:20 (3:22) (Class 4) 4-Y-0+ **£3,302** (£962; £481)

Form RPR
23 **1** **First Look (FR)**[15] [2335] 5-11-2 .... WilsonRenwick 105+
(P Monteith) *prom: led last: rdn and r.o wl* **7/4**[2]
2 *3½* **Nae Bother At All (IRE)** 4-11-2 .... TonyDobbin 101
(N G Richards) *hld up: hdwy whn nt fluent 2 out: kpt on fr last: nt rch wnr* **8/1**[3]
121- **3** *1¼* **Blue Buster**[357] [2790] 5-10-13 .... MrTGreenall(3) 100
(M W Easterby) *hld up midfield: hdwy bef 2 out: edgd lft u.p run in: kpt on* **11/1**
3 **4** *¾* **Third Empire**[26] [2108] 4-11-2 .... RichardMcGrath 99
(C Grant) *keen: led or disp ld to last: rdn and kpt on same pce* **20/1**
5 *4* **Estepona**[29] 4-11-2 .... GrahamLee 95
(J Howard Johnson) *keen in midfield: hdwy 3 out: effrt next: outpcd run in* **6/4**[1]
6 *5* **Fair Shake (IRE)**[29] 5-10-13 .... KeithMercer(3) 90
(Karen McLintock) *hld up: effrt bef 2 out: nvr rchd ldrs* **33/1**
7 *1* **Heversham (IRE)**[29] 4-10-9 .... PatrickMcDonald(7) 89
(J Hetherton) *bhd: rdn 3 out: nvr on terms* **66/1**
8 *4* **Arctic Cove**[55] 4-11-2 .... FinbarKeniry 85
(M D Hammond) *in tch: effrt 3 out: wknd qckly last* **33/1**
50 **9** *10* **Filey Flyer**[11] [2446] 5-10-9 .... AnthonyRoss 68
(J R Turner) *hld up: shortlived effrt bef 2 out: sn wknd* **50/1**
10 *3* **Tinian**[244] 7-11-2 .... PadgeWhelan 72
(Miss Tracy Waggott) *hld up: pushed along after 3 out: btn next* **200/1**
0 **11** *8* **Exit To Saumur (FR)**[199] [424] 4-11-2 .... BrianHarding 64
(B Storey) *disp ld tl wknd after 3 out* **100/1**
5/ **F** **Loaded Gun**[74] [2331] 5-11-2 .... NeilMulholland —
(W Storey) *chsd ldrs: fell heavily 4 out* **100/1**
P **P** **Silloth Spirit**[10] [2447] 5-10-9 .... ThomasBurrows(7) —
(Mrs A M Naughton) *a bhd: struggling 5 out: t.o whn p.u bef 2 out* **200/1**
0 **P** **Acca Larentia (IRE)**[26] [2108] 4-10-4 .... DougieCostello(5) —
(Mrs H O Graham) *chsd ldrs to 4 out: sn wknd: t.o whn p.u bef 2 out* **200/1**
0 **P** **Viking Star (IRE)**[11] [2444] 4-10-13 .... PaddyAspell(3) —
(A D Brown) *keen: hld up: hdwy and prom 3rd: wknd 4 out: t.o whn p.u bef 2 out* **200/1**

4m 13.5s (9.80) **Going Correction** +0.45s/f (Soft) **15** Ran SP% **113.9**
Speed ratings: **94,92,91,91,89 87,86,84,80,78 74,—,—,—,—** CSF £14.34 TOTE £3.00: £1.10, £2.10, £2.70; EX 15.70 Place 6 £60.24, Place 5 £19.01.
Owner P Monteith **Bred** Gestut Ittlingen **Trained** Rosewell, Midlothian

FOCUS
An ordinary event in which the pace was only fair and the winning time was 7.3 seconds slower than the first division, but while the form is suspect this race could throw up a couple of winners.

NOTEBOOK
First Look(FR), surrounded by previous winners when third at Haydock last time, probably did not have to improve too much to get off the mark over hurdles. He travelled strongly and may be capable of better. *(op 13-8 tchd 2-1 in places)*
Nae Bother At All(IRE) ◆, who is related to several National Hunt winners, was easy to back but showed a fair level of ability on this racecourse debut and is entitled to come on for the experience. He looks sure to win a race in this sphere. *(tchd 7-1)*
Blue Buster, a dual bumper winner, was easy to back but showed ability on this hurdle debut and first run for nearly a year. He should stay two and a half miles and is capable of better in this sphere. *(op 10-1)*
Third Empire had the run of the race but, although failing to settle early on, seemed beaten more on merit than through lack of stamina. He may do better in ordinary handicaps in due course.
Estepona, a progressive middle-distance performer on the Flat, was not disgraced on this hurdle debut given he failed to settle early on. He is entitled to come on for the experience and is sure to win a race. *(op 7-4)*
Fair Shake(IRE), an ordinary handicapper up to a mile on the Flat, was not disgraced on this hurdle debut but still has stamina to prove in a truly-run race over this trip.
T/Jkpt: Not won. T/Plt: £274.00 to a £1 stake. Pool: £54,444.00. 145.00 winning tickets. T/Qpdt: £33.10 to a £1 stake. Pool: £4,314.90. 96.20 winning tickets. RY

2419 WARWICK (L-H)
Sunday, December 4

OFFICIAL GOING: Soft (heavy in places on hurdle course)
Wind: Light, across Weather: Overcast

2659 RACING UK "HOME OF QUALITY RACING" H'CAP HURDLE (8 hdls) 2m
12:40 (12:40) (Class 4) (0-105,105) 3-Y-0+ **£3,669** (£1,069; £534)

Form RPR
3-42 **1** **Nagano (FR)**[17] [2298] 7-10-13 **92** .... RobertThornton 101+
(Ian Williams) *hld up: hdwy appr 4th: led after 3 out: rdn out* **9/4**[1]
2 *5* **Corsican Native (USA)**[114] [1068] 4-11-7 **100** .... RichardJohnson 101
(P Bowen) *hld up: hdwy 5th: hrd rdn flat: styd on same pce* **9/2**[2]
60-3 **3** *3* **Signature Tune (IRE)**[209] [265] 6-11-6 **99** .... PhilipHide 97
(P Winkworth) *chsd ldrs: outpcd after 3 out: styd on flat* **11/1**
35-6 **4** *½* **Shaamit The Vaamit (IRE)**[33] [1977] 5-10-7 **93** .... JohnKington(7) 91
(M Scudamore) *hld up in tch: mstke 5th: rdn appr 2 out: styd on same pce* **5/1**[3]
43/0 **5** *hd* **Pawn Broker**[34] [1957] 8-11-7 **100** .... (b) JamieMoore 100+
(Miss J R Tooth) *hld up: plld hrd: hdwy appr 4th: led next: hdd after 3 out : sn hung lft: cl 2nd and rdn whn blnd last: sn wknd* **18/1**
3P3- **6** *8* **Andy Gin (FR)**[252] [4587] 6-11-2 **102** .... CharliePoste(7) 91
(Miss E M England) *chsd ldrs: led after 4th: hdd next: rdn 3 out: sn wknd* **18/1**
2360 **7** *shd* **Sir Walter (IRE)**[23] [2166] 12-11-3 **96** .... ChristianWilliams 85
(D Burchell) *hld up and bhd: nvr nrr* **16/1**
331- **8** *6* **La Marette**[232] [4871] 7-10-13 **97** .... MarkNicolls(5) 80
(John Allen) *hld up: reminders after 3rd: n.d* **14/1**
25FP **9** *4* **Titian Flame (IRE)**[10] [2459] 5-10-11 **97** .... (p) LiamHeard(7) 76
(D Burchell) *hld up: effrt 5th: wknd next* **7/1**
-63P **10** *2* **Magical Liaison (IRE)**[171] [768] 7-11-2 **95** .... (b) CarlLlewellyn 72
(W Jenks) *chsd ldrs: led appr 4th: hdd after 4th: wknd next* **33/1**
-600 **11** *dist* **Cybele Eria (FR)**[28] [2071] 8-10-1 **87** .... AdrianScholes(7) —
(John Allen) *led to appr 4th: wknd next* **50/1**
004- **12** *dist* **Barcelona**[210] 8-10-4 **90** .... MissLBrooke(7) —
(Lady Susan Brooke) *chsd ldrs: lost pl after 3rd: t.o whn blnd 3 out* **66/1**

4m 1.00s (2.70) **Going Correction** +0.25s/f (Yiel)
WFA 4 from 5yo+ 10lb **12** Ran SP% **115.9**
Speed ratings: **103,100,99,98,98 94,94,91,89,88 —,—** CSF £12.51 CT £91.00 TOTE £3.50: £1.40, £2.00, £2.30; EX 13.80.
Owner Allan Stennett & Terry Warner **Bred** Pierre Camus-Denais **Trained** Portway, Worcs

FOCUS
A moderate handicap, run at a fair pace. The form makes sense. The winner was rated value for further and can strike again over timber.

NOTEBOOK
Nagano(FR), raised 5lb for finishing second at Wincanton on his comeback, duly went one better in ready fashion and can be rated value for further. The softer ground was in his favour and, considering that he is currently rated 104 over fences, he should still be fairly treated in this sphere despite another rise in the weights for this. *(tchd 5-2)*
Corsican Native(USA), last seen landing a Flat claimer at Tramore in August and making his debut for new connections, was doing all of his best work at the finish and turned in a pleasing effort. He will not mind the return to faster ground in the future and it would come as a surprise should this one-time very useful Flat performer not be placed to go one better before too long. *(op 5-1 tchd 7-1)*
Signature Tune(IRE) posted a fair effort on this return to action and did more than enough to suggest he is ready to tackle a stiffer test now. *(op 9-1)*
Shaamit The Vaamit(IRE), dropping back in trip, duly improved on the level of his recent comeback at Worcester yet still lacked the pace to get really serious over this distance. He has a race in him off this mark, and may just want faster ground, but is not easy to predict. *(op 11-2 tchd 9-2)*
Pawn Broker, despite failing to settle through the early stages, was booked for a place before meeting the final flight all wrong and can be rated better than the bare form. If he can maintain this current mood, he really should be placed to strike in this sphere off this sort of mark. *(op 16-1)*
Sir Walter(IRE) *Official explanation: jockey said, regarding the apparent tender ride in the closing stages, he had no riding orders and dropped gelding out last as it has won in the past using these tactics; trainer said some of his horses had been out of form (op 20-1)*

2660 NICK REES 50TH BIRTHDAY BEGINNERS' CHASE (20 fncs) 3m 2f
1:10 (1:10) (Class 4) 5-Y-0+ **£3,981** (£1,168; £584; £291)

Form RPR

1 **Royal Corrouge (IRE)**[1008] 7-11-0 .... MickFitzgerald 125+
(N J Henderson) *hld up: hdwy 8th: nt fluent and outpcd 4 out: rallied to chse clr ldr last: r.o wl to ld post* **7/1**

32-3 2 *nk* **Woodlands Genpower (IRE)**[22] 2184 7-11-0 118........ MarkBradburne 125+
(P A Pritchard) *led to 2nd: chsd ldrs: j. slowly 4th: led appr 14th: clr after 3 out: rdn flat: hdd post* **7/2**[2]

P5-5 3 *28* **Ferimon**[33] 1976 6-11-0 .... RichardJohnson 109+
(H D Daly) *hld up: hmpd 2nd: mstke 11th: hdwy next: chsd wnr appr 14th: rdn 3 out: wknd next* **9/2**[3]

1-PP 4 *21* **Sungates (IRE)**[198] 441 9-11-0 .... AndrewTinkler 75
(C Tinkler) *prom to 14th* **12/1**

11-F 5 *dist* **Rowley Hill**[10] 2464 7-11-0 .... RobertThornton 60
(A King) *hld up in tch: blnd 10th: wknd 15th* **9/4**[1]

0-5P F **Cloneybrien Boy (IRE)**[21] 2214 5-10-9 64.................... DerekLaverty(5) —
(Mrs A M Thorpe) *fell 2nd* **100/1**

23 P **Jolejoker**[43] 1829 7-11-0 .... TomDoyle —
(R Lee) *led 2nd to 7th: wknd appr 14th: t.o whn p.u bef 5 out* **10/1**

P06- P **Ashleybank House (IRE)**[274] 4186 8-10-11 .... LeeVickers(3) —
(David Pearson) *hld up: hmpd 2nd: t.o whn p.u bef 14th* **25/1**

0-PF P **Memories Of Gold (IRE)**[32] 1988 5-10-0 83................ RichardSpate(7) —
(J A Danahar) *chsd ldrs: led 7th: hdd: wknd and p.u bef 14th* **150/1**

F0-0 P **Kingsbay**[17] 2297 6-10-7 .... JimCrowley —
(H Morrison) *hld up in tch: lost pl 7th: mstke next: bhd fr 11th: t.o whn p.u bef 14th* **18/1**

6m 53.7s (-10.30) **Going Correction** +0.30s/f (Yiel) **10** Ran SP% **111.2**
Speed ratings: **108,107,99,92,**— —,—,—,—,— CSF £31.01 TOTE £7.50: £2.20, £1.70, £1.50; EX 34.50.

Owner The Royal Corrouge Partnership **Bred** M Banville **Trained** Upper Lambourn, Berks

FOCUS

A decent staying novices' chase that saw the first two finish well clear. The race has been rated through the second to the level of his hurdles form.

NOTEBOOK

Royal Corrouge(IRE) ◆, last seen completing a hat-trick of point wins back in 2003, looked to have a lot to do turning for home - with his rider appearing content to bag a place - yet he picked up when given a smack before the penultimate fence and then flew home to collar the long-time leader near the line. He has plenty of scope, enjoyed the easy ground and is obviously entitled to improve a deal for the outing. Reported by his new trainer to be a lazy type at home, he clearly possesses a decent engine, and he looked a natural over his fences. *(op 11-2)*

Woodlands Genpower(IRE) ◆, third over timber on his recent seasonal bow, looked all over the winner approaching two out, and was still clear jumping the final fence, yet his stride started to shorten on the run-in and he was agonisingly caught by the fast-finishing winner in the dying strides. He can be considered a winner without penalty next time, on this evidence will enjoy reverting to three miles, and still very much rates as the type to do better as a chaser. *(op 4-1 tchd 5-1)*

Ferimon showed the benefit of his chase debut at Worcester and shaped well enough until finding stamina an issue from two out. He is going the right way, will be better off when reverting to three miles, and should find a race over fences before the year is out. However, his future lies very much with the handicapper. *(op 5-1)*

Sungates(IRE), pulled up on his previous two outings and returning from a 198-day break, was not disgraced on this chasing bow and should improve a deal for the outing. *(op 14-1)*

Rowley Hill, who fell at an early stage on his chasing bow at Uttoxeter nine day previously, failed to convice over his fences and was beaten a long way from home. He won over this trip over timber, so would not have wanted for stamina, and it is more likely that his confidence was dented by his previous fall that attributed to this poor effort. *(op 7-4)*

2661 CHARTHAM MARINE "THAT'S THE MARINE BUSINESS" INTRODUCTORY JUVENILE NOVICES' HURDLE (8 hdls) 2m
1:40 (1:40) (Class 2) 3-Y-0 **£9,300** (£2,730; £1,365; £681)

Form RPR

U 1 **Prime Contender**[17] 2286 3-11-0 .... LeightonAspell 113+
(O Sherwood) *hld up in tch: led 2 out: r.o* **10/1**

3 2 *3 ½* **Take A Mile (IRE)**[17] 2286 3-11-0 .... JohnLevins 108
(B G Powell) *hld up: plld hrd: hdwy appr 4th: led after 3 out: hdd next : no ex last* **20/1**

3 *6* **Ostrogoth (FR)**[219] 3-11-0 .... MickFitzgerald 103+
(N J Henderson) *chsd ldrs: ev ch appr 2 out: wknd flat* **4/1**[2]

2 4 *2 ½* **Hawridge King**[17] 2286 3-11-0 .... TomScudamore 99
(W S Kittow) *hld up in tch: rdn appr 2 out: wknd last* **8/1**

5 *13* **Quasimodo (IRE)**[149] 3-11-0 .... NoelFehily 88+
(A W Carroll) *hld up: hdwy 5th: wknd appr 2 out* **25/1**

2 6 *10* **Pocketwood**[34] 1948 3-11-0 .... DaveCrosse 79+
(Jean-Rene Auvray) *led: hit 3 out: sn hdd: wkng whn blnd next* **5/1**[3]

0 7 *6* **Misters Sister**[15] 2345 3-10-7 .... MarkBradburne 64+
(C A Dwyer) *hld up: hdwy appr 4th: sn rdn: wknd after next* **200/1**

8 *2* **Detroit City (USA)**[151] 3-11-0 .... RichardJohnson 75+
(P J Hobbs) *prom: hit 1st: wknd 3 out* **3/1**[1]

P 9 *1* **Rockys Girl**[28] 2069 3-10-7 .... LeeStephens 60
(R Flint) *hit 1st: bhd fr 3rd* **200/1**

U 10 *hd* **Inn For The Dancer**[3] 2597 3-11-0 .... PaddyMerrigan 67
(Mrs H Dalton) *bhd fr 3rd* **40/1**

11 *17* **Darwaz (IRE)**[238] 3-11-0 .... TomDoyle 50
(D R Gandolfo) *prom: rdn after 3rd: wkng whn mstke 4th* **16/1**

P **Christom**[74] 3-11-0 .... JasonMaguire —
(Mrs Tracey Barfoot-Saunt) *bhd fr 3rd: t.o whn p.u bef next* **200/1**

0 P **Aviemore**[3] 2587 3-11-0 .... JosephByrne —
(J R Cornwall) *w ldr tl wknd appr 4th: t.o whn p.u bef 2 out* **80/1**

P **Maxamillion (IRE)**[30] 3-11-0 .... JamieMoore —
(S Kirk) *hld up: hdwy 4th: mstke and wknd next: t.o whn p.u last* **6/1**

P P **Golden Squaw**[19] 2258 3-10-7 .... AnthonyCoyle —
(Miss C J E Caroe) *hld up: bhd fr 4th: t.o whn p.u bef 2 out* **200/1**

P **Salinger (USA)**[40] 3-11-0 .... GinoCarenza —
(Andrew Turnell) *plld hrd and prom: wknd appr 5th: t.o whn p.u bef 2 out* **40/1**

3m 58.9s (0.60) **Going Correction** +0.25s/f (Yiel) **16** Ran SP% **118.7**
Speed ratings: **108,106,103,102,95 90,87,86,86,85 77,**—,—,—,—,— CSF £185.51 TOTE £14.80: £3.50, £2.50, £1.40; EX 185.90.

Owner Matthew Green & Richard Green **Bred** Gecko Bloodstock Ltd **Trained** Upper Lambourn, Berks

FOCUS

This is likely to prove an above-average juvenile event as the season progresses and seems sure to throw up its share of future winners.

NOTEBOOK

Prime Contender ◆, who unseated at the first flight on his recent hurdle debut when well backed at Hereford, made amends and showed his true colours with a ready success on this first outing for his new yard. He is clearly versatile as regards underfoot conditions, proved fluent over his hurdles, and saw out the trip well. A step-up in grade now looks in order. *(op 9-1)*

Take A Mile(IRE) ◆, third at Hereford on his debut in this sphere 17 days previously, enjoyed the softer ground and turned in another promising effort. He may have given the winner a bit more to think about had he consented to settle through the early stages and is clearly up to going one better in due course.

Ostrogoth(FR), a ten-furlong winner on his sole outing on the Flat in France, shaped with definite promise on this British and hurdling bow and only conceded defeat on the run-in. He should be placed to strike before too long by his top stable, and clearly has a future in this sphere, yet may ideally prefer a stiffer test. *(op 10-3 tchd 9-2)*

Hawridge King had his chance yet ultimately struggled see out the trip on this softer ground and failed to confirm his debut form with Take A Mile. This still rates another fair effort, however, and he will be suited by the return to good ground in the future. *(op 10-1)*

Pocketwood saw his jumping fall apart late on and was eventually well beaten. Despite clearly having the engine to win a race or two over hurdles, he really will have to brush up his jumping if he is to progress. *(op 9-2)*

Detroit City(USA), rated 94 on the Flat and a winner of four of his eight outings in that sphere, proved disappointing on this anticipated hurdling bow and never posed a serious threat. However, given that he stayed 14 furlongs so well on the Flat, it may well be that he already wants further over hurdles, and it would be a surprise were he not to leave this form behind in due course. *(op 5-2)*

2662 PETE KENNEDY 60TH BIRTHDAY H'CAP CHASE (22 fncs) 3m 5f
2:10 (2:10) (Class 3) (0-120,120) 5-Y-0+ **£5,497** (£1,613; £806; £403)

Form RPR

-2P0 1 **Moorlands Again**[21] 2210 10-10-13 107....................(t) MarkBradburne 130+
(M Sheppard) *chsd ldrs: led appr 6th: blnd 17th: clr 4 out: eased flat* **9/2**[2]

13-2 2 *17* **Finzi (IRE)**[10] 2465 7-10-0 94 oh3.................................. TomScudamore 95
(M Scudamore) *prom: chsd ldr 16th: wknd appr 2 out* **5/2**[1]

-202 3 *1 ½* **Koquelicot (FR)**[17] 2299 7-11-12 120.......................... RichardJohnson 120
(P J Hobbs) *hld up in tch: mstkes 8th and 12th: jnd wnr next: rdn appr 16th: wknd 3 out* **5/2**[1]

P50U 4 *7* **Happy Hussar (IRE)**[7] 2524 12-9-9 94 oh3.................... DrPPritchard(5) 87
(Dr P Pritchard) *hld up: hdwy 4th: led next: hdd bef 6th: sn lost pl: t.o fr 10th: sme late hdwy* **8/1**[3]

-60P 5 *5* **Follow The Flow (IRE)**[17] 2293 9-10-10 107................ OwynNelmes(3) 100+
(P A Pritchard) *led to 5th: remained handy tl wknd 17th* **8/1**[3]

450- 6 *dist* **Levallois (IRE)**[206] 4518 9-11-0 108.................................... PhilipHide —
(P Winkworth) *hld up: wknd 14th* **16/1**

55PU 7 *3 ½* **Buzybakson (IRE)**[8] 2506 8-10-0 94 oh15........................ JosephByrne —
(J R Cornwall) *chsd ldrs: lost pl 6th: t.o fr 10th* **14/1**

7m 44.3s (-4.60) **Going Correction** +0.30s/f (Yiel) **7** Ran SP% **110.1**
Speed ratings: **99,94,93,91,90** —,— CSF £15.51 CT £30.74 TOTE £5.10: £2.70, £1.60; EX 12.70.

Owner W J Odell **Bred** R Williams **Trained** Eastnor, H'fords

FOCUS

A modest handicap, run at a solid gallop, and the winner has been rated value for 22l.

NOTEBOOK

Moorlands Again, eighth behind Bannow Strand at Cheltenham 21 days previously, found this smaller field much to his liking and registered his first success since 2003 in emphatic style. He enjoyed himself out in front, can be rated value for even further and, on this evidence, should strike again providing the Handicapper does not react excessively to this. *(op 11-2 tchd 4-1)*

Finzi(IRE), third in this last season, again ran close to his mark in defeat yet is flattered by his proximity to the winner. He is a decent benchmark for this form. *(tchd 11-4)*

Koquelicot(FR), with the blinkers left off, did not jump as well as he can and was found out under his big weight. He remains in fair form, however, and still looked to run close to his mark in defeat. *(op 9-4 tchd 11-4)*

Happy Hussar(IRE) was plugging on at the finish and was not totally disgraced from 3lb out of the handicap. *(tchd 9-1)*

Follow The Flow(IRE), winner of this event in 2004 from a 12lb lower mark, was firmly put in his place and really does need some respite from the Handicapper at present. *(tchd 17-2)*

2663 PAUL O'DONOGHUE 40TH BIRTHDAY MAIDEN HURDLE (11 hdls) 2m 5f
2:40 (2:43) (Class 4) 4-Y-0+ **£3,576** (£1,042; £521)

Form RPR

2 1 **Galteemountain Boy (IRE)**[33] 1969 5-11-2 .... ChristianWilliams 112+
(Evan Williams) *hld up: hdwy appr 6th: led last: r.o wl* **6/1**

2-2 2 *2 ½* **Oscatello (USA)**[39] 1889 5-11-2 .... RobertThornton 107+
(Ian Williams) *hld up: mstke 3rd: hdwy appr 6th: led after 8th: rdn and hdd last: unable qck* **9/2**[1]

4 3 *30* **Mick Jerome (IRE)**[10] 2455 4-11-2 .... MatthewBatchelor 82+
(Rune Haugen, Norway) *hld up: hdwy after 6th: hit 3 out: wknd bef next* **5/1**[2]

20-P 4 *dist* **Dare Too Dream**[16] 2311 6-11-2 .... TomDoyle —
(K Bishop) *prom tl wknd after 3 out* **16/1**

5 *3* **Smilingvalentine (IRE)**[22] 8-10-2 .... RyanCummings(7) —
(D J Wintle) *hld up: hdwy after 6th: wknd bef next* **66/1**

44 6 *2* **Blue Hills**[15] 2343 4-11-2 .... JimmyMcCarthy —
(P W Hiatt) *hld up: hdwy after 6th: mstke and wknd next* **25/1**

40 7 *2 ½* **Key In**[12] 2414 4-10-6 ....(t) LeeVickers(3) —
(I W McInnes) *hld up: bhd fr 7th* **66/1**

0-4 8 *½* **Malko De Beaumont (FR)**[38] 1892 5-11-2 .... JohnMcNamara —
(K C Bailey) *hld up in tch: led after 6th: hdd & wknd after 8th* **8/1**

1/ 9 *17* **From Dawn To Dusk**[600] 4816 6-11-2 .... RichardJohnson —
(P J Hobbs) *hld up in tch: wknd 7th* **7/1**

0/3- 10 *dist* **Major Catch (IRE)**[236] 4814 6-10-11 .... AdamPogson(5) —
(C T Pogson) *led to 2nd: wknd appr 7th* **11/2**[3]

00 P **Another Flint (IRE)**[7] 2528 5-10-11 .... LeeStephens(5) —
(R Flint) *prom to 7th: t.o whn p.u bef 3 out* **100/1**

0- P **Katy's Classic (IRE)**[229] 4922 5-11-2 .... LeightonAspell —
(K C Bailey) *hld up: t.o whn p.u bef 7th* **40/1**

6P0 P **Walton Way**[22] 2185 5-10-11 .... MarkNicolls(5) —
(P W Hiatt) *bhd whn hit 1st: t.o whn p.u after 6th* **100/1**

P **Arinos (GER)**[19] 5-11-2 .... PaulMoloney —
(B J Curley) *chsd ldrs: led after 5th: hdd after next: wknd 8th: bhd whn p.u after 3 out* **8/1**

00- P **Ben Belleshot**[273] 4207 6-11-2 .... SeanCurran —
(P W Hiatt) *plld hrd: chsd ldrs: pckd 1st: mstke and wknd 5th: t.o whn p.u bef next* **150/1**

0-3 P **Boardroom Fiddle (IRE)**[34] 1954 6-11-2 .... BarryFenton —
(Miss E C Lavelle) *chsd ldr: led 2nd: hdd after 5th: sn wknd: t.o whn p.u after next* **12/1**

5m 20.8s (4.70) **Going Correction** +0.30s/f (Yiel)
WFA 4 from 5yo+ 11lb **16** Ran SP% **124.7**
Speed ratings: **103,102,90,—,— —,—,—,—,— —,—,—,—,—** — CSF £33.89 TOTE £8.20: £3.10, £2.00, £2.20; EX 42.50.
Owner Philip & Charles Racing **Bred** John And Hugh Naughton **Trained** Cowbridge, Vale Of Glamorgan

FOCUS
Little strength in depth to this modest maiden, but the pace was fair, and first two came well clear. Not an easy race to rate.

NOTEBOOK
Galteemountain Boy(IRE), making his debut for Evan Williams, showed the benefit of his recent change of scenery and scored a first success over hurdles at the third attempt. He showed a good attitude to fend off the runner-up after the last flight, is clearly suited by cut in the gound, and he saw out the longer trip without fuss. This again advertised his trainer's record of improving such characters. *(tchd 13-2)*
Oscatello(USA) ◆, who showed useful form when runner-up in both his bumper outings, again managed to find one too good on this hurdling bow, but again did little wrong in defeat. He may have found this trip a touch too far at this stage of his career, is entitled to improve for the experience, and was a long way clear of the rest in second, so should have little trouble in finding a similar event in due course. *(op 5-1 tchd 11-2)*
Mick Jerome(IRE), fourth on fast ground at Taunton on his hurdle debut ten days previously, failed to see out the longer trip on this much softer ground and was well beaten. He acted on this sort of ground on the Flat in his native Scandinavia, so this has to rate as disappointing, but it would be little surprise to see him leave this behind when reverting in trip. *(op 9-2 tchd 4-1)*
Dare Too Dream showed the benefit of his recent disappointing comeback over fences, where he jumped poorly, and turned in a more encouraging effort. He is another who may have found this trip too far. *(op 25-1)*
From Dawn To Dusk, last seen winning a bumper on his debut in April 2004, proved easy to back ahead of this hurdling bow and ran as through the race was badly needed. *(op 5-1)*
Major Catch(IRE) *(op 15-2)*
Boardroom Fiddle(IRE) *Official explanation: jockey said gelding bled from the nose (tchd 11-1)*

2664 DRIVE VAUXHALL LEAMINGTON SPA COMMERCIAL VEHICLES H'CAP CHASE (12 fncs) 2m 110y

3:10 (3:10) (Class 3) (0-125,121) 5-Y-O+ **£5,578** (£1,637; £818; £409)

Form				Jockey	SP	RPR
4P52	**1**		**Marked Man (IRE)**[26] 2102 9-11-12 **121** — (R Lee) *hld up in tch: chsd ldr 8th: led 2 out: rdn out*	TomDoyle	**4/1**[1]	133+
204-	**2**	*7*	**Lamp's Return**[245] 4721 6-10-13 **108** — (A King) *plld hrd: j.rt: led: clr 3rd: hdd 2 out: wknd flat*	RobertThornton	**4/1**[1]	113+
P-41	**3**	*8*	**Major Euro (IRE)**[33] 1978 8-11-9 **118** — (S J Gilmore) *chsd ldr to 8th: wknd appr 2 out*	JamesDavies	**16/1**	114
12-F	**4**	*1 ¾*	**Tiger Tips Lad (IRE)**[8] 2504 6-11-1 **110** — (N A Twiston-Davies) *chsd ldrs: rdn 3 out: wknd next*	CarlLlewellyn	**9/2**[2]	107+
3431	**5**	*4*	**Amadeus (AUS)**[19] 2257 8-10-1 **96** — (M Scudamore) *hld up: hdwy appr 6th: mstke 9th: wknd next*	TomScudamore	**5/1**[3]	89+
23U3	**6**	*15*	**Saafend Rocket (IRE)**[161] 840 7-11-8 **117** — (H D Daly) *hld up: mstke 4th: a in rr*	RichardJohnson	**11/2**	92
0606	**7**	*shd*	**Blazing Batman**[7] 2527 12-9-9 **95** oh17 — (Dr P Pritchard) *chsd ldrs: lost pl after 5th: bhd fr next*	DrPPritchard(5)	**100/1**	70
	8	*7*	**Lord Gunnerslake (IRE)**[126] 1114 5-10-3 **101** oh6 ow6 — (Miss C J E Caroe) *hld up: sme hdwy appr 6th: wknd 8th: mstke 3 out*	AnthonyCoyle(3)	**33/1**	69
33U-	**9**	*7*	**Flinders Chase**[341] 3056 10-11-9 **118** — (C J Mann) *hld up: hdwy appr 6th: wknd after 8th*	NoelFehily	**15/2**	86+

4m 8.30s (5.70) **Going Correction** +0.475s/f (Soft) **9** Ran SP% **111.8**
Speed ratings: **105,101,97,97,95 88,88,84,81** CSF £20.09 CT £222.84 TOTE £6.30: £2.20, £1.80, £3.40; EX 25.90.
Owner Mr & Mrs C R Elliott **Bred** Patrick Hogan **Trained** Byton, H'fords

FOCUS
A fair handicap, run at a decent pace in the soft ground, and the field came home fairly strung out. The winner is in a different class to these rivals and the form looks pretty solid.

NOTEBOOK
Marked Man(IRE), runner-up at Huntingdon on his recent return from a break, duly went one better with a comfortable success and defied top weight in the process. There was plenty to like about the manner of this success, and on his day he is different class to these rivals, but this was his highest winning mark to date and the Handicapper will likely now make his life a lot more difficult. *(tchd 9-2)*
Lamp's Return, returning from an eight-month break and having her first outing over fences, proved hard to settle through the early parts and ultimately paid for those exertions from the penultimate fence. However, there was little disgrace in this defeat, and she was clear of the remainder of her rivals at the finish, so she looks well up to finding a similar race in due course. *(tchd 9-2)*
Major Euro(IRE), raised 9lb for winning at Worcester 33 days previously, was not disgraced on ground he would have found plenty soft enough. He still has to prove he is up to this higher mark, but the return to fences should be very much in his favour. *(op 12-1)*
Tiger Tips Lad(IRE), who fell when going as well as any on his recent chase and seasonal debut, was found wanting from the penultimate fence and may have found this deep surface against him. *(op 5-1)*
Amadeus(AUS), raised 10lb for winning at Fakenham 19 days previously, was firmly put in his place in this better company. *(tchd 9-2)*
Saafend Rocket(IRE), returning from a 161-day break, failed to make an impact on this unsuitably soft ground. *(op 6-1)*

2665 RACING UK STANDARD OPEN NATIONAL HUNT FLAT RACE 2m

3:40 (3:40) (Class 6) 4-6-Y-O **£2,000** (£583; £291)

Form				Jockey	SP	RPR
	1		**Aux Le Bahnn (IRE)**[21] 4-10-13 — (Noel T Chance) *hld up in tch: led on bit ins fnl f: nt extended*	WilliamKennedy(5)	**3/1**[1]	118+
	2	*1 ½*	**Fast Forward (NZ)** 5-11-4 — (Miss Venetia Williams) *a.p: led 4f out: rdn over 1f out: hdd and unable qck ins fnl f*	SamThomas	**5/1**[2]	110
	3	*8*	**Keenan's Future (IRE)**[294] 4-11-4 — (Ian Williams) *chsd ldrs: led 10f out: rdn and hdd 4f out: wknd over 1f out*	NoelFehily	**14/1**	102
	4	*4*	**Top Ram (IRE)** 5-11-4 — (J A B Old) *hld up in tch: outpcd over 4f out: styd on ins fnl f*	MarkBradburne	**12/1**	98
4-	**5**	*5*	**Principe Azzurro (FR)**[289] 3932 4-10-13 — (H D Daly) *hld up: hdwy 7f out: outpcd over 4f out: n.d after*	TomGreenway(5)	**10/1**	93
	6	*3 ½*	**Beat The Boys (IRE)** 4-11-4 — (N A Twiston-Davies) *chsd ldrs: rdn over 4f out: wknd 3f out*	CarlLlewellyn	**16/1**	89
	7	*3 ½*	**Tisfreetdream (IRE)** 4-11-1 — (P A Pritchard) *sn chsng ldrs: rdn over 4f out: wknd over 3f out*	OwynNelmes(3)	**66/1**	86
	8	*17*	**The Beaming Bandit (IRE)** 5-11-4 — (M G Rimell) *mid-div: hdwy 1/2-way: wknd over 4f out*	JamieMoore	**9/1**	69
6	**9**	*nk*	**Thunder Child**[196] 470 5-10-13 — (John Allen) *hld up: sme hdwy 1/2-way: wknd over 5f out*	MarkNicolls(5)	**80/1**	69
0/	**10**	*1 ½*	**Minster Park**[855] 1019 6-11-4 — (S C Burrough) *hld up: plld hrd: sme hdwy 1/2-way: wknd over 5f out*	RJGreene	**80/1**	67
0-	**11**	*4*	**Murotoevation (IRE)**[228] 4935 6-11-4 — (D G Bridgwater) *hld up: n.d*	VinceSlattery	**100/1**	63
	12	*¾*	**Mister Notorious (IRE)**[419] 1687 6-10-11 — (N A Twiston-Davies) *chsd ldrs: led after 2f: hdd 10f out: rdn and wknd 3f out*	StevenCrawford(7)	**11/1**	62
	13	*7*	**Pangbourne (FR)** 4-11-4 — (A King) *rel to r: bhd fnl 13f*	RobertThornton	**12/1**	55
43	**14**	*16*	**Northern Endeavour**[17] 2288 6-11-4 — (Simon Earle) *led 2f: wknd 4f out*	MickFitzgerald	**25/1**	39
	15	*13*	**Miss Millfield** 4-10-6 — (V J Hughes) *chsd ldrs over 11f*	LeeStephens(5)	**80/1**	19
	16	*dist*	**Dear Oh Dear** 4-11-1 — (David Pearson) *sn drvn along in rr: t.o fnl 10f*	LeeVickers(3)	**80/1**	—
	P		**Saunders Road (IRE)** 4-11-4 — (P J Hobbs) *mid-div: p.u over 12f out: lame*	RichardJohnson	**6/1**[3]	—

3m 59.9s (1.10) **Going Correction** +0.40s/f (Soft) **17** Ran SP% **122.6**
Speed ratings: **97,96,92,90,87 86,84,75,75,74 72,72,68,60,54 —,—** CSF £16.36 TOTE £3.60: £1.50, £2.80, £5.80; EX 26.90 Place 6 £59.83, Place 5 £36.44.
Owner A D Weller **Bred** Padraig Morrissey **Trained** Upper Lambourn, Berks

FOCUS
This should prove a decent bumper as the season progresses and the first two came clear. The winner can be rated for double his winning margin.

NOTEBOOK
Aux Le Bahnn(IRE) ◆, last seen winning an Irish point at the third attempt in November, could not have been much more impressive in scoring on this debut for new connections and was well backed to do so. He made his rivals look pedestrian when scything through to join the pace in the straight, clearly enjoying the deep surface, and his jockey will likely not have an easier ride all season. Value for further, he rates an exciting prospect, and now deserves to take his chance in Graded company in this sphere. *(tchd 7-2)*
Fast Forward(NZ), whose stable took this event last season, was handy throughout and shaped with real promise, despite proving no match for the winner. He may ideally prefer better ground in the future, showed a decent attitude when headed by the winner, and was nicely clear of the rest at the finish. *(op 6-1)*
Keenan's Future(IRE), a facile winner of an Irish point in February, faded after racing handily yet still did enough to suggest he can find a race in this division with the experience under his belt. He was also well suited by the soft ground. *(op 12-1)*
Top Ram(IRE), a 32,000gns purchase whose dam was a smart bumper/hurdles performer, got outpaced when the tempo increased turning for home and was doing all of his best work at the finish. He should improve a deal for the experience. *(op 14-1)*
Pangbourne(FR) *Official explanation: jockey said he had steering problems (op 14-1)*
Northern Endeavour *Official explanation: jockey said gelding finished lame (tchd 22-1)*
Saunders Road(IRE), who cost 55,000euros and whose dam was Grade One-winning hurdler as a juvenile, was well backed yet pulled up lame and is likely to be absent for some time. *(op 9-1 tchd 11-2)*
T/Plt: £57.40 to a £1 stake. Pool: £37,167.85. 471.95 winning tickets. T/Qpdt: £22.00 to a £1 stake. Pool: £2,796.80. 93.65 winning tickets. CR

[2645] FAIRYHOUSE (R-H)

Sunday, December 4

OFFICIAL GOING: Chase course - heavy; hurdle course - soft to heavy

2667a BET @ BLUESQUARE.COM ROYAL BOND NOVICE HURDLE (GRADE 1) (9 hdls) 2m

1:05 (1:06) 4-Y-O+ **£34,574** (£10,106; £4,787; £1,595)

Form				Jockey	SP	RPR
	1		**Iktitaf (IRE)**[22] 2198 4-11-7 118 — (Noel Meade, Ire) *settled 6th: nt fluent 3rd: 4th 3 out: impr into cl 2nd travelling best 2 out: led whn slt mstke last: qcknd clr run-in: ea*	(t) PCarberry	**7/1**	140+
	2	*5*	**O'Muircheartaigh (IRE)**[21] 2228 5-11-12 — (E J O'Grady, Ire) *mod 3rd: tk clsr order bef 1/2-way: cl 2nd 3 out: chal and led 2 out: sn rdn and strly pressed: hdd last: outpcd run-in*	BJGeraghty	**4/5**[1]	140
	3	*3 ½*	**Mounthenry (IRE)**[32] 1993 5-11-12 — (C Byrnes, Ire) *in rr early: prog into 6th bef 4 out: 3rd after 3 out: sn rdn: no imp fr next*	DNRussell	**5/1**[3]	137
	4	*8*	**Alexander Taipan (IRE)**[14] 2399 5-11-12 — (W P Mullins, Ire) *mod 2nd: tk clsr order bef 5th: led bef 3 out: hdd whn bad mstke 2 out: sn no ex*	DJCasey	**4/1**[2]	129+
	5	*8*	**High Priestess (IRE)**[30] 2031 6-11-7 116 — (M J P O'Brien, Ire) *hld up: drvn along 5 out: 5th u.p after 3 out: no imp fr next*	TGMRyan	**25/1**	116
	6	*dist*	**Silent Oscar (IRE)**[15] 2361 6-11-12 — (C P Donoghue, Ire) *trckd ldrs: 4th bef 1/2-way: rdn 3 out: sn no ex*	MrCJSweeney	**14/1**	—
	P		**Up Above (IRE)**[21] 2228 5-11-12 — (S Donohoe, Ire) *led: clr early: mstke 3rd: hdd bef 3 out: sn wknd: p.u bef 2 out*	APMcCoy	**25/1**	—
	P		**Monty Mint (IRE)**[14] 2387 7-11-12 — (Thomas Foley, Ire) *in tch early: dropped to rr 1/2-way: wknd bef 4 out: t.o whn p.u bef 2 out*	GCotter	**66/1**	—

4m 2.30s **Going Correction** +0.55s/f (Soft)
WFA 4 from 5yo+ 10lb **8** Ran SP% **120.6**
Speed ratings: **115,112,110,106,102 —,—,—** CSF £14.24 TOTE £9.50: £1.80, £1.10, £1.80; DF 28.20.
Owner Mrs P Sloan **Bred** Shadwell Estate Company Ltd **Trained** Castletown, Co Meath

NOTEBOOK
Iktitaf(IRE), who travelled well throughout despite a couple of minor mistakes, was able to hold his position on the inside, and his turn of foot on the run-in was impressive. This was a major improvement on what he had demonstrated in five previous runs that had yielded two successes, at Kilbeggan and at Naas three weeks ago. Fitted with a tongue tie on that most recent occasion, he wore that aid again here. He acted well on good to firm when trained by John Gosden and will be of interest in the spring, although he coped well with these conditions. He goes up 15lb to 133. *(op 6/1)*
O'Muircheartaigh(IRE) looked well but failed to live up to the hype. Not particularly fluent at some of his hurdles, he was ridden to lead two out and the winner had taken his measure before readily outpacing him on the run-in. *(op 8/11 tchd 4/5)*
Mounthenry(IRE) could not improve his position from three out and would have preferred better ground. *(op 11/2 tchd 6/1)*

Alexander Taipan(IRE) found this company too much for him once the pace was turned on and was beaten when blundering two out. *(op 3/1)*
High Priestess(IRE) was not a player from three out.
Up Above(IRE) *Official explanation: jockey said gelding jumped and hung left throughout*

2668a PIERSE GROUP DRINMORE NOVICE CHASE (GRADE 1) (15 fncs) 2m 4f
1:35 (1:35) 5-Y-0+ **£41,489** (£12,127; £5,744; £1,914)

RPR
1 **Kill Devil Hill (IRE)**[14] 2396 5-11-10 .... JLCullen 137
(Paul Nolan, Ire) *a.p: 2nd fr 4th: chal and led 2 out: slt mstke and hdd last: rallied u.p to regain ld nr fin* **5/2**[1]
2 *nk* **Father Matt (IRE)**[7] 2540 7-11-12 .... PCarberry 139
(Noel Meade, Ire) *trckd ldrs: 3rd fr 4 out: slt mstkes 9th and 5 out: 4th bef 3 out: 2nd and rdn after 2 out: led after last: kpt on u.p: hdd* **7/1**[3]
3 *6* **Mansony (FR)**[22] 2194 6-11-12 .... CO'Dwyer 133
(A L T Moore, Ire) *hld up: prog into 3rd 7 out: rdn bef 2 out: no imp fr bef last* **5/2**[1]
4 *2* **Mr Babbage (IRE)**[14] 2396 7-11-12 .... DJCasey 131
(W P Mullins, Ire) *led: rdn and strly pressed 3 out: hdd whn mstke 2 out: no ex* **7/1**[3]
5 *dist* **Davenport Milenium (IRE)**[56] 1703 9-11-12 125........ BJGeraghty —
(W P Mullins, Ire) *prom to 4th: last fr 8th: wknd 5 out: t.o fr bef 3 out* **25/1**
U **Church Island (IRE)**[23] 2165 6-11-12 .... TimmyMurphy —
(Michael Hourigan, Ire) *2nd whn mstke and uns rdr 1st* **11/4**[2]

5m 26.3s **Going Correction** +0.55s/f (Soft) **6** Ran SP% **112.7**
Speed ratings: **115,114,112,111,**— — CSF £19.40 TOTE £4.80: £1.90, £2.20; DF 35.90.
Owner Gigginstown House Stud **Bred** Mrs C Ross **Trained** Enniscorthy, Co. Wexford

NOTEBOOK
Kill Devil Hill(IRE) looked in trouble when headed with a mistake at the last but rallied well, without being knocked about, to shade it close home. He is an improver and might be better in a stonger-run race. *(op 9/4)*
Father Matt(IRE) is still prone to mistakes but came from just off the pace to lead landing over the last. He kept on dourly but was touched off in the last couple of strides. His stable has the key to all the best novice form. *(op 6/1)*
Mansony(FR) got into a challenging position before two out but found absolutely nothing and hung right on the run between the last two. *(op 2/1)*
Mr Babbage(IRE) jumped well in front but was headed and tiring when blundering two out. *(op 5/1)*
Davenport Milenium(IRE) *Official explanation: jockey said gelding made an abnormal respiratory noise in running (op 20/1)*

2669a BALLYMORE PROPERTIES HATTON'S GRACE HURDLE (GRADE 1) (11 hdls) 2m 4f
2:05 (2:06) 4-Y-0+ **£41,489** (£12,127; £5,744; £1,914)

RPR
1 **Solerina (IRE)**[21] 2227 8-11-7 158........ GTHutchinson 160+
(James Bowe, Ire) *led: rdn clr after 3 out: strly pressed after 2 out: slt mstke and hdd last: rallied u.p to regain ld nr fin: all out* **6/4**[2]
2 *shd* **Golden Cross (IRE)**[28] 4383 6-11-12 .... JohnnyMurtagh 165
(M Halford, Ire) *hld up in rr: 4th and hdwy 3 out: 2nd 2 out: chal and led last: kpt on wl u.p: hdd nr fin: jst failed* **7/1**
3 *1 ½* **Brave Inca (IRE)**[14] 2397 7-11-12 166........ APMcCoy 163+
(C A Murphy, Ire) *3rd early: 4th whn reminders bef 5 out: drvn along next: 2nd 3 out: 3rd and no imp after next: styd on fr last* **11/8**[1]
4 *25* **Back In Front (IRE)**[21] 2227 8-11-12 161........ BJGeraghty 138
(E J O'Grady, Ire) *trckd ldrs: 3rd fr 3rd: rdn 3 out: sn wknd* **6/1**[3]
5 *6* **Royal Paradise (FR)**[30] 2032 5-11-12 135........ DJCasey 132
(Thomas Foley, Ire) *trckd ldr in 2nd: rdn 4 out: wknd appr next* **25/1**

5m 4.20s **Going Correction** +0.55s/f (Soft) **5** Ran SP% **112.7**
Speed ratings: **116,115,115,105,102** CSF £11.85 TOTE £2.40: £1.80, £2.20; DF 12.80.
Owner John P Bowe **Bred** Michael J Bowe **Trained** Thurles, Co. Tipperary
■ Stewards' Enquiry : Johnny Murtagh caution: used whip with excessive frequency

NOTEBOOK
Solerina(IRE) put up one of her bravest performances in winning this race for the third year. She clipped the third last and the next, and flattened the last, was headed on the run-in, but fought back with tenacity to gain it again close home for a 16th victory over hurdles. This is her time of year and she is on song as usual. *(op 6/4 tchd 11/8)*
Golden Cross(IRE) was having his first run over hurdles since finishing seventh behind Hardy Eustace at Cheltenham last March, but he was an improved performer on the Flat this autumn. Murtagh was hard at work on him before the straight but he began to stay on from the second last and was in front early on the run-in. A half length up at one stage, he could not contain the mare's efffort on his inside and just gave best near the line. The World Hurdle will be the Cheltenham target this time.
Brave Inca(IRE), being scrubbed along before the fifth-last flight, did not jump all that well and never looked like getting there. He has more questions than answers but this is not his trip and he may have had an easy time since Punchestown. *(op 6/4)*
Back In Front(IRE) was trailing after three out and a switch to chasing surely awaits. *(op 5/1)*
Royal Paradise(FR) shows no signs of a return to form.

2666a, 2670 - 2673a (Foreign Racing) - See Raceform Interactive

2494 NEWCASTLE (L-H)
Monday, December 5

OFFICIAL GOING: Heavy (soft in places)
Wind: Almost nil

2674 GOSFORTH DECORATING AND BUILDING SERVICES MARES' ONLY NOVICES' HURDLE (10 hdls 1 omitted) 2m 4f
12:20 (12:21) (Class 4) 4-Y-0+ **£3,448** (£1,012; £506; £252)

Form RPR
F3 1 **Ile Maurice (FR)**[13] 2414 5-10-5 .... PatrickMcDonald[(7)] 100+
(Ferdy Murphy) *in tch: smooth hdwy to ld bef 2 out: clr bef last: easily* **9/4**[1]
3-P5 2 *13* **Sportula**[23] 2186 4-10-12 92........ RichardMcGrath 80
(C Grant) *chsd ldrs: drvn bef 3 out: kpt on fr next: no ch w wnr* **8/1**
U6 3 *hd* **Nowa Huta (FR)**[13] 2412 4-10-5 .... BenOrde-Powlett[(7)] 80
(Jedd O'Keeffe) *cl up: led after 4 out to bef 2 out: one pce* **20/1**
310- 4 *1 ¾* **Treasured Memories**[242] 4753 5-10-12 .... AndrewThornton 83+
(Miss S E Forster) *hld up: hdwy and prom bef 3 out: one pce next* **7/1**[3]
P4 5 *6* **Another Jameson (IRE)**[31] 2024 5-10-12 .... DavidO'Meara 73
(J M Jefferson) *led to after 4 out: wknd after next* **11/2**[2]
-226 6 *½* **Amalfi Storm**[32] 2012 4-10-9 .... MrTGreenall[(3)] 72
(M W Easterby) *hld up midfield: hdwy and prom 4 out: wknd next* **7/1**[3]
20 7 *10* **Political Pendant**[12] 2446 4-10-5 .... GarethThomas[(7)] 62
(R Nixon) *bhd: hdwy and in tch after 4 out: wknd next* **12/1**
0-06 8 *5* **New's Full (FR)**[8] 2515 4-10-12 .... BrianHarding 57
(Ferdy Murphy) *hld up: hdwy and in tch bef 3 out: sn shkn up and wknd* **16/1**
P0 9 *9* **Leonia's Rose (IRE)**[24] 2171 6-10-9 74........(p) PeterBuchanan[(3)] 48
(Miss Lucinda V Russell) *chsd ldrs tl wknd bef 3 out* **40/1**
4650 P **Roadworthy (IRE)**[159] 854 8-10-7 65........ DesFlavin[(5)] —
(W G Young) *a bhd: t.o whn p.u bef 3 out* **66/1**
F50 P **Tanmeya**[23] 2186 4-10-9 ....(e[1]) LarryMcGrath[(3)] —
(R C Guest) *keen in rr: t.o whn p.u after 4th* **33/1**
40 P **Entre Amis**[13] 2414 5-10-12 .... FinbarKeniry —
(G M Moore) *prom tl wknd 6th: t.o whn p.u bef 3 out* **66/1**
03/P P **Rainha**[11] 2447 8-10-12 .... GrahamLee —
(A C Whillans) *towards rr: wknd 6th: t.o whn p.u bef 3 out* **18/1**
05-0 P **Connaught Lady (IRE)**[13] 2412 6-10-7 ow2........ ThomasDreaper[(7)] —
(Ferdy Murphy) *a bhd: taield off whn p.u 4 out* **40/1**
00 P **Redeswire Ruby**[19] 2268 4-10-5 .... TomMessenger[(7)] —
(Mrs H O Graham) *in tch to 6th: sn wknd: t.o whn p.u bef 3 out* **100/1**

5m 25.1s (9.30) **Going Correction** +0.45s/f (Soft)
WFA 4 from 5yo+ 11lb **15** Ran SP% **117.7**
Speed ratings: **99,93,93,93,90 90,86,84,80,**— —,—,—,—,— CSF £18.63 TOTE £2.70: £1.10, £1.60, £10.90; EX 21.00.
Owner N Iveson & F Murphy **Bred** Haras De Reuilly **Trained** West Witton, N Yorks
■ Stewards' Enquiry : Ben Orde-Powlett caution: used whip with excessive frequency

FOCUS
A bit of a procession with Ile Maurice relishing the step up in trip and running out a ready winner. The form does not look strong though.

NOTEBOOK
Ile Maurice(FR) showed no effects of the fall she suffered on her British debut at Sedgefield when third back at the course last month, and this first try at two and a half miles saw her show improved form. Given a confident ride by her young pilot, she had it sewn up long before the last and there is every chance she can defy a penalty if kept to mares'-only contests. *(op 7-4)*
Sportula is only moderate, but she seems fairly consistent and just got the better of Nowa Huta for second. She gives the impressin three miles will be within her compass and a switch to handicaps would make her interesting. *(op 11-1)*
Nowa Huta(FR), who had previously shown little in two starts since arriving from France, held a prominent early position and made a positive move when going on four out. She was ultimately outclassed by the winner, and just lost second, but a similar performance should see her again going close. *(tchd 22-1)*
Treasured Memories, a bumper winner, travelled well into the straight, but she became outpaced from two out and looked to get a little tired on this first start since April. *(op 6-1)*
Another Jameson(IRE) has run better the last twice and will stand more chance in low-gade handicaps. *(op 6-1 tchd 7-1)*
Amalfi Storm ran a bit better than on her hurdling debut, but will need to improve a fair bit if she is to be winning in novice company. *(op 8-1)*
Tanmeya *Official explanation: jockey said filly had a breathing problem (op 33-1)*
Connaught Lady(IRE) *Official explanation: vet said mare pulled up lame (op 33-1)*
Redeswire Ruby *Official explanation: jockey said filly finished distressed (op 33-1)*

2675 BORDER MINSTREL NOVICES' CHASE (14 fncs 4 omitted) 3m
12:50 (12:51) (Class 4) 4-Y-0+ **£4,178** (£1,297; £698)

Form RPR
3053 1 **Nocatee (IRE)**[40] 1888 4-10-7 104........ APMcCoy 102
(P C Haslam) *hld up in tch: hdwy bef 4 out: 1l down whn lft in ld 2 out: r.o wl* **9/2**[3]
-212 2 *1 ¼* **Chabrimal Minster**[23] 2180 8-11-6 105........ GrahamLee 115+
(R Ford) *led: mstke 5 out: nt fluent and hdd next: rdn whn lft cl 2nd 2 out: one pce last* **5/4**[1]
R-PU 3 *dist* **Abzuson**[12] 2441 8-11-6 105........ FinbarKeniry —
(J R Norton) *hld up: effrt u.p 5 out: wknd bef next: lft distant 3rd 2 out* **14/1**
F61- P **Jack Lynch**[306] 3652 9-11-6 93........ BrianHarding —
(Ferdy Murphy) *chsd ldrs to 5 out: sn wknd: t.o whn p.u bef 2 out* **10/1**
3-30 F **Kharak (FR)**[11] 2449 6-11-6 105........ MarkBradburne 115
(Mrs S C Bradburne) *pressed ldr: led 4 out: 1l up and rdn whn fell 2 out* **10/3**[2]
P/0- P **Sir Rowland Hill (IRE)**[388] 2170 6-10-13 100........ ThomasDreaper[(7)] —
(Ferdy Murphy) *hld up: outpcd after 9th: t.o whn p.u bef 2 out* **16/1**

6m 26.7s (1.90) **Going Correction** 0.0s/f (Good)
WFA 4 from 6yo+ 13lb **6** Ran SP% **107.3**
Speed ratings: **96,95,**—,—,— — CSF £10.16 TOTE £5.00: £3.50, £1.10; EX 11.70.
Owner Middleham Park Racing & Middleham Turf **Bred** Major W R Paton-Smith **Trained** Middleham, N Yorks

FOCUS
Ordinary novice form, though the winner recorded a personal best.

NOTEBOOK
Nocatee(IRE), shaped as though this sort of test would suit when a keeping-on third over three furlongs shorter at Sedgefield in October, and the combination of McCoy and the four-year-old weight-for-age allowance proved too much for the favourite on the run-in. Obviously helped by the fall of Kharak, he is clearly going to make a better chaser than hurdler and should prove capable of defying a penalty before a possible move into handicaps. *(op 4-1 tchd 7-2)*
Chabrimal Minster, who escaped a penalty for his Aintree win, was probably a fortunate second and a couple of errors at a crucial time left him vulnerable. He is most effective in these conditions, and plugged on right the way to the line, but was no match for the winner. *(op 11-10 tchd 11-8 and 6-4 in places)*
Abzuson jumped better than on his chasing debut, but lacked the pace to get involved and weakened down the straight. *(op 16-1)*
Jack Lynch is lightly raced for one of his age, and has clearly been hard to train. He did not put up much of a fight once coming under pressure and on this evidence, is going to struggle. *(op 22-1 tchd 25-1)*
Sir Rowland Hill(IRE) was nibbled at in the market beforehand but, like his stablemate, did not show a great deal and got bogged down in the ground. He is entitled to improve back on a sounder surface. *(op 22-1 tchd 25-1)*
Kharak(FR) has some fair placed form over fences to his name and was still in front when coming down two out. He may well have won, but woud not have done so without fending off a fight from the winner. He will find a race as long as this does not affect confidence. *(op 22-1 tchd 25-1)*

2676 JAMES FLETCHER MARQUEE & PAVILION HIRE JUVENILE NOVICES' HURDLE (8 hdls 1 omitted) 2m
1:20 (1:21) (Class 4) 3-Y-0 **£3,409** (£1,000; £500; £249)

Form RPR
21 1 **Gardasee (GER)**[19] 2263 3-11-5 .... JasonMaguire 124+
(T P Tate) *j.w: mde all: drew clr fr 3 out: readily* **4/7**[1]
4P 2 *14* **One More Time (FR)**[23] 2178 3-10-5 .... GrahamLee 92+
(J Howard Johnson) *pressed wnr tl rdn and no ex fr 3 out* **6/1**[2]
2-06 3 *9* **Orki Des Aigles (FR)**[19] 2263 3-10-6 ow1........ ThomasDreaper[(7)] 83
(Ferdy Murphy) *midfield: outpcd 4th: rallied 3 out: no ch w first two* **40/1**

P5 **4** *1* **Woodford Consult**[12] 2442 3-10-5 .... RichardMcGrath 74
(M W Easterby) *keen: hld up: pushed along 4 out: n.d* **33/1**
0522 **5** *7* **Madge**[10] 2477 3-10-5 ....(v) WilsonRenwick 67
(W Storey) *chsd ldrs tl wknd bef 3 out* **16/1**
6 *13* **Elaala (USA)**[51] 3-10-5 .... AlanDempsey 54
(M Todhunter) *a bhd* **40/1**
215 **7** *10* **Royal Master**[15] 2367 3-11-5 .... APMcCoy 58
(P C Haslam) *chsd ldrs: lost pl 3rd: n.d after* **14/1**
P0 **8** *dist* **Mercari**[10] 2477 3-10-2 .... LarryMcGrath(3) —
(A R Dicken) *a bhd: lost tch fr 1/2-way* **200/1**
P **Mccormack (IRE)**[172] 3-10-12 .... TonyDobbin —
(M D Hammond) *hld up: hdwy 3rd: wknd 4 out: t.o whn p.u bef next* **50/1**
2 **F** **Paparaazi (IRE)**[53] 1729 3-10-12 .... AnthonyRoss —
(R A Fahey) *in tch: hdwy 4 out: sn rdn: disputing 5th and btn whn fell next* **9/1**[3]

4m 12.4s (6.10) **Going Correction** +0.45s/f (Soft) **10** Ran SP% **110.8**
Speed ratings: **102,95,90,90,86 80,75,—,—,—** CSF £3.79 TOTE £1.50: £1.02, £2.50, £4.70; EX 5.80.
Owner A S Helaissi **Bred** Gestut Romerhof **Trained** Tadcaster, N Yorks

FOCUS
An uncompetitive affair, but another good display from the front-running Gardasee.

NOTEBOOK
Gardasee(GER) ◆ has been in good form and faced a fairly straightforward task here under his penalty. Sent straight into the lead, he jumped fluently and began to pull away from the modest opposition after the third last. Although beating little here, his style of racing will continue to serve him well and he fully deserves a crack at something a bit better. *(tchd 8-13)*
One More Time(FR), whose two previous outings over hurdles both came at a higher level, faced her best opportunity yet of winning, but she was readily put in her place by the winner. She will find a race if continuing to be campaigned at a modest level. *(op 11-2)*
Orki Des Aigles(FR) had been a bit disappointing on his two previous tries since arriving from France, but this represented a drop in grade and he kept on well enough into third. Further is going to suit in time and he may be better off in handicaps.
Woodford Consult was again putting in some good late work and looks the sort her trainer will do well with once moving into handicaps. *(op 40-1)*
Madge could have been expected to challenge for a place, but she failed to run to form and faded disappointingly down the straight, possibly find the emphasis too much on stamina.
Paparaazi(IRE), who shaped with promise when runner-up on his hurdling debut, had run his race and was well held when coming down three out. *(op 8-1)*

2677 BET365 CALL 08000 322 365 NOVICES' CHASE (10 fncs 3 omitted) 2m 110y
1:50 (1:50) (Class 3) 4-Y-0+ **£7,779** (£2,318; £1,173; £601; £314)

Form RPR
-124 **1** **Portavadie**[40] 1880 6-11-2 .... GrahamLee 125+
(J M Jefferson) *chsd ldrs: wnt 2nd 4th: led bef 5 out: nt fluent next: hit last: rdn and r.o wl* **10/11**[1]
/0-6 **2** *1* **Tusk**[10] 2482 5-11-2 126.............................. DavidO'Meara 120+
(H P Hogarth) *cl up: rdn bef 4 out: effrt bef 2 out: ev ch run in: hld towards fin* **5/1**[3]
45-4 **3** *14* **Master Sebastian**[36] 1942 6-10-13 103.............................. PeterBuchanan(3) 105
(Miss Lucinda V Russell) *chsd ldrs: outpcd bef 4 out: no imp whn lft 3rd 2 out* **14/1**
1043 **4** *dist* **Prince Adjal (IRE)**[30] 2042 5-11-5 96.............................. MrCStorey(3) —
(Miss S E Forster) *led and sn clr: hdd bef 5 out: wknd next* **16/1**
-P50 **5** *dist* **Derainey (IRE)**[44] 1834 6-11-2 .... KennyJohnson —
(R Johnson) *sn bhd and detached: nvr on terms* **100/1**
24-3 **F** **Moonlit Harbour**[24] 2168 6-11-2 .... BrianHarding 105+
(Ferdy Murphy) *hld up in tch: hdwy 5 out: outpcd after next: 10l 3rd whn fell 2 out* **3/1**[2]
4-44 **U** **Ipledgeallegiance (USA)**[106] 1280 9-10-13 85.............................. AnthonyCoyle(3) —
(Miss Tracy Waggott) *hld up: rdn 5 out: 4th but no imp whn uns rdr next* **25/1**

4m 18.5s (-4.70) **Going Correction** 0.0s/f (Good) **7** Ran SP% **111.4**
Speed ratings: **111,110,103,—,—** — CSF £5.89 TOTE £1.70: £1.30, £2.40; EX 4.10.
Owner Ashleybank Investments Limited **Bred** Mrs J M F Dibben **Trained** Norton, N Yorks

FOCUS
A fair time for a race of this class and the front two look useful novices.

NOTEBOOK
Portavadie, who had not raced on ground like this since his bumper days, developed into a useful sort over hurdles last season, winning twice, and on the evidence of this chase debut, he is going to be equally as good over fences. His jumping in the early stages was good, but he made a couple of blunders when asked to go faster and was pressed all the way by the persistent Tusk, but he stayed on to strongly after the last. He has yet to be tested beyond two miles, but gives the impression he will stay further and it is more than likely he can defy a penalty. *(op Evens tchd 11-10 and 6-5 in a place)*
Tusk ◆, a smart juvenile hurdler when with Henrietta Knight, missed last season due to injury and did not show a great deal, admittedly facing a tough task, on his return at Newbury. This was more realistic and he was able to step up significantly in ground he handles. In contrast to the winner, his jumping got better as the contest went on and this 'stocky' tough nut can find success in this sphere. *(op 4-1)*
Master Sebastian, a long way inferior to the front pair over hurdles, again shaped reasonably on this second try over fences and is sure to find easier opportunities. *(tchd 12-1)*
Moonlit Harbour had run his race and was beaten in third when falling at the second last. A disappointment over two and a half miles last time when he raced prominently, he lacked the pace of the front pair here and is worth trying again at further under a more restrained ride.

2678 WEATHERBYS BANK "NATIONAL HUNT" NOVICES' HURDLE (12 hdls 1 omitted) 3m
2:20 (2:20) (Class 4) 4-Y-0+ **£3,116** (£914; £457; £228)

Form RPR
1 **According To John (IRE)**[250] 5-10-12 .... TonyDobbin 126+
(N G Richards) *in tch: smooth hdwy to ld bef 3 out: drew fr next: eased nr fin* **11/8**[1]
-030 **2** *5* **Rathowen (IRE)**[23] 2186 6-10-9 .... MichalKohl(3) 111
(J I A Charlton) *chsd ldrs: effrt after 4 out: chsd wnr next: kpt on: no imp* **5/2**[2]
0-00 **3** *20* **Brundeanlaws**[31] 2028 4-9-12 .... TomMessenger(7) 88+
(Mrs H O Graham) *mde most to bef 3 out: sn outpcd* **33/1**
4 *26* **Bramble Princess (IRE)**[29] 6-10-2 .... PeterBuchanan(3) 58
(Miss Lucinda V Russell) *cl up tl wknd fr 4 out* **6/1**[3]
0- **5** *18* **I'm No Fairy**[363] 2691 6-10-12 .... AnthonyRoss 47
(P Beaumont) *hld up: rdn 4 out: sn btn* **14/1**
P **Tigger Too** 7-10-7 .... MichaelMcAlister(5) —
(B Storey) *sn bhd: t.o whn p.u bef 7th* **22/1**
20 **P** **Musical Chord (IRE)**[181] 671 6-10-12 .... RichardMcGrath —
(B Storey) *in tch tl wknd and p.u 8th* **9/1**
-000 **P** **Rosedale Gardens**[19] 2262 5-10-9 .... MrTGreenall(3) —
(M W Easterby) *a bhd: t.o whn p.u bef 3 out* **33/1**
PPP- **P** **Clan Law (IRE)**[227] 4965 7-10-7 83.............................. DesFlavin(5) —
(Mrs L B Normile) *chsd ldrs to 8th: sn wknd: t.o whn p.u bef 3 out* **66/1**

6m 19.9s (1.50) **Going Correction** +0.45s/f (Soft)
WFA 4 from 5yo+ 13lb **9** Ran SP% **113.4**
Speed ratings: **107,105,98,90,84** —,—,—,— CSF £4.70 TOTE £2.20: £1.10, £1.10, £9.10; EX 6.40.
Owner Sir Robert Ogden **Bred** John P Kiely **Trained** Greystoke, Cumbria

FOCUS
An impressive display by former pointer According To John, who cruised clear to win comfortably and is value for further.

NOTEBOOK
According To John(IRE) ◆, fourth and third in a couple of Irish points earlier in the year, had to be nothing out of the ordinary to make a winning rules debut and he came clear with the minimum of fuss to win easily. A potentialy useful staying hurdler, it will be disappointing if he cannot defy a penalty before going on to bigger and better things, and in the long run he should make a smashing chaser. *(op 2-1 tchd 9-4)*
Rathowen(IRE) set the standard, albeit it was a modest one, and he proved no match for the useful winner. He was clear of the third and should find a northern novice hurdle before going on to handicaps. *(op 9-4 tchd 11-4)*
Brundeanlaws, a moderate sort in bumpers, shaped with plenty of promise on this hurdling debut, considering it was a decent contest, and she will find easier opportunities.
Bramble Princess(IRE), a well-experienced pointer, could have been expected to fare a little better on this Rules debut and shaped with no real promise for the future. *(op 7-2)*
I'm No Fairy has shown little in two starts and is more than likely to develop into a low-grade handicapper. *(op 16-1)*
Rosedale Gardens *Official explanation: jockey said gelding was unsuited by the heavy (soft in places) ground (op 25-1)*

2679 WEATHERBYS INSURANCE H'CAP CHASE (10 fncs 3 omitted) 2m 110y
2:50 (2:50) (Class 4) (0-110,112) 5-Y-0+ **£4,040** (£1,186; £593; £296)

Form RPR
6665 **1** **Kids Inheritance (IRE)**[16] 2339 7-11-5 109.............................. ThomasDreaper(7) 115
(J M Jefferson) *cl up: led 4 out: hld on wl fr last* **4/1**[3]
6-63 **2** *½* **Sands Rising**[27] 2111 8-11-6 103..............................(t) KennyJohnson 109
(R Johnson) *hld up: hdwy 5 out: effrt 3 out: ev ch fr last: jst hld* **3/1**[1]
-65F **3** *3½* **Cusp**[8] 2522 5-10-2 90.............................. DerekLaverty(5) 92
(Mrs A M Thorpe) *chsd ldrs: outpcd 3 out: kpt on fr last* **14/1**
1541 **4** *2½* **Bergerac (NZ)**[5] 2570 7-11-10 112 7ex.............................. PaulO'Neill(5) 112
(R C Guest) *hld up: hdwy to chse ldrs 4 out: outpcd whn shkn up after 2 out: nt qckn* **7/2**[2]
4032 **5** *1½* **The Miner**[31] 2022 7-10-6 92..............................(p) MrCStorey(3) 90
(Miss S E Forster) *keen: chsd ldrs: hit 5th: nt fluent next: rdn and outpcd fr 2 out* **9/2**
/6P4 **6** *1¾* **Moss Bawn (IRE)**[31] 2022 9-9-9 83 oh10..............................(v[1]) MichaelMcAlister(5) 79
(B Storey) *mde most to 4 out: wknd fr next* **25/1**
441/ **7** *8* **Tagar (FR)**[803] 1425 8-10-9 95.............................. MrTGreenall(3) 83
(C Grant) *plld hrd: prom tl wknd bef 4 out* **6/1**

4m 23.6s (0.40) **Going Correction** 0.0s/f (Good) **7** Ran SP% **110.2**
Speed ratings: **99,98,97,95,95 94,90** CSF £15.67 TOTE £7.20: £3.50, £2.70; EX 17.80.
Owner Mr & Mrs J M Davenport **Bred** Jimmy O'Brien **Trained** Norton, N Yorks

FOCUS
A tight though steadily-run handicap with all bar the hard-pulling Tagar having some sort of chance with half of mile to run.

NOTEBOOK
Kids Inheritance(IRE), still 9lb higher than when last winning back in January, received a fine ride from Dreaper and battled on gamely to hold the renewed challenge of Sands Rising. This was his first win in ground anything worse than good to soft, but he will need to raise his game further to defy a higher mark. *(op 7-2 tchd 10-3)*
Sands Rising is beginning to run into form and he stuck on to pose a persistent challenge to the winner. He will remain vulnerable off this sort of mark, but a similar effort will once again see him go close. *(op 7-2)*
Cusp has largely struggled since winning on her chasing debut, but this was a better effort and she seemed well suited by the testing going. Rated only 90, she should be capable of winning off that sort of mark and remains open to a little improvement at the age of five.
Bergerac(NZ), shouldering a 7lb penalty for his Catterick win, travelled well into the straight, but was never really asked for an effort and as a result connections were called in by the Stewards. It was subsequently discovered that he returned slightly lame and it was probably a decent effort considering. *Official explanation: jockey said, regarding running and riding, his orders were to settle gelding in rear on outside to get best ground, and having been settled gelding jumped into contention sooner than desired, turned into the straight full of running but found nothing off the bridle after 2nd last fence; vet said gelding was slightly lame on left fore (op 3-1 tchd 4-1)*
The Miner, who ran poorly in the cheekpieces back in October, had them back on here and again failed to run to form. He is capable of winning off this mark, but it is probably best advised to leave the headgear off next time.
Tagar(FR) did not run to form in ground that was too testing, failing to get home having pulled hard early. *(op 8-1 tchd 5-1)*

2680 ST JAMES SECURITY H'CAP HURDLE (8 hdls 1 omitted) 2m
3:20 (3:21) (Class 4) (0-110,108) 4-Y-0+ **£3,378** (£984; £492)

Form RPR
5P21 **1** **The Names Bond**[31] 2027 7-11-5 108.............................. MissRDavidson(7) 113+
(N G Richards) *hld up: smooth hdwy 4 out: led 2 out: hld on wl* **4/1**[1]
/505 **2** *nk* **Uptown Lad (IRE)**[11] 2452 6-11-2 98.............................. KennyJohnson 103
(R Johnson) *hld up: hdwy to ld bef 3 out: hdd next: kpt on fr last: jst hld* **4/1**[1]
5-20 **3** *17* **Polly Whitefoot**[23] 2186 6-10-8 90.............................. PadgeWhelan 78
(R A Fahey) *hld up: hdwy and prom 1/2-way: outpcd 3 out: lft modest 3rd last* **9/1**
1-33 **4** *6* **North Landing (IRE)**[11] 2453 5-10-6 91.............................. LarryMcGrath(3) 83+
(R C Guest) *keen: cl up: ev ch 4 out: outpcd after next: disputing modest 3rd whn bdly hmpd after last* **11/2**[3]
40U0 **5** *9* **Gospel Song**[11] 2452 13-10-4 93.............................. EwanWhillans(7) 66
(A C Whillans) *led to bef 3 out: sn btn* **25/1**
2-30 **6** *10* **Fearless Foursome**[29] 2064 6-10-10 95.............................. PeterBuchanan(3) 58
(N W Alexander) *hld up towards rr: rdn 4 out: sn btn* **33/1**
24-0 **F** **Leap Year Lass**[13] 2414 5-10-5 87.............................. RichardMcGrath —
(C Grant) *keen: chsd ldrs: fell 3rd* **50/1**
U-03 **F** **Nerone (GER)**[23] 2191 4-11-8 104.............................. WilsonRenwick 102
(P Monteith) *hld up: hdwy bef 3 out: 4l 3rd but no imp whn fell last* **5/1**[2]
-560 **F** **Bollin Thomas**[10] 2478 7-10-12 97..............................(p) PaddyAspell(3) 88+
(R Allan) *prom: effrt ins and ev ch bef 3 out: 3rd and outpcd whn fell next* **13/2**

2-30 **B** **Fairy Skin Maker (IRE)**[27] 2110 7-11-7 **108**...........(p) WilliamKennedy[(5)] 104
(G A Harker) *in tch: outpcd after 3 out: rallied after next: lft 6l 3rd whn b.d last* **9/1**

4m 12.0s (5.70) **Going Correction** +0.45s/f (Soft) **10** Ran SP% **114.1**
Speed ratings: **103,102,94,91,86 81,**—,—,—,— CSF £19.96 CT £133.87 TOTE £5.40: £2.30, £1.90, £3.20; EX 26.20 Place 6 £6.49, Place 5 £ 3.09.
Owner Mr & Mrs Duncan Davidson **Bred** D R Tucker **Trained** Greystoke, Cumbria

FOCUS
An eventful race with the outcome for third place being almost as interesting as the battle for first.

NOTEBOOK
The Names Bond has returned in cracking form this season and seems to have appreciated the return to hurdles. Up 8lb for his reappearance win, he was made to work hard, but held on well under his lady rider and there is no reason why he can not continue to improve. *(op 5-1)*
Uptown Lad(IRE) has slipped back down to a decent mark and he very nearly got back up, having been headed two out. He pulled 17 lengths clear of the third and should not be long in winning. *(op 5-1)*
Polly Whitefoot was a very fortunate third and probably needs some further assistance from the Handicapper before she is winning. *(op 7-1)*
North Landing(IRE) was already well held when being badly hampered after the last, and did not seem particularly suited by the drop in trip. *(op 13-2)*
Gospel Song is a gallant old boy, but continues to be vulnerable and was readily brushed aside here.
Bollin Thomas had run well and looked set for third when coming down two out. It is hoped this does not affect his confidence. *(tchd 9-2 and 11-2)*
Fairy Skin Maker(IRE) had no luck at all and was left in third, only to be brought down. *(tchd 9-2 and 11-2)*
Nerone(GER) was in third when coming down at the last and took Fairy Skin Maker down with him. *(tchd 9-2 and 11-2)*
T/Plt: £10.10 to a £1 stake. Pool: £38,905.80. 2,804.75 winning tickets. T/Qpdt: £5.10 to a £1 stake. Pool: £3,339.20. 477.20 winning tickets. RY

2212 FONTWELL (L-H)
Tuesday, December 6

OFFICIAL GOING: Soft (good to soft in places)
Wind: Moderate, against

2681 SHONE BUILDING LTD JUVENILE NOVICES' HURDLE (9 hdls) 2m 2f 110y
12:40 (12:41) (Class 4) 3-Y-O **£3,233** (£949; £474; £237)

Form RPR
2 **1** **Tora Bora (GER)**[16] 2373 3-10-12 .... TimmyMurphy 102+
(B G Powell) *hdwy 3rd: wnt 2nd after 5th: mstke 3 out: clr w runner-up whn hit next: slt ld last: drvn out* **3/1**[2]
2 **2** *2 ½* **Rosecliff**[20] 2274 3-10-12 .... APMcCoy 100+
(A M Balding) *chsd ldrs: lft in ld appr 6th: drew clr w wnr 2 out: narrowly hdd whn blnd and stmbld last: no ex* **4/7**[1]
0 **3** *9* **Lord Of Adventure (IRE)**[22] 2236 3-10-12 .... LeightonAspell 90
(Mrs L C Jewell) *hld up in midfield: mstke 5th: effrt 3 out: 3rd and styng on whn hit last: nt pce to trble ldng pair* **66/1**
66 **4** *¾* **Come What Augustus**[16] 2373 3-10-5 .... ShaneWalsh[(7)] 89
(R M Stronge) *prom: led briefly 2nd: w ldrs whn blnd 3 out: sn hrd rdn and outpcd* **25/1**
5 *6* **Sturbury**[136] 3-10-2 .... RichardYoung[(3)] 76
(J W Mullins) *towards rr: sme hdwy after 5th: no imp 3 out* **50/1**
6 *2 ½* **Isle De Maurice**[21] 3-10-12 .... JamesDavies 81
(D B Feek) *mid-div: outpcd whn mstke 6th: n.d after* **25/1**
4 **7** *2* **Joli Classical (IRE)**[20] 2274 3-9-12 .... JamesWhite[(7)] 72
(R J Hodges) *in tch: mstke 6th: wknd appr 2 out* **16/1**[3]
04 **8** *21* **Briannie (IRE)**[36] 1948 3-9-12 ....(p) RobertLucey-Butler[(7)] 51
(P Butler) *hld up in last pl: nt fluent 4th and 5th: no ch fr next* **40/1**
60 **9** *5* **Lojo**[16] 2373 3-10-5 .... JamieGoldstein 46
(Miss Sheena West) *a towards rr: n.d fr 6th* **50/1**
0 **10** *dist* **Keresforth**[16] 2373 3-10-12 .... BenjaminHitchcott —
(Mrs L C Jewell) *led to 2nd: prom tl wknd after 5th* **100/1**
0 **P** **Desert Moonbeam (IRE)**[20] 2274 3-10-0 .... JayHarris[(5)] —
(R J Hodges) *sddle slipped early: hdwy to ld after 2nd: mstke next: rrn wd and p.u appr 6th* **100/1**

4m 47.7s (11.70) **Going Correction** +0.525s/f (Soft) **11** Ran SP% **112.1**
Speed ratings: **96,94,91,90,88 87,86,77,75,**— — CSF £4.73 TOTE £4.10: £1.10, £1.10, £7.40; EX 5.90.
Owner D A Johnson **Bred** H Schroer-Dreesmann **Trained** Morestead, Hants

FOCUS
No real strength in depth to this juvenile event and the pace was very steady through the early stages. The two clear market leaders had it to themselves from some way out and the form looks straightforward.

NOTEBOOK
Tora Bora(GER) took advantage of the favourite's final-flight error and stayed on well up the run-in to lose his maiden tag in this sphere at the second attempt. He had been well supported for his debut at Plumpton 16 days previously, and showed the benefit of that run, with this slightly longer trip much to his liking. With improvement likely - especially as he ought to get even further - it will be interesting to see where connections pitch him next, and he clearly enjoys some cut in the ground. *(op 5-2)*
Rosecliff, whose debut second had been well advertised with the third, Spidam, subsequently hacking up at Sandown, was neck-and-neck with the eventual winner prior to meeting the final flight all wrong, and he would have gone very close without that error. He undoubtedly has a similar race within his grasp, and may have found this ground soft enough, but he has often shown temperament in the past on the Flat, so is never one to overly rely on. *(op 8-13 tchd 8-15)*
Lord Of Adventure(IRE) showed the benefit of his recent debut in this sphere and, while he had no chance with the first two, showed a decent attitude under pressure to win the battle for third. He will be of more interest when handicapped in due course.
Come What Augustus was handy throughout and turned in his best effort over hurdles to date. He now qualifies for handicaps and is slowly going the right way. *(op 20-1)*
Sturbury, who showed little in three outings on the Flat and never went off shorter than odds of 100/1, was not given too hard a time on this hurdling bow and should improve for the outing.
Isle De Maurice, a Polytrack maiden winner for Marcus Tregoning in March, was not at all suited by racing so far off the pace on this hurdling introduction and it was no surprise to see him staying on all too late up the hill. He has the scope to do better in this sphere and will be interesting when eligible for handicaps. *(op 33-1)*
Desert Moonbeam(IRE) *Official explanation: jockey said saddle slipped*

2682 WEATHERBYS BANK BEGINNERS' CHASE (16 fncs) 2m 6f
1:10 (1:13) (Class 4) 5-Y-O+ **£4,044** (£1,187; £593; £296)

Form RPR
F-U4 **1** **Balladeer (IRE)**[51] 1761 7-11-0 105.............................. AndrewThornton 112+
(Mrs T J Hill) *settled midfield: hdwy to ld 13th: 2 l up whn stood off too far 3 out: clr next: easily* **7/2**[2]
4-03 **2** *8* **De Blanc (IRE)**[19] 2297 5-10-7 .... SamThomas 97+
(Miss Venetia Williams) *sn towards rr: drvn to chse ldrs 12th: j. slowly and outpcd 4 out: bdly hmpd next: styd on to take 2nd run-in* **9/2**[3]
221/ **3** *1 ¾* **King Triton (IRE)**[1002] 4083 8-10-7 .... JustinMorgan[(7)] 95+
(L Wells) *prom tl lost pl 9th: towards rr whn mstke 11th: styd on again fr 2 out* **20/1**
P/3- **4** *nk* **Rakalackey**[406] 1848 7-11-0 .... RichardJohnson 97+
(H D Daly) *sn chsng ldrs: cl 3rd whn mstke and lft 2nd 3 out: sn outpcd by wnr: lost 2nd run-in* **15/8**[1]
3P64 **5** *17* **Lucky Sinna (IRE)**[6] 2575 9-11-0 92.............................. TimmyMurphy 85+
(B G Powell) *sn cl up: jnd ldrs 12th: wknd 3 out* **8/1**
FP **6** *dist* **Sett Aside**[16] 2376 7-11-0 .... LeightonAspell —
(Mrs L C Jewell) *a in rr div: lost tch 11th* **50/1**
0- **U** **Mr McDellon (IRE)**[525] 836 8-10-7 .... DarylJacob[(7)] 85
(J F Panvert) *led tl 12th: disputing 2 l 2nd whn blnd, stmbld bdly and uns rdr 3 out* **50/1**
P/P0 **P** **Oscar Performance (IRE)**[10] 2502 10-11-0 91......... BenjaminHitchcott —
(R H Buckler) *sn prom: dropped rr and rdn 10th: wl bhd whn p.u bef 4 out* **33/1**
2-06 **U** **Jonanaud**[23] 2213 6-10-7 117.............................. MrJAJenkins[(7)] —
(H J Manners) *nt fluent early: in rr tl hdwy 10th: sn drvn along: outpcd in midfield whn blnd and uns rdr 12th* **13/2**

5m 57.8s (14.00) **Going Correction** +0.525s/f (Soft) **9** Ran SP% **111.3**
Speed ratings: **95,92,91,91,85** —,—,—,— CSF £18.42 TOTE £4.40: £1.60, £1.60, £2.90; EX 22.10.
Owner M McNeil **Bred** Scott Hardy Partnership **Trained** Chinnor, Oxon

FOCUS
This was no more than a fair beginners' chase, run at an average gallop, and the winner won easily.

NOTEBOOK
Balladeer(IRE) ◆ gained a belated first success over fences on this debut for his new connections. Having raced in midfield throughout the first circuit, he moved up smoothly to join the pace, before kicking for home with four to jump full of running. Despite a serious error at the next fence, at which his rider did really well to stay on board, he ultimately ran out an easy winner and his jumping was near faultless to that point. He deserved this success, has joined the right stable to progress as a chaser, and it will be fascinating to see whether he can now fulfil his potential this term as he should be high on confidence now. *(op 4-1)*
De Blanc(IRE) turned in an improved effort, and would have finished closer but for being hampered three out, but never looked a threat to the winner. She will find life easier in handicaps and appreciated this slightly longer trip. *(op 4-1)*
King Triton(IRE), last seen winning over timber off a mark of 82 in March 2003, ran very much as though this was needed and did all of his best work at the finish. He is entitled to improve plenty for this, has the scope to do better as a chaser, and will obviously benefit from a longer trip in the future. *(op 14-1)*
Rakalackey, rated 127 over hurdles, did not prove suited by the soft ground on this chasing bow and was not totally disgraced in the circumstances. He will need to brush up his jumping, but is entitled to improve for the experience, and could prove a different proposition on a faster surface. *(op 9-4)*
Jonanaud turned in a mulish effort, jumping poorly, and it was no surprise when he eventually unshipped his rider. He has it all to prove now. *(op 40-1)*
Mr McDellon(IRE), who showed little on his hurdling bow when last seen in 2004, was still going well enough when unseating three out and would probably have been placed with a clear round. He looks an improver in this shpere. *(op 40-1)*

2683 SIMON TAYLOR 40TH BIRTHDAY NOVICES' HURDLE (10 hdls) 2m 4f
1:40 (1:41) (Class 4) 4-Y-O+ **£3,309** (£964; £482)

Form RPR
6-52 **1** **Dearson (IRE)**[18] 2322 4-10-12 105.............................. NoelFehily 108+
(C J Mann) *hdwy 7th: chsd ldr 3 out: led appr last: drvn out* **13/2**
1-02 **2** *3 ½* **Arumun (IRE)**[20] 2262 4-10-12 .... TomScudamore 105+
(M Scudamore) *led: hit 5th: rdn and hdd appr last: one pce* **11/2**[2]
0-00 **3** *3* **No Way Back (IRE)**[38] 1916 5-10-12 .... BarryFenton 101
(Miss E C Lavelle) *stdd in last pl s and t.k.h: racd wd: hdwy on outside 6th: shkn up and one pce appr 2 out* **10/1**
51-0 **4** *9* **Royal Stardust**[10] 2487 4-10-12 .... JamieMoore 95+
(G L Moore) *mid-div: rdn to chse ldrs 7th: wknd appr 2 out: 4th and btn whn blnd last* **11/1**
230 **5** *5* **Missyl (FR)**[18] 2309 5-10-12 .... RobertWalford 87
(R H Alner) *t.k.h: chsd ldrs tl wknd 3 out* **14/1**
60/6 **6** *14* **Cornish Jester**[39] 1903 6-10-12 .... MarkBradburne 77+
(C J Down) *in tch tl wknd 3 out* **11/2**[2]
00 **7** *6* **Robbie Will**[14] 2423 4-10-12 .... HenryOliver 67
(F Jordan) *a bhd: no ch fr 7th* **66/1**
00/ **8** *10* **Gullivers Travels**[619] 4578 6-10-12 .... LeightonAspell 57
(N J Gifford) *mstkes: a bhd: no ch fr 7th* **25/1**
P **The Stafford (IRE)**[717] 4-10-12 .... MatthewBatchelor —
(L Wells) *t.k.h in midfield: wknd 6th: t.o next: p.u bef 2 out* **66/1**
4P **P** **Break The Ice**[12] 2461 4-10-2 .... ColinBolger[(3)] —
(L A Dace) *towards rr: rdn 6th: no ch fr next: wl bhd whn p.u bef 2 out* **66/1**
6-10 **P** **Slick (FR)**[23] 2211 4-10-12 .... MickFitzgerald —
(N J Henderson) *prom: blnd 7th: wknd appr 3 out: wl bhd whn p.u bef next* **3/1**[1]
5 **P** **Alexander Sapphire (IRE)**[17] 2343 4-10-2 .... OwynNelmes[(3)] —
(N B King) *prom: mstke 7th: wknd after 3 out: wl bhd whn p.u run-in* **66/1**
3-6 **P** **Mooresini (IRE)**[23] 2212 5-10-12 .... PhilipHide —
(N J Gifford) *prom: mstkes 1st and 5th: wknd after 7th: wl bhd whn p.u bef 2 out* **6/1**[3]
6P6 **F** **Pitton Prince**[20] 2269 6-10-5 .... MrDavidTurner[(7)] —
(N R Mitchell) *chsd ldrs: hit 3rd: drvn and wknd 7th: wl bhd whn fell last* **100/1**

5m 8.70s (4.90) **Going Correction** +0.525s/f (Soft) **14** Ran SP% **118.3**
Speed ratings: **111,109,108,104,102 97,94,90,**—,— —,—,—,— CSF £40.93 TOTE £6.40: £2.20, £1.50, £3.90; EX 24.40.
Owner The Whitcoombe Four **Bred** Mull Enterprises Ltd **Trained** Upper Lambourn, Berks

FOCUS
A modest novice event, run at a sound gallop, and the field finished well strung out. The form makes sense and it produced decent winning time for a race of its class.

NOTEBOOK

Dearson(IRE), who improved for this trip when second to Oscar Park at Windsor 18 days previously, duly went one better and got off the mark over timber at the third attempt. He was given a well-judged ride by Fehily, acted on the soft ground, and jumped tidily throughout. While he may look vulnerable in this division under a penalty, he remains open to further improvement, and now looks to have found his optimum trip. *(op 7-1 tchd 6-1)*

Arumun(IRE) ran keenly at the head of affairs, taking the field along at a decent clip, and did well to finish second in the circumstances. He got the longer trip well, indeed he appears to be an out-and-out galloper, and will be eligible for handicaps after his next outing. In the longer term, he is very much a future chaser. *(op 5-1 tchd 9-2)*

No Way Back(IRE) turned in his best effort to date and enjoyed the step up in trip. He is another who will most likely come into his own over fences, but can build on this all the same. *(op 15-2)*

Royal Stardust showed the benefit of his recent comeback in a stronger event at Newbury, but did not look to see out this longer trip on the deep surface. *(op 10-1)*

Missyl(FR) proved free through the early parts and never threatened over this longer trip, but was keeping on at the same pace up the run-in. He already looks to be crying out for fences.

Slick(FR) found nothing when asked to improve approaching the home turn and dropped out very quickly. *Something may well have been amiss with him. Official explanation: trainer had no explanation for the poor form shown (op 7-1 tchd 15-2)*

Mooresini(IRE) *Official explanation: jockey said gelding hung left throughout (op 7-1 tchd 15-2)*

2684 HYDER CONSULTING (UK) LTD H'CAP CHASE (15 fncs) 2m 4f

2:10 (2:13) (Class 4) (0-90,90) 4-Y-0+ **£3,448** (£1,012; £506; £252)

Form / RPR

5P31 **1** **Jolly Boy (FR)**[7] 2561 6-10-7 **71** 7ex........(b) SamThomas 94+
(Miss Venetia Williams) *led 3rd: hit 5th and 4 out: clr next: easily* **9/2**[1]

6-12 **2** *10* **Mystical Star (FR)**[23] 2217 8-11-12 **90**........ LeightonAspell 101+
(M J Hogan) *hdwy 10th: 3rd whn pckd 4 out: wnt mod 2nd 2 out: no ch w wnr* **13/2**

000- **3** *8* **Harbour Point (IRE)**[253] 4604 9-11-7 **85**........ TomScudamore 88+
(M Scudamore) *hdwy 8th: jnd wnr and stmbld 4 out: sn outpcd* **16/1**

5P32 **4** *2 ½* **Walcot Lad (IRE)**[9] 2522 9-11-5 **86**........(p) ColinBolger(3) 83
(A Ennis) *in tch: jnd wnr after 9th: outpcd fr 11th* **14/1**

4531 **5** *7* **Taksina**[5] 2594 6-9-4 **64** oh4........ PaulDavey(10) 54
(R H Buckler) *bhd: hit 5th: mod late hdwy* **5/1**[2]

-3P3 **6** *6* **Woodenbridge Dream (IRE)**[19] 2287 8-11-7 **85**........ RichardJohnson 71+
(R Lee) *led to 3rd: lost pl 8th: n.d after* **14/1**

3526 **7** *11* **Just Reuben (IRE)**[26] 2151 10-11-0 **78**........ JoeTizzard 51
(C L Tizzard) *prom tl wknd qckly 9th* **33/1**

2-11 **8** *5* **Julies Boy (IRE)**[18] 2323 8-11-5 **90**........(t) WillieMcCarthy(7) 58
(T R George) *chsd ldrs to 10th: steadily lost pl* **15/2**

6020 **P** **Borehill Joker**[93] 1405 9-11-8 **86**........ AndrewThornton —
(V R A Dartnall) *a towards rr: wl bhd whn p.u bef 11th* **11/2**[3]

P **Pasghetti Hoops (IRE)**[20] 2279 8-10-5 **69**........(t) APMcCoy —
(A J Martin, Ire) *nt fluent: in tch to 1/2-way: bhd whn p.u bef 10th* **11/2**[3]

0-PP **P** **Ellas Recovery (IRE)**[16] 2378 5-10-11 **75**........ JamesDavies —
(D B Feek) *prom to 7th: 6th and btn whn blnd 10th: t.o whn p.u bef 2 out* **100/1**

5m 17.3s (9.40) **Going Correction** +0.525s/f (Soft) **11 Ran SP% 113.9**

Speed ratings: **102,98,94,93,91 88,84,82,—,— —** CSF £33.33 CT £425.48 TOTE £5.70: £1.90, £2.90, £4.80; EX 42.10.

Owner Favourites Racing **Bred** Georges Lacombe **Trained** Kings Caple, H'fords

FOCUS

A moderate, yet fairly competitive handicap for the class, and it was run at a sound pace.

NOTEBOOK

Jolly Boy(FR) ◆ made most of the running, and followed-up his recent Hereford success in good style under a 7lb penalty. He jumped fluently in the main, had no trouble with the longer trip and softer ground, and was full value for his winning margin. The recent application of blinkers has clearly worked the oracle and, despite the fact the Handicapper will no doubt hike him up again for this, a bold bid for the hat-trick can be expected. *(op 5-1)*

Mystical Star(FR) never looked like getting to the winner, but turned in another sound effort and remains in good form. He helps set the standard for this form and will not mind the return to a faster surface in the future. *(op 7-1)*

Harbour Point(IRE), making his chasing debut for a new yard and returning from a 253-day break, was running a big race until making a crucial error that looked to have cost him the runner-up spot. He should come on for the run and looks to have a race in him over fences. *(op 20-1 tchd 14-1 in a place)*

Walcot Lad(IRE) tended to run in snatches, but kept on under pressure up the straight. He is weighted to win at present, but is clearly tricky. *(op 16-1)*

Taksina *(op 6-1 tchd 9-2)*

Julies Boy(IRE) did not jump fluently on this quest for the hat-trick under top weight and disappointed. *(op 9-2)*

Borehill Joker, well backed on this debut for his new connections, had jumped well enough prior to pulling up. *Official explanation: jockey said gelding bled from the nose (op 9-2)*

Pasghetti Hoops(IRE), whose Irish trainer merits great respect on such raids to Britain, started to tread water passing the stands for the first time and stopped very quickly thereafter. *(op 9-2)*

2685 BET365 CALL 08000 322 365 H'CAP HURDLE (9 hdls) 2m 2f 110y

2:40 (2:40) (Class 4) (0-110,109) 4-Y-0+ **£3,416** (£1,003; £501; £250)

Form / RPR

F003 **1** **Wenger (FR)**[23] 2218 5-10-12 **95**........(b) PhilipHide 97+
(P Winkworth) *prom: led appr 2 out: hung bdly rt run-in: all out* **14/1**

-224 **2** *½* **Coustou (IRE)**[23] 2214 5-10-7 **90**........(p) BarryFenton 91+
(R M Stronge) *hld up in midfield: smooth hdwy on outside 3 out: styd on to press wnr run-in: jst hld* **6/1**[1]

1-04 **3** *1 ¼* **Hail The King (USA)**[16] 2379 5-10-13 **103**........ RobertLucey-Butler(7) 101
(R M Carson) *hld up and wl bhd: mstke 6th: stdy hdwy to chse ldrs 2 out: rdn and styd on same pce run-in* **14/1**

0P23 **4** *3 ½* **Isam Top (FR)**[16] 2379 9-9-9 **83** oh1........ RobertStephens(5) 78+
(M J Hogan) *hld up in midfield: hdwy 6th: no ex appr last* **20/1**

0S65 **5** *4* **Private Benjamin**[16] 2379 5-10-12 **95**........ MatthewBatchelor 86+
(M R Hoad) *hld up and bhd: gd hdwy 3 out: disputing 2nd whn mstke next: wknd appr last* **33/1**

0-26 **6** *21* **Eljutan (IRE)**[8] 2556 7-10-8 **98**........ ShaneWalsh(7) 67
(J Joseph) *in tch: drvn along 5th: sn outpcd* **40/1**

-040 **7** *hd* **Honey's Gift**[23] 2218 6-11-6 **103**........ APMcCoy 72
(G G Margarson) *mid-div: effrt 6th: wknd after 3 out* **13/2**[2]

-P02 **8** *nk* **Jayed (IRE)**[23] 2218 7-10-2 **92**........ PatrickCStringer(7) 72+
(M Bradstock) *led: sn 10 l clr: hdd & wknd appr 2 out* **7/1**[3]

/0-1 **9** *13* **Auetaler (GER)**[26] 2139 11-10-11 **101**........(p) BCByrnes(7) 57
(E McNamara, Ire) *sn chsng ldrs: wknd 6th* **7/1**[3]

053 **10** *dist* **Tytheknot**[12] 2460 4-10-11 **94**........(p) LeightonAspell —
(O Sherwood) *mid-div: outpcd appr 6th: sn bhd* **8/1**

61-P **11** *17* **Szeroki Bor (POL)**[33] 2010 6-11-5 **102**........ TimmyMurphy —
(M Pitman) *prom: hrd rdn after 6th: mstke and wknd 3 out* **15/2**

41F- **P** **Sesame Rambler (IRE)**[293] 3885 6-11-12 **109**........ JamieMoore —
(G L Moore) *a bhd: p.u after 5th* **8/1**

23-F **P** **Barton Gate**[23] 2217 7-11-3 **100**........(v) NoelFehily —
(D P Keane) *chsd ldrs to 5th: wl bhd whn p.u bef 2 out* **20/1**

4m 44.5s (8.50) **Going Correction** +0.525s/f (Soft)

WFA 4 from 5yo+ 10lb **13 Ran SP% 114.8**

Speed ratings: **103,102,102,100,99 90,90,90,84,— —,—,—** CSF £88.91 CT £1206.52 TOTE £18.70: £4.20, £1.60, £5.00; EX 97.40.

Owner P Winkworth **Bred** Ecurie Delbart And Mme Pascale Menard **Trained** Ramsnest Common, Surrey

FOCUS

A modest handicap run at a sound pace thanks to the front-running Jayed, and the field were strung out from an early stage.

NOTEBOOK

Wenger(FR), third behind Jayed over course and distance last time, stalked that rival throughout before sailing past to hit the front in the straight, looking booked for a comfortable success. However, he once again displayed his quirks by hanging badly right towards the stands' rail after the final flight, and ultimately needed all of his rider's strength to score all-out. He travels smoothly in his races, clearly likes this venue as now both of his wins over timber have come over course and distance, and this proved his ability to act on a soft surface. Whether he can follow-up has to be a doubt, however, as he is fiendishly tricky when any pressure is applied. *(op 16-1)*

Coustou(IRE) was gaining at the finish as the winner hung across him on the run-in, but looked a touch reluctant to fully go through with his effort and again found one too good. He is a fair benchmark at this level, but is clearly not one for win-only purposes. *(op 5-1)*

Hail The King(USA) came from a long way off the pace to get involved in the straight and turned in another sound effort. He is well worth riding more positively in the future and will appreciate the return to faster ground in due course.

Isam Top(FR) was far from disgraced from a 1lb out of the handicap and is clearly in decent heart at present. He is on a long losing run, however. *(op 25-1)*

Eljutan(IRE) *Official explanation: jockey said gelding hung right*

Jayed(IRE), 2lb higher than when finishing in front of the winner over course and distance last time, went off too fast for his own good on this softer surface and proved disappointing. He is capable of better. *(op 13-2 tchd 8-1)*

2686 SAM HARRIS BOOKMAKERS H'CAP CHASE (17 fncs 2 omitted) 3m 2f 110y

3:10 (3:10) (Class 4) (0-100,94) 5-Y-0+ **£4,014** (£1,178; £589; £294)

Form / RPR

-622 **1** **Dunbrody Millar (IRE)**[14] 2424 7-11-11 **93**........ RichardJohnson 110+
(P Bowen) *led 2nd: mstke 8th: hdd home turn: cl 2nd whn bmpd by faller 2 out: rallied to ld last: all out: gamely* **10/3**[3]

P251 **2** *½* **Ebony Jack (IRE)**[6] 2575 8-10-2 **70** 7ex........(p) JoeTizzard 86+
(C L Tizzard) *prom: rdn to slt ld home turn: hdd last: rallied gamely* **3/1**[2]

-640 **3** *dist* **Kappelhoff (IRE)**[6] 2575 8-10-3 **71**........(b) MatthewBatchelor 62
(Mrs L Richards) *bhd: rdn 7th: mstkes 13th and 14th: lft modest 3rd 2 out* **50/1**

2230 **4** *dist* **Lost In Normandy (IRE)**[14] 2424 8-10-0 **68** oh1........(b) DaveCrosse —
(Mrs L Williamson) *hdwy 9th: wknd 13th* **25/1**

0F03 **P** **Jazz Du Forez (FR)**[22] 2243 8-9-8 **69**........ AdrianScholes(7) —
(John Allen) *bhd tl p.u bef 5th: dismtd* **33/1**

/P-3 **F** **Tacita**[22] 2248 10-9-7 **68** oh4........ MrMWall(7) —
(M D McMillan) *hld up towards rr: 5th and no ch whn fell 2 out* **66/1**

1P1- **F** **Pewter Light (IRE)**[303] 3722 8-11-0 **85**........ OwynNelmes(3) —
(B J M Ryall) *chsd ldrs: rdn 10th: 5th whn fell next* **20/1**

2-43 **P** **Princesse Grec (FR)**[20] 2267 7-11-10 **92**........ TomScudamore —
(M Scudamore) *chsd ldrs to 8th: bhd whn p.u after 12th* **20/1**

F **Farmer Grant (IRE)**[16] 2392 6-11-4 **86**........ APMcCoy 100+
(A J Martin, Ire) *hld up in midfield: hdwy 12th: chal and fell 2 out* **13/8**[1]

302 **P** **Armageddon**[19] 2282 8-11-1 **83**........ LeightonAspell —
(O Sherwood) *nt jump wl: sn towards rr: wl bhd whn p.u bef last* **16/1**

3-2P **P** **Commanche Jim (IRE)**[3] 2623 9-11-12 **94**........ AndrewThornton —
(R H Alner) *led to 2nd: mstke and rdn 9th: wknd after next: bhd whn p.u after 12th* **16/1**

7m 10.2s (9.10) **Going Correction** +0.525s/f (Soft) **11 Ran SP% 117.7**

Speed ratings: **107,106,—,—,— —,—,—,—,— —** CSF £13.11 CT £419.79 TOTE £5.10: £2.10, £1.50, £10.20; EX 14.90.

Owner Dundon Else Partnership **Bred** Lord Donegall **Trained** Little Newcastle, Pembrokes

FOCUS

This moderate staying handicap was run at a solid pace in the conditions and the first two came well clear in a battling finish. The form makes sense.

NOTEBOOK

Dunbrody Millar(IRE), narrowly denied over this trip at Warwick two weeks previously and with the cheekpieces left off this time, showed tremendous guts to hold off the runner-up up the run-in and score a much-deserved first success over fences. He deserves plenty of credit for giving away so much weight to a progressive rival, has developed into a really consistent performer, and is the type his trainer tends to do excel with, so can strike again over a similar trip despite a future weight rise. *(op 4-1 tchd 9-2)*

Ebony Jack(IRE), whose stable landed this in 2004 with Brave Spirit, went down all guns blazing on the run-in and posted another solid effort. He is progressive and, while he will have to race off a higher mark next time, is capable of resuming winning ways. *(op 7-2 tchd 11-4)*

Kappelhoff(IRE) stayed on without threatening the front pair and managed to get a touch closer to the runner-up than had been the case at Plumpton six days previously. *(op 40-1)*

Farmer Grant(IRE), 5lb higher than when scoring over an inadequate two miles at Cork last time, has to rate unlucky and looked to be relishing this much longer trip. However, he was none too fluent over the fourth and third-last fences, so it was not a total surprise he came to grief. *(op 6-4 tchd 11-8 and 2-1)*

2687 KINGS BEACH HOTEL, PAGHAM CONDITIONAL JOCKEYS' H'CAP HURDLE (11 hdls) 2m 6f 110y

3:40 (3:41) (Class 4) (0-105,102) 4-Y-0+ **£3,282** (£956; £478)

Form / RPR

-U61 **1** **Businessmoney Jake**[6] 2578 4-11-7 **100** 7ex........ LiamHeard(3) 104+
(V R A Dartnall) *hld up: hdwy to ld 2 out: hung lft run-in: rdn out* **4/1**[2]

2 **2** *3 ½* **Moscow Summit (IRE)**[26] 2140 7-10-5 **87**........ BCByrnes(6) 88+
(E McNamara, Ire) *hld up in rr: smooth hdwy whn hit 7th: sn led: hdd 2 out: nt qckn run-in* **11/2**[3]

5-31 **3** *2 ½* **Rosetown (IRE)**[10] 2505 7-11-4 **102**........(b) WillieMcCarthy(8) 100
(T R George) *in tch and wd most of way: rdn to chse ldrs 2 out: one pce* **10/3**[1]

-061 **4** *9* **English Jim (IRE)**[23] 2214 4-10-3 **79**........ ColinBolger 72+
(Miss A M Newton-Smith) *t.k.h: chsd ldrs: lost pl 5th: rallied 3 out: one pce next: 4th and btn whn blnd last* **7/1**

1604 **5** *3* **Penny's Crown**[6] 2576 6-10-9 **88**........ EamonDehdashti(3) 74
(G A Ham) *hld up towards rr: hdwy 8th: hrd rdn and wknd 2 out* **33/1**

0-05 **6** *5* **Killer Cat (FR)**[14] 2419 4-11-2 **95**........(vt[1]) TomMalone(3) 79+
(M C Pipe) *prom: mstke 7th: wknd appr last* **9/1**

-325 **7** *30* **Classical Love**[183] 665 5-10-10 **89**.................................. ShaneWalsh(3) 40
(C J Down) *plld hrd: dropped to rr 5th: blnd 8th: no ch after* **16/1**
0/43 **8** *9* **Rhossili (IRE)**[65] 1616 5-10-4 **90**.................................. MattyRoe(10) 32
(Mrs L Wadham) *rr div most of way: rdn 5th: no ch fr 8th* **16/1**
/304 **P** **Quintus (USA)**[19] 2296 10-11-3 **96**...............................(v) GinoCarenza(3) —
(A King) *t.k.h in midfield: wknd 7th: wl bhd whn p.u bef 2 out* **16/1**
06UP **P** **Geography (IRE)**[8] 2555 5-10-4 **86**...................(v) RobertLucey-Butler(6) —
(P Butler) *prom tl wknd qckly 8th: wl bhd whn p.u bef 2 out* **50/1**
-214 **P** **Saucy Night**[26] 2140 9-10-4 **80**....................................... RobertStephens —
(Simon Earle) *led tl after 7th: wknd after 3 out: bhd whn p.u bef last* **11/2**[3]
33-0 **P** **Knightsbridge King**[199] 451 9-11-6 **96**.............................. MarkNicolls —
(John Allen) *hld up in rr: mstke 2nd: hdwy and mstke 4th: wknd 7th: wl bhd whn p.u bef 2 out* **50/1**

5m 57.8s (13.00) **Going Correction** +0.525s/f (Soft) **12** Ran SP% **120.9**
Speed ratings: **98,96,95,92,91 90,79,76,—,— —,—** CSF £27.09 CT £82.26 TOTE £5.40: £1.70, £3.10, £2.00; EX 42.80 Place 6 £145.04, Place 5 £134.10.
Owner Business Money Limited **Bred** Mrs I Lefroy **Trained** Brayford, Devon

FOCUS
A moderate handicap whcih saw the field come home fairly strung out. The winner is progressive and the form appears fair.

NOTEBOOK
Businessmoney Jake, off the mark at Plumpton six days previously, followed-up in ready fashion under a 7lb penalty and could be rated value for slightly further as he looked to be idling when in front up the run-in. He has taken time to find his feet over hurdles, but is clearly getting his act together, and he had little trouble acting on this softer ground. Further improvement cannot be ruled out and his trainer really does have his horses in great form at present.
Moscow Summit(IRE), who bounced back to form when runner-up in a similar event at Ludlow last time, had every chance and turned in another creditable effort. He would have appreciated a stronger early gallop and looks up to going one better from this mark. *(op 6-1)*
Rosetown(IRE), raised 6lb higher for resuming winning ways at Towcester last time, was far from disgraced over this shorter trip and remains in decent form. However, he really does look in need of a return to further. *(op 4-1)*
English Jim(IRE), 5lb higher than when scoring at odds of 50/1 over course and distance 23 days previously, confirmed that effort to be no fluke and ran respectably. He can find easier assignments. *(op 10-1 tchd 11-1)*
Penny's Crown ran close to her recent level on ground she would have found plenty soft enough. *(tchd 40-1)*
Killer Cat(FR), equipped with a first-time visor, was found out by the longer trip and much softer ground. He still did enough to suggest he can find a race in due course, however. *(op 12-1 tchd 14-1)*
Saucy Night dropped out uncharacteristically and may have been unsuited by the deep surface. *(op 9-2 tchd 4-1 and 6-1)*
T/Plt: £60.90 to a £1 stake. Pool: £44,761.50. 536.40 winning tickets. T/Qpdt: £44.90 to a £1 stake. Pool: £3,138.60. 51.70 winning tickets. LM

2412 SEDGEFIELD (L-H)
Tuesday, December 6

OFFICIAL GOING: Heavy
After 18mm of rain over the four previous days the ground was described as'very testing, probably the worst it has ever been here'.
Wind: Light, half-behind Weather: Cold with heavy shoers.

2688 CANTORSPREADFAIR.COM CLASSIFIED HURDLE (10 hdls) 2m 5f 110y
12:50 (12:52) (Class 4) 4-Y-0+ **£2,932** (£854; £427)

Form RPR
1 **Compo (IRE)**[9] 2547 7-10-11 90........................... AndrewJMcNamara(3) 106+
(E McNamara, Ire) *w ldrs: led 6th: styd on wl fr 2 out: nudged out run-in* **5/1**[2]
5-00 **2** *2* **Nobodys Perfect (IRE)**[22] 2240 5-10-4 90............. PatrickMcDonald(7) 96
(Ferdy Murphy) *w ldrs: chsd wnr after 3 out: kpt on: no real imp* **25/1**
0-42 **3** *21* **Perfect Balance (IRE)**[14] 2416 4-10-11 84..................... KeithMercer(3) 79+
(D W Thompson) *w ldrs: wknd appr 2 out* **5/1**[2]
0P-0 **4** *12* **Sir Lamb**[218] 152 9-10-9 80.. BrianHughes(5) 66
(Miss S E Hall) *prom: effrt 3 out: sn btn* **150/1**
65PP **5** *3/4* **Mikasa (IRE)**[30] 2063 5-10-11 79.................................. PaddyAspell(3) 65
(R F Fisher) *j.lft: in rr: sme hdwy 3 out: nvr on terms* **100/1**
3-0P **6** *nk* **Scotmail Lad (IRE)**[200] 437 11-11-0 90..........................(p) RussGarritty 65
(C A Mulhall) *led to 6th: wknd appr 2 out* **16/1**[3]
-636 **7** *7* **Ireland's Eye (IRE)**[20] 2264 10-10-7 90.......................... MrSFMagee(7) 66+
(J R Norton) *mstke 1st: in rr: hdwy 3 out: mod 5th whn blnd 2 out* **16/1**[3]
5P65 **8** *dist* **Pornic (FR)**[11] 2474 11-10-9 89.................................... DeclanMcGann(5) —
(A Crook) *pominent: lost pl 7th: sn bhd: t.o: btn 32 l* **66/1**
0436 **P** **Oscar's Lady (IRE)**[20] 2262 4-10-6 85........................ DougieCostello(5) —
(G A Swinbank) *prom: wknd 3 out: p.u bef next* **16/1**[3]
3-21 **U** **Osiris (IRE)**[184] 648 10-11-0 90..........................(t) ChristianWilliams —
(Evan Williams) *trckd ldrs: blnd bdly and lost pl 7th* **10/11**[1]
P **Atlantic Point (IRE)**[954] 4804 8-10-11 88............................ TonyDobbin —
(D W Macauley, Ire) *prom to 5th: sn lost pl: t.o whn p.u bef 2 out* **66/1**
F62P **P** **Approaching Land (IRE)**[6] 2567 10-10-11 85............... MrTGreenall(3) —
(M W Easterby) *racd wd: prom to 6th: sn lost pl: t.o whn p.u bef 2 out* **40/1**

5m 36.4s (20.70) **Going Correction** +0.975s/f (Soft)
WFA 4 from 5yo+ 11lb **12** Ran SP% **114.3**
Speed ratings: **101,100,92,88,88 87,85,—,—,— —,—** CSF £112.70 TOTE £6.30: £1.50, £4.70, £2.30; EX 164.20.
Owner R McNamara **Bred** Denis Fahey **Trained** Rathkeale, Co. Limerick

FOCUS
They went a sensible gallop in the very testing conditions, enjoying the best of the ground. The winner was value for at least three times the official margin.

NOTEBOOK
Compo(IRE), back over hurdles, travelled strongly and made light of the very testing conditions. His able rider is nothing if not cool and confident. *(op 11-2)*
Nobodys Perfect(IRE), last of seven at Folkestone three weeks earlier, went in pursuit of the winner but it was virtually a one-horse war. Even so she deserves credit for finishing some way clear of the remainder. *(op 20-1)*
Perfect Balance(IRE) mixed it from the off but he was fighting a losing battle at the top of the hill. *(op 6-1)*
Sir Lamb, absent since May, would not want conditions as testing as they were here.
Mikasa(IRE), back over hurdles, continually gave away ground jumping to his left and basically he continues to be out of sorts.
Osiris(IRE), absent since winning a chase at Perth in June, qualified for this by the skin of his teeth. He looked in tip-top trim and was poised when giving his rider no chance at the fourth last. A good opportunity lost. *(op 10-1)*
Oscar's Lady(IRE) *Official explanation: vet said filly returned lame (op 10-1)*

2689 CANTOR SPREADFAIR MAIDEN CHASE (21 fncs) 3m 3f
1:20 (1:21) (Class 4) 5-Y-0+ **£4,394** (£1,290; £645; £322)

Form RPR
1 **Weapons Inspector (IRE)**[289] 6-11-2 .... GrahamLee 112+
(J Howard Johnson) *hld up: hdwy to trck ldrs 12th: led 16th: j.rt 2 out: styd on wl* **7/1**[3]
-250 **2** *4* **Canavan (IRE)**[14] 2415 6-10-9 ....(p) ThomasDreaper(7) 106+
(Ferdy Murphy) *hld up: hdwy to chse ldrs 15th: wnt 2nd 17th: styd on same pce fr 2 out* **7/1**[3]
/23- **3** *16* **High Cotton (IRE)**[380] 2374 10-11-2 102.............................. JimCrowley 89
(K G Reveley) *chsd ldrs: outpcd and lost pl 15th: styd on fr 3 out: tk remote 3rd last* **3/1**[1]
0U-6 **4** *2 1/2* **Barrons Pike**[190] 594 6-10-11 .... MichaelMcAlister(5) 87
(B Storey) *chsd ldrs: lost pl appr 2 out* **50/1**
4P/4 **5** *dist* **Fisherman Jack**[25] 2165 10-11-2 70................................ JodieMogford —
(G J Smith) *w ldrs: led 15th: hmpd by loose horse and hdd next: lost pl 4 out: sn bhd: t.o: btn 39 l* **25/1**
0 **P** **Dannymolone (IRE)**[14] 2415 6-11-2 .... FinbarKeniry —
(M D Hammond) *in rr: bhd fr 12th: t.o whn p.u bef 3 out* **33/1**
25-0 **U** **Em's Royalty**[25] 2169 8-11-2 105.. AlanDempsey —
(A Parker) *in tch: pushed along whn blnd and uns rdr 4th* **7/2**[2]
-040 **P** **I'm Your Man**[14] 2415 6-11-2 .... BrianHarding —
(Mrs Dianne Sayer) *in rr: reminders 6th: t.o 11th: p.u after 13th* **66/1**
343P **P** **Cirrus (FR)**[14] 2413 6-11-2 95... TonyDobbin —
(K G Reveley) *hld up: hdwy to chse ldrs 5th: lost pl 13th: bhd whn p.u bef 16th* **7/2**[2]
2P-2 **P** **Chris And Ryan (IRE)**[41] 1886 7-10-11 67.......................... DesFlavin(5) —
(Mrs L B Normile) *led: hit 5th: hdd 7th: wknd 11th: bhd whn p.u bef 14th* **14/1**
P **Junior Des Ormeaux (FR)**[255] 8-11-2 .... WilsonRenwick —
(S H Shirley-Beavan) *chsd ldrs: led 7th to 15th: wknd 17th: t.o whn p.u bef 3 out* **20/1**

7m 24.8s (18.00) **Going Correction** +0.75s/f (Soft) **11** Ran SP% **116.1**
Speed ratings: **103,101,97,96,— —,—,—,—,— —** CSF £51.05 TOTE £4.90: £2.40, £1.80, £1.80; EX 48.70.
Owner Andrea & Graham Wylie **Bred** Colm Moran **Trained** Billy Row, Co Durham

FOCUS
A weak novices' chase rated through the runner-up but the winner has potential.

NOTEBOOK
Weapons Inspector(IRE), snapped up after winning an Irish point in February, was very weak in the betting and was offered at 10 in running on the exchanges. He travelled smoothly and jumped well apart from going right two out. He had only to be kept up to his work and, reported to suffer from sore feet, this type of ground suits him ideally. *(op 9-2 tchd 15-2)*
Canavan(IRE), having just his second outing over fences and with the cheekpieces back on, went in pursuit of the winner five out but was never going to finish anything but second best. He finished clear of the others and deserves some credit. *(op 9-1)*
High Cotton(IRE), a long-standing maiden, was having his first outing for over a year. He stays all day but lacks several gears. *(op 11-4 tchd 5-2)*
Barrons Pike, runner-up in points, was having his first outing since May and ran as if it was needed. *(op 40-1)*
Em's Royalty was already being pushed along when departing from the contest at an early stage. *(op 11-2)*
Cirrus(FR) seemed to lose all interest with a circuit to go and his rider soon called it a day. *(op 11-2)*

2690 CANTORSPREADFAIR.COM "NATIONAL HUNT" NOVICES' HURDLE (10 hdls) 2m 5f 110y
1:50 (1:52) (Class 4) 4-Y-0+ **£3,435** (£1,008; £504; £251)

Form RPR
4-41 **1** **Scotmail (IRE)**[20] 2262 4-11-5 114.. GrahamLee 117+
(J Howard Johnson) *mde all: drvn rt out* **3/1**[2]
21F **2** *2 1/2* **Cloudy Lane**[20] 2262 5-10-12 .... JasonMaguire 106
(D McCain) *trckd ldrs: chsd wnr fr 2 out: no ex run-in* **3/1**[2]
3 *3* **Buachaill Eile (IRE)**[22] 2254 5-11-2 .... AndrewJMcNamara(3) 110
(E McNamara, Ire) *hld up in rr: nt fluent: hdwy and in tch 5th: styd on fr 2 out: nvr a real threat* **5/2**[1]
4-26 **4** *5* **Extra Smooth**[19] 2295 4-10-12 .... JohnMcNamara 99+
(C C Bealby) *w ldrs: fdd fr 2 out* **6/1**[3]
00-5 **5** *2 1/2* **Scotmail Too (IRE)**[20] 2262 4-10-7 .... BrianHughes(5) 97+
(J Howard Johnson) *prom: lost pl 7th: poor 5th whn hit 2 out: kpt on run-in* **33/1**
40 **6** *dist* **Bohemian Brook (IRE)**[12] 2448 4-10-12 .... AlanDempsey —
(J Howard Johnson) *prom to 6th: sn outpcd: t.o 2 out: btn 48 l* **33/1**
0-50 **7** *1 1/4* **Flemingstone (IRE)**[9] 2515 5-9-12 .... MrSFMagee(7) —
(J R Norton) *in tch to 5th: sn lost pl: t.o 2 out* **200/1**
00- **8** *5* **Square Dealer**[271] 4276 4-10-9 .... PaddyAspell(3) —
(J R Norton) *prom: lost pl after 4th: t.o 2 out* **200/1**
6 **9** *2* **Dolans Bay (IRE)**[12] 2447 4-10-12 .... FinbarKeniry —
(G M Moore) *lost tch 6th: t.o 2 out* **80/1**
00/0 **10** *3 1/2* **Kicking Bear (IRE)**[37] 1937 7-10-5 69........................... GarethThomas(7) —
(J K Hunter) *lost tch 6th: t.o 2 out* **200/1**
4P-P **P** **Howsham Lad**[19] 2295 6-10-12 .... TomSiddall —
(G P Kelly) *lost tch 6th: t.o whn p.u bef 2 out* **100/1**
P **Bowes Cross** 5-10-5 .... ThomasDreaper(7) —
(Ferdy Murphy) *in rr:bhd fr 6th: t.o whn p.u bef 2 out* **16/1**
P **Colonel James (IRE)** 4-10-12 .... KennyJohnson —
(R Johnson) *hld up in rr: bhd fr 7th: t.o 2 out: p.u bef last* **50/1**
P **P** **Alderclad Lad (IRE)**[218] 147 5-10-7 ....(t) DeclanMcGann(5) —
(J Howard Johnson) *chsd ldrs: wknd qckly after 4th: t.o whn p.u bef 6th* **40/1**

5m 42.2s (26.50) **Going Correction** +1.275s/f (Heav) **14** Ran SP% **112.7**
Speed ratings: **102,101,100,98,97 —,—,—,—,— —,—,—,—** CSF £11.48 TOTE £4.50: £1.50, £1.20, £1.20; EX 10.20.
Owner Gordon Brown/bert Watson **Bred** Paul Smyth **Trained** Billy Row, Co Durham

FOCUS
The slower of the two novice hurdles over this trip, but conditions were deteriorating. The winner is on the up and the fourth backs up the overall value of the form.

NOTEBOOK
Scotmail(IRE) made this a true test, fully appreciating the extended trip, but in the end he had to be kept right up to his work. He will make a chaser in time. *(op 7-2 tchd 11-4 in places)*
Cloudy Lane, meeting the winner on better terms, tried his hardest but could never really get in a telling blow. *(op 9-4 tchd 4-1)*
Buachaill Eile(IRE), who took a maiden hurdle at Limerick, was rather let down by his jumping and the impression he gave is that of an out-and-out stayer. *(op 11-4 tchd 9-4)*
Extra Smooth, warm beforehand on a cold day, stuck to the inner and did not see it out as well in the conditions as the first three.

Scotmail Too(IRE), having just his second start over fences, looks as though no trip will be too far for him. *(op 40-1)*

2691 CANTOR SPREADFAIR H'CAP HURDLE (13 hdls) 3m 3f 110y
2:20 (2:20) (Class 4) (0-110,105) 4-Y-0+ **£3,714** (£1,090; £545; £272)

Form RPR
0431 **1** **General Duroc (IRE)**[12] 2453 9-11-9 102..........................(p) TonyDobbin 115
(B Storey) *chsd ldrs: wnt 2nd appr 2 out: led last: styd on* **8/1**
/5-2 **2** *7* **San Peire (FR)**[28] 2110 8-11-2 95.................................. GrahamLee 102+
(J Howard Johnson) *wnt prom 8th: led after 10th: hdd last: fin v tired* **9/2**[2]
-001 **3** *6* **Jethro Tull (IRE)**[14] 2417 6-10-13 97...................... WilliamKennedy(5) 98+
(G A Harker) *hld up: wnt prom 8th: one pce fr 2 out* **2/1**[1]
4 *1* **Gold Flo (IRE)**[23] 2221 8-10-4 86.......................... AndrewJMcNamara(3) 85
(E McNamara, Ire) *in tch: outpcd after 3 out: styd on one pce fr next* **9/1**
0541 **5** *3* **Villago (GER)**[14] 2416 5-11-0 93.................................. BrianHarding 89
(E W Tuer) *sn trcking ldrs: one pce appr 2 out* **6/1**[3]
23-0 **6** *10* **Sara Monica (IRE)**[20] 2264 8-11-2 105.............................. JohnEnnis(10) 93+
(L Lungo) *chsd ldrs: drvn along 10th: wknd appr 2 out* **12/1**
P4-3 **7** *4* **Forever Eyesofblue**[14] 2417 8-11-7 100........................... AlanDempsey 82
(A Parker) *j.lft: led tl after 10th: sn lost pl* **15/2**
2350 **8** *14* **Toni Alcala**[6] 2461 6-11-3 99....................................(p) KeithMercer(3) 67
(R F Fisher) *hld up in rr: bhd fr 10th* **25/1**
P4UF **9** *nk* **Kidithou (FR)**[13] 2445 7-11-7 105........................... MichaelMcAlister(5) 73
(W T Reed) *w ldrs: lost pl 9th: sn bhd* **66/1**
4456 **P** **Brave Effect (IRE)**[60] 1666 9-11-1 94..................................(t) FinbarKeniry —
(Mrs Dianne Sayer) *in rr: wknd rapidly after 9th: bhd whn p.u after next* **100/1**

7m 25.1s (21.20) **Going Correction** +1.275s/f (Heav) **10 Ran SP% 112.7**
Speed ratings: **103,101,99,99,98 95,94,90,90,—** CSF £42.65 CT £99.04 TOTE £13.80: £3.40, £2.90, £1.60; EX 32.40.
Owner F S Storey **Bred** Frank Burke **Trained** Kirklinton, Cumbria

FOCUS
A severe test of stamina and the winner was once rated a stone and a half higher.

NOTEBOOK
General Duroc(IRE), 6lb higher, was still well in on his old form and his bottomless stamina in the end carried the day. *(op 10-1)*
San Peire(FR) went on but in the end struggled to make the finishing line. He may need time to recover from this. *(op 7-2)*
Jethro Tull(IRE), 5lb higher, found this much tougher. *(op 5-2 tchd 15-8)*
Gold Flo(IRE), lightly-raced of late, stayed on when it was all over and stamina is clearly her strong suit. *(op 12-1)*
Villago(GER), 7lb higher, did not improve for the step up in trip.

2692 CANTORSPREADFAIR.COM H'CAP CHASE (16 fncs) 2m 5f
2:50 (2:51) (Class 4) (0-105,105) 4-Y-0+ **£4,837** (£1,420; £710; £354)

Form RPR
3 **1** **Captain Mac (IRE)**[23] 2223 6-10-13 95.............(b) AndrewJMcNamara(3) 114+
(E McNamara, Ire) *in tch: wnt prom 6th: led 3 out: styd on strly: readily* **7/1**
3F1U **2** *10* **Ornella Speed (FR)**[11] 2476 5-10-4 90...................(t) PatrickMcDonald(7) 94
(J R Weymes) *hld up in rr: gd hdwy 12th: chsng ldrs 3 out: styd on same pce between last 2* **12/1**
011U **3** *2* **Devondale (IRE)**[10] 2495 9-10-12 94.................................. KeithMercer(3) 96
(Ferdy Murphy) *chsd ldrs: rdn 11th: one pce appr 2 out* **6/4**[1]
01-U **4** *29* **Jour De Mee (FR)**[13] 2431 8-10-8 92............................ PaddyMerrigan(5) 69+
(Mrs H Dalton) *in tch: effrt 12th: lost pl appr 3 out* **13/2**[3]
3 **5** *17* **Arctic Cherry (IRE)**[19] 2284 7-10-2 81.................................. GrahamLee 53+
(R Ford) *led to 3 out: wknd and modest 5th whn blnd 2 out* **7/2**[2]
340P **6** *5* **Benefit**[14] 2413 11-10-0 79... TomSiddall 30
(Miss L C Siddall) *blnd 1st: chsd ldrs: drvn along 8th: lost pl next* **16/1**
30SP **F** **Nomadic Blaze**[14] 2415 8-10-7 89................................ LarryMcGrath(3) —
(P G Atkinson) *prom: outpcd whn fell 9th* **16/1**
3-P6 **P** **Tyndarius (IRE)**[9] 2518 14-11-9 105.............................. PaddyAspell(3) —
(A Crook) *in rr: bhd fr 7th: t.o 8th: p.u bef 3 out* **25/1**
P-3P **P** **Classic Lash (IRE)**[41] 1887 9-10-11 90................................ FinbarKeniry —
(P Needham) *chassed ldrs: lost pl 12th: t.o whn p.u bef 3 out* **50/1**
F/01 **P** **Loy's Lad (IRE)**[67] 1592 9-11-10 103.................................. SamStronge —
(Miss V Scott) *trckd ldrs: jnd ldrs 12th: wknd qckly 3 out: bhd whn p.u bef 2 out* **22/1**

5m 44.1s (20.70) **Going Correction** +1.075s/f (Soft) **10 Ran SP% 117.7**
Speed ratings: **103,99,98,87,80 79,—,—,—,—** CSF £82.06 CT £192.40 TOTE £6.60: £1.50, £2.60, £1.30; EX 96.40.
Owner Red Star Syndicate **Bred** P Budds **Trained** Rathkeale, Co. Limerick

FOCUS
The winner, a maiden after 18 previous starts, made this look simple and was value for double the official margin.

NOTEBOOK
Captain Mac(IRE)travelled strongly and was value for at least double the official margin. The *backwash of low-rated Irish-trained jumpers chancing their arm looks like becoming a flood.*
Official explanation: trainer was unable to explain the improved form shown (op 15-2)
Ornella Speed(FR), a stone higher than Hexham, was happy to sit off the pace. She moved up to chase the winner three out but it was soon clear she was fighting a losing battle. *(op 11-1 tchd 14-1)*
Devondale(IRE) was making hard work of this early on the final circuit and was not at his best. *(op 2-1)*
Jour De Mee(FR), 8lb higher than his last success, seems likely to struggle. *(op 6-1 tchd 7-1)*
Arctic Cherry(IRE), an Irish point winner, took them along at a strong gallop but he was out on his feet when blundering two out.

2693 CANTOR SPREADFAIR NOVICES' H'CAP HURDLE (8 hdls) 2m 1f
3:20 (3:20) (Class 4) (0-100,100) 3-Y-0+ **£3,461** (£1,016; £508; £253)

Form RPR
5P4 **1** **Eborarry (IRE)**[30] 2076 3-10-11 99.................................. RussGarritty 93
(T D Easterby) *hld up: wnt prom 5th: led last: rdn out* **12/1**
3334 **2** *6* **Templet (USA)**[29] 1605 5-11-2 90.............................(b) JimmyMcCarthy 93+
(W G Harrison) *racd v wd: led: hdd last: no ex* **15/2**
3-03 **3** *2 ½* **Mr Tim (IRE)**[12] 2448 7-11-11 99.................................. TonyDobbin 99
(L Lungo) *trckd ldrs: chal 5th: rdn after next: kpt on same pce* **13/8**[1]
1 **4** *7* **Tushna (IRE)**[52] 1747 8-11-5 96.......................... AndrewJMcNamara(3) 91+
(E McNamara, Ire) *nt fluent: hdwy to chse ldrs 6th: disputing 4th whn blnd next: sn btn* **4/1**[2]
6-30 **5** *9* **Silver Seeker (USA)**[11] 2475 5-10-5 82.............................. KeithMercer(3) 66
(A R Dicken) *hld up: sme hdwy 5th: lost pl after next* **7/1**[3]
6420 **6** *2* **Bargain Hunt (IRE)**[45] 1836 4-10-12 86.................................. GrahamLee 68
(W Storey) *hld up in rr: hdwa 5th: lost pl after next* **16/1**
-020 **7** *15* **Timbuktu**[14] 2416 4-11-2 90.. BrianHarding 57
(B Storey) *w ldr: lost pl after 5th* **25/1**
4106 **8** *2 ½* **Cheery Martyr**[37] 1937 7-11-1 89.. FinbarKeniry 53
(P Needham) *prom: lost pl after 5th: sn bhd* **33/1**
030- **9** *11* **Savannah River (IRE)**[240] 4783 4-10-3 82..................... MichaelMcAlister(5) 35
(Miss Kate Milligan) *chsd ldrs: drvn along 3rd: lost pl after next* **33/1**
00/P **10** *8* **First Grey**[25] 2171 6-9-13 80.. PhilKinsella(7) 25
(E W Tuer) *in tch: lost pl after 5th: sn bhd* **50/1**
33B0 **U** **Hugs Destiny (IRE)**[11] 2478 4-10-9 90......................... BenOrde-Powlett(7) 85+
(M A Barnes) *chsd ldrs: rdn 6th: disputing 4th whn uns rdr sn after 2 out* **14/1**

4m 26.7s (20.20) **Going Correction** +1.275s/f (Heav)
WFA 3 from 4yo 13lb 4 from 5yo+ 10lb **11 Ran SP% 114.3**
Speed ratings: **103,100,99,95,91 90,83,82,77,73** — CSF £92.56 CT £224.34 TOTE £15.20: £3.60, £1.80, £1.40; EX 97.20 Place 6 £19.03, Place 5 £4.75.
Owner T J Benson **Bred** Calley House Syndicate **Trained** Great Habton, N Yorks

FOCUS
Largely out-of-sorts types in the line-up, but the second and third set the standard.

NOTEBOOK
Eborarry(IRE), having just his fourth start and his first in handicap company, proved ideally suited by this stiff test. *(op 9-1 tchd 14-1)*
Templet(USA), who took the by-pass route, tried hard to make all but had to accept defeat jumping the final flight. *(op 11-1)*
Mr Tim(IRE), making his handicap debut, travelled strongly but was in trouble in a matter of strides *and the response was not 100%. He still looks to have some wort of wind problem.* *(op 11-8 tchd 5-4 and 7-4 in places)*
Tushna(IRE), 1llb higher and racing on totally different ground, was let down by his jumping. *(op 9-2)*
Silver Seeker(USA) a sprinter on the level, did too much and never looked like getting home. *(op 15-2 tchd 8-1)*
Hugs Destiny(IRE) was in the process of running a better race when his rider slipped down his shoulder two out. It will not be a race in his video diary.
T/Plt: £14.80 to a £1 stake. Pool: £42,193.10. 2,071.05 winning tickets. T/Qpdt: £2.20 to a £1 stake. Pool: £4,098.40. 1,375.80 winning tickets. WG

2262 HEXHAM (L-H)
Wednesday, December 7
2694 Meeting Abandoned - Waterlogged

2580 LEICESTER (R-H)
Wednesday, December 7

OFFICIAL GOING: Chase course - good (good to soft in places); hurdle course - heavy
Wind: Light, half-behind Weather: Overcast

2701 SPRUCE BEGINNERS' CHASE (15 fncs) 2m 4f 110y
1:00 (1:00) (Class 4) 5-Y-0+ **£4,934** (£1,448; £724; £361)

Form RPR
62-4 **1** **Alderburn**[39] 1917 6-11-0 .... RichardJohnson 123+
(H D Daly) *hld up in tch: racd keenly: hit 10th: ev ch whn mstke 3 out: styd on u.p to ld towards fin* **8/11**[1]
03-P **2** *nk* **Alfie's Sun**[13] 2464 6-11-0 .... JimmyMcCarthy 120
(D E Cantillon) *trckd ldrs: led 6th: rdn appr last: hdd towards fin* **14/1**
42-P **3** *11* **Bengo (IRE)**[36] 1976 5-11-0 .... NoelFehily 109
(B De Haan) *hld up: hdwy 11th: ev ch 3 out: sn rdn: wknd appr last* **8/1**[3]
012- **4** *11* **Dolmur (IRE)**[242] 4781 5-11-0 .... KeithMercer 98
(Ferdy Murphy) *prom: rdn after 11th: wknd appr 3 out* **9/1**
0 **5** *½* **Launde (IRE)**[32] 2044 6-10-7 .... TomMessenger(7) 99+
(B N Pollock) *led to 6th: ev ch 3 out: wkng whn hmpd next* **20/1**
42-F **6** *dist* **Dramatic Quest**[197] 486 8-11-0 102..................................(p) DaveCrosse —
(A G Juckes) *prom: rdn 8th: wkng whn blnd 4 out* **25/1**
0P/P **P** **Jeanie's Last**[25] 2179 6-10-7 .... JodieMogford —
(G J Smith) *hld up: a bhd: t.o whn p.u bef 4 out* **100/1**
PP/P **P** **Thorpeness (IRE)**[9] 2555 6-11-0 92.. AndrewTinkler —
(P D Cundell) *hld up: a bhd: t.o whn p.u bef 4 out* **66/1**
05U0 **P** **Tails I Win**[129] 1109 6-10-11 61.. AnthonyCoyle(3) —
(Miss C J E Caroe) *chsd ldrs to 6th: t.o whn p.u bef 4 out* **66/1**
12-6 **F** **Monte Vista (IRE)**[39] 1917 8-11-0 .... APMcCoy 123+
(Jonjo O'Neill) *hld up: hdwy appr 6th: jnd ldrs 3 out: disputing ld but gng best whn fell next* **9/2**[2]

5m 12.3s (-11.30) **Going Correction** -0.25s/f (Good) **10 Ran SP% 116.4**
Speed ratings: **111,110,106,102,102 —,—,—,—,—** CSF £11.62 TOTE £1.90: £1.10, £3.80, £2.20; EX 15.50.
Owner Mrs D P G Flory **Bred** Mrs D P G Flory **Trained** Stanton Lacy, Shropshire

FOCUS
A decent winning time for a race of its type with two potentially useful novices pulling clear.

NOTEBOOK
Alderburn, fourth in what was a very decent contest on his chasing debut behind Copsale Lad at Lingfield, was rightly made favourite to win what was a lesser race, but he made particularly hard work of it and only just got the better of Alfie's Sun. He may have been fighting it out for second had Monte Vista stayed on his feet, but his jumping in the main was good and three miles will suit in time. He will probably need to improve on this to defy a penalty, but would make some appeal if switched to handicaps in the new year. *(op 10-11)*
Alfie's Sun ◆ did not quite go on as expected over hurdles, and hardly made the ideal start to his chasing career when pulled up at Uttoxeter, but this big, attractive son of Alflora was much more on his game under a more positive ride here and jumped fluently throughout. He battled back once headed, giving his all, but the winner was always just doing enough. There was a fair gap back to third and if going the right way from this it will be disappointing if he is not winning next time, presuming he is kept to a similar level.
Bengo(IRE), who ran well for a long way before getting tired on his fencing debut, is not the biggest and, although not making any mistakes, he did all his best work in between fences. He made stylish headway to dispute it turning in, but he soon became outpaced and faded out of it in the final quarter mile. Handicaps are likely to represent his best chance of winning in future, but being only five one cannot rule out improvement. *(op 7-1)*
Dolmur(IRE), a modest sort of over hurdles, shaped quite nicely on this chasing debut and ran as *though very much in need of the outing. He is bound to find easier opportunities back up north.* *(op 10-1 tchd 11-1)*
Launde(IRE), outclassed in a decent race on his rules debut at Sandown, appreciated the extra distance here and was able to take them along early. Despite having been headed, he remained on the scene and was bang there taking three out, but class ultimately told and he was left trailing. He *is another who is sure to find easier opportunities in future and three miles may help in time.* *(tchd 22-1)*

Monte Vista(IRE), two places behind Alderburn on his chase debut at Lingfield, had clearly improved for the run and was travelling mightily strongly here when falling at the second-last. One could not guarantee he would have won, but he looked the most likely victor at the time and he *should not be long in gaining compensation as long as this has not affected his confidence. (op 7-2)*

2702 CHESTNUT (S) HURDLE (9 hdls) 2m
1:30 (1:30) (Class 5) 4-7-Y-0 **£2,823** (£822; £411)

Form RPR
-530 **1** **Blackthorn**[7] 2285 6-10-5 86 .... RichardSpate(7) 87+
(M Appleby) *chsd ldrs: led 3rd: clr appr 3 out: hit last: eased flat* **9/4**[2]
-455 **2** *8* **Makandy**[10] 2523 6-10-5 .... MrRArmson(7) 77
(R J Armson) *led to 2nd: hit 4th: chsd wnr 3 out: no imp* **2/1**[1]
P04P **3** *dist* **Blaise Wood (USA)**[8] 2561 4-10-10 82 ....(bt) ThomasBurrows(7) —
(A L Forbes) *led 2nd to next: jnd wnr 5th: wknd bef next* **4/1**[3]
PFP- **4** *27* **Gilded Ally**[252] 4654 5-10-9 .... OwynNelmes(3) —
(N B King) *hld up: hdwy 3rd: wknd appr 3 out* **7/1**
P **P** **Grumpyintmorning**[10] 2523 6-10-5 .... MrMatthewSmith(7) —
(M J Gingell) *bhd fr 4th: t.o whn p.u bef 3 out* **14/1**
P **Bjorling**[288] 4-10-6 ow1 .... MrNPearce(7) —
(M J Gingell) *prom tl rdn and nt run on appr 5th: sn t.o: p.u bef next* **14/1**

4m 9.30s (1.70) **Going Correction** +0.125s/f (Yiel) **6** Ran SP% **109.9**
Speed ratings: **100,96,—,—,—** — CSF £7.08 TOTE £2.60: £1.50, £1.50; EX 5.90.There was no bid for the winner.
Owner C A Cavanagh **Bred** Juddmonte Farms **Trained** Shrewley, Warwicks

FOCUS
Undoubtedly one of the worst races of the year, and possibly of all time.

NOTEBOOK
Blackthorn ran out a ready-enough winner of what was probably one of the worst races of all time. This drop back down in grade clearly helped him, but he beat absolutely nothing and achieved very little. *(op 5-2 tchd 2-1)*
Makandy has been running okay in similar races, but he was readily brushed aside by the winner. He plugged on well enough in second, but as with the winner, little was achieved. *(tchd 9-4)*
Blaise Wood(USA) was hammered back in third and probably found the ground too testing. *(op 9-2)*
Gilded Ally continues to show nothing and trailed in a distance fourth. *(tchd 6-1)*
Bjorling chucked in the towel once coming under pressure. *(op 10-1 tchd 16-1 in a place)*

2703 HOLLY H'CAP CHASE (18 fncs) 2m 7f 110y
2:00 (2:00) (Class 3) (0-125,123) 5-Y-0+ **£7,150** (£2,099; £1,049; £524)

Form RPR
-4P1 **1** **Millenaire (FR)**[23] 2241 6-11-8 **119** .... APMcCoy 136+
(Jonjo O'Neill) *hld up: hmpd 1st: pckd next: hdwy 9th: mstke next: chal 2 out: sn rdn: styd on u.p to ld nr fin* **7/2**[2]
-P36 **2** *hd* **You're Special (USA)**[13] 2451 8-11-1 **119** ....(t) ThomasDreaper(7) 134
(Ferdy Murphy) *hld up in tch: led after 4 out: rdn flat: hdd nr fin* **13/2**
P5-P **3** *15* **Yann's (FR)**[195] 516 9-11-4 **115** .... RichardJohnson 116+
(R T Phillips) *hld up: hdwy 7th: lost pl after next: hdwy 12th: ev ch 3 out: rdn after next: wknd last* **9/1**
33P- **4** *2 ½* **Lord Seamus**[300] 3773 10-10-13 **110** .... JohnMcNamara 108
(K C Bailey) *led to 9th: led next: hdd after 4 out: wknd appr 2 out* **28/1**
1501 **5** *20* **Strong Magic (IRE)**[10] 2524 13-9-9 **96** 7ex........ MarkNicolls(5) 75
(J R Cornwall) *prom to 11th* **40/1**
-2F0 **6** *1* **Harrycone Lewis**[53] 1735 7-11-12 **123** ....(b) WarrenMarston 100
(Mrs P Sly) *hld up: reminders 5th: hdwy 10th: wknd after 4 out* **16/1**
0-FU **7** *½* **Farlington**[7] 2577 8-11-11 **122** .... ChristianWilliams 98
(P Bowen) *chsd ldr: led 9th to next: wknd appr 3 out* **25/1**
3P-5 **8** *21* **King Georges (FR)**[29] 2100 7-10-11 **108** ....(p) JodieMogford 63
(J C Tuck) *hld up: mstke 1st: hit 8th: bhd whn blnd 4 out* **50/1**
1F-4 **F** **Kosmos Bleu (FR)**[36] 1978 7-10-13 **110** .... AndrewThornton —
(R H Alner) *chsd ldrs: disputing cl 4th whn fell 3 out* **6/1**[3]
/403 **P** **One Day (NZ)**[13] 2465 7-9-10 **98** oh1 ow1........(b[1]) PaddyMerrigan(5) —
(R C Guest) *hld up: a in rr: bhd fr 9th: t.o whn p.u bef 3 out* **10/1**
-U12 **U** **Bay Island (IRE)**[34] 2009 9-10-0 **97** oh1........(t) TimmyMurphy —
(M Pitman) *hld up: hdwy 12th: mstke 5 out: cl 6th whn blnd and uns rdr next* **5/2**[1]

5m 55.9s (-9.50) **Going Correction** -0.25s/f (Good) **11** Ran SP% **115.1**
Speed ratings: **105,104,99,99,92 92,91,84,—,—** — CSF £25.30 CT £188.07 TOTE £3.70: £1.60, £2.90, £2.20; EX 31.60 Trifecta £180.50 Pool: £406.82 - 1.60 winning tickets..
Owner The Risky Partnership **Bred** Pierre J Delage **Trained** Cheltenham, Gloucs

FOCUS
A competitive handicap where the pace was sound. The race should produce winners.

NOTEBOOK
Millenaire(FR) made to work really hard for victory, and only really got on top close to the line despite some minor jumping blips on the way around. He has scope for further improvement, and has the option to go back into novice company. Three miles plus should prove no problem to him in the future.
You're Special(USA), who was full of running coming up the home straight, ran right up to his best by harassing Millenaire all the way to the line. The soft ground probably did not suit him last time, and this was much more like his true form. *(op 6-1)*
Yann's(FR) did really well to get as close as he did because he was under strong pressure leaving *the back straight. He is fairly handicapped on his best form and handles more ease in the ground. (op 8-1)*
Lord Seamus made a sound return to the track after a long absence, and shaped well after leading for much of the race. He is still above his highest- winning handicap mark, but gave enough encouragement to suggest he can win off his current rating, given a suitable opportunity. *(tchd 33-1)*
Harrycone Lewis did not look very cooperative passing the stands' for the first time and, despite getting himself back into contention at one stage, looked unenthusiastic. *(tchd 18-1)*
Farlington was always close to the pace early in the race, but does not convince as the most natural jumper of fences.
Bay Island(IRE) was still travelling well within himself when overpitching at the last in the back straight, and coming down. *(op 14-1)*
One Day(NZ) *Official explanation: trainer said gelding had a breathing problem (op 14-1)*
Kosmos Bleu(FR) was still going well within himself when falling at the third-last. This was a much better effort than last time until coming down, and still has some scope for improvement. *(op 14-1)*

2704 "HIMSELF IS SIXTY" MARES' ONLY NOVICES' HURDLE (8 hdls 1 omitted) 2m
2:30 (2:31) (Class 3) 4-Y-0+ **£4,905** (£1,440; £720; £359)

Form RPR
3- **1** **Glory Be**[380] 2399 5-10-10 .... SamThomas 106+
(Miss Venetia Williams) *mde all: clr last: easily* **11/4**[2]
6 **2** *10* **Pont Neuf (IRE)**[18] 2335 5-10-7 ....(t) PaddyAspell(3) 88+
(A Crook) *hld up: hdwy and c wd appr 2 out: styd on to go 2nd flat: no ch w wnr* **20/1**
3-51 **3** *4* **Air Of Affection**[15] 2412 4-11-3 103........ GrahamLee 89
(J R Turner) *chsd wnr: rdn and hit 2 out: no ex last* **9/4**[1]
1000 **4** *½* **Ericas Charm**[25] 2186 5-10-10 .... ChristianWilliams 82
(P Bowen) *hld up in tch: outpcd appr 2 out: styd on towards fin* **9/1**
1- **5** *2* **Sunshine Rays**[560] 512 7-10-10 .... AndrewTinkler 81+
(C Tinkler) *hld up: hdwy after 5th: wknd last f* **5/1**[3]
0-50 **6** *4* **Alderbrook Girl (IRE)**[12] 2486 5-10-10 .... TomDoyle 76
(R Curtis) *prom: pckd 2nd: wknd after 5th* **50/1**
7 *nk* **Louve Heureuse (IRE)**[9] 4-10-10 .... LeightonAspell 76+
(J R Boyle) *hld up: hmpd 2nd: hdwy and hit 2 out: wknd bef last* **12/1**
0 **8** *8* **Knotty Ash Girl (IRE)**[15] 2423 6-10-10 .... WarrenMarston 71+
(D J Wintle) *hld up: hmpd 2nd: wknd after 5th* **33/1**
6 **9** *13* **Stormy Madam (IRE)**[226] 27 5-10-3 .... MrRWakeham(7) 54
(J R Turner) *hld up: hdwy 4th: wknd next* **20/1**
60-0 **10** *5* **Luscious (IRE)**[10] 2515 5-10-10 .... JohnMcNamara 49
(K C Bailey) *prom: mstke 4th: wknd after next* **66/1**
F50P **11** *6* **Tanmeya**[2] 2674 4-10-5 ....(e) PaddyMerrigan(5) 43
(R C Guest) *hld up: plld hrd: effrt appr 2 out: sn wknd* **33/1**
B **Wiz The Dove** 4-10-10 .... AntonyEvans —
(C J Price) *hld up: b.d 2nd* **33/1**
000 **F** **Orions Eclipse**[11] 2501 4-10-3 .... MrMatthewSmith(7) —
(M J Gingell) *prom whn fell 2nd* **100/1**

4m 7.40s (-0.20) **Going Correction** +0.125s/f (Yiel) **13** Ran SP% **114.6**
Speed ratings: **105,100,98,97,96 94,94,90,84,81 78,—,—** CSF £56.90 TOTE £3.00: £2.00, £4.30, £1.10; EX 45.50.
Owner P S & Mrs B M Willcocks **Bred** Exors Of The Late R M West **Trained** Kings Caple, H'fords

FOCUS
A weak mares'-only race. The winner was value for twice the winning distance, while those in behind are not easy to assess.

NOTEBOOK
Glory Be, returning from 308-day absence, was always well positioned during the race, and bounded clear of her rivals up the straight. She won very easily, but the race was particularly weak and she will face much stiffer assignments now under a penalty. *(op 10-3)*
Pont Neuf(IRE) faced a much easier task than she had done on her debut, and shaped with some promise depite being under pressure a long way from home. However, she was easily beaten and may be better off in handicap company in due course. *(op 33-1)*
Air Of Affection, who was carrying a 7lb penalty for her last win, was probably a bit too keen in the early stages for her to get home as well as some of the others. Her victory was on a much quicker surface, and she can be given another chance on better ground. *(op 11-4 after early 3-1 in a place)*
Ericas Charm did not appear to get home in the ground, and looked quite laboured up the straight. *(op 10-1 tchd 8-1)*
Sunshine Rays, who was noticeably weak in the market prior to the race, travelled nicely into contention up the home straight, but floundered when coming under pressure. Her bumper win came on vastly different ground, so she can be given another chance on better going. *(op 5-2)*
Alderbrook Girl(IRE) travelled nicely until coming under pressure, and only kept on at one pace.
Louve Heureuse(IRE) made a couple of jumping errors on her hurdling debut and may be capable of better.

2705 OAK NOVICES' H'CAP CHASE (12 fncs) 2m
3:00 (3:00) (Class 4) (0-105,99) 4-Y-0+ **£4,845** (£1,504; £809)

Form RPR
5335 **1** **Magico (NZ)**[23] 2248 7-11-1 **93** ....(b[1]) PaulO'Neill(5) 108+
(R C Guest) *chsd ldrs: led appr 3 out: clr next: eased flat* **11/2**
5F41 **2** *5* **Rookery Lad**[14] 2429 7-11-12 **99** .... DaveCrosse 104
(C N Kellett) *prom: rdn 8th: hung rt and chsd wnr 2 out: styd on same pce* **9/2**[3]
56P5 **3** *nk* **Kercabellec (FR)**[22] 2257 7-10-4 **82** .... AdamPogson(5) 87
(J R Cornwall) *disp ld tl led 4th: rdn and hdd appr 3 out: styd on same pce fr next* **12/1**
2P44 **U** **Super Dolphin**[12] 2479 6-10-4 **82** .... StephenCraine(5) —
(R Ford) *hld up: blnd and uns rdr 4th* **9/2**[3]
264/ **U** **Spinaround**[605] 4756 7-10-7 **80** .... TomDoyle —
(P R Webber) *hld up inn tch: cl 5th whn blnd and uns rdr 4 out* **5/2**[1]
2-F2 **P** **Call Me Jack (IRE)**[20] 2284 9-9-13 **77** ....(t) LeeStephens(5) —
(M J M Evans) *disp ld to 4th: chsd ldr to appr 3 out: wkng whn blnd next: sn p.u* **4/1**[2]

4m 8.60s (1.00) **Going Correction** -0.25s/f (Good) **6** Ran SP% **108.0**
Speed ratings: **87,84,84,—,—** — CSF £27.41 TOTE £7.50: £2.70, £1.80; EX 29.10.
Owner Paul Beck **Bred** Bardowie Stud Ltd **Trained** Brancepeth, Co Durham

FOCUS
A moderate winning time. The winner appeared to win easily with the application of blinkers. Those in behind were well beaten.

NOTEBOOK
Magico(NZ), wearing first-time blinkers, won his first-ever race very easily and never had to come off the bridle to do so. It appears that the headgear made all the difference to him, and he would be interesting next time if they were guaranteed to work again.
Rookery Lad was under strong pressure a long way from home, but battled on gamely for his jockey's urgings to grab second place. He did, however, never look like winning at any stage of the race. *(tchd 4-1 and 5-1 in places)*
Kercabellec(FR) shared a lot of the early running and, to be fair to him, kept on well when passed up the straight. That said, he was decisively beaten by the time he had passed the line. *(op 9-1)*
Call Me Jack(IRE), who was still moving well at the top of the home straight, readily got left behind *as the pace increased and was well beaten when pulling up. He was too keen in the early stages. (op 7-2)*
Super Dolphin made a really bad error at the fourth and gave his jockey no chance of staying on. *(op 7-2)*
Spinaround, having his first run for 605 days, was still in with a chance when coming down at the last in the back straight. It was too far out to know how he would have fared at the business end of the race. *(op 7-2)*

2706 BIRCH H'CAP HURDLE (12 hdls) 2m 4f 110y
3:30 (3:31) (Class 3) (0-120,120) 4-Y-0+ **£6,701** (£1,996; £1,010; £518; £270)

Form RPR
0-11 **1** **Magot De Grugy (FR)**[19] 2310 5-10-13 **107** .... AndrewThornton 116+
(R H Alner) *led and sn clr: stdd 2nd: hdd 4th: led next: clr 2 out: rdn out* **6/4**[1]
56-1 **2** *2 ½* **Petwick (IRE)**[15] 2419 6-11-0 **108** .... RobertThornton 110+
(A King) *chsd ldrs: racd wd and alone 2nd to 4th: rdn whn mstke 2 out: styd on* **9/4**[2]
P6-4 **3** *17* **Carapuce (FR)**[221] 121 6-11-2 **120** .... JohnEnnis(10) 107+
(L Lungo) *hld up: hdwy appr 3 out: wknd next* **16/1**
-200 **4** *½* **Jockser (IRE)**[24] 2207 4-10-11 **112** .... WayneKavanagh(7) 96
(J W Mullins) *hdwy 2nd: msiatek 7th: sn rdn: wknd bef next* **4/1**[3]
0-P5 **5** *18* **Scarlet Fantasy**[11] 2505 5-10-1 **100** .... TomGreenway(5) 79+
(P A Pritchard) *hdwy 2nd: led 4th to next: wknd 3 out: bhd whn blnd last* **25/1**

111 **P** **Flintoff (USA)**^{191} [596] 4-11-2 **115**.................................. PaulO'Neill$^{(5)}$ —
(R C Guest) *sn chsng ldrs: wknd 3 out: t.o whn p.u after next* **10/1**

5m 41.4s (6.60) **Going Correction** +0.125s/f (Yiel)
WFA 4 from 5yo+ 11lb **6** Ran SP% **109.6**
Speed ratings: **92,91,84,84,77** — CSF £5.19 TOTE £2.70: £1.10, £1.90; EX 5.00 Place 6 £27.36, Place 5 £20.01.
Owner P M De Wilde **Bred** Earl La Grugerie **Trained** Droop, Dorset

FOCUS
A modest winning time for a race of its class. A very muddling affair, as they did not start moving foward for 10 seconds after the tapes went up, and then the pace throughout the race was very uneven.

NOTEBOOK
Magot De Grugy(FR), who was always well placed, got away from his rivals up the home straight and never looked like being caught after that move was made. He remains an interesting prospect but is getting the Handicapper's attention for winning very modest events. *(tchd 13-8)*
Petwick(IRE) was always chasing the pace but never got past the eventual winner at any stage of the race. He was racing off a 12lb higher mark than his success last time, and it was probably enough to stop him. *(op 7-4)*
Carapuce(FR), returning after 221 days off the track, ran a bit better than his final position suggested. He held a chance of sorts until coming under pressure three from home, and should be fully competitive next time.
Jockser(IRE), who was nicely supported in the market prior to the race, was quite disappointing having showed fair form at Cheltenham last time. He is surely suffering with the Handicapper at the moment, and the track and ground conditions were not ideal for him. *(op 13-2)*
Scarlet Fantasy was not too far off the third and fourth-placed horses coming to the last, but made a bad blunder at the final flight and did well to stay on his feet. *(tchd 28-1)*
Flintoff(USA) travelled nicely for much of the race, but stopped as if shot when the pressure was applied. *He was reported to having a breathing problem after the race.Official explanation: jockey said gelding had a breathing problem (op 9-1)*
T/Plt: £36.10 to a £1 stake. Pool: £49,170.20. 993.65 winning tickets. T/Qpdt: £15.30 to a £1 stake. Pool: £4,121.90. 198.40 winning tickets. CR

2707 - 2713a (Foreign Racing) - See Raceform Interactive

^{2341}HUNTINGDON (R-H)

Thursday, December 8

OFFICIAL GOING: Good (good to soft in places on chase course)
Wind: Light, across Weather: Cloudy with sunny spells

2714 SPONSOR AT HUNTINGDON H'CAP HURDLE (10 hdls) 2m 5f 110y

12:30 (12:31) (Class 4) (0-110,110) 4-Y-0+ **£3,919** (£1,150; £575; £287)

Form RPR
B-61 **1** **Welcome To Unos**^{8} [2566] 8-11-2 **107**.................................. PhilKinsella$^{(7)}$ 116+
(K G Reveley) *chsd ldr 3rd: led 7th: drvn out* **9/2**^{3}
662 **2** *8* **Archduke Ferdinand (FR)**^{16} [2421] 7-11-7 **105**............ RobertThornton 106
(A King) *hld up: hdwy 7th: chsd wnr 2 out: styd on same pce last* **4/1**^{2}
143P **3** *2* **Common Girl (IRE)**^{44} [1870] 7-11-9 **107**.......................... JohnMcNamara 106
(O Brennan) *led to 7th: styd on same pce fr 2 out* **33/1**
/2-6 **4** *1* **Shirazi**^{25} [2218] 7-11-2 **105**.. SamCurling$^{(5)}$ 104+
(D R Gandolfo) *hld up: hdwy appr 3 out: wknd last* **25/1**
56-5 **5** *4* **Sherkin Island (IRE)**^{40} [1929] 7-11-6 **104**.............................. APMcCoy 98
(Jonjo O'Neill) *hld up: hdwy and mstke 6th: wknd 2 out* **9/4**^{1}
5F44 **6** *2* **True Mariner (FR)**^{25} [2218] 5-10-13 **97**........................ JimmyMcCarthy 89
(B I Case) *prom: ev ch 3 out: sn rdn: nt fluent and wknd 2 out* **20/1**
0402 **7** *27* **Heisse**^{53} [1750] 5-10-5 **89**..(t) TomScudamore 66+
(Ian Williams) *chsd ldrs tl wknd appr 2 out* **18/1**
0-4F **8** *9* **Courant D'Air (IRE)**^{21} [2296] 4-11-3 **106**..................... RobertStephens$^{(5)}$ 62
(Lucinda Featherstone) *chsd ldrs: lost pl 6th: wknd next* **10/1**
FP-P **9** *6* **Long Shot**^{34} [2027] 8-10-11 **95**.. SeanCurran 45
(Miss L C Siddall) *hld up: a in rr: t.o whn hit 2 out* **80/1**
433- **10** *1 3/4* **Penny Stall**^{33} [4936] 4-10-13 **97**.................................... WarrenMarston 45
(Miss E C Lavelle) *hld up: hdwy 6th: wknd appr 3 out* **10/1**
00P6 **P** **Turkama (FR)**^{22} [2271] 8-11-5 **110**..............................(v^{1}) JustinMorgan$^{(7)}$ —
(L A Dace) *hld up in tch: wknd 7th: t.o whn p.u bef 2 out* **50/1**
0005 **P** **Donie Dooley (IRE)**^{14} [2466] 7-10-9 **93**.......................... JamesDavies —
(P T Dalton) *hld up: rdn and wknd appr 6th: t.o whn p.u bef next* **40/1**
/13- **P** **Beauchamp Gigi (IRE)**^{321} [3460] 7-11-7 **105**.................... GrahamLee —
(J Howard Johnson) *hld up: blnd 1st: hdwy 6th: hit next: sn wknd: bhd whn p.u bef 3 out* **15/2**

5m 27.1s (16.30) **Going Correction** +0.675s/f (Soft)
WFA 4 from 5yo+ 11lb **13** Ran SP% **121.3**
Speed ratings: **97,94,93,93,91 90,81,77,75,74** —,—,— CSF £22.23 CT £543.59 TOTE £5.90: £2.00, £1.70, £6.60; EX 22.20.
Owner J W Andrews **Bred** P D And Mrs Player **Trained** Lingdale, Redcar & Cleveland

FOCUS
They did not seem to go a great pace for much of this contest and the time was ordinary, but the form looks solid enoughh with winner, third and fourth close to their marks.

NOTEBOOK
Welcome To Unos, who escaped a penalty for his recent Catterick success as it came in a conditional jockeys' event, followed up in great style over this extra quarter-mile but he is already due to go up 8lb which will obviously make things a lot tougher and this margin of victory will not get him much sympathy either. *(tchd 4-1)*
Archduke Ferdinand(FR) was keen enough early, though not as bad as he has been on occasions, and was produced at just the right time had he been good enough. The fact that he was not is partly down to the winner, and partly down to the ground looking a little softer than the official description suggests. *(tchd 5-1)*
Common Girl(IRE), running in a handicap for only the second time in her life, was given a positive ride and hung in there for a lot longer than may have been expected. Both her wins to date have come at Fakenham, and she looks better suited by left-handed tracks in general so it was probably no coincidence that she ended up racing against the stands' rail in the closing stages.
Shirazi improved from his recent reappearance from a very long absence, but seemed to get tired on reaching the run-in and this should have put him spot-on.
Sherkin Island(IRE), off a 13lb lower mark than over fences, was very well backed but ran a similar race to last time when returning from a lengthy absence, holding every chance but finding *little off the bridle. It does seem as though a return to the larger obstacles is needed. (op 4-1 tchd 9-2 in place)*
True Mariner(FR) continues to slide down the handicap and was far from disgraced, whilst connections also have the option of putting him back over fences. *(op 18-1)*
Donie Dooley(IRE) *Official explanation: vet said gelding bled from nose (op 11-2)*
Beauchamp Gigi(IRE) *Official explanation: jockey said mare had breathing problem (op 11-2)*

2715 E.B.F./TATTERSALLS (IRELAND) MARES' ONLY NOVICES' CHASE (QUALIFIER) (16 fncs) 2m 4f 110y

1:00 (1:01) (Class 3) 4-Y-0+ **£5,334** (£1,566; £783; £391)

Form RPR
2-44 **1** **Clouding Over**^{13} [2476] 5-11-3 104.................................. GrahamLee 100+
(K G Reveley) *hld up: hdwy to chse ldr 10th: led 2 out: styd on wl* **15/8**^{2}
0-36 **2** *12* **Bonnet's Pieces**^{19} [2344] 6-11-3 .... WarrenMarston 90+
(Mrs P Sly) *hld up in tch: chsd ldr after 5th: led 8th: hdd and pckd 2 out: sn btn* **20/1**
0431 **3** *dist* **Sunny South East (IRE)**^{10} [2553] 5-11-4 .... WilliamKennedy$^{(5)}$ —
(S Gollings) *led to 8th: pckd next: mstke 11th: wknd 13th* **8/1**^{3}
4-FP **4** *dist* **Caballe (USA)**^{9} [2561] 8-11-3 83.................................. TomScudamore —
(M Scudamore) *chsd ldr to 3rd: wknd 11th* **33/1**
FP0/ **U** **Perle De Puce (FR)**^{616} [4629] 6-10-10 .... MrSWaley-Cohen$^{(7)}$ —
(N J Henderson) *chsd ldr 3rd tl pckd and uns rdr 5th* **5/6**^{1}

5m 22.7s (16.60) **Going Correction** +0.925s/f (Soft) **5** Ran SP% **108.2**
Speed ratings: **105,100,—,—,—** CSF £24.32 TOTE £2.90: £1.60, £6.40; EX 28.00.
Owner W D Hockenhull **Bred** Shade Oak Stud **Trained** Lingdale, Redcar & Cleveland

FOCUS
An uncompetitive event, especially after the departure of the odds-on favourite, but the winner did it nicely and with the runner-up sets the standard, while the time was perfectly acceptable.

NOTEBOOK
Clouding Over ◆ faced a straightforward task after the favourite had exited the contest and already looked to be getting the better of the runner-up when jumping the second last much the better of the pair. She still has scope for improvement over fences and should be able to find further success against her own sex. *(op 5-2)*
Bonnet's Pieces, beaten around 70 lengths when 100/1 for her chase debut over course and distance last month, ran much better this time but already looked destined for second when a mistake at the second last removed any lingering doubts. Races like these are often fairly uncompetitive and she showed enough to suggest she can pinch one. *(op 25-1)*
Sunny South East(IRE), dropping in trip, did not jump well enough this time and was eventually beaten out of sight. Also her penalty for her very fortunate win at Folkestone is not doing her any favours. *(op 5-1 tchd 17-2)*
Caballe(USA) does not look a natural chaser at this stage.
Perle De Puce(FR), a very decent hurdler a couple of seasons ago and making her chasing debut on this first start in 20 months, pecked slightly at the fifth but that was enough to send her rider out the side door. *(op 8-11 tchd 10-11 in places)*

2716 BRAMPTON H'CAP HURDLE (8 hdls) 2m 110y

1:30 (1:32) (Class 3) (0-125,124) 4-Y-0+ **£5,530** (£1,217; £1,217; £405)

Form RPR
-142 **1** **Hernando's Boy**^{11} [2519] 4-11-1 **120**................................ PhilKinsella$^{(7)}$ 124+
(K G Reveley) *hld up in tch: led 2 out: nt fluent last: all out* **7/2**^{1}
0-62 **2** *shd* **Silver Prophet (IRE)**^{20} [2324] 6-10-12 **110**........................ SeanCurran 114+
(M R Bosley) *hld up: hdwy after 3rd: led appr 3 out: nt fluent and hdd next: r.o u.p* **15/2**
13P1 **2** *dht* **Irish Wolf (FR)**^{36} [1987] 5-10-11 **114**........................ TomGreenway$^{(5)}$ 117
(P Bowen) *prom: lost pl 3rd: hdwy 5th: rdn and ev ch flat: r.o* **9/2**^{2}
/22- **4** *8* **Sun King**^{50} [444] 8-9-4 **98** oh3................................(t) JamesReveley$^{(10)}$ 93
(K G Reveley) *hld up and bhd: hdwy 2 out: rdn flat: no imp* **25/1**
1P0 **5** *4* **Front Rank (IRE)**^{25} [2218] 5-10-7 **105**........................ JimmyMcCarthy 96
(K C Bailey) *mid-div: dropped rr after 4th: n.d after* **50/1**
14/6 **6** *9* **Salhood**^{19} [2334] 6-11-6 **118**.. TomScudamore 101+
(S Gollings) *chsd ldrs: rdn appr 2 out: wkng whn mstke last* **12/1**
21-6 **7** *1 1/4* **Credit (IRE)**^{11} [2519] 4-11-7 **119**.................................... GrahamLee 100
(J Howard Johnson) *prom: rdn appr 3 out: wkng whn mstke next* **6/1**
2220 **8** *4* **Pirandello (IRE)**^{28} [2150] 7-10-12 **110**........................ JohnMcNamara 91+
(K C Bailey) *led tl after 1st: wknd 3 out* **9/1**
0-02 **9** *hd* **Candarli (IRE)**^{14} [2459] 9-10-9 **112**........................ SamCurling$^{(5)}$ 93+
(D R Gandolfo) *led aftger 1st: hdd appr 3 out: wknd next* **25/1**
-210 **10** *22* **Harrycat (IRE)**^{24} [2247] 4-10-9 **107**................................(p) PhilipHide 61
(V Smith) *mid-div: wknd and lost pl 4th: wknd after next* **20/1**
030- **P** **Atahuelpa**^{243} [4768] 5-11-12 **124**.................................... JosephByrne —
(Jennie Candlish) *hld up: hdwy 4th: wknd after next: bhd whn p.u bef 2 out* **40/1**
-P01 **P** **Barton Park**^{22} [2269] 5-10-2 **100**.................................. RobertThornton —
(D P Keane) *free to post: hld up: plld hrd: hdwy and mstke 4th: wknd and mstke 3 out: p.u bef next* **11/2**^{3}

4m 2.50s (6.80) **Going Correction** +0.675s/f (Soft)
WFA 4 from 5yo+ 10lb **12** Ran SP% **116.4**
Speed ratings: **111,110,110,107,105 101,100,98,98,88** —,—Plc: 1.70, IW 2.10, SP 2.60; Ex: HB/IW 8.20, HB/SP 16.60; CSF: HB/IW 9.08, HB/SP 13.72; Tri: HB/IW/SP 55.54, HB/SP/IW 60.23 TOTE £4.40.
Owner Crack of Dawn Partnership **Bred** T E Pocock **Trained** Lingdale, Redcar & Cleveland

FOCUS
A very tight finish and a fair time for a race of its type. The form looks solid with the first three all close to their pre-race marks.

NOTEBOOK
Hernando's Boy looked likely to win comfortably after taking over at the second last, but was very awkward at the final flight and in the end he only managed to hold on by the skin of his teeth and give his trainer his third win of the afternoon. This trip is probably sharp enough for him now so he deserves a bit of extra credit. *(op 4-1)*
Irish Wolf(FR) raised 6lb for his course-and-distance victory the previous month, put in a determined late effort against the stands' rail but the post just beat him. The fact that the ground may have been a little softer than advertised would not have suited him. *(op 8-1)*
Silver Prophet(IRE), raised 5lb for getting beaten at Windsor, was kept wide throughout in search of better ground and never stopped trying all the way to the line. He deserves to win a race, provided the Handicapper does not put him up again for this. *(op 8-1)*
Sun King, a stable companion of the winner and down the field in a couple of races on the Flat recently after returning from a very long layoff, performed with great credit on this return to hurdles and is another who would not have been suited by any cut in the ground. *(op 33-1)*
Front Rank(IRE) did not improve for the removal of the headgear and does not look particularly well handicapped at present. *(tchd 66-1)*
Credit(IRE) failed to build on his recent return to action and either would have preferred genuinely *fast ground or is badly handicapped on what he has actually achieved over hurdles. (op 13-2 tchd 15-2)*
Barton Park *Official explanation: trainer said gelding found good ground too soft (op 4-1)*

2717 RACING UK NOVICES' H'CAP CHASE (19 fncs) 3m

2:00 (2:00) (Class 3) (0-110,109) 4-Y-0+ **£5,660** (£1,661; £830; £414)

Form RPR
0-66 **1** **Florida Dream (IRE)**^{20} [2325] 6-11-12 **109**....................(b^{1}) AntonyEvans 115
(N A Twiston-Davies) *chsd ldr: lft in ld 8th: rdn appr last: hdd flat: rallied to ld nr fin* **8/1**

/P30 **2** *nk* **Bell Lane Lad (IRE)**[20] 2313 8-11-3 **100**....................(v[1]) RobertThornton 106
(A King) *a.p: chsd wnr 4 out: rdn after next: led flat: hdd nr fin* **15/2**

-364 **3** *19* **Monsieur Georges (FR)**[35] 2010 5-10-4 **90**................. OwynNelmes(3) 79+
(F Jordan) *hld up: hdwy 9th: mstke 15th: wknd 3 out* **25/1**

25-6 **4** *8* **Fullards**[36] 1988 7-11-10 **107**... WarrenMarston 92+
(Mrs P Sly) *led: blnd: rdr lost iron and hdd 8th: sn lost pl: rallied to chse wnr 14th to 4 out: wknd next* **13/2**[3]

3120 **5** *3/4* **Ultimate Limit**[24] 2243 5-11-2 **99**... GrahamLee 77
(A Ennis) *hld up: hdwy 9th: wknd 16th* **5/1**[2]

033 **6** *7* **Ardashir (FR)**[30] 2104 6-10-11 **94**... DaveCrosse 65
(Mrs S J Humphrey) *prom to 16th* **9/1**

-3PP **7** *30* **Penalty Clause (IRE)**[11] 2522 5-9-9 **85**....................... AdrianScholes(7) 26
(Lucinda Featherstone) *a in rr: blnd 7th: bhd fr 13th* **40/1**

0P6 **8** *13* **Fantastic Champion (IRE)**[53] 1760 6-10-0 **83** oh7.......... JosephByrne 11
(J R Cornwall) *prom: mstke 2nd: wknd 10th* **50/1**

560F **9** *20* **Unusual Suspect**[20] 2325 6-11-4 **101**..................................(b) PhilipHide 9
(G L Moore) *prom: hit 6th: wknd 12th: bhd whn blnd 4 out* **25/1**

/05- **P** **Gay Kindersley (IRE)**[376] 2482 7-9-7 **83**.......................... PhilKinsella(7) —
(K G Reveley) *hld up: blnd 9th: sn p.u* **12/1**

0P-F **P** **Galaxy Sam (USA)**[7] 2593 6-11-1 **98**..............................(t) JamesDavies —
(N J Gifford) *mstke 3rd: a bhd: t.o whn p.u after 12th* **20/1**

0-12 **P** **King Of Gothland (IRE)**[11] 2529 6-11-3 **100**.............(p) JohnMcNamara —
(K C Bailey) *prom: mstkes 6th and 8th: lost pl whn hit 10th: bhd whn p.u bef 15th* **11/4**[1]

6m 27.9s (15.60) **Going Correction** +0.925s/f (Soft) **12** Ran SP% **114.1**
Speed ratings: **111,110,104,101,101 99,89,84,78,— —,—** CSF £59.92 CT £1426.38 TOTE £9.50: £2.70, £3.00, £6.10; EX 86.60 TRIFECTA Not won..
Owner D J & S A Goodman **Bred** Mrs Patricia Mackean **Trained** Naunton, Gloucs

FOCUS
An ordinary event of its type and probably not strong form, but a fair winning time for the grade. The first two were both wearing first-time headgear and it obviously made a difference.

NOTEBOOK
Florida Dream(IRE) ♦ found the first-time headgear making the difference. Given a positive ride, he finally realised his potential over fences despite the narrow margin and did well to battle back after looking likely to be beaten. He should be able to build on this and would not mind softer ground. *(op 7-1)*
Bell Lane Lad(IRE) ♦, trying his longest trip to date in the first-time visor, was under pressure some way out. Responding well to his rider's urgings, he looked likely to have timed his effort just right coming to the last but once on the run-in the winner appeared to want it just a little more. He stayed the trip well enough and should be up to winning a similar contest. *(tchd 8-1)*
Monsieur Georges(FR) has been tumbling down the handicap over hurdles recently and was on a very modest mark for this chasing debut. He was not disgraced even though he never had a prayer with the front two, but he lacks pace and is still looking for his first win of any description.
Fullards, whose rider did extremely well to recover from a huge blunder at the eighth, still managed to play an active part until the home bend. There are more races in him when his jumping holds up. *(op 8-1)*
Ultimate Limit did not seem to get home and if the ground was softer than the official description that would not have been ideal for him.
King Of Gothland(IRE) ran a complete shocker, jumping poorly and dropping himself out before being pulled up. He has it all to prove now. *Official explanation: jockey said gelding was unsuited by good to soft ground (op 5-2 tchd 3-1 in places)*

2718 JOHN SMITH'S/E.B.F. MARES' ONLY "NATIONAL HUNT" NOVICES' HURDLE (QUALIFIER) (10 hdls) 2m 4f 110y
2:30 (2:32) (Class 3) 4-Y-0+ **£4,856** (£1,425; £712; £356)

Form RPR

3-32 **1** **Vertical Bloom**[12] 2501 4-10-12 .... WarrenMarston 107+
(Mrs P Sly) *hld up: hdwy and mstke 5th: led last: rdn out* **9/4**[2]

30-5 **2** *4* **Harringay**[35] 2012 5-10-12 97..(t) RobertThornton 101
(Miss H C Knight) *hld up: hdwy 7th: rdn and hit last: styd on same pce* **7/1**

2-14 **3** *2 1/2* **Viciana**[24] 2238 6-11-4 112.. JimmyMcCarthy 106+
(Mrs L Wadham) *trckd ldrs: led after 7th: rdn and hdd last: wknd flat* **2/1**[1]

2-45 **4** *13* **Retro's Girl (IRE)**[14] 2461 4-10-12 .... TomScudamore 86
(M Scudamore) *prom: mstkes 1st and 4th: ev ch 3 out: wknd bef next* **16/1**

06- **5** *6* **The Washerwoman**[255] 4608 5-10-12 .... DaveCrosse 80
(B I Case) *hld up: hdwy 6th: wknd appr 2 out* **40/1**

3400 **6** *9* **Silver Bow**[16] 2412 4-10-9 .... FergusKing(3) 71
(J M Jefferson) *hld up: hdwy 6th: wknd appr 2 out* **40/1**

00-5 **7** *15* **Just Ask**[38] 1954 5-10-12 .... SeanCurran 56
(N R Mitchell) *mid-div: mstke 1st: wknd after 6th* **100/1**

55 **8** *23* **Missy Moscow (IRE)**[14] 2457 7-10-12 .... RichardHobson 33
(H J Evans) *led: hdd & wknd after 7th* **100/1**

60- **9** *5* **Chilly Milly**[270] 4349 4-10-12 .... PhilipHide 28
(V Smith) *mid-div: wknd appr 6th* **80/1**

0-23 **10** *2* **Our Joycey**[34] 2028 4-10-12 .... BrianHarding 26
(Mrs K Walton) *hld up: bhd fr 5th* **40/1**

00-0 **11** *4* **Eveon (IRE)**[20] 2309 5-10-12 .... JamesDavies 22
(Ian Williams) *hld up: bhd fr 5th* **100/1**

0-00 **12** *1* **Burnside Place**[57] 1714 5-10-12 .... JohnMcNamara 21
(C C Bealby) *hld up: nvr nr to chal* **100/1**

0P-4 **P** **Tenko**[18] 2376 6-10-7 .... WilliamKennedy(5) —
(M D McMillan) *hld up: hdwy 6th: wknd and p.u bef 2 out* **40/1**

05 **R** **My Rosie Ribbons (IRE)**[34] 2021 6-10-2 .... CyrilleLeveque(10) —
(B W Duke) *racd wd: chsd ldrs: cl up whn rn out 3 out* **66/1**

2123 **P** **Bonchester Bridge**[13] 2486 4-10-7 .... SamCurling(5) —
(N J Henderson) *chsd ldrs: wknd after 3 out: p.u bef next* **5/1**[3]

02/ **P** **Polyanthus Jones**[644] 4144 6-10-7 .... TomGreenway(5) —
(H D Daly) *chsd ldrs tl rdn and wknd appr 6th: p.u bef next* **16/1**

5m 10.5s (15.20) **Going Correction** +0.675s/f (Soft)
WFA 4 from 5yo+ 11lb **16** Ran SP% **121.5**
Speed ratings: **98,96,95,90,88 84,79,70,68,67 66,65,—,—,— —** CSF £18.12 TOTE £3.80: £1.60, £2.80, £1.20; EX 28.80.
Owner Thorney Racing Club **Bred** Mrs P Sly **Trained** Thorney, Cambs

FOCUS
This looked a weak contest despite the size of the field and little to get excited about outside the first three. The winning time was also modest for the class but the runner-up sets the standard and the winner is value for a bit further.

NOTEBOOK
Vertical Bloom continues her progressive form over hurdles and relished the extra half-mile. She comprehensively turned around last month's Towcester form with the favourite on 6lb better terms and the way she won this does suggest there was enough juice in the ground. This was not a great race, but she is going the right way. *(op 3-1)*
Harringay, running for the first time since her controversial effort at Towcester last month, had the tongue tie on this time and, though she was brought to hold every chance, she hung over to the stands' rail on the run-in and could find no extra. She is no star, but there should be an ordinary novice in her. *(op 5-1)*
Viciana, who had Vertical Bloom just over three lengths behind her when winning at Towcester last month, was always up with the pace and had every chance, but could not confirm the form on 6lb worse terms and the winner does look more progressive. *(op 5-2 tchd 15-8, 11-4 in places)*
Retro's Girl(IRE), who failed to stay three miles last time, did not get home even over this shorter trip but her performances in bumpers suggested she needed further than two miles, so it would probably be worth giving her another go over this sort of trip. *(op 20-1)*
The Washerwoman was not entirely disgraced on this hurdling debut and should come on for this first run in ten months. *(op 33-1)*
Polyanthus Jones *Official explanation: vet said mare was lame (op 4-1)*
Bonchester Bridge ran very poorly and is still to confirm the promise she showed in bumpers. *Official explanation: jockey said filly hung right (op 4-1)*
My Rosie Ribbons(IRE), racing very wide, appeared to nearly run out jumping the third. Still wide, she made no mistake at the same flight on the next circuit when not completely out of it, crashing through the wing and mowing down a member of the groundstaff in the process. She is obviously not completely without ability if her head can be sorted out. *(op 4-1)*

2719 OPEN DITCH CONDITIONAL JOCKEYS' H'CAP CHASE (12 fncs) 2m 110y
3:00 (3:01) (Class 4) (0-105,105) 4-Y-0+ **£4,089** (£1,200; £600; £299)

Form RPR

P311 **1** **Jolly Boy (FR)**[2] 2684 6-9-11 **79** 7ex oh1...................(b) LiamTreadwell(3) 96+
(Miss Venetia Williams) *chsd ldr 3rd: led 8th: shkn up but 3l ahd and looked in command whn lft clr last* **6/4**[1]

-P04 **2** *dist* **Le Royal (FR)**[30] 2100 6-11-4 **105**....................................... PhilKinsella(8) 86
(K G Reveley) *bhd whn hit 3rd: lft remote 3rd whn hit last: nvr nrr* **14/1**

3P33 **3** *7* **Wild Power (GER)**[25] 2217 7-11-0 **93**.............................(p) OwynNelmes 67
(Mrs H R J Nelmes) *hld up: hdwy 6th: wknd 3 out* **16/1**

-P65 **4** *16* **Game On (IRE)**[19] 2342 9-11-3 **104**............................... TomMessenger(8) 62
(B N Pollock) *chsd ldrs: mstke 6th: wknd next* **33/1**

U3-4 **5** *7* **Polish Pilot (IRE)**[32] 2080 10-10-2 **84** oh4 ow5............ AdamPogson(3) —
(J R Cornwall) *led: hdd after 1st: mstke 3rd: wknd 3 out* **25/1**

-523 **P** **Green Gamble**[24] 2239 5-10-11 **93**..................... RobertLucey-Butler(3) —
(D B Feek) *hld up: a in rr: bhd whn p.u bef 9th* **11/2**[3]

3404 **F** **Buffalo Bill (IRE)**[24] 2241 9-11-10 **103**.......................... WilliamKennedy —
(A M Hales) *hld up: hdwy 6th: wkng whn fell 9th* **12/1**

31P4 **P** **Charliemoore**[20] 2323 9-10-5 **90**...............................(b) EamonDehdashti(6) —
(G L Moore) *pckd 1st: bhd fr 3rd: t.o whn p.u bef 2 out* **33/1**

PP-4 **F** **Interstice**[23] 2257 8-10-0 **79** oh7... TomGreenway —
(M J Gingell) *led after 1st: hdd 8th: 5th and wkng whn fell 3 out* **50/1**

4612 **U** **Celtic Legend (FR)**[8] 2570 6-10-5 **92**.......................... JamesReveley(8) 103+
(K G Reveley) *hld up: hdwy 6th: chsd wnr and mstke 3 out: 3l down and rdn whn blnd and uns rdr last* **3/1**[2]

4m 23.6s (14.30) **Going Correction** +0.925s/f (Soft) **10** Ran SP% **112.3**
Speed ratings: **103,—,—,—,— —,—,—,—,—** CSF £20.17 CT £239.74 TOTE £2.50: £1.60, £3.30, £3.20; EX 27.00.
Owner Favourites Racing **Bred** Georges Lacombe **Trained** Kings Caple, H'fords

FOCUS
A moderate contest, especially with only half the field completing, but the winner could do no more than win as he did and is rated as running to recent form.

NOTEBOOK
Jolly Boy(FR) made light of his penalty to complete a nine-day hat-trick and was well on top when his only danger departed at the last. Connections may be tempted into running him again pretty soon, and in his current mood there is no reason why he should not keep the sequence going, provided his exertions do not catch up with him. *(op 13-8)*
Le Royal(FR), dropping in trip, still does not convince with his jumping and only inherited a remote second due to the misfortune of others. *(op 16-1 tchd 12-1)*
Wild Power(GER), a hard horse to win with, added yet another placing to his record but even by his standards this was a poor effort as he would have been well out of the frame had others stood up.
Game On(IRE) achieved nothing in finishing a remote fourth and continues out of form.
Celtic Legend(FR), who goes well on a Flat track, stalked the winner on the home turn and looked to have a big chance of giving his trainer a four-timer at the meeting, but he did not find as much as had looked likely and was well held when ejecting his rider at the last. He is due to go up another 4lb which will leave him 13lb higher than for his last chase win. *(op 11-4)*
Interstice jumped boldly out in front for the first half of the contest, but had run his race when coming down. *(op 11-4)*

2720 RACING UK INTERMEDIATE NATIONAL HUNT FLAT RACE (CONDITIONAL JOCKEYS/AMATEUR RIDERS) 2m 110y
3:30 (3:30) (Class 6) 4-6-Y-0 **£1,843** (£537; £268)

Form RPR

0 **1** **Night Safe (IRE)**[43] 1882 4-10-11 .... MarcGoldstein(7) 105
(N A Twiston-Davies) *chsd ldr tl led 1/2-way: rdn and hdd over 1f out: rallied to ld post* **9/1**

2 *hd* **Kimi (IRE)** 4-10-13 .... WilliamKennedy(5) 105
(Noel T Chance) *hld up: hdwy 1/2-way: rdn over 2f out: led over 1f out: hdd post* **2/1**[1]

3 *1 1/4* **Ellerslie George (IRE)** 5-10-13 .... SamCurling(5) 104
(O Brennan) *hld up: hdwy over 7f out: rdn over 1f out: styd on* **12/1**

0 **4** *3* **Ammunition (IRE)**[214] 241 5-10-11 .... RobertLucey-Butler(7) 101
(M Pitman) *hld up: hdwy 7f out: rdn over 1f out: styd on same pce* **33/1**

0 **5** *5* **John Diamond (IRE)**[11] 2534 4-10-11 .... MrJJarrett(7) 96
(Miss H C Knight) *trckd ldrs: rdn over 2f out: wknd over 1f out* **7/1**[2]

0-0 **6** *1/2* **Golden Crew**[24] 2242 5-11-1 .... ColinBolger(3) 95
(Miss Suzy Smith) *prom: rdn over 4f out: wknd 2f out* **66/1**

4 **7** *29* **Lord Ryeford (IRE)**[21] 2288 5-10-11 .... MrRMcCarthy(7) 66
(T R George) *chsd ldrs over 12f* **12/1**

0 **8** *13* **Kahysera**[15] 2446 4-10-6 .... PaddyMerrigan(5) 46
(Mrs H Dalton) *chsd ldrs over 12f* **8/1**[3]

0- **9** *1 1/4* **Sparklinspirit**[336] 3238 6-10-11 .... TomMessenger(7) 52
(J L Spearing) *hld up: rdn 1/2-way: sn wknd* **100/1**

P0 **10** *7* **Willhebemyguy**[33] 2056 6-11-1 .... OwynNelmes(3) 45
(Mrs H R J Nelmes) *led to 1/2-way: wknd 5f out* **50/1**

11 *1 1/4* **Carroll's O'Tully (IRE)**[222] 5-10-4 .... JustinMorgan(7) 37
(L A Dace) *hld up: a bhd* **33/1**

12 *13* **Nar Valley** 4-10-11 .... MrGTumelty(7) 31
(A King) *mid-div: wknd 1/2-way* **9/1**

13 *4* **Moritz (FR)** 5-10-11 .... PhilKinsella(7) 27
(K G Reveley) *hld up: a bhd* **8/1**[3]

14 *6* **Wot Way Chief** 4-10-13 .... PaulO'Neill(5) —
(J M Jefferson) *hld up: rdn over 6f out: sn wknd* **12/1**

0 **15** *1* **Celtic Flame**[15] 2446 6-10-4 .... DarrenO'Dwyer(7) —
(O Brennan) *hld up: a in rr* **66/1**

16 *18* **Musicalish** 4-10-11 .... SeanQuinlan(7) —
(R Mathew) *mid-div: rdn and wknd over 7f out* **66/1**

0 **17** *dist* **Winsome Wendy (IRE)**[12] 2507 5-10-4 .... EamonDehdashti(7) —
(P A Pritchard) *chsd ldrs to 1/2-way* **100/1**

(3.50) **Going Correction** +0.675s/f (Soft)
WFA 4 from 5yo+ 10lb **17** Ran SP% **125.4**
Speed ratings: **103,102,102,100,98 98,84,78,77,74 74,67,66,63,62 54,—** CSF £27.04 TOTE £8.70: £3.00, £1.30, £7.60; EX 39.50 Place 6 £121.28, Place 5 £48.08.
Owner C B Sanderson **Bred** John Blake **Trained** Naunton, Gloucs
■ Stewards' Enquiry : Owyn Nelmes one-day ban: used whip when out of contention and without giving gelding time to respond (Jan 19)

FOCUS
A fair bumper, but only the first six counted from some way out and a few of them look to have a future with the fifth the best guide to the level.

NOTEBOOK
Night Safe(IRE) confirmed the promise of his Cheltenham debut, but only just, and having the stands' rail to help him in the battle to the line with the favourite may have been the key. This sharp track may not have been totally ideal and he is probably better than this when faced with a stiffer test. *(op 15-2)*
Kimi(IRE), a half-brother to a winning hurdler, a bumper winner and two winning pointers, was well supported to make a winning debut and did little wrong, but just lost out in the battle to the line. Like the winner, this sharp track would not have been ideal given his breeding and he should make amends on a stiffer track. *(op 5-2)*
Ellerslie George(IRE), resold for 46,000euros as a four-year-old and half-brother to a couple of winning hurdlers, ran with plenty of promise and, as one of his siblings won over three-and-a-quarter miles, it will be no surprise if he requires a test of stamina himself. *(op 14-1 tchd 16-1)*
Ammunition(IRE), unplaced on his debut back in May, performed better this time and can be expected to improve with racing.
John Diamond(IRE), a half-brother to a winning hurdler out of a winning hurdler, was bang there until done for foot over the last furlong or so and should come on for the experience. *(tchd 6-1)*
Golden Crew pulled well clear of the others, but had been beaten miles in two previous bumpers so could be a little flattered by this.
T/Jkpt: £10,313.90 to a £1 stake. Pool: £21,790.00. 1.50 winning tickets. T/Plt: £181.00 to a £1 stake. Pool: £38,930.60. 157.00 winning tickets. T/Qpdt: £43.60 to a £1 stake. Pool: £2,841.80. 48.15 winning tickets. CR

2139 LUDLOW (R-H)
Thursday, December 8

OFFICIAL GOING: Chase course - good (good to soft in places); hurdle course - good to soft
Wind: Nil Weather: Mainly fine, a light shower

2721 PERROTT PROPERTIES NOVICES' CLAIMING HURDLE (9 hdls) 2m
12:40 (12:41) (Class 4) 4-Y-0+ **£3,422** (£1,004; £502; £250)

Form RPR

00 **1** **Twist Bookie (IRE)**[8] 2573 5-11-1 .... ShaneWalsh(7) 99+
(J S Moore) *w ldr: led 6th: hit 3 out and 2 out: drvn out* **25/1**

0PP0 **2** *1* **Hunting Lodge (IRE)**[7] 2584 4-10-13 .... MrJAJenkins(7) 95
(H J Manners) *mid-div: lost pl 5th: rallied appr 3 out: swtchd lft flat: r.o* **12/1**

4303 **3** *shd* **Siena Star (IRE)**[9] 2560 7-10-3 86 .... (v1) MrTJO'Brien(7) 85
(P Bowen) *hld up in tch: rdn and r.o flat* **9/2**[1]

040 **4** *6* **Weet Watchers**[9] 2560 5-10-10 .... TonyDobbin 81+
(T Wall) *hld up: hdwy 6th: chsd wnr appr 3 out: mstke last: wknd flat* **20/1**

3431 **5** *5* **Rojabaa**[7] 2582 6-11-4 85 .... LeightonAspell 84+
(B D Leavy) *hld up towards rr: hdwy 3 out: nvr trbld ldrs* **9/2**[1]

P0- **6** *2 1/2* **Night Warrior (IRE)**[4] 3123 5-11-7 .... (b) JohnLevins(5) 88
(K McAuliffe) *led to 6th: wknd 3 out* **20/1**

0U42 **7** *1 1/2* **Canadian Storm**[9] 2560 4-10-12 87 .... (p) AlanO'Keeffe 72
(A G Juckes) *t.k.h towards rr: hit 1st: hdwy 4th: wknd 3 out* **6/1**[2]

3100 **8** *4* **Young Tot (IRE)**[28] 2150 7-11-0 89 .... (p) SamThomas 70
(M Sheppard) *hld up in tch: rdn after 6th: wknd 3 out: j.lft 2 out* **7/1**[3]

/P-0 **9** *4* **Star Wonder**[26] 2179 5-10-1 60 .... AnthonyRoss 53
(G R I Smyly) *nvr nr ldrs* **100/1**

U43 **10** *hd* **Zeis (IRE)**[101] 1362 5-11-0 90 .... (t) MarkBradburne 66
(Miss J R Gibney) *nvr nr ldrs* **6/1**[2]

P/0 **11** *3/4* **Stylish Prince**[16] 2423 5-10-1 .... (t) MrTCollier(7) 59
(R Lee) *hld up: hdwy 5th: rdn and wknd after 6th* **66/1**

6 **12** *3/4* **Rabbit**[193] 574 4-10-11 .... BenjaminHitchcott 61
(Mrs A L M King) *a bhd* **50/1**

13 *11* **Mobo-Baco**[31] 8-10-7 .... JayHarris(5) 51
(R J Hodges) *in rr: mstkes 1st and 3rd: short-lived effrt after 6th* **14/1**

-000 **14** *3 1/2* **Lanos (POL)**[9] 2560 7-10-3 83 .... (t) DerekLaverty(5) 44
(W Davies) *prom tl wknd 6th* **28/1**

P000 **15** *dist* **Pridewood Dove**[14] 2460 6-10-3 59 .... HenryOliver —
(R J Price) *a bhd* **100/1**

/4F- **P** **Balmoral Queen**[355] 2893 5-9-12 .... StephenCraine(5) —
(D McCain) *plld hrd: prom tl p.u bef 3rd: sddle slipped* **66/1**

3m 52.9s (0.60) **Going Correction** +0.10s/f (Yiel)
WFA 4 from 5yo+ 10lb **16** Ran SP% **115.5**
Speed ratings: **102,101,101,98,95 94,93,91,89,89 89,89,83,81,— —** CSF £265.09 TOTE £62.00: £15.20, £2.60, £1.70; EX 781.60.Siena Star was claimed by Naughty Diesel Ltd for £6,000.
Owner Mrs Fitri Hay **Bred** Wolfgang Stiltz **Trained** Upper Lambourn, Berks

FOCUS
Just two runners in this weak claimer could boast a previous win over hurdles. The pace was sound and not many were able to get involved, but the form looks solid enough rated through third, fourth and fifth.

NOTEBOOK
Twist Bookie(IRE) was a winner on the Flat in Germany but had shown little in two previous runs over hurdles. Following a couple of ragged jumps, the healthy lead he had established leaving the back straight was being reduced fast on the run-in but the line came in time. The drop in grade and more prominent ride combined to good effect, but he is not likely to prove easy to place for a follow up. *Official explanation: trainer's representative said, regarding the improved form shown, gelding was suited by being ridden more prominently and by the drop in class*
Hunting Lodge(IRE), a one-time useful performer on the Flat who had shown little previously over hurdles, was lowered in class. After losing his pitch in the back straight, he rallied on the home turn. He was still only fourth over the final flight but stayed on to grab second on the line.
Siena Star(IRE), tried in a visor for the first time, cheekpieces having been used once before, ran his race again but once more had to settle for place money. He was claimed and his new connections might well consider a return to further. *(op 4-1)*
Weet Watchers, found wanting in sellers previously, went after the winner on the turn out of the back straight but was held when diving through the last, losing two places on the run-in. He has stamina limitations. *(op 25-1)*
Rojabaa ran a fair race on his first start since leaving Bill Turner but the sharp two miles was against him. *Official explanation: jockey said gelding slipped going into final bend (op 5-1 tchd 4-1)*
Night Warrior(IRE), a winner in banded company on Fibresand four days earlier, showed more than he had in a couple of novice hurdles a year ago but his stamina did not last out. *Official explanation: jockey said gelding hung badly right*
Zeis(IRE) showed ability in three runs in August but was never within striking distance here. He may need fast ground. *(op 13-2 tchd 7-1 and 11-2)*

2722 VERA DAVIES MEMORIAL TROPHY NOVICES' CHASE (12 fncs 1 omitted) 2m
1:10 (1:10) (Class 4) 4-Y-0+ **£5,298** (£1,719; £969)

Form RPR

P60P **1** **Scotch Corner (IRE)**[12] 2488 7-11-4 95 .... CarlLlewellyn 106+
(N A Twiston-Davies) *chsd ldr tl hmpd 3rd: hld up: lft 2nd 6th: led 3 out: sn rdn: clr appr last: r.o* **4/1**[2]

2 *9* **Solar At'Em (IRE)**[143] 1029 7-11-4 92 .... MarkBradburne 96+
(M Sheppard) *sn chsng ldr: lft in ld 6th: hit and hdd 3 out: sn rdn: one pce* **14/1**

-632 **3** *6* **Humid Climate**[191] 604 5-11-4 102 .... AnthonyRoss 88
(R A Fahey) *hld up in rr: rdn 9th: sn struggling* **11/2**[3]

6P2P **F** **Let's Rock**[21] 2284 7-10-11 67 .... MrRHodges(7) —
(Mrs A Price) *fell 1st* **50/1**

-0F6 **F** **Sunley Future (IRE)**[18] 2379 6-11-4 98 .... BenjaminHitchcott —
(M F Harris) *led tl fell 1st* **12/1**

F-12 **F** **Reseda (GER)**[34] 2018 6-10-11 105 .... PaulMoloney —
(Ian Williams) *lft in ld 1st: 4l clr whn fell 6th* **5/6**[1]

4m 4.80s (0.70) **Going Correction** +0.10s/f (Yiel) **6** Ran SP% **106.3**
Speed ratings: **102,97,94,—,— —** CSF £41.56 TOTE £4.50: £1.70, £3.50; EX 36.90.
Owner H R Mould **Bred** Ollie Brooks **Trained** Naunton, Gloucs

FOCUS
This low-grade novices' handicap was rendered even less competitive by the intervention of the fences, with only three runners left standing after halfway, and the runner-up offers the best guide to the level of the form. The first fence in the home straight was bypassed on the final circuit to avoid an injured jockey.

NOTEBOOK
Scotch Corner(IRE) made a promising chasing debut when bustling up Hasty Prince on this card a year ago but had been a sore disappointment since. Down in both trip and class, he was soon in command after challenging at the third last but this form means little. *(op 5-1)*
Solar At'Em(IRE), previously trained by Joanna Morgan in Ireland, made a satisfactory debut for this stable on his first start since July. A little race could come his way, perhaps in the cheekpieces he often wore for his old yard. *(op 8-1)*
Humid Climate, runner-up at Hexham in May when last in action, has won after a lengthy lay-off in the past but ran as if this was needed. His jumping was a little laborious and he was booked for third from a good way out. *(op 9-2)*
Let's Rock, who has never run anywhere other than here or at Hereford in 14 starts under Rules, hit the deck for the first time in his career. *(op 4-5 tchd 10-11 in places)*
Sunley Future(IRE), making his chasing debut, became a victim of the notorious first fence. *(op 4-5 tchd 10-11 in places)*
Reseda(GER), dropped in trip after a decent chasing bow, seemed to have been found a good opportunity. She was bowling along in front when getting in too close to the first in the back straight and coming down. *(op 4-5 tchd 10-11 in places)*

2723 COSELEY CHRISTMAS CRAIC AMATEUR JOCKEYS NOVICES' H'CAP HURDLE (11 hdls) 2m 5f
1:40 (1:40) (Class 4) (0-105,100) 3-Y-0+ **£3,872** (£1,200; £600; £300)

Form RPR

13P- **1** **She's Our Native (IRE)**[252] 4670 7-11-3 **91** .... MrNWilliams 111+
(Evan Williams) *hld up: hdwy 5th: led on bit appr 3 out: sn clr: easily* **15/2**[3]

0154 **2** *6* **Astyanax (IRE)**[11] 2530 5-11-9 **100** .... MrJSnowden(3) 108
(N J Henderson) *led: rdn and hdd appr 3 out: no ch w wnr* **6/4**[1]

6-P0 **3** *11* **Point**[28] 2144 8-11-12 **100** .... MrTGreenall 98+
(W Jenks) *prom: rdn appr 3 out: wknd 2 out* **20/1**

00-0 **4** *3 1/2* **Salopian**[14] 2455 5-11-3 **96** .... MrPCallaghan(5) 90
(H D Daly) *hld up and bhd: hdwy 8th: sn wknd* **20/1**

60-3 **5** *4* **Waziri (IRE)**[9] 2563 4-10-3 **84** .... MrLRPayter(7) 76+
(M Sheppard) *hld up and bhd: hdwy on ins 6th: rdn appr 3 out: wknd appr 2 out* **10/1**

4P65 **6** *3* **Darko Karim**[14] 2454 3-9-12 **90** .... (b) MissCTizzard(3) 62
(R J Hodges) *hld up in tch: lost pl appr 6th: rallied 7th: mstke 8th: sn wknd* **14/1**

20/5 **7** *14* **Pin High (IRE)**[15] 2427 6-11-9 **100** .... MrTJO'Brien(3) 73
(Miss H C Knight) *hld up in mid-div: hit 3rd: lost pl 5th: rallied 7th: sn wknd* **14/1**

222F **8** *4* **Murphy's Nails (IRE)**[26] 2173 8-11-3 **98** .... (p) MrRQuinn(7) 67
(K C Bailey) *prom: chsd ldr appr 6th to 8th: sn wknd* **11/2**[2]

0- **9** *dist* **Sullivan's Cascade (IRE)**[385] 2293 7-9-11 **78** .... MrTCollier(7) —
(E G Bevan) *a in rr: t.o* **40/1**

05-0 **P** **Shogoon (FR)**[28] 2146 6-9-7 **74** oh5 .... MrRhysHughes(7) —
(N E Berry) *w ldr tl appr 6th: sn wknd: t.o 8th: p.u bef 3 out* **50/1**

P-55 **P** **Kirby's Vic (IRE)**[41] 1910 5-10-9 **90** .... MrWBiddick(7) —
(N A Twiston-Davies) *a bhd: lost tch 5th: t.o whn p.u bef 8th* **14/1**

5m 17.3s (-1.00) **Going Correction** +0.10s/f (Yiel)
WFA 3 from 4yo 14lb 4 from 5yo+ 11lb **11** Ran SP% **110.2**
Speed ratings: **105,102,98,97,95 94,89,87,—,— —** CSF £17.61 CT £200.97 TOTE £7.30: £3.40, £1.10, £4.00; EX 19.50.
Owner Ian Brice **Bred** J Mangan **Trained** Cowbridge, Vale Of Glamorgan

FOCUS
A modest affair that could be rated higher but not totally convincing, although the winner value for double the official margin.

NOTEBOOK
She's Our Native(IRE), who held an entry in the mares' handicap too, ran out a clear-cut winner. She fractured her pelvis in a chase at this course when last seen in March and needed several months' box rest, but showed no ill effects as she won in ready style. A return to fences beckons now. *(op 9-1)*
Astyanax(IRE), whose one hurdling success thus far came over course and distance in October, ran a sound race from the front but had no answer when the mare eased past. *(op 13-8)*
Point ran respectably but does not look especially well handicapped at present. The return to three miles could help. *(op 16-1)*
Salopian, on his handicap debut, took quite a hold over this longer trip. He still appeared to have plenty of running in him on the long home turn but he was not helping his jockey and the leaders soon went away from him. Stronger handling might help and he can improve on this. *Official explanation: jockey said gelding hung left-handed (op 12-1)*
Waziri(IRE) was third in a similar event at Hereford last time but that was over half a mile shorter and the extra yardage seemed to find him out. *(op 11-1 tchd 12-1)*
Darko Karim Plating-class hurdler; probably stays 2m 5f. *(op 12-1)*

Murphy's Nails(IRE) had proved consistent prior to a fall at Cheltenham last time but he was below-par here. *(op 5-1)*

2724 VISCOUNT BOYNE MEMORIAL CHALLENGE TROPHY (HANDICAP CHASE) (22 fncs) 3m 1f 110y

2:10 (2:10) (Class 3) (0-125,126) 5-Y-0+ **£11,434** (£3,407; £1,724; £884; £462)

Form				RPR
-534	**1**		**Le Jaguar (FR)**[21] [2299] 5-11-4 **119**....(bt[1]) LiamHeard[(7)] (P F Nicholls) *hld up in tch: wnt 2nd 16th: led after 18th: rdn 3 out: mstke last: all out* **9/2**[2]	129+
50B2	**2**	*1*	**Tribal Dancer (IRE)**[32] [2077] 11-10-0 **94**.... AlanO'Keeffe (Miss Venetia Williams) *t.k.h: led tl after 18th: rdn 3 out: ev ch flat: styd on* **5/1**[3]	101
11-5	**3**	*16*	**Calvic (IRE)**[33] [2046] 7-11-8 **116**.... PaulMoloney (T R George) *hld up in tch: wkng whn mstke 15th* **6/1**	108+
0U1F	**4**	*2 ½*	**Underwriter (USA)**[26] [2180] 5-11-0 **115**.... ThomasDreaper[(7)] (Ferdy Murphy) *hld up in tch: wknd 18th* **9/2**[2]	104
0P-6	**5**	*dist*	**Zaffamore (IRE)**[21] [2299] 9-11-12 **120**.... SamThomas (Miss H C Knight) *a in rr: j. slowly 4th: rdn appr 15th: t.o whn j.lft 2 out: exhausted whn ref last: completed* **9/2**[2]	—
-1U4	**P**		**You Owe Me (IRE)**[27] [2162] 8-11-9 **117**.... CarlLlewellyn (N A Twiston-Davies) *chsd ldr to 16th: wknd 17th: t.o whn mstke 3 out: p.u bef 2 out: b.b.v* **7/2**[1]	—

6m 37.7s (2.50) **Going Correction** +0.10s/f (Yiel) **6** Ran SP% **107.7**

Speed ratings: **100,99,94,94,—** — CSF £24.17 TOTE £5.20: £2.80, £2.70; EX 25.60.

Owner The Connaught 'Le Jaguar' Syndicate **Bred** M Lille **Trained** Ditcheat, Somerset

■ Stewards' Enquiry : Sam Thomas three-day ban: improper riding - continuing on a horse that appeared to be exhausted and that had refused at the last (Dec 19-21)

FOCUS

A modest handicap but with some of these out of sorts this was a two-horse race from some way out.

NOTEBOOK

Le Jaguar(FR), down in trip after a couple of runs over marathon distances, went to the front on the turn for home but did not win as easily as he had promised to as a couple of errors, notably at the last, took their toll and allowed the runner-up a second bite of the cherry. He is only a five-year-old and has more improvement in him, but it remains to be seen whether the blinkers have a similarly positive effect next time. *(op 7-2)*

Tribal Dancer(IRE), 3lb higher than when pipped at Market Rasen, made the running until headed by the eventual winner and was clawing him back on the run-in. He has his problems and has gone 15 races since gaining his last win, over course and distance in May last year, but is running well at present. *(op 9-2)*

Calvic(IRE), dropped 4lb since his reappearance, was well handicapped with Le Jaguar on Wincanton form in January, but ran as if still short of peak fitness. Softer ground is ideal for him. *(op 13-2 tchd 7-1)*

Underwriter(USA) won a weak novice event two starts back and had his limitations exposed on this handicap bow, but the clear round will not have done any harm. *(tchd 4-1)*

Zaffamore(IRE) has a good record round here and has become attractively handicapped, but he trailed all the way and was a tired horse when refusing at the last. He eventually completed for fifth prize. *(tchd 4-1 and 5-1)*

You Owe Me(IRE) disputed the lead with a circuit to run but began to struggle in the back straight. He has now failed to get home three times over this sort of trip since scoring over two miles five on his chasing debut in May, although there was a valid excuse here. Official explanation: trainer's representative said gelding bled from the nose *(tchd 4-1)*

2725 ALFA AGGREGATES NOVICES' H'CAP CHASE (17 fncs) 2m 4f

2:40 (2:40) (Class 3) (0-120,119) 4-Y-0 **£6,399** (£1,906; £965; £494; £258)

Form				RPR
F4	**1**		**Nayodabayo (IRE)**[14] [2456] 5-11-3 **110**....(v[1]) TonyDobbin (Evan Williams) *mde all: mstke 8th: hit 4 out: hit 2 out and last: drvn out* **8/1**	122+
-312	**2**	*3*	**Winsley**[24] [2239] 7-11-8 **115**.... LeightonAspell (O Sherwood) *hld up in tch: chsd wnr fr 5th: rdn 4 out: one pce fr 2 out* **6/4**[1]	121+
5/62	**3**	*hd*	**It Was'Nt Me (IRE)**[9] [2562] 8-10-6 **99**.... MarkBradburne (M Sheppard) *hld up in tch: outpcd appr 4 out: styd on wl flat* **13/2**[3]	104+
60/1	**4**	*1*	**Detonateur (FR)**[68] [1595] 7-11-8 **115**.... PaulMoloney (Ian Williams) *plld hrd early in rr: hdwy 13th: hit 3 out: sn rdn: no ex flat* **10/1**	120+
0113	**5**	*dist*	**Welsh Main**[16] [2420] 8-10-11 **104**.... CarlLlewellyn (Miss Tor Sturgis) *hld up: blnd 11th: sn struggling: t.o* **4/1**[2]	—
/1P-	**P**		**Fourboystoy (IRE)**[264] [4463] 6-11-3 **110**.... SamThomas (Miss H C Knight) *chsd ldr to 5th: blnd bdly 11th: p.u bef 12th* **7/1**	—

5m 7.60s (-3.10) **Going Correction** +0.10s/f (Yiel) **6** Ran SP% **106.0**

Speed ratings: **110,108,108,108,—** — CSF £19.15 TOTE £8.40: £3.70, £1.60; EX 21.50.

Owner D Tumman & R F Bloodstock **Bred** Mrs Karen Daly **Trained** Cowbridge, Vale Of Glamorgan

FOCUS

A modest contest but a fair winning time for the grade with the winner value for further.

NOTEBOOK

Nayodabayo(IRE), with a first-time visor replacing the cheekpieces, was able to get off the mark over fences. A last-fence faller when in with every chance on his chasing debut at this venue last month, he lacked confidence in his jumping next time and got away with several errors here, including at the final obstacle on both circuits, but stayed on well enough over this longer trip. *(op 5-1)*

Winsley jumped soundly enough and was renewing his effort in the latter stages over this longer trip without getting to the winner. He has yet to match his hurdling form over fences, however. *(op 13-8 tchd 11-8)*

It Was'Nt Me(IRE) ◆ lost his pitch on the long run round to the home straight and was only fourth over the final fence, but came home strongly and nearly snatched second. He is due to go up 2lb in the weights from tomorrow and is going the right way for his new yard. *(op 7-1)*

Detonateur(FR) landed an ordinary race on his return from a long absence two months ago and he was found wanting from this mark, although it was only from the final fence that he conceded defeat. *(op 9-1)*

Welsh Main has been held twice from higher marks since completing a quick double in October. His chance was effectively ended by a blunder at the 11th. *(tchd 9-2)*

Fourboystoy(IRE), formerly with Chris Bealby, had been off since March and was making his chasing debut. He was in touch when sprawling badly after a mistake at the 11th and was pulled up before the next. *(op 8-1)*

2726 MARGARET FLETCHER SPECIAL BIRTHDAY MARES' ONLY H'CAP HURDLE (9 hdls) 2m

3:10 (3:10) (Class 4) (0-110,101) 4-Y-0+ **£4,658** (£1,367; £683; £341)

Form				RPR
31-5	**1**		**Capitana (GER)**[157] [78] 4-11-2 **91**.... AndrewTinkler (N J Henderson) *t.k.h in tch: led on bit appr 3 out: rdn and qcknd clr flat: readily* **3/1**[2]	107+
2434	**2**	*4*	**Don And Gerry (IRE)**[26] [2173] 4-11-9 **98**.... JodieMogford (P D Evans) *a.p: ev ch last: rdn and one pce flat* **11/4**[1]	102+
306-	**3**	*½*	**Ellway Prospect**[237] [3793] 5-10-10 **85**.... JimCrowley (M G Rimell) *chsd ldr: led 5th to 6th: outpcd appr 3 out: rallied 2 out: r.o flat* **9/2**[3]	87+
4F30	**4**	*½*	**Samandara (FR)**[46] [1862] 5-11-5 **97**....(v[1]) GinoCarenza[(3)] (A King) *hld up in tch: rdn appr 3 out: kpt on same pce fr 2 out* **20/1**	99
0P4-	**5**	*7*	**Shady Anne**[242] [4796] 7-11-12 **101**....(p) LeightonAspell (F Jordan) *led to 5th: rdn appr 3 out: wknd flat* **20/1**	96
1604	**6**	*3*	**Margarets Wish**[49] [1793] 5-10-9 **84**.... TonyDobbin (T Wall) *hld up: hdwy on ins after 6th: rdn and wknd 2 out* **8/1**	76
0462	**7**	*2*	**My Sharp Grey**[28] [2139] 6-11-2 **91**.... SamThomas (J Gallagher) *hld up: hdwy after 6th: wknd appr 2 out* **7/1**	82+
-300	**8**	*12*	**Resonance**[63] [1658] 4-11-2 **98**.... StevenCrawford[(7)] (N A Twiston-Davies) *racd keenly: hdwy 3rd: led 6th tl appr 3 out: sn wknd* **28/1**	76
35-P	**9**	*7*	**Soleil D'Hiver**[222] [134] 4-9-10 **78**.... JohnKington[(7)] (C J Drewe) *bhd: rdn after 6th: no rspnse* **50/1**	49

3m 54.1s (1.80) **Going Correction** +0.10s/f (Yiel)

WFA 4 from 5yo+ 10lb **9** Ran SP% **108.4**

Speed ratings: **99,97,96,96,93 91,90,84,81** CSF £10.46 CT £30.11 TOTE £4.20: £1.40, £1.50, £1.90; EX 12.80.

Owner P J D Pottinger **Bred** Gestut Hof Ittlingen **Trained** Upper Lambourn, Berks

FOCUS

This mares' event was run at a modest pace and as a consequence there were plenty in the mix turning for home. The winner is value for treble the winning margin with the placed horses to form.

NOTEBOOK

Capitana(GER) ◆, having her first run since an outing on the Flat in July, travelled well if a little keenly before cruising to the front turning into the straight. The sister to Caracciola quickened away readily to assert on the run-in and, although the Handicapper will step in, she may well be capable of winning again. *(op 5-2)*

Don And Gerry(IRE) made the frame once more but had no answer to the winner's turn of foot. Her turn will come but she does look something of a weak finisher. *(tchd 5-2, 3-1 in places)*

Ellway Prospect ◆ was outpaced on the final bend but was coming home in good style. Formerly with Iona Craig, this was an encouraging debut for this yard on her first start since February. *(op 4-1)*

Samandara(FR) was a little keen in the first-time visor and could not take advantage of being eased 3lb in the weights. *(tchd 18-1)*

Shady Anne, a winner on this card a year ago, ran respectably on this first run since the spring and a return to further should suit her. *(op 16-1)*

My Sharp Grey was close enough turning for home before fading. She is due for a 2lb rise in the weights, which will see her back on the mark from which she landed this event two years ago, her most recent victory. *(op 8-1)*

2727 E.B.F./DONCASTER BLOODSTOCK SALES MARES' ONLY STANDARD OPEN NATIONAL HUNT FLAT RACE 2m

3:40 (3:40) (Class 6) 4-6-Y-0 **£4,059** (£1,191; £595; £297)

Form				RPR
0-0	**1**		**Lady Bling Bling**[11] [2534] 4-10-11 .... GinoCarenza[(3)] (P J Jones) *a.p: rdn over 3f out: led over 2f out: clr 1f out: r.o wl* **9/1**	96
	2	*9*	**Mrs Goldfarb**[592] 6-11-0 .... SamThomas (Miss Venetia Williams) *led 5f: led over 5f out: rdn and edgd lft 3f out: sn hdd: one pce* **5/1**[3]	87
6	**3**	*2*	**Bonnie Blue**[12] [2507] 6-10-7 .... ShaneWalsh[(7)] (Mrs Norma Pook) *mid-div: rdn and outpcd 6f out: hdwy over 3f out: hung lft to stands' rail fr over 1f out: styd on* **11/1**	85
4-	**4**	*¾*	**Dallas Alice**[249] [4720] 5-11-0 .... PaulMoloney (Ian Williams) *hld up in tch: one pce fnl 3f* **14/1**	84
	5	*6*	**Mrs O'Malley** 5-10-9 .... StephenCraine[(5)] (D McCain) *hld up in tch: rdn 7f out: wknd over 4f out* **40/1**	78
51	**6**	*1 ¼*	**She's The Lady**[15] [2446] 5-11-7 .... TomSiddall (R S Brookhouse) *chsd ldr: led after 5f to over 5f out: rdn over 3f out: wknd over 2f out* **7/2**[2]	84
20-	**7**	*½*	**Hiho Silver Lining**[245] [4753] 4-11-0 .... JimCrowley (H Morrison) *hld up and bhd: rdn and hdwy 7f out: wknd over 4f out* **3/1**[1]	76
	8	*13*	**Shoestodiefor** 5-11-0 .... TonyDobbin (S A Brookshaw) *mid-div: wknd over 5f out* **25/1**	63
0-00	**9**	*hd*	**Just Ruby**[169] [817] 4-11-0 .... LeightonAspell (F Jordan) *hld up in mid-div: hdwy after 6f: wknd over 4f out* **66/1**	63
	10	*3*	**Another Burden** 4-11-0 .... MarkBradburne (H D Daly) *a bhd* **10/1**	60
20	**11**	*dist*	**Princess Yum Yum**[183] [685] 5-11-0 .... HenryOliver (J L Spearing) *t.k.h in rr: rdn 6f out: t.o* **20/1**	—
001-	**12**	*18*	**Post It**[262] [4499] 4-11-7 .... AndrewTinkler (R J Hodges) *swvd bdly lft s: hdwy after 4f: wknd 7f out: t.o* **16/1**	—
	13	*5*	**Lile Na Casca (IRE)**[186] 6-10-9 .... DerekLaverty[(5)] (Mrs A M Thorpe) *mid-div: rdn 8f out: sn bhd: t.o* **66/1**	—
	14	*dist*	**Rosemary's Fancy** 4-11-0 .... AlanO'Keeffe (C N Kellett) *a bhd: t.o* **100/1**	—
	P		**Tudor Rose (IRE)** 4-11-0 .... JodieMogford (Mrs N S Evans) *t.k.h: prom tl wknd 7f out: t.o whn p.u over 5f out* **66/1**	—

3m 50.4s (-1.80) **Going Correction** +0.10s/f (Yiel) **15** Ran SP% **120.4**

Speed ratings: **94,89,88,88,85 84,84,77,77,76 —,—,—,—,—** CSF £50.93 TOTE £9.80: £2.20, £2.30, £4.10; EX 103.40 Place 6 £150.26, Place 5 £46.16.

Owner P J Jones **Bred** East Kennett Bloodstock **Trained** East Kennett, Wilts

FOCUS

The form of many of these distaff bumpers is weak and this race looks no exception with the third and fourth setting the level.

NOTEBOOK

Lady Bling Bling, who showed ability in a better race at Newbury, took time to get into full stride but stayed on strongly once in front. She comes from a decent jumping family and should make her mark over obstacles, probably over further. *(op 10-1)*

Mrs Goldfarb , a half-sister to Flat winner Whitewater Boy, showed promise in maiden points in the spring of last year. She ran a decent race from the front on this Rules debut, but she could only keep galloping at the same pace in the straight and was soon cut down by the winner. *(tchd 11-2)*

Bonnie Blue had a lot of ground to make up turning for home but stayed on stoutly in the straight after drifting over to the stands' fence. Stamina appears her strongest suit. *(op 10-1)*

Dallas Alice, withdrawn due to the soft ground from her intended reappearance recently, confirmed the impression of her debut back in the spring that she possesses a degree of ability. *(op 11-1)*

Mrs O'Malley, a half-sister to Heavenly Stride, a winner over hurdles and fences for the McCain yard, out of a winning hurdler, made a satisfactory debut. *(op 33-1)*

She's The Lady made all at Wetherby but was harried for the lead here. Close up when slipping slightly crossing the road crossing on the entrance to the home straight, she soon began to fade and was ultimately well held under the penalty. *(op 4-1 tchd 10-3)*

Hiho Silver Lining, in front of Lady Bling Bling when both were down the field in a hot race of this type at Aintree in the spring, was a disappointment on this first run since. She may need faster ground. *(op 5-2)*
Post It, a winner at Hereford in March when last seen, was well beaten under the penalty. After losing ground when swerving at the start, she was in touch by halfway but soon began to weaken. She may need a sound surface. *(op 14-1)*
T/Plt: £179.50 to a £1 stake. Pool: £31,515.25. 128.15 winning tickets. T/Qpdt: £6.20 to a £1 stake. Pool: £3,193.80. 375.60 winning tickets. KH

2454 TAUNTON (R-H)

Thursday, December 8

OFFICIAL GOING: Good (good to firm in places)
Wind: Mild, across Weather: Dry

2728 "GET FREE TIPS AT GGBET.COM" (S) HURDLE (10 hdls) 2m 3f 110y
12:50 (12:50) (Class 5) 4-7-Y-0 **£2,309** (£672; £336)

Form RPR
F324 **1** **Urban Dream (IRE)**[15] 2428 4-10-12 85 RichardJohnson 86
(R A Farrant) *towards rr: drvn along and hdwy 6th: jnd ldrs 7th: led 2 out: sn rdn: styd on run-in: rdn out* **4/1**[2]
0306 **2** *2 ½* **It's My Party**[8] 2576 4-10-2 97 (v[1]) RichardGordon(10) 84
(W G M Turner) *in tch: hdwy to go 3rd 3 out: rdn appr 2 out: ev ch last: no ex* **5/1**[3]
P65 **3** *7* **Sungio**[26] 1486 7-10-7 82 LeeStephens(5) 79+
(B P J Baugh) *towards rr: drvn appr 6th: hdwy appr 3 out: ev ch whn nt fluent 2 out: sn rdn: wknd last* **13/2**
52-3 **4** *13* **Pedler's Profiles**[28] 2146 5-10-12 73 AndrewThornton 64
(Miss K M George) *sn drvn along in rr: styd on past btn horses fr 2 out: nvr a danger* **4/1**[2]
0006 **5** *8* **Bebe Factual (GER)**[28] 2146 4-10-7 72 ChrisHonour(5) 58+
(J D Frost) *chsd ldrs: led after 5th: nt fluent and hdd next: j.lft 3 out: sn wknd* **12/1**
0P **6** *1* **Zilla (FR)**[5] 2619 4-9-12 MissLucyBridges(7) 50+
(Miss Lucy Bridges) *hld up towards rr: making sme hdwy whn mstke 7th: wknd after 3 out* **40/1**
3-5P **7** *1 ¼* **Killy Beach**[15] 2429 7-10-5 MissSGaisford(7) 58+
(J D Frost) *chsd ldr: led 6th: mstke and hdd 2 out: wknd qckly* **12/1**
PP60 **P** **Gordy's Joy**[9] 2560 5-10-5 65 (bt) RJGreene —
(G A Ham) *led: rdn and hdd after 5th: sn wl bhd: p.u bef 7th* **66/1**
PP-0 **P** **Forest Rail (IRE)**[63] 1654 5-10-0 64 HowieEphgrave(5) —
(L Corcoran) *chsd ldrs tl wknd qckly appr 7th: t.o and p.u bef 2 out* **66/1**
3005 **F** **Nice Baby (FR)**[24] 2244 4-9-12 85 (vt) MrCHughes(7) —
(M C Pipe) *in tch: reminders after 5th: sme hdwy whn broke leg and fell appr 3 out: (dead)* **7/2**[1]

4m 50.7s (4.70) **Going Correction** +0.10s/f (Yiel) **10** Ran SP% **113.0**
Speed ratings: **94,93,90,85,81 81,80,—,—,—** CSF £23.73 TOTE £3.50: £1.10, £1.70, £2.80; EX 25.20.The winner was bought in for 7,200gns.
Owner Barnstaple Racing Club **Bred** Corrin Stud **Trained** Bampton, Devon

FOCUS
A moderate race, even by selling standards, and a good early pace sorted them out.

NOTEBOOK
Urban Dream(IRE) proved suited by this step up in trip and responded well to a strong ride from Johnson to gain his first success over hurdles at the seventh attempt. He looks as though he will stay further still, but this is very much his grade. *(op 10-3)*
It's My Party, with a visor replacing cheekpieces on this drop into selling company, did not look very keen under pressure and that proved his undoing. *(op 6-1)*
Sungio, without the blinkers on his return to hurdling, stayed on from well off the pace to get into a challenging position, but was not clever over the second last and could not sustain his effort. *(op 7-1)*
Pedler's Profiles was never really going and failed to build on the promise he showed when third round here on his previous start. *Official explanation: jockey said gelding was never travelling (op 5-1 tchd 7-2)*
Bebe Factual(GER) continues to run below the required level. *(op 14-1)*
Nice Baby(FR) sadly broke a leg on the Flat and had to be put down. *(op 3-1 tchd 4-1)*

2729 WEATHERBYS INSURANCE BEGINNERS' CHASE (17 fncs) 2m 7f 110y
1:20 (1:20) (Class 3) 5-Y-0+ **£5,907** (£1,734; £867; £433)

Form RPR
4-62 **1** **Cruising River (IRE)**[18] 2377 6-11-0 118 TimmyMurphy 117+
(Miss H C Knight) *mde most: briefly hdd 7th: shkn up to go clr appr 3 out: kpt on: rdn out* **10/11**[1]
03-P **2** *1 ½* **Quid Pro Quo (FR)**[40] 1917 6-11-0 118 JoeTizzard 113+
(P F Nicholls) *w wnr: led briefly 7th: rdn after 4 out: sn slty outpcd by wnr: styd on again run-in: (hung lft on bnds)* **5/2**[2]
436- **3** *9* **Treasulier (IRE)**[242] 4790 8-10-7 95 KeiranBurke(7) 103
(P R Rodford) *in tch: trckd ldrs 10th: outpcd after 4 out: styd on again after next: hit 2 out: wnt 3rd last* **20/1**
0/55 **4** *1 ½* **Wild Oats**[9] 2562 7-10-9 95 MarkNicolls(5) 104+
(B J M Ryall) *hld up: hdwy to trck ldrs 11th: rdn after 13th: chalng for 2nd whn wnt lft and hit 2 out: wknd* **20/1**
4-PP **5** *6* **Wizard Of Edge**[12] 2488 5-10-7 115 JamesWhite(7) 98+
(R J Hodges) *plld hrd early: hld up: hdwy to trck ldrs 7th: blnd 9th: rdn after 14th: wknd 3 out* **18/1**
/0-6 **F** **Goldseam (GER)**[5] 2620 6-11-0 RJGreene —
(S C Burrough) *in tch whn fell 3rd* **66/1**
24-P **B** **Grande Creole (FR)**[38] 1959 6-11-0 AndrewThornton —
(P F Nicholls) *hld up: b.d 3rd* **15/2**[3]
45F- **P** **Dunnicks Field**[280] 4142 9-10-9 79 ChrisHonour(5) —
(F G Tucker) *disp tl 3rd: chsd ldrs: dropped rr 11th: j.lft fr next: t.o and p.u after 4 out* **66/1**

6m 9.10s (4.00) **Going Correction** +0.30s/f (Yiel) **8** Ran SP% **110.5**
Speed ratings: **105,104,101,101,99 —,—,—** CSF £3.20 TOTE £2.00: £1.10, £1.30, £2.30; EX 2.90.
Owner Four Stablemates **Bred** John And Paul Cousins **Trained** West Lockinge, Oxon

FOCUS
Not much strength in depth in this beginners' chase, and not strong form with the third and fourth the best guides.

NOTEBOOK
Cruising River(IRE) ran well when second behind Big Moment over two miles one at Plumpton on his previous start but, being a winning pointer over three miles, this sort of trip was always going to suit much better. Given a positive ride, he made the odd mistake and gave the impression there is plenty of room for improvement in his jumping, but he was too good for these on the Flat and always looked like holding on. There really ought to be more to come. *(op 6-5)*
Quid Pro Quo(FR), a 118-rated hurdler who pulled up on his chasing debut, ran much better this time upped to his furthest trip to date but, although staying on quite well for pressure, was always just being held by the eventual winner. He looks well up to winning races in novice company this season. *(op 3-1 tchd 10-3)*
Treasulier(IRE) probably ran about as well as could have been expected off the back of a 242-day break. He should be suited by a return to handicap company. *(op 16-1 tchd 14-1)*
Wild Oats had a bit to find with the front two and did not run too badly in the circumstances. He is another who is probably better suited to handicap company. *(tchd 16-1)*
Wizard Of Edge, pulled up on both his previous starts over fences, managed to complete this time but was still well below his hurdling form. *(op 16-1)*
Grande Creole(FR) had his race ended when brought down at the third. *(op 6-1 tchd 5-1)*

2730 GRANT RAMNAUTH ST JAMES'S PLACE NOVICES' HURDLE (9 hdls) 2m 1f
1:50 (1:51) (Class 3) 4-Y-0+ **£7,319** (£2,148; £1,074; £536)

Form RPR
1151 **1** **Natal (FR)**[12] 2487 4-11-8 142 (t) MickFitzgerald 130+
(P F Nicholls) *trckd ldrs: nt fluent 5th: hit next: led on bit 3 out: sn clr: eased run-in* **4/11**[1]
2 *5* **Blaeberry**[167] 4-10-5 BarryFenton 102+
(Miss E C Lavelle) *hld up bhd: gd hdwy on outer after 3 out: jnd chsng gp 2 out: r.o to go 2nd run-in: no ch w wnr: improve* **50/1**
10 **3** *½* **Albarino (IRE)**[11] 2533 6-10-12 108 BrianCrowley 107+
(M Scudamore) *hld up towards rr: hdwy and nt clr run on inner after 3 out: styd on to go 2nd after 2 out: lost 2nd run-in* **40/1**
50 **4** *1 ¾* **It's The Limit (USA)**[9] 2559 6-10-7 LeeStephens(5) 105
(W K Goldsworthy) *mid div: hdwy after 3 out: sn rdn: kpt on same pce* **50/1**
0 **5** *9* **Smoothly Does It**[28] 2148 4-10-12 TomDoyle 96
(Mrs A J Bowlby) *keen in midfield: rdn after 3 out: kpt on same pce* **100/1**
43 **6** *½* **Xamborough (FR)**[16] 2423 4-10-12 RichardJohnson 96+
(B G Powell) *mid div: hdwy after 4th: led after next: hdd 3 out: sn rdn: wknd appr last* **11/1**[3]
4/30 **7** *1* **Photographer (USA)**[12] 2487 7-10-12 88 JasonMaguire 94
(S Lycett) *led tl 2nd: prom: rdn and one pced after 3 out* **100/1**
00 **8** *4* **Secret Divin (FR)**[21] 2301 5-10-12 JoeTizzard 90
(Jean-Rene Auvray) *chsd ldrs: drvn along fr 5th: rdn in 3rd after 3 out: wknd next* **250/1**
P0 **9** *10* **Miniperse (FR)**[24] 2249 5-10-7 ChrisHonour(5) 81+
(G R I Smyly) *chsd ldrs: rdn appr 3 out: wkng whn mstke 2 out* **300/1**
22- **10** *3* **Mega D'Estruval (FR)**[365] 2697 5-10-5 TimmyMurphy 70
(M C Pipe) *hld up towards rr: sme hdwy after 4th: wknd 3 out* **6/1**[2]
6-04 **11** *4* **Gotta Get On**[14] 2457 4-9-12 74 DarylJacob(7) 66
(R H Alner) *led 2nd tl after 5th: wknd 3 out* **125/1**
0 **12** *¾* **Tamreen (IRE)**[12] 2487 4-10-12 JamieMoore 72
(G L Moore) *mid div tl wknd after 3 out* **66/1**
3222 **P** **Miss Midnight**[14] 2457 4-9-12 JamesWhite(7) —
(R J Hodges) *mid div: hit 3rd: p.u bef next: lame* **20/1**
0/0- **P** **What A Monday**[330] 3321 7-10-12 NoelFehily —
(M Pitman) *a towards rr: blnd 6th: p.u bef next* **25/1**

4m 4.70s (-4.10) **Going Correction** +0.10s/f (Yiel) **14** Ran SP% **115.9**
Speed ratings: **113,110,110,109,105 105,104,102,98,96 94,94,—,—** CSF £36.89 TOTE £1.20: £1.10, £7.50, £7.80; EX 33.20.
Owner Mrs Monica Hackett **Bred** Yves D'Armaille **Trained** Ditcheat, Somerset

FOCUS
An ordinary race for the grade, but the time was a fair one for the class of contest and the form should work out.

NOTEBOOK
Natal(FR) found this a straightforward enough task to follow up his recent Newbury success and won comfortably. Connections plan to keep him to good ground, and he deserves his chance back in better company when he gets his conditions. *(op 4-9)*
Blaeberry, a 60-rated performer on the Flat who twice won over seven furlongs, made an eye-catching debut over hurdles as she was not subjected to that hard a ride in second. Given her stamina looked pretty limited on the Flat, she was probably ridden to get the trip and, as a result, was never positioned to pose any kind of threat. However, now it is clear she stays this sort of distance, she can be ridden more positively in future and it will be disappointing if she does not progress. *Official explanation: jockey said, regarding the apparent tender ride, his orders were to relax the filly getting her into a rhythm, and to ride her to get the trip having previously been a 7f flat winner; he dropped her out to settle her, ensuring she did not get too competitive and buzzed up early on, and made steady progress around final bend as the pace slackened; he added that she jumped well despite having schooled poorly at home; vet said filly was very lit up and had a high heart-rate after the race (op 40-1)*
Albarino(IRE) did well to keep on for third considering he was denied a clear run when looking to make his move on the turn, and this represented a return to form. *(op 33-1)*
It's The Limit(USA) seemed to run his best race to date over hurdles with a solid effort in fourth, but this was his qualifying run for a handicap mark and he has probably not done himself any favours.
Smoothly Does It was not without promise and only needs one more run for a handicap mark.
Xamborough(FR) ran below the form he showed on both his previous runs over hurdles and was a little disappointing. This run did, though, qualify him for a handicap mark. *(op 10-1 tchd 12-1)*
Mega D'Estruval(FR) did not look one to get carried away with when second on both her previous starts last season, and offered little on her return from a 365-day break. However, this run qualified her for a handicap mark and, given her connections, she cannot be dismissed in future. *(tchd 11-2)*
Miss Midnight *Official explanation: jockey said filly became lame after third hurdle (op 16-1)*

2731 WEATHERBYS BANK H'CAP HURDLE (12 hdls) 3m 110y
2:20 (2:21) (Class 3) (0-120,117) 4-Y-0+ **£5,159** (£1,514; £757; £378)

Form RPR
-555 **1** **Diletia**[36] 1992 8-10-3 **101** DarylJacob(7) 106+
(R H Alner) *chsd ldr: led 9th: rdn after 3 out: edgd rt u.p run-in: all out* **20/1**
-111 **2** *1* **Drumbeater (IRE)**[49] 1796 5-11-5 **110** RichardJohnson 115+
(P J Hobbs) *mid div: tk clsr order after 4th: shkn up and ev ch 2 out and nt fluent: swtchd rt run-in: styd on to go 2nd fnl strides* **11/8**[1]
3033 **3** *hd* **Ingres**[14] 2466 5-10-5 **103** CharlieStudd(7) 106
(B G Powell) *chsd ldrs: rdn after 3 out: styd on run-in* **15/2**[2]
0-UP **4** *½* **Dream Falcon**[36] 1984 5-11-5 **117** JamesWhite(7) 121+
(R J Hodges) *hld up bhd: stdy prog fr 9th: chsd ldrs appr 2 out: wnt 2nd at the last: no ex and hung lft u.p run-in* **25/1**
-P00 **5** *5* **Son Of Greek Myth (USA)**[19] 2347 4-10-12 **103** (b) JamieMoore 101
(G L Moore) *in tch: rdn appr 9th: one pced fr 3 out* **12/1**
213P **6** *1 ½* **Red Dahlia**[10] 2556 8-10-0 **91** TimmyMurphy 87
(M Pitman) *chsd ldrs: rdn and effrt after 3 out: sn one pce* **10/1**
4-06 **7** *3 ½* **Business Traveller (IRE)**[1] 2466 5-9-11 **93** MarkNicolls(5) 86
(R J Price) *mid div: outpcd 7th: styd on again fr 2 out* **25/1**

C5FP **8** *7* **Charango Star**[25] 2215 7-10-7 **105** .... WayneKavanagh(7) 91
(W K Goldsworthy) *chsd ldrs tl wknd after 3 out* **33/1**

5F31 **9** *1/2* **Arm And A Leg (IRE)**[14] 2466 10-11-2 **112** .... LeeStephens(5) 97
(Mrs D A Hamer) *hld up towards rr and nvr a danger* **14/1**

-P60 **10** *3* **Haydens Field**[198] 488 11-10-8 **102** .... TomMalone(3) 84
(Miss H Lewis) *led tl 9th: sn wknd* **40/1**

P-P5 **11** *12* **Dat My Horse (IRE)**[49] 1800 11-10-4 **95** .... VinceSlattery 65
(Tim Vaughan) *a towards rr* **150/1**

1-40 **P** **Turaath (IRE)**[19] 2347 9-11-9 **114** .... JasonMaguire —
(A J Deakin) *hld up and a towards rr: p.u bef 3 out* **25/1**

2463 **P** **Noble Calling (FR)**[6] 2609 8-10-9 **100** .... BarryFenton —
(R J Hodges) *mid div: dropped rr 6th: bhd fr 9th: t.o and p.u bef 2 out* **8/1**[3]

6m 6.90s (-1.70) **Going Correction** +0.10s/f (Yiel)
WFA 4 from 5yo+ 13lb **13** Ran SP% **110.8**
Speed ratings: **106,105,105,105,103 103,102,100,99,98 95,—,—** CSF £43.59 CT £226.32 TOTE £24.00: £4.90, £1.10, £2.70; EX 57.10.
Owner T H Chadney **Bred** T H Chadney **Trained** Droop, Dorset

FOCUS
The form of this handicap hurdle may not be as strong as one might have expected for the grade, with the third and fourth to their marks, but it was still very competitive.

NOTEBOOK
Diletia had not offered a great deal in two runs in similar company recently, but this was much better and she ran out a game winner. She should not go up much for this and can remain very competitive. *(op 16-1)*
Drumbeater(IRE), chasing the four-timer off a mark 10lb higher than when winning at Haydock when last seen 49 days ago, and no less than 27lb higher than when starting his winning run, ran a fine race in defeat and was just held. He may not have stopped improving just yet, but will go up again for this and things will continue to get tougher. *(op 5-4)*
Ingres, back up in trip, again ran right up to his best in third and can have few excuses. *(op 8-1)*
Dream Falcon is probably high enough in the weights, but he stayed on well from off the pace to take fourth and this represented a return to form. *(op 20-1)*
Son Of Greek Myth(USA) shaped as though he would improve for a return to this sort of trip at Huntingdon on his previous start, but it did not work out that way. *(op 9-1)*
Red Dahlia, just as when pulled up at Folkestone on her previous start, travelled strongly before failing to go through with her effort. *(op 12-1)*
Noble Calling(FR) *Official explanation: jockey said gelding hung badly (op 15-2)*

2732 ST JAMES'S PLACE H.B.L.B. NOVICES' CHASE (14 fncs) 2m 3f
2:50 (2:51) (Class 3) 4-Y-0+ **£7,937** (£2,420; £1,264; £687)

Form RPR

3L0/ **1** **Hors La Loi III (FR)**[978] 4478 10-11-3 .... DGallagher 127+
(P F Nicholls) *slowly away: sn rcvrd to trck ldrs 4th: jnd ldr after 4 out: j.big and wnt rt 3 out: sn led: j.big next: easily* **9/4**[1]

4-04 **2** *2 1/2* **Cossack Dancer (IRE)**[33] 2044 7-11-3 114 .... (p) MatthewBatchelor 122+
(M Bradstock) *led: stmbld bdly and hdd sn after 3 out: kpt on but no ch w wnr fr next* **3/1**[2]

45P2 **3** *24* **Kings Brook**[14] 2456 5-11-3 114 .... TomDoyle 104+
(Nick Williams) *chsd ldr: rdn and effrt after 4 out: sn wknd: j.lft fr next: mstke last* **5/1**[3]

153F **4** *dist* **Chase The Sunset (IRE)**[49] 1801 7-11-3 110 .... TimmyMurphy —
(Miss H C Knight) *chsd ldrs tl wknd 9th: sn t.o* **9/4**[1]

F0-4 **F** **Portavo (IRE)**[28] 2144 5-11-3 92 .... JasonMaguire —
(Miss H C Knight) *in tch whn fell heavily 3rd* **16/1**

6/P- **P** **Charalambous (USA)**[576] 283 8-11-3 .... JoeTizzard —
(C L Tizzard) *wl bhd fr 7th: t.o and p.u bef 9th* **40/1**

4m 56.4s (3.60) **Going Correction** +0.30s/f (Yiel) **6** Ran SP% **111.5**
Speed ratings: **104,102,92,—,—** — CSF £9.55 TOTE £3.30: £1.90, £1.60; EX 15.50.
Owner Paul Green **Bred** Francois Cottin **Trained** Ditcheat, Somerset

FOCUS
He may not have beaten a great deal, but the 2002 Champion Hurdler Hors La Loi III showed he retains plenty of ability on his chasing debut off the back of a 978-day absence and is value for more than the official margin.

NOTEBOOK
Hors La Loi III(FR), the 2002 Champion Hurdler, had not been seen for 978 days. Switched to fences for the first time on his debut for Paul Nicholls, he was soon in a rhythm. His jumping was quite big at most of the fences, but he showed he retains plenty of ability with a comfortable success. Unfortunately he returned with quite a nasty cut on a foreleg, so plans are on hold for the time being but it was most encouraging and he deserves his chance in better company if he can get over his latest setback. *(op 2-1 tchd 5-2)*
Cossack Dancer(IRE) probably had little realistic chance of beating the winner despite that one's advancing years, and he was already looking held when making a mistake three out. Still, this was a respectable effort and time should show what the form is worth. *(op 7-2 tchd 11-4)*
Kings Brook ran quite a bit below the form he showed when second over two miles here on his previous start and has to be considered a little disappointing. *(op 9-2 tchd 11-2)*
Chase The Sunset(IRE), who would have won at Ludlow on his previous start but for falling at the last, ran no sort of race this time. On the evidence of this performance, he has to prove that fall has not left its mark. *(op 5-2 tchd 11-4)*

2733 SIS H'CAP CHASE (14 fncs) 2m 3f
3:20 (3:20) (Class 4) (0-110,110) 5-Y-0+ **£4,215** (£1,237; £618; £309)

Form RPR

PF32 **1** **Free Gift**[19] 2342 7-11-5 **110** .... DarylJacob(7) 123+
(R H Alner) *j.w: mde all: rdn appr 3 out: r.o wl* **7/4**[1]

0032 **2** *1 1/2* **Berengario (IRE)**[7] 2593 5-11-5 **106** .... TomMalone(3) 115
(S C Burrough) *hld up towards rr: hdwy fr 5th: wnt 3rd after 7th: rdn and ev ch 3 out: kpt on but a hld fr last* **20/1**

500- **3** *15* **Message Recu (FR)**[230] 4960 9-10-12 **96** .... (b) JoeTizzard 92+
(C L Tizzard) *chsd ldrs: rdn after 4 out: one pced whn lft 4th 3 out: wnt 3rd at the last* **40/1**

/P06 **4** *1* **Ingenu (FR)**[9] 2562 9-10-4 **88** .... (p) JamieGoldstein 81
(P Wegmann) *mid div: rdn after 10th: one pced fr 4 out: lft 4th last* **100/1**

4342 **5** *4* **Jupon Vert (FR)**[16] 2420 8-10-2 **93** .... JamesWhite(7) 83+
(R J Hodges) *t.k.h in tch: wnt 4th after 4 out: sn rdn: lft 3rd next: wknd after 2 out* **7/1**[3]

0/PP **6** *dist* **Lunardi (IRE)**[23] 2260 7-9-7 **84** oh14 .... MissLHorner(7) —
(D L Williams) *hld up and a in rr: t.o* **100/1**

-336 **7** *1 1/4* **Flying Fuselier**[16] 2421 6-11-7 **105** .... RichardJohnson —
(P J Hobbs) *in tch: blnd 7th: wknd after 4 out: t.o* **14/1**

P/1- **8** *5* **Regal Bandit (IRE)**[392] 2153 7-11-6 **104** .... TimmyMurphy —
(Miss H C Knight) *a in rr: t.o fr 10th* **12/1**

3550 **9** *2 1/2* **Kadam (IRE)**[21] 2296 5-11-7 **105** .... (b) MickFitzgerald —
(P F Nicholls) *chsd ldrs tl 7th: sn bhd: t.o* **8/1**

1026 **F** **Master T (USA)**[24] 2239 6-11-5 **103** .... JamieMoore —
(G L Moore) *towards rr whn fell heavily 4th* **20/1**

0-02 **P** **Flower Of Pitcur**[28] 2141 8-10-8 **92** .... JasonMaguire —
(T R George) *hld up towards rr: blnd 8th: p.u bef next* **8/1**[1]

F-05 **F** **Joe Deane (IRE)**[7] 2594 9-10-12 **101** .... (p) ChrisHonour(5) 97+
(M J Coombe) *trckd ldrs: rdn after 4 out: ev ch whn fell next* **66/1**

0P-4 **F** **Semi Precious (IRE)**[15] 2431 7-10-9 **93** .... NoelFehily —
(D P Keane) *hld up towards rr: stdy prog fr 9th: rdn after 4 out: one pced fr next: 5th whn fell last* **6/1**[2]

4m 55.4s (2.60) **Going Correction** +0.30s/f (Yiel) **13** Ran SP% **115.2**
Speed ratings: **106,105,99,98,96 —,—,—,—,— —,—,—** CSF £41.53 CT £1028.67 TOTE £2.30: £1.40, £3.30, £9.00; EX 42.60.
Owner T Chadney, D Guyer, V Howard, P Tozer **Bred** T J Whitley **Trained** Droop, Dorset

FOCUS
A pretty ordinary handicap chase but it could be rated a bit higher.

NOTEBOOK
Free Gift ◆ had been proving a little frustrating this season and did not seem to be fulfilling his potential as quickly as some people might have expected, but he had been running into form in recent efforts and stepped up on his latest second at Huntingdon to run out a decisive winner. If continuing to go the right way, he should be able to defy a rise in the weights. *(op 2-1 tchd 9-4)*
Berengario(IRE) emerges with plenty of credit in second, as the winner is by no means badly handicapped and he finished well clear of the remainder. *(op 16-1)*
Message Recu(FR), returned to fences on his debut for a new yard, made an encouraging return from a 230-day absence and should be able to build on this. *(op 33-1)*
Ingenu(FR) has not shown very much for a long time now but, with cheekpieces fitted for the first time, he ran much better than of late. It is probably worth waiting to see if he can confirm this next time before getting financially involved.
Jupon Vert(FR) had been running quite well in defeat recently, but this was a touch disappointing and he continues on a losing run. *(op 13-2)*
Joe Deane(IRE) looked to be in with every chance when falling three out and was certainly no 66/1 shot. *(op 5-1)*
Semi Precious(IRE) was well beaten when falling and has to be considered a little disappointing. *(op 5-1)*

2734 MERRY CHRISTMAS TO YOU ALL H'CAP HURDLE (10 hdls) 2m 3f 110y
3:50 (3:50) (Class 3) (0-120,120) 4-Y-0+ **£4,827** (£1,417; £708; £353)

Form RPR

221U **1** **Desert Quest (IRE)**[7] 2595 5-11-6 **114** .... (b) RichardJohnson 124+
(P F Nicholls) *hld up towards rr: hit 7th: hdwy next: chal on bit 2 out: hit last: sn narrow advantage and idled: pushed out* **8/11**[1]

0-U1 **2** *1/2* **Direct Flight (IRE)**[21] 2287 7-11-2 **110** .... BrianCrowley 117
(Noel T Chance) *hld up towards rr: hdwy after 7th: led after 3 out: jnd next: narrowly hdd sn after last: kpt on* **10/1**[3]

-0 **3** *13* **Adecco (IRE)**[14] 2459 6-10-0 **94** oh2 .... JamieMoore 88
(G L Moore) *t.k.h in midfield: hdwy after 7th: rdn after 3 out: styd on to go 3rd run-in: nt pce of ldng pair* **7/1**[2]

0400 **4** *5* **Caspian Dusk**[16] 2419 4-9-7 **97** .... (v[1]) RichardGordon(10) 87+
(W G M Turner) *chsd ldrs: rdn and ev ch after 3 out: mstke next: wknd* **80/1**

-101 **5** *hd* **Devito (FR)**[14] 2459 4-11-5 **120** .... MrDEdwards(7) 108
(G F Edwards) *hld up in tch: nt fluent 3 out: sn rdn: one pce* **20/1**

-133 **6** *6* **Dr Cerullo**[30] 2099 4-11-4 **112** .... TomDoyle 94
(C Tinkler) *chsd ldrs: rdn after 3 out: sn wknd* **16/1**

5P-P **7** *6* **Etendard Indien (FR)**[54] 1677 4-11-9 **117** .... MickFitzgerald 93
(N J Henderson) *prom: led 5th: nt fluent and reminders 7th: hdd sn after 3 out: wknd* **12/1**

34-0 **8** *shd* **Monte Cristo (FR)**[22] 109 7-11-0 **108** .... (v) NoelFehily 84
(Mrs L C Taylor) *led tl 5th: w ldr tl wknd after 3 out* **10/1**[3]

0-PP **9** *17* **Musimaro (FR)**[9] 2562 7-10-4 **103** .... (p) MarkNicolls(5) 62
(R J Price) *reminders after 5th: a towards rr* **100/1**

-404 **P** **New Currency (USA)**[150] 959 5-10-3 **97** .... (t) TimmyMurphy —
(M C Pipe) *mstkes: hld up: p.u after 5th* **12/1**

4m 46.0s **Going Correction** +0.10s/f (Yiel) **10** Ran SP% **116.8**
Speed ratings: **104,103,98,96,96 94,91,91,84,—** CSF £9.24 CT £32.71 TOTE £1.80: £1.10, £3.10, £2.50; EX 10.00 Place 6 £12.32, Place 5 £4.04.
Owner Mrs M Findlay **Bred** Ballygallon Stud **Trained** Ditcheat, Somerset

FOCUS
A reasonable enough handicap hurdle in which Desert Quest gained compensation for unseating on his previous start and is value for further.

NOTEBOOK
Desert Quest(IRE), a beaten favourite when unseating his rider a fair way out at Wincanton on his previous start, proved good enough to gain compensation, but had to work harder than he might have liked. Having travelled well, he looked set to win comfortably, but he did not find as much as had looked likely when seriously challenged and only just denied the in-form runner-up. This was, though, just his fifth-ever run over hurdles and, seemingly not badly handicapped, there should be more to come. *(op 4-5 tchd 5-6 in a place)*
Direct Flight(IRE), racing off the same mark as when winning a handicap chase at Hereford on his last start, ran a game race returned to hurdles and was just denied. He should remain competitive under both disciplines. *(op 12-1)*
Adecco(IRE) probably did well to take third considering he was pretty keen for a lot of the way and could well be placed to take advantage off his current lowly rating. *(tchd 8-1)*
Caspian Dusk, with the visor replacing cheekpieces, ran well for a long way and this has to go down as a most encouraging effort. Rated 2lb lower than when last winning, he is not one to underestimate. *(op 66-1)*
Devito(FR) appeared found out by an 11lb rise in the weights for his recent course and distance success. *(op 14-1)*
New Currency(USA) *Official explanation: jockey said gelding felt wrong behind (op 16-1)*
T/Plt: £33.70 to a £1 stake. Pool: £40,763.05. 882.30 winning tickets. T/Qpdt: £15.30 to a £1 stake. Pool: £3,351.90. 161.10 winning tickets. TM

2735 - 2741a (Foreign Racing) - See Raceform Interactive

2206 CHELTENHAM (New Course) (L-H)
Friday, December 9

OFFICIAL GOING: Good to soft
Wind: Nil

2742 DBS BUY AT TONIGHT'S BREEZE-UP SALES E B F "NATIONAL HUNT" NOVICES' HURDLE (QUALIFIER) (8 hdls) 2m 1f
12:10 (12:11) (Class 3) 4-6-Y-0
£8,417 (£2,486; £1,243; £622; £310; £155)

Form RPR

16-3 **1** **Noland**[47] 1857 4-11-0 .... ChristianWilliams 127+
(P F Nicholls) *lw: trckd ldrs in 3rd: disp 2nd fr 2 out: led wl bef last: c clr and reminder run-in: readily* **8/1**[3]

40-3 **2** *5* **Good Citizen (IRE)**[21] 2309 5-11-0 112.......... JasonMaguire 121
(T R George) *bhd: hdwy 3 out: rdn 2 out: styd on u.p to chse wnr run-in but no ch* **20/1**

1112 **3** *1 ½* **Buena Vista (IRE)**[28] 2161 4-11-10 135.......... APMcCoy 130+
(M C Pipe) *lw: led: mstke 3rd: rdn after 2 out and hdd wl bef last: sn one pce* **8/13**[1]

32- **4** *9* **De Soto**[268] 4399 4-11-0.......... TomDoyle 114+
(P R Webber) *lw: chsd ldr: hit 2 out: sn rdn: wknd bef last* **3/1**[2]

0- **5** *8* **Krismas Cracker**[251] 4697 4-11-0.......... MickFitzgerald 102
(N J Henderson) *bhd: hdwy 3 out: rdn and one pce whn mstke 2 out: sn wknd* **20/1**

6303 **6** *10* **Lago D'Oro**[12] 2526 5-10-13 94.......... RJGreene 91
(Dr P Pritchard) *a bhd: rdn and no ch fr 3 out* **150/1**

04-2 **F** **Foxtrot Yankee (IRE)**[23] 2269 6-11-0.......... GrahamLee 80
(Andrew Turnell) *j. modly in rr: hit 2nd: blnd 4th: hdwy and mstke 3 out: wknd 2 out: no ch whn fell last* **50/1**

4m 5.00s (-7.20) **Going Correction** -0.175s/f (Good) 7 Ran SP% **110.2**
Speed ratings: **109,106,105,101,97 93,**— CSF £98.68 TOTE £7.40: £2.50, £4.00; EX 71.50.
Owner J Hales **Bred** The Niarchos Family **Trained** Ditcheat, Somerset

FOCUS
A good novice hurdle but a slightly surprising result with Noland taking advantage of both Buena Vista and De Soto running below expectations. The time was fair and the form may prove reasonable.

NOTEBOOK
Noland ◆ had to be considered disappointing on his hurdling debut at Wincanton given the definite promise he showed in two runs in bumpers last season but, returning from a 47-day break, this was more like it and he ran out a thoroughly convincing winner. While both Buena Vista and De Soto were below their best, they are still two noticeable scalps and this effort marks him down as a potentially smart sort. He clearly deserves his chance in decent company this season. *(tchd 15-2)*

Good Citizen(IRE) has maybe not progressed as one might have expected from his promising debut under Rules when third in a decent race over course and distance, but this was a much better and he clearly likes Cheltenham. He never really looked like winning, but this was still encouraging and surely he can find a race or two in slightly lesser company before embarking on a chasing career.

Buena Vista(IRE) appeared to run very close to his best when second in a Grade Two here last time but, forced to give weight away all round, he was below form this time. Having been made to work to hold off the challenge of De Soto, he could not sustain his effort long enough to see off the fresh challengers and faded on the run-in. Now the better novices are beginning to emerge, he cannot really dominate as easily as he did earlier in the season. *(tchd 4-6)*

De Soto looked a most exciting prospect when second in the Champion Bumper last season, even if that race was not quite of the class of previous years but, making his hurdling debut off the back of a 268-day break, he proved most disappointing. His jumping was fine for most of the way, and he was able to stay well in touch with Buena Vista but, if anything, he was travelling too well and found little when finally asked for his effort. It may be that he was fresher than is ideal, and can surely be given another chance to fulfill his undoubted potential. *(tchd 10-3)*

Krismas Cracker, not unsupported but down the field in a Newbury bumper on his only previous start 251 days ago, had no easy task on his hurdling debut and did not run too badly in the circumstances. He should find easier opportunities and can progress. *(op 16-1)*

2743 DECEMBER NOVICES' CHASE (21 fncs) 3m 1f 110y
12:45 (12:45) (Class 2) 5-Y-0+ **£10,099** (£2,983; £1,491; £746; £372)

Form RPR

-121 **1** **Darkness**[14] 2484 6-11-8 149.......... APMcCoy 156+
(C R Egerton) *lw: hld up rr but in tch: nt fluent 5th: hit 13th: hdwy 16th: hit 4 out: chsd ldr next: slt ld 2 out: c clr last: comf* **13/8**[1]

-341 **2** *8* **Zabenz (NZ)**[10] 2564 8-11-5..........(b) RichardJohnson 143+
(P J Hobbs) *led: nt fluent 8th: hit 11th: rdn after 3 out: narrowly hdd next: outpcd last* **11/4**[2]

24-1 **3** *18* **Billyvoddan (IRE)**[20] 2344 6-11-8.......... RobertThornton 127+
(H D Daly) *lw: chsd ldrs: mstke 2nd: wnt 2nd 12th: hit 14th: blnd and lost 2nd 3 out: sn wknd* **7/2**[3]

1P-2 **4** *¾* **Back Nine (IRE)**[41] 1917 8-11-0 120.......... AndrewThornton 117+
(R H Alner) *lw: bhd: hdwy 15th: wknd 4 out: nt fluent next* **5/1**

0314 **5** *dist* **Goblet Of Fire (USA)**[14] 2484 6-11-8..........(b) ChristianWilliams 100
(P F Nicholls) *chsd ldr: hit 11th: wknd 13th: hit next: sn t.o* **20/1**

6m 32.4s (-13.40) **Going Correction** -0.175s/f (Good) 5 Ran SP% **108.4**
Speed ratings: **113,110,105,104,**— CSF £6.41 TOTE £2.20: £1.30, £1.80; EX 6.30.
Owner Lady Lloyd-Webber **Bred** Heatherwold Stud **Trained** Chaddleworth, Berks

FOCUS
Just the five runners, but Zabenz ensured this was a decent test and Darkness confimed the form of his recent Newbury success with another comfortable victory. He was value for more than the official margin and the race could rate higher.

NOTEBOOK
Darkness ◆, who thrashed Iris's Gift when upped to three miles at Newbury on his previous start, showed that was no fluke with another impressive display. Held up from the start, he jumped well in the main and, having moved into contention pretty easily, only had to be shaken up to see off the runner-up's brave effort. He is developing into a very smart sort indeed, and must be taken seriously in better company. The Royal & SunAlliance Chase will surely be his long-term target. *(tchd 2-1and 6-4 in places)*

Zabenz(NZ), formerly trained in Australia and the US, has seemingly taken a little while to acclimatise to British racing, but he bolted up in a race that ultimately took little winning at Hereford on his previous start and ran gamely in defeat in this tougher heat. *(op 4-1)*

Billyvoddan(IRE) looked potentially useful when winning on his chasing debut over two and a half miles at Huntingdon, but he failed to confirm that promise upped to his furthest trip to date, even allowing for the tougher opposition. This trip appeared to stretch his stamina, but he is better than he showed whatever the case. *(op 5-2)*

Back Nine(IRE) struggled to stay in touch when the pace was increased, which is surprising considering he was trying his furthest trip to date. It may be that he needs softer ground. *(op 11-2 tchd 9-2 and 6-1 in places)*

Goblet Of Fire(USA) did not convince with his jumping under pressure and has to prove he is up to this level over fences. *(op 16-1 tchd 14-1)*

2744 MEARS GROUP CHASE (H'CAP) (LISTED RACE) (21 fncs) 3m 1f 110y
1:20 (1:20) (Class 1) 5-Y-0+
£28,510 (£10,695; £5,355; £2,670; £1,340; £670)

Form RPR

2F-5 **1** **Royal Auclair (FR)**[20] 2337 8-11-5 155..........(t) LiamHeard[(7)] 165+
(P F Nicholls) *trckd ldrs:chal fr 10th: hit 12th: led 16th: rdn after 3 out: styd on strly run-n* **13/2**[3]

-U15 **2** *3 ½* **All In The Stars (IRE)**[13] 2491 7-9-9 131.......... DarylJacob[(7)] 139+
(D P Keane) *lw: bhd: hit 8th: pushed along fr 14th: styd on fr 4 out: chsd wnr after 2 out: kpt on but no imp run-in* **7/1**

211/ **3** *6* **Fork Lightning (IRE)**[633] 4384 9-10-10 139.......... RobertThornton 141+
(A King) *lw: chsd ldrs: hit 8th: mitake 3 out and sn chsng wnr: one pce and hit 2 out: lost 2nd sn* **8/1**

-2U0 **4** *6* **Joes Edge (IRE)**[13] 2491 8-10-8 142.......... ThomasDreaper[(5)] 136
(Ferdy Murphy) *bhd: drvn along fr 16th: styd on fr 3 out: kpt on fr next but nvr gng pce to rch ldrs* **25/1**

1130 **5** *1 ½* **Ballycassidy (IRE)**[13] 2491 9-10-13 142.......... APMcCoy 135+
(P Bowen) *chsd ldr to 10th: styd chsng ldrs: hit 15th: one pce and n.d after* **12/1**

01-0 **6** *11* **Liverpool Echo (FR)**[146] 1013 5-9-11 133.......... RichardSpate[(7)] 120+
(Mrs K Waldron) *in tch tl wknd 4 out* **25/1**

42-4 **7** *dist* **It Takes Time (IRE)**[19] 2370 11-11-9 152.......... TimmyMurphy 139
(M C Pipe) *bhd: hdwy 16th: chsd ldrs fr 4 out: wknd qckly last: eased run-in: t.o* **8/1**

/0-U **P** **Exit Swinger (FR)**[19] 2370 10-10-5 134.......... ChristianWilliams —
(P F Nicholls) *a bhd: t.o whn p.u bef 4 out* **50/1**

10-0 **U** **Liberthine (FR)**[27] 2177 6-9-13 135 ow1.......... MrSWaley-Cohen[(7)] 144+
(N J Henderson) *bhd: stdy hdwy fr 15th:chalng and gng wl whn uns rdr 3 out* **5/1**[2]

3P-5 **P** **Lord Sam (IRE)**[27] 2177 9-11-1 144.......... RichardJohnson —
(V R A Dartnall) *chsd ldrs: chal and blnd 12th: wknd qckly 15th: p.u bef next* **3/1**[1]

11/0 **P** **Lord Maizey (IRE)**[13] 2499 8-10-0 129 oh1.......... CarlLlewellyn —
(N A Twiston-Davies) *lw: led tl hdd 16th: wknd and hit 4 out: mstke next: t.o whn p.u bef 2 out* **16/1**

6m 34.1s (-11.70) **Going Correction** -0.175s/f (Good) 11 Ran SP% **112.9**
Speed ratings: **111,109,108,106,105 102,**—,—,—,— — CSF £48.78 CT £366.82 TOTE £7.70: £2.70, £2.40, £2.40; EX 49.60 Trifecta £561.00 Pool £1,185.42. 1.50 winning units.
Owner Clive D Smith **Bred** Jacky Rauch, Mme Colette Rauch & Patrick Lauer **Trained** Ditcheat, Somerset

FOCUS
A good handicap chase and a decent performance from Royal Auclair to defy top weight. The runner-up sets the standard but the form may not be the strongest for the grade.

NOTEBOOK
Royal Auclair(FR) ◆ was well beaten in the Betfair Chase at Haydock on his reappearance, but that was a tough ask and he clearly benefited a great deal from the outing. Forced to give weight away to some smart rivals, he looked to have it all to do, even taking into account his rider's 7lb claim, but he showed himself as good as ever with a most decisive success. No doubt he will once again contest many of the top chases in the coming months but, if this performance is anything to go by, he could just get a bit closer than he has done in the past. Connections will now choose between the King George and the Welsh National, while they suggested the Grand National is his long-term aim. *(op 7-1)*

All In The Stars(IRE) ◆, a fine fifth having been given plenty to do in the Hennessy on his previous start, was again dropped right out the back. Responding well to pressure, he moved into a threatening position on the home turn but could not quite reach the eventual winner and probably used more energy than was ideal to get into contention. Connections are apparently aiming him at the Scottish National, but can they resist Aintree with this horse? *(op 11-2)*

Fork Lightning(IRE), not seen since winning the National Hunt Handicap Chase at the Festival 633 days ago, made a tremendous reappearance. Always travelling well, he looked set to go very close as the race began to get serious but, although producing an effort, got a little tired and faded close home. If he can go the right way from this, he looks capable of making up for lost time. *(op 17-2 tchd 9-1)*

Joes Edge(IRE) ran much better than when tailed off in the Hennessy on his previous start and could be about to run into form. *(op 22-1)*

Ballycassidy(IRE), ran well for a long way in the Hennessy on his previous start and looked better than the bare form there. This effort confirmed that promise and, given this was just his second run back after a break, there could be even more to come. *(op 11-1)*

It Takes Time(IRE) stopped very quickly having looked as though he might pose a threat and something may have been amiss. *(op 13-2 tchd 6-1)*

Lord Sam(IRE) offered plenty of encouragement in the Paddy Power on his reappearance but, stepped back up in trip, his jumping was never that fluent and he weakened quickly after making a mistake at the 12th. Despite winning in graded company, he has never totally convinced over fences and has plenty to prove off the back of this performance. *Official explanation: jockey said gelding jumped poorly (op 11-4 tchd 5-2)*

Liberthine(FR) ◆, dropped 3lb after finishing well held in the Paddy Power on her reappearance, looked sure to go very close when unseating three out. On the evidence of this performance, she must be respected off her current mark. *(op 11-4 tchd 5-2)*

2745 SPORTING INDEX H'CAP CHASE (CROSS COUNTRY CHASE) (32 fncs) 3m 7f
1:55 (1:55) (Class 2) (0-150,150) 5-Y-0+
£15,294 (£4,517; £2,258; £1,130; £564; £283)

Form RPR

1 **Ivoire De Beaulieu (FR)**[159] 9-10-0 124 oh9.......... AlanO'Keeffe 138+
(Ferdy Murphy) *w'like: lw: bhd: stdy hdwy fr 25th: chsd ldr 2 out: chal last: sn led: drvn out* **16/1**

25-2 **2** *2 ½* **Shady Lad (IRE)**[19] 2394 8-9-11 124 oh4.......... MissNCarberry[(3)] 136
(E Bolger, Ire) *str: chsd ldrs tl led 27th: rdn 3 out: hdd run-in: kpt on same pce* **20/1**

1P **3** *1 ½* **Good Step (IRE)**[13] 2512 7-10-3 127.......... CO'Dwyer 137
(E Bolger, Ire) *bhd: hdwy 26th: drvn to chse ldrs fr 2 out: kpt on appr last but no imp run-in* **7/1**[3]

2023 **4** *10* **Koquelicot (FR)**[5] 2662 7-10-0 124 oh4.......... RichardJohnson 124
(P J Hobbs) *chsd ldrs: led 25th: hdd 27th: wknd 2 out* **14/1**

-561 **5** *1* **Inca Trail (IRE)**[22] 2299 9-10-8 139..........(b) MissCTizzard[(7)] 138
(P F Nicholls) *lw: bhd: hdwy 18th: outpcd 4 out: styd on again appr last* **7/1**[3]

-0P3 **6** *6* **Just In Debt (IRE)**[19] 2370 9-10-9 133.......... AlanDempsey 126
(M Todhunter) *in tch: chsd ldrs fr 20th: hit 28th: wknd 3 out* **10/1**

3250 **7** *4* **Wildfield Rufo (IRE)**[28] 2164 10-10-0 124 oh8.......... MarkBradburne 113
(Mrs K Walton) *prom early: bhd fr 14th: styd on again fr 2 out* **150/1**

211P **8** *½* **Catch The Perk (IRE)**[27] 2189 8-9-11 124 oh4..........(p) PeterBuchanan[(3)] 113
(Miss Lucinda V Russell) *mid-div: mod prog fr 3 out* **40/1**

-P63 **9** *2* **French Executive (IRE)**[12] 2518 10-10-4 128.......... ChristianWilliams 115
(P F Nicholls) *rr tl mod prog fr 3 out* **14/1**

5511 **10** *18* **Comanche War Paint (IRE)**[8] 2596 8-10-8 132 7ex.......... JoeTizzard 101
(P F Nicholls) *chsd ldrs to 22nd: n.d after* **11/2**[2]

10-1 **11** *5* **Spot Thedifference (IRE)**[28] 2164 12-11-12 150.......... MrJTMcNamara 121+
(E Bolger, Ire) *a in rr: mstke 24th* **5/1**[1]

24-0 **12** *14* **Star Performance (IRE)**[50] 1811 10-10-4 128..........(bt) GCotter 78
(Oliver McKiernan, Ire) *bhd whn hmpd 21st: sme hdwy 26th: sn wknd* **20/1**

50U4 **13** *11* **Happy Hussar (IRE)**[5] 2662 12-9-9 124 oh6.......... DrPPritchard[(5)] 63
(Dr P Pritchard) *a in rr* **100/1**

P-52 **14** *5* **Lord Jack (IRE)**[28] 2164 9-11-5 143.......... BrianHarding 77
(N G Richards) *chsd ldrs tl wknd 24th* **7/1**[3]

/0-5 **15** *dist* **Il De Boitron (FR)**[15] 2468 7-10-6 133..........(b) AndrewJMcNamara[(3)] —
(Thomas Gerard O'Leary, Ire) *led: sn clr: hdd 25th: sn wknd: t.o* **33/1**

 The Form Book, Raceform Ltd, Compton, RG20 6NL

P223 **F** **Oh My Lord (IRE)**[28] 2164 7-10-8 **135**.............................(t) DFO'Regan(3) —
(A J Martin, Ire) *lw: chsd ldrs: wkng whn fell 21st* **10/1**

8m 22.2s (-21.10) **Going Correction** -0.45s/f (Good) course record **16** Ran SP% **123.5**
Speed ratings: **109,108,107,105,105 103,102,102,101,97 95,92,89,88,—** — CSF £302.45 CT £2454.93 TOTE £21.00: £3.90, £4.90, £1.80, £3.30; EX 649.80 TRIFECTA Not won..

Owner Ferdy Murphy **Bred** Xavier Blois **Trained** West Witton, N Yorks

■ Stewards' Enquiry : Alan O'Keeffe caution: raised whip arm above shoulder height

FOCUS
A good race as far as these cross-country races go, and the pace was much faster than is often the case. However, the form is not easy to assess.

NOTEBOOK
Ivoire De Beaulieu(FR) ◆, a multiple winner round cross-country courses in France, proved well suited by Cheltenham's version and made a winning British debut from 9lb out of the handicap. Having travelled nicely pretty much throughout, he moved into contention going easily and found enough to win well. On this evidence, he looks like a leading contender for the handicap chase round here at the Festival.

Shady Lad(IRE) would have come on a fair bit for his recent run over two miles six and posted a fine effort in second from 4lb out of the handicap. Having sat just off the strong pace from the start, he sustained his effort all the way to the line and was just held. This was his first run on Cheltenham's cross-country course and it clearly suited well.

Good Step(IRE) was pulled up on his only previous start round this course, but this was much better and he finished a most creditable third. *(op 14-1)*

Koquelicot(FR), a beaten favourite in a conventional chase at Warwick just five days previously, did not take badly to this unique challenge and posted a very respectable effort from 4lb out of the handicap. *(op 16-1)*

Inca Trail(IRE) was 7lb higher than when winning over three miles four at Wincanton his previous start and could not quite repeat that level of form on his first run round this particular course. *(op 13-2)*

Comanche War Paint(IRE) had been in good form in conventional chases recently, but he was 5lb wrong at the weights under his penalty and was below form on his third round this course. *(op 6-1 tchd 5-1)*

Spot Thedifference(IRE) was unbeaten in four previous runs on this cross-country course, but he was faced with very stiff competition this time and, 16lb higher than when winning this last year, was forced to give weight away all round. However, even allowing for that, he was in trouble some way from the finish and posted a lacklustre effort. *(op 7-2 tchd 11-2, 6-1 in a place)*

Lord Jack(IRE) ran nowhere near the level of form he showed to be second to Spot Thedifference round here on his previous start. *(tchd 15-2)*

Il De Boitron(FR) set a very good pace. *(tchd 40-1)*

2746 CFR GROUP (ELECTRICAL SERVICES) H'CAP HURDLE (8 hdls) 2m 1f
2:30 (2:32) (Class 3) (0-135,130) 4-Y-0+

£14,592 (£4,310; £2,155; £1,078; £538; £270)

Form	Pos	Dist	Horse / details	RPR
311	**1**		**Motorway (IRE)**[12] 2533 4-10-6 **110**............................ RichardJohnson (P J Hobbs) *lw: trckd ldrs: wnt 2nd 3 out: led wl bef last: rdn and kpt on strly run-in* **2/1**[1]	124+
400-	**2**	1 ½	**Desert Air (JPN)**[266] 4438 6-11-9 **127**.........................(t) TomScudamore (M C Pipe) *lw: hld up in rr: hdwy 4th: trckd ldrs 2 out: sn rdn: kpt on run-in to take 2nd last strides but a hld by wnr* **20/1**	137
1-05	**3**	nk	**Arrayou (FR)**[33] 2079 4-11-2 **120**..(b) APMcCoy (O Sherwood) *bhd: hdwy 2 out: styd on to chse wnr and hit last: sn one pce: ct for 2nd last strides* **25/1**	130
0-21	**4**	9	**Woody Valentine (USA)**[201] 467 4-10-11 **120**................ PaulO'Neill(5) (Miss Venetia Williams) *chsd ldrs: rdn 2 out: wknd appr last* **14/1**	121
5-32	**5**	2 ½	**Dom D'Orgeval (FR)**[13] 2493 5-11-5 **123**.................. ChristianWilliams (Nick Williams) *bhd: virtually t.o appr 2 out: hdwy appr last: fin fast* **6/1**[2]	122
2340	**6**	½	**Borora**[26] 2209 6-11-7 **130**.. WilliamKennedy(5) (R Lee) *bhd: hdwy 2 out: chsd ldrs and rdn wl bef last: wknd run-in* **12/1**[3]	128
3-P1	**7**	4	**Jake Black (IRE)**[27] 2190 5-11-2 **125**......................... DougieCostello(5) (J J Quinn) *chsd ldrs: rdn and outpcd after 3 out* **16/1**	119
2241	**8**	¾	**Critical Stage (IRE)**[26] 2216 6-10-1 **110**......................... ChrisHonour(5) (J D Frost) *hit 1st: bhd: lost tch 4 out: kpt on fr 2 out but nvr in contention* **33/1**	104+
114B	**9**	2 ½	**Crathorne (IRE)**[19] 2369 5-11-0 **118**...................................... GrahamLee (M Todhunter) *chsd ldr to 3 out: wknd after 2 out* **20/1**	109
1-04	**10**	11	**Always Waining (IRE)**[12] 2519 4-11-2 **120**......................... SamStronge (P L Clinton) *in tch: chsd ldrs fr 4th: wknd and blnd 2 out* **40/1**	105+
11	**11**	11	**Nous Voila (FR)**[8] 2584 4-11-6 **124** 7ex............................ TimmyMurphy (M C Pipe) *lw: led tl hdd wl bef last: sn wknd* **2/1**[1]	109+

4m 3.00s (-9.20) **Going Correction** -0.175s/f (Good)
WFA 4 from 5yo+ 10lb **11** Ran SP% **119.9**
Speed ratings: **114,113,113,108,107 107,105,105,104,98 93** CSF £47.28 CT £804.59 TOTE £2.90: £1.50, £5.00, £4.90; EX 75.10 Trifecta £246.70 Pool £1,077.42. 3.10 winning units..

Owner D Allen **Bred** Epona Bloodstock Ltd **Trained** Withycombe, Somerset

FOCUS
A decent handicap hurdle run in a smart time in which Motorway took advantage of being able to race off a mark 9lb lower than in future to complete the hat-trick. The form looks solid.

NOTEBOOK
Motorway(IRE), 9lb lower than in future following his recent success in a conditional riders' race at Newbury on his previous start, took full advantage to complete the hat-trick. Having looked likely to win pretty well approaching the last, he jumped it big and was forced to work hard to regain his momentum. Things will be harder off higher marks, but he is progressing. *(op 15-8)*

Desert Air(JPN), still 5lb higher than when last winning over a year previously, made a fine return from a 266-day break. However, his overall record suggests one should not take too short a price about him confirming this next time. *(op 25-1)*

Arrayou(FR) has been given something of a chance by the Handicapper since his last run and ran a fine race. He is tough and could do better again.

Woody Valentine(USA), having his first run since winning an intermediate hurdle at Southwell 201 days previously, travelled well for much of the way before flattening out in the straight. He can be expected to be sharper next time. *(op 12-1)*

Dom D'Orgeval(FR), racing off a career-high mark, looked as though he might be pulled up at one stage but he finally responded to his rider's pressure to finish in very eye-catching fashion. If this performance is anything to go by, he is not one to place too much faith in. *(tchd 7-1)*

Nous Voila(FR) looked a useful prospect in winning both his previous starts over hurdles in novice company at Leicester, and was 9lb well-in under his penalty on his handicap debut, but he dropped out quickly after the second last. He is obviously better this, but while he may need softer ground, the disappointing current form of his trainer's horses may well have been the problem. *(op 5-2 tchd 11-4)*

2747 PERTEMPS H'CAP HURDLE (QUALIFIER) (12 hdls) 3m
3:05 (3:06) (Class 2) 4-Y-0+

£14,392 (£4,251; £2,125; £1,063; £530; £266)

Form	Pos	Dist	Horse / details	RPR
40-0	**1**		**Attorney General (IRE)**[48] 1828 6-10-3 **132** ow2............ JasonMaguire (J A B Old) *hld up in rr: stdy hdwy 2 out: qcknd to chal last: drvn and led run-in: hld on wl* **9/1**	138+
-1P2	**2**	½	**Fire Dragon (IRE)**[45] 1872 4-10-3 **132**......................... RichardJohnson (Jonjo O'Neill) *lw: trckd ldrs: chsd wnr after 2 out: drvn to chal last and stl upsides run-in: nt pce of wnr fnl 100yds* **8/1**[3]	137
4-42	**3**	1 ¼	**Oodachee**[27] 2175 6-10-0 **129** oh2... DJCasey (C F Swan, Ire) *in tch: hdwy and hmpd 2 out: slt ld and rdn last: hdd run-in: outpcd nr fin* **4/1**[1]	134+
P12-	**4**	4	**Glacial Sunset (IRE)**[348] 2977 10-10-0 **129** oh2..................... TomDoyle (C Tinkler) *led tl narrowly hdd last: wknd fnl 100yds* **50/1**	130+
-645	**5**	5	**Rambling Minster**[20] 2336 7-9-13 **131**........................ MissNCarberry(3) (K G Reveley) *in tch: chsd ldrs fr 3 out: rdn 2 out: wknd appr last* **6/1**[2]	126
56-4	**6**	2 ½	**Korelo (FR)**[13] 2490 7-11-12 **155**.. APMcCoy (M C Pipe) *bhd: hdwy into mid-div appr 2 out: shkn up and kpt on appr last but nvr gng pce to trble ldrs* **14/1**	148
P-P5	**7**	½	**Sh Boom**[21] 2326 7-11-1 **144**... TomSiddall (S A Brookshaw) *lw: chsd ldrs: rdn 3 out: wknd after 2 out* **33/1**	136
/2-0	**8**	¾	**True Lover (GER)**[20] 2336 8-9-11 **129** oh4................... RichardYoung(3) (J W Mullins) *mid-div: outpcd 3 out: kpt on again appr last* **25/1**	120
01-P	**9**	1 ¾	**The Bajan Bandit (IRE)**[20] 2336 10-11-2 **145**.................... TonyDobbin (L Lungo) *in tch: chsd ldrs after 3 out: sn rdn: wknd after next* **50/1**	135
2-0	**10**	hd	**Don't Be Shy (FR)**[26] 2209 4-10-11 **140**......................... TimmyMurphy (M C Pipe) *bhd: sme hdwy 2 out: nvr rchd ldrs* **11/1**	129
PP-P	**11**	10	**Stormez (FR)**[27] 2176 8-10-11 **140**..(t) RJGreene (M C Pipe) *bhd most of way* **66/1**	119
50P-	**12**	12	**Ravenswood (IRE)**[243] 4791 8-10-0 **129** oh4.............(t) TomScudamore (M C Pipe) *bhd tl hmpd 2 out* **33/1**	101+
PP-3	**13**	7	**Control Man (IRE)**[27] 2176 7-10-2 **134**.........................(v) TomMalone(3) (M C Pipe) *lw: bhd most of way* **16/1**	94
0-P0	**14**	shd	**Your A Gassman (IRE)**[23] 2265 7-10-0 **129** oh9................ BrianHarding (Ferdy Murphy) *bhd most of way* **66/1**	89
0-05	**15**	7	**Zibeline (IRE)**[15] 2456 8-10-0 **129**..................................(p) AlanDempsey (B Ellison) *bhd: sme hdwy 4 out: wknd after next* **66/1**	82
54-1	**P**		**Covent Garden**[19] 2369 7-10-3 **132**.. GrahamLee (J Howard Johnson) *in tch tl p.u bef 6th: dismntd* **6/1**[2]	—
20F-	**P**		**Hirvine (FR)**[245] 4767 7-10-6 **140**................................... TomGreenway(5) (P Bowen) *hit 2nd: chsd ldr to 4th: stl in tch whn p.u bef 3 out* **40/1**	—
1F1/	**F**		**Rosarian (IRE)**[762] 2001 8-9-7 **129** oh9............................(p) MrJJDoyle(7) (V R A Dartnall) *chsd ldr fr 4th: chal 7th: upsides and pushed along whn fell 2 out* **20/1**	128
025-	**U**		**Dancing Bay**[36] 4747 8-11-2 **145**...................................... MickFitzgerald (N J Henderson) *in tch and travelling wl whn mstke, slipped and uns rdr 4 out* **14/1**	—

5m 56.8s (-2.10) **Going Correction** -0.175s/f (Good)
WFA 4 from 5yo+ 13lb **19** Ran SP% **122.6**
Speed ratings: **96,95,95,94,92 91,91,91,90,90 87,83,80,80,78** —,—,—,— CSF £72.68 CT £339.11 TOTE £10.50: £2.50, £2.00, £2.00, £9.00; EX 104.60 Trifecta £596.10 Pool £1,595.22. 1.90 winning units..

Owner W E Sturt **Bred** Sheikh Mohammed Bin Rashid Al Maktoum **Trained** Barbury Castle, Wilts

FOCUS
The winning time was modest for the grade, and the form is only fair. The winner and third improved, but the runner-up and fourth ran pretty close to their marks.

NOTEBOOK
Attorney General(IRE), back up to three miles, stepped up on the form he showed in a good race at Chepstow on his reappearance to run out a narrow winner. This was just the second success of his career over hurdles, but on this evidence there could be more to come. *(op 14-1)*

Fire Dragon(IRE), raised 6lb for his recent second over two miles five round here, ran a fine race upped to three miles for the first time and was just denied. He did not fail through lack of stamina, but the way he travelled suggests he may just want producing later over this kind of trip. *(op 7-1)*

Oodachee, from 2lb out of the handicap, was effectively 7lb higher than when second in a similar event here on his previous start, and this was another fine effort in defeat. He would appear to have a decent race in him, but the Handicapper is unlikely to be making things any easier. *(op 11-2 tchd 7-2 in places)*

Glacial Sunset(IRE), from 2lb out of the handicap, ran a fine race from the front on his return from a 348-day absence. If he can go the right way from this, he could well be in for a good season. *(op 40-1 tchd 66-1)*

Rambling Minster ran a most creditable race, but he again just failed to see out his race. He may need to be produced quite late in his races. *(op 8-1)*

Korelo(FR) stayed on without ever posing a threat, but this was still a good effort considering he was conceding upwards of 10lb to his rivals on his return to handicap company.

Control Man(IRE), returned to hurdles, never posted a threat but did hint that he could do better.

Dancing Bay, returned to hurdling following an unsuccessful but creditable spell on the Flat, did not look out of it when unseating his rider four out. *(op 22-1 tchd 25-1)*

Covent Garden, 5lb higher than when winning gamely at Aintree on his previous start, pulled up and dismounted, suggesting something was amiss. *Official explanation: jockey said gelding was lame (op 22-1 tchd 25-1)*

Hirvine(FR) *Official explanation: jockey said gelding was lame (op 22-1 tchd 25-1)*

Rosarian(IRE), returning from a 762-day absence, ran well for a long way but may just have been beginning to struggle when he fell two out. *(op 22-1 tchd 25-1)*

2748 CHELTENHAM BUSINESS CLUB CONDITIONAL JOCKEYS' H'CAP CHASE (17 fncs) 2m 5f
3:40 (3:41) (Class 4) (0-125,125) 5-Y-0+

£8,492 (£2,508; £1,254; £627; £313; £157)

Form	Pos	Dist	Horse / details	RPR
2100	**1**		**Va Vavoom (IRE)**[13] 2492 7-10-11 **118**.......................... BernieWharfe(8) (N A Twiston-Davies) *lw: chsd ldrs tl outpcd 4 out: plenty to do whn* **mstke next: hdwy and hung lft after 2 out: mstke and slt ld last:drvn and s** **8/1**	127+
3433	**2**	2 ½	**Mark Equal**[12] 2532 9-10-12 **114**......................................(t) TomMalone(3) (M C Pipe) *bhd: hdwy 12th: chal fr 13th tl slt advantage fr 4 out: rdn and wnt lft 2 out: hdd last and sn one pce* **5/1**[2]	121+
03-P	**3**	2	**Sonevafushi (FR)**[13] 2499 7-11-9 **125**................................ PaulO'Neill(3) (Miss Venetia Williams) *lw: chsd ldrs: blnd 10th: lost position 4 out: rn again fr 2 out and fin wl but nvr a danger* **9/2**[1]	131+
2533	**4**	1 ½	**Lord Dundaniel (IRE)**[12] 2529 8-10-8 **107**......................... WilliamKennedy (B De Haan) *lw: led 2nd to 3rd: led again 7th tl narrowly hdd 4 out: styd w ldr next tl wnt lft 2 out: wknd run-in* **8/1**	109

3-62 **5** *16* **Moscow Leader (IRE)**[13] [2495] 7-10-0 **99**........................(p) PaddyAspell 85
(R C Guest) *chsd ldrs: hit 1st: 8th and 10th: rdn 11th: wknd fr next* **13/2**

-PP2 **6** *9* **The Extra Man (IRE)**[16] [2431] 11-10-6 **108**..................(b) LiamHeard(3) 88+
(A King) *led to 2nd: led and hit 3rd: hdd 7th: wknd 4 out* **11/2**[3]

60-0 **P** **Christopher**[26] [2210] 8-11-4 **120**.................................... RobertStephens(3) —
(P J Hobbs) *sn bhd: t.o whn p.u bef 4 out* **9/2**[1]

/6U2 **P** **Blitzy Boy (IRE)**[47] [1855] 11-9-11 **99** oh4........................ JamesWhite(3) —
(G T Lynch, Ire) *bhd tl blnd 4 out: t.o whn p.u bef 2 out* **25/1**

16-5 **P** **Uncle Wallace**[34] [2048] 9-10-9 **111**.............................. MarkNicolls(3) —
(P R Webber) *bhd: sme hdwy and hit 8th: sn wknd: t.o whn p.u bef 2 out* **14/1**

4023 **F** **Ask The Umpire (IRE)**[8] [2594] 10-9-9 **99** oh17............(b) JohnKington(5) —
(N E Berry) *j. slowly and bhd 6th: rdn 8th: no ch whn fell 4 out* **33/1**

5m 24.3s (-2.40) **Going Correction** -0.175s/f (Good) **10** Ran SP% **117.4**
Speed ratings: **97,96,95,94,88 85,—,—,—,—** CSF £49.10 CT £205.14 TOTE £9.30: £2.90, £1.90, £2.10; EX 57.70 Trifecta £283.20 Pool £837.72. 2.10 winning units. Place 6 £976.86, Place 5 £73.13.
Owner H R Mould **Bred** Owen Dermody **Trained** Naunton, Gloucs

FOCUS
A fair handicap chase for conditional jockeys, run at a reasonable pace. However, the form is ordinary for the track

NOTEBOOK
Va Vavoom(IRE) had struggled in both his starts since winning at Chepstow off a 10lb lower mark earlier in the season, and it looked as though he would again finish up well beaten when losing touch as the race got serious, but he finally got going late on and, despite not jumping that well, got up close home. It remains to be seen what sort of performance he will produce next time, but he would avoid a penalty if turned out before he is reassessed. *(op 15-2)*
Mark Equal has not always found that much under pressure but, to be fair, he saw off his main challenger in Lord Dundaniel readily enough, and had little chance of containing the eventual winner's late burst. *(op 11-2 tchd 6-1)*
Sonevafushi(FR), pulled up in a much better race at Newcastle on his reappearance, ran better this time but was held from some way out. Having travelled quite well, he lost his chance when getting outpaced at a crucial stage, and it was all over by the time he got going again. He could well come on again for this. *(op 7-1)*
Lord Dundaniel(IRE) was given every chance but did not quite see out his race. The ability is there; he is just finishing his races a touch weakly and may need holding up. *(op 10-1 tchd 11-1)*
Moscow Leader(IRE) failed to build on the promise of his recent Newcastle second. *(op 6-1 tchd 7-1)*
The Extra Man(IRE) looked as though he was right back in form when second at Chepstow on his previous start, so this has to be considered a little disappointing. *(tchd 13-2)*
Christopher, well beaten on his reappearance, again offered little. *Official explanation: jockey said gelding jumped poorly and never travelled (op 4-1 tchd 7-2)*
T/Jkpt: Not won. T/Plt: £1,739.20 to a £1 stake. Pool: £94,346.85. 39.60 winning tickets. T/Qpdt: £178.30 to a £1 stake. Pool: £13,904.10. 57.70 winning tickets. ST

[2515] DONCASTER (L-H)
Friday, December 9

OFFICIAL GOING: Good (good to soft in places)
Racing went ahead after an inspection due to fog, which steadily cleared during the afternoon. The first open ditch was omitted on all circuits of all chases.
Wind: Nil

2749 INTERCASINO.CO.UK NOVICES' HURDLE (DIV I) (10 hdls) 2m 3f 110y
12:00 (12:01) (Class 4) 4-Y-O+ **£3,822** (£1,122; £561; £280)

Form RPR

2 **1** **Predator (GER)**[176] [764] 4-10-12 .... NoelFehily 102+
(Jonjo O'Neill) *chsd clr ldr: hdwy to ld appr 3 out: rdn last: kpt on wl* **13/8**[2]

4-1 **2** *2* **Menchikov (FR)**[29] [2142] 5-11-5 .... AndrewTinkler 106+
(N J Henderson) *trckd ldrs: hdwy 3 out and sn chsng wnr: rdn appr last: kpt on* **1/1**[1]

F-00 **3** *6* **Franco (IRE)**[12] [2527] 7-10-5 95.. MrRJBarrett(7) 92
(Mrs A E Brooks) *trckd ldrs: hdwy 3 out: rdn along and one pce appr last* **33/1**

0-0P **4** *3/4* **Pearly Star**[10] [2559] 4-10-5 .... MrGTumelty(7) 91
(A King) *trckd ldrs: hdwy appr 3 out: rdn along and one pce appr last* **50/1**

655 **5** *1/2* **Sgt Pepper (IRE)**[29] [2148] 4-10-12 .... LeightonAspell 91
(O Sherwood) *hld up in rr: hdwy 4 out: chsd ldrs next: rdn and no imp appr last* **7/1**[3]

00 **6** *18* **Compton Dragon (USA)**[16] [2444] 6-10-12 .... KennyJohnson 73
(R Johnson) *hld up in rr: hdwy and wd st: sn rdn along and nvr nr ldrs* **66/1**

0P-0 **7** *5* **Muraqeb**[205] [343] 5-10-12 75.. JodieMogford 68
(Mrs Barbara Waring) *chsd ldrs: rdn along appr 3 out: grad wknd* **80/1**

00 **8** *shd* **Theatre Belle**[12] [2515] 4-10-5 .... WarrenMarston 61
(Ms Deborah J Evans) *plld hrd: led 1st and sn clr: hdd & wknd appr 3 out* **80/1**

60 **9** *3* **Mr Albanello (ARG)**[40] [1937] 6-10-5 .... PatrickMcDonald(7) 65
(Ferdy Murphy) *a rr* **100/1**

000- **10** *8* **Nicozetto (FR)**[175] [3466] 5-10-12 .... WilsonRenwick 57
(N Wilson) *midfield: hdwy and in tch 1/2-way: rdn along and wknd bef 3 out* **100/1**

03-0 **11** *dist* **Dormy Two (IRE)**[12] [2515] 5-10-5 .... JimmyMcCarthy —
(P T Midgley) *in tch: pushed along 1/2-way: wknd wl bef 3 out* **50/1**

-0 **12** *dist* **Carpe Momentum (USA)**[16] [2444] 6-10-9 ....(t) LarryMcGrath(3) —
(R C Guest) *a bhd* **200/1**

0 **P** **Makin Air**[16] [2444] 4-10-12 .... BarryFenton —
(J Howard Johnson) *a bhd: p.u bef last* **150/1**

4m 51.4s (-2.20) **Going Correction** -0.20s/f (Good)
WFA 4 from 5yo+ 10lb **13** Ran SP% **114.6**
Speed ratings: **96,95,92,92,92 85,83,83,81,78 —,—,—** CSF £3.44 TOTE £2.70: £1.30, £1.20, £3.50; EX 3.10.
Owner Glencoe Plant Services Ltd **Bred** D Joswich **Trained** Cheltenham, Gloucs

FOCUS
They bet 33/1 bar three in this fair novices' event, which has been rated through the second. Visibility was poor because of the lingering fog and the race was run at a steady pace.

NOTEBOOK
Predator(GER), Listed placed on the Flat in Germany, was just beaten by subsequent scorer Whispered Promises on his debut over hurdles back in June. Having his first run since, he showed ahead at the first flight in the straight and kept up the gallop to score in decent style. *(op 7-4 tchd 6-4 and 15-8 in places)*
Menchikov(FR), whose Ludlow win has not worked out, was stepping up in trip. He travelled well enough but, having gone after the winner on the entrance to the home straight, he could never get to him. *(op 11-10 tchd 5-4 in places)*
Franco(IRE), who ran out on his recent return to hurdles, adopted more patient tactics than usual. He was in third place turning into the home straight and was still in that position when the runners emerged from the fog approaching the final flight. A decent pointer, he is more effective over further.
Pearly Star showed more than he had on his hurdling debut and could be capable of a bit more improvement over further.
Sgt Pepper(IRE), who fell foul of the Stewards last time, was again held up. He could never get to the leaders but was keeping on at the end over this longer trip. *(op 6-1)*
Nicozetto(FR) *Official explanation: jockey said gelding hung left straight*

2750 INTERCASINO.CO.UK CONDITIONAL JOCKEYS' NOVICES' H'CAP HURDLE (8 hdls) 2m 110y
12:30 (12:31) (Class 4) (0-100,98)
3-Y-O+ **£3,614** (£1,061; £530; £264)

Form RPR

0-61 **1** **Caesarean Hunter (USA)**[7] [2605] 6-10-7 **87** 7ex........... SeanQuinlan(8) 98+
(R T Phillips) *hld up in rr: gd hdwy and wd st: chsd ldrs 2 out: rdn to chal last: led flat: drvn out* **6/1**[2]

0-51 **2** *2* **North Lodge (GER)**[10] [2563] 5-11-6 **95** 7ex.................... GinoCarenza(3) 103+
(A King) *trckd ldrs: hdwy to ld after 2 out: sn rdn: drvn and hdd flat: no ex towards fin* **7/2**[1]

22/2 **3** *3* **Rebel Raider (IRE)**[24] [2261] 6-11-4 **98**........................ TomMessenger(8) 103
(B N Pollock) *led: rdn along 3 out: hdd after next: drvn and one pce last* **9/1**

36-P **4** *3/4* **Colophony (USA)**[215] [238] 5-10-8 **85**...................... PatrickMcDonald(5) 89
(K A Morgan) *hld up towards rr: hdwy after 4 out: rdn to chse ldrs 2 out: kpt on same pce last* **50/1**

30-3 **5** *2 1/2* **Ishka Baha (IRE)**[25] [2244] 6-10-7 **87**............................ WillieMcCarthy(8) 89
(T R George) *midfield: hdwy and in tch 4 out: chsd ldrs next: rdn and hit last: kpt on u.p flat* **7/1**[3]

U002 **6** *1 3/4* **Bestam**[8] [2585] 6-10-11 **86**.. ShaneWalsh(3) 86
(Mrs A V Roberts) *hld up in rr: rapid hdwy and wd st: chsd ldrs 3 out: rdn next and sn one pce* **10/1**

1500 **7** *hd* **Uncle John**[12] [2517] 4-10-6 **83**....................................(v) PhilKinsella(5) 83
(M E Sowersby) *hld up: hdwy 4 out: in tch next: sn rdn and kpt on same pce fr 2 out* **33/1**

-0U5 **8** *4* **Pauls Plain**[38] [1975] 4-11-4 **90**.. OwynNelmes 86
(P W Hiatt) *in tch: rdn along appr 3 out: outpcd fr next* **40/1**

000P **9** *5* **Iloveturtle (IRE)**[12] [2517] 5-10-11 **90**........................(t) ThomasBurrows(7) 81
(M C Chapman) *prom: hit 4th: rdn along appr 3 out and grad wknd* **100/1**

603 **10** *2* **Miss Pross**[12] [2525] 5-11-9 **95**... KeithMercer 84
(T D Walford) *trckd ldrs: rdn 3 out: wknd bef next* **10/1**

42U **11** *6* **Step Perfect (USA)**[16] [2444] 4-11-9 **95**................................ GaryBerridge 78
(G M Moore) *prom: effrt and cl up 3 out: sn rdn and wknd* **40/1**

2-04 **12** *4* **Barranco (IRE)**[11] [2552] 4-10-9 **87**............................. EamonDehdashti(6) 66
(G L Moore) *bhd fr 1/2-way* **33/1**

6P-3 **13** *3* **Indian Solitaire (IRE)**[22] [2285] 6-11-4 **90**.................................(p) TJPhelan 66
(B P J Baugh) *midfield: pushed along 4 out: outpcd bef next* **33/1**

3B0U **14** *1/2* **Hugs Destiny (IRE)**[3] [2693] 4-10-12 **90**........................ BenOrde-Powlett(6) 65
(M A Barnes) *towards rr: mstke 2nd: rdn along 4th and sn bhd* **22/1**

464- **15** *2 1/2* **Northern Shadows**[256] [4613] 6-10-10 **90**...................... JamesReveley(8) 63
(K G Reveley) *a rr* **28/1**

3-64 **16** *15* **Schinken Otto (IRE)**[181] [716] 4-10-8 **80**............................ PaddyMerrigan 38
(J M Jefferson) *plld hrd in midfield: sme hdwy after 4 out: rdn next and sn wknd* **11/1**

-003 **17** *17* **Danebank (IRE)**[17] [2419] 5-11-12 **98**................................(p) SamCurling 39
(J Mackie) *prom: rdn along after 4 out: wknd after next* **9/1**

4m 3.00s (-8.40) **Going Correction** -0.20s/f (Good)
WFA 4 from 5yo+ 10lb **17** Ran SP% **120.0**
Speed ratings: **111,110,108,108,107 106,106,104,101,101 98,96,94,94,93 86,78** CSF £24.61 CT £192.91 TOTE £7.70: £2.40, £2.10, £1.70, £5.50; EX 14.00.
Owner A A Wickham **Bred** Lee R Oakford **Trained** Adlestrop, Gloucs
■ Stewards' Enquiry : Sean Quinlan caution: used whip with excessive frequency

FOCUS
A decent time for the class and the fastest of the three hurdle races run over this trip at the meeting. The first two were well in and the race has been rated through the winner to the level of his Exeter win. The form looks pretty solid.

NOTEBOOK
Caesarean Hunter(USA) was officially 8lb well in under the penalty he acquired at Exeter as he was put up 15lb for that win. Back down in trip, he was held up off the pace before joining issue and got on top after the last, appearing to idle a little once in front. He will be up against it from his new mark but there could be a bit more to come. *(op 11-2)*
North Lodge(GER), officially 3lb well in, showed ahead going to the last but was run out of it after a good tussle. He lost little in defeat. *(op 10-3 tchd 3-1)*
Rebel Raider(IRE), raised 5lb after finishing second at Fakenham, ran a decent race from the front but was held by two well-treated rivals. His turn should come. *(op 10-1)*
Colophony(USA), without the tongue tie on this first run for seven months, made a satisfactory return to action.
Ishka Baha(IRE), dropped in trip, travelled well but did not appear to find much when brought under pressure. *(op 9-1 tchd 13-2)*
Bestam briefly looked a threat at the third last but could not sustain the effort. He is due to race off a 5lb higher mark now. *(op 14-1)*

2751 INTERCASINO.CO.UK MAIDEN CHASE (11 fncs 1 omitted) 2m 110y
1:00 (1:00) (Class 3) 4-Y-O+ **£5,517** (£1,619; £607; £607)

Form RPR

20-5 **1** **Amarula Ridge (IRE)**[25] [2249] 4-10-8 115................................ NoelFehily 102+
(P J Hobbs) *hld up in tch: hdwy 5 out: qcknd to ld after 3 out: clr whn mstke last: sn rdn and kpt on* **9/4**[2]

P004 **2** *1 3/4* **Dictator (IRE)**[15] [2460] 4-10-8 ....(t) JohnMcNamara 99+
(D R Gandolfo) *in tch: hit 5th: pushed along and outpcd 4 out: rdn next: styd on wl flat: nrst fin* **33/1**

000F **3** *1/2* **Moorlaw (IRE)**[25] [2246] 4-10-3 107.................................. StephenCraine(5) 97+
(D McCain) *cl up: rdn along 3 out: drvn next and kpt on same pce flat* **14/1**

0-55 **3** *dht* **Ground Breaker**[152] [942] 5-11-2 ....(t) MrTGreenall(3) 107
(M W Easterby) *hld up in tch: hdwy 1/2-way: cl up 5 out: rdn along 3 out: kpt on same pce fr next* **14/1**

00U- **5** *25* **Bel Ombre (FR)**[300] [3805] 5-11-5 96.................................. LeightonAspell 84+
(O Sherwood) *chsd ldrs: rdn along 5 out: lost pl next and bhd fr 3 out* **25/1**

4-04 **6** *7* **Banchory Two (IRE)**[12] [2516] 5-11-5 113......................(b[1]) SamThomas 84+
(P F Nicholls) *prom: mstke 4th: pushed along 5 out: rdn and wkng whn hmpd 3 out: bhd after* **5/1**[3]

5-P **7** *1 1/4* **Perfect Punch**[17] [2415] 6-11-5 .... JimCrowley 74
(K G Reveley) *hld up in rr: mstke 6th: sn pushed along and bhd fr 4 out* **20/1**

5- **F** **Liberia (FR)**[344] 3105 6-11-5 .... AndrewTinkler —
(N J Henderson) *led: hit 3rd: pushed along and hit 5th: rdn 4 out: length up whn fell next* **13/8**[1]

4m 5.90s (-3.10) **Going Correction** 0.0s/f (Good)
WFA 4 from 5yo+ 10lb **8** Ran SP% **110.4**
Speed ratings: **107,106,105,105,94 90,90,—** CSF £63.63 TOTE £3.10: £1.60, £3.60; EX 94.00 TRIFECTA Pl: Groundbreaker 1.40, Moorlaw 1.20.
Owner John P McManus **Bred** S Coughlan **Trained** Withycombe, Somerset

FOCUS
Four-year-olds dominated the finish in a race that should throw up a few winners, with the first two rated better than the bare result. The open ditch in the back straight was omitted.

NOTEBOOK
Amarula Ridge(IRE), a useful maiden over hurdles, made a winning chase bow. He was in command when making an error at the last, when despite clouting the fence and stumbling on landing he did not lose too much momentum. Although he is capable of rating higher he may not be easy to place for a follow up. *(op 5-2)*
Dictator(IRE), on his chasing debut, was only fourth over the last fence but he finished in good style. A step up in trip may suit him.
Moorlaw(IRE) ran a fair race and was keeping on at the end. He would have more chance in novices' handicaps. *(op 16-1 tchd 12-1)*
Ground Breaker, equipped with a tongue tie for this switch to chasing, ran an encouraging race but after taking the last in second place he had to settle for a share of third place. *(op 16-1 tchd 12-1)*
Liberia(FR) was making his chasing debut on his return from nearly a year off. Bowling along in front, he was less than fluent at several fences and was under pressure when coming down at the third last. He should make the grade if he learns from this experience. *(op 6-4 tchd 7-4)*

2752 INTERCASINO.CO.UK (S) HURDLE (8 hdls) 2m 110y
1:35 (1:35) (Class 5) 3-4-Y-0 **£2,891** (£842; £421)

Form RPR
3P62 **1** **Dennick**[13] 2494 3-10-2 .... (t) PaddyMerrigan[(5)] 95+
(P C Haslam) *nt fluent: cl up tl led 3rd: clr whn mstke 5th: hit last: v easily* **2/1**[1]
FP0 **2** *17* **Another Misk**[8] 2587 3-10-4 .... FergusKing[(3)] 70
(M E Sowersby) *hld up and bhd: hdwy 4 out: rdn to chse ldrs next: styd on u.p appr last: no ch w wnr* **150/1**
5 **3** *1* **Grandma's Girl**[14] 2477 3-9-11 .... OwynNelmes[(3)] 64+
(Robert Gray) *hld up in midfield: stdy hdwy 4 out: chsd ldrs and hit next: sn rdn and kpt on same pce: hit last* **8/1**
05 **4** *1 ¾* **Nepal (IRE)**[8] 2587 3-10-0 .... DaveCrosse 61+
(M Mullineaux) *in tch: hdwy to chse ldrs 1/2-way: rdn along bef 3 out and sn one pce* **16/1**
60 **5** *3* **Isitloveyourafter (IRE)**[13] 2501 3-10-0 .... JamieMoore 59+
(G L Moore) *hld up: hit 1st: hit 4th: stdy hdwy 4 out: rdn to chse ldrs next: sn drvn and one pce* **16/1**
005P **6** *2 ½* **Bold Pursuit (IRE)**[16] 2442 3-10-7 90.......... KeithMercer 62
(S B Clark) *rdn along and bhd 1/2-way: hdwy appr 3 out: sn drvn and kpt on: nvr rch ldrs* **7/1**[3]
2P06 **7** *½* **The Wife's Sister**[16] 2428 4-10-9 75.......... (b[1]) StephenCraine[(5)] 68
(D McCain) *chsd ldrs: rdn along after 4 out and grad wknd fr next* **25/1**
0 **8** *9* **Penel (IRE)**[16] 2444 4-11-7 .... KennyJohnson 66
(P T Midgley) *in tch: hdwy to chse ldrs 1/2-way: rdn along after 4 out and grad wknd* **16/1**
000 **9** *1 ¼* **Shinko Femme (IRE)**[12] 2515 4-11-0 .... (t) FinbarKeniry 58
(M E Sowersby) *hld up in tch: hdwy to chse wnr 4 out: rdn along and wknd next* **33/1**
P20 **10** *1 ½* **Crimson Bow (GER)**[16] 2442 3-9-11 .... (b) LeeVickers[(3)] 42
(J G Given) *led to 3rd: mstke next: rdn along 4 out and wknd appr next* **13/2**[2]
00 **11** *18* **Look At The Stars (IRE)**[20] 1802 3-10-7 .... (p) PaulMoloney 31
(R Hollinshead) *bhd fr 1/2-way* **33/1**
P **12** *2 ½* **Harrys House**[9] 2569 3-10-7 .... DavidO'Meara 29
(J J Quinn) *a rr: bhd fr 1/2-way* **28/1**
13 *19* **Alcott (FR)**[17] 3-10-7 .... (t) LeightonAspell —
(J Jay) *bhd fr 1/2-way* **7/1**[3]
14 *dist* **Lady Predominant**[55] 4-10-9 .... DeclanMcGann[(5)] —
(Robert Gray) *a rr: wl bhd fr 1/2-way* **40/1**
440 **15** *dist* **Redditzio**[31] 2112 4-11-0 .... NeilMulholland —
(C W Thornton) *chsd ldrs: hdwy to chse wnr whn blnd 4 out and wknd qckly: sn wl bhd* **50/1**

4m 6.90s (-4.50) **Going Correction** -0.20s/f (Good)
WFA 3 from 4yo 13lb **15** Ran SP% **118.7**
Speed ratings: **102,94,93,92,91 90,89,85,85,84 75,74,65,—,—** CSF £481.36 TOTE £2.70: £1.90, £23.70, £1.60; EX 389.50.The winner was bought in for 12,000gns.
Owner D Browne **Bred** Barton Stud **Trained** Middleham, N Yorks

FOCUS
A weak seller but the winner, who was value for 25l, looks decent for this level with the third setting the standard.

NOTEBOOK
Dennick consented to settle after the first couple of flights and went on to prove far too good for this field. Bought in for 12,000gns, he is better than a plater but his hurdling is not great and might find him out in better company. *(tchd 15-8)*
Another Misk had shown very little previously over hurdles and this was more encouraging, although the favourite was in a different league.
Grandma's Girl, down in the bottom grade for this second run over hurdles, stayed on without ever posing a threat. *(op 7-1)*
Nepal(IRE), dropped into a seller for this third run over hurdles, could never land a blow. *(op 14-1)*
Isitloveyourafter(IRE) looks a very limited performer but is now eligible for handicaps.

2753 INTERCASINO.CO.UK JUVENILE NOVICES' HURDLE (8 hdls) 2m 110y
2:05 (2:05) (Class 3) 3-Y-0 **£5,347** (£1,570; £785; £392)

Form RPR
1 **Shiny Thing (USA)**[88] 3-10-5 .... WarrenMarston 94
(A King) *trckd ldrs: mstke 4th: hdwy 4 out: cl up next: swtchd rt and rdn to chal last: sn led: drvn and jst hld on* **7/1**[3]
1 **2** *shd* **Tritonville Lodge (IRE)**[23] 2274 3-11-4 .... BarryFenton 107
(Miss E C Lavelle) *racd wd: a.p: cl up 4 out: rdn next: led after 2 out: sn drvn and hdd after last: rallied wl flat: jst hld* **1/1**[1]
0 **3** *4* **Darwaz (IRE)**[5] 2661 3-10-12 .... LeightonAspell 98+
(D R Gandolfo) *chsd ldrs: hit 2nd: hdwy 4 out: led next: rdn and hdd after next: drvn and one pce last* **33/1**
4 *2* **Whistle Blowing (IRE)**[94] 3-10-7 .... StephenCraine[(5)] 95
(D McCain) *in tch: hdwy to chse ldrs 4 out: rdn after next and ev ch tl drvn and wknd appr last* **66/1**
0P **5** *23* **Double Ells**[16] 2442 3-10-5 .... DavidO'Meara 65
(J M Jefferson) *bhd tl styd on fr 3 out: nvr a factor* **100/1**
6 *nk* **Fixateur**[102] 3-10-12 .... NoelFehily 72
(C C Bealby) *led: rdn along 4 out: hdd & wknd bef next* **3/1**[2]
04 **7** *1 ½* **Calfraz**[13] 2494 3-10-12 .... NeilMulholland 70
(M D Hammond) *towards rr: hdwy 4 out: rdn along bef next and nvr rch ldrs* **40/1**
5 **8** *5* **Sandysnowing (FR)**[12] 2521 3-10-7 .... BrianHughes[(5)] 65
(J Howard Johnson) *chsd ldrs: rdn along after 4 out and grad wknd* **25/1**
9 *6* **Turtle Bay**[121] 3-10-5 .... KeithMercer 52
(B Storey) *hld up: a rr* **33/1**
P6 **10** *3* **With Honours**[13] 2494 3-10-5 .... PadgeWhelan 49
(T J Fitzgerald) *hit 2nd: a towards rr* **200/1**
0P **11** *1 ¼* **Asteem**[9] 2569 3-10-9 .... FergusKing[(3)] 55
(M E Sowersby) *bhd fr 1/2-way* **200/1**
25 **12** *14* **Jackadandy (USA)**[68] 1601 3-10-7 .... MichaelMcAlister[(5)] 41
(B Storey) *chsd ldrs: rdn along appr 4 out: sn wknd* **11/1**
13 *dist* **Belton**[65] 3-10-9 .... TJPhelan[(3)] —
(Ronald Thompson) *a bhd* **80/1**
FP0 **14** *½* **Champagne Rossini (IRE)**[24] 2258 3-10-12 .... KennyJohnson —
(M C Chapman) *plld hrd: hld up: a bhd* **200/1**

4m 5.80s (-5.60) **Going Correction** -0.20s/f (Good) **14** Ran SP% **113.2**
Speed ratings: **105,104,103,102,91 91,90,88,85,83 83,76,—,—** CSF £13.56 TOTE £7.70: £2.10, £1.10, £6.10; EX 16.70.
Owner H F Morris **Bred** W D Stiff And Gainesway Management Corp **Trained** Barbury Castle, Wilts

FOCUS
A fine tussle between the first two in what was a fair juvenile event. The runner-up ran to his mark but the proximity of the fourth is a worry.

NOTEBOOK
Shiny Thing(USA), a ten-furlong winner on the Flat for this yard, made a winning debut over hurdles. After being switched to the outside rail going to the last, she battled on willingly to gain the verdict. She could struggle under a penalty but her toughness should stand her in good stead. *(op 13-2 tchd 15-2 in places)*
Tritonville Lodge(IRE), whose Wincanton win has been been boosted by the placed horses, had every chance in a hard-fought duel but the filly, who was receiving 13lb, proved just the stronger. *(op 10-11 tchd 11-10 in places)*
Darwaz(IRE), unplaced in two maidens on the Flat in Ireland for John Oxx, showed little on his recent hurdles debut and this was much better, although he could not go with the first two from the final flight. *(op 40-1)*
Whistle Blowing(IRE) was sold out of Michael Bell's yard after showing little in three runs on the Flat. He came under pressure towards the end of the back straight and eventually dropped away going to the final flight.
Double Ells probably achieved little in staying on for a remote fifth, but is at least now eligible for handicaps.
Fixateur, a four-times winner at up to a mile and a half on the Flat in France for Freddie Head, was sold for 130,000 euros in October. He ended up well beaten on this hurdles debut after making the running, but is a dual winner on Polytrack so a switch to the sand could be on the cards. *(op 7-2 tchd 4-1 in places)*
Sandysnowing(FR) *(op 33-1)*

2754 INTERCASINO.CO.UK H'CAP CHASE (11 fncs 1 omitted) 2m 110y
2:40 (2:40) (Class 3) (0-115,115) 5-Y-0+ **£6,798** (£1,995; £997; £498)

Form RPR
60-1 **1** **Lorient Express (FR)**[25] 2239 6-11-0 103.......... SamThomas 115+
(Miss Venetia Williams) *trckd ldrs: hit 6th: swtchd outside and gd hdwy to ld 3 out: clr last: comf* **2/1**[1]
1353 **2** *1 ¾* **Pure Brief (IRE)**[9] 2570 8-10-0 89.......... (p) PaulMoloney 95+
(J Mackie) *trckd ldng pair: effrt 5 out: rdn along and j.lft 3 out: drvn to chse wnr 2 out: kpt on u.p flat* **9/2**[2]
2-F3 **3** *½* **Lewis Island (IRE)**[19] 2377 6-11-12 115.......... JamieMoore 120+
(G L Moore) *keen: hld up in rr: hdwy 5 out: rdn to chse ldng pair 2 out: kpt on flat* **12/1**
-P5P **4** *10* **Jodante (IRE)**[209] 354 8-10-5 97.......... (p) LarryMcGrath[(3)] 93+
(R C Guest) *plld hrd: trckd ldrs: hdwy and cl up 6 out: rdn along 3 out and grad wknd* **15/2**
534 **5** *2* **Bob's Buster**[28] 2172 9-10-3 92.......... (tp) KennyJohnson 87+
(R Johnson) *hld up in tch: hdwy 1/2-way: led 4 out: hdd and rdn next: sn wknd* **5/1**[3]
0-53 **6** *4* **Argento**[16] 2443 8-11-10 113.......... FinbarKeniry 102
(G M Moore) *cl up: led 5th: rdn along and hdd 4 out: sn wknd* **5/1**[3]
633P **7** *27* **Log On Intersky (IRE)**[8] 2588 9-11-10 113.......... JosephByrne 75
(J R Cornwall) *led to 5th: lost pl next and bhd fr 5 out* **16/1**

4m 7.50s (-1.50) **Going Correction** 0.0s/f (Good) **7** Ran SP% **110.2**
Speed ratings: **103,102,101,97,96 94,81** CSF £10.84 TOTE £2.30: £1.80, £2.50; EX 8.70.
Owner Let's Live Racing **Bred** D Laupretre **Trained** Kings Caple, H'fords
■ Stewards' Enquiry : Jamie Moore 10-day ban (reduced from 20 days on appeal): made insufficient effort (Dec 29-Jan 7)

FOCUS
A steadily-run handicap in which the winner was value for more than the official margin. The runner-up ran to form and the third improved considerably on recent efforts.

NOTEBOOK
Lorient Express(FR) ◆, raised 7lb after Folkestone, had little problem following up. He was a bit untidy over the sixth last and again at the next, but after easing to the front three from home he scored with the minimum of fuss. He could go in again. *(op 13-8 tchd 9-4 in places)*
Pure Brief(IRE), whose yard sent out the winner of this a year ago, briefly lost his pitch at the end of the back straight but rallied once in line for home. Keeping on to secure second on the run-in, he was flattered to have been beaten less than two lengths. *(op 11-2)*
Lewis Island(IRE), held up in last place in this steadily-run race, was still pulling for his head at the sixth last, and only began to close in the straight, still apparently going well. Disputing second place with two to jump, his rider made what appeared to be only a token effort from that point as the winner pulled clear, and he was run out of second on the run-in. The Stewards deemed him a *non-trier and imposed stiff penalties, but connections have lodged an appeal.Official explanation: 40-day ban: (Dec 29-Feb 6)*
Jodante(IRE), who has left Peter Beaumont's yard since his last appearance in May, should come on for this return to action. *(op 10-1)*
Bob's Buster, winner of this event two years ago and third last year, was equipped with a tongue tie for the first time to accompany the cheekpieces. He is edging down the weights but is without a win for nearly two years. *(op 11-2)*
Argento, without a victory for two years but just a pound above his last winning mark, set only a moderate pace and had no answers once headed. *(tchd 11-2)*

2755 INTERCASINO.CO.UK NOVICES' HURDLE (DIV II) (10 hdls) 2m 3f 110y
3:15 (3:16) (Class 4) 4-Y-0+ **£3,822** (£1,122; £561; £280)

Form RPR
0-12 **1** **L'Antartique (FR)**[16] 2444 5-11-5 .... KeithMercer 117+
(Ferdy Murphy) *stdd s: sn cl up: led 4th: clr fr 4 out: v easily* **2/1**[2]

2 15 **Calin Royal (FR)** 4-10-12 .... BarryFenton 88+
(J Howard Johnson) *trckd ldrs: pushed along and outpcd 4 out: kpt on fr next: no ch w wnr* **11/1**
0-42 **3** 2 **Jimmy Bedney (IRE)**[22] 2288 4-10-12 .... JamieMoore 85
(M G Rimell) *led to 4th: rdn along 4 out: kpt on same pce u.p fr next* **25/1**
65-6 **4** 1 1/2 **Ballyhale (IRE)**[9] 2571 7-10-12 .... BruceGibson 83
(P D Niven) *midfield: rdn along bef 4 out: plugged on fr next* **100/1**
3 **5** 3/4 **Odiham**[13] 2487 4-10-12 .... JimCrowley 82
(H Morrison) *trckd ldrs: hit 4th: mstke 5th: sn rdn along and wknd fr 4 out* **13/8**[1]
10-3 **6** 3 **The Duke's Speech (IRE)**[16] 2444 4-10-12 .... RussGarritty 81+
(T P Tate) *trckd ldrs: effrt to chse wnr 4 out: rdn next and sn wknd* **7/2**[3]
1-00 **7** 1/2 **Hi Humpfree**[22] 2295 5-10-7 .... PaddyMerrigan(5) 79
(Mrs H Dalton) *a rr* **50/1**
06-0 **8** 1/2 **Ballistigo (IRE)**[22] 2301 6-10-12 .... JimmyMcCarthy 78
(A King) *midfield: rdn along and bhd fr 1/2-way* **50/1**
25/ **9** 29 **Reminiscent (IRE)**[11] 4232 6-10-12 .... JodieMogford 49
(B P J Baugh) *bhd fr 1/2-way* **100/1**
4 **P** **Top Brass (IRE)**[30] 2131 4-10-12 .... AndrewTinkler —
(K G Reveley) *hld up in rr: mstke 4th: bhd fr 1/2-way: p.u bef last* **33/1**
0-00 **P** **Bob's Temptation**[23] 2269 6-10-12 .... (t) WarrenMarston —
(A J Wilson) *in tch: rdn alonga nd wknd 5th: bhd whn p.u bef 3 out* **200/1**
P **Izzyizzenty**[221] 6-10-9 .... FergusKing(3) —
(J M Jefferson) *hld up and bhd: hdwy and in tch 4 out: sn rdn and wknd: p.u bef 2 out* **100/1**

4m 50.8s (-2.80) **Going Correction** -0.20s/f (Good)
WFA 4 from 5yo+ 10lb **12** Ran SP% **116.2**
Speed ratings: **97,91,90,89,89 88,87,87,76,—** —,— CSF £21.85 TOTE £3.00: £1.40, £3.20, £4.70; EX 25.40 Place 6 £13.51, Place 5 £11.85.
Owner Mrs A N Durkan **Bred** T Picard And Phillipe De Maeseneire **Trained** West Witton, N Yorks

FOCUS
The winner was value for much further and the race could have been rated a lot higher, but the fifth and sixth were both well below form.

NOTEBOOK
L'Antartique(FR) bounced back to form with a facile success over this more suitable trip, although there was an anxious moment at the last when he rapped the flight and stumbled a stride or two afterwards. This relentless galloper is a nice chasing prospect but should enjoy further success over hurdles beforehand. *(op 9-4)*
Calin Royal(FR), out of a decent chasing mare in France and from the family of the high-class jumper Mister Banjo, was bought for 185,000gns in May last year. He stayed on into a moderate second before the final flight and should improve as he gains experience. *(op 12-1)*
Jimmy Bedney(IRE), who showed ability in bumpers, ran a satisfactory race on this hurdles debut but was only playing for places once the winner asserted.
Ballyhale(IRE) looks a stayer and has improvement in him over three miles. *(tchd 80-1)*
Odiham made a promising hurdles debut at Newbury and this longer trip should have suited him, but he was struggling before the home straight. *(op 15-8 tchd 2-1 in places)*
The Duke's Speech(IRE) , in trouble a fair way out, finished a lot further behind L'Antartique than he had when they were second and third at Wetherby. *(op 3-1)*
Hi Humpfree, whose bumper win had the look of a flash in the pan, was doing his best work at the end and might need a bit further. *(op 40-1)*
Izzyizzenty *Official explanation: jockey said gelding hung left from four out*
T/Plt: £8.10 to a £1 stake. Pool: £29,693.60. 2,675.90 winning tickets. T/Qpdt: £7.80 to a £1 stake. Pool: £2,286.10. 215.50 winning tickets. JR

2742
CHELTENHAM (New Course) (L-H)
Saturday, December 10

OFFICIAL GOING: Good to soft
Wind: Virtually nil

2756 TOTEPOOL JUVENILE NOVICES' HURDLE (8 hdls) 2m 1f
12:20 (12:21) (Class 2) 3-Y-O

£13,778 (£4,070; £2,035; £1,018; £508; £255)

Form RPR
2 **1** **Afsoun (FR)**[28] 2178 3-11-0 .... MickFitzgerald 134+
(N J Henderson) *lw: trckd ldrs: wnt cl 2nd 4th: hit 2 out: led wl bef last: drvn and kpt on wl whn strly chal run-in* **11/8**[1]
1 **2** 3/4 **Turko (FR)**[15] 2481 3-11-7 .... APMcCoy 139+
(P F Nicholls) *lw: chsd ldr to 4th: styd cl up: chal after 2 out: pressed wnr appr last: str chal run-in: one pce nr fin* **2/1**[2]
1111 **3** 5 **Fair Along (GER)**[20] 2367 3-11-7 141 .... RichardJohnson 134+
(P J Hobbs) *led: sn 10 clr: rdn 2 out: hdd wl bef last: wknd run-in* **10/3**[3]
4 17 **Desert Jim (FR)**[22] 3-11-0 .... (b[1]) RobertThornton 110+
(F Doumen, France) *small: hit 1st: chsd clr ldng gp of 3: hit 3rd: sme hdwy to cl after 3 out but n.d: wknd next* **16/1**
1655 **5** 11 **Wembury Point (IRE)**[8] 2612 3-11-3 115 .... (b) GrahamLee 101
(B G Powell) *bhd: rdn and mod hdwy after 3 out: nvr nr ldng gp of 3 and sn wknd* **40/1**
6 1 1/2 **Shannon Springs (IRE)**[62] 3-11-0 .... TonyDobbin 97
(Andrew Turnell) *hit 4th: bhd: mod effrt after 3 out but nvr nr ldrs and sn bhd* **20/1**
7 15 **Wotchalike (IRE)**[8] 3-11-0 .... HenryOliver 84+
(R J Price) *lw: a in rr* **100/1**
U0 **8** 9 **Ghabesh (USA)**[37] 2001 3-11-0 .... OllieMcPhail 73
(Evan Williams) *a wl bhd* **300/1**
50 **9** 3 1/2 **Mickey Pearce (IRE)**[23] 2286 3-11-0 .... (p) StevenCrawford 69
(J G M O'Shea) *a wl bhd* **300/1**

4m 6.10s (-7.00) **Going Correction** -0.05s/f (Good) **9** Ran SP% **113.3**
Speed ratings: **112,111,109,101,96 95,88,84,82** CSF £4.35 TOTE £2.40: £1.10, £1.30, £1.30; EX 5.20 Trifecta £10.00 Pool £928.98. 65.40 winning units..
Owner Million In Mind Partnership **Bred** S A Aga Khan **Trained** Upper Lambourn, Berks

FOCUS
One of the best juvenile hurdles run this season, but it only concerned three horses from some way out. The first two both showed much improved form, and the third has been rated to the level of his Aintree win. The form should work out.

NOTEBOOK
Afsoun(FR), a promising second to Fair Along on his hurdling debut over course and distance, showed the benefit of that experience to reverse placings on 7lb better terms. Having looked likely to win quite well jumping the last, Turko ensured he had to work very hard on the run-in, and he showed the right attitude. He is likely to come back to Cheltenham for the Finesse Hurdle in January before going for the Triumph. *(op 15-8 tchd 2-1 in places)*
Turko(FR), off the mark in a decent juvenile hurdle on his British debut at Newbury, ran a fine race under his penalty behind the well-regarded winner. He is now likely to be aimed at the Grade One Finale Junior Hurdle at Chepstow, where the likely soft ground should suit, before finding a small race en-route to the Triumph. *(tchd 9-4)*
Fair Along(GER), who was chasing a five-timer, was not ridden as forcefully as on his previous starts despite building up a decent early lead, and let both Afsoun and Turko close up before the race got really serious. In the end though, it probably made little difference and some of the better juveniles appear to have caught up with him now. *(op 11-4)*
Desert Jim(FR), a maiden on the Flat in France at up to a mile seven, was fitted with blinkers for the first time on his hurdling debut. He lacks size and proved no match for the front three, but this was still creditable enough and he ought to be found easier opportunities. *(op 20-1 tchd 25-1 in a place)*
Wembury Point(IRE) looked out of his depth somewhat. *(op 33-1 tchd 50-1)*
Shannon Springs(IRE) was a useful middle-distance winner on the Flat, but this was a stiff introduction to his new role. *(op 18-1 tchd 16-1)*

2757 JENNY MOULD MEMORIAL H'CAP CHASE (14 fncs) 2m 110y
12:55 (12:56) (Class 2) (0-145,145)
5-Y-O+

£13,402 (£3,959; £1,979; £990; £494; £248)

Form RPR
34-4 **1** **Tysou (FR)**[29] 2163 8-11-2 135 .... MickFitzgerald 148+
(N J Henderson) *lw: in tch: hdwy 10th: trckd ldrs after 3 out: drvn to ld last: rdn and r.o strly run-in* **6/1**[3]
12B0 **2** 2 **Tribal Dispute**[21] 2339 8-10-7 126 .... DavidO'Meara 137
(T D Easterby) *in tch: nt fluent 6th (water): hdwy 10th: disp 2nd and rdn after 3 out: styd on to chse wnr run-in: kpt on same pce* **33/1**
-235 **3** 1 3/4 **Bleu Superbe (FR)**[14] 2489 10-10-9 128 .... AlanO'Keeffe 139+
(Miss Venetia Williams) *swtg: led to 5th: hit 7th: styd pressing ldrs: led 10th: sn hdd: chal 3 out: sn led: hdd last: kpt on same pce* **12/1**
1-40 **4** 6 **Ground Ball (IRE)**[39] 1970 8-11-12 145 .... APMcCoy 149+
(C F Swan, Ire) *lw: hld up in rr: j. slowly 5th: sme hdwy 4 out: nt rch ldrs and one pce 3 out: kpt on again run-in but nvr a danger* **10/1**
6-32 **5** 1 3/4 **Made In Japan (JPN)**[14] 2489 5-11-6 139 .... (b) RichardJohnson 141+
(P J Hobbs) *lw: chsd ldrs: wnt 2nd 7th: led 9th to next: chal 4 out: wknd fr 2 out* **5/2**[1]
4422 **6** 3 **Escompteur (FR)**[14] 2488 5-10-0 119 oh4 .... TimmyMurphy 118+
(M C Pipe) *lw: chsd ldr: led 5th to 10th: led again sn after: hdd after 3 out: wknd next* **7/1**
1F31 **7** dist **Feel The Pride (IRE)**[13] 2516 7-10-12 131 .... BrianHarding —
(Jonjo O'Neill) *a bhd: lost tch fr 8th: t.o* **16/1**
2F-1 **P** **Provocative (FR)**[43] 1913 7-11-2 135 .... GrahamLee —
(M Todhunter) *in tch: rdn 9th: hit 10th: wknd qckly and p.u bef 4 out* **12/1**
FP-3 **F** **Le Seychellois (FR)**[14] 2489 5-11-0 133 .... ChristianWilliams —
(P F Nicholls) *bhd: nt fluent 7th: hit 8th: no ch whn fell 4 out* **11/4**[2]

4m 5.20s (-2.30) **Going Correction** -0.05s/f (Good) **9** Ran SP% **115.3**
Speed ratings: **103,102,101,98,97 96,—,—,—** CSF £143.30 CT £2282.02 TOTE £7.00: £2.20, £7.20, £3.20; EX 190.80 Trifecta £656.50 Part won. Pool £924.72. 0.10 winning units..
Owner W J Brown **Bred** Gilles Deroubaix **Trained** Upper Lambourn, Berks

FOCUS
A good handicap chase and the form looks solid. The first two both recorded personal bests.

NOTEBOOK
Tysou(FR) built on the form he showed on his reappearance round here to end a losing run stretching back to April 2003 with a personal best. Having seemingly been in the Handicapper's grip, this was his first success over fences outside novice company, so he looks one to oppose in the immediate future following his reassessment. However, he usually gives his running and his main aim will probably be the Grand Annual, in which he was fourth in March. *(op 11-2 tchd 13-2)*
Tribal Dispute was brought down when just beginning to get involved at Wetherby two starts ago, before blundering his chance away at Haydock on his previous outing. He showed what he is capable of this time with a good effort in defeat, and on this evidence he is not on a bad mark, so he should remain very competitive in similar events. *(op 25-1)*
Bleu Superbe(FR), 4lb lower than when last winning in November 2003, ran yet another creditable race in defeat. He would appear in good enough form to end his losing run, but may benefit from being ridden by a conditional who can take a few pounds off his pack. *(op 14-1)*
Ground Ball(IRE), dropped 7lb after being well beaten at Exeter on his latest outing, stayed on for pressure without ever looking likely to get seriously involved. Although he has won on good ground on the Flat, a softer surface probably suits better. *(op 14-1)*
Made In Japan(JPN), just held off this mark at Newbury on his previous start, ran below that level of form this time and was a touch disappointing. He is proving hard enough to win with, but probably prefers genuinely good ground. *(op 3-1 tchd 10-3 in a place)*
Escompteur(FR), from 4lb out of the handicap, was not at his best and remains winless over fences. *(op 9-1)*
Provocative(FR) *Official explanation: trainer said post-race x-ray had shown gelding to have hairline fracture of splint bone (op 5-2 tchd 3-1)*
Le Seychellois(FR) got kicked by a rival before the tapes went up and should never have been allowed to run. *Unsurprisingly he was never really going, and then got a fall for his troubles.Official explanation: jockey said gelding never travelled (op 5-2 tchd 3-1)*

2758 "RELKEEL" HURDLE (10 hdls) 2m 5f 110y
1:30 (1:31) (Class 2) 4-Y-O+ **£13,389** (£3,989; £2,019; £1,035; £541)

Form RPR
11-0 **1** **Mighty Man (FR)**[27] 2209 5-11-7 138 .... RichardJohnson 145
(H D Daly) *hld up rr but in tch: hdwy fr 3 out:pushed along to chse ldrs after next: r.o gamely u.p run-in to ld cl home* **11/2**[2]
-11 **2** hd **The Market Man (NZ)**[15] 2483 5-11-4 142 .... MickFitzgerald 142
(N J Henderson) *trckd ldrs: wnt 2nd after 2 out: hrd drvn to ld wl bef last: kpt on wl: hdd cl home* **2/1**[1]
241- **3** 6 **Prins Willem (IRE)**[241] 4820 6-11-4 134 .... (t) APMcCoy 136
(J R Fanshawe) *hld up rr but in tch: hdwy to trck ldrs after 3 out: rdn to dispute 2nd after 2 out and effrt appr last: wknd last half f* **8/1**[3]
-110 **4** 3 **Penneyrose Bay**[27] 2207 6-10-11 133 .... BenjaminHitchcott 126
(J A Geake) *lw: led: drvn along after 3 out: hdd wl bef last: sn wknd* **10/1**
1060 **5** 9 **Yes Sir (IRE)**[27] 2209 6-11-4 150 .... ChristianWilliams 124
(P Bowen) *chsd ldr: rdn 3 out: wknd qckly after 2 out* **14/1**
214- **F** **Moulin Riche (FR)**[246] 4765 5-11-7 .... RobertThornton —
(F Doumen, France) *lw: hld up in rr: mstke 3rd: stl last but in tch and travelling ok whn fell 4 out* **2/1**[1]

5m 16.6s **Going Correction** -0.05s/f (Good) **6** Ran SP% **108.9**
Speed ratings: **98,97,95,94,91** — CSF £16.35 TOTE £7.40: £2.70, £1.80; EX 16.60.
Owner E R Hanbury **Bred** Evan Hanbury **Trained** Stanton Lacy, Shropshire

FOCUS
This looked a decent enough renewal of the Relkeel Hurdle, but the pace was just steady for much of the way and the winning time was modest for a race of its class. It has been rated through the runner-up and the form is nothing to get carried away about.

NOTEBOOK

Mighty Man(FR) was a very useful novice over two miles last season, but he was well held in the Greatwood off a mark of 139 on his reappearance, and he improved for this significant step up in trip. He looked likely to be held on jumping the last, but responded most gamely to pressure to get the better of The Market Man, with whom he would have been 7lb better off had this been a handicap. While he is obviously open to more improvement over hurdles and could find further opportunities, he has an awful lot to find to make up into a leading stayer. *(tchd 6-1, 13-2 in places and 7-1 in a place)*

The Market Man(NZ), successful off a mark of 133 in a handicap over three miles at Newbury on his previous start, ran well switched to conditions company and was just denied by the equally progressive winner. He can probably remain competitive back in handicap company off his new mark. *(op 15-8 tchd 7-4 and 9-4 in places)*

Prins Willem(IRE), successful in a weaker race over course and distance when last seen 241 days previously, travelled well and acquitted himself most creditably behind two very progressive sorts, who both had the benefit of previous runs. He is likely to rise in the weights for this, which will make things tougher, but he is open to improvement. *(op 5-1)*

Penneyrose Bay, well held off a mark of 135 round here on his previous start, probably ran out about as well as could have been expected. *(tchd 12-1)*

Yes Sir(IRE) has lost his way for the time being and is best watched until his trainer's horses return to form. *(op 12-1)*

Moulin Riche(FR), reappearing off the back of a 246-day break, was still in with every chance when falling four out. *(op 11-4)*

2759 CHELTENHAM NOVICES' CHASE (17 fncs) 2m 5f

2:05 (2:05) (Class 2) 5-Y-0+ **£9,864** (£2,913; £1,456; £729)

Form				RPR
3-33	**1**		**Exotic Dancer (FR)**[28] [2174] 5-11-0 .... APMcCoy (Jonjo O'Neill) *lw: hld up rr but in tch: hit 13th: hdwy 3 out: drvn to ld last: hld on wl u.p run-in* **4/1**	142+
FP-1	**2**	*1 ¼*	**Bewleys Berry (IRE)**[17] [2441] 7-11-5 .... GrahamLee (J Howard Johnson) *led tl hdd after 2 out: rallied and kpt on gamely run-in to re-take 2nd last strides: no imp on wnr* **5/2**[2]	144+
-131	**3**	*hd*	**Albuhera (IRE)**[13] [2531] 7-11-8 ....(t) JoeTizzard (P F Nicholls) *disp 2nd: blnd 3 out: swtchd lft to chal 2 out: led sn after: hdd last: rallied but no imp on wnr: lost 2nd last strides* **3/1**[3]	147+
P-12	**4**	*dist*	**Celtic Son (FR)**[29] [2165] 6-11-8 ....(t) TimmyMurphy (M C Pipe) *lw: disp 2nd: hit 4 out and next: chal after 3 out: rdn and sn btn next: t.o* **2/1**[1]	132

5m 19.4s (-7.30) **Going Correction** -0.05s/f (Good) **4** Ran SP% **106.9**

Speed ratings: **111,110,110,—** CSF £13.50 TOTE £4.80; EX 11.90.

Owner Sir Robert Ogden **Bred** Gaetan Gilles And Ecurie Jules Ouaki **Trained** Cheltenham, Gloucs

FOCUS

A good novice chase, but with Bewleys Berry not setting that strong a pace, all four runners were in with a chance approaching two out. No obvious stars, and Exotic Dancer was still well short of his best hurdles mark.

NOTEBOOK

Exotic Dancer(FR), fitted with earplugs, confirmed the promise he showed on both his previous starts over fences to run out a narrow winner. He was getting weight from all three of his rivals, but this was still a most encouraging effort and he is developing into a smart novice chaser. He deserves to take his chance in graded company. *(tchd 9-2)*

Bewleys Berry(IRE), an impressive winner of a beginners' chase over three miles one at Wetherby on his debut over fences, ran most creditably stepped up in grade and dropped in trip, but may have been better suited by setting a stronger pace as he is clearly not short of stamina. This effort is all the more creditable given he was reported to have swallowed his tongue several times and, if that problem can be rectified, presumably with the aid of tongue-tie, he looks a fine prospect. *(op 9-4 tchd 11-4 in places)*

Albuhera(IRE), a comfortable winner when upped to two and a half miles at Newbury on his previous start, was produced with every chance to follow up, and travelled as well as anything for most of the way, but he was one paced after the last and found this stretching his stamina. There are plenty more races in him, but he may prove better back over shorter. *(op 5-2)*

Celtic Son(FR), so impressive on his chasing debut at Wincanton but beaten at odds on over three miles round here on his previous start, looked to have every chance of getting back on track, and was still in with a chance on turning in, but he weakened very quickly under pressure and finished up tailed off. His yard is badly out of form and he must be given another chance when all is well again. *Official explanation: trainer was unable to explain the poor form shown (tchd 9-4, 5-2 in places and 13-5 in a place)*

2760 ROBIN COOK MEMORIAL GOLD CUP (A H'CAP CHASE) (SPONSORED BY TOTESPORT) GRADE 3 (17 fncs) 2m 5f

2:40 (2:44) (Class 1) 5-Y-0+

£62,722 (£23,529; £11,781; £5,874; £2,948; £1,474)

Form				RPR
04-6	**1**		**Sir Oj (IRE)**[40] [1965] 8-10-0 **132** oh2........(b) PCarberry (Noel Meade, Ire) *lw: sn bhd: hdwy after 3 out but plenty to do: chsd ldr after 2 out and 8l down appr last: styd on strly to ld nr fin* **16/1**	142+
3-44	**2**	*1*	**Le Passing (FR)**[14] [2492] 6-10-9 **141**........(b) JoeTizzard (P F Nicholls) *chsd ldrs: led 4 out: lft 8l clr next: stl clr 2 out and rdn: one pce run-in and ct nr fin* **20/1**	150+
-161	**3**	*5*	**Lacdoudal (FR)**[8] [2615] 6-11-3 **149** 6ex........ RichardJohnson (P J Hobbs) *chsd ldrs: outpcd after 4 out: sn rdn: styd on again fr 2 out: kpt on run-in but nt rch ldrs* **8/1**	152
1-10	**4**	*shd*	**Brooklyn Breeze (IRE)**[28] [2177] 8-10-9 **141**........ TonyDobbin (L Lungo) *lw: hit 3rd: chsd ldrs: lost position 10th: hdwy 4 out: hmpd next: kpt on fr 2 out but nt pce to rch ldrs* **20/1**	145+
-0P2	**5**	*5*	**Europa**[14] [2492] 9-10-4 **136**........ JasonMaguire (Ferdy Murphy) *bhd: hdwy fr 4 out: kpt on fr next but nvr gng pce to rch ldrs* **16/1**	134
-2F0	**6**	*5*	**Redemption**[14] [2491] 10-10-2 **134**........ CarlLlewellyn (N A Twiston-Davies) *mstkes in rr: blnd 5th: hdwy 4 out: lft chsng ldr after 3 out: no imp after next: wknd and hit last* **17/2**	132+
1-20	**7**	*¾*	**Mixsterthetrixster (USA)**[14] [2492] 9-10-2 **134**........ HenryOliver (Mrs Tracey Barfoot-Saunt) *in tch: hdwy 9th: chsd ldrs 4 out: hmpd next: sn rdn: no imp on ldrs appr next* **66/1**	126
30-0	**8**	*¾*	**Therealbandit (IRE)**[28] [2177] 8-10-8 **150**........(p) AndrewGlassonbury[(10)] (M C Pipe) *slt ld to 5th: styd chsng ldrs: rdn and hmpd 3 out: styd on same pce* **25/1**	146+
5-01	**9**	*3*	**Scots Grey**[24] [2272] 10-10-7 **139**........ AndrewTinkler (N J Henderson) *chsd ldrs: rdn 13th: sn wknd: no ch whn hmpd 3 out* **25/1**	133+
P14/	**10**	*17*	**Our Armageddon (NZ)**[616] [4648] 8-10-0 **135**........ LarryMcGrath[(3)] (R C Guest) *hit 2nd: w ldr tl led 5th: hdd and hit 4 out: wknd next* **15/2**[3]	118+
1-26	**11**	*14*	**Quazar (IRE)**[42] [1924] 7-10-11 **143**........(t) BrianHarding (Jonjo O'Neill) *hmpd 3 out: a in rr* **40/1**	100
1600	**12**	*9*	**Tango Royal (FR)**[63] [1676] 9-10-3 **138**........(t) TomMalone[(3)] (M C Pipe) *a in rr* **50/1**	86
-P62	**S**		**Risk Accessor (IRE)**[14] [2499] 10-10-4 **136**........ APMcCoy (Jonjo O'Neill) *rr whn slipped up bnd appr 4th* **14/1**	—
PP-1	**P**		**Our Vic (IRE)**[28] [2177] 7-11-12 **158**........ TimmyMurphy (M C Pipe) *lw: hit 2nd and 3rd: nvr gng wl: t.o whn p.u after 7th* **9/2**[1]	—
14-3	**F**		**Thisthatandtother (IRE)**[21] [2346] 9-11-11 **157**........ ChristianWilliams (P F Nicholls) *chsd ldrs: length 2nd and styng on wl whn fell 3 out* **15/2**[3]	—
2P-4	**B**		**Fondmort (FR)**[28] [2177] 9-11-6 **152**........ MickFitzgerald (N J Henderson) *lw: in tch: hdwy to trck ldrs 10th: clsng in 3rd and travelling wl whn hmpd and b.d 3 out* **11/2**[2]	—

5m 15.0s (-11.70) **Going Correction** -0.05s/f (Good) **16** Ran SP% **120.3**

Speed ratings: **120,119,117,117,115 113,113,113,112,105 100,96,—,—,— —** CSF £293.09 CT £2747.71 TOTE £17.10: £2.80, £4.20, £2.20, £4.70; EX 521.40 Trifecta £4086.50 Pool £12,662.47. 2.20 winning units..

Owner Brian Keenan **Bred** Gareth Metcalfe **Trained** Castletown, Co Meath

■ A new name for this event, run last year as the bonusprint.com Gold Cup.

FOCUS

A solid renewal, but no stars. There was a shortage of obviously well-handicapped horses and, while the race was run in a very smart winning time, even for such a competitive chase, most are likely to continue to struggle off their current ratings. The first three home all finished in the first five in the Jewson Novices' Handicap at the Festival, highlighting the importance of course form in these types of events.

NOTEBOOK

Sir Oj(IRE), fourth in the Jewson Novices' Handicap over this course and distance at the Festival just two days after finishing down the field in the Arkle, had disappointed on his reappearance, but he had jumped poorly that day and the blinkers, which were missing there, were back in place here. He still had it all to do jumping the last but got up in the final moments to record a thrilling success. Three miles should not pose any problems. *(op 20-1)*

Le Passing(FR), left with a clear lead when Thisthatandtother fell and hampered a number of rivals three out, still held a big advantage jumping the last. He tired on the run-in, though, and failed to hold off the strong-finishing Sir Oj. He has looked held by the Handicapper off this sort of mark this season and, although softer ground will help, he is likely to remain vulnerable to less-exposed types.

Lacdoudal(FR), sixth in the Paddy Power Gold Cup last month, showed he has the stamina for three miles when successful at Sandown last time out, and this effort appeared to confirm the impression that his future lies over the longer trip. The Racing Post Chase is a likely target. *(tchd 10-1 in a place)*

Brooklyn Breeze(IRE), hampered slightly three out, kept on fairly well from then on, but he was another to run as though he needs some help from the Handicapper. *(tchd 25-1 in a place)*

Europa, third in the race last year off a 1lb lower mark, avoided the carnage at the third last and kept on well enough. He is likely to continue to struggle while rated in the mid 130s. *(op 14-1 tchd 20-1 in a place)*

Redemption, going well when falling at the second last in the Paddy Power Gold Cup last month and excused his defeat in the Hennessy on account of the trip, was racing off a 2lb lower mark and was one of very few who could be considered favourably handicapped prior to the race. He has a poor record over fences here, though, often failing to complete, and for that reason he was given a patient ride and plenty of daylight. Having headed the chase of Le Passing after three out he weakened at the last, and a flatter track and slightly shorter trip may help. *(op 15-2)*

Mixsterthetrixster(USA) is another who looks on a stiff enough mark for what he has achieved. *(tchd 100-1)*

Therealbandit(IRE) was under pressure but staying on when Thisthatandtother and Fondmort fell in front of him. He found himself trampling all over the latter and his rider, and his finishing position does not do him justice. *(tchd 28-1)*

Scots Grey, who is proabably at his best fresh, was also under pressure when getting caught up in the melee at the third last.

Our Armageddon(NZ), the 2004 Cathcart winner over this course and distance, looked potentially well handicapped for this return from a 616-day absence. The money came for him, but he ran as though the run would bring him on. *(op 8-1 tchd 10-1 in a place)*

Fondmort(FR) is fairly handicapped on his best form and looked poised to get involved when brought down by the fall of Thisthatandtother at the third last. He has not won for two years but should remain competitive if this incident does not leave its mark. *(op 6-1 tchd 5-1 and 13-2 in a place)*

Thisthatandtother(IRE) was threatening his stablemate Le Passing at the head of affairs when ploughing through the third last. He is another who is high enough in the weights, but a repeat win in what is now the Ryanair Chase at the Festival remains perfectly possible. *(op 6-1 tchd 5-1 and 13-2 in a place)*

Our Vic(IRE) jumped poorly in rear prior to being pulled up. This was not the same horse who won the Paddy Power Gold Cup here in November, and his performance highlighted the poor form of his stable over recent days. *Official explanation: trainer said, regarding the poor form shown, gelding had jumped poorly (op 6-1 tchd 5-1 and 13-2 in a place)*

2761 TOTESPORT BULA HURDLE GRADE 2 (8 hdls) 2m 1f

3:15 (3:17) (Class 1) 4-Y-0+

£42,765 (£16,042; £8,032; £4,005; £2,010; £1,005)

Form				RPR
-213	**1**		**Harchibald (FR)**[20] [2397] 6-11-8 .... PCarberry (Noel Meade, Ire) *lw: hld up in rr: smooth hdwy fr 2 out: nt clr run on rail and swtchd lft appr last: led on bit sn after: easily* **10/11**[1]	171+
0-2P	**2**	*1 ¾*	**Intersky Falcon**[14] [2500] 8-11-0 160........(bt) APMcCoy (Jonjo O'Neill) *led: clr 3rd: rdn and kpt on whn chal appr last: hdd run-in: styd on but no ch w wnr* **14/1**	159
21-2	**3**	*5*	**Faasel (IRE)**[21] [2338] 4-11-4 145........(v) TonyDobbin (N G Richards) *hld up in rr: hdwy 2 out: drvn to chal appr last: wknd u.p run-in* **9/2**[2]	160+
11-3	**4**	*11*	**Penzance**[21] [2338] 4-11-4 145........ RobertThornton (A King) *bit bkwd: hld up in rr: rdn 2 out: nvr gng pce to rch ldrs* **12/1**	147
P132	**5**	*7*	**Royal Shakespeare (FR)**[14] [2500] 6-11-4 153........ TomScudamore (S Gollings) *lw: chsd ldr fr 3rd: wknd after 2 out* **10/1**[3]	140
2-34	**6**	*6*	**Phar Bleu (FR)**[14] [2493] 4-11-4 138........(t) MickFitzgerald (P F Nicholls) *in tch: rdn and effrt appr 2 out: sn wknd* **20/1**	137+
F-4F	**7**	*15*	**Sporazene (IRE)**[7] [2635] 6-11-0 154........ ChristianWilliams (P F Nicholls) *chsd ldrs but nvr fluent: wknd after 3 out: no ch whn hmpd next* **11/1**	119+
R-40	**P**		**Westender (FR)**[27] [2209] 9-11-4 157........(b) TimmyMurphy (M C Pipe) *lw: chsd ldrs tl wknd 3rd: sn t.o: p.u bef 2 out* **25/1**	—
13-3	**U**		**Akilak (IRE)**[226] [88] 4-11-4 .... GrahamLee (J Howard Johnson) *in tch: hdwy 3 out: disputing 5l 2nd and gng wl whn blnd bdly and uns rdr 2 out* **12/1**	142+

4m 0.70s (-11.50) **Going Correction** -0.05s/f (Good)

WFA 4 from 6yo+ 10lb **9** Ran SP% **118.6**

Speed ratings: **125,124,121,116,113 110,103,—,—** CSF £16.53 TOTE £1.90: £1.20, £3.90, £1.60; EX 26.40 Trifecta £90.00 Pool £2,029.79. 16 winning units..

Owner D P Sharkey **Bred** S N C Ecurie Bouchard Jean-Lo **Trained** Castletown, Co Meath

■ Stewards' Enquiry : A P McCoy one-day ban: careless riding (Dec 21)

FOCUS

Intersky Falcon's return to front-running tactics meant they went a good pace for once, resulting in a very smart winning time, even for a Grade Two contest, 5.4 seconds quicker than Afsoun took in the opener. The form looks solid, although the winner faced none of the other big guns here and it is doubtful if we learned anything new.

NOTEBOOK

Harchibald(FR), returning to the scene of his Champion Hurdle defeat, was well backed from 6-4 in the morning and, with none of the other Irish big guns in attendence, nor the promising English-trained pair Arcalis and Lingo, he had a fairly easy task on his plate, even though he had to give weight all round. Having to be switched when tight for room next to the rail on the run to the final flight probably helped Carberry, as it meant he had to delay his challenge even longer, and his mount responded well on the run-in to draw away from the runner-up. This was a performance which oozed class and yet taught us little new about Harchibald. He does not do battling victories and one wonders whether he can win a Champion Hurdle, for which he is now the new favourite, this way. *(op 5-4)*

Intersky Falcon, who had a breathing problem when pulled up on soft ground at Newcastle, had a tongue tie back on this time. Reverting to the front-running tactics which served him well earlier in his career, he ran well in defeat, coming clear of the rest, and he clearly remains capable of smart form on his day. A decent surface is essential to see him at his best. *(op 10-1 tchd 16-1)*

Faasel(IRE), with the visor back on, showed much improved form and ran particularly well considering his age. He had his chance going to the final flight, although under pressure, but weakened on the run-in. On this evidence he will struggle to reverse form with the winner in the Champion Hurdle, but he would be of serious interest for the Arkle if a decision was taken to send him over fences, as he would benefit from the five-year-olds' allowance in that race. *(tchd 5-1)*

Penzance appears to be following in the recent tradition of Triumph Hurdle winners in facing a difficult second season. He has now twice finished behind Faasel, whom he beat in the Triumph, but he too has improved since then. A sounder surface would help, although he did win in softer conditions than these last year en route to the Festival. *(op 10-1 tchd 14-1)*

Royal Shakespeare(FR), who needs a sound surface to be seen at his best, had a tough task at the weights as he was 13lb worse off with Intersky Falcon for a length and a half victory over him at Wincanton last month. *(op 16-1 tchd 20-1)*

Phar Bleu(FR), wearing a tongue tie for the first time, had been beaten in handicaps off marks in the mid to high 130s on his last two starts, and he was out of his depth in this company. *(op 16-1)*

Sporazene(IRE), who is difficult to place both over hurdles and fences, could have done with a confidence-boosting round, but he never really jumped that well at all. *(op 9-1)*

Westender(FR), who declined to go through the gap in the the second last caused by one of the sections being flattened by one of his rivals, was yet another runner from the Pipe stable who failed to run his race. *(op 20-1 tchd 33-1)*

Akilak(IRE) ◆ was towards the fore of the chasing pack when all but falling at the second last. He might well have been involved in the battle for the places. *(op 20-1 tchd 33-1)*

2762 BRIT INSURANCE NOVICES' HURDLE (REGISTERED AS THE BRISTOL NOVICES' HURDLE) GRADE 2 (12 hdls) 3m

3:45 (3:47) (Class 1) 4-Y-0+

£17,106 (£6,417; £3,213; £1,602; £804; £402)

Form	Pos	Dist	Horse	Jockey	RPR
1-11	1		**Black Jack Ketchum (IRE)**[27] [2206] 6-11-7 (Jonjo O'Neill) *lw: hld up in rr: stdy hdwy fr 3 out: trckd ldr after next: chal on bit last: sn led: shkn up and sn in command: readily* **4/6**[1]	APMcCoy	154+
31	2	*2*	**Gungadu**[17] [2427] 5-11-0 (P F Nicholls) *lw: chsd ldrs: led after 3 out: hrd drvn after 2 out: hdd sn after last: kpt on but no ch w wnr* **5/1**[2]	ChristianWilliams	140
2112	3	*24*	**Amicelli (GER)**[15] [2483] 6-11-7 122 (P J Hobbs) *lw: led to 4 out: led again next: hdd sn after: wknd qckly after 2 out* **10/1**	RichardJohnson	123
0-21	4	*7*	**Mister Quasimodo**[17] [2426] 5-11-0 (C L Tizzard) *lw: rr but in tch: sme hdwy after 3 out: nvr rchd ldrs and sn wknd* **9/1**[3]	JoeTizzard	109
	5	*12*	**Contact Dancer (IRE)**[27] [2220] 6-11-0 (C F Swan, Ire) *hit 3rd: rr but in tch: brief effrt after 3 out: nvr rchd ldrs and sn wknd* **16/1**	PCarberry	101+
-110	6	*12*	**Rimsky (IRE)**[29] [2161] 4-11-7 (b[1]) (N A Twiston-Davies) *chsd ldr: chal fr 5th tl led 4 out: mstke and hdd next: sn wknd* **12/1**	CarlLlewellyn	98+

5m 56.3s (-2.60) **Going Correction** -0.05s/f (Good) **6** Ran SP% **109.3**
Speed ratings: **102,101,93,91,87 83** CSF £4.17 TOTE £1.60: £1.40, £2.40; EX 3.70 Place 6 £280.86, Place 5 £264.47.

Owner Mrs Gay Smith **Bred** E Morrissey **Trained** Cheltenham, Gloucs

FOCUS

Another fluent success for Black Jack Ketchum, albeit in a modest time for a race of its type, and he currently sets the standard for the Royal & SunAlliance Hurdle. He has been rated value for a seven-length victory.

NOTEBOOK

Black Jack Ketchum(IRE) looked to have plenty going for him in his bid to extend his unbeaten run in bumpers and hurdle races to five, and he did not disappoint, as he won comfortably and was value for much further at the line. He has a handy change of pace for a stayer and, with his ability to handle decent ground already proven, he has plenty going for him with regard to the Festival. However, at this point his trainer is undecided as to whether to aim him at the Royal & SunAlliance Hurdle or the Spa Novices' Hurdle over this longer trip. *(tchd 8-13 and 8-11)*

Gungadu is flattered by his proximity to the winner but still showed much improved form in finishing well clear of the others. He is clearly a very useful animal himself, though he is perhaps more of a future chaser than the winner and will benefit from softer ground. *(op 4-1)*

Amicelli(GER), beaten in a handicap off a mark of 118 last time out, was the most experienced runner in the line-up. He tried to put that to his advantage by making the running, but was outclassed at the business end. *(op 9-1)*

Mister Quasimodo is a promising five-year-old but this race was a big step up from the Chepstow novice hurdle he won last time out. He will be interesting in staying handicaps when the mud is flying as he was keeping on bravely at the finish and, although well held, his mother Dubacilla will have been proud. *(op 20-1)*

Contact Dancer(IRE), the 2004 Cesarewitch winner, was second over two miles on his hurdling debut and this stiffer test of stamina looked likely to suit him much better. He was a bit disappointing, though, and connections will now need to lower their sights.

Rimsky(IRE), who had Gungadu 14 lengths back in third when successful at Chepstow in October, had subsequently jumped poorly over two miles when tenth of ten behind Boychuck here last month. Connections tried blinkers here, but they failed to have the desired result.

T/Jkpt: Not won. T/Plt: £353.80 to a £1 stake. Pool: £139,921.75. 288.65 winning tickets. T/Qpdt: £62.80 to a £1 stake. Pool: £9,210.00. 108.40 winning tickets. ST

2749 DONCASTER (L-H)

Saturday, December 10

OFFICIAL GOING: Good to soft

The open ditch in the back straight was omitted in all chases.
Wind: Virtually nil.

2763 ADRIAN WELCH GLASS & GLAZING INTRODUCTORY NOVICES' HURDLE (8 hdls) 2m 110y

12:40 (12:40) (Class 3) 4-Y-0+ **£5,504** (£1,615; £807; £403)

Form	Pos	Dist	Horse	Jockey	RPR
0	1		**Huckster (ZIM)**[16] [2455] 6-11-0 (Miss Venetia Williams) *trckd ldrs: hdwy to ld appr 3 out: rdn clr after next drvn flat: all out* **14/1**	SamThomas	112+
	2	*1*	**Fuel Cell (IRE)**[51] 4-11-0 (M E Sowersby) *hld up: hdwy after 4 out: rdn 2 along 2 out: styd on wl flat* **50/1**	KeithMercer	110
10-	3	*14*	**Cracboumwiz (FR)**[245] [4774] 5-10-9 (Mrs H Dalton) *cl up tl lft in ld 3rd: pushed along and hdd bef 3 out: rdn and j.rt 2 out: sn drvn and one pce* **9/2**[1]	PaddyMerrigan(5)	98+
	4	*1 ½*	**Panzer (GER)**[63] 4-10-9 (D McCain) *hld up in tch: smooth hdwy 4 out: cl up appr next: sn rdn and one pce fr 2 out* **16/1**	StephenCraine(5)	95+
0	5	*4*	**Futoo (IRE)**[7] [2627] 4-11-0 (G M Moore) *prom: mstke 4th: rdn along after 4 out and grad wknd fr next* **9/1**	FinbarKeniry	92+
	6	*1 ½*	**Unshakable (IRE)**[57] 6-11-0 (Bob Jones) *hld up in midfield: stdy hdwy to trck ldrs 4 out: rdn next and sn btn* **11/2**[3]	JimmyMcCarthy	89
/36-	7	*7*	**Tank Buster**[308] [3710] 5-10-7 (Mrs E Langley) *towards rr: sme hdwy 1/2-way: rdn along and hit 3 out: sn wknd* **100/1**	MrRLangley(7)	82
3	8	*½*	**Titus Salt (USA)**[71] [1588] 4-11-0 (M D Hammond) *hld up: effrt and sme hdwy 1/2-way: rdn along 4 out and nvr a factor* **66/1**	NeilMulholland	81
0	9	*7*	**Heversham (IRE)**[6] [2658] 4-10-11 (J Hetherton) *a rr* **50/1**	PaddyAspell(3)	74
-	10	*4*	**Adventurist**[808] 5-11-0 (P Bowen) *chsd ldrs on outer: rdn along 4 out and sn wknd* **9/1**	PaulMoloney	70
0-5	11	*5*	**Grand Daum (FR)**[15] [2480] 4-11-0 (T P Tate) *chsd ldrs to 4th: sn lost pl and bhd* **33/1**	DominicElsworth	65
0	12	*dist*	**Red Bluff (IRE)**[32] [2108] 5-11-0 (H Alexander) *mstke 2nd: a bhd* **100/1**	JosephByrne	—
	13	*11*	**Extra Cover (IRE)**[53] 4-11-0 (Ronald Thompson) *a bhd* **50/1**	SamStronge	—
0	14	*½*	**Total Turtle (IRE)**[7] [2627] 6-11-0 (T D Easterby) *in tch: hdwy to trck ldrs 4 out: cl up next: rdn and mstke 2 out: drvn and btn whn blnd bdly last and virtually p.u* **5/1**[2]	RussGarritty	98+
	P		**Doringo**[96] 4-11-0 (J L Spearing) *a rr: bhd whn p.u bef 2 out* **100/1**	AntonyEvans	—
	F		**Leo's Luckyman (USA)**[91] 6-11-0 (R S Brookhouse) *led tl fell 3rd* **9/2**[1]	JohnMcNamara	—
	P		**Bond Millennium**[135] 7-11-0 (B Smart) *a rr: bhd whn p.u bef 3 out* **50/1**	BrianCrowley	—

4m 2.80s (-8.60) **Going Correction** -0.40s/f (Good) **17** Ran SP% **116.2**
Speed ratings: **104,103,96,96,94 93,90,90,86,84 82,—,—,—,— —,—** CSF £562.61 TOTE £22.30: £5.40, £11.80, £2.20; EX 547.10.

Owner P A Deal,Mrs N L Bruss & M E R Allsopp **Bred** And Mrs J D Harris **Trained** Kings Caple, H'fords

FOCUS

A modest novices' run that could be a little high rated through the fifth, but run at a good pace and could work out.

NOTEBOOK

Huckster(ZIM) showed the clear benefit of his recent debut at Taunton and duly got off the mark over hurdles in game style. This softer ground proved no problem, he jumped neatly throughout, and did enough to suggest he may get a bit further in due course. While this may not have been the strongest of novice events, he remains open to improvement and may be able to defy a penalty while his yard remains in decent form.

Fuel Cell(IRE), a dual ten-furlong winner on the Flat and rated 53 in that sphere, was motoring at the finish and turned in a very pleasing hurdles debut for new connections. He was nicely clear of the rest and, granted a more positive ride in the future, looks well up to finding a race in this division.

Cracboumwiz(FR), last seen finishing mid-division in a Grade Two bumper at Aintree in April and making his hurdling debut, was well backed on course, yet was firmly put in his place from the penultimate flight and disappointed. However, he can no doubt do better in this sphere when consenting to settle, and his stable is not in the best of form at present, so he is not one to write off. *(op 11-2)*

Panzer(GER), a 12-furlong winner and rated 71 on the Flat, turned in a respectable debut effort and shaped as though the race would bring him on. It should be noted that his best efforts on the Flat came on fast ground and, as a half-brother to the very useful staying hurdler Quick, it would be no surprise were he to prove better in this sphere. *(op 20-1)*

Futoo(IRE), seventh on his debut at Haydock a week previously, looked to run near to that level *and helps set the standard for this form. He will be eligible for handicaps after his next outing.* *(op 15-2)*

Unshakable(IRE), rated 91 on the Flat, did not jump with any fluency and failed to get home on this hurdling bow. *(op 9-2)*

Adventurist, rated 79 on the level and returning from an 808-day layoff, shaped better than his finishing position suggests and should improve markedly for this debut experience. He has joined a decent yard and is one to keep an eye on in this division. *(tchd 8-1)*

Total Turtle(IRE), ninth at Haydock on his hurdling bow a week previously, appeared booked for third place prior to making a serious error over the final flight and he stopped very quickly on the run-in. This must rate a much-improved effort and, providing he can recover from this experience, *should win in this sphere. Official explanation: jockey said gelding made a mistake at last hurdle and lost its action*

Bond Millennium *Official explanation: jockey said gelding was unsuited by the good to soft ground* *(tchd 5-1)*

Leo's Luckyman(USA), rated 100 and the best of these on the Flat, fell too early to tell how he would have fared on this hurdling debut. *(tchd 5-1)*

2764 WEATHERBYS BANK BEGINNERS' CHASE (14 fncs 1 omitted) 2m 3f
1:15 (1:15) (Class 4) 4-Y-0+ **£5,217** (£1,531; £765; £382)

Form	Pos	Dist	Horse	RPR
P-32	1		**Classic Capers**[23] 2291 6-11-2 112 .... FergusKing(3) (J M Jefferson) *hld up towards rr: stdy hdwy 5 out: rdn to ld appr last drvn flat and kpt on* **8/1**	129
12	2	3/4	**New Alco (FR)**[29] 2169 4-10-7 .... KeithMercer (Ferdy Murphy) *a.p: cl up 5 out: rdn 3 out: led next: hdd appr last: drvn and rallied flat: kpt on wl* **13/8**[1]	116
210-	3	16	**Reel Missile**[259] 4554 6-11-0 .... AdamPogson(5) (C T Pogson) *led: blnd 7th: pushed along and mstke 5 out: rdn next: blnd and hdd 2 out: kpt on same pce* **13/2**[3]	118+
32-3	4	3	**Aleron (IRE)**[205] 420 7-11-5 .... RussGarritty (J J Quinn) *a.p: cl up and rdn along 4 out: swtchd lft next and sn rdn: ev ch tl drvn and wknd after 2 out* **10/1**	112+
	5	6	**Handsuposcar (IRE)**[27] 2224 6-11-5 .... BarryFenton (S Donohoe, Ire) *hld up towards rr: hdwy 5 out: rdn along next: kpt on: nvr rch ldrs* **40/1**	103
5/0-	6	nk	**Mr McAuley (IRE)**[135] 1092 7-10-12 .... MrMJO'Hare(7) (I R Ferguson, Ire) *chsd ldrs: rdn along 5 out: hit next and sn wknd* **8/1**	104+
21P/	7	dist	**Samby**[679] 3604 7-11-2 .... OwynNelmes(3) (O Sherwood) *a rr* **6/1**[2]	—
2P3/	8	nk	**Patriarch (IRE)**[662] 3870 9-11-5 .... PaulMoloney (P Bowen) *trckd ldrs: lost pl 7th: bhd fr 5 out* **14/1**	—
006	9	29	**Zaffiera (IRE)**[18] 2415 4-10-7 .... NeilMulholland (M D Hammond) *hld up in rr: blnd 7th and bhd after* **200/1**	—
51-0	P		**Kings Square**[222] 152 5-11-2 .... MrTGreenall(3) (M W Easterby) *hld up: a rr: bhd whn p.u befd 4 out* **100/1**	—
6-05	U		**Italiano**[16] 2449 6-11-5 108 .... AnthonyRoss (P Beaumont) *in tch on inner: pushed along whn blnd bdly and uns rdr 5 out* **12/1**	—

4m 45.6s (-11.80) **Going Correction** -0.40s/f (Good) course record
WFA 4 from 5yo+ 10lb **11** Ran SP% **115.3**
Speed ratings: **108,107,100,99,97 97,—,—,—,— —** CSF £21.94 TOTE £8.00: £2.30, £1.50, £2.30; EX 23.10.
Owner Richard Collins **Bred** G A Bosley **Trained** Norton, N Yorks

FOCUS
A fair beginners' chase, run at a sound pace, and the first pair came well clear. The form could be rated higher but the third is the best guide to the level.

NOTEBOOK
Classic Capers ground down his rivals from two out and got off the mark over fences at the third attempt under a well-judged ride from King. There was a lot to like about the manner in which he knuckled down when asked to win his race, and he should be high on condidence now. *(op 10-1)*
New Alco(FR) ◆, strongly backed on course ahead of this chasing debut, had every chance yet could not get past the winner on the run-in, try as he might. He has done little wrong since joining connections from France, remains open to further improvement and should have little trouble in getting off the mark in this division. He may also benefit for the return to easier ground in the future. *(op 9-4 tchd 5-2 in a place)*
Reel Missile, making his chasing bow and returning from a 259-day break, made too many mistakes at his fences and was ultimately well held. The fact that he was still in contention prior to another bad error at the penultimate fence is testament to his ability, and he should improve for the outing, but he will need to brush up his jumping if he is to progress in this division. *(op 8-1 tchd 6-1)*
Aleron(IRE), making his chasing bow and notably weak in the betting, had every chance until tiring after the penultimate fence and emerged with credit. He jumped well in the main and, considering he was fifth in the Supreme Novice last season, may prove happiest back over two miles in the future. *(op 4-1)*
Handsuposcar(IRE), whose Irish trainer recently saddled a four-timer at Musselburgh, was given a conservative ride and did all of his best work at the finish. He should get closer next time - now that his confidence should have been restored - and will not mind a stiffer test in the future. *(op 50-1)*
Mr McAuley(IRE), a well-backed Irish-raider, found less than looked likely from the top of the straight and was disappointing. *(op 10-1)*
Samby, returning from a 679-day layoff, was given a considerate introduction to fences and never figured. He is capable of a lot better and should be much sharper next time out. *(tchd 13-2)*
Patriarch(IRE) *Official explanation: jockey said gelding moved poorly throughout (op 12-1)*
Italiano had started to tread water prior to unshipping his rider with five to jump.

2765 INTERCASINO.CO.UK SEA PIGEON H'CAP HURDLE (8 hdls) 2m 110y
1:45 (1:47) (Class 2) (0-140,136) 4-Y-0+ **£10,544** (£3,095; £1,547; £773)

Form	Pos	Dist	Horse	RPR
21U1	1		**Desert Quest (IRE)**[2] 2734 5-10-3 120 6ex .... (b) LiamHeard(7) (P F Nicholls) *trckd ldrs: hdwy on bit 3 out: cl up next: rdn and qckned to ld and hung bdly lft flat: jst hld on* **3/1**[1]	137+
211-	2	hd	**Briareus**[252] 4696 5-11-4 128 .... BarryFenton (A M Balding) *prom: led 4 out: rdn along 2 out: hit last: sn hdd: rallied wl under presure flat: jst hld* **14/1**	141
1-15	3	4	**Into The Shadows**[13] 2533 5-10-1 111 .... JimCrowley (K G Reveley) *hld up: stdy hdwy 4 out: cl up next: rdn and ev ch last: nt qckn flat* **8/1**[3]	120
52-2	4	3/4	**Prairie Moonlight (GER)**[13] 2533 5-10-10 120 .... NoelFehily (C J Mann) *hld up in rr: smooth hdwy 4 out: cl up nmext: rdn and ev ch last: nt qckn flat* **10/1**	128
-010	5	6	**Caracciola (GER)**[14] 2489 8-11-7 136 .... SamCurling(5) (N J Henderson) *hld up: hdwy after 4 out: chsd ldrs 2 out: sn rdn and one pce last* **14/1**	139+
-111	6	nk	**Chef De Cour (FR)**[32] 2106 4-10-12 122 .... RussGarritty (L Lungo) *hld up: hdwy 4 out: cl up whn hit next: sn rdn and grad wknd* **12/1**	125+
0-52	7	2	**Calatagan (IRE)**[21] 2334 6-10-13 126 .... FergusKing(3) (J M Jefferson) *hld up: hdwy 4 out: rdn and ch 2 out: sn drvn and wknd* **15/2**[2]	128+
-112	8	29	**Mexican Pete**[28] 1720 5-11-0 124 .... JohnMcNamara (A W Carroll) *a rr* **16/1**	104+
360-	9	1/2	**Caraman (IRE)**[281] 3277 7-10-4 114 .... AlanDempsey (J J Quinn) *a towards rr* **33/1**	85
0-20	10	11	**Genuine Article (IRE)**[153] 947 9-10-4 114 .... PaulMoloney (M Pitman) *chsd ldng pair: pushed along 1/2-way: lost pl and bhd fr 4 out* **40/1**	74
112-	11	10	**Dont Call Me Derek**[35] 4453 4-10-8 123 .... DougieCostello(5) (J J Quinn) *led to 4 out: rdn along and wknd bef next: sn bhd* **3/1**[1]	73
0206	12	3	**Grave Doubts**[13] 2533 9-10-9 122 .... (t) OwynNelmes(3) (K Bishop) *in tch: rdn along 1/2-way: sn lost pl and bhd* **50/1**	69

4m 1.70s (-9.70) **Going Correction** -0.40s/f (Good)
WFA 4 from 5yo+ 10lb **12** Ran SP% **116.2**
Speed ratings: **106,105,104,103,100 100,99,86,85,80 76,74** CSF £43.53 CT £308.00 TOTE £3.60: £1.90, £3.70, £2.50; EX 56.50.
Owner Mrs M Findlay **Bred** Ballygallon Stud **Trained** Ditcheat, Somerset

FOCUS
A fair handicap, run at a fairly sound gallop, and the form looks solid for the class.

NOTEBOOK
Desert Quest(IRE) ◆, back to winning ways over further at Taunton two days previously, followed-up in typical fashion under his 6lb penalty. He was travelling all over his rivals in the straight, and looked set to win comfortably when leading over the final flight, but once again idled badly on the run-in and was eventually all-out to score. While he is clearly most quirky - and needs to be produced with his challenge as late as possible - he is also the type the Handicapper has trouble in assessing, so can strike again. *(op 7-2 tchd 11-4)*
Briareus ◆, progressive over timber last term, defied market weakness on this seasonal bow, and quest for the hat-trick, with a most game effort in defeat. This has to rate a very promising comeback effort, especially as he was conceding weight to the progressive winner and ran a touch freely, so he really should be placed to go one better before too long. *(op 12-1)*
Into The Shadows held every chance yet was put in her place by the first two on the run-in. She remains in good heart, but could face another weight rise for this improved display. *(op 10-1)*
Prairie Moonlight(GER), runner-up to Motorway at Newbury on her comeback 13 days previously, turned in another solid effort and had every chance. She helps set the standard for this form and may be ready to tackle further now. *(op 9-1)*
Caracciola(GER), whose trainer's previous runners in this event were both successful, was not disgraced yet never really looked like getting to the leaders at any stage. He is better over hurdles, but holds few secrets from the Handicapper.
Chef De Cour(FR), who bagged a hat-trick of novice wins at Sedgefield 32 days previously, would have been a touch closer but for making an error three from home and posted a fair effort on this handicap debut. He has to prove he is up to winning off this mark, but could find easier opportunities in the future. *(tchd 11-1)*
Calatagan(IRE) had his chance, yet failed to see out the race and looks held by the Handicapper at present. *(op 7-1 tchd 8-1)*
Dont Call Me Derek, last seen winning over two miles at this track on the Flat in November, proved a sitting duck at the top of the straight and dropped away disappointingly thereafter. This effort leaves him with a fair amount to prove, but he could better this when returned to softer ground, and *may well be in need of a step-up in trip now. Official explanation: trainer had no explanation for the poor form shown (tchd 4-1)*

2766 SYKES LAWN TURF H'CAP HURDLE (10 hdls) 2m 3f 110y
2:20 (2:21) (Class 3) (0-115,115) 4-Y-0+ **£5,692** (£1,671; £835; £417)

Form	Pos	Dist	Horse	RPR
5-00	1		**Fard Du Moulin Mas (FR)**[200] 488 12-10-10 99 .... BrianCrowley (M E D Francis) *cl up: led after 3rd: rdn along 3 out: drvn last: styd on wl flat* **20/1**	105+
053	2	3	**Backgammon**[15] 2475 4-10-12 101 .... JimCrowley (K G Reveley) *hld up in tch: stdy hdwy on inner 4 out: rdn to chse wnr 2 out and ev ch tl drvn last and one pce flat* **4/1**[1]	103
6345	3	3/4	**Karathaena (IRE)**[13] 2519 5-11-6 109 .... KeithMercer (M E Sowersby) *midfield: hdwy 4 out: rdn to chse ldng pair 2 out: drvn appr last: kpt on same pce flat* **7/1**	110
1300	4	15	**Wally Wonder (IRE)**[10] 2566 7-10-0 99 .... JamesReveley(10) (K G Reveley) *led tl hit 3rd and sn hdd: cl up tl rdn along and wknd 3 out* **28/1**	88+
3005	5	1 1/2	**Flame Phoenix (USA)**[20] 2369 6-11-4 112 .... (t) StephenCraine(5) (D McCain) *hld up: hdwy 4 out: rdn along and in tch next: drvn and no imp 2 out* **8/1**	97
12-0	6	12	**Simply Mystic**[13] 2525 5-11-5 108 .... FinbarKeniry (P D Niven) *hld up towards rr: sme hdwy 1/2-way: rdn along 4 out and sn wknd* **14/1**	81
6-33	7	hd	**Night Sight (USA)**[4] 1642 8-10-3 95 .... (p) LeeVickers(3) (Mrs S Lamyman) *hld up: hdwy on outer whn mstke 6th: rdn along 4 out and btn bef next* **6/1**[3]	68
001-	8	dist	**Krakow Baba (FR)**[309] 3688 5-11-7 110 .... SamThomas (Miss Venetia Williams) *chsd ldrs. mstke 4 out and sn wknd* **9/2**[2]	—
P03P	9	29	**Renvyle (IRE)**[50] 1815 7-11-2 115 .... (e[1]) JohnFlavin(10) (R C Guest) *chsd ldrs: mstke 5th: rdn along and wknd bef 4 out* **28/1**	—
300-	F		**Presumptuous**[243] 4810 5-11-2 105 .... DominicElsworth (Mrs S J Smith) *trckd ldrs: effrt 4 out: cl up and ev ch whn fell next* **13/2**	106
2-P0	P		**County Classic**[9] 2590 6-10-13 102 .... RussGarritty (T D Easterby) *in tch: rdn along 1/2-way: sn lost pl and bhd whn p.u bef 3 out* **22/1**	—

4m 49.0s (-4.60) **Going Correction** -0.40s/f (Good)
WFA 4 from 5yo+ 10lb **11** Ran SP% **112.1**
Speed ratings: **93,91,91,85,84 80,80,—,—,— —** CSF £92.05 CT £625.00 TOTE £29.30: £7.40, £1.90, £2.50; EX 124.80.
Owner Mrs Merrick Francis Iii **Bred** Hubert Carion **Trained** Lambourn, Berks

FOCUS
A moderate winning time for a race like this, but the form makes sense with the winner, third and faller pretty much to their marks.

NOTEBOOK
Fard Du Moulin Mas(FR) is rising 13 and was upwards of four years older than any of his rivals in the field. He could have been expected to need this first start since May, but connections had clearly got him ready and and he steadily drew clear to win with quite a bit in hand. Consistency has never been his strong point however and it would be surprising if he were up to winning off a higher mark. *(op 18-1)*
Backgammon qualified for this when finishing third at Musselburgh last month and left his previous form behind in finishing second. He came from the back to stay on into second and, with his stable in such great form at the moment, it is not hard to see him winning a similar race. *(op 10-3)*
Karathaena(IRE) remains in good form and was again keeping on well in the closing stages. She was tried over two and three quarter miles earlier in her hurdling career and she looks well worth another go. *(op 8-1)*
Wally Wonder(IRE) has largely struggled since winning at Market Rasen in August and needs some further help from the Handicapper. *(op 33-1)*
Flame Phoenix(USA) continues to creep down the weights, but as with Wally Wonder, is in need of some assistance from the Handicapper. *(op 7-1)*
Presumptuous was in the process of running a big race and was upsides going well when falling three out. It is hoped this does not affect confidence. *(op 6-1 tchd 11-2)*

2767 INTERCASINO.CO.UK NEVILLE CRUMP MEMORIAL H'CAP CHASE (18 fncs 1 omitted) 3m 2f
2:55 (2:57) (Class 2) (0-140,131) 5-Y-0+ **£13,948** (£4,095; £2,047; £1,022)

Form	Pos	Dist	Horse	RPR
P362	1		**You're Special (USA)**[3] 2703 8-10-9 119 .... ThomasDreaper(5) (Ferdy Murphy) *trckd ldng pair: pushed along 1/2-way: hdwy to ld 5 out: rdn next: drvn last: styd on wl flat* **7/2**[2]	134+
-0PP	2	3 1/2	**Tribal Venture (FR)**[14] 2491 7-11-12 131 .... (b[1]) KeithMercer (Ferdy Murphy) *led tl mstke and hdd 12th: sn pushed along and sltly outpcd next: rdn to chse wnr 3 out: drvn next: kpt on* **17/2**	143+

4-22 **3** *17* **Lou Du Moulin Mas (FR)**[28] 2176 6-11-4 **130**................(t) LiamHeard(7) 123
(P F Nicholls) *trckd ldrs on inner: pushed along and reminders 12th: rdn and outpcd next: drvn 4 out and plugged on same pce* **6/5**[1]

-522 **4** *3* **The Kew Tour (IRE)**[13] 2518 9-10-12 **117**......................... PadgeWhelan 107
(Mrs S J Smith) *cl up: led 12th: hdd and rdn5 out: drvn next: wknd 3 out* **9/2**[3]

0163 **5** *dist* **Little Big Horse (IRE)**[14] 2499 9-11-10 **129**................ DominicElsworth —
(Mrs S J Smith) *a rr: pushed along 1/2-way: sn outpcd and bhd fr 12th* **7/1**

6m 28.9s (-11.20) **Going Correction** -0.40s/f (Good) **5** Ran SP% **108.9**
Speed ratings: **101,99,94,93,**— CSF £26.55 TOTE £4.10: £1.60, £3.00; EX 34.80.
Owner Mrs Diane O'Rourke **Bred** Ralph C Wilson Jnr Trust Agreement **Trained** West Witton, N Yorks

■ Stewards' Enquiry : Liam Heard four-day ban: using his whip with excessive force (December 21-22 & 26-27)

FOCUS
The Ferdy Murphy-trained pair dominated with You're Special coming out on top. The race could be rated higher but the form is slightly suspect with the hot favourite running below-par.

NOTEBOOK
You're Special(USA) has gradually been coming back to form and was making a quick reappearance having finished second at Leicester only three days previously. He looked in trouble at one stage and was being ridden, but came back on the bridle and went on five out. In receipt on plenty of weight from stable companion Tribal Venture, he kept on right the way to the line and won with a bit to spare, but he is hardly improving and may struggle off a higher mark. *(op 11-4 tchd 4-1)*
Tribal Venture(FR) has faced tough tasks on each of his three previous starts this season, all in graded company, but this was more realistic despite top weight and the blinkers appeared to inject some life back into him. Jumping boldly in front early on, he rallied gamely once headed, but the weight concession to his stablemate proved too much and he had to settle for second. If the headgear continues to have the same affect he will make some appeal off this sort of mark, but that cannot be guaranteed. *(op 8-1)*
Lou Du Moulin Mas(FR), for all that he is consistent, rarely wins and must be beginning to get thoroughly frustrated with the game. He was travelling as one would expect early on, but was in trouble a long way from home and appeared to run flat, being unable to pick up and just plodding on to claim third. On this evidence he is one to avoid. *(op 6-4)*
The Kew Tour(IRE), who has been in decent form, was up with the early gallop, but faded disappointingly down the straight. Although he has not won since March of last year, he remains only 2lb lower and will continue to be vulnerable. *(op 4-1)*
Little Big Horse(IRE) never got into it and was beaten before halfway. He had plenty of weight to shoulder, but has largely struggled since winning on his reappearance at Market Rasen in September and is another who needs some help from the Handicapper. *(op 13-2 tchd 11-2)*

2768 INTERCASINO.CO.UK VULRORY'S CLOWN H'CAP CHASE (14 fncs 1 omitted) 2m 3f

3:30 (3:31) (Class 3) (0-135,133) 5-Y-O+ **£10,608** (£3,114; £1,557; £777)

Form RPR

23-5 **1** **Kelrev (FR)**[14] 2492 7-11-6 **127**.................................. SamThomas 140+
(Miss Venetia Williams) *hld up gng wl: smooth hdwy 5 out: led 3 out: rdn clr after next: comf* **5/1**[2]

1111 **2** *4* **Hakim (NZ)**[20] 2368 11-11-4 **125**.................................. AntonyEvans 130
(J L Spearing) *led: rdn 5 out: hdd 3 out: sn drvn and kpt on same pce* **11/2**[3]

6PU0 **3** *1 ¾* **Turgeonev (FR)**[9] 2590 10-11-6 **127**.......................... RussGarritty 131+
(T D Easterby) *chsd ldrs: hdwy to dispute ld 8th: mstke next: rdn along 5 out: drvn 3 out: kpt on same pce* **20/1**

1-00 **4** *3* **Cregg House (IRE)**[6] 2666 10-11-6 **132**..................... PaddyMerrigan(5) 134+
(S Donohoe, Ire) *in tch: mstke 5th: hdwy 8th: hit next: rdn along to chse ldrs 5 out: kpt on u.p fr 2 out* **22/1**

3-52 **5** *1 ½* **Super Nomad**[17] 2443 10-11-1 **125**............................... MrTGreenall(3) 126+
(M W Easterby) *hld up: hdwy 5 out: rdn along to chse ldrs next: drvn and no imp fr 2 out* **9/1**

-420 **6** *5* **Almaydan**[14] 2489 7-11-12 **133**...................................... JohnMcNamara 130+
(R Lee) *trckd ldrs on inner: rdn along and hit 6 out: nt fluent next: sn drvn and wknd fr 4 out* **11/1**

4356 **7** *12* **Day Du Roy (FR)**[17] 2443 7-10-8 **115**............................ TomSiddall 105+
(Miss L C Siddall) *hld up and bhd: stdy hdwy appr 6 out: rdn to chse ldrs whn blnd 3 out: sn wknd* **50/1**

24-P **8** *1* **Flight Command**[6] 2656 7-11-7 **128**............................... AnthonyRoss 109
(P Beaumont) *hld up and bhd: stdy hdwy on outer 1/2-way: in tch 6 out: rdn along next and sn wknd* **50/1**

P **9** *1 ¾* **Lulumar (FR)**[7] 2622 6-11-1 **125**..............................(t) OwynNelmes(3) 104
(O Sherwood) *midfield: rdn along and rr fr 1/2-way* **33/1**

35F **10** *5* **Cobbet (CZE)**[20] 2368 9-10-7 **121**.............................. WillieMcCarthy(7) 95
(T R George) *a rr: blnd 8th and sn bhd* **20/1**

3511 **F** **Oso Magic**[14] 2498 7-11-5 **126**...................................... DominicElsworth —
(Mrs S J Smith) *cl up tl fell 8th* **7/2**[1]

12-1 **U** **Wicked Nice Fella (IRE)**[32] 2100 7-10-13 **120**.................... NoelFehily —
(C C Bealby) *in tch gng wl tl bdly hmpd and uns rdr 8th* **5/1**[2]

-210 **P** **Encore Cadoudal (FR)**[17] 2443 7-10-5 **119**..................... PhilKinsella(7) —
(H P Hogarth) *hld up: hdwy 1/2-way: chsd ldrs whn blnd 5 out: drvn and mstke next: sn wknd and p.u bef last* **16/1**

4m 48.1s (-9.30) **Going Correction** -0.40s/f (Good) course record **13** Ran SP% **115.9**
Speed ratings: **103,101,100,99,98 96,91,91,90,88** —,—,— CSF £29.24 CT £501.52 TOTE £6.40: £2.40, £2.50, £3.40; EX 34.70 Place 6 £244.37, Place 5 £70.19.
Owner Len Jakeman, Flintham, King & Roberts **Bred** Rene Merlin **Trained** Kings Caple, H'fords

FOCUS
A decent handicap chase that was won in grand style by Kelrev. The winner is value for double the official margin, the form looks solid with the runner-up and fourth to their marks and it is likely the race will work out.

NOTEBOOK
Kelrev(FR) comes from a stable that can do little wrong at present and showed the benefit of his seasonal reappearance with an authoritative display. A strong traveller, he remains open to further improvement, but is sure to go up a fair bit for this and will need to step up again. *(op 9-2)*
Hakim(NZ), a winner over the National fences at Aintree last time, has been on a roll since returning from a lengthy lay-off, winning his last four starts and shooting up 37lb in the ratings. He was fully expected to go close here but, having soon lead, he was passed by the winner three out. He ran his race and battled on well to hold second, but was no match for Kelrev, who is four years his junior.
Turgeonev(FR) ran his best race for some time and may have been helped by a recent confidence-boosting spin over hurdles recently. He is extremely well handicapped on old form, but cannot be relied upon to build on this.
Cregg House(IRE) travelled with his usual fluency on the bit but, as is often the case, his effort off it was unsatisfactory. A few more runs should see him ready for the spring. *(op 20-1)*
Super Nomad was running beyond two miles for the first time in well over a year, but he failed to improve for it and remains hard to win with. *(tchd 8-1)*
Almaydan, a very useful novice last season, offered a bit more here, but failed to see his race out under top weight and needs some further assistance from the Handicapper. *(op 12-1 tchd 14-1)*

Oso Magic has returned an improved performer, winning the last twice, but as a consequence he was up a fair chunk in the weights. He held a prominent early position, and was jumping well, but got the eighth all wrong and came down. It is hoped this does not affect confidence.
T/Plt: £638.70 to a £1 stake. Pool: £60,550.10. 69.20 winning tickets. T/Qpdt: £91.30 to a £1 stake. Pool: £5,665.20. 45.90 winning tickets. JR

2125 LINGFIELD (L-H)

Saturday, December 10

2769 Meeting Abandoned - Frost

2776a, 2778a - 2781a (Foreign Racing) - See Raceform Interactive

2535 NAVAN (L-H)

Saturday, December 10

OFFICIAL GOING: Soft (soft to heavy in places on chase course)

2777a GILTSPUR SCIENTIFIC TARA HURDLE (GRADE 2) 2m 4f

1:00 (1:00) 4-Y-O+ **£26,778** (£7,856; £3,743; £1,275)

RPR

1 **Solerina (IRE)**[6] 2669 8-11-7 158................................ GTHutchinson 160
(James Bowe, Ire) *mde all: edgd clr 3 out: styd on strly: easily* **2/5**[1]

2 *20* **Emotional Moment (IRE)**[27] 2227 8-11-10 148.................. BJGeraghty 143
(T J Taaffe, Ire) *cl up in 2nd: slt mstke 3rd: pushed along 5 out: rdn after 4 out: no ex whn slt mstke 2 out* **3/1**[2]

3 *9* **Baron De Feypo (IRE)**[7] 2650 7-11-8 128............................... JLCullen 132
(Patrick O Brady, Ire) *settled 3rd: rdn bef 3 out: no imp* **16/1**

4 *5* **Jack High (IRE)**[28] 2176 10-11-8 130..................................... GCotter 127
(T M Walsh, Ire) *hld up in 4th: dropped to rr 4 out: kpt on same pce fr next* **14/1**[3]

5 *7* **Macs Valley (IRE)**[1042] 3421 8-11-8 120.............................. MrPJCasey 120
(Miss A M Winters, Ire) *in rr: prog into mod 4th bef 3 out: sn no ex* **50/1**

5m 1.00s
WFA 4 from 7yo+ 11lb **6** Ran SP% **110.9**
CSF £2.06 TOTE £1.40: £1.10, £1.40; DF 1.60.
Owner John P Bowe **Bred** Michael J Bowe **Trained** Thurles, Co. Tipperary

FOCUS
Just as she did after winning the Hatton's Grace the previous two seasons, Solerina followed up in this particular race.

NOTEBOOK
Solerina(IRE) was bidding to follow up a Hatton's Grace success in this particular race for the third successive year, but this time had less than a week to recover, compared with two weeks in the previous two seasons. Despite appearing to have a very hard race just six days previously, she showed no ill-effects and totally outclassed her four rivals. Connections say her ideal conditions are two and a half miles on soft ground, hence the reason she was turned out so quickly, but there is little for her over this trip for the time being and she may be forced to step up or down in distance next time. Having said that, a trip to England has not been ruled out. *(op 1/2)*
Emotional Moment(IRE), behind Solerina in a similar event over course and distance on his previous start, again proved no match for that rival. *(op 7/2)*
Baron De Feypo(IRE) had conditions to suit, but is not up to this class. *(op 14/1)*

2782a BRIAN M. DURKAN & CO.LTD "FUTURE CHAMPIONS" (PRO/AM) INH FLAT RACE (GRADE 2) 2m

3:30 (3:30) 4-Y-O+ **£16,159** (£4,741; £2,258; £769)

RPR

1 **Back To Bid (IRE)**[6] 2671 5-11-7 .... MrJPMcKeown(7) 126+
(Noel Meade, Ire) *trckd ldrs: 4th after 1/2-way: 3rd and rdn early st: impr to ld under 2f out: styd on wl* **5/1**[3]

2 *9* **Once A Brownie (IRE)**[36] 2035 4-11-6 .... MrJPMagnier(3) 114
(Edward U Hales, Ire) *led: rdn early st: hdd under 2f out: no ex fnl f* **9/2**[2]

3 *10* **Bluebyyou (IRE)**[23] 2308 4-11-4 ....(t) MrCJSweeney(5) 106
(T Hogan, Ire) *trckd ldr in 2nd: tk clsr order appr st: rdn to chal over 2 1/2f out: 3rd and no ex fr 2f out* **6/1**

4 *1 ½* **Woodbine Willie (IRE)**[20] 4-11-2 .... MrBTO'Connell(7) 105
(Philip Fenton, Ire) *towards rr: mod 8th early st: kpt on fr 2f out* **33/1**

5 *1 ½* **Ceeawayhome**[672] 3731 6-11-11 .... MrDerekO'Connor(3) 109
(John E Kiely, Ire) *hld up in rr: prog into 7th 5f out: mod 4th early st: no ex fr 2f out* **7/1**

6 *nk* **Your The One (IRE)**[7] 2647 6-11-11 .... MrKEPower(3) 108
(Joseph Crowley, Ire) *settled 3rd: rdn and wknd ent st* **7/1**

7 *5* **Saddleeruppat (IRE)**[7] 2651 4-10-11 .... MrDPFahy(7) 94
(Ms Joanna Morgan, Ire) *trckd ldrs: 5th 6f out: rdn appr st: sn no ex* **9/4**[1]

8 *5* **Some Bob Back (IRE)**[23] 2308 4-10-13 .... MrLPFlynn(5) 90
(C F Swan, Ire) *a towards rr* **12/1**

9 *11* **City Deep (IRE)**[28] 2199 5-11-7 .... MrDRoche(7) 92
(Paul A Roche, Ire) *trckd ldrs: 4th 1/2-way: lost pl 6f out: no ex bef st* **10/1**

10 *2* **Strike An Ark (IRE)**[42] 1936 4-11-1 .... MissNCarberry(3) 80
(Ms Caroline Hutchinson, Ire) *hld up: prog into 6th 5f out: wknd ent st: virtually p.u ins fnl f* **8/1**

4m 10.1s
WFA 4 from 5yo+ 10lb **10** Ran SP% **135.7**
CSF £32.91 TOTE £8.60: £2.40, £3.10, £1.50; DF 44.50.
Owner West Coast Pinner Syndicate **Bred** Burgage Stud **Trained** Castletown, Co Meath

NOTEBOOK
Back To Bid(IRE), who did not jump well on his debut over hurdles last time out, won for the third time on the level. He is clearly a smart horse but, according to his trainer, is a slow learner. Meade plans to send him back over hurdles around Christmas time. *(op 7/1 tchd 4/1)*
Once A Brownie(IRE) tried to make all but found the winner too strong inside the last furlong. *(op 6/1)*
T/Jkpt: @406.50. Pool of @5,420.00 - 10 winning units. T/Plt: Not won. II

2783 - (Foreign Racing) - See Raceform Interactive

2387 CORK (R-H)

Sunday, December 11

OFFICIAL GOING: Heavy

2784a O'CONNELL TRANSPORT CORK STAYERS NOVICE HURDLE (GRADE 3) 3m

1:15 (1:15) 5-Y-0+ **£18,468** (£5,418; £2,581; £879)

RPR

1 **Alpha Royale (IRE)**[22] 2354 5-11-2 ....(b) DNRussell 122+
(C Byrnes, Ire) *hld up in rr: clsr order fr 7 out: 5th fr bef 6 out: chal and led 2 out: sn strly pressed and jnd: styd on wl run-in: all o* **7/4**[1]

2 *shd* **Mister Top Notch (IRE)**[10] 2603 6-11-2 .... JLCullen 122+
(D E Fitzgerald, Ire) *chsd ldrs: clsr in 3rd appr st: 2nd and chal fr 2 out: disp ld and kpt on wl run-in: jst failed* **9/2**[3]

3 *12* **Justpourit (IRE)**[14] 2538 6-11-9 .... NJO'Shea[(7)] 117
(D T Hughes, Ire) *trckd ldrs in 3rd: 2nd fr bef 6 out: led ent st: hit 3 out: strly pressed and hdd next: sn dropped to 3rd and kpt on same p* **5/2**[2]

4 *15* **Court Storm (IRE)**[21] 2393 6-10-11 .... KTColeman[(5)] 95
(F Flood, Ire) *racd mainly 4th: dropped to 5th and no imp u.p fr early st* **6/1**

5 *25* **Liscooney (IRE)**[22] 2356 7-11-5 114 .... JohnnyMurtagh 73
(David A Kiely, Ire) *racd in 2nd: led appr 6 out: rdn after 4 out: strly pressed and hdd ent st: sn wknd* **7/1**

P **Clearly Oscar (IRE)**[22] 2335 6-10-9 .... MrJPO'Farrell[(7)] —
(Seamus O'Farrell, Ire) *chsd ldrs: lost tch in 6th 6 out: sn bhd: p.u after 4 out* **16/1**

P **Onefortheroadpaddy (IRE)**[84] 1493 5-10-8 74 ....(b[1]) WJLee[(3)] —
(F Costello, Ire) *led: clr early: hdd appr 6 out: sn wknd qckly and p.u bef 6 out* **50/1**

6m 27.6s **8** Ran SP% **117.7**
CSF £10.88 TOTE £2.90: £1.80, £2.20; DF 19.40.
Owner Anywhere But Home Syndicate **Bred** Charles Byrnes **Trained** Ballingarry, Co Limerick

NOTEBOOK

Alpha Royale(IRE) had developed a nasty habit of finishing second, but this step up to three miles did the trick and he willingly stuck his neck out to narrowly deny the persistent runner-up. He remains open to further improvement at this sort of distance but, although he is no Grade One horse, he should make a good staying chaser in time. *(op 2/1 tchd 6/4)*

Mister Top Notch(IRE) is gradually getting it together over hurdles, but the fact is he has yet to win in five attempts. He went down narrowly here, giving his all, and this level of form should see him winning an ordinary hurdle. *(op 4/1)*

Justpourit(IRE) was not quite up to it on this first try at graded level, but there are more races for him back at an easier level. *(op 9/4 tchd 11/4)*

2786a O'CONNELL WAREHOUSING HILLY WAY CHASE (GRADE 2) (11 fncs) 2m

2:15 (2:16) 5-Y-0+ **£27,702** (£8,127; £3,872; £1,319)

RPR

1 **Central House**[28] 2230 8-11-12 157 ....(t) RLoughran 150
(D T Hughes, Ire) *led: strly pressed and briefly hdd 4 out: sn regained narrow ld: styd on wl u.p and clr run-in* **6/4**[2]

2 *3* **Rathgar Beau (IRE)**[24] 2304 9-11-12 157 .... JRBarry 147
(E Sheehy, Ire) *in rr: 3rd fr 6 out: pushed along 4 out: slt mstke next: rdn to chal appr last: no imp and kpt on one pce run-in* **9/10**[1]

3 *1 ½* **Mariah Rollins (IRE)**[29] 2177 7-11-7 136 .... JLCullen 141
(P A Fahy, Ire) *trckd ldr in 2nd: led briefly 4 out: sn hdd: dropped to 3rd and kpt on same pce u.p fr bef last* **5/1**[3]

4 *dist* **Alcapone (IRE)**[24] 2304 11-11-12 131 .... BMCash —
(M F Morris, Ire) *racd in 3rd: bad mstke 3rd and rdr lost reins: dropped to rr 6 out: pushed along fr next: sn lost tch* **16/1**

4m 17.1s **4** Ran SP% **115.2**
CSF £3.67 TOTE £2.70; DF 5.00.
Owner John F Kenny **Bred** A J Ilsley **Trained** Osborne Lodge, Co. Kildare

FOCUS

A two-horse contest on paper and so it turned out, but not the winner many expected and the improved Central House continued his climb up the chasing ranks. Rathgar Beau was undoubtedly below par in second, all out to get past the 136-rated Mariah Rollins.

NOTEBOOK

Central House, who became only the second horse to beat Moscow Flyer over fences when winning the Fortria Chase, has clearly returned an improved performer this season and he made most of the running to win cosily from the below-par favourite. He seems to get on particularly well with his jockey, and his fluent jumping made it hard for anything to make ground in the heavy going. He is quickly developing into a leading Irish chaser and will no doubt take the beating in the Grade One at Leopardstown over Christmas. *(op 5/4)*

Rathgar Beau(IRE), the first horse to beat Moscow Flyer over fences, was forced to miss the previous week's Tingle Creek as a result of a dirty scope. He was rightly made favourite to beat Central House, but did not jump with his usual fluency and, having been given plenty to do, he could only plod on at the one pace. With Moscow Flyer not looking at his best on his return, it was hoped this fella could develop into the top Irish two-miler, but he will have to leave this running behind if he is to do so. *(op 4/5 tchd 1/1)*

Mariah Rollins(IRE) started off over three miles on her return and then dropped to two and a half when running a respectable eighth in the Paddy Power. Down another half mile here, she ran way above expectations and it was only the final quarter mile in which her lack of pace began to tell. Evidently effective at a variety of trips, positive tactics seem to suit her best and she is not badly handicapped on some of her novice efforts.

Alcapone(IRE) often runs in these events and collects some place money. A bad blunder at the third took a bit out of him and caused his rider to lose his reins, so it is safe to assume that led to his abysmal display. *(op 14/1)*

2787 - 2792a, 2794a - 2795a (Foreign Racing) - See Raceform Interactive

2394 PUNCHESTOWN (R-H)

Sunday, December 11

OFFICIAL GOING: Soft

2793a JOHN DURKAN MEMORIAL PUNCHESTOWN CHASE (GRADE 1) 2m 4f

2:00 (2:01) 5-Y-0+ **£46,099** (£13,475; £6,382; £2,127)

RPR

1 **Hi Cloy (IRE)**[28] 2230 8-11-12 150 .... AndrewJMcNamara 158+
(Michael Hourigan, Ire) *hld up in tch: 6th 5 out: prog 4 out: 4th 3 out: 3rd after last: styd on wl u.p to ld nr fin* **7/1**[3]

2 *hd* **Jim (FR)**[41] 1965 8-11-12 148 .... RMPower 158+
(J T R Dreaper, Ire) *led: jnd 5 out: hdd after 4 out: imp to dispute ld after 3 out: led appr last: mstke: strly pressed run-in: hdd nr fin* **10/1**

3 *4* **Forget The Past**[29] 2177 7-11-12 150 .... BJGeraghty 154
(M J P O'Brien, Ire) *prom: 2nd fr 4th: disp ld 5 out: led after 4 out: jnd after 3 out: hdd appr last: no ex run-in* **4/1**[2]

4 *3* **Ned Kelly (IRE)**[10] 2599 9-11-12 132 .... PWFlood 151?
(E J O'Grady, Ire) *trckd ldrs in 4th: prog into 3rd 3 out: rdn to chal appr next: no ex fr last* **25/1**

5 *15* **War Of Attrition (IRE)**[24] 2304 6-11-12 157 .... CO'Dwyer 136
(M F Morris, Ire) *trckd ldrs in 5th: impr into 3rd 5 out: rdn and dropped to 5th after next: sn no ex: eased fr last* **4/5**[1]

6 *4 ½* **Strong Project (IRE)**[24] 2304 9-11-12 138 .... JMAllen 131
(Sean O O'Brien, Ire) *settled 3rd: 4th after 4 out: no ex fr next* **25/1**

7 *20* **Native Upmanship (IRE)**[28] 2230 12-11-12 150 .... DJCasey 111
(A L T Moore, Ire) *a bhd: lost tch bef 5 out: t.o* **14/1**

P **Le Coudray (FR)**[246] 4772 11-11-12 150 ....(t) APMcCoy —
(C Roche, Ire) *hld up: 7th and in tch 4 out: sn no ex: p.u bef 2 out* **25/1**

5m 19.0s **Going Correction** +0.275s/f (Yiel) **8** Ran SP% **115.4**
Speed ratings: **115,114,113,112,106 104,96,—** CSF £66.54 TOTE £8.20: £1.90, £1.60, £1.40; DF 38.10.
Owner Mrs S McCloy **Bred** Mrs Paul Finegan **Trained** Patrickswell, Co Limerick

FOCUS

A top event with some of Ireland's leading chasers in opposition, but hot favourite War Of Attrition failed to give his running. The front pair look to hold major claims in the Ryanair Chase at the Festival if the ground is not too fast, while the exciting third-placed Forget The Past stepped up on his reappearance effort.

NOTEBOOK

Hi Cloy(IRE), a high-class chaser who rarely runs a bad race, was well suited to this step back up in trip. Having travelled with his usual fluency, he did leave it rather late but he got there in time, running on strongly after the last. Effective at the highest level from two to three miles, he is the sort who has further improvement in him and it will be interesting to see if connections aim him at the Ryanair Chase in March. *(op 7/1 tchd 8/1)*

Jim(FR), who proved six lengths too strong for Hi Cloy at Galway in October, was 7lb worse off at the weights, but was still able to run a smashing race and it was only in the final strides he was reeled in, not being helped by a mistake at the last. A gallant front-running chaser, he too is effective over a variety of distances and a little further improvement would see him winning at this level. He is another Ryanair Chase possible. *(op 12/1)*

Forget The Past ◆, a high-class novice, faced a very stiff assignment on his reappearance when asked to shoulder 11-11 in the Paddy Power, but he ran well for a long way. Again jumping fluently, he got tired in the straight and was probably outpaced on the run-in, but remains open to masses of further improvement. Three miles is going to suit and, although a long way off, it would not surprise to see him develop into a 2007 Gold Cup contender. *(op 9/2)*

Ned Kelly(IRE), a high-class hurdler a few seasons back, has done well since returning from a lengthy spell on the sidelines, but he has not reached the top over fences and, although running well, was again found wanting. If going to the Festival, it is likely to be for one of the handicaps. *(op 25/1 tchd 33/1)*

War Of Attrition(IRE), perhaps the most promising chaser in Ireland right now, having already claimed two big scalps this season in the form of Kicking King and Rathgar Beau. However, although he has won in this sort of ground before, it has been against vastly inferior opposition and connections had voiced their concerns beforehand over the form of the stable. He travelled well to a point, but dropped away tamely, O'Dwyer wisely looking after him once his chance had gone. This effort was not in keeping with his previous runs and bookmaker reaction in pushing him right *back out to 20/1 for the Gold Cup seems ridiculous. Official explanation: jockey said gelding ran flat throughout; vet said gelding was blowing hard after the race; trainer said gelding was found to have a high bilirubin level when examined at yard post race (op 4/6)*

2796a BEWLEYS HOTELS & ITBA FILLIES BONUS (PRO/AM) FLAT RACE 2m 2f

3:30 (3:30) 4-5-Y-0 **£18,468** (£5,418; £2,581; £879)

RPR

1 **Knockara Luck (IRE)**[241] 4841 4-11-1 .... MissNCarberry[(3)] 101+
(N G Richards) *mid-div: 7th after 1/2-way: 5th 5f out: tk clsr order 4f out: led appr st: sn rdn clr: styd on wl fnl f: comf* **2/1**[1]

2 *3 ½* **Haydens First (IRE)**[28] 2225 5-11-2 .... MrDCO'Connor[(7)] 94
(Thomas Cooper, Ire) *trckd ldrs: 6th after 1/2-way: 4th and prog 4f out: 2nd into st: kpt on wl: nt trble wnr* **7/2**[3]

3 *7* **Berkeley House (IRE)**[42] 1947 5-11-4 .... MrLPFlynn[(5)] 87
(C F Swan, Ire) *trckd ldrs on outer: impr into cl 3rd over 4f out: rdn appr st: no imp fr 2f out* **5/2**[2]

4 *2* **Clover Pearl (IRE)**[63] 1704 5-11-2 .... MrJJDoyle[(7)] 85
(Michael Cullen, Ire) *mid-div: impr into 4th over 6f out: cl 2nd over 4f out: sn led: hdd 2 1/2f out: 4th and no ex st* **25/1**

5 *½* **Mistify Me (IRE)**[21] 2400 4-10-11 .... MissJGeraghty[(7)] 80
(T K Geraghty, Ire) *rr of mid-div: 7th 4f out: kpt on same pce st* **20/1**

6 *12* **Windmill View (IRE)** 5-11-2 .... MrDMacAuley[(7)] 73
(F Flood, Ire) *towards rr: kpt on wl st* **16/1**

7 *10* **Presenting Gayle (IRE)**[39] 2000 4-10-11 .... MrATDuff[(7)] 58
(F Flood, Ire) *chsd ldrs: 7th 5f out: mod 6th under 4f out: no ex st* **20/1**

8 *4* **Overbury Lady**[27] 2252 4-11-4 .... MrJTMcNamara 54
(Daniel O'Connell, Ire) *cl up in 2nd: led 6f out: hdd & wknd under 4f out* **10/1**

9 *½* **Fastnet Light (IRE)**[56] 1771 5-11-2 .... MrRMHennessy[(7)] 58
(D T Hughes, Ire) *cl up in 3rd: 2nd 6f out: rdn and wknd fr 5f out* **25/1**

10 *25* **Deeshan (IRE)**[22] 2359 4-10-13 .... MrRO'Sullivan[(5)] 28
(I Madden, Ire) *nvr a factor: trailing 4f out: t.o st* **50/1**

11 *8* **Sithgaoithe (IRE)** 5-11-2 .... MrMJO'Hare[(7)] 25
(Leonard Whitmore, Ire) *mid-div: wknd over 4f out: eased st: t.o* **25/1**

12 *12* **Tristar (IRE)**[226] 118 5-11-2 .... MrDPFahy[(7)] 13
(Daniel Miley, Ire) *led: hdd 6f out: sn wknd: t.o* **50/1**

13 *dist* **Kates Little Pearl (IRE)**[14] 2548 5-11-4 .... MissEDoyle[(5)] —
(Thomas Gerard O'Leary, Ire) *a in rr: wknd 1/2-way: completely t.o* **50/1**

5m 0.40s
WFA 4 from 5yo 10lb **13** Ran SP% **126.0**
CSF £8.73 TOTE £2.40: £1.50, £1.50, £1.40; DF 8.20.
Owner A Clark/W B Morris/J Dudgeon **Bred** George Durrheim And Mrs Maria Mulcahy Durrheim **Trained** Greystoke, Cumbria

■ Stewards' Enquiry : Mr D C O'Connor caution: excessive use of the whip

NOTEBOOK

Knockara Luck(IRE), a winner on her debut at Cheltenham in the spring, beat a fairly modest field comfortably. She is a promising type and it will be interesting to see how she gets on when faced with a flight of hurdles. *(op 6/4)*

T/Jkpt: @489.10. Pool of @15,000.00 - 23 winning units. T/Plt: @42.60. Pool of @2,106.00 - 37 winning units. II

2573 PLUMPTON (L-H)

Monday, December 12

OFFICIAL GOING: Soft

Wind: Almost nil Weather: Fine

2797 CAROLE & ROY REEVE 40TH ANNIVERSARY JUVENILE NOVICES' HURDLE (9 hdls) 2m

12:50 (12:50) (Class 4) 3-Y-O £3,261 (£950; £475)

Form RPR

5333 1 **Josear**[11] 2597 3-10-5 100 ShaneWalsh(7) 100+
(C J Down) *led tl after 2nd: trckd ldr: led after 5th: sn wl clr: easily* 7/2[2]

5 2 *18* **Dance Hall Diva**[22] 2373 3-9-12 LeeNewnes(7) 68
(M D I Usher) *chsd ldrs: hmpd 3 out: rdn to go 2nd sn after: no ch w wnr* 12/1

3 3 *20* **Laconicos (IRE)**[22] 2373 3-10-9 GinoCarenza(3) 55
(W B Stone) *in tch: rdn after 6th: wnt 2nd briefly after 3 out: wknd next* 4/1[3]

0P 4 *11* **Desert Moonbeam (IRE)**[6] 2681 3-10-0 JayHarris(5) 37
(R J Hodges) *chsd ldrs: mstke and hmpd 3 out: sn rdn and wknd* 66/1

00 5 *11* **Femme D'Avril (FR)**[11] 2597 3-9-12 MissLucyBridges(7) 26
(Miss Lucy Bridges) *a in rr: blnd 3 out* 33/1

6 *12* **Smokincanon**[55] 3-10-2 StuartHaddon(10) 21
(W G M Turner) *a towards rr: t.o* 40/1

6 P **River Role**[10] 2611 3-10-0 RobertStephens(5) —
(J W Tudor) *a bhd: t.o and p.u after 5th* 40/1

0 P **Blazing Ember**[39] 2014 3-10-5 ChristianWilliams —
(J W Tudor) *sn wl bhd: p.u after 5th* 100/1

040 P **Briannie (IRE)**[6] 2681 3-9-12 (p) RobertLucey-Butler(7) —
(P Butler) *sn bhd: t.o and p.u after 5th* 50/1

P **Harry May**[58] 3-10-12 JoeTizzard —
(C L Tizzard) *in tch tl wknd 3 out: bhd and p.u bef 2 out* 6/1

0 P **It's A Hottie**[39] 2014 3-10-12 LeightonAspell —
(P Winkworth) *mid div tl wknd qckly 5th: p.u bef next* 66/1

64 F **Satin Rose**[12] 2569 3-10-0 (p) PaddyMerrigan(5) 37
(K J Burke) *bhd: mstke 2nd: chalng for distant 4th whn fell last* 10/1

U P **Another Mistress**[22] 2373 3-9-12 JayPemberton(7) —
(R M Flower) *wl bhd whn j. bdly lft 3rd: t.o and p.u after 5th* 100/1

F4 F **Ellerslie Tom**[61] 1718 3-10-12 RichardJohnson —
(P Bowen) *trckd wnr: led after 2nd tl after 5th: wkng in 15l 2nd whn fell 3 out* 2/1[1]

4m 5.90s (4.70) **Going Correction** +0.20s/f (Yiel) 14 Ran SP% **121.4**

Speed ratings: **96,87,77,71,66 60,—,—,—,— —,—,—,—** CSF £42.77 TOTE £4.70: £1.30, £2.50, £1.50; EX 44.50.

Owner Mrs L M Edwards **Bred** Peter Barclay **Trained** Mutterton, Devon

FOCUS

A truly awful juvenile hurdle run in a moderate time and is unlikely to produce anything other than the odd winner.

NOTEBOOK

Josear was given an intelligent ride by his young pilot and was able to steal a few lengths at a vital stage before gradually coming clear of a toiling field. He could have won easier had his rider kept going on him, but there was no need and this well-experienced individual will no doubt continue to pay his way at a moderate level, albeit connections said he may be given a rest. *(tchd 4-1)*

Dance Hall Diva, well held on her hurdling debut here last month, obtained a better finishing position this time, comprehensively reversing form with the Laconicos, but she was beaten a long way by the winner and achieved little. She is clearly not very good and it may take a switch to low-grade handicaps for her to win.

Laconicos(IRE) was unable to confirm course form with runner-up, and clearly failed to run to form on this softer surface. He may be worthy of another chance. *(op 9-2)*

Desert Moonbeam(IRE) stepped up on her initial effort and showed a bit more, but was eventually well-beaten and her stamina for hurdling remains suspect.

Femme D'Avril(FR) had run his race and was on his way back to the pack when falling three out. It remains to be seen how this affects confidence.

2798 CORALCASINO.COM NOVICES' CHASE (12 fncs) 2m 1f

1:20 (1:21) (Class 3) 4-Y-O+ £7,857 (£2,341; £1,185; £607; £317)

Form RPR

33-1 1 **Voy Por Ustedes (FR)**[20] 2422 4-11-1 RobertThornton 140+
(A King) *hld up bhd ldrs: jnd ldr after 3 out: shkn up to ld after 2 out: r.o wl: readily* 6/4[1]

515- 2 *5* **My World (FR)**[275] 4329 5-10-9 AndrewThornton 124+
(R H Alner) *prom: led 9th: rdn and hdd after 2 out: kpt on but nt pce of wnr* 16/1

20-1 3 *8* **Big Moment**[22] 2377 7-11-8 JimCrowley 130+
(Mrs A J Perrett) *trckd ldrs: mstke 5th: rdn appr 8th: hit 9th and 3 out: one pced after* 4/1[3]

133/ 4 *½* **Fleet Street**[619] 4638 6-11-2 MickFitzgerald 124+
(N J Henderson) *j.rt thrght: led tl mstke and hdd 9th: rdn after 3 out: wknd next* 2/1[2]

0-20 5 *dist* **Elfkirk (IRE)**[14] 2553 6-10-9 BenjaminHitchcott —
(R H Buckler) *chsd ldrs: nt fluent 2nd: lost tch fr 7th: t.o* 25/1

00 P **Butsadtohavetogo (IRE)**[29] 2211 5-11-2 MatthewBatchelor —
(A E Jones) *lost tch fr 4th: t.o and p.u after 6th* 100/1

1-24 U **Kawagino (IRE)**[16] 2488 5-10-13 110 RichardYoung(3) 120
(J W Mullins) *hld up: tk clsr order 7th: rdn whn nt fluent 3 out: 5th and btn whn blnd and uns rdr last* 12/1

4m 22.2s (-1.90) **Going Correction** +0.40s/f (Soft)

WFA 4 from 5yo+ 10lb 7 Ran SP% **111.7**

Speed ratings: **112,109,105,105,— —,—** CSF £22.66 TOTE £2.60: £1.40, £2.80; EX 28.80.

Owner Sir Robert Ogden **Bred** Ecurie Macaire Guillaume, And Francis Picoulet **Trained** Barbury Castle, Wilts

FOCUS

A decent contest for the course and the winning time was fair. The winner is rated value for further and the form looks solid.

NOTEBOOK

Voy Por Ustedes(FR), a decent hurdler, is quickly making up into a very useful novice and he followed his fencing debut success with another smooth display. A tall, attractive type, he again jumped fluently and had only the mare to worry about as they turned for home. Although undoubtedly a smart prospect, he has yet to beat anything of note and whether at this stage he deserves quotes as low as 16/1 for the Arkle is debatable. That said he will be only five in the new year and will continue to get a weight-for-age allowance, so can pick up a nice prize somewhere. *(op 5-4 tchd 6-5)*

My World(FR), a 112-rated hurdler, was supposed to make her reappearance over the smaller obstacles at the abandoned Lingfield meeting the previous weekend, was allowed to take her chance over fences. As with many Alner runners, she showed greatly improved form for the switch and jumped boldly towards the head of affairs. She had them all beaten off barring the classy winner turning in and was unable to match his change of gear, but it will be surprising if she does not win her share of races this season. *(tchd 14-1)*

Big Moment, the best of these over hurdles, faced a very stiff task conceding weight to some useful sorts and he was readily outpaced. There is room for improvement in the jumping department, but further suits ideally and he may be open to a little further improvement in handicaps. *(tchd 5-1)*

Fleet Street, a smart novice hurdler who placed in both the major Cheltenham and Aintree two-mile novice events back in 2004, was returning from a lengthy lay-off due to injury, but his stable is one of the best at readying a horse first time back and he was strong in the market. However he continually jumped out to the right and made a couple of mistakes, causing him to be left behind in the straight. The match-practice will no doubt do him good, and he may improve for going the other way around, so he should be capable of winning a similar event. In the long-term he should make a decent handicapper. *(op 5-2 tchd 3-1)*

Elfkirk(IRE) *Official explanation: trainer said mare finished distressed (tchd 20-1)*

Kawagino(IRE) was unable to build on the promise of his staying-on chase debut at Newbury, but he did travel well to a point and will probably be more at home back in handicaps.

2799 CORALCASINO.COM "NATIONAL HUNT" NOVICES' HURDLE (12 hdls) 2m 5f

1:50 (1:50) (Class 4) 4-Y-O+ £3,467 (£1,018; £509; £254)

Form RPR

2-1 1 **What A Vintage (IRE)**[30] 2185 5-10-5 RichardJohnson 104+
(R T Phillips) *hld up towards rr: hit 5th: smooth hdwy to trck ldrs after 7th: hit 3 out: shkn up to ld 2 out: kpt on wl: rdn out* 7/2[2]

0620 2 *6* **Double Dizzy**[31] 2166 4-10-7 106 WilliamKennedy(5) 104+
(R H Buckler) *in touch: mstke 7th: rdn and effrt after 3 out: kpt on same pce* 7/2[2]

3 *½* **Something Wells (FR)**[171] 4-11-5 SamThomas 111+
(Miss Venetia Williams) *trckd ldrs: led after 3 out: rdn and hdd next: kpt on same pce* 9/4[1]

4/P- 4 *19* **Tuck In**[373] 2616 8-10-12 PhilipHide 86+
(P Winkworth) *prom: led 3rd: rdn and hdd after 3 out: wknd next: stmbled last* 25/1

-064 5 *4* **Ice Bucket (IRE)**[15] 2528 5-10-12 WarrenMarston 85+
(Miss H C Knight) *t.k.h: trckd ldrs: rdn after 3 out: 5th and btn whn blnd next* 9/1

0- 6 *2* **River Of Light (IRE)**[268] 4463 5-10-5 DarylJacob(7) 78
(D P Keane) *in tch: hit 5th: rdn after 8th: wknd 3 out* 100/1

30 7 *nk* **Joseph Beuys (IRE)**[19] 2426 6-10-12 NoelFehily 78+
(D P Keane) *hld up towards rr: sme hdwy after 9th: wkng whn mstke 3 out* 50/1

2-3U 8 *2 ½* **Scalini'S (IRE)**[15] 2528 5-10-12 APMcCoy 77+
(Jonjo O'Neill) *hld up mid div: trckd ldrs 8th: rdn and wknd after 3 out* 13/2[3]

63/ 9 *29* **The Wooden Spoon (IRE)**[740] 2537 7-10-12 LeightonAspell 46
(L Wells) *a towards rr: t.o fr 9th* 25/1

4P00 10 *2* **Silverio (GER)**[14] 2554 4-10-12 (p) JamieMoore 44
(G L Moore) *prom tl 8th: sn lost tch: t.o* 50/1

00-0 11 *12* **Optimo (GER)**[24] 2322 4-10-12 BrianCrowley 32
(G L Moore) *chsd ldrs: reminders after 4th: bhd fr 6th: t.o* 50/1

-50 12 *7* **Good Call (IRE)**[9] 2631 6-10-5 MrAJBerry(7) 25
(Jonjo O'Neill) *in tch: lost pl and dropped rr 5th: t.o fr 9th* 66/1

0-6 P **Red Granite**[53] 1799 5-10-12 JimmyMcCarthy —
(K C Bailey) *in tch tl 7th: sn wl bhd: p.u bef 2 out* 40/1

5m 18.3s (-6.50) **Going Correction** +0.20s/f (Yiel) 13 Ran SP% **117.0**

Speed ratings: **105,102,102,95,93 93,92,91,80,80 75,72,—** CSF £15.22 TOTE £4.70: £1.90, £2.10, £1.70; EX 21.20.

Owner The Someday's Here Racing Partnership **Bred** John Costello **Trained** Adlestrop, Gloucs

FOCUS

Ordinary novice form, but the front three pulled well clear and are probably up to winning more races at a similar level. The runner-up sets the standard.

NOTEBOOK

What A Vintage(IRE), a winner second time up in bumpers, comes from a stable that is going nicely after a slow start and she was always likely to go well here in receipt of a fair amount of weight. A strong traveller throughout, she made smooth headway into a challenging position before the turn into the straight, and soon swept into the lead to win going away. She clearly has the makings of a useful mare and should be capable of defying a penalty. *(tchd 4-1)*

Double Dizzy found himself a bit outclassed in a decent handicap at Cheltenham last time and this was more his bag. He kept on dourly up the straight and got the better of the well supported favourite for second, but will find life easier back in handicaps at an average level. *(op 9-2 tchd 5-1)*

Something Wells(FR), an ex-French gelding shouldering a penalty, was strong in the market to make it yet another winner for the Williams team, but Thomas seemed determined to keep him towards the inside of the track on what looked the worse ground and away from the other principals. He still travelled well into the lead, but it was clear from turning in that he was not going to win and he was passed for second on the run-in. He rates a fair bit better than the bare result, but his penalty will continue to leave him vulnerable. *(op 7-2)*

Tuck In, who is rising nine, was having the only the fourth start of his career and he ran well to a point. *He will find life easier in low-grade handicaps. Official explanation: jockey said gelding gurgled after last (tchd 22-1)*

Ice Bucket(IRE) had looked to be heading the right way, but this was a step in the wrong direction and maybe the ground was too soft. He is unlikely to be seen at his best until tackling fences. *(op 15-2)*

Scalini'S(IRE) was held when unseating on his hurdling debut, but he had run well to a point that day, something which cannot be said here. He clearly has ability, but needs to leave this showing behind. *(op 4-1 tchd 7-1)*

2800 BARRY DAVIES MEMORIAL H'CAP CHASE (18 fncs) 3m 2f

2:20 (2:20) (Class 3) (0-115,115) 5-Y-O £6,553 (£1,952; £988; £506; £265)

Form RPR

U212 1 **Mon Mome (FR)**[16] 2504 5-11-12 115 SamThomas 135+
(Miss Venetia Williams) *a travelling wl in tch: tk clsr order 14th: led on bit after 3 out: sn clr: easily* 9/2[3]

B-43 2 *6* **Infrasonique (FR)**[14] 2557 9-10-10 99 (v) MarkBradburne 103
(Mrs L C Taylor) *j.rt thrght: led 3rd: rdn and hdd after 3 out: kpt on but no ch w wnr fr next* 13/2

P-56 3 *1* **Dun Locha Castle (IRE)**[12] 2575 10-10-0 89 oh7 TomScudamore 92
(N R Mitchell) *led tl 3rd: chsd ldr: rdn appr 15th: kpt on same pce fr 3 out* 33/1

60P5 4 *1 ¾* **Follow The Flow (IRE)**[8] 2662 9-11-1 107 (p) OwynNelmes(3) 108
(P A Pritchard) *chsd ldrs: rdn after 13th: kpt on same pce fr 4 out* 50/1

0130 5 *dist* **Super Road Train**[100] 1398 6-10-2 91 (b) LeightonAspell —
(O Sherwood) *hld up and a towards rr: lost tch fr 14th: t.o* 12/1

The Form Book, Raceform Ltd, Compton, RG20 6NL

361/ **U** **Mcsnappy**[599] 4930 8-10-0 **92** RichardYoung(3) —
(J W Mullins) *mid div tl blnd and uns rdr 4th* **14/1**

P45- **P** **El Viejo (IRE)**[331] 3355 8-11-0 **110** JustinMorgan(7) —
(L Wells) *chsd ldrs tl 12th: sn lost tch: p.u bef 14th* **25/1**

31P/ **F** **Helixir Du Theil (FR)**[738] 2567 10-10-2 **91** (p) BenjaminHitchcott —
(R H Buckler) *mid div: hdwy 9th: cl up in 6th whn fell 14th* **20/1**

00-3 **P** **Bar Gayne (IRE)**[14] 2555 6-10-3 **92** ow2 JasonMaguire —
(T R George) *in tch: reminders 8th: struggling whn mstke 12th: p.u after next* **11/4**[1]

P26U **P** **Billy Ballbreaker (IRE)**[10] 2610 9-10-6 **95** (tp) JoeTizzard —
(C L Tizzard) *hld up: hdwy 9th: rdn and wknd after 14th: t.o and p.u bef 3 out* **9/1**

52-2 **P** **Majestic Moonbeam (IRE)**[14] 2557 7-10-12 **101** APMcCoy —
(Jonjo O'Neill) *hld up: mstke 10th: hdwy 13th: hit 15th: sn rdn: wknd appr 2 out: p.u bef last* **4/1**[2]

7m 0.90s (6.90) **Going Correction** +0.40s/f (Soft) **11** Ran SP% **116.1**
Speed ratings: **97,95,94,94,**— —,—,—,—,— — CSF £32.21 CT £858.55 TOTE £4.90: £2.10, £2.40, £5.50; EX 34.80.
Owner Mrs Vida Bingham **Bred** A Deschere **Trained** Kings Caple, H'fords

FOCUS
A modest winning time for the grade, but Mon Mome is undoubtedly progressive and is value for more than double the official margin and the form could rate higher.

NOTEBOOK
Mon Mome(FR) has really got his act together since unseating on his chase debut and appreciated this step back up in distance having finished second over two miles at Towcester latest. Always travelling fluently, he cruised into the lead at the third-last and cantered clear under top weight to win with any amount in hand. Still only five, he is likely to be capable of further improvement and a follow up is highly probable. *(op 3-1)*
Infrasonique(FR), racing here off a 21lb lower mark than when last successful, again ran well in defeat, looking helped by the headgear, but it has been some time since he got his head in front and he cannot be backed with any confidence. *(op 8-1)*
Dun Locha Castle(IRE), 7lb out of the handicap, ran a bold race at rewarding each-way odds and kept on right the way to the line. Stamina is his strong suit and he can win again back down in grade where he will be able to race in the handicap proper.
Follow The Flow(IRE), a six-time winner last season, has been shown little leniency by the Handicapper, but the application of cheekpieces injected some life back into him and he plugged on for fourth. He may need some further help before making any appeal.
Super Road Train was the only other to complete, but he came home in his own time. *(op 16-1)*
Helixir Du Theil(FR), nibbled at in the market beforehand, was still going well enough when coming down at the 14th, but it was too early to tell how he would have fared and it is hoped this does not affect his confidence. *(op 10-3 tchd 7-2 in places)*
Bar Gayne(IRE), a staying-on third on his chase debut at Folkestone, was stepping up five furlongs in trip and looked sure to go well off his lowly mark, but he ran very flat and was never really travelling. He has winning form in similar ground, but maybe a sounder surface suits best over fences. *(op 10-3 tchd 7-2 in places)*

2801 CORALPOKER.COM H'CAP CHASE (14 fncs) 2m 4f
2:50 (2:51) (Class 4) (0-90,88) 5-Y-O+ **£4,016** (£1,196; £605; £310; £162)

Form RPR

3111 **1** **Jolly Boy (FR)**[4] 2719 6-11-7 **83** 7ex (b) SamThomas 100+
(Miss Venetia Williams) *trckd ldr: led after 9th: mstke next: a in command after: readily* **4/5**[1]

-P **2** *8* **Minat Boy**[24] 2313 9-10-11 **73** JoeTizzard 72+
(C L Tizzard) *chsd ldrs: lost tch after 9th: styd on again u.p fr 3 out: tk 2nd cl home* **8/1**[3]

042P **3** *nk* **Sitting Duck**[14] 2555 6-10-11 **80** CharlieStudd(7) 80+
(B G Powell) *j. sltly rt thrght: led tl after 9th: chsd wnr: rdn after 3 out: kpt on same pce: lost 2nd cl home* **25/1**

52R4 **4** *8* **Hill Forts Henry**[22] 2378 7-10-7 **69** (tp) AndrewThornton 60+
(J W Mullins) *in tch: outpcd and drvn along fr 10th: 15 l 3rd whn hit 11th: one pced fr 3 out* **11/2**[2]

P-40 **5** *10* **Opportunity Knocks**[14] 2555 5-10-9 **78** KeiranBurke(7) 58
(N J Hawke) *a towards rr* **11/1**

3P-P **P** **Test Of Friendship**[18] 2465 8-11-7 **83** JimCrowley —
(Mrs H Dalton) *in tch: drvn along fr 4th: bhd fr 9th: p.u bef next* **16/1**

-1P5 **P** **Our Jolly Swagman**[16] 2506 10-11-5 **88** (v) WayneKavanagh(7) —
(J W Mullins) *hld up: making hdwy whn mstke 10th and rdr lost iron: p.u bef next* **10/1**

-5PF **P** **Cloneybrien Boy (IRE)**[8] 2660 5-9-11 **64** DerekLaverty(5) —
(Mrs A M Thorpe) *in tch: trckd ldrs after 8th: rdn and wknd after 11th: t.o and p.u bef 2 out* **33/1**

5m 21.6s (3.15) **Going Correction** +0.40s/f (Soft) **8** Ran SP% **112.1**
Speed ratings: **101,97,97,94,90** —,—,— CSF £7.92 CT £86.18 TOTE £1.80: £1.10, £2.40, £3.70; EX 8.10.
Owner Favourites Racing **Bred** Georges Lacombe **Trained** Kings Caple, H'fords

FOCUS
A weak race and an easy opportunity for Jolly Boy to complete the four-timer. He was value for more than double the winning margin with the second setting the level.

NOTEBOOK
Jolly Boy(FR), bidding for his fourth win in the space of 14 days, was shouldering a 7lb penalty and was rightly made a hot favourite. Always well placed, he quickly brushed aside early leader Sitting Duck and had the race sewn up in a matter of strides, again cantering clear to win as he liked. He would be entitled to win again if running at Windsor on Friday, where he will be allowed to run off this mark, but it is worth bearing in mind just how weak a race this was. *(tchd 10-11)*
Minat Boy just got the better of a dual with Sitting Duck for second and ran what was probably his best race to date under Rules. *(op 12-1 tchd 15-2)*
Sitting Duck failed to build on his chasing debut when pulled up at Folkestone last time, but this was a much better effort. He left himself vulnerable to the favourite by going off in front, but kept on well once passed and his fluent jumping will continue to stand him in good stead. *(op 16-1)*
Hill Forts Henry, who has yet to win in 20 starts, was the disappointment of the race, looking incredibly one-paced under pressure. He remains one to avoid. *(op 7-1)*
Our Jolly Swagman *Official explanation: jockey said saddle slipped (op 9-1)*

2802 CORALPOKER.COM H'CAP HURDLE (9 hdls) 2m
3:20 (3:20) (Class 4) (0-105,104) 4-Y-O+ **£3,193** (£930; £465)

Form RPR

0002 **1** **Silistra**[22] 2379 6-10-7 **85** (p) BenjaminHitchcott 87
(Mrs L C Jewell) *hld up: hdwy 6th: led on bit appr 2 out: shkn up and edgd rt run-in: kpt on wl cl home* **12/1**

-P00 **2** *hd* **Amnesty**[9] 2632 6-11-0 **92** (b) JamieMoore 94
(G L Moore) *mid div: hdwy appr 3 out: pressed wnr fr 2 out: hrd rdn and ev ch run-in: no ex cl home* **17/2**

P/PP **3** *4* **Carly Bay**[12] 2576 7-11-8 **100** RichardJohnson 98
(G P Enright) *hld up: hdwy after 6th: rdn and ev ch appr 2 out: cl 4th and hld whn nt fluent last: tk 3rd cl home* **20/1**

-421 **4** *nk* **Nagano (FR)**[8] 2659 7-11-7 **99** 7ex RobertThornton 97
(Ian Williams) *hld up mid div: tk clsr order 6th: pressed wnr appr 2 out: rdn and ev ch last: no ex* **11/10**[1]

-051 **5** *7* **Killing Me Softly**[11] 2585 4-11-12 **104** (v) ChristianWilliams 95
(J Gallagher) *led tl 2nd: chsd ldr: rdn and effrt after 3 out: kpt on same pce* **7/1**[2]

0620 **6** *3/4* **Amanpuri (GER)**[10] 2605 7-10-9 **92** DerekLaverty(5) 82
(Mrs A M Thorpe) *prom: led 2nd: rdn and hdd after 3 out: kpt on same pce* **16/1**

-000 **7** *20* **Greatest By Phar**[17] 2043 4-10-7 **85** AndrewThornton 63+
(J Akehurst) *chsd ldrs: rdn after 3 out: sn wknd* **16/1**

4PPU **8** *5* **Peppershot**[29] 2214 5-10-7 **92** (t) JayPemberton(7) 57
(R Gurney) *hld up and a in rr* **33/1**

0U-0 **9** *12* **The Player**[11] 2584 6-10-12 **90** JoeTizzard 43
(A M Balding) *racd keenly: hld up: rdn after 6th: wknd 3 out: t.o whn blnd 2 out* **16/1**

P6-0 **10** *dist* **Tiger Island (USA)**[55] 1784 5-10-4 **82** MatthewBatchelor —
(A E Jones) *a bhd: t.o fr 5th* **66/1**

F-0F **P** **Buckland Gold (IRE)**[14] 2556 5-10-5 **90** RobertLucey-Butler(7) —
(D B Feek) *mid div tl lost pl qckly appr 5th: p.u bef 6th: b.b.v* **20/1**

4000 **P** **The Gene Genie**[10] 2609 10-10-10 **88** JimCrowley —
(R J Hodges) *chsd ldrs: reminders after 4th: sn bhd: t.o and p.u bef 2 out* **8/1**[3]

4m 3.20s (2.00) **Going Correction** +0.20s/f (Yiel) **12** Ran SP% **121.1**
Speed ratings: **103,102,100,100,97 96,86,84,78,**— —,— CSF £107.32 CT £2042.51 TOTE £13.50: £2.10, £2.70, £5.00; EX 143.60 Place 6 £136.12, Place 5 £60.08.
Owner Mrs P S Donkin **Bred** Sir Eric Parker **Trained** Sutton Valence, Kent
■ Stewards' Enquiry : Benjamin Hitchcott caution: careless riding
Jamie Moore one-day ban: used whip with excessive frequency (Jan 13)

FOCUS
Average form assessed through the second, and could rate a bit higher.

NOTEBOOK
Silistra came into this winless in 33 attempts both on the Flat and over jumps, but he travelled strongly into contention and simply battled on too willingly for the runner-up. This should do his confidence good and there may be more races in him off this sort of mark. *(op 14-1)*
Amnesty has not run a decent race over hurdles for some time, but he was given a good ride and locked in battle with Silistra after the last. He did not get up the hill as well as that one however, and had to settle for second, but this was at least a step in the right direction. The negative however is that he has never been the most consistent and as a result cannot be relied up on to repeat the effort. *(op 10-1 tchd 8-1)*
Carly Bay, who had pulled up in each of her three most recent starts, showed a bit more zip on this occasion and stayed on well on the climb to the line to snatch third. She can find a small race at one of the gaff tracks if building on this. *(op 16-1)*
Nagano(FR), up 7lb for winning at Warwick earlier in the month, held every chance and simply did not look good enough under his penalty. Although a winner in this ground last time, he may be better back on good ground. *(op 5-4 tchd 11-8)*
Killing Me Softly was another who came into this off the back off a 7lb rise for winning and he too struggled from the turn-in. This was not a bad effort under top weight. *(op 13-2 tchd 8-1)*
Buckland Gold(IRE) *Official explanation: jockey said gelding bled from the nose*
T/Plt: £237.40 to a £1 stake. Pool £52,712.15, 162.05 winning tickets T/Qpdt: £56.50 to a £1 stake. Pool £4,175.70, 54.60 winning tickets TM

[2552]FOLKESTONE (R-H)
Tuesday, December 13

OFFICIAL GOING: Chase course - good; hurdle course - soft (good to soft in places)
Wind: Almost nil Weather: Fine but cloudy

2803 SMITH & WILLIAMSON NOVICES' HURDLE (DIV I) (9 hdls) 2m 1f 110y
12:10 (12:10) (Class 4) 3-Y-O+ **£3,526** (£1,035; £517; £258)

Form RPR

5 **1** **Warningcamp (GER)**[23] 2374 4-11-5 LeightonAspell 115+
(Lady Herries) *cl up: led sn after 2 out: rdn and styd on wl bef last* **14/1**[3]

1 **2** *2 1/2* **Siberian Highness (FR)**[21] 2423 4-11-5 RobertThornton 113+
(A King) *hld up midfield: prog 3 out: chsd wnr between fnl 2f: rdn and kpt on same pce* **1/3**[1]

4422 **3** *7* **Corker**[13] 2578 3-9-12 104 RobertLucey-Butler(7) 91
(D B Feek) *hld up in rr: sme prog 3 out: outpcd by ldrs next: kpt on u.p to snatch 3rd nr fin* **8/1**[2]

4 *nk* **Lysander (GER)**[16] 6-10-12 JMarinov(7) 105
(Frau E Mader, Germany) *t.k.h: prom: w ldr 5th: mstkes next 2: upsides after 2 out: sn one pce u.p* **20/1**

0-F3 **5** *12* **Nobel Bleu De Kerpaul (FR)**[13] 2573 4-11-5 RJGreene 93
(P Winkworth) *hld up in rr: outpcd after 3 out: hrd rdn and no prog next: plugged on* **16/1**

25-0 **6** *1* **Lannigans Lock**[29] 2238 4-11-5 BrianCrowley 93+
(R Rowe) *led to 3rd: led 5th tl sn after 2 out: in 4th whn shkn up briefly between last 2: grad wknd: do bttr* **33/1**

31S0 **7** *19* **Trigger Guard**[31] 2178 3-10-12 103 (b) PhilipHide 66
(G L Moore) *settled midfield: hit 2nd: rdn and outpcd after 3 out: wknd after next* **20/1**

P **8** *2* **Crystal Ka (FR)**[43] 1948 3-10-5 MatthewBatchelor 57
(M R Hoad) *t.k.h: sn restrained in rr: lost tch w ldrs after 5th: no ch after* **100/1**

9 *7* **Pharoah's Gold (IRE)**[8] 7-11-5 ChristianWilliams 64
(D Burchell) *plld hrd: pressed ldr: led 3rd: looked like refusing next: hdd 5th : wknd 2 out* **50/1**

0 **10** *17* **Castle Frome (IRE)**[29] 2249 6-11-2 ColinBolger(3) 47
(A E Price) *stdd s: hld up wl in rr: lost tch 5th: sn bhd: t.o* **100/1**

-0PF **11** *19* **Ray Mond**[16] 2523 4-11-0 DerekLaverty(5) 28
(M J Gingell) *plld v hrd: racd wd: in tch to 5th: sn wknd rapidly: t.o* **100/1**

00 **12** *18* **Castletown Lad**[11] 2606 5-11-5 TimmyMurphy 10
(M C Pipe) *nt jump wl: hld up: last: lost tch after 3rd: t.o* **50/1**

4m 27.8s (-1.50) **Going Correction** +0.075s/f (Yiel)
WFA 3 from 4yo+ 13lb **12** Ran SP% **118.0**
Speed ratings: **106,104,101,101,96 95,87,86,83,75 67,59** CSF £19.23 TOTE £17.40: £2.50, £1.10, £1.60; EX 26.80.
Owner Lady Sarah Clutton **Bred** Schwindibode Ag **Trained** Patching, W Sussex

FOCUS
Two potentially useful sorts pulled clear in what was an uncompetitive hurdle. The time was decent and the third is the best guide to the form.

NOTEBOOK
Warningcamp(GER), who caught the eye of many when a staying-on fifth on his hurdles debut, appeared to face a stiff task against the favourite, but he travelled extremely a few places ahead of the favourite and it was evident from half a mile out that he was going best of the pair. He went further clear of her before the second last and, although getting a little weary on the run-in, he won with a fair bit in hand. There is no reason to believe this to be a fluke and he looks a potentially useful sort. *(op 11-1)*
Siberian Highness(FR) created a favourable impression when winning easily on her British/hurdling debut at Warwick last month and was understandably a very short price with a distinct lack of serious opposition. She too travelled well, but was in trouble before the turn into the straight and it emerged after the race she had sustained damage to her knee. A big, scopey filly, it is safe to assume she is a bit better than this and two and a half miles may bring about further improvement. She will make a good chaser in time. *(op 2-7 tchd 4-11 in places)*
Corker is a consistent sort who again ran his race, keeping on late to grab a place. He was not in the same league as the front pair and will remain vulnerable to something less exposed. *(op 15-2)*
Lysander(GER), a German raider, did himself no favours in racing keenly early on and may have held third but for a few jumping errors. There was promise to be gleaned from this and he can probably find a race at an ordinary level. *(op 16-1)*
Nobel Bleu De Kerpaul(FR) kept on late and was at least going forward at the end of his race. Low-grade handicaps will see him in a better light. *(op 14-1)*
Lannigans Lock was not given an overly hard time once beaten and is another likely to be more at home in handicaps, once qualified. *(tchd 40-1)*
Pharoah's Gold(IRE) *Official explanation: trainer said gelding had a breathing problem*

2804 SMITH & WILLIAMSON NOVICES' HURDLE (DIV II) (9 hdls) 2m 1f 110y
12:40 (12:45) (Class 4) 3-Y-0+ **£3,526** (£1,035; £517; £258)

Form RPR
1 **1** **In Media Res (FR)**[201] [515] 4-11-5 .... CharlieStudd(7) 122+
(N J Henderson) *w ldr: led 3rd: mde rest: shkn up and pressed last: drvn clr flat* **4/1**[2]
44 **2** *4* **Eleazar (GER)**[21] [2423] 4-11-5 .... LeightonAspell 105
(Mrs L Wadham) *hld up in tch: prog and cl up 2 out: rdn to chse wnr between fnl 2: chal last: sn outpcd* **4/1**[2]
6 **3** *5* **Saraba (FR)**[13] [2573] 4-10-9 .... ColinBolger(3) 93
(Mrs L J Mongan) *prom: cl up after 2 out: kpt on same pce u.p between last 2* **22/1**
6 **4** *7* **Dance World**[17] [2487] 5-10-12 .... MrMatthewSmith(7) 94+
(Miss J Feilden) *hld up in tch: prog to join wnr 2 out: wknd u.p between fnl 2* **6/1**[3]
0 **5** *9* **Anna Panna**[19] [2455] 4-10-12 .... AndrewThornton 84+
(R H Alner) *prom: w wnr fr 3rd tl after 3 out: losing pl whn sltly hmpd 2 out: eased whn btn* **50/1**
6 *9* **Flamand (FR)**[261] [4593] 4-11-5 .... JimmyMcCarthy 75
(C P Morlock) *t.k.h: hld up in tch: rdn and wknd 2 out* **33/1**
5 **7** *3 ½* **Magic Amigo**[39] [485] 4-11-5 .... JodieMogford 72
(J R Jenkins) *t.k.h: racd wd: hld up: last of main gp 3 out: no prog and btn sn after next* **25/1**
0 **8** *dist* **Nelson Du Ronceray (FR)**[16] [2528] 4-11-5 .... TimmyMurphy —
(M C Pipe) *racd wd: mde most to 3rd: losing pl whn slow jump next: sn t.o: p.u after 2 out: resed and j. last eventually* **20/1**
232- **F** **Le Galactico (FR)**[255] [4697] 4-11-5 .... RobertThornton —
(A King) *hld up midfield: prog 3 out: poised to chal whn fell 2 out: dead* **11/8**[1]
P- **P** **Harbour King (FR)**[284] [3303] 6-11-2 .... OwynNelmes(3) —
(N I M Rossiter) *in tch tl wknd u.p bef 4th: sn t.o: p.u after 2 out: dismntd* **100/1**
60 **P** **Gameset'N'Match**[86] [1480] 4-10-12 .... RobertLucey-Butler(7) —
(Miss M P Bryant) *t.k.h: hld up in rr: wknd 5th: sn wl t.o: p.u bef last* **100/1**

4m 30.4s (1.10) **Going Correction** +0.075s/f (Yiel) **11** Ran SP% **116.2**
Speed ratings: **100,98,96,92,88 84,83,—,—,—** — CSF £19.07 TOTE £4.20: £1.30, £1.60, £5.00; EX 23.40.
Owner Killinghurst Park Stud **Bred** Barron T De Zuylen De Nyevelt **Trained** Upper Lambourn, Berks

FOCUS
The weaker of the two divisions with the winner rated value for ten lengths and the second setting the standard.

NOTEBOOK
In Media Res(FR), a winner on the level in France, made a successful debut over hurdles at Newton Abbot in May, but had a penalty and softer ground to contend with here so could not be backed with any real confidence. However with favourite Le Galactico taking a fatal fall at the second last he was left with only Eleazar to shake off and he asserted on the run-in. He has thus far found a couple of weak opportunities it is likely he will struggle once meeting better opposition, but he may yet improve for a rise in distance. *(tchd 7-2)*
Eleazar(GER) ran his best race yet over hurdles and it looked as though he might claim the winner at the last, but he was unable to stay on as strongly and had to settle for second. There is a small novice at one of the small tracks in him. *(op 7-2 tchd 10-3)*
Saraba(FR) stepped up on her initial effort over obstacles and kept on at the one pace to claim a place. Low-grade handicaps are likely to represent her best chance of winning. *(op 25-1 tchd 28-1)*
Dance World travelled well to a point, but did not quite get home and may be better back on a sounder surface. *(tchd 5-1)*
Anna Panna ran better than her finishing position suggests, but is likely to need more time before she is winning. *Official explanation: jockey said filly was hampered by faller*
Le Galactico(FR), a fair sort in bumpers, was travelling strongly and looked the likeliest winner when taking a fatal fall at the second last. *(op 13-8 tchd 2-1)*

2805 SMITH & WILLIAMSON BEGINNERS' CHASE (18 fncs) 3m 1f
1:10 (1:14) (Class 4) 5-Y-0+ **£4,333** (£1,272; £636; £317)

Form RPR
FP-2 **1** **Lord Olympia (IRE)**[14] [2564] 6-11-0 .... SamThomas 117+
(Miss Venetia Williams) *settled in midfield: trckd ldrs fr 10th: mstke 13th and nt fluent 15th: effrt after 3 out: led next: clr last: styd on strl* **9/4**[2]
2 *8* **Vesuve (FR)**[37] 6-11-0 .... (b) BGicquel 107+
(G Macaire, France) *wl in tch: trckd ldrs fr 10th: chsd ldr 15th: mstke next: rdn and outpcd bef 2 out: mstke last: kpt on* **15/8**[1]
0-PP **3** *2* **Lin D'Estruval (FR)**[12] [2581] 6-11-0 104 .... (b[1]) JimmyMcCarthy 105+
(C P Morlock) *mostly j.w: led: hdd and nt fluent 2 out: btn whn mstke last: wknd flat* **50/1**
55/ **4** *hd* **Backpacker (IRE)**[1328] [4883] 8-10-7 .... CharlieStudd(7) 102
(B G Powell) *prom: chsd ldr 6th to 9th: outpcd after 3 out: styd on again flat* **66/1**
52-4 **5** *3 ½* **Roman Court (IRE)**[41] [1988] 7-11-0 91 .... AndrewThornton 99+
(R H Alner) *wl in tch: prog to trck ldrs 11th: outpcd u.p fr 3 out* **8/1**
03-4 **6** *21* **Murphy's Quest**[24] [2344] 9-11-0 119 .... LeightonAspell 82+
(Lady Herries) *prog fr midfield to chse ldr 9th: mstke 11th: lost 2nd 15th: wknd after 3 out* **6/1**[3]
3P **7** *5* **Murphy's Magic (IRE)**[12] [2581] 7-11-0 .... RobertThornton 72
(Mrs T J Hill) *a in midfield: rdn and nt on terms w ldrs fr 12th: brief effrt 14th: sn btn* **33/1**
FP6 **8** *17* **Sett Aside**[7] [2682] 7-11-0 .... BenjaminHitchcott 55
(Mrs L C Jewell) *a in rr: lost tch 10th: t.o whn blnd 13th: r.o flat* **100/1**
0P/- **9** *½* **Redhouse Chevalier**[598] 6-10-9 .... JohnnyLevins(5) 55
(B G Powell) *chsd ldr to 6th: wkng in midfield whn mstke 11th: t.o fr 14th* **66/1**
5- **10** *20* **Ask Again**[360] [2895] 6-11-0 .... JodieMogford 35
(D G Bridgwater) *mstkes: a in rr: lost tch 10th: t.o whn blnd 13th* **80/1**
P **Good Sort (IRE)**[198] 5-11-0 .... TimmyMurphy —
(B G Powell) *a in last trio: wknd 9th: t.o whn p.u bef 12th* **20/1**
2FP- **U** **Concert Pianist**[235] [4967] 10-11-0 108 .... BrianCrowley —
(P Winkworth) *settled in last pair: mstke and uns rdr 8th* **14/1**
5003 **P** **Kellys Fable**[12] [2593] 5-10-11 80 .... RichardYoung(3) —
(J W Mullins) *nvr beyond midfield: nt fluent 6th: lost tch 10th: poor 8th fnl cirucit: mstke 2 out: p.u bef last* **66/1**

6m 21.6s (-11.80) **Going Correction** -0.225s/f (Good) **13** Ran SP% **114.0**
Speed ratings: **109,106,105,105,104 97,96,90,90,84** —,—,— CSF £6.44 TOTE £2.60: £1.50, £1.80, £17.20; EX 7.30.
Owner Mrs Sally-Anne Ryan **Bred** G Merrigan **Trained** Kings Caple, H'fords

FOCUS
A fair time for a race like this, almost six seconds faster than the handicap over the same trip and the winner is value for further.

NOTEBOOK
Lord Olympia(IRE), who ran well for a long way before getting tired on his chasing debut at Hereford (good race for the course) added his name to the ever-growing list of Williams winners in the past couple of weeks, but was hardly impressive. Although well on top in the end, he took a long time to get going and his jumping was not fluent. He is certain to face stiffer tasks in future, but there may yet be some improvement to come in the jumping department and he will always be a danger when stamina is at a premium. *(op 2-1)*
Vesuve(FR) was the most interesting runner on show, having come over from France, but it was slightly off-putting how he continually swaps between hurdles and fences and his jumping largely compromised his chance. Evidently not the quickest, he may find a small race if coming back over, but could hardly be backed with confidence. *(op 2-1 tchd 9-4 in a place)*
Lin D'Estruval(FR) has lost the plot in the last year or so, but the application of blinkers for the first-time brought about a significantly improved performance and he jumped boldly in front. A slight error two out resulted in him being passed, but he kept on well enough to hold third and he would make some appeal in a low-grade handicap if able to build on this. *(op 40-1)*
Backpacker(IRE), returning from a lengthy layoff, improved greatly on previous form for this switch to fences and just failed to get up for third. He is lightly raced for one of his age and may yet be capable of better.
Roman Court(IRE) jumped soundly enough and will be capable of better once handicapping off his current mark of 91. *(op 9-1 tchd 10-1)*
Murphy's Quest was never going after a bad blunder and can be forgiven his below-par performance. *(tchd 11-2 and 13-2)*

2806 HAGGER'S NEW COAT (S) H'CAP HURDLE (9 hdls) 2m 1f 110y
1:40 (1:41) (Class 5) (0-95,88) 4-Y-0+ **£2,487** (£724; £362)

Form RPR
2641 **1** **Zeloso**[12] [2586] 7-10-10 **79** .... (v) CharliePoste(7) 90+
(M F Harris) *trckd ldr 3rd: gng much bttr than rest after 2 out: led bef last: rdn clr flat* **3/1**[2]
P-00 **2** *8* **Rocket Bleu (FR)**[43] [1957] 5-11-12 **88** .... ChristianWilliams 87+
(D Burchell) *t.k.h: led 2nd and set stdy pce: rdn after 2 out: hdd bef last: one pce* **11/4**[1]
P452 **3** *8* **Maria Bonita (IRE)**[19] [2463] 4-10-6 **73** .... TomGreenway(5) 66+
(C N Kellett) *hld up in tch: effrt 3 out: mstke 2 out and rdn: sn struggling: mstke last: plugged on to take 3rd nr fin* **6/1**
3544 **4** *½* **Chariot (IRE)**[26] [2283] 4-10-10 **79** .... MrJAJenkins(7) 70
(M R Bosley) *hld up in last pair: effrt 3 out: rdn to chse ldng pair after 2 out: no imp* **13/2**
-065 **5** *3* **Lovely Lulu**[19] [2463] 7-10-5 **67** .... JodieMogford 56+
(J C Tuck) *hld up in last pair: effrt 3 out: in tch 2 out: sn rdn and no imp: wknd bef last* **7/2**[3]
6000 **6** *22* **Cybele Eria (FR)**[9] [2659] 8-11-11 **87** .... (b[1]) LeightonAspell 53
(John Allen) *reminder bef s: led to 2nd: cl up tl wknd u.p 2 out* **14/1**
POPO **P** **Zahunda (IRE)**[28] [2256] 6-9-9 **67** .... (v) CareyWilliamson(10) —
(M J Gingell) *t.k.h: racd wd: in tch tl wknd bef 4th: sn wl t.o: p.u bef last* **33/1**

4m 36.5s (7.20) **Going Correction** +0.075s/f (Yiel)
WFA 4 from 5yo+ 10lb **7** Ran SP% **111.1**
Speed ratings: **87,83,79,79,78 68,**— CSF £11.29 TOTE £3.80: £2.10, £2.70; EX 14.60.There was no bid for the winner.
Owner The Paxford Optimists **Bred** Coln Valley Stud **Trained** Edgcote, Northants

FOCUS
A moderate time, even for a seller, and significantly slower than both divisions of the novice hurdle. The winner is value for more than the official margin with the third setting the level.

NOTEBOOK
Zeloso is beginning to blossom over hurdles and followed his Market Rasen win with a smooth display. Travelling strongly from some way out, he eased into the straight and readily came clear. He can complete the hat-trick if kept to similarly moderate level. *(tchd 7-2)*
Rocket Bleu(FR) ran his best race for a while and finished clear of the third, but the weight concession to the winner proved too much. He looks well worth a try back at further. *(op 5-2 tchd 3-1 in a place)*
Maria Bonita(IRE) kept on best of the rest for third, but achieved little and remains below a winning level. *(op 5-1)*
Chariot(IRE) has yet to win in 19 attempts on both the Flat and over jumps and makes little future appeal. *(tchd 6-1)*
Lovely Lulu is not progressing and at this stage her future looks bleak. *(op 9-2)*

2807 BETFREDPOKER.COM NOVICES' H'CAP CHASE (12 fncs) 2m
2:10 (2:10) (Class 4) (0-90,88) 4-Y-0+ **£4,049** (£1,188; £594; £296)

Form RPR
0-42 **1** **Moscow Gold (IRE)**[14] [2561] 8-9-13 **64** .... OwynNelmes(3) 83+
(A E Price) *wl in tch: prog 7th: led 3 out: sn jnd: gained upper hand after 2 out: drvn out* **7/2**[2]
0F2U **2** *4* **Wages**[14] [2561] 5-11-7 **88** .... MrNWilliams(5) 101+
(Evan Williams) *wl in tch: prog 7th: jnd wnr 3 out: stl upsides 2 out: one pce after* **7/4**[1]
4606 **3** *7* **Tyup Pompey (IRE)**[19] [2456] 4-10-13 **86** .... JamieGoldstein 80
(Miss J S Davis) *hld up towards rr: prog 7th: chsd ldrs 3 out: rdn and nt qckn bef next: wnt 2nd bef last: one pce* **12/1**

14P3 **4** ¾ **Terrible Tenant**[14] 2561 6-11-9 **88** RichardYoung(3) 94+
(J W Mullins) *led 2nd: pressed fr 8th: hdd 3 out: btn whn mstke 2 out: sn lost 3rd: kpt on* **9/2**[3]

60P- **5** 19 **Palace (FR)**[344] 3199 9-10-0 **62** oh3 BenjaminHitchcott 47
(R H Buckler) *t.k.h: trckd ldrs: mstke 8th: wknd 3 out: hung bdly lft flat* **18/1**

6605 **6** 1¾ **Dawn Frolics**[16] 2526 4-9-9 **73** oh9 DerekLaverty(5) 46
(M J Gingell) *in tch: rdn 6th: sn struggling: wl off the pce fr 8th* **33/1**

-PPP **7** 12 **Ellas Recovery (IRE)**[7] 2684 5-10-13 **75** (b¹) LeightonAspell 47
(D B Feek) *j.lft: led to 2nd: wknd 7th: sn wl bhd: t.o* **25/1**

0050 **8** 14 **Busy Man (IRE)**[41] 1991 6-10-8 **70** JodieMogford 28
(J R Jenkins) *plld hrd: j. appallingly: in tch to 7th: sn t.o* **16/1**

P-PP **9** 24 **Soroka (IRE)**[163] 891 6-11-2 **85** CharlieStudd(7) 19
(C N Kellett) *stdd s: j. bdly and sn t.o: plodded rnd* **16/1**

P-4F **P** **Interstice**[5] 2719 8-10-10 **72** RJGreene —
(M J Gingell) *stdd s: mstkes and sn t.o: clsd and jst in tch 6th: sn wknd: t.o in 9th whn p.u bef 2 out* **16/1**

4m 4.30s (-2.50) **Going Correction** -0.225s/f (Good)
WFA 4 from 5yo+ 10lb **10** Ran SP% **114.2**
Speed ratings: **97,95,91,91,81 80,74,67,55,—** CSF £10.24 CT £63.06 TOTE £4.40: £1.40, £1.90, £2.30; EX 10.40.
Owner Mrs Carol Davis **Bred** I Williams **Trained** Leominster, H'fords

FOCUS
A weak handicap chase, but it could be rated higher and should produce the odd winner at a similarly lowly level.

NOTEBOOK
Moscow Gold(IRE), who shaped as though a win was imminent when second to Jolly Boy at Hereford, was facing nothing as well handicapped as that one and forged clear off his feather weight. Winning here off a plater's mark, he is open to a fair bit of improvement and it will be both surprising and disappointing if he fails to win again. *(op 11-4)*
Wages has not looked a natural over fences, but he showed he is more than capable of winning off this sort of mark and he finished clear of the third. *(op 15-8 tchd 2-1)*
Tyup Pompey(IRE), who is not yet five, improved on his initial effort over fences and, although well held in third, showed enough to suggest he can find a small race off this sort of mark.
Terrible Tenant ran his race and was simply not good enough. He will remain vulnerable off this sort of mark. *(op 5-1)*
Palace(FR) ran well for a long way on this reappearance and, although eventually well beaten, he showed enough to suggest he can win off this sort of mark. *(op 20-1)*
Soroka(IRE) *Official explanation: jockey said gelding was unsuited by the good ground (op 12-1)*

2808 WEATHERBYS BANK H'CAP CHASE (18 fncs) 3m 1f
2:40 (2:40) (Class 3) (0-115,115) 5-Y-0+ **£6,880** (£2,019; £1,009; £504)

Form RPR

/-P5 **1** **Magic Of Sydney (IRE)**[45] 1920 9-10-6 **95** BrianCrowley 111+
(R Rowe) *tended to jump lft: mde virtually all: mstke 3 out: drew clr fr next: 7l up whn j. bdly lft last: eased flat* **15/2**

2F/U **2** 2½ **Stavordale Lad (IRE)**[23] 2375 7-11-7 **110** ChristianWilliams 117+
(P F Nicholls) *j. slowly 4th: chsd wnr fr 7th to 15th: sn outpcd and rdn : styd on again fr 2 out: wnt 2nd flat: no ch w wnr* **11/2**[1]

3P-P **3** 2½ **Mercato (FR)**[203] 489 9-10-10 **99** RobertThornton 103
(J R Best) *hld up in rr: prog 11th: wnt 2nd after 3 out and looked dangerous: no imp next: wknd last* **7/1**[3]

03P- **4** 1½ **Kohinor**[327] 3438 6-10-1 **90** LeightonAspell 92
(O Sherwood) *wl in tch: chsd wnr 15th tl after 3 out: one pce u.p* **7/1**[3]

1P-6 **5** 5 **Jack Fuller (IRE)**[17] 2502 8-10-9 **98** (b) RJGreene 96+
(P R Hedger) *nt fluent: hld up in rr: prog 11th: rdn to chse ldrs 3 out: fdd fr next* **10/1**

/5P- **6** hd **Misty Future**[534] 828 7-11-12 **115** SamThomas 114+
(Miss Venetia Williams) *wl in tch: mstke 13th: chsng ldrs whn mstke 3 out: drvn and no imp after* **8/1**

U4F- **7** 5 **Gatejumper (IRE)**[371] 2687 7-10-9 **98** RobertWalford 90
(R H Alner) *in tch: outpcd fr 13th: effrt again 3 out but nt on terms w ldrs: n.d after* **6/1**[2]

3003 **8** 4 **Even More (IRE)**[19] 2458 10-11-4 **107** AndrewThornton 98+
(R H Alner) *w wnr to 5th: lost pl fr 9th: bhd whn blnd 3 out: no ch after* **7/1**[3]

0063 **9** 4 **Alfred The Grey**[39] 2019 8-9-13 **91** oh18 ow2 (p) ColinBolger(3) 75
(Miss Suzy Smith) *a wl in rr: lost tch 9th: rdn next: plodded on* **50/1**

P1P- **10** dist **Mulligatawny (IRE)**[254] 4726 11-11-7 **110** (t) PhilipHide —
(N J Gifford) *in tch to 13th: sn wknd: t.o 3 out: btn 76l* **16/1**

6033 **P** **Wayward Melody**[15] 2553 5-10-2 **91** (p) JamieMoore —
(G L Moore) *drvn in rr fr 4th and nt keen: losing tch whn p.u after 12th* **12/1**

6m 27.4s (-6.00) **Going Correction** -0.225s/f (Good) **11** Ran SP% **114.7**
Speed ratings: **100,99,98,97,96 96,94,93,92,—** — CSF £48.20 CT £302.40 TOTE £8.50: £2.60, £3.50, £3.50; EX 69.40 Trifecta £200.20 Pool: £564.02 - 2 winning units..
Owner Ann & John Symes **Bred** Johnson Lyons **Trained** Sullington, W Sussex

FOCUS
A tight handicap and the delicate Magic Of Sydney was able to get back to winning ways. He is value for further rated through the runner-up, but the overall form looks suspect and the time was modest.

NOTEBOOK
Magic Of Sydney(IRE) has long been a delicate horse, but he has always been useful on his day and, despite losing ground in continually jumping out to his left, he proved too strong for favourite. Returning to a left-handed track can only help the nine-year-old and he may now head for a race at Newbury. *(op 8-1 tchd 7-1)*
Stavordale Lad(IRE), perhaps the least exposed in the line-up, threw in several dodgy leaps and never looked confident at his fences, but he kept plugging away and recorded a fair effort considering he was conceding so much weight to the winner. He will be winning once brushing up his jumping. *(tchd 6-1)*
Mercato(FR) made a pleasing reappearance and has clearly returned in better form than when he was last seen. He is currently on a very good mark and capable of winning if going the right way from this. *(op 13-2 tchd 15-2)*
Kohinor, a moderate sort over hurdles, was strongly supported in the market beforehand and improved on her previous efforts. She is only six and is evidently going to make a better chaser than hurdler. *(op 12-1)*
Jack Fuller(IRE) bounced back from a couple of poor efforts, but his jumping was sloppy throughout and he failed to see his race out as one would have hoped. *(tchd 11-1)*
Misty Future, whose stable are going great guns at the minute, would have preferred a faster surface and ran well considering. This was a fair reappearance under top weight. *(op 11-2)*
Gatejumper(IRE), who had jumping problems last term, again failed to jump fluently, but he plugged on late and is going to be a real stayer. *(op 13-2)*
Even More(IRE) *Official explanation: jockey said gelding was unsuited by the track (op 11-2)*

2809 BETFREDCASINO.COM MAIDEN HURDLE (11 hdls) 2m 6f 110y
3:10 (3:11) (Class 4) 4-Y-0+ **£3,643** (£1,069; £534; £267)

Form RPR

1 **Brumous (IRE)**[258] 5-11-0 LeightonAspell 113+
(O Sherwood) *wl in tch: prog 8th: led bef 2 out: pushed clr between last 2: styd on strly* **16/1**

2-B4 **2** 7 **Knighton Lad (IRE)**[25] 2322 5-11-0 RobertThornton 103
(A King) *rn in snatches: in tch: sltly hmpd 7th: mstke next: effrt u.p 2 out: chsd wnr between fnl 2: no imp* **8/1**

522- **3** ½ **Aspiring Actor (IRE)**[296] 3973 5-11-0 ChristianWilliams 103
(P F Nicholls) *wl in tch: drvn 2 out: outpcd by wnr between last 2: plugged on* **15/8**[1]

2-4 **4** 28 **Rotheram (USA)**[30] 2212 5-11-0 BrianCrowley 83+
(C J Mann) *prom: mstke 6th: trckd ldr sn after to 3 out: w wnr 2 out: wknd u.p between last 2* **4/1**[2]

63-P **5** 13 **Dancing Shirley**[15] 2552 7-10-7 77 MatthewBatchelor 55
(Miss A M Newton-Smith) *prom: led 6th to bef 2 out: wknd rapidly* **100/1**

4445 **6** 9 **Hatteras (FR)**[10] 2632 6-10-7 103 RobertLucey-Butler(7) 53
(Miss M P Bryant) *wl in tch: chsd ldrs 8th: u.p after 3 out: sn wknd* **12/1**

0 **7** 11 **Flash Cummins (IRE)**[30] 2206 5-11-0 TimmyMurphy 42
(M C Pipe) *hld up in last: lost tch w ldng gp after 6th: modest prog fr 3 out: eased wl bef last* **10/1**

66 **8** dist **Summer Liric**[43] 1954 4-11-0 AndrewThornton —
(J W Mullins) *mstke 1st: hld up in rr: lost tch fr 6th: t.o* **66/1**

0 **P** **Sistema**[41] 1982 4-10-9 TomGreenway(5) —
(A E Price) *mstke 1st: a in rr: t.o after 7th: p.u bef last* **100/1**

06 **P** **Gold Vic (IRE)**[46] 1909 5-11-0 JamieMoore —
(P Bowen) *mstkes: nvr gng wl: wkng whn hmpd bef 7th: t.o whn p.u bef 8th* **50/1**

53-6 **P** **Farnaheezview (IRE)**[203] 489 7-10-11 115 (p) OwynNelmes(3) —
(O Sherwood) *chsd ldrs tl wknd rapidly 4th: t.o whn p.u bef 6th* **9/2**[3]

0356 **P** **Corrib Drift (USA)**[45] 1921 5-10-11 87 ColinBolger(3) —
(Jamie Poulton) *hld up: prog and prom 6th: wknd rapidly 3 out: t.o whn p.u bef last* **33/1**

3-60 **U** **Orange Street**[15] 2554 5-11-0 PhilipHide —
(Mrs L J Mongan) *led to 6th: pushed along and losing pl in 5th whn stmbld and uns rdr bef 7th* **50/1**

5m 58.9s (-10.20) **Going Correction** +0.075s/f (Yiel) **13** Ran SP% **117.1**
Speed ratings: **109,106,106,96,92 89,85,—,—,— —,—,—** CSF £131.66 TOTE £18.90: £3.10, £2.20, £1.40; EX 70.10 Place 6 £11.29, Place 5 £10.38.
Owner J Dougall **Bred** Patrick McNamara **Trained** Upper Lambourn, Berks

FOCUS
Just an ordinary maiden hurdle, but the winning time was fair and the winner is value for more than the offical margin.

NOTEBOOK
Brumous(IRE), placed in a point over three miles in Ireland, was the lesser fancied of the Sherwood pair according to the betting, but jockey bookings suggested otherwise and he proved good enough to make a winning debut under Rules. There should be plenty more to come and he appeals as one to keep on the right side of. *(op 12-1)*
Knighton Lad(IRE), upped to his furthest trip to date, ran better than at Windsor on his previous start and offered plenty of promise in second. *(tchd 7-1)*
Aspiring Actor(IRE), who showed plenty of ability but was a beaten favourite in two of his three runs in bumpers, again failed to justify his market position on his hurdling debut. Given this was his first run in 296 days, he is open improvement but, even so, he has a bit to prove now. *(op 2-1 tchd 5-2)*
Rotheram(USA) had shown plenty of promise in two runs round Fontwell, but was not at his best this time. Still, he is now qualified for a handicap mark and could do better. *(op 7-2 tchd 9-2)*
Dancing Shirley will be better off in handicaps. *(op 66-1)*
Farnaheezview(IRE), back over fences, and with cheekpieces fitted for the first time off the back of a 203-day break, was a much shorter price than his winning stablemate, so this has to be considered disappointing. *(tchd 4-1)*
T/Jkpt: £28,107.90 to a £1 stake. Pool: £39,588.60. 0.50 winning tickets. T/Plt: £23.10 to a £1 stake. Pool: £37,271.65. 1,175.00 winning tickets. T/Qpdt: £8.80 to a £1 stake. Pool: £3,325.80. 277.40 winning tickets. JN

2659 WARWICK (L-H)
Tuesday, December 13

OFFICIAL GOING: Soft (good to soft in places on chase course)
Wind: Almost nil Weather: Fine

2810 RON GASCOIGNE MEMORIAL AMATEUR RIDERS' NOVICES' H'CAP HURDLE (9 hdls) 2m 3f
12:30 (12:30) (Class 4) (0-95,95) 3-Y-0+ **£2,535** (£779; £389)

Form RPR

406 **1** **Piran (IRE)**[61] 1729 3-10-8 **95** MrJETudor(5) 96+
(Evan Williams) *hld up: hdwy 6th: led 2 out: comf* **7/2**[2]

0F/3 **2** 2 **He's A Rascal (IRE)**[16] 2523 7-10-11 **85** (p) MissZoeLilly(7) 91
(A J Lidderdale) *hld up in rr: rdn after 5th: hdwy to ld after 3 out: hdd 2 out: nt qckn flat* **5/1**[3]

3-05 **3** 11 **Road King (IRE)**[12] 2586 11-10-7 **81** MrRBirkett(7) 77+
(Miss J Feilden) *led tl after 4th: wknd appr last* **11/2**

04P0 **4** 1 **Keepasharplookout (IRE)**[14] 2563 3-9-10 **85** MrTCollier(7) 64
(C W Moore) *a.p: ev ch 3 out: sn rdn: wknd appr last* **66/1**

04-6 **5** ½ **Astral Affair (IRE)**[17] 2503 6-10-0 **74** RyanCummings(7) 68
(P A Pritchard) *hld up and bhd: hdwy 6th: wknd 2 out* **16/1**

356 **6** 6 **Lane Marshal**[12] 2587 3-10-13 **95** MrTGreenall 68
(M E Sowersby) *hld up in tch: rdn and wknd appr 2 out* **9/1**

5-64 **7** 15 **Shaamit The Vaamit (IRE)**[9] 2659 5-11-5 **93** MrJMahot(7) 76+
(M Scudamore) *chsd ldr: led after 4th: mstke 6th: hdd after 3 out: slipped bnd appr 2 out: wkng whn hit 2 out* **3/1**[1]

-065 **8** dist **Ilongue (FR)**[26] 2285 4-9-10 **70** MrCHughes(7) —
(R Dickin) *hld up in tch: wknd appr 5th: sn lost tch: t.o* **6/1**

/P3- **P** **Tweed**[433] 1612 8-10-7 **81** MrDAFitzsimmons(7) —
(D McCain) *hld up: j. slowly 4th: sn struggling: t.o whn p.u bef 6th* **28/1**

4m 41.7s (-2.30) **Going Correction** 0.0s/f (Good)
WFA 3 from 4yo 13lb 4 from 5yo+ 10lb **9** Ran SP% **114.4**
Speed ratings: **104,103,98,98,97 95,89,—,—** CSF £21.51 CT £93.30 TOTE £4.50: £1.90, £2.00, £2.40; EX 21.30.
Owner The Welsh Valleys Syndicate **Bred** Michael Hurley **Trained** Cowbridge, Vale Of Glamorgan

FOCUS
A very moderate novices' handicap run at a steady early pace with the winner value for five times the winning margin. The time was decent for the grade and the form may work out.

NOTEBOOK

Piran(IRE), encountering this surface for the first time over hurdles, was officially joint highest rated and proved too good for his older rivals on this handicap debut. He is nothing special but looks capable of winning again at a similar level. *(tchd 3-1 and 4-1)*

He's A Rascal(IRE) has not had much racing for a horse of his age and looks to be on the upgrade. He came from last to first along the back straight and looked the likely winner turning in but, instead of kicking on, his inexperienced rider spent too much time looking around for dangers and ultimately the pair were outpaced from the second last. He looks capable of winning a similar contest and his rider will know better next time. *(tchd 9-2 and 11-2)*

Road King(IRE), who is just a one-paced galloper, was wisely given a positive ride but could not pick up from the home turn. He will appreciate a return to a longer trip. *(op 6-1)*

Keepasharplookout(IRE), a former sprinter who has yet to start at less than 33/1 in seven starts over hurdles, ran surprisingly well on the softest ground and longest trip he had encountered. He did not appear to get home, but may be worth trying back at the minimum in similar conditions. *(op 50-1)*

Astral Affair(IRE), who has shown her best form on faster ground, did not run too badly and looks as if a step back up in trip will be in her favour.

Shaamit The Vaamit(IRE), who has gone well on this track in the past, was just beginning to feel the pinch when he lost his footing on the home turn, which finished his chance. *(op 7-2 tchd 4-1)*

2811 WATCH SECURITY JUVENILE NOVICES' HURDLE (8 hdls) 2m

1:00 (1:00) (Class 4) 3-Y-O £3,412 (£994; £497)

Form				RPR
16	**1**		**Patman Du Charmil (FR)**[31] 2178 3-11-5 ... AntonyEvans (N A Twiston-Davies) *j.w: chsd ldr: led 4th: rdn whn jinked rt last: drvn out* **8/15**[1]	103+
	2	*2*	**Kickahead (USA)**[169] 3-10-12 ... MickFitzgerald (Ian Williams) *hld up: hdwy appr 5th: hit 3 out: sn rdn and outpcd: rallied appr last: kpt on u.p flat* **25/1**	87+
2F0	**3**	*1 ¼*	**Madam Caversfield**[31] 2178 3-10-0 ... StephenCraine[(5)] (P D Evans) *hld up in tch: hit 1st: rdn to chse wnr 3 out: kpt on same pce fr 2 out* **12/1**	79+
P0	**4**	*14*	**Rockys Girl**[9] 2661 3-10-0 ... LeeStephens[(5)] (R Flint) *hld up in mid-div: dropped rr and mstke 4th: styd on fr appr 2 out: n.d* **100/1**	64
	5	*½*	**Globalized (IRE)**[77] 3-10-12 ... WarrenMarston (Mrs P Sly) *plld hrd: hdwy 5th: wknd after 3 out* **50/1**	72+
00	**6**	*11*	**Picot De Say**[12] 2580 3-10-12 ... OllieMcPhail (C Roberts) *nvr nr ldrs* **80/1**	60
6	**7**	*½*	**Oh Mister Pinceau (FR)**[26] 2286 3-10-12 ... RichardJohnson (H D Daly) *hdwy 3rd: nt fluent 5th: wknd after 3 out* **6/1**[2]	66+
00	**8**	*1 ½*	**Garhoud**[27] 2274 3-10-12 ...(b) TomScudamore (Miss K M George) *led to 4th: wknd after 5th: blnd 2 out* **66/1**	58
2203	**9**	*7*	**Compton Quay**[19] 2454 3-10-12 94 ... TomDoyle (Miss K M George) *prom to 4th* **25/1**	51
	10	*dist*	**General Jist**[63] 3-10-7 ... PaulO'Neill[(5)] (Evan Williams) *t.k.h: bhd fr 3rd: t.o* **50/1**	—
	11	*4*	**Top Man Tee**[14] 3-10-12 ... PaulMoloney (D J Daly) *nt j.w: a bhd: t.o fr 4th* **8/1**[3]	—

3m 57.6s (-0.70) **Going Correction** 0.0s/f (Good) **11** Ran SP% **113.7**
Speed ratings: **101,100,99,92,92 86,86,85,82,—** — CSF £19.70 TOTE £1.50: £1.10, £3.70, £2.50; EX 13.10.
Owner H R Mould **Bred** Mme Guilhaine Le Borgne **Trained** Naunton, Gloucs

FOCUS

Just an ordinary juvenile hurdle with the odds-on favourite making harder work of it that expected, but value for more than the official margin, with the third and fourth the best guides to the level.

NOTEBOOK

Patman Du Charmil(FR), who was out of his depth in a Grade Two contest at Cheltenham last time, had to give weight away all round. He travelled well up with the pace and looked to have matters in control when appearing to think about running out at the final flight and losing momentum. He can be forgiven that and still won well enough, but will not find things easy under a double penalty. *(op 4-7 tchd 8-13)*

Kickahead(USA) ◆, who was tried at distances ranging from sprint trips to ten furlongs on the Flat in France, ran well on this hurdling debut, keeping on well on the run-in to hunt up the winner. This was a promising debut and an ordinary contest should come his way. *(op 16-1)*

Madam Caversfield, who was behind the winner at Cheltenham, finished a lot closer on this occasion. She seems to handle any ground and may be able to profit from a modest mark if switched to handicaps. *(tchd 14-1)*

Rockys Girl, who stayed well on the Flat, looked to be out of contention at the last on the far side, but ran on again from the turn and is likely to appreciate a step up in trip. *(op 66-1)*

Globalized(IRE), a fair handicapper on the Flat in Ireland, had shown form on varying ground. He was too keen early on and paid the penalty from the second last, but this was a fair debut. *(op 40-1 tchd 66-1)*

Oh Mister Pinceau(FR), a middle-distance winner on the Flat in France, showed up in the early stages but dropped away before the home turn and was somewhat disappointing. He may be taking time to adjust to his new surroundings. *(op 13-2 tchd 7-1)*

2812 WATCH SECURITY NOVICES' CHASE (18 fncs) 3m 110y

1:30 (1:30) (Class 3) 5-Y-O+ £5,413 (£1,589; £794; £396)

Form				RPR
PF1-	**1**		**The Duckpond (IRE)**[235] 4964 8-11-0 115 ... JasonMaguire (J A B Old) *j.w: led 2nd: clr 4 out: drvn out flat* **11/1**	126+
3/P2	**2**	*6*	**Howrwenow (IRE)**[23] 2375 7-11-0 115 ... APMcCoy (Miss H C Knight) *hld up: mstke 10th: hdwy 14th: rdn after 3 out: wnt 2nd last: no imp* **6/1**	119+
5-23	**3**	*2 ½*	**Eskimo Pie (IRE)**[19] 2464 6-11-0 120 ... NoelFehily (C C Bealby) *hld up in tch: wnt 2nd and mstke 13th: rdn after 3 out: hit 2 out: one pce* **3/1**[2]	117+
2-32	**4**	*14*	**Woodlands Genpower (IRE)**[9] 2660 7-11-0 118 ... MarkBradburne (P A Pritchard) *prom: nt fluent 12th and 13th: sn rdn and wknd* **7/4**[1]	109+
2112	**5**	*10*	**Avitta (IRE)**[29] 2241 6-10-7 115 ... AlanO'Keeffe (Miss Venetia Williams) *hld up: sme hdwy 10th: hmpd 12th and 13th: n.d after* **4/1**[3]	94+
-153	**6**	*21*	**Hot Weld**[20] 2441 6-10-9 115 ... ThomasDreaper[(5)] (Ferdy Murphy) *prom: lost pl 6th: mstkes 13th and 14th: sn bhd* **16/1**	76+
P-P	**P**		**Bobalong (IRE)**[233] 10 8-11-0 104 ...(t) TomDoyle (C P Morlock) *led tl blnd 2nd: bhd fr 5th: t.o whn p.u bef 9th* **100/1**	—

6m 19.6s (-2.70) **Going Correction** -0.15s/f (Good) **7** Ran SP% **110.9**
Speed ratings: **98,96,95,90,87 80,—** CSF £68.35 TOTE £13.00: £4.10, £2.40; EX 97.40.
Owner W E Sturt **Bred** John Bernard O'Connor **Trained** Barbury Castle, Wilts

FOCUS

A fair novices' chase in which the pace steadied at around halfway and the time was ordinary for the grade. The placed horses set the standard for the form.

NOTEBOOK

The Duckpond(IRE) ◆, who had fallen twice in four outings over hurdles, had nevertheless shown plenty of ability. He obviously appreciated the switch to the bigger obstacles and it was his exuberant jumping down the line of five fences on the run to the straight that helped to seal his victory. If he can repeat this effort he can win more decent races. *(op 7-1)*

Howrwenow(IRE) has now been runner-up on all his completed starts over fences. He stays very well but would have appreciated a stronger gallop to offset his lack of acceleration. *(op 8-1)*

Eskimo Pie(IRE), a dual hurdles winner who was trying his longest trip to date over fences, went in pursuit of the winner down the line of fences before the home turn, but could make no impression and was run out of second place in the straight. He has races in him over fences, but may be best at shorter trips for the time being. *(op 4-1)*

Woodlands Genpower(IRE), who was just caught on his chasing debut here earlier in the month, was disappointing on this occasion and was never travelling that well. In the past he has looked better than this, but has a little to prove now. *(op 15-8 tchd 9-4)*

Avitta(IRE) has taken well to fences, but this was a step up in grade and trip and she was found wanting. She may be better off in races against her own sex. *(op 7-2)*

2813 MITIE H'CAP HURDLE (10 hdls 1 omitted) 2m 5f

2:00 (2:00) (Class 3) (0-125,125) 4-Y-O+ £4,853 (£1,424; £712; £355)

Form				RPR
43-1	**1**		**Jaunty Times**[17] 2503 5-10-12 111 ... RichardJohnson (H D Daly) *a.p: led 4th to 5th: led 7th: rdn and hung rt appr last: drvn out* **2/1**[2]	119+
0P-P	**2**	*1*	**Tana River (IRE)**[17] 2492 9-11-12 125 ... BarryFenton (Miss E C Lavelle) *led: hit 1st: hdd 3rd: led 5th to 7th: rdn appr 2 out: r.o flat* **10/1**	131
332-	**3**	*1 ¾*	**Greenfield (IRE)**[277] 4314 7-11-3 116 ...(b) WarrenMarston (R T Phillips) *hld up: hdwy after 6th: rdn and ev ch whn bmpd appr last: no ex flat* **14/1**	121+
-P3U	**4**	*5*	**Bunkum**[25] 2325 7-10-11 110 ... TomDoyle (R Lee) *hld up: hdwy appr 7th: sn rdn: sltly outpcd 3 out: rallied 2 out: wknd flat* **25/1**	109
14-1	**5**	*1*	**Lady Of Fortune (IRE)**[29] 2240 6-11-2 115 ... MickFitzgerald (N J Henderson) *hld up: hdwy appr 7th: rdn appr 2 out: wkng whn mstke last* **5/1**[3]	115+
61-2	**6**	*15*	**Vic The Piler (IRE)**[27] 2264 6-11-3 116 ... TonyDobbin (N G Richards) *hld up: hdwy appr 4th: reminder 6th: rdn and wknd 3 out* **15/8**[1]	107+
-000	**7**	*10*	**Society Buck (IRE)**[149] 1026 8-10-4 108 ... MarkNicolls[(5)] (John Allen) *hld up in tch: wknd after 6th* **66/1**	83+
1PF-	**8**	*3 ½*	**Cowboyboots (IRE)**[332] 3366 7-10-9 115 ... JustinMorgan[(7)] (L Wells) *w ldr: led 3rd to 4th: wknd after 6th* **40/1**	85
P3-6	**9**	*1*	**Andy Gin (FR)**[9] 2659 6-9-12 102 ... RobertStephens[(5)] (Miss E M England) *hdwy after 3rd: hit 6th: rdn and wknd after 7th* **40/1**	71
6-P0	**10**	*2 ½*	**Marrel**[10] 2621 7-10-9 115 ...(v) LiamHeard[(7)] (D Burchell) *bhd fr 7th* **66/1**	81
15-0	**11**	*dist*	**Waterspray (AUS)**[192] 633 7-10-0 99 ... HenryOliver (Ian Williams) *t.k.h in tch: wknd after 6th: t.o* **25/1**	—

5m 12.7s (-3.40) **Going Correction** 0.0s/f (Good) **11** Ran SP% **116.1**
Speed ratings: **106,105,104,103,102 96,93,91,91,90** — CSF £19.90 CT £220.92 TOTE £3.50: £1.30, £3.70, £2.70; EX 42.60.
Owner J B Sumner **Bred** B J Eckley **Trained** Stanton Lacy, Shropshire

FOCUS

A fair handicap hurdle run at a sound gallop and the form looks solid. The fifth-last flight was bypassed.

NOTEBOOK

Jaunty Times ◆, who had a confidence booster when scoring last time, showed the benefit under a positive ride. He managed to hold off a couple of persistent challenges in the straight and looks to be on the upgrade. *(op 3-1)*

Tana River(IRE), who had failed to complete on his last two starts over fences, seemed happier back over hurdles. After looking likely to drop away turning for home, he rallied really well and made the winner work hard. He is reasonably, if not generously, treated, and may be able to find a similar contest if repeating this. *(op 12-1 tchd 16-1)*

Greenfield(IRE) ◆, making his seasonal debut, ran well from his highest-ever mark. He was done no favours by the winner going to the final flight but, from a yard in good form, looks to have improved again and can gain compensation before long. *(op 16-1)*

Bunkum, another reverting from fences, ran his best race of the year. He has slipped in the handicap and, if running in a similar contest at Chepstow, where he gained his two previous wins over hurdles, could pop up at a decent price.

Lady Of Fortune(IRE) has a good strike rate, having won three of her five previous races. However, those wins were all on right-handed tracks and she may need to go the other way around. *(op 4-1 tchd 11-2)*

Vic The Piler(IRE), touched off on his handicap debut in a similar race last month, was disappointing and was struggling a long way from home. He may have other excuses, but it is less than a year since he made his debut, and his two defeats have come when he has had to travel a quite a long way from his stable. *Official explanation: trainer's representative said gelding was unsuited by the soft ground (tchd 2-1)*

Waterspray(AUS) *Official explanation: trainer said gelding was unsuited by the soft ground (op 33-1)*

2814 WATCH SECURITY H'CAP CHASE (17 fncs) 2m 4f 110y

2:30 (2:31) (Class 3) (0-125,128) 5-Y-O+ £5,347 (£1,570; £785; £392)

Form				RPR
-331	**1**		**Pass Me A Dime**[13] 2574 6-11-3 116 ... JoeTizzard (C L Tizzard) *mde all: mstkes 11th and 3 out: j.rt 2 out and last: hung rt flat: drvn out* **11/4**[1]	126+
P521	**2**	*1 ½*	**Marked Man (IRE)**[9] 2664 9-12-1 128 7ex ... TomDoyle (R Lee) *t.k.h early: hit 9th: hdwy 10th: chsd wnr fr 3 out: rdn appr last: ev ch flat: nt qckn* **7/2**[2]	133+
1/4P	**3**	*7*	**Pietro Vannucci (IRE)**[17] 2498 9-10-12 111 ... APMcCoy (Jonjo O'Neill) *a.p: rdn 13th: wknd aftr 2 out* **9/2**[3]	109+
6U31	**4**	*13*	**Dead Mans Dante (IRE)**[35] 2109 7-10-10 109 ... KeithMercer (Ferdy Murphy) *hld up: hdwy appr 4 out: sltly hmpd 3 out: n.d after* **5/1**	98+
14-0	**5**	*dist*	**Parish Oak**[21] 2419 10-10-6 105 ... GrahamLee (Ian Williams) *prom tl wknd 12th: t.o* **22/1**	—
P/F-	**F**		**Denada**[255] 4688 9-10-5 104 ... WarrenMarston (Mrs Susan Nock) *plld hrd in rr: fell 5th* **15/2**	—
-413	**F**		**Major Euro (IRE)**[9] 2664 8-11-5 118 ... RichardJohnson (S J Gilmore) *prom: rdn and disputing 2l 2nd whn fell 3 out* **8/1**	—

5m 16.2s (-9.30) **Going Correction** -0.15s/f (Good) **7** Ran SP% **111.0**
Speed ratings: **111,110,107,102,— —,—** CSF £12.38 CT £38.35 TOTE £3.80: £1.80, £2.30; EX 15.30.
Owner Cherry Bolberry Partnership **Bred** C Raymond **Trained** Milborne Port, Dorset

FOCUS

A run-of-the-mill handicap chase but a fair winning time for the grade and the form appears reasonably solid.

The Form Book, Raceform Ltd, Compton, RG20 6NL

NOTEBOOK
Pass Me A Dime has taken well to fences and, well suited by forcing tactics, led all the way and stuck on gamely. He should not go up too much for this and can win again at a similar level, with the option to return to novice events still available. *(tchd 3-1)*
Marked Man(IRE), a winner here when dropped back to two miles, had a 7lb rise in the weights to defy over this longer trip. He gave the winner a race and was clear of the rest, but perhaps the Handicapper has his measure now. *(tchd 4-1)*
Pietro Vannucci(IRE) has not really gone on from his promising reappearance following a long absence, and the Champion was niggling along from an early stage. However, he did keep going without ever looking likely to trouble the winner and may appreciate even softer ground. *(op 6-1)*
Dead Mans Dante(IRE), who finally broke his duck at Sedgefield last month, had not been raised for that victory. Ridden patiently, he crept into contention before the home turn but found little from that point. Low-grade novice events probably offer his best chance of adding to his score. *(tchd 11-2)*
Parish Oak *Official explanation: trainer said gelding had a breathing problem (op 16-1)*
Major Euro(IRE), who finished behind the runner-up here last time, was 7lb better off. He ran well for a long way, but was coming to the end of his tether when departing at the third from home. He seems better on a sounder surface. *(op 7-1)*

2815 WATCH SECURITY NOVICES' HURDLE (12 hdls) 3m 1f
3:00 (3:00) (Class 4) 4-Y-0+ **£3,545** (£1,033; £516)

Form RPR
5-23 **1** **Gritti Palace (IRE)**[19] 2461 5-10-7 .... MarkNicolls(5) 112
(John R Upson) *racd wd: a.p: led 7th tl appr 8th: rdn to ld appr 3 out: hdd 2 out: led cl home: all out* **6/1**[2]
/32- **2** *shd* **Brankley Boy**[281] 4230 7-10-12 .... MickFitzgerald 113+
(N J Henderson) *t.k.h: mstke 1st: hdwy appr 5th: rdn to ld 2 out: hit last: hdd cl home* **6/5**[1]
5-4 **3** *15* **Woodview (IRE)**[19] 2461 6-10-12 .... JohnMcNamara 97
(K C Bailey) *hld up in mid-div: hdwy after 7th: rdn and wknd appr 2 out* **7/1**[3]
30-0 **4** *10* **Alfasonic**[227] 128 5-10-12 .... WarrenMarston 88+
(A King) *hld up: hdwy 6th: wknd 3 out* **25/1**
3 **5** *3 1/2* **Surface To Air**[26] 2301 4-10-12 .... MarkBradburne 84
(Mrs P N Dutfield) *hld up: mstke and rdr lost irons briefly appr 2nd: hdwy appr 8th: rdn appr 3 out: wknd appr 2 out* **7/1**[3]
1P **6** *dist* **Dunbell Boy (IRE)**[34] 2130 7-11-4 105.................................. NoelFehily —
(C J Mann) *a bhd: t.o bef 2 out* **7/1**[3]
0004 **P** **Logies Lass**[34] 2125 6-10-5 .... PaulMoloney —
(J S Smith) *a bhd: t.o whn p.u bef 2 out* **80/1**
0 **P** **Oddington (IRE)**[20] 2427 5-10-5 .... StevenCrawford(7) —
(Mrs Susan Nock) *hld up in tch: wknd after 8th: t.o whn p.u bef 2 out* **33/1**
0 **P** **Barney Blue (IRE)**[26] 2301 5-10-12 .... JimCrowley —
(Ian Williams) *prom: rdn after 6th: wknd after 7th: t.o whn p.u bef 2 out* **100/1**
P **With Due Respect** 5-10-12 .... TomScudamore —
(N A Twiston-Davies) *t.k.h: prom tl wknd after 7th: t.o whn p.u bef 2 out* **20/1**
P0-0 **P** **Lunar Fox**[17] 2501 6-10-5 .... JosephByrne —
(J L Needham) *prom: nt fluent 1st: mstke 6th: wknd 7th: t.o whn p.u bef 2 out* **100/1**
40 **P** **Call Me Edward (IRE)**[20] 2426 4-10-12 .... AntonyEvans —
(N A Twiston-Davies) *led to 7th: led appr 8th tl appr 3 out: wknd qckly and p.u bef 2 out* **25/1**

6m 28.9s (-1.40) **Going Correction** 0.0s/f (Good)
WFA 4 from 5yo+ 13lb **12** Ran SP% **115.9**
Speed ratings: **102,101,97,93,92** —,—,—,—,— —,— CSF £13.00 TOTE £8.30: £2.30, £1.20, £1.80; EX 18.00.
Owner Sir Nicholas Wilson **Bred** Patrick McGrath **Trained** Maidford, Northants

FOCUS
A modest staying novice hurdle in which only half of the field completed. Those in the frame behind the winner were close to form and it might work out.

NOTEBOOK
Gritti Palace(IRE), touched off on his hurdling debut in similar ground, had since been beaten by the useful Karanja. Already a proven stayer, he was given a positive ride and rallied strongly to get the better of the favourite in a desperate finish. He should make up into a decent chaser next season, and his attitude is a valuable asset. *(op 7-1 tchd 8-1)*
Brankley Boy ♦, beaten on his two previous outings over hurdles, was nevertheless made a short-priced favourite on this step up in trip. However, he did not help his chances by failing to settle and, although he looked sure to win when taking the advantage at the second last, his reserves of energy ebbed and he was unable to resist the renewed effort of the winner. He was well clear of the rest and, with the freshness out of his system, should be able to find a similar contest. *(op Evens)*
Woodview(IRE), who finished just behind today's winner at Uttoxeter last time, was given a patient ride and was close enough on the turn in. However, he could not pick up from that point, but at least now qualifies for a handicap mark. *(op 11-1)*
Alfasonic failed to build on the promise of his bumper efforts in two outings over hurdles in the spring, but this step up in trip was not the answer. He is another who now qualifies for handicaps and a drop back to two miles may be worth a try. *(op 20-1)*
Surface To Air, who ran well on his hurdling debut, showed up for some way, but gave the impression the combination of the longer trip and fast ground found him out. *(op 15-2 tchd 8-1)*
Dunbell Boy(IRE), who narrowly beat today's winner at Chepstow, was given a patient ride but for the second time since failed to reproduce that form. That win seems to have bottomed him and he has something to prove now. *(tchd 13-2)*

2816 WATCH SECURITY H'CAP HURDLE (8 hdls) 2m
3:30 (3:31) (Class 4) (0-90,90) 4-Y-0+ **£3,110** (£906; £453)

Form RPR
0004 **1** **Darkshape**[12] 2585 5-10-7 76.. PaulO'Neill(5) 88+
(Miss Venetia Williams) *hld up in mid-div: smooth hdwy appr 3 out: led on bit appr 2 out: easily* **5/2**[1]
4315 **2** *2 1/2* **Amadeus (AUS)**[9] 2664 8-11-0 78................................. TomScudamore 79
(M Scudamore) *hld up in tch: mstke 5th: rdn 3 out: kpt on flat: no ch w wnr* **7/2**[2]
-054 **3** *3/4* **Foxmeade Dancer**[21] 2419 7-11-5 83.............................. RichardJohnson 83
(P C Ritchens) *hld up and bhd: hdwy 5th: rdn appr 2 out: r.o one pce flat* **6/1**[3]
2U04 **4** *1 1/4* **Upright Ima**[31] 2182 6-11-0 78.. WarrenMarston 77
(Mrs P Sly) *hld up and bhd: hdwy 5th: rdn and ev ch 2 out: no ex flat* **7/1**
P0U5 **5** *1* **Firstflor**[12] 2585 6-10-4 68.. TomDoyle 66
(F Jordan) *hdwy 3rd: rdn appr 2 out: one pce* **20/1**
-PPP **6** *1* **All Sonsilver (FR)**[10] 2623 8-11-12 90................................. HenryOliver 87
(P Kelsall) *led: rdn and hdd appr 2 out: one pce* **100/1**
P/00 **7** *shd* **Herecomestanley**[16] 2528 6-11-6 84................................ AntonyEvans 81
(M F Harris) *plld hrd in rr: hdwy appr 3 out: rdn and one pce fr 2 out* **66/1**
-060 **8** *3/4* **Ndola**[12] 2585 6-11-7 85.. PaulMoloney 82+
(B J Curley) *hld up in tch: rdn appr 2 out: one pce* **20/1**
0400 **9** *17* **Carnt Spell**[19] 2462 4-11-7 85... AlanO'Keeffe 64
(J T Stimpson) *chsd ldr to 5th: wknd appr 2 out* **25/1**
0501 **10** *1 1/4* **Jug Of Punch (IRE)**[33] 2140 6-11-1 86..................... PatrickCStringer(7) 64
(S T Lewis) *hld up in mid-div: hdwy 4th: eased whn btn appr 2 out* **16/1**
14- **11** *3 1/2* **Just Wiz**[15] 4667 9-10-11 85.. SpikeBolton(10) 59
(J Jay) *t.k.h in rr: nvr nr ldrs* **16/1**
6050 **12** *5* **Europrime Games**[20] 2440 7-10-10 74................................ KeithMercer 43
(M E Sowersby) *chsd ldrs tl wknd 3 out* **33/1**
05/0 **13** *1 3/4* **Plantaganet (FR)**[25] 2309 7-11-10 88................................... GrahamLee 56
(Ian Williams) *prom: mstke 2nd: wnt 2nd 5th: eased whn btn appr last* **8/1**
245- **14** *shd* **All On My Own (USA)**[253] 4602 10-9-11 64..................(v) LeeVickers(3) 32
(I W McInnes) *bhd fr 5th* **20/1**
50 **15** *3* **Alchimiste (FR)**[21] 2419 4-11-5 90.................................... MrRLangley(7) 55
(Mrs E Langley) *chsd ldrs to 4th* **100/1**
504/ **16** *15* **Medkhan (IRE)**[796] 1593 8-10-4 71.. TJPhelan(3) 21
(F Jordan) *mid-div: hit 3rd: bhd fr 4th* **50/1**
00/P **17** *10* **Mount Vernon (IRE)**[10] 2624 9-10-2 66................................ MarkGrant 6
(P Wegmann) *bhd fr 4th* **100/1**

3m 59.4s (1.10) **Going Correction** 0.0s/f (Good)
WFA 4 from 5yo+ 10lb **17** Ran SP% **128.0**
Speed ratings: **97,95,95,94,94 93,93,93,84,84 82,79,79,79,77 70,65** CSF £10.93 CT £50.86 TOTE £3.40: £1.70, £1.50, £1.70, £1.80; EX 16.60 Place 6 £91.12, Place 5 £45.76.
Owner Concertina Racing Four **Bred** Juddmonte Farms **Trained** Kings Caple, H'fords

FOCUS
A moderate handicap hurdle, but the first two home look on reasonable marks with the fourth and seventh running to form and setting the standard.

NOTEBOOK
Darkshape showed his first real signs of encouragement over hurdles when fourth on his return from a break at Leicester on his previous start, and built on that to run out a comfortable winner. On this evidence, there are more races to be won with him and he would have an obvious chance if turned out under a penalty. *(tchd 11-4)*
Amadeus(AUS), returned to hurdles to try and take advantage of a mark 16lb lower than that of his chase rating, ran a decent race in second behind the clearly well-handicapped winner. He looks up to winning a similar race off his current sort of mark. *(op 4-1)*
Foxmeade Dancer has never won outside of selling company but this was a creditable effort considering the front looked on reasonable marks. *(op 5-1 tchd 9-2)*
Upright Ima, dropped half a mile in trip, ran well enough in fourth but remains a maiden and needs dropping into the lowest grade. *(op 14-1)*
Firstflor did not seem to have any major excuses and remains winless over hurdles.
Jug Of Punch(IRE) *Official explanation: jockey said gelding was unsuited by the soft ground (op 14-1)*
T/Plt: £96.20 to a £1 stake. Pool: £41,095.10. 311.55 winning tickets. T/Qpdt: £26.50 to a £1 stake. Pool: £2,686.70. 74.90 winning tickets. KH

1668 BANGOR-ON-DEE (L-H)
Wednesday, December 14

OFFICIAL GOING: Chase course - soft; hurdle course - good (good to soft in places)
Wind: Almost nil Weather: Overcast

2817 CHRISTMAS MEETING NOVICES' CHASE (15 fncs) 2m 4f 110y
12:30 (12:30) (Class 3) 4-Y-0+ **£5,439** (£1,596; £798; £398)

Form RPR
4-25 **1** **Nadover (FR)**[18] 2488 4-10-7 111... NoelFehily 120+
(C J Mann) *a.p: led 10th: clr last: drvn out* **11/2**
1-16 **2** *6* **Von Origny (FR)**[12] 2607 4-10-7 120............................... RobertThornton 114
(H D Daly) *trckd ldrs: rdn appr 11th: chsd wnr bef 2 out: one pce run-in* **9/4**[1]
20-4 **3** *7* **Simon**[20] 2464 6-11-5 118... GrahamLee 124+
(J L Spearing) *in tch: 3rd and rdn whn blnd bdly 2 out: n.d after* **5/1**[3]
1001 **4** *2* **Va Vavoom (IRE)**[5] 2748 7-10-12 118................................ BernieWharfe(7) 117
(N A Twiston-Davies) *in tch: lost pl after 4th: rdn and hung lft 4 out: no imp* **11/4**[2]
16P5 **5** *15* **Bannister Lane**[18] 2503 5-11-2 102................................... PaddyAspell(3) 102
(D McCain) *held up: rdn appr 11th: lost tch 4 out* **40/1**
-351 **6** *12* **Terivic**[18] 2504 5-11-5 117.. JohnMcNamara 102+
(K C Bailey) *led: hdd 10th: wknd after 3 out: eased bef last* **11/2**

5m 22.1s (9.60) **Going Correction** +0.65s/f (Soft)
WFA 4 from 5yo+ 11lb **6** Ran SP% **107.3**
Speed ratings: **107,104,102,101,95 91** CSF £17.22 TOTE £7.10: £2.70, £1.30; EX 17.40.
Owner Tony Hayward And Barry Fulton **Bred** And Mrs J L Couetil **Trained** Upper Lambourn, Berks

FOCUS
A fair novice chase which saw the field finish strung out behind the decisive winner and the form should work out well enough. The two four-year-olds finished first and second.

NOTEBOOK
Nadover(FR) appreciated this return to soft ground and broke his duck over fences with a decisive success, reversing Market Rasen form with Von Origny in the process. The step back up to this trip was also much in his favour, as he looked better the further he went, and his confidence should have been significantly boosted by this. Still only a four-year-old, he should have more to offer. *(op 6-1 tchd 13-2)*
Von Origny(FR), who beat Nadover on his chase debut at Market Rasen yet had been disappointing behind the The Listener at Exeter last time, was ridden from a fair way out and never looked like confirming form with the winner. On this evidence he appears flattered by his official rating, but he may have found this coming a touch too soon and still has time on his side, so is not one to write off just yet. *(op 7-4)*
Simon, fourth on his recent British debut, was in the process of running an improved race prior to an error at the penultimate flight that effectively put paid to his chances. He is versatile as regards trip and, as a former winning pointer, can be expected to fare better in this sphere as he gains further experience. *(op 11-2 tchd 6-1)*
Va Vavoom(IRE), reverting to novice company after his dour success under today's rider at Cheltenham five days previously, failed to get into contention from off the pace and most likely found this coming too soon. *(op 3-1)*
Terivic, off the mark on his chasing bow at Towcester last time, performed a long way below that level of form over this longer trip. He is another who is worthy of another chance, as he still has few miles on the clock, but has a fair amount to prove now nevertheless. *(op 9-2)*

2818 BANGORONDEERACES.CO.UK H'CAP CHASE (15 fncs) 2m 4f 110y
1:00 (1:00) (Class 4) (0-105,105) 5-Y-0+ **£4,167** (£1,223; £611; £305)

Form RPR
2304 **1** **Lost In Normandy (IRE)**[8] 2686 8-10-0 79 oh12......(b) TomScudamore 90+
(Mrs L Williamson) *a.p: led 10th: clr 2 out: eased cl home* **10/1**

/3FU **2** *7* **Toon Trooper (IRE)**^{11} [2630] 8-11-5 **98**.......................... WarrenMarston 101
(R Lee) *bhd: hdwy whn mstke 9th: rdn appr 2 out: wnt 2nd last: no imp on wnr* **16/1**

43PP **3** *3* **Quizzling (IRE)**^{13} [2594] 7-9-11 **79** oh3.......................... OwynNelmes$^{(3)}$ 80+
(B J M Ryall) *in tch: hmpd 1st: chsd wnr 4 out: rdn bef 2 out: hit and lost 2nd last: sn wknd* **16/1**

00-6 **4** *1 ¼* **Lord Oscar (IRE)**^{50} [1875] 6-11-1 **97**.......................... TomMalone$^{(3)}$ 96
(M C Pipe) *hld up in rr: hdwy whn j.lft 11th: rdn appr 2 out: one pce* **14/1**

302 **5** *8* **Alphabetical (IRE)**^{13} [2591] 6-11-5 **98**.......................... NoelFehily 89
(C J Mann) *hld up: hdwy appr 10th: rdn bef 4 out: wknd bef 2 out* **11/4**^{1}

3330 **6** *¾* **Lubinas (IRE)**^{49} [1877] 6-11-1 **94**.......................... HenryOliver 89+
(F Jordan) *midfield: j.lft 1st: effrt 9th: wknd after 10th* **5/1**^{2}

4453 **7** *hd* **Paddy The Optimist (IRE)**^{15} [2562] 9-10-2 **88**.......................... LiamHeard$^{(7)}$ 78
(D Burchell) *midfield: rdn appr 4 out: sn wknd* **7/1**^{3}

65F3 **8** *nk* **Cusp**^{9} [2679] 5-10-6 **90**.......................... DerekLaverty$^{(5)}$ 80
(Mrs A M Thorpe) *trckd ldrs: rdn appr 11th: wknd 2 out* **16/1**

6245 **9** *9* **Jefertiti (FR)**^{38} [2067] 8-10-13 **95**.......................... PeterBuchanan$^{(3)}$ 76
(Miss Lucinda V Russell) *led: hdd 10th: wknd 4 out: mstke whn btn next* **14/1**

/0F- **10** *8* **Mister Dave'S (IRE)**^{375} [2642] 10-11-12 **105**.......................... DavidO'Meara 78
(Mrs S J Smith) *hit 9th: a in rr* **12/1**

-06P **11** *5* **Hawk's Landing (IRE)**^{14} [2577] 8-11-11 **104**.......................... BrianHarding 72
(Jonjo O'Neill) *midfield: pushed along and wknd appr 10th* **8/1**

PP25 **F** **Look To The Future (IRE)**^{21} [2429] 11-9-13 **83**.......................... LeeStephens$^{(5)}$ —
(M J M Evans) *prom: wknd 10th: hmpd whn struggling next: bhd whn fell last* **20/1**

5m 25.8s (13.30) **Going Correction** +0.65s/f (Soft) **12** Ran SP% **119.5**
Speed ratings: **100,97,96,95,92 92,92,92,88,85 83,—** CSF £154.48 CT £2536.85 TOTE £18.00: £4.20, £5.50, £6.70; EX 805.10.
Owner Please Hold UK **Bred** Mrs Ann Maxwell **Trained** Saighton, Cheshire

FOCUS
A moderate handicap, run at a fair pace, which saw the winner score decisively from 12lb out of the handicap. The form could be rated higher but should be treated with a little caution.

NOTEBOOK
Lost In Normandy(IRE), dropping markedly in trip, ran out a suprisingly easy winner from 12lb out of the handicap and he clearly relished racing handily over this shorter distance. It is hard to know quite what to make of this vastly-improved effort, and he could be flattered as the market leaders all ran below expectations, but it was nothing if not deserved. A future hike in the weights is likely, *but he would have to be of interest if turned out under a penalty over this sort of trip.Official explanation: trainer said, regarding improved form shown, gelding was better suited by today's shorter trip on softer ground, and by the return to Bangor (op 12-1)*
Toon Trooper(IRE) stayed on well enough without posing a threat to the winner, and turned in by far his best display of jumping to date in this sphere. His confidence should have been restored after this, and the return to further ought to play more to his strengths, yet he is not one to overly trust.
Quizzling(IRE), pulled up on his previous two starts, would have been a touch closer but for blundering at the final fence and ran close to his mark, despite being 1lb out of the handicap. He ideally needs a less-taxing surface and can build on this.
Lord Oscar(IRE), often a front-runner in the past, was restrained off the gallop for this chasing bow and looked like playing a part when moving through rivals past halfway, but his effort proved short-lived and he was ultimately well held. With his powerful stable notably out of form at present, this was probably not a bad effort, and it would be a surprise were he not to find a race from this mark in due course. *(tchd 16-1)*
Alphabetical(IRE), making his chase and handicap bow, jumped well enough yet failed to improve as expected for the longer trip and softer ground. This was disappointing but, as a former winning *pointer, the step up to three miles in this sphere could see him back in a better light. (op 3-1 tchd 10-3)*
Lubinas(IRE) was unable to sustain his effort when it mattered and ran well below his mark. It is *worth noting that his stable's last winner was back in April. Official explanation: trainer said gelding was unsuited by the soft ground (op 7-1)*
Paddy The Optimist(IRE) *(op 8-1)*
Hawk's Landing(IRE) turned in yet another moody effort and is one to avoid at all costs. *(tchd 9-1)*

2819 TILSTON H'CAP CHASE (21 fncs) 3m 6f
1:35 (1:36) (Class 3) (0-120,118) 5-Y-0+ **£6,113** (£1,794; £897; £448)

Form RPR

-140 **1** **Ebony Light (IRE)**^{24} [2368] 9-11-12 **118**.......................... (p) GrahamLee 139+
(D McCain) *trckd ldrs: led 14th (water): clr 3 out: eased run-in* **9/1**

-231 **2** *5* **Brandy Wine (IRE)**^{21} [2440] 7-10-4 **96**.......................... (p) TonyDobbin 105+
(L Lungo) *midfield: hdwy 13th: rdn to chse wnr after 3 out: no imp* **9/4**^{1}

-00P **3** *1 ½* **Lazy But Lively (IRE)**^{25} [2336] 9-11-7 **113**.......................... KeithMercer 120
(R F Fisher) *hld up: hdwy appr 16th: styd on same pce fr 3 out* **25/1**

2P01 **4** *shd* **Moorlands Again**^{10} [2662] 10-11-3 **114** 7ex.......................... (t) LeeStephens$^{(5)}$ 121+
(M Sheppard) *prom: led 3rd: hdd 14th (water): rdn after 4 out: mstke next: sn wknd* **4/1**^{2}

P-31 **5** *19* **Villair (IRE)**^{13} [2589] 10-11-2 **108**.......................... NoelFehily 104+
(C J Mann) *hld up: mstke 13th: sn rdn: nvr on terms* **9/1**

4-FP **6** *dist* **Briar's Mist (IRE)**^{22} [2413] 8-10-1 **93**.......................... (b) RichardMcGrath —
(C Grant) *led to 3rd: remained prom: rdn after 13th: wknd 15th: t.o* **16/1**

460P **F** **Limerick Leader (IRE)**^{12} [2608] 7-10-12 **111**.......................... (b) MrTJO'Brien$^{(7)}$ —
(P J Hobbs) *trckd ldrs tl fell 6th* **11/1**

-404 **P** **Harlov (FR)**^{28} [2265] 10-11-1 **107**.......................... (p) AlanDempsey —
(A Parker) *hld up: rdn after 14th (water): t.o whn p.u after 3 out* **6/1**^{3}

1-1P **P** **Sir Frosty**^{12} [2608] 12-11-1 **107**.......................... JoeTizzard —
(B J M Ryall) *midfield: bhd fr 6th: struggling after 13th: t.o whn p.u bef 17th* **14/1**

8m 9.30s (-0.40) **Going Correction** +0.65s/f (Soft) **9** Ran SP% **109.8**
Speed ratings: **105,103,103,103,98 —,—,—,—** CSF £28.49 CT £454.04 TOTE £10.60: £2.40, £1.30, £5.70; EX 36.80.
Owner Roger Bellamy **Bred** J Boylson **Trained** Cholmondeley, Cheshire

FOCUS
A fair marathon chase, run at a sound gallop, and the form looks sound enough for the class rated through the placed horses. The winner is value for further.

NOTEBOOK
Ebony Light(IRE) was given a positive ride by Lee on this step-up in distance, and got back to winning ways in grand fashion, despite the burden of top weight. While he had appeared unsuited by the big Aintree fences in the Becher Chase last time, that was clearly over an inadequate trip, and it could be a different story over the National course and distance should he progress to make the cut in April. An inevitable hike in the weights for this will aid his cause for that target. *(op 8-1)*
Brandy Wine(IRE), just 1lb higher than when successful over timber in first-time cheekpieces last time, took an age to hit full stride over this longer trip and is flattered by his proximity to the winner. He is bred to do well over fences and at this sort of marathon trip, so may be capable of better in *this sphere when racing more prominently. No doubt he will go up in the weights for this, however. (op 5-2 tchd 2-1)*
Lazy But Lively(IRE), reverting to fences, was doing his best work from the fourth last and turned in by far his best effort for some time. He is rated 4lb lower in this sphere than over hurdles and could build on this when reverting to around three miles. *(op 20-1)*
Moorlands Again, impressive when scoring over slightly shorter at Warwick ten days previously, would have better served by an uncontested lead and was beaten from the fourth last. This was still a fair effort under his penalty, however. *(op 3-1)*
Harlov(FR), proven over course and distance, never looked particularly happy and performed well below expectations. *(tchd 11-2 and 13-2)*

2820 ALFA AGGREGATE H'CAP HURDLE (12 hdls) 3m
2:05 (2:07) (Class 3) (0-135,133) 4-Y-0+ **£8,334** (£2,446; £1,223; £611)

Form RPR

1-U0 **1** **Valley Ride (IRE)**^{31} [2207] 5-11-11 **132**.......................... TomScudamore 137+
(C Tinkler) *hld up: hdwy after 7th: led 2 out: hit last: rdn out* **10/1**

4042 **2** *1 ¼* **Just Beth**^{11} [2621] 9-10-3 **115**.......................... DerekLaverty$^{(5)}$ 118
(G Fierro) *midfield: hdwy 6th: rdn and ev ch 2 out: sn hung lft: nt qckn run-in* **9/1**^{3}

45P- **3** *2* **Truckers Tavern (IRE)**^{271} [4435] 10-11-0 **121**.......................... PadgeWhelan 122
(Mrs S J Smith) *prom: hit 6th: led appr 8th: rdn and hdd 2 out: styd on same pce* **8/1**^{2}

11-F **4** *1* **Halcon Genelardais (FR)**^{24} [2369] 5-11-12 **133**.......................... RobertThornton 134+
(A King) *midfield: hdwy 4 out: ev ch 3 out: sn rdn: kpt on same pce* **2/1**^{1}

0-3B **5** *nk* **Versus (GER)**^{19} [2483] 5-9-7 **110**.......................... KevinTobin$^{(10)}$ 110
(C J Mann) *in tch: ev ch after 3 out: kpt on same pce* **16/1**

0200 **6** *1 ¼* **Phar From Frosty (IRE)**^{19} [2483] 8-11-2 **123**.......................... PaulMoloney 121
(C R Egerton) *led: hdd 3rd: remained cl up: outpcd after 4 out: rallied appr last: sn one pce* **10/1**

F-0P **7** *7* **Freetown (IRE)**^{20} [2451] 9-11-9 **130**.......................... (b^{1}) TonyDobbin 122+
(L Lungo) *s.s: midfield: hdwy 5th: ev ch 3 out: rdn and wknd appr next* **25/1**

0P-0 **8** *3* **Mobasher (IRE)**^{30} [2247] 6-10-10 **117**.......................... AlanO'Keeffe 107+
(Miss Venetia Williams) *hld up: hdwy whn mstke 7th: rdn after 4 out: wknd appr 2 out* **16/1**

0P-3 **9** *5* **Old Feathers (IRE)**^{18} [2505] 8-10-5 **112**.......................... (b) NoelFehily 95
(Jonjo O'Neill) *midfield: rdn 4 out: wknd bef next* **12/1**

060P **10** *3* **Nick's Choice**^{11} [2621] 9-9-12 **112**.......................... LiamHeard$^{(7)}$ 92
(D Burchell) *a bhd* **40/1**

0-F5 **11** *22* **Rowan Castle**^{53} [1826] 9-10-0 **107** oh12.......................... RichardMcGrath 65
(Sir John Barlow Bt) *midfield: wknd appr 7th* **150/1**

050- **12** *9* **Supreme Piper (IRE)**^{272} [4412] 7-10-8 **122**.......................... MissCDyson$^{(7)}$ 71
(Miss C Dyson) *prom: led 3rd: mstke 7th: hdd appr next: sn wknd* **66/1**

5-UP **13** *2* **Double Header (IRE)**^{12} [2607] 6-10-13 **120**.......................... RJGreene 67
(Mrs S D Williams) *prom: rdn and lost pl 5th: n.d after* **33/1**

11F- **P** **Westmeath Flyer**^{237} [4948] 10-11-8 **129**.......................... BrianHarding —
(N G Richards) *a bhd: t.o whn p.u bef 2 out* **12/1**

31P1 **P** **Vicario**^{11} [2629] 4-11-2 **123**.......................... GrahamLee —
(D McCain) *trckd ldrs tl 5th: bhd 7th: t.o whn p.u bef 4 out* **10/1**

5m 52.6s (-4.20) **Going Correction** -0.10s/f (Good)
WFA 4 from 5yo+ 13lb **15** Ran SP% **120.2**
Speed ratings: **103,102,101,101,101 101,98,97,96,95 87,84,84,—,—** CSF £93.68 CT £767.20 TOTE £10.30: £3.90, £2.00, £3.50; EX 182.30 TRIFECTA Not won..
Owner George Ward **Bred** Patrick Doyle **Trained** Compton, Berks

FOCUS
A decent handicap for the track, run at a sound gallop and the form looks solid.

NOTEBOOK
Valley Ride(IRE) ◆ showed his true colours and bounced back to form with a gritty success on this first outing over three miles. He was given a well-judged ride by Scudamore, had the race in the bag prior to clouting the final flight, and clearly got every yard of the longer trip. Most progressive last term, he remains open to further improvement over timber, and this gives connections plenty of further options know they can be confident that he stays. The Coral Cup at Cheltenham in March appeals a viable future target, yet he still has to truly prove his effectivness *away from a Flat track. Official explanation: trainer had no explanation for the improved form shown*
Just Beth hung under maximum pressure when holding every chance after the penultimate flight, but still turned in another rock-solid effort in defeat. She is a decent benchmark for this form, and really does deserve to find a race, but her consistency dictates that she will get little respite from the Handicapper. *(op 17-2)*
Truckers Tavern(IRE), who lost his way over fences last term and is rated 23lb lower over hurdles, made a very encouraging debut for his new yard on this return to action. He looked at one point like winning, until his lack of a recent run told from two out, and he probably ran right up to his official mark in defeat. Certainly entitled to improve for the outing, it will be fascinating to see whether he can now build on this. *(op 9-1)*
Halcon Genelardais(FR), who was still in with a chance prior to falling on his comeback at Aintree 24 days previously, never looked particularly happy over this longer trip yet still held every chance under top weight. His confidence should have been restored somewhat now, and he remains capable of winning from this mark, but is probably better over shorter. *(op 9-4)*
Versus(GER) showed improved form and ran very close to his mark in defeat. He is yet to fully convince at this trip, but can find easier opportunities from his current rating. *(op 20-1)*
Phar From Frosty(IRE) appreciated the drop in class and posted a more encouraging effort, but still looks held by the Handicapper at present. *(op 11-1)*
Freetown(IRE) *(tchd 28-1)*

2821 NICHOLA JANE "NATIONAL HUNT" NOVICES' HURDLE (9 hdls) 2m 1f
2:40 (2:40) (Class 4) 4-Y-0+ **£3,541** (£1,039; £519; £259)

Form RPR

2 **1** **Fier Normand (FR)**^{48} [1895] 6-10-12.......................... RichardMcGrath 117+
(Jonjo O'Neill) *racd keenly: in tch: nt fluent 2 out: sn led and hung lft: readily* **10/11**^{1}

132 **2** *1 ¾* **Fourty Acers (IRE)**^{26} [2309] 5-10-12.......................... RJGreene 112+
(M C Pipe) *led: nt fluent 2 out: sn hdd: nt qckn run-in* **9/2**^{2}

4 **3** *9* **Nice Try (IRE)**^{12} [2617] 6-10-7.......................... PaulO'Neill$^{(5)}$ 102
(Miss Venetia Williams) *trckd ldrs: wnt 2nd appr 3 out tl bef 2 out: wknd bef last* **20/1**

5-34 **4** *5* **Sabreur**^{43} [1968] 4-10-12.......................... RobertThornton 97
(Ian Williams) *midfield: hdwy appr 2 out: no imp on ldrs* **16/1**

4-33 **5** *1* **Nocturnally**^{28} [2269] 5-10-12.......................... JimCrowley 96
(V R A Dartnall) *hld up: sme hdwy whn mstke 2 out: nvr trbld ldrs* **16/1**

0 **6** *3* **Hatton House (IRE)**^{27} [2288] 5-10-12.......................... GrahamLee 93
(D McCain) *prom tl wknd appr 2 out* **100/1**

30-0 **7** *½* **Easby Mandarin**^{18} [2507] 4-10-12.......................... BarryKeniry 93
(C W Thornton) *hld up: hit 5th: struggling 4 out: nvr a danger* **100/1**

15- **8** *1 ½* **Corals Laurel (IRE)**^{333} [3367] 6-10-12.......................... WarrenMarston 91
(R T Phillips) *bhd: j.rt 2nd: sme hdwy appr 2 out: nvr on terms* **11/2**^{3}

246 **9** *nk* **Paradise Bay (IRE)**^{17} [2528] 4-10-12.......................... NoelFehily 92+
(C J Mann) *in tch: hdwy 5th: blnd 3 out: wknd appr 2 out* **20/1**

3-04 **10** *1 ¼* **Reap The Reward (IRE)**^{20} [2450] 5-10-9.......................... GaryBerridge$^{(3)}$ 89
(L Lungo) *in rr: kpt on fr 2 out: nvr on terms* **33/1**

0-5 **11** *3 ½* **Kilmackilloge**^{27} [2295] 6-10-12.......................... TonyDobbin 86
(M Todhunter) *t.k.h: trckd ldrs tl wknd appr 4 out* **20/1**

00-0 **12** ½ **Saddlers Express**[43] 1974 4-10-0 TomGreenway[(5)] 78
(H D Daly) *midfield: rdn and wknd appr 3 out* **66/1**

/44- **13** 1 **Beluga (IRE)**[422] 1767 6-10-12 PaulMoloney 86+
(M Pitman) *in tch: rdn and wknd appr 2 out* **50/1**

14 hd **China Fare (IRE)**[59] 1769 5-10-2 PeterBuchanan[(3)] 77
(Miss Lucinda V Russell) *midfield tl wknd 3 out* **100/1**

0 **15** 1¾ **Fill The Bunker (IRE)**[15] 2559 5-10-5 StevenCrawford[(7)] 83
(N A Twiston-Davies) *a bhd* **50/1**

40- **16** 8 **Alf's Spinney**[239] 4922 5-10-12 TomScudamore 75
(Ian Williams) *midfield tl wknd 3 out* **100/1**

0- **17** 7 **Cloud Venture**[312] 3710 5-10-12 JoeTizzard 68
(S E H Sherwood) *a bhd* **100/1**

60/ **P** **Steel Warrior**[732] 2742 8-10-5 RobertLucey-Butler[(7)] —
(J S Smith) *a bhd: t.o whn p.u bef 2 out* **100/1**

4m 6.20s (-4.70) **Going Correction** -0.10s/f (Good)
WFA 4 from 5yo+ 10lb **18** Ran SP% **126.3**
Speed ratings: **107,106,101,99,99 97,97,96,96,96 94,94,93,93,92 89,85,—** CSF £4.58 TOTE £1.80: £1.40, £1.70, £3.60; EX 8.70.
Owner John P McManus **Bred** Thierry Picard **Trained** Cheltenham, Gloucs

FOCUS
A fair novice event, run at a decent gallop, and the first two came clear. The form should work out.

NOTEBOOK
Fier Normand(FR), runner-up on his British and hurdling debut when last seen in October, duly went one better in ready fashion despite running freely through the early parts. He jumped neatly, all bar the penultimate flight, and just confirmed his comeback form with the runner-up. As a half-brother to L'Antartique he can be expected to rate higher over timber before the season is out, *but shaped as though he may come into his own when faced with a stiffer test in due course. (op Evens tchd 5-6)*
Fourty Acers(IRE) ◆, well behind the winner in third on his penultimate outing, turned in another sound effort and managed to get a lot closer to that rival this time. He will need to learn to settle better if he is to progress to a higher level, but he was clear of the rest at the finish, and has a similar event within his compass. This was also a welcome boost to the well-advertised poor current form for his powerful stable. *(op 7-1)*
Nice Try(IRE) turned in an improved effort and was not given a hard time once his chance evaporated approaching two from home. He can be expected to do much better when eligible for handicaps and upped to a more suitable trip. *(op 16-1)*
Sabreur was again doing his best work at the finish and posted another encouraging effort. He is another who can be expected to fare better when switching to handicaps and a stiffer test. *(op 20-1)*
Nocturnally stayed on eye-catchingly under a fairly considerate ride and can be rated slightly better than the bare form suggests. He has been a touch disappointing to date, but will be qualified for a handicap mark after his next outing. *(op 14-1)*
Hatton House(IRE), making his hurdling debut, showed improved form and clearly needs a stiffer test to be seen at best. He is one to keep an eye on.
Corals Laurel(IRE), a debut bumper winner last term and returning from a 333-day break, failed to get into contention on this hurdling bow and disappointed. *(op 5-1 tchd 13-2)*

2822 RED DRAGON CONDITIONAL JOCKEYS' H'CAP HURDLE (9 hdls) 2m 1f
3:10 (3:10) (Class 4) (0-100,102) 4-Y-0+ **£2,898** (£844; £422)

Form RPR

P600 **1** **Gustavo**[13] 2584 4-10-7 **82** PaulO'Neill[(3)] 92+
(Miss Venetia Williams) *trckd ldrs: led after 3 out: hit last: rdn out* **5/1**[2]

-611 **2** 1 **Caesarean Hunter (USA)**[5] 2750 6-11-8 **102** 7ex SeanQuinlan[(8)] 109+
(R T Phillips) *hld up: hdwy 3 out: hung lft appr last: r.o run-in: nt rch wnr* **7/4**[1]

0-00 **3** 1 **Speed Venture**[13] 2585 8-11-0 **91** (vt) PhilKinsella[(5)] 97
(J Mackie) *led: hdd after 3 out: rdn and nt qckn run-in* **6/1**[3]

0340 **4** 6 **Spike Jones (NZ)**[13] 2592 7-11-6 **92** DerekLaverty 92
(Mrs A M Thorpe) *hld up: hdwy 5th: ev ch 2 out: wknd run-in* **10/1**

6454 **5** 2½ **West Hill (IRE)**[15] 2563 4-10-0 **72** oh1 PaddyAspell 70
(D McCain) *in tch: rdn and wknd appr 2 out* **7/1**

3040 **6** shd **Pearson Glen (IRE)**[5] 2478 6-10-7 **87** (p) MichaelMcAvoy[(8)] 84
(James Moffatt) *midfield: hit 3rd: rdn and wknd after 3 out* **16/1**

0F20 **7** 8 **Earl Of Spectrum (GER)**[15] 2563 4-11-8 **94** JamesDiment 83
(J L Spearing) *t.k.h: hld up: mstke 3rd: hdwy 4 out: nt clr run after 3 out: wknd bef next* **16/1**

P-66 **8** 5 **Allez Mousson**[1] 2064 7-10-9 **81** (p) KeithMercer 65
(A Bailey) *midfield: hdwy 4th: rdn appr 3 out: wknd bef 2 out* **12/1**

-400 **9** 6 **Moorlands Milly**[52] 1851 4-10-7 **82** LiamHeard[(3)] 60
(D Burchell) *a towards rr* **28/1**

1P30 **10** shd **Irish Blessing (USA)**[29] 2256 8-10-11 **83** (tp) OwynNelmes 61
(F Jordan) *in tch: rdn and wknd 4 out* **16/1**

PP **11** 14 **Koln Stars (IRE)**[11] 2625 7-11-12 **98** LiamTreadwell 62
(Jennie Candlish) *prom to 4th* **66/1**

4m 11.7s (0.80) **Going Correction** -0.10s/f (Good)
WFA 4 from 6yo+ 10lb **11** Ran SP% **119.2**
Speed ratings: **94,93,93,90,89 89,85,82,80,80 73** CSF £14.71 CT £55.14 TOTE £7.00: £2.50, £1.70, £1.90; EX 21.00.
Owner Mrs P A H Hartley **Bred** G Reed **Trained** Kings Caple, H'fords

FOCUS
A modest time for the class and 5.5 seconds slower than the preceding novice hurdle. The first three came clear, however, and the form still looks sound enough.

NOTEBOOK
Gustavo, making his handicap debut in this sphere, maintained the excellent recent form of his stable and got off the mark over hurdles at the fourth attempt. He enjoyed the chance to race handily, appreciated the better ground, and showed a decent attitude to recover from a final flight *error on the run-in. A hike in the weights is now inevitable, but he most likely has more to offer. Official explanation: trainer said, regarding the improved form shown, gelding may have benefited from the drop in class (tchd 6-1)*
Caesarean Hunter(USA), well-backed on this quest for the hat-trick, got going all too late and found the winner gone beyond recall on the run-in. He remains in decent form, however, and while he will find life tougher off his higher future mark, could well add to his tally when reverting to further. *(op 9-4)*
Speed Venture stepped-up markedly on the level of his recent return from a break at Leicester and showed the benefit of a 4lb drop in the weights. This better ground was in his favour and he is capable of building on this when reverting to slightly further. *(op 11-2)*
Spike Jones(NZ) clearly enjoyed the drop back in trip and registered his best effort to date for current connections. *(op 11-1 tchd 12-1)*
West Hill(IRE), 1lb out of the handicap, got markedly outpaced when the tempo increased approaching the third last and would have been seen in a better light off a stronger gallop. *(op 8-1)*

2823 JP SEAFOODS INTERMEDIATE OPEN NATIONAL HUNT FLAT RACE 2m 1f
3:40 (3:40) (Class 6) 4-6-Y-0 **£1,808** (£527; £263)

Form RPR

14 **1** **Unjust Law (IRE)**[34] 2145 4-11-8 MrTGreenall[(3)] 119+
(N J Henderson) *midfield: hdwy 4f out: led 2f out: pushed clr fnl f* **9/1**

2 **2** 6 **Bradley Boy (IRE)**[30] 2242 4-11-4 PaulMoloney 104+
(M Pitman) *led: rdn and hdd 2f out: eased whn no ex fnl f* **9/4**[1]

5-6 **3** 6 **Major Oak (IRE)**[25] 2340 4-11-4 BarryKeniry 97+
(G M Moore) *prom: ev ch whn wnt rt over 3f out: wknd over 1f out* **9/1**

22- **4** 1¼ **Butler's Cabin (FR)**[381] 2519 5-10-11 MrAJBerry[(7)] 95
(Jonjo O'Neill) *in tch: ev ch whn n.m.r and hmpd over 3f out: wknd 2f out* **11/4**[2]

5 hd **Team Leader (IRE)** 5-10-11 StevenCrawford[(7)] 95
(N A Twiston-Davies) *in tch: rdn and ev ch over 3f out: wknd 2f out* **15/2**[3]

6 9 **Glen Omen (IRE)** 5-11-4 AlanO'Keeffe 86
(Jennie Candlish) *hld up: sme hdwy over 6f out: wknd over 4f out* **66/1**

7 2½ **Supremely Gifted (IRE)** 4-11-4 DavidO'Meara 83
(Mrs S J Smith) *midfield: hdwy over 6f out: forced wd over 3f out: wknd over 2f out* **10/1**

0 **8** 9 **Bartercard (USA)**[21] 2432 4-11-4 NoelFehily 78+
(C J Mann) *hld up: rdn and hdwy over 5f out: wknd over 2f out* **12/1**

0 **9** 5 **Royal Attraction**[52] 1849 4-11-4 TomSiddall 69
(W M Brisbourne) *in rr: pushed along over 7f out: nvr on terms* **50/1**

0 **10** ¾ **Prince Ickarus (IRE)**[25] 2340 5-10-8 AndrewAdams[(10)] 68
(Mrs S J Smith) *prom tl wknd over 6f out* **50/1**

0 **11** 12 **Young Rocky (IRE)**[52] 1849 4-11-4 RichardMcGrath 56
(C Grant) *prom: n.m.r and lost pl over 6f out: n.d after* **66/1**

0/ **12** ½ **Benjamin Buckram (IRE)**[662] 3934 6-11-4 RobertThornton 56
(C R Egerton) *hld up: rdn and wknd 3f out* **10/1**

0 **13** 27 **Im A Tanner**[27] 2288 4-10-11 MissCDyson[(7)] 29
(Miss S Dyson) *t.k.h: a bhd* **100/1**

4m 7.50s (-3.60) **Going Correction** -0.10s/f (Good) **13** Ran SP% **123.0**
Speed ratings: **104,101,98,97,97 93,92,88,85,85 79,79,66** CSF £30.23 TOTE £6.70: £2.10, £1.30, £2.40; EX 24.40 Place 6 £175.24, Place 5 £78.98.
Owner The Dover Street Boys **Bred** Simon And Helen Plumbly **Trained** Upper Lambourn, Berks
■ Stewards' Enquiry : Alan O'Keeffe £120 fine: passport irregularity

FOCUS
This was run at a steady early gallop, and the field came home fairly strung out, but it could rate higher and may still prove to be a fair bumper as the season progresses.

NOTEBOOK
Unjust Law(IRE) got back to winning ways with a clear-cut success under his penalty and was given an accomplished ride by Greenall. There was a lot to like about the manner of this success, he looked to have plenty in hand at the finish and rates a decent novice hurdle prospect for his powerful stable. *(op 12-1)*
Bradley Boy(IRE) ◆, a decent runner-up behind a stablemate of the winner on his debut at Folkestone last time, registered another solid effort and clearly has the ability to win in this division. *In the longer term, however, he is most likely going to appreciate a much stiffer test. (op 5-2 tchd 11-4)*
Major Oak(IRE) proved at an advantage by racing handily on the steady early pace and turned in *his best effort to date. He appreciated the good ground and is slowly going the right way. (op 10-1 tchd 11-1)*
Butler's Cabin(FR), runner-up on both his previous outings last season, was very well backed for this seasonal return yet proved very one paced when it mattered from two out. It would be a surprise were he not capable of better in due course. *(op 7-2)*
Team Leader(IRE), half-brother to an Irish bumper winner, showed ability on this debut and would have preferred a stronger gallop. He has a future. *(op 11-2)*
Supremely Gifted(IRE), a half-brother to his stable's smart chaser Simply Supreme, was another who would have been seen in a better light granted a stronger overall gallop. *(op 8-1)*
T/Plt: £945.00 to a £1 stake. Pool: £45,115.40. 34.85 winning tickets. T/Qpdt: £26.00 to a £1 stake. Pool: £4,932.70. 140.20 winning tickets. DO

2528 NEWBURY (L-H)
Wednesday, December 14

OFFICIAL GOING: Good to soft (good in places)
The ground appeared to be riding more testing than the official description of 'good to soft'.
Wind: Almost nil

2824 CANTORSPREADFAIR.COM JUVENILE NOVICES' HURDLE (8 hdls) 2m 110y
12:15 (12:16) (Class 4) 3-Y-0 **£3,721** (£1,092; £546; £272)

Form RPR

3-3 **1** **Restless D'Artaix (FR)**[19] 2481 3-11-5 MickFitzgerald 120+
(N J Henderson) *lw: trckd ldrs: wnt 2nd gng wl 3 out: slt ld last: sn clr: v easily* **11/10**[1]

4P **2** 8 **Desert Secrets (IRE)**[12] 2612 3-10-5 TimmyMurphy 94+
(J G Portman) *led: rdn and mstke 2 out: narrowly hdd last: sn no ch w wnr but kpt on wl for clr 2nd* **25/1**

3 5 **Original Fly (FR)**[90] 3-10-12 ChristianWilliams 91
(P F Nicholls) *lw: chsd ldr tl nt fluent and one pce 3 out: sn rdn: kpt on again fr 2 out to take 3rd last strides* **3/1**[2]

4 hd **Sea Map**[19] 3-10-12 LeightonAspell 91
(D E Cantillon) *lw: leggy: hit 1st: hdwy 4th: chsd ldrs 3 out: sn one pce: lost 3rd last strides* **33/1**

0 **5** 18 **Emile Zola**[24] 2373 3-10-12 SamThomas 85+
(Miss Venetia Williams) *chsd ldrs: wnt 3rd 3 out: sn outpcd: no ch fr 2 out: blnd last* **16/1**

6 5 **Shardakhan (IRE)**[105] 3-10-12 PhilipHide 68
(G L Moore) *wl bhd: stl plenty to do 2 out: sme hdwy whn blnd last: r.o cl home* **66/1**

7 9 **Vigna Maggio (FR)**[58] 3-10-5 AndrewThornton 52
(R H Alner) *w'like: lw: in tch: wknd after 3 out* **8/1**[3]

0 **8** 15 **Ihuru**[22] 2425 3-10-12 AndrewTinkler 44
(J G Portman) *bhd: hit 2nd: sme hdwy after 4 out: wknd bef next* **100/1**

0U **9** 4 **Miss Defying**[20] 2454 3-9-12 CharlieStudd[(7)] 33
(R Curtis) *bhd most of way* **100/1**

10 ¾ **Asaateel (IRE)**[66] 3-10-12 JamieMoore 39
(G L Moore) *mstke 1st: bhd: brief effrt after 4 out: nvr nr ldrs and sn wknd* **16/1**

U6 **11** ½ **Before Time**[13] 2597 3-10-5 DarylJacob[(7)] 39
(Mrs A M Thorpe) *chsd ldrs to 4th: wknd bef 3 out: blnd 2 out* **100/1**

12 3 **Mayadeen (IRE)**[181] 3-10-12 TomDoyle 36
(J G M O'Shea) *swtg: bhd: brief effrt 4 out: sn bhd: no ch whn blnd 2 out* **14/1**

00 **13** 9 **Numidas (POL)**[13] 2597 3-10-12 RichardJohnson 27
(P J Hobbs) *sn bhd* **50/1**

14 4 **Brave Hiawatha (FR)**[59] 3-10-12 JasonMaguire 23
(J A B Old) *unf: leggy: chsd ldrs tl mstke and wknd qckly 4th* **9/1**

15 dist **Kitty**[56] 3-10-5 JamieGoldstein —
(Miss J S Davis) *blnd 1st: in tch to 4th: t.o* **100/1**

P **Troublesome Gerri**[551] 3-10-5 .... VinceSlattery —
(S C Burrough) *w'like: bit bkwd: a bhd: no ch whn blnd 3 out and p.u* **100/1**

4m 3.10s (-0.50) **Going Correction** -0.15s/f (Good) **16** Ran SP% **127.4**
Speed ratings: **95,91,88,88,80 77,73,66,64,64 64,62,58,56,—** — CSF £38.87 TOTE £2.10: £1.10, £4.10, £1.50; EX 44.40.
Owner Lynn Wilson **Bred** H Durand And Lucie Durand **Trained** Upper Lambourn, Berks

FOCUS
They finished well strung out in what was a moderate juvenile hurdle by Newbury's standards, but still a decent enough effort from Restless D'Artaix, who was value for more than the official margin. The winning time was modest, 3.5 seconds slower than the later maiden hurdle.

NOTEBOOK
Restless D'Artaix(FR), successful in a Listed hurdle in his native France before running third in a good novice event on his British debut over this course and distance, would have found this a fair bit easier, even though he was conceding upwards of 7lb to all his rivals, and ran out a comfortable winner. He is clearly progressing, but things will be much tougher back in better company. *(op 11-8)*
Desert Secrets(IRE), a promising fourth on her hurdling debut at Huntingdon before pulling up on heavy ground at Sandown, got the run of the race out in front and ran her best races over obstacles yet. While she may be a touch flattered by the bare result, it will be disappointing if she cannot find a small race. *(op 28-1)*
Original Fly(FR), third in a Listed hurdle in France when last seen 90 days previously, made just a satisfactory British debut. He is likely to be better suited by softer ground, and should stay further. *(op 4-1 tchd 9-2)*
Sea Map, successful three times over middle-distances on the Flat, including in selling company on his last two starts, made a pleasing debut over hurdles on his first start for new connections. However, given he was just moderate on the Flat, he does not do a great deal for the form.
Emile Zola, who ran as though something may have been amiss on his hurdling debut at Plumpton, ran a bit better this time but was still well beaten. *(op 20-1)*
Shardakhan(IRE), down the field in a mile and a half maiden on his one start on the Flat 105 days previously, gave the impression he could do better in time on what was his hurdling debut. *(op 100-1)*
Vigna Maggio(FR), a mile winner on the Flat in France, seemed to travel very well for much of the way, but for whatever reason was never too seriously asked and dropped out of contention. She can probably do a fair bit better. *(op 5-1)*
Brave Hiawatha(FR), a ten-furlong winner on the Flat in France, did not jump that well and can probably improve for the experience. *(tchd 10-1)*

2825 RAFFIN STUD GREATWOOD CARING FOR RETIRED RACEHORSES NOVICES' CHASE (A LIMITED H'CAP) (18 fncs) 3m

12:50 (12:50) (Class 3) (0-125,123)
5-Y-0+ **£7,351** (£2,158; £1,079; £539)

Form RPR

5-1 **1** **Gallant Approach (IRE)**[36] 2099 6-11-7 **120** .... AndrewTinkler 140+
(C R Egerton) *hld up in tch: hdwy to trck ldr 8th: led after 14th: shkn up run-in: styd on wl* **7/2**[2]

-0U2 **2** *1 ½* **He's The Guv'Nor (IRE)**[12] 2609 6-10-11 **110** .... BenjaminHitchcott 125+
(R H Buckler) *trckd ldrs: nt fluent 6th: rdn after 3 out: swtchd rt and wnt 2nd appr last: kpt on but a hld run-in* **12/1**

43P1 **3** *15* **Bob The Builder**[13] 2581 6-10-8 **107** .... AntonyEvans 110+
(N A Twiston-Davies) *led tl stmbld bdly and hdd after 14th: chsd wnr: rdn after 4 out: j.lft fr next: wknd run-in* **7/2**[2]

10/6 **4** *5* **Master Trix (IRE)**[17] 2529 8-10-13 **112** .... RichardJohnson 109+
(P J Hobbs) *lw: hld up in tch: blnd 11th: short lived effrt appr 4 out: wknd 3 out* **10/3**[1]

-0F3 **5** *4* **Victory Gunner (IRE)**[15] 2564 7-11-5 **118** .... LeightonAspell 108
(C Roberts) *trckd ldrs: lost position appr 9th: wknd appr 14th* **20/1**

121F **P** **Bob Ar Aghaidh (IRE)**[11] 2644 9-11-10 **123** .... TomDoyle —
(C Tinkler) *lw: trckd ldr tl 8th: losing pl whn hit 12th: sn bhd: p.u bef 4 out* **7/1**[3]

02-4 **P** **Star Angler (IRE)**[18] 2504 7-11-0 **113** .... MarkBradburne —
(H D Daly) *nt a fluent: hld up: mstke 11th: sn lost tch: hit 13th: t.o and p.u bef 3 out* **14/1**

05-4 **P** **Kyper Disco (FR)**[229] 104 7-10-9 **108** .... MickFitzgerald —
(N J Henderson) *hld up: hdwy into 4th at the 13th: rdn and wknd qckly 4 out: p.u bef 3 out* **20/1**

1P **P** **Nick Junior (IRE)**[49] 1879 6-11-3 **116** .... ChristianWilliams —
(Evan Williams) *mstke 1st: hld up: hdwy to chse ldrs 9th: wknd after 11th: bhd and p.u bef 13th: lame* **8/1**

6m 3.10s (-1.90) **Going Correction** +0.10s/f (Yiel) **9** Ran SP% **115.0**
Speed ratings: **107,106,101,99,98** —,—,—,— CSF £42.97 CT £154.58 TOTE £4.10: £1.50, £3.10, £1.50; EX 53.10.
Owner Byrne Bros (Formwork) Limited **Bred** N J Connors **Trained** Chaddleworth, Berks

FOCUS
A decent novices' handicap in which the first two came clear. The third and fourth set the standard and the form looks reasonable.

NOTEBOOK
Gallant Approach(IRE) appeared to have plenty of weight for this chasing debut. Stepping up almost a mile in trip, although he is a winning pointer in Ireland, he eased to the front on the home turn and stayed on strongly. He jumped nicely and can win more races over fences. *(op 3-1 tchd 11-4)*
He's The Guv'Nor(IRE), back over fences, ran a solid race and was certainly not stopping at the end of three miles. He should soon be found a winning opportunity. *(op 14-1)*
Bob The Builder jumped soundly in front until getting the cross fence all wrong, Evans having to pick him up off the floor. Jumping left in the latter stages, he lost second place going to the final fence and was soon left behind by the first two. *(op 9-2)*
Master Trix(IRE), eased 3lb after his recent return, could never get into the action. He has yet to prove he wants this far. *(op 5-1)*
Victory Gunner(IRE) has yet to show any great aptitude for chasing but has not encountered truly testing conditions so far. *(tchd 22-1)*
Bob Ar Aghaidh(IRE) lost his pitch in the back straight and was tailed off when pulled up before *the home turn. He might have been feeling the effects of his Wetherby fall.Official explanation: jockey said gelding never travelled (op 6-1 tchd 11-2)*
Kyper Disco(FR), effectively making his seasonal debut, was still close enough in fourth place at the cross fence but his stamina then seemed to ebb away. *(op 6-1 tchd 11-2)*
Nick Junior(IRE) *Official explanation: jockey said gelding pulled up lame (op 6-1 tchd 11-2)*

2826 CANTOR GAMING MAIDEN HURDLE (8 hdls) 2m 110y

1:20 (1:23) (Class 4) 4-Y-0+ **£4,293** (£1,260; £630; £314)

Form RPR

-1 **1** **Craven (IRE)**[39] 2056 5-11-2 .... MickFitzgerald 123+
(N J Henderson) *lw: in tch: hdwy 4th: trckd ldrs 3 out: chsd wnr next: stl 5l down last: drvn and styd on strly to ld cl home* **9/2**[3]

22 **2** *½* **Private Be**[43] 1968 6-11-2 .... RichardJohnson 123
(P J Hobbs) *lw: led: sn clr: stl 5l ahd last: hrd rdn run-in: ct cl home* **7/2**[2]

3 *23* **Vinando**[32] 4-11-2 ....(bt) AndrewTinkler 103+
(C R Egerton) *lw: chsd ldrs: wnt 2nd 4th: rdn after 3 out: one pce and lost 2nd next: so no ch w 1st pair* **5/2**[1]

4 *6* **Cruise Director**[81] 5-11-2 .... AndrewThornton 96+
(W J Musson) *in tch: chsd ldrs appr 3 out: sn one pce: no ch whn nt fluent last* **14/1**

20 **5** *2* **Tech Eagle (IRE)**[14] 2573 5-11-2 .... TomDoyle 92
(R Curtis) *in tch: nt fluent 4th: lost position appr 3 out: styd on again appr last but nvr a danger* **66/1**

6 *3 ½* **Stocking Island**[463] 4-10-9 .... MarkGrant 84+
(C R Egerton) *bhd tl mod prog fr 2 out* **100/1**

7 *8* **Roussea (IRE)**[199] 7-10-11 ....(t) RobertStephens[(5)] 80
(S G Griffiths) *lw: chsd ldrs: rdn and wknd 3 out* **50/1**

05 **8** *hd* **Smoothly Does It**[6] 2730 4-10-9 .... ShaneWalsh[(7)] 80
(Mrs A J Bowlby) *bhd: mod prog fr 2 out* **50/1**

P **9** *2 ½* **High Charter**[38] 2082 4-11-2 ....(t) MarkBradburne 77
(J R Fanshawe) *chsd ldrs tl wknd appr 3 out* **25/1**

0-04 **10** *1 ½* **Talikos (FR)**[28] 2269 4-11-2 .... SamThomas 76
(Miss H C Knight) *mid-div 3rd: pushed along after 4 out: sn wknd* **50/1**

11 *½* **Once (FR)**[359] 5-11-2 .... JamieMoore 75
(M G Rimell) *w'like: chsd ldrs: rdn after 4 out: wknd next* **11/1**

P **12** *2 ½* **Pure Magic (FR)**[11] 2618 4-11-2 .... JamieGoldstein 73
(Miss J S Davis) *hit 1st: in tch to 4th* **100/1**

44 **13** *3* **Herakles (GER)**[18] 2487 4-10-11 .... SamCurling[(5)] 70
(N J Henderson) *nvr bttr than mid-div* **14/1**

14 *10* **Naja De Billeron (FR)**[39] 4-10-6 .... AndrewGlassonbury[(10)] 60
(M C Pipe) *mid-div: hdwy 4th: chsd ldrs appr 3 out: sn wknd* **20/1**

15 *12* **Fleet Anchor**[22] 4-11-2 .... VinceSlattery 48
(J M Bradley) *mstke 2nd: a bhd* **100/1**

16 *1 ½* **Harcourt (USA)**[114] 5-11-2 .... PhilipHide 46
(M Madgwick) *chsd ldrs to 4 out* **40/1**

17 *13* **Vibe**[14] 4-10-11 .... MarkNicolls[(5)] 33
(R J Price) *chsd ldrs to 4th* **100/1**

1 **18** *15* **Tell Henry (IRE)**[62] 1730 5-11-2 .... ChristianWilliams 18
(Evan Williams) *lw: s.i.s: blnd 1st: a in rr* **20/1**

0 **19** *shd* **Go Commercial (IRE)**[31] 2211 4-11-2 .... TimmyMurphy 18
(M C Pipe) *a bhd* **40/1**

154- **F** **Back Among Friends**[266] 4519 6-11-2 .... JasonMaguire —
(J A B Old) *fell 1st* **14/1**

P **Prizeman (USA)**[228] 7-11-2 .... JimmyMcCarthy —
(J A Geake) *hit 3rd: a bhd: t.o whn p.u bef 2 out* **40/1**

0 **P** **Valleyofthekings (IRE)**[62] 1730 4-11-2 .... LeightonAspell —
(O Sherwood) *a bhd: t.o whn p.u bef 3 out* **66/1**

F **Heathers Girl**[382] 6-9-13 .... JosephStevenson[(10)] —
(R Dickin) *w'like: a bhd: no ch whn fell last* **100/1**

P **Gimmeabreak (IRE)**[269] 5-11-2 .... BarryFenton —
(Miss E C Lavelle) *w'like: bit bkwd: a in rr: t.o whn p.u bef 3 out* **20/1**

0-0 **P** **Judge'N'Thomas**[203] 507 5-10-9 .... MrJAJenkins[(7)] —
(M R Bosley) *blnd 3rd and bhd: no ch whn blnd 3 out: t.o whn p.u bef next* **100/1**

3m 59.6s (-4.00) **Going Correction** -0.15s/f (Good) **25** Ran SP% **137.6**
Speed ratings: **103,102,91,89,88 86,82,82,81,80 80,79,77,73,67 66,60,53,53,—** —,—,—,—,— CSF £19.81 TOTE £4.40: £2.10, £2.00, £2.10; EX 17.50.
Owner Sir Robert Ogden **Bred** Mrs Ann Cunningham **Trained** Upper Lambourn, Berks

FOCUS
A reasonable maiden hurdle and, although they were well strung out behind, there should be a few winners among them.

NOTEBOOK
Craven(IRE) probably had a hard enough race when getting up to justify short-price favouritism on his debut in a Wincanton bumper, and he was far from convincing on this hurdling debut despite again doing enough to win. Having travelled well throughout, he did not respond immediately when asked to produce an effort and, still well behind the leader in the straight, wandered around under pressure looking a far from straightforward ride. His mind was made up for him after the last and he did well to get up close home, but this effort still leaves him with a bit to prove. Connections suggested he is still very green, and that is probably the case but, even so, he does not appeal as one to take a short price about until he matures. *(op 11-2)*
Private Be, as on his two previous outings, just found one too good. This represented a good effort in defeat though, and he should not he long in winning. *(op 3-1 tchd 4-1 in a place)*
Vinando, successful three times over middle-distances and rated 101 on the Flat, made a pleasing enough debut over hurdles in third. Given how well he travelled, it was a touch disappointing to see *him beaten so far, but he is open to plenty of improvement and should make his mark.Official explanation: jockey said colt had a breathing problem (op 10-3 tchd 7-2)*
Cruise Director, four times a winner on the Flat at up to a mile and a half and rated 88, ran most respectably on his hurdling debut. He did not find quite as much as had looked likely at one stage, but was not given too hard a time by Thornton and should improve plenty. *(tchd 16-1)*
Tech Eagle(IRE), a promising second on his hurdling debut at Taunton before running down the field at Plumpton, ran creditably in fifth and clearly possess the ability to make his mark over hurdles. Now qualified for a handicap mark, connections should have more options.
Stocking Island *Official explanation: jockey said, regarding running and riding, his orders were to get filly settled, adding that filly jumped sticking early on before staying on past tired horses in home straight; trainer said filly was very free at home and would probably want further in the future when she learned to settle (op 66-1)*
Roussea(IRE) *Official explanation: trainer said gelding ran without the declared tongue strap because it had become adrift and could not be re-fitted (tchd 66-1 and 100-1 in a place)*
Back Among Friends took an horrendous fall at the first and, although he got up and galloped with the others for a little while, this experience could take some getting over.

2827 CANTORSPREADFAIR.COM H'CAP CHASE (14 fncs 1 omitted) 2m 2f 110y

1:55 (1:58) (Class 4) (0-110,107) 5-Y-0+ **£5,696** (£1,672; £836; £417)

Form RPR

02F1 **1** **Soeur Fontenail (FR)**[14] 2577 8-11-11 **106** .... AndrewThornton 117+
(N J Hawke) *a.p: led 9th: blkd 11th: rdn appr next: in command whn idled bdly and jnd 150yds out: r.o again cl home* **6/1**[3]

4-45 **2** *1* **Ballyrobert (IRE)**[30] 2239 8-11-12 **107** .... AndrewTinkler 115+
(C R Egerton) *keen trcking ldrs: wnt prom 6th tl mstke 8th: rdn to chse wnr 3 out: 2nd whn blnd last: r.o to jn wnr 150y out: no ex cl ho* **4/1**[2]

-061 **3** *3* **Hiers De Brouage (FR)**[21] 2431 10-11-8 **103** ....(tp) TimmyMurphy 106+
(J G Portman) *prom: nt fluent 6th: j.lft 11th: rdn in 3rd whn hit 3 out: drvn and renewed effrt run-in: no ex fnl 100yds* **4/1**[2]

P-P0 **4** *4* **Cloudy Blues (IRE)**[27] 2296 7-10-0 **81** oh14 .... BenjaminHitchcott 80+
(R H Buckler) *chsd ldrs: hit 6th: mstke next: rdn and lost pl after 10th: styd on again fr 3 out* **33/1**

026F **5** *6* **Master T (USA)**[6] 2733 6-11-8 **103** .... PhilipHide 99+
(G L Moore) *hld up: mstke 9th: hit 11th: short lived effrt appr 3 out: no further imp fr 2 out* **16/1**

0-P0 **6** *19* **Kadito**[22] [2419] 9-10-9 **90** JamieMoore 62
(R Dickin) *led tl 9th: prom tl wknd appr 3 out* **33/1**

3-02 **7** *½* **Acertack (IRE)**[14] [2577] 8-11-5 **100** BrianCrowley 72
(R Rowe) *lw: hld up in tch: rdn appr 3 out: sn wknd* **7/1**

2/2- **P** **Gaora Bridge (IRE)**[580] [324] 7-11-10 **105** RichardJohnson —
(C J Mann) *blnd 1st: hld up: broke leg and p.u bef 4th: dead* **3/1**[1]

50F/ **P** **Victory Roll**[670] [3807] 9-11-5 **100** BarryFenton —
(Miss E C Lavelle) *hld up: reminders after 9th: sn lost tch: t.o and p.u bef 2 out* **14/1**

4m 45.1s (3.70) **Going Correction** +0.10s/f (Yiel) **9** Ran SP% **110.2**
Speed ratings: **96,95,94,92,90 82,81,—,—** CSF £28.86 CT £99.98 TOTE £6.40: £2.00, £1.80, £1.90; EX 28.70.
Owner La Connection Francaise **Bred** S Dupuy **Trained** Hewish, Somerset

FOCUS
An ordinary affair and a moderate winning time for a race of its class. The last fence was bypassed due to a stricken horse.

NOTEBOOK
Soeur Fontenail(FR), 7lb higher than when third in this event last year, followed up her Plumpton win. Taking up the running in the back straight, she was around six lengths to the good passing the omitted final fence but then began to stop, only to consent to get going again as the runner-up reached her quarters. *(op 5-1)*
Ballyrobert(IRE) went after the leader at the first in the home straight but looked held when getting the final obstacle all wrong. The mare invited him to have another go at her on the extended run-in and he closed to within half a length before she pulled out a bit more. *(tchd 9-2)*
Hiers De Brouage(FR), 5lb higher than when winning at Chepstow, was prominent throughout and, after coming back into the equation as the leader stopped on the long run-in, only conceded defeat in the final 100 yards. He really needs further than this. *(op 5-1)*
Cloudy Blues(IRE), a stone out of the handicap, stayed on for fourth but in truth was flattered to finish as close as he did. *(op 40-1 tchd 28-1)*
Master T(USA) would not have found this sticky ground suitable.
Gaora Bridge(IRE), making his chasing debut on his first start since May last year, sadly broke a hind leg in the early stages. *(op 4-1 tchd 5-2)*

2828 POWERSOLVE ELECTRONICS GREATWOOD CHARITY H'CAP CHASE (21 fncs) 3m 2f 110y
2:25 (2:27) (Class 3) (0-130,129) 5-Y-0+ **£7,286** (£2,139; £1,069; £534)

Form RPR

1P-4 **1** **Eurotrek (IRE)**[39] [2046] 9-11-5 **122** ChristianWilliams 140+
(P F Nicholls) *chsd ldrs: wnt 2nd 3td: slt ld 17th: drvn clr fr 3 out: wl clr whn heavily eased run-in* **9/2**[1]

-P40 **2** *25* **Spring Grove (IRE)**[18] [2492] 10-11-8 **125** AndrewThornton 123+
(R H Alner) *bhd: hdwy 13th: chsd wnr fr 4 out but sn no ch: kpt on for clr 2nd* **11/2**[3]

3 *16* **Bica (FR)**[563] [590] 5-10-13 **123** MrSWaley-Cohen[(7)] 100
(R Waley-Cohen) *w'like: leggy: lw: in tch: hdwy 8th: trckd ldrs fr 14th: outpcd 16th: hdwy again after next: wknd 4 out: no ch whn mstke 3* **9/1**

P24- **4** *dist* **Bubble Boy (IRE)**[245] [4824] 6-10-12 **115** TimmyMurphy —
(B G Powell) *chsd ldr 6th to 13th: wknd 16th: blnd next: eased whn no ch fr 3 out: t.o* **5/1**[2]

PPP- **P** **Gingembre (FR)**[242] [4861] 11-11-8 **125** MarkBradburne —
(Mrs L C Taylor) *prom early: wknd 11th: p.u bef 13th* **12/1**

2-04 **P** **Beau Supreme (IRE)**[19] [2485] 8-11-4 **121** (p) MickFitzgerald —
(C J Down) *in tch: reminders in rr after 11th: wknd 13th: t.o whn p.u bef 17th* **9/2**[1]

0-46 **P** **Supreme Developer (IRE)**[18] [2499] 8-11-7 **129** ThomasDreaper[(5)] —
(Ferdy Murphy) *lw: mstks in rr: rdn 11th: sn lost tch: t.o whn p.u bef 17th* **9/2**[1]

26-P **U** **Lord Who (IRE)**[33] [2162] 8-11-9 **126** (b) RichardJohnson —
(P J Hobbs) *led: sn clr: mstke 7th: hit 14th: mstke and hdd 17th: poor 4th whn blnd and uns rdr 3 out* **9/1**

6m 43.9s (-2.70) **Going Correction** +0.10s/f (Yiel) **8** Ran SP% **114.3**
Speed ratings: **108,100,95,—,— —,—,—** CSF £29.55 CT £212.17 TOTE £5.60: £1.80, £2.40, £2.90; EX 37.90.
Owner Paul Green **Bred** Mrs D Molony **Trained** Ditcheat, Somerset

FOCUS
A fair handicap and an easy victory for the lightly-raced Eurotrek in a good time.

NOTEBOOK
Eurotrek(IRE), who has suffered leg, heart and breathing problems, had been dropped 3lb since his comeback run and the tongue tie was left off. He came clear in the straight for a facile win, value for even further, and while it may be wise not to get too carried away with this performance it was only the ninth run of his life and he should be able to build on this. *(op 7-2)*
Spring Grove(IRE) continues to fall down the handicap and was racing off 3lb lower than when gaining his last victory at Windsor a year ago. Tackling three miles for the first time this campaign, he ran respectably but was no match at all for the winner. *(op 6-1)*
Bica(FR) made a winning chase debut for Guillaume Macaire at Auteuil in May last year but was well beaten in a Grade One event behind Cyrlight there later the same month. Having his first run since, he went well for a long way before his stamina appeared to run out. Entitled to come on for the outing, a drop back in trip, coupled with genuine soft ground, could be what he requires. *(op 10-1 tchd 8-1)*
Bubble Boy(IRE), who returned lame from Cheltenham in April, was taking on handicappers for the first time on this seasonal debut. He was beaten a long way in the end but might have needed the run. *(tchd 11-2)*
Gingembre(FR), who did not look right in his coat, was 15lb lower than when last seen in the Scottish Grand National in April but the outcome was the same. He has had a fine career and it would seem a shame to persevere with him. *(tchd 11-2)*
Supreme Developer(IRE) jumped sketchily in rear and was pulled up before his stamina could be seriously tested. This was disappointing. *Official explanation: vet said gelding bled from the nose (tchd 11-2)*
Lord Who(IRE), previously trained by Pat Doyle in Ireland, adopted new tactics on his debut for this yard and went off in front. He jumped stickily however and, beaten after a mistake at the cross fence, it was no surprise to see him shed his rider at the final open ditch. *(tchd 11-2)*
Beau Supreme(IRE), fitted with cheekpieces and tackling his longest trip to date, did not jump particularly fluently and was in trouble with a lap to go. *Official explanation: jockey said gelding jumped poorly throughout (tchd 11-2)*

2829 EUROPEAN BREEDERS FUND "NATIONAL HUNT" NOVICES' HURDLE (QUALIFIER) (11 hdls) 2m 3f
3:00 (3:04) (Class 3) 4-6-Y-0 **£5,692** (£1,671; £835; £417)

Form RPR

0-22 **1** **Wee Robbie**[25] [2343] 5-11-0 LeightonAspell 123+
(N J Gifford) *lw: a in tch: nt fluent 4th: tk clsr order 7th: led after 2 out: styd on wl* **12/1**

1-11 **2** *3½* **Oscar Park (IRE)**[26] [2322] 6-11-10 TomDoyle 128
(C Tinkler) *lw: trckd ldrs: nt fluent 6th: jnd ldr after 7th: led next: sn edgd lft: rdn and hdd after next: kpt on* **11/8**[1]

4-2 **3** *shd* **Dream Alliance**[49] [1882] 4-11-0 RichardJohnson 118
(P J Hobbs) *chsd ldrs: lost pl and dropped into midfield 5th: styd on fr 3 out: tk 3rd after 2 out* **14/1**

14-1 **4** *11* **Mr Pointment (IRE)**[27] [2295] 6-11-6 AndrewTinkler 116+
(C R Egerton) *in tch: rdn to chse ldng pair 3 out: 4th and wkng whn mstke 2 out* **15/8**[2]

01-3 **5** *3* **Sunley Shines**[16] [2554] 5-10-2 JohnnyLevins[(5)] 98+
(B G Powell) *prom: led and hit 7th: rdn and hdd next: wknd appr last* **100/1**

3-21 **6** *¾* **Pirate Flagship (FR)**[17] [2528] 6-11-6 ChristianWilliams 109
(P F Nicholls) *lw: in tch: rdn after 7th: one pced fr 3 out* **11/2**[3]

7 *5* **Keswick (IRE)** 5-11-0 MickFitzgerald 98
(N J Henderson) *w'like: mid div: sme hdwy appr 3 out: no further imp after* **40/1**

-456 **8** *hd* **Letsplay (IRE)**[53] [1827] 5-10-7 RyanCummings[(7)] 98
(K J Burke) *hld up towards rr: sme hdwy after 7th: no further imp fr 3 out* **100/1**

4 **9** *21* **Saddlers Cloth (IRE)**[40] [2021] 5-10-7 BenjaminHitchcott 70
(J A Geake) *mid div tl 7th* **100/1**

04 **10** *3½* **Finsbury Fred (IRE)**[35] [2127] 4-11-0 AntonyEvans 73
(N A Twiston-Davies) *a towards rr* **100/1**

0-U0 **11** *17* **Nice Horse (FR)**[22] [2423] 4-10-4 AndrewGlassonbury[(10)] 56
(M C Pipe) *a towards rr* **33/1**

0 **12** *2* **Secured (IRE)**[55] [1799] 5-11-0 JimmyMcCarthy 54
(Ian Williams) *mid div tl 7th* **100/1**

4-0 **13** *2* **Lordington Lad**[18] [2507] 5-11-0 TimmyMurphy 52
(B G Powell) *a towards rr* **66/1**

610- **14** *8* **Little Saltee (IRE)**[309] [3747] 5-11-0 JasonMaguire 44
(J A B Old) *chsd ldrs tl 6th* **40/1**

15 *9* **Icomb (IRE)** 5-11-0 RobertWalford 35
(Mrs Susan Nock) *w'like: lengthy: bit bkwd: a bhd* **100/1**

65-0 **16** *10* **King Louis (FR)**[17] [2534] 4-11-0 BrianCrowley 25
(R Rowe) *racd on outer: towards rr: hit 2nd: t.o fr 7th* **100/1**

4 **P** **Stoney Drove (FR)**[39] [2049] 5-11-0 SamThomas —
(Miss H C Knight) *a bhd: t.o and p.u bef last* **100/1**

/2-0 **P** **Sativa Bay**[12] [2606] 6-11-0 AndrewThornton —
(J W Mullins) *led: nt fluent 3rd: hdd 7th: sn bhd: p.u bef 3 out* **66/1**

4m 39.5s (-7.30) **Going Correction** -0.15s/f (Good)
WFA 4 from 5yo+ 10lb **18** Ran SP% **125.4**
Speed ratings: **109,107,107,102,101 101,99,99,90,88 81,80,79,76,72 68,—,—** CSF £29.83 TOTE £14.00: £2.60, £1.50, £2.90; EX 40.60.
Owner P H Betts (holdings) Ltd **Bred** R Aston **Trained** Findon, W Sussex

FOCUS
A good novice hurdle and, although Oscar Park getting beaten was something of a surprise, the form still looks decent and, with the second and fourth to their marks, Wee Robbie should not be underestimated.

NOTEBOOK
Wee Robbie ◆, down the field in the Champion Bumper, showed a fair level of form when second on his first two starts over hurdles this season and stepped up on those efforts to run out a decisive winner. He won his bumper on a soft surface and was well suited by the ground appearing to rider more testing than the official description. This effort should not be underestimated and he looks well worth following when he gets his conditions. It would represent a big step up in class, but something like the Challow Hurdle back here over two miles five at the end of the month could well suit.
Oscar Park(IRE) ◆ looked potentially smart in winning two bumpers and two novice hurdles, so he could be considered a touch disappointing in failing to complete the five-timer, but he was conceding 10lb to the useful winner and the form is probably a fair bit better than one might immediately think. *(op 6-4 tchd 5-4)*
Dream Alliance, a beaten favourite when second in a Cheltenham bumper on his reappearance, made a pleasing debut over hurdles. This was not a bad race and, with normal improvement, he really should be winning before long. *(op 12-1 tchd 16-1)*
Mr Pointment(IRE) finished in front of Wee Robbie in a good bumper here last season, and won well on his hurdling debut at Market Rasen, so this could be considered a little disappointing. Still, the form in front of him is not bad at all and he did have a penalty. *(op 5-2 tchd 11-4 in places)*
Sunley Shines ran well for a long way under a positive ride and could do well in mares-only company.
Pirate Flagship(FR) would have found this tougher the maiden hurdle he won round here on his previous start, and was probably not far off the level of form he showed that day. *(op 5-1 tchd 9-2 and 6-1)*
Little Saltee(IRE) *Official explanation: jockey said gelding had a breathing problem (op 50-1)*

2830 E B F KENTFORD RACING FILLIES' ONLY "JUNIOR" STANDARD OPEN NATIONAL HUNT FLAT RACE 1m 4f 110y
3:30 (3:35) (Class 6) 3-Y-0 **£2,685** (£782; £391)

Form RPR

34 **1** **Inherent (IRE)**[17] [2521] 3-10-12 MarkBradburne 90+
(C G Cox) *w'like: trckd ldrs: led ins fnl 4f: drvn and styd on strly fnl 2f* **7/1**[3]

2 *1½* **Tambourine Davis (FR)** 3-10-12 OllieMcPhail 87
(N J Henderson) *unf: scope: unf: in tch: rdn and styd on fr over 2f out: r.o ins last to take 2nd last strides: nt rch wnr* **13/2**[2]

3 *shd* **Piper Paddy** 3-10-12 MickFitzgerald 87
(P R Chamings) *neat: prom: rdn to chse wnr fnl f and no imp: ct for 2nd last strides* **25/1**

4 *3½* **She's Humble (IRE)** 3-10-12 RichardJohnson 82
(P D Evans) *w'like: chsd ldrs: led 6f out: hdd ins fnl 4f: styd chalng tl outpcd fnl f* **8/1**

5 *¾* **Forest Emerald (IRE)** 3-10-9 RichardYoung[(3)] 81
(J W Mullins) *unf: scope: mid-div: hdwy 5f out: styd on fnl 2f but nvr gng pce to chal* **33/1**

6 *2* **Nitelite** 3-10-5 MrAMO'Brien[(7)] 79+
(Edward U Hales, Ire) *lengthy: scope: lw: trckd ldrs: chal over 3f out: sn rdn: hung bdly lft fr over 2f out: wknd fnl f* **2/1**[1]

7 *8* **Papswoodmoss** 3-10-12 TomDoyle 67
(Mrs A L M King) *bhd: hdwy 4f out: styd on same pce fnl 2f* **50/1**

8 *2* **Falcon Beneficial (IRE)** 3-10-12 JamieMoore 64
(G L Moore) *leggy: bhd: styd on fnl 2f: n.d* **50/1**

9 *6* **Jamadast Roma** 3-10-12 AntonyEvans 56
(N A Twiston-Davies) *lengthy: bhd: sme hdwy over 3f out: sn wknd* **16/1**

10 *3* **Shuil A Maidin (IRE)** 3-10-12 ChristianWilliams 52
(Peter M Kiely, Ire) *str: bit bkwd: bhd: rdn 5f out: mod hdwy fnl 2f* **14/1**

11 *14* **Heavenly Chorus** 3-10-2 JamesReveley[(10)] 32
(K G Reveley) *w'like: bhd: drvn and hdwy into mid-div over 5f out: sn wknd* **8/1**

12 *hd* **Little Laurita** 3-10-12 TimmyMurphy 32
(B De Haan) *bhd: sme hdwy over 5f out: nvr rchd ldrs and sn wknd* **16/1**

13 ½ **Silverick Lady** 3-10-5 CharlieStudd(7) 31
(B G Powell) *rangy: bhd tl mod prog fnl 2f* **40/1**

S 14 1 ½ **Scots Brook Terror**[57] [1785] 3-10-12 JodieMogford 29
(Mrs N S Evans) *w'like: leggy: led tl hdd 6f out: wknd ins fnl 4f* **100/1**

2 15 13 **Over The Flow**[12] [2611] 3-10-12 BenjaminHitchcott 11
(R H Buckler) *w'like: chsd ldrs: rdn 5f out: sn wknd* **9/1**

16 2 ½ **Run To Me** 3-10-12 AndrewTinkler 7
(Miss Gay Kelleway) *w'like: in tch: rdn 5f out: sn wknd* **66/1**

34 17 16 **Reveal (IRE)**[12] [2611] 3-10-5 MrGTumelty(7) —
(H E Haynes) *w'like: leggy: chsd ldrs to 1/2-way* **50/1**

18 ½ **Rosenfirth (IRE)** 3-10-12 BrianCrowley —
(R Rowe) *w'like: leggy: a in rr* **100/1**

19 4 **Lady Toff** 3-10-12 MatthewBatchelor —
(B R Johnson) *str: bit bkwd: chsd ldrs: rdn 5f out: sn wknd* **100/1**

3m 2.80s (0.60) 19 Ran SP% **129.4**
CSF £51.98 TOTE £8.50: £2.60, £2.70, £5.70; EX 77.20 Place 6 £25.20, Place 5 £18.70.
Owner Elite Racing Club **Bred** Burns Farm Stud **Trained** Lambourn, Berks

FOCUS
This looked a decent event of its type and very few got into the race from the home turn. The winner looks progressive and her previous form could have been underrated.

NOTEBOOK
Inherent(IRE), one of the most experienced in the line-up, seemed to appreciate the easier ground this time and, getting the measure of the favourite when that rival hung fire, ran on strongly to score. *She does not have the size and scope of the runner-up, but clearly has an engine. (op 5-1 tchd 15-2)*
Tambourine Davis(FR) ◆, from the family of Klairon Davis, was making her debut but was well backed. She was well enough placed for much of the way but, after getting outpaced when the leaders kicked on early in the straight, kept on strongly in the closing stages. She will appreciate a stronger pace or a longer trip and should progress with this under her belt. *(op 9-2)*
Piper Paddy, with more of a speedy Flat pedigree, travelled well in the pack and picked up steadily from the turn in. She looks as if she will benefit from the experience. *(op 20-1)*
She's Humble(IRE), a half-sister to a dual bumper winner, was close up throughout and went with the winner and the favourite when they quickened. However, she could not sustain the effort and weakened in the last quarter-mile.
Forest Emerald(IRE), related to Irish Flat winners, was doing her best work in the closing stages and should be better for the run.
Nitelite, a well-backed Irish raider, travelled well and looked sure to win when taking the advantage early in the straight. However, she appeared to falter and jink left when the winner challenged, and dropped away as if something was amiss. She clearly has ability and if none the worse can make amends for this defeat. *(op 7-2)*
Shuil A Maidin(IRE), another Irish raider, looked to run green, was being ridden along some way out and never got into contention. *(op 11-1 tchd 16-1)*
Over The Flow, who ran well on her debut, showed up for some way but this was a tougher ask and she was left behind when the pace quickened. *(op 8-1)*
Reveal(IRE) *Official explanation: jockey said filly had a breathing problem (op 40-1)*
T/Jkpt: Not won. T/Plt: £17.50 to a £1 stake. Pool: £50,832.70. 2,112.10 winning tickets. T/Qpdt: £8.00 to a £1 stake. Pool: £3,509.60. 323.00 winning tickets. ST

2831a -2837a (Foreign Racing) - See Raceform Interactive

2566
CATTERICK (L-H)
Thursday, December 15

OFFICIAL GOING: Good
The ground was described as 'generally good, good to soft in places'.
Wind: Moderate; half against Weather: Fine but on the cold side

2838 WATCH RACING UK LIVE ON 432 NOVICES' HURDLE (9 hdls 1 omitted) 2m 3f
12:20 (12:20) (Class 4) 4-Y-0+ **£3,575** (£1,049; £524; £262)

Form RPR

4 1 **Turnstile**[11] [2652] 4-10-12 GrahamLee 104+
(J Howard Johnson) *trckd ldrs: shkn up to ld appr 2 out: styd on run-in* **5/4**[1]

04-2 2 10 **Edgehill (IRE)**[11] [2652] 4-10-12 TonyDobbin 94+
(R Ford) *trckd ldrs: t.k.h: led bef 2 out: sn hdd: wl hld whn eased last 100yds* **7/4**[2]

02- 3 6 **Double Gin**[264] [4552] 5-10-9 GaryBerridge(3) 85
(W Amos) *chsd ldrs: one pce appr 2 out* **20/1**

6R-0 4 ¾ **Ring The Boss (IRE)**[26] [2340] 4-10-12 RichardMcGrath 84
(K G Reveley) *hld up in rr: hdwy 7th: sn chsng ldrs: kpt on same pce appr 2 out* **40/1**

0 5 ½ **Sparkling Taff**[26] [2340] 6-10-12 DavidO'Meara 87+
(Mrs S J Smith) *nt fluent: trckd ldrs: led 3 out: hdd appr next: disputing 3rd whn j. bdly lft 2 out: one pce* **33/1**

6 6 **Double Turn**[171] 5-10-12 PadgeWhelan 78
(Mrs S J Smith) *chsd ldrs: lost pl appr 2 out* **40/1**

0 7 6 **Fillameena**[18] [2515] 5-10-2 AnthonyCoyle(3) 65
(P T Midgley) *in rr: sme hdwy 6th: lost pl after next* **100/1**

8 2 ½ **Koodoo**[411] 4-10-12 AlanDempsey 69
(M Todhunter) *chsd ldrs: lost pl after 3 out* **100/1**

9 2 ½ **When Your Readyles (IRE)** 5-10-12 RussGarritty 67
(M Todhunter) *a in rr* **40/1**

00 10 3 ½ **Penel (IRE)**[6] [2752] 4-10-12 KennyJohnson 63
(P T Midgley) *hld up in rr: bhd fr 7th* **80/1**

0 11 16 **Lethem Present (IRE)**[217] [323] 5-10-5 BrianHarding 40
(T Butt) *led to 3 out: wknd qckly* **66/1**

P 12 6 **Chanteuse**[37] [2106] 5-9-12 PhilKinsella(7) 34
(Mrs Marjorie Fife) *prom tl lost pl after 5th: bhd fr 3 out* **100/1**

120F U **Dubonai (IRE)**[33] [2191] 5-11-0 100 (t) DougieCostello(5) —
(G M Moore) *mid-div whn hit 1st and uns rdr* **7/1**[3]

0 P **The Frisky Friar**[15] [2571] 7-10-5 MrSFMagee(7) —
(G A Harker) *in rr whn mstke 7th: bhd whn p.u bnd bef 2 out* **40/1**

PP P **Silloth Spirit**[11] [2658] 5-10-5 (p) ThomasBurrows(7) —
(Mrs A M Naughton) *j. poorly: in rr: t.o whn p.u bef 7th* **200/1**

600 P **Cottam Phantom**[33] [2192] 4-10-9 MrTGreenall(3) —
(M W Easterby) *hld up in rr: reminders after 5th: sn bhd: t.o whn p.u bef 2 out* **100/1**

4m 47.8s (-2.70) **Going Correction** -0.15s/f (Good)
WFA 4 from 5yo+ 10lb 16 Ran SP% **118.0**
Speed ratings: **99,94,92,91,91 89,86,85,84,83 76,73,—,—,—,—** — CSF £3.16 TOTE £2.00: £1.10, £1.50, £3.00; EX 3.60.
Owner Andrea & Graham Wylie **Bred** The Queen **Trained** Billy Row, Co Durham

FOCUS
20/1 bar three and the third favourite out at at the first flight. They went very steady and in the end it rested between the two market leaders. The fourth and fifth set the level for the form.

NOTEBOOK
Turnstile, suited by this much better ground, made quite hard work of it but came clear in the end. A real stayer, a much stronger gallop would have suited him even better. *(op 13-8 tchd 7-4 in a place)*
Edgehill(IRE), who finished ahead of the winner at Kelso, in the end did not see out the extended trip anywhere near as well and on the run-in his rider threw in the towel. *(tchd 15-8)*
Double Gin, runner-up in a bumper when last seen out in March, made a satisfactory hurdling bow and should come on for the outing. *(op 14-1)*
Ring The Boss(IRE), who refused to race on the second of his three starts in bumpers, is a fair sort and made a pleasing hurdling bow. He was certainly not knocked about. *(op 25-1)*
Sparkling Taff, who had just one previous outing in a bumper, did not jump too well but revealed ability showing ahead at the third last. *(op 25-1)*
Double Turn, unplaced in eight outings on the Flat, was having his first outing for his new stable.
Dubonai(IRE) dislodged his rider at the very first flight. *(op 6-1 tchd 11-2)*

2839 CHEQUERS INN AND BRIDGEWATER ARMS MAIDEN CHASE (15 fncs) 2m 3f
12:50 (12:51) (Class 4) 5-Y-0+ **£3,146** (£923; £461; £230)

Form RPR

4 1 **King Barry (FR)**[23] [2415] 6-11-0 RichardMcGrath 106+
(Miss P Robson) *chsd ldrs: effrt 2 out: styd on wl to ld cl home* **9/2**[2]

/305 2 ¾ **Lord Payne (IRE)**[11] [2654] 7-11-0 105 TomDoyle 102
(P Monteith) *led: rdn 4 out: j.rt 2 out: kpt on fr last: hdd cl home* **9/1**

3/-3 3 15 **The Frosty Ferret (IRE)**[14] [2591] 7-10-11 FergusKing(3) 89+
(J M Jefferson) *cl up tl rdn and outpcd fr 2 out* **9/1**

00/ 4 3 ½ **Been Here Before**[271] 5-10-7 PhilKinsella(7) 84
(G A Harker) *hld up towards rr: outpcd 8th: kpt on fr 2 out: no imp* **50/1**

6323 5 nk **Humid Climate**[7] [2722] 5-11-0 102 AnthonyRoss 85+
(R A Fahey) *prom tl rdn and outpcd after 2 out* **10/1**

P-00 6 5 **Hot Air (IRE)**[54] [1834] 7-10-11 (t) MichalKohl(3) 78
(J I A Charlton) *hld up: outpcd 1/2-way: sme late hdwy: nvr on terms* **100/1**

P-P 7 15 **Thorsgill**[34] [2169] 7-11-0 AlanDempsey 63
(M Todhunter) *racd wd in midfield: rdn and outpcd 8th: n.d after* **100/1**

P-5P 8 nk **Bobsourown (IRE)**[12] [2639] 6-10-9 StephenCraine(5) 63
(D McCain) *j.rt: hld up: mstke 6th: nvr on terms* **33/1**

0P-P 9 dist **Viking Song**[15] [2571] 5-11-0 KennyJohnson —
(F Kirby) *sn wl bhd: no ch fr 1/2-way* **100/1**

00/P U **Tolcea (IRE)**[21] [2453] 6-10-7 62 EwanWhillans(7) —
(A C Whillans) *bhd whn uns rdr 2nd* **100/1**

PPPP P **Loch Torridon**[12] [2631] 6-10-11 64 (p) PaddyAspell(3) —
(James Moffatt) *sn wl bhd: t.o whn p.u bef 3 out* **100/1**

00/3 U **More Flair**[19] [2496] 8-10-0 BenOrde-Powlett(7) —
(J B Walton) *nt fluent: bhd whn mstke and uns rdr 8th* **40/1**

2005 P **King's Protector**[20] [2475] 5-11-0 GrahamLee —
(M D Hammond) *mstkes: in tch: blnd and wknd 9th: p.u bef 3 out* **7/1**

-553 U **Ground Breaker**[6] [2751] 5-10-11 (t) MrTGreenall(3) —
(M W Easterby) *hld up: hdwy and in tch whn blnd and uns rdr 10th* **11/2**[3]

433- U **The Outlier (IRE)**[262] [4605] 7-11-0 AlanO'Keeffe —
(Miss Venetia Williams) *keen: chsng ldrs whn blnd and uns rdr 2nd* **11/4**[1]

U450 F **Fencote (IRE)**[12] [2630] 8-11-0 97 RussGarritty 89
(P Beaumont) *in tch: effrt bef 3 out: 6l down and no imp whn fell last* **16/1**

4m 51.3s (-2.30) **Going Correction** -0.15s/f (Good) 16 Ran SP% **120.0**
Speed ratings: **98,97,91,89,89 87,81,81,—,— —,—,—,—,— —** CSF £43.26 TOTE £5.60: £1.10, £2.60, £3.20; EX 60.60.
Owner Mr & Mrs Raymond Anderson Green **Bred** Mme Gilbert Gallot **Trained** Kirkharle, Northumberland

FOCUS
Just ordinary form, rated through the placed horses, but the winner has the potential to build on this initial success under Rules.

NOTEBOOK
King Barry(FR), who chipped a knee after winning two points in 2004, showed the benefit of his Sedgefield outing. He made hard work of it but showed a willing attitude to get there in the end. From a handicap mark in the low 100s, he has the ability to progress. *(op 5-1 tchd 4-1)*
Lord Payne(IRE), an Irish point winner, took them along and was only worn down near the finish. He can surely find an opening. *(op 10-1)*
The Frosty Ferret(IRE) made a satisfactory chasing bow but in the end the first two ran right away from him. *(op 12-1)*
Been Here Before, who won a point in March, stayed on when it was all over but was afterwards *reported to have a breathing problem. Official explanation: jockey said, regarding running and riding, his orders were to jump the gelding out, get a clear view of fences and obtain the best possible place without being too hard on his mount, adding that gelding developed a breathing problem approaching the last fence in the back straight which cleared itself approaching the second last before staying on past beaten horses; trainer said gelding had a history of breathing problems*
Humid Climate, having his second outing in a week after being absent since May, is not a certain stayer. *(op 11-1 tchd 9-1)*
Hot Air(IRE), unplaced in seven previous starts, was making his chasing bow and looks a real stayer.
King's Protector was badly let down by his jumping on his chase debut. *(op 5-2 tchd 3-1)*
The Outlier(IRE) did not get any further than the first ditch. *(op 5-2 tchd 3-1)*
Fencote(IRE) was in the process of running a much better race over fences when he fell with fatal consequences at the last. *(op 5-2 tchd 3-1)*
Ground Breaker was bang in the firing line when giving his rider no chance six out, a ditch. His stamina had not been tested at the point. *(op 5-2 tchd 3-1)*

2840 CHRISTMAS TIME H'CAP HURDLE (12 hdls) 3m 1f 110y
1:20 (1:25) (Class 3) (0-115,113) 4-Y-0+ **£4,931** (£1,447; £723; £361)

Form RPR

1420 1 **River Mist (IRE)**[15] [2566] 6-11-0 **101** RichardMcGrath 112+
(Karen McLintock) *hld up in rr: hdwy 3 out: led next: styd on strly* **14/1**

-45P 2 1 ½ **Totally Scottish**[12] [2633] 9-11-0 **111** JamesReveley(10) 117
(K G Reveley) *trckd ldrs: chal appr 2 out: no ex run-in* **11/1**

-551 3 11 **Tobesure (IRE)**[54] [1838] 11-10-13 **103** MichalKohl(3) 98
(J I A Charlton) *hld up in rr: hdwy 6th: one pce fr 2 out* **17/2**

-542 4 1 ¾ **Water Taxi**[20] [2475] 4-11-1 **102** KeithMercer 95
(Ferdy Murphy) *trckd ldrs: led 9th: hdd 2 out: sn btn* **13/2**[1]

2512 5 hd **Red Perk (IRE)**[34] [2170] 8-10-8 **95** (p) KennyJohnson 88
(R C Guest) *mid-div: hdwy to chse ldrs 5th: wknd appr 2 out* **13/2**[1]

U-P4 6 ½ **The Weaver (FR)**[20] [2474] 6-10-9 **99** GaryBerridge(3) 93+
(L Lungo) *chsd ldrs: blnd 5th: lost pl appr 2 out* **8/1**[3]

F-03 7 8 **Lucky Judge**[22] [2440] 8-10-4 **96** DougieCostello(5) 83+
(G A Swinbank) *hld: hdwy after 9th: wknd appr 2 out* **15/2**[2]

-30B 8 6 **Fairy Skin Maker (IRE)**[10] [2680] 7-11-7 **108** (p) BrianHarding 90+
(G A Harker) *hld up in rr: hdwy 9th: nvr rchd ldrs: eased towards fin* **20/1**

F0P4 9 1 **Pottsy's Joy**[23] [2413] 8-10-8 **95** PadgeWhelan 73
(Mrs S J Smith) *bhd and drvn along 7th: nvr on terms* **22/1**

0-PP **10** *4* **Darab (POL)**^{210} [425] 5-10-1 **98**.................................. MichaelO'Connell(10) 72
(Mrs S J Smith) *in rr: nvr a factor* **40/1**
6663 **11** *1* **Old Nosey (IRE)**^{20} [2474] 9-9-7 **87** oh2..................... PatrickMcDonald(7) 60
(B Mactaggart) *w ldr: lost pl after 3 out* **11/1**
5006 **12** *10* **Political Sox**^{20} [2474] 11-10-6 **100**.................................. GarethThomas(7) 63
(R Nixon) *chsd ldrs: lost pl 3 out* **50/1**
-6PP **13** *4* **Simlet**^{23} [2417] 10-11-3 **111**..................................(p) PhilKinsella(7) 70
(E W Tuer) *in rr: drvn along 8th: bhd fr 3 out* **66/1**
1433 **14** *¾* **Altitude Dancer (IRE)**^{151} [1026] 5-11-2 **108**............... DeclanMcGann(5) 66
(A Crook) *chsd ldrs: drvn along 4th: bhd fr 7th* **12/1**
F00P **F** **Minivet**^{20} [2474] 10-10-10 **100**.................................. PaddyAspell(3) —
(R Allan) *led to 9th: struggling whn fell heavily next* **50/1**
5-5P **P** **Neidpath Castle**^{41} [2024] 6-11-0 **101**.................................. TonyDobbin —
(A C Whillans) *rr-divsion: nt fluent: bhd whn hmpd 3 out: sn p.u* **33/1**
P-PP **U** **Grattan Lodge (IRE)**^{21} [2451] 8-11-12 **113**.................. GrahamLee —
(J Howard Johnson) *chsd ldrs: drvn along whn mstke and uns rdr 8th* **12/1**

6m 24.2s (-7.50) **Going Correction** -0.15s/f (Good)
WFA 4 from 5yo+ 13lb **17** Ran SP% **118.7**
Speed ratings: **105,104,101,100,100 100,97,96,95,94 94,91,89,89,— —,—** CSF £145.37 CT £1400.78 TOTE £19.40: £3.60, £2.40, £2.50, £1.40; EX 179.10.
Owner Mrs H Scotto **Bred** Mrs Hilary Scotto **Trained** Ingoe, Northumberland

FOCUS
A moderate contest but a sound gallop and in the end the first two came clear. The runner-up and fourth set the standard.

NOTEBOOK
River Mist(IRE), better for her outing here two weeks earlier, benefited from a patient ride and the extended trip was no problem at all. She is not that big but may now go over fences.
Totally Scottish, who is not easy to win with, ran his best race for some time and if anything improved for the severe test of stamina. *(op 12-1)*
Tobesure(IRE), 8lb higher than when winning at Kelso in October, seems to reserve his best for that track and now may be the time to revert to fences. *(op 9-1 tchd 8-1)*
Water Taxi, having just his fifth start over hurdles, travelled strongly on his handicap bow but he faded badly when headed at the second last flight. *(op 6-1 tchd 7-1)*
Red Perk(IRE), back over hurdles from a 7lb higher mark, was having his first outing for nearly five weeks and he ran as if in need of it. *(op 6-1)*
Neidpath Castle *Official explanation: jockey said gelding lost its action (op 28-1)*

2841 BUY YOUR 2006 YORKSHIRE RACING SEASON TICKET H'CAP CHASE (19 fncs) 3m 1f 110y
1:50 (1:56) (Class 3) (0-120,118) 5-Y-0+ **£6,993** (£2,053; £1,026; £512)

Form RPR
-P30 **1** **Robbo**^{19} [2499] 11-11-8 **117**..................................(p) FergusKing(3) 127+
(K G Reveley) *chsd ldrs: effrt 3 out: led bef last: styd on wl* **11/1**
2P41 **2** *2½* **Lothian Falcon**^{18} [2518] 6-10-7 **102**.................................. GinoCarenza(3) 115+
(P Maddison) *hld up in tch: nt fluent and bdly hmpd 12th: rallied bef 3 out: chsd wnr run in: kpt on* **9/2**^{1}
/4-0 **3** *2½* **Virgin Soldier (IRE)**^{82} [1550] 9-11-12 **118**.............................. TomDoyle 122+
(G A Swinbank) *cl up: hit 15th: effrt 2 out: kpt on same pce last* **25/1**
0-61 **4** *4* **Forest Dante (IRE)**^{15} [2568] 12-10-3 **95**.....................(p) KennyJohnson 96+
(F Kirby) *cl up: led 4th to bef last: edgd lft and outpcd run in* **13/2**^{3}
051- **5** *6* **Monty's Quest (IRE)**^{248} [4811] 10-10-13 **110**........... MichaelMcAlister(5) 111+
(M Smith) *led to 4th: chsd ldrs: hit and rdn fr 10th: rallied: wknd fr 2 out* **7/1**
1-65 **6** *8* **The Merry Mason (IRE)**^{207} [468] 9-11-8 **114**................. DavidO'Meara 99
(Mrs S J Smith) *chsd ldrs: lost pl 6th: n.d after* **10/1**
2633 **7** *6* **Beat The Heat (IRE)**^{28} [2294] 7-11-2 **108**........................(p) BrianHarding 90+
(Jedd O'Keeffe) *hld up in tch: rdn and wknd fr 13th* **9/1**
-130 **U** **Prince Of Slane**^{11} [2653] 6-10-5 **102**........................... DougieCostello(5) —
(G A Swinbank) *uns rdr 1st* **5/1**^{2}
430- **F** **Celioso (IRE)**^{446} [1506] 8-11-8 **114**.................................. PadgeWhelan —
(Mrs S J Smith) *prom whn fell 12th* **14/1**
P-13 **P** **Alfy Rich**^{41} [2022] 9-10-9 **101**.................................. TonyDobbin —
(M Todhunter) *in tch: outpcd 12th: p.u after next* **7/1**
20-0 **P** **Green Finger**^{40} [2037] 7-11-0 **106**.................................. RichardMcGrath —
(J J Quinn) *hld up: hdwy and prom 1/2-way: wknd fr 15th: t.o whn p.u bef last* **25/1**

6m 34.1s (-14.30) **Going Correction** -0.15s/f (Good) **11** Ran SP% **115.0**
Speed ratings: **108,107,106,105,103 100,99,—,—,— —** CSF £60.18 CT £1206.33 TOTE £15.70: £3.60, £2.00, £5.70; EX 100.90.
Owner The Scarth Racing Partnership **Bred** Godolphin Management Co Ltd **Trained** Lingdale, Redcar & Cleveland

FOCUS
Robbo rolled back the years but he had luck on his side and the second, who is rated a three-length winner, must go down as an unlucky loser and the form is not strong.

NOTEBOOK
Robbo recorded his 16th career succes having slipped to a lenient mark. He took a lot more interest than usual but on the day looked only second best. *(op 12-1)*
Lothian Falcon, virtually brought to a standstill at the first fence in the back straight on the final circuit, did very well to get back into the contest and must surely go down as an unlucky loser. The problem might be the ground in the coming weeks, he does not really handle the soft. *(op 5-1)*
Virgin Soldier(IRE), 2lb lower than his last win over two years ago, shaped a lot better fully appreciating the much better ground. *(op 18-1)*
Forest Dante(IRE), 4lb higher, looked in command at one stage but in the end did not see the trip out anywhere near as well as the first three home. *(op 11-2)*
Monty's Quest(IRE), well supported in the ring, was having his first outing since taking a hunter chase at Kelso in April and he ran as if it was very much needed. *(op 11-1)*
Alfy Rich *Official explanation: jockey said gelding had a breathing problem (op 5-1 tchd 15-2)*
Green Finger *Official explanation: jockey said horse lost its action (op 5-1 tchd 15-2)*
Prince Of Slane, a positive on all fronts, did not get beyond the very first fence. In view of the support he must be worth bearing in mind. *(op 5-1 tchd 15-2)*

2842 "JOIN THE 2006 CATTERICK CLUB TODAY" H'CAP CHASE (12 fncs) 2m
2:20 (2:24) (Class 4) (0-105,103) 5-Y-0+ **£4,114** (£1,207; £603; £301)

Form RPR
3-54 **1** **Mexican (USA)**^{17} [2111] 6-10-5 **82**..................................(b) NeilMulholland 99+
(M D Hammond) *hld up in rr: hit 5th: gd hdwy to go 3rd 3 out: led last: rdn rt out* **11/2**
U023 **2** *8* **Polyphon (FR)**^{20} [2479] 7-11-12 **103**.................................. TomDoyle 113+
(P Monteith) *w ldr: led and qcknd 5th: hdd 7th: led appr 2 out: hdd last: no ex* **7/2**^{2}
66-2 **3** *7* **Good Outlook (IRE)**^{14} [2583] 6-11-6 **100**..................... LarryMcGrath(3) 104+
(R C Guest) *led to 5th: led 7th: 3rd and btn whn blnd 2 out* **5/1**^{3}
400 **4** *½* **Reach The Clouds (IRE)**^{114} [1299] 13-10-7 **89**................ MarkNicolls(5) 92+
(John R Upson) *in tch: outpcd 5th: 4th whn blnd 9th: kpt on same pce fr next* **33/1**
-3PP **5** *1¼* **Classic Lash (IRE)**^{9} [2692] 9-10-13 **90**..............................(p) BarryKeniry 90
(P Needham) *chsd ldng pair: one pce appr 3 out* **14/1**
612U **6** *7* **Celtic Legend (FR)**^{7} [2719] 6-11-5 **96**........................... RichardMcGrath 89
(K G Reveley) *lost pl appr 5th: sme hdwy appr 3 out: nvr a factor* **7/4**^{1}
/01P **7** *4* **Loy's Lad (IRE)**^{9} [2692] 9-11-12 **103**.................................. SamStronge 92
(Miss V Scott) *in tch: hit 4th: lost pl appr next: detached whn mstke 9th* **16/1**
41PU **8** *dist* **Longdale**^{11} [2655] 7-11-8 **99**.................................. AlanDempsey —
(M Todhunter) *sn bhd: t.o 7th: btn 40l* **22/1**

4m 0.10s (-2.90) **Going Correction** -0.15s/f (Good) **8** Ran SP% **110.5**
Speed ratings: **101,97,93,93,92 89,87,—** CSF £24.03 CT £95.60 TOTE £6.50: £1.60, £1.50, £1.80; EX 26.20.
Owner Malcolm McCarthy **Bred** Wimborne Farm Inc **Trained** Middleham, N Yorks

FOCUS
The two clear leaders took each other on and they played into the hands of the doubtful battler Mexican. Overall though the form has a sound look if at just a modest level.

NOTEBOOK
Mexican(USA), whose sole win over fences was here a year ago from a stone higher mark, is something of a reluctant hero but the cards were played just right for him. His rider gave him no chance to change his mind and kept him up to his work all the way to the line. *(op 8-1)*
Polyphon(FR), winner of just two of his previous twenty two starts, needs two miles on a sharp track but, taken on for the lead, in the end was a sitting duck for the winner.
Good Outlook(IRE), having his second outing in two weeks after 15 months on the sidelines, went at it hammer and tongs with the runner-up but he was cooked when he met the second last all wrong. *(tchd 11-2 in a place)*
Reach The Clouds(IRE), 14 on New Year's Day, ran a shade better but his glory days are history now. *(op 25-1)*
Classic Lash(IRE), in first-time cheekpieces, had been pulled up on his two most recent starts and this was an insufficient test for him.
Celtic Legend(FR), a quirky horse, had one of his off days and seemed to lose interest going out onto the final circuit. *Official explanation: jockey said gelding ran flat (op 15-8 tchd 13-8)*

2843 GORACING.CO.UK AMATEUR RIDERS' H'CAP HURDLE (10 hdls) 2m 3f
2:50 (2:50) (Class 4) (0-100,98) 4-Y-0+ **£3,450** (£1,070; £534; £267)

Form RPR
-334 **1** **North Landing (IRE)**^{10} [2680] 5-11-2 **91**........................... MrCMulhall(3) 101+
(R C Guest) *hld up midfield: hdwy to ld bef 2 out: pushed out* **9/1**^{2}
3561 **2** *2½* **You Do The Math (IRE)**^{11} [2657] 5-11-3 **94** 7ex............. MrGTumelty(5) 100+
(L Lungo) *prom: bhd 6th: effrt bef 2 out: hung lft and chsd wnr between last two: kpt on run in* **10/11**^{1}
-000 **3** *3* **Welsh Dream**^{21} [2452] 8-10-13 **92**.................................. MissJRiding(7) 94
(Miss S E Forster) *bhd: and in tch bef 2 out: edgd lft and no imp run in* **25/1**
40-P **4** *1¾* **Oscar The Boxer (IRE)**^{222} [215] 6-10-5 **84**.................. MrOWilliams(7) 86+
(J M Jefferson) *led to bef 2 out: sn rdn: no ex whn n.m.r run in* **12/1**^{3}
P0-6 **5** *10* **Armentieres**^{15} [2567] 4-10-8 **87**.......................................(v) MrCJCallow(7) 77
(Mrs E Slack) *hld up: outpcd 6th: kpt on fr 2 out: no imp* **25/1**
-0P5 **6** *½* **Pucks Court**^{15} [2567] 8-9-9 **74**.................................. MrHHaynes(7) 64
(I A Brown) *bhd: hdwy and prom 3 out: wknd next* **40/1**
0000 **7** *1¼* **Merryvale Man**^{12} [2625] 8-11-4 **95**.................................. MrBKing(5) 86+
(Miss Kariana Key) *prom: hit 6th: effrt bef 2 out: sn no ex* **33/1**
0105 **8** *1½* **Acceleration (IRE)**^{11} [2657] 5-11-0 **86**........................... MrTGreenall 73
(R Allan) *in tch: effrt 3 out: wknd after next* **9/1**^{2}
06-6 **9** *7* **Major Royal (FR)**^{40} [2042] 5-10-0 **79**........................... MrSFMagee(7) 59
(A Parker) *chsd ldrs tl wknd bef 2 out* **40/1**
5000 **10** *¾* **Star Trooper (IRE)**^{11} [2657] 9-9-12 **77**.....................(p) MissCarlyFrater(7) 56
(Miss S E Forster) *hld up midfield: hdwy and cl up bef 6th: wknd bef 2 out* **40/1**
2-06 **11** *hd* **Quarry Island (IRE)**^{198} [602] 4-11-5 **94**..................... MissRDavidson(3) 73
(M Todhunter) *hld up: hdwy to chse ldrs 3 out: wknd fr next* **25/1**
00-0 **12** *4* **Darialann (IRE)**^{30} [2256] 10-10-13 **92**........................... MrDGreenway(7) 67
(O Brennan) *bhd: short-lived effrt bef 2 out: sn btn* **40/1**
10P3 **13** *4* **Macreater**^{30} [2256] 7-9-11 **46** ow2..................................(p) MrSWByrne(7) 47
(K A Morgan) *chsd ldrs tl wknd fr 3 out* **16/1**
-PP0 **14** *2* **Washington Pink (IRE)**^{11} [2657] 6-9-9 **74**.................. MrBenHamilton(7) 43
(C Grant) *a bhd: no ch fr 1/2-way* **100/1**
0 **15** *dist* **Turn The Corner (IRE)**^{11} [2657] 6-10-9 **88**..................... MrSClements(7) —
(J Clements, Ire) *bhd: drvn but no imp whn bdly hmpd 3 out: wknd* **12/1**^{3}
4-P0 **F** **Tunes Of Glory (IRE)**^{12} [2625] 9-11-5 **98**.............. MrDAFitzsimmons(7) —
(D McCain) *chsd ldrs: wkng whn fell 3 out* **50/1**
P00P **P** **Friedhelmo (GER)**^{15} [2567] 9-10-6 **85**........................ MissRachelClark(7) —
(S B Clark) *plld hrd: chsd ldrs: wknd 6th: t.o whn p.u bef 2 out* **50/1**
0P/P **U** **Ilton**^{28} [2290] 6-10-1 **76**..................................(p) MissADeniel(3) —
(M E Sowersby) *plld hrd: chsd ldrs to 1/2-way: no ch whn blnd: bdly hmpd and uns rdr 3 out* **100/1**

4m 46.8s (-3.70) **Going Correction** -0.15s/f (Good) **18** Ran SP% **123.8**
Speed ratings: **101,99,98,97,93 93,93,92,89,89 89,87,85,84,— —,—,—** CSF £16.33 CT £224.18 TOTE £7.00: £1.40, £1.20, £6.40, £3.30; EX 28.10.
Owner James S Kennerley And Miss Jenny Hall **Bred** M P B Bloodstock Ltd **Trained** Brancepeth, Co Durham

■ Stewards' Enquiry : Miss J Riding caution: careless riding

FOCUS
Plenty of out of form horses and in the end the first four pulled clear. the third and fourth are the best guides to the level.

NOTEBOOK
North Landing(IRE), whose sole previous success over hurdles was in selling company, had an experienced rider aboard and made this look pretty straight sailing. He might be able to find a low-grade race over fences.
You Do The Math(IRE), hoisted 13lb after Kelso, had a 7lb penalty to overcome but he made on bad mistake and in truth never really looked like seriously troubling the winner. Connections will be hoping for a re-think from the assessors. *(op 5-4)*
Welsh Dream, out of sorts since winning at Kelso in February, gave his young rider real problems hanging violently left on the run-in.
Oscar The Boxer(IRE), pulled up when last seen out at Hexham in May, took them along but was well held when left very short of room on the run-in.
Armentieres, tried in a visor this time, stayed on over the last two after coming from a different parish. The extra distance certainly seemed to suit him.

2844 "COME RACING AGAIN ON 28TH DECEMBER" INTERMEDIATE OPEN NATIONAL HUNT FLAT RACE — 2m

3:20 (3:20) (Class 6) 4-6-Y-0 **£2,240** (£653; £326)

Form	Pos	Btn	Horse	Jockey	RPR
300	**1**		**Topwell**[37] 2112 4-10-12 ow1 — (R C Guest) *hld up in rr: stdy hdwy 6f out: led over 1f out: sn clr: heavily eased towards fin* **66/1**	CiaranEddery(7)	113+
3-11	**2**	4	**According To Pete**[15] 2572 4-11-9 — (J M Jefferson) *hld up in tch: led on bit over 2f out: hdd whn rdr lost whip over 1f out: no ex* **5/4**[1]	ThomasDreaper(5)	115+
35-1	**3**	3	**Custom Design**[37] 2112 4-11-11 — (G A Harker) *led: drvn along 6f out: hdd over 2f out: kpt on same pce* **5/1**[2]	BrianHarding	108
	4	6	**Aldea (FR)** 4-11-4 — (Mrs S J Smith) *trckd ldrs: drvn along 4f out: chal over 2f out: wknd over 1f out* **6/1**[3]	PadgeWhelan	95
20-	**5**	9	**Kerrs Whin**[320] 3598 5-11-1 — (P G Atkinson) *w ldr: drvn along 7f out: wknd fnl 2f* **20/1**	LarryMcGrath(3)	86
	6	6	**Executive Friend (IRE)** 6-11-4 — (O Brennan) *mid-div: effrt 4f out: nvr nr ldrs* **28/1**	TomDoyle	80
0	**7**	hd	**Overfields**[33] 2192 5-10-13 — (S R Bowring) *in tch: t.k.h: lost pl 4f out* **80/1**	AdamPogson(5)	80
30-3	**8**	1 1/4	**Geraldine**[60] 1762 4-10-8 — (Mrs S Lamyman) *in tch: reminders 5f out: sn outpcd* **25/1**	LeeVickers(3)	72
	9	3	**Hedchester** 4-11-1 — (Mrs A Hamilton) *in rr: sn drvn along: nvr on terms* **33/1**	PeterBuchanan(3)	76
	10	1 1/4	**Highland Brief**[292] 5-11-4 — (Mrs A Duffield) *chsd ldrs: drvn along 7f out: lost pl 5f out* **40/1**	KeithMercer	74
5	**11**	3 1/2	**Boulders Beach (IRE)**[33] 2192 5-10-11 — (Mrs S J Smith) *chsd ldrs: drvn 7f out: wknd 4f out* **10/1**	NickCarter(7)	71
0	**12**	1/2	**Stormy Bay (IRE)**[26] 2340 4-10-8 — (R C Guest) *mid-div: drvn and lost pl 5f out* **66/1**	JohnFlavin(10)	70
3	**13**	2 1/2	**Opera Singer**[103] 1401 4-11-4 — (R A Fahey) *hld up in rr: sme hdwy 5f out: lost pl over 2f out* **10/1**	AnthonyRoss	68
	14	shd	**Watch The Wind** 4-10-4 — (J B Walton) *hld up in rr: sme hdwy 6f out: lost pl over 4f out* **50/1**	BenOrde-Powlett(7)	61

3m 49.8s (-5.50) **Going Correction** -0.15s/f (Good) **14** Ran SP% **117.2**
Speed ratings: **107,105,103,100,96 93,92,92,90,90 88,88,86,86** CSF £138.60 TOTE £40.30: £6.90, £1.20, £1.60; EX 160.30 Place 6 £58.22, Place 5 £50.48.
Owner Malcolm Penney **Bred** Red House Stud **Trained** Brancepeth, Co Durham

FOCUS
A surprise winner of an ordinary bumper but it was definitely no fluke, with the placed horses setting an above-average standard.

NOTEBOOK
Topwell, a medium-sized individual, was having his fourth start and came from way off the pace to *doddle up in the end, value at least ten lengths. It may have been a surprise but it was no fluke. Official explanation: trainer said, regarding improved form shown, gelding may have been suited by the better ground, but was suited by being dropped out*
According To Pete, under his double penalty, travelled best but the winner had shot past him when his rider dropped his stick. *(op 11-8 tchd 11-10)*
Custom Design cut out the pace but was making hard work of it some way out and in the end did well to hunt up the first two. He looks to have a lot more stamina than speed. *(op 9-2 tchd 11-2)*
Aldea(FR), who stands over plenty of ground, mixed it from the off but hard at work starting the home turn in the end he finished leg weary. There should be a fair bit better to come. *(tchd 13-2)*
Kerrs Whin took on the leader but was under pressure at the halfway mark and he has disappointed twice now since finishing runner-up to a useful sort on his debut at Wetherby a year ago. *(tchd 16-1)*
Executive Friend(IRE), making his racecourse debut rising seven, looks a very weak and unfurnished individual. *(op 25-1 tchd 33-1)*
T/Plt: £90.20 to a £1 stake. Pool: £28,919.75. 233.95 winning tickets. T/Qpdt: £23.70 to a £1 stake. Pool: £2,640.00. 82.15 winning tickets. RY

2605 EXETER (R-H)

Thursday, December 15

OFFICIAL GOING: Good to soft (soft in places)
Wind: Moderate against Weather: Fine

2845 GG.COM AMATEUR RIDERS' H'CAP HURDLE (10 hdls 1 omitted) — 2m 6f 110y

12:40 (12:40) (Class 4) (0-100,100) 4-Y-0+ **£3,415** (£1,050; £525)

Form	Pos	Btn	Horse	Jockey	RPR
02-6	**1**		**Kings Rock**[12] 2619 4-11-7 **100** — (P A Blockley) *t.k.h: a.p: rdn appr 3 out: led last: r.o wl* **28/1**	MissFayeBramley(5)	106+
0-0P	**2**	3	**Kingsbay**[11] 2660 6-11-7 **100** — (H Morrison) *hld up in mid-div: hdwy 6th: rdn appr 3 out: kpt on flat* **11/1**	MrSWaley-Cohen(5)	102
3P-1	**3**	1/2	**She's Our Native (IRE)**[7] 2723 7-11-5 **98** 7ex — (Evan Williams) *hld up in mid-div: hdwy 6th: led after 2 out: hdd last: one pce* **7/4**[1]	MrJETudor(5)	102+
6054	**4**	1	**Ashgan (IRE)**[21] 2459 12-10-2 **76** — (Dr P Pritchard) *led to 2nd: lost pl appr 5th: rallied 3 out: styd on flat* **25/1**	DrPPritchard	77
4505	**5**	3 1/2	**Tizi Ouzou (IRE)**[22] 2428 4-10-3 **84** (v) — (M C Pipe) *led 2nd: clr 6th: blnd and rdr lost iron briefly 2 out: sn hdd: wknd flat* **33/1**	MrDPick(7)	84+
0/14	**6**	12	**Frosty Jak**[44] 1973 7-10-6 **83** — (J D Frost) *hld up in mid-div: sltly hmpd 7th: no hdwy fr 3 out* **8/1**[3]	MissSGaisford(3)	68
34P4	**7**	1 1/4	**Denarius Secundus**[13] 2605 8-9-9 **76** — (N R Mitchell) *hld up in mid-div: rdn and hdwy appr 5th: wknd 6th* **25/1**	MrNJTerry(7)	60
-54P	**8**	2	**Mrs Pickles**[13] 2609 10-10-8 **87** — (M D I Usher) *sn w ldrs: wknd appr 3 out* **20/1**	MissEALalor(5)	69
0322	**9**	18	**Prayerful**[26] 2341 6-10-12 **93** — (J G M O'Shea) *prom tl wknd 3 out* **13/2**[2]	MrRQuinn(7)	72+
6P3/	**10**	23	**Better Thyne (IRE)**[731] 2775 9-11-5 **100** — (Mrs S D Williams) *prom: rdn 2nd: lost pl 4th: t.o fr 7th* **12/1**	MrJJDoyle(7)	41
3241	**11**	8	**Urban Dream (IRE)**[7] 2728 4-10-11 **92** 7ex — (R A Farrant) *a bhd: t.o fr 7th* **14/1**	RyanCummings(7)	25
1550	**12**	1/2	**Spirit Of Tenby (IRE)**[132] 1152 8-10-3 **84** — (W K Goldsworthy) *a bhd: t.o fr 7th* **16/1**	MissPMHearn(7)	16
-P14	**P**		**The Pecker Dunn (IRE)**[14] 2582 11-10-11 **90** — (Mrs N S Evans) *a bhd: t.o whn p.u bef 3 out* **25/1**	MrPCallaghan(5)	—
4004	**P**		**Caspian Dusk**[7] 2734 4-11-6 **97** (b1) — (W G M Turner) *prom tl wknd 6th: t.o whn p.u bef last* **22/1**	MrJSnowden(3)	—
0	**P**		**They Grabbed Me (IRE)**[22] 2427 4-10-5 **86** — (M C Pipe) *nt j.w: t.o 5th: p.u bef last: rdr lost irons* **100/1**	MrCWallis(7)	—
P0-0	**P**		**Skye Blue (IRE)**[28] 2296 8-9-8 **75** — (M J Weeden) *mid-div: rdn 4th: sn bhd: t.o whn p.u bef last* **100/1**	MrSPJones(7)	—
566-	**P**		**Karoo**[378] 2595 7-11-0 **91** — (K Bishop) *hld up in tch: wkng whn j.lft 7th: t.o whn p.u bef 3 out* **22/1**	MrDEdwards(3)	—
F0-P	**P**		**Mr Micky (IRE)**[25] 2377 7-10-7 **86** — (M B Shears) *mid-div: rdn appr 5th: sn struggling: t.o whn p.u bef 7th* **100/1**	MrDavidTurner(5)	—
F560	**P**		**Hunter Pudding**[18] 2523 5-9-7 **74** — (C L Popham) *hld up and bhd: hdwy appr 5th: sn rdn: wknd 6th: t.o whn p.u bef last* **100/1**	MrTCollier(7)	—

5m 51.5s (12.20) **Going Correction** +0.55s/f (Soft) **19** Ran SP% **124.7**
Speed ratings: **100,98,98,98,97 93,92,91,85,77 74,74,—,—,— —,—,—,—** CSF £280.79 CT £837.33 TOTE £32.80: £8.20, £3.30, £1.10, £6.00; EX 269.50.
Owner J T Billson **Bred** M S Anderson **Trained** Coedkernew, Newport

FOCUS
This moderate handicap hurdle turned into quite a slog up the straight, but Kings Rock ran out a cosy winner and the form looks reasonably solid.

NOTEBOOK
Kings Rock, runner-up in a slightly better contest than this at Haydock in March, was well held in a non-handicap on his reappearance at Chepstow, but this was more realistic and he showed improved form to score off this mark. He will need to improve again to defy a rise, but is unexposed at this sort of trip and, in being only four, that is entirely possible. Connections plan to *send him chasing at some time in the near future.Official explanation: trainer said, regarding the improved form shown, gelding was better suited by being ridden more prominently and from today's going (op 25-1)*
Kingsbay, who looked a potentially useful sorts at the start of last season, has been regressive of late, losing her form completely, but this was a step back in the right direction and she stayed on to claim second. She may have given the winner a bit more to do had her rider got her going earlier and a return to three miles may see her back winning.
She's Our Native(IRE), shouldering a 7lb penalty for winning a weak race at Ludlow earlier in the month, travelled strongly into the straight and held every chance, but did not see her race out as strongly as the front two and faded into third. She may continue to be vulnerable off this sort of mark. *(tchd 13-8 and 2-1)*
Ashgan(IRE), who took a clear early lead, ran on again down the straight to claim fourth and would have finished much closer under stronger handling. He is obviously not getting any better and will be 13 in the New Year.
Tizi Ouzou(IRE) ran a big race for the out-of-sorts Pipe team and held a clear lead before the turn-in, but he was already looking vulnerable when blundering two out and he eventually faded into fifth.
The Pecker Dunn(IRE) *Official explanation: jockey said gelding never travelled (tchd 25-1)*
Karoo, formerly with Paul Nicholls, ran well to a point before getting tired and is entitled to come on for this first run of the season. *(tchd 25-1)*
Caspian Dusk *Official explanation: vet said gelding returned lame (tchd 25-1)*

2846 EUROPEAN BREEDERS FUND/TATTERSALLS (IRELAND) MARES' ONLY NOVICES' CHASE (QUALIFIER) (15 fncs) — 2m 3f 110y

1:10 (1:10) (Class 4) 4-Y-0+ **£4,781** (£1,403; £701; £350)

Form	Pos	Btn	Horse	Jockey	RPR
0-22	**1**		**Supreme Serenade (IRE)**[28] 2297 6-11-3 — (P J Hobbs) *hld up and bhd: stdy hdwy fr 11th: led on bit 3 out: lft clr last* **8/11**[1]	RichardJohnson	126+
40-F	**2**	10	**Horcott Bay**[15] 2574 5-11-3 95 — (M G Rimell) *led to 9th: rdn appr 4 out: wknd 3 out: lft 2nd last* **50/1**	JamieMoore	104
P-6P	**3**	1 1/2	**Priscilla**[13] 2610 7-11-3 91 — (K Bishop) *hld up and bhd: stdy hdwy 10th: wknd appr 2 out* **20/1**	JohnMcNamara	103
2265	**4**	1 1/2	**Latin Queen (IRE)**[14] 2595 5-11-3 — (J D Frost) *prom tl wknd after 4 out* **16/1**	JoeTizzard	101
1P05	**5**	3	**Fallout (IRE)**[20] 2486 4-10-2 — (J W Mullins) *hld up in tch: lost pl and hit 9th: n.d after* **40/1**	RichardYoung(3)	87+
5-55	**6**	dist	**Burnt Out (IRE)**[31] 2240 6-10-12 — (B G Powell) *prom early: lost pl 4th: t.o fr 5th* **14/1**[3]	JohnnyLevins(5)	—
P0/U	**F**		**Perle De Puce (FR)**[7] 2715 6-10-10 — (N J Henderson) *j.rt: prom: led 9th: mstke 4 out: hdd 3 out: ev ch whn fell last* **5/2**[2]	MrSWaley-Cohen(7)	121+
PP/	**P**		**Ringagold**[227] 6-10-10 — (N J Hawke) *hld up in tch: wnt 2nd 6th: rdn 8th: pckd 9th: wknd 11th: t.o whn p.u bef 4 out* **200/1**	KeiranBurke(7)	—

5m 3.90s (10.00) **Going Correction** +0.55s/f (Soft)
WFA 4 from 5yo+ 10lb **8** Ran SP% **108.7**
Speed ratings: **102,98,97,96,95 —,—,—** CSF £40.53 TOTE £1.60: £1.02, £7.60, £3.60; EX 59.20.
Owner Mrs Karola Vann **Bred** Mervyn Kidd **Trained** Withycombe, Somerset

FOCUS
Although without a win between them over fences coming into this, the meeting of formerly smart hurdling pair Supreme Serenade and Perle De Puce made for a fascinating clash in what was a good mares-only event. The fifth and sixth help set the level.

NOTEBOOK
Supreme Serenade(IRE), marginally inferior to Perle De Puce over hurdles, set the standard on what we had seen of the pair over fences and was going marginally the better when being left clear at the last. Often a strong traveller, she has not always found it off the bridle in the past and it would have been interesting had she been pressed for maximum effort, but she deserves the benefit of the doubt and connections will no doubt be relieved to see her get off the mark. There are not many better in this sphere and she will no doubt be a big player in the final of the series at Uttoxeter in March. *(op 10-11)*
Horcott Bay, who herself was a faller on her chasing debut at Plumpton, was given a clear sight of her fences out in front, but was soon brushed aside as the principals went on. She got the better of the weakening Priscilla for second and will find easier opportunities. *(op 40-1 tchd 66-1)*
Priscilla had shown significantly more than her form figures suggest in her two previous attempts over fences, but having travelled strongly once again, she stopped to nothing and it would not surprise to learn she has some sort of problem. There is definitely ability there and she would make plenty of appeal in handicaps. *(tchd 22-1)*
Fallout(IRE), a moderate hurdler, showed enough on this fencing debut to suggest she is going to make a better chaser and she is another who is sure to find easier opportunities. *(op 25-1)*
Burnt Out(IRE) comes from a stable who continue to struggle to find some form and she offered little. *Official explanation: jockey said mare hung badly throughout (op 10-1)*
Perle De Puce(FR) made a far from ideal start to her fencing career when unseating early at Huntingdon and faced much stiffer opposition here, but she was tried at the highest level over hurdles and was in the process of pushing the favourite close when getting the last all wrong. She was not done with, but whether her rider would have been able to get the better of Johnson in a finish is doubtful. There is a similar race in her as long as this does not affect her confidence too severely. *(op 2-1)*

2847 SOUTH-WEST RACING CLUB H'CAP CHASE (19 fncs) 3m 1f 110y
1:40 (1:40) (Class 3) (0-135,126) 5-Y-0+ **£10,344** (£3,036; £1,518; £758)

Form RPR

2-23 **1** **Reflected Glory (IRE)**[27] [2311] 6-11-6 **120** ChristianWilliams 134+
(P F Nicholls) *a.p: wnt 2nd 9th: led appr 4 out: clr 3 out: drvn out* **7/2**[1]

P0-6 **2** *6* **Wain Mountain**[25] [2368] 9-11-10 **124** JasonMaguire 130+
(J A B Old) *a.p: ev ch appr 4 out: btn whn j.rt 3 out* **7/1**

PU-6 **3** *5* **Native Emperor**[33] [2175] 9-11-11 **125** NoelFehily 126+
(Jonjo O'Neill) *hld up: rdn and hdwy 13th: wknd appr 4 out* **11/2**[3]

101- **4** *3* **Indalo (IRE)**[264] [4548] 10-11-7 **126** PaulO'Neill[(5)] 124+
(Miss Venetia Williams) *led tl appr 4 out: sn wknd* **5/1**[2]

U-P4 **5** *19* **Kittenkat**[13] [2608] 11-10-1 **101** TomScudamore 79
(N R Mitchell) *w ldr to 9th: wknd after 13th* **18/1**

6-12 **6** *hd* **Mioche D'Estruval (FR)**[186] [728] 5-11-8 **122** RJGreene 100
(M C Pipe) *hld up and bhd: mstke 8th: rdn 12th: short-lived effrt 15th* **20/1**

0115 **7** *19* **Saffron Sun**[28] [2299] 10-10-13 **113** RichardJohnson 84+
(J D Frost) *hld up in mid-div: mstke 5th: hdwy 11th: wknd 14th* **9/1**

2-F2 **P** **Noble Baron**[29] [2273] 9-10-11 **111** (t) MarkBradburne —
(C G Cox) *a bhd: no ch whn mstke 4 out: p.u bef 3 out* **5/1**[2]

3P-P **P** **Fox In The Box**[28] [2299] 8-11-9 **123** AndrewThornton —
(R H Alner) *hld up in mid-div: short-lived effrt 15th: bhd whn p.u bef 3 out* **14/1**

1-26 **P** **Jaloux D'Estruval (FR)**[12] [2621] 8-11-10 **124** AndrewTinkler —
(Mrs L C Taylor) *hld up and bhd: nt fluent 7th: stmbld bdly 8th: sn struggling: t.o whn p.u bef 14th* **33/1**

6m 42.6s (14.60) **Going Correction** +0.55s/f (Soft) **10** Ran SP% **113.1**
Speed ratings: **99,97,95,94,88 88,82,—,—,—** CSF £27.73 CT £130.22 TOTE £3.60: £1.40, £1.90, £2.70; EX 24.60 Trifecta £392.00 Part won. Pool: £552.18 - 0.70 winning units. Roll over to Saturday of £165.65..
Owner Jeffrey Hordle **Bred** P J Fenton **Trained** Ditcheat, Somerset

FOCUS
A good effort by novice Reflected Glory who forged clear in the straight to win tidily. The form could rate higher but has been rated cautiously.

NOTEBOOK
Reflected Glory(IRE), placed in a fair event behind Lord Killeshanra at the course last month, was a fascinating contender on this handicap debut having only had two previous outings over fences, but he jumped fluently throughout and forged clear from the third last. Yet to finish outside the three in nine starts, he is the type his trainer will find a decent prize for later in the season and, as he is not yet seven, it is hoped there is further improvement to come. *(op 9-2)*
Wain Mountain, although without a win in nearly four years, has run many good races in defeat and was entitled to respect with his stable having recently begun to hit top form. A strong stayer who likes soft ground, conditions were ideal for him and he travelled well just in behind the leaders before being unable to match the winner. He beat the remainder well enough and it is tempting to say he can find a similar race, but the fact is he has yet to win outside novice company. *(op 5-1)*
Native Emperor, winner of the four-mile National Hunt Chase at the Festival back in 2004, has done very little since and, as with many from the stable, had a bad time of things last season. His reappearance over hurdles at Cheltenham was pleasing and he came into this looking one of the likelier winners, but he failed to race with any real zest and basically looks slow. There is no denying he is well-handicapped and he may be worth one more chance given a severe test of stamina. *(op 9-2)*
Indalo(IRE) had a good time of it last term, winning three of his final four starts, and the hot form of his stable was an obvious plus. He led for a long way, but it was evident from half a mile out he was not going to be winning and in the end he faded into fourth. There was enough promise gleamed from this to suggest he can win off this mark. *(op 9-2)*
Kittenkat knows the course inside out but is not as good as she used to be and was struggling some way from the finish. A drop in grade may help. *(op 16-1 tchd 20-1)*
Jaloux D'Estruval(FR) *Official explanation: jockey said gelding never travelled after bad mistake (op 6-1 tchd 9-2)*
Noble Baron has recorded his last four successes at this venue, but was racing off a 21lb higher mark than when last winning and was already held when blundering four out. *(op 6-1 tchd 9-2)*
Fox In The Box was on a retrieval mission having been pulled up the last twice, and he momentarily looked set to play a part under a mile out, but his effort came to nothing and he was eventually pulled up once more. His two chase wins have come on a sound surface, so he may be *worthy of another chance, but hardly has the profile of a horse screaming to be backed next time. (op 6-1 tchd 9-2)*

2848 CHRISTINE LOZE BIRTHDAY BEGINNERS' CHASE (17 fncs) 2m 7f 110y
2:10 (2:11) (Class 3) 4-Y-0+ **£5,926** (£1,740; £870; £434)

Form RPR

1-2F **1** **Lough Derg (FR)**[20] [2484] 5-11-6 TomScudamore 140+
(M C Pipe) *w ldr: led 12th: rdn appr 4 out: styd on wl* **9/4**[1]

10/F **2** *6* **Tighten Your Belt (IRE)**[21] [2464] 8-11-6 SamThomas 135+
(Miss Venetia Williams) *a.p: ev ch 2 out: sn hrd rdn: no ex flat* **7/1**

4-5U **3** *3 ½* **Bob Bob Bobbin**[34] [2165] 6-11-6 JoeTizzard 132+
(C L Tizzard) *hld up in mid-div: hdwy 8th: mstke 11th: one pce fr 4 out* **5/2**[2]

4 *20* **The Spieler (IRE)**[271] 6-11-6 MickFitzgerald 112+
(N J Henderson) *prom tl wknd appr 4 out* **12/1**

6 **5** *26* **Squires Lane (IRE)**[27] [2311] 6-11-6 JasonMaguire 84
(Andrew Turnell) *hld up in mid-div: mstke 8th: bhd fr 11th* **200/1**

-33P **6** *1 ¼* **Gola Supreme (IRE)**[19] [2506] 10-11-6 89 RichardJohnson 82
(R Lee) *hld up: hdwy whn j.rt fr 10th: sn struggling* **40/1**

1P-5 **7** *4* **Loup Charter (FR)**[27] [2311] 6-11-6 TimmyMurphy 98+
(Miss H C Knight) *led to 12th: wknd 4 out* **4/1**[3]

0/P **8** *14* **Stars'N'Stripes (IRE)**[49] [1891] 7-10-13 MrTDennis[(7)] 64
(W W Dennis) *hdwy 4th: wknd 13th* **50/1**

233- **9** *dist* **Lesdream**[237] [4960] 8-11-1 ChrisHonour[(5)] —
(J D Frost) *sn towards rr: lost tch fr 9th: t.o* **25/1**

1-36 **P** **Ardaghey (IRE)**[40] [2052] 6-11-6 AntonyEvans —
(N A Twiston-Davies) *hld up: p.u after 7th* **10/1**

/P00 **P** **Battling Buster (IRE)**[12] [2619] 8-11-1 RobertStephens[(5)] —
(R H Buckler) *prom tl wknd 8th: t.o whn p.u bef 10th* **200/1**

5 **P** **Smilingvalentine (IRE)**[11] [2663] 8-10-13 JodieMogford —
(D J Wintle) *a bhd: rdn 7th: t.o whn p.u bef 4 out* **150/1**

PP-P **P** **Peveril Pride**[13] [2607] 7-11-6 88 JimmyMcCarthy —
(J A Geake) *a bhd: pckd 1st: t.o whn p.u bef 4 out* **100/1**

02-P **P** **Bayoss (IRE)**[19] [2506] 9-11-1 81 MrGBarfoot-Saunt[(5)] —
(Mrs Tracey Barfoot-Saunt) *prom tl wknd 9th: t.o whn p.u bef 13th* **250/1**

6m 7.10s (8.50) **Going Correction** +0.55s/f (Soft) **14** Ran SP% **119.9**
Speed ratings: **107,105,103,97,88 88,86,82,—,— —,—,—,—** CSF £18.76 TOTE £4.40: £1.50, £2.60, £1.50; EX 40.30.
Owner W Frewen **Bred** Patrick Gouesnard **Trained** Nicholashayne, Devon

FOCUS
A good beginners' chase that is likely to produce its share of winners rated through the winner.

NOTEBOOK
Lough Derg(FR), despite coming into this with a bit to prove over his well being (fell last time, stable out of sorts) boasted the best single piece of form having finished second to Crozan at the Paddy Power meeting, with recent winner Exotic Dancer back in third. Prominent throughout, he looked set to come off worse after Tighten Your Belt came there travelling strongly, but kept finding and outstayed the runner-up in the final quarter mile. A tough and thoroughly genuine youngster, he is unlikely to be good enough for Royal & SunAlliance Chase, but may find an opportunity in one of the Festival handicaps, with his ability to handle good ground well proven. *(op 5-2 tchd 3-1)*
Tighten Your Belt(IRE), whose only defeat over hurdles came in the Royal & SunAlliance Hurdle behind Fundamentalist, got no further than the sixth fence on his return from injury at Uttoxeter last month, but he showed no signs of being affected by the fall. He travelled strongly, but the winner was too good for him on the day and, although it looked a case of him being outstayed by the winner in the end, there is a chance he may still have needed this. *(op 15-2)*
Bob Bob Bobbin, a useful hurdler who failed to shine on his fencing debut at Lingfield, was in the process of improving on that when unseating behind Church Island in a better race at Cheltenham last month, so it was somewhat disappointing he did not put up more of a show here. Although ultimately not beaten far in third, he looked paceless and failed to jump with any fluency. The best of him may not be seen until moving into handicaps, where he will have a chance to race over extreme distances. *(tchd 2-1)*
The Spieler(IRE), hailing from the in-form Henderson camp, won his point on vastly different going and, as a result, made a quite a pleasing Rules debut. He travelled well to a point, but was racing against several useful types and struggled to go with them down the straight. He will find easier opportunities. *Official explanation: vet said gelding returned lame (op 10-1)*
Squires Lane(IRE), well held on his Rules debut at the course last month, was again some way adrift of the principals, but faced no realistic chance against this opposition and is young enough to improve. *(op 150-1)*
Loup Charter(FR), a useful hurdler who was always going to improve for fences, disappointed badly on his chase debut at the course last month when failing to jump fluently and getting tired very quickly. This time however he put in a vastly improved round of fencing under a more aggressive ride, but he once again capitulated too quickly for comfort once beaten. Twice a winner at three miles over hurdles, stamina is not the problem and it is hoped that the likeable grey just takes some getting fit. *(op 9-2 tchd 5-1)*
Ardaghey(IRE), who has been crying out for this sort of test, never got going and was pulled up at an early stage, looking as though something may have been amiss. He looked the type to make a decent chaser and, if none the worse, may be capable of leaving this form behind once handicapping. *Official explanation: jockey said saddle slipped (op 8-1)*

2849 JEAN BROWNING HAPPY RETIREMENT NOVICES' HURDLE (9 hdls 1 omitted) 2m 3f
2:40 (2:43) (Class 3) 4-Y-0+ **£5,835** (£1,713; £856; £427)

Form RPR

0-P4 **1** **Dare Too Dream**[11] [2663] 6-10-12 JohnMcNamara 106
(K Bishop) *hld up in tch: led 3 out: sn rdn: all out* **25/1**

12/3 **2** *½* **The Sawyer (BEL)**[19] [2507] 5-10-12 BenjaminHitchcott 105
(R H Buckler) *a.p: rdn and ev ch fr 3 out: r.o flat* **10/1**

1 **3** *3* **Border Castle**[12] [2627] 4-11-4 SamThomas 110+
(Miss Venetia Williams) *hld up in mid-div: hdwy whn hit 7th: rdn appr 2 out: mstke last: one pce* **8/11**[1]

0-44 **4** *11* **Spring Junior (FR)**[44] [1969] 4-10-12 RichardJohnson 91
(P J Hobbs) *led to 3rd: led after 6th to 3 out: wknd 2 out* **25/1**

60 **5** *hd* **Our Girl Kaz (IRE)**[83] [1543] 5-10-0 HowieEphgrave[(5)] 84
(L Corcoran) *hld up in tch: rdn and lost pl 5th: rallied after 6th: wknd 2 out* **100/1**

55 **6** *11* **Wee Anthony (IRE)**[12] [2619] 6-10-12 NoelFehily 80
(Jonjo O'Neill) *nvr nr ldrs* **28/1**

7 *3 ½* **Nietzsche (IRE)**[169] 4-10-12 JimCrowley 76
(R J Hodges) *hld up and bhd: hdwy 6th: wknd 2 out* **66/1**

5 **8** *¾* **Happy Shopper (IRE)**[13] [2606] 5-10-12 TomScudamore 76
(M C Pipe) *prom tl wknd appr 3 out* **25/1**

30 **9** *2 ½* **Whatcanisay**[13] [2606] 6-10-7 ChrisHonour[(5)] 73
(J D Frost) *a bhd* **200/1**

00 **10** *7* **Barathea Blue**[12] [2624] 4-10-12 TimmyMurphy 66
(M C Pipe) *a bhd* **40/1**

-122 **11** *9* **Malaga Boy (IRE)**[201] [549] 8-11-4 107 JoeTizzard 63
(C L Tizzard) *bhd fr 4th* **13/2**[2]

54-P **12** *9* **Alright Now M'Lad (IRE)**[35] [2142] 5-10-12 MickFitzgerald 48
(Jonjo O'Neill) *bhd fr 4th* **33/1**

50-0 **13** *shd* **Tuesday Club (IRE)**[31] [2249] 6-10-12 JasonMaguire 48
(J A B Old) *bhd fr 4th* **100/1**

P **Lorrelini (IRE)** 4-10-12 AndrewThornton —
(R H Alner) *a bhd: t.o whn p.u bef 3 out* **66/1**

0/0 **P** **The Gerry Man (IRE)**[22] [2426] 6-10-12 WarrenMarston —
(D J Wintle) *a bhd: nt fluent 3rd: t.o whn p.u bef 3 out* **150/1**

P **Negociant (FR)**[184] 4-10-12 BarryFenton —
(R M Stronge) *wnt lft s: prom: hit 4th: wknd after 5th: t.o whn p.u bef 3 out* **20/1**

P **Four In Hand**[312] 7-9-12 LiamHeard[(7)] —
(Mrs K M Sanderson) *hld up in mid-div: hdwy 4th: wknd appr 3 out: p.u bef 2 out* **50/1**

24-2 **P** **Wellpict One (IRE)**[22] [2427] 5-10-12 AntonyEvans —
(N A Twiston-Davies) *prom: led 3rd tl after 6th: cl up whn p.u lame bef 3 out* **9/1**[3]

4m 46.7s (5.80) **Going Correction** +0.55s/f (Soft) **18** Ran SP% **123.5**
Speed ratings: **109,108,107,102,102 98,96,96,95,92 88,84,84,—,— —,—,—** CSF £236.28 TOTE £35.60: £6.00, £2.70, £1.10; EX 671.90.
Owner Henry T Cole **Bred** H T Cole **Trained** Spaxton, Somerset

FOCUS
An ordinary affair that went the way of an outsider, but the time was decent and the form should work out well enough.

NOTEBOOK
Dare Too Dream, whose two previous outings this season had seen him fail to see out the trip, was helped by this drop in distance and found what was required to hold the challenge of the persistent runner-up. It will be interesting to see what sort of mark he gets for handicaps and he looks best kept to trips of around this distance for the time being. *(tchd 33-1)*
The Sawyer(BEL), a fair sort in bumpers, looked ready for a switch to hurdles and he relished every yard of the distance, rallying gamely after the last to hassle the winner close home. A further rise in distance should bring about improvement and he can find a small race if kept to a modest level. *(op 9-1)*
Border Castle did it stylishly when winning on his hurdling debut at Haydock, but he did not jump as fluently and was already held when blundering at the last. The 6lb penalty may have proved too much for him, but there is also the possibility the extra three furlongs was beyond him and he deserves another chance. *(op 5-6 tchd 10-11, evens in a place)*
Spring Junior(FR) kept plugging away once headed and one more run will see him qualified for handicaps, a sphere he should do well in. *(op 20-1)*

Our Girl Kaz(IRE) failed to build on her mildly promising bumper debut when down the field at Worcester, but this switch to hurdles saw her in a better light and she was noted travelling well down the back straight. She ultimately weakened out of it, but would be interesting in mares-only company. *(op 33-1)*
Negociant(FR) *Official explanation: jockey said gelding weakened badly at end of back straight (tchd 16-1)*

2850 HAPPY CHRISTMAS H'CAP HURDLE (7 hdls 1 omitted) 2m 1f
3:10 (3:10) (Class 3) (0-125,119) 4-Y-0+ **£5,123** (£1,504; £752; £375)

Form RPR
313- **1** **Gods Token**[571] 482 7-11-6 **113**........ SamThomas 116
(Miss Venetia Williams) *led: rdn and hdd 3 out: rallied to ld nr fin* **3/1**[1]
-111 **2** ½ **Magot De Grugy (FR)**[8] 2706 5-11-10 **117** 7ex........ AndrewThornton 119+
(R H Alner) *a.p: led on bit 3 out: hrd rdn flat: hdd nr fin* **5/1**[3]
553- **3** 1½ **Idiome (FR)**[267] 4518 9-11-1 **115**........ LiamHeard[(7)] 116
(Mrs L C Taylor) *hld up: hdwy appr 3 out: sn rdn: r.o flat* **11/1**
3P12 **4** hd **Irish Wolf (FR)**[7] 2716 5-11-2 **114**........ TomGreenway[(5)] 115
(P Bowen) *hld up: hdwy appr 3rd: rdn appr 3 out: kpt on flat* **7/2**[2]
PP02 **5** ¾ **Hunting Lodge (IRE)**[7] 2721 4-9-13 **99** ow2........ MrJAJenkins[(7)] 99
(H J Manners) *hld up: rdn and hdwy 3 out: styd on flat* **16/1**
-230 **6** nk **Bonny Grey**[25] 2379 7-10-7 **107**........ MrNPearce[(7)] 107
(D Burchell) *t.k.h early: hld up in tch: rdn appr 3 out: kpt on same pce* **33/1**
-UF6 **7** 12 **Charlton Kings (IRE)**[14] 2595 7-11-6 **113**........ RichardJohnson 105+
(R J Hodges) *prom: eased whn btn after 3 out* **8/1**
8 19 **Idian Mix (FR)**[29] 4-10-10 **113**........ AndrewGlassonbury[(10)] 82
(M C Pipe) *hld up: rdn after 4th: bhd fr 3 out* **12/1**
505 **9** 1¾ **Xila Fontenailles (FR)**[27] 2309 4-9-9 **95**........ KeiranBurke[(7)] 62
(N J Hawke) *chsd ldr to 4th: wknd appr 3 out* **9/1**

4m 16.5s (7.30) **Going Correction** +0.55s/f (Soft)
WFA 4 from 5yo+ 10lb **9** Ran SP% **109.8**
Speed ratings: **104,103,103,102,102 102,96,87,87** CSF £17.22 CT £130.22 TOTE £3.80: £1.90, £2.00, £3.70; EX 21.70 Place 6 £11.24, Place 5 £5.15.
Owner The Silver Cod Partnership **Bred** C I Ratcliffe **Trained** Kings Caple, H'fords

FOCUS
A decent handicap to finish in which the outcome changed dramatically on the run-in. The form looks pretty solid.

NOTEBOOK
Gods Token, off-track since May 2004 with injury, was evidently straight for this return and stayed on right the way to the line to nail Magot De Grugy. He looked set for second at best when the Alner runner nosed ahead three out and was around two lengths down, going nowhere, when the leader started to hang fire. Lightly-raced and fully unexposed, he is versatile with regards to going and shapes as though two and a half will not prove a problem, so should be placed to win again if given time to recover from these exertions. *(op 7-2)*
Magot De Grugy(FR) has returned an improved performer this season and was chasing a four-timer here having won comfortably at Leicester last time. Up another 10lb, he travelled strongly into the straight and looked to have done enough when going a couple clear after the last, but started to hang fire and was nailed by the winner. He is due to go up another 1lb in future and is clearly not going to find things easy, but connections have the option of sending him chasing and the five-year-old remains open to a certain amount of further improvement. *(op 3-1 tchd 11-4)*
Idiome(FR) is a horse who has had his problems, but as he showed here he is more than capable of winning off this sort of mark and he stayed on well under his young pilot to grab third close home. He has the option of returning to fences. *(op 8-1 tchd 12-1)*
Irish Wolf(FR), 6lb higher than when winning at Huntingdon in early November, went down narrowly off this mark back there last time and was again far from disgraced, keeping on well for pressure to challenge for third. This was only his sixth start over obstacles and he may be capable of winning again when his stable finds some form. *(tchd 4-1)*
Hunting Lodge(IRE), although arguably holding the form down, may well be an improved performer and showed his Ludlow running to be no fluke, while Bonny Grey offered a bit more in a close-up sixth. *(tchd 20-1)*
Idian Mix(FR), a well-campaigned gelding in France considering he is only four (24 runs), was always in rear and did not offer a great deal of encouragement for the future, although it is worth remembering that many of the Pond House inmates are out of sorts at the minute. *(op 9-1)*
T/Jkpt: Not won. T/Plt: £9.00 to a £1 unit stake. Pool: £52,905.10 - 4,275.65 winning units.
T/Qpdt: £3.80 to a £1 unit stake. Pool: £3,377.30 - 647.40 winning units. KH

2460 UTTOXETER (L-H)
Friday, December 16

OFFICIAL GOING: Heavy
There were four flights in the home straight and one less in the back straight.
Wind: Fresh against Weather: Fine and sunny

2858 RACING POST "HANDS AND HEELS" JUMPS SERIES NOVICES' H'CAP HURDLE FOR CONDITIONAL JOCKEYS (10 hdls) 2m
12:20 (12:23) (Class 4) (0-90,90) 3-Y-0+ **£2,610** (£760; £380)

Form RPR
4F-P **1** **Balmoral Queen**[8] 2721 5-10-4 **68**........ MrGTumelty 80+
(D McCain) *hld up: hdwy 6th: led 3 out: styd on* **50/1**
000 **2** 8 **Prairie Law (GER)**[15] 2584 5-11-12 **90**........ TomMessenger 93
(B N Pollock) *prom: effrt 3 out: styd on same pce fr next* **25/1**
P010 **3** shd **Before The Mast (IRE)**[16] 2567 8-11-1 **79**........ JohnKington 84+
(M F Harris) *hld up: hdwy 5th: ev ch 2 out: wknd flat* **15/2**
0-00 **4** 25 **Nabir (FR)**[1] 2027 5-11-1 **79**........ EwanWhillans 57
(P D Niven) *hld up: hdwy 5th: wknd 3 out* **16/1**
4P04 **5** 5 **Keepasharplookout (IRE)**[3] 2810 3-10-5 **85**........ MrTCollier[(3)] 45
(C W Moore) *chsd ldrs: mstke 2nd: wknd 3 out* **16/1**
1442 **6** 6 **Runaway Bishop (USA)**[20] 2502 10-11-0 **83**........ MissUMoore[(5)] 50
(J R Cornwall) *prom: lost pl after 3rd: sn bhd* **13/2**[3]
0404 **7** 2 **Weet Watchers**[8] 2721 5-10-10 **79**........ MrLEdwards[(5)] 44
(T Wall) *bhd 4th: effrt appr 6th: sn wknd* **14/1**
0-0 **8** 13 **Sullivan's Cascade (IRE)**[8] 2723 7-10-9 **78**........ MissIPickard[(5)] 30
(E G Bevan) *hld up: a bhd* **66/1**
04 **9** 15 **Secluded**[149] 1036 5-11-6 **84**........(p) MrDEdwards 21
(N G Ayliffe) *prom tl wknd after 6th* **25/1**
-002 **10** 21 **City Palace**[17] 2563 4-10-12 **76**........ MrJETudor —
(Evan Williams) *trckd ldrs: led 5th: hdd & wknd 3 out* **3/1**[2]
053 **P** **Kalawoun (FR)**[20] 2494 3-10-11 **88**........ PatrickMcDonald —
(Ferdy Murphy) *bhd fr 4th: t.o whn p.u bef 2 out* **11/4**[1]
00-0 **P** **Okayman (FR)**[75] 1605 4-10-3 **67**........ PhilKinsella —
(A Parker) *mstke 2nd: bhd fr 4th: t.o whn p.u after 6th* **20/1**
-640 **P** **Schinken Otto (IRE)**[7] 2750 4-10-11 **80**........ MrOWilliams[(5)] —
(J M Jefferson) *led: j.rt and hdd 5th: wknd after next: t.o whn p.u bef 2 out* **14/1**

4m 13.9s (13.50) **Going Correction** +0.925s/f (Soft)
WFA 3 from 4yo 13lb 4 from 5yo+ 10lb **13** Ran SP% **117.8**
Speed ratings: **103,99,98,86,83 80,79,73,65,55** —,—,— CSF £917.64 CT £10008.52 TOTE £86.50: £14.10, £6.60, £2.60; EX 1894.10.
Owner Mrs S K Maan **Bred** H S Maan **Trained** Cholmondeley, Cheshire

FOCUS
A poor contest but run at a good pace in the conditions and resulting in a surprise outcome. The third is the best guide to the level.

NOTEBOOK
Balmoral Queen had shown some ability in her first bumper but has shown no form over hurdles having suffered a series of mishaps. She is not overly big but revelled in these conditions under her light weight, making smooth progress around the bottom bend to lead and finding more to go away from the last as her rivals tired. Given similar conditions she can follow up.
Prairie Law(GER), a faist ground middle-distance winner on the Flat, handled these very different conditions on this handicap debut and stayed on to catch the tiring Before The Mast on the line. *(op 20-1)*
Before The Mast(IRE), a previous course and distance winner, looked a big threat early in the straight but hit the last two as he tired and was caught for the runner-up spot. He will be better off back in selling comapny.\n\x\x Before The Mast nearly followed up last month's course and distance win which was in a seller and has not paid much with the handicapper and showed again he can be found an opening at the low level. He was exhausted on the run-in *(op 8-1)*
Nabir(FR), who has been running on the sand of late, had been well beaten at Southwell the previous day. *(op 14-1)*
Keepasharplookout(IRE), who appeared not to get home over three furlongs further three days previously, should have been helped by the trip but did not last in the conditions.
Runaway Bishop(USA), better known as a chaser and having his first run over hurdles for the best part of two years, was struggling after his rider lost an iron and he dropped back at the third. *(op 8-1)*
City Palace, who has run mainly on a sound surface previously, helped set the pace and was A spent force before the third last and the conditions drained his limited stamina. *(tchd 11-4)*
Kalawoun(FR), a three-year-old making his handicap debut, never went a yard and connections could not offer an immediate explanation. *Official explanation: trainer had no explanation for the poor form shown (op 3-1)*

2859 HEATHYARDS ENGINEERING NOVICES' HURDLE (12 hdls) 2m 4f 110y
12:50 (12:51) (Class 4) 4-Y-0+ **£3,566** (£1,039; £519)

Form RPR
UP16 **1** **Vingis Park (IRE)**[19] 2530 7-10-12 **115**........(b) MrJJDoyle[(7)] 116+
(V R A Dartnall) *nt fluent: mde most tl mstke and hdd 7th: rallied 3 out: led next: styd on wl: eased run-in* **5/4**[1]
P **2** 8 **Izzyizzenty**[7] 2755 6-10-9........ FergusKing[(3)] 96
(J M Jefferson) *mid-div: hdwy 6th: sn chsng ldrs: led 3 out: hdd next: sn btn* **25/1**
1- **3** 3½ **Arnold Layne (IRE)**[258] 4690 6-10-12........ WarrenMarston 95+
(R T Phillips) *towards rr: pushed along and hdwy 5th: chsng ldrs 7th: 4th whn blnd 3 out: one pce* **5/2**[2]
/3-0 **4** 5 **Major Catch (IRE)**[12] 2663 6-10-7 **114**........ AdamPogson[(5)] 88
(C T Pogson) *sn bhd: sme hdwy 7th: kpt on fr 2 out* **16/1**
6 **5** 14 **Noir Et Vert (FR)**[22] 2450 4-10-12........ KeithMercer 74
(Ferdy Murphy) *hld up in rr: sme hdwy 7th: nvr a factor* **10/1**[3]
P56/ **6** ½ **Dickie Lewis**[671] 3820 7-10-7 **59**........ StephenCraine[(5)] 73
(D McCain) *in tch: drvn along 6th: sn lost pl* **100/1**
-0F0 **7** 1¼ **Thievery**[13] 2631 4-10-12........ MarkBradburne 72
(H D Daly) *mid-div: reminders 4th: hdwy 6th: wknd after next* **50/1**
5F20 **8** 23 **Imperial Royale (IRE)**[29] 2285 4-10-2 **95**........ ThomasBurrows[(10)] 54+
(P L Clinton) *chsd ldrs: led 7th: hdd 3 out: sn wknd* **50/1**
433U **9** 8 **Sarahs Quay (IRE)**[18] 2553 6-9-12........ RyanCummings[(7)] 34
(K J Burke) *sn bhd: t.o 7th* **100/1**
6 **P** **Mr Smithers Jones**[13] 2624 5-10-12........ JodieMogford —
(Dr P Pritchard) *sn bhd: t.o whn p.u after 5th* **50/1**
0-0P **P** **My Good Lord (IRE)**[22] 2460 6-10-12........ TonyDobbin —
(B D Leavy) *reminders 4th: sn bhd: t.o whn p.u bef 7th* **80/1**
0-06 **P** **Glen Thyne (IRE)**[13] 2631 5-10-12........ JohnMcNamara —
(K C Bailey) *reminders and bhd 3rd: t.o whn p.u after 5th* **100/1**
0/66 **P** **Cornish Jester**[10] 2683 6-10-9........ OwynNelmes[(3)] —
(C J Down) *w ldrs: wknd qckly after 6th: bhd whn p.u bef 2 out* **14/1**
0 **P** **Noun De La Thinte (FR)**[20] 2501 4-10-5........ AlanO'Keeffe —
(Miss Venetia Williams) *mid-div: hdwy to chse ldrs after 5th: lost pl next: bhd whn p.u bef 3 out* **10/1**[3]

5m 27.8s (15.70) **Going Correction** +0.925s/f (Soft)
WFA 4 from 5yo+ 11lb **14** Ran SP% **117.7**
Speed ratings: **107,103,102,100,95 95,94,85,82,**— —,—,—,— CSF £38.71 TOTE £2.60: £1.10, £7.40, £1.90; EX 50.90.
Owner Nick Viney **Bred** Victor Robinson **Trained** Brayford, Devon

FOCUS
An uncompetitive affair but at least another real test, although the winner is value for more than the official margin.

NOTEBOOK
Vingis Park(IRE)looked beaten as Imperial Royale went six lengths clear around the bottom bend but he looks a different proposition now, not only from the application of blinkers but also having undergone a wind operation. He has risen in the ratings and this success under a winner's penalty probably does not amount to any more than his weak Aintree win last month. *(op 6-4)*
Izzyizzenty, a maiden pointer having only his second outing under Rules, came out of the pack in the last six furlongs and never gave up the chase. This was in complete contrast to his pulled-up debut effort and he looks to be going the right way.
Arnold Layne(IRE), who won a bumper on his sole previous outing, made a promising move into the home straight on this hurdling debut but like most of these he looked to be galloping in treacle from the third last. This chasing type should win his novice in similar company given less testing ground. *(op 9-4)*
Major Catch(IRE), who won his bumper on heavy, has not appeared as effective on soft ground over hurdles and, although staying on, may be better off in handicaps on a sounder surface.
Imperial Royale(IRE) helped to force the pace and not surprisingly was legless before the third last. He may be worth trying back at the minimum trip given testing ground. *(tchd 40-1)*
Mr Smithers Jones *Official explanation: vet said gelding was lame behind*

2860 PETER J DOUGLAS MAIDEN HURDLE (10 hdls) 2m
1:20 (1:22) (Class 4) 4-Y-0+ **£2,898** (£844; £422)

Form RPR
36 **1** **Livingonaknifedge (IRE)**[50] 1892 6-10-11........ PaulO'Neill[(5)] 107+
(Ian Williams) *hld up: hdwy 5th: led appr 3 out: styd on wl* **16/1**
4-2 **2** 6 **Magnesium (USA)**[15] 2584 5-11-2 **109**........ JohnMcNamara 101+
(B G Powell) *hld up: hdwy after 5th: ev ch 2 out: sn rdn: no ex last* **4/5**[1]
4-02 **3** 6 **Haunted House**[34] 2179 5-11-2........ MarkBradburne 96+
(H D Daly) *hld up: hdwy 5th: ev ch whn mstke 3 out: wknd last* **7/2**[2]
0-20 **4** 1¼ **Thenameescapesme**[37] 2131 5-11-2........ JasonMaguire 94
(T R George) *hld up: hdwy appr 6th: wknd bef last* **25/1**

U6F- **5** 2 ½ **Tudor Buck (IRE)**[238] [4958] 5-11-2 100 .... WayneHutchinson 91
(R Dickin) *hld up: hdwy appr 3 out: wknd bef last* **20/1**

4-40 **6** 10 **Negus De Beaumont (FR)**[24] [2423] 4-11-2 .... HenryOliver 81
(F Jordan) *hld up: hdwy appr 3 out: wknd bef next* **66/1**

P00 **7** 14 **Miniperse (FR)**[8] [2730] 5-10-13 .... GinoCarenza(3) 67
(G R I Smyly) *prom: chsd ldr 5th to next: wknd appr 3 out* **100/1**

-00P **8** 1 ¾ **Times Up Barney**[49] [1903] 5-11-2 .... JosephByrne 66
(C W Moore) *hld up: hdwy appr 3 out: sn wknd* **100/1**

P00 **9** 9 **Tashkandi (IRE)**[27] [2343] 5-11-2 .... TonyDobbin 57
(P Bowen) *chsd ldrs: mstke 1st: reminders after 4th: wknd appr 3 out* **22/1**

10 14 **Fisby**[55] 4-10-13 .... TJPhelan(3) 43
(K J Burke) *hld up: hdwy after 6th: wknd next* **12/1**[3]

0-20 **11** 3 **Celtic Jem (IRE)**[20] [2487] 5-11-2 .... NoelFehily 40
(P Bowen) *chsd ldrs tl wknd appr 3 out* **16/1**

00 **U** **Spanish Tan (NZ)**[16] [2573] 5-10-9 .... MrAJBerry(7) —
(Jonjo O'Neill) *j.big and uns rdr 1st* **28/1**

0-00 **P** **Luscious (IRE)**[9] [2704] 5-10-9 .... AlanO'Keeffe —
(K C Bailey) *hld up: t.o whn p.u after 6th* **100/1**

P **P** **Musical Shares**[15] [2584] 4-11-2 ....(t) JimmyMcCarthy —
(J A Geake) *bhd fr 4th: t.o whn p.u bef 6th* **100/1**

P **P** **Dandygrey Russett (IRE)**[22] [2462] 4-10-9 .... JamesDavies —
(B D Leavy) *led: wknd hdd and p.u bef 3 out* **50/1**

P **Osorno**[759] 5-11-2 .... AndrewTinkler —
(W M Brisbourne) *prom: blnd 2nd: lost pl 4th: sn bhd: t.o whn p.u bef 6th* **80/1**

PP- **P** **Golden Key**[379] [2589] 4-10-13 .... ColinBolger(3) —
(J Gallagher) *chsd ldr to 5th: sn rdn: wknd after next: t.o whn p.u bef 3 out* **100/1**

4m 15.9s (15.50) **Going Correction** +0.925s/f (Soft) **17** Ran SP% **123.3**
Speed ratings: **98,95,92,91,90 85,78,77,72,65 64,—,—,—,— —,—** CSF £28.62 TOTE £26.80: £4.10, £1.10, £1.30; EX 62.90.
Owner Concertina Racing Five **Bred** Denis Ring **Trained** Portway, Worcs

FOCUS
A moderate maiden hurdle, but a steadier pace saw the principals come home stronger than in the first two races. The third sets the standard for the form which does not look that sound.

NOTEBOOK
Livingonaknifedge(IRE), whose connections were worried about how he would cope with this ground, was always travelling supremely well and only had to be shaken up after the last. This maiden point winner had not made any show in a bumper and over hurdles in two starts under Rules but won this with something to spare and there should be more to come. *(op 20-1)*
Magnesium(USA) travelled every bit as well as the winner but could not live with that rival after three out, despite staying on well enough. He looks to have a race in him and now qualifies for handicaps. *(tchd 10-11, evens in a place)*
Haunted House, runner-up in a similar contest here on testing geround last month, kept tabs on the first two until the second last from where he could only plod on at one pace. A step up in trip may be of benefit. *(op 4-1)*
Thenameescapesme, making his hurdling debut, had run his best previous race on this track but the conditions appeared to find him out. He can be given another chance on better ground.
Tudor Buck(IRE) caught the eye on this first run of the season after 238 days off. His last run ended in a fall but he showed no ill effects and this five-year-old should build on this sound effort and will be interesting once contesting handicaps. *(op 14-1)*

2861 ST MOWDENS PROPERTIES BEGINNERS' CHASE (12 fncs) 2m
1:55 (1:56) (Class 4) 4-Y-0+ **£4,196** (£1,231; £615; £307)

Form RPR

110- **1** **Villon (IRE)**[276] [4381] 6-11-3 .... TonyDobbin 136+
(L Lungo) *hld up: hdwy appr 4 out: mstke next: led 2 out: styd on wl* **7/2**[2]

00-U **2** 6 **Roman Ark**[26] [2371] 7-11-0 .... FergusKing(3) 126+
(J M Jefferson) *hld up: hdwy 7th: outpcd appr 4 out: rallied 2 out: styd on same pce flat* **9/2**[3]

PP-F **3** 4 **Muhtenbar**[29] [2291] 5-11-3 115 .... PaulMoloney 122+
(Miss H C Knight) *led to 4th: led next: hdd 2 out: wknd last* **25/1**

0-64 **4** 1 ¼ **Sharp Rigging (IRE)**[14] [2607] 5-11-3 .... JimmyMcCarthy 122+
(A M Hales) *chsd ldr tl led 4th: hdd next: ev ch 3 out: wknd appr last* **7/1**

24-2 **5** 2 **Tamarinbleu (FR)**[33] [2208] 5-11-3 .... APMcCoy 118
(M C Pipe) *chsd ldrs tl wknd 2 out* **1/1**[1]

6-P **6** dist **Oh Golly Gosh**[24] [2422] 4-10-0 ....(p) MarcGoldstein(7) —
(N P Littmoden) *hld up: hdwy 5th: blnd 4 out: wkng whn blnd and uns rdr next: rmntd* **100/1**

1/ **F** **Billesey (IRE)**[635] [4495] 7-11-3 .... AndrewTinkler —
(S E H Sherwood) *fell 2nd* **40/1**

5-60 **P** **Konker**[28] [2323] 10-10-12 88 .... MarkNicolls(5) —
(J R Cornwall) *chsd ldrs: hit 6th: sn wknd* **100/1**

5-P5 **P** **Greenawn (IRE)**[13] [2620] 6-11-3 .... SamStronge —
(M Sheppard) *hld up: bhd whn hit 6th: t.o whn p.u bef 3 out* **100/1**

06-P **P** **Ashleybank House (IRE)**[12] [2660] 8-11-0 105 .... LeeVickers(3) —
(David Pearson) *chsd ldrs: j.lft 2nd: lost pl next: bhd fr 5th: t.o whn p.u bef 7th* **100/1**

4m 10.1s (5.10) **Going Correction** +0.375s/f (Yiel)
WFA 4 from 5yo+ 10lb **10** Ran SP% **113.1**
Speed ratings: **102,99,97,96,95** —,—,—,—,— CSF £18.49 TOTE £3.60: £1.50, £1.30, £3.80; EX 14.50.
Owner R A Bartlett **Bred** Mrs Margaret Flavin **Trained** Carrutherstown, D'fries & G'way

FOCUS
A decent novice chase run at a sound gallop with the winner value for more than the official margin and the third and fourth setting the level in a contest that should produce future winners.

NOTEBOOK
Villon(IRE), amking his chasing debut, was quick and efficient over his fences and cruised up to the leaders on the home turn and he won in good style. He stays further than two miles and has plenty of options in the coming months, but will be avoiding fast ground, having struggled on it in the Supreme Novices' Hurdle last season.
Roman Ark stepped up considerably on his chasing debut behind Cerium last month. He was slightly outpaced around the home turn, but stayed on steadily and was clear second best without troubling the winner. He should win his share of races. *(op 11-2)*
Muhtenbar, who fell on his chasing debut, jumped well up with the pace before weakening in the closing stages. He looks progressive, having achieved more here than he was entitled to do on hurdle ratings with the first two. *(op 20-1)*
Sharp Rigging(IRE), dropped in trip following a decent chasing debut, ran well enough but only paid for his early exuberance in this testing ground going to the last. If settling better he can prove as good over fences as he did over hurdles. *(tchd 13-2)*
Tamarinbleu(FR) did not jumps as well as he had done on his debut, when just caught by Accordion Etoile at Cheltenham last month. He seems best when fresh and was not seen to best effect on this testing ground, and can win decent races if given plenty of time between races. *(tchd 11-10, 6-5 in places)*
Oh Golly Gosh ran a fine race for a four-year-old, still being in the mix when hitting four out and getting rid of his jockey at the next. He is very unexposed but he still has stamina to prove.

2862 DAVID FITZGERALD MEMORIAL H'CAP HURDLE (14 hdls) 3m
2:30 (2:30) (Class 4) (0-110,109) 4-Y-0+ **£4,313** (£1,266; £633; £316)

Form RPR

-215 **1** **Moustique De L'Isle (FR)**[19] [2529] 5-11-2 99 ....(b[1]) NoelFehily 112+
(C C Bealby) *w ldrs: led 2nd to 3rd: led 3 out: drew clr between last 2* **13/2**[3]

U-11 **2** 11 **Young Lorcan**[22] [2465] 9-9-13 89 .... RichardSpate(7) 90+
(Mrs K Waldron) *hld up and bhd: reminder and hdwy 8th: styd on to take 2nd last: no ch of getting anywhere nr wnr* **5/2**[1]

21/6 **3** nk **Euradream (IRE)**[29] [2296] 7-11-8 105 .... JamesDavies 106
(Jean-Rene Auvray) *hld up in rr-div: hdwy 4th: sn chsng ldrs: wandered appr 3 out: kpt on fr next* **12/1**

50-0 **4** 9 **Smeathe's Ridge**[48] [1921] 7-10-2 85 .... WayneHutchinson 79+
(J A B Old) *in rr: hdwy 8th: rdn appr 3 out: no imp* **12/1**

023F **5** 7 **Ask The Umpire (IRE)**[7] [2748] 10-10-9 92 ....(b) HenryOliver 82+
(N E Berry) *trckd ldrs: led appr 3 out: sn blnd and hdd: 2nd and btn whn mstke 2 out: wknd* **20/1**

3345 **6** 19 **The Flyer (IRE)**[13] [2621] 8-11-11 108 ....(t) JimmyMcCarthy 74
(Miss S J Wilton) *in rr: reminders 2nd: sn drvn along: hdwy into mid-field 4th: lost pl after 8th* **16/1**

5-P0 **7** 8 **Ironside (IRE)**[20] [2505] 6-11-0 97 .... MarkBradburne 55
(H D Daly) *led to 3rd: chsd ldrs: lost pl 8th* **25/1**

P1-3 **8** 1 ¾ **General Gossip (IRE)**[227] [168] 9-11-5 109 .... SeanQuinlan(7) 65
(R T Phillips) *hld up in rr: hdwy 6th: lost pl after 8th* **9/2**[2]

/1FP **9** 2 **Infini (FR)**[35] [2170] 9-10-11 104 .... MichaelO'Connell(10) 58
(Mrs S J Smith) *w ldrs: led 4th: qcknd 7th: hdd appr 3 out: sn lost pl* **33/1**

F136 **10** 6 **Bustisu**[20] [2505] 8-9-13 89 .... RyanCummings(7) 37
(D J Wintle) *in rr: drvn along and reluctant after 7th: sn bhd* **25/1**

0-04 **11** dist **Starry Mary**[22] [2466] 7-9-12 86 oh2 ow3 ....(p) MarkNicolls(5) —
(R J Price) *in rr: reminders 7th: t.o 9th* **12/1**

-30P **P** **Be Telling (IRE)**[18] [2556] 6-10-7 90 .... PaulMoloney —
(B J Curley) *bhd whn p.u bef 9th* **20/1**

50PR **P** **Idlewild (IRE)**[56] [1819] 10-10-7 95 .... AdamPogson(5) —
(C T Pogson) *in tch: lost pl 4th: wl bhd 6th: t.o whn p.u bef 8th* **66/1**

2U0/ **P** **Ocean Tide**[43] [3843] 8-10-12 95 ....(v) TonyDobbin —
(R Ford) *chsd ldrs: drvn along 8th: lost pl next: bhd whn p.u bef 3 out* **8/1**

P-1P **P** **Brisbane Road (IRE)**[14] [2610] 8-10-5 95 ....(bt) MrRMcCarthy(7) —
(B J Llewellyn) *chsd ldrs to 3rd: reminders and lost pl next: t.o whn p.u after 7th* **66/1**

6m 35.6s (30.60) **Going Correction** +0.925s/f (Soft) **15** Ran SP% **123.3**
Speed ratings: **86,82,82,79,76 70,67,67,66,64** —,—,—,—,— CSF £22.19 CT £199.20 TOTE £7.80: £2.30, £1.70, £4.00; EX 29.60.
Owner Michael Hill **Bred** Philippe Sayet **Trained** Barrowby, Lincs
■ Stewards' Enquiry : Michael O'Connell three-day ban: improper riding - failing to pull up an exhausted horse (Dec 27-29)

FOCUS
Another severe test of stamina that few really handled, despite a very moderate winning time. The runner-up and fourth were close to their marks and set the level.

NOTEBOOK
Moustique De L'Isle(FR), a winning chaser on heavy ground, was backed on this return to hurdles with blinkers fitted. He came clear up the straight to take advantage of his lower hurdle rating and his stamina proved a major asset.\n\x\x He has performed best on similarly heavy ground but connections feel his fluent action suggests he is equally effective on a sounder surface\n *(op 10-1)*
Young Lorcan, who mixes hurdling with running over fences, was also coming back to hurdles in attempting a course hat-trick and had a more favourable mark to exploit. He was again held up but found plenty of trouble as he was kept to the inside rail. He made inroads turning for home but was tired by the run-in and only just held second. Tactics looked to be over-exaggerated but the impression was that he would not have given the winner a race if ridden closer to the pace. *(op 11-4 tchd 3-1 in places)*
Euradream(IRE) was always on the premises and ran another sound race seeing out the trip well enough, but the Handicapper has not eased him despite his 18-month absence and this second run back confirmed he needs some help from the assessor. *(op 14-1)*
Smeathe's Ridge had shown only moderate form, mainly at shorter trips, prior to this but the stamina test and the fact that his yard is in good form contributed to a performance that was close to his best. *(tchd 14-1)*
Ask The Umpire(IRE) travelled well for a long way before his stamina clearly ran out. *(op 25-1)*

2863 TRENTHAM GARDEN CONSERVATORIES H'CAP CHASE (FOR THE FRED DIXON MEMORIAL TROPHY) (18 fncs) 3m
3:00 (3:01) (Class 4) (0-105,105) 5-Y-0+ **£4,973** (£1,460; £730; £364)

Form RPR

4-5P **1** **Major Benefit (IRE)**[20] [2502] 8-11-5 105 .... RichardSpate(7) 125+
(Mrs K Waldron) *chsd ldrs: led 8th: clr 3 out: comf* **20/1**

4-54 **2** 14 **Full On**[43] [2011] 8-11-1 94 .... NoelFehily 96+
(A M Hales) *nt jump wl: hld up: hdwy 9th: hit next: chsd wnr 4 out: hit next: sn wknd* **16/1**

2146 **3** 2 **Southerndown (IRE)**[24] [2424] 12-10-3 82 .... AlanO'Keeffe 80
(R Lee) *hld up: mstke 4th: hdwy 5 out: nt rch ldrs* **33/1**

PP0 **4** 3 **Rosses Point (IRE)**[17] [2564] 6-10-0 79 oh2 ....(p) PaulMoloney 74
(Evan Williams) *prom: chsd wnr 11th to 4 out: wknd after next* **14/1**

3123 **5** 2 **Anflora**[29] [2282] 8-9-9 79 oh3 .... StephenCraine(5) 72
(B J Llewellyn) *hld up: hdwy 11th: wknd after 3 out* **13/2**[2]

P-00 **6** 21 **Celtic Pride (IRE)**[36] [2143] 10-11-7 100 ....(v) JohnMcNamara 72
(Jennie Candlish) *led 2nd to 8th: wknd appr 4 out* **20/1**

0-06 **7** ½ **Zimbabwe (FR)**[14] [2610] 5-10-2 88 ....(p) KeiranBurke(7) 60
(N J Hawke) *chsd ldrs: j.lft 2nd: mstke 8th: blnd 13th: sn wknd* **16/1**

364- **8** 1 ¼ **Jackem (IRE)**[272] [4449] 11-10-11 90 .... WayneHutchinson 60
(Ian Williams) *hld up: effrt appr 5 out: sn wknd* **25/1**

24-5 **9** 3 **Dalus Park (IRE)**[20] [2502] 10-10-12 96 .... MrSMorris(5) 63
(C C Bealby) *hld up: rdn after 10th: a bhd* **9/1**

3533 **10** 2 ½ **Good Potential (IRE)**[18] [2556] 9-10-9 88 ....(t) WarrenMarston 53
(D J Wintle) *hld up: rdn 10th: a bhd* **14/1**

4PP- **F** **Gaye Dream**[288] [4134] 7-10-6 85 .... JasonMaguire —
(T R George) *hld up: hdwy 10th: fell next* **14/1**

-241 **P** **Cool Song**[24] [2424] 9-9-11 79 oh5 .... ColinBolger(3) —
(Miss Suzy Smith) *prom: hit 4th: wknd 11th: t.o whn p.u bef 4 out* **8/1**[3]

24-P **P** **Be Upstanding**[222] [240] 10-10-4 88 ....(p) ThomasDreaper(5) —
(Ferdy Murphy) *hld up: bhd fr 8th: t.o whn p.u bef 5 out* **10/1**

P-42 **P** **To The Future (IRE)**[24] [2413] 9-10-5 84 .... AlanDempsey —
(A Parker) *prom: msiatke 12th: sn wknd: t.o whn p.u bef 3 out* **10/1**

636- **P** **Potoffairies (IRE)**[339] [3316] 10-10-9 88 ....(b) TonyDobbin —
(Mrs S A Bramall, Ire) *prom: wknd qckly 10th: bhd whn p.u bef next* **12/1**

000 **P** **Sidcup's Gold (IRE)**[13] 2619 5-10-12 **94**........................ OwynNelmes(3) —
(M Sheppard) *prom: mstke and lost pl 7th: bhd fr 11th: t.o whn p.u bef 3 out* **40/1**

3524 **P** **Sir Cumference**[24] 2424 9-10-13 **97**................................(b) PaulO'Neill(5) —
(Miss Venetia Williams) *led: hdd and hmpd 2nd: mstke 4th: blnd and wknd 5 out: bhd whn p.u bef next* **6/1**[1]

6m 39.4s (6.90) **Going Correction** +0.375s/f (Yiel) **17** Ran SP% **125.1**
Speed ratings: **103,98,97,96,96 89,88,88,87,86** —,—,—,—,— —,— CSF £295.24 CT £10082.09 TOTE £30.90: £4.60, £5.20, £8.90, £3.70; EX 509.20.

Owner Nick Shutts **Bred** Robert McCarthy **Trained** Stoke Bliss, Worcs

FOCUS

A moderate race but another soundly-run contest considering the conditions. The form is not easy to rate, but the winner is value for more than the official margin.

NOTEBOOK

Major Benefit(IRE), carrying top weight, took over before halfway and turned this into a procession. He was able to coast in the straight and in being eased up the run-in the official margin did not do him justice. *Official explanation: trainer said, regarding the improved form shown, gelding was better suited by today's slower ground and by being able to race prominently*

Full On hardly jumped a fence, being very awkward in the last mile, and did well to finish where he did. He is easing to the bottom of the ratings and if able to brush up his jumping can take full advantage.

Southerndown(IRE) was well behind at halfway but made headway down the back straight and ran strongly to the line on ground that was not certain to suit, having shown his best form on a sounder surface. He needs even further and his stamina was clearly a factor. *(op 25-1)*

Rosses Point(IRE), a maiden making his handicap debut, did well to finish so close having made a bad mistake down the back straight. He has not shown much but is lightly raced and on this showing can win a modest staying handicap.

Anflora, who has run well on similar ground this autumn, would be interesting against her own sex but there are few races over this sort of trip in that division. *(op 6-1)*

Good Potential(IRE) *Official explanation: jockey said gelding finished lame*

Cool Song *Official explanation: jockey said gelding pulled up lame (tchd 13-2)*

Sir Cumference *Official explanation: trainer's representative said gelding finished lame (tchd 13-2)*

2864 ROBERT TAYLOR ON BEHALF OF CDC-LIMITED.CO.UK NH FLAT RACE (FOR CONDITIONALS AND AMATEURS) 2m

3:30 (3:35) (Class 6) 4-6-Y-O **£2,007** (£585; £292)

Form RPR

1 **Baron Romeo (IRE)**[306] 5-10-11 .... SeanQuinlan(7) 108+
(R T Phillips) *hld up: hdwy 6f out: led over 3f out: rdn over 1f out: rn green: styd on* **6/1**

2 **2** *½* **Kealshore Lad**[34] 2192 4-10-13 .... DougieCostello(5) 103
(G M Moore) *led 4f: chsd ldrs: ev ch over 3f out: rdn over 1f out: styd on* **5/1**[3]

5 **3** *6* **Le Briar Soul (IRE)**[27] 2340 5-10-11 .... MrJJDoyle(7) 98+
(V R A Dartnall) *plld hrd and prom: chsd ldr 10f out: outpcd 3f out: rallied over 1f out: wknd ins fnl f* **4/1**[2]

3- **4** *10* **Lord Kernow (IRE)**[253] 4760 5-11-1 .... OwynNelmes(3) 87
(C J Down) *hld up in tch: rdn over 3f out: sn wknd* **25/1**

5 *12* **Mange Tout (IRE)** 6-11-1 .... TJPhelan(3) 75
(K J Burke) *hld up: hdwy 6f out: wknd over 3f out* **14/1**

6 *2 ½* **Flemens River (IRE)** 4-11-1 .... TomMalone(3) 73
(C J Down) *got loose prior to r: hld up: nvr nrr* **40/1**

0- **7** *1 ½* **Where's Sally**[286] 4172 5-10-4 .... MrGTumelty(7) 64
(J Mackie) *hld up: plld hrd: hdwy to ld 12f out: clr 10f out: hdd & wknd over 3f out* **25/1**

2 **8** *2* **Deep Moon (IRE)**[20] 2507 5-10-11 .... MrJJarrett(7) 69
(Miss H C Knight) *hld up: hdwy 7f out: wknd over 4f out* **11/4**[1]

9 *16* **Harpurs Girl** 4-10-4 .... PhilKinsella(7) 46
(J Mackie) *hld up: hdwy 5f out: sn wknd* **25/1**

0 **10** *shd* **Lindamarie (IRE)**[23] 2446 4-10-4 .... TomMessenger(7) 46
(C C Bealby) *chsd ldrs 6f* **33/1**

5 **11** *9* **Grand Slam Hero (IRE)**[44] 1985 4-10-13 .... StephenCraine(5) 44
(P Bowen) *mid-div: plld hrd: rdn and wknd over 6f out* **14/1**

6 **12** *25* **Tooka**[222] 242 4-10-13 .... RobertStephens(5) 19
(J Gallagher) *hld up: a in rr* **50/1**

13 *9* **Guess What**[264] 5-10-11 .... MrMSollitt(7) 10
(Mrs S J Smith) *chsd ldrs: rdn 1/2-way: wknd over 5f out* **40/1**

320 **14** *19* **Back With A Bang (IRE)**[113] 1323 6-10-13 .... PaulO'Neill(5) —
(Mrs N S Evans) *chsd ldrs 10f* **10/1**

15 *19* **Lord Saxbury**[216] 6-10-8 .... ThomasBurrows(10) —
(P L Clinton) *chsd ldrs 6f* **50/1**

4m 15.7s (15.90) **Going Correction** +0.925s/f (Soft) **15** Ran SP% **123.3**
Speed ratings: **97,96,93,88,82 81,80,79,71,71 67,54,50,40,31** CSF £33.80 TOTE £7.50: £3.80, £2.00, £1.40; EX 29.90 Place 6 £ 390.81, Place 5 £40.40.

Owner Mrs R J Skan **Bred** Michael F Condon **Trained** Adlestrop, Gloucs

FOCUS

Another steadily-run bumper but the winner looks better than the official margin with the third setting the level.

NOTEBOOK

Baron Romeo(IRE), a winning Irish pointer, looked set to stroll clear early in the straight but he idled and/or ran green and had to be ridden out, at the same time suggesting there was something left even though it was getting tight in the final 100 yards. *(op 5-1)*

Kealshore Lad, who does not impress in his slower paces, did nothing wrong in finishing second again. He rallied to chase the winner all the way and looks a staying prospect *(op 6-1)*

Le Briar Soul(IRE) ran a similar race to the runner-up, but both are slightly flattered with the winner idling.However, he still finished well clear of the remainder. *(op 10-3)*

Lord Kernow(IRE), making his seasonal reappearance having raced on fast ground on his sole previous bumper outing, made the running without threatening to land a telling blow.

Mange Tout(IRE), a half-brother to Your A Gassman from the family of Addington Boy, took a strong grip against the early crawl and can build on this debut, although he will probably not be seen at his best until tackling fences. *(tchd 11-1)*

Flemens River(IRE), from the family of staying chaser Father Dowling, was green to post having *unshipped his jockey and jogged loose, but showed some promise on this racecourse debut. (op 33-1)*

Where's Sally kicked clear down the back straight but tired once in line for home. She may do better against her own sex. *Official explanation: jockey said mare ran too keenly*

Deep Moon(IRE), a chasing type, travelled well towards the back of the pack but could not find the pace to get competitive in the last five furlongs. *(tchd 3-1)*

T/Plt: £622.50 to a £1 stake. Pool: £42,300.25. 49.60 winning tickets. T/Qpdt: £64.70 to a £1 stake. Pool: £4,111.60. 47.00 winning tickets. CR

[2322] WINDSOR (R-H)

Friday, December 16

OFFICIAL GOING: Good to soft

With Saturday's card abandoned and Ascot reopening next year, this might well have been Windsor's last ever jumps meeting.

Wind: Fresh behind Weather: Sunny becoming cold

2865 ATTHERACES.COM "NATIONAL HUNT" MAIDEN HURDLE (DIV I) (10 hdls) 2m 4f

12:30 (12:30) (Class 4) 4-Y-0+ **£3,298** (£968; £484; £241)

Form RPR

1 **Pedros Brief (IRE)**[254] 4743 7-11-0 .... RobertThornton 114+
(R T Phillips) *tall: str: lw: mde all: pressed 2 out: shkn up and drew clr fr last* **13/2**

34 **2** *3 ½* **Aztec Warrior (IRE)**[19] 2534 4-11-0 .... TimmyMurphy 109+
(Miss H C Knight) *lw: hld up: prog to trck ldrs 6th: outpcd next: gd hdwy again 3 out: tried to chal 2 out: btn last: kpt on* **7/2**[2]

2 **3** *5* **Art Virginia (FR)**[41] 2049 6-11-0 .... MickFitzgerald 105+
(N J Henderson) *prom: chsd wnr 6th to 7th: drvn to chal 2 out: wknd and mstke last* **10/3**[1]

4 *23* **Witness Run (IRE)**[48] 5-11-0 .... LeightonAspell 83+
(N J Gifford) *rangy: lw: wl in tch: prog to trck wnr 7th: rdn and wknd after 3 out: mstke 2 out* **4/1**[3]

0 **5** *29* **Candlelight Valley (IRE)**[29] 2301 6-11-0 .... RichardJohnson 52
(P J Hobbs) *bit bkwd: t.k.h: mstke 2nd: prom: lost pl 6th: struggling and btn 3 out* **12/1**

50/ **6** *12* **Bosworth Gypsy (IRE)**[706] 3285 7-10-7 .... JamieGoldstein 33
(Miss J S Davis) *in tch to 6th: wl adrift of ldrs bef 3 out* **100/1**

3130 **7** *11* **Mr Ex (ARG)**[26] 2374 4-10-9 .... JamieMoore 24
(G L Moore) *hld up in rr: lost tch after 6th: t.o after next: plodded on* **16/1**

4 **8** *5* **Hambaphambili**[32] 2242 5-11-0 .... TomDoyle 24
(O Sherwood) *bit bkwd: a wl in rr: lost tch fr 7th: wl bhd next* **22/1**

0 **9** *6* **Loose Morals (IRE)**[41] 2056 4-10-7 .... BarryFenton 11
(Miss E C Lavelle) *stdd s: t.k.h and sn trckd wnr to 6th: wknd and eased bef 3 out* **40/1**

2-20 **10** *14* **Earl Of Forestry (GER)**[36] 2152 4-11-0 .... ChristianWilliams —
(P F Nicholls) *lw: prom tl wknd after 7th: wl bhd 3 out* **15/2**

P **Tigu (IRE)** 4-11-0 .... JimCrowley —
(A Ennis) *in tch to 5th: sn wknd: t.o after next: p.u bef 2 out* **100/1**

0-0 **P** **Murotoevation (IRE)**[12] 2665 6-11-0 .... VinceSlattery —
(D G Bridgwater) *nt jump wl: t.o fr 5th: ms bhd whn p.u bef 3 out* **100/1**

0- **U** **Allborn Lad (IRE)**[344] 3238 5-11-0 .... BrianCrowley —
(C J Mann) *blnd 4th: chsd ldrs to 6th: sn struggling: disputing 30l 5th whn blnd and uns rdr 2 out* **40/1**

5m 6.90s (5.20) **Going Correction** +0.55s/f (Soft) **13** Ran SP% **116.2**
Speed ratings: **111,109,107,98,86 82,77,75,73,67** —,—,— CSF £28.35 TOTE £7.60: £2.40, £1.90, £1.60; EX 40.00.

Owner Mr & Mrs F C Welch **Bred** Peter Sherry **Trained** Adlestrop, Gloucs

FOCUS

They went steadily early, though the pace picked up and it ended up with a decent winning time for a race like this, 5.7 seconds faster than the second division. The contest only concerned the front four in the market from a long way out and the form looks decent rated through the placed horses.

NOTEBOOK

Pedros Brief(IRE) ◆, winner of a point and a bumper in Ireland, was making his British debut following an eight-month break. Allowed an uncontested lead from the start, he found plenty when eventually pressed and ran out a clear winner. He looks a useful recruit and should win more races over hurdles, though it is likely that chasing will eventually be his game. *(op 7-1 tchd 6-1)*

Aztec Warrior(IRE), making his hurdling debut after showing ability in a couple of bumpers, had moved into a challenging position on the long run approaching the second last but the winner kept on finding more and he could make little impression. He has a future at this game, but may need a stiffer test than this. *(tchd 4-1)*

Art Virginia(FR), another making his hurdling debut, appeared to have every chance coming to the second last but was firmly put in his place by the front pair and there seemed to be no real excuses. *(op 5-2 tchd 7-2)*

Witness Run(IRE), winner of an Irish point and yet another making his hurdling debut, had every chance jumping three from home. He was the first of the leading quartet to fold, however, and the way he then stopped very quickly was slightly worrying. Even though his last outing in Ireland was at the end of October, perhaps he just needed it. *(op 7-2)*

Candlelight Valley(IRE) was beaten a very long way and achieved little. *(op 16-1)*

Earl Of Forestry(GER), well backed for this hurdling debut, was easily beaten off and this was another disappointing effort. *(op 8-1 tchd 10-1 and 7-1)*

2866 ATTHERACES.COM "NATIONAL HUNT" MAIDEN HURDLE (DIV II) (10 hdls) 2m 4f

1:00 (1:03) (Class 4) 4-Y-0+ **£3,288** (£965; £482; £241)

Form RPR

6-0 **1** **Kaldouas (FR)**[33] 2211 4-11-0 .... ChristianWilliams 103+
(P F Nicholls) *lw: hld up in midfield: mstke 3rd: prog to trck ldrs 6th: rdn to ld narrowly 2 out: drvn and styd on wl flat* **7/4**[1]

3-F6 **2** *1 ½* **Boberelle (IRE)**[50] 1898 5-10-7 .... TomDoyle 94+
(C Tinkler) *wl plcd: effrt 3 out: rdn and mstke 2 out: sn chsd wnr: chal flat: no imp last 100yds* **7/1**

2 **3** *7* **Ballyshan (IRE)**[19] 2527 7-11-0 .... CarlLlewellyn 95+
(N A Twiston-Davies) *lw: w ldrs: str reminder after 6th: drvn 3 out: kpt on one pce* **5/1**[3]

33-5 **4** *2* **Original Thought (IRE)**[19] 2528 5-11-0 .... MickFitzgerald 91
(B De Haan) *lw: mde most to 7th: stl cl up 2 out: fdd u.p* **9/2**[2]

050 **5** *½* **My Rosie Ribbons (IRE)**[8] 2718 6-10-0 .... MrMWall(7) 84
(B W Duke) *cl up: lost pl 7th: rdn 3 out: nt rch ldrs after: kpt on* **50/1**

3-64 **6** *7* **Follow Your Heart (IRE)**[18] 2554 5-11-0 .... TimmyMurphy 88+
(N J Gifford) *racd wd: w ldrs: led 7th: hdd and mstke 2 out: wknd* **8/1**

5-1 **7** *14* **Gentleman Jimmy**[36] 2152 5-11-0 .... JimCrowley 70
(H Morrison) *lw: w ldrs tl wknd fr 3 out* **8/1**

45-0 **8** *10* **Classic Ruby**[49] 1903 5-10-2 ....(v[1]) JamesDiment(5) 63+
(M R Bosley) *lw: mstkes in rr: lost tch w ldng gp 7th: prog next: nvr on terms: abt 15l 7th at last: virtually p.u: dismntd* **100/1**

9 *29* **Gneeve Hill (IRE)**[613] 4809 7-11-0 .... LeightonAspell 31
(O Sherwood) *tall: str: wl in tch: mstke 5th: mstke 7th and wknd: t.o* **22/1**

00/ **10** *3 ½* **Blind Smart (IRE)**[919] 617 7-10-7 .... CharliePoste(7) 27
(M F Harris) *a towards rr: lost tch fr 7th: t.o* **100/1**

00-P **11** *5* **Ben Belleshot**[12] 2663 6-11-0 .... MatthewBatchelor 22
(P W Hiatt) *settled in last: mstke 2nd: lost tch fr 5th: t.o* **100/1**

5 **12** *dist* **Bally Rainey (IRE)**[16] 2579 6-11-0 .... BenjaminHitchcott —
(Mrs L C Jewell) *w ldrs tl wknd rapidly 6th: t.o* **66/1**

0P/ **P** **O Cinza (IRE)**[694] 3447 7-10-9 .... JohnnyLevins(5) —
(B G Powell) *wl in tch to 5th: wknd rapidly: t.o whn p.u bef 7th: dismntd* **66/1**

P **P** **Ballykiln (IRE)**[46] 1950 4-11-0 .... SamThomas —
(Miss H C Knight) *bit bkwd: terrible blunder 1st: in tch to 6th: sn bhd: t.o whn p.u bef 2 out* **50/1**

5m 12.6s (10.90) **Going Correction** +0.55s/f (Soft) **14** Ran SP% **120.2**
Speed ratings: **100,99,96,95,95 92,87,83,71,70 68,—,—,—** CSF £14.41 TOTE £2.50: £1.30, £3.10, £1.70; EX 22.50.
Owner J Hales **Bred** Mme Evelyne Van Haaren **Trained** Ditcheat, Somerset
■ Stewards' Enquiry : Carl Llewellyn caution: used whip arm from above shoulder height

FOCUS
The winning time was 5.7 seconds slower than the first division and the form looks pretty ordinary, but there were still a couple of interesting types for the future.

NOTEBOOK
Kaldouas(FR) ◆, who showed some promise in two bumpers without setting the world alight, found this a totally different kettle of fish. A massive gelding, he dwarfed the mare in their battle over the last couple of flights and was always doing just enough. Whatever more he achieves over hurdles, he is really going to come into his own over fences. *(op 9-4)*
Boberelle(IRE), on much easier ground than at Taunton, ran better but she is only tiny and so big is the winner that it made her look like a rabbit taking on a buffalo. She lost nothing in defeat, but her best chance of winning over hurdles may be in races confined to her own sex. *(op 10-1)*
Ballyshan(IRE) was inclined to run in snatches and though he was not at all disgraced in the circumstances, he will probably need to go up in trip in order to break his duck. *(op 10-3)*
Original Thought(IRE), stepping up half a mile in trip, ran with plenty of credit under a positive ride and was not beaten off until after jumping the second last. There should be a novice hurdle in him. *(tchd 4-1)*
My Rosie Ribbons(IRE) did not duplicate her errant performance at Huntingdon and once again showed that she is not completely without ability.
Follow Your Heart(IRE), kept wide of his rivals, was disputing second place when ploughing through the second last and ending any remote chance he may have had. He now qualifies for a handicap mark and that may be a better option. *(op 9-1)*

2867 SPORTING INDEX NOVICES' H'CAP CHASE (12 fncs) 2m
1:30 (1:32) (Class 4) (0-105,105) 4-Y-0+ **£4,124** (£1,210; £605; £302)

Form RPR

1111 **1** **Jolly Boy (FR)**[4] 2801 6-10-4 **83** 7ex .... (b) SamThomas 97+
(Miss Venetia Williams) *lw: lft in ld after 3rd: mde rest: in command after 3 out: eased flat* **8/11**[1]

404F **2** *6* **Buffalo Bill (IRE)**[8] 2719 9-11-10 **103** .... RobertThornton 109+
(A M Hales) *wl in tch: chsd wnr and blnd 8th: only danger 3 out: sn no imp and easily hld* **16/1**

-5P6 **3** *8* **Flying Patriarch**[16] 2578 4-10-4 **93** .... (p) JamieMoore 77
(G L Moore) *prom: chsd wnr after 3rd to 8th: bdly outpcd 3 out: plugged on : j.lft last* **14/1**

-512 **4** *5* **Touch Of Fate**[15] 2592 6-11-7 **100** .... BrianCrowley 91+
(R Rowe) *in tch: blnd 6th and dropped to last: lost tch 9th: plugged on* **7/1**[3]

5PPP **5** *10* **Rutland (IRE)**[14] 2605 6-9-7 **79** oh3 .... RobertLucey-Butler(7) 61+
(C J Drewe) *in tch in rr: outpcd fr 8th: no ch whn hmpd next* **66/1**

0F6F **R** **Sunley Future (IRE)**[8] 2722 6-10-12 **98** .... CharliePoste(7) —
(M F Harris) *set off at furious pce: w ldr whn rn out 2nd* **33/1**

450- **F** **Roznic (FR)**[267] 4533 7-11-3 **96** .... PhilipHide —
(P Winkworth) *in tch: effrt after 8th: disputing 2nd and in tch whn fell next* **14/1**

03P- **P** **Raven's Last**[353] 3053 6-11-12 **105** .... RichardJohnson —
(R T Phillips) *lw: set off at furious pce: led and blnd 1st: rdr lost reins: lft clr 2nd: nrly rn out bnd after 3rd: p.u bef next* **11/2**[2]

4m 11.5s (6.40) **Going Correction** +0.55s/f (Soft)
WFA 4 from 6yo+ 10lb **8** Ran SP% **109.4**
Speed ratings: **106,103,99,96,91 —,—,—** CSF £11.93 CT £80.70 TOTE £1.60: £1.10, £2.10, £2.10; EX 13.20.
Owner Favourites Racing **Bred** Georges Lacombe **Trained** Kings Caple, H'fords

FOCUS
A race full of drama, with the favourite colliding with a rival as the tape was released and two horses running out in separate incidents in the early stages. Even so, the final result was very predictable with the first two running to previous marks.

NOTEBOOK
Jolly Boy(FR), despite colliding with Sunley Future as the tape was released, found himself in front after the third fence thanks to all the shenanigans concerning both that rival and Raven's Last. He only had one rival to worry about from a long way out, but never looked in any real danger and completed the five-timer in great style. He has risen 19lb since the sequence started, but is now likely to be given a break. *(tchd 4-6, 4-5 in a place)*
Buffalo Bill(IRE) did his best to get on terms with the favourite over the final line of fences, but could never do so and there is still room for improvement in the jumping department. *(op 14-1)*
Flying Patriarch, making his chasing debut, may not have achieved much and is yet to win a race, but he is still young enough to improve a bit with experience. *(tchd 12-1)*
Touch Of Fate, another making his chasing debut, has been running well over hurdles lately but did not jump well enough even allowing for this trip probably being too sharp. *(op 6-1)*
Roznic(FR), another switching to fences, was still battling away for second when crashing out at the fourth last. *(tchd 16-1)*
Raven's Last, trying fences for the first time, basically bolted as the tape went across and took the first fence by the roots. Unfortunately in doing so he managed to get the reins wrapped around his off-fore and, with no steering as a result, he crashed into the rail by the paddock exit and sustained a very nasty-looking cut before he was able to be pulled up. *Official explanation: jockey said gelding blundered and lost reins at first fence (tchd 16-1)*
Sunley Future(IRE), after colliding with the favourite as the tape went across, seemed to get lit up by Raven's Last bolting and decided to go with him. Unfortunately, he decided he did not want to jump the second fence and swerved past it. *Official explanation: jockey said saddle slipped (tchd 16-1)*

2868 EXECUTIVE HIRE NEWS H'CAP HURDLE (10 hdls) 2m 4f
2:05 (2:05) (Class 4) (0-110,108) 5-Y-0+ **£3,438** (£1,009; £504; £252)

Form RPR

63-P **1** **Silkwood Top (IRE)**[45] 1973 6-10-9 **91** .... (p) MickFitzgerald 101+
(V R A Dartnall) *trckd ldrs: prog 3 out: rdn to chse ldr bef next: narrow ld last: drvn out* **5/1**[1]

5500 **2** *1 ½* **Kadam (IRE)**[8] 2733 5-11-9 **105** .... (b) ChristianWilliams 111
(P F Nicholls) *lw: led 5th: mde most after: kicked on after 3 out: hdd last: kpt on wl flat* **20/1**

-201 **3** *11* **Assoon**[16] 2576 6-11-9 **105** .... (b[1]) JamieMoore 100
(G L Moore) *lw: trckd ldrs: hit 4th: rdn bef 3 out: outpcd bef 2 out: kpt on* **10/1**

PF-P **4** *1 ¼* **Chanticlier**[14] 2609 8-11-9 **105** .... (t) RobertThornton 99+
(R T Phillips) *hld up wl in rr: stdy prog bef 3 out but nvr on terms: shkn up 2 out: wnt 4th last: rdn and styd on flat: do bttr* **16/1**

0400 **5** *2 ½* **Honey's Gift**[10] 2685 6-11-0 **103** .... LiamHeard(7) 94
(G G Margarson) *hld up in midfield: rdn and effrt 3 out: sn outpcd: one pce fr 2 out* **20/1**

0161 **6** *hd* **Pardon What**[18] 2556 9-11-10 **106** .... (b) RJGreene 100+
(S Lycett) *stmbld bdly 2nd: wl in rr and nt gng wl: effrt u.p 7th: plugged on: n.d* **10/1**

5-03 **7** *nk* **Maximinus**[29] 2296 5-11-1 **97** .... JamieGoldstein 89+
(M Madgwick) *lw: chsd ldrs: mstke 6th: u.p and btn after 3 out: mstke 2 out* **6/1**[2]

-P5P **8** *6* **Gan Eagla (IRE)**[35] 2166 6-11-9 **105** .... (b) SamThomas 91+
(Miss Venetia Williams) *racd freely: led to 5th: w ldr to 3 out: wknd next* **12/1**

23-4 **9** *5* **Le Rochelais (FR)**[13] 2619 6-11-12 **108** .... AndrewThornton 90+
(R H Alner) *lw: hld up midfield: brief effrt after 7th: pushed along and no prog after 3 out: nvr nr ldrs* **7/1**[3]

6-PP **10** *3* **Alpha Gamble (IRE)**[18] 2556 5-11-1 **97** .... BrianCrowley 76+
(R Rowe) *lw: hld up in rr: gng wl enough but plenty to do bef 3 out: nvr on terms w ldrs after: blnd last: shkn up briefly flat* **12/1**

55-5 **11** *3* **M'Lord**[28] 2310 7-11-6 **102** .... (t) BenjaminHitchcott 76
(J A Geake) *j. bdly rt 2nd: in tch: effrt after 7th: struggling whn blnd 3 out: wknd* **17/2**

0-00 **12** *dist* **Galant Eye (IRE)**[14] 2609 6-10-6 **88** .... VinceSlattery —
(R J Baker) *in tch to 6th: sn bhd: t.o after next: btn 74l* **40/1**

400 **13** *7* **Dream Merchant (IRE)**[24] 2423 5-11-8 **104** .... RichardJohnson —
(P J Hobbs) *wl in tch: effrt 6th: wknd bef 3 out: t.o: btn 81l* **14/1**

0-00 **14** *6* **Batswing**[16] 2576 10-11-7 **103** .... PhilipHide —
(G L Moore) *in tch: nt gng wl after 4th: sn bhd: wl t.o fr 7th: btn 87l* **33/1**

P-FP **15** *1 ¾* **Galaxy Sam (USA)**[8] 2717 6-11-4 **100** .... (b[1]) LeightonAspell —
(N J Gifford) *lw: mstkes: prom to 6th: sn wknd: t.o: btn 89l* **14/1**

5m 12.3s (10.60) **Going Correction** +0.55s/f (Soft) **15** Ran SP% **121.7**
Speed ratings: **100,99,95,94,93 93,93,90,88,87 86,—,—,—,—** CSF £106.70 CT £981.06 TOTE £5.80: £2.30, £6.90, £3.40; EX 171.80.
Owner O C R Wynne & Mrs S J Wynne **Bred** Mrs Cecily Purcell **Trained** Brayford, Devon

FOCUS
An ordinary if competitive handicap in which the front two pulled well clear. The winner is value for further and the runner-up is rated to his mark.

NOTEBOOK
Silkwood Top(IRE), pulled up on his Exeter reappearance, was nonetheless very well backed for this. Given a patient ride, he was delivered with his effort after jumping the third last and came right away from the field along with the runner-up. There are not too many miles on the clock and he may be capable of a bit more. *Official explanation: trainer said, regarding the improved form shown, gelding was better suited by today's ground and trip, and was having its second run back after a long lay off (op 8-1)*
Kadam(IRE), back over hurdles, was always up with the pace and looked at one point as though he might have stolen it when establishing a decent advantage on the long run to the second last, but the winner proved just too strong for him despite his best efforts. He does look much happier over hurdles than fences and is capable of winning a race like this. *(op 16-1)*
Assoon, blinkered for the first time, is a notoriously hard ride and again came off the bridle a good seven furlongs from the finish. Unlike at Plumpton, his rider's persistence only helped him grab third at a respectable distance, but he still deserves a medal. *(tchd 11-1)*
Chanticlier, who has failed to complete in his last four starts, three of them over fences, was the eye-catcher of the race as he was never closer than at the line. The application of the tongue tie seemed to do him no harm and, as this was only his second outing for the yard, he is definitely one to keep an eye on.
Honey's Gift was not disgraced, but this trip is right on the limit of her stamina and as she has now been unplaced off this mark for four races in a row, she is surely entitled to drop a bit more.
Pardon What, raised 5lb for his Folkestone victory, was probably not helped by the drop in trip on this sharp track and never looked like taking a hand. *(op 8-1 tchd 7-1)*
Maximinus, whose last win came over course and distance 13 months ago off a 2lb lower mark, seemed to be hanging badly on the home bend and did not run his race this time. *(op 11-2)*
Gan Eagla(IRE) raced enthusiastically out in front and did well to hang on until the second last under the circumstances.

2869 ARENA LEISURE PLC NOVICES' CHASE (REGISTERED AS NOEL NOVICES' CHASE) GRADE 2 (14 fncs) 2m 4f
2:40 (2:40) (Class 1) 4-Y-0+ **£20,050** (£7,580; £3,842; £1,962; £1,031)

Form RPR

1S-1 **1** **The Listener (IRE)**[14] 2607 6-11-10 .... AndrewThornton 156+
(R H Alner) *lw: j.w: led 3rd: mde rest: drew clr fr 11th: impressive* **5/4**[1]

P-21 **2** *13* **Lord Killeshanra (IRE)**[28] 2311 6-11-10 .... JoeTizzard 138+
(C L Tizzard) *lw: settled in rr: prog 10th: outpcd and btn next: styd on to take 2nd after 2 out: no ch w wnr* **8/1**

-142 **3** *14* **Stance**[26] 2371 6-11-8 .... JamieMoore 127+
(G L Moore) *lw: t.k.h: hld up in tch: rdn 10th: sn struggling: no ch fr 3 out: tk 3rd nr fin* **12/1**

4 *1 ¾* **Turthen (FR)**[175] 837 4-10-13 .... ChristianWilliams 110
(P F Nicholls) *str: lw: cl up: disp 2nd fr 10th: no ch w wnr whn lft clr in 2nd 3 out: wknd after next* **3/1**[2]

P5 **5** *dist* **Deltic Arrow**[31] 2260 7-11-4 .... MrJAJenkins —
(D L Williams) *nt jump wl: t.o fr 6th: stl appr 2 out as wnr fin* **100/1**

4 **P** **No Full (FR)**[24] 2422 4-10-13 122 .... (p) MickFitzgerald —
(P R Webber) *led tl mstke 3rd: lost pl 9th: wl btn whn p.u bef 3 out* **40/1**

1-41 **F** **Mount Clerigo (IRE)**[22] 2464 7-11-4 .... RichardJohnson 131+
(V R A Dartnall) *lw: prom: mostly chsd wnr fr 7th: mstke 10th: disputing 2nd and btn whn fell 3 out* **4/1**[3]

5m 4.90s
WFA 4 from 6yo+ 11lb **7** Ran SP% **111.7**
CSF £11.52 TOTE £2.10: £1.50, £3.50; EX 9.50.
Owner Old Moss Farm **Bred** Daniel C And Patrick Keating **Trained** Droop, Dorset

FOCUS
Some decent novices on show in this, but the winner treated them with contempt and is value for more than the official margin with the runner-up close to form.

NOTEBOOK
The Listener(IRE) ◆, who created such a big impression when winning on his chasing debut at Exeter, was at least as impressive here and, after making the majority of the running, pulled right away from a decent field. The main point about this victory is how accurate his jumping was and that will always stand him in good stead, but he does appear to relish soft ground which may limit his options with the spring festivals in mind. Still, he stays much further than this and until then there should be plenty more decent chases to be won with him. *(op 11-8 tchd 6-5, 6-4 in places)*
Lord Killeshanra(IRE) probably found this trip too sharp, but even so he was taking on something a bit special in the winner and he achieved as much as could be expected under the circumstances. He will not always come across such a smart rival. *(op 7-1)*
Stance faced a stiff task in this field and only inherited third thanks to the misfortune of others. There should be more opportunities for him at a more modest level. *(tchd 9-1)*

Turthen(FR), a winner over hurdles and fences in France making his British debut, ran well for a long way but found taking on these rivals after a six-month break too much and he got very tired late on. He should strip fitter next time. *(op 11-4 tchd 7-2)*

Mount Clerigo(IRE) was close enough when a slow jump five from home seemed to put him on the back foot, and he was only fighting for second place when coming down at the third last. He probably needs a stiffer test than this. *(op 9-2 tchd 5-1)*

2870 MITIE CHRISTMAS H'CAP CHASE (14 fncs) 2m 4f

3:10 (3:10) (Class 3) (0-125,117) 5-Y-O+ **£6,857** (£2,013; £1,006; £502)

Form RPR

1P-2 **1** **Saintsaire (FR)**[236] 2 6-11-12 **117**.............................. MickFitzgerald 132+
(N J Henderson) *lw: hld up: nt fluent 2nd: prog to chal 3 out: led next: clr whn blnd last: comf* **1/1**[1]

P-24 **2** *9* **Macmar (FR)**[28] 2312 5-11-6 **111**.............................. AndrewThornton 114+
(R H Alner) *in tch in rr: rdn after 10th: rousted along and gd prog to ld bef 3 out: hdd 2 out: no ch w wnr after* **16/1**

5-33 **3** *8* **Neltina**[29] 2300 9-11-10 **115**.............................. LeightonAspell 109
(Mrs J E Scrase) *disp ld to 5th: styd prom: outpcd fr 3 out: n.d after* **10/3**[2]

520- **4** *6* **Jarro (FR)**[239] 4944 9-11-12 **117**.............................. SamThomas 106+
(Miss Venetia Williams) *t.k.h: prog to ld 5th: hdd bef 3 out: sn btn: j.lft last 2* **11/2**[3]

-B1P **5** *15* **Haafel (USA)**[16] 2577 8-11-6 **111**..............................(b) PhilipHide 90+
(G L Moore) *lw: disp ld to 5th: styd prom tl wknd 11th* **22/1**

231/ **P** **Inaki (FR)**[712] 3201 8-10-11 **102**..............................(b) BrianCrowley —
(P Winkworth) *bit bkwd: mstkes and often j.rt: in tch tl wknd after 10th: p.u bef 3 out* **16/1**

1F/P **P** **Be My Destiny (IRE)**[19] 2532 8-11-12 **117**.............................. TimmyMurphy —
(Miss H C Knight) *lw: hld up in last: mstke 2nd: lost tch 10th: wl bhd whn p.u bef 3 out* **11/1**

5m 9.40s **7** Ran SP% **112.9**
CSF £16.11 TOTE £1.80: £1.20, £4.90; EX 16.30.
Owner Anthony Speelman **Bred** Robert-Edmond Schwab & Philippe Lefevre **Trained** Upper Lambourn, Berks

FOCUS
Not the most competitive of handicaps and the time was 4.5 seconds slower than the novices in the previous race. The runner-up is the best guide to the form, which does not look that strong.

NOTEBOOK
Saintsaire(FR) ◆ is rated 23lb lower over fences than he is over hurdles, but that is because he has not being showing the same level of form. He seemed to face a straightforward task though and so it proved, his only moment of anguish coming when he hardly took off at the last with the race won. If this victory helps with his confidence, then he could still look a very well handicapped horse even after he has been reassessed. *(op 11-10 tchd 5-4 and 10-11, 6-4 in a place and 11--8 in places)*

Macmar(FR) was rushed right around the outside of the field to take it up after jumping the fourth last, but once the winner arrived on the scene there was nothing he could do about it. He may have been taking on a very well handicapped horse here and should be up to winning an ordinary handicap, but his best trip is still to be identified. *(op 12-1)*

Neltina, back up to a more suitable trip, might have been better off having more use made of her as she was keen enough in merely disputing the lead and was well and truly exposed for foot when the race started in earnest. *(op 3-1 tchd 7-2)*

Jarro(FR), who is yet to win over as far as this, was reappearing from an eight-month break. One of several to take a keen hold up with the pace, that severely limited his finishing effort but at least the run should have brought him on. *(op 9-2)*

Haafel(USA), with the blinkers back on, was another to do too much too soon over a trip possibly beyond his best. *(op 20-1)*

Inaki(FR) was off the same mark as when successful on his last start almost two years ago, but he jumped badly out to his right at several fences and eventually seemed to blow up. *(op 20-1)*

2871 Q EQUINE LTD H'CAP HURDLE (8 hdls) 2m

3:40 (3:41) (Class 3) (0-135,135) 4£16,795 (£4,960; £2,480; £1,240; £620)

Form RPR

1 **1** **Acambo (GER)**[22] 2455 4-10-9 **118**.............................. TimmyMurphy 130+
(M C Pipe) *lw: pckd 1st: hld up in last: stdy prog fr 4th: effrt 2 out: rdn to ld last: r.o wl* **15/2**[3]

/02- **2** *2* **Chief Yeoman**[405] 2050 5-11-12 **135**.............................. SamThomas 140
(Miss Venetia Williams) *hld up in tch: prog 5th: led sn after 3 out and gng strly: hdd last: outpcd flat* **16/1**

1U11 **3** *3 ½* **Desert Quest (IRE)**[6] 2765 5-10-5 **121** 7ex..............................(b) LiamHeard[(7)] 124+
(P F Nicholls) *hld up in midfield: smooth prog 3 out: rdn and nt qckn 2 out: one pce after* **7/4**[1]

0-51 **4** *2 ½* **Manorson (IRE)**[20] 2493 6-11-9 **132**.............................. LeightonAspell 132+
(O Sherwood) *pressed ldr: led bef 3 out to sn after 3 out: one pce after: mstke last* **8/1**

2-00 **5** *3* **Salut Saint Cloud**[33] 2207 4-11-4 **127**.............................. BrianCrowley 123
(G L Moore) *in tch: mstke 5th: sn rdn: struggling 3 out: effrt u.p bef next: kpt on* **25/1**

3-36 **6** *2 ½* **Cool Roxy**[21] 2483 8-11-0 **128**.............................. ChrisHonour[(5)] 122
(A G Blackmore) *chsd ldrs: mstke 4th: sn rdn: stl cl up bef 3 out: grad fdd* **66/1**

-622 **7** *5* **Silver Prophet (IRE)**[8] 2716 6-10-2 **111** ow1.............................. SeanCurran 102+
(M R Bosley) *prom: drvn and lost pl after 5th: no imp ldrs after* **16/1**

1-20 **8** *10* **Guru**[13] 2636 7-10-8 **117**.............................. PhilipHide 96
(G L Moore) *chsd ldrs: rdn bef 5th: struggling whn mstke 3 out: wknd* **8/1**

01-1 **9** *3 ½* **Priors Dale**[28] 2324 5-11-5 **128**.............................. BarryFenton 108+
(Miss E C Lavelle) *led: hdd bef 3 out: eased whn btn bef 2 out* **7/1**[2]

2-0F **10** *9* **Kalca Mome (FR)**[20] 2492 7-11-7 **130**.............................. RichardJohnson 106+
(P J Hobbs) *prom: rdn and wknd 3 out* **40/1**

00-P **11** *1 ½* **New Entic (FR)**[13] 2636 4-10-11 **120**.............................. JamieMoore 85
(G L Moore) *lw: hld up in rr: rdn after 5th: wknd 3 out* **50/1**

-F0F **12** *6* **Montevideo**[15] 2595 5-10-0 **109** oh3..............................(b) DJCasey 68
(Jonjo O'Neill) *prom tl wknd after 5th* **10/1**

-015 **13** *5* **Come Bye (IRE)**[33] 2218 9-10-3 **112**..............................(bt) MatthewBatchelor 66
(Miss A M Newton-Smith) *mstke 3rd: sn lost pl and struggling: t.o fr 5th* **100/1**

0-20 **F** **Frontier**[13] 2636 8-10-8 **117**..............................(t) OllieMcPhail —
(B J Llewellyn) *in tch to 4th: struggling whn fell next* **66/1**

-053 **P** **Arrayou (FR)**[7] 2746 4-10-11 **120**.............................. MickFitzgerald —
(O Sherwood) *lw: struggling in rr fr 4th: sn t.o: p.u bef 2 out* **9/1**

3m 55.0s (-4.20) **Going Correction** +0.55s/f (Soft)
WFA 4 from 5yo+ 10lb **15** Ran SP% **125.9**
Speed ratings: **112,111,109,108,106 105,102,97,96,91 90,87,85,—,—** CSF £118.28 CT £309.42 TOTE £7.00: £2.80, £5.00, £1.20; EX 122.30 Trifecta £585.90 Pool: £990.32 - 1.20 winning units. Place 6 £13.33, Place 5 £8.70.
Owner D A Johnson **Bred** A Groschler **Trained** Nicholashayne, Devon

FOCUS
A very competitive handicap hurdle run at a decent pace, but won by the least-exposed horse in the race. The form looks strong.

NOTEBOOK
Acambo(GER) ◆, given a typically confident Murphy ride, looked the likely winner from some way out and saw his race out in impression fashion. His victory in a Taunton maiden hurdle in his only previous outing over timber meant that the Handicapper had to apply a certain amount of guesswork to allocate his rating and, on this evidence, the mark he was given was lenient. He is likely to pay for it now, but we still do not know how much more there is to come from him. *(op 6-1)*

Chief Yeoman ◆, last seen finishing runner-up off a 7lb higher mark in the Grade Two Elite Hurdle at Wincanton 13 months ago, made a highly encouraging return to action and just bumped into an unexposed and progressive winner. He may need a little time to get over this, but should be winning again when he does.

Desert Quest(IRE), carrying a 7lb penalty in his hat-trick bid, was only 1lb higher than when winning his second race within the space of 48 hours six days previously. After travelling really well for most of the way, he was still on the bridle approaching two out, but once the gun was put to his head he found very little. His busy schedule may have caught up with him, but he is due to go up another 7lb in future so life is going to get even harder. *(tchd 2-1)*

Manorson(IRE), raised 7lb for his Newbury victory, ran up to form but his hurdle wins have come on a sounder surface, so he may not find too many opportunities until the spring. *(tchd 9-1)*

Salut Saint Cloud ran with plenty of credit in such a competitive race, but may prefer a stiffer test these days.

Cool Roxy, very much suited by a sharp left-handed track, probably ran too well for the Handicapper to give him much help, which does appear to be what he needs.

Silver Prophet(IRE) looks high enough in the weights now. *(op 14-1)*

Priors Dale, raised 8lb for his course-and-distance victory last month, tried the same positive tactics but they were not as effective in this hotter contest.

T/Jkpt: £5,255.40 to a £1 stake. Pool: £62,917.80. 8.50 winning tickets. T/Plt: £14.10 to a £1 stake. Pool: £49,806.25. 2,563.70 winning tickets. T/Qpdt: £11.90 to a £1 stake. Pool: £3,438.20. 212.40 winning tickets. JN

2625 HAYDOCK (L-H)

Saturday, December 17

OFFICIAL GOING: Soft
Wind: Almost nil Weather: Fine, cold

2872 H.B.L.B. NOVICES' CHASE (12 fncs) 2m

12:25 (12:26) (Class 3) 4-Y-O+ **£7,877** (£2,460; £1,324)

Form RPR

321 **1** **Le Volfoni (FR)**[14] 2620 4-10-12 .... JoeTizzard 131+
(P F Nicholls) *chsd ldr: mstke 4 out: led 3 out: rdn clr after last: eased cl home* **8/11**[1]

0-62 **2** *11* **Tusk**[12] 2677 5-11-2 126.............................. DavidO'Meara 120
(H P Hogarth) *j.lft: led: hdd 3 out: dropped to rr and btn appr 2 out: regained poor 2nd towards fin* **11/2**[3]

1241 **3** *1* **Portavadie**[12] 2677 6-11-12 .... TonyDobbin 129
(J M Jefferson) *hld up in rr: impr to chse wnr appr 2 out: rdn and btn after last: wknd run-in: lost 2nd towards fin* **9/4**[2]

-456 **U** **Mr Lewin**[23] 2462 4-10-1 .... StephenCraine[(5)] —
(D McCain) *blnd and uns rdr 1st* **40/1**

4m 13.0s (6.00) **Going Correction** +0.30s/f (Yiel)
WFA 4 from 5yo+ 10lb **4** Ran SP% **106.5**
Speed ratings: **85,79,79,—** CSF £4.80 TOTE £1.70; EX 3.20.
Owner Million In Mind Partnership **Bred** I Plessis And Bertrand Plessis **Trained** Ditcheat, Somerset

FOCUS
They did not go a great gallop early on for this fair novice chase, and the result was a moderate winning time for the grade.

NOTEBOOK
Le Volfoni(FR) had conditions to suit and was receiving a generous weight allowance from the other two main protagonists. He jumped well for the most part and drew clear after the last, and should get further, but this sort of ground looks essential to him. *(op 4-6 tchd 4-5 in places)*

Tusk, who jumped badly out to his left at a number of fences, managed to reverse Newcastle form with Portavadie on 10lb better terms, but he was well held in second and handicaps may offer greater opportunities. *(op 5-1)*

Portavadie raced keenly enough in the early stages of the race but was brought to have every chance going to the second last. The weight concession of a stone to the winner proved too much, though, and he got quite tired in the closing stages, surrendering second to Tusk. *(op 3-1)*

2873 CENTROL RECYCLING GROUP NOVICES' HURDLE (8 hdls) 2m

1:00 (1:00) (Class 3) 4-Y-O+ **£5,465** (£1,604; £802; £400)

Form RPR

26 **1** **Circassian (IRE)**[34] 2206 4-11-0 .... TonyDobbin 120+
(J Howard Johnson) *trckd ldrs: led 3 out: nt fluent 2 out and whn wnt clr last: eased cl home* **8/15**[1]

10-4 **2** *12* **Yaboya (IRE)**[25] 2421 6-11-0 .... RichardJohnson 100
(P J Hobbs) *trckd ldrs: chsd wnr appr 2 out: wl btn fr last* **5/1**[2]

F **3** *8* **Leo's Luckyman (USA)**[7] 2763 6-11-0 .... JohnMcNamara 94+
(R S Brookhouse) *led: hdd 4th: regained ld 4 out: hdd 3 out: wknd after 2 out* **7/1**[3]

56 **4** *7* **Trust Rule**[14] 2627 5-10-11 .... MrTGreenall[(3)] 85+
(M W Easterby) *hld up: hdwy appr 3 out: nvr trbld ldrs* **20/1**

0-PP **5** *½* **Pinkerton Mill**[23] 2460 5-10-2 .... LiamTreadwell[(5)] 78
(J T Stimpson) *midfield: mstke 1st: hdwy after 4 out: rdn and wknd appr 2 out* **125/1**

-000 **6** *2* **Sharp Rally (IRE)**[16] 2584 4-11-0 90..............................(t) WayneHutchinson 83
(A J Wilson) *hld up: shkn up whn hit 2 out: nvr trbld ldrs* **200/1**

62 **7** *7* **Pont Neuf (IRE)**[10] 2704 5-10-4 ....(t) PaddyAspell[(3)] 69
(A Crook) *prom: led 4th: hdd 4 out: wknd next: btn whn mstke 2 out* **16/1**

U **8** *11* **Guymur (FR)**[14] 2624 5-11-0 .... JoeTizzard 68+
(P J Hobbs) *midfield: hdwy appr 4 out: wknd 2 out* **33/1**

6 **9** *nk* **Lone Rider (IRE)**[33] 2242 4-11-0 .... NoelFehily 64
(Jonjo O'Neill) *hld up: sme hdwy appr 4 out: wknd bef next* **50/1**

1/0 **10** *2* **From Dawn To Dusk**[13] 2663 6-10-4 .... DarrenO'Dwyer[(10)] 62
(P J Hobbs) *in tch: rdn and wknd after 4 out: no ch whn blnd last* **25/1**

-00P **11** *12* **Bob's Temptation**[8] 2755 6-11-0 ....(t) AntonyEvans 50
(A J Wilson) *a bhd* **250/1**

000- **12** *13* **Explode**[287] 4166 8-11-0 82.............................. TomSiddall 37
(Miss L C Siddall) *a bhd* **100/1**

0005 **13** *6* **Gunship (IRE)**[14] 2618 4-10-9 .... RobertStephens[(5)] 31
(P J Hobbs) *prom: settled midfield after 2nd: pushed along after 3rd: bhd after* **100/1**

00 **P** **Cryfield**[16] 2584 8-11-0 .... JamesDavies —
(N Tinkler) *hld up: pushed along after 3rd: t.o whn p.u bef 2 out* **125/1**

The Form Book, Raceform Ltd, Compton, RG20 6NL

P **Devolution (IRE)**[871] 7-10-7 .... MissCDyson(7) —
(Miss C Dyson) *t.k.h: handy: mstke 4 out: sn wknd: t.o whn p.u bef 2 out* **125/1**

4m 2.90s (3.80) **Going Correction** +0.30s/f (Yiel) **15** Ran SP% **119.0**
Speed ratings: **90,84,80,76,76 75,71,66,66,65 59,52,49,—,—** CSF £3.16 TOTE £1.60: £1.10, £1.80, £1.80; EX 5.80.
Owner Andrea & Graham Wylie **Bred** Barouche Stud Ireland Ltd **Trained** Billy Row, Co Durham

FOCUS
Despite the numbers this was not a very competitive heat and it was run in a moderate time for a race of its class.

NOTEBOOK
Circassian(IRE) held strong claims having run well in better races than this on his first two starts over hurdles. He duly outclassed this field, being value for much further than the official winning margin, and he looks sure to win more races. *(op 8-11 tchd 4-5 in places)*
Yaboya(IRE), disappointing when a beaten favourite on his hurdling debut, was dropping back in trip here and, given the way he raced a touch keenly, it was probably to his advantage that he did not have another half a mile or so to go at the end this time. *(op 9-2)*
Leo's Luckyman(USA), who fell on his hurdling debut, showed he has a future at this game with a sound effort to finish third. He will improve for this and a sharper track might suit his front-running style better. *(tchd 15-2)*
Trust Rule, who came from off the pace to secure fourth place, was not given a hard time and is *now eligible to run in handicaps, where he will surely do better.Official explanation: jockey said gelding had a breathing problem (op 14-1)*
Pinkerton Mill, pulled up in her first two starts over hurdles, shaped with more promise this time but her future lies in modest handicap company. *(tchd 100-1)*
Pont Neuf(IRE), given a more positive ride this time, was soon seen off in the straight. She is another who now qualifies for a handicap mark. *(op 14-1)*
Guymur(FR) ◆, formerly trained in France and having his second start for his new stable, appeared to be going well approaching the third last, and even going to two out his rider had yet to put him under any serious pressure. He weakened out of contention from that point on, still without having been asked a serious question, and the impression left was that he could have achieved a better placing with a more vigorous ride. He needs one more run for a handicap mark. *(tchd 28-1)*

2874 BET365 NOVICES' H'CAP CHASE (15 fncs) 2m 4f
1:35 (1:35) (Class 3) (0-120,113) 4-Y-0+ **£5,543** (£1,627; £813; £406)

Form				RPR
/4-5	**1**		**Another Native (IRE)**[29] [2323] 7-10-9 **96** ow1 .... NoelFehily (C J Mann) *hld up: hdwy 11th: wnt 2nd 3 out: rdn after last: led fnl 100 yds: styd on wl* **20/1**	112+
-1P5	**2**	*3 ½*	**Itsuptoharry (IRE)**[44] [2003] 6-11-7 **113** .... StephenCraine(5) (D McCain) *hld up: chsd ldrs appr 4th: wnt 2nd 11th: led after 4 out: rdn after last: hdd and no ex fnl 100 yds* **16/1**	125
/112	**3**	*21*	**Precious Bane (IRE)**[14] [2623] 7-10-10 **97** ....(p) MarkBradburne (M Sheppard) *led: clr after 3rd: mstkes fnl circ: hdd after 4 out: wknd appr 2 out* **7/2**[2]	94+
4/52	**4**	*2 ½*	**Algarve**[31] [2266] 8-10-5 **92** .... KeithMercer (Ferdy Murphy) *chsd ldr to 11th: wknd after 4 out* **2/1**[1]	81
P042	**5**	*10*	**Le Royal (FR)**[9] [2719] 6-11-2 **103** .... DavidO'Meara (K G Reveley) *bhd: mstke 7th (water): mstke whn struggling 3 out: nvr on terms* **14/1**	86+
0314	**6**	*22*	**Donovan (NZ)**[13] [2655] 6-10-5 **95** ....(p) LarryMcGrath(3) (R C Guest) *mstke 7th (water): a bhd* **14/1**	68+
/433	**7**	*7*	**Valleymore (IRE)**[14] [2630] 9-10-11 **98** ....(t) TomSiddall (S A Brookshaw) *hld up in tch: lost pl 6th: mstke 8th: struggling whn hmpd 9th: bhd after* **8/1**	48
/F3-	**P**		**Alphabetic**[282] [4285] 8-10-13 **105** .... SamCurling(5) (N J Henderson) *a bhd: rdn after 4 out: t.o whn p.u bef 3 out* **7/1**[3]	—
	U		**Madison Du Berlais (FR)**[31] 4-10-4 **112** .... AndrewGlassonbury(10) (M C Pipe) *chsd ldrs: hit 3rd: cl 3rd whn blnd bdly and uns rdr 9th* **10/1**	—
P-56	**P**		**Lord Rodney (IRE)**[203] [549] 6-11-7 **108** .... RichardMcGrath (P Beaumont) *chsd ldrs: losing pl whn mstke 6th: sn bhd: t.o whn p.u bef 4 out* **33/1**	—

5m 18.8s (-5.40) **Going Correction** +0.30s/f (Yiel)
WFA 4 from 6yo+ 11lb **10** Ran SP% **115.2**
Speed ratings: **110,108,100,99,95 86,83,—,—,—** CSF £280.21 CT £1389.76 TOTE £13.30: £2.90, £3.50, £1.90; EX 169.80.
Owner The Sport of Kings Partnership **Bred** Mrs Brid McCrea **Trained** Upper Lambourn, Berks

FOCUS
An ordinary handicap run at a decent pace and in a fair time for the grade. The fifth, who is struggling for form, sets the level.

NOTEBOOK
Another Native(IRE), given a patient ride in a race run at a decent pace considering the conditions, came through to score a shade cosily, seeing the trip out strongly. He hails from a stable that is going quite well at present. *(op 16-1)*
Itsuptoharry(IRE), who ran as though needing the race over the course and distance last month, had clearly benefited from that outing, and he once again travelled well. He could not quite hold off the winner but the effort suggests he can win a race off this sort of mark. *(op 18-1 tchd 20-1)*
Precious Bane(IRE), wearing cheekpieces for the first time, made the running at a decent pace but he began to pay the price along the back straight for the last time, making mistakes that cost him the lead. He still did not run badly off what looks a fairly stiff mark now. *(op 9-2)*
Algarve could not reverse Hexham form with the eventual third despite being weighted to do so. He also paid for going off too fast in the early stages. *(op 5-2)*
Le Royal(FR) is well handicapped on his hurdling form but he has yet to show he is capable of taking advantage of that.
Lord Rodney(IRE) *Official explanation: jockey said gelding failed to jump fluently (op 6-1)*
Madison Du Berlais(FR) unseated too far out to know whether he would have played a part in the finish, but he was going well enough just behind the leaders at the time. *(op 6-1)*

2875 TIM MOLONY H'CAP CHASE (22 fncs) 3m 4f 110y
2:05 (2:05) (Class 3) (0-135,135) 5-Y-0+ **£13,506** (£3,965; £1,982; £990)

Form				RPR
264F	**1**		**Double Honour (FR)**[27] [2370] 7-11-12 **135** ....(b) RichardJohnson (P J Hobbs) *rdn along several stages: led 2nd to 3rd: led 9th to 11th: led again appr 2 out: all out* **9/2**[3]	149+
0P-4	**2**	*hd*	**Artic Jack (FR)**[35] [2189] 9-10-10 **119** .... DominicElsworth (Mrs S J Smith) *prom whn mstke 1st: sn lost pl: prom again 7th: led after 14th (water): hdd appr 2 out: rallied cl home* **10/3**[1]	131+
P1-1	**3**	*7*	**Native Ivy (IRE)**[42] [2046] 7-11-3 **126** .... TomDoyle (C Tinkler) *led tl slipped 2nd: sn lost pl: hdwy 11th: rdn whn chsd ldrs appr 2 out: no ex fnl 100 yds* **9/2**[3]	134+
6311	**4**	*dist*	**Silver Knight**[14] [2644] 7-11-5 **128** .... RussGarritty (T D Easterby) *in tch: rdn appr 16th: wknd bef 18th: t.o* **7/2**[2]	102
61-P	**R**		**Coursing Run (IRE)**[237] [12] 9-11-0 **123** .... MarkBradburne (H D Daly) *hld up in tch: lost pl 7th: t.o 13th: ref 15th* **16/1**	—
0-26	**F**		**Merchants Friend (IRE)**[35] [2176] 10-11-8 **131** ....(p) NoelFehily (C J Mann) *in rr: blnd 17th: sme hdwy 3 out: no imp in 4th whn fell 2 out* **11/2**	115
1/PP	**P**		**Over The Storm (IRE)**[20] [2518] 8-10-4 **113** .... DavidO'Meara (H P Hogarth) *hld up: rdn 16th: hdwy u.p 4 out: wknd appr next: t.o whn p.u bef 2 out* **20/1**	—
-1P0	**P**		**Naunton Brook**[14] [2628] 6-11-1 **124** .... AntonyEvans (N A Twiston-Davies) *led 3rd: pckd 7th: hdd 9th: led 11th tl after 14th (water): wknd 17th: t.o whn p.u bef 3 out* **20/1**	—

7m 35.4s (2.70) **Going Correction** +0.30s/f (Yiel) **8** Ran SP% **112.5**
Speed ratings: **107,106,105,—,— —,—,—** CSF £19.84 CT £69.34 TOTE £6.30: £2.00, £1.30, £2.00; EX 16.70.
Owner The 4th Middleham Partnership **Bred** Symboli And Co Ltd **Trained** Withycombe, Somerset
■ Stewards' Enquiry : Dominic Elsworth caution: used whip with excessive frequency
Richard Johnson one-day ban: used whip with excessive frequency (Dec 28)

FOCUS
A fairly competitive handicap that provided a true test of stamina and the winner sets the standard.

NOTEBOOK
Double Honour(FR) did not always jump fluently and needed plenty of encouragement from his rider to keep going, but he responded well and his stamina and guts saw him through in the end. He is in the Welsh National, and that would seem a natural target, but that might come a bit soon after this hard race. *(op 11-2 tchd 6-1 in places)*
Artic Jack(FR) beat Kingscliff at this track less than two years ago but he fell in the 2004 Grand National and has struggled since, dropping over 30lb in the handicap as a result. His efforts this term suggest he is steadily regaining his form though, and he should be capable of winning off this sort of mark. *(op 3-1 tchd 7-2 in places)*
Native Ivy(IRE) ran well against some old pros on only his third start over fences and is clearly *progressive. He has a decent strike-rate and looks sure to record further success this season. (tchd 5-1)*
Silver Knight kept on without being a threat to the first three and was the final finisher. He might have found the race coming a bit soon after his successful slog in the mud at Wetherby a fortnight earlier. *(tchd 10-3 and 4-1 in places)*
Merchants Friend(IRE) found his jumping letting him down along the back straight for the final time but he was only keeping on at the one pace when falling at the second last. *(op 13-2)*

2876 TOTESCOOP6 H'CAP HURDLE (10 hdls) 2m 4f
2:35 (2:35) (Class 2) 4-Y-0+ **£13,584** (£3,988; £1,994; £995)

Form				RPR
123-	**1**		**Jazz D'Estruval (FR)**[241] [4925] 8-10-9 **128** .... TonyDobbin (N G Richards) *midfield: smooth hdwy 4 out: led appr 3 out: clr last: readily* **9/4**[1]	142+
440/	**2**	*4*	**Mughas (IRE)**[624] [4643] 6-11-7 **140** .... WayneHutchinson (A King) *midfield: hdwy 5th: wnt 2nd 3 out: no ch w wnr run-in* **10/1**	144+
2-25	**3**	*3 ½*	**Haut De Gamme (FR)**[27] [2370] 10-10-6 **125** .... KeithMercer (Ferdy Murphy) *hld up: hdwy appr 3 out: rdn bef next: styd on: nt rch ldrs* **11/1**	124
B-2F	**4**	*¾*	**Turtle Soup (IRE)**[211] [207] 9-11-5 **145** .... WillieMcCarthy(7) (T R George) *midfield: hdwy 5th: one pce fr 2 out* **16/1**	143
3211	**5**	*6*	**Nathos (GER)**[30] [2292] 8-10-13 **132** .... NoelFehily (C J Mann) *hld up: hdwy after 4 out: sn chsd ldrs: wknd run-in* **6/1**[2]	125+
-016	**6**	*10*	**Flying Enterprise (IRE)**[21] [2493] 5-11-3 **136** .... SamThomas (Miss Venetia Williams) *in tch: rdn appr 2 out: wknd bef last* **7/1**[3]	120+
-P50	**7**	*3 ½*	**Sh Boom**[8] [2747] 7-11-9 **142** .... TomSiddall (S A Brookshaw) *led after 1st: hdd after 4th: regained ld 6th: hdd appr 3 out: wknd bef next* **18/1**	121
-302	**8**	*4*	**Better Days (IRE)**[14] [2629] 9-10-1 **120** .... DominicElsworth (Mrs S J Smith) *led: hdd after 1st: chsd ldr: led again after 4th: hdd 6th: rdn and wknd appr 3 out* **10/1**	99+
4-30	**9**	*3*	**Spring Pursuit**[28] [2336] 9-10-11 **130** .... TomDoyle (E G Bevan) *hld up: hdwy 4 out: sn chsd ldrs: wknd appr 2 out* **12/1**	109+
51-P	**10**	*21*	**Supreme Leisure (IRE)**[23] [2449] 8-9-9 **119** oh8 .... BrianHughes(5) (J Howard Johnson) *midfield: rdn and lost pl 6th: bhd after* **40/1**	70
-U0P	**11**	*10*	**Seebald (GER)**[28] [2346] 10-11-9 **142** ....(v) APMcCoy (M C Pipe) *chsd ldrs: rdn after 4 out: wknd after 3 out* **33/1**	83
-053	**12**	*dist*	**St Pirran (IRE)**[14] [2641] 10-10-0 **122** .... LarryMcGrath(3) (R C Guest) *a bhd: t.o* **40/1**	—
34P-	**F**		**Paperprophet**[253] [4767] 7-10-6 **132** .... ScottMarshall(7) (N G Richards) *in rr: fell 4th* **16/1**	—

5m 3.10s (-6.10) **Going Correction** +0.30s/f (Yiel) **13** Ran SP% **116.6**
Speed ratings: **112,110,109,108,106 102,100,99,98,89 85,—,—** CSF £24.45 CT £203.84 TOTE £3.70: £1.70, £3.90, £3.60; EX 49.10 Trifecta £353.20 Pool £6,567.99 - 13.20 winning units..
Owner Ashleybank Investments Limited **Bred** Bernard Le Gentil **Trained** Greystoke, Cumbria

FOCUS
A number of these, including the winner, are better known as chasers. They went a decent pace and the winner is value for ten lengths, with the first five close to their marks, and the form should work out.

NOTEBOOK
Jazz D'Estruval(FR), who had ground conditions to suit and has gone well fresh before, looked a smart sort in the first half of his novice chasing season but he disappointed somewhat in the spring. Returning to hurdling off a very favourable mark in comparison with his chase rating, he took this field apart and won easily. His trainer plans to send him over fences again next, but he might travel to Ireland for that as Richards believes the gelding does not cope with open ditches well, and the regulation fences in Ireland take less jumping. *(op 5-2 tchd 11-4 in places)*
Mughas(IRE) ◆ ran a promising race on his return from a 624-day absence, travelling well for most of the way. The well-handicapped winner was just too good but he looks rated to win himself with this run under his belt. *(tchd 11-1)*
Haut De Gamme(FR), who ran well on his only previous start over hurdles in this country at Wetherby on his seasonal debut, had a 5lb higher mark to deal with here. Staying on at the finish, he could find a race over timber if stepped up in trip. *(op 10-1 tchd 12-1)*
Turtle Soup(IRE) won this race last year but he had a 10lb higher mark to defy this time and, unlike last season, did not arrive here race-fit.
Nathos(GER) has shot up a stone in the handicap since the first of his two wins last month, and the Handicapper might just have his measure for the time being. *(op 5-1 tchd 13-2)*
Flying Enterprise(IRE) is another who needs some leniency from the Handicapper.
Sh Boom, who set a decent pace, continues to struggle to regain his best form. *(op 16-1)*

2877 SODEXHO PRESTIGE H'CAP CHASE (17 fncs) 2m 6f
3:05 (3:10) (Class 3) (0-115,108) 5-Y-0+ **£8,581** (£2,519; £1,259; £629)

Form				RPR
-341	**1**		**Blunham Hill (IRE)**[21] [2502] 7-10-7 **94** .... MarkNicolls(5) (John R Upson) *in tch: rdn to ld after 4 out: j.lft 3 out: styd on* **11/2**[2]	108+
6605	**2**	*4*	**Pardini (USA)**[20] [2524] 6-10-10 **92** .... JohnMcNamara (M F Harris) *hld up: rdn and hdwy appr 3 out: styd on wl fr last: snatched 2nd post* **25/1**	100+

-220 **3** *shd* **Lochiedubs**[23] 2453 10-10-3 **85**....................(p) NeilMulholland 94+
(Mrs L B Normile) *hld up: mstke 3rd: rdn 7th: hdwy 11th: mstke 4 out: blnd 2 out: chsd wnr last: no ex cl home: lost 2nd post* **14/1**

-001 **4** *6* **Almire Du Lia (FR)**[21] 2495 7-11-5 **101**....................(v) JimmyMcCarthy 103+
(Mrs S C Bradburne) *cl up: rdn appr 4 out: wknd run-in* **7/1**

FFP- **5** *6* **Cyborsun (FR)**[244] 4880 8-10-5 **94**.................... CharliePoste(7) 91+
(M F Harris) *hld up: hdwy appr 9th (water): rdn after 4 out: wknd after last* **33/1**

4-6P **6** *19* **Falchion**[23] 2451 10-11-2 **98**....................(t) RichardMcGrath 74
(J R Bewley) *hld up: rdn 6th: lost tch 10th* **14/1**

PP26 **7** *21* **The Extra Man (IRE)**[8] 2748 11-11-12 **108**....................(b) WayneHutchinson 63
(A King) *prom: reminders after 9th (water): wknd 11th: t.o* **13/2**[3]

1034 **P** **Lutin Du Moulin (FR)**[16] 2589 6-11-3 **99**....................(b) TonyDobbin —
(L Lungo) *in rr: sn niggled along: p.u bef 7th* **9/2**[1]

31-2 **P** **Jballingall**[49] 1928 6-10-2 **84**.................... DNolan —
(N Wilson) *led: slipped 2nd: hdd after 4 out: sn rdn: wkng whn j. slowly 2 out: wl bhd whn p.u bef last* **9/2**[1]

210/ **P** **Heron's Ghyll (IRE)**[637] 4449 8-11-11 **107**.................... SamThomas —
(Miss Venetia Williams) *hld up: hit 8th: rdn after 9th (water): struggling whn stmbld 12th: nt rcvr: p.u bef next* **9/2**[1]

5m 53.4s (4.60) **Going Correction** +0.30s/f (Yiel) **10** Ran SP% **115.9**
Speed ratings: **91,89,89,87,85 78,70,—,—,—** CSF £115.86 CT £1818.62 TOTE £6.50: £2.40, £4.70, £3.30; EX 189.90.
Owner The Reserved Judgment Partnership **Bred** Oliver McDonnell **Trained** Maidford, Northants

FOCUS
A modest handicap but solid enough form. The time was moderate for the grade, though.

NOTEBOOK
Blunham Hill(IRE), whose stamina was not in doubt having won over this trip at Towcester last time, did not look badly treated on a 3lb higher mark and saw this trip out strongly to win well. He is only modest but is notching up the wins over fences. *(op 6-1 tchd 13-2)*
Pardini(USA) had his ground for the first time this season and put up a better effort as a result. His form figures over fences in soft or heavy ground now read P2122.
Lochiedubs ran a better race back over fences, but he has only ever won one race from 28 career starts. *Official explanation: jockey said gelding hung right; trainer said gelding pulled up sore (op 16-1)*
Almire Du Lia(FR) found the 7lb higher mark for his shock Newcastle win holding him back. *(op 6-1)*
Cyborsun(FR), who bled when last seen at Stratford in April, is on a good mark now if he can be brought back to his best.
Lutin Du Moulin(FR) *Official explanation: jockey said gelding never travelled (op 15-2)*
Jballingall ran well for a long way but tired badly in the straight. *(op 15-2)*

2878 RED SQUARE VODKA "FIXED BRUSH" NOVICES' HURDLE (10 hdls) 2m 4f
3:35 (3:39) (Class 3) 4-7-Y-0 **£5,237** (£1,537; £768; £383)

Form RPR

3-1 **1** **Don't Push It (IRE)**[84] 1554 5-10-12 .... APMcCoy 125+
(Jonjo O'Neill) *hld up: hdwy appr 4 out: led 2 out: drew clr run-in* **2/1**[1]

3/1F **2** *4* **Hoh Viss**[20] 2527 5-11-5 120.................... NoelFehily 123+
(C J Mann) *hld up: hdwy appr 5th: led briefly bef 2 out and mstke: no ex run-in* **5/2**[2]

1-4 **3** *6* **Calusa Charlie (IRE)**[24] 2426 6-10-12 .... TomDoyle 108
(B G Powell) *prom: led 6th: rdn and hdd appr 2 out: wknd bef last* **10/1**

12 **4** *dist* **Best Profile (IRE)**[23] 2461 5-11-5 .... CarlLlewellyn 85
(N A Twiston-Davies) *led: hdd 6th: rdn and wknd appr 2 out* **6/1**

5-42 **5** *6* **Winapenny (IRE)**[23] 2448 6-10-12 105.................... KeithMercer 76
(Ferdy Murphy) *midfield: hdwy whn mstke 6th: wkng whn mstke 3 out* **5/1**[3]

F **6** *2½* **Ben Tally Ho**[38] 2127 4-10-12 .... JimmyMcCarthy 70
(Ian Williams) *hld up: mstke 6th: sn rdn and n.d* **50/1**

5-00 **7** *14* **Mokum (FR)**[35] 2173 4-10-12 106.................... WayneHutchinson 56
(A W Carroll) *in tch tl wknd 4 out* **50/1**

8 *2½* **Koral Bay (FR)**[197] 4-10-1 112 ow3.................... MrSWaley-Cohen(7) 50
(R Waley-Cohen) *hld up: hdwy appr 5th: mstke 4 out: sn wknd* **18/1**

0/F- **P** **Run Atim**[405] 2068 7-10-12 .... JohnMcNamara —
(K C Bailey) *midfield: rdn and wknd 5th: t.o whn p.u bef 3 out* **50/1**

50-P **P** **Turnnocard (IRE)**[30] 2295 6-10-5 .... JoffretHuet —
(Ian Williams) *towards rr: rdn after 4th: t.o whn p.u bef 3 out* **125/1**

00P5 **P** **Yankee Holiday (IRE)**[23] 2448 5-10-12.................... RichardMcGrath —
(Mrs S C Bradburne) *prom tl wknd 5th: t.o whn p.u bef 3 out* **125/1**

5m 8.70s (-0.50) **Going Correction** +0.30s/f (Yiel)
WFA 4 from 5yo+ 11lb **11** Ran SP% **114.7**
Speed ratings: **101,99,97,—,—,—,—,—,—,—,—** CSF £7.02 TOTE £2.80: £1.30, £1.40, £2.20; EX 8.00 Place 6 £114.53, Place 5 £65.53.
Owner John P McManus **Bred** Dominick Vallely **Trained** Cheltenham, Gloucs

FOCUS
This looked a fair race and could be rated higher and the winner, value for 9l, is probably a decent novice.

NOTEBOOK
Don't Push It(IRE), off the track since a bumper victory back in September, made a winning debut over obstacles. Tracking the favourite through before outjumping him to lead two out, he was awkward at the last but came away in good style on the flat before being eased down with his race won. Still inexperienced, he is capable of rating higher. *(op 7-2 tchd 4-1 in places)*
Hoh Viss travelled strongly before moving to the front going to the second last, but an awkward jump at the flight lost him the initiative and he was second best from that point. Although flattered to be beaten only four lengths, he was facing a stiff task conceding 7lb to the favourite. *(op 15-8 tchd 11-4 and 3-1 in a place)*
Calusa Charlie(IRE) stuck on quite well when headed and finished a distance clear of the rest. He is going the right way and should stay three miles. *(tchd 12-1 in a place)*
Best Profile(IRE), put in his place by Karanja over three miles at Uttoxeter, set a decent pace under his penalty but faded badly from the second last. *(op 9-2)*
Winapenny(IRE) was expected to appreciate this longer trip, but he did not jump these unconventional obstacles very well and ended up well beaten. *(op 9-2 tchd 11-2 in a place)*
T/Plt: £152.80 to a £1 stake. Pool: £96,622.30. 461.35 winning tickets. T/Qpdt: £65.10 to a £1 stake. Pool: £9,038.50. 102.70 winning tickets. DO

2674 NEWCASTLE (L-H)
Saturday, December 17
2879 Meeting Abandoned - Frost

2865 WINDSOR (R-H)
Saturday, December 17
2886 Meeting Abandoned - Frost

2893 - 2899a (Foreign Racing) - See Raceform Interactive

2474 MUSSELBURGH (R-H)
Sunday, December 18
OFFICIAL GOING: Good to firm (firm in places) changing to firm (good to firm in places) after race 3 (1.20)
Wind: Virtually nil

2900 "WATCH LIVE ON RACING UK" AMATEUR RIDERS' H'CAP CHASE (16 fncs) 2m 4f
12:20 (12:20) (Class 4) (0-95,95) 5-Y-0+ **£3,310** (£1,026; £513; £256)

Form RPR

-223 **1** **Bohemian Spirit (IRE)**[26] 2416 7-11-9 **95**.................... MissRDavidson(3) 120+
(N G Richards) *j.w: mde all: clr fr 1/2-way: easily* **13/8**[1]

13/0 **2** *18* **Balakar (IRE)**[43] 2058 9-10-7 **79**....................(tp) MrROHarding(3) 86+
(J J Lambe, Ire) *trckd ldrs: hdwy to chse wnr 6 out: rdn along and clsd up 3 out: hit next: drvn and 8l down whn blnd last* **20/1**

5/0P **3** *9* **Some Trainer (IRE)**[67] 1723 9-9-7 **69** oh2....................(t) MrCJCallow(7) 63
(J G Cromwell, Ire) *hld up and bhd: stdy hdwy 6 out: rdn along whn mstke 4 out: styd on fr next: nrst fin* **10/1**

02P1 **4** *nk* **Swallow Magic (IRE)**[21] 2522 7-11-1 **91**....................(v) MrSWByrne(7) 85
(Ferdy Murphy) *cl up: pushed along fr 5 out: rdn along appr next and sn outpcd* **6/1**[3]

3352 **5** *3* **Mr Laggan**[71] 1684 10-10-4 **80**.................... MrHHaynes(7) 71
(Miss Kate Milligan) *hld up towards rr: hdwy 6 out: sn rdn along and nvr a factor* **8/1**

P650 **6** *9* **Pornic (FR)**[12] 2688 11-9-13 **75**.................... MrSFMagee(7) 57
(A Crook) *in tch: rdn along 6 out and sn outpcd* **25/1**

4PP0 **7** *½* **Helvetius**[22] 2495 9-11-5 **95**.................... MrJARichardson(7) 76
(W T Reed) *chsd ldrs to 1/2-way: sn outpcd* **25/1**

44P5 **8** *3* **Jallastep (FR)**[22] 2498 8-11-3 **93**.................... MrGGoldie(7) 71
(J S Goldie) *chsd ldrs: rdn along 6 out and sn wknd* **11/2**[2]

6P **9** *8* **Closed Orders (IRE)**[18] 2570 8-10-9 **85**.................... MrDAFitzsimmons(7) 55
(Robert Gray) *a rr* **33/1**

3-14 **10** *8* **Red Flyer (IRE)**[77] 1602 6-11-3 **93**.................... MrRQuinn(7) 55
(Ronald Thompson) *in tch: rdn along 1/2-way: sn lost pl and bhd* **7/1**

4m 44.5s (-14.90) **Going Correction** -0.625s/f (Firm) course record **10** Ran SP% **115.9**
Speed ratings: **104,96,93,93,91 88,88,86,83,80** CSF £36.51 CT £256.24 TOTE £2.60: £1.30, £8.30, £3.20; EX 39.60.
Owner Mr & Mrs Duncan Davidson **Bred** Patrick J Connolly **Trained** Greystoke, Cumbria

FOCUS
Not a competitive heat but the winner impressed in setting a new course record and is likely to rate higher in time.

NOTEBOOK
Bohemian Spirit(IRE) ◆, who had a pipe-opener over hurdles last time, was making his handicap debut over fences having tasted success in the hunting ranks. He raced keenly but jumped well in front and proved much too good for this lot off a mark of 95, winning with his head in his chest. He looks worth following. *(op 7-4 tchd 6-4 and 15-8 in a place)*
Balakar(IRE), formerly trained in Ireland, is well handicapped on his best hurdling form. He was well held in second when blundering the last, losing more ground to the easy winner in the process. *(op 16-1)*
Some Trainer(IRE), who only has one win in 78 starts under both codes to his name, was not disgraced from 2lb out of the handicap, but he is not sure to reproduce this effort next time. *(op 14-1)*
Swallow Magic(IRE) has won from off the pace but he likes to make the running, as when successful at Leicester last time, and the winner never let him dominate here. *(op 4-1 tchd 7-1)*
Mr Laggan was back on the same mark as when successful in this race two years ago, but he never got competitive from off the pace this time. *(op 7-1)*

2901 MUSSELBURGH ANNUAL MEMBERS MAIDEN HURDLE (12 hdls) 2m 4f
12:50 (12:50) (Class 4) 4-Y-0+ **£3,042** (£886; £443)

Form RPR

2-5 **1** **Some Touch (IRE)**[22] 2487 5-11-0 .... GrahamLee 115+
(J Howard Johnson) *mde all: shkn up appr last: rdn and kpt on flat* **4/9**[1]

0 **2** *4* **Rajayla (IRE)**[44] 2031 4-10-2 .... WilliamKennedy(5) 101
(T G McCourt, Ire) *trckd ldrs: hdwy to chse wnr 8th: rdn along 3 out: drvn appr last: one pce flat* **4/1**[2]

1-64 **3** *11* **Powerlove (FR)**[26] 2412 4-10-7 .... MarkBradburne 90
(Mrs S C Bradburne) *chsd wnr: rdn along 4 out and outpcd fr next* **14/1**[3]

06 **4** *2½* **Ballyhurry (USA)**[23] 2475 8-11-0.................... RichardMcGrath 95
(J S Goldie) *hld up in midfield: hdwy to chse ldrs 4 out: rdn along next and sn no imp* **16/1**

2200 **5** *15* **Dalawan**[23] 2475 6-10-11 .... PaddyAspell(3) 80
(Mrs J C McGregor) *chsd ldng pair tl j. bdly rt 8th and sn outpcd* **25/1**

060 **6** *14* **Fly Tipper**[14] 2652 5-11-0 .... NeilMulholland 66
(W Storey) *chsd ldrs: rdn along 4 out: outpcd fr next* **100/1**

P0 **7** *3* **Chanteuse**[3] 2838 5-10-0 .... PhilKinsella(7) 56
(Mrs Marjorie Fife) *midfield: hdwy 8th: sn rdn along and nvr nr ldrs* **100/1**

-00 **8** *14* **Carpe Momentum (USA)**[9] 2749 6-10-11 ....(t) LarryMcGrath(3) 49
(R C Guest) *hld up in rr: sme hdwy 1/2-way: rdn along bef 4 out and nvr a factor* **66/1**

340 **9** *17* **Lord Baskerville**[24] 2448 4-11-0 .... BrianHarding 32
(W Storey) *a bhd* **25/1**

4P **10** *2* **Top Brass (IRE)**[9] 2755 4-11-0 .... JimCrowley 30
(K G Reveley) *hld up in rr: pushed along 1/2-way: a bhd* **33/1**

0 P **Moscow Ali (IRE)**[42] 2062 5-10-11 PeterBuchanan[(3)] —
(Miss Lucinda V Russell) *in tch: rdn along and outpcd fr 1/2-way: bhd whn p.u bef last* **100/1**

4m 52.2s (-2.30) **Going Correction** -0.275s/f (Good)
WFA 4 from 5yo+ 11lb **11** Ran SP% **116.9**
Speed ratings: **93,91,87,86,80 74,73,67,60,60** — CSF £2.33 TOTE £1.50: £1.02, £1.70, £2.40; EX 2.30.
Owner Andrea & Graham Wylie **Bred** Walter Fennell **Trained** Billy Row, Co Durham

FOCUS
An ordinary race and the winner has still to run to the level of his bumper form. The form does not look strong and could be a few pounds higher or lower.

NOTEBOOK
Some Touch(IRE), who shaped with promise on his hurdling debut in a better race than this, made every yard on this step up to two and a half miles. He will probably be happier on easier ground and there is room for improvement in the jumping department. *(op 4-7)*
Rajayla(IRE), an Irish raider, has far more experience over hurdles than the winner but is pretty exposed as a result. She got the longer trip well but the winner always had her measure. *(op 7-2)*
Powerlove(FR) probably found the ground on the fast side as she was easily seen off by the front two in the latter stages. *(op 9-1)*
Ballyhurry(USA) once again appeared to find the trip stretching his stamina. His only start to date over two miles was on soft ground but he preferred a sounder surface on the level and perhaps it will be under those conditions that he will be seen at his best in handicap company. *(tchd 20-1)*
Dalawan finished further behind Ballyhurry this time than he did over the course and distance last *month. He too now qualifies for a handicap mark. Official explanation: jockey said gelding hung right-handed throughout (tchd 33-1)*
Lord Baskerville *Official explanation: jockey said gelding hung left-handed throughout (op 16-1)*

2902 EAST LOTHIAN COUNCIL NOVICES' CHASE (16 fncs) 2m 4f
1:20 (1:20) (Class 4) 5-Y-0+ **£4,098** (£1,203; £601; £300)

Form RPR
-441 **1** **Clouding Over**[10] 2715 5-10-6 106 RichardMcGrath 98+
(K G Reveley) *hld up towards rr: stdy hdwy 9th: led 3 out: easily* **2/5**[1]
-5P3 **2** *4* **El Andaluz (FR)**[23] 2476 5-10-12 78 AlanDempsey 92+
(M Todhunter) *j.lft thrght: led: rdn along and hdd 3 out: blnd last: kpt on: no ch w wnr* **10/1**[3]
5600 **3** *3* **Ton-Chee**[72] 1665 6-10-12 99 TonyDobbin 88
(F P Murtagh) *trckd ldng pair: hdwy 9th: effrt and ev ch 3 out: rdn next and kpt on same pce* **10/1**[3]
1456 **4** *8* **Goodbadindiferent (IRE)**[23] 2476 9-10-12 84 KeithMercer 81+
(Mrs J C McGregor) *chsd ldr: pushed along 5 out: sn rdn and wknd 4 out: mstke next* **11/2**[2]
-060 **F** **Sandy Bay (IRE)**[14] 2657 6-10-12 72 PadgeWhelan —
(W G Harrison) *in tch tl fell 5th* **33/1**
036- **P** **Magic Box**[435] 1658 7-10-7 76 DeclanMcGann[(5)] —
(A M Crow) *a rr: mstke 7th and sn bhd: p.u bef 4 out* **25/1**

4m 57.5s (-1.90) **Going Correction** -0.625s/f (Firm) **6** Ran SP% **111.8**
Speed ratings: **78,76,75,72,—** — CSF £5.47 TOTE £1.50: £1.10, £2.20; EX 4.00.
Owner W D Hockenhull **Bred** Shade Oak Stud **Trained** Lingdale, Redcar & Cleveland

FOCUS
An uncompetitive heat in which the favourite won with plenty in hand and has been rated value for a 12-length victory.

NOTEBOOK
Clouding Over travelled well in behind the pace before taking it up in the straight and drawing away for a very easy win. She was, however, heavily favoured by the weights and did no more than should have been expected. *(op 1-2)*
El Andaluz(FR), who raced a shade keenly and tended to jump out to his left at his fences, had a very difficult task at the weights with the winner, and in the circumstances he ran well. *(tchd 11-1)*
Ton-Chee, running over fences for the first time, went well for most of the way and was bang there early in the straight, but his stamina appeared to give out and a drop back to two miles ought to see him finish his race better. *(op 7-1)*
Goodbadindiferent(IRE) had conditions to suit but he had a stiff task at the weights and, of the four remaining, he was the first beaten early in the straight. *(op 5-1)*

2903 WATCH LIVE ON "THEBETTINGSITE.CO.UK" NOVICES' HURDLE (9 hdls) 2m
1:50 (1:51) (Class 4) 4-Y-0+ **£3,519** (£1,033; £516; £258)

Form RPR
2 **1** **Masafi (IRE)**[64] 1740 4-10-12 GrahamLee 107+
(J Howard Johnson) *a.p: led after 4 out: rdn along after 2 out: styd on u.p fr last: clr towards fin* **2/7**[1]
31 **2** *6* **Spring Breeze**[59] 1794 4-11-5 (v) BrianHarding 109+
(M Dods) *led to after 3rd: cl up 4 out: rdn along and hit 2 out: ev ch tl drvn and one pce flat* **9/2**[2]
0-0 **3** *9* **Ebac (IRE)**[23] 2475 4-10-12 (t) AlanDempsey 91+
(J Howard Johnson) *chsd ldrs: pushed along and lost pl 1/2-way: hdwy 2 out: styng on whn mstke last: kpt on flat* **66/1**
500 **4** *7* **Filey Flyer**[14] 2658 5-10-5 AnthonyRoss 75
(J R Turner) *midfield: hdwy 4 out: chsd ldrs next: sn rdn and one pce* **50/1**
0 **5** *2 1/2* **Tinian**[14] 2658 7-10-9 AnthonyCoyle[(3)] 80
(Miss Tracy Waggott) *in tch: rdn along to chse ldrs 4 out: drvn and hit 2 out: one pce and mstke last* **100/1**
0-00 **6** *5* **What's Ahead**[23] 2480 5-10-2 PaddyAspell[(3)] 68
(Mrs J C McGregor) *hld up towards rr: sme hdwy 4 out: nvr a factor* **100/1**
P **7** *2* **Matthew My Son (IRE)**[40] 2108 5-10-12 TonyDobbin 73
(F P Murtagh) *a towards rr* **66/1**
0-0 **8** *9* **Bint Sesaro (IRE)**[218] 349 4-10-1 ow1 DesFlavin[(5)] 58
(Mrs L B Normile) *a rr* **66/1**
34 **9** *3/4* **Mae Moss**[171] 876 4-10-5 DavidO'Meara 56
(W S Coltherd) *a rr* **50/1**
0 **10** *5* **Auburn Lodge (IRE)**[71] 1683 4-10-0 BrianHughes[(5)] 51
(J J Lambe, Ire) *midfield: hdwy and in tch 4 out: rdn along and outpcd fr next* **50/1**
10F0 **11** *4* **Virtus**[43] 2042 5-11-0 82 (b) DougieCostello[(5)] 61
(Mrs B K Thomson) *a rr: bhd fr 1/2-way* **100/1**
5 **12** *22* **Charlie George**[43] 2040 4-10-2 DavidDaSilva[(10)] 32
(P Monteith) *t.k.h: chsd ldng pair tl led after 3rd: hdd after 4 out: wkng whn mstke next and sn bhd* **100/1**
0/ **P** **Tony Tie**[36] 1958 9-10-12 RichardMcGrath —
(J S Goldie) *towards rr tl p.u bef 4 out* **16/1**[3]

3m 46.5s (-4.70) **Going Correction** -0.275s/f (Good) **13** Ran SP% **116.1**
Speed ratings: **100,97,92,89,87 85,84,79,79,76 74,63,—** CSF £1.75 TOTE £1.40: £1.10, £1.10, £7.10; EX 1.70.
Owner Andrea & Graham Wylie **Bred** G D Waters **Trained** Billy Row, Co Durham

FOCUS
Another uncompetitive affair and the first two, who looked the main contenders beforehand, did not have to be at their best to dominate.

NOTEBOOK
Masafi(IRE), not at all disgraced on his hurdling debut behind a very useful rival, had much less to do in this company. He only had Spring Breeze to beat in the straight and did it easily enough without running to his best. This sort of ground suits and he can only improve. *(op 1-3 tchd 4-11)*
Spring Breeze loves this sort of ground and, although rated as having not quite run to his best, he was having to give weight to a potentially smart performer in the winner. He stays two miles on the Flat and should get further than that over hurdles. *(op 4-1 tchd 5-1)*
Ebac(IRE) ◆, who may have needed his reappearance over two and a half miles on his hurdling debut here last month, kept on well in the latter stages over this shorter trip. He cost 160,000euros and is out of a half-sister to Morley Street and Granville Again, so will be very interesting once he qualifies for a handicap mark after one more run.
Filey Flyer improved for her debut effort over hurdles and perhaps the quicker ground suited. *Official explanation: trainer said mare lost a front shoe*
Tinian, well beaten on his hurdling debut in soft ground, was another to show improved form on this quicker surface. He was only a banded-class performer on the Flat, though.
Charlie George mixed it with the first two to the turn into the straight, and he paid the price, dropping out tamely to be last of the 12 finishers.
Tony Tie *Official explanation: jockey said gelding was unsuited by the firm (good to firm in places) ground (op 20-1)*

2904 FAMOUS GROUSE H'CAP HURDLE (9 hdls) 2m
2:20 (2:20) (Class 3) (0-125,125) 4-Y-0+ **£7,494** (£2,200; £1,100; £549)

Form RPR
-6U1 **1** **Saif Sareea**[23] 2478 5-10-3 102 PadgeWhelan 107+
(R A Fahey) *hld up: hdwy 3 out: n.m.r next: rdn last: qcknd flat to ld last 100 yds* **7/2**[2]
21P- **2** *1* **Motive (FR)**[123] 4749 4-11-0 113 GrahamLee 116+
(J Howard Johnson) *hld up: gd hdwy appr 3 out: led next: rdn last: drvn flat hdd last 100 yds* **9/4**[1]
265 **3** *1 1/2* **George Stubbs (USA)**[25] 2444 7-10-0 99 BrianHarding 100
(B Ellison) *trckd ldrs: effrt and led briefly after 3 out: rdn next: kpt on u.p flat* **9/1**
4-13 **4** *3/4* **Millagros (IRE)**[45] 873 5-11-0 113 JimCrowley 113
(I Semple) *hld up in tch: smooth hdwy on outer after 4 out: n.m.r next: hdwy and hit 2 out: rdn last and kpt on same pce* **5/1**[3]
312P **5** *shd* **Gone Too Far**[45] 1913 7-11-7 120 (v) TimmyMurphy 120
(P Monteith) *led: rdn along 3 out: sn hdd and drvn: rallied flat and kpt on wl towards fin* **10/1**
1550 **6** *2* **Overstrand (IRE)**[22] 2500 6-11-4 117 AlanDempsey 115
(Robert Gray) *trckd ldr: hdwy and cl up 4 out: rdn along next and outpcd fr 2 out* **7/1**
2000 **7** *1 1/4* **Bodfari Signet**[23] 2478 9-10-8 107 MarkBradburne 105+
(Mrs S C Bradburne) *chsd ldrs: hit 4 out: sn rdn along and rr fr next* **20/1**
660 **8** *1* **Royal Glen (IRE)**[23] 2478 7-9-9 99 oh5 BrianHughes[(5)] 95
(W S Coltherd) *trckd ldng pair: cl up 4 out: rdn next and sn wknd* **66/1**

3m 44.9s (-6.30) **Going Correction** -0.275s/f (Good)
WFA 4 from 5yo+ 10lb **8** Ran SP% **107.5**
Speed ratings: **104,103,102,102,102 101,100,100** CSF £10.64 CT £52.02 TOTE £3.90: £1.20, £1.80, £2.40; EX 23.70 Trifecta £96.40 Pool £380.42. 2.80 winning units.
Owner The Ipso Facto Syndicate **Bred** Mrs M Beddis **Trained** Musley Bank, N Yorks

FOCUS
A competitive handicap run at just a fair gallop early on, which meant that each of the runners was in with a chance early in the straight. The third and fourth set the standard for the form, which looks solid enough.

NOTEBOOK
Saif Sareea was raised 12lb for his win here last month but that was not enough to stop him following up. He found the best turn of foot in the straight, is clearly a progressive performer and will bid for the hat-trick here on the 29th of this month. *(op 2-1)*
Motive(FR), last seen finishing third in a handicap at the Ebor meeting in August, was entitled to need this reappearance but he ran well in defeat, only finding the in-form and progressive Saif Sareea too strong. He should be capable of winning a handicap off this sort of mark, but he does need decent ground to show his best. *(op 2-1)*
George Stubbs(USA), making his handicap debut, was keeping on well at the finish. He has won over this trip on the level and should get further than this over timber. *(op 10-1)*
Millagros(IRE), fit from the Flat, travelled well but may have been better suited by a stronger-run race. She probably ran to her mark. *(op 10-1)*
Gone Too Far is on a pretty stiff mark over hurdles now but he still ran creditably, rallying well after being headed. *(tchd 11-1)*
Overstrand(IRE), missing the headgear he has worn recently, continues to struggle in handicap company. *(op 9-1)*

2905 EAST LOTHIAN COUNCIL H'CAP CHASE (18 fncs) 3m
2:50 (2:50) (Class 4) (0-110,107) 5-Y-0+ **£6,251** (£1,940; £1,044)

Form RPR
2514 **1** **Snowy (IRE)**[43] 2037 7-11-10 105 GrahamLee 117+
(J I A Charlton) *trckd ldng pair: hdwy to ld 12th: rdn along and j.lft 3 out and next: kpt on strly appr last* **11/4**[1]
26P5 **2** *7* **World Vision (IRE)**[36] 2143 8-11-12 107 (p) BrianHarding 114+
(Ferdy Murphy) *trckd ldr: cl up 12th: ev ch 4 out: sn pushed along and one pce fr 2 out* **7/2**[2]
5253 **3** *9* **Ideal Du Bois Beury (FR)**[14] 2655 9-9-11 81 oh4 PaddyAspell[(3)] 77
(P Monteith) *hld up: lft 3rd at 12th: rdn along and no imp fr 3 out* **7/1**[3]
/P1- **U** **Gallion's Reach (IRE)**[557] 694 10-9-9 83 oh7 ow2 (b) CharliePoste[(7)] —
(M F Harris) *blnd and uns rdr 1st* **20/1**
4634 **F** **She's My Girl (IRE)**[38] 2141 10-10-13 94 (p) JamesDavies —
(John G Carr, Ire) *led tl hdd and fell 12th* **7/2**[2]
2342 **U** **Pessimistic Dick**[57] 1837 12-9-11 83 DougieCostello[(5)] —
(Mrs J C McGregor) *hld up in rr: pushed along and sme hdwy whn hmpd and uns rdr 12th* **7/2**[2]

5m 47.7s (-17.30) **Going Correction** -0.625s/f (Firm) course record **6** Ran SP% **110.6**
Speed ratings: **103,100,97,—,—** — CSF £12.59 CT £55.03 TOTE £2.70: £1.70, £2.60; EX 9.40.

Owner Mr & Mrs Raymond Anderson Green **Bred** Mrs Mary Clarke **Trained** Stocksfield, Northumberland

FOCUS
A modest handicap in which only half the field completed. The form of the winner's second at Perth in May has been upgraded and he ran to that level here.

NOTEBOOK
Snowy(IRE) , whose three previous wins were all at Kelso, was 5lb higher than when gaining the latest victory. He kicked on the home turn and, despite jumping out to his left at the first two fences in the straight, stayed on too well for the runner-up. This ground was right up his street. *(op 3-1 tchd 10-3)*
World Vision(IRE), 6lb lower, ran a better race but never really looked like he wanted to get past the winner in the straight, although he was not helped by that rival jumping across him at a couple of fences. *(op 4-1)*
Ideal Du Bois Beury(FR), who was 4lb out of the handicap, was struggling on the final circuit. He remains without a win since leaving Martin Pipe in the summer of 2002. *(op 9-2)*

Pessimistic Dick was in touch when unseating his rider while trying to avoid a fallen rival. *(op 12-1)*
She's My Girl(IRE), upped in trip, had just been headed when she came down. She had jumped soundly up to then, if slightly out to her left. *(op 12-1)*
Gallion's Reach(IRE) did not get far on this first run since winning a selling chase for Ian Williams in June last year. *(op 12-1)*

2906 SCOTTISH RACING "YOUR BEST BET" STANDARD OPEN NATIONAL HUNT FLAT RACE — 2m

3:20 (3:20) (Class 6) 4-6-Y-0 **£2,199** (£641; £320)

Form			Horse	Jockey	RPR
00/	**1**		**Winter Star**[615] [4787] 5-10-11	MrROHarding(7)	100
			(J J Lambe, Ire) *hld up in tch: gd hdwy over 4f out: chsd wnr 3f out: sn rdn and styd on to ld 2f out: drvn out* **20/1**		
1/	**2**	3	**Lockstockandbarrel (IRE)**[603] [4962] 6-11-11	(t) KeithMercer	104
			(R Shiels) *led and sn clr: rdn along and qcknd over 3f out: drvn and hdd 2f out: kpt on wl u.p ins last* **4/1**[1]		
	3	2 ½	**Still Solvent** 4-11-4	GrahamLee	95
			(J R Turner) *hld up in midfield: hdwy 1/2-way: rdn to chse ldrs 3f out: sn drvn and kpt on same pce fnl 2f* **4/1**[1]		
	4	9	**Turbulent Flight** 4-10-6	DesFlavin(5)	79
			(Mrs L B Normile) *midfield: hdwy to trck ldrs 1/2-way: rdn along 4f out: wknd 3f out* **5/1**[2]		
	5	hd	**Sparky Rocket** 4-10-11	BrianHarding	79
			(B Storey) *hld up: hdwy 6f out: rdn to chse ldrs over 3f out: sn one pce* **12/1**		
	6	11	**Flemington House** 4-10-6	DeclanMcGann(5)	68
			(A M Crow) *nvr nr ldrs* **8/1**[3]		
	7	7	**Harloes Coffee (IRE)**[134] [1169] 5-11-11	TonyDobbin	75
			(Ronald Thompson) *chsd clr ldr: rdn along 6f out: wknd over 4f out* **5/1**[2]		
5	**8**	3 ½	**Nonotreally**[213] [431] 4-11-4	AlanDempsey	64
			(B Mactaggart) *chsd clr ldr: rdn along over 5f out: wknd over 3f out* **17/2**		
	9	9	**Domesday (UAE)** 4-11-4	PadgeWhelan	55
			(W G Harrison) *a rr* **14/1**		
0-0	**10**	29	**Rab Cee**[23] [2480] 5-11-1	GaryBerridge(3)	26
			(W G Young) *chsd ldrs: lost pl over 6f out: bhd fnl 4f* **66/1**		

3m 44.2s (-7.10) **Going Correction** -0.275s/f (Good)
WFA 4 from 5yo+ 10lb **10 Ran SP% 115.6**
Speed ratings: **106,104,103,98,98 93,89,87,83,68** CSF £97.72 TOTE £30.70: £9.80, £2.50, £1.90; EX 333.10 Place 6 £3.66, Place 5 £1.96.
Owner J J Lambe **Bred** Miss Kerry Lane **Trained** Dungannon, Co. Tyrone
■ The first winner in Britain for Richard Harding, brother of Brian.

FOCUS
Probably a weak bumper, and the race has been given a token rating through the second.

NOTEBOOK
Winter Star, out of an unraced half-sister to 1990 Champion Hurdle winner Kribensis, showed little in two runs for Venetia Williams early in 2004. He picked up well in the home straight to land what looked a weak bumper.
Lockstockandbarrel(IRE) landed a Market Rasen bumper in April last year but was sold out of Michael Banks's yard for only 4,000gns the following autumn. Soon in a clear lead on this first run for 20 months, he stayed on too well for most of his rivals but could not repel the winner. *(op 9-2)*
Still Solvent, a half-brother to a winning selling hurdler, changed hands for just 2,000gns in May. This was a satisfactory start and he is entitled to come on for the run. *(op 6-1)*
Turbulent Flight was supported at big odds and ran respectably. She is bred for stamina, being a half-sister to winning chaser pointer Charango Star out of a winner between the flags. *(op 12-1)*
Sparky Rocket, whose dam won over fences, shaped with a bit of promise on this racecourse debut. *(op 10-1)*
Harloes Coffee(IRE) was sold out of Dessie Hughes's yard for 5,000gns at Doncaster in October, having landed a weak Kilbeggan bumper in August. Under a penalty and with the tongue tie left off, he was found wanting. *Official explanation: jockey said gelding had a breathing problem (op 7-4)*
Nonotreally, who faded once in line for home, is out of the smart Wellwotdouthink which makes him a half-brother to Clouding Over, a winner earlier on this card. *(op 8-1 tchd 9-1)*
T/Jkpt: £92.20 to a £1 stake. Pool: £10,000.00. 77.00 winning tickets. T/Plt: £5.00 to a £1 stake. Pool: £38,939.10. 5,627.15 winning tickets. T/Qpdt: £2.30 to a £1 stake. Pool: £4,063.60. 1,269.35 winning tickets. JR

2907 - 2908a (Foreign Racing) - See Raceform Interactive

2776 NAVAN (L-H)
Sunday, December 18

OFFICIAL GOING: Soft (soft to heavy in places on chase course)

2909a BARRY & SANDRA KELLY MEMORIAL NOVICE HURDLE (GRADE 1) — 2m 4f

1:35 (1:35) 4-Y-0+ **£41,489** (£12,127; £5,744; £1,914)

		Horse	Jockey	RPR
1		**Travino (IRE)**[21] [2536] 6-11-12	JLCullen	140+
		(Ms Margaret Mullins, Ire) *mde all: sn clr: reduced advantage 5 out: rdn and strly pressed after 3 out: slt mstke last: kpt on u.p run-in: all out* **4/1**[3]		
2	nk	**Nicanor (FR)**[21] [2536] 4-11-7	PCarberry	135
		(Noel Meade, Ire) *hld up towards rr: 3rd & hdwy after 4 out: 2nd travelling best 3 out: disp ld whn mstke 2 out: styd on wl u.p fr last: jst* **5/2**[1]		
3	8	**Mossbank (IRE)**[29] [2356] 5-11-12	CO'Dwyer	132
		(Michael Hourigan, Ire) *mod 4th: impr into 2nd after 4 out: 3rd and rdn next: sn no ex* **4/1**[3]		
4	1 ½	**Powerstation (IRE)**[21] [2536] 5-11-12	DNRussell	131
		(C Byrnes, Ire) *hld up: last and trailing 1/2-way: prog into mod 4th 3 out: kpt on same pced fr next* **4/1**[3]		
5	25	**Forty Licks (IRE)**[36] [2193] 8-11-12	APMcCoy	106
		(E J O'Grady, Ire) *mod 2nd: slt mstke 5 out: wknd next: eased fr 2 out* **7/2**[2]		
6	¾	**Ballyagran (IRE)**[35] [2228] 5-11-12	DFO'Regan	105
		(Noel Meade, Ire) *mod 3rd: slt mstke 6th: wknd fr 4 out: eased fr 2 out* **25/1**		

4m 55.8s
WFA 4 from 5yo+ 11lb **6 Ran SP% 114.6**
CSF £15.16 TOTE £6.60: £2.60, £1.60; DF 18.30.
Owner P C Kilroy **Bred** James Treacy **Trained** Gowran, Co. Kilkenny
■ Stewards' Enquiry : J L Cullen caution: used whip with excessive frequency

NOTEBOOK
Travino(IRE) really stretched these in what was arguably the best novice hurdle of the season so far. He made a slight mistake at the last and at the end was all out to hold on, having a harder race than at one stage might have seemed necessary as he returned with a minor cut on his off-fore. Cheltenham options include both the novice stayers' events but he might sidestep Leopardstown at Christmas.
Nicanor(FR) looked to be going best when getting on terms three out but a mistake at the next knocked him back a bit and going through the flattened flight at the last did not help. He stayed on strongly uphill, though. Having the four-year-old allowance so late in the year is unique to Ireland *and was nearly the decisive factor. He finished well clear of the remainder and is worth following. (op 3/1 tchd 9/4)*
Mossbank(IRE), supplemented for 9,000euros, had his limitations rather ruthlessly exposed. *(op 7/2)*
Powerstation(IRE) could not go the early pace and trailed the field. Unable to make any impression over the last three flights, this run has to be viewed questionably. *(op 4/1 tchd 5/1)*
Forty Licks(IRE), weak in the market, lost his unbeaten record. He dropped away before the straight and was eased. *(op 5/2 tchd 4/1)*

2910 - 2915a (Foreign Racing) - See Raceform Interactive

2598 THURLES (R-H)
Sunday, December 18

OFFICIAL GOING: Yielding

2916a HORSE AND JOCKEY HOTEL HURDLE (LISTED RACE) — 2m

1:45 (1:45) 4-Y-0+ **£16,159** (£4,741; £2,258; £769)

		Horse	Jockey	RPR
1		**Pom Flyer (FR)**[15] [2650] 5-11-4 119	KTColeman(5)	125
		(F Flood, Ire) *chsd ldrs: impr into 2nd appr 6 out: chal and led 2 out: sn rdn clr: reduced ld run-in: all out* **10/1**		
2	hd	**High Priestess (IRE)**[14] [2667] 6-11-1 116	(p) TGMRyan(3)	120
		(M J P O'Brien, Ire) *chsd ldr in 2nd: 3rd appr 6 out: rdn bef 3 out: 4th bef st: wnt mod 2nd bef last: styd on wl run-in: jst failed* **10/3**[2]		
3	1 ½	**Rocket Ship (IRE)**[44] [2032] 5-11-2 127	NPMadden	117
		(Noel Meade, Ire) *racd in 5th: sltly slow 2nd: wnt 3rd bef st: sn 2nd: no imp u.p fr after 2 out: kpt on same pce* **7/4**[1]		
4	10	**Sauterelle (IRE)**[28] [2398] 5-10-6 98	(t) JRRyan(5)	102
		(Thomas Mullins, Ire) *led: clr for much: hit 3rd: mstke 3 out: strly pressed and hdd next: sn no ex* **25/1**		
5	shd	**Lissbonney Project (IRE)**[10] [2738] 7-11-2 119	AndrewJMcNamara	106
		(Philip Fenton, Ire) *racd in 3rd: mstke 5th: 4th appr 6 out: rdn after 3 out: no imp u.p fr next* **7/4**[1]		
6	dist	**High Reef (FR)**[99] [1158] 7-10-11 109	DJCasey	101
		(C F Swan, Ire) *a in rr: lost tch 4 out: sn no imp u.p* **6/1**[3]		

4m 1.30s
WFA 4 from 5yo+ 10lb **8 Ran SP% 123.0**
CSF £47.15 TOTE £19.90: £7.20, £2.70; DF 76.90.
Owner Madfish Syndicate **Bred** Mme Elaine Brien **Trained** Grange Con, Co Wicklow

NOTEBOOK
Pom Flyer(FR) is as inconsistent as they come. Tailed off in a Fairyhouse handicap of 121 a *fortnight previously, he went on here after the second last and battled well.Official explanation: trainer's representative said, regarding the improved form shown, gelding benefited for the return to an easier track and for running in non-handicap company, adding that gelding has had more success in conditions races in the past and may enjoy the less competitive nature of these races (op 10/1 tchd 11/1)*
High Priestess(IRE) finds it difficult to get her head in front but finished willingly enough.
Rocket Ship(IRE) was not altogether fluent. He had his chance after the last but there was only a lukewarm response. *(op 6/4)*
Lissbonney Project(IRE), whose most recent run, over fences, saw his rider suspended for "insufficient effort", was under pressure before the straight and never looked a possibility. *(op 13/8)*

2917 - 2920a (Foreign Racing) - See Raceform Interactive

2763 DONCASTER (L-H)
Monday, December 19

OFFICIAL GOING: Chase course - good (good to firm in places); hurdle course - good to firm (good in places)
The ground was described as 'good to firm'.
Wind: Light, half-against Weather: Fine and sunny

2921 TOP CAT JUVENILE NOVICES' HURDLE (8 hdls) — 2m 110y

12:15 (12:15) (Class 4) 3-Y-0 **£4,333** (£1,272; £636; £317)

Form			Horse	Jockey	RPR
2	**1**		**Gidam Gidam (IRE)**[18] [2587] 3-10-12	(p) TomSiddall	98
			(J Mackie) *cl up: led 2nd: rdn and hit 2 out: mstke last: r.o wl u.p flat* **7/1**		
	2	3 ½	**Daldini**[71] 3-10-12	DominicElsworth	95
			(Mrs S J Smith) *led tl hit 2nd and hdd: cl up: effrt and ev ch 3 out: rdn and hit next: drvn and hit last: kpt on same pce flat* **25/1**		
20	**3**	½	**Knightsbridge Hill (IRE)**[86] [1551] 3-10-12	RobertThornton	94
			(A King) *hld up towards rr: hdwy 5th: chsd ldng pair 3 out: rdn next and kpt on same pce appr last* **12/1**		
	4	15	**Linnet (GER)**[71] 3-10-5	PaulMoloney	72
			(Ian Williams) *hmpd and nt fluent 1st: trckd ldrs on inner: rdn along appr 3 out and outpcd fr next* **5/1**[2]		
652P	**5**	shd	**Dock Tower (IRE)**[26] [2442] 3-10-9	(t) PeterBuchanan(3)	79
			(M E Sowersby) *in tch: rdn along and outpcd 4 out: styd on fr 2 out* **9/1**		
2313	**6**	3	**Finland (UAE)**[51] [1923] 3-11-5 113	JoeTizzard	84+
			(Mrs A Duffield) *nt fluent 1st: trckd ldrs: hit 4th: sn rdn along and lost pl: bhd appr 3 out: styd on u.p fr next* **4/1**[1]		
	7	1 ¼	**Estate**[178] 3-10-12	TomDoyle	75
			(P R Webber) *keen: in tch: hit 3rd and sn pushed along: hdwy after 4 out: chsd ldrs next: sn rdn and wknd 2 out* **11/1**		
050	**8**	1 ½	**Esquillon**[18] [2587] 3-10-5	KeithMercer	66
			(S Parr) *in tch: rdn along appr 3 out and sn btn* **50/1**		
03	**9**	nk	**Darwaz (IRE)**[10] [2753] 3-10-12	NoelFehily	73
			(D R Gandolfo) *cl up: blnd 2nd: hit next: rdn along and lost pl 4th: bhd appr 3 out* **6/1**[3]		
	10	1 ½	**Raffish**[149] 3-10-12	TomScudamore	71
			(M Scudamore) *chsd ldrs: hit 2nd: rdn along 4 out: wknd next* **66/1**		
6	**11**	nk	**Elaala (USA)**[14] [2676] 3-10-5	GrahamLee	64
			(M Todhunter) *midfield: hit 2nd: j. slowly 5th: hdwy on inner appr 3 out: rdn and chsng ldrs next: grad wknd* **50/1**		
	12	4	**Maneki Neko (IRE)**[84] 3-10-12	NeilMulholland	67
			(E W Tuer) *in tch: hdwy to chse ldrs 5th: rdn along next and sn wknd* **25/1**		
P6	**13**	17	**Tarkar (IRE)**[24] [2477] 3-10-12	AlanDempsey	50
			(J Howard Johnson) *midfield: rdn along 5th: sn wknd* **100/1**		
P	**14**	8	**Salinger (USA)**[15] [2661] 3-10-12	TonyDobbin	42
			(Andrew Turnell) *a rr* **66/1**		

0 **15** *11* **Belton**[10] 2753 3-10-12 KennyJohnson 31
(Ronald Thompson) *a rr* **200/1**
P **Autumn Dream**[203] 3-10-2 PaddyAspell(3) —
(Miss J E Foster) *s.s: a rr: bhd whn p.u bef 3 out* **100/1**
1 **P** **Baie Des Flamands (USA)**[32] 2286 3-11-5 HenryOliver —
(Miss S J Wilton) *prom: rdn along and wknd after 4 out: blnd next and sn p.u* **8/1**

4m 1.20s (-10.20) **Going Correction** -0.75s/f (Firm) **17** Ran SP% **117.7**
Speed ratings: **94,92,92,85,85 83,83,82,82,81 81,79,71,67,62** —,— CSF £168.91 TOTE £7.50: £2.00, £10.10, £3.70; EX 381.30.
Owner Mrs Jennifer Woodward **Bred** Gerrardstown House Stud **Trained** Church Broughton , Derbys

FOCUS
Just an ordinary juvenile hurdle run at a steady pace and the first three well clear in the end. The winner sets the standard but the modest time limits the form.

NOTEBOOK
Gidam Gidam(IRE), again fitted with cheekpieces, made the best of his way home and though his jumping was not fault free his attitude could not be questioned. *(op 10-1)*
Daldini, a winner at two, is rated 18lb better than the winner on the level. Fitted with a cross noseband, he was in the thick of things from the off but after clouting the final two flights had to admit defeat on the run-in.
Knightsbridge Hill(IRE), absent for two months, is quite a keen type. He ran a lot better than Market Rasen but this may be as good as he is. *(op 14-1)*
Linnet(GER), twice a winner on the Flat and rated 74 in that sphere, had an unhappy experience at the first flight and found the first three leaving her for dead up the home straight. She ought to be capable of better than this. *(op 11-2)*
Dock Tower(IRE), pulled up a month earlier, continually swished his tail in the paddock and his Wetherby second probably flatters him. *(tchd 8-1)*
Finland(UAE) was badly let down by his jumping and was out of contention from the halfway *mark. This was simply too bad to be true. Official explanation: jockey said gelding jumped poorly throughout (op 7-2 tchd 9-2 in places)*
Tarkar(IRE) *Official explanation: jockey said gelding finished lame but returned sound (op 80-1)*
Baie Des Flamands(USA) stopped to nothing after hitting three out when on the retreat and was *found to have suffered an over-reach. Official explanation: jockey said colt never travelled and over reached itself (op 15-2 tchd 7-1)*

2922 SANDS VENUE NOVICES' H'CAP CHASE (17 fncs 1 omitted) 3m
12:45 (12:46) (Class 3) (0-120,112)
5-Y-O+ **£6,915** (£2,030; £1,015; £507)

Form RPR
12-4 **1** **Dolmur (IRE)**[12] 2701 5-11-10 **110** KeithMercer 113+
(Ferdy Murphy) *chsd ldrs: lft 2nd 10th: 1l down whn lef infront 4 out: rdn next: hld on wl run-in* **15/2**
63-3 **2** *1 1/4* **The Grocers Curate (IRE)**[19] 2574 5-11-12 **112** MickFitzgerald 114+
(N J Henderson) *trckd ldrs: drvn along 13th: lft 2nd next: chal 2 out: no ex run-in* **6/1**[3]
63P **3** *20* **Waynesworld (IRE)**[22] 2517 7-10-8 **94** TomScudamore 81+
(M Scudamore) *chsd ldrs: outpcd fr 12th: lft mod 3rd 4 out* **6/1**[3]
43PP **4** *dist* **Cirrus (FR)**[13] 2689 6-10-9 **95** (b[1]) RichardMcGrath —
(K G Reveley) *chsd ldrs: wkng whn mstke 11th: sn bhd: t.o 13th: btn 42l* **25/1**
133U **F** **Pebble Bay**[15] 2654 10-11-8 **108** DominicElsworth —
(Mrs S J Smith) *w ldrs: fell heavily 10th: dead* **11/4**[2]
6221 **F** **Dunbrody Millar (IRE)**[13] 2686 7-11-1 **101** RichardJohnson —
(P Bowen) *led: stl travelling strly and 1 l up whn fell heavily 4 out* **5/2**[1]
4-PB **P** **Grande Creole (FR)**[11] 2729 6-11-9 **109** ChristianWilliams —
(P F Nicholls) *t.k.h in rr: blnd bdly 2nd: mstke 9th: sn rdn: t.o 11th: p.u bef 13th* **12/1**

5m 58.5s (-18.30) **Going Correction** -0.75s/f (Firm) **7** Ran SP% **107.1**
Speed ratings: **100,99,92**,—,— —,— CSF £44.20 CT £245.22 TOTE £8.80: £4.30, £2.10; EX 55.90.
Owner Sean J Murphy **Bred** Kawanin Partnership **Trained** West Witton, N Yorks
■ Stewards' Enquiry : Mick Fitzgerald one-day ban: used whip with excessive force (Dec 30)

FOCUS
A modest novices' handicap in which jumping was the name of the game and in the end the first two slogged it out.

NOTEBOOK
Dolmur(IRE), handed the race on a plate four out, would not be denied. He seems to just jump and stay. *(op 10-1)*
The Grocers Curate(IRE), a big type, had to be rousted along to keep tabs on the leaders but eventually landing upsides at the second last, he then simply proved too slow. He stays all right but lacks a couple of gears. *(op 4-1 tchd 7-1)*
Waynesworld(IRE), back over fences, seems to have gone right off the boil since his two wins over fences in the autumn. *(op 15-2 tchd 11-2)*
Cirrus(FR), tried in blinkers, seemed to lose all interest and in the end could do no more than complete in his own time. *(op 22-1)*
Dunbrody Millar(IRE), 8lb higher, seemed to find the totally different surface no problem and was still travelling strongly in front when he smashed the rail at the fourth last fence. *(op 9-4)*
Pebble Bay sadly fell with fatal consequences. *(op 9-4)*

2923 THE-SANDS.CO.UK NOVICES' HURDLE (10 hdls) 2m 3f 110y
1:20 (1:21) (Class 3) 4-Y-0+ **£5,543** (£1,627; £813; £406)

Form RPR
56 **1** **Napoleon (IRE)**[31] 2309 4-10-12 RichardJohnson 112+
(P J Hobbs) *trckd ldrs: hdwy 6th: cl up 3 out: sn led and hit next: rdn last: drvn and edgd rt flat: kpt on wl* **7/2**[2]
3-61 **2** *1* **Cloudless Dawn**[22] 2515 5-10-11 RussGarritty 109
(P Beaumont) *a cl up: led 3 out: sn rdn and hdd: ev ch tl drvn and n.m.r flat: no ex towards fin* **9/4**[1]
00-2 **3** *3* **Beau De Turgeon (FR)**[20] 2559 4-10-12 NoelFehily 107
(Ian Williams) *hld up: stdy hdwy 6th: chsd ldrs 3 out: sn rdn and kpt on same pce appr last* **6/1**
-0 **4** *1 3/4* **Adventurist**[9] 2763 5-10-12 ChristianWilliams 105
(P Bowen) *in tch: hdwy to trck ldrs 1/2-way: rdn along 3 out: kpt on same pce fr next* **12/1**
2 **5** *2 1/2* **Fuel Cell (IRE)**[9] 2763 4-10-12 KeithMercer 103
(M E Sowersby) *midfield: hdwy 6th: rdn along to chse ldrs 3 out: drvn and no imp fr next* **11/2**[3]
5-6P **6** *20* **Cash King (IRE)**[16] 2631 5-10-12 DominicElsworth 83
(Mrs S J Smith) *a.p: rdn along appr 3 out and sn wknd* **33/1**
6-00 **7** *1/2* **Willies Way**[16] 2627 5-10-12 PadgeWhelan 82
(Mrs S J Smith) *keen: cl up: rdn along 4 out: wknd appr next* **25/1**
60 **8** *3/4* **Majorca**[43] 2081 4-10-12 GrahamLee 82
(J Howard Johnson) *keen: led: rdn along and hdd 3 out: sn wknd* **22/1**
0-50 **9** *3/4* **Hialeah**[78] 1611 4-10-9 MrTGreenall(3) 81
(M W Easterby) *hld up: sme hdwy appr 3 out: nvr a factor* **66/1**

PF-P **10** *5* **Mad Max Too**[54] 1888 6-10-9 (p) PeterBuchanan(3) 76
(N Wilson) *a rr: bhd whn mstkes 3 out and next* **100/1**
0 **11** *5* **Field Spark**[26] 2444 5-10-9 (p) LeeVickers(3) 71
(J G Given) *bhd fr 1/2-way: blnd 2 out and hit last* **100/1**
0/P **12** *3 1/2* **Pride Of Finewood (IRE)**[16] 2638 7-10-12 BruceGibson 67
(E W Tuer) *a bhd* **100/1**
0 **13** *4* **Nigwell Forbees (IRE)**[26] 2444 4-10-7 BrianHughes(5) 63
(J Howard Johnson) *midfield: nmstke 1st: pushed along and in tch 6th: rdn next and sn wknd* **100/1**
10- **14** *12* **Coolawarra (IRE)**[254] 4774 6-10-12 TonyDobbin 51
(D M Forster) *midfield on outer: blnd 4th: mstke next: sn rdn along and lost pl: bhd fr 4 out* **14/1**
P **15** *1 1/2* **Bowes Cross**[13] 2690 5-10-7 ThomasDreaper(5) 50
(Ferdy Murphy) *a bhd* **100/1**
0 **16** *21* **Vrisaki (IRE)**[43] 2081 4-10-12 AlanDempsey 29
(M E Sowersby) *chsd ldrs: rdn along 6th: sn lost pl and bhd* **100/1**
00 **17** *6* **Red Bluff (IRE)**[9] 2763 5-10-9 AnthonyCoyle(3) 23
(H Alexander) *a bhd* **125/1**

4m 43.0s (-10.60) **Going Correction** -0.75s/f (Firm)
WFA 4 from 5yo+ 10lb **17** Ran SP% **116.4**
Speed ratings: **91,90,89,88,87 79,79,79,78,76 74,73,71,67,66 58,55** CSF £10.75 TOTE £5.00: £1.50, £1.60, £2.40; EX 17.20.
Owner M J Tuckey **Bred** Premier Bloodstock **Trained** Withycombe, Somerset

FOCUS
Plenty of dead wood in just an ordinary novices' hurdle with the first five a long way clear in the end. The winning time was 6.8 seconds slower than the later handicap over the same trip and the form is rated through the runner-up.

NOTEBOOK
Napoleon(IRE), a reformed character since being gelded, had to dig deep but in the end did just enough. *(op 4-1 tchd 3-1)*
Cloudless Dawn, carrying a penalty in a better races, made the best of her way home and went down fighting. She looks sure to make a nice chaser in time. *(op 2-1)*
Beau De Turgeon(FR) showed his much-improved Hereford outing was no fluke and the livelier ground did not seem to bother him. *(tchd 13-2)*
Adventurist showed a lot more than on his debut a week ago and, once a fair tool on the Flat, there ought to be even better to come. *(op 16-1)*
Fuel Cell(IRE), a burly individual, found this company much tougher and never really threatened. *(op 5-1)*

2924 RICHARD SHELTON NOVICES' CHASE (12 fncs 3 omitted) 2m 3f
1:55 (1:56) (Class 3) 4-Y-0+ **£8,000** (£2,440; £1,274; £692)

Form RPR
1P-2 **1** **Kasthari (IRE)**[30] 2344 6-11-2 GrahamLee 135+
(J Howard Johnson) *led to 2nd: chsd ldr: lft in ld 9th: wnt clr between last 2: easily* **9/4**[2]
10-3 **2** *8* **Reel Missile**[9] 2764 6-10-11 AdamPogson(5) 123+
(C T Pogson) *led 2nd: blnd and hdd 9th: outpcd by wnr 2 out* **25/1**
300- **3** *2* **Red Ruffles (IRE)**[278] 4397 6-10-11 WilliamKennedy(5) 118
(Noel T Chance) *lft mod 3rd 6th: prom 9th: kpt on same pce fr next* **22/1**[3]
24-F **4** *dist* **Go For Bust**[30] 2344 6-11-2 120 AndrewTinkler 88
(N J Henderson) *last whn mstke 1st: sme hdwy 6th: j. slowly 3 out: sn lost tch: t.o: btn 36l* **40/1**
-125 **F** **Chilling Place (IRE)**[36] 2208 6-11-8 RichardJohnson —
(P J Hobbs) *trckd ldrs: handy 3rd whn fell 6th* **15/8**[1]
13-1 **U** **Taranis (FR)**[23] 2488 4-11-1 136 (t) ChristianWilliams —
(P F Nicholls) *trckd ldrs: handy 3rd whn blnd and uns rdr 5th* **9/4**[2]

4m 38.6s (-18.80) **Going Correction** -0.75s/f (Firm) course record
WFA 4 from 6yo 10lb **6** Ran SP% **107.0**
Speed ratings: **109,105,104**,—,— — CSF £36.22 TOTE £3.30: £2.10, £4.80; EX 37.30.
Owner Elliott Brothers **Bred** His Highness The Aga Khan's Studs S C **Trained** Billy Row, Co Durham

FOCUS
A decent chase rated through the winner; it was a strongly-run race and the winner jumped like an old hand. The fourth last fence had to be omitted after being damaged in the previous chase.

NOTEBOOK
Kasthari(IRE) ◆, suited by going left-handed, has a fine record here. After being left in front, he sprinted clear between the last two bouncing off the fast ground. He dead-heated in the 2004 Doncaster Cup and clearly has the potential to go quite some way over fences when conditions are in his favour. *(op 5-2)*
Reel Missile, rated 24lb behind the winner over hurdles, made a bad blunder and lost the advantage but he deserves credit for the way he stuck to his guns. He can surely make his mark over fences against lesser opposition.
Red Ruffles(IRE) took the eye in the paddock and making his debut over fences on his first outing *since March, he will have learnt plenty and will surely make his mark at a slightly lower level. (op 20-1)*
Go For Bust, an early faller on his chase debut a month earlier, lacked any confidence at his fences and clearly has a lot to learn. *(op 33-1)*
Chilling Place(IRE) was on the heels of the leaders and travelling strongly when crashing out at a relatively early stage. Hopefully this will simply prove a blip. *(tchd 2-1, 9-4 in places)*
Taranis(FR) took quite a grip and seemed unlucky to put his rider on the floor at an early stage. He will soon wipe this off his record. *(tchd 2-1, 9-4 in places)*

2925 SANDS LIVE H'CAP HURDLE (10 hdls) 2m 3f 110y
2:30 (2:33) (Class 3) (0-120,120) 4-Y-0+ **£6,554** (£1,924; £962; £480)

Form RPR
2-20 **1** **Down's Folly (IRE)**[32] 2285 5-10-6 **100** WayneHutchinson 105
(H D Daly) *hld up in tch: hdwy 4 out: led next: sn rdn and hdd appr last: rallied to ld flat: styd on wl* **5/1**[2]
2012 **2** *hd* **Sunday City (JPN)**[30] 2347 4-10-5 **104** TomGreenway(5) 110+
(P Bowen) *hld up in tch: hdwy 4 out: cl up next: rdn to ld appr last: hdd flat: drvn and kpt on* **13/2**[3]
31 **3** *3* **Texas Holdem (IRE)**[33] 2264 6-11-4 **117** MichaelMcAlister(5) 119
(M Smith) *c hased ldrs: rdn along 4 out: dxriven after next and kpt on same pce* **12/1**
14P **4** *1* **Thedublinpublican (IRE)**[59] 1818 5-10-3 **100** LeeVickers(3) 103+
(C C Bealby) *prom: led 4th: rdn along and hdd 3 out: cl up whn hit next: sn drvn and wknd appr last* **40/1**
00-F **5** *3/4* **Presumptuous**[9] 2766 5-10-11 **105** DominicElsworth 106+
(Mrs S J Smith) *trckd ldrs: rdn along: blnd and outpcd 3 out: swtchd rt next: drvn and kpt on fr last* **7/1**
2-64 **6** *hd* **Shirazi**[11] 2714 7-10-5 **104** (t) SamCurling(5) 104
(D R Gandolfo) *hld up in rr: hdwy 4 out: rdn along to chse ldrs next: drvn and no imp fr 2 out* **16/1**
-001 **7** *hd* **Fard Du Moulin Mas (FR)**[9] 2766 12-10-11 **105** BrianCrowley 106+
(M E D Francis) *led to 4th: cl up: rdn along 4 out: wknd after next* **16/1**

3-41 **8** *21* **Euro American (GER)**[16] [2639] 5-11-2 **110** .... AlanDempsey 89
(E W Tuer) *hld up and bhd: stdy hdwy 4 out: chsd ldrs next: sn rdn and btn* **8/1**

U00P **9** *1 ½* **Migration**[52] [1912] 9-11-2 **110** .... JoeTizzard 87
(Mrs S Lamyman) *hld up: a rr* **100/1**

2310 **10** *¾* **Mister Arjay (USA)**[32] [2292] 5-11-7 **120** .... ThomasDreaper(5) 96
(B Ellison) *in tch: rdn along appr 4 out and sn wknd* **16/1**

1640 **11** *5* **Tiger Frog (USA)**[112] [1366] 6-10-8 **102** ....(b) WarrenMarston 73
(J Mackie) *hld up towards rr: pushed along and bhd fr 1/2-way* **33/1**

050 **12** *1 ½* **Border Tale**[7] [2478] 5-10-13 **107** .... JamesDavies 77
(James Moffatt) *chsd ldrs: rdn along 4 out: wknd after next* **40/1**

03P0 **13** *26* **Renvyle (IRE)**[9] [2766] 7-10-8 **112** ....(e) JohnFlavin(10) 56
(R C Guest) *nt fluent: mstke 6th: a bhd* **100/1**

412 **R** **Shining Strand**[22] [2530] 6-11-5 **113** .... AndrewTinkler —
(N J Henderson) *ref to r: tk no part* **11/4**[1]

100/ **P** **Little Sport (IRE)**[991] [4456] 8-11-9 **117** .... SamStronge —
(Miss V Scott) *trckd ldrs: hdwy and cl up 4 out: rdn along and wknd bef next: bhd whn p.u bef last* **33/1**

4m 36.2s (-17.40) **Going Correction** -0.75s/f (Firm) course record
WFA 4 from 5yo+ 10lb **15** Ran SP% **118.4**
Speed ratings: **104,103,102,102,102 101,101,93,92,92 90,89,79,—,—** CSF £35.57 CT £373.08 TOTE £5.90: £2.10, £2.60, £3.70; EX 40.30 Trifecta £233.00 Part won. Pool: £328.30 - 0.20 winning tickets..
Owner Strachan,Gabb,Clarke,Griffith & Barlow **Bred** Oliver Maguire **Trained** Stanton Lacy, Shropshire

FOCUS
No hanging about in this moderate contest and plenty still in with a chance at the second last flight. The form looks solid with the first seven running close to their marks.

NOTEBOOK
Down's Folly(IRE), who lost a front and back shoe at Hereford, looked in tremendous trim in the paddock. He showed a real fighting spirit to regain the lead on the run-in and never flinched under a powerful ride. *(op 9-2)*
Sunday City(JPN), having just his fifth start over hurdles, looked to be travelling the better when going a neck up at the last but crowded on the run-in the winning combination in the end proved just too strong. *(op 15-2)*
Texas Holdem(IRE), 5lb higher, seemed to find the much quicker ground no problem. *(op 16-1)*
Thedublinpublican(IRE), absent for two months, went on and stepped up what was already a sound pace but he was struggling for reserves after clouting the second last.
Presumptuous came again and finished best of all but was found to have bled from the nose. *Official explanation: jockey said gelding had bled from the nose (op 6-1 tchd 15-2)*
Shirazi continues in his uphill battle with the assessors.
Fard Du Moulin Mas(FR), 6lb higher, was unable to make it three from three over this course and distance. *(op 12-1)*
Border Tale *Official explanation: jockey said gelding had a breathing problem (op 33-1)*
Shining Strand, led to post very early, became warm and agitated at the start and, after two or *three attempts to get them under way, he finally stuck his toes in and refused to jump off. (op 10-3 tchd 7-2)*

2926 SANDS RECORDS H'CAP CHASE (12 fncs 3 omitted) 2m 3f
3:00 (3:04) (Class 4) (0-110,109) 5-Y-O+ **£5,562** (£1,633; £816; £407)

Form RPR

0-14 **1** **Lindsay (FR)**[27] [2420] 6-11-4 **106** .... TomGreenway(5) 114
(H D Daly) *t.k.h: trckd ldrs: slt ld 2 out: hld on nr fin* **9/2**[3]

1-25 **2** *hd* **Alcopop**[26] [2431] 6-11-5 **107** .... PaulO'Neill(5) 116+
(Miss Venetia Williams) *led to 7th: led 9th: hit next: hdd 2 out: rallied run-in: jst hld* **7/2**[2]

56-6 **3** *1 ½* **Sound Of Cheers**[23] [2498] 8-11-10 **107** ....(t) KennyJohnson 115+
(F Kirby) *hld up in tch: hdwy to join ldrs 7th: outpcd 2 out: styd on wl run-in* **25/1**

3532 **4** *¾* **Pure Brief (IRE)**[10] [2754] 8-10-6 **89** ....(p) PaulMoloney 95
(J Mackie) *trckd ldrs: hit 9th: kpt on same pce fr 2 out* **6/1**

12-0 **5** *1 ½* **Kew Jumper (IRE)**[44] [2051] 6-11-12 **109** .... GrahamLee 114+
(Andrew Turnell) *sn w ldrs: led 7th to 9th: nt qckn fr 2 out* **5/2**[1]

P/60 **6** *2 ½* **Prairie Minstrel (USA)**[22] [2522] 11-10-4 **87** ....(p) WayneHutchinson 91+
(R Dickin) *in tch: hdwy to chse ldrs appr 3 out: 4th and one pce whn hit last* **33/1**

3-33 **P** **Tipp Top (IRE)**[218] [368] 8-10-4 **87** ....(t) RichardMcGrath —
(O Brennan) *prom: lost pl after 6th: sn bhd: t.o whn pulld up bef 3 out* **8/1**

0-05 **P** **Captains Table**[18] [2583] 12-10-7 **90** .... TomDoyle —
(F Jordan) *w ldrs: reminders after 3rd: mstke 5th: lost pl next: sn bhd: t.o whn p.u bef 3 out* **12/1**

4m 42.6s (-14.80) **Going Correction** -0.75s/f (Firm) course record **8** Ran SP% **108.9**
Speed ratings: **101,100,100,99,99 98,—,—** CSF £19.18 CT £309.12 TOTE £5.40: £2.40, £1.50, £3.60; EX 22.40.
Owner John R Wilson **Bred** Rene Ricous And Mrs Ricous **Trained** Stanton Lacy, Shropshire

FOCUS
Not a strong pace resulting in all six finishers still being in with a shout two out making the form look suspect. The first fence in the home straight, four out, again had to be omitted after being damaged in the first chase.

NOTEBOOK
Lindsay(FR) took quite a grip as a result of the moderate pace. He jumped to the front at the second last and would simply not be denied. *(tchd 4-1)*
Alcopop enjoyed himself in front and, after being collared, to his credit he fought back hard all the *way to the line. His attitude does not always impress but he did nothing at all wrong this time. (op 3-1)*
Sound Of Cheers, 2lb high than the last of his four victories last term, was tapped for toe at a vital stage but showed that he is back on song with a gritty effort on the run-in. *(op 14-1)*
Pure Brief(IRE), back up in trip, battled away over the last two without ever looking a real threat. *(tchd 13-2)*
Kew Jumper(IRE) ran much better than on his return. Three miles round Wetherby is his cup of tea. *(op 11-4 tchd 3-1)*
Prairie Minstrel(USA) ran much much better than on his two previous starts this time after a lengthy abscence. *(op 20-1)*

2927 E B F PLONG AND TRAVES "JUNIOR" STANDARD OPEN NATIONAL HUNT FLAT RACE 1m 5f
3:30 (3:32) (Class 6) 3-Y-O **£2,768** (£806; £403)

Form RPR

1 **Dand Nee (USA)** 3-10-5 .... TonyDobbin 96+
(G A Swinbank) *hld up: hdwy 4f out: chal over 2f out: led over 1f out: hld on towards fin* **11/2**

2 *nk* **Bleak House (IRE)** 3-10-12 .... JasonMaguire 101
(T P Tate) *trckd ldrs: led over 2f out: hrd rdn and hdd over 1f out: no ex nr fin* **5/1**[3]

3 *10* **Sybarite Chief (IRE)** 3-10-12 .... AnthonyRoss 88
(R A Fahey) *mid-div: effrt 4f out: styd on one pce fnl 2f* **18/1**

4 *2 ½* **Sundarbob (IRE)** 3-10-12 .... TomDoyle 85
(P R Webber) *hld up in rr: effrt over 4f out: kpt on one pce fnl 2f* **16/1**

5 *hd* **La Dame Brune (FR)** 3-10-5 .... AndrewTinkler 78
(N J Henderson) *trckd ldrs: rdn: edgd lft and outpcd over 3f out: kpt on fnl f* **3/1**[1]

0 **6** *¾* **Lilian Alexander**[27] [2425] 3-10-0 .... AdamPogson(5) 77
(J R Holt) *led: hrd rdn 4f out: hdd over 2f out: wknd over 1f out* **40/1**

7 *1* **Dr Flight** 3-10-12 .... JoeTizzard 83
(H Morrison) *mid-div: reminders 6f out: sn outpcd: kpt on fnl 3f* **9/2**[2]

8 *8* **Jose Bove** 3-10-2 .... JosephStevenson(10) 72
(R Dickin) *in tch: effrt 4f out: wknd over 2f out* **100/1**

9 *1 ½* **Flowerpotman** 3-10-9 .... MrTGreenall(3) 70
(M W Easterby) *mid-div: outpcd over 3f out* **25/1**

10 *shd* **Commanche Sioux** 3-10-2 .... PaddyAspell(3) 63
(M W Easterby) *in tch on outer: lost pl over 4f out* **33/1**

0 **11** *¾* **Cold Call**[22] [2521] 3-10-12 .... NeilMulholland 69
(C W Thornton) *in rr: hdwy 4f out: lost pl over 2f out* **100/1**

12 *2* **Mightymuller (IRE)** 3-10-7 .... SamCurling(5) 67
(D R Gandolfo) *mid-div: hdwy 5f out: sn chsng ldrs: wknd over 2f out* **28/1**

5 **13** *4* **Ember Dancer**[41] [2105] 3-10-12 .... WayneHutchinson 61
(Ian Williams) *trckd ldrs: lost pl over 2f out* **12/1**

14 *5* **Kaddasan** 3-10-12 .... PaulMoloney 55
(D E Cantillon) *hld up in rr: hdwy to chse ldrs 7f out: lost pl over 4f out* **18/1**

6 **15** *2 ½* **Whatsinitforme (IRE)**[46] [2014] 3-10-12 .... WarrenMarston 52
(Mrs D A Hamer) *chsd ldrs: drvn 7f out: lost pl 5f out* **28/1**

16 *¾* **La Bonne Vie** 3-10-12 .... ChristianWilliams 51
(C Roberts) *trckd ldrs: lost pl over 4f out* **66/1**

17 *9* **Freshford (IRE)** 3-10-12 .... RussGarritty 39
(N Tinkler) *a in rr: bhd fnl 4f* **66/1**

18 *22* **Royal Spell** 3-9-12 .... RichardSpate(7) 3
(M Appleby) *stdd s: a in rr: wl bhd fnl 3f* **80/1**

3m 2.50s **18** Ran SP% **121.7**
CSF £30.38 TOTE £7.10: £3.00, £1.60, £5.70; EX 66.30 Place 6 £767.70, Place 5 £114.76.
Owner Miss Sally R Haynes **Bred** Darley **Trained** Melsonby, N Yorks
■ Stewards' Enquiry : Jason Maguire two-day ban: used whip with excessive force (Dec 30-31)

FOCUS
A better than average pace for this bumper, in the end the first two pulling well clear. They could prove better than average and the race could work out.

NOTEBOOK
Dand Nee(USA), who had trouble with the stalls on the Flat, had to dig deep to keep the runner-up, seemingly twice her size, at bay near the line. She looks a cut above average. *(op 9-2)*
Bleak House(IRE), a half-brother to The Duke's Speech a winner of two bumpers for this yard, is a grand, big type. He responded to severe pressure and was only just held. Suited by this type of ground, he thoroughly deserves to go one better. *(op 6-1 tchd 4-1)*
Sybarite Chief(IRE) showed ability on his debut but he looks to have more stamina than speed and will be better suited by two miles. *(op 14-1)*
Sundarbob(IRE), out of a mare than won over two miles over hurdles, looks as though he might improve a bit given more time.
La Dame Brune(FR), out of a winning jumper in France, stayed on after getting outpaced and ought to be capable of better in due course. *(op 11-4 tchd 10-3, 7-2 in places)*
Lilian Alexander made this a relatively true test but her rider was free with his use of the stick and she might remember this.
Dr Flight, the first two come under pressure, stayed on when it was all over. The market confidence suggests he had shown a bit more at home beforehand. *(op 6-1)*
T/Jkpt: Not won. T/Plt: £745.80 to a £1 stake. Pool: £48,839.80. 47.80 winning tickets. T/Qpdt: £36.00 to a £1 stake. Pool: £5,589.60. 114.80 winning tickets. JR

2681 FONTWELL (L-H)
Tuesday, December 20

OFFICIAL GOING: Good (good to soft in places)
The meeting survived three inspections, and with the frost coming out of the ground the jockeys reported the going to be sticky.
Wind: Virtually nil

2928 PACKHAM CONSTRUCTION CHRISTMAS PARTY NOVICES' HURDLE (10 hdls 1 omitted) 2m 6f 110y
12:40 (12:40) (Class 4) 4-Y-O+ **£3,419** (£996; £498)

Form RPR

0-33 **1** **Glasker Mill (IRE)**[27] [2426] 5-10-12 .... APMcCoy 105+
(Miss H C Knight) *trckd ldrs: led after 6th: clr 2 out: eased run-in* **4/11**[1]

00 **2** *6* **Flash Cummins (IRE)**[7] [2809] 5-10-12 .... TimmyMurphy 93+
(M C Pipe) *led to 6th: rdn appr 2 out: styd on to chse wnr run-in* **12/1**[3]

00P- **3** *3 ½* **Chamacco (FR)**[291] [4158] 5-10-12 .... PaulMoloney 88+
(M F Harris) *hld up: hdwy to trck ldrs 6th: chsd wnr 3 out tl rdn and mstke last: one pce run-in* **80/1**

33 **4** *3* **Coeur D'Alene**[81] [963] 4-10-12 .... AndrewThornton 84
(Dr J R J Naylor) *hld up in mid-div: hdwy after 7th: rdn 3 out: kpt on one pce after* **25/1**

0-40 **5** *16* **Walter (IRE)**[36] [2238] 6-10-12 .... RJGreene 71+
(P Winkworth) *hld up in rr: hmpd 4th: styd on one pce fr 3 out* **20/1**

6 *dist* **Trebello**[56] 4-10-12 .... LeightonAspell —
(J R Boyle) *hld up: hdwy whn hmpd 4th: nvr on terms after: t.o* **50/1**

3-6P **7** *4* **Mooresini (IRE)**[14] [2683] 5-10-12 .... PhilipHide —
(N J Gifford) *mid-div: wknd appr 3 out: t.o* **10/1**[2]

P **8** *7* **Good Sort (IRE)**[7] [2805] 5-10-5 .... CharlieStudd(7) —
(B G Powell) *hmpd 4th: hdwy 6th: disputing 2nd whn rn wd on bnd after 3 out: wknd rapidly: t.o* **33/1**

3 **9** *26* **Persian Genie (IRE)**[122] [1266] 4-10-5 ....(t) JamieGoldstein —
(Miss J S Davis) *a bhd: t.o* **50/1**

0/ **10** *13* **My Big Sister**[632] [4608] 6-9-12 .... WayneKavanagh(7) —
(J W Mullins) *hld up: hdwy to chse ldrs after 7th: wknd qckly 3 out: t.o* **100/1**

5-00 **11** *20* **Lord Leonardo (IRE)**[20] [2579] 5-10-5 .... JustinMorgan(7) —
(L Wells) *bhd whn hmpd 4th: t.o fr next* **50/1**

P **12** *dist* **Tom Tobacco**[32] [2309] 8-10-7 .... ChrisHonour(5) —
(A S T Holdsworth) *prom to 6th: sn wknd t.o* **100/1**

0 **F** **Galandora**[24] [2501] 5-10-5 .... JodieMogford —
(Dr J R J Naylor) *t.k.h: prom tl fell 4th* **33/1**

0 **F** **Lord Musgrave (IRE)**[50] [1954] 6-10-12 .... MatthewBatchelor —
(L Wells) *t.k.h: prom tl fell 4th* **100/1**

The Form Book, Raceform Ltd, Compton, RG20 6NL

P **Chasing The Stars (IRE)** 5-10-5 .... TomDoyle —
(D R Gandolfo) *chsd eladers to 7th: t.o whn p.u bef 2 out* **100/1**
0 P **Carroll's O'Tully (IRE)**[12] 2720 5-10-2 .... ColinBolger(3) —
(L A Dace) *in tch whn hmpd 4th: t.o whn p.u bef 2 out* **100/1**

5m 50.2s (5.40) **Going Correction** +0.325s/f (Yiel) **16** Ran SP% **116.7**
Speed ratings: **103,100,99,98,93** —,—,—,—,— —,—,—,—,— — CSF £4.03 TOTE £1.40: £1.02, £2.40, £34.50; EX 7.00.
Owner Trevor Hemmings **Bred** Noel Murphy **Trained** West Lockinge, Oxon

FOCUS
This is not strong form but the winner was value for further. The last flight on the far side was bypassed on the final circuit.

NOTEBOOK
Glasker Mill(IRE) took advantage of this modest opposition to get off the mark over hurdles with a fluent success. The longer trip suited him and he should go on to better things now. *(tchd 2-5)*
Flash Cummins(IRE), who showed little in two previous runs over hurdles, lost his pitch on the final circuit but rallied in the latter stages. He is a winning pointer and the step up to three miles should suit him. *(op 9-1)*
Chamacco(FR) did not show much in three runs for Keith Reveley, the latest in March, so this was a step in the right direction. *(op 100-1)*
Coeur D'Alene, third in both his bumpers in the summer, did not build on that in three starts on the Flat proper. He showed ability on this hurdles debut but will have to improve if he is to win a race. *(op 33-1)*
Walter(IRE), held up at the rear of the field this time, did plug on but was never really a factor. He now qualifies for handicaps. *(op 22-1)*
Good Sort(IRE) was trying hurdles for the first time after two runs in Irish points and one in a chase. He showed he possesses some ability, but proved reluctant to continue rounding the home turn, probably more due to tiredness than recalcitrance. *(op 28-1)*
My Big Sister, down the field in a bumper for the Tony Carroll yard in March last year, showed a bit of promise on this hurdles debut but failed to get home.

2929 P.S. BRAMMER FORESTRY NOVICES' CHASE (15 fncs) 2m 4f
1:10 (1:10) (Class 4) 4-Y-0+ **£4,801** (£1,490; £802)

Form RPR
00-P **1** **Wenceslas (IRE)**[42] 2100 5-11-4 101 .... TimmyMurphy 112+
(Miss H C Knight) *mde all: srtrly chal fr 3 out: drvn out run-in* **13/2**
0042 **2** 2 **Dictator (IRE)**[11] 2751 4-10-7 103 ....(t) TomDoyle 99+
(D R Gandolfo) *a.p: outpcd and 4th whn mstke 12th: rallied 3 out: lft cl 2nd 2 out: rdn and no imp run-in* **9/2**[3]
6603 **3** dist **Brooklyn's Gold (USA)**[40] 2141 10-10-13 104 .... PaulO'Neill(5) —
(Ian Williams) *prom tl wknd appr 10th: t.o* **5/1**
6063 **U** **Tyup Pompey (IRE)**[7] 2807 4-10-7 86 .... JamieGoldstein —
(Miss J S Davis) *bhd whn mstke and uns rdr 5th* **40/1**
1/4- **F** **Ranelagh Gray (IRE)**[588] 280 8-11-4 105 .... AlanO'Keeffe 109+
(Miss Venetia Williams) *chsd wnr for most of r: cl 2nd whn fell 2 out* **10/3**[2]
-216 **U** **Master D'Or (FR)**[32] 2313 5-11-4 105 .... RichardJohnson 109+
(P J Hobbs) *hld up in rr: hdwy 11th: cl 4th and chalng whn blnd bdly and uns rdr 3 out* **2/1**[1]

5m 20.5s (12.60) **Going Correction** +0.75s/f (Soft)
WFA 4 from 5yo+ 11lb **6** Ran SP% **107.0**
Speed ratings: **104,103**,—,—,— — CSF £31.62 TOTE £6.40: £2.60, £2.20; EX 20.40.
Owner Jim Lewis **Bred** David Geoghegan **Trained** West Lockinge, Oxon

FOCUS
This was run at only a steady pace. Fair form without being anything special, the second running to his mark.

NOTEBOOK
Wenceslas(IRE) made every yard and saw off his remaining challenger in gritty style. On the downside, he was rather novicey at his fences, although he did not make any serious mistakes. *(op 15-2 tchd 6-1)*
Dictator(IRE), duly upped in trip for this second run over fences, could never quite get to the winner and might need a bit further still. *(op 5-1 tchd 11-2)*
Brooklyn's Gold(USA), back up in trip, was soundly beaten and fortunate to pick up third prize. This ground was probably against him. *(op 7-2)*
Ranelagh Gray(IRE) was making his chasing bow on this first start for more than 18 months. After an error at the third last, he was breathing down the winner's neck when crashing out at the next. *(op 9-2)*
Master D'Or(FR), back in novice company, was one of four in contention when parting company at the final ditch. This completed a miserable day for connections, whose former champion hurdler Rooster Booster died on the gallops in the morning. *(op 9-2)*

2930 SGS CONSTRUCTION LTD (S) HURDLE (9 hdls) 2m 2f 110y
1:40 (1:40) (Class 5) 4-7-Y-0 **£2,322** (£676; £338)

Form RPR
4-12 **1** **Indian Star (GER)**[23] 2523 7-11-4 99 ....(t) JodieMogford 106+
(J C Tuck) *hld up: a gng wl: hdwy after 6th: led appr 2 out: styd on* **11/4**[2]
-550 **2** 4 **Kildee Lass**[19] 2595 6-10-0 98 .... ChrisHonour(5) 89
(J D Frost) *a in tch: ev ch 3 out: kpt on one pce fr next* **11/8**[1]
0-P4 **3** 10 **Scarlet Mix (FR)**[37] 2216 4-10-12 98 .... TimmyMurphy 86
(B G Powell) *chsd ldr: led after 6th: rdn, hdd & wknd appr 2 out* **11/2**[3]
4R30 **4** 18 **Spiders Web**[93] 1483 5-10-12 91 ....(b) JamieMoore 68
(G L Moore) *reluctant to s but in tch fr 2nd: wknd qckly 3 out* **12/1**
6-52 **5** dist **Monsal Dale (IRE)**[235] 102 6-10-12 84 .... LeightonAspell —
(Mrs L C Jewell) *hld up: lost tch appr 6th: t.o* **14/1**
P/P- **U** **Premier Cheval (USA)**[303] 3968 6-10-12 .... MatthewBatchelor —
(P R Hedger) *hld up: last whn blnd and uns rdr 4th* **66/1**
F/PP **P** **Breuddwyd Lyn**[17] 2619 7-10-12 .... TomDoyle —
(Mrs D A Hamer) *chsd ldrs tl wknd after 6th: t.o whn p.u bef last* **25/1**
5301 **P** **Blackthorn**[13] 2702 6-10-11 93 .... RichardSpate(7) —
(M Appleby) *led tl hdd sn after mstke 6th: wknd qckly: t.o whn p.u bef last* **14/1**

4m 42.9s (6.90) **Going Correction** +0.325s/f (Yiel)
WFA 4 from 5yo+ 10lb **8** Ran SP% **110.5**
Speed ratings: **98,96,92,84**,— —,—,— CSF £6.63 TOTE £4.20: £1.30, £1.20, £2.00; EX 7.80.There was no bid for the winner.
Owner D J Neale **Bred** Gestut Schlenderhan **Trained** Oldbury on the Hill, Gloucs
■ Stewards' Enquiry : Chris Honour two-day ban: used whip with excessive frequency and unnecessarily (Dec 31-Jan 1)

FOCUS
This seller was run at a fair pace. The winner is progressive but the next two home were below par.

NOTEBOOK
Indian Star(GER) is a useful tool in this grade and he won this weak event a shade comfortably. He was dismounted quickly on pulling up but was found to be sound and the Stewards fined Mogford £150. *(tchd 5-2)*
Kildee Lass, dropped into this grade for the first time, kept trying but found the gelding too strong. She prefers better ground. *(op 15-8 tchd 2-1 in places)*
Scarlet Mix(FR), without the blinkers, ran his race but again it seemed as if was a bit far for him. *(op 5-1)*
Spiders Web was reluctant to exert himself and Moore did well to get him round. *(op 15-2)*
Monsal Dale(IRE) *Official explanation: jockey said gelding hung right (op 12-1)*
Blackthorn, penalised for his Leicester win, paid in the end for setting a fair pace. *(op 12-1)*

2931 JOHN ROGERSON MEMORIAL H'CAP CHASE (16 fncs) 2m 6f
2:10 (2:11) (Class 4) (0-110,110) 5-Y-0+ **£4,122** (£1,210; £605; £302)

Form RPR
1525 **1** **Alcatras (IRE)**[167] 916 8-9-11 84 oh2 .... OwynNelmes(3) 97+
(B J M Ryall) *a in tch: hit 9th: wnt 2nd appr 11th: drvn to ld 2 out: styd on run-in* **16/1**
32P- **2** 1 ¾ **Hever Road (IRE)**[333] 3454 6-11-6 104 .... TimmyMurphy 113+
(M C Pipe) *hld up: reminders 11th: hdwy to go 3rd after 4 out: styd on to snatch 2nd post* **9/2**[2]
P214 **3** shd **Channahrlie (IRE)**[19] 2583 11-10-3 87 ....(p) WayneHutchinson 95
(R Dickin) *led 2nd: rdn and hdd 2 out: one pce and lost 2nd post* **9/1**
-333 **4** 15 **Myson (IRE)**[20] 2577 6-11-3 101 .... JamesDavies 94
(D B Feek) *in tch: trckd ldrs 7th: rdn after 4 out: wknd next* **4/1**[1]
2/25 **5** 1 **Umbrella Man (IRE)**[36] 2243 9-11-1 99 .... BarryFenton 97+
(Miss E C Lavelle) *led to 2nd: blnd and slipped on landing next: bhd tl effrt 4 out: wknd bef next* **5/1**[3]
/1-5 **6** 27 **Rainbows Aglitter**[79] 1617 8-11-12 110 .... TomDoyle 75
(D R Gandolfo) *a bhd: brief effrt 4 out* **16/1**
2-2F **P** **Galapiat Du Mesnil (FR)**[37] 2215 11-11-1 99 .... AndrewThornton —
(R Gurney) *trckd ldr: wknd appr 4 out: p.u bef next* **33/1**
2413 **P** **Eau Pure (FR)**[23] 2522 8-10-12 96 ....(b) JamieMoore —
(G L Moore) *mid-div: whn mstkes 8th and 9th: bhd whn mstke 11th: p.u bef 2 out* **6/1**
P-P3 **P** **Mercato (FR)**[7] 2808 9-11-1 99 .... RobertThornton —
(J R Best) *hld up: hdwy whn mstke 12th: sn rdn: wknd appr 3 out: p.u bef last* **4/1**[1]

5m 58.5s (14.70) **Going Correction** +0.75s/f (Soft) **9** Ran SP% **113.8**
Speed ratings: **103,102,102,96,96 86**,—,—,— CSF £86.89 CT £697.31 TOTE £20.20: £4.70, £1.40, £2.50; EX 130.40.
Owner I & Mrs K G Fawcett **Bred** Anthony O'Mahony **Trained** Rimpton, Somerset

FOCUS
A low-grade handicap in which the winner was well in on his best form and the third sets the standard.

NOTEBOOK
Alcatras(IRE) had been off the track since July and has had treatment on a back problem, which seems to have cured his habit of jumping out to the right. In front at the second last, he idled quite badly on the run-in but the line came in time. *(op 20-1)*
Hever Road(IRE), making his chasing debut, improved on the long home turn. Never quite looking like getting to the front, he briefly threatened to duck out between the last two fences before staying on well up the final hill to grab second on the line. He stayed three miles in points and a real test of stamina is what he needs. *(op 5-1 tchd 4-1)*
Channahrlie(IRE), soon in front, put in a good round of jumping but had no answers when headed at the third last. He needs further and better ground. *(op 8-1)*
Myson(IRE), still 6lb above his last winning mark, found his stamina stretched in this sticky ground. *Official explanation: jockey said gelding hung left (op 7-2)*
Umbrella Man(IRE) did well to stay on his feet at the third where he lost his prominent pitch. He remained in touch until fading on the home turn. *(op 15-2)*
Mercato(FR) ran well enough up to a point, but dropped out of contention on the run round to the home straight and was eventually pulled up. *Official explanation: jockey said gelding ran flat (op 7-2)*

2932 DAVID AND GILL BIRTHDAY CELEBRATION MARES' ONLY H'CAP HURDLE (9 hdls) 2m 2f 110y
2:40 (2:40) (Class 4) (0-105,98) 4-Y-0+ **£3,409** (£1,000; £500; £249)

Form RPR
2-15 **1** **Novacella (FR)**[23] 2530 4-11-9 95 .... AndrewThornton 105
(R H Alner) *chsd ldr: rdn 2 out: styd on to ld run-in* **1/1**[1]
1F22 **2** 3 **Hi Laurie (IRE)**[26] 2466 10-11-0 86 .... TomScudamore 93
(M Scudamore) *led: rdn 2 out: no ex and hdd run-in* **3/1**[2]
3-60 **3** 30 **Esplendidos (IRE)**[17] 2632 6-10-11 90 .... DarylJacob(7) 67
(D P Keane) *chsd ldrs: lost tch w ldng pair 6th* **6/1**[3]
-451 **4** 22 **Ballyhoo (IRE)**[25] 2486 5-11-5 98 .... WayneKavanagh(7) 53
(J W Mullins) *a bhd: lost tch 6th* **16/1**
0P-2 **5** 19 **Forest Fauna**[25] 2486 5-11-7 96 .... RichardYoung(3) 32
(J W Mullins) *chsd ldrs tl wknd rapidly after 5th* **14/1**
000- **P** **Tilla**[22] 4029 5-10-6 78 .... AndrewTinkler —
(Mrs A J Hamilton-Fairley) *hld up: lost tch after 5th: t.o whn p.u bef 2 out* **25/1**
041P **P** **Distant Romance**[26] 2457 8-9-12 77 .... RobertLucey-Butler(7) —
(Miss Z C Davison) *hld up in rr: lost tch 6th: poor 4th whn blnd bdly 2 out: p.u bef next* **33/1**

4m 44.2s (8.20) **Going Correction** +0.325s/f (Yiel) **7** Ran SP% **108.6**
Speed ratings: **95,93,81,71,63** —,— CSF £4.08 CT £8.53 TOTE £2.00: £1.80, £1.60; EX 3.50.
Owner Mrs Norma Kelly **Bred** F Cottin And Mme Gilberte Chaignon **Trained** Droop, Dorset

FOCUS
An uncompetitive mares' handicap which was a two-horse race from a long way out. Both the first two showed improved form.

NOTEBOOK
Novacella(FR) looked held on the home turn, but her proven stamina came into play and she stayed on to wear down the long-time leader on the flat to win going away. A return to further will suit. *(op 11-10 tchd 6-5)*
Hi Laurie(IRE) made this a decent test over this shorter trip and most of her rivals were cooked with a circuit to run. She seemed to have the favourite's measure too on the turn into the straight, but although she kept galloping she was collared on the flat. *(op 7-2 tchd 11-4)*
Esplendidos(IRE) was in a remote third place for much of the final circuit and remains disappointing. *(op 8-1)*
Ballyhoo(IRE) was beaten a long way on this first run in handicap company and really needs further than this. *(op 9-1)*
Distant Romance looked set to finish a poor fourth when almost coming to a standstill at the second last. *(op 25-1)*

2933 PAUL AND NICKY BRAMMER WEDDING DAY H'CAP CHASE (13 fncs) 2m 2f
3:10 (3:10) (Class 4) (0-90,88) 5-Y-0+ **£3,409** (£1,000; £500; £249)

Form RPR
P324 **1** **Walcot Lad (IRE)**[14] 2684 9-11-9 88 ....(p) ColinBolger(3) 97+
(A Ennis) *a front rnk: rdn after 4 out: led appr last: styd on run-in* **6/1**
65-P **2** 2 **Bewleys Guest (IRE)**[50] 1949 6-10-3 65 .... AlanO'Keeffe 72+
(Miss Venetia Williams) *led: blnd 3 out: rdn and hdd appr last: no imp run-in* **7/1**
3041 **3** 13 **Lost In Normandy (IRE)**[6] 2818 8-10-12 74 7ex ....(b) APMcCoy 66
(Mrs L Williamson) *trckd ldrs: rdn appr 3 out: wknd next* **2/1**[1]

2600 **4** *13* **Kaikovra (IRE)**^{20} [2570] 9-11-4 **80**.................... JohnMcNamara 62+
(M F Harris) *bhd: hdwy after 7th: mstke 9th: wknd after 3 out* **16/1**
P064 **5** *14* **Ingenu (FR)**^{12} [2733] 9-11-6 **82**....................(p) SeanCurran 47
(P Wegmann) *hld up: hdwy after 8th: chsd ldrs tl wknd appr 3 out* **33/1**
00-3 **F** **Harbour Point (IRE)**^{14} [2684] 9-11-9 **85**.................... TomScudamore —
(M Scudamore) *trckd ldrs: cl 3rd whn fell 8th* **4/1**^{2}
-5P0 **P** **Killy Beach**^{12} [2728] 7-10-11 **73**.................... JoeTizzard —
(J D Frost) *mid-div whn blnd 9th: t.o whn p.u bef 3 out* **33/1**
PPP0 **P** **Ellas Recovery (IRE)**^{7} [2807] 5-10-6 **68**....................(b) JamesDavies —
(D B Feek) *prom tl wknd after 6th: t.o whn p.u after 4 out* **66/1**
-PP0 **P** **Shannon Quest (IRE)**^{17} [2620] 9-10-13 **82**....................(bt) TomMessenger$^{(7)}$ —
(C L Popham) *hld up: lost tch 7th: t.o whn p.u bef 3 out* **50/1**
0-53 **P** **Irish Grouse (IRE)**^{30} [2378] 6-10-7 **69**.................... TimmyMurphy —
(Miss H C Knight) *bhd: sme hdwy 7th: sn bhd: t.o whn p.u bef 2 out* **9/2**^{3}

4m 52.7s (17.60) **Going Correction** +0.75s/f (Soft) **10** Ran SP% **113.5**
Speed ratings: **90,89,83,77,71** —,—,—,—,— CSF £44.60 CT £112.17 TOTE £7.10: £2.30, £2.60, £1.10; EX 65.50.
Owner Camis Burke Middleton Heaps **Bred** Jim Ruane **Trained** Beare Green, Surrey

FOCUS
A moderate winning time, even for this grade. This was a weak handicap, rated through the winner.

NOTEBOOK
Walcot Lad(IRE) was hard at work on the home turn but responded to pressure to show ahead between the last two fences. His last three wins have all come over this course and distance, *although he had been beaten on his seven most recent visits before today. (op 11-2 tchd 5-1 and 13-2)*
Bewleys Guest(IRE), from a yard in fine form, generally jumped well in the lead on this chasing debut until getting the final ditch wrong. He could not counter when headed between the last two fences but this was a better performance from this winning pointer. *(op 8-1 tchd 9-1)*
Lost In Normandy(IRE), 5lb lower than when scoring at Bangor despite the penalty, could not take *advantage. It could have been that this came too soon or that he found the drop in trip against him. (tchd 85-40 in a place)*
Kaikovra(IRE), normally a tearaway, was held up this time and looked a threat turning into the straight before failing to get home. Similar tactics could bear fruit over a truly-run two miles on better ground. *(tchd 20-1)*
Ingenu(FR), down 6lb, again ran a respectable race although he was beaten a good way in the end. *(op 20-1)*
Harbour Point(IRE) was in the hunt when his fencing let him down again. *(op 5-1)*

2934 EVECHANGE LTD CHRISTMAS PARTY NOVICES' H'CAP HURDLE (10 hdls) 2m 4f
3:40 (3:40) (Class 4) (0-95,95) 4-Y-O+ **£2,960** (£862; £431)

Form RPR
-040 **1** **Hilarious (IRE)**^{36} [2244] 5-11-0 **83**.................... AndrewThornton 86
(Dr J R J Naylor) *mde all: rdn appr 2 out: styd on wl* **16/1**
-040 **2** *3* **Barranco (IRE)**^{11} [2750] 4-11-2 **85**....................(b) JamieMoore 85
(G L Moore) *mid-div: gd hdwy to go 2nd appr 2 out: no imp on wnr after* **16/1**
-063 **3** *1 ¼* **Laharna**^{18} [2617] 5-11-10 **93**.................... BarryFenton 93+
(Miss E C Lavelle) *a.p: chsd wnr appr 3 out tl rdn and one pce fr next* **5/2**^{1}
P2/P **4** *1 ¾* **Instant Appeal**^{17} [2632] 8-11-7 **90**.................... PhilipHide 87
(P Winkworth) *mid-div: hdwy 3 out: styd on one pce* **20/1**
04P- **5** *18* **Quatrain (IRE)**^{271} [4531] 5-11-12 **95**....................(t) TomDoyle 77+
(D R Gandolfo) *in tch: effrt 3 out: sn wknd* **10/1**
-P50 **6** *8* **Peggy's Prince**^{18} [2605] 7-10-10 **79**.................... JoeTizzard 50
(J D Frost) *a bhd* **66/1**
0-2P **7** *3* **Deo Gratias (POL)**^{22} [2552] 5-11-4 **87**....................(t) CarlLlewellyn 55
(M Pitman) *mid-div: hdwy after 6th: rdn and wknd 3 out* **12/1**
004 **8** *9* **Secret Jewel (FR)**^{23} [2527] 5-10-8 **80**.................... AnthonyCoyle$^{(3)}$ 39
(Miss C J E Caroe) *trckd ldrs tl wknd 7th* **50/1**
PPU0 **9** *14* **Peppershot**^{8} [2802] 5-11-9 **92**....................(p) LeightonAspell 37
(R Gurney) *hld upo: sme hdwy 3 out: sn wknd* **100/1**
4P40 **10** *22* **Denarius Secundus**^{5} [2845] 8-10-4 **76**.................... RichardYoung$^{(3)}$ —
(N R Mitchell) *prom tl wknd 7th* **25/1**
62P/ **P** **Cougar (IRE)**^{633} [4573] 5-11-5 **88**....................(t) BrianCrowley —
(R Rowe) *hld up: t.o whn p.u bef 3 out* **20/1**
/B-3 **F** **Lady Maranzi**^{26} [2463] 6-11-0 **83**.................... AlanO'Keeffe —
(Mrs D A Hamer) *hld up in rr: fell 7th* **12/1**
004- **P** **Yes My Lord (IRE)**^{323} [3620] 6-11-10 **93**.................... TimmyMurphy —
(M C Pipe) *nt fluent: t.o 5th: p.u after next* **7/2**^{2}
-000 **P** **Hi Humpfree**^{11} [2755] 5-11-12 **95**.................... APMcCoy —
(Mrs H Dalton) *in tch: rdn and wknd 3 out: p.u bef next* **13/2**^{3}
0-4F **P** **Portavo (IRE)**^{12} [2732] 5-11-9 **92**.................... MatthewBatchelor —
(Miss H C Knight) *trckd ldrs to 7th: t.o whn p.u bef 2 out* **16/1**
330- **P** **Ockley Flyer**^{303} [3968] 6-10-2 **78**....................(p) RobertLucey-Butler$^{(7)}$ —
(Miss Z C Davison) *in tch: rdn after 4th: sn bhd: t.o whn p.u bef 3 out* **50/1**

5m 9.50s (5.70) **Going Correction** +0.325s/f (Yiel) **16** Ran SP% **126.0**
WFA 4 from 5yo+ 11lb
Speed ratings: **101,99,99,98,91 88,87,83,77,69** —,—,—,—,—,— CSF £238.58 CT £871.01 TOTE £25.10: £5.40, £2.10, £1.30, £3.70; EX 98.20 Place 6 £39.65, Place 5 £34.28.
Owner Miles Electronics Ltd **Bred** Airlie Stud **Trained** Shrewton, Wilts

FOCUS
This was an ordinary race but the form looks fairly solid at a low level. The winner was well in on her Worcester form two runs back and has been rated to a similar level, with the second running to his mark.

NOTEBOOK
Hilarious(IRE) was given an enterprising ride by Thornton who decided that the place to be was out in front. To her credit the mare kept up the gallop to break her duck.
Barranco(IRE) ran a better race back in the blinkers and returning to this more suitable trip. He was 2lb lower here but still looks high enough in the weights. *(op 14-1)*
Laharna, on his handicap debut, was still seemingly travelling well in second place on the run round to the home straight, but when let down he could only keep on at the same pace. This winning pointer probably needs three miles. *(tchd 9-4)*
Instant Appeal, back over a more suitable trip for this second run after a lengthy absence, confirmed that he does retain ability. *(op 25-1)*
Quatrain(IRE), equipped with a tongue strap for this first run in March, was close enough leaving the back straight but was soon left behind by the principals. *(op 14-1)*
Yes My Lord(IRE), off the track for the best part of 11 months, jumped stickily at the back of the *field and, soon struggling, was pulled up before halfway. Official explanation: trainer said gelding finished lame (op 6-1 tchd 3-1)*
T/Plt: £42.60 to a £1 stake. Pool: £45,147.10. 772.25 winning tickets. T/Qpdt: £14.70 to a £1 stake. Pool: £3,779.80. 189.80 winning tickets. JS

2721 LUDLOW (R-H)
Wednesday, December 21

OFFICIAL GOING: Good
Wind: Almost nil Weather: Fine

2935 TANNERS CLARET JUVENILE NOVICES' (S) HURDLE (9 hdls) 2m
12:40 (12:40) (Class 5) 3-Y-O **£3,441** (£1,010; £505; £252)

Form RPR
1 **Parsley's Return**^{14} 3-10-11.................... WayneHutchinson 85+
(M Wigham) *a.p: j.rt 1st: j.rt and led 3 out: rdn out* **7/1**
60 **2** *1 ½* **Elaala (USA)**^{2} [2921] 3-10-4.................... GrahamLee 76
(M Todhunter) *hld up: hdwy after 4 out: hit 3 out: rdn appr next: j.rt last: sn chsd wnr: styd on: a hld* **5/1**^{2}
002 **3** *9* **Jamaaron**^{27} [2454] 3-10-1.................... RichardGordon$^{(10)}$ 75+
(W G M Turner) *t.k.h: hld up: hdwy 3rd: blnd 4 out: rdn and ev ch fr 2 out tl stmbld last: wknd run-in* **6/1**^{3}
6F **4** *6* **Methodical**^{20} [2597] 3-10-2 ow3.................... JohnnyLevins$^{(5)}$ 66+
(B G Powell) *hld up: blnd 4 out: rdn and kpt on u.p fr 3 out: no imp* **11/1**
605 **5** *½* **Isitloveyourafter (IRE)**^{12} [2752] 3-10-4 76.................... JamieMoore 62+
(G L Moore) *midfield: hdwy appr 4 out: rdn whn chsd ldrs bef 2 out: wknd run-in* **8/1**
0 **6** *3 ½* **Colonel Bilko (IRE)**^{16} [1729] 3-10-11....................(t) JimmyMcCarthy 65+
(Miss S J Wilton) *t.k.h: hld up: hdwy to ld after 3rd: hit 4 out: hdd 3 out: wknd bef last* **16/1**
0400 **7** *2 ½* **Swallow Falls (IRE)**^{21} [2569] 3-9-13.................... StephenCraine$^{(5)}$ 54
(D McCain) *in tch: tk clsr order 5th: rdn and wknd appr 3 out* **10/1**
6 **8** *10* **Smokey The Bear**^{27} [2454] 3-10-6.................... DerekLaverty$^{(5)}$ 51
(A P Jones) *t.k.h: midfield: hdwy 5th: rdn and wknd appr 3 out* **33/1**
R **9** *28* **Lightening Fire (IRE)**^{27} [2454] 3-10-11....................(b) OllieMcPhail 23
(B J Llewellyn) *sn trckd ldrs: lost pl after 3rd: n.d after* **100/1**
0P46 **10** *1 ¾* **Hamburg Springer (IRE)**^{39} [2076] 3-10-11 92.................... RJGreene 21
(M J Polglase) *prom tl rdn and wknd after 4 out* **12/1**
P **11** *13* **Christom**^{17} [2661] 3-10-11....................(b) JasonMaguire 8
(Mrs Tracey Barfoot-Saunt) *behdind: j.lft 1st: mstke 5th: nvr on terms* **66/1**
0 **12** *3 ½* **Maenflora**^{19} [2611] 3-10-4.................... ChristianWilliams —
(B J Llewellyn) *hld up: j.rt 1st: blnd 2nd: struggling after 4th: nvr on terms* **66/1**
0 **P** **Balgarth (USA)**^{21} [2569] 3-10-11.................... SeanCurran —
(K J Burke) *bhd: p.u after 4th* **80/1**
0216 **P** **Strathtay**^{18} [2632] 3-10-11 95....................(v) TonyDobbin —
(M Appleby) *led: hdd after 3rd: mstke and j. slowly 5th: sn wknd: t.o whn p.u bef 3 out* **7/2**^{1}

3m 48.4s (-3.90) **Going Correction** -0.375s/f (Good) **14** Ran SP% **115.9**
Speed ratings: **94,93,88,85,85 83,82,77,63,62 56,54** [illegible] TOTE £10.10: £3.40, £2.40, £2.[illegible]
Owner D T L Limited **Bred** Baydon House Stud **Trained** Newmarket, Suffolk

FOCUS
A poor seller in which the first two finished clear. The third to sixth all ran to within a few lengths of their pre-race marks.

NOTEBOOK
Parsley's Return, a banded winner on the Flat, made a successful hurdling debut. He jumped badly to his right at the first flight, and again when leading at the same obstacle on the next circuit, but landed this poor event with a bit up his sleeve. *(tchd 15-2)*
Elaala(USA), who finished down the field in a better race just two days earlier, finished nicely clear of the rest and her turn should come. *(op 6-1)*
Jamaaron ran his race again but was held in second when stumbled on landing over the last. He has yet to prove he stays. *(op 7-1)*
Methodical survived a bad blunder at the last flight down the far side before staying on quite nicely past beaten rivals late on. She is only moderate but is going the right way. *(op 15-2 tchd 12-1)*
Isitloveyourafter(IRE) ran respectably but was beaten when making an error at the last. *(tchd 15-2)*
Colonel Bilko(IRE) has had run three times on sand since his hurdling debut here in October. He is a keen sort and will have to settle better if he is to see out the trip.
Strathtay dropped away down the back straight and was found to have put her pelvis out. *Official explanation: vet said filly was lame (op 3-1 tchd 4-1)*

2936 MERRY XMAS TO ALL NOVICES' H'CAP CHASE (17 fncs) 2m 4f
1:10 (1:11) (Class 4) (0-95,95) 4-Y-O+
£3,989 (£1,178; £589; £294; £147; £73)

Form RPR
-421 **1** **Moscow Gold (IRE)**^{8} [2807] 8-9-13 **71** 7ex.................... OwynNelmes$^{(3)}$ 87+
(A E Price) *chsd ldrs: led bef 4 out: pricked ears and idled run in: drvn out* **4/1**^{1}
42P3 **2** *2 ½* **Sitting Duck**^{9} [2801] 6-10-4 **80**.................... CharlieStudd$^{(7)}$ 87
(B G Powell) *set decent gallop tl hdd bef 4 out: kpt on fr next: nt rch wnr* **9/1**
03-4 **3** *1 ¼* **Uncle Max (IRE)**^{28} [2429] 5-11-11 **94**.................... CarlLlewellyn 100
(N A Twiston-Davies) *keen in tch: effrt and hdwy to chse ldrs bef 2 out: rdn and edgd rt 2 out: one pce run in* **8/1**^{3}
-P03 **4** *2* **Point**^{13} [2723] 8-11-12 **95**.................... WarrenMarston 101+
(W Jenks) *mstkes: hld up: hdwy whn hit 11th: effrt bef 4 out: kpt on fr 2 out: no imp* **20/1**
-U66 **5** *4* **Tianyi (IRE)**^{22} [2561] 9-10-3 **72**....................(v) TomScudamore 74+
(M Scudamore) *prom tl rdn and one pce fr 4 out* **22/1**
0030 **6** *2 ½* **Reflex Blue**^{3} [2561] 8-10-9 **78**....................(v) AlanO'Keeffe 77+
(R J Price) *nt fluent in rr: drvn 1/2-way: rallying whn mstkes 4 out and next: nrst fin* **20/1**
4316 **7** *1* **Seveneightsix (IRE)**^{20} [2585] 5-10-6 **75**....................(b) LeightonAspell 75+
(D J Wintle) *hld up: rdn 12th: eased fr 3 out: lame* **7/1**^{2}
-P60 **8** *2* **Runshan (IRE)**^{29} [2421] 5-11-10 **93**.................... AntonyEvans 88
(D G Bridgwater) *midfield: hdwy to chse ldrs 5 out: wknd fr next* **16/1**
424U **9** *2 ½* **Sailor A'Hoy**^{24} [2522] 9-10-10 **82**....................(p) AnthonyCoyle$^{(3)}$ 74
(M Mullineaux) *towards rr: struggling 10th: n.d* **14/1**
52 **10** *shd* **Pristeen Spy**^{55} [1897] 8-9-10 **70**.................... StephenCraine$^{(5)}$ 62
(R Ford) *chsd ldr to 10th: wknd fr 12th* **12/1**
4-P5 **11** *5* **Lucky Luk (FR)**^{23} [2555] 6-10-12 **81**.................... JohnMcNamara 68
(K C Bailey) *mstkes: in tch to 1/2-way: sn lost pl* **10/1**
04-P **12** *11* **Colwyn Jake (IRE)**^{18} [2639] 6-11-2 **85**.................... WayneHutchinson 61
(Ian Williams) *mstkes towards rr: nvr on terms* **20/1**
2055 **13** *14* **Pollensa Bay**^{22} [2561] 6-10-0 **69**....................(b) TomSiddall 31
(S A Brookshaw) *nt fluent: a bhd: struggling fr 1/2-way* **7/1**^{2}
/PP6 **14** *2* **Lunardi (IRE)**^{13} [2733] 7-9-8 **70**.................... MissLHorner$^{(7)}$ 30
(D L Williams) *a towards rr: no ch fr 1/2-way* **66/1**

PUP4 **15** *20* **Cool Carroll (IRE)**[47] [2018] 7-11-3 **86**.................................... HenryOliver 26
(Mrs Tracey Barfoot-Saunt) *mstkes in rr: struggling fr 1/2-way* **100/1**

6/20 **F** **Justino**[20] [2592] 7-11-2 **85**.................................... BenjaminHitchcott —
(J A Geake) *in tch: rdn and wkng whn fell 5 out* **14/1**

5m 5.00s (-5.70) **Going Correction** -0.375s/f (Good) **16** Ran SP% **123.2**
Speed ratings: **96,95,94,93,92 91,90,89,88,88 86,82,76,76,68** — CSF £37.13 CT £284.86 TOTE £6.00: £1.90, £2.60, £1.50, £4.90; EX 29.50.
Owner Mrs Carol Davis **Bred** I Williams **Trained** Leominster, H'fords

FOCUS
This was a moderate race but the winner was value for further and is on the upgrade. The second and third ran to their marks.

NOTEBOOK
Moscow Gold(IRE), back up in trip, had no problem following up his Folkestone win under his penalty. He idled on the run-in and there is more to come. *(tchd 9-2)*
Sitting Duck, third off the same mark last time, set a decent pace but could not counter when headed by the favourite on the turn into the straight.
Uncle Max(IRE), a winner over this trip in his hurdling days, ran a fair race on this second run over fences.
Point, down 5lb, got away with a number of errors and was staying on at the end. *(op 16-1)*
Tianyi(IRE), back up in trip, ran his best race over fences so far although that is not saying a great deal. *(op 25-1 tchd 20-1)*
Reflex Blue, third in a banded race on Fibresand earlier in the week, did not jump well on his return to fences, but for which he might have finished closer. *(op 25-1)*
Seveneightsix(IRE), with blinkers replacing cheekpieces, was making her chasing debut. Held together from the home turn, she was reported to have finished lame. She could be capable of better if none the worse. *Official explanation: jockey said, regarding the apparent tender ride, his orders were to settle the mare two thirds of the way back and get her jumping as she had been schooling poorly at home; however, he started further back than he wanted, due to early pace, and mare jumped deliberately and found nothing over 2nd last, adding that he nursed her over last to get her home; vet said mare finished lame*

2937 JOHN SMITH'S/E.B.F. MARES' ONLY "NATIONAL HUNT" NOVICES' HURDLE (QUALIFIER) (11 hdls) 2m 5f

1:40 (1:42) (Class 3) 4-Y-0+

£5,166 (£1,526; £763; £381; £190; £95)

Form RPR

0-52 **1** **Harringay**[13] [2718] 5-10-12 105.......................................(t) TimmyMurphy 102+
(Miss H C Knight) *prom: wnt 2nd after 4 out: led 2 out: drew clr run-in* **11/10**[1]

-521 **2** *16* **Purple Patch**[25] [2501] 7-11-4 105.. TonyDobbin 100+
(C L Popham) *prom: led appr 3rd: hdd after 5th: regained ld after 4 out: edgd rt after 3 out: hdd next: eased whn btn run-in* **9/4**[2]

000/ **3** *15* **Sparkling Sabrina**[670] [3927] 5-10-12 .... ChristianWilliams 69
(P Bowen) *in tch: rdn after 4 out: tk mod 3rd appr 3 out: nt trble ldng pair* **50/1**

056 **4** *7* **Little Word**[28] [2427] 6-10-5 .... MrRhysHughes[(7)] 62
(P D Williams) *chsd ldrs to 7th: sn struggling: n.d after* **100/1**

654- **5** *1 3/4* **Thenford Star (IRE)**[251] [4841] 4-10-12 ....(t) MarkBradburne 60
(D J S Ffrench Davis) *midfield: rdn whn outpcd appr 4 out: nvr on terms* **8/1**[3]

S-00 **6** *11* **She's Our Daisy (IRE)**[25] [2501] 5-10-2 .... PaulDavey[(10)] 49
(R H Buckler) *plld hrd: hld up: gd hdwy to ld after 5th: sn clr: hdd after 4 out: wknd qckly* **33/1**

00-0 **7** *2 1/2* **Biscay Wind (IRE)**[50] [1974] 5-10-5 .... MrRMcCarthy[(7)] 47
(T R George) *hld up: rdn whn mstke 4 out: nvr on terms* **100/1**

50- **8** *nk* **School Class**[251] [4841] 5-10-5 .... JohnKington[(7)] 46
(M Scudamore) *in tch: rdn and wknd 4 out* **25/1**

5330 **9** *1/2* **One Wild Night**[20] [2592] 5-10-7 95............................... WilliamKennedy[(5)] 46
(J L Spearing) *t.k.h: chsd ldrs tl rdn and wknd appr 3 out* **12/1**

B **P** **Wiz The Dove**[14] [2704] 4-10-12 .... OllieMcPhail —
(C J Price) *a bhd: t.o whn p.u bef 7th* **66/1**

\- **P** **Bens Lady (IRE)**[623] [4711] 6-10-12 .... JasonMaguire —
(T R George) *a bhd: t.o whn p.u bef 4 out* **20/1**

0 **P** **Casalani (IRE)**[80] [1611] 6-10-12 .... AlanO'Keeffe —
(Jennie Candlish) *led: hdd appr 3rd: wknd 6th: t.o whn p.u bef 3 out* **66/1**

0/0P **P** **Ellie Moss**[39] [2179] 7-10-12 .... WayneHutchinson —
(A W Carroll) *midfield tl wknd after 7th: t.o whn p.u bef 3 out* **50/1**

5m 14.2s (-4.10) **Going Correction** -0.375s/f (Good)
WFA 4 from 5yo+ 11lb **13** Ran SP% **117.6**
Speed ratings: **92,85,80,77,76 72,71,71,71,— —,—,—** CSF £3.28 TOTE £2.00: £1.10, £1.10, £7.20; EX 3.40.
Owner Mrs R Vaughan **Bred** Mrs R I Vaughan **Trained** West Lockinge, Oxon

FOCUS
The pace was very steady in the early parts, leading to a a very moderate winning time for a race of its class. A poor race of its type, and it only concerned two from a long way out.

NOTEBOOK
Harringay, at the centre of controversy over her running at Towcester last month, gained her first win since her bumper debut. Stalking the leader leaving the back straight, she went to the front at the second last and only needed to be shaken up to pull clear. The winning margin flatters her and it is debatable how much she would have found had she needed to come under pressure, so she could be vulnerable under her penalty. *(op 10-11)*
Purple Patch, penalised for her Towcester win, regained the lead turning out of the back straight but there was no way back for her when she was headed two from home. *(op 5-2 tchd 11-4)*
Sparkling Sabrina was well beaten in three bumpers for Rod Millman, the last of them 22 months ago. On her hurdles bow, she stayed on over the last three flights to finish a remote third.
Little Word, a dual winning pointer in the spring, has been well beaten on all starts under Rules.
Thenford Star(IRE), who showed ability in bumpers for Jeff King, was tongue tied for this hurdles debut and first run since April. *(op 10-1 tchd 15-2)*
She's Our Daisy(IRE), a keen mare who pulled her way into a clear lead, was headed on the long home turn and quickly on the retreat. *(op 25-1)*
Bens Lady(IRE) *Official explanation: vet said mare bled from the nose*

2938 TANNERS WINES H'CAP CHASE (19 fncs) 3m

2:10 (2:11) (Class 3) (0-125,124) 5-Y-0+

£9,544 (£2,819; £1,409; £705; £352; £176)

Form RPR

0532 **1** **Ede'Iff**[21] [2568] 8-9-10 **101**.. RobertLucey-Butler[(7)] 112+
(W G M Turner) *towards rr: hit 8th: hdwy 13th: led after 2 out: styd on strly fr last* **10/1**

F41 **2** *4* **Nayodabayo (IRE)**[13] [2725] 5-11-4 **116**....................(v) WayneHutchinson 124+
(Evan Williams) *keen: cl up: hit 12th: led after 5 out: clr next: hdd after 2 out: no ch w wnr* **14/1**

5040 **3** *3 1/2* **Benrajah (IRE)**[31] [2368] 8-11-1 **113**.. GrahamLee 117
(M Todhunter) *prom: outpcd bef 4 out: rallied fr last: no ch w first two* **20/1**

P-14 **4** *2 1/2* **Dancer Life (POL)**[19] [2615] 6-11-12 **124**.............................. PaulMoloney 125+
(Evan Williams) *towards rr: effrt u.p fr 6 out: kpt on fr 2 out: n.d* **16/1**

5331 **5** *3* **Luneray (FR)**[41] [2143] 6-11-7 **119**.............................(bt) ChristianWilliams 118+
(P F Nicholls) *in tch: effrt and wnt 2nd briefly 4 out: no ex 2 out: btn run in* **7/1**[3]

0B22 **6** *12* **Tribal Dancer (IRE)**[13] [2724] 11-10-0 **98** oh4...................... AlanO'Keeffe 89+
(Miss Venetia Williams) *led at decent gallop to after 5 out: rdn and wknd bef next* **6/1**[2]

-034 **7** *8* **Hazeljack**[18] [2623] 10-9-9 **98** oh4................................. WilliamKennedy[(5)] 76
(A J Whiting) *prom: rdn 11th: wknd fr bef 5 out* **16/1**

3051 **8** *1 3/4* **Cassia Heights**[20] [2583] 10-10-13 **111**...............................(t) TonyDobbin 87
(S A Brookshaw) *midfield: rdn 13th: wknd next* **9/1**

41F3 **9** *5* **Mini Dare**[19] [2610] 8-10-1 **99** oh1 ow1............................... LeightonAspell 82+
(O Sherwood) *towards rr: drvn fr 11th: shortlived effrt u.p 15th: sn btn* **4/1**[1]

/623 **F** **It Was'Nt Me (IRE)**[13] [2725] 8-10-3 **101**........................... MarkBradburne —
(M Sheppard) *in tch whn fell 7th: broke leg: dead* **16/1**

P-1P **P** **Icy Prospect (IRE)**[43] [2102] 7-11-0 **112**.............................. CarlLlewellyn —
(N A Twiston-Davies) *nt fluent: sn bhd: t.o whn p.u 10th* **25/1**

4-P2 **P** **Putup Or Shutup (IRE)**[23] [2556] 9-10-3 **101**................. JimmyMcCarthy —
(K C Bailey) *sn bhd: struggling 1/2-way: no ch whn p.u bef 4 out* **12/1**

6/P- **P** **Supreme Catch (IRE)**[413] [1982] 8-11-10 **122**.................. TimmyMurphy —
(Miss H C Knight) *a bhd: struggling 1/2-way: t.o whn p.u bef 4 out* **15/2**

5m 56.2s (-15.90) **Going Correction** -0.375s/f (Good) **13** Ran SP% **118.3**
Speed ratings: **111,109,108,107,106 102,100,99,97,— —,—,—** CSF £138.29 CT £2735.35 TOTE £11.60: £3.20, £4.70, £6.60; EX 195.80 Trifecta £418.00 Part won. Pool: £588.80 - 0.70 winning tickets..
Owner Hawks And Doves Racing Syndicate **Bred** A J Smith And M Rogers **Trained** Sigwells, Somerset

FOCUS
A decent winning time for the grade. This was a fair handicap and the form looks pretty solid.

NOTEBOOK
Ede'Iff, who has shown a liking for this track in the past, gained her first win since March last year. *Under a patient ride, she struck the front between the last two fences and quickly asserted. (tchd 11-1)*
Nayodabayo(IRE), raised 6lb for his win here last time, ran a sound race but the mare was too strong in the latter stages. He stayed this longer trip but may prove most effective back at two and a half miles. *(op 12-1)*
Benrajah(IRE), only a pound above his last winning mark, ran his best race of the campaign and was renweing his effort at the end. *(op 16-1)*
Dancer Life(POL), a stablemate of the runner-up, caught the eye keeping on steadily in the latter stages having been outpaced by the leaders on the home turn. When dropped a few pounds there could be a race for him. *(tchd 20-1)*
Luneray(FR), raised 6lb for her course-and-distance win a month ago, looked a threat at the first in *the home straight but could not get to the leader and she faded in the endOfficial explanation: vet said mare bled from the nose (op 6-1)*
Tribal Dancer(IRE), who was 4lb out of the handicap, set a decent pace until headed by the eventual runner-up on the home turn. *(op 7-1)*
Mini Dare did not jump with any great fluency and could never get into the action. *(op 9-2)*
Supreme Catch(IRE) was supported for this first run for over a year, having won after a similarly lengthy absence before, but he was always trailing before being pulled up. *(op 9-1)*

2939 TANNERS CHAMPAGNE H'CAP CHASE (13 fncs) 2m

2:40 (2:41) (Class 3) (0-125,121) 5-Y-0+

£6,369 (£1,881; £940; £470; £234; £117)

Form RPR

0-23 **1** **Demi Beau**[94] [1487] 7-11-12 **121**.................................... ChristianWilliams 143+
(Evan Williams) *prom fr 2nd: led 4th: hdd 9th: regained ld 3 out: readily* **4/1**[3]

0-11 **2** *4* **Lorient Express (FR)**[12] [2754] 6-10-11 **111**......................... PaulO'Neill[(5)] 125+
(Miss Venetia Williams) *hld up: hdwy 7th: led 9th: hdd 3 out: one pce run-in* **2/1**[1]

-310 **3** *9* **Toulouse (IRE)**[46] [2051] 8-11-7 **116**.............................. AndrewThornton 119
(R H Alner) *prom: led 2nd to 4th: settled in tch after 5th: effrt to chse ldrs after 9th: wknd 2 out* **8/1**

3U36 **4** *5* **Saafend Rocket (IRE)**[17] [2664] 7-11-7 **116**.................. RichardJohnson 114
(H D Daly) *hld up: sme hdwy appr 4 out: no imp fr 2 out* **10/3**[2]

020P **5** *3 1/2* **Golly (IRE)**[45] [2077] 9-9-9 **97**... MissLHorner[(7)] 92
(D L Williams) *in tch: lost pl 4th (water): n.d after* **50/1**

5421 **6** *shd* **Runner Bean**[22] [2562] 11-10-11 **106**.................................. RobertThornton 103+
(R Lee) *in tch: wknd after 4 out* **9/1**

2 **7** *10* **Solar At'Em (IRE)**[13] [2722] 7-10-0 **95** oh3......................... MarkBradburne 79
(M Sheppard) *chsd ldrs: lost pl after 5th (water): n.d after* **28/1**

053/ **8** *8* **Pro Dancer (USA)**[27] [2470] 7-11-1 **117**..............................(b) MrJJDoyle[(7)] 93
(P M J Doyle, Ire) *midfield: hdwy 4th: rdn and wknd appr 4 out* **12/1**

U **Rocksham (IRE)**[10] [2787] 5-10-0 **95** oh1.....................(b) TomScudamore —
(E Sheehy, Ire) *led to 2nd: remained cl up tl rdn and wkng whn blnd and uns rdr 8th* **20/1**

3m 55.5s (-8.60) **Going Correction** -0.375s/f (Good) **9** Ran SP% **115.4**
Speed ratings: **106,104,99,97,95 95,90,86,—** CSF £12.76 CT £60.01 TOTE £5.40: £1.50, £1.50, £1.90; EX 20.30.
Owner Cunningham Racing **Bred** Lord Howard De Walden **Trained** Cowbridge, Vale Of Glamorgan

FOCUS
A decent event of its type. The winner was value for double the margin and looks a useful novice, while the runner-up showed improved form in defeat.

NOTEBOOK
Demi Beau ◆, who picked up an injury on his last start in September, was back in front at the third from home and skipped away from the favourite for a comfortable win. He will go up for this but should be capable of winning again. *(op 9-2 tchd 5-1)*
Lorient Express(FR) was bidding for a hat-trick off an 8lb higher mark. Not particularly fluent at his fences, he travelled well and had every chance but was put in his place by the winner from the third last. This was still a decent effort. *(op 9-4 tchd 5-2 in a place)*
Toulouse(IRE), fitter for his recent return to the fray after over five months off, ran respectably but was no match in the end for a couple of progressive performers. *(op 10-1)*
Saafend Rocket(IRE) ran a decent race on his favourite track but does look high enough in the weights at present. *(op 3-1)*
Golly(IRE), pulled up in heavy ground last time, was the first of these under pressure but was keeping on when it was all over.
Runner Bean, who is more effective over the minimum trip, could not defy the 7lb rise for his win at Hereford. *(op 8-1)*

2940 TANNERS CAVA H'CAP HURDLE (9 hdls) 2m

3:10 (3:10) (Class 4) (0-105,104) 4-Y-0+ **£5,081** (£1,491; £745; £372)

Form RPR

6001 **1** **Gustavo**[7] 2822 4-9-13 82 ..... PaulO'Neill(5) 97+
(Miss Venetia Williams) *prom: led 3 out: sn hrd pressed: drvn out fr last* **11/4**[2]

1-51 **2** *4* **Capitana (GER)**[13] 2726 4-11-9 101 ..... MickFitzgerald 109+
(N J Henderson) *hld up midfield: smooth hdwy to disp ld bef 2 out: rdn and kpt on same pce fr last* **15/8**[1]

0-06 **3** *6* **Theatre Tinka (IRE)**[67] 1745 6-9-12 86 ..... AdamHawkins(10) 88
(R Hollinshead) *hld up: hdwy 1/2-way: led briefly bef 3 out: one pce fr next* **16/1**

6555 **4** *1 3/4* **Sgt Pepper (IRE)**[12] 2749 4-11-2 94 ..... LeightonAspell 96+
(O Sherwood) *hld up: hdwy bef 4 out: keeping on whn nt fluent 2 out: no imp* **11/1**

0-41 **5** *1/2* **Blue Mariner**[22] 2560 5-11-7 99 ..... (t) TomScudamore 99
(J Jay) *hld up: hdwy to chse ldrs appr 3 out: sn rdn and no ex: lost 3rd run in* **14/1**

-03 **6** *4* **Adecco (IRE)**[13] 2734 6-11-0 92 ..... JamieMoore 88
(G L Moore) *keen in midfield: effrt bef 3 out: wknd next* **17/2**[3]

P020 **7** *3 1/2* **Jayed (IRE)**[15] 2685 7-10-7 92 ..... PatrickCStringer(7) 85
(M Bradstock) *keen: led to bef 3 out: sn wknd* **25/1**

4620 **8** *1 1/2* **My Sharp Grey**[13] 2726 6-10-12 90 ..... RobertThornton 81
(J Gallagher) *racd wd: hld up midfield: hdwy and prom 1/2-way: rdn and wknd bef 3 out* **50/1**

6-10 **9** *nk* **Silver City**[29] 2419 5-11-4 96 ..... RichardJohnson 87
(P J Hobbs) *chsd ldrs: ev ch bef 3 out: sn rdn and wknd* **14/1**

6046 **10** *6* **Margarets Wish**[13] 2726 5-10-4 82 ..... RJGreene 67
(T Wall) *chsd ldrs tl wknd bef 3 out* **28/1**

P4-5 **11** *1 3/4* **Shady Anne**[13] 2726 7-11-5 100 ..... (p) OwynNelmes(3) 83
(F Jordan) *prom to 1/2-way: sn lost pl* **28/1**

P05 **12** *shd* **Front Rank (IRE)**[13] 2716 5-11-11 103 ..... JimmyMcCarthy 86
(K C Bailey) *a bhd* **50/1**

0/6- **13** *1 1/4* **Late Claim (USA)**[585] 363 5-11-1 103 ..... ShaunJohnson(10) 85
(R T Phillips) *a bhd* **40/1**

-03P **14** *21* **Cashel Dancer**[62] 1804 6-11-4 96 ..... TomSiddall 57
(S A Brookshaw) *in tch to 1/2-way: sn wknd* **50/1**

04-0 **15** *3* **Barcelona**[17] 2659 8-10-2 87 ..... (t) MissLBrooke(7) 45
(Lady Susan Brooke) *a bhd* **100/1**

63P0 **16** *21* **Magical Liaison (IRE)**[17] 2659 7-11-3 95 ..... CarlLlewellyn 32
(W Jenks) *chsd ldrs to 1/2-way: sn wknd* **100/1**

2-66 **17** *2* **Forest Chief (IRE)**[125] 1249 9-11-12 104 ..... (t) ChristianWilliams 39
(Evan Williams) *a bhd: no ch fr 1/2-way* **66/1**

-P30 **U** **A Monk Swimming (IRE)**[70] 1717 4-9-11 82 ..... (t) MarcGoldstein(7) —
(Miss J S Davis) *nt fluent: hld up: rdn but no imp whn blnd and uns rdr 4 out* **100/1**

3m 44.9s (-7.40) **Going Correction** -0.375s/f (Good)
WFA 4 from 5yo+ 10lb **18 Ran SP% 123.1**
Speed ratings: **103,101,98,97,96 94,93,92,92,89 88,88,87,77,75 65,64,—** CSF £7.78 CT £70.36 TOTE £4.10: £1.50, £1.40, £3.90, £2.40; EX 7.20.
Owner Mrs P A H Hartley **Bred** G Reed **Trained** Kings Caple, H'fords

FOCUS
Quite a well contested handicap, run at a decent pace, and the form should work out. The winner is rated value for further.

NOTEBOOK
Gustavo ◆, unpenalised for his win in a conditionals' race a week earlier, followed up in a style of *a progressive performer. He is due to go up 6lb now but that may not be enough to stop him. (op 10-3 tchd 7-2 in a place)*
Capitana(GER), put up 10lb for a fluent win against her own sex here, travelled strongly and came there with every chance but found one too good at the weights. *(op 2-1 tchd 85-40 in a place)*
Theatre Tinka(IRE), making his handicap debut on only his fourth start over hurdles, ran well and can find a small race from this mark.
Sgt Pepper(IRE), in handicap company for the first time, confirmed the promise of his last two runs and definitely has a race in him, although he looks the sort who will not find much off the bridle. *(op 8-1)*
Blue Mariner was bought in for a tidy sum after landing a seller last time and he ran a sound race in this better company. This was only his fourth run over hurdles and he is capable of further improvement. *(op 12-1)*
Adecco(IRE), down to two miles and dropped a couple of pounds, shaped as if he does need a bit further. *(op 9-1 tchd 8-1)*
Jayed(IRE) set a sound pace and was not given a hard time when headed. *(op 20-1)*
Silver City, just a pound lower, was right in the action at the first flight in the straight before fading out of contention. *(op 12-1)*

2941 TANNERS BURGUNDY STANDARD NATIONAL HUNT FLAT RACE (CONDITIONAL JOCKEYS/AMATEUR RIDERS) 2m

3:40 (3:40) (Class 6) 4-6-Y-0 **£2,452** (£720; £360; £179)

Form RPR

1 **Ringaroses** 4-10-13 ..... PaulO'Neill(5) 107+
(Miss H C Knight) *hld up: hdwy 9f out: wnt 2nd 4f out: led over 2f out: drew clr fnl f* **10/3**[1]

2 *7* **Magical Harry**[297] 5-10-11 ..... MissRAGreen(7) 98+
(P F Nicholls) *midfield: hdwy 7f out: ev ch 2f out: one pce fnl f* **18/1**

1 **3** *1/2* **The Hollow Bottom**[41] 2145 4-11-4 ..... BernieWharfe(7) 105+
(N A Twiston-Davies) *in tch: rdn 5f out: hung bdly lft whn chsd ldrs 3f out: styd on same pce fnl 2f* **9/1**

4 *2* **The Rocking Dock (IRE)**[17] 2672 4-11-1 ..... MDarcy(3) 95
(E Sheehy, Ire) *a.p: led 6f out: hung lft over 3f out: hdd over 2f out: no ex fnl f* **11/2**[3]

5 *2 1/2* **Mister Chatterbox (IRE)** 4-10-13 ..... RobertStephens(5) 92+
(P J Hobbs) *midfield: rdn and lost pl after 5f out: rn green and kpt on fr 3f out* **16/1**

2 **6** *3 1/2* **Dateldoo (IRE)**[66] 1755 6-10-4 ..... MrRhysHughes(7) 82
(P D Williams) *led early: settled in tch: lost pl 1/2-way: kpt on fr 3f out: no imp on ldrs* **50/1**

-2 **7** *hd* **Gold Beach (IRE)**[41] 2145 5-11-1 ..... MrMRimell(3) 88+
(M G Rimell) *rn green early: t.k.h: midfield: hdwy 9f out: wknd over 3f out* **7/2**[2]

3 **8** *nk* **Miss Chippy (IRE)**[23] 2558 5-10-4 ..... WillieMcCarthy(7) 81
(T R George) *sn led: hdd after 2f: remained prom: rdn over 3f out: wknd over 2f out* **8/1**

9 *1* **William Butler (IRE)**[409] 5-11-1 ..... MrRBurton(3) 87
(S A Brookshaw) *prom after 3f: rdn and wknd over 3f out* **12/1**

3-0 **10** *4* **Midnight Star**[32] 2340 4-10-11 ..... TomMessenger(7) 83
(M Mullineaux) *hld up: struggling 1/2-way: nvr on terms* **100/1**

0 **11** *5* **Kadanza**[22] 2565 4-11-1 ..... TomMalone(3) 78
(P Bowen) *midfield: lost pl after 4f: no imp after* **66/1**

3- **12** *1* **Kilkilian (IRE)**[323] 3640 5-10-13 ..... JohnnyLevins(5) 87+
(B G Powell) *hld up: hdwy 3f out: no imp whn hung bdly lft over 1f out: wl btn after* **10/1**

0 **13** *12* **Dryliner**[49] 1985 5-11-1 ..... OwynNelmes(3) 65
(A E Price) *t.k.h: midfield: pushed along 7f out: wknd over 5f out* **100/1**

14 *1 1/2* **Golden Inca** 5-10-4 ..... ShaneWalsh(7) 57
(J Gallagher) *midfield: struggling 1/2-way: sn btn* **66/1**

0 **15** *2* **Swete Deva**[22] 2565 5-10-13 ..... TomGreenway(5) 62
(C Roberts) *in tch: rdn 1/2-way: sn wknd* **100/1**

0- **16** *dist* **Percy Jay (NZ)**[352] 3210 6-10-13 ..... StephenCraine(5) —
(W Jenks) *led after 2f: hdd 6f out: wknd 5f out: t.o* **100/1**

17 *26* **Come On Jim (IRE)** 4-10-13 ..... ThomasDreaper(5) —
(A J Whiting) *in tch: wknd 9f out: t.o* **66/1**

18 *1 1/2* **Tanners Grove** 4-10-11 ..... (t) MissCDyson(7) —
(Miss C Dyson) *plld hrd: a bhd: t.o* **100/1**

3m 44.9s (-7.30) **Going Correction** -0.375s/f (Good) **18 Ran SP% 121.1**
Speed ratings: **103,99,99,98,97 95,95,95,94,92 90,89,83,82,81 —,—,—** CSF £62.46 TOTE £4.00: £2.10, £6.40, £3.00; EX 61.40 Place 6 £95.59, Place 5 £33.76.
Owner Mrs Nicholas Jones/Martin Broughton **Bred** Coln Valley Stud **Trained** West Lockinge, Oxon

FOCUS
The winner could be useful and with the third, sixth and tenth running close to their pre-race marks this could have been a reasonable bumper.

NOTEBOOK
Ringaroses, whose dam was a high-class staying hurdler, is a half-brother to several winners including smart staying chaser Frosty Canyon, smart but quirky staying hurdler Red Cardinal and Alvino, who was successful for this yard. Getting on top in the last quarter-mile, he pulled away for a decisive success and he should go on to better things. *(op 4-1)*
Magical Harry, out of a winning jumper who stayed three miles, showed ability in a maiden point over two and a half in February. Coming from off the pace to dispute the lead with two furlongs to run, he soon found the favourite too strong but this was a promising effort. *(op 16-1 tchd 20-1)*
The Hollow Bottom, penalised for his debut win here, ran his race despite hanging early in the home straight. *(op 13-2)*
The Rocking Dock(IRE) was well held on his debut in testing ground earlier in the month. This was better and he has ability.
Mister Chatterbox(IRE), out of a winning Irish pointer, stayed on in encouraging fashion in the latter stages.
Dateldoo(IRE), runner-up in a weak race on her debut, probably ran up to that form.
Gold Beach(IRE), second to The Hollow Bottom on his debut here, paid the price for pulling too hard. *(op 3-1)*
T/Jkpt: Not won. T/Plt: £83.00 to a £1 stake. Pool: £61,621.90. 541.75 winning tickets. T/Qpdt: £19.30 to a £1 stake. Pool: £4,883.10. 186.50 winning tickets. DO

2062 AYR (L-H)

Thursday, December 22

OFFICIAL GOING: Soft (good to soft in places)
Wind: Breezy, half-against

2942 NEW YEAR AT AYR RACECOURSE NOVICES' HURDLE (9 hdls) 2m

12:30 (12:32) (Class 4) 4-Y-0+ **£4,381** (£1,286; £643; £321)

Form RPR

3P **1** **Up Above (IRE)**[18] 2667 5-11-2 ..... (p) AndrewJMcNamara(3) 123+
(S Donohoe, Ire) *led and sn clr: rdn 3 out: edgd lft: styd on strly* **3/1**[2]

F **2** *5* **Double Vodka (IRE)**[29] 2444 4-10-12 ..... RichardMcGrath 107
(C Grant) *midfield: hdwy 4 out: chsd wnr last: kpt on* **5/1**[3]

0-1 **3** *12* **Planters Punch (IRE)**[28] 2448 4-11-5 ..... BarryKeniry 104+
(G M Moore) *chsd ldrs: drvn bef 3 out: sn one pce* **12/1**

1-10 **4** *3 1/2* **Malt De Vergy (FR)**[39] 2211 5-10-12 ..... TonyDobbin 98+
(L Lungo) *hld up in tch: smooth hdwy to press ldr and 1l down whn mstke 3 out: sn no ex: lost 2nd last* **11/4**[1]

2112 **5** *3* **Rare Coincidence**[12] 2566 4-11-5 109 ..... (p) KeithMercer 96
(R F Fisher) *cl up: outpcd after 4 out: no imp fr next* **8/1**

6 *3 1/2* **Hawkwell (IRE)** 4-10-12 ..... BrianHarding 85+
(N G Richards) *hld up: stdy hdwy whn nt fluent 4 out: nvr nrr* **50/1**

0 **7** *5* **It's No Easy (IRE)**[63] 1799 4-10-12 ..... DominicElsworth 80
(N G Richards) *hld up: shkn up 4 out: n.d* **100/1**

-U00 **8** *5* **Cloudmor (IRE)**[26] 2497 4-10-9 ..... GaryBerridge(3) 75
(L Lungo) *hld up: stdy hdwy 5th: outpcd fr next* **100/1**

P **9** *1 3/4* **Inch High**[115] 1291 7-10-9 ..... PaddyAspell(3) 73
(J S Goldie) *bhd tl sme late hdwy: nvr on terms* **100/1**

102- **10** *hd* **Golden Measure**[73] 3078 5-10-12 ..... DNRussell 73
(G A Swinbank) *bad mstkes 1st and 2nd: wl bhd tl sme late hdwy: nvr on terms* **11/1**

02-L **11** *2* **Baffling Secret (FR)**[28] 2448 5-10-12 ..... BruceGibson 71
(L Lungo) *hld up: hit 5th: n.d* **100/1**

0 **12** *18* **Zandeed (IRE)**[28] 2448 7-10-5 ..... EwanWhillans(7) 53
(A C Whillans) *towards rr: rdn whn hit 4 out: sn btn* **100/1**

4-04 **13** *15* **Silver Dollars (FR)**[22] 2571 4-10-12 ..... GrahamLee 38
(J Howard Johnson) *in tch tl wknd fr 4 out* **16/1**

60 **14** *8* **Stormy Madam (IRE)**[15] 2704 5-10-2 ow4 ..... MrRWakeham(7) 27
(J R Turner) *towards rr: struggling fr 4th* **100/1**

0/P **15** *1 1/2* **Tony Tie**[4] 2903 9-10-12 ..... NeilMulholland 29
(J S Goldie) *chsd ldrs to 4 out: sn rdn and wknd* **100/1**

16 *15* **Beardie's Dream (IRE)**[214] 5-10-5 ..... TimmyMurphy 7
(Miss P Robson) *a wl bhd* **33/1**

17 *14* **Phone Tapping**[269] 4-10-7 ..... DesFlavin(5) —
(Mrs L B Normile) *nvr on terms* **100/1**

0-50 **F** **Kilmackilloge**[8] 2821 6-10-12 ..... RussGarritty —
(M Todhunter) *fell 2nd* **50/1**

6 **P** **Auenmoon (GER)**[18] 2652 4-10-12 ..... WilsonRenwick —
(P Monteith) *prom tl wknd 4 out: p.u bef next* **33/1**

0- **P** **Caymanas Bay**[298] 4086 5-10-12 ..... AlanDempsey —
(A Parker) *midfield: wknd 5th: p.u and dismntd next* **100/1**

3m 59.7s (2.40) **Going Correction** +0.175s/f (Yiel) **20 Ran SP% 120.1**
Speed ratings: **101,98,92,90,89 87,85,82,81,81 80,71,64,60,59 51,44,—,—,—** CSF £17.31 TOTE £3.50: £2.10, £2.80, £3.20; EX 27.40.
Owner K Kerrigan **Bred** Mrs D H Clyde **Trained** Cootehill Road, Co. Cavan

FOCUS
An ordinary event in which the pace was sound throughout and this bare form should prove reliable.

NOTEBOOK
Up Above(IRE), tried in cheekpieces, did not have to improve too much to win his second race over hurdles in workmanlike fashion. He should stay two and a half, has room for improvement with his hurdling and is the type to win again. *(op 11-4 tchd 5-2)*

The Form Book, Raceform Ltd, Compton, RG20 6NL

Double Vodka(IRE) fully confirmed the promise shown before falling on his debut and, on this evidence, should have no problem winning a run of the mill event in the north this winter. *(op 4-1 tchd 11-2)*
Planters Punch(IRE) was not totally disgraced under his penalty but is likely to continue to look vulnerable in this grade and may do better in ordinary handicaps when upped to two and a half miles. *(op 11-1)*
Malt De Vergy(FR) ◆, a dual bumper winner, shaped better than the bare form on this hurdle debut as he ploughed through the first in the home straight when looking dangerous on ground that may have been too soft. He is one to bear in mind in similar company. *(tchd 5-2 and 3-1)*
Rare Coincidence was not totally disgraced under his penalty but may be better when able to dominate on less testing ground in ordinary handicap company. He is well worth another chance. *(tchd 9-1)*
Hawkwell(IRE) ◆, a half-brother to a winning pointer and hurdler, caught the eye without being knocked about on this racecourse debut. Although this bare form is only moderate, he appeals strongly as the type to do better in due course. *(op 33-1)*
It's No Easy(IRE) was another from this stable to catch the eye on this hurdle debut and he too should fare better with time and experience.

2943 WEDDINGS AT WESTERN HOUSE BEGINNERS' CHASE (11 fncs 1 omitted) 2m
1:00 (1:01) (Class 3) 4-Y-0+ **£5,371** (£1,576; £788; £393)

Form				RPR
-620	**1**		**Shares (IRE)**[28] [2452] 5-10-8 105 .... DavidDaSilva(10) *(P Monteith) hld up: hdwy to take mod 4th 4th: smooth hdwy to ld 2 out: styd on run-in* **16/1**	112
/0-6	**2**	1 ¾	**Mr McAuley (IRE)**[12] [2764] 7-11-4 .... DNRussell *(I R Ferguson, Ire) hld up in rr: hdwy 8th: j.rt last 3: wnt 2nd between last 2: no ex run-in* **4/1**[3]	110
6/26	**3**	17	**Albertino Lad**[48] [2026] 8-11-1 91 .... PeterBuchanan(3) *(Miss Lucinda V Russell) w ldrs: lft in ld 6th: hdd after 2 out: sn wknd* **20/1**	95+
0-PF	**4**	3	**Skenfrith**[18] [2654] 6-11-1 112 .... MrCStorey(3) *(Miss S E Forster) outpcd and in rr: mstke 5th: hdwy and prom 7th: wknd appr 3 out* **25/1**	90
00P-	**5**	dist	**Fleetfoot Mac**[204] [4928] 4-10-3 .... MichaelMcAlister(5) *(B Storey) prom to 3rd: bhd fr 7th* **50/1**	—
021/	**F**		**Armaguedon (FR)**[650] [4292] 7-11-4 .... TonyDobbin *(L Lungo) led tl fell 6th* **15/8**[2]	—
0030	**U**		**Named At Dinner**[22] [2567] 4-10-8 .... WilsonRenwick *(Miss Lucinda V Russell) bhd fr 4th: 6th whn fell 2 out* **66/1**	—
F5P-	**P**		**Astronomic**[258] [4762] 5-11-4 .... GrahamLee *(J Howard Johnson) chsd ldr: sltly hmpd 6th: chal 3 out: 4th and wkng whn blnd next: 5th whn p.u sn after last* **13/8**[1]	—

4m 6.40s (1.90) **Going Correction** +0.025s/f (Yiel)
WFA 4 from 5yo+ 10lb **8** Ran SP% **110.8**
Speed ratings: **96,95,86,85,—** —,—,— CSF £72.72 TOTE £18.30: £2.70, £1.50, £2.30; EX 69.20.
Owner The Dregs Of Humanity **Bred** Patrick Farrell **Trained** Rosewell, Midlothian

FOCUS
A modest time for a race of its class. The first fence in the home straight had to be omitted because of a bad patch of ground.

NOTEBOOK
Shares(IRE), who had plenty to find with the two market leaders on hurdle-race ratings, jumped soundly on his chase debut and, after taking it up on the bridle, in the end did enough. His stamina is strictly limited and he is suited by going left-handed. *(op 14-1)*
Mr McAuley(IRE), rated 11lb better than the winner over hurdles, was backed to step up on his chase debut dropped back in trip. But for jumping right over the final three fences he would have given the winner more to do. *(op 11-2 tchd 6-1)*
Albertino Lad, who had plenty to find, was left in command but he tired badly on the run to the final fence. *(tchd 22-1)*
Skenfrith, who failed to get round on his two previous outings over fences, at least shaped a bit better and managed to complete if only in his own time. *(op 28-1)*
Armaguedon(FR), winner of two bumpers, was having his first outing since taking a maiden hurdle here in March 2004. A grand big type, he made the running at his own pace before coming down. Hopefully it will prove just a blip. *(op 7-4 tchd 5-2)*
Astronomic still seems to be remembering his crashing fall over hurdles at Sandown in January. On his first try over fences, he raced up with the pace but, after challenging, he emptied in a matter of strides and went right through the second last. Legless when pulled up soon after the last, there *must be a big question mark over him now. Official explanation: jockey said gelding was stiff behind (op 7-4 tchd 5-2)*

2944 SUBSCRIBE TO RACING UK ON 08700 860 432 H'CAP HURDLE (11 hdls) 2m 4f
1:30 (1:31) (Class 4) (0-105,105) 4-Y-0+ **£4,840** (£1,421; £710; £354)

Form				RPR
-31P	**1**		**Topanberry (IRE)**[46] [2066] 6-11-9 102 .... TonyDobbin *(N G Richards) in tch: effrt 3 out: led run in: edgd rt: hld on wl* **10/1**[3]	107
4460	**2**	1 ¼	**Chief Dan George (IRE)**[27] [2475] 5-10-7 89 .... PaddyAspell(3) *(D R MacLeod) in tch: drvn 7th: rallied bef 3 out: kpt on wl fr last: nt rch wnr* **50/1**	93
-224	**3**	nk	**Jolika (FR)**[28] [2453] 8-10-10 99 .... JohnEnnis(10) *(L Lungo) trckd ldrs: led after 4 out: hdd after last: kpt on same pce* **12/1**	103+
65/3	**4**	5	**Zoltano (GER)**[32] [2372] 7-10-13 92 .... GrahamLee *(M Todhunter) trckd ldrs: effrt bef 3 out: one pce fr next* **13/2**[2]	91+
3	**5**	1 ½	**My Lucky Rose (IRE)**[8] [2831] 7-10-6 88 .... (b) AndrewJMcNamara(3) *(S Donohoe, Ire) midfield: hdwy bef 4 out: effrt next: one pce fr 2 out* **12/1**	85
-305	**6**	5	**Silver Seeker (USA)**[16] [2693] 5-10-1 80 .... KeithMercer *(A R Dicken) midfield: drvn 7th: kpt on fr 2 out: nrst fin* **25/1**	72
5F20	**7**	½	**Silver Sedge (IRE)**[28] [2453] 6-10-6 88 .... PeterBuchanan(3) *(Mrs A Hamilton) midfield: hdwy to ld briefly 4 out: outpcd fr next* **16/1**	79
333-	**8**	12	**Brave Thought (IRE)**[285] [4322] 10-11-7 100 .... TimmyMurphy *(P Monteith) hld up: stdy hdwy bef 3 out: shkn up and no imp* **14/1**	79
03/3	**9**	¾	**Castle Richard (IRE)**[28] [2452] 8-11-10 103 .... BarryKeniry *(G M Moore) midfield on outside: drvn 7th: no imp fr 3 out* **12/1**	82
3-06	**10**	5	**Sara Monica (IRE)**[16] [2691] 8-11-7 103 .... GaryBerridge(3) *(L Lungo) chsd ldrs tl wknd fr 4 out* **20/1**	77
0U05	**11**	1 ¼	**Gospel Song**[17] [2680] 13-10-4 90 .... EwanWhillans(7) *(A C Whillans) mde most to 4 out: sn rdn and wknd* **50/1**	62
-306	**12**	nk	**Fearless Foursome**[17] [2680] 6-10-11 90 .... AndrewThornton *(N W Alexander) towards rr: outpcd 6th: nvr on terms* **50/1**	62
F5-4	**13**	8	**Random Native (IRE)**[28] [2448] 7-11-2 95 .... BrianHarding *(N G Richards) hld up: hdwy and in tch 7th: wknd bef 3 out* **16/1**	59
4202	**14**	hd	**Time To Roam (IRE)**[19] [2625] 5-10-13 102 .... (b) NeilWalker(10) *(Miss Lucinda V Russell) chsd ldrs: ev ch 4 out: sn rdn and wknd* **25/1**	66
PU0	**15**	9	**Winds Supreme (IRE)**[28] [2453] 6-9-11 83 .... (t) MissAngelaBarnes(7) *(M A Barnes) hld up: gd hdwy to join ldrs 1/2-way: wknd 4 out* **100/1**	38
0325	**16**	1 ¼	**The Miner**[17] [2679] 7-10-8 90 .... MrCStorey(3) *(Miss S E Forster) a bhd* **50/1**	44
52-P	**17**	21	**Political Cruise**[61] [1838] 7-9-12 84 ow2 .... GarethThomas(7) *(R Nixon) a bhd* **66/1**	17
140-	**18**	hd	**Lady Past Times**[246] [4928] 5-10-3 82 .... DominicElsworth *(D W Whillans) chsd ldrs to 6th: sn rdn and wknd* **33/1**	15
1/1-	**B**		**Sobraon (IRE)**[432] [1726] 6-11-5 105 .... ScottMarshall(7) *(N G Richards) hld up: b.d bnd after 5th* **6/1**[1]	—
13/4	**B**		**Jexel (FR)**[19] [2629] 8-11-7 100 .... RichardMcGrath *(B Storey) keen: hld up: b.d bnd after 5th* **20/1**	—
6422	**S**		**Bywell Beau (IRE)**[18] [2653] 6-11-6 102 .... (t) MichalKohl(3) *(J I A Charlton) midfield whn slipped and fell bnd after 5th* **10/1**[3]	—
05-4	**P**		**Silken Pearls**[47] [2042] 9-11-9 102 .... BruceGibson *(L Lungo) chsd ldrs to 6th: sn lost pl: t.o whn p.u bef 3 out* **25/1**	—
0-05	**P**		**Stravonian**[28] [2447] 5-9-11 81 .... DougieCostello(5) *(G A Swinbank) nt fluent in rr: struggling 6th: t.o whn p.u bef 3 out* **16/1**	—

5m 14.6s (1.90) **Going Correction** +0.175s/f (Yiel) **23** Ran SP% **127.5**
Speed ratings: **103,102,102,100,99 97,97,92,92,90 89,89,86,86,82 82,74,74,—,—** —,—,— CSF £455.77 CT £5984.73 TOTE £10.10: £2.20, £7.90, £4.20, £2.30; EX 972.50.
Owner Mrs D McGawn **Bred** Miss E Hamilton **Trained** Greystoke, Cumbria

FOCUS
An ordinary handicap in which the pace was fair

NOTEBOOK
Topanberry(IRE), who disappointed after a break at this course last time, fared much better this time and showed the right attitude in the closing stages. She is well worth another chance to prove *herself effective over three miles. Official explanation: trainer said, regarding the improved form shown, mare may have been suited by today's better ground (op 12-1)*
Chief Dan George(IRE) duly proved well suited by the step into handicap company and ran his best race yet. He left the impression that he will stay three miles and looks sure to win a run-of-the-mill event away from progressive sorts.
Jolika(FR) is a reliable and versatile sort who again gave it her best shot and she looks a good guide to the worth of this form. She should continue to give a good account in ordinary company.
Zoltano(GER), having his second run back after a very long break, again confirmed that he retains plenty of ability and he should be placed to best advantage in due course. *(op 6-1)*
My Lucky Rose(IRE), a chase winner, has yet to win over hurdles but again ran creditably and left the impression that the step up to three miles would be in her favour.
Silver Seeker(USA) left the impression that an even stiffer test of stamina would have suited but, given a losing run that stretches back to a Flat maiden win in 2002 shows he is not one to place much faith in.
Brave Thought(IRE), reverted to hurdles, caught the eye on this first start for over seven months. His stable is now in better form and the drop to two miles and the return to fences should see him in a better light.

2945 ABSOLUTE MORTGAGES NOVICES' H'CAP CHASE (15 fncs 3 omitted) 2m 5f 110y
2:00 (2:02) (Class 4) (0-105,105) 5-Y-0+ **£4,958** (£1,539; £828)

Form				RPR
23-3	**1**		**Fountain Brig**[46] [2063] 9-10-0 79 .... BrianHarding *(N W Alexander) chsd ldrs: chalng whn lft in ld 2 out: hld on run-in* **10/1**[3]	85
5PP5	**2**	1 ¾	**Mikasa (IRE)**[16] [2688] 5-10-0 79 oh8 .... KeithMercer *(R F Fisher) in rr: hdwy 9th: cl up 3 out: almost upsides last: kpt on grimly* **20/1**	83
-3PP	**3**	24	**Oliverjohn (IRE)**[150] [1062] 8-10-11 100 ow8 .... NeilWalker(10) *(Miss Lucinda V Russell) chsd ldrs: led 10th: hdd 2 out: sn wknd* **20/1**	84+
P2-4	**U**		**Do Keep Up**[41] [2168] 8-9-9 79 oh6 .... DougieCostello(5) *(J R Weymes) in rr whn blnd and uns rdr 2nd* **25/1**	—
/U4-	**F**		**True North (IRE)**[318] [3739] 10-11-7 105 .... DerekLaverty(5) *(D R MacLeod) chsd ldrs: 4th whn fell 9th* **40/1**	—
-000	**P**		**Another Taipan (IRE)**[48] [2024] 5-10-0 79 oh5 .... BarryKeniry *(A C Whillans) in rr: blnd 10th: p.u bef next* **50/1**	—
53-4	**P**		**Not A Trace (IRE)**[76] [1663] 6-10-6 85 .... AndrewThornton *(Mrs S C Bradburne) in rr: bhd whn p.u after 8th* **14/1**	—
5-0U	**P**		**Em's Royalty**[16] [2689] 8-11-12 105 .... AlanDempsey *(A Parker) lost pl 7th: t.o whn j. slowly 10th: sn p.u* **20/1**	—
3-31	**F**		**Corrib Lad (IRE)**[48] [2026] 7-11-9 102 .... BruceGibson *(L Lungo) hld up: wnt prom 8th: led on bit and fell 2 out* **2/1**[1]	110+
0-5P	**P**		**Jofi (IRE)**[28] [2450] 6-9-11 79 oh6 .... PeterBuchanan(3) *(Miss Lucinda V Russell) j. slowly: sn bhd: t.o whn p.u after 8th* **100/1**	—
1	**P**		**Lanaken (IRE)**[27] [2476] 5-11-5 101 .... (b) AndrewJMcNamara(3) *(S Donohoe, Ire) led: blnd 6th: hdd 10th: wkng whn blnd next: p.u bef 13th* **12/1**	—
F56U	**P**		**Northern Minster**[22] [2568] 6-11-2 100 .... MichaelMcAlister(5) *(F P Murtagh) hiut 5th: sn chsng ldrs: 4th and outpcd whn p.u after 13th* **25/1**	—
-313	**P**		**Silver Jack (IRE)**[28] [2451] 7-11-12 105 .... TonyDobbin *(M Todhunter) chsd ldrs: mstke 7th: rdn after next: sn lost pl: in rr whn p.u bef 12th* **9/4**[2]	—

5m 52.1s (-1.60) **Going Correction** +0.025s/f (Yiel) **13** Ran SP% **114.9**
Speed ratings: **103,102,93,—,—** —,—,—,—,— —,—,— CSF £174.87 CT £3855.81 TOTE £9.00: £2.30, £6.70, £4.10; EX 142.70.
Owner Alexander Family **Bred** Exors Of The Late C J T Alexander **Trained** Kinneston, Perth & Kinross

FOCUS
A severe test in the deteriorating conditions. In all three fences were omitted including two of the four in the final straight.

NOTEBOOK
Fountain Brig, 12lb better off with Silver Jack, proved ideally suited by the testing conditions and opened his account at the 16th attempt. Basically big and slow, the more emphasis on stamina the better for him. *(op 8-1)*
Mikasa(IRE), 8lb out of the handicap, was in effect 9lb higher than his sole previous success in a novices' handicap at Cartmel in May. One thing he did prove is that he is a genuine stayer, refusing to lay down arms all the way to the line.
Oliverjohn(IRE), pulled up on quick ground on his last two starts the latest in July, stopped to nothing when headed and his rider's use of the whip on the run-in ought to have come under scrutiny.
Corrib Lad(IRE) ◆, raised 8lb after winning on his chase debut at Hexham, travelled strongly and had just taken command when he crashed out at what is normally the third last fence. A big, strong type, he will surely gain compensation. *(tchd 5-2 and 11-4 in places)*
Silver Jack(IRE), 9lb higher than when winning by a wide margin here last month, was not in the *same sort of form this time and was struggling with a full circuit to go. Official explanation: trainer had no explanation for the poor form shown (tchd 5-2 and 11-4 in places)*

2946 BETFAIR H'CAP CHASE (15 fncs 4 omitted) 3m 1f

2:30 (2:32) (Class 3) (0-125,120) 5-Y-0+ **£6,792** (£1,994; £997; £497)

Form				RPR
0-42	**1**		**D J Flippance (IRE)**[28] 2453 10-10-0 **94** oh2 .... TimmyMurphy (A Parker) *chsd ldrs: outpcd appr 2 out: rallied to ld last: styd on* **15/2**	105
15-5	**2**	*1 ¼*	**Kerry Lads (IRE)**[29] 2445 10-11-9 **120** .... (p) PeterBuchanan(3) (Miss Lucinda V Russell) *led: mstke 3 out: mstke and hdd last: kpt on towards fin* **6/1**[2]	133+
2P-5	**3**	*hd*	**Cordilla (IRE)**[19] 2629 7-11-4 **112** .... TonyDobbin (N G Richards) *prom: hit 11th: effrt bef 2 out: ev ch last: one pce towards fin* **3/1**[1]	123+
-563	**4**	*26*	**Harrovian**[19] 2644 8-11-6 **114** .... AlanDempsey (Miss P Robson) *trckd ldrs tl wknd bef 2 out* **7/1**	104+
00P3	**5**	*dist*	**Lazy But Lively (IRE)**[8] 2819 9-11-5 **113** .... KeithMercer (R F Fisher) *hld up: outpcd 9th: nvr on terms* **12/1**	—
6422	**6**	*1 ½*	**Jungle Jinks (IRE)**[19] 2644 10-11-6 **114** .... FinbarKeniry (G M Moore) *chsd ldrs tl wknd 10th* **6/1**[2]	—
P630	**P**		**Hollows Mill**[29] 2443 9-10-3 **100** .... PaddyAspell(3) (F P Murtagh) *mstkes in rr: struggling 9th: p.u bef 2 out* **100/1**	—
-F63	**P**		**Behavingbadly (IRE)**[21] 2589 10-10-0 **94** .... BrianHarding (A Parker) *bhd: outpcd 9th: nvr on terms: t.o whn p.u bef 2 out* **8/1**	—
40-0	**P**		**Harry Hooly**[36] 2265 10-9-11 **98** .... MissRDavidson(7) (Mrs H O Graham) *hld up: blnd 8th: wknd next: t.o whn p.u bef 3 out* **100/1**	—
5P1	**P**		**Magnificent Seven (IRE)**[21] 2588 6-10-4 **98** .... GrahamLee (J Howard Johnson) *in tch: outpcd and reminders 9th: t.o whn p.u bef 2 out* **13/2**[3]	—

6m 41.8s (-3.90) **Going Correction** +0.025s/f (Yiel) **10** Ran SP% **112.0**
Speed ratings: **107,106,106,98,**— —,—,—,—,— CSF £50.58 CT £163.14 TOTE £9.10: £2.00, £2.10, £2.10; EX 61.00 Trifecta £351.20 Pool: £494.70 - 1.00 winning ticket..

Owner Mr & Mrs Raymond Anderson Green **Bred** Capt D Foster And B Corscadden **Trained** Ecclefechan, D'fries & G'way

FOCUS
A fair handicap in which the pace was sound. Two fences in the home straight were omitted, the first and the open ditch.

NOTEBOOK
D J Flippance(IRE) ◆, back up in trip and back over fences, looks a dour stayer but showed a good attitude in the closing stages. Whether he would have beaten the runner-up had that jumped the last cleanly is open to debate, but he is certainly capable of winning more races over either hurdles or fences when the emphasis is on stamina. *(op 8-1)*

Kerry Lads(IRE), who seems to reserve his best efforts for the track, ran up to his best and would have gone very close had he jumped the last cleanly. He is capable of winning from this sort of mark when his jumping holds up. *(op 15-2)*

Cordilla(IRE), back over fences, ran as well as he has ever done in this sphere. He is effective over *two and a half miles, is in good hands and he is sure to win more races over the larger obstacles. (op 7-2)*

Harrovian, who had shaped better at Wetherby on his previous start, was disappointing this time and has not really progressed in the anticipated manner since winning twice over fences in January. *(op 6-1)*

Lazy But Lively(IRE), turned out quickly after a fair run over three miles and six at Bangor last week, was a long way below that level and consistency is not his strongest suit. *(tchd 14-1)*

Jungle Jinks(IRE), who has only won once since February 2003, was a long way below his recent best and he does not look one to place too much faith in. *(op 7-1)*

2947 A NEW DAWN AT CUMBERNAULD NOVICES' HURDLE (11 hdls) 2m 4f

3:00 (3:04) (Class 3) 4-Y-0+ **£4,964** (£1,457; £728; £363)

Form				RPR
	1		**Hard Act To Follow (IRE)**[280] 4425 6-10-12 .... GrahamLee (J Howard Johnson) *trckd ldrs: led appr 3 out: rdn clr after last: readily* **6/4**[1]	120+
0-10	**2**	*5*	**Supreme's Legacy (IRE)**[33] 2340 6-10-12 .... RichardMcGrath (K G Reveley) *hld up in rr div: stdy hdwy 6th: wnt 2nd 2 out: kpt on: no imp* **7/1**	110+
3-3	**3**	*8*	**Windy Hills**[36] 2262 5-10-12 .... TonyDobbin (N G Richards) *hld up in mid-div: hdwy to chse ldrs 8th: one pce fr 2 out* **4/1**[2]	105+
1-53	**4**	*6*	**Sotovik (IRE)**[18] 2652 4-10-5 .... EwanWhillans(7) (A C Whillans) *chsd ldrs: rdn appr 3 out: one pce* **8/1**	99+
	5	*4*	**Great Approach (IRE)** 4-10-12 .... BrianHarding (N G Richards) *hld up towards rr: hdwy 6th: kpt on fr 3 out: will improve* **33/1**	94+
10-2	**6**	*½*	**Witch Wind**[28] 2447 5-10-7 .... DeclanMcGann(5) (A M Crow) *led after 2nd: hdd appr 3 out: wknd appr 2 out* **13/2**[3]	94+
51-6	**7**	*9*	**Allegedly So (IRE)**[36] 2268 4-10-9 .... PeterBuchanan(3) (D W Whillans) *in tch: drvn along 8th: sn wknd* **50/1**	83
10-4	**8**	*½*	**Treasured Memories**[17] 2674 5-10-5 .... AndrewThornton (Miss S E Forster) *t.k.h: hdwy to trck ldrs 5th: lost pl after 8th* **20/1**	75
0-05	**9**	*30*	**Norminster**[18] 2652 4-10-5 .... GarethThomas(7) (R Nixon) *chsd ldrs: rdn and lost pl 6th: sn bhd* **100/1**	52
05	**10**	*nk*	**Futoo (IRE)**[12] 2763 4-10-12 .... RussGarritty (G M Moore) *chsd ldrs: lost pl after 8th* **25/1**	52
0	**11**	*7*	**Koodoo**[7] 2838 4-10-12 .... AlanDempsey (M Todhunter) *prom: lost pl 6th: sn bhd* **100/1**	45
-003	**12**	*4*	**Brundeanlaws**[17] 2678 4-10-0 .... TomGreenway(5) (Mrs H O Graham) *led tl after 2nd: lost pl 7th: sn bhd* **66/1**	34
00-P	**P**		**Moffied (IRE)**[46] 2062 5-10-7 .... MichaelMcAlister(5) (J Barclay) *sn bhd: t.o whn p.u after 8th* **100/1**	—
0	**P**		**Bishop's Brig**[36] 2268 5-10-7 .... DesFlavin(5) (N W Alexander) *sn bhd: reminders 5th: t.o whn p.u bef 8th* **100/1**	—
0/P-	**P**		**Tallahassee (IRE)**[372] 2834 7-10-7 .... DerekLaverty(5) (D R MacLeod) *bhd and drvn along 5th: p.u bef 3 out* **150/1**	—
0-0P	**F**		**Romanov Rambler (IRE)**[27] 2475 5-10-5 .... DavidDaSilva(7) (Mrs S C Bradburne) *in rr: last whn fell heavily 3 out* **100/1**	—
436	**P**		**Mulligan's Pride (IRE)**[44] 2112 4-10-7 .... DougieCostello(5) (G A Swinbank) *sn bhd: drvn along 6th: sn t.o: p.u bef 8th* **33/1**	—

5m 13.3s (0.60) **Going Correction** +0.175s/f (Yiel) **17** Ran SP% **120.5**
Speed ratings: **105,103,99,97,95 95,92,91,79,79 76,75,**—,—,— —,— CSF £11.42 TOTE £2.20: £1.40, £2.30, £1.80; EX 16.00.

Owner Andrea & Graham Wylie **Bred** Mrs Linda Gault **Trained** Billy Row, Co Durham

FOCUS
No strength in depth but the winner looks a very useful recruit and the second and third should be able to make their mark.

NOTEBOOK
Hard Act To Follow(IRE), winner of a Down Royal bumper in March, is an old-fashioned raw-boned chasing type. He travelled strongly up with the pace and, very accurate over the final two flights, in the end proved different gear. He is sure to build on this but he will not go over fences until next winter. *(tchd 13-8 in places)*

Supreme's Legacy(IRE), a Wetherby bumper winner, has had his problems but is another who *looks every inch a potential chaser. He finished clear second best and can surely go one better. (tchd 13-2 and 8-1)*

Windy Hills, third in modest company at Hexham, seemed to step up on that. He looks every inch a chaser but hopefully will make his mark over hurdles before then. *(tchd 9-2)*

Sotovik(IRE), a dual bumper winner, was having his third start over hurdles and so far at least he is proving a shade disapointing. *(tchd 10-1)*

Great Approach(IRE), bred to make a chaser, made a highly satisfactory racecourse bow and there should be a fair bit of improvement in time. *(op 25-1)*

Witch Wind helped take them along, but his jumping was not good and he eventually dropped right away. *(op 6-1 tchd 7-1)*

2948 SIMPSON AND SHAW STANDARD OPEN NATIONAL HUNT FLAT RACE 2m

3:30 (3:35) (Class 6) 4-6-Y-0 **£1,891** (£551; £275)

Form				RPR
	1		**Young Albert (IRE)** 4-11-4 .... BrianHarding (N G Richards) *hld up: smooth hdwy to chse ldrs 4f out: effrt over 2f out: led ins fnl f: hld on wl* **8/1**	103
2-2	**2**	*hd*	**My Final Bid (IRE)**[36] 2268 6-11-1 .... PeterBuchanan(3) (Mrs A C Hamilton) *keen early: cl up: led and rdn over 3f out: hdd ins fnl f: rallied: jst hld* **10/1**	103
1-2	**3**	*7*	**Oakapple Express**[49] 2007 5-11-6 .... WilliamKennedy(5) (G A Harker) *hld up and bhd: hdwy over 2f out: kpt on wl: nt rch first two* **7/2**[2]	103
3	**4**	*½*	**Bedlam Boy (IRE)**[33] 2340 4-11-4 .... TonyDobbin (N G Richards) *hld up: hdwy and prom over 3f out: rdn and one pce fr 2f out* **11/4**[1]	97+
	5	*6*	**Bally Brakes (IRE)**[250] 5-11-1 .... PaddyAspell(3) (J N R Billinge) *led to over 3f out: rdn and edgd lft over 2f out: nt qckn* **66/1**	90
	6	*3*	**Lucky Angler (IRE)** 6-10-13 .... DerekLaverty(5) (Mark Campion) *prom tl rdn and outpcd over 2f out* **100/1**	87
	7	*1 ½*	**Special Ballot (IRE)** 4-10-11 .... DNRussell (G A Swinbank) *hld up: hdwy on outside over 3f out: sn rdn and no imp* **5/1**[3]	78
	8	*1 ¾*	**Monifieth** 5-10-11 .... DominicElsworth (D W Whillans) *prom tl lost pl over 3f out: n.d after* **33/1**	76
	9	*2*	**Colonel Hayes (IRE)** 5-11-1 .... GaryBerridge(3) (J I A Charlton) *hld up: hdwy and prom on outside 6f out: rdn and outpcd fr 3f out* **50/1**	81
	10	*¾*	**The Last Viking** 5-11-4 .... TimmyMurphy (A Parker) *bhd: rdn over 4f out: n.d* **33/1**	81
34	**11**	*shd*	**Phantom Major (FR)**[194] 719 4-10-11 .... MissRDavidson(7) (Mrs R L Elliot) *in tch tl wknd fr 3f out* **66/1**	80
	12	*1 ¼*	**Van Cleef (IRE)** 4-11-4 .... GrahamLee (M Todhunter) *midfield tl wknd fr 4f out* **33/1**	79
25	**13**	*2 ½*	**Super Revo**[49] 2007 4-11-4 .... RichardMcGrath (Mrs K Walton) *in tch tl wknd over 3f out* **33/1**	77
3	**14**	*2 ½*	**Tory Island (IRE)**[27] 2480 4-11-1 .... AndrewJMcNamara(3) (S Donohoe, Ire) *midfield tl wknd over 4f out* **14/1**	74
	15	*14*	**Ad Murum (IRE)** 6-11-4 .... FinbarKeniry (G M Moore) *chsd ldrs tl wknd over 4f out* **100/1**	60
4	**16**	*1*	**Witch Power**[48] 2028 4-10-6 .... DeclanMcGann(5) (A M Crow) *in tch to 6f out: sn lost pl* **33/1**	52
	17	*1 ½*	**Grand In The Hand (IRE)** 5-10-11 .... MrRWakeham(7) (J R Turner) *a bhd* **100/1**	58
	18	*8*	**Rash Leader (IRE)** 6-11-4 .... BruceGibson (L Lungo) *midfield: rdn 5f out: sn wknd* **10/1**	50
	19	*9*	**Native Coll** 5-11-4 .... AndrewThornton (N W Alexander) *a bhd* **100/1**	41

4m 1.00s (1.80) **Going Correction** +0.175s/f (Yiel)
WFA 4 from 5yo+ 10lb **19** Ran SP% **125.1**
Speed ratings: **102,101,98,98,95 93,92,92,91,90 90,89,88,87,80 79,79,75,70** CSF £80.95 TOTE £11.10: £2.90, £2.30, £2.30; EX 121.80 Place 6 £316.97, Place 5 £166.76.

Owner Trevor Hemmings **Bred** S G And W R Deacon **Trained** Greystoke, Cumbria

FOCUS
An ordinary event in which the pace was steady. However the winner looks a fair staying prospect.

NOTEBOOK
Young Albert(IRE) ◆, who is related to winners, turned in a pleasing display on this racecourse debut. He showed the right attitude, despite his apparent greenness, and he appeals as the type to win races over obstacles.

My Final Bid(IRE) had the run of the race and again gave it his best shot. He showed the right attitude and looks sure to win a small event over obstacles in due course. *(op 14-1)*

Oakapple Express ◆ caught the eye in a race that was not really run to suit and is one to keep on *the right side in ordinary company when upped to two and a half miles over hurdles in due course. (op 3-1)*

Bedlam Boy(IRE) ran to a similar level as on his debut at Haydock. He is capable of winning an *ordinary event in this sphere but will be seen to best effect over further when sent over obstacles. (op 10-3 tchd 7-2 and 5-2)*

Bally Brakes(IRE), a winning pointer, had the run of the race and was not disgraced on this *bumper debut, but the best will not be seen of him until he is in modest company over obstacles. (op 50-1)*

Lucky Angler(IRE) was not totally disgraced on this racecourse debut and left the impression that a stiffer test of stamina would suit when sent over hurdles. *(op 66-1)*

Special Ballot(IRE), who is related to winners on the Flat and over hurdles, was not totally disgraced in a race that was not run to suit on this racecourse debut. She is from a stable that does well in this type of race and is worth keeping an eye on. *(tchd 9-2)*

T/Jkpt: Not won. T/Plt: £953.70 to a £1 stake. Pool: £50,367.95. 38.55 winning tickets. T/Qpdt: £100.70 to a £1 stake. Pool: £5,418.50. 39.80 winning tickets. RY

[2256]FAKENHAM (L-H)

Thursday, December 22

OFFICIAL GOING: Good

Wind: Light, across Weather: Cloudy

2949 NORFOLK ARC JUVENILE MAIDEN HURDLE (DIV I) (8 hdls 1 omitted) 2m

12:20 (12:22) (Class 4) 3-Y-O **£3,203** (£933; £467)

Form	Pos	Btn	Horse	Jockey / SP	RPR
32	1		**Take A Mile (IRE)**[18] 2661 3-10-7 (B G Powell) *a.p: jnd ldr 6th: led last: clr fnl f: eased nr fin*	JohnLevins(5) **4/5**[1]	103+
53	2	9	**Best Game**[27] 2477 3-10-12 (D W Thompson) *led: rdn and hdd last: styd on same pce*	(p) RichardJohnson **9/1**[3]	91+
2	3	11	**Knock Bridge (IRE)**[37] 2258 3-10-5 (P D Evans) *hld up: hdwy 4th: wknd appr last*	AntonyEvans **3/1**[2]	71
U0	4	hd	**Inn For The Dancer**[18] 2661 3-10-7 (Mrs H Dalton) *hld up: r.o flat: nvr nr to chal*	PaulO'Neill(5) **66/1**	78
0454	5	½	**Ghaill Force**[32] 2373 3-10-5 95 (P Butler) *hld up: hdwy after 6th: wknd appr last*	(t) RobertLucey-Butler(7) **22/1**	77
	6	12	**Tancredi (SWE)**[203] 3-10-9 (N B King) *prom: rdn appr 2 out: wknd bef last*	OwynNelmes(3) **33/1**	69+
0	7	23	**Top Man Tee**[9] 2811 3-10-12 (D J Daly) *hld up: mstke 2 out: n.d*	PaulMoloney **16/1**	42
0	8	4	**Karrnak**[38] 2236 3-10-5 (Miss J Feilden) *prom to 6th*	(bt1) MrMatthewSmith(7) **66/1**	38
	9	3	**Annals**[222] 3-10-2 (R C Guest) *hld up: hdwy appr 6th: sn wknd*	(p) LarryMcGrath(3) **28/1**	28
	10	28	**Montcalm (IRE)**[22] 3-10-2 (J G Given) *prom: lost pl 3rd: bhd fr 6th*	LeeVickers(3) **50/1**	—
	11	18	**E Bride (USA)**[31] 3-9-12 (T T Clement) *hld up: a in rr: bhd fr 5th*	TomMessenger(7) **100/1**	—
04	P		**Lobengula (IRE)**[12] 2258 3-10-7 (I W McInnes) *chsd ldr: sddle slipped after 2nd: p.u after next*	ThomasDreaper(5) **50/1**	—
00	P		**Keresforth**[16] 2681 3-10-2 (Mrs L C Jewell) *bhd fr 2nd: t.o whn hung rt after 5th: p.u bef next*	CraigMessenger(10) **100/1**	—
	F		**Ball Boy**[216] 3-10-12 (G Haine) *plld hrd and prom: chsd ldr 3rd tl after 5th: cl 3rd whn fell next*	WarrenMarston **22/1**	—

4m 3.90s (-5.00) **Going Correction** -0.15s/f (Good) **14** Ran SP% **120.4**

Speed ratings: **106,101,96,95,95 89,78,76,74,60 51,—,—,—** CSF £8.50 TOTE £1.50: £1.30, £2.00, £1.02; EX 8.40.

Owner R E Williams **Bred** Gerry Flannery **Trained** Morestead, Hants

FOCUS

The winning time was fair for the class and over seven seconds faster than the second division. The last flight was bypassed as a section was missing.

NOTEBOOK

Take A Mile(IRE) was suited by racing up with the decent pace before moving smoothly to the front at the last obstacle. Soon clear, he was eased up with his race won in the final 100 yards. *(op 10-11 tchd evens in places)*

Best Game, equipped with cheekpieces for the first time, made the running to the final flight - normally the second last - and could only plug on at the same pace afterwards. *(op 12-1)*

Knock Bridge(IRE) finished in front of today's runner-up on her hurdling debut but was unable to confirm that form.

Inn For The Dancer, a plating-class maiden on the Flat, had shown little in two starts over hurdles. *He was in the rear division until keeping on past tired opponents on the extended run-inOfficial explanation: trainer said gelding had a breathing problem*

Ghaill Force, the most experienced hurdler in the line-up, is no great shakes but may do better in handicaps. *(op 16-1)*

Tancredi(SWE), a winner over five and a half furlongs on dirt in Norway at two, seems likely to have trouble staying the trip over hurdles. *(op 25-1)*

Ball Boy, a fair middle-distance performer on the Flat for Mick Channon who had been off the track since May, was on the heels of the leaders when coming down at the last in the back straight. He would probably have made the frame. *(op 20-1)*

Lobengula(IRE) *Official explanation: jockey said saddle slipped (op 20-1)*

2950 CHRISTMAS NOVICES' HURDLE (9 hdls) 2m

12:50 (12:51) (Class 4) 4-Y-O+ **£3,405** (£992; £496)

Form	Pos	Btn	Horse	Jockey / SP	RPR
5	1		**Arry Dash**[21] 2584 5-10-12 (M J Wallace) *hld up: hdwy 6th: led 2 out: styd on*	BarryFenton **4/1**[2]	108+
64	2	2	**Dance World**[9] 2804 5-10-5 (Miss J Feilden) *hld up: hdwy and mstke 5th: chsd wnr after 2 out: hit last: styd on*	MrMatthewSmith(7) **11/2**[3]	106+
6-	3	5	**Fabulous Jet (FR)**[392] 2441 5-10-12 (Miss Venetia Williams) *led: hit 4th: hdd 2 out: wknd appr last*	SamThomas **7/2**[1]	101+
5	4	6	**Grand Bay (USA)**[58] 1875 4-10-12 (Jonjo O'Neill) *hld up: nt fluent 1st: hit 4th: hdwy 6th: wknd 2 out*	APMcCoy **4/1**[2]	94
001	5	2	**Twist Bookie (IRE)**[14] 2721 5-10-12 101 (J S Moore) *prom: chsd ldr 5th tl wknd appr 2 out*	ShaneWalsh(7) **14/1**	99
	6	27	**Cottingham (IRE)**[93] 4-10-12 (M C Chapman) *hld up: hit 5th: n.d*	KennyJohnson **100/1**	65
4-1	7	10	**Charlie Tango (IRE)**[44] 2108 4-11-5 (D W Thompson) *chsd ldrs tl wknd after 3 out*	RichardJohnson **6/1**	62
-610	8	½	**Cappanrush (IRE)**[37] 2261 5-11-2 94 (A Ennis) *chsd ldr to 5th: wkng whn mstke next*	ColinBolger(3) **33/1**	62
5	9	nk	**Wychbury (USA)**[7] 2070 4-10-7 (Mrs H Dalton) *chsd ldrs to 3 out*	PaulO'Neill(5) **25/1**	54
54	10	1	**Stroom Bank (IRE)**[62] 1820 5-10-9 (C C Bealby) *hld up: bhd fr 5th*	LeeVickers(3) **100/1**	53
	11	8	**Cabrillo (IRE)**[89] 4-10-2 (John A Quinn, Ire) *a in rr: bhd fr 5th*	TomMalone(3) **50/1**	38
PP-0	12	9	**Bright Present (IRE)**[50] 1990 7-10-5 (B N Pollock) *prom: sn drvn along: lost pl whn mstke 3rd: bhd fr 5th*	(b1) TomMessenger(7) **100/1**	36
F0	P		**Charm Indeed**[22] 2579 5-10-9 (N B King) *a bhd: t.o whn p.u bef 6th*	(t) OwynNelmes(3) **100/1**	—
3P	P		**Monsieur Delage**[57] 1885 5-10-12 (S Gollings) *hld up in tch: wknd 6th: t.o whn p.u bef 2 out*	RobertThornton **20/1**	—

4m 3.30s (-5.60) **Going Correction** -0.15s/f (Good) **14** Ran SP% **116.0**

Speed ratings: **108,107,104,101,100 87,82,81,81,81 77,72,—,—** CSF £24.19 TOTE £4.10: £1.40, £1.80, £1.50; EX 24.00.

Owner Mike & Denise Dawes **Bred** Miletrian P L C **Trained** Newmarket, Suffolk

FOCUS

An ordinary novice event, run at a good pace.

NOTEBOOK

Arry Dash, sharper for his recent hurdles debut, appreciated this better ground and scored in workmanlike style. He might well prove vulnerable under a penalty, especially on a stiffer track. *(op 11-4)*

Dance World ran a decent race and was keeping on at the end of this sharp two miles after paddling through the final flight. *(op 8-1)*

Fabulous Jet(FR), off the track since his hurdles debut 13 months ago, set a decent pace until headed by the winner with two to jump. He should come on for the experience and can win in ordinary novice company. *(op 4-1 tchd 9-2)*

Grand Bay(USA) was never able to quicken and may have found tight track against him. *(op 7-2)*

Twist Bookie(IRE), winner of a seller last time, ran a decent race in this better company but was well held from the second last.

Cottingham(IRE), a moderate performer on the Flat, did not shape without a bit of promise on this hurdles debut and first run since September.

Charlie Tango(IRE) faced a stiffer task under his penalty but it was still disappointing the way he faded out of contention. *(op 7-1)*

2951 GG.COM NOVICES' H'CAP CHASE (16 fncs) 2m 5f 110y

1:20 (1:20) (Class 4) (0-100,100) 4-Y-O+ **£4,835** (£1,419; £709; £354)

Form	Pos	Btn	Horse	Jockey / SP	RPR
3621	1		**New Perk (IRE)**[37] 2259 7-10-5 **84** (M J Gingell) *chsd ldrs: led 2 out: drvn out*	ChrisHonour(5) **5/1**[3]	100+
002	2	2½	**Kyno (IRE)**[25] 2517 4-10-10 **95** (M G Quinlan) *led: j.rt: hdd 4th: ev ch fr 4 out tl rdn after 2 out: styd on same pce*	(t) PaulMoloney **9/2**[2]	96
4444	3	15	**Sconced (USA)**[30] 2416 10-10-11 **88** (R C Guest) *hld up: hdwy 5th: lost pl and pckd 7th: bhd and drvn 9th: styd on flat*	(b) LarryMcGrath(3) **11/1**	85
2364	4	3	**Tommy Spar**[35] 2287 5-11-12 **100** (P Bowen) *hld up in tch: rdn 3 out: wkng whn hmpd next*	APMcCoy **5/1**[3]	96+
-0U4	5	1¾	**Ah Yeah (IRE)**[26] 2506 8-9-11 **74** oh1 (N B King) *prom: rdn after 11th: disputing cl 3rd whn hmpd next: sn wknd*	OwynNelmes(3) **7/1**	72+
6550	6	5	**Spider Boy**[23] 2561 8-9-7 **74** oh7 (Miss Z C Davison) *hld up: hmpd 5 out: sn wknd*	(p) RobertLucey-Butler(7) **25/1**	63+
00P0	7	4	**Iloveturtle (IRE)**[13] 2750 5-10-13 **87** (M C Chapman) *hld up: hit 1st: a bhd*	(t) KennyJohnson **33/1**	70
F/-2	F		**Ashwell (IRE)**[62] 1819 6-11-7 **95** (C C Bealby) *hld up: hit 6th: hdwy 9th: disputing cl 3rd whn fell 5 out*	NoelFehily **4/1**[1]	—
-362	F		**Bonnet's Pieces**[14] 2715 6-11-4 **92** (Mrs P Sly) *plld hrd: trckd ldr: mstke 3rd: led next: mstke 5th: blnd 11th: hdd whn fell 2 out*	WarrenMarston **7/1**	89

5m 46.1s (1.60) **Going Correction** +0.025s/f (Yiel)

WFA 4 from 5yo+ 11lb **9** Ran SP% **111.6**

Speed ratings: **98,97,91,90,89 88,86,—,—** CSF £27.10 CT £229.29 TOTE £3.80: £2.10, £1.30, £3.20; EX 33.70.

Owner A White **Bred** Tim Mulhare **Trained** North Runcton, Norfolk

FOCUS

A modest event run at an ordinary pace.

NOTEBOOK

New Perk(IRE), who broke his duck last time over course and distance when a long way out of the handicap, was raised 18lb after that but was effectively just 2lb higher. He jumped soundly and showed the right attitude to see off the runner-up.

Kyno(IRE), tongue tied for the first time, made a satisfactory chasing debut although his attitude did not please everyone. The return to three miles should suit him. *(op 4-1)*

Sconced(USA) was pulled up on his one previous attempt over fences, back in March. He never looked particularly keen and merely stayed on past beaten rivals late on for a remote third. *(op 10-1 tchd 12-1)*

Tommy Spar was held in fourth place when having to sidestep a faller at the second last. *(op 9-2)*

Ah Yeah(IRE), ideally served by further, lost what chance he had when badly hampered with five to jump. *(op 11-1)*

Bonnet's Pieces was in front when getting away with a diabolical error at the last fence on the second circuit. She had just been headed when crashing out at the second last, a ditch. *(op 7-2)*

Ashwell(IRE) has reportedly had sore shins since his promising chasing debut here two months ago. Raised 5lb, he was very much in contention when departing five from home. *(op 7-2)*

2952 SIS H'CAP HURDLE (11 hdls) 2m 4f

1:50 (1:50) (Class 3) (0-120,119) 4-Y-O+ **£5,569** (£1,634; £817; £408)

Form	Pos	Btn	Horse	Jockey / SP	RPR
2130	1		**Brooklyn Brownie (IRE)**[33] 2347 6-10-8 **106** (J M Jefferson) *a.p: chsd ldr after 3 out: led appr last: drvn out*	ThomasDreaper(5) **6/1**[3]	109+
2	2	¾	**Corsican Native (USA)**[18] 2659 4-10-10 **103** (P Bowen) *hld up: hdwy appr 8th: led 3 out: hit next: rdn and hdd bef last: styd on*	RichardJohnson **7/2**[1]	107+
2310	3	2½	**Festive Chimes (IRE)**[33] 2347 4-11-0 **110** (N B King) *hld up: hdwy 5th: rdn after 3 out: styd on same pce last*	OwynNelmes(3) **14/1**	110
3341	4	12	**North Landing (IRE)**[7] 2843 5-10-1 **97** 7ex (R C Guest) *hld up: reminders 2nd: hdwy 8th: wknd 2 out*	LarryMcGrath(3) **7/2**[1]	85
4654	5	8	**Siegfrieds Night (IRE)**[22] 2566 4-10-0 **93** oh1 (M C Chapman) *w ldr to appr 4th: lost pl after next: wknd 8th*	(t) KennyJohnson **14/1**	73
0000	6	1¼	**Merryvale Man**[7] 2843 8-10-2 **95** (Miss Kariana Key) *prom: chsd ldr 5th: led after 8th: hdd next: sn wknd*	AlanO'Keeffe **33/1**	74
6252	7	2	**Sovereign State (IRE)**[27] 2478 8-11-7 **114** (D W Thompson) *racd keenly: prom to 8th*	(p) RobertThornton **7/1**	92+
P005	8	10	**Son Of Greek Myth (USA)**[14] 2731 4-10-9 **102** (G L Moore) *hld up: rdn whn mstke 7th: sn wknd*	(b) WarrenMarston **10/1**	69
1051	9	7	**Smart Boy Prince (IRE)**[21] 2590 4-11-12 **119** (C Smith) *led: rdn and hdd after 8th: wknd next*	APMcCoy **5/1**[2]	79

5m 9.10s (-3.10) **Going Correction** -0.15s/f (Good) **9** Ran SP% **113.3**

Speed ratings: **100,99,98,93,90 90,89,85,82** CSF £27.31 CT £279.54 TOTE £7.70: £2.00, £1.10, £3.00; EX 53.00.

Owner P Gaffney & J N Stevenson **Bred** John P A Kenny **Trained** Norton, N Yorks

FOCUS

An ordinary handicap hurdle, run at a decent pace.

NOTEBOOK

Brooklyn Brownie(IRE) was behind two of today's opponents when down the field at Huntingdon last time. This tight track did not entirely suit him, but the ground did and he battled well to score. *(op 7-1)*

Corsican Native(USA), 3lb higher than at Warwick but suited by this better ground, showed ahead at the third from home but after flattening the next flight he could not hold off the winner. He stayed well enough, albeit on this sharp track. *(tchd 10-3)*

Festive Chimes(IRE), given a break since a below-par effort a month back, returned to form with a sound enough run and finished clear of the rest. *(op 16-1)*

North Landing(IRE) was officially 3lb well in under the 7lb penalty incurred at Catterick. After receiving early reminders, he was not given a hard time when held in the last half-mile. *(op 4-1)*

Siegfrieds Night(IRE), who continues to fall in the handicap, again failed to get home over this trip. *(op 12-1)*
Merryvale Man briefly showed ahead before weakening pretty quickly. He has become well handicapped during a winless run stretching back to April 2004.
Smart Boy Prince(IRE) has had a good season but the 9lb rise for his latest win told. *Official explanation: jockey said gelding ran very flat (tchd 11-2)*

2953 INDEPENDENT RACECOURSE GROUP NOVICES' CHASE (18 fncs) 3m 110y
2:20 (2:20) (Class 3) 5-Y-0+ **£8,072** (£2,369; £1,184; £591)

Form RPR
3-42 **1** **Briery Fox (IRE)**[29] [2441] 7-11-0 .... MarkBradburne 132+
(H D Daly) *a.p: chsd ldr 9th: rdn to chal 2 out: led flat: styd on u.p* **6/1**
0605 **2** 2 ½ **Yes Sir (IRE)**[12] [2758] 6-11-0 .... ChristianWilliams 130+
(P Bowen) *led: j.lft 5th: mstkes 7th and 13th: rdn appr 2 out: hdd and no ex flat* **6/1**
-321 **3** 6 **Classic Capers**[12] [2764] 6-11-1 127 .... ThomasDreaper(5) 129
(J M Jefferson) *hld up: hdwy 13th: styd on same pce fr 4 out* **5/1**[3]
3-15 **4** 11 **The Dark Lord (IRE)**[27] [2484] 8-11-10 .... LeightonAspell 132+
(Mrs L Wadham) *chsd ldr tl mstke 9th: j. slowly next: wknd 13th: mstke last: eased* **9/4**[2]
4P11 **F** **Millenaire (FR)**[15] [2703] 6-11-10 126 .... APMcCoy —
(Jonjo O'Neill) *hld up: nt fluent: fell 11th* **15/8**[1]

6m 35.7s (-1.90) **Going Correction** +0.025s/f (Yiel) **5** Ran SP% **110.8**
Speed ratings: **104,103,101,97,—** CSF £36.45 TOTE £6.00: £1.40, £3.50; EX 25.20.
Owner Vicky Jeyes Helen Plumbly Jane Trafford **Bred** Simon And Helen Plumbly **Trained** Stanton Lacy, Shropshire

FOCUS
A decent little race but a number of these made jumping errors.

NOTEBOOK
Briery Fox(IRE) went after the leader at halfway and briefly looked in trouble after the last down the back, but he stayed on to join issue two from home and eventually got the better of a drawn-out tussle. He jumped soundly, unlike most of his rivals, and this is his trip. *(op 7-1)*
Yes Sir(IRE), much the best of these over hurdles, spoilt his chance with some sloppy jumping on his chase debut early last month and he put in a less than flawless round here. Tackling three miles for the first time, he attempted to make all but eventually had to admit defeat on the run-in. *(op 9-2)*
Classic Capers, tackling this trip for the first time, did seem to see it out but in truth was only playing for third prize at best on the final circuit. *(tchd 9-2)*
The Dark Lord(IRE) looks to have lost his confidence since his successful chase debut here and again jumped sketchily. He was well beaten a long way out but might have been third had he not made another mistake at the last. *(op 10-3)*
Millenaire(FR), back against novices, jumped deliberately and it was no real surprise to see him end up on the deck *(op 13-8 tchd 2-1 and 85-40 in a place)*

2954 NORFOLK ARC JUVENILE MAIDEN HURDLE (DIV II) (9 hdls) 2m
2:50 (2:50) (Class 4) 3-Y-O **£3,203** (£933; £467)

Form RPR
4 **1** **Prize Fighter (IRE)**[27] [2481] 3-10-12 .... APMcCoy 101+
(Jonjo O'Neill) *chsd ldrs: hit 4th: led 2 out: sn clr: eased nr fin* **8/11**[1]
4 **2** 8 **Sea Map**[8] [2824] 3-10-12 .... LeightonAspell 86
(D E Cantillon) *a.p: led appr 3 out: hdd next: sn outpcd* **4/1**[2]
03 **3** 1 **Lord Of Adventure (IRE)**[16] [2681] 3-10-12 .... RobertThornton 85
(Mrs L C Jewell) *mid-div: hdwy u.p 5th: nt rch ldrs* **14/1**
P **4** 7 **Maxamillion (IRE)**[18] [2661] 3-10-7 .... PaulO'Neill(5) 78
(S Kirk) *mid-div: mstke 2nd: hdwy 3 out: nt fluent and wknd next* **25/1**
00 **5** 1 ¼ **Trackattack**[9] [2258] 3-10-5 .... RobertLucey-Butler(7) 77
(P Howling) *hld up: hdwy 3 out: wknd bef next* **100/1**
00 **6** 17 **Misters Sister**[18] [2661] 3-10-5 .... (v[1]) MarkBradburne 53
(C A Dwyer) *hld up: bhd fr 5th* **100/1**
0 **7** hd **Asaateel (IRE)**[8] [2824] 3-10-12 .... SamThomas 60
(G L Moore) *hld up: hdwy 5th: wknd appr 3 out* **28/1**
00 **8** 5 **Rashida**[22] [2569] 3-9-12 .... (tp) TomMessenger(7) 48
(M Appleby) *sn prom: wkng whn hit 2 out* **100/1**
33 **9** 7 **Laconicos (IRE)**[10] [2797] 3-10-9 .... GinoCarenza(3) 48
(W B Stone) *chsd ldrs tl wknd appr 3 out* **16/1**
2F **10** 6 **Paparaazi (IRE)**[17] [2676] 3-10-12 .... (v[1]) AnthonyRoss 42
(R A Fahey) *hld up: hdwy appr 4th: rdn and hit 3 out: sn wknd* **12/1**
60 **11** ¾ **Oh Mister Pinceau (FR)**[9] [2811] 3-10-12 .... RichardJohnson 41
(H D Daly) *led: hdd appr 3 out: sn wknd* **11/1**[3]
P **Moment Of Clarity**[108] 3-10-9 .... (e[1]) LarryMcGrath(3) —
(R C Guest) *hld up and bhd: p.u after 3 out* **50/1**
0 **P** **Sterling Supporter**[27] [2477] 3-10-2 .... OwynNelmes(3) —
(D W Thompson) *prom to 5th: t.o whn p.u bef last* **100/1**
P **P** **Swell Lad**[26] [2494] 3-10-12 .... TomScudamore —
(S Gollings) *chsd ldrs tl rdn and wknd after 5th: t.o whn p.u bef last* **100/1**

4m 11.0s (2.10) **Going Correction** -0.15s/f (Good) **14** Ran SP% **120.7**
Speed ratings: **88,84,83,80,79 70,70,68,64,61 61,—,—,—** CSF £3.55 TOTE £1.70: £1.10, £1.70, £2.70; EX 3.80.
Owner Diamond Racing Ltd **Bred** G Dunne **Trained** Cheltenham, Gloucs

FOCUS
A moderate winning time, over seven seconds slower than the first division.

NOTEBOOK
Prize Fighter(IRE) was found a nice opportunity to get off the mark and he made no mistake with a facile victory. He generally jumped well and should be able to handle a step up the ladder. *(tchd 4-6 and 4-5)*
Sea Map tried to kick on once in front and exploit his stamina, but was no match for the winner who like him had been fourth at Newbury on his hurdles debut. An ordinary race should come his way. *(op 6-1)*
Lord Of Adventure(IRE) never looked like being involved at the business end, but he now qualifies for handicaps and a return to further will help. *(op 16-1)*
Maxamillion(IRE), a seven-furlong winner on the Flat for this yard, was sent off fourth favourite on his recent hurdles debut but was pulled up. This was more like it, but he was beaten a good way in the end. *(tchd 28-1)*
Trackattack, a winning plater for Martin Pipe on the Flat, showed more than on his first two runs over hurdles last month but looks short on the requisite stamina.
Moment Of Clarity *Official explanation: jockey said gelding lost his action*

2955 GGBET.COM H'CAP CHASE (18 fncs) 3m 110y
3:20 (3:20) (Class 3) (0-115,109) 5-Y-0+ **£6,131** (£1,800; £900; £449)

Form RPR
4314 **1** **Reverse Swing**[23] [2562] 8-10-0 83 .... JodieMogford 101+
(Mrs H Dalton) *led 3rd: clr 14th: eased flat* **8/1**
62P- **2** 8 **Fireaway**[243] [4976] 11-11-1 98 .... JohnMcNamara 98
(O Brennan) *prom: chsd wnr appr 14th: wknd 4 out* **9/1**
0-64 **3** ¾ **Standing Bloom**[26] [2505] 9-10-11 94 .... PaulMoloney 95+
(Mrs P Sly) *prom: mstke 5th: chsd wnr 8th to appr 14th: wknd 4 out* **12/1**
632 **4** 2 ½ **Mick Divine (IRE)**[28] [2458] 7-10-8 91 .... (t) RobertThornton 89+
(C J Mann) *hld up: nt fluent: hit 8th: hdwy 10th: wknd 4 out: hit next* **9/4**[1]
-625 **5** 1 ¾ **Moscow Leader (IRE)**[13] [2748] 7-10-13 99 .... (p) LarryMcGrath(3) 94
(R C Guest) *hld up: hdwy 10th: wknd 13th* **11/2**[3]
F1-3 **6** 8 **Dickens (USA)**[42] [2143] 5-11-8 105 .... SamThomas 92
(Miss Venetia Williams) *hld up: wknd 13th* **7/2**[2]
-5P3 **7** 16 **Bold Investor**[21] [2588] 8-11-12 109 .... (v[1]) APMcCoy 80
(Jonjo O'Neill) *chsd ldrs tl wknd 13th* **13/2**
0-P6 **P** **Colmcille (IRE)**[33] [2341] 5-10-3 89 .... (b) LeeVickers(3) —
(C C Bealby) *led to 3rd: chsd wnr to 8th: wknd bef next: t.o whn p.u after 13th* **25/1**

6m 47.3s (9.70) **Going Correction** +0.025s/f (Yiel) **8** Ran SP% **114.4**
Speed ratings: **85,82,82,81,80 78,73,—** CSF £73.75 CT £858.16 TOTE £9.70: £2.30, £2.70, £2.90; EX 72.70 Place 6 £74.94, Place 5 £68.82.
Owner The Herons Partnership **Bred** Mrs P Sly **Trained** Norton, Shropshire

FOCUS
An ordinary handicap. The winning time was very moderate for a race of its type, 11.7 seconds slower than the earlier novice chase.

NOTEBOOK
Reverse Swing, without the tongue tie, ran her rivals ragged and was never seriously challenged. She jumped soundly and the longer trip was not a problem on this sharp track.
Fireaway, making his first run for eight months, ran creditably but never looked like getting to the mare. *(op 12-1)*
Standing Bloom, who was running over fences for the first time since February, weakened some way from home and lost out in the tussle for second.
Mick Divine(IRE), who had his tongue tied for the first time since coming to Britain, did not jump well and could never get into the action as a consequence. *(tchd 5-2)*
Moscow Leader(IRE) did not seem at home round this tight track and was never going sufficiently well enough. *(op 5-1 tchd 6-1)*
Dickens(USA), still minus the visor, was always at the back of the field. *(op 9-2 tchd 10-3)*
Bold Investor has become most disappointing and the visor failed to bring about any improvement. *(op 11-2)*
Colmcille(IRE) *Official explanation: trainer said gelding finished distressed*
T/Plt: £56.60 to a £1 stake. Pool: £45,809.15. 590.80 winning tickets. T/Qpdt: £26.50 to a £1 stake. Pool: £3,303.10. 92.10 winning tickets. CR

2714 HUNTINGDON (R-H)
Monday, December 26

OFFICIAL GOING: Good (good to soft in places)
Wind: Light, across Weather: Sunny spells

2956 STANJAMESUK.COM "NATIONAL HUNT" NOVICES' HURDLE (12 hdls) 3m 2f
12:45 (12:45) (Class 4) 4-Y-0+ **£3,309** (£964; £482)

Form RPR
2F06 **1** **Harrycone Lewis**[19] [2703] 7-10-12 117 .... PaulMoloney 118+
(Mrs P Sly) *a.p: chsd ldr appr 6th: led 3 out: hung lft flat: rdn out* **15/2**
2-11 **2** 1 ¼ **King Of Confusion (IRE)**[51] [2036] 6-10-11 120 .... PatrickMcDonald(7) 123+
(Ferdy Murphy) *hld up: hdwy 8th: styd on flat: nt rch wnr* **5/4**[1]
P **3** 1 **Two Hoots**[31] [2486] 7-9-9 .... KevinTobin(10) 109
(C J Mann) *hld up: hdwy appr 3 out: chsd wnr next: ev ch last: styd on same pce* **50/1**
1106 **4** 8 **Rimsky (IRE)**[16] [2762] 4-11-10 130 .... (b) TomSiddall 122+
(N A Twiston-Davies) *hld up: hdwy 7th: ev ch 3 out: wknd last* **7/1**[3]
B-41 **5** 1 ¾ **In Accord**[23] [2619] 6-10-13 118 .... TomGreenway(5) 113+
(H D Daly) *hld up: hdwy 7th: rdn 2 out: wknd last* **9/4**[2]
30-5 **6** 19 **The Bo'sun**[28] [2556] 8-10-12 91 .... BrianCrowley 87
(A E Jessop) *hld up: hdwy 8th: wknd after next* **50/1**
3 **7** 1 **Caveman**[33] [2427] 5-10-12 .... TomDoyle 86
(P R Webber) *led to 3 out: wknd bef next* **25/1**
36-0 **8** 2 **Tank Buster**[16] [2763] 5-10-5 .... MrRLangley(7) 84
(Mrs E Langley) *chsd ldrs: lost pl 3rd: wknd after 9th* **66/1**
4560 **9** 19 **Letsplay (IRE)**[12] [2829] 5-10-5 97 .... RyanCummings(7) 65
(K J Burke) *hld up: hmpd bnd after 7th: mstke and wknd 9th* **33/1**
3 **10** 26 **Debris (IRE)**[71] [1755] 6-10-12 .... JimmyMcCarthy 39
(Miss E C Lavelle) *hld up: hdwy 8th: wknd appr 3 out* **16/1**
-050 **11** 2 **Gaining Ground (IRE)**[30] [2503] 5-10-12 64 .... RichardHobson 37
(John R Upson) *chsd ldrs: rdn after 7th: wknd 9th* **100/1**
/00P **P** **It's Official (IRE)**[28] [2555] 6-10-12 79 .... (b) HenryOliver —
(Miss A M Newton-Smith) *chsd ldr to appr 6th: wknd next: t.o whn p.u after 8th* **100/1**

6m 25.4s (3.00) **Going Correction** +0.20s/f (Yiel) **12** Ran SP% **119.5**
Speed ratings: **103,102,102,99,99 93,93,92,86,78 78,—** CSF £17.65 TOTE £9.70: £2.20, £1.30, £6.50; EX 19.60.
Owner The Craftsmen **Bred** Mrs P Sly **Trained** Thorney, Cambs

FOCUS
A fair novice event, run at a sound pace, and the first three came clear of a decent benchmark.

NOTEBOOK
Harrycone Lewis, reverting to hurdles with the blinkers left off, ran out a determined winner to lose his maiden tag in this sphere at the 12th attempt. This has to rate a big improvement on his recent level of form and, now that his confidence should be restored, he may be able to add to this when returned to fences at around this trip in the coming weeks. *(op 17-2 tchd 9-1)*
King Of Confusion(IRE), an easy winner of both his previous outings this term, just failed to reel in the winner in this quest for the hat-trick and probably just found this longer trip stretching his stamina. This must still rate a decent effort under his double penalty and he remains a progressive sort.
Two Hoots left behind the disappointment of her Newbury debut for connections and showed her true colours in defeat. She is another who probably found this trip just stretching her and she can find a race in this division when dropped to three miles. As a former winning pointer, however, her future lies very much as a novice chaser.
Rimsky(IRE) appreciated the drop in class, and had every chance, but was ultimately held by his big weight. He is not going to prove easy to place now, but is a decent benchmark for this form all the same. *(op 13-2 tchd 8-1)*
In Accord failed to see out this longer trip and can defy his penalty in this division when reverting to shorter. *(op 5-2)*

2957 STANJAMESUK.COM H'CAP CHASE (19 fncs) 3m
1:20 (1:24) (Class 4) (0-100,99) 5-Y-0+ **£4,115** (£1,208; £604; £301)

Form RPR
316 **1** **Regal Vision (IRE)**[29] [2522] 8-10-2 82 .... MissCDyson(7) 94+
(Miss C Dyson) *mid-div: hit 3rd: hdwy 5th: led 15th: j.lft last 2: all out* **16/1**
0630 **2** shd **Alfred The Grey**[13] [2808] 8-9-11 73 oh2 .... (p) TJPhelan(3) 83
(Miss Suzy Smith) *hld up: hdwy 13th: rdn and ev ch last: styd on* **25/1**

The Form Book, Raceform Ltd, Compton, RG20 6NL

65-P **3** *3* **Shoulton (IRE)**[32] 2464 8-10-0 **73**........................ JodieMogford 81+
(G H Yardley) *prom: lost pl 5th: hdwy 3 out: styd on same pce flat* **22/1**

6P-2 **4** *7* **Extra Cache (NZ)**[50] 2080 12-10-0 **73** oh1.................. HenryOliver 73
(O Brennan) *chsd ldrs: lost pl 7th: hdwy 14th: wknd last* **7/1**[2]

P645 **5** *9* **Lucky Sinna (IRE)**[20] 2682 9-10-10 **88**.................. JohnLevins[(5)] 79
(B G Powell) *hld up: hdwy 16th: wknd appr 2 out* **8/1**[3]

F- **6** *3/4* **Ballyfin (IRE)**[284] 4424 7-11-0 **87**.................. JimmyMcCarthy 77
(J A Geake) *hld up: hdwy 8th: wknd after 2 out* **10/3**[1]

P1-U **7** *11* **Gallion's Reach (IRE)**[8] 2905 10-9-8 **74**..........(b) MarcGoldstein[(7)] 59+
(M F Harris) *led after 1st: hit 8th and 9th: hdd and blnd 15th: wknd appr 2 out* **16/1**

U45 **U** **Ah Yeah (IRE)**[4] 2951 8-9-11 **73**.................. OwynNelmes[(3)] —
(N B King) *mid-div: blnd and uns rdr 10th* **7/1**[2]

3RP- **P** **Jollyshau (IRE)**[285] 4402 7-11-0 **90**.................. ColinBolger[(3)] —
(Miss A M Newton-Smith) *bhd fr 5th: bhd whn p.u bef 11th* **16/1**

0-5P **P** **Jaybejay (NZ)**[39] 2294 10-11-5 **99**..........(p) WillieMcCarthy[(7)] —
(T R George) *hld up: bhd whn hmpd 12th: t.o whn p.u bef 3 out* **20/1**

P-3P **F** **The Tall Guy (IRE)**[31] 2485 9-11-8 **95**..........(t) TomSiddall —
(N A Twiston-Davies) *chsd ldrs: 6th and wkng whn fell 12th: dead* **14/1**

1P-P **P** **Red Alert Man (IRE)**[32] 2465 9-9-9 **73** oh5..........(b) TomGreenway[(5)] —
(Mrs L Williamson) *chsd ldr 2nd: wknd 13th: t.o whn p.u bef 16th* **20/1**

/00- **P** **Gathering Storm (IRE)**[597] 232 7-10-8 **81**.................. JohnMcNamara —
(P R Hedger) *hld up: mstke 2nd: hit 10th: t.o whn p.u bef 15th* **12/1**

3643 **P** **Monsieur Georges (FR)**[18] 2717 5-11-1 **88**..........(p) TomDoyle —
(F Jordan) *hld up: hdwy 12th: blnd and wknd 15th: bhd whn p.u bef 2 out* **8/1**[3]

336 **P** **Ardashir (FR)**[18] 2717 6-11-2 **89**.................. BrianCrowley —
(Mrs S J Humphrey) *led: hdd after 1st: remained handy: blnd and wknd 3 out: p.u bef next* **11/1**

6m 16.8s (4.50) **Going Correction** +0.30s/f (Yiel) **15** Ran SP% **128.4**
Speed ratings: **104,103,102,100,97 97,93,—,—,— —,—,—,—,—** CSF £376.23 CT £8528.06 TOTE £27.20: £6.80, £6.10, £15.10; EX 894.30.
Owner Miss C Dyson **Bred** B Freiha **Trained** Lower Bentley, Worcs

FOCUS
A moderate handicap, but the pace was decent and the form looks fair for the grade.

NOTEBOOK
Regal Vision(IRE) resumed winning ways with a most game effort back over this more suitable longer trip. He enjoyed the decent pace, plus the good ground, and a bold bid for a follow-up bid should be expected at this level while he is in this current mood. *(op 14-1)*
Alfred The Grey, with the blinkers re-applied, only just failed to get the better of the winner and did nothing wrong in defeat. He is very hard to predict, but this was much his best effort for some time and he was nicely clear of the rest, so he could be about to end his long losing run.
Shoulton(IRE) produced a much more encouraging effort and did enough to suggest that he should improve a touch again for this outing. *(op 20-1 tchd 25-1)*
Extra Cache(NZ) ran well until his stamina gave way approaching the final flight and can get closer again when reverting in trip. *(op 11-2)*
Ballyfin(IRE), last seen winning an Irish hunter chase 284 days previously, showed ability on this debut for new connections, but shaped as though this outing was very much needed. He is capable of a deal better. *(op 4-1)*
Red Alert Man(IRE) *Official explanation: jockey said gelding suffered an over-reach on its near hind (op 16-1)*

2958 STANSPOKER.CO.UK H'CAP HURDLE (10 hdls) 2m 5f 110y
1:50 (1:56) (Class 4) (0-100,100) 4-Y-0+ **£2,816** (£820; £410)

Form RPR

F446 **1** **True Mariner (FR)**[18] 2714 5-11-7 **95**..........(t) SamStronge 102+
(B I Case) *hld up: hdwy 6th: drvn to ld flat: styd on* **14/1**

-P61 **2** *1 1/4* **Paddy Boy (IRE)**[28] 2552 4-10-6 **80**.................. PhilipHide 86+
(J R Boyle) *chsd ldrs: led appr 2 out: rdn and hdd flat: styd on* **7/2**[1]

6-P4 **3** *3* **Colophony (USA)**[17] 2750 5-10-7 **86**.................. JohnLevins[(5)] 90+
(K A Morgan) *hld up: hdwy appr 3 out: rdn appr last: styd on same pce flat* **7/1**[3]

22F0 **4** *6* **Murphy's Nails (IRE)**[18] 2723 8-11-8 **96**..........(p) JohnMcNamara 94+
(K C Bailey) *led to 2nd: led 7th: hdd appr 2 out: wknd last* **7/1**[3]

U044 **5** *3 1/2* **Upright Ima**[13] 2816 6-9-11 **78**.................. MarcGoldstein[(7)] 73+
(Mrs P Sly) *hld up: hdwy 6th: n.m.r appr 2 out: wknd bef last* **5/1**[2]

4315 **6** *1 1/2* **Rojabaa**[18] 2721 6-11-2 **90**.................. RichardHobson 83+
(B D Leavy) *hdwy 3rd: ev ch whn hit 3 out: wkng whn mstke next* **12/1**

-606 **7** *10* **There Is No Doubt (FR)**[24] 2606 4-11-3 **98**.......... MissLucyBridges[(7)] 80
(Miss Lucy Bridges) *chsd ldrs tl wknd appr 2 out* **11/1**

2-44 **8** *16* **Rotheram (USA)**[13] 2809 5-11-12 **100**..........(p) BrianCrowley 66
(C J Mann) *hld up: hit 5th: effrt appr next: wkng whn hit 7th* **7/1**[3]

0-00 **9** *3 1/2* **Magic Red**[28] 2555 5-10-3 **80**..........(b) ColinBolger[(3)] 42
(J Ryan) *led 2nd to 7th: wknd bef next* **33/1**

6566 **10** *1 1/2* **Stopwatch (IRE)**[38] 2323 10-9-6 **76**..........(p) CraigMessenger[(10)] 37
(Mrs L C Jewell) *chsd ldrs tl hit 6th: sn wknd* **40/1**

-345 **11** *1* **Breezer**[25] 2582 5-10-11 **85**..........(p) JimmyMcCarthy 45
(J A Geake) *hld up: rdn after 5th: in rr whn hit 7th* **14/1**

000 **12** *dist* **Robbie Will**[20] 2683 4-11-2 **90**.................. HenryOliver —
(F Jordan) *hld up: effrt 6th: wknd next: bhd whn mstke 3 out* **33/1**

U430 **P** **Zeis (IRE)**[18] 2721 5-10-13 **90**..........(t) OwynNelmes[(3)] —
(Miss J R Gibney) *hld up: a in rr: t.o whn p.u bef 3 out* **20/1**

U00- **P** **Bronhallow**[346] 3340 12-9-11 **74** oh5..........(t) TJPhelan[(3)] —
(Mrs Barbara Waring) *bhd fr 5th: t.o whn p.u bef 3 out* **50/1**

-02P **P** **Flower Of Pitcur**[18] 2733 8-11-4 **99**.................. WillieMcCarthy[(7)] —
(T R George) *hld up: hdwy 6th: wknd 3 out: p.u bef next* **14/1**

PP4- **P** **Orchard Fields (IRE)**[285] 4404 8-11-3 **91**.................. JodieMogford —
(Mrs A V Roberts) *prom: lost pl 3rd: bhd whn p.u and dismntd after 5th* **16/1**

5m 16.4s (5.60) **Going Correction** +0.20s/f (Yiel)
WFA 4 from 5yo+ 11lb **16** Ran SP% **133.3**
Speed ratings: **97,96,95,93,92 91,87,82,80,80 79,—,—,—,— —** CSF £66.83 CT £401.12 TOTE £30.50: £5.80, £1.60, £2.40, £1.40; EX 149.30.
Owner D Allen **Bred** J P Philippe And Classic Breeding Sarl **Trained** Edgcote, Northants

FOCUS
A moderate handicap, run at a solid gallop and the field came home fairly strung out. It is fair form for the grade.

NOTEBOOK
True Mariner(FR), in a first-time tongue tie, finally took advantage of his declining handicap mark and got back to winning ways in ready fashion. The tongue tie clearly had the desired effect, as he saw out his race really well this time, and he should go close if turned out under a penalty. *(op 12-1)*
Paddy Boy(IRE), raised 8lb for getting off the mark at Folkestone last time, turned in a respectable *effort and is clearly still going the right way. He is probably happier over slightly shorter, however. (op 4-1)*
Colophony(USA) turned in another sound effort and looks to be slowly coming right again now, but again he did little to convince that he stays this far. *(op 13-2)*
Murphy's Nails(IRE), well backed, had his chance but was eventually put in his place from the penultimate flight. This was a better effort, but he really is hard to catch right. *(op 12-1)*
Orchard Fields(IRE) *Official explanation: vet said gelding was lame (op 20-1)*

2959 STANJAMESUK.COM NOVICES' CHASE (16 fncs) 2m 4f 110y
2:25 (2:27) (Class 3) 5-Y-0+ **£5,478** (£1,608; £804; £401)

Form RPR

-000 **1** **Migwell (FR)**[23] 2633 5-10-12 120.................. JimmyMcCarthy 123+
(Mrs L Wadham) *disp ld tl led 12th: hdd last: rallied to ld towards fin* **6/1**

130- **2** *1 1/4* **Pardishar (IRE)**[247] 4982 7-10-12 120.................. PhilipHide 122
(G L Moore) *chsd ldrs: led last: rdn and hdd towards fin* **7/1**

1-32 **3** *2 1/2* **Carthys Cross (IRE)**[29] 2516 6-10-5 119.................. WillieMcCarthy[(7)] 121+
(T R George) *hld up in tch: mstke 3 out: no ex last* **4/1**[2]

0-43 **4** *6* **Simon**[12] 2817 6-10-12 118.................. BrianCrowley 117+
(J L Spearing) *prom: wkng whn hit 2 out* **5/1**[3]

0005 **5** *28* **Mac's Elan**[27] 2563 5-10-5 93.................. MrMatthewSmith[(7)] 86
(A B Coogan) *sn bhd* **33/1**

2-1U **6** *13* **Wicked Nice Fella (IRE)**[16] 2768 7-10-12 120.......... JohnMcNamara 106+
(C C Bealby) *hit 7th: mde most to 12th: wknd appr 2 out* **5/4**[1]

5m 13.6s (7.50) **Going Correction** +0.30s/f (Yiel) **6** Ran SP% **110.8**
Speed ratings: **97,96,95,93,82 77** CSF £42.07 TOTE £7.90: £2.60, £2.70; EX 57.70.
Owner DGM Partnership **Bred** Mme Brigitte Ricous **Trained** Newmarket, Suffolk
■ Stewards' Enquiry : Jimmy McCarthy two-day ban: used whip with excessive force and in an incorrect place (Jan 6,9)

FOCUS
A fair novice chase, run at an average pace, and the form looks reasonable.

NOTEBOOK
Migwell(FR), rated 120 over hurdles, got his chase career off to a perfect start in game fasion and jumped well for a debutant. He had rather lost his way over hurdles this term, but this will serve as a welcome confidence booster, and he ought to be capable of even better in a more truly-run race over fences in the future. This ground would also have been plenty quick enough for him. *(op 5-1)*
Pardishar(IRE) ◆, making his seasonal and chasing bow, turned in a decent effort and was only denied on the run-in. He is clearly up to going one better in this division, should improve for the experience, and looks to have resumed this season in decent heart. However, a slight drop in trip ought to be to his advantage in the future.
Carthys Cross(IRE) would have been closer without making an error three from home and ran another fair race. He helps set the level for this form. *(op 7-2)*
Simon was starting to tread water prior to clouting the penultimate fence and he really looks in need of a step up in trip. *(op 13-2 tchd 7-1)*
Wicked Nice Fella(IRE) dropped out tamely when push came to shove approaching two out and has to rate disappointing. He has it to prove now. *(op 11-10)*

2960 STAN JAMES H'CAP CHASE (12 fncs) 2m 110y
3:00 (3:00) (Class 4) (0-105,102) 4-Y-0+ **£3,792** (£1,113; £556; £278)

Form RPR

3425 **1** **Jupon Vert (FR)**[18] 2733 8-11-1 **91**.................. JodieMogford 98
(R J Hodges) *hld up: sme hdwy appr 2 out: no ch whn lft in ld flat: styd on* **9/2**[3]

3P36 **2** *9* **Woodenbridge Dream (IRE)**[20] 2684 8-10-9 **85**.......... JohnMcNamara 94+
(R Lee) *hld up: hdwy to chse clr ldr appr 2 out: no ch whn lft in ld and blnd last: sn hdd and nt rcvr* **6/1**

P-UF **3** *10* **Randolph O'Brien (IRE)**[59] 1914 5-11-6 **96**.................. TomSiddall 84
(N A Twiston-Davies) *bhd: hit 4th: nvr nrr* **12/1**

-PPF **4** *12* **Fantasmic**[27] 2562 9-11-6 **99**.................. OwynNelmes[(3)] 77+
(O Sherwood) *hld up: no ch whn hmpd 3 out* **8/1**

3-P0 **5** *7* **Cool Chilli**[41] 2257 7-10-5 **88** ow3..........(t) MrNPearce[(7)] 57
(N J Pomfret) *sn chsng clr ldrs: lft 2nd and hmpd 3 out: sn wknd* **12/1**

41/2 **U** **Afro Man**[33] 2429 7-11-12 **102**.................. BrianCrowley —
(C J Mann) *hit 1st: hld up: mstke 5th: blnd and uns rdr next* **3/1**[1]

33-0 **F** **Penny Stall**[18] 2714 4-10-11 **97**.................. TomDoyle —
(Miss E C Lavelle) *led after 1st: hdd 3rd: mod 2nd whn fell 3 out* **9/1**

0-00 **F** **Major Belle (FR)**[236] 180 6-10-5 **81**.................. HenryOliver 86+
(John R Upson) *bhd 3rd: hdwy appr 2 out: lft 3rd and hld whn fell last* **16/1**

F-14 **F** **French Direction (IRE)**[180] 862 6-10-7 **83**.................. PhilipHide 104+
(R Rowe) *led: hdd after 1st: led 3rd: clr 6th: in command whn fell last* **7/2**[2]

4m 16.4s (7.10) **Going Correction** +0.30s/f (Yiel)
WFA 4 from 5yo+ 10lb **9** Ran SP% **122.1**
Speed ratings: **95,90,86,80,77 —,—,—,—** CSF £33.90 CT £312.26 TOTE £4.90: £1.60, £2.40, £5.00; EX 18.60.
Owner Mrs J B Jenkins **Bred** Scea La Chaussee **Trained** Charlton Adam, Somerset

FOCUS
An accident-packed handicap and the form is clearly going to prove unreliable. French Direction has been rated as a 14-length winner.

NOTEBOOK
Jupon Vert(FR) posted his first success since 2004, but he has to rate as a very fortunate winner as he was well held prior to rivals falling at the final fence. He is never that far away in his races, however, so this slice of luck was at least deserved. *(op 4-1)*
Woodenbridge Dream(IRE), very well backed, looked set to take advantage of French Direction's fall at the final fence, but he made a serious error at the fence himself and failed to recover. He is in fair form at present, but is never one to trust too much. *(op 8-1)*
Randolph O'Brien(IRE) never figured and is flattered by his finishing position, but at least he completed this time. *(op 10-1)*
Afro Man never looked happy over his fences and it was not a surprise when he unshipped his rider. *(tchd 18-1)*
Major Belle(FR) looked set to finish ahead of the winner until she too blundered and fell at the final fence. *(tchd 18-1)*
French Direction(IRE) had the race in the bag prior to coming to grief at the final flight and has to rate as most unlucky. *(tchd 18-1)*

2961 STAN JAMES TELEBETTING STANDARD OPEN NATIONAL HUNT FLAT RACE 2m 110y
3:35 (3:35) (Class 6) 4-6-Y-0 **£2,041** (£595; £297)

Form RPR

1 **Apollo Lady** 4-10-4.................. MrGTumelty[(7)] 95+
(A King) *trckd ldrs: plld hrd: led over 2f out: rdn out* **9/1**

2 *1* **Theatre Dance (IRE)** 4-11-4.................. TomDoyle 99
(C Tinkler) *hld up: hdwy 1/2-way: rdn over 1f out: styd on* **11/4**[1]

6- **3** *2* **Adlestrop**[288] 4349 5-10-11.................. JimmyMcCarthy 90
(R T Phillips) *hld up: hdwy over 4f out: rdn and ev ch over 1f out: styd on same pce fnl f* **8/1**

4 *5* **Maryscross (IRE)**[288] 5-10-11.................. HenryOliver 85
(O Brennan) *plld hrd and prom: outpcd 3f out: styd on u.p appr fnl f* **14/1**

5 *2* **Carnival Town** 4-10-11.................. MrAJBerry[(7)] 90
(Jonjo O'Neill) *hld up: hdwy 1/2-way: wknd over 1f out* **5/1**[2]

- 6 4 **Navelina** 5-10-4 DavidCullinane[7] 79
(T J Fitzgerald) *hld up: hdwy over 3f out: rdn and wknd over 1f out* **100/1**
0 7 2 **Persian Native (IRE)**[26] 2572 5-11-4 JohnMcNamara 84
(C C Bealby) *hld up in tch: led over 4f out: hdd over 2f out: hung rt and wknd over 1f out* **20/1**
2 8 nk **Blackbriery Thyne (IRE)**[33] 2446 6-10-6 TomGreenway[5] 77
(H D Daly) *led 13f out: hdd over 4f out: wknd over 2f out* **11/2**[3]
9 6 **Hunters Ridge (IRE)** 4-11-1 OwynNelmes[3] 79+
(O Sherwood) *prom: lost pl 1/2-way: rallied over 5f out: wknd over 2f out* **33/1**
10 2½ **Reflector (IRE)** 4-11-4 SamStronge 77+
(Miss H C Knight) *hld up: hdwy 6f out: wknd over 2f out* **7/1**
5 11 6 **Mange Tout (IRE)**[10] 2864 6-11-1 TJPhelan[3] 69
(K J Burke) *led 3f: wknd 3f out* **20/1**
0 12 ½ **Latin Player (IRE)**[42] 2242 6-11-4 VinceSlattery 69
(B G Powell) *prom: lost pl after 2f: n.d after* **66/1**
13 1¾ **Just Touch Wood** 4-10-13 JohnLevins[5] 67
(B G Powell) *hld up: bhd fnl 4f* **25/1**
14 3½ **The Piker (IRE)** 4-10-11 WillieMcCarthy[7] 63
(T R George) *prom over 12f* **10/1**
15 dist **Master Tanner** 5-10-11 MissCDyson[7] —
(Miss C Dyson) *plld hrd: jnd ldr after 3f: wknd over 5f out* **66/1**
16 dist **Charley Brown (IRE)** 5-10-8 MattyRoe[10] —
(Mrs L Wadham) *sn prom: lost pl over 6f out: sn bhd* **20/1**

3m 59.4s (2.90) **Going Correction** +0.20s/f (Yiel) **16** Ran SP% **133.1**
Speed ratings: **101,100,99,97,96 94,93,93,90,89 86,86,85,83,—** — CSF £34.25 TOTE £13.70: £3.00, £1.80, £4.10; EX 55.10 Place 6 £5,045.05, Place 5 £2,667.97.
Owner Jerry Wright & Andy Longman **Bred** Mrs J M Bailey **Trained** Barbury Castle, Wilts

FOCUS
A fair bumper which saw the field fairly strung out at the finish. The form looks sound.

NOTEBOOK
Apollo Lady, a 7,200gns purchase whose dam was a winning hurdler, got her career off to a perfect start with a ready success. She can be rated better than the bare form, as she ran very freely early on, and looked better the further she went.
Theatre Dance(IRE), a half-brother to several winners, most notably smart chaser Celibate and Balla Sola, showed definite ability on this debut and it would be a surprise were he not soon placed to go one better in this sphere. *(op 3-1)*
Adlestrop, sixth on her debut last season, emerged to hold every chance on this return to action and posted a pleasing effort. She has a future and looks ready to tackle hurdles now.
Maryscross(IRE), a winner of a mares' point in Ireland, did not settle in the early stages but she was keeping on at the finish and looks capable of better. *(op 20-1)*
Carnival Town, a 92,000gns purchase whose dam is an unraced half-sister to decent hurdlers Anzum, Jazilah and Sh Boom, looked in need of the experience and can be expected to do much better in due course. *(op 4-1)*
T/Plt: £8,439.60 to a £1 stake. Pool: £16,763.60. 1.45 winning tickets. T/Qpdt: £244.30 to a £1 stake. Pool: £759.40. 2.30 winning tickets. CR

2586 MARKET RASEN (R-H)

Monday, December 26

OFFICIAL GOING: Hurdle course - good to soft; chase course - soft (good to soft in places)
The going was described as 'soft, very tacky and hard work'.
Wind: Almost nil Weather: Cold, mixture of sunshine and showers.

2962 HENSON FRANKLYN (S) H'CAP HURDLE (8 hdls) 2m 1f 110y
12:25 (12:25) (Class 5) (0-95,89) 4-Y-0+ **£2,281** (£665; £332)

Form RPR
0103 1 **Before The Mast (IRE)**[10] 2858 8-10-9 **79** CharliePoste[7] 83
(M F Harris) *hld up in rr: hdwy 4th: w ldrs 6th: styd on to ld last 75yds* **9/2**[1]
06P4 2 ¾ **Seraph**[25] 2586 5-10-11 **77** LeeVickers[3] 80
(O Brennan) *chsd ldrs fr 4th: slt advantage last: hdd and no ex towards fin* **15/2**[3]
U250 3 1¾ **Munaawesh (USA)**[80] 1663 4-10-12 **75** NeilMulholland 77
(Mrs Marjorie Fife) *chsd ldrs: led 5th to last: no ex* **12/1**
0-00 4 10 **Darialann (IRE)**[11] 2843 10-11-4 **88** DarrenO'Dwyer[7] 80
(O Brennan) *in rr: sn drvn along: kpt on fr 5th: nvr nr ldrs* **16/1**
0004 5 4 **Southern Bazaar (USA)**[26] 2567 4-10-0 **70** (p) JohnEnnis[7] 58
(M E Sowersby) *chsd ldrs: wknd appr 2 out* **9/1**
62PP 6 9 **Approaching Land (IRE)**[20] 2688 10-11-2 **82** MrTGreenall[3] 61
(M W Easterby) *chsd ldrs: lost pl after 6th* **11/1**
2000 7 2½ **Protocol (IRE)**[66] 1814 11-11-11 **88** (tp) MarkBradburne 64
(Mrs S Lyman) *mid-div: lost pl on fr 6th: nvr a factor* **8/1**
0000 8 1½ **Shinko Femme (IRE)**[17] 2752 4-10-2 **72** ow6 (t) GarethThomas[7] 47
(M E Sowersby) *hld up in rr: hdwy 5th: lost pl after next* **25/1**
0606 9 10 **Tiger Talk**[32] 2463 9-11-4 **84** (b) LarryMcGrath[3] 49
(R C Guest) *a towards rr* **9/1**
F056 10 nk **La Muette (IRE)**[23] 2625 5-10-5 **73** (p) ChrisHonour[5] 37
(M Appleby) *chsd ldrs: wkng whn mstke 6th* **20/1**
4P0P 11 15 **Macchiato**[23] 2639 4-10-12 **80** DerekLaverty[5] 29
(I W McInnes) *chsd ldrs: drvn along 4th: lost pl after 5th* **18/1**
PP-P 12 1½ **Palais (IRE)**[148] 1109 10-10-9 **77** DesFlavin[5] 25
(John A Harris) *led to 5th: lost pl after next* **33/1**
P/PU 13 1¼ **Ilton**[11] 2843 6-10-2 **72** (v[1]) ScottMarshall[7] 18
(M E Sowersby) *in rr: t.o 2 out* **66/1**
000 14 3½ **Penel (IRE)**[11] 2838 4-11-12 **89** (b) DavidO'Meara 32
(P T Midgley) *a in rr: t.o 2 out* **22/1**
00PP 15 3 **Friedhelmo (GER)**[11] 2843 9-10-10 **80** (t) MissRachelClark[7] 20
(S B Clark) *in rr: blnd 5th: sn bhd: t.o 2 out* **25/1**
3226 P **Samson Des Galas (FR)**[25] 2586 7-10-3 **66** (t) OllieMcPhail —
(Robert Gray) *bhd fr 6th: t.o whn p.u bef last* **5/1**[2]
0-0P P **Okayman (FR)**[10] 2858 4-10-1 **64** JimCrowley —
(A Parker) *chsd ldrs: lost pl and mstke 3rd: sn bhd: t.o whn p.u bef 6th* **20/1**

4m 12.1s (-4.30) **Going Correction** -0.05s/f (Good) **17** Ran SP% **130.9**
Speed ratings: **107,106,105,101,99 95,94,93,89,89 82,81,81,79,78** —,— CSF £37.46 CT £402.84 TOTE £3.60: £1.20, £2.20, £4.20, £5.30; EX 24.80.There was no bid for the winner.
Owner Walk The Plank Partnership **Bred** John McGuinness **Trained** Edgcote, Northants

FOCUS
There were three almost in line jumping the final flight. The form looks rock solid and could be rated a little higher.

NOTEBOOK
Before The Mast(IRE), who has twice suffered pelvic injuries, was 7lb higher than when scoring at Uttoxeter in November. He likes soft ground and in the end did just enough. *(op 5-1)*
Seraph confirmed his improved effort last time was no fluke and, after taking a narrow advantage at the final flight, just missed out in the end. *(op 7-1)*
Munaawesh(USA), a long-standing maiden on the Flat, was having just his fifth start over hurdles and his second for this yard. In the end he was just found wanting.
Darialann(IRE), well beaten on both his two previous starts this year, soon seemed to be struggling to handle the conditions.
Southern Bazaar(USA), who finished ahead of the winner at Catterick last month, was one of four in contention rounding the home turn but he was the first of the principals to crack. He does not want the ground as testing as this.

2963 GARTHWEST NOVICES' CHASE (12 fncs) 2m 1f 110y
12:55 (12:56) (Class 3) 4-Y-0+ **£5,531** (£1,717; £924)

Form RPR
4112 1 **Bishop's Bridge (IRE)**[25] 2595 7-11-0 114 GinoCarenza[3] 115+
(Andrew Turnell) *chsd ldr: lft in ld 3rd: hdd 5th: led 2 out: drvn rt out* **3/1**[3]
0/14 2 1¾ **Detonateur (FR)**[18] 2725 7-11-3 115 JimCrowley 112+
(Ian Williams) *trckd ldrs: led 5th to 2 out: no ex run-in* **5/2**[2]
20/0 3 ¾ **Thistlecraft (IRE)**[29] 2530 6-11-0 110 LeeVickers[3] 114+
(C C Bealby) *trckd ldrs: hmpd 3rd: hit 7th: drvn 9th: 5 l 3rd whn blnd 2 out: rallied run-in: fin best* **5/1**
1113 U **Parisienne Gale (IRE)**[32] 2457 6-10-10 112 (t) DavidO'Meara —
(R Ford) *led: j.lft: blnd and uns rdr 3rd* **2/1**[1]
5U3F C **Vigoureux (FR)**[47] 2128 6-11-3 95 (p) NeilMulholland —
(S Gollings) *w ldrs: blnd: bdly hmpd 3rd and sn carried off trck* **12/1**

4m 38.4s (7.30) **Going Correction** +0.40s/f (Soft) **5** Ran SP% **111.3**
Speed ratings: **99,98,97,—,—** CSF £11.20 TOTE £3.70: £2.00, £1.50; EX 16.00.
Owner S Kimber **Bred** F Fennelly **Trained** Broad Hinton, Wilts

FOCUS
With the favourite out at an early stage this did not take that much winning and the third was overhauling the first two at the line. The form is difficult to evaluate but for the time being it has been rated through the hurdling form of the first and third.

NOTEBOOK
Bishop's Bridge(IRE), having just his second start over fences, was a bit hesitant in his jumping, but after travelling best the needle was almost on empty at the line. He prefers much better ground than he encountered here. *(op 7-2)*
Detonateur(FR), dropping back in trip, stuck to his task when headed and had the winner virtually all out at the line. *(op 9-4 tchd 11-4)*
Thistlecraft(IRE), a soft-ground bumper winner in the past, looked cooked when blundering two out but he came again strongly on the run-in and was fast closing down the first two at the line. *(op 6-1)*
Parisienne Gale(IRE), wearing a tongue strap for the first time, went sideways at the first fence in the home straight and gave her rider no chance. *(op 7-4)*

2964 ROSELAND GROUP KILVINGTON H'CAP HURDLE (10 hdls) 2m 3f 110y
1:30 (1:30) (Class 3) (0-125,115) 4-Y-0+ **£5,048** (£1,482; £741; £370)

Form RPR
10 1 **Star Member (IRE)**[44] 2173 6-11-2 **105** JimCrowley 122+
(Ian Williams) *trckd ldrs 4th: led 8th: wnt clr appr next: coasted home* **9/2**[2]
2304 2 6 **Openide**[37] 2338 4-11-5 **115** (b) MrMWall[7] 117
(B W Duke) *led to 2nd: chsd ldrs: kpt on to take 2nd last: no ch w wnr* **20/1**
-235 3 1 **Marsh Run**[25] 2590 6-11-3 **109** (b[1]) MrTGreenall[3] 110
(M W Easterby) *chsd ldrs: kpt on same pce fr 2 out* **6/1**
3453 4 6 **Karathaena (IRE)**[16] 2766 5-11-0 **110** JohnEnnis[7] 107+
(M E Sowersby) *chsd ldrs: wnt 2nd 2 out: wknd last* **5/1**[3]
6545 5 7 **Siegfrieds Night (IRE)**[4] 2952 4-9-13 **93** ow1 (t) ChrisHonour[5] 82+
(M C Chapman) *in rr: sme hdwy 8th: nvr a factor* **16/1**
00P0 6 9 **Migration**[7] 2925 9-11-7 **110** MarkBradburne 95+
(Mrs S Lyman) *hld up in last: sme hdwy 8th: nvr nr ldrs* **50/1**
06F6 7 1¾ **All Bleevable**[21] 1816 8-10-2 **98** (p) ScottMarshall[7] 75
(Mrs S Lyman) *led 2nd to 8th: sn wknd* **33/1**
P000 8 nk **Isellido (IRE)**[32] 2452 6-11-1 **107** (e) LarryMcGrath[3] 84
(R C Guest) *hld up in mid-div: lost pl after 6th* **20/1**
20-P 9 4 **Bollin Annabel**[23] 2629 4-11-8 **111** DavidO'Meara 84
(T D Easterby) *chsd ldrs: lost pl 3 out* **16/1**
4/66 10 5 **Salhood**[18] 2716 6-11-12 **115** NeilMulholland 83
(S Gollings) *chsd ldrs: wknd 3 out* **14/1**
6210 11 14 **Nick The Silver**[48] 2110 4-10-8 **102** (p) DesFlavin[5] 56
(Robert Gray) *in rr: bhd fr 8th* **10/1**
60-0 U **Caraman (IRE)**[16] 2765 7-11-8 **111** OllieMcPhail —
(J J Quinn) *chsd ldrs: outpcd whn blnd and uns rdr 6th* **12/1**
6411 U **Zeloso**[13] 2806 7-9-7 **89** oh1 (v) CharliePoste[7] —
(M F Harris) *hld up towards rr: bdly hmpd and uns rdr 6th* **4/1**[1]
03P- P **Kaparolo (USA)**[261] 4777 6-10-9 **103** LeeStephens[5] —
(John A Harris) *chsd ldrs: lost pl 6th: t.o whn p.u bef 8th* **40/1**
0/P- F **Fred's In The Know**[604] 114 10-11-4 **110** AnthonyCoyle[3] 87
(Miss Tracy Waggott) *t.k.h in rr: bhd fr 7th: fell last* **28/1**

4m 46.0s (-4.00) **Going Correction** -0.05s/f (Good)
WFA 4 from 5yo+ 10lb **15** Ran SP% **124.7**
Speed ratings: **106,103,103,100,98 94,93,93,91,89 84,—,—,—,—** CSF £99.41 CT £562.10 TOTE £6.10: £2.40, £5.90, £2.10; EX 280.40.
Owner A L R Morton **Bred** Killeen Castle Stud **Trained** Portway, Worcs

FOCUS
The winner simply trounced them and, nine lengths clear at the final flight, was value for at least 15. The form looks solid with the placed horses right up to their marks.

NOTEBOOK
Star Member(IRE), rated 88 on the Flat, was having just his third start over hurdles. He travelled supremely well and, quickening right away going to two out, was full value for 15 lengths. His trainer would be well advised to run him again soon under a penalty. *(tchd 4-1)*
Openide, with the blinkers fitted again, stuck on to follow home the winner and will be suited by a stiffer test. *(op 16-1)*
Marsh Run, tried in blinkers, ran creditably without showing any real zest. She may need some relief from the Handicapper. *(op 11-2)*
Karathaena(IRE) went in pursuit of the winner but was very leg-weary on the run-in. *(op 11-2)*
Siegfrieds Night(IRE) ran his usual sort of race, taking little interest until deciding to try a bit harder late on.
Migration, anchored at the back, is steadily slipping back to a more attractive mark. *(op 33-1)*
Zeloso, 10lb higher and out of selling grade, was put out of the contest at the first flight in the back straight. *(op 5-1)*

The Form Book, Raceform Ltd, Compton, RG20 6NL

2965 CLUGSTON LINCOLNSHIRE NATIONAL (A H'CAP CHASE) (19 fncs) 3m 4f 110y

2:00 (2:03) (Class 3) (0-125,117) 5-Y-0+ **£6,001** (£1,761; £880; £440)

Form RPR

0F35 **1** **Victory Gunner (IRE)**[12] 2825 7-11-4 **114** LeeStephens(5) 125+
(C Roberts) *j. slowly 1st circ: hdwy to chse ldrs 10th: wnt 2nd 15th: led 2 out: styd on* **10/1**

-P53 **2** *7* **Fin Bec (FR)**[30] 2502 12-10-5 **101** (b) DerekLaverty(5) 106+
(A P Jones) *j.rt: led 5th: blnd 4 out: hdd 2 out: kpt on same pce* **10/1**

0435 **3** *1* **Waterberg (IRE)**[38] 2325 10-10-8 **99** (b) MarkBradburne 101
(H D Daly) *hld up: wnt prom 10th: one pce fr 3 out* **5/1**[2]

0-P1 **4** *3 ½* **Supreme Breeze (IRE)**[40] 2265 10-11-12 **117** JimCrowley 117+
(Mrs S J Smith) *chsd ldrs: one pce fr 3 out* **5/1**[2]

2-13 **5** *9* **Capybara (IRE)**[40] 2265 7-11-10 **115** DavidO'Meara 106+
(H P Hogarth) *a.p: one pce fr 4 out* **6/1**[3]

4426 **6** *hd* **Runaway Bishop (USA)**[10] 2858 10-9-9 **93** MrDGreenway(7) 82
(J R Cornwall) *in rr: outpcd fr 13th: nvr a factor* **14/1**

P-4P **7** *¾* **Bob's The Business (IRE)**[24] 2608 11-10-0 **101** DavidBoland(10) 90
(Ian Williams) *led to 3rd: hrd drvn 13th: lost pl after 15th* **10/1**

404P **8** *3* **Harlov (FR)**[12] 2819 10-10-13 **107** (v[1]) MrTGreenall(3) 94+
(A Parker) *chsd ldrs: wknd appr 3 out* **16/1**

-P52 **9** *24* **Heidi III (FR)**[39] 2293 10-11-7 **112** (p) NeilMulholland 83+
(M D Hammond) *led 3rd to 5th: drvn 13th: lost pl 4 out: sn bhd* **8/1**

0F-0 **P** **Mister Dave'S (IRE)**[12] 2818 10-10-8 **102** LarryMcGrath(3) —
(Mrs S J Smith) *detached in last: nt fluent: t.o whn p.u after 13th* **25/1**

2151 **P** **Moustique De L'Isle (FR)**[10] 2862 5-10-10 **104** (b) LeeVickers(3) —
(C C Bealby) *lost pl 6th: sn in rr: bhd fr 12th: sn t.o: p.u bef 4 out* **9/2**[1]

7m 44.5s (6.50) **Going Correction** +0.40s/f (Soft) **11** Ran SP% **120.6**
Speed ratings: **107,105,104,103,101 101,101,100,93,— —** CSF £107.15 CT £568.66 TOTE £15.00: £3.80, £3.30, £2.20; EX 119.30.
Owner Ron Bartlett & F J Ayres **Bred** J Neville **Trained** Newport, Newport

FOCUS
A severe test in the conditions but a decisive and unexposed winner who was stepping up greatly on his three previous starts over fences.

NOTEBOOK
Victory Gunner(IRE), 4lb below his hurdles mark, turned in a much improved effort, suited by this stiff test of stamina. There might be even better to come. *(op 12-1)*
Fin Bec(FR), who has not tasted success for over two years, continually gave away ground by jumping to his right. *(tchd 9-1)*
Waterberg(IRE), who has not won for over two years, had the blinkers on again. He moved up *looking a danger at one stage but could only plug on in his own time over the final three fences.* *(op 11-2)*
Supreme Breeze(IRE), 6lb higher than at Hexham, was not disgraced but this may be as good as he is. *(op 11-2)*
Capybara(IRE), meeting Supreme Breeze on 5lb better terms, was unable to turn the tables. *(op 9-2)*
Moustique De L'Isle(FR), with the blinkers fitted on just his fourth start over fences, ran a stinker for no obvious reason. *Official explanation: trainer said gelding was never travelling* *(op 5-1)*

2966 GRANGE & LINKS HOTEL AND SANDILANDS GOLF CLUB NOVICES' H'CAP CHASE (16 fncs 1 omitted) 3m 1f

2:35 (2:38) (Class 4) (0-105,103) 5-Y-0+ **£3,900** (£1,145; £572; £285)

Form RPR

5P32 **1** **El Andaluz (FR)**[8] 2902 5-10-3 **80** ow2 OllieMcPhail 90+
(Robert Gray) *tk fierce hold: blnd bdly 1st: hdwy and prom 5th: styd on to ld 1f out: hld on towards fin* **5/1**[2]

302- **2** *½* **Blackergreen**[248] 4967 6-11-3 **94** MarkBradburne 102+
(Mrs S J Smith) *chsd ldrs: mstke 8th: led 12th tl after 14th: blnd next: styd on: no ex towards fin* **4/1**[1]

32P/ **3** *4* **Roddy The Vet (IRE)**[675] 3926 7-10-2 **79** JimCrowley 82+
(A Ennis) *hld up in rr: jnd ldrs 7th: led after 14th: hdd 1f out: no ex* **11/2**[3]

4443 **4** *7* **Sconced (USA)**[4] 2951 10-10-8 **88** (b) LarryMcGrath(3) 83+
(R C Guest) *prom: j.lft and lost pl 5th: hdwy and wl in tch 11th: outpcd fr 14th* **9/1**

0/P0 **P** **Bedford Leader**[30] 2505 7-9-13 **81** DerekLaverty(5) —
(A P Jones) *bhd fr 8th: t.o whn p.u after 10th* **22/1**

0P00 **F** **Iloveturtle (IRE)**[4] 2951 5-10-5 **87** (t) ChrisHonour(5) —
(M C Chapman) *in rr: hdwy to chse ldrs 7th: fell 10th* **16/1**

P425 **P** **Valley Warrior**[47] 2126 8-10-1 **83** oh7 ow6 LeeStephens(5) —
(J S Smith) *j. slowly: sn bhd: t.o whn p.u after 10th* **7/1**

PP50 **R** **John Rich**[26] 2568 9-10-0 **84** oh14 ow7 (tp) GarethThomas(7) —
(M E Sowersby) *prom: hmpd and lost pl 10th: bhd whn ref 13th* **12/1**

-P06 **P** **Back De Bay (IRE)**[41] 2260 5-9-13 **79** oh4 ow2 LeeVickers(3) —
(J R Cornwall) *chsd ldrs: blnd and lost pl 9th: sn bhd: p.u after 11th* **25/1**

-6F1 **P** **One Five Eight**[22] 2655 6-11-9 **103** MrTGreenall(3) —
(M W Easterby) *in tch: bdly hmpd and lost pl 10th: bhd whn p.u after next* **6/1**

3336 **P** **Jonny's Kick**[23] 2630 5-11-3 **94** (b[1]) DavidO'Meara —
(T D Easterby) *led: blnd 7th: hdd 12th: blnd next: wknd 14th: bhd whn p.u bef last* **11/2**[3]

6m 45.3s (7.90) **Going Correction** +0.40s/f (Soft) **11** Ran SP% **126.0**
Speed ratings: **103,102,101,99,— —,—,—,—,— —** CSF £28.18 CT £119.91 TOTE £5.30: £1.90, £1.90, £2.40; EX 28.90.
Owner Naughty Diesel Ltd **Bred** Pierre Bourdon **Trained** Malton, N Yorks

FOCUS
Weak form with a much-improved effort from the winner and the fourth possibly the best guide to the overall value of the form. The final fence had to be omitted so a stricken rider could receive treatment.

NOTEBOOK
El Andaluz(FR), almost out of the contest at the first fence where his saddle temporarily shifted, went ahead passing the omitted final fence but at the line there was precious little to spare. This was his first outing for this yard and clearly the soft ground suited him. *(tchd 11-2)*
Blackergreen, absent since April, was making his chase debut. But for a blunder at what is normally the third last, here two out, he would probably have prevailed. *(tchd 9-2)*
Roddy The Vet(IRE), having his first run for almost two years after finishing lame, went on starting the final turn and in the end was only run out of it in the dash to the line. *(op 5-1)*
Sconced(USA), a long-standing maiden, looks to just go through the motions.
One Five Eight *Official explanation: jockey said gelding was never travelling* *(op 11-2)*

2967 AC OFFICE SUPPLIES MAIDEN HURDLE (DIV I) (10 hdls) 2m 3f 110y

3:05 (3:09) (Class 4) 4-Y-0+ **£2,220** (£647; £323)

Form RPR

2-22 **1** **Oscatello (USA)**[22] 2663 5-11-0 JimCrowley 110+
(Ian Williams) *nt fluent: hdwy to chse ldrs 6th: led appr 2 out: forged clr run-in: v readily* **10/11**[1]

0-00 **2** *4* **Seymar Lad (IRE)**[23] 2631 5-11-0 MarkBradburne 100
(P Beaumont) *in rr: hdwy to chse ldrs 6th: wnt 2nd appr 2 out: kpt on: no real imp* **16/1**

-423 **3** *8* **Perfect Balance (IRE)**[20] 2688 4-10-7 84 JohnEnnis(7) 92
(D W Thompson) *in rr: hdwy to chsee ldrs after 7th: one pce appr 2 out* **8/1**[3]

31P **4** *1 ¾* **Schumann**[24] 2617 4-11-0 MarkGrant 90
(M Pitman) *chsd ldrs: rdn after 8th: wl outpcd appr next* **8/1**[3]

134- **5** *5* **Caulkleys Bank**[375] 2852 5-10-11 MrTGreenall(3) 87+
(M W Easterby) *trckd ldrs: led 6th: hdd appr 2 out: sn wknd* **4/1**[2]

P0/ **6** *28* **Saxon Mill**[659] 4219 10-11-0 OllieMcPhail 57
(T J Fitzgerald) *in rr: sme hdwy 7th: lost pl after next* **25/1**

0/P0 **7** *9* **Captain Smoothy**[25] 2584 5-10-9 DerekLaverty(5) 48
(M J Gingell) *jnd ldr 4th: wknd after 7th: sn bhd* **20/1**

0500 **U** **Europrime Games**[13] 2816 7-10-11 72 (b[1]) LarryMcGrath(3) —
(M E Sowersby) *led tl blnd and uns rdr 2nd* **66/1**

P **Eamon An Chnoic (IRE)**[86] 4-10-4 CyrilleLeveque(10) —
(B W Duke) *in rr: bhd fr 6th: sn t.o: p.u bef last* **16/1**

UP00 **P** **Government (IRE)**[22] 2517 4-10-7 64 ThomasBurrows(7) —
(M C Chapman) *in rr: bhd fr 5th: t.o whn p.u after 7th* **66/1**

5-00 **P** **Commemoration Day (IRE)**[26] 2566 4-11-0 80 (v) DavidO'Meara —
(M E Sowersby) *lft in ld 2nd: hdd 6th: wknd next: bhd whn p.u bef 2 out* **50/1**

P/P- **P** **Crazy Like A Fool (IRE)**[539] 332 6-10-6 ow2 TimothyBailey(10) —
(M G Quinlan) *sn in rr and drvn along: bhd fr 5th: t.o whn p.u bef next* **25/1**

4m 50.0s **Going Correction** -0.05s/f (Good)
WFA 4 from 5yo+ 10lb **12** Ran SP% **123.8**
Speed ratings: **98,96,93,92,90 79,75,—,—,— —,—** CSF £17.94 TOTE £1.90: £1.10, £5.40, £1.50; EX 28.90.
Owner Rye Braune **Bred** Highland Farms Inc **Trained** Portway, Worcs

FOCUS
The winner was not winning out of turn and value at least ten lengths. The third is perhaps the best guide to the overall value of the race.

NOTEBOOK
Oscatello(USA), runner-up on his three previous career starts, did not jump well but still proved much too good for this lot. He is by no means the finished article. *(op 5-6 tchd Evens and 4-5 in places)*
Seymar Lad(IRE), who took a bumper at Wetherby in February, ran a lot better and should be able to win a modest heat.
Perfect Balance(IRE), having his eighth start over hurdles, is starting to look fully exposed. *(op 10-1)*
Schumann, having just his second start over hurdles, may be capable of something better given a decent racing surface. *(op 9-1)*
Caulkleys Bank, a useful bumper horse, was having his first outing for a year. He went on and looked the threat to the winner but stopped to nothing over the last two. The ground was probably against him and he may do better back over two miles. *(op 7-2)*

2968 AC OFFICE SUPPLIES MAIDEN HURDLE (DIV II) (10 hdls) 2m 3f 110y

3:35 (3:38) (Class 4) 4-Y-0+ **£2,213** (£645; £322)

Form RPR

0-00 **1** **Waterloo Son (IRE)**[55] 1968 5-11-0 MarkBradburne 112+
(H D Daly) *chsd ldrs: led appr 2 out: hit last: styd on strly* **20/1**

21-3 **2** *6* **Blue Buster**[22] 2658 5-10-11 MrTGreenall(3) 100
(M W Easterby) *trckd ldrs: wnt 2nd appr 2 out: kpt on: no real imp* **11/4**[1]

-460 **3** *10* **It's Bertie**[29] 2528 5-11-0 DavidO'Meara 93+
(Mrs S J Smith) *w ldr: led 3 out: hdd: 3rd and one pce whn blnd next* **20/1**

-422 **4** *5* **Di's Dilemma**[25] 2590 7-10-4 95 LeeVickers(3) 79+
(C C Bealby) *chsd ldrs: 5th and outpcd whn hit 8th* **7/2**[2]

25 **5** *1 ¾* **Fuel Cell (IRE)**[7] 2923 4-10-11 LarryMcGrath(3) 83
(M E Sowersby) *mid-div: hdwy 7th: sn rdn: one pce* **7/2**[2]

0- **6** *1* **Hermano Cordobes (IRE)**[357] 3210 5-10-9 DesFlavin(5) 83+
(Mrs J R Buckley) *s.s: w.w in rr: effrt and sme hdwy 8th: nvr nr ldrs* **100/1**

F200 **7** *dist* **Imperial Royale (IRE)**[10] 2859 4-10-4 90 ThomasBurrows(10) —
(P L Clinton) *mde most to 8th: lost pl appr next: t.o: btn 37 l* **20/1**

8 *9* **Gran Dana (IRE)**[74] 5-10-9 LeeStephens(5) —
(G Prodromou) *bhd fr 7th: t.o* **40/1**

0P-5 **9** *4* **Protective**[23] 2627 4-11-0 104 JimCrowley —
(J G Given) *racd wd: in tch: drvn 6th: lost pl 3 out: t.o* **6/1**[3]

00 **10** *shd* **Vrisaki (IRE)**[7] 2923 4-10-7 GarethThomas(7) —
(M E Sowersby) *hld up in rr: bhd fr 7th: t.o* **100/1**

00 **11** *3 ½* **Tickhill Tom**[53] 2007 5-11-0 NeilMulholland —
(C W Fairhurst) *chsd ldrs: drvn 6th: lost pl next: t.o* **50/1**

12 *2 ½* **El Corredor (IRE)**[731] 2972 6-10-7 CharliePoste(7) —
(M F Harris) *in rr: bhd fr 7th: t.o* **66/1**

13 *hd* **Bucks**[24] 8-10-11 JoffretHuet(3) —
(Ian Williams) *bhd and drvn 7th: t.o* **13/2**

0PF0 **14** *dist* **Ray Mond**[13] 2803 4-10-9 DerekLaverty(5) —
(M J Gingell) *s.s: a bhd: t.o 7th: virtually p.u: btn 41 l* **66/1**

4m 49.5s (-0.50) **Going Correction** -0.05s/f (Good)
WFA 4 from 5yo+ 10lb **14** Ran SP% **122.4**
Speed ratings: **99,96,92,90,89 89,—,—,—,— —,—,—,—** CSF £74.07 TOTE £17.50: £3.80, £2.20, £5.10; EX 71.30 Place 6 £111.66, Place 5 £46.01.
Owner Trevor Hemmings **Bred** Walter Zieg **Trained** Stanton Lacy, Shropshire
■ Stewards' Enquiry : Des Flavin seven-day ban: in breach of Rule 157 - made insufficient effort (Jan 17-24)

FOCUS
The winner looked value for double the official margin and the runner-up sets the standard.

NOTEBOOK
Waterloo Son(IRE), unplaced in four previous starts, came good in a big way, being value for double the official margin. He should go on from here. *(tchd 18-1)*
Blue Buster went in pursuit of the winner but it was soon very clear that he was only going to be second best. *(op 5-2)*
It's Bertie ran easily his best race over hurdles on just his third attempt.
Di's Dilemma has yet to hit the target in 17 outings under national hunt rules.
Fuel Cell(IRE) has not really built on his sound debut effort in two subsequent starts. *(op 4-1 tchd 9-2)*
Hermano Cordobes(IRE), well beaten in a bumper on his only previous start almost a year ago, was dropped in at the start. He paddled through the first flight and his rider seemed pretty keen to keep a strong hold on his head. Staying on starting the final turn, his finishing effort did not go down well with the Stewards who came down with a heavy hand. Clearly very inexperienced, it *remains to be seen what he can actually achieve when ridden a lot more positively. Official explanation: 40-day ban (Jan 17-Feb 25)*

T/Plt: £103.50 to a £1 stake. Pool: £17,851.90. 125.85 winning tickets. T/Qpdt: £37.60 to a £1 stake. Pool: £905.10. 17.80 winning tickets. WG

2632 SANDOWN (R-H)

Monday, December 26

OFFICIAL GOING: Chase course - good (good to firm in places in the back straight); hurdle course - good to soft (good in places)

Meeting switched from Kempton Park, which is being redeveloped.

Wind: Moderate, across Weather: Overcast, becoming fine

2969 STANJAMESUK.COM H'CAP HURDLE (8 hdls) 2m 110y

12:35 (12:35) (Class 3) (0-125,119) 4-Y-0+

£6,576 (£1,942; £971; £486; £242; £121)

Form				RPR
103	1		**Albarino (IRE)**[18] 2730 6-11-0 **107** ..... TomScudamore (M Scudamore) *hld up in rr: prog to trck ldrs 3 out and gng easily: led 2 out: clr last: comf* **16/1**	125+
-314	2	9	**Nanga Parbat (FR)**[29] 2533 4-11-10 **117** ..... (t) RWalsh (P F Nicholls) *hld up: mstke 3rd and rr of main gp after: drvn and styd on fr 2 out: kpt on to take 2nd nr fin* **8/1**	123+
-F26	3	½	**Tanikos (FR)**[30] 2489 6-11-1 **113** ..... SamCurling(5) (N J Henderson) *prom: rdn and lost pl sn after 3 out: rallied u.p and w wnr 2 out: sn brushed aside: wknd and lost 2nd nr post* **16/1**	118+
16-6	4	2	**Foodbroker Founder**[38] 2324 5-11-6 **113** ..... TonyDobbin (D R C Elsworth) *lw: nt a fluent: prom: hrd rdn after 3 out: btn 2 out: fdd* **10/1**	116+
0-P0	5	*hd*	**New Entic (FR)**[10] 2871 4-11-9 **116** ..... JamieMoore (G L Moore) *hld up in tch: bdly hmpd 5th: hrd rdn after 3 out: no prog: keeping on again nr fin* **33/1**	120+
13-1	6	1 ½	**Gods Token**[11] 2850 7-11-11 **118** ..... APMcCoy (Miss Venetia Williams) *cl up: effrt and w ldr after 3 out: wknd 2 out* **6/1**[3]	119
-200	7	15	**Genuine Article (IRE)**[16] 2765 9-11-4 **111** ..... CarlLlewellyn (M Pitman) *led: hit 5th: hdd & wknd 2 out* **33/1**	108+
3111	F		**Motorway (IRE)**[17] 2746 4-11-12 **119** ..... RichardJohnson (P J Hobbs) *blnd 1st: trckd ldrs: nt fluent 3rd: cl up whn fell 5th* **7/4**[1]	—
-000	P		**Batswing**[10] 2868 10-10-7 **100** ..... TimmyMurphy (G L Moore) *settled in last: lost tch after 3rd: t.o 3 out: 9th whn p.u bef next* **40/1**	—
P2P-	P		**Mambo (IRE)**[255] 4848 7-11-12 **119** ..... MickFitzgerald (N J Henderson) *fit: trckd ldrs tl wknd rapidly 3 out: t.o in 8th whn p.u bef 2 out* **7/2**[2]	—
41P-	P		**Montesino**[358] 3177 6-11-1 **108** ..... BarryFenton (M Madgwick) *bit bkwd: hld up in rr: lost tch after 3rd: wl t.o 3 out: 10th whn p.u bef 2 out* **100/1**	—

4m 0.10s (-8.80) **Going Correction** -0.325s/f (Good) **11** Ran SP% **114.1**

Speed ratings: **107,102,102,101,101 100,93,—,—,—** — CSF £129.98 CT £2079.78 TOTE £24.90: £3.50, £2.40, £4.30; EX 194.60.

Owner Mrs N M Watkins **Bred** Michael And Fiona O'Connor **Trained** Bromsash, Herefordshire

FOCUS

Jockeys reported the ground on the hurdles course to be 'dead'. Improved form from the winner, who has been rated as value for 12 lengths. The form looks pretty solid, with the second, fourth and fifth all close to their marks.

NOTEBOOK

Albarino(IRE) has improved out of recognition since arriving from Ireland and travelled strongly throughout before settling the issue quickly when allowed a bit of rein and winning in great style. This ground suited him well and he looks to be on the upgrade. *(op 14-1)*

Nanga Parbat(FR), only fourth over the final flight, stayed on well up the hill but in truth never looked a likely winner. *(op 15-2)*

Tanikos(FR), who got very warm in the preliminaries, had not run over hurdles since April 2003. Currently rated 9lb higher over fences, he did best of those to race up with the pace.

Foodbroker Founder ran a respectable race on what was only his fourth appearance over hurdles but was a spent force with two to jump.

New Entic(FR) stayed on after having to jump the fallen favourite on the landing side of the fifth, but he was never going well enough to be a factor.

Gods Token faded from the second last as the 5lb rise for his Exeter win began to tell.

Mambo(IRE), who looked fit for this first run since April, was well treated on the best of his chase form, but he dropped right away at the end of the back straight and has now been pulled up on four of his last five starts. *(op 4-1 tchd 9-2 and 10-3)*

Motorway(IRE), bidding for a four-timer off a 9lb higher mark, had already put in a couple of less than fluent jumps before he succumbed at the fifth. *(op 4-1 tchd 9-2 and 10-3)*

2970 STAN JAMES WAYWARD LAD NOVICES' CHASE GRADE 2 (13 fncs) 2m

1:05 (1:07) (Class 1) 4-Y-0+ **£30,227**

Form				RPR
12	1		**Hoo La Baloo (FR)**[23] 2634 4-10-13 ..... RWalsh (P F Nicholls) *led: outj and hdd 4th: lft in ld 6th: rdn 3 out: 3 l clr and looked in command whn lft alone 2 out* **10/11**[1]	145+
-331	F		**Exotic Dancer (FR)**[16] 2759 5-11-9 ..... APMcCoy (Jonjo O'Neill) *3rd whn fell 1st* **7/2**[3]	—
1216	F		**Flying Spirit (IRE)**[44] 2174 6-11-9 136 ..... (b) TimmyMurphy (G L Moore) *trckd wnr: led 4th tl fell heavily 6th* **16/1**	—
-31B	F		**Crossbow Creek**[23] 2634 7-11-7 ..... JamieMoore (M G Rimell) *nt fluent: hld up: fft last of 2 remaining 6th: rdn after 10th: 3 l down and no imp whn fell 2 out: winded* **5/2**[2]	148

4m 0.20s (-2.30) **Going Correction** -0.325s/f (Good)

WFA 4 from 5yo+ 10lb **4** Ran SP% **109.1**

Speed ratings: **92,—,—,—** CSF £1.91 TOTE £1.90; EX 1.30.

Owner The Stewart Family **Bred** N P Bloodstock **Trained** Ditcheat, Somerset

FOCUS

The defection of morning favourite Racing Demon took some of the gloss from this Grade 2 event. Hoo La Baloo finished alone and has been rated to his mark, with Crossbow Creek rated as finishing 5l second.

NOTEBOOK

Hoo La Baloo(FR), already faced with an easier task following the withdrawal of Racing Demon, who beat him here in the Henry VIII, ended up coming home alone as his three opponents all hit the deck. He jumped well and liked this quicker ground, but he is regarded as a much better horse going this way round so is far from certain to be aimed at the Arkle. *(op 4-5)*

Flying Spirit(IRE), back at two miles, was in front when coming down at the open ditch in the back straight. *(op 22-1)*

Crossbow Creek was apparently held when he took off too soon at the second last and came down. Winded before eventually getting to his feet, he had an unfortunate experience at the same obstacle on his last visit to Sandown. *(op 22-1)*

Exotic Dancer(FR) dropped back to two miles for this rather than tackle three in the Feltham, but it became immaterial when he departed at the first. *(op 22-1)*

2971 STAN JAMES CHRISTMAS HURDLE GRADE 1 (8 hdls) 2m 110y

1:40 (1:41) (Class 1) 4-Y-0+

£57,020 (£21,390; £10,710; £5,340; £2,680; £1,340)

Form				RPR
11	1		**Feathard Lady (IRE)**[23] 2650 5-11-0 ..... RWalsh (C A Murphy, Ire) *lengthy: settled in rr: prog after 3 out: led bef 2 out: readily drew clr bef last: shkn up and styd on strly flat: impress* **6/4**[1]	160+
2-04	2	12	**Self Defense**[30] 2500 8-11-7 149 ..... MickFitzgerald (Miss E C Lavelle) *lw: trckd ldrs: rdn and nt qckn bef 2 out: styd on to take 2nd last 100yds: no ch w wnr* **13/2**[3]	152
1325	3	3	**Royal Shakespeare (FR)**[16] 2761 6-11-7 152 ..... TomScudamore (S Gollings) *prom: pressed ldr fr 3rd: led briefly bef 2 out: mstke 2 out: no ch w wnr after: lost 2nd last 100yds* **12/1**	150+
1511	4	7	**Natal (FR)**[18] 2730 4-11-7 142 ..... (t) BJGeraghty (P F Nicholls) *pressed ldr to 3rd: styd wl in tch: effrt and cl up bef 2 out: hanging lft and sn btn* **8/1**	143+
3-3U	5	13	**Akilak (IRE)**[16] 2761 4-11-7 137 ..... TonyDobbin (J Howard Johnson) *hld up in rr: drvn after 5th: struggling sn after 3 out: wl btn bef next* **13/2**[3]	129
F-P4	6	2	**Cloudy Grey (IRE)**[23] 2636 8-11-7 135 ..... BarryFenton (Miss E C Lavelle) *racd wd: in tch to 5th: sn bhd* **20/1**	127
-2P2	7	1 ¼	**Intersky Falcon**[16] 2761 8-11-7 158 ..... (bt) APMcCoy (Jonjo O'Neill) *led at str pce: hdd bef 2 out: wkng whn blnd bdly 2 out* **7/2**[2]	131+

3m 55.3s (-13.60) **Going Correction** -0.325s/f (Good) **7** Ran SP% **112.5**

Speed ratings: **119,113,111,108,102 101,101** CSF £11.50 TOTE £2.20: £2.00, £3.10; EX 13.70.

Owner Lord of the Ring Syndicate **Bred** J C Condon **Trained** Gorey, Co Wexford

FOCUS

Not a great renewal, but Feathard Lady took another big step up in class readily in her stride and improved by around 13lb to a figure which puts her right in the picture for the Champion Hurdle with her mare's allowance. The runner-up ran his best race of the season, and the third ran to his Newcastle mark.

NOTEBOOK

Feathard Lady(IRE) ◆, stepping up in grade, maintained her unbeaten record in impressive fashion, scything through the field to strike the front going to the second last and soon coming well clear. A fine jumper who appears to act on most types of ground, she is a genuine Champion Hurdle contender but before then will take on stablemate Brave Inca in the Irish version. *(op 11-8 tchd 13-8)*

Self Defense could not go with the leading pair from the second last but stayed on well up the hill. He has a fine record here, having never been out of the first three in seven visits, and this was his best run of the campaign so far. *(tchd 7-1)*

Royal Shakespeare(FR), put in his place by the mare from the penultimate flight, where he made a mistake, was run out of second on the run-in. This was a sound effort but he really needs better ground. *(op 14-1)*

Natal(FR) ran respectably considering he is a novice and was taking on classy performers. *(op 17-2)*

Akilak(IRE) was always at the rear of the field and this was disappointing. The ground might have been against him. *(op 8-1)*

Cloudy Grey(IRE), the Lavelle second string, is normally a front-runner and he seemed to resent being held up. Although he was the first beaten, he was not entirely disgraced. *(op 25-1)*

Intersky Falcon, twice a winner of this event at Kempton, made the running at a good pace, but was collared on the run to the second last and already in fifth place when fortunate to stay on his feet at that obstacle. *(op 10-3)*

2972 STAN JAMES KING GEORGE VI CHASE GRADE 1 (20 fncs 2 omitted) 3m 110y

2:15 (2:20) (Class 1) 4-Y-0+

£114,040 (£42,780; £21,420; £10,680; £5,360; £2,680)

Form				RPR
-123	1		**Kicking King (IRE)**[37] 2337 7-11-10 ..... BJGeraghty (T J Taaffe, Ire) *trckd ldrs fr 8th: wnt 2nd briefly 13th: trckd ldr again 4 out: led 2 out: rdn last: jst hld on* **11/8**[1]	172+
1224	2	*nk*	**Monkerhostin (FR)**[23] 2635 8-11-10 154 ..... TomScudamore (P J Hobbs) *hld up in tch: nt fluent 11th: prog to trck ldng pair 3 out: rdn next: chsd wnr last: styd on strly flat: jst failed* **22/1**	171
2211	3	5	**Impek (FR)**[37] 2346 9-11-10 145 ..... APMcCoy (Miss H C Knight) *lw: led to 4th: led again 12th: rdn and hdd 2 out: one pce* **13/2**[3]	166
43-2	4	6	**L'Ami (FR)**[30] 2491 6-11-10 ..... TimmyMurphy (F Doumen, France) *lw: hld up in tch: cl enough 3 out: sn rdn: wnt 4th on long run to 2 out but sn outpcd: plugged on* **10/1**	160
F-51	5	9	**Royal Auclair (FR)**[17] 2744 8-11-10 155 ..... (t) RWalsh (P F Nicholls) *trckd ldng pair to 12th: styd chsng ldrs: rdn 3 out: fdd on long run bef next* **8/1**	152+
2-10	6	20	**Ollie Magern**[37] 2337 7-11-10 163 ..... CarlLlewellyn (N A Twiston-Davies) *w ldr: led 4th to 12th: upsides again 15th: wknd after 3 out* **11/1**	135+
1305	7	17	**Ballycassidy (IRE)**[17] 2744 9-11-10 145 ..... BarryFenton (P Bowen) *lw: nt fluent 1st and sn detached in last: jst in tch 10th: bhd again fr 12th: continued t.o* **100/1**	114
P/3-	P		**Irish Hussar (IRE)**[286] 4384 9-11-10 153 ..... MickFitzgerald (N J Henderson) *fit: wl in tch tl wknd rapidly 17th: t.o whn p.u bef 2 out* **28/1**	—
-421	P		**Kingscliff (IRE)**[37] 2337 8-11-10 162 ..... TonyDobbin (R H Alner) *lw: trckd ldrs: blnd 10th and dropped to last pair: nvr gng wl after: t.o fr 13th: mstke 4 out: p.u bef 2 out* **10/3**[2]	—

6m 11.9s (-19.60) **Going Correction** -0.325s/f (Good) **9** Ran SP% **115.8**

Speed ratings: **118,117,116,114,111 105,99,—,—** CSF £32.12 TOTE £2.30: £1.70, £3.60, £2.00; EX 44.50 Trifecta £239.50 Pool: £7,727.03 - 22.90 winning tickets..

Owner Conor Clarkson **Bred** Sunnyhill Stud **Trained** Straffan, Co Kildare

■ Stewards' Enquiry : Tom Scudamore one-day ban: used whip out of stride pattern (Jan 6)

FOCUS

The Pond fence was omitted on both circuits because of the low sun. The strong early pace slackened off and allowed the field to bunch up passing the stands for the first time before it picked up again down the far side. Kicking King failed to reproduce the level of form he showed at Kempton or Cheltenham last season and has been assessed 4lb below the 10-year average winning mark for the King George. Monkerhostin showed career best form at the longer trip in second, but he did not improve as much as first impressions suggest.

The Form Book, Raceform Ltd, Compton, RG20 6NL

NOTEBOOK

Kicking King(IRE), who had excuses for his two defeats this autumn, returned to winning ways to land his second King George but was around 7lb below the form he showed at Kempton a year ago. Travelling strongly and jumping with great fluency, he eased to the front at the second last but could never get more than a length or so clear, and in the end the line only just arrived in time as Monkerhostin closed him down fast up the hill. His preparation for this was somewhat rushed as he recovered from pricking a foot at Haydock, and he remains the one to beat at Cheltenham again in March, when he should be in the peak of condition. *(op 6-4 tchd 13-8 in places)*

Monkerhostin(FR) had 11lb to find on Racing Post Ratings and was running over this trip for the first time over fences, having landed last year's Rendlesham Hurdle on his only previous run at around three miles. Travelling well under a patient ride from Scudamore, a late replacement for the injured Richard Johnson, he was asked to go after the favourite at the second last. Not as fluent as Kicking King over the final fence, he stayed on very strongly up the hill and would have got there with a little further to run. On this evidence the longer trip at Cheltenham would not be a problem and the Gold Cup looks the logical target now, while connections will also be mindful of his position at the top of the BHB's Order of Merit. *(op 25-1)*

Impek(FR), always up with the pace, was back in front at the twelfth but could not repel the winner's challenge at the second last, fading in the end as the trip in this company told. He is more likely to go for the Ryanair Chase over two miles five furlongs at the Festival than the Gold Cup. *(op 7-1 tchd 15-2)*

L'Ami(FR), bidding to give his trainer his sixth King George winner, ran well for a long way but could not match the leaders for pace on the long run past the omitted Pond fence. Still only six, he is capable of further improvement. Interestingly, his performance suggested that Trabolgan, who beat him in the Hennessy, would have gone close here. *(op 11-1 tchd 12-1)*

Royal Auclair(FR) became outpaced as the pace hotted up over the Railway fences on the final circuit and he lost touch with the principals on the extended run to the second last. He is ideally suited by a stiffer test. *(op 11-1tchd 12-1 in a place)*

Ollie Magern, taken on for the lead by Impek, eventually dropped away turning out of the back straight. He is at his best when able to dominate. *(op 10-1)*

Ballycassidy(IRE) was taken off his feet in the early stages. He did close to race in touch with a circuit to run but was soon dropped again. *(op 66-1)*

Irish Hussar(IRE), who looked fit for this first run since the Cheltenham Festival, was on the scene until dropping out of contention quickly towards the end of the back straight. *(op 33-1 tchd 25-1)*

Kingscliff(IRE), attempting leg two of a potential £1m treble, travelled well enough until leaving his hind legs in the open ditch with a circuit to run, from which point he was struggling. Eventually *pulled up, he suffered cuts to his hind legs but was essentially sound after the race.Official explanation: jockey said gelding made mistake at 10th fence first time around and was never travelling thereafter; vet said gelding suffered cuts to hind legs (op 33-1 tchd 25-1)*

2973 STAN JAMES FELTHAM NOVICES' CHASE GRADE 1 (20 fncs 2 omitted) 3m 110y

2:50 (2:55) (Class 1) 4-Y-0+ **£39,914** (£14,973; £7,497; £3,738; £1,876)

Form				RPR
1211	**1**		**Darkness**[17] 2743 6-11-7 154 ... APMcCoy (C R Egerton) *several minor errors and nvr looked to be gng wl: mostly 4th: drvn and in trble after 3 out: rallied fr next: r.o to ld las* **13/8**[1]	148+
3412	**2**	3	**Zabenz (NZ)**[17] 2743 8-11-7 ... (b) RWalsh (P J Hobbs) *lw: pressed ldr: nt fluent 5th: effrt to ld 3 out: pckd 2 out: sn hrd rdn: hdd and outpcd last 150yds* **8/1**	143+
P-12	**3**	hd	**Bewleys Berry (IRE)**[16] 2759 7-11-7 ... TonyDobbin (J Howard Johnson) *lw: led: hdd and nt qckn 3 out: rallied next: drvn to chal last: one pce flat* **7/2**[3]	143+
1	**4**	25	**Crozan (FR)**[44] 2174 5-11-7 ... MickFitzgerald (N J Henderson) *nt a fluent in 3rd: mstke 13th: effrt after 3 out: cl 3rd whn mstke 2 out: btn whn mstke last: wknd and eased* **2/1**[2]	132+
4111	**5**	dist	**State Of Play**[36] 2375 5-11-7 128 ... PaulMoloney (Evan Williams) *nt fluent: mostly in last: stl in tch after 3 out: sn wknd: no ch whn stmbld bdly 2 out: t.o* **20/1**	—

6m 16.2s (-15.30) **Going Correction** -0.325s/f (Good) **5** Ran SP% **109.5**
Speed ratings: **111,110,109,101,**— CSF £13.28 TOTE £2.30: £1.50, £2.60; EX 12.00.
Owner Lady Lloyd-Webber **Bred** Heatherwold Stud **Trained** Chaddleworth, Berks

FOCUS

The Pond Fence was omitted on both circuits. The winner has been rated 8lb off his Cheltenham mark in this slightly below average renewal of the Feltham, which has been rated through the second and third. Crozan was 15lb off his Cheltenham mark.

NOTEBOOK

Darkness, the clear form choice, was below-par in notching his fourth win in five starts over fences. Putting in a sticky round of jumping and looking beaten leaving the back straight, he was still only third over the last but swept through on the uphill run-in to win going away. Probably happier going left-handed, he is unlikely to run again before the Royal & SunAlliance. *(op 7-4 tchd 15-8 in places)*

Zabenz(NZ), always in the first two but unable to have his own way in front, went on at the last in the back straight. He was still in front over the final fence, but was cut down by the favourite up the hill and only just held on for second. This was a solid run. *(op 14-1)*

Bewleys Berry(IRE), back up in trip, set a steady pace until collared at the last down the far side. Rallying in the straight, he was held at the final fence but stayed on up the hill and would have been second with a bit further to run. He looks a real stayer. *(op 7-2 tchd 4-1)*

Crozan(FR), whose Cheltenham win has worked out really well, was a disappointment. A mistake in the back straight first set the alarm bells ringing and another error two from home ended his chance. The longer trip was not the sole reason for this lacklustre run and he is better than this. *(op 6-4)*

State Of Play had a lot to find on official figures. Always at the rear of the field, he was still in touch turning out of the back straight but was soon in trouble and was well adrift when nearly coming down at the second last. *(op 20-1)*

2974 STANSPOKER.CO.UK H'CAP HURDLE (9 hdls) 2m 4f 110y

3:25 (3:31) (Class 3) (0-135,135) 4-Y-0+

£6,717 (£1,984; £992; £496; £247; £124)

Form				RPR
-245	**1**		**Afrad (FR)**[30] 2493 4-11-4 127 ... BJGeraghty (N J Henderson) *t.k.h early: prom: led bef 2 out: pushed clr bef last: eased fnl 75yds* **6/1**[2]	144+
05-3	**2**	5	**Only Vintage (USA)**[30] 2493 5-11-12 135 ... TimmyMurphy (Miss H C Knight) *lw: mostly chsd ldr: led briefly bef 2 out: no ch w wnr sn after 2 out: hld on for 2nd* **4/1**[1]	140+
2/33	**3**	1 ¾	**Pepe Galvez (SWE)**[29] 2533 8-10-12 121 ... APMcCoy (Mrs L C Taylor) *settled midfield: effrt after 3 out: rdn to chse ldng pair 2 out: kpt on same pce* **6/1**[2]	123
60-P	**4**	2 ½	**Back To Ben Alder (IRE)**[233] 207 8-10-11 120 ... MickFitzgerald (N J Henderson) *mstke 2nd: hld up in tch: rdn sn after 3 out: outpcd and btn bef next: plugged on* **6/1**[2]	120
1243	**5**	1 ½	**Mouseski**[23] 2621 11-10-9 118 ... RWalsh (P F Nicholls) *trckd ldrs: lost pl after 3rd: sn detached in last: t.o 3 out: styd on again fr 2 out* **13/2**[3]	116
1P02	**6**	14	**Nonantais (FR)**[23] 2633 8-10-13 129 ... PatrickCStringer[(7)] (M Bradstock) *led and sn 5l clr: hdd & wknd bef 2 out* **16/1**	117+
	7	16	**Sunrise Spirit (FR)**[15] 4-10-6 120 ow5 ... ADuchene[(5)] (F Doumen, France) *t.k.h early: cl up: rdn and outpcd in 4th pl sn after 2 out: wknd bdly: virtually p.u nr fin* **8/1**	108+
32-3	**P**		**Greenfield (IRE)**[13] 2813 7-10-9 118 ... (b) PaulMoloney (R T Phillips) *t.k.h early: hit 1st: prom: wkng rapidly whn mstke 6th: wl t.o whn p.u bef 2 out* **7/1**	—
P-P2	**P**		**Tana River (IRE)**[13] 2813 9-11-6 129 ... BarryFenton (Miss E C Lavelle) *hld up in rr: terrible blunder 3rd: rdn and lost tch bef 3 out: sn t.o: p.u bef last* **12/1**	—

5m 1.70s (-11.70) **Going Correction** -0.325s/f (Good)
WFA 4 from 5yo+ 11lb **9** Ran SP% **113.4**
Speed ratings: **109,107,106,105,104 99,93,**—,— CSF £30.18 CT £149.30 TOTE £6.70: £2.20, £1.80, £2.40; EX 35.30 Place 6 £75.12, Place 5 £8.02.
Owner The Not Afraid Partnership **Bred** S A Aga Khan **Trained** Upper Lambourn, Berks

FOCUS

A decent handicap in which the winner has been rated as value for 12l with a performance in line with his improved Flat form. The next four were all close to their marks.

NOTEBOOK

Afrad(FR), whose attitude was called into question after his defeat at Newbury, had not tackled this far over hurdles before but he is a winner at around this trip on the Flat. Coming clear pretty effortlessly between the last two flights, he was eased down with his race won on the run-in, allowing the second and third to close. He picks up a 4lb penalty for the Ladbroke here next month, back at two miles. *(op 9-2)*

Only Vintage(USA) beat today's winner just under three lengths at Newbury last time and was 2lb worse off here. Always prominent, he was in front for a few strides going to the second last but the winner soon eased away from him and he was flattered to be beaten only five lengths in the end. *(tchd 9-2 in places)*

Pepe Galvez(SWE), keeping on at the end over this longer trip, has now run three solid races since returning after missing the 2004/5 campaign. *(op 7-1)*

Back To Ben Alder(IRE), a stablemate of the winner, ran a respectable race on his first start since May, finding a second wind after looking well held turning into the home straight. *(tchd 13-2)*

Mouseski, the first beaten, was staying on past beaten rivals at the end. He needs a stiffer test but looks too high in the weights at the moment. *(op 15-2 tchd 6-1)*

Nonantais(FR), raised 7lb after finishing second over further here earlier in the month, held a clear lead for a good deal of the way but was headed early in the home straight and weakened pretty tamely. *(op 20-1)*

Sunrise Spirit(FR), whose rider's claim was cancelled out by the overweight, looked like making the frame on the approach to the final flight but he weakened badly. *(op 15-2)*

Greenfield(IRE) *Official explanation: trainer said gelding had a breathing problem (op 16-1)*

Tana River(IRE) *Official explanation: jockey said gelding was never travelling (op 16-1)*

T/Jkpt: £12,318.30 to a £1 stake. Pool: £34,699.50. 2.00 winning tickets. T/Plt: £190.10 to a £1 stake. Pool: £128,928.10. 495.05 winning tickets. T/Qpdt: £8.90 to a £1 stake. Pool: £7,714.00. 635.60 winning tickets. JN

2688 SEDGEFIELD (L-H)

Monday, December 26

OFFICIAL GOING: Soft

Wind: Light, half-against

2975 32RED.COM BEGINNERS' CHASE (DIV I) (16 fncs) 2m 5f

12:20 (12:20) (Class 4) 4-Y-0+ **£3,783** (£1,110; £555; £277)

Form				RPR
122	**1**		**New Alco (FR)**[16] 2764 4-10-2 ... ThomasDreaper[(5)] (Ferdy Murphy) *led to 2nd: w ldrs: led after 4 out: drew clr bef 2 out: easily* **8/15**[1]	111+
-23P	**2**	17	**Dark Ben (FR)**[48] 2110 5-10-13 ... DougieCostello[(5)] (Miss Kate Milligan) *a.p: hdwy 1/2-way: rdn after 4 out: chsd wnr last: no imp* **17/2**[3]	97
PP-0	**3**	¾	**Kingfisher Sunset**[26] 2566 9-10-11 85 ... NickCarter[(7)] (Mrs S J Smith) *cl up: led 2nd: hit 10th: hdd after 4 out: one pce fr next* **100/1**	96
45-0	**4**	5	**Mr Prickle (IRE)**[212] 545 5-11-4 90 ... AnthonyRoss (P Beaumont) *hld up: stdy hdwy bef 4 out: rdn after next: sn no imp* **25/1**	91
0425	**5**	14	**Le Royal (FR)**[9] 2874 6-10-11 98 ... PhilKinsella[(7)] (K G Reveley) *in tch: lost pl whn nt fluent 9th: n.d after* **8/1**[2]	77
30B0	**6**	½	**Fairy Skin Maker (IRE)**[11] 2840 7-11-1 ... GaryBerridge[(3)] (G A Harker) *hld up: rdn after 10th: nvr rchd ldrs* **9/1**	79+
0/3U	**7**	1 ¼	**More Flair**[11] 2839 8-10-4 ... BenOrde-Powlett[(7)] (J B Walton) *chsd ldrs: mstke 12th: sn rdn: wknd fr 3 out* **100/1**	73+
00-0	**8**	18	**Valeureux**[17] 2590 7-11-1 ... PaddyAspell[(3)] (J Hetherton) *hld up in tch: hdwy to chse ldrs 5th: wknd 10th* **20/1**	58
0P40	**P**		**Cody**[52] 2025 6-11-4 ... (p) FinbarKeniry (James Moffatt) *chsd ldrs to 1/2-way: sn lost pl: t.o whn p.u bef 3 out* **40/1**	—
1-0P	**P**		**Kings Square**[16] 2764 5-11-4 83 ... AlanDempsey (M W Easterby) *hld up: hdwy 1/2-way: outpcd whn hit 11th: t.o whn p.u bef 2 out* **40/1**	—

5m 32.3s (8.90) **Going Correction** +0.475s/f (Soft)
WFA 4 from 5yo+ 11lb **10** Ran SP% **112.3**
Speed ratings: **102,95,95,93,88 87,87,80,**—,— CSF £4.85 TOTE £2.20: £1.20, £1.50, £13.50; EX 6.70.
Owner D McGowan and S Murphy **Bred** Vicomte Roger De Soultrait **Trained** West Witton, N Yorks

FOCUS

Little strength in depth but the winner, who won with plenty in hand, being value for 25 lengths, and looks the type to progress over fences.

NOTEBOOK

New Alco(FR) ◆, upped further in trip, jumped soundly and turned in his best effort over fences. Although this was not much of a race, there was plenty to like about the manner of the win and he is the type to hold his own in better company. *(op 8-13)*

Dark Ben(FR), a 112-rated hurdler, jumped soundly and shaped well on this chasing debut. Although he may remain vulnerable to the better types in this sort of race, he showed more than enough to suggest he can win over the larger obstacles. *(op 8-1 tchd 9-1)*

Kingfisher Sunset, whose form over obstacles has been very patchy, ran arguably his best race returned to fences. His proximity confirms this bare form is nothing special but he may do better over further in modest handicaps. *(op 66-1)*

Mr Prickle(IRE), who has been a keen type in the past, travelled well under restraint for a long way on this chasing debut and first run since May and he is another that may do better in ordinary handicap company.

Le Royal(FR), still not foot-perfect, was again below the pick of his hurdles form and he looks one to tread carefully with at present. *(op 15-2)*

Fairy Skin Maker(IRE), a hurdle winner over this trip at this course, was again disappointing returned to the larger obstacles and, although it is too early to be writing him off, he does not look anywhere near as effective in this sphere.

2976 32RED.COM BEGINNERS' CHASE (DIV II) (14 fncs 2 omitted) 2m 5f
12:50 (12:53) (Class 4) 4-Y-0+ **£3,783** (£1,110; £555; £277)

Form RPR
132- **1** **Kinburn (IRE)**[400] [2359] 6-11-4 101 .... AlanDempsey 125+
(J Howard Johnson) *mde all: styd on strly to go clr bef 2 out* **3/1**[1]
322- **2** *17* **Ryders Storm (USA)**[403] [2295] 6-11-1 110 .... PaddyAspell(3) 108
(Mrs S J Smith) *prom: rdn 4 out: chsd wnr bef 2 out: no imp* **5/1**[3]
2-3F **3** *13* **Kitski (FR)**[39] [2294] 7-10-13 113 .... ThomasDreaper(5) 97+
(Ferdy Murphy) *nt fluent: hld up: hdwy and prom 3 out: wknd bef next* **4/1**[2]
4201 **4** *5* **River Mist (IRE)**[11] [2840] 6-10-11 .... WilsonRenwick 86+
(Karen McLintock) *bhd: blnd 2nd: rdn whn hit 10th: n.d* **6/1**
2104 **5** *11* **Emmasflora**[30] [2501] 7-10-6 105 .... AdamPogson(5) 72
(C T Pogson) *chsd ldrs to 9th: sn wknd* **12/1**
2546 **6** *7* **Rifleman (IRE)**[29] [2523] 5-10-13 .... (t) StephenCraine(5) 76+
(Robert Gray) *prom: chsd wnr 1/2-way to bef 2 out: wknd* **20/1**
0/ **7** *12* **Le Millenaire (FR)**[238] 6-10-13 .... MichaelMcAlister(5) 60
(S H Shirley-Beavan) *nt jump wl: bhd after blunder at 2nd: no ch fr 1/2-way* **33/1**
62R4 **P** **Iris's Prince**[33] [2441] 6-10-13 109 .... DougieCostello(5) —
(A Crook) *a bhd: t.o whn p.u bef 2 out* **20/1**
6-F0 **P** **Beamish Prince**[44] [2190] 6-11-4 115 .... FinbarKeniry —
(G M Moore) *cl up: tl wknd 7th: t.o whn p.u 9th* **12/1**
12-4 **P** **Kimbambo (FR)**[65] [1835] 7-11-1 .... GaryBerridge(3) —
(J P L Ewart) *prom: outpcd bef 10th: sn wknd: t.o whn p.u bef last* **6/1**
00/4 **P** **Been Here Before**[11] [2839] 5-10-11 .... PhilKinsella(7) —
(G A Harker) *midfield: struggling 10th: t.o whn p.u bef 2 out* **12/1**

5m 29.1s (5.70) **Going Correction** +0.475s/f (Soft) **11** Ran SP% **125.8**
Speed ratings: **108,101,96,94,90 87,83,—,—,— —** CSF £19.60 TOTE £4.80: £2.50, £3.00, £2.70; EX 26.00.
Owner W M G Black **Bred** Mrs A Kirkwood **Trained** Billy Row, Co Durham

FOCUS
Another race lacking strength but, as in the first division, an easy winner in a decent time who looks the type to hold his own in better company.

NOTEBOOK
Kinburn(IRE) ◆, a steadily progressive hurdler last year, always looked the sort to do better over fences and created a favourable impression on this chasing debut and first run after a long break. He jumped soundly, will be suited by the return to three miles and is the type to win again. *(op 4-1)*
Ryders Storm(USA) was no match for a potentially fair sort but showed enough on this first start for over a year to suggest an ordinary handicap could be found, especially when upped to three miles. *(op 9-2)*
Kitski(FR), who took a heavy fall at Market Rasen, is still far from the finished article in the jumping department and was disappointing after looking threatening at the end of the back straight. He is not one to write off just yet, though.
River Mist(IRE), a dual winner over hurdles this year, will have to jump with a lot more fluency than she did on her chasing debut this time if she is to win races in this sphere. *(op 7-1)*
Emmasflora, who had run creditably on three of her four starts this term, did not get home over this trip on this chasing debut and is likely to continue to look vulnerable in this type of event.
Rifleman(IRE), a frustrating maiden hurdler, travelled in his customary strong fashion for a long way but did not get home in the conditions on this chasing debut. Although less of a test may help, *he is not one to place much faith in. Official explanation: jockey said gelding had a breathing problem*
Beamish Prince *Official explanation: vet said gelding bled from nose (op 16-1)*
Been Here Before *Official explanation: jockey said gelding was never travelling (op 16-1)*

2977 HAPPY 40TH BIRTHDAY STUART TAYLOR CONDITIONAL JOCKEYS' H'CAP HURDLE (10 hdls) 2m 5f 110y
1:25 (1:25) (Class 4) (0-105,104) 3-Y-0+ **£3,194** (£937; £468; £234)

Form RPR
2613 **1** **Chickapeakray**[22] [2653] 4-9-13 80 .... StephenCraine(3) 93+
(D McCain) *cl up: led bef 3 out: clr bef next: pressed last: kpt on wl* **9/1**
3-34 **2** *1* **Zaffaran Express (IRE)**[53] [2004] 6-11-4 104 .... EwanWhillans(8) 114
(N G Richards) *hld up: hdwy u.p bef 3 out: chsd wnr bef next: hung lft bef last: kpt on fr last* **5/1**[3]
5415 **3** *7* **Villago (GER)**[20] [2691] 5-11-1 93 .... GaryBerridge 96
(E W Tuer) *hld up: drvn after 4 out: rallied bef 2 out: sn one pce* **4/1**[2]
5534 **4** *14* **True Temper (IRE)**[23] [2639] 8-10-1 79 .... DeclanMcGann 68
(A M Crow) *hld up: drvn 4 out: sme late hdwy: nvr rchd ldrs* **20/1**
1465 **5** *¾* **Red Man (IRE)**[26] [2566] 8-11-4 104 .... StevenGagan(8) 93+
(Mrs E Slack) *led to bef 3 out: wknd bef next* **10/1**
5424 **6** *½* **Water Taxi**[11] [2840] 4-11-7 102 .... ThomasDreaper(3) 90
(Ferdy Murphy) *hld up: hdwy to chse ldrs bef 3 out: rdn and wknd bef next* **6/1**
-PP0 **7** *5* **Darab (POL)**[11] [2840] 5-10-7 95 .... MichaelO'Connell(10) 78
(Mrs S J Smith) *midfield: reminders 4th: outpcd next: no ch after* **25/1**
13P **8** *1 ¼* **Alfy Rich**[11] [2841] 9-11-3 95 .... (t) PaddyAspell 77
(M Todhunter) *hld up in tch: rdn after 4 out: wknd bef next* **16/1**
5-22 **9** *2* **San Peire (FR)**[20] [2691] 8-11-3 98 .... BrianHughes(3) 78
(J Howard Johnson) *chsd ldrs tl dropped rr 5th: sn n.d* **5/2**[1]
3U **10** *18* **Astronaut**[39] [2290] 8-10-0 88 .... JohnFlavin(10) 50
(R C Guest) *midfield: rdn bef 3 out: sn btn* **16/1**
600- **11** *dist* **Baby Sister**[250] [4923] 6-9-11 85 .... GarryWhillans(10) —
(D W Whillans) *keen: chsd ldrs to 4 out: sn rdn and btn* **25/1**
040P **P** **I'm Your Man**[20] [2689] 6-11-0 92 .... DougieCostello —
(Mrs Dianne Sayer) *a bhd: t.o whn p.u after 4 out* **66/1**
U63 **P** **Nowa Huta (FR)**[21] [2674] 4-10-11 92 .... BenOrde-Powlett(3) —
(Jedd O'Keeffe) *chsd ldrs tl wknd bef 3 out: t.o whn p.u bef next* **20/1**

5m 31.9s (16.20) **Going Correction** +0.65s/f (Soft) **13** Ran SP% **129.1**
Speed ratings: **96,95,93,88,87 87,85,85,84,78** —,—,— CSF £55.21 CT £219.39 TOTE £11.50: £2.60, £2.80, £1.70; EX 88.20.
Owner Ray Pattison **Bred** J Singleton **Trained** Cholmondeley, Cheshire
■ Stewards' Enquiry : Ewan Whillans caution: used whip in the incorrect position
Stephen Craine two-day ban: used whip with excessive force (Jan 6, 17)

FOCUS
An ordinary handicap but one in which the pace was sound and this bare form, rated through the runner-up, should prove reliable.

NOTEBOOK
Chickapeakray seems a tough sort who showed the right attitude in the closing stages to record her second win over hurdles. She will go up in the weights again for this but should continue to go well away from progressive sorts. *(op 10-1)*
Zaffaran Express(IRE) has had problems with her jumping but fared better in that department this time and ran up to her best over hurdles. She pulled clear of the remainder and can win a similar event away from progressive sorts when her jumping holds up. *(op 9-2)*
Villago(GER) back in trip to the distance he scored over in November, was not disgraced, but on *this occasion he left the impression that a stiffer test of stamina would have been in his favour. (op 9-2 tchd 5-1)*
True Temper(IRE), an inconsistent maiden hurdler, was again below the level she showed at Kelso in October and she remains one to tread carefully with until she has put her head in front where it matters. *(op 18-1)*
Red Man(IRE), back on a soft surface, was again below the pick of his efforts over hurdles and consistency remains his weak point. *(op 12-1)*
Water Taxi, back in distance but on softer ground, again failed to get home having travelled strongly for a long way and, although capable of winning an ordinary event, he looks one to have a few reservations about at present. *(op 7-1)*
San Peire(FR) ran as though still feeling the effects of a very hard race over three miles and three *furlongs in bad ground at this course last time, and he is not one to write off just yet. Official explanation: jockey said gelding was never travelling (op 3-1)*

2978 32RED ONLINE CASINO H'CAP CHASE (21 fncs) 3m 3f
1:55 (1:55) (Class 4) (0-95,95) 5-Y-0+ **£3,763** (£1,104; £552; £275)

Form RPR
041F **1** **Bang And Blame (IRE)**[25] [2589] 9-10-4 78 .... MichaelMcAlister(5) 104+
(M W Easterby) *mde all: clr 13th: unchal* **6/1**[3]
5-14 **2** *23* **Getinbybutonlyjust**[40] [2266] 6-11-5 93 .... DougieCostello(5) 94
(Mrs Dianne Sayer) *hld up: hdwy 7th: outpcd 12th: rallied to chse wnr run in: no imp* **11/2**[2]
P/1F **3** *3* **Twotiming Gent (IRE)**[51] [2039] 12-10-0 69 .... AnthonyRoss 70+
(P D Niven) *a cl up: rdn 4 out: wknd after 2 out: lost 2nd run in* **10/1**
-013 **4** *4* **Celtic Flow**[34] [2413] 7-9-9 69 oh3 .... BrianHughes(5) 65+
(C R Wilson) *prom: outpcd 14th: n.d after* **6/1**[3]
-P6P **P** **Fifteen Reds**[32] [2449] 10-10-0 76 ow1 .... EwanWhillans(7) —
(J C Haynes) *a bhd: t.o whn p.u 12th* **33/1**
6-PF **P** **Missoudun (FR)**[48] [2109] 5-10-5 81 .... PhilKinsella(7) —
(J R Weymes) *a bhd: t.o whn p.u after 15th* **25/1**
0P-0 **P** **Celia's High (IRE)**[22] [2653] 6-9-11 71 .... (t) StephenCraine(5) —
(D McCain) *a bhd: t.o whn p.u bef 17th* **16/1**
522P **U** **Farington Lodge (IRE)**[131] [1232] 7-10-10 86 .... NickCarter(7) —
(Mrs S J Smith) *cl up whn mstke and uns rdr 10th* **7/1**
F0P **P** **Roman Rebel**[40] [2266] 6-11-12 95 .... AlanDempsey —
(Mrs K Walton) *prom to 1/2-way: sn wknd: t.o whn p.u appr 4 out* **14/1**
14P- **P** **Recent Edition (IRE)**[253] [4875] 7-11-1 87 .... (p) PaddyAspell(3) —
(J Wade) *chsd ldrs to 15th: sn wknd: t.o whn p.u bef 3 out* **10/1**
10-P **P** **Jumbo's Dream**[52] [2022] 14-10-0 74 .... (p) DeclanMcGann(5) —
(J E Dixon) *chsd ldrs tl lost pl qckly 6th: t.o whn p.u after 13th* **25/1**
64 **P** **Place Above (IRE)**[29] [2524] 9-11-11 94 .... WilsonRenwick —
(E A Elliott) *midfield: reminders 4th: sn lost pl: t.o whn p.u bef 12th* **10/1**
31UU **P** **Dark Thunder (IRE)**[34] [2413] 8-10-4 78 .... (b) ThomasDreaper(5) —
(Ferdy Murphy) *hld up: hdwy bef 12th: wknd 14th: t.o whn p.u bef 3 out* **4/1**[1]

7m 18.1s (11.30) **Going Correction** +0.475s/f (Soft) **13** Ran SP% **126.9**
Speed ratings: **102,95,94,93,**— —,—,—,—,— —,—,— CSF £41.71 CT £339.81 TOTE £4.70: £2.00, £2.40, £8.70; EX 43.50.
Owner Edward C Wilkin **Bred** Miss Sandra Hunter **Trained** Sheriff Hutton, N Yorks

FOCUS
A run-of-the-mill handicap but a decent gallop ensured this was a thorough test of stamina in the conditions. The form is rated through the runner-up but could be too high.

NOTEBOOK
Bang And Blame(IRE) jumped soundly and showed himself none-the-worse for his latest fall to notch his second course and distance win from his last three starts. Stamina is his strong suit and, although he will go up in the weights for this, he may be capable of winning another ordinary event when the emphasis is on stamina. *(op 5-1)*
Getinbybutonlyjust, having only his second run over fences, turned in a laboured effort and never really threatened at any stage. A similar trip at a more galloping course may help, though, and he is not one to write off just yet. *(op 5-1)*
Twotiming Gent(IRE), another coming here on the back of a fall, jumped soundly in the main and, although he did not get home in the conditions, he should be placed to best advantage around three miles on less testing ground this winter. *(op 8-1)*
Celtic Flow, who won a poor race over course and distance in October, was 3lb out of the handicap and finished a bit further behind the winner than she had done at this course last time. She may be suited by less testing ground. *(op 5-1)*
Dark Thunder(IRE) seems to reserve his best form for this course and was closely matched with the winner on a recent run. Although getting round this time, he proved disappointing after a brief splutter and is not one for maximum faith.

2979 PLAY ROULETTE AT 32RED NOVICES' HURDLE (13 hdls) 3m 3f 110y
2:25 (2:25) (Class 4) 4-Y-0+ **£3,402** (£998; £499; £249)

Form RPR
1 **1** **Ivoire De Beaulieu (FR)**[17] [2745] 9-10-7 .... ThomasDreaper(5) 105+
(Ferdy Murphy) *hld up: smooth hdwy to ld after 3 out: rdn next: hld on wl fr last* **4/6**[1]
3500 **2** *¾* **Toni Alcala**[20] [2691] 6-10-9 95 .... PaddyAspell(3) 101
(R F Fisher) *in tch: outpcd appr 3 out: rallied and chsd wnr next: kpt on fr last: hld towards fin* **14/1**
3623 **3** *12* **Nevada Red**[32] [2450] 4-10-7 101 .... StephenCraine(5) 91+
(D McCain) *chsd ldrs: ev ch 3 out: no ex bef next* **6/1**[2]
4 **4** *1* **Bramble Princess (IRE)**[21] [2678] 6-10-5 .... WilsonRenwick 81
(Miss Lucinda V Russell) *led to 3 out: sn one pce* **33/1**
0-55 **5** *½* **Scotmail Too (IRE)**[20] [2690] 4-10-7 116 .... BrianHughes(5) 88
(J Howard Johnson) *hld up: hdwy to ld briefly 3 out: wknd bef next* **8/1**[3]
3-04 **6** *28* **Major Catch (IRE)**[10] [2859] 6-10-7 110 .... AdamPogson(5) 60
(C T Pogson) *chsd ldrs to 3 out: sn wknd* **6/1**[2]
05 **7** *13* **Doris's Gift**[30] [2497] 4-10-12 .... AlanDempsey 47
(J Howard Johnson) *hld up: outpcd 4 out: sn btn* **20/1**
-0PP **8** *dist* **Inmate (IRE)**[57] [1938] 4-10-9 .... GaryBerridge(3) —
(Mrs E Slack) *a bhd: struggling fnl circ* **50/1**
0-5 **P** **I'm No Fairy**[21] [2678] 6-10-12 .... AnthonyRoss —
(P Beaumont) *chsd ldrs tl wknd bef 9th: p.u after next* **50/1**

7m 21.5s (17.60) **Going Correction** +0.65s/f (Soft) **9** Ran SP% **118.0**
Speed ratings: **100,99,96,96,95 87,84,**—,— CSF £11.68 TOTE £2.10: £1.50, £3.70, £1.50; EX 300.10.
Owner I Todd F Murphy **Bred** Xavier Blois **Trained** West Witton, N Yorks

FOCUS
Another race lacking strength in depth and one in which the pace was just ordinary. The winner offers the best guide to the level of the form and the winner should be able to score again over hurdles.

NOTEBOOK
Ivoire De Beaulieu(FR) ◆, reverting to hurdles after a useful performance in a cross-country chase last time, did not have to reproduce that form to beat a 95-rated rival back over hurdles. However, he travelled strongly for a long way and, although his main targets this year are in the cross-country races at the big Festivals, he can win again over hurdles.

Toni Alcala, who has become frustrating on the Flat, returned to something like his best back over hurdles but, given his losing run, would not be one to take too short a price about under either code next time.
Nevada Red had no problems with the longer distance in a race run at just an ordinary gallop, but he remains the type to do better in ordinary handicap company in due course. *(op 9-2)*
Bramble Princess(IRE) had the run of the race and was not disgraced but is another that is likely to remain vulnerable to the more progressive types in this grade.
Scotmail Too(IRE) is in good hands and, although seeming to find this trip too far on this occasion, may do better in modest handicaps in the North.
Major Catch(IRE) could have been expected to fare better in this company and, while he may not have lasted home over this trip in the ground, he may not be one to make too many excuses for. *(op 7-1)*

2980 32RED.COM H'CAP CHASE (13 fncs) 2m 110y
2:55 (2:55) (Class 4) (0-105,97) 4-Y-0+ **£4,453** (£1,307; £653; £326)

Form RPR
1PU0 **1** **Longdale**[11] [2842] 7-11-9 **94** AlanDempsey 108+
(M Todhunter) *hld up: smooth hdwy 4 out: led between last two: hung lft: kpt on fr last* **33/1**
P/P6 **2** *¾* **Gohh**[26] [2570] 9-10-8 **79** (t) WilsonRenwick 90+
(M W Easterby) *hld up: effrt after 3 out: rallied to chse wnr run in: edgd lft: r.o* **4/1**[2]
012F **3** *5* **Loulou Nivernais (FR)**[22] [2655] 6-11-6 **96** ThomasDreaper[(5)] 102+
(Robert Gray) *j.w: led to between last two: no ex* **5/4**[1]
P56 **4** *19* **Little Flora**[40] [2267] 9-10-13 **89** MichaelMcAlister[(5)] 75
(S J Marshall) *chsd ldrs tl wknd fr 3 out* **7/1**
-44U **5** *2* **Ipledgeallegiance (USA)**[21] [2677] 9-10-11 **85** PaddyAspell[(3)] 69
(Miss Tracy Waggott) *prom to 4 out: sn wknd* **10/1**
PP3U **6** *hd* **Twist N Turn**[22] [2655] 5-9-11 **73** StephenCraine[(5)] 59+
(D McCain) *chsd ldrs tl wknd fr 3 out* **11/2**[3]
3235 **7** *dist* **Humid Climate**[11] [2839] 5-11-12 **97** AnthonyRoss —
(R A Fahey) *in tch to 8th: sn wknd* **7/1**
456P **8** *22* **Brave Effect (IRE)**[20] [2691] 9-11-1 **91** DougieCostello[(5)] —
(Mrs Dianne Sayer) *a bhd: lost tch fr 1/2-way* **14/1**

4m 28.9s (14.70) **Going Correction** +0.475s/f (Soft) **8** Ran SP% **123.5**
Speed ratings: **84,83,81,72,71 71,—,—** CSF £174.12 CT £303.79 TOTE £36.20: £4.70, £2.30, £1.70; EX 92.80.
Owner David Curr **Bred** David Curr **Trained** Orton, Cumbria
■ Stewards' Enquiry : Wilson Renwick three-day ban: used whip with excessive force and frequency (Jan 6-7,9)

FOCUS
An ordinary event in which the pace was steady and the winner is the best guide to the level.

NOTEBOOK
Longdale, back on a soft surface, turned in easily his best effort over fences and, although looking less than an easy ride off the bridle, travelled strongly for a long way and he may well be capable of better. *Official explanation: trainer had no explanation for the improved form shown (op 25-1)*
Gohh ◆ has slipped to a potentially lenient mark and fully confirmed the hint of promise of his previous start and showed more than enough to suggest he can win a similar race over fences in the coming weeks.
Loulou Nivernais(FR) jumped really well given that he took a crashing fall at Kelso on his previous start and was far from disgraced against an unexposed and potentially well-treated sort. He looks a good guide to the worth of this form. *(op 13-8)*
Little Flora, down in trip, was again below the pick of her Kelso win in April and she is one to have reservations about at present.
Ipledgeallegiance(USA) is an inconsistent sort and infrequent winner who was again below his best returned to handicap company, and he remains one to tread carefully with. *(op 9-1)*
Twist N Turn, having only her second start over fences, is an inconsistent sort who had her limitations exposed in this ordinary event, and the fact that she has yet to win a race of any description is a concern. *(op 6-1 tchd 13-2)*

2981 32REDPOKER.COM H'CAP HURDLE (8 hdls) 2m 1f
3:25 (3:25) (Class 4) (0-110,110) 3-Y-0+ **£3,799** (£1,115; £557; £278)

Form RPR
1P-0 **1** **Torkinking (IRE)**[44] [2190] 6-11-5 **110** (t) BenOrde-Powlett[(7)] 124+
(M A Barnes) *mde all: rdn bef 2 out: 5l up whn lft wl clr last* **10/1**
1243 **2** *23* **Teme Valley**[26] [2566] 11-11-1 **109** (p) JohnFlavin[(10)] 100
(R C Guest) *hld up: hdwy 4 out: outpcd after next: 20l 3rd and no imp whn lft 2nd last* **7/2**[2]
-002 **3** *5* **Nobodys Perfect (IRE)**[20] [2688] 5-10-2 **91** ow1 ThomasDreaper[(5)] 79+
(Ferdy Murphy) *trckd ldrs: rdn after 3 out: outpcd whn hung rt after next: lft modest 3rd last* **9/2**[3]
3033 **4** *22* **Siena Star (IRE)**[18] [2721] 7-10-0 **87** (v) GaryBerridge[(3)] 51
(Robert Gray) *chsd ldrs tl wknd bef 3 out* **8/1**
30-0 **5** *3* **Only Words (USA)**[246] [9] 8-10-0 **89** BrianHughes[(5)] 50
(A J Lockwood) *in tch: outpcd 4 out: n.d after* **25/1**
15-5 **6** *2* **Emperor's Monarch**[57] [1940] 6-11-1 **102** PaddyAspell[(3)] 61
(J Wade) *chsd ldrs tl wknd 4 out* **16/1**
4653 **7** *14* **Calomeria**[23] [2625] 4-11-0 **103** (b) StephenCraine[(5)] 48
(D McCain) *hld up: rdn after 4 out: btn after next* **8/1**
R3/6 **P** **Dark Character**[33] [2444] 6-10-12 **96** WilsonRenwick —
(G A Swinbank) *prom tl wknd bef 3 out: t.o whn p.u bef next* **7/4**[1]
0006 **F** **Merryvale Man**[4] [2952] 8-10-9 **93** AlanDempsey 97
(Miss Kariana Key) *trckd ldrs: effrt bef 2 out: 5l down and one pce whn fell last* **14/1**

4m 19.6s (13.10) **Going Correction** +0.65s/f (Soft) **9** Ran SP% **124.5**
WFA 4 from 5yo+ 10lb
Speed ratings: **95,84,81,71,70 69,62,—,—** CSF £49.46 CT £188.75 TOTE £11.20: £4.10, £1.60, £1.70; EX 26.00 Place 6 £19.10, Place 5 £15.03.
Owner J G Graham, Scott Lowther **Bred** James Browne **Trained** Farlam, Cumbria

FOCUS
Another ordinary event but a fair gallop to a race where the winner was left 20 lengths clear at the last. The faller looks well treated on his old form.

NOTEBOOK
Torkinking(IRE), a prolific winner over hurdles earlier this year, put two below-par performances firmly behind him with the tongue-tie back on, and he looked in control when his nearest pursuer came to grief at the final flight. Life will be tougher in a better grade after reassessment but he should continue to go well when allowed to dominate. *(op 8-1)*
Teme Valley was below his recent best back at his favourite course but he is likely to fare better when dropped a few pounds in the handicap and when reverting to his favoured fast ground.
Nobodys Perfect(IRE), who has run her best races over two miles and five furlongs at this course, was not suited by the drop in distance and she is one to bear in mind for a similar event when stepped back up in distance.
Siena Star(IRE), having his first run for his current stable, did not get home and, although he may prefer less testing conditions, has yet to win over hurdles and is not one to be place maximum faith in. *(op 6-1)*
Only Words(USA), who has not won since January of last year, has form over this course and distance and in bad ground but was again well beaten. Consistency is not his strongest suit.
Emperor's Monarch, well beaten on his handicap debut on his previous start after a break in October, again had his limitations exposed. A more galloping course may suit but he is best watched for now. *(tchd 18-1)*
Merryvale Man has slipped to a fair mark and was in the process of running his best race for some time when coming to grief. He would not have beaten the winner but is capable of scoring again when his jumping holds up. *(op 12-1)*
Dark Character, who shaped well on his first start after a long break last time (missed whole of last year), proved a big disappointment on this handicap debut. However, he has not had much racing and is worth another chance. *Official explanation: jockey said gelding had a breathing problem (op 12-1)*
T/Plt: £15.60 to a £1 stake. Pool: £19,382.15. 905.25 winning tickets. T/Qpdt: £10.10 to a £1 stake. Pool: £964.20. 70.10 winning tickets. RY

2501 TOWCESTER (R-H)
Monday, December 26

OFFICIAL GOING: Good to soft (good in places)
Wind: Moderate, across Weather: Overcast

2982 GG-POKER.COM NOVICES' CHASE (16 fncs) 2m 6f
12:30 (12:32) (Class 4) 5-Y-0+ **£4,128** (£1,211; £605; £302)

Form RPR
P-00 **1** **Mighty Matters (IRE)**[31] [2482] 6-11-0 105 WayneHutchinson 115+
(T R George) *hld up in tch: trckd ldrs 9th: blnd 3 out: led next: drvn out* **15/2**
-522 **2** *5* **Superrollercoaster**[25] [2581] 5-11-0 100 (v[1]) LeightonAspell 108
(O Sherwood) *led briefly after 1st: remained prom: led after 7th: hdd 2 out: one pce run-in* **10/3**[1]
/-33 **3** *dist* **The Frosty Ferret (IRE)**[11] [2839] 7-10-9 94 PaulO'Neill[(5)] 83
(J M Jefferson) *prom: ev ch 3 out: wknd next: blnd bdly and rdr lost iron last* **5/1**[2]
-P55 **4** *15* **Scarlet Fantasy**[19] [2706] 5-11-0 95 GerrySupple 58
(P A Pritchard) *a bhd: t.o* **33/1**
0144 **F** **Celtic Blaze (IRE)**[29] [2526] 6-10-2 100 (t) MarkNicolls[(5)] —
(B S Rothwell) *hld up: fell 8th* **7/1**[3]
61-P **U** **Jack Lynch**[21] [2675] 9-10-7 93 MrGTumelty[(7)] —
(Ferdy Murphy) *hld up: blnd bdly and uns rdr 8th* **14/1**
54-1 **F** **Blame The Ref (IRE)**[59] [1914] 8-11-0 105 WarrenMarston —
(C C Bealby) *prom: lost pl bef 8th: wknd 11th: btn whn fell 3 out* **10/3**[1]
21/3 **P** **King Triton (IRE)**[20] [2682] 8-10-7 103 JustinMorgan[(7)] —
(L Wells) *j. slowly 2nd: niggled along thrght: towards rr: t.o whn p.u bef last* **8/1**
5P36 **P** **Rash Moment (FR)**[25] [2583] 6-10-7 99 (b[1]) RichardSpate[(7)] —
(Mrs K Waldron) *led: pckd bdly 1st: hdd briefly: hdd and rdn after 7th: losing pl whn blnd 8th: t.o whn p.u bef 12th* **16/1**

5m 51.0s (-15.00) **Going Correction** -0.20s/f (Good) **9** Ran SP% **113.7**
Speed ratings: **108,106,—,—,— —,—,—,—** CSF £33.27 TOTE £14.50: £3.60, £1.80, £1.60; EX 48.90.
Owner Slad Valley Racing Partnership **Bred** Miss Elizabeth Kennedy **Trained** Slad, Gloucs

FOCUS
A moderate novices' chase run at a decent pace and concerning only the first three from some way out. The form should work out at a similar level.

NOTEBOOK
Mighty Matters(IRE), a lightly-raced ex-pointer whose best effort under Rules had been in a bumper at the beginning of the year, had been taking on some decent company and this was a drop in class. He travelled well throughout and overcame a blunder at the last ditch to win nicely. He appreciated the step up in trip and looks likely to pay his way at a similar level. *(op 7-1 tchd 8-1)*
Superrollercoaster, with a visor replacing the cheekpieces, did not appear to hit a flat spot this time and ran well, although no match for the winner. He has been second on all three starts over fences and deserves a change of luck. *(op 9-2)*
The Frosty Ferret(IRE), stepping up in trip, had his chance but was left behind from the last ditch and was out on his feet when hitting the final fence. *(op 4-1 tchd 11-2)*
Scarlet Fantasy, making his chasing debut, was out the back throughout but at least got round.
Blame The Ref(IRE), who got off the mark on his 20th start over fences last time, was well beaten when departing at the last ditch. *(op 3-1 tchd 7-2)*

2983 EUROPEAN BREEDERS FUND "NATIONAL HUNT" NOVICES' HURDLE (QUALIFIER) (8 hdls) 2m
1:00 (1:02) (Class 3) 4-6-Y-0 **£5,604** (£1,645; £822; £410)

Form RPR
6 **1** **Shaka's Pearl**[28] [2554] 5-10-12 JamesDavies 92+
(N J Gifford) *midfield: hdwy 4th: led 2 out: hdd briefly run-in: r.o* **25/1**
5-1 **2** *nk* **Major Miller**[42] [2242] 4-10-12 AndrewTinkler 92+
(N J Henderson) *trckd ldrs: led after 3 out: hdd 2 out: regained ld briefly run- in: r.o: hld towards fin* **3/1**[1]
22-4 **3** *3* **Butler's Cabin (FR)**[12] [2823] 5-10-5 MrAJBerry[(7)] 89+
(Jonjo O'Neill) *midfield: hdwy after 3rd: led 3 out: sn hdd: stl ev ch 2 out: nt qckn run-in* **15/2**[3]
-006 **4** *2* **Kayceecee (IRE)**[25] [2584] 4-10-12 JosephByrne 86
(H D Daly) *hld up: hdwy appr 2 out: sn rdn: styd on: nt rch ldrs* **12/1**
10-U **5** *1* **Grenfell (IRE)**[31] [2486] 6-10-5 WarrenMarston 78
(R T Phillips) *hld up: hdwy 3 out: rdn appr 2 out: styd on: nt rch ldrs* **14/1**
-0P4 **6** *3 ½* **Pearly Star**[17] [2749] 4-10-12 WayneHutchinson 84+
(A King) *midfield: effrt whn hmpd 2 out: one pce after* **14/1**
16/5 **7** *shd* **Scaramouche**[28] [2554] 5-10-12 DaveCrosse 82+
(B De Haan) *trckd ldrs: rdn whn j.lft 2 out: kpt on same pce* **16/1**
36-6 **8** *2* **Ballybawn House**[31] [2486] 4-10-5 SeanCurran 76+
(J C Fox) *hld up: hdwy 4 out: rdn in 5th whn hmpd 2 out and rdr lost iron: btn after* **14/1**
23 **9** *2 ½* **River Ripples (IRE)**[36] [2376] 6-10-5 MrRMcCarthy[(7)] 77
(T R George) *hld up: hdwy after 3rd: rdn and wknd appr 2 out* **11/2**[2]
1/ **10** *6* **Something Gold (FR)**[646] [4454] 5-10-12 MatthewBatchelor 71
(M Bradstock) *prom: led 4 out: hdd next: wknd appr 2 out* **8/1**
10- **11** *2 ½* **Creinch**[317] [3810] 4-10-12 LeightonAspell 68
(O Sherwood) *t.k.h: midfield: hdwy 4th: ev ch 3 out: wknd appr next* **11/2**[2]
00/0 **12** *½* **Gullivers Travels**[20] [2683] 6-10-5 RobertLucey-Butler[(7)] 68
(N J Gifford) *bhd after 3rd* **100/1**
0-0P **13** *½* **Star Galaxy (IRE)**[23] [2624] 5-10-12 GerrySupple 67
(Andrew Turnell) *midfield: wknd appr 4 out* **100/1**
10-0 **14** *18* **Little Saltee (IRE)**[12] [2829] 5-10-12 VinceSlattery 49
(J A B Old) *prom tl wknd appr 3 out* **40/1**

2P **15** ½ **Thyne Spirit (IRE)**[62] 1870 6-10-7 .... MarkNicolls(5) 49
(S T Lewis) *led: hdd 4 out: wknd next* **66/1**

4m 10.0s (-1.40) **Going Correction** -0.40s/f (Good)
WFA 4 from 5yo+ 10lb **15** Ran SP% **122.0**
Speed ratings: **84,83,82,81,80 79,79,78,76,73 72,72,72,63,62** CSF £100.69 TOTE £45.20: £10.60, £1.60, £3.30; EX 110.60.
Owner Mrs Bridget Biddlecombe **Bred** Mrs B M Biddlecombe **Trained** Findon, W Sussex

FOCUS
A moderate contest run at a very steady pace that resulted in something of a sprint from the home turn, and as a result the form does not look strong.

NOTEBOOK
Shaka's Pearl, having just his second outing, clearly benefited from that initial experience and, having travelled well for most of the way, took over at the second last and ran on well to resist the renewed effort of the runner-up. He looks to have the scope to progress over hurdles and should eventually make his mark over fences.
Major Miller ◆, winner of a Folkestone bumper in November, ran a race full of promise on this hurdling debut, battling back after being headed between the last two flights and going down narrowly. He should not be long in finding a race. *(tchd 11-4)*
Butler's Cabin(FR), who had shown fair form in three bumper outings, tended to run around going into his hurdles, but had every chance before being outpaced from the turn in. A stronger pace should suit him better. *(op 8-1 tchd 7-1)*
Kayceecee(IRE), who is bred to be a jumper, had more previous experience than most in this line-up. He was doing his best work late, having been held up, and may appreciate a longer trip. *(tchd 14-1)*
Grenfell(IRE), who was hampered when unseating on her hurdling debut, ran quite well and would have appreciated a stronger gallop. She can win races against her own sex. *(op 12-1)*
Pearly Star, dropped in trip, seems to be gradually finding his feet over hurdles. He would have been closer but for being knocked sideways by the errant Scaramouche at the second last.
Scaramouche, a bumper winner on this track, showed prominently but was tiring when going badly left at the second-last flight. *(op 20-1)*
Creinch was quite keen early, but looked a big threat climbing the hill before stopping quickly turning in. *(op 4-1)*

2984 READ MALCOLM HEYHOE @ GG.COM H'CAP CHASE (14 fncs) 2m 3f 110y
1:35 (1:38) (Class 4) (0-100,100) 5-Y-0+ **£3,604** (£1,058; £529; £264)

Form RPR
-P1P **1** **Yassar (IRE)**[32] 2465 10-11-2 90 .... WarrenMarston 97+
(D J Wintle) *led tl after 2nd: led again 5th tl bef next: wnt 2nd bef 8th: rdn 7l down and hld whn lft in ld after last: drvn out* **12/1**
P654 **2** 7 **Game On (IRE)**[18] 2719 9-11-5 100 .... TomMessenger(7) 99
(B N Pollock) *prom: rdn and btn appr 2 out: lft mod 2nd last* **9/1**
5315 **3** 5 **Taksina**[20] 2684 6-10-7 81 .... LeightonAspell 75
(R H Buckler) *trckd ldrs: lost pl 4th: hit 6th: lft mod 3rd last: no imp* **7/1**
4P34 **4** 5 **Terrible Tenant**[13] 2807 6-10-9 86 .... RichardYoung(3) 75
(J W Mullins) *prom: mstke 7th: hit 8th and lost pl: no imp after* **5/1**[3]
-PP0 **P** **Soroka (IRE)**[13] 2807 6-10-7 81 .... VinceSlattery —
(C N Kellett) *bhd: rdn after 3rd: t.o whn p.u bef 10th* **33/1**
-4 **F** **Gerrard (IRE)**[28] 2555 7-9-11 78 .... (v) RobertLucey-Butler(7) —
(Mrs A Barclay) *cl up whn blnd 1st: sn lost pl: hdwy appr 5th: fell 9th* **4/1**[2]
P-41 **P** **Eggmount (IRE)**[25] 2594 7-11-11 99 .... WayneHutchinson —
(T R George) *hld up: hdwy 10th: disputing 4th whn eased and p.u after 3 out* **5/2**[1]
PP54 **P** **Auditor**[50] 2074 6-9-12 77 ow2 .... (b) MarkNicolls(5) —
(S T Lewis) *prom: led after 2nd: hdd 5th: regained ld bef next: hdd bef 8th: sn wknd: t.o whn p.u bef 10th* **12/1**
P-P4 **R** **Merry Storm (IRE)**[25] 2581 6-9-7 74 oh6 .... RichardSpate(7) 92+
(Mrs K Waldron) *hld up: hdwy 7th: led bef next: clr appr 3 out: 7l up and in command whn rn out run-in: unlucky* **7/1**

5m 25.7s (7.50) **Going Correction** -0.20s/f (Good) **9** Ran SP% **118.6**
Speed ratings: **74,71,69,67,— —,—,—,—** CSF £114.20 CT £824.39 TOTE £9.50: £2.30, £2.20, £2.10; EX 76.80.
Owner Lavender Hill Stud L L C **Bred** Francis Small **Trained** Naunton, Gloucs

FOCUS
A very moderate handicap chase with a very fortunate winner and the form looks suspect.

NOTEBOOK
Yassar(IRE), who normally either wins or is pulled up, ran his race but was well held when left in front by the recalcitrant Merry Storm. He is not one to rely on, but this is his level. *(op 10-1)*
Game On(IRE), who saves his best efforts for Market Rasen, had every chance but was beaten turning in. He has dropped in the weights and will be of interest if returned to the Lincolnshire track. *(op 16-1 tchd 8-1)*
Taksina was out the back throughout and merely ran on past beaten rivals. *(op 8-1)*
Terrible Tenant ran reasonably, but is much better on a sound surface. *(op 7-1)*
Gerrard(IRE) will need to jump better than he did here if he is to make his mark. *(tchd 6-1)*
Eggmount(IRE), who dead-heated with today's third last time, was meeting that rival on the same terms. He made a short-lived effort at the end of the back straight, but was pulled up after the last ditch. Easier tracks may suit him better. *Official explanation: jockey said gelding was lame behind (tchd 6-1)*
Merry Storm(IRE), a winning pointer who had not made much impression under Rules, took the race by the scruff of the neck in the back straight and had the race won when he tried to turn sharp left into the exit gate halfway up the run-in, giving his rider no chance. He can gain compensation at a similar level, although he clearly has his quirks. *(tchd 6-1)*

2985 GG.COM CHRISTMAS "NATIONAL HUNT" NOVICES' H'CAP HURDLE (11 hdls) 2m 5f
2:05 (2:06) (Class 3) (0-110,110) 3-Y-0+ **£5,211** (£1,529; £764; £382)

Form RPR
-003 **1** **Franco (IRE)**[17] 2749 7-10-4 95 .... MrRJBarrett(7) 98+
(Mrs A E Brooks) *mde all: mstke 2 out: all out* **8/1**
022 **2** *nk* **Love Of Classics**[38] 2327 5-11-12 110 .... (v[1]) LeightonAspell 113+
(O Sherwood) *trckd ldrs: wnt 2nd 3rd: rdn appr 2 out: ch last: r.o cl home* **8/1**
3421 **3** 22 **The Gangerman (IRE)**[23] 2621 5-11-1 106 .... StevenCrawford(7) 91+
(N A Twiston-Davies) *prom: rdn whn mstke 4 out: wknd appr 2 out* **7/2**[1]
2/42 **4** 10 **Elvis Returns**[23] 2638 7-11-7 110 .... PaulO'Neill(5) 80
(J M Jefferson) *in tch: rdn and wknd appr 3 out* **4/1**[2]
6/0- **5** 22 **Flexible Concience (IRE)**[326] 3664 10-10-0 84 .... WayneHutchinson 32
(J A B Old) *hit 5th: a bhd* **10/1**
4-65 **6** 15 **Astral Affair (IRE)**[13] 2810 6-9-7 84 oh10 .... TomMessenger(7) 17
(P A Pritchard) *hld up: hdwy 4th: wknd after 7th* **33/1**
-454 **7** *dist* **Retro's Girl (IRE)**[18] 2718 4-10-6 90 .... JamesDavies —
(M Scudamore) *trckd ldrs: lost pl 4th: n.d after: t.o* **10/1**
P-24 **P** **Amber Starlight**[23] 2621 7-11-1 99 .... MatthewBatchelor —
(R Rowe) *a bhd: t.o whn p.u bef 3 out* **9/2**[3]
-506 **P** **Alderbrook Girl (IRE)**[19] 2704 5-10-4 88 .... DaveCrosse —
(R Curtis) *midfield: rdn and wknd appr 3 out: t.o whn p.u bef 2 out* **25/1**
-506 **U** **Royal Cliche**[33] 2426 6-11-2 100 .... AndrewTinkler —
(R T Phillips) *in tch: wknd after 7th: wl bhd whn tried to refuse and uns rdr 2 out* **8/1**

5m 31.9s (-9.30) **Going Correction** -0.40s/f (Good)
WFA 4 from 5yo+ 11lb **10** Ran SP% **118.7**
Speed ratings: **98,97,89,85,77 71,—,—,—,—** CSF £71.48 CT £268.27 TOTE £10.40: £2.60, £2.00, £1.80; EX 131.90.
Owner T L Brooks **Bred** Andrew Pierce **Trained** Towcester, Northamptonshire
■ The first winner for Anna Brooks, and at her local track.

FOCUS
A modest handicap hurdle run at an even pace, with the first two clear from the home turn and producing a good finish and could be rated higher.

NOTEBOOK
Franco(IRE), three times a winner in points, was given a positive ride again and showed a really good attitude to resist the persistent challenge of the runner-up. He looks capable of winning more races in this sphere and the switch back to chasing gives connections another alternative.
Love Of Classics, with a first-time visor replacing cheekpieces, gave the winner a good race and was miles clear of the rest. He has now been runner-up in his last three hurdle races, but judged on this effort deserves to win one.
The Gangerman(IRE), whose win last time was a slog in the mud, may have found this an insufficient test, although the stiff track should have helped compensate for that. *(op 4-1)*
Elvis Returns travelled well off the pace and moved up onto the heels of the leaders at the end of the back straight. However, from that point he found disappointingly little.
Retro's Girl(IRE) *Official explanation: jockey said filly hung left (op 11-1)*
Amber Starlight has form over further on heavy ground, but never figured on this easier surface and this was a below-par effort. *Official explanation: jockey said mare finished lame (op 4-1)*

2986 FREE TIPS @ GG.COM CLASSIFIED CHASE (18 fncs) 3m 110y
2:40 (2:41) (Class 4) 5-Y-0+ **£3,516** (£1,032; £516; £257)

Form RPR
/21- **1** **Graceful Dancer**[271] 4655 8-10-11 85 .... JamesDavies 102+
(B G Powell) *led to 3rd: remained handy: led 2 out: pushed clr after last* **9/2**[1]
P134 **2** 9 **Five Alley (IRE)**[26] 2575 8-11-0 88 .... LeightonAspell 97+
(R H Buckler) *in rr: hdwy 10th: chsd wnr appr last: one pce run-in* **15/2**
-1PP **3** 21 **Heartache**[25] 2594 8-11-0 67 .... (b) MatthewBatchelor 84+
(R Mathew) *in tch: led 6th to 8th: lft in ld 10th: clr 13th: rdn and hdd whn mstke 2 out: wkng whn blnd last* **40/1**
1-U4 **4** *dist* **Jour De Mee (FR)**[20] 2692 8-11-0 90 .... GerrySupple —
(Mrs H Dalton) *in rr: hit 13th: nvr on terms* **10/1**
02 **5** 6 **Hazel Bank Lass (IRE)**[24] 2610 9-10-11 90 .... AndrewTinkler —
(Andrew Turnell) *hld up: hdwy 10th: 2nd whn stmbld 4 out: wknd after next* **7/1**[3]
3P-P **6** 6 **The River Joker (IRE)**[61] 1884 9-10-9 83 .... MarkNicolls(5) —
(John R Upson) *a bhd* **25/1**
56P0 **7** *dist* **Chocolate Bombe (IRE)**[29] 2522 8-10-7 64 .... MrJAJenkins(7) —
(S Lycett) *in tch: rdn and lost pl after 8th: sn bhd: t.o* **25/1**
005 **P** **Joe McHugh (IRE)**[36] 2376 6-11-0 71 .... DaveCrosse —
(C J Mann) *prom tl wknd 12th: t.o whn p.u bef 3 out* **16/1**
P-F1 **F** **Trenance**[24] 2610 7-11-0 90 .... WayneHutchinson —
(T R George) *midfield: hdwy after 9th: 4th whn fell 4 out* **6/1**[2]
11-3 **P** **Just Anvil (IRE)**[26] 2575 7-10-7 83 .... JustinMorgan(7) —
(L Wells) *in tch: lost pl after 8th: t.o whn p.u bef 13th* **8/1**
4-PP **P** **Be Upstanding**[10] 2863 10-11-0 88 .... (p) SeanCurran —
(Ferdy Murphy) *in tch: mstke 1st: wknd 12th: t.o whn p.u bef 3 out* **20/1**
3P0 **F** **Murphy's Magic (IRE)**[13] 2805 7-10-11 82 .... (b[1]) MissPGundry(3) —
(Mrs T J Hill) *chsd ldrs: pushed along and losing pl whn fell 10th* **20/1**
2R44 **U** **Hill Forts Henry**[14] 2801 7-10-11 67 .... (tp) RichardYoung(3) —
(J W Mullins) *in tch: lost pl 6th: bhd whn blnd and uns rdr 2 out* **50/1**
P011 **U** **Never Awol (IRE)**[30] 2506 8-10-7 86 .... (p) TomMessenger(7) —
(B N Pollock) *prom: led 3rd to 6th: led again 8th tl blnd and uns rdr 10th* **9/2**[1]

6m 39.1s (-7.50) **Going Correction** -0.20s/f (Good) **14** Ran SP% **122.6**
Speed ratings: **101,98,91,—,— —,—,—,—,— —,—,—,—** CSF £35.64 TOTE £5.60: £1.80, £2.90, £12.70; EX 58.80.
Owner The Fairway Connection **Bred** Auldyn Stud Ltd **Trained** Morestead, Hants

FOCUS
A selling-class chase but a decisive winner who appears well handicapped and the form rated through the placed horses at their best.

NOTEBOOK
Graceful Dancer ◆, better known as a staying hurdler, was having just her third start over fences from a 21lb lower mark than her hurdles rating. Jumping was not a problem and in the end she asserted early in the straight to win with a bit to spare. She will go up a fair bit but looks capable of winning off a higher mark. *(op 7-2)*
Five Alley(IRE), who is something of a Plumpton specialist, did not have the pace to trouble the winner but remains in decent form. *(tchd 8-1)*
Heartache, who has a moderate completion record of late, ran well for a long way, but stopped very quickly once the winner asserted and this trip on such a stiff track seemed to find him out. *(op 33-1)*
Jour De Mee(FR) was always at the back and merely stayed on past beaten rivals.
Hazel Bank Lass(IRE) , who was narrowly beaten on her chasing debut last time, had moved into contention and was in pursuit of the winner when a mistake at the last on the far side stopped her in her tracks. *(op 6-1)*
Never Awol(IRE), who loves this track and seems to be something of a reformed character of late, was up with the pace as usual and going well enough when making a mistake and giving his rider no chance just after halfway. *(op 14-1)*
Trenance, who got off the mark last time, found his previous jumping problems resurfacing on this occasion. *(op 14-1)*
Joe McHugh(IRE) *Official explanation: jockey said gelding was unsuited by good to soft, good in places, ground (op 14-1)*

2987 COMPARE ODDS @ GG-ODDS.COM INTERMEDIATE OPEN NATIONAL HUNT FLAT RACE (DIV I) 2m
3:10 (3:10) (Class 6) 4-6-Y-0 **£2,521** (£740; £370; £184)

Form RPR
1 **Victor Daly (IRE)** 4-11-4 .... AndrewTinkler 98+
(Mrs H Dalton) *midfield: hdwy 5f out: led over 3f out: rdn out* **10/1**
05- **2** 3½ **Cloudina**[256] 4841 4-10-8 .... EmmettStack(3) 86
(P T Dalton) *hld up: hdwy bef 1/2-way: wnt 2nd over 3f out: kpt on u.p* **25/1**
3 2 **Rapallo (IRE)** 4-11-4 .... WayneHutchinson 91
(M Pitman) *towards rr: hdwy over 4f out: rdn over 3f out: kpt on same pce fnl 2f* **15/2**
20 **4** 9 **Even Flo**[29] 2534 4-10-11 .... JamesDavies 75
(Jean-Rene Auvray) *hld up: rdn and hdwy 4f out: wknd 2f out* **14/1**

5 2½ **Nobile (FR)** 4-11-4 ...... MatthewBatchelor 80
(M Bradstock) *chsd ldrs: rdn 1/2-way: wknd over 3f out* **5/1**[3]
1 **6** 2 **Long Road Home (IRE)**[127] 1274 6-11-1 ...... WayneJones(10) 85
(Jonjo O'Neill) *in tch: rdn and wknd over 3f out* **9/4**[1]
7 20 **Just Jaffa (IRE)** 6-10-13 ...... PaulO'Neill(5) 58
(Miss Venetia Williams) *t.k.h: cl up: rdn 4f out: sn wknd* **3/1**[2]
- **8** 11 **Green Collar** 6-10-11 ...... MrNMoore(7) 47
(M Salaman) *t.k.h: led: hdd over 3f out: wknd qckly* **33/1**
5 **9** 7 **Double Spread**[232] 242 6-11-4 ...... DaveCrosse 40
(M Mullineaux) *midfield: hdwy after 6f: wknd 5f out* **16/1**
0 **10** 5 **Rosemary's Fancy**[18] 2727 4-10-11 ...... JosephByrne 28
(C N Kellett) *cl up: rdn 1/2-way: wknd 5f out* **66/1**
11 7 **Hoober** 4-11-4 ...... LeightonAspell 28
(J Gallagher) *a towards rr* **33/1**
12 16 **All Fun And Games (IRE)** 4-10-13 ...... MarkNicolls(5) 12
(John R Upson) *a bhd* **16/1**
0 **13** 27 **Wot Way Chief**[18] 2720 4-10-11 ...... MrOWilliams(7) —
(J M Jefferson) *midfield: wknd 5f out* **25/1**
000 **14** 21 **Mr Parson (IRE)**[173] 917 5-10-11 ...... MrRMcCarthy(7) —
(S T Lewis) *a bhd: t.o over 6f out* **66/1**

4m 4.00s (-7.90) **Going Correction** -0.40s/f (Good) **14** Ran SP% **128.3**
Speed ratings: **100,98,97,92,91 90,80,75,71,69 65,57,44,33** CSF £253.84 TOTE £21.20: £4.30, £9.70, £3.30; EX 619.60.
Owner C B Compton **Bred** Joseph O'Dwyer **Trained** Norton, Shropshire
■ Stewards' Enquiry : Emmett StackM two-day ban: used whip with excessive frequency (Jan 6,9)

FOCUS
An ordinary bumper fractionally slower than the second division and rated through the fourth to her mark.

NOTEBOOK
Victor Daly(IRE), a half-brother to the staying chaser Willie John Daly, travelled well and, kicking on climbing the hill, the move proved decisive. He looks capable of making his mark over hurdles. *(op 9-1)*
Cloudina, from the family of Teeton Mill, looks to have improved for her two outings last season. Although always being held by the winner, she ran well and looks capable of winning races over hurdles, probably over longer trips.
Rapallo(IRE), related to a pointing/hurdles winner in Ireland, ran a nice race on this debut and looks capable of improvement with this experience under his belt. *(op 9-1 tchd 7-1)*
Even Flo, whose best previous effort was on much faster ground, ran a fair race and will be better suited by mares-only handicaps once switched to hurdles.
Nobile(FR) showed some promise on this racecourse debut before weakening. *(op 7-1)*
Long Road Home(IRE), under a penalty for his win on fast ground at Newton Abbot in the summer, found this a very different test and never looked likely to follow up. *(tchd 2-1)*
Just Jaffa(IRE), bred to be a stayer, was too keen in the early stages and paid the penalty up the hill. *(op 11-4)*

2988 COMPARE ODDS @ GG-ODDS.COM INTERMEDIATE OPEN NATIONAL HUNT FLAT RACE (DIV II) 2m
3:40 (3:40) (Class 6) 4-6-Y-0 **£2,521** (£740; £370; £184)

Form RPR
6 **1** **Senora Snoopy (IRE)**[29] 2534 4-10-11 ...... JosephByrne 98
(Ferdy Murphy) *hld up: hdwy 1/2-way: led 1f out: edgd rt ins fnl f: rdn out* **7/2**[2]
33 **2** 3½ **Kobai (IRE)**[42] 2242 6-11-4 ...... WayneHutchinson 101
(A King) *midfield: hdwy after 6f: outpcd 3f out: styd on to take 2nd towards fin* **7/1**
2 **3** 1¼ **Fast Forward (NZ)**[22] 2665 5-10-13 ...... PaulO'Neill(5) 100
(Miss Venetia Williams) *prom: led over 6f out: rdn over 2f out: hdd 1f out: no ex towards fin* **9/4**[1]
2 **4** 2½ **Sydney Greenstreet (GER)**[26] 2579 4-11-4 ...... LeightonAspell 97
(C R Egerton) *midfield: hdwy after 6f: rdn over 2f out: kpt on same pce fnl f* **11/2**
0 **5** 18 **Something Cristal (FR)**[29] 2534 4-11-4 ...... MatthewBatchelor 79
(M Bradstock) *in rr: sme hdwy over 4f out: nvr on terms* **9/2**[3]
00/ **6** ¾ **Dutch Star**[631] 4670 6-10-1 ...... JayPemberton(10) 72
(G P Enright) *hld up: hdwy after 6f: wknd 5f out* **50/1**
7 1¼ **Silver Rosa** 4-10-4 ...... TomMessenger(7) 70
(C C Bealby) *in rr: rdn 1/2-way: nvr on terms* **50/1**
8 2½ **Bob Mountain (IRE)** 4-11-4 ...... JamesDavies 75
(C Tinkler) *prom: rdn over 5f out: sn wknd* **14/1**
9 ½ **Another Chat (IRE)**[246] 5-11-4 ...... SeanCurran 74
(R T Phillips) *led: hdd over 6f out: rdn over 4f out: wknd over 3f out* **14/1**
0 **10** 13 **Tisfreetdream (IRE)**[22] 2665 4-11-4 ...... GerrySupple 61
(P A Pritchard) *a bhd* **40/1**
6 **11** 6 **Hue And Cry**[27] 2565 4-11-4 ...... AndrewTinkler 55
(N J Henderson) *in tch: rdn and wknd over 3f out* **20/1**
0/3- **12** 26 **Harbour Rock (IRE)**[532] 938 6-10-11 ...... WayneJones(7) 29
(D J Wintle) *midfield to 1/2-way: n.d after* **20/1**
P **Sherman Bay** 5-11-4 ...... DaveCrosse —
(G F Bridgwater) *trckd ldrs: lost pl after 5f: sn bhd: t.o whn p.u 4f out* **66/1**

4m 3.90s (-8.00) **Going Correction** -0.40s/f (Good)
WFA 4 from 5yo+ 10lb **13** Ran SP% **129.8**
Speed ratings: **101,99,98,97,88 88,87,86,85,79 76,63,—** CSF £29.25 TOTE £5.90: £2.20, £2.40, £1.70; EX 30.00 Place 6 £1,075.78, Place 5 £593.56.
Owner Racegoers Club Owners Group **Bred** Mrs M Doran **Trained** West Witton, N Yorks

FOCUS
This looked the slightly stronger division, but the time was only 0.10sec faster. The runner-up, fifth and sixth give the form a solid enough appearance.

NOTEBOOK
Senora Snoopy(IRE), who showed plenty of promise in a decent Newbury bumper, had clearly benefited from the outing and was always travelling well. She looks the type to go on from this and should make a decent hurdler. *(op 11-4 tchd 4-1)*
Kobai(IRE) gives a fair guide to the form, but looks the sort who needs a stamina test, as he was running on best of all up the hill. *(op 14-1 tchd 13-2)*
Fast Forward(NZ), who was narrowly beaten on softer ground on his debut, was up with the pace from the start but weakened up the hill. He may be better back on a flatter track. *(op 2-1)*
Sydney Greenstreet(GER), a half-brother to Seebald, ran a fair race without appearing to improve on his debut effort. He may need easier conditions. *Official explanation: jockey said gelding hung left (op 9-2 tchd 6-1)*
Something Cristal(FR) ran almost to the pound with the winner compared with their Newbury efforts. *(op 11-1 tchd 4-1)*
Bob Mountain(IRE) *Official explanation: jockey said colt hung left (op 16-1)*
Sherman Bay *Official explanation: jockey said gelding had steering problems*
T/Plt: £3,951.80 to a £1 stake. Pool: £22,736.90. 4.20 winning tickets. T/Qpdt: £157.60 to a £1 stake. Pool: £1,022.60. 4.80 winning tickets. DO

2638 WETHERBY (L-H)
Monday, December 26

OFFICIAL GOING: Soft (good to soft in places)
Wind: Virtually nil

2989 SKYBET 4 WAYS TO BET - ONE ACCOUNT BEGINNERS' CHASE (12 fncs) 2m
12:50 (12:50) (Class 3) 4-Y-0+ **£5,614** (£1,648; £824; £411)

Form RPR
2-1F **1** **Coat Of Honour (USA)**[71] 1758 5-11-4 ...... GrahamLee 123+
(J Howard Johnson) *cl up: led 5th: rdn along 2 out: kpt on flat* **5/6**[1]
3-44 **2** 2½ **Show Me The River**[52] 2023 6-11-4 109 ...... KeithMercer 116
(Ferdy Murphy) *led to 5th: cl up: rdn along 3 out and ev ch tl drvn and one pce flat* **5/1**[3]
2-F2 **3** 9 **Steppes Of Gold (IRE)**[23] 2620 8-11-4 ...... NoelFehily 111+
(Jonjo O'Neill) *trckd ldrs: hdwy 5 out: cl up next: sn rdn and wknd fr 2 out* **9/4**[2]
P5-P **4** 5 **Vanormix (FR)**[24] 2609 6-10-11 ...... (v) BernieWharfe(7) 103+
(C J Gray) *cl up: rdn along 4 out: sn wknd and carried bdly lft next* **33/1**
5-P0 **5** 12 **Perfect Punch**[17] 2751 6-11-4 ...... RichardMcGrath 97+
(K G Reveley) *hld up: hdwy 1/2-way: cl up 4 out: sn rdn and wkng whn j. bdly lft next: blnd 2 out* **33/1**
P/FP **6** 6 **Jerom De Vindecy (FR)**[32] 2449 8-11-1 ...... PeterBuchanan(3) 84
(Miss Lucinda V Russell) *a rr: rdn along 5th: outpcd and bhd fr 5 out* **40/1**

4m 15.5s (8.90) **Going Correction** +0.80s/f (Soft) **6** Ran SP% **110.3**
Speed ratings: **109,107,103,100,94 91** CSF £5.34 TOTE £1.80: £1.30, £2.30; EX 6.50.
Owner Andrea & Graham Wylie **Bred** Makio Shimo Yashki **Trained** Billy Row, Co Durham

FOCUS
With Steppes Of Gold quite a way below the pick of his form, Coast Of Honour's task was made easier and he won decisively. The race has been rated through the first two.

NOTEBOOK
Coat Of Honour(USA), a 143-rated hurdler who took a heavy fall on his chasing debut at Market Rasen, showed he was none the worse for that experience and ran out a decisive winner. This was just an ordinary race, but he is held in pretty high regard and his trainer thinks he could be an Arkle horse, especially as better ground should suit. He did, though, say that he may be best on a flat track. *(op 10-11)*
Show Me The River, a beaten favourite in a maiden chase over three miles one at Hexham on his previous start, proved quite well suited by this significant drop in trip and probably did well to get so close to the highly-regarded winner. *(op 13-2)*
Steppes Of Gold(IRE) had not run badly in defeat at Chepstow on his previous start, but he was well below the pick of his form this time and is just not progressing as one might have hoped. *(op 2-1)*
Vanormix(FR), with the visor re-fitted on his return to fences, probably ran about as well as could have been expected. *(tchd 25-1)*
Perfect Punch *Official explanation: jockey said gelding hung left-handed (op 40-1)*

2990 "IT MATTERS MORE WHEN THERE'S MONEY ON IT" H'CAP HURDLE (12 hdls) 2m 7f
1:20 (1:21) (Class 3) (0-130,127) 4-Y-0+ **£6,987** (£2,051; £1,025; £512)

Form RPR
3222 **1** **Russian Sky**[34] 2417 6-10-2 110 ...... MissRDavidson(7) 118+
(Mrs H O Graham) *made all: rdn clr 3 out: kpt on wl flat* **12/1**
1-63 **2** 1¼ **Hidden Bounty (IRE)**[31] 2483 9-11-10 125 ...... RichardMcGrath 130+
(K G Reveley) *hld up in tch: hdwy 4 out: rdn after next: styng on whn bmpd last: drvn and r.o wl flat* **7/1**[2]
45P2 **3** 2 **Totally Scottish**[11] 2840 9-10-4 115 ...... JamesReveley(10) 117
(K G Reveley) *hld up: stdy hdwy appr 3 out: rdn next: styd on last: nrst fin* **10/1**
13 **4** 11 **Day Of Claies (FR)**[38] 2327 4-10-9 110 ...... AntonyEvans 105+
(N A Twiston-Davies) *trckd ldrs on inner: hdwy 4 out: chsd wnr next: sn rdn: mstke 2 out: j. bdly rt last: wknd flat* **14/1**
2-06 **5** 2½ **Simply Mystic**[16] 2766 5-10-5 106 ...... PadgeWhelan 95
(P D Niven) *midfield: hdwy and in tch 1/2-way: rdn along and outpcd after 4 out: styd on fr 2 out* **66/1**
-253 **6** ½ **Haut De Gamme (FR)**[9] 2876 10-11-10 125 ...... KeithMercer 113
(Ferdy Murphy) *hld up: hdwy to chse ldrs 4 out: rdn along next and sn btn* **7/2**[1]
6316 **7** 21 **Cantgeton (IRE)**[43] 2207 5-11-2 127 ...... AndrewGlassonbury(10) 110+
(M C Pipe) *hld up and bhd: gd hdwy on inner 4 out: rdn to chse ldrs next: sn drvn and wknd 2 out* **11/1**
2-61 **8** 5 **Like A Lord (IRE)**[180] 861 7-10-11 112 ...... DominicElsworth 76+
(Mrs S J Smith) *prom on outer: mstke 7th: rdn along 4 out: sn wknd and bhd whn hit last* **9/1**[3]
/5-0 **9** nk **Great As Gold (IRE)**[23] 2629 6-11-2 117 ...... (p) RussGarritty 79
(B Ellison) *chsd ldrs: rdn along 4 out: wkng whn mstke next* **33/1**
11/0 **10** 5 **Corbie Lynn**[34] 2417 8-10-6 107 ...... BruceGibson 64
(W S Coltherd) *prom tl rdn along 4 out and sn wknd* **50/1**
4330 **11** 9 **Altitude Dancer (IRE)**[11] 2840 5-10-0 108 ...... AdrianScholes(7) 56
(A Crook) *a rr: bhd fr 1/2-way* **40/1**
3-31 **12** 3½ **River Alder**[221] 422 7-10-13 117 ...... PeterBuchanan(3) 61
(J M Dun) *in tch: rdn along after 4 out and wknd bef next* **7/1**[2]
2-20 **13** 25 **Roobihoo (IRE)**[58] 1929 6-10-9 110 ...... JoeTizzard 29
(C Grant) *midfield: pushed along 4 out: sn wknd* **11/1**
35 **14** 12 **Burren Moonshine (IRE)**[40] 2271 6-10-0 101 oh1 ...... BrianHarding 8
(P Bowen) *chsd ldrs: rdn along appr 4 out and sn wknd* **25/1**
6-PP **P** **Ashleybank House (IRE)**[10] 2861 8-10-2 110 ...... BernieWharfe(7) —
(David Pearson) *a rr: bhd whn p.u bef 3 out* **100/1**
P-30 **P** **Old Feathers (IRE)**[12] 2820 8-10-9 110 ...... (b) NoelFehily —
(Jonjo O'Neill) *rr: rdn along 1/2-way: bhd whn p.u bef 7th* **25/1**
P-00 **P** **Mobasher (IRE)**[12] 2820 6-11-0 115 ...... (b) AlanO'Keeffe —
(Miss Venetia Williams) *midfield: hit 6th: mstke 8th and sn p.u* **20/1**
PR-P **P** **Ballybough Rasher (IRE)**[30] 2499 10-11-7 122 ...... GrahamLee —
(J Howard Johnson) *rr and reminders 5th: bhd whn p.u bef 3 out* **20/1**

5m 58.7s (2.00) **Going Correction** +0.80s/f (Soft)
WFA 4 from 5yo+ 11lb **18** Ran SP% **124.4**
Speed ratings: **107,106,105,102,101 101,93,91,91,90 86,85,77,72,— —,—,—** CSF £86.06 CT £895.18 TOTE £19.10: £2.80, £2.20, £1.90, £2.90; EX 175.20.
Owner H G Racing **Bred** Mrs Susan Corbett **Trained** Philip Law, Borders

FOCUS
A fair handicap hurdle and pretty competitive. It has been rated through the third.

NOTEBOOK

Russian Sky, racing off a career-high mark despite having not won in over a year, deserved to end that losing run having posted many creditable efforts in defeat, and did do so under a good ride from the front. Things will be tougher next time, but this could well have boosted his confidence and the follow up cannot be ruled out. *(op 14-1)*

Hidden Bounty(IRE) confirmed the promise he showed when third at Newbury on his previous start with another good effort in defeat. He looks well up to winning a similar event. *(tchd 8-1)*

Totally Scottish, 4lb higher than when second at Catterick on his previous start, ran well off his new mark and was clear of the remainder in third. *(op 11-1)*

Day Of Claies(FR), switched to handicap company for the first time, showed he is not on a bad mark with a respectable enough effort. Given this was only his second run in this country, and his third over hurdles in total, there ought to be more to come.

Simply Mystic ◆ caught the eye in fifth and could be running into form.

Haut De Gamme(FR) gave the impression a return to this sort of trip would suit when third at Haydock on his previous start, but failed to build on that and has to be considered a little disappointing. *(tchd 4-1in places)*

2991 ROCOM NOVICES' HURDLE (9 hdls) 2m

1:55 (1:58) (Class 4) 4-Y-0+ **£3,809** (£1,110; £555)

Form RPR

1P **1** **Percussionist (IRE)**[24] 2614 4-11-5 .... GrahamLee 113+
(J Howard Johnson) *disp ld: rdn along 3 out: drvn to ld appr last: kpt on flat* **2/1**[1]

3-43 **2** *3* **Tous Chez (IRE)**[26] 2572 6-10-12 .... PadgeWhelan 100+
(Mrs S J Smith) *trckd ldrs: hdwy 4 out: rdn to chse wnr whn hit last: kpt on flat* **16/1**

F04 **3** *3 ½* **Millennium Hall**[23] 2627 6-10-9 103 .... PeterBuchanan(3) 97+
(Miss Lucinda V Russell) *hld up: stdy hdwy 3 out: rdn enxt: styng on whn hmpd and n.m.r flat* **16/1**

0 **4** *3 ½* **Springvic (IRE)**[33] 2444 5-10-12 .... RussGarritty 94+
(G M Moore) *disp ld: rdn along 3 out: drvn next: wknd appr last: hung bdly lft flat* **66/1**

114 **5** *5* **High Day**[37] 2335 5-11-12 .... KeithMercer 101
(Ferdy Murphy) *in tch: hdwy to chse ldrs 4 out: rdn along next: edgd lft and btn 2 out* **5/2**[3]

21 **6** *4* **Predator (GER)**[17] 2749 4-11-5 .... NoelFehily 91+
(Jonjo O'Neill) *trckd ldrs: effrt 3 out: sn rdn and outpcd fr next* **9/4**[2]

00U **7** *3* **Spanish Tan (NZ)**[10] 2860 5-10-12 .... RichardMcGrath 80
(Jonjo O'Neill) *midfield: hdwy to chse ldrs 4 out: sn rdn and outpcd fr next* **50/1**

F- **8** *17* **Patrixtoo (FR)**[292] 4259 4-10-12 .... AlanO'Keeffe 63
(T J Fitzgerald) *midfield: mstke 5th: sn in rr* **25/1**

50 **9** *5* **Boris The Spider**[16] 2448 4-10-12 .... DominicElsworth 58
(M D Hammond) *prom: mstke 4th: rdn along bef 4 out and sn wknd* **33/1**

00 **10** *¾* **Swahili Dancer (USA)**[22] 2652 4-10-12 .... KennyJohnson 57
(M D Hammond) *a rr* **100/1**

2266 **11** *6* **Amalfi Storm**[21] 2674 4-10-5 .... BruceGibson 44
(M W Easterby) *a bhd* **50/1**

3400 **12** *6* **Lord Baskerville**[8] 2901 4-10-5 .... LiamBerridge(7) 45
(W Storey) *bhd fr 1/2-way* **33/1**

13 *12* **Fourswainby (IRE)**[35] 4-10-12 .... BrianHarding 33
(B Ellison) *bhd fr 1/2-way* **100/1**

0 **P** **Oulan Bator (FR)**[67] 1794 5-10-12 .... AntonyEvans —
(R A Fahey) *a rr: bhd whn p.u bef 3 out* **33/1**

4m 10.4s (11.00) **Going Correction** +0.80s/f (Soft)
WFA 4 from 5yo+ 10lb **14** Ran SP% **124.5**
Speed ratings: **104,102,100,99,96 94,93,84,82,81 78,75,69,—** CSF £33.44 TOTE £3.20: £1.60, £2.50, £3.40; EX 28.10.

Owner Andrea & Graham Wylie **Bred** Swettenham Stud **Trained** Billy Row, Co Durham

FOCUS

Just an ordinary novice hurdle in which Percussionist was able to get back on track having flopped in a much better race at Sandown on his previous start. His task was made easier by the disappointing runs of High Day and Predator. The race has been rated around the second, who is credited as having run to his bumper mark.

NOTEBOOK

Percussionist(IRE), a comfortable enough winner of a minor race on his hurdling debut at Carlisle before pulling up in a hot contest over two and a half miles at Sandown, appreciated the drop in class and got back on track with a straightforward success. Things will be much harder back up in grade, and he still has plenty to prove, but Graham Lee thinks he can do better on a sounder surface, despite soft ground appearing to suit best on the Flat. *(tchd 9-4)*

Tous Chez(IRE), who showed plenty of ability in four runs in bumpers, looked to improve for the switch to hurdles and ran well behind the classy winner. There should be plenty more to come. *(op 18-1)*

Millennium Hall would have been even closer had he not met with trouble when staying on for pressure and emerged with plenty of credit in third. On this evidence, he could be worth a try in handicap company off his current sort of mark.

Springvic(IRE), well beaten over course and distance on hurdling debut, stepped up on that effort despite hanging quite badly under pressure. In the longer term, he is likely to do better when handicapped and needs one more run for a mark.

High Day, below form in a Listed hurdle at Haydock on his previous start, failed to take advantage of this drop in class and was again short of his best. *(op 11-4 tchd 9-4)*

Predator(GER) won well in a similar event at Doncaster on his previous start, but was well below that level of form this time and proved disappointing. Perhaps this ground was soft enough. *(op 11-4)*

2992 SKYBET.COM ROWLAND MEYRICK H'CAP CHASE GRADE 3 (18 fncs) 3m 1f

2:30 (2:30) (Class 1) 5-Y-0+ **£29,012** (£11,197; £5,857; £3,172)

Form RPR

0-00 **1** **Therealbandit (IRE)**[16] 2760 8-9-10 149 .... (p) AndrewGlassonbury(10) 157
(M C Pipe) *hld up in tch: stdy hdwy 6 out: led after next: rdn appr 2 out: drvn last: kpt on wl* **9/1**

-536 **2** *1 ½* **Take The Stand (IRE)**[37] 2337 9-10-12 155 .... BrianHarding 162+
(P Bowen) *trckd ldrs: smooth hdwy and cl up 5 out: chsd wnr next: rdn to chal 2 out: ev ch tl drvn and one pce flat* **6/1**[3]

-202 **3** *15* **My Will (FR)**[24] 2615 5-10-4 147 .... JoeTizzard 143+
(P F Nicholls) *hld up in tch: pushed along 10th: hdwy to join ldrs 5 out: rdn and hit next: mstke 3 out and sn wknd: wl hld 3rd whn hit la* **11/4**[1]

2U04 **4** *dist* **Joes Edge (IRE)**[17] 2744 8-10-0 143 oh2 .... KeithMercer —
(Ferdy Murphy) *in tch: rdn along and outpcd fr 6 out* **10/1**

1P-3 **P** **Malek (IRE)**[23] 2628 9-10-0 143 oh17 .... RichardMcGrath —
(K G Reveley) *sn outpcd and bhd: p.u after 10th* **33/1**

5110 **F** **St Matthew (USA)**[30] 2491 7-10-0 143 oh10 .... PadgeWhelan —
(Mrs S J Smith) *chsd ldrs: hit 5th: fell 10th* **16/1**

5-UP **P** **Forest Gunner**[22] 2656 11-9-11 143 oh3 .... PeterBuchanan(3) —
(R Ford) *chsd ldrs tl lost pl 1/2-way: bhd whn p.u bef 10th* **33/1**

216- **P** **Baron Windrush**[310] 3935 7-10-0 143 oh6 .... AntonyEvans —
(N A Twiston-Davies) *hld up in tch: hdwy 10th: chsd ldrs 14th: rdn along and wknd 5 out: bhd whn p.u bef 3 out* **8/1**

51-P **P** **Grey Abbey (IRE)**[58] 1926 11-11-12 169 .... GrahamLee —
(J Howard Johnson) *cl up: hit 1st: led after 5th: rdn along 12th: hdd and blnd 6 out: sn drvn:wknd bef 4 out: bhd whn p.u bef last* **6/1**[3]

5P-3 **P** **Truckers Tavern (IRE)**[12] 2820 10-10-1 144 .... DominicElsworth —
(Mrs S J Smith) *led tl after 5th: hit 7th: cl up tl led again 6 out: rdn and hdd after next: wkng whn mstke 4 out: p.u bef last* **9/2**[2]

6m 38.5s (-1.50) **Going Correction** +0.80s/f (Soft) **10** Ran SP% **115.4**
Speed ratings: **113,112,107,—,— —,—,—,—,—** CSF £62.22 CT £187.39 TOTE £11.50: £3.20, £2.70, £2.00; EX 84.60.

Owner D A Johnson **Bred** R J Whitford **Trained** Nicholashayne, Devon

■ Andrew Glassonbury, partnering only his fifth winner, sweated off 8lb to make the weight.

FOCUS

This looked a reasonable renewal of the Rowland Meyrick, but it proved quite a test and only four finished. Therealbandit had run better than his finishing position suggested in the Robin Cook Memorial at Cheltenham on his previous start and built on that to deny the frustrating Take The Stand. The winner has been rated 5lb off his best form of last season.

NOTEBOOK

Therealbandit(IRE), much better than his finishing position would suggest in the Robin Cook Memorial at Cheltenham on his previous start, showed what he is really capable of to end a year-long losing run in determined fashion under a good ride from his 10lb claimer. This is likely to provide him with a welcome boost to his confidence boost and he could well go on from this. *(op 8-1)*

Take The Stand(IRE) was produced with every chance, but his jumping was yet again not up to scratch and he found one too good. He is better suited by decent ground, but one cannot keep making excuses for him and a horse of his ability really should win more races. *(tchd 13-2 in places)*

My Will(FR), trying this trip for the second time, travelled quite well for a lot of the way, but dropped out of contention after making mistakes at both the fourth and third last. He is obviously better than this and can be given another chance. *(tchd 5-2)*

Joes Edge(IRE) shaped as though about to hit form when fourth at Cheltenham on his previous start, but this was disappointing and he looks best watched for the time being. *(tchd 11-1)*

Grey Abbey(IRE) had no easy task off a mark of 169 and, as on his reappearance, pulled up. He could be hard to place now. *(tchd 11-2)*

Truckers Tavern(IRE) shaped quite well when third over hurdles on his reappearance, but failed to build on that returned to fences and this may have come soon enough. *(tchd 11-2)*

2993 "YOU'RE EITHER VEGAS OR YOU'RE NOT" H'CAP CHASE (15 fncs) 2m 4f 110y

3:05 (3:06) (Class 3) (0-125,125) 5-Y-0+ **£5,728** (£1,681; £840; £420)

Form RPR

6444 **1** **Sir Storm (IRE)**[23] 2640 9-11-0 113 .... (p) FinbarKeniry 125+
(G M Moore) *led to 4th: cl up tl led again 10th: rdn along and 3 l up whn lft wl clr 2 out: eased flat* **16/1**

-P11 **2** *5* **Sharp Belline (IRE)**[33] 2445 8-10-13 112 .... DominicElsworth 114
(Mrs S J Smith) *chsd ldrs tl rdn along and lost pl 1/2-way: bhd 5 out: styd on fr 3 out: no ch w wnr* **5/1**[2]

3-32 **3** *17* **Posh Stick**[30] 2498 8-10-8 107 .... BruceGibson 92
(J B Walton) *chsd ldrs: rdn along 5 out and outpcd bef next* **9/1**

4-P0 **4** *11* **Flight Command**[16] 2768 7-11-9 125 .... PeterBuchanan(3) 99
(P Beaumont) *prom tl rdn along and outpcd fr 5 out* **50/1**

4-1P **5** *3* **Gatorade (NZ)**[30] 2498 13-11-3 116 .... (p) PadgeWhelan 87
(R C Guest) *hld up: hdwy 9th: chsd ldrs 5 out: sn rdn along and outpcd fr next* **25/1**

F-P6 **P** **Per Amore (IRE)**[85] 1617 7-10-13 119 .... (b) BernieWharfe(7) —
(David Pearson) *a bhd: p.u bef 8th* **100/1**

PP-0 **P** **Historg (FR)**[45] 2164 10-10-7 106 .... BrianHarding —
(Ferdy Murphy) *sn outpcd and bhd: t.o fr 1/2-way: p.u bef 4 out* **25/1**

-042 **F** **Green Ideal**[23] 2640 7-10-6 105 .... (b) KeithMercer —
(Ferdy Murphy) *a.p: effrt to chse wnr and cl 2nd whn fell 4 out* **10/1**

1-22 **P** **Manbow (IRE)**[33] 2445 7-10-13 112 .... GrahamLee —
(M D Hammond) *midfield: rdn along 8th: sn lost pl and bhd whn p.u bef 4 out* **5/1**[2]

F13- **P** **Cruise Leader (IRE)**[365] 2968 10-11-4 117 .... RichardMcGrath —
(C Grant) *chsd ldrs on outer: mstke 9th: sn wknd and bhd whn p.u bef 4 out* **10/1**

PU03 **P** **Turgeonev (FR)**[16] 2768 10-11-12 125 .... RussGarritty —
(T D Easterby) *trckd ldrs on inner: led 4th: hdd 10th: rdn along and wknd 5 out: bhd whn p.u bef next* **6/1**[3]

05-3 **F** **Windsor Boy (IRE)**[51] 2054 8-10-12 121 .... AndrewGlassonbury(10) 131+
(M C Pipe) *hld up: stdy hdwy 10th: chsd wnr appr 3 out: sn rdn and 3 l down in 2nd whn fell 2 out* **4/1**[1]

0-3F **B** **Be My Better Half (IRE)**[36] 2368 10-11-10 123 .... NoelFehily 128
(Jonjo O'Neill) *in tch: mstke 5th: pushed along to chse ldrs 5 out: hdwy next: 3rd and styng on u.p whn b.d 2 out* **9/1**

5m 36.6s (15.90) **Going Correction** +0.80s/f (Soft) **13** Ran SP% **122.3**
Speed ratings: **101,99,92,88,87 —,—,—,—,— —,—,—** CSF £96.32 CT £789.16 TOTE £25.80: £6.70, £2.40, £2.60; EX 211.80.

Owner J R F (management Consultants) Ltd **Bred** D And Mrs Noonan **Trained** Middleham, N Yorks

FOCUS

A fair handicap chase, but it is hard to know what the form is worth given the likes of Green Ideal, Windsor Boy and Be My Better Half would surely have gone close had they managed to complete. As it was, Sir Storm, who was value for ten lengths, was able to take advantage and end a losing run stretching back to April 2004.

NOTEBOOK

Sir Storm(IRE), with the cheekpieces re-fitted, stepped up on his recent efforts to end a losing run stretching back to April 2004, but his task was made a whole lot easier with several of his main rivals failing to complete, and the way he finished suggests he was no sure thing to have won had some of the others got round. *Official explanation: trainer said, regarding the improved form shown, gelding was refitted with cheekpieces and enjoyed the run of the race today (op 12-1)*

Sharp Belline(IRE), chasing the hat-trick off an 11lb higher mark than when winning over two miles seven here on his previous start, got going far too late to pose a serious threat, and the bare result obviously flatters him given the trouble some of his rivals met with. *(op 9-2)*

Posh Stick may be high enough in the weights, but she was still entitled to finish a little closer. *(op 8-1)*

Flight Command, on this evidence, still looks high enough in the weights. *(op 33-1)*

Gatorade(NZ) ran better than when pulled up on his return from a break at Newcastle last time.

Turgeonev(FR) failed to build on the promise of his recent Doncaster third. *Official explanation: jockey said gelding was unsuited by soft, good to soft in places (tacky) ground (tchd 9-2)*

Windsor Boy(IRE), dropped half a mile in trip, was staying on and still in with a chance when falling two out. *(tchd 9-2)*

Be My Better Half(IRE) was staying on and not out of it when brought down two out. *(tchd 9-2)*

Green Ideal was in second and still in with every chance when falling four out. *(tchd 9-2)*

Manbow(IRE), second on both his starts this season, was below form this time with no obvious *excuse. Official explanation: jockey said gelding was unsuited by soft, good to soft in places (tacky) ground* *(tchd 9-2)*

2994 SKYBET IN-PLAY BETTING ON ALL PREMIERSHIP GAMES NOVICES' H'CAP HURDLE (10 hdls) 2m 4f 110y

3:35 (3:40) (Class 3) (0-110,106) 3-Y-0+ **£5,393** (£1,583; £791; £395)

Form RPR

-512 **1** **Aston Lad**[23] 2639 4-11-12 **106** GrahamLee 114
(M D Hammond) *hld up in rr: stdy hdwy 4 out: chsd ldr 2 out: sn rdn: drvn flat and styd on wl to ld last 50 yds* **11/2**[3]

PU-1 **2** *shd* **Birdwatch**[29] 2523 7-11-0 **94** (b) RichardMcGrath 103+
(K G Reveley) *led: pushed along appr 3 out: rdn and hit last: drvn flat: hdd and no ex last 50 yds* **8/1**

030 **3** *11* **Miss Pross**[17] 2750 5-10-11 **94** PeterBuchanan(3) 91
(T D Walford) *hld up in tch: hdwy 4 out: chsd ldrs next: sn rdn: kpt on u.p appr last* **33/1**

U2P- **4** *1* **Fromragstoriches (IRE)**[578] 528 9-11-10 **104** DominicElsworth 102+
(Mrs S J Smith) *bhd: hit 4th and sn rdn along: hdwy after 4 out: styd on u.p fr 2 out: nrst fin* **50/1**

0250 **5** *1 ¾* **Flake**[26] 2566 5-11-3 **97** PadgeWhelan 92+
(Mrs S J Smith) *midfield: hit 6th: hdwy to chse ldrs 4 out: rdn along next: drvn and wknd bef last* **25/1**

24 **6** *3* **Amazing Valour (IRE)**[26] 2578 3-10-11 **105** (b) NoelFehily 84+
(P Bowen) *trckd ldrs: hdwy to chse ldr 5th: rdn along appr 3 out and grad wknd* **14/1**

P323 **7** *13* **Notanotherdonkey (IRE)**[23] 2623 5-11-4 **98** JoeTizzard 76
(M Scudamore) *chsd ldr: rdn along appr 4 out and sn wknd* **14/1**

5125 **8** *5* **Red Perk (IRE)**[11] 2840 8-11-1 **95** (p) KennyJohnson 68
(R C Guest) *in tch: rdn along 4 out and sn wknd* **16/1**

33-0 **9** *17* **Le Forezien (FR)**[24] 2605 6-9-11 **84** BernieWharfe(7) 40
(C J Gray) *chsd ldrs: rdn along 4 out and sn wknd* **66/1**

424 **10** *19* **Mac Dargin (IRE)**[23] 2638 6-11-4 **98** AntonyEvans 35
(N A Twiston-Davies) *midfield: rdn along and lost pl 1/2-way: sn bhd* **25/1**

-063 **P** **Orki Des Aigles (FR)**[21] 2676 3-10-5 **99** KeithMercer —
(Ferdy Murphy) *a rr: bhd whn p.u bef 2 out* **10/1**

-P22 **F** **Sergio Coimbra (IRE)**[36] 2372 6-11-5 **99** BrianHarding —
(N G Richards) *chsd ldrs: rdn along and lost pl 6th: fell next* **9/2**[2]

45/6 **P** **Batto**[23] 2639 5-10-3 **83** FinbarKeniry —
(G M Moore) *chsd ldng pair: rdn along and wknd 6th: bhd whn p.u bef 2 out* **50/1**

5-64 **P** **Ballyhale (IRE)**[17] 2755 7-11-8 **102** BruceGibson —
(P D Niven) *chsd ldrs: rdn along 4 out: sn wknd: p.u and dismntd bef 3 out* **16/1**

6P-3 **P** **Greek Star**[23] 2639 4-11-1 **95** RussGarritty —
(K A Morgan) *midfield: effrt and pushed along whn hmpd 4 out: nt rcvr and bhd whn p.u bef 2 out* **16/1**

0041 **P** **Darkshape**[13] 2816 5-10-7 **87** AlanO'Keeffe —
(Miss Venetia Williams) *hld up on inner in midfield: effrt 6th: sn rdn along and btn: bhd whn p.u bef 3 out* **5/2**[1]

5m 23.5s (14.60) **Going Correction** +0.80s/f (Soft)
WFA 3 from 4yo+ 14lb **16** Ran SP% **129.4**
Speed ratings: **104,103,99,99,98 97,92,90,84,77** —,—,—,—,— — CSF £49.94 CT £1383.91 TOTE £6.40: £1.70, £2.40, £8.60, £3.80; EX 48.00 Place 6 £240.74, Place 5 £161.25.
Owner S T Brankin **Bred** Micky Hammond Racing Ltd And S Branklin **Trained** Middleham, N Yorks

FOCUS
A moderate handicap hurdle for novices rated around the winner, who seems to have run to his recent course and distance mark.

NOTEBOOK
Aston Lad, off the mark at Ayr before running a creditable second in a similar event over course and distance on his previous start, defied a 4lb rise in the weights to run out a game winner. He took a while to get the hang of things over hurdles, but is progressing now and there could be even more to come. *(op 6-1)*
Birdwatch, off the mark in a selling hurdle over two miles at Leicester on his previous start, ran well in this more competitive heat and was just denied. *(op 7-1)*
Miss Pross is still a maiden, but she seemed well suited by this step up to her furthest trip to date and ran respectably.
Fromragstoriches(IRE), from an in-form yard, offered plenty of promise on his return from a 578-day absence. *(op 66-1)*
Flake did not run badly but he may just need dropping into the lowest grade.
Darkshape, 11lb higher than when winning over two miles at Warwick on his previous start, ran *well below that form and was beaten before this longer trip could be used as an excuse.Official explanation: jockey said gelding hung violently right (op 6-1 tchd 7-1 in places)*
Ballyhale(IRE) *Official explanation: jockey said gelding lost its action (op 6-1 tchd 7-1 in places)*
Sergio Coimbra(IRE) looked in trouble when falling, which is a little disappointing given the promise he had shown in recent starts. *(op 6-1 tchd 7-1 in places)*
T/Plt: £253.20 to a £1 stake. Pool: £52,938.55. 152.60 winning tickets. T/Qpdt: £69.80 to a £1 stake. Pool: £2,483.90. 26.30 winning tickets. JR

2592 WINCANTON (R-H)

Monday, December 26

OFFICIAL GOING: Good (good to soft in places)
Wind: Nil

2995 BATHWICK TYRES YEOVIL NOVICES' H'CAP HURDLE (8 hdls) 2m

12:30 (12:31) (Class 4) (0-95,95) 3-Y-0+ **£2,966** (£864; £432)

Form RPR

0-35 **1** **Ishka Baha (IRE)**[17] 2750 6-11-4 **87** PaddyBrennan 100+
(T R George) *chsd ldrs: led appr 2 out: drvn and r.o wl run-in* **5/1**[2]

3-24 **2** *1 ½* **Sweet Oona (FR)**[42] 2244 6-11-12 **95** SamThomas 103+
(Miss Venetia Williams) *chaed ldrs: wnt 2nd appr 2 out: kpt on u.p and styd on cl home but nt rch wnr* **4/1**[1]

33/0 **3** *10* **Munadil**[25] 2585 7-10-6 **78** (t) TomMalone(3) 75+
(A M Hales) *hld up in rr: stdy hdwy after 3 out: shkn up and kpt on fr 2 out: nvr gng pce to rch ldrs* **33/1**

0-35 **4** *3* **Waziri (IRE)**[18] 2723 4-10-12 **81** AndrewThornton 75
(M Sheppard) *chsd ldrs: chal 3 out: sn led: rdn and hdd appr 2 out: sn wknd* **10/1**

005P **5** *1* **Sunset King (USA)**[24] 2605 5-10-4 **78** JayHarris(5) 71
(R J Hodges) *chsd ldrs: rdn 3 out: wknd bef next* **50/1**

0040 **6** *9* **Bollitree Bob**[24] 2606 4-11-2 **92** JohnKington(7) 76
(M Scudamore) *bhd: hdwy appr 2 out but nvr a danger* **16/1**

0023 **7** *nk* **Jamaaron**[5] 2935 3-10-3 **95** RichardGordon(10) 66
(W G M Turner) *bhd: sme hdwy 3 out: nvr in contention* **12/1**

000 **8** *4* **Secret Divin (FR)**[18] 2730 5-11-1 **89** (v1) WilliamKennedy(5) 69
(Jean-Rene Auvray) *in tch: chsd ldrs 4 out: wknd after next* **22/1**

5050 **9** *7* **Xila Fontenailles (FR)**[11] 2850 4-11-0 **90** KeiranBurke(7) 63
(N J Hawke) *bhd most of way* **16/1**

-044 **10** *1 ½* **The Rip**[39] 2298 4-10-8 **84** ShaneWalsh(7) 55
(R M Stronge) *hld up: hit 3rd: hdwy next: chsd ldrs 3 out: wknd and mstke next* **9/1**

11 *½* **Barella (IRE)**[14] 1347 6-11-5 **95** CharlieStudd(7) 66
(B G Powell) *chsd ldr 3rd: chal 4 out: slt lded next: sn hdd & wknd* **28/1**

-200 **12** *9* **Kentford Lady**[31] 2486 4-11-0 **90** WayneKavanagh(7) 52
(J W Mullins) *chsd ldrs: blnd 4th: wknd after next* **25/1**

P000 **13** *6* **Tashkandi (IRE)**[10] 2860 5-10-6 **75** (v1) ChristianWilliams 31
(P Bowen) *blnd 2nd: nvr jumping after and sn wl bhd* **7/1**

/P-P **P** **Charalambous (USA)**[18] 2732 8-10-9 **78** (t) RJGreene —
(C L Tizzard) *a bhd: blnd 3 out: t.o whn p.u bef 2 out* **66/1**

0000 **P** **My Retreat (USA)**[27] 2563 8-10-6 **75** (b) JamieGoldstein —
(R Fielder) *chsd ldrs to 4th: t.o whn p.u bef last* **66/1**

2F03 **P** **Madam Caversfield**[13] 2811 3-10-12 **94** (p) RobertThornton —
(P D Evans) *chsd ldrs to 4th: t.o whn p.u bef 2 out* **11/2**[3]

50-0 **P** **Alasil (USA)**[52] 2015 5-10-13 **82** (b) BenjaminHitchcott —
(Mrs N Smith) *led to 3 out: sn wknd: t.o whn p.u bef 2 out* **40/1**

3m 43.8s (-5.30) **Going Correction** -0.15s/f (Good)
WFA 3 from 4yo 13lb 4 from 5yo+ 10lb **17** Ran SP% **125.1**
Speed ratings: **107,106,101,99,99 94,94,92,89,88 88,83,80**,—,— —,— CSF £24.32 CT £618.99 TOTE £6.00: £1.70, £1.50, £8.40, £2.90; EX 17.60.
Owner Miss Judith Wilson **Bred** Mrs E Tector **Trained** Slad, Gloucs

FOCUS
Not a bad race for the grade and the front two pulled well clear. A step up in form for the winner, who has been rated value for further.

NOTEBOOK
Ishka Baha(IRE) shaped well when dropped to this distance at Doncaster earlier in the month and proved good enough to provide Paddy Brennan with a return winner. Given a positive ride, she went on two out and ground out the result. Although effective at further, she seems best kept to this distance for the time being.
Sweet Oona(FR) has seen her mark gradually decline of late, despite having run some good races in defeat, and she was rightly made favourite here with her stable continuing in good form. She ran her race and had every chance, pulling ten lengths clear of the third, but the winner proved too strong. She can find a race off this sort of mark. *(op 9-2)*
Munadil, well held on his return to hurdles at Leicester, stepped up significantly on that effort and did best of the rest back in third. He showed enough to make him of interest off a similar mark. *(op 25-1)*
Waziri(IRE) held a good early position and went ahead soon after the third last, but he did not last long and faded in the final furlong or so. *(op 12-1)*
Sunset King(USA) ran one of his better races and left behind a recent poor effort. He has a race in him off this lowly mark if building on this.
Tashkandi(IRE) has thus far disappointed over hurdles and failed to improve for this move into *handicaps. The first-time visor was of little help and his jumping was once again a hindrance. Official explanation: jockey said horse did not face the visor (op 8-1)*
Madam Caversfield *Official explanation: jockey said filly had bled from the nose (op 5-1 tchd 6-1)*

2996 WISE CATERING HARRY DUFOSEE H'CAP CHASE (17 fncs) 2m 5f

1:00 (1:01) (Class 3) (0-115,114) 5-Y-0+ **£5,608** (£1,646; £823; £411)

Form RPR

1- **1** **Preacher Boy**[25] 2593 6-11-9 **111** ChristianWilliams 128+
(R J Hodges) *led to 4th: led again 8th: wnt lft fr 10th: wnt bdly lft and hit 3 out: kpt on run-in: readily* **5/1**[3]

/1-0 **2** *3 ½* **Regal Bandit (IRE)**[18] 2733 7-10-13 **101** SamThomas 107+
(Miss H C Knight) *chsd ldrs: nt fluent 13th: chaallenged fr 2nd 3 out: chsd wnr next but a hld* **7/1**

00-3 **3** *3 ½* **Message Recu (FR)**[18] 2733 9-10-7 **95** (b) RobertThornton 96
(C L Tizzard) *chsd ldrs: rdn and lost position 9th: hdwy 12th: chsd ldrs and rdn 4 out: narrow 2nd 3 out: one pce and mstke next* **10/1**

0-32 **4** *9* **Lizzie Bathwick (IRE)**[28] 2555 6-10-0 **95** DarylJacob(7) 90+
(D P Keane) *chsd ldrs: wnt 2nd 13th: rdn 4 out: wknd next: no ch whn mstke 2 out* **3/1**[2]

3321 **5** *8* **Lord Nellsson**[39] 2296 9-10-2 **90** RJGreene 74
(Andrew Turnell) *led and blnd 4th: hdd next: styd chalng: led 7th: hdd next: rdn fr 9th: sn bhd* **5/2**[1]

-43P **P** **Princesse Grec (FR)**[20] 2686 7-9-10 **91** JohnKington(7) —
(M Scudamore) *hit 4th: bhd 6th: t.o whn p.u bef 2 out* **11/1**

0-30 **P** **Ideal Jack (FR)**[39] 2296 9-9-8 **89** oh6 ow1 (t) EamonDehdashti(7) —
(G A Ham) *hit 2nd: led and hit 5th: hdd 7th: wknd qckly 8th: t.o whn p.u after 9th* **16/1**

521F **P** **Forever Dream**[26] 2577 7-11-12 **114** (b) PaddyBrennan —
(P J Hobbs) *hit 1st: hld up in rr: hdwy 8th: chsd ldrs 11th: styng on and 6l 4th whn blnd 4 out: p.u bef next* **8/1**

5m 21.2s (-1.90) **Going Correction** -0.05s/f (Good) **8** Ran SP% **117.2**
Speed ratings: **101,99,98,94,91** —,—,— CSF £40.11 CT £339.68 TOTE £4.50: £1.50, £2.30, £3.50; EX 70.10.
Owner Hunt & Co (bournemouth) Ltd **Bred** M H Ings **Trained** Charlton Adam, Somerset

FOCUS
An ordinary handicap chase, but Preacher Boy has the makings of a useful sort and won nicely. He was value for much further here. The form looks sound enough.

NOTEBOOK
Preacher Boy, who made a successful transition to Rules racing when winning over course and distance earlier in the month, was trying his luck in handicaps for the first time, but his relative inexperience did not set him back and he jumped fluently under a positive ride from Williams. A blunder at the third-last cost him momentum, but he was soon in control once more and won with something in hand. Evidently a potentially useful chaser, he remains open to further improvement and is one to keep on the right side. *(op 7-2)*
Regal Bandit(IRE) showed very little on his reappearance at Taunton, but with the run under his belt he was able to step up on that and stayed on well into second. He may go up a little for this effort, but that should not prevent him finding a similar race if building on this. *(op 9-1)*
Message Recu(FR) is on a handy mark over fences and may have been closer here had he not made an error at he second last. He should soon be back winning. *(op 12-1)*
Lizzie Bathwick(IRE) has yet to win in three attempts over fences, but she has run some reasonable races and finding a race off this lowly mark should not prove to be too much of a problem. *(op 11-4 tchd 7-2)*
Lord Nellsson, who has the size to make a chaser, did not take that well to fences when last tried over them and in all honesty was disappointing. He jumped well enough in the main, but failed to see out his race in the manner he usually does and for the time being has a bit to prove. *(op 11-4 tchd 3-1)*
Forever Dream ruined his chance by making several minor errors and a more serious mistake four out knocked the stuffing out of him. He may be worth another chance. *(op 9-1)*

2997 BATHWICK TYRES BRIDGWATER MARES' ONLY "NATIONAL HUNT" NOVICES' HURDLE (8 hdls) 2m

1:30 (1:32) (Class 4) 4-Y-0+ **£3,446** (£1,004; £502)

Form RPR

30 **1** **Treaty Flyer (IRE)**[30] 2501 4-10-10 .... SamThomas 100
(P G Murphy) *bhd: hit 2nd: hday fr 4th: chsd ldrs but plenty to do 2 out: styd on to go 2nd last: kpt on u.p to ld cl home* **40/1**

4342 **2** *1* **Don And Gerry (IRE)**[18] 2726 4-10-5 98.................... WilliamKennedy(5) 99
(P D Evans) *led: rdn fr 2 out: one pce: no ex and hdd cl home* **6/1**[2]

1-U1 **3** *11* **Senorita Rumbalita**[28] 2554 4-11-3 .... RobertThornton 101+
(A King) *bdly bumped 1st: sn trcking ldrs: wnt 2nd 4th: rdn and no imp on ldr appr 2 out: no ch whn nt fluent last* **1/3**[1]

21 **4** *4* **Fountain Crumble**[131] 1237 4-10-10 .... ChristianWilliams 84
(P F Nicholls) *bhd: sme hdwy fr 3 out: nvr gng pce to rch ldrs* **9/1**[3]

-040 **5** *6* **Gotta Get On**[18] 2730 4-10-3 74..................................... DarylJacob(7) 78
(R H Alner) *chal 2nd to next: wknd appr 2 out* **100/1**

222P **6** *3 ½* **Miss Midnight**[18] 2730 4-10-7 .... TomMalone(3) 76+
(R J Hodges) *in tch early: bhd fr 4th* **25/1**

0-0 **7** *3* **Tanzanite Dawn**[33] 2432 4-10-10 .... PaddyBrennan 72
(Andrew Turnell) *a in rr* **100/1**

-006 **8** *¾* **She's Our Daisy (IRE)**[5] 2937 5-10-10 .... RJGreene 71
(R H Buckler) *mstke 1st: a bhd* **66/1**

01-0 **9** *10* **Post It**[18] 2727 4-10-10 .... AndrewThornton 61
(R J Hodges) *hit 4 out: a bhd* **50/1**

0- **10** *1* **Shambolina**[350] 3306 4-10-3 .... SimonElliott(7) 60
(J W Mullins) *a in rr* **150/1**

0-50 **11** *2 ½* **Mialyssa**[159] 1042 5-10-5 .... JamesDiment(5) 57
(M R Bosley) *chsd ldrs to 4th* **100/1**

0-0 **12** *1 ¾* **Will She Spin**[28] 2558 4-10-3 .... WayneKavanagh(7) 56
(J W Mullins) *veered bdly rt 1st: chsd ldrs tl after 4 out: no ch whn blnd 2 out* **150/1**

3m 45.8s (-3.30) **Going Correction** -0.15s/f (Good) **12** Ran SP% **113.3**
Speed ratings: **102,101,96,94,91 89,87,87,82,81 80,79** CSF £247.24 TOTE £70.60: £9.50, £1.40, £1.10; EX 340.80.
Owner Mrs Dianne Murphy **Bred** Mrs M Brophy **Trained** East Garston, Berks

FOCUS
An uncompetitive race and a shock result with hot favourite Senor Rumbalita running a long way below par back in third. The winner improved 9lb on her best bumper form, and the race has been rated through the fifth.

NOTEBOOK
Treaty Flyer(IRE), who ran a little better than her finishing position suggested on her hurdling debut at Towcester, looked to face little realistic chance here of defeating hot favourite Senorita Rumbalita, but with that one underperforming back in third, she came out best of the rest and stayed on strongly on the run-in to claim the gallant Don And Gerry. Quite what the form is worth is open to debate, but she is unexposed and it will be interesting to see whether she is up to defying a penalty in mares-only company. *Official explanation: trainer said, regarding the improved form shown, filly had been better suited by today's faster ground and track* (op 33-1)
Don And Gerry(IRE) has been on the go a long time and has had many hard races, but she shows no signs of losing her form and ran another cracker in second, being unfortunate to be reeled in by the winner close home. She was clear of the below-par favourite back in third and can probably win over hurdles once returned to handicaps. (op 5-1)
Senorita Rumbalita, off the mark over hurdles in impressive fashion at Folkestone last month, appeared to face the most simple of tasks here in a bid to defy a penalty, but she was left labouring down the straight, looking weary back in third. It is possible she got upset after being badly bumped jumping the first and it is safe to assume she was not at her best, but this was not the performance of a Festival contender. *Official explanation: vet said filly finished wrong behind* (op 2-5)
Fountain Crumble, a winner on her second and final start in bumpers, could have been expected to fill one of the placings, but she could only plod on at the one pace having been held up. There were enough positives to take from this to suggest she can find a race in mares-only company. (tchd 10-1)
Gotta Get On is a poor performer who does little for the form. A switch to handicaps will help.
Post It *Official explanation: jockey said, regarding the running and riding, his orders had been to drop mare in and get her switched off as she is very keen, adding that filly had been keen over the first two flights but when the field quickened she dropped her bridle and tensed up; trainer added that filly had been very keen when running in a bumper and schooling at home*

2998 BATHWICK TYRES TAUNTON MID SEASON CHASE (A H'CAP) (13 fncs) 2m

2:05 (2:05) (Class 3) (0-130,130) 5-Y-0+ **£10,253** (£3,010; £1,505; £751)

Form RPR

-112 **1** **Lorient Express (FR)**[5] 2939 6-10-7 111........................... SamThomas 129+
(Miss Venetia Williams) *hld up rr but in tch: hdwy 9th: qckknd to ld 4 out: c clr fr next: v easily* **11/8**[1]

5-60 **2** *7* **Master Rex**[30] 2489 10-11-12 130...................................... RobertThornton 136+
(B De Haan) *led 3rd to next: styd prom: pushed along 7th to 8th: chsd wnr fr 3 out but nvr any ch* **4/1**[2]

-314 **3** *7* **Serpentine Rock**[23] 2622 5-11-7 125.................................. PaddyBrennan 123+
(P J Hobbs) *led 2nd to 3rd: led again 4th to 6th: wknd 3 out* **15/2**

4332 **4** *2* **Mark Equal**[17] 2748 9-10-8 115..................................(vt) TomMalone(3) 110
(M C Pipe) *chsd ldrs: led 6th: hdd and hit 4 out: sn wknd* **5/1**[3]

-601 **5** *hd* **Roofing Spirit (IRE)**[39] 2300 7-10-7 118........................... DarylJacob(7) 113
(D P Keane) *rr but in tch: hday to chse ldrs fr 7th: rdn and wakened 4 out* **6/1**

-3U6 **P** **Another Joker**[51] 2048 10-10-12 116................................. AndrewThornton —
(J L Needham) *led to 2nd: styd prom tl wknd rapidly 7th: t.o whn p.u bef 3 out* **13/2**

3m 58.0s (-3.90) **Going Correction** -0.05s/f (Good) **6** Ran SP% **118.2**
Speed ratings: **107,103,100,99,98** — CSF £8.20 TOTE £2.50: £1.50, £3.20; EX 11.50.
Owner Let's Live Racing **Bred** D Laupretre **Trained** Kings Caple, H'fords

FOCUS
Another smooth display by the highly progressive Lorient Express, who was value for 12l. The runner-up was 11lb off his form in winning this a year ago.

NOTEBOOK
Lorient Express(FR) has returned an improved performer this season and had little difficulty making it three wins in his last four with an authoritative display. In receipt of plenty of weight from the runner-up, he cruised clear down the straight and it is not hard to envisage him win again, albeit a further rise will follow. (op 7-4 tchd 2-1)
Master Rex is a very useful performer on his day and was the best horse in the line up, hence top weight, but he proved no match for the progressive winner and could only keep on at the one pace. He did not travel with his usual fluency, but is still up to winning at a good level. (tchd 9-2)
Serpentine Rock has looked vulnerable off this mark the last twice now and he had every chance back in third. He is open to improvement as he has yet to have his sixth birthday, but a little help from the handicapper would not go amiss. (op 13-2 tchd 8-1)
Mark Equal travelled with his usual fluency before finding little off the bridle and he will remain vulnerable until shown some further leniency by the handicapper. (op 4-1)
Roofing Spirit(IRE), up 7lb for his course and distance win last month, was ridden with restraint in rear and made a brief forward move down the back, but he was soon struggling to go with the front pair and faded in the straight. (op 15-2)
Another Joker was up on the pace from an early stage, but the manner in which he stopped once coming under pressure suggested there may have been something amiss. (op 10-1)

2999 PERTEMPS H'CAP HURDLE (SERIES QUALIFIER) (11 hdls) 2m 6f

2:40 (2:40) (Class 2) 4-Y-0+
£12,404 (£3,664; £1,832; £917; £457; £229)

Form RPR

10-0 **1** **Pretty Star (GER)**[43] 2207 5-11-0 126............................. RobertThornton 133
(A King) *chsd ldrs: chal 2 out: sn rdn to ld: hld on all out* **10/1**

1P22 **2** *¾* **Fire Dragon (IRE)**[17] 2747 4-11-12 138.............................. PaddyBrennan 144
(Jonjo O'Neill) *chsd ldrs: led appr 2 out: hdd sn after: edgd lft run-in: rallied cl home but a hld* **7/2**[1]

-UP4 **3** *10* **Dream Falcon**[18] 2731 5-10-1 120..................................... JamesWhite(7) 117+
(R J Hodges) *bhd: pushed along and hdwy appr 2 out: kpt on run-in but nvr gng pce to rch ldrs* **16/1**

0/1- **4** *1 ¼* **Its Wallace Jnr**[596] 251 6-10-2 114..................................(t) JamieGoldstein 109
(Miss Sheena West) *rr but in tch: hday 7th: rdn to chse ldrs appr 2 out: sn outpcd* **16/1**

0003 **5** *hd* **Anatar (IRE)**[23] 2633 7-9-12 113...................................(v) TomMalone(3) 108
(M C Pipe) *rr but in tch: hday 7th: pressed ldrs 3 out: sn rdn: wknd 2 out* **14/1**

0333 **6** *7* **Ingres**[18] 2731 5-9-7 112 oh5.. CharlieStudd(7) 100
(B G Powell) *chsd ldrs: chal 3 out: sn rdn: wknd bef next* **22/1**

5-50 **7** *shd* **Le Roi Miguel (FR)**[37] 2346 7-11-2 128......................... ChristianWilliams 116
(P F Nicholls) *bhd: pushed along and sme hdwy fr 3 out: nvr gng pce to rch ldrs* **4/1**[2]

2002 **8** *2 ½* **Penny Pictures (IRE)**[36] 2369 6-11-4 137.............................. MrRQuinn(7) 125+
(M C Pipe) *led 2nd: hdd & wknd appr 2 out* **15/2**

/05- **9** *dist* **His Nibs (IRE)**[329] 3631 8-11-12 138................................... SamThomas —
(Miss Venetia Williams) *chsd ldrs: bhd whn rdn and hit 7th: t.o* **7/1**

2060 **10** *25* **Grave Doubts**[16] 2765 9-10-7 119...(t) RJGreene —
(K Bishop) *nt fluent: a in rr: t.o* **16/1**

/F-P **F** **Perfect Liaison**[23] 2621 8-10-8 120.............................. AndrewThornton —
(R H Alner) *led to 2nd: cl up whn fell 4th* **22/1**

14F1 **R** **Water King (USA)**[45] 2166 6-9-12 117.................................. ShaneWalsh(7) —
(R M Stronge) *prom early: bhd fr 6th: no ch whn rn out bnd appr 2 out* **11/2**[3]

5m 19.6s (-5.50) **Going Correction** -0.15s/f (Good) **12** Ran SP% **124.0**
Speed ratings: **104,103,100,99,99 97,96,96,—,— —,—** CSF £47.98 CT £572.66 TOTE £14.00: £3.40, £1.90, £3.80; EX 44.80.
Owner Exterior Profiles Ltd **Bred** Gestut Auenquelle **Trained** Barbury Castle, Wilts

FOCUS
Not an easy race to rate and probably just an ordinary race for the grade, but the front two were 10 lengths clear of the third and are clearly on good terms with themselves at present.

NOTEBOOK
Pretty Star(GER) faced a stiff task in a highly competitive race on his reapearance at Cheltenham last month, and with the run under his belt it was reasonable to expect a markedly improved effort here. Just off the early leaders, he had to fight hard to hold Fire Dragon, but he stayed on too strongly for the runner-up and was always holding on. Still only five, he remains open to a deal of *further improvement and it will be interesting to see how he gets on if/when tried at three miles. Official explanation: trainer said, regarding the improved form shown, gelding had been better suited by the slower pace and less competitive race* (tchd 9-1 and 11-1)
Fire Dragon(IRE) has had a good season of it thus far, barring a poor run at Chepstow back in October, and he again ran well here, coming through to lead two out and finding only the winner too strong. As with the winner, he is only a young horse and this was a fine effort under joint top weight. (op 9-2)
Dream Falcon got a bit behind before plugging on again to claim a never-nearer third, staying on through beaten horses. This was quite a good race for him to be contesting and it is likely he will find life easier back down a grade.
Its Wallace Jnr, not seen since winning a lesser race at Plumpton in May, was clearly in fine fettle and looked fit enough, so it was no surprise to see him run such a bold race. He will find easier opportunities. (op 14-1)
Anatar(IRE) is hardly renowned as a strong finisher and he once again failed to get home having travelled strongly. He often keeps good company and is another who may benefit from a drop in grade. (op 12-1)
Le Roi Miguel(FR), a high-class chaser on his day, has found things tough over fences of late and was understandably fancied on this return to hurdles, but he failed to live up to expectations and never really got going. He was keeping on late, but to no real effect and this has to go down as a disappointment. (op 7-2 tchd 9-2)
Water King(USA) *Official explanation: jockey said gelding hit the third-last hurdle and lost its action* (op 5-1 tchd 6-1)

3000 BATHWICK TYRES LORD STALBRIDGE MEMORIAL CUP (A H'CAP CHASE) (21 fncs) 3m 1f 110y

3:15 (3:16) (Class 3) (0-125,125) 5-Y-0+ **£6,896** (£2,024; £1,012; £505)

Form RPR

01/P **1** **Yardbird (IRE)**[44] 2174 6-11-0 113.................................. RobertThornton 126+
(A King) *in tch:chsd ldrs 11th:lost pl 17th: mstke 4 out: plenty to do next:styd on u.p fr 2 out: r.o gamely to ld last stride* **20/1**

1213 **2** *shd* **Black De Bessy (FR)**[30] 2492 7-11-9 122......................... AndrewThornton 133+
(D R C Elsworth) *trckd ldrs:chal 3 out:sn led:hit next: 3l clr last: rdn run-in: styd on same pce and ct last stride* **5/2**[2]

-P42 **3** *1 ¼* **Dante Citizen (IRE)**[25] 2596 7-10-2 104.............................. TomMalone(3) 113
(T R George) *chsd ldrs: lost pl and rr 13th: hdwy 4 out: stl plenty to do next: r.o wl fr 2 out: chsd ldrs run-in: one pce cl home* **7/1**[3]

P211 **4** *4* **Lord Anner (IRE)**[40] 2273 6-10-13 112......................(bt) ChristianWilliams 120+
(P F Nicholls) *chsd ldrs: led 14th: hit 16th: rdn and blnd 3 out: sn hdd and btn* **9/4**[1]

1-P2 **5** *1* **Gray's Eulogy**[24] 2616 7-9-9 99 oh3..........................(b) WilliamKennedy(5) 103
(D R Gandolfo) *chsd ldrs: lost position 14th: rallied to chse ldrs after next: one pce whn hit 3 out* **16/1**

226P **6** *3* **Jiver (IRE)**[24] 2608 6-10-7 113.. JohnKington(7) 114
(M Scudamore) *bhd: rdn fr 14th: styd on fr 4 out but nvr rchd ldrs* **50/1**

P-65 **7** *½* **Zaffamore (IRE)**[18] 2724 9-11-3 116.................................. SamThomas 120+
(Miss H C Knight) *chsd ldrs: rdn 17th: wknd 3 out* **16/1**

0234 **8** *2* **Koquelicot (FR)**[17] 2745 7-11-6 119...............................(b) PaddyBrennan 120+
(P J Hobbs) *led: hdd 14th: wknd 4 out* **10/1**

253F **9** *10* **Tom Sayers (IRE)**[25] 2596 7-11-0 118.......................... RobertStephens(5) 114+
(P J Hobbs) *bhd: sme hdwy 12th: wknd 4 out* **16/1**

6-13 **10** *12* **Snowy Ford (IRE)**[58] 1920 8-11-6 119..................................... RJGreene 104+
(N J Gifford) *nt jump wl: rdn fr 8th: chsd ldrs u.p 17th: wknd and blnd 4 out* **12/1**

1105 **F** **I Hear Thunder (IRE)**[23] 2628 7-11-12 125 BenjaminHitchcott —
(R H Buckler) *chsd ldrs: hit 6th: stl prom whn fell 14th* **14/1**

6m 35.2s (-4.70) **Going Correction** -0.05s/f (Good) **11** Ran SP% **119.7**
Speed ratings: **105,104,104,103,103 102,101,101,98,94** — CSF £73.89 CT £406.71 TOTE £27.90: £4.70, £1.70, £2.30; EX 110.70.
Owner Gilco **Bred** T Horgan **Trained** Barbury Castle, Wilts

FOCUS
A good handicap chase that produced a cracking finish and it is likely to be a race that produces winners. It has been rated through the third, fourth and fifth.

NOTEBOOK
Yardbird(IRE) ◆ faced a stiff task against some useful types on his chasing debut at Cheltenham last month, his first start since April 2004, but this was a much more realistic task off a rating of 113 and he put up a really decent effort considering he was nearer last than first turning in after a blunder four out. Thornton got a strong run out of him on the outside of runners and he really knuckled down after the last to nail Black De Bessy in the dying stride. Unexposed and open to significant improvement, he is evidently a dour stayer and is one to keep on the right side. *(op 22-1 tchd 25-1)*
Black De Bessy(FR), who is regarded as still being well handicapped by connections, continued his highly consistent run of form, but he had looked set to make it another win when jumping the last as he still held a three-length lead over the winner, but he was unable to hang on and lost out by the narrowest of margins. He is undoubtedly capable of winning off this sort of mark, but a further rise is probable after this. *(op 2-1)*
Dante Citizen(IRE) has a decent record at this venue and he put in some good late work to claim third. He is relatively well handicapped at present and should be capable of scoring again back down in grade. *(op 8-1 tchd 9-1)*
Lord Anner(IRE), a really progressive gelding, put up an improved performance in the first-time blinkers at the course last month, but they did not have quite the same effect here and he flattened out under pressure, the 12lb hike probably telling as well. He has plenty of size and scope about him and may be capable of winning off this mark in time. *(op 5-2 tchd 11-4)*
Gray's Eulogy seemed to find this company a little too hot and he struggled despite having to shoulder a mere feather-weight. He gave his all in fairness and kept on right the way to the line, but simply found the opposition too good for him. *(op 20-1)*
Jiver(IRE) ran way above market expectations and stayed on past tiring rivals to claim a never-nearer sixth. He has yet to win over fences, but should have little trouble on this evidence. *(op 66-1)*
I Hear Thunder(IRE) has seen his progressive profile level out in recent starts, but he was far from done with here when falling. It remains to be seen how this affects his confidence. *(op 16-1)*

3001 GOOD LUCK STEPHEN INTERMEDIATE OPEN NATIONAL HUNT FLAT RACE 2m
3:45 (3:52) (Class 6) 4-6-Y-0 **£2,357** (£686; £343)

Form RPR
1 **Pepperoni Pete (IRE)** 4-11-4 ChristianWilliams 122+
(P F Nicholls) *in tch: hdwy 5f out: chal over 3f out: led over 2f out: c clr fnl f: easily* **7/4**[1]
0 **2** *5* **Pangbourne (FR)**[22] 2665 4-11-4 (be[1]) RobertThornton 112+
(A King) *w ldr tl led 1/2-way: rdn 4f out: hdd over 2f out: hung lft u.p over 1f out and sn no ch w wnr* **16/1**
3 *11* **Warlord** 4-11-4 BenjaminHitchcott 100
(R H Buckler) *chsd ldrs: rdn 3f out: styd on same pce* **50/1**
4 *1 3/4* **Petitjean** 5-11-4 PaddyBrennan 98
(P J Hobbs) *chsd ldrs: rdn 4f out: one pce fr over 2f out* **6/1**
5 *hd* **Captain Marlon (IRE)** 4-11-4 RJGreene 98
(C L Tizzard) *chsd ldrs: rdn 4f out: styd on same pce fnl 2f* **10/1**
6 *1/2* **Rhacophorus** 4-10-6 RobertStephens(5) 90
(C J Down) *bhd: kpt on wl fr over 2f out: n.d* **100/1**
7 *hd* **Portland Bill (IRE)** 5-10-11 MrJSnowden(7) 97
(R H Alner) *chsd ldrs: rdn over 4f out: one pce fnl 2f* **33/1**
4/ **8** *5* **Return Ticket**[613] 4934 6-10-11 SeanQuinlan(7) 93+
(R T Phillips) *mid-div: hdwy 1/2-way: nvr rchd ldrs and wknd fnl 2f* **20/1**
9 *3* **Single Player (IRE)** 5-10-13 WilliamKennedy(5) 91+
(Noel T Chance) *sn pushed along in mid-div: n.d* **9/2**[2]
00 **10** *7* **Fairlight Express (IRE)**[74] 1730 5-10-11 DarylJacob(7) 82
(D P Keane) *chsd ldrs to 4f out* **50/1**
1 **11** *5* **Legal Glory (IRE)**[39] 2288 5-11-4 CharlieStudd(7) 84
(B G Powell) *nvr trbld ldrs* **12/1**
12 *1* **La Cuenta (IRE)** 5-11-4 SamThomas 76
(Miss Venetia Williams) *bhd fnl 5f* **5/1**[3]
0- **13** *14* **Red Raptor**[314] 3864 4-10-11 (t) SimonElliott(7) 62
(J A Geake) *bhd most of way* **66/1**
0 **14** *1 3/4* **Hold That Thought (IRE)**[27] 2565 5-11-4 AndrewThornton 60
(Miss H C Knight) *a in rr* **12/1**
15 *1/2* **Kyliemoss** 4-10-4 KeiranBurke(7) 53
(N R Mitchell) *a in rr* **100/1**
16 *dist* **That's Final** 4-11-1 TomMalone(3) —
(J C Tuck) *t.o after 7f* **100/1**
00/0 **P** **Valderrama**[50] 2075 5-10-11 (t) ShaneWalsh(7) —
(C J Down) *led: hdd 1/2-way: sn wknd: t.o whn p.u 6f out* **100/1**

3m 37.0s (-14.70) **Going Correction** -0.15s/f (Good) **17** Ran SP% **132.9**
WFA 4 from 5yo+ 10lb
Speed ratings: **110,107,102,101,101 100,100,98,96,93 90,90,83,82,82** —,— CSF £38.17 TOTE £2.40: £1.10, £5.40, £8.00; EX 42.10 Place 6 £59.48, Place 5 £28.37.
Owner C G Roach **Bred** M W And Mrs M Doran **Trained** Ditcheat, Somerset

FOCUS
An ordinary bumper in all truth, but Pepperoni Pete was most impressive, value for double the winning margin, and looks well worth his place in a better contest.

NOTEBOOK
Pepperoni Pete(IRE) ◆, representing top connections who took this event last year, travelled strongly under Williams and assumed control two out before clearing away with the minimum of fuss. Impressive on the eye, he looks a potentially useful sort and is no doubt set to step up in grade now. A pacey sort, it would not surprise to see him line up in one of the Championship Bumpers, with Aintree likely to suit best. *(tchd 2-1)*
Pangbourne(FR), who looked most unwilling when down the field on his debut, had headgear fitted today and raced much more sweetly. He is clearly not straightforward however, and hung when pressed for maximum effort, but he was a long way clear of the third and clearly has the ability to win a similar race. *(op 50-1)*
Warlord, representing connections who are hardly renowned for their success in this sphere, recorded a highly pleasing effort back in third and, although well held by the front two, it is unlikely he will be seen at his best until tackling hurdles. *(op 66-1)*
Petitjean has the makings of a decent sort and he kept on steadily under pressure to claim fourth. It is safe to assume he will come on for this and there is no doubt a race for him in this sphere. *(tchd 13-2)*
Captain Marlon(IRE) ◆ comes from a stable whose horses tend to do well under a test of stamina and it is highly likely he would not have been ready for this first time up. Taking this into consideration, he made a pleasing debut and looks one to watch out for next time. *(op 16-1)*
Rhacophorus, one of only two mares in the race, ran above market expectations and was putting in some good late work. She will stay further once hurdling, but for the moment will be helped by a move into mares-only company. *(op 66-1)*
Single Player(IRE), whose stable have an excellent record in National Hunt Flat races, was unsurprisingly short in the betting, but he failed to live up to expectations and was in trouble some way from home. He may lack the speed for bumpers, in which case a switch to hurdles could be on the horizon. *(op 5-1 tchd 6-1)*
La Cuenta(IRE), whose stable have had a brilliant time of it in the past few weeks, never got involved and was unable to add his name to the list of winners. He may need more time. *(op 11-2 tchd 6-1 and 9-2)*
T/Plt: £92.50 to a £1 stake. Pool: £34,348.70. 270.85 winning tickets. T/Qpdt: £7.90 to a £1 stake. Pool: £1,537.50. 143.90 winning tickets. ST

3002 - (Foreign Racing) - See Raceform Interactive

LEOPARDSTOWN (L-H)
Monday, December 26
OFFICIAL GOING: Yielding (yielding to soft in places)

3003a DURKAN NEW HOMES MAIDEN HURDLE (9 hdls) 2m 2f
12:55 (12:56) 4-Y-O **£7,106** (£1,655; £730; £421)

RPR
1 **Finger Onthe Pulse (IRE)**[30] 2508 4-11-4 SMMcGovern(3) 123
(T J Taaffe, Ire) *mde virtually all: strly pressed after 2 out: styd on wl fr last to draw clr run-in* **4/1**[2]
2 *4* **Akarem**[23] 2627 4-11-7 NPMadden 120
(K R Burke) *trckd ldrs: 5th 4 out: impr into 2nd after 2 out: sn chal and ev ch: no ex whn slt mstke last* **8/1**
3 *14* **Line Ball (IRE)**[36] 2400 4-11-7 CO'Dwyer 107
(C Roche, Ire) *trckd ldrs: 6th whn slt mstke 4th: 3rd whn slt mstke 4 out: 2nd bef 2 out: 3rd and no ex bef last* **5/2**[1]
4 *9* **Well Mounted (IRE)**[22] 2671 4-11-7 DNRussell 99
(A L T Moore, Ire) *mid-div: 10th appr 1/2-way: 5th bef 3 out: rdn next: kpt on same pce* **5/1**
5 *2* **Mercuric** 4-11-7 TPTreacy 97
(Mrs John Harrington, Ire) *towards rr: hdwy into mod 7th 2 out: kpt on* **33/1**
6 *2 1/2* **Dinarobin (USA)**[11] 2855 4-11-7 (bt) PCarberry 95
(Noel Meade, Ire) *settled 3rd: 2nd fr 5th: rdn and lost pl bef 2 out: sn no ex* **9/2**[3]
7 *1/2* **Beau Bridget (IRE)**[22] 2672 4-10-9 MrJEBurns(7) 89
(Henry De Bromhead, Ire) *towards rr: 7th and hdwy 4 out: 6th next: no imp fr 2 out* **50/1**
8 *20* **Tudorvic (IRE)**[36] 2393 4-11-0 MrMDHickey(7) 76
(John Joseph Murphy, Ire) *rr of mid-div: kpt on one pce fr 3 out* **33/1**
9 *2* **Ballyfinney (IRE)**[22] 4-11-4 RLoughran(3) 75
(D T Hughes, Ire) *mid-div: 9th 1/2-way: wknd fr 4 out* **20/1**
10 *1/2* **Snow Patrol**[185] 4-11-7 DJCasey 74
(C F Swan, Ire) *trckd ldrs: 4th at 4th: 6th next: wknd 3 out* **14/1**
11 *2* **Williamtown Lad (IRE)**[19] 2708 4-11-0 MrDRoche(7) 72
(Paul A Roche, Ire) *nvr a factor* **33/1**
12 *8* **Eight Fifty Six (IRE)**[48] 2115 4-11-7 MrJTMcNamara 65
(Michael Hourigan, Ire) *hld up: prog into mod 8th bef 3 out: sn no ex* **50/1**
13 *3* **Yeoman (FR)**[9] 2899 4-11-2 KTColeman(5) 62
(D J Ryan, Ire) *a bhd* **100/1**
14 *1/2* **Warpath (IRE)** 4-11-0 MPWatts(7) 62
(Anthony Mullins, Ire) *nvr a factor* **25/1**
15 *25* **Muslin**[8] 2907 4-11-2 APCrowe 35
(Liam McAteer, Ire) *mid-div: no ex fr bef 3 out* **50/1**
16 *dist* **Fanling Lady**[75] 4-11-2 GCotter —
(Martin Brassil, Ire) *a bhd: completely t.o fr 4 out* **33/1**
17 *1* **Nechouka (FR)**[303] 4077 4-11-4 AJDonoghue(3) —
(Seamus Neville, Ire) *a bhd: completely t.o fr 4 out* **66/1**
F **Barrell Rose (IRE)**[8] 2918 4-11-2 PACarberry —
(Paul Magnier, Ire) *bhd: fell 4 out* **50/1**
F **Mickataine (IRE)**[11] 2855 4-11-4 MDarcy(3) —
(M F Morris, Ire) *trckd ldrs: 4th whn fell 5th* **8/1**
B **Parliament Square (IRE)**[50] 4-11-7 JohnnyMurtagh —
(M J P O'Brien, Ire) *mid-div: 8th whn b.d 5th* **8/1**
P **Serusier (IRE)**[178] 4077 4-11-0 RJKiely(7) —
(T J Arnold, Ire) *2nd and disp ld: wknd fr 5th: p.u after 3 out* **100/1**

4m 28.1s **Going Correction** -0.90s/f (Hard) **21** Ran SP% **155.1**
Speed ratings: **99,97,91,87,86 85,84,75,75,74 73,70,69,68,57** —,—,—,—,— — CSF £42.74 TOTE £4.80: £1.60, £2.50, £1.50, £1.30; DF 53.70.
Owner Conor Clarkson **Bred** Mary Fanning McCormack **Trained** Straffan, Co Kildare

NOTEBOOK
Akaremwent in pursuit of the winner after the second last and had every chance early in the straight although he was looking held when making a slight blunder at the last. This was an above-average maiden hurdle, the first pair drawing right away. *(op 7/1)*

3004a DURKAN NEW HOMES JUVENILE HURDLE (GRADE 2) (8 hdls) 2m
1:25 (1:29) 3-Y-O **£23,085** (£6,773; £3,226; £1,099)

RPR
1 **Clear Riposte (IRE)**[11] 2851 3-10-4 DJCasey 114
(W P Mullins, Ire) *trckd ldrs on inner: 4th 4 out: led next: strly pressed after 2 out: styd on wl fr last* **14/1**
2 *3* **Artist's Muse (IRE)**[9] 2893 3-10-4 DNRussell 111
(T M Walsh, Ire) *hld up: hdwy 3 out: 3rd travelling 2 out: rdn and no imp fr last: kpt on same pce* **7/2**[1]
3 *shd* **Dreux (FR)**[25] 2601 3-10-9 NPMadden 116
(Thomas Cooper, Ire) *in tch: 6th 4 out: 4th next: 2nd and chal 2 out: ev ch appr last: no ex cl home* **8/1**
4 *7* **Miss Caruso**[11] 2851 3-10-4 GCotter 104
(P J Prendergast, Ire) *towards rr: prog into 5th 2 out: mod 4th bef last: kpt on same pce* **16/1**
5 *hd* **First Row (IRE)**[107] 3-10-9 RLoughran 109
(D T Hughes, Ire) *hld up: 10th 3 out: 8th 2 out: kpt on u.p* **16/1**
6 *20* **Kells Castle**[11] 2851 3-10-9 95 (b) JLCullen 89
(Ms F M Crowley, Ire) *trckd ldrs on outer: 5th 3 out: 4th and rdn next: sn no ex: eased fr last* **12/1**
7 *1/2* **Quinmaster (USA)**[98] 3-10-9 JohnnyMurtagh 88
(M Halford, Ire) *hld up: prog 3 out: 6th 2 out: sn no ex: eased fr last* **8/1**

8 *25* **King Of Merlia (USA)**[11] 2851 3-10-9 .... JRBarry 63
(E Sheehy, Ire) *hld up: impr into 5th and rdn bef 2 out: sn no ex: eased fr last* **6/1**[3]

9 *15* **The Last Stand**[23] 2645 3-10-12 109 .... MPWatts 51
(Anthony Mullins, Ire) *led: hdd 3 out: sn wknd: t.o whn eased bef last* **7/1**

10 *2 1/2* **Orpen Guama (IRE)**[18] 2735 3-10-9 95 .... MDarcy 46
(John F Gleeson, Ire) *settled 2nd: rdn and wknd fr 3 out: eased fr 2 out: t.o* **20/1**

11 *1 1/2* **Ballygally Bay**[23] 2645 3-10-9 .... PCarberry 44
(S J Mahon, Ire) *trckd ldrs: reminders 3rd: impr into 3rd next: slt mstke 4 out: wknd after 3 out: eased next: t.o* **4/1**[2]

12 *3 1/2* **Packie Tam (IRE)**[9] 2893 3-10-9 .... (t) TPTreacy 41
(Patrick O Brady, Ire) *prom tl mstke 4th: dropped to rr next: t.o and eased fr 2 out* **33/1**

3m 55.0s **Going Correction** -0.90s/f (Hard) **12** Ran SP% **125.1**
Speed ratings: **105,103,103,99,99 89,89,77,69,68 67,65** CSF £67.32 TOTE £26.00: £5.50, £1.60, £1.80; DF 59.10.
Owner Heritage Syndicate **Bred** Miss Honora Corridan **Trained** Muine Beag, Co Carlow

NOTEBOOK
Clear Riposte(IRE) emerged as best of what appears a moderate bunch of juvenile hurdlers. Leading three out, she had her opposition struggling from the next and, having gained first run, maintained her advantage to the line.
Artist's Muse(IRE) looked very one paced when asked to quicken before the last.
Dreux(FR) almost certainly improved on his Thurles win but could not take on the winner with a serious challenge.
Miss Caruso has had her chances and this represents her form.
King Of Merlia(USA) was eased on the run-in as though something was amiss. *Official explanation: jockey said colt went badly lame in the closing stages*
The Last Stand *Official explanation: jockey said gelding ran freely and found little off the bridle*
Ballygally Bayfailed to build on the promise of his two previous efforts, which included a Punchestown win. *(op 4/1 tchd 7/2)*

3005a DURKAN NEW HOMES H'CAP HURDLE (9 hdls) 2m 2f
1:55 (1:58) (81-116,117) 4-Y-0+ **£7,106** (£1,655; £730; £421)

RPR

1 **Buck Whaley (IRE)**[51] 2719 5-10-11 99 .... DNRussell 118+
(Jonjo O'Neill) *mid-div: 7th after 3 out: 4th and smooth hdwy 2 out: led ent st: clr fr last: eased cl home* **7/2**[1]

2 *6* **Shifting Alliance (IRE)**[15] 2792 5-10-8 96 .... JLCullen 106
(Paul Nolan, Ire) *rr of mid-div: hdwy 2 out: styd on to go mod 2nd fr last* **14/1**

3 *3 1/2* **Game Ball Ali (IRE)**[15] 2783 4-10-4 92 .... JohnnyMurtagh 99
(M Halford, Ire) *settled 2nd: led after 3 out: hdd after 2 out: 3rd and no ex fr last* **12/1**

4 *2 1/2* **Bold As Brass (IRE)**[30] 2513 6-9-7 84 .... AJDonoghue(3) 88
(James Keegan, Ire) *trckd ldrs: 6th appr 2 out: kpt on same pce fr bef last* **50/1**

5 *3/4* **Maralan (IRE)**[16] 2778 4-10-11 102 .... SMMcGovern(3) 105
(Patrick O Brady, Ire) *trckd ldrs: 5th 3 out: 2nd and chal appr next: no ex bef last* **14/1**

6 *1 1/2* **Sea To Sky (FR)**[30] 2511 5-10-9 102 .... (t) MrJPO'Farrell(5) 104
(Michael Joseph Fitzgerald, Ire) *mid-div: kpt on fr 2 out* **16/1**

7 *1/2* **Coconut Beach**[40] 2277 4-10-12 100 .... APCrowe 101
(C Roche, Ire) *prom: 2nd 4 out: 3rd next: 4th and no ex after 2 out: wknd fr last* **5/1**[3]

8 *3* **Malthouse Master (IRE)**[9] 2898 5-10-9 97 .... DTEvans 95
(Oliver Finnegan, Ire) *towards rr: prog into mid-div 3 out: no imp fr 2 out* **14/1**

9 *4* **Max Time**[16] 2778 8-9-13 87 .... PACarberry 81
(I Madden, Ire) *hld up: 10th and effrt 2 out: no imp st* **14/1**

10 *3* **Syroco (FR)**[37] 2363 6-10-7 95 .... DJCasey 86
(A L T Moore, Ire) *mid-div: 10th 1/2-way: no imp fr bef 2 out* **9/2**[2]

11 *3/4* **Ballard Lad (IRE)**[9] 2896 6-11-8 110 .... JRBarry 101
(Miss S Cox, Ire) *trckd ldrs: 5th 4 out: 4th next: sn rdn: wknd fr next* **10/1**

12 *shd* **Aqua Breezer (IRE)**[15] 2787 6-11-6 108 .... GCotter 95
(Ms Caroline Hutchinson, Ire) *chsd ldrs: 9th appr 1/2-way: no ex bef 2 out* **20/1**

13 *3 1/2* **Mac Robin's Lass (IRE)**[37] 2363 5-9-7 86 .... KTColeman(5) 73
(Gerard Keane, Ire) *hld up: 11th and effrt 2 out: sn no ex* **33/1**

14 *3* **Freddie Foster (IRE)**[16] 2778 6-11-3 105 .... PCarberry 89
(Noel Meade, Ire) *nvr a factor* **14/1**

15 *2* **Loughanelteen (IRE)**[140] 1183 7-11-7 116 .... JPFortune(7) 98
(P J Rothwell, Ire) *hld up: hdwy 3 out: 4th appr 2 out: sn wknd* **16/1**

16 *8* **Lagudin (IRE)**[19] 2710 7-10-6 97 .... (b) RLoughran(3) 71
(Paul John Gilligan, Ire) *towards rr: mstke 3rd: no ex fr bef 3 out* **25/1**

17 *4* **Dream Castle (IRE)**[9] 2898 11-11-3 112 .... (p) MPWatts(7) 82
(Barry Potts, Ire) *led: hdd & wknd 3 out* **25/1**

18 *14* **Tragic Lover**[16] 2778 9-10-13 101 .... TPTreacy 57
(Donal Kinsella, Ire) *prom: 4th 1/2-way: wknd fr 3 out* **12/1**

19 *1 1/2* **Greywell (IRE)**[19] 2710 8-10-2 95 .... (t) MissEDoyle(5) 49
(Miss Elizabeth Doyle, Ire) *mid-div: 8th and effrt appr 2 out: sn no ex* **16/1**

20 *2 1/2* **Happiest Days (IRE)**[32] 2467 7-10-9 97 .... (b) NPMadden 49
(Oliver McKiernan, Ire) *a bhd: trailing fr bef 3 out* **20/1**

21 *1/2* **Penny Rich (IRE)**[9] 2898 11-11-8 117 .... (t) MrJJRyan(7) 68
(T Hogan, Ire) *a bhd: trailing thrght* **16/1**

F **She'll Be Lucky (IRE)**[15] 2787 7-11-1 106 .... (p) MDarcy(3) —
(Michael Hourigan, Ire) *mid-div: rdn bef 2 out: no imp whn fell last* **14/1**

4m 25.6s **Going Correction** -0.90s/f (Hard)
WFA 4 from 5yo+ 10lb **22** Ran SP% **167.2**
Speed ratings: **104,101,99,98,98 97,97,96,94,93 92,91,91,89,88 85,83,77,76,75 75,—** CSF £67.87 CT £626.82 TOTE £4.50: £1.90, £3.40, £2.60, £18.40; DF 79.30.
Owner Barry Connell **Bred** Mileshan Nominees Pty Ltd **Trained** Cheltenham, Gloucs
■ Stewards' Enquiry : J R Barry caution: used whip with excessive frequency

NOTEBOOK
Buck Whaley(IRE) looked well handicapped and made a nonsense of his assessment. He drew clear before the last and won unchallenged, earning a 14lb rise in the process. *(op 3/1)*

3006a DURKAN NEW HOMES NOVICE CHASE (GRADE 1) (11 fncs) 2m 1f
2:30 (2:35) 4-Y-0+ **£46,099** (£13,475; £6,382; £2,127)

RPR

1 **Missed That**[16] 2776 6-11-12 .... DJCasey 156
(W P Mullins, Ire) *trckd ldrs in 4th: rdn to chal after 2 out: led ent st: hdd after last: rallied u.p run-in to regain ld cl home* **10/1**

2 *1 1/2* **Wild Passion (GER)**[36] 2395 5-11-10 .... PCarberry 152
(Noel Meade, Ire) *cl 2nd: pushed along after 4 out: chal after 2 out: led after last: kpt on u.p: hdd and no ex cl home* **7/2**[2]

3 *25* **Kill Devil Hill (IRE)**[22] 2668 5-11-10 .... JLCullen 127
(Paul Nolan, Ire) *settled 3rd: slt mstke 4 out: 4th after 2 out: no ex whn lft mod 3rd last* **6/1**[3]

4 *nk* **Arteea (IRE)**[36] 2395 6-11-12 .... MrJTMcNamara 129
(Michael Hourigan, Ire) *hld up: mod 6th 3 out: lft 5th next: lft 4th fr last* **20/1**

5 *dist* **Baron De Feypo (IRE)**[8] 2908 7-11-12 .... NPMadden —
(Patrick O Brady, Ire) *a bhd: mstke 5th: trailing fr 4 out: t.o* **25/1**

U **Justified (IRE)**[36] 2395 6-11-12 .... JRBarry —
(E Sheehy, Ire) *ldng whn blnd and uns rdr 1st* **5/4**[1]

F **Doctor Linton (IRE)**[15] 2795 6-11-12 133 .... DNRussell —
(M J P O'Brien, Ire) *hld up: mod 5th 3 out: no imp whn fell next* **12/1**

F **Mansony (FR)**[22] 2668 6-11-12 .... CO'Dwyer 141+
(A L T Moore, Ire) *lft in ld fr 1st: hdd after 2 out: 3rd and no ex whn fell last* **7/1**

4m 12.1s **Going Correction** -0.90s/f (Hard) **8** Ran SP% **118.8**
Speed ratings: **107,106,94,94,— —,—,—** CSF £47.87 TOTE £15.90: £2.70, £1.10, £1.60; DF 121.10.
Owner Mrs Violet O'Leary **Bred** Exors Of The Late T F M Corrie **Trained** Muine Beag, Co Carlow

NOTEBOOK
Missed That continues his education over fences and this was a real result, incomparable with his initial effort in a Thurles novice chase early in December. He relished the battle from the last after *being headed. He will come back here next month and the Arkle is his intended Cheltenham race (op 8/1)*
Wild Passion(GER) looked to have the race won when leading after the last but the winner showed greater determination. *(op 7/2 tchd 100/30)*
Kill Devil Hill(IRE) left his Grade One Fairyhouse win in tatters after this. He needs the extra half mile but was beaten a long way out, and possibly prefers going the other way around.

3007 - 3011a (Foreign Racing) - See Raceform Interactive

2250 LIMERICK (R-H)
Monday, December 26

OFFICIAL GOING: Soft changing to heavy after race 2 (1.10)

3012a GUINNESS GREENMOUNT PARK NOVICE CHASE (GRADE 2) 2m 4f
2:20 (2:26) 5-Y-0+ **£25,393** (£7,450; £3,549; £1,209)

RPR

1 **Baily Breeze (IRE)**[25] 2599 6-11-5 .... (p) PWFlood 142+
(M F Morris, Ire) *chsd ldr in 2nd: led bef st: strly pressed and jnd bef 2 out: sn in front again: kpt on wl run-in* **10/1**

2 *5* **Coljon (IRE)**[19] 2712 7-11-5 120 .... (p) RMMoran 137
(Paul Nolan, Ire) *led and clr early: reduced ld and hdd bef st: sn dropped to 3rd: no imp u.p appr 2 out: wnt 2nd again cl home* **9/1**

3 *1/2* **On The Net (IRE)**[19] 2712 7-11-5 125 .... DFO'Regan 136
(Eoghan O'Grady, Ire) *chsd ldrs: impr into 2nd ent st: sn chal and disp ld 2 out: hdd appr last and sn no ex: dropped to 3rd cl home* **5/2**[2]

4 *3* **Sher Beau (IRE)**[241] 116 6-11-5 .... DJCondon 133
(Philip Fenton, Ire) *chsd ldrs: dropped to rr 4 out: rdn to go 4th bef st: sn no imp: kpt on same pce* **7/2**[3]

5 *7* **Kerryhead Windfarm (IRE)**[37] 2364 7-11-5 .... AndrewJMcNamara 126
(Michael Hourigan, Ire) *trckd ldrs: slt mstke 4th: lost pl u.p appr st: sn no imp* **6/4**[1]

6 *dist* **Django (IRE)**[25] 2598 6-11-5 .... RMPower —
(Mrs John Harrington, Ire) *racd mainly in rr: no imp u.p fr bef st* **12/1**

U **American Jennie (IRE)**[15] 2787 7-11-0 .... GTHutchinson —
(Michael Cullen, Ire) *mstke and uns rdr 3rd* **10/1**

5m 44.6s **7** Ran SP% **126.7**
CSF £96.16 TOTE £9.70: £3.00, £6.40; DF 144.10.
Owner R A Scott **Bred** A W Buller **Trained** Fethard, Co Tipperary

NOTEBOOK
Baily Breeze(IRE) sprang a surprise here, relishing the ground and going on a second time between the last two fences for an easy win. *(op 10/1 tchd 12/1)*
Coljon(IRE) soon built up a clear lead and despite giving way before the straight came back again from third place over the last. He needs further. *(op 7/1)*
On The Net(IRE) disputed it two out but floundered on the run-in. *(op 3/1)*
Sher Beau(IRE) ran indifferently, dropping away four out and then staying on again in the straight *(op 5/2)*
Kerryhead Windfarm(IRE) was another to disappoint, fading before the straight with no apparent excuse. *(op 2/1)*

3013 - 3016a (Foreign Racing) - See Raceform Interactive

2618 CHEPSTOW (L-H)
Tuesday, December 27

OFFICIAL GOING: Good to soft (soft in places)
Wind: Light across Weather: Snow showers race 7.

3017 JIM NEVILLE MEMORIAL BEGINNERS' CHASE (16 fncs) 2m 3f 110y
12:00 (12:01) (Class 3) 4-Y-0+ **£6,128** (£1,799; £899; £449)

Form RPR

5-24 **1** **Lustral Du Seuil (FR)**[32] 2482 6-11-4 130 .... MickFitzgerald 140+
(N J Henderson) *a.p: mstke 7th: led 3 out: clr next: comf* **4/1**[2]

05 **2** *9* **Launde (IRE)**[20] 2701 6-11-4 .... AndrewThornton 125+
(B N Pollock) *led: mstke 5 out: hdd 3 out: styd on same pce fr next* **50/1**

2654 **3** *13* **Latin Queen (IRE)**[12] 2846 5-10-6 .... ChrisHonour(5) 102
(J D Frost) *hld up: hdwy 6th: outpcd 9th: sme late hdwy* **33/1**

-032 **4** *1* **Very Optimistic (IRE)**[39] 2311 7-11-4 .... BrianHarding 110+
(Jonjo O'Neill) *chsd ldr tl rdn after 4 out: hit next: sn wknd* **11/8**[1]

/3-4 **5** *8* **Rakalackey**[21] 2682 7-11-4 .... TonyDobbin 100
(H D Daly) *chsd ldrs tl wknd after 11th* **12/1**

444P **6** *5* **Windy Spirit (IRE)**[33] 2458 10-11-4 106 .... ChristianWilliams 95
(Evan Williams) *hld up: a bhd* **33/1**

-543 **U** **Give Me Love (FR)**[24] 2620 5-11-4 119 .... (t) RWalsh —
(P F Nicholls) *hld up: blnd and uns rdr 7th* **9/2**[3]

0 **P** **Roussea (IRE)**[13] 2826 7-10-13 .... LeeStephens(5) —
(S G Griffiths) *hld up: mstke 2nd: t.o whn p.u bef 5 out* **100/1**

113/ **P** **Special Rate (IRE)**[668] 4045 8-11-4 .... RobertThornton —
(A King) *hld up in tch: wknd 7th: t.o whn p.u bef 5 out* **7/1**

0/P0 **P** **Stars'N'Stripes (IRE)**[12] 2848 7-11-4 .... TomDoyle —
(W W Dennis) *prom: mstke 2nd: wknd after 7th: t.o whn p.u bef 5 out* **66/1**

5m 1.90s (-9.40) **Going Correction** -0.425s/f (Good) **10** Ran SP% **110.8**
Speed ratings: **101,97,92,91,88 86,—,—,—,—** CSF £153.65 TOTE £5.20: £1.70, £11.90, £6.00; EX 101.20.
Owner W J Brown **Bred** M Boudot **Trained** Upper Lambourn, Berks

FOCUS
Not much strength in depth to this beginners' chase, run at a fair pace, but it is probably form to be positive about with easy winner value for 15l.

NOTEBOOK
Lustral Du Seuil(FR) enjoyed the step up in trip and ultimately ran out an easy winner to lose his maiden tag over fences at the third attempt. He remains open to improvement as a chaser, and could defy a penalty, but he looks slightly flattered by this and is not going to prove easy to place from his current official rating.
Launde(IRE) was given a positive ride and, despite proving no match for the winner, managed to finish closer to that rival than had been the case on his debut under Rules at Sandown in November. He now becomes eligible for handicaps, should prove suited by the return to a stiffer test in the future, and he is going the right way. *(op 33-1)*
Latin Queen(IRE) was doing all of her best work at the finish having struggled to go the pace turning for home, and turned in another fair effort. She will be happier when reverting to a faster surface. *(op 25-1 tchd 40-1)*
Very Optimistic(IRE), back up in trip, looked a big player at the top of the straight, but he quickly started to tread water when asked to win his race and faded most disappointingly from the third-last fence. He has questions to answer regarding his attitude now. *(tchd 6-4)*
Rakalackey never looked happy on this tacky ground and again ran way below his best. He has made a disappointing start to life over fences, but all of his best form is on a decent surface and he could leave this behind when getting his ground in the future. *(op 9-1)*

3018 ATTHERACES.COM FREE ARCHIVE VIDEO H'CAP HURDLE (12 hdls) 3m
12:30 (12:34) (Class 3) (0-120,117)
4-Y-0+
£6,059 (£1,789; £894; £447; £223; £112)

Form				RPR
1112	**1**		**Drumbeater (IRE)**[19] 2731 5-11-9 **114** .... PaddyBrennan (P J Hobbs) *hld up in mid-div: hdwy 6th: led appr last: drvn out* **13/2**[2]	118
6P31	**2**	*nk*	**Keepers Mead (IRE)**[25] 2609 7-11-6 **111** .... TimmyMurphy (R H Alner) *led: rdn and hdd appr last: r.o* **7/1**[3]	115
45P1	**3**	*2 ½*	**Three Lions**[175] 906 8-10-11 **102** .... RobertThornton (R S Brookhouse) *hld up and bhd: hdwy after 8th: rdn appr last: no ex flat* **16/1**	103
2-43	**4**	*5*	**Albert House (IRE)**[38] 2341 7-10-11 **102** .... AndrewThornton (R H Alner) *a.p: rdn appr 2 out: wknd appr last* **12/1**	99+
1616	**5**	*3 ½*	**Pardon What**[11] 2868 9-11-1 **106** ....(b) KeithMercer (S Lycett) *hld up in mid-div: styd on fr 3 out: nvr trbld ldrs* **20/1**	99
P3U4	**6**	*shd*	**Bunkum**[14] 2813 7-11-4 **109** .... TomDoyle (R Lee) *hld up and bhd: hdwy 7th: hit 2 out: sn rdn and wknd* **16/1**	103+
-4F0	**7**	*7*	**Courant D'Air (IRE)**[19] 2714 4-11-1 **106** .... LeightonAspell (Lucinda Featherstone) *hld up and bhd: hdwy appr 4 out: wknd appr 3 out* **33/1**	93+
5FP0	**8**	*6*	**Charango Star**[19] 2731 7-10-12 **103** .... TonyDobbin (W K Goldsworthy) *hld up in mid-div: hdwy 6th: rdn appr 4 out: sn wknd* **33/1**	83
4-04	**9**	*11*	**Dere Lyn**[25] 2609 7-10-7 **103** ....(v) LeeStephens(5) (Mrs D A Hamer) *hld up in mid-div: short-lived effrt appr 4 out* **22/1**	72
-3B5	**10**	*13*	**Versus (GER)**[13] 2820 5-10-10 **111** .... KevinTobin(10) (C J Mann) *hld up in tch: rdn and lost pl after 5th: n.d after* **14/1**	67
033P	**11**	*1 ½*	**Wayward Melody**[14] 2808 5-9-11 **91** ....(b) ColinBolger(3) (G L Moore) *hld up in mid-div: rdn appr 8th: sn bhd* **40/1**	45
	12	*½*	**Lusaka De Pembo (FR)**[99] 6-11-12 **117** .... AntonyEvans (N A Twiston-Davies) *t.k.h in mid-div: hdwy 5th: wknd appr 3 out* **16/1**	71
60P0	**13**	*5*	**Nick's Choice**[13] 2820 9-10-12 **110** .... MrRMcCarthy(7) (D Burchell) *bhd fr 8th* **40/1**	59
5002	**14**	*2*	**Kadam (IRE)**[11] 2868 5-11-5 **110** ....(b) RWalsh (P F Nicholls) *prom tl rdn and wknd appr 3 out* **11/2**[1]	57
-006	**15**	*10*	**Miss Fahrenheit (IRE)**[25] 2609 6-11-5 **110** .... ChristianWilliams (C Roberts) *prom tl wknd 6th* **11/1**	47
/1P-	**P**		**Monteforte**[272] 4655 7-11-11 **116** .... JasonMaguire (J A B Old) *prom tl wknd rapidly and p.u after 7th* **11/2**[1]	—
-PPU	**P**		**Grattan Lodge (IRE)**[12] 2840 8-11-8 **113** .... GrahamLee (J Howard Johnson) *a towards rr: t.o whn p.u bef 4 out* **20/1**	—
P-3P	**P**		**Lalagune (FR)**[48] 2130 6-11-8 **113** .... BarryFenton (Miss E C Lavelle) *hld up in rr: sme prog appr 4 out: p.u bef 2 out* **50/1**	—

6m 0.90s (-15.90) **Going Correction** -0.425s/f (Good)
WFA 4 from 5yo+ 13lb **18** Ran SP% **123.5**
Speed ratings: **109,108,108,106,105 105,102,100,97,92 92,92,90,89,86 —,—,—** CSF £46.78 CT £717.26 TOTE £6.00: £2.20, £1.70, £2.90, £3.30; EX 24.90.
Owner D Allen **Bred** Paul McDonnell **Trained** Withycombe, Somerset

FOCUS
A fair handicap, run at a sound gallop, in which the first two were the best handiacpped horses in the race and ran close to their marks.

NOTEBOOK
Drumbeater(IRE) got back to winning ways with a gritty success and registered a personal-best in the process. He handled the deeper surface without fuss, showed a very willing attitude on the run-in, and is clearly in the form of his life at present. Further improvement cannot be ruled out. *(op 5-1)*
Keepers Mead(IRE), raised 6lb for winning at Exeter last time, turned in another very brave effort from the front and only just failed. He saw out the longer trip well and was nicely clear of the rest, so he could add to his tally from this mark in the coming weeks. *(op 8-1)*
Three Lions, last seen winning from an 8lb lower mark 175 days previously, posted a very pleasing return to action and is entitled to improve a deal for this outing.
Albert House(IRE) was found out after the penultimate flight but still turned in another sound effort on ground he would have found plenty soft enough. It would come as little surprise to see him reverting to fences in the coming weeks. *(op 10-1)*
Pardon What, as has often been the case in the past, did not appear the easiest of rides and was doing all of his best work at the finish. He has been improved this season, however, and could still be capable of getting closer from this mark when in the mood.
Kadam(IRE) looked in with a real shout at the top of the straight, but he found little when push came to shove and faded disappointingly from two out. He is clearly one to have reservations about. *Official explanation: trainer said gelding bled from the nose (op 13-2)*
Monteforte, returning from a 272-day absence, was disappointing and has now been pulled up in his last two outings. *Official explanation: vet said gelding had a breathing problem (op 5-1)*
Lalagune(FR) *Official explanation: jockey said mare had a breathing problem (op 5-1)*

3019 AT THE RACES RED BUTTON BETTING H'CAP CHASE (16 fncs) 2m 3f 110y
1:00 (1:06) (Class 3) (0-135,135) 5-Y-0+
£9,682 (£2,860; £1,430; £715; £357; £179)

Form				RPR
1/0P	**1**		**Lord Maizey (IRE)**[18] 2744 8-10-13 **122** .... AntonyEvans (N A Twiston-Davies) *prom: mstke 3rd: rdn at several stages: hrd rdn 5 out: led 2 out: styd on u.p* **10/1**	136+
42-1	**2**	*2*	**Edmo Yewkay (IRE)**[24] 2640 5-11-4 **127** ....(b) DavidO'Meara (T D Easterby) *chsd ldrs: led 6th: hit 5 out: hdd 2 out: no ex towards fin* **9/1**	139+
214/	**3**	*2 ½*	**Patricksnineteenth (IRE)**[650] 4395 8-11-12 **135** .... TomDoyle (P R Webber) *prom: jnd ldr 6th: ev ch whn mstke 4 out: outpcd 2 out: styd on towards fin* **7/1**[3]	142
44/3	**4**	*1 ¼*	**No Visibility (IRE)**[24] 2622 10-10-9 **118** .... AndrewThornton (R H Alner) *led to 6th: hmpd next: outpcd 3 out: styd on towards fin* **16/1**	125+
1-F3	**5**	*3*	**Almost Broke**[24] 2619 8-11-7 **130** .... RWalsh (P F Nicholls) *hld up: hdwy 5 out: wknd last* **9/2**[1]	134+
-0F0	**6**	*14*	**Kalca Mome (FR)**[11] 2871 7-11-7 **130** .... PaddyBrennan (P J Hobbs) *hld up: mstkes 1st and 11th: sn rdn: n.d* **33/1**	119
-200	**7**	*8*	**Mixsterthetrixster (USA)**[17] 2760 9-11-10 **133** .... HenryOliver (Mrs Tracey Barfoot-Saunt) *chsd ldrs: mstke 11th: hit 4 out: wknd next* **14/1**	117+
5212	**F**		**Marked Man (IRE)**[14] 2814 9-11-7 **130** .... RobertThornton (R Lee) *hld up: fell 1st* **11/1**	—
0-40	**P**		**Shamawan (IRE)**[24] 2621 10-11-5 **128** .... RichardMcGrath (Jonjo O'Neill) *hld up: effrt after 11th: p.u bef next* **14/1**	—
2F11	**P**		**Soeur Fontenail (FR)**[13] 2827 8-10-3 **112** .... TimmyMurphy (N J Hawke) *chsd ldrs tl wknd 5 out: bhd whn p.u bef 3 out* **10/1**	—
3-51	**U**		**Kelrev (FR)**[17] 2768 7-11-7 **135** .... PaulO'Neill(5) (Miss Venetia Williams) *hld up in tch: cl 5th whn blnd and uns rdr 7th* **13/2**[2]	—
P2-1	**F**		**Island Faith (IRE)**[38] 2339 8-11-9 **132** .... GrahamLee (J Howard Johnson) *hld up: rdn appr 5 out: no ch whn fell 2 out* **13/2**[2]	—
-P32	**P**		**Wrags To Riches (IRE)**[24] 2622 8-10-13 **127** .... ChrisHonour(5) (J D Frost) *in rr whn mstke 4th and next: bhd whn p.u bef 6th* **33/1**	—

5m 1.20s (-10.10) **Going Correction** -0.425s/f (Good) **13** Ran SP% **119.0**
Speed ratings: **103,102,101,100,99 93,90,—,—,— —,—,—** CSF £97.14 CT £675.66 TOTE £11.20: £4.20, £3.50, £3.30; EX 115.90.
Owner Mr & Mrs Peter Orton **Bred** Mick Berry **Trained** Naunton, Gloucs

FOCUS
A decent handicap for the class, run at just an average gallop, and the form looks pretty solid.

NOTEBOOK
Lord Maizey(IRE) dug deep under pressure approaching the top of the straight, before staying on dourly to mow down his rivals and ultimately score a touch comfortably. He had slipped to an identical mark as when last successful - in this race in 2003 - and it was just his third outing since, but he clearly loves this venue, and his trainer is adept at getting his horses back on track after injury. He is entitled to improve now he has got his head back in front, and he looks better kept to this sort of trip, but whether he can build on this back at a higher level remains to be seen. *(op 9-1)*
Edmo Yewkay(IRE), raised 9lb for winning on his seasonal bow at Wetherby last time, ran another solid race under a positive ride and has resumed this term in decent heart. He stuck to his task gamely once headed by the winner, finishing nicely clear in second, and further improvement looks likely over fences as he will still only be six at the turn of the year. *(op 8-1 tchd 10-1)*
Patricksnineteenth(IRE) ◆, last seen finishing fourth in the Royal & SunAlliance Chase at Cheltenham 650 days previously, turned in a blinder under his big weight and really looks the horse to take from the race. Considering he took the Scilly Isles Novices' Chase in 2004, he looks to be on a decent handicap mark at present, providing connections can keep him sound, and he looks ready to tackle a stiffer test now. It would not be a surprise were he to make up into a contender for the Ryanair Chase at the Festival come March. *(op 5-1)*
No Visibility(IRE) again showed he retains all of his ability with a brave effort and, providing he is not raised too much in the weights for this, appears capable of ending his losing run before too long. *(tchd 20-1)*
Almost Broke, who took this race last season off an 18lb lower mark, was not totally disgraced on this return to chasing. However, he looked reluctant to fully go through with his effort when push came to shove, and it would not be a surprise to see some headgear applied for his next outing. *(op 6-1)*
Wrags To Riches(IRE) *Official explanation: jockey said gelding was never travelling (tchd 28-1)*

3020 TOTESPORT LONG WALK HURDLE GRADE 1 (12 hdls) 3m
1:35 (1:39) (Class 1) 4-Y-0+
£28,510 (£10,695; £5,355; £2,670; £1,340; £670)

Form				RPR
02-2	**1**		**My Way De Solzen (FR)**[38] 2336 5-11-7 149 .... RobertThornton (A King) *hld up in tch: led 2 out: rdn out* **12/1**[3]	154+
141	**2**	*5*	**Neptune Collonges (FR)**[25] 2614 4-11-7 .... RWalsh (P F Nicholls) *led to 2 out: sn hrd rdn: 2 l 2nd and hld whn mstke last* **6/1**[2]	150+
054/	**3**	*12*	**Starzaan (IRE)**[613] 4954 6-11-7 149 .... TimmyMurphy (H Morrison) *t.k.h in rr: hdwy on ins 4 out: j.rt 3 out: sn btn* **66/1**	140+
-5U3	**4**	*8*	**Bob Bob Bobbin**[12] 2848 6-11-7 142 .... MickFitzgerald (C L Tizzard) *prom: rdn 4 out: wknd 3 out* **33/1**	129
32-5	**5**	*8*	**Brewster (IRE)**[59] 1925 8-11-7 150 .... TonyDobbin (Ian Williams) *prom: tl rdn and wknd appr 4 out* **14/1**	123+
1P05	**6**	*½*	**Carlys Quest**[31] 2490 11-11-7 140 .... KeithMercer (Ferdy Murphy) *hld up in rr: rdn after 5th: sn struggling* **66/1**	121
/12-	**7**	*2 ½*	**Mistanoora**[409] 2186 6-11-7 155 ....(b) AntonyEvans (N A Twiston-Davies) *w ldr tl after 8th: wknd 4 out* **28/1**	118
2-11	**F**		**Inglis Drever**[31] 2490 6-11-7 163 .... GrahamLee (J Howard Johnson) *hld up: rdn after 7th: j.lft 4 out: 10 l 4th and no imp whn fell 2 out* **2/5**[1]	140

5m 55.6s (-21.20) **Going Correction** -0.425s/f (Good) **8** Ran SP% **109.4**
Speed ratings: **118,116,112,109,107 106,106,—** CSF £70.65 TOTE £13.70: £2.20, £1.50, £9.80; EX 72.40.
Owner B Winfield,A Longman,J Wright & C Fenton **Bred** C Ricous-Guerin & Jacques Guerin **Trained** Barbury Castle, Wilts
■ This race, which will be back at Ascot in 2006, was rescheduled after Windsor's meeting on December 17 was abandoned.

FOCUS
With Inglis Drever well below-par and Baracouda an absentee, this did not look a vintage renewal. The winner's performance on time only 19lb better than that of Drumbeater in an earlier race and this is probably not form to get carried away with.

NOTEBOOK

My Way De Solzen(FR), runner-up in a handicap on his first try at this sort of trip last time, confirmed himself a smart stayer, keeping on too well for his only serious challenger from the second last, but luck was with him to a certain extent as he was not among the original field for this event at Windsor, while Inglis Drever had an off-day. His chasing career will now be deferred and he will go for the World Hurdle, but he is unlikely to get the soft conditions he needs at Cheltenham. *(op 10-1)*

Neptune Collonges(FR), only a four-year-old, ran a big race on his first try at three miles but was held when making a mistake at the last. The Spa Novices' Hurdle over three miles and a furlong could be the race for him at Cheltenham, but this mudlark may not get his ground at the Festival.

Starzaan(IRE) ran a satisfactory race on his first start since April 2004. Held up off the pace, he improved once into the home straight, staying on the inside of the track where the ground was less poached. Brought right over to the stands' side at the third last, he soon faded as his stamina began to wane. *(op 50-1)*

Bob Bob Bobbin, back over hurdles after his chasing career failed to ignite as hoped, ran a decent race but is going to remain hard to place. *(op 50-1)*

Brewster(IRE) was reported to have a sinus infection when beaten on his return at Wetherby. He was again a little disappointing, weakening on the long home turn.

Carlys Quest faced another stiff task and was found wanting. *(op 50-1 tchd 80-1)*

Mistanoora, who had been off the track for over a year, raced prominently until dropping away at the first in the home straight. He should come on for the run. *(op 25-1 tchd 20-1 and 33-1)*

Inglis Drever has a tendency to hit flat spots in his races, but this time he came under pressure down the back and Lee was still working hard on the home turn. He made some progress in the straight, but was held in fourth when falling at the second last. This was very disappointing and a long and abortive trip to Windsor earlier in the month appears to have left its mark. A little shaken and sore after his fall, he will run in the Cleeve Hurdle at Cheltenham in a month's time all being *well, and it would be no surprise to see him bounce back to form.Official explanation: jockey said gelding was never travelling (tchd 4-9)*

3021 AT THE RACES 1.2 MILLION VIEWERS FINALE JUVENILE HURDLE GRADE 1 (8 hdls) 2m 110y

2:05 (2:12) (Class 1) 3-Y-O

£28,510 (£10,695; £5,355; £2,670; £1,340; £670)

Form				Jockey	SP	RPR
5-	**1**		**Blue Shark (FR)**[51] [2083] 3-11-0 (N J Henderson) *a.p: chsd ldr 5th: led after 3 out: clr next: rdn whn nt fluent last: styd on*	MickFitzgerald	**7/1**[3]	138+
12	**2**	*8*	**Turko (FR)**[17] [2756] 3-11-0 (P F Nicholls) *hld up: hdwy appr 5th: rdn to chse wnr appr 2 out: no imp*	RWalsh	**11/10**[1]	129
161	**3**	*11*	**Patman Du Charmil (FR)**[14] [2811] 3-11-0 112 (N A Twiston-Davies) *chsd ldrs: hmpd bnd after 4th: rdn appr 3 out: wknd after next*	AntonyEvans	**40/1**	119+
1113	**4**	*nk*	**Fair Along (GER)**[17] [2756] 3-11-0 138 (P J Hobbs) *led: blnd 3 out: sn hdd: wknd next*	PaddyBrennan	**11/2**[2]	122+
61	**5**	*10*	**Twist Magic (FR)**[26] [2597] 3-11-0 (P F Nicholls) *hld up in tch: rdn 5th: wknd after 3 out*	ChristianWilliams	**12/1**	108
2	**6**	*1*	**My Immortal**[32] [2481] 3-11-0 (M C Pipe) *plld hrd and prom: wknd 3 out*	TimmyMurphy	**8/1**	107
211	**7**	*7*	**Gardasee (GER)**[22] [2676] 3-11-0 (T P Tate) *chsd ldr to 5th: wkng whn hit next*	JasonMaguire	**8/1**	103+
14	**8**	*1*	**Flaming Weapon**[37] [2367] 3-11-0 (G L Moore) *hld up in tch: rdn and wknd 5th*	ColinBolger	**100/1**	99
042	**9**	*8*	**Cava Bien**[26] [2580] 3-11-0 106 (B J Llewellyn) *hld up: sme hdwy after 4th: wknd bef next*	BrianHarding	**100/1**	91
21	**10**	*1*	**Equilibria (USA)**[37] [2373] 3-11-0 (G L Moore) *hld up: mstke 2nd: a in rr*	LeightonAspell	**66/1**	90
51	**11**	*6*	**Barnbrook Empire (IRE)**[63] [1873] 3-10-7 (B J Llewellyn) *hld up: reminders after 2nd: a in rr*	OllieMcPhail	**100/1**	77
222	**12**	*4*	**Kanpai (IRE)**[25] [2612] 3-11-0 (J G M O'Shea) *hld up: a in rr*	TomDoyle	**100/1**	80
	13	*23*	**Form And Beauty (IRE)**[165] 3-11-0 (C Roberts) *sn wl bhd*	LeeStephens	**200/1**	57
3331	**P**		**Josear**[15] [2797] 3-11-0 110 (C J Down) *prom to 4th: bhd whn p.u bef next*	TonyDobbin	**100/1**	—
	P		**Solarias Quest**[133] 3-11-0 (A King) *hld up: in rr and rdn 3rd: bhd fr next: p.u bef 3 out*	RobertThornton	**25/1**	—

3m 58.0s (-12.40) **Going Correction** -0.425s/f (Good) **15** Ran SP% **118.6**
Speed ratings: **112,108,103,102,98 97,94,93,90,89 86,85,74,—,—** CSF £15.03 TOTE £7.90: £2.50, £1.20, £7.30; EX 24.20 Trifecta £676.70 Part won. Pool: £953.10. 0.50 winning tickets..

Owner Trevor Hemmings **Bred** G Gayet **Trained** Upper Lambourn, Berks

FOCUS

A decent event of its type in which they finished well strung out. This is good juvenile form, which could be rated a fair bit higher, but the 2nd and 4th were both below par while the modest 8th to 10th horses ran to their marks.

NOTEBOOK

Blue Shark(FR) ran five times for Bernard Secly at Auteuil, getting off the mark in the latest of them in a Listed handicap early last month. Coming clear from the second last and staying on really well, he looks more of a galloper than stablemate Afsoun and may miss the Triumph Hurdle in favour of the longer Royal & SunAlliance, in which he would get the four-year-old's allowance. *(op 6-1)*

Turko(FR) was the form pick on his second at Cheltenham to Afsoun, who was receiving 7lb. He ran his race, but having moved into second place after the third-last he was never able to close the gap on the winner. *(op 5-4)*

Patman Du Charmil(FR) belied his big price and ran well, but could not go with the first two over the final two flights. This ground seemed to suit him. *(tchd 50-1)*

Fair Along(GER) made the running as expected, but never attempted to get clear. A blunder three from home when hard pressed saw him drop back to fourth place, and although he did rally a little in the latter stages he finished further behind Turko than he did at Cheltenham. *(op 6-1)*

Twist Magic(FR), a stable companion of the beaten favourite, ran a decent race but was found out in this company. *(op 11-1 tchd 12-1 in places)*

My Immortal was 6lb worse off with Turko from their meeting at Newbury. Rather keen through the first part of the race, he was nudged along leaving the back straight before weakening with three to jump. *(op 15-2)*

Gardasee(GER), an all-the-way winner of two minor events, could never reach the front in this top company and was already on the retreat when rapping the third last.

Josear *Official explanation: jockey said gelding lost its action (op 20-1)*

Solarias Quest *Official explanation: vet said gelding had bled from the nose (op 20-1)*

3022 CORAL WELSH NATIONAL (A H'CAP CHASE) GRADE 3 (22 fncs) 3m 5f 110y

2:40 (2:46) (Class 1) 5-Y-O+

£57,020 (£21,390; £10,710; £5,340; £2,680; £1,340)

Form				Jockey	SP	RPR
0-64	**1**		**L'Aventure (FR)**[46] [2164] 6-10-4 **131** (P F Nicholls) *a.p: jnd ldr 3 out: rdn to ld 2 out: lft wl clr last*	(bt) LeightonAspell	**14/1**	151+
P0-6	**2**	*dist*	**Heros Collonges (FR)**[37] [2370] 10-10-11 **138** (P F Nicholls) *hdwy 6th: hrd rdn and wknd appr 3 out: rallied to take poor 2nd nr fin*	ChristianWilliams	**25/1**	124
32-3	**3**	*nk*	**Cornish Rebel (IRE)**[31] [2491] 8-11-12 **153** (P F Nicholls) *nt fluent: mid-div: lost pl 9th: hdwy 16th: rdn and outpcd 5 out: lft modest 2nd last: wknd flat*	RWalsh	**9/2**[1]	138
3-43	**4**	*1 3/4*	**Crystal D'Ainay (FR)**[31] [2490] 6-11-0 **141** (A King) *hld up in mid-div: hdwy 12th: wknd 16th*	RobertThornton	**12/1**	124
0-62	**5**	*3*	**Wain Mountain**[12] [2847] 9-10-3 **130** oh3 ow3 (J A B Old) *bhd: mstke 6th: stdy hdwy after 11th: 5th and no ch whn blnd 3 out*	JasonMaguire	**20/1**	110
U3-P	**6**	*1 1/2*	**Granit D'Estruval (FR)**[58] [1941] 11-10-0 **127** oh2 (Ferdy Murphy) *prom tl wknd 4 out*	KeithMercer	**40/1**	106
-P2F	**7**	*12*	**Strong Resolve (IRE)**[37] [2370] 9-10-4 **134** (Miss Lucinda V Russell) *led to 1st: led 2nd to 4th: prom tl wknd 14th*	PeterBuchanan(3)	**16/1**	101
/PF-	**P**		**Present Bleu (FR)**[263] [4764] 10-9-12 **128** (M C Pipe) *bhd tl p.u bef 16th*	(t) TomMalone(3)	**100/1**	—
P6-4	**P**		**Comply Or Die (IRE)**[31] [2491] 6-11-7 **148** (M C Pipe) *bhd tl p.u bef 15th*	TimmyMurphy	**12/1**	—
U-63	**P**		**Native Emperor**[12] [2847] 9-10-0 **127** oh2 (Jonjo O'Neill) *nvr gng wl: bhd tl p.u bef 13th*	BrianHarding	**20/1**	—
0-0F	**P**		**Philson Run (IRE)**[37] [2370] 9-10-6 **133** ow5 (Nick Williams) *a bhd: mstke 15th: t.o whn p.u bef 17th*	TomDoyle	**25/1**	—
221U	**P**		**Mckelvey (IRE)**[24] [2643] 6-10-8 **135** (P Bowen) *mid-div: mstke 16th: sn bhd: t.o whn p.u bef 5 out*	TonyDobbin	**8/1**[3]	—
U-05	**P**		**World Wide Web (IRE)**[32] [2483] 9-10-0 **127** oh2 (Jonjo O'Neill) *bhd: reminders 8th: p.u bef 14th*	RichardMcGrath	**7/1**[2]	—
2U0/	**P**		**Shardam (IRE)**[612] [4965] 8-10-11 **138** (N A Twiston-Davies) *bhd: mstke 1st: t.o whn p.u bef 4 out*	AntonyEvans	**40/1**	—
P-30	**U**		**Control Man (IRE)**[18] [2747] 7-9-12 **135** (M C Pipe) *n.m.r whn stmbld and uns rdr bnd after s*	(v) AndrewGlassonbury(10)	**14/1**	—
F/1-	**F**		**One Knight (IRE)**[388] [2619] 9-11-8 **149** (P J Hobbs) *led 4th: rdn and hdd 2 out: 2 l 2nd whn fell last*	PaddyBrennan	**9/2**[1]	165
P-PP	**F**		**Sir Rembrandt (IRE)**[24] [2628] 9-11-10 **151** (R H Alner) *hld up in tch: rdn and disputing 3 l 4th whn fell 5 out*	AndrewThornton	**33/1**	—
01-4	**P**		**Indalo (IRE)**[12] [2847] 10-10-0 **127** oh1 (Miss Venetia Williams) *t.k.h: led 1st to 2nd: prom tl blnd bdly and rdr lost iron 15th: nt rcvr: t.o whn p.u bef 5 out*	AlanO'Keeffe	**33/1**	—

7m 38.9s (-25.90) **Going Correction** -0.425s/f (Good) **18** Ran SP% **123.5**
Speed ratings: **117,—,—,—,— —,—,—,—,— —,—,—,—,— —,—,—** CSF £324.26 CT £1840.37 TOTE £16.90: £3.10, £4.70, £1.40, £2.80; EX 214.30 Trifecta £630.30 Pool £4,350.20 - 4.90 winning units..

Owner C J Harriman **Bred** F Cottin **Trained** Ditcheat, Somerset

■ A 1-2-3 for trainer Paul Nicholls and a big boost for his championship hopes.

■ Stewards' Enquiry : Leighton Aspell caution: used whip in an incorrect place

FOCUS

A competitive renewal, run at a strong pace. The form of last season's Rehearsal Chase, in which One Knight beat L'Aventure, has been upgraded, and the former looks Gold Cup class. The remainder were upwards of 9lb off their best, and there is a case to be made for rating this form higher.

NOTEBOOK

L'Aventure(FR), a staying-on fourth off this mark to stablemate Silver Birch in this last year, must have plenty of time between her races and came into this fresh. With the blinkers back in place, she jumped to the front two from home and would probably have won even if One Knight's fall at the last had not left her a distance clear. This was her first win since taking a hurdle at this track in October 2004. She did not enjoy the Aintree experience last season and is unlikely to be entered for the Grand National.

Heros Collonges(FR), fitter for his return to action last month, ran well for a long way but faded with three to jump. He plugged on past an equally tired Cornish Rebel to snatch second close home and is unlikely to run again before the Grand National, in which he was eighth last season. *(tchd 28-1)*

Cornish Rebel(IRE), raised 3lb for his fine effort in the Hennessy, ran here rather than in the King George the previous day. Unable to go with the leaders from the turn into the home straight, he was tired when left a remote second at the final fence and was caught for that position near the line. This was a decent effort under top-weight on a track which did not really suit him. *(op 11-2)*

Crystal D'Ainay(FR) ran here instead of in the Long Walk Hurdle, the fact that he is currently rated 18lb lower over fences obviously swaying connections. After dropping out of contention down the far side, he did rally a bit at the end. There are plenty of options for him in the remainder of the season.

Wain Mountain, who was 3lb out of the handicap and whose rider put up the same amount of overweight, latched on to the back of the leading group on the long home turn but was beaten when blundering at the third last. He is performing respectably at present but is without a win for the best part of four years.

Granit D'Estruval(FR), has been lightly raced and largely out of form since the spring of 2004, but he was reportedly laid out for this and he gave his supporters a run for their money before weakening after a mistake at the first in the home straight. *(op 33-1 tchd 50-1)*

Strong Resolve(IRE), runner-up last year and 3lb higher this time, soon lost his early lead and faded in the back straight before coming home last of seven finishers.

Indalo(IRE) was unable to lead for long, but was not entirely out of it when he blundered badly and nearly unshipped O'Keeffe down the far side. *(op 5-1)*

One Knight(IRE) had been sidelined with a back problem since winning the Rehearsal Chase here at this track over a year ago, but he was only 3lb higher here and has a good record first time out. Soon in front, generally jumping well, he was headed with two to jump but was switched right to renew his challenge and was not quite out of it when getting in too close to the last. He would probably have finished second, which is scant consolation for Brennan who got off L'Aventure in order to ride him. *(op 5-1)*

World Wide Web(IRE) has been lightly raced and without a win since taking the Paddy Power Chase at Leopardstown two years ago. Running over fences for the first time this season, and 2lb out of the handicap, he ran a lacklustre race and was always towards the rear of the field before being pulled up. *(op 5-1)*

Sir Rembrandt(IRE), without the visor, was being niggled along at an early stage but was still in with a shout when coming down at the first fence in the home straight. A blunder at the same obstacle arguably cost him victory in the 2003 renewal in which he was second to Bindaree. This was more encouraging but he has now failed to complete the course in four runs since finishing third in the Gold Cup. *(op 5-1)*

Mckelvey(IRE), facing his toughest task so far, was close enough when making an error at the second last in the back straight and soon began to struggle. *(op 5-1)*

3023 PONTINS BLUECOAT FLYER NOVICES' HURDLE (11 hdls) 2m 4f
3:15 (3:21) (Class 4) 4-Y-0+ £3,919 (£1,150; £575; £287)

Form RPR
25-1 **1** **Be Be King (IRE)**[38] [2343] 6-11-5 122 .... RWalsh 128+
(P F Nicholls) *chsd ldr tl chal 4 out: led 2 out: rdn whn j.lft and mstke last: drvn out* **13/8**[1]
P-10 **2** *5* **Miko De Beauchene (FR)**[24] [2633] 5-11-5 117 .... AndrewThornton 121+
(R H Alner) *a.p: led 8th: hdd 2 out: j.lft last: styd on same pce* **13/2**[3]
F1 **3** *4* **Killaghy Castle (IRE)**[43] [2238] 5-11-5 .... LeightonAspell 117+
(N J Gifford) *hld up: hdwy 5th: rdn 3 out: styng on same pce whn nt fluent last* **11/4**[2]
1/F **4** *¾* **Billesey (IRE)**[11] [2861] 7-10-12 .... BarryFenton 107
(S E H Sherwood) *led to 8th: styd on same pce fr 2 out* **66/1**
2/32 **5** *2* **The Sawyer (BEL)**[12] [2849] 5-10-12 .... BenjaminHitchcott 105
(R H Buckler) *chsd ldrs: outpcd 3 out: styd on appr last* **8/1**
6- **6** *1 ¼* **Alformasi**[595] [284] 6-10-12 .... ChristianWilliams 104
(P F Nicholls) *chsd ldrs tl wknd 2 out* **50/1**
0-51 **7** *6* **Biscar Two (IRE)**[24] [2624] 4-11-5 125 .... (b) OllieMcPhail 105
(B J Llewellyn) *bhd 4th: nvr nrr* **12/1**
8 *3* **Silent Dream** 7-10-12 .... BrianHarding 95
(Simon Earle) *hld up: hit 1st: nvr nrr* **100/1**
54- **9** *1 ¼* **Sharajan (IRE)**[590] [383] 5-10-12 .... RobertThornton 94
(A King) *hld up: hdwy 7th: wknd 3 out* **14/1**
30 **10** *14* **Winter Sport (IRE)**[27] [2579] 4-10-12 .... PaddyBrennan 80
(P J Hobbs) *prom to 8th* **33/1**
36 **11** *5* **Absolutelythebest (IRE)**[51] [2070] 4-10-12 .... TomDoyle 75
(J G M O'Shea) *hld up: sme hdwy after 7th: wknd bef next* **100/1**
4 **12** *8* **What'sonyourmind (IRE)**[45] [2179] 5-10-12 .... RichardMcGrath 67
(Jonjo O'Neill) *prom: lost pl after 4th: n.d after* **20/1**
13 *13* **Ocean Of Storms (IRE)**[123] 10-10-5 .... MrRMcCarthy(7) 54
(N I M Rossiter) *hld up: sme hdwy after 7th: rdn and wknd bef next* **100/1**
02 **P** **Nagam (FR)**[24] [2619] 4-10-9 .... ColinBolger(3) —
(A Ennis) *hld up: hdwy 6th: wknd appr 8th: bhd whn p.u bef last* **20/1**
P **Financial Future**[216] 5-10-12 .... JasonMaguire —
(C Roberts) *hld up: plld hrd: a in rr: t.o whn p.u bef 4 out* **100/1**

4m 58.0s (-4.70) **Going Correction** -0.425s/f (Good)
WFA 4 from 5yo+ 11lb **15** Ran SP% **123.4**
Speed ratings: **92,90,88,88,87 86,84,83,82,77 75,71,66,—,—** CSF £12.44 TOTE £2.80: £1.40, £2.70, £2.00; EX 14.80.
Owner C G Roach **Bred** P E Atkinson **Trained** Ditcheat, Somerset

FOCUS
A decent novice event, run in a snowstorm. Not an easy race to assess, this has been rated through the second, with the winner still 7lb off his best bumper form

NOTEBOOK
Be Be King(IRE) followed up his Huntingdon win, this stiffer track suiting him. In front at the second last, he was in command when going out to his left over the final flight, his nearest pursuer following suit. His jumping still lacks fluency but he is a promising stayer. *(op 2-1 tchd 9-4)*
Miko De Beauchene(FR), back in novice company, ran a sound race but found the favourite too strong from the penultimate flight. This trip is a bare minimum for him. *(op 9-1 tchd 6-1)*
Killaghy Castle(IRE) ◆, back up in trip, was close enough when making an error at the third last and was not knocked about from then on as the first two appeared to have his measure. He is capable of winning again over hurdles before switching codes. *(op 2-1 tchd 7-2)*
Billesey(IRE), an early faller on his recent chase debut, ran a good race on his first run over hurdles and could win a novice event before going back over fences. *(op 50-1)*
The Sawyer(BEL) was keeping on stoutly at the end over this longer trip, suggesting that ideally he needs further still. *(op 9-1 tchd 10-1)*
Alformasi had only made the racecourse once before, when sixth in a bumper in May 2004. A stablemate of the winner, he was held from the second last but this was still a promising run. *(tchd 66-1)*
Biscar Two(IRE), runner-up in the Finale Hurdle on this card a year ago, blundered at the fourth and was soon looking less than keen in rear. Over this longer trip, he did stay on well when it was all over, but he is one to be wary of. *(op 16-1)*
Sharajan(IRE) made a pleasing hurdles debut on this first run since May of last year and should be ready to build on this now. *(tchd 16-1)*

3024 PONTINS CAPTAIN CROCODILE STANDARD OPEN NATIONAL HUNT FLAT RACE 2m 110y
3:50 (3:51) (Class 6) 4-6-Y-0 £2,343 (£682; £341)

Form RPR
2 **1** **Hot 'N' Holy**[28] [2565] 6-11-4 .... RWalsh 103+
(P F Nicholls) *hld up in tch: led over 2f out: drvn out* **4/6**[1]
1 **2** *2 ½* **Baron Romeo (IRE)**[11] [2864] 5-11-4 .... SeanQuinlan(7) 107
(R T Phillips) *hld up: hdwy over 5f out: rdn over 2f out: ev ch over 1f out: edgd lft and no ex ins fnl f* **10/3**[2]
3 *nk* **Goscar Rock (IRE)** 4-11-4 .... PaddyBrennan 100
(P J Hobbs) *a.p: led briefly over 2f out: sn rdn: kpt on towards fin* **8/1**[3]
34 **4** *3* **Bring Me Sunshine (IRE)**[27] [2579] 4-11-4 .... MickFitzgerald 97
(C L Tizzard) *led 2f: led 6f out tl over 2f out: wknd over 1f out* **14/1**
0 **5** *3* **Mo Chailin**[51] [2075] 6-10-11 .... LeightonAspell 87
(D A Rees) *hld up and bhd: styd on fnl 2f: nt rch ldrs* **100/1**
00 **6** *19* **Schindler's List**[205] [655] 5-11-4 .... AndrewThornton 75
(C Roberts) *plld hrd early: hld up in tch: hdwy over 5f out: wknd over 2f out* **33/1**
00 **7** *5* **Shinjiru (USA)**[230] [300] 5-10-8 .... AngharadFrieze(10) 70
(P A Blockley) *hld up: rdn 4f out: sn btn* **100/1**
0- **8** *dist* **Hazel Mere**[550] [822] 5-10-11 .... SeanCurran —
(A P Jones) *plld hrd: led 2f: prom tl rdn and wknd over 4f out: t.o* **100/1**
9 *17* **Hope Hill** 4-10-11 .... ChristianWilliams —
(M Salaman) *a bhd: t.o fnl 5f* **50/1**
0 **10** *1 ¼* **Miss Millfield**[23] [2665] 4-10-6 .... LeeStephens(5) —
(V J Hughes) *sddle slipped: led after 2f to 6f out: sn wknd: t.o* **100/1**
4 **P** **Top Ram (IRE)**[23] [2665] 5-11-4 .... JasonMaguire —
(J A B Old) *hld up: hdwy 5f out: rdn 3f out: wknd over 1f out: p.u ins fnl f: lame* **12/1**

4m 6.20s (-4.00) **Going Correction** -0.425s/f (Good) **11** Ran SP% **117.4**
Speed ratings: **92,90,90,89,87 78,76,—,—,— —** CSF £2.94 TOTE £1.60: £1.10, £1.60, £2.60; EX 3.70 Place 6 £837.79, Place 5 £181.76.
Owner Paul K Barber & C G Roach **Bred** R Chugg **Trained** Ditcheat, Somerset

FOCUS
This looked a reasonable bumper, rated around the second and fourth.

NOTEBOOK
Hot 'N' Holy, narrowly beaten on his debut at Hereford, went one better. He came under pressure passing the thee pole but soon showed ahead and, with the rail alongside him to help, he stayed on willingly. *(op Evens)*
Baron Romeo(IRE) relinquished his unbeaten record, but this was a good effort and he only gave best in the last half-furlong. *(op 4-1)*
Goscar Rock(IRE) ◆, the first foal of a half-sister to useful chasers Old Bridge and Eastshaw who was placed in Irish points, ran a nice race on this debut and was keeping on at the end. He should not be long in winning. *(op 11-2)*
Bring Me Sunshine(IRE) handled the easier conditions well enough and ran a third solid race in as many starts. *(op 12-1)*
Mo Chailin, who has left Peter Bowen since finishing tailed off on her debut early last month, stayed on steadily through beaten rivals late in the day and obviously has her share of ability. *(op 66-1)*
Top Ram(IRE) ran well for a long way and was still fifth going to the final furlong, before being eased to a walk and pulled up lame. *Official explanation: vet said gelding returned lame (op 8-1 tchd 14-1)*
T/Jkpt: Not won. T/Plt: £1,193.20 to a £1 stake. Pool: £98,729.40. 60.40 winning tickets. T/Qpdt: £119.60 to a £1 stake. Pool: £11,045.10. 68.30 winning tickets. KH

2956 HUNTINGDON (R-H)
Tuesday, December 27
3025 Meeting Abandoned - Snow

2701 LEICESTER (R-H)
Tuesday, December 27
3031 Meeting Abandoned - Frost

2989 WETHERBY (L-H)
Tuesday, December 27
OFFICIAL GOING: Soft (good to soft in places)
Wind: Nil

3037 SKYBET.COM TONY DICKINSON NOVICES' H'CAP CHASE (15 fncs) 2m 4f 110y
12:50 (12:51) (Class 3) (0-110,108) 4-Y-0+ £5,712 (£1,676; £838; £418)

Form RPR
04/2 **1** **Jimmy Bond**[45] [2187] 6-10-2 84 .... NeilMulholland 94+
(M D Hammond) *trckd ldrs: hit 8th: hdwy to chse ldr 4 out: chal next: rdn to ld after 2 out: wandered last: drvn clr flat* **11/4**[1]
5F44 **2** *5* **Assumetheposition (FR)**[34] [2440] 5-10-6 88 .... (p) LarryMcGrath 92+
(R C Guest) *trckd ldng pair: led 8th: pushed along and jnd 3 out: hdd after next: sn rdn: n.m.r and hit last: one pce flat* **9/1**
-610 **3** *12* **Spring Gamble (IRE)**[24] [2630] 6-11-9 105 .... FinbarKeniry 96
(G M Moore) *cl up: hit 8th: rdn along after 5 out: drvn and outpcd after next* **9/1**
-05U **4** *3 ½* **Italiano**[17] [2764] 6-11-12 108 .... RussGarritty 96
(P Beaumont) *hld up in tch: hit 7th: hdwy and mstke 6 out: chsd ldr 4 out: sn rdn and grad wknd fr next* **6/1**[3]
16/0 **5** *10* **Corroboree (IRE)**[24] [2629] 8-11-6 102 .... CarlLlewellyn 80
(N A Twiston-Davies) *led to 8th: cl up: rdn along 5 out: wkng whn hit next and sn bhd* **7/1**
05-P **6** *17* **Gay Kindersley (IRE)**[19] [2717] 7-10-1 83 .... JimCrowley 44
(K G Reveley) *nt fluent: a bhd* **6/1**[3]
-222 **F** **Rare Society (IRE)**[35] [2415] 7-11-9 105 .... DominicElsworth —
(Mrs S J Smith) *trckd ldrs tl fell 2nd* **7/2**[2]

5m 41.6s (20.90) **Going Correction** +0.90s/f (Soft) **7** Ran SP% **110.0**
Speed ratings: **96,94,89,88,84 77,—** CSF £24.10 CT £179.08 TOTE £3.00: £1.80, £3.70; EX 41.70.
Owner Mrs A J Findlay **Bred** Mrs A J Findlay **Trained** Middleham, N Yorks

FOCUS
A moderate chase and probably not strong form, but won by a potential improver at the bottom of the weights.

NOTEBOOK
Jimmy Bond ◆ fulfilled the promise of his last effort, after a long break, to win nicely. He is at the right end of the handicap to win again. *(op 5-2 tchd 3-1 in places)*
Assumetheposition(FR), well behind Jimmy Bond the last time they met, ran up to his best over fences but did not get home as well as the winner. *(op 12-1)*
Spring Gamble(IRE) stays the trip well but is almost certainly finding his current handicap mark too much, as he could not go with the front two when the pace increased. *(op 10-1)*
Italiano ran better than his final position suggests, as he faced an impossible task giving so much weight away to a potentially progressive type at the bottom of the handicap. *(op 8-1)*
Corroboree(IRE) travelled nicely in the early stages but found nothing when let down. The current form of the stable is of a slight concern. *(op 11-2 tchd 5-1)*
Gay Kindersley(IRE) never managed to get into a challenging position and looked awkward jumping his fences. *(op 10-1)*

3038 SKYBET PRESS RED TO BET ON CH4 INTRODUCTORY JUVENILE NOVICES' HURDLE (9 hdls) 2m
1:25 (1:25) (Class 2) 3-Y-0 £9,355 (£2,746; £1,373; £685)

Form RPR
2 **1** **Ortolan Bleu (FR)**[37] [2367] 3-11-0 .... JoeTizzard 112+
(J Howard Johnson) *hld up towards rr: stdy hdwy 5th: cl up 4 out: led and hit 2 out: rdn clr appr last: kpt on* **5/4**[1]
1 **2** *6* **Dan's Heir**[164] [1011] 3-11-5 .... FinbarKeniry 107
(P C Haslam) *led: rdn along after 4 out: hdd 2 out: sn drvn and kpt on same pce appr last* **9/1**
3 **3** *10* **Copper Bay (IRE)**[26] [2580] 3-11-0 .... WayneHutchinson 93+
(A King) *hld up towards rr: hdwy 4 out: effrt and ev ch 2 out: sn rdn and wknd appr last* **3/1**[2]
2 **4** *hd* **Dafarabad (IRE)**[34] [2442] 3-11-0 .... DominicElsworth 92
(Jonjo O'Neill) *chsd ldr: rdn along and outpcd appr 3 out:drvn next and plugged on u.p fr last* **7/2**[3]
5 **5** *½* **Quasimodo (IRE)**[23] [2661] 3-11-0 .... CarlLlewellyn 92+
(A W Carroll) *hld up: hdwy on inner appr 3 out: rdn along bef next: kpt on: nrst fin* **20/1**
2 **6** *2 ½* **Orang Outan (FR)**[41] [2263] 3-11-0 .... (t) GaryBerridge 89
(J P L Ewart) *chsd ldrs: rdn along bef 3 out and grad wknd* **33/1**
6 **7** *14* **Fixateur**[18] [2753] 3-11-0 .... LeeVickers 81+
(C C Bealby) *trckd ldrs: effrt and pushed along whn hit 3 out: rdn and wkng whn blnd next: sn bhd* **28/1**

P **8** *dist* **Mccormack (IRE)**[22] 2676 3-11-0 .... NeilMulholland —
(M D Hammond) *a rr: outpcd and bhd fr 4 out* **200/1**

P **C'Est La Vie**[99] 3-10-7 .... PadgeWhelan —
(Miss J E Foster) *chsd ldrs: rdn along and wknd 4 out: bhd whn p.u bef last* **100/1**

4m 17.0s (17.60) **Going Correction** +0.90s/f (Soft) **9** Ran SP% **114.3**
Speed ratings: **92,89,84,83,83 82,75,—,—** CSF £12.81 TOTE £2.40: £1.50, £1.70, £1.30; EX 9.10.

Owner Andrea & Graham Wylie **Bred** V R De Soultrait **Trained** Billy Row, Co Durham

FOCUS
No great pace on in the early stages but a pleasing performance from the winner who was value for ten lengths with the third and fifth setting the level for the form.

NOTEBOOK
Ortolan Bleu(FR), who ran a highly promising race against a very useful performer in Fair Along on his British debut, found nothing of that gelding's calibre against him here. Having travelled well, he drew clear in the closing stages for a tidy win, and his trainer expects him to be seen to better effect on a sounder surface. He looks open to further improvement. *(op 6-4)*
Dan's Heir, a winner on his hurdling debut, was saddled with a penalty as a result, and probably achieved the best he could in finishing second. He enjoyed the run of the race, setting just a steady pace in front, and kept on stoutly. *(op 8-1 tchd 15-2)*
Copper Bay(IRE) looked to have every chance going to the second last, but he appeared not to get home in the ground. He might be helped by better ground or a sharper track. *(op 4-1 tchd 9-2)*
Dafarabad(IRE) was disappointing, but after one more run handicaps will become an option, and *faster ground in that sphere may bring about the improvement necessary to see him off the mark. (op 11-4)*
Quasimodo(IRE), who has been set stiff tasks on his first two starts over timber, will not be without hope at a more realistic level. *(op 28-1)*

3039 SKYBET.COM CASTLEFORD CHASE GRADE 2 (12 fncs) 2m
2:00 (2:00) (Class 1) 5-Y-0+ **£28,845** (£11,030; £5,690; £3,005)

Form RPR

-654 **1** **Mister McGoldrick**[31] 2499 8-11-8 153 .... DominicElsworth 165+
(Mrs S J Smith) *cl up: led after 5 out: rdn after next: lft clr 3 out* **11/2**[3]

1313 **2** *12* **Albuhera (IRE)**[17] 2759 7-11-3 ....(t) JoeTizzard 148+
(P F Nicholls) *trckd ldrs: mstke 4th: effrt 4 out: rdn to chse wnr next: drvn and hit 2 out: sn no imp: hit last* **6/1**

14-3 **3** *dist* **Oneway (IRE)**[24] 2635 8-11-2 157 .... JamieMoore 117
(M G Rimell) *hld up in rr: effrt and sme hdwy 5 out: rdn along next and sn btn: lft modest 3rd 3 out* **5/4**[1]

12U- **4** *17* **Fundamentalist (IRE)**[360] 3150 7-11-3 154 .... CarlLlewellyn —
(N A Twiston-Davies) *trckd ldrs: poushed along 6 out: rdn and wknd next: bhd whn mstke 4 out and sn t.o* **3/1**[2]

1-P3 **U** **El Vaquero (IRE)**[25] 2615 7-11-3 147 .... JimCrowley —
(J Howard Johnson) *led: hdd 8th: cl up tl rdn along and outpcd 4 out: wkng whn blnd and uns rdr next* **12/1**

4m 13.5s (6.90) **Going Correction** +0.90s/f (Soft) **5** Ran SP% **106.8**
Speed ratings: **118,112,—,—,—** CSF £31.62 TOTE £6.40: £2.30, £1.90; EX 22.30.

Owner Richard Longley **Bred** Mrs J Key **Trained** High Eldwick, W Yorks

FOCUS
An interesting renewal but the form is open to question with the front two in the market both failing to run to their best and the second sets the standard.

NOTEBOOK
Mister McGoldrick loves soft ground and had been successful in six of his previous seven starts around here, including in this race last year, but the punters did not want to know him under his 10lb penalty. He was always going to handle the ground better than his opponents, though, and with both Oneway and Fundamentalist failing to show their true form, he probably did not have to be at his very best to prevail. *(tchd 5-1)*
Albuhera(IRE) ran well considering he is only a novice and is happier on better ground. A flat track such as this suits him, and this tough performer takes his racing well. He will be winning again soon. *(op 7-1)*
Oneway(IRE) did not travel in the soft ground and failed to run his race. He improved through the handicapping ranks to stand on the verge of being a high-class two-miler last season but has so far failed to take that next step up the ladder. He might be a different proposition on a sounder surface, though. *Official explanation: trainer had no explanation for the poor form shown (op 11-8)*
Fundamentalist(IRE), an exciting novice last term who had his season curtailed by injury, was having his first outing for almost a year. He had never before in his previous seven starts run on ground described as anything but good, and he looked a long way short of his best here. He looked an unlikely finisher at one stage but Llewellyn kept him up to his work and he completed a well-beaten last of four finishers. It remains to be seen if he retains his ability, but he deserves another chance on faster ground. *(op 11-4 tchd 5-2 and 10-3)*
El Vaquero(IRE), dropping back from an extended three miles, tended to jump out to his right and he was beating a retreat when unseating at the third last. He has plenty of talent but it is worrying that he is not seeing his races out at any distance, and the assumption must be that he has a problem of some sort. *(op 10-1)*

3040 PLAY ROULETTE ON CH4 - PRESS RED H'CAP HURDLE (9 hdls) 2m
2:35 (2:36) (Class 3) (0-115,113) 4-Y-0+ **£5,074** (£1,489; £744; £372)

Form RPR

511F **1** **Oso Magic**[17] 2768 7-10-4 91 .... DominicElsworth 105+
(Mrs S J Smith) *trckd ldrs gng wl: smooth hdwy to ld 3 out: hit 2 out: rdn and styd on wl flat* **15/8**[2]

1P-1 **2** *2* **Diamond Sal**[33] 2452 7-11-6 112 .... BrianHughes[(5)] 121+
(J Howard Johnson) *hld up in tch: hit 3rd: hdwy 4 out: chsd wnr 2 out: sn rdn and kpt on same pce flat* **13/8**[1]

-03F **3** *8* **Nerone (GER)**[22] 2680 4-11-3 104 .... JimCrowley 103
(P Monteith) *hld up in tch: hdwy 3 out: rdn next: kpt on same pce appr last* **9/1**

-644 **4** *1* **Dance Party (IRE)**[24] 2625 5-10-8 98 .... MrTGreenall[(3)] 96
(M W Easterby) *hld up towards rr: hdwy and hit 3 out: rdn to chse ldng pair next: sn drvn and one pce* **14/1**

5052 **5** *1 1/2* **Uptown Lad (IRE)**[22] 2680 6-11-2 103 .... KennyJohnson 100
(R Johnson) *racd wd: hld up and bhd: hdwy 3 out: rdn next and kpt on same pce* **8/1**[3]

-000 **6** *10* **Mokum (FR)**[10] 2878 4-11-2 103 .... CarlLlewellyn 90
(A W Carroll) *led: rdn along and hdd 3 out: sn drvn and wknd* **28/1**

-P0P **7** *dist* **County Classic**[17] 2766 6-10-13 100 ....(b[1]) RussGarritty —
(T D Easterby) *cl up: effrt to dispute ld 4 out: rdn bef next and sn wknd* **33/1**

11-0 **8** *4* **Fair Spin**[45] 2190 5-11-12 113 ....(v) FinbarKeniry —
(M D Hammond) *chsd ldrs: rdn along 4 out: wknd bef next* **33/1**

4m 13.5s (14.10) **Going Correction** +1.025s/f (Soft)
WFA 4 from 5yo+ 10lb **8** Ran SP% **110.0**
Speed ratings: **105,104,100,99,98 93,—,—** CSF £4.98 CT £16.49 TOTE £3.00: £1.30, £1.40, £2.30; EX 6.20.

Owner Michael Thompson **Bred** M H Ings **Trained** High Eldwick, W Yorks

FOCUS
Just a modest contest but the well-handicapped winner was value for more than the official margin and could go in again while in this sort of form.

NOTEBOOK
Oso Magic ◆, who fell over fences last time, took advantage of a 35lb lower hurdles mark. He travelled well and there was never going to be any doubt that he would see the trip out strongly as he had done all his previous winning over further. This should have done his confidence some *good, and he could well pick up another race over hurdles prior to returning to chasing. (tchd 7-4 and 2-1)*
Diamond Sal, raised 8lb for her Carlisle success, looked like a pony next to the winner and, as it turned out, had a stiff task against a well-handicapped rival. She lost little in defeat. *(tchd 2-1)*
Nerone(GER), who is still searching for his first win over hurdles, is running to a fairly consistent level at present but is going to have to find some improvement from somewhere to defy his current mark. *(op 8-1)*
Dance Party(IRE) won two races as a novice and she has struggled since as a result, including in handicap company this year. She has dropped 7lb from her highest mark but needs even more leniency. *(op 12-1)*
Uptown Lad(IRE), who ran well in defeat at Newcastle last time, was put up 5lb in the handicap for that, meaning that he is now once again saddled with a three-figure mark, something he has been unable to defy in eight attempts.
Mokum(FR), who has been set some stiff tasks in the past, has shown very little this season. *(op 25-1)*

3041 ROCOM BEGINNERS' CHASE (18 fncs) 3m 1f
3:05 (3:05) (Class 4) 5-Y-0+ **£4,279** (£1,555)

Form RPR

-2F2 **1** **Rebel Rhythm**[33] 2449 6-11-0 .... DominicElsworth 137+
(Mrs S J Smith) *mde most: rdn clr fr 3 out: easily* **4/5**[1]

01-4 **2** *25* **Trisons Star (IRE)**[33] 2449 7-10-9 .... DesFlavin[(5)] 112
(Mrs L B Normile) *cl up: effrt and ev ch 5 out tl rdn and outpcd fr 3 out* **15/2**[3]

-PU3 **U** **Abzuson**[22] 2675 8-11-0 105 .... FinbarKeniry —
(J R Norton) *in tch tl blnd bdly and uns rdr 6th* **40/1**

1/33 **U** **Tees Components**[38] 2336 10-11-0 ....(t) JimCrowley —
(K G Reveley) *trckd ldng pair tl blnd and uns rdr 8th* **15/8**[2]

7m 3.00s (23.00) **Going Correction** +1.15s/f (Heav) **4** Ran SP% **104.5**
Speed ratings: **109,101,—,—** CSF £6.00 TOTE £1.70; EX 4.40.

Owner The Fees R Us Syndicate **Bred** Five Horses Ltd **Trained** High Eldwick, W Yorks

FOCUS
Rebel Rhythm won like a classy performer, with the two to complete running close to their Carlisle marks.

NOTEBOOK
Rebel Rhythm readily disposed of his only remaining opponent after the other two had departed, and won with any amount in hand. He is clearly a decent prospect and more races will come his way, but he did slightly suggest he has some quirks, as he needed a slap down the neck to go out for his final circuit, and had a good look at the last fence before jumping it. However, with plenty of time on his side, he has time to mature and the stable do hold him in high regard, so it would be surprising if he does not land a decent event at some stage, and he now heads for the valuable Towton Chase back here in February. *(op 8-11 tchd 5-6 in a place)*
Trisons Star(IRE) did very little wrong but was completely outclassed by the winner, who had already thrashed him at Carlisle. There will be easier opportunities for him, as he was no mug over hurdles, and a stiffer test at three miles in lesser company will suit him. *(op 8-1 tchd 7-1)*
Tees Components jumped adequately until hardly getting off the ground at the eighth fence. The slow pace may not have helped him have a cut at the fence, and he can easily be given another chance. *(tchd 33-1)*
Abzuson made a terrible mistake at the sixth and gave his jockey no chance of staying aboard. *(tchd 33-1)*

3042 SKYBET IN-PLAY BETTING ON ALL PREMIERSHIP GAMES NOVICES' H'CAP HURDLE (12 hdls) 3m 1f
3:35 (3:36) (Class 4) (0-95,95) 3-Y-0+ **£2,799** (£815; £408)

Form RPR

00-4 **1** **Spectested (IRE)**[45] 2186 4-11-11 94 .... WayneHutchinson 96+
(A W Carroll) *hld up and bhd: hit 3rd: pushed along 1/2-way: hdwy 3 out: rdn and styd on fr next: drvn flat to ld last 50 yds* **5/1**[2]

530 **2** *3* **Joe Brown**[24] 2631 5-11-12 95 .... JimCrowley 95+
(Mrs H Dalton) *trckd ldrs on inner: hdwy to ld 3 out: rdn next: drvn flat: hdd and no ex last 50 yds* **9/2**[1]

3005 **3** *3/4* **Network Oscar (IRE)**[26] 2591 4-11-5 91 .... MrTGreenall[(3)] 89
(M W Easterby) *hld up towards rr: stdy hdwy 4 out: chsd ldrs next: rdn and hung lft 2 out and last: kpt on same pce flat* **11/1**

06-0 **4** *3/4* **Cragg Prince (IRE)**[27] 2571 6-11-4 87 .... DominicElsworth 87+
(Mrs S J Smith) *a.p on outer: effrt 3 out and ev ch: hit next and sn drvn: kpt on same pce fr last* **12/1**

2000 **5** *6* **Northern Rambler (IRE)**[26] 2586 8-9-5 70 ....(b) JamesReveley[(10)] 62
(K G Reveley) *cl up: led 6th: hdd next: rdn along 4 out: wknd fr next* **14/1**

2056 **6** *8* **Minster Abbi**[23] 2653 5-10-4 73 ....(p) NeilMulholland 59+
(W Storey) *midsfield: steadsy hdwy to chse ldrs 4 out: rdn along bef next and sn wknd* **8/1**

0-03 **7** *8* **Avanti Tiger (IRE)**[40] 2290 6-9-11 69 oh1 ....(b) LeeVickers[(3)] 45
(C C Bealby) *chsd ldrs: rdn along after 4 out: wknd fr next* **13/2**

50P2 **8** *15* **That's Racing**[23] 2657 5-10-7 76 .... JamieMoore 37
(J Hetherton) *midfield: hdwy 7th: rdn along and in tch appr 4 out: sn drvn and wknd bef next* **6/1**[3]

00-P **9** *3 1/2* **Paperchaser**[58] 1938 5-9-11 71 .... DougieCostello[(5)] 28
(F P Murtagh) *m idfield: effrt and hdwy 4 out: rdn and btn bef next* **33/1**

P3P **10** *9* **Kiss The Girls (IRE)**[30] 2517 6-10-5 74 ....(v[1]) JosephByrne 22
(Jennie Candlish) *led to 6th: led again and blnd 7th: hit next: sn rdn: hdd & wknd after 4 out* **20/1**

-2P5 **11** *15* **Iron Warrior (IRE)**[24] 2639 5-11-7 90 .... FinbarKeniry 23
(G M Moore) *chsd ldrs: rdn along after 4 out: sn wknd* **12/1**

540/ **12** *10* **Troysgreen (IRE)**[927] 644 7-9-9 69 oh6 .... BrianHughes[(5)] —
(P D Niven) *chsd ldrs: rdn along bef and wknd bef 4 out* **50/1**

400 **P** **Key In**[23] 2663 4-11-5 88 ....(t) AlanDempsey —
(I W McInnes) *midfield: lost pl and bhd fr 1/2-way: puleld up bef 3 out* **33/1**

3-00 **P** **Dormy Two (IRE)**[18] 2749 5-11-7 90 ....(p) KennyJohnson —
(P T Midgley) *midfield: pushed along and hit 7th: sn rdn and wknd: bhd whn p.u bef 3 out* **40/1**

6m 57.8s (43.30) **Going Correction** +1.275s/f (Heav)
WFA 4 from 5yo+ 13lb **14** Ran SP% **119.0**
Speed ratings: **81,80,79,79,77 75,72,67,66,63 58,55,—,—** CSF £26.44 CT £240.60 TOTE £5.80: £1.80, £2.70, £3.80; EX 18.50 Place 6 £55.01, Place 5 £20.58.

Owner Bezwell Fixings Limited **Bred** Don Commins **Trained** Cropthorne, Worcs

FOCUS
A poor race for the track run in a very slow time, and probably not strong form

NOTEBOOK

Spectested(IRE), having his first run in handicap company over hurdles, finished behind Joe Brown last time but was much better suited by the step up in trip than he was. However, you would have wanted really long odds about him getting placed jumping two from home, as he appeared to be going nowhere quickly. It is hard to say whether he quickened or the front four slowed badly after the last, but he is certainly not a horse to take short odds about before a race.

Joe Brown, who finished in front of Spectested last time, did not quite get home over the extra distance. He should be better suited by slightly shorter in the future. *(op 5-1)*

Network Oscar(IRE) ran his best race to date, but is either still green and needs more time, or has *a few quirks under pressure because he tended to veer badly left approaching the final few* hurdles. *(op 10-1 tchd 12-1)*

Cragg Prince(IRE), trying handicap company for the first time, kept plugging away but is very moderate indeed. *(tchd 11-1)*

Northern Rambler(IRE) did not appear to see out the three-mile trip as well as others despite the refitting of blinkers. *(op 12-1)*

That's Racing was under considerable pressure some way from home and was never seen with any chance. *(op 8-1)*

Key In *Official explanation: jockey said filly lost her action (op 25-1)*

T/Plt: £72.50 to a £1 stake. Pool: £74,676.05. 751.75 winning tickets. T/Qpdt: £25.70 to a £1 stake. Pool: £4,876.30. 139.90 winning tickets. JR

3043 - 3050a (Foreign Racing) - See Raceform Interactive

3002 **LEOPARDSTOWN** (L-H)

Tuesday, December 27

OFFICIAL GOING: Yielding to soft

3051a PADDY POWER DIAL-A-BET CHASE (GRADE 1) (11 fncs) 2m 1f

1:30 (1:30) 5-Y-0+ **£32,269** (£9,432; £4,468; £1,489)

RPR

1 **Hi Cloy (IRE)**[16] [2793] 8-11-12 151 AndrewJMcNamara 162+
(Michael Hourigan, Ire) *hld up in rr: slow 4 out: prog after 2 out: 4th last: styd on wl to ld cl home* **8/1**[3]

2 3/4 **Fota Island (IRE)**[243] [89] 9-11-12 150 APMcCoy 161
(M F Morris, Ire) *trckd ldrs in 4th: mstke 5th: impr into 2nd after 2 out: sn chal: slt ld last: hdd early run-in: kpt on u.p* **9/1**

3 1 1/2 **Central House**[16] [2786] 8-11-12 159 (t) RLoughran 163+
(D T Hughes, Ire) *led: rdn and strly pressed after 2 out: narrowly hdd last: sn regained ld: rdr mistk winng post & eased: hdd cl home* **11/4**[2]

4 2 1/2 **Moscow Flyer (IRE)**[44] [2230] 11-11-12 180 BJGeraghty 157
(Mrs John Harrington, Ire) *cl up in 2nd: slt mstke 4th: 3rd and rdn to chal after 2 out: no imp fr last: kpt on same pce* **8/11**[1]

5 15 **Mariah Rollins (IRE)**[16] [2786] 7-11-7 143 JLCullen 137
(P A Fahy, Ire) *trckd ldrs in 3rd: cl up 3 out: 4th and rdn after 2 out: sn no ex* **16/1**

4m 16.0s **Going Correction** -0.40s/f (Good) **5** Ran SP% **111.6**
Speed ratings: **118,117,116,115,108** CSF £60.53 TOTE £12.20: £3.00, £1.90; DF 62.20.
Owner Mrs S McCloy **Bred** Mrs Paul Finegan **Trained** Patrickswell, Co Limerick
■ Stewards' Enquiry : R Loughran 14-day ban: mistook winning post (Jan 5,7-8,12,14-15,19,21-22,26,28-29, Feb 2,4)

NOTEBOOK

Hi Cloy(IRE) stayed on up the far rail from what appeared an impossible position to gain the day close home *(op 7/1)*

Fota Island(IRE) went second after two out and gained a marginal advantage at the last. Headed on the run-in, he fought back and looked a winner until headed again close home. This was his first start of the season and he will improve, especially on better ground, and might be a candidate for the Queen Mother Champion Chase.

Central House turned the finish into a farce. Having made virtually all the running and beaten off his challengers, his rider mistook the winning post, stood up in the saddle and waved his whip in premature celebration. The penny did not drop until all too late and he has to be counted an unlucky loser. The hapless Loughran got a 14-days ban but apparently retains the ride on the horse. *(op 5/2)*

Moscow Flyer(IRE) again raced close to the pace but was in trouble soon after the second last and in the straight was just going through the motions, unable to take advantage of what happened on the run-in. It looks as if age has caught up with him and it will be a surprise if he comes back to anything resembling his best. *(op 4/5 tchd 10/11)*

3052a PADDYPOWER.COM FUTURE CHAMPIONS NOVICE HURDLE (GRADE 2) (8 hdls) 2m

2:00 (2:00) 4-Y-0+ **£23,085** (£6,773; £3,226; £1,099)

RPR

1 **Mr Nosie (IRE)**[72] [1763] 4-10-13 PCarberry 131+
(Noel Meade, Ire) *trckd ldrs: 3rd fr 3rd: 2nd and rdn 2 out: led appr last: styd on wl run-in* **7/2**[2]

2 5 **Blueberry Boy (IRE)**[16] [2790] 6-11-4 BJGeraghty 131
(Paul Stafford, Ire) *led: slt mstke 3rd: strly pressed after 2 out: hdd bef last: kpt on* **2/1**[1]

3 15 **Wanango (GER)**[38] [2335] 4-10-13 WJLee 111
(T Stack, Ire) *3rd early: dropped to 5th 1/2-way: impr into 3rd appr 2 out: sn rdn and outpcd: no ex bef last* **2/1**[1]

4 14 **County Final (IRE)**[16] [2790] 6-11-4 119 APMcCoy 112
(Noel Meade, Ire) *trckd ldr in 2nd: 4th and rdn bef 2 out: sn outpcd: no ex fr last* **4/1**[3]

5 10 **Hardwick**[86] [1623] 6-11-4 MrCJSweeney 102
(Adrian Maguire, Ire) *hld up in tch: 4th fr 4 out: rdn after 3 out: no ex fr next: eased fr last* **22/1**

6 25 **Dancing Water**[10] [2898] 6-11-4 90 JLCullen 77
(Patrick O Brady, Ire) *a in rr: rdn and lost tch fr 4 out* **66/1**

3m 57.5s **Going Correction** -0.40s/f (Good)
WFA 4 from 6yo 10lb **6** Ran SP% **114.7**
Speed ratings: **119,116,109,107,102 102** CSF £11.63 TOTE £4.10: £1.70, £1.90; DF 7.30.
Owner Mrs P Sloan **Bred** Miss Josephine O'Flynn **Trained** Castletown, Co Meath

NOTEBOOK

Mr Nosie(IRE) put up a solid performance, overcoming a slight mistake at the second last to take it up approaching the final flight. He drew clear on the flat and improvement is guaranteed. *(op 3/1)*

Blueberry Boy(IRE) is luckless but was well held by the winner when eased in the closing stages. *(op 5/2)*

Wanango(GER) was outpaced very quickly in the straight. *(op 7/4)*

County Final(IRE) was another to struggle with no response after the second last. *(op 9/2 tchd 5/1)*

3053a PADDY POWER CHASE (GRADE B H'CAP) (17 fncs) 3m

2:35 (2:35) (0-145,137) 5-Y-0+

£77,021 (£25,886; £12,411; £4,326; £2,978; £1,631)

RPR

1 **Black Apalachi (IRE)**[37] [2390] 6-10-5 118 ow1 JLCullen 128+
(P J Rothwell, Ire) *trckd ldrs on inner: 3rd 4 out: cl 2nd next: led 2 out: sn rdn and strly pressed: kpt on wl u.p fr last* **25/1**

2 1 **Camden Tanner (IRE)**[38] [2365] 9-10-8 126 RMMoran(5) 135
(Robert Tyner, Ire) *hld up: prog on outer 11th: 4th 4 out: 2nd travelling best 2 out: sn rdn to chal: kpt on u.p fr last* **20/1**

3 1 1/2 **Ross River**[24] [2650] 9-10-12 125 DNRussell 133
(A J Martin, Ire) *mid-div: 9th 6 out: 7th 2 out: styd on wl fr last* **8/1**[2]

4 2 **Adarma (IRE)**[30] [2539] 7-10-10 123 APMcCoy 129
(C Roche, Ire) *hld up: mstke 5th: rdn after 3 out: 11th and hdwy 2 out: kpt on fr last* **12/1**

5 hd **G V A Ireland (IRE)**[17] [2781] 7-10-4 122 KTColeman(5) 127
(F Flood, Ire) *trckd ldrs: 5th 3 out: 8th and rdn next: kpt on fr last* **16/1**

6 4 **Like A Bee (IRE)**[16] [2794] 7-9-10 109 APCrowe 110
(C Roche, Ire) *towards rr: prog into mid-div after 3 out: kpt on u.p fr next* **33/1**

7 1 **Lost Time (IRE)**[23] [2666] 8-10-12 125 CO'Dwyer 125
(C Roche, Ire) *hld up towards rr: prog 5 out: 6th 3 out: kpt on same pce fr next* **9/1**[3]

8 shd **A New Story (IRE)**[30] [2539] 7-10-7 120 AndrewJMcNamara 120
(Michael Hourigan, Ire) *hld up: prog on inner 2 out: 10th bef last: kpt on same pce* **12/1**

9 1/2 **Fatherofthebride (IRE)**[24] [2649] 9-9-13 115 (b) JMAllen(3) 115
(Joseph Crowley, Ire) *sn led: slow and hdd 3 out: 3rd u.p bef next: no ex bef last* **40/1**

10 4 **Point Barrow (IRE)**[30] [2539] 7-11-4 131 (t) JPElliott 127
(P Hughes, Ire) *hld up: 11th 1/2-way: prog into 6th appr 2 out: kpt on same pce* **20/1**

11 2 **Pearly Jack**[16] [2785] 7-10-3 121 MrMJO'Connor(5) 115
(D E Fitzgerald, Ire) *towards rr: prog into 8th 3 out: no ex fr next* **14/1**

12 3 **Mullacash (IRE)**[24] [2649] 7-10-4 120 (b) MissNCarberry(3) 111
(Noel Meade, Ire) *prom: 4th 3 out: wknd u.p bef next* **25/1**

13 2 **Lincam (IRE)**[79] [1700] 9-10-2 118 (p) WJLee(3) 107
(P O'Keeffe, Ire) *settled 2nd: led 3 out: hdd next: wknd u.p bef last* **50/1**

14 2 **Doodle Addle (IRE)**[16] [2794] 9-10-7 125 AELynch(5) 112
(J T R Dreaper, Ire) *a towards rr* **25/1**

15 7 **Carneys Cross (IRE)**[16] [2794] 7-10-5 121 RLoughran(3) 101
(S J Treacy, Ire) *trckd ldrs: 7th 6 out: wkng whn mstke 4 out: no ex* **25/1**

16 9 **Joint Agreement (IRE)**[13] [2834] 8-9-10 115 6ex GCotter 80
(T M Walsh, Ire) *nvr a factor* **25/1**

17 7 **Well Presented (IRE)**[30] [2539] 7-11-3 130 RMPower 94
(Mrs John Harrington, Ire) *mid-div: 8th 6 out: no ex fr 4 out: trailing fr 2 out* **40/1**

18 7 **Jaquouille (FR)**[23] [2670] 8-10-10 123 DJCasey 80
(A L T Moore, Ire) *mid-div: no ex fr 3 out: eased bef last* **11/2**[1]

19 7 **Star Clipper**[30] [2539] 8-10-13 126 PCarberry 76
(Noel Meade, Ire) *towards rr: slt mstke 9th: trailing fr 3 out* **16/1**

20 5 **Marcus Du Berlais (FR)**[30] [2539] 8-11-10 137 TPTreacy 82
(A L T Moore, Ire) *a bhd: trailing fr 2 out* **33/1**

21 3/4 **What Odds (IRE)**[17] [2781] 9-10-11 124 RGeraghty 68
(T K Geraghty, Ire) *in tch: 8th 1/2-way: wknd fr 5 out: trailing after 3 out* **25/1**

F **Knock Knock (IRE)**[17] [2781] 8-10-9 122 DFO'Regan —
(David Wachman, Ire) *hld up: fell 7th* **9/1**[3]

F **Solar System (IRE)**[38] [2365] 8-10-6 122 SMMcGovern(3) —
(T J Taaffe, Ire) *hld up: 11th 6 out: fell next* **25/1**

B **Numbersixvalverde (IRE)**[23] [2670] 9-11-8 135 NPMadden —
(Martin Brassil, Ire) *hld up in tch: b.d 5 out* **20/1**

P **Prince Of Tara (IRE)**[30] [2539] 8-11-1 128 BJGeraghty —
(S J Mahon, Ire) *mid-div: dropped to rr and p.u 1/2-way* **8/1**[2]

P **Cane Brake (IRE)**[37] [2390] 6-11-1 131 (p) MrKEPower(3) —
(David Wachman, Ire) *chsd ldrs: 9th 1/2-way: wknd 5 out: p.u bef 3 out* **33/1**

6m 18.6s **Going Correction** -0.40s/f (Good) **27** Ran SP% **148.3**
Speed ratings: 111,110,110,109,109 108,108,108,108,108 108,108,108,108,108 108,108,108,108,108 108,—,—, CSF £462.72 CT £4381.70 TOTE £18.70: £3.90, £11.40, £2.40, £4.00; DF 703.70.
Owner G Burke **Bred** Thomas Hatton **Trained** Tinahely, Co. Wicklow

NOTEBOOK

Black Apalachi(IRE) was having only his third start over fences but jumped well and took it up with two left. He repelled all and stayed on in tremendous fashion, and The Irish National is the target.

Camden Tanner(IRE) left his previous runs this season well behind but he caught a real tartar in *the winner Official explanation: trainer said, regarding the improved form shown, gelding was having only its third run back after a long break due to injury and, while disappointing at Punchestown last time, its two runs prior to this had been over a much shorter trip; he added that gelding had worked well since last running and the hope was that today's extra distance would bring about some improvement*

Ross River was another for whom this race had been a long-term objective. He will gain compensation quickly enough. *(op 12/1)*

Adarma(IRE) came through beaten horses in eyecatching style.

G V A Ireland(IRE) showed more than a spark of his old form. *(op 14/1)*

Lost Time(IRE) acquitted himself well enough for one so inexperienced. *(op 12/1)*

A New Story(IRE) likes passing horses at the end but was set an impossible task in the straight. *(op 10/1)*

Jaquouille(FR) was in trouble with three to jump and the position was accepted in the straight. *Official explanation: jockey said gelding ran too keen in the early stages (op 6/1)*

Prince Of Tara(IRE) *Official explanation: jockey said horse was never travelling; vet said horse finished lame (op 7/1)*

3054 - 3062a (Foreign Racing) - See Raceform Interactive

2838 CATTERICK (L-H)
Wednesday, December 28
3063 Meeting Abandoned - Snow

2824 NEWBURY (L-H)
Wednesday, December 28
3070 Meeting Abandoned - Frost

3077 - 3078a (Foreign Racing) - See Raceform Interactive

3049 LEOPARDSTOWN (L-H)
Wednesday, December 28

OFFICIAL GOING: Yielding to soft

3079a ASCON/ROHCON NOVICE CHASE (GRADE 1) (17 fncs) 3m
1:25 (1:27) 5-Y-O+ **£34,574** (£10,106; £4,787; £1,595)

RPR

1 **Southern Vic (IRE)**[10] 2908 6-11-10 130 RWalsh 145+
(T M Walsh, Ire) *a cl up: led fr 3rd: jnd 6th: hdd 10th: led again fr 5 out: drew clr after 2 out: styd on strly fr last* **5/2**[1]

2 *15* **Homer Wells (IRE)**[11] 2894 7-11-10 DJCasey 124
(W P Mullins, Ire) *trckd ldrs: 6th and drvn along after 4 out: 4th next: 3rd after 2 out: mod 2nd bef last: no ex run-in* **7/1**[2]

3 *4 ½* **Tumbling Dice (IRE)**[46] 2174 6-11-10 BJGeraghty 120
(T J Taaffe, Ire) *hld up in tch: slt mstke 5 out: 5th and drvn along next: 3rd 3 out: 2nd 2 out: sn no ex* **7/1**[2]

4 *20* **Coast To Coast (IRE)**[40] 2331 6-11-10 (bt) MrKEPower 100
(E J O'Grady, Ire) *hld up in tch: prog 10th: 4th 4 out: 2nd next: wknd fr 2 out* **20/1**

5 *2 ½* **Romaha (IRE)**[10] 2908 9-11-10 (t) LJFleming 97
(S J Mahon, Ire) *cl up: disp ld 6th: led bef 10th: hdd 5 out: no ex after 4 out* **50/1**

6 *7* **Oulart**[25] 2648 6-11-10 CO'Dwyer 90
(D T Hughes, Ire) *trckd ldrs on outer: reminders 6th: impr into 3rd 4 out: 5th whn slow next: sn no ex* **20/1**

F **Slim Pickings (IRE)**[39] 2364 6-11-10 DNRussell —
(Robert Tyner, Ire) *fell 1st* **7/1**[2]

F **Mr Babbage (IRE)**[24] 2668 7-11-10 JRBarry —
(W P Mullins, Ire) *hld up in tch: fell 6 out* **10/1**[3]

F **Tigerlion (IRE)**[25] 2648 7-11-10 MDarcy —
(J Bleahen, Ire) *trckd ldrs in 4th: 3rd fr 10th tl fell 5 out* **10/1**[3]

U **Church Island (IRE)**[24] 2668 6-11-10 PCarberry —
(Michael Hourigan, Ire) *led: hdd 3rd: mstke 10th: in tch whn bdly hmpd and uns rdr 5 out* **5/2**[1]

6m 25.2s **Going Correction** -0.075s/f (Good) **10** Ran SP% **124.3**
Speed ratings: **113,108,106,99,99 96,—,—,—,—** CSF £22.19 TOTE £4.10: £1.80, £2.50, £1.90; DF 61.00.
Owner Mrs Brenda Graham **Bred** Neil R Tector **Trained** Kill, Co Kildare

NOTEBOOK
Southern Vic(IRE) appreciated this trip and travelled well throughout. Going on after the second last, he had no challengers in the straight and won as he pleased. There are a couple of more steps to be taken before Cheltenham comes into the equation. *(op 9/4 tchd 11/4)*
Homer Wells(IRE) improved under pressure from four out but could never get in any sort of a challenge.
Tumbling Dice(IRE) flattered briefly two out but was soon beaten. *(op 6/1)*
Coast To Coast(IRE) went second three out but was struggling before the next.
Church Island(IRE) wasn't too clever at a couple of the early fences but it was hardly his fault that he was badly hampered five out giving Carberry no chance of staying on board *(op 3/1)*

3080a WOODIESDIY.COM CHRISTMAS HURDLE (GRADE 2) (12 hdls) 3m
2:00 (2:00) 4-Y-O+ **£23,085** (£6,773; £3,226; £1,099)

RPR

1 **Rosaker (USA)**[201] 703 8-11-8 139 PCarberry 151
(Noel Meade, Ire) *settled 3rd: drvn along after 3 out: outpcd after 2 out: rallied last: styd on wl run-in to ld cl home* **7/1**

2 *2* **Emotional Moment (IRE)**[18] 2777 8-11-8 146 BJGeraghty 149
(T J Taaffe, Ire) *cl 2nd: led bef 4 out: strly pressed 2 out: jnd ent st: regnd ld appr last: 3l clr early run-in: hrd rdn & no ex whn hdd cl* **11/4**[2]

3 *1 ½* **Strangely Brown (IRE)**[45] 2235 4-11-4 RWalsh 143
(E McNamara, Ire) *trckd ldrs in 4th: outpcd 2 out: kpt on wl fr last* **13/2**[3]

4 *1* **Solerina (IRE)**[18] 2777 8-11-5 158 GTHutchinson 143
(James Bowe, Ire) *led: hdd bef 4 out: chal after 2 out: disp ld ent st: hdd bef last: no ex run-in* **4/5**[1]

5 *9* **Holy Orders (IRE)**[45] 2227 8-11-10 (b) DJCasey 139
(W P Mullins, Ire) *trckd ldrs in 5th: lost tch after 3 out: trailing next: kpt on fr last* **25/1**

6m 3.00s **Going Correction** -0.55s/f (Firm)
WFA 4 from 8yo 13lb **5** Ran SP% **111.9**
Speed ratings: **104,103,102,102,99** CSF £26.57 TOTE £8.00: £2.60, £1.70; DF 22.60.
Owner High Street Ceathar Syndicate **Bred** Morgans Ford Stud **Trained** Castletown, Co Meath

NOTEBOOK
Rosaker(USA) regained winning form to gain a first success since February 2004. He looked to have no chance in the straight but the complexion of the race changed dramatically on the run-in and he stayed on doggedly to wrest it close home. *(op 7/1 tchd 8/1)*
Emotional Moment(IRE) came back at Solerina to take the lead a second time approaching the last and went clear on the run-in. But he emptied quickly as the winner stayed on to catch him close home. *(op 5/2)*
Strangely Brown(IRE) was struggling two out and had no chance early in the straight. But he stayed on late with such effect from the last that he grabbed third place. *(op 11/2 tchd 7/1)*
Solerina(IRE) does not stay three miles and doesn't like Leopardstown. Headed by the winner before four out after a mistake at the previous flight, she came back in the inner turning for home but was headed again before the last. On the flat she had nothing more to give. *(op 4/5 tchd 9/10)*

3081a LEXUS CHASE (GRADE 1) (17 fncs) 3m
2:35 (2:35) 5-Y-O+ **£69,148** (£20,212; £9,574; £3,191)

RPR

1 **Beef Or Salmon (IRE)**[39] 2337 9-11-12 170 PCarberry 174+
(Michael Hourigan, Ire) *hld up in 4th: slt mstke 5 out: tk clsr order 3 out: 2nd travlng best after 2 out: led early st: clr fr last: heavily eased* **9/10**[1]

2 *4* **War Of Attrition (IRE)**[17] 2793 6-11-12 157 CO'Dwyer 167
(M F Morris, Ire) *settled 3rd: drvn along to cl appr 2 out: mod 2nd bef last: kpt on wout troubling wnr* **11/4**[2]

3 *11* **Forget The Past**[17] 2793 7-11-12 148 DNRussell 163+
(M J P O'Brien, Ire) *cl 2nd: led 3 out: rdn and strly pressed after 2 out: hdd early st: 3rd and no ex bef last* **11/2**[3]

4 *2* **Hedgehunter (IRE)**[24] 2670 9-11-12 160 RWalsh 154
(W P Mullins, Ire) *led: hdd 3 out: dropped to 4th and rdn after 2 out: sn no ex* **7/1**

5 *20* **Jack High (IRE)**[18] 2777 10-11-12 138 GCotter 134
(T M Walsh, Ire) *hld up in rr: pushed along and lost tch after 4 out: trailing fr next* **66/1**

6m 23.1s **Going Correction** -0.075s/f (Good) **5** Ran SP% **108.7**
Speed ratings: **117,115,112,111,104** CSF £3.79 TOTE £2.10: £1.30, £1.90; DF 3.10.
Owner B J Craig **Bred** John Murphy **Trained** Patrickswell, Co Limerick

NOTEBOOK
Beef Or Salmon(IRE) was not fluent at the fifth from home but was going best of all when closing three out. He led before the straight and had everything well sewn up before the last, allowing Carberry to ease him right down on the run-in. Small field races at Leopardstown suit him ideally and he will be back for the Hennessy here in February. *(op Evens)*
War Of Attrition(IRE) proved absolutely no match for the winner from two out and is flattered by his proximity. However, he put his recent disappointing Punchestown display behind him and might yet prove capable of answering bigger questions. *(op 11/4 tchd 3/1)*
Forget The Past was under pressure to hold his advantage two out and was beaten in the straight, losing second place before the last and struggling home. He was reported as having burst a blood-vessel. *Official explanation: trainer's representative said gelding broke a blood vessel*
Hedgehunter(IRE) was having his first run over fences since Aintree and his jumping in front was a joy to watch. He dropped away on the approach to two out and returned with a nick on a hind leg, but is still on course for a tilt at the Hennessy next month.

3082 - 3085a (Foreign Racing) - See Raceform Interactive

3056 LIMERICK (R-H)
Wednesday, December 28

OFFICIAL GOING: Hurdle course - heavy; chase course - soft to heavy

3086a LADBROKES.IE DORANS PRIDE NOVICE HURDLE (GRADE 3) 2m 6f
1:45 (1:45) 4-Y-O+ **£18,468** (£5,418; £2,581; £879)

RPR

1 **Vic Venturi (IRE)**[31] 2536 5-10-7 (t) MrBTO'Connell(7) 123
(Philip Fenton, Ire) *chsd ldrs: mainly 5th: clsd into 3rd bef st: led bef 2 out: styd on wl u.p fr bef last* **12/1**

2 *3* **Mister Top Notch (IRE)**[17] 2784 6-11-0 JLCullen 120
(D E Fitzgerald, Ire) *a.p: travelling wl in 2nd bef st: rdn 2 out: clsd bef last: no imp and kpt on same pce run-in* **5/1**[3]

3 *10* **Purple Shuffle (IRE)**[41] 2306 7-11-0 105 (t) DJHoward 110
(P A Fahy, Ire) *sn led: strly pressed bef st: hdd bef 2 out: sn no imp: kpt on same pce* **33/1**

4 *3* **Letterman (IRE)**[56] 1995 5-11-0 PWFlood 107
(E J O'Grady, Ire) *trckd ldrs: 4th bef st: no imp u.p and kpt on same pce fr bef 2 out* **9/2**[2]

5 *13* **Marbeuf (USA)**[13] 2853 4-10-9 111 DFO'Regan 89+
(Noel Meade, Ire) *mid-div: clsr in 6th fr 4 out: 5th bef st: sn no imp u.p: bad mstke last* **11/2**

6 *2 ½* **The Spoonplayer (IRE)**[45] 2206 6-10-11 118 JMAllen(3) 92
(Henry De Bromhead, Ire) *trckd ldrs: dropped to 6th and rdn bef st: sn no imp* **14/1**

7 *8* **Alpha Royale (IRE)**[17] 2784 5-11-6 (b) RMPower 90
(C Byrnes, Ire) *towards rr: clsr order fr 6 out: 7th 3 out: no imp u.p and kpt on same pce fr bef st* **11/2**

8 *25* **Oscar's Advance (IRE)**[34] 2471 6-11-3 APCrowe 62
(C Roche, Ire) *mid-div: 8th whn slt mstke 4 out: rdn fr next: sn no imp u.p* **9/4**[1]

9 *25* **Kerryhead Sunshine (IRE)**[27] 2602 5-10-9 AndrewJMcNamara 47
(Michael Hourigan, Ire) *towards rr: rdn after 6 out: sn lost tch* **50/1**

P **Sir Frederick (IRE)**[34] 2470 5-11-0 116 BMCash —
(W J Burke, Ire) *chsd ldrs: rdn and lost pl 3 out: sn bhd: p.u bef last* **12/1**

P **Il Mulino (IRE)**[21] 2711 5-10-13 ow2 MrDerekO'Connor(3) —
(Denis Ahern, Ire) *towards rr: lost tch appr 6 out: sn no imp: bhd whn p.u bef 3 out* **14/1**

6m 19.7s
WFA 4 from 5yo+ 11lb **11** Ran SP% **130.0**
CSF £79.51 TOTE £21.20: £3.90, £2.00, £7.90; DF 137.40.
Owner J P Dunne **Bred** Mrs P & C Brabazon **Trained** Carrick-On-Suir, Co Waterford

NOTEBOOK
Vic Venturi(IRE) showed improved form with an effort that if taken literally would place him very high in the staying novice ranks. He showed a tendency to edge left from the last, excusable in the bad ground. *(op 10/1)*
Mister Top Notch(IRE) found little once the winner went on two out but was still nicely clear of the remainder and kept on to the line.
Purple Shuffle(IRE) ran in front but was totally outpaced when headed.
Letterman(IRE) was toiling before the turn-in. *(op 4/1 tchd 5/1)*
Marbeuf(USA) was absolutely no threat when blundering badly at the last. *(op 5/1)*
Alpha Royale(IRE) failed to run anywhere near his form. *(op 5/1 tchd 6/1)*
Oscar's Advance(IRE) was toiling when clipping the fourth last and was not going to be involved from the next. *Official explanation: jockey said gelding was never travelling (op 5/2 tchd 11/4)*
Sir Frederick(IRE) *Official explanation: trainer said gelding was found to have mucus on its lungs (op 10/1)*

3087 - 3090a (Foreign Racing) - See Raceform Interactive

[2900]MUSSELBURGH (R-H)
Thursday, December 29

3091 Meeting Abandoned - Frost and snow

[2824]NEWBURY (L-H)
Thursday, December 29

3098 Meeting Abandoned - Frost

3105 - 3108a (Foreign Racing) - See Raceform Interactive

[3077]LEOPARDSTOWN (L-H)
Thursday, December 29

OFFICIAL GOING: Soft

3109a BEWLEYSHOTELS.COM DECEMBER FESTIVAL HURDLE (GRADE 1) (8 hdls) 2m
2:25 (2:25) 4-Y-O+ **£41,489** (£12,127; £5,744; £1,914)

RPR

1 **Brave Inca (IRE)**[25] [2669] 7-11-12 166 .... APMcCoy 169
(C A Murphy, Ire) *mod 2nd early: tk clsr order bef 1/2-way: nt fluent 3 out: drvn along bef next: led appr last: styd on wl run-in* **9/4**[2]

2 *3* **Harchibald (FR)**[19] [2761] 6-11-12 166 .... PCarberry 166
(Noel Meade, Ire) *hld up in rr: smooth hdwy after 2 out: 3rd appr last: 2nd early run-in: sn rdn and no imp: kpt on same pce* **9/10**[1]

3 *4 ½* **Newmill (IRE)**[39] [2397] 7-11-12 140 .... AndrewJMcNamara 161
(John Joseph Murphy, Ire) *led: clr early: rdn after 2 out: hdd appr last: 3rd and no ex early run-in* **40/1**

4 *2 ½* **Macs Joy (IRE)**[39] [2397] 6-11-12 164 .... BJGeraghty 159
(Mrs John Harrington, Ire) *mod 3rd: tk clsr order 3 out: 4th and rdn after 2 out: kpt on same pce* **8/1**

5 *9* **Essex (IRE)**[39] [2397] 5-11-12 158 .... DNRussell 150
(M J P O'Brien, Ire) *mod 4th: tk clsr order 3 out: no ex fr next* **6/1**[3]

4m 2.90s **Going Correction** +0.05s/f (Yiel) 5 Ran SP% **111.2**
Speed ratings: **123,121,119,118,113** CSF £4.93 TOTE £3.20: £1.60, £1.30; DF 3.90.
Owner Novices Syndicate **Bred** D W Macauley **Trained** Gorey, Co Wexford

NOTEBOOK
Brave Inca(IRE) was back to his best and McCoy got a much sweeter tune out of him than at Fairyhouse. He was not clever at the third last but was responding well from the next. Leading approaching the final flight, he found plenty on the flat and drew away. *(op 9/4 tchd 2/1)*
Harchibald(FR) was given plenty to do but came to win his race from the last, a length and a half down jumping it, he went second on the flat but found nothing as the winner stayed on much the better. He was subsequently found to have a piece of birch embedded in a tendon and was operated on, which could possibly mean he misses the rest of the season. *(op 4/5 tchd Evens)*
Newmill(IRE) tried to make all and was soon clear. Headed approaching the last, he just found the one pace on the run-in. He goes up 7lb to 147. *(op 33/1)*
Macs Joy(IRE) was fourth and going nowhere after two out. His stable remains under a cloud *(op 7/1)*
Essex(IRE) was another unable to run anywhere near his best. *(op 6/1 tchd 7/1)*

3110a BEWLEYS HOTEL DUBLIN AIRPORT EUROPEAN BREEDERS FUND MARES HURDLE (LISTED RACE) (10 hdls) 2m 4f
2:55 (2:55) 4-Y-O+ **£20,776** (£6,095; £2,904; £989)

RPR

1 **Celestial Wave (IRE)**[21] [2736] 5-11-3 .... MissNCarberry 130+
(Adrian Maguire, Ire) *mde all: clr to 1/2-way: rdn clr again after 2 out: styd on wl: easily* **9/4**[2]

2 *9* **Brogella (IRE)**[11] [2910] 5-11-6 121 .... (b) RWalsh 124
(Ms F M Crowley, Ire) *mod 2nd: tk clsr order 1/2-way: effrt 2 out: no imp fr bef last* **7/4**[1]

3 *10* **Mrs Wallensky (IRE)**[33] [2510] 7-11-6 122 .... JLCullen 114
(Paul Nolan, Ire) *mod 4th: 5th 3 out: rdn next: kpt on to go mod 3rd fr last* **13/2**

4 *8* **Molly Massini (IRE)**[35] [2470] 5-11-3 113 .... MPButler 103
(Gerard Quirk, Ire) *mod 5th: 6th 6 out: prog 2 out: 4th bef last: sn no ex* **12/1**

5 *1* **Princess Commanche (IRE)**[18] [2792] 6-11-3 98 .... PCarberry 102
(S J Mahon, Ire) *mod 3rd: 2nd briefly 3 out: sn rdn: 6th next: kpt on same pce* **16/1**

6 *5* **Berkeley House (IRE)**[18] [2796] 5-10-13 .... DJCasey 93
(C F Swan, Ire) *in rr: 7th and no imp fr bef 2 out* **10/1**

7 *9* **Outlaw Princess (IRE)**[40] [2356] 5-11-3 .... JMAllen 88
(Sean O O'Brien, Ire) *towards rr early: prog into 5th 4 out: 3rd 2 out: wknd bef last* **4/1**[3]

8 *dist* **Lala Nova (IRE)**[1] [3082] 6-11-6 97 .... DFO'Regan —
(John Joseph Murphy, Ire) *a bhd: wknd fr 3 out: t.o* **20/1**

5m 5.90s **Going Correction** +0.05s/f (Yiel) 8 Ran SP% **127.9**
Speed ratings: **108,104,100,97,96 94,91,—** CSF £7.89 TOTE £3.00: £1.40, £1.30, £1.80; DF 4.40.
Owner Cahir Racing Syndicate **Bred** Sean Casey **Trained** Lombardstown, Co Cork

NOTEBOOK
Celestial Wave(IRE) appreciated ground and distance and made all to win virtually unchallenged. *(op 9/4 tchd 5/2)*
Brogella(IRE) has bits of form but the winner is altogether a tougher mare. *(op 7/4 tchd 2/1)*
Mrs Wallensky(IRE) has been novice chasing without success and she might as well return to that sphere *(op 7/1)*
Molly Massini(IRE) was never on terms.
Outlaw Princess(IRE) *Official explanation: trainer said mare was found to have mucus in its trachea post race (op 9/2)*

3111 - 3118a (Foreign Racing) - See Raceform Interactive

[2872]HAYDOCK (L-H)
Friday, December 30

3119 Meeting Abandoned - Frost

[2728]TAUNTON (R-H)
Friday, December 30

OFFICIAL GOING: Good (good to firm in places) changing to good (good to soft in places) after race 4 (2.20)
Wind: Mild, across

3125 TOTEPLACEPOT (S) H'CAP HURDLE (12 hdls) 3m 110y
12:50 (12:52) (Class 5) (0-90,87) 4-Y-O+ **£2,377** (£692; £346)

Form RPR

6045 1 **Penny's Crown**[24] [2687] 6-11-3 85 .... EamonDehdashti[(7)] 88+
(G A Ham) *hld up towards rr: hdwy appr 8th: trckd ldr 9th: led appr 2 out: styd on wl* **6/1**[2]

6443 2 *4* **Buz Kiri (USA)**[29] [2582] 7-11-7 82 .... (t) WayneHutchinson 80
(A W Carroll) *mid div: tk clsr order 8th: rdn after 3 out: wnt 2nd next: kpt on but no further imp on wnr* **7/1**[3]

0544 3 *3 ½* **Ashgan (IRE)**[15] [2845] 12-10-11 77 .... DrPPritchard[(5)] 72+
(Dr P Pritchard) *racd wd: prom: lost position after 8th: styd on again fr 2 out: wnt 3rd run-in* **6/1**[2]

0060 4 *6* **Holly Walk**[43] [2283] 4-10-5 73 .... (p) CharliePoste[(7)] 62
(A G Juckes) *hld up towards rr: hdwy appr 8th: hit 9th: sn rdn: kpt on same pce* **20/1**

PP-0 5 *3 ½* **Kiwi Riverman**[34] [2503] 5-10-3 64 .... PaddyBrennan 50+
(D P Keane) *hld up towards rr: hdwy 8th: rdn after 3 out: one pced fr next* **11/2**[1]

532/ 6 *1 ½* **Jorodama King**[664] 11-9-10 64 .... KeiranBurke[(7)] 48
(N J Hawke) *prom: led 7th tl appr 2 out: one pced fr next* **16/1**

P506 7 *16* **Peggy's Prince**[10] [2934] 7-11-4 79 .... (t) JoeTizzard 47
(J D Frost) *hld up and a towards rr* **7/1**[3]

4-00 8 *2 ½* **Barcelona**[9] [2940] 8-11-5 87 .... (t) MissLBrooke[(7)] 52
(Lady Susan Brooke) *chsd ldrs tl 8th: wknd after 3 out* **33/1**

P653 9 *3* **Sungio**[22] [2728] 7-11-7 82 .... JodieMogford 44
(B P J Baugh) *in tch: rdn appr 8th: sn bhd* **7/1**[3]

560P 10 *14* **Hunter Pudding**[15] [2845] 5-10-9 70 .... JimmyMcCarthy 18
(C L Popham) *mid div: hdwy to trck ldrs after 7th: wknd 3 out* **28/1**

-040 11 *6* **Starry Mary**[14] [2862] 7-11-1 81 .... (p) MarkNicolls[(5)] 23
(R J Price) *mid div: reminders after 7th: sn bhd* **6/1**[2]

P-00 P **Another Windfall**[204] [697] 6-10-2 63 .... (t) RJGreene —
(C P Morlock) *led tl 7th: wknd 3 out: p.u after 2 out* **66/1**

-PPR P **Kadlass (FR)**[64] [1900] 10-10-7 75 .... RyanCummings[(7)] —
(Mrs D Thomas) *chsd ldrs tl 5th: sn reminders in tch: bhd fr 8th: t.o and p.u bef 3 out* **66/1**

6m 18.3s (9.70) **Going Correction** +0.425s/f (Soft)
WFA 4 from 5yo+ 13lb 13 Ran SP% **115.8**
Speed ratings: **101,99,98,96,95 95,89,89,88,83 81,—,—** CSF £44.11 CT £262.34 TOTE £8.40: £2.30, £2.30, £2.10; EX 30.10.There was no bid for the winner.
Owner The Browns And Brats **Bred** D J And Mrs Deer **Trained** Rooks Bridge, Somerset

FOCUS
A typically weak contest but the pace was sound and the form looks solid enough with the first two close to their marks.

NOTEBOOK
Penny's Crown, who has only won in selling company, could be called the winner some way from home, and saw the three-mile trip out really well. She had never tried the distance before but suggested more success can come her way at the trip. *(op 5-1 tchd 9-2)*
Buz Kiri(USA), yet to win a race over hurdles, kept on well for his jockey but never got to the easy winner. He often runs well but is finding it impossible to win. *(op 4-1)*
Ashgan(IRE) was pretty keen and prominent throughout the early part of the race, but lost his place down the back straight on the final circuit. However, he picked up again turning for home and was closing again as the line approached, something he has done in his recent races, and stronger handling may help him when he hits a 'flat spot'. *(tchd 11-2 and 13-2)*
Holly Walk, who had never raced at further than two miles one, pulled hard towards the rear of the field early in the race, and did not get home.
Kiwi Riverman, dropped in class and stepped up in trip, moved slowly into contention throughout the race, after being held up at the back of the field, but did not appear to get home. He has shown very little to date on the track. *(op 6-1)*
Jorodama King pulled plenty hard enough on his first run for 664 days - his last run came in a point-to-point - and did not shape without promise for the future. However, he will need to settle much better to fully get home over three miles. *(op 25-1)*
Peggy's Prince, wearing a tongue tie for the first time, was well supported in the market before the race, but shown next to nothing during it. *(op 20-1)*

3126 TOTESPORT 0800 221 221 NOVICES' H'CAP CHASE (14 fncs) 2m 3f
1:20 (1:28) (Class 4) (0-95,95) 4-Y-O+ **£3,708** (£1,088; £544; £271)

Form RPR

6420 1 **He's The Gaffer (IRE)**[36] [2456] 5-11-2 85 .... (b) RobertThornton 101+
(R H Buckler) *mid div: hdwy after 8th: chsd ldr after 4 out: rdn after 3 out: styd on wl to led last: lft wl clr* **9/2**[3]

-PP5 2 *17* **Wizard Of Edge**[22] [2729] 5-11-11 94 .... ChristianWilliams 95+
(R J Hodges) *trckd ldrs: hit 10th: rdn in 3rd appr 3 out: kpt on same pce: lft 2nd at the last* **11/4**[1]

4P-5 3 *13* **Quatrain (IRE)**[10] [2934] 5-11-12 95 .... (t) TomDoyle 84+
(D R Gandolfo) *led tl 4th: w ldr: rdn after 4 out: wknd appr next: blnd 2 out: lft 3rd last* **7/1**

4202 4 *dist* **Moorland Monarch**[42] [2313] 7-10-8 82 .... ChrisHonour[(5)] —
(J D Frost) *chsd ldrs tl 5th: bhd fr 8th: t.o* **7/2**[2]

P-PP 5 *3 ½* **Baudolino**[38] [2424] 8-9-12 72 ow2 .... (p) MarkNicolls[(5)] —
(R J Price) *in tch: rdn appr 8th: wknd 10th: t.o* **33/1**

060F 6 *17* **Only For Gold**[27] [2620] 10-9-10 70 ow1 .... DrPPritchard[(5)] —
(Dr P Pritchard) *a towards rr: t.o fr 9th* **33/1**

5PFP F **Cloneybrien Boy (IRE)**[18] [2801] 5-9-12 72 oh10 ow3 .... DerekLaverty[(5)] —
(Mrs A M Thorpe) *fell 2nd* **50/1**

063U F **Tyup Pompey (IRE)**[10] [2929] 4-10-4 84 .... JamieGoldstein —
(Miss J S Davis) *mid div tl fell 8th* **8/1**

0P-P P **A Pound Down (IRE)**[58] [1980] 8-10-3 72 .... JodieMogford —
(N G Ayliffe) *bhd fr 7th: t.o and p.u after 8th* **20/1**

-PFP **P** **Memories Of Gold (IRE)**[26] 2660 5-10-7 **83**................ RichardSpate(7) —
(J A Danahar) *hld up: mstke 2nd: wknd 8th: p.u bef 10th* **50/1**

5F-P **P** **Dunnicks Field**[22] 2729 9-10-3 **79**.................................. SimonElliott(7) —
(F G Tucker) *in tch: blnd bdly 9th: nt rcvr and p.u bef 4 out* **25/1**

P344 **U** **Terrible Tenant**[4] 2984 6-11-0 **86**.................................. RichardYoung(3) 98
(J W Mullins) *prom: led 4th: rdn appr 3 out: narrowly hdd whn stmbld : slipped and uns rdr last* **11/2**

5m 1.30s (8.50) **Going Correction** +0.425s/f (Soft)
WFA 4 from 5yo+ 10lb **12** Ran SP% **124.5**
Speed ratings: **99,91,86,—,—,—,—,—,—,—,—,—** CSF £17.75 CT £89.05 TOTE £4.90: £2.00, £1.60, £2.90; EX 18.80.
Owner M J Hallett **Bred** Pat O'Donovan **Trained** Melplash, Dorset

FOCUS
A very moderate novices' handicap, but a sound gallop and a clear-cut winner, helped by the faller at the last. The second is the best guide to the level of the form.

NOTEBOOK
He's The Gaffer(IRE), having only his second outing over fences, was in the process of taking the lead jumping the last when his closest rival came down at that fence. He has the scope for improvement and he should stay a bit further as well, but might need turning out quickly before the assessor can adjust his handicap mark. *(op 7-1)*
Wizard Of Edge has still to translate the best of his hurdling ability to fences, but probably ran his best race to date over the larger obstacles, despite being only third-best until the last-fence fall of Terrible Tennant. *(op 9-2 tchd 11-2)*
Quatrain(IRE), making his chasing debut, regularly gets beaten a long way and did not buck that trend at this discipline, despite racing up with the leaders until the end of the back straight. *(tchd 8-1)*
Moorland Monarch never got involved in the race at any stage, and was already receiving reminders with a circuit to go. He was the second well-fancied horse from the Frost stable to disappoint on the card. *(op 4-1 tchd 9-2)*
Dunnicks Field was still travelling well when making an awful blunder in the back straight. However, it was too far out to know how he would have fared without the jumping error. *(op 33-1 tchd 40-1)*
Terrible Tenant, making a quick reappearance after a run on Boxing Day, was only just giving way to the winner, after getting a positive ride, when slipping after the last and losing his jockey. He is most consistent horse in his grade, and was unlucky not to complete. *(op 33-1 tchd 40-1)*

3127 TOTESPORT.COM NOVICES' HURDLE (9 hdls) 2m 1f
1:50 (1:55) (Class 3) 4-Y-O+ **£6,489** (£1,905; £952; £475)

Form RPR

1 **Neveesou (FR)**[37] 4-11-4 .... TimmyMurphy 116+
(M C Pipe) *a travelling wl: trckd ldrs: led appr 2 out: r.o wl: comf* **6/4**[1]

2 *7* **Vaughan**[77] 4-10-12 .... MarkBradburne 95+
(H D Daly) *in tch: stdy hdwy appr 3 out: jnd wnr and ev ch 2 out: sn rdn: nt pce of wnr* **7/2**[2]

4/3 **3** *6* **Landescent (IRE)**[50] 2148 5-10-12 .... AndrewThornton 89
(Miss K M George) *led: rdn and hdd appr 2 out: kpt on same pce: mstke last* **33/1**

6 **4** *7* **Flamand (FR)**[17] 2804 4-10-12 .... JimmyMcCarthy 82
(C P Morlock) *hld up towards rr: styd on appr 2 out: wnt 4th run-in: nvr trbld ldrs* **100/1**

5- **5** *1 1/4* **Storm Of Applause (IRE)**[286] 4451 4-10-12 .... RichardJohnson 81
(P J Hobbs) *in tch: rdn to chse ldng trio after 3 out: one pce fr next* **12/1**

-012 **6** *2* **Red Moor (IRE)**[144] 1182 5-11-4 114.............. BenjaminHitchcott 85
(Mrs D A Hamer) *mid div: rdn after 3 out: wknd next* **14/1**

0 **7** *6* **Once (FR)**[16] 2826 5-10-12 .... APMcCoy 73
(M G Rimell) *mid div: rdn appr 3 out: sn wknd* **16/1**

564P **8** *1* **Redlynch Spirit (IRE)**[27] 2619 5-10-12 .... JoeTizzard 72
(C L Tizzard) *mid div: mstke 2nd: rdn after 3 out: sn wknd* **100/1**

9 *hd* **Clare Galway**[11] 4-10-0 .... JohnLevins(5) 65
(B G Powell) *chsd ldrs: mstke 3rd: rdn and wknd after 3 out* **100/1**

30 **10** *22* **Selective**[38] 2423 6-10-12 .... WayneHutchinson 50
(A W Carroll) *t.k.h and a towards rr* **11/1**

6P0P **11** *3* **Walton Way**[26] 2663 5-10-12 .... HenryOliver 47
(P W Hiatt) *chsd ldrs: rdn after 5th: sn btn* **100/1**

0P/ **12** *10* **Lady Wurzel**[229] 6-10-2 .... MissPGundry(3) 30
(J G Cann) *a bhd* **100/1**

13 *dist* **Mr Tambourine Man (IRE)**[77] 4-10-12 .... OllieMcPhail —
(B J Llewellyn) *chsd ldrs tl 5th: sn wl bhd* **50/1**

2 **P** **Blaeberry**[22] 2730 4-10-5 .... BarryFenton —
(Miss E C Lavelle) *t.k.h: hld up in rr: sddle slipped and p.u after 4th* **4/1**[3]

4m 11.7s (2.90) **Going Correction** +0.25s/f (Yiel) **14** Ran SP% **120.6**
Speed ratings: **103,99,96,93,93 92,89,88,88,78 76,72,—,—** CSF £6.61 TOTE £2.80: £1.40, £1.80, £4.00; EX 11.40.
Owner D A Johnson **Bred** Gilles & Jean-Pierre Deroubaix **Trained** Nicholashayne, Devon

FOCUS
A decent race of its type for the track, run at a fair gallop but 1.7sec slower than the following handicap. The third, fourth and eighth were all close to their marks.

NOTEBOOK
Neveesou(FR), carrying a penalty after already winning in very soft ground in France, may well have won on his racecourse debut - as a three-year-old in August 2004 - but came down at the last in a Listed hurdle won by another successful French import Napolitain. Sure to be suited by ease in the ground, he sped away from his rivals when asked to quicken clear, and looks sure to go on to much better things. The only minus is that he does not look overly big in stature. *(op 15-8)*
Vaughan, claimed for £50,000 after scoring at Newmarket in October, came to have every chance jumping the second last, but landed slightly awkwardly and did not get home as well as the winner. His fluency over hurdles has room for improvement, but he may have caught a tartar here and should be able to win races. *(op 4-1 tchd 10-3)*
Landescent(IRE) led the field for much of the race at a decent pace, and stuck to his task fairly well under pressure. He will now be handicapped and might be suited by a little bit further over hurdles given his Flat form. *(op 25-1)*
Flamand(FR) is gradually improving with racing and is one to keep and eye on for the future. He might be interesting if given a low handicap mark and tried in that company. *(op 66-1)*
Storm Of Applause(IRE), making his hurdling debut, shaped with a little promise and has plenty of time on his side. *(op 11-1 tchd 14-1)*
Blaeberry, who caught the eye on her jumping debut, was pulled up just after the fourth flight when her saddle slipped. *Official explanation: jockey said saddle slipped (op 5-2)*

3128 STEVE LOGAN MEMORIAL COUNTY CONTRACTORS H'CAP HURDLE (9 hdls) 2m 1f
2:20 (2:22) (Class 3) (0-115,113) 3-Y-O+ **£6,375** (£1,871; £935; £467)

Form RPR

21F0 **1** **Nippy Des Mottes (FR)**[33] 2530 4-11-3 **111**..................(t) LiamHeard(7) 125+
(P F Nicholls) *mid div: gd hdwy after 3 out to ld next: rdn after last: all out* **11/4**[2]

3404 **2** *shd* **Spike Jones (NZ)**[16] 2822 7-10-0 **92**............................. DerekLaverty(5) 104
(Mrs A M Thorpe) *hld up towards rr: stdy hdwy fr 6th: rdn to go 2nd appr last: r.o gamely u.p: jst failed* **33/1**

-512 **3** *11* **Capitana (GER)**[9] 2940 4-11-0 **101**................................ AndrewTinkler 105+
(N J Henderson) *in tch: tk clsr order 4th: led 6th: nt fluent and hdd 2 out: sn rdn: no ex* **6/4**[1]

000P **4** *3* **The Gene Genie**[18] 2802 10-9-9 **87** oh3.............................. JayHarris(5) 85
(R J Hodges) *towards rr: styd on fr 3 out: nvr trbld ldrs* **66/1**

0031 **5** *8* **Wenger (FR)**[24] 2685 5-10-13 **100**..................................(b) PhilipHide 92+
(P Winkworth) *hld up towards rr: hdwy 5th: rdn to press ldrs appr 2 out: wknd appr last* **12/1**

10-4 **6** *3* **Redi (ITY)**[55] 2047 4-11-12 **113**..(t) APMcCoy 100
(A M Balding) *in tch: rdn after 3 out: wknd next* **7/1**[3]

13P6 **7** *3 1/2* **Red Dahlia**[22] 2731 8-9-10 **90**.. MissZoeLilly(7) 73
(M Pitman) *chsd ldrs: mstke 5th: wknd 3 out* **33/1**

-646 **8** *2* **Shirazi**[11] 2925 7-11-3 **104**..(t) TimmyMurphy 85
(D R Gandolfo) *hld up towards rr: hdwy after 5th: short lived effrt after 3 out* **16/1**

35P0 **9** *8* **Nuit Sombre (IRE)**[60] 1958 5-11-9 **110**..........................(p) DaveCrosse 83
(J G M O'Shea) *in tch: rdn and effrt after 3 out: sn btn* **66/1**

-000 **10** *9* **Galant Eye (IRE)**[14] 2868 6-10-0 **87** oh2..........................(p) VinceSlattery 51
(R J Baker) *mid div tl 5th* **150/1**

3600 **11** *1 3/4* **Sir Walter (IRE)**[26] 2659 12-10-9 **96**..................................... RJGreene 59
(D Burchell) *led tl 6th: sn wknd* **66/1**

-F40 **12** *1 3/4* **Fame**[29] 2595 5-11-6 **107**.. RichardJohnson 68
(P J Hobbs) *a bhd* **10/1**

2410 **13** *20* **Critical Stage (IRE)**[21] 2746 6-11-2 **108**.......................(t) ChrisHonour(5) 49
(J D Frost) *a towards rr* **25/1**

162P **14** *23* **Imperial Rocket (USA)**[132] 1263 8-11-3 **104**...........(t) ChristianWilliams 22
(W K Goldsworthy) *chsd ldrs tl 5th: sn bhd* **40/1**

4m 10.0s (1.20) **Going Correction** +0.25s/f (Yiel) **14** Ran SP% **119.1**
Speed ratings: **107,106,101,100,96 95,93,92,88,84 83,82,73,62** CSF £93.86 CT £185.84 TOTE £3.20: £1.60, £13.00, £1.10; EX 147.50.
Owner Paul Green **Bred** Mme J Poirier **Trained** Ditcheat, Somerset

FOCUS
A modest handicap run at a decent pace and the time was 1.7sec faster than the preceding contest over the same trip. The winner is rated value for more than the official margin and to his mark.

NOTEBOOK
Nippy Des Mottes(FR), who seems suited by a right-handed track and a little cut in the ground, travelled well off the pace and once he asserted at the second last looked likely to win easily. However, he had to contend with the late effort of the runner-up, who pressed him all the way to the line. This is about as good as he is, but he should make a chaser in time. *(op 5-2)*
Spike Jones(NZ) has gradually been finding some form for new connections since being picked up cheaply earlier in the year. He put up is best effort yet and, pushing the winner all the way to the line, he looks capable of finding a small race from his current mark.
Capitana(GER), who is suited by a sharp track and good ground, ran her race but was soon in trouble once taken on by the winner. The only excuse could be that the morning rain may have made the ground too soft for her. *(op 2-1 tchd 9-4 in places)*
The Gene Genie has not shown much of late, but has run well here in the past and was doing his best work at the finish. He is well handicapped on his old form. *(op 50-1)*
Wenger(FR) travelled well enough but was left behind from the home turn. He seems to reserve his best efforts for Fontwell. *(tchd 11-1)*
Redi(ITY) was reluctant to line up, but then raced up with the pace until fading from the last on the far side *(tchd 13-2)*
Critical Stage(IRE) *Official explanation: jockey said gelding had bled from the nose*

3129 TOTEPOOL H'CAP CHASE (17 fncs) 2m 7f 110y
2:50 (2:50) (Class 4) (0-105,99) 5-Y-O+ **£4,905** (£1,440; £720; £359)

Form RPR

3-21 **1** **Presenting Express (IRE)**[32] 2555 6-10-13 **86**................. BarryFenton 111+
(Miss E C Lavelle) *trckd ldrs: led 10th tl next: led 12th: styd on wl: readily* **11/4**[1]

43-0 **2** *3 1/2* **Boddidley (IRE)**[29] 2592 7-11-5 **99**................................... LiamHeard(7) 108
(P F Nicholls) *mid div: trckd ldrs 10th: rdn and effrt on outer after 4 out: kpt on same pce fr next* **10/1**

5251 **3** *7* **Alcatras (IRE)**[10] 2931 8-10-13 **89** 7ex.......................... OwynNelmes(3) 93+
(B J M Ryall) *hld up: hdwy after 11th: cl 2nd and rdn whn pckd 3 out: kpt on same pce* **7/1**

P-6P **4** *13* **Boardroom Dancer (IRE)**[218] 511 8-10-8 **81**................. PaulMoloney 73+
(Miss Suzy Smith) *hld up bhd: hdwy to trck ldrs appr 4 out: rdn after 3 out: sn wknd* **25/1**

3141 **5** *24* **Reverse Swing**[8] 2955 8-11-3 **90** 7ex................................... JodieMogford 67+
(Mrs H Dalton) *led tl 10th: led and hit next: mstke and hdd 12th: chsd ldr tl wknd appr 3 out* **9/2**[3]

-233 **F** **Kimono Royal (FR)**[170] 977 7-11-12 **99**.......................... RobertThornton —
(A King) *fell 1st* **5/1**

PP0P **P** **Shannon Quest (IRE)**[10] 2933 9-10-9 **82**.................(bt) JimmyMcCarthy —
(C L Popham) *in tch: rdn after 11th: sn wknd: p.u bef 13th* **66/1**

50-U **P** **Huw The News**[28] 2610 6-10-12 **85**.. RJGreene —
(S C Burrough) *hld up bhd: mstke 10th: wknd appr 13th: p.u bef 4 out* **50/1**

2512 **P** **Ebony Jack (IRE)**[24] 2686 8-10-4 **77**..................................(p) JoeTizzard —
(C L Tizzard) *w ldr tl nt fluent and lost position 8th: lost tch 13th: t.o and p.u bef 3 out* **3/1**[2]

6m 22.1s (17.00) **Going Correction** +0.775s/f (Soft) **9** Ran SP% **115.4**
Speed ratings: **102,100,98,94,86 —,—,—,—** CSF £28.95 CT £175.02 TOTE £3.90: £1.70, £3.10, £1.90; EX 62.10.
Owner N Mustoe **Bred** Patrick O'Dwyer **Trained** Wildhern, Hants

FOCUS
A moderate contest but an authoritative winner with the third and fourth setting the standard.

NOTEBOOK
Presenting Express(IRE) ◆, raised 6lb for his win at Folkestone, defied that in the manner of an improving chaser. Pulling his way to the front at halfway, he had several challengers at the first in the straight, but picked up well when asked and won with authority. He looks capable of completing the hat-trick in similar company. *(tchd 10-3)*
Boddidley(IRE), a winning pointer making his chasing debut under Rules off top weight, was given a patient ride and looked a threat to the winner turning in, but was brushed aside from the first in the straight. He did nothing wrong though and there are small races to be won with him over fences. *(op 9-1)*
Alcatras(IRE), under a 7lb penalty and stepping up in trip, settled nicely off the pace and, like the runner-up looked to be going as well as the winner straightening up for home. However, he made a mistake at the first in the straight and could not find an extra gear from that point, so may not quite have stayed. *(op 8-1)*
Boardroom Dancer(IRE), returning from a break, has been very lightly raced recently. He was given a patient ride but could never get into contention, and he should benefit from the outing. *(op 40-1)*

Reverse Swingset the pace until halfway, and disputed the lead until dropping out after jumping the last ditch, four out. *(op 7-2)*
Ebony Jack(IRE) *Official explanation: jockey said gelding hung badly left throughout (op 7-2 tchd 11-4)*

3130 GREENSLADE TAYLOR HUNT CHARITY STKS "NATIONAL HUNT" NOVICES' HURDLE (DIV I) (10 hdls) — 2m 3f 110y

3:20 (3:20) (Class 4) 4-Y-0+ — **£3,890** (£1,142; £571; £285)

Form	Pos	Dist	Horse / Comment	Jockey	SP	RPR
222	1		**Private Be**[16] [2826] 6-10-12 — (P J Hobbs) *led: hit 2nd: tried to run off crse and hdd after 5th: sn bk trcking ldrs: led 7th: hung lft but drew clr fr 2 out: rdn out*	RichardJohnson	4/9[1]	114+
00-	2	6	**Michigan D'Isop (FR)**[282] [4519] 5-10-12 — (B J M Ryall) *mid div tl hung bdly lft on bnd appr 6th and dropped rr : hdwy 3 out: rdn and styd on wl run-in: tk 2nd cl home*	JoeTizzard	200/1	100+
0P-1	3	1	**Pearly Bay**[36] [2457] 7-10-12 100 — (M G Rimell) *chsd ldrs: rdn and effrt appr 2 out: kpt on same pce: lost 2nd cl home*	APMcCoy	7/2[2]	95
P-62	4	19	**Earth Moving (IRE)**[37] [2432] 5-10-12 — (P F Nicholls) *hld up towards rr: hdwy appr 7th: rdn to chse wnr after 3 out: wknd 2 out*	ChristianWilliams	8/1[3]	78+
004P	5	1 1/4	**Logies Lass**[17] [2815] 6-10-5 — (J S Smith) *a towards rr*	WarrenMarston	150/1	68
00	6	13	**Nelson Du Ronceray (FR)**[17] [2804] 4-10-12 — (M C Pipe) *trckd ldrs: lft in ld after 5th: hdd 7th: sn wknd*	TimmyMurphy	33/1	62
PP/P	7	2	**Ringagold**[15] [2846] 6-9-12 — (N J Hawke) *mid div tl 7th: sn bhd*	KeiranBurke(7)	200/1	57+
2/4-	8	14	**Dodger McCartney**[541] [902] 7-10-12 — (K Bishop) *hld up towards rr: wkng whn mstke 7th*	(t) RJGreene	40/1	46
UPP-	9	dist	**Powra**[302] [4143] 5-10-5 — (R J Hodges) *chsd ldrs tl 5th: sn t.o*	JamesWhite(7)	200/1	—
000	F		**Castletown Lad**[17] [2803] 5-10-9 — (M C Pipe) *hld up bhd: fell 6th*	TomMalone(3)	100/1	—
06F-	F		**Aber Gale**[264] [4795] 6-10-5 — (Mrs S M Johnson) *mid div: hit 5th: fell 7th*	JamesDavies	100/1	—

(14.00) **Going Correction** +0.775s/f (Soft) — **11** Ran SP% **112.1**
Speed ratings: **103,100,100,92,92 86,86,80,—,—** — CSF £158.05 TOTE £1.40: £1.02, £19.90, £1.10; EX 105.00.
Owner David and Daphne Walsh **Bred** Mrs C W Middleton **Trained** Withycombe, Somerset

FOCUS
A modest hurdle race but the winner is rated value for further and he and and the third set a reasonable standard.

NOTEBOOK
Private Be, runner-up in his three previous attempts over hurdles, was a hot favourite and stole a few lengths at the start. However, he relinquished that when appearing to try to make for the exit gate passing the stands and his rider did well to keep him in the race. He was in front again halfway down the back straight and from that point had matters in safe keeping. His rider reported that he is not quirky but prefers going the other way around. *(tchd 1-2 tchd 8-15 in a place)*
Michigan D'Isop(FR), well beaten in two bumpers earlier in the year, was making his hurdling debut. Totally unfancied, he looked to be pulling up after a circuit but apparently he cocked his jaw on the turn. Once racing on an even keel he picked up steadily and was doing his best work at the *finish. If he can repeat this effort he looks capable of winning over hurdles.Official explanation: jockey said gelding cocked its jaw and tried to run out on the stable bend (op 100-1)*
Pearly Bay, who won a mares' race over course and distance last month, seemed to run her race. She may be better off back against her own sex. *(op 4-1)*
Earth Moving(IRE), making his hurdling debut, travelled well off the pace and was close enough on the home turn but faded rather tamely as if he did not get home. He is a half-brother to a two-mile chaser and may be better at that trip for the time being. *(op 7-1)*
Aber Gale, having her first run since the spring, travelled quite well behind the leaders before departing. She has fallen on both her starts over hurdles, but looks to have ability if she can get her act together. *(tchd 150-1)*

3131 GREENSLADE TAYLOR HUNT CHARITY STKS "NATIONAL HUNT" NOVICES' HURDLE (DIV II) (10 hdls) — 2m 3f 110y

3:50 (3:50) (Class 4) 4-Y-0+ — **£3,880** (£1,139; £569; £284)

Form	Pos	Dist	Horse / Comment	Jockey	SP	RPR
6P0-	1		**Prestbury Knight**[283] [4511] 5-10-12 — (N A Twiston-Davies) *prom: sltly outpcd after 3 out: rallied 2 out: led last: drvn out*	CarlLlewellyn	7/1	103+
0-3	2	4	**Loita Hills (IRE)**[33] [2528] 5-10-12 — (P J Hobbs) *led tl after 3 out: sn rdn: led next: hdd last: no ex*	RichardJohnson	6/5[1]	98
22P6	3	2 1/2	**Miss Midnight**[4] [2997] 4-10-2 — (R J Hodges) *trckd ldrs: rdn to ld after 3 out: mstke and hdd next: kpt on same pce*	(b[1]) TomMalone(3)	6/1[3]	90+
11P6	4	14	**Hill Forts Timmy**[40] [2374] 5-10-12 — (J W Mullins) *hld up: hdwy 5th: rdn and effrt after 3 out: wknd next*	AndrewThornton	8/1	83+
0P-0	5	20	**Lyrical Lily**[134] [1246] 7-10-5 — (B J Llewellyn) *prom tl wknd appr 7th*	OllieMcPhail	50/1	54
1300	6	1	**Twelve Paces**[37] [2426] 4-10-12 — (M C Pipe) *a towards rr*	TimmyMurphy	7/2[2]	60
00P	7	dist	**Another Flint (IRE)**[26] [2663] 5-10-5 — (R Flint) *a towards rr: t.o fr 7th*	(t) AngharadFrieze(7)	66/1	—
0P	P		**Valleyofthekings (IRE)**[16] [2826] 4-10-12 — (O Sherwood) *mid div tl 6th: sn bhd: p.u after 7th*	(t) LeightonAspell	25/1	—
P0-0	P		**Kossies Mate**[34] [2507] 6-10-5 — (P W Hiatt) *t.k.h towards rr: lost tch 7th: t.o and p.u bef last*	HenryOliver	100/1	—

4m 59.3s (13.30) **Going Correction** +0.775s/f (Soft)
WFA 4 from 5yo+ 10lb — **9** Ran SP% **113.9**
Speed ratings: **104,102,101,95,87 87,—,—,—** CSF £16.06 TOTE £6.60: £2.20, £1.10, £1.70; EX 17.60 Place 6 £76.77, Place 5 £29.68.
Owner Cheltenham Racing Ltd **Bred** D McCain **Trained** Naunton, Gloucs

FOCUS
The slightly faster of the two divisions but just an ordinary contest although the form looks reasonable, with the four immediately behind the winner close to their marks.

NOTEBOOK
Prestbury Knight, placed in bumpers last autumn, had not shown much in soft-ground hurdles earlier in the year. He seemed to appreciate the sounder surface, looks to have improved a little over the summer, and came through after being slightly outpaced to collar the two leaders at the last and win going away. He has scope for improvement. *(op 10-1 tchd 13-2)*
Loita Hills(IRE) was made favourite following the withdrawal of the horse who beat him on his hurdling debut at Newbury. He was given a positive ride but got involved in a tussle with the third from the home turn, and the pair of them were cut down by the rallying winner. He has a race in him on this evidence, possibly back at two miles. *(op 5-4 tchd 11-8 and 6-4 in places)*
Miss Midnight, runner-up to the third in the first division of this contest when they met last month, ran well enough in the first-time blinkers and helps set the standard, but continues to find at least one or two too good. *(tchd 11-2 and 7-1)*
Hill Forts Timmy, a dual bumper winner in the summer, ran his best race over hurdles so far on this faster surface but was left behind in the straight. *(op 10-1)*
Twelve Paces, a bumper winner on fast ground in the summer, has shown very little over hurdles since and was struggling after a circuit. He may need fast going and longer trips to be seen at his best. *(op 5-2)*
T/Plt: £22.70 to a £1 stake. Pool: £89,426.20. 2,864.60 winning tickets. T/Qpdt: £4.30 to a £1 stake. Pool: £6,482.60. 1,097.30 winning tickets. TM

[2125] LINGFIELD (L-H)

Saturday, December 31

OFFICIAL GOING: Chase course - soft (good to soft in places); hurdle course - soft (heavy in places); all-weather - standard
Wind: Moderate across

3132 ROR SECOND CAREER FOR RACEHORSES JUVENILE NOVICES' HURDLE (8 hdls) — 2m 110y

12:20 (12:20) (Class 3) 3-Y-0 — **£5,178** (£1,520; £760; £379)

Form	Pos	Dist	Horse / Comment	Jockey	SP	RPR
	1		**Heathcote**[138] 3-10-12 — (G L Moore) *a in tch: nt fluent whn drvn to ld 2 out: styd on wl run-in*	PhilipHide	18/1	114+
3	2	2 1/2	**Victorias Groom (GER)**[56] [2045] 3-10-12 — (Mrs L Wadham) *hmpd 1st: sn in tch: t.k.h: ev ch whn j.lft 2 out: styd on run-in*	JimmyMcCarthy	7/1[3]	108
3	3	6	**Original Fly (FR)**[17] [2824] 3-10-12 — (P F Nicholls) *trckd ldrs: ev ch 2 out: rdn and one pce run-in*	ChristianWilliams	10/3[2]	103+
623	4	8	**Mahogany Blaze (FR)**[38] [2442] 3-10-12 — (N A Twiston-Davies) *chsd ldr to 3 out: wknd after 2 out*	AntonyEvans	11/1	95+
54	5	2	**Golden Square**[30] [2580] 3-10-12 — (A W Carroll) *led: briefly hdd whn mstke 3 out: hdd & wknd 2 out*	WayneHutchinson	33/1	94+
40	6	5	**Joli Classical (IRE)**[25] [2681] 3-9-12 — (R J Hodges) *a towards rr: no ch fr 5th*	JamesWhite(7)	66/1	80
15	7	4	**Reaching Out (IRE)**[42] [2345] 3-11-4 110 — (N J Henderson) *chsd ldrs tl rdn and wknd appr 2 out*	MickFitzgerald	8/1	89
	8	16	**Beauchamp Twist**[119] 3-10-5 — (M R Hoad) *a bhd: t.o whn p.u bef 2 out*	MatthewBatchelor	66/1	60
U1	B		**Prime Contender**[27] [2661] 3-11-4 — (O Sherwood) *b.d 1st*	LeightonAspell	6/4[1]	—
	P		**Altenburg (FR)**[124] 3-10-12 — (Mrs N Smith) *t.o fr 2nd: p.u bef 2 out*	JimCrowley	33/1	—
40	F		**David's Symphony (IRE)**[31] [2286] 3-10-12 — (A W Carroll) *prom whn fell 1st*	PaddyBrennan	100/1	—
0	U		**Greenacre Legend**[29] [2611] 3-10-12 — (D B Feek) *bhd: rdn whn blnd and uns rdr 3rd*	JamesDavies	100/1	—
F	P		**A Qui Le Tour**[47] [2236] 3-10-12 — (M R Hoad) *bhd whn blnd 5th: t.o whn p.u bef 2 out*	SeanCurran	100/1	—
00	U		**Asaateel (IRE)**[9] [2954] 3-10-12 — (G L Moore) *prom tl wknd 5th: wl bhd and tired whn uns rdr last*	KeithMercer	25/1	—

4m 11.0s (4.90) **Going Correction** +0.525s/f (Soft) — **14** Ran SP% **116.0**
Speed ratings: **109,107,105,101,100 97,96,88,—,— —,—,—,—** CSF £129.22 TOTE £19.50: £4.90, £1.90, £1.40; EX 113.80.
Owner B Siddle & B D Haynes **Bred** Miss K Rausing **Trained** Woodingdean, E Sussex

FOCUS
A fair juvenile event and a positive view has been taken of the form. The winner's Flat form entitles him to be above average, and improvement was anticipated from both the second and third.

NOTEBOOK
Heathcote, a fair middle-distance performer on the Flat, was sold out of Charles Cyzer's yard for 15,000gns. He has reportedly not proved a natural while schooling, but he jumped well enough and, in front two out, he stayed on to score decisively. This ground suited him. *(op 14-1 tchd 20-1)*
Victorias Groom(GER), who was caught up in the melee at the first, ran another sound race but found the winner too strong from the second last. *(op 13-2)*
Original Fly(FR) again looked short of a change of gear, although he handled this testing ground well enough. He is now eligible for handicaps. *(op 7-2 tchd 3-1)*
Mahogany Blaze(FR) eventually paid the price for chasing the pace in this testing ground *(op 12-1)*
Golden Square was rather keen in front and unsurprisingly he failed to last home. He was a miler on the Flat and his three hurdles runs have been over stiff tracks, so a sharp two miles could be what he needs now he is qualified for handicaps.
Reaching Out(IRE) lost his pitch towards the end of the back straight, and although he tried to stay on again from the home turn he was soon on the retreat again. He has now been held twice under the penalty for his debut win. *(op 15-2)*
Prime Contender has now departed at the first on two of his three runs over hurdles, but on this occasion it was hardly his fault. *(tchd 7-4 and 15-8 in a place)*

3133 GOLF AND RACING AT LINGFIELD PARK NOVICES' HURDLE (8 hdls) — 2m 110y

12:50 (12:51) (Class 3) 4-Y-0+ — **£5,204** (£1,528; £764; £381)

Form	Pos	Dist	Horse / Comment	Jockey	SP	RPR
F	1		**Blu Teen (FR)**[28] [2618] 5-11-0 — (P F Nicholls) *a in tch: hdwy to ld sn after 2 out: rdn and styd on run-in*	ChristianWilliams	8/13[1]	106+
	2	3 1/2	**Amour Multiple (IRE)**[52] 6-11-7 128 — (S Lycett) *trckd ldr: ev ch appr last: hung rt run-in: no imp*	KeithMercer	8/1[2]	109+
422-	3	1 1/4	**Master Mahogany**[126] [4852] 4-11-0 113 — (R J Hodges) *led tl hdd sn after 2 out: wknd run-in*	APMcCoy	8/1[2]	101
2-	4	5	**Sheriff Roscoe**[282] [4540] 5-11-0 — (P Winkworth) *hld up: styd on appr 2 out: nvr nrr*	LeightonAspell	25/1	97+
1-04	5	3	**Royal Stardust**[25] [2683] 4-10-7 — (G L Moore) *chsd ldr: outpcd 3 out: styd on*	EamonDehdashti(7)	50/1	94+
00	6	nk	**Tamreen (IRE)**[23] [2730] 4-11-0 — (G L Moore) *hld up towards rr: styd on appr 2 out*	PhilipHide	66/1	93
P/3	7	2	**Buddhi (IRE)**[37] [2462] 7-11-0 — (M Pitman) *trckd ldrs tl rdn and wknd appr 2 out*	AndrewTinkler	20/1	91
5-00	8	4	**King Louis (FR)**[17] [2829] 4-11-0 — (R Rowe) *mid-div: hdwy 3 out: one pce fr next*	BrianCrowley	100/1	88+
	9	4	**Glimmer Of Light (IRE)**[484] 5-11-0 — (A King) *mid-div: bhd fr 5th*	WayneHutchinson	25/1	83
0/00	10	1 1/2	**Phazar**[33] [2554] 5-11-0 — (N J Hawke) *a bhd*	JimmyMcCarthy	100/1	81
	11	23	**Doctored**[83] 4-11-0 — (D C O'Brien) *a bhd*	MatthewBatchelor	100/1	58
	12	1 1/2	**Rapscallion (GER)**[770] 6-11-0 — (Mrs H Dalton) *in rr: rdn 3 out and lost tch*	JimCrowley	20/1	57
0-	13	6	**Cartier Opera**[574] [643] 5-11-0 — (Miss Venetia Williams) *nvr bttr than mid-div*	AlanO'Keeffe	33/1	51

0P-P **14** 1 1/2 **Fortanis**[49] 2179 6-10-2 .... LeeStephens(5) 42
(P C Ritchens) *a bhd* **200/1**

4-00 **15** 1 1/4 **Lordington Lad**[17] 2829 5-11-0 .... JamesDavies 48
(B G Powell) *a bhd* **100/1**

P **16** 15 **Lorrelini (IRE)**[16] 2849 4-11-0 .... AndrewThornton 33
(R H Alner) *trckd ldrs tl wknd 5th* **100/1**

0-5 **17** 1 1/4 **Krismas Cracker**[22] 2742 4-11-0 .... MickFitzgerald 32
(N J Henderson) *trckd ldrs tl rdn and wknd 3 out: eased bef next* **12/1**[3]

F **P** **Little Gannet**[31] 2573 4-10-4 .... ColinBolger(3) —
(T D McCarthy) *a bhd: t.o whn p.u bef 2 out* **100/1**

P **Belshazzar (USA)**[513] 4-10-11 .... TJPhelan(3) —
(D C O'Brien) *trckd ldrs tl wknd appr 5th: t.o whn p.u bef 2 out* **100/1**

4m 13.1s (7.00) **Going Correction** +0.525s/f (Soft)
WFA 4 from 5yo+ 10lb **19** Ran SP% **122.9**
Speed ratings: **104,102,101,99,98 97,96,95,93,92 81,80,78,77,76 69,69,—,—** CSF £4.82 TOTE £1.80: £1.30, £2.00, £2.90; EX 9.10.
Owner The Stewart Family **Bred** Bertrand Compignie **Trained** Ditcheat, Somerset

FOCUS
The time was slightly slower than for the opening juvenile hurdle. The third, fifth, sixth and seventh all appeared to run within a couple of pounds of their pre-race marks, but the winner has been rated 10lb below what he looked set to achieve when falling at Chepstow.

NOTEBOOK
Blu Teen(FR), unlucky at Chepstow on his British debut, made amends, but was merely workmanlike and ran below the level he looked set to achieve that day. Yet to tackle anything other than testing conditions, he looks a chasing type and will not be given a hard campaign over hurdles. *(op 4-6)*
Amour Multiple(IRE) was much the most experienced member of this field, having had 13 starts over hurdles in France, winning a Listed event on the last of them before a couple of defeats over fences. He made a promsing British debut under his penalty but was held when hanging over to the near-side rail on the flat. *(op 9-1)*
Master Mahogany has enjoyed a fruitful campaign on the Flat since his last hurdles run in the spring. Making the running as usual, he was collared by the winner after the second last but did stick on to secure third. *(op 9-1 tchd 10-1)*
Sheriff Roscoe, runner-up to The Cool Guy in a bumper last term, stayed on steadily once in line for home on this hurdles debut. He should come on for the run.
Royal Stardust, down in trip, ran as well as he was entitled to.
Tamreen(IRE) ◆, a twelve-furlong winner in France, ran an eye-catching race on this third appearance over hurdles and gave the impression he should be capable of better over a slightly longer trip.
Buddhi(IRE) ran well for a long way but was a tired horse from the penultimate flight. This was his second run back after a three-year absence and he might still have needed it. *(op 12-1)*

3134 PLAY POKER AT LADBROKES.COM NOVICES' CHASE (14 fncs) 2m 4f 110y
1:20 (1:22) (Class 3) 5-Y-0+ **£8,317** (£2,582; £1,390)

Form RPR

3-12 **1** **Copsale Lad**[34] 2531 8-11-6 136 .... MickFitzgerald 142+
(N J Henderson) *trckd ldr: blnd 8th: rcvrd to ld 4 out: in command whn lft long way clr 2 out: eased run-in* **1/1**[1]

6F0- **2** dist **Phone Back (IRE)**[393] 2615 6-11-0 .... PhilipHide —
(G L Moore) *in tch tl outpcd 10th: lft remote 2nd 2 out* **11/1**[3]

FP60 **3** 6 **Sett Aside**[18] 2805 7-11-0 .... LeightonAspell —
(Mrs L C Jewell) *in tch whn mstke 9th: lft distant 3rd 2 out* **50/1**

304- **U** **Twenty Degrees**[278] 4622 7-10-11 100 .... ColinBolger(3) —
(G L Moore) *in last pl whn blnd and uns rdr 6th* **12/1**

P-24 **F** **Back Nine (IRE)**[22] 2743 8-11-0 120 .... AndrewThornton 129
(R H Alner) *led tl hdd 4 out: rdn and 2l down whn fell 2 out* **6/4**[2]

5m 27.2s (8.20) **Going Correction** +0.20s/f (Yiel) **5** Ran SP% **108.0**
Speed ratings: **92,—,—,—,—** CSF £10.63 TOTE £1.70: £1.10, £3.90; EX 10.40.
Owner Swallow Partnership **Bred** G G A Gregson **Trained** Upper Lambourn, Berks

FOCUS
An easy win for Copsale Lad, who already looked set to confirm his course and distance superiority over Back Nine when he was left a long way clear. The winner and faller are rated to their marks.

NOTEBOOK
Copsale Lad, runner-up in a Grade 2 event last time, did not like this ground and would have been taken out had chief rival Foreman not been withdrawn. His jumping was sticky in the back straight but he gradually got his act together, led four from home, and was set for a fairly comfortable win when he was left virtually alone at the second last. Connections intend to avoid this sort of ground in future. *(op 11-10 tchd 10-11)*
Phone Back(IRE), making his chase debut after an absence of over a year, did not jump fluently and was left well behind by the two market leaders. He was fortunate to inherit a distant runner-up spot two from home. *(op 12-1 tchd 10-1)*
Sett Aside is a dual winning pointer but he has shown next to nothing in his ventures under Rules so far. *(op 40-1)*
Back Nine(IRE), beaten 13l by Copsale Lad here in October and 6lb better off today, looked the likelier winner as his rival jumped stickily down the back, but he was headed with four to jump and held in second when taking an ugly fall two from home. *(tchd 7-4)*

3135 BET WITH LADBROKES ON 0800 524524 H'CAP HURDLE (10 hdls) 2m 3f 110y
1:50 (1:52) (Class 2) (0-140,132) 4-Y-0+
£9,845 (£2,908; £1,454; £727; £363; £182)

Form RPR

-325 **1** **Dom D'Orgeval (FR)**[22] 2746 5-11-3 123 .... PaddyBrennan 135+
(Nick Williams) *hld up: mstke 4th: chalng whn mstke 3 out: led appr next: kpt up to work* **4/1**[2]

2115 **2** 5 **Nathos (GER)**[14] 2876 8-11-2 132 .... KevinTobin(10) 136+
(C J Mann) *mid-div: hdwy to go 2nd 7th: ev ch 2 out: kpt on one pce* **9/1**

-366 **3** 3 1/2 **Cool Roxy**[15] 2871 8-11-0 127 .... AndrewGlassonbury(7) 127
(A G Blackmore) *trckd ldrs: rdn 6th: rallied and styd on one pce fr 2 out* **25/1**

102- **4** 2 1/2 **Papini (IRE)**[262] 4826 4-11-5 125 .... MickFitzgerald 125+
(N J Henderson) *led tl rdn and hdd & wknd appr 2 out* **10/1**

P6-4 **5** 3/4 **L'Oudon (FR)**[30] 2595 4-10-7 120 .... LiamHeard(7) 116
(P F Nicholls) *hld up: hdwy 6th: one pce fr 3 out* **6/1**[3]

53-3 **6** 9 **Idiome (FR)**[16] 2850 9-10-10 116 .... JimmyMcCarthy 103
(Mrs L C Taylor) *hld up: hmpd 5th: n.d after* **14/1**

1112 **7** 13 **Magot De Grugy (FR)**[16] 2850 5-11-0 120 .... AndrewThornton 94
(R H Alner) *trckd ldr tl appr 5th: wknd appr 2 out* **7/2**[1]

-005 **8** 3 **Salut Saint Cloud**[15] 2871 4-11-5 125 .... BrianCrowley 96
(G L Moore) *racd wd: a bhd* **6/1**[3]

U-0 **9** 24 **Maletton (FR)**[28] 2629 5-11-4 124 .... (b) AlanO'Keeffe 71
(Miss Venetia Williams) *wnt 2nd appr 5th: wknd bef 7th* **20/1**

UF60 **F** **Charlton Kings (IRE)**[16] 2850 7-10-5 111 .... JimCrowley —
(R J Hodges) *t.k.h: sn prom: fell 5th* **16/1**

520- **P** **Downpour (USA)**[274] 4678 7-10-7 123 .... DavidBoland(10) —
(Ian Williams) *hld up in tch: rdn 6th: sn bhd: p.u after 3 out* **50/1**

0045 **P** **Constantine**[34] 2525 5-10-5 111 .... (b) PhilipHide —
(G L Moore) *in tch: wknd 6th: sddle slipped and wl bhd whn p.u bef last* **12/1**

5m 8.50s (5.80) **Going Correction** +0.525s/f (Soft) **12** Ran SP% **120.7**
Speed ratings: **109,107,105,104,104 100,95,94,84,—** —,— CSF £40.01 CT £812.12 TOTE £5.40: £1.40, £3.70, £9.90; EX 54.30.
Owner Mrs Jane Williams **Bred** Max De Minden **Trained** George Nympton, Devon

FOCUS
A reasonably competitive handicap in which the emphasis was on stamina and not many got home. Dom D'Orgeval and Nathos had the race to themselves from the second last and both ran personal bests, although the latter's 10lb claim was no doubt a factor.

NOTEBOOK
Dom D'Orgeval(FR) was suited by the step up in trip and his attitude could not be faulted this time as he was required to work hard for his victory. He reportedly needs a bit of time between his races. *(op 9-2)*
Nathos(GER) ran a solid race and his rider's claim was a big help, but he may remain vulnerable from this mark. *(tchd 10-1)*
Cool Roxy lost his pitch in the back straight and was only sixth turning into the straight, but rallied from the second last. The handicapper is unlikely to drop him after this. *(op 20-1)*
Papini(IRE), who had a good season as a juvenile, made the running as usual on this first run since April. Headed going the second last, he looked out on his feet but did keep going for fourth. This was an encouraging enough reappearance, as he had a stiffish task at the weights. *(op 8-1)*
L'Oudon(FR), stepping up in trip, improved running downhill to the home turn but the effort then flattened out. *(op 5-1)*
Magot De Grugy(FR), up a further 3lb after a narrow defeat on his bid for a four-timer, was beaten *at the top of the hill having not jumped too well.Official explanation: jockey said gelding became tired after two mistakes on far side (op 5-1)*
Salut Saint Cloud was struggling a long way out and ran disappointingly. *(tchd 13-2)*
Constantine *Official explanation: jockey said saddle slipped*

3136 LADBROKES.COM H'CAP CHASE (12 fncs) 2m
2:20 (2:20) (Class 2) 5-Y-0+ **£18,858** (£5,619; £2,844; £1,458; £762)

Form RPR

6-15 **1** **Armaturk (FR)**[50] 2163 8-11-12 153 .... ChristianWilliams 164
(P F Nicholls) *trckd ldr: rdn and chalng whn hit last: r.o gamely to ld post* **4/1**[2]

2353 **2** nk **Bleu Superbe (FR)**[21] 2757 10-10-1 128 .... AlanO'Keeffe 140+
(Miss Venetia Williams) *j.lft thrght: led: hrd rdn run-in: hdd post* **9/2**[3]

00-4 **3** 5 **Non So (FR)**[35] 2489 7-10-11 138 .... MickFitzgerald 144
(N J Henderson) *hld up: nt fluent 4th: hdwy to go 3rd 4 out: ev ch appr 2 out: wknd bef last* **7/2**[1]

40-0 **4** 1 **Claymore (IRE)**[35] 2492 9-10-7 134 .... LeightonAspell 140+
(O Sherwood) *bhd: styd on fr 3 out: nvr nr to chal* **6/1**

2-0P **5** 16 **Kadount (FR)**[35] 2489 7-11-1 142 .... WayneHutchinson 134+
(A King) *in tch tl outpcd appr 4 out* **13/2**

P-3F **P** **Le Seychellois (FR)**[21] 2757 5-10-1 135 ow2 .... LiamHeard(7) —
(P F Nicholls) *trckd ldrs tl wknd 8th: t.o whn p.u bef last* **7/2**[1]

4m 6.20s (-1.70) **Going Correction** +0.20s/f (Yiel) **6** Ran SP% **110.2**
Speed ratings: **112,111,109,108,100** — CSF £21.08 TOTE £4.60: £2.20, £2.40; EX 13.20.
Owner Trevor Hemmings **Bred** Rene Collet And Mme Catherine Auniac **Trained** Ditcheat, Somerset

FOCUS
An interesting handicap and a valuable prize, although there were question marks over several of the runners. Armaturk remains unbeaten at Lingfield and put up a performance bordering on championship class.

NOTEBOOK
Armaturk(FR) has now won on all three of his visits to Lingfield, each time at the chief expense of Bleu Superbe, who was in receipt of no less than 25lb here. He looked just held when making a mistake at the last, but ran on very willingly despite his big weight to put his head in front close on the line. This was a new personal best and he now heads to Cheltenham for the Victor Chandler Chase. *(op 9-2)*
Bleu Superbe(FR) remains without a win for over two years, but he has been running well in defeat and looked to have cracked it this time only to be caught by his old rival right on the post. Like the winner he is set to run in the Victor Chandler now. *(op 5-1)*
Non So(FR) looked a threat in third place turning for home, but when shaken up after the third last he did not find much of a response. He is certainly handicapped to win but is going to need everything to fall right for him. *(tchd 4-1)*
Claymore(IRE)has become well handicapped and had ground conditions to suit, but found this too sharp and was never able to get in a challenge. *(op 11-2)*
Kadount(FR) was struggling going up the hill to the fourth last and now has plenty to prove. *(tchd 6-1)*
Le Seychellois(FR) had an excuse for his lacklustre showing at Cheltenham but there was no obvious reason for this poor run. *(op 3-1)*

3137 LINGFIELD-RACECOURSE.CO.UK NOVICES' H'CAP HURDLE (10 hdls) 2m 3f 110y
2:55 (2:55) (Class 4) (0-100,99) 3-Y-0+ **£3,467** (£1,018; £509; £254)

Form RPR

556- **1** **Play The Melody (IRE)**[354] 3307 4-11-3 90 .... MickFitzgerald 95+
(C Tinkler) *racd wd and j.rt thrght: ld appr 3rd: hdd bef 5th: led 3 out: rdr lost iron after last: wnt lft: all out* **11/4**[1]

033 **2** 1 **Lord Of Adventure (IRE)**[9] 2954 3-10-12 99 .... LeightonAspell 85
(Mrs L C Jewell) *led tl hdd appr 3rd: wnt 2nd 3 out: pressed wnr fr 2 out* **3/1**[2]

0402 **3** 10 **Barranco (IRE)**[11] 2934 4-11-1 88 .... (b) PhilipHide 80+
(G L Moore) *in tch: mstke 7th: one pce after 3 out* **11/4**[1]

006- **4** 18 **Little Saxtead (IRE)**[331] 3662 5-10-0 73 oh1 .... JimCrowley 45
(J A Supple) *hld up in rr: sme hdwy after 3 out: hld whn blnd last* **10/1**

0 **5** dist **Barella (IRE)**[5] 2995 6-11-8 95 .... (v[1]) JamesDavies —
(B G Powell) *hld up: chal 6th: wknd after 3 out: blnd next: t.o* **11/1**

2460 **6** 2 1/2 **Paradise Bay (IRE)**[17] 2821 4-11-2 99 .... KevinTobin(10) —
(C J Mann) *prom: ld appr 5th: hdd 3 out: wknd qckly and blnd next: t.o* **11/2**[3]

5m 19.0s (16.30) **Going Correction** +0.525s/f (Soft)
WFA 3 from 4yo 13lb 4 from 5yo+ 10lb **6** Ran SP% **111.1**
Speed ratings: **88,87,83,76,—** — CSF £11.39 CT £22.36 TOTE £4.00: £1.90, £1.70; EX 13.40.
Owner Doubleprint **Bred** Gatebest Ltd **Trained** Compton, Berks

FOCUS
A very weak event, run more than ten seconds slower than Dom d'Orgeval's handicap and rated through the runner-up.

NOTEBOOK

Play The Melody(IRE) won the second of only two starts on the Flat and looked on a potentially lenient mark, but he was having his first run for the best part of a year and jumped to his right all the way. In front for a second time at the third last, he just held on despite his rider losing an iron at the final flight which caused him to edge left. This did not take much winning, but he might improve going right handed. *(tchd 3-1)*

Lord Of Adventure(IRE), on his handicap debut, found a second wind to challenge on the downhill run to the home turn, but could never quite get past the winner who did him no favours when edging left on the run-in. *(op 7-2)*

Barranco(IRE) is an exposed performer who has been found wanting plenty of times from this sort of mark. *(op 10-3)*

Little Saxtead(IRE), the first to look beaten, did stage a brief rally running to the home straight before weakening. He appears to be a very limited performer. *(op 8-1)*

Barella(IRE) showed fair form in cheekpieces when trained in Ireland, but failed to get home in the first-time visor. *(op 10-1 tchd 12-1)*

3138 LINGFIELD-RACECOURSE.CO.UK STANDARD OPEN NATIONAL HUNT FLAT RACE 2m

3:30 (3:30) (Class 6) 4-6-Y-O **£2,220** (£647; £323)

Form RPR

1 **Deep Reflection** 5-11-4 .... AlanO'Keeffe 102+
(J A Supple) *hld up in rr: stdy hdwy on outside over 3f out: led 1f out: rdn clr* **33/1**

2 *7* **Parish House (IRE)** 5-10-11 .... MrMWall(7) 95
(B W Duke) *chsd ldrs: led over 2f out: rdn and hdd 1f out: no ex* **7/1[3]**

0 3 *nk* **Kalamazoo (IRE)**[34] 2534 4-11-4 .... PaddyBrennan 94
(Nick Williams) *prom: rdn and outpcd 2f out: styd on to go 3rd ins fnl f* **3/1[2]**

0/0 4 *1 3/4* **Benjamin Buckram (IRE)**[17] 2823 6-11-4 .... APMcCoy 93
(C R Egerton) *trckd ldr: led over 4f out: rdn and hdd over 2f out: no ex appr fnl f* **8/1**

0-62 5 *1/2* **Flyingwithoutwings**[52] 2131 6-11-4 .... WayneHutchinson 92
(A King) *hld up in rr: hdwy 4f out: styd on fnl 2f: nvr nrr* **6/4[1]**

6 *9* **King Of Java** 4-10-11 .... LeeNewnes(7) 83
(M Bradstock) *racd wd: t.k.h: prom tl wknd over 2f out* **12/1**

06 7 *2* **Berkeley Court**[192] 817 4-11-4 .... PhilipHide 81
(G L Moore) *mid-div: wknd over 2f out* **14/1**

8 *7* **Kathleen Kennet** 5-10-11 .... JamesDavies 67
(Mrs H Sweeting) *mid-div: rdn 6f out: sn bhd* **25/1**

0- 9 *15* **Judy's Lad**[570] 698 6-11-4 .... MatthewBatchelor 59
(Mrs H R J Nelmes) *led tl hdd over 4f out: wknd qckly sn after* **66/1**

10 *dist* **Santa Sheva** 4-10-11 .... AndrewGlassonbury(7) —
(K F Clutterbuck) *bhd whn rdn 1/2-way: sn lost tch: t.o* **25/1**

00 11 *1 3/4* **Ilringuback (IRE)**[38] 2432 5-11-4 .... SeanCurran —
(A J Chamberlain) *mid-div: wknd over 5f out: t.o* **25/1**

3m 29.8s **11** Ran SP% **118.9**
CSF £241.42 TOTE £47.80: £8.30, £2.30, £1.90; EX 295.30 Place 6 £74.19, Place 5 £32.02.
Owner J J M Bailey **Bred** Mrs C J C Bailey **Trained** Worlingworth, Suffolk

FOCUS
A pretty modest Polytrack bumper, but it was run at a fair pace and the form should work out with the fifth the best guide.

NOTEBOOK

Deep Reflection is out of a winning Irish hurdler who was a half-sister to one-time smart jumper Dawn Leader. Improving from off the pace to strike the front with a furlong to run, he stayed on strongly. He should go on from here.

Parish House(IRE) is out of a mare who was unplaced in an Irish bumper on her only run. He showed ability, but having had to work to get to the front he had nothing left in the tank when headed at the furlong pole. *(op 8-1 tchd 6-1)*

Kalamazoo(IRE) ran respectably but this track did not really play to his strengths. He looks a stayer. *(op 5-2 tchd 7-2)*

Benjamin Buckram(IRE), who recently returned to the track after nearly 22 months out, looks the type to need a stiffer test when he goes over hurdles. *(op 9-1)*

Flyingwithoutwings was proven on the surface, having been runner-up in a similar race here last time, but failed to step up on that. *(op 7-4 tchd 2-1 and 15-8 in places)*

T/Plt: £88.70 to a £1 stake. Pool: £55,841.70. 459.50 winning tickets. T/Qpdt: £22.10 to a £1 stake. Pool: £3,926.80. 131.45 winning tickets. JS

2858 UTTOXETER (L-H)

Saturday, December 31

OFFICIAL GOING: Heavy

The meeting had to survive a morning inspection and the ground was 'desperate'. Middle two fences in bk st, and 3rd & last flights in bk st omitted.
Wind: Moderate, half-against Weather: Mainly fine but cold.

3139 A.P.H. EARTHWORKS LTD NOVICES' HURDLE (8 hdls 4 omitted) 2m 4f 110y

12:40 (12:41) (Class 4) 4-Y-O+ **£3,566** (£1,039; £519)

Form RPR

/1F2 1 **Hoh Viss**[14] 2878 5-11-5 120 .... NoelFehily 132+
(C J Mann) *trckd ldrs: led and qcknd 6th: clr appr 3 out: 18l up last: heavily eased* **1/3[1]**

2 *22* **Palm Island (FR)**[230] 4-10-12 .... JohnMcNamara 100+
(Noel T Chance) *chsd ldrs: wnt 2nd appr 3 out: no ch w wnr: eased run-in* **12/1[3]**

-406 3 *19* **Negus De Beaumont (FR)**[15] 2860 4-10-12 .... HenryOliver 75
(F Jordan) *chsd ldrs: outpcd 7th: kpt on to take remote 3rd run-in* **16/1**

0/0 4 *3* **Minster Park**[27] 2665 6-10-12 .... RJGreene 72
(S C Burrough) *hld up in rr: outpcd 6th: kpt on fr 3 out: nvr a factor* **100/1**

300 5 *3* **Joseph Beuys (IRE)**[19] 2799 6-10-5 .... DarylJacob(7) 72+
(D P Keane) *hld up in rr: sme hdwy 7th: 4th whn blnd next: sn wknd* **16/1**

44-0 6 *21* **Beluga (IRE)**[17] 2821 6-10-12 .... MarkGrant 48
(M Pitman) *set stdy pce: hdd 6th: wknd appr 3 out: fin tired* **9/1[2]**

P **Jacobin (USA)**[63] 4-10-5 .... JohnKington(7) —
(M Scudamore) *bhd fr 6th: mstke 2 out: sn p.u* **80/1**

060 P **Ol' Man River (IRE)**[28] 2619 5-10-12 .... BarryFenton —
(H D Daly) *bhd: sme hdwy 5th: sn lost pl and bhd: p.u bef 3 out* **20/1**

5m 31.9s (19.80) **Going Correction** +1.125s/f (Heav)
WFA 4 from 5yo+ 11lb **8** Ran SP% **111.5**
Speed ratings: **107,98,91,90,89 81,—,—** CSF £5.06 TOTE £1.40: £1.10, £2.00, £2.30; EX 5.20.

Owner D F Allport **Bred** D F Allport **Trained** Upper Lambourn, Berks

FOCUS
A one-sided event and a facile winner who was value for 25l.

NOTEBOOK

Hoh Viss was left with a simple task after the withdrawals and took this in facile fashion. He will now be given a short break. *(tchd 3-10 tchd 4-11 in places and 2-5 in a place)*

Palm Island(FR), who is not very big, won three times in the French Provinces. He finished clear second best but what he actually achieved is uncertain.

Negus De Beaumont(FR), having his third start over hurdles, looks much more of a chaser.

Minster Park, on his toes beforehand, was making his hurdling debut after showing little in two starts in bumper races.

Joseph Beuys(IRE), a big type, looks much more of a chaser. *(op 14-1)*

3140 HEATHYARDS ENGINEERING H'CAP HURDLE (10 hdls 4 omitted) 3m

1:10 (1:10) (Class 4) (0-100,100) 4-Y-O+ **£2,569** (£748; £374)

Form RPR

56/6 1 **Dickie Lewis**[15] 2859 7-9-13 78 .... StephenCraine(5) 96+
(D McCain) *w ldr: led 9th: hit last 3: heavily eased: walked over line: won by 42l* **10/1**

-112 2 *dist* **Young Lorcan**[15] 2862 9-10-8 89 .... RichardSpate(7) 72
(Mrs K Waldron) *in tch: reminders after 8th: chsd wnr after next: sn rdn: btn after 3 out* **11/8[1]**

12P- 3 *12* **Desert Tommy**[462] 1507 4-11-7 100 .... PaulO'Neill(5) 58
(Evan Williams) *in tch: reminders 6th: one pce fr 9th* **12/1**

PPP6 4 *dist* **All Sonsilver (FR)**[18] 2816 8-11-1 89 .... HenryOliver —
(P Kelsall) *led racing wd: hdd 9th: sn lost pl and bhd: t.o* **9/1**

61/U 5 *dist* **Mcsnappy**[19] 2800 8-11-3 98 .... WayneKavanagh(7) —
(J W Mullins) *chsd ldrs: rdn and lost pl after 7th: sn bhd: t.o whn p.u bef next* **11/1**

122 P **Potts Of Magic**[35] 2505 6-11-7 95 .... (b) JohnMcNamara —
(R Lee) *in tch: lost pl 8th: t.o whn p.u bef next* **4/1[2]**

0P-P P **Gamma-Delta (IRE)**[46] 2256 10-10-12 91 .... AdamPogson(5) —
(C T Pogson) *bhd and reminders 4th: sn t.o: p.u bef next* **25/1**

3220 P **Prayerful**[16] 2845 6-11-2 93 .... OwynNelmes(3) —
(J G M O'Shea) *rdn and lost pl after 7th: sn bhd: t.o whn p.u after 3 out* **15/2[3]**

0-00 P **Redde (IRE)**[29] 2609 10-11-5 100 .... CharlieStudd(7) —
(Mrs J G Retter) *chsd ldrs: lost pl 9th: sn wl bhd: virtually p.u: hopelessly t.o* **33/1**

6m 35.4s (30.40) **Going Correction** +1.125s/f (Heav)
WFA 4 from 6yo+ 13lb **9** Ran SP% **115.8**
Speed ratings: **108,—,—,—,— —,—,—,—** CSF £25.06 CT £174.48 TOTE £6.60: £2.20, £1.40, £4.10; EX 21.70.
Owner L A Morgan **Bred** Col J L Parkes **Trained** Cholmondeley, Cheshire

FOCUS
A very moderate race but the winner is value for at least 35 lengths.

NOTEBOOK

Dickie Lewis, raised 19lb, fell through the last three flights yet still finished in glorious isolation turning in a vastly improved effort and carrying the race sponsor's colours.

Young Lorcan lay a lot handier this time but, flat out starting the home turn, he found the winner running away from him going to two out. This possibly came too soon after his punishing race here two weeks earlier. *(op 13-8 tchd 15-8 in places)*

Desert Tommy, absent since pulling up lame 15 months ago, should improve for the outing. *(op 11-1)*

All Sonsilver(FR), keen to post, set the pace racing away from the running rail but he stopped to nothing when headed.

3141 PETER J DOUGLAS ENGINEERING CHRISTMAS (S) HURDLE (8 hdls 2 omitted) 2m

1:40 (1:41) (Class 5) 4-Y-O+ **£2,226** (£649; £324)

Form RPR

3-FP 1 **Barton Gate**[25] 2685 7-10-5 97 .... (b) DarylJacob(7) 94
(D P Keane) *chsd ldrs: led appr 2 out: rdn rt out* **11/2**

P060 2 *8* **The Wife's Sister**[22] 2752 4-10-0 75 .... (b) StephenCraine(5) 79
(D McCain) *chsd ldrs: one pce fr 3 out* **6/1**

4500 3 *7* **Pilca (FR)**[28] 2625 5-10-12 96 .... BarryFenton 81+
(R M Stronge) *chsd ldr: led 6th: hdd appr 2 out: btn whn hit last* **9/2[2]**

200- 4 *1 1/2* **The Last Mohican**[308] 4058 6-10-12 107 .... OllieMcPhail 79+
(A G Juckes) *hdwy to chse ldrs 6th: rdn appr 3 out: 4th and btn whn mstke 2 out* **4/1[1]**

P00- 5 *1 3/4* **Knockrigg (IRE)**[345] 3444 11-10-5 87 .... CharlieStudd(7) 76
(Dr P Pritchard) *in tch: effrt 5th: wknd after next* **14/1**

P535 6 *15* **Oulton Broad**[31] 2576 9-10-12 95 .... (p) HenryOliver 61
(F Jordan) *in tch: drvn along 5th: lost pl after next* **5/1[3]**

0PRP 7 *2 1/2* **Idlewild (IRE)**[15] 2862 10-11-0 93 .... AdamPogson(5) 65
(C T Pogson) *prom: lost pl 4th: sn bhd: t.o 5th* **9/1**

40P 8 *dist* **Weldiva**[35] 2503 5-10-4 ow6 .... MrRJBarrett(7) —
(B N Pollock) *in rr: bhd fr 4th: t.o next: btn 41l* **50/1**

F/ P **Bold Century**[787] 1951 8-10-12 .... RJGreene —
(S C Burrough) *plld hrd in rr: lost pl and p.u bef 7th* **40/1**

PP- P **Don't Matter**[303] 4132 5-9-12 .... RichardSpate(7) —
(A E Price) *in tch: lost pl 6th: t.o whn p.u bef next* **40/1**

0P/5 P **Paradise Garden (USA)**[104] 1485 8-10-2 .... ThomasBurrows(10) —
(P L Clinton) *led to 6th: wknd qckly: t.o whn p.u bef next* **20/1**

50P/ P **Secret Dell (IRE)**[26] 9-10-5 .... (b) MrGTumelty(7) —
(R Brotherton) *prom: reminders 3rd: lost pl after next: sn bhd: t.o whn p.u bef 3 out* **33/1**

4m 24.1s (23.70) **Going Correction** +1.125s/f (Heav)
WFA 4 from 5yo+ 10lb **12** Ran SP% **115.7**
Speed ratings: **99,95,91,90,89 82,81,—,—,— —,—** CSF £35.86 TOTE £6.70: £2.30, £2.00, £2.00; EX 44.40.The winner was bought in for 4,500gns. Oulton Broad was claimed by D. W. Watson for £6,000.
Owner Lady Clarke **Bred** John James **Trained** North End, Dorset

FOCUS
A moderate contest as is typical for the grade, and the runner-up sets the standard.

NOTEBOOK

Barton Gate, who had plenty to prove, revelled in the testing conditions and his rider left nothing to chance. *(op 7-1)*

The Wife's Sister, in first-time blinkers, ran better than of late but in the end the winner proved simply too strong. *(op 7-1 tchd 8-1)*

Pilca(FR), out of form on his last three starts, went on but was out on his feet when hitting the last hard. *(tchd 4-1)*

The Last Mohican, absent for ten months, would have made short work of these at his peak but his chance had slipped when getting the second last wrong. *(op 7-2)*

Knockrigg(IRE) has not won for over four years now and time is not on his side.

Oulton Broad was in trouble at halfway. He was claimed by his former owner and may now join Richard Ford. *(op 9-2)*

Secret Dell(IRE) *Official explanation: jockey said gelding was never travelling*

3142 BETFRED BEGINNERS' CHASE (14 fncs 4 omitted) 3m
2:10 (2:11) (Class 4) 5-Y-O+ **£5,142** (£1,509; £754; £377)

Form RPR
0U22 **1** **He's The Guv'Nor (IRE)**[17] 2825 6-11-0 113............ BenjaminHitchcott 125+
(R H Buckler) *trckd ldrs: wnt 2nd 10th: led appr 4 out: j.rt 2 out: styd on run-in* **9/4**[1]
2-13 **2** *4* **Admiral Peary (IRE)**[41] 2375 9-11-0 118................................ MarkGrant 120
(C R Egerton) *j.rt: led to 6th: swtchd lft and almost upsides last: no ex* **3/1**[2]
PP0P **3** *dist* **Soroka (IRE)**[5] 2984 6-10-7 81.................................(b) CharlieStudd(7) —
(C N Kellett) *outpcd 7th: bhd and reminders 10th: wnt poor 3rd appr 2 out: t.o: btn 57l* **66/1**
P302 **4** *dist* **Bell Lane Lad (IRE)**[23] 2717 8-11-0 105.............................. HenryOliver —
(D J Wintle) *chsd ldrs: 4th and wkng whn blundered 10th: t.o next: btn 37l* **8/1**
-PP4 **U** **Sungates (IRE)**[27] 2660 9-11-0 .... BarryFenton —
(C Tinkler) *wl in tch tl mstke and uns rdr 5th* **11/1**
6200 **U** **Mythical King (IRE)**[28] 2633 8-11-0 .... JohnMcNamara —
(R Lee) *hld up: in tch whn stmbld and uns rdr 3rd* **4/1**[3]
P **The Mighty Dunne (IRE)**[294] 5-10-9 .... PaulO'Neill(5) —
(Evan Williams) *trckd ldrs: bmpd 2nd: led 6th: hdd appr 4 out: sn wknd: poor 3rd whn blnd 3 out: 4th whn p.u bef next* **7/1**

6m 46.9s (14.40) **Going Correction** +0.675s/f (Soft) **7** Ran SP% **109.2**
Speed ratings: **103,101,—,—,— —,—** CSF £8.75 TOTE £2.80: £2.10, £2.20; EX 6.80.
Owner M J Hallett **Bred** Mrs Maureen Ring **Trained** Melplash, Dorset

FOCUS
A fair novices' chase where stamina played its part. The first two set the standard to recent marks.

NOTEBOOK
He's The Guv'Nor(IRE) travelled strongly and had to dig deep but was firmly in command at the line. This was only his third start over fences and there should be even better to come. *(op 2-1)*
Admiral Peary(IRE), having just his second start over fences, continually lost ground jumping to his right. He stuck to his guns but had to give best on the run-in. A right-handed track will surely suit him better. *(tchd 11-4)*
Soroka(IRE) is struggling to make any impact at all over fences.
Bell Lane Lad(IRE), with the visor left off on his first start for this stable, ran poorly and finished nearly 100 lengths behind the winner. *(op 9-1)*
Mythical King(IRE), making a belated debut over fences, departed somewhat unluckily at an early stage.

3143 BETFREDCASINO H'CAP HURDLE (8 hdls 4 omitted) 2m 4f 110y
2:45 (2:45) (Class 3) (0-125,124) 4-Y-O+ **£7,010** (£2,058; £1,029; £513)

Form RPR
0515 **1** **Killing Me Softly**[19] 2802 4-10-5 103...............................(v) BarryFenton 119+
(J Gallagher) *a.p: drvn along 7th: led appr next: clr 2 out: drvn out* **9/1**
004 **2** *24* **Jockser (IRE)**[24] 2706 4-10-5 110............................. WayneKavanagh(7) 101
(J W Mullins) *a in tch: kpt on to go 2nd after 3 out: no ch w wnr* **7/1**
1015 **3** *24* **Devito (FR)**[23] 2734 4-10-13 118...................................... MrDEdwards(7) 94+
(G F Edwards) *racd wd: wnt prom 6th: wnt 3rd after 3 out: wl btn whn hit last* **12/1**
1P1P **4** *15* **Vicario**[17] 2820 4-11-6 123... StephenCraine(5) 75
(D McCain) *chsd ldrs: led after 6th: hdd appr 3 out: wkng whn hit 3 out* **7/1**
P-50 **5** *14* **King Georges (FR)**[24] 2703 7-10-5 103.......................(v[1]) JodieMogford 41
(J C Tuck) *led: reminders 5th: hdd after next: wknd qckly and sn bhd* **20/1**
-040 **P** **Always Waining (IRE)**[22] 2746 4-11-5 117.......................... SamStronge —
(P L Clinton) *prom: wknd after 7th: bhd whn p.u bef last* **5/1**[3]
-40P **P** **Turaath (IRE)**[23] 2731 9-11-0 112.....................................(b) NoelFehily —
(A J Deakin) *in rr and rdn 6th: sn bhd: t.o whn p.u bef 3 out* **33/1**
11 **P** **In Media Res (FR)**[18] 2804 4-11-5 124................................ CharlieStudd(7) —
(N J Henderson) *chsd ldrs: wknd qckly and eased sn after 7th: bhd whn p.u up bef next* **7/2**[1]
F310 **P** **Arm And A Leg (IRE)**[23] 2731 10-11-0 112............... BenjaminHitchcott —
(Mrs D A Hamer) *chsd ldrs: rdn and lost pl after 5th: sn bhd: t.o whn p.u bef 3 out* **12/1**
52-P **P** **Mazzareme (IRE)**[248] 61 7-10-7 110................................ PaulO'Neill(5) —
(Miss Venetia Williams) *chsd ldrs: wnt 2nd after 7th: wknd next: 5th and v tired whn p.u bef 2 out* **9/2**[2]

5m 35.5s (23.40) **Going Correction** +1.125s/f (Heav) **10** Ran SP% **115.2**
Speed ratings: **100,90,81,76,70 —,—,—,—,—** CSF £69.87 CT £761.66 TOTE £14.90: £4.10, £3.50, £5.10; EX 72.80 TRIFECTA Not won..
Owner Stuart Prior **Bred** S R Prior **Trained** Chastleton, Oxon

FOCUS
A fair handicap with the field finishing well strung out and the runner-up to recent mark setting the standard.

NOTEBOOK
Killing Me Softly, much improved by the fitting of a visor, is very willing and revelling in the conditions, in the end came right away, his rider leaving nothing to chance.
Jockser(IRE) put a poor effort last time behind him and kept on to finish clear second best. *(op 6-1)*
Devito(FR), who went wide in search of less testing ground, was out on his feet when falling through the final flight.
Vicario, 8lb higher than his last success, seems happiest these days at Haydock. *(op 8-1)*
Arm And A Leg(IRE) *Official explanation: jockey said gelding was never travelling (tchd 4-1)*
Mazzareme(IRE), having his first outing since April, has changed stables. He looked a real threat when taking second spot travelling comfortably, but the way he emptied in a matter of strides must be a cause for concern. *(tchd 4-1)*
In Media Res(FR) stopped to nothing in a matter of strides and connections blamed the very testing ground. *Official explanation: trainer's representative said gelding was unsuited by heavy ground (tchd 4-1)*

3144 BETFREDPOKER H'CAP CHASE (12 fncs 4 omitted) 2m 6f 110y
3:20 (3:20) (Class 3) (0-120,117) 5-Y-O+ **£6,912** (£2,029; £1,014; £506)

Form RPR
4-51 **1** **Another Native (IRE)**[14] 2874 7-10-13 104............................ NoelFehily 126+
(C J Mann) *trckd ldrs gng wl: led on bit 3 out: v cheekily* **15/8**[1]
-5P1 **2** *nk* **Major Benefit (IRE)**[15] 2863 8-11-5 117........................ RichardSpate(7) 125
(Mrs K Waldron) *led to 3rd: led 6th: kpt on fr 4 out: greatly flattered* **4/1**[3]
34P5 **3** *dist* **Thyne Man (IRE)**[39] 2415 7-10-9 100.............................(p) PaulMoloney —
(J Mackie) *in tch: wnt prom 6th: wnt 3rd 4 out: sn wknd: t.o: btn 31l* **11/1**
-F30 **4** *20* **Charlies Future**[43] 2325 7-11-6 111...................................... RJGreene —
(S C Burrough) *chsd ldrs: drvn 7th: lost pl appr 4 out: sn bhd: t.o* **17/2**
321- **5** *dist* **Jordans Lad (IRE)**[265] 4799 9-11-0 112.......................... JohnKington(7) —
(M Scudamore) *trckd ldrs: lost pl 8th: sn wl bhd: hopelessly t.o: btn 38l* **7/1**
052 **F** **Pardini (USA)**[14] 2877 6-10-1 92................................ BenjaminHitchcott —
(M F Harris) *chsd ldr: led 3rd to 6th: wknd 4 out: poor 4th whn fell 2 out* **7/2**[2]

6m 15.0s **6** Ran SP% **108.4**
CSF £9.24 TOTE £2.60: £2.00, £2.20; EX 8.80.
Owner The Sport of Kings Partnership **Bred** Mrs Brid McCrea **Trained** Upper Lambourn, Berks

FOCUS
A modest contest but the narrow winner was value for 15 lengths and the runner-up sets the level.

NOTEBOOK
Another Native(IRE), a big type, was racing from an 8lb higher mark on only his fourth start. He went round in third gear and scored in cheeky fashion with any amount in hand. The Tophan will be his spring target. *(op 2-1)*
Major Benefit(IRE), 12lb higher, ran his heart out but the winner was simply toying with him. *(op 10-3)*
Thyne Man(IRE), in first-time cheekpieces, does not get very high at his fences and his attitude does not impress. *(op 10-1)*
Charlies Future, 10lb higher than his last success, was in trouble early on the final circuit and he dropped right away on the turn for home. *(op 11-1 tchd 8-1)*
Jordans Lad(IRE) stopped to nothing five out and was found to be lame afterwards. *Official explanation: vet said gelding finished lame (op 11-2 tchd 5-1)*
Pardini(USA) was a tired fourth when taking a crashing fall. *(op 4-1)*

3145 LAURA GLENDINING MAIDEN OPEN NATIONAL HUNT FLAT RACE 2m
3:50 (3:51) (Class 6) 4-6-Y-O **£2,000** (£583; £291)

Form RPR
00- **1** **Suprendre Espere**[287] 4451 5-11-4 .... JohnMcNamara 94
(Jennie Candlish) *mde all: clr over 1f out: drvn out* **28/1**
2 *11* **Herons Cove (IRE)**[251] 19 6-11-4 .... BenjaminHitchcott 83
(W M Brisbourne) *trckd ldrs: chal over 3f out: regained 2nd over 1f out: one pce* **14/1**
3 *3* **Classic Harry** 4-11-4 .... RussGarritty 80
(P Beaumont) *chsd ldrs: rdn to go 2nd over 2f out: one pce over 1f out* **9/2**[2]
00 **4** *nk* **Overfields**[16] 2844 5-10-13 .... AdamPogson(5) 80
(S R Bowring) *trckd ldrs: effrt over 3f out: one pce* **10/1**
5 *4* **Mrs Higham (IRE)** 4-10-4 .... JohnKington(7) 69
(M Scudamore) *in rr: hdwy 7f out: one pce fnl 3f* **8/1**
-0 **6** *9* **Huron (FR)**[35] 2507 4-11-4 .... JosephByrne 67
(H D Daly) *chsd ldrs: drvn along 5f out: wknd over 2f out* **5/1**[3]
0 **7** *8* **Harpurs Girl**[15] 2864 4-10-11 .... PaulMoloney 52
(J Mackie) *rr div: hdwy 6f out: wknd over 3f out:* **16/1**
8 *2 1/2* **Bleak Friday** 6-10-4 .... ChrisDavies(7) 50
(J G M O'Shea) *sn wl bhd: nvr a factor* **25/1**
0- **9** *19* **Bobble Wonder**[293] 4349 4-10-11 .... JodieMogford 31
(J G M O'Shea) *in rr: hdwy 5f out: sn prom: lost pl 3f out* **28/1**
10 *dist* **Perfectly Posh** 4-10-4 .... DarylJacob(7) —
(J K Cresswell) *bhd and drvn 10f out: t.o 4f out* **18/1**
0- **11** *nk* **Nasstar**[329] 3710 4-11-1 .... MrTGreenall(3) —
(M W Easterby) *in tch: drvn 6f out: lost pl over 4f out: t.o* **8/1**
12 *dist* **Tight Corner (IRE)**[245] 6-11-1 .... JoffretHuet(3) —
(Ian Williams) *t.k.h in mid-div: drvn and floundered 7f out: sn bhd: wl t.o 4f out: virtually p.u* **7/2**[1]
0 **P** **Vincere**[49] 2192 6-11-4 .... RJGreene —
(L R James) *stdd s: bhd: p.u after 5f* **66/1**

4m 25.0s (25.20) **Going Correction** +1.125s/f (Heav) **13** Ran SP% **118.4**
Speed ratings: **96,90,89,88,86 82,78,77,67,— —,—,—** CSF £365.61 TOTE £43.90: £7.70, £4.00, £1.70; EX 1309.30 Place 6 £58.42, Place 5 £49.61.
Owner Ricochet Management Limited **Bred** T A F Neal **Trained** Basford Green, Staffs

FOCUS
As usual a very steady gallop to past halfway. The winner was kept right up to his work and the form looks very ordinary, rated through the fourth.

NOTEBOOK
Suprendre Espere, absent since March, has changed stables and, making all, his rider left nothing to chance. *(op 25-1 tchd 33-1)*
Herons Cove(IRE), who cut no ice in points, showed nothing in a bumper start at Cork in April. Keeping to the inner, he stuck to his task to regain second spot but the winner had flown.
Classic Harry, bred to stay all day, went in pursuit of the winner but in the end tired slightly and missed out on second spot. *(op 5-1)*
Overfields ran perhaps his best race so far on his third start.
Mrs Higham(IRE), fitted with a cross noseband, is out of a mare that won two bumpers and she showed a glimmer of ability.
Huron(FR), who looks a long-term chasing prospect, was in trouble the moment the pace increased and in the end he dropped right away. *(op 4-1)*
Tight Corner(IRE), runner-up in three points, changed hands for just 15,000gns in May. He took a keen grip then seemed to flounder badly in the ground before dropping right away and in the end struggling to complete. *(op 4-1)*
Vincere *Official explanation: jockey said gelding was unsteerable around paddock bend (tchd 50-1)*
T/Plt: £68.90 to a £1 stake. Pool: £58,151.45. 615.95 winning tickets. T/Qpdt: £30.50 to a £1 stake. Pool: £3,804.10. 92.20 winning tickets. WG

2810 WARWICK (L-H)
Saturday, December 31

OFFICIAL GOING: Soft (heavy in places on hurdle course)
The last hurdle in the back straight was omitted after the 1st race because of a patch of false ground.
Wind: Moderate behind Weather: Fine

3146 RACING UK CONDITIONAL JOCKEYS' H'CAP HURDLE (12 hdls) 3m 1f
12:30 (12:30) (Class 4) (0-105,103) 4-Y-O+ **£3,269** (£959; £479; £239)

Form RPR
4/1- **1** **Passenger Omar (IRE)**[599] 296 7-11-2 96............(t) WilliamKennedy(3) 98+
(Noel T Chance) *hld up: hdwy appr 7th: led 2 out: edgd lft nr fin: drvn out* **5/1**[3]
-004 **2** *1/2* **Dundridge Native**[30] 2592 7-10-0 80..................... RobertLucey-Butler(3) 82+
(M Madgwick) *hld up in mid-div: hdwy on ins 5th: outpcd 8th: rallied appr 3 out: mstke 2 out: rdn and ev ch last: r.o* **12/1**
-0P2 **3** *2* **Kingsbay**[16] 2845 6-11-12 103... TomMalone 102
(H Morrison) *a.p: mstke 3rd: led 8th: rdn and hdd 2 out: no ex flat* **11/4**[1]
4005 **4** *15* **Honey's Gift**[15] 2868 6-11-11 102................................ RobertStephens 88+
(G G Margarson) *hld up and bhd: hdwy 8th: wknd 2 out* **11/1**
045- **5** *15* **Dr Mann (IRE)**[443] 1716 7-10-5 82.................................... SamCurling 51
(Miss Tor Sturgis) *led after 1st to 8th: wknd appr 2 out* **15/2**

The Form Book, Raceform Ltd, Compton, RG20 6NL

0-04 **6** ½ **Smeathe's Ridge**[15] 2862 7-10-6 **83** .... GinoCarenza 52
(J A B Old) *hld up in tch: wknd after 3 out* **9/2**[2]

0-54 **7** 21 **Protagonist**[33] 2556 7-11-1 **100** .... TomMessenger[(8)] 48
(B N Pollock) *prom: led after 7th to 8th: rdn 9th: wknd 3 out* **15/2**

0050 **8** 5 **Silver Gift**[88] 1630 8-10-0 **77** .... DerekLaverty 20
(G Fierro) *hld up: hdwy after 4th: lost pl 7th: rdn and rallied appr 8th: wknd 9th* **28/1**

3340 **9** ¾ **Half Inch**[88] 1631 5-11-4 **98** .... ShaneWalsh[(3)] 40
(B I Case) *racd wd: prom tl wknd after 7th* **16/1**

0-0P **U** **Cosi Celeste (FR)**[33] 2552 8-10-13 **93** ....(p) CharliePoste[(3)] —
(John Allen) *hld up in mid-div: mstke and uns rdr 7th* **66/1**

150- **P** **Razzamatazz**[410] 2263 7-10-8 **93** .... JosephStevenson[(8)] —
(R Dickin) *hld up and bhd: hdwy appr 7th: wknd 8th: t.o whn p.u bef 2 out* **40/1**

000/ **P** **Golden Tamesis**[622] 4887 8-9-6 **77** oh11 .... JohnPritchard[(8)] —
(R Dickin) *plld hrd: prom tl lost pl appr 5th: struggling whn mstke 7th: t.o whn p.u bef 8th* **40/1**

6m 33.6s (3.30) **Going Correction** +0.125s/f (Yiel) **12** Ran SP% **116.8**
Speed ratings: **99,98,98,93,88 88,81,80,79,— —,—** CSF £59.84 CT £198.31 TOTE £4.80: £1.50, £4.70, £1.60; EX 95.00.
Owner Mrs V Griffiths **Bred** Matt O'Hara **Trained** Upper Lambourn, Berks

FOCUS
A modest handicap run at a steady pace in some proper winter ground. The third is the best guide to the level.

NOTEBOOK
Passenger Omar(IRE) was off the same mark as when winning over an extra quarter of a mile at Newton Abbot when last seen in May 2004. He should come on for the outing and looks a staying chaser in the making. *(op 13-2 tchd 7-1)*
Dundridge Native fought back well after quite a bad error at the penultimate hurdle and lost nothing in defeat.
Kingsbay, back up in distance, could not overcome a 3lb hike in the ratings on ground that may have been softer than she prefers. *(op 10-3 tchd 7-2)*
Honey's Gift did not get home in these conditions on her first attempt at three miles. *(tchd 12-1)*
Dr Mann(IRE), a winner of an Irish point in soft ground, was having his first run since October last year. *(tchd 8-1)*

3147 2006 ANNUAL MEMBERSHIP NOVICES' H'CAP HURDLE (7 hdls 2 omitted) 2m 3f
1:00 (1:03) (Class 4) (0-90,88) 3-Y-0+ **£2,799** (£815; £408)

Form RPR

0- **1** **Return Home**[42] 2363 6-11-5 **81** .... PaulMoloney 92+
(J S Smith) *hld up in mid-div: smooth hdwy on ins appr 4th: hrd rdn to ld last strides* **15/8**[1]

/000 **2** *hd* **Herecomestanley**[18] 2816 6-11-1 **84** ....[1] CharliePoste[(3)] 94+
(M F Harris) *hld up and bhd: rdn appr 4th: hdwy appr 5th: led appr 2 out: sn rdn: hit last: hdd last strides* **33/1**

6302 **3** 11 **Brigadier Du Bois (FR)**[46] 2257 6-10-13 **85** .... MattyRoe[(10)] 83
(Mrs L Wadham) *hld up in tch: rdn appr 2 out: wknd appr last* **10/1**

F/32 **4** 1¼ **He's A Rascal (IRE)**[18] 2810 7-11-12 **88** ....(p) TomDoyle 85
(A J Lidderdale) *hld up and bhd: hdwy 5th: rdn and wknd appr last* **5/1**[3]

2141 **5** 9 **Romany Dream**[39] 2420 7-11-2 **78** ....(b) RobertThornton 68+
(R Dickin) *a.p: led 5th: rdn and hdd appr 2 out: sn wknd* **9/2**[2]

P/05 **6** 13 **Baron Blitzkrieg**[30] 2592 7-10-12 **74** .... WarrenMarston 49
(D J Wintle) *hld up and bhd: hdwy after 3rd: wknd after 5th* **7/1**

46P **7** ½ **Safe To Blush**[49] 2181 7-10-13 **80** ....(t) TomGreenway[(5)] 54
(P A Pritchard) *hld up in mid-div: rdn and wknd 4th* **12/1**

-060 **8** ½ **Elle Roseador**[30] 2592 6-10-1 **70** .... RobertLucey-Butler[(7)] 44
(M Madgwick) *hld up in tch: wknd appr 4th* **66/1**

0-00 **9** 2½ **Sullivan's Cascade (IRE)**[15] 2858 7-10-6 **75** .... WillieMcCarthy[(7)] 46
(E G Bevan) *hld up in tch: rdn appr 5th: sn wknd* **40/1**

B-3F **10** 3 **Lady Maranzi**[11] 2934 6-11-1 **82** .... RobertStephens[(5)] 50
(Mrs D A Hamer) *hld up and bhd: hdwy after 3rd: wknd after 4th* **20/1**

-600 **11** 14 **Too Posh To Share**[31] 2578 7-10-8 **70** .... JodieMogford 24
(D J Wintle) *led to 4th: rdn and wknd appr 2 out* **28/1**

P000 **P** **Miniperse (FR)**[15] 2860 5-11-5 **84** .... GinoCarenza[(3)] —
(G R I Smyly) *bhd fr 5th: t.o whn p.u bef 2 out* **66/1**

-0UP **P** **Casas (IRE)**[30] 2582 8-10-2 **71** ....(t) MrSFMagee[(7)] —
(J R Norton) *a bhd: rdn and struggling appr 4th: t.o whn p.u bef 2 out* **66/1**

016P **P** **Faraway Echo**[170] 987 4-11-2 **78** .... GrahamLee —
(James Moffatt) *prom: led 4th: hdd and hit 5th: sn wknd: t.o whn p.u bef 2 out* **20/1**

4m 42.1s (-1.90) **Going Correction** +0.125s/f (Yiel)
WFA 4 from 5yo+ 10lb **14** Ran SP% **121.7**
Speed ratings: **109,108,104,103,99 94,94,94,93,91 85,—,—,—** CSF £74.72 CT £517.84 TOTE £2.50: £1.10, £9.60, £3.40; EX 74.90.
Owner Donald Smith **Bred** A Munnis And K Helliwell **Trained** Tirley, Gloucs

FOCUS
They went a reasonable gallop for the conditions in this modest handicap and the winner can rate a bit higher.

NOTEBOOK
Return Home, a recent Irish import, was the subject of an old-fashioned gamble having been available at 12/1 in the morning. He had to work really hard to land the spoils after travelling strongly for most of the race. *(op 11-4)*
Herecomestanley was fitted with a hood despite not being disgraced over two miles here last time. Just touched off after rapping the final flight, he does seem to be on the upgrade. *(op 20-1)*
Brigadier Du Bois(FR), reverting to hurdles, seems to stay this trip on this sort of ground over fences. *(op 8-1 tchd 11-1)*
He's A Rascal(IRE) had gone up 3lb for his good second over course and distance last time. *(op 9-2)*
Romany Dream, 21lb lower than when successful over fences here last month, had never scored *on ground worse than good. Official explanation: jockey said mare was unsuited by soft, heavy in places ground (op 4-1)*

3148 RURAL STRESS INFORMATION NETWORK 10TH ANNIVERSARY BEGINNERS' CHASE (20 fncs) 3m 2f
1:30 (1:30) (Class 4) 4-Y-0+ **£3,942** (£1,157; £578; £289)

Form RPR

2-03 **1** **Basilea Star (IRE)**[247] 90 8-11-6 ....(t) TimmyMurphy 142+
(M C Pipe) *hld up: stdy hdwy 6th: led appr last: idled flat: drvn out* **6/4**[1]

-36P **2** ¾ **Ardaghey (IRE)**[16] 2848 6-11-6 .... CarlLlewellyn 135
(N A Twiston-Davies) *hld up and bhd: hdwy after 13th: hit 15th: led 4 out: rdn and hdd appr last: styd on flat* **4/1**[3]

1 **3** 14 **Super Lord (IRE)**[43] 2327 7-11-6 .... MarkBradburne 125+
(J A B Old) *w ldr: led 5th to 4 out: rdn and wknd appr 2 out* **10/3**[2]

1-F5 **4** *dist* **Rowley Hill**[27] 2660 7-11-6 .... RobertThornton 95
(A King) *prom: blnd 15th: rdn and wknd 4 out* **5/1**

P3/0 **5** *dist* **Patriarch (IRE)**[21] 2764 9-11-6 .... PaulMoloney —
(P Bowen) *hld up in mid-div: sme hdwy 11th: wknd 14th: t.o* **20/1**

P/U- **P** **There Goes Wally**[435] 1799 7-11-3 .... RichardYoung[(3)] —
(A Ennis) *a bhd: t.o whn p.u bef 14th* **66/1**

PP/4 **P** **Toy Boy (IRE)**[30] 2593 7-11-6 80 .... DaveCrosse —
(P W Hiatt) *hld up in tch: rdn and wknd appr 14th: p.u bef 15th* **66/1**

P/-0 **P** **Redhouse Chevalier**[18] 2805 6-11-1 .... JohnLevins[(5)] —
(B G Powell) *led to 5th: rdn appr 9th: sn wknd: t.o whn p.u bef 14th* **66/1**

F600 **P** **Witness Time (IRE)**[32] 2564 9-11-1 .... MarkNicolls[(5)] —
(B J Eckley) *hld up in tch: lost pl 6th: bhd fr 9th: t.o whn p.u bef 14th* **33/1**

6m 53.7s (-10.30) **Going Correction** -0.10s/f (Good) **9** Ran SP% **111.9**
Speed ratings: **103,102,98,—,— —,—,—,—** CSF £7.43 TOTE £2.50: £1.80, £1.70, £1.30; EX 7.50.
Owner D A Johnson **Bred** Bruno Buser **Trained** Nicholashayne, Devon

FOCUS
Quite an interesting contest with a few potentially promising recruits to the novice chasing ranks. The winner is rated value for further with the placed horses to recent marks.

NOTEBOOK
Basilea Star(IRE) made a successful start to his chasing career having progressed into a useful staying hurdler for Ferdy Murphy when completing a four-timer last winter. He seemed set for a clear cut victory until apparently thinking he had done enough on the run-in. *(op 6-5 tchd 11-10)*
Ardaghey(IRE), whose saddle slipped when pulled up last time, really appreciated this stamina test and is capable of going one better in this sort of ground. *(op 5-1 tchd 7-2)*
Super Lord(IRE) was quickly switched to fences having won an Irish point in heavy ground. *(op 11-4 tchd 9-2)*
Rowley Hill was in trouble after making a mess of the final ditch. *(op 15-2)*
There Goes Wally *Official explanation: jockey said gelding lost its action*

3149 JOHN SMITH'S/E.B.F. MARES' ONLY "NATIONAL HUNT" NOVICES' HURDLE (QUALIFIER) (9 hdls 2 omitted) 2m 5f
2:00 (2:02) (Class 3) 4-Y-0+ **£4,876** (£1,431; £715; £357)

Form RPR

111 **1** **Ben's Turn (IRE)**[33] 2558 4-10-10 .... RobertThornton 110+
(A King) *t.k.h: a.p: led on bit appr 2 out: rdn appr last: drvn out* **11/4**[2]

1-3 **2** *nk* **Cash And New (IRE)**[35] 2503 6-10-10 .... WarrenMarston 104
(R T Phillips) *hld up in mid-div: hdwy appr 6th: nt fluent 7th: rdn appr 2 out: ev ch last: r.o* **5/1**

-F62 **3** 19 **Boberelle (IRE)**[15] 2866 5-10-10 .... TomDoyle 89+
(C Tinkler) *chsd ldrs: rdn appr 6th: led 7th: rdn and hdd whn mstke 2 out: wknd appr last* **4/1**[3]

55 **4** 19 **Riffles**[33] 2558 5-10-3 .... ShaneWalsh[(7)] 66
(Mrs A J Bowlby) *hld up in mid-div: wkng whn mstke 5th* **66/1**

50/6 **5** *dist* **Bosworth Gypsy (IRE)**[15] 2865 7-10-3 .... MarcGoldstein[(7)] —
(Miss J S Davis) *nvr nr ldrs* **66/1**

5633 **6** ½ **Lets Get Busy (IRE)**[29] 2605 5-10-7 83 .... RichardYoung[(3)] —
(J W Mullins) *mid-div: j.lft 3rd: mstke 5th: sn struggling* **33/1**

3-1 **7** 6 **Glory Be**[24] 2704 5-11-3 115 .... SamThomas —
(Miss Venetia Williams) *led: hdd and hit 7th: sn wknd* **15/8**[1]

8 7 **Gulshique** 5-10-10 .... CarlLlewellyn —
(N A Twiston-Davies) *j. slowly 1st: sn mid-div: rdn and hdwy appr 6th: wknd 7th* **14/1**

9 12 **Atlantic Jane** 5-10-7 .... TomMalone[(3)] —
(Mrs H Dalton) *a bhd* **40/1**

0-50 **10** 5 **Just Ask**[23] 2718 5-10-10 .... MarkBradburne —
(N R Mitchell) *a bhd* **125/1**

5P **11** 12 **Smilingvalentine (IRE)**[16] 2848 8-10-3 .... RyanCummings[(7)] —
(D J Wintle) *prom: nt fluent 5th: wknd appr 6th* **100/1**

0-00 **12** 15 **Eveon (IRE)**[23] 2718 5-10-5 .... RobertStephens[(5)] —
(Ian Williams) *a bhd* **100/1**

P **Dargin's Lass (IRE)** 4-10-3 .... TomMessenger[(7)] —
(B N Pollock) *a bhd: t.o whn p.u bef 6th* **100/1**

/00- **P** **Top Gale (IRE)**[602] 232 6-10-0 .... JosephStevenson[(10)] —
(R Dickin) *bhd fr 5th: t.o whn p.u bef 6th* **100/1**

0-S0 **P** **Georgie Girl Dove**[245] 138 5-10-10 .... VinceSlattery —
(C J Price) *a bhd: mstke 5th: t.o whn p.u bef 6th* **100/1**

04 **P** **Cresswell Willow (IRE)**[119] 1401 5-10-10 .... GrahamLee —
(W K Goldsworthy) *hld up in tch: wkng whn nt fluent 6th: p.u bef 7th* **66/1**

5m 18.4s (2.30) **Going Correction** +0.125s/f (Yiel)
WFA 4 from 5yo+ 11lb **16** Ran SP% **120.4**
Speed ratings: **100,99,92,85,— —,—,—,—,— —,—,—,—,— —** CSF £16.67 TOTE £5.20: £1.90, £2.30, £1.50; EX 24.70.
Owner C B Brookes **Bred** Miss E Violet Sweeney **Trained** Barbury Castle, Wilts

FOCUS
Quantity rather than quality and the field was soon quite well strung out. The winner is rated value for further and should rate higher.

NOTEBOOK
Ben's Turn(IRE), unbeaten in three ordinary bumpers, showed signs of inexperience after striking the front and did not score anything like as easily as had seemed likely. She will be aimed at the Newbury final of this series in March. *(op 9-4)*
Cash And New(IRE) ◆ appeared to hurdle better this time but could not quite take advantage of the winner's greenness. A similar contest would appear there for the taking. *(op 6-1)*
Boberelle(IRE) had already been headed when missing out at the penultimate flight. This ground could have been on the soft side for her. *(op 6-1)*
Riffles had not shown a lot in a couple of Folkestone bumpers last month including one won by Ben's Turn. *(op 50-1)*

3150 BETFREDPOKER NOVICES' CHASE (12 fncs) 2m
2:30 (2:31) (Class 3) 4-Y-0+ **£7,140** (£2,096; £1,048; £523)

Form RPR

3-11 **1** **Voy Por Ustedes (FR)**[19] 2798 4-11-2 .... RobertThornton 134+
(A King) *hld up: hdwy to ld appr 6th: qcknd after 4 out: shkn up appr last: rdn and r.o wl flat* **5/6**[1]

0-1P **2** 4 **Royal Hector (GER)**[34] 2531 6-11-8 128 .... RichardJohnson 130
(Jonjo O'Neill) *hld up: outpcd after 4 out: rdn appr 2 out: rallied and wnt 2nd last: one pce* **14/1**

00-P **3** 5 **Medison (FR)**[28] 2636 5-11-2 .... TimmyMurphy 121+
(M C Pipe) *led to 2nd: led 4th tl appr 6th: rdn appr 2 out: wknd flat* **6/1**[3]

1-21 **4** 20 **Cornish Sett (IRE)**[36] 2482 6-11-8 137 ....(b) JoeTizzard 105
(P F Nicholls) *led 2nd to 4th: hit 7th: rdn whn mstke 4 out: sn struggling* **9/4**[2]

4m 53.9s
WFA 4 from 5yo+ 10lb **4** Ran SP% **106.3**
CSF £9.11 TOTE £1.70; EX 10.40.

Owner Sir Robert Ogden **Bred** Ecurie Macaire Guillaume, And Francis Picoulet **Trained** Barbury Castle, Wilts

FOCUS

A decent contest but a farcical race with the runners only breaking into a trot 50 seconds after the tape went back. The race is rated around the first two.

NOTEBOOK

Voy Por Ustedes(FR) completed a hat-trick in pretty good style but the value of the form is obviously questionable. He remains on course for a crack at the Arkle. *(op 4-5 tchd 10-11)*

Royal Hector(GER), highly tried last time, did not mind the conditions under foot. He was not suited by the way things worked out on this drop back to the minimum trip. *(op 12-1)*

Medison(FR) did not help his rider in the short home straight on this chasing debut and perhaps better ground will help. *(op 11-2)*

Cornish Sett(IRE) is another who could have found conditions too testing and, given the way the race panned out, this run might be best forgotten. *(op 5-2)*

3151 BETFREDCASINO H'CAP CHASE (18 fncs) 3m 110y

3:00 (3:00) (Class 3) (0-120,110) 5-Y-0+ **£5,530** (£1,623; £811; £405)

Form				RPR
/6-3	1		**King Bee (IRE)**[38] 2445 8-11-8 **106** ... RichardJohnson (H D Daly) *led to 13th: led 2 out: sn rdn and hung rt: styd on* **2/1**[1]	119+
1P-1	2	3	**Datito (IRE)**[28] 2623 10-11-7 **105** ... WarrenMarston (R T Phillips) *hld up: hdwy 8th: rdn and outpcd appr 4 out: rallied 2 out: one pce flat* **7/2**[3]	113+
2FP4	3	24	**Jaoka Du Gord (FR)**[43] 2325 8-11-5 **103** ... TomDoyle (P R Webber) *hld up in rr: hdwy 8th: led 13th: rdn and hdd 2 out: wknd flat: fin tired* **10/3**[2]	90+
1-3U	4	2 ½	**Calcot Flyer**[33] 2557 7-11-0 **98** ... RobertThornton (A King) *hld up: stmbld bdly 3rd: hdwy 8th: mstke 12th: wknd 4 out: j. slowly 3 out* **4/1**	84+
5-PP	P		**Spinofski**[59] 1989 10-11-3 **106** ... MarkNicolls(5) (D R Stoddart) *chsd ldr to 9th: rdn 11th: sn lost tch: t.o whn p.u bef 2 out* **14/1**	—

6m 37.8s (15.50) **Going Correction** -0.10s/f (Good) **5** Ran SP% **105.3**

Speed ratings: **84,83,75,74,—** CSF £8.52 TOTE £2.20: £1.60, £1.80; EX 6.70 Trifecta £24.20 Pool: £255.90 - 7.50 winning tickets.

Owner Trevor Hemmings **Bred** Lawson Burriss **Trained** Stanton Lacy, Shropshire

■ Stewards' Enquiry : Richard Johnson two-day ban: used whip with excessive frequency (Jan 11-12)

FOCUS

A weak affair for its type with the top weight rated 106 but reasonably sound rated around the principals to their marks.

NOTEBOOK

King Bee(IRE) built on the promise of his comeback run at Wetherby. He did not help his rider by hanging after hitting the front and Johnson was handed a two-day ban for excessive use of the whip. *(op 6-4)*

Datito(IRE), raised 8lb for his win at Chepstow confirmed his liking for the mud but he may not have been ideally suited by this sharper course. *(op 5-2)*

Jaoka Du Gord(FR) needs a sounder surface to be at his best over this trip. *(op 4-1)*

Calcot Flyer is another who probably wants better ground. *(op 6-1)*

3152 BETFRED H'CAP HURDLE (7 hdls 1 omitted) 2m

3:35 (3:36) (Class 4) (0-110,105) 4-Y-0+ **£3,350** (£976; £488)

Form				RPR
45-1	1		**The Hairy Lemon**[69] 1856 5-11-8 **101** ... RobertThornton (A King) *a.p: led 2 out: drvn out* **1/1**[1]	114+
360-	2	½	**Make My Hay**[31] 4813 6-10-10 **89** ... (b) RichardJohnson (J Gallagher) *led: rdn and hdd 2 out: kpt on flat* **9/1**	98
-003	3	4	**Speed Venture**[17] 2822 8-10-7 **93** ... (vt) PhilKinsella(7) (J Mackie) *a.p: rdn appr 2 out: one pce* **9/2**[2]	98
500P	4	14	**Reservoir (IRE)**[155] 1099 4-11-5 **105** ... ShaneWalsh(7) (J Joseph) *prom tl rdn and wknd 2 out* **66/1**	96
31-0	5	5	**La Marette**[27] 2659 7-10-13 **97** ... MarkNicolls(5) (John Allen) *hld up: hdwy 3rd: wknd appr 2 out* **14/1**	85+
0406	6	5	**Pearson Glen (IRE)**[17] 2822 6-10-7 **86** ... (p) GrahamLee (James Moffatt) *hld up in tch: wknd appr 2 out* **25/1**	70+
-203	7	2	**Polly Whitefoot**[26] 2680 6-10-9 **88** ... (t) PadgeWhelan (R A Fahey) *hld up: rdn after 5th: sn struggling* **7/1**[3]	67
6400	8	4	**Tiger Frog (USA)**[12] 2925 6-11-8 **101** ... (b) WarrenMarston (J Mackie) *reminders 4th: a bhd* **16/1**	76
P-U3	9	¾	**Presenter (IRE)**[28] 2618 5-10-13 **99** ... MrLRPayter(7) (M Sheppard) *hld up: rdn after 5th: no rspnse* **25/1**	73
F6F0	10	16	**Sunley Future (IRE)**[15] 2867 6-10-12 **98** ... CharliePoste(7) (M F Harris) *hld up in rr: sme hdwy whn nt fluent 3rd: sn bhd* **50/1**	56

3m 57.7s (-0.60) **Going Correction** +0.125s/f (Yiel) **10** Ran SP% **114.4**

WFA 4 from 5yo+ 10lb

Speed ratings: **106,105,103,96,94 91,90,88,88,80** CSF £10.21 CT £29.43 TOTE £1.70: £1.20, £2.50, £1.80; EX 15.60 Trifecta £128.90 Pool: £4,542.23 - 25 winning units. Place 6 £14.16, Place 5 £7.71.

Owner The Hairy Lemon Partnership **Bred** Houston Mill Stud **Trained** Barbury Castle, Wilts

FOCUS

This was arguably the worst and most uncompetitive Scoop 6 bonus race ever, but the form looks solid rated through the third.

NOTEBOOK

The Hairy Lemon defied a 10lb rise in the weights for his win at Towcester in October. He was not the first winner of the meeting who had to work a lot harder than had seemed likely for much of the race despite the fact that he had the stands' rail to help. *(op 5-4)*

Make My Hay, who had three runs on the All-Weather in November, went backwards over hurdles last term after finishing second at Towcester in this sort of ground in February. *(op 10-1 tchd 11-1)*

Speed Venture, with the visor refitted, is proven in this sort of ground. *(op 7-2 tchd 5-1)*

Reservoir(IRE), pulled up when last seen in July, wants a much sounder surface than this. *(op 50-1)*

T/Jkpt: £3,913.30 to a £1 stake. Pool: £46,850.50. 8.50 winning tickets. T/Plt: £51.30 to a £1 stake. Pool: £65,241.85. 927.00 winning tickets. T/Qpdt: £5.70 to a £1 stake. Pool: £3,931.30. 506.60 winning tickets. KH

3153a, 3155a - 3166a (Foreign Racing) - See Raceform Interactive

2790 PUNCHESTOWN (R-H)

Saturday, December 31

OFFICIAL GOING: Soft (soft to heavy in places on hurdle course; heavy in places on chase course)

3154a HAPPY NEW YEAR HURDLE 2m 4f

1:15 (1:17) 4-Y-0+ **£8,408** (£1,826; £805)

			RPR
1		**Hardy Eustace (IRE)**[291] 4383 8-11-12 167 ... CO'Dwyer (D T Hughes, Ire) *led: hdd briefly 7th: edgd 2 l clr 3 out: nt extended: hrd hld* **1/8**[1]	143+
2	1	**Native Upmanship (IRE)**[20] 2793 12-11-4 ... DJCasey (A L T Moore, Ire) *a cl up: 3rd whn slt mstke 5 out: rdn 2 out: 2nd and kpt on wl fr last: no ch w wnr* **8/1**[2]	114
3	4 ½	**Tawrific Laois (IRE)**[4] 3057 5-11-1 114 ... JPSullivan(7) (Seamus Fahey, Ire) *cl up: racd freely: led briefly 7th: 2nd and rdn to chal after 2 out: 3rd and no ex fr last* **33/1**[3]	113

5m 33.7s **3** Ran SP% **102.9**

CSF £1.42 TOTE £1.20; DF 1.60.

Owner Laurence Byrne **Bred** Patrick Joyce **Trained** Osborne Lodge, Co. Kildare

■ The first running of this event, restricted to horses who had not won more than two hurdle races since May 2004.

NOTEBOOK

Hardy Eustace(IRE), making his reappearance and carrying plenty of condition, had an easy task and won on the bridle. He might have been expected to extend his advantage in the straight but remained hard held after the last. The AIG at Leopardstown and then the Red Mills at Gowran will be his pre-Cheltenham agenda again.

Native Upmanship(IRE) showed himself to be in good form and despite his age will be placed to win.

Tawrific Laois(IRE) has only a maiden success to his credit but was not disgraced against two much superior opponents. *(op 25/1)*

2838 CATTERICK (L-H)

Sunday, January 1

OFFICIAL GOING: Good (good to soft in places)

After the snow and frost the ground was described as 'on the soft side, quite tacky'.

Wind: Almost nil Weather: Fine but cold.

3167 PETER PAN NOVICES' HURDLE (DIV I) (9 hdls 1 omitted) 2m 3f

12:15 (12:15) (Class 4) 4-Y-0+ **£2,927** (£859; £429; £214)

Form				RPR
	1		**Zeitgeist (IRE)**[137] 5-11-6 ... GrahamLee (J Howard Johnson) *hld up in rr: hdwy 3rd: shkn up 8th: led at omitted 2 out: hung lft: styd on* **1/3**[1]	96+
4	2	nk	**Panzer (GER)**[22] 2763 5-11-6 ... DominicElsworth (D McCain) *trckd ldrs: led 7th: kpt on wl run-in: no ex towards fin* **9/1**[2]	93+
42U0	3	3 ½	**Step Perfect (USA)**[23] 2750 5-11-6 93 ... FinbarKeniry (G M Moore) *chsd ldr: led 6th to next: 4th whn slipped bnd bef omitted 2 out: hit last: kpt on* **25/1**	89+
1060	4	¾	**Cheery Martyr**[26] 2693 8-10-13 87 ... PhilKinsella(7) (P Needham) *chsd ldrs: outpcd 8th: styd on run-in* **33/1**	87
R-04	5	6	**Ring The Boss (IRE)**[17] 2838 5-11-6 ... RichardMcGrath (K G Reveley) *mid-div: wnt prom 5th: w ldrs appr omitted 2 out: wknd and eased last 150yds* **16/1**	84+
4145	6	3	**Jontys'Lass**[35] 2515 5-10-8 ... ThomasDreaper(5) (A Crook) *led to 5th: wknd 8th* **25/1**	71
1-2F	7	9	**Dancing Partner (USA)**[46] 2262 5-11-3 ... MrTGreenall(3) (M W Easterby) *nt jump wl: in rr: hdwy 7th: lost pl next* **14/1**[3]	69
00	8	2 ½	**Fillameena**[17] 2838 6-10-10 ... AnthonyCoyle(3) (P T Midgley) *in tch: outpcd 7th: wknd next* **50/1**	60
-000	9	dist	**Carpe Momentum (USA)**[14] 2901 7-11-6 ... (t) KennyJohnson (R C Guest) *hld up in rr: racd wd: bhd fr 7th: t.o: btn 41l* **200/1**	—
340	10	hd	**Mae Moss**[14] 2903 5-10-13 ... AlanDempsey (W S Coltherd) *chsd ldrs: drvn 5th: bhd fr 8th: t.o* **200/1**	—
	P		**Etching (USA)**[53] 6-10-13 ... WilsonRenwick (W Storey) *in rr: bhd fr 7th: t.o whn p.u bef last* **66/1**	—
0	P		**Bally Abbie**[85] 1674 5-10-13 ... RussGarritty (P Beaumont) *sn prom: lost pl after 7th: t.o whn p.u bef last* **200/1**	—
5/F	U		**Loaded Gun**[28] 2658 6-10-13 ... LiamBerridge(7) (W Storey) *t.k.h in rr: bhd whn stmbld landing and uns rdr 8th* **100/1**	—

4m 54.0s (3.50) **Going Correction** +0.075s/f (Yiel) **13** Ran SP% **114.1**

Speed ratings: **95,94,93,93,90 89,85,84,—,— —,—,—** CSF £3.14 TOTE £1.40: £1.10, £1.20, £6.90; EX 4.00.

Owner Andrea & Graham Wylie **Bred** Sir Eric Parker **Trained** Billy Row, Co Durham

FOCUS

The winner had to struggle to account for a rival 20lb inferior on the Flat but the four immediately behind the winner ran close to their marks. Second-last fence bypassed.

NOTEBOOK

Zeitgeist(IRE), rated 98 on the level, looked to have been found a golden opportunity but his jumping was not up to scratch. He showed a marked tendency to hang but in the end was persuaded to do just enough. He can surely do a lot better than this. *(op 1-2 tchd 8-15 in places)*

Panzer(GER), rated a stone and a half inferior to the winner on the level, stuck to his guns and gave him a real fright. He deserves to go one better. *(op 7-1)*

Step Perfect(USA), a 50-rated maiden on the Flat, seemed to run out of his skin but his proximity puts a question mark over the overall value of the form. *(op 22-1)*

Cheery Martyr, struggling to get back on the rails, stuck on in determined fashion and will be suited by three miles.

Ring The Boss(IRE) found this tougher and was leg-weary late in the day. *(op 12-1)*

3168 PETER PAN NOVICES' HURDLE (DIV II) (8 hdls 2 omitted) 2m 3f

12:45 (12:45) (Class 4) 4-Y-0+ **£2,927** (£859; £429; £214)

Form				RPR
41	1		**Turnstile**[17] 2838 5-11-13 ... GrahamLee (J Howard Johnson) *trckd ldrs: led after omitted 3 out: clr last: coasted home* **2/5**[1]	122+

50- **2** *5* **That's Rhythm (FR)**^{295} [4323] 6-11-1 ThomasDreaper$^{(5)}$ 100+
(M Todhunter) *nt fluent: hld up: hdwy 7th: styd on to go 2nd last: no ch w wnr* **25/1**

066 **3** *5* **Tiger King (GER)**^{29} [2638] 5-11-6 WilsonRenwick 96+
(P Monteith) *sn trcking ldrs: wnt 2nd appr omitted 2 out: wknd last* **25/1**

34-5 **4** *14* **Caulkleys Bank**^{6} [2967] 6-11-3 MrTGreenall$^{(3)}$ 81
(M W Easterby) *trckd ldrs: rdn and wknd appr omitted 2 out* **17/2**^{2}

0-4 **5** *1* **Big Bertha**^{35} [2515] 8-10-13 NeilMulholland 73
(M D Hammond) *sn trcking ldrs: rdn and wknd appr omitted 2 out* **12/1**^{3}

5146 **6** *4* **Rising Tempest**^{40} [2414] 5-10-13 DominicElsworth 69
(Mrs S J Smith) *sn trcking ldrs: led appr 6th: hdd after omitted 3 out: sn lost pl* **12/1**^{3}

7 *19* **The Wizard Mul**^{74} 6-11-1 BrianHughes$^{(5)}$ 57
(W Storey) *hld up in rr: hdwy 7th: rdn and lost pl bef omitted 2 out* **50/1**

00 **8** *6* **Barney (IRE)**^{56} [2062] 5-11-3 GaryBerridge$^{(3)}$ 51
(Mrs E Slack) *hld up in rr: sme hdwy 7th: sn wknd* **100/1**

60 **9** *2 1/2* **Dolans Bay (IRE)**^{26} [2690] 5-11-6 FinbarKeniry 49
(G M Moore) *nt jump wl in rr: bhd fr 7th* **80/1**

00 **10** *14* **Field Spark**^{13} [2923] 6-11-3 (p) LeeVickers$^{(3)}$ 35
(J G Given) *mstkes: led blnd 5th: hdd appr next: lost pl after 7th: sn bhd* **66/1**

0-00 **11** *1 1/2* **Rosina Copper**^{218} [549] 6-10-13 AnthonyRoss 26
(P Beaumont) *chsd ldrs: lost pl appr 6th: sn bhd* **100/1**

4m 50.2s (-0.30) **Going Correction** +0.075s/f (Yiel)
WFA 4 from 5yo+ 11lb **11** Ran SP% **111.7**
Speed ratings: **103,100,98,92,92 90,82,80,79,73 72** CSF £15.54 TOTE £1.50: £1.02, £4.40, £6.10; EX 17.30.
Owner Andrea & Graham Wylie **Bred** The Queen **Trained** Billy Row, Co Durham

FOCUS
Much the quicker of the two divisions and the progressive winner had plenty to spare, rated value for 15 lengths.

NOTEBOOK
Turnstile made this look relatively simple and, simply coasting home, was value at least double the *official margin. He does not want the ground too soft and is now ready for a step up in grade. (op 4-9)*
That's Rhythm(FR), absent since March after a couple of efforts in bumpers, benefited from a patient ride and stayed on to finish clear second best in the end. The experience will have done him a power of good. *(op 33-1)*
Tiger King(GER), a winner twice on the Flat in Germany, ran easily his best race over hurdles so far. *(op 28-1)*
Caulkleys Bank, making a quick return to action after a lengthy break, ran out of petrol completely once in line for home. *(op 7-1)*
Big Bertha, having just her second start over hurdles, may do better on much quicker ground. *(op 14-1)*
Rising Tempest, having just his second start over hurdles, took his bumper at Hexham on quick ground. *(op 11-1)*

3169 CINDERELLA (S) H'CAP HURDLE (10 hdls) 2m 3f
1:20 (1:20) (Class 5) (0-90,86) 4-Y-O+ **£2,740** (£798; £399)

Form RPR

5000 **1** **Uncle John**^{23} [2750] 5-11-1 **82** (v) PhilKinsella$^{(7)}$ 91+
(M E Sowersby) *chsd ldrs: wnt 2nd appr 2 out: led last: styd on* **11/2**^{2}

0-65 **2** *3 1/2* **Armentieres**^{17} [2843] 5-11-2 **86** (v) StevenGagan$^{(10)}$ 92+
(Mrs E Slack) *w ldrs: led 4th: hit 2 out: hdd last: no ex* **8/1**^{3}

P40 **3** *12* **Moyne Pleasure (IRE)**^{28} [2652] 8-11-5 **79** KennyJohnson 72
(R Johnson) *stdd s: hld up in rr: hdwy 7th: styd on fr 2 out: tk modest 3rd sn after last* **10/1**

5-66 **4** *2 1/2* **Power And Demand**^{216} [592] 9-10-7 **72** DougieCostello$^{(5)}$ 63
(C W Thornton) *hld up towards rr: stdy hdwy 3 out: one pce fr next* **16/1**

/060 **5** *10* **Colway Ritz**^{28} [2657] 12-11-0 **74** (p) GrahamLee 55
(W Storey) *in tch: smooth hdwa to chse ldrs 7th: wknd appr 2 out* **17/2**

0030 **6** *1* **Silver Dagger**^{28} [2657] 8-10-9 **69** (vt) FinbarKeniry 49
(J C Haynes) *chsd ldrs: reminders 5th: lost pl appr 2 out* **25/1**

6060 **7** *3 1/2* **Tiger Talk**^{6} [2962] 10-11-0 **84** (p) JonathanMoorman$^{(10)}$ 60
(R C Guest) *chsd ldrs: wknd appr 2 out* **12/1**

FP02 **8** *3 1/2* **Another Misk**^{23} [2752] 4-10-10 **86** PeterBuchanan$^{(3)}$ 46
(M E Sowersby) *mid-div: sme hdwy 7th: nvr on terms* **14/1**

0645 **9** *2 1/2* **Phase Eight Girl**^{47} [2256] 10-10-4 **67** PaddyAspell$^{(3)}$ 37
(J Hetherton) *chsd ldrs: hrd drvn 5th: sn lost pl: t.o 3 out* **9/1**

-P06 **10** *1/2* **Purr**^{31} [2582] 5-10-3 **70** MrSRees$^{(7)}$ 40
(M Wigham) *bhd fr 5th* **40/1**

P-43 **11** *22* **Flemming (USA)**^{31} [2586] 9-10-12 **72** AlanO'Keeffe 20
(I A Brown) *in rr: drvn 6th: nvr on terms* **9/2**^{1}

500U **12** *14* **Europrime Games**^{6} [2967] 8-10-7 **72** (b) ThomasDreaper$^{(5)}$ 6
(M E Sowersby) *led to 4th: wknd qckly appr 2 out* **40/1**

0/00 **13** *10* **Kicking Bear (IRE)**^{26} [2690] 8-10-2 **69** GarethThomas$^{(7)}$ —
(J K Hunter) *bhd fr 6th: t.o 3 out* **33/1**

/03- **14** *dist* **Milan King (IRE)**^{513} [1128] 13-10-9 **74** BrianHughes$^{(5)}$ —
(A J Lockwood) *in rr: bhd fr 7th: t.o next: virtually p.u: btn 35l* **33/1**

4206 **R** **Bargain Hunt (IRE)**^{26} [2693] 5-11-5 **86** LiamBerridge$^{(7)}$ —
(W Storey) *prom: lost pl: rn out and uns rdr 7th* **11/1**

4m 52.8s (2.30) **Going Correction** +0.075s/f (Yiel)
WFA 4 from 5yo+ 11lb **15** Ran SP% **117.5**
Speed ratings: **98,96,91,90,86 85,84,82,81,81 72,66,62,—,—** CSF £45.37 CT £428.32 TOTE £6.80: £2.60, £2.20, £4.30; EX 45.00.There was no bid for the winner.
Owner R D Seldon **Bred** Aramstone Stud **Trained** Goodmanham, E Yorks

FOCUS
A routine seller, the first two clear and they came home well strung out. The third sets the level for the form.

NOTEBOOK
Uncle John, back in the right grade, went in pursuit of the leader and thoroughly appreciating the extra trip, ran out a decisive winner in the end. *(op 6-1 tchd 13-2)*
Armentieres went on and soon had them strung out but in the end he had to settle for second spot. *(tchd 9-1)*
Moyne Pleasure(IRE), dropped in at the start, came from a different parish despite some *indifferent jumping to take a remote third spot on the run-in.Official explanation: jockey said, regarding the running and riding, his orders were to settle gelding as it has a tendency to be keen, and creep into the race and win if possible, adding that gelding failed to jump fluently and merely stayed on at one pace (op 9-1)*
Power And Demand , back after a break, as usual travelled strongly but when asked a question he was found very much wanting.
Colway Ritz moved up on the bridle, but when asked a question the old boy soon decided this was too much of struggle. *(op 7-1)*
Flemming(USA) likes soft ground but he ran no race at all and was struggling soon after halfway. *Official explanation: jockey said gelding was unsuited by good, good to soft in places ground (op 4-1 tchd 5-1)*

3170 DICK WHITTINGTON BEGINNERS' CHASE (19 fncs) 3m 1f 110y
1:50 (1:51) (Class 4) 5-Y-O+ **£3,903** (£1,146; £573; £286)

Form RPR

6455 **1** **Rambling Minster**^{23} [2747] 8-11-5 RichardMcGrath 110+
(K G Reveley) *hld up: stdy hdwy to trck ldrs 15th: led 2 out: drvn rt out* **4/5**^{1}

3F1/ **2** *1 1/2* **Tufty Hopper**^{1015} [4340] 9-11-0 105 ThomasDreaper$^{(5)}$ 104+
(Ferdy Murphy) *j.lft in rr: hdwy and prom 11th: 3rd whn stmbld 3 out: lft 2nd next: kpt on wl run-in* **12/1**

1-1P **3** *6* **Bellaney Jewel (IRE)**^{45} [2291] 7-10-12 GrahamLee 89
(J J Quinn) *chsd ldrs: outpcd appr 3 out: styd on run-in* **8/1**^{3}

U-64 **4** *6* **Barrons Pike**^{26} [2689] 7-11-0 (p) MichaelMcAlister$^{(5)}$ 92+
(B Storey) *mde most: j.rt: hdd 4 out: outpcd fr next* **40/1**

25 **5** *23* **Wee William**^{51} [2168] 6-11-2 PeterBuchanan$^{(3)}$ 67
(T D Walford) *prom: hit 15th: wknd next* **25/1**

0/4P **6** *7* **Been Here Before**^{6} [2976] 6-10-12 PhilKinsella$^{(7)}$ 60
(G A Harker) *in tch: pushed along 11th: bhd fr 14th* **33/1**

2-4U **7** *dist* **Do Keep Up**^{10} [2945] 9-11-0 73 DougieCostello$^{(5)}$ —
(J R Weymes) *hld up in rr: hmpd 4th: prom 11th: lost pl 15th: sn bhd: t.o: btn 40l* **50/1**

-PFP **F** **Missoudun (FR)**^{6} [2978] 6-10-12 81 (b^{1}) PatrickMcDonald$^{(7)}$ —
(J R Weymes) *t.k.h: w ldrs: fell 4th* **80/1**

0P40 **U** **Pottsy's Joy**^{17} [2840] 9-11-5 79 PadgeWhelan —
(Mrs S J Smith) *hld up towards rr: blnd and uns rdr 2nd* **25/1**

222F **F** **Rare Society (IRE)**^{5} [3037] 8-11-5 105 DominicElsworth 110+
(Mrs S J Smith) *trckd ldrs: blnd 12th: led 4 out: hdd and fell 2 out* **7/2**^{2}

P/P- **P** **Just Jed**^{288} 7-11-5 WilsonRenwick —
(R Shiels) *t.k.h: wnt prom 11th: wkng whn blnd 14th: sn bhd: t.o whn p.u bef 3 out* **80/1**

6m 44.0s (-4.40) **Going Correction** -0.10s/f (Good) **11** Ran SP% **114.1**
Speed ratings: **102,101,99,97,90 88,—,—,—,— —** CSF £10.39 TOTE £1.70: £1.40, £2.40, £2.30; EX 16.80.
Owner The Lingdale Optimists **Bred** J K M Oliver **Trained** Lingdale, Redcar & Cleveland

FOCUS
An eventful contest with the winner making a satisfactory chasing bow. Rare Society is rated as dead-heating with the winner, the proximity of the fourth is something of a worry.

NOTEBOOK
Rambling Minster, a 130-rated hurdler, jumped rather carefully but once in front he seemed to run very lazily and had to be kept up to the task in hand. He is a real stayer and can only climb the chasing ladder. *(op 5-6 tchd 10-11 and 8-11)*
Tufty Hopper, having his first outing for 1015 days, tended to jump left-handed. He lost ground three out but stuck to his guns on the run-in, without ever looking likely to overhaul the winner. Hopefully he will come back after this none the worse. *(op 10-1)*
Bellaney Jewel(IRE), a winning pointer, was let down by her jumping and pulled up on her first try over fences. This was a lot more encouraging and she can do even better. *(op 7-1 tchd 9-1)*
Barrons Pike, in first-time cheekpieces, took them along at a sound gallop but he continually jumped right. One more outing will see him qualified for novices' handicap chases.
Wee William, a winning pointer, is struggling to make any impression under Rules. *(op 18-1 tchd 16-1)*
Rare Society(IRE), making a quick return, went on and was still upsides when he took an unlucky looking fall two out. He richly deserves a change of luck. *(op 9-2)*

3171 ALADDIN H'CAP HURDLE (8 hdls) 2m
2:20 (2:21) (Class 3) (0-120,116) 4-Y-O+ **£5,204** (£1,528; £764; £381)

Form RPR

1P-2 **1** **Motive (FR)**^{14} [2904] 5-11-12 **116** GrahamLee 124+
(J Howard Johnson) *hld up: smooth hdwy 5th: 2nd and j.lft 2 out: upsides last: hung lft and kpt on to ld last 75yds* **2/1**^{1}

1-2U **2** *1 1/4* **Andre Chenier (IRE)**^{65} [1912] 5-11-1 **115** DavidDaSilva$^{(10)}$ 118
(P Monteith) *trckd ldrs: led on bit appr 2 out: hdd and no ex run-in* **9/2**^{2}

4655 **3** *3* **Red Man (IRE)**^{6} [2977] 9-10-4 **104** (p) StevenGagan$^{(10)}$ 105+
(Mrs E Slack) *led: hdd and 3rd whn hit 2 out: kpt on same pce* **8/1**

4-21 **4** *3 1/2* **Farne Isle**^{192} [647] 7-11-8 **112** (p) AlanDempsey 110+
(G A Harker) *trckd ldrs: chal appr 2 out: kpt on same pce* **7/1**^{3}

1040 **5** *7* **Cumbrian Knight (IRE)**^{23} [1412] 8-11-2 **111** ThomasDreaper$^{(5)}$ 101
(J M Jefferson) *a in tch: effrt appr 2 out: sn outpcd* **16/1**

600 **6** *1* **Royal Glen (IRE)**^{14} [2904] 8-10-4 **94** RichardMcGrath 83
(W S Coltherd) *stdd s: hld up in rr: effrt 3 out: no imp and eased fr next* **25/1**

4000 **7** *1 3/4* **Lord Baskerville**^{6} [2991] 5-10-3 **93** NeilMulholland 80
(W Storey) *hld up in rr: hdwy and prom 5th: lost pl appr 2 out* **40/1**

-240 **8** *4* **Coming Again (IRE)**^{47} [2261] 5-10-8 **98** (bt^{1}) DominicElsworth 81
(D McCain) *chsd ldrs: lost pl appr 2 out* **20/1**

130 **9** *5* **Diamond Cutter (NZ)**^{189} [841] 7-10-12 **107** BrianHughes$^{(5)}$ 85
(R C Guest) *stdd s: hld up in rr: hdwy 3 out: sn rdn and btn* **16/1**

5P41 **10** *7* **Eborarry (IRE)**^{26} [2693] 4-10-6 **108** FinbarKeniry 67
(T D Easterby) *t.k.h: sn trcking ldrs: lost pl after 5th: sn in rr* **9/1**

521- **11** *8* **Cha Cha Cha Dancer**^{421} [2035] 6-10-3 **98** DougieCostello$^{(5)}$ 61
(G A Swinbank) *chsd ldrs: drvn 4th: lost pl after 3 out: sn bhd* **9/1**

3m 55.7s (-0.60) **Going Correction** +0.075s/f (Yiel)
WFA 4 from 5yo+ 11lb **11** Ran SP% **117.9**
Speed ratings: **104,103,101,100,96 96,95,93,90,87 83** CSF £11.45 CT £59.99 TOTE £3.20: £1.50, £1.30, £2.80; EX 12.90.
Owner Andrea & Graham Wylie **Bred** Darley Stud Management **Trained** Billy Row, Co Durham

FOCUS
A competitive handicap hurdle. The winner tested Graham Lee's patience, the third and fourth are possibly the keys to the form.

NOTEBOOK
Motive(FR)has plenty of ability but is not entirely straightfoward. Lee had to earn his fee but, a horse with a good engine, he can hold his own in stronger handicaps than this, especially on better ground. *(op 9-4 tchd 5-2 in a place)*
Andre Chenier(IRE) ◆ travelled strongly and looked the likelier winner when taking it up on the *bridle but in the end he had to settle for second spot. He richly deserves to go one better. (tchd 5-1 and 4-1 in a place)*
Red Man(IRE), wikth the cheekpieces back on, took them along at a strong pace and deserves credit for the way he kept going all the way to the line. *(op 10-1)*
Farne Isle, 8lb higher than her last win at Perth in June, was having her first outing since then. *(op 8-1)*
Cumbrian Knight(IRE) was having his first run over hurdles for over a year but in the meantime has taken two chases and a Flat race three weeks ago. *(op 11-1)*
Royal Glen(IRE) needs much better ground and she was certainly not over-punished. *Official explanation: jockey said mare was unsuited by good, good to soft in places ground (op 22-1)*
Eborarry(IRE) *Official explanation: trainer was unable to offer any explanation for poor form shown (op 8-1)*

3172 GO RACING AT WETHERBY THIS THURSDAY H'CAP CHASE (15 fncs) 2m 3f

2:55 (2:55) (Class 3) (0-120,115) 5-Y-0+ **£6,506** (£1,910; £955; £477)

Form RPR

6-23 **1** **Good Outlook (IRE)**[17] [2842] 7-10-10 **99** DominicElsworth 108+
(R C Guest) *trckd ldr: led 4th: styd on u.p run-in: hld on towards fin* **6/1**[3]

-611 **2** ½ **Welcome To Unos**[24] [2714] 9-11-6 **109** RichardMcGrath 116
(K G Reveley) *trckd ldrs: wnt 2nd 2 out: styd on run-in: no ex towards fin* **7/2**[1]

-134 **3** 1¼ **Cyborg De Sou (FR)**[29] [2626] 8-11-4 **107** AlanDempsey 113
(G A Harker) *hld up: smooth hdwy 10th: chsng ldrs 3 out: kpt on same pce run-in* **16/1**

-536 **4** 9 **Argento**[23] [2754] 9-11-7 **110** FinbarKeniry 108+
(G M Moore) *chsd ldrs: wknd appr last* **12/1**

6651 **5** 8 **Kids Inheritance (IRE)**[27] [2679] 8-11-5 **113** ThomasDreaper(5) 104+
(J M Jefferson) *led to 4th: chsd ldrs: wknd appr 2 out* **8/1**

6-63 **6** ¾ **Sound Of Cheers**[13] [2926] 9-11-5 **108** (t) KennyJohnson 96
(F Kirby) *prom: outpcd 11th: n.d after* **9/2**[2]

/54- **7** 1¾ **Pillaging Pict**[256] [4927] 11-11-1 **111** BenOrde-Powlett(7) 98
(J B Walton) *in rr: hdwy to chse ldrs 8th: wknd appr 3 out* **16/1**

-60P **8** 3½ **Alam (USA)**[36] [2498] 7-11-12 **115** WilsonRenwick 98
(P Monteith) *in tch: hit 5th: outpcd 11th: sn lost pl* **20/1**

6061 **F** **Scarrabus (IRE)**[101] [1521] 5-10-3 **105** PaddyAspell(3) —
(A Crook) *in rr whn hit 8th: bhd whn fell 11th* **25/1**

U413 **F** **Fiery Peace**[37] [2478] 9-11-6 **112** MrTGreenall(3) —
(C Grant) *keen: blnd and rdr lost iron 2nd: fell next* **16/1**

0/ **P** **Native Heights (IRE)**[246] [144] 8-10-9 **98** GrahamLee —
(M Todhunter) *in tch: reminders 7th: bhd fr 9th: t.o whn p.u bef 3 out* **9/2**[2]

4m 49.6s (-4.00) **Going Correction** -0.10s/f (Good)
WFA 5 from 7yo+ 8lb **11** Ran SP% **117.9**
Speed ratings: **104,103,103,99,96 95,95,93,—,—** — CSF £28.32 CT £324.54 TOTE £5.70: £2.50, £3.00, £3.40; EX 20.10.

Owner Gerald Tyrrell and John Tyrrell **Bred** Kenneth William Quinn **Trained** Brancepeth, Co Durham

FOCUS

A strongly-run race with the first three clear in the end. The first three are rated to their marks but the winner has been rated higher in the past and there could be better to come if his problems are behind him.

NOTEBOOK

Good Outlook(IRE) went on travelling strongly and well held together, in the end did just enough. He was rated higher in the past and hopefully his problems are behind him now. *(op 7-1 tchd 15-2)*

Welcome To Unos, having just his fifth start over fences, came into this on the back of two hurdle-race wins. He tended to spend a little too much time in the air but sticking to the task in hand, in the end was just denied. This will have sharpened him up. *(op 4-1 tchd 9-2 in a place)*

Cyborg De Sou(FR) came there travelling strongly but in the end had to settle for third spot. He seems to need everything to fall just right to get his head in front. *(tchd 14-1)*

Argento, who has not tasted success for over two years, seems to find this trip the very limit of his stamina. *(op 10-1 tchd 14-1)*

Kids Inheritance(IRE), 4lb higher, seems better over two miles.

Sound Of Cheers for some reason or other did not shine on the day. *(tchd 4-1)*

3173 JACK & THE BEANSTALK NOVICES' HURDLE (12 hdls) 3m 1f 110y

3:30 (3:30) (Class 4) 5-Y-0+ **£3,253** (£955; £477; £238)

Form RPR

31P1 **1** **Nine De Sivola (FR)**[29] [2638] 5-11-3 **122** PatrickMcDonald(7) 125+
(Ferdy Murphy) *in tch: wnt prom 8th: wnt 2nd 2 out: chalng whn lft clr last: styd on strly* **7/4**[2]

-6P6 **2** 9 **Cash King (IRE)**[13] [2923] 6-10-12 DominicElsworth 104
(Mrs S J Smith) *trckd ldrs: chal appr 2 out: one pce whn lft clr 2nd last* **12/1**

1302 **3** 17 **Brave Rebellion**[32] [2571] 7-10-12 RichardMcGrath 94+
(K G Reveley) *t.k.h: nt fluent: trckd ldrs: effrt appr 2 out: wknd and eased whn blnd and lft mod 3rd last* **9/2**[3]

-00P **4** dist **Commemoration Day (IRE)**[6] [2967] 5-10-9 **80** (v) PeterBuchanan(3) —
(M E Sowersby) *chsd ldrs: outpcd 9th: sn bhd: t.o: btn 57l* **150/1**

0P-0 **5** 8 **Team Resdev (IRE)**[40] [2414] 6-9-12 PhilKinsella(7) —
(F P Murtagh) *in rr: bhd fr 8th: t.o 3 out* **200/1**

P **Chisel**[190] 5-10-5 MrSRees(7) —
(M Wigham) *bhd fr 5th: t.o whn p.u after 7th* **100/1**

06P- **P** **Kituhwa (USA)**[575] [637] 6-10-12 WilsonRenwick —
(R Shiels) *led to 7th: sn bhd: t.o whn p.u after 3 out* **200/1**

0-P **P** **Lade Braes (IRE)**[51] [2169] 5-10-12 AlanDempsey —
(J Howard Johnson) *in rr: bhd and reminders 6th: t.o whn p.u after next* **125/1**

2F **F** **Unexplored (IRE)**[38] [2450] 6-10-12 GrahamLee 111
(J Howard Johnson) *wnt prom 5th: led 7th: qcknd 9th: jnd and rdn whn fell heavily last* **6/5**[1]

P **P** **Abbotsford (IRE)**[29] [2638] 6-10-7 BrianHughes(5) —
(J Howard Johnson) *chsd ldrs: lost pl after 7th: t.o 3 out: hopelessly detached whn p.u bef last* **100/1**

6m 32.1s (0.40) **Going Correction** +0.075s/f (Yiel) **10** Ran SP% **112.1**
Speed ratings: **102,99,94,—,— —,—,—,—,—** CSF £19.79 TOTE £3.20: £1.10, £2.50, £1.50; EX 13.00 Place 6 £10.71, Place 5 £9.50.

Owner The DPRP Sivola Partnership **Bred** G Trapenard **Trained** West Witton, N Yorks

FOCUS

A fair contest in which the winner is on the up and has been rated a two lengths winner from the last-flight faller Unexplored.

NOTEBOOK

Nine De Sivola(FR) went in pursuit of the leaders and the suspicion was that he was just starting *to get the better of the argument when presnted with the prize at the last. He is progressing nicely. (op 2-1 tchd 5-2)*

Cash King(IRE), who did not go without market support, looked a big danger going to two out but in the end was handed second spot. *(op 20-1)*

Brave Rebellion, too keen for his own good, does not respect his hurdles and with no more to give his rider accepted things going to the last. *(op 7-2 tchd 5-1)*

Unexplored(IRE) went on and pressed for home but he had been joined at the last and looked booked for second spot when for the second time running he crashed out, taking a heavy fall. His luck must surely change. *(tchd 11-10 and 5-4, 11-8 in places)*

T/Plt: £27.60 to a £1 stake. Pool: £29,861.85. 788.65 winning tickets. T/Qpdt: £19.20 to a £1 stake. Pool: £2,366.30. 91.10 winning tickets. WG

[2756] CHELTENHAM (L-H)

Sunday, January 1

OFFICIAL GOING: Good to soft (good in places)

Wind: Slight, behind

3174 STANJAMESUK.COM CHALLOW NOVICES' HURDLE GRADE 1 (12 hdls) 2m 4f 110y

11:55 (11:55) (Class 1) 5-Y-0+

£22,808 (£8,556; £4,284; £2,136; £1,072; £536)

Form RPR

11 **1** **Denman (IRE)**[45] [2301] 6-11-7 RWalsh 157+
(P F Nicholls) *disp ld tl def advantage 2 out: pushed clr wl bef last: easily* **5/2**[1]

-211 **2** 21 **The Cool Guy (IRE)**[29] [2631] 6-11-7 CarlLlewellyn 135+
(N A Twiston-Davies) *slt advantage although pressed by wnr tl mstke and hdd 2 out: sn no ch: j.lft and mstke last: jst hld on for 2nd* **7/2**[3]

111 **3** ¾ **Boychuk (IRE)**[51] [2161] 5-11-7 RichardJohnson 131
(P J Hobbs) *hld up in tch: rdn appr 2 out: styd on u.p to cl on 2nd run-in but nvr any ch w wnr* **3/1**[2]

112 **4** ¾ **Ungaro (FR)**[36] [2497] 7-11-7 128 JimCrowley 132+
(K G Reveley) *hld up rr but in tch: rdn after 3 out: kpt on u.p after 2 out to cl on 2nd and 3rd run-in but nvr any ch w wnr* **14/1**

1-11 **5** 5 **Its A Dream (IRE)**[30] [2617] 6-11-7 MickFitzgerald 126
(N J Henderson) *chsd ldrs: rdn and outpcd after 3 out: styd on again u.p fr next and kpt on run-in but nvr a danger* **7/2**[3]

3/11 **6** ½ **Ask The Gatherer (IRE)**[40] [2421] 8-11-7 118 TimmyMurphy 126+
(M Pitman) *mstke 3rd: in tch: rdn 3 out: outpcd next: styd on u.p fr 2 out but n.d* **20/1**

6202 **7** 17 **Double Dizzy**[20] [2799] 5-11-7 106 RobertThornton 109+
(R H Buckler) *in tch: rdn after 3 out: wknd next* **150/1**

-510 **8** 24 **Biscar Two (IRE)**[5] [3023] 5-11-7 125 (b) ChristianWilliams 84
(B J Llewellyn) *mstke 3rd: bhd tl lost tch fr 6th* **80/1**

4m 59.5s **8** Ran SP% **111.3**
CSF £11.14 TOTE £4.00: £1.60, £1.80, £1.10; EX 16.50.

Owner Paul K Barber & Mrs M Findlay **Bred** Colman O'Flynn **Trained** Ditcheat, Somerset

■ This Grade One was transferred from the abandoned meeting at Newbury.

FOCUS

A high-class renewal of this Grade One run at a good gallop, being 2.4secs faster than the later conditions hurdle, and a runaway winner. The form looks rock-solid with the runner-up, fourth and seventh to their marks, and it looks sure to work out.

NOTEBOOK

Denman(IRE), an unbeaten former point winner who thrashed the useful Karanja at Wincanton last time, was well fancied on this step into graded company and, always travelling well, asserted at the bottom of the hill and won impressively despite wandering going to the final flight. He is going to take a deal of beating on this evidence and was unsurprisingly made favourite for the Royal and SunAlliance Hurdle at the Festival after this, but will not run if the ground is fast. He looks an exciting prospect for chasing next season. *(op 11-4 tchd 3-1)*

The Cool Guy(IRE), winner of both his previous hurdle races, tried to dictate the pace but was given no peace by the winner and did not help his chances by making several mistakes in the second half of the race. He held on for second and can win a graded event if he can jump more accurately.

Boychuk(IRE), winner of all his three previous hurdles including a Grade Two here, was stepping up in trip but got left behind running down the hill and could not pick up from the turn. He may be better back at the minimum trip for now. *(op 11-4 tchd 100-30 in places)*

Ungaro(FR), who has been progressive this season, was taking a big step up in grade and ran as well as could have been expected. He can win more races in slightly lesser company.

Its A Dream(IRE), a dual bumper winner who scored on ordinary company on his hurdling debut, was well backed but appeared to find the step up in grade too much at this stage of his career. He is another who should win more races at a lower level and a return to shorter trips will not be an inconvenience. *(tchd 3-1)*

Ask The Gatherer(IRE), who has done well since his return from a long absence, was held up off the pace but gives the impression that he will be suited by a step up to three miles and may have been better off ridden close to the pace.

3175 HIGH SHERIFF OF GLOUCESTERSHIRE'S "CRIME BEAT" "NATIONAL HUNT" NOVICES' H'CAP HURDLE (8 hdls) 2m 1f

12:25 (12:28) (Class 3) (0-120,118) 4-Y-0+

£10,333 (£3,052; £1,526; £763; £381; £191)

Form RPR

-216 **1** shd **Pirate Flagship (FR)**[18] [2829] 7-11-9 **115** RWalsh 124+
(P F Nicholls) *in tch: rdn and hdwy fr 2 out: swtchd rt after last: str chal whn hmpd fnl 100yds: rallied: jst failed: fin 2nd, shd: awrdd* **7/1**[3]

4-33 **2** **Armariver (FR)**[42] [2374] 6-11-2 **108** ChristianWilliams 116
(P F Nicholls) *chsd ldrs: wnt 2nd appr 2 out: led wl bef last: hung rt whn chal fnl 100yds: jst hld on fin 1st: disq: plcd 2nd* **20/1**

/321 **3** 3½ **Green Iceni**[29] [2632] 7-11-4 **110** MickFitzgerald 114
(N J Henderson) *prom: hit 3rd: hrd drvn fr 2 out: styd on run-in but nvr gng pce to rch ldrs* **5/1**[2]

0-32 **4** 3 **Good Citizen (IRE)**[23] [2742] 6-11-6 **112** JasonMaguire 114+
(T R George) *chsd ldrs: rdn 2 out: styd on same pce appr last* **5/1**[2]

1U-1 **5** 3 **The Mick Weston**[38] [2460] 7-11-12 **118** RichardJohnson 116+
(R T Phillips) *hld up in rr: hdwy appr 2 out: hrd drvn sn after: kpt on but nvr gng pce to rch ldrs* **3/1**[1]

-521 **6** 3 **Dearson (IRE)**[26] [2683] 5-11-6 **112** NoelFehily 107
(C J Mann) *chsd ldr 2nd: slt ld 4th: rdn appr 2 out: hdd wl bef last: sn btn* **20/1**

7 ½ **Spiritual Society (IRE)**[45] [2303] 6-10-10 **109** JohnKington(7) 104
(M Scudamore) *plld hrd: hld up in rr: hdwy appr 2 out: rdn and effrt wl bef last: nvr gng pce to chal and sn wknd* **16/1**

00-4 **8** 1½ **River Indus**[30] [2606] 6-10-3 **95** BenjaminHitchcott 88
(R H Buckler) *chsd ldrs: rdn after 3 out: outpcd next: kpt on u.p again last* **50/1**

-21 **9** ½ **Fleurette**[53] [2127] 6-10-6 **98** TomDoyle 91
(D R Gandolfo) *slt ld to 4th: wknd 2 out* **9/1**

44-5 **10** 11 **High Altitude (IRE)**[66] [1895] 5-11-4 **110** WayneHutchinson 92
(A King) *bhd: rdn after 3 out: n.d* **25/1**

04-0 **11** ½ **Cousin Nicky**[35] [2530] 5-11-1 **112** RobertStephens(5) 93
(P J Hobbs) *chsd ldrs: hit 4 out: sn rdn: one pce fr 2 out* **100/1**

5210 **12** ½ **Theocritus (GER)**[35] [2533] 5-11-1 **107** AndrewThornton 93+
(Nick Williams) *bhd: sme hdwy after 3 out: wknd after next* **33/1**

The Form Book, Raceform Ltd, Compton, RG20 6NL

P0-1 **13** *6* **Mikado Melody (IRE)**[64] 1916 7-11-8 **114**.................... RobertThornton 89
(A King) *bhd most of way* **11/1**
-U00 **14** *29* **Nice Horse (FR)**[18] 2829 5-11-8 **114**................................ TimmyMurphy 60
(M C Pipe) *a bhd: lost tch fr 4 out* **25/1**
6/0- **P** **June's River (IRE)**[432] 1846 13-9-10 **93** oh7 ow1........... DrPPritchard(5) —
(Dr P Pritchard) *sn bhd: t.o whn p.u bef 2 out* **100/1**

4m 13.5s (1.30) **Going Correction** +0.325s/f (Yiel) **15** Ran SP% **119.1**
Speed ratings: **108,109,107,105,104 103,102,102,101,96 96,96,93,79,**— CSF £137.51 CT £767.19 TOTE £9.80: £2.90, £6.40, £2.20; EX 169.00.
Owner Mr & Mrs Mark Woodhouse **Bred** Haras De Preaux **Trained** Ditcheat, Somerset

FOCUS
A solid novice handicap which should produce winners. It has been rated around the third.

NOTEBOOK
Pirate Flagship(FR) was given the prize in the Stewards' room after they decided that Armariver had hampered him sufficiently on the run-in to have cost him the race. Like his stablemate, he was making his handicap debut, and he can find more success providing the ground is not too soft. *(op 6-1)*
Armariver(FR), making his handicap debut having shown promise in his first three starts over timber, was demoted from first place having been considered by the Stewards to have stopped his stablemate Pirate Flagship in his run after jumping the last. The distance by which he 'won' was so short that the Stewards ruled against him, but he finished clear of the rest and can make up for this in the near future.
Green Iceni, 6lb higher than when successful in heavy ground at Sandown last time, was keeping on well at the finish, and this better ground was probably not ideal for him. The race can be rated around his performance, though. *(op 9-2)*
Good Citizen(IRE) did not get home when tried over further last spring, but he has shaped this season as though he will appreciate a return to two and a half miles. *(tchd 11-2 and 6-1 in places)*
The Mick Weston, a smart bumper performer who made a winning debut over hurdles last time, was saddled with top-weight. On Racing Post Ratings he improved 5lb on his Uttoxeter effort, but he was still a bit disappointing as he struggled to get competitive from off the pace. He can do better in time and with more experience. *(op 7-2)*
Dearson(IRE), who won over two and a half miles in soft ground last time, found this too much of a test of speed. *(op 25-1)*
Spiritual Society(IRE), making his debut for his new stable having been successful twice in Ireland in the autumn, looked to have a stiff task at the weights, and failing to settle in the early stages - something he has done in Ireland - did not help his chances. A hold-up horse who tends to pull hard, he has ability but does not look an easy ride. *(op 20-1)*
June's River(IRE) *Official explanation: jockey said gelding was never travelling*

3176 CHELTENHAM RACING LIMITED H'CAP CHASE (22 fncs) 3m 2f 110y
1:00 (1:00) (Class 2) (0-145,143) 5-Y-0+

£16,910 (£4,995; £2,497; £1,250; £623; £313)

Form RPR
12F- **1** **Joaaci (IRE)**[254] 4959 6-11-12 **143**.................................... TimmyMurphy 159+
(M C Pipe) *hld up rr: stl plenty to do whn stdy hdwy after 3 out: chsd wnr appr last: styd on strly to ld run-in: readily* **12/1**
1-P0 **2** *1 ¾* **Lord Of Illusion (IRE)**[36] 2491 9-11-5 **136**....................... JasonMaguire 151+
(T R George) *led: 4l clr 2 out and rdn: hdd and no ex run-in* **8/1**[3]
11/3 **3** *10* **Fork Lightning (IRE)**[23] 2744 10-11-8 **139**.................... RobertThornton 143+
(A King) *in tch: hdwy and hit 13th: chsd ldr appr 2 out but no imp: wknd last* **7/2**[1]
1-10 **4** *½* **Run For Paddy**[36] 2491 10-11-7 **138**....................................... NoelFehily 141
(M Pitman) *hld up in rr: gd hdwy fr 4 out: chsd ldrs after next: kpt on same pce* **8/1**[3]
P **5** *nk* **Holy Joe (FR)**[35] 2532 9-10-11 **128**...................................... SamThomas 131+
(Miss Venetia Williams) *chsd ldrs: wnt 2nd 16th to next: hit 3 out: outpcd next* **25/1**
0014 **6** *13* **Va Vavoom (IRE)**[18] 2817 8-10-6 **123**................................ CarlLlewellyn 115+
(N A Twiston-Davies) *bhd: hit 11th hdwy and hit next: chsd ldr 17th: hit 3 out: wknd bef next* **20/1**
146- **7** *15* **Longshanks**[260] 4861 9-11-2 **133**.................................... JohnMcNamara 107
(K C Bailey) *chsd ldrs: rdn 18th: sn wknd* **12/1**
24-F **P** **Gingerbread House (IRE)**[29] 2644 8-10-7 **124**............ MarkBradburne —
(R T Phillips) *hit 16th: bhd most of way tl t.o and p.u bef 2 out* **33/1**
0-UP **P** **Exit Swinger (FR)**[23] 2744 11-10-10 **127**..................... ChristianWilliams —
(P F Nicholls) *bhd: hdwy 11th: wknd 15th: t.o whn p.u bef 4 out* **66/1**
16-0 **P** **Nil Desperandum (IRE)**[42] 2370 9-11-7 **138**...................(p) TonyDobbin —
(Ms F M Crowley, Ire) *chsd ldrs: reminders 8th: wknd 12th: p.u bef 15th* **16/1**
-631 **P** **Willie John Daly (IRE)**[29] 2637 9-10-13 **130**................ RichardJohnson —
(P J Hobbs) *chsd ldr: hit 3rd and 10th: blnd 13th: mstke next: sn wknd and p.u bef 15th* **8/1**[3]
0PP2 **R** **Tribal Venture (FR)**[22] 2767 8-11-0 **131**...........................(b) KeithMercer 105
(Ferdy Murphy) *chsd ldrs: hit 3rd and 11th: mstke 18th and sn wknd: no ch whn hmpd and ref last* **9/1**
0-02 **U** **Le Duc (FR)**[42] 2370 7-11-7 **138**.. RWalsh 144+
(P F Nicholls) *rr and blnd 7th: last at 11th: blnd bdly 14th (water):hdwy 16th: styng on one pce in 4th whn blnd and uns rdr 2 out* **5/1**[2]

7m 0.70s (3.60) **Going Correction** +0.175s/f (Yiel) **13** Ran SP% **116.5**
Speed ratings: **101,100,97,97,97 93,88,**—,—,— —,—,— CSF £98.82 CT £411.76 TOTE £14.70: £3.60, £2.60, £2.20; EX 175.10.
Owner D A Johnson **Bred** John Mangan **Trained** Nicholashayne, Devon

FOCUS
Solid handicap form and a potentially top-class winner in the lightly-raced Joaaci.

NOTEBOOK
Joaaci(IRE) ♦, who had four starts under Rules last season, all in the space of three and a half weeks in the spring, shot what had looked a favourable handicap mark to bits when running My Will to a short-head at Perth, but he showed here that he is potentially top class, jumping well to defy a mark of 143 off top weight. He has a number of options in the next few weeks, the best of which could be the Red Square Vodka Gold Cup at Haydock, and he should be kept on side wherever he appears. *(op 14-1)*
Lord Of Illusion(IRE), who was a 12-length winner of this race last year off a mark of 126, was 10lb higher this time around. He did nothing wrong in defeat, putting behind him a fairly disappointing effort in the Hennessy, and was unlucky to run into an unexposed, well-handicapped rival who could be anything. He finished well clear of the rest and, granted a sound surface, can win off this sort of mark. *(op 7-1)*
Fork Lightning(IRE), third behind Royal Auclair here on his reappearance, has been rated by Racing Post Ratings as having done marginally better this time, but there was not the sizeable improvement expected by some on the back of his seasonal return. His next outing should help clarify whether the Handicapper has his measure or not. *(tchd 4-1 in places)*
Run For Paddy rarely runs a bad race but the Handicapper seems to know where he is with him, and he gets no respite as a result.
Holy Joe(FR) showed the sort of form he could have achieved on his British debut at Newbury had he not made a bad blunder which forced his rider to pull him up that time.
Va Vavoom(IRE) did not get home on this step up in trip.
Le Duc(FR) was staying on in fourth when giving his rider no chance at the second last. A difficult horse to win with anyway, he continues to look held by the Handicapper at present. *(op 9-2)*

3177 STEEL PLATE AND SECTIONS HURDLE (12 hdls) 2m 4f 110y
1:35 (1:36) (Class 2) 4-Y-0+

£13,152 (£3,885; £1,942; £972; £485; £243)

Form RPR
00-3 **1** **The French Furze (IRE)**[36] 2500 12-11-4 144.................. BrianHarding 151
(N G Richards) *mde all: 16l clr 2nd: 12l clr 4 out: 9l ahd 2 out: rdn appr last: hld on gamely cl home* **12/1**
1-01 **2** *¾* **Mighty Man (FR)**[22] 2758 6-11-12 149.......................... RichardJohnson 159+
(H D Daly) *in tch: hdwy to chse 9l ldr and ultimate wnr after 3 out: stl 9l down 2 out: edgd lft and r.o gamely run-in: nt quite rch w* **7/4**[1]
25-U **3** *8* **Dancing Bay**[23] 2747 9-11-4 145....................................... MickFitzgerald 142
(N J Henderson) *hld up rr but in tch: hdwy fr 5th: disp 9l 2nd 2 out: sn rdn: outpcd appr last* **15/2**
-40P **4** *5* **Westender (FR)**[22] 2761 10-11-8 157............................(b) TimmyMurphy 141
(M C Pipe) *chsd ldrs: rdn and lost position 5th: recovred after next but n.d: wknd after 2 out* **6/1**[3]
0-25 **5** *26* **Howle Hill (IRE)**[49] 2209 6-11-4 139................................ RobertThornton 111
(A King) *prom: chsd clr ldr and ultimate wnr 5th: nt fluent 3 out: sn wknd* **11/2**[2]
41-3 **6** *¾* **Prins Willem (IRE)**[22] 2758 7-11-8 140............................(t) CarlLlewellyn 123+
(J R Fanshawe) *chsd ldrs: rdn and bhd fr 5th: no ch whn bdly hmpd 2 out* **11/2**[2]
-P00 **7** *11* **Marrel**[19] 2813 8-11-4 110...(v) ChristianWilliams 100
(D Burchell) *chsd wnr to 5th: wknd and hit 6th* **200/1**
-4F0 **F** **Sporazene (IRE)**[22] 2761 7-11-4 149... RWalsh 105
(P F Nicholls) *hld up rr: hdwy 3 out: disputing 4th and styng on whn fell 2 out* **8/1**

5m 1.90s **8** Ran SP% **112.5**
CSF £33.41 TOTE £16.50: £2.90, £1.50, £1.60; EX 44.90 Trifecta £474.50 Pool: £1,203.10 - 1.80 winning tickets..
Owner Jim Ennis **Bred** Stonethorn Stud Farms Ltd **Trained** Greystoke, Cumbria

FOCUS
The form of this decent race looks suspect as the winner was ignored in front and is flattered by the bare result.

NOTEBOOK
The French Furze(IRE) is thoroughly exposed but remains a capable performer when allowed an uncontested lead. Soon taking a clear advantage, the other riders made a mistake in allowing him such leeway and, although he got tired in the closing stages, he was never going to get caught. *(tchd 14-1)*
Mighty Man(FR) comes out as the best horse in the race and, given the way the race was run, did well in the circumstances to finish so close. He is still improving. *(op 5-2)*
Dancing Bay, a hold-up performer best seen in a strongly-run race, did not have this contest run to suit. *(op 6-1)*
Westender(FR) made all in this race last year but it was The French Furze who successfully adopted those tactics this time around. *(op 11-2 tchd 7-1)*
Howle Hill(IRE), like most in this race, is a difficult horse to place, and he might have better opportunities on the All-Weather this winter. *(op 5-1)*
Sporazene(IRE), whose confidence cannot have been that high anyway, took another fall, and he looks one to leave alone for the time being. *(tchd 9-1)*

3178 UNICOIN HOMES "DIPPER" NOVICES' CHASE GRADE 2 (17 fncs) 2m 5f
2:10 (2:10) (Class 1) 5-Y-0+

£19,957 (£7,486; £3,748; £1,869; £938; £469)

Form RPR
S-11 **1** **The Listener (IRE)**[16] 2869 7-11-11 .... AndrewThornton 148+
(R H Alner) *chal 4th: led next: slt advantage tl hdd 10th: led 4 out tl after next: led 2 out: drvn and r.o strly run-in* **8/11**[1]
-12F **2** *¾* **Napolitain (FR)**[43] 2344 5-10-8 138........................... ChristianWilliams 129+
(P F Nicholls) *hit 3rd: in tch: chsd ldrs 6th: hit 8th: r.o u.p fr 3 out: chsd wnr last: styd on wl but a jst hld* **20/1**
3-12 **3** *1 ¼* **Star De Mohaison (FR)**[30] 2607 5-10-12 .... MickFitzgerald 132+
(P F Nicholls) *chsd ldrs: hit 12th: outpcd 13th: plenty to do after 3 out: r.o wl u.p fr 2 out: clsng on ldrs nr fin* **4/1**[2]
4-13 **4** *1* **Billyvoddan (IRE)**[23] 2743 7-11-8 .... RichardJohnson 141+
(H D Daly) *led to 5th: styd w ldr: led 10th: hdd 4 out: chal next: led sn after: hdd 2 out: sn one pce* **8/1**[3]
1-31 **5** *11* **Leading Man (IRE)**[29] 2643 6-11-11 132............................ KeithMercer 132
(Ferdy Murphy) *bhd: rdn 11th: some hdwy fr 2 out but nvr in contention* **25/1**
0-F1 **6** *18* **King Killone (IRE)**[36] 2496 6-11-8 125.............................. DavidO'Meara 111
(H P Hogarth) *chsd ldrs to 6th: bhd 8th: lost tch fr 10th* **25/1**
11- **P** **Knowhere (IRE)**[428] 1892 8-11-4 .... CarlLlewellyn —
(N A Twiston-Davies) *a bhd and nt fluent: tailed of 10th: p.u bef 2 out* **8/1**[3]

5m 22.4s (-4.30) **Going Correction** +0.175s/f (Yiel)
WFA 5 from 6yo+ 9lb **7** Ran SP% **112.6**
Speed ratings: **115,114,114,113,109 102,**— CSF £16.91 TOTE £1.70: £1.30, £6.00; EX 16.70.
Owner Old Moss Farm **Bred** Daniel C And Patrick Keating **Trained** Droop, Dorset
■ Stewards' Enquiry : Christian Williams two-day ban: used whip with excessive frequency (Jan 12-13)

FOCUS
They went a fair gallop in this Grade Two and it produced a good finish. The form is solid enough with the third the best guide to the level.

NOTEBOOK
The Listener(IRE) ♦, who stays further, was unable to dominate with Billyvoddan taking him on for the lead, but he showed real determination to fight his way back in front at the second last and then resist the challenges for the Nicholls pair up the hill. His sound jumping, staying power and good attitude make him a leading Royal and SunAlliance Chase fancy, but there are plenty of other good races on the way to the Festival. *(tchd 5-6 and 10-11 in places)*
Napolitain(FR) ♦ bounced back from his early fall last time and, always on the heels of the leaders, picked up from the turn to push the winner all the way to the line. He should not be long in winning again at around this trip. *(tchd 16-1)*
Star De Mohaison(FR), runner-up to today's winner at Exeter last month was 9lb better off an close the gap. Having tracked the leaders until losing his place running down the hill to the third last, but then stayed on well under pressure up the hill. He may be happier on a flatter track and may be best aimed for Aintree rather than the Festival. *(tchd 9-2)*
Billyvoddan(IRE) made a bold bid to stretch his rivals having taken on the winner for the lead but, after kicking clear on the home turn, he could not respond when the winner rallied and he was run out of the places up the hill. This was a decent effort and it may be that good ground suits him better than this sticky going. *(op 17-2)*
Leading Man(IRE) who prefers longer trips and softer ground, was rather taken off his feet in the early stages and could never get competitive. He is likely to do better when conditions are more in his favour. *(op 33-1)*
King Killone(IRE) was out of his depth in this company and was left behind in the second half of the race.

Knowhere(IRE) was set a stiff task on his chasing debut following a 14 month absence, and was *struggling from an early stage.* *Official explanation: jockey said gelding was distressed (op 9-1 tchd 15-2)*

3179 INTERCASINO.CO.UK H'CAP HURDLE (12 hdls) 3m
2:45 (2:45) (Class 2) 4-Y-0+

£16,910 (£4,995; £2,497; £1,250; £623; £313)

Form				RPR
0-01 **1**		**Attorney General (IRE)**[23] 2747 7-11-12 **139** .... JasonMaguire	151+
	(J A B Old) *hld up in rr: pushed along 3 out: hdwy to trck ldrs next: led wl bef last and sn clr: easily* **15/2**

0-01 **1** **Attorney General (IRE)**[23] 2747 7-11-12 **139** .... JasonMaguire 151+
(J A B Old) *hld up in rr: pushed along 3 out: hdwy to trck ldrs next: led wl bef last and sn clr: easily* **15/2**

P-P0 **2** *10* **Stormez (FR)**[23] 2747 9-11-8 **135** ....(t) TimmyMurphy 135+
(M C Pipe) *bhd: pushed along 6th: plenty to do and wl in rr 2 out: swtchd lft and hdwy bef last: r.o wl to take 2nd: no ch w wnr* **20/1**

0422 **3** *nk* **Just Beth**[18] 2820 10-10-1 **119** .... DerekLaverty[(5)] 118
(G Fierro) *chsd ldrs: drvn along fr 7th: kpt on wl u.p fr 2 out but no ch w wnr sn after: ct for 2nd run-in* **16/1**

1613 **4** *2 ½* **Lacdoudal (FR)**[22] 2760 7-11-11 **138** .... RichardJohnson 135+
(P J Hobbs) *chsd ldrs: led appr 2 out: heded wl bef last and sn one pce* **11/4**[1]

-63P **5** *shd* **Native Emperor**[5] 3022 10-11-3 **130** .... NoelFehily 126
(Jonjo O'Neill) *in tch: rdn and outpcd 4 out: kpt on u.p fr 2 out: r.o run-in and gng on cl home* **25/1**

1-2F **6** *3* **Il Duce (IRE)**[37] 2483 6-11-10 **137** .... RobertThornton 130
(A King) *hld up rr but in tch: hdwy 3 out: chsd ldrs next: wknd last* **7/2**[2]

1263 **7** *1 ½* **Saltango (GER)**[35] 2530 7-10-2 **115** .... ChristianWilliams 107
(A M Hales) *in tch: hdwy to chse ldrs 3 out: chal next: wknd bef last* **7/1**[3]

0020 **8** *7* **Penny Pictures (IRE)**[6] 2999 7-11-3 **137** .... AndrewGlassonbury[(7)] 122
(M C Pipe) *chsd ldrs: led 8th: hdd appr 2 out: wknd sn after* **25/1**

1/20 **9** *1 ¼* **Tramantano**[29] 2636 7-11-10 **137** .... CarlLlewellyn 121+
(N A Twiston-Davies) *hit 2nd: bhd: hdwy 3 out: chsd ldrs next: sn wknd* **17/2**

2006 **10** *28* **Phar From Frosty (IRE)**[18] 2820 9-10-10 **123** .... AndrewTinkler 78
(C R Egerton) *chsd ldr: led 5th to 7th: wknd after 3 out* **33/1**

-2F6 **11** *2* **Blue Business**[33] 2564 8-11-11 **138** ....(b) MickFitzgerald 91
(P F Nicholls) *chsd ldrs tl mstke and rdn 6th: sn bhd and n.d* **12/1**

50-0 **12** *hd* **Supreme Piper (IRE)**[18] 2820 8-10-2 **122** .... MissCDyson[(7)] 75
(Miss C Dyson) *led to 5th: led 7th to 8th: sn wknd* **100/1**

4-F0 **13** *3 ½* **Visibility (FR)**[29] 2621 7-10-0 **120** ....(p) MrCHughes[(7)] 70
(M C Pipe) *rr: effrt 6th: sn bhd* **66/1**

P6/ **14** *10* **Garde D'Estruval (FR)**[82] 12-10-11 **124** ....(v[1]) RJGreene 64
(M C Pipe) *hit 1st and 7th: bhd most of way* **33/1**

6m 4.20s (5.30) **Going Correction** +0.325s/f (Yiel) **14** Ran SP% **118.1**
Speed ratings: **104,100,100,99,99 98,98,95,95,86 85,85,84,80** CSF £143.68 CT £2323.61 TOTE £8.60: £2.60, £5.40, £3.30; EX 276.90 TRIFECTA Not won..
Owner W E Sturt **Bred** Sheikh Mohammed Bin Rashid Al Maktoum **Trained** Barbury Castle, Wilts

FOCUS
A competitive-looking handicap and quite an impressive performance from the winner, who needs to find around a stone to reach the level of an average World Hurdle winner. The race has been rated around the runner-up.

NOTEBOOK
Attorney General(IRE) ran on strongly up the hill to follow up his course and distance win last month. He still has a stone to find to be considered World Hurdle-winning material, but this trip at this track clearly brings out the best in him - his record now reads 22011 - so further improvement is not out of the question. *(op 7-1 tchd 8-1)*
Stormez(FR), unco-operative as usual for much of the race, consented to run on after the second last and was never nearer than at the finish. He has the ability to win off this sort of mark over hurdles and is fairly favourably rated over fences too, but he is not easy to predict. *(tchd 25-1)*
Just Beth last won a race off a mark of 94 and was running off a rating of 119. Improving without winning, she ran another fine race in defeat.
Lacdoudal(FR), 5lb higher than when successful over timber at Chepstow in October, never runs a bad race and once again he went down fighting. He will have his chance in the Racing Post Chase next month, but it will be a surprise if he well enough handicapped to win it. *(tchd 3-1)*
Native Emperor ran a shocker in the Welsh National but showed much better form here back over timber only five days later. He is not easy to predict but he is well handicapped on his best hurdling form and might be able to find a race if building on this. *(op 28-1 tchd 33-1)*
Il Duce(IRE), beaten when falling last time out, again failed to get home. He will be of far more interest when he drops back to a trip around two and a half miles.
Saltango(GER) will be seen to better effect on a sharper track. *(op 8-1)*
Penny Pictures(IRE) remains in the grip of the Handicapper.
Tramantano did not get home on this step up to three miles. *(op 9-1 tchd 10-1)*

3180 UNICOIN HOMES CHASE H'CAP (LISTED RACE) (11 fncs 6 omitted) 2m 5f
3:20 (3:21) (Class 1) 5-Y-0+

£22,808 (£8,556; £4,284; £2,136; £1,072; £536)

Form RPR

P-4B **1** **Fondmort (FR)**[22] 2760 10-11-12 **152** .... MickFitzgerald 165+
(N J Henderson) *trckd ldrs: nt fluent 4th: led next: drvn and styd on strly fr bypassed 2nd last* **10/3**[1]

5-01 **2** *¾* **Too Forward (IRE)**[35] 2532 10-10-9 **135** .... TimmyMurphy 146
(M Pitman) *hit 2nd: bhd: hdwy 6th: chsd wnr appr bypassed 2nd last: swtchd lft and kpt on wl fnl f: no ex nr fin* **17/2**

-325 **3** *2* **Made In Japan (JPN)**[22] 2757 6-10-12 **138** .... RichardJohnson 147
(P J Hobbs) *in tch: hdwy 6th: one pce 3 out: kpt on again after bypassed 2nd last: kpt on cl home* **9/1**

2F06 **4** *1 ¾* **Redemption**[42] 2760 11-10-8 **134** .... CarlLlewellyn 145+
(N A Twiston-Davies) *rr: mstke 4th and 7th: hdwy and blnd 3 out: hdwy appr bypassed 2nd last: kpt on but no imp fnl 100yds* **8/1**[3]

PFP- **5** *14* **Limerick Boy (GER)**[254] 4961 8-11-3 **143** .... SamThomas 137+
(Miss Venetia Williams) *in tch: hdwy 6th: wknd after bypassed 2nd last* **16/1**

-442 **6** *6* **Le Passing (FR)**[22] 2760 7-11-6 **146** ....(b) ChristianWilliams 134
(P F Nicholls) *hit 1st: chsd ldrs: wnt 2nd 7th: rdn 3 out: wknd appr bypassed 2nd last* **13/2**[2]

P2/6 **7** *3* **Iris Royal (FR)**[43] 2346 10-10-13 **139** .... AndrewTinkler 125+
(N J Henderson) *chsd ldrs: rdn 4 out: wknd and mstke last* **12/1**

2-3P **8** *¾* **Kandjar D'Allier (FR)**[36] 2491 8-10-11 **137** .... RobertThornton 122+
(A King) *hit 1st: sn in tch: blnd and wknd 3 out* **13/2**[2]

0-50 **9** *¾* **Whereareyounow (IRE)**[42] 2368 9-10-0 **126** oh2 .... AntonyEvans 110+
(N A Twiston-Davies) *led tl after 3rd: wknd and blnd 3 out* **14/1**

2-45 **10** *20* **See You Sometime**[30] 2615 11-11-2 **142** .... AndrewThornton 105
(J W Mullins) *led after 3rd to 5th: hit 6th: wknd next* **33/1**

15-1 **11** *8* **Noisetine (FR)**[29] 2622 8-10-6 **137** .... PaulO'Neill[(5)] 92
(Miss Venetia Williams) *prom early: bhd fr 6th* **20/1**

5-05 **12** *7* **Alexanderthegreat (IRE)**[28] 2656 8-10-0 **126** oh2 .... KeithMercer 74
(Ferdy Murphy) *wl bhd fr 7th* **33/1**

-260 **P** **Quazar (IRE)**[22] 2760 8-11-0 **140** .... NoelFehily —
(Jonjo O'Neill) *bhd tl p.u bef 8th* **40/1**

5m 13.9s (-12.80) **Going Correction** +0.175s/f (Yiel) **13** Ran SP% **114.7**
Speed ratings: **113,112,111,111,105 103,102,102,101,94 91,88,—** CSF £29.45 CT £232.32 TOTE £3.50: £1.70, £2.80, £2.90; EX 30.60 Trifecta £289.20 Pool: £2,322.00 - 5.70 winning tickets..
Owner W J Brown **Bred** Hubert Carion **Trained** Upper Lambourn, Berks

FOCUS
A good handicap but the low sun resulted in all the fences in the home straight being omitted, four on the first circuit and two on the second. This had a significant effect on the final time, which was 8.5 seconds quicker than The Listener took earlier in the afternoon. In order to be able to allocate speed figures for this race, an estimated time has been calculated as though all 17 fences had been jumped.

NOTEBOOK
Fondmort(FR), brought down at the third last when looking a potential winner in the Robin Cook, gained compensation. Going better than anything running down the hill, he held on well up the long run-in, once again showing his liking for the track. He looks sure to be a major player again in the Ryanair Chase at the Festival. Before that, though, he is likely to take in the Ladbroke Trophy Handicap Chase here towards the end of the month. *(op 3-1)*
Too Forward(IRE), 8lb higher for his Newbury success, ran a personal-best in second, staying on well up the hill. An improving sort, he looks sure to be winning again soon, and the Mildmay Of Flete looks the obvious Festival target. *(op 8-1 tchd 9-1)*
Made In Japan(JPN), without the blinkers he had worn on his last five starts, somewhat surprisingly got this longer trip well, although the bypassing of six of the intended 15 fences may have helped in that regard. *(tchd 10-1)*
Redemption could only benefit from the bypassing of six of the intended 15 fences given his record around here but he still hit a few. It was, however, no surprise to see him record his best placing of the season so far over fences. *(tchd 17-2)*
Limerick Boy(GER) made a promising return to action, going well until lack of race fitness found him out. If he improves for the run he could be dangerous off his current mark. *(op 20-1)*
Le Passing(FR), raised 5lb in the handicap for his second place in the Robin Cook, ideally wants *the ground softer than this, but the Handicapper looks to have his measure anyway. (op 7-1 tchd 15-2)*
Iris Royal(FR) again dropped out tamely, and it remains to be seen whether he retains the ability that saw him win the Tripleprint Gold Cup and finish runner-up in the Cathcart in the 2003-04 season.
Kandjar D'Allier(FR) should have had a serious chance on the form of his third in the Paddy Power Gold Cup off a 2lb lower mark, but he was disappointing. The bypassing of six of the fences *probably did not help, and he might need proper soft ground to be seen at his best. (op 5-1 tchd 7-1 in places)*
Whereareyounow(IRE), back down to his last winning mark, was not left alone in front as he would have liked. *(op 16-1)*

3181 EBF CHELTENHAM AND THREE COUNTIES CLUB "JUNIOR" STANDARD OPEN NH FLAT RACE (LISTED RACE) 1m 4f
3:50 (3:52) (Class 1) 4-Y-0

£9,819 (£3,676; £1,836; £917)

Form RPR

31 **1** **Burnt Oak (UAE)**[35] 2521 4-11-2 .... MickFitzgerald 115+
(C W Fairhurst) *hld up in rr: hdwy 3f out: str run to ld appr fnl f: drvn clr* **4/1**[1]

1 **2** *7* **Belita**[40] 2425 4-10-9 .... JamieGoldstein 95
(Miss Sheena West) *chsd ldrs: slt advantage 4f out: rdn over 2f out: hdd appr fnl f: styd on: nt pce of wnr* **13/2**

2 **3** *¾* **Modicum (USA)**[56] 2068 4-10-5 .... MissRDavidson[(7)] 97
(N G Richards) *in tch: chsd ldrs 3f out: r.o u.p fr over 1f out: nvr gng pce to trble wnr* **5/1**[3]

4 *1 ½* **Dark Corner** 4-10-12 .... CarlLlewellyn 95+
(N A Twiston-Davies) *chsd ldrs: rdn 3f out: one pce fr over 1f out* **7/1**

6 **5** *½* **Golden Streak (IRE)**[29] 2642 4-10-12 .... AndrewTinkler 94
(C R Egerton) *mid-div: drvn along 1/2-way: kpt on fr over 1f out: styd on cl home* **10/1**

2 **6** *nk* **Tooting (IRE)**[35] 2520 4-10-12 .... RobertThornton 94
(J Nicol) *in tch: chsd ldrs 1/2-way: one pce fnl 2f* **14/1**

11 **7** *½* **Sword Of Damascus (IRE)**[59] 2014 4-11-0 .... StephenCraine[(5)] 100
(D McCain) *chsd ldrs: chal fr 4f out tl 2f out: wknd fnl f* **12/1**

0 **8** *1 ¾* **Dr Flight**[13] 2927 4-10-12 .... JimCrowley 91
(H Morrison) *chsd ldrs: outpcd and drvn 1/2-way: kpt on again fnl f: fin wl* **20/1**

1 **9** *½* **Dand Nee (USA)**[13] 2927 4-10-9 .... TonyDobbin 87
(G A Swinbank) *chsd ldrs: rdn over 3f out: one pce fnl 2f* **9/2**[2]

10 *6* **Entrelechambre** 4-10-5 .... MrDavidTurner[(7)] 82
(A J Chamberlain) *chsd ldrs: rdn 5f out: wknd over 2f out* **100/1**

11 *12* **A Sea Commander (GER)** 4-10-9 .... RichardYoung[(3)] 65
(J W Mullins) *bhd: sme hdwy fnl 2f* **33/1**

35 **12** *2* **Themanfromfraam**[30] 2611 4-10-12 .... RichardJohnson 62
(Mrs S M Johnson) *narrow advantage tl hdd 4f out: sn wknd* **25/1**

55 **13** *3* **Ballinger Venture**[35] 2520 4-10-2 ....(b[1]) TJPhelan[(3)] 51
(N M Babbage) *bhd: mod late prog* **50/1**

14 *5* **Hakumatata** 4-10-12 .... AndrewThornton 51
(Miss Z C Davison) *a in rr* **50/1**

5 **15** *22* **Lansdowne Princess**[59] 2014 4-10-5 .... RJGreene 13
(G A Ham) *chsd ldrs to 1/2-way* **66/1**

0 **16** *30* **Bora Shaamit (IRE)**[29] 2642 4-9-12 .... JohnKington[(7)] —
(M Scudamore) *chsd ldrs to 1/2-way* **100/1**

2m 46.6s **16** Ran SP% **123.1**
CSF £28.38 TOTE £4.90: £2.20, £2.70, £2.30; EX 37.80 Place 6 £179.93, Place 5 £132.69.
Owner Glasgow House Racing Syndicate **Bred** Darley **Trained** Middleham, N Yorks

FOCUS
A decent bumper run at a fair pace and a race which should produce a few winners. Burnt Oak has been rated value for a ten-length success.

NOTEBOOK
Burnt Oak(UAE) came from off the pace and ran on strongly up the hill for an impressive victory. He looks a decent juvenile on this evidence and will deserve to take his chance in the Champion Bumper here at the Festival, although on a word of caution, his age group has a poor record in the race, Dato Star being the last four-year-old to win in 1995. *(op 7-2)*
Belita, a winner over a mile six on her debut, ran well under her penalty and brought home the chasing pack. She should pay her way when sent over hurdles. *(op 7-1)*
Modicum(USA) had Burnt Oak behind him on his debut and was better off at the weights this time, but he was unable to confirm the places. A bigger type than the winner, he has the scope to improve when faced with a flight of hurdles. *(tchd 9-2)*
Dark Corner, whose dam is a half-sister to useful two and a half mile hurdler Arkley Royal and staying hurdler/chaser Buck's Palace, is bred to improve with time and distance when he goes over obstacles. *(op 14-1)*
Golden Streak(IRE), disappointing on his debut, ran a better race on this sounder surface, staying on well up the hill. *(op 8-1)*

Tooting(IRE) had run a fair race in a division of a bumper at Doncaster on his debut, but the other division, won by Burnt Oak, was run in a faster time, and the impression that that race was the stronger of the two was upheld here.
Sword Of Damascus(IRE) had plenty on his plate giving weight all round in this stronger contest, and it proved too much for him. *(tchd 11-1)*
T/Jkpt: Not won. T/Plt: £131.50 to a £1 stake. Pool: £103,476.90. 574.35 winning tickets. T/Qpdt: £32.10 to a £1 stake. Pool: £8,800.00. 202.80 winning tickets. ST

2797 PLUMPTON (L-H)

Sunday, January 1

OFFICIAL GOING: Soft (heavy in places)
Wind: Light, half-behind

3182 SKY BET PRESS RED TO BET NOW JUVENILE NOVICES' HURDLE (9 hdls) 2m

12:20 (12:20) (Class 4) 4-Y-0 **£2,927** (£859; £429; £214)

Form RPR
132 **1** **Pace Shot (IRE)**[31] [2597] 4-11-5 115 PaddyBrennan 121+
(G L Moore) *a in tch: wnt 2nd appr 6th: led appr 2 out: r.o wl* **3/1**[2]
2 *2* **Slew Charm (FR)**[57] 4-10-7 WilliamKennedy(5) 110
(Noel T Chance) *racd keenly: hld up: hdwy to go 3rd 3 out: styd on wl to go 2nd last* **16/1**
321 **3** *3 ½* **Take A Mile (IRE)**[10] [2949] 4-11-0 119 JohnLevins(5) 115+
(B G Powell) *hld up in tch: hld whn mstke 2 out: one pce after* **5/2**[1]
1 **4** *2 ½* **Caribou (FR)**[31] [2580] 4-11-5 LeightonAspell 112+
(O Sherwood) *led to 2nd and again 4th tl hdd appr 2 out: rdn and wknd run-in* **5/2**[1]
3 **5** *10* **Sole Agent (IRE)**[48] [2236] 4-10-12 PhilipHide 94
(G L Moore) *trckd ldr: led 2nd to 4th: lost pl 5th: sn bhd* **9/1**[3]
52 **6** *9* **Dance Hall Diva**[20] [2797] 4-9-12 LeeNewnes(7) 78
(M D I Usher) *t.k.h: sn prom: wknd appr 6th* **25/1**
3 **7** *3 ½* **Willy The Slip**[30] [2611] 4-10-5 DarylJacob(7) 85+
(R H Alner) *in tch: 3rd whn blnd bdly 3 out: no ch after* **16/1**
6 **8** *shd* **Isle De Maurice**[26] [2681] 4-10-12 JamesDavies 81
(D B Feek) *prom tl outpcd appr 6th: sn bhd* **33/1**
4545 **9** *6* **Ghaill Force**[10] [2949] 4-10-5 95 (t) RobertLucey-Butler(7) 75
(P Butler) *mstke 5th: a bhd* **40/1**
P0 **10** *21* **Crystal Ka (FR)**[19] [2803] 4-10-12 MatthewBatchelor 54
(M R Hoad) *t.k.h: a bhd* **100/1**
0 **11** *9* **Camerons Future (IRE)**[75] [1785] 4-10-12 JimmyMcCarthy 45
(J A Geake) *a in rr* **25/1**

4m 10.0s (8.80) **Going Correction** +0.45s/f (Soft) **11** Ran SP% **118.0**
Speed ratings: **96,95,93,92,87 82,80,80,77,67 62** CSF £44.16 TOTE £4.00: £2.00, £3.00, £2.00; EX 69.20.
Owner R A Green **Bred** Joe Rogers **Trained** Woodingdean, E Sussex

FOCUS
A reasonable juvenile hurdle by course standards rated through the winner and could go higher.

NOTEBOOK
Pace Shot(IRE) took over on the home turn and was always in control from then on. He looked a tricky ride last time at Wincanton but apart from wandering going into the second last he did nothing wrong, and his trainer believes he is growing up. *(tchd 11-4 and 100-30 in places)*
Slew Charm(FR) showed ability over middle distances on the Flat in France but was tailed off on his debut for this yard on Polytrack last month. He stayed on very well from the second last and should not be long in getting off the mark. *(tchd 14-1)*
Take A Mile(IRE), a smooth winner of a weak race at Fakenham, let the leading pair get away from him in the back straight and could only keep on at the same pace once in line for home. *(tchd 3-1)*
Caribou(FR) could not fight off the eventual winner on the home turn and was run out of the places as he weakened from the final flight. He is a strapping sort and this sharp track did not really suit him. *(op 11-4 tchd 3-1)*
Sole Agent(IRE), the Moore second string, lost his prominent pitch in the back straight but did plug on again in the latter stages.
Dance Hall Diva was a well beaten second in a weak race over course and distance and probably ran to a similar level here.
Willy The Slip, a half-brother to the yard's fair hurdler Diletia, showed ability on this hurdling debut but was soon on the retreat after a bad blunder at the last flight on the far side.

3183 SKY BET PRESS RED TO PLAY ROULETTE NOVICES' CHASE (12 fncs) 2m 1f

12:50 (12:51) (Class 3) 5-Y-0+ **£7,543** (£2,247; £1,137; £583; £305)

Form RPR
3211 **1** **Le Volfoni (FR)**[15] [2872] 5-11-3 JoeTizzard 140+
(P F Nicholls) *trckd ldrs: wnt 2nd 3 out: rdn to ld bef hit 2 out: lft 5l clr last: drvn out* **10/11**[1]
-644 **2** *5* **Sharp Rigging (IRE)**[16] [2861] 6-11-2 JimmyMcCarthy 132
(A M Hales) *hld up in tch: styd on fr 3 out: lft 2nd last: one pce run-in* **13/2**[3]
15-2 **3** *8* **My World (FR)**[20] [2798] 6-10-2 DarylJacob(7) 119+
(R H Alner) *trckd ldr: chal 8th: hit 4 out: wknd sn after* **5/2**[2]
4-2P **4** *13* **Jacks Craic (IRE)**[29] [2622] 7-11-2 117 PaddyBrennan 116+
(J L Spearing) *in tch: wkng whn blnd bdly 3 out* **20/1**
P/4P **5** *19* **Incorporation**[179] [912] 7-10-9 RichardSpate(7) 95+
(M Appleby) *hld up in rr: outpcd appr 7th: sn wl bhd* **100/1**
1-10 **F** **Priors Dale**[16] [2871] 6-11-2 BarryFenton 136
(Miss E C Lavelle) *mde most tl hdd bef mstke 2 out: swtchd rt and rallied gamely: 1l down whn fell last* **8/1**

4m 30.9s (6.80) **Going Correction** +0.45s/f (Soft) **6** Ran SP% **111.2**
Speed ratings: **102,99,95,89,80** — CSF £7.43 TOTE £2.00: £1.70, £2.50; EX 8.90.
Owner Million In Mind Partnership **Bred** I Plessis And Bertrand Plessis **Trained** Ditcheat, Somerset

FOCUS
A decent novice chase with the winner setting the standard.

NOTEBOOK
Le Volfoni(FR), conceding just a pound to his rivals despite having won twice over fences, completed the hat-trick. He had to work to get the measure of Priors Dale but looked just in command when that one fell at the last. This ground was ideal but a more galloping track suits him. *(tchd Evens and 11-10 in places)*
Sharp Rigging(IRE) settled better, but was unable to go with the leaders leaving the back straight and could only stick on at the same pace. He has yet to match his hurdling form in three tries over fences but needs a step back up in trip. *(op 8-1 tchd 6-1)*
My World(FR), close up when clouting the fourth last, was soon in trouble. This was a little disappointing as she had run well behind Voy Por Ustedes on her chasing debut at this track and was in receipt of plenty of weight. *(tchd 11-4)*
Jacks Craic(IRE), back down in trip, was fifth and beginning to feel the pinch when he blundered three from home. *(op 25-1)*
Priors Dale made a bold bid on this chasing debut. Headed at the second last, he was switched and trying to renew his effort when he took a nasty fall at the final fence. He had jumped soundly enough before his fall and can win a novice chase if his confidence has not been too badly affected.

3184 PLAY POKER KENO ON SKY CHANNEL 272 "NATIONAL HUNT" NOVICES' HURDLE (12 hdls) 2m 5f

1:25 (1:25) (Class 3) 4-Y-0+ **£5,204** (£1,528; £764; £381)

Form RPR
0-P3 **1** **Zipalong Lad (IRE)**[36] [2497] 6-11-6 PaddyBrennan 114+
(P Bowen) *a.p: led 3 out: styd on wl* **9/2**[3]
2-11 **2** *8* **What A Vintage (IRE)**[20] [2799] 6-11-5 WarrenMarston 105
(R T Phillips) *hld up: hdwy fr 8th: wnt 2nd 3 out: rdn and no imp fr next* **1/1**[1]
2/2- **3** *9* **New Mischief (IRE)**[406] [2373] 8-11-1 WilliamKennedy(5) 100+
(Noel T Chance) *hld up: hdwy 8th: stmbld on landing 2 out: sn wknd* **4/1**[2]
40 **4** *19* **Hambaphambili**[16] [2865] 6-11-6 (t) LeightonAspell 78
(O Sherwood) *trckd ldr to 3rd: stl prom whn blnd 6th: wknd appr 9th* **28/1**
0-6 **5** *shd* **River Of Light (IRE)**[20] [2799] 6-10-13 DarylJacob(7) 78
(D P Keane) *in tch tl lost pl after 7th* **100/1**
/P-4 **6** *8* **Tuck In**[20] [2799] 9-11-6 (t) PhilipHide 70
(P Winkworth) *sn led: hdd 3 out: wknd qckly* **25/1**
506P **7** *20* **Alderbrook Girl (IRE)**[6] [2985] 6-10-10 87 (p) ColinBolger(3) 43
(R Curtis) *prom tl wknd qckly appr 9th* **80/1**
6- **P** **Fort Royal (IRE)**[543] [902] 7-10-13 MrGPewter(7) —
(G R Pewter) *hld up: wknd appr 6th: t.o whn p.u after 8th* **80/1**
2-F3 **P** **Edgar Wilde (IRE)**[220] [514] 8-11-6 105 BrianCrowley —
(R Rowe) *trckd ldr to 3rd: wknd bef 3 out: t.o whn p.u bef next* **12/1**
4-3P **P** **Cruising Clyde**[36] [2503] 7-11-6 100 DaveCrosse —
(C J Mann) *mid-div: hdwy appr 5th: rdn 8th: sn wknd: t.o whn p.u bef 2 out* **12/1**

5m 30.0s (5.20) **Going Correction** +0.45s/f (Soft) **10** Ran SP% **114.3**
Speed ratings: **108,104,101,94,94 91,83,—,—,—** CSF £9.34 TOTE £4.10: £1.30, £1.10, £1.80; EX 10.30.
Owner A P Davies **Bred** James Larkin **Trained** Little Newcastle, Pembrokes

FOCUS
The testing ground placed the emphasis on stamina, but the first two set the level and the form looks solid.

NOTEBOOK
Zipalong Lad(IRE), who showed improved form on his latest start, was in front three out and kept galloping for a clear-cut victory. There could be more to come and he will stay further. *(op 4-1)*
What A Vintage(IRE), a comfortable winner over course and distance on her hurdling debut, was held under her penalty and appeared to have no obvious excuse. *(op 10-11 tchd 11-10)*
New Mischief(IRE) began his career back in November 2002 but this was only his seventh start, and his first for over a year. He retains his ability, and there should be a small race for him with this outing behind him. *(op 5-1)*
Hambaphambili was tongue tied for this second run over hurdles. This winning Irish pointer was left behind by the leading three in the back straight but shaped as if a return to three miles would suit.
River Of Light(IRE) has been well beaten on each of his three starts.
Tuck In, tried in a tongue tie after reportedly gurgling on his reappearance, made the running but stopped quickly once headed.
Cruising Clyde *Official explanation: jockey said gelding was never travelling (op 10-1 tchd 14-1)*

3185 PLAY ELVIS 5 REEL SLOTS - PRESS RED H'CAP HURDLE (9 hdls) 2m

1:55 (1:56) (Class 4) (0-110,108) 4-Y-0+ **£3,253** (£955; £477; £238)

Form RPR
-413 **1** **Alph**[29] [2632] 9-11-10 106 MatthewBatchelor 116+
(B R Johnson) *hld up in rr: hdwy appr 4 out: led after 3 out: drvn clr fr next* **11/4**[1]
1413 **2** *7* **Polished**[73] [1795] 7-11-5 108 (b) MrJJDoyle(7) 108+
(V R A Dartnall) *trckd ldrs: led briefly after mstke 3 out: rdn and nt pce of wnr fr 2 out* **8/1**
0-33 **3** *1 ¼* **Signature Tune (IRE)**[28] [2659] 7-11-3 99 PhilipHide 97
(P Winkworth) *led tl hdd 4 out: rdn and styd on one pce fr next* **12/1**
-043 **4** *1 ½* **Hail The King (USA)**[26] [2685] 6-11-2 105 RobertLucey-Butler(7) 101
(R M Carson) *hld up: hdwy fr 3 out: nvr nrr* **20/1**
06-3 **5** *1 ¼* **Ellway Prospect**[24] [2726] 6-10-3 85 OllieMcPhail 82+
(M G Rimell) *in tch tl blnd 3 out: styd on again fr next* **5/1**[3]
P025 **6** *1 ½* **Hunting Lodge (IRE)**[17] [2850] 5-10-10 99 MrJAJenkins(7) 93
(H J Manners) *in tch: rdn 3 out: one pce after* **25/1**
0021 **7** *7* **Silistra**[20] [2802] 7-10-9 91 (p) PaddyBrennan 78
(Mrs L C Jewell) *a bhd* **16/1**
6620 **8** *2 ½* **Shaman**[31] [2595] 9-10-12 94 BrianCrowley 79+
(G L Moore) *prom: led briefly appr 3 out: wknd sn after* **25/1**
P002 **9** *2 ½* **Amnesty**[20] [2802] 7-11-1 97 (b) LeightonAspell 79
(G L Moore) *chsd ldr: led 4 out tl bef next: wknd qckly sn after* **12/1**
/PP3 **10** *9* **Carly Bay**[20] [2802] 8-10-9 101 JayPemberton(10) 74
(G P Enright) *mid-div: wknd appr 4 out* **16/1**
14 **11** *4* **Vale De Lobo**[71] [1821] 4-10-4 105 LiamHeard(7) 62
(P F Nicholls) *hld up in tch: wknd appr 3 out* **4/1**[2]
0026 **P** **Bestam**[23] [2750] 7-10-8 90 JodieMogford —
(Mrs A V Roberts) *a bhd: t.o whn p.u bef 2 out: lame* **16/1**

4m 10.2s (9.00) **Going Correction** +0.45s/f (Soft)
WFA 4 from 5yo+ 11lb **12** Ran SP% **119.9**
Speed ratings: **95,91,90,90,89 88,85,84,82,78 76,—** CSF £25.08 CT £227.79 TOTE £3.40: £1.80, £3.20, £2.70; EX 30.50.
Owner Andy Chard Boris Thompson Alan Jackson **Bred** G A And Mrs Antill **Trained** Ashtead, Surrey

FOCUS
A fair race of its type with the winner value for more than the official margin and the second and fourth to their marks.

NOTEBOOK
Alph defied a further 3lb rise with a fluent victory. Built for chasing, he has had a very light career and, despite his relatively advanced age, is very much on the upgrade. *(tchd 5-2)*
Polished, successful over fences last time, ran a sound race on his return to hurdles following a break. He has made big strides since landing a seller off an official mark of 84 back in May. *(op 15-2)*
Signature Tune(IRE), sharper for his recent reappearance, was clear in the early stages but the field soon closed up on him. Headed at the fourth last, he deserves some credit for sticking on for third. He is ready for a step up in trip. *(op 16-1)*
Hail The King(USA), ridden from off the pace as usual, ran well from a 2lb higher mark on ground which is probably not ideal for him. *(tchd 25-1)*
Ellway Prospect dropped back through the field after a blunder three from home but did stay on again in the straight. She has run two decent races since joining this yard and a slightly longer trip could pay dividends. *(op 6-1)*
Hunting Lodge(IRE), not for the first time, was doing his best work when it was all over.

Silistra, 6lb higher for her course win last month, was never within striking distance but did confirm the form with Amnesty and Carly Bay.
Shaman, who gained his sole win over hurdles in the equivalent race two years ago off a 6lb higher mark, showed ahead briefly at the last down the back but was soon in trouble. *(op 20-1)*
Vale De Lobo, without the tongue tie, was taking on established handicappers on only her third start over hurdles. After improving up the inside in the back straight, she dropped away quickly *from the third last. Official explanation: jockey said filly was unsuited by soft, heavy in places going (tchd 9-2)*
Bestam *Official explanation: vet said gelding was lame (tchd 18-1)*

3186 SKY BET SUSSEX NATIONAL (HANDICAP CHASE) (21 fncs) 3m 5f

2:25 (2:25) (Class 3) (0-130,125) 5-Y-0+

£18,789 (£5,550; £2,775; £1,389; £693; £348)

Form				RPR
221F	**1**		**Dunbrody Millar (IRE)**[13] 2922 8-9-13 **101**...... TomMalone(3) *(P Bowen) led 2nd: mde rest: drew clr fr 3 out* **6/1**[2]	121+
2-12	**2**	*10*	**Toulouse-Lautrec (IRE)**[30] 2608 10-11-5 **125**...... WillieMcCarthy(7) *(T R George) trckd wnr 2nd to 11th: wnt 2nd again 3 out: drvn out run-in to hold 2nd pl* **6/1**[2]	132
1-53	**3**	*1 ¼*	**Calvic (IRE)**[24] 2724 8-11-0 **113**...... PaulMoloney *(T R George) hld up: hdwy to go 2nd 5 out: chalng whn blnd next: rdn and one pce fr 2 out* **15/2**	120+
PF-0	**4**	*6*	**Cowboyboots (IRE)**[19] 2813 8-11-5 **125**...... JustinMorgan(7) *(L Wells) dropped rr after blnd bdly 4th: in tch again 7th: 3rd fr 9th: wknd after 3 out* **50/1**	128+
50-6	**5**	*18*	**Levallois (IRE)**[28] 2662 10-10-4 **103**...... PhilipHide *(P Winkworth) prom tl wknd qckly 3 out* **25/1**	88+
-P21	**6**	*23*	**Midnight Gunner**[62] 1960 12-10-6 **105**...... JimmyMcCarthy *(A E Price) led to 2nd: mid-div: lost pl 12th: t.o 5 out* **12/1**	64
P0	**P**		**Lulumar (FR)**[22] 2768 7-11-4 **120**...... (t) OwynNelmes(3) *(O Sherwood) mid-div: bhd whn p.u bef 4 out* **66/1**	—
5341	**P**		**Le Jaguar (FR)**[24] 2724 6-11-3 **123**...... (bt) LiamHeard(7) *(P F Nicholls) hld up in rr: a bhd: t.o whn p.u bef last* **12/1**	—
1P-0	**P**		**Mulligatawny (IRE)**[19] 2808 12-10-7 **106**...... (b[1]) JamesDavies *(N J Gifford) prom tl wknd qckly 12th: p.u bef 14th* **20/1**	—
-142	**P**		**Brave Spirit (FR)**[29] 2637 8-11-10 **123**...... (p) JoeTizzard *(C L Tizzard) nt fluent 3rd: dropped rr 6th: taile off whn p.u bef 13th* **6/1**[2]	—
-116	**P**		**Kausse De Thaix (FR)**[37] 2485 8-11-2 **115**...... LeightonAspell *(O Sherwood) w.w: hdwy 8th: chsd wnr 11th: wkng whn blnd 4 out: sn p.u* **13/2**[3]	—
P630	**P**		**French Executive (IRE)**[23] 2745 11-11-7 **120**...... PaddyBrennan *(P F Nicholls) hld up in rr: mstke 13th: blnd 15th: t.o whn p.u bef 2 out* **9/2**[1]	—

7m 47.6s (-3.50) **Going Correction** +0.45s/f (Soft) **12** Ran SP% **113.6**
Speed ratings: **113,110,109,108,103 96,—,—,—,— —,—** CSF £39.24 CT £272.25 TOTE £8.50: £2.80, £2.40, £2.60; EX 47.00.
Owner Dundon Else Partnership **Bred** Lord Donegall **Trained** Little Newcastle, Pembrokes

FOCUS
A real stamina test for this valuable prize and big step up from the winner with the runner-up and fourth to their marks.

NOTEBOOK
Dunbrody Millar(IRE), going well when falling at Doncaster last time, was able to race off the same mark. Soon in front, he kicked away on the home turn and was never seriously challenged. He is really getting his act together now and this was a fine staying performance. *(op 13-2 tchd 7-1)*
Toulouse-Lautrec(IRE), a winner of the equivalent event on this card a year ago, was 20lb higher. He ran another solid race and has only been out of the first two once in his last ten starts. *(op 9-2)*
Calvic(IRE), a stablemate of the runner-up, had the ground to suit and ran well, but he was held after hitting the fourth from home when the winner jumped across him. *(op 8-1 tchd 17-2)*
Cowboyboots(IRE) had a recent spin over hurdles after 11 months on the sidelines. He did remarkably well to get back into contention after a bad early blunder, from which Morgan made a good recovery, but he was held from the home turn.
Levallois(IRE)was sharper for his recent reappearance but his stamina seemed to give way with three to jump.
Mulligatawny(IRE), in blinkers for the first time, but minus the tongue strap, was prominent until dropping back quickly through the field at halfway. *(tchd 13-2)*
French Executive(IRE) was always at the rear of the field before pulling up, marring a course *record which previously read four wins and a second from six visits. He needs better ground. (tchd 13-2)*
Kausse De Thaix(FR) was a stone higher than when winning at Windsor in November. He moved into second place at halfway, but had begun to weaken when he blundered at the fourth last and was pulled up. He has yet to prove his stamina for marathon trips. *(tchd 13-2)*
Brave Spirit(FR) was never going, and an extremely hard race at Sandown a month ago seemed to have left its mark. *Official explanation: jockey said gelding was never travelling (tchd 13-2)*
Le Jaguar(FR), raised 4lb after his win at Ludlow, was never happy on this slower ground and the *effect of the blinkers appeared to have worn off. Official explanation: jockey said gelding was unsuited by soft, heavy in places going (tchd 13-2)*

3187 YOU'RE EITHER VEGAS OR YOU'RE NOT H'CAP CHASE (14 fncs) 2m 4f

3:00 (3:00) (Class 4) (0-105,99) 5-Y-0+**£3,771** (£1,123; £568; £291; £152)

Form				RPR
0P-P	**1**		**Barton Nic**[29] 2636 13-11-5 **99**...... (b) DarylJacob(7) *(D P Keane) hld up in tch: hdwy to go 3rd 6 out: led 3 out: sn clr: styd on wl* **10/1**	124+
-122	**2**	*15*	**Mystical Star (FR)**[26] 2684 9-11-5 **92**...... LeightonAspell *(M J Hogan) hld up: hdwy 8th: wnt 2nd 2 out: no ch w wnr* **11/8**[1]	99
F412	**3**	*13*	**Rookery Lad**[25] 2705 8-11-12 **99**...... DaveCrosse *(C N Kellett) trckd ldr: led briefly 4th: led 8th tl mstke next: wknd after next* **8/1**	93
P2	**4**	*7*	**Minat Boy**[20] 2801 10-10-0 **73**...... PaddyBrennan *(C L Tizzard) led to 4th: led 9th: hdd whn blnd bdly 4 out: wl hld whn blnd again 2 out* **7/2**[2]	65+
31/P	**5**	*25*	**Inaki (FR)**[16] 2870 9-11-11 **98**...... (b) PhilipHide *(P Winkworth) hld up in tch: mstke 7th: wkng whn blnd 4 out* **11/1**	70+
00-U	**P**		**Banaluso (IRE)**[53] 2126 6-9-13 **79**...... CharlieStudd(7) *(B G Powell) a bhd: t.o whn p.u bef 3 out* **14/1**	—
-020	**P**		**Acertack (IRE)**[18] 2827 9-11-12 **99**...... BrianCrowley *(R Rowe) trckd ldr: led appr 5th: hdd 8th: wknd after next: p.u bef 4 out* **7/1**[3]	—

5m 26.9s (8.45) **Going Correction** +0.45s/f (Soft) **7** Ran SP% **112.0**
Speed ratings: **101,95,89,87,77** —,— CSF £24.51 CT £117.28 TOTE £13.40: £4.90, £1.90; EX 31.20.
Owner Proverbial Optimists **Bred** Barton Stallion Partnership **Trained** North End, Dorset

FOCUS
An ordinary handicap with the winner value for more than the official margin but the overall form is not strong.

NOTEBOOK
Barton Nic is well treated over fences, currently 23lb lower than over hurdles, and was sharper for his recent run over the smaller obstacles. Coming away from the third last for a comfortable success, he is unbeaten in his last four runs at Plumpton, although he did lose the first of those wins after testing positive for morphine. *(tchd 11-1)*
Mystical Star(FR), successful off a 17lb lower mark on his chase debut over course and distance in October, has now found one too good for him on his last three starts with Julies Boy and Jolly Boy, who both beat him at Fontwell, having gone in again since. On this occasion he was outpaced *by the leaders in the back straight but plugged on without threatening the easy winner. (tchd 5-4 and 6-4 in places)*
Rookery Lad ran his race again but this longer trip told from the home turn.
Minat Boy, runner-up over course and distance last time, had just been headed when he left a hole in the fourth last, and he was beaten when somehow getting away with another major error two fences later. *(op 4-1 tchd 9-2)*
Inaki(FR) has gained both his British wins at Plumpton in the month of January, but was out of action for nearly two years after scoring on this card in 2004. He has yet to prove he is as good as he was. *(op 14-1)*
Acertack(IRE) usually runs his best races at Plumpton but failed to fire this time. *(op 11-2)*

3188 SKY BET PRESS RED TO BET NOW STANDARD OPEN NATIONAL HUNT FLAT RACE 2m 2f

3:35 (3:36) (Class 6) 4-6-Y-0 **£1,713** (£499; £249)

Form				RPR
	1		**Safari Adventures (IRE)** 4-10-7...... PhilipHide *(P Winkworth) plld hrd: racd wd and hld up in rr: hdwy to ld over 2f out: kpt up to work: r.o* **10/1**	99+
1	**2**	*2*	**Ice Tea (IRE)**[32] 2579 6-11-5...... LiamHeard(7) *(M G Rimell) in tch: rdn and outpcd 1/2-way: kpt on u.p to chse wnr fnl 2f but hung lft and no imp* **11/8**[1]	113+
22	**3**	*6*	**Bradley Boy (IRE)**[18] 2823 5-10-12...... RobertLucey-Butler(7) *(M Pitman) led tl hdd over 4f out: kpt on one pce after* **3/1**[2]	100
0	**4**	*7*	**Romney Marsh**[34] 2558 5-10-12...... DaveCrosse *(R Curtis) prom: led over 4f out: hdd over 2f out: sn btn* **50/1**	87+
0	**5**	*1 ½*	**Falcon Beneficial (IRE)**[18] 2830 4-9-7...... EamonDehdashti(7) *(G L Moore) trckd ldr tl rdn over 4f out: plugged on one pce after* **4/1**[3]	73
	6	*13*	**That Man Fox** 5-11-5...... AntonyProcter *(Lucinda Featherstone) hld up in tch: wknd over 3f out* **40/1**	79
326	**7**	*10*	**Twist The Facts (IRE)**[34] 2558 6-10-5...... MrNMoore(7) *(N P Littmoden) chsd ldrs tl wknd 4f out* **12/1**	65+
	8	*2 ½*	**Popsleebobross (IRE)** 5-10-12...... LeightonAspell *(P Butler) hld up: lost tch 6f out* **50/1**	59
	9	*10*	**Cool Society** 4-10-0...... DarylJacob(7) *(R H Alner) plld hrd: prom tl wknd over 3f out* **16/1**	44
	10	*dist*	**Montanah Jet** 4-10-2...... TomGreenway(5) *(C N Kellett) chsd ldrs tl wknd 4f out: t.o* **50/1**	—
0	**11**	*dist*	**Spring Chick**[62] 1961 6-10-7...... WilliamKennedy(5) *(A J Whiting) hld up: lost tch 1/2-way: t.o* **66/1**	—

4m 52.3s (27.55) **Going Correction** +0.45s/f (Soft)
WFA 4 from 5yo+ 11lb **11** Ran SP% **119.6**
Speed ratings: **56,55,52,49,48 42,38,37,32,— —** CSF £24.32 TOTE £9.90: £1.60, £1.20, £1.50; EX 34.80 Place 6 £17.50, Place 5 £10.47.
Owner Mrs Tessa Winkworth **Bred** Mrs James Wigan And London Thoroughbred Services L **Trained** Ramsnest Common, Surrey

FOCUS
A pedestrian time, even for a bumper, although the form looks reasonable rated through the runner-up.

NOTEBOOK
Safari Adventures(IRE) ◆ is a half-brother to high-class hurdler Royal Shakespeare. Kept out wide on the best of the ground, he travelled well, if a little keenly, and came away in taking style in the straight. A more truly-run race will see him in an even better light and he could be up to defying a penalty. *(op 14-1)*
Ice Tea(IRE), a course and distance winner on his debut, became outpaced when the pace finally lifted but did stay on for pressure from the home turn, although he hung and never looked like catching the winner. *(op 7-4 tchd 9-4)*
Bradley Boy(IRE) made the frame for the third time in as many starts. A trip of around two and a half miles shoud suit him over hurdles. *(op 5-2)*
Romney Marsh, whose dam was a decent servant to the Curtis yard on the Flat and over hurdles, showed nothing on her debut but this was much more encouraging. She should make the grade in time.
Falcon Beneficial(IRE) showed promise on her debut at Newbury and was well supported over this longer trip, but did not prove good enough. *(op 5-1 tchd 10-3)*
Cool Society, a half-brother to fair hurdler Cool Spice, refused to settle in this slowly-run affair and could be worth another chance. *(op 14-1)*
T/Plt: £13.50 to a £1 stake. Pool: £44,067.90. 2,375.80 winning tickets. T/Qpdt: £6.50 to a £1 stake. Pool: £3,805.90. 432.60 winning tickets. JS

3189 - 3202a (Foreign Racing) - See Raceform Interactive

2942 AYR (L-H)

Monday, January 2

OFFICIAL GOING: Soft (good to soft in places)

The going was described as 'holding'.
Wind: Light, half-behind Weather: Overcast and cold

3203 PHENOMENAL JUVENILE NOVICES' HURDLE (8 hdls 1 omitted) 2m

12:35 (12:36) (Class 4) 4-Y-0 **£2,927** (£859; £429; £214)

Form				RPR
040	**1**		**Calfraz**[24] 2753 4-10-11...... FinbarKeniry *(M D Hammond) in tch: hit 6th: styd on to go 2nd appr last: led last 150yds: kpt on* **100/1**	97+
U31	**2**	*2 ½*	**Lankawi**[40] 2442 4-11-4...... BrianHarding *(Jedd O'Keeffe) w ldr: led 3rd: hit last: sn hdd and no ex* **8/1**[3]	102+
50	**3**	*3*	**Rossin Gold (IRE)**[37] 2494 4-10-1...... DavidDaSilva(10) *(P Monteith) hld up in rr: hdwy 6th: chsng ldrs next: edgd lft and nt qckn run-in* **33/1**	91
	4	*3*	**Clueless**[93] 4-10-11...... TonyDobbin *(N G Richards) mid-div: hdwy 4th: drvn to go 2nd after 6th: one pce between last 2* **2/5**[1]	90+
	5	*2*	**Oscar D'Hyrome (FR)**[54] 4-10-8...... MrTGreenall(3) *(C Grant) in tch: one pce whn hit 2 out* **50/1**	86
4	**6**	*¾*	**Whistle Blowing (IRE)**[24] 2753 4-10-6...... StephenCraine(5) *(D McCain) chsd ldrs: 3rd and rdn whn blnd 2 out: sn wknd* **14/1**	90+
P4	**7**	*3 ½*	**Lerida**[38] 2477 4-10-8...... PeterBuchanan(3) *(Miss Lucinda V Russell) chsd ldrs: swtchd lft to avoid omitted 2 out: wknd appr last* **100/1**	82

	8	19	**William Tell (IRE)**[199] 4-10-11 .... NeilMulholland	72+
			(M D Hammond) *rr-div: sme hdwy whn blnd 5th: n.d after* **33/1**	
0	9	6	**Turtle Bay**[24] 2753 4-10-4 .... RichardMcGrath	50
			(B Storey) *in rr whn blnd 6th* **100/1**	
532	10	10	**Best Game**[11] 2949 4-10-11 107 .... (p) DominicElsworth	47
			(D W Thompson) *t.k.h: led to 3rd: lost pl appr 2 out: sn bhd* **25/1**	
	U		**Mighty Fella** 4-10-8 .... GaryBerridge(3)	—
			(Mrs E Slack) *in rr whn mstke and uns rdr 1st* **100/1**	
	P		**Power Glory**[29] 4-10-11 .... AnthonyRoss	—
			(R A Fahey) *in rr: lost pl 6th: t.o whn p.u bef next* **66/1**	
P00	P		**Mercari**[28] 2676 4-10-4 .... KeithMercer	—
			(A R Dicken) *in tch: lost pl 5th: t.o whn p.u bef 2 out* **150/1**	
1	P		**Renada**[37] 2494 4-10-11 .... GrahamLee	—
			(J Howard Johnson) *chsd ldrs: lost pl after 6th: t.o whn p.u bef next* **7/1**[2]	
	P		**King Henrik (USA)**[169] 4-10-6 .... ThomasDreaper(5)	—
			(A Crook) *stdd s: bhd and pushed along 3rd: t.o whn p.u bef 2 out* **150/1**	

4m 1.20s (3.90) **Going Correction** +0.35s/f (Yiel) 15 Ran SP% **120.2**
Speed ratings: **104,102,101,99,98 98,96,87,84,79** —,—,—,—,— CSF £759.68 TOTE £140.00: £30.80, £2.10, £7.00; EX 327.50.
Owner J McAllister **Bred** G G A Gregson **Trained** Middleham, N Yorks

FOCUS
A modest juvenile hurdle and a shock result. The runner-up sets the level for the form. Second-last flight bypassed.

NOTEBOOK
Calfraz, whose best previous effort over hurdles was when encountering similar ground, was 7lb better off with Renada, who won that race. He came out of the pack to collar the leader on the flat and won going away. This was clearly a shock and what the form amounts to is open to question.
Lankawi, who has been steadily progressive over hurdles, did his best to make most of the running, and he looked like holding on before the winner arrived on the scene. He is capable of winning more races in this grade. *(op 13-2)*
Rossin Gold(IRE)came through on the heels of the winner and stuck to his task, but never looked like winning. He had been well behind Calfraz at Newcastle so this was an improvement, and he now qualifies for a handicap mark.
Clueless, a decent middle-distance handicapper on the Flat, was unsurprisingly odds-on for this hurdling debut. He never travelled particularly smoothly but had every chance when making a slight mistake at the first in the straight and could not pick up from that point. Although he handled soft ground on the Flat his wins were on fast going and so he may prefer a sounder surface over hurdles. *(op 1-2 tchd 4-7 in places)*
Oscar D'Hyrome(FR), making his British debut, had form on heavy ground in France. He may be suited by a longer trip.
Whistle Blowing(IRE) had the winner behind him when running well on his hurdling debut, but could not build on that effort on this much softer ground. He can be given another chance on a faster surface, which he handled on the Flat. *(op 16-1)*
William Tell(IRE) *Official explanation: jockey said gelding was unsuited by the soft, good to soft in places ground (tchd 40-1)*
Renada *Official explanation: jockey said filly was unsuited by the soft, good to soft in places ground (op 13-2)*

3204 FINDLAYS NOVICES' H'CAP CHASE (17 fncs 2 omitted) 3m 1f
1:05 (1:07) (Class 4) (0-110,110) 5-Y-0+ **£3,578** (£1,050; £525; £262)

Form				RPR
2312	1		**Brandy Wine (IRE)**[19] 2819 8-11-0 98 .... (b1) TonyDobbin	110+
			(L Lungo) *chsd ldrs: mstke 11th: led next: drew clr appr 2 out: heavily eased towards fin* **2/1**[1]	
16-2	2	8	**See You There (IRE)**[64] 1939 7-11-9 110 .... PeterBuchanan(3)	113+
			(Miss Lucinda V Russell) *nt fluent in rr: jnd wnr 12th: disp ld 14th to next: sn btn* **12/1**	
06-1	3	12	**Theatre Knight (IRE)**[41] 2415 8-11-8 106 .... GrahamLee	94+
			(J Howard Johnson) *hld up: wnt prom 9th: hmpd 12th: chsd 1st 2 14th: rdn and wknd bef next* **5/1**[3]	
-30F	4	3	**Kharak (FR)**[28] 2675 7-11-7 105 .... WilsonRenwick	91+
			(Mrs S C Bradburne) *prom: hit 10th and 11th: lost pl 14th* **13/2**	
P	5	dist	**Trovaio (IRE)**[47] 2266 9-9-10 85 .... (p) DeclanMcGann(5)	—
			(Miss Lucinda V Russell) *led: hdd and j.rt 12th: sn wknd: t.o: btn 36l* **50/1**	
/524	P		**Algarve**[16] 2874 9-10-8 92 .... KeithMercer	—
			(Ferdy Murphy) *chsd ldrs: j.lft 12th: wknd next: t.o whn p.u bef 2 out* **7/2**[2]	
/0-P	P		**Sir Rowland Hill (IRE)**[28] 2675 7-10-11 100 .... ThomasDreaper(5)	—
			(Ferdy Murphy) *in rr: blnd 8th: bhd fr 11th: t.o whn p.u bef 3 out* **33/1**	
3-31	P		**Fountain Brig**[11] 2945 10-10-0 84 .... BrianHarding	—
			(N W Alexander) *chsd ldrs: reminders 8th: lost pl after 10th: t.o whn p.u bef 13th* **15/2**	

6m 41.7s (-4.00) **Going Correction** +0.025s/f (Yiel) 8 Ran SP% **109.9**
Speed ratings: **107,104,100,99**,— —,—,— CSF £23.13 CT £96.56 TOTE £3.40: £1.90, £1.80, £1.02; EX 21.20.
Owner Ashleybank Investments Limited **Bred** Joel McCleary **Trained** Carrutherstown, D'fries & G'way

FOCUS
A modest novices' handicap where stamina played an important part and the form could rate higher. The first in the home straight was omitted on both circuits.

NOTEBOOK
Brandy Wine(IRE), a thorough stayer but having only his third run over fences, was equipped with blinkers for the first time. He basically galloped his rivals into the ground and it would be no surprise to see him contesting races like the Eider and the Midlands National in the future. *(op 5-2)*
See You There(IRE), an ex-pointer who is well suited by the trip and ground, was having only his second outing over fences. He drew clear of the rest with the winner, but began to tire from the *third last and was well beaten in the end. He looks capable of winning races in similar company. (op 10-1)*
Theatre Knight(IRE), another ex-pointer who was a narrow winner on his chasing debut, was up in trip and on softer ground. He was left behind by the first two from the last on the far side. *(op 4-1)*
Kharak(FR), who looked an unlucky loser last time, ran his race but a couple of mistakes on the final circuit did not help his chance. *(op 7-1)*
Algarve was rather disappointing but may prefer better ground or a shorter trip in any case. *Official explanation: trainer's representative had no explanation for the poor form shown (tchd 4-1)*
Fountain Brig *Official explanation: jockey said race come too soon after its previous outing 11 days ago (tchd 4-1)*

3205 TIZER "NATIONAL HUNT" NOVICES' HURDLE (12 hdls) 2m 6f
1:35 (1:39) (Class 4) 5-Y-0+ **£2,927** (£859; £429; £214)

Form				RPR
1	1		**According To John (IRE)**[28] 2678 6-11-4 .... TonyDobbin	120+
			(N G Richards) *hld up: wnt prom 6th: led 2 out: rdn and styd on run-in* **1/1**[1]	
P034	2	1 1/2	**Morgan Be**[30] 2631 6-10-12 107 .... RichardMcGrath	111
			(Mrs K Walton) *prom: chal 3 out: kpt on same pce run-in* **8/1**[3]	
1633	3	1 3/4	**Ball O Malt (IRE)**[33] 2571 10-10-12 117 .... AnthonyRoss	111+
			(R A Fahey) *hld up: hdwy and prom 8th: chsng ldrs and rdn 3 out: kpt on same pce appr last* **3/1**[2]	
2-54	4	4	**Kirkside Pleasure (IRE)**[37] 2497 5-10-12 .... WilsonRenwick	107+
			(Mrs S C Bradburne) *reluctant ldr: j. slowly 2nd: hdd 3 out: j.lft last: wknd last 150yds* **66/1**	
31-4	5	17	**Regal Heights (IRE)**[71] 1847 5-10-7 .... StephenCraine(5)	88
			(D McCain) *chsd ldrs: rdn 9th: sn wknd* **16/1**	
65	6	13	**Noir Et Vert (FR)**[17] 2859 5-10-12 .... KeithMercer	75
			(Ferdy Murphy) *in tch: outpcd 9th: sn lost pl* **66/1**	
0-26	7	dist	**Witch Wind**[11] 2947 6-10-7 .... DeclanMcGann(5)	—
			(A M Crow) *chsd ldrs: rdn 9th: sn wknd: t.o: btn 39l* **12/1**	
50-P	8	10	**Bubba Boy (IRE)**[131] 1307 6-10-2 .... DavidDaSilva(10)	—
			(P Monteith) *hld up in rr: sme hdwy 8th: sn lost pl and bhd: t.o* **100/1**	
-430	9	8	**Ambition Royal (FR)**[37] 2497 6-10-9 97 .... (v1) PeterBuchanan(3)	—
			(Miss Lucinda V Russell) *chsd ldr: rdn 8th: lost pl next: sn bhd: t.o* **66/1**	
35-	10	1 1/2	**Cash Bonanza (IRE)**[274] 4707 6-10-12 .... BrianHarding	—
			(N G Richards) *hld up towards rr: effrt 8th: sn lost pl and bhd: t.o* **12/1**	
/PP-	11	1	**Goodandplenty**[575] 653 8-10-7 .... ThomasDreaper(5)	—
			(Mrs J C McGregor) *bhd and struggling 6th: t.o 9th* **200/1**	
P0	P		**Whatcanyasay**[57] 2062 5-10-2 .... StevenGagan(10)	—
			(Mrs E Slack) *mstkes in rr: bhd fr 7th: t.o whn p.u bef 3 out* **200/1**	
/P-0	P		**Lethem Air**[236] 301 8-10-7 .... DougieCostello(5)	—
			(T Butt) *chsd ldrs: rdn and lost pl 7th: t.o whn p.u bef 3 out* **200/1**	
	P		**Silver Chancelor (IRE)** 5-10-12 .... GrahamLee	—
			(J Howard Johnson) *hdwy and in tch whn mstke 4th: reminders and lost pl after 6th: sn bhd: t.o whn p.u bef 9th* **20/1**	

6m 2.20s (20.60) **Going Correction** +0.35s/f (Yiel) 14 Ran SP% **119.1**
Speed ratings: **76,75,74,73,67 62**,—,—,—,— —,—,—,— CSF £10.00 TOTE £2.10: £1.40, £2.50, £1.50; EX 16.70.
Owner Sir Robert Ogden **Bred** John P Kiely **Trained** Greystoke, Cumbria

FOCUS
A modest novices' hurdle run in a slow time after the field stood still for almost six seconds when the tape went across. There were only four in contention from the home turn and the runner-up sets the standard in a fair event form-wise.

NOTEBOOK
According To John(IRE), an ex-pointer who won over three miles at Newcastle on his debut under Rules, put his stamina to good use in the straight after looking as if he might struggle to score. There looks to be more to come. *(op 5-4 tchd 11-8 in places)*
Morgan Be has been quietly progressive over shorter trips and ran well again, keeping on steadily to hunt up the winner. He looks more than capable of winning a similar contest. *(op 7-1)*
Ball O Malt(IRE) is better known as a chaser who goes well on fast ground. He does handle this surface but his best form is at shorter trips and his stamina ran out in the straight. *(op 7-2)*
Kirkside Pleasure(IRE), another stepping up in trip, was leader on sufferance but kept going well and only faded out of contention after going badly left at the final flight. A drop back in trip may be required for the moment.
Cash Bonanza(IRE) *Official explanation: trainer said gelding was found to be coughing post race*

3206 BARR H'CAP HURDLE (9 hdls) 2m
2:05 (2:10) (Class 4) (0-115,115) 4-Y-0+ **£3,578** (£1,050; £525; £262)

Form				RPR
006F	1		**Merryvale Man**[7] 2981 9-10-1 90 .... GrahamLee	97+
			(Miss Kariana Key) *led tl blnd and hdd 1st: w ldr: led after 4th: styd on fr 3 out: drvn rt out* **9/4**[2]	
0200	2	3 1/2	**Timbuktu**[27] 2693 5-10-0 89 oh2 .... RichardMcGrath	90+
			(B Storey) *w ldr: lft in ld 1st: hdd after 4th: blnd 6th: rallied next: styd on same pce run-in* **18/1**	
10-0	3	3/4	**Mr Midaz**[250] 64 7-10-11 100 .... DominicElsworth	101+
			(D W Whillans) *nt fluent: chsd ldrs: outpcd 6th: 4th and styng on whn blnd last* **12/1**	
-F23	4	13	**Hollywood Critic (USA)**[39] 2447 5-10-8 107 .... DavidDaSilva(10)	94+
			(P Monteith) *s.s: hdwy to chse ldrs 4th: j.lft last 2: wknd run-in* **10/1**	
F043	5	5	**Millennium Hall**[7] 2991 7-10-11 103 .... PeterBuchanan(3)	84
			(Miss Lucinda V Russell) *trckd ldrs: rdn 3 out: hung lft and sn btn* **7/2**[3]	
P0P/	6	nk	**Maradan (IRE)**[1011] 4394 10-10-0 89 .... KeithMercer	70
			(Mrs J C McGregor) *in tch: outpcd 6th: n.d after* **100/1**	
P211	7	6	**The Names Bond**[28] 2680 8-11-5 115 .... MissRDavidson(7)	90
			(N G Richards) *chsd ldrs: outpcd 6th: sn lost pl* **2/1**[1]	

4m 3.70s (6.40) **Going Correction** +0.35s/f (Yiel) 7 Ran SP% **109.4**
Speed ratings: **98,96,95,89,86 86,83** CSF £33.33 TOTE £3.30: £2.20, £5.00; EX 58.40.
Owner Miss Kariana Key **Bred** Arthur Symons Key **Trained** Knaresborough, N Yorks
■ Stewards' Enquiry : Miss R Davidson caution: used whip when out of contention

FOCUS
A moderate handicap run at an ordinary gallop, but a welcome return to form for the winner who could rate higher with the runner-up setting the standard.

NOTEBOOK
Merryvale Man, who ran well at Sedgefield last time before falling at the last, was none the worse for that and gained compensation under a forceful ride. This was his first win since April 2004, but *he is 20lb below his last winning mark and even with a rise for this could prove well handicapped. (tchd 5-2 and 11-4 in places)*
Timbuktu has shown bits and pieces of form but is basically plating class. He looked beaten after a mistake on the far side, but came again in the straight and was running on quite strongly. He has a small race in him on this evidence. *(op 16-1)*
Mr Midaz hit form about this time last year but lost his way in the spring. This was a better effort, and he rallied after losing his place down the far side, but he is still 5lb above his last winning mark. He looks to need the extra half mile nowadays. *(op 10-1)*
Hollywood Critic(USA) overcame a slow start to get in contention on the far side, but gradually faded in the straight. He may get the trip better on a sounder surface. *(op 8-1 tchd 11-1 in a place)*
Millennium Hall, a most modest middle-distance handicapper on the Flat, did not build on recent hurdles efforts. All his wins on the Flat were at Hamilton, so he may be worth a try on a stiff right-handed track such as Carlisle. *(tchd 9-2)*
The Names Bond, bidding for a hat-trick but 7lb higher in the weights, ran no sort of race in *conditions that should have suited and must have had an excuse for this effort. Official explanation: trainer had no explanation for the poor form shown (op 7-4)*

3207 IRN BRU H'CAP CHASE (15 fncs 2 omitted) 2m 4f
2:35 (2:36) (Class 3) (0-130,128) 5-Y-0+ **£6,506** (£1,910; £955; £477)

Form				RPR
5-43	1		**Master Sebastian**[28] 2677 7-10-5 110 .... PeterBuchanan(3)	110
			(Miss Lucinda V Russell) *j.rt: chsd ldrs: led after 7th: hdd next: led 11th: jst hld on* **8/1**	
41	2	nk	**King Barry (FR)**[18] 2839 7-10-5 107 .... RichardMcGrath	109+
			(Miss P Robson) *wnt prom 5th: jnd wnr 11th: kpt on towards fin: jst hld* **7/4**[1]	

44-6 **3** *11* **Through The Rye**[30] 2641 10-11-12 **128**........................... BrianHarding 119+
(E W Tuer) *hld up: nt fluent: blnd 6th: hdwy 10th: chal 3 out: rdn and wknd after next* **16/1**

0412 **4** *4* **South Bronx (IRE)**[29] 2654 7-11-4 **120**...................(t) WilsonRenwick 105
(Mrs S C Bradburne) *chsd ldrs: j. ahd 8th: hdd 11th: wknd 3 out* **5/1**[3]

3-P5 **5** *1 1/4* **Hugo De Grez (FR)**[39] 2451 11-10-4 **106**........................ AlanDempsey 89
(A Parker) *w ldrs: lft in ld 7th: sn hdd: lost pl 9th: detached tl kpt on run-in* **20/1**

0-52 **P** **Mistral De La Cour (FR)**[30] 2626 6-10-13 **115**................(p) TonyDobbin —
(R Ford) *led: blnd and hdd 7th: lost pl 11th: p.u bef next* **9/2**[2]

/24- **P** **Tollbrae (IRE)**[407] 2363 9-11-2 **118**............................ GrahamLee —
(J Howard Johnson) *wnt prom and hit 5th: lost pl 11th: bhd whn p.u bef next* **5/1**[3]

5m 23.6s (0.70) **Going Correction** +0.025s/f (Yiel) **7** Ran SP% **109.6**
Speed ratings: **99,98,94,92,92** —,— CSF £21.59 TOTE £10.00: £3.30, £1.50; EX 40.50.
Owner Mrs J M Grimston **Bred** Mrs J Key **Trained** Arlary, Perth & Kinross

FOCUS
A fair handicap in which fortunes changed several times in the closing stages and the race is rated around the first two. First fence in the straight omitted both circuits.

NOTEBOOK
Master Sebastian, stepping up in trip on this third run over fences, was left in front at the seventh and, pushing on from the last on the far side, looked likely to be collared by the favourite after jumping right at the second last , but proved the stronger on the run-in. He still looks to have room for improvement and likes testing ground.
King Barry(FR), a dual winning pointer, looked all set to add to his maiden chase win when upsides at the last, but failed to find as much as looked likely and was outbattled. This ground may have been too soft for him. *(op 2-1 tchd 9-4 in places)*
Through The Rye, back over fences after a spell on the Flat in the spring, was settled out the back *and moved up looking a big threat to all. However, he did not find quite as much as expected. (op 12-1)*
South Bronx(IRE) handled the step up to two miles six and soft ground last time, but was unable to *build on that effort this time. Official explanation: jockey said gelding had a breathing problem (tchd 9-2)*
Hugo De Grez(FR) is better over further and likes going the other way around, so it was not surprising when he dropped away.
Tollbrae(IRE), a delicate sort who had been absent for over a year, was struggling and behind when his rider wisely drew stumps. *(op 9-2)*
Mistral De La Cour(FR) set the pace but was pulled up soon after making an almighty blunder on the far side. *Official explanation: jockey said gelding jumped poorly throughout (op 9-2)*

3208 DIET IRN BRU H'CAP HURDLE (11 hdls) 2m 4f
3:10 (3:10) (Class 3) (0-135,134) 4-Y-0+ **£5,204** (£1,528; £764; £381)

Form RPR

-400 **1** **Habitual Dancer**[30] 2629 5-10-7 **115**................................ BrianHarding 114
(Jedd O'Keeffe) *mde most to 8th: outpcd next: rallied and wnt 2nd between last 2: styd on to ld nr fin* **11/2**[3]

6-43 **2** *3/4* **Carapuce (FR)**[26] 2706 7-10-10 **118**.................................. RussGarritty 117+
(L Lungo) *trckd ldrs: led 3 out: 4 l up last: hdd and no ex towards fin* **7/1**

1F/6 **3** *6* **Thosewerethedays**[39] 2452 13-10-7 **115**........................ RichardMcGrath 107
(Miss P Robson) *trckd ldrs: outpcd appr 3 out: kpt on: nvr a real threat* **6/1**

P000 **4** *9* **Culcabock (IRE)**[39] 2452 6-9-11 **108** oh8.................... PeterBuchanan[(3)] 91
(Miss Lucinda V Russell) *trckd ldrs: led 8th to next: wknd appr last: hung rt run-in* **16/1**

-640 **5** *3* **Crackleando**[39] 2452 5-10-0 **108**.. KeithMercer 88
(A R Dicken) *chsd ldrs: outpcd 8th: sn lost pl* **25/1**

4P-F **6** *15* **Paperprophet**[16] 2876 8-11-10 **132**.................................... TonyDobbin 102+
(N G Richards) *nvr gng wl: hit 3rd: reminders next: drvn along to go prom 7th: lost pl next: sn bhd* **2/1**[1]

/4-4 **7** *hd* **Inching Closer**[44] 2336 9-11-12 **134**................................... GrahamLee 104+
(J Howard Johnson) *prom: drvn along 7th: outpcd whn hit next: sn lost pl and bhd* **5/2**[2]

5m 14.8s (2.10) **Going Correction** +0.35s/f (Yiel) **7** Ran SP% **113.8**
Speed ratings: **109,108,106,102,101 95,95** CSF £41.50 TOTE £8.00: £3.40, £2.50; EX 30.70.
Owner The Country Stayers **Bred** Mrs A Yearley **Trained** Coverham, N Yorks

FOCUS
A fair handicap hurdle in which the first two in the betting ran below expectations, which tends to limit the form.

NOTEBOOK
Habitual Dancer, who had some fair form as a novice last year but had struggled in decent company this season, appreciated this easier task and a drop in the weights and, after making the *running, came again and got the better of the runner-up late on. This is more his grade.Official explanation: trainer had no explanation for the improved form shown (op 6-1 tchd 13-2 in places)*
Carapuce(FR), better for his outing at Leicester last month, looked sure to win when taking the lead at the first in the straight, but he could not hold the renewed effort of the winner on the flat. This was the second race in succession where his owners had victory snatched away after looking sure to collect. *(op 11-2 tchd 8-1 in places)*
Thosewerethedays, a lightly-raced veteran who is better known as a chaser, seems happier over the smaller obstacles these days and performed with credit. He looks reasonably treated and another couple of furlongs may be within his compass these days. *(op 9-2)*
Culcabock(IRE), who likes this track, moved up from the rear going well but his effort petered out in the straight. He is more effective on good ground. *(tchd 18-1)*
Paperprophet was never going from an early stage and his fall last time may have dented his enthusiasm. *Official explanation: jockey said gelding was never travelling (op 10-3 tchd 7-2)*
Inching Closer, who returned from a long absence last time, may have bounced despite having *had over six weeks to recover from that run. Official explanation: trainer's representative had no explanation for the poor form shown (tchd 9-4)*

3209 ORANGINA H'CAP HURDLE (11 hdls 1 omitted) 3m 110y
3:40 (3:42) (Class 5) (0-95,91) 4-Y-0+ **£2,398** (£698; £349)

Form RPR

0246 **1** **Caesar's Palace (GER)**[41] 2417 9-11-9 **91**............(p) PeterBuchanan[(3)] 94
(Miss Lucinda V Russell) *sn bhd and drvn along: detached fr 3rd: hdwy 9th: mod 4th 2 out: styd on to ld towards fin* **5/1**[1]

10-5 **2** *1* **Moon Mist**[47] 2267 8-10-9 **74**.. RichardMcGrath 76
(N W Alexander) *led to 6th: rdn and lost pl next: rallied to ld 9th: hdd nr fin: fin tired* **6/1**[3]

00-0 **3** *3 1/2* **Seeking Shelter (IRE)**[29] 2653 7-10-2 **67**......................... BrianHarding 67+
(N G Richards) *chsd ldrs: wnt clr 2nd 9th: one pce between last 2* **10/1**

650P **4** *18* **Roadworthy (IRE)**[28] 2674 9-10-0 **65**............................ WilsonRenwick 50+
(W G Young) *bhd: gd hdwy to chse ldrs 8th: one pce fr next* **66/1**

0-54 **5** *17* **Generals Laststand (IRE)**[29] 2653 8-10-3 **73**..............(p) DesFlavin[(5)] 37
(Mrs L B Normile) *hdwy to chse ldrs 6th: wknd after 9th* **11/2**[2]

0-00 **6** *1/2* **Top Dawn (IRE)**[55] 2108 6-10-7 **72**.................................. BruceGibson 35
(L Lungo) *rn in snatches: jnd ldrs 7th: lost pl after next* **9/1**

3056 **7** *18* **Silver Seeker (USA)**[11] 2944 6-10-13 **78**............................ KeithMercer 23
(A R Dicken) *chsd ldrs to 6th: bhd fr 8th* **6/1**[3]

P6PP **8** *1 3/4* **Fifteen Reds**[7] 2978 11-10-8 **80**.................................(p) EwanWhillans[(7)] 23
(J C Haynes) *w ldrs: led 6th to 9th: sn lost pl* **100/1**

P405 **P** **Hapthor**[29] 2653 7-10-9 **74**.. TonyDobbin —
(F Jestin) *mid-div: lost pl 7th: t.o whn p.u after 9th* **10/1**

P-04 **P** **Sir Lamb**[27] 2688 10-10-10 **80**.. BrianHughes[(5)] —
(Miss S E Hall) *bhd and drvn 7th: t.o whn p.u after 9th* **20/1**

0-00 **P** **Blue Morning**[29] 2657 8-10-9 **74**......................................(p) GrahamLee —
(Mrs J C McGregor) *hdwy 6th: in tch 8th: wkng whn p.u after next* **33/1**

322- **U** **Alice's Old Rose**[393] 2650 9-10-11 **81**........................ DougieCostello[(5)] —
(Mrs H O Graham) *hld up towards rr: blnd and uns rdr 4th* **9/1**

5-FP **P** **Hollow Flight (IRE)**[57] 2063 8-10-10 **75**......................... NeilMulholland —
(Mrs L B Normile) *w ldrs: wknd after 6th: sn bhd: p.u bef 8th* **40/1**

-40P **P** **You'Re The Man (IRE)**[57] 2066 9-10-9 **84**................(p) StevenGagan[(10)] —
(Mrs E Slack) *chsd ldrs: sn drvn along: bhd and rdn 6th: t.o whn p.u bef 9th* **14/1**

P00 **U** **Leonia's Rose (IRE)**[28] 2674 7-10-4 **74**...................... TomGreenway[(5)] —
(Miss Lucinda V Russell) *hld up: gd hdwy and prom 7th: 4th whn blnd and uns rdr 9th* **33/1**

6m 40.5s (8.70) **Going Correction** +0.35s/f (Yiel) **15** Ran SP% **121.0**
Speed ratings: **100,99,98,92,87 87,81,80,**—,— —,—,—,—,— CSF £33.35 CT £296.15 TOTE £5.90: £2.50, £2.40, £4.50; EX 27.90 Place 6 £418.30, Place 5 £46.81.
Owner Peter J S Russell **Bred** Frau B Limmer **Trained** Arlary, Perth & Kinross

FOCUS
A very ordinary stayers' handicap that developed into a war of attrition and the quirky winner passed all his rivals on the final circuit to score and is probalbt the best guide to the form rated through recent efforts on the track. The third-last flight was omitted on the final circuit.

NOTEBOOK
Caesar's Palace(GER) is a quirky old devil, but has ability and in the distant past was rated 31lb higher. He showed no interest in the early stages and was tailed off with a circuit to go but, after passing a few rivals on the far side, he consented to race and collared the tiring leaders on the flat. He does not win very often but is clearly capable if he puts his mind to it. *(op 6-1 tchd 13-2)*
Moon Mist, having her first run over hurdles since April 2004 off a mark 12lb below her chase rating, relishes a stamina test and galloped most of her rivals into submission. She was *unfortunate to come up against the winner on a going day and deserves to gain compensation. (op 13-2 tchd 7-1)*
Seeking Shelter(IRE), who has shown a glimmer of ability in a handful of outings, ran well but was very tired in the straight. She is only very moderate but may have improvement in her.
Roadworthy(IRE) had not shown much, sometimes in plating company, since coming from Ireland last spring, but this was the longest trip she has tried to date and she ran quite well until fading in the straight.
Silver Seeker(USA), up in trip, did not figure in the latter stages and probably did not stay in the *testing conditions. Official explanation: trainer said gelding was found to be lame on returning home (op 7-1)*
Leonia's Rose(IRE), a stable companion of the winner, had shown little in her previous starts in this country but had just moved onto the heels of the leaders when departing at the last on the far side.
T/Plt: £382.50 to a £1 stake. Pool: £40,846.65. 77.95 winning tickets. T/Qpdt: £49.90 to a £1 stake. Pool: £3,572.80. 52.95 winning tickets. WG

2845 EXETER (R-H)
Monday, January 2

OFFICIAL GOING: Good to soft (soft in places)
The hurdle going away from the stands was again omitted because of false ground.
Wind: Almost nil Weather: Fine

3210 HAPPY NEW YEAR "NATIONAL HUNT" NOVICES' HURDLE (9 hdls 1 omitted) 2m 3f
12:55 (12:55) (Class 4) 5-Y-0+ **£2,927** (£859; £429; £214)

Form RPR

-214 **1** **Mister Quasimodo**[23] 2762 6-11-5 115........................ JoeTizzard 120+
(C L Tizzard) *hld up in tch: led on bit 3 out: rdn appr last: drvn out* **6/1**[3]

42 **2** *1 3/4* **The Luder (IRE)**[30] 2624 5-10-12 .... ChristianWilliams 112+
(P F Nicholls) *hld up and bhd: rdn and hdwy appr 3 out: pckd last: wandered u.p flat: nt qckn* **10/1**

4-F1 **3** *4* **Sea The Light**[45] 2309 6-11-5 .... RobertThornton 114
(A King) *a.p: rdn 3 out: one pce flat* **11/2**[2]

3-4F **4** *1 3/4* **Duncliffe**[58] 2054 9-10-12 .... AndrewThornton 106
(R H Alner) *led: rdn and hdd 3 out: one pce fr 2 out* **11/2**[2]

-344 **5** *3 1/2* **Sabreur**[19] 2821 5-10-12 .... WayneHutchinson 102
(Ian Williams) *hld up: hdwy 5th: ev ch 3 out: sn rdn: wknd appr last* **50/1**

342 **6** *1* **Aztec Warrior (IRE)**[17] 2865 5-10-12 .... APMcCoy 101
(Miss H C Knight) *hld up: hdwy appr 6th: rdn appr 3 out: wknd 2 out* **9/2**[1]

5212 **7** *7* **Purple Patch**[12] 2937 8-10-12 105.................................. MickFitzgerald 95+
(C L Popham) *prom: ev ch 3 out: sn rdn: wknd 2 out* **33/1**

2-13 **8** *2* **Black Hills**[31] 2606 7-11-5 ....(t) MarkBradburne 102+
(J A Geake) *hld up: hit and lost pl 4th: rdn and hdwy 6th: wknd 3 out: eased appr last* **8/1**

23-0 **9** *19* **Here We Go (IRE)**[86] 1681 7-10-12 .... CarlLlewellyn 73
(W K Goldsworthy) *a bhd* **66/1**

-444 **10** *3/4* **Spring Junior (FR)**[18] 2849 5-10-12 .... RichardJohnson 72
(P J Hobbs) *prom to 4th* **50/1**

11 *nk* **Doc Row (IRE)**[36] 6-10-12 .... TimmyMurphy 72
(M C Pipe) *bhd fr 4th* **6/1**[3]

-022 **12** *10* **Arumun (IRE)**[27] 2683 5-10-12 .... BrianCrowley 62
(M Scudamore) *plld hrd in rr: hdwy appr 3rd: wknd 6th* **20/1**

0-3 **P** **Il Capriccio (IRE)**[247] 138 6-10-7 .... MarkNicolls[(5)] —
(B J M Ryall) *bhd tl p.u lame after 3rd: dead* **250/1**

-P41 **P** **Dare Too Dream**[18] 2849 7-11-5 .... JohnMcNamara —
(K Bishop) *a bhd: mstke 2nd: p.u bef 3 out* **20/1**

51/ **P** **Marchensis (IRE)**[963] 263 8-10-9 .... OwynNelmes[(3)] —
(O Sherwood) *hld up and bhd: hdwy 4th: nt fluent 5th: sn rdn and wknd: bhd whn p.u bef 2 out* **150/1**

4m 45.8s (4.90) **Going Correction** +0.575s/f (Soft) **15** Ran SP% **116.7**
Speed ratings: **112,111,109,108,107 106,104,103,95,94 94,90,**—,—,— CSF £57.89 TOTE £8.00: £2.80, £4.30, £2.10; EX 41.70.
Owner J M Dare, T Hamlin, J W Snook **Bred** H T Cole **Trained** Milborne Port, Dorset

FOCUS
A decent time for a race like this, four seconds quicker than the later handicap over the same trip, and the form looks solid rated through the third and seventh.

NOTEBOOK

Mister Quasimodo, highly tried over three miles last time, went smoothly to the front and proved more resolute than the runner-up. He is now likely to graduate to handicaps rather than shoulder a double penalty, but it is considered essential that he has give in the ground. *(tchd 13-2)*

The Luder(IRE) does not look straightforward and hung both ways away from the whip when his rider did his best to keep him straight on the run-in. *(op 8-1)*

Sea The Light ran very respectably over this extra quarter-mile under a penalty. *(op 5-1)*

Duncliffe ◆ was running for the first time over hurdles after falling on his previous outing. This should have restored his confidence and he may even be capable of taking a similar event over a longer trip. *(tchd 6-1)*

Sabreur appeared to get found out by a combination of a longer trip and dead ground. *(tchd 40-1)*

Aztec Warrior(IRE) was a bit disappointing following his hurdle debut at Windsor. *(tchd 5-1)*

3211 SIS NOVICES' H'CAP HURDLE (10 hdls 1 omitted) 2m 6f 110y

1:25 (1:25) (Class 4) (0-100,100) 4-Y-0+ £3,083 (£898; £449)

Form				RPR
-500	1		**Sandmartin (IRE)**[45] 2309 6-10-11 **85**.........................(b[1]) PaddyBrennan (P J Hobbs) *a.p: led appr 7th: clr fr 3 out: v easily* **16/1**	98+
0050	2	10	**Gunship (IRE)**[16] 2873 5-10-2 **76**.................................. RichardJohnson (P J Hobbs) *hld up in mid-div: rdn and lost pl 5th: hdwy after 7th: wnt 2nd 3 out: no ch w wnr* **7/1**[3]	69
0401	3	5	**Hilarious (IRE)**[13] 2934 6-11-1 **89**................................. AndrewThornton (Dr J R J Naylor) *led: hdd appr 7th: wknd 3 out: hit last* **5/1**[2]	77
30/-	4	7	**Mizinky**[656] 4401 6-9-8 **78**... RichardGordon(10) (W G M Turner) *bhd: styd on u.p appr 3 out: hit 2 out: n.d* **33/1**	59
0P/5	5	hd	**Stakeholder (IRE)**[31] 2605 8-9-10 **77** oh8 ow3................. DarylJacob(7) (Mrs H E Rees) *prom tl wknd after 3 out* **33/1**	58
356	6	5	**Micky Cole (IRE)**[34] 2559 6-11-5 **100**................................ LiamHeard(7) (P F Nicholls) *hld up and bhd: hdwy appr 5th: rdn appr 7th: wknd appr 3 out* **8/1**	76
P400	7	3	**Denarius Secundus**[13] 2934 9-10-0 **74**............................... DaveCrosse (N R Mitchell) *prom tl wknd 6th* **20/1**	47
2/P4	8	7	**Instant Appeal**[13] 2934 9-11-2 **90**.. RJGreene (P Winkworth) *t.k.h in mid-div: rdn appr 5th: hdwy 6th: wknd appr 3 out* **7/1**[3]	56
0036	9	4	**Classic Clover**[32] 2592 6-10-3 **77**.. JoeTizzard (C L Tizzard) *hld up in tch: lost pl after 4th: sn bhd* **10/1**	39
000	10	dist	**Garhoud**[20] 2811 4-10-0 **88** oh12..............................(b) BenjaminHitchcott (Miss K M George) *bhd fr 6th: t.o* **25/1**	—
5F	P		**Case Equal (IRE)**[173] 978 6-10-5 **86**............................... KeiranBurke(7) (N J Hawke) *a bhd: nt fluent 5th: p.u bef 3 out* **33/1**	—
/146	P		**Frosty Jak**[18] 2845 8-10-7 **81**... RobertThornton (J D Frost) *a bhd: reminder after 4th: p.u bef 3 out* **4/1**[1]	—
000	P		**Barathea Blue**[18] 2849 5-11-9 **97**...................................(t) TimmyMurphy (M C Pipe) *bhd: short-lived effrt appr 7th: p.u bef 3 out* **10/1**	—
PF5-	P		**Lady Alderbrook (IRE)**[267] 4789 6-10-6 **80**.................. MarkBradburne (C J Down) *hld up in tch: wknd 6th: bhd whn p.u bef 3 out* **20/1**	—

5m 57.2s (17.90) **Going Correction** +0.575s/f (Soft)
WFA 4 from 5yo+ 12lb **14** Ran SP% **119.0**
Speed ratings: **91,87,85,83,83 81,80,78,76,— —,—,—,—** CSF £112.42 CT £646.27 TOTE £36.30: £9.30, £4.50, £1.02; EX 79.30.
Owner D Allen **Bred** T A Johnsey **Trained** Withycombe, Somerset

FOCUS

An ordinary handicap with few appreciating the stamina test in tacky ground. The winner is value for double the official margin with the second and fourth setting the level for the form.

NOTEBOOK

Sandmartin(IRE) had given the impression he might not be in love with the game in his last two outings. Transformed by the blinkers over a longer trip, the Handicapper is likely to take a dim view of this win in a canter. Whether the headgear will work again remains to be seen and he could be one to take on next time.

Gunship(IRE) appreciated the step up in distance but proved no match for his stable companion. *(op 8-1)*

Hilarious(IRE), raised 6lb for her Fontwell win, was tackling a longer distance on more demanding ground. *(op 6-1)*

Mizinky gave her connections some cause for optimism having been off course since March 2004. *(op 20-1)*

Stakeholder(IRE), 8lb out of the handicap, has yet to show he possesses the sort of stamina that was required here. *(op 25-1)*

Micky Cole(IRE) has failed to come up to his debut over three miles at Chepstow. *(tchd 15-2)*

Frosty Jak did not give favourite backers a run for their money. *Official explanation: jockey said gelding was never travelling (op 6-1)*

3212 THURLESTONE HOTEL H'CAP CHASE (17 fncs) 2m 7f 110y

1:55 (1:57) (Class 4) (0-115,115) 5-Y-0+ £5,204 (£1,528; £764; £381)

Form				RPR
42P-	1		**Nas Na Riogh (IRE)**[289] 4459 7-11-7 **110**......................... MickFitzgerald (N J Henderson) *a.p: led after 6th: rdn after 2 out: all out* **7/2**[1]	122+
0030	2	½	**Even More (IRE)**[20] 2808 11-11-4 **107**........................... AndrewThornton (R H Alner) *led after 2nd to 3rd: lost pl after 10th: rallied appr 4 out: styd on u.p flat* **25/1**	118
-65P	3	1¼	**Lucky Leader (IRE)**[30] 2623 11-9-11 **89** oh7..............(b) OwynNelmes(3) (N R Mitchell) *hld up: hdwy appr 10th: hit 13th: rdn appr 4 out: ev ch whn nt fluent last: nt qckn* **28/1**	100+
1FU6	4	10	**Moscow Whisper (IRE)**[30] 2633 9-11-12 **115**.............. RichardJohnson (P J Hobbs) *hld up: hdwy 7th: hit 4 out: sn rdn: hit 3 out: ev ch whn mstke 2 out: wknd last* **7/1**[3]	118+
-563	5	1¼	**Dun Locha Castle (IRE)**[21] 2800 11-9-7 **89** oh4............ KeiranBurke(7) (N R Mitchell) *led 3rd tl after 6th: rdn appr 4 out: wknd 3 out* **20/1**	88
1P44	6	3	**Mandica (IRE)**[31] 2613 8-10-8 **97**...................................... JasonMaguire (T R George) *hld up and bhd: mstke 9th: hdwy appr 10th: wknd 4 out* **15/2**	95+
-06P	7	1¼	**Auburn Spirit**[31] 2608 11-11-6 **109**...................................... DaveCrosse (M D I Usher) *hld up in tch: rdn 6th: lost pl 12th: no real prog fr 13th* **25/1**	105+
-F2P	8	27	**Noble Baron**[18] 2847 10-11-6 **109**...............................(tp) MarkBradburne (C G Cox) *prom tl wknd 3 out* **13/2**[2]	77
P3	9	12	**Yann's (FR)**[26] 2703 10-11-11 **114**................................... WarrenMarston (R T Phillips) *reminders after 6th: a bhd* **7/1**[3]	70
P640	10	11	**Twisted Logic (IRE)**[50] 2215 13-11-1 **111**......................... DarylJacob(7) (R H Alner) *led: hit 2nd: sn hdd: lost pl and mstke 5th: bhd whn blnd 9th* **12/1**	56
-61R	P		**Athnowen (IRE)**[210] 666 14-11-1 **104**...................................... RJGreene (J R Payne) *v rel to r: wl t.o tl p.u after 9th* **50/1**	—
F3-5	P		**Grandee Line**[248] 106 11-10-0 **89** oh8.............................. TomSiddall (R H Alner) *a bhd: rdn after 7th: t.o whn p.u bef 4 out* **66/1**	—
1P/F	P		**Helixir Du Theil (FR)**[21] 2800 11-10-2 **91**...............(p) BenjaminHitchcott (R H Buckler) *hld up in tch: p.u lame after 11th* **18/1**	—
4-00	F		**Tribal King (IRE)**[43] 2368 11-11-6 **109**............................ RobertThornton (A King) *hld up and bhd: hdwy 10th: 6th and in tch whn hmpd and fell 12th* **7/1**[3]	—
P3-P	P		**L'Orphelin**[62] 1978 11-11-5 **115**...(b) LiamHeard(7) (C L Tizzard) *sn prom: j.lft fr 6th: mstke 11th: wknd 12th: t.o whn p.u bef 4 out* **33/1**	—

6m 13.5s (14.90) **Going Correction** +0.575s/f (Soft) **15** Ran SP% **120.1**
Speed ratings: **98,97,97,94,93 92,92,83,79,75 —,—,—,—,—** CSF £91.08 CT £2143.73 TOTE £2.10: £1.02, £10.90, £17.70; EX 121.00.
Owner Brian J Griffiths and John Nicholson **Bred** Eric Simian **Trained** Upper Lambourn, Berks

FOCUS

This very ordinary handicap turned out to be pretty competitive especially considering the prevailing conditions. The form looks sound with the first five close to their marks.

NOTEBOOK

Nas Na Riogh(IRE) was 9lb lower than when pulled up in the mares-only final at Uttoxeter on her previous outing last March. She put up a brave display but may need a little time to get over a hard race. *(tchd 4-1 in a place)*

Even More(IRE) bounced back to form but could not quite peg back the winner after finding a second wind in the home straight. *(op 22-1 tchd 33-1)*

Lucky Leader(IRE), 7lb 'wrong', jumped well by his standards but he put in a short one at the final fence just at the wrong time. *(op 25-1)*

Moscow Whisper(IRE) looked a big danger early in the home straight but then got let down by his suspect jumping. *(op 6-1)*

Dun Locha Castle(IRE) again ran well for a long way this time from 4lb out of the handicap.

Mandica(IRE) remains unproven at this sort of distance. *(op 10-1)*

3213 HATCH MARQUEE HIRE NOVICES' CHASE (19 fncs) 3m 1f 110y

2:25 (2:26) (Class 3) 5-Y-0+ £7,807 (£2,292; £1,146; £572)

Form				RPR
1P-1	1		**Idle Talk (IRE)**[62] 1976 7-11-10 .... JasonMaguire (T R George) *chsd ldr: led briefly 8th: led 4 out: hrd rdn appr last: all out* **4/1**[3]	139+
-231	2	2½	**Reflected Glory (IRE)**[18] 2847 7-12-0 129.................. ChristianWilliams (P F Nicholls) *hld up: hdwy 4th: rdn and ev ch 2 out: no ex flat* **7/2**[2]	139+
-2F1	3	1	**Lough Derg (FR)**[18] 2848 6-11-10 .... APMcCoy (M C Pipe) *led: mstke 7th: hdd 8th: sn led again: rdn and hdd 4 out: no ex fr 2 out* **6/4**[1]	137+
1123	4	1¼	**Amicelli (GER)**[23] 2762 7-11-4 .... RichardJohnson (P J Hobbs) *hld up: hdwy 4th: blnd and lost pl 3 out: styd on flat* **12/1**	127+
-621	P		**Cruising River (IRE)**[25] 2729 7-11-10 118...................... TimmyMurphy (Miss H C Knight) *hld up in rr: hit 5th: struggling 13th: p.u bef 15th* **20/1**	—
-212	P		**Lord Killeshanra (IRE)**[17] 2869 7-12-0 130............................ JoeTizzard (C L Tizzard) *hld up: rdn after 12th: bhd fr 15th: t.o whn p.u bef 2 out* **5/1**	—

6m 43.0s (15.00) **Going Correction** +0.575s/f (Soft) **6** Ran SP% **111.3**
Speed ratings: **99,98,97,97,— —** CSF £18.16 TOTE £4.20: £2.70, £2.20; EX 17.70.
Owner Mrs M J George **Bred** Roland Rothwell **Trained** Slad, Gloucs
■ Stewards' Enquiry : Jason Maguire two-day ban: used whip with excessive force (Jan 13-14)

FOCUS

There were some promising sorts in what looked to be a good contest and the form should work out.

NOTEBOOK

Idle Talk(IRE), who made such a favourable impression when successful on his chasing debut at Worcester in November, was pulled out of the Feltham on Boxing Day because the ground was on the fast side at Sandown. Finding what was required under pressure, he will be aimed at the Royal & SunAlliance Chase at Cheltenham providing that the going is soft enough. *(op 3-1)*

Reflected Glory(IRE) lost little in defeat and could be the type for the four-mile National Hunt Chase at the Cheltenham Festival. *(op 9-2)*

Lough Derg(FR) could not raise his game sufficiently from the penultimate fence but got the longer trip well enough. *(op 13-8 tchd 7-4)*

Amicelli(GER) ◆ had a tough task on his chasing debut and looked in big trouble when making a hash of the third last. The way he fought back in the closing stages augurs well for the future. *(op 16-1)*

Cruising River(IRE) *Official explanation: jockey said gelding had been unsuited by the good to soft, soft in places ground (tchd 18-1)*

3214 THURLESTONE HOTEL H'CAP HURDLE (9 hdls 1 omitted) 2m 3f

2:55 (2:56) (Class 4) (0-115,113) 4-Y-0+ £4,554 (£1,337; £668; £333)

Form				RPR
-201	1		**Down's Folly (IRE)**[14] 2925 6-11-4 **105**......................... RichardJohnson (H D Daly) *hld up and bhd: gd hdwy after 6th: rdn whn nt fluent last: drvn out* **10/3**[2]	114+
F0-P	2	¾	**Cockatoo Ridge**[62] 1968 9-10-7 **94**.. JoeTizzard (N R Mitchell) *led to 6th: rdn to ld appr 3 out: sn hdd: hit 2 out: rallied flat* **100/1**	100+
3-P1	3	7	**Silkwood Top (IRE)**[17] 2868 7-10-11 **98**......................(p) MickFitzgerald (V R A Dartnall) *prom: outpcd appr 3 out: styd on flat* **9/2**[3]	96
101	4	¾	**Star Member (IRE)**[7] 2964 7-11-11 **112** 7ex......................... JimCrowley (Ian Williams) *hld up: hdwy 6th: rdn and ev ch 2 out: wknd flat* **15/8**[1]	110+
6-12	5	9	**Petwick (IRE)**[26] 2706 7-11-12 **113**................................ RobertThornton (A King) *hld up and bhd: hdwy appr 6th: wknd 3 out* **13/2**	101
0	6	4	**Idian Mix (FR)**[18] 2850 5-11-4 **108**...................................... TomMalone(3) (M C Pipe) *hld up: hdwy 4th: led 6th tl appr 3 out: sn wknd* **20/1**	92
1-36	7	½	**Dickens (USA)**[11] 2955 6-11-5 **111**...................................... PaulO'Neill(5) (Miss Venetia Williams) *hld up and bhd: hdwy appr 5th: wknd appr 3 out* **16/1**	95
4-P0	8	2½	**Bak To Bill**[31] 2609 11-11-0 **108**.. MissLGardner(7) (Mrs S Gardner) *prom tl wknd after 6th* **40/1**	89
P020	9	6	**Middleham Park (IRE)**[39] 2459 6-11-0 **108**............. WayneKavanagh(7) (J W Mullins) *prom tl wknd appr 3 out* **33/1**	83
2-00	10	29	**Damarisco (FR)**[39] 2459 6-10-7 **94**................................. PaddyBrennan (P J Hobbs) *prom tl rdn and wknd appr 3 out* **20/1**	40
0P-P	11	1½	**Kiwi Babe**[31] 2609 7-11-2 **110**.. DarylJacob(7) (D P Keane) *bhd fr 6th* **50/1**	55
506-	P		**Big Max**[301] 4235 11-10-8 **95**... AndrewThornton (Miss K M George) *bhd fr 4th: p.u bef 3 out* **40/1**	—
/6-0	P		**Late Claim (USA)**[12] 2940 6-10-3 **100**...................... ShaunJohnson(10) (R T Phillips) *sn prom: wknd 4th: bhd whn p.u bef 3 out* **66/1**	—

4m 49.8s (8.90) **Going Correction** +0.575s/f (Soft) **13** Ran SP% **117.0**
Speed ratings: **104,103,100,100,96 94,94,93,91,78 78,—,—** CSF £301.29 CT £1526.41 TOTE £3.90: £1.90, £16.40, £2.40; EX 138.40 TRIFECTA Not won..
Owner Strachan,Gabb,Clarke,Griffith & Barlow **Bred** Oliver Maguire **Trained** Stanton Lacy, Shropshire

FOCUS

There were a few unexposed types in this handicap. The winner is better than the bare result with the second setting the level.

NOTEBOOK

Down's Folly(IRE) had already shown he could handle these sort of conditions and again displayed *his battling qualities off a mark 6lb higher than when scoring on much faster ground at Doncaster. (op 4-1)*

Cockatoo Ridge ran by far his best race over hurdles but could not quite pull it out of the fire. Only time will tell if this was merely a flash in the pan. *(op 66-1)*

Silkwood Top(IRE), raised 7lb for landing a touch at Windsor, was not beaten as far as had seemed likely early in the home straight. *(tchd 5-1)*

Star Member(IRE), turned out again quickly under a penalty, was supported by the offices. This stiffer course should not have been against him because he has won over further. *(op 7-4 tchd 2-1)*

Petwick(IRE) was anchored by another 5lb rise in the weights. *(op 6-1 tchd 7-1)*

Idian Mix(FR), a winner over this trip in the heavy at Auteuil, had been dropped 5lb. *(tchd 22-1)*

3215 AT THE RACES BEGINNERS' CHASE (15 fncs) — 2m 3f 110y

3:25 (3:25) (Class 4) 5-Y-O+ **£3,903** (£1,146; £573; £286)

Form — RPR

223 **1** **Montgermont (FR)**[37] 2488 6-11-3 124 .... MarkBradburne 145+
(Mrs L C Taylor) *hld up and bhd: hdwy 9th: led appr 4 out: rdn appr last: r.o wl* **7/2**[3]

116- **2** *10* **Reveillez**[292] 4394 7-11-3 .... APMcCoy 140+
(J R Fanshawe) *hld up: hmpd 2nd: hdwy 7th: chsd wnr fr 4 out: wknd flat* **7/4**[1]

06-0 **3** *28* **Marcel (FR)**[58] 2055 6-11-3 .... TimmyMurphy 115+
(M C Pipe) *mde most tl rdn and hdd appr 4 out: hld whn mstke 3 out* **5/2**[2]

P56- **4** *23* **Matthew Muroto (IRE)**[377] 2927 7-10-10 .... DarylJacob[(7)] 84
(R H Alner) *hld up: short-lived effrt 8th* **100/1**

P055 **5** *3 ½* **Fallout (IRE)**[18] 2846 5-9-7 .... WayneKavanagh[(7)] 64
(J W Mullins) *mstke 8th: a bhd* **100/1**

0-6P **6** *8* **Diamond Merchant**[74] 1801 7-11-3 105 .... WayneHutchinson 73
(Ian Williams) *chsd ldr to 10th: wknd appr 4 out* **100/1**

/PP- **F** **Jasper Rooney**[361] 3245 7-10-10 .... KeiranBurke[(7)] —
(C W Mitchell) *mstke 1st: fell 2nd* **250/1**

1220 **U** **Malaga Boy (IRE)**[18] 2849 9-11-3 .... JoeTizzard —
(C L Tizzard) *sltly hmpd 2nd: blnd and uns rdr 3rd* **50/1**

2 **U** **Ballez (FR)**[50] 2213 5-10-7 ....(b[1]) ChristianWilliams —
(P F Nicholls) *in tch: 6th whn blnd and uns rdr 6th* **12/1**

3/1- **P** **Grey Brother**[615] 31 8-11-3 .... RichardJohnson —
(P J Hobbs) *bdly hmpd 2nd: nt rcvr: p.u after 4th* **6/1**

5m 0.30s (6.40) **Going Correction** +0.575s/f (Soft)
WFA 5 from 6yo+ 8lb **10** Ran SP% **114.5**
Speed ratings: **110,106,94,85,84 81,—,—,—,—** CSF £10.45 TOTE £5.10: £1.50, £1.60, £1.70; EX 14.10.
Owner Mrs L C Taylor **Bred** D Allard **Trained** Upper Lambourn, Berks

FOCUS

An interesting contest which featured the chasing debuts of some decent hurdlers.

NOTEBOOK

Montgermont(FR) really got his act together with the help of some improved jumping and put his previous experience to good use. He can defy a penalty. *(op 10-3)*

Reveillez ◆ had not been seen since finishing sixth in the Royal & SunAlliance Hurdle at Cheltenham last March. He could make no impression on the winner and stiff finish eventually took its toll. There will be other days for him. *(op 6-4)*

Marcel(FR), a high-class novice hurdler last season, appeared to be getting the worst of the argument when missing out at the third last on this chasing bow. He was a big flop when odds-on here over hurdles last February. *(tchd 7-2)*

Grey Brother was a springer in the market on this switch to fences, and his supporters must have been cursing their luck when he was effectively put out of the contest at the second through no fault of his own. *(op 14-1)*

3216 GG.COM MAIDEN OPEN NATIONAL HUNT FLAT RACE — 2m 1f

3:55 (3:55) (Class 6) 4-6-Y-O **£2,055** (£599; £299)

Form — RPR

23 **1** **Leading Authority (IRE)**[40] 2432 5-11-5 .... JoeTizzard 103
(C L Tizzard) *a.p: hrd rdn over 2f out: led and hung lft ins fnl f: r.o* **9/2**[3]

04 **2** *1 ½* **Ammunition (IRE)**[25] 2720 6-11-5 .... TimmyMurphy 101
(M Pitman) *a.p: led over 4f out: rdn over 2f out: hdd ins fnl f: no ex cl home* **10/1**

3 **3** *1 ¼* **Graphex**[36] 2520 4-10-7 .... RobertThornton 88
(A King) *hld up in mid-div: hdwy over 4f out: rdn over 2f out: r.o one pce fnl f* **13/2**

4 *4* **Man Of Mine** 5-11-5 .... APMcCoy 96
(Mrs H Dalton) *t.k.h towards rr: rdn over 4f out: hdwy over 3f out: one pce fnl f* **5/1**

6 **5** *6* **Flemens River (IRE)**[17] 2864 5-11-2 .... TomMalone[(3)] 90
(C J Down) *prom: led over 5f out tl over 4f out: rdn over 3f out: wknd fnl f* **66/1**

0 **6** *hd* **Supreme Copper (IRE)**[65] 1922 6-11-5 .... TomDoyle 90
(Miss E C Lavelle) *hld up in rr: stdy hdwy over 6f out: rdn over 2f out: wknd fnl f* **22/1**

0 **7** *10* **Lagan Gunsmoke**[60] 2014 4-10-7 .... AndrewThornton 68
(Dr J R J Naylor) *hld up and bhd: sme hdwy 3f out: n.d* **50/1**

8 *½* **Mokujin (FR)**[254] 6-11-5 .... ChristianWilliams 79
(P F Nicholls) *hld up in tch: bmpd over 3f out: wknd over 2f out* **9/4**[1]

0 **9** *2 ½* **Marlowe (IRE)**[31] 2611 4-10-0 .... JamesWhite[(7)] 65
(R J Hodges) *led: hdd over 5f out: rdn whn edgd rt over 3f out: sn wknd* **33/1**

10 *1 ½* **Just Poppytee** 4-9-10 ow3 .... DarylJacob[(7)] 59
(R H Alner) *bhd fnl 6f* **33/1**

11 *dist* **Crystal Hollow** 6-11-5 .... SeanCurran —
(N R Mitchell) *bhd fnl 6f: t.o* **66/1**

0 **12** *dist* **King's Silver (IRE)**[36] 2534 5-11-5 .... VinceSlattery —
(N I M Rossiter) *hld up in tch: lost pl and rdn 8f out: t.o* **50/1**

0 **13** *25* **Knapp Bridge Boy**[236] 300 6-11-5 .... RJGreene —
(J R Payne) *t.k.h in rr: a bhd: t.o* **100/1**

4 **P** **Templer (IRE)**[74] 1799 5-11-5 .... RichardJohnson —
(P J Hobbs) *led into s: swvd bdly lft and rn off crse s: continued: t.o whn p.u after 5f* **4/1**[2]

4m 20.0s (13.20) **Going Correction** +0.575s/f (Soft)
WFA 4 from 5yo+ 11lb **14** Ran SP% **126.2**
Speed ratings: **91,90,89,87,85 84,80,79,78,78 —,—,—,—** CSF £48.77 TOTE £5.80: £1.60, £2.70, £2.30; EX 32.40 Place 6 £141.41, Place 5 £49.96.
Owner R G Tizzard **Bred** Jerry Murphy **Trained** Milborne Port, Dorset

FOCUS

An ordinary bumper with the first two to their marks.

NOTEBOOK

Leading Authority(IRE) was suited by the stiff course and found what was required despite turning out to be a difficult ride in the closing stages. *(op 6-1 tchd 7-1)*

Ammunition(IRE) was not inconvenienced by the soft ground and only got out-gunned towards the finish. *(op 8-1)*

Graphex eventually found his stamina coming into play over this stiffer test. *(op 6-1 tchd 15-2)*

Man Of Mine, out of a bumper winning half-sister to The Tsarevich, shaped fairly well on his debut. *(tchd 8-1)*

Flemens River(IRE) failed to get home after having far more use made of him this time.

Supreme Copper(IRE) was another who ran out of steam in the closing stages. *(op 20-1 tchd 25-1)*

T/Jkpt: Not won. T/Plt: £177.90 to a £1 stake. Pool: £82,977.80. 340.45 winning tickets. T/Qpdt: £20.40 to a £1 stake. Pool: £5,064.20. 183.20 winning tickets. KH

2803 FOLKESTONE (R-H)

Monday, January 2

OFFICIAL GOING: Chase course - soft (heavy in places); hurdle course - heavy

Wind: Light across Weather: Overcast

3217 BARRETTS ASHFORD FOR LANDROVER MARES' ONLY NOVICES' H'CAP HURDLE (9 hdls) — 2m 1f 110y

12:40 (12:40) (Class 4) (0-100,100) 4-Y-O+ **£3,253** (£955; £477; £238)

Form — RPR

F222 **1** **Hi Laurie (IRE)**[13] 2932 11-10-8 89 .... RichardSpate[(7)] 101+
(M Scudamore) *j.lft: mde all: drew clr bef last: easily* **10/11**[1]

0033 **2** *19* **Flower Haven**[33] 2569 4-10-0 91 ow3 .... ChrisHonour[(5)] 71
(M J Gingell) *in tch: chsd wnr sn after 2 out: rdn and no imp wl bef last* **7/1**[3]

22-0 **3** *28* **Mega D'Estruval (FR)**[25] 2730 6-11-5 100 .... AndrewGlassonbury[(7)] 64
(M C Pipe) *t.k.h: hld up in last: prog to dispute 2nd fr 4th: rdn and nt keen 2 out: sn wl btn: t.o* **7/4**[2]

600 **4** *5* **Lojo**[27] 2681 4-10-0 86 oh10 .... JamieGoldstein 33
(Miss Sheena West) *last fr 2nd: lost tch 5th: no ch after: wknd after 2 out: t.o* **33/1**

64F **P** **Satin Rose**[21] 2797 4-9-11 86 .... TJPhelan[(3)] —
(K J Burke) *mostly chsd wnr tl sn after 2 out: wknd rapidly: disputing poor 3rd whn p.u bef last* **20/1**

4m 35.6s (6.30) **Going Correction** +0.25s/f (Yiel)
WFA 4 from 6yo+ 11lb **5** Ran SP% **109.0**
Speed ratings: **96,87,75,72,—** CSF £7.36 TOTE £1.50: £1.02, £4.10; EX 6.80.
Owner Mrs N M Watkins **Bred** J J O'Neill **Trained** Bromsash, Herefordshire

FOCUS

Uncompetitive stuff and moderate form and the winner ran up to previous marks.

NOTEBOOK

Hi Laurie(IRE), who seems to go on any ground, is kept busy but she holds her form well. She tended to jump out to her left, but with her only serious market rival Mega D'Estruval failing to make an impact, it made little difference and she won easily. *(tchd Evens)*

Flower Haven, who had it to prove in the ground, did not get home in the conditions as well as the winner. *(tchd 6-1)*

Mega D'Estruval(FR) was expected to show more on this handicap debut but she looked far from enthusiastic and is probably one to have reservations about. *(op 2-1)*

Satin Rose *Official explanation: trainer's representative said filly had bled from the nose (op 14-1)*

3218 HOBBS PARKER TELECOMS BEGINNERS' CHASE (18 fncs) — 3m 1f

1:10 (1:10) (Class 4) 5-Y-O+ **£3,903** (£1,146; £573; £286)

Form — RPR

FP-U **1** **Concert Pianist**[20] 2805 11-11-5 108 .... PhilipHide 113+
(P Winkworth) *nt fluent: in tch: mstke 14th and looked to be struggling: effrt and lft 2nd 3 out: clsd to ld 2 out: sn clr* **10/1**

F/U2 **2** *8* **Stavordale Lad (IRE)**[20] 2808 8-11-5 110 ....(b[1]) SamThomas 105+
(P F Nicholls) *nt fluent: chsd ldr: upsides 13th: mstke next: 8l down whn lft in ld 3 out: sn drvn and nt look keen: hdd 2 out: one pce* **7/4**[1]

55/4 **3** *6* **Backpacker (IRE)**[20] 2805 9-10-12 104 .... CharlieStudd[(7)] 102+
(B G Powell) *chsd ldrs: rdn and 3rd whn terrible blunder 3 out: no ch after: plugged on fr 2 out* **15/2**[3]

0-31 **4** *dist* **Just A Splash (IRE)**[43] 2376 6-11-5 106 .... AndrewTinkler —
(N J Gifford) *hld up: effrt 12th: struggling fr 14th: hmpd 3 out: tired and no ch after: scrambled over last and virtually p.u* **7/2**[2]

2-00 **P** **True Lover (GER)**[24] 2747 9-11-2 .... RichardYoung[(3)] —
(J W Mullins) *in tch tl p.u suddenly bef 9th* **7/2**[2]

40 **P** **Saddlers Cloth (IRE)**[19] 2829 6-10-12 .... JimmyMcCarthy —
(J A Geake) *a in last pair: lost tch after mstke 12th: wknd rapidly and p.u bef 14th* **20/1**

-556 **U** **Burnt Out (IRE)**[18] 2846 7-10-12 .... JamesDavies —
(B G Powell) *led: jnd 12th: sn drew clr: 8 l ahd and gng strly whn ploughed through 3 out and uns rdr* **20/1**

6m 42.1s (8.70) **Going Correction** +0.475s/f (Soft) **7** Ran SP% **111.2**
Speed ratings: **105,102,100,—,— —,—** CSF £27.65 TOTE £8.50: £3.30, £1.20; EX 16.90.
Owner Ms J Segal, Mrs C Barber **Bred** Shade Oak Stud **Trained** Ramsnest Common, Surrey

FOCUS

A modest handicap best rated through the third.

NOTEBOOK

Concert Pianist, who had failed to complete in his last three starts, bounced back to post a personal best over fences. He is not as good as he used to be over hurdles but has always been capable when the mud is flying. *(op 12-1)*

Stavordale Lad(IRE), who is one-paced, was blinkered for the first time in an attempt to help him jump better. He was once again far from fluent, though. *(op 6-4 tchd 15-8)*

Backpacker(IRE), who blundered away his chance at the fence which caught out his stablemate Burnt Out, kept on but was never going to be a threat thereafter. *(op 8-1 tchd 7-1)*

Just A Splash(IRE), who was later reported to have been struck into, was struggling at the back *from a fair way out on his chasing debut. Official explanation: vet said gelding had been struck into on the right hand (op 4-1)*

Burnt Out(IRE), aided by the soft ground, was in the process of running her best race so far for her current trainer and looked the likeliest winner when diving through the third last and giving her rider no chance. Running to the level of her best hurdles form in Ireland would have been good enough to win this, and she can be given another chance.

3219 EASTWELL MANOR NOVICES' HURDLE (11 hdls) — 2m 6f 110y

1:40 (1:40) (Class 4) 5-Y-O+ **£3,253** (£955; £477; £238)

Form — RPR

1 **1** **Magnifico (FR)**[34] 2559 5-11-5 .... AndrewGlassonbury[(7)] 125+
(M C Pipe) *chsd ldr: nt fluent 7th: led 2 out: hrd rdn and steadily forged clr: all out* **4/6**[1]

FP-5 **2** *8* **Stoop To Conquer**[62] 1969 6-10-12 .... NoelFehily 105+
(A W Carroll) *led: narrowly hdd whn blnd 2 out: sn drvn: grad wknd bef last* **6/1**[3]

The Form Book, Raceform Ltd, Compton, RG20 6NL

43 **3** *11* **Nice Try (IRE)**[19] [2821] 7-10-12 .... SamThomas 92
(Miss Venetia Williams) *t.k.h early: trckd ldrs: mstke 8th: rdn and no imp after 3 out: eased after 2 out: kpt on again bef last* **11/4**[2]

0 **4** *dist* **Gran Dana (IRE)**[7] [2968] 6-10-7 .... LeeStephens(5) —
(G Prodromou) *in tch to 8th: sn wknd: t.o: btn 53l* **33/1**

P **Captain's Legacy** 5-10-5 .... RobertLucey-Butler(7) —
(D B Feek) *nt jump wl: a last: lost tch 6th: t.o whn p.u bef 3 out* **25/1**

/PP- **P** **Trooper Kit**[409] [2319] 7-10-12 .... LeightonAspell —
(Mrs L Richards) *in tch: niggled along after 5th: reluctant and lost tch bef 7th: ref to go rnd bnd bef 3 out and p.u* **66/1**

6m 9.20s (0.10) **Going Correction** +0.25s/f (Yiel) **6** Ran SP% **109.2**
Speed ratings: **109,106,102,—,—** — CSF £4.96 TOTE £1.50: £1.20, £1.20; EX 5.80.
Owner Nick Shutts **Bred** J De Muynck **Trained** Nicholashayne, Devon

FOCUS
Another uncompetitive race in which the first two have been rated as running to their pre-race marks.

NOTEBOOK
Magnifico(FR) made the less serious error of the two main players at the second last and that helped him to go clear on the run to the final flight. He coped with the ground and got the longer trip well enough, but he did not win in the manner that many had expected. *(op 4-7 tchd 1-2 in a place)*
Stoop To Conquer put his nose in the turf at the second last where the eventual winner also made a mistake, albeit less serious, and that error seemed to do it for him. He stayed well on the Flat and handles soft ground, so this sort of trip should suit him. *(op 11-2 tchd 7-1)*
Nice Try(IRE) was bred to appreciate this longer trip but he began to lose touch with the front two from the third last. He is now eligible for a handicap mark and better ground might see him in a better light. *(op 7-2)*
Gran Dana(IRE) was a banded-class middle-distance performer on the Flat.

3220 DVDKING.CO.UK MAIDEN CHASE (12 fncs) 2m
2:10 (2:10) (Class 4) 5-Y-0+ **£3,903** (£1,146; £573; £286)

Form RPR
32 **1** **Smart Cavalier**[33] [2574] 7-11-2 .... (t) SamThomas 113+
(P F Nicholls) *tended to jump lft: trckd ldrs: led 6th: lft clr 3 out: in command after: pushed out* **10/11**[1]

5P63 **2** *3* **Flying Patriarch**[17] [2867] 5-10-7 91 .... (b) PhilipHide 94
(G L Moore) *led to 4th: lost pl next: drvn and nt keen after 6th: lft modest 3rd 3 out: r.o fr next: chsd wnr last: unable to chal* **7/1**[3]

5-F **3** *14* **Liberia (FR)**[24] [2751] 7-11-2 .... AndrewTinkler 96+
(N J Henderson) *w ldr: led 4th to 6th: mstke 7th: 3rd whn mstke next: lft 2nd again 3 out: wknd 2 out: fin tired* **15/8**[2]

0U-5 **4** *20* **Bel Ombre (FR)**[24] [2751] 6-11-2 96 .... LeightonAspell 99+
(O Sherwood) *hld up: trckd ldrs fr 5th: chsd wnr 8th: 3l down whn tried to demolish 3 out: great rcvry by jockey but no ch after* **20/1**

P-PP **5** *2 ½* **Peveril Pride**[18] [2848] 8-11-2 83 .... (t) JimmyMcCarthy 67
(J A Geake) *a in rr: last and pushed along 5th: t.o fr 8th* **66/1**

6-P6 **6** *18* **Oh Golly Gosh**[17] [2861] 5-10-0 .... (p) MarcGoldstein(7) 40
(N P Littmoden) *t.k.h: nt fluent: hld up in last pair: jst in tch 8th: hanging lft after: wknd after 3 out: fin v tired* **25/1**

4m 13.2s (6.40) **Going Correction** +0.475s/f (Soft)
WFA 5 from 6yo+ 8lb **6** Ran SP% **109.8**
Speed ratings: **103,101,94,84,83** **74** CSF £7.20 TOTE £1.80: £1.20, £2.00; EX 7.30.
Owner J M dare **Bred** D F Sumpter **Trained** Ditcheat, Somerset

FOCUS
A modest maiden chase but the winner, rated value for ten lengths, did it nicely enough despite not looking altogether happy going this way round.

NOTEBOOK
Smart Cavalier, who did not get home over further because he failed to settle, appreciated the drop back to two miles and, although he jumped left handed, it did not stop him getting off the mark under Rules. He won easily enough but might be happier going the other way round when taking on better opposition. *(op 11-10 tchd 5-6)*
Flying Patriarch, back in the blinkers having worn cheekpieces last time, stepped up on his debut effort over fences and has been rated as having run to within 7lb of his best hurdles form. He stays further than this and that helped him see the trip out well. *(op 8-1)*
Liberia(FR) followed the winner by jumping out to his left over the last few fences and finished *pretty tired. He might do better back on a sounder surface.Official explanation: jockey said gelding hung badly left throughout (op 6-4 tchd 2-1)*
Bel Ombre(FR) did not pick his feet up at all at the third last and, although his rider did well to retain the partnership, his chance went there. He is capable of better than his finishing position suggests. *(op 25-1)*

3221 TED LONG CHALLENGE CUP AMATEUR RIDERS' H'CAP CHASE (15 fncs) 2m 5f
2:40 (2:40) (Class 5) (0-90,88) 5-Y-0+ **£3,435** (£1,065; £532; £266)

Form RPR
P40 **1** **Merry Storm (IRE)**[7] [2984] 7-10-3 68 .... MrJSnowden(3) 87+
(Mrs K Waldron) *trckd ldrs gng wl: led 2 out: clr last: pushed out* **5/2**[1]

6455 **2** *7* **Lucky Sinna (IRE)**[7] [2957] 10-11-5 88 .... MrSPJones(7) 97
(B G Powell) *trckd ldng pair: reminder after 9th: effrt to ld 3 out: hdd next: immediately btn* **9/1**

5506 **3** *nk* **Spider Boy**[11] [2951] 9-9-10 65 .... (p) MrTCollier(7) 74
(Miss Z C Davison) *towards rr but in tch: effrt 3 out: cl up bef 2 out: sn outpcd: wnt 3rd bef last: kpt on* **20/1**

P/45 **4** *2 ½* **Fisherman Jack**[27] [2689] 11-10-1 70 .... (p) RyanCummings(7) 77+
(G J Smith) *pressed ldr: led 9th to 3 out: btn whn mstke next: one pce* **16/1**

P3-4 **5** *3 ½* **Tallow Bay (IRE)**[54] [2129] 11-9-11 62 oh2 .... MrGTumelty(3) 65
(Mrs S Wall) *wl in rr: j. slowly 3rd and reminders: struggling fr 10th: plugged on again after 3 out: nrst fin* **9/1**

FP10 **6** *dist* **New Leader (IRE)**[35] [2555] 9-10-0 69 .... MrDGreenway(7) —
(Mrs L Richards) *settled in rr: wl adrift fr 8th: rapid prog to join ldrs after 3 out: wknd rapidly next: clambered over last: btn 44l* **6/1**[3]

U4-P **7** *4* **Monsieur Rose (IRE)**[239] [231] 10-10-12 81 .... MrSPHanson(7) —
(N J Gifford) *first ride: pottered rnd in last: t.o fr 11th: snatched 7th on line: btn 48l* **12/1**

6004 **8** *½* **Kaikovra (IRE)**[13] [2933] 10-10-8 77 .... (p) MrRQuinn(7) —
(M F Harris) *hld up off the pce: effrt 11th: nvr on terms: wknd rapidly after 3 out: t.o: btn 49l* **16/1**

5-P2 **P** **Bewleys Guest (IRE)**[13] [2933] 7-10-2 71 ow5 .... MrWBiddick(7) —
(Miss Venetia Williams) *blnd bdly 1st: led: j.lft and hdd 9th: mstke next: wknd 3 out: last whn p.u bef 2 out* **3/1**[2]

5m 37.7s (13.30) **Going Correction** +0.475s/f (Soft) **9** Ran SP% **112.1**
Speed ratings: **93,90,90,89,87** —,—,—,— CSF £24.24 CT £358.72 TOTE £3.20: £1.70, £2.00, £5.70; EX 27.70.
Owner Nick Shutts **Bred** Jim Healy **Trained** Stoke Bliss, Worcs

FOCUS
Low-grade stuff but the form might work out alright. The winner, value for a ten-length success, was very well handicapped.

NOTEBOOK
Merry Storm(IRE), who looked sure to score at Towcester on Boxing Day until running out on the run-in, was very well in as he got to race off a 6lb lower mark. He was always going well in behind *the leaders and ran out an easy winner in the end. He could well win again at a moderate level. (op 11-4 tchd 9-4)*
Lucky Sinna(IRE) has still to win a race but in all fairness second place was as good as he could have hoped for with the well-handicapped winner on his best behaviour. *(op 10-1)*
Spider Boy, another who remains a maiden, looked a danger turning into the straight but he found little for pressure. *(op 25-1)*
Fisherman Jack, fitted with cheekpieces this time, ran his best race so far under Rules, appreciating the drop back in trip.
New Leader(IRE), who prefers quicker ground, dropped out tamely in the straight. *(op 15-2)*

3222 PADDOCK (S) H'CAP HURDLE (11 hdls) 2m 6f 110y
3:15 (3:15) (Class 5) (0-90,90) 4-Y-0+ **£2,740** (£798; £399)

Form RPR
064- **1** **Roman Rampage**[441] [1763] 11-10-13 84 .... (p) RobertLucey-Butler(7) 83
(Miss Z C Davison) *settled in last: pushed along 7th: hrd drvn in remote 6th after 3 out: styd on fr 2 out: led last: plugged on* **7/1**

P656 **2** *1 ½* **Darko Karim**[25] [2723] 4-10-4 87 .... (b) JayHarris(5) 71+
(R J Hodges) *nt a fluent: prom: pressed ldr 6th: clr of rest next: led after 2 out: 5l clr between last 2: collared last: plugged on* **9/2**[2]

5003 **3** *12* **Better Moment (IRE)**[33] [2576] 9-11-5 90 .... (v) AndrewGlassonbury(7) 77+
(M C Pipe) *pressed ldr: led 4th: t.k.h in ld: drvn and hdd after 2 out: fnd little and sn btn* **5/1**[3]

4432 **4** *29* **Buz Kiri (USA)**[3] [3125] 8-11-4 82 .... (t) NoelFehily 38
(A W Carroll) *in tch: chsd clr ldng pair 7th to 3 out: sn wknd: t.o* **11/8**[1]

P0-0 **5** *7* **Exclusive Air (USA)**[231] [384] 7-9-7 64 oh2 .... TomMessenger(7) 13
(H H G Owen) *t.k.h: hld up: prog to trck clr ldng pair 3 out: wknd rapidly sn after 2 out: t.o* **28/1**

06P- **6** *9* **Darcy**[259] [4914] 12-10-3 67 .... PhilipHide 7
(D C O'Brien) *cl up to 6th: struggling fr 8th: mstke 3 out: t.o* **16/1**

3-P5 **P** **Dancing Shirley**[20] [2809] 8-10-13 77 .... MatthewBatchelor —
(Miss A M Newton-Smith) *led to 4th: wknd bef 7th: t.o whn mstke 3 out: p.u bef last* **7/1**

6m 17.0s (7.90) **Going Correction** +0.40s/f (Soft)
WFA 4 from 7yo+ 12lb **7** Ran SP% **111.3**
Speed ratings: **102,101,97,87,84** **81**,— CSF £36.23 TOTE £7.70: £3.60, £3.30; EX 70.70.There was no bid for the winner.
Owner Barry Ward **Bred** Mrs K Walton **Trained** Hammerwood, E Sussex

FOCUS
A poor race featuring a gambled-on winner and the form rated around the runner-up, but there is little to take from it for the future.

NOTEBOOK
Roman Rampage came in for some support in the market beforehand and landed the gamble on his first start for 441 days. Held up off the pace, he picked up those who had raced more prominently as they began to tire in the latter stages. He has had leg and wind problems and there was no bid for him at the subsequent auction. *(op 12-1)*
Darko Karim, running over the longest trip he has ever competed over, did not get home in the testing conditions, and his handicap mark looks too stiff for the time being. *(tchd 4-1)*
Better Moment(IRE) had not shown a liking for this sort of ground in the past and this longer trip in these conditions proved too taxing. *(op 7-2)*
Buz Kiri(USA), not for the first time this season, gave the impression that he could achieve more in banded contests on the All-Weather. *(op 6-4 tchd 13-8)*
Dancing Shirley *Official explanation: trainer said mare finished with a sore mouth (tchd 8-1)*

3223 HAPPY NEW YEAR H'CAP HURDLE (9 hdls) 2m 1f 110y
3:45 (3:45) (Class 4) (0-105,103) 4-Y-0+ **£4,228** (£1,241; £620; £310)

Form RPR
P234 **1** **Isam Top (FR)**[27] [2685] 10-10-0 82 .... RobertStephens(5) 84+
(M J Hogan) *chsd ldr: led after 2 out: rdn and jnd bef last: forged away again flat* **4/1**[3]

510- **2** *3 ½* **Misbehaviour**[258] [4579] 7-10-13 95 .... ChristopherMurray(5) 94
(Jim Best) *hld up in tch: smooth prog after 2 out: jnd wnr bef last: rdn and fnd nil flat* **11/2**

-525 **3** *12* **Monsal Dale (IRE)**[13] [2930] 7-10-7 84 .... (tp) LeightonAspell 71
(Mrs L C Jewell) *reluctant to line up and led in: hld up: clsd on ldrs after 2 out: sn rdn and outpcd: plugged on to take 3rd nr fin* **8/1**

1031 **4** *shd* **Before The Mast (IRE)**[7] [2962] 9-10-2 86 7ex .... CharliePoste(7) 72
(M F Harris) *hld up in tch: clsd on ldrs after 2 out: rdn and outpcd bef last: lost 3rd nr fin* **2/1**[1]

00P4 **5** *18* **The Gene Genie**[3] [3128] 11-10-2 84 .... JayHarris(5) 58+
(R J Hodges) *cl up: rdn 2 out: tried to rally u.p between last 2: sn wknd* **11/4**[2]

6F00 **6** *dist* **Sunley Future (IRE)**[2] [3152] 7-11-7 98 .... SamStronge —
(M F Harris) *tore off in clr ld: j.lft: thought abt refusing to go out on fnl circ: hdd sn after 2 out: stopped to nil: t.o* **22/1**

4m 36.1s (6.80) **Going Correction** +0.40s/f (Soft) **6** Ran SP% **110.8**
Speed ratings: **100,98,93,93,85** — CSF £24.52 TOTE £4.90: £2.30, £1.90; EX 28.70 Place 6 £41.81, Place 5 £25.44.
Owner Mrs Barbara Hogan **Bred** Mrs Jean Besnouin **Trained** North End, W Sussex

FOCUS
A moderate handicap in which the winner did not have to improve on the level of form he showed in his last two starts to score.

NOTEBOOK
Isam Top(FR) found extra on the run-in to see off Misbehaviour, who had looked a big danger jumping the final flight, and end a losing run stretching back to August 2002. He did not have to improve on his recent form to win and would not be great interest in a follow-up bid. *(op 9-2)*
Misbehaviour, a first runner for Jim Best, was running off a rating just 1lb lower than his career-high mark. He looked a serious danger early in the straight, but he found disappointingly little after the final flight. While the run might just have been needed on this return from a 258-day absence, he has shown a reluctant streak before. *(tchd 13-2)*
Monsal Dale(IRE), whose only career win over hurdles came over this course and distance, had the headgear back on. He looks badly handicapped at present. *(op 6-1)*
Before The Mast(IRE) seemed to be found out by the 7lb penalty he had to carry for his win in a selling handicap on Boxing Day. *(tchd 9-4 in a place)*
The Gene Genie was unable to take advantage of being able to run off a career-low mark. *(tchd 7-2 in a place)*

T/Plt: £94.70 to a £1 stake. Pool: £38,495.80. 296.50 winning tickets. T/Qpdt: £27.60 to a £1 stake. Pool: £2,521.70. 67.60 winning tickets. JN

3224 - 3230a (Foreign Racing) - See Raceform Interactive

3203 AYR (L-H)

Tuesday, January 3

OFFICIAL GOING: Soft (heavy in places)
After overnight rain the ground was very testing.
Wind: Almost nil Weather: Fine but on the cold side

3231 MEMBERSHIP AT AYR "NATIONAL HUNT" MAIDEN HURDLE (DIV I) (8 hdls 1 omitted) 2m

12:30 (12:31) (Class 4) 4-Y-O+ **£3,485** (£1,029; £514; £257; £128)

Form				RPR
2-42	**1**		**Harmony Brig (IRE)**[31] 2631 7-11-5 115 TonyDobbin (N G Richards) *mde all: hung lft extended run-in: styd on wl* **2/9**[1]	105+
-50F	**2**	3 ½	**Kilmackilloge**[12] 2942 7-11-5 AlanDempsey (M Todhunter) *hld up in rr: stdy hdwy 5th: wnt 2nd last: kpt on: no real imp* **20/1**[3]	97
0-34	**3**	2 ½	**Chateau Rouge (IRE)**[34] 2572 5-11-5 GrahamLee (M D Hammond) *sn chsng ldrs: wnt 2nd 2 out: one pce extended run-in* **8/1**[2]	94
3060	**4**	3	**Fearless Foursome**[12] 2944 7-11-2 85 PeterBuchanan(3) (N W Alexander) *chsd ldrs: one pce fr 2 out* **33/1**	91
00-0	**5**	15	**Buffy**[38] 2497 6-10-12 NeilMulholland (B Mactaggart) *chsd ldrs: wknd 2 out* **100/1**	69
	6	6	**Stand On Me**[233] 7-11-5 TimmyMurphy (P Monteith) *hld up in rr: hdwy 4th: lost pl 6th* **33/1**	70
/F00	**7**	5	**Datbandito (IRE)**[31] 2627 7-11-5 BruceGibson (L Lungo) *chsd ldrs: mstke 2nd: lost pl after 6th* **50/1**	65
0P	**8**	dist	**Glenisla Mist**[42] 2414 5-10-5 (t) DavidDaSilva(7) (Mrs S C Bradburne) *prom: lost pl 4th: t.o 6th: btn 36l* **100/1**	—
0P0	**U**		**Galahad (FR)**[31] 2627 5-11-5 BrianHarding (B Storey) *hld up in rr: hdwy and in tch whn blnd and uns rdr 5th* **66/1**	—
0-PP	**P**		**Moffied (IRE)**[12] 2947 6-11-0 MichaelMcAlister(5) (J Barclay) *t.k.h: trckd ldrs: lost pl 6th: bhd whn p.u bef next* **100/1**	—

4m 3.10s (5.80) **Going Correction** +0.225s/f (Yiel)
WFA 4 from 5yo+ 11lb **10** Ran SP% **110.0**
Speed ratings: **94,92,91,89,82 79,76,—,—,—** CSF £7.25 TOTE £1.20: £1.02, £2.30, £1.30; EX 5.00.
Owner It's A Bargain Syndicate **Bred** Mrs O E Matthews **Trained** Greystoke, Cumbria
■ The final flight had to be omitted.

FOCUS
A modest time for a race of its class and 3.1 seconds slower than the second division. No strength in depth with the first four well clear in the end.

NOTEBOOK
Harmony Brig(IRE), an exciteable type, had two handlers in the paddock. He set his own pace and still looked inexperienced on the extended run-in but was always doing more than enough. It will be one step at a time with him. *(op 1-5 tchd 1-4 in places)*
Kilmackilloge, a moderate walker, was put to sleep at the back. He went in pursuit of the winner at what is normally two out but, as hard as he tried, he was never going to finish anything but second best. This was much his best effort over hurdles so far. *(op 14-1)*
Chateau Rouge(IRE), who also had two handlers in the paddock, made a satisfactory start to his hurdling career but he looks to have a lot more stamina than speed. *(op 7-1 tchd 9-1)*
Fearless Foursome ran better on his fourth start after a break but he looks basically slow. *(op 25-1)*
Moffied(IRE) *Official explanation: vet said gelding had bled from the nose (op 66-1)*

3232 MEMBERSHIP AT AYR "NATIONAL HUNT" MAIDEN HURDLE (DIV II) (8 hdls 1 omitted) 2m

1:00 (1:00) (Class 4) 4-Y-O+ **£3,485** (£1,029; £514; £257; £128)

Form				RPR
0-36	**1**		**The Duke's Speech (IRE)**[25] 2755 5-11-5 JasonMaguire (T P Tate) *mde all: 10l clr whn blnd 2 out: clumsy last: easily* **1/2**[1]	115+
0/0	**2**	11	**Le Millenaire (FR)**[8] 2976 7-11-5 WilsonRenwick (S H Shirley-Beavan) *chsd ldrs: wnt 2nd 5th: kpt on fr 3 out: no ch w wnr* **33/1**	95
3	**3**	1 ½	**Triple Mint (IRE)**[52] 2185 5-11-0 StephenCraine(5) (D McCain) *chsd ldrs: blnd 5th: one pce fr 3 out* **15/2**[2]	96+
000	**4**	17	**Cedar Rapids (IRE)**[38] 2497 6-11-5 DavidO'Meara (H P Hogarth) *hld up: hdwy to chse ldrs 5th: wknd 2 out* **17/2**[3]	82+
00-P	**5**	6	**Kempski**[65] 1937 6-10-12 90 (p) GarethThomas(7) (R Nixon) *chsd ldrs: drvn along 4th: lost pl next* **25/1**	71
0-	**6**	10	**The Right People (IRE)**[297] 4323 6-11-5 BruceGibson (L Lungo) *nt jump wl: sn bhd: nvr a factor* **12/1**	61
00	**7**	3	**Turn The Corner (IRE)**[19] 2843 7-10-12 MrSClements(7) (J Clements, Ire) *chsd ldrs: drvn 5th: sn lost pl and bhd* **16/1**	58
0P	**8**	dist	**Claudia May**[30] 2652 5-10-9 PeterBuchanan(3) (Miss Lucinda V Russell) *in tch: lost pl after 4th: t.o 3 out: btn 76l* **100/1**	—
0-P	**P**		**Border Craic (IRE)**[59] 2036 6-11-5 NeilMulholland (B Mactaggart) *j. bdly 1st 2: t.o whn p.u after 3rd* **100/1**	—
0	**P**		**Native Coll**[12] 2948 6-11-5 RichardMcGrath (N W Alexander) *chsd ldrs: lost pl 4th: sn bhd: t.o whn p.u bef 3 out* **100/1**	—

(2.70) **Going Correction** +0.225s/f (Yiel) **10** Ran SP% **112.3**
Speed ratings: **102,96,95,87,84 79,77,—,—,—** CSF £26.21 TOTE £1.50: £1.10, £4.10, £2.40; EX 22.60.
Owner The Ivy Syndicate **Bred** Eamonn Delaney **Trained** Tadcaster, N Yorks
■ The fourth last flight was omitted on both circuits.

FOCUS
The sort of time you would expect for a race like this in the conditions, despite being 3.1 seconds faster than the first division. The winner outclassed the opposition but his jumping will need to improve.

NOTEBOOK
The Duke's Speech(IRE), who did not seem to stay the extended trip at Doncaster, made this a true test and had it in the bag when he almost failed to rise at the second last. Despite a clumsy jump at the final flight he outclassed the opposition but his hurdling technique will need to improve is he is to progress. *(tchd 4-7 in places)*
Le Millenaire(FR), a dual point winner, was making a quick return and over hurdles this time. He tried hard to keep tabs on the winner but it was clear some way from home that second best was the most he could hope for.
Triple Mint(IRE), making his debut over hurdles, stuck on after a blunder four out. A potential chaser, he probably just stays. *(op 8-1)*
Cedar Rapids(IRE), who ran out when in front last time, was heavily restrained and the basic idea was to try and teach him to settle. *(op 8-1)*
Kempski wore cheekpieces on his second outing after a six-month break but he is still some way short of the form that saw him finish runner-up twice last term. *(tchd 33-1)*

3233 FIRST FOOT H'CAP CHASE (11 fncs 1 omitted) 2m

1:30 (1:30) (Class 4) (0-115,113) 5-Y-O+ **£5,070** (£1,497; £748; £374; £187)

Form				RPR
3PP3	**1**		**Oliverjohn (IRE)**[12] 2945 9-10-2 92 PeterBuchanan(3) (Miss Lucinda V Russell) *mde virtually all: j. slowly 8th: styd on wl run-in* **4/1**[1]	105+
51B-	**2**	5	**Moment Of Madness (IRE)**[283] 4554 8-11-5 106 PadgeWhelan (T J Fitzgerald) *jnd ldrs 5th: upsides last: nt qckn* **8/1**	113
41/0	**3**	1 ¼	**Tagar (FR)**[29] 2679 9-10-3 93 MrTGreenall(3) (C Grant) *chsd wnr: drvn 8th: kpt on same pce appr last* **14/1**	99
5-F4	**4**	1 ¾	**Do L'Enfant D'Eau (FR)**[38] 2498 7-11-11 112 BrianHarding (B Storey) *wnt prom 5th: cl 3rd and rdn whn blnd last: kpt on same pce* **5/1**[2]	118+
-541	**5**	23	**Mexican (USA)**[19] 2842 7-10-5 92 (b) NeilMulholland (M D Hammond) *trckd ldrs 5th: lost grnd 7th: wknd 2 out* **4/1**[1]	73
PU01	**B**		**Longdale**[8] 2980 8-11-0 101 7ex AlanDempsey (M Todhunter) *wnt prom 5th: b.d next* **7/1**[3]	—
33-0	**F**		**Brave Thought (IRE)**[12] 2944 11-11-12 113 TimmyMurphy (P Monteith) *hld up: wnt prom 5th: fell next* **4/1**[1]	—

4m 11.1s (6.60) **Going Correction** +0.55s/f (Soft) **7** Ran SP% **106.9**
Speed ratings: **105,102,101,101,89 —,—** CSF £29.68 CT £338.38 TOTE £3.50: £2.70, £3.80; EX 26.90.
Owner Thoroughbred Leisure Racing Club **Bred** Joseph J O'Connor **Trained** Arlary, Perth & Kinross

FOCUS
The winner, a major market mover, was able to dominate and in the end won going away but overall it was a weak handicap. The fourth-last fence was bypassed.

NOTEBOOK
Oliverjohn(IRE), a 12/1 shot on the morning line and, from a stable back amongst the winners here the previous day, made this a true test. A slow jump four out put him on the back foot, but he deserves credit for the way he dug deep and came clear on the run-in. He is possibly better over two and a half miles but the conditions made this quite a test. *(op 11-2)*
Moment Of Madness(IRE), absent since being brought down over hurdles at Haydock in March, ran well especially as conditions were probably more testing than he really appreciates. He had won on his only previous start over fences and there is surely better to come. *(op 10-1)*
Tagar(FR), having his second run in a month after over two years on the sidelines, shaped a lot better and should improve again. *(tchd 16-1)*
Do L'Enfant D'Eau(FR), dropping back in trip, was still in with a shout when he made a horlicks of the last. He could well have finished runner-up. *(op 11-2)*
Mexican(USA), who had everything in his favour at Catterick, was not in the same sort of mood and folded tamely. *(tchd 9-2 and 5-1 in places)*
Brave Thought(IRE) was out of the contest at an early stage. *(op 3-1)*

3234 NEW GRANDSTAND SEASON TICKET H'CAP HURDLE (9 hdls 2 omitted) 2m 4f

2:05 (2:06) (Class 4) (0-115,110) 4-Y-O **£4,436** (£1,310; £655; £327; £163)

Form				RPR
U-12	**1**		**Birdwatch**[8] 2994 8-10-11 95 (b) RichardMcGrath (K G Reveley) *mde all: styd on fr 3 out: hrd rdn and kpt on run-in* **2/1**[1]	103+
5612	**2**	¾	**You Do The Math (IRE)**[19] 2843 6-10-8 99 MrGTumelty(7) (L Lungo) *hld up: stdy hdwy 5th: 5l 2nd and styng on wl whn blnd 3 out: clumsy next: styd on run-in: nt quite rch wnr* **11/4**[2]	107+
6454	**3**	10	**Speed Kris (FR)**[42] 2417 7-10-9 100 (v) DavidDaSilva(7) (Mrs S C Bradburne) *chsd ldrs: one pce fr 3 out* **12/1**	97+
/F1-	**4**	1 ¼	**Letitia's Loss (IRE)**[405] 2428 8-11-3 101 TonyDobbin (N G Richards) *wnt prom 4th: one pce fr 3 out* **10/1**	96
U-60	**5**	dist	**Brave Vision**[235] 332 10-11-7 110 ThomasDreaper(5) (A C Whillans) *in tch: outpcd 5th: lost pl after next: sn bhd: t.o: btn 46l* **50/1**	—
0/P	**6**	23	**Native Heights (IRE)**[2] 3172 8-11-10 108 (b) AlanDempsey (M Todhunter) *w ldrs: rdn 6th: wknd: bhd fr next: t.o* **25/1**	—
41-P	**F**		**Aberdare**[48] 2264 7-10-13 104 EwanWhillans(7) (J R Bewley) *mid-div whn fell 2nd* **25/1**	—
1-10	**B**		**Muckle Flugga (IRE)**[34] 2566 7-10-9 100 ScottMarshall(7) (N G Richards) *rr-div whn b.d 2nd* **14/1**	—
3/4B	**P**		**Jexel (FR)**[12] 2944 9-11-2 100 TimmyMurphy (B Storey) *chsd ldrs to 5th: outpcd after next: bhd whn p.u bef 2 out* **11/1**	—
FPP-	**P**		**Cambrian Dawn**[275] 4708 12-11-2 105 DesFlavin(5) (Mrs L B Normile) *sn struggling and detached: t.o whn p.u after 5th* **100/1**	—
4602	**P**		**Chief Dan George (IRE)**[12] 2944 6-10-10 94 GrahamLee (D R MacLeod) *in rr: reminders 4th: lost tch 6th: t.o whn p.u bef next* **6/1**[3]	—

5m 15.0s (2.30) **Going Correction** +0.225s/f (Yiel) **11** Ran SP% **116.7**
Speed ratings: **104,103,99,99,— —,—,—,—,— —** CSF £7.79 CT £50.76 TOTE £3.10: £1.30, £1.40, £1.90; EX 9.30.
Owner Jeremy Mitchell And Janet Powney **Bred** W R Lewis **Trained** Lingdale, Redcar & Cleveland
■ The fourth last hurdle was omitted on each circuit.

FOCUS
A true test in the conditions but the best horse on the day was only second best at the line.

NOTEBOOK
Birdwatch made this a true test and, stepping up the gallop in the final three quarters of a mile, simply would not be denied but he definitely had luck on his side. *(op 9-4 tchd 5-2)*
You Do The Math(IRE) moved through in smooth fashion to chase the winner but he made a nonsense of the third last flight. Losing ground to a lesser extent at the next, he really knuckled down on the run-in and would have made it with a bit further to go. The trouble is he is likely to go up in the ratings again. *(op 3-1 tchd 7-2 in a place)*
Speed Kris(FR) ran another respectable race but finds it very hard to add to his sole career hurdle-race win. *(tchd 14-1)*
Letitia's Loss(IRE), absent for over a year, took a walk in the market. She kept on in her own time and the outing will not be lost on her. *(op 6-1)*
Chief Dan George(IRE), 5lb higher, seemed to take little intest in the rear and was hopelessly tailed off when his rider called it a day. *Official explanation: trainer said gelding appeared to sulk when not getting run of race (op 8-1)*

3235 WEE DRAM MARES' ONLY NOVICES' HURDLE (9 hdls 2 omitted) 2m 4f

2:35 (2:35) (Class 4) 4-Y-O+ **£3,802** (£1,123; £561; £280; £140)

Form				RPR
6-12	**1**		**Camden Bella**[42] 2412 6-11-0 TonyDobbin (N G Richards) *hld up: hdwy and prom 6th: chalng whn blnd 3 out: upsides last: styd on wl to ld last 150yds* **4/1**[2]	99+
2-42	**2**	2	**Diklers Rose (IRE)**[37] 2515 7-11-0 RichardMcGrath (K G Reveley) *hdwy to trck ldrs 4th: styd on to take slt advantage between last 2: hdd and no ex run-in* **1/1**[1]	96+
	3	9	**Cinema (FR)**[7] 3045 6-10-9 ThomasDreaper(5) (B R Hamilton, Ire) *trckd ldrs: led appr 3 out: hdd between last 2: sn btn* **9/2**[3]	87

200 **4** *5* **Political Pendant**[29] [2674] 5-10-7 .... GarethThomas(7) 82
(R Nixon) *in rr: hdwy to chse ldrs after 5th: led after next: hdd appr 3 out: one pce* **100/1**

-035 **5** *2* **August Rose (IRE)**[60] [2024] 6-10-11 81 .... PeterBuchanan(3) 80
(Miss Lucinda V Russell) *prom: jnd ldrs 5th: lost pl appr 3 out* **20/1**

4006 **6** *5* **Silver Bow**[26] [2718] 5-11-0 .... GrahamLee 75
(J M Jefferson) *in rr: hdwy 5th: sn chsng ldrs: lost pl appr 3 out* **33/1**

0- **7** *27* **Fast And Fiery (IRE)**[7] [3046] 6-11-0 .... AnthonyRoss 48
(I A Duncan, Ire) *mde most tl after 6th: lost pl appr next* **50/1**

0F50 **8** *5* **Gemini Lady**[93] [1605] 6-11-0 74 .... KeithMercer 43
(Mrs J C McGregor) *in rr: sme hdwy 6th: sn lost pl and bhd* **66/1**

66 **P** **Two Good (IRE)**[103] [1532] 6-11-0 .... BrianHarding —
(P D Niven) *w ldrs: lost pl after 5th: sn bhd: t.o whn p.u bef 3 out* **50/1**

-P52 **P** **Sportula**[29] [2674] 5-10-11 92 .... MrTGreenall(3) —
(C Grant) *w ldrs: lost pl after 5th: sn bhd: t.o whn p.u bef 3 out* **10/1**

00 **P** **Lethem Present (IRE)**[19] [2838] 6-10-9 .... DougieCostello(5) —
(T Butt) *w ldrs: lost pl after 5th: sn bhd: t.o whn p.u bef 3 out* **100/1**

P3PP **P** **Aba Gold (IRE)**[188] [854] 6-10-7 .... MrSClements(7) —
(J Clements, Ire) *hld up in rr: drvn along 5th: sn bhd: t.o whn p.u bef 3 out* **100/1**

5m 16.0s (3.30) **Going Correction** +0.225s/f (Yiel) **12** Ran SP% **113.4**
Speed ratings: **102,101,97,95,94 92,82,80,—,— —,—** CSF £7.95 TOTE £4.50: £2.20, £1.10, £1.30; EX 6.30.
Owner Mrs Carole Stephenson **Bred** Mrs C Stephenson **Trained** Greystoke, Cumbria

FOCUS
No strength in depth in this mares-only novices hurdle. The first two should continue to hold their own at a similar level. Last flight in back straight omitted.

NOTEBOOK
Camden Bella survived a blunder three out and showed a very good attitude to gain the upper hand on the run-in. Her willingness to battle should stand her in good stead. *(op 3-1 tchd 9-2 in places)*
Diklers Rose(IRE) looked to be travelling slightly better when going on between the last two but in the end the winner proved the tougher nut. She may not have appreciated the ground as testing as this. *(op 5-4 tchd 11-8 in places)*
Cinema(FR) looked a real threat when taking it up turning for home, but in the end she did not see out the extended trip anywhere near as well as the first two. *(op 4-1 tchd 5-1 in places)*
Political Pendant stepped up on her initial effort over hurdles but basically she looks slow.

3236 HAPPY NEW YEAR BEGINNERS' CHASE (15 fncs 2 omitted) 2m 4f
3:10 (3:10) (Class 4) 5-Y-0+ **£5,070** (£1,497; £748; £374; £187)

Form RPR

0-U2 **1** **Roman Ark**[18] [2861] 8-11-3 .... GrahamLee 126+
(J M Jefferson) *hld up: hdwy 6th: trckd ldrs 8th: led appr 3 out: rdn and styd on run-in* **8/11**[1]

P **2** *3½* **Junior Des Ormeaux (FR)**[28] [2689] 9-11-3 .... WilsonRenwick 117
(S H Shirley-Beavan) *led tl appr 3 out: rallied last: no ex* **66/1**

1-42 **3** *8* **Trisons Star (IRE)**[7] [3041] 8-10-12 .... DesFlavin(5) 112+
(Mrs L B Normile) *chsd ldrs: blnd 3rd and 11th: kpt on fr 3 out to take mod 3rd last* **11/2**[3]

-622 **4** *6* **Tusk**[17] [2872] 6-11-3 124 .... DavidO'Meara 111+
(H P Hogarth) *trckd ldrs: 6l 3rd whn blnd 3 out: mstke next: 4th and wl btn whn blnd last: eased* **3/1**[2]

-PF4 **5** *26* **Skenfrith**[12] [2943] 7-11-0 107 .... MrCStorey(3) 77
(Miss S E Forster) *in rr: outpcd and bhd fr 8th* **33/1**

P **6** *12* **The Associate (IRE)**[53] [2168] 9-11-0 .... PeterBuchanan(3) 65
(Miss Lucinda V Russell) *last whn blnd 4th: bhd tl sme hdwy 9th: sn lost pl* **100/1**

45P- **7** *1¾* **Blackout (IRE)**[261] [4875] 11-10-12 53 .... MichaelMcAlister(5) 63
(J Barclay) *sn pushed along: chsd ldrs: outpcd 8th: bhd fr 12th* **200/1**

0P **P** **Dannymolone (IRE)**[28] [2689] 7-11-3 .... FinbarKeniry —
(M D Hammond) *in tch: lost pl 8th: p.u after next* **100/1**

P **The Ample Hamper**[290] 8-11-3 .... NeilMulholland —
(Mrs L B Normile) *in tch: blnd 5th: in rr whn p.u after 7th* **100/1**

3052 **P** **Lord Payne (IRE)**[19] [2839] 8-11-3 105 .... TimmyMurphy —
(P Monteith) *wnt prom 5th: lost pl 8th: bhd fr 12th: p.u bef 2 out* **16/1**

5m 29.8s (6.90) **Going Correction** +0.55s/f (Soft) **10** Ran SP% **112.1**
Speed ratings: **108,106,103,101,90 85,85,—,—,—** CSF £54.89 TOTE £1.70: £1.10, £4.60, £1.40; EX 57.60.
Owner Richard Collins **Bred** Miss Deborah J Baker **Trained** Norton, N Yorks

FOCUS
The winner struggled in the end and the second deserves to find a race. First fence in home straight omitted.

NOTEBOOK
Roman Ark, heavily backed, travelled strongly jumping well on the whole. He took it up on the bridle but made hard work of it in the end. The ground might have been more testing than he prefers and, judged on the way he travels, a drop back to two miles will not be a problem. *(tchd 10-11)*
Junior Des Ormeaux(FR), a point winner, made this a true test and deserves credit for the way he stuck to his guns, giving the winner a fight in the end. He can surely go one better.
Trisons Star(IRE), having just his third start over fences, shaped better and will be suited by a return to three miles. *(op 7-1)*
Tusk had leeway to make up when hitting the third last low and hard. He met the last two wrong and in the end his rider let him finish in his own time. Two miles might suit him better but he still has plenty to prove over fences. *(tchd 11-4)*
The Ample Hamper *Official explanation: jockey said gelding was unsuited by the soft (heavy in places) ground*

3237 CONFERENCES AT AYR RACECOURSE STANDARD NATIONAL HUNT FLAT RACE (CONDITIONAL JOCKEYS/AMATEURS) 2m
3:40 (3:40) (Class 6) 4-6-Y-0 **£2,055** (£599; £299)

Form RPR

0 **1** **Stolen Moments (FR)**[34] [2572] 5-11-2 .... MrTGreenall(3) 100
(P D Niven) *chsd ldrs: rdn and outpcd over 3f out: styd on to ld last 150yds: hld on towards fin* **20/1**

32 **2** *nk* **Character Building (IRE)**[34] [2572] 6-11-0 .... DougieCostello(5) 100
(J J Quinn) *trckd ldrs: effrt over 3f out: kpt on to ld 1f out: no ex towards fin* **1/1**[1]

0 **3** *7* **Scarlet Cloak (USA)**[45] [2340] 5-11-5 .... KeithMercer 93+
(Mrs L B Normile) *hld up in mid-div: hdwy to trck ldrs 7f out: led over 2f out tl 1f out: fdd* **25/1**

4 *1½* **Open De L'Isle (FR)** 4-10-2 .... StephenCraine(5) 80
(J P L Ewart) *led: qcknd 5f out: hdd over 2f out: one pce* **25/1**

5 *6* **Benny The Piler (IRE)** 6-10-12 .... EwanWhillans(7) 86
(N G Richards) *hld up towards rr: hdwy 7f out: sn chsng ldrs: outpcd over 3f out: n.d after* **4/1**[2]

6 **6** *9* **Classy Chav (IRE)**[58] [2068] 4-9-11 .... DavidDaSilva(10) 65
(P Monteith) *mid-div: wnt prom after 5f: lost pl over 3f out* **14/1**

0- **7** *6* **Mountain Mix**[597] [384] 6-11-0 .... DesFlavin(5) 71
(Mrs L B Normile) *hld up in rr: hdwy 7f out: sn pushed along: lost pl over 4f out* **20/1**

8 *9* **Windygate (IRE)** 6-11-0 .... ThomasDreaper(5) 62
(A Parker) *hld up in rr: sme hdwy 7f out: sn lost pl* **33/1**

4 **9** *8* **Tahaddi Turtle (IRE)**[31] [2642] 4-10-2 .... WilliamKennedy(5) 42
(T P Tate) *prom: drvn along 6f out: lost pl over 5f out* **5/1**[3]

10 *2½* **Ansa The Question** 5-10-5 .... PhilKinsella(7) 44
(A H Mactaggart) *in rr: hdwy 7f out: sn lost pl* **100/1**

0-00 **11** *dist* **Rab Cee**[16] [2906] 6-10-12 .... MrMSollitt(7) —
(W G Young) *prom 5f: sn lost pl: t.o 7f out: btn 95l* **200/1**

12 *7* **Red Rain (IRE)** 4-9-9 .... BrianHughes(5) —
(J Clements, Ire) *sn drvn along: lost pl after 5f: t.o 7f out* **50/1**

35 **13** *2½* **Overnight**[56] [2112] 6-10-12 .... PatrickMcDonald(7) —
(Mrs A C Hamilton) *t.k.h: jnd ldr after 3f: hung rt and rn v wd bnd after 4f: sn eased and bhd: t.o fnl 9f* **50/1**

4m 0.70s (1.50) **Going Correction** +0.225s/f (Yiel)
WFA 4 from 5yo+ 11lb **13** Ran SP% **118.9**
Speed ratings: **105,104,101,100,97 93,90,85,81,80 —,—,—** CSF £38.29 TOTE £17.20: £3.00, £1.10, £4.90; EX 72.50 Place 6 £3.77, Place 5 £3.76.
Owner The Poppet Partnership **Bred** Elevage Des Chartreux **Trained** Barton-le-Street, N Yorks

FOCUS
They stood still for about five seconds when the tap went across and the early pace was funereal. The first two pulled clear in the end but those behind might struggle.

NOTEBOOK
Stolen Moments(FR), on the leg, had clearly learnt plenty and after being tapped for toe did just enough to upset the favourite.
Character Building(IRE), again heavily supported, looked to have done enough when going half a length up with just a furlong to go but in the end he was edged out of it. He is proving expensive to follow. *(op 5-4)*
Scarlet Cloak(USA) travelled supremely well and took it up still on the bridle but the way he faded suggested the outing was still needed.
Open De L'Isle(FR), who stands over a fair amount of ground, wound the gallop up from the front but in the end had his limitations ruthlessly exposed. *(tchd 33-1)*
Benny The Piler(IRE), a big type who stands over plenty of ground, made a satisfactory debut but basically he looks a long-term chasing prospect. *(op 3-1 tchd 9-2)*
Tahaddi Turtle(IRE) wanted to do nothing but hang right in the back straight and something may have been amiss. *Official explanation: jockey said gelding hung badly right-handed back straight (op 11-2)*
Overnight *Official explanation: jockey said saddle slipped*
T/Plt: £14.60 to a £1 stake. Pool: £43,043.55. 2,137.90 winning tickets. T/Qpdt: £11.70 to a £1 stake. Pool: £3,903.95. 246.70 winning tickets. WG

2995 WINCANTON (R-H)
Wednesday, January 4

OFFICIAL GOING: Soft
Wind: Virtually nil Weather: Fine

3238 MORRIS FURNITURE GROUP MAIDEN HURDLE (DIV I) (11 hdls) 2m 6f
1:00 (1:00) (Class 4) 4-Y-0+ **£4,228** (£1,241; £620; £310)

Form RPR

1 **Geeveem (IRE)**[220] 6-11-6 .... ChristianWilliams 117+
(P F Nicholls) *trckd ldrs: wnt 2nd 6th: drvn along after 3 out: chal next: rdn to ld appr last: styd on strly* **13/2**[3]

1- **2** *9* **Hobbs Hill**[338] [3633] 7-11-6 .... APMcCoy 110+
(C R Egerton) *trckd ldr: led 3rd: pckd 5th: hit 4 out: pushed along appr 2 out: hdd appr last: kpt on same pce* **10/11**[1]

0-2P **3** *8* **Sir Pandy (IRE)**[64] [1975] 6-11-6 .... AndrewThornton 99
(R H Alner) *chsd ldrs: hit 2nd: outpcd and lost position after 4 out: plenty to do appr 2 out: kpt on again appr last* **14/1**

41-6 **4** *1* **Barton Legend**[63] [1980] 6-10-13 .... DarylJacob(7) 98
(D P Keane) *chsd ldrs: rdn after 3 out: wknd fr next* **28/1**

315/ **5** *11* **Historic Place (USA)**[68] [4649] 6-11-6 .... MarkBradburne 93+
(J A Geake) *chsd ldrs: disp cl 2nd 3 out: rdn sn after: wknd 2 out: no ch whn blnd last* **7/2**[2]

334 **6** *24* **Coeur D'Alene**[15] [2928] 5-11-6 .... RobertThornton 63
(Dr J R J Naylor) *a in rr* **20/1**

56-0 **7** *2½* **Harrival**[55] [2148] 6-10-13 .... MrGTumelty(7) 61
(Miss M Bragg) *a in rr* **200/1**

8 *10* **Heavy Weather (IRE)**[256] 8-11-6 .... JasonMaguire 51
(Miss Joanne Priest) *hit 3rd: a in rr* **25/1**

0-6 **9** *1¾* **Northern Link (IRE)**[45] [2376] 7-11-6 .... MatthewBatchelor 49
(Miss Tor Sturgis) *blnd 5th: a in rr* **200/1**

53-0 **10** *19* **Freeline Fury**[55] [2144] 6-11-6 .... TomDoyle 30
(P R Webber) *led to 3rd: wknd 6th: blnd 7th* **125/1**

P **Jeffslottery**[196] 4-10-7 .... DaveCrosse —
(D W Lewis) *j. slowly and bhd 6th: p.u after next* **250/1**

3 **P** **Outside Half (IRE)**[101] [1563] 4-10-2 .... HowieEphgrave(5) —
(L Corcoran) *in tch to 6th: t.o whn p.u bef 3 out* **33/1**

P **Fair View (GER)**[74] 5-10-13 .... JodieMogford —
(Dr P Pritchard) *prom early: bhd fr 6th: t.o whn p.u bef 2 out* **66/1**

0 **P** **First Centurion**[43] [2423] 5-11-6 .... (v[1]) WayneHutchinson —
(Ian Williams) *in tch: hit 3 out and wknd sn after: p.u bef last* **40/1**

5m 36.4s (11.30) **Going Correction** +0.525s/f (Soft)
WFA 4 from 5yo+ 12lb **14** Ran SP% **115.7**
Speed ratings: **100,96,93,93,89 80,79,76,75,68 —,—,—,—** CSF £12.06 TOTE £8.40: £1.80, £1.60, £3.70; EX 11.30.
Owner Paul Barber,Colin Lewis,Malcolm Calvert **Bred** James Barry **Trained** Ditcheat, Somerset

FOCUS
A modest maiden hurdle, run at an average pace, and the field came home strung out on the deep surface. The form looks fair rated through the third, and it was the stonger of the two divisions.

NOTEBOOK
Geeveem(IRE), last seen taking an Irish point 220 days previously and very easy to back in the betting ring, responded gamely for pressure from three out and gradually wore down the runner-up before the final flight to make a winning debut for new connections. He is entitled to improve a deal for the experience, should be seen in a better light when faced with a stiffer test in the future, and can win again in this division before ultimately going novice chasing. *(op 5-1)*
Hobbs Hill, an impressive bumper winner on debut for connections at Kempton 338 days previously, looked most likely to score at the top of the straight, but his stride shortened approaching the penultimate flight and he was ultimately outstayed by the winner. He will have better claims of staying the trip with this outing under his belt, and may prefer a less-taxing surface in the future, so is not one to write off on the back of this display. *(tchd 11-8 in a place)*
Sir Pandy(IRE) failed to threaten at any stage, but was doing all of his best work at the finish and turned in a more encouraging effort. He now becomes eligible for a handicap mark and shaped as though an even stiffer test will be to his advantage in the future. *(op 10-1)*

Barton Legend posted a much more encouraging effort, but failed to see out this longer trip. He should be of more interest when eligible for handicaps after his next outing. *(op 25-1)*
Historic Place(USA), not at all disgraced on the Flat in 2005 and making his hurdling debut, showed up well enough until running out of gas after the third last. This could be deemed a touch disappointing, but his yard is struggling for form at present, and it would be a surprise were he not to leave this form behind in due course. *(op 4-1 tchd 10-3)*
Jeffslottery *Official explanation: jockey said gelding bled from the nose (op 100-1)*

3239 HAPPY NEW YEAR H'CAP CHASE (17 fncs) 2m 5f
1:30 (1:30) (Class 4) (0-105,105) 5-Y-O+ **£5,704** (£1,684; £842; £421; £210)

Form RPR

0-26 **1** **First De La Brunie (FR)**[37] 2555 5-10-5 **94** .... RobertThornton 103+
(A King) *trckd ldrs: clsd up 4 out: chal next: sn ld and clr: v easily* **11/2**[2]

2-40 **2** *8* **Sargasso Sea**[32] 2632 9-11-12 **105** .... JasonMaguire 114+
(J A B Old) *chsd ldrs: nt fluent 9th (water): led 13th: nt fluent 4 out: hdd after next and sn outpcd: hld on for 2nd run-in* **20/1**

0613 **3** *1* **Hiers De Brouage (FR)**[21] 2827 11-11-5 **103** ....(tp) StephenCraine(5) 112+
(J G Portman) *led 3rd tl after next: styd pressing ldrs tl hit 11th: rdn next: one pce fr 4 out* **12/1**

4F0F **4** *4* **Roschal (IRE)**[45] 2368 8-11-12 **105** .... RichardJohnson 108+
(P J Hobbs) *bhd: hdway fr 3 out: styd on fr next but nvr in contention* **10/1**

F-6 **5** *½* **Ballyfin (IRE)**[9] 2957 8-10-8 **87** .... JimmyMcCarthy 89
(J A Geake) *hit 10th: nvr nr ldrs* **6/1**[3]

4251 **6** *½* **Jupon Vert (FR)**[9] 2960 9-11-5 **98** 7ex .... JimCrowley 100+
(R J Hodges) *chsd ldrs: led after 4th: hdd 13th: wknd and mstke 3 out* **25/1**

3153 **7** *7* **Taksina**[9] 2984 7-9-6 **81** .... PaulDavey(10) 77+
(R H Buckler) *led to 3rd: wknd 9th* **25/1**

2P/4 **F** **Predestine (FR)**[32] 2630 6-11-11 **104** .... JohnMcNamara —
(K C Bailey) *in tch whn fell 11th* **14/1**

3PP3 **P** **Quizzling (IRE)**[21] 2818 8-9-11 **79** oh3 .... OwynNelmes(3) —
(B J M Ryall) *a in rr: rdn 8th: t.o whn p.u bef 13th* **33/1**

-324 **P** **Lizzie Bathwick (IRE)**[9] 2996 7-11-2 **95** .... NoelFehily —
(D P Keane) *in tch: hdway 10th: one pce in 5th whn p.u bef 4 out* **9/2**[1]

53-3 **P** **Tradingup (IRE)**[42] 2431 7-10-13 **92** .... PaddyBrennan —
(Andrew Turnell) *hit 1st and 5th: bhd and nvr gng: t.o whn p.u bef 13th* **9/2**[1]

/0-2 **P** **Manawanui**[65] 1953 8-11-10 **103** .... AndrewThornton —
(R H Alner) *chsd ldrs: hit 3rd and 5th: sn bhd: bdly hmpd 11th and p.u* **9/1**

5m 30.3s (7.20) **Going Correction** +0.525s/f (Soft)
WFA 5 from 6yo+ 9lb **12** Ran SP% **114.9**
Speed ratings: **107,103,103,102,101 101,99,—,—,— —,—** CSF £106.56 CT £1260.39 TOTE £9.70: £2.80, £6.00, £2.40; EX 199.40.
Owner Mr & Mrs F C Welch **Bred** J Crouzillac Et Al **Trained** Barbury Castle, Wilts

FOCUS
A modest handicap and probably not strong form, but run at a decent pace, and the winner is progressive.

NOTEBOOK
First De La Brunie(FR) ◆ ran out a most convincing winner and landed his first race over jumps at the ninth attempt. He has taken time to find his feet since switching from France, but this softer ground was clearly right up his street, and his jumping was particularly assured. This looked about as far as he wanted to go, indeed he may just prove happiest over shorter in the future, and he will prove very hard to beat if found a suitable opportunity under a penalty. *(op 7-1)*
Sargasso Sea, pulled up on his only two previous outings over fences, showed much his best form for some time and performed with credit under his big weight. He still has to improve his jumping in this sphere, and while consistency is far from his strong suit, he remains open to further imrpovement over this sort of trip. *(tchd 16-1)*
Hiers De Brouage(FR) kept to his task gamely under pressure, enjoying the return to this longer trip, and clearly remains in decent heart at present. *(op 7-1)*
Roschal(IRE) never seriously threatened, yet kept on well enough under his big weight, and this should help to restore his confidence. *(op 16-1)*
Lizzie Bathwick(IRE) was looking laboured prior to pulling up with something presumably amiss. *Official explanation: jockey said mare lost its action, but returned sound (tchd 4-1)*
Tradingup(IRE) *Official explanation: jockey said gelding never travelled (tchd 4-1)*

3240 MORRIS FURNITURE GROUP MAIDEN HURDLE (DIV II) (11 hdls) 2m 6f
2:00 (2:01) (Class 4) 4-Y-O+ **£4,228** (£1,241; £620; £310)

Form RPR

04 **1** **Nero West (FR)**[32] 2624 5-10-13 .... MissLucyBridges(7) 90+
(Miss Lucy Bridges) *hld up in rr: stdy hdwy fr 4 out: pushed along to ld appr 2 out: c clr sn after: comf* **33/1**

2 *10* **Just For Men (IRE)**[248] 6-11-6 .... ChristianWilliams 81+
(P F Nicholls) *j.big 1st: chsd ldrs: wnt 2nd 7th: chal 3 out: sn led: rdn and hdd bef next: sn no ch: hung rt run-in* **10/11**[1]

5 **3** *5* **Black And Tan (IRE)**[36] 2565 6-11-6 .... RichardJohnson 72
(P J Hobbs) *hld up mid-div: hdwy fr 4 out: chsd ldrs and pushed along after next: one pce fr 2 out* **7/1**[3]

6 **4** *2½* **Coleraine (IRE)**[48] 2288 6-11-6 .... LeightonAspell 70
(O Sherwood) *in tch: pushed along and hday to chse ldrs 7th: one pce fr 3 out* **22/1**

10/0 **5** *1¾* **Alf Lauren**[38] 2528 8-11-6 .... RobertThornton 68
(A King) *bhd: hdwy 7th: chsd ldrs and rdn after 3 out: wknd bef next* **9/2**[2]

P0 **6** *3* **Pure Magic (FR)**[21] 2826 5-11-6 .... JamieGoldstein 65
(Miss J S Davis) *chsd ldrs: rdn 3 out: wknd bef next* **66/1**

P **7** *12* **Four In Hand**[20] 2849 8-10-6 .... LiamHeard(7) 46
(Mrs K M Sanderson) *bhd: hdwy 5th: chsd ldrs 7th: wknd sn after 3 out* **100/1**

8 *8* **Mylord Collonges (FR)**[255] 6-11-6 .... PaddyBrennan 45
(Mrs Susan Nock) *led to 5th: led again 6th: hdd after 3 out: wknd qckly* **10/1**

0P/0 **9** *13* **Lady Wurzel**[5] 3127 7-10-10 .... MissPGundry(3) 25
(J G Cann) *prom early: bhd fr 6th* **125/1**

00 **10** *2½* **The Laying Hen (IRE)**[37] 2558 6-10-6 .... DarylJacob(7) 22
(D P Keane) *a in rr* **100/1**

330 **11** *5* **Milanshan (IRE)**[37] 2558 6-10-13 .... RJGreene 17
(J W Mullins) *a in rr* **50/1**

00 **12** *2* **Go Commercial (IRE)**[21] 2826 5-11-6 .... TimmyMurphy 22
(M C Pipe) *chsd ldrs to 6th: sn bhd* **20/1**

00 **13** *4* **Royal Hilarity (IRE)**[43] 2421 6-11-6 .... PaulMoloney 18
(Ian Williams) *bhd: sme hdwy 6th: sn wknd* **22/1**

\- **P** **Pine Marten** 7-11-6 ....(t) JimmyMcCarthy —
(J A Geake) *a in rr: t.o whn p.u bef 7th* **50/1**

0-U **P** **Allborn Lad (IRE)**[19] 2865 6-11-6 .... NoelFehily —
(C J Mann) *led 5th to 6th: wknd 7th: t.o whn p.u bef 2 out* **100/1**

5m 43.5s (18.40) **Going Correction** +0.525s/f (Soft) **15** Ran SP% **117.7**
Speed ratings: **87,83,81,80,80 78,74,71,66,66 64,63,62,—,—** CSF £61.56 TOTE £43.50: £5.00, £1.20, £2.30; EX 92.00.
Owner Cdre Richard Bridges **Bred** Ecurie Pelder **Trained** Shaftesbury, Dorset

FOCUS
A moderate winning time for the grade, 7.1 seconds slower than the first division, and the field came home strung out due to the frenetic early pace. The form looks weak.

NOTEBOOK
Nero West(FR), ridden to get the longer trip, sycthed through rivals to lead before the penultimate flight and ultimately opened his account over hurdles in grand style. The combination of this stiffer test and softer ground certainly played to his strengths, and it will be interesting to see whether he can now progress again, as he shaped as though he will stay even further in due course.
Just For Men(IRE), bought by connections for 18,000euros after winning an Irish point 248 days previously, had no answer to the winner's challenge and finished very tired in second. He was very well backed for this, so is presumably thought capable of much better, and it may have been a different story had he been given a more patient ride Very much a future chasing type, he is not one to write off just yet. *(op 11-8 tchd 6-4 in places)*
Black And Tan(IRE), who showed ability when fifth on his recent bumper debut, appeared one paced and did not totally convince over this stiffer test. He can do better as he gains further experience, however. *(op 9-2)*
Coleraine(IRE) was not given too hard a time on this hurdling debut and is another who did not look totally at home over this trip. He is going to need more time. *(op 20-1)*
Alf Lauren failed to improve for this recent comeback effort at Newbury and looked a non-stayer over this longer trip. He has plenty to prove now. *(op 5-1)*
Royal Hilarity(IRE) *Official explanation: trainer said gelding was unsuited by the soft ground (op 33-1)*

3241 CONNAUGHT CUP DAY 21ST JANUARY H'CAP CHASE (21 fncs) 3m 1f 110y
2:30 (2:32) (Class 4) (0-105,105) 5-Y-O+ **£5,704** (£1,684; £842; £421; £210)

Form RPR

2P-P **1** **Boundary House**[42] 2431 8-10-6 **85** .... TimmyMurphy 94+
(J A B Old) *hld up in rr: stdy hdwy to trck ldrs 17th: chal 3 out: led next: drvn and styd on wl run-in* **16/1**

36-3 **2** *3½* **Treasulier (IRE)**[27] 2729 9-10-11 **97** .... KeiranBurke(7) 103+
(P R Rodford) *in tch: chal 11th: led 15th: blnd 17th: hdd 2 out: kpt on same pce* **17/2**

P **3** *4* **Nykel (FR)**[73] 1845 5-10-13 **104** .... RobertThornton 94+
(A King) *chsd ldrs fr 8th: blnd 15th: rallied fr 4 out: one pce fr 3 out* **9/1**

140- **4** *½* **Walter's Destiny**[302] 4239 14-11-8 **101** .... PaddyBrennan 103+
(C W Mitchell) *led to 4th: lost pl and rdn 12th: hdwy 14th: hmpd 16th: rallied u.p fr 4 out: one pce fr next* **33/1**

/P0P **5** *10* **Oscar Performance (IRE)**[29] 2682 11-10-0 **79** oh5(b[1])
BenjaminHitchcott 73+
(R H Buckler) *led 4th to 8th: led again 12th tl blnd and hdd 15th: drvn to chal 17th: wknd 3 out* **100/1**

-432 **6** *¾* **Infrasonique (FR)**[23] 2800 10-11-6 **99** ....(v) MarkBradburne 91+
(Mrs L C Taylor) *chsd ldsrs tl: rdn and bdly hmpd 15th: n.d after* **11/2**[2]

B226 **7** *4* **Tribal Dancer (IRE)**[14] 2938 12-11-1 **94** .... SamThomas 78
(Miss Venetia Williams) *chsd ldrs: led 8th to 12th: wknd 17th* **15/2**[3]

U1F2 **P** **Supreme Tadgh (IRE)**[33] 2613 9-11-5 **105** .... SimonElliott(7) —
(J A Geake) *a in rr: t.o whn p.u bef 14th* **8/1**

3P4/ **P** **Lord Broadway (IRE)**[630] 4837 10-10-13 **95** .... TJPhelan(3) —
(N M Babbage) *a in rr: t.o whn p.u bef 2 out* **33/1**

2-10 **F** **Motcombe (IRE)**[38] 2529 8-11-7 **100** ....(v) AndrewThornton —
(R H Alner) *chsd ldrs to 6th: bhd whn fell 14th* **5/1**[1]

6605 **U** **Multi Talented (IRE)**[37] 2557 10-11-1 **94** ....(b) LeightonAspell —
(L Wells) *in rr tl mstke and uns rdr 17th* **12/1**

1P-5 **P** **Roky Star (FR)**[223] 518 9-11-3 **96** .... JasonMaguire —
(T R George) *w ldrs to 4th: wknd 7th: t.o whn p.u after 13th* **8/1**

P532 **U** **Fin Bec (FR)**[9] 2965 13-11-3 **101** ....(b) DerekLaverty(5) —
(A P Jones) *hit 3rd: chsd ldrs 10th: wkng whn mstke and uns rdr 15th* **9/1**

0-40 **F** **Malko De Beaumont (FR)**[31] 2663 6-11-2 **95** .... JohnMcNamara 96
(K C Bailey) *hit 1st: bhd: hdwy 13th: chsd ldrs 15th: blnd next: pressed ldrs 3 out: one pce in 4th whn hmpd and fell 2 out* **20/1**

6m 49.6s (9.70) **Going Correction** +0.525s/f (Soft)
WFA 5 from 6yo+ 12lb **14** Ran SP% **121.8**
Speed ratings: **106,104,103,103,100 100,99,—,—,— —,—,—,—** CSF £143.93 CT £1321.50 TOTE £18.90: £5.30, £3.70, £3.40; EX 448.20 TRIFECTA Not won..
Owner Mrs C H Antrobus **Bred** Mrs D Jenks **Trained** Barbury Castle, Wilts

FOCUS
A weak handicap, despite the generous gallop, and the form is worth treating with caution.

NOTEBOOK
Boundary House, pulled up on his prevous two outings, found things go very much his way and ultimately landed his first event at the 11th attempt under a typically patient ride by Murphy. The step-up to this trip clearly worked the oracle, but while he has talent, he also has his problems, and was given oxygen straight after this victory, so whether he can build on this remains to be seen. *(op 14-1)*
Treasulier(IRE) turned in another sound effort and, while he looks to hold few secrets from the Handicapper, he was nicely clear of the rest at the finish and does have a similar race within his compass. *(op 10-1 tchd 12-1)*
Nykel(FR), pulled up on his British debut last time and making his handicap bow, showed more enthusiasm yet did not look to really get home over this longer trip. He could be capable of defying this sort of mark when reverting in trip. *(op 7-1 tchd 10-1)*
Walter's Destiny posted a satisfactory return from a 302-day break and looks to have retained his ability. *(op 20-1)*
Roky Star(FR) *Official explanation: jockey said gelding pulled up lame (tchd 11-2)*
Supreme Tadgh(IRE) failed to show much and is another of his yard's runners of late to perform below expectations. *(tchd 11-2)*
Motcombe(IRE) was held prior to departing and looks to be going the wrong way. *(tchd 11-2)*

3242 KINGWELL LODGE NOVICES' H'CAP HURDLE (8 hdls) 2m
3:00 (3:02) (Class 4) (0-105,105) 4-Y-O+ **£4,554** (£1,337; £668; £333)

Form RPR

0-1 **1** **Return Home**[4] 3147 7-10-9 **88** 7ex .... PaulMoloney 100+
(J S Smith) *trckd ldrs: slt ld 2 out: drvn and hld on wl run-in* **15/8**[1]

-640 **2** *½* **Shaamit The Vaamit (IRE)**[22] 2810 6-10-6 **92** .... JohnKington(7) 101
(M Scudamore) *chsd ldrs: led after 3 out: narrowly hdd 2 out: stl pressing wnr last: no ex nr fin* **20/1**

05P5 **3** *10* **Sunset King (USA)**[9] 2995 6-9-9 **79** oh1 .... JayHarris(5) 78
(R J Hodges) *chsd ldrs: led after 4 out: hdd after 3 out: sn rdn and one pce* **100/1**

0015 **4** *½* **Twist Bookie (IRE)**[13] 2950 6-11-1 **101** .... ShaneWalsh(7) 99
(J S Moore) *led tl after 4 out: one pce appr next* **33/1**

-100 **5** *2 ½* **Silver City**^{14} [2940] 6-11-2 **95** RichardJohnson 91
(P J Hobbs) *chsd ldrs: hrd drvn after 3 out and sn one pce* **20/1**

-242 **6** *5* **Sweet Oona (FR)**^{9} [2995] 7-11-2 **95** SamThomas 91+
(Miss Venetia Williams) *bhd: sme hdwy whn blnd 4 out: n.d after* **15/8**^{1}

-603 **7** *3 ½* **Esplendidos (IRE)**^{15} [2932] 7-10-3 **89** (p) DarylJacob$^{(7)}$ 76
(D P Keane) *chsd ldrs to 4th: n.d after* **20/1**

223P **8** *6* **The Castilian (FR)**^{32} [2632] 4-10-4 **98** (p) TomMalone$^{(3)}$ 67
(M C Pipe) *j. slowly in rr 3rd and 4th: sme hdwy fr 2 out but nvr in contention* **11/1**^{2}

0-50 **9** *13* **Simonovski (USA)**^{53} [2173] 5-11-12 **105** RJGreene 73
(S C Burrough) *chsd ldrs: rdn 4th: bhd wknd 3 out* **66/1**

0006 **10** *5* **Sharp Rally (IRE)**^{18} [2873] 5-10-11 **90** (t) WarrenMarston 53
(A J Wilson) *a in rr* **50/1**

5F04 **11** *1 ½* **Able Charlie (GER)**^{34} [2587] 4-10-7 **98** HenryOliver 48
(Mrs Tracey Barfoot-Saunt) *in tch to 4 out* **40/1**

660 **P** **Nobelmann (GER)**^{34} [2584] 7-11-4 **97** WayneHutchinson —
(A W Carroll) *a in rr: t.o whn p.u bef 2 out* **28/1**

-003 **P** **No Way Back (IRE)**^{29} [2683] 6-11-12 **105** NoelFehily —
(Miss E C Lavelle) *sn bhd: t.o whn p.u bef last* **16/1**^{3}

P21P **P** **Meadow Hawk (USA)**^{32} [2632] 6-11-7 **100** TimmyMurphy —
(A W Carroll) *prom early: t.o whn p.u after 3 out* **20/1**

3m 54.4s (5.30) **Going Correction** +0.525s/f (Soft)
WFA 4 from 5yo+ 11lb **14** Ran SP% **116.1**
Speed ratings: **107,106,101,101,100 97,96,93,86,84 83,—,—,—** CSF £41.77 CT £2786.63 TOTE £3.20: £1.80, £4.80, £23.10; EX 55.00.
Owner Donald Smith **Bred** A Munnis And K Helliwell **Trained** Tirley, Gloucs

FOCUS
A moderate handicap, yet the pace was generous and the first two came clear, so the form looks fair for the grade.

NOTEBOOK
Return Home, who just got up to land a big gamble at Warwick on his British debut four days previously, raced more prominently over this shorter trip and shook off the persistent challenge of the runner-up in the straight to follow-up under his 7lb penalty. Considering that he was most likely idling when in front, he can be rated value for further, and really has found his form with a vengeance since switching from Ireland. However, he will need to keep improving, as a likely hike in the weights is now assured. *(op 9-4)*
Shaamit The Vaamit(IRE) went down with all guns blazing and posted his best effort of the current campaign. He is a touch flattered by his proximity to the idling winner, and has yet to get his head in front in ten attempts now, but his attitude could not be faulted this time.
Sunset King(USA) was firmly put in his place when the first two asserted at the top of the straight, but this must still rate a personal-best effort over timber, and he is clearly going the right way. He can find easier opportunities from his current mark. *(op 50-1)*
Twist Bookie(IRE) eventually paid for his early exertions, but was not disgraced on this step-up in class. *(op 20-1)*
Sweet Oona(FR) lost any chance with a bad blunder four from home, but was already looking held and this must rate very disappointing. She remains winless over hurdles and is one to avoid. *(tchd 2-1, 9-4 in places)*
No Way Back(IRE) *Official explanation: jockey said gelding was unsuited by the soft ground (op 14-1)*

3243 DR FREDDIE BUCKLER NOVICES' H'CAP CHASE (13 fncs) 2m
3:30 (3:32) (Class 4) (0-110,108) 5-Y-O **£6,338** (£1,872; £936; £468; £234)

Form RPR

021/ **1** **Crimson Pirate (IRE)**^{1029} [4117] 9-11-12 **108** NoelFehily 119+
(B De Haan) *blnd 3rd: chsd ldrs: lft in ld 9th: drvn and mstke 2 out and last: kpt on wl run-in* **7/2**^{2}

PP52 **2** *¾* **Wizard Of Edge**^{5} [3126] 6-10-12 **94** (b^{1}) ChristianWilliams 101
(R J Hodges) *chsd ldrs tl lost pl 7th: hit next: rallied fr 4 out to press wnr 2 out: stl ch last: one pce run-in* **7/1**

3-04 **3** *11* **Megapac (IRE)**^{228} [451] 8-10-12 **97** WilliamKennedy$^{(3)}$ 93
(Noel T Chance) *bhd: rdn and styd on fr 3 out: nvr gng pce to rch ldrs* **8/1**

-351 **4** *3 ½* **Ishka Baha (IRE)**^{9} [2995] 7-10-5 **87** JasonMaguire 81+
(T R George) *in tch: hdwy 7th: chsd ldrs and rdn 4 out: sn wknd* **6/4**^{1}

4P2- **5** *7* **Fantastic Arts (FR)**^{272} [4756] 6-11-12 **108** SamThomas 94
(Miss Venetia Williams) *bhd: hdwy 6th: drvn to chal 4 out: wknd next* **14/1**

0U6P **6** *7* **Kinkeel (IRE)**^{36} [2561] 7-9-9 **82** StephenCraine$^{(5)}$ 61
(A W Carroll) *chsd ldrs to 4 out: sn wknd* **20/1**

0422 **P** **Dictator (IRE)**^{15} [2929] 5-10-12 **103** (t) TomDoyle —
(D R Gandolfo) *nvr gng wl in rr: p.u bef 9th* **4/1**^{3}

0P-5 **F** **Palace (FR)**^{22} [2807] 10-10-0 **82** oh23 (p) BenjaminHitchcott —
(R H Buckler) *led tl rdn and fell 9th* **66/1**

4m 7.40s (5.50) **Going Correction** +0.525s/f (Soft)
WFA 5 from 6yo+ 8lb **8** Ran SP% **118.8**
Speed ratings: **107,106,101,99,95 92,—,—** CSF £29.11 CT £186.24 TOTE £5.90: £1.60, £2.10, £2.00; EX 44.10.
Owner Duncan Heath **Bred** P G McGillion **Trained** Lambourn, Berks

FOCUS
A modest novices' handicap, run at a fair gallop, and the first two came clear. The third sets the standard and the race could rate higher.

NOTEBOOK
Crimson Pirate(IRE) ◆, absent with injury since winning over timber at Huntingdon 1029 days previously, made winning return to action and has clearly begun handicap life on a decent mark. He made a few mistakes, but is entitled to improve his jumping for this debut experience and, providing he remains sound, looks be one to follow as he has few miles on the clock and has always been well-regarded by connections. *(new market op 9-2 tchd 5-1)*
Wizard Of Edge, equipped with first-time blinkers, posted another improved display and enjoyed the drop back to this trip. He is currently rated 125 over the smaller obstacles, and while he is not an easy ride, can be found a race in this sphere in the coming weeks. *(new market op 10-1)*
Megapac(IRE), having his first outing for 228 days, was doing his best work at the finish and shaped as though he would improve a deal for the outing. *(new market tchd 11-1)*
Ishka Baha(IRE), off the mark over timber at this venue nine days previously and able to race off the same mark on this chasing bow, failed to find all that much when it mattered and has to rate disappointing. She may just prefer further in this sphere, however, and is entitled to improve for the experience. *(new market new market op 2-1)*

3244 BRUTON BUMPER (AN INTERMEDIATE NATIONAL HUNT FLAT RACE) (CONDITIONAL JOCKEYS/AMATEUR RIDERS) 2m
4:00 (4:00) (Class 6) 4-6-Y-O **£2,055** (£599; £299)

Form RPR

1 **Kicks For Free (IRE)** 5-10-12 LiamHeard$^{(7)}$ 125+
(P F Nicholls) *hld up rr: stdy hdwy 5f out: led on bit over 2f out: c clr: impressive* **3/1**^{3}

2 *10* **Wyldello** 5-10-5 MrGTumelty$^{(7)}$ 98+
(A King) *in tch: drvn to chse ldrs 3f out: styd on and edgd rt 1f out: kpt on wl for 2nd: no ch w wnr* **11/4**^{2}

2 **3** *2 ½* **Kimi (IRE)**^{27} [2720] 5-11-2 WilliamKennedy$^{(3)}$ 104+
(Noel T Chance) *in tch: rdn 5f out: styd on u.p fnl 2f to take 3rd ins last: nt rch ldrs* **2/1**^{1}

2- **4** *½* **Boston Strong Boy (IRE)**^{456} [1599] 6-11-0 StephenCraine$^{(5)}$ 102
(C Tinkler) *chsd ldrs: pushed along 6f out: led over 3f out: hdd and rdn over 2f out: edgd lft over 1f out:carried rt jst ins last: one* **8/1**

3-4 **5** *8* **Lord Kernow (IRE)**^{19} [2864] 6-11-2 OwynNelmes$^{(3)}$ 98+
(C J Down) *led tl rn v wd and lost many lengths after 5f: rcvrd to press ldrs and chal over 3f out: wknd 2f out* **33/1**

00 **6** *3 ½* **So Wise So Young**^{35} [2579] 5-10-9 PaulDavey$^{(10)}$ 91
(R H Buckler) *chsd ldrs: rdn 6f out: wknd 3f out* **100/1**

-20 **7** *1 ½* **Gold Beach (IRE)**^{14} [2941] 6-11-2 MrMRimell$^{(3)}$ 89
(M G Rimell) *chsd ldrs: lft in ld ater 5f: hdd over 3f out and sn btn* **14/1**

8 *3* **Lagan Legend** 5-10-5 WayneKavanagh$^{(7)}$ 79
(Dr J R J Naylor) *chsed ldrs: rdn 6f out: wknd over 4f out* **100/1**

0 **9** *7* **Jomelamin**^{33} [2611] 4-9-7 JamesWhite$^{(7)}$ 60
(R J Hodges) *chsd ldrs over 10f* **100/1**

0-30 **10** *dist* **Katy Jones**^{37} [2558] 6-10-5 (t) MrJJenkinson$^{(7)}$ —
(Noel T Chance) *nvr bttr than mid-div: t.o* **50/1**

11 *dist* **Pats Last** 4-10-0 KeiranBurke$^{(7)}$ —
(P R Rodford) *chsd ldrs 10f: t.o* **100/1**

12 *17* **Sky By Night** 5-10-9 TomMalone$^{(3)}$ —
(B J M Ryall) *sn bhd: t.o* **50/1**

3m 52.1s **Going Correction** +0.525s/f (Soft)
WFA 4 from 5yo+ 11lb **12** Ran SP% **113.6**
Speed ratings: **99,94,92,92,88 86,86,84,81,— —,—** CSF £10.92 TOTE £4.50: £2.00, £1.20, £1.10; EX 15.80 Place 6 £247.69, Place 5 £182.80.
Owner Mark Tincknell **Bred** Martin Cullinane **Trained** Ditcheat, Somerset

FOCUS
This should prove an above-average bumper as the season progresses. The winner was most impressive, being rated value for twice the official margin, and the first four home all look capable of rating higher in due course.

NOTEBOOK
Kicks For Free(IRE) ◆, whose dam is half-sister to fair hurdler/chaser Cigarello, could not have been any more impressive in making a winning debut and should be rated value for even further than his wide winning margin. He rates an exciting prospect for his powerful stable and, as this was most likely an above-average bumper, it is little surprise that he is likely to head next for the Champion Bumper at Cheltenham in March. *(op 5-2 tchd 10-3)*
Wyldello ◆, bred to be useful over jumps, stayed on to post an encouraging debut effort, despite proving no match for the winner. She has scope and can soon go one better in this sphere. *(op 9-4 tchd 3-1)*
Kimi(IRE), just touched off when a well-backed favourite on his debut last time, was doing his best work at the finish and gives the form a very sound look. He is going to appreciate further in time, but does have a race of this nature within his compass before the season's end. *(op 9-4 tchd 5-2 and 15-8)*
Boston Strong Boy(IRE), runner-up on his debut at Huntingdon in 2004, had his chance and shaped as though he would improve a deal for the outing. He would have found this ground plenty soft enough and will no doubt be sent over timber before too long. *(op 10-1)*
Lord Kernow(IRE) *Official explanation: jockey said gelding failed to handle bend into back straight (tchd 40-1)*

T/Jkpt: Not won. T/Plt: £1,317.60 to a £1 stake. Pool: £55,323.60. 30.65 winning tickets. T/Qpdt: £421.80 to a £1 stake. Pool: £4,788.10. 8.40 winning tickets. ST **Race 3245 void**

2559 HEREFORD (R-H)
Thursday, January 5

OFFICIAL GOING: Soft (good to soft in places)
Wind: Almost nil Weather: Overcast and cold

3246 EUROPEAN BREEDERS FUND "NATIONAL HUNT" NOVICES' HURDLE (QUALIFIER) (DIV I) (10 hdls) 2m 3f 110y
12:30 (12:33) (Class 4) 4-7-Y-O **£4,228** (£1,241; £620; £310)

Form RPR

112 **1** **Tokala**^{53} [2211] 5-11-4 APMcCoy 114+
(B G Powell) *mde virtually all: clr 3 out: easily* **5/4**^{1}

3-00 **2** *9* **Here We Go (IRE)**^{3} [3210] 7-10-13 LeeStephens$^{(5)}$ 94+
(W K Goldsworthy) *hld up: hdwy appr 4 out: wnt 2nd bef last: no ch w wnr* **50/1**

2-6 **3** *16* **Campaign Charlie**^{256} [7] 6-11-4 MarkBradburne 79+
(H D Daly) *plld hrd: midfield: hmpd 5th: hdwy next: chsd wnr 3 out: no imp: lost 2nd and wknd bef last* **33/1**

0-0P **4** *11* **Cadtauri (FR)**^{123} [1407] 5-11-4 PaulMoloney 65
(Miss H C Knight) *hld up: hdwy 6th: wkng whn sltly hmpd 2 out* **80/1**

00- **5** *shd* **Cornish Orchid (IRE)**^{421} [2123] 5-11-4 PhilipHide 65
(C J Down) *hld up: niggled along 3 out: sme hdwy next: no imp* **100/1**

-455 **6** *3* **Highland Chief (IRE)**^{49} [2301] 6-11-4 RobertThornton 62
(Miss H C Knight) *trckd ldrs: hmpd 5th: wknd bef 4 out* **9/1**

50 **7** *25* **Happy Shopper (IRE)**^{21} [2849] 6-11-1 TomMalone$^{(3)}$ 37
(M C Pipe) *prom: hmpd 6th: wknd appr 4 out: n.d whn hmpd 2 out* **33/1**

1/00 **8** *16* **From Dawn To Dusk**^{19} [2873] 7-11-4 RichardJohnson 21
(P J Hobbs) *midfield: effrt appr 4 out: sn btn* **33/1**

4-3 **9** *10* **Wotashambles (IRE)**^{256} [7] 5-10-13 MarkNicolls$^{(5)}$ 11
(P R Webber) *midfield: pckd 2nd: hmpd 6th: wknd 4 out* **33/1**

000F **10** *dist* **Castletown Lad**^{6} [3130] 6-11-4 (v^{1}) TimmyMurphy —
(M C Pipe) *bhd and rdn fr 4th: t.o* **66/1**

00 **P** **Ourcarl**^{49} [2288] 6-11-4 MatthewBatchelor —
(G Brown) *a bhd: t.o whn p.u bef 6th* **125/1**

00 **P** **Maenflora**^{15} [2935] 4-10-0 VinceSlattery —
(B J Llewellyn) *a bhd: t.o after 4th: p.u after 6th* **200/1**

6P **P** **River Role**^{24} [2797] 4-9-11 OwynNelmes$^{(3)}$ —
(J W Tudor) *midfield early: bhd fr 4th: t.o whn p.u bef 2 out* **200/1**

25 **U** **Commander Kev (IRE)**^{39} [2534] 5-11-1 WilliamKennedy$^{(3)}$ —
(Noel T Chance) *midfield: hdwy whn blnd and uns rdr 5th* **11/2**^{3}

0- **P** **Oyster Pearl (IRE)**^{396} [2665] 7-11-4 ChristianWilliams —
(P Bowen) *trckd ldrs tl wknd 4 out: t.o whn p.u bef last* **3/1**^{2}

5 **F** **Hardybuck (IRE)**^{72} [1870] 5-11-4 AntonyEvans 65
(N A Twiston-Davies) *prom: blnd 3rd: wknd 3 out: 4th and btn whn fell 2 out* **20/1**

4m 54.4s (6.50) **Going Correction** +0.475s/f (Soft)
WFA 4 from 5yo+ 11lb **16** Ran SP% **118.8**
Speed ratings: **106,102,96,91,91 90,80,73,69,— —,—,—,—,— —** CSF £89.04 TOTE £2.30: £1.02, £23.80, £7.40; EX 105.40.

Owner John P McManus **Bred** Greenfield Stud S A **Trained** Morestead, Hants

FOCUS

A cracking novice hurdle for the track, won the previous season by Star De Mohaison. However, the race lost some of its interest with Commander Kev coming down fairly early. The winning time was slightly faster than the second division and the winner is value for more than double the official margin and the form could rate higher.

NOTEBOOK

Tokala ♦, who had some really good bumper form coming into the race, fully deserved his place at the head of the market, despite a lack of hurdling experience, and handled the ground well. He won with tons in hand and looks a very exciting prospect. His rider reported that he was not doing much in front. *(tchd 11-10 and 11-8)*

Here We Go(IRE) had shown nothing in two starts for his current stable, but this was a big improvement on his most recent efforts and he might be returning to the form of his opening two performances in bumpers behind some decent types. He will get further.

Campaign Charlie, behind Highland Chief in a bumper, is related to that nice staying chaser of the past Roberty Bob and will no doubt make more effective over the bigger obstacles. He pulled plenty hard enough in the early stages and is another that should get further. *(op 25-1)*

Cadtauri(FR) ran his best race to date and is probably improving with experience. *(op 66-1)*

Cornish Orchid(IRE) also ran by far his best race to date and seemed to appreciate this longer trip.

Highland Chief(IRE) seemed to get outpaced as the gallop increased, but stayed on up the straight. He finished a fairly close fourth in his only Irish point behind now prominent Gold Cup hope Joaaci, and will no doubt make his mark next season when tried over fences. *(op 8-1)*

From Dawn To Dusk *Official explanation: trainer's representative said gelding had a breathing problem*

Oyster Pearl(IRE), a long-time absentee, was well supported in the market but was beaten very early. *(op 5-1)*

3247 LETHEBY AND CHRISTOPHER MARES' ONLY H'CAP HURDLE (10 hdls) 2m 3f 110y

1:00 (1:02) (Class 4) (0-115,107) 4-Y-0+

£5,010 (£1,480; £740; £370; £184; £92)

Form | | | | RPR
P-13 **1** **She's Our Native (IRE)**[21] [2845] 8-11-1 **101**.................. LeeStephens(5) 115+
(Evan Williams) *hld up: hdwy 4th: lost pl 6th: hdwy 8th: rdn to ld after 2 out: j.rt last: styd on* **10/3**[2]
-211 **2** *3 ½* **Magical Legend**[82] [1745] 5-10-12 **98**........................... HowieEphgrave(5) 108+
(L Corcoran) *chsd ldrs: j.lft: led 6th: hdd next: led 2 out: sn hdd: styd on same pce* **5/1**[3]
5502 **3** *8* **Kildee Lass**[16] [2930] 7-10-8 **94**.. ChrisHonour(5) 94+
(J D Frost) *hld up in tch: effrt appr 2 out: wknd bef last* **14/1**
6/6- **4** *1 ¼* **Precious Mystery (IRE)**[33] [2688] 6-11-11 **106**.............. RobertThornton 104
(A King) *prom: rdn 8th: wknd next* **14/1**
-151 **5** *2 ½* **Novacella (FR)**[16] [2932] 5-11-7 **102**.............................. AndrewThornton 97
(R H Alner) *chsd ldrs: led 7th: rdn and hdd 2 out: sn wknd* **15/8**[1]
31-5 **6** *2 ½* **White Dove (FR)**[228] [462] 8-10-10 **91**................................ PaulMoloney 84
(Ian Williams) *hld up in tch: wknd after 8th* **16/1**
2136 **7** *shd* **Tirikumba**[43] [2430] 10-11-6 **101**.. PaddyBrennan 94
(S G Griffiths) *led to 6th: wknd appr 2 out* **22/1**
03P0 **8** *6* **Cashel Dancer**[15] [2940] 7-10-13 **94**...................................... TomSiddall 81
(S A Brookshaw) *hld up: hdwy 7th: wknd after next* **50/1**
2306 **9** *2 ½* **Bonny Grey**[21] [2850] 8-11-5 **107**... MrNPearce(7) 91
(D Burchell) *hld up: reminders 6th: in rr whn hmpd next* **20/1**
5FP0 **10** *4* **Titian Flame (IRE)**[32] [2659] 6-10-6 **94**..........................(p) LiamHeard(7) 74
(D Burchell) *hld up: hdwy and hmpd 7th: sn wknd* **20/1**
11 *dist* **Drive On Driver (IRE)**[308] [4150] 9-9-11 **85**.................... MissLBrooke(7) —
(Lady Susan Brooke) *prom: lost pl 4th: bhd fr 6th* **66/1**
0-30 **F** **Simple Glory (IRE)**[230] [441] 7-11-1 **96**.................... WayneHutchinson —
(R Dickin) *chsd ldrs: cl up whn fell 7th* **25/1**

4m 59.4s (11.50) **Going Correction** +0.475s/f (Soft) **12** Ran SP% **114.9**
Speed ratings: **96,94,91,90,89 88,88,86,85,83** —,— CSF £17.93 CT £203.74 TOTE £4.80: £1.30, £2.40, £4.60; EX 21.90.
Owner Ian Brice **Bred** J Mangan **Trained** Cowbridge, Vale Of Glamorgan

FOCUS

An interesting but modest mares-only event, with a couple of potential blots on the handicap. The early pace was modest due to the ground, which resulted in plenty holding chances exiting the back straight. The third sets the standard but the form does not look strong.

NOTEBOOK

She's Our Native(IRE), dropping slightly in trip, was soundly beaten last time when carrying a penalty, but she has done really well to be racing at all after fracturing her pelvis when running over fences in March. Under a strong ride, she was forced into the lead down the side of the course and sped away from her rivals from that point. Presumably connections will be keen to return her to fences soon in an attempt to make use of her better mark. *(op 7-2 tchd 4-1)*

Magical Legend, taking the handicap hurdle option rather than contesting one of the novice races on the card, had shown most progressive form since joining her current yard. She beat the boys last time on her hurdling debut when receiving plenty of weight and that race has already produced three individual winners. She gave away her chance by jumping out to the left badly at some of the flights, but remains an interesting sort if her jumping can be ironed out. *(op 11-2)*

Kildee Lass, whose two victories had come on a sounder surface, appeared to run up to her best on this softer ground. *(op 16-1 tchd 20-1)*

Precious Mystery(IRE) stayed on well after becoming outpaced down the far side. *(op 10-1)*

Novacella(FR), who appeared to have plenty in her favour, took up the lead in the back straight but was back-pedalling shortly afterwards and for some reason did not appear to get home. This was disappointing. *(op 2-1 tchd 7-4)*

3248 EUROPEAN BREEDERS FUND "NATIONAL HUNT" NOVICES' HURDLE (QUALIFIER) (DIV II) (10 hdls) 2m 3f 110y

1:30 (1:32) (Class 4) 4-7-Y-0 **£4,228** (£1,241; £620; £310)

Form | | | | RPR
P- **1** **Five Colours (IRE)**[444] [1765] 6-11-4 .... RobertThornton 119+
(A King) *in tch: tk clsr order after 4th: led after 2 out: clr last: rdn out* **50/1**
4-5 **2** *10* **Principe Azzurro (FR)**[32] [2665] 5-11-4 .... MarkBradburne 110+
(H D Daly) *midfield: hdwy 6th: rdn and ev ch after 2 out: one pce fr last* **28/1**
1 **3** *2 ½* **College Ace (IRE)**[70] [1895] 5-11-11 .... RichardJohnson 114
(P J Hobbs) *midfield: hdwy 4th: led after 3 out: hdd after 2 out: sn rdn and hung lft: wknd bef last* **11/8**[2]
6-05 **4** *½* **Reach For The Top (IRE)**[34] [2617] 5-11-4 .... PaulMoloney 106
(Miss H C Knight) *in tch: mstke 4th: trcking ldrs whn mstke 3 out: sn rdn: kpt on same pce fr next* **33/1**
1000 **5** *16* **Flying Spur (IRE)**[58] [2099] 5-11-1 .... TomMalone(3) 91+
(M C Pipe) *hld up: rdn after 2 out: no imp* **80/1**
40-0 **6** *6* **Alf's Spinney**[22] [2821] 6-11-4 .... WayneHutchinson 87+
(Ian Williams) *prom: led 4 out: hdd after 3 out: wknd after next: n.d whn blnd last* **125/1**
-423 **7** *6* **Jimmy Bedney (IRE)**[27] [2755] 5-11-4 .... APMcCoy 78
(M G Rimell) *j.lft: led: hit and hdd 4 out: rdn and wknd 2 out* **10/1**[3]
250- **8** *1* **Barclay Boy**[267] [4820] 7-11-4 .... JimmyMcCarthy 77
(A J Lidderdale) *midfield: hdwy 6th: rdn and wknd 2 out* **25/1**
21/1 **9** *½* **Here's Johnny (IRE)**[61] [2049] 7-11-4 .... JimCrowley 77
(V R A Dartnall) *midfield: reminder after 3rd: hdwy 6th: rdn appr 3 out: wkng whn mstke 2 out* **6/5**[1]
040 **10** *14* **Brave Jo (FR)**[56] [2152] 5-10-11 .... KeiranBurke(7) 63
(N J Hawke) *a bhd* **150/1**
002 **11** *11* **Flash Cummins (IRE)**[16] [2928] 6-11-4 .... TimmyMurphy 52
(M C Pipe) *a bhd* **16/1**
40- **12** *5* **Freddie Ed**[346] [3520] 5-11-4 .... JasonMaguire 47
(R N Bevis) *mstke 5th: a bhd* **125/1**
5-00 **13** *2 ½* **Ellandshe (IRE)**[44] [2421] 6-11-4 .... JamesDavies 44
(P R Webber) *midfield: wknd 6th* **66/1**
F0P- **14** *6* **Valuso (IRE)**[279] [4680] 6-11-1 .... WilliamKennedy(3) 38
(Noel T Chance) *prom tl wknd after 4th* **100/1**
-200 **P** **Celtic Jem (IRE)**[20] [2860] 6-11-4 .... ChristianWilliams —
(P Bowen) *trckd ldrs tl wknd after 4th: t.o whn p.u after 2 out* **100/1**
00-0 **P** **Bonny Grove**[43] [2432] 6-11-4 .... VinceSlattery —
(H J Evans) *mstkes: midfield early: sn bhd: t.o whn p.u bef 3 out* **200/1**

4m 54.8s (6.90) **Going Correction** +0.475s/f (Soft) **16** Ran SP% **122.2**
Speed ratings: **105,101,100,99,93 91,88,88,88,82 78,76,75,72,**— — CSF £952.67 TOTE £75.80: £11.50, £6.60, £1.10; EX 822.90.
Owner Knightsbridge BC & J Sigler **Bred** Patrick Doyle **Trained** Barbury Castle, Wilts

FOCUS

On paper this appeared to be the weaker of the two divisions and it turned up a huge shock, but the winning time was only slightly slower. The fifth and sixth set the level for the form

NOTEBOOK

Five Colours(IRE), the slowest horse in his yard according to his trainer, was apparently though fit after his 444 day absence and that almost certainly made the difference, as he stayed on in dogged style after being pushed into the lead after the second last. He will probably get further than this. *(op 33-1)*

Principe Azzurro(FR) shaped most encouragingly and, although he did not get home as well as the winner, he has plenty of scope for improvement. *(tchd 33-1)*

College Ace(IRE), not seen since winning a race that worked out respectably at Stratford in October, still looked a bit green under pressure. Hanging slightly left coming to the home turn, he stayed on well under his penalty. *(op 6-4 tchd 5-4)*

Reach For The Top(IRE) looks every inch a chaser in the making and ran his best race to date. Given more time to mature, it is not difficult to envisage him making up into a nice chaser next season like his half-brother Rosslea.

Flying Spur(IRE) ran an interesting race. He slowly made his way through the pack after taking a *grip early and despite being beaten a long way, shaped as though he is capable of better. (tchd 100-1)*

Alf's Spinney finished very weary after racing up with the early pace. *(op 100-1)*

Jimmy Bedney(IRE) also finished tired after making much of the early running. *(tchd 11-1)*

Here's Johnny(IRE) never looked to be enjoying himself and his jockey was already showing signs of distress with a circuit to go. The ground was apparently the problem and he is worth another chance given his good quality bumper form. *Official explanation: jockey said gelding never travelled (op 13-8)*

3249 LETHEBY AND CHRISTOPHER NOVICES' HURDLE (13 hdls) 3m 2f

2:05 (2:06) (Class 4) 4-Y-0+ **£4,228** (£1,241; £620; £310)

Form | | | | RPR
230/ **1** **Before Dark (IRE)**[677] [4050] 8-11-5 .... RichardJohnson 103+
(Mrs H Dalton) *hld up: hdwy after 7th: outpcd bef 10th: rallied appr last: led flat: drvn out* **40/1**
6323 **2** *4* **Seeador**[35] [2592] 7-10-12 100...................................... WayneKavanagh(7) 99+
(J W Mullins) *chsd ldrs: outpcd and mstke 2 out: rallied and ev ch last: no ex flat* **16/1**
FP00 **3** *½* **Charango Star**[9] [3018] 8-11-11 103..............................(b[1]) TimmyMurphy 104+
(W K Goldsworthy) *chsd ldrs: mstke and outpcd 9th: rallied appr last: styd on u.p* **33/1**
412- **4** *¾* **Northern Deal (IRE)**[419] [2169] 11-11-5 .... ChristianWilliams 96+
(Evan Williams) *led to 10th: rdn to ld after 2 out: hdd and no ex flat* **12/1**[3]
-B42 **5** *dist* **Knighton Lad (IRE)**[23] [2809] 6-11-5 .... RobertThornton —
(A King) *hld up in tch: lost pl 5th: hdwy appr 7th: rdn and wknd after 9th* **8/1**[2]
30 **6** *½* **Elegant Eskimo**[37] [2559] 7-10-12 .... JoeTizzard —
(S E H Sherwood) *hld up: plld hrd: bhd whn hmpd 7th: effrt appr 9th: sn wknd* **66/1**
F **Justice Jones**[38] 5-11-2 .... RichardYoung(3) —
(Mrs P Ford) *hld up: fell 9th* **200/1**
/F-P **P** **Run Atim**[19] [2878] 8-11-5 .... SamStronge —
(K C Bailey) *hld up: a bhd: t.o whn p.u bef 9th* **125/1**
P **Leave It To You**[291] 8-10-12 .... MarkBradburne —
(M Sheppard) *prom to 7th: t.o whn p.u bef 9th* **250/1**
P **Run To The King (IRE)**[81] 8-11-5 .... AndrewThornton —
(P C Ritchens) *chsd ldrs to 5th: t.o whn p.u bef 9th* **25/1**
P **Havit**[285] 8-10-12 .... MissLBrooke(7) —
(Lady Susan Brooke) *mstke 1st: bhd fr next: t.o whn p.u after 7th* **250/1**
0P **P** **Blazing Ember**[24] [2797] 4-9-11 .... OwynNelmes(3) —
(J W Tudor) *prom: reminders 6th: wknd appr 8th: bhd whn p.u bef next* **250/1**
P **Tano (CZE)**[550] 5-10-12 .... MrRJBarrett(7) —
(Mrs A E Brooks) *mid-div: lost pl whn mstke 4th: bhd fr next: t.o whn p.u after 7th* **150/1**
01-0 **P** **Sommelier**[35] [2584] 6-11-5 .... AntonyEvans —
(N A Twiston-Davies) *hld up: hdwy 7th: rdn next: wknd after 9th: t.o whn p.u bef 2 out* **25/1**
F **Olchons Debut (IRE)**[257] 8-11-5 .... PhilipHide —
(Miss A E Broyd) *mid-div: plld hrd: hdwy 4th: wknd after next: mstke 6th: in rr whn fell next* **200/1**
-221 **P** **Karanja**[42] [2461] 7-11-11 .... PaddyBrennan —
(V R A Dartnall) *hld up in tch: jnd ldr 9th: led next: rdn and hdd after 2 out: wknd qckly and p.u* **2/5**[1]

6m 43.4s (15.40) **Going Correction** +0.575s/f (Soft)
WFA 4 from 5yo+ 13lb **16** Ran SP% **114.3**
Speed ratings: **99,97,97,97,**— —,—,—,—,— —,—,—,—,— — CSF £510.70 TOTE £29.80: £6.00, £3.20, £5.60; EX 198.70.
Owner C B Compton **Bred** Mrs D R Lonergan **Trained** Norton, Shropshire

FOCUS

The ground appeared to be getting progressively worse as the day went on and nearly half the field were starting to struggle with a circuit to go. The odds-on favourite pulled up late on and the first four home were a distance clear of the remainder.

NOTEBOOK

Before Dark(IRE) stayed on in determined fashion to defy a 677-day layoff. Given a really patient ride by his pilot, he crept through the field during the final circuit and won going away after taking the last just in front. The obvious concern will now be if he can reproduce this effort next time and he would certainly not be one to go overboard about unless given time to get over his exertions. *(op 50-1)*

Seeador, scrubbed along from a long way out, kept finding for pressure and should make a nice staying chaser in his grade when tried over the bigger obstacles again. *(op 25-1)*

Charango Star, wearing first-time blinkers, stays really well and gave the impression he was flying home at the end, but that was only because those in front were stopping. He has been noted as being a bit mulish in the past and has form between the flags over four miles, so a return to chasing over extreme distances would make him interesting, especially if Murphy took the ride again.

Northern Deal(IRE), a classy pointer in his time, has been hard to train but possesses ability. Trying hurdles for the first time, presumably as a warm up for chasing again, he was always close up before getting very tired late on. As long as he remains sound, more races can be won with him. *(op 10-1)*

Karanja nudged his way into the lead on the back straight, but never got away from Northern Deal after going past him and was weakening quickly when pulled up on the home turn. He reportedly had swallowed his tongue. *(op 1-2 tchd 8-15)*

3250 LETHEBY AND CHRISTOPHER CLASSIFIED HURDLE (13 hdls) 3m 2f

2:40 (2:42) (Class 5) 4-Y-0+ **£2,927** (£859; £429; £214)

Form				RPR
0-3P	**1**		**Bar Gayne (IRE)**[24] 2800 7-11-5 90 JasonMaguire *(T R George) a.p: mstke 2 out: sn led: drvn out* **7/1**	91+
5330	**2**	*3*	**Good Potential (IRE)**[20] 2863 10-11-5 88 (t) PaddyBrennan *(D J Wintle) midfield: hdwy 7th: ev ch 2 out: sn rdn and chsd wnr: no ex cl home* **8/1**	87
U0/P	**3**	*6*	**Ocean Tide**[20] 2862 9-10-12 90 (v) RobertLucey-Butler(7) *(R Ford) trckd ldrs: rdn and outpcd whn hit 3 out: rallied bef last: styd on run-in* **16/1**	81
0543	**4**	*2 ½*	**Foxmeade Dancer**[23] 2816 8-11-5 84 AndrewThornton *(P C Ritchens) bhd: stdy hdwy appr 4 out: kpt on u.p run-in* **16/1**	79
00-0	**5**	*¾*	**Radnor Lad**[60] 2073 6-11-5 74 RichardJohnson *(Mrs S M Johnson) led: hdd after 2 out: wknd appr last* **50/1**	78
3S23	**6**	*2 ½*	**Sissinghurst Storm (IRE)**[44] 2424 8-11-2 89 WayneHutchinson *(R Dickin) chsd ldrs: mstke 9th: rdn after 3 out: wknd after 2 out* **6/1**[3]	72
P14P	**7**	*dist*	**The Pecker Dunn (IRE)**[21] 2845 12-11-5 88 JodieMogford *(Mrs N S Evans) midfield: mstke 7th: hdwy after 9th: rdn and wknd appr 2 out* **33/1**	—
1421	**8**	*1 ½*	**Temper Lad (USA)**[60] 2073 11-10-12 85 MissSGaisford(7) *(J D Frost) trckd ldrs to 4th: sn bhd* **5/1**[2]	—
0P	**9**	*3 ½*	**They Grabbed Me (IRE)**[21] 2845 5-10-9 85 MrCHughes(7) *(M C Pipe) mstke 3rd: hmpd 4 out: a bhd* **66/1**	—
6P00	**10**	*23*	**Chocolate Bombe (IRE)**[10] 2986 9-11-2 64 TJPhelan(3) *(S Lycett) hld up: rdn after 9th: struggling whn hmpd 4 out: t.o* **100/1**	—
-21U	**P**		**Osiris (IRE)**[30] 2688 11-11-5 90 (t) ChristianWilliams *(Evan Williams) a bhd: t.o whn p.u bef 4 out* **7/4**[1]	—
3P00	**F**		**Magical Liaison (IRE)**[15] 2940 8-11-5 90 (b) NoelFehily *(W Jenks) midfield: hdwy 9th: in tch whn fell 4 out* **20/1**	—
/06-	**P**		**New Diamond**[592] 482 7-11-2 77 RichardYoung(3) *(Mrs P Ford) t.k.h: hld up: hdwy after 2nd: wknd 8th: t.o whn p.u after 9th* **100/1**	—

6m 53.3s (25.30) **Going Correction** +0.575s/f (Soft) **13** Ran SP% **115.8**

Speed ratings: **84,83,81,80,80 79,—,—,—,— —,—,—** CSF £57.19 TOTE £5.30: £1.50, £2.40, £6.50; EX 58.60.

Owner M R C Opperman **Bred** Martin J Dibbs **Trained** Slad, Gloucs

FOCUS

A weak classified hurdle over a staying trip in which they went a sedate early pace. The winning time was slow even for a race like this, nearly ten seconds slower than the novice hurdle. The second sets the standard but the race could be too high.

NOTEBOOK

Bar Gayne(IRE), returning to hurdles after frightening himself over fences, had not had as many chances as a few of the others and, from the stable that landed last year's renewal, won under strong driving. He had winning form in heavy ground when taking a bumper on his racecourse debut, so clearly relished underfoot conditions. *Official explanation: trainer said, regarding the improved form shown, gelding had lost its confidence over fences and was suited by the return to hurdling (op 8-1 tchd 12-1)*

Good Potential(IRE) has never lived up to his name and had no conclusive proof in the form book that this was his ideal trip. However, he stuck on really well for pressure and the trip did not appear to pose him any problems. *(op 11-1 tchd 7-1)*

Ocean Tide is on a good mark given his best hurdling form and ran a much more encouraging race than he had done on his return to hurdling last time following a spell on the Flat.

Foxmeade Dancer was not particularly well in at the weights with some of his rivals given the nature of the race and has yet to win outside selling company. He made good headway throughout the final circuit, but never got to the leaders.

Radnor Lad probably ran his best race after making a lot of the early running, but he regularly gets beaten a long way. *(op 66-1)*

Temper Lad(USA), a proven stayer, could never get into contention this time. *(op 7-2)*

Osiris(IRE) was well backed prior to the race, but was pulled up before making any impact having bled from the nose and suffering an over-reach on his off-fore. *Official explanation: trainer said gelding bled from nose and suffered an overreach of the off-fore (op 6-4 tchd 2-1)*

3251 LETHEBY AND CHRISTOPHER BEGINNERS' CHASE (14 fncs) 2m 3f

3:15 (3:17) (Class 4) 5-Y-0+

£6,263 (£1,850; £925; £463; £231; £116)

Form				RPR
0-42	**1**		**Green Tango**[41] 2482 7-11-3 RichardJohnson *(H D Daly) hld up: hdwy 6th: led 2 out: drvn out* **7/2**[3]	151+
2-00	**2**	*1 ¼*	**Don't Be Shy (FR)**[27] 2747 5-10-7 TimmyMurphy *(M C Pipe) a.p: led after 10th: hdd 2 out: sn rdn: styd on* **9/4**[1]	140+
P-F3	**3**	*22*	**Muhtenbar**[20] 2861 6-11-3 122 PaulMoloney *(Miss H C Knight) chsd ldrs tl wknd appr 2 out* **14/1**	128
4443	**4**	*5*	**Keepthedreamalive**[34] 2607 8-11-3 123 BenjaminHitchcott *(R H Buckler) led to 3rd: remained handy tl wknd appr 3 out* **7/1**	123
6052	**5**	*16*	**Yes Sir (IRE)**[14] 2953 7-11-3 ChristianWilliams *(P Bowen) chsd ldrs: led 7th: hdd after 10th: wknd next* **5/1**	109+
614-	**6**	*8*	**Idole First (IRE)**[273] 4747 7-11-3 AlanO'Keeffe *(Miss Venetia Williams) hld up: hdwy 8th: wknd next* **11/4**[2]	99
P2PF	**7**	*20*	**Let's Rock**[28] 2722 8-10-10 67 MrRHodges(7) *(Mrs A Price) hld up: mstke 2nd: a bhd* **200/1**	79
3-P0	**8**	*2 ½*	**Mnason (FR)**[39] 2525 6-10-12 JamesDiment(5) *(S J Gilmore) prom to 8th* **100/1**	77
P-3P	**9**	*dist*	**The Muratti**[89] 1671 8-11-3 MatthewBatchelor *(G Brown) j. slowly 1st: a bhd* **100/1**	—
-P5P	**10**	*2*	**Greenawn (IRE)**[20] 2861 7-11-3 SamStronge *(M Sheppard) hld up: bhd whn blnd 4th* **200/1**	—
P	**P**		**Ballybean (IRE)**[66] 1950 6-11-3 JohnMcNamara *(K C Bailey) hld up: hdwy 7th: wknd 9th: t.o whn p.u bef last* **66/1**	—
	U		**Glenkill (IRE)**[205] 755 8-10-3 MissIsabelTompsett(7) *(S M Jacobs) led 3rd: mstke next: hdd whn blnd and uns rdr 7th* **200/1**	—
P/P-	**P**		**Miss Colmesnil (FR)**[612] 143 6-10-10 (p) HenryOliver *(A E Jessop) hld up: in rr whn mstke 5th: t.o whn p.u bef 2 out* **200/1**	—
P/00	**P**		**Stylish Prince**[28] 2721 6-11-0 (t) WilliamKennedy(3) *(R Lee) hld up: hit 6th: in rr whn hmpd next: t.o whn p.u bef 4 out* **150/1**	—

4m 46.7s (0.10) **Going Correction** +0.30s/f (Yiel)

WFA 5 from 6yo+ 8lb **14** Ran SP% **121.6**

Speed ratings: **111,110,101,99,92 89,80,79,—,— —,—,—,—** CSF £12.80 TOTE £4.40: £2.20, £1.50, £2.70; EX 19.20.

Owner Mrs Strachan,Gabb,Lady Barlow & Harford **Bred** Southill Stud **Trained** Stanton Lacy, Shropshire

FOCUS

A really good beginners' chase for the course, run at a decent pace. The first two finished well clear of the remainder and the form might be useful, with the third setting the level, especially as the winning time was good for a race of its class.

NOTEBOOK

Green Tango ◆, who had already faced a couple of tough tasks over fences, was always travelling well and won this with a little bit in hand. He has form on soft, but is much better suited by better ground and might be the type for a race such as the Grand Annual. *(op 4-1)*

Don't Be Shy(FR) ◆ had arguably been a shade disappointing since his arrival from France, having shown a good level of form in Graded hurdles, and this probably presented him with his most realistic task to date in receipt of the weight allowance. He jumped well and looked the most likely winner exiting the back straight before weakening late on. Time may show two miles is his trip and he can be given another chance. *(op 3-1 tchd 10-3)*

Muhtenbar did not seem to see the trip out, but gives the form a solid look as he was beaten ten lengths by another decent prospect in Villon last time in similarly bad ground. He is on a fair mark over fences, one he looks capable of exploiting if tried in that company.

Keepthedreamalive set the standard, having already received an official mark of 123, but was beaten a long way by a couple of unexposed sorts. *(op 8-1)*

Yes Sir(IRE) did his customary job from the front, but weakened right out of contention once the pace increased. *(op 4-1)*

Idole First(IRE) was a huge disappointment on this chasing debut, never going with any enthusiasm from an early stage. The jury is out to whether he enjoyed his first experience over fences or not. *(op 3-1 tchd 7-2)*

Ballybean(IRE) *Official explanation: jockey said he lost reins when gelding made a mistake (tchd 80-1)*

3252 LETHEBY AND CHRISTOPHER H'CAP CHASE (19 fncs) 3m 1f 110y

3:50 (3:51) (Class 5) (0-85,85) 5-Y-0+

£3,444 (£1,017; £508; £254; £127; £63)

Form				RPR
P401	**1**		**Merry Storm (IRE)**[3] 3221 7-10-9 75 7ex RichardSpate(7) *(Mrs K Waldron) hld up: hdwy 13th (water): led 2 out: clr last: comf* **5/2**[2]	99+
3023	**2**	*12*	**Brigadier Du Bois (FR)**[5] 3147 7-11-4 77 LeightonAspell *(Mrs L Wadham) midfield: hdwy after 11th: led 3 out: mstke and hdd 2 out: sn btn* **12/1**	89+
-3PP	**3**	*1 ½*	**Supreme Sir (IRE)**[33] 2623 8-11-1 77 ColinBolger(3) *(P G Murphy) j.lft: led after 1st: hdd 3 out: wknd after next* **50/1**	86+
-313	**4**	*13*	**Rosetown (IRE)**[30] 2687 8-11-3 76 (b) JasonMaguire *(T R George) led: hdd after 1st: remained prom: rdn appr 4 out: wknd 3 out: btn whn j.lft 2 out* **9/4**[1]	79+
-144	**5**	*5*	**Up The Pub (IRE)**[34] 2610 8-11-9 82 AndrewThornton *(R H Alner) in tch tl wknd 4 out* **6/1**[3]	72
P1-F	**6**	*2 ½*	**Pewter Light (IRE)**[30] 2686 9-11-10 83 PaddyBrennan *(B J M Ryall) prom: pushed along bef 12th: wknd 14th* **15/2**	70
1463	**7**	*6*	**Southerndown (IRE)**[20] 2863 13-11-6 82 WilliamKennedy(3) *(R Lee) midfield: rdn and lost pl 12th: bhd after* **20/1**	63
550	**8**	*5*	**Missy Moscow (IRE)**[28] 2718 8-11-1 74 RichardHobson *(H J Evans) rdn bef 14th: a bhd* **100/1**	50
-060	**F**		**Zimbabwe (FR)**[20] 2863 6-11-8 81 (p) JoeTizzard *(N J Hawke) prom tl fell 12th* **16/1**	—
5-P3	**F**		**Shoulton (IRE)**[10] 2957 9-11-0 73 JodieMogford *(G H Yardley) midfield: fell 3rd* **14/1**	—
P6-0	**P**		**Star Time (IRE)**[60] 2073 7-10-12 78 (v) JohnKington(7) *(M Scudamore) a bhd: t.o whn p.u bef 13th (water)* **33/1**	—
000P	**F**		**Sidcup's Gold (IRE)**[20] 2863 6-11-9 85 OwynNelmes(3) *(M Sheppard) trckd ldrs: losing pl whn fell 12th* **125/1**	—
-P06	**U**		**Kadito**[22] 2827 10-11-10 83 WayneHutchinson *(R Dickin) hld up: hdwy 10th: blnd and uns rdr 12th* **125/1**	—
2-PP	**P**		**Bayoss (IRE)**[21] 2848 10-11-0 78 (b1) MrGBarfoot-Saunt(5) *(Mrs Tracey Barfoot-Saunt) a bhd: hmpd 3rd: t.o whn p.u after 10th* **100/1**	—
-P04	**P**		**Cloudy Blues (IRE)**[22] 2827 8-11-1 74 BenjaminHitchcott *(R H Buckler) midfield: hit 7th: sn bhd: t.o whn p.u bef 13th (water)* **25/1**	—
F-PP	**P**		**Dunnicks Field**[6] 3126 10-11-1 79 ChrisHonour(5) *(F G Tucker) hld up: sme hdwy 14th: no imp: mstke next: sn wknd: t.o whn p.u bef last* **66/1**	—

6m 46.2s (12.00) **Going Correction** +0.30s/f (Yiel) **16** Ran SP% **124.2**

Speed ratings: **93,89,88,84,83 82,80,79,—,— —,—,—,—,— —** CSF £31.19 CT £1252.53 TOTE £4.00: £2.20, £2.40, £7.20, £1.10; EX 57.50 Place 6 £1,712.16, Place 5 £811.05.

Owner Nick Shutts **Bred** Jim Healy **Trained** Stoke Bliss, Worcs

FOCUS

Mainly exposed sorts in this 73-85 handicap chase, but it did contain a couple of horses that had the potential to be extremely well-in judged on the best of their form. The winning time was moderate, however, but the form looks solid, rated through the placed horses.

NOTEBOOK

Merry Storm(IRE), turned out quickly under his penalty, landed this in good style. A giant of a horse, he won fairly much as he liked at Folkestone earlier in the week after looking a bit of a monkey the time before at Towcester when crashing through the paddock gate after jumping the last clear. He is still at the right end of the handicap to land another race or two at this level. *(op 11-4 tchd 7-2)*

Brigadier Du Bois(FR) was returning to fences after a reasonable effort over hurdles last time. Trying a trip far in excess of anything he had previously attempted, he ran really well but he almost certainly bumped into a horse running off a mark below his true ability. There should be more options for him now. *(op 14-1)*

Supreme Sir(IRE) ran his best race under Rules, but is clearly very moderate. If connections can find a race for him off his lowly handicap mark at a stiffer track, he would be of some interest. *(op 33-1)*

Rosetown(IRE), a winner over hurdles on this card 12 months ago, was really well in over fences compared with the best of his hurdling form. Running off a mark 20lb lower than when winning over hurdles at Towcester in November, he threatened briefly in the back straight before not seeming to get home after making a mistake at the third last. *(tchd 2-1 and 5-2)*

Up The Pub(IRE) clung to the front four as long as he could, but was dropped exiting the back straight. *(op 7-1)*
Cloudy Blues(IRE) *Official explanation: jockey said gelding was unsuited by the soft (good to soft in places) ground (op 28-1)*

T/Plt: £5,322.90 to a £1 stake. Pool: £42,656.35. 5.85 winning tickets. T/Qpdt: £213.80 to a £1 stake. Pool: £3,872.10. 13.40 winning tickets. DO

3037 WETHERBY (L-H)

Thursday, January 5

OFFICIAL GOING: Soft (heavy in places)
On the back of the two day Christmas meeting the ground was described as 'awful, testing and loose, it could hardly be any worse'.
Wind: Almost nil Weather: Dry but cold

3253 PHEASANT "NATIONAL HUNT" MAIDEN HURDLE (12 hdls) 2m 7f
12:15 (12:15) (Class 5) 4-Y-O+ £2,740 (£798; £399)

Form				RPR
-102	1		**Supreme's Legacy (IRE)**[14] [2947] 7-11-7 .... RichardMcGrath (K G Reveley) *hld up in mid-div: smooth hdwy 7th: led on bit 3 out: rdn and kpt on run-in* **5/2**[1]	114+
23	2	*1*	**Ballyshan (IRE)**[20] [2866] 8-11-7 .... CarlLlewellyn (N A Twiston-Davies) *hld up: hdwy 7th: chal 3 out: styd on wl run-in* **11/1**	111
1-43	3	*13*	**Calusa Charlie (IRE)**[19] [2878] 7-11-7 .... TomDoyle (B G Powell) *trckd ldrs: led 6th: hdd 3 out: wknd between last 2* **7/2**[2]	99+
2P-4	4	*1 ½*	**Fromragstoriches (IRE)**[10] [2994] 10-11-7 104 .... DominicElsworth (Mrs S J Smith) *chsd ldrs: hit 3 out: one pce* **6/1**	99+
F-P4	5	*¾*	**Chanticlier**[20] [2868] 9-11-7 104 .... (t) MickFitzgerald (R T Phillips) *trckd ldrs: rdn 3 out: sn wknd* **10/1**	96
F-P0	6	*14*	**Mad Max Too**[17] [2923] 7-11-4 .... (p) PeterBuchanan[(3)] (N Wilson) *sn in rr: sme hdwy 3 out: nvr a factor* **200/1**	82
0-23	7	*3 ½*	**Beau De Turgeon (FR)**[17] [2923] 5-11-7 .... GrahamLee (Ian Williams) *hld up: hdwy 7th: mstke next: rdn and wknd after 9th* **4/1**[3]	79+
23-	8	*¾*	**Lost Boy (IRE)**[404] [2485] 7-11-7 .... TonyDobbin (R Bastiman) *in rr: sme hdwy 9th: sn chsng ldrs: wknd next* **25/1**	78
5004	9	*dist*	**Filey Flyer**[18] [2903] 6-11-0 .... AnthonyRoss (J R Turner) *in rr: hit 9th: sn bhd: t.o* **100/1**	—
05	10	*17*	**Candlelight Valley (IRE)**[20] [2865] 7-11-2 .... RobertStephens[(5)] (P J Hobbs) *in rr: bhd fr 9th: t.o* **33/1**	—
00	11	*1*	**Northern Quest (IRE)**[36] [2572] 5-11-7 .... DavidO'Meara (H P Hogarth) *t.k.h in mid-field: lost pl 9th: sn bhd: t.o* **200/1**	—
0	P		**When Your Readyles (IRE)**[21] [2838] 6-11-7 .... FinbarKeniry (M Todhunter) *sn in rr: t.o whn blnd 9th: sn p.u* **200/1**	—
0-50	P		**Grand Daum (FR)**[26] [2763] 5-11-7 .... BrianHarding (T P Tate) *led to 6th: lost pl next: t.o whn p.u bef 3 out* **100/1**	—
P-PP	P		**Howsham Lad**[30] [2690] 7-11-7 .... DaveCrosse (G P Kelly) *w ldrs: mstke 6th: blnd and lost pl 8th: sn bhd: t.o whn p.u bef 3 out* **100/1**	—

6m 21.3s (24.60) **Going Correction** +1.125s/f (Heavy) **14** Ran SP% **113.8**
Speed ratings: **102,101,97,96,96 91,90,90,—,— —,—,—,—** CSF £29.34 TOTE £3.10: £1.30, £2.30, £1.60; EX 24.90.
Owner The Supreme Alliance **Bred** J Mernagh **Trained** Lingdale, Redcar & Cleveland

FOCUS
A steady gallop until the final three quarters of a mile but in the testing conditions they came home well strung out. The form could be rated higher but those with form may have had excuses for below-par efforts.

NOTEBOOK
Supreme's Legacy(IRE), patiently ridden, took it up running away but, idling on the run-in, he had to be kept up to his work. If anything the extended trip suited him. *(op 11-4 tchd 3-1)*
Ballyshan(IRE) seemed to thoroughly appreciate the extended trip and was coming back for more at the line. He deserves to go one better. *(op 8-1)*
Calusa Charlie(IRE) went on and soon stepped up the pace but in the end he did not see out the trip anywhere near as well as the first two. *(op 11-4)*
Fromragstoriches(IRE) was having his second outing in less than two weeks after missing a year and a half after finishing lame. *(tchd 13-2)*
Chanticlier seemed to find a combination of the extra distance and the testing conditions overtaxing. *(tchd 11-1)*
Beau De Turgeon(FR), after a mistake, dropped away in a matter of strides starting the home turn. *He seemed not to handle the dire conditions.Official explanation: jockey said gelding was unsuited by the soft (heavy in places) ground (op 5-1 tchd 7-2)*

3254 PARTRIDGE MARES' ONLY NOVICES' HURDLE (9 hdls) 2m
12:45 (12:47) (Class 4) 4-Y-O+ £3,426 (£998; £499)

Form				RPR
3/22	1		**Sabreflight**[44] [2414] 6-11-0 .... GrahamLee (J Howard Johnson) *trckd ldrs: mstke 3rd: led next: qcknd 3 out: drew clr appr last: eased towards fin* **2/1**[2]	105+
1	2	*11*	**Charlotte Vale**[44] [2414] 5-11-7 112 .... TonyDobbin (M D Hammond) *trckd ldrs: wnt 2nd appr 3 out: 3l 2nd whn hit 2 out: 8l 3rd last: tired run-in* **7/4**[1]	97+
	3	*nk*	**Dayoff (IRE)**[17] 5-11-0 .... RussGarritty (P D Evans) *mde most to 4th: outpcd appr 3 out: styd on run-in* **40/1**	87
4-0F	4	*3*	**Leap Year Lass**[31] [2680] 6-11-0 87 .... RichardMcGrath (C Grant) *hld up towards rr: hdwy 5th: kpt on fr 3 out: nvr trbld ldrs* **40/1**	84
3422	5	*17*	**Don And Gerry (IRE)**[10] [2997] 5-10-9 98 .... StephenCraine[(5)] (P D Evans) *t.k.h: trckd ldrs: wknd appr 2 out* **11/4**[3]	69+
U500	6	*7*	**Thorn Of The Rose (IRE)**[44] [2412] 5-10-4 80 .... MichaelMcAvoy[(10)] (James Moffatt) *sn bhd: t.o 4th: nvr on terms* **100/1**	60
600	7	*23*	**Stormy Madam (IRE)**[14] [2942] 6-10-7 .... MrRWakeham[(7)] (J R Turner) *in tch: sn pushed along: outpcd and bhd fr 6th: virtually p.u run-in* **100/1**	37
10	8	*¾*	**Granny Shona (IRE)**[39] [2515] 5-11-0 .... TomDoyle (P R Webber) *w ldrs: lost pl after 4th: bhd fr 3 out: virtually p.u run-in* **16/1**	36
	F		**Lady Sunrize**[23] 7-11-0 .... BrianHarding (P D Evans) *sn in rr: bhd fr 4th: t.o whn fell heavily 6th* **100/1**	—

4m 23.5s (24.10) **Going Correction** +1.125s/f (Heavy) **9** Ran SP% **110.1**
Speed ratings: **84,78,78,76,68 64,53,52,—** CSF £5.57 TOTE £3.00: £1.10, £1.10, £5.10; EX 5.80.
Owner D S Coates **Bred** A Saccomando **Trained** Billy Row, Co Durham

FOCUS
A very moderate winning time even in these conditions, 12.3 seconds slower than the later handicap. It seemed a case of only the winner handling the very testing ground and the form is not strong.

NOTEBOOK
Sabreflight, closely matched with Charlotte Vale on course running, handled the ground much the better and, sent clear going to the last, she was able to take things very easily in the closing stages. *(tchd 7-4)*
Charlotte Vale, meeting the winner on 7lb worse terms, went in pursuit but she became stuck in the mud and, very leg-weary near the line, just clung on to second spot. *(tchd 15-8)*
Dayoff(IRE), fit after an All-Weather outing on the Flat, took them along but after getting left behind she stayed on to some effect late in the day and almost snatched the runner-up spot. *(tchd 50-1)*
Leap Year Lass put three poor runs behind her and ran her best race since finishing runner-up in a similar event here a year ago. *(tchd 50-1)*
Don And Gerry(IRE) would not settle and ran herself into the ground in these arduous conditions. *(op 3-1 tchd 7-2)*

3255 WOODCOCK NOVICES' H'CAP CHASE (12 fncs) 2m
1:20 (1:20) (Class 3) (0-125,115) 5-Y-O+ £8,457 (£2,483; £1,241; £620)

Form				RPR
U3FC	1		**Vigoureux (FR)**[10] [2963] 7-10-7 95 .... (p) KeithMercer (S Gollings) *chsd ldrs: led after 2 out: hld on towards fin* **20/1**	105
/263	2	*¾*	**Albertino Lad**[14] [2943] 9-10-0 91 .... PeterBuchanan[(3)] (Miss Lucinda V Russell) *keen early: trckd ldrs: wnt 2nd appr last: kpt on wl: no ex towards fin* **9/1**	100
12F3	3	*3*	**Loulou Nivernais (FR)**[10] [2980] 7-10-8 96 .... OllieMcPhail (Robert Gray) *led to 3rd: w ldrs: led and hit 8th: j.lft 2 out: sn hdd: kpt on same pce* **7/1**	104+
0-51	4	*6*	**Amarula Ridge (IRE)**[27] [2751] 5-11-4 115 .... MickFitzgerald (P J Hobbs) *hld up in tch: hit 7th: effrt 4 out: kpt on same pce: 5th and no imp whn hit last* **9/2**[3]	108+
4/21	5	*5*	**Jimmy Bond**[9] [3037] 7-10-3 91 7ex .... NeilMulholland (M D Hammond) *in tch: pushed along 4th: lost pl appr 4 out* **5/2**[2]	88+
1P52	F		**Itsuptoharry (IRE)**[19] [2874] 7-11-7 114 .... StephenCraine[(5)] (D McCain) *t.k.h: led 3rd to 8th: cl 3rd but looked hld whn fell heavily last* **15/8**[1]	122

4m 27.2s (20.60) **Going Correction** +0.80s/f (Soft)
WFA 5 from 7yo+ 8lb **6** Ran SP% **108.8**
Speed ratings: **94,93,92,89,86** — CSF £150.92 TOTE £19.80: £5.50, £3.80; EX 69.00.
Owner Ian Hesketh **Bred** Exors Of The Late H Le Baron & Dominique Le Baron **Trained** Scamblesby, Lincs
■ Stewards' Enquiry : Stephen Craine caution: used whip with excessive force

FOCUS
An ordinary novices' handicap rated through the runner-up to his mark and with the third and fourth close to form.

NOTEBOOK
Vigoureux(FR), who lacks size and scope, has been out of luck but he came good in a battling way. *(op 16-1)*
Albertino Lad, from a stable back in top form, kept battling away and made the winner pull out all the stops. *(op 10-1)*
Loulou Nivernais(FR) ran a lot better than Sedgefield but his jumping is not yet fault free. *(tchd 13-2)*
Amarula Ridge(IRE), a negative, was hunted round but when called on for an effort never looked to be enjoying himself in the ground and he was making no impression at all when clouting the final fence. *(op 7-2)*
Jimmy Bond, under his penalty, was soon struggling and dropped right way on the final turn. This possibly came just too soon for him. *(op 3-1 tchd 10-3 in a place)*
Itsuptoharry(IRE), keen to get on with it, was bang there in third but looking held when he took a bone-crunching fall at the last. Fortunately he seemed to walk away none the worse. *(tchd 2-1)*

3256 ROCOM SIEMENS H'CAP HURDLE (9 hdls) 2m
1:55 (1:55) (Class 3) (0-130,127) 4-Y-£0,922 (£2,340; £1,170; £585; £292)

Form				RPR
-621	1		**Town Crier (IRE)**[40] [2489] 11-11-1 116 .... DominicElsworth (Mrs S J Smith) *racd wd: trckd ldrs gng wl: jnd ldr 4th: led on bit 3 out: drew clr run-in: easily* **11/4**[1]	139+
1116	2	*11*	**Chef De Cour (FR)**[26] [2765] 5-11-5 120 .... TonyDobbin (L Lungo) *hld up towards rr: smooth hdwy 6th: sn chsng ldrs: wnt 2nd 2 out: kpt on: no ch w wnr* **7/1**[3]	125+
-214	3	*8*	**Woody Valentine (USA)**[27] [2746] 5-11-5 120 .... SamThomas (Miss Venetia Williams) *blnd and lost pl 2nd: hdwy 5th: styd on fr 2 out to take 3rd run-in* **11/2**[2]	116
62P2	4	*2*	**Kentucky Blue (IRE)**[33] [2641] 6-11-10 125 .... (p) RussGarritty (T D Easterby) *chsd ldrs: one pce fr 2 out* **16/1**	120+
-P10	5	*3*	**Jake Black (IRE)**[27] [2746] 6-11-3 123 .... DougieCostello[(5)] (J J Quinn) *t.k.h: trckd ldrs: lost pl 6th: kpt on same pce fr next* **10/1**	115+
FP-P	6	*8*	**Stormy Lord (IRE)**[69] [1913] 10-10-10 111 .... BrianHarding (J Wade) *led to 6th: lost pl appr 2 out* **50/1**	94
0-2P	7	*2 ½*	**Adopted Hero (IRE)**[33] [2636] 6-11-7 127 .... BrianHughes[(5)] (J Howard Johnson) *hld up: hdwy 6th: hmpd and stmbld after next: sn btn* **12/1**	110+
-032	8	*3 ½*	**Haditovski**[39] [2525] 10-9-8 102 .... (v) MrGTumelty[(7)] (J Mackie) *chsd ldrs: led 6th to next: sn btn* **12/1**	79
3100	9	*10*	**Mister Arjay (USA)**[17] [2925] 6-11-4 119 .... KeithMercer (B Ellison) *in rr: drvn along 4th: nvr a factor* **50/1**	86
P/5-	10	*½*	**Albany (IRE)**[411] [2335] 6-11-6 121 .... GrahamLee (J Howard Johnson) *chsd ldrs: wknd 3 out: bhd whn eased between last 2* **33/1**	88
2-22	11	*2*	**Dhehdaah**[33] [2627] 5-10-11 112 .... WarrenMarston (Mrs P Sly) *chsd ldrs: lost pl after 3 out* **11/2**[2]	77
P301	12	*8*	**Honest Endeavour**[39] [2525] 7-10-7 113 .... (p) ThomasDreaper[(5)] (J M Jefferson) *chsd ldrs: lost pl 5th: sn bhd* **28/1**	70

4m 11.2s (11.80) **Going Correction** +1.125s/f (Heav) **12** Ran SP% **110.6**
Speed ratings: **115,109,105,104,103 99,97,96,91,90 89,85** CSF £20.09 CT £92.03 TOTE £3.00: £1.60, £2.20, £2.20; EX 23.60 Trifecta £81.60 Pool: £839.32 - 7.30 winning tickets..
Owner Trevor Hemmings **Bred** Frank Tobin **Trained** High Eldwick, W Yorks

FOCUS
A very smart time for the class, 12.3 seconds faster than the earlier novice event. A competitive handicap turned into a procession by the leniently-weighted winner but the second deserves some credit.

NOTEBOOK
Town Crier(IRE), a late developer, was able to run from a mark 29lb below his chase rating. Kept wide, he travelled supremely well and after taking charge running away he had only to be shaken up to pull clear. He will revert to fences in the Victor Chandler Chase at Cheltenham later this month. *(op 2-1)*
Chef De Cour(FR), having just his second outing in handicap company, travelled almost as well as the winner but, when sent in pursuit of him, it was soon very clear that it was a one-sided argument. He is not that big but deserves to go one better. *(op 8-1 tchd 13-2)*
Woody Valentine(USA), having his second outing in the space of a month after a break, ploughed through the second flight. He stuck to his guns up the straight to secure third spot on the run-in. He looks weighted to the hilt now. *(op 6-1 tchd 13-2)*

Kentucky Blue(IRE) keeps running well but as a result gets no relief from the Handicapper. *(op 20-1)*
Jake Black(IRE), absent for a month, was a shade too keen and was struggling leaving the back straight. He is still 11lb higher than his last success. *(op 9-1)*
Stormy Lord(IRE), out of form over fences, was having his first outing since October and this will have put him right. *(op 66-1)*
Adopted Hero(IRE), hard to predict, was in the process of running a sound race when badly interfered with on the run between three out and two out.

3257 TEAL NOVICES' HURDLE (10 hdls) 2m 4f 110y
2:30 (2:30) (Class 4) 4-Y-0+ **£3,253** (£955; £477; £238)

Form				RPR
52-	1		**Ballyjohnboy Lord (IRE)**[74] 1863 7-11-13 ...... BrianCrowley (M Scudamore) *led tl after 1st: w ldrs: led appr 3 out: styd on wl run-in* **7/2**[2]	120+
361	2	1 3/4	**Livingonaknifedge (IRE)**[20] 2860 7-11-8 ...... PaulO'Neill[(5)] (Ian Williams) *hld up: smooth hdwy to trck ldrs 6th: upsides 3 out tl hit last: no ex* **11/4**[1]	120+
3-	3	21	**Best Accolade**[360] 3298 7-11-6 ...... GrahamLee (J Howard Johnson) *trckd ldrs: led 5th tl appr 3 out: one pce fr next* **4/1**[3]	90
0/P0	4	5	**Pride Of Finewood (IRE)**[17] 2923 8-10-13 ...... PhilKinsella[(7)] (E W Tuer) *trckd ldrs: led 4th to next: outpcd appr 3 out: kpt on* **100/1**	85
6642	5	6	**Shady Baron (IRE)**[131] 1337 7-11-6 87 ...... BrianHarding (J Wade) *chsd ldrs: outpcd appr 3 out: n.d after* **50/1**	79
436	6	dist	**Xamborough (FR)**[28] 2730 5-11-6 110 ...... MickFitzgerald (B G Powell) *hld up in tch: blnd 5th: rdn and lost pl appr 3 out: sn bhd: t.o* **5/1**	—
0-13	7	27	**Planters Punch (IRE)**[14] 2942 5-11-13 109 ...... FinbarKeniry (G M Moore) *chsd ldrs: hit 6th: lost pl appr 3 out: sn bhd: t.o* **9/2**	—
0	F		**Fourswainby (IRE)**[10] 2991 5-11-6 ...... KeithMercer (B Ellison) *led after 1st: hdd 4th: drvn 6th: lost pl after next: last and bhd whn fell heavily 3 out* **100/1**	—

5m 43.7s (34.80) **Going Correction** +1.125s/f (Heav) **8** Ran SP% **107.7**
Speed ratings: **78,77,69,67,65** —,—,— CSF £12.20 TOTE £4.50: £1.50, £1.40, £1.80; EX 9.90.

Owner F K Jennings **Bred** Mrs Ada McConnell **Trained** Bromsash, Herefordshire

FOCUS
A very steady gallop resulting in a very slow time, even in these conditions. The first two finished some way clear and could be rated higher, but the fourth limits the form.

NOTEBOOK
Ballyjohnboy Lord(IRE), followed home by two subsequent winners when off the mark at Clonmel in October, showed real battling qualities. He will be even better suited by three miles and will make a chaser next term.
Livingonaknifedge(IRE), already a point winner, moved upsides seemingly travelling the better, but after a sustained dual he was just getting the worst of the argument when he clouted the last. He too looks sure to make up into a chaser. *(op 7-2)*
Best Accolade, a dual point winner and third in a bumper, was having his first outing for a year and found the first two leaving him for dead over the final three flights. He too looks more of a chasing prospect.
Pride Of Finewood(IRE) ran his best race over hurdles on his third start but he is another that has the make and shape of a potential chaser.
Shady Baron(IRE), absent since finishing runner-up on fast ground at Cartmel in August, is from a stable struggling to find form at present. *(op 33-1)*
Xamborough(FR) blundered at halfway and dropped away in a matter of strides turning for home. The conditions were probably all against him. *(op 9-2)*
Planters Punch(IRE), who is not very big, ran poorly for no obvious reason. *Official explanation: jockey said gelding was unsuited by the soft (heavy in places) ground (op 7-2)*

3258 SNIPE H'CAP CHASE (18 fncs) 3m 1f
3:05 (3:05) (Class 3) (0-130,127) 5-Y-0+ **£9,594** (£2,895; £1,491; £789)

Form				RPR
5-52	1		**Kerry Lads (IRE)**[14] 2946 11-11-6 **124** ......(p) PeterBuchanan[(3)] (Miss Lucinda V Russell) *w ldrs: led 4 out: styd on fr 2 out: edgd lft run-in: kpt on* **7/1**	139+
5224	2	2 1/2	**The Kew Tour (IRE)**[26] 2767 10-11-2 **117** ...... DominicElsworth (Mrs S J Smith) *trckd ldrs: ev ch fr 4 out: upsides whn hit 2 out: kpt on same pce* **8/1**	129+
-061	3	3/4	**Ossmoses (IRE)**[32] 2656 9-11-8 **123** ...... TonyDobbin (D M Forster) *w ldrs: hit 5th: led 8th to 4 out: kpt on same pce fr 2 out* **4/1**[1]	134+
P-3P	4	dist	**Malek (IRE)**[10] 2992 10-11-11 **126** ...... RichardMcGrath (K G Reveley) *j.rt: reminders 2nd: j. bdly rt and lost tch 12th: t.o fr 14th* **11/2**[3]	—
1401	F		**Ebony Light (IRE)**[22] 2819 10-11-12 **127** ......(p) GrahamLee (D McCain) *trckd ldrs: upsides whn fell 11th* **5/1**[2]	—
0P-6	P		**Hussard Collonges (FR)**[253] 62 11-11-6 **121** ...... RussGarritty (P Beaumont) *chsd ldrs: lost pl appr 10th: bhd whn p.u bef next* **16/1**	—
413-	F		**Glen Warrior**[281] 4657 10-11-10 **125** ...... WarrenMarston (J S Smith) *hld up in last: hdwy to chse ldrs 8th: outpcd whn fell 11th* **12/1**	—
-661	F		**Florida Dream (IRE)**[28] 2717 7-11-1 **116** ......(b) CarlLlewellyn (N A Twiston-Davies) *mde most to 8th: 4th and sing to struggle whn fell 13th* **15/2**	—
13-5	P		**Devil's Run (IRE)**[61] 2037 10-10-13 **114** ...... BrianHarding (J Wade) *chsd ldrs: reminders 6th: drvn and lost tch 9th: bhd whn p.u bef next* **9/1**	—

6m 54.3s (14.30) **Going Correction** +0.80s/f (Soft) **9** Ran SP% **111.0**
Speed ratings: **109,108,107**,—,— —,—,—,— CSF £57.55 CT £244.64 TOTE £8.90: £2.50, £2.50, £1.70; EX 44.90.
Owner Mrs C G Greig **Bred** S O'Donoghue **Trained** Arlary, Perth & Kinross

FOCUS
A fair contest rated through the third to his mark.

NOTEBOOK
Kerry Lads(IRE), 4lb higher, managed to avoid any serious jumping errors and his battling *qualities carried the day in the end. His stable has really turned the corner in the New Year. (tchd 15-2)*
The Kew Tour(IRE), without a win for two years, ran out of his skin and would have given the winner even more to do but for clouting two out. The drought will surely end soon. *(op 7-1)*
Ossmoses(IRE), creeping up the handicap, took them along at a sound pace but was found lacking over the last two. All he does is jump and stay and the further he goes the better. *(op 9-2)*
Malek(IRE) continually gave away ground jumping out to his right and a violent manoeuvre a mile out saw him waving goodbye to the other three. *(tchd 5-1)*
Ebony Light(IRE), 9lb higher, was bang in the firing line when coming to grief but it was still a mile from home. *(op 4-1)*

3259 DUCK FILLIES' ONLY "JUNIOR" STANDARD OPEN NATIONAL HUNT FLAT RACE 1m 6f
3:40 (3:42) (Class 5) 4-Y-0 **£2,740** (£798; £399)

Form				RPR
	1		**Barton Belle** 4-10-12 ...... TonyDobbin (G A Swinbank) *in tch: jnd ldrs 6f out: led over 2f out: shkn up and wnt clr over 1f out: easily* **5/2**[1]	104+
	2	12	**Ruby Joy** 4-10-5 ...... TomMessenger[(7)] (Mrs H O Graham) *chsd ldrs: upsides 3f out: kpt on same pce appr fnl f* **33/1**	86
	3	8	**Dance The Mambo** 4-10-9 ...... MrTGreenall[(3)] (M W Easterby) *in rr: hdwy 4f out: n.m.r over 1f out: styd on* **6/1**[3]	77
4	4	1 1/4	**Asrar**[60] 2068 4-10-9 ...... PeterBuchanan[(3)] (Miss Lucinda V Russell) *chsd ldrs: one pce fnl 4f* **8/1**	75
	5	4	**Aqua** 4-10-9 ...... AnthonyCoyle[(3)] (P T Midgley) *in tch: hdwy to chse ldrs 6f out: fdd over 1f out* **50/1**	71+
6	6	2 1/2	**Now Then Katie**[39] 2520 4-10-12 ...... RichardMcGrath (C Grant) *chsd ldr: led 8f out tl over 2f out: lost pl over 1f out* **22/1**	67
	7	2	**Maylee (IRE)** 4-10-12 ...... KeithMercer (Mrs H O Graham) *sn in rr: t.o 6f out: sme hdwy 3f out: nvr a factor* **16/1**	65
4	8	9	**She's Humble (IRE)**[22] 2830 4-10-12 ...... GrahamLee (P D Evans) *trckd ldrs: chal 5f out: rdn and wknd over 3f out* **3/1**[2]	54
0	9	nk	**Amadores**[39] 2520 4-10-12 ...... DominicElsworth (J Ryan) *rr-div: nvr a factor* **33/1**	54
	10	15	**Ailsa** 4-10-7 ...... DougieCostello[(5)] (C W Thornton) *in tch: hdwy to chse ldrs 6f out: lost pl over 3f out* **8/1**	36
06	11	15	**Lilian Alexander**[17] 2927 4-10-7 ...... AdamPogson[(5)] (J R Holt) *t.k.h: reluctant ldr: sddle slipped after 3f: hdd 8f out: lost pl 5f out* **25/1**	18
	12	24	**Gessecapade** 4-10-5 ...... MrMatthewSmith[(7)] (P S McEntee) *sn bhd: t.o 5f out* **50/1**	—
	13	18	**Marton Jubilee** 4-10-9 ...... LeeVickers[(3)] (A D Brown) *sn bhd: t.o 6f out* **100/1**	—
	14	26	**Bella Cosa (IRE)** 4-10-7 ...... DesFlavin[(5)] (Mrs L B Normile) *mid-div: lost pl 6f out: sn bhd: t.o 4f out: virtually p.u* **50/1**	—

3m 45.9s **14** Ran SP% **116.9**
CSF £98.01 TOTE £2.90: £1.50, £7.40, £2.30; EX 101.40 Place 6 £199.00, Place 5 £121.44.
Owner Bellwood Rewinds Limited **Bred** Woodcote Stud Ltd **Trained** Melsonby, N Yorks

FOCUS
No strength in depth but a very modest mares-only bumper won in some style by a filly of some potential. The race is rated through the fourth and could rate higher.

NOTEBOOK
Barton Belle, who has plenty of size and scope, went clear in a matter of strides when put about her job and proved totally different class. She beat little of any consequence but could hardly have made a brighter start. *(op 2-1)*
Ruby Joy, bred for speed rather than stamina, was upsides once in line for home but in the end the winner proved different class. *(op 25-1)*
Dance The Mambo, who did not go without support, is quite a big filly. She looked fairly clueless *but stayed on late in the day after being messed about. The experience will not be lost on her. (op 10-1)*
Asrar did not seem to improve on her debut effort in a bumper that has worked out well at Ayr in November. *(op 13-2 tchd 6-1)*
Aqua, bred for speed rather than stamina, could not find a buyer when offered for sale as a yearling. *(op 40-1)*
She's Humble(IRE) was in the thick of things, but she struggled badly turning in and soon dropped right away and in the end her rider gave up. *(op 11-4 tchd 10-3)*
Lilian Alexander *Official explanation: jockey said saddle slipped*
T/Jkpt: Part won. £7,100.00 to a £1 stake. Pool: £10,000.00. 0.50 winning tickets. T/Plt: £223.50 to a £1 stake. Pool: £46,725.45. 152.55 winning tickets. T/Qpdt: £71.50 to a £1 stake. Pool: £3,452.60. 35.70 winning tickets. WG

3260a, 3262a - 3266a (Foreign Racing) - See Raceform Interactive

2914 THURLES (R-H)
Thursday, January 5

OFFICIAL GOING: Hurdle course - yielding; chase course - yielding to soft

3261a PHIL SWEENEY MEMORIAL CHASE (LISTED RACE) 2m 2f
1:25 (1:25) 5-Y-0+ **£13,468** (£3,951; £1,882; £641)

			RPR
1		**Strong Project (IRE)**[25] 2793 10-11-6 138 ...... JMAllen[(3)] (Sean O O'Brien, Ire) *mde all: clr early: mstke 6th: strly pressed 4 out: styd on wl fr 2 out* **4/1**[2]	146
2	8	**Doctor Linton (IRE)**[10] 3006 7-11-2 133 ...... BJGeraghty (M J P O'Brien, Ire) *trckd ldrs in 3rd: rdn 4 out: 2nd after 3 out: rdn to chal after next: no imp whn slt mstke last* **6/4**[1]	131
3	8	**Public Reaction**[25] 2795 8-11-2 ...... CO'Dwyer (Edward U Hales, Ire) *mod 2nd: slt mstke 5th: tk clsr order 1/2-way: chal 4 out: 3rd and no ex after next* **13/2**	123
4	7	**Kahuna (IRE)**[25] 2795 9-11-2 128 ......(p) JRBarry (E Sheehy, Ire) *trckd ldrs: slt mstke 2nd: 4th 5 out: in tch whn bad mstke 3 out: sn no ex* **5/1**	116+
5	25	**Mandm (IRE)**[39] 2547 8-11-2 ...... GCotter (P C O'Connor, Ire) *hld up: mstke 4th: trailing fr 1/2-way* **33/1**	91
P		**Green Belt Flyer (IRE)**[10] 3007 8-11-9 136 ...... TPTreacy (Mrs John Harrington, Ire) *trckd ldrs: cl 5th 5 out: no ex after 4 out: p.u bef 2 out* **9/2**[3]	—

4m 40.6s **6** Ran SP% **111.1**
CSF £10.74 TOTE £6.00: £2.60, £1.80; DF 14.60.
Owner J Patrick O'Brien **Bred** John J Buckley **Trained** Kilworth, Co. Cork

NOTEBOOK
Strong Project(IRE), by far the most experienced in the field, made all in determined fashion. He was not always fluent, but went clear again before the last, and this must rate a personal-best over fences. It is most likely that he will be given an entry for the Grand National. *(op 7/2)*
Doctor Linton(IRE) chased the winner from three out, but was never able to get on terms. His confidence should have been restored by this, however, and he was a clear-second best. *(op 7/4)*
Public Reaction, who had Missed That behind when making a winning chase debut over course and distance in December, could offer no more from three out. He may be best when able to dominate. *(op 8/1)*
Kahuna(IRE) makes too many mistakes to be effective in this company and over the trip. *(op 9/2)*
Green Belt Flyer(IRE), like so many from his stable these days, ran well below par. He was actually responsible for providing his stable with their latest success, back in October.

[2900] MUSSELBURGH (R-H)

Friday, January 6

OFFICIAL GOING: Good to firm

The going was described as 'on the fast side of good'.

Wind: Virtually nil Weather: Fine but cold

3267 TOM MCCONNELL NOVICES' HURDLE (9 hdls) 2m

12:40 (12:40) (Class 4) 4-Y-0+ **£3,253** (£955; £477; £238)

Form RPR

5 **1** **Estepona**[33] [2658] 5-11-5 GrahamLee 105+
(J Howard Johnson) *hld up: stdy hdwy to trck ldrs after 4 out: effrt 2 out: led last: rdn and styd on wl flat* **15/8**[2]

2 *3* **Premier Dane (IRE)**[145] 4-10-7 TonyDobbin 90+
(N G Richards) *trckd ldrs: hdwy to chse ldr 3 out: led next: sn rdn: hdd last: drvn and edgd lft flat: sn one pce* **4/5**[1]

064 **3** *3 ½* **Ballyhurry (USA)**[19] [2901] 9-11-5 104 RichardMcGrath 95
(J S Goldie) *in tch: hdwy appr 3 out: sn rdn and kpt on appr last* **20/1**

2653 **4** *2* **George Stubbs (USA)**[19] [2904] 8-11-5 100 BrianHarding 94+
(B Ellison) *cl up: hit 4th: led after 4 out: rdn clr next: drvn and hdd 2 out: wknd appr last* **9/1**[3]

6502 **5** *14* **Loner**[37] [2567] 8-11-5 83 AlanDempsey 79
(W S Coltherd) *trckd ldrs: effrt appr 3 out: sn rdn and one pce fr next* **50/1**

0-00 **6** *nk* **Bint Sesaro (IRE)**[19] [2903] 5-10-7 DesFlavin[(5)] 72
(Mrs L B Normile) *led to 2nd: cl up tl rdn along and wknd after 4 out* **200/1**

0P **7** *1 ¾* **Acca Larentia (IRE)**[33] [2658] 5-10-7 DougieCostello[(5)] 70
(Mrs H O Graham) *hit 2nd: a towards rr* **200/1**

0 **8** *4* **Logistical**[33] [2652] 6-11-5 KeithMercer 73
(Ferdy Murphy) *in tch: rdn along 5th and sn wknd* **100/1**

P0-0 **9** *12* **Cashema (IRE)**[200] [302] 5-10-7 69 DeclanMcGann[(5)] 54
(D R MacLeod) *cl up: led 2nd: rdn along and hdd after 4 out: sn wknd* **150/1**

10 *24* **Mr Marucci (USA)**[280] 4-9-11 CraigLidster[(10)] 25
(B Ellison) *in tch: racd wd: pushed along and bhd fr 4 out* **100/1**

0P **11** *4* **Peggy Naylor**[34] [2627] 5-10-5 PhilKinsella[(7)] 26
(Miss J E Foster) *a bhd* **200/1**

3060 **P** **Howards Dream (IRE)**[61] [2064] 8-11-5 80 (t) DominicElsworth —
(D A Nolan) *a rr: bhd whn p.u bef 4th* **200/1**

P6P/ **F** **Lucky Largo (IRE)**[64] [4440] 6-11-0 BrianHughes[(5)] 50
(D A Nolan) *keen: in tch to 1/2-way: sn wknd and bhd whn fell last* **200/1**

3m 52.6s (1.40) **Going Correction** 0.0s/f (Good) **13** Ran SP% **112.2**
WFA 4 from 5yo+ 11lb
Speed ratings: **96,94,92,91,84 84,83,81,75,63 61,—,—** CSF £3.51 TOTE £3.60: £1.40, £1.10, £2.50; EX 5.60.
Owner Andrea & Graham Wylie **Bred** Mrs S Camacho **Trained** Billy Row, Co Durham

FOCUS
An above average novices' hurdle with the first two both good prospects and Ballyhurry running his best race on his third start over hurdles, dropped in trip.

NOTEBOOK
Estepona, put to sleep at the back, came between horses to lead at the final flight and in the end won going away, showing much improved form. The much better ground suited him and he looks a fair prospect. *(op 2-1 tchd 9-4)*
Premier Dane(IRE) ◆, rated 11lb ahead of the winner on the level, was having his first outing since August, during which time he has been gelded. Giving the flights plenty of air, in the end he was outpaced by the race-fit winner on the run-in. He will improve a bundle for the outing and will probably have a bit more use made of his proven stamina next time. *(tchd 8-11 and 5-6)*
Ballyhurry(USA) ◆, having his fourth outing and dropped in trip, travelled strongly and, by no means knocked about, did just enough to secure third spot. His rating of 104 will hopefully not increase after this, if it stays the same he can surely find a handicap. *(op 16-1)*
George Stubbs(USA) went on and stepped up the pace but, having been readily picked off by the first two, he then lost third spot on the run-in. He is starting to look fully exposed. *(op 6-1)*
Loner, runner-up in selling company last time, found this much too tough.
Howards Dream(IRE) *Official explanation: jockey said gelding pulled up lame (op 100-1)*

3268 COUNTRY REFRESHMENTS NOVICES' CHASE (18 fncs) 3m

1:10 (1:10) (Class 4) 5-Y-0+ **£3,903** (£1,146; £573; £286)

Form RPR

5P1P **1** **Magnificent Seven (IRE)**[15] [2946] 7-11-5 98 GrahamLee 100+
(J Howard Johnson) *trckd ldrs: hdwy 6 out: rdn 2 out: led last: drvn and kpt on wl flat* **10/3**[3]

3-4P **2** *1* **Not A Trace (IRE)**[15] [2945] 7-11-5 80 MarkBradburne 98+
(Mrs S C Bradburne) *led to 3rd cl up tl led 4 out: rdn along 2 out: hdd last: drvn and kpt wl flat* **10/1**

P321 **3** *17* **El Andaluz (FR)**[11] [2966] 6-11-12 80 OllieMcPhail 92+
(Robert Gray) *hld up: j. slowly 3rd: hit 7th: hdwy and cl up 1/2-way: rdn along 5 out and outpcd fr next* **5/1**

634F **4** *9* **She's My Girl (IRE)**[19] [2905] 11-10-12 94 (b) NeilMulholland 67+
(John G Carr, Ire) *cl up: led 3rd: clr 5th: rdn along and hdd appr 4 out: sn wknd* **3/1**[2]

0SPF **5** *¾* **Nomadic Blaze**[31] [2692] 9-10-12 89 PhilKinsella[(7)] 72+
(P G Atkinson) *trck ldrs: rdn along 5 out: outpcd fr next* **12/1**

4033 **6** *24* **Arctic Lagoon (IRE)**[51] [2266] 7-11-2 76 (t) OwynNelmes[(3)] 47
(Mrs S C Bradburne) *cl up: rdn along 12th: sn lost pl and bhd* **11/4**[1]

6m 1.00s (-4.00) **Going Correction** 0.0s/f (Good) **6** Ran SP% **108.2**
Speed ratings: **106,105,100,97,96 88** CSF £29.40 TOTE £4.30: £2.30, £4.00; EX 21.50.
Owner George Tobitt **Bred** Kilian Farm **Trained** Billy Row, Co Durham

FOCUS
A modest novices' chase, rated through the third.

NOTEBOOK
Magnificent Seven(IRE), happiest going right-handed, had to work hard to get on level terms and had to be kept up to his work all the way to the line. This form has been rated 6lb off his Market Rasen win. *(op 5-2 tchd 7-2)*
Not A Trace(IRE), pulled up on his debut over regulation fences in bad ground two weeks earlier, jumped for fun and battled back all the way to the line. Runner-up in an Irish point, this was much better than anything he achieved over hurdles and he deserves to go one better. *(tchd 12-1)*
El Andaluz(FR), racing on much quicker ground, had 18lb to find with the winner on official ratings and he was struggling to keep up turning for home approaching four out. *(tchd 11-2)*
She's My Girl(IRE), who had failed to complete in three of her five previous tries over fences, had the best chance on official ratings but after forcing the pace her stamina seemed to give out altogether. She has come to fences late in life. *(op 5-2)*
Nomadic Blaze, who failed to get round on his three most recent starts, was struggling to keep up when he clouted the fourth last.
Arctic Lagoon(IRE) started favourite despite having the least chance on official ratings. He was *struggling to keep up a mile out and his chance soon evaporated.Official explanation: jockey said gelding hung left-handed throughout (op 4-1)*

3269 COUNTRY REFRESHMENTS NOVICES' H'CAP HURDLE (11 hdls 1 omitted) 2m 4f

1:40 (1:40) (Class 4) (0-100,100) 4-Y-0+ **£3,253** (£955; £477; £238)

Form RPR

-653 **1** **Nobel (FR)**[50] [2289] 5-11-5 100 MissRDavidson[(7)] 110+
(N G Richards) *trckd ldrs: smooth hdwy 4 out: cl up 2 out: led last: rdn and styd on wl flat* **7/1**

0-P4 **2** *3* **Oscar The Boxer (IRE)**[22] [2843] 7-10-5 84 ThomasDreaper[(5)] 89+
(J M Jefferson) *led: pushed along and hit 4 out: rdn next: drvn and hdd last: kpt on same pce* **9/2**[2]

5254 **3** *2* **Reem Two**[47] [2372] 5-11-10 98 DominicElsworth 100
(D McCain) *prom: hit 1st: pushed along and hit 6th: rdn 3 out: kpt on same pce appr last* **8/1**

-P46 **4** *7* **The Weaver (FR)**[22] [2840] 7-11-9 97 (p) BrianHarding 93+
(L Lungo) *hld up in tch gng wl: smooth hdwy to trck ldrs 3 out: sn shkn up: wknd bef last* **4/1**[1]

-424 **5** *2 ½* **We'll Meet Again**[10] [520] 6-10-12 86 AlanDempsey 79
(M W Easterby) *hld up: hdwy 8th: rdn along 3 out: kpt on same pce* **9/2**[2]

-643 **6** *shd* **Powerlove (FR)**[19] [2901] 5-11-11 99 MarkBradburne 92+
(Mrs S C Bradburne) *trckd ldrs: lost pl and bhd 4 out: sn rdn: styd on appr last* **16/1**

-060 **7** *12* **Quarry Island (IRE)**[22] [2843] 5-11-4 92 GrahamLee 72
(M Todhunter) *trckd ldrs: hit 3rd: pushed along and hit 4 out: rdn next and sn wknd* **20/1**

0000 **8** *2 ½* **Durba (AUS)**[136] [1302] 6-9-9 74 (t[1]) BrianHughes[(5)] 55+
(R C Guest) *trckd ldr: effrt and hit 4 out: rdn along next and sn wknd* **12/1**

0000 **9** *20* **Bromley Abbey**[63] [2027] 8-10-0 77 oh3 ow3 MrCStorey[(3)] 35
(Miss S E Forster) *bhd fr 5th* **100/1**

-532 **F** **Handa Island (USA)**[33] [2146] 7-10-13 90 MrTGreenall[(3)] —
(M W Easterby) *hld up: fell 5th* **6/1**[3]

4m 50.8s (-3.70) **Going Correction** 0.0s/f (Good) **10** Ran SP% **113.6**
Speed ratings: **107,105,105,102,101 101,96,95,87,—** CSF £38.12 CT £256.99 TOTE £5.90: £1.60, £1.70, £1.70; EX 46.30.
Owner Mr & Mrs Duncan Davidson **Bred** Yvon Alcan **Trained** Greystoke, Cumbria
■ The second last flight had to be omitted.

FOCUS
A much improved effort by the winner, who seemed to appreciate the much quicker ground. The second and third ran pretty much to their marks and the form looks solid.

NOTEBOOK
Nobel(FR) ◆, suited by this much quicker ground, travelled smoothly and had only to be kept up to his work. Thisi was a massive step up on his previous form and he can win again. *(op 9-1)*
Oscar The Boxer(IRE), having his second outing after a break, had conditions to suit. Attempting *to pinch it from the front, he was readily outspeeded by the unexposed winner on the run-in. (tchd 5-1)*
Reem Two, absent since November, had conditions in her favour and this is as good as she is. *(op 7-1)*
The Weaver(FR), in cheekpieces, travelled strongly but not for the first time he found little when pressure was applied. *(tchd 9-2)*
We'll Meet Again, who ran badly on the All-Weather ten days earlier, has yet to prove conclusively that he stays this far. *(op 5-1)*
Powerlove(FR), a bumper winner, she looks plenty high enough in the ratings on what she has achieved over hurdles so far. *(op 20-1 tchd 25-1)*

3270 COUNTRY REFRESHMENTS NOVICES' H'CAP CHASE 2m 1f

2:10 (2:10) (Class 5) (0-95,95) 5-Y-0+ **£3,253** (£955; £477; £238)

Form RPR

05P2 **1** **Word Gets Around (IRE)**[42] [2476] 8-11-12 95 BrianHarding 101+
(L Lungo) *trckd ldrs: hdwy 6 out: cl up next: led 3 out: rdn and jnd last: drvn out* **5/6**[1]

620 **2** *2* **Upswing**[36] [2585] 9-10-13 82 KennyJohnson 87+
(R C Guest) *hld up: smooth hdwy 4 out: hit next: effrt to chal and ev ch whn hit last: nt qckn flat* **8/1**[3]

P3U6 **3** *17* **Twist N Turn**[11] [2980] 6-10-4 73 DominicElsworth 59
(D McCain) *cl up: rdn along after 5 out: drvn 2 out and sn outpcd* **14/1**

4340 **4** *1* **Lascar De Ferbet (FR)**[42] [2476] 7-11-4 87 RichardMcGrath 73+
(R Ford) *led: rdn along 4 out: hdd next and wknd fr 2 out* **8/1**[3]

0000 **5** *10* **Star Trooper (IRE)**[22] [2843] 10-10-10 82 (p) MrCStorey[(3)] 57
(Miss S E Forster) *prom tl rdn along & lost pl 5 out: sn bhd* **25/1**

2533 **U** **Ideal Du Bois Beury (FR)**[19] [2905] 10-9-12 77 DavidDaSilva[(10)] —
(P Monteith) *hld up: hdwy 5 out: cl up whn blnd and uns rdr next* **10/3**[2]

4m 17.1s **6** Ran SP% **110.4**
CSF £7.83 TOTE £1.70: £1.30, £2.50; EX 6.70.
Owner Mr & Mrs Raymond Anderson Green **Bred** William O'Keeffe **Trained** Carrutherstown, D'fries & G'way
■ They started with their backs to the final fence in the back straight and not at the usual two-mile start.

FOCUS
A weak race in which the winner was the form pick on his best form. The second ran to around the level of his Market Rasen hurdles second.

NOTEBOOK
Word Gets Around(IRE), treated for a fibrillating heart, was dropping back in trip. He travelled strongly but in the end had to be kept right up to his work, getting off the mark on his third attempt over fences. *(tchd Evens)*
Upswing, given a patient ride on his return to fences, had joined the winner when he overjumped at the final fence. He gave his all on the run-in but was never going to come off anything but second best. He can surely break his duck at some point. *(op 7-1)*
Twist N Turn, struggling to keep up starting the home turn, was left for dead over the final two fences. *(tchd 16-1)*
Lascar De Ferbet(FR) took them along but was flat out on the turn for home and dropped away tamely two out.
Ideal Du Bois Beury(FR) hasn't won for nearly four years and has yet to hit the target over fences in 26 attempts and was out of the contest here at an early stage. *(op 7-2)*

3271 COUNTRY REFRESHMENTS H'CAP HURDLE 3m 110y

2:40 (2:40) (Class 4) (0-105,103) 4-Y-0+ **£3,253** (£955; £477; £238)

Form RPR

-140 **1** **Tickateal**[40] [2517] 6-11-4 95 GrahamLee 97
(R D E Woodhouse) *hld up in tch: hdwy 4 out: led 2 out: rdn last: styd on wl u.p flat* **11/2**[2]

0000 **2** *¾* **Bodfari Signet**[19] [2904] 10-11-9 103 OwynNelmes[(3)] 104
(Mrs S C Bradburne) *hld up towards rr: hdwy 9th: pushed along to chse ldrs 3 out: rdn next: styd on wl fr last* **7/1**

-PP5 **3** *nk* **Kyber**[56] 2171 5-10-6 **83**........ DominicElsworth 84
(R F Fisher) *prom: led briefly 10th: led again appr 3 out: rdn and hdd next:drvn last: n.m.r and switch rt flat: kpt on wl* **10/1**
PP00 **4** *4* **Washington Pink (IRE)**[22] 2843 7-9-7 **77** oh8........ MrBenHamilton(7) 75+
(C Grant) *hld up and bhd: hdwy 10th: sn pushed along: rdn after 3 out: hit next: styd on wl appr last: nrst fin* **100/1**
56-4 **5** *7* **I Got Rhythm**[205] 319 8-11-4 **95**........ RichardMcGrath 86+
(K G Reveley) *hld up towards rr: stdy hdwy on inner 4 out: chsd ldrs next: rdn 2 out and kpt on same pce* **6/1**[3]
4434 **6** *2½* **Sconced (USA)**[11] 2966 11-9-8 **81**........(b) JohnFlavin(10) 69
(R C Guest) *led to 2nd: cl up tl led again 8th: rdn along and hdd 10th: wd st and wknd fr 3 out* **7/1**
0-02 **7** *shd* **Lorio Du Misselot (FR)**[42] 2474 7-10-4 **81**........ KeithMercer 69+
(Ferdy Murphy) *cl up: led 2nd: hdd 8th: rdn along and hit next: blnd 10th and sn wknd* **3/1**[1]
-464 **8** *5* **Opal's Helmsman (USA)**[233] 410 7-10-8 **85**........ AlanDempsey 67
(W S Coltherd) *cl up: led 4 out: sn rdn along: hdd bef next and grad wknd* **20/1**
2100 **9** *shd* **Nick The Silver**[11] 2964 5-11-11 **102**........(p) OllieMcPhail 84
(Robert Gray) *in tch: mstkes and rdn along whn hit 8th: wkng whn blnd 3 out and bhd after* **14/1**
5050 **10** *1¾* **Now Then Auntie (IRE)**[37] 2571 5-10-5 **85**........ PeterBuchanan(3) 66
(Mrs S A Watt) *chsd ldrs: rdn along 4 out and sn wknd* **25/1**
4UF0 **11** *8* **Kidithou (FR)**[31] 2691 8-11-4 **100**........ MichaelMcAlister(5) 73
(W T Reed) *midfield tl lost pl and bhd fr 10th* **50/1**
0060 **12** *3½* **Political Sox**[22] 2840 12-10-13 **97**........ GarethThomas(7) 66
(R Nixon) *nt fluent 5th: a rr* **25/1**
1P-0 **13** *1½* **Top The Bill (IRE)**[37] 2566 6-11-7 **103**........ ThomasDreaper(5) 71
(Mrs S A Watt) *a bhd* **16/1**
00PF **P** **Minivet**[22] 2840 11-11-4 **95**........ BrianHarding —
(R Allan) *a bhd: p.u bef 2 out* **50/1**

5m 59.9s (-121.9) **Going Correction** 0.0s/f (Good) **14** Ran SP% **118.7**
Speed ratings: **103,102,102,101,99 98,98,96,96,96 93,92,91,—** CSF £40.53 CT £380.28 TOTE £6.80: £2.20, £2.50, £3.70; EX 40.80.
Owner R D E Woodhouse **Bred** R D E Woodhouse And Mrs C Woodhouse **Trained** Welburn, N Yorks

FOCUS
This was run at a sound gallop, but it is just ordinary handicap form, rated through the winner and the third.

NOTEBOOK
Tickateal, having his second outing after a break, likes quick ground and did just enough. *(op 5-1)*
Bodfari Signet, a close fourth in this race two years ago, loves it round here and showed a return to form, just found wanting in the end. *(op 6-1)*
Kyber, having his second outing in two months after a break, came again when headed and would *have finished even closer but for running out of racing room on the run-in.Official explanation: vet said gelding was lame*
Washington Pink(IRE), 8lb out of the handicap, ran easily his best race in a long time, if anything relishing the extended trip.
I Got Rhythm, third last year, was having his first outing since June and should come on for it.
Lorio Du Misselot(FR), who has yet to make his mark over hurdles, had no more to give when blundering four out. *(op 5-1)*

3272 COUNTRY REFRESHMENTS KILMANY CUP H'CAP CHASE (16 fncs) 2m 4f
3:10 (3:10) (Class 4) (0-110,110) 5-Y-0+ **£5,204** (£1,528; £764; £381)

Form RPR
2231 **1** **Bohemian Spirit (IRE)**[19] 2900 8-11-5 **110**........ MissRDavidson(7) 129+
(N G Richards) *mde all: blnd 5th: rdn 2 out: styd on wl* **4/6**[1]
P5P4 **2** *1¼* **Jodante (IRE)**[28] 2754 9-10-11 **95**........ DominicElsworth 109+
(R C Guest) *hld up and bhd: smooth hdwy 5 out: effrt on bit to chse wnr whn mstke 2 out: tenderly rdn after: kpt on wl flat* **10/1**
12U6 **3** *8* **Celtic Legend (FR)**[22] 2842 7-10-12 **96**........ RichardMcGrath 103+
(K G Reveley) *trckd ldrs: hdwy 5 out: rdn along 3 out and outpcd fr next* **9/2**[2]
3-50 **4** *15* **Sargon**[40] 2519 7-11-5 **103**........(b) OllieMcPhail 96+
(Robert Gray) *hld up: hdwy to chse wnr 6th: mstke 8th: rdn along after 5 out and wknd fr next* **16/1**
3P00 **5** *13* **Renvyle (IRE)**[18] 2925 8-10-9 **103**........(e) JohnFlavin(10) 80
(R C Guest) *chsd wnr to 6th: rdn along and bhd fr 5 out* **40/1**
-533 **6** *dist* **Gangsters R Us (IRE)**[37] 2568 10-10-11 **95**........ AlanDempsey —
(A Parker) *hld up in tch: hdwy 6 out: rdn along after next: sn wknd* **5/1**[3]

4m 56.2s (-3.20) **Going Correction** 0.0s/f (Good) **6** Ran SP% **112.2**
Speed ratings: **106,105,102,96,91** — CSF £8.09 TOTE £1.50: £1.10, £3.30; EX 7.00.
Owner Mr & Mrs Duncan Davidson **Bred** Patrick J Connolly **Trained** Greystoke, Cumbria
■ A first double for amateur Rose Davidson.

FOCUS
The winner looked well in again and has been rated value for further. The second is just as interesting and should win soon.

NOTEBOOK
Bohemian Spirit(IRE), 15lb higher, jumps for fun on the whole and sticking on willingly, he looked to be really enjoying himself. He can improve again. *(op 8-11)*
Jodante(IRE) ◆, having just his second outing for this stable, had the cheekpieces left off and seemed to be ridden with an eye on conserving his stamina. He survived a mistake two out to pursue the winner but was never going to quite get on level terms. He was certainly not knocked about and perhaps next time will be given a more positive ride. *(tchd 12-1)*
Celtic Legend(FR) had the ground and the trip in his favour but he has never been one to put up much of a fight and it was the same story here. *(op 7-2)*
Sargon, having his third outing for this yard, continues some way off peak form. *(op 12-1)*
Gangsters R Us(IRE) *Official explanation: trainer said gelding finished distressed (op 7-1)*

3273 COUNTRY REFRESHMENTS INTERMEDIATE OPEN NATIONAL HUNT FLAT RACE 2m
3:40 (3:40) (Class 6) 4-6-Y-0 **£2,055** (£599; £299)

Form RPR
0 **1** **Insurgent (IRE)**[34] 2642 4-9-11........ JohnFlavin(10) 64+
(R C Guest) *hld up: gd hdwy on inner over 3f out: rdn to ld wl over 1f out: edgd lft and kpt on ins last* **25/1**
2 *¾* **Mister Jungle (FR)** 4-10-7........ MarkBradburne 63
(Mrs S C Bradburne) *hld up in tch: hdwy 3f out: swtchd lft and rdn wl over 1f out kpt on wl fnl f* **7/1**[3]
3 *shd* **James Bay (IRE)** 5-11-5........ BrianHarding 75
(N G Richards) *trckd ldrs: pushed along 4f out: hdwy to ld over 2f out: sn rdn: hdd wl over 1f out: kpt on same pce* **4/6**[1]
/0 **4** *3½* **Watercress**[82] 1762 6-10-12........(t) GrahamLee 64
(Miss M E Rowland) *in tch: effrt to chse ldrs 3f out: sn rdn and kpt on same pce fnl 2f* **16/1**
00 **5** *shd* **Young Rocky (IRE)**[23] 2823 5-11-5........ DominicElsworth 71
(C Grant) *cl up: rdn along over 3f out: kpt on same pce fnl 2f* **33/1**
0 **6** *shd* **Celtic Saloon (IRE)**[34] 2642 4-10-7........ RichardMcGrath 59
(K G Reveley) *keen: trckd ldrs: hdwy and ev ch 3f out: sn rdn and one pce fnl 2f* **6/1**[2]
7 *4* **Floral Rhapsody** 5-10-12........ RussGarritty 60
(P Beaumont) *set stdy pce: qcknd 3f out: sn rdn and hdd: grad wknd* **9/1**
5 **8** *16* **Sparky Rocket**[19] 2906 5-10-7........ DougieCostello(5) 44
(B Storey) *trckd ldrs: rdn along over 3f out and sn wknd* **16/1**
6 **9** *12* **Flemington House**[19] 2906 5-10-7........ DeclanMcGann(5) 32
(A M Crow) *hld up: hdwy on outer to press ldrs 6f out: rdn along 4f out and sn wknd* **25/1**

4m 4.90s (13.60) **Going Correction** 0.0s/f (Good)
WFA 4 from 5yo+ 11lb **9** Ran SP% **119.2**
Speed ratings: **66,65,65,63,63 63,61,53,47** CSF £191.85 TOTE £26.60: £4.40, £1.50, £1.10; EX 280.10 Place 6 £63.08, Place 5 £56.94.
Owner Richard Guest Racing Club **Bred** Swettenham Stud **Trained** Brancepeth, Co Durham
■ A first winner for 20-year-old John Flavin who has partnered five point winners in Ireland.

FOCUS
As usual, no gallop at all in the early stages. There was not that much between the first six at the line and the form is pretty meaningless.

NOTEBOOK
Insurgent(IRE), having his second outing, was given a patient ride. He made his effort on the inner once in line for home and in the end did just enough.
Mister Jungle(FR), a tall, narrow type, came in for plenty of support. He was making hard work of it turning in but stuck to his task to snatch second spot on the line. A stronger gallop would have suited him much better. *(op 14-1)*
James Bay(IRE), a rangy, well-made type, was heavily backed to make a winning debut. He made hard work of getting to the front only to be run out of it in the closing stages. A stronger gallop and stiffer track would have seen him in a better light. *(op Evens tchd 11-10 in a place)*
Watercress, unplaced on his previous outing in October, showed a fair bit more this time. *(op 14-1)*
Young Rocky(IRE), having his third start, is a big boy who will not be seen at his best until he goes over fences.
Celtic Saloon(IRE), on the leg, wouldn't settle and had no more to give in the final quarter mile. *(op 5-1 tchd 7-1 in a place)*
T/Plt: £53.80 to a £1 stake. Pool: £39,386.45. 534.00 winning tickets. T/Qpdt: £24.80 to a £1 stake. Pool: £3,440.40. 102.40 winning tickets. JR

2982 TOWCESTER (R-H)
Friday, January 6

OFFICIAL GOING: Soft (good to soft in places)
Wind: Almost nil Weather: Overcast

3274 SIS H'CAP CHASE (12 fncs) 2m 110y
1:20 (1:21) (Class 5) (0-95,95) 5-Y-0+ **£3,253** (£955; £477; £238)

Form RPR
F2U2 **1** **Wages**[24] 2807 6-11-2 **90**........ MrNWilliams(5) 108+
(Evan Williams) *hld up: mstke 4th: hdwy 7th: mstke next: led last: drvn out* **7/1**[3]
4215 **2** *15* **Avadi (IRE)**[34] 2630 8-11-2 **85**........ AndrewThornton 95+
(P T Dalton) *hld up: hdwy 6th: outpcd 8th: rallied after next: led appr 2 out: rdn and hdd last: wknd and eased last 75 yds* **4/1**[1]
-110 **3** *6* **Julies Boy (IRE)**[31] 2684 9-11-0 **90**........(t) WillieMcCarthy(7) 86
(T R George) *led 3rd: hdd appr 2 out: wknd bef last* **4/1**[1]
P54P **4** *15* **Auditor**[11] 2984 7-10-1 **75**........(b) MarkNicolls(5) 56
(S T Lewis) *chsd ldrs tl wknd appr 2 out* **14/1**
535P **5** *6* **Apadi (USA)**[56] 2172 10-11-2 **88**........ LarryMcGrath(3) 64+
(R C Guest) *hld up: mstke 2nd: hdwy 9th: wknd after 3 out* **16/1**
563- **6** *5* **Smurfit (IRE)**[262] 4917 7-10-10 **86**........ TomMessenger(7) 56
(C C Bealby) *led to 3rd: chsd ldrs tl wknd after 3 out* **16/1**
5U0P **7** *22* **Tails I Win**[30] 2701 7-10-2 **74** oh8 ow5........ AnthonyCoyle(3) 22
(Miss C J E Caroe) *chsd ldrs tl wknd after 3 out* **25/1**
5100 **F** **Walsingham (IRE)**[40] 2527 8-11-7 **90**........ TomDoyle —
(R Lee) *fell 2nd* **28/1**
5F30 **P** **Cusp**[23] 2818 6-11-1 **89**........ DerekLaverty(5) —
(Mrs A M Thorpe) *p.u bef 3rd* **14/1**
-440 **P** **Jacarado (IRE)**[45] 2424 8-9-11 **69** oh4........ TomMalone(3) —
(R Dickin) *bhd whn hmpd 2nd: t.o whn p.u bef 2 out* **12/1**
P-3P **P** **Advance East**[43] 2465 14-10-0 **74**........ LeeStephens(5) —
(M J M Evans) *hld up: bhd fr 4th: t.o whn p.u bef 2 out* **25/1**
3-43 **U** **Uncle Max (IRE)**[16] 2936 6-11-12 **95**........ AntonyEvans —
(N A Twiston-Davies) *chsd ldrs: mstke 8th: cl up whn uns rdr next* **13/2**[2]
PPP5 **P** **Rutland (IRE)**[21] 2867 7-9-11 **71**........ RobertLucey-Butler(5) —
(C J Drewe) *hld up: hmpd 2nd: in rr whn mstke 4th: t.o whn p.u bef 2 out* **50/1**

4m 23.9s (4.60) **Going Correction** +0.325s/f (Yiel) **13** Ran SP% **111.7**
Speed ratings: **102,94,92,85,82 79,69,—,—,— —,—,—** CSF £32.34 CT £124.98 TOTE £8.80: £3.10, £1.70, £2.00; EX 33.00.
Owner Paul Morgan **Bred** Miss June Frankham **Trained** Cowbridge, Vale Of Glamorgan

FOCUS
There was a decent pace on here for this moderate handicap chase. Improved form from the winner

NOTEBOOK
Wages, given a patient ride in a race run at a decent pace, came there going well approaching the final fence and drew clear on the run-in. This was his first success over jumps in 19 starts but he had shown improved form since switching to chasing this season, and he seemed to thrive on the strong pace and soft ground as he gained his reward here. *(tchd 8-1)*
Avadi(IRE), outpaced by the winner from the last, is likely to appreciate a return to further, so this was not a bad run off what looks quite a stiff mark now.
Julies Boy(IRE) helped set the decent gallop so finishing third was a fair effort in the *circumstances. He should be seen to better effect when allowed to set a less frantic pace in front. (op 9-2)*
Auditor could not take advantage of being much better off at the weights with Wages than when they met at Hereford in November.
Apadi(USA), keen in the early stages as usual, is back on the mark off which he last won a handicap, but he is struggling to find his form at present.
Smurfit(IRE) did not get home on his first start since April.
Uncle Max(IRE) made slight blunders at a couple of fences on the trot and, in a rather undignified manner, Evans exited stage right at the second of them. He looked like taking part in the finish at the time. *(op 6-1 tchd 11-2)*
Cusp *Official explanation: jockey said mare pulled up lame (op 6-1 tchd 11-2)*

3275 HAPPY 40TH BIRTHDAY CLARE FOGARTY NOVICES' HURDLE (8 hdls) 2m
1:50 (1:51) (Class 3) 4-Y-0+ **£5,387** (£1,591; £795; £397; £198)

Form | | | | RPR
2P5- **1** **Montecorvino (GER)**[272] 4775 5-11-5 .... AntonyEvans 92+
(N A Twiston-Davies) *chsd clr ldr tl led 4th: drvn out* **4/1**[2]
6-60 **2** *1 1/4* **Ballybawn House**[11] 2983 5-11-1 ow3 .... SeanFox 84
(J C Fox) *hld up: hdwy 4th: chsd wnr 2 out: mstke last: styd on* **12/1**
61 **3** *1 1/4* **Shaka's Pearl**[11] 2983 6-11-10 .... JamesDavies 92
(N J Gifford) *hld up in tch: rdn appr last: styd on* **7/2**[1]
3 **4** *7* **Count Boris**[34] 2624 5-11-5 .... BenjaminHitchcott 83+
(J A Geake) *chsd ldrs: ev ch 3 out: rdn whn blnd next: sn wknd* **4/1**[2]
5 *1 3/4* **Robeson**[86] 4-10-4 .... TJPhelan(3) 66
(G Haine) *hld up: hdwy after 3 out: styd on same pce fr next* **66/1**
35 **6** *2 1/2* **Proprioception (IRE)**[50] 2286 4-10-0 .... RobertThornton 57
(A King) *chsd ldrs tl wknd appr 2 out* **9/2**[3]
0/ **7** *3/4* **Regal Term (IRE)**[1099] 2947 8-10-9 .... JosephStevenson(10) 78+
(R Dickin) *hld up: blnd 3 out: nt trble ldrs* **100/1**
6 **8** *hd* **Trebello**[17] 2928 5-11-5 .... LeightonAspell 75
(J R Boyle) *hld up: hdwy 3 out: nt trble ldrs* **50/1**
230 **9** *1 1/4* **River Ripples (IRE)**[11] 2983 7-11-5 .... JasonMaguire 74
(T R George) *hld up: nvr nr to chal* **9/1**
6 **10** *13* **Molly's Spirit (IRE)**[243] 235 5-10-12 .... TomDoyle 57+
(P R Webber) *hld up: hdwy after 5th: rdn and wknd appr 2 out* **20/1**
00 **11** *12* **Fill The Bunker (IRE)**[23] 2821 6-11-5 .... TomSiddall 49
(N A Twiston-Davies) *prom to 5th* **33/1**
PP **12** *dist* **A One (IRE)**[34] 2618 7-10-12 .... MrJAJenkins(7) —
(H J Manners) *led and sn clr: hdd 4th: wknd after next* **150/1**
0-P4 **P** **Roseville (IRE)**[224] 531 6-10-7 .... MarkNicolls(5) —
(S T Lewis) *chsd ldrs tl wknd appr 3 out: t.o whn p.u bef next* **150/1**
P **Benefit Fund (IRE)**[320] 6-11-5 .... HenryOliver —
(D J Wintle) *hld up: hdwy after 5th: sn wknd: t.o whn p.u bef last* **66/1**
0-0P **P** **Murotoevation (IRE)**[21] 2865 7-11-0 ....(v[1]) RobertLucey-Butler(5) —
(D G Bridgwater) *hld up: wknd 5th: t.o whn p.u bef 2 out* **150/1**
F **P** **Heathers Girl**[23] 2826 7-10-12 .... WayneHutchinson —
(R Dickin) *hld up: plld hrd: hdwy 4th: wknd 3 out: t.o whn p.u bef next* **66/1**

4m 20.5s (9.10) **Going Correction** +0.40s/f (Soft)
WFA 4 from 5yo+ 11lb **16** Ran SP% **115.2**
Speed ratings: **93,92,91,88,87 86,85,85,85,78 72,—,—,—,— —** CSF £16.94 TOTE £5.00: £1.50, £1.90, £2.60.
Owner Three Off The Tee Partnership **Bred** A Steigenberger **Trained** Naunton, Gloucs

FOCUS
This was quite a test in the ground, but the form does not look that strong.

NOTEBOOK
Montecorvino(GER), debuting for his new stable, shrugged off a 272-day absence and saw the trip out well to get off the mark over hurdles. A chasing sort, he will get further in time. *(op 11-2)*
Ballybawn House chased the winner home without ever looking likely to pass him, but this was still an improvement on her last two efforts, and it is noticeable that her three best runs to date in bumpers and over hurdles have all come in soft ground.
Shaka's Pearl, who won over the course and distance on Boxing Day, had worse ground to cope with this time and a penalty to shoulder. He did not run badly in the circumstance and is another who will get further in time. *(tchd 4-1 and 9-2 in places)*
Count Boris, going well at the bottom of the hill, found less than looked likely under pressure, and this former Flat horse found the first three – all jumps-bred – too strong up the hill. He will be suited by an easier track. *(tchd 7-2)*
Robeson, up against his elders on his hurdling debut, stayed on quite well given that he was bred to be a sprinter. A sounder surface should suit him.
Proprioception(IRE) had never run on soft ground before and, although she received all the allowances for being a filly and a four-year-old, it was not enough. *(op 4-1)*
Regal Term(IRE), off the track since finishing lame behind Ashley Brook in a bumper three years ago, made a promising return to action. She almost lost her rider at the third last but kept on quite well afterwards. She should come on quite a bit for this outing.
River Ripples(IRE), a half-brother to bumper winner/very smart staying hurdler Brewster, is likely *to be seen to better effect when stepped up in trip in handicap company.Official explanation: jockey said gelding had breathing problem; jockey said, regarding running and riding, his orders were to drop gelding in and switch him off, as he failed to get home on previous starts; he added gelding made a noise at third-last hurdle and he didn't want to give him a hard race thereafter; trainer said gelding had travelled well in previous race and found nothing (op 8-1)*
Benefit Fund(IRE) *Official explanation: jockey said gelding was unsuited by soft, good to soft in places ground*

3276 TONY FANNING HAPPY 75TH BIRTHDAY H'CAP CHASE (18 fncs) 3m 110y
2:20 (2:22) (Class 4) (0-100,96) 5-Y-0+ **£4,436** (£1,310; £655; £327; £163)

Form | | | | RPR
1PP3 **1** **Heartache**[11] 2986 9-10-0 70 oh3 ....(b) WayneHutchinson 83+
(R Mathew) *led 2nd to 6th: led 7th to next: led 11th: hdd after 3 out: rallied to ld flat: drvn out* **13/2**[3]
011U **2** *2* **Never Awol (IRE)**[11] 2986 9-10-9 86 ....(p) TomMessenger(7) 96
(B N Pollock) *led to 2nd: led 6th to next: 8th to 11th: led after 3 out: rdn appr last: hdd and nt qckn flat* **8/1**
P-P6 **3** *6* **The River Joker (IRE)**[11] 2986 10-10-8 83 .... MarkNicolls(5) 88+
(John R Upson) *chsd ldrs: outpcd and mstke 12th: rallied after 15th: styd on same pce appr last* **33/1**
PP-F **4** *9* **Gaye Dream**[21] 2863 8-11-1 85 .... JasonMaguire 80
(T R George) *hld up: hdwy 15th: wknd after 2 out* **6/1**[2]
6403 **5** *1/2* **Kappelhoff (IRE)**[31] 2686 9-10-0 70 oh2 ....(b) MatthewBatchelor 67+
(Mrs L Richards) *hld up: hdwy 10th: wknd appr 2 out* **16/1**
P-65 **6** *8* **Jack Fuller (IRE)**[24] 2808 9-11-12 96 ....(b) LeightonAspell 83
(P R Hedger) *hld up: hdwy 7th: ev ch 3 out: wknd next* **8/1**
PPP3 **7** *3 1/2* **Maybeseven**[41] 2506 12-9-7 70 oh7 .... JohnPritchard(7) 55+
(R Dickin) *prom: rdn 10th: wkng whn hmpd 12th* **33/1**
4-50 **8** *13* **Dalus Park (IRE)**[21] 2863 11-11-1 90 ....(b[1]) MrSMorris(5) 60
(C C Bealby) *mid-div: hdwy 7th: wknd 10th* **10/1**
4240 **9** *27* **Mac Dargin (IRE)**[11] 2994 7-11-12 96 .... AntonyEvans 39
(N A Twiston-Davies) *hld up: mstke 1st: hdwy 12th: wknd 15th* **16/1**
F **Shrove Tuesday (IRE)**[29] 2739 7-9-10 71 .... RCColgan(5) —
(A J Martin, Ire) *hld up: mstke 1st: in rr whn fell 7th* **4/1**[1]
52F **P** **Pardini (USA)**[6] 3144 7-11-8 92 ....(b) JohnMcNamara —
(M F Harris) *hld up: hdwy 7th: wknd 15th: p.u bef next* **16/1**
P-04 **U** **Indian Laburnum (IRE)**[43] 2465 9-10-0 73 ....(b) LeeVickers(3) —
(C C Bealby) *chsd ldrs: wkng whn blnd and uns rdr 9th* **9/1**
-350 **P** **It's Rumoured**[49] 2325 6-11-1 85 .... JamesDavies —
(Jean-Rene Auvray) *prom: j. slowly and lost pl 2nd: bhd whn p.u bef 9th* **16/1**

6m 51.7s (5.10) **Going Correction** +0.325s/f (Yiel) **13** Ran SP% **118.3**
Speed ratings: **104,103,101,98,98 95,94,90,81,— —,—,—** CSF £57.91 CT £1588.70 TOTE £7.50: £2.20, £2.60, £8.60; EX 51.80.
Owner Robin Mathew **Bred** Robin Mathew **Trained** Little Barrington, Gloucs
■ Stewards' Enquiry : Wayne Hutchinson four-day ban: used whip with excessive frequency (Jan 17-20)

FOCUS
This featured a number of course regulars and the form might not be that relevant elsewhere. The first and second both looked nicely treated.

NOTEBOOK
Heartache did not get home over the course and distance last time, but he had a stiff task at the weights that day. Although 3lb out of the handicap here, his chance was clearer and he saw it out well, rallying to lead on the run-in. *(op 7-1 tchd 6-1)*
Never Awol(IRE), a course regular who has his own ideas about things, did not appear to do *anything wrong this time, but he is on a career-high mark now so things are not getting any easier. (op 7-1 tchd 9-1)*
The River Joker(IRE) was behind Heartache here last time in a classified heat and found himself worse off at the weights with that rival in this handicap. *(op 28-1)*
Gaye Dream, who fell on his chasing debut, came in for some support in the morning and did not run too badly. Having failed to complete on his previous three starts, this should have done his confidence some good. *(op 5-1)*
Kappelhoff(IRE) again gave the impression that he finds this trip too far. *(op 14-1)*
Jack Fuller(IRE) was back on the same mark as when successful under top weight over the course and distance in March, but the ground was softer this time and he did not get up the hill, having looked a player three out. *(tchd 9-1)*

3277 GG.COM NOVICES' HURDLE (12 hdls) 3m
2:50 (2:53) (Class 4) 5-Y-0+ **£4,436** (£1,310; £655; £327; £163)

Form | | | | RPR
0-04 **1** **Alfasonic**[24] 2815 6-10-12 .... RobertThornton 107
(A King) *mid-div: hdwy 6th: led appr 2 out: drvn out* **20/1**
-231 **2** *3/4* **Gritti Palace (IRE)**[24] 2815 6-10-13 116 .... MarkNicolls(5) 112
(John R Upson) *hld up in tch: led after 3 out: hdd bef next: ev ch whn mstke last: styd on* **5/1**[3]
3 *7* **Exceptionnel (FR)**[258] 7-10-5 .... MrJNewbold(7) 99
(Lady Connell) *hld up: hdwy 8th: nt rch ldrs* **50/1**
-046 **4** *6* **Major Catch (IRE)**[11] 2979 7-10-7 110 .... AdamPogson(5) 93
(C T Pogson) *prom tl wknd appr 2 out* **50/1**
6-32 **5** *dist* **Royal Coburg (IRE)**[43] 2450 6-10-12 .... AntonyEvans —
(N A Twiston-Davies) *hld up in tch: rdn and wknd appr 2 out* **4/1**[1]
0-42 **6** *7* **Kildonnan**[44] 2426 7-10-12 .... WayneHutchinson —
(J A B Old) *led: hdd & wknd after 3 out* **4/1**[1]
30-0 **7** *3/4* **Coltscroft**[40] 2528 6-11-1 ow3 .... SeanFox —
(J C Fox) *plld hrd: hung lft: jnd ldr whn tried to run out 2nd: sn lost pl bhd fr next* **66/1**
/325 **8** *1 1/4* **The Sawyer (BEL)**[10] 3023 6-10-12 .... BenjaminHitchcott —
(R H Buckler) *chsd ldrs tl wknd 3 out* **6/1**
P/5- **P** **Arceye**[348] 9-10-7 .... DerekLaverty(5) —
(W Davies) *hld up: rdn and wknd appr 8th: t.o whn p.u bef 2 out* **66/1**
60-0 **P** **Chilly Milly**[29] 2718 5-10-5 .... JamesDavies —
(V Smith) *hld up: in rr whn hmpd 5th: t.o whn p.u bef 3 out* **150/1**
P **Senor Set (GER)**[51] 5-10-2 .... AngharadFrieze(10) —
(P A Blockley) *hld up: hdwy 7th: wknd 3 out: bhd whn p.u bef next* **150/1**
2P0 **P** **Thyne Spirit (IRE)**[11] 2983 7-10-12 .... AlanO'Keeffe —
(S T Lewis) *chsd ldrs: rdn and lost pl 6th: t.o whn p.u bef 8th* **50/1**
P **P** **With Due Respect**[24] 2815 6-10-12 .... TomSiddall —
(N A Twiston-Davies) *mid-div: j.rt and lost pl 5th: t.o whn p.u bef 2 out* **100/1**
50-2 **P** **Optimistic Alfie**[41] 2503 6-10-12 .... JohnMcNamara —
(B G Powell) *hld up: hdwy appr 8th: wknd 3 out: bhd whn p.u bef last* **7/1**
0210 **P** **Lyes Green**[40] 2530 5-11-4 107 .... LeightonAspell —
(O Sherwood) *hld up: hdwy after 6th: wknd appr 3 out: bhd whn p.u bef 2 out* **9/2**[2]

6m 36.6s (5.60) **Going Correction** +0.40s/f (Soft) **15** Ran SP% **117.6**
Speed ratings: **98,97,95,93,— —,—,—,—,— —,—,—,—,—** CSF £113.82 TOTE £23.70: £5.20, £3.10, £10.00; EX 108.10.
Owner Mrs S Warren **Bred** Mrs E M Charlton **Trained** Barbury Castle, Wilts

FOCUS
They went a fair pace in the conditions and it proved a real stamina test for these novices.

NOTEBOOK
Alfasonic, 25 lengths behind the match-fit Gritti Palace at Warwick last time, managed to reverse that form on 6lb better terms with the benefit of that run underneath his belt. He looks a chaser in the making and could well go that route this season. *(op 25-1)*
Gritti Palace(IRE) had the benefit of fitness on his side when finishing 25 lengths in front of Alfasonic at Warwick, and the concession of 6lb to that rival this time proved just too great. He still finished nicely clear of the rest, though. *(tchd 9-2)*
Exceptionnel(FR), a half-brother to 2000 Grand National runner-up Mely Moss, won a point-to-point in the spring and ran a promising race on his debut under Rules, keeping on well under his inexperienced rider. Cleary not short of stamina, he should come on for this and be capable of winning a similar race. *(op 40-1)*
Major Catch(IRE) did not run badly given that he raced prominently throughout at a fair pace given the conditions. He finished well clear of the remainder, but he has still to run to the level of form he showed for his previous stable. *(op 66-1)*
Royal Coburg(IRE) was expected to appreciate the step up in trip but he was beaten at the bottom of the hill. *(op 9-2)*
Kildonnan set a fair pace given the conditions and, although he looked to be going well enough *jumping the third last, he soon paid the price as they began the climb for home. (op 9-2 tchd 5-1 in places)*
Coltscroft *Official explanation: jockey had difficulty steering gelding on right-handed track*
Lyes Green *Official explanation: trainer said gelding was unsuited by ground (soft, good to soft in places) and course (op 4-1)*

3278 FREE TIPS @GG.COM MARES' ONLY BEGINNERS' CHASE (14 fncs) 2m 3f 110y
3:20 (3:23) (Class 4) 6-Y-0+ **£3,802** (£1,123; £561; £280; £140)

Form | | | | RPR
-032 **1** **De Blanc (IRE)**[31] 2682 6-10-12 98 .... SamThomas 115+
(Miss Venetia Williams) *j.lft: mde all: clr 10th: rdn appr last: unchal* **7/4**[2]
0/UF **2** *4* **Perle De Puce (FR)**[22] 2846 7-10-5 ....(b[1]) MrSWaley-Cohen(7) 111+
(N J Henderson) *prom: chsd wnr 5th: rdn and mstke last: nt rch wnr* **4/5**[1]
5F-4 **3** *26* **Scratch The Dove**[39] 2553 9-10-12 100 .... WayneHutchinson 85
(A E Price) *chsd ldrs to 10th* **12/1**[3]
3036 **4** *1* **Lago D'Oro**[28] 2742 6-10-7 93 .... TJPhelan(5) 84
(Dr P Pritchard) *hld up: nvr nr to chal* **16/1**
UP40 **5** *dist* **Cool Carroll (IRE)**[16] 2936 8-10-12 81 .... HenryOliver —
(Mrs Tracey Barfoot-Saunt) *prom to 6th* **40/1**

The Form Book, Raceform Ltd, Compton, RG20 6NL

F P **The Sneakster (IRE)**[194] 843 8-10-12 .... TomSiddall —
(S A Brookshaw) *prom: blnd and wknd 7th: t.o whn p.u bef 11th* **66/1**
/P0P P **Bedford Leader**[11] 2966 8-10-7 81..............................(p) DerekLaverty(5) —
(A P Jones) *chsd ldrs: lost pl 2nd: bhd and rdn 4th: t.o whn p.u after next* **66/1**

5m 33.0s (14.80) **Going Correction** +0.825s/f (Soft) **7** Ran SP% **110.9**
Speed ratings: **103,101,91,90,— —,—** CSF £3.44 TOTE £2.60: £1.80, £1.10; EX 4.90.
Owner Jeremy Hancock **Bred** Pat Galavan **Trained** Kings Caple, H'fords

FOCUS
The two market leaders dominated. The beaten favourite was rated a stone higher than the winner over hurdles and wasn't seen to best effect. Dodgy form overall.

NOTEBOOK
De Blanc(IRE) enjoyed the run of the race in front and got to the bottom of the hill with an eight-length lead. That proved enough of a gap to defend in the straight and she won fairly comfortably. She tended to jump out to her left here so will perhaps be happier going the other way round in future. *(op 9-4 tchd 13-8)*
Perle De Puce(FR) ◆, wearing blinkers for the first time, was given too much to do by her rider, who allowed his main market rival to extend into an eight-length lead rounding the turn into the straight. By the line he had halved that deficit, but the impression left was that had he kept his rival closer to him when the run for home began the finish would have been tighter. *(op 4-6 tchd 10-11)*
Scratch The Dove is flattered by her official mark. Unable to go with the front two from the fifth last, she only just held on to third place from the staying-on Lago D'Oro. *(op 10-1)*
Lago D'Oro, given a patient ride, stayed on without threatening the first two. Whether she really wants the ground this soft is open to question.

3279 SIS AMATEUR RIDERS' H'CAP HURDLE (10 hdls) 2m 3f 110y
3:50 (3:51) (Class 5) (0-90,90) 4-Y-0+ **£2,734** (£854; £427; £213; £106)

Form RPR
23F5 **1** **Ask The Umpire (IRE)**[21] 2862 11-11-12 **90**..........(b) MrGBarfoot-Saunt 95+
(N E Berry) *chsd ldrs: led 3 out: rdn clr appr last: eased nr fin* **14/1**
2 *6* **Mayoun (IRE)**[53] 2253 9-11-6 **84**.......................................(p) MrNWilliams 84+
(Evan Williams) *hld up: hdwy whn hmpd 3 out: chsd wnr next: rdn and hung rt appr last: hung lft flat: no imp* **4/1**[2]
-6P0 **3** *¾* **Mooresini (IRE)**[17] 2928 6-11-5 **90**..............................(p) MrSPHanson(7) 87
(N J Gifford) *hld up in tch: rdn appr 2 out: styd on same pce* **28/1**
4 *13* **Bonnell (IRE)**[19] 2919 7-11-5 **88**.............................. MrATDuff(5) 72
(K J Burke) *hld up: hdwy 8th: chsd wnr after 3 out: wknd next* **20/1**
0306 **5** *18* **Reflex Blue**[16] 2936 9-10-9 **80**...(v) MrMPrice(7) 46
(R J Price) *prom to 3 out* **14/1**
-000 **6** *3 ½* **Kaid (IRE)**[61] 2073 11-10-1 **72**.. MrTCollier(7) 35
(R Lee) *hld up: n.d* **66/1**
7 *3 ½* **The Small Farmer (IRE)**[229] 9-10-3 **74**........................... MrJBarrett(7) 33
(Mrs A E Brooks) *hld up: nvr nrr* **15/2**[3]
-053 **8** *4* **Road King (IRE)**[24] 2810 12-10-9 **80**.................................(p) MrRBirkett(7) 35
(Miss J Feilden) *hld up: hdwy 4th: wknd 3 out* **12/1**
411U **9** *12* **Zeloso**[11] 2964 8-11-3 **88**..(v) MrRQuinn(7) 31
(M F Harris) *hld up: effrt 8th: wknd next* **8/1**
3450 **10** *30* **Breezer**[11] 2958 6-11-0 **85**..(p) MrDHannig(7) —
(J A Geake) *led to 2nd: led appr 6th: hdd 3 out: sn wknd: bhd whn blnd last* **18/1**
P-P0 **P** **Palais (IRE)**[11] 2962 11-10-9 **80** ow3.............................. MrMMackley(7) —
(John A Harris) *chsd ldrs: mstke 5th: wknd next* **100/1**
5-P0 **F** **Soleil D'Hiver**[29] 2726 5-10-6 **75**.. MrBKing(5) —
(C J Drewe) *hld up: hdwy 7th: ev ch whn fell 3 out* **66/1**
6360 **P** **Ireland's Eye (IRE)**[31] 2688 11-11-0 **85**........................(v) MrSFMagee(7) —
(J R Norton) *chsd ldrs to 7th: t.o whn p.u bef 2 out* **20/1**
1360 **P** **Bustisu**[21] 2862 9-11-3 **88**.. RyanCummings(7) —
(D J Wintle) *hld up: sme hdwy 8th: sn wknd: t.o whn p.u bef 2 out* **33/1**
005P **P** **Impero**[161] 1100 8-9-12 **69**...(b) MrDanielChinn(7) —
(G F Bridgwater) *led 2nd: hdd after 5th: wknd 7th: t.o whn p.u bef 2 out* **100/1**
P612 **P** **Paddy Boy (IRE)**[11] 2958 5-10-13 **80**.............................. MrGTumelty(3) —
(J R Boyle) *hld up in tch: led after 5th: hdd bef next: wknd 7th: t.o whn p.u bef last* **15/8**[1]

5m 16.3s (-1.80) **Going Correction** +0.40s/f (Soft) **16** Ran SP% **124.8**
Speed ratings: **101,98,98,93,85 84,83,81,76,64 —,—,—,—,— —** CSF £68.10 CT £1602.63 TOTE £18.80: £2.00, £1.40, £6.60, £3.60; EX 73.50 Place 6 £223.69, Place 5 £151.76.
Owner Craig Davies **Bred** Michael Conroy **Trained** Llanishen, Monmouths

FOCUS
This looked a weak race beforehand, but it was run at a fair pace and proved a real slog in the mud.

NOTEBOOK
Ask The Umpire(IRE) was in the process of running a good race at Uttoxeter last time before his stamina ran out. He appreciated the drop back in trip and won easily enough in what was quite a slog in the mud. This will not do him any good with the Handicapper, though, and he might have to return to chasing now. *(op 16-1)*
Mayoun(IRE), formerly trained in Ireland, has not won a race since his debut in a bumper at Downpatrick in March 2002, but this was not a bad effort in defeat. This was a poor race but he is nicely handicapped on some of his old form and his new trainer may be able to get some improvement out of him. *(op 5-1)*
Mooresini(IRE), wearing cheekpieces for the first time on this handicap debut, looked to have quite a stiff tast under top weight and achieved a new personal best, albeit only marginally. *(op 25-1)*
Bonnell(IRE), another ex-Irish performer making his debut for a stable on this side of the Irish Sea, got tired up the hill, and he looks to need help from the Handicapper.
Reflex Blue has shown his best form on better ground than this.
Soleil D'Hiver, who had conditions to suit, was bang there, although they had yet to hit the climb to the line, when she departed at the third last. *(op 5-2 after early 11-4)*
Paddy Boy(IRE) *Official explanation: jockey said gelding was unsuited by the soft, good to soft in places ground (op 5-2 after early 11-4)*
T/Plt: £257.00 to a £1 stake. Pool: £59,922.80. 170.20 winning tickets. T/Qpdt: £119.40 to a £1 stake. Pool: £4,343.80. 26.90 winning tickets. CR

[2928]FONTWELL (L-H)
Saturday, January 7

OFFICIAL GOING: Good to soft
Wind: Virtually nil

3280 CORTAFLEX FOR HORSES MARES' ONLY NOVICES' HURDLE (DIV I) (9 hdls) 2m 2f 110y
12:20 (12:20) (Class 4) 4-Y-0+ **£3,253** (£716; £716; £238)

Form RPR
1-35 **1** **Sunley Shines**[24] 2829 6-10-9 .... JohnLevins(5) 105+
(B G Powell) *w ldr: led after 3rd: hit 3 out: nt fluent next: sn rdn: drvn out* **9/4**[2]
0P **2** *3 ½* **Noun De La Thinte (FR)**[22] 2859 5-10-9 .... PaulO'Neill(5) 99
(Miss Venetia Williams) *mid div: tk clsr order 6th: rdn and effrt appr 2 out: kpt on run-in* **16/1**
63 **2** *dht* **Saraba (FR)**[25] 2804 5-10-11 .... ColinBolger(3) 99
(Mrs L J Mongan) *chsd ldrs: chsd wnr fr 6th: hit 3 out: sn rdn: chal 2 out: ev ch last: no ex* **8/1**[3]
33-2 **4** *¾* **Tessanoora**[62] 2070 5-11-0 .... AndrewTinkler 101+
(N J Henderson) *mid div: hdwy to trck ldrs 5th: rdn appr 2 out: ev ch whn hit last: wknd fnl 100yds* **1/1**[1]
0P0 **5** *8* **Dream On Maggie**[39] 2559 6-11-0 .... JimCrowley 90
(P Bowen) *towards rr: gd hdwy after 5th: hit 3 out: sn rdn and effrt: one pced fr next* **50/1**
/6P- **6** *16* **Grey Mistral**[338] 3667 8-11-0 .... RJGreene 74
(P R Chamings) *a towards rr* **50/1**
5 **7** *¾* **Sturbury**[32] 2681 4-9-8 .... WayneKavanagh(7) 60
(J W Mullins) *towards rr: hdwy 6th: wknd after 3 out* **16/1**
006 **8** *10* **Winter Coral (FR)**[37] 2580 4-10-1 ....(p) PaulMoloney 50
(Mrs N S Evans) *led tl after 3rd: chsd ldr tl appr 6th: sn wknd* **33/1**
00 **9** *23* **Overjoyed**[40] 2558 5-10-11 .... TJPhelan(3) 40
(Miss Suzy Smith) *mstke 1st: mid div tl 3rd: sn bhd: t.o* **100/1**
63 **10** *3 ½* **Bonnie Blue**[30] 2727 7-11-0 .... SeanCurran 37
(Mrs Norma Pook) *a bhd* **16/1**
P **P** **Chasing The Stars (IRE)**[18] 2928 6-11-0 .... MatthewBatchelor —
(D R Gandolfo) *in tch: blnd 2nd: lost tch 4th: t.o and p.u bef 6th* **50/1**
PFP- **P** **River Of Wishes**[270] 4814 8-10-7 .... KeiranBurke(7) —
(C W Mitchell) *chsd ldr until hit 2nd: bhd fr next: t.o and p.u bef 6th* **100/1**

4m 45.0s (9.00) **Going Correction** +0.60s/f (Soft)
WFA 4 from 5yo+ 11lb **12** Ran SP% **120.3**
Speed ratings: **105,103,103,103,99 93,92,88,78,77 —,—** TOTE £3.41: £1.30 TRIFECTA Pl: NLT 4.20, SA 2.20; Ex: SS/NLT 14.20, SS/SA 9.40; CSF: SS/NLT 17.63, SS/SA 10.25.
Owner John B Sunley **Bred** Sunley Stud Ltd **Trained** Morestead, Hants

FOCUS
The quicker of the two divisions by 2.3sec and the form of this race looked the stronger.

NOTEBOOK
Sunley Shines had run with promise against the geldings on her first two starts over hurdles and competing against her own sex proved far less of a test. Leading for much of the contest at a track where it often pays to race prominently, she drew clear from the last. She is expected to appreciate better ground. *(op 7-4)*
Noun De La Thinte(FR) had not shown much on her first two starts over hurdles in this country, but this was far more promising. She shapes as though she will get further. *(tchd 20-1)*
Saraba(FR) plugged on well and was only outpointed on the run-in. She looks to be steadily improving with racing and can now race in handicaps. *(tchd 20-1)*
Tessanoora looked likely to take a bit of beating in this company but she was disappointing. A mistake at the last ensured that Sunley Shines got away from her, and she will have to find improvement to get off the mark in novice company. *(op 11-8 tchd 6-4 in places)*
Dream On Maggie ran her best race to date on her first start against other mares, but she was still well held by the principals in the end.

3281 CORTAFLEX FOR HORSES MARES' ONLY NOVICES' HURDLE (DIV II) (9 hdls) 2m 2f 110y
12:50 (12:50) (Class 4) 4-Y-0+ **£3,253** (£955; £477; £238)

Form RPR
4P2 **1** **Desert Secrets (IRE)**[24] 2824 4-10-1 98........................ AndrewTinkler 81+
(J G Portman) *racd wd: trck ldrs: led after 3rd: hdd briefly after 3 out: kpt on wl run-in: drvn out* **10/11**[1]
5P **2** *8* **Alexander Sapphire (IRE)**[1] 2683 5-10-9 ....(t) ChrisHonour(5) 86
(N B King) *in tch: jnd ldrs 4th: led briefly after 3 out: rdn and ev ch next: no ex* **33/1**
0P **3** *18* **Carroll's O'Tully (IRE)**[18] 2928 6-10-7 .... JustinMorgan(7) 68
(L A Dace) *bhd: styd on past btn horses fr after 3 out: wnt poor 3rd run-in* **40/1**
0 **4** *5* **Clare Galway**[8] 3127 5-10-7 .... CharlieStudd(7) 63
(B G Powell) *hld up towards rr: hdwy 4th: jnd ldrs 6th: wknd after 3 out: lft 3rd at the last* **14/1**
05 **5** *7* **Falcon Beneficial (IRE)**[6] 3188 4-10-1 .... PaulMoloney 43
(G L Moore) *towards rr: hdwy 5th: wknd 3 out* **6/1**[3]
04P **6** *3* **Cresswell Willow (IRE)**[7] 3149 6-10-7 .... ShaneWalsh(7) 53
(W K Goldsworthy) *chsd ldrs tl 5th: sn bhd* **33/1**
00-0 **7** *6* **She's No Muppet**[52] 2269 6-11-0 .... SeanCurran 47
(N R Mitchell) *racd freely on outer: j.rt: led tl after 5th: w ldrs: hit next: wknd 3 out* **33/1**
8 *25* **Charmatic (IRE)**[90] 5-10-11 .... GinoCarenza(3) 22
(Andrew Turnell) *mid div: blnd 3rd: wknd after 6th* **7/2**[2]
P **9** *3 ½* **Fair View (GER)**[3] 3238 5-10-11 .... TJPhelan(3) 19
(Dr P Pritchard) *prom tl 5th: sn wl bhd* **25/1**
P **On The Fairway (IRE)**[388] 7-10-9 ....(t) RobertLucey-Butler(5) —
(Miss M P Bryant) *a bhd: t.o and p.u after 6th* **66/1**
506- **F** **Floragalore**[263] 3946 5-10-11 .... OwynNelmes(3) 76
(O Sherwood) *mid div: hdwy appr 6th: ev ch 2 out: wkng in 3rd whn fell last* **12/1**

4m 47.3s (11.30) **Going Correction** +0.60s/f (Soft)
WFA 4 from 5yo+ 11lb **11** Ran SP% **119.9**
Speed ratings: **100,96,89,86,84 82,80,69,68,— —** CSF £46.62 TOTE £2.00: £1.10, £6.00, £8.90; EX 61.70.
Owner M J Vandenberghe **Bred** Patrick F Kelly **Trained** Compton, Berks

FOCUS
This looked the weaker of the two divisions, and that was reflected in a time 2.3 sec slower.

NOTEBOOK
Desert Secrets(IRE), runner-up at Newbury on her last start, has a mark of 98, so the fact that she was sent off at odds-on for this and ran out a clear winner suggests there was not much strength to the race. Handicaps look the best option now as she is likely to find trying to defy a penalty too difficult. *(op Evens tchd 11-10 and 6-5 in a place)*
Alexander Sapphire(IRE), reappearing quickly following an outing on the All-Weather the previous day, ran well in defeat, but those behind her are not up to much so she will have to improve to win a similar contest.
Carroll's O'Tully(IRE), whose rider appeared to have more or less given up heading to the third last, was able to pick up places steadily as those in front of her got tired, and she was eventually *gifted third place with the fall of Floragalore at the last. She did not achieve much in terms of form. (op 33-1 tchd 50-1)*
Clare Galway, who won over a mile on the Flat, did not get home.
Falcon Beneficial(IRE), who showed modest ability in bumpers, failed to distinguish herself on her hurdling debut. *(op 9-2)*
Charmatic(IRE) *Official explanation: trainer said mare gurgled (op 11-2)*
On The Fairway(IRE) *Official explanation: jockey said mare hung right throughout (op 11-1 tchd 10-1)*

Floragalore, last seen in a maiden on the Flat in April, was held in third but clear of the rest when crashing out at the final flight. She could step up on this next time providing the fall has not left its mark. *(op 11-1 tchd 10-1)*

3282 CANINE & FELINE CORTAFLEX NOVICES' CHASE (13 fncs) 2m 2f
1:25 (1:25) (Class 4) 5-Y-0+ **£5,530** (£1,623; £811; £405)

Form RPR
3351 **1** **Magico (NZ)**[31] 2705 8-10-11 102 (b) PaulO'Neill(5) 112+
(Miss Venetia Williams) *t.k.h: trckd ldrs: led appr 4 out tl next: lft in ld after 2 out: sn clr: kpt on: pushed out* **5/4**[1]
5-4P **2** *6* **Kyper Disco (FR)**[24] 2825 8-11-2 103 (t) AndrewTinkler 110+
(N J Henderson) *trckd ldrs: drew clr w wnr appr 4 out: led 3 out: narrow advantage whn stmbld bdly and hdd after 2 out: no ch after* **7/2**[2]
0-F3 **3** *15* **Lough Rynn (IRE)**[225] 532 8-11-2 103 PaulMoloney 91
(Miss H C Knight) *chsd ldrs tl outpcd after 9th: tk mod 3rd appr last* **9/2**[3]
-004 **4** *6* **I D Technology (IRE)**[38] 2574 10-10-11 98 EamonDehdashti(5) 85
(G L Moore) *led: j.rt fr 6th: hit 9th and sn hdd: wknd 3 out* **12/1**
04F2 **5** *dist* **Buffalo Bill (IRE)**[22] 2867 10-11-2 103 RJGreene 80
(A M Hales) *hld up bhd ldrs: hit 6th: outpcd appr 4 out: wknd 3 out : virtually p.u run-in* **9/2**[3]

4m 50.1s (15.00) **Going Correction** +1.025s/f (Soft) **5** Ran SP% **110.7**
Speed ratings: **107,104,97,95,—** CSF £6.19 TOTE £2.30: £1.50, £1.80; EX 7.50.
Owner Paul Beck **Bred** Bardowie Stud Ltd **Trained** Kings Caple, H'fords

FOCUS
A modest novice chase which concerned only two from before the third last.

NOTEBOOK
Magico(NZ) was debuting for his new stable having left Richard Guest after winning at Leicester in first-time blinkers. The headgear was retained by his new trainer and he looked to be going marginally better than Kyper Disco when that one stumbled on landing at the second last, handing the race to him. *(op 15-8 tchd 2-1)*
Kyper Disco(FR) was under pressure but upsides the eventual winner when stumbling after jumping the second last, putting his nose in the turf in the process. The drop back in trip suited him and he might be able to find a similarly modest heat. *(op 3-1)*
Lough Rynn(IRE) had a fair chance in this company judged on official marks, but the trip may have been on the short side and he continues to frustrate. *(op 6-1 tchd 4-1)*
I D Technology(IRE), who is happier on a sounder surface, tended to jump out to his right. *(op 15-2)*

3283 MERVYN WESTON 60TH BIRTHDAY CELEBRATION (S) HURDLE (10 hdls) 2m 4f
1:55 (1:55) (Class 5) 4-Y-0+ **£2,192** (£639; £319)

Form RPR
-114 **1** **Kings Castle (IRE)**[217] 633 11-11-9 110 JamesWhite(7) 92+
(R J Hodges) *hld up bhd: smooth hdwy 7th: led sn after 2 out: styd on: rdn out* **11/10**[1]
0 **2** *5* **Ocean Of Storms (IRE)**[11] 3023 11-10-10 MarkHunter(10) 77
(N I M Rossiter) *mid div: hdwy to trck ldr 6th: led appr 2 out: rdn and hdd appr last: kpt on same pce* **25/1**
3 *10* **Lets Try Again (IRE)**[30] 2737 9-11-6 RJGreene 67
(R A Farrant) *trckd ldrs: rdn and ev ch 2 out: wknd appr last* **12/1**
PU00 **4** *4* **Peppershot**[18] 2934 6-10-13 89 JayPemberton(7) 63
(R Gurney) *hld up towards rr: styd on past btn horses fr 3 out: nvr trbld ldrs* **25/1**
5443 **5** *1* **Ashgan (IRE)**[8] 3125 13-11-6 77 DrPPritchard(5) 67
(Dr P Pritchard) *led tl 5th: outpcd 7th: nt a danger after* **10/1**
0/-4 **6** *11* **Mizinky**[5] 3211 6-10-3 78 RichardGordon(10) 44
(W G M Turner) *chsd ldrs: rdn and effrt after 3 out: wknd next* **7/1**[3]
0-00 **7** *3* **Will She Spin**[12] 2997 5-10-6 WayneKavanagh(7) 41
(J W Mullins) *a towards rr* **20/1**
/P-U **8** *11* **Premier Cheval (USA)**[18] 2930 7-11-6 HenryOliver 37
(P R Hedger) *a bhd* **50/1**
2-02 **9** *dist* **Bekstar**[38] 2576 11-10-13 88 BenjaminHitchcott —
(J C Tuck) *chsd ldrs: rdn after 7th: sn wknd* **4/1**[2]
P0 **P** **Tom Tobacco**[18] 2928 9-11-1 ChrisHonour(5) —
(A S T Holdsworth) *chsd ldrs: mstke 4th: lost tch next: p.u bef 7th* **40/1**
/00- **P** **Native Commander (IRE)**[217] 641 11-11-1 97 ChristopherMurray(5) —
(Jim Best) *plld hrd: restrained in rr: hdwy to ld 5th: hdd & wknd qckly appr 2 out: p.u bef last* **12/1**

5m 15.4s (11.60) **Going Correction** +0.60s/f (Soft) **11** Ran SP% **121.4**
Speed ratings: **100,98,94,92,92 87,86,82,—,— —** CSF £40.63 TOTE £2.40: £1.10, £5.10, £3.70; EX 53.50.The winner was bought in for 6,500gns.
Owner R J Hodges **Bred** Miss Katie Thorner And Joseph Kent **Trained** Charlton Adam, Somerset

FOCUS
A couple of 11-year-olds showed them the way home in a race lacking in any strength.

NOTEBOOK
Kings Castle(IRE), fourth in a handicap off 110 last time, had an obvious chance back in this modest grade, and he eventually ran out a comfortable winner. His record in selling company now reads 22111. *(op 6-4)*
Ocean Of Storms(IRE), who did not show a lot on the Flat in the summer and was well held on his hurdling debut at Chepstow, albeit in a decent novice contest, ran a better race in this lower grade. He found the hot favourite too strong in the end but he was clear of the rest and a reproduction of this effort could be good enough to win a similarly weak heat. *(op 20-1)*
Lets Try Again(IRE), a winner of a handicap hurdle in Ireland on good to firm ground, might have found this surface more testing than ideal, but he still showed some ability on his debut for his new stable. *(op 10-1)*
Peppershot, missing the headgear this time and dropping into a seller for the first time, kept on without seriously threatening to get involved. *(op 20-1 tchd 28-1)*
Ashgan(IRE) is happier on faster ground. *(op 11-1 tchd 9-1)*
Bekstar *Official explanation: jockey said mare was never travelling (op 9-2 tchd 5-1)*
Native Commander(IRE), better known as a chaser in recent years in Ireland, was having his first start for his new stable. He was in front swinging into the straight but stopped very quickly soon afterwards. *(op 11-1)*
Tom Tobacco *Official explanation: jockey said gelding swallowed its tongue (op 11-1)*

3284 CLINICALLY PROVEN CORTAFLEX H'CAP CHASE (15 fncs) 2m 4f
2:25 (2:25) (Class 4) (0-115,113) 5-Y-0+ **£5,530** (£1,623; £811; £405)

Form RPR
3025 **1** **Alphabetical (IRE)**[24] 2818 7-10-11 98 DaveCrosse 118+
(C J Mann) *hld up: hdwy 8th: led after 10th: drew clr fr 3 out: shkn up after 2 out: stmbld last: kpt on wl* **13/2**[3]
3241 **2** *17* **Walcot Lad (IRE)**[18] 2933 10-10-2 92 (p) ColinBolger(3) 100+
(A Ennis) *prom: led 7th tl mstke and hdd 10th: chsd ldrs: rdn after 4 out: kpt on same pce: regained 2nd run-in: no ch w wnr* **13/2**[3]
0-11 **3** *2* **Harris Bay**[36] 2613 7-11-8 109 (t) PaulMoloney 109
(Miss H C Knight) *trckd ldrs: chsd wnr after 4 out: rdn after 3 out: sn no ch w wnr: lost 2nd run-in* **6/5**[1]
0P1F **4** *2 1/2* **Stormy Skye (IRE)**[40] 2557 10-10-7 99 (b) EamonDehdashti(5) 97
(G L Moore) *chsd ldrs: drvn along in tch fr 7th: one pced fr 4 out* **7/1**
0-13 **5** *1 1/4* **King Coal (IRE)**[36] 2613 7-11-7 108 BrianCrowley 104
(R Rowe) *led tl 7th: chsd ldrs: rdn after 4 out: sn one pced: 4th whn mstke last* **5/1**[2]
PPP- **6** *22* **Native Performance (IRE)**[307] 4205 11-11-12 113 JimCrowley 87
(N J Gifford) *bhd fr 7th* **20/1**
0046 **7** *dist* **The Newsman (IRE)**[38] 2577 14-10-8 100 DerekLaverty(5) —
(G Wareham) *chsd ldrs tl 8th: sn bhd: t.o* **22/1**

5m 24.3s (16.40) **Going Correction** +1.025s/f (Soft) **7** Ran SP% **110.4**
Speed ratings: **108,101,100,99,98 90,—** CSF £43.21 CT £79.02 TOTE £9.20: £3.60, £2.10; EX 50.50.
Owner Hugh Villiers **Bred** Peter O'Dwyer **Trained** Upper Lambourn, Berks
■ Stewards' Enquiry : Eamon Dehdashti two-day ban: careless riding (Jan 18-19)

FOCUS
A good jumping display from Alphabetical, who was a disappointing favourite on his chasing debut, but showed his true form here.

NOTEBOOK
Alphabetical(IRE) had clearly learnt from his chasing debut as this performance was far more like that which had been expected when he made the switch to the larger obstacles. Drawing clear from the third last, he won in good style, and he might well be up to defying a penalty. *(op 5-1 tchd 15-2)*
Walcot Lad(IRE), something of a course specialist and running off a career-high mark, took second place off Harris Bay on the run-in, and that was about as much as he could expect to achieve as the lightly-raced winner was clearly well handicapped here. *(op 7-1)*
Harris Bay, seeking a hat-trick and to remain unbeaten over fences, did not look at all handicapped out of things on a 7lb higher mark than when successful last time at Sandown, but he could not keep tabs on the winner from the third last and the way he weakened hinted that perhaps his old breathing problem had returned. *(op 11-8 tchd 6-4 and 11-10)*
Stormy Skye(IRE) needs a longer trip on better ground to be seen at his best. *(tchd 13-2 and 15-2)*
King Coal(IRE) was 22 lengths behind Harris Bay at Sandown and 7lb better off at the weights this time. He clawed back just over 18 lengths of that deficit. *(op 9-2)*

3285 CORTAFLEX FOR PEOPLE H'CAP CHASE (16 fncs) 2m 6f
3:00 (3:00) (Class 5) (0-95,95) 5-Y-0+ **£3,578** (£1,050; £525; £262)

Form RPR
PP04 **1** **Rosses Point (IRE)**[22] 2863 7-10-8 77 (p) PaulMoloney 97+
(Evan Williams) *hld up: smooth hdwy to trck ldrs 11th: led and hit 3 out: in command fr next: eased run-in* **3/1**[1]
130- **2** *3* **Smart Guy**[337] 3685 14-10-9 78 (p) BenjaminHitchcott 88+
(Mrs L C Jewell) *led: stmbld 10th: hdd 3 out: sn rdn: kpt on but no ch w wnr fr next* **9/1**
-05F **3** *3 1/2* **Joe Deane (IRE)**[30] 2733 10-11-12 95 (p) RJGreene 101
(M J Coombe) *rn in snatches: in tch: trckd ldrs after 7th: dropped rr 10th: rdn and hdwy appr 13th: kpt on same pce* **9/2**[3]
6060 **4** *3* **Blazing Batman**[34] 2664 13-10-4 78 DrPPritchard(5) 81
(Dr P Pritchard) *hld up bhd: styd on fr 3 out: nvr a danger* **25/1**
-542 **5** *14* **Full On**[22] 2863 9-11-6 94 PaulO'Neill(5) 87+
(A M Hales) *in tch: stmbld on bnd after 7th: chsd ldr 10th: rdn and effrt after 4 out: wknd next* **4/1**[2]
-405 **6** *29* **Opportunity Knocks**[26] 2801 6-9-13 75 (p) KeiranBurke(7) 35
(N J Hawke) *w ldr: hit 2nd: wkng whn pckd 12th* **12/1**
-U04 **P** **Royale Acadou (FR)**[40] 2557 8-11-8 94 ColinBolger(3) —
(Mrs L J Mongan) *chsd ldrs tl 10th: sn bhd: t.o and p.u bef 3 out* **20/1**
025 **P** **Hazel Bank Lass (IRE)**[12] 2986 10-11-4 90 GinoCarenza(3) —
(Andrew Turnell) *chsd ldrs: rdn appr 4 out: wknd qckly: p.u bef 3 out* **8/1**
421/ **P** **Designer Label (IRE)**[850] 1330 10-11-5 93 RobertLucey-Butler(5) —
(M Pitman) *pckd bdly 1st: nvr travelling and a in rr after: p.u bef 8th* **13/2**

6m 9.90s (26.10) **Going Correction** +1.025s/f (Soft) **9** Ran SP% **113.9**
Speed ratings: **93,91,90,89,84 73,—,—,—** CSF £29.48 CT £118.92 TOTE £4.20: £1.90, £2.80, £2.30; EX 45.40.
Owner W Ralph Thomas **Bred** Simon Kearney Jnr **Trained** Cowbridge, Vale Of Glamorgan

FOCUS
A moderate handicap but the winner, who landed a gamble, looks capable of better.

NOTEBOOK
Rosses Point(IRE), who ran with promise at Uttoxeter last time, was a well-backed favourite and won easily, the margin of victory failing to reflect his superiority. Lightly raced, he showed himself to be a well-handicapped horse and he will remain so if turned out under a penalty. *(op 6-1)*
Smart Guy is a course specialist and had won first time out following a summer break the past two years. Had he not run into a gambled-on unexposed and well-handicapped rival in Rosses Point he may well have won his fifth race at the track. *(op 8-1 tchd 10-1)*
Joe Deane(IRE), racing off a double-digit mark for the first time since successful at Plumpton two years ago, is handicapped to win if he can find his form. *(op 11-2)*
Blazing Batman is dropping in the weights but is struggling to regain his form. *(op 20-1)*
Full On was only 1lb worse off with Rosses Point compared with when he finished five lengths in front of him at Uttoxeter last time.While that rival undoubtedly had more scope for improvement, he really should have finished closer.
Designer Label(IRE) *Official explanation: jockey said gelding was never travelling (op 9-1 tchd 7-1)*
Hazel Bank Lass(IRE) *Official explanation: trainer said mare bled from nose (op 9-1 tchd 7-1)*

3286 EQUINE AMERICA H'CAP HURDLE (10 hdls) 2m 4f
3:35 (3:35) (Class 4) (0-115,111) 4-Y-0+ **£3,903** (£1,146; £573; £286)

Form RPR
0150 **1** **Come Bye (IRE)**[22] 2871 10-11-11 110 (bt) MatthewBatchelor 112+
(Miss A M Newton-Smith) *mde all: styd on gamely: rdn out* **12/1**
4061 **2** *1 3/4* **Piran (IRE)**[25] 2810 4-10-6 104 PaulMoloney 91+
(Evan Williams) *hld up: hdwy after 7th: rdn after 3 out: styd on u.p to go 2nd cl home* **7/2**[1]
U611 **3** *1 1/2* **Businessmoney Jake**[32] 2687 5-11-8 107 JamieGoldstein 105
(V R A Dartnall) *chsd ldrs tl lost pl 3rd: in tch: drvn along fr 7th: hdwy after 3 out: wnt 2nd appr last: kpt on same pce* **7/2**[1]
504 **4** *1 1/2* **It's The Limit (USA)**[30] 2730 7-10-12 104 (t) ShaneWalsh(7) 101+
(W K Goldsworthy) *in tch: chsd wnr and n.m.r on bnd after 3 out: sn rdn: kpt on same pce fr last* **7/1**[2]
2013 **5** *8* **Assoon**[22] 2868 7-11-3 105 (b) ColinBolger(3) 94+
(G L Moore) *chsd ldrs: rdn after 3 out: one pced fr next* **12/1**
6100 **6** *9* **Capparush (IRE)**[16] 2950 6-10-4 94 RobertLucey-Butler(5) 73
(A Ennis) *a towards rr* **33/1**
01-0 **7** *3/4* **Krakow Baba (FR)**[28] 2766 6-11-4 108 PaulO'Neill(5) 87
(Miss Venetia Williams) *chsd ldrs tl wknd after 3 out* **10/1**[3]
F60F **8** *nk* **Charlton Kings (IRE)**[7] 3135 8-11-12 111 JimCrowley 89
(R J Hodges) *racd freely w wnr: ev ch 3 out: wknd next* **10/1**[3]

The Form Book, Raceform Ltd, Compton, RG20 6NL

25 **9** *dist* **Danse Macabre (IRE)**[35] 2633 7-11-1 **100** ..... RJGreene —
(A W Carroll) *chsd ldrs tl wknd appr 3 out* **7/2**[1]

5m 11.5s (7.70) **Going Correction** +0.60s/f (Soft)
WFA 4 from 5yo+ 12lb **9** Ran SP% **115.7**
Speed ratings: **108,107,106,106,102 99,99,98,—** CSF £54.96 CT £182.09 TOTE £14.30: £2.20, £1.70, £1.60; EX 44.90 Place 6 £58.47, Place 5 £19.18.
Owner Pps Racing **Bred** Timothy Coffey **Trained** Jevington, E Sussex
■ Stewards' Enquiry : Matthew Batchelor three-day ban: careless riding (Jan 18-20)

FOCUS
A competitive-looking handicap but course specialist Come Bye dominated throughout.

NOTEBOOK
Come Bye(IRE) showed his younger rivals the way it is done around here, making every yard for his fourth course success. At his best with some cut in the ground, he is always dangerous when allowed an uncontested lead. *(op 11-1)*
Piran(IRE), whose trainer won the previous race and whose stable is in fine form at present, justified the Handicapper's decision to put him up 9lb for winning a moderate amateurs' handicap last time. *(op 11-4)*
Businessmoney Jake, going for the hat-trick off a 7lb higher mark than for the latest of his wins here last month, ran well but was not quite up to it. *(op 4-1)*
It's The Limit(USA), wearing a tongue strap for the first time, was hampered by the winner and stumbled on the turn out of the back straight, without which he may have finished slightly closer. A fast-ground horse on the Flat, it would be surprising if he was at his best in these conditions, and he might be one to bear in mind for a handicap on a sounder surface. *(op 8-1)*
Assoon is not an easy ride and needs plenty of assistance from the saddle. *(op 11-1 tchd 14-1)*
Cappanrush(IRE) *Official explanation: jockey said gelding hung right*
Danse Macabre(IRE), whose Sandown efforts earlier this season had suggested that he should be *competitive off this sort of mark, failed to run his race for one reason or another.Official explanation: jockey said gelding made a noise (op 5-1 tchd 11-2)*
T/Plt: £137.30 to a £1 stake. Pool: £37,436.00. 198.95 winning tickets. T/Qpdt: £36.00 to a £1 stake. Pool: £3,733.20. 76.60 winning tickets. TM

[2872] HAYDOCK (L-H)
Saturday, January 7

OFFICIAL GOING: Soft (heavy in places)
Wind: Light behind Weather: Wintry showers

3287 JOHN SMITH'S/E B F MARES' ONLY "NATIONAL HUNT" NOVICES' HURDLE (QUALIFIER) (12 hdls) 2m 6f
12:45 (12:48) (Class 4) 4-Y-0+ **£4,554** (£1,337; £668; £333)

Form RPR
-F1F **1** **Heltornic (IRE)**[43] 2486 6-11-6 ..... TonyDobbin 115+
(M Scudamore) *mde all: j.rt fr 7th: rdn clr after last: eased cl home* **9/4**[1]
-612 **2** *7* **Cloudless Dawn**[19] 2923 6-11-6 ..... AnthonyRoss 107+
(P Beaumont) *trckd ldrs: lft 2nd 7th: rdn and 4 l down whn mstke last: btn whn hung lft run-in* **7/2**[2]
1045 **3** *12* **Emmasflora**[12] 2976 8-11-1 105 ..... AdamPogson(5) 95+
(C T Pogson) *hld up: hdwy after 6th: rdn appr 2 out: wknd bef last* **12/1**
0505 **4** *5* **My Rosie Ribbons (IRE)**[22] 2866 7-10-7 ..... MrMWall(7) 84+
(B W Duke) *racd keenly: cl up: nt fluent 5th: rdn and ev ch appr 3 out: wknd bef last* **16/1**
-4 **5** *8* **Little Venus (IRE)**[45] 2446 6-11-0 ..... RichardJohnson 74
(H D Daly) *hld up: hit 7th: effrt 3 out: rdn whn hung lft and wknd appr 2 out* **9/2**[3]
/0-5 **6** *dist* **Black Collar**[42] 2501 7-11-0 ..... AlanO'Keeffe —
(K C Bailey) *j.rt: hld up in rr: hmpd 7th: struggling 4 out: t.o* **20/1**
23 **7** *14* **Dillay Brook (IRE)**[45] 2446 6-11-0 ..... JasonMaguire —
(T R George) *in tch: lost pl after 6th: bdly hmpd next: sn t.o* **6/1**
43P3 **F** **Common Girl (IRE)**[30] 2714 8-11-12 106 ..... NoelFehily —
(O Brennan) *racd keenly: prom tl fell 7th* **14/1**

5m 55.6s (12.10) **Going Correction** +0.70s/f (Soft) **8** Ran SP% **110.5**
Speed ratings: **106,103,99,97,94 —,—,—** CSF £9.59 TOTE £3.20: £1.20, £2.00, £2.50; EX 10.80.
Owner Stephen W Molloy **Bred** A W Buller **Trained** Bromsash, Herefordshire

FOCUS
A fair event of it's type and the winner is capable of rating higher.

NOTEBOOK
Heltornic(IRE), who took a nasty fall at Newbury last time, made amends for that effort and showed her true colours with a comfortable success from the front. She will be high on confidence again now, should be rated value for further, and remains open to further improvement this term. *(op 5-2 tchd 2-1, 11-4 in places)*
Cloudless Dawn was the only one to make the winner work in the straight, but while she blundered the final flight, it ultimately made no difference to the result. She would have found this ground plenty soft enough and lost little in defeat this time. *(op 11-4 tchd 4-1 in a place)*
Emmasflora found this too stiff a test and was not disgraced at the weights. She is better over shorter and would look better off in handicaps from her current official mark. *(op 16-1)*
My Rosie Ribbons(IRE)
Little Venus(IRE) failed to improve on her recent debut in a Wetherby bumper and did little to convince she is ready for this trip. *(op 4-1)*
Dillay Brook(IRE) proved disappointing and failed to confirm her bumper form with Little Venus. Something may well have been amiss. *(op 8-1)*

3288 32RED ONLINE CASINO NOVICES' CHASE (15 fncs) 2m 4f
1:15 (1:15) (Class 3) 5-Y-0+ **£6,506** (£1,910; £955; £477)

Form RPR
6-12 **1** **Bannow Strand (IRE)**[49] 2339 6-11-5 127 ..... AndrewGlassonbury(7) 140+
(M C Pipe) *mde all: mstke 9th: hung lft run-in: drvn out* **6/4**[1]
-221 **2** *1 ¾* **Supreme Serenade (IRE)**[23] 2846 7-11-1 125 ..... RichardJohnson 128+
(P J Hobbs) *hld up in rr: hdwy whn mstke 2 out: nt fluent last: rallied to snatch 2nd cl home* **15/8**[2]
4 **3** *½* **Turthen (FR)**[22] 2869 5-11-2 ..... JoeTizzard 126
(P F Nicholls) *a.p: mstke 9th: nt fluent 10th: rdn and ev ch last: no ex cl home* **7/2**[3]
5-13 **4** *18* **Without A Doubt**[41] 2531 7-11-8 ..... CarlLlewellyn 118+
(M Pitman) *cl up tl rdn and wknd 2 out* **7/1**

5m 29.7s (5.50) **Going Correction** +0.45s/f (Soft)
WFA 5 from 6yo+ 9lb **4** Ran SP% **109.5**
Speed ratings: **107,106,106,98** CSF £4.86 TOTE £2.00; EX 4.50.
Owner D A Johnson **Bred** W E McCluskey **Trained** Nicholashayne, Devon
■ Stewards' Enquiry : Joe Tizzard one-day ban: used whip with excessive frequency, sometimes with excessive force (Jan 18)

FOCUS
A decent little novice event, and while the pace was uneven, the form still looks solid.

NOTEBOOK
Bannow Strand(IRE), who found two miles too sharp at this track when beaten at odds on last time, made all under a stop-start ride from his improving rider and scored with a fair amount up his sleeve. He remains open to plenty of further progression as a chaser, does jump well, and is clearly better suited by this sort of trip. *(tchd 7-4)*
Supreme Serenade(IRE), off the mark over fences at Exeter last time, did not particularly impress with her jumping, yet still turned in another improved effort and looked to run right up to her official rating in defeat. While she may not be the easiest of rides, she clearly does have a decent engine, and she has only finished out of the frame once from 14 career starts. *(op 9-4 tchd 7-4 in a place)*
Turthen(FR) ◆, fourth in a Grade Two novice event at Windsor on his British debut last time, got this longer trip well and was not at all disgraced in defeat. He should soon be found an opening in this division and clearly enjoys soft ground. *(tchd 4-1, 9-2 in a place)*
Without A Doubt was put in his place when the race became serious two out and is going to continue to be hard to place over fences.

3289 32REDPOKER.COM H'CAP HURDLE (12 hdls) 2m 7f 110y
1:45 (1:46) (Class 3) (0-135,135) 4-Y-0+ **£7,807** (£2,292; £1,146; £572)

Form RPR
1-UR **1** **Huka Lodge (IRE)**[52] 2265 9-10-0 **109** oh5 ..... RichardMcGrath 123+
(Mrs K Walton) *led 1st to 3rd: remained prom: led after 4 out: rdn clr whn mstke 2 out: eased cl home* **25/1**
-004 **2** *7* **Vicars Destiny**[37] 2590 8-10-7 **116** ..... (p) TomSiddall 118+
(Mrs S Lamyman) *hld up: hmpd bef 3rd: rdn after 4 out: hdwy aprroaching 2 out: styd on to take 2nd run-in: no ch w wnr* **12/1**
-0P0 **3** *2* **Freetown (IRE)**[24] 2820 10-11-5 **128** ..... (b) TonyDobbin 128+
(L Lungo) *in tch: rdn to chse wnr whn blnd 3 out: wknd and lost 2nd run-in* **12/1**
3-11 **4** *6* **Jaunty Times**[25] 2813 6-10-7 **116** ..... RichardJohnson 108
(H D Daly) *cl up: rdn whn hit 3 out: one pce after* **9/2**[1]
3-U6 **5** *6* **Sharp Jack (IRE)**[35] 2629 8-9-10 **112** ..... SeanQuinlan(7) 98
(R T Phillips) *hld up: mstke 3rd: rdn whn mstke 4 out: sme hdwy appr next: no real imp: wknd last* **33/1**
11-1 **6** *¾* **Overserved**[56] 2184 7-10-6 **115** ..... AlanDempsey 100
(A Parker) *in tch: rdn appr 3 out: sn wknd* **6/1**[3]
5-64 **7** *1 ½* **Fullards**[30] 2717 8-10-1 **115** ..... StephenCraine(5) 99
(Mrs P Sly) *led to 1st: led 3rd: hdd after 4 out: sn rdn: wknd appr 2 out* **22/1**
PU3U **8** *8* **Abzuson**[11] 3041 9-9-11 **109** oh4 ..... PeterBuchanan(3) 85
(J R Norton) *midfield: hdwy after 6th: rdn and wknd 4 out* **66/1**
F1/F **9** *nk* **Rosarian (IRE)**[29] 2747 9-10-11 **120** ..... (p) JoeTizzard 98+
(V R A Dartnall) *trckd ldrs: lost pl after 6th: n.d after* **11/2**[2]
54-6 **10** *11* **Hawadeth**[63] 2055 11-11-12 **135** ..... VinceSlattery 99
(V R A Dartnall) *a bhd* **25/1**
11-0 **11** *5* **Alagon (IRE)**[55] 2207 6-10-6 **115** ..... (v) NoelFehily 74
(Ian Williams) *midfield: hdwy 8th: rdn appr 3 out: wknd bef last* **33/1**
-26P **12** *4* **Jaloux D'Estruval (FR)**[23] 2847 9-10-6 **115** ..... MarcusFoley 70
(Mrs L C Taylor) *hld up: rdn after 4 out: nvr on terms* **16/1**
13-4 **13** *dist* **Manx Royal (FR)**[55] 2207 7-11-2 **132** ..... AndrewGlassonbury(7) —
(M C Pipe) *hld up: hdwy after 6th: wkng whn blnd 3 out: t.o* **10/1**
-300 **P** **Spring Pursuit**[21] 2876 10-11-1 **129** ..... LeeStephens(5) —
(E G Bevan) *hld up: p.u bef 3rd: sddle slipped* **22/1**
0P00 **P** **Nick's Choice**[11] 3018 10-10-0 **109** oh2 ..... BrianHarding —
(D Burchell) *a bhd: rdn after 5th: t.o whn p.u bef 4 out* **50/1**
U4-F **P** **True North (IRE)**[16] 2945 11-9-9 **109** oh4 ..... DeclanMcGann(5) —
(D R MacLeod) *prom: rdn and lost pl appr 7th: t.o whn p.u bef 2 out* **66/1**
/0-4 **P** **Derivative (IRE)**[35] 2633 8-10-11 **120** ..... AlanO'Keeffe —
(Miss Venetia Williams) *prom tl after 2nd: struggling after: t.o whn p.u bef 7th* **17/2**

6m 22.3s (18.10) **Going Correction** +0.70s/f (Soft) **17** Ran SP% **116.0**
Speed ratings: **97,94,94,92,90 89,89,86,86,82 81,79,—,—,— —,—** CSF £261.10 CT £3750.11 TOTE £30.90: £6.30, £2.80, £2.80, £1.80; EX 208.20.
Owner Mrs J M Jones **Bred** Michael Lysaght **Trained** Middleham, N Yorks

FOCUS
A fair handicap, run in testing conditions, and the field came home strung out. The overall form may be suspect, but the winner can be rated value for further all the same.

NOTEBOOK
Huka Lodge(IRE), making his debut for a new yard, relished the deep surface and ran his rivals ragged to come home an easy winner from 5lb out of the weights. Considering he is rated 13lb higher over fences, this cannot be considered a total surprise, and the change of scenery has clearly had a positive effect. A hike in the weights over hurdles is now assured, but his confidence will have been significantly boosted for an impending return to the bigger obstacles, and he may have more to offer.
Vicars Destiny is flattered by her proximity to the winner, but enjoyed the step up in trip and still posted a decent effort. She is worth trying over even further and is well suited to this sort of testing ground.
Freetown(IRE), supported in the betting ring, would have been closer but for blundering three out and turned in a much more encouraging effort. He is rated 3lb lower over fences and may be better off when reverting to that sphere. *(op 16-1)*
Jaunty Times, raised 5lb for winning at Warwick last time, was treading water after a blunder three from home and was well held in this quest for the hat-trick. This represented much his stiffest task to date, however, and he was not disgraced in defeat. *(op 7-2)*
Overserved, bidding for a four-timer from a career-high mark, never looked particularly happy on the testing surface and proved disappointing. He has it to prove now, but remains relatively lightly raced, and is not one to write off just yet. *(op 9-2)*
Rosarian(IRE) looked all at sea on this ground and is capable of a deal better when reverting to a faster surface. *(tchd 6-1, 5-1 in places)*
Alagon(IRE) *Official explanation: trainer said gelding choked (op 28-1)*
Spring Pursuit *Official explanation: jockey said saddle slipped (op 20-1)*

3290 32RED.COM NOVICES' H'CAP CHASE (18 fncs) 3m
2:20 (2:21) (Class 3) (0-120,123) 5-Y-0+ **£6,506** (£1,910; £955; £477)

Form RPR
15P- **1** **Lord Brock**[294] 4450 7-11-2 **110** ..... CarlLlewellyn 125+
(N A Twiston-Davies) *hld up: hdwy 12th: led 2 out: drvn clr run-in* **16/1**
3FU2 **2** *10* **Toon Trooper (IRE)**[24] 2818 9-9-13 **98** ..... MarkNicolls(5) 101
(R Lee) *hld up: hdwy after 10th (water): led 13th: hdd 2 out: sn rdn: hung lft and wknd run-in* **12/1**
-P00 **3** *3* **Ironside (IRE)**[22] 2862 7-10-0 **94** ..... RichardJohnson 94
(H D Daly) *chsd ldrs: pushed along whn lft 2nd after 14th: styd on u.p run- in* **10/1**[3]
12PP **4** *10* **Special Conquest**[41] 2529 8-10-8 **105** ..... RichardYoung(3) 100+
(J W Mullins) *led to 2nd: led after 5th to 7th: led 10th (water) to 13th: j.lft 4 out: rdn and ev ch next: wknd 2 out: btn whn mstke last* **20/1**
F351 **6** *4* **Victory Gunner (IRE)**[12] 2965 8-11-10 **123** ..... LeeStephens(5) 103
(C Roberts) *mstke 6th: a bhd* **8/1**[2]
6P55 **7** *¾* **Bannister Lane**[24] 2817 6-10-3 **102** ..... StephenCraine(5) 81
(D McCain) *hld up: mstke 8th: rdn along after: mstke 12th: n.d* **50/1**

4330 **8** *23* **Valleymore (IRE)**[21] 2874 10-10-1 **95**.................................. TomSiddall 51
(S A Brookshaw) *led 2nd tl after 5th: led 7th to 10th (water): wknd 14th* **14/1**

1201 **9** *5* **Koumba (FR)**[41] 2529 8-11-4 **117**.................................. MrNWilliams(5) 68
(Evan Williams) *trckd ldrs: lost pl appr 11th: mstke next: n.d after* **11/1**

P034 **P** **Point**[17] 2936 9-10-3 **95** ow2.................................. JasonMaguire —
(W Jenks) *bhd: blnd bdly 2nd: nt rcvr: p.u after 3rd* **11/1**

6m 37.7s (9.40) **Going Correction** +0.45s/f (Soft) **10** Ran SP% **116.2**
Speed ratings: **102,98,97,94,92 91,90,83,81,**— CSF £185.48 CT £2019.11 TOTE £10.60: £3.50, £2.30, £2.50; EX 220.00.
Owner Graham And Alison Jelley **Bred** Mrs P Badger **Trained** Naunton, Gloucs

FOCUS
A modest handicap, run at a fair gallop, won in great style by the winner.

NOTEBOOK
Lord Brock, making his chasing debut and returning from a 294-day layoff, got his season off to a perfect start with an authoritative display. He jumped particularly well throughout, saw out the trip without fuss, and is clearly right at home on a soft surface. A hike in the weights is inevitable, and his next outing will reveal more, but he is totally unexposed over fences and is the type his trainer excels with. *(op 14-1)*
Toon Trooper(IRE) was made to look very one-paced when the winner went for home, yet still posted another sound effort, and is well up to finding a race when dropping back in trip from his current mark. *(op 11-1)*
Ironside(IRE), having his first outing over fences, was doing his best work at the finish and showed his best form of the current campaign. He is open to improvement in this sphere and looks a dour stayer. *(op 12-1)*
Special Conquest, pulled up on his previous two outings, was just starting to fold prior to losing any chance with a serious error three out, but this still represents a much-improved effort and he can build on this.
Another Native(IRE), raised 11lb for winning at Uttoxeter a week previously, appeared to be found out by the longer trip in this bid for the hat-trick. He may have found this test coming a touch too soon and is not one to write off from his new mark just yet. *(op 6-5 tchd 5-4 in places)*

3291 RED SQUARE VODKA "FIXED BRUSH" NOVICES' HURDLE (10 hdls) 2m 4f
2:50 (2:51) (Class 4) 4-7-Y-0 **£4,554** (£1,337; £668; £333)

Form RPR

21F2 **1** **Cloudy Lane**[32] 2690 6-11-6 .... JasonMaguire 107+
(D McCain) *in tch: hdwy 5th: rdn 3 out: led last: edgd lft towards fin: drvn out* **4/1**[2]

2 *1/2* **Master Wells (IRE)**[84] 5-11-6 .... RichardJohnson 108+
(P J Hobbs) *cl up: led 2 out: hit and hdd last: stl ev ch whn rdr dropped whip run-in: styd on* **4/1**[2]

-233 **3** *11* **No Guarantees**[36] 2614 6-11-6 .... CarlLlewellyn 98+
(N A Twiston-Davies) *led: rdn appr 3 out: hdd 2 out: wknd run-in* **11/4**[1]

6/50 **4** *11* **Scaramouche**[12] 2983 6-11-6 .... MarcusFoley 89+
(B De Haan) *hld up: hdwy after 6th: rdn appr 3 out: wknd 2 out* **20/1**

5 *29* **Parkinson (IRE)**[258] 5-11-6 .... NoelFehily 56
(Jonjo O'Neill) *a bhd: lost tch after 4 out: t.o* **22/1**

63 **P** **Carraig (IRE)**[42] 2501 4-10-0 .... BrianHarding —
(Evan Williams) *a bhd: t.o whn p.u bef 2 out* **10/1**[3]

0-63 **P** **Keen Warrior**[37] 2591 6-11-3 .... LeeVickers(3) —
(Mrs S Lamyman) *midfield: wknd after 4 out: t.o whn p.u bef 3 out* **50/1**

U00 **P** **Ghabesh (USA)**[28] 2756 4-10-7 .... OllieMcPhail —
(Evan Williams) *prom: nt fluent 3rd: wkng whn mstke 5th: t.o whn p.u bef 2 out* **66/1**

26 **P** **Hockenheim (FR)**[57] 2169 5-11-6 .... TonyDobbin —
(J Howard Johnson) *midfield: hdwy 5th: hit 4 out: sn wknd: t.o whn p.u bef 3 out* **4/1**[2]

2100 **P** **West End Wonder (IRE)**[67] 1975 7-11-7 108................. MrNWilliams(5) —
(D Burchell) *hld up: hdwy after 4th: wknd after 5th: t.o whn p.u bef 4 out* **33/1**

5m 16.3s (7.10) **Going Correction** +0.50s/f (Soft)
WFA 4 from 5yo+ 12lb **10** Ran SP% **111.3**
Speed ratings: **105,104,100,96,84** —,—,—,—,— CSF £18.43 TOTE £3.90: £1.30, £1.80, £2.00; EX 16.60.
Owner Trevor Hemmings **Bred** Gleadhill House Stud Ltd **Trained** Cholmondeley, Cheshire
■ Stewards' Enquiry : Jason Maguire caution: careless riding

FOCUS
A fair novice event, run at a sound pace, and the first two came clear.

NOTEBOOK
Cloudy Lane gradually ground down the runner-up in the straight to get off the mark over timber at the third time of asking. He has done little wrong in his career to date, clearly enjoys this testing ground, and does stay very well. In the long term he is very much a staying chaser, but he could defy a penalty in this division when the emphasis is on stamina. *(op 9-2 tchd 5-1 in a place)*
Master Wells(IRE) ◆, rated 68 on the Flat, posted a very pleasing debut effort and things could have been different had his rider not lost his whip after jumping the final flight. He is clearly capable of rating higher in this sphere and should stay further than this in time. *(tchd 9-2, 5-1 in a place)*
No Guarantees failed to improve for this drop back in class and was left behind when the front two *asserted before the final flight. He may be better off in novice handicaps.* *(op 4-1 tchd 5-1 and 9-2 in places)*
Hockenheim(FR)proved disappointing and was pulled up soon after hitting the fourth last. *(op 9-4)*

3292 SPORTING INDEX STANDARD OPEN NATIONAL HUNT FLAT RACE 2m
3:25 (3:26) (Class 6) 4-6-Y-0 **£1,713** (£499; £249)

Form RPR

1 **1** **Albertas Run (IRE)**[49] 2340 5-11-12 .... NoelFehily 103
(Jonjo O'Neill) *trckd ldrs: rdn to chal over 3f out: led ins fnl f: all out* **1/1**[1]

0 **2** *hd* **Jobsworth (IRE)**[45] 2432 6-11-5 .... TonyDobbin 96
(Evan Williams) *in tch: rdn over 3f out: r.o cl home* **25/1**

3 *3/4* **Saxon Leader (IRE)** 4-10-7 .... JasonMaguire 83
(T P Tate) *led: hdd 5f out: regained ld over 3f out: hdd ins fnl f: nt qckn cl home* **5/1**[3]

0 **4** *17* **William Butler (IRE)**[17] 2941 6-11-5 .... TomSiddall 78
(S A Brookshaw) *hld up: rdn 4f out: hung lft and wknd over 1f out* **16/1**

5 *10* **The Otmoor Fox (IRE)** 6-11-5 .... RichardJohnson 68
(P J Hobbs) *w ldr: led 5f out: rdn and hdd over 3f out: wknd over 1f out* **9/2**[2]

6 *3/4* **Don Castille (USA)** 4-10-7 .... JamesDavies 55
(P R Webber) *in tch: rdn and ev ch 3f out: wknd over 1f out* **6/1**

60- **7** *dist* **Just Posin**[355] 3395 5-10-9 .... LeeVickers(3) —
(Mrs S Lamyman) *in tch tl pushed along and wknd 6f out: t.o* **66/1**

4m 5.30s (8.90) **Going Correction** +0.70s/f (Soft)
WFA 4 from 5yo+ 11lb **7** Ran SP% **110.4**
Speed ratings: **105,104,104,96,91 90,**— CSF £27.88 TOTE £2.00: £1.70, £2.60; EX 15.30.
Owner Trevor Hemmings **Bred** Oliver And Salome Brennan **Trained** Cheltenham, Gloucs

FOCUS
A fair bumper, run in testing ground, which saw the first three come clear.

NOTEBOOK
Albertas Run(IRE) followed up his course and distance success with a gritty effort under his penalty. He took time to warm to his task, and is clearly going to need further when sent over hurdles, but looks a fine prospect for connections all the same. *(op 11-10)*
Jobsworth(IRE), who showed little on his Chepstow debut last time, produced a vastly-improved display and made the winner fight to the line. He is clearly going the right way and, with further progression likely, can go one better in a race of this nature.
Saxon Leader(IRE), a 26,000euros purchase whose dam was a winner over hurdles, fences and on the Flat, was only run out of it in the final 50 yards and posted a pleasing debut effort. He looks a nice prospect for his capable yard, handled the ground well, and is clearly up to winning a bumper this term. *(tchd 6-1)*
William Butler(IRE) ran near to the level of his Ludlow bumper and helps set the standard of this form. *(tchd 14-1 in a place)*
The Otmoor Fox(IRE), an 18,000euros half-brother to Irish bumper winner Aran Dawn, showed ability yet could not sustain his effort when it mattered on this deep surface. He is entitled to improve. *(op 5-1 tchd 11-2)*
Don Castille(USA), related to Flat winners in the US, was another who failed to find much for *pressure on this testing ground. He will do better when faced with good ground in the future.* *(op 5-1)*

3293 DRINK J.W. LEES BITTER H'CAP CHASE (15 fncs) 2m 4f
3:55 (3:56) (Class 3) (0-135,130) 5-Y-0+ **£8,783** (£2,578; £1,289; £643)

Form RPR

6-14 **1** **Schuh Shine (IRE)**[35] 2628 9-11-7 **125**.............................. AlanO'Keeffe 138+
(Miss Venetia Williams) *mde all: rdn appr last: kpt on* **11/2**[3]

P-P1 **2** *1 1/4* **Barton Nic**[6] 3187 13-9-9 **106** 7ex..................................(b) DarylJacob(7) 115
(D P Keane) *hld up: bmpd 2nd: hdwy after 4 out: chsd wnr run-in: styd on* **8/1**

5-25 **3** *nk* **Aristoxene (FR)**[41] 2532 6-11-12 **130**................................ MarcusFoley 141+
(N J Henderson) *hld up: hdwy after 4 out: rdn and outpcd after 2 out: styd on towards fin* **11/4**[1]

0-0P **4** *5* **Christopher**[29] 2748 9-11-0 **118**....................................... RichardJohnson 124+
(P J Hobbs) *in tch: tk clsr order 4th: rdn and ev ch 2 out: no ex run-in* **12/1**

P0-5 **5** *20* **The Villager (IRE)**[55] 2210 10-10-11 **115**.......................... JasonMaguire 106+
(T R George) *in tch: pckd 1st: lost pl 6th: clsd 3 out: rdn bef next: wknd last* **3/1**[2]

1U4P **6** *22* **You Owe Me (IRE)**[30] 2724 9-10-12 **116**............................ CarlLlewellyn 78
(N A Twiston-Davies) *hld up: mstke 3rd: hdwy 10th: wknd 3 out* **16/1**

4441 **7** *3* **Sir Storm (IRE)**[12] 2993 10-11-1 **119**..............................(p) FinbarKeniry 78
(G M Moore) *prom tl rdn and wknd appr 3 out* **14/1**

1-30 **P** **General Gossip (IRE)**[22] 2862 10-10-13 **117**.................... TonyDobbin —
(R T Phillips) *bmpd 2nd: a bhd: t.o whn p.u bef 3 out* **16/1**

06P1 **P** **Nowator (POL)**[35] 2626 9-11-4 **122**...................................... OllieMcPhail —
(Robert Gray) *midfield: hdwy 4th: hit 5th: rdn and wknd appr 3 out: t.o whn p.u bef 2 out* **25/1**

U624 **P** **Fiori**[42] 2502 10-10-2 **111**...(p) LeeStephens(5) —
(P C Haslam) *trckd ldrs: mstke 5th: pushed along after 6th: wknd 8th: t.o whn p.u bef 3 out* **12/1**

5m 28.6s (4.40) **Going Correction** +0.45s/f (Soft) **10** Ran SP% **115.8**
Speed ratings: **109,108,108,106,98 89,88,**—,—,— CSF £48.64 CT £146.65 TOTE £4.90: £2.00, £2.90, £1.80; EX 49.60 Place 6 £94.88, Place 5 £61.05.
Owner Mrs Gill Harrison **Bred** Mrs Maria Mulcahy **Trained** Kings Caple, H'fords

FOCUS
A fair handicap and the first three came clear. The form looks sound for the class.

NOTEBOOK
Schuh Shine(IRE) resumed winning ways by making all in most game fashion and clearly relished this drop back in trip. He is a very likeable character, clearly likes this venue, and further improvement cannot be ruled out just yet. *(op 5-1)*
Barton Nic, easily back to winning ways at Plumpton six days previously, was not at all disgraced under his penalty and posted another solid display. He is clearly not ready to retire yet. *(op 6-1)*
Aristoxene(FR) was staying on dourly towards the finish and was not disgraced under top weight. He is well worth another try over three miles on this evidence. *(op 7-2 tchd 4-1)*
Christopher looked a big player before the penultimate fence, but failed to sustain his effort when it really mattered. This was a more encouraging display, however.
The Villager(IRE), well backed, found less than looked likely when push came to shove and was disappointing. *(op 4-1 tchd 9-2 in places)*
T/Plt: £354.60 to a £1 stake. Pool: £59,482.75. 122.45 winning tickets. T/Qpdt: £168.10 to a £1 stake. Pool: £3,977.20. 17.50 winning tickets. DO

2969 SANDOWN (R-H)
Saturday, January 7

OFFICIAL GOING: Hurdle course - soft (good to soft in back straight); chase course - good to soft (good in back straight)
Wind: Virtually nil

3294 PLAY POKER AT LADBROKES.COM JUVENILE NOVICES' HURDLE (8 hdls) 2m 110y
1:00 (1:00) (Class 3) 4-Y-0 **£6,506** (£1,910; £955; £477)

Form RPR

55 **1** **Quasimodo (IRE)**[11] 3038 4-10-12 .... WayneHutchinson 104+
(A W Carroll) *mde virtually all: 4l clr after 2 out: nt fluent last: hrd drvn run-in: jst hld on* **50/1**

3 **2** *shd* **Ostrogoth (FR)**[34] 2661 4-10-12 .... MickFitzgerald 103
(N J Henderson) *lw: hmpd 1st: chsd ldrs: rdn to go 2nd appr last: styd on strly run-in: jst failed* **7/2**[2]

31 **3** *3 1/2* **Spidam (FR)**[36] 2612 4-11-6 .... ChristianWilliams 109+
(P F Nicholls) *veered bdly rt 1st: chsd ldrs: rdn to chse wnr appr last: one pce appr last* **10/11**[1]

U1B **4** *2* **Prime Contender**[7] 3132 4-11-6 .... LeightonAspell 106+
(O Sherwood) *mstke 1st: chsd ldrs: rdn to chse wnr 2 out but no imp: one pce run-in* **5/1**[3]

5 *1 1/2* **Illuminati**[245] 4-10-7 .... HowieEphgrave(5) 97+
(L Corcoran) *hmpd 1st: bhd: hdwy 4 out: chsd ldrs and rdn 2 out: sn one pce* **100/1**

6 *1/2* **Ortega (FR)**[244] 4-10-12 .... PaddyBrennan 95
(P J Hobbs) *w'like: hmpd 1st: bhd: hdwy 4th: chsd ldrs appr 2 out: wknd and mstke last* **25/1**

7 *5* **Love Angel (USA)**[89] 4-10-12 .... GerrySupple 90
(J J Bridger) *bhd tl stdy hday to trck ldrs appr 2 out: wknd appr last* **50/1**

8 *8* **Hereditary**[136] 4-10-12 .... JohnMcNamara 82
(Mrs L C Jewell) *bhd: hday 4th: wknd 2 out* **100/1**

9 *13* **Love Beauty (USA)**[143] 4-10-12 .... SamThomas 69
(M F Harris) *w ldr to 3rd: styd chalng to 3 out: wknd bef next* **66/1**

6 **10** *7* **Shardakhan (IRE)**[24] 2824 4-10-12 .... PhilipHide 62
(G L Moore) *a in rr* **33/1**

5 **11** *shd* **Garibaldi (GER)**[43] 2481 4-10-12 .... AndrewThornton 85+
(D R C Elsworth) *lw: hmpd 1st: chsd ldrs: wknd 2 out no ch whn blnd last* **14/1**

12 *7* **Benedict Bay**[162] 4-10-5 ....(v) SimonElliott(7) 56+
(J A Geake) *hmpd and mstke 1st: bhd: hdwy 4th: wknd bef 2 out* **100/1**

13 *17* **Beauchamp Trump**[23] 4-10-5 ....(t) StevenCrawford(7) 38
(G A Butler) *bdly bmpd 1st: bhd and j.v.slowly 3rd: nvr in contention after* **50/1**

60 **U** **Isle De Maurice**[6] 3182 4-10-9 .... WilliamKennedy(3) —
(D B Feek) *mstke and uns rdr 2nd* **100/1**

0 **U** **E Bride (USA)**[16] 2949 4-9-12 .... TomMessenger(7) —
(T T Clement) *chsd ldrs to 4th: bhd whn mstke and uns rdr 3 out* **100/1**

4m 8.30s (-0.60) **Going Correction** +0.025s/f (Yiel) **15** Ran SP% **117.1**
Speed ratings: **102,101,100,99,98 98,96,92,86,82 82,79,71,—,—** CSF £214.13 TOTE £45.00: £5.90, £1.40, £1.40; EX 114.60.
Owner R G Owens **Bred** Gerard Hayes **Trained** Cropthorne, Worcs

FOCUS
Vastly improved form from the winner, but not a strong race of its type overall. The form has been rated through the third and fourth.

NOTEBOOK
Quasimodo(IRE) was there to be shot at throughout but he kept finding more and, jumping the second last, bounded four lengths clear. He bungled the last, causing him to lose momentum, and that allowed the eventual runner-up to close right up on the run-in and force a photo, but he was a worthy winner, improving greatly for the switch to front-running tactics.
Ostrogoth(FR) finished over 15 lengths in front of Quasimodo at Warwick on his hurdling debut but was unable to confirm the form with that rival adopting different tactics this time. In another yard or two he would have been in front, and he should not be long in going one better. *(op 10-3)*
Spidam(FR), a course and distance winner last month, jumped out to his right at a few of the *flights. He kept plugging away, though, without quite looking up to defying his 8lb penalty.Official explanation: jockey said gelding jumped right (op 11-10 tchd 5-4 in a place)*
Prime Contender, another with an 8lb penalty to shoulder, had every chance. He went in pursuit of the winner after the second last but did not see the trip out as strongly as some. *(op 4-1)*
Illuminati showed little in two starts on the level but he is a half-brother to top-class middle-distance filly Ouija Board and useful hurdler Spectrometer. This effort suggests he will achieve a bit more over timber than he did on the Flat.
Ortega(FR), a winner of a ten-furlong good-ground maiden on the Flat in the French Provinces, threatened to get involved early in the straight but, once asked to pick up, looked all at sea on the ground. He should be seen to better effect on a sounder surface.
Love Angel(USA) has a couple of ten-furlong successes on the level to his name on good to firm and hard ground, so these conditions are unlikely to have been to his liking. He still showed ability, though, and he will have better chances when the ground dries up. *(op 40-1)*
Love Beauty(USA), a fair maiden on the Flat, was with the winner turning into the straight but could not pick up in the ground. He will be happier on faster ground in the spring.
Garibaldi(GER) *Official explanation: jockey said colt had breathing problem (op 12-1)*

3295 PLAY CASINO AT LADBROKES.COM MARES' ONLY H'CAP HURDLE (8 hdls) 2m 110y
1:30 (1:31) (Class 3) (0-130,124) 4-Y-0+
£9,394 (£2,775; £1,387; £694; £346; £174)

Form RPR
1111 **1** **Refinement (IRE)**[63] 2050 7-11-11 **123** .... APMcCoy 129+
(Jonjo O'Neill) *trckd ldrs: wnt 2nd 4 out to next: led wl bef 2 out: wnt lft last: drvn and kpt on wl run-in* **5/6**[1]

2-42 **2** *4* **Pay Attention**[44] 2452 5-11-12 **124** .... RussGarritty 124
(T D Easterby) *hld up rr but in tch: hdwy to chse ldrs 2 out: styd on wl for 2nd cl home but no imp on wnr* **11/4**[2]

00-P **3** *shd* **Dancing Pearl**[33] 1444 8-11-11 **123** .... MarkBradburne 123
(C J Price) *chsd ldrs: wnt 2nd 3 out: w wnr wl bef 2 out: rdn sn after: kpt on wl to press for 2nd run-in: nt imp on wnr* **25/1**

13 **4** *3/4* **Miss Pebbles (IRE)**[39] 2559 6-11-2 **114** .... WayneHutchinson 114+
(R Dickin) *hld up rr but in tch: hdwy and nt fluent 3 out: styng on whn hit 2 out: kpt on same pce u.p run-in* **8/1**[3]

5644 **5** *2* **Sardagna (FR)**[41] 2532 6-11-5 **117** .... TimmyMurphy 114
(M C Pipe) *chsd ldr tl j. slowly 4th: outpcd appr 2 out: kpt on again run-in but nvr gng pce to rch ldrs* **8/1**[3]

0-U6 **6** *1/2* **Sword Lady**[40] 2553 8-11-7 **119** ....(b) PaddyBrennan 117+
(Mrs S D Williams) *led: rdn after 3 out: hdd wl bef 2 out: kpt on u.p sn after and rallied run-in but nt trble ldrs* **25/1**

4m 8.50s (-0.40) **Going Correction** +0.025s/f (Yiel) **6** Ran SP% **111.1**
Speed ratings: **101,99,99,98,97 97** CSF £3.63 TOTE £1.80: £1.60, £1.60; EX 3.10.
Owner Michael Tabor **Bred** M Tabor **Trained** Cheltenham, Gloucs

FOCUS
A fair race and Refinement continues to win without suggesting she is as good over hurdles as her bumper form promised she might be. The form has been rated through the second, but the time was slow and it could be suspect.

NOTEBOOK
Refinement(IRE) won her fifth start on the trot and her first handicap, but she was entitled to win off this mark and she was not impressive in beating opponents of no more than fair ability. She is a 25-1 shot for the Supreme Novices', but her trainer is inclined to swerve the Festival and opt instead to try and mop up prizes with her in mares-only company. *(op 10-11 tchd Evens in a place)*
Pay Attention won the race for second but only confirmed the impression left by her Carlisle effort, which was that the Handicapper has a fairly good idea about her ability now. *(op 5-2)*
Dancing Pearl, who had a spin on the All-Weather last month, is another about whom the Handicapper knows all too much. Third in this event in 2005 and second in 2004, she ran her usual game race. *(op 20-1)*
Miss Pebbles(IRE) looked on a stiff enough mark beforehand for her handicap debut, and clattering the second last did not help. Better ground in future might, though. *(op 7-1)*
Sardagna(FR), returning to hurdling, finished slightly further behind Dancing Pearl than she did in this race last year. *(op 14-1)*
Sword Lady is a stayer and she found this trip too much of a test of speed. *(op 20-1)*

3296 BET WITH LADBROKES ON 0800 524 524 H'CAP CHASE (22 fncs) 3m 110y
2:05 (2:06) (Class 2) (0-140,138) 5-Y-0+
£25,052 (£7,400; £3,700; £1,852; £924; £464)

Form RPR
3U-2 **1** **Graphic Approach (IRE)**[41] 2532 8-11-6 **132** .... APMcCoy 145+
(C R Egerton) *lw: hld up mid-div: hdwy 12th:drvn to chse ldr and 3l down but styng on whn lft in ld 2 out: rdn and r.o wl run-in* **7/1**[3]

2522 **2** *3 1/2* **Shalako (USA)**[43] 2485 8-10-4 **116** .... PaddyBrennan 123
(P J Hobbs) *chsd ldrs: rdn and styd on fr 3 out: swtchd lft run-in: r.o u.p but no imp on wnr cl home* **10/1**

P-0P **3** *1 1/2* **Jakari (FR)**[42] 2492 9-11-4 **130** .... MarkBradburne 137+
(H D Daly) *lw: led to 7th: led again 11th: rdn and hdd appr 3 out: rallied and kpt on run-in* **22/1**

-223 **4** *8* **Lou Du Moulin Mas (FR)**[28] 2767 7-11-4 **130** ....(bt[1]) GrahamLee 129+
(P F Nicholls) *chsd ldrs: hit 13th: kpt on same pce u.p fr 3 out* **11/1**

0-0U **5** *4* **Liberthine (FR)**[29] 2744 7-11-1 **134** .... MrSWaley-Cohen(7) 129+
(N J Henderson) *in tch: hdwy 12th: chsd ldrs next: wknd 3 out* **9/2**[2]

10-4 **6** *2 1/2* **Gunther McBride (IRE)**[76] 1861 11-11-5 **134** .... RobertStephens(3) 125
(P J Hobbs) *hit 1st: chsd ldrs: rdn 4 out: wknd after 4 out* **25/1**

U331 **7** *2* **Latimer's Place**[36] 2616 10-11-2 **128** .... JimmyMcCarthy 119+
(J A Geake) *rr: hit 4th: blnd 10th: nvr rchd ldrs* **12/1**

P-23 **8** *5* **Durlston Bay**[36] 2616 9-10-1 **113** oh5 ow1 .... LeightonAspell 100+
(S Dow) *chsd ldr: led 7th to 11th: styd chalng 13th to next: wknd 4 out* **50/1**

20-6 **P** **Horus (IRE)**[35] 2628 11-11-9 **138** .... TomMalone(3) —
(M C Pipe) *lw: hit 9th: a bhd: t.o whn p.u bef 17th* **25/1**

20-P **P** **Zeta's River (IRE)**[73] 1879 8-11-8 **134** .... TimmyMurphy —
(M C Pipe) *lw: sn bhd: rdn 12th: t.o whn p.u bef 15th* **14/1**

1-25 **P** **Ken'tucky (FR)**[41] 2518 8-10-12 **124** .... RobertThornton —
(A King) *bhd: sme hdwy 9th: wknd 13th: t.o whn p.u bef 3 out* **16/1**

1-PP **P** **Distant Thunder (IRE)**[42] 2491 8-11-5 **131** .... AndrewThornton —
(R H Alner) *lw: sprawled 9th: a bhd: t.o whn p.u bef 3 out* **9/1**

P5 **P** **Holy Joe (FR)**[6] 3176 9-11-2 **128** .... SamThomas —
(Miss Venetia Williams) *in tch: blnd 10th: j. slowly 12th: blnd 15th and bhd: t.o whn p.u bef 3 out* **16/1**

-331 **F** **Ladalko (FR)**[43] 2485 7-11-5 **131** .... ChristianWilliams 147+
(P F Nicholls) *chsd ldrs: chal fr 16th tl led appr 3 out: 3l clr and styng on whn fell 2 out* **7/2**[1]

6m 24.9s (-6.60) **Going Correction** +0.025s/f (Yiel) **14** Ran SP% **120.5**
Speed ratings: **111,109,109,106,105 104,104,102,—,— —,—,—,—** CSF £72.09 CT £1478.41 TOTE £8.30: £2.10, £4.10, £6.70; EX 76.40 Trifecta £1033.90 Part won. Pool: £1,456.22 - 0.70 winning tickets..
Owner Mr & Mrs Peter Orton **Bred** Walter Connors **Trained** Chaddleworth, Berks

FOCUS
A competitive handicap likely to produce future winners. Ladalko was heading for a new personal best when he fell, but Graphic Approach is progressive too and can win again. The second ran to hsi mark and the third is well treated now.

NOTEBOOK
Graphic Approach(IRE), put up 2lb for his promising reappearance effort at Newbury, still looked fairly handicapped here. He travelled well and looked to be Ladalko's only danger when that one fell at the second last. Idling in front, he found more on the run-in, and he looks a progressive type. He may come back here for the Racing Post Chase next month or go to Newbury for the Vodafone Gold Cup. *(tchd 13-2)*
Shalako(USA), who has a poor strike-rate, is a horse the Handicapper knows plenty about. *Runner-up to Ladalko last time, both horses gave a boost to that form here. (op 9-1 tchd 11-1 in a place)*
Jakari(FR) ◆ returned to form having struggled since being pulled up in the Grand National. He is well handicapped on his best form – 9lb lower than when fifth in the William Hill Handicap Chase at *the Festival – and he should be capable of winning soon. A sounder surface would suit him* ideally. *(op 25-1)*
Lou Du Moulin Mas(FR) is a difficult horse to win with and the blinkers did not help. The Handicapper has had plenty of chances to assess his ability and he remains opposable. *(op 10-1)*
Liberthine(FR) is fairly handicapped at the moment on a mark 6lb higher than when successful in the Mildmay of Flete, but she did not find the leaders coming back to her this time. *(op 4-1 tchd 5-1)*
Gunther McBride(IRE) looked fit on his return from a 76-day break but is not getting any younger and needs some help from the Handicapper. *(op 20-1)*
Distant Thunder(IRE) sprawled badly on landing over the Pond Fence first time round which did not help his cause, and was always towards the rear of the field. Eventually pulled up - third time this season - he clearly has some sort of problem as he is well handicapped on his novice form and really should be competitive in this type of race. *(tchd 16-1 in a place)*
Ladalko(FR) ◆ was going well in front and looked the likeliest winner when coming down at the second last. This was only his fourth start over fences and he looks an improving type, so hopefully this tumble will not have affected his confidence. The Racing Post Chase here next *month and the William Hill Handicap Chase at the Festival look ideal targets for him. (tchd 16-1 in a place)*
Zeta's River(IRE) *Official explanation: trainer's representative said gelding bled from nose (tchd 16-1 in a place)*

3297 ANGLO IRISH BANK CORPORATE TREASURY TOLWORTH HURDLE GRADE 1 (8 hdls) 2m 110y
2:35 (2:40) (Class 1) 4-Y-0+ **£28,510** (£10,695; £5,355; £2,670; £1,340)

Form RPR
6-31 **1** **Noland**[29] 2742 5-11-7 .... ChristianWilliams 136+
(P F Nicholls) *lw: trckd ldr: chal 2 out: sn led: drvn out* **6/4**[1]

141 **2** *5* **Whispered Promises (USA)**[45] 2444 5-11-7 132 .... JohnMcNamara 131
(R S Brookhouse) *led: rdn bef 2 out: hdd sn after: kpt on but no ch w wnr* **15/2**

1031 **3** *9* **Albarino (IRE)**[12] 2969 7-11-7 107 .... TomScudamore 122
(M Scudamore) *in tch 3rd: chsd ldrs and rdn after 3 out: wknd next* **9/1**

0-21 **4** *14* **Lennon (IRE)**[37] 2591 6-11-7 116 .... GrahamLee 108
(J Howard Johnson) *chsd ldrs: rdn appr 2 out: sn btn* **15/8**[2]

5 *7* **Compton Bolter (IRE)**[22] 9-11-7 .... APMcCoy 104+
(G A Butler) *bhd: j. slowly 4th: sme hdwy after 3 out: nvr rchd ldrs and wknd bef next* **7/1**[3]

4m 6.70s (-2.20) **Going Correction** +0.025s/f (Yiel) **5** Ran SP% **109.0**
Speed ratings: **106,103,99,92,89** CSF £12.05 TOTE £2.50: £1.40, £2.80; EX 11.50.
Owner J Hales **Bred** The Niarchos Family **Trained** Ditcheat, Somerset

FOCUS
With Irish raider Iktitaf a non-runner, this looked no more than a fair renewal. The winner improved again, but is still some way short of the level required to make him a serious contender at Cheltenham. The second and third ran to their marks.

NOTEBOOK
Noland coped with the soft ground rather than enjoyed it and drew clear in the closing stages for a comfortable success. Now 16-1 for the Supreme Novices', he will apparently have one more run *before Cheltenham, but he should be much happier when he gets a decent surface. (op 11-8 tchd 13-8)*
Whispered Promises(USA) is probably flattered by his official rating of 132 but he ran well in defeat, albeit having enjoyed the run of the race in front. Winning opportunities are likely to be difficult to come by from now on, though. *(op 8-1)*
Albarino(IRE), a winner of a handicap over the course and distance on Boxing Day off a mark of 107, had a lot more on his plate in this company and was far from disgraced. Left behind on the run to the last, he nevertheless posted a performance which, when assessed by the Handicapper, might make things very difficult for him in future. *(tchd 10-1)*
Lennon(IRE) was well supported but let his backers down, failing to pick up in the straight. A winner of bumpers on good and good to firm ground, a sounder surface might see him to better effect. *(op 11-4)*

Compton Bolter(IRE), a smart performer on the Flat, had apparently schooled well, but he never showed his best form on the level on soft ground and it was not a great surprise to see him drift in *the market beforehand and struggle in the race itself. He might do better on a sounder surface. (op 9-2)*

3298 LADBROKE H'CAP HURDLE (LISTED RACE) (8 hdls) 2m 110y
3:10 (3:11) (Class 1) (0-150,149) 4-Y-0+

£57,020 (£21,390; £10,710; £5,340; £2,680; £1,340)

Form RPR

00-2 **1** **Desert Air (JPN)**29 2746 7-10-9 **132**.......................(t) TomScudamore 141+
(M C Pipe) *lw: chsd ldrs: led bef 2 out: sn rdn: hld on all out* **25/1**

1152 **2** *1¼* **Nathos (GER)**7 3135 9-9-13 **132**.......................... KevinTobin(10) 139+
(C J Mann) *bhd: stl plenty to do whn c wd bnd bef 2 out: str run sn after: chsd wnr sn last: r.o strly: gng on cl home* **25/1**

-P30 **3** *6* **Fenix (GER)**35 2636 7-10-4 **127**.......................(b) LeightonAspell 130+
(Mrs L Wadham) *hld up in rr: stdy hday 3 out: chsd wnr 2 out: no imp appr last and sn outpcd* **14/1**

02-2 **4** *3* **Chief Yeoman**22 2871 6-11-3 **140**.......................... SamThomas 140+
(Miss Venetia Williams) *chsd ldrs: rdn and styd on same pce fr 2 out* **16/1**

0502 **5** *4* **Cherub (GER)**35 2636 6-10-12 **135**.......................... APMcCoy 129
(Jonjo O'Neill) *bhd: hdwy after 3 out: chsd ldrs and rdn appr 2 out: wknd sn after* **12/1**

3406 **6** *1* **Borora**29 2746 7-10-6 **129**.......................... TomDoyle 122
(R Lee) *bhd: rdn appr 2 out: styd on run-in but nvr gng pce to rch ldrs* **100/1**

1303 **7** *½* **Fait Le Jojo (FR)**41 2519 9-10-10 **138**.................. HowieEphgrave(5) 131
(L Corcoran) *led after 2nd to 4th: rdn 3 out: wknd next* **100/1**

2451 **8** *½* **Afrad (FR)**12 2974 5-10-8 **131** 4ex.......................... MickFitzgerald 124+
(N J Henderson) *mid-div: hdwy 4th: rdn 3 out: no ch w ldrs next and sn wknd* **3/1**1

053P **9** *½* **Arrayou (FR)**22 2871 5-10-2 **125**.......................(v) PaddyBrennan 117
(O Sherwood) *bhd: rdn 3 out: sme prog fr 2 out but n.d* **50/1**

-042 **10** *½* **Self Defense**12 2971 9-11-5 **149**.......................... LiamHeard(7) 140
(Miss E C Lavelle) *chsd ldrs to 3 out: wknd next* **14/1**

413- **11** *1½* **Miss Academy (FR)**262 4930 5-10-2 **128**.................. TomMalone(3) 118
(M C Pipe) *bhd: hdwy 3 out: sn rdn: nvr rchd ldrs and wknd 2 out* **16/1**

0-12 **12** *4* **Not Left Yet (IRE)**51 2292 5-10-0 **123** oh1.................. TimmyMurphy 109
(M C Pipe) *lw: bhd: sme hdwy 3 out: nvr rchd ldrs and sn btn* **9/2**2

11-2 **13** *2½* **Briareus**28 2765 6-10-10 **133**.......................... JimmyMcCarthy 116
(A M Balding) *lw: in tch: hdwy andf rdn 3 out: wknd bef next* **10/1**3

-110 **14** *2* **Admiral (IRE)**42 2500 5-11-0 **147**.......................... JohnFlavin(10) 128
(R C Guest) *led tl: after 2nd: styd w ldr tl led 4th: hdd & wknd appr 2 out* **33/1**

-011 **15** *8* **Verasi**35 2636 5-10-11 **134**.......................(p) PhilipHide 107
(G L Moore) *chsd ldrs to 3 out* **14/1**

-P46 **16** *3½* **Cloudy Grey (IRE)**12 2971 9-10-12 **135**.................. AndrewThornton 121+
(Miss E C Lavelle) *chsd ldrs: rdn after 3 out: sn wknd: no ch whn blnd last* **25/1**

4215 **17** *nk* **All Star (GER)**35 2636 6-10-2 **130**.......................... SamCurling(5) 99
(N J Henderson) *chsd ldrs to 3 out* **16/1**

3-40 **18** *28* **Dalaram (IRE)**55 2209 6-11-0 **137**.......................(t) GrahamLee 78
(J Howard Johnson) *rdn 4 out: a in rr* **25/1**

050P **19** *dist* **Fontanesi (IRE)**35 2636 6-10-12 **135**.......................... GerrySupple —
(M C Pipe) *t.o fr 4th* **100/1**

5-06 **P** **Handy Money**55 2209 9-10-7 **130**.......................... RobertThornton —
(A King) *in tch: hdwy to trck ldrs 4th: wknd qckly 2 out: p.u bef last* **16/1**

3m 58.8s (-10.10) **Going Correction** +0.025s/f (Yiel) **20** Ran SP% **126.8**
Speed ratings: 121,120,117,116,114 113,113,113,113,112 112,110,109,108,104 102,102,89,—,— CSF £524.56 CT £8774.84 TOTE £22.00: £4.90, £5.30, £3.30, £3.70; EX 821.80 Trifecta £7713.40 Part won. Pool: £10,863.97 - 0.30 winning units..

Owner Mrs Belinda Harvey **Bred** B B A Ireland Ltd **Trained** Nicholashayne, Devon

FOCUS

A decent, competitive handicap run in a cracking time, even for a hot contest like this, around eight to nine seconds faster than the other three hurdle races over the same trip. Strong form.

NOTEBOOK

Desert Air(JPN) took it up early in the straight, responded well to pressure and stayed on strongly up the hill. He was fourth in the race last year off a 7lb lower mark but he came here this year on the back of a lighter campaign and was ridden more prominently. That seemed to help, and this was a personal best by around 8lb. The totesport Trophy Hurdle at Newbury, in which he finished in mid-division last year, looks the logical next target.

Nathos(GER) usually runs over further than this but the strong pace played to his strengths over this stiff two miles and he made up a lot of ground over the final two flights. This was his best effort yet, and by some way. *(tchd 28-1)*

Fenix(GER), runner-up in the Imperial Cup here in March and a faller at the second last while in the process of running a good race in this event 12 months ago, once again showed that this track suits him well. He could hardly be described as well handicapped, though. *(tchd 16-1)*

Chief Yeoman, whose reappearance run at Windsor was a promising effort, was travelling best of all early in the straight but did not find as much as promised off the bridle. This stiff track in this ground proved just too much and he might be of more interest on a flatter course, the totesport Trophy Hurdle at Newbury being an obvious target, but it might just be that he is high enough in the weights at present. *(tchd 18-1)*

Cherub(GER), 6lb higher for finishing runner-up here in the William Hill Handicap last month, did *best of those who contested that race, but the Handicapper probably has his measure now. (tchd 14-1)*

Borora did not run badly considering he is probably happier on a sounder surface. *(op 66-1)*

Fait Le Jojo(FR) helped set a strong pace out in front and paid for his effort in the closing stages. He would have been happier being given an uncontested lead. *(op 66-1)*

Afrad(FR), 7lb well in at the weights under his 4lb penalty, was struggling from a fair way out, but *he did have an excuse as it was later discovered that he was lame behind. Official explanation: vet said gelding was lame behind (op 7-2 tchd 4-1 in a place)*

Miss Academy(FR) looked fit for her first run in 262 days but could not get competitive from off the pace. She might need better ground to show her best. *(op 14-1)*

Not Left Yet(IRE), running off a 15lb higher mark than when successful at Cheltenham at the Paddy Power meeting, was well backed but could not get into it from off the pace. He may need further now. *(op 4-1 tchd 5-1 in a place)*

Briareus did not appreciate the testing conditions. *Official explanation: jockey said gelding was unsuited by soft ground (op 8-1)*

Admiral(IRE) got into a battle for the lead with Fait Le Jojo and they cut each other's throats.

Verasi, who came from well off the pace to win the William Hill Handicap here last month, had a stiff task on his plate this time off a 10lb higher mark.

3299 LADBROKES.COM H'CAP CHASE (13 fncs) 2m
3:45 (3:46) (Class 2) (0-145,142) 5-Y-0+

£12,526 (£3,700; £1,850; £926; £462; £232)

Form RPR

U13- **1** **Dempsey (IRE)**273 4769 8-11-12 **142**.......................... AndrewTinkler 153+
(M Pitman) *t.k.h early: trckd ldrs: led 6th: c clr after 2 out: pushed along run-in: readily* **17/2**

461- **2** *¾* **Tikram**260 4972 9-11-12 **142**.......................... APMcCoy 150
(G L Moore) *chsd ldrs: rdn and styd on to chse wnr sn after last: kpt on u.p but a hld* **15/2**

4-41 **3** *4* **Tysou (FR)**28 2757 9-11-10 **140**.......................... MickFitzgerald 144
(N J Henderson) *lw: prom: chsd wnr 9th: rdn and no imp fr 3 out: lost 2nd sn after last* **4/1**1

-540 **4** *10* **Palua**70 1918 9-11-1 **131**.......................... TimmyMurphy 125
(Miss E C Lavelle) *led 2nd to 6th: styd chsng ldrs tl wknd fr 3 out* **33/1**

1121 **5** *10* **Lorient Express (FR)**12 2998 7-10-8 **124**.......................... SamThomas 111+
(Miss Venetia Williams) *bhd: hdwy 6th: chsd ldrs 8th: rdn after 4 out: wknd next* **9/2**2

-F1P **6** *1¾* **Full House (IRE)**56 2177 7-11-6 **136**.......................... TomDoyle 118
(P R Webber) *in tch 4th: rdn and one pce 4 out: styng on whn blnd 3 out: sme hdwy again run-in* **14/1**

2B02 **7** *¾* **Tribal Dispute**28 2757 9-10-12 **128**.......................... RussGarritty 110
(T D Easterby) *bhd: sme hdwy 4 out: nvr rchd ldrs and sn wknd* **5/1**3

1423 **8** *3½* **Stance**22 2869 7-11-0 **130**.......................... PhilipHide 108
(G L Moore) *bhd tl mod hdwy fr 3 out* **14/1**

213- **9** *5* **Executive Decision (IRE)**287 4555 12-10-1 **117** oh4 ow1(v) LeightonAspell 90
(Mrs L Wadham) *bhd most of way* **14/1**

35F0 **10** *9* **Cobbet (CZE)**28 2768 10-10-4 **120**.......................... PaddyBrennan 84
(T R George) *chsd ldrs tl rdn and wknd 4 out: no ch whn mstke next* **16/1**

-4F4 **11** *5* **Duncliffe**5 3210 9-11-8 **138**.......................... AndrewThornton 97
(R H Alner) *lw: led to 2nd: chsd ldr to 5th: wknd after 4 out* **12/1**

6-30 **12** *2* **Kadarann (IRE)**67 1970 9-11-5 **142**.......................... LiamHeard(7) 99
(P F Nicholls) *hit 1st: in tch and hit 4th: wknd 8th* **16/1**

4m 0.10s (-2.40) **Going Correction** +0.025s/f (Yiel) **12** Ran SP% **119.5**
Speed ratings: **107,106,104,99,94 93,93,91,89,84 82,81** CSF £72.23 CT £299.19 TOTE £10.60: £3.10, £3.20, £1.80; EX 66.20 Trifecta £712.90 Pool: £1,506.22 - 1.50 winning units. Place 6 £163.56, Place 5 £126.68.

Owner Mrs T Brown **Bred** Seamus Larkin **Trained** Upper Lambourn, Berks

FOCUS

A decent handicap and again they went a good pace. The form looks pretty solid and Dempsey has been assessed as having improved by around 10lb. While Tikram ran to his mark, Tysou was a few pounds off his Cheltenham form.

NOTEBOOK

Dempsey(IRE), who looked fit for his return from a 273-day break, jumped well once out in front and defied top weight and a mark of 142 with a degree of ease. He is clearly a smart performer but happier going this way round, so the fact that the Victor Chandler Chase, while an obvious target, takes place at Cheltenham this year, may not be ideal for him. *(op 8-1 tchd 15-2 and 9-1 in a place)*

Tikram looked fit for his reappearance having been operated on for a tumour on the back of his head during the off-season and, given that the ground was softer than he would ideally have liked, he put up a very creditable effort. All his wins over jumps have come on good ground and a return to further will suit him - each of his wins over fences has come over two and a half miles or further, but he is likely to take on the winner again in the Victor Chandler Chase. *(op 7-1)*

Tysou(FR), 5lb higher for his Cheltenham win, ran a solid race off his highest ever chase mark. He rarely runs a bad race and is a reliable yardstick for the form. *(tchd 9-2 in a place)*

Palua, an in-and-out performer who is happier on a sounder surface, ran one of his better races, but the Handicapper still looks to have his measure for the present time. *(tchd 40-1)*

Lorient Express(FR), 13lb higher than when an easy winner at Wincanton last time, found himself taking on much better opposition here and was found out. He might do better on a sounder surface but he has it to prove now off his revised mark. *(op 5-1 tchd 11-2 in a place)*

Full House(IRE) is a fast-ground horse. *(op 12-1)*

Tribal Dispute has shown of late that he can be competitive off this sort of mark, so this was a disappointing effort. *(op 6-1)*

T/Jkpt: Not won. T/Plt: £195.20 to a £1 stake. Pool: £117,094.50. 437.85 winning tickets. T/Qpdt: £114.40 to a £1 stake. Pool: £6,717.80. 43.45 winning tickets. ST

3300 - 3308a (Foreign Racing) - See Raceform Interactive

2193 NAAS (L-H)
Sunday, January 8

OFFICIAL GOING: Soft

3309a WOODLANDS PARK 100 SLANEY NOVICE HURDLE (GRADE 2) 2m 4f
1:50 (1:50) 5-Y-0+ **£26,039** (£7,639; £3,639; £1,240)

RPR

1 **Toofarback (IRE)**28 2791 6-11-5 119.......................... NPMadden 126+
(Noel Meade, Ire) *cl up in 2nd: led 2 out: strly pressed bef last: styd on wl u.p* **7/1**3

2 *1½* **Vic Venturi (IRE)**11 3086 6-11-8.......................(t) AndrewJMcNamara 127
(Philip Fenton, Ire) *settled 4th: rdn 2 out: 3rd last: 2nd and kpt on wl run-in* **12/1**

3 *1½* **Merdeka (IRE)**35 2671 6-11-5.......................... BJGeraghty 123
(T J Taaffe, Ire) *trckd ldrs in 3rd: 2nd and chal after 2 out: ev ch appr last: no ex run-in* **15/8**2

4 *1* **Wild Ocean (IRE)**10 3112 5-11-1.......................... JRBarry 118
(E Sheehy, Ire) *led: slt mstke 3 out: sn rdn and strly pressed: hdd 2 out: 5th appr last: kpt on u.p* **14/1**

5 *1½* **Thyne Again (IRE)**6 3227 5-11-1.......................... DNRussell 116
(W J Burke, Ire) *in tch: slt mstke 5th: rdn 2 out: 4th appr last: no ex run-in* **12/1**

6 *4½* **Mister Top Notch (IRE)**11 3086 7-11-5.......................... JLCullen 116
(D E Fitzgerald, Ire) *hld up in rr: prog into 4th 3 out: 6th and rdn next: kpt on same pce* **12/1**

7 *3½* **Alexander Taipan (IRE)**35 2667 6-11-5.......................... DJCasey 112
(W P Mullins, Ire) *hld up in tch: slt mstke 5 out: dropped to rr after slt mstke 3 out: rdn and no imp bef next: eased bef last* **7/4**1

5m 7.90s **7** Ran SP% **113.4**
CSF £76.41 TOTE £8.40: £3.10, £2.10; DF 70.70.

Owner Mrs M Cahill **Bred** John Magee **Trained** Castletown, Co Meath

NOTEBOOK

Toofarback(IRE), whose Punchestown maiden win has not been advertised as anything out of the ordinary, took this step up in class in his stride and produced a fair staying performance to score. While he will need to keep improving to rate Cheltenham material, he is likely to be aimed at the Brit Insurance Novices' Hurdle. *(op 6/1 tchd 8/1)*

Vic Venturi(IRE) posted another solid effort and showed that his Limerick win was no fluke. However, he really needs further than this trip to be seen at best. *(op 8/1)*
Merdeka(IRE) ran below expectations, yet still turned in a personal best over hurdles, and he looks like he has more to offer still. In the long term, he should make a decent chaser. *(op 7/4 tchd 2/1)*
Wild Ocean(IRE) again employed front running tactics, but was not particularily fluent. He kept on after a mistake three out and remains interesting, even at this level. *(op 12/1)*
Thyne Again(IRE) ran creditably, only tapped for foot between the last two flights and then staying on again. He would have appreciated a stronger overall gallop. *(op 10/1)*
Mister Top Notch(IRE) did not run to his Limerick form with the runner-up, but is still an above-average staying maiden, and did not get the race run to suit this time. *(op 10/1)*
Alexander Taipan(IRE), back up in trip, made mistakes and was beaten two out. It transpired that *he pulled a muscle in his hind-quarters. Official explanation: vet said gelding pulled a muscle in its hind quarter (op 7/4 tchd 13/8)*

3310 - 3313a (Foreign Racing) - See Raceform Interactive

2674 NEWCASTLE (L-H)

Monday, January 9

OFFICIAL GOING: Soft (heavy in places)

Wind: Almost nil

3314 NITEX.CO.UK "NATIONAL HUNT" NOVICES' HURDLE (9 hdls) 2m

12:40 (12:40) (Class 4) 4-Y-0+ **£3,083** (£898; £449)

Form				RPR
5-13	**1**		**Etched In Stone (IRE)**[68] 1990 7-11-5 .... TonyDobbin (N G Richards) *mde all: j.rt and hit 4 out: hrd pressed next: drvn out* **1/1**[1]	107+
50	**2**	*2 ½*	**Boulders Beach (IRE)**[25] 2844 6-11-5 .... PadgeWhelan (Mrs S J Smith) *prom: effrt and ev ch 2 out: kpt on same pce last* **50/1**	102
-432	**3**	*2 ½*	**Tous Chez (IRE)**[14] 2991 7-11-5 .... DominicElsworth (Mrs S J Smith) *nt fluent: cl up: effrt bef 3 out: one pce after next* **7/4**[2]	101+
P-0P	**4**	*1*	**Lethem Air**[7] 3205 8-11-0 81 .... DougieCostello(5) (T Butt) *chsd ldrs tl rdn and wknd fr 2 out* **200/1**	98
U000	**5**	*10*	**Cloudmor (IRE)**[18] 2942 5-11-2 .... GaryBerridge(3) (L Lungo) *hld up: effrt and pushed along 4 out: kpt on but no imp fr next* **100/1**	88
2-L0	**6**	*5*	**Baffling Secret (FR)**[18] 2942 6-11-5 .... BruceGibson (L Lungo) *hld up: hdwy whn hit 4th: rdn after 4 out: no ex bef next* **50/1**	83
-500	**7**	*6*	**Hialeah**[21] 2923 5-10-12 .... MrOGreenall(7) (M W Easterby) *bhd tl sme late hdwy: nvr on terms* **50/1**	77
P	**8**	*9*	**Colonel James (IRE)**[34] 2690 5-11-5 .... KennyJohnson (R Johnson) *a bhd* **200/1**	68
04	**9**	*15*	**Springvic (IRE)**[14] 2991 6-11-5 .... FinbarKeniry (G M Moore) *prom tl wknd fr 3 out* **10/1**[3]	53
5-34	**10**	*7*	**Trafalgar Man (IRE)**[58] 2192 5-11-5 .... GrahamLee (M D Hammond) *nt fluent: hld up: pushed along 4 out: wknd bef next* **20/1**	46
0-	**11**	*6 ½*	**Dusky Dame**[293] 4513 6-10-5 .... TomMessenger(7) (S B Bell) *a bhd* **200/1**	33
0	**12**	*7*	**Beardie's Dream (IRE)**[18] 2942 6-10-12 .... BrianHarding (Miss P Robson) *a bhd* **200/1**	26
0	**U**		**Commanche Sioux**[21] 2927 4-10-0 .... AlanDempsey (M W Easterby) *uns rdr 1st* **100/1**	—
	P		**Lord Rex (IRE)**[303] 6-10-12 .... MrAJFindlay(7) (S G Waugh) *midfield: wknd 4th: p.u 4 out* **33/1**	—
6-	**P**		**Platinum Point (IRE)**[374] 3126 7-10-12 .... PhilKinsella(7) (E W Tuer) *chsd ldrs tl wknd 4 out: p.u bef next* **50/1**	—

4m 13.1s (6.80) **Going Correction** +0.325s/f (Yiel)
WFA 4 from 5yo+ 11lb **15** Ran SP% **115.0**
Speed ratings: **96,94,93,93,88 85,82,78,70,67 63,60,—,—,—** CSF £64.94 TOTE £2.00: £1.20, £7.10, £1.20; EX 66.30.
Owner Mr & Mrs Duncan Davidson **Bred** Vincent Finn **Trained** Greystoke, Cumbria

FOCUS
A race lacking strength in depth, this was tricky to assess and has been rated through the modest fifth and sixth.

NOTEBOOK
Etched In Stone(IRE) did not enjoy the rub of the green on his hurdling debut in November and made amends on this drop in trip. Setting a decent gallop throughout, he showed a tendency to jump away to his right a couple of times in the back straight and briefly looked in trouble approaching the third last. The further he went the more he dug deep, and this headstrong sort can handle a return to a longer trip. *(op 6-5 tchd 5-4)*
Boulders Beach(IRE), much the bigger priced of the Smith pair, shaped well on this hurdling debut and seemed to appreciate this ground. The experience should do him good. *(op 40-1)*
Tous Chez(IRE), a stablemate of the runner-up, did not jump that fluently and was put in his place from the third last. This was slightly disappointing after his promising hurdles debut behind Percussionist. *(op 2-1)*
Lethem Air had shown nothing in two previous runs under Rules but is a former winning pointer.
Cloudmor(IRE) had been well beaten at big prices on all his previous starts and this was slightly more encouraging.
Baffling Secret(FR) is now qualified for handicaps and a step up in trip might help. *(op 66-1)*
Beardie's Dream(IRE) *Official explanation: jockey said horse hung right-handed from halfway*

3315 BBC RADIO NEWCASTLE H'CAP CHASE (23 fncs) 3m 6f

1:10 (1:11) (Class 4) (0-110,110) 5-Y-0+ **£3,903** (£1,146; £573; £286)

Form				RPR
-FP6	**1**		**Briar's Mist (IRE)**[26] 2819 9-10-5 **89** .... (b) RichardMcGrath (C Grant) *a cl up: led 16th: mde rest: kpt on wl fr last* **8/1**	102+
23-3	**2**	*¾*	**High Cotton (IRE)**[34] 2689 11-11-4 **102** .... GrahamLee (K G Reveley) *in tch: chsd wnr 16th: effrt 4 out: kpt on fr last* **13/2**[2]	115+
2500	**3**	*16*	**Wildfield Rufo (IRE)**[31] 2745 11-11-7 **110** .... (p) ThomasDreaper(5) (Mrs K Walton) *in tch: outpcd 15th: rallied 4 out: kpt on: no ch w first two* **12/1**	105
-42P	**4**	*2 ½*	**To The Future (IRE)**[24] 2863 10-10-0 **84** oh2 .... (p) AlanDempsey (A Parker) *cl up: blnd 14th: rdn bef 5 out: outpcd fr next* **15/2**[3]	79+
-6P6	**5**	*2*	**Falchion**[23] 2877 11-10-5 **92** .... (t) PeterBuchanan(3) (J R Bewley) *in tch: drvn after 17th: outpcd bef 4 out* **11/1**	85+
0P35	**6**	*25*	**Lazy But Lively (IRE)**[18] 2946 10-11-12 **110** .... DominicElsworth (R F Fisher) *hld up: stdy hdwy whn hmpd 16th: rdn after next: btn bef 4 out* **13/2**[2]	76
P-0P	**P**		**Historg (FR)**[14] 2993 11-10-12 **96** .... KeithMercer (Ferdy Murphy) *sn detached: t.o whn p.u 9th* **9/1**	—
P002	**F**		**Gimme Shelter (IRE)**[39] 2589 12-10-0 **89** .... MichaelMcAlister(5) (S J Marshall) *led: rdn 13th: jst hdd whn fell 16th* **13/2**[2]	—
0014	**P**		**Almire Du Lia (FR)**[23] 2877 8-11-2 **100** .... (v) TonyDobbin (Mrs S C Bradburne) *prom: reminders and lost pl 5th: t.o whn p.u 9th* **9/2**[1]	—
405P	**U**		**Ta Ta For Now**[44] 2495 9-9-12 **89** ow3 .... DavidDaSilva(7) (Mrs S C Bradburne) *hit and lost pl 2nd: in tch whn blnd and uns rdr 8th* **16/1**	—

8m 18.2s (-2.20) **Going Correction** +0.10s/f (Yiel) **10** Ran SP% **113.0**
Speed ratings: **106,105,101,100,100 93,—,—,—,—** CSF £57.83 CT £618.44 TOTE £8.80: £2.30, £1.80, £3.10; EX 40.90.
Owner Trevor Hemmings **Bred** Oliver Loughlin **Trained** Newton Bewley, Co Durham

FOCUS
A poor race which concerned only two in the home straight both of whom were well in on their best form.

NOTEBOOK
Briar's Mist(IRE) had shown little in three previous runs this term but a recent day's hunting had *freshened him up. Going best some way out, he stayed on too strongly for the runner-up. Official explanation: trainer said, regarding the improved form shown, gelding is inconsistent and got the run of the race today (op 12-1)*
High Cotton(IRE), back up in trip, was closing the gap on the winner up the run-in but was always being held. He has made the first four 22 times in a 28-race career but is still a maiden. *(op 6-1)*
Wildfield Rufo(IRE), with the cheekpieces back on, ran in snatches and plugged on for a pretty remote third place. He is still 5lb above his last winning mark. *(op 9-1)*
To The Future(IRE), wearing cheekpieces for the first time - he has worn a visor once - faded under pressure in the straight and remains without a win for three years. *(op 7-1)*
Falchion has dropped 20lb in the space of a year but remains out of sorts. *(op 12-1 tchd 10-1)*
Almire Du Lia(FR) was unhappy from an early stage and was pulled up before his stamina for this *longer trip could be tested. This was disappointing as Newcastle is his track. Official explanation: vet said gelding finished distressed (op 4-1)*

3316 PHOENIX SECURITY NOVICES' HURDLE (13 hdls) 3m

1:40 (1:42) (Class 4) 4-Y-0+ **£3,083** (£898; £449)

Form				RPR
0302	**1**		**Rathowen (IRE)**[35] 2678 7-11-7 97 .... GrahamLee (J I A Charlton) *cl up: led 7th: mde rest: drew clr bef 2 out* **8/1**[3]	117+
16P2	**2**	*18*	**Notaproblem (IRE)**[47] 2440 7-12-0 105 .... AlanDempsey (G A Harker) *hld up in tch: hdwy bef 4 out: chsd wnr appr next: sn rdn and one pce* **12/1**	104
-112	**3**	*9*	**King Of Confusion (IRE)**[14] 2956 7-11-9 121 .... ThomasDreaper(5) (Ferdy Murphy) *prom: rdn bef 3 out: sn btn* **8/13**[1]	95
1-3	**4**	*19*	**Arnold Layne (IRE)**[24] 2859 7-11-7 .... JimCrowley (R T Phillips) *nt fluent: chsd ldrs tl wknd fr 4 out* **9/2**[2]	69
5-P6	**5**	*9*	**Gay Kindersley (IRE)**[13] 3037 8-10-11 .... JamesReveley(10) (K G Reveley) *cl up tl wknd fr 8th* **40/1**	60
P0	**F**		**Bowes Cross**[21] 2923 6-11-7 .... KeithMercer (Ferdy Murphy) *bhd: fell after 7th* **100/1**	—
/22-	**P**		**Sports Express**[429] 2035 8-10-11 .... PeterBuchanan(3) (Miss Lucinda V Russell) *bhd: lost tch and p.u bef 7th* **16/1**	—
-F50	**P**		**Rowan Castle**[26] 2820 10-11-7 95 .... RichardMcGrath (Sir John Barlow Bt) *led to 7th: wknd next: t.o whn p.u bef 3 out* **100/1**	—

6m 20.0s (1.60) **Going Correction** +0.325s/f (Yiel) **8** Ran SP% **109.2**
Speed ratings: **110,104,101,94,91 —,—,—** CSF £81.18 TOTE £8.90: £1.80, £2.00, £1.10; EX 52.10.
Owner J I A Charlton **Bred** Patrick Roche **Trained** Stocksfield, Northumberland

FOCUS
This was run at a steady pace. A seemingly huge step up in form from the winner, who could be rated a bit higher, but the form is dubious with the favourite well below-par.

NOTEBOOK
Rathowen(IRE), runner-up over course and distance last time to According To John, who has won again since at Ayr, had 24lb to find with the favourite on official figures but that opponent was *below-par. Proven in testing conditions, he got off the mark with a very comfortable success. (op 15-2)*
Notaproblem(IRE) went after the winner early in the home straight but was soon left toiling. He stays well and this was a fair run under a big weight in the conditions.
King Of Confusion(IRE) was also third in this event last year but he has improved in the interim. This was very disappointing, as he had upwards of 8lb in hand on official figures, and something might have been amiss. *Official explanation: jockey said gelding ran flat (tchd 4-6)*
Arnold Layne(IRE) dropped away rather tamely at the head of the straight and might not have stayed, although as a son of Roselier stamina should not be a problem for him. *(tchd 4-1)*
Gay Kindersley(IRE) looks a very limited performer and the return to hurdles did not bring about any improvement. *(op 50-1)*
Bowes Cross unfortunately sustained an injury and fell just after landing over the seventh.

3317 PIMMS WINTER NOVICES' CHASE (13 fncs) 2m 110y

2:10 (2:10) (Class 3) 5-Y-0+ **£7,807** (£2,292; £1,146; £572)

Form				RPR
21/F	**1**		**Armaguedon (FR)**[18] 2943 8-11-2 .... TonyDobbin (L Lungo) *keen: mde most to 3 out: rallied and ev ch whn lft in ld last: sn hdd: kpt on to ld post* **9/4**[2]	116+
6201	**2**	*shd*	**Shares (IRE)**[18] 2943 6-10-12 111 .... DavidDaSilva(10) (P Monteith) *keen: hld up: hdwy to dispute ld 3 out: hit next: led run in: kpt on: hdd post* **12/1**	123+
3-13	**3**	*7*	**Ever Present (IRE)**[37] 2629 8-11-2 .... BrianHarding (N G Richards) *chsd ldrs tl rdn and outpcd fr 3 out* **15/8**[1]	108
2-34	**4**	*½*	**Aleron (IRE)**[30] 2764 8-11-2 .... RussGarritty (J J Quinn) *w ldr: led 3 out: blnd bdly and hdd last: nt rcvr* **7/2**[3]	115+
44U5	**5**	*dist*	**Ipledgeallegiance (USA)**[14] 2980 10-11-2 81 .... DavidO'Meara (Miss Tracy Waggott) *prom to 6th: sn outpcd* **40/1**	—
/FP6	**6**	*½*	**Jerom De Vindecy (FR)**[14] 2989 9-10-13 .... PeterBuchanan(3) (Miss Lucinda V Russell) *chsd ldrs to 1/2-way: sn wknd: btn whn nt fluent 5 out* **40/1**	—
2-P0	**7**	*4*	**Political Cruise**[18] 2944 8-10-9 .... GarethThomas(7) (R Nixon) *a bhd: no ch whn blnd 5 out* **100/1**	—
P505	**8**	*¾*	**Derainey (IRE)**[35] 2677 7-11-2 .... KennyJohnson (R Johnson) *sn wl bhd* **100/1**	—
1343	**U**		**Cyborg De Sou (FR)**[8] 3172 8-11-3 107 .... ThomasDreaper(5) (G A Harker) *hld up: hdwy 5 out: 5l down and styng on steadily whn blnd and uns rdr next* **8/1**	—

4m 23.4s (0.20) **Going Correction** +0.10s/f (Yiel) **9** Ran SP% **113.4**
Speed ratings: **103,102,99,99,— —,—,—,—** CSF £26.14 TOTE £3.50: £1.30, £2.30, £1.10; EX 22.60.
Owner Ashleybank Investments Limited **Bred** Olivier Tricot **Trained** Carrutherstown, D'fries & G'way

FOCUS
A fair novice chase which could be rated bit higher using the winner, third and fourth, all of whom could be rated 10lb higher on hurdle form.

NOTEBOOK

Armaguedon(FR), always up with the pace, just looked held halfway up the run-in but rallied to snatch the race on the post, the relative experience of the two riders involved perhaps the telling factor. *He fell on his recent chasing debut but jumped well here, if a shade extravagantly at times.* *(op 5-2 tchd 11-4)*

Shares(IRE), penalised for his chasing debut win, was again keen under restraint but steadily worked his way into the race. Just about in front when pecking at the second last, he rallied to go half a length up on the flat but was pipped on the line. *(op 14-1)*

Ever Present(IRE) made one or two minor jumping errors on this chasing debut. He found this too sharp and was outpaced by the leaders in the home straight, but did keep on up the run-in to grab third. *(op 9-4)*

Aleron(IRE), back down in trip, was headed between the last two fences but was coming back for more when a bad blunder at the last ended his chance. There should be a race for him. *(op 11-4)*

Cyborg De Sou(FR), the most experienced over fences in this field, was keeping on and by no means out of it when he paddled through the final ditch and unshipped his rider.

3318 NGI H'CAP HURDLE (11 hdls) 2m 4f
2:40 (2:41) (Class 3) (0-125,120) 4-Y-0+ **£5,204** (£1,528; £764; £381)

Form RPR

-410 **1** **Euro American (GER)**[21] 2925 6-11-2 **110** .... AlanDempsey 127+
(E W Tuer) *hld up: smooth hdwy to ld 2 out: wnt clr last: v easily* **11/2**[3]

/P-F **2** *4* **Fred's In The Know**[14] 2964 11-10-11 **108** .... AnthonyCoyle(3) 110+
(Miss Tracy Waggott) *hld up in tch: hdwy to ld 3 out: hdd next: no ch w wnr* **100/1**

-415 **3** *7* **Tynedale (IRE)**[54] 2264 7-11-7 **120** .... ThomasDreaper(5) 115+
(Mrs A Hamilton) *chsd ldrs: rdn 1/2-way: outpcd 4 out: kpt on fr 2 out: no ch w first two* **4/1**[2]

413/ **4** *1 1/2* **Big-And-Bold (IRE)**[1360] 4836 10-10-13 **107** .... (t) TonyDobbin 100
(N G Richards) *keen: led to 3 out: outpcd next* **2/1**[1]

1425 **5** *3 1/2* **Tandava (IRE)**[37] 2638 8-10-9 **110** .... DavidDaSilva(7) 100+
(Mrs S C Bradburne) *hld up: blnd and rdn 5th: hdwy 2 out: nvr nrr* **16/1**

-065 **6** *1 3/4* **Simply Mystic**[14] 2990 6-10-11 **105** .... GrahamLee 94+
(P D Niven) *hld up: rdn whn hit 4 out: sn n.d* **10/1**

-200 **7** *1/2* **Roobihoo (IRE)**[14] 2990 7-10-13 **107** .... RichardMcGrath 94
(C Grant) *chsd ldrs: outpcd 7th: n.d after* **12/1**

4U-1 **8** *6* **October Mist (IRE)**[43] 2519 12-10-11 **115** .... JamesReveley(10) 96
(K G Reveley) *chsd ldrs tl wknd fr 4 out* **7/1**

0110 **9** *4* **Longstone Lass**[48] 2417 6-9-12 **99** .... MissCMetcalfe(7) 76
(Miss Tracy Waggott) *hld up: hdwy to join ldrs 1/2-way: wknd 3 out* **14/1**

144F **10** *3/4* **Celtic Blaze (IRE)**[14] 2982 7-10-6 **100** .... (t) AnthonyRoss 76
(B S Rothwell) *a bhd* **50/1**

5m 24.8s (9.00) **Going Correction** +0.325s/f (Yiel) **10** Ran SP% **113.5**
Speed ratings: **95,93,90,90,88 87,87,85,83,83** CSF £282.45 CT £2405.67 TOTE £6.00: £1.90, £15.80, £2.20; EX 436.70.
Owner Shore Property **Bred** Euro-American Bet Verm Gmbh **Trained** Great Smeaton, N Yorks

FOCUS

A moderate winning time for the class. The winner is rated value for 15l, although the form is probably not that solid.

NOTEBOOK

Euro American(GER) ◆ was held from this mark last time, but that was on fast ground and he is much more at home in testing conditions. Quickening right away and value for a much greater margin of victory, he will always be of interest when the mud is flying and can follow up if turned out under a penalty. *(op 5-1)*

Fred's In The Know has rarely completed the course in recent outings and fell on Boxing Day on his first start since May 2004. This was much better, but after travelling well for a long way he was put in his place by the easy winner.

Tynedale(IRE) put in a fair effort from a career-high mark but really needs further than this. *(op 5-1)*

Big-And-Bold(IRE), who beat Harbour Pilot in the Group One Powers Gold Cup Novices' Chase at Fairyhouse in April 2002, has been sidelined since later that year with niggling problems. Having his first run for this yard, having previously been trained by Ger Lyons, he made a satisfactory return to action but his Cheltenham Gold Cup entry does look ambitious. *(op 7-4)*

Tandava(IRE), on his handicap debut, made a blunder at the fifth and could never really get into it the race afterwards. He was probably unsuited by this drop in trip. *(op 14-1)*

Simply Mystic, who has shown a preference for better ground, was struggling after a mistake at the last flight in the back straight. *(op 9-1)*

October Mist(IRE) *Official explanation: trainer said gelding pulled up stiff behind (op 9-1 tchd 10-1)*

Longstone Lass *Official explanation: jockey said mare hung left-handed throughout (op 16-1)*

3319 SALTWELL SIGNS MAIDEN NATIONAL HUNT FLAT RACE (CONDITIONAL JOCKEYS' AND AMATEUR RIDERS' RACE) 2m
3:10 (3:11) (Class 6) 5-6-Y-0 **£1,713** (£499; £249)

Form RPR

1 **Spitfire Sortie (IRE)** 5-11-1 .... MrTGreenall(3) 110+
(M W Easterby) *hld up midfield: smooth hdwy to ld over 3f out: drew clr fr 2f out* **11/2**[3]

54 **2** *8* **Nevertika (FR)**[51] 2340 5-11-4 .... KeithMercer 97
(Mrs K Walton) *hld up midfield: hdwy and ev ch over 2f out: kpt on: no ch w wnr* **11/8**[1]

3 *1 1/4* **Hush Tiger** 5-10-11 .... MrMEllwood(7) 96
(R Nixon) *bhd tl kpt on fr 2f out: nrst fin* **66/1**

0 **4** *8* **More Likely**[47] 2446 5-10-6 .... DougieCostello(5) 81
(Mrs A F Tullie) *chsd ldrs: lost pl 1/2-way: kpt on fr 2f out: nrst fin* **25/1**

5 *3/4* **Unfair Dismissal (IRE)** 5-10-11 .... MrGTumelty(7) 87
(M D Hammond) *chsd ldrs tl rdn and wknd over 2f out* **16/1**

4 **6** *12* **Aldea (FR)**[25] 2844 5-10-8 .... MichaelO'Connell(10) 75
(Mrs S J Smith) *chsd ldrs: outpcd over 3f out: n.d after* **7/2**[2]

7 *7* **Tuatara Bay (IRE)** 6-10-11 .... MrBMcHugh(7) 68
(R A Fahey) *hld up: hdwy to chse ldrs 1/2-way: rdn and wknd over 2f out* **9/1**

8 *1* **High Five**[260] 6-10-11 .... MrAJFindlay(7) 67
(S G Waugh) *led to over 4f out: wknd over 3f out* **28/1**

0-5 **9** *5* **Sticky End**[54] 2268 5-10-11 .... BenOrde-Powlett(7) 62
(J B Walton) *prom: led over 4f to over 3f out: wknd* **16/1**

10 *dist* **Tangoroch (FR)** 5-11-1 .... GaryBerridge(3) —
(J P L Ewart) *bhd: reminders 1/2-way: sn lost tch* **22/1**

00- **11** *12* **Paper Classic**[305] 4276 6-10-4 .... EwanWhillans(7) —
(A C Whillans) *towards rr: strugging fr 7f out: t.o* **100/1**

4m 9.90s (-2.70) **Going Correction** +0.325s/f (Yiel) **11** Ran SP% **115.6**
Speed ratings: **101,97,96,92,92 86,82,82,79,—** — CSF £12.60 TOTE £6.00: £2.10, £1.10, £14.90; EX 16.50.
Owner M P Burke **Bred** M P B Bloodstock Ltd **Trained** Sheriff Hutton, N Yorks

FOCUS

Not much pace on, and it turned into a sprint. Spitfire Sortie has been rated value for further and is an above-average bumper winner. The race has been rated around the second and fourth.

NOTEBOOK

Spitfire Sortie(IRE), out of a French Group Three winner, is a half-brother to amongst others Prix de Diane runner-up Mousse Glacee and last season's progressive handicapper Sound Breeze. He has reportedly been very hard to train, but ran out an impressive winner on this debut, drawing right away in the last quarter-mile, and can win again if remaining sound. *(op 7-2)*

Nevertika(FR), who has put in two fair efforts at Haydock, ran his race again but the winner was far too good. *(op 15-8)*

Hush Tiger, whose dam won a maiden hurdle for the Nixon yard, made a promising debut and was not given too hard a time. *(op 33-1)*

More Likely showed more than she had on her debut against her own sex in November. *(op 50-1)*

Unfair Dismissal(IRE), who made a satisfactory debut, is out of a grand-daughter of top-class two-mile chaser Anaglogs Daughter. *(tchd 20-1)*

Aldea(FR) was disappointing, and the softer ground might have been to blame. *(tchd 10-3)*

3320 WEATHERBYS INSURANCE H'CAP CHASE (13 fncs) 2m 110y
3:40 (3:40) (Class 5) (0-90,90) 5-Y-0+ **£2,740** (£798; £399)

Form RPR

5345 **1** **Bob's Buster**[31] 2754 10-11-12 **90** .... KennyJohnson 99+
(R Johnson) *racd wd: hld up: smooth hdwy to ld 2 out: rdn out* **5/1**[2]

030 **2** *3* **Glenfarclas Boy (IRE)**[44] 2495 10-11-7 **88** .... (p) PeterBuchanan(3) 92+
(Miss Lucinda V Russell) *chsd ldrs: mstke and lost pl 4th: rallied 3 out: chsd wnr run in: kpt on* **5/1**[2]

30P- **3** *1 1/2* **Gaucho**[279] 4734 9-10-7 **78** .... (p) MissTJackson(7) 81+
(Miss T Jackson) *chsd ldrs: led 4 out to 2 out: one pce last* **40/1**

533U **4** *1 3/4* **Ideal Du Bois Beury (FR)**[3] 3270 10-10-3 **77** .... DavidDaSilva(10) 79+
(P Monteith) *bhd tl kpt on fr 2 out: n.d* **9/2**[1]

6506 **5** *4* **Pornic (FR)**[22] 2900 12-10-2 **71** .... (b[1]) ThomasDreaper(5) 67
(A Crook) *trckd ldrs tl outpcd fr 3 out* **14/1**

030U **6** *nk* **Named At Dinner**[18] 2943 5-10-6 **84** .... (v) DougieCostello(5) 70
(Miss Lucinda V Russell) *prom: outpcd bef 4 out: n.d after* **11/1**

35 **7** *6* **Arctic Cherry (IRE)**[34] 2692 8-11-1 **79** .... RichardMcGrath 70+
(R Ford) *led 3rd to 4 out: mstke next and sn btn* **9/2**[1]

PP52 **8** *dist* **Mikasa (IRE)**[18] 2945 6-11-1 **79** .... KeithMercer —
(R F Fisher) *nt fluent: hld up: rdn whn mstke 5 out: nvr on terms* **5/1**[2]

54PP **P** **Lion Guest (IRE)**[36] 2655 9-10-2 **73** .... TomMessenger(7) —
(Mrs S C Bradburne) *led to 3rd: chsd ldrs tl wknd 8th: p.u bef 4 out* **10/1**[3]

4m 29.3s (6.10) **Going Correction** +0.10s/f (Yiel)
WFA 5 from 6yo+ 8lb **9** Ran SP% **112.9**
Speed ratings: **89,87,86,86,84 84,81,—,—** CSF £30.03 CT £883.61 TOTE £4.40: £1.70, £2.30, £8.00; EX 27.40 Place 6 £27.42, Place 5 £24.03.
Owner Mrs Geraldine Jones **Bred** Miss H K Monteith **Trained** Newburn, Tyne & Wear

FOCUS

A slow winning time for the grade, almost six seconds slower than the novice chase. Run in gloomy conditions, this was a poor race, contested by some serial losers. The winner was value for six lengths and to the level of his best form of the last 18 months.

NOTEBOOK

Bob's Buster, who was without the tongue tie and cheekpieces he wore last time, took it up going comfortably at the second last and was in control when not fluent over the final fence. He needs things to fall right ansd this was his first win for two years. *(tchd 11-2)*

Glenfarclas Boy(IRE) extended his losing run to 20, but he acts on this type of ground and this was a better effort. *(op 9-2)*

Gaucho, a long-standing maiden under Rules, ran well on this first start since April and was only run out of second place on the Flat.

Ideal Du Bois Beury(FR) passed beaten rivals from the second last but was never a factor. He is without a win in 35 starts. *(op 5-1 tchd 4-1)*

Arctic Cherry(IRE) was down in trip, but after making the running as usual he still failed to get home. He is a very moderate performer. *(op 4-1)*

T/Plt: £21.90 to a £1 stake. Pool: £33,906.95. 1,129.00 winning tickets. T/Qpdt: £8.10 to a £1 stake. Pool: £3,098.00. 280.20 winning tickets. RY

3125 TAUNTON (R-H)
Monday, January 9

OFFICIAL GOING: Good (good to soft in places)

Wind: Virtually nil

3321 NEW YEAR CONDITIONAL JOCKEYS' (S) H'CAP HURDLE (10 hdls) 2m 3f 110y
12:50 (12:51) (Class 5) (0-90,90) 4-7-Y-0 **£2,192** (£639; £319)

Form RPR

6F4 **1** **Methodical**[19] 2935 4-10-6 **83** .... JohnLevins 88+
(B G Powell) *hld up towards rr: hdwy 7th: led after 3 out: sn clr: v easily* **7/1**[3]

2 *12* **Gotontheluckyone (IRE)**[143] 1256 6-10-8 **80** .... KeiranBurke(8) 80
(P R Rodford) *w ldr: led 4th tl after 3 out: kpt on but no ch w wnr fr next* **20/1**

4023 **3** *3 1/2* **Barranco (IRE)**[9] 3137 5-11-4 **88** .... (b) EamonDehdashti(6) 85+
(G L Moore) *in tch: reminders after 5th: rdn appr 3 out: kpt on same pce* **7/2**[1]

0000 **4** *1 3/4* **Garhoud**[7] 3211 4-9-9 **77** oh1 .... (p) RichardGordon(5) 58
(Miss K M George) *towards rr: styd on past btn horses fr 2 out: nvr trbld ldrs* **9/1**

0P6 **5** *2 1/2* **Zilla (FR)**[32] 2728 5-10-0 **64** oh4 .... StephenCraine 56
(Miss Lucy Bridges) *in tch: rdn appr 3 out: sn wknd* **25/1**

5055 **6** *6* **Tizi Ouzou (IRE)**[25] 2845 5-11-3 **84** .... (p) TomMalone(3) 70
(M C Pipe) *in tch: jnd ldr 4th: rdn appr 3 out: sn btn* **7/2**[1]

0065 **7** *3* **Bebe Factual (GER)**[32] 2728 5-10-0 **67** .... (t) ShaneWalsh(3) 50
(J D Frost) *in tch: rdn after 6th: wknd after 3 out* **12/1**

P-05 **8** *26* **Kiwi Riverman**[10] 3125 6-9-9 **65** ow1 .... DarylJacob(6) 22
(D P Keane) *a towards rr* **5/1**[2]

0U0 **9** *28* **Miss Defying**[26] 2824 4-9-9 **77** oh3 .... (v[1]) JohnKington(5) —
(R Curtis) *mid div tl 5th: sn wl bhd* **66/1**

4000 **P** **Moorlands Milly**[26] 2822 5-11-1 **79** .... WilliamKennedy —
(D Burchell) *a towards rr: t.o and p.u bef 2 out* **20/1**

5040 **P** **Duke's View (IRE)**[153] 1188 5-10-7 **74** .... LiamHeard(3) —
(D C Turner) *stmbld 4th: a in rr: t.o and p.u bef 7th* **33/1**

-040 **F** **Griffin's Legacy**[217] 665 7-11-9 **90** .... JamesWhite(3) —
(N G Ayliffe) *mid div: mstke 3rd: sn in rr: fell 6th* **25/1**

36-P **P** **Kynance Cove**[43] 2517 7-9-11 **64** .... RichardSpate(3) —
(C P Morlock) *led tl 4th: chsd ldrs: wknd 3 out: p.u bef 2 out* **25/1**

00-P **P** **Tilla**[20] 2932 6-10-6 **75** .... (b[1]) AndrewGlassonbury(5) —
(Mrs A J Hamilton-Fairley) *sn trcking ldrs: rdn and wknd 3 out: p.u bef 2 out* **25/1**

4m 51.1s (5.10) **Going Correction** +0.375s/f (Yiel)
WFA 4 from 5yo+ 11lb **14** Ran SP% **120.6**
Speed ratings: **104,99,97,97,96 93,92,82,70,— —,—,—,—** CSF £136.69 CT £579.35 TOTE £8.50: £2.60, £7.20, £2.30; EX 191.90.There was no bid for the winner.

Owner Woodhaven Racing Syndicate **Bred** The Woodhaven Stud **Trained** Morestead, Hants

FOCUS

A very moderate affair, run at a fair gallop, and the winner came home as she pleased. She is rated value for much more than the winning margin and the form appears sound with the placed horses close to their marks.

NOTEBOOK

Methodical scored with any amount in hand on her handicap bow. She had been a frustrating maiden on the Flat when with the Ian Wood stable, and her stamina for hurdling was far from assured, but this decisive career-first success proves she stays the trip very well. While she may have beaten little, and now faces a hike in the weights, she enjoyed racing off the decent pace and will be high on confidence for her next assignment. *(op 6-1 tchd 11-2)*

Gotontheluckyone(IRE), making his debut for new connections after a 143-days absence, showed arguably his best form to date and finished a clear second-best. He is entitled to improve on this and has found his level now.

Barranco(IRE) failed to improve for this drop back in class and was disappointing as he never seriously threatened to hit the front. He is not one to rely on, but he does have the ability to win at this level, and may prefer reverting to a stiffer test in the future. *(op 9-2 tchd 5-1)*

Garhoud was doing his best work at the finish and improved on his latest dismal effort over further. *(op 11-1 tchd 12-1)*

Tizi Ouzou(IRE), with cheekpieces replacing a visor this time, ran her usual race and helps set the level of this form. *(op 3-1)*

Kiwi Riverman is somewhat of an enigma and looks in need of the sharpest possible test in order to have better claims of getting home over timber. *(op 11-2 tchd 13-2)*

3322 SOUTHWESTRACING.COM MARES' ONLY NOVICES' HURDLE (10 hdls) 2m 3f 110y

1:20 (1:20) (Class 4) 4-Y-0+ **£3,903** (£1,146; £573; £286)

Form				RPR
-521	1		**Harringay**[19] [2937] 6-11-9 109 .... (t) TimmyMurphy (Miss H C Knight) *trckd ldrs: drvn along to hold position after 6th: j.lft 3 out : stmbld on bnd appr 2 out: led sn after last: rdn out* **11/8**[1]	111+
51-5	2	½	**Makeabreak (IRE)**[69] [1974] 7-11-2 .... NoelFehily (C J Mann) *mid div: hdwy 6th: led 2 out: sn rdn: hdd sn after last: kpt on but no ex cl home* **5/1**[3]	99
6	3	6	**Stocking Island**[26] [2826] 5-11-2 .... APMcCoy (C R Egerton) *t.k.h: settled in rr: hdwy 7th: chal appr 2 out: sn rdn: kpt on same pce* **9/2**[2]	93
05	4	2	**Anna Panna**[27] [2804] 5-11-2 .... AndrewThornton (R H Alner) *led: blnd 5th: rdn and hdd 2 out: wknd run-in* **14/1**	93+
214	5	6	**Fountain Crumble**[14] [2997] 5-11-2 .... ChristianWilliams (P F Nicholls) *mid div: tk clsr order 6th: rdn and effrt after 3 out: one pced* **6/1**	85
4	6	14	**Quotable**[42] [2558] 5-11-2 .... LeightonAspell (O Sherwood) *hld up towards rr: mstke 5th: hdwy 7th: wknd after 3 out* **10/1**	71
1-00	7	13	**Post It**[14] [2997] 5-11-2 .... TomScudamore (R J Hodges) *trckd ldr: rdn and wknd 3 out* **100/1**	58
063-	8	5	**Lurid Affair (IRE)**[312] [4138] 5-10-9 .... MissLGardner[(7)] (Mrs S Gardner) *prom tl 6th: sn bhd* **33/1**	53
	9	11	**Venetian Romance (IRE)**[51] 5-11-2 .... MarkBradburne (D J S Ffrench Davis) *chsd ldrs tl wknd 7th* **100/1**	42
0-0	10	2	**Miss Sirius**[259] [27] 6-10-9 .... MrJNewbold[(7)] (John R Upson) *towards rr: lost tch fr 6th* **100/1**	40
-500	11	dist	**Mialyssa**[14] [2997] 6-10-11 .... JamesDiment[(5)] (M R Bosley) *chsd ldrs: mstke 3rd: wknd after 6th* **100/1**	—
40/	12	17	**Irenie**[1002] 11-11-2 .... SeanCurran (N R Mitchell) *a bhd* **100/1**	—
	P		**Cultured**[20] 5-11-2 .... AndrewTinkler (Mrs A J Bowlby) *a towards rr: t.o and p.u bef 2 out* **50/1**	—

4m 53.2s (7.20) **Going Correction** +0.375s/f (Yiel) **13** Ran SP% **116.8**

Speed ratings: **100,99,97,96,94 88,83,81,77,76** —,—,— CSF £8.18 TOTE £2.30: £1.10, £1.70, £2.10; EX 11.10.

Owner Mrs R Vaughan **Bred** Mrs R I Vaughan **Trained** West Lockinge, Oxon

FOCUS

A modest winning time to this mares' event, 2.1 seconds slower than the seller, but the first two came clear on the run-in. The third and fourth set the level for the form.

NOTEBOOK

Harringay, finally off the mark at Ludlow last time, showed a decent attitude under pressure to repel the runner-up and score all-out under her penalty. She needed all of her rider's urgings to get to the front in the straight, but this track would have been plenty sharp enough for her, and she is probably slightly better than the bare form suggests. The recent application of a tongue-tie has clearly worked the oracle, and while she will find life tougher under a double penalty in the future, the mares' division lacks strength at present, and she is reportedly to be aimed at the EBF Mares Only Final at Newbury in March. *(op 7-4)*

Makeabreak(IRE) went down with all guns blazing and improved on the level of her recent hurdling debut for connections. She got this longer trip well enough and, considering she was nicely clear of the rest, she should be placed to go one better in this sphere before long.

Stocking Island, who caught the eye of the stewards at Newbury on her debut last time when staying on in a better contest, looked a big player when scything through rivals to join the leaders turning for home, yet found just the one pace when it really mattered over this longer trip. She certainly looks like proving better in this sphere than she was on the Flat, and has a similar event well within her compass, but may prove best when eligible for handicaps. *(op 5-1)*

Anna Panna turned in a brave effort from the front and only tired out of things approaching the final flight. She improved for this stiffer test and now has the option of handicaps.

Fountain Crumble failed to really improve for this step-up in distance, but would have found this ground plenty soft enough. *(op 5-1)*

3323 CORFE NOVICES' H'CAP CHASE (14 fncs) 2m 3f

1:50 (1:50) (Class 3) (0-130,128) 5-Y-0+ **£6,665** (£2,069; £1,114)

Form				RPR
-1P2	1		**Royal Hector (GER)**[9] [3150] 7-11-12 128 .... APMcCoy (Jonjo O'Neill) *hld up in 3rd: hdwy after 4 out: led briefly appr 2 out: 2nd and hld whn lft clr last* **7/1**[3]	130+
305-	2	6	**Big Bone (FR)**[292] [4518] 6-10-10 112 .... PaddyBrennan (P J Hobbs) *led: sn clr: rdn appr 3 out: hdd appr 2 out: sn no ex: lft 2nd at the last* **10/1**	107+
30-2	3	26	**Pardishar (IRE)**[14] [2959] 8-11-4 120 .... JamieMoore (G L Moore) *hld up: drvn along fr 8th: wknd after 4 out: lft poor 3rd at the last* **17/2**	89
3142	U		**Nanga Parbat (FR)**[14] [2969] 5-10-5 117 .... (t) ChristianWilliams (P F Nicholls) *blnd and uns rdr 2nd* **3/1**[1]	—
-U41	U		**Balladeer (IRE)**[34] [2682] 8-10-13 115 .... AndrewThornton (Mrs T J Hill) *blnd bdly and uns rdr 2nd* **7/1**[3]	—
/1-P	F		**Grey Brother**[7] [3215] 8-10-13 115 .... RichardJohnson (P J Hobbs) *hld up: j.lft 3rd: mstke 9th: wknd after 4 out: fell next* **5/1**[2]	—
-U12	F		**Direct Flight (IRE)**[32] [2734] 8-11-1 120 .... WilliamKennedy[(3)] (Noel T Chance) *hld up in 4th: hit 6th: hdwy after 3 out: led 2 out: 6l clr whn fell last* **5/1**[2]	130+
1121	U		**Bishop's Bridge (IRE)**[14] [2963] 8-11-2 118 .... JasonMaguire (Andrew Turnell) *chsd ldr: mstke 9th: rdn after 4 out: chalng for 3rd whn stmbld bdly and uns rdr last* **9/1**	109

4m 56.2s (3.40) **Going Correction** +0.375s/f (Yiel)

WFA 5 from 6yo+ 8lb **8** Ran SP% **113.0**

Speed ratings: **107,104,93,**—,— —,—,— CSF £68.49 CT £599.90 TOTE £5.80: £2.30, £2.30, £3.10; EX 111.60.

Owner Three Counties Racing 2 **Bred** Gestut Katharinenhof **Trained** Cheltenham, Gloucs

FOCUS

An accident-packed handicap, run at a sound pace thanks to the front-running Big Bone, that saw changing fortunes in the home straight. The winner sets the standard and the last-fence faller is rated an eight-length winner.

NOTEBOOK

Royal Hector(GER) was held by Direct Flight prior to that rival departing at the last fence, and who has to rate a very fortunate winner. This was his handicap debut over fences, and while he may be better off reverting to two miles in the future, he could struggle if the Handicapper takes this form literally. *(op 5-1 tchd 15-2)*

Big Bone(FR), making his chase debut after a 292-day break, showed promise for the future with a creditable effort from the front, and impressed with his jumping. He is obviously entitled to improve for this experience and will no doubt prove better in this sphere than he was over timber. *(op 18-1 tchd 20-1)*

Pardishar(IRE) did not look to enjoy the switch to more patient tactics and disappointed. *(op 9-1)*

Balladeer(IRE), raised 10lb for winning at Fontwell previously, gave Thornton little chance of staying aboard at the second fence. *(tchd 11-2)*

Grey Brother, pulled up early on when hampered at Exeter last time, was careful over his jumps prior to falling and has it all to prove as a chaser now. *(tchd 11-2)*

Bishop's Bridge(IRE) was running a respectable race prior to unseating, but appears to be in the Handicapper's grip on this evidence. *(tchd 11-2)*

Direct Flight(IRE), reverting from hurdles, looked to have the race in the bag prior to getting in too low at the final fence and agonisingly coming to grief. If his confidence is none too badly dented by this, he is clearly capable of making amends from his current mark. *(tchd 11-2)*

Nanga Parbat(FR) was well backed to make a winning chase debut, but unseated too early to tell how he would have fared. *(tchd 11-2)*

3324 STAPLE FITZPAINE INTRODUCTORY NOVICES' HURDLE (9 hdls) 2m 1f

2:20 (2:20) (Class 2) 4-Y-0+ **£13,012** (£3,820; £1,910; £954)

Form				RPR
1	1		**Kalmini (USA)**[51] [2345] 4-10-5 .... JamieGoldstein (Miss Sheena West) *prom: led 2nd tl next: w ldr: led after 3 out: rdn and hdd after 2 out: r.o wl to ld fnl 100yds: rdn out* **4/1**[3]	105+
	2	1	**Opera Mundi (FR)**[79] 4-10-7 .... ChristianWilliams (P F Nicholls) *trckd ldr: led 3rd tl after 3 out: rdn to regain ld after 2 out: no ex whn hdd fnl 100yds* **11/4**[2]	105
	3	5	**Tarlac (GER)**[135] 5-11-5 .... APMcCoy (N J Henderson) *t.k.h: hld up in tch: trckd ldrs on bit after 3 out: rdn and ev ch appr last: kpt on same pce* **5/2**[1]	114+
6	4	2½	**Shannon Springs (IRE)**[30] [2756] 4-10-7 .... JasonMaguire (Andrew Turnell) *hld up: hdwy after 6th: trckd ldrs appr 2 out: sn rdn: kpt on same pce* **15/2**	97
	5	3½	**Sakenos (POL)**[456] 6-11-5 .... RichardJohnson (P J Hobbs) *led tl 2nd: trckd ldrs: rdn and effrt appr 2 out: kpt on same pce* **20/1**	106
3	6	1½	**Legally Fast (USA)**[76] [1873] 4-10-7 .... RJGreene (S C Burrough) *in tch: rdn after 6th: one pced fr next* **25/1**	92
6	7	22	**Smokincanon**[28] [2797] 4-10-7 .... RichardGordon (W G M Turner) *hld up: hdwy 6th: blnd 3 out: sn wknd* **250/1**	70
P	8	2½	**Harry May**[28] [2797] 4-10-7 .... JoeTizzard (C L Tizzard) *t.k.h: hld up: hdwy 6th: wknd after 3 out* **125/1**	68
	9	10	**Barjou (NZ)**[379] 5-11-5 .... RobertThornton (A King) *trckd ldrs: pckd 6th: sn rdn: wknd after 3 out* **9/2**	70
P-	10	24	**Primeshade Promise**[144] [2288] 5-10-12 .... OllieMcPhail (D Burchell) *t.k.h: hld up: lost tch fr 3 out* **200/1**	39

4m 16.9s (8.10) **Going Correction** +0.375s/f (Yiel)

WFA 4 from 5yo+ 11lb **10** Ran SP% **115.5**

Speed ratings: **95,94,92,91,89 88,78,77,72,61** CSF £15.31 TOTE £4.00: £2.00, £1.40, £1.30; EX 17.10.

Owner W R B Racing 58 (wrbracing.com) **Bred** Darley **Trained** Falmer, E Sussex

FOCUS

This novices' event is often won by a decent future prospect - Penzance made a winning debut in this last term en-route to landing the Triumph Hurdle - and this year's renewal looked a decent heat. It was run at an average pace and saw the first two pull clear on the run-in. The fourth and sixth are the best guides to the form.

NOTEBOOK

Kalmini(USA), a facile winner on debut at Huntingdon in November, duly followed-up with a tenacious display under her penalty and looked better the further she went. There was a lot to like about the manner in which she knuckled down to her task and hinted that she would prefer the return to a faster surface in the future. She will most likely get quicker ground at the Cheltenham Festival - where the Triumph Hurdle remains very much her target - and that stiffer course is likely to suit her better than the sharp track she encountered this time. While she still has to prove herself in Graded company, further improvement cannot be ruled out, and she is likely to have a crack at the Finesse Hurdle at Cheltenham later this month in her quest for the hat-trick. *(op 7-2 tchd 3-1)*

Opera Mundi(FR) ♦, runner-up on his sole outing over hurdles in France, created a very favourable impression and finished a clear second-best. He has plenty of scope, jumped neatly throughout, and should have no trouble in getting off the mark when racing on a suitably stiffer track. *(op 7-2 tchd 4-1)*

Tarlac(GER) ♦, who won three of his nine outings on the Flat in Germany, including a Group Three over ten furlongs, ran freely on this British and hurdling bow and ultimately paid for that when it mattered from two out. He will be seen to much better effect when racing off a stronger pace and looks a nice prospect for his leading connections. *(op 13-8)*

Shannon Springs(IRE), sixth in Graded company on his hurdling bow last time, did not look overly suited by this sharper track and would have ideally preferred a stronger pace. He is capable of better, and it will be interesting to see how the Handicapper reacts after his next outing, as he could be an interesting sort for the Juvenile Handicap at Cheltenham in March. *(op 8-1)*

Sakenos(POL), who boasted a Listed event among his seven victories on the Flat in Poland, looked in need of the experience and can improve on this. *(tchd 22-1)*

Barjou(NZ), a dual winner on the Flat in New Zealand, but he dropped away tamely from halfway after a couple of deliberate jumps. He is presumably thought capable of a deal better than this as he met plenty of support in the betting ring. *(op 10-1 tchd 11-1)*

3325 COMPARE PRICES AT GG-ODDS.COM H'CAP HURDLE (12 hdls) 3m 110y

2:50 (2:50) (Class 4) (0-105,105) 4-Y-0+ **£3,578** (£1,050; £525; £262)

Form				RPR
5-2P	**1**		**Squantum (IRE)**[219] 630 9-10-8 **87** .... JasonMaguire	89+
			(Miss Joanne Priest) *mid div: hdwy 7th: rdn to chse ldrs after 3 out: styd on strly u.p to ld cl home* **33/1**
3333	**2**	*1*	**Welsh Dane**[43] 2517 6-10-6 **85** ....(p) WayneHutchinson	85
			(M Sheppard) *w ldr: led 5th: rdn after 3 out: narrow advantage last: kpt on but no ex whn hdd cl home* **6/1**[2]
246	**3**	*½*	**Amazing Valour (IRE)**[14] 2994 4-10-10 **103** ....(b) APMcCoy	89
			(P Bowen) *prom tl 7th: sn drvn along in tch: styd on again after 3 out: ev ch last: swtchd rt run-in: kpt on cl home* **7/1**[3]
0F-0	**4**	*13*	**Emphatic (IRE)**[51] 2341 11-11-2 **100** ....(b) StephenCraine[(5)]	87
			(J G Portman) *led tl after 5th: outpcd after 8th: styd on again after 3 out: wnt 4th run-in* **20/1**
-154	**5**	*nk*	**Azzemour (FR)**[176] 1026 7-11-1 **101** ....(t) LiamHeard[(7)]	87
			(P F Nicholls) *hld up towards rr: hdwy after 7th: rdn to chse ldrs after 3 out: wknd run-in* **7/1**[3]
463P	**6**	*2*	**Noble Calling (FR)**[32] 2731 9-11-12 **105** .... TomScudamore	89
			(R J Hodges) *in tch tl outpcd after 8th: styd on again fr 3 out* **20/1**
0451	**7**	*7*	**Penny's Crown**[10] 3125 7-10-6 **90** .... EamonDehdashti[(5)]	67
			(G A Ham) *mid div: rdn appr 3 out: one pced after* **14/1**
PP0	**8**	*dist*	**Koln Stars (IRE)**[26] 2822 8-11-2 **95** .... JosephByrne	—
			(Jennie Candlish) *in tch tl wknd after 3 out* **66/1**
5FP	**9**	*3 ½*	**Case Equal (IRE)**[7] 3211 6-10-0 **86** .... KeiranBurke[(7)]	—
			(N J Hawke) *a bhd* **66/1**
0P	**10**	*½*	**Open Range (IRE)**[46] 2466 6-11-12 **105** .... AlanO'Keeffe	—
			(Jennie Candlish) *a bhd: blnd 2 out* **50/1**
0/	**P**		**Old Splendour (IRE)**[26] 2831 8-9-11 **79** oh1 .... TomMalone[(3)]	—
			(D J Ryan, Ire) *in tch tl 8th: sn wknd: t.o and p.u bef 2 out* **25/1**
P30U	**P**		**A Monk Swimming (IRE)**[19] 2940 5-10-3 **82** ....(t) JamieGoldstein	—
			(Miss J S Davis) *a bhd: lost tch 7th: t.o and p.u bef 3 out* **100/1**
5001	**P**		**Sandmartin (IRE)**[7] 3211 6-10-13 **92** 7ex........(b) RichardJohnson	74+
			(P J Hobbs) *in tch: trckd ldrs 7th: nt fluent next: jnd ldr and hit 3 out: rdn and wknd qckly appr 2 out: p.u run-in* **1/1**[1]

6m 9.25s (0.65) **Going Correction** +0.375s/f (Yiel)
WFA 4 from 5yo+ 13lb **13** Ran SP% **118.2**
Speed ratings: **103,102,102,98,98 97,95,—,—,— —,—,—** CSF £208.65 CT £1574.98 TOTE £34.70: £6.60, £1.10, £2.10; EX 233.50.

Owner The Leppington Partnership **Bred** David Fenton **Trained** Stourport, Worcs
■ Joanne Priest's first training success under Rules.

FOCUS
A modest handicap, run at a fair pace, which saw the first three come clear. The form is very ordinary, rated around the placed horses.

NOTEBOOK
Squantum(IRE), having his first outing for 219 days, did enough to get his head in front under pressure on the run-in and record a first success since joining connections from Ireland. This easier ground was much to his liking, as was the trip, and he could have more to offer now he has resumed winning ways. It would also come as little surprise to see him back over fences soon and, considering he was successful on his only previous outing over the bigger obstacles in Ireland, he could be well treated in that sphere off a mark of 90. *(op 40-1)*
Welsh Dane fared the best of those to force the early gallop and was only just denied. He is a very consistent performer, but never one to rely on for win-only purposes.
Amazing Valour(IRE) was staying on again at the finish under a typically strong ride from McCoy. He is a very tricky ride, and while this was an improved effort over the longer trip, he has been disappointing since joining current connections. *(op 8-1)*
Emphatic(IRE) got outpaced before keeping on again in the straight and looks in need of further respite from the Handicapper *(op 18-1)*
Azzemour(FR) appeared a threat turning for home, but failed to sustain his effort when push came to shove. He may improve for the outing and probably wants faster ground. *(op 13-2)*
Sandmartin(IRE), a clear-cut winner at Exeter on his handicap bow a week previously, stopped very quickly at the top of the straight and was most disappointing under his penalty. He was *eventually pulled up as though something was amiss. Official explanation: jockey said gelding felt wrong behind* *(op 6-5 tchd 5-4 in places)*

3326 ORCHARD RESTAURANT H'CAP CHASE (17 fncs) 2m 7f 110y

3:20 (3:20) (Class 4) (0-115,114) 5-Y-0+ **£5,530** (£1,623; £811; £405)

Form				RPR
161P	**1**		**Glacial Delight (IRE)**[43] 2529 7-11-11 **113** .... MarcusFoley	121+
			(Miss E C Lavelle) *hld up bhd: stdy hdwy after 10th: jnd ldrs 12th: pckd 13th : led appr 3 out: slt advantage whn lft clr last* **4/1**[1]
5P-6	**2**	*3*	**Misty Future**[27] 2808 8-11-11 **113** .... SamThomas	118+
			(Miss Venetia Williams) *led tl after 3rd: w ldr: rdn after 4 out: ev ch next: 3rd and hld whn lft 2nd and hmpd at the last* **14/1**
/P1-	**3**	*7*	**Frosty Run (IRE)**[497] 1331 8-10-10 **98** .... AndrewTinkler	97+
			(Mrs H Dalton) *mid div: hit 10th: hdwy 12th: effrt whn nt fluent 3 out: nt fluent 2 out: kpt on same pce: lft 3rd at the last* **14/1**
2-45	**4**	*6*	**Roman Court (IRE)**[27] 2805 8-10-10 **98** .... AndrewThornton	88
			(R H Alner) *chsd ldrs: rdn after 4 out: kpt on same pce: lft 4th at the last* **10/1**
5321	**5**	*1 ½*	**Ede'Iff**[19] 2938 9-11-2 **109** .... RobertLucey-Butler[(5)]	98
			(W G M Turner) *hld up towards rr: rdn after 4 out: styd on past btn horses fr next* **9/1**
5-P3	**6**	*5*	**Tom Costalot (IRE)**[45] 2485 11-10-2 **97** .... StevenCrawford[(7)]	82+
			(Mrs Susan Nock) *in tch: hit 12th: sn rdn: one pced fr 4 out* **6/1**[3]
P30	**7**	*½*	**Yann's (FR)**[7] 3212 10-11-12 **114** .... TomSiddall	97
			(R T Phillips) *mid div: rdn appr 4 out: sn btn* **16/1**
4530	**8**	*hd*	**Paddy The Optimist (IRE)**[26] 2818 10-9-11 **88** oh2. WilliamKennedy[(3)]	71
			(D Burchell) *mid div tl 13th: wknd after 4 out* **14/1**
2-F4	**9**	*½*	**Tiger Tips Lad (IRE)**[36] 2664 7-11-6 **108** .... CarlLlewellyn	91+
			(N A Twiston-Davies) *hld up towards rr: sme hdwy after 10th: nvr a danger* **11/2**[2]
-253	**10**	*10*	**Adelphi Theatre (USA)**[39] 2583 9-11-3 **105** .... BrianCrowley	96+
			(R Rowe) *chsd ldrs: mstke 8th: wnt 3rd appr 11th: rdn and effrt 4 out: sn wknd* **14/1**
4/PP	**11**	*11*	**Master Billyboy (IRE)**[38] 2607 8-11-8 **110** .... JoeTizzard	76+
			(Mrs S D Williams) *mid divison tl wknd 12th* **33/1**
000-	**P**		**Montu**[292] 4516 9-9-11 **88** oh3........ RobertStephens[(3)]	—
			(Miss K M George) *mid div tl wknd after 11th: t.o and p.u bef 3 out* **40/1**
F/PP	**P**		**Be My Destiny (IRE)**[24] 2870 9-11-8 **110** .... TimmyMurphy	—
			(Miss H C Knight) *hld up bhd: lost tch fr 11th: t.o and p.u bef 4 out* **16/1**
4-1F	**P**		**Splash Out Again**[51] 2344 8-11-8 **110** .... RichardJohnson	—
			(P Bowen) *prom: led after 3rd tl 8th: bhd fr 11th: t.o whn blnd 13th: p.u bef next* **20/1**
F304	**F**		**Charlies Future**[9] 3144 8-11-8 **110** .... TomDoyle	116
			(S C Burrough) *chsd ldrs: led 8th: hit 10th: rdn and hdd appr 3 out: rallied gamely u.p: ev ch whn fell last* **20/1**

6m 14.6s (9.50) **Going Correction** +0.375s/f (Yiel) **15** Ran SP% **122.1**
Speed ratings: **99,98,95,93,93 91,91,91,91,87 84,—,—,—,—** CSF £56.29 CT £732.87 TOTE £3.80: £2.20, £2.60, £6.90; EX 66.60 Trifecta £279.20 Part won. Pool: £393.30 - 0.20 winning tickets..

Owner The Friday Night Racing Club **Bred** Patrick Tarrant **Trained** Wildhern, Hants

FOCUS
A modest handicap rated around the fourth and the last fence faller, although the winner looks progressive.

NOTEBOOK
Glacial Delight(IRE), off the mark as a chaser over course and distance on his penultimate outing, made amends for an unlucky effort at Newbury with a ready success under a fine ride. This ground would have been soft enough for him, and he impressed with his jumping this time, so may be capable of even further improvement now his confidence will have been fully restored. *(op 9-2)*
Misty Future jumped well throughout and posted an improvement on his recent comeback effort at Folkestone. The return to further can see him go one better in this class. *(op 10-1)*
Frosty Run(IRE), last seen winning over hurdles 497 days previously, produced a fine comeback effort and only tired out of things approaching the final fence. He should come on a deal for this debut experience, will not mind a return to further, and has a race or two in him over fences.
Roman Court(IRE) ran another fair race and helps set the level of this form.
Ede'Iff, raised 8lb for winning at Ludlow last time, lacked the pace to get to the leaders yet was not disgraced considering she ideally prefers a faster surface. *(op 8-1)*
Tiger Tips Lad(IRE) found nothing from off the pace when push came to shove and disappointed. *(op 7-1)*
Splash Out Again *Official explanation: jockey said gelding bled from the nose and was lame (op 16-1)*
Charlies Future, runner-up in this event last term, was still in with every chance when falling at the final fence and has to rate as unlucky. *(op 16-1)*

3327 TAUNTON COURSE WEBSITE STANDARD OPEN NATIONAL HUNT FLAT RACE 2m 1f

3:50 (3:50) (Class 6) 4-6-Y-0 **£1,713** (£499; £249)

Form				RPR
1		**Willie Pep (IRE)** 5-11-5 .... APMcCoy	107
			(C R Egerton) *mid div: hdwy over 4f out: rdn wl over 2f out: swtchd rt 1f out: str run to ld fnl 50yds: drvn out* **11/2**[3]
1	**2**	*nk*	**Hennessy (IRE)**[73] 1909 5-11-12 .... CarlLlewellyn	113
			(M Pitman) *trckd ldrs: led 3f out: sn briefly hdd and rdn: kpt on u.p: no ex whn hdd fnl 50yds* **4/1**[2]
2	**3**	*½*	**Presentandcorrect (IRE)**[43] 2534 5-11-5 .... RichardJohnson	106
			(P J Hobbs) *trckd clr ldr: led briefly over 2f out: sn hrd rdn: ev ch ins fnl f: no ex cl home* **1/1**[1]
4	*1 ¼*	**Classic Fantasy** 5-10-12 .... ChristianWilliams	98
			(P F Nicholls) *trckd ldrs: rdn and ev ch over 2f out: swtchd rt over 1f out: kpt on* **12/1**
5	*11*	**Picts Hill** 6-10-12 .... LiamHeard[(7)]	94
			(P F Nicholls) *mid div: tk clsr order 5f out: rdn over 3f out: kpt on same pce* **20/1**
4P	**6**	*1 ½*	**Templer (IRE)**[7] 3216 5-11-5 .... PaddyBrennan	92
			(P J Hobbs) *in tch: rdn and effrt over 3f out: kpt on same pce* **25/1**
7	*4*	**Swift Half (IRE)** 4-10-0 .... WayneKavanagh[(7)]	76
			(J W Mullins) *hld up towards rr: hdwy over 5f out: wknd 3f out* **66/1**
440	**8**	*½*	**Phriapatius**[44] 2507 5-11-5 .... AndrewThornton	88
			(Dr J R J Naylor) *racd wd: led: sn clr: rdn and hdd 3f out: sn wknd* **80/1**
9	*7*	**Lucent (IRE)** 5-11-5 .... TimmyMurphy	81
			(Miss H C Knight) *hld up and a towards rr* **14/1**
10	*5*	**Wednesday Country (IRE)** 5-11-5 .... MarcusFoley	76
			(J A T De Giles) *in tch tl wknd over 5f out* **66/1**
11	*3*	**Inching West** 4-9-11 .... OwynNelmes[(3)]	54
			(C J Down) *mid div tl 5f out* **100/1**
0	**12**	*19*	**At Loggerheads**[68] 1985 5-10-2 .... RichardKilloran[(10)]	47
			(B G Powell) *chsd ldrs tl wknd over 5f out* **100/1**
5	**P**		**April Showers**[245] 266 6-10-9 .... TomMalone[(3)]	—
			(J C Tuck) *a bhd: t.o fr 1/2-way: p.u ins fnl f* **100/1**

4m 6.20s (-2.40) **Going Correction** +0.375s/f (Yiel)
WFA 4 from 5yo+ 11lb **13** Ran SP% **115.5**
Speed ratings: **109,108,108,108,102 102,100,100,96,94 92,84,—** CSF £25.72 TOTE £10.70: £3.90, £1.10, £1.10; EX 36.70 Place 6 £188.30, Place 5 £74.41.

Owner Rhydian Morgan-Jones **Bred** Olympic Bloodstock Ltd **Trained** Chaddleworth, Berks

FOCUS
This was a warm heat for the division; it was run at a solid pace, and with the first four coming nicely clear the form appears solid and above average. A very decent winning time for a bumper, 10.7 seconds quicker than the earlier valuable novice hurdle over the same trip.

NOTEBOOK
Willie Pep(IRE) ◆, who cost 27,000gns and is related to winners on the Flat and over jumps, needed all of McCoy's urgings to get up in the straight, but duly did so to make a winning debut. He looked ready for this, and had a fairly hard race, so may well need time to get over these exertions. However, he clearly has a decent engine and will be suited by a stiffer test in the future, so connections look to have an exciting prospect on their hands. *(op 7-1 tchd 15-2)*
Hennessy(IRE) ◆, impressive when winning on his debut at Uttoxeter in October, showed a decent attitude and only just missed out under his 7lb penalty. Like the winner, he did not appear too happy on this tight track, so should be rated as the best horse in the race and it will be interesting to see whether connections persevere with him in bumpers. *(op 9-2 tchd 10-3)*
Presentandcorrect(IRE) ◆, runner-up to leading Champion Bumper candidate Wichita Lineman on his Newbury debut last time, was still hard on the bridle turning for home and looked the most likely winner. However, he lacked the resolution of the front pair and was eventually just held. This was another solid effort, and he is clearly useful, but it is a touch disappointing he failed to find just what looked likely when it mattered. *(tchd 10-11 and 11-10 in a place)*
Classic Fantasy ◆, a 76,000euros purchase who is a half-sister to high-class two-mile chaser Central Hoursе among others, ran a race full of promise and was only run out of contention late in the day. She looks a sure-fire winner of a similar event. *(op 7-1)*
Picts Hill, a brother to bumper winner Rye Brook, was doing his best work at the finish and shaped as though he would improve a deal for the experience. *(op 16-1)*
Templer(IRE)showed no signs of trouble at the start this time and looked to run his race. He is ready to tackle hurdles now. *(op 18-1)*

T/Jkpt: Not won. T/Plt: £183.80 to a £1 stake. Pool: £44,484.80. 176.60 winning tickets. T/Qpdt: £88.20 to a £1 stake. Pool: £2,791.75. 23.40 winning tickets. TM

2701 LEICESTER (R-H)

Tuesday, January 10

OFFICIAL GOING: Hurdles course - soft (heavy in places); chase course - good (good to soft in places)

Wind: Fresh, behind Weather: Raining

3328 NOMAD NOVICES' HURDLE (9 hdls) 2m

1:30 (1:30) (Class 3) 4-Y-0+ **£5,070** (£1,497; £748; £374; £187)

Form RPR

1 **Straw Bear (USA)**[468] 5-11-5 .... APMcCoy 142+
(N J Gifford) *hld up: hdwy 5th: led 2 out: clr last: eased flat* **9/2**[2]

2 *7* **Nikola (FR)**[95] 5-11-5 .... CarlLlewellyn 124
(N A Twiston-Davies) *chsd ldrs: ev ch 2 out: styd on same pce appr last* **20/1**

11 3 *1* **Acambo (GER)**[25] [2871] 5-11-13 129.......... TimmyMurphy 133+
(M C Pipe) *hld up in tch: hit 3 out: sn led: hdd next: styd on same pce appr last* **8/15**[1]

4 *21* **Cordial (IRE)**[81] 6-11-5 .... RussGarritty 104+
(J J Quinn) *chsd ldrs: mstke 3rd: led 3 out: sn hdd: wknd after next* **22/1**

54-F 5 *8* **Back Among Friends**[27] [2826] 7-11-5 .... JasonMaguire 97+
(J A B Old) *led: j.lft: clr 4th: hdd 3 out: sn wknd* **40/1**

4/0 6 *3 ½* **Return Ticket**[15] [3001] 7-11-5 .... RichardJohnson 90
(R T Phillips) *hld up: nvr nr to chal* **40/1**

50 7 *10* **Street Life (IRE)**[45] [2487] 8-11-5 .... LeightonAspell 80
(W J Musson) *hld up: effrt appr 3 out: sn wknd* **50/1**

24 8 *8* **Dafarabad (IRE)**[14] [3038] 4-10-7 .... MickFitzgerald 60
(Jonjo O'Neill) *hld up in tch: rdn appr 5th: wknd bef next* **12/1**[3]

9 *2 ½* **Nemetan (FR)**[107] 5-11-5 .... AndrewThornton 70
(R H Alner) *hld up: mstke 3rd: n.d* **33/1**

556 10 *5* **Wee Anthony (IRE)**[26] [2849] 7-11-5 .... NoelFehily 65
(Jonjo O'Neill) *chsd ldrs tl wknd after 5th* **66/1**

F-0 11 *½* **Patrixtoo (FR)**[15] [2991] 5-11-5 .... AlanO'Keeffe 64
(T J Fitzgerald) *hld up: riden appr 3 out: n.d* **80/1**

4-06 12 *1* **Beluga (IRE)**[10] [3139] 7-11-5 .... PaulMoloney 63
(M Pitman) *hld up: hdwy appr 3 out: sn wknd* **100/1**

04 13 *1 ½* **Gran Dana (IRE)**[8] [3219] 6-11-0 .... LeeStephens(5) 62
(G Prodromou) *hld up: rdn after 5th: a in rr* **200/1**

P 14 *3 ½* **Financial Future**[14] [3023] 6-11-2 .... RobertStephens(3) 58
(C Roberts) *hld up: a in rr* **100/1**

0 15 *3 ½* **Another Chat (IRE)**[15] [2988] 6-10-12 .... SeanQuinlan(7) 55
(R T Phillips) *hld up: a in rr* **100/1**

30 16 *½* **Caveman**[15] [2956] 6-11-5 .... TomDoyle 54
(P R Webber) *chsd ldr tl wknd appr 3 out* **66/1**

17 *17* **Ermine Grey**[167] 5-11-5 .... WayneHutchinson 37
(A W Carroll) *hld up: mstke 5th: a in rr* **66/1**

0-P0 18 *14* **Ben Belleshot**[25] [2866] 7-11-5 .... SeanCurran 23
(P W Hiatt) *hld up: hdwy appr 5th: sn rdn and wknd* **200/1**

P 19 *3* **Chisel**[9] [3173] 5-10-12 .... MrSRees(7) 20
(M Wigham) *a bhd* **200/1**

20 *23* **Royal Sailor (IRE)**[27] 4-10-7 .... AntonyProcter —
(Lucinda Featherstone) *hld up: bhd fr 5th* **150/1**

0- P **Assumptalina**[290] [4559] 6-10-12 .... TomSiddall —
(R T Phillips) *hld up: a in rr: t.o whn p.u bef 2 out* **100/1**

P F **Devolution (IRE)**[24] [2873] 8-10-12 .... MissCDyson(7) —
(Miss C Dyson) *prom: blnd 2nd: wknd appr 3 out: in rr whn fell next* **150/1**

3m 58.8s (-8.80) **Going Correction** +0.35s/f (Yiel)
WFA 4 from 5yo+ 11lb 22 Ran SP% 122.5
Speed ratings: **116,112,112,101,97 95,90,86,85,83 82,82,81,79,78 77,69,62,60,49** —,—
CSF £87.75 TOTE £4.80: £1.80, £5.40, £1.10; EX 117.40.
Owner John P McManus **Bred** Cyril Humphris **Trained** Findon, W Sussex

FOCUS
This should prove to be a decent event for the division and the field finished well strung out behind the impressive debut winner who is value for 18 lengths. It was an outstanding winning time for a race of its type given the conditions and the form should work out, with the third setting the standard.

NOTEBOOK
Straw Bear(USA) ♦, rated 96 on the Flat and bought out of Sir Mark Prescott's yard in 2005, got his hurdling career off to a perfect start and could hardly have been any more impressive. He jumped neatly throughout and there was an awful lot to like about the manner in which he settled the race. Granted that he is entitled to improve a deal for the experience, and had a solid benchmark in Acambo back in third, it is little surprise that he was introduced near the top of many an ante-post list for the Supreme Novices' Hurdle. It is also interesting that last term's winner of this race, Dusky Warbler, went on to place in that event at Cheltenham. However, while he was placed on fast ground on the Flat, he looked well at home on this deep surface, and his ability to act so well on the likely ground come March has to be taken on trust. *(op 11-2)*
Nikola(FR) ♦, a dual good-ground winner at around 12 furlongs in France, ran a race full of promise on this British and hurdling bow for his new trainer. He handled this soft ground without fuss and, given that he had yet to be asked a serious question prior to finding just the one pace nearing the last flight, it is safe to assume he can improve a deal for this experience. He rates a potentially useful recruit and may want a little further in due course.
Acambo(GER), well backed for the Supreme Novices' Hurdle after winning on his handicap bow at Windsor last time, found just the same pace when it mattered in the straight and was well held under his double penalty. While this could be deemed as disappointing, time may tell that there was no disgrace in this defeat, and he may have been at a disadvantage in sticking to the inside rail during the course of the race. He does jump well, and may be happier on better ground, so it is too soon to write him off just yet. *(op 4-7)*
Cordial(IRE), rated 85 on the Flat and like the winner bought out of Sir Mark Prescott's academy, failed to sustain his effort when pressed from the penultimate flight and was ultimately well beaten. However, he still shaped with promise, and can better this when encountering a faster surface in the future. *(op 20-1)*
Back Among Friends, who took a heavy fall on his hurdling bow last time, was firmly put in his place when the principals asserted and finished a tired horse. However, this will have helped restore his confidence, and he gives the form a sound look. *(op 33-1)*
Return Ticket, who showed just modest form in two previous bumper outings, was given a fairly conservative ride and should be seen in a better light when eligible for handicaps and upped in trip.
Street Life(IRE) *Official explanation: jockey said gelding had breathing problem*

3329 GROBY BEGINNERS' CHASE (12 fncs) 2m

2:00 (2:00) (Class 4) 5-Y-0+ **£5,070** (£1,497; £748; £374; £187)

Form RPR

-520 1 **Calatagan (IRE)**[31] [2765] 7-10-11 .... ThomasDreaper(5) 124+
(J M Jefferson) *chsd ldrs: mstke 6th and next: outpcd 5 out: lft 2nd next: rallied 3 out: hung rt and styd on u.p to ld nr fin* **6/1**[3]

-042 2 *hd* **Cossack Dancer (IRE)**[33] [2732] 8-11-2 114..........(p) MatthewBatchelor 122+
(M Bradstock) *led: rdn 2 out: hung rt flat: hung lft: hmpd and hdd nr fin* **8/1**

00P- 3 *18* **Meehan (IRE)**[384] [2939] 6-11-2 90.......... SeanCurran 103
(Miss J S Davis) *hld up: hmpd 4th: hdwy next: outpcd 7th: lft 3rd 4 out: no imp* **100/1**

4 4 *28* **Beaufort County (IRE)**[38] [2620] 9-11-2 120.......... ChristianWilliams 81+
(Evan Williams) *hld up: sme hdwy appr 3 out: sn wknd* **25/1**

50 5 *13* **Bally Rainey (IRE)**[25] [2866] 7-11-2 .... LeightonAspell 62
(Mrs L C Jewell) *hld up: a bhd* **50/1**

244- F **Pole Star**[278] [4752] 8-11-2 .... APMcCoy —
(J R Fanshawe) *trckd ldrs: racd keenly: fell 4th* **11/10**[1]

/0PP P **Ellie Moss**[20] [2937] 8-10-9 .... WayneHutchinson —
(A W Carroll) *prom to 7th: t.o whn p.u bef 2 out* **100/1**

1213 F **Phar Out Phavorite (IRE)**[46] [2482] 7-11-2 ....(v) NoelFehily —
(Miss E C Lavelle) *chsd ldr: ev ch whn fell 4 out* **9/4**[2]

00P P **Butsadtohavetogo (IRE)**[29] [2798] 6-10-11 .... DerekLaverty(5) —
(A E Jones) *hld up: a in rr: bhd whn blnd 4 out: p.u bef next* **100/1**

60P P **Konker**[25] [2861] 11-10-11 88.......... JamesDiment(5) —
(J R Cornwall) *hld up: j.big and rdr lost iron 2nd: bhd fr 6th: hit 3 out: t.o whn p.u bef next* **100/1**

4m 8.20s (0.60) **Going Correction** +0.225s/f (Yiel) 10 Ran SP% 113.6
Speed ratings: **107,106,97,83,77** —,—,—,—,— CSF £45.87 TOTE £8.10: £1.70, £2.60, £13.90; EX 34.40.
Owner Mr & Mrs J M Davenport **Bred** Mrs S Camacho **Trained** Norton, N Yorks

FOCUS
A fair beginners' chase, which saw the two clear market leaders both fall, and the first two eventually came clear. The runner-up sets the standard but the form is suspect.

NOTEBOOK
Calatagan(IRE) ran out a game winner to open his account over fences at the first time of asking. He did not appear comfortable when under maximum pressure late on, and most likely needs faster ground, but he is clearly flattered by this victory all the same and will look vulnerable under a penalty next time. *(op 13-2)*
Cossack Dancer(IRE), well held in second by Hors La Loi III at Taunton last time, lost his chance by hanging into the winner on the run-in and just missed out. He again jumped with aplomb, however, and has developed into a consistent sort, so does deserve to find a race in this sphere. *(op 15-2)*
Meehan(IRE), making his chase debut after a 384-day layoff, ran as well as could have been expected at the weights and should improve for the experience.
Beaufort County(IRE) proved disappointing and looks flattered by his official rating.
Pole Star, by far the best of these over hurdles, took a crashing fall at the fourth fence and his confidence is going to need boosting after this debut experience. *(op 2-1)*
Phar Out Phavorite(IRE), with the visor back on for this, looked to have a fairly straightforward task when Pole Star departed early on and was still going best of all prior to falling four from home. This has to rate a missed opportunity, but he can make amends. *(op 2-1)*

3330 DOVE (S) H'CAP HURDLE (9 hdls) 2m

2:30 (2:30) (Class 5) (0-90,87) 4-Y-0+ **£2,602** (£764; £382; £190)

Form RPR

P300 1 **Irish Blessing (USA)**[27] [2822] 9-11-6 81..........(tp) TomDoyle 84+
(F Jordan) *hld up: pushed along 3rd: hdwy to chse ldr 3 out: led next: clr whn hit last: eased flat* **6/1**[1]

4552 2 *3 ½* **Makandy**[34] [2702] 7-11-2 84.......... MrRArmson(7) 74+
(R J Armson) *hld up: hdwy 5th: sn rdn: outpcd whn hit 2 out: styd on u.p flat: no ch w wnr* **13/2**[2]

-000 3 *4* **John Jorrocks (FR)**[90] [1717] 7-10-5 69..........(p) TomMalone(3) 55+
(J C Tuck) *led after 2nd: hdd 4th: led next: rdn and hdd 2 out: wknd bef last* **7/1**[3]

6-00 4 *2 ½* **Needwood Spirit**[41] [2567] 11-10-7 71.......... OwynNelmes(3) 54
(Mrs A M Naughton) *hld up in tch: outpcd 5th: styd on flat* **7/1**[3]

0560 5 *1* **La Muette (IRE)**[15] [2962] 6-10-3 71.......... RichardSpate(7) 53
(M Appleby) *chsd ldrs: rdn after 5th: wknd appr 2 out* **10/1**

P3P0 6 *1 ¼* **Kiss The Girls (IRE)**[14] [3042] 7-10-9 70..........(v) AlanO'Keeffe 50
(Jennie Candlish) *chsd ldrs: rdn 3 out: wknd after next* **13/2**[2]

1P20 7 *2 ½* **Aleemdar (IRE)**[53] [2314] 9-11-1 81..........(p) DerekLaverty(5) 59
(A E Jones) *hld up: hdwy appr 5th: wknd after 3 out* **6/1**[1]

0000 8 *14* **Protocol (IRE)**[15] [2962] 12-11-9 87..........(tp) LeeVickers(3) 51
(Mrs S Lamyman) *chsd ldrs: mstke 3rd: sn lost pl: bhd fr 5th* **16/1**

P060 9 *3 ½* **Purr**[9] [3169] 5-10-2 70.......... MrSRees(7) 30
(M Wigham) *hit 5th: a bhd* **33/1**

054 P **Nepal (IRE)**[32] [2752] 4-10-7 80.......... DaveCrosse —
(M Mullineaux) *prom to 5th: t.o whn p.u bef next* **7/1**[3]

0-05 P **Exclusive Air (USA)**[8] [3222] 7-9-12 62.......... RobertStephens(3) —
(H H G Owen) *mid-div: effrt 5th: wknd bef next: bhd whn p.u bef 2 out* **33/1**

3P-P P **Comete Du Lac (FR)**[247] [238] 9-11-0 75.......... BrianCrowley —
(Mrs N Macauley) *led: hdd after 2nd: led 4th to next: wknd bef next: bhd whn p.u bef 2 out* **14/1**

4m 11.9s (4.30) **Going Correction** +0.625s/f (Soft)
WFA 4 from 5yo+ 11lb 12 Ran SP% 120.3
Speed ratings: **94,92,90,89,88 87,86,79,77,**— —,— CSF £45.91 CT £281.72 TOTE £7.00: £2.30, £2.40, £3.60; EX 36.10.There was no bid for the winner.
Owner The Bhiss Partnership **Bred** Kenneth L Ramsey And Sarah K Ramsey **Trained** Adstone, Northants

FOCUS
A weak affair, run at an average pace, and the field finished fairly strung out on the deep surface. The winner is value for almost four times the official margin.

NOTEBOOK
Irish Blessing(USA) bounced right back to form and, having taken time to hit his stride, ultimately ran out an easy winner. He handled this soft ground better than his rivals, and while he should be rated value for double his winning margin, he may struggle off a higher mark next time.
Makandy failed to quicken when it mattered, and again managed to find one too good, but still finished a clear second-best. He is a decent benchmark for this form and deserves a change of luck. *(op 7-1)*
John Jorrocks(FR), returning from a 90-day break in first-time cheekpieces, showed up well from the front and only tired nearing the final flight. He is entitled to build on this, will appreciate faster ground in the future, and looks to have found his level now. *(op 8-1)*
Needwood Spirit found this an inadequate test, but still enjoyed the deeper surface and can get closer from this sort of mark when reverting to further. *(op 9-1)*
Aleemdar(IRE) could not sustain his effort when asked to improve on this deep surface and can be given another chance when encountering faster ground. *(op 7-2)*
Comete Du Lac(FR) *Official explanation: trainer said mare lost an off-fore shoe during the race (op 12-1)*
Nepal(IRE) *Official explanation: jockey said filly was never travelling (op 12-1)*

3331 GG.COM NOVICES' CHASE (18 fncs) 2m 7f 110y
3:00 (3:00) (Class 3) 6-Y-O+
£6,263 (£1,850; £925; £463; £231; £116)

Form RPR
1 **Mort De Rire (FR)**55 6-10-7 .... DarylJacob(7) 130+
(R H Alner) *chsd ldrs: led 3 out: styd on wl* 20/1
2-6F 2 6 **Monte Vista (IRE)**34 2701 9-11-0 .... APMcCoy 123+
(Jonjo O'Neill) *hld up: stmbld 8th: mstke 12th: hdwy appr 3 out: ev ch whn nt fluent 2 out: styd on same pce last* 2/1[1]
-41F 3 15 **Mount Clerigo (IRE)**25 2869 8-11-6 .... AndrewThornton 112
(V R A Dartnall) *led to 14th: ev ch 3 out: wknd next* 2/1[1]
PP4U 4 2 1/2 **Sungates (IRE)**10 3142 10-11-0 .... AndrewTinkler 105+
(C Tinkler) *prom to 3 out: in rr whn hmpd last* 33/1
-154 5 1 **The Dark Lord (IRE)**19 2953 9-11-10 125 .... LeightonAspell 112
(Mrs L Wadham) *hld up in tch: mstkes: wknd 3 out: j.rt last* 6/1[3]
0 6 12 **Lord Gunnerslake (IRE)**37 2664 6-10-11 89 .... AnthonyCoyle(3) 90
(Miss C J E Caroe) *hld up: a in rr: lost tch 4 out* 100/1
243/ 7 8 **Isotop (FR)**632 4888 10-10-9 95 .... MarkNicolls(5) 85+
(John Allen) *prom: chsd ldr 6th tl led 14th: hdd whn hit 3 out: sn wknd* 100/1
2-41 F **Alderburn**34 2701 7-11-6 .... RichardJohnson —
(H D Daly) *fell 1st* 9/2[2]
-06U F **Jonanaud**35 2682 7-10-7 117 .... MrJAJenkins(7) —
(H J Manners) *hld up: fell 7th* 50/1
0 P **Lookafterme (IRE)**59 2192 6-11-0 .... WayneHutchinson —
(A W Carroll) *hld up: hdwy 7th: wknd 3 out: blnd next: p.u bef last* 50/1
P **Barrshan (IRE)**241 7-11-0 .... (t) MickFitzgerald —
(N J Henderson) *chsd ldr to 6th: wknd after 10th: t.o whn p.u bef 3 out* 16/1

6m 11.1s (5.70) **Going Correction** +0.225s/f (Yiel) **11 Ran SP% 118.6**
Speed ratings: **99,97,92,91,90 86,84,—,—,—** — CSF £62.20 TOTE £35.30: £5.20, £1.40, £1.20; EX 160.70.
Owner Andrew Wiles **Bred** Haras De Saint-Voir **Trained** Droop, Dorset

FOCUS
A fair novice chase, run at an average gallop, and the field came home well strung out. The form, rated through the runner-up, should be treated with a degree of caution.

NOTEBOOK
Mort De Rire(FR), making his British debut, stepped up markedly on his French chase form and lost his maiden tag in great style. He was handy throughout, clearly enjoyed the testing surface, and hardly put a foot wrong over his fences. The step-up to three miles in the future could bring about more improvement and he has the potential to make into a nice handicapper for his new connections. *(op 25-1 tchd 33-1)*
Monte Vista(IRE) was none too fluent under restraint through the first half of the race, but still made smooth headway to join the leaders turning for home, and would have finished a touch closer but for blundering two out. He is a frustrating horse to follow, but he finished well clear of the rest this time, and has the ability to land a similar event. *(op 5-2)*
Mount Clerigo(IRE), who fell when booked for place behind the Listener in a Grade Two at Windsor last time, found disappointingly little when push came to shove at the top of the straight and was well beaten. His jumping was much more assured this time, and his yard are notably struggling for form at present, so it would be wise to assume he can leave this form behind again in the future. It may also be that this trip stretches his stamina. *(tchd 9-4 after early 5-2)*
Sungates(IRE), who unseated at Uttoxeter last time, turned in a more encouraging effort yet has still to convince he is a natural over fences. *(op 25-1)*
The Dark Lord(IRE) was none too fluent throughout and was disappointingly well beaten. He faced no easy task under his big weight, and probably found this ground too testing, but is not progressing over fences as looked likely at the start of the current campaign. *(op 11-2 tchd 5-1)*
Alderburn, who just got up to open his account over fences at this venue last time, took a heavy fall at the first flight and his confidence could be markedly dented by this experience. *(op 10-1)*
Barrshan(IRE) *Official explanation: trainer said gelding was distressed (op 10-1)*

3332 CHIEFTAIN CLAIMING HURDLE (12 hdls) 2m 4f 110y
3:30 (3:30) (Class 4) 5-Y-O+ £3,903 (£1,146; £573; £286)

Form RPR
5100 1 **Biscar Two (IRE)**9 3174 5-11-3 120 .... (p) ChristianWilliams 101+
(B J Llewellyn) *sn pushed along in rr: hdwy appr 3 out: led last: sn clr* 5/2[2]
1F-P 2 10 **Westmeath Flyer**27 2820 11-11-6 129 .... TonyDobbin 95+
(N G Richards) *hld up: hdwy 6th: hit 3 out: led next: sn hrd rdn and hung rt: hdd last: sn wknd* 4/5[1]
0-65 3 2 1/2 **Desertmore Chief (IRE)**43 2552 7-10-11 75 .... (v[1]) NoelFehily 83
(B De Haan) *led: hdd after 1st: led 4th: rdn and hdd 2 out: wknd flat* 33/1
P050 4 4 **Front Rank (IRE)**20 2940 6-11-4 101 .... MarkNicolls(5) 92+
(K C Bailey) *hld up: hdwy 7th: wknd appr last* 11/1
3156 5 7 **Rojabaa**15 2958 7-11-6 90 .... LeightonAspell 81
(B D Leavy) *hld up: hdwy 6th: wkng whn mstke 2 out* 10/1[3]
-PPP 6 dist **Ashleybank House (IRE)**15 2990 9-10-8 105 .... RichardHobson —
(David Pearson) *prom to 6th* 33/1
0 7 9 **Silverpro**79 1851 5-10-10 .... HenryOliver —
(D J Wintle) *plld hrd: led after 1st: hdd 4th: mstke and wknd 7th* 66/1
0040 P **Secret Jewel (FR)**21 2934 6-10-4 77 .... AnthonyCoyle(3) —
(Miss C J E Caroe) *prom to 6th: t.o whn p.u bef 3 out* 50/1
3062 R **It's My Party**33 2728 5-10-7 90 .... (b[1]) RichardGordon(10) —
(W G M Turner) *hld up: hdwy 6th: wknd after next: in rr whn rn out 3 out* 14/1

5m 35.9s (1.10) **Going Correction** +0.625s/f (Soft) **9 Ran SP% 117.6**
Speed ratings: **102,98,97,95,93** —,—,—,— CSF £5.05 TOTE £2.60: £1.50, £1.60, £5.20; EX 9.20.The winner was claimed by A. E. Jones for £8,000. Desertmore Chief was the subject of a friendly claim. Westmeath Flyer was claimed by P. A. Blockley for £9,000.
Owner Maenllwyd Racing Club **Bred** Michael O'Dwyer **Trained** Fochriw, Caerphilly

FOCUS
A weak affair, run at a fair gallop, and the form looks fairly straightforward.

NOTEBOOK
Biscar Two(IRE) ran in snatches throughout, and looked like folding when under maximum pressure down the back straight, but he stuck to his task dourly and ultimately ran out a comfortable winner. He is very much at home on this ground, and while he is a tricky ride, is certainly capable of further success in this grade. *(tchd 9-4)*
Westmeath Flyer eventually won the battle with the third horse approaching the penultimate flight, and looked like going on to score, but his stride soon shortened nearing the final flight and he had no answer to the winner's challenge. While he may have paid for his exertions in the straight, and should always rate a threat in contests of this nature, he could have just been holding something back for himself when passed by the winner on the run-in. *(tchd 5-6 in places and 10-11 in a place)*
Desertmore Chief(IRE), dropped in grade, showed his best form to date and the application of a first-time visor clearly had a positive effect. He is a tricky customer, but could build on this.
Front Rank(IRE) found this trip too testing on the deep surface and was never a serious threat. *(op 10-1 tchd 12-1)*

3333 COMPARE ODDS @ GG-ODDS.COM AMATEUR RIDERS' H'CAP HURDLE (9 hdls) 2m
4:00 (4:00) (Class 4) (0-110,110) 4-Y-O£3,646 (£1,138; £569; £284; £142)

Form RPR
5-11 1 **The Hairy Lemon**10 3152 6-11-7 108 .... MrGTumelty(3) 113+
(A King) *hld up: hdwy 4th: chsd ldr 3 out: led on bit whn hit last: hung rt flat: drvn out* 1/1[1]
P526 2 1 1/4 **Billyandi (IRE)**39 2617 6-10-9 100 .... MrRMcCarthy(7) 98
(N A Twiston-Davies) *led after 2nd: hdd 4th: led appr 3 out: rdn and hdd last: styd on* 7/1
24/0 3 1 1/2 **Mirant**38 2629 7-11-5 110 .... MrDPick(7) 107
(M C Pipe) *prom: led 4th to appr 3 out: outpcd next: styd on flat* 18/1
2-31 4 nk **Coach Lane**38 2618 5-11-2 107 .... MrWBiddick(7) 103
(Miss Venetia Williams) *chsd ldrs: rdn approaching 2 out: styd on same pce last* 7/1
4266 5 3 **Runaway Bishop (USA)**15 2965 11-9-7 84 oh1 .... MissUMoore(7) 77
(J R Cornwall) *led tl after 2nd: sn lost pl: r.o flat* 28/1
-U30 6 6 **Presenter (IRE)**10 3152 6-10-8 99 .... MrLRPayter(7) 87+
(M Sheppard) *hld up and bhd: mstke 3rd: rdn appr 3 out: n.d* 33/1
4132 7 12 **Polished**9 3185 7-11-5 108 .... (b) MrJJDoyle(5) 83
(V R A Dartnall) *hld up: hdwy 4th: hmpd 3 out: sn rdn: wknd after next* 7/2[2]
41F 8 dist **Random Quest**59 2173 8-11-0 105 .... MrRQuinn(7) —
(B J Llewellyn) *plld hrd and prom: rdn and wknd after 5th* 4/1[3]
66/U P **Caroline's Rose**233 279 8-9-13 90 oh20 ow6 .... MrElmelov(7) —
(A P Jones) *hld up: plld hrd: hdwy 3rd: rdn and wknd after 5th: p.u bef next* 33/1

4m 9.20s (1.60) **Going Correction** +0.625s/f (Soft) **9 Ran SP% 131.8**
Speed ratings: **101,100,99,99,97 94,88,—,—** CSF £10.83 CT £95.80 TOTE £2.30: £1.10, £3.00, £4.60; EX 14.40 Place 6 £22.85, Place 5 £20.18.
Owner The Hairy Lemon Partnership **Bred** Houston Mill Stud **Trained** Barbury Castle, Wilts

FOCUS
A moderate handicap, run at a modest gallop, and the in-form winner can be rated value for a touch further. The form appears solid enough, rated through the second, fourth and sixth.

NOTEBOOK
The Hairy Lemon put the race to bed when quickening into the lead approaching the final flight and, despite tiring when on the run-in, was always going to get up to land the hat-trick from a 7lb higher mark. Clearly most progressive, he is well suited by a soft surface, and looks the type to defy another weight rise. *(op 11-8 after early 6-4 in a place)*
Billyandi(IRE) was coming back at the winner near the finish and showed just about his best form over timber to date. With a step-up in trip, he could be ready to break his duck in this sphere. *(op 9-1 tchd 10-1)*
Mirant posted an encouraging effort and was another doing his best work at the finish. This was a creditable effort under top weight and he can be placed to advantage when encountering less taxing ground in the future. *(op 16-1)*
Coach Lane, not raised by the Handicapper for winning a maiden last time, could only find the same pace when it mattered and this is probably about as good as he is.
Runaway Bishop(USA) *Official explanation: jockey said, regarding the apparent tender ride, her orders were to ride the race from a handy position, and try to keep the gelding away from kickback on the best available ground, adding that gelding, on turning into the straight, hung right, rendering it very difficult to ride; trainer added that gelding is on the list of previously-wealed horses and cannot be encouraged with the whip too vigorously (op 20-1)*
Polished found nothing for pressure after being the meat in the sandwich three from home and has to rate disappointing. His yard is not firing at present and he is capable of better than this.
Random Quest turned in a mulish effort on this handicap bow and has definite questions to answer after this. *(op 9-2)*
T/Plt: £72.00 to a £1 stake. Pool: £44,558.20. 451.45 winning tickets. T/Qpdt: £4.40 to a £1 stake. Pool: £4,159.60. 684.70 winning tickets. CR

2975 SEDGEFIELD (L-H)
Tuesday, January 10

OFFICIAL GOING: Soft (heavy in places)
The ground was described as 'very holding'. The middle two fences in the back straight had to be omitted because of the ground.
Wind: Fresh, half-behind Weather: Overcast and windy

3334 GG.COM NOVICES' CHASE (10 fncs 3 omitted) 2m 110y
1:10 (1:10) (Class 4) 5-Y-O+ £4,228 (£1,241; £620; £310)

Form RPR
F200 1 **Silver Sedge (IRE)**19 2944 7-10-13 85 .... PeterBuchanan(3) 110+
(Mrs A Hamilton) *chsd ldrs: led after 2 out: stmbld landing last: styd on* 4/1[3]
6444 2 2 1/2 **Dance Party (IRE)**14 3040 6-10-6 97 .... MrTGreenall(3) 99+
(M W Easterby) *hld up in rr: hdwy 7th: wnt 2nd between last 2: kpt on same pce* 10/3[2]
U01B 3 3 **Longdale**7 3233 8-11-2 101 .... GrahamLee 105+
(M Todhunter) *trckd ldrs: effrt after 3 out: kpt on same pce between last 2* 11/4[1]
6003 4 11 **Ton-Chee**23 2902 7-11-2 99 .... BrianHarding 92+
(F P Murtagh) *led: qcknd 5th: hdd after 2 out: sn wknd* 8/1
5466 5 1 **Rifleman (IRE)**15 2976 6-11-2 94 .... (t) OllieMcPhail 90
(Robert Gray) *chsd ldrs: pushed along 5th: wknd appr 2 out* 12/1
-052 6 1 **Persian Point**37 2655 10-10-13 82 .... MrCStorey(3) 89
(Miss S E Forster) *chsd ldrs: outpcd whn mstke 5th: n.d after* 14/1
3FC1 7 16 **Vigoureux (FR)**5 3255 7-11-9 95 .... (p) KeithMercer 80
(S Gollings) *chsd ldr: lost pl after 3 out* 6/1
/PP- 8 dist **Magic Bengie**307 4257 7-11-2 68 .... KennyJohnson —
(F Kirby) *mstkes: a last: detached fr 7th: t.o: btn 47 l* 100/1

4m 22.3s (8.10) **Going Correction** +0.625s/f (Soft) **8 Ran SP% 110.5**
Speed ratings: **105,103,102,97,96 96,88,—** CSF £17.07 TOTE £5.80: £1.80, £2.00, £1.40; EX 25.80.
Owner Ian Hamilton **Bred** David Mooney **Trained** Great Bavington, Northumbland

FOCUS
A modest novices' chase but the first two may progress further and the fourth holds the key to the overall value of the form.

NOTEBOOK
Silver Sedge(IRE), who came down at the first on his chase debut, jumped soundly on the whole. He surged to the front between the last two and survived over-jumping at the last. Soft ground brings out the best in him and two and a half miles will play to his strengths even better. *(op 11-2)*
Dance Party(IRE), rated 11lb ahead of the winner over hurdles, went in pursuit between the last two and stuck on all the way to the line. She deserves to go one better. *(op 3-1 tchd 5-2)*
Longdale travelled strongly but when called on for an effort under his penalty he could only stay on in his own time. *(op 7-2 tchd 4-1)*

Ton-Chee, having just his second try over fences for his new stable, tried to pinch it from the front but in the end he could not keep up the gallop in the testing conditions. *(tchd 11-1)*
Rifleman(IRE), having just his second start over fences, makes it hard work for his rider and he seemed to throw in the towel very readily. *(op 9-1 tchd 14-1)*
Vigoureux(FR), making a quick return, is not that big and he dropped away tamely after three out. *This almost certainly came too soon after Wetherby and the bad ground there.Official explanation: jockey said, gelding ran flat (op 4-1)*

3335 JOHN WADE FOR EQUINE FIBRE AND RUBBER CONDITIONAL JOCKEYS' (S) H'CAP HURDLE (QUALIFIER) (8 hdls) 2m 1f

1:40 (1:40) (Class 5) (0-85,85) 4-Y-O+ **£2,192** (£639; £319)

Form | | | | RPR
0005 **1** **Star Trooper (IRE)**[4] [3270] 10-10-10 **74**..................(p) TomMessenger(5) 74
(Miss S E Forster) *hmpd 1st: bhd and drvn 3rd: hdwy 5th: wnt 2nd last: styd on wl to ld last 75yds* **6/1**[2]
2503 **2** *1* **Munaawesh (USA)**[15] [2962] 5-10-13 **77**.......................... PhilKinsella(5) 77+
(Mrs Marjorie Fife) *sn trcking ldrs: led 3 out: 15 l clr next: 7 l clr last: wknd and hdd run-in* **7/1**
0500 **3** *5* **Vulcan Lane (NZ)**[229] [520] 9-10-11 **78**..........................(p) JohnFlavin(8) 72
(R C Guest) *racd wd: hdwy to chse ldrs 5th: wnt 2nd 2 out: wknd last* **8/1**
3PPP **4** *15* **Comfortable Call**[40] [2586] 8-11-12 **85**..........................(t) BrianHughes 64
(H Alexander) *in rr: drvn 4th: kpt on fr 3 out: nvr on terms* **16/1**
/000 **5** *hd* **Kicking Bear (IRE)**[9] [3169] 8-10-5 **69**..........................(p) StevenGagan(5) 48
(J K Hunter) *chsd ldrs: wknd 3 out* **50/1**
P006 **6** *4* **Just Sal**[37] [2657] 10-10-9 **73**.. EwanWhillans(5) 50+
(R Nixon) *mid-div: outpcd after 5th: sn lost pl* **8/1**
0602 **7** *3 ½* **The Wife's Sister**[10] [3141] 5-11-9 **85**..........................(b) StephenCraine(3) 56
(D McCain) *chsd ldrs: wknd appr 2 out* **5/1**[1]
00U0 **8** *1 ¾* **Europrime Games**[9] [3169] 8-10-13 **72**..........................(b) DougieCostello 42
(M E Sowersby) *led to 3 out: wknd qckly next* **28/1**
0PP0 **9** *dist* **Friedhelmo (GER)**[15] [2962] 10-10-11 **75**..........................(t) JohnEnnis(5) —
(S B Clark) *prom: lost pl 5th: sn bhd: t.o: btn 32 l* **28/1**
000 **F** **Red Bluff (IRE)**[22] [2923] 6-10-12 **71**.................................... GaryBerridge —
(H Alexander) *bhd whn fell 3 out* **25/1**
0600 **P** **New Wish (IRE)**[41] [2567] 6-10-9 **68**.................................... KeithMercer —
(S B Clark) *blnd 1st: p.u bef next* **20/1**
/PU0 **P** **Ilton**[15] [2962] 7-10-5 **67**..(v) PatrickMcDonald(3) —
(M E Sowersby) *bhd: t.o 5th: p.u bef next* **40/1**
-P0P **P** **Grafton Truce (IRE)**[47] [2453] 9-10-10 **77** ow10................ NeilWalker(8) —
(Miss Lucinda V Russell) *bhd: t.o 5th: p.u bef next* **50/1**
-0P0 **P** **Culbann (IRE)**[46] [2474] 7-10-13 **72**............................... MichaelMcAlister —
(C Rae) *chsd ldrs: lost pl 5th: sn bhd: t.o whn p.u bef 2 out* **33/1**
0000 **P** **Shinko Femme (IRE)**[15] [2962] 5-10-2 **66**....................(t) LiamBerridge(5) —
(M E Sowersby) *hld up in rr: lost tch 3 out: t.o whn p.u bef next* **14/1**
226P **P** **Samson Des Galas (FR)**[15] [2962] 8-10-7 **66**.................. TomGreenway —
(Robert Gray) *chsd ldrs: drvn along after 2nd: lost pl and p.u after 5th* **13/2**[3]

4m 27.7s (21.20) **Going Correction** +1.275s/f (Heav) **16** Ran SP% **116.4**
Speed ratings: **101,100,98,91,91 89,87,86,—,— —,—,—,—,— —** CSF £41.23 CT £337.36 TOTE £7.20: £2.10, £1.30, £2.10, £5.80; EX 26.20.There was no bid for the winner.
Owner C Storey **Bred** Martin Ryan **Trained** Kirk Yetholm, Borders

FOCUS
Run-of-the-mill selling race form, the first three well clear. The race has been rated through the runner-up.

NOTEBOOK
Star Trooper(IRE), on a losing run stretching back 30 outings, was on the back foot after becoming the meat in the sandwich at the very first flight. Flat out with a full circuit to go, his rider deserves full marks and they wore down the leader near the line. *(op 7-1)*
Munaawesh(USA), attempting to break his duck at the 38th attempt, looked to have it in the bag two out but he slowed up after the last and the final hill proved his undoing. *(op 9-2 tchd 15-2)*
Vulcan Lane(NZ), kept wide, was having his first outing since May and, after being sent in pursuit of the leader, he was leg-weary jumping the final flight. *(op 9-1)*
Comfortable Call, who has lost the plot, was soon being driven along and this trip is much too short for him.
Kicking Bear(IRE), in first-time cheepieces, has now finished unplaced in nine starts over hurdles.
The Wife's Sister, hoisted 10lb, dropped right away once in line for home. *(op 6-1 tchd 13-2)*
New Wish(IRE) *Official explanation: jockey said saddle slipped (op 6-1 tchd 7-1)*
Samson Des Galas(FR) *Official explanation: jockey said gelding lost its action (op 6-1 tchd 7-1)*

3336 RAMSIDE EVENT CATERING H'CAP CHASE (16 fncs 5 omitted) 3m 3f

2:10 (2:10) (Class 4) (0-105,105) 5-Y-O+ **£4,424** (£1,298; £649; £324)

Form | | | | RPR
41F1 **1** **Bang And Blame (IRE)**[15] [2978] 10-10-9 **93**........... MichaelMcAlister(5) 115+
(M W Easterby) *mde all: qcknd clr 11th: 14 l clr last: eased run-in* **6/1**[2]
1 **2** *20* **Weapons Inspector (IRE)**[35] [2689] 7-11-12 **105**................. GrahamLee 107+
(J Howard Johnson) *hld up in rr: hdwy to chse ldrs 10th: wnt 2nd 3 out: wknd and eased run-in: fin tired* **2/1**[1]
0-0P **3** *20* **Harry Hooly**[19] [2946] 11-10-3 **89**.................................. MissRDavidson(7) 67
(Mrs H O Graham) *a.p: outpcd 11th: kpt on fr 2 out: tk remote 3rd run-in* **50/1**
4P-P **4** *1 ¼* **Recent Edition (IRE)**[15] [2978] 8-10-5 **84**........................(p) AlanDempsey 61
(J Wade) *prom: hit 2nd: rdn and mstke 11th: wknd 13th* **25/1**
2122 **5** *6* **Chabrimal Minster**[36] [2675] 9-11-12 **105**...................... RichardMcGrath 76
(R Ford) *chseed ldrs: mstke 8th: 4th and wkng whn mstke 13th* **6/1**[2]
0013 **6** *1 ¼* **Jethro Tull (IRE)**[35] [2691] 7-11-1 **97**.......................... WilliamKennedy(3) 67
(G A Harker) *hld up in rr: bhd fr 11th* **6/1**[2]
/PPP **P** **Over The Storm (IRE)**[24] [2875] 9-11-1 **101**...................... PhilKinsella(7) —
(H P Hogarth) *in rr: bhd whn p.u bef 13th* **10/1**[3]
P40U **P** **Pottsy's Joy**[9] [3170] 9-10-0 **79**.. PadgeWhelan —
(Mrs S J Smith) *in rr: bhd fr 10th: t.o whn p.u bef 2 out* **25/1**
4P **P** **Place Above (IRE)**[15] [2978] 10-10-12 **91**....................(b[1]) WilsonRenwick —
(E A Elliott) *prom: lost pl 4th: bhd whn p.u bef 9th* **40/1**
F63P **P** **Behavingbadly (IRE)**[19] [2946] 11-10-8 **87**.......................... BrianHarding —
(A Parker) *in rr: reminders 8th: sn bhd: p.u after 12th* **11/1**
3P1- **P** **Secret Drinker (IRE)**[268] [4875] 10-10-8 **87**....................(b) JimmyMcCarthy —
(N P McCormack) *chsd ldrs: lost pl 6th: wl bhd whn p.u bef 11th* **28/1**
P-03 **F** **Kingfisher Sunset**[15] [2975] 10-10-11 **90**...................... DominicElsworth 82
(Mrs S J Smith) *chsd ldrs: disputing 2nd but wkng whn fell heavily 2 out* **20/1**

7m 15.9s (9.10) **Going Correction** +0.625s/f (Soft) **12** Ran SP% **113.9**
Speed ratings: **105,99,93,92,91 90,—,—,—,— —,—** CSF £16.90 CT £544.19 TOTE £8.60: £2.20, £1.40, £12.60; EX 21.40 TRIFECTA Not won..
Owner Edward C Wilkin **Bred** Miss Sandra Hunter **Trained** Sheriff Hutton, N Yorks
■ Stewards' Enquiry : Dominic Elsworth one-day ban: improper riding - kicked out at gelding as it ran off track (21 Jan)

FOCUS
No hanging about and the front-running winner goes from strength to strength. The race has been rated through the runner-up but both the first two could be even higher.

NOTEBOOK
Bang And Blame(IRE), put up 15lb after his Boxing Day success, cocked another snook at the Handicapper. Stepping up the gallop going out on to the final circuit, he kept going strongly and was able to ease off on the run-in. He will take another big step up in the ratings. *(op 5-1)*
Weapons Inspector(IRE) went in pursuit of the winner but was never going to get on terms and he was very leg-weary up the final hill. *(tchd 15-8 and 9-4)*
Harry Hooly, struggling to keep up early on the final circuit, in the end did just enough to secure a remote third spot. He is struggling to make much of an impact over fences.
Recent Edition(IRE), pulled up behind the winner here on Boxing Day, is from a stable starting to emerge from the doldrums. He is back on a winning mark and all he does is stay. *(op 20-1)*
Chabrimal Minster, trying to keep tabs on the winner, was out on his feet when he ploughed through the fourth last. *(op 9-2)*
Jethro Tull(IRE), a point winner, was having his first try over regulation fences and he never entered the argument. *(op 8-1)*
Kingfisher Sunset, making his handicap debut, was still in a share of second spot but looking to have no more to give when he took a crashing fall two out. His rider looked displeased and his temper earned him a one-day ban. *(tchd 16-1)*

3337 GG ODDS MARES' ONLY NOVICES' HURDLE (10 hdls) 2m 5f 110y

2:40 (2:41) (Class 4) 4-Y-O+ **£3,253** (£955; £477; £238)

Form | | | | RPR
F31 **1** **Ile Maurice (FR)**[36] [2674] 6-11-8 110.................................... KeithMercer 110+
(Ferdy Murphy) *wnt prom 5th: drvn along 8th: led appr next: 8 l clr last: styd on strly* **5/6**[1]
336P **2** *11* **Verstone (IRE)**[45] [2494] 4-10-3 89.................................. JimmyMcCarthy 74+
(R F Fisher) *hld up in rr: hdwy to chse ldrs 7th: sn led: hdd appr 2 out: kpt on: no ch w wnr* **33/1**
-230 **3** *¾* **Our Joycey**[33] [2718] 5-11-2 .... RichardMcGrath 85
(Mrs K Walton) *chsd ldrs: one pce fr 2 out* **40/1**
2004 **4** *shd* **Political Pendant**[7] [3235] 5-10-9 .... GarethThomas(7) 85
(R Nixon) *wnt prom 5th: one pce fr 2 out* **16/1**
303- **5** *12* **Fortuna Favente (IRE)**[282] [4720] 6-10-11 .... BrianHughes(5) 75+
(J Howard Johnson) *prominet: chsng ldrs 8th: wknd after next* **15/2**[3]
0500 **6** *½* **Esquillon**[22] [2921] 4-9-10 87.. PhilKinsella(7) 61+
(S Parr) *led tl after 7th: wknd appr 2 out* **20/1**
-500 **7** *7* **Flemingstone (IRE)**[35] [2690] 6-10-9 .... MrSFMagee(7) 66
(J R Norton) *prom: w ldrs 8th: wknd appr next* **150/1**
0-10 **8** *14* **Zaffie Parson (IRE)**[48] [2446] 5-10-13 .... WilliamKennedy(3) 52
(G A Harker) *chsd ldrs: lost pl after 8th* **8/1**
5-00 **9** *15* **Penney Lane**[49] [2412] 5-10-13 .... PeterBuchanan(3) 37
(Miss Kate Milligan) *bhd fr 5th* **100/1**
6-06 **10** *30* **Beau Peak**[219] [643] 7-11-2 .... DominicElsworth —
(D W Whillans) *in rr: bhd fr 5th: t.o* **50/1**
P0 **P** **Books Delight**[95] [1661] 6-11-2 .... BrianHarding —
(J Wade) *chsd ldrs: lost pl and hit 7th: bhd whn p.u bef next* **100/1**
620 **P** **Pont Neuf (IRE)**[24] [2873] 6-11-2 .... GrahamLee —
(A Crook) *quite keen in rr: hdwy 7th: lost pl next: bhd whn p.u bef 2 out* **13/2**[2]
4400 **P** **Redditzio**[32] [2752] 5-11-2 ....(b[1]) NeilMulholland —
(C W Thornton) *in rr: hdwy 5th: lost pl after 7th: t.o whn p.u bef 2 out* **150/1**

5m 49.6s (33.90) **Going Correction** +1.275s/f (Heav)
WFA 4 from 5yo+ 12lb **13** Ran SP% **112.1**
Speed ratings: **89,85,84,84,80 80,77,72,67,56 —,—,—** CSF £38.84 TOTE £1.60: £1.10, £10.30, £5.60; EX 36.50.
Owner N Iveson & F Murphy **Bred** Haras De Reuilly **Trained** West Witton, N Yorks

FOCUS
A moderate winning time, more than ten seconds slower than the later handicap over the same trip. In the end the winner found it plain sailing against some mediocre opponents. The second and fourth hold the key to the overall value of the form.

NOTEBOOK
Ile Maurice(FR) made hard work of it for a few strides but in the end her stamina carried her clear. All she looks to do is to stay. *(op 4-5 tchd 8-11 and evens in a place)*
Verstone(IRE), pulled up on her previous start, went on and stepped up the gallop but it was soon evident the winner was much too strong.
Our Joycey, having just her second start over hurdles, looks to have a lot more stamina than speed.
Political Pendant is gradually finding her feet over hurdles and will be suited by a step up to three miles. *(op 14-1)*
Fortuna Favente(IRE), absent for nine months, moved up looking a threat on her hurdling debut at the fourth last flight but she dropped right out jumping the next. The outing may well have been needed. *(op 8-1 tchd 9-1)*
Esquillon took them along in her own time but she stopped to nothing turning into two out. On the level she was suited by two miles so stamina ought not to have been a problem. *(op 14-1)*
Pont Neuf(IRE), keen to get on with it, ran without the usual tongue strap and she is happier going *the other way round. Official explanation: trainer said mare may have missed its tongue strap and could have been unsuited by left-handed track (op 6-1 tchd 7-1)*

3338 GG.COM H'CAP CHASE (12 fncs 4 omitted) 2m 5f

3:10 (3:12) (Class 5) (0-90,89) 5-Y-O+ **£3,513** (£1,031; £515; £257)

Form | | | | RPR
FP-5 **1** **Cyborsun (FR)**[24] [2877] 9-11-5 **89**.................................... CharliePoste(7) 106+
(M F Harris) *hld up in rr: hdwy 8th: chsng ldrs 10th: led between last 2: styd on wl* **10/1**
1-2P **2** *12* **Jballingall**[24] [2877] 7-11-7 **84**..(b) WilsonRenwick 92+
(N Wilson) *led tl between last 2: kpt on same pce* **5/1**[2]
-3PF **3** *20* **Wild About Harry**[55] [2266] 9-10-7 **70**.............................. JimmyMcCarthy 55
(A R Dicken) *sn chsng ldrs: wknd 10th: lft mod 3rd 2 out* **16/1**
0-PP **4** *27* **Jumbo's Dream**[15] [2978] 15-10-3 **71**........................(p) DeclanMcGann(5) 29
(J E Dixon) *chsd ldrs: drvn along 6th: mstke and lost pl 8th* **40/1**
65U6 **5** *24* **Get Smart (IRE)**[45] [2495] 9-10-12 **75**................................... KeithMercer 9
(Ferdy Murphy) *chsd ldr: wknd 9th: sn bhd* **5/1**[2]
P-P0 **P** **Viking Song**[26] [2839] 6-10-1 **64**.. KennyJohnson —
(F Kirby) *mstkes: sn bhd: t.o 8th: p.u bef last* **100/1**
F-0P **P** **Jupsala (FR)**[227] [555] 9-10-11 **74**.. JLCullen —
(S B Bell) *wnt prom 4th: lost pl 9th: bhd whn p.u bef 2 out* **16/1**
605P **P** **Sea Maize**[45] [2495] 8-9-11 **63** oh7.................................. PeterBuchanan(3) —
(C R Wilson) *reminders 5th: sn bhd: t.o whn p.u bef 3 out* **66/1**
4-00 **P** **Terramarique (IRE)**[60] [2171] 7-11-1 **78**............................ BrianHarding —
(L Lungo) *chsd ldrs: lost pl bef 9th: t.o whn p.u bef 2 out* **11/2**[3]
10-P **P** **Lantern Lad (IRE)**[47] [2465] 10-11-7 **84**.......................(p) RichardMcGrath —
(R Ford) *chsd ldrs: lost pl 7th: bhd whn p.u after 8th* **14/1**

24F4 **P** **Another Club Royal**[66] 2039 7-10-12 **75**..........................(b[1]) GrahamLee —
(D McCain) *wnt prom 4th: lost pl 9th: bhd whn p.u bef 2 out* **7/2**[1]
56P0 **P** **Brave Effect (IRE)**[15] 2980 10-11-9 **86**.......................... BarryKeniry —
(Mrs Dianne Sayer) *in rr: lost tch after 6th: t.o whn p.u after 9th* **40/1**
40PP **F** **You'Re The Man (IRE)**[8] 3209 9-10-1 **69**..............(p) MichaelMcAlister(5) —
(Mrs E Slack) *sn drvn along: chsd ldrs: lost pl after 5th: sn bhd: fell 3 out* **16/1**
-4U0 **U** **Do Keep Up**[9] 3170 9-10-5 **73**.......................... DougieCostello(5) —
(J R Weymes) *hld up: hdwy 8th: chsng ldrs whn mstke 3 out: 2 l down and disputing 2nd whn blnd bdly and uns rdr 2 out* **16/1**

5m 35.9s (12.50) **Going Correction** +0.625s/f (Soft) **14** Ran SP% **117.6**
Speed ratings: **101,96,88,78,69** —,—,—,—,— —,—,—,— CSF £58.81 CT £805.68 TOTE £8.90: £3.10, £1.60, £5.70; EX 49.30.
Owner C J Leech **Bred** J Thoreau **Trained** Edgcote, Northants
■ A first chase success for Charlie Poste, aboard his 16th career winner.

FOCUS
A modest handicap run at a sound pace and they came home in indian file. The winner has had his problems, the runner-up is the key to the form.

NOTEBOOK
Cyborsun(FR), who has broken blood-vessels in the past, benefited from a patient ride and he came clear up the final hill. At one time he was rated 122 so there should be plenty to play with. *(op 8-1)*
Jballingall, with the blinkers back on, took them along but in the end he had no answer as the winner swept by him. *(op 8-1)*
Wild About Harry, second behind the runner-up at Carlisle in April, is not in the same form now and had failed to get round on his two most recent starts. *(op 14-1)*
Jumbo's Dream, third in this last year, brings his pension book to the races with him now. *(op 20-1)*
Get Smart(IRE), who last won in Ireland over two years ago, has been tried over a variety of distances lately without connections discovering the secret. *(tchd 9-2)*
Do Keep Up, dropping back in trip, ran a lot better and would have finished third at worst but for giving his rider no chance two out. *(op 20-1 tchd 25-1)*
Another Club Royal stopped to nothing four out before calling it a day. He was reported to have a breathing problem. *Official explanation: jockey said gelding had a breathing problem (op 20-1 tchd 25-1)*

3339 JOHN SMITH'S EXTRA SMOOTH H'CAP HURDLE (10 hdls) 2m 5f 110y
3:40 (3:41) (Class 4) (0-110,105) 4-Y-0+ **£3,383** (£993; £496; £248)

Form RPR
5302 **1** **Joe Brown**[14] 3042 6-11-7 **100**.......................... JimCrowley 104+
(Mrs H Dalton) *chsd ldr fr 3rd: led after 6th: 3 l up last: hld on wl towards fin* **3/1**[1]
4150 **2** *3/4* **Primitive Poppy**[37] 2653 7-10-1 **83**.......................... PeterBuchanan(3) 83
(Mrs A Hamilton) *in rr: gd hdwy 7th: wnt 2nd appr 2 out: styd on run-in: no ex towards fin* **10/1**
0303 **3** *29* **Miss Pross**[15] 2994 6-11-0 **93**.......................... RobertWalford 64
(T D Walford) *wnt prom 4th: chsd wnr 7th tl appr 2 out: regained remote 3rd last* **9/2**[2]
00P2 **4** *3/4* **Why The Long Face (NZ)**[72] 1940 9-11-2 **105**.............. JohnFlavin(10) 75
(R C Guest) *hld up: hdwy to chse ldrs 7th: wnt modest 3rd next: one pce* **7/1**[3]
0023 **5** *8* **Nobodys Perfect (IRE)**[15] 2981 6-10-11 **90**.......................... KeithMercer 52
(Ferdy Murphy) *prom: outpcd appr 8th* **9/2**[2]
034P **6** *15* **Lutin Du Moulin (FR)**[24] 2877 7-11-7 **100**.......................... WilsonRenwick 47
(L Lungo) *chsd ldrs: lost pl after 7th: sn bhd* **7/1**[3]
1FP0 **7** *19* **Infini (FR)**[25] 2862 10-10-11 **100**.......................... MichaelO'Connell(10) 28
(Mrs S J Smith) *led: sn clr: hdd after 6th: wkng whn mstke next: sn bhd: t.o 2 out* **20/1**
40PP **P** **I'm Your Man**[15] 2977 7-10-10 **89**.......................... BrianHarding —
(Mrs Dianne Sayer) *in rr: bhd whn reminders 4th: t.o whn p.u bef 6th* **100/1**
40-0 **P** **Lady Past Times**[19] 2944 6-10-3 **82**.......................... GrahamLee —
(D W Whillans) *reminders and lost pl 4th: sn bhd: t.o whn p.u bef 6th* **16/1**
3101 **P** **Sheer Guts (IRE)**[63] 2107 7-11-9 **102**..........................(vt) OllieMcPhail —
(Robert Gray) *chsd ldrs: drvn along 5th: lost pl next: t.o 7th: p.u bef 2 out* **14/1**

5m 39.3s (23.60) **Going Correction** +1.275s/f (Heavy) **10** Ran SP% **113.8**
Speed ratings: **108,107,97,96,94 88,81**,—,—,— CSF £32.25 CT £132.18 TOTE £4.20: £2.20, £3.40, £1.70; EX 48.40 Place 6 £46.19, Place 5 £35.70.
Owner Miss C A Owen **Bred** R C Owen **Trained** Norton, Shropshire

FOCUS
They raced all over the track searching for less cut-up ground. In the end the first two were out on their own in a very ordinary contest, and the race is rated through the temperamental runner-up.

NOTEBOOK
Joe Brown, a maiden point winner, was racing from a 5lb higher mark over a shorter trip. He landed flat-footed at the final flight but in the end did just enough. Fences will not be a problem. *(tchd 7-2 in a place and 10-3 in places)*
Primitive Poppy, who is a worrier, improved from the rear to go in pursuit of the winner and was clawing him back all the way to the line. The problem is with her temperament she is not sure to run as well next time. *(op 14-1)*
Miss Pross, a maiden after a dozen previous starts, likes soft ground but the first two ran clean away from her over the final two flights. *(op 11-2)*
Why The Long Face(NZ), absent since October, ran without the usual headgear.
Nobodys Perfect(IRE) did not improve one iota for the step up in trip. *(op 5-1)*
T/Jkpt: Part won. £25,477.60 to a £1 stake. Pool: £35,884.00. 0.50 winning tickets. T/Plt: £37.60 to a £1 stake. Pool: £47,274.10. 915.45 winning tickets. T/Qpdt: £11.90 to a £1 stake. Pool: £3,112.60. 192.10 winning tickets. WG

2824 NEWBURY (L-H)
Wednesday, January 11
OFFICIAL GOING: Good to soft (good in places)
Wind: Slight, ahead

3340 BERKSHIRE STAND BOOKSHOP JUVENILE NOVICES' HURDLE (7 hdls 1 omitted) 2m 110y
12:45 (12:51) (Class 4) 4-Y-0 **£2,927** (£859; £429; £214)

Form RPR
0 **1** **Detroit City (USA)**[38] 2661 4-10-12 .... PJBrennan 124
(P J Hobbs) *hmpd 1st: hdwy 3rd: chsd ldrs 4th: led 2 out: drvn and r.o strly run-in* **8/1**
4 **2** *1 1/2* **Royals Darling (GER)**[110] 4-11-5 .... MickFitzgerald 129
(N J Henderson) *angular: lw: chsd ldrs: chal 2 out: stl ev ch at bypassed fnl flight: one pce run-in* **3/1**[1]
32 **3** *8* **Victorias Groom (GER)**[11] 3132 4-10-12 .... LeightonAspell 116+
(Mrs L Wadham) *in tch whn hmpd 4th: chsd ldrs sn after: rdn and one pce appr bypassed fnl flight* **9/2**[3]
4 *7* **Jack Rolfe**[8] 4-10-12 .... JamieMoore 107
(G L Moore) *in tch: hdwy 5th: styd on one pce fr next* **20/1**
0 **5** *5* **Estate**[23] 2921 4-10-12 .... TomDoyle 102
(P R Webber) *in tch: hdwy 4th: rdn and wknd 2 after 2 out* **100/1**
1 **6** *8* **Shiny Thing (USA)**[33] 2753 4-10-12 .... RobertThornton 94
(A King) *lw: chsd ldrs: rdn and wknd 2 out* **12/1**
7 *7* **Kryena**[30] 4-10-5 .... JimmyMcCarthy 80
(Mrs P Robeson) *rr whn hmpd 4th: sn in tch: wknd after 3 out* **100/1**
0 **8** *10* **Brave Hiawatha (FR)**[28] 2824 4-10-12 .... JasonMaguire 77
(J A B Old) *chsd ldrs: lft in ld 4th: hdd & wknd 2 out* **50/1**
5 **9** *7* **Globalized (IRE)**[29] 2811 4-10-12 .... AntonyEvans 70
(Mrs P Sly) *rr: hdwy 4th: sn wknd* **100/1**
10 *7* **Kofi**[254] 4-10-12 .... AndrewThornton 63
(Miss K M George) *hmpd 1st: bhd most of way* **100/1**
0 **11** *7* **Innpursuit**[41] 2580 4-10-12 .... MarkBradburne 56
(J M P Eustace) *chsd ldrs to 5th* **100/1**
0P4 **12** *7* **Desert Moonbeam (IRE)**[30] 2797 4-10-0 .... JayHarris(5) 42
(R J Hodges) *led tl after 1st: hmpd 4th and sn wknd* **100/1**
13 *8* **Danzare**[22] 4-10-5 .... PhilipHide 34
(Mrs A J Hamilton-Fairley) *hmpd 4th: a in rr* **100/1**
F **14** *24* **Ball Boy**[20] 2949 4-10-12 ....(t) PaulMoloney 17
(G Haine) *hmpd 1st: a in rr* **50/1**
F **Love Affair (IRE)**[16] 4-10-5 .... RJGreene —
(R Hannon) *fell 1st* **100/1**
0 **F** **Form And Beauty (IRE)**[15] 3021 4-10-7 .... LeeStephens(5) —
(C Roberts) *fell 1st* **100/1**
B **Maya's Prince** 4-10-12 ....(b[1]) DaveCrosse —
(M D I Usher) *bdly hmpd and b.d 1st* **100/1**
41 **B** **Prize Fighter (IRE)**[20] 2954 4-11-5 .... APMcCoy —
(Jonjo O'Neill) *lw: hmpd and b.d 1st* **4/1**[2]
F4F **F** **Ellerslie Tom**[30] 2797 4-10-12 .... TimmyMurphy —
(P Bowen) *led after 1st tl fell 4th* **25/1**
P **Spear Thistle**[69] 4-10-12 .... JimCrowley —
(Mrs N Smith) *hmpd 1st: sn t.o: p.u bef last* **8/1**
B **Son Of Bathwick (IRE)**[128] 4-10-12 .... SeanCurran —
(Mrs Norma Pook) *bdly hmpd and b.d 1st* **100/1**
00 **P** **Ihuru**[8] 2824 4-10-12 .... AndrewTinkler —
(J G Portman) *rr: rdn 3rd: t.o whn p.u bef 2 out* **100/1**
P **Akram (IRE)**[167] 4-10-12 .... NoelFehily —
(Jonjo O'Neill) *chsd ldrs to 5th: t.o whn p.u bef last* **14/1**
F **Oakley Absolute**[25] 4-10-12 .... BrianCrowley —
(R Hannon) *lw: in tch: hdwy 4th: sn wknd: no ch whn fell last* **66/1**

3m 59.7s (-3.90) **Going Correction** -0.05s/f (Good) **24** Ran SP% **125.7**
Speed ratings: **107,106,102,99,96 93,89,85,81,78 75,71,68,56**,— —,—,—,—,— —,—,—,— CSF £30.75 TOTE £9.20: £3.40, £2.10, £1.80; EX 50.20.
Owner Terry Warner **Bred** E J Kelly **Trained** Withycombe, Somerset

FOCUS
There was total melee at the first flight with two fallers and three others being brought down. The carnage also resulted in that hurdle, which would have been the final obstacle, being omitted next time around. The pace was decent and the field finished well strung out, so the form looks reasonable.

NOTEBOOK
Detroit City(USA) proved a completely different proposition compared with his hurdling debut, but although Warwick is a stiff-enough track, this more galloping course suited him down to the ground. He and the runner-up had the race to themselves on the very long run-in and his Flat speed was an asset under the circumstances. This looked a decent contest and he should continue to progress. *(tchd 7-1)*
Royals Darling(GER) ◆, a winner over hurdles in Germany and placed in a Listed hurdle in France, made a very encouraging British debut. Only the winner was able to stay with him after jumping what proved to be the final flight, but his rival's Flat speed on the long run-in probably proved decisive. Despite having to carry a penalty in races like this, he should not take long in going one better. *(tchd 10-3 in places)*
Victorias Groom(GER), although eventually well held by the front pair, ran another decent race over hurdles on ground that may have been faster than ideal, but he appears to lack finishing speed and may be worth a try over further. *(op 5-1 tchd 11-2)*
Jack Rolfe ◆, winner of a 12-furlong Polytrack maiden eight days earlier, was making his hurdling debut and offered plenty of encouragement. A novice hurdle should come his way before too long.
Estate ran with credit considering his price, though he may not have improved much from his Doncaster hurdling debut and he was still firmly put in his place by the principals. Considering his breeding, he has been a disappointing sort.
Shiny Thing(USA) found this much tougher under her penalty and will need her sights lowered. *(op 11-1)*
Prize Fighter(IRE) was given no chance to build on his easy Fakenham victory and hopefully this experience will not leave its mark. *(op 3-1 tchd 9-2, 5-1 in places)*
Ellerslie Tom, who was very keen to get on with things and broke the tape at the first attempt for a start, was again keen when the race got under way for real and was still in front when crumpling on landing at the fourth. He has now fallen in three of his four starts over hurdles, but still gives the impression that a sharp track and fast ground could see him land a small event. *(op 3-1 tchd 9-2, 5-1 in places)*

3341 PHEASANT INN NOVICES' CHASE (13 fncs) 2m 1f
1:20 (1:23) (Class 3) 5-Y-0+ **£7,807** (£2,292; £1,146; £572)

Form RPR
-11U **1** **Justified (IRE)**[16] 3006 7-11-12 .... APMcCoy 151+
(E Sheehy, Ire) *lw: j.w: mde all: shkn up run-in: kpt on wl* **8/13**[1]
-214 **2** *2 1/2* **Cornish Sett (IRE)**[11] 3150 7-11-8 137..........................(b) ChristianWilliams 144+
(P F Nicholls) *lw: j. sltly rt thrght: hld up but in tch: tk clsr order appr 9th: chsd wnr fr 4 out: hit last: kpt on same pce* **9/2**[2]
L0/1 **3** *7* **Hors La Loi III (FR)**[34] 2732 11-11-12 .... DGallagher 142+
(P F Nicholls) *hld up: hdwy to chse wnr 4th: rdn appr 4 out: one pced fr 3 out: hit last* **11/1**
-124 **4** *dist* **Celtic Son (FR)**[32] 2759 7-11-12 ....(t) TimmyMurphy —
(M C Pipe) *lw: chsd ldrs: sn niggled along to go pce: lost tch after 8th* **5/1**[3]
0-6F **5** *dist* **Goldseam (GER)**[34] 2729 7-11-2 .... MarkBradburne —
(S C Burrough) *reminders after 5th: bhd fr 8th* **300/1**
F-PF **P** **Perfect Liaison**[16] 2999 9-11-2 120.......................... AndrewThornton —
(R H Alner) *j.rt thrght: chsd wnr tl 4th: sn bhd: mstke 7th: t.o whn blnd 4 out: p.u bef next* **33/1**

4m 14.8s (5.40) **Going Correction** +0.30s/f (Yiel) **6** Ran SP% **108.4**
Speed ratings: **99,97,94**,—,— — CSF £3.70 TOTE £1.60: £1.10, £2.10; EX 3.80.

Owner Braybrook Syndicate **Bred** Miss Maura McGuinness **Trained** Graiguenamanagh, Kilkenny

FOCUS

A fascinating novice chase, but even though Justified set a decent early pace the eventual winning time was very ordinary for a race of its class. With the favourite not winning in the style many expected and Celtic Son running so badly, the precise merit of the form is hard to evaluate.

NOTEBOOK

Justified(IRE) put his first-fence blemish at Leopardstown behind him and jumped very well under a positive ride, but he had to be put under pretty serious pressure to hold the persistent runner-up at bay, and things would have been even harder had that rival not missed out the last. In his defence, he apparently had a very difficult trip over from Ireland and remains a major player for this year's Arkle. *(op 4-6 tchd 8-11 in places)*

Cornish Sett(IRE), like the winner attempting to put the record straight following his dismal Warwick effort, was a completely different proposition back on a sounder surface and back on a track he is proven on. He made sure the favourite never had things easy and may have given him even more to think about had he jumped the last better. He may be just below the very top novices and it will be interesting to see if his trainer considers the handicap option, with a race like the Grand Annual an intriguing possibility. *(op 11-2)*

Hors La Loi III(FR), who cut his leg when winning on his chasing debut at Taunton last month, was close enough at halfway but he was awkward at the cross-fence and could never make much impression after that. He does not look up to this level at his time of life and it will be interesting to see what route he takes next. *(op 8-1 tchd 12-1)*

Celtic Son(FR), dropped right down in trip, was never travelling from an early stage and again proved bitterly disappointing. His stable is going better now than it was, so that can hardly be used as an excuse this time and he has plenty of questions to answer now. *(op 9-2)*

Perfect Liaison *Official explanation: jockey said gelding had breathing problems (op 40-1)*

3342 FABULOUS FAKES NOVICES' HURDLE (11 hdls) 2m 3f

1:55 (1:58) (Class 4) 5-Y-0+ **£3,253** (£955; £477; £238)

Form / RPR

2-2 **1** **Wogan**[45] 2528 6-10-12 MickFitzgerald 123+
(N J Henderson) *lw: trckd ldrs: wnt 2nd 3 out: sn rdn: styd on to ld last: drvn and kpt on wl* **9/4**[1]

412R **2** *3 ½* **Shining Strand**[23] 2925 7-11-5 113 AndrewTinkler 124
(N J Henderson) *slt ld fr 3rd: pushed along 2 out: rdn and hdd last: no ex run-in* **8/1**

35 **3** *7* **Odiham**[33] 2755 5-10-12 (v) JimCrowley 111+
(H Morrison) *mid-div: rdn and hdwy whn hit 3 out: nvr gng pce to rch ldrs but kpt on to take 3rd last* **9/2**[2]

561 **4** *6* **Napoleon (IRE)**[23] 2923 5-11-5 120 PJBrennan 112+
(P J Hobbs) *chsd ldrs: rdn appr 3 out: wknd next* **7/1**

34- **5** *6* **Killenaule (IRE)**[313] 4160 6-10-12 TomDoyle 100+
(B G Powell) *led to 3rd: chsd ldr 4 out to next: sn wknd* **11/2**[3]

6 *13* **Champion's Day (GER)**[444] 5-10-12 APMcCoy 85
(Jonjo O'Neill) *lw: w'like: bhd: hdwy 4 out: trckd ldrs appr next: sn wknd* **9/1**

7 *10* **Darn Good**[107] 5-10-12 RobertThornton 75
(A King) *bhd tl mod prog fr 2 out* **40/1**

PU **8** *3 ½* **Irish Raptor (IRE)**[74] 1917 7-10-12 AntonyEvans 72
(N A Twiston-Davies) *chsd ldrs: rdn 4 out: wknd next* **50/1**

/3-0 **9** *3* **Harbour Rock (IRE)**[16] 2988 7-10-12 CarlLlewellyn 69
(D J Wintle) *lw: a in rr* **150/1**

10 *24* **Grenoli (FR)**[213] 5-10-12 ChristianWilliams 45
(P F Nicholls) *w'like: chsd ldrs to 4 out* **25/1**

40 **11** *shd* **Lord Ryeford (IRE)**[34] 2720 6-10-12 JasonMaguire 44
(T R George) *a in rr: no ch whn blnd 2 out* **100/1**

12 *dist* **Clanrye (IRE)**[88] 5-10-12 LeightonAspell —
(P G Murphy) *a in rr: t.o* **80/1**

05- **F** **Mrs Fizziwig**[266] 4935 7-10-5 JimmyMcCarthy —
(R T Phillips) *in rr tl fell 5th* **66/1**

-04 **P** **Adventurist**[23] 2923 6-10-12 NoelFehily —
(P Bowen) *lw: in tch to 5th: t.o whn p.u bef 3 out* **14/1**

00 **P** **Country Rally**[220] 656 7-10-12 JohnMcNamara —
(Mrs S Gardner) *nt fluent in rr: t.o whn p.u after 6th* **200/1**

P **Teal Saqqara (FR)** 7-10-12 SamThomas —
(Miss Venetia Williams) *w ldr after 3rd to 6th: wknd 4 out: t.o whn p.u bef 2 out* **50/1**

4m 45.2s (-1.60) **Going Correction** -0.05s/f (Good) **16** Ran SP% **119.7**
Speed ratings: **101,99,96,94,91 86,81,80,79,69 68,—,—,—,— —** CSF £20.00 TOTE £3.40: £1.60, £2.80, £1.90; EX 25.70.

Owner P A Deal **Bred** Mrs Helen Plumbly **Trained** Upper Lambourn, Berks

FOCUS

The early pace did not appear to be that strong, but they still finished well strung out and the race provided a one-two for the Henderson yard. The winner looks a nice prospect and the race could be rated higher.

NOTEBOOK

Wogan did not appear to be travelling as well as his stable companion starting up the home straight and had to be hard ridden to get on terms with him, but the further they went the better he was going and despite landing on all-fours at the last, he was well on top on the run-in. The step up in trip obviously suited and he should go on from here. *(op 11-4)*

Shining Strand fortunately did not repeat his Doncaster antics. Given a positive ride, he still seemed to be travelling much better than his rivals out in front starting up the home straight, but although he did nothing wrong he found his less-exposed stable companion too strong from the final flight. His penalty will always make him vulnerable to improvers in races like this and a return to handicaps looks to be in order. *(tchd 9-1)*

Odiham, with the visor back on for the first time over hurdles, stayed on at the one pace over the last half-mile without ever looking likely to get on terms with the Henderson duo. He shaped as though even this trip was insufficient and, as we know he stays so well on the Flat, another step up in trip over timber could make him interesting. *(op 5-1 tchd 11-2)*

Napoleon(IRE) faced a stiff task under his penalty against some unexposed sorts and was not completely disgraced, but he did not appear to get home on this easier surface. *(op 15-2 tchd 8-1)*

Killenaule(IRE), reappearing from a ten-month break, was nonetheless well supported in the market and showed up for a long way, but gradually dropped away up the home straight as though the run was needed. He will strip fitter next time. *(op 9-1)*

Champion's Day(GER), placed in Group and Listed company on the Flat in Germany, was racing for the first time in 15 months and although he looked at one stage like getting into it starting up the home straight, his effort came to nothing. The market suggested the run was needed and that is how it looked. *(op 5-1)*

Darn Good *Official explanation: jockey said gelding had breathing problems (op 33-1)*

3343 THREE SWANS H'CAP CHASE (FOR THE HARWELL TROPHY) (18 fncs) 3m

2:25 (2:29) (Class 3) (0-125,125) 5-Y-0+ **£6,506** (£1,910; £955; £477)

Form / RPR

3-P3 **1** **Sonevafushi (FR)**[33] 2748 8-11-12 **125** SamThomas 152+
(Miss Venetia Williams) *j.w: mde all: drew clr fr 3 out: easily* **9/2**[1]

5220 **2** *17* **Bee An Bee (IRE)**[47] 2485 9-11-7 **120** (b) JasonMaguire 130+
(T R George) *trckd ldrs: cl 3rd whn hit 4 out: sn rdn to chse wnr: 2nd and hld whn hit 2 out* **7/1**

-132 **3** *6* **Admiral Peary (IRE)**[11] 3142 10-11-3 **116** APMcCoy 117+
(C R Egerton) *chsd wnr: nt fluent 5th: rdn whn stmbld 5 out: wknd after 3 out* **6/1**

-P51 **4** *2* **Magic Of Sydney (IRE)**[29] 2808 10-10-7 **106** BrianCrowley 101
(R Rowe) *chsd ldrs: hit 13th: rdn after next: wknd 4 out* **9/1**

3P-4 **5** *18* **Lord Seamus**[35] 2703 11-10-10 **109** JohnMcNamara 86
(K C Bailey) *chsd ldrs: losing pl whn hit 10th: sn bhd* **16/1**

4 **6** *26* **Lord Archie (IRE)**[41] 2599 8-11-1 **114** (tp) MarkBradburne 65
(M Sheppard) *sn mid div: trckd ldrs 9th: rdn after 14th: wkng whn sltly hmpd 3 out* **14/1**

-1P3 **7** *8* **Trust Fund (IRE)**[40] 2608 8-11-6 **119** RobertWalford 62
(R H Alner) *swtg: a bhd: lost tch fr 12th* **13/2**

-00P **P** **Redde (IRE)**[11] 3140 11-9-7 **99** oh8 CharlieStudd[(7)] —
(Mrs J G Retter) *sn bhd: t.o fr 8th: p.u bef 4 out* **100/1**

3411 **P** **Blunham Hill (IRE)**[25] 2877 8-9-11 **101** MarkNicolls[(5)] —
(John R Upson) *nvr travelling: towards rr: drvn into midfield 7th: bhd fr 11th: t.o and p.u bef 3 out* **5/1**[2]

FP43 **U** **Jaoka Du Gord (FR)**[11] 3151 9-10-2 **101** TomDoyle —
(P R Webber) *hld up bhd: hdwy 12th: trckd ldrs 14th:cl 2nd whn blnd bdly and rdr lost irons 4 out: mstke and uns rdr next* **11/2**[3]

6m 6.50s (1.50) **Going Correction** +0.30s/f (Yiel) **10** Ran SP% **113.9**
Speed ratings: **109,103,101,100,94 86,83,—,—,—** CSF £35.50 CT £188.98 TOTE £5.10: £2.50, £2.30, £2.10; EX 22.80.

Owner B C Dice **Bred** Gil M Protti **Trained** Kings Caple, H'fords

FOCUS

A fair handicap, which saw the field finish strung out, and the winner turned in a fine front-running display under top weight and the race could rate higher.

NOTEBOOK

Sonevafushi(FR), reverting to three miles, put in an exemplary round of fencing and never saw another rival en-route to a most decisive success under top weight. He has always looked happiest when able to dominate over fences, which is more feasible for him over this longer trip, and he should be rated value for even further than his already wide winning margin. However, he has struggled off higher marks in the past so while his confidence should be sky high now, he is not one to bank on for a follow-up bid after an inevitable hike in the weights. *(op 7-2)*

Bee An Bee(IRE), with the blinkers back on, emerged as the clear danger to the winner approaching three out, but despite a bad mistake at the penultimate fence, it made little difference to the overall result and he was well held. His tendency to make mistakes at a crucial stage is his downfall, and he receives little respite from the Handicapper due to his consistent profile, but he is a sound benchmark for this form nevertheless. *(op 13-2)*

Admiral Peary(IRE) rather spoilt his chance with some sloppy jumping, but this was just his third outing over fences to date, and he is still entitled to improve in that department. It may also be that he needs a deeper surface to be seen at best. *(op 4-1)*

Magic Of Sydney(IRE), raised 11lb for winning easily at Folkestone last time, was found out by this higher mark yet was not disgraced in defeat. He can find easier opportunities to regain the winning thread. *(op 8-1)*

Trust Fund(IRE) turned in a tame effort and failed to pick up at any stage from off the pace. He has something to prove now. *(op 8-1)*

Jaoka Du Gord(FR) made a serious error four out and then gave his rider no chance of maintaining their partnership when getting the third last all wrong. He was still going well at the time, however, and would most likely have bagged a place with a clear round. *(op 13-2 tchd 7-1)*

Blunham Hill(IRE), up in trip and bidding for a hat-trick from a 7lb higher mark, never looked happy at any stage and proved most disappointing. *Official explanation: trainer said gelding was unsuited by the good to soft (good in places) ground (op 13-2 tchd 7-1)*

3344 M AND C CARPETS H'CAP CHASE (15 fncs) 2m 2f 110y

3:00 (3:01) (Class 3) (0-120,116) 5-Y-0+ **£6,506** (£1,910; £955; £477)

Form / RPR

156- **1** **Rubberdubber**[337] 3747 6-11-8 **112** APMcCoy 125+
(C R Egerton) *lw: hld up in tch: hdwy 10th: led 4 out: lft 8l clr next: easily* **10/3**[1]

-F50 **2** *3 ½* **Key Phil (FR)**[42] 2577 8-11-12 **116** HenryOliver 120
(D J Wintle) *chsd ldrs: chal 11th: sn one pce: rallied to chse wnr 2 out: kpt on run-in but a readily hld* **40/1**

2-05 **3** *½* **Kew Jumper (IRE)**[23] 2926 7-11-4 **108** JasonMaguire 118+
(Andrew Turnell) *hld up rr: hdwy 10th: trckd ldrs next: chsd wnr and styng on whn sprawled on landing 3 out: kpt on wl run-in: but nt rcvr* **12/1**

F11P **4** *14* **Soeur Fontenail (FR)**[15] 3019 9-11-8 **112** MickFitzgerald 101
(N J Hawke) *chsd ldrs: rdn and hit 4 out: wknd fr next* **20/1**

-141 **5** *2 ½* **Lindsay (FR)**[23] 2926 7-11-2 **111** TomGreenway[(5)] 98
(H D Daly) *chsd ldrs: wknd and hit 4 out: mstke next* **12/1**

4226 **6** *2 ½* **Escompteur (FR)**[32] 2757 6-11-4 **115** AndrewGlassonbury[(7)] 100+
(M C Pipe) *hit 2nd: chsd ldrs 5th: led 8th: hdd 4 out and sn wknd* **11/2**[3]

3560 **7** *5* **Day Du Roy (FR)**[32] 2768 8-11-8 **112** TomSiddall 91
(Miss L C Siddall) *in tch: hdwy 7th: trckd ldrs 11th: wknd 4 out* **80/1**

F-4F **8** *14* **Kosmos Bleu (FR)**[35] 2703 8-11-6 **110** AndrewThornton 75
(R H Alner) *led 3rd to 8th: mstke 9th: wknd 4 out: no ch whn blnd last* **9/1**

3103 **9** *3* **Toulouse (IRE)**[21] 2939 9-11-4 **115** DarylJacob[(7)] 77
(R H Alner) *chsd ldrs: hit 8th: ev ch 11th: wknd and hit next* **25/1**

-452 **10** *¾* **Ballyrobert (IRE)**[28] 2827 9-11-6 **110** AndrewTinkler 71
(C R Egerton) *hit 2nd: blnd 11th: a bhd* **12/1**

P40- **11** *shd* **Wakeup Smiling (IRE)**[396] 2760 8-10-11 **101** MarcusFoley 62
(Miss E C Lavelle) *hit 11th: bhd most of way* **12/1**

B1P5 **12** *dist* **Haafel (USA)**[26] 2870 9-11-6 **110** (b) PhilipHide —
(G L Moore) *hit 6th: a bhd: t.o* **66/1**

P-26 **F** **New Bird (GER)**[53] 2339 11-11-5 **109** WayneHutchinson —
(Ian Williams) *bhd tl fell 8th* **66/1**

04-2 **P** **Lamp's Return**[38] 2664 7-11-4 **108** RobertThornton —
(A King) *prom early: t.o whn p.u bef 11th* **9/2**[2]

611- **P** **Laurier D'Estruval (FR)**[310] 4234 7-11-2 **106** JoeTizzard —
(S E H Sherwood) *prom early: bhd fr 7th: t.o whn p.u bef 11th* **20/1**

21FP **P** **Forever Dream**[16] 2996 8-11-10 **114** (b) PJBrennan —
(P J Hobbs) *in tch:blnd 7th: mstkes ninth and 10th: sn wknd: t.o whn p.u bef last* **80/1**

4m 44.6s (3.20) **Going Correction** +0.30s/f (Yiel) **16** Ran SP% **118.7**
Speed ratings: **105,103,103,97,96 95,93,87,86,85 85,—,—,—,— —** CSF £136.08 CT £1443.78 TOTE £5.00: £2.20, £12.60, £2.40, £4.40; EX 327.70 Trifecta £798.30 Part won. Pool: £1,124.38 - 0.30 winning tickets..

Owner Mr & Mrs Peter Orton **Bred** Mrs Susan Orton **Trained** Chaddleworth, Berks

FOCUS

A modest handicap for the grade, which saw the first three come clear and, although not strong form, the winner can rate higher in due course.

NOTEBOOK

Rubberdubber ◆, making his chase and handicap debut after a 337-day absence, got his campaign off to a perfect start with a most decisive success. His jumping was very assured for a first-timer, he looked very much at home on this ground, and shaped as though he should have no trouble in staying a bit further. Lightly-raced, he is open to plenty of further improvement over fences - despite looking fit for his run after an absence - and appeals as one to follow. *(tchd 7-2)*

Key Phil(FR) was handy throughout and posted a very creditable effort under top weight in defeat. He never rated a serious threat to the winner, but this was still his best effort of the current campaign, and he could build on this if found an opportunity on softer ground in the coming weeks.

Kew Jumper(IRE) ◆ did very well to recover from a terrible error three from home, and the manner in which he finished his race suggests he would have gone close with a clear round. He was progressive last term, and this was much more like his true form, so he looks one to side with next time providing the Handicapper does not raise him too much for this. *(op 11-1)*

Soeur Fontenail(FR), pulled up at Cheptsow when seaching for the hat-trick last time, showed her true colours in defeat and would have been a touch closer, but for making an error four from home. She still looks held by her current mark, however.

Lindsay(FR), raised 5lb for winning at Doncaster last time, ran below his best and saw his jumping fall apart from four out.

Escompteur(FR) was another to run below his recent level and he has become a frustrating customer. *(op 5-1)*

Lamp's Return stopped quickly and was pulled up as though something was amiss. *Official explanation: jockey said mare boiled over prior to race (tchd 11-2 in places and 6-1 in places)*

3345 WEATHERBYS INSURANCE CONDITIONAL JOCKEYS' H'CAP HURDLE (13 hdls) 3m 110y

3:30 (3:32) (Class 4) (0-110,109) 4-Y-O+ **£3,083** (£898; £449)

Form				RPR
325	**1**		**Kilty Storm (IRE)**[64] [2099] 7-10-13 **104**................ AndrewGlassonbury(8) *(M C Pipe) in tch: wnt 2nd at the 8th: led appr 3 out: sn rdn: edgd lft fr 2 out: styd on: rdn out* **4/1**[2]	111+
4213	**2**	*5*	**The Gangerman (IRE)**[16] [2985] 6-11-1 **106**.................... BernieWharfe(8) *(N A Twiston-Davies) lw: chsd ldrs: rdn after 9th: lft 2nd 3 out and j.lft thereafter : kpt on same pce* **8/1**[3]	106
P-01	**3**	*2 ½*	**Captain Corelli**[39] [2628] 9-11-7 **107**............................ RobertStephens(3) *(P J Hobbs) hld up towards rr: stdy hdwy fr 6th to chse ldrs after 9th: rdn and mstke 3 out: styd on same pce* **5/6**[1]	105
64-1	**4**	*23*	**Roman Rampage**[9] [3222] 11-10-5 **91** 7ex..........(p) RobertLucey-Butler(5) *(Miss Z C Davison) hld up in rr: mstke 6th: wnt poor 4th after last: nvr a danger* **25/1**	66
3456	**5**	*1 ¾*	**The Flyer (IRE)**[26] [2862] 9-11-5 **105**........................(t) RichardSpate(3) *(Miss S J Wilton) hld up towards rr: sme hdwy 8th: wknd after 3 out* **33/1**	78
0200	**6**	*½*	**Middleham Park (IRE)**[9] [3214] 6-11-3 **108**............... WayneKavanagh(8) *(J W Mullins) hld up towards rr: stdy hdwy fr 6th to chse ldrs after 9th: sn rdn: wkng in 4th whn mstke 2 out* **40/1**	80
-32P	**7**	*dist*	**Baikaline (FR)**[58] [2243] 7-10-9 **100**.................................... DavidBoland(8) *(Ian Williams) chsd ldrs tl wknd after 7th* **33/1**	—
000P	**F**		**Hi Humpfree**[22] [2934] 6-10-12 **95**...............................(b[1]) KeithMercer *(Mrs H Dalton) led tl narrowly hdd and fell 3 out* **25/1**	—
-500	**P**		**Simonovski (USA)**[7] [3242] 5-11-8 **105**......................... TomMalone *(S C Burrough) a towards rr: t.o and p.u bef 3 out* **33/1**	—
6P5-	**P**		**Bright Green**[426] [2153] 7-10-13 **96**.............................. DerekLaverty *(C J Gray) mid div tl 7th: sn bhd: p.u bef 3 out* **100/1**	—
PP	**P**		**Bobalong (IRE)**[29] [2812] 9-11-12 **109**...............................(t) OwynNelmes *(C P Morlock) chsd ldrs tl 5th: sn wl bhd: p.u bef 8th* **100/1**	—
0000	**F**		**Society Buck (IRE)**[29] [2813] 9-11-8 **105**............................(p) MarkNicolls *(John Allen) mid div: reminders after 4th: fell next* **100/1**	—
0P-5	**P**		**Celtic Major (IRE)**[63] [2130] 8-11-2 **99**...................... WilliamKennedy *(P Bowen) w ldr tl wknd after 9th: bhd and p.u bef 3 out* **12/1**	—
P-24	**P**		**Rudolf Rassendyll (IRE)**[40] [2616] 11-11-5 **105**................ LiamHeard(3) *(Miss Venetia Williams) mid div tl 7th: sn bhd: p.u bef 3 out* **16/1**	—
1P-P	**P**		**Montesino**[16] [2969] 7-11-5 **105**................................(v[1]) EamonDehdashti(3) *(M Madgwick) in tch: wnt 2nd appr 6th: wknd after 8th: t.o and p.u bef 3 out* **66/1**	—

6m 10.2s (8.10) **Going Correction** -0.05s/f (Good) **15** Ran SP% **122.7**

Speed ratings: **85,83,82,75,74 74,—,—,—,— —,—,—,—,—** CSF £33.89 CT £51.08 TOTE £6.40: £2.00, £1.90, £1.30; EX 45.30.

Owner Sean Lucey **Bred** Denis O'Donnell **Trained** Nicholashayne, Devon

FOCUS

A slow winning time, even for a race like this, and the field finished well strung out. The form looks fair for the class rated through the runner-up.

NOTEBOOK

Kilty Storm(IRE) ◆ was aided by Hi Humpfree falling three out, but looked to be on top of that rival at the time, and still ran out a very convincing winner. He was well backed for this handicap bow, clearly stays very well, and looks a typical improver for his powerful yard. As a former winning pointer, it would come as little surprise to see him sent over fences before too long. *(op 5-1)*

The Gangerman(IRE) could only muster the same pace when it really mattered on this return to three miles, but stuck to his task gamely all the same, and has developed into a consistent performer. He looks a dour stayer, probably needs more testing ground, and is a good benchmark for this form. *(op 10-1)*

Captain Corelli, who took the Tommy Whittle at Haydock in grand style last time and is rated two and a half stone lower over hurdles, has to rate as disappointing. However, he is undoubtedly better over fences - and is presumably only racing timber to protect his chasing mark until the National weights are declared - so is not one to write off on the back of this effort. *(op 10-11 tchd evens in a place)*

Roman Rampage

Hi Humpfree, equipped with first-time blinkers, was only just being held by the eventual winner when departing three from home. He was running much his best race to date over hurdles prior to falling, the headgear looked to have a positive effect, and he can build on this providing his confidence has not been too badly dented.

3346 GORDON PASSEY MEMORIAL "JUNIOR" STANDARD OPEN NATIONAL HUNT FLAT RACE 1m 4f 110y

4:05 (4:06) (Class 5) 4-Y-O **£2,398** (£698; £349)

Form				RPR
	1		**Pressgang** 4-11-0 .... TomDoyle *(P R Webber) unf: scope: hld up in tch: hdwy 4f out: chsd ldr over 2f out: led wl over 1f out: c clr ins last: readily* **9/2**[1]	113+
	2	*5*	**Crofters Lad (IRE)** 4-11-0 .... SamThomas *(Miss Venetia Williams) trckd ldr: led ins fnl 5f: rdn over 2f out: hdd wl over 1f out: no ch w wnr ins last but kpt on wl for clr 2nd* **6/1**[2]	103
	3	*11*	**Otantique (FR)** 4-11-0 .... MarcusFoley *(Miss E C Lavelle) w/l: b.bkwd: bhd: hdwy 4f out: chsd ldrs over 2f out: styd on one pce* **10/1**	89+
5	**4**	*6*	**Forest Emerald (IRE)**[28] [2830] 4-10-4 .... RichardYoung(3) *(J W Mullins) mid-div: hdwy to chse ldrs over 3f out: wknd ins fnl 2f* **6/1**[2]	72
	5	*nk*	**Fleur Des Pres (FR)** 4-10-0 .... CharlieStudd(7) *(B G Powell) bhd: rdn and hdwy to chse ldrs over 3f out: one pce fnl 2f* **7/1**	72
	6	*½*	**Handel With Care (IRE)** 4-10-11 .... RobertStephens(3) *(R A Farrant) chsd ldrs: rdn 3f out: sn btn* **16/1**	78
	7	*3*	**Gentle John (FR)** 4-11-0 .... APMcCoy *(R M Stronge) keen hold: chsd ldrs: rdn 3f out: wknd 2f out* **6/1**[2]	74
	8	*2*	**Trooper Lee (IRE)** 4-11-0 .... JimCrowley *(Mrs H Dalton) in tch: rdn 3f out: hung lft and wknd over 2f out* **16/1**	71
	9	*2*	**Auburn Grey** 4-10-7 .... LeeNewnes(7) *(M D I Usher) leggy: bhd: pushed along 6f out: styd on through btn horses fnl f* **80/1**	68
0	**10**	*½*	**Hakumatata**[10] [3181] 4-10-9 .... RobertLucey-Butler(5) *(Miss Z C Davison) tall: w'like: bhd: hdwy 4f out: chsd ldrs and rn green ins fnl 3f: wknd fnl 2f* **33/1**	68
	11	*1*	**Lord Raffles** 4-11-0 .... JamesDavies *(P R Webber) w'like: b.bkwd: chsd ldrs tl wknd fr 3f out* **20/1**	66
	12	*4*	**Secret Moment** 4-11-0 .... MarkBradburne *(C G Cox) chsd ldrs: disp 2nd 4f out to 3f out: sn wknd* **13/2**[3]	61
0	**13**	*8*	**La Bonne Vie**[23] [2927] 4-11-0 .... ChristianWilliams *(C Roberts) led tl hdd ins fnl 5f: wknd 3f out* **80/1**	49
	14	*3 ½*	**Kilmeena Magic** 4-10-7 .... SeanCurran *(J C Fox) unf: a in rr* **100/1**	37
0	**15**	*2 ½*	**Rosenfirth (IRE)**[28] [2830] 4-10-7 .... BrianCrowley *(R Rowe) nvr bttr than mid-div* **100/1**	34
	16	*dist*	**Palaver** 4-10-7 .... TomScudamore *(G R I Smyly) w'like: b.bkwd: chsd ldrs 7f: t.o* **50/1**	—
	P		**Stingray (IRE)** 4-11-0 .... LeightonAspell *(N I M Rossiter) in tch 1m: wknd 3f out: p.u fnl f* **20/1**	—

3m 5.80s (3.60) **17** Ran SP% **126.6**

CSF £29.85 TOTE £5.70: £2.40, £2.40, £3.50; EX 35.30 Place 6 £9.01, Place 5 £5.90.

Owner Mrs Anthony West **Bred** Juddmonte Farms **Trained** Mollington, Oxon

FOCUS

As is often the case with such events, the form is difficult to assess, but there was a lot to like about the winner's display.

NOTEBOOK

Pressgang ◆, who failed to make the racecourse when owned by Khalid Abdulla, looked fit enough to do himself justice and was well supported on course to make a belated winning debut and duly landed the odds with an impressive display. He was given time to find his stride before creeping into contention four out and, after running green when asked to win his race, ultimately pulled clear and should be rated value for further. As a half-brother to the smart dual-purpose performer Big Moment, he clearly has a bright future, and it will be interesting to see whether connections persevere with him in bumpers. *(op 5-1)*

Crofters Lad(IRE) ◆, who cost 20,000euros as a two-year-old, looked fit for his debut and ran a race full of promise despite proving no match for the winner. He was a clear second-best, and is entitled to improve for this debut experience, so looks a likely winner of a similar event before the season is out. *(op 7-1)*

Otantique(FR), a 21,000euros purchase by a leading French National Hunt sire, posted a sound effort on this debut yet already looks in need of two miles. He is one to keep an eye on. *(tchd 11-1)*

Forest Emerald(IRE), fifth on debut in a fillies' equivalent of this event 28 days previously, did not obviously improve on that effort yet still helps to set the level of this form. She may be in need of a stiffer test now. *(tchd 7-1)*

Fleur Des Pres(FR), an athletic filly related to winners in France over hurdles and on the Flat, failed to sustain her effort when it mattered and was well held. She ought to improve a deal for this experience, however. *(op 8-1 tchd 9-1)*

Secret Moment, out of a fair 12-furlong winner, found little under pressure and looks modest. *(op 6-1 tchd 7-1)*

T/Jkpt: Part won. £17,975.40 to a £1 stake. Pool: £25,317.50. 0.50 winning tickets. T/Plt: £14.00 to a £1 stake. Pool: £63,948.75. 3,318.95 winning tickets. T/Qpdt: £7.60 to a £1 stake. Pool: £4,375.20. 421.40 winning tickets. ST

3167 CATTERICK (L-H)

Thursday, January 12

OFFICIAL GOING: Good

The going was described as 'generally good but very loose on top'.

Wind: Fresh, half-behind Weather: Overcast and breezy

3347 HALIFAX NOVICES' HURDLE (8 hdls) 2m

12:50 (12:51) (Class 4) 5-Y-O+ **£3,253** (£955; £477; £238)

Form				RPR
41-	**1**		**Industrial Star (IRE)**[223] [4981] 5-10-12 .... NeilMulholland *(M D Hammond) trckd ldrs: wnt 2nd 3 out: hung lft and led appr last: styd on wl towards fin* **11/1**	106+
	2	*1 ¼*	**Balyan (IRE)**[159] 5-10-12 .... GrahamLee *(J Howard Johnson) trckd ldrs: led appr 2 out: hdd appr last: crowded: no ex last 75yds* **6/4**[1]	104+
2	**3**	*5*	**Quartier Latin (USA)**[43] [2573] 5-10-12 .... JamieMoore *(C Von Der Recke, Germany) chsd ldrs: rdn appr 2 out: kpt on same pce* **5/2**[2]	99
6331	**4**	*2 ½*	**Sunisa (IRE)**[24] [2625] 5-10-2 99..................................(t) WilliamKennedy(3) *(J Mackie) chsd ldrs: 4th and one pce whn nt fluent last 2* **4/1**[3]	93+
20FU	**5**	*3 ½*	**Dubonai (IRE)**[28] [2838] 6-11-5 100.......................................(t) BarryKeniry *(G M Moore) set mod pce to 3rd: led 3 out: hdd appr next: wknd between last 2* **16/1**	100
34	**6**	*4*	**Third Empire**[39] [2658] 5-10-12 .... RichardMcGrath *(C Grant) trckd ldrs: mstke 1st: outpcd 3 out: n.d after* **11/1**	89
00	**7**	*1 ¾*	**Wot Way Chief**[17] [2987] 5-10-7 .... ThomasDreaper(5) *(J M Jefferson) hld up towards rr: sme hdwy 3 out: nvr trbld ldrs* **66/1**	87
3-06	**8**	*9*	**Clifford T Ward**[70] [2007] 6-10-7 .... StephenCraine(5) *(D McCain) sn trcking ldrs: lost pl appr 2 out* **40/1**	78
30	**9**	*7*	**Titus Salt (USA)**[33] [2763] 5-10-2 .... CWilliams(10) *(M D Hammond) hld up in rr: sme hdwy 3 out: nvr on terms* **40/1**	71
P	**10**	*nk*	**Etching (USA)**[11] [3167] 6-10-0 ....(t) BrianHughes(5) *(W Storey) chsd ldrs: hrd drvn 3 out: sn btn* **150/1**	64
0P	**11**	*13*	**Bally Abbie**[11] [3167] 5-10-5 .... AnthonyRoss *(P Beaumont) a in rr* **200/1**	51
0-0	**12**	*dist*	**Nasstar**[12] [3145] 5-10-9 .... MrTGreenall(3) *(M W Easterby) in rr and reminders after 3rd: bhd fr 5th: t.o: btn 39 l* **100/1**	—

000 **13** *2* **Barney (IRE)**[11] 3168 5-10-12 .... BrianHarding —
(Mrs E Slack) *plld hrd in rr: bhd fr 5th: t.o* **200/1**

00 **14** *1 1/4* **Logistical**[6] 3267 6-10-12 .... KeithMercer —
(Ferdy Murphy) *trckd ldrs: led and qcknd 3rd: hdd 3 out: sn lost pl: t.o* **100/1**

0P **F** **Whitsun**[78] 1889 6-10-7 .... MichaelMcAlister[(5)] —
(Miss Kate Milligan) *hld up towards rr: sme hdwy 4th: lost pl 3 out: bhd whn fell next* **200/1**

3m 54.7s (-1.60) **Going Correction** -0.175s/f (Good) **15** Ran SP% **121.6**
Speed ratings: **97,96,93,92,90 88,88,83,80,79 73,—,—,—,—** CSF £29.17 TOTE £14.70: £2.60, £1.30, £1.70; EX 60.40.
Owner Racing Management & Training Ltd **Bred** Emanuele Patruno **Trained** Middleham, N Yorks

FOCUS
A modest novice hurdle but the first two came clear and look capable of notching further success.

NOTEBOOK
Industrial Star(IRE), a bumper winner in 2005 and last seen running a fair race in a Haydock maiden on the Flat in June, made a winning debut over hurdles, seeing off the favourite in a duel to the line. He sustained a nasty injury to his near-hind leg in a horsebox accident in the summer which meant he had to have three months' box rest, but he has made a full recovery and this effort suggests he could be worth following in handicap company on decent ground. A Flat campaign over staying trips is the plan later in the year. *(op 10-1)*
Balyan(IRE), who won of a couple of middle-distance races in Ireland for John Oxx, did not run badly on his debut for his current yard in the Chester Cup, but he failed to build on that promise in two subsequent starts. Making his hurdling debut, he looked the likeliest winner jumping the second-last, but he was eventually outbattled. Nevertheless, he was clear of the rest and should soon be going one better. *(op 11-4)*
Quartier Latin(USA) again performed as though he will appreciate a stiffer track as he wa running on at the finish. *(op 9-4 tchd 2-1)*
Sunisa(IRE), who had a run on the All-Weather after winning a minor contest at Haydock last month, is exposed and fairly consistent, so her performance is probably a good guide to the level of the form. Softer ground would have suited her better, though. *(op 7-2)*
Dubonai(IRE) is another who looks pretty exposed now, and trying to give weight away all round proved too much for him. *(tchd 20-1 in a place)*
Third Empire may do better now that he is eligible to run in handicaps. *(op 8-1)*

3348 W. L. AND HECTOR CHRISTIE MEMORIAL TROPHY (A NOVICES' H'CAP CHASE) (12 fncs) 2m
1:20 (1:20) (Class 4) (0-105,96) 5-Y-0+ **£3,903** (£1,146; £573; £286)

Form RPR

01P- **1** **Whaleef**[474] 1504 8-11-12 **96** ....(p) TonyDobbin 109+
(B J Llewellyn) *trckd ldrs: led bef 3 out: kpt on wl* **9/2**

32-5 **2** *2* **Waltzing Along (IRE)**[48] 2479 8-10-10 **80** .... BrianHarding 88
(L Lungo) *led to 3 out: sn drvn: kpt on fr last to take 2nd nr fin* **4/1**[3]

/P62 **3** *1 1/4* **Gohh**[17] 2980 10-10-11 **84** ....(t) MrTGreenall[(3)] 91
(M W Easterby) *hld up in tch: hdwy 5th: rdn to chse wnr 3 out: no ex last: lost 2nd cl home* **5/2**[1]

3146 **4** *19* **Donovan (NZ)**[26] 2874 7-11-7 **94** ....(p) LarryMcGrath[(3)] 88+
(R C Guest) *chsd ldrs: blnd 4th: outpcd whn mstke 8th: btn whn hit 3 out* **3/1**[2]

00P- **5** *3* **Taipo Prince (IRE)**[276] 4810 6-11-7 **96** ....(p) MichaelMcAlister[(5)] 81
(Miss Kate Milligan) *mstkes: in tch to 5th: sn outpcd* **25/1**

0456 **6** *3/4* **Drumossie (AUS)**[97] 1663 6-11-0 **84** .... KennyJohnson 68
(R C Guest) *a bhd: no ch fr 1/2-way* **10/1**

0434 **F** **Prince Adjal (IRE)**[38] 2677 6-11-9 **96** .... MrCStorey[(3)] —
(Miss S E Forster) *nt fluent: prom tl wknd bef 5th: btn whn fell heavily 7th* **7/1**

4m 0.10s (-2.90) **Going Correction** -0.20s/f (Good) **7** Ran SP% **117.2**
Speed ratings: **99,98,97,87,86 86,—** CSF £24.01 TOTE £4.60: £2.10, £3.00; EX 16.50.
Owner Jason Parfitt **Bred** Gainsborough Stud Management Ltd **Trained** Fochriw, Caerphilly

FOCUS
A moderate handicap but a good race between the first three home. The winner has been rated value for five lengths.

NOTEBOOK
Whaleef, off the track since September 2004, has suffered from tendon problems but he was produced fit for this reappearance. Supported in the market, he looked well handicapped on his hurdling form, and he duly landed the money. *(op 6-1)*
Waltzing Along(IRE) stepped up on his effort at Musselburgh in November when returning from almost a year's absence, and has the ability to go one better in similar company. *(tchd 9-2)*
Gohh was a shade disappointing but he might have preferred easier ground. *(op 11-4 tchd 3-1)*
Donovan(NZ) remains on a 6lb higher mark than when successful in a weak race at Towcester in the autumn. He probably needs some kindness from the Handicapper. *(op 10-3 tchd 7-2)*

3349 BRADFORD JUVENILE NOVICES' (S) HURDLE (8 hdls) 2m
1:50 (1:50) (Class 5) 4-Y-0 **£2,740** (£798; £399)

Form RPR

050 **1** **No Commission (IRE)**[43] 2569 4-10-12 .... RichardMcGrath 83
(R F Fisher) *prom: drvn 3 out: rallied to ld next: hung lft fr last: r.o* **11/1**

503 **2** *2* **Rossin Gold (IRE)**[10] 3203 4-10-2 .... DavidDaSilva[(10)] 83+
(P Monteith) *midfield: hdwy to ld briefly bef 2 out: edgd lft and kpt on same pce last* **11/4**[1]

0230 **3** *1 3/4* **Jamaaron**[17] 2995 4-10-7 93 .... RobertLucey-Butler[(5)] 84+
(W G M Turner) *hld up: bdly hmpd 4th: hdwy whn n.m.r between last two: kpt on run in: nt rch first two* **9/1**[3]

P **4** *nk* **Power Glory**[10] 3203 4-10-12 .... AnthonyRoss 79
(R A Fahey) *hld up: hdwy 1/2-way: ev ch bef 2 out: sn one pce* **25/1**

3566 **5** *5* **Lane Marshal**[30] 2810 4-10-5 92 .... PatrickMcDonald[(7)] 74
(M E Sowersby) *cl up: led 4th to bef 2 out: outpcd whn nt fluent last* **12/1**

P020 **6** *shd* **Another Misk**[11] 3169 4-10-9 86 .... PeterBuchanan[(3)] 74
(M E Sowersby) *midfield: hdwy and ev ch bef 2 out: wknd between last two* **33/1**

300F **7** *1/2* **Maunby Reveller**[9] 2416 4-10-9 91 ....(p) RobertStephens[(3)] 73
(P C Haslam) *chsd ldrs: rdn and ev ch bef 2 out: sn btn* **5/1**[2]

56PP **8** *16* **Emerald Destiny (IRE)**[57] 2263 4-10-12 .... BrianHarding 57
(Jedd O'Keeffe) *hld up: hdwy bef 3 out: wknd bef next* **14/1**

P0 **9** *26* **Cadogen Square**[48] 2477 4-9-12 .... PhilKinsella[(7)] 24
(Mrs Marjorie Fife) *led to 4th: cl up tl rdn and wknd after 3 out* **50/1**

U **10** *3 1/2* **Jenna Stannis**[59] 2245 4-10-5 .... NeilMulholland 21
(W Storey) *bhd: hdwy and in tch 3 out: wknd bef next* **50/1**

11 *3/4* **Cabopino Lad (USA)**[51] 4-10-9 .... AnthonyCoyle[(3)] 27
(Miss Tracy Waggott) *chsd ldrs: ev ch 3 out: sn rdn and wknd* **50/1**

602 **B** **Elaala (USA)**[22] 2935 4-10-5 95 .... GrahamLee —
(M Todhunter) *midfield whn b.d 4th* **11/4**[1]

0 **U** **Annals**[21] 2949 4-10-2 ....(p) LarryMcGrath[(3)] —
(R C Guest) *bhd whn hmpd and uns rdr 4th* **20/1**

6S00 **F** **Bellalou**[33] 2001 4-10-5 74 ....(t) KeithMercer —
(Mrs S A Watt) *in tch whn fell 4th* **25/1**

P **Jules Lee**[458] 4-10-2 .... RichardGordon[(10)] —
(W G M Turner) *a bhd: t.o whn p.u bef 2 out* **100/1**

3m 55.3s (-1.00) **Going Correction** -0.175s/f (Good) **15** Ran SP% **125.0**
Speed ratings: **95,94,93,92,90 90,90,82,69,67 67,—,—,—,—** CSF £40.88 TOTE £14.60: £3.10, £1.30, £2.40; EX 61.90.There was no bid for the winner.
Owner Bishopthorpe Racing Two **Bred** N D Cronin **Trained** Ulverston, Cumbria

FOCUS
Weak form but solid enough for the grade.

NOTEBOOK
No Commission(IRE) found improvement for the drop in grade and saw the trip out strongly. He is clearly no star but he might be able to hold his own in minor handicap company. *(op 12-1)*
Rossin Gold(IRE) finished behind No Commission at Newcastle in November but appeared to have *progressed since and was sent off the shorter priced of the pair. He had every chance.* *(op 3-1 tchd 10-3)*
Jamaaron is fairly exposed at this level but he was very badly hampered in the incident at the *fourth flight and did well to finish as close as he did. He will surely find a race of this kind soon.* *(op 10-1 tchd 12-1)*
Power Glory, pulled up on his only previous start over timber, ran a better race on this sounder surface. *(op 20-1)*
Lane Marshal has shown a preference for softer ground. *(op 11-1)*
Maunby Reveller, wearing cheekpieces for the first time over timber, did not get home. *(op 6-1)*

3350 CATTERICKBRIDGE.CO.UK H'CAP CHASE (19 fncs) 3m 1f 110y
2:20 (2:21) (Class 3) (0-120,118) 5-Y-0+ **£6,506** (£1,910; £955; £477)

Form RPR

130U **1** **Prince Of Slane**[28] 2841 7-10-5 **102** .... DougieCostello[(5)] 118+
(G A Swinbank) *hld up in rr: blnd 7th: hdwy 11th: mstke 14th: lft 5 l 2nd 3 out: styd on to ld last 75yds* **4/1**[2]

0403 **2** *1 3/4* **Benrajah (IRE)**[22] 2938 9-11-1 **112** .... ThomasDreaper[(5)] 122
(M Todhunter) *led: hdd and no ex run-in* **9/4**[1]

5234 **3** *12* **Shannon's Pride (IRE)**[40] 2644 10-11-1 **110** .... LarryMcGrath[(3)] 112+
(R C Guest) *chsd ldr: rdn along 4 out: 5 l 2nd whn blnd 3 out: no ch after* **8/1**

4-03 **4** *shd* **Virgin Soldier (IRE)**[28] 2841 10-11-12 **118** .... TonyDobbin 116
(G A Swinbank) *chsd ldrs: outpcd fr 14th* **11/2**[3]

3U4P **5** *9* **Cill Churnain (IRE)**[40] 2640 13-11-1 **107** .... DominicElsworth 99+
(Mrs S J Smith) *chsd ldrs: handy 3rd whn hit 15th: wknd appr 3 out* **10/1**

/5-6 **6** *17* **Sea Drifting**[41] 2616 9-10-5 **102** ow4 .... AdamPogson[(5)] 74
(Miss M E Rowland) *chsd ldrs: outpcd whn hmpd 12th: sn lost pl* **25/1**

33-P **F** **Dumadic**[259] 83 9-9-12 **97** .... PhilKinsella[(7)] —
(R E Barr) *chsd ldrs: 4th whn fell 12th* **8/1**

-P6P **P** **Tyndarius (IRE)**[37] 2692 15-9-10 **95** .... PatrickMcDonald[(7)] —
(A Crook) *sn detached in last: t.o 6th: p.u bef 12th* **33/1**

6P52 **P** **World Vision (IRE)**[25] 2905 9-11-0 **106** ....(p) BrianHarding —
(Ferdy Murphy) *nt fluent: chsd ldrs: lost pl 14th: sn bhd: p.u bef 3 out* **13/2**

6m 35.6s (-12.80) **Going Correction** -0.20s/f (Good) **9** Ran SP% **117.6**
Speed ratings: **111,110,106,106,103 98,—,—,—** CSF £14.34 CT £68.96 TOTE £6.80: £1.90, £1.70, £1.90; EX 29.20.
Owner J H Richardson **Bred** J Richardson **Trained** Melsonby, N Yorks

FOCUS
A fairly competitive handicap run in a good time.

NOTEBOOK
Prince Of Slane wore down Benrajah after the last to get on top close home. A horse who can take chances with his fences - he did so, on occasions, again here - he appreciates being given time to warm up. A thorough stayer who likes decent ground, he is pretty good at this level when he gets his act together. *(op 5-1 tchd 11-2)*
Benrajah(IRE) did nothing wrong in defeat and, after jumping well, was only worried out of it late on. He deserves to find compensation after this gallant effort. *(op 5-2 tchd 11-4, 3-1 in places)*
Shannon's Pride(IRE) was comfortably held in third after blundering badly three out, when his measure had already been taken.
Virgin Soldier(IRE), a stablemate of the winner, was unable to get to grips with the principals when the chips were down. *(op 5-1 tchd 9-2)*
Cill Churnain(IRE) ran well for a long way before weakening. *(op 8-1)*
Dumadic, appearing for the first time since April, was in the process of running a sound race when he came to grief. *(tchd 7-1)*

3351 LEEDS H'CAP HURDLE (10 hdls) 2m 3f
2:50 (2:51) (Class 4) (0-110,109) 4-Y-0+ **£3,253** (£955; £477; £238)

Form RPR

0122 **1** **Sunday City (JPN)**[24] 2925 5-11-6 **108** .... TomGreenway[(5)] 124+
(P Bowen) *in tch: hdwy 1/2-way: led 3 out: clr bef next: edgd lft: unchal* **6/4**[1]

6553 **2** *8* **Red Man (IRE)**[11] 3171 9-10-9 **102** ....(p) StevenGagan[(10)] 105+
(Mrs E Slack) *led to 3 out: sn rdn: no imp whn hit last* **7/1**[2]

-0PP **3** *1 1/2* **Kings Square**[17] 2975 6-10-0 **83** .... AlanDempsey 84
(M W Easterby) *in tch: outpcd bef 3 out: rallied next: no imp* **33/1**

0001 **4** *2* **Uncle John**[11] 3169 5-9-13 **89** 7ex ....(v) PhilKinsella[(7)] 88
(M E Sowersby) *hld up: hdwy bef 2 out: sn no imp* **11/1**

0000 **5** *4* **Lord Baskerville**[11] 3171 5-10-7 **90** .... NeilMulholland 86+
(W Storey) *keen: chsd ldrs tl wknd fr 2 out* **100/1**

0604 **6** *12* **Cheery Martyr**[11] 3167 8-10-4 **87** .... BarryKeniry 70
(P Needham) *in tch: outpcd bef 3 out: no imp fr next* **16/1**

0003 **7** *3* **Welsh Dream**[28] 2843 9-10-8 **94** .... MrCStorey[(3)] 74
(Miss S E Forster) *bhd: rdn whn blnd 3 out: nvr rchd ldrs* **10/1**

4000 **8** *3* **Tiger Frog (USA)**[12] 3152 7-11-1 **101** ....(b) WilliamKennedy[(3)] 78
(J Mackie) *midfield: outpcd 1/2-way: n.d after* **25/1**

02P0 **9** *4* **Talarive (USA)**[46] 2525 10-11-0 **97** ....(tp) TonyDobbin 70
(P D Niven) *midfield: outpcd 1/2-way: sn n.d* **33/1**

3004 **10** *3* **Wally Wonder (IRE)**[33] 2766 8-10-5 **98** .... JamesReveley[(10)] 68
(K G Reveley) *chsd ldrs tl wknd bef 4 out* **16/1**

-010 **11** *7* **Time Marches On**[192] 451 8-11-3 **100** .... RichardMcGrath 63
(K G Reveley) *bhd: rdn 4 out: nvr on terms* **25/1**

2030 **12** *1/2* **Polly Whitefoot**[12] 3152 7-10-2 **85** ....(t) PadgeWhelan 47
(R A Fahey) *hld up midfield: effrt 4 out: wknd bef 2 out* **16/1**

343- **13** *5* **Hue**[16] 4084 5-11-7 **104** .... RussGarritty 61
(B Ellison) *hld up: hit 2nd: hdwy 3 out: wkng whn blnd next: eased* **14/1**

-652 **14** *4* **Armentieres**[11] 3169 5-10-3 **86** ....(v) BrianHarding 39
(Mrs E Slack) *in tch to 1/2-way: sn lost pl* **9/1**[3]

P-P0 **15** *1 1/2* **Long Shot**[35] 2714 9-10-7 **90** .... TomSiddall 42
(Miss L C Siddall) *sn wl bhd: no ch fr 1/2-way* **80/1**

10-0 **P** **Gift Voucher (IRE)**[54] 2334 5-11-7 **109** .... MarkNicolls[(5)] —
(P R Webber) *chsd ldrs: mstke 4th: wknd 3 out: p.u bef next* **16/1**

4m 42.1s (-8.40) **Going Correction** -0.175s/f (Good) **16** Ran SP% **125.9**
Speed ratings: **110,106,106,105,103 98,97,95,94,92 90,89,87,86,85** — CSF £12.15 CT £270.28 TOTE £2.30: £1.10, £1.90, £9.10, £3.60; EX 16.10.

Owner R Greenway **Bred** Shiraoi Farm **Trained** Little Newcastle, Pembrokes

FOCUS

The winner has been rated value for 13 lengths and to the level of his Flat form. The placed horses have been rated close to their recent form.

NOTEBOOK

Sunday City(JPN) gained a decisive success. He is progressing well at this game and was hardly winning out of turn after two solid efforts in defeat on his latest starts. Skipping clear leaving the back straight, he had only to be kept up to his work to remain clear. He has the scope to climb further up the ladder. *(op 2-1)*

Red Man(IRE) made a gallant attempt, but was unable to mix it with the winner from the third last. He looks on good terms with himself and will not always come across a rival as progressive as the winner. *(op 8-1 tchd 10-1)*

Kings Square, pulled up in two attempts over fences, shaped encouragingly over a trip short of his best and on this more favourable ground. *(op 25-1)*

Uncle John ran creditably under the penalty for his course-and-distance win on New Year's Day. *(op 10-1)*

Lord Baskerville, a long-standing maiden, was far from disgraced.

3352 WAKEFIELD BEGINNERS' CHASE (15 fncs) 2m 3f

3:20 (3:20) (Class 4) 5-Y-O+ £3,903 (£1,146; £573; £286)

Form RPR

6112 **1** **Welcome To Unos**[11] [3172] 9-11-3 109 .... RichardMcGrath 116+
(K G Reveley) *cl up: led 7th: hit 11th: kpt on wl fr 3 out* **13/8**[1]

23P2 **2** *2* **Dark Ben (FR)**[17] [2975] 6-10-12 .... DougieCostello(5) 109
(Miss Kate Milligan) *prom: effrt fr 4 out: kpt on fr 2 out: nt rch wnr* **25/1**

14-F **3** *dist* **Prato (GER)**[43] [2574] 6-11-3 ....(b) JamieMoore 74
(C Von Der Recke, Germany) *mstkes: in tch: effrt bef 4 out: wknd after next* **25/1**

1100 **4** *5* **Longstone Lass**[3] [3318] 6-10-3 .... MissCMetcalfe(7) 57
(Miss Tracy Waggott) *sn wl bhd: kpt on fr 4 out: nvr on terms* **40/1**

11-P **5** *1* **Galero**[47] [2496] 7-10-12 110 .... BrianHughes(5) 70
(J Howard Johnson) *in tch: rdn and outpcd whn hmpd 8th: n.d after* **9/2**[3]

-006 **6** *5* **Hot Air (IRE)**[28] [2839] 8-11-3 ....(t) BrianHarding 60
(J I A Charlton) *in tch: outpcd whn hit 8th: sn btn* **66/1**

/P-P **7** *23* **Just Jed**[11] [3170] 7-11-3 .... KennyJohnson —
(R Shiels) *hld up: hdwy to chse ldrs 7th: outpcd fr 11th: btn whn blnd bdly 2 out* **100/1**

/424 **8** *4* **Elvis Returns**[17] [2985] 8-10-12 .... ThomasDreaper(5) —
(J M Jefferson) *sn wl bhd: nvr on terms* **15/2**

0-62 **P** **Mr McAuley (IRE)**[21] [2943] 8-11-3 .... TonyDobbin —
(I R Ferguson, Ire) *nt fluent in rr: p.u after 6th* **7/2**[2]

05U4 **P** **Italiano**[16] [3037] 7-11-3 106 .... RussGarritty —
(P Beaumont) *in tch whn bdly hmpd and p.u after 8th* **11/1**

666- **F** **Lucky Duck**[438] [1930] 9-11-0 .... PeterBuchanan(3) —
(Mrs A Hamilton) *led 4th to 7th: upsides whn fell next* **25/1**

0P-5 **F** **Fleetfoot Mac**[21] [2943] 5-10-2 ....(b) MichaelMcAlister(5) —
(B Storey) *led to 4th: chsd ldrs tl wknd 7th: wl btn whn fell 3 out* **100/1**

4m 50.1s (-3.50) **Going Correction** -0.20s/f (Good)
WFA 5 from 6yo+ 8lb **12 Ran SP% 116.0**
Speed ratings: **99,98,—,—,— —,—,—,—,— —,—** CSF £45.27 TOTE £2.10: £1.10, £4.80, £6.70; EX 31.40.

Owner J W Andrews **Bred** P D And Mrs Player **Trained** Lingdale, Redcar & Cleveland

FOCUS

A modest beginners' chase in which the winner has been rated value for seven lengths.

NOTEBOOK

Welcome To Unos, who has been in terrific form this season, did his job well to add a chasing success to his two hurdling wins. An athletic individual who travels strongly, he should continue to pay his way. *(op 7-4 tchd 6-4, 2-1 and 15-8 in places)*

Dark Ben(FR) made a bold bid and was the only danger to the winner from a fair way out. He should go one better in a run-of-the-mill race. *(tchd 33-1)*

Prato(GER), a German raider who was blinkered for the first time over obstacles, was beaten an awful long way into third.

Longstone Lass stayed on late, very late. *(op 33-1)*

Galero showed little on his second start over fences. *(op 4-1)*

3353 HUDDERSFIELD INTERMEDIATE NATIONAL HUNT FLAT RACE (CONDITIONAL JOCKEYS' & AMATEUR RIDERS' RACE) 2m

3:50 (3:50) (Class 6) 4-6-Y-O £2,055 (£599; £299)

Form RPR

2 **1** **Astarador (FR)**[40] [2642] 4-10-2 .... BrianHughes(5) 101+
(J Howard Johnson) *trckd ldrs: led over 3f out: rdn clr over 1f out: styd on strly* **8/13**[1]

2 *10* **Medic (IRE)** 5-10-12 .... DavidCullinane(7) 103+
(T J Fitzgerald) *trckd ldrs: led over 4f out tl over 3f out: kpt on to take modest 2nd over 1f out: no ch w wnr* **14/1**

4 **3** *3* **Mohayer (IRE)**[70] [2013] 4-10-2 .... StephenCraine(5) 86
(D McCain) *in rr: hdwy 7f out: wnt 2nd 3f out: wknd fnl f* **10/1**[3]

10 **4** *4* **Star Shot (IRE)**[60] [2211] 5-11-7 .... MarkNicolls(5) 101
(P R Webber) *mid-div: hdwy 7f out: outpcd over 4f out: n.d after* **9/2**[2]

5 *8* **Mr Viaillie (IRE)** 4-10-2 .... DougieCostello(5) 74
(Karen McLintock) *in rr: hdwy 5f out: kpt on fnl 3f* **33/1**

004 **6** *8* **Overfields**[12] [3145] 6-11-0 .... AdamPogson(5) 78
(S R Bowring) *chsd ldrs: led 6f out tl over 4f out: wknd fnl 2f* **33/1**

0 **7** *½* **Tuckers Bay**[61] [2185] 5-10-5 .... ChrisGlenister(7) 71
(J R Holt) *mid-div: outpcd 6f out: sn btn* **100/1**

0 **8** *nk* **Guess What**[27] [2864] 6-10-12 .... MrMSollitt(7) 77
(Mrs S J Smith) *in tch: outpcd 5f out: sn lost pl* **80/1**

9 *12* **Arctic Ghost** 6-11-0 .... ThomasDreaper(5) 65
(N Wilson) *chsd ldrs: lost pl 5f out: sn bhd* **28/1**

0 **10** *12* **Crackpot (IRE)**[48] [2480] 6-11-0 .... MichaelMcAlister(5) 53
(C Rae) *led tl 6f out: sn lost pl* **100/1**

11 *19* **Georgedoubleyou (IRE)** 5-10-12 .... MissTJackson(7) 34
(Miss T Jackson) *keen: sn trcking ldrs: lost pl 6f out: sn bhd* **16/1**

0 **12** *dist* **Marton Jubilee**[7] [3259] 4-9-7 .... MrBMcHugh(7) —
(A D Brown) *bhd and reminders after 4f: t.o 7f out: virtually p.u* **100/1**

13 *2* **Wold Top** 5-10-9 .... MrTGreenall(3) —
(M W Easterby) *in rr: t.o 7f out: virtually p.u* **20/1**

0 **14** *6* **The Bay Bogle**[48] [2480] 5-10-12 ....(t) BenOrde-Powlett(7) —
(M A Barnes) *lost pl after 4f: sn wl bhd: t.o 7f out* **100/1**

P **Bannow Beach (IRE)** 5-10-9 .... WilliamKennedy(3) —
(J Mackie) *t.k.h and jnd ldr after 3f: sddle sn slipped: taken wd paddock bnd and sn p.u* **20/1**

3m 49.5s (-5.80) **Going Correction** -0.175s/f (Good)
WFA 4 from 5yo+ 11lb **15 Ran SP% 125.8**
Speed ratings: **107,102,100,98,94 90,90,90,84,78 68,—,—,—,—** CSF £11.01 TOTE £1.60: £1.02, £5.40, £4.70; EX 21.60 Place 6 £40.57, Place 5 £29.63.

Owner Alderclad Roofing Ltd And S V Rutter **Bred** J C Haimet And Jean-Pascal Liberge **Trained** Billy Row, Co Durham

FOCUS

Not a lot of strength in depth in this bumper and they were well strung out behind the clear winner, who has been rated to his Wetherby mark.

NOTEBOOK

Astarador(FR) fulfilled the promise he showed at Wetherby on his debut, by posting a wide-margin win, being driven clear in the straight. Out of a French jumping winner, he has already been schooled over hurdles and he looks the type to come into his own when faced with some obstacles. *(op 10-11 tchd evens in places)*

Medic(IRE), a 75,000euros yearling and related to Le Corvee, shaped nicely on his debut although he was no match for the winner. He is entitled to improve and looks a promising sort. *(op 10-1 tchd 16-1 in a place)*

Mohayer(IRE), a Maktoum cast-off who is a half-brother to three winners, again showed signs of ability on this second start. *(op 8-1)*

Star Shot(IRE), the only previous winner in the field, had to give a fair amount of weight away and was well held. *(op 4-1 tchd 5-1)*

Georgedoubleyou(IRE), a springer in the market, showed up well for a long way, racing keenly, but dropped out tamely. From the family of The Grey Monk, he should do better with this experience under his belt, providing he settles better. *(op 80-1)*

Bannow Beach(IRE) *Official explanation: jockey said saddle slipped (op 14-1 tchd 22-1)*

T/Plt: £31.90 to a £1 stake. Pool: £36,852.10. 843.25 winning tickets. T/Qpdt: £5.50 to a £1 stake. Pool: £2,543.80. 342.15 winning tickets. RY

2935 LUDLOW (R-H)

Thursday, January 12

OFFICIAL GOING: Good

Wind: Light, across Weather: Fine

3354 SUNSHINE 855 MAIDEN HURDLE (DIV I) (9 hdls) 2m

1:00 (1:01) (Class 4) 4-Y-O+ £3,903 (£1,146; £573; £286)

Form RPR

22 **1** **Rosecliff**[37] [2681] 4-10-7 .... APMcCoy 112+
(A M Balding) *hld up in mid-div: hdwy 4th: led after 3 out: clr last: easily* **15/8**[1]

1-53 **2** *2½* **Call Oscar (IRE)**[76] [1908] 7-11-5 .... TomScudamore 112
(C Tinkler) *a.p: ev ch appr 3 out: sn hung lft: no ch w wnr fr 2 out* **12/1**

2- **3** *11* **Wellbeing**[390] [2880] 9-11-5 .... PJBrennan 102+
(P J Hobbs) *a.p: led after 6th tl after 3 out: wknd 2 out* **5/2**[2]

2P **4** *1¾* **Blaeberry**[13] [3127] 5-10-12 .... MarcusFoley 93+
(Miss E C Lavelle) *hld up and bhd: hdwy after 6th: mstke 2 out: r.o flat* **15/2**

P **5** *10* **The Iron Giant (IRE)**[42] [2580] 4-10-7 .... SamThomas 78+
(Miss H C Knight) *led to 2nd: prom: rdn appr 6th: wknd appr 3 out* **50/1**

6 **6** *10* **Wenlocks Wonder**[68] [2049] 5-11-5 .... JohnMcNamara 79
(K C Bailey) *mid-div: sme hdwy appr 3 out: no further prog* **125/1**

5- **7** *6* **Ile Facile (IRE)**[345] [3635] 5-11-5 .... DaveCrosse 78+
(B De Haan) *t.k.h: prom: led appr 4th tl after 6th: wkng whn blnd 3 out* **33/1**

2-50 **8** *1¼* **Miller's Monarch**[41] [2606] 6-11-5 .... JasonMaguire 72
(Andrew Turnell) *hld up in mid-div: short-lived effrt 6th:* **66/1**

9 *25* **Highland Games (IRE)**[89] 6-11-5 .... TomDoyle 47
(P R Webber) *hld up in tch: wknd appr 6th: t.o* **7/1**[3]

10 *4* **Lucky Turf (IRE)**[648] 9-11-0 .... LeeStephens(5) 43
(W K Goldsworthy) *bhd fr 5th: t.o fr 3 out* **150/1**

10-0 **P** **Creinch**[17] [2983] 5-11-5 .... LeightonAspell —
(O Sherwood) *a bhd: t.o whn p.u bef 3 out* **20/1**

P **Jigsaw Jumper (IRE)** 6-10-10 ow1 .... GinoCarenza(3) —
(Andrew Turnell) *a bhd: t.o whn p.u bef 3 out* **100/1**

46- **P** **Introduction**[478] [1461] 5-11-5 .... AlanO'Keeffe —
(R J Price) *a bhd: t.o 5th: p.u bef 3 out* **125/1**

P **Liberty Run (IRE)**[70] 4-10-7 .... JimmyMcCarthy —
(Mrs A J Hamilton-Fairley) *a bhd: t.o whn p.u bef 3 out* **100/1**

P **Habanero**[104] 5-11-5 .... NoelFehily —
(Miss S J Wilton) *led 2nd tl appr 4th: wknd appr 6th: bhd whn p.u bef 3 out* **25/1**

P **Bombaybadboy (NZ)** 7-11-5 .... HenryOliver —
(Ian Williams) *hld up and bhd: short-lived effrt appr 5th: t.o whn p.u bef 3 out* **80/1**

3m 47.8s (-4.50) **Going Correction** -0.15s/f (Good)
WFA 4 from 5yo+ 11lb **16 Ran SP% 115.8**
Speed ratings: **105,103,98,97,92 87,84,83,71,69 —,—,—,—,— —** CSF £22.93 TOTE £2.50: £1.20, £3.10, £1.20; EX 16.90.

Owner Michael Tabor **Bred** Britton House Stud Ltd **Trained** Kingsclere, Hants

FOCUS

Riders in the first reported the hurdles track to be good to soft and tacky. This was an interesting maiden hurdle with which to open the card, run at a sound pace. The time was two seconds faster than the second division and the winner has been rated value for 12 lengths, 5lb higher than his previous best.

NOTEBOOK

Rosecliff had been in front too far out at Fontwell but made no mistake here with a very fluent victory. He jumped nicely and may be up to tackling better things, although his appetite for a fight has been questioned in the past. The Fred Winter Juvenile Handicap at the Festival is a possibility depending on the Handicapper's reaction. *(op 9-4 tchd 5-2 in places)*

Call Oscar(IRE) was attempting to concede 12lb to the favourite and ran a sound race in the circumstances. This chasing type hung slightly on the home turn and was no match for the winner in the end, flattered to get within two and a half lengths, but his turn should come.

Wellbeing, a smart Flat performer who was runner-up on his only previous hurdles run 13 months ago, had every chance but could not find a change of gear. He is nothing like as good at this game as he was on the level but an ordinary race should come his way, perhaps over further. *(op 3-1 tchd 100-30 in places)*

Blaeberry was a real eye-catcher back in fourth. The mare, who seemed to resent being anchored in the rear, was given a good deal to do and never looked like getting near the leaders, although *she did keep on in a taking manner from the second last. She is now eligible for handicaps.Official explanation: jockey said, regarding running and riding, his orders were to drop the mare in and get her switched off, as she had been very keen in previous races; the mare again ran keenly in the early stages before getting outpaced when the leaders quickened in the back straight; trainer said the mare is a difficult ride and needs to learn to settle (op 11-2)*

The Iron Giant(IRE), an Aidan O'Brien cast-off, shaped much more encouragingly than he had on his hurdling debut and should improve for the experience. *(op 66-1)*

Highland Games(IRE), a useful stayer on the Flat for Luca Cumani, did not jump too well on this *hurdles debut but might have found things happening too quickly for him.Official explanation: trainer said gelding was found to have swallowed its tongue (tchd 15-2)*

Creinch *Official explanation: trainer said gelding finished distressed (op 16-1)*

3355 SUNSHINE 855 MAIDEN HURDLE (DIV II) (9 hdls) 2m
1:30 (1:33) (Class 4) 4-Y-0+ £3,903 (£1,146; £573; £286)

Form				RPR
6-3	1		**Fabulous Jet (FR)**[21] 2950 6-11-5 SamThomas (Miss Venetia Williams) *led: blnd 4th: hdd and hit 3 out: lft 6 l 2nd and btn whn lft in ld last: rdn out* 7/4[1]	105+
	2	3 ½	**The Composer**[111] 4-10-7 JimmyMcCarthy (M Blanshard) *hld up: hdwy 5th: mstke 6th: rdn appr 3 out: kpt on same pce* 20/1	91+
	3	3	**Avalon**[105] 4-10-7 APMcCoy (Jonjo O'Neill) *chsd clr ldrs: rdn and one pce fr 6th* 9/2[3]	86+
	4	16	**Helmac (GER)**[40] 5-11-5 RobertThornton (C Von Der Recke, Germany) *bhd tl styd on fr 3 out: nvr nr ldrs* 16/1	82
	5	2 ½	**After Lent (IRE)**[84] 5-11-5 TimmyMurphy (M C Pipe) *bhd tl styd on fr 3 out: n.d* 20/1	79
4-2F	6	nk	**Foxtrot Yankee (IRE)**[34] 2742 7-11-5 JasonMaguire (Andrew Turnell) *mid-div: nt fluent 4th: n.d* 16/1	79
0	7	14	**El Corredor (IRE)**[17] 2968 7-10-12 CharliePoste(7) (M F Harris) *a bhd* 100/1	65
60	8	3	**Rabbit**[35] 2721 5-10-12 JoeTizzard (Mrs A L M King) *a bhd* 66/1	55
0-0P	9	dist	**Judge'N'Thomas**[29] 2826 6-10-12 (p) MrRBliss(7) (M R Bosley) *a bhd: t.o 3 out: blnd last* 100/1	—
	R		**Oohourboo (IRE)** 6-10-12 DavidVerco (G J Smith) *bhd tl tried to refuse and rn out 5th* 80/1	—
P	P		**Jacobin (USA)**[12] 3139 5-11-5 TomScudamore (M Scudamore) *a bhd: t.o whn p.u bef 3 out* 100/1	—
	P		**Bubbling Fun**[93] 5-10-12 RJGreene (T Wall) *mid-div: mstke 5th: bhd whn p.u after 6th* 100/1	—
	P		**Chaplin**[454] 5-11-5 (t) TomDoyle (P R Webber) *hld up in tch: wknd appr 6th: bhd whn p.u bef 3 out* 14/1	—
	F		**Double Ransom**[38] 7-11-5 CarlLlewellyn (Mrs L Stubbs) *towards rr: no ch whn mstke 3 out: fell 2 out* 66/1	—
	F		**Bureaucrat**[111] 4-10-7 PJBrennan (P J Hobbs) *t.k.h: chsd ldr: led 3 out: mstke 2 out: 6 l clr whn fell last* 3/1[2]	103+
0-0	P		**Red Raptor**[17] 3001 5-11-5 (t) MarkBradburne (J A Geake) *t.k.h in tch: hit 4th: sn wknd: mstke 2 out: p.u bef last* 100/1	—

3m 49.8s (-2.50) **Going Correction** -0.15s/f (Good)
WFA 4 from 5yo+ 11lb 16 Ran SP% 116.7
Speed ratings: **100,98,96,88,87 87,80,78,—,— —,—,—,—,— —** CSF £40.12 TOTE £2.80: £1.10, £6.00, £2.00; EX 77.40.
Owner Malcolm Edwards **Bred** Jean Biraben And Mme Jean Biraben **Trained** Kings Caple, H'fords

FOCUS
The winner set a strong pace and the field quickly became strung out, but the time was two seconds slower than the first division. Not many got into it and Bureaucrat has been rated value for a 12-length success.

NOTEBOOK
Fabulous Jet(FR), sharper for his reappearance last month, set a strong gallop and survived a couple of errors, but could never shake off Bureaucrat, who had taken his measure and looked in command when falling at the last. He was fortunate to collect but second place would still have been a creditable effort. He may prove vulnerable under a penalty unless he settles better. *(op 11-4)*
The Composer, who was useful but regressive on the Flat, made a pleasing hurdling debut although his jumping has room for improvement. He stayed a mile and a half on the Flat and a step up in trip could suit him at this game. *(op 25-1)*
Avalon, a 1,000,000gns yearling out of Oaks winner Lady Carla, failed to live up to expectations at Ballydoyle but his third in the Great Voltigeur was very smart form. Weak in the market for this hurdles debut, he raced in third place, some way off the two leaders, but came under pressure turning out of the back straight and was not given a hard time when it became obvious he would not catch them. He was slow over the fourth but otherwise jumped quite well, and gave the impression that he will improve for the experience. *(op 2-1)*
Helmac(GER), a German Flat winner, stayed on from out of the pack to finish a fairly remote fourth.
After Lent(IRE) kept on from the rear of the field on his hurdles debut and first start for Pipe. He may well do better, but he was a very limited performer on the Flat for Paul Blockley.
Bureaucrat ◆ was rather free on this hurdling debut, but he was able to keep tabs on the leader before easing past him three from home. Awkward over the next, he had the race apparently in safe keeping when coming down at the last. A useful performer at around ten furlongs for John Gosden, *he should have no problems winning races in this sphere and better ground would be a plus. (op 7-2 tchd 4-1)*

3356 CONCHA Y TORO WINES NOVICES' CHASE (17 fncs) 2m 4f
2:00 (2:01) (Class 3) 5-Y-0+ £7,619 (£2,324; £1,214; £659)

Form				RPR
3-1U	1		**Taranis (FR)**[24] 2924 5-11-3 136 (t) APMcCoy (P F Nicholls) *hld up in tch: rdn appr 3 out: led 2 out: r.o* 4/7[1]	121+
/14-	2	3	**Dickensbury Lad (FR)**[609] 326 6-11-3 AntonyEvans (J L Spearing) *chsd ldr: rdn whn lft in ld 3 out: hdd 2 out: one pce* 14/1[3]	115
6-00	3	dist	**Tank Buster**[17] 2956 6-10-10 MrRLangley(7) (Mrs E Langley) *a bhd: lost tch 6th: tk poor 3rd last* 33/1	75
20	4	2	**Solar At'Em (IRE)**[22] 2939 8-11-3 90 (p) MarkBradburne (M Sheppard) *hld up: hdwy 9th: wknd 11th* 20/1	73
FP	F		**The Sneakster (IRE)**[6] 3278 8-10-5 DerekLaverty(5) (S A Brookshaw) *fell 3rd* 50/1	—
0	F		**Desertmore King (IRE)**[67] 2075 6-10-10 RichardSpate(7) (J A Danahar) *bhd tl fell 10th* 40/1	—
-060	R		**Business Traveller (IRE)**[35] 2731 6-11-3 AlanO'Keeffe (R J Price) *j. bdly in rr: ref and uns rdr 4th* 20/1	—
00-4	F		**Team Tassel (IRE)**[44] 2564 8-11-3 TomScudamore (M C Pipe) *led: rdn appr 4 out: narrow advantage whn fell 3 out* 11/4[2]	115
/00P	U		**Stylish Prince**[7] 3251 6-10-10 (t) MrTCollier(7) (R Lee) *prom: hit 5th and 8th: wknd 11th: no ch whn mstke 4 out: blnd and uns rdr 3 out* 40/1	—

5m 0.50s (-10.20) **Going Correction** -0.325s/f (Good)
WFA 5 from 6yo+ 9lb 9 Ran SP% 116.3
Speed ratings: **107,105,—,—,— —,—,—,—** CSF £8.15 TOTE £1.60: £1.10, £1.40, £5.10; EX 8.60.
Owner Foster Yeoman Limited **Bred** P De Maleissye Melun **Trained** Ditcheat, Somerset

FOCUS
The jockeys reported the ground on the chase course to be good, as per the official description. Although stripped of much of its interest by the defection of Racing Demon, whose trainer took him out because she felt the ground was too quick, this was still a fair novice chase.

NOTEBOOK
Taranis(FR) came under pressure in third approaching the home straight, but he stuck to his task and eventually won quite decisively. While this performance was nothing to get excited about, this sharp track did not really suit a horse who ought to get three miles in time and he is capable of better. *(op 8-13)*
Dickensbury Lad(FR) jumped soundly on this chasing debut and his new yard will be very pleased with his first run since May 2004. A race should come his way provided his sights are not set too high. *(op 12-1)*
Tank Buster trailed throughout on this chasing bow but plugged on to claim an unlikely third prize. *(tchd 40-1)*
Solar At'Em(IRE), a long-standing maiden, made an error two from home and was caught for third at the final fence. *(tchd 16-1)*
Team Tassel(IRE) seemed to appreciate being allowed to lead and showed much more aptitude for chasing than he had on his debut. He actually jumped pretty well prior to coming down at the last ditch, but it is unlikely that he would have held on. Still, this was a more encouraging run after some lacklustre efforts. *(op 10-3 tchd 5-2)*

3357 LUDLOW CLUB H'CAP CHASE (13 fncs) 2m
2:30 (2:32) (Class 3) (0-135,133) 5-Y-0+
£10,960 (£3,237; £1,618; £810; £404; £203)

Form				RPR
5404	1		**Palua**[5] 3299 9-11-10 131 TimmyMurphy (Miss E C Lavelle) *j.lft: mde all: rdn appr 2 out: r.o* 7/1[3]	140+
-2P4	2	1 ½	**Jacks Craic (IRE)**[11] 3183 7-10-10 117 AntonyEvans (J L Spearing) *hld up and bhd: hdwy 9th: ev ch whn hit last: swtchd lft flat: nt qckn* 25/1	125+
1215	3	3 ½	**Lorient Express (FR)**[5] 3299 7-11-3 124 SamThomas (Miss Venetia Williams) *hld up in mid-div: hdwy 7th: rdn appr 2 out: one pce* 4/1[1]	129+
-602	4	10	**Master Rex**[17] 2998 11-11-9 130 NoelFehily (B De Haan) *hld up in tch: wnt 2nd and hit 4 out: rdn and wknd 2 out* 5/1[2]	124+
-156	5	nk	**O'Toole (IRE)**[47] 2488 7-10-7 114 PJBrennan (P J Hobbs) *prom: rdn appr 2 out: wkng whn swtchd lft appr last* 11/1	107+
46/1	6	2	**Joey Tribbiani (IRE)**[131] 1399 9-10-1 108 WayneHutchinson (T Keddy) *nvr nr ldrs* 14/1	98
4206	7	1 ¼	**Almaydan**[33] 2768 8-11-11 132 RobertThornton (R Lee) *prom tl rdn and wknd 9th* 8/1	121+
U364	8	1 ½	**Saafend Rocket (IRE)**[22] 2939 8-10-8 115 MarkBradburne (H D Daly) *hld up: rdn after 9th: sn struggling* 8/1	103+
1215	9	3	**Harry Potter (GER)**[75] 1919 7-9-13 109 ColinBolger(3) (Evan Williams) *mstke 3 out: a bhd* 16/1	93
P-0P	10	5	**Hot Shots (FR)**[54] 2346 11-11-12 133 (p) PaulMoloney (M Pitman) *prom tl wknd appr 4 out* 16/1	112
-3FP	U		**Le Seychellois (FR)**[12] 3136 6-11-4 132 (t) LiamHeard(7) (P F Nicholls) *hld up and bhd: hdwy 9th: wknd 3 out: blnd and uns rdr 2 out* 7/1[3]	121

3m 54.7s (-9.40) **Going Correction** -0.325s/f (Good) 11 Ran SP% 114.5
Speed ratings: **110,109,107,102,102 101,100,99,98,95** CSF £147.28 CT £791.74 TOTE £7.40: £2.50, £3.60, £2.00; EX 202.30 TRIFECTA Not won..
Owner R J Lavelle **Bred** David Jamison Bloodstock And J Dohle **Trained** Wildhern, Hants

FOCUS
A fairly competitive handicap in which the winner, running right up to his best, was able to make all. The form should prove sound.

NOTEBOOK
Palua, who ran quite well in a better race than this at Sandown at the weekend, appreciated being able to dominate and was able to make every yard. He jumped out to his left throughout but had sufficient in reserve to hold off the runner-up. *(op 9-1)*
Jacks Craic(IRE) lacked the chasing experience of most of his rivals but he ran a good race and the result might have been different had he not got in too close to the final fence when challenging. He rallied on the run-in but the damage had been done.
Lorient Express(FR), a place behind Palua five days earlier, has twice been held from this mark now but he remains in good heart. He does have a tendency to get rather low over his fences and that contributed to his defeat. *(op 9-2 tchd 5-1 in places)*
Master Rex was 13lb better off with Lorient Express from their meeting at Wincanton on Boxing Day, but after looking a real danger turning for home he clouted the first fence in the home straight and could not sustain his challenge. *(op 9-2 after 4-1 in places)*
O'Toole(IRE), dropped 3lb, ran respectably on only his third run over fences. *(op 10-1)*
Joey Tribbiani(IRE), raised 8lb after a winning reappearance in September, was never nearer on this first run since. *(op 12-1 tchd 16-1 in places)*
Le Seychellois(FR), tried in a tongue-strap, was close enough on the home turn but was a beaten sixth when unseating his rider at the second last. There were no real excuses here and he has quickly become disappointing. *(tchd 15-2)*

3358 AMATEUR JOCKEYS ASSOCIATION AMATEUR RIDERS' NOVICES' H'CAP HURDLE (11 hdls) 2m 5f
3:00 (3:00) (Class 4) (0-110,108) 4-Y-0+ £4,059 (£1,259; £629; £314)

Form				RPR
-131	1		**She's Our Native (IRE)**[7] 3247 8-11-11 108 7ex MrJETudor(5) (Evan Williams) *hld up: hdwy after 8th: led on bit and j.rt 3 out: v easily* 7/2[2]	124+
6206	2	8	**Amanpuri (GER)**[31] 2802 8-10-7 90 MrsLucyRowsell(5) (Mrs A M Thorpe) *t.k.h: prom: led 3rd tl after 8th: one pce fr 3 out* 66/1	93
4211	3	1	**Miss Shakira (IRE)**[46] 2526 8-10-12 97 MrRMcCarthy(7) (N A Twiston-Davies) *chsd ldr: led after 8th to 3 out: one pce* 6/1	99
0-04	4	5	**Salopian**[35] 2723 6-10-13 96 MrPCallaghan(5) (H D Daly) *prom tl wknd appr 3 out* 25/1	93
1542	5	4	**Astyanax (IRE)**[35] 2723 6-11-6 101 MrJSnowden(3) (N J Henderson) *led to 3rd: nt fluent 6th: rdn and wknd appr 3 out: mstke 2 out* 9/4[1]	94
0P46	6	8	**Pearly Star**[17] 2983 5-11-0 95 MrGTumelty(3) (A King) *hld up in tch: rdn and wknd appr 3 out* 5/1[3]	80
0006	7	1 ½	**Mokum (FR)**[16] 3040 5-11-1 100 MrCHughes(7) (A W Carroll) *bhd: rdn after 8th: nvr nr ldrs* 25/1	84
6F-6	8	1 ½	**Red Lion (FR)**[44] 2563 9-10-7 92 MrDAFitzsimmons(7) (D McCain) *plld hrd: hdwy 3rd: wknd appr 7th* 33/1	74
000P	9	nk	**Barathea Blue**[10] 3211 5-10-12 97 (t) MrRQuinn(7) (M C Pipe) *hld up: hdwy appr 8th: rdn and wknd appr 3 out* 16/1	79
PFPP	10	17	**Memories Of Gold (IRE)**[13] 3126 6-9-12 83 (p) MrCHolman(7) (J A Danahar) *bhd fr 4th* 100/1	48
0-24	11	hd	**Teorban (POL)**[57] 2271 7-11-6 98 MrNWilliams (D J S Ffrench Davis) *prom tl rdn and wknd after 8th* 10/1	63
-053	12	½	**Deliceo (IRE)**[46] 2524 13-9-12 83 MrLRPayter(7) (M Sheppard) *rdn appr 7th: a bhd* 22/1	47

5m 14.8s (-3.50) **Going Correction** -0.15s/f (Good) 12 Ran SP% 116.4
Speed ratings: **100,96,96,94,93 90,89,88,88,82 82,82** CSF £222.80 CT £1352.37 TOTE £4.70: £1.80, £18.80, £2.00; EX 457.30.
Owner Ian Brice **Bred** J Mangan **Trained** Cowbridge, Vale Of Glamorgan

FOCUS
A competitive handicap run at a decent gallop. The winner has been rated value for 13 lengths and could well win again.

NOTEBOOK

She's Our Native(IRE), 5lb well in under her 7lb penalty, ended up winning easily. The fact that the ground appeared to be riding easier than the official description suited her and, although she jumped out to her right at the three flights in the straight, it made no difference as she was going strongly at the time. Another quick reappearance looks on the cards. *(op 9-2)*

Amanpuri(GER) , an inconsistent type and still a maiden over timber, was one of three to take each other on at the head of affairs and stuck on for second, if no match for the winner.

Miss Shakira(IRE), last seen winning a couple of novice chases in the autumn, looked on a fair mark for her return to hurdling, but to get this trip properly she probably needs a sound surface. Although last to capitulate to the winner, she weakened in the straight and had to give up second place to fellow pacesetter Amanpuri. *(tchd 13-2)*

Salopian, over a stone better off with She's Our Native on their course-and-distance form in December, gives the impression he has started life in handicap company on a high enough mark. *(op 28-1)*

Astyanax(IRE), had a pull of over a stone with the winner compared with their meeting here last time, but this ground was not as quick as he would have liked. *(tchd 2-1 and 5-2)*

Pearly Star might do better back over a shorter trip. *(op 4-1 tchd 11-2 in places)*

Barathea Blue, a one-time fair Flat performer having his third run over hurdles, hinted at a little ability and might be seen to better effect on faster ground. *(op 14-1)*

3359 SAVE LUDLOW COMMUNITY HOSPITAL H'CAP CHASE (19 fncs) 3m

3:30 (3:31) (Class 5) (0-85,90) 5-Y-0+

£3,444 (£1,017; £508; £254; £127; £63)

Form — RPR

-6P4 **1** **Boardroom Dancer (IRE)**[13] [3129] 9-11-3 **81** .... DarylJacob(7) 97+
(Miss Suzy Smith) *mde all: hit 4 out: clr 2 out: comf* **16/1**

241P **2** *7* **Cool Song**[27] [2863] 10-11-0 **74** .... ColinBolger(3) 81
(Miss Suzy Smith) *a.p: rdn appr 3 out: styd on to take 2nd towards fin: no ch w wnr* **6/1**[2]

4011 **3** *1 ¼* **Merry Storm (IRE)**[7] [3252] 7-11-12 **90** 7ex .... RichardSpate(7) 98+
(Mrs K Waldron) *hld up: hdwy 9th: wnt 2nd and hit 4 out: rdn appr last: one pce* **2/1**[1]

425P **4** *9* **Valley Warrior**[17] [2966] 9-10-13 **70** .... PJBrennan 69+
(J S Smith) *hld up and bhd: hdwy 12th: rdn after 15th: wknd 2 out* **12/1**

3065 **5** *16* **Reflex Blue**[6] [3279] 9-11-5 **76** ....(v) AlanO'Keeffe 57
(R J Price) *hld up and bhd: rdn and hdwy 15th: wknd 3 out* **16/1**

6302 **6** *1 ¼* **Alfred The Grey**[17] [2957] 9-11-2 **76** ....(p) TJPhelan(3) 56
(Miss Suzy Smith) *hld up in mid-div: reminder after 9th: struggling 15th: no ch whn mstke 4 out* **7/1**[3]

3-PP **7** *11* **Jesnic (IRE)**[67] [2073] 6-11-10 **81** .... WayneHutchinson 50
(R Dickin) *hld up in mid-div: 5th and no imp whn blnd 3 out* **50/1**

/05 **8** *4* **Constant Husband**[46] [2522] 13-10-9 **73** .... MrGTumelty(7) 38
(R N Bevis) *hdwy 3rd: wknd 14th* **33/1**

3P-5 **9** *12* **Shuffling Pals (IRE)**[41] [2610] 9-11-1 **72** ....(b[1]) JoeTizzard 25
(S E H Sherwood) *prom tl wknd 14th* **25/1**

-06P **10** *dist* **Glen Thyne (IRE)**[27] [2859] 6-11-0 **71** .... JohnMcNamara —
(K C Bailey) *a bhd: t.o* **28/1**

306/ **P** **Dome**[1281] [642] 8-11-0 **71** .... PaulMoloney —
(M Pitman) *bhd fr 14th: p.u bef 3 out* **14/1**

312P **U** **Petolinski**[220] [669] 8-11-1 **79** ....(p) TomMessenger(7) —
(C L Popham) *bhd tl hmpd and uns rdr 14th* **11/1**

-PP5 **F** **Peveril Pride**[10] [3220] 8-11-12 **83** ....(t) JimmyMcCarthy —
(J A Geake) *bhd: mstke 9th: fell 14th* **50/1**

P **P** **Aisjem (IRE)**[82] [1832] 7-11-4 **75** .... AntonyEvans —
(Evan Williams) *bhd: pckd 2nd (water): p.u bef 14th* **9/1**

-4PU **P** **Monster Mick (FR)**[47] [2506] 8-11-1 **72** ....(b[1]) CarlLlewellyn —
(N A Twiston-Davies) *hld up in mid-div: reminder after 6th: bhd fr 9th: p.u bef 14th* **16/1**

6m 5.00s (-7.10) **Going Correction** -0.325s/f (Good) **15** Ran SP% **124.6**
Speed ratings: **98,95,95,92,86 86,82,81,77,— —,—,—,—,—** CSF £109.83 CT £283.71 TOTE £17.60: £3.70, £2.50, £1.50; EX 128.40.

Owner Dr D J Meecham Jones **Bred** Patrick Higgins **Trained** Lewes, E Sussex

■ A one-two for trainer Suzy Smith.

FOCUS

A weak handicap chase that is unlikely to throw up many winners in the near future. Rated through the second, the form looks sound enough, though.

NOTEBOOK

Boardroom Dancer(IRE) had not shown much in the last couple of years, albeit from few opportunities, but he ran a better race on his latest start and the switch to front-running tactics here paid off. *He jumped soundly throughout and stayed on too well for his pursuers.Official explanation: trainer said, regarding the improved form shown, gelding had been better suited by making all the running here*

Cool Song, a stablemate of the winner, scored off a 5lb lower mark at Warwick two starts back and there were excuses last time. He ran a solid race and plugged on to claim second on the run-in. *(op 13-2)*

Merry Storm(IRE), seeking a hat-trick, was 4lb well in under the penalty for his latest win at Hereford and was able to get in this 0-85 affair off a mark of 90. After looking to be travelling best on the home turn, he hit the first fence in the straight and could never get to the winner, losing second on the run-in. On this evidence he will struggle when his new mark comes into operation, but this ground was faster than he would like. *(op 5-2 tchd 11-4 in places)*

Valley Warrior is a very limited performer and still a maiden, but he turned in a better run after his moody effort on Boxing Day. *(op 14-1)*

Reflex Blue failed to see out this longer trip. *(op 14-1)*

Alfred The Grey, 3lb higher, could never get into the action in a race in which his stablemates finished first and second. *(tchd 13-2)*

3360 1871 H'CAP HURDLE (9 hdls) 2m

4:00 (4:01) (Class 3) (0-125,125) 4-Y-0+

£7,828 (£2,312; £1,156; £578; £288; £145)

Form — RPR

4-F4 **1** **Go For Bust**[24] [2924] 7-11-7 **120** .... MarcusFoley 122
(N J Henderson) *hld up: hdwy 6th: led 2 out: r.o* **18/1**

-331 **2** *1 ¼* **Armariver (FR)**[11] [3175] 6-10-2 **108** .... LiamHeard(7) 109
(P F Nicholls) *hld up in tch: led 3 out to 2 out: nt qckn flat* **11/8**[1]

0126 **3** *1 ½* **Red Moor (IRE)**[13] [3127] 6-10-12 **111** .... RobertThornton 113+
(Mrs D A Hamer) *hld up in mid-div: rdn and hdwy 3 out: kpt on flat* **33/1**

3160 **4** *shd* **Cantgeton (IRE)**[17] [2990] 6-11-12 **125** .... TimmyMurphy 125+
(M C Pipe) *hld up and bhd: hdwy on ins appr 3 out: sltly hmpd last: one pce* **9/2**[2]

0-PP **5** *½* **Broke Road (IRE)**[131] [1087] 10-11-0 **113** ....(t) JimCrowley 112
(Mrs H Dalton) *led to 3rd: w ldr: ev ch appr 3 out: one pce fr 2 out* **20/1**

6220 **6** *1 ¼* **Silver Prophet (IRE)**[27] [2871] 7-11-0 **113** .... SeanCurran 111+
(M R Bosley) *prom: led briefly appr 3 out: btn whn hit last* **16/1**

241- **7** *5* **Sir Brastias**[469] [1541] 7-10-11 **110** .... JohnMcNamara 103+
(K C Bailey) *hld up in tch: rdn appr 3 out: wknd 2 out* **25/1**

1336 **8** *4* **Dr Cerullo**[35] [2734] 5-10-11 **110** .... TomDoyle 99+
(C Tinkler) *prom tl rdn and wknd 3 out* **16/1**

P-P0 **9** *1 ¾* **Etendard Indien (FR)**[35] [2734] 5-11-0 **113** .... MickFitzgerald 101+
(N J Henderson) *hld up in tch: rdn and wknd appr 3 out* **12/1**

0-46 **10** *3* **Redi (ITY)**[13] [3128] 5-10-12 **111** ....(tp) APMcCoy 99+
(A M Balding) *s.s: sme hdwy 3 out: no imp whn hit and hmpd last* **9/1**[3]

1201 **11** *5* **Sunnyarjun**[55] [2314] 8-9-11 **99** oh1 .... TomMalone(3) 78
(J C Tuck) *hld up and bhd: hdwy appr 5th: rdn and wknd after 6th* **14/1**

30-P **12** *11* **Atahuelpa**[35] [2716] 6-11-8 **121** ....(t) AlanO'Keeffe 89
(Jennie Candlish) *plld hrd: a bhd* **66/1**

62P0 **13** *20* **Imperial Rocket (USA)**[13] [3128] 9-9-12 **102** ....(t) LeeStephens(5) 50
(W K Goldsworthy) *w ldr: led 3rd tl appr 3 out: wknd appr 2 out: eased flat* **100/1**

0FUP **P** **A Bit Of Fun**[84] [1804] 5-10-4 **108** .... LiamTreadwell(5) —
(J T Stimpson) *bhd tl p.u bef last* **100/1**

4042 **F** **Spike Jones (NZ)**[13] [3128] 8-9-11 **101** ow1 .... DerekLaverty(5) 101+
(Mrs A M Thorpe) *hld up and bhd: hdwy appr 6th: rdn appr 3 out: cl 3rd whn fell last* **11/1**

3m 48.8s (-3.50) **Going Correction** -0.15s/f (Good)
WFA 4 from 5yo+ 11lb **15** Ran SP% **125.0**
Speed ratings: **102,101,100,100,100 99,97,95,94,92 90,84,74,—,—** CSF £43.97 CT £905.08 TOTE £23.30: £6.10, £1.50, £13.30; EX 72.80 Place 6 £21.90, Place 5 £16.53.

Owner Mrs E Roberts & Nick Roberts **Bred** Stetchworth Park Stud Ltd **Trained** Upper Lambourn, Berks

FOCUS

Quite a competitive handicap, this was run at a strong pace and the form is likely to prove sound for the grade.

NOTEBOOK

Go For Bust, back hurdling after losing his confidence over fences, had no problem with the drop to the minimum trip on this sharp track and he was always holding his challengers after edging ahead at the second last. He is still relatively unexposed over hurdles and looks the type to make a nice chaser sooner or later. *(op 16-1)*

Armariver(FR), able to race off the same mark as when first past the post (subsequently demoted) at Cheltenham on New Year's Day, had every chance but was just held. This was an opportunity missed as he will race off 7lb higher in future handicaps. *(op 6-4 tchd 13-8 in places)*

Red Moor(IRE) was shuffled back as the field bunched on the approach to the home straight but stayed on well up the run-in to claim third. This was his second run after a break and he should be spot-on next time. *(op 40-1)*

Cantgeton(IRE), back at two miles, showed something of a return to form. Sticking to the inner throughout, he was impeded by the faller at the last but his measure had already been taken. *(op 6-1)*

Broke Road(IRE), equipped with a tongue tie, ran well considering he was up with the strong pace throughout and that this was his first run since an outing on the Flat in September. *(op 16-1)*

Silver Prophet(IRE) ran his race but will remain beatable from this sort of mark.

Sir Brastias, appearing for the first time since landing a novice hurdle in September 2004, made an error at the last flight in the back straight which left him with work to do. The return to a longer trip will suit him.

Atahuelpa had his tongue tied down for this second run for the yard. He was not knocked about and gave the impression that he is capable of better.

Spike Jones(NZ), raised 8lb for his good second at Taunton, was in the process of running another fine race when falling at the last. He had to be switched going into the flight, but was staying on and would definitely have been placed at least. *(tchd 12-1)*

T/Jkpt: Not won. T/Plt: £7.50 to a £1 stake. Pool: £48,383.30. 4,682.20 winning tickets. T/Qpdt: £6.40 to a £1 stake. Pool: £3,123.20. 359.40 winning tickets. KH

3361 - 3366a (Foreign Racing) - See Raceform Interactive

2956 HUNTINGDON (R-H)

Friday, January 13

OFFICIAL GOING: Good to soft

Wind: Moderate, half-against Weather: Overcast

3367 RACING POST - MORE THAN JUST RACING CONDITIONAL JOCKEYS' H'CAP HURDLE (10 hdls) 2m 5f 110y

1:00 (1:01) (Class 5) (0-95,97) 4-Y-0+ **£2,192** (£639; £319)

Form — RPR

5505 **1** **Golden Feather**[44] [2569] 4-10-5 **82** .... PhilKinsella 83+
(Miss Venetia Williams) *hld up: hdwy 5th: led on bit appr 2 out: styd on wl* **3/1**[1]

64-0 **2** *9* **Northern Shadows**[35] [2750] 7-11-3 **87** .... JamesReveley(6) 89+
(K G Reveley) *hld up: hdwy appr 3 out: styd on same pce fr next: mstke last* **8/1**

/056 **3** *¾* **Baron Blitzkrieg**[13] [3147] 8-10-3 **73** .... RyanCummings(6) 73
(D J Wintle) *chsd ldrs: led and hit 7th: hdd appr 2 out: no ex last* **15/2**

-004 **4** *7* **Darialann (IRE)**[18] [2962] 11-11-7 **88** .... DarrenO'Dwyer(3) 81
(O Brennan) *sn pushed along in rr: hdwy and mstke 3 out: no imp fr next* **20/1**

U0 **5** *14* **Astronaut**[18] [2977] 9-11-3 **87** .... JohnFlavin(6) 70+
(R C Guest) *hld up: swtchd lft after 5th: sn jnd main gp again: hdwy and mstke next: hit 3 out: sn wknd* **14/1**

3F51 **6** *6* **Ask The Umpire (IRE)**[7] [3279] 11-12-5 **97** 7ex ....(b) JohnKington 70
(N E Berry) *prom tl wknd appr 2 out* **5/1**[2]

30PP **7** *1 ¼* **Be Telling (IRE)**[28] [2862] 7-11-6 **87** .... TimothyBailey(3) 59
(B J Curley) *hld up: hmpd after 5th: hdwy next: wknd after 7th* **14/1**

055 **8** *7* **Chigorin**[41] [2624] 5-11-9 **87** .... WayneKavanagh 52
(Miss S J Wilton) *hld up: hdwy 6th: wknd 3 out* **20/1**

06-4 **9** *¾* **Little Saxtead (IRE)**[13] [3137] 6-10-5 **69** .... SimonElliott 33
(J A Supple) *a bhd* **25/1**

400P **10** *29* **Key In**[17] [3042] 5-11-10 **88** ....(v[1]) TomMessenger 23
(I W McInnes) *led to 7th: wknd qckly* **50/1**

00-P **11** *1* **Bronhallow**[18] [2958] 13-10-2 **69** ....(bt) KeiranBurke(3) 3
(Mrs Barbara Waring) *prom: j. slowly and lost pl 2nd: wknd appr 6th* **100/1**

P04 **12** *15* **Rockys Girl**[31] [2811] 4-10-3 **80** .... AndrewGlassonbury —
(R Flint) *mid-div: mstke and dropped rr 3rd: effrt appr 3 out: no ch whn hit next* **12/1**

-55P **13** *dist* **Kirby's Vic (IRE)**[36] [2723] 6-11-4 **85** .... BernieWharfe(3) —
(N A Twiston-Davies) *hld up in tch: rdn and wknd appr 6th* **33/1**

-2P0 **P** **Deo Gratias (POL)**[24] [2934] 6-11-8 **86** ....(t) WillieMcCarthy —
(M Pitman) *chsd ldrs tl wknd after 7th: bhd whn p.u bef 2 out* **7/1**[3]

46P0 **P** **Safe To Blush**[13] [3147] 8-11-0 **78** ....(tp) DavidCullinane —
(P A Pritchard) *chsd ldrs tl wknd after 7th: bhd whn p.u bef 2 out* **22/1**

5m 23.8s (13.00) **Going Correction** +0.625s/f (Soft)
WFA 4 from 5yo+ 12lb **15** Ran SP% **121.7**
Speed ratings: **101,97,97,94,89 87,87,84,84,73 73,68,—,—,—** CSF £25.08 CT £170.87 TOTE £4.30: £1.90, £3.00, £2.90; EX 27.00.

Owner Paul Beck **Bred** Newgate Stud Co **Trained** Kings Caple, H'fords

■ Stewards' Enquiry : John Flavin one-day ban: careless riding (Jan 24)

FOCUS

A poor race and Golden Feather ran out a ready winner on this handicap debut. The race has been rated through the runner-up.

NOTEBOOK

Golden Feather ◆, disappointing in four starts for previous trainer Richard Guest, found the combination of the switch to the Williams stable and move into handicaps off only 82 enabling him to get off the mark and, although beating a poor field, he could hardly have done it more easily. His stable continues to churn out the winners and he may go to Musselburgh in a bid for a quick follow up. *Official explanation: trainer's representative said, regarding the improved form shown, gelding was having its first run for the yard (tchd 4-1)*

Northern Shadows, whose stable have an excellent record at this course, made good headway down the back straight, but she was unable to go in pursuit of the winner when asked and took her time in getting the better of Baron Blitzkrieg on the run-in. She has yet to win in 11 starts and shaped here as though worth a try at three miles.

Baron Blitzkrieg has not been running too badly since returning from a layoff and stepped up again with a gallant effort in third. This return to a better surface clearly suited and he can probably find a race at a similarly lowly level. *(op 8-1)*

Darialann(IRE) was unable to improve on his recent fourth at Market Rasen. He is not getting any younger and will find his best opportunities coming at selling level these days.

Astronaut, although well-beaten, showed a little more than when down the field at Sedgefield on Boxing Day, but still remain below his early form. *(op 16-1)*

Ask The Umpire(IRE)faced a tough task under such a big weight and it was no surprise to see him struggle. *(op 7-1 tchd 15-2)*

3368 RPSPORT FREE WITH RACING POST EVERY SATURDAY H'CAP CHASE (16 fncs) 2m 4f 110y

1:30 (1:33) (Class 4) (0-100,101) 5-Y-0+ **£3,578** (£1,050; £525; £262)

Form RPR

3306 **1** **Lubinas (IRE)**[30] 2818 7-11-5 **92** AndrewThornton 111+
(F Jordan) *in tch: hdwy 7th: chsd ldrs 9th: hit 12th: chal last: sn led: drvn and r.o strly* **20/1**

/255 **2** *4* **Umbrella Man (IRE)**[24] 2931 10-11-10 **97** MarcusFoley 108
(Miss E C Lavelle) *hld up in rr: hdwy 13th: drvn and one pce after 3 out: styd on to chse wnr run-in but no imp* **7/1**[3]

P362 **3** *1 3/4* **Woodenbridge Dream (IRE)**[18] 2960 9-10-12 **85** RichardJohnson 94
(R Lee) *led to 5th: led again next: rdn and narrowly hdd 2 out: one pce run-in* **16/1**

64/U **4** *1 1/2* **Spinaround**[37] 2705 8-10-7 **80** TomDoyle 90+
(P R Webber) *hld up rr: stdy hdwy 10th: drvn and slt ld 2 out: mstke last and sn hdd: wknd run-in* **7/1**[3]

3/05 **5** *7* **Patriarch (IRE)**[13] 3148 10-11-8 **95** PJBrennan 97+
(P Bowen) *hit 1st: chsd ldrs: hit 10th: chsd ldr 11th: rdn 3 out: wknd after 2 out* **40/1**

661/ **6** *dist* **Longstone Loch (IRE)**[679] 4164 9-10-9 **89** TomMessenger(7) —
(C C Bealby) *chsd ldrs: hit 7th: wknd 4 out: t.o* **40/1**

-33P **7** *6* **Tipp Top (IRE)**[25] 2926 9-10-11 **84** (t) JohnMcNamara —
(O Brennan) *hit 1st: bhd: hdwy 8th: chsd ldrs next: wknd qckly 4 out: t.o* **50/1**

-646 **8** *1 1/4* **Follow Your Heart (IRE)**[28] 2866 6-11-10 **97** APMcCoy —
(N J Gifford) *hmpd 1st: rr mstke next (water): rdn 10th: mstke 11 (water): nvr in contention: t.o* **5/1**[2]

-4F **9** *1* **Gerrard (IRE)**[18] 2984 8-10-5 **78** (v) AntonyEvans —
(Mrs A Barclay) *bhd: hdwy to chse ldrs 9th: hit 13th: sn wknd: t.o* **12/1**

P632 **10** *2 1/2* **Flying Patriarch**[11] 3220 5-10-8 **91** (b) PhilipHide —
(G L Moore) *hit 5th: chsd ldrs 7th: rdn 9th: sn wknd: t.o* **12/1**

-643 **11** *13* **Standing Bloom**[22] 2955 10-11-4 **91** PaulMoloney —
(Mrs P Sly) *hit 4th: a bhd: t.o* **20/1**

6/05 **12** *3* **Corroboree (IRE)**[17] 3037 9-11-12 **99** CarlLlewellyn —
(N A Twiston-Davies) *led 5th: styd w ldr to 10th: wknd next: t.o* **28/1**

F442 **F** **Assumetheposition (FR)**[17] 3037 6-11-0 **90** (p) LarryMcGrath(3) —
(R C Guest) *fell 1st* **25/1**

-261 **P** **First De La Brunie (FR)**[9] 3239 5-11-4 **101** 7ex RobertThornton —
(A King) *bhd: rdn 9th: no rspnse: t.o whn p.u bef 2 out* **9/4**[1]

5m 15.7s (9.60) **Going Correction** +0.625s/f (Soft)
WFA 5 from 6yo+ 9lb **14** Ran SP% **117.4**
Speed ratings: **106,104,103,103,100** —,—,—,—,— —,—,—,— CSF £143.51 CT £2311.63 TOTE £25.10: £5.10, £2.00, £3.90; EX 177.60.

Owner Paul Ratcliffe **Bred** Gestut Fahrhof Stiftung **Trained** Adstone, Northants

FOCUS

A tight handicap run at a decent gallop and there were still five in with a chance on the run towards the second-last. It is probably solid form and should work out.

NOTEBOOK

Lubinas(IRE) ◆, although winless over fences coming into this, had done more than enough to suggest a race such as this would come his way and ran out a deserved winner under a fine ride, coming clear after the last. A highly consistent gelding, who will stay further, he looks the type to win again. *(op 16-1)*

Umbrella Man(IRE) travelled well in rear and made headway down the back straight, but got going all too late and was arguably given a bit too much to do. He does not win very often, but a slightly more positive ride in future will at least give him more of a chance. *(op 8-1 tchd 17-2)*

Woodenbridge Dream(IRE) was disputing the lead with Corroboree from an early stage and went on when that one blundered badly early in the back straight, but it was clear from two out that a place was the best he could hope for and he battled on to regain third from Spinaround. *(op 18-1)*

Spinaround ◆, who was probably a little unlucky when unseating at Leicester on his chasing debut, looked set to gain compensation here when going to the front two out, but Lubinas soon had his move covered and a blunder at the last ended his chance. Racing here off a mark of 80, it is only a matter of time before he strikes. *(op 8-1)*

Patriarch(IRE) had shown very little in two starts since returning from a layoff, but it was possible he still needed his most recent run (decent race) and this move into handicap company brought about an improved effort. He was a fair hurdler a few seasons back and is lightly raced enough to find some further improvement.

Standing Bloom *Official explanation: jockey said mare never travelled (op 25-1)*

First De La Brunie(FR), shouldering a 7lb penalty for winning easily at Wincanton, was beaten with fully a circuit to go and threw in a rather moody display. His trainer reported he may well have *found the race coming too soon, but he nonetheless has a bit to prove after this.Official explanation: trainer said, regarding the poor form shown, gelding never travelled and may have been feeling effects of previous run (tchd 5-2 in places)*

3369 EBF RPSPORT "NATIONAL HUNT" NOVICES' HURDLE (QUALIFIER) (8 hdls) 2m 110y

2:00 (2:03) (Class 4) 4-7-Y-0 **£5,204** (£1,528; £764; £381)

Form RPR

-263 **1** **Idris (GER)**[50] 2455 5-11-5 110 PhilipHide 121
(G L Moore) *led: hdd after 1st: chsd ldr: led 5th: hit 2 out: drvn out* **14/1**[3]

-11 **2** *3/4* **Craven (IRE)**[30] 2826 6-11-11 MickFitzgerald 127+
(N J Henderson) *hld up in tch: chsd wnr and nt fluent 3 out: ev ch last: rdn and hung lft flat: nt qckn towards fin* **6/5**[1]

42-U **3** *19* **Easter Present (IRE)**[97] 1669 7-11-5 106 RobertThornton 101
(Miss H C Knight) *hld up in tch: ev ch 3 out: wknd next* **22/1**

21 **4** *1* **Fier Normand (FR)**[30] 2821 7-11-11 APMcCoy 107+
(Jonjo O'Neill) *hld up: hdwy 4th: wknd 2 out* **6/4**[2]

05 **5** *shd* **John Diamond (IRE)**[36] 2720 5-11-5 SamThomas 100
(Miss H C Knight) *hld up: hdwy after 5th: hmpd 3 out: sn wknd* **66/1**

4 **6** *hd* **Witness Run (IRE)**[28] 2865 6-11-5 LeightonAspell 100
(N J Gifford) *prom tl wknd 3 out* **18/1**

7 *11* **Take Time** 7-11-5 TomScudamore 89
(M G Rimell) *hld up: plld hrd: hdwy 4th: wknd after next* **100/1**

-204 **8** *3 1/2* **Thenameescapesme**[28] 2860 6-11-5 NoelFehily 89+
(T R George) *hld up: hdwy 5th: ev ch 3 out: sn wknd* **50/1**

9 *23* **Sapient** 5-10-12 MrJMahot(7) 62
(M Scudamore) *bhd fr 3rd* **200/1**

10 *1* **Posh Act** 6-11-5 PaulMoloney 61
(Miss H C Knight) *hld up: bhd fr 4th* **100/1**

4-30 **11** *shd* **Wotashambles (IRE)**[8] 3246 5-11-5 TomDoyle 61
(P R Webber) *prom: mstke 4th: wknd bef next* **100/1**

3-0 **12** *dist* **Kilkilian (IRE)**[23] 2941 6-11-5 (t) JohnMcNamara —
(B G Powell) *hld up: a in rr* **100/1**

0 **13** *18* **Just Touch Wood**[18] 2961 5-10-12 CharlieStudd(7) —
(B G Powell) *hld up: effrt after 5th: sn wknd: in rr whn hmpd next* **200/1**

-000 **F** **Lordington Lad**[13] 3133 6-11-5 JamesDavies —
(B G Powell) *racd keenly: led after 1st: hdd 5th: ev ch whn fell next* **150/1**

4m 4.50s (8.80) **Going Correction** +0.625s/f (Soft) **14** Ran SP% **110.8**
Speed ratings: **104,103,94,94,94 94,88,87,76,75 75,—,—,—** CSF £29.81 TOTE £9.10: £3.10, £1.02, £3.70; EX 27.60.

Owner Rdm Racing **Bred** Darley **Trained** Woodingdean, E Sussex

FOCUS

A decent race on paper, but a disappointing outcome with neither Craven nor Fier Normand proving good enough to beat the seemingly exposed Idris. It has been rated around the third.

NOTEBOOK

Idris(GER), third behind the useful Acambo at Taunton back in November, looked booked for a placing at best here, but he stepped up on previous efforts and galloped on resolutely, proving too battle-hardened for Craven on the run-in. In receipt of 6lb from the runner-up, he will be doing well to defy a penalty, but would make some appeal in handicaps with the possibility of further improvement to come. He is viewed as a chaser in the long term. *(op 12-1 tchd 11-1)*

Craven(IRE), who had been made to work hard in winning both his bumper and novice hurdle, again looked unsure of what was required of him under pressure and was outbattled by the winner. He was simply not up to conceding the winner weight on the day, but is going to stay further and is a fine-looking animal who looks sure to make a chaser in time. *(op Evens tchd 5-4)*

Easter Present(IRE) was no match for the front two and ended up being beaten a long way in *third, but that was always likely to be the case and a return to fences is imminent. (op 25-1 tchd 20-1)*

Fier Normand(FR), who created a favourable impression when winning at Bangor, faced a stiffer task in what was a markedly better race, but he should still have done an awful lot better and was simply found wanting under the penalty. Being a son of Cyborg, however, a stiffer test should suit and he could be worth another chance. *(op 15-8 tchd 2-1 in a place)*

John Diamond(IRE) is clearly learning with experience and put in some good late work, looking a tad unfortunate not to get fourth having been impeded at the third last. Although very much a *chasing type, he may be capable of winning a small race over hurdles before going fencing. (op 50-1)*

Witness Run(IRE), an Irish point winner who failed to see out his race on his hurdling debut at Windsor, raced too keenly for his own good, reverting to two miles, and again failed to get home. He was a negative in the market beforehand and the best of him may not be seen until he tackles handicaps. *(op 20-1 tchd 25-1)*

Lordington Lad was still bang there when he came down three out. It will be interesting to see what the Handicapper makes of him. *(op 100-1)*

3370 WEATHERBYS BANK H'CAP CHASE (12 fncs) 2m 110y

2:30 (2:31) (Class 4) (0-105,104) 5-Y-0+ **£3,903** (£1,146; £573; £286)

Form RPR

225- **1** **Just A Touch**[361] 3397 10-11-3 **95** LeightonAspell 104
(P Winkworth) *bhd: hdwy 7th: chsd ldrs 4 out: stmbld 3 out: drvn to ld last: pushed clr run-in* **12/1**

2516 **2** *7* **Jupon Vert (FR)**[9] 3239 9-11-1 **93** TomScudamore 95
(R J Hodges) *led: kpt slt advantage and rdn after 3 out: hdd last: styd on same pce u.p to hold 2nd but no ch w wnr* **8/1**

0-15 **3** *hd* **Madison De Vonnas (FR)**[66] 2103 6-11-12 **104** (t) MarcusFoley 107+
(Miss E C Lavelle) *trckd ldr: chal fr 5th: stl upsides and rdn appr last: one pce u.p run-in* **8/1**

2U63 **4** *2 1/2* **Celtic Legend (FR)**[7] 3272 7-10-8 **96** JamesReveley(10) 97+
(K G Reveley) *in tch: pushed along and one pce 4 out: mod prog whn mstke last: nvr a danger* **5/1**[3]

2U21 **5** *1 1/2* **Wages**[7] 3274 6-11-0 **97** 7ex MrNWilliams(5) 100+
(Evan Williams) *hld up in rr: hit 4th: mstke 6th: hit 8th: sme hdwy appr 2 out but nvr gng pce to rch ldrs* **15/8**[1]

6202 **6** *2* **Upswing**[7] 3270 9-9-11 **85** ow3 JohnFlavin(10) 83+
(R C Guest) *bhd: hit 2nd: sme hdwy 6th: never dangerous: wknd 4 out: no ch whn hit last* **7/2**[2]

-00F **7** *23* **Major Belle (FR)**[18] 2960 7-10-3 **81** HenryOliver 67+
(John R Upson) *hit 1st and 2nd: bhd and rdn 6th: no ch whn hit last* **11/1**

3-45 **8** *4* **Polish Pilot (IRE)**[36] 2719 11-9-11 **80** oh3 ow2 MarkNicolls(5) 49
(J R Cornwall) *chsd ldrs to 4 out: sn wknd* **40/1**

4m 21.7s (12.40) **Going Correction** +0.625s/f (Soft) **8** Ran SP% **114.4**
Speed ratings: **95,91,91,90,89 88,77,76** CSF £99.89 CT £817.84 TOTE £10.50: £2.60, £2.10, £2.70; EX 75.80.

Owner R N Scott, R G Robinson, Peter Broste **Bred** Shade Oak Stud **Trained** Ramsnest Common, Surrey

FOCUS

Ordinary form, rated around the third who has run to his hurdles mark, and a modest winning time, but a good training performance by Peter Winkworth.

NOTEBOOK

Just A Touch, off since suffering an injury at Plumpton nearly a year ago, was given a fine ride by Aspell, making gradual headway into a promising position as they turned for home and outstaying both Jupon Vert and Madison De Vonnas from two out. Expected to stay further by connections, he has gone well fresh in the past and this did not come as a total surprise, but he will need to step up on it if he is to defy a penalty. *(op 10-1)*

Jupon Vert(FR) led or disputed it for a long way and got into a fine jumping rhythm under Scudamore, but he had no answer as the winner swooped by. He gave his all in defeat, sticking his neck out to hold Madison De Vonnas for second, but he will remain vulnerable to anything less exposed. *(op 15-2)*

Madison De Vonnas(FR), a modest hurdler, made a highly pleasing start to his chasing career and harried Jupon Vert for the lead throughout, but his big weight took its toll in the end and he was just run out of second. There are races in him over fences on this evidence. *(tchd 9-1)*

Celtic Legend(FR), a winner over hurdles on his reappearance back in November, has thus far been unable to supplement it in five subsequent starts back over fences, but he has been running adequately and will no doubt continue to pay his way.

Wages, shouldering a 7lb penalty for winning at Towcester, was let down by his jumping and never got into it. He is better than this, but needs to be more fluent. *(op 13-8 tchd 2-1, 9-4 and 6-4 in places)*

Upswing came into this off the back of a good second at Musselburgh and was open to some improvement as this was only his third outing over fences, but, like the favourite, he could never get going and also made a few errors. *(op 9-2)*

3371 RPSPORT - READ, WATCH, WIN NOVICES' H'CAP HURDLE (8 hdls) 2m 110y

3:00 (3:00) (Class 4) (0-100,100) 4-Y-O+ **£3,083** (£898; £449)

Form				RPR
60-2	**1**		**Make My Hay**[13] 3152 7-11-5 **93**................................(b) RichardJohnson (J Gallagher) *led to 2 out: rallied to ld nr fin* **13/2**[3]	98
205	**2**	*shd*	**Tech Eagle (IRE)**[30] 2826 6-11-7 **95**.................................... TomDoyle (R Curtis) *hld up: hdwy 4th: led 2 out: hit last: rdn and hdd nr fin* **10/1**	100
0445	**3**	*11*	**Upright Ima**[18] 2958 7-9-13 **78**........................ StephenCraine[(5)] (Mrs P Sly) *hld up: hdwy 5th: sn rdn: wknd 2 out* **11/1**	72
0/0	**4**	*6*	**Monroe Gold**[43] 2585 6-10-5 **79**.................................... JosephByrne (Jennie Candlish) *hld up: hdwy 4th: rdn after next: hit 2 out: sn wknd: hung rt flat* **100/1**	70+
050	**5**	*1*	**Smoothly Does It**[30] 2826 5-11-7 **95**........................... AndrewTinkler (Mrs A J Bowlby) *hld up: gd hdwy appr 3 out: wknd next* **20/1**	82
6402	**6**	*19*	**Shaamit The Vaamit (IRE)**[9] 3242 6-10-11 **92**............... JohnKington[(7)] (M Scudamore) *chsd wnr: j.lft: ev ch 3 out: sn wknd* **4/1**[2]	69+
0-0F	**7**	*9*	**Salt Cellar (IRE)**[76] 1917 7-11-7 **100**......................... MarkNicolls[(5)] (P R Webber) *mid-div: rdn after 3rd: sn lost pl: n.d after* **50/1**	59
0030	**8**	*6*	**Danebank (IRE)**[35] 2750 6-11-10 **98**................................(p) PJBrennan (J Mackie) *prom to 5th* **20/1**	51
0406	**9**	*1 1/4*	**Bollitree Bob**[18] 2995 5-11-2 **90**.............................. TomScudamore (M Scudamore) *hld up: a in rr* **25/1**	42
00-0	**10**	*7*	**Explode**[27] 2873 9-10-5 **79**... TomSiddall (Miss L C Siddall) *hld up: bhd fr 4th* **100/1**	24
0-00	**11**	*2 1/2*	**Lake Imperial (IRE)**[72] 1991 5-10-5 **79**........................ AlanO'Keeffe (Mrs H Dalton) *hld up: effrt appr 5th: sn wknd* **11/1**	21
-415	**P**		**Blue Mariner**[23] 2940 6-11-10 **98**...............................(t) LeightonAspell (J Jay) *hld up: bhd whn p.u bef 4th* **12/1**	—
0600	**P**		**Ndola**[31] 2816 7-10-10 **84**.. PaulMoloney (B J Curley) *prom to 5th: bhd whn p.u bef 2 out* **33/1**	—
0020	**P**		**Amnesty**[12] 3185 7-11-9 **97**..(b) APMcCoy (G L Moore) *hld up: wknd after 4th: bhd whn p.u bef 2 out* **16/1**	—
3300	**P**		**One Wild Night**[23] 2937 6-10-13 **90**.......................... WilliamKennedy[(3)] (J L Spearing) *hld up: a in rr: bhd whn p.u bef 2 out* **50/1**	—
-045	**P**		**Pick Of The Crop**[59] 2261 5-10-13 **87**.............................. NoelFehily (J R Jenkins) *chsd ldrs to 4th: bhd whn p.u bef 2 out* **66/1**	—
-512	**P**		**North Lodge (GER)**[35] 2750 6-11-12 **100**..................... RobertThornton (A King) *chsd ldrs: mstke and wknd 3 out: p.u bef next* **7/2**[1]	—

4m 6.30s (10.60) **Going Correction** +0.625s/f (Soft) **17** Ran SP% **118.6**

Speed ratings: **100,99,94,91,91 82,78,75,74,71 70,—,—,—,— —,—** CSF £61.40 CT £708.20 TOTE £7.10: £1.80, £2.80, £2.00, £22.00; EX 64.80.

Owner Mrs Irene Clifford **Bred** The Valentines **Trained** Chastleton, Oxon

FOCUS

A race likely to produce the odd winner at a similarly moderate level.

NOTEBOOK

Make My Hay, beaten only by the in-form The Hairy Lemon on his reappearance at Warwick, has long been searching for an elusive first win. He looked set to come off second-best again for much of the straight, with Tech Eagle seemingly going just the better, but he pulled it out after the last and just shaded it. A tough individual who goes particularly well for Johnson, he will need to improve again to defy a rise, but that is not out of the question. *(op 8-1)*

Tech Eagle(IRE), who did not shape without promise in three novice hurdles, made smooth headway to stalk the winner turning in and took a narrow lead jumping two out, but he did not find as much as had looked likely and was claimed on the line. His stable has gone a long time without a winner, but it will be disappointing if this scopey type cannot find a race sooner rather than later. *(op 9-1)*

Upright Ima is still seeking her first win and, although running well in third, failed to do enough to suggest she is about to strike. A drop into selling company may be the answer. *(op 12-1)*

Monroe Gold ◆, an ex-Irish performer who showed little on his first start over hurdles in Britain at Leicester, stepped up massively on that effort and it was only in the final quarter mile that his effort petered out. There is a race in him on this evidence and he would make plenty of appeal dropped to selling company.

Smoothly Does It, behind Tech Eagle at Newbury, did not shape without promise, but was unable to bridge the gap on the runner-up. He may improve with further experience, but needs to. *(op 22-1 tchd 25-1)*

Shaamit The Vaamit(IRE) gave a bold sighter in front, but he was readily brushed aside and failed to build on his recent Wincanton second, while favourite North Lodge found the ease in the ground against him and can be given another chance back on a sound surface. *(op 9-2)*

Blue Mariner *Official explanation: jockey said gelding pulled up lame (op 10-3)*

North Lodge(GER) *Official explanation: jockey said gelding was unsuited by the good to soft ground (op 10-3)*

3372 RPSPORT - NO1 FOR SPORTS BETTING NOVICES' CHASE (19 fncs) 3m

3:30 (3:30) (Class 4) 5-Y-O+ **£3,903** (£1,146; £573; £286)

Form				RPR
3F20	**1**		**Party Games (IRE)**[49] 2485 9-11-5 105................................(p) PhilipHide (G L Moore) *trckd ldrs: wnt 2nd and nt fluent 3 out: led appr next: clr last: readily* **5/1**[2]	120+
/F-F	**2**	*9*	**Denada**[31] 2814 10-10-12 104.............................. StevenCrawford[(7)] (Mrs Susan Nock) *chsd ldrs: hit 7th and 10th: led 15th: hdd appr 2 out: sn no ch w wnr* **20/1**	110
0022	**3**	*10*	**Kyno (IRE)**[22] 2951 5-10-7 99..(t) PaulMoloney (M G Quinlan) *bhd: hit 4th and 5th: hdwy 14th: rdn sn after and wknd qckly* **5/1**[2]	88
5-43	**4**	*10*	**Woodview (IRE)**[31] 2815 7-11-5 105............................... JohnMcNamara (K C Bailey) *mid-div: hdwy 12th: sn rdn and wknd* **5/1**[2]	90
60P1	**5**	*1/2*	**Scotch Corner (IRE)**[36] 2722 8-11-5 102............................ CarlLlewellyn (N A Twiston-Davies) *bhd: pushed along and sme hdwy 13th: nvr nr ldrs* **11/1**	90
2-4P	**P**		**I'm For Waiting**[46] 2555 10-11-0 68.................................. MarkNicolls[(5)] (John Allen) *hit 2nd: t.o 8th: p.u bef 10th* **100/1**	—
1F2P	**P**		**Supreme Tadgh (IRE)**[9] 3241 9-10-12 105....................... SimonElliott[(7)] (J A Geake) *in tch: wknd 14th: t.o whn p.u bef 3 out* **10/1**[3]	—
F3-P	**P**		**Alphabetic**[27] 2874 9-11-5 100... MarcusFoley (N J Henderson) *chsd ldrs: hit 4th: wknd 13th: t.o whn p.u bef 3 out* **22/1**	—
00/1	**P**		**Martin Ossie**[248] 281 9-11-5 100.................................. MickFitzgerald (J M Bradley) *mde most tl hdd 15th: sn wknd: t.o whn p.u bef 3 out* **7/2**[1]	—
2U-0	**P**		**General Grey (IRE)**[44] 2574 6-11-5 104............................. SamThomas (Miss H C Knight) *chsd ldrs: hit 8th and 9th and sn bhd: t.o whn p.u bef 3 out* **14/1**	—
-PP3	**P**		**Lin D'Estruval (FR)**[31] 2805 7-11-5 104.....................(b) JimmyMcCarthy (C P Morlock) *chsd ldr: hit 6th: chal 12th to 15th: wknd sn after: t.o whn p.u bef 2 out* **11/1**	—

6m 28.2s (15.90) **Going Correction** +0.625s/f (Soft)

WFA 5 from 6yo+ 12lb **11** Ran SP% **114.7**

Speed ratings: **98,95,91,88,88 —,—,—,—,— —** CSF £91.43 TOTE £7.60: £1.70, £6.10, £2.20; EX 156.90.

Owner Goldfingers **Bred** G N Cannon **Trained** Woodingdean, E Sussex

FOCUS

Modest novice chase form and a race unlikely to produce many winners. It has been rated around the third, who has run to the level of his previous two starts.

NOTEBOOK

Party Games(IRE), evidently freshened up by a break, was always ideally positioned and jumped well barring a mistake at the third last. Left with only Denada to pick off as they turned into the straight, that rival got tired over the last two and he ran out an authoritative winner. He may yet be open to some further improvement and remains an interesting handicap prospect. *(op 7-1)*

Denada has obviously been a hard horse to train, this being only his seventh start, but he clearly has a good deal of ability and showed no ill-effects from a fall on his reappearance at Warwick, jumping boldly. He will remain a risky betting proposition.

Kyno(IRE) ran well for a long way on his chasing debut at Fakenham last month and was understandably fancied here, but he did not jump with the same fluency under hold-up tactics and failed to build on that effort. *(op 6-1 tchd 13-2)*

Woodview(IRE) is not the quickest, but he stepped up on his hurdling form with a one-paced fourth and is going to find life easier once contesting handicaps. *(op 6-1)*

Scotch Corner(IRE) began to stay on leaving the back straight, but his effort did not last long and he was floundering again before the second-last. A winner last time over two miles, this return to three clearly did not suit and he is going to find life easier back in handicaps. *(op 8-1)*

Martin Ossie was a truly fascinating contender, having won his last seven races in points, plus a hunter chase more recently at this course. Usually a bold jumper, this better class of rival appeared to find him out and a few mistakes down the back straight were enough to see him pulled up. He *may be worth another chance, but could not be backed with confidence.Official explanation: jockey said gelding was unsuited by the good to soft ground (op 3-1 tchd 11-4 and 4-1)*

3373 BUY YOUR ANNUAL MEMBERSHIP TODAY MAIDEN OPEN NATIONAL HUNT FLAT RACE 2m 110y

4:00 (4:00) (Class 6) 5-6-Y-O **£1,713** (£499; £249)

Form				RPR
02	**1**		**Pangbourne (FR)**[18] 3001 5-11-4 ....(be) RobertThornton (A King) *chsd ldr: led 6f out: hdd over 3f out: rallied to ld nr fin* **9/4**[2]	103+
2	**2**	*3/4*	**Theatre Dance (IRE)**[18] 2961 5-11-4 .... TomDoyle (C Tinkler) *hld up in tch: chsd ldr over 4f out: led over 3f out: rdn and hdd nr fin* **2/1**[1]	102
6	**3**	*16*	**Glen Omen (IRE)**[30] 2823 6-11-4 .... AlanO'Keeffe (Jennie Candlish) *hld up in tch: wknd over 3f out* **14/1**	86
4	**4**	*12*	**Maryscross (IRE)**[18] 2961 6-10-8 .... LeeVickers[(3)] (O Brennan) *hld up: hdwy 1/2-way: wknd over 3f out* **9/2**[3]	67
	5	*2 1/2*	**Earn A Buck** 5-10-4 .... TomMessenger[(7)] (B I Case) *hld up: hdwy 1/2-way: wknd over 4f out* **33/1**	65
0-	**6**	*25*	**Incandescence (IRE)**[300] 4465 5-11-4 .... JimmyMcCarthy (Mrs P Robeson) *hld up: hdwy 7f out: wknd 5f out* **28/1**	47
60	**7**	*12*	**Tooka**[28] 2864 5-11-4 .... TomScudamore (J Gallagher) *chsd ldrs: rdn 1/2-way: wknd 6f out* **40/1**	35
0-0	**8**	*2 1/2*	**Barons Knight**[47] 2534 5-11-4 .... JamesDavies (P R Webber) *chsd ldrs: lost pl after 5f: bhd fr 1/2-way* **33/1**	32
	9	*1 3/4*	**Bowdlane Barb** 5-10-11 .... AndrewThornton (John A Harris) *bhd fnl 10f* **80/1**	23
60	**10**	*3*	**Supreme Nova**[46] 2558 6-10-6 .... MarkNicolls[(5)] (John Allen) *hld up: hdwy 1/2-way: wknd 6f out* **50/1**	20
	11	*22*	**Miss Domino** 5-10-6 .... JamesDiment[(5)] (S J Gilmore) *hld up: bhd fr 1/2-way* **100/1**	—
0-0	**12**	*3*	**Where's Sally**[28] 2864 6-10-11 .... PJBrennan (J Mackie) *led 10f: wknd over 4f out* **14/1**	—
0	**13**	*dist*	**Master Tanner**[18] 2961 6-10-11 .... MissCDyson[(7)] (Miss C Dyson) *a in rr: bhd fr 1/2-way* **250/1**	—

3m 59.2s (2.70) **Going Correction** +0.625s/f (Soft) **13** Ran SP% **112.0**

Speed ratings: **103,102,95,89,88 76,70,69,68,67 57,55,—** CSF £6.16 TOTE £2.90: £1.60, £1.40, £3.10; EX 5.70 Place 6 £814.59, Place 5 £387.88.

Owner P E Atkinson **Bred** Haras De Reuilly And Gerard Ben Lassin **Trained** Barbury Castle, Wilts

FOCUS

Ordinary bumper form, but Pangbourne and Theatre Dance pulled 16 lengths clear of the third and look fair hurdling prospects.

NOTEBOOK

Pangbourne(FR) is clearly not straightforward, but he gave a vastly improved performance last time in the headgear and it again had the desired affect here. Having chased the clear early leader, he and the runner-up began to draw clear, but he was demoted to second starting the turn into the straight. He stuck to the task well though and, despite looking awkward under pressure, was driven to regain the lead close home. He is sure to stay further over hurdles and is a nice prospect. *(op 5-2)*

Theatre Dance(IRE), a keeping-on second in a course and distance bumper on his debut on Boxing Day, looked set to go one better when going on turning in, but the winner was too strong in the finish. He can win a race in this sphere before going hurdling. *(op 11-8)*

Glen Omen(IRE) did best of the rest and showed a fair deal of improvement on his initial effort, making steady headway before plugging on at the one pace for a remote third. He will not be winning until tackling hurdles.

Maryscross(IRE), a winning pointer who ran well behind Theatre Dance on his debut at the course on Boxing Day, again shaped promisingly to a point, but she was toiling in the straight and may find life easier in mares' only company. *(op 9-1)*

Earn A Buck, who has some Flat speed in her pedigree, is probably the other to take from the race, having ran a little better than her finishing position suggests on this racecourse debut. *(op 25-1)*
Where's Sally *Official explanation: jockey said mare ran too free (op 11-1 tchd 9-1)*
T/Jkpt: Not won. T/Plt: £832.10 to a £1 stake. Pool: £54,259.60. 47.60 winning tickets. T/Qpdt: £116.30 to a £1 stake. Pool: £3,772.50. 24.00 winning tickets. CR

2652 KELSO (L-H)

Friday, January 13

OFFICIAL GOING: Good to soft

Wind: Fresh, half against

3374 GG.COM INTRODUCTORY NOVICES' HURDLE (8 hdls) 2m 110y

1:10 (1:11) (Class 2) 4-Y-0+ **£13,012** (£3,820; £1,910; £954)

Form — RPR

1 **1** **Alfred The Great (IRE)**[69] [2045] 4-10-12 ..... BarryKeniry 101+
(P C Haslam) *chsd ldrs: lft in ld 3 out: sn rdn clr: kpt on wl fr last* **5/2**[1]

4 **2** *5* **Lysander (GER)**[31] [2803] 7-11-5 ..... SamStronge 101+
(M F Harris) *hld up: hdwy on outside bef 2 out: chsd wnr last: kpt on* **16/1**[3]

0 **3** *4* **Maneki Neko (IRE)**[25] [2921] 4-10-7 ..... NeilMulholland 84
(E W Tuer) *prom: ev ch 3 out: one pce after next* **100/1**

4 *3 ½* **Acropolis (IRE)**[110] 5-11-5 ..... WilsonRenwick 93+
(J Howard Johnson) *hld up: hdwy and prom 3 out: sn rdn: one pce fr next* **5/2**[1]

5 *19* **Temple Place (IRE)**[125] 5-11-5 ..... DominicElsworth 78+
(D McCain) *trckd ldrs: ev ch 3 out: wknd fr next* **10/1**[2]

3 **6** *1 ½* **Hush Tiger**[4] [3319] 5-11-5 ..... GarethThomas 72
(R Nixon) *cl up: ev ch 3 out: wknd fr next* **80/1**

6 **7** *1* **Stand On Me**[10] [3231] 7-11-5 ..... TimmyMurphy 71
(P Monteith) *led to 1st: sn stdd in midfield: wknd fr 4 out* **66/1**

-104 **8** *4* **Malt De Vergy (FR)**[22] [2942] 6-11-5 ..... TonyDobbin 70+
(L Lungo) *hld up: hdwy and in tch bef 3 out: rdn and wknd bef next* **5/2**[1]

0-6 **9** *3* **The Right People (IRE)**[10] [3232] 6-11-5 ..... BruceGibson 64
(L Lungo) *hld up: pushed along 4 out: n.d* **100/1**

10 *dist* **Mr Attitude**[292] 6-11-5 ..... AlanDempsey —
(W S Coltherd) *chsd ldrs to 1/2-way: sn wknd* **200/1**

11 *dist* **Le Chiffre (IRE)**[93] 4-10-7 ..... BrianHarding —
(N G Richards) *hld up: shkn up 1/2-way: nvr on terms* **25/1**

60 **12** *¾* **Alisons Treasure (IRE)**[44] [2572] 7-11-5 ..... KennyJohnson —
(R Johnson) *nt fluent: a bhd* **200/1**

0-0 **F** **Kiwijimbo (IRE)**[44] [2572] 6-11-5 ..... RichardMcGrath —
(A C Whillans) *plld hrd: led 1st tl fell heavily 3 out* **100/1**

3001 **F** **Topwell**[29] [2844] 5-11-5 ..... PadgeWhelan —
(R C Guest) *towards rr: struggling bef 3 out: btn whn fell next* **20/1**

P **Romantique (GER)**[18] 5-10-12 ..... JimCrowley —
(C Von Der Recke, Germany) *towards rr: rdn 4 out: btn next: t.o whn p.u bef 2 out* **16/1**[3]

4m 12.0s (8.30) **Going Correction** +0.40s/f (Soft)
WFA 4 from 5yo+ 11lb **15** Ran SP% **121.9**
Speed ratings: **96,93,91,90,81 80,80,78,76,— —,—,—,—,—** CSF £49.33 TOTE £3.20: £1.40, £3.20, £51.80; EX 28.50.
Owner Les Buckley **Bred** Mrs Rebecca Philipps **Trained** Middleham, N Yorks

FOCUS
A couple of interesting runners but, with two of the three market leaders failing to come up to expectations, this race did not take as much winning as seemed likely. Nevertheless, the winner is the type to improve again.

NOTEBOOK
Alfred The Great(IRE) ◆, who jumped with much more fluency than on his debut, had the run of the race and showed the right attitude. Although a couple of his market rivals disappointed, this represented an improved effort and there should be more to come. *(op 4-1)*
Lysander(GER) ◆, ridden with more patience than on his debut, shaped as though a bit better than the bare form in a race in which it paid to race prominently. He looks sure to win a small race when handicapped. *(tchd 14-1)*
Maneki Neko(IRE), a dual Flat winner last year, bettered the form of his hurdle debut. He travelled strongly for a long way and is the type to win a small race when handicapped.
Acropolis(IRE), a very smart performer over middle distances on the Flat, fourth in the 2004 Prix de l'Arc de Triomphe, was disappointing on this hurdle debut but, given a stiffer test would have *suited and the fact he finished lame, he deserves another chance.Official explanation: vet said horse returned lame left-fore (op 13-8 tchd 10-3)*
Temple Place(IRE), a 91-rated performer on the Flat, did not get home on this first run after a break and on this first run for new connections. He may continue to look vulnerable in this type of event. *(op 12-1)*
Hush Tiger, who made his debut only four days earlier in a bumper, was not totally disgraced on this hurdle debut but is another that is going to be seen to better advantage in low-grade handicap company in due course. *(op 100-1)*
Malt De Vergy(FR), who shaped better than the bare form on his hurdle debut, proved a *disappointment this time. A sound surface may suit him better but he has a bit to prove at present. (op 3-1)*
Le Chiffre(IRE) *Official explanation: trainer said gelding finished distresed (op 33-1)*

3375 E B F/TATTERSALLS IRELAND MARES' ONLY NOVICES' CHASE (QUALIFIER) (17 fncs) 2m 6f 110y

1:40 (1:40) (Class 4) 5-Y-0+ **£4,554** (£1,337; £668; £333)

Form — RPR

0000 **1** **Isellido (IRE)**[18] [2964] 7-11-8 107 ..... BrianHarding 109+
(R C Guest) *led 2nd: mde rest: r.o strly fr 3 out* **7/2**[1]

P-0P **2** *13* **Cool Dessa Blues**[68] [2066] 7-10-13 76 ..... GaryBerridge(3) 90+
(W Amos) *prom: chsd wnr 4 out: rdn and one pce fr 2 out* **50/1**

5-P2 **3** *6* **Glenogue (IRE)**[46] [2553] 8-11-2 94 ..... (b) TonyDobbin 82
(K C Bailey) *chsd ldrs: outpcd 4 out: no imp fr next* **7/2**[1]

0224 **4** *1 ½* **Uneven Line**[40] [2657] 10-10-13 76 ..... (p) MrCStorey(3) 83+
(Miss S E Forster) *hld up: hdwy and prom 11th: outpcd whn blnd 2 out: sn btn* **12/1**

P2-P **F** **Minster Fair**[260] [80] 8-10-9 ..... EwanWhillans(7) —
(A C Whillans) *hld up: fell 4th* **10/1**

P6P- **P** **Freydis (IRE)**[286] [4694] 8-11-2 98 ..... MarkBradburne —
(S Gollings) *prom: blnd 1st: mstke 10th: sn wknd: t.o whn p.u 3 out* **13/2**[3]

44 **P** **Bramble Princess (IRE)**[18] [2979] 7-11-2 ..... WilsonRenwick(3) —
(Miss Lucinda V Russell) *led to 2nd: chsd ldrs tl wknd 10th: t.o whn p.u bef 12th* **6/1**[2]

F1U2 **U** **Ornella Speed (FR)**[38] [2692] 6-11-1 90 ..... (t) PatrickMcDonald(7) —
(J R Weymes) *hld up: stdy hdwy 11th: 8l down and no imp whn blnd and uns rdr 3 out* **7/2**[1]

6m 5.00s (8.40) **Going Correction** +0.50s/f (Soft) **8** Ran SP% **113.0**
Speed ratings: **105,100,98,97,— —,—,—** CSF £108.18 TOTE £5.90: £2.40, £12.30, £1.20; EX 165.00.
Owner C J Cookson **Bred** Hugh J Holohan **Trained** Brancepeth, Co Durham

FOCUS
A race lacking strength and one in which the pace was only fair, but the winner has been rated as back to his best.

NOTEBOOK
Isellido(IRE) is not the most consistent and had not been in much form over hurdles, but she had a good chance at the weights and enjoyed the run of the race. She won an ordinary race with *plenty in hand, but her record suggests she would be no certainty to follow up next time. (op 4-1 tchd 9-2)*
Cool Dessa Blues, a modest and inconsistent maiden hurdler, looks like becoming a much better chaser and turned in her best effort yet over obstacles. She stays three miles and could win a small race over fences in due course.
Glenogue(IRE), an Irish point winner, had a decent chance at the weights but shaped as though she needs a much stiffer test of stamina. She does not look one to be taking a short price about, though. *(op 10-3 tchd 3-1)*
Uneven Line was not totally disgraced in the face of a stiff task and will be suited by the return to modest handicaps. However lack of consistency and the fact that she has yet to win a race under Rules are the concerns. *(op 14-1)*
Ornella Speed(FR) is capable of winning a race from this mark when things fall right, but it has to be a worry that she has either fallen or unseated on five of her nine starts over fences. *(tchd 4-1)*
Bramble Princess(IRE) *Official explanation: jockey said mare lost its action (tchd 4-1)*

3376 EUROPEAN BREEDERS FUND "NATIONAL HUNT" NOVICES' HURDLE (QUALIFIER) (10 hdls) 2m 2f

2:10 (2:10) (Class 4) 4-7-Y-0 **£3,253** (£955; £477; £238)

Form — RPR

1 **Money Trix (IRE)**[286] [4703] 6-11-5 ..... TonyDobbin 104+
(N G Richards) *midfield: effrt 3 out: led run in: styd on wl* **9/2**[2]

2-22 **2** *¾* **My Final Bid (IRE)**[22] [2948] 7-11-5 ..... AlanDempsey 103+
(Mrs A C Hamilton) *chsd ldrs: hit 3 out: led bef next: hit last: hdd run in: kpt on* **9/1**

04 **3** *5* **More Likely**[4] [3319] 5-10-7 ..... DougieCostello(5) 90+
(Mrs A F Tullie) *chsd ldrs: outpcd 3 out: rallying whn rdr dropped whip after last: kpt on: no ch w first two* **100/1**

602P **4** *11* **Chief Dan George (IRE)**[10] [3234] 6-11-0 94 ..... DeclanMcGann(5) 86+
(D R MacLeod) *prom: outpcd 3 out: one pce fr next* **33/1**

-534 **5** *6* **Sotovik (IRE)**[22] [2947] 5-11-5 103 ..... JimCrowley 81+
(A C Whillans) *chsd ldrs: drvn 4 out: outpcd bef 2 out* **7/1**[3]

14-6 **6** *3* **Troll (FR)**[76] [1927] 5-11-2 ..... GaryBerridge(3) 76
(L Lungo) *keen: nt fluent: hld up: hdwy bef 3 out: rdn and btn bef next* **9/1**

2-51 **7** *9* **Some Touch (IRE)**[26] [2901] 6-11-7 ..... BrianHughes(5) 79+
(J Howard Johnson) *plld hrd and sddle slipped early: chsd ldrs: led bef 4th to bef 2 out: wknd* **4/6**[1]

340 **8** *¾* **Phantom Major (FR)**[22] [2948] 5-10-12 ..... MissRDavidson(7) 66
(Mrs R L Elliot) *hld up: rdn 4 out: n.d* **100/1**

-050 **9** *20* **Norminster**[22] [2947] 5-10-12 ..... GarethThomas(7) 46
(R Nixon) *bhd: rdn 1/2-way: nvr on terms* **200/1**

0-P0 **10** *13* **Bubba Boy (IRE)**[11] [3205] 6-11-5 ..... TimmyMurphy 33
(P Monteith) *hld up: nvr on terms* **66/1**

11 *1* **Bafana Boy**[251] 6-11-5 ..... BrianHarding 32
(N G Richards) *bhd: drvn 1/2-way: nvr on terms* **66/1**

00 **12** *5* **Nigwell Forbees (IRE)**[25] [2923] 5-11-5 ..... WilsonRenwick 27
(J Howard Johnson) *hld up: rdn bef 4 out: sn btn* **100/1**

-05P **13** *21* **Crofton Arch**[222] [643] 6-10-13 85 ow1 ..... MrTDavidson(7) 7
(J E Dixon) *led to bef 4th: wknd next* **150/1**

20P **P** **Musical Chord (IRE)**[39] [2678] 7-11-0 ..... MichaelMcAlister(5) —
(B Storey) *towards rr: struggling 1/2-way: t.o whn p.u bef 2 out* **200/1**

4m 39.5s (-0.40) **Going Correction** +0.40s/f (Soft) **14** Ran SP% **121.2**
Speed ratings: **103,102,100,95,92 91,87,87,78,72 72,69,60,—** CSF £43.68 TOTE £6.00: £2.00, £2.30, £17.80; EX 20.70.
Owner Craig Bennett **Bred** John R Cox **Trained** Greystoke, Cumbria

FOCUS
An ordinary event in which the pace was fair. The second has been rated as running to the level of his bumper form.

NOTEBOOK
Money Trix(IRE) ◆, who showed ability on his bumper debut last April, showed the right attitude on this hurdle debut and first run for connections. Stepping up to two and a half miles will suit and he is sure to win more races. *(op 5-1)*
My Final Bid(IRE) finished second for the fourth outing in succession on this hurdle debut but once again did nothing wrong. He should stay two and a half miles and is sure to win a race over hurdles.
More Likely left her bumper form well behind on this hurdle debut. Her proximity appears to hold the form down, but she may well be a better performer over obstacles and again shaped as though two and a half miles would suit.
Chief Dan George(IRE) an inconsistent and exposed performer, fared better than at Ayr earlier in the month but left the impression that the return to handicaps and the return to two and a half miles would suit.
Sotovik(IRE) has not really progressed in the anticipated manner over hurdles but may benefit from switching to ordinary handicaps and returning to two and a half miles plus. *(op 13-2)*
Troll(FR) remains a fair way below below the pick of his bumper form but has time on his side and is sure to do better over further in due course when his hurdling technique improves. *(op 7-1)*
Some Touch(IRE)'s run is best ignored as his saddle slipped in the early stages. He is well worth *another chance, especially back on a sound surface. Official explanation: jockey said saddle slipped after first flight (op 10-11 tchd evens and 11-10 in places)*

3377 RICCALTON SHETLANDS H'CAP CHASE (19 fncs) 3m 1f

2:40 (2:40) (Class 4) (0-110,110) 5-Y-0+ **£4,554** (£1,337; £668; £333)

Form — RPR

-32P **1** **Interdit (FR)**[58] [2265] 10-11-12 **110** ..... WilsonRenwick 120
(Mrs B K Thomson) *led or disp ld thrght: rdn and styd on wl fr 2 out* **7/1**

3124 **2** *3* **Miss Mattie Ross**[40] [2656] 10-11-7 **110** ..... MichaelMcAlister(5) 117
(S J Marshall) *led or disp ld to 4 out: cl up: effrt bef 3 out: kpt on u.p* **9/2**[2]

5634 **3** *6* **Harrovian**[22] [2946] 9-11-12 **110** ..... AlanDempsey 117+
(Miss P Robson) *rn in snatches: prom: effrt and a length down whn blnd bdly 2 out: rallied bef last: hung rt and no ex run in* **10/3**[1]

51-5 **4** *10* **Monty's Quest (IRE)**[29] [2841] 11-11-10 **108** ..... TonyDobbin 105+
(M Smith) *chsd ldrs: disp ld 10th to 13th: cl up tl outpcd fr 3 out* **13/2**

-14P **5** *4* **Diamond Cottage (IRE)**[48] [2495] 11-10-1 **85** ..... PadgeWhelan 72
(S B Bell) *prom tl rdn and wknd bef 3 out* **20/1**

1250 **6** *1* **Red Perk (IRE)**[18] [2994] 9-10-5 **89** ..... (p) KennyJohnson 75
(R C Guest) *bhd: drvn 1/2-way: nvr on terms* **5/1**[3]

052P **7** *1 ½* **Lord Payne (IRE)**[10] [3236] 8-11-7 **105** ..... TimmyMurphy 90
(P Monteith) *hld up: rdn 12th: wknd 15th* **20/1**

U314 **8** *30* **Dead Mans Dante (IRE)**[31] [2814] 8-11-5 **108**........... ThomasDreaper(5) 63
(Ferdy Murphy) *hld up: hdwy 15th: rdn and wknd fr bef 2 out* **9/1**

342U **P** **Pessimistic Dick**[26] [2905] 13-9-9 **84** oh1..................... DougieCostello(5) —
(Mrs J C McGregor) *nt fluent in rr: struggling 1/2-way: t.o whn p.u 2 out* **10/1**

-0U3 **F** **The Tinker**[48] [2498] 11-10-12 **96**...................................... MarkBradburne —
(Mrs S C Bradburne) *sn lost pl and bhd: struggling fnl circ: no ch whn fell heavily last* **33/1**

6m 37.3s (7.70) **Going Correction** +0.50s/f (Soft) **10** Ran SP% **115.3**
Speed ratings: **107,106,104,100,99 99,98,89,—,—** CSF £37.92 CT £124.72 TOTE £9.00: £3.20, £1.80, £1.80; EX 43.30.
Owner Mrs B K Thomson **Bred** Gilles Chaignon **Trained** Lambden, Borders
■ Stewards' Enquiry : Timmy Murphy two-day ban: used whip whilst out of contention (Jan 24-25)

FOCUS
A race featuring exposed performers, but the pace seemed sound and the form should prove reliable. The winner has been rated back to his best.

NOTEBOOK
Interdit(FR), who did not stay four miles on his previous start, was allowed to dominate for much of the way and ran up to his best back at his favourite course. He should continue to give a good account. *(op 6-1)*
Miss Mattie Ross, bidding for her fifth course win, gave it her best shot and is a good guide to the worth of this form, but she has little margin for error from her current mark. *(tchd 4-1, 5-1 in places)*
Harrovian, who has been essentially disappointing since his win in this race a year ago, shaped as though better than the bare form as he ploughed through the penultimate fence. However he is not one to keep making excuses for. *(op 4-1 tchd 9-2 and 3-1)*
Monty's Quest(IRE) was far from disgraced on this second start after a break and, given he is on a fair mark at present, will be of interest in similar company back on a sound surface. *(op 5-1 tchd 7-1)*
Diamond Cottage(IRE), who is suited by a good test of stamina, was not totally disgraced on this second start after a break and should be spot on next time. *(op 25-1)*
Red Perk(IRE), returned to fences, did not travel with much fluency and failed to show enough to suggest he is of any short term interest. *(tchd 6-1)*

3378 WEATHERBYS INSURANCE MOREBATTLE H'CAP HURDLE (8 hdls) 2m 110y
3:10 (3:13) (Class 3) (0-125,125) 4-Y-0+ **£7,807** (£2,292; £1,146; £572)

Form RPR

0004 **1** **Culcabock (IRE)**[11] [3208] 6-9-10 **100**........................ DougieCostello(5) 112+
(Miss Lucinda V Russell) *in tch: led 3 out: r.o strly fr next* **14/1**

P03- **2** *10* **Crazy Horse (IRE)**[285] [4711] 13-11-7 **120**......................... BruceGibson 120
(L Lungo) *hld up and bhd: stdy hdwy on bit bef 2 out: shkn up and kpt on wl run in: no ch w wnr* **33/1**

03F3 **3** *3/4* **Nerone (GER)**[17] [3040] 5-10-5 **104**.................................... TimmyMurphy 103
(P Monteith) *hld up: hdwy on ins to chse wnr 2 out: kpt on same pce run in* **9/2**[2]

0213 **4** *1* **Rising Generation (FR)**[55] [2334] 9-11-12 **125**.................. BrianHarding 123
(N G Richards) *cl up: led after 3rd to 3 out: one pce next* **8/1**[3]

5364 **5** *shd* **Argento**[12] [3172] 9-10-11 **110**.. BarryKeniry 108
(G M Moore) *prom tl rdn and no ex bef 2 out* **33/1**

1162 **6** *3 1/2* **Chef De Cour (FR)**[8] [3256] 5-11-7 **120**................................ TonyDobbin 117+
(L Lungo) *hld up bhd: smooth hdwy and prom 3 out: sn rdn: no ex next* **11/8**[1]

3342 **7** *2* **Templet (USA)**[25] [2693] 6-9-8 **100** oh6 ow1.................(b) RichardSpate(7) 93
(W G Harrison) *hld up bhd: hdwy and prom bef 3 out: rdn and outpcd last* **33/1**

6405 **8** *2* **Crackleando**[11] [3208] 5-10-2 **108**............................... PatrickMcDonald(7) 99
(A R Dicken) *bhd: struggling 1/2-way: sme late hdwy: n.d* **100/1**

0525 **9** *2 1/2* **Uptown Lad (IRE)**[17] [3040] 7-10-3 **102**.........................(p) KennyJohnson 91+
(R Johnson) *chsd ldrs: ev ch 3 out: wknd bef next: btn whn hmpd last* **14/1**

2-4P **10** *6* **Kimbambo (FR)**[18] [2976] 8-11-4 **120**.........................(p) GaryBerridge(3) 102
(J P L Ewart) *keen: sn midfield: outpcd bef 3 out: n.d after* **20/1**

101/ **11** *8* **The Joker (IRE)**[776] [2456] 8-10-5 **111**................................. MrEMagee(7) 85
(J K Magee, Ire) *racd wd: hdwy and prom after 3rd: wknd fr 3 out* **14/1**

06F1 **12** *4* **Merryvale Man**[11] [3206] 9-10-5 **104** 7ex............................ AlanDempsey 74
(Miss Kariana Key) *led to after 3rd: lost pl after next: sn no ch* **20/1**

1-60 **13** *3 1/2* **Credit (IRE)**[36] [2716] 5-11-1 **119**....................................... BrianHughes(5) 90+
(J Howard Johnson) *prom: rdn bef 3 out: sn btn* **33/1**

0530 **14** *11* **St Pirran (IRE)**[27] [2876] 11-11-7 **120**..........................(p) DominicElsworth 76
(R C Guest) *chsd ldrs: ev ch 3 out: rdn and wknd bef next* **25/1**

12P5 **F** **Gone Too Far**[26] [2904] 8-10-11 **120**.............................. DavidDaSilva(10) 110
(P Monteith) *hld up: hdwy after 4 out: wknd after next: btn whn fell last* **28/1**

-605 **F** **Brave Vision**[10] [3234] 10-10-4 **110**................................. EwanWhillans(7) 110
(A C Whillans) *in tch: effrt and ev ch 3 out: rdn bef next: 5th and hld whn fell last* **25/1**

4m 5.70s (2.00) **Going Correction** +0.40s/f (Soft) **16** Ran SP% **124.8**
Speed ratings: **111,106,105,105,105 103,102,101,100,97 94,92,90,85,—** — CSF £401.97 CT £2422.00 TOTE £15.90: £2.70, £10.60, £1.40, £2.70; EX 897.30 TRIFECTA Not won..
Owner Mrs Elizabeth Ferguson **Bred** Lee Kwai Sang **Trained** Arlary, Perth & Kinross

FOCUS
Few progressive sorts, but a competitive race run at a decent gallop and so the form should stand up. The winner has been rated value for a 12-length success.

NOTEBOOK
Culcabock(IRE), down in the weights and in distance, has not been the most consistent in recent times but turned in a career best effort. However he may have to improve to follow up as the handicapper is unlikely to be over generous after this rout. *(tchd 16-1)*
Crazy Horse(IRE) is at the veteran stage but, despite being set a mammoth task by his rider, who was having his last ride in public, shaped as though retaining a good deal of ability. He is capable of winning a race from this mark - especially over further - but the fact that he has not won for nearly five years has to be a concern. *(op 25-1)*
Nerone(GER) had the race run to suit and ran creditably. He remains worth a try over further but has been expensive to follow so far and has yet to win a race over hurdles. *(op 11-2)*
Rising Generation(FR) was not disgraced but has little margin for error from his current mark and will always be seen to best effect when allowed to dominate. *(tchd 17-2)*
Argento, who is on a losing run, was not disgraced returned to hurdles but may need more assistance from the handicapper before he does get his head in front where it matters.
Chef De Cour(FR), who had improved steadily over hurdles, travelled strongly for much of the way but proved a disappointment when let down. He is not one to write off yet, but nor is he is one to take short odds about from this mark. *(op 7-4 tchd 2-1 in a place)*
The Joker(IRE), having his first run since late 2003, shaped as though retaining ability, having raced wide throughout. He has a good strike-rate in bumpers and over hurdles, and he should be all the better for this outing. *(op 12-1)*
Brave Vision was in the process of running his best race for some time when coming to grief. Although high enough in the weights at present, he is one to keep an eye on back on a sound surface in ordinary company. *(tchd 22-1)*

3379 GET HITCHED AT THE RACECOURSE H'CAP CHASE (12 fncs) 2m 1f
3:40 (3:42) (Class 4) (0-110,109) 5-Y-0+ **£3,708** (£1,088; £544; £271)

Form RPR

121- **1** **Moor Spirit**[380] [3074] 9-11-8 **105**... RussGarritty 111+
(P Beaumont) *cl up: led 7th: blnd and hdd 2 out: sn rcvrd: led run in: kpt on wl* **11/1**

124- **2** *5* **Reivers Moon**[273] [4848] 7-11-9 **109**.................................. GaryBerridge(3) 110+
(W Amos) *keen: hld up in tch: hdwy bef 3 out: led last: hdd and no ex run in* **8/1**

3/5 **3** *8* **Grand Slam (IRE)**[40] [2655] 11-10-1 **84**................................ BarryKeniry 75
(A C Whillans) *prom: outpcd 4 out: kpt on fr 2 out: no ch w first two* **16/1**

P564 **4** *1* **Little Flora**[18] [2980] 10-9-12 **86**................................. MichaelMcAlister(5) 76
(S J Marshall) *mde most to 7th: cl up tl wknd fr 2 out* **6/1**

1B-2 **5** *nk* **Moment Of Madness (IRE)**[10] [3233] 8-11-9 **106**............. PadgeWhelan 96
(T J Fitzgerald) *keen: hld up in tch: hdwy 4 out: wknd bef 2 out* **4/1**[2]

35P5 **6** *nk* **Apadi (USA)**[7] [3274] 10-10-5 **88**................................ DominicElsworth 78+
(R C Guest) *plld hrd: hld up in tch: hdwy whn hit 5th: lft in ld 2 out: hdd last: wknd run in* **7/1**

3250 **7** *7* **The Miner**[22] [2944] 8-10-4 **90**.....................................(v[1]) MrCStorey(3) 74+
(Miss S E Forster) *chsd ldrs tl wknd fr 8th* **9/2**[3]

-632 **F** **Sands Rising**[39] [2679] 9-11-8 **105**................................(t) KennyJohnson —
(R Johnson) *hld up: fell 2nd* **3/1**[1]

4m 35.9s (12.70) **Going Correction** +0.50s/f (Soft) **8** Ran SP% **115.3**
Speed ratings: **90,87,83,83,83 83,79,—** CSF £92.57 CT £1407.07 TOTE £9.10: £3.30, £1.60, £3.50; EX 107.10 Place 6 £960.52, Place 5 £307.18.
Owner Mrs C M Clarke **Bred** J W Walmsley **Trained** Stearsby, N Yorks

FOCUS
An ordinary event in which the pace was just fair and the winning time modest, but the winner looks the sort to score again over fences. The first two have been rated close to their pre-race marks.

NOTEBOOK
Moor Spirit ◆, off the course for nearly 400 days, did well to survive a penultimate fence blunder to record a career-best effort. This was not much of a race, but he has plenty of size and is versatile enough to have won over three miles, so he looks likely to win more races. *(op 8-1)*
Reivers Moon, back in a more suitable grade after a seven-month break, failed to settle in a race run at just an ordinary gallop but shaped as though retaining plenty of ability and should be suited by a return to two and a half miles. *(op 6-1)*
Grand Slam(IRE), only lightly raced in recent times, has not won since 2001 but shaped as though a stiffer test of stamina would have been in his favour. His record suggests he may not put it all in next time, though. *(op 14-1)*
Little Flora is undoubtedly on a fair mark but she had the run of the race and did not show enough to suggest she is one to be on in similar company next time. *(op 8-1)*
Moment Of Madness(IRE) was a shade disappointing but did not really get the race run to suit and, in any case, this may have come too quickly after his latest outing after a break. *(op 7-2)*
Apadi(USA), an inconsistent and hard-pulling chaser, fared a bit better than the bare form suggests. He is slipping back to a fair mark, but is not one to be placing maximum faith in. *(op 9-1 tchd 10-1)*

T/Plt: £503.30 to a £1 stake. Pool: £51,537.25. 74.75 winning tickets. T/Qpdt: £50.00 to a £1 stake. Pool: £4,581.60. 67.80 winning tickets. RY

[2447] CARLISLE (R-H)
Saturday, January 14

OFFICIAL GOING: Heavy (soft in places)
This meeting was transferred from Kempton as that track is closed for re-development. First fence after winning post omitted all chases.
Wind: Light, half-against

3380 TOTEPLACEPOT NOVICES' CHASE (11 fncs 1 omitted) 2m
1:10 (1:10) (Class 3) 5-Y-0+ **£6,506** (£1,910; £955; £477)

Form RPR

2U-4 **1** **Iron Man (FR)**[42] [2634] 5-10-7 .... TonyDobbin 123+
(J Howard Johnson) *mde all: 7l up whn mstke 2 out: eased towards fin* **4/7**[1]

5-00 **2** *6* **Great As Gold (IRE)**[8] [2990] 7-11-2 ....(b) WilsonRenwick 117
(B Ellison) *prom: outpcd 1/2-way: rallied 2 out: kpt on to take 2nd towards fin: no ch w wnr* **20/1**

2413 **3** *1 3/4* **Portavadie**[28] [2872] 7-11-7 .... ThomasDreaper(5) 129+
(J M Jefferson) *chsd ldrs: wnt 2nd 6th: effrt whn hit 3 out and next: lost 2nd towards fin* **5/2**[2]

2F33 **4** *23* **Loulou Nivernais (FR)**[9] [3255] 7-11-12 96......................... OllieMcPhail 105+
(Robert Gray) *chsd wnr to 6th: rdn and outpcd fr bef 4 out: btn whn j.lft last* **16/1**

5U4P **5** *12* **Italiano**[2] [3352] 7-11-2 106... RussGarritty 80
(P Beaumont) *chsd ldrs tl wknd fr 7th* **14/1**[3]

-P00 **6** *7* **Political Cruise**[5] [3317] 8-10-9 .... GarethThomas(7) 73
(R Nixon) *in tch to 4th: sn wknd* **100/1**

P6 **7** *4* **The Associate (IRE)**[11] [3236] 9-10-13 .... PeterBuchanan(3) 69
(Miss Lucinda V Russell) *bhd: lost tch fr 4th* **100/1**

4m 21.6s (4.50) **Going Correction** +0.375s/f (Yiel)
WFA 5 from 7yo+ 8lb **7** Ran SP% **111.5**
Speed ratings: **103,100,99,87,81 78,76** CSF £11.45 TOTE £1.60: £1.10, £8.60; EX 17.80.
Owner Andrea & Graham Wylie **Bred** Earl Detouillon Raphael & Frederique **Trained** Billy Row, Co Durham
■ Stewards' Enquiry : Gareth Thomas two-day ban: careless riding (Jan 25-26)

FOCUS
A straightforward sucess for the useful Iron Man, who looked value for 15 lengths, and solid novice form.

NOTEBOOK
Iron Man(FR), thrown in against crack two-mile novices Racing Demon and Hoo La Baloo on his chasing debut at Sandown, finished a respectable fourth that day and faced a vastly different test here with him appearing only to have to negotiate the fences safely to win. Given a positive ride by Dobbin, he won easily enough in the end, but will have to raise his game when again faced with better opposition and it would not be a surprise to see him take the handicap route, with the Grand Annual looking a feasible target. *(op 4-5)*
Great As Gold(IRE) plugged on again to reclaim second and recorded a fair effort in finishing ahead of Portavadie. He will find easier opportunities. *(op 16-1)*
Portavadie was a little disappointing and should really have finished second on form, but he was tired on the run-in and Great As Gold came through late on to claim him. He has not yet built on his Newcastle win, but may be capable of further improvement in handicaps. *(op 2-1)*
Loulou Nivernais(FR) faced a very stiff task trying to concede weight all round and it was not surprising that he floundered. *(tchd 14-1)*
Italiano has yet to convince over fences and will be more at home in low-grade handicaps. *(tchd 16-1)*

The Form Book, Raceform Ltd, Compton, RG20 6NL

3381 TOTEPOOL "A BETTER WAY TO BET" NOVICES' HURDLE (12 hdls) 3m 1f
1:45 (1:47) (Class 3) 5-Y-0+ **£6,506** (£1,910; £955; £477)

Form RPR
1 **1** **Hard Act To Follow (IRE)**[23] [2947] 7-11-3 .... TonyDobbin 120+
(J Howard Johnson) *in tch: hdwy to ld after 8th: rdn and kpt on wl fr 2 out* **2/7**[1]
1 **2** *5* **Numero Un De Solzen (FR)**[51] [2450] 5-10-12 .... ThomasDreaper(5) 110
(J P L Ewart) *in tch: hdwy and ev ch after 8th: kpt on same pce fr 2 out* **4/1**[2]
P005 **3** *9* **Matmata De Tendron (FR)**[144] [1294] 6-10-7 90...... MichaelMcAlister(5) 96
(A Crook) *led or disp ld to after 8th: outpcd bef 3 out: no imp fr next* **40/1**
0-P5 **4** *26* **Kempski**[11] [3232] 6-10-5 87..(p) GarethThomas(7) 70
(R Nixon) *led or disp ld to after 8th: wknd fr next* **33/1**[3]
40 **5** *2* **Witch Power**[23] [2948] 5-10-0 .... DeclanMcGann(5) 61
(A M Crow) *keen: hld up: effrt u.p after 4 out: no imp fr next* **50/1**
50P4 **6** *2* **Roadworthy (IRE)**[12] [3209] 9-10-5 64............................. WilsonRenwick 59
(W G Young) *chsd ldrs to 8th: sn wknd* **50/1**
3400 **P** **Mae Moss**[13] [3167] 5-10-5 .... AlanDempsey —
(W S Coltherd) *chsd ldrs tl wknd 8th: t.o whn p.u bef 2 out* **100/1**
0-0 **P** **Tees Mill**[237] [470] 7-10-5 .... BenOrde-Powlett(7) —
(D W Thompson) *keen and sn cl up: lost pl 5th: t.o whn p.u bef 7th* **100/1**

6m 40.4s **8** Ran SP% **109.0**
CSF £1.47 TOTE £1.30: £1.10, £1.10, £3.00; EX 1.60.
Owner Andrea & Graham Wylie **Bred** Mrs Linda Gault **Trained** Billy Row, Co Durham

FOCUS
An uncompetitive novice hurdle in which Hard Act To Follow, who as value for further, continued his progress with a straightforward success.

NOTEBOOK
Hard Act To Follow(IRE), off the mark on his debut in a Downpatrick bumper before winning on his hurdling debut on his first start for these connections over two and a half miles at Ayr, got this longer trip well and defied his penalty in pretty straightforward fashion. He is worth his place in better company. *(tchd 1-4 and 1-3)*
Numero Un De Solzen(FR), who could be considered a touch fortunate when winning here on his debut over two and a half miles, would have found this tougher under his penalty and the winner was basically too good. *(op 7-2 tchd 5-1)*
Matmata De Tendron(FR), a 90-rated maiden, was outclassed by the front two but was still able to finish third. His proximity holds the value of the form down. *(op 33-1 tchd 50-1)*
Kempski did not really improve for this longer trip and will be better off in handicaps and sellers. *(op 20-1)*

3382 TOTESPORT.COM NOVICES' H'CAP CHASE (16 fncs 2 omitted) 3m 110y
2:15 (2:16) (Class 3) (0-120,115) 5-Y-0+ **£6,506** (£1,910; £955; £477)

Form RPR
32-1 **1** **Kinburn (IRE)**[19] [2976] 7-11-12 115.................................... AlanDempsey 132+
(J Howard Johnson) *j.lft: mde all: mstke 5th: hrd pressed whn lft 3l clr last: styd on wl* **3/1**[2]
235U **2** *6* **Pass Me By**[41] [2656] 7-10-12 111.....................................(e) JohnFlavin(10) 120+
(R C Guest) *a cl up: effrt bef 3 out: 3l down and one pce whn lft 2nd last: no ex run in* **9/1**
02-2 **3** *27* **Blackergreen**[19] [2966] 7-10-10 99....................................... DavidO'Meara 80
(Mrs S J Smith) *hld up: outpcd 1/2-way: kpt on fr 2 out: no ch w first two* **7/1**
5222 **4** *nk* **Superrollercoaster**[19] [2982] 6-10-11 100......................(v) LeightonAspell 81
(O Sherwood) *cl up tl rdn and wknd after 4 out* **15/2**
-P4P **5** *13* **Good Judgement (IRE)**[42] [2623] 8-11-0 103.................. NoelFehily 71
(Jonjo O'Neill) *in tch: outpcd 5 out: hung rt and no imp fr next* **16/1**
3121 **P** **Brandy Wine (IRE)**[12] [3204] 8-11-6 109.............................(b) TonyDobbin —
(L Lungo) *prom: outpcd bef 10th: t.o whn p.u bef 2 out* **11/4**[1]
PF45 **P** **Skenfrith**[11] [3236] 7-9-12 90 oh1 ow1..................................... MrCStorey(3) —
(Miss S E Forster) *a bhd: struggling 1/2-way: t.o whn p.u bef 4 out* **12/1**
6-22 **F** **See You There (IRE)**[12] [3204] 7-11-4 110.................... PeterBuchanan(3) 124+
(Miss Lucinda V Russell) *in tch: hdwy 1/2-way: effrt after 4 out: 1l down and styng on whn fell last* **6/1**[3]

6m 42.6s **8** Ran SP% **113.8**
CSF £28.99 CT £172.80 TOTE £3.90: £1.70, £2.70, £1.80; EX 46.60 Trifecta £181.60 Part won. Pool £255.80 - 0.20 winning units..
Owner W M G Black **Bred** Mrs A Kirkwood **Trained** Billy Row, Co Durham

FOCUS
Kinburn was being challenged and possibly about to be headed by See You There when the latter came down two out, leaving him clear.

NOTEBOOK
Kinburn(IRE), who won in taking style on his chasing debut at Sedgefield, faced a stiffer task here under top weight and had a fight on his hands when left clear by the fall of See You There, who was maybe just ahead taking two out. Undoubtedly progressive, he will need to improve again to defy a rise, but that is possible, and his fluent jumping will continue to stand him in good stead. *(op 11-4)*
Pass Me By ran his race and was a long way clear of the eventual third, but he failed to see his race out quite as strongly as the winner. He should continue to pay his way. *(op 12-1)*
Blackergreen failed to build on his chasing debut second and it was rather disappointing that he failed to get closer to the principals. A dour stayer, he is probably a bit better than this, but needs to up his game. *(op 8-1)*
Superrollercoaster, who found the visor working well for him at Towcester, did not race as sweetly in it on this occasion and turned in a disappointing effort. *(op 8-1)*
Brandy Wine(IRE), who finished ahead of See You There at Ayr earlier in the month, was way below that form on this occasion and ran a lacklustre race. This was out of charatcer and he may be worth another chance. *Official explanation: trainer had no explanation for the poor form shown (op 13-2 tchd 7-1)*
See You There(IRE) was in the process of taking it up when clipping the top of the second last and coming down. He had jumped well to that point and it is hoped that this does not affect his confidence. *(op 13-2 tchd 7-1)*

3383 TOTESPORT LANZAROTE HURDLE (H'CAP) (9 hdls) 2m 1f
2:45 (2:45) (Class 2) (0-140,137) 4-Y-0+
£14,197 (£14,197; £3,237; £1,620; £808; £406)

Form RPR
01-0 **1** **Rayshan (IRE)**[262] [67] 6-10-7 125............................ MissRDavidson(7) 135+
(N G Richards) *hld up: hmpd bef 4th: effrt 3 out: swtchd lft run in: kpt on wl to deadheat post* **22/1**
14-1 **1** *dht* **Buck Whaley (IRE)**[19] [3005] 6-10-6 117.................................... NoelFehily 128+
(Jonjo O'Neill) *hld up: mstke 1st: hdwy bef 4 out: rdn next: led run in: jnd post* **5/2**[1]
P-01 **3** *nk* **Torkinking (IRE)**[19] [2981] 7-10-2 120......................(t) BenOrde-Powlett(7) 130+
(M A Barnes) *led: rdn 3 out: hdd run in: kpt on gamely* **13/2**[3]
5506 **4** *6* **Overstrand (IRE)**[27] [2904] 7-10-4 115.................................. OllieMcPhail 118
(Robert Gray) *in tch: nt fluent and outpcd 4th: rallied 3 out: kpt on same pce bef last* **33/1**
-3U5 **5** *3 1/2* **Akilak (IRE)**[19] [2971] 5-11-12 137....................................... AlanDempsey 138+
(J Howard Johnson) *chsd ldrs: hit 4 out: ev ch next: wknd after 2 out* **9/1**
313 **6** *2 1/2* **Texas Holdem (IRE)**[26] [2925] 7-10-2 118................ MichaelMcAlister(5) 115
(M Smith) *chsd ldrs: effrt bef 3 out: wknd next* **10/1**
031- **7** *16* **Mr President (GER)**[330] [3928] 7-11-0 125.......................... SamThomas 114+
(Miss Venetia Williams) *hld up: effrt after 4 out: wknd 2 out* **3/1**[2]
/UP- **8** *25* **Benbyas**[359] [3296] 9-11-5 135... JohnnyLevins(5) 91
(D Carroll) *pressed ldr to 4 out: sn wknd* **50/1**
4163 **P** **Thoutmosis (USA)**[44] [2590] 7-10-7 118.............................. TonyDobbin —
(L Lungo) *prom tl wknd bef 4 out: p.u bef next* **14/1**
2P24 **P** **Kentucky Blue (IRE)**[9] [3256] 6-10-12 123.......................(b[1]) RussGarritty —
(T D Easterby) *hld up in tch: wknd 4 out: p.u next* **33/1**
2 **P** **Amour Multiple (IRE)**[14] [3133] 7-11-3 128.................. RichardMcGrath —
(S Lycett) *prom tl wknd after 4 out: t.o whn p.u bef last* **22/1**
-2U2 **P** **Andre Chenier (IRE)**[13] [3171] 5-9-11 118..................... DavidDaSilva(10) —
(P Monteith) *hld up: hdwy to chse ldrs 1/2-way: wknd bef 3 out: t.o whn p.u bef last* **14/1**

4m 28.6s (2.90) **Going Correction** +0.375s/f (Yiel) **12** Ran SP% **115.9**
Speed ratings: **108,108,107,105,103 102,94,82,—,— —,—**WIN: Rayshan £14.30, Buck Whaley £1.70. PL: Ray £3.50, BW £1.70, Torkinking £2.10. EX: Ray/BW £44.40, BW/Ray £63.50. CSF: Ray/BW £36.98, BW/Ray £30.57. TRIC: Ray/BW/Tor £207.70, BW/Ray/Tor £162.64. TRIF: Ray/BW/Tor £132.30, BW/Ray/Tor £132.30. T27 Owner.
Owner Mr & Mrs D Davidson/B Connell **Bred** H H Aga Khan's Studs/Mileshan Nominees Pty Ltd **Trained** Greystoke, Cumbria/Cheltenham, Glos

FOCUS
The form of this year's Lanzarote Hurdle looks solid but, with just 12 runners in the line-up compared with last year when there were 21 (held at Kempton), there was obviously not as much strength in depth as has been the case in the past.

NOTEBOOK
Rayshan(IRE), well beaten at Punchestown when last seen 262 days previously but still 7lb higher than when winning at Wetherby before that, produced his best performance yet over hurdles to share the prize, and received a good ride from his amateur in the process. He is open to further improvement and is one to respect in future. *(tchd 9-4, 11-4 in places)*
Buck Whaley(IRE), raised no less than 18lb for his very easy success at Leopardstown, showed his new mark was justified by gaining a share of this valuable prize. Although he had nothing in hand, further improvement cannot be ruled out and connections also have the option of going back on the Flat. *(tchd 9-4, 11-4 in places)*
Torkinking(IRE), raised 10lb to a career-high mark following his recent Sedgefield success, ran a fine race in third in this much tougher contest. He is clearly still improving and should be kept on the right side. *(op 7-1)*
Overstrand(IRE) has been quite highly tried by his current connections since winning a claimer at Perth much earlier in the season, but he has actually been holding his form quite well and this was another decent effort.
Akilak(IRE), although carrying top weight, looked to have a very realistic chance off a mark of 137 on his handicap debut, but he was well held and has not really progressed as one might have hoped. *(op 8-1)*
Mr President(GER), not seen since winning a novice hurdle at Sandown 330 days previously, had no easy task for his handicap debut, especially considering his absence, and finished up well beaten. He can probably do a fair bit better. *(op 10-3 tchd 7-2)*
Amour Multiple(IRE) *Official explanation: jockey said gelding was unsuited by the heavy (soft in places) ground (op 20-1)*

3384 TOTEEXACTA H'CAP HURDLE (11 hdls) 2m 4f
3:15 (3:16) (Class 3) (0-130,124) 4-Y-0+ **£6,506** (£1,910; £955; £477)

Form RPR
0050 **1** **Corlande (IRE)**[56] [2347] 6-10-12 110.................................. DavidO'Meara 121+
(Mrs S J Smith) *chsd ldrs: led bef 3 out: drew clr fr next* **15/2**
-612 **2** *11* **Wild Is The Wind (FR)**[69] [2079] 5-11-12 124.......................... NoelFehily 123
(Jonjo O'Neill) *hld up: hdwy and prom 4 out: rdn bef next: kpt on to chse wnr run in: no imp* **7/2**[2]
U-00 **3** *7* **Maletton (FR)**[14] [3135] 6-11-8 120... SamThomas 112
(Miss Venetia Williams) *cl up: led 4th to 3 out: outpcd fr next* **16/1**
-121 **4** *2* **Birdwatch**[11] [3234] 8-10-4 102.......................................(b) RichardMcGrath 92
(K G Reveley) *chsd ldrs tl rdn and wknd bef 3 out* **7/2**[2]
-432 **5** *11* **Carapuce (FR)**[12] [3208] 7-11-10 122.................................... TonyDobbin 101
(L Lungo) *hld up in tch: hdwy whn nt fluent 7th: sn rdn: btn after next* **13/2**[3]
0P-0 **6** *2 1/2* **Jack Martin (IRE)**[58] [2292] 9-10-10 113...................... ThomasDreaper(5) 90
(S Gollings) *in tch: hdwy bef 6th: wknd 4 out* **14/1**
1000 **7** *22* **Mister Arjay (USA)**[9] [3256] 6-11-5 117............................ WilsonRenwick 72
(B Ellison) *hld up: struggling 7th: sn btn* **14/1**
4311 **8** *7* **General Duroc (IRE)**[39] [2691] 10-10-12 110...................(p) RussGarritty 58
(B Storey) *led to 4th: hit and reminders next: lost pl 6th: sn t.o* **3/1**[1]

5m 20.8s (3.70) **Going Correction** +0.375s/f (Yiel) **8** Ran SP% **113.8**
Speed ratings: **107,102,99,99,94 93,84,82** CSF £34.16 CT £408.21 TOTE £10.10: £2.30, £1.90, £3.10; EX 69.10.
Owner Crow Partnership **Bred** Dr Paschal Carmody **Trained** High Eldwick, W Yorks

FOCUS
A welcome return to form for Corlande, who has been dropping in the weights and was very well in on the form of his second to Thames at Haydock last February.

NOTEBOOK
Corlande(IRE) has steadily been dropping in the weights and made it two wins from two in heavy ground with a resolute galloping performance. Having only just turned six, he remains open to a fair amount of improvement and should jump a fence next season. *(op 8-1)*
Wild Is The Wind(FR) has shot up 14lb in the weights this season despite only winning once and, although keeping on late here, was no match for the winner. Testing conditions suit him well and he may be ready for three miles. *(op 10-3 tchd 4-1)*
Maletton(FR) ran his best race since arriving in Britain, showing up prominently before tiring in the final quarter mile. His stable continue to have winners and he is one to be interested in next time. *(op 14-1)*
Birdwatch has been in good form this season, winning twice, but he was a bit below his best here and may have been found out by a 7lb rise.
Carapuce(FR) is still 10lb higher than when last winning over hurdles and needs some further help from the Handicapper. *(op 7-1)*
General Duroc(IRE), in search of a hat-trick, should have found this slog in the mud right up his street, but he was never going after a mistake at the fifth and appeared to throw in the towel. *Official explanation: trainer had no explanation for the poor form shown (op 7-2 tchd 4-1 in places)*

3385 TOTESPORT 0800 221 221 H'CAP CHASE (15 fncs 1 omitted) 2m 4f
3:45 (3:46) (Class 2) (0-140,139) 5-Y-0+
£12,526 (£3,700; £1,850; £926; £462; £232)

Form				RPR
-3FB	1		**Be My Better Half (IRE)**[19] 2993 11-10-9 **122** .... NoelFehily (Jonjo O'Neill) *a cl up: led bef 4 out: edgd rt and hld on wl run in* **11/1**	135
3020	2	nk	**Better Days (IRE)**[28] 2876 10-10-10 **123** .... RichardMcGrath (Mrs S J Smith) *keen: a cl up: disp ld 5 out: kpt on wl fr last* **20/1**	136
0-04	3	7	**Claymore (IRE)**[14] 3136 10-11-6 **133** .... LeightonAspell (O Sherwood) *hld up: hdwy and prom 11th: ev ch 2 out: one pce last* **7/2**[1]	139
FP-2	4	9	**Backbeat (IRE)**[91] 1735 9-11-12 **139** .... TonyDobbin (J Howard Johnson) *hld up: hdwy and prom 9th: rdn after 4 out: one pce after next* **15/2**	136
2-12	5	1 3/4	**Edmo Yewkay (IRE)**[18] 3019 6-11-3 **130** ....(b) RussGarritty (T D Easterby) *chsd ldrs: led 8th to bef 4 out: wknd 2 out* **11/2**[3]	125
PP/	6	5	**Tyneandthyneagain**[637] 4861 11-11-10 **137** .... AlanDempsey (J Howard Johnson) *hld up in tch: outpcd 9th: n.d after* **28/1**	127
14/0	7	14	**Our Armageddon (NZ)**[35] 2760 9-11-4 **134** .... LarryMcGrath(3) (R C Guest) *chsd ldrs: led 4th to 8th: wknd bef 4 out* **5/1**[2]	110
0225	8	11	**Vandas Choice (IRE)**[49] 2499 8-11-7 **137** .... PeterBuchanan(3) (Miss Lucinda V Russell) *hld up: struggling 8th: sn btn* **8/1**	102
-51U	9	dist	**Kelrev (FR)**[18] 3019 8-11-8 **135** .... SamThomas (Miss Venetia Williams) *hld up: hdwy 9th: chsng ldrs tl wknd 4 out* **8/1**	—
/0P1	10	dist	**Lord Maizey (IRE)**[18] 3019 9-11-3 **130** .... AntonyEvans (N A Twiston-Davies) *led to 4th: cl up: reminders 7th: wknd 9th: t.o* **9/1**	—
-323	P		**Posh Stick**[19] 2993 9-9-12 **118** oh8 ow5 .... BenOrde-Powlett(7) (J B Walton) *sn wl bhd: p.u 9th* **25/1**	

5m 23.6s (3.70) **Going Correction** +0.375s/f (Yiel) **11 Ran SP% 118.7**
Speed ratings: **107,106,104,100,99 97,92,87,—,—** — CSF £196.90 CT £934.33 TOTE £14.30: £3.30, £5.30, £2.30; EX 129.60 Trifecta £279.10 Part won. Pool £393.20 - 0.30 winning units. Place 6 £58.33, Place 5 £38.05.
Owner John P McManus **Bred** Gerard Mullins **Trained** Cheltenham, Gloucs
■ Stewards' Enquiry : Antony Evans three-day ban: improper riding - failed to pull up gelding having become totally tailed off (Jan 25-27)

FOCUS
A decent handicap chase in which Be My Better Half, who ran to a 4lb higher rating than this in Ireland, gained compensation for being brought down at Wetherby on his previous start.

NOTEBOOK
Be My Better Half(IRE), who was still going quite well when brought down at Wetherby on his previous start, gained compensation under a good ride from the impressive Noel Fehily. He only just held on, but should not go up much as a result. *(tchd 12-1)*
Better Days(IRE), back over fences, stayed on strongly for pressure and was just held. He has not won since December 2003, but must have a chance of ending that losing run whilst in this form.
Claymore(IRE) had every chance and ran a solid third. He tends to give his running but is not the easiest to win with these days. *(tchd 9-2)*
Backbeat(IRE) was racing off a career-high mark following his promising reappearance 91 days previously and was well held in fourth. *(tchd 7-1, 8-1 in places)*
Edmo Yewkay(IRE) had no easy task off a career-high mark, but was a little bit below his best in any case. *(op 6-1 tchd 7-1 in places)*
Our Armageddon(NZ) gave the impression he would come on a fair bit for his reappearance at Cheltenham, but failed to build on that and was disappointing. *(op 11-2 tchd 9-2)*
T/Plt: £68.60 to a £1 stake. Pool: £60,785.55. 646.60 winning tickets. T/Qpdt: £58.60 to a £1 stake. Pool: £4,567.70. 57.60 winning tickets. RY

3146 WARWICK (L-H)
Saturday, January 14

OFFICIAL GOING: Hurdle course - soft; chase course - good to soft (soft in places), changing to soft (good to soft in places) after race 2 (1.25)
Wind: Light, behind Weather: Rain clearing

3386 TOTEJACKPOT NOVICES' H'CAP HURDLE (8 hdls) 2m
12:55 (12:55) (Class 4) (0-110,109) 4-Y-0+
£4,554 (£1,337; £668; £333)

Form				RPR
0064	1		**Kayceecee (IRE)**[19] 2983 5-11-2 **99** .... RichardJohnson (H D Daly) *a.p: led 2 out: drvn out* **13/2**	106+
100F	2	4	**Walsingham (IRE)**[8] 3274 8-10-7 **90** .... TomDoyle (R Lee) *led: hdd 2 out: styd on same pce last* **25/1**	94+
4-22	3	12	**Magnesium (USA)**[29] 2860 6-11-12 **109** ....(t) JohnMcNamara (B G Powell) *chsd ldr: ev ch 3 out: wkng whn mstke last* **9/2**[1]	103+
3/05	4	2 1/2	**Pawn Broker**[41] 2659 9-11-3 **100** ....(b) JamieMoore (Miss J R Tooth) *hld up: mstke 5th: hdwy bef next: wknd appr 2 out* **6/1**[3]	90+
2P63	5	2	**Miss Midnight**[15] 3131 5-10-10 **93** ....(b) MickFitzgerald (R J Hodges) *chsd ldrs tl wknd after 3 out* **16/1**	80
0002	6	8	**Herecomestanley**[14] 3147 7-10-0 **90** .... CharliePoste(7) (M F Harris) *in rr whn blnd and rdr lost irons 2nd: n.d after* **5/1**[2]	77+
0	7	28	**Spiritual Society (IRE)**[13] 3175 6-11-12 **109** .... TomScudamore (M Scudamore) *hld up: a in rr* **8/1**	60
0154	8	7	**Twist Bookie (IRE)**[10] 3242 6-10-11 **101** .... ShaneWalsh(7) (J S Moore) *hld up: bhd fr 4th* **10/1**	45
660P	9	11	**Nobelmann (GER)**[10] 3242 7-10-12 **95** .... PaulMoloney (A W Carroll) *hld up: hdwy after 5th: wknd next* **40/1**	28
203	P		**Knightsbridge Hill (IRE)**[26] 2921 4-11-0 **109** .... RobertThornton (A King) *prom: stmbld and wknd 5th: bhd whn p.u bef 2 out* **8/1**	—
4063	P		**Negus De Beaumont (FR)**[14] 3139 5-10-7 **90** .... HenryOliver (F Jordan) *mid-div: mstke 1st: rdn and wknd appr 4th: bhd whn p.u bef 2 out* **14/1**	—

3m 57.6s (-0.70) **Going Correction** +0.10s/f (Yiel)
WFA 4 from 5yo+ 11lb **11 Ran SP% 112.6**
Speed ratings: **105,103,97,95,94 90,76,73,67,—** — CSF £139.88 CT £798.81 TOTE £8.20: £2.70, £5.90, £1.90; EX 248.20.
Owner Michael Lowe **Bred** J F C Maxwell **Trained** Stanton Lacy, Shropshire

FOCUS
Not a strong pace, but the time was all right. The winner stepped up significantly on his previous muddling form.

NOTEBOOK
Kayceecee(IRE), making his handicap debut over hurdles, stepped up on previous form and reversed novice running with Magnesium on 11lb better terms. He handled the ground well and his future will be governed by how the Handicapper reacts.
Walsingham(IRE), reverting to hurdles after falling over fences last time, handled the ground surprisingly well for a horse who had winning form on much quicker ground. He was allowed an easy lead but shaped well all the same at a trip short of his best.
Magnesium(USA) failed to confirm Leicester running with the winner on 11lb worse terms. He remains 10lb off the level of last year's best form. *(op 4-1 tchd 5-1)*
Pawn Broker ran nicely up to a point but failed to land a blow when the race began in earnest. Most of his best Flat form was on much better ground and he is probably one to watch out for in the spring.
Miss Midnight was with the leaders until finding the ground all against her in the closing stages. All of her previous form had come on vastly different ground. *(op 12-1)*
Herecomestanley lost his chance when his jockey lost his irons after the second flight. This run can be ignored. *(op 11-2 tchd 4-1)*
Twist Bookie(IRE) *Official explanation: jockey said gelding was unsuited by the soft ground (op 11-1)*

3387 TOTEEXACTA H'CAP CHASE (FOR THE EDWARD COURAGE CUP) (12 fncs) 2m
1:25 (1:25) (Class 3) (0-135,131) 5-Y-0+ £6,506 (£1,910; £955; £477)

Form				RPR
F263	1		**Tanikos (FR)**[19] 2969 7-11-3 **122** .... MickFitzgerald (N J Henderson) *mid-div: hdwy 8th: led last: drvn out* **8/1**	138
0F06	2	1 1/2	**Kalca Mome (FR)**[18] 3019 8-11-9 **128** .... RichardJohnson (P J Hobbs) *hld up: hdwy 6th: outpcd 9th: rallied appr 2 out: nt clr run and swtchd rt bef last: r.o* **9/1**	142
U	3	8	**Madison Du Berlais (FR)**[28] 2874 5-9-11 **114** oh2 .... TomMalone(3) (M C Pipe) *chsd ldrs: led after 4 out: rdn and hdd 2 out: wknd flat* **9/2**[2]	112+
6-31	4	6	**The Local**[44] 2595 6-11-1 **120** .... AndrewTinkler (C R Egerton) *chsd ldr tl led 5th: mstke 4 out: sn hdd: rdn to ld 2 out: hdd & wknd last* **11/4**[1]	123+
F310	5	8	**Feel The Pride (IRE)**[35] 2757 8-11-12 **131** .... APMcCoy (Jonjo O'Neill) *chsd ldrs: rdn and wknd appr last* **14/1**	125+
4/34	6	25	**No Visibility (IRE)**[18] 3019 11-10-12 **117** .... AndrewThornton (R H Alner) *hld up: a in rr* **11/2**[3]	84
1415	7	9	**Romany Dream**[14] 3147 8-10-0 **105** oh1 ....(b) JamieMoore (R Dickin) *s.s: bhd: effrt appr 6th: sn wknd* **10/1**	63
4203	P		**Jericho III (FR)**[42] 2626 9-10-5 **113** ....(b) PaulO'Neill(3) (Miss Venetia Williams) *led: j.rt 1st and 3rd: mstke next: hdd 5th: wknd qckly bef 6th: bhd whn p.u bef 5 out* **6/1**	—

4m 5.60s
WFA 5 from 6yo+ 8lb **8 Ran SP% 111.4**
CSF £70.18 CT £354.82 TOTE £6.80: £2.90, £3.10, £1.60; EX 43.50.
Owner Studwell Two Partnership **Bred** G Blasco **Trained** Upper Lambourn, Berks

FOCUS
A fair handicap run at a strong gallop. The two leaders went too fast and horses coming from behind were at an obvious advantage. The first two were both well in on last year's form.

NOTEBOOK
Tanikos(FR), still 10lb higher than when last winning over fences, ran a cracking race back over hurdles at Sandown on Boxing Day and carried that form back to the larger obstacles. Given a patient ride by Fitzgerald, he was on hand to pounce when the leaders began to stop in the straight and quickly went clear after the last. He seems to have been around for a long time, but has only just turned seven and may be improving. *(op 7-1)*
Kalca Mome(FR) is back on a decent mark, but his previous efforts this season meant he could not be backed and he surprised a few in coming through to grab the runner-up spot. This was better. *(op 12-1)*
Madison Du Berlais(FR) ◆, still going nicely enough when unseating on his British debut at Haydock last month, put in an excellent round of jumping and went ahead after another fluent leap four from home. He poured on the pressure but began to tire as they turned for home and had nothing left after the last, paying for chasing the fast early pace. There were plenty of positives to be taken from this and it will be both disappointing and surprising if connections do not get their moneys worth out of him this season. *(op 4-1)*
The Local ◆ is from a stable that introduced a chasing debutant to win a handicap at Newbury in the week, and was attempting to repeat the trick, but he likes to dominate and that was not possible with Jericho III in opposition. His jumping was sound enough and he deserves another chance. *(op 3-1 tchd 7-2)*
Feel The Pride(IRE) ran well under her big weight and looked a threat turning in, but those coming from behind had the legs of her and she tied up in the final quarter mile. *(op 12-1)*
No Visibility(IRE) should have done better given he was held up right at the back, but he could never get into it and was some way below form.
Romany Dream was never going and ran a lifeless race. *(tchd 12-1)*
Jericho III(FR), part of a large shipment of horses transfered by owner Paul Beck to the Williams yard, was unable to maintain the new partnership's 100% record and simply went too fast in his urgency to lead. *Official explanation: jockey said gelding had choked (op 7-1)*

3388 TOTESCOOP6 LEAMINGTON NOVICES' HURDLE GRADE 2 (11 hdls) 2m 5f
2:00 (2:03) (Class 1) 4-Y-0+
£22,808 (£8,556; £4,284; £2,136; £1,072; £536)

Form				RPR
5-11	1		**Be Be King (IRE)**[18] 3023 7-11-10 122 .... RWalsh (P F Nicholls) *hld up in tch: led after 3 out: j.lft next: rdn and j.lft last: styd on u.p* **2/1**[1]	135+
-112	2	3 1/2	**Oscar Park (IRE)**[31] 2829 7-11-10 126 .... TomDoyle (C Tinkler) *hld up: hdwy 7th: rdn to chse wnr appr 2 out: styd on same pce last* **9/4**[2]	128
-102	3	13	**Miko De Beauchene (FR)**[18] 3023 6-11-12 117 .... AndrewThornton (R H Alner) *chsd ldrs: mstkes 7th and 8th: blnd 3 out: wknd next: j.lft last* **25/1**	121+
F1F1	4	8	**Heltornic (IRE)**[7] 3287 6-11-3 .... TomScudamore (M Scudamore) *led to 2nd: chsd ldr tl led 6th: hdd after 3 out: wknd bef next* **11/1**	103+
261	5	4	**Circassian (IRE)**[28] 2873 5-11-10 125 .... RichardJohnson (J Howard Johnson) *prom: chsd ldr and mstke 7th: hit 3 out: wknd bef next* **7/2**[3]	105+
	6	20	**Wins Now**[52] 5-11-6 .... APMcCoy (T Doumen, France) *hld up: mstke 3rd: effrt 7th: wknd after 3 out* **16/1**	87+
2/	P		**How Is The Lord (IRE)**[920] 832 10-11-6 .... PhilipHide (C J Down) *hld up: blnd 5th: wknd next: t.o whn p.u bef 8th* **150/1**	—
	P		**Stag Party (FR)**[47] 5-11-6 .... ADuchene (F Doumen, France) *hld up: effrt 7th: wknd after 3 out: bhd whn p.u bef next* **33/1**	—
1	P		**Pedros Brief (IRE)**[29] 2865 8-11-10 .... RobertThornton (R T Phillips) *led 2nd: blnd 5th: hdd next: wknd appr 7th: t.o whn p.u bef next* **16/1**	—

5m 19.0s (2.90) **Going Correction** +0.20s/f (Yiel) **9 Ran SP% 113.9**
Speed ratings: **102,100,95,92,91 83,—,—,—** — CSF £6.73 TOTE £3.00: £1.20, £1.10, £6.20; EX 8.10 Trifecta £77.40 Pool £655.70, 6.10 w/u.

Owner C G Roach **Bred** P E Atkinson **Trained** Ditcheat, Somerset

FOCUS

Just an average Grade Two event, and certainly not s atrong renewal of this particular race. The form looks solid enough, but while the front two are useful prospects, neither look likely to make it at Grade One level over hurdles.

NOTEBOOK

Be Be King(IRE), placed in graded company in bumpers, has not looked back since a poor hurdling debut at Uttoxeter and confirmed the promise of his Huntingdon and Chepstow wins by beating another useful novice in Oscar Park, despite edging left again under pressure. A strong traveller throughout, he is clearly talented and a nice prospect. Whether he can emulate the last two winners of this race and go on to figure prominently in the Royal & SunAlliance hurdle is doubtful however, as there are surely a good few better than this fellow. *(op 9-4)*

Oscar Park(IRE), winner of the Listed bumper on this card last year, lost his unbeaten record under the double penalty at Newbury last month, but the winner that day is no mug. Despite running in snatches, he gave chase to Be Be King in the straight and ensured he did not have it all his own way. A useful type, he may deserve to take his chance in the Royal & SunAlliance, but has next to no realistic chance of winning it and the handicap route may be the wiser option. *(op 5-2)*

Miko De Beauchene(FR), whose sole win thus far came off a mark of 109 in a handicap hurdle at Lingfield earlier in the season, had to give weight all round, but he covered himself in glory back in third and it was only in the straight that he really began to struggle. His rating will no doubt go up a bit now, but he will not be seen at his best until tackling fences next season anyway and he is very much one for the future. *(tchd 33-1)*

Heltornic(IRE), a cosy winner at Haydock the previous weekend, faced a vastly stiffer task here and ran pretty much as expected. She is a fair mare and will find things a lot easier back against *her own sex, with the Mares' Final at Newbury later in the season no doubt the long term aim.* *(op 12-1 tchd 10-1)*

Circassian(IRE), whose owner/trainer had been responsible for the last two winners of this with Inglis Drever and No Refuge, had not looked in the same league as those two in three previous starts and confirmed it here with a disappointing display. He may make a useful handicapper in time, but is not Cheltenham bound on this evidence. *(tchd 4-1)*

Wins Now, an interesting French raider, travelled really strongly despite jumping stickily and losing momentum at most of his hurdles. However, he stopped as though shot after the third-last and there may have been something amiss. *(op 12-1)*

Stag Party(FR), a multiple winner on the Flat in France, faced a very tough introduction to hurdles and it was no surprise to see him fail to complete. *(tchd 40-1)*

Pedros Brief(IRE), an attractive type, is every inch a chaser and, although pulling up here, can be *given another chance once tackling the larger obstacles.Official explanation: jockey said gelding bled from the nose* *(tchd 40-1)*

3389 PERTEMPS H'CAP HURDLE (SERIES QUALIFIER) (12 hdls) 3m 1f

2:30 (2:31) (Class 2) 5-Y-O+ **£13,012** (£3,820; £1,910; £954)

Form					RPR
1P11	**1**		**Nine De Sivola (FR)**[13] 3173 5-9-7 **127**.................... PatrickMcDonald(7) (Ferdy Murphy) *hld up: hdwy 9th: rdn to ld flat: r.o*	**9/2**[1]	127+
05-0	**2**	*1¾*	**His Nibs (IRE)**[19] 2999 9-10-3 **133**.................................... PaulO'Neill(3) (Miss Venetia Williams) *led: hdd after 1st: chsd ldr tl led 6th: hdd after 3 out: led again next: hdd and unable qck flat*	**14/1**	132+
6-46	**3**	*1½*	**Korelo (FR)**[36] 2747 8-11-12 **153**.................................... TimmyMurphy (M C Pipe) *hld up: racd wd: nt fluent 3 out: r.o flat: nvr nrr*	**13/2**[3]	151+
UP43	**4**	*nk*	**Dream Falcon**[19] 2999 6-9-7 **127** oh7................................ JamesWhite(7) (R J Hodges) *hld up: hdwy 3 out: rdn appr last: styd on*	**40/1**	123
-U01	**5**	*2½*	**Valley Ride (IRE)**[31] 2820 6-10-11 **138**................................ TomDoyle (C Tinkler) *hld up: hdwy 3 out: styd on same pce fr next*	**5/1**[2]	133+
-436	**6**	*5*	**Hasty Prince**[49] 2500 8-11-3 **144**.. APMcCoy (Jonjo O'Neill) *hld up: hdwy 3 out: rdn appr last: wknd flat*	**12/1**	133+
40-P	**7**	*2½*	**Chives (IRE)**[77] 1926 11-10-0 **127** oh6.......................... DominicElsworth (Mrs S J Smith) *chsd ldrs: mstke 4th: wknd 3 out*	**10/1**	113
5P0-	**8**	*shd*	**Be My Royal (IRE)**[315] 4189 12-10-0 **127** oh4................. RobertWalford (R H Alner) *chsd ldrs tl wknd appr 2 out*	**50/1**	113
	9	*hd*	**Naos De Mirande (FR)**[41] 5-10-0 **127** oh3......................... MarcusFoley (T Doumen, France) *hld up: hdwy 8th: led on bit after 3 out: hdd next: wknd last*	**11/1**	115+
P056	**10**	*15*	**Carlys Quest**[18] 3020 12-10-10 **137**.................................(b) BrianHarding (Ferdy Murphy) *hld up: rdn after 7th: sn lost tch*	**16/1**	108
13/P	**11**	*nk*	**Special Rate (IRE)**[18] 3017 9-10-1 **128**........................... RobertThornton (A King) *chsd ldrs: mstke 2nd: wknd 3 out*	**20/1**	99
0F-P	**12**	*1½*	**Hirvine (FR)**[36] 2747 8-10-13 **140**... PJBrennan (P Bowen) *chsd ldrs: rdn and mstke 8th: wknd after 3 out*	**25/1**	110+
512	**13**	*3½*	**Mikado**[67] 2099 5-9-11 **127** oh2... TJPhelan(3) (Jonjo O'Neill) *prom: wknd after 9th*	**9/1**	93
1P12	**14**	*3*	**Irishkawa Bellevue (FR)**[52] 2430 8-9-11 **127** oh4.(b) WilliamKennedy(3) (Jean-Rene Auvray) *led after 1st: hdd 5th: mstke 9th: sn wknd*	**33/1**	90
P61/	**P**		**Creon**[669] 4386 11-9-9 **129** oh7 ow2................................. ShaneWalsh(7) (Jonjo O'Neill) *prom: mstke 3rd: lost pl next: bhd fr 7th: t.o whn p.u bef 2 out*	**28/1**	—

6m 30.5s (0.20) **Going Correction** +0.20s/f (Yiel) **15** Ran SP% **115.2**
Speed ratings: **107,106,105,105,105 103,102,102,102,97 97,97,96,95,**— CSF £56.72 CT £408.13 TOTE £5.10: £2.30, £3.40, £2.60; EX 73.00 Trifecta £478.90 Part won. Pool £674.60 - 0.20 winning units..

Owner The DPRP Sivola Partnership **Bred** G Trapenard **Trained** West Witton, N Yorks

FOCUS

A highly competitive qualifier taken in great style by the improving Nine De Sivola. The form looks solid enough with a back-to-form His Nibs in second and top-weight Korelo coming through late to claim third.

NOTEBOOK

Nine De Sivola(FR) ◆, in search of a four-timer having won twice at Wetherby and Catterick, just gets better and better, and his young rider deserves much credit for what appeared to be a perfectly judged ride, sweeping past the gallant His Nibs after the last. Evidently a highly progressive young hurdler, he will go up again for this win, but looks sure to rank highly in the final of the series at the Festival. *(op 5-1 tchd 4-1)*

His Nibs(IRE), a tough, consistent individual who often pays his way, showed enough in a limited campaign last season to suggest he still had plenty of ability and the support in the market throughout the day was obviously a plus. Soon disputing the lead, he kept tabs on the strong travelling Naos De Mirande as they swung into the straight and battled his way to the front before being swallowed up late on by the winner. This was a good effort and he may be capable of improving on his fourth in the 2004 final of the series. *(op 20-1)*

Korelo(FR) is hard to win with, as he is not quite up to graded level and is forced to carry big weights in handicaps, but he continues to run well and give his all nonetheless. This was a fine effort, but he will remain hard to place. *(op 6-1)*

Dream Falcon ◆ ran an absolute blinder from 7lb out of the handicap and just lost out on a place back in fourth. He has been quietly progressive despite failing to win and should continue to head the right way.

Valley Ride(IRE) got his season back on track at Bangor last month, but he was found out here off a 6lb higher mark, being unable to get going in time. He has a progressive profile and will be better suited by a more galloping track. *(tchd 11-2)*

Hasty Prince ◆ is slipping back down to a decent mark and ran well over a trip that stretches him. He would make some appeal back down in trip. *(tchd 11-1)*

Chives(IRE), a formerly very smart chaser, got tired in the final quarter mile, but made a pleasing return nonetheless and will no doubt come on for the outing. *(op 12-1)*

Be My Royal(IRE), another former decent chaser, had been off the track since March but travelled well until getting understandably tired.

Naos De Mirande(FR) ◆, an interesting French raider, made smooth headway from the rear before tanking into the lead three from the finish, but he tired badly on the run-in and may have made his move too soon. He is clearly a useful prospect and ran a lot better than his finishing position suggests. *(op 10-1)*

3390 TOTESPORT CLASSIC CHASE (A H'CAP) GRADE 3 (22 fncs) 3m 5f

3:00 (3:02) (Class 1) 6-Y-O+

£42,765 (£16,042; £8,032; £4,005; £2,010; £1,005)

Form					RPR
P-41	**1**		**Eurotrek (IRE)**[31] 2828 10-10-9 **135**.. RWalsh (P F Nicholls) *hld up: hdwy 11th: led appr 2 out: rdn clr*	**6/1**[2]	154+
-PPF	**2**	*15*	**Sir Rembrandt (IRE)**[18] 3022 10-11-7 **147**.................. AndrewThornton (R H Alner) *hld up: hdwy 16th: styd on same pce fr 3 out*	**10/1**	152+
-30U	**3**	*1½*	**Control Man (IRE)**[18] 3022 8-10-0 **133**.............(v) AndrewGlassonbury(7) (M C Pipe) *led 2nd to 4th: led appr 6th: rdn and hdd bef 2 out: wknd last*	**10/1**	137+
-434	**4**	*8*	**Crystal D'Ainay (FR)**[18] 3022 7-11-0 **140**....................(v) RobertThornton (A King) *led to 2nd: chsd ldrs: rdn and wknd after 3 out*	**6/1**[2]	135+
13-F	**5**	*dist*	**Glen Warrior**[9] 3258 10-10-0 **126** oh2.................................. PaulMoloney (J S Smith) *hld up: effrt 13th: wknd after 15th*	**33/1**	91
P-42	**6**	*3½*	**Artic Jack (FR)**[28] 2875 10-10-0 **126** oh3...................... DominicElsworth (Mrs S J Smith) *prom: wknd after 15th: in rr whn mstke 17th*	**8/1**	89
64F1	**7**	*dist*	**Double Honour (FR)**[28] 2875 8-11-0 **140**..................(b) RichardJohnson (P J Hobbs) *prom to 14th*	**10/1**	—
2F-1	**B**		**Joaaci (IRE)**[13] 3176 6-11-12 **152**....................................... TimmyMurphy (M C Pipe) *hld up: b.d 7th*	**3/1**[1]	—
1411	**F**		**Dead-Eyed Dick (IRE)**[43] 2608 10-10-0 **126**.......................... PJBrennan (Nick Williams) *hld up: fell 7th*	**7/1**[3]	—
U0/P	**P**		**Shardam (IRE)**[18] 3022 9-10-7 **133**....................................... CarlLlewellyn (N A Twiston-Davies) *prom to 15th: t.o whn p.u bef 2 out*	**33/1**	—
3516	**P**		**Victory Gunner (IRE)**[7] 3290 8-9-9 **126** oh3.................. LeeStephens(5) (C Roberts) *chsd ldrs: hit 4th: sn lost pl: t.o whn p.u bef 4 out*	**33/1**	—
-P45	**P**		**Kittenkat**[30] 2847 12-10-0 **126** oh27................................. TomScudamore (N R Mitchell) *chsd ldrs: lost pl 3rd: bhd whn hmpd 7th: t.o whn p.u bef 5 out*	**100/1**	—
3-P6	**P**		**Granit D'Estruval (FR)**[18] 3022 12-10-0 **126** oh5.............. BrianHarding (Ferdy Murphy) *chsd ldrs: j.rt: led 4th to appr 6th: lost pl 9th: bhd whn p.u bef 13th*	**16/1**	—

7m 55.3s (6.40) **Going Correction** +0.50s/f (Soft) **13** Ran SP% **120.2**
Speed ratings: **111,106,106,104,**— —,—,—,—,— —,—,— CSF £63.18 CT £599.51 TOTE £6.30: £2.20, £2.40, £3.00; EX 66.20 Trifecta £690.20 Pool £38,889.63, 40.00 w/u.

Owner Paul Green **Bred** Mrs D Molony **Trained** Ditcheat, Somerset

FOCUS

A top staying handicap, and solid form, with the 'right' horses dominating, although the early departure of favourite and potential Gold Cup contender Joaaci was a shame. The winner has been raised a stone, and while Sir Rembrandt was still 10lb off his Gold Cup mark he is coming right again now.

NOTEBOOK

Eurotrek(IRE) ◆, a useful but lightly-raced horse over the years, had been put up 13lb for his Newbury romp, but was rightly one of the market leaders with such a test looking right up his alley. Restrained in rear by Walsh, he jumped fluently and had crept into a challenging position to stalk Control Man before finally being allowed to go on before the second-last. He really impressed was the way he put distance between himself and the others and, although another hefty rise will follow, this progressive 10-year-old is likely to be a leading contender for all the big staying handicap chases, ground permitting (likes it soft). On the negative side though, he has had plenty of physical problems over the years and is hardly one to back ante-post for something like the National, especially as it is unlikely he would be risked on anything without 'soft' in the going description. *(op 5-1)*

Sir Rembrandt(IRE) ◆, a high-class stayer on his day and placed in the last two runnings of the Gold Cup, is having a typical season by his standards and beginning to run into form at the right time. Pulled up on his first two outings of the campaign, he was in the process of running a huge race under 11st10lb in the Welsh National when coming down four out, but showed no ill-effects of that fall here and put up a fine weight-carrying performance to come through for second. A resolute galloper who gets on well with Thornton, he has dropped 21lb in the ratings in the last 14 months and is undoubtedly weighted to win a big handicap, but his record in the big race at the Festival cannot be ignored and 40/1 currently available looks almost too good to be true, with Kicking King out for the season and big question marks hanging over current favourites Beef Or Salmon (never been seen to best effect at Cheltenham), stablemate Kingscliff (ran lifeless race in King George) and Monkerhostin (judged on second to below-par Kicking King at Sandown). He looks certain to run his race on the day. *(op 11-1)*

Control Man(IRE), unfortunate to unseat his rider on the flat in the Welsh National, is not the most consistent but he is a very useful stayer when conditions are right and the positive tactics employed by the impressive Glassonbury suited the gelding down to the ground. He kept finding, but it was clear once the winner went on he was playing for second-place only and there was no shame in being passed on the run-in by dual Gold Cup-placed Sir Rembrandt. There is a big staying handicap in him off this sort of mark. *(op 8-1)*

Crystal D'Ainay(FR), a high-class staying hurdler back in 2003, has not quite proved as good over fences as some expected, but he has done rather well this season considering the chases he won on France as a youngster ruled him out of novice events and he has been forced to run in he some tough races. Winner of last season's Rendelsham Hurdle in the visor, this was the first time he had the headgear reapplied and he raced sweetly for a long way before simply failing through lack of stamina. A little help from the Handicapper could see him land a nice prize back at three miles, and it is worth remembering he has only just turned seven, so it would be folly to rule out a little improvement. *(op 8-1)*

Glen Warrior, who took a nasty fall at Wetherby only nine days previously, was a long way adrift of the leading quartet, but that was to be expected and he ran as well as he was entitled to. There will be easier opportunities.

Artic Jack(FR), although showing more signs of life when just denied at Haydock last time, is a shadow of the horse that beat Kingscliff two years ago and he again fell away without putting up much of a fight. *(op 9-1)*

Double Honour(FR), who again showed great tenacity to deny Artic Jack at Haydock last month, stopped very quickly here and there was presumably something amiss. Although better than this, his current rating will continue to make life hard for him in the big handicaps.

Dead-Eyed Dick(IRE), a highly progressive handicapper who looked sure to go well here, fell too early to determine how he would have fared, but his bottomless stamina would have been a massive asset. *(tchd 15-2)*

Shardam(IRE), a useful staying handicap chaser a couple of seasons back, was set a masive task on his reappearance in the Welsh National and showed a lot more on this occasion. He is not one to give up on yet, despite ultimately being pulled up. *(tchd 15-2)*

Victory Gunner(IRE) *Official explanation: trainer said gelding had gurgled during the race* *(tchd 15-2)*

Joaaci(IRE) quickly made up into a useful novice last spring, and a taking reappearance win at Cheltenham led to quotes of 20/1 for the Gold Cup. Raised 9lb for that victory, he faced no simple task here under top weight of 11st12lb, but was made favourite nonetheless and was strongly fancied to enhance his Gold Cup claims. Sadly however he got no further than the seventh with the fall of Dead-Eyed Dick bringing him down, but it would have taken a performance of Gold Cup proportions to beat the winner and we will have to wait for another day to see what he can do. It would not surprise to see him take his chance in either of the Pillar or the AON Chase, with the latter looking the likelier option as connections already have Celestial Gold pencilled in for the former. *(tchd 15-2)*

3391 TOTEPOOL "A BETTER WAY TO BET" NOVICES' CHASE (18 fncs) 3m 110y
3:30 (3:31) (Class 2) 5-Y-O+ **£12,793** (£3,861; £1,989; £1,053)

Form — RPR

1-F4 **1** **Halcon Genelardais (FR)**[31] [2820] 6-11-5 .... RobertThornton 147+
(A King) *hld up in tch: chsd ldr after 11th: mstke 5 out: rdn to chal whn lft clr 4 out: drvn out* **5/1**[3]

4P **2** *26* **No Full (FR)**[29] [2869] 5-11-1 120 .... MickFitzgerald 118+
(P R Webber) *prom tl wknd appr 12th: lft poor 2nd 4 out* **50/1**

2F21 **3** *13* **Rebel Rhythm**[18] [3041] 7-11-10 .... DominicElsworth 113
(Mrs S J Smith) *chsd ldr tl wknd after 11th: lft poor 3rd 4 out* **11/4**[2]

-315 **4** *9* **Leading Man (IRE)**[13] [3178] 6-11-13 132 .... BrianHarding 107
(Ferdy Murphy) *hld up in tch: wknd appr 12th* **14/1**

1112 **F** **Iris's Gift**[50] [2484] 9-11-13 147 .... APMcCoy —
(Jonjo O'Neill) *led: mstke 12th: jnd whn fell 4 out* **4/5**[1]

6m 33.2s (10.90) **Going Correction** +0.50s/f (Soft)
WFA 5 from 6yo+ 12lb **5** Ran SP% **107.5**
Speed ratings: **102,93,89,86,**— CSF £75.45 TOTE £6.30: £2.80, £6.10; EX 113.40.
Owner Ian Payne & Kim Franklin **Bred** G Descours & Mlle Constance Descours **Trained** Barbury Castle, Wilts

FOCUS
An unsatisfactory outcome, with Iris's Gift hitting the deck four from home when looking as though he could have a battle on his hands. The form can not be assessed with any confidence, but the winner looks a smart recruit.

NOTEBOOK
Halcon Genelardais(FR) ◆, a useful hurdler who was always likely make a better chaser, had been jumping well and was going nicely alongside Iris's Gift when left clear. It is impossible to say how he would have fared had the favourite stayed on his feet, but he looked a big danger, admittedly in receipt of 8lb, and deserves plenty of credit for this winning debut over fences. Connections reportedly see him as a Royal & SunAlliance type, but he would only go there if the ground was suitable. *(tchd 11-2)*
No Full(FR) has shown little since arriving from France and cheekpieces failed to help last time. With neither the third or fourth running to form it is debatble what he achieved and he may still be in need of more time. *(op 40-1)*
Rebel Rhythm looked the one most likely to serve it up to the favourite, having boasted very useful form in several previous efforts, notably a close second to the smart Turpin Green at Carlisle. However, he ran a lifeless race, finding nothing for pressure, and was struggling a long way from home. This was hugely disappointing and he may need freshening up.
Leading Man(IRE), outclassed in graded company at Cheltenham at the start of the month, had to concede weight to all bar the favourite, but could still have been expected to fare a little better. He may continue to struggle under his penalty. *(op 10-1)*
Iris's Gift, whose comprehensive defeat by Darkness at Newbury had been made to look better by the subsequent efforts of the winner, hardly came into this off the back of an ideal prep, having fallen in a schooling session at Haydock the previous weekend. Despite connections trying to put a positive spin on things in saying the spill may have bucked his ideas up, his jumping flaws were once again evident and he had been joined by the winner when coming down at the fourth from home. The Gold Cup reportedly remains the target, but with Inglis Drever out for the season now connections may find it hard to resist the temptation to supplement him in a bid for another win in the World Hurdle. If he stays over fences it may be worth trying headgear in an attempt to get him concentrating at his fences. *(op 5-6)*

3392 TOTESPORTCASINO.COM STANDARD OPEN NATIONAL HUNT FLAT RACE (LISTED RACE) 2m
4:00 (4:01) (Class 1) 4-6-Y-O **£8,926** (£3,342; £1,669; £834)

Form — RPR

/1-1 **1** **Roll Along (IRE)**[85] [1820] 6-11-12 .... TimmyMurphy 123+
(M Pitman) *hld up: hdwy over 3f out: swtchd lft over 1f out: rdn to ld ins fnl f: styd on* **15/8**[1]

1 **2** *1 1/4* **Spartacus Bay (IRE)**[83] [1849] 5-11-4 .... LiamTreadwell(5) 117
(Miss Venetia Williams) *trckd ldrs: led over 3f out: rdn over 1f out: hdd and unable qck ins fnl f* **13/2**

1- **3** *2 1/2* **Round The Horn (IRE)**[352] [3558] 6-11-9 .... PJBrennan 116+
(J A B Old) *hld up: hdwy 5f out: rdn and hung lft over 1f out: styd on same pce* **11/2**[3]

2 **4** *9* **Marshalls Run (IRE)**[56] [2340] 6-11-5 .... RobertThornton 102
(A King) *hld up: hdwy over 6f out: rdn and wknd over 1f out* **11/4**[2]

0-1 **5** *2* **Not For Diamonds (IRE)**[90] [1762] 6-11-9 .... APMcCoy 104
(Mrs H Dalton) *led 3f: chsd ldr: rdn and ev ch 3f out: wknd over 1f out* **12/1**

6 *3 1/2* **Sexy Rexy (IRE)** 5-11-5 .... CarlLlewellyn 97+
(N A Twiston-Davies) *chsd ldrs: led over 6f out: hdd over 3f out: hung lft and wknd over 2f out* **12/1**

7 *30* **Glorious Castlebar** 5-11-5 .... SeanFox 66
(J C Fox) *hld up: wknd 4f out* **100/1**

8 *6* **Westgate (IRE)** 4-10-7 .... TomScudamore 48
(S Gollings) *chsd ldr: led after 3f: hung lft 1/2-way: hdd over 6f out: sn lost pl* **50/1**

4m 9.60s (10.80) **Going Correction** +0.475s/f (Soft)
WFA 4 from 5yo 11lb 5 from 6yo 8lb **8** Ran SP% **108.5**
Speed ratings: **92,91,90,85,84 82,67,64** CSF £13.07 TOTE £2.00: £1.10, £2.30, £1.80; EX 13.90 Place 6 £855.72, Place 5 £297.20.
Owner Bryan & Philippa Burrough **Bred** Mrs M Brennan **Trained** Upper Lambourn, Berks

FOCUS
A useful bumper in which three drew clear, but the lack of pace counted against the third and fourth and would have suited the speedy winner better than any.

NOTEBOOK
Roll Along(IRE), impressive in each of his first two victories at lesser tracks, was facing his first real test here and put up a smart performance under his big weight. Ridden for a change of pace by Murphy, he took his time to get on top, but was going away at the end and ultimately won readily. He is clearly a useful sort, but as his stable has Hennessy for the Festival bumper he may instead head to Aintree, where his speed will be an obvious asset. *(op 6-4 tchd 11-8)*
Spartacus Bay(IRE), a tidy winner on his debut at Aintree, stepped up on that initial effort in defeat and ensured the favourite had no easy time of it. Sent into the lead three out, he stayed on right the way to the line despite being unable to match the winner's acceleration and is going to stay further over hurdles. *(op 8-1)*
Round The Horn(IRE) ◆ had been off since winning impressively in a course bumper almost a year ago, but his stable are more than capable of readying one to win first time up and he would have given the winner much more to think about had there been a stronger gallop. He will improve greatly for two and a half miles over hurdles and remains a useful prospect. *(op 6-1)*
Marshalls Run(IRE) found himself readily outpaced by the leading trio as the kick for home began and he too would have preferred a sounder gallop. He will require further than two miles over hurdles. *(tchd 7-2)*
Not For Diamonds(IRE) was unable to step up on his Market Rasen win and was readily brushed aside by the principals. *(op 9-1 tchd 8-1)*
Sexy Rexy(IRE) faced a stiff introduction and struggled badly once the pace quickened. He showed distinct signs of inexperience, but that was only to be expected and it is safe to assume he will be capable of better in due course. *(op 14-1)*
T/Jkpt: Not won. T/Plt: £407.60 to a £1 stake. Pool: £102,074.05. 182.80 winning tickets. T/Qpdt: £76.90 to a £1 stake. Pool: £7,234.60. 69.60 winning tickets. CR

3253 WETHERBY (L-H)
Saturday, January 14

OFFICIAL GOING: Heavy
The meeting had to survive two morning inspections. The ground was described as 'deep and tacky, horrendous'.
Wind: Almost nil Weather: Fine

3393 EUROPEAN BREEDERS FUND "NATIONAL HUNT" NOVICES' HURDLE (QUALIFIER) (10 hdls) 2m 4f 110y
12:35 (12:35) (Class 3) 4-7-Y-O **£5,855** (£1,719; £859; £429)

Form — RPR

3 **1** **Keenan's Future (IRE)**[41] [2665] 5-11-6 .... WayneHutchinson 114+
(Ian Williams) *hld up in rr: hdwy to chse ldrs 5th: led 2 out: drew clr after last: eased nr fin* **5/1**

-002 **2** *14* **Seymar Lad (IRE)**[19] [2967] 6-11-6 92 .... MarkBradburne 100
(P Beaumont) *trckd ldrs: led 7th: rdn next: hdd 2 out: kpt on same pce* **7/2**[1]

15-0 **3** *3/4* **Corals Laurel (IRE)**[31] [2821] 7-11-6 .... JimCrowley 99
(R T Phillips) *hld up in rr: hdwy to trck ldrs 5th: upsides 3 out: kpt on same pce appr last* **4/1**[2]

4-54 **4** *11* **Caulkleys Bank**[13] [3168] 6-11-3 .... MrTGreenall(3) 94+
(M W Easterby) *j.lft: led to 7th: wknd last* **10/1**

40 **5** *12* **What'sonyourmind (IRE)**[18] [3023] 6-11-6 .... JoeTizzard 76
(Jonjo O'Neill) *nt jump wl: prom: mstke and lost pl 6th: kpt on fr 3 out: n.d* **6/1**

6 *3* **Buy Onling (IRE)**[58] [2308] 5-11-6 .... DaveCrosse 73
(C J Mann) *trckd ldrs: lost pl appr 3 out* **16/1**

4435 **7** *4* **Delightful Cliche**[45] [2571] 5-11-1 105 .... StephenCraine(5) 69
(Mrs P Sly) *chsd ldrs: wknd appr 3 out* **9/2**[3]

-P06 **8** *25* **Mad Max Too**[9] [3253] 7-11-6 93 ....(p) BarryKeniry 44
(N Wilson) *hld up in rr: wnt prom 5th: hit next: lost pl after 6th: t.o 2 out* **50/1**

9 *8* **Jago's Girl** 5-10-6 .... TomMessenger(7) 29
(B N Pollock) *chsd ldrs: lost pl after 6th: sn bhd: t.o 2 out* **150/1**

000 **P** **Rosina Copper**[13] [3168] 6-10-13 .... AnthonyRoss —
(P Beaumont) *in rr: wkng whn blnd 7th: sn bhd: t.o whn p.u bef next* **150/1**

5m 42.4s (33.50) **Going Correction** +1.35s/f (Heav) **10** Ran SP% **109.6**
Speed ratings: **90,84,84,80,75 74,72,63,60,**— CSF £21.41 TOTE £5.10: £1.50, £2.00, £2.00; EX 19.50.
Owner Dsm Demolition Limited **Bred** Charles Micheal Gildea **Trained** Portway, Worcs

FOCUS
A modest event run at just a steady pace in the ground. In the end the winner came right away and clearly stamina is his forte. Overall the form looks reliable, with the winner rated to his bumper form.

NOTEBOOK
Keenan's Future(IRE), who looks every inch a potential chaser, already has an Irish point to his name. In the end he came right away, and he looks a real stayer. *(op 4-1)*
Seymar Lad(IRE), well supported, went on four out but in the end proved no match. *(op 6-1 tchd 13-2 in a place)*
Corals Laurel(IRE), who has a real soft-ground action, travelled strongly and looked a real threat *when landing upsides three out, but in the end he could not even get the better of the runner-up.* *(op 7-2)*
Caulkleys Bank continually gave away ground jumping to his left and in the end this trip in these conditions seemed to stretch his stamina. *(op 9-1)*
What'sonyourmind(IRE), who took his bumper at Navan in similar ground, fell through the majority *of his hurdles and his jumping will need to improve a good deal if he is to come up to scratch.* *(op 5-1)*
Delightful Cliche ran below par for a second time and he has yet to prove he can handle ground as testing as this. *(op 5-1)*

3394 WETHERBY "SMALL RACECOURSE OF THE YEAR 2005" NOVICES' CHASE (15 fncs) 2m 4f 110y
1:05 (1:07) (Class 3) 5-Y-O+ **£7,807** (£2,292; £1,146)

Form — RPR

-251 **1** **Nadover (FR)**[31] [2817] 5-10-13 124 .... DaveCrosse 120+
(C J Mann) *disp ld: def advantage 7th: styd on strly fr 3 out: eased towards fin* **1/2**[1]

-F54 **2** *7* **Rowley Hill**[14] [3148] 8-11-3 .... WayneHutchinson 112+
(A King) *disp ld: mstke 4th: outj. 4 out: untidy next: sn btn* **15/8**[2]

3 *dist* **Delaware Trail**[286] 7-11-3 .... KennyJohnson —
(R Johnson) *t.k.h in detached 3rd: blnd 8th: sn lost tch: t.o whn mstke 10th: completed in own time: btn 48 l* **33/1**[3]

5m 52.8s (32.10) **Going Correction** +1.575s/f (Heav)
WFA 5 from 7yo+ 9lb **3** Ran SP% **104.4**
Speed ratings: **101,98,**— CSF £1.74 TOTE £1.60; EX 1.80.
Owner Tony Hayward And Barry Fulton **Bred** And Mrs J L Couetil **Trained** Upper Lambourn, Berks

FOCUS
A pathetic turnout for a novices' chase carrying £12,000 added money and suspect form. In the end the winner had only to jump round safely to collect.

NOTEBOOK
Nadover(FR) has shown he can handle this type of ground and, jumping much the better, in the end found this easy. *(op 4-9 tchd 2-5)*
Rowley Hill, rated 133 over hurdles, is finding it difficult to adapt to fences. Completely outjumped at the big ditch four out, he was getting much the worst of the argument when losing ground at the next. *(op 9-4 tchd 5-2)*
Delaware Trail, who failed to get round in two points last year, was soon detached and, after a bad blunder at the eighth, the priority was to make sure he completed and earn a handy £1,146. Unplaced in nine starts on the Flat, this was his big payday. *(op 16-1)*

The Form Book, Raceform Ltd, Compton, RG20 6NL

3395 RACING POST "HANDS AND HEELS" JUMPS SERIES H'CAP HURDLE (FOR CONDITIONAL JOCKEYS/AMATEUR RIDERS)(9 hdls) 2m

1:35 (1:35) (Class 4) (0-105,98) 4-Y-0+ **£3,253** (£955; £477; £238)

Form RPR
6-41 **1** **Polar Gunner**[52] 2443 9-10-9 **86** MrOWilliams(5) 102+
(J M Jefferson) *t.k.h: trckd ldr: led 5th: pushed clr between last 2: hit last: r.o wl* **13/8**[1]

U050 **2** *14* **Gospel Song**[23] 2944 14-11-0 **86** EwanWhillans 87
(A C Whillans) *led: hdd 5th: sn drvn along: kpt on to regain 2nd after last: no ch w wnr* **10/1**

F-P1 **3** *1* **Balmoral Queen**[29] 2858 6-10-5 **77** MrGTumelty 77
(D McCain) *hdwy and in tch 5th: outpcd appr 3 out: styd on between last 2: tk 3rd run-in* **8/1**[3]

0314 **4** *3* **Before The Mast (IRE)**[12] 3223 9-10-13 **85** JohnKington 84+
(M F Harris) *hld up in tch: hdwy 5th: wnt 2nd between last 2: wknd run-in* **11/1**

4436 **5** *5* **Truckle**[45] 2569 4-10-11 **95** PhilKinsella 75
(C W Fairhurst) *hld up in tch: wnt prom 4th: wknd 2 out* **6/1**[2]

366- **6** *2 ½* **Baby Gee**[274] 4847 12-11-7 **98** GarryWhillans(5) 88
(D W Whillans) *in rr: outpcd 5th: kpt on fr 3 out: nvr on terms* **40/1**

0002 **7** *hd* **Prairie Law (GER)**[29] 2858 6-11-4 **90** TomMessenger 79
(B N Pollock) *w ldrsm pushed along 4th: lost pl appr 3 out* **10/1**

0-05 **8** *12* **Only Words (USA)**[19] 2981 9-10-11 **86** FearghalDavis(3) 63
(A J Lockwood) *in rr: outpcd after 5th: lost pl appr 3 out* **16/1**

4 **9** *7* **Bonnell (IRE)**[8] 3279 7-11-2 **88** MrATDuff 58
(K J Burke) *trckd ldrs: lost pl appr 3 out* **16/1**

0P20 **10** *30* **That's Racing**[18] 3042 6-10-4 **76** LiamBerridge 16
(J Hetherton) *prom: lost pl after 6th: sn bhd: t.o* **11/1**

641F **11** *9* **Peter's Imp (IRE)**[91] 1334 11-11-6 **95** JohnEnnis(3) 26
(A Berry) *in rr: bhd fr 5th: sn t.o* **50/1**

4m 17.1s (17.70) **Going Correction** +1.35s/f (Heav)
WFA 4 from 6yo+ 11lb **11** Ran SP% **114.5**
Speed ratings: **109,102,101,100,97 96,96,90,86,71 67** CSF £18.34 CT £101.92 TOTE £2.50: £1.60, £2.90, £1.80; EX 15.60.
Owner Mrs M E Dixon **Bred** Mrs P Nicholson **Trained** Norton, N Yorks
■ A first success for 21-year-old Oliver Williams, who has two point wins to his credit.

FOCUS
The winner was able to race from a mark 29lb lower than his chase rating and he took full advantage. They went a sound pace and the form, rated through the third and fourth, should be sound.

NOTEBOOK
Polar Gunner, two stone below his chase mark, loves this type of ground and, keen to get on with the task in hand, was out on his own when he had a disagreement with his rider at the last. He *should continue to give a good account of himself whether it be over hurdles or fences. (op 7-4 tchd 2-1 and 15-8 in places)*
Gospel Song, winner of this race for the last two years, was able to race from a 5lb lower mark than last time but he is now into his 15th year. Suited by the ground, he ran his heart out but the leniently treated winner, five years younger, was far too good. *(op 9-1 tchd 11-1)*
Balmoral Queen, 9lb higher, showed her improved Uttoxeter success was no fluke and she might well appreciate an even stiffer test. *(op 6-1)*
Before The Mast(IRE), third behind Balmoral Queen at Uttoxeter, showed in a clear second between the last two but he became very leg-weary indeed on the run-in.
Truckle, well supported on his handicap debut, tends to want to get on with things and this type of ground will not have suited him. *(op 9-1)*

3396 TRINIDAD & TOBAGO H'CAP CHASE (18 fncs) 3m 1f

2:10 (2:10) (Class 3) (0-135,133) 5-Y-0+ **£8,457** (£2,483; £1,241; £620)

Form RPR
4226 **1** **Jungle Jinks (IRE)**[23] 2946 11-10-5 **112** BarryKeniry 127+
(G M Moore) *w ldrs: led 10th: kpt on fr 4 out: hld on towards fin* **4/1**[3]

P014 **2** *½* **Moorlands Again**[31] 2819 11-10-7 **114** (t) MarkBradburne 127
(M Sheppard) *w ldrs: led 4th to 10th: upsides fr 4 out: no ex towards fin* **9/2**

21UP **3** *17* **Mckelvey (IRE)**[18] 3022 7-11-12 **133** ChristianWilliams 133+
(P Bowen) *nvr gng wl: nt fluent: in tch: reminders 5th: chsng ldrs whn hit 10th: lost pl 14th: tk remote 3rd run-in* **11/4**[1]

P112 **4** *¾* **Sharp Belline (IRE)**[19] 2993 9-10-5 **112** PadgeWhelan 107
(Mrs S J Smith) *led to 4th: w ldrs: reminders 11th: lost pl after 14th: sn bhd* **3/1**[2]

P-21 **F** **Lord Olympia (IRE)**[32] 2805 7-11-0 **121** AlanO'Keeffe —
(Miss Venetia Williams) *hld up wl in tch: mstke 5th: smooth hdwy and handy 3rd whn fell heavily 14th* **5/1**

7m 0.90s (20.90) **Going Correction** +1.575s/f (Heav) **5** Ran SP% **106.5**
Speed ratings: **109,108,103,103,—** CSF £19.52 TOTE £5.10: £2.00, £1.90; EX 22.50.
Owner Mrs Mary And Miss Susan Hatfield **Bred** Stephen McCarthy **Trained** Middleham, N Yorks

FOCUS
The favourite was in an uncooperative mood and the novice Lord Olympia crashed out when looking a big threat, leaving the first two to engage in battle over the final four fences. The race could be rated 3lb higher.

NOTEBOOK
Jungle Jinks(IRE), meeting Mckelvey on much better terms compared with November, had to work hard to achieve his fourth course and distance success. He loves soft ground but this may be as good as he is now. *(tchd 9-2)*
Moorlands Again, 7lb higher than Warwick, just stays, and he had the mud and the left-handed track he needs. He went at it head to head with the winner over the last four fences and was coming back for more at the line. *(op 11-2)*
Mckelvey(IRE), meeting the winner on 1llb worse terms, was not in the same mood and his rider was soon cajoling him along to keep in the contest. *(op 10-3 tchd 7-2)*
Sharp Belline(IRE), who is not very big, was unable to dominate and was struggling early on the final circuit, finally missing out on third spot on the run-in. He is still 1llb higher than for his last success. *(op 11-4)*
Lord Olympia(IRE), having just his third start over fences, was on the heels of the first two and seemingly full of running when he took a crashing fall five out. Thankfully, he hacked back looking none the worse. *(op 7-2)*

3397 ANTIGUA & BARBUDA H'CAP HURDLE (10 hdls) 2m 4f 110y

2:40 (2:40) (Class 2) 4-Y-0+ **£11,315** (£3,371; £1,706; £875; £457)

Form RPR
2536 **1** **Haut De Gamme (FR)**[19] 2990 11-10-1 **125** MrGTumelty(7) 130+
(Ferdy Murphy) *stdd s: hld up: hdwy 5th: sltly hmpd 7th: led appr last: rdn out* **7/2**[2]

5151 **2** *2* **Killing Me Softly**[14] 3143 5-9-11 **117** oh2 (v) RobertStephens(3) 119+
(J Gallagher) *chsd ldr: lft in ld 7th: hdd appr last: kpt on wl* **6/1**[3]

40/2 **3** *11* **Mughas (IRE)**[28] 2876 7-11-12 **143** WayneHutchinson 137+
(A King) *trckd ldrs: hmpd 7th: outpcd appr 2 out: lft mod 3rd last* **6/4**[1]

P1P4 **4** *18* **Vicario**[14] 3143 5-10-0 **122** StephenCraine(5) 100+
(D McCain) *chsd ldrs: rdn 7th: wknd appr 2 out* **14/1**

4F10 **5** *8* **Water King (USA)**[19] 2999 7-10-0 **117** JamesDavies 81
(R M Stronge) *chsd ldrs: lost pl appr 3 out: bhd whn j.lft 2 out: hmpd last* **9/1**

1-P0 **F** **The Bajan Bandit (IRE)**[36] 2747 11-11-9 **143** (b) GaryBerridge(3) —
(L Lungo) *led tl fell 7th* **8/1**

300P **F** **Spring Pursuit**[7] 3289 10-10-12 **129** JimCrowley 125+
(E G Bevan) *stdd s: hdwy 5th: wnt handy 3rd 3 out: 6 l 3rd and wl hld whn fell last* **14/1**

5m 33.4s (24.50) **Going Correction** +1.35s/f (Heav) **7** Ran SP% **111.0**
Speed ratings: **107,106,102,95,92 —,—** CSF £22.90 CT £41.08 TOTE £5.80: £2.20, £1.80; EX 21.70.
Owner The Haut De Gamme Partnership **Bred** Haras De Saint-Voir **Trained** West Witton, N Yorks

FOCUS
A sound gallop. The winner is heading for the Grand National and the runner-up is improving at a rate of knots. The winner is rated almost a stone higher over fences and the race could be rated a few pounds higher.

NOTEBOOK
Haut De Gamme(FR), who has already shown that the big Aintree fences hold no terrors for him, is a Grand National entry. He came there travelling strongly but in the end had to be kept up to his work. He will have another outing over fences before the big one, but not before the weights are published as his trainer wants to protect his handicap mark. *(op 4-1)*
Killing Me Softly, a stone higher, was handed the adavantage four out and went down fighting. He is vastly improved. *(tchd 13-2)*
Mughas(IRE), 3lb higher, was closely matched with the winner on Haydock running but he was *not in the same sort of form this time and, on the day, looked only fourth-best. (op 11-8 tchd 13-8 in places)*
Vicario, 7lb higher than his last success, is hardly a model of consistency. *(op 16-1)*
Water King(USA), 10lb higher than Cheltenham, dropped away in a matter of strides and was well out of contention when almost brought to a standstill at the final flight. *(op 10-1)*
Spring Pursuit is not at the top of his game at present and was booked for just a modest third when crashing out at the last. *(op 13-2)*
The Bajan Bandit(IRE) loves these conditions. He set a sound pace and had not been asked any sort of question when he hit the deck four out. He might well have given the first two a run for their money. *(op 13-2)*

3398 JAMAICA H'CAP CHASE (15 fncs) 2m 4f 110y

3:10 (3:10) (Class 4) (0-115,110) 5-Y-0+ **£4,554** (£1,337; £668; £333)

Form RPR
-636 **1** **Sound Of Cheers**[13] 3172 9-11-9 **107** (t) KennyJohnson 110+
(F Kirby) *in tch: wnt prom 7th: wnt 3rd between last 2: styd on strly to ld last strides* **6/1**[2]

0413 **2** *½* **Lost In Normandy (IRE)**[25] 2933 9-10-2 **86** (b) DaveCrosse 90+
(Mrs L Williamson) *wnt promient 3rd: led 3 out: 6 l clr last: eased last 50yds: jst ct* **15/2**[3]

2152 **3** *7* **Avadi (IRE)**[8] 3274 8-10-1 **85** JimCrowley 79
(P T Dalton) *promient: outpcd appr 4 out: wnt 2nd after 2 out: kpt on one pce* **7/2**[1]

P-20 **4** *25* **Flaming Heck**[55] 2372 9-10-8 **92** NeilMulholland 66+
(Mrs L B Normile) *mstkes: led: hit 6th and 7th: blnd 10th: hdd 3 out: wknd next: clambered over last* **14/1**

624P **5** *½* **Fiori**[7] 3293 10-11-7 **110** PaddyMerrigan(5) 79
(P C Haslam) *promient: lost pl 10th: sn bhd* **8/1**

2P2 **P** **Jballingall**[4] 3338 7-10-0 **84** BarryKeniry —
(N Wilson) *chsd ldrs: wknd after 10th: bhd whn p.u bef 4 out* **7/2**[1]

-635 **P** **Imaginaire (USA)**[42] 2626 11-11-11 **109** AlanO'Keeffe —
(Miss Venetia Williams) *chsd ldrs: lost pl after 10th: bhd whn p.u bef 4 out* **10/1**

6F1P **P** **One Five Eight**[19] 2966 7-11-2 **103** MrTGreenall(3) —
(M W Easterby) *hdwy to chse ldrs 7th: lost pl 10th: 6th and last whn p.u bef 2 out* **10/1**

0-0P **P** **Green Finger**[30] 2841 8-11-3 **106** DougieCostello(5) —
(J J Quinn) *lost pl 6th: sn drvn and in rr: bhd fr 10th: blnd next: t.o whn p.u bef 4 out* **22/1**

5m 48.6s (27.90) **Going Correction** +1.575s/f (Heav) **9** Ran SP% **110.8**
Speed ratings: **109,108,106,96,96 —,—,—,—** CSF £47.03 CT £172.64 TOTE £8.80: £2.50, £2.70, £1.50; EX 65.60.
Owner Fred Kirby **Bred** Pendley Farm **Trained** Streetlam, N Yorks
■ Stewards' Enquiry : Dave Crosse 28-day ban: dropped hands and lost 1st place (Jan 25-Feb 21)

FOCUS
Lost In Normandy ought to have won by about four lengths and David Crosse was handed the mandatory 28-day ban for throwing away a race he should definitely have won. Overall, though, the form has a weak look about it.

NOTEBOOK
Sound Of Cheers put a below-par effort last time behind him but in truth he was only second best. His rider deserves full marks, however, for seizing the opportunity handed to him. *(op 7-1)*
Lost In Normandy(IRE) had it in the bag jumping the last but his rider rather vainly concentrated on admiring his own style on the big screen on the inside of the track just past the winning post. The camera concentrated on him and did not show Sound Of Cheers catching him fast as he eased up and the prize was thrown away near the line. Crosse was given a hostile reception by angry punters but at least he was honest enough to hold up his hands and admit the error. He certainly was not the first to commit such a sin and nor will he be the last. *(op 7-1)*
Avadi(IRE), struggling to keep up going to four out, stayed on in his own time and seems to lack anything in the way of a turn of foot. The stiffer the track the better it is for him. *(op 4-1)*
Flaming Heck, back over fences, showed the obstacles no respect and his rider deserves a gold medal for getting him round in one piece. *(op 16-1)*
Fiori, without the cheekpieces, seems to have gone off the boil for the time being at least.
Jballingall, making a quick return without the blinkers, was unable to dominate this time and he dropped right out on the home turn before being pulled up. *(op 9-2)*

3399 BARBADOS STANDARD OPEN NATIONAL HUNT FLAT RACE 1m 6f

3:40 (3:41) (Class 5) 4-6-Y-0 **£2,398** (£698; £349)

Form RPR
1 **1** **Wind Instrument (IRE)**[46] 2565 5-11-5 MrRMcCarthy(7) 106+
(T R George) *w ldrs: led 3f out: kpt on wl fnl f* **1/1**[1]

4 **2** *1* **Old Benny**[46] 2565 5-11-5 WayneHutchinson 98+
(A King) *mid-div: hdwy 6f out: chal 3f out: no ex ins last* **11/4**[2]

3 *3 ½* **Lord Collingwood (IRE)** 5-11-5 NeilMulholland 94
(M D Hammond) *hdwy 6f out: sn chsng ldrs: one pce fnl 2f* **9/1**[3]

05 **4** *7* **Intersky Emerald (IRE)**[99] 1667 5-11-0 DougieCostello(5) 88+
(G A Swinbank) *hld up in rr: hdwy 6f out: chsng ldrs whn hmpd and stmbld 4f out: fdd fnl 2f* **20/1**

	5	6	**Young Bobby** 6-11-5 .... AnthonyRoss (P Beaumont) *trckd ldrs: led over 3f out: sn hdd: wknd fnl 2f* **20/1**	78
	6	9	**Young Smokey (IRE)** 5-11-5 .... MarkBradburne (P Beaumont) *w ldrs: rdn and outpcd 4f out: sn lost pl* **12/1**	67
	7	1	**Lowsha Green** 5-11-5 .... KennyJohnson (R Johnson) *hld up in rr: stdy hdwy 6f out: nvr nr ldrs* **40/1**	66
0	8	15	**Incalotte**[53] 2425 4-10-0 .... AlanO'Keeffe (J A Supple) *t.k.h towards rr: bhd fnl 4f* **100/1**	29
00-	9	½	**Primitive Cove**[298] 4513 5-11-5 .... JimCrowley (G A Swinbank) *set stdy pce: hdd over 3f out: sn wknd and eased* **22/1**	48
0	10	3	**Freshford (IRE)**[26] 2927 4-10-5 ow1 .... MrTGreenall(3) (N Tinkler) *chsd ldrs: outpcd 6f out: lost pl over 3f out: sn bhd* **66/1**	33
	11	dist	**Nightmare Bud (IRE)** 5-11-5 .... PadgeWhelan (T J Fitzgerald) *prom: lost pl over 5f out: sn bhd: taiuled off: btn 70 l* **40/1**	—
0-	12	dist	**Silver Hill Lad**[266] 4981 5-11-5 .... BarryKeniry (C W Fairhurst) *lost pl 6f out: sn bhd: t.o: virtually p.u: btn 42 l* **100/1**	—

3m 58.5s **12 Ran SP% 116.6**
CSF £3.11 TOTE £2.30: £1.10, £1.40, £2.60; EX 4.80 Place 6 £55.87, Place 5 £39.38.
Owner Ryder Racing Ltd **Bred** John P Kiely **Trained** Slad, Gloucs

FOCUS
They went no gallop at all until halfway but in the end they came home well strung out. The runner-up improved on his Hereford debut run and the winner is a tough sort whose record now reads two wins from two starts.

NOTEBOOK
Wind Instrument(IRE), dropping back in trip and racing on much slower ground, battled hard and was in command at the line. *(op 11-8)*
Old Benny, who looks every inch a chaser, finished a whole lot closer to the winner this time. He looked to be travelling the better when moving upsides but in the end he looked by far more the inexperienced. *(op 3-1 tchd 5-2)*
Lord Collingwood(IRE), who stands over plenty of ground, kept on in his own time and looks to have a lot more stamina than speed. *(tchd 10-1)*
Intersky Emerald(IRE), who has changed stables, is quite a keen type. He was left short of room once in line for home but in the end did not truly see it out in the bad ground. *(op 11-1)*
Young Bobby, whose dam was a winning staying hurdler, is a sturdy, well-made type. He will improve both for the outing and the experience.
Young Smokey(IRE) looks very unfurnished and will not be seen at his best for a while yet. *(op 14-1)*
T/Plt: £43.40 to a £1 stake. Pool: £37,786.10. 634.85 winning tickets. T/Qpdt: £25.30 to a £1 stake. Pool: £1,964.20. 57.40 winning tickets. WG

3400 - (Foreign Racing) - See Raceform Interactive

3153 PUNCHESTOWN (R-H)

Saturday, January 14

OFFICIAL GOING: Soft to heavy

3401a PUNCHESTOWN JUVENILE HURDLE (GRADE 3) 2m

1:00 (1:00) 4-Y-0 **£14,366** (£4,215; £2,008; £684)

				RPR
1		**Marhaba Million (IRE)**[9] 3262 4-10-9 .... BCByrnes(5) (E McNamara, Ire) *trckd ldrs in 5th: impr into 2nd after 3 out: chal after next: led last: kpt on wl u.p* **6/1**[3]	123
2	¾	**Dreux (FR)**[19] 3004 4-11-0 .... NPMadden (Thomas Cooper, Ire) *trckd ldrs: 4th 1/2-way: slt mstke 4 out: impr to ld after 3 out: rdn & strly pressed after next: hdd last: rallied u.p: no* **9/2**[2]	122
3	13	**First Row (IRE)**[19] 3004 4-10-9 .... NJO'Shea(5) (D T Hughes, Ire) *trckd ldrs: 5th and pushed along 1/2-way: 6th and rdn 3 out: kpt on to go mod 3rd fr last* **6/1**[3]	109
4	3 ½	**Clear Riposte (IRE)**[19] 3004 4-10-11 .... RJKiely(7) (W P Mullins, Ire) *cl 2nd: led briefly 4 out: hdd next: sn outpcd: 3rd whn slt mstke 2 out: no ex bef last* **9/2**[2]	110
5	3 ½	**Artist's Muse (IRE)**[19] 3004 4-10-9 ....(b) DNRussell (T M Walsh, Ire) *trckd ldrs in 6th: cl 5th 3 out: 4th and rdn next: sn no ex: one pced* **6/4**[1]	97
6	15	**Ballygally Bay**[19] 3004 4-10-7 .... MrKBBowens(7) (S J Mahon, Ire) *sn led: rn off bnd after 3rd: slt mstke and hdd 4 out: rdn and wknd after 3 out* **9/1**	87
7	9	**Abraham (IRE)**[14] 3157 4-11-0 .... JPElliott (Michael Cunningham, Ire) *hld up towards rr: no ex fr 3 out* **33/1**	78
8	13	**Dream Of Tomorrow (IRE)**[17] 3084 4-10-9 .... RMPower (John Joseph Murphy, Ire) *hld up towards rr: slt mstke 4th: no ex after 4 out* **25/1**	60
9	dist	**Virtue**[9] 3262 4-10-9 .... DJCasey (C F Swan, Ire) *trckd ldrs on outer: slow 3rd: dropped to rr bef 1/2-way: trailing 4 out: t.o whn bad mstke last* **10/1**	—

4m 23.3s **9 Ran SP% 130.8**
CSF £38.29 TOTE £5.30: £1.40, £1.90, £1.60; DF 58.90.
Owner E McNamara **Bred** Gainsborough Stud Management L **Trained** Rathkeale, Co. Limerick

NOTEBOOK
Marhaba Million(IRE) looks progressive in what increasingly appears a moderate collection of juvenile hurdlers this season. Twenty lengths behind Mister Hight here last month and a faller at Thurles last time, he drew clear with the runner-up after two out and stayed on best from the last. The stable won this race last season with Strangely Brown and this one will follow a similarly ambitious route with Leopardstown on February 12th next on the schedule. *(op 5/1)*
Dreux(FR) had no difficulty in turning around Leopardstown form with Clear Riposte and Artist's Muse and, further in front of First Row here, this was an effort that suggests he is improving too. *(op 7/2)*
First Row(IRE) was struggling three out, but stayed on in the straight. *(op 5/1)*
Clear Riposte(IRE), with her 9lb penalty, was in trouble before three out and a mistake at the next put paid to her chance. *(op 9/2 tchd 4/1)*
Artist's Muse(IRE) looked to have plenty going for her at the weights, but she had had enough of it before the second last and dropped away. This sort of winter ground might be taking a toll on her enthusiasm and first-time blinkers had no effect. *(op 9/4 tchd 5/2)*
Virtue *Official explanation: trainer said filly was never travelling from an early stage (op 8/1)*

3402 - 3407a (Foreign Racing) - See Raceform Interactive

3105 LEOPARDSTOWN (L-H)

Sunday, January 15

OFFICIAL GOING: Heavy

3408a P.B.S HURDLE (10 hdls) 2m 4f

12:50 (12:54) 4-Y-0+ **£8,979** (£2,634; £1,255; £427)

				RPR
1		**Night Bridge (IRE)**[10] 3262 4-10-1 ow1 .... RMPower (John Joseph Murphy, Ire) *hld up in 4th: 3rd fr 4 out: hdwy after 2 out: led bef last: styd on wl* **11/2**[2]	105+
2	4 ½	**Openide**[20] 2964 5-10-11 ....(b) MrMWall(7) (B W Duke) *led: drvn along fr 5 out: rdn and jnd 2 out: rallied u.p: hdd bef last: kpt on* **9/1**[3]	117
3	5	**Back To Bid (IRE)**[20] 3002 6-11-8 .... NPMadden (Noel Meade, Ire) *settled 3rd: slt mstke 2nd: impr into cl 2nd travelling wl 3 out: disp ld next: sn rdn: dropped to 3rd and no ex appr last* **4/11**[1]	116
4	dist	**Monsieur Monet (IRE)**[19] 3057 7-11-8 .... CO'Dwyer (Michael Flynn, Ire) *cl 2nd: drooped to 4th and no ex 4 out: t.o* **12/1**	—
5	3 ½	**Boher Storm (IRE)**[84] 1866 6-11-8 109 .... RWalsh (P A Fahy, Ire) *a bhd: lost tch bef 1/2-way: t.o* **12/1**	—
6	25	**Jakers (IRE)**[63] 2223 9-11-12 113 .... BJGeraghty (P A Fahy, Ire) *nvr a factor: lost tch bef 1/2-way: completely t.o* **16/1**	—

5m 10.8s **Going Correction** +0.325s/f (Yiel)
WFA 4 from 5yo+ 12lb **7 Ran SP% 120.0**
Speed ratings: **109,107,105,—,—** — CSF £50.77 TOTE £9.10: £2.50, £2.00; DF 42.50.
Owner O Finetto **Bred** Moat View Stud **Trained** Upton, Co. Cork

NOTEBOOK
Openide ran with a lot of credit under a positive ride and the testing conditions obviously held no fears for him. *(op 7/1)*

3409a PADDY FITZPATRICK MEMORIAL NOVICE CHASE (GRADE 2) (12 fncs 2 omitted) 2m 5f

1:20 (1:29) 5-Y-0+ **£26,937** (£7,903; £3,765; £1,282)

				RPR
1		**Nickname (FR)**[17] 3108 7-11-5 .... CO'Dwyer (Martin Brassil, Ire) *sn led: clr bef 4th: j. v wl: pushed out fr last: impressive* **1/1**[1]	142+
2	11	**Father Matt (IRE)**[28] 2908 8-11-5 .... BJGeraghty (Noel Meade, Ire) *mod 2nd fr 4th: no imp whn bad mstke 4 out: 3rd whn slt mstke next: styd on fr 2 out* **10/3**[2]	131+
3	5	**Romaha (IRE)**[18] 3079 10-11-5 ....(t) LJFleming (S J Mahon, Ire) *prom: mod 3rd 1/2-way: 2nd rdn and no imp 3 out: kpt on same pce fr next* **100/1**	126
4	nk	**Kerryhead Windfarm (IRE)**[20] 3012 8-11-5 .... AndrewJMcNamara (Michael Hourigan, Ire) *cl up early: dropped to rr after bad mstke 6th: trailing bef 4 out: kpt on fr 2 out* **16/1**	126
5	15	**Major Vernon (IRE)**[29] 2895 7-11-5 .... RWalsh (W P Mullins, Ire) *hld up in rr: slt mstke 3rd: mod 4th 4 out: effrt 2 out: sn no ex* **5/1**[3]	111
P		**The Railway Man (IRE)**[63] 2231 7-11-5 .... DJCasey (A L T Moore, Ire) *hld up: 4th whn blnd 7th: p.u after 8th* **5/1**[3]	—

6m 2.70s **Going Correction** +0.75s/f (Soft) **7 Ran SP% 113.3**
Speed ratings: **113,108,106,106,101** — CSF £5.08 TOTE £1.90: £1.40, £1.70; DF 3.90.
Owner Mrs Claudia Jungo-Corpataux **Bred** Sylvie Wildenstein **Trained** Dunmurray, Co Kildare

FOCUS
Two fences in the back straight were omitted.

NOTEBOOK
Nickname(FR) was hugely impressive. Taking a strong hold, he made all and was never seriously challenged and his rider claimed that he was being run away with for the first two miles. Twenty five lengths clear from four out, his stride was shortening a bit when he ran across to the left at the last fence. Soft ground is the essential, a fact which leaves Cheltenham with a big question mark, but he will come back here on February 12th for the Dr P J Moriarty Novice Chase over this trip, rather than the shorter Arkle a fortnight earlier. He is certainly the most exciting of the current crop of novice chasers. *(op 5/4)*
Father Matt(IRE) clouted the fourth last and made another mistake at the next. He had no chance of getting on terms over the last two. *(op 7/2)*
Romaha(IRE), second or third throughout, he held out no hope from three out. *(op 50/1)*
Kerryhead Windfarm(IRE) blundered at the sixth and dropped right out. He stayed on again from two out, but with no prospect of getting on terms. *(op 14/1)*
Major Vernon(IRE) was never on terms. *(op 4/1)*
The Railway Man(IRE) blundered badly six out and was soon pulled up. *(op 7/2)*

3411a PIERSE HURDLE (EXTENDED H'CAP) (GRADE B) (8 hdls) 2m

2:20 (2:35) (0-145,135) 4-Y-0+
£54,241 (£17,482; £8,517; £3,137; £2,241; £1,344)

				RPR
1		**Studmaster**[18] 3082 6-10-3 114 .... TPTreacy (Mrs John Harrington, Ire) *cl up in 2nd: disp ld 3 out: led after 2 out: rdn clr bef last: slt mstke: styd on wl* **12/1**	130+
2	2 ½	**No Where To Hyde (IRE)**[43] 2650 6-10-8 119 .... APMcCoy (C Roche, Ire) *mid-div: 9th and rdn after 2 out: hdwy appr last: 2nd and styd on wl run-in* **6/1**[2]	133
3	2 ½	**Pom Flyer (FR)**[28] 2916 6-10-6 122 .... KTColeman(5) (F Flood, Ire) *hld up: hdwy after 3 out: 5th after 2 out: 2nd last: 3rd and no ex cl home* **25/1**	133
4	3 ½	**Charlies First (IRE)**[15] 3155 6-9-7 111 .... OCasey(7) (Peter Casey, Ire) *hld up: rdn and styd on wl fr 2 out* **25/1**	119
5	1	**Bon Temps Rouler (FR)**[115] 1534 7-10-4 115 .... PACarberry (A L T Moore, Ire) *led: jnd 3 out: rdn and hdd after 2 out: no ex appr last* **33/1**	122
6	shd	**Escrea (IRE)**[18] 3082 7-10-7 123 9ex .... RMMoran(5) (Paul Nolan, Ire) *prom: 5th 3 out: 3rd and rdn after 2 out: no imp fr bef last* **7/1**[3]	129
7	3 ½	**Allez Petit Luis (FR)**[36] 2778 8-9-13 113 .... AJDonoghue(3) (C A Murphy, Ire) *towards rr: r.o fr 2 out* **20/1**	117+
8	9	**On Your Way**[77] 1945 7-9-7 109 .... LJFleming(5) (Miss Elizabeth Doyle, Ire) *chsd ldrs: 8th 3 out: 7th and rdn 2 out: kpt on same pce* **20/1**	103
9	4	**Inch Island (IRE)**[18] 3077 6-9-10 107 ow1 .... DJCasey (W P Mullins, Ire) *hld up towards rr: kpt on fr bef 2 out* **14/1**	97

10	1	**The Fingersmith (IRE)**[20] 3013 7-9-10 107 ow2 PWFlood *(A J McNamara, Ire) trckd ldrs: imrpoved into 4th 3 out: 3rd bef next: wknd bef last* **14/1**	96
11	½	**Adamant Approach (IRE)**[63] 2209 12-11-6 131 RWalsh *(W P Mullins, Ire) towards rr: prog after 3 out: 10th and rdn after 2 out: sn no ex* **20/1**	119
12	2	**Rocket Ship (IRE)**[17] 3107 6-10-7 123 (b) RJMolloy(5) *(Noel Meade, Ire) in tch: 6th appr 2 out: sn rdn and wknd* **25/1**	109
13	¾	**Fortmassini (IRE)**[28] 2910 5-10-10 121 (b) APCrowe *(C Roche, Ire) mid-div: 12th 1/2-way: effrt on outer after 2 out: sn no ex* **14/1**	107
14	4½	**Arch Rebel (USA)**[20] 3010 5-11-5 130 (b) JMurtagh *(Noel Meade, Ire) rr of mid-div: no ex appr 2 out* **14/1**	111
15	3½	**Atlantic Rhapsody (FR)**[17] 3107 9-9-9 111 MsKWalsh(5) *(T M Walsh, Ire) rr of mid-div thrght* **50/1**	89
16	1	**Kilbeggan Lad (IRE)**[18] 3082 8-10-6 117 AndrewJMcNamara *(Michael Hourigan, Ire) rr of mid-div: no ex fr bef 2 out* **12/1**	94
17	2	**Steel Band**[20] 3007 8-9-12 109 (t) GTHutchinson *(Paul A Roche, Ire) nvr a factor* **50/1**	84
18	14	**Cherub (GER)**[8] 3298 6-11-10 135 (t) CO'Dwyer *(Jonjo O'Neill) nvr a factor* **25/1**	96
19	nk	**Ennistown Lady (IRE)**[18] 3082 7-10-2 113 RGeraghty *(R P Burns, Ire) cl up: 3rd 1/2-way: 4th appr 2 out: sn wknd* **50/1**	73
20	25	**Sirius Storm (IRE)**[17] 3107 6-10-11 122 JLCullen *(Paul Nolan, Ire) rr of mid-div: no ex after 3 out: t.o* **20/1**	57
21	11	**Levitator**[17] 3107 5-10-5 116 BJGeraghty *(M J P O'Brien, Ire) in tch: 7th 3 out: wknd next: t.o* **16/1**	40
22	9	**Barati (IRE)**[19] 3050 5-10-10 128 RTDunne(7) *(M J P O'Brien, Ire) trckd ldrs: 6th 3 out: rdn and wknd fr next: eased bef last: t.o* **33/1**	43
23	¾	**Blue Corrig (IRE)**[18] 3082 6-10-5 119 MDarcy(3) *(Joseph Crowley, Ire) nvr a factor: mstke 4th: t.o* **100/1**	34
24	25	**Masrahi (IRE)**[43] 2650 5-10-0 111 NPMadden *(Noel Meade, Ire) prom early: 7th 1/2-way: wknd fr 3 out: t.o* **50/1**	—
25	3½	**High Reef (FR)**[28] 2916 8-9-3 107 DGHogan(7) *(C F Swan, Ire) nvr a factor: t.o* **50/1**	—
F		**Loughanelteen (IRE)**[20] 3005 8-10-5 116 JMAllen *(P J Rothwell, Ire) towards rr: fell 3 out* **20/1**	—
P		**Victram (IRE)**[43] 2636 6-10-0 111 TimmyMurphy *(Adrian McGuinness, Ire) hld up towards rr: no ex 2 out: p.u bef last* **4/1**[1]	—

4m 14.8s **Going Correction** +0.625s/f (Soft) **27** Ran SP% **150.6**
Speed ratings: 117,115,114,112,112 112,110,105,103,103 103,102,101,99,97 97,96,89,89,76 71,66,66,53,52 —, CSF £79.85 CT £1894.81 TOTE £12.40: £3.00, £2.90, £10.00, £10.20; DF 110.50.
Owner Mothership Racing Club **Bred** Martyn Arbib **Trained** Moone, Co Kildare

NOTEBOOK
Studmaster ended a long losing run for his stable and built on his Christmas effort here. Always in the first two, he kept to the inner and led before the straight. A slight mistake at the last did not hinder him and he stayed on strongly. Now 10lb higher, Newbury could be next.
No Where To Hyde(IRE) got going all too late and now goes up 5lb. *(op 5/1)*
Pom Flyer(FR) chased the winner going into the last but could not raise his effort on the flat. *(op 20/1)*
Charlies First(IRE) came from far back to be nearest at the finish. He was beaten eight-and-a-half lengths, but still goes up 1lb.
Bon Temps Rouler(FR) tried to make all and kept on once headed by the winner. For an animal purportedly unsuited by the ground, this was a good effort.
Escrea(IRE) struggled in third place early in the straight under her 9lb penalty and was done with well before the last. *(op 7/1 tchd 8/1)*
Cherub(GER) never showed with any chance.
Victram(IRE) skinned a hind leg after a mistake at the first flight and was always in the rear before *being pulled up in the straight. Official explanation: jockey said gelding did not jump or travel throughout (op 9/2)*

3410 - 3414a (Foreign Racing) - See Raceform Interactive

2949 FAKENHAM (L-H)
Monday, January 16

OFFICIAL GOING: Good
Wind: Almost nil Weather: Gloomy

3415 EDP MARIE CURIE NOVICES' HURDLE (11 hdls) 2m 4f
12:50 (12:50) (Class 4) 4-Y-0+ **£4,554** (£1,337; £668; £333)

Form				RPR
12	1		**Dan's Heir**[20] 3038 4-10-9 PaddyMerrigan(5) *(P C Haslam) led tl after 1st: prom: mstke 8th: led again next: drew clr appr last: easily* **11/10**[1]	110+
50	2	7	**Magic Amigo**[34] 2804 5-11-5 RichardJohnson *(J R Jenkins) hld up: prog gng wl 8th: chsd wnr next: rdn and outpcd appr last* **28/1**	103
442	3	10	**Eleazar (GER)**[34] 2804 5-11-5 110 LeightonAspell *(Mrs L Wadham) w.w: prog 6th: cl up whn pckd 3 out: sn outpcd* **15/8**[2]	98+
5P2	4	23	**Alexander Sapphire (IRE)**[9] 3281 5-10-9 91 (t) OwynNelmes(3) *(N B King) in tch: rdn 8th: wknd next: tired and t.o* **20/1**	68+
-34P	5	10	**Zouave (IRE)**[67] 2147 5-11-5 94 (b) NoelFehily *(C J Mann) prom: chsd ldr 4th: led after 6th: hdd 3 out: immediately btn* **16/1**	60
4	6	dist	**Water Pistol**[116] 1519 4-10-7 KennyJohnson *(M C Chapman) mstke 1st: hld up: j.rt 2nd: lost tch 6th: sn t.o: btn 90l* **40/1**	—
2/3	P		**Top Of The Agenda**[47] 2579 7-11-5 CarlLlewellyn *(M Pitman) chsd ldrs tl 4th: rdn and lost pl after next: bhd whn p.u 7th* **12/1**[3]	—
0PP-	P		**Barbilyrifle (IRE)**[390] 2934 5-10-12 (b) TomMessenger(7) *(H H G Owen) plld hrd: hld up and bhd: rdn and mstke 5th: sn t.o: p.u 3 out* **200/1**	—
-05P	P		**Exclusive Air (USA)**[6] 3330 7-10-12 62 (b) MrJOwen(7) *(H H G Owen) keen: led after 1st tl hdd after 6th: wknd qckly: hit next: t.o and p.u 3 out* **200/1**	—

5m 15.2s (3.00) **Going Correction** +0.275s/f (Yiel)
WFA 4 from 5yo+ 12lb **9** Ran SP% **107.6**
Speed ratings: **105,102,98,89,85** —,—,—,— CSF £33.11 TOTE £1.80: £1.10, £3.10, £1.40; EX 38.70.
Owner Peter W Tomlinson **Bred** R P Williams **Trained** Middleham, N Yorks

FOCUS
The pace was a fair one and the favourite scored easily.

NOTEBOOK
Dan's Heir, up against older novices for the first time, had no problem with this step up in trip and came away between the last two flights for a pretty easy victory. On the debit side, he beat little and his jumping has room for improvement. *(op Evens)*
Magic Amigo ran his best race to date over hurdles on his third start, and in doing so turned around Folkestone form with today's third. Softer ground will not inconvenience him.
Eleazar(GER), who finished in front of today's second when runner-up at Folkestone, lost his *chance with a mistake three from home. He did not shape as if this longer trip was required. (op 2-1)*
Alexander Sapphire(IRE), runner-up against her own sex last time, was put in her place in this slightly stronger company.
Top Of The Agenda, who showed ability in both his bumpers, had an excuse for this disappointing first attempt over hurdles. *Official explanation: vet said gelding had bled from the nose (op 10-1)*

3416 HORSERACE BETTING LEVY BOARD H'CAP HURDLE (12 hdls 1 omitted) 2m 7f 110y
1:20 (1:20) (Class 4) (0-100,100) 4-Y-0+ **£4,554** (£1,337; £668; £333)

Form				RPR
6211	1		**New Perk (IRE)**[25] 2951 8-10-3 **82** ChrisHonour(5) *(M J Gingell) j.big 1st: chsd ldr: led bef 3 out: sn clr: 7l ahd last: rdn and hung rt: all out* **5/2**[1]	93+
5455	2	1	**Siegfrieds Night (IRE)**[21] 2964 5-11-2 **90** (t) KennyJohnson *(M C Chapman) hld up: pushed along 7th: prog 9th: wnt 2nd bef last: styd on wl u.p* **8/1**	96
4461	3	28	**True Mariner (FR)**[21] 2958 6-11-12 **100** (t) SamStronge *(B I Case) t.k.h: hld up last: mstke 3rd: prog 8th: rdn bef 3 out: sn wl outpcd: tk poor 3rd after last* **13/2**	78
6131	4	2½	**Chickapeakray**[21] 2977 5-10-7 **86** StephenCraine(5) *(D McCain) led and keen: clr 2nd: hdd bef 3 out: sn rdn and btn* **11/4**[2]	62
F-01	5	3½	**In The Hat (IRE)**[58] 2341 10-10-13 **87** RichardJohnson *(J R Jenkins) hld up: prog 5th: mstke 8th: rdn 10th: sn wknd* **7/2**[3]	59
40P0	P		**Weldiva**[16] 3141 6-9-7 **74** oh10 TomMessenger(7) *(B N Pollock) chsd ldrs: drvn and lost pl 4th: rr next: t.o after 7th: p.u 10th* **66/1**	—
14P/	P		**Commanche General (IRE)**[797] 2080 9-10-13 **87** PJBrennan *(J F Panvert) chsd ldrs: mstkes 5th and 7th: rdn and fdd bef next: blnd bdly 9th and p.u* **20/1**	—

6m 15.7s (9.30) **Going Correction** +0.275s/f (Yiel) **7** Ran SP% **108.2**
Speed ratings: **95,94,85,84,83** —,— CSF £19.66 TOTE £3.00: £1.40, £3.20; EX 29.20.
Owner A White **Bred** Tim Mulhare **Trained** North Runcton, Norfolk

FOCUS
A modest time for a race of its class. The second-last flight was bypassed on the final circuit as it was damaged.

NOTEBOOK
New Perk(IRE), a winner twice over fences here, completed a course hat-trick off his lower hurdles mark. He looked set for a comfortable win when clear on the home turn but only scrambled home in the end. *(tchd 9-4, 11-4 in places)*
Siegfrieds Night(IRE) began to stay on once in sight of home and, after moving into second skirting round the bypassed second last he finished strongly and would have embarrassed the favourite with a bit further to run. He is a character but is well handicapped now.
True Mariner(FR) was 5lb higher than when winning at Huntingdon. Weak in the market, his measure had been taken with three to jump. *(op 5-1 tchd 7-1)*
Chickapeakray, raised 6lb for her win on Boxing Day, set the pace but had no answers when the winner went by. A return to slightly shorter should suit her. *(tchd 3-1)*
In The Hat(IRE) still looked on a decent mark based on his old form in Ireland despite the 5lb rise *for his Huntingdon win two months ago, but was struggling with a circuit to run. (op 4-1 tchd 9-2 in a place)*

3417 FAKENHAM NATIONAL HUNT CLUB FAREWELL "NATIONAL HUNT" NOVICES' HURDLE (9 hdls) 2m
1:50 (1:51) (Class 4) 4-Y-0+ **£4,554** (£1,337; £668; £333)

Form				RPR
141	1		**Unjust Law (IRE)**[33] 2823 5-11-1 MrTGreenall(3) *(N J Henderson) trckd ldrs: forced through on inner to ld 2 out: sn clr: rdn last: idled flat: jst hld on* **5/4**[1]	107+
0220	2	shd	**Arumun (IRE)**[14] 3210 5-11-4 TomScudamore *(M Scudamore) taken down early: plld hrd in ld: rdn and j.rt 3 out: hdd and wnt rt next: rallied u.p flat: jst failed* **4/1**[3]	105+
65-3	3	8	**Finely Tuned (IRE)**[75] 1991 7-11-4 102 CarlLlewellyn *(M Pitman) chsd ldrs: rdn bef 3 out: outpcd next* **13/8**[2]	99+
50	4	dist	**Mange Tout (IRE)**[21] 2961 7-11-1 TJPhelan(3) *(K J Burke) t.k.h: hld up midfield: rdn and fdd qckly bef 3 out: btn 50l* **50/1**	—
-63P	5	8	**Keen Warrior**[9] 3291 6-11-1 LeeVickers(3) *(Mrs S Lamyman) chsd ldrs: rdn and fdd rapidly bef 3 out: fin tired: btn 58l* **33/1**	—
0-PP	6	10	**The Rainbow Man**[79] 1916 6-11-4 WayneHutchinson *(J Ryan) hld up towards rr: rdn and lost tch bef 6th: sn t.o: btn 68l* **50/1**	—
PF00	7	2	**Ray Mond**[21] 2968 5-10-13 ChrisHonour(5) *(M J Gingell) hld up last: brief hdwy 4th: wknd after next: t.o* **150/1**	—
	U		**Nellie The Nod**[261] 7-10-1 CareyWilliamson(10) *(M J Gingell) bhd tl stmbld and uns rdr 3rd* **150/1**	—
60-0	P		**Just Posin**[9] 3292 5-10-11 TomSiddall *(Mrs S Lamyman) sn bhd: rdn and lost tch qckly 4th: t.o and p.u next* **150/1**	—

4m 10.8s (1.90) **Going Correction** +0.275s/f (Yiel) **9** Ran SP% **111.4**
Speed ratings: **106,105,101**,—,— —,—,—,— CSF £6.40 TOTE £1.80: £1.40, £1.10, £1.10; EX 8.70.
Owner The Dover Street Boys **Bred** Simon And Helen Plumbly **Trained** Upper Lambourn, Berks

FOCUS
This was run at a reasonable pace and the race might rate higher than at first glance.

NOTEBOOK
Unjust Law(IRE), successful twice in bumpers, made a winning hurdling debut. Trapped on the inner on the approach to the second last, he rather barged his way through to lead and came clear on the turn. He did not do much after the last and was fortunate that the run-in was so short, as he would have been caught with slightly further to go. *(tchd 11-8 and 6-4 in places)*
Arumun(IRE), taken to post very early, raced keenly in the lead. He jumped markedly to his right at the second last, forfeiting the lead to the favourite who challenged him on his inside, but rallied from the final flight and nearly snatched victory. *(op 7-2)*
Finely Tuned(IRE), whose Huntingdon running has been boosted by the two who finished in front of him, ran his race but could not go with the leading pair from the second last. *(op 15-8)*
Mange Tout(IRE), making his hurdling debut, was again somewhat keen and he faded to be beaten a long way into fourth.
Keen Warrior is a very modest performer who was flattered to have got within five lengths of Lennon at Market Rasen two runs back. *(op 25-1)*

3418 L.L. FIRTH AND PAT FIRTH MEMORIAL NOVICES' H'CAP CHASE (12 fncs) 2m 110y

2:20 (2:20) (Class 4) (0-110,107) 5-Y-O+ £6,506 (£1,910; £955; £477)

Form RPR

2-1P **1** **Glengarra (IRE)**[115] [1542] 9-11-9 **104** TomDoyle 122+
(D R Gandolfo) *mde all: gng wl 3 out: pushed clr after next: comf* **9/2**[1]

-2P0 **2** *2 ½* **Lord On The Run (IRE)**[50] [2528] 7-11-3 **101** RichardYoung(3) 114
(J W Mullins) *chsd wnr thrght: rdn bef 2 out: nt qckn after* **8/1**

6P53 **3** *9* **Kercabellec (FR)**[40] [2705] 8-9-10 **82** MarkNicolls(5) 87+
(J R Cornwall) *taken down early: cl up: rdn and ev ch 3 out: wknd next: lft 3rd at last* **8/1**

4123 **4** *3* **Rookery Lad**[15] [3187] 8-11-4 **99** DaveCrosse 100
(C N Kellett) *midfield: prog 5th: rdn bef 3 out: sn btn: lft 4th at last* **7/1**[3]

553U **5** *9* **Ground Breaker**[32] [2839] 6-11-4 **102** (t) MrTGreenall(3) 106+
(M W Easterby) *hld up: hdwy 7th. rdn 2 out: sn wknd: disputing 3rd whn blnd last* **10/1**

U-54 **6** *11* **Bel Ombre (FR)**[14] [3220] 6-11-1 **96** LeightonAspell 80+
(O Sherwood) *hld up towards rr: j. slowly 8th: no ch whn mstke next* **17/2**

40 **7** *16* **Bonnell (IRE)**[2] [3395] 7-10-7 **88** SeanCurran 53
(K J Burke) *hld up: effrt 5th: j.lft next: rdn bef 8th: no ch after: t.o* **14/1**

P2-5 **8** *6* **Fantastic Arts (FR)**[12] [3243] 6-11-12 **107** SamThomas 66
(Miss Venetia Williams) *chsd ldng trio: mstke 8th: sn rdn and btn: blnd 3 out: eased flat: t.o* **9/2**[1]

U0P0 **9** *4* **Tails I Win**[10] [3274] 7-10-1 **82** oh20 ow1 MarkGrant 37
(Miss C J E Caroe) *a wl bhd: blnd 8th: sn t.o* **50/1**

-4FP **10** *7* **Interstice**[13] [2807] 9-9-11 **81** oh14 OwynNelmes(3) 29
(M J Gingell) *hld up last and wl off pce: t.o 8th* **66/1**

362F **F** **Bonnet's Pieces**[25] [2951] 7-10-11 **92** PaulMoloney —
(Mrs P Sly) *hld up: mstke 3rd: 10th whn fell next* **6/1**[2]

4m 16.6s (-4.00) **Going Correction** 0.0s/f (Good) **11 Ran SP% 115.1**
Speed ratings: **109,107,103,102,97 92,85,82,80,77** — CSF £39.86 CT £279.38 TOTE £4.50: £1.70, £4.00, £2.40; EX 85.00 Trifecta £161.20 Pool: £340.72 - 1.50 winning tickets..

Owner Starlight Racing **Bred** T J Whitley **Trained** Wantage, Oxon

FOCUS
The winner set a decent gallop and few got into this.

NOTEBOOK
Glengarra(IRE) had been let down by his jumping on his last run in September, when he suffered a slight back injury, but he put in a good round here. Travelling nicely in front, he burnt off his pursuers from the second last and scored in the manner of a progressive chaser.

Lord On The Run(IRE), reverting to fences, jumped soundly and was in second place all the way, although he could not go with the winner from the second last. He is reported to be a nervous individual and this should have boosted his confidence. *(tchd 9-1)*

Kercabellec(FR) raced in third place for much of the way and was back in that position at the final fence. This was a respectable effort but he remains hard to win with. *(op 9-1)*

Rookery Lad, back over this more suitable trip, kept on in the latter stages without posing a threat. He will continue to prove vulnerable off this mark. *(op 8-1 tchd 17-2)*

Ground Breaker would probably have finished third had he not blundered at the final fence, but in truth he was never really a factor. *(op 17-2 tchd 11-1)*

Fantastic Arts(FR) chased the leading trio, who filled the first three places at the finish, but was dropped by them after an error at the eighth. *(op 5-1)*

3419 BETTY JARROD 60TH BIRTHDAY CELEBRATION BEGINNERS' CHASE (18 fncs) 3m 110y

2:50 (2:50) (Class 3) 5-Y-O+ £6,506 (£1,910; £955; £477)

Form RPR

0/03 **1** **Thistlecraft (IRE)**[21] [2963] 7-11-5 115 NoelFehily 120+
(C C Bealby) *t.k.h: settled in tch: led 10th: gng best fr 3 out: rdn clr bef last: idled flat: fnd ex whn pressed* **9/2**

1155 **2** *1 ¼* **Jackson (FR)**[48] [2564] 9-11-5 WayneHutchinson 116+
(A King) *chsd ldrs: wnt 2nd after 14th: 2l down whn blnd bdly 2 out: rallied and ch after last: a hld* **9/4**[1]

02-3 **3** *9* **Bohemian Boy (IRE)**[247] [353] 8-11-5 CarlLlewellyn 108+
(M Pitman) *in tch: rdn 15th: chsd ldng pair after next: no imp* **3/1**[3]

3-45 **4** *23* **Rakalackey**[20] [3017] 8-11-5 RichardJohnson 87+
(H D Daly) *hld up in tch: mstke and drvn 10th: rallied 12th: mstke 13th and rdn: blnd next: no ch after* **11/4**[2]

45U **5** *dist* **Ah Yeah (IRE)**[21] [2957] 9-11-2 69 OwynNelmes(3) —
(N B King) *j.rt: led tl hdd and reminders 7th: rdn 11th: fdd qckly next: sn t.o: btn 76l* **22/1**

P00F **6** *7* **Iloveturtle (IRE)**[21] [2966] 6-11-5 82 (t) KennyJohnson —
(M C Chapman) *detached in last and nt fluent: t.o 14th: btn 83l* **100/1**

-305 **U** **The Holy Bee (IRE)**[47] [2574] 7-11-5 97 JohnMcNamara 98
(Mrs S J Humphrey) *chsd ldr tl led 7th: hdd 10th: rdn after 14th: sn wknd: poor 4th whn blnd and uns rdr last* **14/1**

6m 32.9s (-4.70) **Going Correction** 0.0s/f (Good) **7 Ran SP% 112.6**
Speed ratings: **107,106,103,96,—** —,— CSF £15.20 TOTE £4.60: £2.00, £1.90; EX 15.70.

Owner The Wally Partnership **Bred** Hugh Harley **Trained** Barrowby, Lincs

FOCUS
The late withdrawal of favourite Tighten Your Belt somewhat detracted from the event, but there were still one or two fair sorts on show and Thistlecraft excelled under a fine front-running ride from Noel Fehily. The winning time was three seconds faster than the handicap over the same trip.

NOTEBOOK
Thistlecraft(IRE), a highly creditable third over an inadequate trip on his chasing debut at Market Rasen last month, was made more use of on this occasion and picked up again when Jackson came to him after the last, seeing out the three-mile trip well. His jumping was fluent and connections are now eyeing the Jewson Novices' Handicap Chase at the Festival, although he will need to improve a fair bit on this to play any sort of a hand in that event. *(op 5-1)*

Jackson(FR), who jumped abysmally when down the field on his fencing debut at Hereford, may well have won had he not blundered at the second-last, but his jumping in the main was sound and he should improve with further experience. Good, fast ground suits him ideally and it would not be the end of the world if connections kept him for a summer campaign as he would be a smart type for that time of year. *(op 11-4)*

Bohemian Boy(IRE), making his chasing and seasonal reappearance, spoiled his chance with several sloppy jumps and did well to get as close as he did considering. Although his stable can ready one, it is likely the run will bring him on a little and he can find a small race when the ground is soft, possibly in a novices' handicap if his jumping can be improved. *(tchd 11-4 and 10-3)*

Rakalackey continually lost ground at his fences and has yet to convince as a chaser. He was a decent hurdler and it has been somewhat surprising this brother to smart chaser Young Spartacus has yet to transfer his ability to the larger obstacles. *(op 5-2 tchd 3-1)*

3420 AT THE RACES H'CAP CHASE (18 fncs) 3m 110y

3:20 (3:20) (Class 3) (0-125,125) 5-Y-~~£7,605~~ (£2,246; £1,123; £561; £280)

Form RPR

P10 **1** **Melford (IRE)**[57] [2368] 8-10-13 **112** NoelFehily 120+
(C J Mann) *hld up: mstke 3rd: rdn 13th: 9l 5th 3 out: styd on for driving to ld bef last: forged clr* **6/1**

F061 **2** *3 ½* **Harrycone Lewis**[21] [2956] 8-11-7 **120** PaulMoloney 126+
(Mrs P Sly) *keen: trckd ldrs: rdn 14th: mstke 3 out: effrt bef last: nt qckn* **11/4**[2]

1-02 **3** *3* **Regal Bandit (IRE)**[21] [2996] 8-10-3 **102** PJBrennan 105+
(Miss H C Knight) *trckd ldrs: led 10th: clr 14th: 5l ahd 3 out: wknd and hdd bef last: fin lame* **11/2**

-550 **4** *16* **Spring Lover (FR)**[50] [2530] 7-11-9 **122** SamThomas 111+
(Miss Venetia Williams) *led tl 10th: chsd ldr: mstke 15th: wknd bef next* **16/1**

U2-4 **5** *15* **Menphis Beury (FR)**[53] [2458] 6-10-7 **106** MarkBradburne 86+
(H D Daly) *keen and hld up: 4th and rdn after 13th: wknd qckly bef 2 out* **4/1**[3]

5015 **6** *dist* **Strong Magic (IRE)**[40] [2703] 14-9-9 **99** oh3 MarkNicolls(5) —
(J R Cornwall) *pressed ldr tl 9th: mstke 10th: wkng whn mstke 13th: sn t.o: btn 98l* **33/1**

3621 **P** **You're Special (USA)**[37] [2767] 9-11-7 **125** (t) ThomasDreaper(5) —
(Ferdy Murphy) *hld up: mstke and pushed along 8th: nvr gng wl after: t.o 14th: p.u 2 out* **5/2**[1]

6m 35.9s (-1.70) **Going Correction** 0.0s/f (Good) **7 Ran SP% 113.7**
Speed ratings: **102,100,99,94,90** —,— CSF £23.32 TOTE £6.90: £2.90, £2.20; EX 30.20.

Owner Mrs J M Mayo **Bred** Mrs Nuala Delaney **Trained** Upper Lambourn, Berks

FOCUS
They went a fair pace here and stamina won the day in the end, but the form probably does not amount to much.

NOTEBOOK
Melford(IRE) came through from off the pace to take it up turning into the straight. He did not look particularly well handicapped beforehand and this tight track would not have been ideal, but the step up in trip proved right up his street and he added to his stable's recent run of good form. *(op 7-1)*

Harrycone Lewis, back over fences following a hurdles win on Boxing Day, had won on his two previous visits here. He did not see the trip out as strongly as the winner but again showed his liking for the track. *(op 10-3)*

Regal Bandit(IRE) took on Spring Lover at the head of affairs and eventually won the battle. He weakened quickly after the second last, though, as though he had hit the wall, but was later found to be lame. Making the running on this sharp track seemed to suit him and he can be given another chance. *Official explanation: jockey said gelding pulled up lame (op 5-1)*

Spring Lover(FR) would have been happier being left alone in front, but he is also high in the handicap and has yet to prove he truly stays three miles. *(op 9-1)*

Menphis Beury(FR) was expected to step up on his reappearance at Taunton but proved disappointing. *(op 9-2)*

You're Special(USA) was always struggling after a mistake at the eighth fence. *Official explanation: jockey said gelding never travelled (tchd 11-4)*

3421 FAKENHAM STANDARD OPEN NATIONAL HUNT FLAT RACE 2m

3:50 (3:50) (Class 5) 4-6-Y-O £2,912 (£848; £424)

Form RPR

1 **Golden Parachute (IRE)** 5-11-4 NoelFehily 110+
(C C Bealby) *chsd ldr tl led 4f out: sn rdn clr: styd on strly* **12/1**

6 **2** *13* **Aubigny (FR)**[55] [2425] 4-10-7 WayneHutchinson 87+
(A King) *in tch: prgress to 2nd 6f out: rdn 4f out: no ch w wnr after* **7/2**[3]

3 *16* **Raven Hall Lady (IRE)** 5-10-11 RichardJohnson 74
(M G Rimell) *hld up: in tch: prog 6f out: ev ch 4f out: sn rdn and btn* **9/2**

4 *9* **Karrie** 5-10-4 TomMessenger(7) 65
(C C Bealby) *in tch: rdn 1/2-way: sn outpcd: sme late prog* **25/1**

4 **5** *11* **The Rocking Dock (IRE)**[26] [2941] 5-11-4 TomScudamore 61
(M Scudamore) *led at stdy pce: hdd 4f out: immediately btn* **5/2**[1]

60 **6** *2 ½* **Bradders**[69] [2105] 4-10-7 CarlLlewellyn 48
(J R Jenkins) *keen: hld up: in tch: rdn 1/2-way: sn wl bhd: t.o* **28/1**

30-6 **7** *dist* **Bright Spirit**[71] [2075] 5-11-4 AndrewTinkler —
(N J Henderson) *trckd ldrs: rdn 6f out: sn floundering: eased: btn 150l* **11/4**[2]

4m 6.00s (-4.20) **Going Correction** +0.275s/f (Yiel)
WFA 4 from 5yo 11lb **7 Ran SP% 110.6**
Speed ratings: **102,95,87,83,77 76,—** CSF £50.06 TOTE £11.90: £4.80, £3.50; EX 39.60 Place 6 £25.13, Place 5 £21.57.

Owner Irvin S Naylor **Bred** Mrs L Eadie **Trained** Barrowby, Lincs

FOCUS
Just the seven runners and not a very strong bumper, but they went a reasonable enough pace - certainly better than is often the case in these type of races.

NOTEBOOK
Golden Parachute(IRE) ◆ ran out a ready winner on his racecourse debut. A 12,000gns half-brother to moderate maiden hurdler Cintra Ruby, he galloped on strongly when sent to the front by the in-form Noel Fehily and had this won a long way out. He looks the sort who could well defy a penalty in this type of race, even though he could be faced with tougher opposition, and should have a future over obstacles in the longer term. *(op 10-1 tchd 16-1)*

Aubigny(FR) was not without promise on his debut when sixth of 17 over a mile six at Warwick and looked to step up on that effort in second. He was no match for the winner, but kept on well enough for pressure and is clearly going the right way. *(op 10-3)*

Raven Hall Lady(IRE) is from the family of Florida Pearl, but she cost just 4,000gns and came home a modest third on her racecourse debut. *(op 4-1)*

Karrie, a stablemate of the winner, finished up well held in fourth but can be expected to show improvement in time. *(op 22-1)*

The Rocking Dock(IRE) seemed to be going the right way when fourth at Ludlow on his previous start but, making his debut for new connections, he was well beaten after showing up well early on. *(op 7-2 tchd 4-1)*

Bright Spirit, as on all three of his previous career starts when a beaten favourite, ran *disappointingly. It almost goes without saying that he is one to avoid. Official explanation: jockey said gelding never travelled (op 5-2 tchd 9-4)*

T/Plt: £42.30 to a £1 stake. Pool: £36,997.35. 637.90 winning tickets. T/Qpdt: £12.20 to a £1 stake. Pool: £3,709.40. 224.80 winning tickets. IM

[3182]PLUMPTON (L-H)

Monday, January 16

OFFICIAL GOING: Soft (heavy in places)

Wind: Light, against Weather: Overcast and raining

3422 SKY BET PRESS RED TO BET ON ATR NOVICES' HURDLE (DIV I) (9 hdls) 2m

1:00 (1:03) (Class 4) 4-Y-0+ **£4,228** (£1,241; £620; £310)

Form RPR

4-P0 **1** **Alright Now M'Lad (IRE)**[32] 2849 6-11-4 .... APMcCoy 117+
(Jonjo O'Neill) *hld up off the pce: clsd on ldrs fr 6th: led 2 out: sn in command: easily* **33/1**

331P **2** *9* **Josear**[20] 3021 4-10-6 110 .... ShaneWalsh[(7)] 97+
(C J Down) *led at decent pce: pressed fr 3 out: hdd next: kpt on but no ch w wnr* **8/1**

4 **3** *4* **Cruise Director**[33] 2826 6-11-4 .... AndrewThornton 98+
(Ian Williams) *trckd ldr and sn clr of rest: effrt to chal 3 out: btn next: fdd* **11/4**[2]

4 *3 1/2* **Ridjit (FR)**[270] 4951 6-11-4 .... TimmyMurphy 93
(N J Gifford) *chsd clr ldng pair: blnd 1st: mstke 6th: drvn and outpcd sn after 3 out: plugged on again bef last: hung rt flat* **25/1**

0 **5** *1* **Harcourt (USA)**[12] 2826 6-11-4 .... PhilipHide 93+
(M Madgwick) *hld up off the pce: gng wl enough but plenty to do after 6th: tried to cl after 3 out: hmpd after last: styd on flat: do bt* **100/1**

6 *2 1/2* **Mystery Lot (IRE)**[72] 4-10-0 .... RobertThornton 72
(A King) *hld up bhd clr ldrs: clsd and wl in tch after 5th: rdn and btn bef 2 out: wknd last* **9/4**[1]

04 **7** *3/4* **Najca De Thaix (FR)**[46] 2584 5-11-1 .... ColinBolger[(3)] 89
(Mrs L Wadham) *hld up in last trio: gng wl enough 5th: sn lost tch: pushed along after 6th: nvr nr ldrs: plugged on* **6/1**

210 **8** *1 3/4* **Equilibria (USA)**[20] 3021 4-10-13 .... JamieMoore 82
(G L Moore) *chsd clr ldng pair: wl in tch after 6th: rdn and wknd 3 out* **11/2**[3]

64 **9** *dist* **Flamand (FR)**[17] 3127 5-11-4 .... JimmyMcCarthy —
(C P Morlock) *hld up in last pair and wl off the pce: brief effrt after 6th: sn wknd: t.o: btn 57 l* **50/1**

20 **10** *29* **Haloo Baloo**[47] 2573 6-11-4 .... MickFitzgerald —
(Jonjo O'Neill) *off the pce in midfield: pushed along after 4th: sn struggling: no ch after 6th: t.o: btn 86 l* **25/1**

/02- **11** *6* **Armagh South (IRE)**[416] 2462 7-11-1 .... TomMalone[(3)] —
(J C Tuck) *chaased clr ldrs to 4th: wknd next: t.o: btn 92 l* **66/1**

P-U **12** *21* **Red Jester**[59] 2309 5-10-13 .... DerekLaverty[(5)] —
(A E Jones) *a in rr: wknd 5th: sn wl t.o: btn 113 l* **100/1**

FP **P** **Little Gannet**[16] 3133 5-10-11 .... JimCrowley —
(T D McCarthy) *mstke 2nd: a in rr: wknd 5th: t.o whn p.u bef next* **100/1**

4m 11.5s (10.30) **Going Correction** +0.775s/f (Soft) 13 Ran SP% **115.3**
WFA 4 from 5yo+ 11lb
Speed ratings: **105,100,98,96,96 95,94,93,—,— —,—,—** CSF £259.33 TOTE £36.30: £5.10, £2.80, £1.20; EX 320.70.

Owner John P McManus **Bred** John Fowler **Trained** Cheltenham, Gloucs

■ After over 13 years of riding, Tony McCoy partnered his first-ever 33/1 winner.

■ Stewards' Enquiry : Timmy Murphy caution: careless riding

FOCUS

Just a moderate novice hurdle in terms of depth, but an impressive winner in Alright Now M'lad who left his previous form behind.

NOTEBOOK

Alright Now M'Lad(IRE) had shown very limited form on his previous four starts but, given a patient ride, he moved into contention going well and found plenty when asked to run out an easy winner. This performance left his previous efforts behind, but it remains to be seen whether he can *repeat this next time. Official explanation: jockey said, regarding the improved form shown, gelding was better suited by the soft (heavy in places) ground and rode a waiting race in a fast-run contest*

Josear, totally outclassed when pulled up in a Grade One at Chepstow on his previous start, found this much easier and posted a creditable effort behind the shock winner. *(op 7-1)*

Cruise Director looked to have every chance but proved unable to build on the promise he showed when fourth on his debut at Newbury. *(op 5-2 tchd 9-4)*

Ridjit(FR) was pulled up in a point-to-point and finished well beaten in a bumper when trained in Ireland. Making his debut for new connections off the back of a 270-day absence, and without a tongue-tie this time, he ran to just a moderate level of form in fourth. *(op 20-1)*

Harcourt(USA) ran better than on his debut over hurdles, and gave the impression he can do even better when handicapped - he needs one more run. *(op 80-1)*

Mystery Lot(IRE), an 80-rated ten-furlong winner on the Flat, looked a potentially decent recruit to hurdling but finished up well held on her debut. She really should do better. *(op 10-3 tchd 7-2 in a place)*

Najca De Thaix(FR) failed to build on the promise he showed when fourth at Leicester last time, but needed this run for a handicap mark and could do better. *(op 13-2)*

Equilibria(USA) probably ran about as well as could have been expected in a Grade One at Chepstow on his previous start, but this was disappointing. *(tchd 5-1)*

Flamand(FR) *Official explanation: jockey said gelding was unsuited by the soft (heavy in places) ground (op 40-1)*

Haloo Baloo *Official explanation: jockey said gelding never travelled (op 16-1)*

3423 SKY BET PRESS RED TO BET ON ATR NOVICES' HURDLE (DIV II) (9 hdls) 2m

1:30 (1:30) (Class 4) 4-Y-0+ **£4,228** (£1,241; £620; £310)

Form RPR

1 **Temoin**[80] 6-11-4 .... MickFitzgerald 108+
(N J Henderson) *nrly ref 1st: w ldr: mstke 6th: jnd new ldr after 3 out: rn green after next: drvn to ld flat: styd on wl* **1/1**[1]

0 **2** *2 1/2* **Glimmer Of Light (IRE)**[16] 3133 6-11-4 .... RobertThornton 101
(A King) *racd on inner: trckd ldrs: slipped through on inner to ld after 3 out: sn jnd: hdd and one pce after last* **8/1**[3]

0020 **3** *11* **Flash Cummins (IRE)**[11] 3248 6-11-4 .... TimmyMurphy 92+
(M C Pipe) *led at stdy pce: hdd after 3 out: nudged along and outpcd by first pair: reminder after last and styd on: can do bttr* **9/1**

U04 **4** *1 1/4* **Inn For The Dancer**[25] 2949 4-10-7 .... JimCrowley 78
(Mrs H Dalton) *hld up in rr but wl in tch: prog on outer 3 out: outpcd after 3 out and reminder: r.o again flat: do bttr* **12/1**

04 **5** *1 3/4* **Clare Galway**[9] 3281 5-10-6 .... JohnnyLevins[(5)] 80
(B G Powell) *trckd ldrs: hit 4th: outpcd after 3 out: bmpd along and one pce fr 2 out* **16/1**

0 **6** *1 1/4* **Sapient**[3] 3369 5-10-11 .... MrJMahot[(7)] 86
(M Scudamore) *hld up in rr: wl in tch 6th: rdn bef 3 out: sn outpcd* **40/1**

00/ **7** *13* **Dirty Sanchez**[1282] 725 8-11-1 .... ColinBolger[(3)] 73
(Miss A M Newton-Smith) *t.k.h: wl in ntouch tl wknd after 3 out* **66/1**

0-0P **8** *dist* **Can Can Flyer (IRE)**[236] 504 5-11-1 .... TomMalone[(3)] —
(J C Tuck) *t.k.h: hld up: mstke 2nd: lost tch 5th: wknd after next: t.o* **40/1**

0-0 **P** **Confluence (IRE)**[55] 2421 5-11-4 .... APMcCoy —
(Jonjo O'Neill) *hld up: prog whn pckd 6th: wl in tch whn stmbld 3 out and broke down: p.u* **10/3**[2]

4m 27.7s (26.50) **Going Correction** +0.95s/f (Soft) 9 Ran SP% **114.1**
WFA 4 from 5yo+ 11lb
Speed ratings: **71,69,64,63,62 62,55,—,—** CSF £9.84 TOTE £1.60: £1.20, £1.40, £1.90; EX 9.70.

Owner The Unemployables **Bred** Bloomsbury Stud **Trained** Upper Lambourn, Berks

FOCUS

The bare form of this novice hurdle is nothing special, but there was still much more strength in deoth than in the first division. They went a steady pace and the winning time was slow, over 16 seconds slower than the first division.

NOTEBOOK

Temoin, three times a winner at up to a mile five on the Flat in France, proved good enough to make a winning debut over hurdles. Never too far away, he showed signs of inexperience when put under pressure, and looked as though he might have to settle for second, but he responded well and was nicely on top at the line. He has a fair way to go to get competitive in a significantly higher grade, but looks up to defying a penalty in the meantime. *(op 11-8 tchd 6-4 in places)*

Glimmer Of Light(IRE), a 67-rated mile winner on the Flat, stepped up on the form he showed on his hurdling debut and ensured the favourite had a proper race. With more improvement possible, he looks up to winning a similar event. *(op 13-2)*

Flash Cummins(IRE) looked likely to drop right out when seriously challenged, but he responded well enough to pressure to keep on for third and can probably do a fair bit better when stepped back up in trip. *(op 11-2)*

Inn For The Dancer offered some promise in fourth and could do better over further. *Official explanation: jockey said gelding made a noise (op 16-1)*

Clare Galway has yet to really prove her stamina for hurdling and better ground may suit. *(op 20-1)*

Can Can Flyer(IRE) *Official explanation: jockey said gelding was unsuited by the soft (heavy in places) ground (tchd 33-1)*

Confluence(IRE) was not out of it when stumbling and sadly breaking down three from home. *(op 3-1 tchd 7-2)*

3424 PLAY MONOPOLY @ SKYBETVEGAS.COM NOVICES' H'CAP HURDLE (14 hdls) 3m 1f 110y

2:00 (2:01) (Class 4) (0-105,96) 4-Y-0+ **£3,253** (£955; £477; £238)

Form RPR

-366 **1** **Strolling Vagabond (IRE)**[50] 2517 7-10-2 **72** .... JamieGoldstein 77+
(John R Upson) *wl in tch: rdn to chse ldr 4 out: led sn after next: drvn and kpt on fr 2 out* **4/1**[2]

0614 **2** *2* **English Jim (IRE)**[41] 2687 5-10-9 **79** .... MatthewBatchelor 80+
(Miss A M Newton-Smith) *hld up in rr: pushed along 9th: prog after next: chsd wnr sn after 3 out: hld whn mstke last: kpt on* **9/2**[3]

3-22 **3** *23* **Finzi (IRE)**[43] 2662 8-11-0 **91** .... JohnKington[(7)] 68
(M Scudamore) *led to 4th: chsd ldr to 4 out: sn outpcd u.p: plugged on to take modest 3rd bef last* **7/2**[1]

4000 **4** *11* **Denarius Secundus**[14] 3211 9-9-7 **70** oh2 .... (b) KeiranBurke[(7)] 36
(N R Mitchell) *t.k.h: w ldr: led 4th: drew 4 l clr 4 out: hdd & wknd sn after 3 out* **16/1**

P-05 **5** *11* **Lyrical Lily**[17] 3131 8-10-4 **74** .... OllieMcPhail 29
(B J Llewellyn) *in tch: blnd bdly 9th: sn bhd: wl t.o 4 out: j. bdly rt 2 out: r.o after* **28/1**

06P0 **6** *2 1/2* **Alderbrook Girl (IRE)**[15] 3184 6-10-12 **85** .... (p) ColinBolger[(3)] 38
(R Curtis) *in touh: reminders after 7th: struggling after 10th: wknd 3 out* **25/1**

0-00 **7** *8* **Optimo (GER)**[35] 2799 5-10-0 **70** oh2 .... (p) JamieMoore 15
(G L Moore) *prom: drvn fr 9th: steadily wknd fr 4 out* **8/1**

30-P **P** **Ockley Flyer**[27] 2934 7-10-3 **78** .... (p) RobertLucey-Butler[(5)] —
(Miss Z C Davison) *wl in tch: rdn 8th: wknd after next: t.o whn p.u bef 4 out* **33/1**

4514 **P** **Ballyhoo (IRE)**[27] 2932 6-11-5 **96** .... WayneKavanagh[(7)] —
(J W Mullins) *hld up in tch: rdn 9th: struggling 4 out: wkng whn mstke 3 out: p.u bef next* **10/1**

6P03 **P** **Mooresini (IRE)**[10] 3279 6-11-6 **90** .... (p) JamesDavies —
(N J Gifford) *in tch in rr: rdn after 9th: sn struggling: wknd 4 out: wl bhd whn p.u bef 2 out* **7/2**[1]

7m 1.30s (25.40) **Going Correction** +0.95s/f (Soft) 10 Ran SP% **118.9**
Speed ratings: **98,97,90,86,83 82,80,—,—,—** CSF £22.83 CT £69.88 TOTE £6.50: £2.40, £1.80, £1.50; EX 35.70.

Owner Jim Bath **Bred** Mrs A Mansfield **Trained** Maidford, Northants

FOCUS

A very moderate handicap hurdle, and it prove quite a test.

NOTEBOOK

Strolling Vagabond(IRE), back down to the lowest mark he has ever raced off, responded gamely to pressure and basically saw this stamina test out best to get off the mark at the tenth attempt. He will still be at the right end of the handicap when reassessed. *(op 6-1)*

English Jim(IRE), stepped up to his furthest trip to date, stayed every yard and was only just held. Although he will go up in the weights for not winning, he is in fine form and is one to keep on the right side of in similar events. *(tchd 5-1)*

Finzi(IRE)'s only previous win came over fences and, returned to hurdles, he was just a moderate third. *(op 3-1)*

Denarius Secundus, with headgear fitted for the first time over hurdles (he has worn them on the Flat), did not run that badly but remains a maiden under all codes.

Lyrical Lily, upped to her furthest trip to date, never threatened. *(op 25-1 tchd 33-1)*

Mooresini(IRE), upped significantly in trip, failed to confirm the promise he showed when third *over just short of two and a half miles at Towcester on his previous start. Official explanation: trainer had no explanation for the poor form shown (op 6-1)*

3425 EBF PLAY ELVIS 5 REEL SLOTS - PRESS RED CH272 "NATIONAL HUNT" NOVICES' HURDLE (QUALIFIER) (12 hdls) 2m 5f

2:30 (2:30) (Class 3) 4-7-Y-0 **£5,204** (£1,528; £764; £381)

Form RPR

20- **1** **Dunsfold Duke**[299] 4519 6-11-5 .... PhilipHide 116+
(P Winkworth) *racd wd: cl up: mstke 4th and nt fluent next: effrt to join ldr after 3 out: led 2 out: sn clr: easily* **8/1**[3]

2 *12* **Rare Gold (IRE)**[57] 6-11-5 .... AndrewThornton 104+
(R H Alner) *hld up wl in tch: effrt and hit 3 out: chsd ldng pair sn after : kpt on to take 2nd last: no ch w wnr* **9/1**

2-43 **3** *6* **Butler's Cabin (FR)**[21] 2983 6-11-5 .... APMcCoy 95+
(Jonjo O'Neill) *cl up: led 3 out: sn jnd: hdd 2 out: wknd and lost 2nd last* **3/1**[1]

54-0 **4** *10* **Sharajan (IRE)**[20] 3023 6-11-5 .... RobertThornton 84
(A King) *hld up in rr but wl in tch: prog 9th: cl up gng wl 3 out: sn rdn and fnd nil* **13/2**[2]

0P-3 **5** *11* **Chamacco (FR)**[27] 2928 6-10-12 .... CharliePoste(7) 73
(M F Harris) *hld up in rr but wl in tch: stl cl up 3 out: rdn and wknd bef next* **16/1**

6P6F **6** *6* **Pitton Prince**[41] 2683 7-10-12 .... MrDavidTurner(7) 67
(N R Mitchell) *led: set stdy pce to 8th: hdd 3 out: wknd bef next* **66/1**

5-06 **7** *29* **Lannigans Lock**[34] 2803 5-11-5 .... BrianCrowley 38
(R Rowe) *hld up wl in rr: lost tch 8th: t.o next: plugged on again fr 2 out* **9/1**

10-4 **8** *3 1/2* **Best Actor (IRE)**[51] 2507 7-11-5 .... MickFitzgerald 35
(M Pitman) *prom: lost pl 9th: brief rally bef 3 out: sn wknd and eased: t.o* **3/1**[1]

12 **9** *12* **Pan The Man (IRE)**[57] 2376 5-10-12 .... WayneKavanagh(7) 23
(J W Mullins) *t.k.h: cl up: mstke 8th: wknd rapidly after next: t.o* **8/1**[3]

P **10** *4* **Tigu (IRE)**[31] 2865 5-11-5 .... ChristianWilliams 19
(A Ennis) *in tch to 8th: sn struggling: t.o fr next* **100/1**

0/ **P** **Catfish Hunter**[670] 4407 6-10-12 .... MarcGoldstein(7) —
(Mrs L P Baker) *bhd fr 4th: wl t.o whn p.u bef 8th* **100/1**

P **Redneck Girl (IRE)**[365] 7-10-7 .... DerekLaverty(5) —
(A E Jones) *t.k.h early: in tch tl wknd 8th: t.o next: p.u bef 2 out* **40/1**

P0 **P** **Good Sort (IRE)**[27] 2928 6-10-12 .... CharlieStudd(7) —
(B G Powell) *mostly chsd ldr to 9th: wknd v rapidly 3 out: t.o whn p.u bef last* **33/1**

5m 43.6s (18.80) **Going Correction** +0.95s/f (Soft) **13** Ran SP% **120.3**
Speed ratings: **102,97,95,91,87 84,73,72,67,66** —,—,— CSF £76.73 TOTE £8.10: £1.90, £3.20, £1.50; EX 48.50.
Owner P Winkworth **Bred** Peter Winkworth **Trained** Ramsnest Common, Surrey

FOCUS
Not a great deal of strength in depth for this novice hurdle, but a decent effort from the highly-promising Dunsfold Duke, who was chased home by another reasonable sort.

NOTEBOOK
Dunsfold Duke ◆, second on his debut in a Sandown bumper but down the field when favourite at Chepstow on his next start, was always going to be suited by jumping obstacles and, returning from a 299-day break, ran out a pretty impressive winner. A big, imposing sort, his long-term future could well be over fences, but there is plenty more for him to achieve over hurdles in the meantime. *(op 15-2)*
Rare Gold(IRE), a three-mile point-to-point winner in Ireland, made a pleasing debut under Rules behind the promising winner and should make his mark before going chasing. *(op 8-1)*
Butler's Cabin(FR), third on his hurdling debut over two miles at Towcester, ran creditably in third but was stepping up significantly in trip and was beaten by two potentially stout stayers. *(tchd 11-4 and 10-3 in places)*
Sharajan(IRE) did not really progress from what was quite a promising debut over hurdles at Chepstow. He needs one more run for a handicap mark and may do better in time. *(tchd 7-1)*
Chamacco(FR) failed to build on the promise he showed at Fontwell on his previous start and may not have been suited by the testing conditions. *(tchd 20-1)*
Best Actor(IRE) showed a fair level of form when winning on his debut in a bumper, but disappointed next time and was again below form on his reappearance. Switched to hurdles and stepped up in trip, he proved pretty disappointing and has something to prove now, but better ground could well suit. *(tchd 7-2 and 4-1 in a place)*

3426 FREE CASINO CHIPS @ SKYBETVEGAS.COM NOVICES' H'CAP CHASE (13 fncs 1 omitted) 2m 4f
3:00 (3:01) (Class 4) (0-110,109) 5-Y-0+ **£5,079** (£1,549; £809; £439)

Form RPR

-205 **1** **Elfkirk (IRE)**[35] 2798 7-11-12 **109** .... BenjaminHitchcott 118+
(R H Buckler) *trckd ldr: mstke 9th: led next: clr 2 out: drvn out* **8/1**

33-U **2** *5* **The Outlier (IRE)**[32] 2839 8-11-10 **107** .... AlanO'Keeffe 110
(Miss Venetia Williams) *t.k.h: hld up in rr: prog 9th: chsd wnr 4 out: cl up after next: rdn and btn bef 2 out* **15/2**

04-U **3** *dist* **Twenty Degrees**[16] 3134 8-11-3 **100** ....(b) JamieMoore 65
(G L Moore) *chsd ldrs: rdn whn blnd 10th: btn after: mstke 4 out: wnt poor 3rd and j.lft 2 out* **16/1**

5-P4 **4** *3/4* **Vanormix (FR)**[21] 2989 7-10-10 **100** ....(v) BernieWharfe(7) 64
(C J Gray) *chsd ldrs: rdn and wknd bef 4 out: t.o: jst hld for remote 3rd flat* **14/1**

F **Georges Boy (IRE)**[254] 224 8-10-11 **97** .... GinoCarenza(3) —
(P J Jones) *in tch in rr tl fell 8th* **9/1**

F **Rosamio (IRE)**[16] 3162 10-10-0 **83** oh1 .... JamesDavies —
(R Donohoe, Ire) *led: narrowly hdd and rdn whn fell 10th* **6/1**[3]

-500 **P** **Good Call (IRE)**[35] 2799 7-11-3 **100** .... APMcCoy —
(Jonjo O'Neill) *nt a fluent: in tch to 8th: wknd rapidly: p.u after next* **20/1**

043 **P** **Megapac (IRE)**[12] 3243 8-10-10 **96** .... WilliamKennedy(3) —
(Noel T Chance) *in tch in rr: tried to demolish 8th and hmpd sn after: wknd: t.o whn p.u after 10th* **5/2**[1]

3-40 **U** **Le Rochelais (FR)**[31] 2868 7-11-8 **105** .... AndrewThornton 70
(R H Alner) *cl up: lft 2nd at 10th: lost pl next: wkng and disputing poor 3rd whn bmpd and uns rdr 2 out* **3/1**[2]

5m 28.2s (9.75) **Going Correction** +0.60s/f (Soft) **9** Ran SP% **118.0**
Speed ratings: **104,102**,—,—,— —,—,—,— CSF £67.22 CT £945.78 TOTE £11.90: £3.30, £1.90, £6.20; EX 81.80.
Owner Mrs D A La Trobe **Bred** Mrs Teresa Thornton **Trained** Melplash, Dorset

FOCUS
A modest handicap chase for novices, and with several of the principals failing to complete, the front two came home alone. The last fence was bypassed on the final circuit.

NOTEBOOK
Elfkirk(IRE) would have found this easier than the novice chase she contested over slightly shorter here last time and gained deserved compensation for an unfortunate incident at Folkestone two starts previously - she had the race won but crashed through the wing of the final fence due to her dislike of going right-handed. A rise in the weights will make things tougher, though. *(op 10-1)*
The Outlier(IRE) soon unseated when favourite for his debut over fences in a maiden at Catterick, but he got round this time and ensured the reasonably-handicapped winner had to be kept up to her work. He looks up to finding a similar race. *(op 7-1 tchd 6-1)*
Twenty Degrees, with the blinkers back on having unseated on his chasing debut, was beaten a long way into third and will need to step up considerable on this form. *(op 12-1)*
Vanormix(FR), back up in trip, looked to have a realistic enough chance but never posed a serious threat and is hard to win with. *(op 12-1)*
Rosamio(IRE), an Irish raider making her chasing debut on her first start in this country, was still in with a chance when falling. *(op 7-2 tchd 4-1)*
Le Rochelais(FR), a maiden over hurdles, was well beaten when unseating. *(op 7-2 tchd 4-1)*
Megapac(IRE) shaped well enough on his chasing debut at Wincanton, but hit the eighth and was hampered on landing. He can do better. *(op 7-2 tchd 4-1)*

3427 YOU'RE EITHER VEGAS OR YOU'RE NOT H'CAP CHASE (15 fncs 3 omitted) 3m 2f
3:30 (3:31) (Class 5) (0-90,88) 5-Y-0+
£3,131 (£925; £462; £231; £115; £58)

Form RPR

3-45 **1** **Tallow Bay (IRE)**[14] 3221 11-9-7 **62** oh2 .... MrGTumelty(7) 82+
(Mrs S Wall) *prom: pressed ldr bef 12th: shkn up to ld bef last and sn in command: rdn out* **10/1**

512P **2** *9* **Ebony Jack (IRE)**[17] 3129 9-11-1 **77** ....(p) JoeTizzard 87+
(C L Tizzard) *led to 8th: led again 11th: sn rdn: hdd bef last: tired and wl btn last 150yds* **4/1**[1]

1342 **3** *8* **Five Alley (IRE)**[21] 2986 9-11-12 **88** .... BenjaminHitchcott 91+
(R H Buckler) *in tch: pushed along fr 6th: prog to chse ldrs 10th: sn outpcd u.p: kpt on to take 3rd bef last: nrst fin* **4/1**[1]

45-5 **4** *7* **Dr Mann (IRE)**[16] 3146 8-11-6 **82** .... MarcusFoley 76
(Miss Tor Sturgis) *hld up in rr: prog to chse clr ldng pair 12th: no imp: lost 3rd bef last* **12/1**

0-65 **5** *17* **River Of Light (IRE)**[15] 3184 6-11-3 **84** .... DarylJacob(5) 61
(D P Keane) *settled towards rr: rdn after 10th: effrt 12th but sn no imp on ldrs: wl btn after* **16/1**

1235 **6** *1/2* **Anflora**[31] 2863 9-10-13 **75** .... ChristianWilliams 52
(B J Llewellyn) *in tch: outpcd fr 11th: wl btn after next* **13/2**[3]

P-PP **7** *28* **Red Alert Man (IRE)**[21] 2957 10-10-1 **68** ....(b) DerekLaverty(5) 17
(Mrs L Williamson) *prom: mstke 7th: u.p and wkng 9th: t.o* **50/1**

3P0F **F** **Murphy's Magic (IRE)**[21] 2986 8-11-6 **82** ....(b) RobertThornton —
(Mrs T J Hill) *in tch: fell 2nd* **66/1**

1-3P **P** **Just Anvil (IRE)**[21] 2986 8-11-0 **83** .... JustinMorgan(7) —
(L Wells) *pressed ldr: led 8th to 11th: sn btn u.p: mstke 3 out: wl bhd whn p.u bef last* **10/1**

2P/3 **P** **Roddy The Vet (IRE)**[21] 2966 8-11-3 **79** .... JimCrowley —
(A Ennis) *hld up in last: rdn and brief effrt after 10th: sn wknd: t.o whn p.u bef 12th* **9/1**

00-P **P** **Gathering Storm (IRE)**[21] 2957 8-11-0 **76** .... AndrewThornton —
(P R Hedger) *reluctant to line up: prom to 5th: sn lost pl and in rr: wkng in last whn p.u bef 11th* **25/1**

R44U **R** **Hill Forts Henry**[21] 2986 8-9-8 **63** ....(vt[1]) WayneKavanagh(7) —
(J W Mullins) *nt keen: j. slowly 6th and urged along: wknd 10th: t.o whn nrly ref 12th and next: ref 2 out* **6/1**[2]

7m 25.6s (31.60) **Going Correction** +0.775s/f (Soft) **12** Ran SP% **116.7**
Speed ratings: **82,79,76,74,69 69,60**,—,—,— —,— CSF £49.96 CT £190.23 TOTE £8.60: £3.30, £2.10, £2.30; EX 79.70.
Owner Mrs S Wall **Bred** Mrs S P H Oliver **Trained** Dallington, E Sussex

FOCUS
A pretty moderate handicap chase and they finish well strung out. The winning time was very slow indeed, even allowing for the conditions. Last fence omitted on each circuit.

NOTEBOOK
Tallow Bay(IRE) had gone three years without a win, and was racing from 2lb out of the handicap, but the testing conditions suited ideally and he responded well to a determined ride from his amateur to end that losing run. He could hardly have been any lower in the weights, so will not exactly look badly handicapped when reassesed, and could continue to go well when faced with similar conditions. *(op 9-1)*
Ebony Jack(IRE) returned to form having been pulled up at Plumpton on his previous start, and found only one too good under a positive ride. Both his point win, and his only success to date under Rules came on good ground, but these conditions did not seem to pose a problem. *(op 7-2 tchd 9-2 in a place)*
Five Alley(IRE) looked to have everything in his favour, but made hard work of it and never threatened the front two when it mattered.
Dr Mann(IRE), an Irish point winner who failed to make the frame in four runs over hurdles, made a respectable enough debut over fences without picking up sufficiently to throw down a serious challenge. *(op 14-1)*
River Of Light(IRE), well beaten in three runs over hurdles, offered some hope on his debut over fences but will clearly need to improve. *(op 14-1)*
Roddy The Vet(IRE) *Official explanation: jockey said gelding was unsuited by the soft (heavy in places) ground (op 15-2)*
Hill Forts Henry did not appear to be on a going day. *(op 15-2)*

3428 PLAY ROULETTE & BLACKJACK @ SKYBETVEGAS.COM H'CAP HURDLE (12 hdls) 2m 5f
4:00 (4:00) (Class 4) (0-115,115) 4-Y-0+ **£4,554** (£1,337; £668; £333)

Form RPR

32-2 **1** **Brankley Boy**[34] 2815 8-11-12 **115** .... MickFitzgerald 116+
(N J Henderson) *hld up in tch: prog to trck ldr bef 3 out: led narrowly 2 out: drvn out flat* **1/1**[1]

-266 **2** *3 1/2* **Eljutan (IRE)**[41] 2685 8-10-2 **98** .... ShaneWalsh(7) 94
(J Joseph) *in tch: rdn after 8th and struggling: rallied 3 out: styd on to take 2nd flat: nt rch wnr* **33/1**

63-5 **3** *1* **At The Double**[254] 218 10-10-1 **90** ....(b) PhilipHide 86+
(P Winkworth) *pressed ldr: led 4th: mde rest tl narrowly hdd 2 out: wknd last* **16/1**

1501 **4** *dist* **Come Bye (IRE)**[9] 3286 10-11-12 **115** ....(bt) MatthewBatchelor 81
(Miss A M Newton-Smith) *led tl nt fluent and hdd 4th: chsd ldr to bef 3 out: wkng whn blnd 2 out: btn 40 l* **10/1**

26P0 **5** *26* **Jaloux D'Estruval (FR)**[9] 3289 9-11-10 **113** .... AndrewThornton 74
(Mrs L C Taylor) *cl up: rdn bef 9th: wknd 3 out: eased: t.o: btn 66 l* **6/1**[3]

6UPP **P** **Geography (IRE)**[41] 2687 6-9-9 **89** oh6 ....(v) RobertLucey-Butler(5) —
(P Butler) *racd on inner: lost tch fr 6th: t.o whn p.u bef 9th* **50/1**

0-6P **P** **Midnight Gold**[86] 1833 6-10-11 **100** .... RobertThornton —
(A King) *racd on inner: mstke 3rd: in tch to 8th: wknd next: t.o whn p.u bef 2 out* **5/2**[2]

5m 40.7s (15.90) **Going Correction** +0.95s/f (Soft) **7** Ran SP% **112.7**
Speed ratings: **107,105,105**,—,— —,— CSF £27.31 TOTE £2.30: £2.10, £14.70; EX 44.80 Place 6 £123.72, Place 5 £33.33.
Owner Gary Stewart **Bred** C D Harrison **Trained** Upper Lambourn, Berks

FOCUS
The majority of the runners took a wide route throughout and the pair that stayed on the inside were both pulled up. Despite the deteriorating ground, the winning time was almost three seconds faster than the novice hurdle.

NOTEBOOK
Brankley Boy, down in trip and making his handicap debut, was given a patient ride before moving up on the final circuit. He did not seem to be travelling quite as well as the leader starting up the home straight but his stamina came to his aid and he was well on top at the line. Despite his age he does still have a bit of scope. *(tchd 5-4 in a place and 11-10 in places)*
Eljutan(IRE) ran with a deal of credit on ground much softer than ideal. Stamina did not seem to be a problem and a modest handicap can come his way on better ground. *(op 25-1)*

At The Double, a winner over course and distance and proven in this ground, was returning from an eight-month break. Given a positive ride, he still seemed to be travelling best of the leaders coming to the second last, but lack of a recent run then appeared to take its toll.
Come Bye(IRE), raised 5lb for his recent Fontwell victory, was never given an easy lead and that almost certainly contributed to his rapid capitulation. *(op 8-1)*
Jaloux D'Estruval(FR) ran poorly on ground that should have suited and now has questions to answer. *(op 13-2)*
Midnight Gold was kept towards the inside of the track which may not have been ideal as things turned out, but this was the second successive time he has failed to complete and perhaps he *does not want the ground as testing as this. Official explanation: jockey said gelding was unsuited by the soft (heavy in places) ground (op 4-1)*
T/Jkpt: Not won. T/Plt: £47.00 to a £1 stake. Pool: £48,877.10. 757.55 winning tickets. T/Qpdt: £19.90 to a £1 stake. Pool: £3,843.70. 142.90 winning tickets. JN

3217 FOLKESTONE (R-H)

Tuesday, January 17

OFFICIAL GOING: Hurdle course - heavy; chase course - soft
Wind: Light, across Weather: Overcast with drizzle

3429 JOHN DEXTER 40TH BIRTHDAY JUVENILE MAIDEN HURDLE (DIV I) (9 hdls) 2m 1f 110y

1:00 (1:00) (Class 4) 4-Y-O **£2,927** (£859; £429; £214)

Form | | | | RPR

1 **Dear Villez (FR)**[233] 583 4-11-2 ... RWalsh 120+
(P F Nicholls) *prom in chsng gp: trckd ldr after 3 out: clsd to chal between last 2: rdn to ld last: styd on* **10/11**[1]

0 **2** *5* **Grasp**[53] 2481 4-11-2 ...(bt[1]) JamieMoore 113+
(G L Moore) *trckd clr ldng pair: led 5th: kicked on 2 out: sn rdn: hdd last: no ex flat* **25/1**

2 **3** *11* **Slew Charm (FR)**[16] 3182 4-11-2 ... TomDoyle 103+
(Noel T Chance) *in tch in chsng gp: prog to chse ldng pair bef 2 out: rdn and grad lost tch on long run to last* **13/2**[3]

4 *dist* **Shamayoun (FR)**[84] 4-11-2 ... APMcCoy 63
(C R Egerton) *j.lft 1st: hld up in tch: prog to chse ldng trio bef 2 out: sn rdn and btn: wknd bef last: btn 50 l* **5/2**[2]

0 **5** *5* **Beauchamp Twist**[17] 3132 4-10-9 ... MatthewBatchelor 46
(M R Hoad) *hld up in last trio: sme prog 5th: nt on terms w ldrs bef 2 out: grad wknd: btn 55 l* **100/1**

0 **6** *3 ½* **Hereditary**[10] 3294 4-11-2 ... JohnMcNamara —
(Mrs L C Jewell) *stdd s: hld up in last pair: stdy prog 5th: nt on terms w ldrs after 3 out: steadily wknd: btn 59 l* **33/1**

7 *28* **Zolash (IRE)**[29] 4-11-2 ... BenjaminHitchcott —
(Mrs L C Jewell) *t.k.h: hld up in rr: wknd 3 out: t.o: btn 87 l* **100/1**

30 **8** *1 ½* **Willy The Slip**[16] 3182 4-11-2 ... RobertWalford —
(R H Alner) *chsd clr ldrs: j. slowly 4th and reminders: j. slowly 3 out and wknd: eased bef last: t.o: btn 89 l* **28/1**

B **9** *dist* **Son Of Bathwick (IRE)**[6] 3340 4-11-2 ... LeightonAspell —
(Mrs Norma Pook) *stdd s: t.k.h: hld up in last: wknd 3 out: t.o : btn 122 l* **100/1**

00 **10** *20* **Brave Hiawatha (FR)**[6] 3340 4-11-2 ... TimmyMurphy —
(J A B Old) *mstke 1st: chsd ldrs: lost pl 3rd: wknd 5th: t.o: btn 142 l* **33/1**

PP0 **P** **Goose Chase**[53] 2481 4-11-2 ...(b[1]) NoelFehily —
(C J Mann) *racd freely: led to 4th: wknd rapidly: t.o whn p.u bef 3 out* **50/1**

3355 **U** **Dusty Dane (IRE)**[47] 2597 4-10-6 99...(t) RichardGordon[(10)] —
(W G M Turner) *7th whn j. into bk of rival: slipped and uns rdr 2nd* **25/1**

U00P **P** **Ghabesh (USA)**[10] 3291 4-10-13 ... PaulO'Neill[(3)] —
(Evan Williams) *racd freely: chsd ldr: led 4th to 5th: wknd: tailing off whn p.u bef 2 out* **100/1**

4m 26.2s (-3.10) **Going Correction** +0.10s/f (Yiel) **13** Ran SP% **117.2**
Speed ratings: **110,107,102**,—,— —,—,—,—,— —,—,— CSF £30.10 TOTE £2.10: £1.30, £4.40, £1.10; EX 32.00.
Owner Mr and Mrs J D Cotton **Bred** Mme E Haye & Mlle Sandrine Gosfeild **Trained** Ditcheat, Somerset

FOCUS
Not a great deal of strength in depth in this juvenile maiden, but the front two appeared to put up good efforts and the winning time was decent, almost nine seconds faster than the second division.

NOTEBOOK
Dear Villez(FR) ◆, placed in a Listed hurdle in France, defied a 233-day break to make a successful British debut. Having travelled well for much of the way, he had to work harder than one might have expected to see off the eventual runner-up, but was ultimately well on top. There was plenty to like about this performance, not least the winning time, and there should be even better to come. *(op Evens tchd 11-10 in places)*
Grasp ◆, well held on his British debut at Newbury, stepped up significantly on that performance and clearly appreciated the testing ground. He gives the impression he can keep improving, especially as he steps up in trip, and looks one to follow. *(tchd 33-1)*
Slew Charm(FR) shaped well when second on his hurdling at Plumpton and gives this form a pretty solid look. He could find a similar race, but should find his level when handicapped. *(op 6-1)*
Shamayoun(FR), a winner at up to a mile six on the Flat in France, looked an interesting prospect, and appeared to have conditions to suit for his hurdling debut, but he was beaten a very long way. *(tchd 11-4)*

3430 EASTWELL MANOR H'CAP CHASE (15 fncs) 2m 5f

1:30 (1:30) (Class 5) (0-95,95) 5-Y-0+ **£3,578** (£1,050; £525; £262)

Form | | | | RPR

-046 **1** **Smeathe's Ridge**[17] 3146 8-10-11 80 ... MarkBradburne 93
(J A B Old) *chsd ldrs: effrt 10th: rdn to chse ldng pair after 3 out: styd on fr next: tk narrow ld and lft clr last: drvn out* **9/2**[1]

-40F **2** *3 ½* **Malko De Beaumont (FR)**[13] 3241 6-11-12 95 ... JohnMcNamara 105
(K C Bailey) *hld up in rr: stdy prog 10th: mstke 12th: chsd ldr after 3 out: no imp next and dropped to 3rd: lft 2nd again last: kpt on* **10/1**

1/P5 **4** *1* **Inaki (FR)**[16] 3187 9-11-9 92 ...(b) PhilipHide 83+
(P Winkworth) *nt fluent: in tch: 5th whn mstke 11th: effrt after 3 out and looked to be gng wl enough: sn btn: lft 3rd last: wknd* **7/1**[3]

-2FP **5** *dist* **Galapiat Du Mesnil (FR)**[28] 2931 12-11-7 90...(p) LeightonAspell —
(R Gurney) *prom: j.lft 7th: mstke next and sn wknd: t.o: btn 60 l* **20/1**

31P- **P** **Twotensforafive**[299] 4539 13-11-0 90 ... KeiranBurke[(7)] —
(P R Rodford) *a in rr: wknd after 6th: t.o whn p.u bef 11th* **33/1**

21/P **P** **Designer Label (IRE)**[10] 3285 10-11-10 93 ... PaulMoloney —
(M Pitman) *led to 8th: chsd ldr tl mstke 12th: wknd: poor 5th whn p.u bef last* **12/1**

00U0 **P** **Spanish Tan (NZ)**[22] 2991 6-11-7 90 ... APMcCoy —
(Jonjo O'Neill) *nt fluent: prom: mstke 10th: chsd ldr 12th: wknd and eased after 3 out: p.u bef next* **6/1**[2]

-43U **P** **Uncle Max (IRE)**[11] 3274 6-11-12 95 ... CarlLlewellyn —
(N A Twiston-Davies) *chsd ldrs: lost pl and rdn 9th: mstke next: sn wknd: wl bhd whn p.u bef 2 out* **6/1**[2]

P24 **P** **Minat Boy**[16] 3187 10-10-4 73 ... JoeTizzard —
(C L Tizzard) *nt jump wl: hld up: lost tch fr 8th: sn toiling: t.o whn clambered over 3 out: p.u bef next* **6/1**[2]

P603 **U** **Sett Aside**[17] 3134 8-10-4 73 ...(p) BenjaminHitchcott 82
(Mrs L C Jewell) *w ldr: led 8th: kicked on 3 out: 4 l clr 2 out: tired and jst hdd whn blnd and uns rdr last* **25/1**

5m 42.2s (17.80) **Going Correction** +0.925s/f (Soft) **11** Ran SP% **114.4**
Speed ratings: **103,101,94,94**,— —,—,—,—,— — CSF £45.76 CT £309.63 TOTE £6.80: £1.90, £1.90, £2.70; EX 113.10.
Owner Smeathes Ridge Partnership **Bred** David Knox **Trained** Barbury Castle, Wilts

FOCUS
A moderate handicap chase.

NOTEBOOK
Smeathe's Ridge, a moderate maiden over hurdles, improved for the switch to fences to gain his first career success at the ninth attempt. He probably would have won even if Sett Aside had not unseated at the last, but was still making hard work of it and is likely to do even better back over further. *(op 11-2)*
Malko De Beaumont(FR), held in fourth when falling on his chasing debut over three miles one at Wincanton, got round this time and ran with promise in second. He should continue to go the right way and may do even better back over further. *(tchd 11-1)*
Spider Boy is still a maiden and was not seriously involved in the finish.
Inaki(FR) has yet to recapture his best form since returning from a long absence, but this was a step in the right direction. *(op 9-1)*
Minat Boy, just as when fourth at Plumpton on his previous start, did not jump well enough and needs to improve in that department. *(op 5-1)*
Uncle Max(IRE) might have gone close had he not unseated at Towcester on his previous start, but this was a poor effort and something could have been amiss. *(op 5-1)*
Sett Aside, had not shown a great deal on his previous starts under Rules but, with cheekpieces on for the first time, this was much better. He was in front when unseating at the last and clearly running a massive race, although it looked as though he might just have been about to give way. *(op 5-1)*
Spanish Tan(NZ), very limited over hurdles, ran no sort of race upped significantly in trip on his chasing debut. *Official explanation: vet said gelding was lame on the right fore (op 5-1)*

3431 JOHN DEXTER 40TH BIRTHDAY JUVENILE MAIDEN HURDLE (DIV II) (9 hdls) 2m 1f 110y

2:00 (2:00) (Class 4) 4-Y-O **£2,927** (£859; £429; £214)

Form | | | | RPR

35 **1** **Sole Agent (IRE)**[16] 3182 4-11-2 ... PhilipHide 112+
(G L Moore) *w ldr tl hit 3rd: styd chsng tl led 2 out: pressed between fnl 2: drew clr bef last: 10 l up flat: eased* **12/1**

P **2** *3* **Spear Thistle**[6] 3340 4-11-2 ... MarcusFoley 105+
(Mrs N Smith) *trckd ldrs: nt fluent 2 out: effrt to chal between fnl 2: sn outpcd: wnt 2nd and blnd last: no ch w wnr* **8/1**[3]

33 **3** *3 ½* **Original Fly (FR)**[17] 3132 4-11-2 ... RWalsh 100+
(P F Nicholls) *prom: chsd wnr after 2 out and sn clsd to chal: btn and lost 2nd last* **6/5**[1]

4 *22* **Backbord (GER)**[79] 4-11-2 ... LeightonAspell 84+
(Mrs L Wadham) *trckd ldrs: cl enough in 4th 2 out: sn wknd* **9/4**[2]

450 **5** *30* **Just Beware**[19] 2101 4-10-4 ...(p) RobertLucey-Butler[(5)] 40
(Miss Z C Davison) *last and rdn 3rd: struggling after: plugged on fr 2 out to snatch remote 5th nr fin* **100/1**

0 **6** *1* **Love Beauty (USA)**[10] 3294 4-11-2 ... SamStronge 46
(M F Harris) *racd wd: mde most: drew clr and mstke 4th: hdd 2 out: wknd rapidly* **50/1**

P **7** *¾* **Akram (IRE)**[6] 3340 4-11-2 ... APMcCoy 45
(Jonjo O'Neill) *hld up in rr: sme prog after 3 out: tried to cl 2 out: sn no imp: wknd and eased* **16/1**

P **Edith Bankes**[428] 4-9-13 ... RichardGordon[(10)] —
(W G M Turner) *j. bdly: rdn in last pair 3rd: t.o whn p.u bef 3 out* **100/1**

00 **P** **Top Man Tee**[26] 2949 4-11-2 ... PaulMoloney —
(D J Daly) *in tch in rr to 5th: sn wknd and t.o: 11th whn p.u bef last* **100/1**

05 **U** **Halcyon Express (IRE)**[70] 2101 4-10-9 ...(t) CharlieStudd[(7)] —
(Mary Meek) *prom: rdn and losing pl whn uns rdr sme way after 4th* **100/1**

60 **P** **Fixateur**[21] 3038 4-11-2 ... NoelFehily —
(C C Bealby) *mstke 2nd: struggling in rr fr 4th: t.o 3 out: 10th whn p.u bef last* **25/1**

6 **P** **Tancredi (SWE)**[26] 2949 4-10-13 ... OwynNelmes[(3)] —
(N B King) *hld up towards rr: sme prog and in tch 3 out: sn wknd: t.o in 8th whn p.u bef last* **100/1**

0332 **P** **Lord Of Adventure (IRE)**[17] 3137 4-11-2 103 ... TimmyMurphy —
(Mrs L C Jewell) *in tch to 5th: wkng whn mstke 2 out: t.o in 9th whn p.u bef last* **9/1**

4m 35.1s (5.80) **Going Correction** +0.10s/f (Yiel) **13** Ran SP% **121.7**
Speed ratings: **91,89,88,78,65 64,64**,—,—,— —,—,— CSF £103.94 TOTE £8.60: £2.00, £2.50, £1.20; EX 108.50.
Owner B & J Crainey **Bred** J Costello **Trained** Woodingdean, E Sussex

FOCUS
Probably just a modest maiden hurdle, and possibly not as strong as the first division. The time was moderate for the grade, almost nine seconds slower than the first division though the winner could have won by further..

NOTEBOOK
Sole Agent(IRE) stepped up on the form he showed on his two previous starts over hurdles at the third attempt and was probably value for around double the winning margin. Clearly now progressing, he must have every chance of defying a penalty. *(op 16-1)*
Spear Thistle ◆ was pulled up on his hurdling debut at Newbury, but a Flat rating of 86 suggested he was going to be capable of a fair bit better and this was promising. Although flattered by the margin of defeat given the winner was eased, he looks capable of going on again and finding a similar race at least. *(tchd 7-1)*
Original Fly(FR), just as on his three previous starts over hurdles (one in France, two in this country), found a couple too good. He will need to improve to find a similar race, but is now qualified for a handicap mark and could well be capable of better. *(op 5-4 tchd 6-4, 13-8 in a place)*
Backbord(GER), a winner on the Flat in France, Germany and Italy at up to a mile six, including in Listed company, proved disappointing on his hurdling debut and reportedly had a breathing problem. *For that reason, he is one to be cautious about. Official explanation: jockey said colt had a breathing problem (op 5-2)*
Just Beware will surely be better off in handicaps.
Top Man Tee *Official explanation: jockey said colt had a breathing problem (op 66-1)*

3432 HYTHE BAY FISH AND SEAFOOD RESTAURANT NOVICES' H'CAP CHASE (12 fncs) 2m

2:30 (2:30) (Class 4) (0-100,99) 5-Y-O+ **£4,228** (£1,241; £620; £310)

Form RPR

50-F **1** **Roznic (FR)**[32] 2867 8-11-9 **96**.......................... PhilipHide 108+
(P Winkworth) *sn trckd ldr: clsd to chal after 3 out: led bef last: sn in command: readily* **9/4**[1]

0F/P **2** *4* **Victory Roll**[34] 2827 10-11-11 **98**.......................... MarcusFoley 104+
(Miss E C Lavelle) *led: rdn and hdd bef last: sn outpcd and btn* **7/2**[3]

356P **3** *6* **Corrib Drift (USA)**[35] 2809 6-10-11 **87**.......................... ColinBolger(3) 86
(Jamie Poulton) *hld up: clsd on ldrs 8th: wl in tch bef 2 out: sn rdn and nt qckn* **6/1**

3144 **4** *20* **Before The Mast (IRE)**[3] 3395 9-10-12 **85**.......................... JohnMcNamara 69+
(M F Harris) *t.k.h: hld up: effrt 8th: rdn and wknd after 3 out* **11/4**[2]

5P-4 **5** *8* **Squeeze (IRE)**[247] 364 8-11-5 **99**.......................... TomMessenger(7) 70
(B N Pollock) *t.k.h: prom tl wknd 9th* **10/1**

PP5P **P** **Rutland (IRE)**[11] 3274 7-9-9 **73** oh7.......................... RobertLucey-Butler(5) —
(C J Drewe) *prom to 5th: sn struggling: t.o and mstkes fr 8th: p.u bef 2 out* **20/1**

4m 18.3s (11.50) **Going Correction** +0.925s/f (Soft) **6** Ran SP% **107.8**
Speed ratings: **108,106,103,93,89** — CSF £9.87 TOTE £3.00: £1.90, £2.30; EX 15.00.
Owner Etoile Racing **Bred** Francis Faure **Trained** Ramsnest Common, Surrey

FOCUS
A modest event and not much to go on, but the comfortable winner improved by 9lb on his hurdles form.

NOTEBOOK
Roznic(FR), who might well have finished second on his chasing debut had he produced a clear round, did this nicely. While he did not have much to beat, he looks to be on the upgrade. *(op 11-4 after 10-3 and 3-1 in places)*
Victory Roll, having only his second run since February 2004, made a brave bid to lead all the way but the winner was much too good for him from the final fence. *(op 11-4)*
Corrib Drift(USA) found this too sharp, but all told this was a fairly satisfactory chasing debut. *(op 7-1 tchd 8-1)*
Before The Mast(IRE), whose two hurdles wins came in sellers, was making his chasing debut. He travelled well enough but found little when brought under pressure. *(op 2-1)*
Squeeze(IRE) *Official explanation: vet said gelding finished lame (tchd 11-1)*

3433 WESTENHANGER (S) HURDLE (11 hdls) 2m 6f 110y

3:00 (3:00) (Class 5) 4-Y-O+ **£2,740** (£798; £399)

Form RPR

1-12 **1** **Graffiti Tongue (IRE)**[176] 1067 13-12-13 110.......................(p) APMcCoy 108+
(Evan Williams) *hld up in tch: prom fr 6th: mstke 8th: chsd ldr after 3 out: rdn to ld bef last: forged clr: 15 l up flat: eased* **9/4**[1]

-030 **2** *9* **Avanti Tiger (IRE)**[21] 3042 7-11-6 68.......................(b) NoelFehily 67
(C C Bealby) *trckd ldr: led 6th: clr whn hit 2 out: hdd & wknd bef last* **4/1**[2]

60P- **3** *20* **Lavenoak Lad**[395] 2895 6-10-13.......................(p) JamesWhite(7) 47
(P R Rodford) *cl up: trckd ldr after 6th: clattered through 3 out: sn rdn and outpcd: plugged on again flat* **100/1**

U004 **4** *4* **Peppershot**[10] 3283 6-11-6 85.......................(t) LeightonAspell 43
(R Gurney) *hld up: trckd ldrs fr 7th: rdn after 3 out and sn outpcd: struggled into 3rd bef last: wknd flat* **6/1**[3]

0233 **5** *2* **Barranco (IRE)**[8] 3321 5-11-6 87.......................(b) JamieMoore 41
(G L Moore) *hld up: chsd ldrs after 6th: u.p fr next: wl outpcd fr 2 out* **9/4**[1]

P **Bagwell Ben** 9-10-13.......................... MrsMRoberts(7) —
(M J Coombe) *nt jump wl: last fr 2nd: t.o after 6th: p.u bef 2 out* **66/1**

2P **P** **Somewhere My Love**[18] 2216 5-10-8.............(p) RobertLucey-Butler(5) —
(P Butler) *a wl in rr: wknd 6th: t.o whn p.u bef 8th* **25/1**

-000 **P** **Magic Red**[14] 2958 6-11-3 77.......................(b) ColinBolger(3) —
(J Ryan) *prom: drvn and wknd bef 7th: wl bhd 3 out: p.u bef last* **14/1**

500- **P** **Final Lap**[381] 3142 10-10-13 60.......................(p) MrJOwen(7) —
(H H G Owen) *prom tl wknd rapidly after 6th: sn t.o: p.u bef 2 out* **100/1**

F0P **P** **Charm Indeed**[26] 2950 6-11-3.......................... OwynNelmes(3) —
(N B King) *racd freely: led to 6th: wknd rapidly: t.o whn p.u after next* **50/1**

/60- **P** **Baileys Prize (USA)**[616] 294 9-10-13.......................... KeiranBurke(7) —
(P R Rodford) *prom: mstke 2nd: wknd rapidly after 6th: t.o whn p.u bef 8th* **12/1**

6m 19.1s (10.00) **Going Correction** +0.375s/f (Yiel) **11** Ran SP% **119.5**
Speed ratings: **97,93,86,85,84** —,—,—,—,— — CSF £11.81 TOTE £2.80: £1.20, £1.60, £9.20; EX 13.70.There was no bid for the winner.
Owner Patrick Heffernan **Bred** Mrs M Farrell **Trained** Cowbridge, Vale Of Glamorgan

FOCUS
An uncompetitive event and a stamina test, with the winner rated value for 20l.

NOTEBOOK
Graffiti Tongue(IRE), absent since July, was fit from hunting. He defied his huge weight in decisive style in the end, although he needed a fair amount of stoking up from McCoy with whom he has developed a good partnership. He has been largely campaigned on fast ground since joining Williams but handled this sort of ground in his Irish days. *(op 2-1 tchd 3-1)*
Avanti Tiger(IRE), back in more suitable grade, tried to steal a march at one stage but was no match for the veteran in the end. He can win a seller although he may not be the most reliable. *(op 7-2)*
Lavenoak Lad is a very modest performer indeed but at least the drop into the bottom grade enabled him to collect a little prize money. *(op 66-1)*
Peppershot, re-fitted with a tongue tie, was beaten in the back straight on the final circuit but did look like taking a remote third place at one stage. *(op 15-2 tchd 8-1)*
Barranco(IRE) came under pressure early on the final circuit and remains costly to follow. *(op 5-2 tchd 11-4)*

3434 HYTHE H'CAP CHASE (18 fncs) 3m 1f

3:30 (3:30) (Class 4) (0-110,105) 5-Y-O+ **£6,506** (£1,910; £955; £477)

Form RPR

-211 **1** **Presenting Express (IRE)**[18] 3129 7-11-6 **99**.......................... MarcusFoley 120+
(Miss E C Lavelle) *hld up in last pair: mstke 2nd: smooth prog 12th: led 15th and sn clr: breather after 3 out: shkn up and readily drew clr a* **7/4**[1]

/3P- **3** *1 1/2* **Hobbycyr (FR)**[612] 360 11-10-1 **87** ow4.......................... MrPMason(7) 94+
(J A T De Giles) *cl up: rdn 13th: struggling whn mstke 15th: rallied bef 2 out: tk 3rd last: one pce flat* **14/1**

-P25 **4** *3* **Gray's Eulogy**[22] 3000 8-11-3 **96**.......................(b) TomDoyle 100+
(D R Gandolfo) *cl up: mstke 13th: rdn after 3 out: one pce and wl hld fr next* **6/1**[2]

0214 **5** *1/2* **Tommy Carson**[80] 1920 11-11-2 **98**.......................... ColinBolger(3) 101+
(Jamie Poulton) *prom: disp ld fr 10th: drvn fr 12th: hdd and mstke 15th: fdd u.p fr 2 out* **16/1**

0-65 **6** *5* **Levallois (IRE)**[16] 3186 10-11-3 **96**.......................... PhilipHide 97+
(P Winkworth) *hld up in tch: effrt after 3 out to press ldrs: disp 2nd and btn 2 out: wknd* **8/1**

1P5P **P** **Our Jolly Swagman**[36] 2801 11-10-2 **88**...............(v) WayneKavanagh(7) —
(J W Mullins) *cl up: rdn 10th: wknd 12th: t.o whn p.u bef 15th* **20/1**

2-2P **P** **Majestic Moonbeam (IRE)**[36] 2800 8-11-8 **101**.......................... APMcCoy —
(Jonjo O'Neill) *prom: lost pl 11th: wkng whn blnd 13th: t.o whn p.u bef 15th* **8/1**

P/4F **P** **Predestine (FR)**[13] 3239 6-11-11 **104**.......................... JohnMcNamara —
(K C Bailey) *nt fluent: hld up in last: effrt 12th: wknd 15th: t.o whn p.u bef 2 out* **16/1**

-20P **P** **Meggie's Beau (IRE)**[52] 2502 10-11-7 **103**.......................... PaulO'Neill(3) —
(Miss Venetia Williams) *disp ld: mstke 13th: hdd 15th: wknd after next: wl btn in 7th whn p.u bef last* **13/2**[3]

6m 56.6s (23.20) **Going Correction** +0.925s/f (Soft) **10** Ran SP% **115.3**
Speed ratings: **99,97,96,95,95 94**,—,—,—,— CSF £29.16 CT £303.82 TOTE £2.70: £1.70, £3.20, £4.50; EX 31.20.
Owner N Mustoe **Bred** Patrick O'Dwyer **Trained** Wildhern, Hants

FOCUS
A weak race, but the progressive winner did it well and has been rated value for 14l.

NOTEBOOK
Presenting Express(IRE) completed the hat-trick in taking style despite being nearly a stone higher. Well at home in this deep ground, he went on four from home and allowed the chasing bunch to close on the home turn before pulling away from them with little problem. He is progressing nicely but the handicapper will be stepping in again. *(op 7-4 after 2-1 in places, tchd 15-8)*
Stormy Skye(IRE), back over a more suitable trip, kept on dourly to finish best of the rest. He is only 3lb higher than when last successful and another minor handicap could come his way. *(op 14-1)*
Hobbycyr(FR) made a couple of errors in the back straight but stayed on once in line for home for a slice of the prize money. This was a pleasing effort on his first run since pulling up in a hunter chase in May 2004.
Gray's Eulogy ran a solid race without quite looking like getting his head in front. *(op 11-2)*
Tommy Carson, who missed out the middle fence in the back straight when about to take the lead, made a satisfactory return to action on this first start since October.
Levallois(IRE), patiently ridden, looked a potential threat on the home turn only to fade from the second last. *(op 10-1)*
Meggie's Beau(IRE), who made much of the running, was still in with a chance of a place turning for home but soon weakened. *(op 7-1)*

3435 ASHFORD MARES' ONLY MAIDEN OPEN NATIONAL HUNT FLAT RACE 2m 1f 110y

4:00 (4:00) (Class 6) 4-6-Y-O **£1,713** (£499; £249)

Form RPR

-52 **1** **Colline De Fleurs**[50] 2558 6-11-2.......................... MarkBradburne 97+
(J A B Old) *t.k.h: hld up in tch: effrt 3f out: led 2f out: drvn and styd on wl fnl f* **5/2**[2]

2 *2* **Rowlands Dream (IRE)**[630] 41 6-11-2.......................... TimmyMurphy 95+
(R H Alner) *hld up in rr of clly bunched field: prog on inner 4f out: chsd wnr over 1f out: edgd lft and nt qckn fnl f* **9/2**[3]

6 **3** *7* **Lady Wilde (IRE)**[55] 2446 6-11-2.......................... TomDoyle 89+
(Noel T Chance) *t.k.h: cl up: effrt to ld 3f out: drvn and hdd 2f out: fdd* **9/2**[3]

4 *6* **Two Shillings** 6-10-13.......................... TomMalone(3) 82
(R Curtis) *racd wd: w ldrs: stl wl there 3f out: outpcd sn after* **33/1**

5 *1 1/2* **Etoilerouge** 5-11-2.......................... RWalsh 81
(P F Nicholls) *hld up in rr but wl in tch: rdn 5f out and sn struggling: sme prog 3f out: nvr rchd ldrs* **7/4**[1]

6 *4* **Hazzard A Guess** 5-10-9.......................... WayneKavanagh(7) 77
(J W Mullins) *hld up in rr: rdn 5f out: outpcd 4f out: plugged on fnl 2f* **33/1**

7 *8* **Migigi** 6-10-13.......................... PaulO'Neill(3) 69
(M J Roberts) *t.k.h: cl up: effrt over 3f out: wknd over 2f out* **50/1**

0 **8** *1 1/4* **Silver Rosa**[22] 2988 5-10-9.......................... TomMessenger(7) 67
(C C Bealby) *disp ld at v stdy pce: def advantage 7f out: hdd 3f out : sn wknd* **33/1**

5 **9** *3* **Mrs Higham (IRE)**[17] 3145 5-10-9.......................... JohnKington(7) 64
(M Scudamore) *t.k.h: prom tl wknd over 2f out* **25/1**

0 **10** *7* **Silverick Lady**[34] 2830 4-9-12.......................... CharlieStudd(7) 46
(B G Powell) *disp ld at v stdy pce to 7f out: struggling in rr 5f out: no ch after* **66/1**

11 *24* **Rambling Allie** 5-11-2.......................... LeightonAspell 33
(B I Case) *t.k.h: cl up tl wknd rapidly 4f out* **66/1**

0 **12** *21* **Popsleebobross (IRE)**[16] 3188 5-10-11.............. RobertLucey-Butler(5) 12
(P Butler) *a in rr: lost tch 5f out: t.o* **100/1**

4m 38.9s (4.80) **Going Correction** +0.375s/f (Yiel)
WFA 4 from 5yo+ 11lb **12** Ran SP% **119.9**
Speed ratings: **104,103,100,97,96 94,91,90,89,86 75,66** CSF £13.55 TOTE £4.90: £1.70, £1.90, £1.90; EX 20.40 Place 6 £19.73, Place 5 £13.75.
Owner The Wheels Have Come Off **Bred** J A B Old **Trained** Barbury Castle, Wilts

■ Stewards' Enquiry : John Kington caution: used whip when out of contention

FOCUS
This was probably a decent event of its type, but it turned into something of a sprint from the home turn.

NOTEBOOK
Colline De Fleurs, beaten a head by subsequent hurdles winner Ben's Turn here in November, put her experience to good use and produced the best turn of foot in a sprint finish to this falsely-run event. *(op 3-1)*
Rowlands Dream(IRE) ran once for Charlie Swan, when third in a valuable fillies' bumper at the Punchestown Festival in 2004. She ran a promising race after her long absence and connections will be keen to put this strapping half-sister to Ground Ball over obstacles sooner rather than later. *(tchd 4-1)*
Lady Wilde(IRE), a disappointment on her debut, tried to kick on in the straight but was cut down. She possesses her share of ability. *(op 11-2)*
Two Shillings, out of a winning pointer, was kept wide in search of better ground and this was a respectable start to her career.
Etoilerouge, whose dam was a smart hurdler and winning chaser, looked set to finish well out the back when coming under pressure in the back straight, but did keep on past some toiling rivals. A more truly-run race on better ground should suit her. *(op 13-8 tchd 2-1)*
Silverick Lady *Official explanation: jockey said filly had been hanging very badly left*

T/Plt: £18.50 to a £1 stake. Pool: £39,460.15. 1,552.15 winning tickets. T/Qpdt: £5.60 to a £1 stake. Pool: £3,364.00. 442.50 winning tickets. JN

[3280]FONTWELL (L-H)

Tuesday, January 17

OFFICIAL GOING: Soft (heavy in places)

Wind: Almost nil Weather: Fair, mild

3436 BET365 CALL 08000 322 365 JUVENILE NOVICES' HURDLE (9 hdls) 2m 2f 110y

1:40 (1:40) (Class 4) 4-Y-O **£4,554** (£1,337; £668; £333)

Form RPR

1 **Blazing Bailey**[108] 4-10-12 RobertThornton 116+
(A King) *t.k.h: chsd ldrs: led after 3 out: drvn out* **11/1**

4 2 9 **Desert Jim (FR)**[38] [2756] 4-10-9 ow2 ADuchene(5) 110+
(F Doumen, France) *hld up in tch: chsd wnr appr 2 out: hrd rdn: kpt on same pce* **5/4**[1]

0420 3 13 **Cava Bien**[21] [3021] 4-10-12 106 ChristianWilliams 95+
(B J Llewellyn) *wd most of way: w ldr: led 2nd tl after 3 out: 3rd and btn whn mstke last* **5/1**[3]

33 4 2 **Cave Of The Giant (IRE)**[46] [2612] 4-10-12 JimCrowley 92+
(T D McCarthy) *t.k.h: settled in midfield: styd on fr 3 out: gng on steadily at fin* **14/1**

0 5 18 **Benedict Bay**[10] [3294] 4-10-5 (v) SimonElliott(7) 74
(J A Geake) *t.k.h in tch: hrd rdn and btn after 6th* **66/1**

6 9 **Cold Mountain (IRE)**[139] 4-10-9 RichardYoung(3) 65
(J W Mullins) *hld up towards rr: nvr rchd chalng position* **66/1**

7 1 ½ **Llamadas**[43] 4-10-12 OllieMcPhail 64
(C Roberts) *plld hrd: hld up and bhd: mstke 4th: nvr in chalng position* **33/1**

60 8 1 **Shardakhan (IRE)**[10] [3294] 4-10-7 EamonDehdashti(5) 63
(G L Moore) *pushed along 3rd: a bhd* **25/1**

0 9 4 **Next Lord (FR)**[47] [2580] 4-10-12 MickFitzgerald 59
(C Von Der Recke, Germany) *mid-div: mstke 5th: wknd appr next* **25/1**

551 10 16 **Quasimodo (IRE)**[10] [3294] 4-11-5 118 PJBrennan 50
(A W Carroll) *led: j. slowly and hdd 2nd: w ldr after tl wknd 3 out* **11/4**[2]

00 11 10 **Brendan's Surprise**[53] [2481] 4-10-12 SeanCurran 33
(K J Burke) *t.k.h: a bhd: no ch fr 6th* **100/1**

P **Opera Villevert (FR)**[79] 4-10-7 HowieEphgrave(5) —
(L Corcoran) *in tch: outpcd whn mstke 6th: wkng in midfield whn p.u bef 2 out* **66/1**

0F P **Form And Beauty (IRE)**[6] [3340] 4-10-7 LeeStephens(5) —
(C Roberts) *chsd ldrs: j.lft 1st: mstke 5th: sn wknd: t.o whn p.u bef 2 out* **100/1**

4m 54.0s (18.00) **Going Correction** +1.15s/f (Heav) **13** Ran SP% **119.9**
Speed ratings: **108,104,98,97,90 86,85,85,83,77 72,—,—** CSF £25.32 TOTE £15.30: £3.70, £1.10, £1.60; EX 38.90.
Owner Three Line Whip **Bred** A M Tombs **Trained** Barbury Castle, Wilts

FOCUS
Rated through the third, the winner would appear above average and the form should work out.

NOTEBOOK
Blazing Bailey, a moderate stayer on the Flat who had never before run on ground other than good to firm on turf, coped well with conditions on his hurdling debut, seeing the trip out strongly. Things will be tougher for him under a penalty but he looks capable of progressing. *(op 12-1)*
Desert Jim(FR), missing the blinkers that he wore at Cheltenham, might be happier on better ground, but he finished clear of the third, who appears to have run his race, so this might not have been a bad effort with his rider putting up 2lb overweight. *(op 11-8 tchd 6-4)*
Cava Bien has his limitations and his performance is probably a fair guide to the level of the form. *(op 6-1)*
Cave Of The Giant(IRE) was keeping on at the finish and looks to be steadily improving with experience.
Quasimodo(IRE), up there for a long way, had a penalty to defy. He may have found the race coming too soon after his hard-fought Sandown success as he dropped out tamely from the third last. *(tchd 3-1)*

3437 JOHN SMITH'S/EBF MARES' ONLY "NATIONAL HUNT" NOVICES' HURDLE (QUALIFIER) (10 hdls) 2m 4f

2:10 (2:10) (Class 4) 4-Y-O+ **£4,749** (£1,394; £697; £348)

Form RPR

301 1 **Treaty Flyer (IRE)**[22] [2997] 5-11-7 SamThomas 101+
(P G Murphy) *wd most of way: hld up in tch: led appr 2 out: mstke last: fnd ex whn chal run-in: all out* **5/1**[3]

-210 2 ½ **Fleurette**[16] [3175] 6-11-7 97 MickFitzgerald 99
(D R Gandolfo) *hld up towards rr: hdwy 6th: drvn to chal run-in: jst hld* **15/8**[1]

230 3 1 ¾ **Dillay Brook (IRE)**[10] [3287] 6-11-1 JasonMaguire 91
(T R George) *prom: led briefly after 3 out: kpt on u.p* **5/1**[3]

-602 4 6 **Ballybawn House**[11] [3275] 5-11-1 97 SeanFox 85
(J C Fox) *hld up in rr: j. slowly 3rd: stdy hdwy 7th: chsd ldrs appr 2 out: rdn and nt qckn* **4/1**[2]

0600 5 4 **Elle Roseador**[17] [3147] 7-11-1 70 (p) JamieGoldstein 81
(M Madgwick) *mde most tl after 3 out: sn outpcd* **100/1**

F5-P 6 1 ½ **Lady Alderbrook (IRE)**[15] [3211] 6-11-1 80 JimmyMcCarthy 80
(C J Down) *prom tl wknd appr 2 out* **66/1**

54-5 7 9 **Thenford Star (IRE)**[27] [2937] 5-11-1 (t) PJBrennan 73+
(D J S Ffrench Davis) *mid-div: tk clsr order 5th: wknd after 3 out* **20/1**

0P3 8 dist **Carroll's O'Tully (IRE)**[10] [3281] 6-10-8 JustinMorgan(7) —
(L A Dace) *mstke 4th: a bhd* **40/1**

0 9 8 **Silver Seline**[267] [27] 5-11-1 RJGreene —
(B N Pollock) *pressed ldrs tl 3rd: in tch after tl wknd 7th* **66/1**

0-0 10 1 ½ **Shambolina**[22] [2997] 5-11-1 AndrewThornton —
(J W Mullins) *mid-div: outpcd whn j. slowly 7th: sn bhd* **50/1**

-500 11 30 **Just Ask**[17] [3149] 6-11-1 SeanCurran —
(N R Mitchell) *in tch: mstke 3rd: wknd next: sn wl bhd* **100/1**

605 F **Our Girl Kaz (IRE)**[33] [2849] 6-10-10 HowieEphgrave(5) —
(L Corcoran) *in tch: hrd rdn and wknd 6th: bhd whn fell next* **12/1**

000 F **The Laying Hen (IRE)**[13] [3240] 6-10-10 DarylJacob(5) 65
(D P Keane) *in tch: jnd ldrs 6th: wknd 3 out: 8th and no ch whn fell last* **100/1**

0555 P **Fallout (IRE)**[15] [3215] 5-11-4 93 RichardYoung(3) 1
(J W Mullins) *t.k.h towards rr: sme hdwy 6th: wknd next: wl bhd whn p.u bef 2 out* **14/1**

00/6 P **Dutch Star**[22] [2988] 7-10-5 JayPemberton(10) —
(G P Enright) *towards rr: sme hdwy 5th: wknd next: no ch whn j. slowly 7th: t.o whn p.u bef 2 out* **40/1**

5m 28.3s (24.50) **Going Correction** +1.15s/f (Heav) **15** Ran SP% **120.0**
Speed ratings: **97,96,96,93,92 91,87,—,—,— —,—,—,—,—** CSF £14.38 TOTE £8.50: £2.50, £1.20, £2.20; EX 14.60.
Owner Mrs Dianne Murphy **Bred** Mrs M Brophy **Trained** East Garston, Berks

FOCUS
A modest winning time and, rated around the fourth, this is not strong form.

NOTEBOOK
Treaty Flyer(IRE) was not sure to like this soft ground but she coped with the conditions well enough to beat a modest bunch. She showed an admirable attitude when challenged on the run-in *and connections are now likely to aim her at the final of this series at Newbury in March. (tchd 11-2, 6-1 in places)*
Fleurette put up a better effort back against her own sex and stayed on well up the run-in. She seems to appreciate plenty of cut in the ground. *(op 13-8 tchd 2-1 in places)*
Dillay Brook(IRE), disappointing on her hurdling debut, showed more like her true form, although her efforts in bumpers suggest she is capable of slightly better still. *(op 8-1 tchd 9-1)*
Ballybawn House acts on soft ground but this longer trip in the conditions found her out. She will be happier back over shorter. *(op 5-1)*
Elle Roseador, whose performance does not do a lot for the value of the form, appeared to run better in the first-time cheekpieces. *(op 66-1)*

3438 WEATHERBYS BANK NOVICES' CHASE (19 fncs) 3m 2f 110y

2:40 (2:40) (Class 3) 5-Y-O+ **£10,159** (£3,098; £1,618; £879)

Form RPR

2121 1 **Mon Mome (FR)**[36] [2800] 6-12-1 125 SamThomas 140+
(Miss Venetia Williams) *led to 2nd: led 9th: steadily drew clr fr 13th: unchal* **8/13**[1]

P003 2 9 **Charango Star**[12] [3249] 8-11-11 102 (v[1]) RichardJohnson 111
(W K Goldsworthy) *4th most of way tl wnt 15 l 3rd after 14th: kpt on to take 2nd run-in: no ch w wnr* **15/2**[3]

620- 3 3 ½ **Matelot (FR)**[46] 6-11-0 ADuchene(5) 105+
(F Doumen, France) *sn chsng ldng pair: wnt 8 l 2nd at 14th: nt pce to trble wnr: lost 2nd run-in* **15/2**[3]

1/3P 4 dist **King Triton (IRE)**[22] [2982] 9-10-12 103 JustinMorgan(7) —
(L Wells) *bhd fr 7th: hrd rdn and no ch fr 12th: remote 4th whn blnd last: walked up run-in* **16/1**

4/ P **All Bart Native (IRE)**[1163] [1870] 11-11-5 BrianCrowley —
(L Wells) *nt fluent in rr: sn bhd: p.u after 13th* **66/1**

P-U1 U **Concert Pianist**[15] [3218] 11-11-11 113 RJGreene —
(P Winkworth) *towards rr: blnd 3rd: j. slowly and uns rdr 5th (ditch)* **6/1**[2]

33U0 P **Sarahs Quay (IRE)**[32] [2859] 7-10-12 78 (b[1]) SeanCurran —
(K J Burke) *chsd ldr: led and stmbld 2nd: mstke next: hdd 9th: blnd 11th: wknd after 13th: 4th and losing pl whn p.u after next* **100/1**

7m 40.3s (39.20) **Going Correction** +1.425s/f (Heav) **7** Ran SP% **108.1**
Speed ratings: **98,95,94,—,— —,—** CSF £5.31 TOTE £1.50: £1.30, £2.00; EX 4.50.
Owner Mrs Vida Bingham **Bred** A Deschere **Trained** Kings Caple, H'fords

FOCUS
A moderate winning time for the grade of contest and a weak race for the money on offer. The winner has been rated value for 25 lengths and to the form of his recent Plumpton win.

NOTEBOOK
Mon Mome(FR) had very little to beat in this uncompetitive heat and did not have to show any improvement to win as he liked. He clearly handles soft ground well but it remains to be seen whether he copes with a faster surface. *(op 4-6 tchd 8-11 in places)*
Charango Star, visored for the first time on his return to chasing, will hopefully have done his confidence some good with this completion. *(op 8-1 tchd 7-1)*
Matelot(FR), who ran well in a bumper here last year, was having his first start over fences in this country. A mistake at the last when tired probably cost him second place, and he might do better when dropped back in distance. *(op 6-1)*
King Triton(IRE) ran quite well here on his chasing debut but he was pulled up last time and never featured in this contest. *(op 22-1)*
Concert Pianist had already blundered badly at the third fence before his rider was unseated at the fifth. Far from fluent when winning at Folkestone last time, he might be happier reverting to hurdling. *(tchd 11-2 and 13-2, 7-1 in a place)*

3439 CROWN RACING CHAMPION TIPSTER "COLIN SHEPPARD" MARES' ONLY H'CAP HURDLE (9 hdls) 2m 2f 110y

3:10 (3:10) (Class 4) (0-115,115) 4-Y-O+ **£5,204** (£1,528; £764; £381)

Form RPR

-351 1 **Sunley Shines**[10] [3280] 6-10-10 104 JohnnyLevins(5) 122+
(B G Powell) *wd most of way: w ldr: led 3rd to 4th: led 6th: wnt 5 l clr 2 out: hung lft in st: rdn and styd on* **3/1**[2]

2221 2 8 **Hi Laurie (IRE)**[15] [3217] 11-10-7 96 TomScudamore 101
(M Scudamore) *hdwy 3rd: chsd ldng pair appr 2 out: wnt 2nd at the last: nt pce to trble wnr* **11/4**[1]

0/3- 3 5 **Lady Harriet**[425] [2301] 7-10-0 89 oh1 DaveCrosse 89
(C J Mann) *wd most of way: hld up in rr: smooth hdwy fr 5th: trckd wnr after 3 out: outpcd appr next* **20/1**

0054 4 5 **Honey's Gift**[17] [3146] 7-10-9 101 RobertStephens(3) 96
(G G Margarson) *hld up in rr: mod effrt whn mstke 6th: nvr rchd ldrs* **7/1**

-U66 5 ½ **Sword Lady**[10] [3295] 8-11-5 115 (b) MrDEdwards(7) 110
(Mrs S D Williams) *drvn to ld after 1st: hdd 3rd: led 4th to 6th: wknd appr 2 out* **10/1**

4013 6 15 **Hilarious (IRE)**[15] [3211] 6-10-0 89 oh1 JamieGoldstein 74+
(Dr J R J Naylor) *led tl after 1st: prom tl wknd 3 out* **5/1**[3]

2120 P **Purple Patch**[15] [3210] 8-11-2 105 MickFitzgerald —
(C L Popham) *bhd fr 1/2-way: p.u bef 6th* **17/2**

510 P **Barnbrook Empire (IRE)**[21] [3021] 4-10-0 101 oh1 OllieMcPhail —
(B J Llewellyn) *hdwy 4th: wknd appr 6th: t.o whn p.u bef last* **10/1**

P-P0 P **Kiwi Babe**[15] [3214] 7-10-13 107 (b) DarylJacob(5) —
(D P Keane) *in tch: mstke 2nd: reminder next: bhd and rdn 4th: p.u bef 6th* **40/1**

4m 55.9s (19.90) **Going Correction** +1.15s/f (Heav)
WFA 4 from 6yo+ 11lb **9** Ran SP% **116.7**
Speed ratings: **104,100,98,96,96 89,—,—,—** CSF £12.21 CT £137.93 TOTE £4.00: £1.70, £1.60, £6.00; EX 11.30 Trifecta £276.20 Pool: £544.74 - 1.40 winning tickets..
Owner John B Sunley **Bred** Sunley Stud Ltd **Trained** Morestead, Hants

FOCUS
A fairly competitive mares' handicap in which the winner has been rated value for 13 lengths and the placed horses rated close to their pre-race marks. The form should work out well enough.

NOTEBOOK
Sunley Shines had won over the course and distance ten days earlier and, stepping into a handicap for the first time, showed herself to have got in lightly off a mark of 104. Wisely kept wide for most of the race, avoiding the worst of the ground, she hung over to the far rail in the straight but always had plenty in hand. A progressive performer, it would not be a surprise to see her out again quickly under a penalty. *(op 7-2 tchd 4-1 in places)*
Hi Laurie(IRE) won easily at Folkestone last time and probably ran to a similar level here. She was *just unlucky to run into a younger, more favourably rated rival making her handicap debut. (op 3-1 tchd 10-3 in places)*

Lady Harriet ◆, returning from a 425-day absence, looked to be going just as well as the eventual winner turning out of the back straight, and although she could not go with her in the closing stages this was still a very promising return. Her stable is in good form at present and, providing she avoids bouncing next time, she looks capable of winning off this sort of mark. *(op 16-1)*

Honey's Gift, twice a winner over this course and distance in the past and only on a 1lb higher mark than when last successful, was running on at the finish. *(op 6-1 tchd 8-1)*

Sword Lady, who looks high in the handicap at present, has done her most recent winning over three miles. *(op 8-1)*

Hilarious(IRE) probably found the ground too testing. *(op 6-1)*

Purple Patch *Official explanation: trainer said mare lost a hind shoe (op 9-1 tchd 8-1)*

3440 CLINICALLY PROVEN CORTAFLEX H'CAP CHASE (15 fncs) 2m 4f

3:40 (3:40) (Class 3) (0-125,120) 5-Y-£7,605 (£2,246; £1,123; £561; £280)

Form RPR

2412 **1** **Walcot Lad (IRE)**[10] [3284] 10-9-11 **94** oh2..............(p) RobertStephens(3) 100+
(A Ennis) *prom: led 3rd: rdn and hld on wl fr 3 out: gamely* **4/1**[2]

/4P3 **2** *2 ½* **Pietro Vannucci (IRE)**[35] [2814] 10-11-2 **110**................ RichardJohnson 115+
(Jonjo O'Neill) *cl up: mstke 7th: rdn to press wnr 2 out: nt fluent last: nt qckn* **9/2**[3]

U41U **3** *nk* **Balladeer (IRE)**[8] [3323] 8-11-7 **115**.............................. RobertThornton 118+
(Mrs T J Hill) *hld up in tch: hdwy 4 out: 3rd whn nt fluent last: one pce* **5/1**

1125 **4** *dist* **Avitta (IRE)**[35] [2812] 7-11-7 **115**.. SamThomas 93
(Miss Venetia Williams) *led to 3rd: stmbld bdly 4th and lost pl: rallied 11th: wknd 3 out* **6/1**

-242 **5** *17* **Macmar (FR)**[32] [2870] 6-11-3 **111**..............................(v¹) AndrewThornton —
(R H Alner) *in tch: pushed along to chse ldrs appr 10th: wknd 3 out* **7/2**[1]

11P- **6** *dist* **Translucid (USA)**[255] 8-11-12 **120**..................................... MickFitzgerald —
(C Von Der Recke, Germany) *in tch tl wknd 4 out* **15/2**

-F35 **U** **East Lawyer (FR)**[60] [2312] 7-11-2 **110**.......................... ChristianWilliams —
(P F Nicholls) *hld up in tch in rr: bdly hmpd and uns rdr 4th* **8/1**

5m 33.8s (25.90) **Going Correction** +1.425s/f (Heav) **7** Ran SP% **114.2**
Speed ratings: **105,104,103,—,—** —,— CSF £22.40 TOTE £6.10: £1.60, £3.90; EX 35.50.

Owner Camis Burke Middleton Heaps **Bred** Jim Ruane **Trained** Beare Green, Surrey

FOCUS

Another course win for Walcot Lad. The form has been handicapped around the runner-up, who has been rated as running to the best of this season's form.

NOTEBOOK

Walcot Lad(IRE) was strongly challenged from some way out but he knows how to win at this track and held off his pursuers for a fifth course win, and his first over this longer trip of two and a half miles. He also defied a career-high mark. *(op 5-1 tchd 11-2, 6-1 in a place)*

Pietro Vannucci(IRE) could never quite get past the eventual winner despite jumping the last upsides. This was still his best run since his reappearance at Huntingdon, though. *(op 4-1)*

Balladeer(IRE), a winner of a beginners' event over two furlongs further here last month, was not done any favours by the Handicapper for that win, and this was probably a career-best effort in defeat. *(op 6-1)*

Avitta(IRE) stumbled badly after jumping the fourth fence and it was remarkable that she came back to have her chance jumping three out. She weakened soon afterwards but that was understandable and she deserves another opportunity. *(op 13-2)*

Macmar(FR), who wore blinkers when he scored his only success over fences to date in the *French Provinces, was disappointing in the first-time visor and may need better ground.Official explanation: jockey said gelding was unsuited by the track (op 4-1)*

3441 RACECOURSE VIDEO SERVICES H'CAP HURDLE (10 hdls) 2m 4f

4:10 (4:10) (Class 4) (0-110,106) 4-Y-0+ **£4,554** (£1,337; £668; £333)

Form RPR

2062 **1** **Amanpuri (GER)**[5] [3358] 8-10-10 **90**........................ ChristianWilliams 94
(Mrs A M Thorpe) *prom: rdn to ld 2 out: hrd drvn run-in: all out* **8/1**

-434 **2** *nk* **Albert House (IRE)**[21] [3018] 8-11-7 **101**..................... AndrewThornton 105
(R H Alner) *led tl 2 out: rallied gamely run-in: jst hld* **7/2**[1]

5253 **3** *16* **Monsal Dale (IRE)**[15] [3223] 7-10-4 **84**.................................(tp) PJBrennan 72
(Mrs L C Jewell) *hld up towards rr: effrt 3 out: nt pce to rch ldrs* **25/1**

/2-3 **4** *2 ½* **New Mischief (IRE)**[16] [3184] 8-11-5 **102**.................. WilliamKennedy(3) 90+
(Noel T Chance) *chsd ldrs: rdn and mstke 2 out: wknd appr last* **9/2**[2]

56-1 **5** *1* **Play The Melody (IRE)**[17] [3137] 5-11-2 **96**..................... MickFitzgerald 80
(C Tinkler) *chsd ldrs tl wknd appr 2 out* **7/2**[1]

5PP1 **P** **Past Heritage**[68] [2146] 7-9-10 **81** oh7 ow1...................... DerekLaverty(5) —
(A E Jones) *bhd fr 4th: p.u after 6th* **28/1**

044 **F** **It's The Limit (USA)**[10] [3286] 7-11-10 **104**.................(t) RichardJohnson —
(W K Goldsworthy) *sn prom: rdn 7th: wknd 3 out: bhd whn fell last: winded* **11/2**[3]

041 **P** **Nero West (FR)**[13] [3240] 5-11-1 **102**........................ MissLucyBridges(7) —
(Miss Lucy Bridges) *r alone on inner most of way: bhd fr 4th: t.o whn p.u bef last* **11/2**[3]

5m 23.9s (20.10) **Going Correction** +1.15s/f (Heav) **8** Ran SP% **111.8**
Speed ratings: **105,104,98,97,97** —,—,— CSF £35.13 CT £660.43 TOTE £8.20: £2.60, £1.40, £2.50; EX 37.70 Place 6 £18.75, Place 5 £12.89.

Owner Mrs A M Thorpe **Bred** H Von Finck **Trained** Bronwydd Arms, Carmarthens

FOCUS

A moderate heat but the best finish of the day. The winner has been rated as having run 5lb better than at Ludlow last time.

NOTEBOOK

Amanpuri(GER) had the stands'-side rail to help him in the closing stages and that was probably what enabled him to hang on as he was strongly challenged by Albert House. This was his first success under either code in this country. *(op 12-1)*

Albert House(IRE) adopted the front-running tactics that can be so effective around here and rallied really well in the closing stages, as befits a horse who stays beyond three miles. *(tchd 4-1 in places)*

Monsal Dale(IRE) kept on from off the pace but was never a threat to the first two. His best form is on quicker ground. *(op 16-1)*

New Mischief(IRE) had his chance turning into the straight but he weakened over the final two flights. Perhaps this run came too soon after his promising reappearance from a lengthy absence at Plumpton on New Year' Day. *(op 4-1 tchd 5-1 in a place)*

Play The Melody(IRE) could not cope with a 6lb higher mark following his win in a weak Lingfield handicap for novices on New Year's Eve. *(tchd 4-1 and 9-2 in a place)*

T/Jkpt: Not won. T/Plt: £41.20 to a £1 stake. Pool: £55,956.50. 991.10 winning tickets. T/Qpdt: £22.50 to a £1 stake. Pool: £3,305.00. 108.30 winning tickets. LM

3314 NEWCASTLE (L-H)

Wednesday, January 18

OFFICIAL GOING: Soft (heavy in places, good to soft last 3f)

Wind: Almost nil

3442 CONTINENTAL FINANCE MARES' ONLY MAIDEN HURDLE (9 hdls) 2m

12:50 (12:53) (Class 4) 4-Y-0+ **£2,927** (£859; £429; £214)

Form RPR

P54 **1** **Woodford Consult**[29] [2676] 4-10-4 .... MrTGreenall(3) 83
(M W Easterby) *in tch: hdwy whn pushed along bef 3 out: rallied and led bef last: kpt on wl* **11/2**[2]

0235 **2** *1 ¾* **Nobodys Perfect (IRE)**[8] [3339] 6-10-11 90............. PatrickMcDonald(7) 92
(Ferdy Murphy) *chsd ldrs: effrt and ev ch bef 3 out: kpt on fr last* **8/1**[3]

0-05 **3** *3 ½* **Buffy**[15] [3231] 6-11-4 .... NeilMulholland 90+
(B Mactaggart) *racd wd: hld up: hdwy and prom whn nt fluent 3 out: edgd rt and one pce last* **100/1**

0355 **4** *4* **August Rose (IRE)**[15] [3235] 6-11-1 90................... PeterBuchanan(3) 85
(Miss Lucinda V Russell) *chsd ldrs: outpcd bef 3 out: rallied next: no imp* **20/1**

4P2 **5** *¾* **One More Time (FR)**[44] [2676] 4-10-7 .... GrahamLee 77+
(J Howard Johnson) *chsd ldrs: led bef 4 out: hdd whn mstke last: btn whn flashed tail nr fin* **11/10**[1]

-0F4 **6** *shd* **Leap Year Lass**[13] [3254] 6-11-4 92.......................... RichardMcGrath 84
(C Grant) *hld up: hdwy and in tch 4 out: rdn and outpcd fr next* **18/1**

0-40 **7** *7* **Treasured Memories**[27] [2947] 6-11-4 .... AndrewThornton 77
(Miss S E Forster) *bhd: rdn 1/2-way: kpt on fr 2 out: n.d* **8/1**[3]

0600 **8** *1 ¼* **Quarry Island (IRE)**[12] [3269] 5-10-11 90......................... PhilKinsella(7) 76
(M Todhunter) *hld up: drvn bef 4 out: wknd bef next* **20/1**

5 **9** *¾* **Olmetta (FR)**[46] [2642] 4-10-4 .... GaryBerridge(3) 64
(J P L Ewart) *towards rr: outpcd whn hit 4 out: sn btn* **50/1**

10-0 **10** *dist* **Arctic Moss (IRE)**[203] [854] 7-11-4 .... JimCrowley —
(E W Tuer) *keen: chsd ldrs tl wknd bef 3 out: t.o* **10/1**

620P **11** *2* **Pont Neuf (IRE)**[8] [3337] 6-10-13 98............................(t) ThomasDreaper(5) —
(A Crook) *bhd: hmpd 3rd: nvr on terms* **20/1**

06S **R** **Teutonic (IRE)**[19] [1908] 5-11-4 .... TonyDobbin —
(R F Fisher) *ref to r* **100/1**

0-0 **F** **Dusky Dame**[9] [3314] 6-11-4 .... PadgeWhelan —
(S B Bell) *midfield whn fell 3rd* **200/1**

P **Archerfield (IRE)**[109] 5-11-4 .... KennyJohnson —
(R Johnson) *a bhd: t.o whn p.u bef 3 out* **100/1**

0U **P** **Commanche Sioux**[9] [3314] 4-10-7 .... AlanDempsey —
(M W Easterby) *sn wl bhd: t.o whn p.u 4 out* **200/1**

P **One And Only (GER)**[74] 5-10-11 .... BenOrde-Powlett(7) —
(D W Thompson) *bhd: struggling 1/2-way: p.u bef 3 out* **66/1**

P200 **P** **Crimson Bow (GER)**[40] [2752] 4-10-4 87............................(b) LeeVickers(3) —
(J G Given) *led to bef 4 out: sn wknd: t.o whn p.u bef next* **40/1**

4m 10.7s (4.40) **Going Correction** +0.275s/f (Yiel)
WFA 4 from 5yo+ 11lb **17** Ran SP% **123.7**
Speed ratings: **100,99,97,95,95 94,91,90,90,**— —,—,—,—,— —,— CSF £46.11 TOTE £8.90: £1.90, £2.00, £19.20; EX 64.30.

Owner Woodford Group Plc **Bred** Hesmonds Stud Ltd **Trained** Sheriff Hutton, N Yorks

FOCUS

A typically ordinary mares-only hurdle rated through the fourth, but the race should produce the odd winner at a similarly modest level.

NOTEBOOK

Woodford Consult, who has been gradually improving with experience over hurdles, finished a creditable fourth when reverting to the All-Weather last month and ran out a ready winner on this return to hurdles, quickening well to come through and lead approaching the last before staying on strongly. In receipt of weight from all bar two of her rivals, she will find life tougher under a penalty, but rates an interesting handicap prospect and is in good hands. *(op 10-1 tchd 11-1)*

Nobodys Perfect(IRE) has had plenty of experience of hurdles and is well exposed, but she recorded one of her better efforts here and looks best kept to mares'-only novice hurdles for the time being. *(op 7-1)*

Buffy stepped up on her initial effort over hurdles when running well to a point at Ayr and this was another improvement, keeping on for third having been outpaced by the front two. Two and a half miles may bring about further improvement and she is not one to underestimate in future.

August Rose(IRE) was not necessarily helped by this drop in distance, but she ran well nonetheless and would make some appeal in low-grade handicaps. *(tchd 22-1)*

One More Time(FR) has faced some stiffish tasks since going hurdling, but ran well at a more sensible level last time and was expected to take some beating in what looked a softer race. Having travelled well into the straight, she tired badly after the last and looked awkward under pressure. *She is clearly not one to have total faith in and has a bit to prove at this stage. (op Evens tchd 6-5 tchd 5-4 in a place)*

Leap Year Lass has yet to win in 20 starts under either code, but she has the form to pick up a small race and is likely to benefit from a step back up in distance. *(op 16-1)*

Treasured Memories got a bit behind before keeping on in the straight and is now qualified for handicaps, a sphere she is likely to do well in. *(op 10-1 tchd 11-1)*

3443 BET365.COM NOVICES' HURDLE (13 hdls) 3m

1:20 (1:21) (Class 3) 4-Y-0+
£5,010 (£1,480; £740; £370; £184; £92)

Form RPR

1-32 **1** **Cash And New (IRE)**[18] [3149] 7-11-6 .... RichardJohnson 90+
(R T Phillips) *hld up in tch: hdwy and ev ch bef 3 out: sn rdn: rallied to ld run in: styd on wl* **4/6**[1]

/P04 **2** *2 ½* **Pride Of Finewood (IRE)**[13] [3257] 8-11-13 .... NeilMulholland 94
(E W Tuer) *cl up: ev ch bef 3 out: rdn and hung lft next: kpt on fr last* **50/1**

6P22 **3** *½* **Notaproblem (IRE)**[9] [3316] 7-12-5 105.............................. AlanDempsey 101+
(G A Harker) *hld up in tch: smooth hdwy to ld whn nt fluent 3 out: hdd run in: no ex* **8/1**[3]

-P65 **4** *dist* **Gay Kindersley (IRE)**[9] [3316] 8-11-3 .... JamesReveley(10) 65
(K G Reveley) *led to bef 3 out: sn wknd* **80/1**

-604 **5** *17* **Ro Eridani**[74] [2040] 6-11-3 64.. MrCStorey(3) —
(Miss S E Forster) *bhd: struggling fr 9th: t.o* **200/1**

006 **6** *15* **Compton Dragon (USA)**[40] [2749] 7-11-13 .... KennyJohnson —
(R Johnson) *a bhd: no ch fnl circ* **66/1**

0-0P **P** **Tees Mill**[4] [3381] 7-11-6 .... MrCDawson(7) —
(D W Thompson) *a bhd: t.o whn p.u 4 out* **500/1**

P **Conemara Breeze** 8-11-13 .... TomSiddall —
(Miss L C Siddall) *towards rr: struggling fnl circ: p.u bef 3 out* **100/1**

P6 **P** **Mist Opportunity (IRE)**[56] [2442] 4-10-4 .... GaryBartley(10) —
(P C Haslam) *in tch to 9th: sn wknd: t.o whn p.u bef 3 out* **66/1**

2 P **Calin Royal (FR)**[40] 2755 5-11-13 GrahamLee —
(J Howard Johnson) *nt fluent: chsd ldrs: ev ch 4 out: sn lost action and p.u* 9/4[2]

6m 21.8s (3.40) **Going Correction** +0.275s/f (Yiel) **10** Ran SP% **109.7**
WFA 4 from 5yo+ 13lb
Speed ratings: **105,104,104,—,—** —,—,—,—,— CSF £32.31 TOTE £1.50: £1.10, £4.00, £1.20; EX 36.10.
Owner The 23rd Floor **Bred** Mrs John Noonan **Trained** Adlestrop, Gloucs
■ Stewards' Enquiry : Richard Johnson one-day ban: used whip with excessive frequency (Jan 29)

FOCUS
An uncompetitive novices' hurdle and Cash And New ultimately made hard work of winning after her only credible rival Calin Royal was pulled up before the home turn. The winner is rated some way below her best with the third the best guide to the form.

NOTEBOOK
Cash And New(IRE), who showed fair placed form in two previous hurdling attempts, made hard enough work of landing the odds, especially with Calin Royal failing to run any sort of a race. Evidently a strong stayer, she will need to raise her game if she is to defy a penalty, but this was only her fourth racecourse outing and she is entitled to improve as she gains further experience. *(op 5-6 tchd 11-10 in a place)*
Pride Of Finewood(IRE) did not have the form to suggest he could sneak a place, but he kept galloping under pressure and came through for second close home. He is lightly-raced for his age and remains open to a little improvement at this distance. *(op 40-1)*
Notaproblem(IRE) ran as well as could have been expected under his big weight, which began to tell after the last. A consistent gelding, he travelled strongly and will be of interest back in handicaps, with a drop in trip likely to help. *(op 15-2)*
Gay Kindersley(IRE) is a largely disappointing sort and he found himself readily brushed aside once the race for home began. He is bred to be a chaser, but has not looked a natural in any of his three starts over fences thus far. *(op 100-1)*
Calin Royal(FR), who made a highly pleasing debut when chasing home the useful L'Antartique on his racecourse debut at Doncaster last month, was never in a decent rhythm here and continually lost momentum at his hurdles, but still appeared to be going well enough when losing his action and being pulled up before the turn for home. This was obviously not his running and he is worthy of another chance back on good ground. *(op 15-8)*

3444 MILLER HOMES H'CAP CHASE (18 fncs) 3m
1:50 (1:53) (Class 4) (0-100,99) 5-Y-0+ **£3,936** (£1,200; £627; £340)

Form RPR
22PU **1** **Farington Lodge (IRE)**[23] 2978 8-10-13 **86** DominicElsworth 99+
(Mrs S J Smith) *a cl up: led bef 2 out: styd on strly* 5/1[3]
0134 **2** 8 **Celtic Flow**[23] 2978 8-10-0 **73** oh7 BrianHarding 75
(C R Wilson) *lft in ld 5th: hdd bef 2 out: one pce* 5/1[3]
5-04 **3** 12 **Mr Prickle (IRE)**[23] 2975 6-11-3 **90** RussGarritty 82+
(P Beaumont) *hld up in tch: hdwy bef 4 out: rdn and hung lft after next: sn outpcd* 9/2[2]
3PF3 **4** 9 **Wild About Harry**[8] 3338 9-10-1 **74** oh3 ow1 SeanCurran 58+
(A R Dicken) *chsd ldrs tl wknd bef 4 out* 10/1
0-52 **F** **Moon Mist**[16] 3209 8-10-13 **86** RichardMcGrath —
(N W Alexander) *led tl fell 5th* 3/1[1]
34P6 **U** **Lutin Du Moulin (FR)**[8] 3339 7-11-12 **99** (b) WilsonRenwick —
(L Lungo) *hit: stmbld and uns rdr 1st* 9/1
P-P4 **P** **Recent Edition (IRE)**[8] 3336 8-10-11 **84** (b[1]) AlanDempsey —
(J Wade) *in tch: drvn 1/2-way: struggling 12th: p.u bef 4 out* 9/2[2]

6m 23.4s (-1.40) **Going Correction** +0.025s/f (Yiel) **7** Ran SP% **113.8**
Speed ratings: **103,100,96,93,—** —,— CSF £29.60 TOTE £6.00: £2.60, £2.80; EX 32.60.
Owner The Shaw Hall Partnership **Bred** Mrs Patricia Mackean **Trained** High Eldwick, W Yorks

FOCUS
A poor handicap ratedf through the runner-up. Those that finished were well strung out and the trip clearly took a bit of getting.

NOTEBOOK
Farington Lodge(IRE), still going well when unseating on his reappearance at Sedgefield, never put a foot wrong on this occasion and galloped on relentlessly having gone to the front before the second-last. This was only his fourth chase start under Rules and he is in the right hands to progress further, assuming the Handicapper treats him fairly. *(op 9-2 tchd 11-2)*
Celtic Flow, who is often forced to race from out of the handicap over fences, was left in front by the fall of favourite Moon Mist as early as the fifth fence and she made a good fist of it, leading until passed by the winner two out. She kept on well for a clear second and should continue to pay her way. *(op 11-2 tchd 6-1 and 9-2)*
Mr Prickle(IRE) has taken quite well to fences and shown enough in two starts this season to suggest there is a small race in him. This was his first try at three miles and he appeared to see it out well enough. *(op 4-1 tchd 5-1)*
Wild About Harry has yet to win in 19 starts in bumpers, hurdles or over fences and he did not do enough here to suggest he is about to put an end to that. *(op 8-1 tchd 7-1)*
Moon Mist has been in decent form and looked to hold strong claims here, but she got no further than the fifth and it is hoped this does not affect her confidence. *(op 8-1 tchd 9-1)*
Recent Edition(IRE) is more than capable of throwing in a stinker and the first-time blinkers had anything but the desired effect. *(op 8-1 tchd 9-1)*

3445 GUINNESS H'CAP HURDLE (9 hdls) 2m
2:20 (2:21) (Class 4) (0-105,105) 4-Y-0+ **£3,253** (£955; £477; £238)

Form RPR
0-03 **1** **Mr Midaz**[16] 3206 7-11-4 **100** PeterBuchanan(3) 107+
(D W Whillans) *prom: effrt 3 out: led run in: styd on wl* 13/2[3]
0320 **2** 1 1/4 **Haditovski**[13] 3256 10-11-7 **100** (v) GrahamLee 106+
(J Mackie) *led to 2nd: led bef 3 out to run in: kpt on* 5/1[2]
141- **3** 12 **Inn From The Cold (IRE)**[419] 2440 10-10-0 **86** MrGWilloughby(7) 81+
(L Lungo) *hld up: nt fluent 3 out: shkn up and kpt on fr next: nvr nr to chal* 9/1
0005 **4** 8 **Lord Baskerville**[6] 3351 5-10-11 **90** NeilMulholland 77+
(W Storey) *keen: led 2nd to bef 3 out: wknd next* 33/1
2020 **5** 2 **Time To Roam (IRE)**[27] 2944 6-10-13 **102** (b) NeilWalker(10) 85
(Miss Lucinda V Russell) *prom tl rdn and wknd bef 3 out* 9/1
0000 **6** 14 **Nifty Roy**[68] 2171 6-10-2 **80** ow6 PaddyMerrigan(5) 55
(I McMath) *hld up: outpcd 1/2-way: n.d after* 8/1
3/30 **7** 3 1/2 **Castle Richard (IRE)**[27] 2944 9-11-10 **103** BarryKeniry 69
(G M Moore) *chsd ldrs to 5th: sn rdn and btn* 8/1
5-40 **8** 6 **Random Native (IRE)**[27] 2944 8-10-11 **90** BrianHarding 50
(N G Richards) *hld up: hdwy 5th: wknd next* 9/1
6112 **9** 7 **Caesarean Hunter (USA)**[35] 2822 7-11-5 **105** SeanQuinlan(7) 58
(R T Phillips) *nt fluent: hld up: hit and rdn 5th: nvr on terms* 11/4[1]

4m 8.50s (2.20) **Going Correction** +0.275s/f (Yiel) **9** Ran SP% **111.8**
Speed ratings: **105,104,98,94,93 86,84,81,78** CSF £37.71 CT £288.40 TOTE £7.20: £2.20, £1.50, £2.40; EX 27.20.
Owner Chas N Whillans, Dr Doreen M Steele **Bred** G E Amey **Trained** Hawick, Borders

FOCUS
The front two pulled well clear in what was an ordinary race, but the pace was decent and the form looks solid enough.

NOTEBOOK
Mr Midaz showed a bit more when third at Ayr last time and, although still 5lb higher than when last winning at Musselburgh in February of last year, proved too strong for Haditovski after the last. His stable have not had the best of times of it thus far this season, but things are getting better and he may yet be capable of a bit better. *(op 6-1)*
Haditovski, 17lb lower than when last successful, is not as good as he used to be but he is evidently still capable of a bold showing every now and then and he gave his all in second. He was a fair way clear of the third and is likely to go up a little for this, but a similar effort could see him back winning again. *(op 9-2 tchd 11-2)*
Inn From The Cold(IRE) ◆, in good form when last seen towards the end of 2004, found this drop back to two miles against him and simply lacked the pace of the front two. This was an ideal starting point however, and he showed more than enough to suggest he will soon resume winning ways once back up in trip. *(op 10-1 tchd 8-1)*
Lord Baskerville is a longstanding maiden under both codes and this was his 41st visit to the racecourse without a win. *(op 20-1)*
Time To Roam(IRE) failed to last home over two and a half miles at Ayr last month and this drop back in distance brought about a marginally better effort. *(op 10-1)*
Random Native(IRE) *Official explanation: jockey said gelding, regarding the running and riding, his orders were to drop gelding in as it can be keen, get it jumping and thereafter creep away and do his best, adding that gelding began making a noise halfway down back straight, made a mistake at the final hurdle in back straight, and gurgled throughout in home straight; he further added that this was the tackiest ground gelding had raced on this season; trainer said gelding had had a breathing problem (tchd 10-1)*
Caesarean Hunter(USA) has been in cracking form, but was unable to complete the hat-trick off his new mark when second at Bangor last month and ran significantly below-par here without any obvious excuse. *Official explanation: jockey said gelding never travelled (op 9-4 tchd 3-1)*

3446 GOSFORTH DECORATING AND BUILDING SERVICES CONDITIONAL JOCKEYS' (S) H'CAP HURDLE (11 hdls) 2m 4f
2:50 (2:55) (Class 5) (0-95,90) 4-Y-0+ **£2,081** (£611; £305; £152)

Form RPR
0560 **1** **Silver Seeker (USA)**[16] 3209 6-10-11 **78** PatrickMcDonald(3) 86+
(A R Dicken) *bhd and sn pushed along: hdwy bef 3 out: led bef last: kpt on strly* 9/2
30U6 **2** 10 **Named At Dinner**[9] 3320 5-10-12 **84** (b) NeilWalker(8) 83+
(Miss Lucinda V Russell) *prom: hdwy 1/2-way: led bef 3 out: hdd bef last: no ch w wnr* 10/1
5216 **3** 1/2 **Maunby Rocker**[49] 2566 6-11-9 **90** (p) PaddyMerrigan(3) 88+
(P C Haslam) *hld up: rdn dropped whip 4 out: hdwy and prom whn lft 2nd 3 out: one pce after next* 5/2[1]
-004 **4** 14 **Needwood Spirit**[8] 3330 11-10-7 **71** OwynNelmes 56+
(Mrs A M Naughton) *in tch: outpcd 4 out: rallied 2 out: no imp* 4/1[3]
30-0 **5** 5 **Savannah River (IRE)**[43] 2693 5-11-1 **79** MichaelMcAlister 57
(Miss Kate Milligan) *chsd ldrs: outpcd bef 4 out: n.d after* 33/1
5065 **6** 6 **Pornic (FR)**[9] 3320 12-11-7 **85** (b) ThomasDreaper 57
(A Crook) *mde most to bef 3 out: sn rdn and btn* 20/1
5L52 **7** nk **Joe Malone (IRE)**[48] 2586 7-10-9 **81** FearghalDavis(8) 52+
(N G Richards) *whipped rnd repeatedly s: nt fluent: hdwy to bk of main gp 4th: rdn and wknd bef 3 out* 11/4[2]
P-05 **F** **Team Resdev (IRE)**[17] 3173 6-10-8 **77** (p) PhilKinsella(5) —
(F P Murtagh) *prom: effrt after 4 out: 3l down and chsng ldr whn fell next* 50/1

5m 33.5s (17.70) **Going Correction** +0.925s/f (Soft) **8** Ran SP% **112.2**
Speed ratings: **101,97,96,91,89 86,86,—** CSF £43.40 CT £134.24 TOTE £5.90: £1.70, £2.80, £1.50; EX 52.10.There was no bid for the winner
Owner A R Dicken **Bred** Darley Stud Management, L L C **Trained** West Barns, E Lothian

FOCUS
A poor race, not strong form and very little to enthuse about for the future.

NOTEBOOK
Silver Seeker(USA) last won a race as a two-year-old on the Flat, but he found this race dropping into his lap as those at the head of affairs stopped. His last two efforts at Ayr suggested a race such as this was within his ability, but he would not be an obvious candidate to follow up. *(op 5-1 tchd 11-2 and 4-1)*
Named At Dinner, who has done most of his running over two miles, took up the running apparently going well entering the straight, but he probably went for home too soon as he was eventually outstayed. *(op 8-1 tchd 11-1)*
Maunby Rocker, whose rider lost his whip with four to jump, did not run badly in the circumstances off a 7lb higher mark than when successful at Hexham in November. *(op 9-4 tchd 11-4)*
Needwood Spirit continues to have a regressive profile. *(tchd 9-2)*
Pornic(FR), who is rated higher over hurdles than he is over fences, went well for a long way but stopped pretty quickly once they turned into the straight. *(tchd 16-1)*
Joe Malone(IRE), who has refused to race in the past, played up badly at the start and gave away plenty of ground to his rivals. He is not one to trust. *(op 3-1 tchd 10-3)*

3447 SALTWELL SIGNS H'CAP CHASE (16 fncs) 2m 4f
3:20 (3:25) (Class 4) (0-105,97) 5-Y-0+ **£3,918** (£1,182; £609; £322)

Form RPR
P520 **1** **Mikasa (IRE)**[9] 3320 6-10-11 **79** RichardMcGrath 83
(R F Fisher) *in tch: effrt 4 out: led jst after last: kpt on wl* 4/1[3]
3451 **2** 3 **Bob's Buster**[9] 3320 10-12-1 **97** 7ex KennyJohnson 99+
(R Johnson) *hld up and wl bhd: smooth hdwy to chse ldrs bef 4 out: led 2 out: mstke last: sn hdd: nt qckn* 9/2
1/03 **3** 3 1/2 **Tagar (FR)**[15] 3233 9-11-8 **93** MrTGreenall(3) 92+
(C Grant) *keen: mde most to 11th: one pce after 2 out: lft 3rd last: no imp* 9/4[1]
-0P6 **4** 22 **Scotmail Lad (IRE)**[43] 2688 12-11-12 **94** (p) RussGarritty 77+
(C A Mulhall) *prom tl wknd bef 4 out* 8/1
2632 **U** **Albertino Lad**[13] 3255 9-11-9 **94** PeterBuchanan(3) 96+
(Miss Lucinda V Russell) *cl up: led 6 out: hdd and hit 2 out: 3rd and hld whn hit: stmbld and uns rdr last* 5/2[2]

5m 35.4s (6.70) **Going Correction** +0.425s/f (Soft) **5** Ran SP% **108.6**
Speed ratings: **103,101,100,91,—** CSF £20.27 TOTE £4.90: £2.10, £2.40; EX 21.80.
Owner Sporting Occasions 7 **Bred** Michael Fleming **Trained** Ulverston, Cumbria

FOCUS
Moderate handicap form and the winner was probably the only one to get home. He sets the standard but the form does look suspect.

NOTEBOOK
Mikasa(IRE) jumped better this time and responded well to pressure, getting the best jump at the last to seal the win. An inconsistent type, he would not be guaranteed to repeat this effort next time. *(op 7-2 tchd 3-1)*
Bob's Buster was going best four out but his stamina was in doubt over this longer trip and in the end he did not see it out as well as Mikasa. He will appreciate a drop back to trips of around two miles. *(op 4-1 tchd 6-1)*
Tagar(FR) kept on well after being headed and, given that he raced keenly, did not run too badly. His only previous win came on good ground, though, and perhaps he will be happier on a decent surface. *(op 5-2 tchd 11-4)*

Albertino Lad, having his first start over a trip as far as this, was held in third when losing his rider at the final fence. He might prefer a drop back to two miles. *(tchd 11-4)*

3448 E.B.F./DONCASTER BLOODSTOCK SALES MARES' ONLY STANDARD OPEN NATIONAL HUNT FLAT RACE (QUALIFIER) 2m

3:50 (3:55) (Class 6) 4-6-Y-0 **£1,626** (£477; £238; £119)

Form RPR

1 **Scarvagh Diamond (IRE)** 5-10-9 MissRDavidson[7] 96+
(Mrs R L Elliot) *chsd ldrs: led and hrd pressed over 3f out: styd on strly fnl f* **14/1[3]**

6-3 **2** *4* **Adlestrop**[23] 2961 6-11-2 RichardJohnson 92
(R T Phillips) *hld up: hdwy to chse ldrs over 2f out: sn rdn: kpt on: nt pce of wnr fnl f* **3/1[2]**

61 **3** *3 ½* **Senora Snoopy (IRE)**[23] 2988 5-11-4 ThomasDreaper[5] 95
(Ferdy Murphy) *plld hrd: hld up in tch: hdwy to dispute ld over 3f out: sn rdn: no ex 2f out* **4/6[1]**

0 **4** *7* **Monifieth**[27] 2948 6-11-2 DominicElsworth 81
(D W Whillans) *hld up in tch: outpcd over 3f out: kpt on fnl f: no ch w first three* **14/1[3]**

5 **5** *3 ½* **Mrs O'Malley**[41] 2727 6-11-2 GrahamLee 78
(D McCain) *led after 2f to over 3f out: sn wknd* **14/1[3]**

6 *8* **Falcon's Cliche** 5-11-2 RussGarritty 70
(P Beaumont) *led 2f: chsd ldrs tl wknd wl over 2f out* **33/1**

7 *17* **Roman Gypsy** 5-11-2 RichardMcGrath 53
(Mrs K Walton) *chsd ldrs to over 4f out: sn rdn and btn* **33/1**

8 *½* **Wiljen (IRE)** 6-11-2 AnthonyRoss 52
(B S Rothwell) *hld up: rdn over 4f out: sn btn* **100/1**

9 *1 ¾* **Supreme Prospect** 5-11-2 KennyJohnson 50
(R Johnson) *racd wd: hld up: wknd over 4f out* **80/1**

10 *dist* **Bonny Blink (IRE)** 6-11-2 PadgeWhelan —
(S B Bell) *hld up: rdn and wknd fr 4f out* **100/1**

4m 31.4s (18.80) **Going Correction** +1.20s/f (Heavy) **10** Ran SP% **114.1**
Speed ratings: **101,99,97,93,92 88,79,79,78,**— CSF £54.14 TOTE £10.00: £1.60, £1.50, £1.20; EX 71.40 Place 6 £429.14, Place 5 £131.90.
Owner M S Borders Racing Club **Bred** Edwin Carlisle **Trained** Hownam, Borders

FOCUS
They crawled in the early stages suggesting the form is not reliable, but the winner, who was well backed and is bred to make a staying chaser in time, did it well.

NOTEBOOK
Scarvagh Diamond(IRE), a half-sister to winning hurdler/useful staying chaser Toulouse-Lautrec and to a winning pointer, was supported in from 33-1 and landed a bit of a touch for her small stable. This was not a great bumper but she did it well and has a future over obstacles. *(op 33-1)*
Adlestrop could not get to the gambled-on winner but ran another fair race in defeat. A stronger pace and better ground would have been in her favour. *(op 7-2 tchd 4-1)*
Senora Snoopy(IRE) did not settle off the slow pace and basically used up too much energy early in the race. She too would have been seen to better effect in a more strongly-run race. *(op 4-5 tchd 8-13)*
Monifieth probably only improved slightly on the form that saw her finish eighth at Ayr on her debut. *(op 12-1 tchd 16-1)*
Mrs O'Malley had her chance but was outpaced in the straight. A sharper track might suit her. *(op 9-1)*
T/Plt: £220.60 to a £1 stake. Pool: £53,202.50. 176.05 winning tickets. T/Qpdt: £38.50 to a £1 stake. Pool: £5,746.00. 110.20 winning tickets. RY

3139 UTTOXETER (L-H)

Wednesday, January 18

3449 Meeting Abandoned - Waterlogged

3354 LUDLOW (R-H)

Thursday, January 19

OFFICIAL GOING: Good (good to soft in places)
Wind: Light, across Weather: Fine, drizzle later

3456 LUDLOW FOR FUNCTIONS (S) H'CAP HURDLE (9 hdls) 2m

1:20 (1:20) (Class 5) (0-95,95) 4-Y-0+ **£2,602** (£764; £382; £190)

Form RPR

05 **1** **Barella (IRE)**[19] 3137 7-11-0 **90** (p) CharlieStudd[7] 94+
(B G Powell) *hld up in mid-div: hdwy appr 3 out: led and hit last: drvn out* **25/1**

23P0 **2** *1 ¾* **The Castilian (FR)**[15] 3242 4-10-8 **95** (v) AndrewGlassonbury[7] 85
(M C Pipe) *hld up in tch: led appr 3 out: rdn appr 2 out: hdd last: nt qckn* **6/1[1]**

P026 **3** *hd* **So Cloudy**[51] 2560 5-10-0 **69** PaulMoloney 71+
(D McCain) *hld up and bhd: sltly hmpd 3rd: hdwy after 6th: mstke 2 out: kpt on flat* **20/1**

U420 **4** *½* **Canadian Storm**[42] 2721 5-10-12 **88** (p) RichardSpate[7] 90+
(A G Juckes) *hld up and bhd: hdwy appr 3 out: hmpd and stmbld sn after 2 out: swtchd rt appr last: kpt on towards fin* **11/1**

4040 **5** *3* **Weet Watchers**[34] 2858 6-10-10 **79** JohnMcNamara 77+
(T Wall) *hld up and bhd: hdwy appr 3 out: rdn appr 2 out: no ex flat* **12/1**

5444 **6** *4* **Chariot (IRE)**[37] 2806 5-10-9 **78** (t) SeanCurran 71
(M R Bosley) *hld up and bhd: sme hdwy 5th: rdn after 6th: styd on fr 3 out* **16/1**

2303 **7** *1 ¼* **Jamaaron**[7] 3349 4-10-8 **93** RobertLucey-Butler[5] 74
(W G M Turner) *hld up and bhd: hdwy 6th: rdn appr 3 out: sn wknd* **13/2[2]**

5P53 **8** *2 ½* **Sunset King (USA)**[15] 3242 6-10-3 **77** JayHarris[5] 67
(R J Hodges) *prom: ev ch appr 3 out: sn rdn: wknd 2 out* **15/2[3]**

-354 **9** *2 ½* **Waziri (IRE)**[24] 2995 5-10-11 **80** (t) PJBrennan 67
(M Sheppard) *led: nt fluent 4th: rdn and hdd appr 3 out: wknd 2 out* **6/1[1]**

6P0 **10** *¾* **Life Estates**[62] 2309 6-10-0 **74** ow2 ChrisHonour[5] 60
(J D Frost) *hld up in tch: mstke 6th: wknd appr 3 out* **33/1**

5003 **11** *nk* **Pilca (FR)**[19] 3141 6-11-12 **95** SamStronge 81
(R M Stronge) *prom tl rdn and wknd after 6th* **8/1**

050P **12** *8* **Simiola**[51] 2560 7-9-13 **75** PatrickCStringer[7] 53
(S T Lewis) *hld up in tch: ev ch appr 3 out: sn wknd* **40/1**

-00P **13** *7* **Another Windfall**[20] 3125 7-10-0 **69** oh6 (t) MarkGrant 40
(C P Morlock) *hld up in tch: wknd after 6th* **50/1**

0003 **14** *2* **John Jorrocks (FR)**[9] 3330 7-10-0 **69** (v[1]) JimCrowley 38
(J C Tuck) *a bhd* **9/1**

0655 **15** *½* **Lovely Lulu**[37] 2806 8-10-0 **69** oh5 JodieMogford 38
(J C Tuck) *a bhd* **25/1**

6000 **U** **Sir Walter (IRE)**[20] 3128 13-11-4 **94** MrRMcCarthy[7] —
(D Burchell) *hld up and bhd: blnd and uns rdr 3rd* **16/1**

3m 51.2s (-1.10) **Going Correction** -0.05s/f (Good)
WFA 4 from 5yo+ 11lb **16** Ran SP% **122.4**
Speed ratings: **101,100,100,99,98 96,95,94,93,92 92,88,85,84,83** — CSF £162.59 CT £3104.64 TOTE £40.70: £5.90, £1.70, £3.80, £3.10; EX 248.90.There was no bid for the winner. Canadian Storm was the subject of a friendly claim. The Castilian was the subject of a friendly claim.
Owner Con Harrington **Bred** Mrs Chris Harrington **Trained** Morestead, Hants

FOCUS
A reasonably competitive event of its type and plenty were in with a chance turning into the home straight. The form looks solid enough, rated through the first two.

NOTEBOOK
Barella(IRE), down in the basement level for the first time, scored a shade readily, idling a little after striking the front at the last. The shorter trip and a 5lb lower mark presumably helped, as did *the return of cheekpieces. Official explanation: trainer said, regarding the improved form shown, gelding may benefited from the drop in class*
The Castilian(FR), lowered into selling company, ran a sound race with the visor re-applied, but after edging to his left at the second last he could not hold off the winner. *(tchd 13-2)*
So Cloudy settled a bit better this time before improving on the turn, but a slight error at the second last ended what chance she had.
Canadian Storm would have finished closer had he not stumbled after the second last when appearing to clip heels. He is capable of landing a seller when things go his way. *(op 12-1)*
Weet Watchers travelled well but again betrayed stamina limitations. *(tchd 10-1)*
Jamaaron, not for the first time, failed to get home. *(tchd 6-1)*
Waziri(IRE), in a tongue tie for the first time, was another taking a drop in grade but after making the running he faded in the straight. *(tchd 11-2)*

3457 CLIVE PAVILION BEGINNERS' CHASE (13 fncs) 2m

1:50 (1:51) (Class 4) 5-Y-0+
£4,384 (£1,295; £647; £324; £161; £81)

Form RPR

4-25 **1** **Tamarinbleu (FR)**[34] 2861 6-11-1 TomScudamore 135+
(M C Pipe) *led to 1st: w ldr: led and lft clr 3rd: j.lft 7th and 2 out: unchal* **8/15[1]**

2P42 **2** *14* **Jacks Craic (IRE)**[7] 3357 7-11-1 115 PJBrennan 125+
(J L Spearing) *hld up and bhd: hdwy 8th: chsd wnr 9th: rdn after 2 out: eased whn btn flat* **11/4[2]**

/P-P **3** *22* **Miss Colmesnil (FR)**[14] 3251 6-10-8 (p) HenryOliver 88
(A E Jessop) *hld up: hdwy 5th: no imp fr 9th* **66/1**

2P00 **4** *9* **Imperial Rocket (USA)**[7] 3360 9-10-10 (t) LeeStephens[5] 86
(W K Goldsworthy) *hld up towards rr: hdwy 4th: wknd 9th* **20/1[3]**

2PF0 **5** *11* **Let's Rock**[14] 3251 8-10-8 67 MrRHodges[7] 75
(Mrs A Price) *hld up: hdwy 4th: rdn after 8th: wknd after 9th* **50/1**

/5-P **6** *2 ½* **Arceye**[13] 3277 9-10-8 TomMessenger[7] 73
(W Davies) *a bhd: lost tch 7th* **66/1**

2P0P **7** *7* **Thyne Spirit (IRE)**[13] 3277 7-11-1 MarkGrant 66
(S T Lewis) *prom: mstke 2nd: wknd appr 5th: lost tch 7th* **50/1**

PP-P **8** *5* **Don't Matter**[19] 3141 6-10-1 MrMWall[7] 54
(A E Price) *mstkes: t.k.h in tch: wknd after 9th* **80/1**

PP **9** *dist* **Ballybean (IRE)**[14] 3251 6-11-1 JohnMcNamara —
(K C Bailey) *prom: wkng whn hit 9th: t.o* **20/1[3]**

PP-0 **F** **Powra**[20] 3130 6-10-10 JayHarris[5] —
(R J Hodges) *plld hrd: led: j.rt 2nd: hdd and fell 3rd* **66/1**

3m 58.5s (-5.60) **Going Correction** -0.40s/f (Good) **10** Ran SP% **111.1**
Speed ratings: **98,91,80,75,70 68,65,62,—,—** CSF £1.90 TOTE £1.50: £1.10, £1.10, £7.70; EX 2.10.
Owner The Arthur White Partnership **Bred** E A R L Lucy **Trained** Nicholashayne, Devon

FOCUS
No strength in depth in this novices' chase and the time was modest, but Tamarinbleu accomplished a straightforward task with little fuss. The eased down second sets the level with the winner value for less than the official margin.

NOTEBOOK
Tamarinbleu(FR) was found a good opportunity to restore a reputation dented a little after his defeat in bad ground at Uttoxeter. Left in a clear lead at the third, he jumped cleanly throughout, if showing a tendency to go out to his left, and was never seriously challenged. Last season's Ladbroke winner is now on course for a crack at the Arkle, having shown smart form on his chasing debut at Cheltenham when splitting leading Arkle contenders Accordion Etoile and Albuhera. He does look a better horse when given time between his races, though. *(op 4-9)*
Jacks Craic(IRE), runner-up in a decent handicap at the last Ludlow meeting, went after the favourite at the end of the back straight but, although closing the gap a little, he faced a thankless task. After appearing to hang slightly when the pressure was on, he was eased on the run-in to accentuate the margin of defeat. *(op 3-1 tchd 10-3)*
Miss Colmesnil(FR)was merely best of the rest. She had placed form over hurdles in France but had shown very little in this country, including on her recent chasing debut. *(tchd 80-1)*
Imperial Rocket(USA) has been out of sorts in his recent runs over hurdles and he was well held on this return to fences, albeit in light of a pretty stiff task.

3458 LUDLOWRACECOURSE.CO.UK H'CAP HURDLE (12 hdls) 3m

2:20 (2:20) (Class 4) (0-115,114) 4-Y-0+ **£5,204** (£1,528; £764; £381)

Form RPR

0612 **1** **Piran (IRE)**[12] 3286 4-10-6 **107** PaulMoloney 108+
(Evan Williams) *hld up towards rr: hdwy after 9th: led after 3 out: drvn out* **8/1[3]**

3336 **2** *2* **Ingres**[24] 2999 6-10-12 **107** CharlieStudd[7] 115
(B G Powell) *hld up in mid-div: hdwy appr 3 out: rdn appr 2 out: styd on flat* **12/1**

1-00 **3** *12* **Krakow Baba (FR)**[12] 3286 6-11-1 **106** PaulO'Neill[3] 103+
(Miss Venetia Williams) *hld up in tch: led after 9th: sn rdn: hdd after 3 out: hit 2 out: wknd flat* **18/1**

3-21 **4** *½* **Present Glory (IRE)**[70] 2147 7-11-7 **109** JasonMaguire 106+
(C Tinkler) *prom tl wknd appr 3 out* **5/1[2]**

3251 **5** *1 ¼* **Kilty Storm (IRE)**[8] 3345 7-10-9 **104** AndrewGlassonbury[7] 100+
(M C Pipe) *t.k.h in mid-div: hdwy appr 8th: rdn after 9th: ev ch 3 out: wkng whn hit last* **2/1[1]**

060R **6** *2 ½* **Business Traveller (IRE)**[7] 3356 6-10-3 **91** (bt[1]) MarcusFoley 83+
(R J Price) *hld up in mid-div: hdwy after 9th: wknd 3 out* **25/1**

-30P **7** *1 ¾* **Old Feathers (IRE)**[24] 2990 9-11-4 **106** (v) NoelFehily 97+
(Jonjo O'Neill) *led: hit 9th: sn rdn and hdd: wknd appr 2 out* **22/1**

1360 **8** *17* **Tirikumba**[14] 3247 10-10-4 **99** MrTJO'Brien[7] 72
(S G Griffiths) *hld up in tch: wknd 7th* **20/1**

P600 **9** *3* **Haydens Field**[42] 2731 12-10-8 **101** (t) LeeStephens[5] 71
(Miss H Lewis) *prom to 7th* **28/1**

136- **10** *3* **Proper Squire (USA)**[571] 828 9-11-2 **114** KevinTobin[10] 81
(C J Mann) *prom to 3rd* **16/1**

06-P **11** *8* **Big Max**[17] [3214] 11-10-4 **92** TomScudamore 51
(Miss K M George) *prom tl wknd 8th* **50/1**

-P2P **12** *1* **Putup Or Shutup (IRE)**[29] [2938] 10-10-8 **101** ChrisHonour[(5)] 59
(K C Bailey) *a bhd* **16/1**

P000 **13** *3 ½* **Marrel**[18] [3177] 8-11-1 **110** (v) MrGTumelty[(7)] 65
(D Burchell) *hld up in tch: wknd 8th* **40/1**

652- **14** *5* **Metal Detector (IRE)**[342] [3796] 9-11-7 **109** JohnMcNamara 59
(K C Bailey) *a bhd* **33/1**

40PP **15** *14* **Turaath (IRE)**[19] [3143] 10-11-8 **110** PJBrennan 46
(A J Deakin) *hld up in mid-div: hdwy appr 8th: wkng whn mstke 3 out* **33/1**

134 **P** **Day Of Claies (FR)**[24] [2990] 5-11-8 **110** CarlLlewellyn —
(N A Twiston-Davies) *bhd fr 5th: p.u bef 2 out* **9/1**

242- **P** **Factor Fifteen**[324] [4110] 7-11-6 **108** JodieMogford —
(J C Tuck) *a bhd: tailed of whn p.u bef 3 out* **28/1**

P00P **P** **Nick's Choice**[12] [3289] 10-10-12 **107** MrRMcCarthy[(7)] —
(D Burchell) *bhd fr 7th: t.o whn p.u bef 2 out* **40/1**

5m 50.0s (-4.60) **Going Correction** -0.05s/f (Good)
WFA 4 from 5yo+ 13lb **18** Ran SP% **128.4**
Speed ratings: **106,105,101,101,100 99,99,93,92,91 89,88,87,85,81** —,—,— CSF £92.48 CT £1717.74 TOTE £10.80: £2.10, £2.00, £5.10, £1.90; EX 167.10.
Owner The Welsh Valleys Syndicate **Bred** Michael Hurley **Trained** Cowbridge, Vale Of Glamorgan

FOCUS
An ordinary handicap, run at a fair pace and the form has been rated positively, with the winner value for three times the official margin.

NOTEBOOK
Piran(IRE) sat off the pace before improving on the long turn round to the home straight. He came back on the bit before taking up the running but had to be driven out to hold on. Having only his sixth run over hurdles, he is on the upgrade but he gave the impression that three miles on a stiffer track than this might find him out. *(op 7-1)*

Ingres, who stayed on well to bustle up the winner, has been performing creditably of late without getting his head in front. As he finished 12 lengths clear of the rest, he is unlikely to be coming down the weights after this.

Krakow Baba(FR) had not shown much in two previous outings this term but ran better here, if not quite seeing out this half-mile longer trip. *(op 20-1 tchd 22-1)*

Present Glory(IRE), an easy novice winner, weakened out of contention on his handicap debut. The best will not be seen of him until he tackles fences. *(op 9-2)*

Kilty Storm(IRE) escaped a penalty for his win in a conditionals' race last week and was officially 6lb ahead of the Handicapper, but he was rather keen through the race and did not have much left at the business end. *(op 15-8 tchd 7-4)*

Business Traveller(IRE), who refused on his chasing debut a week earlier, was equipped with blinkers and a tongue tie for the first time and was not disgraced. There could be a small race to be won with him.

Old Feathers(IRE) set a reasonable pace but did not last too long once headed. *(op 20-1)*

3459 RACING UK H'CAP CHASE (17 fncs) 2m 4f

2:50 (2:50) (Class 4) (0-115,115) 5-Y-0+

£6,263 (£1,850; £925; £463; £231; £116)

Form RPR

3P13 **1** **Bob The Builder**[36] [2825] 7-11-3 **106** CarlLlewellyn 134+
(N A Twiston-Davies) *led 2nd: j.lft fr 10th: lft clr 4 out: hung lft fr 2 out: eased towards fin* **4/1**[1]

21-3 **2** *12* **Jaffa**[265] [97] 14-11-5 **115** MrRArmson[(7)] 126+
(Miss J Wormall) *hld up and bhd: hdwy 10th: lft 2nd 4 out: no ch w wnr* **12/1**

F0F4 **3** *9* **Roschal (IRE)**[15] [3239] 8-11-0 **103** PJBrennan 105+
(P J Hobbs) *bhd: rdn 10th: styd on fr 4 out: n.d* **11/2**[3]

3640 **4** *¾* **Saafend Rocket (IRE)**[7] [3357] 8-11-12 **115** MarkBradburne 117+
(H D Daly) *hld up: pckd 1st: hdwy 9th: rdn after 13th: wkng whn mstke 2 out* **9/1**

2216 **5** *2 ½* **Kind Sir**[186] [1028] 10-11-6 **109** NoelFehily 107+
(A W Carroll) *led to 2nd: w ldr: mstke 11th: wknd 13th* **20/1**

0530 **6** *1 ¼* **Deliceo (IRE)**[7] [3358] 13-10-12 **101** (p) JimmyMcCarthy 97
(M Sheppard) *hld up: hdwy 9th: wknd 11th* **20/1**

2513 **7** *shd* **Alcatras (IRE)**[20] [3129] 9-10-2 **91** JimCrowley 86
(B J M Ryall) *a bhd* **9/2**[2]

4216 **8** *2 ½* **Runner Bean**[29] [2939] 12-11-2 **105** JohnMcNamara 98
(R Lee) *hld up: hdwy 9th: wknd 10th* **18/1**

1-56 **9** *1* **Rainbows Aglitter**[30] [2931] 9-11-4 **107** MarcusFoley 99
(D R Gandolfo) *a bhd: rdn appr 13th: hit 2 out* **12/1**

-252 **F** **Alcopop**[31] [2926] 7-11-5 **111** PaulO'Neill[(3)] —
(Miss Venetia Williams) *prom: chsd wnr 12th: rdn and 6l 2nd whn fell 4 out* **9/2**[2]

-P0F **P** **Tunes Of Glory (IRE)**[35] [2843] 10-11-9 **112** JasonMaguire —
(D McCain) *hld up: hdwy 9th: wknd appr 11th: t.o whn p.u bef 4 out* **40/1**

5m 0.50s (-10.20) **Going Correction** -0.40s/f (Good) **11** Ran SP% **114.4**
Speed ratings: **104,99,95,95,94 93,93,92,92,**— — CSF £47.24 CT £263.94 TOTE £5.00: £1.70, £3.50, £2.20; EX 63.60.
Owner Mr & Mrs Peter Orton **Bred** Mrs Susan Orton **Trained** Naunton, Gloucs

FOCUS
A fair handicap in which they were soon strung out. The winner is value for more than the official margin and, with the placed horses close to their marks, the form looks solid enough.

NOTEBOOK
Bob The Builder won the early tussle for the lead with Kind Sir and set a decent pace. Jumping out to his left throughout, a trait he has shown before, he was left clear four from home and was well in command when going alarmingly out to his left at the final fence. The return to this trip suited and he is probably capable of better still. *(tchd 9-2 in places)*

Jaffa stayed on steadily in the latter stages on this first start April without ever threatening the winner. He has not had much racing and retains plenty of zest despite his advanced age. *(op 10-1)*

Roschal(IRE) kept on in the latter stages without getting to grips with the leaders. A second successive clear round will have done him good and he could be worth a try at three miles. *(tchd 5-1)*

Saafend Rocket(IRE), having the 19th run of his career at the Shropshire track, is perhaps more effective over the minimum trip. He has not been firing this winter but this was better and he is due to race off a 2lb lower mark in future

Kind Sir is happiest when able to dominate but could not do so with the winner in opposition. He should come on for this first run for six months but is currently 8lb above his last winning mark. *(op 14-1)*

Deliceo(IRE), winner of this event two years ago, is on the decline now. *(op 25-1)*

Alcopop was in second place, but not looking like catching the eventual winner, when he paddled through the first fence in the home straight and came down. He remains in good heart. *(op 4-1)*

3460 LUDLOW FOR CONFERENCES NOVICES' H'CAP CHASE (19 fncs) 3m

3:20 (3:23) (Class 4) (0-100,99) 5-Y-0+

£5,323 (£1,572; £786; £393; £196; £98)

Form RPR

3134 **1** **Rosetown (IRE)**[14] [3252] 8-10-1 **74** (b) PJBrennan 86+
(T R George) *a.p: led 13th: rdn appr 4 out: hdd 3 out: rallied to ld flat: r.o* **3/1**[1]

2 *1 ¾* **Fieldsofclover (IRE)**[91] [1809] 9-10-10 **83** MarcusFoley 90
(Miss E C Lavelle) *hld up in mid-div: hdwy 12th: led 3 out: sn rdn: hdd and no ex flat* **7/1**[2]

440P **3** *5* **Jacarado (IRE)**[13] [3274] 8-9-7 **73** oh8 (v) JohnPritchard[(7)] 77+
(R Dickin) *hld up in tch: pckd 13th (water): rdn after 15th: hit 4 out: hung lft flat: one pce* **25/1**

33F **4** *11* **Kimono Royal (FR)**[20] [3129] 8-11-9 **99** GinoCarenza[(3)] 96+
(A King) *hld up in mid-div: hdwy appr 12th: 4 l 3rd whn blnd and rdr lost iron 2 out: wknd last* **8/1**[3]

P-00 **5** *1* **Bright Present (IRE)**[28] [2950] 8-9-7 **73** oh9 (tp) TomMessenger[(7)] 64+
(B N Pollock) *led to 2nd: prom: rdn after 11th: hit 15th: wknd appr 4 out* **40/1**

P-0P **6** *3* **Celia's High (IRE)**[24] [2978] 7-9-7 **73** oh7 (t) MrGTumelty[(7)] 60
(D McCain) *hld up: hdwy 10th: wknd appr 4 out* **28/1**

F-43 **7** *2 ½* **Scratch The Dove**[13] [3278] 9-11-8 **95** JasonMaguire 82+
(A E Price) *hld up and bhd: hdwy 14th: wknd appr 4 out* **16/1**

3300 **8** *5* **Valleymore (IRE)**[12] [3290] 10-11-4 **91** TomSiddall 71
(S A Brookshaw) *mid-div: rdn after 14th: sn struggling* **12/1**

00PF **9** *3 ½* **Sidcup's Gold (IRE)**[14] [3252] 6-10-5 **78** JimmyMcCarthy 54
(M Sheppard) *a bhd* **40/1**

P-P5 **10** *1 ¾* **Cleymor House (IRE)**[53] [2517] 8-9-11 **73** oh19 (b) LeeVickers[(3)] 47
(John R Upson) *prom tl rdn and wknd after 15th: j. bdly lft 2 out* **12/1**

1F30 **11** *10* **Mini Dare**[29] [2938] 9-11-10 **97** LeightonAspell 61
(O Sherwood) *mid-div: pushed along 10th: bhd fr 15th* **8/1**[3]

-PP0 **P** **Jesnic (IRE)**[7] [3359] 6-10-8 **81** CarlLlewellyn —
(R Dickin) *a bhd: t.o whn p.u bef 4 out* **25/1**

-53P **P** **Irish Grouse (IRE)**[30] [2933] 7-10-0 **73** oh7 PaulMoloney —
(Miss H C Knight) *a bhd: t.o whn p.u bef 4 out* **11/1**

U665 **P** **Tianyi (IRE)**[29] [2936] 10-10-0 **73** oh3 (v) TomScudamore —
(M Scudamore) *prom: hit 9th: wknd 10th: t.o whn p.u bef 4 out* **14/1**

3PP5 **P** **Alexander Musical (IRE)**[63] [2284] 8-10-0 **73** oh11 (b) MarkGrant —
(S T Lewis) *led 2nd to 13th: wknd after 15th: bhd whn p.u bef 3 out* **33/1**

/5-4 **P** **Rohan**[267] [51] 10-11-3 **90** MarkBradburne —
(R F Johnson Houghton) *mid-div: j. slowly and lost pl 3rd: reminders after 6th: t.o whn p.u bef 4 out* **14/1**

6m 4.80s (-7.30) **Going Correction** -0.40s/f (Good) **16** Ran SP% **121.6**
Speed ratings: **96,95,93,90,89 88,87,86,85,84 81,**—,—,—,— — CSF £22.84 CT £449.80 TOTE £3.20: £1.50, £2.70, £11.50, £2.10; EX 31.60.
Owner Timothy N Chick **Bred** Mrs F Harrington **Trained** Slad, Gloucs

FOCUS
There was only one previous chase winner in this distinctly modest affair. The winner did not need to run up to his hurdles form to score, with the second rated to his Irish form.

NOTEBOOK
Rosetown(IRE) ◆ was the most prolific scorer in the field with five hurdles wins to his name and was able to get in here off no less than 29lb lower than his current hurdles mark. He looked in trouble when headed after a slow jump at the fourth from home, but rallied to lead on the flat and won with a bit up his sleeve. There could be more to come from him even after he is re-assessed, especially on softer ground. *(op 11-4)*

Fieldsofclover(IRE), who showed little in three attempts over fences when trained in Ireland, looked like making a winning debut for the Lavelle yard on his first run for three months but was run out of it after the last. This longer trip looks the key to him, on relatively sharp tracks such as this anyway. *(op 8-1)*

Jacarado(IRE), with the visor refitted, ran his best race to date on this step back up in trip despite being 8lb out of the handicap. *(op 20-1)*

Kimono Royal(FR) got no further than the first on his recent chasing debut and this was effectively his first run since July. He ran respectably on ground that was easier than he would like but was just held when making a hash of the second last. *(op 11-2)*

Bright Present(IRE), equipped with blinkers and a tongue tie for this return to fences, was not disgraced from 9lb out of the handicap.

Mini Dare, the only winning chaser in the field, has now run lacklustre races on his last two starts, both at this track. *(tchd 15-2)*

3461 ENTERTAIN AT LUDLOW MARES' ONLY MAIDEN HURDLE (11 hdls) 2m 5f

3:50 (3:52) (Class 4) 4-Y-0+ **£3,903** (£1,146; £573; £286)

Form RPR

0 **1** **Atlantic Jane**[19] [3149] 6-11-2 TJPhelan[(3)] 101
(Mrs H Dalton) *hld up in tch: lost pl appr 6th: rdn appr 7th: rallied appr 3 out: styd on to ld flat* **40/1**

F304 **2** *1 ½* **Samandara (FR)**[42] [2726] 6-11-2 97 (v) GinoCarenza[(3)] 99
(A King) *hld up towards rr: hdwy appr 7th: rdn to ld last: hdd flat: nt qckn* **8/1**

1-52 **3** *hd* **Makeabreak (IRE)**[10] [3322] 7-11-5 NoelFehily 99
(C J Mann) *hld up in tch: rdn to ld 2 out: hdd last: nt qckn* **3/1**[2]

5P0 **4** *2 ½* **Smilingvalentine (IRE)**[19] [3149] 9-11-5 JodieMogford 97+
(D J Wintle) *a.p: led after 8th to 2 out: no ex flat* **100/1**

F623 **5** *20* **Boberelle (IRE)**[19] [3149] 6-11-5 105 JasonMaguire 76
(C Tinkler) *hld up in mid-div: hdwy on ins 6th: rdn and wknd appr 3 out* **11/4**[1]

02/P **6** *2 ½* **Polyanthus Jones**[42] [2718] 7-11-0 TomGreenway[(5)] 74
(H D Daly) *hld up in tch: rdn after 6th: wknd appr 3 out* **20/1**

2145 **7** *11* **Fountain Crumble**[10] [3322] 5-10-12 MissRAGreen[(7)] 63
(P F Nicholls) *hld up and bhd: mstkes 1st and 5th: hdwy appr 7th: wknd appr 3 out* **10/1**

0 **8** *¾* **Koral Bay (FR)**[33] [2878] 5-10-12 112 (b[1]) MrSWaley-Cohen[(7)] 62
(R Waley-Cohen) *led: clr 5th: hdd after 8th: wkng whn j.rt 3 out* **16/1**

0P2 **9** *6* **Noun De La Thinte (FR)**[12] [3280] 5-11-2 100 PaulO'Neill[(3)] 56
(Miss Venetia Williams) *prom tl rdn and wknd appr 3 out* **4/1**[3]

04P6 **10** *2 ½* **Cresswell Willow (IRE)**[12] [3281] 6-11-0 LeeStephens[(5)] 54
(W K Goldsworthy) *mid-div: bhd whn hit 6th* **50/1**

30 **11** *dist* **Miss Chippy (IRE)**[29] [2941] 6-11-5 CarlLlewellyn —
(T R George) *t.k.h: chsd ldr: pckd 4th: wknd after 8th: t.o* **20/1**

12 *dist* **Eva's Edge (IRE)** 5-10-12 TomMessenger[(7)] —
(B N Pollock) *nvr gng wl: a bhd: mstke 1st: t.o whn blnd 3 out* **40/1**

05 **P** **Mo Chailin**[23] [3024] 7-11-5 LeightonAspell —
(D A Rees) *bhd tl p.u lame after 7th* **33/1**

FPF **P** **The Sneakster (IRE)**[7] [3356] 8-11-5 TomSiddall —
(S A Brookshaw) *a bhd: t.o whn p.u bef 3 out* **100/1**

50-0 **P** **School Class**[29] [2937] 6-10-12 .... JohnKington(7) —
(M Scudamore) *mid-div: bhd fr 7th: t.o whn p.u bef 3 out* **66/1**

P **P** **Leave It To You**[14] [3249] 8-11-5 ....(t) MarkBradburne —
(M Sheppard) *t.k.h in mid-div: mstke 7th: bhd whn p.u after 8th* **100/1**

5m 18.9s (0.60) **Going Correction** -0.05s/f (Good) **16** Ran SP% **121.5**
Speed ratings: **97,96,96,95,87 86,82,82,80,79** —,—,—,—,— CSF £320.93 TOTE £76.00: £13.00, £2.20, £1.90; EX 1052.20.
Owner P J Hughes Developments Ltd **Bred** G G A Gregson **Trained** Norton, Shropshire

FOCUS
A surprise outcome to this ordinary mares' event. The runner-up is the best guide to the level of the form.

NOTEBOOK
Atlantic Jane, well beaten on her debut, looked set to finish out the back when adrift down the far side and still had a lot to do on the long home turn, but after jumping the last in fourth place she *picked up really well to win going away. Official explanation: trainer said, regarding improved form shown, that in mare's first outing at Warwick she made a mistake at the first flight and was never able to make up ground thereafter (op 33-1)*
Samandara(FR), upped in trip after a fair effort in a mares' handicap over two miles here, looked the likeliest scorer up the straight but, although battling on to hold off the third, could not contain the winner's strong run. *(tchd 15-2)*
Makeabreak(IRE), runner-up to Harringay at Taunton over a slightly shorter trip, had every chance but could not quicken up on the run to the line. *(tchd 100-30 in places)*
Smilingvalentine(IRE) is a winner between the flags in Ireland but this was her first worthwhile form under Rules. She finished a long way ahead of the remainder and there could be a little race for her if she is able to reproduce this.
Boberelle(IRE), who had today's winner a long way behind at Warwick last time, faded to finish a rather remote fifth. This was disappointing. *(op 3-1 tchd 10-3)*
Noun De La Thinte(FR) ran well behind subsequent winner Sunley Shines at Fontwell but failed to see out this longer trip. *(tchd 9-2)*
Mo Chailin, who showed promise in a bumper last time, unfortunately sustained a serious injury on this hurdles debut. *(tchd 40-1)*

3462 RACING POST "HANDS AND HEELS" JUMPS SERIES INTERMEDIATE NH FLAT RACE (CONDITIONAL/AMATEUR RIDERS) 2m
4:20 (4:27) (Class 5) 4-6-Y-0 **£2,602** (£764; £382; £190)

Form RPR

1 **Sir Jimmy Shand (IRE)** 5-11-4 .... MrSWaley-Cohen 109+
(N J Henderson) *a gng wl: led over 1f out: qckn d clr ins fnl f: readily* **1/1**[1]

0 **2** *5* **Just Smudge**[58] [2425] 4-10-7 .... AndrewGlassonbury 88+
(A E Price) *hld up in tch: sltly outpcd over 1f out: styd on to take 2nd post* **28/1**

13 **3** *shd* **The Hollow Bottom**[29] [2941] 5-11-11 .... BernieWharfe 105
(N A Twiston-Davies) *led: rdn and edgd lft over 2f out: hdd over 1f out: one pce* **7/1**[3]

4 *7* **Hollandia (IRE)** 5-10-13 .... MrJJarrett(5) 91
(Miss H C Knight) *hld up: stdy hdwy over 6f out: wknd over 3f out* **9/1**

2 **5** *13* **Magical Harry**[29] [2941] 6-11-1 .... MissRAGreen(3) 81+
(P F Nicholls) *prom tl wknd over 3f out* **11/4**[2]

6 *3 ½* **Tiger Rock** 5-11-1 .... MissSSharratt(3) 75
(Ms N M Hugo) *chsd ldr tl over 5f out: wknd 4f out* **40/1**

0 **7** *nk* **Native Forest (IRE)**[53] [2534] 5-11-4 .... JohnKington 74
(Miss H C Knight) *hld up in tch: rdn over 6f out: wknd 5f out* **20/1**

8 *½* **Coorbawn Vic (IRE)** 5-10-13 .... MrJMahot(5) 74
(S A Brookshaw) *a bhd* **16/1**

0 **9** *12* **Perfectly Posh**[19] [3145] 5-10-11 .... MrGTumelty 55
(J K Cresswell) *hld up: hdwy 9f out: rdn over 6f out: wknd over 5f out* **66/1**

00 **10** *23* **Im A Tanner**[36] [2823] 5-11-4 .... MissCDyson 39
(Miss C Dyson) *a bhd: t.o* **100/1**

3m 47.3s (-4.90) **Going Correction** -0.05s/f (Good)
WFA 4 from 5yo+ 11lb **10** Ran SP% **118.2**
Speed ratings: **103,100,100,96,90 88,88,88,82,70** CSF £43.51 TOTE £2.00: £1.30, £4.00, £1.30; EX 41.40 Place 6 £121.70, Place 5 £35.17.
Owner W H Ponsonby **Bred** C Morgan **Trained** Upper Lambourn, Berks

FOCUS
Probably a fair little race of its type and the market got it spot-on. The winner was value for double the winning margin and looks above average, with the third and seventh setting the level for the form.

NOTEBOOK
Sir Jimmy Shand(IRE) made an impressive winning debut. Out of a half-sister to the smart Redundant Pal, he was always travelling supremely well just behind the leaders before sweeping to the front over a furlong from home with his rider looking around for dangers. He looks to have a bright future. *(op 11-8)*
Just Smudge, out of the 1994 Champion Hurdler Flakey Dove, improved a ton from his debut in a 14-furlong junior bumper at Warwick in November and may have finished a little bit closer had he not become short of room between the winner and the eventual third around two furlongs from home. There are certainly races to be won with him. *(op 25-1)*
The Hollow Bottom, whose three runs have all been here, tried to make every yard of the running but had no answer when the favourite arrived on the scene. His penalty will continue to make him *vulnerable to unexposed sorts in races like this and now may be the time to put him over hurdles. (op 5-1)*
Hollandia(IRE), a half-brother to a winning Irish pointer out of an Irish bumper winner, was close enough on the home bend but then appeared to run green and could make no further impression. He should come on for this debut. *(tchd 10-1)*
Magical Harry dropped tamely away in the home straight and was very disappointing in view of his promising effort here last month. He is surely better than this. *(op 3-1 tchd 100-30)*
T/Plt: £67.70 to a £1 stake. Pool: £38,772.00. 417.95 winning tickets. T/Qpdt: £22.00 to a £1 stake. Pool: £3,332.50. 111.60 winning tickets. KH

[3321] TAUNTON (R-H)
Thursday, January 19

OFFICIAL GOING: Good to soft (soft in places)
Wind: Mild, across

3463 SOUTHWESTRACING.COM NOVICES' HURDLE (DIV I) (9 hdls) 2m 1f
1:00 (1:00) (Class 4) 4-Y-0+ **£3,578** (£1,050; £525; £262)

Form RPR

1 **Princelet (IRE)**[106] 4-10-7 .... APMcCoy 101+
(N J Henderson) *racd freely: a.p: led 6th: shkn up run-in: kpt on wl* **13/8**[1]

2 *1 ½* **Traprain (IRE)**[106] 4-10-7 .... RichardJohnson 96+
(P J Hobbs) *t.k.h: hld up towards rr: stdy hdwy fr 4th: chsd wnr appr 2 out: kpt on but a hld by wnr* **2/1**[2]

U60 **3** *7* **Before Time**[36] [2824] 4-10-2 81 .... DerekLaverty(5) 86
(Mrs A M Thorpe) *mid div: hdwy 6th: rdn after 3 out: wnt 3rd after 3 out: kpt on same pce* **33/1**

4 *8* **Megaton**[473] 5-11-4 .... ChristianWilliams 89
(P Bowen) *chsd ldrs: rdn and effrt after 3 out: wknd next* **20/1**

5 *7* **Wee Dinns (IRE)**[90] 5-10-8 .... TomMalone(3) 75+
(M C Pipe) *hld up bhd: drvn along fr 6th: styd on past btn horses fr 2 out: nvr trbld ldrs* **10/1**[3]

P0 **6** *5* **Financial Future**[9] [3328] 6-11-4 .... AndrewThornton 77
(C Roberts) *nt fluent 4th: towards rr: sme late hdwy: nvr a danger* **100/1**

-000 **7** *5* **Post It**[10] [3322] 5-10-11 .... JamieMoore 65
(R J Hodges) *chsd ldrs: rdn appr 6th: sn btn* **50/1**

400 **8** *3* **Lord Ryeford (IRE)**[8] [3342] 6-10-11 .... WillieMcCarthy(7) 69
(T R George) *mid div tl wknd appr 3 out* **33/1**

0 **9** *5* **Mr Tambourine Man (IRE)**[20] [3127] 5-11-4 .... OllieMcPhail 64
(B J Llewellyn) *led tl 6th: wknd after 3 out* **66/1**

060 **10** *7* **Berkeley Court**[19] [3138] 5-11-4 .... PhilipHide 59+
(G L Moore) *chsd ldrs tl wknd 3 out* **28/1**

60 **11** *4* **Lone Rider (IRE)**[33] [2873] 5-11-4 .... MickFitzgerald 53
(Jonjo O'Neill) *mid div tl wknd 3 out* **40/1**

12 *10* **Windyx (FR)**[551] 5-11-4 .... RJGreene 43
(M C Pipe) *hld up and a bhd* **10/1**[3]

000 **P** **Eudyptes**[57] [2428] 7-11-4 ....(b[1]) BenjaminHitchcott —
(N E Berry) *bhd fr 4th: t.o and p.u after 3 out* **200/1**

P **P** **The Stafford (IRE)**[44] [2683] 5-10-11 .... JustinMorgan(7) —
(L Wells) *mid div: mstke 5th: sn bhd: t.o and p.u after 3 out* **200/1**

4m 7.00s (-1.80) **Going Correction** +0.05s/f (Yiel)
WFA 4 from 5yo+ 11lb **14** Ran SP% **111.6**
Speed ratings: **106,105,102,98,94 92,90,88,86,83 81,76,**—,— CSF £4.15 TOTE £2.70: £1.60, £1.40, £5.70; EX 5.70.
Owner John P McManus **Bred** Kilfrush Stud **Trained** Upper Lambourn, Berks

FOCUS
A decent novices' hurdle in which former stablemates from the Flat, Princelet and Traprain, pulled clear from the turn in. There is little to go on form-wise, and the race has been rated around time compared with the later handicap.

NOTEBOOK
Princelet(IRE), successful in a Nottingham maiden on his third and final start for Michael Jarvis on the level, had been purchased by top connections and was rightly made favourite in what looked a relatively uncompetitive race. He gave the impression he was always wanting to go a little quicker than McCoy would allow, but he had enough energy in reserve and stayed on well after the last, always holding the persistent runner-up. It is unlikely he will prove good enough to take his chance *in graded company at the Festival, and it may well be he is aimed at the juvenile handicap hurdle. (op 15-8 tchd 5-2)*
Traprain(IRE), a stablemate of the winner on the Flat, made steady headway at past halfway and had reached a challenging position before they turned for home, but he was never quite getting to the winner. This was still a fair effort, with a gap back to the third, and he is in the right hands to win races. *(tchd 15-8)*
Before Time ran his best race to date, but does little for the form. He has acquired a rating of 81 and, on this evidence, will be capable of exploiting that in handicaps. *(op 25-1 tchd 40-1)*
Megaton, successful in one of his eight starts on the Flat in France, was never far from the lead and kept on well enough for pressure without being able to go on with the principals. He should benefit from the experience. *(op 12-1 tchd 11-1)*
Wee Dinns(IRE), a modest sort on the Flat, never got into it on this hurdles debut, but was putting in some good late work and should know more next time. She may be a useful sort in mares-only races. *(op 9-1 tchd 12-1)*
Windyx(FR) was perhaps the most interesting runner on show, having won two of his four starts for Andre Fabre in France, but he jumped poorly in rear and was always trailing. It will be both disappointing, and surprising if he cannot step up on this next time. *(op 8-1 tchd 13-2)*
Eudyptes *Official explanation: vet said gelding was lame (op 100-1)*

3464 SOUTHWESTRACING.COM NOVICES' HURDLE (DIV II) (9 hdls) 2m 1f
1:30 (1:30) (Class 4) 4-Y-0+ **£3,578** (£1,050; £525; £262)

Form RPR

12 **1** **Siberian Highness (FR)**[37] [2803] 5-11-4 113 .... RobertThornton 122+
(A King) *trckd ldrs: led 3 out: sn clr: mstke last: readily* **11/10**[1]

2 *11* **Dark Parade (ARG)**[167] 5-11-4 .... JamieMoore 104+
(G L Moore) *in tch: tk clsr order 6th: rdn appr 2 out: kpt on to go 2nd and blnd last: no ch w wnr* **33/1**

5 **3** *½* **Topkat (IRE)**[56] [2455] 5-11-1 ....(t) TomMalone(3) 102
(M C Pipe) *hld up bhd: styd on strly u.p fr 2 out: tk 3rd cl home* **11/2**[3]

36 **4** *hd* **Legally Fast (USA)**[10] [3324] 4-10-7 .... AndrewThornton 91
(S C Burrough) *prom: led 3rd tl 6th: chsd ldrs: rdn after 3 out: kpt on* **12/1**

0256 **5** *3* **Hunting Lodge (IRE)**[18] [3185] 5-10-11 98 .... MrJAJenkins(7) 99
(H J Manners) *in tch: tk clsr order 5th: rdn and effrt after 3 out: one pcd fr next* **40/1**

6 *5* **Investment Wings (IRE)**[137] 4-10-7 .... RJGreene 83
(M C Pipe) *mid div: rdn after 3 out: sn one pce* **25/1**

54 **7** *1* **Grand Bay (USA)**[28] [2950] 5-11-4 .... APMcCoy 94+
(Jonjo O'Neill) *hld up towards rr: hdwy 4th: trckd ldrs 6th: outpcd after 3 out: nt a danger after* **12/1**

006 **8** *dist* **Nelson Du Ronceray (FR)**[20] [3130] 5-11-4 .... TimmyMurphy —
(M C Pipe) *mid div tl 5th: sn bhd* **66/1**

0F **9** *9* **Island Light (USA)**[56] [2455] 6-11-4 ....(p) JamieGoldstein —
(P Wegmann) *mid div: rdn and wknd after 3 out* **200/1**

40/0 **10** *dist* **Irenie**[10] [3322] 11-10-8 .... RichardYoung(3) —
(N R Mitchell) *led tl 3rd: fdd fr 5th: t.o* **200/1**

P **P** **Chaplin**[7] [3355] 5-11-4 ....(vt[1]) TomDoyle —
(P R Webber) *chsd ldrs tl 5th: sn t.o: p.u bef 2 out* **66/1**

0 **P** **Danzare**[8] [3340] 4-10-0 .... AndrewTinkler —
(Mrs A J Hamilton-Fairley) *wnt lft 2nd: a bhd: t.o and p.u bef 2 out* **200/1**

P **Danehill Prince (IRE)**[1135] 7-11-4 .... ChristianWilliams —
(P Bowen) *plld hrd in rr: lost tch 5th: t.o and p.u after 3 out* **80/1**

U **Massif Centrale**[116] 5-11-4 .... RobertWalford —
(D R C Elsworth) *t.k.h: trckd ldrs: led 6th tl 3 out: sn rdn: 4th and hld whn nt fluent and uns rdr 2 out* **7/2**[2]

4m 8.00s (-0.80) **Going Correction** +0.05s/f (Yiel)
WFA 4 from 5yo+ 11lb **14** Ran SP% **115.5**
Speed ratings: **103,97,97,97,96 93,93,**—,—,— —,—,—,— CSF £47.74 TOTE £2.20: £1.10, £9.20, £1.90; EX 39.50.
Owner Million In Mind Partnership **Bred** Haras De Manneville Et Al **Trained** Barbury Castle, Wilts

FOCUS
The lesser of the two divisions, but the winner is value for more than the official margin and with a number close behind the principals running to their marks, the race should still produce winners.

NOTEBOOK

Siberian Highness(FR), who reportedly damaged a knee when turned over at short odds last month, showed her true form and disposed of a modest field as she was entitled to. She has yet to do anything to suggest she is up to running well in the Supreme Novices, but there are not many better mares around and she is open to further improvement. *(op 10-11)*

Dark Parade(ARG), a modest sort on the Flat, is evidently going to make a better hurdler and really got going in the straight to claim second. He was never near the winner, but will not always bump into one as useful as her and is sure to find a small race this season, probably over further.

Topkat(IRE), down the field behind smart stablemate Acambo on his debut at this course, improved on that initial effort and kept on strongly for third, shaping like a horse in need of further. He is the type to do well handicapping in time. *(tchd 7-1)*

Legally Fast(USA) appeared to run his race and tried to stretch the winner, but did not have the engine and was run out of the places close home. He can find an ordinary novice event before going handicapping. *(op 20-1)*

Hunting Lodge(IRE) kept on at his own pace to claim a reasonable fifth and will find better opportunities back in handicaps.

Investment Wings(IRE), a fair maiden for Mark Johnston on the Flat, looked the type who would *jump a hurdle, but market vibes were not great and he made a quiet start. (op 28-1 tchd 33-1 and 22-1)*

Grand Bay(USA) ran a little better than his finishing position suggests and is now qualified for handicaps. *(op 10-1)*

Massif Centrale, a huge gelding who did not quite live up to expectations on the Flat, raced too keenly for his own good, refusing to settle, and he was held when unseating at the second-last. There were enough positives to take from this and he will hopefully settle better in future. *(op 5-1)*

3465 TAUNTON RACECOURSE SEMINAR CENTRE NOVICES' H'CAP CHASE (13 fncs 1 omitted) 2m 3f

2:00 (2:00) (Class 4) (0-110,105) 5-Y-0+ **£5,204** (£1,528; £764; £381)

Form RPR

P522 **1** **Wizard Of Edge**[15] [3243] 6-11-4 **97**............................(b) ChristianWilliams 102+
(R J Hodges) *led: rdn whn pckd 3 out: hit next: sn hdd: 2nd and hld whn lft clr last* **10/3**[1]

UF3 **2** *1 ½* **Randolph O'Brien (IRE)**[24] [2960] 6-11-0 **93**...................... AntonyEvans 95
(N A Twiston-Davies) *in tch: tk clsr order 9th: rdn and outpcd after 4 out: styd on again fr 2 out: lft 2nd at the last* **10/1**

56-4 **3** *1 ½* **Matthew Muroto (IRE)**[17] [3215] 7-11-2 **100**...................... DarylJacob[(5)] 100
(R H Alner) *in tch: reminders after 7th: wnt 3rd after 8th: rdn and ev ch after 4 out: kpt on same pce: lft 3rd at the last* **16/1**

-4P2 **4** *16* **Kyper Disco (FR)**[12] [3282] 8-11-12 **105**..........................(t) MickFitzgerald 93+
(N J Henderson) *prom tl 8th: chsd wnr: ev ch after 4 out: wknd next* **9/2**[3]

-P00 **5** *dist* **Mnason (FR)**[14] [3251] 6-11-4 **102**................................... JamesDiment[(5)] —
(S J Gilmore) *chsd ldrs: mstke 5th: weaknd 8th: t.o whn blnd last* **40/1**

-30P **P** **Ideal Jack (FR)**[24] [2996] 10-10-0 **82**...........................(t) RichardYoung[(3)] —
(G A Ham) *in tch tl 7th: t.o and p.u bef 3 out* **25/1**

-030 **P** **Maximinus**[34] [2868] 6-11-4 **97**... JamieGoldstein —
(M Madgwick) *bhd fr 5th: blnd 8th: t.o and p.u bef 4 out* **10/1**

6150 **P** **Money Line (IRE)**[64] [2262] 7-11-12 **105**................................ APMcCoy —
(Jonjo O'Neill) *nvr fluent: bhd fr 7th: t.o and p.u after 8th* **6/1**

3-5P **P** **Grandee Line**[17] [3212] 11-10-2 **81**.................................... RobertWalford —
(R H Alner) *blnd bdly and virtually fell 2nd: immediately p.u* **20/1**

-6P3 **U** **Priscilla**[35] [2846] 8-11-1 **94**... TomDoyle 103+
(K Bishop) *hld up: smooth hdwy to trck ldrs 4 out: chsd wnr 3 out: rdn to ld sn after 2 out: 1 1/2 l clr whn pckd bdly and ur last* **4/1**[2]

4m 56.5s (3.70) **Going Correction** +0.05s/f (Yiel) **10** Ran SP% **110.7**

Speed ratings: **94,93,92,86,—** —,—,—,—,— CSF £33.04 CT £438.02 TOTE £4.60: £1.30, £3.90, £5.00; EX 45.90.

Owner Mrs C Taylor & K Small **Bred** R G Percival And R Kent **Trained** Charlton Adam, Somerset

FOCUS

A race that changed quickly with Priscilla in front and looking set to score when unseating at the last, leaving Wizard Of Edge to score. The winning time was moderate and although the form makes sense it is moderate. The first open ditch on the second circuit was bypassed.

NOTEBOOK

Wizard Of Edge has really got his act together since being fitted with blinkers, but had been passed and looked booked for second again until luckily left clear at the last. He was given a fine ride and should not go up too much for this, so should have chance of following up. *(op 7-2)*

Randolph O'Brien(IRE) has not taken to fences with the relish many from his stable do, but he is gradually improving and battled on for second. A return to further may see him off the mark and, is being only six, he has time to improve. *(op 7-1 tchd 11-1)*

Matthew Muroto(IRE) ran his best race thus far in three attempts over fences and would probably have found this trip on the sharp side. He is in good hands and Alner may be capable of extracting some improvement from him. *(op 14-1)*

Kyper Disco(FR) was always likely to struggle under top weight and he stopped quickly in the straight. He has yet to win in 14 starts and and does not have the soundest framework. *(op 4-1)*

Mnason(FR) was the only other to complete, but he was beaten too far for it to matter. *(op 28-1)*

Money Line(IRE) *Official explanation: jockey said gelding had never been travelling (op 7-1 tchd 15-2 and 11-2)*

Priscilla, who had run better than her finishing position suggested on all three previous starts over fences, appreciated the slightly better ground and jumped well throughout to hold a strong position turning in. Sent on before the last, she pecked on landing and her rider was unable to maintain the partnership, looking most unlucky. Racing here off a mark of 94, she is capable of winning off higher than that and is one to keep on the right side. *(op 7-1 tchd 15-2 and 11-2)*

3466 EUROPEAN BREEDERS FUND "NATIONAL HUNT" NOVICES' HURDLE (QUALIFIER) (10 hdls) 2m 3f 110y

2:30 (2:30) (Class 3) 4-7-Y-0 **£5,204** (£1,528; £764; £381)

Form RPR

1 **1** **Au Courant (IRE)**[79] [1979] 6-11-5 .... MickFitzgerald 104+
(N J Henderson) *trckd ldrs: wnt 2nd appr 6th: hrd rdn appr 2 out: led sn after last: drvn out* **11/2**[3]

1-64 **2** *1 ¼* **Barton Legend**[15] [3238] 6-11-0 .... DarylJacob[(5)] 103
(D P Keane) *led: rdn after 2 out: hdd sn after last: kpt on* **9/2**[2]

4/ **3** *9* **Caged Tiger**[679] [4277] 7-11-5 .... DaveCrosse 94
(C J Mann) *mid div: hdwy after 7th to chse ldrs: mstke 3 out: sn rdn: styd on* **33/1**

21 **4** *½* **Hot 'N' Holy**[23] [3024] 7-11-5 .... ChristianWilliams 94
(P F Nicholls) *chsd ldrs: outpcd appr 7th: styd on same pce u.p fr 3 out* **5/4**[1]

0 **5** *12* **Portland Bill (IRE)**[24] [3001] 6-11-5 .... TimmyMurphy 82
(R H Alner) *chsd ldrs: mstke 6th: outpcd next: styd on again past btn horses after 3 out* **40/1**

0-0 **6** *7* **Sparklinspirit**[42] [2720] 7-11-5 .... PhilipHide 75
(J L Spearing) *mstke 3rd: a towards rr* **200/1**

5 **7** *9* **Mister Chatterbox (IRE)**[29] [2941] 5-11-5 .... RichardJohnson 66
(P J Hobbs) *chsd ldrs tl 7th* **14/1**

2-24 **8** *½* **Dan's Man**[54] [2503] 5-11-5 .... AntonyEvans 65
(N A Twiston-Davies) *in tch: rdn appr 7th: wknd after 3 out* **15/2**

00 **9** *½* **Another Chat (IRE)**[9] [3328] 6-10-12 .... SeanQuinlan[(7)] 65
(R T Phillips) *a towards rr* **66/1**

0/04 **10** *1 ¾* **Minster Park**[19] [3139] 7-11-5 .... RJGreene 63
(S C Burrough) *mid div: hdwy 7th: sn rdn: wknd after 3 out* **66/1**

20 **11** *dist* **Deep Moon (IRE)**[34] [2864] 6-11-5 .... SamThomas —
(Miss H C Knight) *mid div tl 7th* **16/1**

0F **12** *2 ½* **Lord Musgrave (IRE)**[30] [2928] 7-10-12 .... JustinMorgan[(7)] —
(L Wells) *chsd ldrs tl wknd after 7th: mstke next* **200/1**

200 **P** **Princess Yum Yum**[42] [2727] 6-10-7 .... JamesDiment[(5)] —
(J L Spearing) *j.rt thrght: a bhd: t.o and p.u bef 3 out* **150/1**

0-P **P** **Assumptalina**[9] [3328] 6-10-12 ....(t) RobertThornton —
(R T Phillips) *racd wd: a towards rr: t.o and p.u after 3 out* **100/1**

4m 47.4s (1.40) **Going Correction** +0.05s/f (Yiel) **14** Ran SP% **113.3**

Speed ratings: **99,98,94,94,89 87,83,83,83,82** —,—,—,— CSF £28.70 TOTE £6.40: £2.20, £1.40, £4.50; EX 45.50.

Owner Michael Buckley **Bred** Miss Hilary Gibson **Trained** Upper Lambourn, Berks

FOCUS

Average hurdling form, but solid enough and the race should still produce the odd winner at the 'lesser' tracks.

NOTEBOOK

Au Courant(IRE), winner of a weak bumper on his debut back in November, made a successful transition to hurdles and won in workmanlike fashion, getting on top after the last under a power-packed Fitzgerald ride. This was an average affair and he will find it much tougher going under a penalty, but he could do no more than win and will make a chaser in time. *(op 9-2 tchd 6-1)*

Barton Legend travelled strongly into the straight, looking the likely winner, but he was unable to pick up again when the winner joined him and he was made to settle for second. He has gradually *been coming down in trip and the way he ran suggests a return to two miles may not go amiss. (op 7-1)*

Caged Tiger, an average fourth on his bumper debut at Carlisle, ran way above market expectations and got the better of favourite Hot'N'Holy for third. A rise in distance is going to help and he can probably find a race at a moderate level. *(op 40-1)*

Hot 'N' Holy, off the mark at the second attempt in bumpers, proved bitterly disappointing on this hurdles debut and it was clear some way from the finish he was not going to be winning. The way *he kept on suggests a rise in distance will help, but he has a little to prove after this. (op 11-10 tchd 10-11)*

Portland Bill(IRE) made a pleasing hurdles debut, travelling well until outpaced by the principals, and he is definitely one to be interested in once tackling trip in excess of this. *(op 33-1)*

Assumptalina *Official explanation: jockey said mare had had breathing problem*

3467 CARLSBERG UK CHALLENGE TROPHY H'CAP HURDLE (9 hdls) 2m 1f

3:00 (3:00) (Class 3) (0-120,120) 4-Y-0+ **£5,204** (£1,528; £764; £381)

Form RPR

1F01 **1** **Nippy Des Mottes (FR)**[20] [3128] 5-11-5 **120**..................(t) LiamHeard[(7)] 130+
(P F Nicholls) *hld up towards rr: stdy hdwy fr 5th: trckd ldrs 3 out: led on bit at the last: shkn up flat: comf* **6/4**[1]

F6P- **2** *5* **Goldbrook**[287] [4755] 8-11-5 **120**.. JamesWhite[(7)] 122+
(R J Hodges) *trckd ldrs: jnd ldr 3 out: led next: rdn and hdd at the last: nt pce of wnr* **40/1**

4/33 **3** *10* **Landescent (IRE)**[20] [3127] 6-10-1 **95**......................... BenjaminHitchcott 90+
(Miss K M George) *chsd clr ldr: led sn after 3 out: rdn and hdd next: 3rd and hld whn hit last* **12/1**

0153 **4** *5* **Devito (FR)**[19] [3143] 5-11-0 **115**...................................... MrDEdwards[(7)] 103+
(G F Edwards) *racd wd: hld up towards rr: hdwy appr 3 out: sn rdn: styd on to go 4th appr 2 out* **10/1**

5-63 **5** *10* **Westernmost**[49] [2595] 8-10-1 **95**.. RJGreene 72
(K Bishop) *mid div: outpcd after 5th: nvr on terms after* **9/1**[3]

P000 **6** *6* **Maclean**[53] [2533] 5-10-10 **104**...(b) JamieMoore 75
(G L Moore) *mid div: hdwy u.p appr 3 out:wknd appr 2 out* **12/1**

-F00 **7** *2* **Visibility (FR)**[18] [3179] 7-11-0 **115**.................................(p) MrCHughes[(7)] 84
(M C Pipe) *a towards rr: lost tch 5th* **40/1**

13 **8** *9* **Sasso**[49] [2587] 4-11-0 **119**.. APMcCoy 68
(Jonjo O'Neill) *hld up towards rr: nt fluent 1st and 2nd: sme hdwy after 6th: wknd after 3 out* **3/1**[2]

1PU/ **9** *15* **Geri Roulette**[381] [4727] 8-9-13 **98**..................................... DarylJacob[(5)] 43
(S C Burrough) *in tch tl wknd after 6th* **100/1**

1636 **10** *13* **Alva Glen (USA)**[187] [1016] 9-10-8 **102**............................ ChristianWilliams 34
(B J Llewellyn) *a towards rr: lost tch fr 5th* **40/1**

/2-P **P** **Ilabon (FR)**[49] [2595] 10-10-10 **107**...................................(v) TomMalone[(3)] —
(M C Pipe) *led and set gd pce: sn clr: rdn appr 6th: hdd & wknd qckly after 3 out: p.u bef next* **12/1**

4m 5.10s (-3.70) **Going Correction** +0.05s/f (Yiel)

WFA 4 from 5yo+ 11lb **11** Ran SP% **115.5**

Speed ratings: **110,107,102,100,95 93,92,87,80,74** — CSF £65.51 CT £549.86 TOTE £2.30: £1.10, £9.20, £2.90; EX 63.60.

Owner Paul Green **Bred** Mme J Poirier **Trained** Ditcheat, Somerset

FOCUS

A fair handicap run in a good time in which the two class horses pulled clear. The winner is value for more than the official margin and the form, assessed through the third, could be rated higher.

NOTEBOOK

Nippy Des Mottes(FR), 9lb higher than when scoring here last month, had to work hard that day, but enjoyed a much smoother route to victory on this occasion and came clear after the last under a confident ride. Having only just turned five it is safe to assume this speedy individual has more to offer and he will continue to be a threat when the emphasis is on speed. *(op 13-8 tchd 11-8)*

Goldbrook, a useful hurdler who failed to translate his form to fences last season, could have been expected to need this reappearance run, but he put up a bold showing and pulled clear with the favourite before being done for toe after the last. This was a highly pleasing return and he is on a fair mark if staying hurdling for the time being. *(op 33-1)*

Landescent(IRE), making his handicap debut after three fair efforts, was well held in third, but he was beaten by two useful sorts and had the remainder comfortably behind. He will find easier opportunities and is one to keep on the right side of.

Devito(FR), who has raced here on five of his six starts this term, winning twice, stayed on past tiring rivals down the straight to claim fourth and may benefit from a slightly more positive ride in future. *(tchd 11-1)*

Westernmost is back on a good mark and it would not surprise to see him pop up in a similar race, although it would have been preferable had he shown a little more here. *(op 12-1)*

Sasso made errors at both the first and second and, despite attempting to get into it, he was always facing an uphill struggle. *(tchd 7-2)*

3468 E.B.F./DONCASTER BLOODSTOCK SALES MARES' ONLY STANDARD OPEN NATIONAL HUNT FLAT RACE (QUALIFIER) 2m 1f

3:30 (3:30) (Class 6) 4-7-Y-0 **£1,713** (£499; £249)

Form RPR

6 **1** **Rhacophorus**[24] [3001] 5-11-0 .... PhilipHide 102+
(C J Down) *trckd ldrs: led wl over 2f out: r.o wl: readily* **8/1**

	Pos	Dist	Horse / Comment	Jockey	RPR
	2	3 ½	**Karello Bay** 5-11-0 (N J Henderson) *trckd ldrs: drew clr w wnr and ev ch over 2f out: sn rdn: nt qckn* **2/1**[1]	MickFitzgerald	97
	3	10	**Marigolds Way** 4-9-10 (R J Hodges) *hld up towards rr: hdwy 6f out: styd on fnl 2f* **33/1**	JamesWhite(7)	76
	4	7	**Nefertari** 4-10-3 (P R Webber) *chsd ldrs: rdn 4f out: kpt on same pce fnl 2f* **4/1**[2]	TomDoyle	69
0	5	½	**Rosewater Bay**[75] 2056 5-10-7 (P F Nicholls) *t.k.h: hld up in rr: hdwy 5f out: outpcd over 3f out: styd on again fr over 1f out* **10/1**	LiamHeard(7)	79
	6	½	**Delena** 5-11-0 (P F Nicholls) *mid div: hdwy to ld over 4f out: rdn and hdd wl over 2f out: one pced after* **15/2**	ChristianWilliams	79
	7	5	**Pyleigh Lady** 5-11-0 (S C Burrough) *t.k.h: hld up towards rr: hdwy over 5f out: ev ch over 3f out: one pced after* **100/1**	RJGreene	74
	8	1 ½	**Poppy Smith** 4-9-12 (B J Eckley) *chsd ldrs tl 5f out* **33/1**	MarkNicolls(5)	61
0	9	1 ¾	**Lagan Legend**[15] 3244 5-11-0 (Dr J R J Naylor) *led tl over 4f out: wknd 3f out* **14/1**	AndrewThornton	70
0	10	shd	**Just Poppytee**[17] 3216 4-9-12 (R H Alner) *in tch tl 5f out* **33/1**	DarylJacob(5)	59
	11	16	**Ebony Queen** 5-11-0 (Miss H C Knight) *hld up towards rr: gd hdwy over 7f out: ev ch 3f out: wknd qckly: eased fnl f* **7/1**[3]	TimmyMurphy	54
	12	6	**Fine Edge** 5-11-0 (H E Haynes) *mid div tl 7f out* **66/1**	DaveCrosse	48
0	13	dist	**Spring Ice**[53] 2521 4-10-3 (M Scudamore) *mid div tl 7f out* **66/1**	JamesDavies	—
	P		**Around Nassau Town** 6-11-0 (C J Gray) *dwlt: a bhd: t.o 9f out: p.u over 4f out* **100/1**	RichardHobson	—

4m 10.0s (1.40) **Going Correction** +0.05s/f (Yiel) **14** Ran SP% **118.3**
WFA 4 from 5yo+ 11lb
Speed ratings: **98,96,91,88,88 87,85,84,84,83 76,73,—,—** CSF £23.16 TOTE £7.30: £1.40, £1.80, £5.30; EX 29.40.
Owner W A Bromley **Bred** Wood Farm Stud **Trained** Mutterton, Devon

FOCUS
Not the worst mares' bumper of all time and it is likely the front pair are capable of better. The fifth sets the standard.

NOTEBOOK
Rhacophorus, who put in some good late work when sixth on her debut at Wincanton on Boxing Day, was ridden more prominently on this occasion and galloped on relentlessly to win with something in hand. With ten lengths back to the third it is likely this was a decent effort and there is no reason why she can not defy a penalty in this sphere. *(op 12-1 tchd 7-1)*
Karello Bay comes from a stable that is always to be feared in this sphere, but she was unable to cope with the winner and was left trailing in the final furlong. Finding a similar race should not prove too hard and she is sure to pay her way at a sensible level. *(op 9-4 tchd 5-2)*
Marigolds Way was in receipt of plenty of weight from the front pair, but she was unable to make it tell and got going too late. This was a pleasing debut however and the experience can only do her good.
Nefertari was perhaps a little disappointing, failing to live up to market expectation, and she will need to improve a fair deal on this if she is to be winning next time. *(tchd 5-1)*
Rosewater Bay improved a little on her initial effort, but does not look to have the pace to win in this sphere and it is likely the best of her will not be seen until tackling trips in excess of two and a half miles over hurdles. *(tchd 11-1)*
Delena came to the front travelling well with half a mile to run, but her spell in front did not last long and she was readily left behind in the final quarter mile. *(op 6-1 tchd 8-1)*
Ebony Queen, like so many from her stable this season, failed to find it off the bridle and stopped quickly under pressure. *Official explanation: jockey said mare had breathing problem (tchd 11-2)*

3469 GET PRICE AT GG-ODDS.COM H'CAP CHASE (17 fncs 2 omitted) 3m 3f

4:00 (4:00) (Class 3) (0-130,132) 5-Y-0+ **£7,807** (£2,292; £1,146; £572)

Form	Pos	Dist	Horse / Comment	Jockey	RPR
-P31	1		**Sonevafushi (FR)**[8] 3343 8-12-5 **132** 7ex (Miss Venetia Williams) *j.w: mde all: drew clr after 4 out: unchal* **7/2**[1]	SamThomas	152+
142P	2	6	**Brave Spirit (FR)**[18] 3186 8-11-8 **121** (C L Tizzard) *chsd ldrs: pckd 3rd: outpcd in 3rd after 13th: styd on again fr 3out: wnt 2nd at the last: no ch w wnr* **8/1**	(v[1]) JoeTizzard	129
F-04	3	1 ¼	**Cowboyboots (IRE)**[18] 3186 8-11-2 **122** (L Wells) *hld up: hdwy after 12th: rdn appr 4 out: styd on: wnt 3rd at the last* **12/1**	JustinMorgan(7)	130+
1/P1	4	2	**Yardbird (IRE)**[24] 3000 7-11-5 **118** (A King) *in tch: chsd wnr after 12th: rdn after 4 out: wknd next: tired whn mstke and lost 2nd at the last* **4/1**[2]	RobertThornton	125+
2340	5	1 ¾	**Koquelicot (FR)**[24] 3000 8-11-3 **116** (P J Hobbs) *in tch: reminders after 11th: wnt 3rd after next: rdn appr 4 out: styd on same pce* **9/2**[3]	(b) RichardJohnson	119
1P0P	6	20	**Naunton Brook**[33] 2875 7-11-8 **121** (N A Twiston-Davies) *chsd wnr tl 12th: sn wknd* **22/1**	AntonyEvans	104
0302	7	nk	**Even More (IRE)**[17] 3212 11-10-11 **110** (R H Alner) *sn outpcd and towards rr: sme hdwy whn mstke 13th: no ch after* **5/1**	AndrewThornton	93
53F0	8	8	**Tom Sayers (IRE)**[24] 3000 8-10-13 **115** (P J Hobbs) *in tch: rdn and effrt after 13th: wknd after 4 out* **20/1**	RobertStephens(3)	90
PF-P	9	dist	**Present Bleu (FR)**[23] 3022 11-11-3 **123** (M C Pipe) *a bhd: t.o fr 12th* **66/1**	(t) MrCHughes(7)	—
26P6	F		**Jiver (IRE)**[24] 3000 7-10-10 **109** (M Scudamore) *fell 2nd* **9/1**	BrianCrowley	—

7m 3.40s (-12.00) **Going Correction** +0.05s/f (Yiel) **10** Ran SP% **116.5**
Speed ratings: **109,107,106,106,105 99,99,97,—,—** CSF £30.82 CT £303.77 TOTE £4.10: £1.70, £2.30, £2.30; EX 25.70 Trifecta £153.10 Pool: £517.80 - 2.40 winning tickets. Place 6 £37.70, Place 5 £29.28.
Owner B C Dice **Bred** Gil M Protti **Trained** Kings Caple, H'fords

FOCUS
A competitive-looking staying handicap chase, as the market indicated, but the winner did it comfortably and is value for double the official margin.

NOTEBOOK
Sonevafushi(FR), officially 6lb well in but carrying a big weight over this far, had no trouble in following up his victory at Newbury over this longer trip. He seems to be heading in the right direction and it is not too fanciful to suggest that he could play a leading role in one of the Nationals this spring. He stays well, jumps well and is rising up the handicap. *(op 10-3 tchd 4-1)*
Brave Spirit(FR) won this contest off a 10lb lower mark a year earlier, but had a question mark against him after an unusually poor effort at Plumpton earlier this month. With a visor replacing cheekpieces, he put that behind him with a solid effort against a bang in-form rival. *(op 15-2)*
Cowboyboots(IRE) has yet to win away from Fontwell and was never going to reel in the first two. This was a good effort, though. *(op 9-1)*
Yardbird(IRE) was one of the less exposed members of the line-up but one of the more in-form having scored at Wincanton last time, where he had three of today's rivals behind. Racing off 5lb higher here, he was inclined to hit one or two fences, but is obviously a stayer with a future and will benefit from this experience. *(op 7-2)*
Koquelicot(FR) was a further 3lb lower but continues to prove hard to win with. *(op 6-1 tchd 13-2)*
Even More(IRE) was always being niggled at and in the end finished well beaten. *(op 12-1)*
T/Jkpt: £7,100.00 to a £1 stake. Pool: £10,000.00. 1.00 winning ticket. T/Plt: £68.20 to a £1 stake. Pool: £47,126.80. 504.25 winning tickets. T/Qpdt: £54.90 to a £1 stake. Pool: £3,227.80. 43.45 winning tickets. TM

3470 - 3471a (Foreign Racing) - See Raceform Interactive

3260 THURLES (R-H)

Thursday, January 19

OFFICIAL GOING: Yielding to soft

3472a MACLOCHLAINN ROAD MARKINGS LTD. KINLOCH BRAE CHASE (GRADE 2) 2m 4f

2:05 (2:05) 6-Y-0+ **£22,448** (£6,586; £3,137; £1,068)

Pos	Dist	Horse / Comment	Jockey	RPR
1		**Newmill (IRE)**[21] 3109 8-11-10 135 (John Joseph Murphy, Ire) *hld up in rr: smooth hdwy into 3rd 6 out: 2nd after 3 out: led after next: styd on wl u.p fr last* **5/1**[3]	RMPower	155+
2	4	**Mossy Green (IRE)**[18] 3199 12-11-8 142 (W P Mullins, Ire) *slow 1st: settled 2nd: led after 3 out: slt mstke 2 out: sn hdd: rallied u.p: no imp fr last* **11/2**	RWalsh	149
3	3 ½	**Strong Project (IRE)**[14] 3261 10-11-8 145 (Sean O O'Brien, Ire) *sn led: mstke 7th: mstke 6 out: rdn and hdd after 3 out: 3rd and no ex fr next: kpt on* **9/2**[2]	JMAllen	146
4	25	**Hi Cloy (IRE)**[23] 3051 9-11-12 158 (Michael Hourigan, Ire) *hld up in tch: impr into 4th 6 out: drvn along after next: no ex fr 3 out* **1/1**[1]	AndrewJMcNamara	125
5	20	**Native Upmanship (IRE)**[19] 3154 13-11-12 147 (A L T Moore, Ire) *hld up towards rr: mod 5th 5 out: t.o fr 3 out* **12/1**	(p) CO'Dwyer	105
6	25	**Alcapone (IRE)**[39] 2786 12-11-12 131 (M F Morris, Ire) *trckd ldrs: wkng whn slt mstke 6 out: completely t.o* **25/1**	BJGeraghty	80
P		**The Galway Man (IRE)**[341] 3817 9-11-8 137 (Anthony Mullins, Ire) *mod 3rd: wknd 6 out: completely t.o whn p.u bef 2 out* **25/1**	RGeraghty	—

5m 22.6s **7** Ran SP% **115.6**
CSF £32.70 TOTE £4.70: £2.00, £2.50; DF 46.30.
Owner Mrs Mary T Hayes **Bred** Mrs Veronica O'Farrell **Trained** Upton, Co. Cork

NOTEBOOK
Newmill(IRE), returning to chasing following a spell over hurdles, travelled best and asserted going to the final flight. He is thought to be best fresh and happier on good ground, so he might not run again before the Champion Chase.
Mossy Green(IRE), who is in the veteran stage of his career now, ran right up to his best at a track where he has run well in the past. *(op 5/1)*
Strong Project(IRE) is usually found out in Graded company but he still made a good fist of it, jumping well in the main up front. *(op 4/1)*
Hi Cloy(IRE) performed well below his best and his rider was inclined to blame the tacky ground. *(op 1/1 tchd 5/4)*

3473 - 3476a (Foreign Racing) - See Raceform Interactive

3017 CHEPSTOW (L-H)

Friday, January 20

OFFICIAL GOING: Soft (heavy in places)
First flight in home straight omitted all hurdle races.
Wind: Moderate, across Weather: Sunny periods

3477 LETHEBY & CHRISTOPHER MAIDEN HURDLE (DIV I) (10 hdls 2 omitted) 3m

1:00 (1:00) (Class 5) 4-Y-0+ **£2,277** (£668; £334; £166)

Form	Pos	Dist	Horse / Comment	Jockey	RPR
232	1		**Ballyshan (IRE)**[15] 3253 8-11-6 117 (N A Twiston-Davies) *hld up in tch: led 3 out: sn clr: easily* **5/2**[1]	CarlLlewellyn	118+
-426	2	7	**Kildonnan**[14] 3277 7-11-6 117 (J A B Old) *hld up in mid-div: hdwy appr 6th: chsd wnr fr 2 out: no imp* **7/1**[3]	JasonMaguire	110+
5-5	3	10	**Geordie Peacock (IRE)**[95] 1777 7-11-6 (Miss Venetia Williams) *chsd ldr: led after 7th to 3 out: wknd after 2 out* **16/1**	SamThomas	100+
63/0	4	19	**The Wooden Spoon (IRE)**[39] 2799 8-10-13 (L Wells) *hld up: hdwy 3rd: wknd appr 3 out* **50/1**	JustinMorgan(7)	80
0	5	1 ¼	**Silent Dream**[24] 3023 8-11-6 (Simon Earle) *hld up in mid-div: wknd after 7th* **25/1**	MickFitzgerald	79
0222	6	17	**Love Of Classics**[25] 2985 6-11-6 115 (O Sherwood) *hld up: stdy hdwy 3rd: wknd appr 3 out: eased whn no ch flat* **3/1**[2]	(v) LeightonAspell	74+
030/	P		**Born Leader (IRE)**[665] 4560 8-11-6 (A King) *a bhd: t.o whn p.u bef 3 out* **20/1**	RobertThornton	—
P	P		**Havit**[15] 3249 8-10-13 (Lady Susan Brooke) *a bhd: t.o fr 5th: p.u after 7th* **100/1**	MissLBrooke(7)	—
240-	P		**Kayleigh (IRE)**[319] 4233 8-10-6 90 (P R Rodford) *a bhd: t.o fr 5th: p.u bef 3 out* **33/1**	KeiranBurke(7)	—
6106	P		**Surfboard (IRE)**[48] 2618 5-11-6 (P A Blockley) *led tl after 7th: wknd qckly: p.u bef 3 out* **50/1**	PJBrennan	—
R	R		**Grey Court**[172] 1123 11-10-13 (P D Purdy) *rn out and crashed through wing and uns rdr 1st* **100/1**	MarkHunter(7)	—
000/	P		**See More Jock**[648] 4787 8-11-6 (Dr J R J Naylor) *a bhd: hit 1st: t.o whn p.u bef 3 out* **100/1**	AndrewThornton	—
P0P	P		**Tom Tobacco**[13] 3283 9-10-13 (A S T Holdsworth) *a bhd: j. slowly 5th: sn t.o: p.u bef 7th* **100/1**	(tp) JamesWhite(7)	—
6-6	P		**Alformasi**[24] 3023 7-11-6 (P F Nicholls) *hld up in tch: lost pl 5th: rallied after 7th: wknd and p.u bef 3 out* **3/1**[2]	RWalsh	—
P06	P		**Pure Magic (FR)**[16] 3240 5-11-6 (Miss J S Davis) *prom: j.lft 1st: rdn appr 7th: sn wknd: t.o whn p.u bef 2 out* **80/1**	JamieGoldstein	—

6m 31.2s (14.40) **Going Correction** +0.65s/f (Soft) **15** Ran SP% **117.6**
Speed ratings: **102,99,96,90,89 83,—,—,—,— —,—,—,—,—** CSF £19.08 TOTE £3.30: £1.10, £2.20, £5.70; EX 22.70.

Owner Jump For Fun Racing **Bred** C Black **Trained** Naunton, Gloucs

FOCUS

This proved quite a test for these novices and, with only six managing to complete, the form is obviously just modest. The race has been rated through the second.

NOTEBOOK

Ballyshan(IRE) proved well suited by this extreme stamina test and confirmed the promise he showed when placed on his three previous starts over hurdles to get off the mark at the fourth attempt. He looked set for a prolonged battle with Geordie Peacock at the top of the straight, but galloped on too strongly for that one and was always holding the eventual runner-up. He is clearly one to be with when the emphasis is on stamina and, placed in an Irish point, should make a nice staying chaser in time. *(op 11-4 tchd 7-2)*

Kildonnan was ridden more patiently than when a beaten favourite under similar conditions at Towcester on his previous start, and saw his race out well. He is still a maiden, but clearly has a similar race in him. *(op 15-2 tchd 8-1)*

Geordie Peacock(IRE), returning from a 95-day break, would have found this a very different test to the bumpers he contested on his only two previous starts, and ran creditably in the circumstances. He looked likely to go close at the top of the straight, but not surprisingly failed to sustain his effort, and should be a lot better for the experience. *(op 20-1)*

The Wooden Spoon(IRE), who hinted at ability in a couple of bumpers back in 2003, improved on the form he showed on his return from a two-year absence at Plumpton and seems to be going the right way.

Silent Dream showed up well for a lot of the way and could be one to keep an eye on when handicapped.

Love Of Classics failed to run to the level of form he had shown when second on his last three starts over hurdles, and the headgear may not have been as effective this time. *(op 11-4)*

Alformasi offered promise over two and a half miles round here on his hurdling debut, but failed to confirm that and was beaten a long way out. He can be given another chance. *Official explanation: trainer's representative said gelding was unsuited by the soft (heavy in places) ground* *(op 5-2 tchd 9-4)*

3478 LETHEBY & CHRISTOPHER MAIDEN HURDLE (DIV II) (10 hdls 2 omitted) 3m

1:30 (1:33) (Class 5) 4-Y-0+ **£2,277** (£668; £334; £166)

Form				RPR
	1		**Teeton Babysham**[306] 6-11-6 ..... RWalsh (P F Nicholls) *hld up and bhd: smooth hdwy fr 7th: disputing ld whn lft wl clr 2 out* **4/1**[2]	114+
3232	2	28	**Seeador**[15] 3249 7-10-13 100 ..... WayneKavanagh[(7)] (J W Mullins) *hld up: sn in tch: rdn and 3rd whn blnd 3 out: lft 2nd 2 out: no ch w wnr* **6/1**[3]	88+
223-	3	1 3/4	**Call Me Anything (IRE)**[451] 1851 7-11-6 ..... TomScudamore (D Brace) *hld up: hdwy 5th: rdn and one pce fr 3 out* **14/1**	84
002	4	11	**Here We Go (IRE)**[15] 3246 7-11-1 ..... LeeStephens[(5)] (W K Goldsworthy) *hld up and bhd: hdwy 7th: wknd after 3 out* **8/1**	73
03	5	4	**Blue Splash (FR)**[212] 816 6-11-6 ..... ChristianWilliams (Evan Williams) *chsd ldr: led appr 5th to 6th: led after 7th tl appr 3 out: sn wknd* **10/1**	69
3346	6	dist	**Coeur D'Alene**[16] 3238 5-11-6 ..... AndrewThornton (Dr J R J Naylor) *a bhd: t.o* **25/1**	—
-06	P		**Huron (FR)**[20] 3145 5-11-6 ..... RichardJohnson (H D Daly) *a bhd: t.o whn p.u after 6th* **25/1**	—
0/0-	P		**Gwens Girl**[499] 1395 6-10-6 ..... RichardSpate[(7)] (J Rudge) *a bhd: t.o whn p.u after 6th* **100/1**	—
054/	P		**Idbury (IRE)**[791] 2277 8-11-6 ..... NoelFehily (V J Hughes) *prom: wkng whn blnd 5th: p.u bef 6th* **50/1**	—
-0	U		**Green Collar**[25] 2987 7-10-13 ..... (t) MrNMoore[(7)] (M Salaman) *plld hrd in tch: blnd and uns rdr 2nd* **100/1**	—
/F-P	P		**Edgar Gink (IRE)**[252] 333 12-11-1 ..... (t) HowieEphgrave[(5)] (L Corcoran) *a bhd: mstke 5th: t.o whn p.u after 6th* **100/1**	—
554	P		**Riffles**[20] 3149 6-10-13 ..... AndrewTinkler (Mrs A J Bowlby) *hld up in tch: wknd 5th: t.o whn p.u bef 2 out* **25/1**	—
05	P		**Buffers Lane (IRE)**[59] 2421 7-11-6 ..... CarlLlewellyn (N A Twiston-Davies) *prom tl wknd appr 3 out: p.u after 2 out* **9/1**	—
1/F4	F		**Billesey (IRE)**[24] 3023 8-11-6 ..... JoeTizzard (S E H Sherwood) *led tl appr 5th: led 6 tl after 7th: led appr 3 out tl fell 2 out* **11/4**[1]	108+
0	P		**Heavy Weather (IRE)**[16] 3238 8-11-6 ..... JasonMaguire (Miss Joanne Priest) *reluctant to line up and lost sme grnd s: j. slowly 1st: a bhd: t.o whn p.u bef 3 out* **33/1**	—

6m 32.0s (15.20) **Going Correction** +0.65s/f (Soft) **15** Ran SP% **117.2**
Speed ratings: **100,90,90,86,85** —,—,—,—,— —,—,—,—,— CSF £25.74 TOTE £4.40: £2.20, £1.80, £5.00; EX 26.10.

Owner Derek Millard **Bred** And Mrs A D Sansome **Trained** Ditcheat, Somerset

FOCUS

Like the first division, this proved quite a test for these novices, and again only six finished. Only the winner got home, but for which the race could be rated higher, and the faller has been rated as finishing 6l second.

NOTEBOOK

Teeton Babysham proved well suited by the strong pace and got a perfect ride from Ruby Walsh in the circumstances. Held up early, he moved into contention going easily and was still under a hold when his main challenger Billesey, whom he was upsides at the time, fell at the second last. He would almost certainly have won in any case and, although obviously flattered by the winning margin, this was a most promising introduction to Rules. A winning pointer over three miles, his future is very much in staying chases and he will apparently not be given too hard a time over hurdles. *(op 11-4)*

Seeador ran his usual sort of race without proving good enough to win and remains a maiden after 18 starts under National Hunt Rules. *(tchd 9-2)*

Call Me Anything(IRE), having just his second start over hurdles, was racing over a mile further than he had ever tried before, and ran with credit on his return from a 451-day break.

Here We Go(IRE) made very promising-looking headway before the turn into the straight, but could not sustain his effort in what was his first run beyond two miles three. *(tchd 15-2)*

Blue Splash(FR) showed promise in two runs in bumpers, but would have found this a different test altogether and unsurprisingly failed to last home. *(op 14-1)*

Buffers Lane(IRE) won a point-to-point on easy ground in Ireland, so should really have handled conditions, but he failed to complete and was a little disappointing. *(op 7-1)*

Billesey(IRE), who offered plenty of promise on his hurdling debut over two and a half miles round here on his previous start, would almost certainly have finished second had he not fallen at the penultimate hurdle. He was still upsides the eventual winner when crashing out, and was responding gamely to pressure. If this has not left its mark, he really should find a similar race. *(op 7-1)*

Riffles *Official explanation: jockey said mare had a breathing problem* *(op 7-1)*

3479 LETHEBY & CHRISTOPHER JUVENILE NOVICES' CLAIMING HURDLE (7 hdls 1 omitted) 2m 110y

2:00 (2:05) (Class 5) 4-Y-0 **£2,081** (£611; £305; £152)

Form				RPR
P621	1		**Dennick**[9] 2752 4-12-0 110 ..... (t) APMcCoy (P C Haslam) *a.p: led 4th: clr whn rdn appr 2 out: jst hld on* **11/4**[2]	95+
6204	2	shd	**Inchcape Rock**[57] 2454 4-10-10 105 ..... RichardJohnson (J G M O'Shea) *hld up and bhd: plenty to do whn rdn and hdwy appr 3 out: r.o flat: jst failed* **15/8**[1]	78+
40F	3	2	**David's Symphony (IRE)**[20] 3132 4-11-4 ..... NoelFehily (A W Carroll) *hld up: sn in tch: rdn appr 3 out: kpt on same pce flat* **12/1**	83
640	4	12	**Theflyingscottie**[50] 2597 4-10-9 81 ..... ChrisHonour[(5)] (J D Frost) *hld up in tch: rdn appr 3 out: wkng whn blnd last* **25/1**	72+
0P40	5	7	**Desert Moonbeam (IRE)**[9] 3340 4-10-0 ..... JayHarris[(5)] (R J Hodges) *led to 2nd: led 3rd tl hit 4th: rdn and wkng whn blnd 3 out* **33/1**	53+
1P	6	6	**Etoile Russe (IRE)**[90] 1821 4-11-7 ..... (t) MrTJO'Brien[(7)] (P C Haslam) *hld up: short-lived effrt after 4th: no ch whn blnd last* **10/1**	72+
0004	7	3 1/2	**Garhoud**[11] 3321 4-10-10 76 ..... (v[1]) AndrewThornton (Miss K M George) *hld up in mid-div: short-lived effrt after 4th* **12/1**	47
00	8	12	**Innpursuit**[9] 3340 4-11-0 ..... (b[1]) MarkBradburne (J M P Eustace) *bhd fr 4th* **20/1**	39
216P	P		**Strathtay**[7] 2935 4-10-1 95 ..... (b) PJBrennan (M Appleby) *a bhd: t.o whn p.u bef 3 out* **9/1**[3]	—
60	P		**Whatsinitforme (IRE)**[32] 2927 4-10-10 ..... BenjaminHitchcott (Mrs D A Hamer) *wl bhd fr 3rd: t.o whn p.u bef 3 out* **40/1**	—
60	P		**Smokincanon**[11] 3324 4-10-4 ..... RichardGordon[(10)] (W G M Turner) *hld up: hdwy appr 2nd: wknd appr 3 out: t.o whn p.u bef 2 out* **33/1**	—
500	P		**Mickey Pearce (IRE)**[41] 2756 4-11-2 80 ..... (p) DaveCrosse (J G M O'Shea) *w ldr: led 2nd to 3rd: rdn 4th: sn wknd: t.o whn p.u bef 3 out* **66/1**	—

4m 33.5s (23.10) **Going Correction** +0.975s/f (Soft) **12** Ran SP% **114.3**
Speed ratings: **84,83,83,77,74 71,69,63**,—,— —,— CSF £7.51 TOTE £2.90: £1.40, £1.20, £3.50; EX 6.50.Inchcape Rock was claimed by K. Goldsworthy for £6,000.

Owner D Browne **Bred** Barton Stud **Trained** Middleham, N Yorks

FOCUS

A moderate claiming hurdle restricted to juveniles. The early pace was pretty strong given the testing conditions, but they paid for it later and final time was moderate.

NOTEBOOK

Dennick, returned to hurdling following a recent third over a mile on the Flat, followed up his easy success in a Doncaster seller, but was made to work much harder this time. Always going well, he looked set to win pretty decisively when sent to the front, but this proved quite a test and he ultimately had nothing in hand over the runner-up, who had been held up well off the pace from the start. This was a good effort at the weights considering he would have been 13lb better off with the second had this been a handicap. *(op 2-1 tchd 3-1)*

Inchcape Rock was given a sensible ride allowing for the testing conditions and, although taking longer to pick up than one might have expected, would still have won had he not blundered his way through the last hurdle. Even so, given he was 13lb clear of the eventual winner at the weights, he was not at his best in defeat and may be best watched until stepping up in trip. *(op 2-1 tchd 5-2)*

David's Symphony(IRE) would have appreciated the drop in grade and did enough to suggest he could eventually find a similar race for his currently in-form yard. *(op 16-1)*

Theflyingscottie would have been suited by the drop in class and offered some hope. *(tchd 28-1)*

Etoile Russe(IRE), a stablemate of the winner, could not take advantage of this drop in grade.

Strathtay proved disappointing on her return to hurdling and may not have appreciated the testing conditions. *(op 15-2)*

3480 LETHEBY & CHRISTOPHER BEGINNERS' CHASE (22 fncs) 3m 2f 110y

2:35 (2:35) (Class 4) 5-Y-0+ **£4,127** (£1,258; £657; £357)

Form				RPR
5U34	1		**Bob Bob Bobbin**[24] 3020 7-11-5 ..... JoeTizzard (C L Tizzard) *led 2nd to 9th: led 12th: clr 3 out: easily* **11/10**[1]	132+
65	2	15	**Squires Lane (IRE)**[36] 2848 7-11-5 ..... PJBrennan (Andrew Turnell) *a.p: chsd wnr fr 16th: rdn 4 out: no imp* **50/1**	107
-324	3	11	**Woodlands Genpower (IRE)**[38] 2812 8-11-5 118 ..... MarkBradburne (P A Pritchard) *hld up: hdwy 11th: rdn and outpcd 15th: styd on to take 3rd 5 out: no imp* **7/2**[3]	99+
6-32	4	21	**Treasulier (IRE)**[16] 3241 9-10-12 99 ..... KeiranBurke[(7)] (P R Rodford) *prom: led 9th to 12th: wknd appr 5 out* **12/1**	75
0	U		**Drive On Driver (IRE)**[15] 3247 9-10-5 ..... MissLBrooke[(7)] (Lady Susan Brooke) *hmpd and uns rdr 2nd* **150/1**	—
5-0	P		**Ask Again**[38] 2805 7-11-5 ..... (p) JodieMogford (D G Bridgwater) *a bhd: j.rt 7th: sn t.o: p.u bef 12th* **150/1**	—
/U-P	P		**There Goes Wally**[20] 3148 8-11-2 ..... ColinBolger[(3)] (A Ennis) *prom: lost pl 9th: t.o whn p.u bef 12th* **150/1**	—
13	P		**Super Lord (IRE)**[20] 3148 8-11-5 ..... JasonMaguire (J A B Old) *hld up: hdwy 11th: mstke 13th: pckd 17th: wknd appr 5 out: p.u bef 4 out* **5/2**[2]	—
2-F6	P		**Dramatic Quest**[44] 2701 9-11-5 100 ..... (p) DaveCrosse (A G Juckes) *led to 2nd: lost pl appr 7th: bhd fr 12th: t.o whn p.u bef 14th* **50/1**	—
06UF	P		**Jonanaud**[10] 3331 7-10-12 117 ..... MrJAJenkins[(7)] (H J Manners) *bhd: short-lived effrt 17th: j.rt 13th: blnd 15th: t.o whn p.u bef 17th* **50/1**	—
30-P	P		**Beauchamp Prince (IRE)**[131] 1456 5-10-7 113 ..... TomScudamore (M Scudamore) *hld up: hit 4th: hdwy appr 12th: blnd 13th: wknd after 17th: p.u bef 5 out* **22/1**	—

7m 40.0s (22.90) **Going Correction** +0.975s/f (Soft)
WFA 5 from 7yo+ 12lb **11** Ran SP% **118.3**
Speed ratings: **105,100,97,91**,— —,—,—,—,— — CSF £61.53 TOTE £2.50: £1.10, £6.20, £1.30; EX 57.70.

Owner Mrs Sarah Tizzard **Bred** M H Ings **Trained** Milborne Port, Dorset

FOCUS

An intriguing beginners' chase on paper but, with Woodlands Genpower again running below expectations, and Super Lord also not at his best, Bob Bob Bobbin's task was a pretty simple one. He has been rated value for 25l.

NOTEBOOK

Bob Bob Bobbin had his task made much easier with Woodlands Genpower again running below expectations, and Super Lord also below form, and comfortably gained his first success over fences at the fourth attempt. He is ideally suited by a proper test of stamina, particularly round here, and his trainer rightly sees the Welsh National as a good long-term target, but there really ought to be more to come this season in the meantime - a tilt at the Royal & SunAlliance has not been ruled out. *(op 11-8 tchd 6-4)*

Squires Lane(IRE) was 46 lengths behind today's winner on his previous start, but is clearly going the right way and was a creditable second.

Woodlands Genpower(IRE) looked a potential chaser from the moment he won a Newton Abbot bumper on his debut in June 2003, but he has not taken to the larger obstacles as one might have hoped and this was disappointing. *(op 9-2)*
Treasulier(IRE) was not at his best but would have been better off in handicap company in any case. *(op 14-1 tchd 11-1)*
Super Lord(IRE) shaped well enough on his chasing debut at Warwick having won a novice hurdle at Windsor on his first start under Rules but, after appearing to travel quite well, he stopped pretty quickly. *Official explanation: jockey said gelding was unsuited by the soft (heavy in places) ground (op 9-4)*

3481 WEATHERBYS BANK H'CAP CHASE (18 fncs) 3m
3:10 (3:12) (Class 4) (0-115,113) 5-Y-0 **£4,400** (£1,311; £663; £340; £177)

Form RPR
1123 **1** **Precious Bane (IRE)**[34] 2874 8-10-10 **97** AndrewThornton 114+
(M Sheppard) *mde all: hit 12th: clr 4 out: hit 2 out: drvn out* **6/1**[3]
0-0P **2** *1 1/4* **Earl's Kitchen**[48] 2623 9-11-8 **109** (t) JoeTizzard 121
(C L Tizzard) *a.p: chsd wnr fr 8th: disp ld 12th: hung lft and outpcd appr 4 out: rallied flat* **14/1**
5635 **3** *19* **Dun Locha Castle (IRE)**[18] 3212 11-10-0 **87** oh2 TomScudamore 80
(N R Mitchell) *chsd wnr to 8th: wknd 13th* **20/1**
3-3P **4** *1/2* **Tradingup (IRE)**[16] 3239 7-10-5 **92** PJBrennan 87+
(Andrew Turnell) *prom: rdn 11th: wknd appr 5 out* **17/2**
12-P **5** *dist* **Cinnamon Line**[56] 2485 10-11-3 **104** RobertThornton —
(R Lee) *hld up and bhd: hdwy appr 8th: mstke 11th: wknd appr 5 out: eased flat* **25/1**
1U4- **U** **Miss Mailmit**[278] 4876 9-10-9 **96** MarkBradburne —
(J A B Old) *hld up: blnd and uns rdr 4th* **15/2**
P-12 **P** **Datito (IRE)**[20] 3151 11-11-4 **105** JimmyMcCarthy —
(R T Phillips) *a bhd: t.o whn p.u bef 4 out* **11/2**[2]
4/PP **F** **Chateau Rose (IRE)**[53] 2556 10-10-12 **99** (p) MarcusFoley —
(Miss E C Lavelle) *a bhd: no ch whn fell 4 out* **16/1**
6-31 **F** **King Bee (IRE)**[20] 3151 9-11-12 **113** RichardJohnson —
(H D Daly) *hld up: mstke 4th: lost pl appr 8th: fell 9th* **9/2**[1]
21-1 **U** **Graceful Dancer**[25] 2986 9-11-2 **103** JamesDavies —
(B G Powell) *hld up: towards rr whn bdly hmpd and uns rdr 9th* **6/1**[3]
24-4 **P** **Bubble Boy (IRE)**[37] 2828 7-11-10 **111** JohnMcNamara —
(B G Powell) *prom tl wknd 9th: sn hung rt: j. slowly 13th: sn p.u* **8/1**
65P3 **P** **Lucky Leader (IRE)**[18] 3212 11-10-1 **91** (b) RichardYoung[(3)] —
(N R Mitchell) *hld up: hdwy 7th: wknd 13th: t.o whn p.u bef 3 out* **28/1**

6m 47.2s (32.30) **Going Correction** +1.475s/f (Heavy) **12** Ran SP% **120.1**
Speed ratings: **105,104,98,98,**—,—,—,—,—,—,—,— CSF £83.05 CT £1591.95 TOTE £7.90: £2.40, £3.40, £4.20; EX 97.70 TRIFECTA Not won..
Owner M W & A N Harris **Bred** Rowanstown Stud **Trained** Eastnor, H'fords

FOCUS
A modest but competitive handicap chase.

NOTEBOOK
Precious Bane(IRE) made pretty much every yard under a good ride from Andrew Thornton. His task was admittedly made easier with the likes of King Bee, Graceful Dancer and Miss Mailmit failing to complete, but he still had to work hard to hold off the relatively fast-finishing runner-up and showed himself every bit as effective without cheekpieces (they were fitted when third at Haydock on his previous start). Clearly still improving, he may not look too badly treated when reassessed and appeals as one to keep on the right side of. *(op 13-2 tchd 7-1)*
Earl's Kitchen was pulled up in a similar event over course and distance on his previous start, but had the tongue-tie re-fitted this time and ran much better. He was closing all the way to the line and is probably better suited by even further. *(op 20-1 tchd 25-1)*
Dun Locha Castle(IRE), from 2lb out of the handicap, ran a solid enough race in defeat. His handicap mark enables him to race in a lower grade, and that could provide him with best chance of gaining a deserved success. *(tchd 25-1)*
Tradingup(IRE) was disappointing when pulled up and a beaten favourite at Wincanton on his previous start, but he goes well at Chepstow and this was better. *(op 8-1 tchd 9-1)*
Cinnamon Line, who pulled up on his reappearance, did not see his race out after moving into contention going quite well. *(tchd 33-1)*
Datito(IRE) won a similar race over course and distance under these sorts of conditions just two starts previously, so this was disappointing. *(op 13-2 tchd 7-1)*
King Bee(IRE), a recent winner at Warwick, fell too early to know how he might have fared. *(op 13-2 tchd 7-1)*
Graceful Dancer, chasing a hat-trick, was badly hampered by King Bee and unseated her rider at the ninth. *(op 13-2 tchd 7-1)*
Miss Mailmit parted company with her rider a long way from home on her return from a 278-day break. *(op 13-2 tchd 7-1)*

3482 LETHEBY & CHRISTOPHER H'CAP CHASE (12 fncs) 2m 110y
3:45 (3:46) (Class 5) (0-95,95) 5-Y-0+ **£3,253** (£955; £477; £238)

Form RPR
-3PP **1** **Advance East**[14] 3274 14-10-2 **70** RichardJohnson 79
(M J M Evans) *hld up and bhd: hdwy 7th: wnt 2nd appr 5 out: r.o u.p to ld towards fin* **10/1**
5162 **2** *1* **Jupon Vert (FR)**[7] 3370 9-11-11 **93** APMcCoy 101
(R J Hodges) *led: hrd rdn and hdd towards fin* **3/1**[1]
0604 **3** *14* **Blazing Batman**[13] 3285 13-10-3 **76** DrPPritchard[(5)] 72+
(Dr P Pritchard) *hld up and bhd: hdwy appr 3 out: nvr nr ldrs* **12/1**
PP **4** *14* **Aisjem (IRE)**[8] 3359 7-10-0 **75** (p) MrRhysHughes[(7)] 55
(Evan Williams) *sn prom: mstke 2nd: rdn appr 5 out: nt fluent and wknd 4 out* **16/1**
2024 **5** *9* **Moorland Monarch**[21] 3126 8-10-7 **80** ChrisHonour[(5)] 51
(J D Frost) *prom tl wknd appr 4 out* **7/2**[2]
-P43 **6** *25* **Scarlet Mix (FR)**[31] 2930 5-11-0 **95** JohnnyLevins[(5)] 33
(B G Powell) *prom: mstke 7th: hrd rdn and wknd appr 4 out* **11/2**[3]
0-UP **7** *22* **Huw The News**[21] 3129 7-10-12 **80** RJGreene 4
(S C Burrough) *hld up in tch: wknd appr 5 out: blnd 4 out: t.o* **40/1**
0-33 **P** **Message Recu (FR)**[25] 2996 10-11-12 **94** (b) JoeTizzard —
(C L Tizzard) *a bhd: t.o whn p.u bef 6th* **7/2**[2]
54P4 **P** **Auditor**[14] 3274 7-10-0 **73** (b) MarkNicolls[(5)] —
(S T Lewis) *prom: rdn 3rd: wknd 6th: t.o whn p.u bef 4 out* **12/1**

4m 37.7s (14.80) **Going Correction** +1.475s/f (Heavy)
WFA 5 from 7yo+ 8lb **9** Ran SP% **117.6**
Speed ratings: **103,102,95,89,85 73,63,**—,— CSF £42.35 CT £374.29 TOTE £13.00: £2.50, £1.20, £2.80; EX 60.60.
Owner Mrs J Z Munday **Bred** Chippenham Lodge Stud **Trained** Kidderminster, Worcs

FOCUS
Just a moderate handicap chase which did not take much winning, but the 14-year-old Advance East produced a fine performance.

NOTEBOOK
Advance East had been pulled up on his last two starts, but was back on a winning mark as a result and responded most gamely to pressure to pick up the leader on the run-in. This success is a credit to his connections, and afterwards they took the decision to give him a much-deserved retirement. *(tchd 12-1)*
Jupon Vert(FR) ran his race under a positive ride and only just gave way on the run-in to a horse back on a winning mark. He is holding his form well. *(op 9-4 tchd 7-2)*
Blazing Batman finished well without posing a threat to the front two, but this was a creditable effort from a horse who is clearly better suited by further. *(op 10-1 tchd 14-1)*
Aisjem(IRE), a maiden over hurdles in Ireland who had been pulled up on her two previous runs over fences, ran better in first-time cheekpieces and offered some hope at least. *(op 14-1)*
Moorland Monarch seemed to be positioned with every chance but did not see his race out and remains a maiden. *(op 5-1)*
Message Recu(FR) had been shaping as though about ready to win, but put in a disappointing performance and this ground may have been soft enough. *Official explanation: jockey said gelding never travelled (op 9-2)*

3483 LETHEBY & CHRISTOPHER MARES' ONLY H'CAP HURDLE (7 hdls 1 omitted) 2m 110y
4:15 (4:17) (Class 5) (0-95,94) 4-Y-0+ **£2,602** (£764; £382; £190)

Form RPR
0-42 **1** **Bally Bolshoi (IRE)**[49] 2605 6-11-3 **85** RichardJohnson 103+
(Mrs S D Williams) *w ldrs: led after 4th: hit 2 out: clr last: r.o wl* **7/2**[2]
6F41 **2** *9* **Methodical**[11] 3321 4-9-13 **83** JohnnyLevins[(5)] 80+
(B G Powell) *hld up: hdwy appr 3 out: ev ch 2 out: sn rdn: one pce* **9/4**[1]
50-0 **3** *6* **Royal Niece (IRE)**[59] 2419 7-10-5 **83** RyanCummings[(10)] 85+
(D J Wintle) *a in tch: rdn appr 3 out: hit 2 out: btn whn hit last* **9/2**[3]
406 **4** *1 1/2* **Joli Classical (IRE)**[20] 3132 4-10-6 **85** NoelFehily 74
(R J Hodges) *hld up and bhd: hdwy appr 3 out: wknd 2 out* **13/2**
5023 **5** *2 1/2* **Kildee Lass**[15] 3247 7-11-7 **94** ChrisHonour[(5)] 91
(J D Frost) *ev ch appr 3 out: wknd 2 out* **10/1**
6 *5* **Tinvane Rose (IRE)**[203] 883 7-10-6 **81** ChrisDavies[(7)] 73
(J G M O'Shea) *hld up and bhd: sme hdwy whn lost pl on ins bnd after 4th: n.d after* **40/1**
005 **7** *2 1/2* **Femme D'Avril (FR)**[39] 2797 4-9-7 **79** oh4 MissLucyBridges[(7)] 58
(Miss Lucy Bridges) *hld up: hdwy 4th: ev ch appr 3 out: wknd qckly appr 2 out* **20/1**
-3F0 **8** *3/4* **Lady Maranzi**[20] 3147 7-10-12 **80** BenjaminHitchcott 69
(Mrs D A Hamer) *t.k.h: a bhd* **33/1**
4-50 **9** *5* **Shalati Princess**[168] 1156 5-10-3 **78** MrRhysHughes[(7)] 62
(D Burchell) *prom tl wknd appr 3 out* **28/1**
500 **10** *9* **Alchimiste (FR)**[38] 2816 5-10-8 **83** MrRLangley[(7)] 58
(Mrs E Langley) *racd wd: prom: wknd appr 3 out* **100/1**
-P0F **P** **Soleil D'Hiver**[14] 3279 5-10-0 **75** JohnKington[(7)] —
(C J Drewe) *bhd fr 4th: p.u bef last* **25/1**
P04/ **P** **Probus Lady**[908] 970 9-9-11 **68** oh4 RobertStephens[(3)] —
(C J Down) *mde most to 4th: wknd appr 3 out: p.u bef last* **66/1**
0P43 **R** **Court Empress**[133] 1445 9-10-7 **75** CarlLlewellyn —
(P D Purdy) *prom tl dropped rr 4th: t.o whn ref and uns rdr 2 out* **40/1**
5605 **P** **La Muette (IRE)**[10] 3330 6-9-10 **71** (b) RichardSpate[(7)] —
(M Appleby) *hld up: short-lived effrt after 4th: bhd whn p.u bef last* **33/1**

4m 29.2s (18.80) **Going Correction** +0.975s/f (Soft)
WFA 4 from 5yo+ 11lb **14** Ran SP% **118.9**
Speed ratings: **94,89,86,86,85 82,81,81,78,74** —,—,—,— CSF £10.76 CT £36.25 TOTE £4.80: £1.80, £1.70, £1.40; EX 18.20 Place 6 £102.05, Place 5 £44.44.
Owner Mrs Rowena Cotton **Bred** Stephen Lanigan-O'Keeffe **Trained** Mariansleigh, Devon

FOCUS
A moderate mares-only handicap hurdle. The time was fair compared to the earlier claimer. A personal best from the winner, with the runner-up 11lb off her recent Taunton win on better ground.

NOTEBOOK
Bally Bolshoi(IRE) clearly relished the conditions and ran on strongly under pressure to ultimately win well having looked as though she might have to settle for second when challenged by Methodical. On this evidence, she can prove every bit as effective back over further and is one to have on your side when the ground is testing. *(op 6-1)*
Methodical looked to have an obvious chance of following up her recent success in a Taunton seller given she was due to be raised 17lb but, racing against her elders on very testing ground, she finished up well held in second. Her new mark may need looking at again. *(op 2-1 tchd 5-2)*
Royal Niece(IRE), returning from a two-month break, ran better than on her reappearance and is clearly going in the right direction. *(op 11-2)*
Joli Classical(IRE) ◆ was not without promise both on the Flat and in three runs in novice hurdles, and there was enough encouragement in this effort to suggest she can make her mark in similar company. *(op 9-2)*
Kildee Lass has been holding her form well enough, but has not won for over a year. *(op 8-1)*
T/Plt: £48.30 to a £1 stake. Pool: £50,280.30. 759.10 winning tickets. T/Qpdt: £12.50 to a £1 stake. Pool: £5,165.70. 304.00 winning tickets. KH

3267 MUSSELBURGH (R-H)
Friday, January 20

OFFICIAL GOING: Good
Wind: Virtually nil

3484 RABBIE BURNS TRIBUTE MARES' ONLY NOVICES' HURDLE (12 hdls) 2m 4f
12:50 (12:50) (Class 4) 4-Y-0+ **£3,253** (£955; £477; £238)

Form RPR
2543 **1** **Reem Two**[14] 3269 5-11-2 98 StephenCraine[(5)] 98+
(D McCain) *a.p: hit 7th: rdn to ld appr 2 out: mstke last: drvn and kpt on wl flat* **9/2**[2]
6436 **2** *1 3/4* **Powerlove (FR)**[14] 3269 5-10-12 99 OwynNelmes[(3)] 88
(Mrs S C Bradburne) *in tch: pushed along after 7th: hdwy to chse ldrs after 4 out: effrt 2 out: chsd wnr last: swtchd lft flat and kpt on* **9/1**
0000 **3** *1* **Bromley Abbey**[14] 3269 8-10-8 71 (p) TomMessenger[(7)] 87
(Miss S E Forster) *led: rdn along 3 out: hdd appr next: drvn appr last: kpt on* **100/1**
0500 **4** *17* **Now Then Auntie (IRE)**[14] 3271 5-10-12 83 (p) PeterBuchanan[(3)] 70
(Mrs S A Watt) *prom: rdn along after 4 out: hit 3 out: drvn and wkng whn mstke next* **50/1**
100 **5** *5* **Granny Shona (IRE)**[15] 3254 5-11-1 TomDoyle 65
(P R Webber) *trckd ldrs: effrt and cl up 8th: rdn along and hit next: sn wknd* **25/1**
-121 **6** *29* **Camden Bella**[17] 3235 6-11-7 TonyDobbin 42
(N G Richards) *trckd ldrs: pushed along 1/2-way: rdn 7th: hit next and sn btn* **8/11**[1]
P **Minnesinger**[107] 4-10-3 AlanDempsey —
(M Todhunter) *a rr: bhd fr 7th: p.u bef 2 out* **12/1**
03-5 **P** **Fortuna Favente (IRE)**[10] 3337 6-11-1 GrahamLee —
(J Howard Johnson) *hld up in rr: slipped bdly on landing 6th: pushed along next: sn outpcd and bhd whn p.u bef 2 out* **8/1**[3]

The Form Book, Raceform Ltd, Compton, RG20 6NL

5m 4.70s (10.20) **Going Correction** +0.475s/f (Soft)
WFA 4 from 5yo+ 12lb **8** Ran SP% **111.7**
Speed ratings: **98,97,96,90,88 76,—,—** CSF £39.82 TOTE £5.00: £1.40, £1.70, £11.80; EX 27.70.
Owner Dave Ellis **Bred** Darley **Trained** Cholmondeley, Cheshire

FOCUS
A modest event for mares and the winner probably only had to run to her official mark to win.

NOTEBOOK
Reem Two appreciated the return to novice company having been held in handicaps on her previous two starts. She did not need to improve to win this. *(op 4-1)*
Powerlove(FR), three places behind Reem Two over the course and distance earlier in the month, got closer to her this time but was unable to reverse the places. *(tchd 8-1 and 10-1)*
Bromley Abbey ran by far her best race to date, appreciating the switch to front-running tactics.
Camden Bella looked to have been found a good opportunity to follow up her Ayr success, but she was beaten a long way out. Clearly this was not her true form and she should be forgiven this below-par effort. *Official explanation: trainer had no explanation for the poor form shown (op 4-5 tchd 10-11 in places)*

3485 PETER YOUNG MEMORIAL JUVENILE NOVICES' H'CAP HURDLE (9 hdls) 2m
1:20 (1:20) (Class 4) (0-105,105) 4-Y-O **£3,253** (£955; £477; £238)

Form RPR
5051 **1** **Golden Feather**[7] 3367 4-10-1 **83** ow1 .... PaulO'Neill(3) 89+
(Miss Venetia Williams) *hld up: hdwy to trck ldrs 1/2-way: chal 3 out: sn led: shkn up and kpt on flat* **1/2**[1]
1 **2** *1 ½* **Parsley's Return**[30] 2935 4-11-12 **105** .... TonyDobbin 104
(M Wigham) *keen: a.p: led after 3rd: hit next: rdn along and jnd 3 out: sn hdd: hit next and sn drvn: kpt on flat* **10/1**[3]
602B **3** *20* **Elaala (USA)**[8] 3349 4-11-2 **95** .... GrahamLee 74
(M Todhunter) *hld up in rr: hdwy to trck ldrs 3 out: rdn next and sn outpcd* **20/1**
P40 **4** *13* **Lerida**[18] 3203 4-10-13 **95** .... PeterBuchanan(3) 61
(Miss Lucinda V Russell) *chsd ldrs: rdn along appr 3 out and sn outpcd* **33/1**
P60 **5** *3 ½* **Tarkar (IRE)**[32] 2921 4-10-4 **83** .... AlanDempsey 46
(J Howard Johnson) *in tch: hdwy to chse ldrs 4 out: sn rdn and wknd fr next* **40/1**
6 *10* **Quarrelsome Queen (IRE)**[12] 3311 4-10-13 **95**. AndrewJMcNamara(3) 48
(S Donohoe, Ire) *hld up: hmpd 2nd: sn bhd* **25/1**
0206 **7** *¾* **Another Misk**[8] 3349 4-10-2 **86** .... DougieCostello(5) 42+
(M E Sowersby) *in tch: pushed along 5th: outpcd fr 3 out* **66/1**
3212 **U** **Comical Errors (USA)**[51] 2569 4-11-7 **105** .... PaddyMerrigan(5) —
(P C Haslam) *cl up whn bdly hmpd and uns rdr 2nd* **5/1**[2]
0P0 **P** **Asteem**[42] 2753 4-9-7 **79** oh15 .... PhilKinsella(7) —
(M E Sowersby) *puleld hrd: led and j. bdly rt 2nd: hdd after next: bhd appr 4 out: p.u bef 2 out* **100/1**

3m 56.2s (5.00) **Going Correction** +0.475s/f (Soft) **9** Ran SP% **108.9**
Speed ratings: **106,105,95,88,87 82,81,—,—** CSF £4.69 CT £37.58 TOTE £1.60: £1.10, £1.80, £2.70; EX 5.90.
Owner Paul Beck **Bred** Newgate Stud Co **Trained** Kings Caple, H'fords

FOCUS
A modest handicap in which the winner has been rated value for five lengths.

NOTEBOOK
Golden Feather was not inconvenienced by the drop back in trip and continued his improvement since switching stables. The pound overweight his rider put up made no difference and he looked value for a five-length success. Things will be tougher in future, though, as he is already due to go up 13lb. *(tchd 2-5)*
Parsley's Return, successful in a seller on his hurdling debut, was the only danger to the eventual winner turning into the straight and pulled clear of the third, whom he beat by only a length and a half at Ludlow. He is clearly on the upgrade. *(tchd 11-1)*
Elaala(USA), close behind Parsley's Return at Ludlow two starts ago, was beaten much further by that rival this time but looks to have run close to the level of her Ludlow form herself. *(tchd 25-1)*
Lerida achieved little. *(tchd 40-1)*
Comical Errors(USA), who finished nicely clear of Golden Feather the last time they met in November, was unlucky to lose his rider early in the race. *(op 4-1)*

3486 FORTH ONE CONDITIONAL JOCKEYS' H'CAP CHASE (18 fncs) 3m
1:50 (1:50) (Class 5) (0-95,95) 5-Y-O+ **£3,253** (£955; £477; £238)

Form RPR
4F4P **1** **Another Club Royal**[10] 3338 7-10-3 **75** .... (bt) StephenCraine(3) 98+
(D McCain) *a.p: mstke 12th: hdwy to ld 5 out: rdn clr after next: hit 2 out: styd on wl* **7/1**
336 **2** *13* **Gangsters R Us (IRE)**[14] 3272 10-11-5 **93** .... PhilKinsella(5) 104+
(A Parker) *hld up towards rr: stdy hdwy 12th: chsd ldrs after 4 out: chsd wnr and blnd 3 out: sn rdn and no imp* **13/2**[3]
33U4 **3** *9* **Ideal Du Bois Beury (FR)**[11] 3320 10-10-0 **77** .... DavidDaSilva(8) 77
(P Monteith) *hld up and bhd: hdwy 5 out: rdn along next: plugged on same pce* **13/2**[3]
P005 **4** *1 ¾* **Renvyle (IRE)**[14] 3272 8-11-4 **95** .... (e) JohnFlavin(8) 93
(R C Guest) *cl up: lft in ld 12th: hdd 5 out: sn rdn along and wknd after next* **11/1**
5-PF **5** *11* **No Kidding**[56] 2479 12-10-9 **78** .... BrianHughes 65
(J I A Charlton) *hld up: hdwy and in tch 12th: rdn along next and outpcd fr 5 out* **40/1**
-0PP **6** *5* **Jupsala (FR)**[10] 3338 9-10-5 **74** .... (p) OwynNelmes 56
(S B Bell) *hld up towards rr: hdwy to chse ldrs 10th: rdn along after 5 out and sn wknd* **25/1**
-333 **7** *2 ½* **The Frosty Ferret (IRE)**[25] 2982 8-11-11 **94** .... PaddyMerrigan 74
(J M Jefferson) *in tch: rdn along 6 out: wknd fr next* **6/1**[2]
3525 **8** *hd* **Mr Laggan**[33] 2900 11-10-9 **78** .... MichaelMcAlister 58
(Miss Kate Milligan) *mstkes: a bhd: t.o fr 12th* **16/1**
P5OR **P** **John Rich**[25] 2966 10-9-11 **69** oh8 .... (bt[1]) PatrickMcDonald(3) —
(M E Sowersby) *a bhd: t.o whn p.u bef 4 out* **20/1**
-00P **U** **Terramarique (IRE)**[10] 3338 7-10-6 **78** .... (p) GaryBerridge(3) —
(L Lungo) *cl up: led 5th tl blnd and uns rdr 12th* **10/1**
5P-3 **P** **Bobby Brown (IRE)**[84] 1905 6-9-11 **69** oh4 .... (t) ShaneWalsh(3) —
(Mrs H Dalton) *in tch: lost pl 8th and sn rdn along: bhd whn p.u after 12th* **11/2**[1]
42UP **P** **Pessimistic Dick**[7] 3377 13-11-0 **83** .... DougieCostello —
(Mrs J C McGregor) *in tch: pushed along and lost pl 1/2-way:m bhd fr 12th: p.u bef 4 out* **9/1**
4PPP **P** **Lion Guest (IRE)**[11] 3320 9-9-13 **73** .... (v[1]) TomMessenger(5) —
(Mrs S C Bradburne) *led to 5th: pushed along and wkng whn hit 12th: sn bhd and p.u bef 3 out* **20/1**

6m 8.10s (3.10) **Going Correction** +0.225s/f (Yiel) **13** Ran SP% **118.0**
Speed ratings: **103,98,95,95,91 89,88,88,—,— —,—,—** CSF £49.50 CT £313.81 TOTE £9.60: £3.20, £2.60, £2.10; EX 75.00.
Owner Halewood International Ltd **Bred** Halewood International Ltd **Trained** Cholmondeley, Cheshire

FOCUS
An ordinary chase rated around the third and fourth.

NOTEBOOK
Another Club Royal, wearing blinkers and a tongue strap together for the first time, appreciated the sounder surface and ran out a clear winner of this ordinary contest. His stable can do little wrong at present. *(tchd 8-1)*
Gangsters R Us(IRE) is finally down to a mark lower than when last successful almost two years ago. Putting behind him a poor effort at this track last time when he finished distressed, he was back to the level of his best form this season. *(tchd 7-1)*
Ideal Du Bois Beury(FR) was happier back over this longer trip but his long losing run continues and he remains opposable. *(op 5-1)*
Renvyle(IRE), given a chance by the Handicapper, did not see his race out but this was still a little more encouraging. *(op 12-1)*
Bobby Brown(IRE) had travelled a long way to run here and the better ground and fitting of the tongue tie offered hope of a better showing. As a result he was backed into favouritism, but he let his supporters down. *Official explanation: jockey said gelding had never been travelling (op 6-1 tchd 13-2)*
Terramarique(IRE), pulled up on his chasing debut, was wearing cheekpieces for the first time. Enjoying himself out in front, he was still going well when unseating. *(op 6-1 tchd 13-2)*

3487 COSMIC CASE H'CAP HURDLE 3m 110y
2:25 (2:26) (Class 4) (0-105,105) 4-Y-O+ **£3,253** (£955; £477; £238)

Form RPR
1 **1** **Not Today Sir (IRE)**[34] 2897 8-11-9 **105** .... AndrewJMcNamara(3) 121+
(S Donohoe, Ire) *hld up in tch: smooth hdwy 4 out: led appr 2 out: clr last: comf* **4/1**[2]
4153 **2** *5* **Villago (GER)**[25] 2977 6-11-0 **93** .... TonyDobbin 97
(E W Tuer) *in tch: pushed along 9th: hdwy after 4 out: rdn next: styd on appr last: no ch w wnr* **7/2**[1]
P464 **3** *3 ½* **The Weaver (FR)**[14] 3269 7-10-13 **95** .... GaryBerridge(3) 97+
(L Lungo) *in tch: hdwy 4 out: rdn along next: kpt on same pce u.p fr 2 out* **12/1**
-P42 **4** *7* **Oscar The Boxer (IRE)**[14] 3269 7-10-2 **86** .... PaddyMerrigan(5) 80
(J M Jefferson) *cl up: rdn along after 4 out: kpt on same pce u.p fr 2 out* **7/1**[3]
0002 **5** *¾* **Bodfari Signet**[14] 3271 10-11-9 **105** .... OwynNelmes(3) 99+
(Mrs S C Bradburne) *towards rr: rdn along 9th: styd on u.p fr 2 out: nrst fin* **9/1**
5513 **6** *1 ½* **Tobesure (IRE)**[36] 2840 12-11-7 **103** .... MichalKohl(3) 94
(J I A Charlton) *hld up and bhd: hdwy after 4 out: styd on fr 2 out: nrst fin* **14/1**
13-P **7** *6* **Beauchamp Gigi (IRE)**[43] 2714 8-11-12 **105** .... GrahamLee 90
(J Howard Johnson) *hld up and bhd: stdy hdwy 10th: styd on fr 3 out: no imp whn hit last* **14/1**
3300 **8** *½* **Altitude Dancer (IRE)**[25] 2990 6-11-7 **105** .... DeclanMcGann(5) 90
(A Crook) *in tch: pushed along 9th: rdn next and sn outpcd* **33/1**
00PF **9** *nk* **Hi Humpfree**[9] 3345 6-11-2 **95** .... (b) JimCrowley 84+
(Mrs H Dalton) *j. persistently lft: cl up tl led 3rd: mstke 5 out: blnd next: sn rdn and hdd appr 2 out: grad wknd* **9/1**
21-0 **10** *hd* **Cha Cha Cha Dancer**[19] 3171 6-11-0 **98** .... DougieCostello(5) 87+
(G A Swinbank) *chsd ldrs: rdn along appr 3 out and grad wknd fr next* **12/1**
P004 **11** *¾* **Washington Pink (IRE)**[14] 3271 7-9-7 **79** oh4 .... MrBenHamilton(7) 63
(C Grant) *in tch: pushed along and lost pl 5th: bhd fr 4 out* **33/1**
2-00 **12** *1 ½* **Valerun (IRE)**[76] 2038 10-10-6 **95** .... JohnFlavin(10) 77
(R C Guest) *hld up towards rr: sme haedway 1/2-way: rdn along and outpcd fr 4 out* **25/1**
4543 **13** *4* **Speed Kris (FR)**[17] 3234 7-10-13 **99** .... (v) DavidDaSilva(7) 77
(Mrs S C Bradburne) *chsd ldrs: rdn along 10th: wknd appr 4 out* **14/1**
4640 **14** *dist* **Opal's Helmsman (USA)**[14] 3271 7-10-6 **85** .... AlanDempsey —
(W S Coltherd) *hld up in rr: a bhd* **50/1**
0600 **15** *11* **Political Sox**[14] 3271 12-10-8 **94** .... GarethThomas(7) —
(R Nixon) *a bhd* **66/1**
13P0 **16** *3* **Alfy Rich**[25] 2977 10-10-9 **93** .... (t) ThomasDreaper(5) —
(M Todhunter) *midfield: rdn along 1/2-way: sn outpcd and bhd fr 10th* **50/1**

6m 15.3s (13.50) **Going Correction** +0.475s/f (Soft) **16** Ran SP% **125.2**
Speed ratings: **97,95,94,92,91 91,89,89,89,89 88,88,87,—,— —** CSF £18.34 CT £162.84 TOTE £5.30: £1.80, £1.40, £2.70, £2.30; EX 22.80.
Owner Seamus Ross **Bred** John Bourke **Trained** Cootehill Road, Co. Cavan

FOCUS
This looked a competitive handicap beforehand but the winner won in style and has been rated value for 12 lengths. The race should work out.

NOTEBOOK
Not Today Sir(IRE), who won here in November, was not overburdened on a 5lb higher mark, although this appeared a more competitive race. He actually won easily though, being value for 12 lengths, and there are more races to be won with him, including over fences. Indeed, his trainer has a good novice at Fairyhouse over Easter in mind for him. *(tchd 9-2)*
Villago(GER) probably ran up to his best in second and was unlucky to run into a winner who is improving all the time. He can find a similar contest himself off this sort of mark. *(op 9-2)*
The Weaver(FR) was weighted to reverse course and distance form with Not Today Sir but that rival has improved since their last meeting. In the circumstances he did not run badly in third, but a question remains over his temperament. *(op 14-1)*
Oscar The Boxer(IRE) was pulled up the last time he tried three miles but he coped with the distance better this time. He still did not run to the same level of form as he has over shorter this winter, though, and perhaps he is at his best at around two and a half miles. *(op 6-1)*
Bodfari Signet, who has done all his winning over hurdles on ground officially described as good to firm, is a regular around here, but this was not one of his best runs of recent times. *(op 8-1)*
Tobesure(IRE), who looks high enough in the handicap now, never got competitive. *(op 16-1)*
Hi Humpfree did not look happy going this way round. *(op 7-1)*
Cha Cha Cha Dancer *Official explanation: jockey said gelding lost its action (op 16-1)*

3488 LAURA TODD AGENT OF THE MONTH NOVICES' HURDLE (9 hdls) 2m
3:00 (3:00) (Class 3) 4-Y-O+ **£6,506** (£1,910; £955; £477)

Form RPR
21 **1** **Masafi (IRE)**[33] 2903 5-11-10 .... GrahamLee 117+
(J Howard Johnson) *trckd ldr: led approach 3 out: jnd and hit next: rdn: rdr lost whip and j.rt last: styd on u.p flat* **4/11**[1]
F2 **2** *3* **Double Vodka (IRE)**[29] 2942 5-11-4 .... RichardMcGrath 105+
(C Grant) *hld up in tch: smooth hdwy after 4 out: chal and hit 2 out: rdn and ev ch whn bmpd last: drvn and no ex flat* **4/1**[2]

26 **3** *1 1/2* **Orang Outan (FR)**[24] 3038 4-10-4 ....(t) GaryBerridge(3) 91
(J P L Ewart) *chsd ldrs: rdn along 3 out: kpt on same pce fr next* **16/1**[3]
4 *10* **Easibet Dot Net**[98] 6-11-4 .... BrianHarding 95+
(I Semple) *hld up: gd hdwy 4 out: chsd ldrs whn blnd 2 out: sn rdn and one pce appr last* **20/1**
000 **5** *1/2* **Vrisaki (IRE)**[25] 2968 5-10-13 .... DougieCostello(5) 92
(M E Sowersby) *in tch: hit 3rd: effrt 4 out: sn rdn along and outpcd bef next* **150/1**
05 **6** *19* **Tinian**[1] 2903 8-11-1 .... AnthonyCoyle(3) 73
(Miss Tracy Waggott) *bhd tl styd on fr 3 out: n.d* **150/1**
0P **7** *5* **Oulan Bator (FR)**[25] 2991 6-11-4 .... AnthonyRoss 68
(R A Fahey) *hld up: a towards rr* **50/1**
8 *4* **Rightful Ruler**[134] 4-10-7 .... AlanDempsey 53
(M Todhunter) *nvr nr ldrs* **33/1**
0-00 **9** *2* **Cashema (IRE)**[14] 3267 5-10-6 69.................... DeclanMcGann(5) 55
(D R MacLeod) *bhd fr 1/2-way* **150/1**
00 **10** *8* **Power Strike (USA)**[16] 1432 5-11-1 .... PeterBuchanan(3) 54
(Mrs L B Normile) *bhd fr 1/2-way* **150/1**
P44P **11** *nk* **King's Envoy (USA)**[56] 2478 7-10-13 84.............. ThomasDreaper(5) 53
(Mrs J C McGregor) *in tch: pushed along and lost pl after 3rd: bhd fr 1/2-way* **66/1**
6-P **12** *1/2* **Platinum Point (IRE)**[11] 3314 7-11-4 .... TonyDobbin 53
(E W Tuer) *a rr* **100/1**
0-0 **13** *4* **Nicozetto (FR)**[42] 2749 6-11-4 .... WilsonRenwick 49
(N Wilson) *led: rdn along 4 out: hdd & wknd bef next* **150/1**
14 *16* **Palamedes**[60] 7-11-4 .... OllieMcPhail 33
(Robert Gray) *midfield: pushed along and lost pl 1/2-way: sn bhd* **28/1**
P0 **15** *8* **Mccormack (IRE)**[24] 3038 4-10-7 .... NeilMulholland 14
(M D Hammond) *midfield: pushed along and lost pl 1/2-way: sn bhd* **150/1**

3m 58.8s (7.60) **Going Correction** +0.475s/f (Soft)
WFA 4 from 5yo+ 11lb **15** Ran SP% **118.8**
Speed ratings: **100,98,97,92,92 83,80,78,77,73 73,73,71,63,59** CSF £1.85 TOTE £1.50: £1.10, £1.40, £2.10; EX 1.90.
Owner Andrea & Graham Wylie **Bred** G D Waters **Trained** Billy Row, Co Durham

FOCUS
Masafi was expected to win easily but the ground was not in his favour and he was unimpressive. The form looks sound enough, but the proximity of the fifth is worrying.

NOTEBOOK
Masafi(IRE) was not impressive but he got the job done, despite his rider losing his whip approaching the final flight. He will be better suited by a sound surface, and he remains a 33-1 shot for the Supreme Novices' Hurdle. *(op 2-5 tchd 4-9 in places)*
Double Vodka(IRE) had already shown enough to be capable of winning an ordinary novice event, and this effort confirmed that view. Connections now have, however, the option of going the handicap route. *(tchd 9-2)*
Orang Outan(FR), whose dam is a half-sister to Azertyuiop, was another having his third run to qualify him for a mark. He finished nicely clear of the rest and appears to be progressing.
Easibet Dot Net, a winner over middle distances on the Flat in fair handicap company, did not shape too badly on his hurdling debut, although the conditions would not have been entirely suitable. He was better on quick ground on the level. *(op 33-1)*
Vrisaki(IRE), who is only plating class, is flattered by his proximity to the winner. *(op 100-1)*
Nicozetto(FR) *Official explanation: jockey said gelding hung left-handed from the back straight (op 100-1)*

3489 EDINBURGH EVENING NEWS NOVICES' H'CAP CHASE (16 fncs) 2m 4f
3:35 (3:35) (Class 4) (0-110,110) 5-Y-0+ **£5,204** (£1,528; £764; £381)

Form RPR
1-P5 **1** **Galero**[8] 3352 7-11-12 **110**.................................... GrahamLee 122+
(J Howard Johnson) *chsd ldr: led 6 out: rdn 3 out: drvn last: styd on gamely flat* **9/1**
-4P2 **2** *3/4* **Not A Trace (IRE)**[14] 3268 7-10-4 **88**........................ WilsonRenwick 98
(Mrs S C Bradburne) *trckd ldrs: effrt to chse wnr 4 out: rdn along next: drvn and ev ch last tl no ex towards fin* **7/2**[2]
4411 **3** *15* **Clouding Over**[33] 2902 6-11-8 **106**........................ RichardMcGrath 103+
(K G Reveley) *hld up towards rr: gd hdwy 5 out: chsd ldrs next: effrt 2 out: rdn and wknd appr last* **11/4**[1]
34F4 **4** *1 3/4* **She's My Girl (IRE)**[14] 3268 11-10-5 **89**...................(p) NeilMulholland 84+
(John G Carr, Ire) *in tch: effrt and hdwy 5 out: rdn along next and wknd fr 3 out* **20/1**
1P **5** *4* **Lanaken (IRE)**[29] 2945 6-11-0 **101**...............(b) AndrewJMcNamara(3) 90
(S Donohoe, Ire) *led: rdn along and hdd 6 out: sn wknd* **11/2**[3]
4564 **6** *28* **Goodbadindiferent (IRE)**[33] 2902 10-9-11 **84** oh4.... PeterBuchanan(3) 45
(Mrs J C McGregor) *in tch: rdn along 10th and sn outpcd* **16/1**
-504 **7** *7* **Sargon**[14] 3272 7-10-13 **97**..............................(b) OllieMcPhail 51
(Robert Gray) *a rr: bhd fr 1/2-way* **33/1**
061F **8** *1/2* **Scarrabus (IRE)**[19] 3172 5-10-7 **105**.................. MichaelMcAlister(5) 50
(A Crook) *nt fluent: a bhd* **50/1**
0531 **9** *5* **Nocatee (IRE)**[46] 2675 5-10-10 **108**....................... PaddyMerrigan(5) 48
(P C Haslam) *midfield: pushed along 1/2-way: sn lost pl and bhd* **6/1**
5P21 **P** **Word Gets Around (IRE)**[14] 3270 8-11-3 **101**................. BrianHarding —
(L Lungo) *j.lft: chsd ldrs: rdn along and wknd 5 out: p.u bef next* **13/2**

5m 2.30s (2.90) **Going Correction** +0.225s/f (Yiel)
WFA 5 from 6yo+ 9lb **10** Ran SP% **117.4**
Speed ratings: **103,102,96,96,94 83,80,80,78,—** CSF £41.45 CT £111.99 TOTE £10.70: £2.60, £2.20, £1.10; EX 63.60.
Owner Andrea & Graham Wylie **Bred** B J And Mrs Crangle **Trained** Billy Row, Co Durham

FOCUS
Rated around the runner-up and third, this looks fair form.

NOTEBOOK
Galero, successful over hurdles here last year, appeared suited by the positive tactics and put two *lacklustre efforts over fences behind him. A sounder surface should be even more to his liking. Official explanation: trainer said, regarding improved form shown, gelding was better suited by the more forceful ride given today (op 8-1 tchd 10-1)*
Not A Trace(IRE) looks a better horse over fences than he ever was over timber, and this was *another step in the right direction. He should find a handicap before too long off this sort of mark. (tchd 4-1)*
Clouding Over, beaten in a handicap off a 2lb lower mark than this prior to her two wins in novice company against lesser opposition, was found out by the return to handicaps. She will have a better chance of winning again in uncompetitive mares' novice chases. *(op 9-2 tchd 5-2)*
She's My Girl(IRE) had the sheepskin back on having worn blinkers last time but, although she got closer to Not A Trace this time, she has still to convince over fences. *(op 16-1)*
Lanaken(IRE) went too fast in the conditions and paid for the effort in the latter part of the race. He would have been happier on quicker ground. *(op 6-1)*
Word Gets Around(IRE) *Official explanation: jockey said gelding was unsuited by the good to soft going (op 4-1)*

3490 BOOGIE IN THE MORNING INTERMEDIATE OPEN NATIONAL HUNT FLAT RACE 2m
4:05 (4:05) (Class 6) 4-6-Y-O **£2,055** (£599; £299)

Form RPR
1 **Rocca's Boy (IRE)** 4-10-2 .... StephenCraine(5) 82+
(M Wigham) *trckd ldrs: hdwy to ld 4f out: rdn and hdd over 2f out: styng on whn hmpd and swtchd rt ent last: led last 100 yds* **20/1**
2 *1* **Dundock** 5-10-11 .... EwanWhillans(7) 90
(A C Whillans) *hld up: stdy hdwy 5f out: effrt on inner over 3f out: led 2f out: sn rdn and edgd lft ent last: hdd and no ex last 100 yds* **16/1**
3 *2* **Top Dressing (IRE)** 5-11-4 .... GrahamLee 88
(J Howard Johnson) *trckd ldrs: pushed along and sltly outpcd 6f out: hdwy over 3f out: sn rdn to chse ldng pair: kpt on same pce appr last* **11/4**[1]
206 **4** *1* **Rothbury**[51] 2572 6-11-1 .... MichalKohl(3) 87+
(J I A Charlton) *keen: trckd ldrs tl sddle slipped and hdwy to ld 1/2-way: hdd 4f out: kpt on u.p fnl 2f* **9/2**
5 *nk* **Rien A Perdre (FR)**[264] 5-11-1 .... AndrewJMcNamara(3) 87
(S Donohoe, Ire) *hld up towards rr: stdy hdwy over 4f out: rdn to chse ldrs over 2f out:one pce appr last* **4/1**[3]
0 **6** *2* **Special Ballot (IRE)**[29] 2948 5-10-11 .... TonyDobbin 78
(G A Swinbank) *hld up: hdwy 6f out: chsd ldrs 3f out: sn rdn and one pce fnl 2f* **7/2**[2]
7 *12* **Blast The Past** 4-9-11 .... PeterBuchanan(3) 55
(T D Walford) *bhd: hdwy over 3f out: rdn 3f out and sn no imp* **25/1**
0 **8** *3* **Tuatara Bay (IRE)**[11] 3319 6-11-4 .... AnthonyRoss 70
(R A Fahey) *hld up: hdwy on outer over 5f out: rdn along over 3f out and sn wknd* **12/1**
4 **9** *28* **Turbulent Flight**[33] 2906 5-10-11 .... NeilMulholland 35
(Mrs L B Normile) *led to 1/2-way: rdn along 6f out and sn wknd* **25/1**
10 *1 1/4* **Clovella** 5-10-11 .... BrianHarding 34
(R Allan) *a rr* **66/1**
11 *2* **Falcon's Tribute (IRE)** 4-10-0 .... RichardMcGrath 21
(P Beaumont) *keen: chsd ldrs: rdn along over 6f out and sn wknd* **40/1**
50 **12** *9* **Talisker Rock (IRE)**[246] 424 6-11-4 ....(t) AlanDempsey 30
(A Parker) *keen: chsd ldrs: cl up over 6f out tl rdn over 3f out and sn wknd* **50/1**
13 *2 1/2* **Blizzard Beach (IRE)** 5-10-11 .... WilsonRenwick 20
(J Parkes) *cl up: pushed along 1/2-way: rdn 6f out and sn wknd* **50/1**

4m 6.90s (15.60) **Going Correction** +0.475s/f (Soft)
WFA 4 from 5yo 11lb 5 from 6yo 8lb **13** Ran SP% **121.0**
Speed ratings: **80,79,78,78,77 76,70,69,55,54 53,49,47** CSF £293.60 TOTE £18.10: £6.70, £3.70, £1.10; EX 208.10 Place 6 £29.28, Place 5 £5.19.
Owner D Hassan **Bred** Hammarsfield Bloodstock And Stuart Mullion **Trained** Newmarket, Suffolk

FOCUS
They went no pace here and the result was a slow time, even for a bumper, and dodgy form, rated for the time being through the fifth and eighth.

NOTEBOOK
Rocca's Boy(IRE), whose dam is a half-sister to Yorkshire Oaks winner Key Change, is himself a half-brother to Park Hill winner Discreet Brief. Despite being short of room inside the last furlong, he picked up well to win in taking style, and connections now have ambitious plans to go for the Cheltenham Bumper with him. *(op 16-1)*
Dundock, unlike the winner, is bred to get a trip in time as he is a half-brother to winning hurdler/chaser Paxford Jack, who has won at up to three miles. The way the race was run would not have suited him as much and in the circumstances this was a creditable debut effort. *(op 33-1)*
Top Dressing(IRE), who is a brother to the smart hurdler/chaser Full Irish, shaped with promise and is the type to improve when faced with a flight of hurdles. *(tchd 5-2)*
Rothbury, the most experienced in the line-up, did well considering his saddle slipped in the first half of the race. He now goes over hurdles. *Official explanation: jockey said saddle slipped (op 4-1)*
Rien A Perdre(FR), fifth in an Irish point in May, looks the type to do better with time and experience. *(op 5-1 tchd 11-2)*
Special Ballot(IRE) would not have been suited by the way the race was run, and this sister to *smart Flat stayer/jumper First Ballot should be seen to better effect in a more strongly-run affair. (op 3-1)*
Talisker Rock(IRE) *Official explanation: jockey said gelding had a breathing problem*
T/Jkpt: £7,100.00 to a £1 stake. Pool: £10,000.00. 1.00 winning ticket. T/Plt: £45.30 to a £1 stake. Pool: £51,062.42. 821.40 winning tickets. T/Qpdt: £5.10 to a £1 stake. Pool: £4,796.70. 687.20 winning tickets. JR

3287 HAYDOCK (L-H)
Saturday, January 21

OFFICIAL GOING: Heavy
Wind: Almost nil Weather: Fine

3491 ANGLO IRISH BANK NOVICES' HURDLE (REGISTERED AS THE ROSSINGTON MAIN NOVICES' HURDLE RACE) GRADE 2 (8 hdls) 2m
1:10 (1:11) (Class 1) 4-Y-0+ **£17,106** (£6,417; £3,213; £1,602; £804)

Form RPR
110 **1** **Nous Voila (FR)**[43] 2746 5-11-8 133.......................... TimmyMurphy 142+
(M C Pipe) *mde all: clr 2 out: easily* **7/4**[1]
612 **2** *12* **Livingonaknifedge (IRE)**[16] 3257 7-11-8 116.............. RobertThornton 120
(Ian Williams) *cl up: wnt 2nd 4 out: no ch w wnr fr 2 out* **4/1**[3]
1P1 **3** *15* **Percussionist (IRE)**[26] 2991 5-11-8 .... GrahamLee 108+
(J Howard Johnson) *sweating: prom: mstke 1st: rdn and wknd appr 3 out* **5/2**[2]
252- **4** *4* **Accordello (IRE)**[289] 4753 5-10-11 .... RichardMcGrath 90+
(K G Reveley) *hld up: n.d fr 3 out* **7/1**
F3 **5** *dist* **Leo's Luckyman (USA)**[35] 2873 7-11-4 .... JohnMcNamara —
(R S Brookhouse) *a bhd: lost tch after 4 out: t.o* **12/1**

4m 7.40s (8.30) **Going Correction** +0.75s/f (Soft) **5** Ran SP% **105.1**
Speed ratings: **109,103,95,93,—** CSF £8.15 TOTE £2.80: £3.20, £1.10; EX 7.40.
Owner D A Johnson **Bred** Haras De Saint-Voir **Trained** Nicholashayne, Devon

FOCUS
With Percussionist running below expectations, there was very little strength in depth in this Grade Two novice hurdle, and Nous Voila was able to get back on track following a disappointing run at Cheltenham. He has been rated as value for 22 lengths and looks one of the better two-mile novices. The form should work out.

The Form Book, Raceform Ltd, Compton, RG20 6NL

NOTEBOOK

Nous Voila(FR) ◆ disappointed at Cheltenham on his latest start when his stable were out of form, but the Pipe horses are running better now and he was able to confirm the promise he showed when winning on his first two starts over hurdles. With Percussionist running below expectations, he did not have that much to beat and duly looked a class apart. He obviously deserves his chance in better company, and could well go for the Totesport Trophy at Newbury, before the Cheltenham Festival. The only imponderable is how effective he will be on decent ground, as all three of his wins over hurdles have come on a soft surface. *(tchd 13-8 and 2-1)*

Livingonaknifedge(IRE), dropped half a mile in trip, had conditions to suit and probably ran about as well as could have been expected behind the classy winner. He should make a nice chaser. *(op 9-2 tchd 7-2)*

Percussionist(IRE), despite winning on two of his three previous starts over hurdles, had been far from convincing and it was a surprise to see him turn up here on heavy ground given Graham Lee suggested after his latest outing that a sounder surface may actually suit best. In any case, he looked to lose his race before the conditions could even become an issue, as he got very wound up before the start, and then made a mistake at the first that he would have done very well to recover from. While there were excuses, he has it all to prove now, not least his attitude.*Official explanation: jockey said gelding had a breathing problem* *(tchd 2-1, 11-4 in places)*

Accordello(IRE) showed useful form in four runs in bumpers, including in a Listed race at Aintree when last seen 289 days previously, but this was a tough enough ask for her hurdling debut and she finished up well held. The experience ought to do her good and she can find easier opportunities. *(op 11-2 tchd 8-1)*

Leo's Luckyman(USA) should not have minded the ground, but was well below form. *(tchd 14-1)*

3492 COMMHOIST LOGISTICS CHAMPION HURDLE TRIAL GRADE 2 (8 hdls) 2m

1:40 (1:41) (Class 1) 4-Y-0+

£28,510 (£10,695; £5,355; £2,670; £1,340; £670)

Form RPR

301- **1** **Al Eile (IRE)**[217] [4771] 6-11-12 .... TimmyMurphy 140+
(John Queally, Ire) *hld up: gd hdwy bef 3rd: wnt 2nd 3 out: j.lft 2 out and whn mstke last: sn edgd lft: led run-in: hld on wl cl home* **5/1**

6541 **2** *nk* **Mister McGoldrick**[25] [3039] 9-11-4 140 .... PadgeWhelan 133+
(Mrs S J Smith) *prom: led 4th: mstke last: hdd run-in: rallied cl home* **4/1**[3]

1-23 **3** *5* **Faasel (IRE)**[42] [2761] 5-11-8 154 ....(v) TonyDobbin 132+
(N G Richards) *hld up: hdwy 3 out: effrt whn bmpd 2 out: one pce run-in* **2/1**[1]

3253 **4** *1* **Royal Shakespeare (FR)**[26] [2971] 7-11-8 151 .... TomScudamore 130
(S Gollings) *handy: effrt 2 out: one pce after* **18/1**

406F **5** *17* **Milligan (FR)**[88] [1871] 11-11-4 113 .... DrPPritchard 109
(Dr P Pritchard) *led: hdd 4th: rdn and wknd after 4 out* **250/1**

5064 **6** *½* **Overstrand (IRE)**[7] [3383] 7-11-4 115 .... OllieMcPhail 109
(Robert Gray) *prom: rdn after 4 out: wknd next: btn whn mstke 2 out* **200/1**

31-1 **P** **Arcalis**[56] [2500] 6-11-12 159 .... GrahamLee —
(J Howard Johnson) *hld up: hdwy whn mstke 3 out: p.u qckly bef next: dismntd* **9/4**[2]

4m 12.0s (12.90) **Going Correction** +0.75s/f (Soft) 7 Ran SP% **106.9**
Speed ratings: **97,96,94,93,85 85,—** CSF £22.14 TOTE £5.40: £2.30, £2.40; EX 20.20.
Owner M A Ryan **Bred** Michael Ryan **Trained** Dungarvan, Co Waterford

FOCUS

A somewhat muddling renewal of the Champion Hurdle Trial, as not only was the pace very steady for much of the way, but the ground was far more testing than it is likely to be at Cheltenham in March. Not surprisingly, the winning time was moderate for a race like this, 4.6 seconds slower than the novices in the first. The first four were all upwards of 18lb off their best.

NOTEBOOK

Al Eile(IRE), who had two runs on the Flat during the summer following his neck defeat of Inglis Drever over two and a half miles at Aintree, defied a 217-day break to follow up that success on his return to hurdling. He could be considered a touch fortunate, as the eventual second looked the most likely winner until making a mess of the last, but this was still a fine effort on his seasonal reappearance. The plan now is to go for the Totesport Trophy, and a decision on the Champion Hurdle will be made after he runs at Newbury. *(tchd 11-2, 6-1 and 9-2 in places)*

Mister McGoldrick, winner of the Castleford Chase at Wetherby on his previous start, was having his first run over hurdles since finishing second to Inglis Drever in this race last year, and may well have won had he jumped the last better. Another fine effort from this admirable performer. *(tchd 9-2)*

Faasel(IRE) managed to win on heavy ground during his juvenile season, but that was in minor company and connections reported he could not handle these conditions. He will now go straight for the Champion Hurdle, but will have it all to do there. *(tchd 7-4)*

Royal Shakespeare(FR), chasing the Order Of Merit and being kept busy as a result, was below his best in fourth and is another who was probably unsuited by the testing conditions. *(op 20-1 tchd 16-1)*

Arcalis, an impressive winner of the Fighting Fifth on his only previous start this season, was a surprise runner given he is at his best on a decent surface, and he looked beaten when his rider pulled him up, thinking he had gone lame. It turned out there were no serious problems, and he must not be underestimated in the Champion Hurdle if the ground is on the 'good' side, but this was hardly an ideal preparation. *Official explanation: jockey said gelding lost its action from 3rd last* *(op 2-1 tchd 5-2)*

3493 PETER MARSH CHASE (A LIMITED H'CAP) GRADE 2 (18 fncs) 3m

2:10 (2:10) (Class 1) 5-Y-0+ **£43,267** (£16,545; £8,535; £4,507)

Form RPR

401F **1** **Ebony Light (IRE)**[16] [3258] 10-9-13 **149** oh22 ....(p) StephenCraine[(5)] 148+
(D McCain) *prom: led 14th: clr 3 out: rdn appr last: styd on* **33/1**

421P **2** *9* **Kingscliff (IRE)**[26] [2972] 9-11-10 **169** .... RobertWalford 162+
(R H Alner) *prom: mstke 7th: rdn and lost pl after 10th (water): struggling and bhd whn blnd next: past btn horses after 3 out:* **5/2**[2]

P-3P **3** *14* **Truckers Tavern (IRE)**[26] [2992] 11-10-4 **149** oh6 .... DavidO'Meara 130+
(Mrs S J Smith) *nt fluent: hld up: rdn 14th: wknd 4 out: btn whn hit 3 out* **10/1**[3]

-3P0 **4** *dist* **Kandjar D'Allier (FR)**[20] [3180] 8-10-4 **149** oh13 .... RobertThornton 110
(A King) *hld up: hdwy 11th: blnd 4 out: sn rdn and wknd: t.o* **11/1**

F1-2 **P** **Lord Transcend (IRE)**[49] [2628] 9-10-5 **150** .... GrahamLee 143
(J Howard Johnson) *led: mstke 7th: hdd 14th: wknd after 3 out: 2nd and btn whn p.u bef last* **8/11**[1]

6m 37.7s (9.40) **Going Correction** +0.85s/f (Soft) 5 Ran SP% **106.8**
Speed ratings: **118,115,110,—,—** CSF £106.43 TOTE £24.60: £2.90, £1.50; EX 77.20.
Owner Roger Bellamy **Bred** J Boylson **Trained** Cholmondeley, Cheshire

FOCUS

An impossible race to assess with confidence. With the 'form' horses Kingscliff and Lord Transcend failing to give their true running, it did not take as much winning as usual, and Ebony Light proved good enough despite racing from 22lb out of the handicap. He threatened this sort of figure as a novice, however, and now looks a worthy Grand National contender. The winning time was creditable, even for a race of this class.

NOTEBOOK

Ebony Light(IRE) ◆ has been progressing into a pretty useful staying chaser this term, but few could have expected him to be good enough to take this valuable prize from 22lb out of the handicap. However, with Kingscliff and, more noticeably, Lord Transcend failing to give their true running, he took full advantage and ran out a most decisive winner. The Handicapper will hit him hard for this, but that will ensure he gets into the Grand National and he looks yet another serious contender for Aintree maestro Ginger McCain. However, it's worth remembering he made a series of mistakes when tried there in November. *(op 25-1)*

Kingscliff(IRE), pulled up in the King George on his last start, had since been the subject rumours (emphatically denied by connections) that all was not right. Out to prove a point, he never travelled with any enthusiasm and looked as though he might be pulled up when becoming detached at one point, but he eventually responded to pressure and kept on in the straight. Although well below what he is capable of, there is clearly nothing physically wrong with him to stop his galloping and jumping for three miles, so he can not be written off for the Gold Cup, especially as better ground should suit. *Official explanation: jockey said gelding was unsuited by the heavy ground* *(op 9-4 tchd 11-4 in places)*

Truckers Tavern(IRE), disappointing when pulled up in the Rowland Meyrick on his previous start, managed to complete this time but was still well below form. On recent evidence, he cannot be followed with much confidence. *(tchd 9-1)*

Kandjar D'Allier(FR) had the ground to suit, but he is unproven over this sort of trip and was well held from 13lb out of the handicap. He did not help his chance by hitting the fourth last fence, but still has plenty to prove now. *(op 9-1)*

Lord Transcend(IRE), having just his second start since winning this race last year off a 10lb lower mark, was a disappointing second and well held when he appeared to go wrong and was pulled up before the last. His owners' first horse, he has always been fragile and was immediately retired. *Official explanation: jockey said gelding pulled up lame* *(op 4-5 tchd 5-6)*

3494 SPORTING INDEX NOVICES' CHASE (15 fncs) 2m 4f

2:45 (2:45) (Class 2) 5-Y-0+ **£16,265** (£4,775; £2,387; £1,192)

Form RPR

-002 **1** **Don't Be Shy (FR)**[16] [3251] 5-10-7 .... TimmyMurphy 148+
(M C Pipe) *led 2nd: sn hdd: led again 4th: mde rest: pckd 10th: clr bef 2 out: easily* **8/11**[1]

1221 **2** *8* **New Alco (FR)**[26] [2975] 5-10-12 .... ThomasDreaper 128+
(Ferdy Murphy) *led to 2nd: remained prom: wnt 2nd 6th: hit 9th: btn whn hit 2 out* **11/2**[3]

-233 **3** *25* **Eskimo Pie (IRE)**[39] [2812] 7-11-2 119 .... TonyDobbin 103
(C C Bealby) *in tch tl wknd 9th* **13/2**

0364 **4** *½* **Lago D'Oro**[15] [3278] 6-10-9 93 .... TJPhelan 95
(Dr P Pritchard) *led after 2nd: hdd 4th: remained handy tl wknd after 7th (water)_* **100/1**

43 **5** *1* **Turthen (FR)**[14] [3288] 5-11-1 ....(t) ChristianWilliams 103+
(P F Nicholls) *hld up: hdwy 8th: 3rd whn blnd 4 out: sn wknd* **7/2**[2]

5m 34.9s (10.70) **Going Correction** +0.85s/f (Soft)
WFA 5 from 6yo+ 9lb 5 Ran SP% **109.8**
Speed ratings: **112,108,98,98,98** CSF £5.31 TOTE £1.70: £1.10, £2.20; EX 4.80.
Owner D A Johnson **Bred** P Talvard, P Deshayes And J P Deshayes **Trained** Nicholashayne, Devon

FOCUS

Not much strength in depth in this novice chase and Don't Be Shy ran out a very easy winner, rated value for 25l. The runner-up improved to the level of his hurdling form.

NOTEBOOK

Don't Be Shy(FR) ◆, a promising second on his chasing debut at Hereford, improved on that effort to get off the mark over the larger obstacles with any amount in hand. While this race lacked real strength in depth for the class, he could do no more than win as he liked and deserves his chance in a higher grade. He won at around two miles in France, and there is every reason to believe he still has the speed for that sort of trip, so 16/1 for the Arkle seems very fair indeed. *(tchd 5-6, 10-11 in a place)*

New Alco(FR), an easy winner of a minor race at Sedgefield last time, found this tougher and was no match whatsoever for the easy winner - the margin of defeat flatters him. *(op 6-1 tchd 5-1)*

Eskimo Pie(IRE) had run some encouraging races over fences, and looked to have conditions in his favour, so this was pretty disappointing. He was certainly nowhere near his official mark of 119. *(op 8-1)*

Turthen(FR), a winner over hurdles and fences in France, had shaped well on both his starts to date in this country, and looked to have conditions in his favour, but he was fitted with a tongue-tie for the first time and posted a pretty poor effort. *(tchd 10-3, 4-1 in a place)*

3495 KEVIN MOORE H'CAP CHASE (12 fncs) 2m

3:15 (3:16) (Class 3) (0-135,135) 5-Y-0+ **£8,132** (£2,387; £1,193; £596)

Form RPR

-P12 **1** **Barton Nic**[14] [3293] 13-10-0 **112** ....(b) PeterBuchanan[(3)] 124+
(D P Keane) *bhd: hdwy 8th: led appr last: rdn clr run-in* **7/1**[3]

6P1P **2** *10* **Nowator (POL)**[14] [3293] 9-10-13 **122** .... TonyDobbin 124+
(Robert Gray) *in tch: rdn after 4 out: led bef 2 out: hdd appr last: no ex run-in* **28/1**

-P04 **3** *8* **Flight Command**[26] [2993] 8-10-11 **120** .... RussGarritty 112
(P Beaumont) *midfield bef 3rd: hdwy 7th: ev ch 3 out: rdn and wknd next* **18/1**

411P **4** *¾* **Dangerousdanmagru (IRE)**[49] [2622] 10-11-4 **127** .... ChristianWilliams 118
(A E Jones) *hld up: struggling appr 3 out: kpt on u.p run-in* **11/1**

4410 **5** *nk* **Sir Storm (IRE)**[14] [3293] 10-10-10 **119** ....(p) BarryKeniry 110
(G M Moore) *prom: rdn appr 8th: wknd after 4 out* **16/1**

6515 **6** *1* **Kids Inheritance (IRE)**[20] [3172] 8-10-0 **114** ow1 .... PaddyMerrigan[(5)] 104
(J M Jefferson) *led 2nd to 3rd: remained cl up: mstke and rdr lost iron briefly 5th: regained ld 4 out: sn hdd & wknd* **7/1**[3]

11F1 **7** *11* **Oso Magic**[25] [3040] 8-11-3 **126** .... DavidO'Meara 108+
(Mrs S J Smith) *cl up: led after 4 out: hdd appr 2 out: wkng whn blnd last* **3/1**[1]

0 **8** *2½* **Lusaka De Pembo (FR)**[25] [3018] 7-11-1 **124** .... CarlLlewellyn 100
(N A Twiston-Davies) *led to 2nd: led again 3rd: hdd 4 out: wknd appr next* **10/1**

33-0 **9** *shd* **Simply Gifted**[269] [69] 11-11-12 **135** .... BrianHarding 111
(Jonjo O'Neill) *a bhd* **10/1**

210P **10** *10* **Encore Cadoudal (FR)**[42] [2768] 8-10-8 **117** .... RichardMcGrath 83
(H P Hogarth) *a bhd* **22/1**

P **Nostra (FR)**[66] 5-10-2 **119** .... TimmyMurphy —
(M C Pipe) *in tch: wknd 6th: t.o whn p.u bef 3 out* **9/2**[2]

4m 18.2s (11.20) **Going Correction** +0.85s/f (Soft)
WFA 5 from 7yo+ 8lb 11 Ran SP% **113.6**
Speed ratings: **106,101,97,96,96 95,90,89,89,84** — CSF £158.81 CT £3320.79 TOTE £8.10: £2.70, £7.70, £4.30; EX 213.80.
Owner Proverbial Optimists **Bred** Barton Stallion Partnership **Trained** North End, Dorset

FOCUS

A sound gallop throughout and 13-year-old Barton Nic cleared away on the run-in to record a career-best effort over fences. This is not form to get carried away with but it looks solid enough.

NOTEBOOK

Barton Nic, 13lb higher than when winning at Plumpton on New Year's Day, put up a career-best effort over fences at the age of 13, coming right away on the run-in to destroy a decent field. He had next to no weight to carry, but that may change in future as he is sure to go up a fair bit for this and will need to hold this level of form if he is to have a chance of following up. *(op 8-1)*

Nowator(POL), a winner at the course in December, failed to repeat that form off a 5lb higher mark when pulling up here earlier in the month, but he showed that to be all wrong with a respectable second. He came through to have a crack at it approaching the second last, but was readily brushed aside after the final fence. *(op 25-1)*

Flight Command ◆, racing off a 2lb higher mark than when last winning a year ago, would have found two miles on the sharp side, but he showed further signs of a return to winning form and could slip a further few pounds in the weights after this. A return to two and a half miles will help and he is one to watch in future. *(op 20-1)*

Dangerousdanmagru(IRE), whose good spell came to an end when pulled up at Chepstow in December, has clearly benefited from a short break and put in some strong late running to claim a never-nearer fourth. He is the type who will continue to run well, without looking up to winning off this sort of mark. *(op 8-1 tchd 12-1)*

Sir Storm(IRE) is not the biggest, but he wins in his turn and will be capable of doing so once more when dropping a few pounds in the handicap.

Kids Inheritance(IRE) was up there disputing it from an early stage, but he tired badly in the final three furlongs or so and did not get home. *(op 9-1)*

Oso Magic, winner of his last three completed starts, looked to hold strong claims of following up his Wetherby win over hurdles, but he failed to live up to expectations and weakened badly after the second last. He may have been found out by this mark, but deserves another chance to prove otherwise. *(op 5-2)*

Nostra(FR) was one of the more interesting runners of the afternoon having won six races over obstacles in France, three of which were over fences, and she did not look to have been overburdened with a mark of 119. She was claimed for £11,418 after winning on her final start at Auteuil in November, but connections will have to wait for another day to see some of that repaid as she was never travelling here and was wisely pulled up by Murphy before taking the third last. Obviously better than this, she should show this running to be all wrong in time and it is worth bearing in mind she has only just turned five. *(tchd 5-1)*

3496 RED SQUARE VODKA "FIXED BRUSH" NOVICES' HURDLE (9 hdls 1 omitted) 2m 4f

3:50 (3:51) (Class 4) 4-7-Y-O **£4,554** (£1,337; £668; £333)

Form — RPR

-331 **1** **Glasker Mill (IRE)**[32] [2928] 6-11-11 .... TimmyMurphy 120+
(Miss H C Knight) *midfield: hdwy 5th: led appr 3 out: rdn out* **5/2**[1]

41-2 **2** *5* **Liathroidisneachta (IRE)**[54] [2554] 6-11-5 .... TonyDobbin 110+
(Jonjo O'Neill) *hld up: hdwy 6th: ev ch 2 out: rdn appr last: edgd lft run-in: no ex towards fin* **3/1**[2]

1- **3** *dist* **Pontiff (IRE)**[341] [3857] 6-11-5 .... CarlLlewellyn 80+
(M Pitman) *midfield: hdwy after 4th: ev ch appr 3 out: wknd qckly bef next* **9/2**[3]

/000 **4** *¾* **From Dawn To Dusk**[16] [3246] 7-10-9 .... DarrenO'Dwyer(10) 77
(P J Hobbs) *hld up: rdn and sme hdwy appr 3 out: btn bef next* **100/1**

5 **5** *15* **Parkinson (IRE)**[14] [3291] 5-11-5 .... RichardMcGrath 62
(Jonjo O'Neill) *in tch: hdwy appr 5th: wknd bef 3 out* **50/1**

P **6** *13* **Cooldine Lad (IRE)**[49] [2638] 6-11-5 .... GrahamLee 49
(J Howard Johnson) *cl up: rdn appr 3 out: sn wknd* **20/1**

23-5 **7** *5* **Master Of The Ward (IRE)**[49] [2631] 6-11-0 .... StephenCraine(5) 44
(D McCain) *chsd ldrs tl rdn and wknd after 6th* **14/1**

6 **8** *2½* **Champion's Day (GER)**[10] [3342] 5-11-5 .... BrianHarding 42
(Jonjo O'Neill) *hld up: n.d* **14/1**

12 **F** **Baron Romeo (IRE)**[25] [3024] 6-11-5 .... RobertThornton —
(R T Phillips) *fell 1st* **9/2**[3]

3-00 **P** **Harbour Rock (IRE)**[10] [3342] 7-11-0 .... PaddyMerrigan(5) —
(D J Wintle) *bdly hmpd 1st: sn p.u* **100/1**

0/5 **P** **John's Treasure (IRE)**[230] [645] 6-10-12 ....(t) BenOrde-Powlett(7) —
(M A Barnes) *chsd ldrs tl wknd bef 5th: t.o whn p.u bef 3 out* **125/1**

2 **P** **Herons Cove (IRE)**[21] [3145] 7-11-5 .... TomScudamore —
(W M Brisbourne) *led: hdd after 1st: remained cl up tl wknd bef 5th: t.o whn p.u bef 2 out* **50/1**

P-50 **P** **Protective**[26] [2968] 5-11-5 98........(b[1]) RussGarritty —
(J G Given) *racd keenly: led after 1st: hdd appr 3 out and wknd qckly: t.o whn p.u bef 2 out* **33/1**

10-0 **P** **Gay Gladys**[268] [93] 6-10-5 .... BernieWharfe(7) —
(T H Caldwell) *racd keenly: prom early: j.lft and lost pl qckly 2nd: sn bhd: t.o whn p.u bef 3 out* **25/1**

5m 19.7s (10.50) **Going Correction** +0.75s/f (Soft) **14** Ran SP% **121.5**
Speed ratings: **109,107,—,—,— —,—,—,— —,—,—,—** CSF £9.77 TOTE £3.60: £1.10, £2.10, £2.30; EX 14.10.

Owner Trevor Hemmings **Bred** Noel Murphy **Trained** West Lockinge, Oxon

■ Stewards' Enquiry : Paddy Merrigan one-day ban: improper behaviour at start (Feb 1)
Bernie Wharfe caution: used whip on a mare showing no response

FOCUS

Not a very competitive novice hurdle, but still a good effort from Glasker Mill and Liathroidisneachta to pull so far clear. Both seem to have improved for the heavy ground and brush hurdles and look capable of better still. The final flight in the back straight was omitted on the final circuit due to a stricken horse.

NOTEBOOK

Glasker Mill(IRE) ◆ is beginning to fulfil his potential and followed up his recent Fontwell success in decent enough style. Progressing nicely, he deserves his chance in better company. *(tchd 3-1)*

Liathroidisneachta(IRE) ◆, who had no chance with Senorita Rumbalita when second at Folkestone on his previous start, basically ran into another very useful sort. A mile clear of the rest, he should be a good thing for an ordinary novice hurdle. *(op 7-2 tchd 4-1, 9-2 in a place)*

Pontiff(IRE), off the mark on his only previous start in a Plumpton bumper, travelled well for much of the way on his hurdling debut off the back of a 341-day break. He was ultimately well beaten, but the front two are decent sorts and he can be expected to improve. *(op 4-1)*

From Dawn To Dusk had not gone on at all from his winning debut in a Chepstow bumper but, although beaten a long way, this offered some hope for the future. *(op 80-1)*

Parkinson(IRE) will probably be seen to best effect when handicapped.

Harbour Rock(IRE) was unfortunately injured when hampered landing over the first. *(op 80-1)*

Baron Romeo(IRE), a fair bumper performer, made a far from ideal start to his hurdling career. *(op 80-1)*

3497 E.B.F./DONCASTER BLOODSTOCK SALES MARES' ONLY STANDARD OPEN NATIONAL HUNT FLAT RACE (QUALIFIER) 2m

4:20 (4:20) (Class 6) 4-7-Y-O **£1,713** (£499; £249)

Form — RPR

1 **Larkbarrow** 5-10-8 .... StevenCrawford(7) 90+
(N A Twiston-Davies) *prom: led over 5f out: rdn 3f out: r.o gamely towards fin* **3/1**[2]

05-2 **2** *1¼* **Cloudina**[26] [2987] 5-11-1 .... RobertThornton 88
(P T Dalton) *in tch: rdn to take 2nd over 1f out: ev ch ins fnl f: nt qckn towards fin* **5/2**[1]

3 *5* **Nannys Gift (IRE)** 7-10-12 .... LeeVickers(3) 83
(O Brennan) *racd keenly: hld up: rdn 6f out: hdwy over 3f out: one pce fnl 2f* **16/1**

4 **4** *1¾* **Solent Sunbeam**[82] [1961] 6-11-1 .... JohnMcNamara 81
(K C Bailey) *racd wd: sn prom: led after 4f: hdd over 5f out: sn outpcd: n.d after* **11/2**

00 **5** *1¼* **Harpurs Girl**[21] [3145] 5-11-1 .... GrahamLee 80
(J Mackie) *prom: ev ch over 2f out: rdn and hung lft over 1f out: sn wknd* **18/1**

55 **6** *13* **Mrs O'Malley**[3] [3448] 6-10-10 .... StephenCraine(5) 67
(D McCain) *led: hdd after 4f: remained prom: wknd 2f out* **15/2**

7 *14* **Lucky Third Time** 4-10-4 .... TomScudamore 42
(M Scudamore) *racd keenly: hld up: racd wd: struggling 5f out: sn btn* **9/2**[3]

4m 22.1s (25.70) **Going Correction** +0.75s/f (Soft)
WFA 4 from 5yo+ 11lb **7** Ran SP% **110.0**
Speed ratings: **65,64,61,61,60 53,46** CSF £10.06 TOTE £3.90: £2.40, £1.70; EX 7.70 Place 6 £204.88, Place 5 £117.85.

Owner N A Twiston-Davies **Bred** R D And Mrs J S Chugg **Trained** Naunton, Gloucs

■ Stewards' Enquiry : Steven Crawford one-day ban: careless riding (Feb 1); two-day ban: used whip with excessive frequency (Feb 2-3)

FOCUS

A moderate bumper and, with the pace steady as usual, the winning time was slow.

NOTEBOOK

Larkbarrow, the first foal of a sister to a two-mile hurdling winner, showed the right attitude under pressure to make a winning debut. This was just an ordinary race, but she is obviously open to improvement and should make a jumper. *(op 2-1 tchd 10-3)*

Cloudina looked to have every chance and basically just found one too good. She should find a mares-only hurdle. *(op 3-1 tchd 9-4 and 7-2 in a place)*

Nannys Gift(IRE), a half-sister to a winning Irish pointer, made a satisfactory debut but would probably want to be going over obstacles sooner rather than later. *(op 20-1)*

Solent Sunbeam ran with credit in fourth, but probably failed to improve a great deal on her debut effort. *(op 7-1 tchd 15-2 in a place)*

Harpurs Girl gradually seems to be going the right way. *(op 10-1)*

T/Plt: £228.50 to a £1 stake. Pool: £67,996.45. 217.15 winning tickets. T/Qpdt: £41.90 to a £1 stake. Pool: £3,907.80. 68.90 winning tickets. DO

3132 LINGFIELD (L-H)

Saturday, January 21

OFFICIAL GOING: Chase course - soft (heavy in places); hurdle course - heavy; all-weather - standard

The open ditch at the end of the back straight was omitted in all chases.

Wind: Almost nil Weather: Fine

3498 INTERCASINO.CO.UK JUVENILE NOVICES' HURDLE (8 hdls) 2m 110y

12:40 (12:40) (Class 4) 4-Y-O **£3,253** (£955; £477; £238)

Form — RPR

1 **Onnix (FR)**[54] 4-10-10 ow1 .... ADuchene(5) 114+
(F Doumen, France) *athletic, good-bodied: swtg: hld up in 4th: clsd on ldrs 2 out: chal gng wl whn outjumped last: hrd rdn and r.o to ld nr fi* **5/4**[1]

1 **2** *¾* **Heathcote**[21] [3132] 4-11-7 .... JamieMoore 116+
(G L Moore) *lw: trckd ldng pair: wnt 2nd after 3 out: led and hit 2 out: sn rdn and hanging: hdd and nt qckn nr fin* **2/1**[2]

3 *5* **Brads House (IRE)**[92] 4-11-0 .... DaveCrosse 104+
(J G M O'Shea) *cl up: led to 5th: hdd 2 out: btn whn j.rt last* **7/2**[3]

4 *3½* **Monash Lad (IRE)**[7] 4-11-0 .... LeightonAspell 100
(M H Tompkins) *lw: led to 5th: outpcd bef 2 out: no imp after* **16/1**

5 *dist* **Rose Bien**[72] 4-10-7 .... MatthewBatchelor —
(P J McBride) *j.bdly rt: a last: lost tch 3 out: t.o: btn 41 l* **40/1**

4m 17.4s (11.30) **Going Correction** +0.45s/f (Soft) **5** Ran SP% **108.3**
Speed ratings: **91,90,88,86,—** CSF £4.03 TOTE £1.90: £1.10, £2.80; EX 4.40.

Owner Haras D'Ecouves **Bred** M Trinquet & Exors Of B Trinquet **Trained** Bouce, France

FOCUS

Only the runner-up had run over hurdles before. The early pace was very ordinary, resulting in a moderate winning time even for a race of its type. They finished in market order, with the winner value for further.

NOTEBOOK

Onnix(FR), a dual-winner at around a mile and a half on the Flat in France, was given a patient ride but seemed to get a bit outpaced on the downhill run into the straight. He managed to get back into contention though, and despite not jumping the final flight as quickly as the runner-up still had enough time to utilise his Flat speed on the run-in. Given a stronger pace, he is probably even better than he showed here. *(op 6-4 tchd 6-5 and 13-8 in a place)*

Heathcote, under a penalty for his course-and-distance victory last month, like the favourite was probably not suited by the modest pace and came off the bridle a long way out. He responded to the pressure to get to the front at the second last and it looked as though he might prevail when he jumped the last quicker than the favourite and gained a length, but when it came down to a test of speed on the run-in he was definitely second best. There should be more races in him given a more generous pace. *(op 6-4 tchd 9-4)*

Brads House(IRE), an 85-rated performer on the Flat making his hurdling debut, raced up with the pace for a long way but was done for foot from the second last. He stayed 14 furlongs on the level so probably needs a stronger pace or longer trip. *(op 9-2)*

Monash Lad(IRE), a maiden on the Flat after 17 attempts and rated some 16lb below Brads House, had a bit to do against that rival on this hurdling debut let alone the two market principals. Given a positive ride until put in his place turning for home, he probably achieved as much as could be expected. He is rather lightly-made for this game, but may do better under less taxing conditions. *(tchd 14-1)*

Rose Bien, a maiden after six attempts on the Flat and rated just 52, was always trailing and *jumped alarmingly out to her right at several flights. She hardly looks a natural at this game. (op 33-1)*

3499 INTERCASINO.CO.UK NOVICES' H'CAP CHASE (16 fncs 2 omitted) 3m

1:15 (1:15) (Class 4) (0-100,95) 5-Y-O+ **£3,903** (£1,146; £573; £286)

Form — RPR

-F1F **1** **Trenance**[26] [2986] 8-11-7 90 .... JasonMaguire 104+
(T R George) *lw: mstke 1st: in tch: prog to join ldrs 10th: rdn bef 3 out: led sn after 2 out: drvn and kpt on flat* **9/2**[3]

P041 **2** *3* **Rosses Point (IRE)**[14] [3285] 7-11-8 91 ....(p) PaulMoloney 104+
(Evan Williams) *mstkes: hld up in last pair: prog after 12th: rdn bef 3 out: effrt to chal 2 out: nt qckn and hld flat* **11/4**[1]

P-3P **3** *shd* **Mandingo Chief (IRE)**[49] [2623] 7-11-9 **92**................. WayneHutchinson 103+
(R T Phillips) *prom: pressed ldr 11th: abt 2 l down whn lft in ld 3 out: blnd next and hdd: one pce flat* **7/1**

3005 **4** *14* **Joseph Beuys (IRE)**[21] [3139] 7-10-10 **84**.......................... DarylJacob(5) 79
(D P Keane) *swtg: t.k.h: hld up in last pair: prog to press ldrs 13th: wknd bef 3 out* **9/1**

P/4P **5** *14* **Toy Boy (IRE)**[21] [3148] 8-10-11 **80**............................... MatthewBatchelor 61
(P W Hiatt) *hld up in last trio: prog 10th: trckd ldng pair 12th to next: sn lost pl rapidly: t.o 3 out* **25/1**

P-5P **F** **Celtic Major (IRE)**[10] [3345] 8-11-12 **95**............................... DaveCrosse —
(P Bowen) *fell 3rd* **16/1**

0-UP **P** **Banaluso (IRE)**[20] [3187] 6-10-3 **72**....................................... JamesDavies —
(B G Powell) *reminder 2nd: led next to 10th: wknd 12th: t.o whn p.u bef 3 out* **33/1**

-PR0 **P** **Mr Crawford**[64] [2313] 7-10-0 **69** oh5....................................... HenryOliver —
(Nick Williams) *led tl nrly fell 3rd: mstkes after: wknd after 8th: t.o whn p.u after 11th* **66/1**

P003 **P** **Ironside (IRE)**[14] [3290] 7-11-10 **93**................................... MarkBradburne —
(H D Daly) *prom: mstke 3rd: j. slowly 5th: wknd after 12th: mstke next: t.o whn p.u bef 3 out* **4/1**[2]

500 **F** **Happy Shopper (IRE)**[16] [3246] 6-11-3 **93**.......... AndrewGlassonbury(7) 100+
(M C Pipe) *pressed ldr fr 3rd: led 10th: rdn after 13th: abt 2 l clr whn fell 3 out* **11/2**

6m 32.8s (9.10) **Going Correction** +0.25s/f (Yiel) **10** Ran SP% **116.9**
Speed ratings: **94,93,92,88,83** —,—,—,—,— CSF £17.81 CT £85.86 TOTE £5.80: £3.10, £1.80, £2.20; EX 20.20.
Owner Mr & Mrs D A Gamble **Bred** D A Gamble **Trained** Slad, Gloucs

FOCUS
A modest novices' handicap and jumping ability played its part. The finish was almost in slow motion, so perhaps it was not surprising that the winning time was moderate for the class. Weakish form, although The first three ran close to their marks.

NOTEBOOK
Trenance has been having real problems with his jumping, but apart from the first fence his jumping was adequate this time and that proved the key. One of four with any chance turning for home, his task was helped by one of his rivals coming down three out and another making a mistake at the next. He took full advantage to record his second victory over fences, but given his jumping record he is never going to be one to lump on. *(tchd 5-1)*
Rosses Point(IRE), raised a stone for his Fontwell romp, did not jump with any great fluency but still had a chance as good as any coming to the third last. He was quite badly hampered when the leader came down at that fence and a sloppy jump at the last confirmed that this was not going to be his day. *(op 3-1 tchd 10-3 and 7-2 in a place)*
Mandingo Chief(IRE), minus the tongue tie he wore when pulling up at Chepstow, was presented with a real chance when left in front at the third last, but then wasted the opportunity by banking the next fence and losing the advantage. He is tumbling down the handicap and may be able to find a race like this. *(op 13-2 tchd 15-2)*
Joseph Beuys(IRE), making his chasing debut and trying his longest trip to date, emerged with a bit of credit but may not have achieved much. *(tchd 10-1)*
Happy Shopper(IRE), a winning pointer making his chasing debut under Rules after three spins over hurdles, was always up with the pace and was in front, though being hard pressed, when landing too steep at the third last and coming down. It is difficult to say what would have happened had he stood up, but he is probably worth another chance. *(op 13-2 tchd 5-1)*
Banaluso(IRE) *Official explanation: jockey said gelding hung and jumped to the left (op 13-2 tchd 5-1)*

3500 E.B.F./INTERCASINO.CO.UK "NATIONAL HUNT" NOVICES' HURDLE (QUALIFIER) (10 hdls) 2m 3f 110y

1:50 (1:51) (Class 4) 4-7-Y-0 **£3,253** (£955; £477; £238)

Form RPR

20-2 **1** **Snakebite (IRE)**[68] [2238] 6-11-4 .... PaulMoloney 116+
(M Pitman) *mde all: clr fr 6th: in n.d fr 2 out: comf* **5/2**[2]

-251 **2** *6* **Inaro (IRE)**[50] [2606] 5-11-10 .... APMcCoy 112+
(Jonjo O'Neill) *lw: hld up in tch: prog after 3 out to chse clr wnr next: no imp: rdn out to hold on for 2nd nr fin* **4/1**[3]

0 **3** *3/4* **Doc Row (IRE)**[19] [3210] 6-11-4 .... RJGreene 105+
(M C Pipe) *lw: ch type: nt fluent: towards rr: rdn 7th: struggling 3 out: r.o after next: wnt 3rd flat: nrst fin* **25/1**

U000 **4** *1 1/2* **Nice Horse (FR)**[20] [3175] 5-10-11 110....................................... MrCHughes(7) 108+
(M C Pipe) *lw: rel to r and lft 15 l: mostly last tl prog bef 3 out: styd on to chse ldng pair last: one pce flat* **40/1**

2-4 **5** *4* **Sheriff Roscoe**[21] [3133] 6-11-4 .... LeightonAspell 98
(P Winkworth) *lw: prom: mstke 3rd: chsd wnr 6th to 2 out: wknd* **7/1**

-023 **6** *12* **Haunted House**[36] [2860] 6-11-4 .... MarkBradburne 88+
(H D Daly) *t.k.h: wl plcd: effrt to dispute 2nd whn mstke 3 out: wknd next* **14/1**

012- **7** *7* **Bumper (FR)**[301] [4559] 5-10-11 .... AndrewGlassonbury(7) 79
(M C Pipe) *hmpd 3rd: in tch: rdn and struggling after 7th: wknd 2 out* **20/1**

0-2P **8** *11* **Optimistic Alfie**[15] [3277] 6-11-4 .... JamesDavies 68
(B G Powell) *chsd wnr to 6th: wknd u.p after next* **25/1**

0-00 **9** *1/2* **Coltscroft**[15] [3277] 6-11-4 .... SeanFox 68
(J C Fox) *mstkes: in tch to 7th: wknd 3 out* **100/1**

10 *dist* **Rioja Rally (IRE)**[370] 6-10-11 .... SeanQuinlan(7) —
(R T Phillips) *big, chasing type: hld up: stl jst in tch whn blnd and almost c to a halt 3 out : nt rcvr: t.o* **100/1**

-324 **F** **Good Citizen (IRE)**[20] [3175] 6-11-4 112.................................. JasonMaguire —
(T R George) *in tch whn fell 3rd* **7/4**[1]

5m 12.2s (9.50) **Going Correction** +0.45s/f (Soft) **11** Ran SP% **121.0**
Speed ratings: **99,96,96,95,94 89,86,82,81**,— — CSF £12.80 TOTE £4.30: £1.50, £2.00, £4.60; EX 13.20.
Owner Malcolm C Denmark **Bred** Harry Boyle **Trained** Upper Lambourn, Berks

FOCUS
In effect a four-horse race, which became a three-horse race after the favourite departed at the third. The winner proved different class to those remaining and has been rated value for 10 lengths, but he is nowhere near Cheltenham class yet.

NOTEBOOK
Snakebite(IRE), given his usual positive ride, had his task made easier by the early departure of the favourite, but still disposed of what was left very easily. This longer trip held no fears for him and he remains a decent prospect. *(tchd 11-4)*
Inaro(IRE) finished almost three lengths behind Snakebite at Folkestone in November and was 6lb worse off, having picked up a penalty for his Exeter win in the meantime. Given a waiting ride, he tried to get closer starting up the home straight, but it was noticeable that his rider did not get stuck into him and he never looked like bridging the gap. In fact it was all he could do to hang on for second so the conclusion may be that he did not stay.
Doc Row(IRE) performed much better than on his hurdling debut at Exeter and this former Irish point winner looks to be crying out for a greater test of stamina. *(op 33-1)*
Nice Horse(FR) lost a huge amount of ground at the start and it could be argued that he would have finished second at least had he broken on terms, but that could be misleading as he was beginning to look a bit disappointing.
Sheriff Roscoe, promising on his hurdling debut here last month, failed to build on that over this longer trip. *(op 5-1)*
Haunted House didn't get home after being on edge in the preliminaries and taking a keen hold. *(op 20-1)*
Optimistic Alfie *Official explanation: jockey said gelding hung right*
Good Citizen(IRE), who is still looking for his first win over hurdles despite running some fine races in decent company recently, was in about fifth place when diving at the third flight and paying the penalty. *(op 9-4 tchd 5-2 in places)*

3501 INTERCASINO.CO.UK NOVICES' CHASE (REGISTERED AS THE LIGHTNING NOVICES' CHASE) GRADE 2 (11 fncs 1 omitted) 2m

2:20 (2:20) (Class 1) 5-Y-0+ **£19,957** (£7,486; £3,748; £1,869)

Form RPR

/22- **1** **Foreman (GER)**[50] 8-11-3 .... APMcCoy 154+
(T Doumen, France) *hld up bhd ldng pair: chsd ldr 3 out: led 3 out: easily* **11/8**[2]

2111 **2** *3* **Le Volfoni (FR)**[20] [3183] 5-10-13 137...................................... JoeTizzard 140
(P F Nicholls) *trckd ldr: led 3 out: pressed next: hdd last: styd on but no ch w wnr* **1/1**[1]

6-03 **3** *12* **Marcel (FR)**[19] [3215] 6-11-3 .... RJGreene 134+
(M C Pipe) *hld up bhd ldng pair: clsd 8th: rdn bef 3 out: sn btn* **9/1**[3]

2F64 **4** *dist* **Kahuna (IRE)**[16] [3261] 9-11-7 .... MickFitzgerald —
(E Sheehy, Ire) *lengthy: led at gd pce: nt fluent 8th and pressed: hdd & wknd 3 out: t.o: btn 64 l* **12/1**

4m 7.80s (-0.10) **Going Correction** +0.25s/f (Yiel)
WFA 5 from 6yo+ 8lb **4** Ran SP% **109.8**
Speed ratings: **110,108,102**,— CSF £3.33 TOTE £2.20; EX 2.80.
Owner John P McManus **Bred** Mrs B Neumann **Trained** France
■ This race is traditionally run at Ascot but took place at Uttoxeter last year.

FOCUS
Despite there only being four runners, this was a fascinating novice chase and the pace was very respectable in view of the small field. The form looks very solid. The winner, rated value for 10 lengths, is a class act and can rate higher still.

NOTEBOOK
Foreman(GER) ◆, a top-class hurdler who showed plenty of ability in two outings over fences at Newbury and Leopardstown a year ago, could hardly have been more impressive on this return to chasing, travelling supremely well and finding plenty without being put under maximum pressure. He is now likely to head for the Arkle and he must be considered a serious candidate for that, as the likely better ground there should suit him even better. *(op 13-8, 7-4 in places)*
Le Volfoni(FR), bidding for a four-timer, went to the front turning for home but had no answer to the winner's turn of foot from the last fence. He was taking on a decent sort here and this was another personal best, but the penalties are mounting up. He could be an intriguing prospect if switched to handicaps. *(tchd 11-10, 5-4 in a place and 6-5 in places)*
Marcel(FR), dropped back in trip, stepped up on his chase debut but had every chance and never really picked up. This was more encouraging, but he does not look in the same league as the front pair over fences. *(op 8-1)*
Kahuna(IRE), from the same stable as the smart Justified though hardly in the same league, may have been on a reconnaissance mission to see where they stand with the likes of Foreman. He made the early running, but as soon as his three rivals gathered around him straightening up for home he was in trouble and whether the yard will have learnt much from this is anyone's guess. *(tchd 14-1)*

3502 INTERCASINO.CO.UK HURDLE (LIMITED H'CAP) (REGISTERED AS THE CHURCHILL ROAD HURDLE) GRADE 2 (10 hdls) 2m 3f 110y

2:50 (2:52) (Class 1) 4-Y-0+

£22,808 (£8,556; £4,284; £2,136; £1,072; £536)

Form RPR

3251 **1** **Dom D'Orgeval (FR)**[21] [3135] 6-10-11 **132**............................. APMcCoy 138
(Nick Williams) *lw: settled in rr: rdn after 3 out: prog on inner fr 2 out: jnd ldr last: drvn to ld flat: hld on* **5/2**[1]

P303 **2** *nk* **Fenix (GER)**[14] [3298] 7-9-11 **128**.......................................(b) MattyRoe(10) 134
(Mrs L Wadham) *pressed ldrs: led bef 2 out: hdd flat: stl nrly upsides nr fin: nt qckn* **10/1**

-2F4 **3** *5* **Turtle Soup (IRE)**[35] [2876] 10-11-3 **145**........................ WillieMcCarthy(7) 146
(T R George) *trckd ldr tl after 3 out: lost pl: effrt again 2 out: one pce bef last* **11/2**[3]

1522 **4** *1 3/4* **Nathos (GER)**[14] [3298] 9-10-8 **139**...................................... KevinTobin(10) 140+
(C J Mann) *trckd ldrs: lost pl 7th: effrt again on wd outside to chal and mstke 2 out: one pce bef last* **5/1**[2]

P500 **5** *3 1/2* **Sh Boom**[35] [2876] 8-11-7 **142**.. TomSiddall 138
(S A Brookshaw) *in tch: prog to trck ldr after 3 out: upsides new ldr 2 out: sn rdn and btn* **20/1**

5-U3 **6** *3* **Dancing Bay**[20] [3177] 9-11-5 **145**.. SamCurling(5) 138
(N J Henderson) *hld up: prog after 3 out: trcking ldrs gng wl 2 out: sn rdn and fnd nil* **12/1**

11B- **7** *4* **Victom's Chance (IRE)**[295] [4679] 8-10-4 **125**........................... TomDoyle 115+
(Noel T Chance) *mstke 1st: hld up in last: rdn after 3 out: effrt but no real imp whn hit 2 out: fdd* **12/1**

103- **8** *14* **Blushing Bull**[275] [4945] 7-10-4 **125**.. JoeTizzard 106+
(P F Nicholls) *trckd ldrs: rdn and struggling after 7th: last and losing tch bef 2 out: no ch after* **7/1**

32-0 **9** *3 1/2* **Dusky Warbler**[56] [2493] 7-11-2 **137**.. JamieMoore 118+
(G L Moore) *led but nvr looked that keen in front: hdd and btn bef 2 out: wkng and being eased whn blnd last* **8/1**

5m 6.40s (3.70) **Going Correction** +0.45s/f (Soft) **9** Ran SP% **113.5**
Speed ratings: **110,109,107,107,105 104,102,97,95** CSF £27.04 CT £125.04 TOTE £3.70: £1.60, £3.10, £2.30; EX 37.40.
Owner Mrs Jane Williams **Bred** Max De Minden **Trained** George Nympton, Devon

FOCUS
The early pace was very ordinary, but they really picked up in the later stages and eight of the nine runners jumped the second last within a couple of lengths of each other. The winning time was not bad considering, almost six seconds faster than the novice hurdle over the same trip.

NOTEBOOK
Dom D'Orgeval(FR), raised 9lb for his course-and-distance victory last month, got outpaced on the downhill run into the straight and looked more likely to finish last, but he picked up in good style against the inside rail on straightening up and maintained the effort to prevail in a driving finish. The margin may only have been narrow, but there is probably more to come from him given a truly run race. *(op 11-4 tchd 3-1)*
Fenix(GER), back up in trip, took over in front turning for home and battled his heart out all the way to the line, but was just held at bay. After a game effort like this it seems remarkable that he has only won one race over hurdles from 19 attempts. *(op 9-1)*

Turtle Soup(IRE) ran his race under conditions that suit and had every chance, but a stronger pace would probably have suited him better. He remains 10lb higher than his last winning mark, but is running too well for the Handicapper to drop him. *(op 7-1)*

Nathos(GER), raised 7lb for his cracking effort in the Ladbroke and only 2lb better off with the winner for a five-length beating here last month, was inclined to run in snatches but would have been a bit closer but for a mistake at the second last. Considering he has won over further than this, the way the race was run probably did not suit him. *(op 11-2)*

Sh Boom was still bang there jumping the second last and this was his best effort on his third outing for his new yard, but he still has some way to go to match the sort of form he was showing two years ago. *(tchd 22-1)*

Dancing Bay was close enough two out, but did not find much off the bridle and was one of several not suited by the way the race was run. *(op 10-1)*

Victom's Chance(IRE) had been off the course nearly 10 months and faced a stiffish task on his handicap debut. *(op 11-1)*

Blushing Bull had been off the track nine months and was a long way below his best. *(op 6-1)*

Dusky Warbler found himself a reluctant leader and looked awkward as a result. He eventually *stopped to nothing and has not had the race run to suit him in either outing since returning. (op 15-2)*

3503 INTERCASINO.CO.UK H'CAP CHASE (13 fncs 1 omitted) 2m 4f 110y

3:25 (3:25) (Class 2) (0-150,140) 5-Y-0+**£16,265** (£4,775; £2,387; £1,192)

Form				RPR
-625	1		**Wain Mountain**[25] [3022] 10-10-8 **122** ..... (b[1]) JasonMaguire (J A B Old) *prog to ld 4th: mde rest and a gng strly: pressed after 10th: drew clr again next: styd on wl* **7/2**[3]	134
3FB1	2	*6*	**Be My Better Half (IRE)**[7] [3385] 11-10-13 **127** ..... APMcCoy (Jonjo O'Neill) *disp ld at str pce to 4th: styd handy: chsd ldng pair and rdn bef 3 out: chalng for 2nd whn lft 2nd last: kpt on* **4/1**	133
4/3	3	*26*	**Patricksnineteenth (IRE)**[25] [3019] 9-11-7 **135** ..... TomDoyle (P R Webber) *lw: j.rt: disp ld at str pce to 4th: styd prom tl rdn and btn after 10th: wknd last: fin tired* **10/3**[2]	115
P-21	4	*3/4*	**Saintsaire (FR)**[36] [2870] 7-11-2 **130** ..... MickFitzgerald (N J Henderson) *hld up: nt a fluent: niggled along fr 6th: hrd rdn and btn sn after 10th: wl bhd next* **2/1**[1]	109
-0P5	F		**Kadount (FR)**[21] [3136] 8-11-12 **140** ..... WayneHutchinson (A King) *lw: in tch: rdn 9th: prog to join wnr after next: btn bef 3 out: stl jst 2nd whn fell heavily last* **9/1**	147
5-10	P		**Noisetine (FR)**[20] [3180] 8-11-9 **137** ..... AlanO'Keeffe (Miss Venetia Williams) *tried to ld but unable to gain advantage: dropped to rr and nt gng wl after 5th: lost tch 7th: t.o whn p.u bef 10th* **20/1**	—

5m 18.2s (-0.80) **Going Correction** +0.25s/f (Yiel) **6** Ran SP% **113.4**

Speed ratings: **111,108,98,98,**— — CSF £18.12 TOTE £5.30: £2.20, £3.00; EX 21.70.

Owner W J Smith And M D Dudley **Bred** Hesmonds Stud Ltd **Trained** Barbury Castle, Wilts

FOCUS

A valuable prize and a talented field, some of whom had questions to answer. The pace was strong though, so the form looks reliable.

NOTEBOOK

Wain Mountain, whose last win was four years ago though he had been placed on several occasions in the meantime, had been given a chance by the handicapper and the application of first-time blinkers obviously did him no harm. In front with over a circuit to go, he kept on finding enough to keep his rivals at bay and the race was already his when his nearest pursuer fell at the last. He will still be reasonably handicapped under a penalty and the only question is whether the headgear will work again. *(op 9-2)*

Be My Better Half(IRE), raised 5lb for his Carlisle victory, had every chance but lacked pace over the last half-mile and only inherited a clear second place at the final fence. He may prefer a stiffer track or longer trip.

Patricksnineteenth(IRE), following his promising return from a very long layoff at Chepstow last *month, showed up for a long way but eventually blew up. There must be a suspicion he bounced. Official explanation: trainer said gelding was later found to have pulled muscles in its back (op 11-4)*

Saintsaire(FR), raised 13lb for his Windsor victory, never looked happy at all and made no impression at any stage. He may be the sort that needs everything to fall right for him, but in any case he cannot be supported with any real confidence. *(op 9-4 tchd 5-2)*

Noisetine(FR) seemed to resent being unable to dominate early and eventually gave up. *(op 17-2 tchd 10-1)*

Kadount(FR), disappointing in three previous starts this season, needed plenty of persuading to get himself into a challenging position running down the hill into the straight, but he could never get on *top of the winner and was just hanging on to second when taking the last by the roots. (op 17-2 tchd 10-1)*

3504 INTERCASINO.CO.UK STANDARD OPEN NATIONAL HUNT FLAT RACE 2m

3:55 (3:56) (Class 6) 4-6-Y-O **£1,713** (£499; £249)

Form				RPR
	1		**Dubai Sunday (JPN)** 5-11-4 ..... JamieMoore (P S McEntee) *w'like: hld up in midfield: smooth prog 5f out: trckd ldrs over 2f out: effrt to ld over 1f out: sn clr: rdn out* **9/2**[3]	97+
00	2	*2 1/2*	**Persian Native (IRE)**[26] [2961] 6-11-4 ..... WayneHutchinson (C C Bealby) *prom: cl up on inner 2f out: n.m.r over 1f out and sn outpcd: styd on to take 2nd nr fin* **20/1**	92
	3	*nk*	**Trafalgar Night** 5-11-4 ..... JimCrowley (H Morrison) *lengthy: unf: prom: chsd ldr 7f out: rdn to chal 2f out: outpcd 1f out: styd on* **7/2**[1]	92
3	4	*1 1/4*	**Warlord**[26] [3001] 5-11-4 ..... BenjaminHitchcott (R H Buckler) *w'like: mde most: kicked on 4f out: hdd over 1f out: wknd last 75yds* **8/1**	91
	5	*1/2*	**Cleric** 5-10-11 ..... JustinMorgan[(7)] (N A Dunger) *big, chasing type: hld up in rr: prog to chse ldrs 3f out: sn outpcd: styd on fr over 1f out: nrst fin* **50/1**	90
04	6	*3*	**William Butler (IRE)**[14] [3292] 6-11-4 ..... TomSiddall (S A Brookshaw) *w'like: hld up: prog to trck ldrs and gng wl 4f out: rdn and outpcd over 2f out: one pce after* **25/1**	87
00	7	*2 1/2*	**Dr Flight**[20] [3181] 4-10-7 ..... MickFitzgerald (H Morrison) *pressed ldr to 7f out: lost pl rapidly u.p and wl in rr 4f out: plugged on again fnl 2f* **4/1**[2]	74
1	8	*3*	**Deep Reflection**[21] [3138] 6-11-11 ..... AlanO'Keeffe (J A Supple) *w'like: hld up wl in rr: effrt on outer 7f out: rdn and struggling 3f out: no prog after* **9/2**[3]	89
	9	*7*	**My Little Molly (IRE)** 4-9-7 ..... WayneKavanagh[(7)] (J W Mullins) *neat: hld up in rr: rdn 7f out: sn struggling: hmpd 4f out: no ch after* **20/1**	57
	10	*19*	**Wild Lass** 5-10-11 ..... SeanCurran (J C Fox) *leggy: unf: chsd ldrs tl lost pl rapidly u.p over 5f out: hung rt bnd 4f out: t.o* **100/1**	49
	11	*1 3/4*	**Son Of Samson (IRE)** 5-11-4 ..... JoeTizzard (R J Price) *str: bit bkwd: in tch tl wknd rapidly 4f out: t.o* **9/1**	54
0	12	*30*	**Equivocate**[50] [2611] 4-10-0 ..... MatthewBatchelor (R Mathew) *athletic type: t.k.h: cl up tl wknd v rapidly over 4f out: wl t.o* **100/1**	6

3m 40.0s

WFA 4 from 5yo 11lb 5 from 6yo 8lb **12** Ran SP% **117.0**

CSF £96.19 TOTE £6.20: £2.40, £5.30, £2.10; EX 86.60 Place 6 £55.11, Place 5 £47.02.

Owner Mrs R L McEntee **Bred** Northern Farm **Trained** Newmarket, Suffolk

■ Winning jockey Jamie Moore knows his way around here having won three Flat races on this track as an amateur.

FOCUS

Probably a modest event and won by a horse bred to relish this surface. How the form will work out on turf remains to be seen.

NOTEBOOK

Dubai Sunday(JPN), by the brilliant American colt Sunday Silence and a full-brother to two winners on the Flat in Japan, was bred to go on this surface and was the subject of a morning gamble. He was running all over his rivals from some way out, and when it came down to finishing speed it was no contest. However, he does not strike as a natural for hurdling so it will be *interesting to see if he is given a Flat campaign - he was in training with David Loder but unraced. (op 4-1 tchd 5-1 in a place)*

Persian Native(IRE) improved on his two previous efforts in turf bumpers, but whether the progress is natural or was down to the different surface will not be known until he races again.

Trafalgar Night, a full-brother to the smart chaser Frenchman's Creek and half-brother to three other winners over hurdles and fences, showed plenty of ability on this debut but is not really bred for these conditions and his lack of finishing pace showed. He is likely to improve a good deal when he switches to turf. *(op 10-3 tchd 3-1)*

Warlord had at least already shown ability on a sharp track and tried to make it count under a positive ride, but was found wanting for toe at the end.

Cleric is a half-brother to winning sprinter Physical and bred for speed, but he is a jumper on looks and finished strongly after getting outpaced.

Dr Flight, a half-brother to Busy Flight and Borora, was more likely than many to cope with these conditions but got completely caught flat-footed when the tempo increased over half a mile out and there was no way back. He is probably capable of better. *(op 9-2)*

Deep Reflection, surprise winner of an identical race over course and distance last month, failed to *run up to that and was beaten too far for the penalty to have been the only reason. (op 5-1 tchd 13-2 in places)*

T/Plt: £61.20 to a £1 stake. Pool: £52,445.35. 625.35 winning tickets. T/Qpdt: £31.40 to a £1 stake. Pool: £3,518.35. 82.70 winning tickets. JN

[3238]WINCANTON (R-H)

Saturday, January 21

OFFICIAL GOING: Good to soft (soft in places)

Paul Nicholls made history as the first trainer to win six races on one card in Britain, Flat or jumps. Ruby Walsh rode five of them.

Wind: Almost nil

3505 CONNAUGHT "NATIONAL HUNT" NOVICES' HURDLE (DIV I) (8 hdls) 2m

1:00 (1:00) (Class 4) 4-Y-0+ **£3,083** (£898; £449)

Form				RPR
	1		**Raffaello (FR)**[59] 5-11-10 ..... RWalsh (P F Nicholls) *trckd ldrs: led 2 out: r.o wl: pushed out* **10/11**[1]	121+
1P64	2	*2 1/2*	**Hill Forts Timmy**[22] [3131] 6-11-4 ..... AndrewThornton (J W Mullins) *hld up mid div: hdwy appr 2 out: sn rdn: styd on to go 2nd run-in* **40/1**	109
2631	3	*nk*	**Idris (GER)**[8] [3369] 5-11-10 115 ..... PhilipHide (G L Moore) *w ldr: led briefly appr 2 out: sn rdn to chse wnr: kpt on same pce: lost 2nd run-in* **15/8**[2]	116+
4	4	*17*	**Great Memories**[59] [2432] 7-11-4 ..... NoelFehily (Jonjo O'Neill) *hld up: hdwy appr 3 out: rdn and effrt approachong 2 out: wknd appr last* **25/1**	92
1-	5	*5*	**Fibre Optics (IRE)**[558] [938] 6-10-11 ..... ShaneWalsh[(7)] (Jonjo O'Neill) *trckd ldrs: rdn and effrt appr 2 out: wknd appr last* **20/1**	87
0-32	6	*20*	**Loita Hills (IRE)**[22] [3131] 6-11-4 ..... RichardJohnson (P J Hobbs) *led: rdn and hdd appr 2 out: wknd* **7/1**[3]	77+
P-P0	7	*5*	**Fortanis**[21] [3133] 7-10-6 ..... LeeStephens[(5)] (P C Ritchens) *in tch tl wknd appr 2 out* **250/1**	55
00-5	8	*7*	**Cornish Orchid (IRE)**[16] [3246] 5-11-1 76 ..... OwynNelmes[(3)] (C J Down) *nt fluent and rdr lost iron briefly 1st: a bhd: t.o* **66/1**	55
P/P0	P		**Ringagold**[22] [3130] 7-10-4 ..... KeiranBurke[(7)] (N J Hawke) *a bhd: t.o and p.u bef 3 out* **250/1**	—
0/0-	P		**The Trojan Horse (IRE)**[620] [284] 6-11-4 ..... SamThomas (Miss H C Knight) *bhd: lost tch 5th: t.o and p.u bef 2 out* **80/1**	—

3m 52.8s (3.70) **Going Correction** +0.425s/f (Soft) **10** Ran SP% **114.2**

Speed ratings: **107,105,105,97,94 84,82,78,**—,— CSF £43.43 TOTE £2.10: £1.10, £4.50, £1.10; EX 53.60.

Owner Tony Hayward And Barry Fulton **Bred** Mme Isabelle Boireau **Trained** Ditcheat, Somerset

FOCUS

The winning time was fair for the class and more than eight seconds faster than the second division. Probably decent form, which could be rated a few pounds higher.

NOTEBOOK

Raffaello(FR) faced no simple task on this British debut in shouldering 11-10 but he was undoubtedly the one in the line-up with the most potential having won his sole start over hurdles in France, and he gradually edged clear under Walsh. This was not the strongest of fields, but he could do no more and the EBF Final at Sandown in March was mooted as a probable long-term target. *(op 11-10 tchd 6-5)*

Hill Forts Timmy, a dual winner in bumpers, has yet to win over hurdles, but this was easily his best effort thus far and he just got the better of 115-rated Idris on the run-in. On this evidence he should have no trouble finding a small race at one of the lesser tracks, with a return to further likely to help. *(op 33-1)*

Idris(GER) finally got off the mark at Huntingdon earlier in the month, beating a useful sort into second, but the penalty was enough to stop him here and he was run out of second by outsider Hill Forts Timmy. A move into handicaps is surely on the agenda now, and he may yet be capable of better in that sphere. *(op 9-4 tchd 5-2)*

Great Memories, a mildly promising fourth on his bumper debut at Chepstow, worked his way into a challenging position before the turn in, but was soon left trailing and was ultimately well beaten. Further is likely to suit in time and he is the sort to do better once handicapped. *(tchd 20-1)*

Fibre Optics(IRE) was weak in the market and the fact an unbeaten O'Neill gelding was allowed to go off 20/1 was a good guide to his chance of maintaining that 100% record. He is clearly one for the future, and another likely sort for handicaps. *(op 11-1)*

Loita Hills(IRE) failed to run to form and stopped disappointingly quickly once headed. His previous form over hurdles was fair and he may be worth giving another chance to. *(op 6-1)*

Ringagold *Official explanation: jockey said gelding bled from the nose (op 200-1)*

The Form Book, Raceform Ltd, Compton, RG20 6NL

3506 CONNAUGHT NOVICES' CHASE (17 fncs) 2m 5f
1:30 (1:30) (Class 4) 5-Y-0+ **£7,222** (£2,626)

Form				RPR
-434	**1**		**Simon**[26] 2959 7-11-2 115 .... PJBrennan (J L Spearing) *w ldr tl 10th: chsd ldr tl outpcd after 13th: 12 l 3rd and hld whn hit 3 out: lft 2nd next: lft clr last* **9/1**	112
2-P3	**2**	*11*	**Bengo (IRE)**[45] 2701 6-11-2 115 .... NoelFehily (B De Haan) *chsd ldrs: hit 7th and 13th: sn outpcd: 20 l 4th whn lft 3rd 2 out: styng on whn lft 2nd and blnd last* **11/2**	108+
-323	**P**		**Carthys Cross (IRE)**[26] 2959 7-11-2 117 .... AndrewThornton (T R George) *chsd ldrs: rdn after 4 out: wknd qckly and p.u bef next* **11/2**	—
F412	**F**		**Nayodabayo (IRE)**[31] 2938 6-11-2 118 ....(v) AntonyEvans (Evan Williams) *led: hit 6th: drew clr 10th: rdn appr 3 out: lft wl clr 2 out: fell last* **4/1**[2]	135+
2U	**P**		**Ballez (FR)**[19] 3215 5-10-7 120 ....(b) RWalsh (P F Nicholls) *nvr travelling in rr: hit 7th: reminders after next: lost tch 10th: t.o and p.u bef 3 out* **9/2**[3]	—
-162	**F**		**Von Origny (FR)**[38] 2817 5-10-7 120 .... RichardJohnson (H D Daly) *hld up: mstke 11th: hdwy to chse wnr after 13th: rdn after next: styng on and 3 l 2nd whn fell 2 out* **2/1**[1]	123+

5m 34.9s (11.80) **Going Correction** +0.425s/f (Soft)
WFA 5 from 6yo+ 9lb **6** Ran SP% **112.3**
Speed ratings: **94,89,—,—,—,—** — CSF £54.12 TOTE £10.80: £2.50, £2.50; EX 73.50.
Owner Mrs Mercy Rimell **Bred** Mrs Mercy Rimell **Trained** Kinnersley, Worcs

FOCUS
A particularly eventful affair run in a slow time. The fall of Von Origny two out left Nayodabayo in a clear lead, but he declined the gift-wrapped race and came down himself at the final fence, leaving outsider Simon to come through and collect. Nayodabayo would have won by at least 20l.

NOTEBOOK
Simon had shown only average form in three previous starts over fences and he was booked for a well-beaten third here until events unfolded and he was eventually gifted the race on a plate. He was the third best horse on the day, but negotiated the course safely and the wisest move now is surely handicaps as defying a penalty is going to prove a very stiff task. *(op 8-1 tchd 10-1)*
Bengo(IRE) is not the biggest and gives the impression jumping fences is quite an effort. He had run his race and looked booked for fourth when the front two at the time came down, leaving him in second, but any chance of him catching the winner went when he clipped the last and sprawled on landing. He will continue to find winning tough over fences. *(op 15-2 tchd 8-1)*
Nayodabayo(IRE), for the second time this season, came down at the last when looking set to score and was most unlucky. Having turned in with a healthy advantage, he had to fight off the attentions of favourite Von Origny, and looked to be doing so when left clear, but luck soon deserted him and he himself came to grief at the last. It is hoped this does not affect his confidence too severely. *(tchd 7-2)*
Carthys Cross(IRE) had a solid profile and looked sure to run his race, but the manner in which he stopped suggested there may have been something amiss and he is worthy of another chance if nothing too serious comes to surface. *(tchd 7-2)*
Ballez(FR) has hardly been one of team-Nicholls' best French acquisitions and the blinkers appear to have made little difference. He was never going here and as things turned out, it was he who spoiled the party for Nicholls on a day when he trained all six other winners on the card. *(tchd 7-2)*
Von Origny(FR) has not gone on since his winning chase debut at Market Rasen, turning in a laboured effort at Exeter and racing lazily when second at Bangor last time. He was again in rear having to be shoved along from some way out, but was edging nearer to the winner when taking a clumsy fall at the second last. He may need headgear to buck his ideas up. *(tchd 7-2)*

3507 GASFORCE H'CAP CHASE (17 fncs) 2m 5f
2:05 (2:05) (Class 3) (0-125,125) 5-Y-0+ **£11,060** (£3,247; £1,623; £810)

Form				RPR
F35U	**1**		**East Lawyer (FR)**[4] 3440 7-10-11 110 .... RWalsh (P F Nicholls) *hld up bhd: smooth hdwy after 4 out: led 2 out: r.o wl: readily* **12/1**	124+
2132	**2**	*6*	**Black De Bessy (FR)**[26] 3000 8-11-12 125 .... AndrewThornton (D R C Elsworth) *t.k.h: trckd ldrs: hit 3rd: led appr 3 out: sn rdn: hdd 2 out: kpt on but no ch w wnr* **11/4**[1]	133
-0P4	**3**	*2*	**Christopher**[14] 3293 9-11-4 117 .... RichardJohnson (P J Hobbs) *mid div: tk clsr order 8th: rdn after 12th: kpt on same pce fr 3 out* **9/2**[2]	123
-001	**4**	*3 ½*	**Mighty Matters (IRE)**[26] 2982 7-10-11 110 .... SamThomas (T R George) *trckd ldrs: led appr 4 out: rdn and hdd appr 3 out : kpt on same pce* **12/1**	113
5115	**5**	*12*	**Another Native (IRE)**[14] 3290 8-11-2 115 .... NoelFehily (C J Mann) *mid div: hit 13th: sn rdn and effrt: one pced fr 3 out* **7/1**	106
2P-1	**6**	*1 ¼*	**Nas Na Riogh (IRE)**[19] 3212 7-11-3 116 ....(t) AndrewTinkler (N J Henderson) *trckd ldr: led after 10th: hdd appr 4 out: sn rdn: wkng whn wnt lft 2 out* **11/2**[3]	108+
6015	**7**	*10*	**Roofing Spirit (IRE)**[26] 2998 8-11-4 117 .... PJBrennan (D P Keane) *hld up: hdwy after 13th: rdn and effrt after 4 out: wknd after next* **33/1**	98+
3511	**8**	*1 ¾*	**Magico (NZ)**[14] 3282 8-10-8 110 ....(b) PaulO'Neill[(3)] (Miss Venetia Williams) *chsd ldrs: rdn after 4 out: wknd next* **9/2**[2]	90+
415-	**9**	*1 ¼*	**Kim Fontenail (FR)**[391] 2944 6-11-1 114 .... PhilipHide (N J Hawke) *hld up and a bhd* **40/1**	90
05-2	**P**		**Barren Lands**[263] 170 11-9-13 105 .... JamesWhite[(7)] (K Bishop) *mid div tl 8th: sn bhd: p.u bef 12th* **33/1**	—
11/6	**P**		**Biliverdin (IRE)**[66] 2272 12-11-9 122 .... BrianCrowley (J A Geake) *led tl blnd and hdd 10th: grad fdd: p.u bef 3 out* **40/1**	—

5m 30.0s (6.90) **Going Correction** +0.425s/f (Soft) **11** Ran SP% **117.1**
Speed ratings: **103,100,99,98,94 93,89,89,88,—** — CSF £45.55 CT £175.06 TOTE £15.80: £3.10, £2.10, £1.20; EX 64.70 Trifecta £293.80 Pool £662.26. 1.60 winning units.
Owner Champneys Partnership **Bred** A Guyennot And Jean Paul Guyennot **Trained** Ditcheat, Somerset

FOCUS
A fair handicap chase won in excellent fashion by East Lawyer, who put in a good round of jumping and ran out a ready winner. He ran to the level of last year's form, and this form looks pretty solid.

NOTEBOOK
East Lawyer(FR), who has gradually been slipping in the weights, put in a sound round of jumping (often been his downfall) and, on a day where it all fell right for the Nicholls camp, ran out a ready winner. He has never been the most reliable however and, as a result, cannot be relied on to repeat the form next time, but on the plus side the extensive schooling he has undergone at home has clearly helped. *(op 10-1)*
Black De Bessy(FR), narrowly foiled at the course on Boxing Day, again found one too good, but this time his defeat was more emphatic. A strong traveller throughout, he did not find a great deal once going to the front, but beat the rest well enough and may be better suited to carrying smaller weights in better races. *(op 4-1)*
Christopher has slipped back down to a fair mark and offered hopes of a return to winning ways in the near future, keeping on well for third. He has not won for a year however and is hardly the sort to make a habit of backing. *(tchd 5-1)*
Mighty Matters(IRE) faced stiffish tasks on each of his first two outings over fences, but got off the mark when faced with a more realistic challenge at Towcester on Boxing Day and stepped up on that form on this first venture into handicaps. A proficient jumper, he will stay three miles and is lightly raced enough to find some improvement. *(op 8-1)*
Another Native(IRE) has struggled since winning at Uttoxeter two starts back, the 11lb rise seemingly proving too much. This was not a bad effort, but it will be a surprise if he proves capable of winning off this sort of mark.
Nas Na Riogh(IRE), who had a tough race when winning at Exeter earlier in the month, failed to build on that and may still have been feeling the effects. She had a first-time tongue on here, but how well it worked proved inconclusive. *(op 9-2)*
Roofing Spirit(IRE) travelled strongly and looked likely to play a part before the turn into the straight, but he failed to find as much as anticipated and faded out of it. He may be interesting down in grade. *(tchd 40-1)*
Magico(NZ) has been transformed by the fitting of blinkers and was on a hat-trick following wins at Leicester and Fontwell, but he ran below-par and was unable to maintain his progression. *(op 13-2)*
Biliverdin(IRE) has been some way below his best in two starts thus far this season and really needs to brush up his jumping. *Official explanation: jockey said gelding bled from the nose (op 33-1)*

3508 GASFORCE H'CAP HURDLE (11 hdls) 2m 6f
2:35 (2:38) (Class 3) (0-120,118) 4-Y-0+ **£7,807** (£2,292; £1,146; £572)

Form				RPR
422	**1**		**The Luder (IRE)**[19] 3210 5-11-5 111 .... RWalsh (P F Nicholls) *hld up in tch: nt fluent 5th: hdwy after 3 out: led next: kpt on wl: rdn out* **6/4**[1]	123+
2630	**2**	*1 ½*	**Saltango (GER)**[20] 3179 7-11-6 115 .... WilliamKennedy[(3)] (A M Hales) *towards rr: gd hdwy 3 out: pressed wnr and ever ch 2 out: kpt on but no ex flat* **11/2**[3]	122
1141	**3**	*13*	**Kings Castle (IRE)**[14] 3283 11-10-11 110 .... JamesWhite[(7)] (R J Hodges) *hld up towards rr: hdwy after 3 out: sn rdn: lft 3rd at the last: styd on* **12/1**	105+
2011	**4**	*23*	**Down's Folly (IRE)**[19] 3214 6-11-7 113 .... RichardJohnson (H D Daly) *hld up towards rr: hdwy 3 out: rdn and effrt appr 2 out: sn wknd: lft 4th at the last* **4/1**[2]	88+
0-00	**5**	*9*	**Supreme Piper (IRE)**[20] 3179 8-11-2 115 .... MissCDyson[(7)] (Miss C Dyson) *chsd ldrs tl 8th: wknd after 3 out* **50/1**	77
350	**6**	*nk*	**Burren Moonshine (IRE)**[26] 2990 7-10-2 97 .... TomMalone[(3)] (P Bowen) *in tch: rdn after 3 out: wknd next* **40/1**	59
4-00	**7**	*15*	**Cousin Nicky**[20] 3175 5-11-0 109 .... RobertStephens[(3)] (P J Hobbs) *mid div tl wknd 3 out* **40/1**	56
0-4P	**8**	*8*	**Derivative (IRE)**[14] 3289 8-11-11 117 ....(b) SamThomas (Miss Venetia Williams) *led tl after 6th: chsd ldr tl wknd after 3 out: mstke last* **12/1**	56
30-0	**9**	*28*	**Siyaran (IRE)**[101] 1714 5-10-3 95 ....(t) PhilipHide (D R Gandolfo) *a bhd: t.o fr 6th* **66/1**	—
1P-P	**P**		**Fourboystoy (IRE)**[44] 2725 7-11-4 110 .... PJBrennan (Miss H C Knight) *mid div tl wknd after 6th: bhd and p.u bef 3 out* **25/1**	—
131-	**P**		**Igloo D'Estruval (FR)**[445] 1972 10-11-8 114 .... AndrewThornton (Mrs L C Taylor) *mid div tl wknd 6th: bhd and p.u bef 8th* **16/1**	—
0-2P	**P**		**Manawanui**[17] 3239 8-10-1 93 .... AndrewTinkler (R H Alner) *chsd ldrs: blnd 2nd and rdr lost irons: wknd 8th: p.u bef 2 out* **25/1**	—
0-P2	**F**		**Cockatoo Ridge**[19] 3214 9-10-8 100 .... NoelFehily (N R Mitchell) *chsd ldrs: led after 6th: rdn and hdd 2 out: 3rd and hld whn fell last* **16/1**	99+

5m 33.4s (8.30) **Going Correction** +0.425s/f (Soft) **13** Ran SP% **118.6**
Speed ratings: **101,100,95,87,84 83,78,75,65,—,—,—,—** CSF £9.55 CT £74.57 TOTE £2.10: £1.70, £2.00, £2.40; EX 12.40 Trifecta £173.20 Pool £3,928.11. 16.10 winning units.
Owner Derek Millard **Bred** T Lynch **Trained** Ditcheat, Somerset

FOCUS
The front two pulled clear in what was a fair handicap hurdle. The form, rated through the second, does not look that strong.

NOTEBOOK
The Luder(IRE), successful on his sole start in the pointing field, had created a good impression in three starts in novice company, travelling strongly on each occasion, and this step up in trip for his handicap debut brought about the improvement required. He had looked tricky on occasions in the past, but found what was required once Walsh asked him to go on and win his race, giving the impression he could have pulled out more had he been pressed. A promising sort, he will stay further and his ability to travel will continue to stand him in good stead. He can be expected to follow up. *(tchd 13-8)*
Saltango(GER) has had a pretty good season of it thus far, running several good races in defeat and winning once. He made smooth headway to challenge before the second last and kept on right to the line, but the winner always appeared to have him covered. Clear of the third, this was a decent effort and he is the sort who will continue to pay his way. *(op 7-1)*
Kings Castle(IRE) returned in good form when winning at Fontwell earlier in the month, albeit in a much lesser race, but he was still capable of putting in a reasonable effort here, coming through for third after the fall of Cockatoo Ridge. *(tchd 11-1)*
Down's Folly(IRE), on a hat-trick following wins at Doncaster and Exeter, was up another 8lb here and never got into the contest, fading in the final quarter-mile having made his effort. He now has a bit to prove.
Supreme Piper(IRE) has faced some stiff tasks of late, but he has been dropping in the weights as a consequence there were positives to be taken from this.
Derivative(IRE) has not built on a pleasing reappearance at Sandown and he was unable to keep up the gallop here. *(op 14-1)*
Cockatoo Ridge pulled a big run from out of nowhere when second at Exeter earlier in the month, and he was in the process of building on it, looking booked for third, when falling at the final flight. He seems to have suddenly improved at a late stage of his career, as did his brother Rooster Booster, and it is hoped this fall does not affect his confidence. *(op 33-1 tchd 40-1)*
Fourboystoy(IRE) *Official explanation: jockey said gelding had a breathing problem (op 33-1 tchd 40-1)*

3509 CONNAUGHT CUP (A H'CAP CHASE) (21 fncs) 3m 1f 110y
3:10 (3:10) (Class 3) (0-135,132) 5-Y-0+
£18,789 (£5,550; £2,775; £1,389; £693; £348)

Form				RPR
-F35	**1**		**Almost Broke**[25] 3019 9-11-9 129 .... RWalsh (P F Nicholls) *hld up bhd: stdy hdwy fr 15th: trckd ldrs appr 4 out : chal 2 out: rdn flat: led fnl 50yds: all out* **6/1**[3]	143
21F1	**2**	*hd*	**Dunbrody Millar (IRE)**[20] 3186 8-10-6 115 .... TomMalone[(3)] (P Bowen) *led after 3rd: blnd 14th: rdn appr 3 out: hrd pressed fr 2 out: kpt on gamely u.p: narrowly hdd fnl 50yds* **6/1**[3]	131+
P423	**3**	*dist*	**Dante Citizen (IRE)**[26] 3000 8-10-0 106 .... PJBrennan (T R George) *prom: rdn and effrt 4 out: wknd next: lft 3rd at the last* **7/2**[1]	88

F201 **4** *1* **Party Games (IRE)**[8] 3372 9-10-9 **115**.................................(p) PhilipHide 96
(G L Moore) *mid div: hdwy 14th: rdn after 17th: wknd next: lft 4th at the last* **11/1**

P402 **5** *12* **Spring Grove (IRE)**[38] 2828 11-11-3 **123**...................... AndrewThornton 92
(R H Alner) *in tch: tk clsr order and hit 12th: mstke 16th: wknd next* **13/2**

40-4 **6** *2 ½* **Walter's Destiny**[17] 3241 14-9-7 **106** oh5......................... KeiranBurke(7) 72
(C W Mitchell) *in tch tl 6th: sn drvn along towards rr and nvr a danger after* **50/1**

/P-P **P** **Supreme Catch (IRE)**[31] 2938 9-11-0 **120**........................ MarcusFoley —
(Miss H C Knight) *a towards rr: mstke 13th (water): bhd and p.u bef 3 out* **25/1**

35-0 **P** **Parsons Legacy (IRE)**[55] 2532 8-11-6 **126**.................. RichardJohnson —
(P J Hobbs) *a towards rr: blnd 10th: bhd whn mstke 2 out: p.u bef last* **14/1**

12P- **P** **Bathwick Annie**[308] 4461 10-11-12 **132**................................. NoelFehily —
(B G Powell) *led tl after 3rd: chsd ldrs: nt fluent 4th (water): losing pl whn p.u bef 16th* **12/1**

-21F **F** **Lord Olympia (IRE)**[7] 3396 7-11-1 **121**............................ SamThomas 128
(Miss Venetia Williams) *chsd ldrs: jnd ldr 4 out: sn rdn and ev ch: hit 3 out: 3rd and hld whn fell last* **4/1**[2]

6m 43.0s (3.10) **Going Correction** +0.425s/f (Soft) **10** Ran SP% **112.6**
Speed ratings: **112,111,—,—,—** —,—,—,—,— CSF £40.99 CT £143.63 TOTE £5.60: £2.10, £1.80, £2.10; EX 36.50 Trifecta £110.00 Pool £806.00. 5.20 winning units.
Owner A G Fear **Bred** Mrs Kin Lundberg-Young **Trained** Ditcheat, Somerset
■ The fourth of six winners on the card for Paul Nicholls and his 100th of the season, his fastest century.

FOCUS
A decent winning time for a race of its class and the front two ended up finishing a distance clear of the third. The first two could both have been rated a good deal higher.

NOTEBOOK
Almost Broke, tackling this sort of distance for the first time in over a year, was noted travelling strongly some way out and it looked a case of Walsh merely having to press the button as they swung into the straight, but it turned out to be hard work in the end, with him needing all of his rider's strength to get him across the line in front. He was conceding plenty of weight to the runner-up and, although a nine-year-old, is lightly-raced enough to improve further. *(op 5-1)*
Dunbrody Millar(IRE), up 14lb for winning at Plumpton, set off in front in his usual fashion and really served it up to the winner, sticking his neck out gamely but proving unable to hold on. This was a cracking effort considering he did not look entirely happy going this way around, and he remains one to keep on the right side. *(op 4-1)*
Dante Citizen(IRE) came through in his own time to claim a fortunate third, benefiting from the fall of Lord Olympia. He did not appear to get home and may be worthy of another chance back down in trip. *(op 5-1)*
Party Games(IRE), a ready winner at Huntingdon in the first-time cheekpieces, again had the headgear on, but he was not as effective on this occasion and the 10lb rise appeared to find him out. *(op 10-1)*
Spring Grove(IRE) is back on a decent mark, but he is not showing enough to suggest he can capitalise on it. *(op 8-1)*
Lord Olympia(IRE), travelling strongly and looking the likeliest winner when falling at Wetherby the previous weekend, had shown no ill-effects of that and had run a decent race, looking booked for third, when again coming down. He may require a confidence booster after this.

3510 CONNAUGHT H'CAP HURDLE (7 hdls 1 omitted) 2m
3:45 (3:49) (Class 3) (0-125,127) 4-Y-0+
£7,515 (£2,220; £1,110; £555; £277; £139)

Form RPR

F011 **1** **Nippy Des Mottes (FR)**[2] 3467 5-11-7 **127** 7ex.............(t) LiamHeard(7) 131+
(P F Nicholls) *hld up mid div: hdwy on outer after 2 out: led last: qcknd clr: readily* **2/1**[1]

111- **2** *2 ½* **Silencio (IRE)**[473] 1605 5-11-5 **125**.................................. MrGTumelty(7) 124
(A King) *trckd ldrs: led sn after 2 out: sn rdn and edgd rt: hdd last: nt pce of wnr* **14/1**

3060 **3** *1 ¼* **Bonny Grey**[16] 3247 8-10-3 **105**.................................. WilliamKennedy(3) 104+
(D Burchell) *chsd ldrs: rdn after 3 out: kpt on gamely* **25/1**

1-F4 **4** *2* **Predicament**[55] 2525 7-10-12 **111**...................................... NoelFehily 108+
(Jonjo O'Neill) *in tch: tk clsr order 3 out: rdn and ev ch after 2 out: nt fluent last: nt qckn and hung lft run-in* **20/1**

0434 **5** *2 ½* **Hail The King (USA)**[20] 3185 6-10-0 **104**............ RobertLucey-Butler(5) 97
(R M Carson) *hld up: tk clsr order appr 2 out: sn rdn: kpt on same pce* **25/1**

22-3 **6** *½* **Master Mahogany**[21] 3133 5-11-0 **113**.............................. PJBrennan 106
(R J Hodges) *led: blnd bdly 1st: rdn and hdd sn after 2 out: kpt on same pce* **14/1**

05-0 **7** *¾* **Noble Request (FR)**[105] 1677 5-11-7 **120**................... RichardJohnson 112
(P J Hobbs) *mid div: hdwy after 3 out: rdn and ev ch appr last : wknd run-in* **20/1**

-24U **8** *4* **Kawagino (IRE)**[40] 2798 6-10-8 **110**........................ RichardYoung(3) 102+
(J W Mullins) *nvr fluent and j.lft thrght: a towards rr* **15/2**

1263 **9** *1 ¼* **Red Moor (IRE)**[9] 3360 6-10-13 **112**................................ SamThomas 99
(Mrs D A Hamer) *chsd ldrs tl wknd 2 out* **12/1**

0313 **10** *8* **Albarino (IRE)**[14] 3297 7-11-7 **120**................................ BrianCrowley 99
(M Scudamore) *hld up: short lived effrt appr 2 out* **11/2**[3]

U01- **11** *15* **Island Stream (IRE)**[415] 2593 7-11-5 **118**..............................(b) RWalsh 82
(P F Nicholls) *hld up: rdn and wknd appr 2 out* **4/1**[2]

3m 52.8s (3.70) **Going Correction** +0.425s/f (Soft) **11** Ran SP% **118.7**
Speed ratings: **107,105,105,104,102 102,102,100,99,95 88** CSF £28.25 CT £540.29 TOTE £2.80: £1.40, £4.50, £6.30; EX 39.20 Trifecta £441.10 Pool £994.10. 1.60 winning units.
Owner Paul Green **Bred** Mme J Poirier **Trained** Ditcheat, Somerset

FOCUS
Another good display by the improving Nippy Des Mottes, who killed off his rivals with a telling burst of speed after the last. The form might not be that strong. First flight after stands omitted because of the low sun.

NOTEBOOK
Nippy Des Mottes(FR), who has really flourished since being dropped back to this sort of distance, was shouldering a 7lb penalty having won easily at Taunton two days previously and he made light work of it, travelling with his usual fluency and quickening up smartly once asked to settle the matter. A real speed-ball, he continues to improve and the fact he gets on so well with his 7lb claimer will continue to be of great benefit. *(tchd 9-4 and 5-2 in a place)*
Silencio(IRE), off since completing a four-timer in 2004, could have been expected to need this quite badly, but he put up a bold show and it was only the winner's late burst that found him out. Obviously a promising sort, it is hoped he goes the right way from this and, with further likely to suit in time, connections can look forward to his future. *(op 16-1)*
Bonny Grey ran above market expectation and stayed on well without really threatening the winner. She is on a decent mark and capable of capitalising on it back down in grade. *(tchd 28-1)*
Predicament did not quite see his race out, but this was his first outing since November and hr may have needed the outing. He is lightly raced and open to some improvement. *(tchd 22-1)*
Hail The King(USA), who would have found this competition a bit hot, ran above himself in fifth and may be one to watch out back down in grade. *(op 33-1)*
Master Mahogany ran well enough under a positive ride from Brennan and may be ready for a step up in distance. *(tchd 12-1)*
Noble Request(FR) ◆ showed signs of a return to form and this well-experienced hurdler is one of the more interesting ones to take fom the race. *(tchd 16-1)*
Kawagino(IRE) *Official explanation: trainer said gelding was found to be lame following the race (op 7-1 tchd 8-1)*
Island Stream(IRE), the Nicholls second string, was not up to it on this first start since December 2004, but he deserves at least another chance to show what he can do, with the outing sure to bring him forward. *(op 9-2 tchd 7-2 and 6-1 in a place)*

3511 CONNAUGHT "NATIONAL HUNT" NOVICES' HURDLE (DIV II) (7 hdls 1 omitted) 2m
4:15 (4:18) (Class 4) 4-Y-0+ **£3,083** (£898; £449)

Form RPR

1 **Bold Fire**[77] 2059 4-10-6 127.. RWalsh 86+
(P F Nicholls) *led tl after 2nd: led after 3rd: j.rt fr 2 out: clr last: easily* **4/11**[1]

32 **2** *6* **Busy Henry**[81] 1979 6-10-11 .... MrAJBerry(7) 86+
(Jonjo O'Neill) *in tch: hdwy to chse wnr appr 2 out: sn rdn: kpt on same pce* **7/1**[2]

5-5 **3** *6* **Storm Of Applause (IRE)**[22] 3127 5-11-4 .... RichardJohnson 80
(P J Hobbs) *w wnr: led after 2nd tl after next: prom: rdn appr 2 out: sn one pced* **10/1**[3]

00 **4** *2* **Loose Morals (IRE)**[36] 2865 5-10-11 .... MarcusFoley 73+
(Miss E C Lavelle) *hld up: hdwy after 3 out: chalng for 3rd whn blnd last* **33/1**

0/3- **5** *1* **Ten Pressed Men (FR)**[399] 2905 6-11-4................................ NoelFehily 77
(Jonjo O'Neill) *in tch: rdn and effrt appr 2 out: sn btn* **12/1**

6 *17* **Lordsbridge (USA)** 4-10-2 .... DarylJacob(5) 54+
(D P Keane) *stmbld bdly 1st: bhd: hdwy after 3 out: wknd next* **66/1**

0 **7** *11* **The Piker (IRE)**[26] 2961 5-11-4 .... PJBrennan 49
(T R George) *chsd ldrs tl wknd appr 2 out* **40/1**

0-0 **8** *30* **Judy's Lad**[21] 3138 7-11-1 .... OwynNelmes(3) 19
(Mrs H R J Nelmes) *chsd ldrs tl wknd after 3 out* **100/1**

0 **P** **Crystal Hollow**[19] 3216 6-11-1 .... RichardYoung(3) —
(N R Mitchell) *hld up: wknd after 3 out: p.u bef 2 out* **200/1**

0- **U** **Gay Millenium**[436] 2150 6-10-1 .... MarkHunter(10) —
(N I M Rossiter) *mid div tl mstke 3rd: sn bhd: blnd and uns 5th* **100/1**

4m 0.90s (11.80) **Going Correction** +0.425s/f (Soft)
WFA 4 from 5yo+ 11lb **40** Ran SP% **111.9**
Speed ratings: **87,84,81,80,79 71,65,50,—,—** CSF £3.12 TOTE £1.40: £1.10, £1.30, £1.90; EX 3.50 Place 6 £58.77, Place 5 £49.78.
Owner Mrs Sue Craven **Bred** Theakston Stud **Trained** Ditcheat, Somerset

FOCUS
A very slow time and unreliable form. Bold Fire did not need to run anywhere near her French level to win easily. The runner-up has been rated well off his bumper form. First flight after stands omitted - low sun.

NOTEBOOK
Bold Fire, placed in Graded company on her final outing in France, could hardly have been found an easier opportunity to launch her British career and she made no mistake, cantering clear with the minimum of fuss to make it a historic six-timer on the card for trainer Paul Nicholls, and a five-timer for Walsh. She beat little, so it is debatable just what she achieved, but there was a lot to like about the display and it will be disappointing if she cannot follow up, especially as she has the option of mares-only races. *(op 1-3)*
Busy Henry showed modest form in two bumpers, but there was enough promise to be taken from *this first start for current connections to suggest he can win races over hurdles at the right level. (op 16-1)*
Storm Of Applause(IRE) appeared to step up on his Taunton effort and will be qualified for handicaps after one more start, a sphere he will be capable of winning in. *(op 9-1)*
Loose Morals(IRE) was fighting it out for third when blundering at the last, showing enough to suggest she can find a small race in mares-only company.
Ten Pressed Men(FR) showed only moderate form and failed to build on his bumper form as much as anticipated.
T/Jkpt: Not won. T/Plt: £143.90 to a £1 stake. Pool: £76,072.25. 385.75 winning tickets. T/Qpdt: £6.80 to a £1 stake. Pool: £6,375.30. 687.60 winning tickets. TM

3512 - (Foreign Racing) - See Raceform Interactive

3307 NAAS (L-H)
Saturday, January 21

OFFICIAL GOING: Soft

3513a CEDAR BUILDING HURDLE 2m 3f
1:45 (1:46) 5-Y-0+ **£11,224** (£3,293; £1,568; £534)

RPR

1 **Solerina (IRE)**[24] 3080 9-11-7 158.................................... GTHutchinson 146+
(James Bowe, Ire) *settled 2nd: disp ld 4 out: led bef next: drvn out fr last: comf* **1/6**[1]

2 *2* **Florida Coast (IRE)**[51] 2602 11-10-9 128...................... MrNMcParlan(7) 135
(James Bowe, Ire) *trckd ldrs in 3rd: tk clsr order 3 out: 2nd next: rdn after last: kpt on* **12/1**[3]

3 *25* **Up Above (IRE)**[30] 2942 6-11-9 ....(p) AndrewJMcNamara 127+
(S Donohoe, Ire) *led: jnd 4 out: hdd next: rdn and wknd appr 2 out: mstke last* **8/1**[2]

4 *dist* **Biennale (IRE)**[7] 3400 10-10-9 ....(t) MrNTSlevin(7) —
(Patrick O Brady, Ire) *trckd ldrs in 4th: slt mstke 4th: reminders and lost tch bef next: completely t.o* **50/1**

P **Star Performance (IRE)**[20] 3192 11-10-9 ....(t) DMBean(7) —
(Oliver McKiernan, Ire) *p.u after 1st* **50/1**

4m 45.0s **Going Correction** -0.05s/f (Good) **5** Ran SP% **108.4**
Speed ratings: **111,110,99,—,—** CSF £3.13 TOTE £1.10: £1.10, £1.70; DF 2.40.
Owner John P Bowe **Bred** Michael J Bowe **Trained** Thurles, Co. Tipperary

NOTEBOOK
Solerina(IRE) had little to beat here and was sent off at prohibitive odds as a result. She won, but was not at her best, and her rider reported that she did not show her normal enthusiasm. Her next race is likely to be either the Red Mills at Gowran Park on February 18 or a two and a half mile contest at Fairyhouse a week later. *(op 1/7)*
Florida Coast(IRE), who apparently works better than Solerina at home, is officially rated 30lb inferior to her. His amateur rider came in for criticism for not giving him the hardest of rides but the Stewards were happy that the gelding obtained his best possible position.
Up Above(IRE) probably put up a personal best, despite being well held in the end.
Star Performance(IRE) *Official explanation: jockey said his stirrup leather slipped after the start*

3514a WOODLANDS PARK 100 CLUB NOVICE CHASE (GRADE 2) 3m

2:15 (2:15) 5-Y-O+ **£24,693** (£7,244; £3,451; £1,175)

RPR

1 **Southern Vic (IRE)**[24] [3079] 7-11-12 138 CO'Dwyer 155+
(T M Walsh, Ire) *mde all: drew clr bef 2 out: nt extended: impressive* **4/5**[1]

2 *12* **Church Island (IRE)**[24] [3079] 7-11-8 AndrewJMcNamara 141
(Michael Hourigan, Ire) *in tch: 5th u.p bef 5 out: kpt on same pce to go mod 2nd fr last* **5/1**[2]

3 *20* **Homer Wells (IRE)**[24] [3079] 8-11-5 127 DJCasey 123
(W P Mullins, Ire) *settled 3rd: slow 6th: 4th u.p bef 5 out: kpt on same pce: lft mod 3rd fr last* **6/1**[3]

4 *dist* **Slim Pickings (IRE)**[24] [3079] 7-11-8 BMCash 125+
(Robert Tyner, Ire) *hld up in tch: drvn along 1/2-way: 2nd whn slt mstke 3 out: sn rdn & outpcd: no ex whn bad mstke & uns rdr last: rmntd to f* **9/1**

F **Tigerlion (IRE)**[24] [3079] 8-11-5 BJGeraghty —
(J Bleahen, Ire) *trckd ldrs: 4th whn fell 6 out* **8/1**

F **That's An Idea (IRE)**[69] [2224] 8-11-5 123 MrKEPower —
(David Wachman, Ire) *settled 2nd: bad mstke 5th: 3rd 3 out: sn no ex: 5th whn fell last* **11/1**

6m 49.0s **Going Correction** +0.475s/f (Soft) **7** Ran SP% **116.0**
Speed ratings: **117,113,106,—,—** — CSF £5.87 TOTE £2.10: £1.40, £2.50; DF 5.80.
Owner Mrs Brenda Graham **Bred** Neil R Tector **Trained** Kill, Co Kildare

NOTEBOOK

Southern Vic(IRE) jumped well throughout and ran out an impressive winner in the soft ground. Progressing with every run, he is clearly a very smart staying novice, but the obvious target of the Royal & SunAlliance Chase, for which he is a 16-1 shot, will not figure in his campaign according to his trainer unless the ground is testing at Cheltenham. The Ten Up Novice Chase at Navan is likely to be his next assignment. *(op 9/10 tchd 11/10)*

Church Island(IRE), who unseated on his previous two starts, put those disappointing performances behind him with this solid effort. Unlike the winner, he has proven himself on quicker ground, and around Cheltenham. He is a tough and experienced novice, and could well be a big player in the Royal & SunAlliance Chase, for which he is currently a 40-1 chance. *(op 4/1)*

Homer Wells(IRE), runner-up to Southern Vic at Leopardstown last month, ran a fair race but could not match that level of form this time around. *(op 5/1)*

Slim Pickings(IRE), given a waiting ride, chased the winner into the straight but was dropping back when making a bad mistake at the final fence and unseating his rider. *(op 7/1)*

3515a IRISH STALLION FARMS EUROPEAN BREEDERS FUND IRISH RACING WRITERS NOVICE HURDLE 2m

2:45 (2:46) 4-Y-O+ **£12,795** (£3,754; £1,788; £609)

RPR

1 **Sweet Wake (GER)**[25] [3050] 5-11-2 PCarberry 134+
(Noel Meade, Ire) *plld hrd early: a cl up: disp ld 4 out: led appr next: qcknd clr bef 2 out: nt extended* **1/2**[1]

2 *3 ½* **Conscript (IRE)**[113] 4-10-0 DJHoward 96+
(A L T Moore, Ire) *trckd ldrs: 4th 4 out: 3rd next: mod 2nd bef last: kpt on same pce* **50/1**

3 *4* **Jomacomi**[180] [919] 5-11-2 (t) DNRussell 108
(C Byrnes, Ire) *settled 5th: prog appr 2 out: mod 3rd and no imp fr last* **14/1**[3]

4 *1* **Sky To Sea (FR)**[179] [1071] 8-10-11 103 AO'Shea[(3)] 105
(Mrs A M O'Shea, Ire) *trckd ldrs in 3rd: mod 2nd briefly 2 out: sn no ex* **66/1**

5 *nk* **Mont Saint Michel (IRE)**[129] 4-9-11 RCColgan[(3)] 91
(Miss Clare Judith Macmahon, Ire) *hld up in rr: kpt on same pce fr 2 out* **66/1**

6 *shd* **Albert Mooney (IRE)**[42] [2780] 6-11-6 DJCasey 111
(David Wachman, Ire) *reluctant ldr: jnd 4 out: hdd whn slt mstke next: rdn wknd 2 out* **15/8**[2]

7 *1 ½* **Fiery Lord (IRE)** 5-10-7 RMMoran[(3)] 99
(Paul Nolan, Ire) *hld up in tch: effrt whn slt mstke 2 out: no ex* **50/1**

4m 30.9s **Going Correction** +0.475s/f (Soft) **7** Ran SP% **115.0**
WFA 4 from 5yo+ 11lb
Speed ratings: **50,48,46,45,45 45,44** CSF £27.91 TOTE £1.60: £1.20, £7.00; DF 38.50.
Owner High Street Ceathar Syndicate **Bred** Gestut Wittekindshof **Trained** Castletown, Co Meath

NOTEBOOK

Sweet Wake(GER) ◆, a Group performer on the Flat in Germany, has quickly developed into the leading two-mile novice hurdler and rightfully heads the Supreme Novices' market. Most impressive when scoring on his debut at Leopardstown, he again showed a telling burst of speed here that surely no horse he is likely to face at the Festival can handle. He has a tendency to race keenly, but in a big field at Cheltenham Carberry will be able to get him settled, and at this stage he rates as the most likely winner of the curtain raiser. *(op 4/7 tchd 4/6)*

Conscript(IRE), in receipt of plenty of weight from the winner, did best of the rest but was no match for the favourite and will find easier opportunities. *(op 40/1)*

Jomacomi was having his first outing under either code since July and was always likely to struggle against a horse of the winner's ability. *(op 12/1)*

Albert Mooney(IRE), twice a winner in bumpers, did it well when winning on his hurdling debut at Navan back in December, but looked to be facing a stiff task here in attempting to give the favourite 4lb. Forced to make his own running due to a lack of pace, he recoiled sharply in the final quarter mile and was readily outspeeded. *(op 13/8 tchd 6/4)*

3189 FAIRYHOUSE (R-H)

Sunday, January 22

OFFICIAL GOING: Chase course - soft; hurdle course - yielding to soft (soft in places)

3527a NORMANS GROVE CHASE (GRADE 2) 2m 1f

2:15 (2:15) 5-Y-O+ **£20,203** (£5,927; £2,824; £962)

RPR

1 **Fota Island (IRE)**[26] [3051] 10-11-7 157 APMcCoy 154+
(M F Morris, Ire) *cl 3rd: 4th 4 out: hdwy to ld next: styd on wl fr 2 out: comf* **11/8**[2]

2 *4* **Old Flame (IRE)**[27] [3007] 7-11-4 132 JLCullen 139
(Paul Nolan, Ire) *hld up in tch: tk clsr order 4 out: 2nd and chal appr 3 out: no imp fr next: kpt on* **14/1**[3]

3 *1* **Strike Back (IRE)**[27] [3007] 8-11-4 130 RMPower 138
(Mrs John Harrington, Ire) *trckd ldr in 2nd: disp ld briefly 5 out: rdn to chal after next: 3rd and no imp fr 2 out* **16/1**

4 *20* **Central House**[26] [3051] 9-11-12 159 (t) PCarberry 126
(D T Hughes, Ire) *led: jnd briefly 5 out: drvn along and strly after 4 out: hdd next: bad mstke 2 out: sn eased* **4/5**[1]

4m 29.2s **Going Correction** +0.475s/f (Soft) **5** Ran SP% **110.2**
Speed ratings: **118,116,115,106** CSF £13.51 TOTE £2.70; DF 16.90.
Owner John P McManus **Bred** E Morrissey **Trained** Fethard, Co Tipperary

NOTEBOOK

Fota Island(IRE) ◆ developed into a smart novice last season, winning the Grand Annual in impressive fashion before defying a 12lb higher mark at Aintree, but his season ended on a sour note with him unseating in the Grade One Swordlestown Cup behind War Of Attrition at Punchestown. What with the likes of Azertyuiop and Well Chief being out for the season, and Moscow Flyer not looking at his best, there was room for him to develop into a leading two-miler this term. Despite being effective in soft ground, he is at his very best on a sound surface and it is safe to assume that he won with a fair amount in hand here, as he does not always find a great deal once hitting the front. Kauto Star is obviously going to be a tough nut to crack, but this 10-year-old is definitely one of his main challengers and it is not hard to see him going close come March. He may now head for the Newlands Chase at Naas next month as a final prep for the Festival. *(op 11/10)*

Old Flame(IRE) ran above himself in second, but is not a Graded horse and will obviously find things easier back in handicaps. *(op 16/1 tchd 20/1)*

Strike Back(IRE) comes from a stable which is beginning to find its form again and he would make some interest in one of the handicaps at the Festival.

Central House has really improved this season and was set to record his third career win at Grade One level at Leopardstown over Christmas until the well advertised incident in which his very good regular jockey Roger Loughran had a moment of madness and mistook the winning line when in front. He looked set to take the beating here with the ground more in his favour than Fota Island's, but he failed to run his race under Carberry and failed to jump with his usual fluency. Better can be expected with his regular jockey back on board and, if getting back on track in the Newlands Chase at Naas next month, he will go to the Champion Chase with major claims. *Official explanation: jockey said gelding was never travelling and ran flat throughout; vet said gelding finished lame* *(op 9/10)*

3528a IRISH STALLION FARMS EUROPEAN BREEDERS FUND BEGINNERS CHASE 2m 1f

2:45 (2:45) 5-Y-O+ **£9,054** (£2,109; £930; £537)

RPR

1 **Our Ben**[24] [3108] 7-11-12 RWalsh 123+
(W P Mullins, Ire) *a.p: sltly hmpd 3rd: nt fluent 5 out: led after 4 out: rdn and styd on wl fr 2 out* **4/6**[1]

2 *2 ½* **Lissbonney Project (IRE)**[21] [3200] 8-11-12 BJGeraghty 121+
(Philip Fenton, Ire) *trckd ldrs: 4th 3 out: 2nd after 2 out: kpt on wout troubling wnr* **7/2**[2]

3 *2 ½* **Some Timbering (IRE)**[8] [3406] 7-11-12 JRBarry 118
(E Sheehy, Ire) *a.p: 2nd 5 out: chal next: 3rd and rdn 3 out: 2nd whn hit next: kpt on same pce* **6/1**[3]

4 *12* **Native Cooper (IRE)**[26] [3061] 8-11-12 (t) PWFlood 106
(Miss A M Lambert, Ire) *mid-div: 7th 1/2-way: prog after 4 out: kpt on to go mod 4th fr last* **50/1**

5 *½* **Wills Wilde (IRE)**[22] [3153] 7-11-9 APLane[(3)] 106
(P A Fahy, Ire) *mid-div: 6th 4 out: 7th bef next: kpt on* **50/1**

6 *2* **Hang Seng (IRE)**[36] [2894] 8-11-7 MJFerris[(5)] 104
(Eugene M O'Sullivan, Ire) *mid-div: 8th 1/2-way: 6th 3 out: no imp fr next* **25/1**

7 *4* **Swordlestown (IRE)**[43] [2776] 8-11-12 GCotter 100
(T M Walsh, Ire) *prom: led after 5th: hdd after 4 out: wknd fr next* **20/1**

8 *25* **Last Minute Goal (IRE)**[21] [3194] 7-11-12 DFO'Regan 75
(Noel Meade, Ire) *nvr a factor: kpt on one pce fr 4 out* **25/1**

9 *nk* **Depth Perception (IRE)**[52] [2602] 6-11-12 APCrowe 74
(Paul John Gilligan, Ire) *cl up: lft in ld 3rd: hdd bef 6th: in tch to 4 out: wknd bef next* **66/1**

10 *10* **Thejamman (IRE)**[21] [3194] 7-11-12 PCarberry 64
(Noel Meade, Ire) *nvr a factor* **20/1**

11 *7* **Ballyfourlass (IRE)**[105] [1704] 6-11-7 GTHutchinson 52
(James Cousins, Ire) *nvr a factor* **66/1**

12 *nk* **In The Morning (IRE)**[7] [3412] 7-11-12 DTEvans 57
(A J Martin, Ire) *rr of mid-div: no ex fr 5 out* **33/1**

13 *dist* **Habitual (IRE)**[8] [3406] 5-11-3 RGeraghty —
(John A Quinn, Ire) *a bhd: t.o fr 5 out* **33/1**

P **Coogans Bluff (IRE)**[8] [3406] 6-11-9 (tp) MPWalsh[(3)] —
(Gerard Keane, Ire) *a bhd: p.u* **100/1**

F **Dosco (IRE)**[21] [3194] 7-11-7 (t) NJO'Shea[(5)] —
(D T Hughes, Ire) *nvr a factor: bhd whn fell last* **66/1**

F **Lucifer Du Montceau (FR)**[26] [3043] 7-11-12 DJHoward —
(A L T Moore, Ire) *led tl fell 3rd* **33/1**

B **Eko Deauville (DEN)**[35] [2919] 11-11-12 JPElliott —
(I Madden, Ire) *towards rr whn b.d after 1st* **50/1**

S **Dont Askim (IRE)**[21] [3194] 6-11-12 PACarberry —
(Patrick G Kelly, Ire) *towards rr whn slipped up after 1st* **66/1**

4m 31.4s **Going Correction** +0.475s/f (Soft) **18** Ran SP% **135.4**
WFA 5 from 6yo+ 8lb
Speed ratings: **113,111,110,105,104 103,101,90,90,85 82,81,—,—,— —,—,—** CSF £3.06 TOTE £1.70: £1.10, £1.40, £1.10, £8.00; DF 3.90.
Owner Trevor Hemmings **Bred** Granham Farms **Trained** Muine Beag, Co Carlow

NOTEBOOK

Our Ben ◆, third in last season's Royal & SunAlliance Hurdle, made a highly satisfactory start to his chasing career when second to the potentially high-class Nickname at Leopardstown and was the obvious winner of what looked nothing more than an ordinary affair. The one question he did have to answer, though, was his ability to cope with two miles, but he had the class and put in a sound round of jumping to win in workmanlike fashion. Three miles is going to see him in a totally different light and the way he flew up the hill at the Festival last season suggests he will have no trouble with the demands of the Royal & SunAlliance Chase, a race for which he looks a major contender at this stage. *(op 1/2)*

In The Morning(IRE) *Official explanation: jockey said gelding made a respiratory noise in running and tired in closing stages; vet said gelding suffered an overreach in running*

3529 - 3531a (Foreign Racing) - See Raceform Interactive

3231 AYR (L-H)

Monday, January 23

OFFICIAL GOING: Heavy

Racing was abandoned and the course evacuated after race three after a shed caught fire in a nearby garden.

Wind: Breezy, across

3532 E B F POSTER PLUS "NATIONAL HUNT" NOVICES' HURDLE (QUALIFIER) (9 hdls 2 omitted) 2m 4f

1:10 (1:10) (Class 4) 4-7-Y-O **£3,578** (£1,050; £525; £262)

Form RPR

0342 **1** **Morgan Be**[21] [3205] 6-11-3 107 .... TonyDobbin 105+
(Mrs K Walton) *trckd ldrs: led 4 out: drew clr fr 2 out* **1/4**[1]

-P54 **2** *8* **Kempski**[9] [3381] 6-10-10 87 ....(b[1]) GarethThomas(7) 90
(R Nixon) *cl up: led 5th to next: ev ch and rdn bef 3 out: no ex appr next* **14/1**[3]

60 **3** *dist* **Stand On Me**[10] [3374] 7-11-3 .... MarkBradburne —
(P Monteith) *led to 5th: hit next: sn lost tch* **20/1**

00P **4** *dist* **Lethem Present (IRE)**[20] [3235] 6-10-5 .... DougieCostello(5) —
(T Butt) *in tch to 5th: sn btn* **33/1**

00 **P** **Stormy Bay (IRE)**[39] [2844] 5-11-3 .... PadgeWhelan —
(R C Guest) *hld up: wknd 5th: t.o whn p.u bef 4 out* **33/1**

0-PP **P** **Border Craic (IRE)**[20] [3232] 6-11-3 ....(v[1]) AlanDempsey —
(B Mactaggart) *j.v.slowly and wl bhd fr 1st: p.u after 4th* **50/1**

0 **P** **Van Cleef (IRE)**[32] [2948] 5-11-3 .... GrahamLee —
(M Todhunter) *hld up: reminders 4th: lost tch next: t.o whn p.u bef 3 out* **10/1**[2]

0P **P** **Moscow Ali (IRE)**[36] [2901] 6-10-12 .... DeclanMcGann(5) —
(Miss Lucinda V Russell) *towards rr: drvn 3rd: lost tch fr 5th: p.u bef 4 out* **50/1**

5m 20.8s (8.10) **Going Correction** +0.55s/f (Soft) **8** Ran SP% **110.3**
Speed ratings: **105,101**,—,—,— —,—,— CSF £3.68 TOTE £1.20: £1.10, £1.40, £2.70; EX 3.50.

Owner S Breakspeare **Bred** Martin Blandford **Trained** Middleham, N Yorks

■ Stewards' Enquiry : Gareth Thomas one-day ban: used whip whilst gelding was showing no response (Feb 3)

FOCUS

Testing conditions and a one-horse race according to the market. Apart from the winner, rated value for 15l, this looked a weak contest. The middle flight in the back straight was omitted on both circuits.

NOTEBOOK

Morgan Be, who has been running with plenty of credit behind some useful sorts in his last three outings, had little to beat this time and at no stage did he not look like winning. He will not find too many other opportunities like this over hurdles, especially under a penalty, and he is seen as a *chaser in the making, but he could be interesting if tried in a handicap off this sort of mark. (after early 1-3 in a place)*

Kempski, with first-time blinkers replacing cheekpieces, was always up with the pace and was the only one to give the red-hot favourite any kind of a race. He would have been getting 20lb from the winner in a handicap, so probably ran a bit above himself and should be capable of making his mark at a modest level with the headgear retained. *(op 12-1)*

Stand On Me, stepping up in trip, stopped to nothing after making much of the early running and ran as though not staying the trip in the testing conditions. This efforts suggests the point he won last spring must have been a very poor affair. *(op 12-1)*

Lethem Present(IRE), runner-up in a couple of points but well beaten in a bumper and two hurdles since, is going to have a form figure next to her name that grossly flatters her. *(op 25-1 tchd 40-1)*

Van Cleef(IRE), a full-brother to Calling Brave but beaten out of sight in a bumper here on his debut, did not look happy with over a circuit left to race and looks very poor at this stage.

3533 GILES INSURANCE CONDITIONAL JOCKEYS' H'CAP CHASE (13 fncs 4 omitted) 2m 4f

1:40 (1:40) (Class 4) (0-110,105) 5-Y-O+ **£6,506** (£1,910; £955; £477)

Form RPR

042F **1** **Green Ideal**[28] [2993] 8-11-9 **105** ....(b) ThomasDreaper(3) 113+
(Ferdy Murphy) *trckd ldrs: led bef 3 out: styd on strly fr next* **13/2**

-31P **2** *1* **Fountain Brig**[21] [3204] 10-10-5 **84** .... MichaelMcAlister 89
(N W Alexander) *in tch: drvn bef 3 out: rallied to chse wnr last: kpt on* **10/1**

-31F **3** *6* **Corrib Lad (IRE)**[32] [2945] 8-11-9 **105** .... GaryBerridge(3) 104
(L Lungo) *prom: j. slowly 7th: rallied 9th: ev ch bef 3 out: rdn and edgd lft bef next: one pce between last two* **7/4**[1]

-231 **4** *3* **Good Outlook (IRE)**[22] [3172] 7-11-4 **105** .... JohnFlavin(8) 101
(R C Guest) *led to 7th: cl up: outpcd bef 3 out: n.d after* **8/1**

35 **5** *3* **My Lucky Rose (IRE)**[32] [2944] 8-11-1 **94** ....(b) AndrewJMcNamara 89+
(S Donohoe, Ire) *hld up: effrt and rdn 4 out: btn bef next* **11/2**[3]

1111 **P** **Jolly Boy (FR)**[38] [2867] 7-11-7 **103** ....(b) LiamTreadwell(3) —
(Miss Venetia Williams) *cl up: led 7th to bef 3 out: sn btn and p.u* **3/1**[2]

4-FP **P** **True North (IRE)**[16] [3289] 11-11-12 **105** .... DeclanMcGann —
(D R MacLeod) *sn bhd: struggling fr 1/2-way: t.o whn p.u bef 2 out* **66/1**

5m 33.8s (10.90) **Going Correction** +0.725s/f (Soft) **7** Ran SP% **111.8**
Speed ratings: **107,106,104,103,101** —,— CSF £59.87 TOTE £5.10: £2.50, £4.30; EX 68.30.

Owner Mrs J Morgan **Bred** Juddmonte Farms **Trained** West Witton, N Yorks

FOCUS

A modest event that turned into a real test of stamina. The winner was value for 3l, the second ran to his best and the form looks pretty solid. The second last fence in the back straight and the first in the home straight wee omitted on each circuit.

NOTEBOOK

Green Ideal, who was in the process of running a better race before toppling over at Wetherby last time, confirmed that he is back in form with a very game victory. The testing conditions made this a thorough test of stamina, which suited him, and he showed plenty of spirit to hold on after looking certain to be overhauled on the run-in. He is always worthy of respect when the mud is flying. *(op 5-1 tchd 7-1)*

Fountain Brig, pulled up over the extended three miles here earlier this month, was much happier over this shorter trip and it looked as though he might catch the winner after jumping the last, but he found an extra spurt beyond him. He is consistent even though he has only won once and is a real course specialist as 16 of his 18 outings have been here.

Corrib Lad(IRE) was possibly unlucky not to be unbeaten in two starts over fences coming into this, but he was taking on more experienced chasers this time and running in snatches would not have helped him either. He might well have won off a 3lb lower mark here last time, but the fact remains he was off an 11lb higher mark than when making a successful chasing debut in a novices' handicap at Hexham in November. *(op 13-8 tchd 2-1 in a place)*

Good Outlook(IRE), raised 6lb for his Catterick victory, was given a positive ride, but he was encountering much softer ground here and did not get home in the conditions. *(tchd 9-1)*

My Lucky Rose(IRE), running over the fences for the first time since May, never got involved and has shown nothing over the larger obstacles since winning a beginners' chase at Down Royal last March. *(op 13-2)*

Jolly Boy(FR), bidding for a six-timer, was racing off a whopping 20lb higher mark than when last seen, but he appeared to travel well enough until suddenly coming off the bridle jumping the fourth last and soon stopped to nothing. Even allowing for the weight rise, the way he blew out here *suggested there were other reasons for this dismal effort.Official explanation: trainer had no explanation for the poor form shown (op 11-4 tchd 7-2 in a place)*

3534 KENNEDY CONSTRUCTION MAIDEN HURDLE (8 hdls 1 omitted) 2m

2:10 (2:25) (Class 4) 4-Y-O+ **£4,111** (£1,198; £599)

Form RPR

1-45 **1** **Regal Heights (IRE)**[21] [3205] 5-10-13 .... StephenCraine(5) 111
(D McCain) *prom: drvn bef 3 out: rallied: kpt on to ld towards fin* **12/1**[3]

6P **2** *1* **Auenmoon (GER)**[32] [2942] 5-11-4 .... MarkBradburne 110
(P Monteith) *mde most: rdn bef 2 out: kpt on: hdd towards fin* **80/1**

32 **3** *5* **Akarem**[28] [3003] 5-11-4 .... BarryKeniry 108+
(K R Burke) *mstkes: chsd ldrs: rdn bef 3 out: kpt on same pce fr last* **2/5**[1]

43-0 **4** *5* **Hue**[11] [3351] 5-11-4 102 .... WilsonRenwick 101+
(B Ellison) *cl up: ev ch bef 3 out: one pce fr next* **14/1**

3 **5** *3/4* **Cinema (FR)**[20] [3235] 6-10-6 .... ThomasDreaper(5) 92
(B R Hamilton, Ire) *in tch: outpcd bef 3 out: n.d after* **13/2**[2]

-0P4 **6** *nk* **Lethem Air**[14] [3314] 8-10-13 103 .... DougieCostello(5) 99
(T Butt) *prom: outpcd after 4 out: rallied next: sn no imp* **40/1**

30-0 **7** *16* **Fiddlers Creek (IRE)**[7] [2657] 7-11-4 88 ....(t) GrahamLee 83
(R Allan) *prom tl wknd bef 3 out* **33/1**

0044 **8** *1 1/4* **Political Pendant**[13] [3337] 5-10-4 94 .... GarethThomas(7) 75
(R Nixon) *midfield: struggling 4 out: sn n.d* **40/1**

-L06 **9** *13* **Baffling Secret (FR)**[14] [3314] 6-11-1 .... GaryBerridge(3) 69
(L Lungo) *j.lft: a bhd* **66/1**

10 *11* **Saw Doctor (IRE)**[169] [1175] 6-10-11 .... MrEMagee(7) 58
(J K Magee, Ire) *a bhd* **100/1**

0P **11** *2 1/2* **Bishop's Brig**[32] [2947] 6-10-13 .... MichaelMcAlister(5) 55
(N W Alexander) *a bhd: no ch fr 1/2-way* **200/1**

12 *26* **Imlaak**[187] 4-10-7 .... AnthonyRoss 18
(James Moffatt) *a bhd: nvr on terms* **100/1**

P0 **13** *3 1/2* **Matthew My Son (IRE)**[36] [2903] 6-10-11 .... PhilKinsella(7) 26
(F P Murtagh) *a bhd* **100/1**

5- **P** **Red Cedar (USA)**[320] [4259] 6-11-4 95 .... AlanDempsey —
(J Wade) *a bhd: t.o whn p.u bef 3 out* **33/1**

6P/F **P** **Lucky Largo (IRE)**[17] [3267] 6-10-11 85 .... EwanWhillans(7) —
(D A Nolan) *a bhd: t.o whn p.u bef 3 out* **150/1**

0P0U **S** **Galahad (FR)**[20] [3231] 5-11-4 .... DavidO'Meara —
(B Storey) *a bhd: no imp whn slipped up after 4 out* **100/1**

00 **P** **It's No Easy (IRE)**[32] [2942] 5-11-4 .... TonyDobbin —
(N G Richards) *midfield: outpcd 1/2-way: t.o whn p.u bef 3 out* **20/1**

P **Hezaam (USA)**[114] 5-11-4 .... TomSiddall —
(C W Fairhurst) *midfield: outpcd 4 out: btn whn blnd 2 out: p.u bef last* **50/1**

4m 6.10s (8.80) **Going Correction** +0.55s/f (Soft)
WFA 4 from 5yo+ 11lb **18** Ran SP% **124.5**
Speed ratings: **100,99,97,94,94 93,85,85,78,73 72,59,57**,—,— —,—,— CSF £696.68 TOTE £12.80: £2.30, £14.00, £1.10; EX 871.90 Place 6 £12.41, Place 5 £11.21.

Owner Mrs Janet Heler **Bred** Mrs R Deane **Trained** Cholmondeley, Cheshire

FOCUS

Not as competitive as the size of the field would suggest with only five of the 18 runners starting at less than 33/1. A surprise result with the favourite disappointing, but despite the pace not looking that strong the front six still pulled miles clear of the rest. Those that raced up with the pace seemed favoured. The winner has been rated up to the level of his bumper form and the race has been rated through the sixth. The middle flight in the back straight was omitted.

NOTEBOOK

Regal Heights(IRE), dropped in trip on this third outing over hurdles, was always thereabouts and grabbed an unlikely-looking victory on the run-in. He still has a bit of scope and gives the impression that a stiff two miles suits him best.

Auenmoon(GER) ran by far his best race since arriving from Germany and looked like winning starting up the run-in, only to wilt in the last 50 yards. He may have been helped by being given a positive ride under conditions in which it seemed difficult to make up ground, but ought to find an ordinary novice event nonetheless.

Akarem was extremely disappointing in view of his efforts over timber so far and on several occasions his jumping was modest to say the least. The ground should not have bothered him, so he now has plenty of questions to answer. *(op 4-9)*

Hue ran better than on his return to hurdling earlier this month, but was another who may be flattered by racing up with the pace in a race where it was very hard to come from behind. He is beginning to look exposed under both codes. *(tchd 16-1)*

Cinema(FR), not unbacked, was probably not helped by the drop in trip even in these conditions. *(op 8-1)*

Lethem Air rather ran in snatches, but still managed to finish a long way clear of the others. Despite him being a winning pointer, it is proving very difficult isolating his best trip over hurdles.

It's No Easy(IRE) *Official explanation: vet said gelding coughed (op 10-1)*

3535 GILES INSURANCE NOVICES' CHASE (19 fncs) 3m 1f

() (Class 2) 5-Y-O+ £

3536 DAWN CONSTRUCTION NOVICES' H'CAP HURDLE (11 hdls) 2m 4f

() (Class 5) (0-90,) 4-Y-O+ £

3537 JOHNSTONE WATERFRONT H'CAP HURDLE (9 hdls) 2m

() (Class 4) (0-110,) 4-Y-O+ £

3538 SPONSOR'S LUNCH AT AYR RACECOURSE STANDARD OPEN NATIONAL HUNT FLAT RACE 2m

() (Class 6) 4-6-Y-O £

T/Jkpt: £246.50 to a £1 stake. Pool: £15,451.00. 44.50 winning tickets. T/Plt: £5.80 to a £1 stake. Pool: £36,032.70. 4,529.40 winning tickets. T/Qpdt: £1.10 to a £1 stake. Pool: £3,024.00. 2,305.40 winning tickets. RY

3393 WETHERBY (L-H)

Monday, January 23

OFFICIAL GOING: Heavy

The going was described as 'a gluepot, very tacky and holding'. The rails on both bends were on the extreme outside, maximism the distances.

Wind: Moderate, half-behind Weather: Overcast and cold

3539 LORD RIMMER MEMORIAL JUVENILE NOVICES' HURDLE (9 hdls) 2m

1:30 (1:30) (Class 4) 4-Y-O **£3,415** (£1,002; £501; £250)

Form RPR

2110 **1** **Gardasee (GER)**[27] 3021 4-11-12 .... JasonMaguire 121+
(T P Tate) *mde virtually all: hit 2 out: styd on wl run-in* **11/10**[1]

P410 **2** *6* **Eborarry (IRE)**[22] 3171 4-11-5 108 .... RussGarritty 105
(T D Easterby) *hld up: hdwy to chse ldrs 6th: wnt 2nd approachintg next: upsides 2 out: no ex run-in* **25/1**

0401 **3** *5* **Calfraz**[21] 3203 4-11-5 103 .... NeilMulholland 100
(M D Hammond) *chsd ldrs: one pce fr 3 out* **14/1**

U312 **4** *5* **Lankawi**[21] 3203 4-11-5 107 .... BrianHarding 95
(Jedd O'Keeffe) *chsd ldrs: rdn appr 3 out: one pce* **7/1**[3]

52P5 **5** *1 ½* **Dock Tower (IRE)**[35] 2921 4-10-9 ....(t) PeterBuchanan(3) 87
(M E Sowersby) *hdwy to chse ldrs 5th: fdd appr 3 out* **25/1**

2 **6** *14* **Daldini**[35] 2921 4-10-12 .... DominicElsworth 77+
(Mrs S J Smith) *trckd ldrs: wknd 3 out: no ch whn hit last* **7/1**[3]

0 **7** *dist* **Mr Marucci (USA)**[17] 3267 4-10-5 .... PatrickMcDonald(7) —
(B Ellison) *mstkes: prom: mstke 6th: sn lost pl and bhd: t.o: btn 32 l* **200/1**

0U **8** *11* **Annals**[11] 3349 4-10-5 ....(e[1]) KennyJohnson —
(R C Guest) *stdd s: a in rr: t.o* **200/1**

P **9** *dist* **Moment Of Clarity**[32] 2954 4-10-9 ....(e) LarryMcGrath(3) —
(R C Guest) *staedied s: in rr whn mstke 4th: sn bhd: hopelessly t.o: btn 43 l* **200/1**

64 **U** **John Forbes**[27] 1011 4-10-2 .... CraigLidster(10) —
(B Ellison) *hld up in rr: blnd and uns rdr 1st* **50/1**

P **Jeune Loup**[11] 4-10-12 .... SamThomas —
(P C Haslam) *nt fluent: chsd ldrs: lost pl 5th: sn bhd: t.o 9th whn p.u bef last* **50/1**

121 **P** **Dan's Heir**[7] 3415 4-11-7 .... PaddyMerrigan(5) —
(P C Haslam) *chsd ldrs: pushed along after 3rd: lost pl 6th: bhd whn p.u bef next* **10/3**[2]

4m 18.9s (19.50) **Going Correction** +1.375s/f (Heav) **12** Ran SP% **115.5**
Speed ratings: **106,103,100,98,97 90,—,—,—,— —,—** CSF £34.01 TOTE £2.00: £1.20, £3.20, £3.90; EX 40.90.
Owner A S Helaissi **Bred** Gestut Romerhof **Trained** Tadcaster, N Yorks

FOCUS
A true test in the conditions but a two-horse race in the end. Fair juvenile form for the track. The winner did not have to be at his very best while the runner-up is now getting his act together over hurdles.

NOTEBOOK
Gardasee(GER) made sure there was no hanging about and in the end he stayed on much the better to record his third success. Rated just 51 on the level, he could be interesting in that sphere with his stamina tested. *(op 11-8, tchd 6-4 in places)*
Eborarry(IRE), suited by the give, moved upsides looking a real threat but he was very definitely second best at the line. He will make a better chaser next term. *(op 28-1)*
Calfraz showed his 100/1 Ayr win was no fluke but this may be as good as he is. *(op 11-1)*
Lankawi, closely matched with Calfraz on Ayr running, was unable to turn the tables.
Dock Tower(IRE), flattered by his second in a Listed event here in October, looks to have some sort of problem, as he seems unable to finish his races now.
Daldini travelled strongly and was taken wide but he fell in a heap three out. He doesn't want the ground as testing as this.
Dan's Heir was struggling at an early stage and this gluepot ground was alien to him. *Official explanation: jockey said gelding lost its action rounding home turn (op 3-1 tchd 7-2, 4-1 in places)*

3540 SCAFELL PIKE AMATEUR RIDERS' H'CAP HURDLE (12 hdls) 2m 7f

2:00 (2:00) (Class 5) (0-90,90) 4-Y-0+ **£2,966** (£912; £456)

Form RPR

/1F3 **1** **Twotiming Gent (IRE)**[28] 2978 13-10-3 74 .... MissLHaagensen(7) 83+
(P D Niven) *led tl appr 3 out: led appr last: edgd lft and styd on wl* **15/2**

6/61 **2** *3* **Dickie Lewis**[23] 3140 8-11-5 90 .... MrDAFitzsimmons(7) 96+
(D McCain) *trckd ldrs: chal 2 out: no ex run-in* **5/2**[1]

1456 **3** *11* **Jontys'Lass**[22] 3167 5-11-7 88 .... MrMSeston(3) 84+
(A Crook) *trckd ldrs: slt ld 2 out: hdd appr last: sn wknd* **14/1**

0302 **4** *6* **Avanti Tiger (IRE)**[6] 3433 7-10-4 68 ....(b) MrSMorris 59+
(C C Bealby) *chsd ldrs: rdn to ld appr 3 out: hdd & wknd 2 out* **7/2**[2]

F000 **5** *dist* **Datbandito (IRE)**[20] 3231 7-10-11 78 .... MrGTumelty(3) —
(L Lungo) *in tch: hdwy to chse ldrs 7th: sn rdn: lost pl after 9th: t.o: btn 54 l* **8/1**

0PP3 **6** *8* **Kings Square**[11] 3351 6-10-13 84 .... MrOGreenall(7) —
(M W Easterby) *chsd ldrs: rdn and lost pl 9th: t.o* **4/1**[3]

0530 **U** **Road King (IRE)**[17] 3279 12-10-8 79 ....(p) MrRBirkett(7) —
(Miss J Feilden) *hdwy 4th: in tch whn blnd and uns rdr 7th* **16/1**

6000 **P** **Stormy Madam (IRE)**[18] 3254 6-10-3 74 .... MrRWakeham(7) —
(J R Turner) *in tch: drvn 6th: sn bhd: t.o whn p.u after 9th* **33/1**

00P4 **P** **Commemoration Day (IRE)**[22] 3173 5-10-6 77 ....(v) MrCJCallow(7) —
(M E Sowersby) *sn detached in last: t.o 3rd: p.u after 6th* **50/1**

6m 25.5s (28.80) **Going Correction** +1.375s/f (Heav) **9** Ran SP% **111.1**
Speed ratings: **104,102,99,97,— —,—,—,—** CSF £25.79 CT £248.03 TOTE £8.30: £2.10, £1.60, £2.90; EX 21.90.
Owner Miss L Haagensen **Bred** M Nolan **Trained** Barton-le-Street, N Yorks
■ Stewards' Enquiry : Mr D A Fitzsimmons two-day ban: used whip with excessive force and above shoulder height (Feb 5,8)

FOCUS
A low-grade amateur riders' handicap but overall the form looks sound. The veteran winner, capably handled, looks to just stay.

NOTEBOOK
Twotiming Gent(IRE) made this a true test. His rider never panicked and he knuckled down in willing fashion to gain the upper hand on the run-in. *(op 8-1)*
Dickie Lewis, 12lb higher, travelled best but, despite his rider's efforts, in the end he was very much second best. *(op 9-4 tchd 11-4)*
Jontys'Lass jumped ahead two out but her stamina seemed to ebb away to nothing in the end. *(op 15-2)*
Avanti Tiger(IRE), runner-up in a seller a week ago, is running well in blinkers but in the end he found this much too tough. *(op 5-1)*

Stormy Madam(IRE) *Official explanation: jockey said mare was unsuited by the heavy ground (tchd 40-1)*

3541 ROCOM SAMSUNG BEGINNERS' CHASE (18 fncs) 2m 7f 110y

2:35 (2:35) (Class 4) 5-Y-0+ **£5,204** (£1,528; £764; £381)

Form RPR

1-44 **1** **Olney Lad**[83] 1976 7-11-6 .... RussGarritty 137+
(Mrs P Robeson) *mde virtually all: styd on wl fr 2 out: hld on towards fin* **4/1**[2]

0/F2 **2** *½* **Tighten Your Belt (IRE)**[39] 2848 9-11-6 .... SamThomas 138+
(Miss Venetia Williams) *trckd ldrs: chalng whn hit 3 out: outj. last 2: styd on towards fin* **4/9**[1]

P550 **3** *dist* **Bannister Lane**[16] 3290 6-11-6 97 .... JasonMaguire 108
(D McCain) *w ldrs: blnd 11th: wknd 3 out: t.o: btn 33 l* **33/1**

F1/2 **4** *9* **Tufty Hopper**[22] 3170 9-11-6 113 .... BrianHarding 101
(Ferdy Murphy) *hld up in last but wl in tch: pushed along 14th: wknd 3 out: t.o* **11/1**[3]

3-2P **5** *15* **Onyourheadbeit (IRE)**[58] 2502 8-11-6 105 ....(p) JohnMcNamara 86
(K C Bailey) *w ldrs: rdn 14th: lost pl next: bhd 2 out: t.o* **12/1**

6m 28.5s (30.00) **Going Correction** +1.375s/f (Heav) **5** Ran SP% **108.2**
Speed ratings: **105,104,—,—,—** CSF £6.40 TOTE £7.70: £1.80, £1.10; EX 11.10.
Owner The Tyringham Partnership **Bred** T H Rossiter **Trained** Tyringham, Milton Keynes

FOCUS
The first two are decent novices and have been rated pretty much to their hurdles marks. Olney Lad jumped better than Tighten Your Belt and that made the difference in the end.

NOTEBOOK
Olney Lad made this a true test and his jumping was very accurate. Revelling in the ground, in the end he did just enough. *(op 9-2)*
Tighten Your Belt(IRE) didn't jump as well as the winner but he stuck to his task and in the end was just held at bay. *(tchd 1-2, 8-15 in places)*
Bannister Lane seemed to find the extended trip and very testing ground all too much. *(op 28-1 tchd 25-1)*
Tufty Hopper, a negative on the exchanges, raced in last place but his head carriage was not encouraging and he stopped to nothing three out. He will bounce back. *(op 8-1)*

3542 WETHERBY RACECOURSE & CONFERENCE CENTRE H'CAP HURDLE (9 hdls) 2m

3:05 (3:05) (Class 3) (0-125,115) 4-Y-0+ **£6,506** (£1,910; £955; £477)

Form RPR

1-P0 **1** **Supreme Leisure (IRE)**[37] 2876 9-11-3 111 .... BrianHughes(5) 117+
(J Howard Johnson) *trckd ldrs: j. ahd 6th: drvn clr after next: hit 2 out: kpt on wl* **9/1**

-036 **2** *4* **Imtihan (IRE)**[78] 2071 7-10-6 95 .... DominicElsworth 95
(Mrs S J Smith) *chsd ldrs: outpcd appr 3 out: styd on to take 2nd last 150yds* **7/2**[1]

6-0P **3** *hd* **Aldiruos (IRE)**[65] 2347 6-11-2 105 .... WayneHutchinson 105
(A W Carroll) *hld up in tch: effrt 6th: wnt 2nd 2 out: kpt on same pce* **8/1**

P-P6 **4** *25* **Stormy Lord (IRE)**[18] 3256 10-11-7 110 .... BrianHarding 85
(J Wade) *nt fluent: led to 6th: wknd next* **6/1**[3]

0041 **5** *1 ¼* **Culcabock (IRE)**[10] 3378 6-11-9 115 .... PeterBuchanan(3) 89
(Miss Lucinda V Russell) *chsd ldrs: lost pl appr 3 out* **5/1**[2]

-214 **6** *9* **Farne Isle**[22] 3171 7-11-8 111 ....(p) RichardMcGrath 76
(G A Harker) *wnt prom 4th: pushed along 6th: lost pl appr next* **7/2**[1]

4534 **U** **Karathaena (IRE)**[28] 2964 6-11-0 110 .... JohnEnnis(7) 68
(M E Sowersby) *in tch: drvn along 6th: sn wknd: last whn mstke and uns rdr 2 out* **6/1**[3]

4m 18.1s (18.70) **Going Correction** +1.375s/f (Heav) **7** Ran SP% **110.8**
Speed ratings: **108,106,105,93,92 88,—** CSF £38.35 TOTE £9.60: £3.20, £2.90; EX 68.20.
Owner Mrs Mary Bird & J Howard Johnson **Bred** Donal Murphy **Trained** Billy Row, Co Durham

FOCUS
A sound pace and in the end the first three were a long way clear. The winner was well in on his best form but this was still a slight step up from him while the runner-up has become well handicapped.

NOTEBOOK
Supreme Leisure(IRE) has already shown he can handle ground such as he encountered here and his rider left nothing to chance after he had jumped ahead four out. Though no youngster, he will make an even better chaser. *(op 10-1)*
Imtihan(IRE), who has changed stables, was having his first outing for eleven weeks. He stuck on after getting outpaced and will be sharper next time. *(op 4-1 tchd 10-3)*
Aldiruos(IRE), back after a two-month break, went in pursuit of the winner, but was never going to get in a serious blow and in the end just missed out on second spot.
Stormy Lord(IRE) treated his hurdles as if they were fences. From a stable struggling to find form, this will put him spot on for a return to chasing.
Culcabock(IRE), raised a harsh 15lb, was a major negative and he was beaten on the turn for home. *Official explanation: jockey said gelding ran flat (op 4-1 tchd 11-2)*
Farne Isle dropped right out and was reported to have a breathing problem. *Official explanation: jockey said mare had a breathing problem*

3543 BOW FELL NOVICES' H'CAP CHASE (12 fncs) 2m

3:40 (3:40) (Class 4) (0-110,110) 5-Y-0+ **£5,204** (£1,528; £764; £381)

Form RPR

PP31 **1** **Oliverjohn (IRE)**[20] 3233 9-11-0 101 .... PeterBuchanan(3) 107+
(Miss Lucinda V Russell) *j.lft: mde all: lft 6 l clr 2 out: drvn out* **1/1**[1]

FP66 **2** *4* **Jerom De Vindecy (FR)**[14] 3317 9-9-9 84 oh3 .... TomGreenway(5) 84
(Miss Lucinda V Russell) *chsd ldrs: hrd drvn 8th: lft 6 l 2nd 2 out: kpt on same pce* **17/2**

250 **3** *5* **College City (IRE)**[50] 2657 7-11-9 110 ....(p) LarryMcGrath(3) 105
(R C Guest) *racd in last but in tch: drvn and outpcd appr 4 out: lft mod 3rd 2 out: kpt on* **8/1**

U6P6 **4** *19* **Kinkeel (IRE)**[19] 3243 7-10-0 84 oh6 .... WayneHutchinson 60
(A W Carroll) *chsd wnr: wknd after 4 out* **13/2**[3]

2001 **5** *24* **Silver Sedge (IRE)**[13] 3334 7-11-9 107 .... BrianHarding 110+
(Mrs A Hamilton) *hdwy 4th: sn chsng ldrs: 1/2 l 2nd and styng on wl whn stmbld bdly and wnt lft 2 out: nt rcvr: virtually p.u* **3/1**[2]

4m 29.5s (22.90) **Going Correction** +1.375s/f (Heav) **5** Ran SP% **110.0**
Speed ratings: **97,95,92,83,71** CSF £9.25 TOTE £1.70: £1.20, £4.20; EX 7.90.
Owner Thoroughbred Leisure Racing Club **Bred** Joseph J O'Connor **Trained** Arlary, Perth & Kinross
■ Lucinda Russell originally entered seven to make sure the race filled and she was rewarded with a one-two.

FOCUS
A low-grade handicap, with the winner recording a slight personal best over fences. Silver Sedge was heading for a figure up around 4lb on his Sedgefield win.

NOTEBOOK
Oliverjohn(IRE)followed up from a 9lb higher mark, but he would have had a lot more on his plate but for Silver Sedge's mishap at the second last. *(tchd 11-10)*

Jerom De Vindecy(FR), who has cut no ice since arriving from France, was racing from 3lb out of the handicap. In the end he was handed second spot. *(op 14-1)*
College City(IRE), back over fences, never looked at all happy in the testing conditions but deserves credit for the way he stuck to his task to secure a never-dangerous third spot. *(op 5-1)*
Kinkeel(IRE), 6lb out of the handicap, is struggling to make any impact. *(op 8-1)*
Silver Sedge(IRE), hoisted 22lb after Sedgefield, was upsides and a real threat when he lost his legs on landing two out. He was looking a serious threat at the time. *(op 10-3)*

3544 WETHERBY RACES NEXT SATURDAY 4TH FEBRUARY MARES' ONLY NOVICES' HURDLE (10 hdls) 2m 4f 110y

4:10 (4:10) (Class 4) 4-Y-0+ **£3,415** (£1,002; £501; £250)

Form RPR
-422 **1** **Diklers Rose (IRE)**[20] 3235 7-11-1 105........................ RichardMcGrath 105+
(K G Reveley) *mde all: styd on wl between last 2: hld on towards fin* **11/10**[1]
F311 **2** *½* **Ile Maurice (FR)**[13] 3337 6-11-6 115........................ PatrickMcDonald[(7)] 115+
(Ferdy Murphy) *chsd wnr: chal 3 out: styd on wl towards fin: jst hld* **6/5**[2]
203- **3** *13* **Classic Sight**[323] 4210 6-11-1 ....(b) NoelFehily 89
(C C Bealby) *chsd ldrs: one pce fr 3 out* **16/1**
36P2 **4** *dist* **Verstone (IRE)**[13] 3337 4-10-3 95........................ JimmyMcCarthy 57
(R F Fisher) *hld up in last: hdwy 7th: sn chsng ldrs: wknd appr next: virtually p.u run-in: t.o: btn 34 l* **14/1**[3]
P **Deep Rising** 8-10-12 .... AnthonyCoyle[(3)] —
(S P Griffiths) *wnt prom 6th: rdn and wknd next: sn bhd: t.o whn p.u bef 3 out* **66/1**

5m 46.1s (37.20) **Going Correction** +1.375s/f (Heavy)
WFA 4 from 6yo+ 12lb **5** Ran SP% **107.1**
Speed ratings: **84,83,78,—,—** CSF £2.65 TOTE £1.80: £1.40, £1.10; EX 3.00 Place 6 £11.17, Place 5 £5.91.
Owner The Mary Reveley Racing Club **Bred** James O'Keeffe **Trained** Lingdale, Redcar & Cleveland

FOCUS
Diklers Rose was always in the right place in a race run at a very steady pace. The runner-up would have appreciated a stronger gallop and she deserves credit for this. The first two ran to their marks.

NOTEBOOK
Diklers Rose(IRE) enjoyed herself in front but in the end did just enough. She is set to return to her breeder in Ireland in the spring having now won a bumper and a hurdle race. *(op 5-4)*
Ile Maurice(FR) could have done with a much stronger pace. She stuck to her guns and in the end was just held at bay. She deserves credit for this. *(tchd 5-4 in places)*
Classic Sight tried hard to keep tabs on the big two but was left behind from three out.
Verstone(IRE), meeting her Sedgefield conqueror on 5lb better terms, dropped right out once in line for home and eventually completed in her own time. *(op 12-1)*
T/Plt: £60.40 to a £1 stake. Pool: £37,950.15. 458.35 winning tickets. T/Qpdt: £19.20 to a £1 stake. Pool: £2,593.20. 99.80 winning tickets. WG

3328 LEICESTER (R-H)

Tuesday, January 24

OFFICIAL GOING: Hurdle course - heavy (soft in places); chase course - good to soft (good in places)
Wind: Light, behind Weather: Overcast

3545 GG.COM NOVICES' HURDLE (12 hdls) 2m 4f 110y

1:50 (1:50) (Class 3) 4-Y-0+
£6,263 (£1,850; £925; £463; £231; £116)

Form RPR
1 **1** **Brumous (IRE)**[42] 2809 6-11-10 .... LeightonAspell 116+
(O Sherwood) *hld up: hdwy 5th: led 3 out: drvn out* **10/3**[2]
0464 **2** *1 ½* **Major Catch (IRE)**[18] 3277 7-11-0 102........................ AdamPogson[(5)] 108
(C T Pogson) *chsd ldrs: ev ch 3 out: sn rdn: styd on same pce flat* **8/1**
2 **3** *3* **Palm Island (FR)**[24] 3139 5-11-5 .... TomDoyle 105
(Noel T Chance) *chsd ldrs: ev ch 3 out: rdn appr last: styd on same pce* **6/1**
12F **4** *18* **Baron Romeo (IRE)**[3] 3496 6-11-5 .... RichardJohnson 90+
(R T Phillips) *hld up: hdwy after 6th: wknd appr 2 out* **11/4**[1]
0/65 **5** *4* **Bosworth Gypsy (IRE)**[24] 3149 8-10-5 .... MarcGoldstein[(7)] 76
(Miss J S Davis) *led to 2nd: led next to 3 out: wknd bef next* **300/1**
33/ **6** *6* **Pertemps Timmy**[1325] 517 8-11-5 .... RobertThornton 77
(R T Phillips) *hld up: hdwy appr 7th: wknd after 3 out* **25/1**
-433 **7** *¾* **Butler's Cabin (FR)**[8] 3425 6-11-5 ....(t) APMcCoy 76
(Jonjo O'Neill) *hld up: hdwy 7th: rdn and wknd bef next* **4/1**[3]
8 *7* **Cayman Calypso (IRE)**[20] 5-11-5 .... PaulMoloney 69
(Mrs P Sly) *hld up: mstke 4th: hdwy next: wknd appr 2 out* **50/1**
0 **9** *dist* **Nemetan (FR)**[14] 3328 5-11-5 .... AndrewThornton —
(R H Alner) *hld up: hdwy 5th: wknd appr 3 out* **16/1**
P0 **10** *28* **Chisel**[14] 3328 5-10-12 ....(t) MrSRees[(7)] —
(M Wigham) *hld up: bhd fr 4th* **300/1**
00P0 **11** *3* **Bob's Temptation**[38] 2873 7-11-5 .... AntonyEvans —
(A J Wilson) *hld up: hdwy appr 5th: wknd next: bhd whn blnd last* **200/1**
6 **12** *10* **Cleverality (IRE)**[75] 2145 6-11-5 .... ChristianWilliams —
(Evan Williams) *chsd ldr: j.big 1st: led next to 3rd: wknd 7th* **40/1**
00-1 **P** **Suprendre Espere**[24] 3145 6-11-5 .... AlanO'Keeffe —
(Jennie Candlish) *prom to 5th: t.o whn p.u bef 3 out* **20/1**

5m 24.0s (-10.80) **Going Correction** -0.325s/f (Good) **13** Ran SP% **115.2**
Speed ratings: **107,106,105,98,96 94,94,91,—,— —,—,—** CSF £27.90 TOTE £2.70: £2.10, £2.50, £2.80; EX 35.90.
Owner J Dougall **Bred** Patrick McNamara **Trained** Upper Lambourn, Berks

FOCUS
An ordinary novices' hurdle for the prizemoney but run at an even pace and the first three came clear in the straight. The winner was rated value for a bit further and the form looks reasonably solid.

NOTEBOOK
Brumous(IRE) was the only previous hurdles winner in the field and proved good enough to give weight all round. He travelled well throughout and found extra when his rider got serious after the last. He will appreciate better ground and may take his chance in the Brit Insurance Novices' Hurdle at the Festival, and next season should make a chaser. *(op 7-2 tchd 4-1)*
Major Catch(IRE) had some fair form for Nick Gifford, but had struggled for his current stable prior to this. The drop back in trip seemed to help and, if he can repeat this performance, he may have a small race in him. *(op 11-1)*
Palm Island(FR) has already shown he handles testing ground and looked to run his race without being able to find an extra gear in the straight. He may be worth trying back at two miles and racing up with the pace. *(op 11-2)*
Baron Romeo(IRE) was careful at his hurdles after his first-flight fall at the weekend and could never quite get to the front rank. He showed plenty of ability in bumpers and can be given another chance. *(tchd 5-2 and 3-1)*
Bosworth Gypsy(IRE) ran much better ridden from the front and, although she dropped away from the first in the straight, was not disgraced. She has not had much racing and may be worth a try in a mares-only handicap.
Pertemps Timmy, a stable companion of the favourite, looked fit enough on this return from over three and a half years off the track and only got tired on the climb to the second last. He should be better for the outing if given time to recover.
Butler's Cabin(FR), wearing a first-time tongue tie, reverted to waiting tactics but was *disappointing as he never landed a blow, although he may not have handled the heavy ground. Official explanation: jockey said gelding hung left-handed (tchd 7-2)*
Cayman Calypso(IRE) settled in rear and moved up travelling well turning in but appeared not to stay; somewhat surprising for a two-mile Fibresand winner.
Suprendre Espere *Official explanation: jockey said gelding hung right-handed*

3546 BROOK CONDITIONAL JOCKEYS' H'CAP CHASE (12 fncs) 2m

2:20 (2:20) (Class 4) (0-100,96) 5-Y-0+ **£3,578** (£1,050; £525; £262)

Form RPR
1103 **1** **Julies Boy (IRE)**[18] 3274 9-10-11 **89**........................(t) WillieMcCarthy[(8)] 102+
(T R George) *led to 3rd: chsd ldr tl led 4 out: drvn clr flat* **11/8**[1]
3/03 **2** *7* **Munadil**[29] 2995 8-10-8 **78**........................(t) TomMalone 84
(A M Hales) *hld up: hdwy 4 out: ev ch next: no ex last* **9/2**[2]
0P-3 **3** *1 ¾* **Meehan (IRE)**[14] 3329 6-11-7 **96**........................ AndrewGlassonbury[(5)] 101+
(Miss J S Davis) *chsd ldrs: ev ch 3 out: mstke next: sn rdn: styd on same pce* **13/2**[3]
P533 **4** *5* **Kercabellec (FR)**[8] 3418 8-10-12 **82**........................ MarkNicolls 82+
(J R Cornwall) *chsd ldr tl led 3rd: hdd 4 out: rdn and wknd after next* **9/2**[2]
0020 **U** **Prairie Law (GER)**[10] 3395 6-10-11 **89**........................ TomMessenger[(8)] —
(B N Pollock) *mstke and uns rdr 1st* **10/1**
0P-0 **P** **Valuso (IRE)**[19] 3248 6-9-11 **70** oh3........................ WilliamKennedy[(3)] —
(Noel T Chance) *hld up: hit 5th: mstke next: sn bhd: hit 4 out: t.o whn p.u bef 2 out* **11/1**

4m 8.50s (0.90) **Going Correction** -0.15s/f (Good) **6** Ran SP% **109.2**
Speed ratings: **91,87,86,84,— —** CSF £7.72 TOTE £2.10: £1.70, £2.20; EX 6.80.
Owner R P Foden **Bred** Patrick Slattery **Trained** Slad, Gloucs

FOCUS
A very moderate conditionals' chase run in a very modest time that fell to the only previous winner over fences. The form looks solid enough, rated through the third.

NOTEBOOK
Julies Boy(IRE) has established a good partnership with McCarthy, and the pair gained their fourth win together and third this season. He put in a bold display, regaining the advantage at the last *ditch and then running on too strongly for his rivals, who were right on his heels at the third last. (op 6-5)*
Munadil travelled well for a long way on this chasing debut under Rules on ground that was softer *than he prefers. His current mark gives him a chance of picking up a similar small handicap. (tchd 4-1)*
Meehan(IRE), who made his chasing debut here two weeks previously following a year's absence, *looked a big threat early in the straight but faded rather tamely and may have 'bounced' (op 8-1 tchd 6-1)*
Kercabellec(FR) took on the winner for the lead but capitulated quickly in the straight and is yet to score in 21 starts over fences. *(tchd 5-1)*
Valuso(IRE), making his chasing debut, spoilt his chance with some sloppy jumping. *(op 14-1)*

3547 RABBIT H'CAP CHASE (18 fncs) 2m 7f 110y

2:50 (2:50) (Class 4) (0-100,100) 5-Y-0 **£4,436** (£1,310; £655; £327; £163)

Form RPR
-160 **1** **Monger Lane**[73] 2184 10-10-12 **86**........................ PJBrennan 109+
(K Bishop) *mid-div: hdwy 5th: styd on u.p to ld nr fin* **14/1**
56-1 **2** *1 ¼* **Thedreamstillalive (IRE)**[54] 2592 6-11-7 **95**........................ JasonMaguire 116
(J A B Old) *hld up: hdwy 10th: led after 2 out: rdn and hdd nr fin* **3/1**[1]
532U **3** *6* **Fin Bec (FR)**[20] 3241 13-11-12 **100**........................(b) AndrewThornton 115
(A P Jones) *led 2nd: rdn and hdd after 2 out: no ex last* **14/1**
6P41 **4** *4* **Boardroom Dancer (IRE)**[12] 3359 9-10-10 **89**........................ DarylJacob[(5)] 100
(Miss Suzy Smith) *led and j.lft 1st: hdd next: chsd ldr tl rdn 4 out: styd on same pce fr next* **15/2**[2]
U12U **5** *1 ½* **Bay Island (IRE)**[48] 2703 10-11-8 **96**........................(t) NoelFehily 108+
(M Pitman) *hld up in tch: lost pl 10th: hit 13th: hdwy 4 out: wknd 2 out* **3/1**[1]
5300 **6** *2 ½* **Paddy The Optimist (IRE)**[15] 3326 10-10-6 **83**........ WilliamKennedy[(3)] 91+
(D Burchell) *hld up: hit 11th: effrt appr 3 out: no imp fr next* **20/1**
-656 **7** *½* **Jack Fuller (IRE)**[18] 3276 9-11-3 **91**........................(v) LeightonAspell 98
(P R Hedger) *hld up: hdwy 12th: wknd 2 out* **10/1**
P4/P **8** *11* **Lord Broadway (IRE)**[20] 3241 10-11-2 **90**........................ JamesDavies 86
(N M Babbage) *chsd ldrs to 14th* **33/1**
40P6 **9** *6* **Benefit**[49] 2692 12-10-4 **78**........................ TomSiddall 68
(Miss L C Siddall) *hld up: hdwy 7th: wknd 10th* **50/1**
06P0 **10** *8* **Glen Thyne (IRE)**[12] 3359 6-10-0 **74** oh8........................(b[1]) TomScudamore 56
(K C Bailey) *hld up: a in rr* **100/1**
P0P3 **11** *hd* **Soroka (IRE)**[24] 3142 7-9-7 **74**........................(b) CharlieStudd[(7)] 55
(C N Kellett) *bhd fr 6th* **66/1**
5-66 **12** *24* **Sea Drifting**[12] 3350 9-11-2 **95**........................(p) AdamPogson[(5)] 52
(Miss M E Rowland) *mid-div: hit 5th: wknd 9th* **33/1**
P10/ **U** **Silent Snipe**[665] 4615 13-10-0 **74** oh4........................ SeanCurran —
(Miss L C Siddall) *mstke and uns rdr 1st* **66/1**
P/3P **P** **Roddy The Vet (IRE)**[8] 3427 8-10-5 **79**........................(p) JimCrowley —
(A Ennis) *hld up: in rr whn hit 10th: t.o whn p.u bef 2 out* **8/1**[3]
643P **P** **Monsieur Georges (FR)**[29] 2957 6-10-8 **82**........................ TomDoyle —
(F Jordan) *prom: j. slowly 5th: lost pl next: bhd whn p.u bef 10th* **25/1**

5m 59.6s (-5.80) **Going Correction** -0.15s/f (Good) **15** Ran SP% **115.7**
Speed ratings: **103,102,100,99,98 97,97,94,92,89 89,81,—,—,—** CSF £51.99 CT £614.60 TOTE £14.10: £3.60, £1.70, £3.60; EX 71.70.
Owner Slabs And Lucan **Bred** K Bishop **Trained** Spaxton, Somerset

FOCUS
A big field for this staying handicap and solid form, rated through the third and fourth.

NOTEBOOK
Monger Lane ◆ is better known as a hurdler, but won on her chasing debut two years ago and showed plenty of determination to prevail. She is currently rated 27lb lower over fences than over hurdles, and will clearly remain well handicapped, even after re-assessment. *(tchd 16-1)*
Thedreamstillalive(IRE) looked sure to win, as he had jumped and travelled well on this chasing debut. However, he seemed to run out of stamina after the last and succumbed to the renewed *challenge of the winner. He should be able to gain compensation, probably over a shorter trip. (op 11-4 tchd 10-3)*
Fin Bec(FR) took them along at a good gallop and did not give way until after jumping the second *last. He is getting on in years but has shown in the past that he is capable of winning off this mark. (op 10-1)*

Boardroom Dancer(IRE), who made all when scoring at Ludlow, was unable to dominate this time with Fin Bec in the field and that, combined with the softer ground, probably contributed to a slightly disappointing effort. *(tchd 7-1 and 8-1)*
Bay Island(IRE) was held up off the pace and, despite an error at the last on the far side, was close enough early in the straight before fading. *(op 11-4)*
Jack Fuller(IRE) travelled well in the pack in the re-applied visor, but failed to pick up in the straight and may have found the ground too soft for him. *(op 12-1)*
Roddy The Vet(IRE) *Official explanation: jockey said gelding was unsuited by the good to soft (good in places) ground (op 9-1)*

3548 SIS H'CAP HURDLE (12 hdls) 2m 4f 110y
3:20 (3:20) (Class 4) (0-110,110) 4-Y-0+ **£3,903** (£1,146; £573; £286)

Form RPR
FP00 **1** **Titian Flame (IRE)**[19] 3247 6-10-4 **91**......................(p) WilliamKennedy(3) 98+
(D Burchell) *chsd ldr tl led 4th: 2l up whn lft clr 2 out* **40/1**
5054 **2** *12* **My Rosie Ribbons (IRE)**[17] 3287 7-10-5 **96**......................... MrMWall(7) 91+
(B W Duke) *hld up: hdwy 4th: rdn and wkng whn lft 2nd 2 out* **33/1**
U3U0 **3** *5* **Abzuson**[17] 3289 9-11-4 **105**.. LeeVickers(3) 94
(J R Norton) *chsd ldrs: mstke 6th: chal next: wkng whn lft 3rd 2 out* **50/1**
6165 **4** *hd* **Pardon What**[28] 3018 10-11-7 **105**...(b) APMcCoy 94
(S Lycett) *hld up: hdwy 7th: wknd 3 out* **12/1**
4-50 **5** *½* **High Altitude (IRE)**[23] 3175 5-11-9 **107**......................... RobertThornton 95
(A King) *mid-div: rdn 7th: wknd next* **14/1**
-333 **6** *13* **Signature Tune (IRE)**[23] 3185 7-11-1 **99**................................ PhilipHide 77+
(P Winkworth) *hld up: hdwy 6th: wknd appr 3 out* **6/1**[2]
3021 **7** *18* **Joe Brown**[14] 3339 6-11-10 **108**.. JimCrowley 65
(Mrs H Dalton) *hld up in tch: rdn and wknd appr 3 out* **9/2**[1]
2353 **8** *7* **Marsh Run**[29] 2964 7-11-9 **110**..(b) MrTGreenall(3) 60
(M W Easterby) *led to 4th: chal 7th: wknd bef next* **7/1**[3]
250 **9** *1* **Danse Macabre (IRE)**[17] 3286 7-11-2 **100**................. WayneHutchinson 49
(A W Carroll) *hld up: a in rr: bhd whn hit last* **8/1**
520 **10** *6* **Backstreet Lad**[108] 1679 4-9-7 **96** oh4............................. MrTJO'Brien(7) 27
(Evan Williams) *hld up: hdwy 7th: wknd bef next* **15/2**
0-40 **11** *½* **River Indus**[23] 3175 6-10-10 **94**.................................... BenjaminHitchcott 37
(R H Buckler) *prom to 6th* **12/1**
PPP6 **12** *dist* **Ashleybank House (IRE)**[14] 3332 9-11-2 **100**............(t) RichardHobson —
(David Pearson) *mid-div: mstke 3rd: sn rdn: wknd 6th* **150/1**
0060 **13** *10* **Miss Fahrenheit (IRE)**[28] 3018 7-11-9 **107**.............. ChristianWilliams —
(C Roberts) *n.m.r 1st: chsd ldrs: mstke and wknd 5th* **20/1**
4565 **P** **The Flyer (IRE)**[13] 3345 9-11-5 **103**..(t) NoelFehily —
(Miss S J Wilton) *hld up: a in rr: t.o whn p.u bef 2 out* **22/1**
0060 **P** **Sharp Rally (IRE)**[20] 3242 5-10-3 **87**.. PJBrennan —
(A J Wilson) *hld up: sme hdwy 7th: sn wknd: t.o whn p.u bef 2 out* **66/1**
42-0 **F** **Durante (IRE)**[52] 2619 8-11-2 **100**.. JasonMaguire 101
(J A B Old) *hld up: hdwy 7th: chsd wnr 3 out: 2l 2nd and rdn whn fell next* **7/1**[3]

5m 24.2s (-10.60) **Going Correction** -0.325s/f (Good)
WFA 4 from 5yo+ 12lb **16** Ran SP% **121.0**
Speed ratings: **107,102,100,100,100 95,88,85,85,83 82,—,—,—,—** — CSF £954.79 CT £48294.70 TOTE £64.10: £10.90, £8.80, £8.10, £2.40; EX 1287.90.
Owner Don Gould, W Gorman **Bred** M Ervine **Trained** Briery Hill, Blaenau Gwent

FOCUS
A modest but competitive handicap hurdle that few got into from off the pace. The winner was back to the level of his best form for his previous trainer and the form looks solid enough at a low level.

NOTEBOOK
Titian Flame(IRE) was up with the pace from the start and, after taking over with a circuit to go, kept up the gallop and may still have won even if Durante had stayed on his feet. She gained her only previous win around this time last year, but the stable is just coming out of a period with the virus and that may be the reason for the improved performance.*Official explanation: trainer said, regarding improved form shown, mare was badly hampered on previous run at Hereford (tchd 50-1)*
My Rosie Ribbons(IRE) was another to produce an improved effort on this handicap debut. She seems to be improving with experience and the testing ground appears to suit her.
Abzuson, like the first two, was in the front rank throughout, and kept galloping to the line. He seems happier over hurdles than he was over fences.
Pardon What was kept wide throughout, but could not pick up from the turn in and may prefer less-testing conditions.
High Altitude(IRE) was never going well and his jockey was niggling from an early stage; in the circumstances he did well to finish as close as he did. *(op 12-1)*
Signature Tune(IRE) was stepping up in trip and may not have got home in the conditions. *(op 5-1)*
Joe Brown should have had no problem with the trip or the ground, but faded after appearing to have every chance turning for home. *(op 11-2)*
Marsh Run , with the blinkers again fitted, was too keen in the early stages and faded in the straight. *(op 15-2 tchd 8-1)*
Durante(IRE) was the only one to come from off the pace and was on the heels of the winner when taking a crashing fall two out. He looked somewhat unlucky but the winner was not stopping. *(op 8-1 tchd 17-2 in a place)*

3549 DICK CHRISTIAN NOVICES' CHASE (15 fncs) 2m 4f 110y
3:50 (3:50) (Class 3) 5-Y-0+
£7,515 (£2,220; £1,110; £555; £277; £139)

Form RPR
-134 **1** **Billyvoddan (IRE)**[23] 3178 7-11-12 .... RichardJohnson 138+
(H D Daly) *chsd ldrs: led 4th to appr 6th: led 4 out: drvn out* **7/4**[2]
16-2 **2** *½* **Reveillez**[22] 3215 7-11-2 .... APMcCoy 128+
(J R Fanshawe) *hld up: hdwy and mstke 3 out: chsd wnr appr last: r.o* **4/5**[1]
P-24 **3** *13* **Simoun (IRE)**[259] 286 8-11-2 .... AndrewThornton 114
(B N Pollock) *chsd ldrs: rdn 3 out: wknd flat* **50/1**
4434 **4** *3½* **Keepthedreamalive**[19] 3251 8-11-2 121.............. BenjaminHitchcott 111
(R H Buckler) *led to 4th: led appr 6th: hdd next: led 9th to 4 out: wknd last* **7/1**[3]
200U **5** *7* **Mythical King (IRE)**[24] 3142 9-11-2 .... TomDoyle 107+
(R Lee) *hld up in tch: wkng whn hit 2 out* **25/1**
/4P5 **6** *6* **Incorporation**[23] 3183 7-10-9 .... RichardSpate(7) 98
(M Appleby) *hld up: rdn after 4 out: sn wknd* **400/1**
06 **7** *dist* **Lord Gunnerslake (IRE)**[14] 3331 6-10-13 89.............. AnthonyCoyle(3) —
(Miss C J E Caroe) *chsd ldrs tl led 7th: hdd 9th: wknd appr 3 out: bhd whn hit last* **200/1**
60PP **P** **Konker**[14] 3329 11-11-2 88.. RichardHobson —
(J R Cornwall) *hld up: blnd 9th: sn p.u* **300/1**
0-00 **P** **Moving On Up**[247] 458 12-11-2 ....(b) DavidVerco —
(C N Kellett) *bhd fr 3rd: t.o whn p.u bef 11th* **200/1**

5m 18.4s (-5.20) **Going Correction** -0.15s/f (Good) **9** Ran SP% **111.8**
Speed ratings: **103,102,97,96,93 91,—,—,—** CSF £3.52 TOTE £2.00: £1.20, £1.10, £4.10; EX 4.80.
Owner Trevor Hemmings **Bred** D P O'Brien **Trained** Stanton Lacy, Shropshire

FOCUS
A decent prize for this novices' chase attracted a couple of interesting runners, and they fought out the finish. The form looks sound enough, although the proximity of the sixth is a concern, and the first two could be heading for the big spring meetings.

NOTEBOOK
Billyvoddan(IRE), under a 10lb penalty, again raced and jumped with enthusiasm, and that enabled him to hold off the strong finish of Reveillez. He is entered in both the Arkle and Royal & SunAlliance Chases at the Festival and will also be entered in the Jewson Novices' Handicap, and is likely to go to Cheltenham but may have another run before then. *(op 15-8 tchd 2-1)*
Reveillez was not quite as fluent as the winner at his fences, but looked to be travelling best in the straight. He was unable to get past the winner but lost little in defeat and is sure to win races, especially on better ground, although connections may opt to preserve his novice status until next season by switching him back to hurdles. *(tchd 8-11, Evens in places)*
Simoun(IRE) travelled well throughout, but was left behind when the principals got serious going to the last. This was his first outing since the spring and he looks sure to win races over fences with this run under his belt. *(op 40-1)*
Keepthedreamalive ran another good race against useful opponents, but has not got the pace to trouble good novices over this trip and, being by Roselier, may well appreciate stepping up to three miles. *(op 13-2 tchd 6-1)*
Mythical King(IRE), having only his second outing over the bigger obstacles, ran well enough and would have finished closer but for making a mess of the second last. *(op 16-1)*

3550 CROXTON PARK MARES' ONLY NOVICES' HURDLE (9 hdls) 2m
4:20 (4:21) (Class 3) 4-Y-0+
£6,263 (£1,850; £925; £463; £231; £116)

Form RPR
1 **Nevsky Bridge**[51] 4-10-0 .... StephenCraine(5) 94+
(D McCain) *hld up in tch: hit 5th: led 3 out: clr whn nt fluent last: eased nr fin* **11/1**
2 *2½* **Sonnengold (GER)**[177] 5-11-2 .... LeightonAspell 97+
(Mrs L Wadham) *hld up: hdwy 5th: outpcd appr 2 out: styd on fr last: no ch w wnr* **5/1**[3]
054 **3** *¾* **Anna Panna**[15] 3322 5-11-2 .... AndrewThornton 94
(R H Alner) *chsd ldrs: rdn appr 2 out: styd on same pce* **7/2**[2]
0060 **4** *2* **Winter Coral (FR)**[17] 3280 4-10-5 81...............................(p) JodieMogford 81
(Mrs N S Evans) *led after 2nd: hdd 4th: led next: hdd 3 out: styd on same pce fr next* **25/1**
50 **5** *11* **Flirty Jill**[60] 2486 5-11-2 ....(t) TomDoyle 81
(P R Webber) *hld up: hdwy 3rd: wknd appr 2 out* **20/1**
6 *nk* **Al Alba (USA)**[138] 4-9-12 .... AndrewGlassonbury(7) 70
(Mrs H Dalton) *hld up: hdwy appr 3 out: wknd bef next* **10/1**
P0 **7** *2* **Fair View (GER)**[17] 3281 5-11-2 .... TomScudamore 79
(Dr P Pritchard) *hld up: effrt appr 3 out: sn wknd* **40/1**
FP **8** *17* **Heathers Girl**[18] 3275 7-11-2 .... WayneHutchinson 62
(R Dickin) *hld up: sme hdwy appr 3 out: sn wknd* **33/1**
3-1 **9** *dist* **Alaskan Fizz**[254] 375 5-11-2 .... RichardJohnson —
(R T Phillips) *hld up: hdwy 5th: rdn and wknd next* **5/2**[1]
P **10** *19* **Dargin's Lass (IRE)**[24] 3149 5-10-9 .... TomMessenger(7) —
(B N Pollock) *chsd ldrs to 5th* **150/1**
60 **11** *9* **Molly's Spirit (IRE)**[18] 3275 5-10-11 .... MarkNicolls(5) —
(P R Webber) *bhd fr 4th* **28/1**
U **P** **Nellie The Nod**[8] 3417 7-10-9 .... MrMatthewSmith(7) —
(M J Gingell) *hld up: mstke 3rd: a in rr: t.o whn p.u bef 2 out* **100/1**
4- **P** **One Alone**[523] 1217 5-11-2 ....(b) JamesDavies —
(Jean-Rene Auvray) *hld up: hit 2nd: hdwy appr 5th: sn rdn and wknd: t.o whn p.u bef 2 out* **40/1**
63P **P** **Carraig (IRE)**[17] 3291 4-10-5 100.................................(p) ChristianWilliams —
(Evan Williams) *led: j.lft 1st: hdd next: chsd ldrs tl wknd after 3 out: bhd whn p.u bef last* **5/1**[3]
0F- **P** **Panama Royale (IRE)**[390] 3105 8-10-11 .... AdamPogson(5) —
(J R Holt) *hld up: plld hrd: hdwy after 2nd: led 4th to next: wknd qckly: t.o whn p.u bef 3 out* **100/1**

4m 5.90s (-1.70) **Going Correction** -0.325s/f (Good)
WFA 4 from 5yo+ 11lb **15** Ran SP% **124.1**
Speed ratings: **91,89,89,88,82 82,81,73,—,— —,—,—,—,—** CSF £63.10 TOTE £15.40: £4.10, £2.00, £1.50; EX 88.50 Place 6 £231.90, Place 5 £100.91 .
Owner B Dunn **Bred** Burton Agnes Stud Co Ltd **Trained** Cholmondeley, Cheshire

FOCUS
There was not a lot of previous form to go on in this mares' contest and the time was moderate, but the winner scored much more easily than the official margin suggests, value for around 8l. The form does not look easy to rate.

NOTEBOOK
Nevsky Bridge, a hurdling debutante whom connections acquired out of a maiden claimer on the Flat, something they did with Calomeria last season, was value for much more than the official distance and looks capable of winning more races against her own sex. *(op 12-1)*
Sonnengold(GER), a Flat winner in Germany, was making her hurdling debut after six months off and overcame an early error to chase home the winner, but the margin of defeat flatters her. *(op 11-2)*
Anna Panna is progressing steadily with experience over hurdles and will be interesting once switched to handicaps. *(op 4-1)*
Winter Coral(FR) had not shown much in previous outings and, rated just 81, tends to limit the form. *(op 33-1)*
Flirty Jill, a former pointer, was fancied to improve on her disappointing effort last time, but after having every chance early in the straight, faded and may need a longer trip. *(op 12-1)*
Alaskan Fizz, the only previous winner, had not run since May but could have been expected to do better than this. *(op 10-3 tchd 7-2)*
T/Plt: £317.80 to a £1 stake. Pool: £52,449.35. 120.45 winning tickets. T/Qpdt: £104.40 to a £1 stake. Pool: £4,094.90. 29.00 winning tickets. CR

3334 SEDGEFIELD (L-H)
Tuesday, January 24

OFFICIAL GOING: Soft (heavy in places)
The ground was described as 'very deep, very tiring'.
Wind: Almost nil Weather: Fine and sunny becoming overcast and cold

3551 P & C MORRIS EXPRESS CATERING UNITS MARES' ONLY "NATIONAL HUNT" NOVICES' HURDLE (10 hdls) 2m 5f 110y
1:40 (1:40) (Class 4) 4-Y-0+ **£3,578** (£1,050; £525; £262)

Form RPR
/221 **1** **Sabreflight**[19] 3254 6-11-8 .... GrahamLee 104+
(J Howard Johnson) *trckd ldrs: led after 3 out: drvn rt out towards fin* **4/11**[1]

1U2U **2** 1 ¼ **Ornella Speed (FR)**[11] 3375 6-10-9 74..................(t) PatrickMcDonald(7) 94
(J R Weymes) *hld up in rr: hdwy 3rd: sn trcking ldrs: wnt 2nd after 3 out: chal next: kpt on wl run-in* **10/1**[2]

2303 **3** 13 **Our Joycey**[14] 3337 5-11-2 .... RichardMcGrath 82+
(Mrs K Walton) *chsd ldrs: j. slowly 7th: led next: sn hdd: one pce* **10/1**[2]

0- **4** dist **Losing Grip (IRE)**[472] 1657 7-11-2 .... DominicElsworth —
(Mrs S J Smith) *keen in front: hdd 3 out: wl btn 4th whn blnd next: t.o: btn 34 l* **25/1**[3]

-100 **5** 4 **Zaffie Parson (IRE)**[14] 3337 5-11-2 .... AlanDempsey —
(G A Harker) *nt jump wl in rr: bhd fr 7th: t.o* **10/1**[2]

0-0F **6** dist **Dusky Dame**[6] 3442 6-11-2 .... PadgeWhelan —
(S B Bell) *a in rr: bhd and drvn 6th: hopelessly t.o: btn 44 l* **100/1**

P **Merits Pride** 6-10-11 .... MichaelMcAlister(5) —
(B Storey) *t.k.h: chsd ldr: lost pl 6th: sn bhd: t.o whn p.u after 3 out* **50/1**

5m 33.7s (18.00) **Going Correction** +0.875s/f (Soft) 7 Ran SP% **107.4**
Speed ratings: **102,101,96,—,— —,—** CSF £3.97 TOTE £1.30: £1.10, £3.10; EX 5.60.
Owner D S Coates **Bred** A Saccomando **Trained** Billy Row, Co Durham

FOCUS
A weak mares-only novices' hurdle run at just a steady pace, the first two clear in the end. The form seems to make sense.

NOTEBOOK
Sabreflight looked in total command when taking up the running but in the end she had to be kept right up to her work. She didn't seem to improve for the step up in trip. *(op 1-3)*
Ornella Speed(FR), last seen over hurdles in selling company a year ago, has improved over fences since and she made the winner work hard in the end. Her hurdle-race rating of just 74 will shoot up as a result, but she can surely go one better in a similar event.
Our Joycey went on four out but she was soon struggling in the wake of the first two. *(tchd 9-1)*
Losing Grip(IRE), awarded a mares-only point in Ireland in 2004, is a very lean type. The reluctant leader, she was out on her feet when making a mess of two out. *(op 16-1)*
Zaffie Parson(IRE), on her toes beforehand, will need to brush up her jumping if she is to make any impression over hurdles at all. *(op 11-1)*

3552 JOHN WADE FOR EQUINE FIBRE AND RUBBER (S) H'CAP HURDLE (QUALIFIER) 2m 4f
2:10 (2:12) (Class 5) (0-90,87) 4-Y-0+ **£2,192** (£639; £319)

Form RPR
P403 **1** **Moyne Pleasure (IRE)**[23] 3169 8-11-4 79..................... KennyJohnson 88+
(R Johnson) *hld up: hdwy 7th: led between last 2: styd on wl* **5/1**[2]

0P46 **2** 5 **Roadworthy (IRE)**[10] 3381 9-10-3 64........................ WilsonRenwick 66
(W G Young) *in rr: gd hdwy to ld after 5th: hdd 3 out: kpt on same pce appr last* **15/2**

0066 **3** 2 ½ **Just Sal**[14] 3335 10-10-3 71.............................. GarethThomas(7) 73+
(R Nixon) *chsd ldrs: led appr 2 out: hdd between last 2: kpt on same pce* **15/2**

0051 **4** 1 **Star Trooper (IRE)**[14] 3335 10-10-13 81....................(p) MissJRiding(7) 81+
(Miss S E Forster) *chsd ldrs: led and blnd 3 out: hdd appr next: one pce* **11/2**[3]

-436 **5** 3 ½ **Tioga Gold (IRE)**[70] 2256 7-11-2 80...........................(p) OwynNelmes(3) 76+
(L R James) *in rr: hdwy to chse ldrs 7th: one pce fr next* **13/2**

6 23 **Florazine (IRE)**[19] 3265 5-11-1 81............................ TomGreenway(5) 53
(F J Bowles, Ire) *chsd ldrs: blnd 5th: wknd 3 out: sn bhd* **9/1**

0005 **7** 1 ¼ **Kicking Bear (IRE)**[14] 3335 8-9-10 64.......................(p) StevenGagan(7) 35
(J K Hunter) *led tl after 5th: lost pl next: sn bhd* **9/1**

6PP0 **P** **Fifteen Reds**[22] 3209 11-11-1 76..............................(p) GrahamLee —
(J C Haynes) *w ldrs: rdn 5th: sn lost pl: bhd whn p.u after next* **25/1**

0502 **P** **Gospel Song**[10] 3395 14-11-5 87................................ EwanWhillans(7) —
(A C Whillans) *w ldrs: lost pl after 4th: sn struggling: t.o 3 out: p.u bef next* **4/1**[1]

5m 8.20s (15.60) **Going Correction** +0.875s/f (Soft) 9 Ran SP% **112.8**
Speed ratings: **103,101,100,99,98 89,88,—,—** CSF £40.92 CT £276.00 TOTE £5.80: £1.50, £3.00, £2.20; EX 31.30.There was no bid for the winner.
Owner Robert C Whitelock **Bred** Castlemartin Stud **Trained** Newburn, Tyne & Wear
■ A new distance for Sedgefield. Because of problems with the tape they were started by flag and they were back from the line.
■ Stewards' Enquiry : Steven Gagan caution: improper iding - used whip whilst out of contention
Tom Greenway one-day ban: improper iding - used whip whilst out of contention (Feb 5)

FOCUS
A weak race, rated around the third. The winner is unexposed over hurdles and may be capable of even better.

NOTEBOOK
Moyne Pleasure(IRE), dropped in, jumped better and took this with the minimum of fuss, the ground no problem at all. *(op 11-2 tchd 9-2)*
Roadworthy(IRE), unplaced in twenty previous starts under Rules, had hinted at something better on her last two outings but in the end the winner had far too much speed for her. *(op 10-1 tchd 11-1)*
Just Sal, who has tumbled down the ratings, finds this trip stretching her stamina to the very limit. *(op 9-1 tchd 10-1)*
Star Trooper(IRE), 7lb higher, was in the thick of things from start to finish this time and a blunder when taking charge three out did not exactly help his cause. *(op 9-2 tchd 6-1)*
Tioga Gold(IRE), absent for ten weeks, has yet to shine on this type of ground. *(op 5-1)*
Gospel Song, who is not built to carry big weights, was never happy and was struggling to keep up *with a full circuit to go. Connections will surely retire him sooner rather than later.Official explanation: jockey said gelding never travelled (op 7-2 tchd 5-1)*

3553 CAMERONS BREWERY MAIDEN CHASE (18 fncs 3 omitted) 3m 3f
2:40 (2:40) (Class 4) 5-Y-0+ **£4,554** (£1,337; £668; £333)

Form RPR
2502 **1** **Canavan (IRE)**[49] 2689 7-11-0 95.............................. ThomasDreaper(5) 110+
(Ferdy Murphy) *chsd ldrs: led 3 out: clr appr next: hung rt and drvn out run-in* **11/8**[1]

0053 **2** 16 **Matmata De Tendron (FR)**[10] 3381 6-11-0 78....(t) MichaelMcAlister(5) 90
(A Crook) *chsd ldrs: outpcd 13th: wnt mod 3rd after 3 out: styd on to take 2nd nr line* **11/2**[3]

2244 **3** 1 ¾ **Uneven Line**[11] 3375 10-10-9 76..............................(p) MrCStorey(3) 83+
(Miss S E Forster) *chsd ldrs: wnt clr 2nd after 3 out: tired and lost 2nd nr line* **15/2**

-644 **4** dist **Barrons Pike**[23] 3170 7-11-5 .... TonyDobbin —
(B Storey) *j. bdly rt: led to 3 out: wknd qckly: t.o: btn 42 l* **10/3**[2]

44P **5** 30 **Bramble Princess (IRE)**[11] 3375 7-10-9 .... PeterBuchanan(3) —
(Miss Lucinda V Russell) *chsd ldr: wknd appr 3 out: sn bhd: t.o* **8/1**

P **U** **The Ample Hamper**[21] 3236 8-10-12 .... PatrickMcDonald(7) —
(Mrs L B Normile) *chsd ldrs: blnd and uns rdr 10th* **50/1**

0060 **P** **Zaffiera (IRE)**[45] 2764 5-10-7 69...................................... NeilMulholland —
(M D Hammond) *mstkes: struggling 11th: sn bhd: t.o whn p.u after 3 out* **25/1**

0 **P** **Highland Brief**[40] 2844 6-11-5 .... RichardMcGrath —
(Mrs A Duffield) *in rr: struggling 11th: sn lost tch: t.o 14th: p.u after 3 out* **66/1**

7m 14.5s (7.70) **Going Correction** +0.875s/f (Soft)
WFA 5 from 6yo+ 12lb 8 Ran SP% **110.7**
Speed ratings: **104,99,98,—,— —,—,—** CSF £8.91 TOTE £2.10: £1.40, £1.50, £1.50; EX 11.40.
Owner John Duddy **Bred** Pat Tobin **Trained** West Witton, N Yorks

FOCUS
A very modest maiden chase and in the end a clear-cut winner, who probably ran to the level of his recent course-and-distance second. Third last fence omitted eace circuit - low sun.

NOTEBOOK
Canavan(IRE), weak on the exchanges, ran without cheekpieces this time. He went on and galloped the opposition into the ground, though it was disconcerting the way he hung right on the run-in. All he looks to do is stay. *(op 10-11 tchd 13-8)*
Matmata De Tendron(FR), with his tongue tied down, was back over fences. After being left behind his stamina came into play and he snatched a remote second spot near the line. With him it is a case of the further the better. *(op 13-2)*
Uneven Line, a point winner four years ago, went in pursuit of the winner but she was very leg-weary up the final hill. *(op 9-1)*
Barrons Pike again jumped badly right and will surely be better served racing the other way round. *(op 4-1 tchd 11-4)*

3554 WEATHERBYS INSURANCE H'CAP HURDLE (13 hdls) 3m 3f 110y
3:10 (3:10) (Class 4) (0-105,101) 4-Y-0+ **£3,903** (£1,146; £573; £286)

Form RPR
-220 **1** **San Peire (FR)**[29] 2977 9-11-9 98.................................. GrahamLee 105+
(J Howard Johnson) *hld up: hdwy 10th: sn trcking ldrs: led after 2 out: styd on wl* **4/1**[1]

F1-4 **2** 6 **Letitia's Loss (IRE)**[21] 3234 8-11-12 101.......................... TonyDobbin 105+
(N G Richards) *trckd ldrs: led after 3 out: hdd after next: no ex* **5/1**[3]

002F **3** 15 **Gimme Shelter (IRE)**[15] 3315 12-9-11 77............... MichaelMcAlister(5) 62
(S J Marshall) *mde most: mstke 7th: hdd after 3 out: one pce* **6/1**

-421 **4** 3 **D J Flippance (IRE)**[33] 2946 11-11-6 100................ ThomasDreaper(5) 82
(A Parker) *chsd ldrs: rdn 3 out: sn btn* **9/2**[2]

6-04 **5** 1 ¼ **Cragg Prince (IRE)**[28] 3042 7-11-1 90........................ DominicElsworth 71
(Mrs S J Smith) *in tch: rdn after 10th: btn next* **5/1**[3]

14P5 **6** 23 **Diamond Cottage (IRE)**[11] 3377 11-10-6 81................... PadgeWhelan 39
(S B Bell) *chsd ldrs: wknd 3 out* **14/1**

32UP **7** 3 ½ **Chancers Dante (IRE)**[63] 2413 10-10-5 87............. PatrickMcDonald(7) 41
(Ferdy Murphy) *in rr: rdn after 10th: sn bhd* **33/1**

6045 **8** dist **Ro Eridani**[6] 3443 6-9-12 76 oh11 ow1.......................... MrCStorey(3) —
(Miss S E Forster) *t.k.h in rr: wnt prom 10th: lost pl next: sn bhd: t.o: btn 55 l* **80/1**

-0P3 **U** **Harry Hooly**[14] 3336 11-11-2 98.................................. MissRDavidson(7) —
(Mrs H O Graham) *chsd ldrs: blnd and uns rdr 3 out* **10/1**

6-6F **P** **Sylviesbuck (IRE)**[54] 2589 9-10-10 85.............................. BarryKeniry —
(G M Moore) *w ldr: reminders 4th: wknd qckly: t.o whn p.u after next* **18/1**

7m 11.0s (7.10) **Going Correction** +0.875s/f (Soft) 10 Ran SP% **111.0**
Speed ratings: **105,103,99,98,97 91,90,—,—,—** CSF £23.30 CT £112.18 TOTE £5.00: £2.10, £2.50, £1.20; EX 20.40 Trifecta £89.60 Pool: £303.10 - 2.40 winning tickets..
Owner Ellenvalley Optimists & J Howard Johnson **Bred** Francois-Xavier Cordier And Mme Hans Rhyn **Trained** Billy Row, Co Durham

FOCUS
A strong gallop. The winner was back to his best and the second deserves plenty of credit under her big weight. The form looks reasonable enough.

NOTEBOOK
San Peire(FR) returned to form and a spectacular leap at the final flight sealed it. All four of his career wins have been here and he rarely runs elsewhere. *(op 7-2 tchd 9-2)*
Letitia's Loss(IRE), better for her Ayr outing, went on but in the end the winner simply proved the *stronger. This was a game effort under top weight and she deserves to find another opening. (op 7-2)*
Gimme Shelter(IRE), reverting to hurdles from a much lower mark, made this a true test but in the end the first two were simply too sharp for this tough veteran. Hexham in March is getting closer now. *(tchd 11-2)*
D J Flippance(IRE), hoisted 10lb after Carlisle, was back over hurdles but he was going nowhere fully three out. *(tchd 4-1)*
Cragg Prince(IRE) doesn't seem the type to progress from one race to another. *(op 7-1)*
Harry Hooly, suited by the trip and the ground, looked much happier over hurdles and was bang in the firing line when giving his rider little chance three out. *(op 16-1)*
Sylviesbuck(IRE) *Official explanation: jockey said gelding bled from the nose (op 16-1)*

3555 JOHN SMITH'S EXTRA SMOOTH H'CAP CHASE (13 fncs) 2m 110y
3:40 (3:40) (Class 5) (0-90,90) 5-Y-0+ **£3,578** (£1,050; £525; £262)

Form RPR
-204 **1** **Flaming Heck**[10] 3398 9-11-12 90..................................... NeilMulholland 99+
(Mrs L B Normile) *mde all: styd on gamely fr 2 out* **10/1**

5003 **2** 5 **Vulcan Lane (NZ)**[14] 3335 9-11-4 85............................(p) LarryMcGrath(3) 90+
(R C Guest) *in rr: hdwy 5th: sn chsng ldrs: wnt 2nd 9th: no ex between last 2* **5/1**[2]

53 **3** 4 **Grand Slam (IRE)**[11] 3379 11-10-11 82........................ EwanWhillans(7) 82+
(A C Whillans) *chsd ldrs: drvn along 5th: sn lost pl: hdwy 3 out: wnt 3rd next: kpt on same pce* **8/1**

P0/6 **4** 6 **Saxon Mill**[29] 2967 11-11-6 84.. OllieMcPhail 77
(T J Fitzgerald) *chsd ldrs: one pce fr 10th* **25/1**

SPF5 **5** 5 **Nomadic Blaze**[18] 3268 9-10-13 84.................................. PhilKinsella(7) 72
(P G Atkinson) *in tch: hdwy to chse ldrs 10th: lost pl appr 2 out* **14/1**

5644 **6** 6 **Little Flora**[11] 3379 10-11-1 84................................ MichaelMcAlister(5) 66
(S J Marshall) *chsd ldrs: outpcd after 5th: n.d after* **8/1**

4U55 **7** 3 **Ipledgeallegiance (USA)**[15] 3317 10-11-3 81.................. DavidO'Meara 60
(Miss Tracy Waggott) *in rr: lost tch 5th: sn bhd* **11/1**

P006 **F** **Political Cruise**[10] 3380 8-10-4 75............................... GarethThomas(7) —
(R Nixon) *in rr: struggling whn fell 9th* **13/2**[3]

0P-3 **P** **Gaucho**[15] 3320 9-10-7 78.......................................(p) MissTJackson(7) —
(Miss T Jackson) *prom: outpcd 9th: bhd whn p.u bef last* **8/1**

5624 **P** **Pavey Ark (IRE)**[55] 2570 8-10-9 73.............................(p) GrahamLee —
(James Moffatt) *wiyth ldrs: lost pl appr 3 out: bhd whn p.u bef next* **7/2**[1]

4m 26.8s (12.60) **Going Correction** +0.875s/f (Soft) 10 Ran SP% **113.5**
Speed ratings: **105,102,100,97,95 92,91,—,—,—** CSF £58.99 CT £421.73 TOTE £10.50: £3.90, £2.00, £3.50; EX 55.40.
Owner D A Whitaker **Bred** R L Green **Trained** Duncrievie, Perth & Kinross
■ Stewards' Enquiry : Ollie McPhail caution: careless riding

FOCUS
A bold jumping, front-running performance from the back-on-song winner. This is unlikely to throw up many winners.
NOTEBOOK
Flaming Heck jumped much better and made every yard to win going away in the end. His rider deserves full marks. *(op 9-1)*
Vulcan Lane(NZ), back over fences, went in pursuit of the winner but in truth was never going to finish anything but second best.
Grand Slam(IRE), who last tasted success five year ago, struggled on the ground but deserves credit for keeping on in his own time all the way to the line. *(op 7-1)*
Saxon Mill, having his second outing after a long break, has come to fences very late in life. This trip is basically on the sharp side for him.
Nomadic Blaze, who usually tries his hand over further, is a long-standing maiden and likely to remain so. *(op 11-1)*
Gaucho *Official explanation: jockey said gelding hung to the right (op 4-1 tchd 9-2 in places)*
Pavey Ark(IRE) stopped in a matter of strides and connections reckoned the ground was against him. *Official explanation: jockey said gelding was unsuited by the soft (heavy in places) ground (op 4-1 tchd 9-2 in places)*

3556 SIS MARES' ONLY INTERMEDIATE OPEN NATIONAL HUNT FLAT RACE — 2m 1f
4:10 (4:10) (Class 6) 4-6-Y-0 — **£1,713** (£499; £249)

Form — RPR
0- **1** **Sparron Hawk (FR)**[304] 4559 6-11-2 .... TonyDobbin 95+
(N G Richards) *mid-div: hdwy to chse ldrs over 4f out: led over 2f out: styd on wl* **11/2**[2]
2 *2½* **Riodan (IRE)** 4-10-0 .... DougieCostello[(5)] 81
(J J Quinn) *trckd ldrs: led over 4f out tl over 2f out: kpt on same pce* **11/2**[2]
3 *3½* **The Music Queen** 5-11-2 .... GrahamLee 89+
(G A Swinbank) *hld up in rr: hdwy 7f out: rdn 3f out: kpt on same pce* **10/11**[1]
4 *8* **Maura's Legacy (IRE)**[28] 3048 6-10-9 .... MrMJO'Hare[(7)] 81+
(I A Duncan, Ire) *trckd ldrs: chal over 4f out: wknd fnl 2f* **14/1**
5 *18* **Stormont Dawn (IRE)** 5-11-2 .... NeilMulholland 62
(Mrs L B Normile) *mid-div: rdn and lost pl over 4f out* **25/1**
6 *5* **Is There More** 5-10-11 .... ThomasDreaper[(5)] 57
(J M Jefferson) *s.i.s: sn drvn along: sme hdwy 7f out: lost pl 5f out* **9/1**[3]
7 *2½* **Hooky's Quest** 4-10-2 .... OwynNelmes[(3)] 44
(Mrs H O Graham) *promient: lost pl over 3f out* **50/1**
0 **8** *21* **Watch The Wind**[40] 2844 5-10-9 .... BenOrde-Powlett[(7)] 34
(J B Walton) *bhd: hdwy to chse ldrs 7f out: lost pl 5f out* **100/1**
60-0 **9** *13* **Only Millie**[255] 349 5-10-6 .... MichaelMcAvoy[(10)] 21
(James Moffatt) *led tl over 4f out: sn lost pl and bhd* **50/1**
10 *dist* **Mary Casey** 5-11-2 .... DominicElsworth —
(C A Mulhall) *prom: lost pl after 7f out: sn bhd: t.o 5f out: btn 37 l* **20/1**
11 *nk* **Fairfield** 5-10-11 .... MichaelMcAlister[(5)] —
(B Storey) *w ldrs: lost pl over 5f out: sn wl bhd: t.o* **25/1**

4m 15.9s (9.00) **Going Correction** +0.875s/f (Soft)
WFA 4 from 5yo+ 11lb — **11** Ran SP% **117.2**
Speed ratings: **101,99,98,94,85 83,82,72,66,—** — CSF £33.03 TOTE £6.90: £2.70, £1.40, £1.10; EX 33.50 Place 6 £25.67, Place 5 £20.99.
Owner R Haggas **Bred** Dora Bloodstock Ltd **Trained** Greystoke, Cumbria
FOCUS
A steady gallop to halfway but in the end the first three pulled clear. Probably a fair bumper by mares-only standards.
NOTEBOOK
Sparron Hawk(FR), whose only previous outing was in March, is a well-made mare and she took this in convincing fashion. *(op 9-2 tchd 6-1)*
Riodan(IRE), a medium-sized, narrow filly, was well supported. After seizing the initiative, she did not go down without a fight and deserves to go one better in a similar event. *(op 11-1 tchd 12-1)*
The Music Queen, a rangy, well-made mare, was easily the pick of the paddock. She travelled strongly but, coming under pressure at the top of the hill, she could only stay on in her own time. The outing will have done her no harm at all. *(tchd Evens in places)*
Maura's Legacy(IRE), well beaten in two bumpers in Ireland, was left for dead by the first three down the final hill. *(op 11-1)*
T/Plt: £27.90 to a £1 stake. Pool: £38,073.10. 996.15 winning tickets. T/Qpdt: £4.90 to a £1 stake. Pool: £3,007.00. 451.30 winning tickets. WG

3347 CATTERICK (L-H)
Wednesday, January 25
OFFICIAL GOING: Good (good to firm in places)
The ground was described as 'mainly good but a bit dead and tacky in places'.
Wind: Moderate; half against. Weather: Changeable, occasional showers

3557 BEDALE (S) H'CAP HURDLE (8 hdls) — 2m
1:00 (1:00) (Class 5) (0-90,89) 4-Y-0+ — **£2,740** (£798; £399)

Form — RPR
0605 **1** **Colway Ritz**[24] 3169 12-10-9 72 .... (p) GrahamLee 76+
(W Storey) *trckd ldrs: smooth hdwy and cl up whn blnd 2 out: rdn last: styd on to ld last 100 yds* **8/1**[2]
6P42 **2** *1½* **Seraph**[30] 2962 6-11-1 81 .... LeeVickers[(3)] 81
(O Brennan) *trckd ldrs: hdwy 3 out: led next: rdn appr last: drvn flat: hdd and no ex last 100 yds* **7/1**[1]
6520 **3** *nk* **Armentieres**[13] 3351 5-11-2 89 .... (v) StevenGagan[(10)] 89
(Mrs E Slack) *led tl after 3rd: cl up tl rdn and outpcd after 3 out: hdwy on inner and cl up next: ev ch tl drvn and one pce flat* **9/1**[3]
0045 **4** *1* **Southern Bazaar (USA)**[30] 2962 5-10-6 69 .... AlanDempsey 69+
(M E Sowersby) *keen: hld up towards rr: smooth hdwy appr 3 out: cl up next rdn and ev ch last: drvn and one pce flat* **11/1**
-664 **5** *3½* **Power And Demand**[24] 3169 9-10-4 72 .... DougieCostello[(5)] 67+
(C W Thornton) *hld up: hdwy after 3 out: rdn to chse ldrs appr last: hung rt flat and no imp* **8/1**[2]
2060 **6** *13* **Bargain Hunt (IRE)**[24] 3169 5-11-9 86 .... NeilMulholland 68
(W Storey) *bhd tl styd on fr 2 out* **18/1**
5665 **7** *1¾* **Lane Marshal**[13] 3349 4-10-6 87 .... PatrickMcDonald[(7)] 56
(M E Sowersby) *bhd tl styd on fr 2 out* **8/1**[2]
0600 **8** *nk* **Tiger Talk**[24] 3169 10-10-9 82 .... (p) JonathanMoorman[(10)] 62
(R C Guest) *in tch: pushed along 3 out and sn wknd* **25/1**
2PP6 **9** *5* **Approaching Land (IRE)**[30] 2962 11-11-0 80 .... MrTGreenall[(3)] 55
(M W Easterby) *chsd ldrs: rdn along after 3 out and sn wknd* **25/1**
0-P0 **10** *hd* **Karyon (IRE)**[56] 2567 6-9-12 66 .... MichaelMcAlister[(5)] 44+
(Miss Kate Milligan) *trckd ldrs tl led after 3rd: hit next and sn hdd: mstkes 5th and 6th: rdn and wknd whn bl8undered 2 out and sn bhd* **33/1**
16PP **11** *3½* **Faraway Echo**[25] 3147 5-10-12 75 .... MarkBradburne 46
(James Moffatt) *nvr nr ldrs* **25/1**
000 **12** *½* **Fillameena**[24] 3167 6-11-4 84 .... AnthonyCoyle[(3)] 55
(P T Midgley) *a rr* **8/1**[2]
0303 **13** *½* **Nutley Queen (IRE)**[19] 2567 7-10-2 72 .... (t) RichardSpate[(7)] 42
(M Appleby) *midfield: effrt and rdn along bef 3 out: nvr a factor* **12/1**
054P **14** *5* **Nepal (IRE)**[15] 3330 4-10-1 80 .... StephenCraine[(5)] 34
(M Mullineaux) *chsd ldrs tl rdn along 5th and sn wknd* **16/1**
600P **15** *nk* **New Wish (IRE)**[15] 3335 6-9-12 68 .... PhilKinsella[(7)] 33
(S B Clark) *keen: hld upo in tch: hdwy to ld after 4th: clr after 3 out: rdn and hdd appr next: sn wknd* **33/1**
3040 **16** *7* **Dubai Dreams**[41] 2419 6-11-4 86 .... (b) AdamPogson[(5)] 44
(S R Bowring) *cl up: pushed along and hit 4th: sn lost pl and bhd fr 3 out* **14/1**
5P6 **P** **Bold Pursuit (IRE)**[47] 2752 4-10-11 85 .... RussGarritty —
(S B Clark) *a bhd: p.u bef 2 out* **14/1**
0306 **P** **Silver Dagger**[24] 3169 8-10-4 67 .... (vt) BarryKeniry —
(J C Haynes) *in tch: effrt to chse ldrs 4th: rdn along and wknd bef 3 out: bhd whn p.u bef next* **50/1**

3m 48.6s (-7.70) **Going Correction** -0.425s/f (Good)
WFA 4 from 5yo+ 11lb — **18** Ran SP% **126.8**
Speed ratings: **102,101,101,100,98 92,91,91,88,88 86,86,86,83,83 80,—,—** CSF £60.72 CT £533.30 TOTE £9.20: £2.10, £1.80, £2.40, £4.40; EX 61.00.There was no bid for the winner.
Owner D Tindale **Bred** R P Williams **Trained** Muggleswick, Co Durham
FOCUS
A poor race, but a decent pace and there were various leaders during the contest. The race is rated through the runner-up and there was a very healthy gap after the first five which does not bode well for the sixth horse backwards.
NOTEBOOK
Colway Ritz, who failed to get home over an extra three furlongs here last time, proved well suited by this drop to the minimum trip and would probably have won more easily had he not missed out the second last. This is his ground and he does seem to like it here, under both codes. *(op 9-1)*
Seraph, raised 4lb for his Market Rasen effort, did not seem to do much wrong but the winner's Flat speed proved decisive on the run-in. He may prefer the ground a little easier than this. *(op 13-2)*
Armentieres, who finished in front of Colway Ritz here two runs ago, was given a positive ride but this drop in trip did not seem to suit her so well and she was just found wanting for toe where it mattered. *(tchd 10-1)*
Southern Bazaar(USA), less exposed than most over hurdles, was one of four in with every chance between the last two flights but could not quicken where it mattered. The ground was suitable for him, but he may need a bit further. *(op 14-1)*
Power And Demand, not for the first time, looked like getting involved when the dash for home began but failed to deliver. He is still looking for his first win of any sort in 45 attempts, Flat and jumps, plus another five in points.
Fillameena was the subject of a real gamble, but was never in the race. *(op 28-1)*

3558 RICHMOND BEGINNERS' CHASE (15 fncs) — 2m 3f
1:30 (1:30) (Class 4) 5-Y-0+ — **£5,204** (£1,528; £764; £381)

Form — RPR
-344 **1** **Aleron (IRE)**[16] 3317 8-11-2 .... (p) RussGarritty 120+
(J J Quinn) *led to 3rd: lft in ld 7th: styd on wl fr 2 out: readily* **10/3**[2]
2-23 **2** *6* **Martha's Kinsman (IRE)**[69] 2291 7-11-2 .... MarkBradburne 115+
(H D Daly) *prom: chsd wnr fr 10th: kpt on fr 2 out: no imp* **7/2**[3]
P4 **3** *19* **Sandy Gold (IRE)**[101] 1758 8-11-2 .... DominicElsworth 94
(Miss J E Foster) *w ldrs: outpcd 8th: kpt on to take mod 3rd 2 out* **200/1**
4665 **4** *8* **Rifleman (IRE)**[15] 3334 6-11-2 94 .... (t) OllieMcPhail 86
(Robert Gray) *chsd ldrs: hmpd 7th: lost pl and lft mod 3rd 3 out: wknd next* **40/1**
3010 **5** *28* **Honest Endeavour**[20] 3256 7-10-11 105 .... ThomasDreaper[(5)] 78+
(J M Jefferson) *in rr: bdly hmpd 7th: t.o 12th* **16/1**
0P **6** *2½* **Lookafterme (IRE)**[15] 3331 6-10-11 .... StephenCraine[(5)] 56
(A W Carroll) *in tch: wnt prom 8th: lost pl 10th: t.o 12th* **33/1**
0525 **F** **Yes Sir (IRE)**[20] 3251 7-11-2 127 .... ChristianWilliams —
(P Bowen) *led 3rd: fell 7th* **11/8**[1]
4-3F **F** **Moonlit Harbour**[51] 2677 7-11-2 118 .... BrianHarding —
(Ferdy Murphy) *chsd ldrs: 3rd and wl outpcd whn fell 3 out* **9/1**

4m 42.6s (-11.00) **Going Correction** -0.50s/f (Good) — **8** Ran SP% **109.2**
Speed ratings: **103,100,92,89,77 76,—,—** CSF £14.31 TOTE £5.00: £1.60, £1.50, £12.60; EX 15.40.
Owner Grahame Liles **Bred** Sheikh Mohammed Bin Rashid Al Maktoum **Trained** Settrington, N Yorks
FOCUS
An ordinary beginners' chase and the race became less competitive after the exit of the favourite with over a circuit left. The fourth sets the standard and the form could rate higher.
NOTEBOOK
Aleron(IRE), with the cheekpieces back on, was left in front when the favourite came down with over a circuit to go and showed plenty of resolution to keep the rest at bay from that point. He goes on any ground and should be able to find another ordinary novice event this term. *(op 5-2)*
Martha's Kinsman(IRE) kept on trying to bridge the gap to the winner from a long way out, but lacked the pace to do so and probably found this trip on this tight circuit too sharp, especially on this ground.
Sandy Gold(IRE) plodded on over the last half-mile to snatch the minor berth, but it is probably fair to say his final placing was down to the misfortune of others. *(op 100-1)*
Rifleman(IRE) was done few favours by the fall of the favourite at the seventh, but it is hard to blame that too much and he continues to look a weak finisher. *(op 33-1)*
Honest Endeavour, pulled up in his only previous try over fences, was brought to a standstill by the fall of the favourite at the seventh and this effort should be ignored. *(op 25-1)*
Moonlit Harbour found the front pair running away from him, but was safe in third, when knuckling over at the third last. *(op 13-8)*
Yes Sir(IRE) was taking the field along when crumpling on landing at the seventh. *(op 13-8)*

3559 HIPSWELL NOVICES' HURDLE (12 hdls) — 3m 1f 110y
2:00 (2:00) (Class 4) 5-Y-0+ — **£3,253** (£955; £477; £238)

Form — RPR
6P62 **1** **Cash King (IRE)**[24] 3173 6-10-12 107 .... DominicElsworth 101+
(Mrs S J Smith) *trckd ldrs: hdwy 8th: cl up 3 out: led next: rdn clr appr last: styd on* **5/4**[1]
6 **2** *10* **Double Turn**[41] 2838 6-10-12 .... PadgeWhelan 91+
(Mrs S J Smith) *trckd ldrs: hdwy to ld after 3 out: rdn along and hdd next sn drvn and wknd appr last* **7/1**
6425 **3** *¾* **Shady Baron (IRE)**[20] 3257 7-10-12 87 .... BrianHarding 88
(J Wade) *cl up: led 2nd: rdn along 9th: hdd after next and outpcd bef 2 out* **20/1**

0-41 **4** *7* **Spectested (IRE)**[19] [3042] 5-11-4 102........................ WayneHutchinson 88+
(A W Carroll) *bhd: hdwy appr 3 out: sn rdn along and plugged on same pce fr 2 out: hit last* **9/2**[3]

3P3F **5** *2* **Common Girl (IRE)**[18] [3287] 8-11-3 106................ JohnMcNamara 84
(O Brennan) *led to 2nd: cl up tl rdn along 8th and wknd after next* **4/1**[2]

500 **6** *1 3/4* **Nearly Never**[69] [2295] 11-10-2 .... MichaelO'Connell[(10)] 78
(Mrs S J Smith) *a towards rr* **100/1**

0 **7** *10* **Ad Murum (IRE)**[34] [2948] 7-10-12 .... BarryKeniry 68
(G M Moore) *hld up in rr: hdwy 8th: chsd ldrs next: rdn 3 out and sn wknd* **50/1**

10 **8** *10* **Moscow Blue**[143] [1410] 5-11-4 ....(t) OllieMcPhail 67+
(Robert Gray) *trckd ldrs: hit 8th: sn poushed along: rdn and wknd 3 out: rr whn mstke next* **16/1**

/P-P **9** *11* **Tallahassee (IRE)**[34] [2947] 8-10-7 .... DeclanMcGann[(5)] 47
(D R MacLeod) *bhd fr 1/2-way: t.o fr 3 out* **200/1**

P **P** **Red Wharf**[78] [2106] 5-10-12 .... AlanDempsey —
(J Wade) *a bhd: p.u bef 8th* **80/1**

0 **F** **Callingwood (IRE)**[262] [241] 6-10-5 .... PatrickMcDonald[(7)] —
(Ferdy Murphy) *towards rr: fell 5th* **50/1**

20PP **P** **Musical Chord (IRE)**[12] [3376] 7-10-12 ....(p) GrahamLee —
(B Storey) *midfield: poushed along 8th: rdn next and sn wknd: bhd whn p.u bef 3 out* **50/1**

0PF **P** **Whitsun**[13] [3347] 6-10-7 ....(p) MichaelMcAlister[(5)] —
(Miss Kate Milligan) *in rr: plld hrd and hdwy to chse ldrs 4th: lost pl 7th: bhd whn p.u bef 8th* **200/1**

6m 25.0s (-6.70) **Going Correction** -0.425s/f (Good) **13** Ran SP% **114.9**
Speed ratings: **93,89,89,87,86 86,83,80,76,— —,—,—** CSF £10.06 TOTE £2.30: £1.30, £1.80, £2.60; EX 9.30.
Owner A D Dick and A J Duckworth **Bred** Frank Cuddihy **Trained** High Eldwick, W Yorks

FOCUS
A modest staying novice hurdle and not as competitive as the numbers would suggest. The early pace was ordinary and those that raced prominently were favoured. The winning time was also modest for the class which tempers confidence.

NOTEBOOK
Cash King(IRE), whose effort when runner-up over course and distance earlier this month has already been boosted by the winner going in again since, probably only needed to repeat the performance to collect and was running all over his stable companion from the home turn. He obviously stays well and seems to have improved for a sounder surface. *(op 11-8 tchd 6-4)*
Double Turn, taking a big step up in trip on this second outing over hurdles, was always up there and although he did not see his race out as well as his stable companion, this was still a fair effort. He could be interesting when dropped back a little in distance. *(op 18-1 tchd 13-2)*
Shady Baron(IRE), another trying a longer trip, was never far away before getting caught out for toe from the home bend. His proximity does not do a lot for the form given his official rating, but he has at least already been placed over hurdles and may be interesting in a novices' handicap off his current mark. *(op 25-1)*
Spectested(IRE), already a winner over this trip, found this sharp track on a quicker surface an insufficient test, especially given the ordinary early pace, and all he could do was plod on over the last half-mile. His win came in a novices' handicap and he may be better off back in that sort of company. *(op 5-2)*
Common Girl(IRE) was given a positive ride, but seemed to find this trip beyond her. She is totally exposed and will always be vulnerable to progressive types in races like this. *(op 5-1)*

3560 WEATHERBYS BANK NORTH YORKSHIRE GRAND NATIONAL (HANDICAP CHASE) (22 fncs 1 omitted) 3m 6f
2:30 (2:30) (Class 3) (0-130,130) 5-Y-0+
£6,263 (£1,850; £925; £463; £231; £116)

Form RPR

30U1 **1** **Prince Of Slane**[13] [3350] 7-9-13 **108**...................... DougieCostello[(5)] 128+
(G A Swinbank) *hld up in rr: hdwy 16th: shkn up 4 out: led 2 out: styd on wl* **8/1**[2]

04P0 **2** *3 1/2* **Harlov (FR)**[30] [2965] 11-10-2 **106**..................................(v) RichardMcGrath 120
(A Parker) *rr-div: hdwy 17th: sn chsng ldrs: wnt 2nd last: no imp* **33/1**

3-32 **3** *1 3/4* **High Cotton (IRE)**[16] [3315] 11-10-0 **104** oh2.................... JimCrowley 116
(K G Reveley) *reminders and lost tch 15th: hdwy 17th: styd on fr 2 out: tk 3rd nr fin* **8/1**[2]

0-46 **4** *5* **Gunther McBride (IRE)**[18] [3296] 11-11-12 **130**............ RichardJohnson 139+
(P J Hobbs) *chsd ldrs: drvn 4 out: led next: hdd 2 out: wknd appr last* **9/2**[1]

-034 **5** *1 3/4* **Virgin Soldier (IRE)**[13] [3350] 10-10-13 **117**................... JohnMcNamara 122
(G A Swinbank) *prom: effrt appr 3 out: wknd between last 2* **33/1**

1F11 **6** *2 1/2* **Bang And Blame (IRE)**[15] [3336] 10-9-11 **106**......... MichaelMcAlister[(5)] 113+
(M W Easterby) *led: hit 5th: blnd 9th: reminders after 15th: hdd and mstke 3 out: sn btn* **9/1**[3]

P216 **7** *2* **Midnight Gunner**[24] [3186] 12-10-1 **105**........................ TomScudamore 106
(A E Price) *chsd ldrs: wknd 3 out* **11/1**

4032 **8** *6* **Benrajah (IRE)**[13] [3350] 9-10-10 **114**.. GrahamLee 112+
(M Todhunter) *trckng ldrs: blnd 6th: wknd appr 3 out* **9/1**[3]

-135 **9** *19* **Capybara (IRE)**[30] [2965] 8-10-11 **115**............................... DavidO'Meara 91
(H P Hogarth) *j.rt: a in rr: lost tch 15th* **10/1**

1-54 **P** **Monty's Quest (IRE)**[12] [3377] 11-10-0 **104**.............................. BarryKeniry —
(M Smith) *in rr: bhd whn p.u bef 8th* **10/1**

-P6P **F** **Granit D'Estruval (FR)**[11] [3390] 12-11-0 **118**..................... BrianHarding —
(Ferdy Murphy) *chsd ldrs: fell 10th* **14/1**

-P14 **U** **Supreme Breeze (IRE)**[30] [2965] 11-10-12 **116**.................. PadgeWhelan —
(Mrs S J Smith) *mid-div whn blnd and uns rdr 4th* **16/1**

P301 **P** **Robbo**[41] [2841] 12-10-13 **124**..(p) PhilKinsella[(7)] —
(K G Reveley) *dropped rr and drvn 7th: bhd: t.o whn p.u bef 2 out* **20/1**

30-F **U** **Celioso (IRE)**[41] [2841] 9-10-10 **114**................................ DominicElsworth 123+
(Mrs S J Smith) *chsd ldrs: 3rd and keeping on same pce whn blnd and uns rdr last* **12/1**

7m 38.4s course record **14** Ran SP% **117.8**
CSF £238.53 CT £2162.10 TOTE £10.20: £2.60, £8.80, £2.60; EX 459.60 TRIFECTA Not won..
Owner J H Richardson **Bred** J Richardson **Trained** Melsonby, N Yorks

FOCUS
Just a fair handicap for the grade, run at an above-average gallop, and the form appears sound enough rated through the third and fourth. The sixth last fence was bypassed on the final circuit.

NOTEBOOK
Prince Of Slane, raised 6lb for swooping late under today's rider to score over shorter at this track 13 days previously, advertised his current rude health and followed up with another authoritative success. The longer trip was much to his liking, as was the good ground, and he was given another well-judged ride by Costello. He is clearly in the form of his life at present, and his jumping has been much-improved of late, so a bold bid for the hat-trick looks likely despite another future rise in the weights. His connections also still have the option of reverting to novice company.
Harlov(FR), winner of this event in 2004 from a 1lb lower mark, came from a similar position as the winner and produced by far his best effort of the current campaign. This has to rate a commendable effort considering he would have preferred a softer surface, yet while he is on a fair mark at present, he really is hard to predict these days. *(op 40-1)*
High Cotton(IRE) again displayed his quirks by running in snatches for most of the race, before finally responding all too late in the day and flying home to bag third place. Incredibly, he remains a maiden and he must rate one of the most frustrating horses in training.
Gunther McBride(IRE) turned in his usual brave effort and was not at all disgraced under top weight. However, while he shaped as though he needed a longer trip at Sandown last time, this trip may just have stretched his stamina, and he probably needs further respite from the Handicapper before getting his head back in front. *(tchd 5-1)*
Virgin Soldier(IRE) travelled and jumped sweetly for a long way, but his stamina limitations told from the penultimate fence and he was ultimately well held. When reverting in distance, he could well be capable of ending his long losing run from this mark. *(op 25-1)*
Bang And Blame(IRE) spoilt his chance of landing the hat-trick with some sloppy jumping, so did well to finish where he did in the circumstances off this much higher mark. He can strike again when returning to Sedgefield. *(op 7-1)*
Celioso(IRE) was still in with definite place prospects when coming to grief at the final fence. He is fairly handicapped at present, but his confidence will surely have been severely dented by this. *(op 11-1)*

3561 WATT FENCES RACECOURSE SUPPLIERS H'CAP HURDLE (10 hdls) 2m 3f
3:00 (3:01) (Class 3) (0-130,123) 4-Y-0+ **£5,204** (£1,528; £764; £381)

Form RPR

3136 **1** **Texas Holdem (IRE)**[11] [3383] 7-11-2 **118**................ MichaelMcAlister[(5)] 124+
(M Smith) *trckd ldrs: hdwy 3 out: led next: sn rdn and styd on wl flat* **11/2**[2]

0-11 **2** *2 1/2* **Return Home**[21] [3242] 7-10-0 **97** oh1.................................... PaulMoloney 101
(J S Smith) *trckd ldrs on inner: smooth hdwy after 3 out: cl up next: shkn up flat and kpt on same pce* **13/2**[3]

P24P **3** *3* **Kentucky Blue (IRE)**[11] [3383] 6-11-4 **120**.................... StephenCraine[(5)] 121
(T D Easterby) *hld up in tch: gd hdwy on inner appr 2 out: sn rdn and ev ch tl drvn and one pce last* **20/1**

22-4 **4** *1 1/2* **Sun King**[48] [2716] 9-9-4 **97** oh2..................................(t) JamesReveley[(10)] 96
(K G Reveley) *hld up: gd hdwy 3 out: chsd ldrs next: sn rdn and one pce last* **16/1**

1301 **5** *3 1/2* **Brooklyn Brownie (IRE)**[34] [2952] 7-10-8 **110**............ ThomasDreaper[(5)] 106
(J M Jefferson) *a cl up: led after 3 out: rdn and hdd next: drvn and wknd appr last* **11/1**

1-00 **6** *3* **Full Irish (IRE)**[75] [2163] 10-11-12 **123**.................................... TonyDobbin 118+
(L Lungo) *hld up: stdy hdwy 1/2-way: effrt to chse ldrs 2 out: sn rdn and wknd appr last* **11/1**

312 **7** *7* **Spring Breeze**[38] [2903] 5-11-7 **118**...............................(v) RichardMcGrath 104
(M Dods) *cl up: led 6th: rdn along and hit 3 out: sn hdd & wknd fr 2 out* **7/1**

1012 **8** *8* **Wet Lips (AUS)**[102] [1739] 8-11-4 **118**.................................(p) PaulO'Neill[(3)] 96
(R C Guest) *midfield: hdwy on outer 7th: rdn along appr 2 out and sn wknd* **16/1**

44F0 **9** *1 1/4* **Celtic Blaze (IRE)**[16] [3318] 7-9-8 **98**...........................(t) DavidCullinane[(7)] 74
(B S Rothwell) *led to 6th: cl up tl rdn along after 3 out and grad wknd* **66/1**

1-11 **10** *5* **Bogus Dreams (IRE)**[263] [213] 9-11-0 **114**.................... GaryBerridge[(3)] 85
(L Lungo) *a rr* **12/1**

5614 **11** *3* **Napoleon (IRE)**[14] [3342] 5-11-7 **118**.............................. RichardJohnson 86
(P J Hobbs) *in tch: pushed along 1/2-way: sn lost pl and bhd fr 7th* **9/2**[1]

300 **12** *1 3/4* **Diamond Cutter (NZ)**[24] [3171] 7-10-5 **105**.................... LarryMcGrath[(3)] 72
(R C Guest) *bhd fr 1/2-way* **33/1**

2362 **13** *3 1/2* **Izzykeen**[157] [1275] 7-10-13 **110**... DominicElsworth 73
(Mrs S J Smith) *chsd ldrs to 4th: sn lost pl and bhd fr 6th* **12/1**

005P **14** *15* **King's Protector**[41] [2839] 6-10-3 **100**................................ NeilMulholland 48
(M D Hammond) *a rr* **33/1**

0FU5 **F** **Dubonai (IRE)**[13] [3347] 6-10-5 **102**.....................................(t) BarryKeniry 98
(G M Moore) *hld up: gd hdwy 3 out: cl up and ev ch whn fell next* **28/1**

4m 39.5s (-11.00) **Going Correction** -0.425s/f (Good) **15** Ran SP% **118.8**
Speed ratings: **106,104,103,103,101 100,97,94,93,91 90,89,87,81,—** CSF £38.46 CT £673.81 TOTE £5.40: £2.00, £3.00, £9.80; EX 61.00.
Owner Michael Smith **Bred** Burren Racing Syndicate **Trained** Kirkheaton, Northumberland

FOCUS
A very competitive event for the grade, run at a solid pace, and the field came home fairly strung out. The form looks solid.

NOTEBOOK
Texas Holdem(IRE), sixth in the Lanzarote at Carlisle last time, duly resumed winning ways in ready fashion on this drop back in class and was full value for his winning margin. The better ground proved right up his street and, as he has relatively few miles on the clock for a seven-year-old, he probably has more to offer over timber this term. *(op 7-1)*
Return Home, winner of both his previous outings since joining connections from Ireland, was travelling every bit as well as the winner two out, yet ultimately failed to see out the race as well as that rival despite the big weight concession. This must still rate another improved effort, however, and while another weight rise is now inevitable, he is clearly still in great heart at present. *(op 5-1)*
Kentucky Blue(IRE) had his chance and kept to his task well under maximum pressure from the penultimate flight. This was a much more encouraging effort, but he is a hard horse to predict and appears weighted right up to his best at present.
Sun King failed to see out the longer trip all that well, but posted another sound effort all the same, and can find easier opportunities from this mark. *(op 20-1)*
Brooklyn Brownie(IRE), raised 4lb for winning a weaker heat at Fakenham a month or so ago, ran his race and now looks held by the Handicapper. *(tchd 12-1)*
Napoleon(IRE) was never happy at any stage and proved disappointing on this handicap bow. *Official explanation: jockey said gelding was never travelling (op 5-1 tchd 11-2 in places)*
Izzykeen *Official explanation: jockey said gelding had a breathing problem (op 20-1)*
Dubonai(IRE) took a crashing fall when still holding every chance and has to rate unlucky. *(op 25-1)*

3562 COME RACING AGAIN ON 3RD FEBRUARY NOVICES' H'CAP CHASE (12 fncs) 2m
3:30 (3:30) (Class 4) (0-105,105) 5-Y-0+ **£3,903** (£1,146; £573; £286)

Form RPR

0004 **1** **Cedar Rapids (IRE)**[22] [3232] 6-10-11 **90**.............................. DavidO'Meara 96+
(H P Hogarth) *t.k.h: trckd ldrs: led 6th: hdd 2 out: lft 4 l clr last: hld on* **9/1**

5532 **2** *1 3/4* **Red Man (IRE)**[13] [3351] 9-11-2 **105**...........................(p) StevenGagan[(10)] 108+
(Mrs E Slack) *led to 6th: lft 2nd last: kpt on* **9/2**[2]

0526 **3** *1 1/2* **Persian Point**[15] [3334] 10-10-1 **83**.. MrCStorey[(3)] 85+
(Miss S E Forster) *chsd ldrs: outpcd appr 3 out: styd on same pce fr 2 out* **12/1**

4566 **4** *5* **Drumossie (AUS)**[13] [3348] 6-10-3 **82**..............................(p) DominicElsworth 78
(R C Guest) *in rr: sme hdwy 8th: one pce fr 3 out* **11/1**

2350 **5** *17* **Humid Climate**[30] 2980 6-11-1 **94** AnthonyRoss 73
(R A Fahey) *nt fluent: bhd fr 5th* **9/1**

450P **6** *27* **Barneys Reflection**[80] 2080 6-9-7 **79** oh9 (b) AdrianScholes(7) 31
(A Crook) *chsd ldrs: lost pl 6th: bhd fr 8th* **33/1**

1P-1 **F** **Whaleef**[13] 3348 8-11-9 **102** (p) ChristianWilliams —
(B J Llewellyn) *hld up: wl in tch whn fell 4th* **9/4**[1]

01B3 **P** **Longdale**[15] 3334 8-11-8 **101** GrahamLee —
(M Todhunter) *in rr: reminders 3rd: bhd fr 6th: t.o whn p.u bef 3 out* **6/1**[3]

0034 **F** **Ton-Chee**[15] 3334 7-11-1 **94** TonyDobbin 101+
(F P Murtagh) *wnt prom 5th: led 2 out: 2 l up whn fell heavily last* **13/2**

0P-5 **P** **Taipo Prince (IRE)**[13] 3348 6-10-9 **93** (p) MichaelMcAlister(5) —
(Miss Kate Milligan) *w ldrs: lost pl 4th: blnd next: sn bhd: t.o whn p.u bef 3 out* **50/1**

3m 59.0s (-4.00) **Going Correction** -0.50s/f (Good) **10** Ran SP% **117.5**
Speed ratings: **90,89,88,85,77 63,—,—,—,—** CSF £50.86 CT £496.24 TOTE £11.90: £2.80, £1.60, £4.00; EX 90.70.
Owner Hogarth Racing **Bred** W Stafford **Trained** Stillington, N Yorks

FOCUS
A moderate winning time for a race of its type and with the favourite falling the form must rate as suspect.

NOTEBOOK
Cedar Rapids(IRE), despite again refusing to settle early on, got his chase career under Rules off to a perfect start yet has to rate a very fortunate winner nevertheless. He would have finished second to Ton-Chee had that rival not fallen at the last, but on the plus side his jumping was assured, and he is at the right end of the handicap to progress further in this sphere. *(op 12-1)*
Red Man(IRE), making his chase debut, had his chance from the front and looked to run very close to his official rating. He helps set the level of this form and deserves to find a race over fences. *(tchd 4-1)*
Persian Point was not disgraced and again did more than enough to suggest he needs a stiffer test.
Whaleef fell too early to tell how he would have fared. *(op 9-2 tchd 13-2)*
Ton-Chee had the race at his mercy prior to coming to grief at the final fence and must rate very unlucky. He is clearly capable of making amends on this sort of ground in the future, but his fall was particularly heavy and he may need time to recover from this experience. *(op 9-2 tchd 13-2)*
Longdale did not look happy at any stage and proved most disappointing. *(op 9-2 tchd 13-2)*

3563 LEYBURN MAIDEN NATIONAL HUNT FLAT RACE (CONDITIONAL JOCKEYS' AND AMATEUR RIDERS' RACE) 2m
4:00 (4:00) (Class 6) 4-7-Y-O **£2,055** (£599; £299)

Form RPR

1 **Mumbles Head (IRE)** 5-10-12 MrTJO'Brien(7) 92+
(P Bowen) *trckd ldrs: led 2f out: styd on* **11/2**[2]

0 **2** *3* **Arctic Ghost**[13] 3353 6-11-0 MarkNicolls(5) 85
(N Wilson) *led tl 3f out: kpt on: nt qckn fnl f* **22/1**

0 **3** *2 ½* **Heavenly Chorus**[42] 2830 4-9-5 JamesReveley(10) 65
(K G Reveley) *trckd ldrs: chal over 2f out: kpt on same pce appr fnl f* **13/2**

4 *3 ½* **The Saltire Tiger** 5-11-0 DesFlavin(5) 80+
(Mrs L B Normile) *in tch: led 3f out: hdd 2f out: one pce* **25/1**

0 **5** *6* **Floral Rhapsody**[19] 3273 5-10-7 ThomasDreaper(5) 66
(P Beaumont) *w ldrs: chal over 3f out: wknd 2f out* **12/1**

6 *2* **Madam Killeshandra** 6-10-5 PhilKinsella(7) 64
(A Parker) *hld up in rr: bhd 9f out: stdy hdwy 4f out: styng on nicely at fin* **16/1**

0 **7** *2 ½* **Darcy Wells**[74] 2192 5-11-0 StephenCraine(5) 69
(T D Easterby) *chsd ldrs: drvn along after 5f: one pce fnl 4f* **4/1**[1]

8 *1 ½* **Teviot Brig** 5-11-2 GaryBerridge(3) 67
(L Lungo) *mid-div: hdwy to chse ldrs 9f out: outpcd over 3f out: n.d after* **6/1**[3]

00 **9** *1 ½* **Freshford (IRE)**[11] 3399 4-10-3 DougieCostello(5) 55
(N Tinkler) *w ldrs: wknd over 3f out* **100/1**

0- **10** *21* **Teen Lady**[639] 28 7-10-5 MrSWByrne(7) 38
(Ferdy Murphy) *in rr: lost tch 7f out: sn bhd* **10/1**

11 *3 ½* **Harbour Buoy** 5-10-12 MrCDawson(7) 41
(J Wade) *bhd: lost tch 7f out* **50/1**

12 *29* **On Tilt** 5-10-12 MrOGreenall(7) 12
(M W Easterby) *a in rr: bhd fnl 9f: t.o* **8/1**

0 **13** *3* **Nightmare Bud (IRE)**[11] 3399 5-10-12 (t) DavidCullinane(7) —
(T J Fitzgerald) *chsd ldrs: lost pl 9f out: sn wl bhd: t.o* **66/1**

U **Eden Linty** 5-10-7 BrianHughes(5) —
(W Storey) *swvd lft s: unruly and sn uns rdr* **18/1**

3m 54.3s (-1.00) **Going Correction** -0.425s/f (Good)
WFA 4 from 5yo+ 11lb **14** Ran SP% **114.7**
Speed ratings: **85,83,82,80,77 76,75,74,73,63 61,47,45,—** CSF £126.34 TOTE £6.80: £2.50, £6.30, £2.00; EX 145.20 Place 6 £216.94, Place 5 £90.12.
Owner Ms Jill Day **Bred** John Sweeney **Trained** Little Newcastle, Pembrokes

FOCUS
A very moderate winning time when compared to the earlier selling hurdle and the field came home strung out, suggesting it is a race that is unlikely to produce many winners.

NOTEBOOK
Mumbles Head(IRE), a half-brother to Irish bumper winner Sonnerschien and Irish hurdle winner Crooked Mile, made a winning debut in good fashion despite running distinctly green in the home straight. He looks a nice prospect for connections and, considering his dam - who also won a bumper - finished fourth in the 1992 National Hunt Chase at Cheltenham, he can be expected to relish a stiffer test when sent over timber. *(op 5-1)*
Arctic Ghost stepped up markedly on the level of his recent debut over course and distance and finished a clear second best to the winner. He has scope, probably needs softer ground, and looks very much a future chaser.
Heavenly Chorus, well beaten on her debut over 12 furlongs at Newbury last time, improved *considerably for this stiffer test and shaped as though she would improve again for the experience. (tchd 6-1)*
The Saltire Tiger, whose dam was a fair hurdler/chaser, showed up well enough from the front and posted a pleasing debut effort. He has a future and is another who will need further over jumps.
Madam Killeshandra, reported to have been very difficult to handle, was doing her best work at the finish and can be rated better than the bare form. As a half-sister to the useful Lord Killeshandra, and considering that her dam is a half-sister to Earthmover, she looks a nice prospect for connections. *Official explanation: jockey said, regarding running and riding, his orders were to hold up the mare and try to get her to relax as she has had a wind operation and is liable not to breathe properly if tensing up, and to finish as close as he could without resorting to the whip; he said mare did not settle well initially getting detached from leaders in back straight when he felt mare could not have gone any faster without becoming unbalanced, and when he rode hands and heels in straight she stayed on through tired horses but didn't quicken up; trainer said mare is highly strung and liable to a breathing problem (tchd 18-1)*
Darcy Wells, a half-brother to Simply Dashing, was well backed to improve on his Wetherby debut 74 days previously and duly did just that, but never looked like getting to the leaders at any stage and again ran below expectations. *(op 13-2 tchd 7-2)*
Teviot Brig, half-brother to fair bumper/hurdles/chase winner Reivers Moon, proved easy to back and shaped as though he is already in need of a stiffer test. His stable are struggling for form at present and he can do better in time. *(op 3-1)*
T/Jkpt: Not won. T/Plt: £468.40 to a £1 stake. Pool: £54,385.25. 84.75 winning tickets. T/Qpdt: £128.90 to a £1 stake. Pool: £5,106.40. 29.30 winning tickets. JR

3367 HUNTINGDON (R-H)
Wednesday, January 25
3564 Meeting Abandoned - Frost

3422 PLUMPTON (L-H)
Thursday, January 26
3571 Meeting Abandoned - Frost

3386 WARWICK (L-H)
Thursday, January 26

OFFICIAL GOING: Soft (heavy in places on hurdle course) changing to soft after race 2 (1.50)
Wind: Moderate, half-against Weather: Fine

3577 ENTERTAIN CLIENTS AT WARWICK RACECOURSE CLASSIFIED HURDLE (11 hdls) 2m 5f
1:20 (1:20) (Class 5) 4-Y-0+ **£2,740** (£798; £399)

Form RPR

0026 **1** **Herecomestanley**[12] 3386 7-10-12 90 CharliePoste(7) 94+
(M F Harris) *hld up and bhd: hdwy 8th: rdn and hit 2 out: led sn after last: r.o* **12/1**

P632 **2** *2* **Mistified (IRE)**[59] 2552 5-11-2 90 RichardYoung(3) 92+
(J W Mullins) *hld up in tch: hit 4th: led 8th: rdn whn hit 2 out: nt fluent last: sn hdd: nt qckn* **10/1**

/324 **3** *3 ½* **He's A Rascal (IRE)**[26] 3147 8-11-5 88 (tp) TomDoyle 89+
(A J Lidderdale) *hld up and bhd: mstke 3 out: rdn and hdwy appr 2 out: no ex flat* **13/2**[3]

5434 **4** *8* **Foxmeade Dancer**[21] 3250 8-11-5 84 AndrewThornton 79
(P C Ritchens) *hld up in mid-div: hdwy 7th: ev ch 3 out: sn rdn: wknd appr last* **13/2**[3]

6562 **5** *3 ½* **Darko Karim**[24] 3222 4-10-2 90 (b) JayHarris(5) 64+
(R J Hodges) *prom: rdn appr 7th: ev ch whn hit 3 out: wkng whn hit 2 out* **20/1**

060P **6** *10* **Ol' Man River (IRE)**[26] 3139 6-11-5 90 MarkBradburne 65
(H D Daly) *hld up in tch: rdn 7th: wknd sn after 3 out* **33/1**

006 **7** *1 ¾* **Picot De Say**[44] 2811 4-10-7 78 OllieMcPhail 51
(C Roberts) *hld up in mid-div: hdwy 7th: ev ch 3 out: sn rdn: eased whn btn appr 2 out* **50/1**

3302 **8** *6* **Good Potential (IRE)**[21] 3250 10-11-5 90 (t) PJBrennan 57
(D J Wintle) *prom: rdn 7th: wknd 8th* **6/1**[2]

-421 **9** *20* **Bally Bolshoi (IRE)**[6] 3483 6-11-9 85 RichardJohnson 41
(Mrs S D Williams) *led: mstke 5th: hdd 8th: sn wknd* **7/4**[1]

05-0 **10** *7* **Homelife (IRE)**[73] 2249 8-10-12 MrRJBarrett(7) 30
(Mrs J A Saunders) *t.k.h: sn w ldrs: wknd after 6th* **33/1**

0604 **11** *shd* **Sandywell George**[112] 1656 11-11-5 83 (t) SamThomas 30
(L P Grassick) *nt fluent: a in rr: rdn appr 6th: lost tch 8th* **66/1**

P00F **U** **Magical Liaison (IRE)**[21] 3250 8-11-5 90 (b) CarlLlewellyn —
(W Jenks) *blnd and uns rdr 2nd* **16/1**

5m 17.8s (1.70) **Going Correction** +0.20s/f (Yiel)
WFA 4 from 5yo+ 12lb **12** Ran SP% **114.1**
Speed ratings: **90,89,87,84,83 79,79,76,69,66 66,—** CSF £113.39 TOTE £11.80: £3.20, £2.90, £2.50; EX 116.40.
Owner T Hart **Bred** Roy Matthews **Trained** Edgcote, Northants

FOCUS
A fairly competitive affair on paper, but low on quality. The form appears solid enough, rated through the second and the third close to his best.

NOTEBOOK
Herecomestanley, who had an excuse last time, ran on best of all in the closing stages while those around him were getting tired. Described by his trainer as a worrier, the seven-year-old hardly deserves much of a hike in the weights for this success. *(op 8-1)*
Mistified(IRE), a frustrating sort who often places but has yet to win a race, was not fluent at the last two flights and perhaps had he jumped those obstacles more cleanly he would have made things more difficult for the eventual winner. *(tchd 11-1)*
He's A Rascal(IRE), fitted with a tongue strap for the first time, got the longer trip well enough but was unable to reverse recent course form with Herecomestanley, despite being 4lb better off with that rival. He does not look all that genuine. *(op 5-1)*
Foxmeade Dancer, whose only successes to date have come in selling grade, would be better employed back in that sort of company. He is running to a fairly consistent level at present. *(op 8-1)*
Darko Karim did not get home having raced fairly keenly towards the head of affairs. *(tchd 22-1)*
Bally Bolshoi(IRE), giving weight all round, was a solid favourite but she failed to get home over this longer trip. *Official explanation: jockey said mare was never travelling (op 2-1 tchd 9-4 in a place)*

3578 DRIVE VAUXHALL LEAMINGTON AND VAUXHALL LEASING H'CAP CHASE (20 fncs) 3m 2f
1:50 (1:50) (Class 4) (0-110,110) 5-Y-0+ **£3,578** (£1,050; £525; £262)

Form RPR

-223 **1** **Finzi (IRE)**[10] 3424 8-10-7 **91** TomScudamore 101
(M Scudamore) *a.p: rdn 16th: led flat: all out* **9/2**[3]

2PP4 **2** *hd* **Special Conquest**[19] 3290 8-11-5 **103** AndrewThornton 113
(J W Mullins) *led to 9th: rdn to ld appr 14th: hdd flat: r.o* **12/1**

2P-2 **3** *17* **Hever Road (IRE)**[37] 2931 7-11-9 **107** (p) APMcCoy 110+
(M C Pipe) *hld up and bhd: hdwy 12th: mstke 14th: rdn 16th: ev ch 3 out: wnt rt and wknd last* **11/4**[1]

52FP **4** *23* **Pardini (USA)**[20] 3276 7-10-8 **92** (v[1]) JohnMcNamara 62
(M F Harris) *sn w ldr: led 9th tl appr 14th: wknd 16th* **16/1**

06P0 **5** *7* **Auburn Spirit**[24] 3212 11-11-7 **105** NoelFehily 68
(M D I Usher) *hld up in tch: wknd appr 14th* **7/1**

P300 **6** *shd* **Yann's (FR)**[17] 3326 10-11-10 **108** TomSiddall 71
(R T Phillips) *mid-div: lost pl 4th: n.d after* **16/1**

P06U **7** *nk* **Kadito**[21] 3252 10-10-0 **84** oh1 WayneHutchinson 46
(R Dickin) *mid-div: mstke 6th: bhd fr 13th* **25/1**

1122 **R** **Young Lorcan**[26] 3140 10-10-10 **101** .... RichardSpate(7) —
(Mrs K Waldron) *swvd rt s: ref to r: tk no part* **15/2**

FP0- **P** **Flying Trix (IRE)**[390] 3151 10-11-1 **99** .... RichardJohnson —
(P J Hobbs) *prom tl mstke 12th: t.o whn p.u bef 2 out* **4/1**[2]

P4U4 **P** **Sungates (IRE)**[16] 3331 10-11-12 **110** .... AndrewTinkler —
(C Tinkler) *hld up and bhd: hdwy 12th: rdn after 13th: wknd appr 14th: t.o whn p.u bef 2 out* **14/1**

6m 52.7s (-11.30) **Going Correction** +0.20s/f (Yiel) **10** Ran SP% **119.1**
Speed ratings: **103,102,97,90,88 88,88,—,—,—** CSF £56.91 CT £177.72 TOTE £4.50: £1.70, £3.50, £1.30; EX 55.30.
Owner The Meld Partnership **Bred** A W Buller **Trained** Bromsash, Herefordshire

FOCUS
A modest handicap but they went a fair pace and it proved a proper test in the ground. The form looks sound enough with the first two rated to their marks.

NOTEBOOK
Finzi(IRE), dropped 3lb since his last start over fences, had conditions in his favour and just held on from the rallying runner-up. He stays well but whether he can find the improvement to compete off a higher mark remains to be seen. *(op 4-1)*
Special Conquest is happier on better ground so this was a good performance in the circumstances. There to be shot at throughout, he kept responding to pressure and even rallied once headed on the run-in. He should be capable of winning a minor contest again once the ground turns in his favour. *(op 7-1)*
Hever Road(IRE), wearing cheekpieces for the first time, made a bad mistake at the 14th when threatening the leader, and that seemed to knock the stuffing out of him temporarily. He came back from that mistake to challenge turning into the straight though, but then looked less than keen about going past the leader, carrying his head awkwardly. A final fence blunder sealed his fate and he is clearly one to have reservations about. *(op 3-1 tchd 7-2 in places)*
Pardini(USA), pulled up in blinkers last time, had a visor on for the first time. He had not proved his stamina for this trip beforehand, and this race, which was run at a good pace, exposed his limitations on that front.
Auburn Spirit is currently on a 5lb lower mark than when last successful but he is not getting any younger and is struggling to find his best form at present. *(op 9-1 tchd 10-1)*

3579 RACING UK JUVENILE NOVICES' HURDLE (8 hdls) 2m
2:20 (2:21) (Class 4) 4-Y-O **£3,253** (£955; £477; £238)

Form RPR

1 **Opera De Coeur (FR)**[256] 4-10-12 .... MarkBradburne 107+
(H D Daly) *hld up in tch: hit 3 out: led 2 out: rdn whn lft clr last: r.o* **12/1**

2 *3 ½* **Screen Test**[144] 4-10-5 .... RobertThornton 95
(A King) *hld up: hdwy after 3rd: rdn 3 out: btn whn lft 2nd last* **20/1**

3 *5* **Trompette (USA)**[101] 4-10-5 .... AndrewTinkler 90
(N J Henderson) *a.p: rdn and ev ch appr 2 out: wknd appr last* **5/1**[3]

6 **4** *1 ½* **Ortega (FR)**[19] 3294 4-10-12 .... RichardJohnson 95
(P J Hobbs) *hld up and bhd: hdwy 3 out: sn rdn: wknd 2 out* **15/8**[1]

0 **5** *10* **Llamadas**[9] 3436 4-10-12 .... OllieMcPhail 87+
(C Roberts) *chsd ldrs: rdn appr 4th: wknd appr 2 out* **40/1**

6 *11* **Aberdeen Park**[58] 4-10-5 .... PhilipHide 67
(Mrs H Sweeting) *prom: nt fluent 3 out: wknd appr 2 out* **50/1**

50 **7** *15* **Globalized (IRE)**[15] 3340 4-10-12 .... PaulMoloney 59
(Mrs P Sly) *t.k.h in rr: nt fluent 3rd: nvr nr ldrs* **50/1**

2 **8** *¾* **Kickahead (USA)**[44] 2811 4-10-12 .... MickFitzgerald 58
(Ian Williams) *t.k.h: prom: rdn appr 2 out: sn wknd and eased* **5/2**[2]

0FP **9** *1 ¼* **Form And Beauty (IRE)**[9] 3436 4-10-12 .... JimmyMcCarthy 57
(C Roberts) *hld up and bhd: reminder after 3rd: hdwy appr 4th: wknd 3 out* **100/1**

606 **10** *16* **Bradders**[10] 3421 4-10-12 .... CarlLlewellyn 41
(J R Jenkins) *mstke 3rd: a bhd* **66/1**

40 **11** *hd* **Cape Guard**[65] 2425 4-10-12 .... HenryOliver 41
(F Jordan) *prom: nt fluent 3rd: rdn 4th: sn wknd* **33/1**

P **Viniyoga**[9] 4-10-12 .... TomScudamore —
(M H Tompkins) *a bhd: hmpd 3rd: t.o whn p.u bef 4th* **100/1**

6 **F** **Investment Wings (IRE)**[7] 3464 4-10-12 .... APMcCoy 105
(M C Pipe) *led: rdn and hdd 2 out: cl 2nd whn fell last* **5/1**[3]

P4 **P** **Maxamillion (IRE)**[35] 2954 4-10-12 .... JimCrowley —
(S Kirk) *a bhd: j. slowly 2nd: t.o whn p.u bef 3 out* **25/1**

0 **P** **Trappeto (IRE)**[23] 2345 4-10-9 .... WilliamKennedy(3) —
(C Smith) *hld up in tch: hit 1st: wknd appr 4th: t.o whn p.u bef 2 out* **100/1**

3m 56.5s (-1.80) **Going Correction** +0.20s/f (Yiel) **15** Ran SP% **126.8**
Speed ratings: **98,96,93,93,88 82,75,74,74,66 65,—,—,—,—** CSF £214.20 TOTE £12.90: £3.10, £5.80, £2.30; EX 178.80.
Owner The Hon Mrs A E Heber-Percy **Bred** N Burlot, Olivier Burlot,& Michel Le Bris **Trained** Stanton Lacy, Shropshire

FOCUS
An ordinary juvenile contest but the winner is value for further and the race could rate higher.

NOTEBOOK
Opera De Coeur(FR), a winner on the Flat in the French Provinces on his only previous start, appeared to just have the edge on Investment Wings when that one fell at the final flight. He looks the type to progress, but Cheltenham is apparently not on the agenda this year. *(op 11-1)*
Screen Test inherited second place when Investment Wings took a fall at the final flight. A modest performer on the level, if this debut effort is anything to go by she looks likely to achieve more over timber. Better ground might suit her.
Trompette(USA), a half-sister to the smart hurdler Ambobo, was twice a winner over middle distances on the Flat in the French Provinces. She travelled well into the straight but weakened over the final two flights on this hurdling debut and should prove stronger next time. *(op 4-1 tchd 11-2)*
Ortega(FR) got tired in the closing stages having raced keenly earlier in the race. Once again the impression left was that he would do better on a sounder surface. *(tchd 2-1)*
Llamadas settled better this time and ran a bit better as a result. He will have better chances in minor handicap company after one more run.
Kickahead(USA), a promising runner-up over this course and distance on his hurdling debut, failed to run his race. He was under pressure turning out of the back straight and was eased when held, the suspicion being that something was amiss. *(op 11-4 tchd 3-1)*
Investment Wings(IRE), who was well backed, was still fighting it out with the eventual winner when taking a crashing fall at the last. It is to be hoped that this tumble does not leave its mark but for now it would probably be wise not to back him. *(op 9-1)*

3580 RAY COOPER NOVICES' H'CAP CHASE (12 fncs) 2m
2:50 (2:50) (Class 3) (0-120,120) 5-Y-0+ **£6,506** (£1,910; £955; £477)

Form RPR

0-F1 **1** **Roznic (FR)**[9] 3432 8-10-9 **103** 7ex .... PhilipHide 115+
(P Winkworth) *hld up: hdwy after 5th: mstke 4 out: rdn to ld cl home* **7/2**[3]

-1P1 **2** *1* **Glengarra (IRE)**[10] 3418 9-11-3 **111** 7ex .... TomDoyle 122+
(D R Gandolfo) *chsd ldr: led 8th to 2 out: rdn to ld last: hdd cl home* **4/1**

-314 **3** *9* **The Local**[12] 3387 6-11-11 **119** .... APMcCoy 122+
(C R Egerton) *led: rdn appr 6th: hdd 8th: hit 4 out and 3 out: led 2 out to last: wknd flat* **3/1**[2]

321 **4** *17* **Smart Cavalier**[24] 3220 7-11-4 **112** .... (t) ChristianWilliams 103+
(P F Nicholls) *hld up in tch: stmbld appr 6th: mstke 8th: sn wknd* **9/4**[1]

3516 **5** *10* **Terivic**[43] 2817 6-11-9 **117** .... JohnMcNamara 98+
(K C Bailey) *t.k.h in rr: hdwy 8th: wknd after 3 out* **20/1**

0116 **R** **Lord Lington (FR)**[60] 2525 7-11-12 **120** .... HenryOliver —
(D J Wintle) *ref to r: tk no part* **20/1**

FC10 **P** **Vigoureux (FR)**[16] 3334 7-10-3 **100** .... (p) WilliamKennedy(3) —
(S Gollings) *prom tl wknd appr 6th: t.o whn p.u bef 7th* **25/1**

4m 6.30s **7** Ran SP% **111.4**
CSF £16.80 TOTE £4.30: £2.60, £1.90; EX 23.10.
Owner Etoile Racing **Bred** Francis Faure **Trained** Ramsnest Common, Surrey

FOCUS
A modest handicap, run at a decent clip, and the first two came clear. The form appears solid with the placed horses close to their marks.

NOTEBOOK
Roznic(FR), off the mark over fences at Folkestone in a similar event nine days previously, survived an error four out and found plenty for his rider's urgings to ultimately mow down the runner-up and win going away. He has clearly been much-improved since being sent over fences recently, is well suited by a soft surface, and will be capable of even better when reverting to a stiffer track in the future. His stable has made a bright start to the year. *(op 5-1)*
Glengarra(IRE), back to winning ways at Fakenham ten days previously, was only pegged back on the run-in and finished nicely clear of the rest. This was a solid effort under his penalty and, while he is due to go up another 2lb in the future, he could be capable of defying that rise if able to maintain this current mood. *(op 7-2 tchd 9-2)*
The Local saw his jumping deteriorate with bad mistakes at the fourth and third-last fences and that effectively ended his chance of success. He has started life over fences from a career-high mark, but he remains open to improvement in this sphere, and can win races providing he brushes up his jumping. *(op 5-2 tchd 10-3)*
Smart Cavalier, making his handicap debut, found things happening all too quickly for his liking and was never a serious threat. This has to rate slightly disappointing, and he clearly has his limitations, but ought to be better off when faced with a stiffer test in the future. *(op 85-40 tchd 2-1)*
Lord Lington(FR), returning from a 60-day break, disgraced himself at the start by refusing to take part and has it all to prove after this. *(op 25-1)*

3581 GRAHAM HOSKIN RACEGOERS CLUB H'CAP HURDLE (12 hdls) 3m 1f
3:20 (3:20) (Class 3) (0-120,120) 4-Y-0+ **£5,204** (£1,528; £764; £381)

Form RPR

/1-1 **1** **Passenger Omar (IRE)**[26] 3146 8-10-4 **101** ....(t) WilliamKennedy(3) 111+
(Noel T Chance) *hld up and bhd: hdwy 7th: sn rdn: led 2 out: nt fluent and hdd last: rallied to ld cl home* **4/1**[1]

6P6F **2** *½* **Jiver (IRE)**[7] 3469 7-11-2 **110** .... (v[1]) TomScudamore 117
(M Scudamore) *j. slowly and lost pl 1st: hdwy 2nd: led 3 out: sn rdn: hdd 2 out: led last: hdd cl home* **25/1**

4C-5 **3** *12* **Clan Royal (FR)**[55] 2609 11-11-1 **109** .... APMcCoy 105+
(Jonjo O'Neill) *hld up and bhd: hdwy appr 8th: rdn after 3 out: wknd appr last* **13/2**[2]

111- **4** *hd* **Silver Birch (IRE)**[394] 3049 9-11-5 **113** .... ChristianWilliams 108
(P F Nicholls) *led appr 2nd to 3 out: sn rdn: wknd appr last* **4/1**[1]

-P45 **5** *3 ½* **Chanticlier**[21] 3253 9-10-10 **104** .... (t) RobertThornton 95
(R T Phillips) *hld up and bhd: hdwy 8th: rdn after 3 out: wknd 2 out* **25/1**

1654 **6** *hd* **Pardon What**[2] 3548 10-10-11 **105** .... (b) MickFitzgerald 96
(S Lycett) *hld up and bhd: hdwy on ins after 7th: wknd 2 out* **20/1**

2-4P **7** *18* **Star Angler (IRE)**[43] 2825 8-11-5 **113** .... RichardJohnson 86
(H D Daly) *hld up and bhd: carried lft 5th: reminders after 6th: hdwy after 7th: wknd appr 2 out* **25/1**

61-3 **8** *shd* **Sunset Light (IRE)**[87] 1959 8-11-12 **120** .... TomDoyle 93
(C Tinkler) *hld up in mid-div: hdwy after 7th: wknd after 3 out* **8/1**[3]

P312 **9** *6* **Keepers Mead (IRE)**[30] 3018 8-11-8 **116** .... RobertWalford 83
(R H Alner) *led tl appr 2nd: prom tl wknd after 3 out* **10/1**

1/63 **10** *7* **Euradream (IRE)**[41] 2862 8-10-11 **105** .... JamesDavies 65
(Jean-Rene Auvray) *hld up towards rr: rdn after 6th: wknd appr 8th* **8/1**[3]

151P **11** *2* **Moustique De L'Isle (FR)**[31] 2965 6-10-13 **107** ....(b) NoelFehily 65
(C C Bealby) *prom: nt fluent 7th: wknd 8th* **10/1**

0P23 **P** **Kingsbay**[26] 3146 7-10-11 **105** .... JimCrowley —
(H Morrison) *prom to 7th: bhd whn p.u bef 2 out* **12/1**

-3PP **P** **Lalagune (FR)**[30] 3018 7-11-5 **113** .... MarcusFoley —
(Miss E C Lavelle) *a bhd: mstke 3rd: hmpd 5th: t.o whn p.u bef 3 out* **50/1**

P3/0 **P** **Better Thyne (IRE)**[42] 2845 10-10-0 **101** ow1 ....(p) LiamHeard(7) —
(Mrs S D Williams) *bhd: rdn 2nd: j.lft 5th: t.o whn p.u bef 8th* **25/1**

-U1U **P** **Concert Pianist**[9] 3438 11-11-9 **117** .... PhilipHide —
(P Winkworth) *hld up in tch: wknd after 7th: t.o whn p.u bef 2 out* **20/1**

/1P- **P** **Mike Simmons**[599] 662 10-10-1 **95** .... OllieMcPhail —
(L P Grassick) *prom: rdn after 6th: wknd after 7th: t.o whn p.u bef 9th* **66/1**

6m 22.0s (-8.30) **Going Correction** +0.20s/f (Yiel) **16** Ran SP% **129.8**
Speed ratings: **107,106,103,102,101 101,95,95,94,91 91,—,—,—,— —** CSF £112.64 CT £671.14 TOTE £6.10: £1.50, £5.50, £2.40, £1.60; EX 260.60.
Owner Mrs V Griffiths **Bred** Matt O'Hara **Trained** Upper Lambourn, Berks

FOCUS
A fair handicap, run at a solid pace, and the first two pulled clear. The third sets the standard and the race was notable for the running of leading Grand National hopefuls Clan Royal and Silver Birch who both shaped with promise.

NOTEBOOK
Passenger Omar(IRE), raised 5lb for winning on his recent comeback over course and distance 26 days previously, followed-up and landed the hat-trick in typically game fashion under a strong ride from Kennedy. While he clearly resumed this season on a lenient handicap mark, he is the type of horse the Handicapper has trouble assessing, as he only looks to do just enough in his races and therefore could still be on a fair mark when reassessed after this. In the long term he looks a nice staying chaser in the making, and he has very few miles on the clock for his age. *(op 5-1 tchd 11-2 in places)*
Jiver(IRE), reverting to hurdles after falling at Chepstow last time and equipped with a first-time visor, failed to cope with the renewed challenge of the winner on the run-in and was just held. Considering he was well clear of the rest at the finish, this must rate a very pleasing effort, and his confidence should have been nicely restored by this. *(tchd 33-1)*
Clan Royal(FR) again caught the eye travelling nicely under a patient ride and, while he was ultimately well beaten by the front pair, it can be considered little surprise that he got outpaced rounding the turn for home. This will have provided a further step up the ladder towards his preparation for another crack at the Grand National in April and he looks to be in good heart at present. *(op 6-1)*
Silver Birch(IRE), last seen landing a hat-trick over fences with a ready success in the Welsh Grand National in 2004, was making his comeback over timber in order to protect his chase mark ahead of a tilt at the Grand National in April. He showed up nicely from the front until tiring from three out and, considering he should improve a deal for the outing and is currently rated 29lb lower over hurdles, he can certainly be placed to advantage if connections opt to find another opportunity in this sphere. As regards the National in April, he certainly appeals as a leading player if taking his chance, and his most likely next target is the County Gentleman's Chase at Wincanton, shortly after the National weights are published. *(op 7-2 tchd 9-2)*

Chanticlier was doing his best work at the finish and ran another sound enough race. He remains a maiden, but the recent application of a tongue tie has helped him and he can find easier assignments from his current rating.

3582 BANBURY H'CAP CHASE (17 fncs) 2m 4f 110y
3:50 (3:50) (Class 4) (0-105,105) 5-Y-0+ **£3,578** (£1,050; £525; £262)

Form RPR

433 **1** **Nice Try (IRE)**^{24} [3219] 7-11-12 **105** SamThomas 116+
(Miss Venetia Williams) *hld up: mstke 6th: hdwy 13th: led 3 out: mstke 2 out: sn hung lft: rdn out* **4/1**^{2}

0461 **2** *2* **Smeathe's Ridge**^{9} [3430] 8-10-8 **87** 7ex MarkBradburne 93
(J A B Old) *hld up in tch: led 13th to 3 out: sn rdn: ev ch last: nt qckn* **11/10**^{1}

2FP5 **3** *15* **Galapiat Du Mesnil (FR)**^{9} [3430] 12-10-11 **90** PhilipHide 83+
(R Gurney) *led to 4th: led 7th tl appr 11th: mstke 12th: wknd 4 out* **25/1**

-U44 **4** *3* **Jour De Mee (FR)**^{31} [2986] 9-10-11 **90** JimCrowley 78
(Mrs H Dalton) *prom: led appr 11th to 13th: wknd 3 out* **5/1**^{3}

P5PP **5** *13* **Our Jolly Swagman**^{9} [3434] 11-10-9 **88** (v) AndrewThornton 63
(J W Mullins) *hld up: rdn after 13th: sn struggling* **8/1**

P25F **6** *½* **Look To The Future (IRE)**^{43} [2818] 12-9-9 **79** LeeStephens$^{(5)}$ 54
(M J M Evans) *chsd ldr: led 4th to 7th: prom: hit 13th: sn wknd* **8/1**

5m 26.5s (1.00) **Going Correction** +0.20s/f (Yiel) **6** Ran SP% **110.4**
Speed ratings: **92,91,85,84,79 79** CSF £9.02 TOTE £3.90: £1.90, £1.30; EX 9.70.
Owner The Juggins Partnership **Bred** Gregory And Margaret Rossiter **Trained** Kings Caple, H'fords

FOCUS
A moderate handicap, run at just an average gallop, and the form makes sense although the form is not strong.

NOTEBOOK
Nice Try(IRE) ◆ clouted the penultimate fence, and hung left when asked for maximum effort, but it was still not enough to stop him from registering a first success under Rules under top weight. He had left the impression on his three previous outings over hurdles that he was capable of better and, as a well-bred former point winner, it was not a surprise that he was sent straight over fences for this handicap bow. The manner of this success suggests he has a fair bit more to offer yet in this sphere and he should improve again when reverting to a stiffer test. *(op 10-3)*
Smeathe's Ridge, under a 7lb penalty for making a successful chase debut at Folkestone nine days previously, had every chance of following-up and finished well clear of the remainder of his rivals. He will not be inconvenienced a return to a longer trip on this evidence and can find compensation in the coming weeks. *(tchd 6-5 and 5-4 in places)*
Galapiat Du Mesnil(FR) continues to look regressive and really is a shadow of his former self.
Jour De Mee(FR), back in trip, was found wanting approaching the third last fence and again disappointed. *(op 9-2 tchd 4-1)*

3583 RACING UK STANDARD OPEN NATIONAL HUNT FLAT RACE 2m
4:20 (4:21) (Class 6) 5-6-Y-0 **£1,713** (£499; £249)

Form RPR

1 **Mam Ratagan** 5-11-4 MickFitzgerald 95+
(N J Henderson) *hld up in tch: led over 1f out: drvn out* **6/4**^{1}

2 *1 ½* **Somedo Somedont**^{263} 6-11-4 ChristianWilliams 94
(P F Nicholls) *unruly s: a.p: ev ch 1f out: hrd rdn: nt qckn* **11/2**^{3}

3 *2* **Hopkins (IRE)** 5-11-4 RichardJohnson 92
(H D Daly) *hld up in mid-div: hdwy 8f out: led over 5f out: rdn and hdd over 1f out: no ex ins fnl f* **7/2**^{2}

4 *1 ¼* **For All Mankind** 5-11-4 CarlLlewellyn 90
(M Pitman) *hld up in tch: rdn and outpcd over 3f out: styd on fnl f* **10/1**

5 *1 ¼* **Nougat De L'Isle (FR)** 5-11-4 JoeTizzard 89
(C L Tizzard) *hld up: hdwy over 5f out: rdn and outpcd over 3f out: styd on fnl f* **12/1**

06 **6** *11* **Supreme Copper (IRE)**^{24} [3216] 6-11-4 TomDoyle 81+
(Miss E C Lavelle) *hld up and bhd: stmbld 9f out: hdwy 4f out: wknd over 1f out* **9/1**

65 **7** *dist* **Flemens River (IRE)**^{24} [3216] 5-11-4 MarkBradburne —
(C J Down) *hld up: hdwy over 7f out: rdn over 6f out: sn wknd: t.o* **20/1**

0 **8** *8* **All Fun And Games (IRE)**^{31} [2987] 5-11-4 HenryOliver —
(John R Upson) *t.k.h: set modest pce: hdd over 5f out: wknd over 4f out: t.o* **66/1**

0 **9** *21* **Hoober**^{31} [2987] 5-11-1 RobertStephens$^{(3)}$ —
(J Gallagher) *prom 9f: t.o* **100/1**

0- **10** *nk* **Marys Moment**^{305} [4589] 6-10-6 TomGreenway$^{(5)}$ —
(P A Pritchard) *a bhd: t.o* **66/1**

U **Worth A Glance** 5-10-11 MrPCallaghan$^{(7)}$ —
(H D Daly) *bhd fnl 8f: t.o whn hmpd and uns rdr over 1f out* **20/1**

P **Ballycross (IRE)** 6-10-11 StevenCrawford$^{(7)}$ —
(N A Twiston-Davies) *hld up: hdwy over 6f out: wknd over 3f out: p.u over 1f out: broke leg: dead* **10/1**

3m 54.4s (-4.40) **Going Correction** +0.20s/f (Yiel) **12** Ran SP% **127.0**
Speed ratings: **101,100,99,98,98 92**,—,—,—,— —,— CSF £10.52 TOTE £2.30: £1.50, £2.00, £1.70; EX 16.10 Place 6 £222.19, Place 5 £52.68.
Owner N J Henderson **Bred** Cyril Humphris **Trained** Upper Lambourn, Berks
■ Stewards' Enquiry : Christian Williams four-day ban: used whip with excessive force and without giving time to respond (Feb 6-9)

FOCUS
A potentially above-average bumper, run at a fair gallop, and the first five came clear at the finish.

NOTEBOOK
Mam Ratagan, a half-brother to this season's promising novice hurdler Straw Bear, dug deep when for maximum effort by Fitzgerald approaching two out and duly responded to make a winning debut in ready fashion. His dam stayed 12 furlongs on the Flat, so he will probably be suited by further when sent over hurdles in due course, yet appeals as the type to defy a penalty in this sphere with the experience under his belt. *(op 15-8 tchd 2-1)*
Somedo Somedont, a former winning pointer and half-brother to winning Irish hurdler Purple Patch, had every chance on this debut for new connections and posted a pleasing debut effort. He not surprisingly lacked the same finishing kick as the winner and, while he has the ability to go one better in this division, he already looks to be crying out for the return to a longer trip. *(op 6-1)*
Hopkins(IRE), a 67,000euros purchase and a half-brother to his yard's smart novice chaser Billyvoddan, had his chance and was only found wanting approaching the final furlong. This must rate a promising effort, he clearly has an engine, and looks a nice future prospect for novice hurdles where he will no doubt enjoy being faced with a longer trip. *(op 4-1 tchd 9-2)*
For All Mankind, a 12,000gns purchase whose dam was a fair chaser at up to three miles, was doing all of his best work at the finish and looks bound to improve plenty from this debut experience. He is another who is going to relish further in time. *(op 8-1)*
Nougat De L'Isle(FR), who cost 18,000gns and is related to three winning French Jumpers, was another doing his best work at the finish and posted a satisfactory debut display. His yard's *runners invariably improve for their first outing and he can be expected to better this in due course. (op 9-1)*
T/Plt: £208.90 to a £1 stake. Pool: £56,124.95. 196.05 winning tickets. T/Qpdt: £39.10 to a £1 stake. Pool: £5,174.70. 97.90 winning tickets. KH

3584 - (Foreign Racing) - See Raceform Interactive

^{2851}GOWRAN PARK (R-H)
Thursday, January 26

OFFICIAL GOING: Hurdle course - yielding; chase course - good to yielding

3585a ALO DUFFIN MEMORIAL GALMOY HURDLE (GRADE 3) 3m
1:45 (1:45) 5-Y-0+ **£17,958** (£5,268; £2,510; £855)

RPR

1 **Emotional Moment (IRE)**^{29} [3080] 9-11-10 145 BJGeraghty 154
(T J Taaffe, Ire) *mde all: nt fluent 5th: rdn clr after 3 out: slt mstke next: styd on wl* **4/5**^{1}

2 *8* **Strangely Brown (IRE)**^{29} [3080] 5-11-7 RWalsh 144+
(E McNamara, Ire) *trckd ldrs in 3rd: impr into 2nd 1/2-way: rdn and outpcd after 3 out: no imp fr next* **11/8**^{2}

3 *6* **Jack High (IRE)**^{29} [3081] 11-11-8 128 GCotter 138+
(T M Walsh, Ire) *hld up: mod 4th 4 out: mod 3rd after 2 out: kpt on same pce* **20/1**

4 *8* **Holy Orders (IRE)**^{11} [3413] 9-11-12 135 (b) DJCondon 134
(W P Mullins, Ire) *hld up towards rr: prog into mod 3rd 4 out: no ex after next* **12/1**^{3}

5 *2* **Yogi (IRE)**^{67} [2388] 10-11-8 133 DNRussell 128
(Thomas Foley, Ire) *settled 2nd: dropped to 3rd 1/2-way: lost tch whn slt mstke 4 out: kpt on same pce fr next* **20/1**

6 *dist* **Arkadian (IRE)**^{4} [3519] 7-10-13 71 (p) AO'Shea$^{(3)}$ —
(Mrs A M O'Shea, Ire) *a towards rr: wknd 5 out: completely t.o* **300/1**

6m 18.7s **Going Correction** -0.10s/f (Good) **6** Ran SP% **115.2**
Speed ratings: **113,110,108,105,105** — CSF £2.34 TOTE £1.90: £1.60, £1.70; DF 2.40.
Owner Watercork Syndicate **Bred** Tom Taaffe **Trained** Straffan, Co Kildare

NOTEBOOK
Emotional Moment(IRE), who won this race last year, made every yard for a repeat victory. He appreciated this track more than Leopardsotwn, which is a bit sharp for him, and the plan is now to either go straight to Cheltenham for the World Hurdle or take in the Boyne Hurdle. *(op 4/5 tchd 9/10)*
Strangely Brown(IRE) finished behind Emotional Moment at Leopardstown and, with the track favouring his older rival better this time, the distance he was beaten was even further. Perhaps he would appreciate being raced over a little shorter. *(op 5/4 tchd 6/4)*
Jack High(IRE), last year's Betfred Gold Cup winner, was staying on at the finish, and perhaps better ground in the spring will see an upturn in his fortunes. *(op 16/1)*
Holy Orders(IRE) is a difficult horse to place off his current rating. *(op 16/1)*

3587a ELLEN CONSTRUCTION THYESTES H'CAP CHASE (GRADE A) 3m
2:45 (2:46) 5-Y-0+ **£44,827** (£13,103; £6,206; £2,068)

RPR

1 **Dun Doire (IRE)**^{25} [3192] 7-9-10 115 PCarberry 134+
(A J Martin, Ire) *hld up in rr: smooth hdwy 4 out: 4th next: rdn to ld 2 out: bad mstke last: kpt on wl* **9/4**^{1}

2 *1 ½* **Coljon (IRE)**^{31} [3012] 8-10-1 123 (p) RMMoran$^{(3)}$ 137+
(Paul Nolan, Ire) *attempted to make all: rdn after 4 out: strly pressed after 3 out: hdd next: kpt on wl u.p* **12/1**

3 *3* **A New Story (IRE)**^{11} [3410] 8-9-7 119 DGHogan$^{(7)}$ 130+
(Michael Hourigan, Ire) *hld up: 8th 3 out: kpt on wl u.p fr next* **7/1**^{3}

4 *hd* **Barrow Drive**^{25} [3199] 10-11-5 138 (t) BJGeraghty 149
(Anthony Mullins, Ire) *a.p: 4th 4 out: 2nd and chal next: 3rd and no ex last: kpt on same pce* **16/1**

5 *4* **Colnel Rayburn (IRE)**^{25} [3193] 10-11-3 136 DNRussell 143
(Paul Nolan, Ire) *mid-div: prog into 5th 4 out: cl up and chal 2 out: no ex bef last* **10/1**

6 *1 ½* **Coolnahilla (IRE)**^{11} [3410] 10-10-8 127 (b) DFO'Regan 132
(W J Burke, Ire) *trckd ldrs in 5th: prog 5 out: 3rd after next: rdn bef 3 out: no ex fr 2 out* **16/1**

7 *¾* **Randwick Roar (IRE)**^{30} [3061] 7-9-12 117 PWFlood 122
(P M J Doyle, Ire) *mid-div: 7th appr 1/2-way: 5th after 4 out: no ex fr next* **14/1**

8 *hd* **Doodle Addle (IRE)**^{30} [3053] 10-10-0 122 RCColgan$^{(3)}$ 126
(J T R Dreaper, Ire) *mid-div: 9th 1/2-way: no ex 4 out* **33/1**

9 *4* **Jaquouille (FR)**^{30} [3053] 9-10-3 122 DJCasey 122
(A L T Moore, Ire) *mid-div: mstke 8 out: prog bef 4 out: 7th 3 out: sn no ex* **9/1**

10 *3 ½* **Point Barrow (IRE)**^{30} [3053] 8-10-9 128 (t) NPMadden 125
(P Hughes, Ire) *towards rr and reminders early: prog into mid-div 1/2-way: no ex bef 4 out* **10/1**

11 *nk* **Livingstonebramble (IRE)**^{243} [561] 10-10-10 129 RWalsh 126
(W P Mullins, Ire) *hld up: bad mstke 9th: no ex fr bef 4 out* **12/1**

12 *20* **Fatherofthebride (IRE)**^{30} [3053] 10-9-10 115 (b) JMAllen 92
(Joseph Crowley, Ire) *sn cl up in 2nd: blnd 4 out: wknd bef next: t.o* **25/1**

P **Catalpa Cargo (IRE)**^{25} [3199] 12-10-8 127 (b^{1}) JRBarry —
(E Sheehy, Ire) *chsd ldrs early: bhd whn p.u bef 7th* **33/1**

P **Kymandjen (IRE)**^{25} [3199] 9-11-2 135 JLCullen —
(Paul Nolan, Ire) *chsd ldrs to 1/2-way: sn no ex: p.u bef 5 out* **13/2**^{2}

P **Cane Brake (IRE)**^{30} [3053] 7-10-12 131 RMPower —
(David Wachman, Ire) *chsd ldrs to 1/2-way: wknd 6 out: p.u bef 3 out* **33/1**

P **Howaya Pet (IRE)**^{18} [3310] 10-10-1 123 (t) MPWalsh$^{(3)}$ —
(Gerard Keane, Ire) *towards rr: reminders 8th: t.o 5 out: p.u bef 3 out* **33/1**

P **Marcus Du Berlais (FR)**^{30} [3053] 9-11-3 136 CO'Dwyer —
(A L T Moore, Ire) *nvr a factor: reminders 7th: trailing whn p.u bef 3 out* **25/1**

P **The Premier Cat (IRE)**^{25} [3199] 10-10-10 129 (b^{1}) GCotter —
(T Cahill, Ire) *chsd ldrs in 3rd: lost pl 6 out: wknd 4 out: p.u bef 3 out* **25/1**

6m 10.7s **Going Correction** -0.10s/f (Good) **18** Ran SP% **141.9**
Speed ratings: **109,108,107,107,106 105,105,105,103,102 102,96**,—,—,— —,—,— CSF £33.15 CT £184.61 TOTE £3.60: £2.20, £2.40, £2.00, £3.50; DF 37.90.
Owner Dunderry Racing Syndicate **Bred** Mrs Sarah Martin **Trained** Summerhill, Co. Meath

NOTEBOOK
Dun Doire(IRE), who got into the race as a reserve, was a well-backed favourite and completed a five-timer in good style, travelling well off the pace and winning with more in hand than the margin of victory would suggest. He has progressed a long way since starting over fences and it would be a surprise if there was not more improvement to come. He has a number of options at Cheltenham, of which the Kim Muir might be the likeliest, but he will demand respect wherever he turns up.
Coljon(IRE) tried to make all but the progressive and still well-handicapped winner proved too good on the day. He still ran well, though, seeing out the trip stongly, and there are more races to be won with him over this sort of distance.
A New Story(IRE) ran a solid race but would ideally have preferred another half mile.

Barrow Drive ran well under top weight but the Handicapper will not give cut him any slack on the back of this effort.
Colnel Rayburn(IRE), having his first start over fences since last year's Grand National, ran a solid race. He will be hoping for softer ground at Aintree this time around.
Coolnahilla(IRE) had the blinkers back on for the first time in over a year, but he really wants softer ground than this.
Kymandjen(IRE) came here on the back of an interrupted preparation and he failed to run to his race.

3588 - 3590a (Foreign Racing) - See Raceform Interactive

3415 FAKENHAM (L-H)

Friday, January 27

OFFICIAL GOING: Good

The ground was described as 'mainly good but loose on top'.
Wind: Almost nil Weather: Overcast and cold

3591 THE PRINCE OF WALES STAND FOR PRIVATE FUNCTIONS NOVICES' HURDLE (DIV I) (9 hdls) 2m

1:10 (1:11) (Class 4) 5-Y-0+ **£2,927** (£859; £429; £214)

Form				RPR
0	1		**Muntami (IRE)**[15] 2249 5-10-12 ... AndrewTinkler (John A Harris) *midfield: drvn along 3 out: 5l 3rd next: styd on u.p to ld after last: forged clr* **22/1**	95+
	2	1 1/4	**Easy Laughter (IRE)**[62] 5-10-12 ... RobertThornton (A King) *trckd ldrs: lft cl 3rd at 6th: rdn to ld 2 out: bmpd last: sn hdd: nt qckn* **3/1**[2]	94+
5-0	3	1 1/2	**Ile Facile (IRE)**[15] 3354 5-10-12 ... NoelFehily (B De Haan) *set gd pce: drvn and hdd 2 out: ev ch last: wknd cl home* **12/1**[3]	92+
P5	4	11	**Zonic Boom (FR)**[7] 2423 6-10-9 ... TJPhelan[(3)] (Mrs H Dalton) *cl up: hit 4th: lft 2nd 6th: rdn whn blnd 2 out: wknd qckly* **12/1**[3]	82+
06-0	5	shd	**Petrovka (IRE)**[155] 1323 6-10-2 ... WilliamKennedy[(3)] (S Gollings) *midfield: u.p 5th: nvr on terms after* **100/1**	73
0-10	6	1 1/2	**Clydeoneeyed**[73] 2256 7-10-12 70 ... ShaneWalsh[(7)] (K F Clutterbuck) *midfield: rdn 5th: sn struggling* **100/1**	86
6	7	1 3/4	**That Man Fox**[26] 3188 5-10-12 ... AntonyProcter (Lucinda Featherstone) *towards rr: lost tch 6th* **150/1**	77
450	8	22	**Butler Services (IRE)**[64] 2455 6-10-12 ... APMcCoy (Jonjo O'Neill) *a bhd: rdn and lost tch v tamely after 5th* **25/1**	55
0-	9	1 3/4	**Quest On Air**[45] 1909 7-10-12 ... (v[1]) JodieMogford (J R Jenkins) *j.rt and v slow 1st and 2nd: last most of way: t.o 6th* **100/1**	53
-0P0	P		**Judge'N'Thomas**[15] 3355 6-10-12 ... SeanCurran (M R Bosley) *prom tl wknd bef 6th: t.o and p.u 2 out* **250/1**	—
4	F		**Cordial (IRE)**[17] 3328 6-10-12 ... RussGarritty (J J Quinn) *pressed ldr: drew level and fell heavily 6th: dead* **4/6**[1]	—
P	P		**Bjorling**[3] 2702 5-10-2 ... (tp) CareyWilliamson[(10)] (M J Gingell) *bhd: struggling bdly 5th: t.o and p.u 3 out* **250/1**	—

4m 2.90s (-6.00) **Going Correction** -0.15s/f (Good) 12 Ran SP% **113.0**
Speed ratings: **109,108,107,102,102 101,100,89,88,— —,—** CSF £85.21 TOTE £28.80: £3.60, £1.50, £2.50; EX 109.00.
Owner Dermot Owens **Bred** Shadwell Estate Company Limited **Trained** Eastwell, Leics

FOCUS
A strong gallop and the winning time was good, 7.6 seconds faster than the second division, but a weak event after Cordial's fatal departure and the form is not easy to rate.

NOTEBOOK
Muntami(IRE) travelled strongly under a patient ride and in the end his superior stamina carried the day. *(op 20-1)*
Easy Laughter(IRE), who ended up wearing blinkers on the Flat, took charge at the second last but could not quite last out. His stamina is suspect and he will need to stick to sharp tracks. *(op 10-3 tchd 7-2)*
Ile Facile(IRE), very warm at the start, took them along at a good gallop but the needle was on empty near the line. At least this qualifies him for a handicap mark.
Zonic Boom(FR), back over hurdles, was on the heels of the leaders when he blundered his chance away two out. *(op 17-2)*
Petrovka(IRE), making her hurdling debut, could never muster the pace to enter the argument.
Clydeoneeyed, off the mark in selling company here last May, had an impossible task under his penalty. *(op 150-1)*
Cordial(IRE) was bang in the firing line when falling with fatal consequences four out. *(op 8-11 tchd 5-6 in a places and 4-5 in places)*

3592 FAKENHAM HUNTER'S LODGE ACCOMMODATION CONDITIONAL JOCKEYS' H'CAP HURDLE (9 hdls) 2m

1:40 (1:41) (Class 4) (0-100,98) 4-Y-0+ **£3,253** (£955; £477; £238)

Form				RPR
2/4-	1		**Beau Torero (FR)**[515] 1326 8-10-10 90 ... TomMessenger[(8)] (B N Pollock) *mde all: rdn and hit 2 out: outbattled rival fr last* **14/1**	94
3P02	2	nk	**The Castilian (FR)**[8] 3456 4-10-4 95 ... (v) AndrewGlassonbury[(8)] (M C Pipe) *prom: nt fluent fr 3 out: wnt 2nd next: chal last: declined to overtake* **4/1**[2]	90+
F006	3	7	**Sunley Future (IRE)**[25] 3223 7-11-0 92 ... [1] CharliePoste[(6)] (M F Harris) *keen: sn pressing wnr: rdn bef 3 out: demoted next: sn btn: hit last* **40/1**	90+
6F60	4	9	**All Bleevable**[10] 2964 9-11-5 96 ... (p) JohnKington[(5)] (Mrs S Lamyman) *prom: rdn 5th: outpcd bef 3 out* **25/1**	84
160P	5	3	**Bayadere (GER)**[46] 2552 6-11-1 90 ... ShaneWalsh[(3)] (K F Clutterbuck) *midfield: rdn and lost tch 6th* **33/1**	75
5P56	6	7	**Apadi (USA)**[14] 3379 10-11-4 96 ... CiaranEddery[(6)] (R C Guest) *j.big 1st: pld hrd in rr: lost tch 6th* **20/1**	77+
-3FP	7	11	**Tignasse (FR)**[41] 1987 5-11-9 95 ... (b) ColinBolger (G L Moore) *bhd: rdn after 5th: sn lost tch* **14/1**	62
16P	8	11	**Kristinor (FR)**[29] 2632 4-10-9 98 ... EamonDehdashti[(6)] (G L Moore) *chsd ldrs tl rdn bef 3 out: nt keen and sn btn* **13/2**[3]	43
4FP0	9	12	**Interstice**[11] 3418 9-10-10 85 ... MrJAJenkins[(3)] (M J Gingell) *plld v hrd in rr tl c off bridle bef 6th: nt keen and sn remote* **100/1**	29
006-	10	1	**Ethan Snowflake**[337] 4030 7-11-3 89 ... OwynNelmes (N B King) *midfield: rdn 6th: lost tch qckly: t.o 2 out* **25/1**	32
/P00	P		**Captain Smoothy**[32] 2967 6-11-12 98 ... StephenCraine (M J Gingell) *dropped rr and rdn 4th: hopelessly t.o whn plld 3 out* **33/1**	—
0011	P		**Gustavo**[37] 2940 5-11-2 91 ... LiamTreadwell[(3)] (Miss Venetia Williams) *rdn and nvr gng wl in rr: lost tch 5th: t.o whn mstke 3 out: sn p.u* **11/10**[1]	—

4m 4.00s (-4.90) **Going Correction** -0.15s/f (Good)
WFA 4 from 5yo+ 11lb 12 Ran SP% **116.1**
Speed ratings: **106,105,102,97,96 92,87,81,75,75 —,—** CSF £64.35 CT £2210.90 TOTE £12.80: £2.80, £1.30, £8.30; EX 62.70 TRIFECTA Not won..
Owner Mrs K Lloyd Mrs L Pollock L Stilwell **Bred** Armand Khaida **Trained** Medbourne, Leics

FOCUS
A moderate race and a sound gallop set by the winner but the runner-up looked to throw it away. The winner is the best guide to the level.

NOTEBOOK
Beau Torero(FR), absent for a year and a half, travelled strongly in front but in the end he was handed the success on a plate. *(op 12-1)*
The Castilian(FR) travelled easily best and looked nailed on when moving into the leader's wake two out. However, when asked to put his head in front on the run-in he refused point blank. *(tchd 9-2)*
Sunley Future(IRE), who has rather lost his way, had the headgear reapplied but with only limited effect. *(op 33-1)*
All Bleevable, back over hurdles, is from a stable struggling for form at present.
Bayadere(GER) looks to be going backwards and had finished last on the All-Weather on her previous start seven weeks ago.
Gustavo, 9lb higher, never went a yard and soon under pressure was a long way behind when his rider eventually called it a day. This was simply too bad to be true. Official explanation: trainer's representative had no explanation for the poor form shown *(op 5-4 tchd 11-8 in places)*

3593 FAKENHAM RACECOURSE FOR SUMMER EQUESTRIAN HOLIDAYS NOVICES' H'CAP CHASE (18 fncs) 3m 110y

2:10 (2:10) (Class 4) (0-105,99) 5-Y-0+ **£4,879** (£1,432; £716; £357)

Form				RPR
4346	1		**Sconced (USA)**[21] 3271 11-10-5 81 ... (b) LarryMcGrath[(3)] (R C Guest) *nt a fluent: led 2nd tl 6th: rdn 10th: chsd ldr tl bad mstke 2 out: chal last: dashed ahd nr fin* **7/2**[3]	85+
1234	2	1 1/4	**Rookery Lad**[11] 3418 8-11-12 99 ... NoelFehily (C N Kellett) *j.w: led 6th: rdn and 3l clr 2 out: wknd and hdd nr fin* **3/1**[1]	99+
305U	3	nk	**The Holy Bee (IRE)**[11] 3419 7-11-10 97 ... JohnMcNamara (Mrs S J Humphrey) *chsd ldng pair 8th: j. slowly 14th and rdn: lft 2nd 2 out: drvn and ev ch after last: v one pced* **7/2**[3]	98+
00F6	4	6	**Iloveturtle (IRE)**[11] 3419 6-10-9 82 ... (t) KennyJohnson (M C Chapman) *nt jump wl in last pair: effrt 13th: in tch whn mstke 15th: nrly fell next: kpt on steadily* **18/1**	78+
P60	5	dist	**Fantastic Champion (IRE)**[50] 2717 7-9-10 74 ow1 ... MarkNicolls[(5)] (J R Cornwall) *j. slowly and reluctantly in last pair: many reminders: t.o 13th: btn 56l* **13/2**	—
4313	P		**Sunny South East (IRE)**[50] 2715 6-11-9 99 ... WilliamKennedy[(3)] (S Gollings) *led tl 2nd: already struggling whn mstke 9th: mstke 12th and rdn: t.o and j. slowly 15th: p.u next* **10/3**[2]	—

6m 44.5s (6.90) **Going Correction** 0.0s/f (Good) 6 Ran SP% **111.1**
Speed ratings: **88,87,87,85,— —** CSF £14.40 TOTE £4.90: £2.60, £1.80; EX 13.30.
Owner James S Kennerley And Miss Jenny Hall **Bred** Whitewood Stable Inc **Trained** Brancepeth, Co Durham

FOCUS
A weak race and a moderate winning time. Just three in it throughout the final circuit and in the end it was a case of the second running out of stamina near the line. The third is the best guide to the form.

NOTEBOOK
Sconced(USA), a real monkey, made his rider earn his fee. Five lengths down when blundering two out, he decided to put his best foot foward and caught the flagging second near the line. His rider looked exhausted afterwards. *(op 10-3)*
Rookery Lad jumped for fun and looked nailed on when jumping the last with a three lengths advantage, but his stamina seemed to give out completely causing his downfall in the final strides. *(op 10-3 tchd 7-2)*
The Holy Bee(IRE) kept tabs on the leader but lacked that vital bit of speed to pull it out of the fire on the run-in. *(tchd 10-3)*
Iloveturtle(IRE), a hesitant jumper, was almost on the floor three out and his proximity at the line suggests all of the first three were slowing up. *(op 12-1)*
Fantastic Champion(IRE) would not have a cut at his fences at all and was out of contention on the final circuit. *(op 7-1)*
Sunny South East(IRE) was struggling to keep up with a circuit to go and, with her jumping deteriorating, she was tailed off when calling it a day. *(tchd 7-2)*

3594 THE PRINCE OF WALES STAND FOR BUSINESS MEETINGS JUVENILE NOVICES' HURDLE (8 hdls 1 omitted) 2m

2:45 (2:45) (Class 3) 4-Y-O **£6,506** (£1,910; £955; £477)

Form				RPR
21	1		**Bayard (USA)**[73] 2258 4-11-4 110 ... PJBrennan (J R Fanshawe) *settled in 3rd pl: rdn bef 3 out: 4th and outpcd next: 10l 3rd whn lft in ld at omitted last: all out: fin 3rd, hd & 1l: awrdd r* **22/1**	98
6	2	2 3/4	**Mystery Lot (IRE)**[11] 3422 4-10-5 ... RobertThornton (A King) *keen: pressed ldrs: rdn bef 3 out: sn outpcd: lft 2nd at omitted last: nt qckn: fin 4th, hd, 1l & 1 1/2l: plcd 2nd* **20/1**	83
4	3	11	**Monash Lad (IRE)**[6] 3498 4-10-9 ... ColinBolger[(3)] (M H Tompkins) *hld up and bhd: lost tch 6th: fin 5th: plcd 3rd* **40/1**	79
	4	2	**Daraybad (FR)**[164] 4-10-12 ... APMcCoy (N J Henderson) *prom: nt fluent 6th and rdn: 3rd and btn after next: fin weakly: fin 6th: plcd 4th* **5/4**[1]	80+
0	5	7	**Mightymuller (IRE)**[39] 2927 4-10-12 ... TomDoyle (D R Gandolfo) *a bhd: lost tch 6th: fin 7th: plcd 5th* **150/1**	71+
	6	dist	**Kirin**[26] 4-10-12 ... (t) PaulMoloney (D E Cantillon) *hld up in last pair: t.o after 6th: btn 90l: fin 8th: plcd 6th* **100/1**	—
	7	3 1/2	**Turn On The Style**[147] 4-10-9 ... LeeVickers[(3)] (M J Polglase) *hld up and wl bhd: t.o 6th: btn 94l: fin 9th: plcd 7th* **100/1**	—
0P	8	3 1/2	**Aviemore**[54] 2661 4-10-12 ... RichardHobson (J R Cornwall) *midfield: mstke 2nd: rdn and lost tch 5th: sn t.o: btn 97l: fin 10th: plcd 8th* **250/1**	—
P0	9	4	**Moment Of Clarity**[4] 3539 4-10-12 ... (e) JohnMcNamara (R C Guest) *midfield tl 5th: t.o after next: btn 101l: fin 11th: plcd 9th* **250/1**	—
26	D		**My Immortal**[31] 3021 4-10-12 ... RJGreene (M C Pipe) *led at fast pce: hrd rdn bef 3 out: hdd and hit next: tk wrong crse at omitted last: fin 2nd, hd: disq* **11/8**[2]	104+
41B	D		**Prize Fighter (IRE)**[16] 3340 4-11-4 ... NoelFehily (Jonjo O'Neill) *pressed ldr: led gng best 2 out: 2l ahd whn jockey missed 3 dolls in omitted fnl flight: fin 1st, hd: disq* **9/1**[3]	113+

0U0 **P** **Annals**[4] [3539] 4-10-5 ....(e) KennyJohnson —
(R C Guest) *mstkes in rr: blnd 4th: t.o after next: p.u 3 out* **250/1**

U **P** **Beaumont Girl (IRE)**[8] [2286] 4-10-2 ow2.................. AdamPogson[(5)] —
(Miss M E Rowland) *bhd after mstke 3rd: p.u and dismntd 6th* **250/1**

4m 7.30s (-1.60) **Going Correction** -0.15s/f (Good) **13** Ran SP% **112.3**
Speed ratings: **97,96,91,90,86** —,—,—,—,**98 97**,—,— CSF £274.39 TOTE £14.10: £3.70, £2.90, £4.10; EX 76.40.
Owner Mr & Mrs G Middlebrook/Mr & Mrs P Brain **Bred** And Mrs G Middlebrook & Brain International Lt **Trained** Newmarket, Suffolk

■ Stewards' Enquiry : Noel Fehily nine-day ban (reduced from 10 on appeal): in breach of Rule 156 - jumped dolled-off hurdle (Feb 7-15)
R J Greene nine-day ban (reduced from 10 on appeal): in breach of Rule 156 - jumped dolled-off hurdle (Feb 7-15)

FOCUS
The last flight was omitted on the final circuit as a section was damaged. A controversial finish but the first two riders were not looking ahead and they cannot blame anyone but themselves. The disqualified pair are rated value for further with the original third the best guide to the form.

NOTEBOOK
Bayard(USA), pushed along with a circuit to go, was booked for a modest third spot when presented with the race when his rider made the right decision and bypassed the dolled-off final flight. His proximity to the first two past the post at the line is due to them being eased up once the penny dropped. *(op 16-1 tchd 25-1)*
Mystery Lot(IRE), too keen for her own good, will have to learn to settle if she is to make any impact. *At least her rider made the right decision and she was promoted to second spot. (op 16-1 tchd 14-1)*
Monash Lad(IRE), running on much quicker ground, could never go the pace. *(op 33-1)*
Daraybad(FR), a winner on the Flat in France and now a gelding, is a big type and his jumping was *hesitant. He dropped right away but can surely do a lot better especially on a less sharp track. (op 6-5 tchd 11-8)*
Prize Fighter(IRE) travelled strongly and had it in the bag when his rider missed the chequered flag man on the inside once in line for home and he went through the final flight on the inner where the *damaged panel was missing after the previous circuit. He richly deserves compensation. (op 10-1 tchd 12-1)*
My Immortal set a strong pace and his rider was hard at work with a full circuit to go. He was clear second when his rider made the same mistake as the winner. *(op 10-1 tchd 12-1)*
Beaumont Girl(IRE) *Official explanation: jockey said saddle slipped (op 150-1)*

3595 E B F FAKENHAM RACECOURSE OUTDOOR EVENTS SITE "NATIONAL HUNT" NOVICES' HURDLE (QUALIFIER) (11 hdls) 2m 4f
3:20 (3:20) (Class 3) 4-7-Y-0 **£5,204** (£1,528; £764; £381)

Form				RPR

1121 **1** **Tokala**[22] [3246] 5-11-8 .... APMcCoy 113+
(B G Powell) *j. slowly 1st: led tl 2nd: led again 6th: blnd next: drvn and nt fluent 2 out: sn outpcd: rallied u.p to ld flat* **4/9**[1]

25U **2** 3/4 **Commander Kev (IRE)**[22] [3246] 5-11-0 .... WilliamKennedy[(3)] 108+
(Noel T Chance) *hld up: prog and nt fluent 8th: sn 2nd: rdn to ld after 2 out: 3l clr whn blnd last: hdd nr fin* **12/1**[3]

-321 **3** 16 **Vertical Bloom**[50] [2718] 5-10-10 113.............. StephenCraine[(5)] 88+
(Mrs P Sly) *chsd ldrs: drvn bef 7th: outpcd and mstke next: no ch whn stmbld after 3 out* **7/2**[2]

2-33 **4** 5 **Autumn Red (IRE)**[66] [2421] 6-11-3 .... TomDoyle 86+
(P R Webber) *trckd ldrs: effrt 7th: sn rdn and fdd tamely: mstke 2 out* **14/1**

-3U0 **5** 8 **Scalini'S (IRE)**[46] [2799] 6-11-3 .... NoelFehily 77+
(Jonjo O'Neill) *last pl: niggled 5th: sn struggling: remote whn mstke 2 out* **50/1**

PP **P** **Monsieur Delage**[36] [2950] 6-11-3 .... JohnMcNamara —
(S Gollings) *keen: led and hit 2nd: hdd 6th: stopped to nil bef 3 out: t.o and p.u 2 out* **100/1**

5m 12.6s (0.40) **Going Correction** -0.15s/f (Good) **6** Ran SP% **108.8**
Speed ratings: **93,92,86,84,81** — CSF £6.58 TOTE £1.30: £1.10, £3.40; EX 7.50.
Owner John P McManus **Bred** Greenfield Stud S A **Trained** Morestead, Hants

FOCUS
The winning time was modest and what looked beforehand plain sailing for Tokala turned out to be a real battle. The winner sets the level judged on previous form.

NOTEBOOK
Tokala seemed to lose confidence in his jumping and, after looking well cooked, a vintage ride from the champion saw him snatch the prize from out of the fire near the line. He impressed at Hereford and is surely a lot better than he showed on this day.
Commander Kev(IRE) looked to have it in the bag when three lengths up at the final flight, but he blundered and lost momentum and that gave the champion jockey another bite at the cherry and he was not to be denied. *(op 11-1)*
Vertical Bloom, who defeated a subsequent dual winner in a mares-only race at Huntingdon, found this open company much too strong and she was beaten off some way from home.
Autumn Red(IRE) did not improve on his first two efforts over hurdles. *(op 12-1)*

3596 ROGER LYLES, FAKENHAM RACECOURSE DIRECTOR 1970-2005 H'CAP CHASE (16 fncs) 2m 5f 110y
3:50 (3:50) (Class 3) (0-130,125) 5-Y-0+ **£7,807** (£2,292; £1,146; £572)

Form				RPR

5-3F **1** **Windsor Boy (IRE)**[32] [2993] 9-11-8 **121** .... APMcCoy 134+
(M C Pipe) *settled in 3rd: j. slowly 2nd: chsd ldr after 13th tl led bef 2 out: in command bef last* **7/4**[1]

1112 **2** 6 **Hakim (NZ)**[48] [2768] 12-11-12 **125** .... PJBrennan 130
(J L Spearing) *led: nt fluent 7th: drvn and hdd bef 2 out: kpt on gamely but no ch w wnr* **4/1**[2]

252F **3** 3/4 **Alcopop**[8] [3459] 7-10-9 **111** .... PaulO'Neill[(3)] 116+
(Miss Venetia Williams) *pressed ldr tl after 13th: 3rd and gng wl 3 out: tk 2nd but outpcd between last two: nt run on fr last* **9/2**[3]

P-06 **4** 7 **Jack Martin (IRE)**[13] [3384] 9-11-7 **120** .... JohnMcNamara 118+
(S Gollings) *nt fluent in last: rdn 9th: outpcd 13th: impeded next* **40/1**

5600 **5** 1 1/4 **Day Du Roy (FR)**[16] [3344] 8-10-8 **107** .... TomSiddall 103
(Miss L C Siddall) *hld up towards rr: mstke 10th: effrt to press ldrs briefly 13th: sn fnd nil* **20/1**

2P-2 **6** 21 **Fireaway**[36] [2955] 12-9-11 **99** oh3.................. LeeVickers[(3)] 74
(O Brennan) *towards rr: hit 8th: drvn 11th: sn lost tch: t.o 2 out* **10/1**

2343 **7** 9 **Shannon's Pride (IRE)**[15] [3350] 10-10-6 **110**.............. StephenCraine[(5)] 76
(R C Guest) *midfield: 4l 4th and effrt 13th: 5th and fading whn almost fell next: t.o* **13/2**

4121 **P** **Walcot Lad (IRE)**[10] [3440] 10-9-12 **100** 7ex ow1...........(p) ColinBolger[(3)] —
(A Ennis) *nt fluent and nvr gng wl: last and rdn after 11th: t.o and pckd next and sn p.u* **9/1**

5m 39.0s (-5.50) **Going Correction** 0.0s/f (Good) **8** Ran SP% **114.2**
Speed ratings: **110,107,107,105,104 96,93**,— CSF £9.63 CT £26.09 TOTE £2.50: £1.10, £1.60, £2.50; EX 12.30.
Owner Byrne Bros (Formwork) Limited **Bred** Wickfield Stud And Hartshill Stud **Trained** Nicholashayne, Devon

FOCUS
A fair handicap and solid form, with those in the frame behind the winner running to their marks.

NOTEBOOK
Windsor Boy(IRE), happy to get a good lead, jumped ahead two out and had this in the bag in a matter of strides. He will have a lot more on his plate in future. *(op 13-8 tchd 2-1)*
Hakim(NZ) enjoyed himself in front but the winner had him in his sights and in the end he proved no match. He is not the biggest and may be better suited by carrying lower weights in better company. *(op 9-2)*
Alcopop, unable to dominate, joined contention travelling smoothly but he has never been one for a fight and in the end seemed content to accept third spot. *(op 4-1 tchd 7-2)*
Jack Martin(IRE), who has plenty to mprove back over fences, would not have a cut at his fences and was soon in trouble on ground a good deal quicker than he prefers. *(op 33-1)*
Day Du Roy(FR), on a long losing run, joined issue four out but when called in for an effort he soon very readily threw in the towel.

3597 THE PRINCE OF WALES STAND FOR PRIVATE FUNCTIONS NOVICES' HURDLE (DIV II) (9 hdls) 2m
4:20 (4:20) (Class 4) 5-Y-0+ **£2,927** (£859; £429; £214)

Form				RPR

642 **1** **Dance World**[14] [2950] 6-10-5 107.................. MrMatthewSmith[(7)] 110+
(Miss J Feilden) *trckd ldrs gng wl: led 3 out: sn qckdnd clr: 7l ahd whn hit next: unchal* **9/2**[3]

63 **2** 10 **Stocking Island**[18] [3322] 5-10-5 .... AndrewTinkler 93
(C R Egerton) *pressed tl led 5th: rdn and hdd 3 out: sn outpcd by wnr: hit last* **11/1**

1 **3** 7 **Cold Turkey**[20] [2374] 6-11-5 .... JamieMoore 100
(G L Moore) *keen: trckd ldrs: effrt and cl up bef 3 out: sn rdn: disp mod between last two: wknd* **4/5**[1]

6 **4** 1 **Cottingham (IRE)**[36] [2950] 5-10-12 .... KennyJohnson 92
(M C Chapman) *plld hrd: prom: ev ch 3 out: rdn and btn bef next* **100/1**

5 17 **Master Theo (USA)**[21] 5-10-12 ....(t) JohnMcNamara 75
(Lucinda Featherstone) *hld up bhd: short lived effrt 6th* **20/1**

045P **6** 19 **Pick Of The Crop**[14] [3371] 5-10-12 84..................(v) JodieMogford 56
(J R Jenkins) *plld hrd: chsd ldrs tl rdn 6th: nt run on: t.o* **100/1**

000F **7** 10 **Orions Eclipse**[51] [2704] 5-10-2 .... OwynNelmes[(3)] 39
(M J Gingell) *a struggling in last trio: t.o fr 6th* **100/1**

600 **8** 24 **Lone Rider (IRE)**[8] [3463] 5-10-12 .... NoelFehily 22
(Jonjo O'Neill) *a wl bhd: last and rdn after 5th and no rspnse: continued t.o* **100/1**

6-P **9** 2 1/2 **Fort Royal (IRE)**[26] [3184] 7-10-5 .... MrGPewter[(7)] 20
(G R Pewter) *led tl blnd 5th: hopelessly t.o after next* **100/1**

42 **F** **Lysander (GER)**[14] [3374] 7-10-12 .... PJBrennan —
(M F Harris) *hld up towards rr: effrt 6th: cl 5th whn fell next* **10/3**[2]

4m 10.5s (1.60) **Going Correction** -0.15s/f (Good) **10** Ran SP% **114.9**
Speed ratings: **90,85,81,81,72 63,58,46,44**,— CSF £44.48 TOTE £4.60: £1.50, £2.40, £1.10; EX 39.60 Place 6 £591.72, Place 5 £181.61.
Owner Stowstowquickquickstow Partnership **Bred** Juddmonte Farms **Trained** Exning, Suffolk

FOCUS
Much the slower of the two divisions and the winner seemed to steal first run. The second is the best guide to the form but it does not look reliable.

NOTEBOOK
Dance World travelled strongly and seemed to steal a march on his rivals. He had it in the bag when clouting the last. He looked easily best on the day anyway. *(tchd 5-1)*
Stocking Island, in the firing line throughout, was left for dead in a matter of strides when the winner increased the tempo. *(op 9-1)*
Cold Turkey took a keen grip. He rather gave the winner first run but when called on for a serious effort between the last two flights the response was limited to say the very least. He prefers a lot more give underfoot. *(op 10-11 tchd Evens in places)*
Cottingham(IRE) would not settle and, after matching strides, was on the retreat going to two out.
Lysander(GER) was bang there in the mix and full of running when crashing out three from home.
T/Jkpt: Not won. T/Plt: £157.20 to a £1 stake. Pool: £46,961.65. 218.00 winning tickets. T/Qpdt: £12.60 to a £1 stake. Pool: £4,356.20. 254.40 winning tickets. IM

3436 FONTWELL (L-H)
Friday, January 27

OFFICIAL GOING: Good to soft
Wind: Virtually nil

3598 CROWN RACING "NATIONAL HUNT" NOVICES' HURDLE (13 hdls) 3m 3f
1:30 (1:30) (Class 4) 5-Y-0+ **£4,554** (£1,337; £668; £333)

Form				RPR

-041 **1** **Alfasonic**[21] [3277] 6-11-4 110.................. WayneHutchinson 114+
(A King) *chsd ldrs: rdn to press ldrs after 3 out: led sn after 2 out: styd on wl: rdn out* **9/4**[1]

30/1 **2** 5 **Before Dark (IRE)**[22] [3249] 8-11-4 104.................. RichardJohnson 109
(Mrs H Dalton) *hld up: tk clsr order after 9th: ev ch 2 out: sn rdn: kpt on same pce: tk 2nd fnl stride* **11/2**[3]

52-1 **3** hd **Ballyjohnboy Lord (IRE)**[22] [3257] 7-11-10 117........... TomScudamore 118+
(M Scudamore) *trckd ldrs: led appr 10th: rdn and hdd sn after 2 out: 2nd and hld whn mstke last: lost 2nd fnl stride* **9/4**[1]

0032 **4** 6 **Charango Star**[10] [3438] 8-11-4 105..................(v) TimmyMurphy 104+
(W K Goldsworthy) *rn in snatches in rr: reminders after 1st: mstke 4th: hdwy to ld after 7th tl 10th: sn drvn: one pced fr 2 out* **7/2**[2]

P55 **5** dist **Deltic Arrow**[42] [2869] 8-10-12 .... AndrewThornton —
(D L Williams) *racd keenly: led after 1st: mstke 6th: hdd after 7th: chsd ldr tl wknd appr 10th: t.o* **20/1**

RP-P **6** 4 **Jollyshau (IRE)**[32] [2957] 8-10-12 .... MatthewBatchelor —
(Miss A M Newton-Smith) *led tl after 1st: chsd ldr tl 7th: grad fdd: t.o fr 10th* **40/1**

P **Germany Park (IRE)**[655] 8-10-9 .... GinoCarenza[(3)] —
(W B Stone) *chsd ldrs tl 7th: sn t.o: p.u after 9th* **100/1**

7m 3.60s (29.30) **Going Correction** +0.475s/f (Soft) **7** Ran SP% **107.3**
Speed ratings: **75,73,73,71**,— —,— CSF £13.13 TOTE £2.70: £1.40, £3.10; EX 15.50.
Owner Mrs S Warren **Bred** Mrs E M Charlton **Trained** Barbury Castle, Wilts

FOCUS
A fair novice for the track, run over an extreme trip but at a steady early pace, which resulted in a pedestrian time. The winner and second both showed improved form, but the third looks better at shorter.

NOTEBOOK
Alfasonic is a progressive gelding whose main asset is stamina, and he put it to good use to draw away from his rivals after the last over this extreme trip. He may have to contest handicaps rather than try to carry a double penalty. *(op 5-2)*

Before Dark(IRE), another with plenty of stamina judged on previous efforts, had every chance but found the winner too strong from the last flight. *(op 5-1 tchd 6-1 in a place)*
Ballyjohnboy Lord(IRE) was held up in the early stages but then pushed the pace until a mistake at the last caused him to lose the advantage. He was just outstayed for second over this extreme trip, but this was a fair effort under a double penalty. *(op 7-4)*
Charango Star required early reminders and made Murphy earn his fee. However, he was left behind from the final turn. *(op 9-2)*

3599 CROWN RACING FIRST FOR SERVICE BEGINNERS' CHASE (13 fncs) 2m 2f
2:00 (2:01) (Class 4) 5-Y-O+ **£5,204** (£1,528; £764; £381)

Form RPR
5-23 **1** **My World (FR)**^{26} [3183] 6-10-11 112 .... AndrewThornton 124+
(R H Alner) *chsd clr ldr: led sn after 9th: rdn and qcknd pce appr 3 out: narrow advantage whn mstke last: all out* **7/4**^{2}
0-P3 **2** *nk* **Medison (FR)**^{27} [3150] 6-11-4 .... TimmyMurphy 131+
(M C Pipe) *veered rt s: bhd: blnd 2nd: tk clsr order after 7th: hit 9th: wnt 2nd after next: ev ch and hrd rdn flat: no ex* **5/6**^{1}
-200 **3** *16* **Guru**^{42} [2871] 8-11-4 .... PhilipHide 118+
(G L Moore) *hld up but in tch: tk clsr order 8th: outpcd appr 3 out: btn whn mstke 2 out* **8/1**^{3}
P-46 **4** *dist* **Tuck In**^{26} [3184] 9-11-4 .... (t) LeightonAspell —
(P Winkworth) *chsd ldrs: hit 3rd: fdd fr 7th: sn wl bhd* **20/1**
5/PP **P** **Neophyte (IRE)**^{76} [2179] 7-11-4 .... (b^{1}) WayneHutchinson —
(B De Haan) *led and sn clr: pckd 2nd: hit 8th: hdd sn after next: wknd qckly: p.u bef 3 out* **100/1**

4m 44.0s (8.90) **Going Correction** +0.65s/f (Soft) **5** Ran SP% **107.8**
Speed ratings: **106,105,98,—,—** CSF £3.60 TOTE £3.40: £1.30, £1.20; EX 4.00.
Owner Nicky Turner, Penny Tozer, Lotte Schicht **Bred** J E Dubois And Frederic Sauque **Trained** Droop, Dorset
■ Stewards' Enquiry : Timmy Murphy one-day ban: used whip with excessive force and frequency (Feb 5)

FOCUS
This was run at a decent pace and concerned only three for much of the final circuit. The winner was back to the level of her debut and the second ran his best race yet over fences, although still well below his hurdles form.

NOTEBOOK
My World(FR) had come up against decent sorts in Voy Por Ustedes and Le Volfoni in her previous starts and, after taking the advantage at the ninth, did her best to stretch the favourite. She rallied well after that rival got upsides on the flat and deserved her victory. She can find more opportunities on soft ground, and the mares' final at Uttoxeter could suit her, although she will need to qualify. *(op 15-8 tchd 6-4 and 2-1 in places)*
Medison(FR) had a bit to find on a strict line through Voy Por Ustedes, and he did not help himself by being reluctant to start and then looking less than enthusiastic from the final fence. He clearly *has the ability to win chases, but his temperament may count against him.* *(op 10-11 tchd Evens, 11-10 in places and 6-5 in a place)*
Guru, who has been lightly raced in recent seasons, ran quite well on this chasing debut but was left behind from the third last. He should benefit from the experience and can win a race over fences. *(op 11-2 tchd 17-2 in places)*
Neophyte(IRE) was too keen in the first-time blinkers and had run himself out early on the final circuit. *(op 66-1)*

3600 CROWN RACING "YOUR BEST BET" H'CAP HURDLE (11 hdls) 2m 6f 110y
2:35 (2:35) (Class 3) (0-125,125) 4-Y-0 **£6,338** (£1,872; £936; £468; £234)

Form RPR
030- **1** **Golden Bay**^{322} [4314] 7-10-0 **104** .... DarylJacob$^{(5)}$ 114+
(Miss Suzy Smith) *chsd clr ldr: shkn up to ld after 3 out: clr next: wnt rt last: styd on: comf* **5/1**^{2}
110- **2** *11* **Rosemauve (FR)**^{413} [2746] 6-11-12 **125** .... (b) TomScudamore 125+
(M C Pipe) *led and sn clr: rdn and hdd after 3 out: no ch w wnr fr next* **9/2**^{1}
55-5 **3** *4* **Alfa Sunrise**^{96} [1858] 9-10-8 **107** .... BenjaminHitchcott 101
(R H Buckler) *j.rt thrght: chsd ldrs: outpcd and dropped rr 8th: styd on again fr 2 out: tk 3rd run-in* **20/1**
10/P **4** *2 ½* **Heron's Ghyll (IRE)**^{41} [2877] 9-10-8 **107** .... SamThomas 99
(Miss Venetia Williams) *chsd ldrs: sltly outpcd after 8th: 3rd whn wnt lft 2 out: kpt on same pce: lost 3rd run-in* **11/2**^{3}
1413 **5** *10* **Kings Castle (IRE)**^{6} [3508] 11-10-4 **110** .... JamesWhite$^{(7)}$ 92
(R J Hodges) *hld up bhd: sme hdwy after 7th: outpcd next: nvr on terms after* **9/2**^{1}
F105 **6** *1* **Water King (USA)**^{13} [3397] 7-11-2 **115** .... SamStronge 96
(R M Stronge) *mid div: rdn and mstke 3 out: one pced after* **8/1**
4F00 **7** *dist* **Courant D'Air (IRE)**^{31} [3018] 5-10-5 **104** .... RichardJohnson —
(Lucinda Featherstone) *hld up towards rr: hdwy 6th: trckd ldrs 8th: rdn and wknd after 3 out* **7/1**
F-P2 **8** *24* **Westmeath Flyer**^{17} [3332] 11-11-12 **125** .... MickFitzgerald —
(P A Blockley) *hld up towards rr: brief effrt after 8th: sn wknd: t.o* **14/1**
0-56 **P** **The Bo'sun**^{32} [2956] 9-10-0 **99** oh8 .... WayneHutchinson —
(A E Jessop) *in tch tl 4th: sn bhd: t.o and p.u bef 8th* **40/1**
2030 **P** **Global Challenge (IRE)**^{63} [2483] 7-11-12 **125** .... (p) LeightonAspell —
(P G Murphy) *mid div tl 4th: sn struggling and bhd: t.o and p.u after 7th* **16/1**

5m 51.7s (6.90) **Going Correction** +0.475s/f (Soft) **10** Ran SP% **111.8**
Speed ratings: **107,103,101,100,97 97,—,—,—,—** CSF £27.01 CT £402.81 TOTE £6.60: £1.70, £2.30, £3.90; EX 32.00.
Owner Goldie's Friends **Bred** Mrs S D Watts **Trained** Lewes, E Sussex

FOCUS
A fair handicap run at a good gallop but very few got into it from off the pace.

NOTEBOOK
Golden Bay, having her first run since last March, due to pelvic and hock problems, and her first start for the yard, likes soft ground and was ridden positively. She chased the leader throughout, but closed him down and took the advantage three out. She was soon clear, won very much as she liked and could prove well handicapped if, as suggested by this performance, she has improved since last season. *(op 11-2)*
Rosemauve(FR), who was returning from nearly 14 months off, set off in front but probably ran too free. He was brushed aside by the winner, but was able to keep going well enough to hold off the rest. He is likely to need a little while to recover from this. *(tchd 5-1 in places)*
Alfa Sunrise, who has been chasing of late, was another returning from a break and chased the principals throughout. He never looked likely to catch them but could be interesting over further off his current mark.
Heron's Ghyll(IRE), pulled up on his chasing debut last time after 21 months off, ran better on this return to the smaller obstacles and is now 7lb below his last winning mark. *(op 6-1)*
Kings Castle(IRE), who has been in good form of late, was held up out the back and never got into contention in a race which the first two held those positions throughout. *(op 5-1)*
Water King(USA) was another who never figured and would probably have preferred faster ground. *(op 6-1)*
The Bo'sun *Official explanation: vet said gelding was lame on its left fore (tchd 50-1)*

3601 CROWN RACING FREEPHONE 08000 724624 NOVICES' CHASE (16 fncs) 2m 6f
3:10 (3:10) (Class 3) 5-Y-O+ **£9,394** (£2,775; £1,387; £694; £346; £174)

Form RPR
-123 **1** **Star De Mohaison (FR)**^{26} [3178] 5-11-3 .... (t) BJGeraghty 144+
(P F Nicholls) *j. and travelled wl: trckd ldr: led 6th: in command fr 3 out: readily* **1/3**^{1}
-F23 **2** *13* **Steppes Of Gold (IRE)**^{32} [2989] 9-11-2 128 .... MickFitzgerald 131+
(Jonjo O'Neill) *trckd ldrs: niggled along after 10th: rdn after 4 out: wnt 2nd after next: kpt on but no ch w wnr fr 2 out* **5/1**^{2}
240F **3** *11* **One Cornetto (IRE)**^{55} [2634] 7-11-8 127 .... LeightonAspell 125+
(L Wells) *trckd ldrs: chsd wnr fr 8th: rdn and effrt appr 3 out: wknd 2 out* **12/1**^{3}
30-1 **4** *26* **Dedrunknmunky (IRE)**^{84} [2018] 7-11-1 109 .... MarcusFoley 89
(Miss Tor Sturgis) *led tl 6th: chsd wnr tl 8th: outpcd fr 11th* **18/1**
P **5** *18* **Run To The King (IRE)**^{22} [3249] 8-11-2 .... AndrewThornton 72
(P C Ritchens) *bhd: mstke 6th: sn lost tch: t.o* **66/1**
3U0P **6** *dist* **Sarahs Quay (IRE)**^{10} [3438] 7-10-8 78 ow2 .... (b) GinoCarenza$^{(3)}$ —
(K J Burke) *j.lft thrght: hit 2nd: a bhd: t.o fr 7th* **100/1**

5m 50.3s (6.50) **Going Correction** +0.65s/f (Soft)
WFA 5 from 7yo+ 9lb **6** Ran SP% **107.1**
Speed ratings: **114,109,105,95,89** — CSF £2.29 TOTE £1.10: £1.20, £1.50; EX 2.40.
Owner Sir Robert Ogden **Bred** J Veau **Trained** Ditcheat, Somerset

FOCUS
A reasonable contest for the track. The favourite was a convincing winner in a good time, but the placed horses weren't proven at the trip and neither of them looked well handicapped.

NOTEBOOK
Star De Mohaison(FR) has made a good start to his career over fences, and his two recent defeats were at the hands of the very useful The Listener. This was a nice confidence booster, and he jumped well and came away in the straight. The time was good and he looks a likely sort for the *Jewson Novices' Chase at the Festival, although he is in the Royal & SunAlliance Chase.* *(op 4-11 tchd 2-5 in places)*
Steppes Of Gold(IRE), trying his longest trip to date, again encountered a useful opponent. He did not travel that well on this sharp track, but was close enough turning in before the winner found another gear. *(op 9-2)*
One Cornetto(IRE) has been highly tried since making a good start to his chasing career on fast ground in the summer. He travelled well for a long way on this sharper track, but the first two left him behind from the third last. He looks capable of winning a novices' handicap on a sound surface.
Dedrunknmunky(IRE), a course winner on her chasing debut here in November, set the early pace *on this first outing since. However, she was struggling for most of the final circuit.* *(op 14-1 tchd 20-1)*

3602 CROWN RACING H'CAP CHASE (15 fncs) 2m 4f
3:40 (3:40) (Class 5) (0-85,82) 5-Y-O+ **£3,578** (£1,050; £525; £262)

Form RPR
0232 **1** **Brigadier Du Bois (FR)**^{22} [3252] 7-11-7 **77** .... LeightonAspell 92+
(Mrs L Wadham) *chsd ldrs: wnt 2nd at the 8th: led appr 10th: pckd 4 out: 6l clr 2 out: sn rdn: tired cl home: drvn out* **9/4**^{1}
2P32 **2** *3 ½* **Sitting Duck**^{37} [2936] 7-11-5 **82** .... CharlieStudd$^{(7)}$ 89
(B G Powell) *j.rt thrght: led 2nd tl 10th: chsd wnr: rdn after 3 out: 6l 2nd 2 out: rallied briefly run-in* **5/2**^{2}
3PP0 **3** *11* **Penalty Clause (IRE)**^{50} [2717] 6-11-8 **78** .... AndrewThornton 75+
(Lucinda Featherstone) *hld up: hdwy to chse ldrs after 9th: rdn appr 4 out: one pced after* **12/1**
2-26 **4** *23* **Miss Wizadora**^{268} [181] 11-11-10 **80** .... MickFitzgerald 59+
(Simon Earle) *led tl 2nd: chsd ldr: nt fluent 6 and 7th: sn lost pl but in tch: rdn after 11th: wknd 3 out* **3/1**^{3}
5U5 **5** *20* **Ah Yeah (IRE)**^{11} [3419] 9-10-8 **69** .... (b^{1}) ChrisHonour$^{(5)}$ 22
(N B King) *chsd ldrs: rdn after 8th: wknd after 11th* **12/1**
-6F5 **6** *dist* **Goldseam (GER)**^{16} [3341] 7-11-0 **70** .... MarkBradburne —
(S C Burrough) *a towards rr: lost tch fr 10th* **33/1**
-UP0 **P** **Huw The News**^{7} [3482] 7-11-10 **80** .... (b^{1}) PhilipHide —
(S C Burrough) *hit 2nd and 3rd: a bhd: t.o and p.u bef 10th* **100/1**
PP/P **R** **Renaloo (IRE)**^{57} [2594] 11-10-12 **68** .... (b) BrianCrowley —
(R Rowe) *chsd ldrs: wkng whn blnd 10th: t.o whn ref 3 out* **20/1**

5m 20.8s (12.90) **Going Correction** +0.65s/f (Soft) **8** Ran SP% **108.4**
Speed ratings: **100,98,94,85,77 —,—,—** CSF £7.66 CT £43.48 TOTE £3.50: £1.10, £1.30, £3.50; EX 6.30.
Owner Hebomapa **Bred** G Gilles And Maurice Blin **Trained** Newmarket, Suffolk

FOCUS
A very moderate chase in which the first two had it to themselves for much of the way.

NOTEBOOK
Brigadier Du Bois(FR), six times runner-up in nine previous starts over fences, finally broke his duck. Given a good lead by the eventual second, he took the advantage halfway around the final circuit and looked sure to win easily before tiring on the flat. This success should help his confidence, and he should not go up the handicap too much. *(op 7-4)*
Sitting Duck, less experienced than the winner, set off in front again but jumped to the right. He tends to set races up for others, but rallied after looking well held and ought to win a small race one day.
Penalty Clause(IRE) has not really gone on from his chasing debut in October, but a drop in the weights and sharper track seemed to produce something of a return to form. He was, however, never a threat to the principals. *(op 10-1)*
Miss Wizadora, returning from a nine-month absence, has not had much racing in the last four years but she generally performs better than this. She did not help her cause with some sloppy jumping. *(op 4-1)*

3603 CROWN RACING NOVICES' H'CAP HURDLE (9 hdls) 2m 2f 110y
4:10 (4:10) (Class 4) (0-110,107) 4-Y-O+ **£4,879** (£1,432; £716; £357)

Form RPR
-F35 **1** **Nobel Bleu De Kerpaul (FR)**^{45} [2803] 5-10-11 **92** .... LeightonAspell 93
(P Winkworth) *mid div: hdwy to join ldrs 4th: led appr 2 out: sn rdn: hrd pressed run-in: all out* **7/2**^{2}
4456 **2** *hd* **Hatteras (FR)**^{45} [2809] 7-11-0 **100** .... RobertLucey-Butler$^{(5)}$ 101
(Miss M P Bryant) *hld up towards rr: rdn and stdy hdwy after 3 out: wnt 2nd at the last: ev ch run-in: kpt on but no ex cl home* **20/1**
006 **3** *8* **Tamreen (IRE)**^{27} [3133] 5-11-10 **105** .... PhilipHide 100+
(G L Moore) *mid div: nt fluent 2nd: rdn to chse ldrs after 3 out: kpt on same pce* **9/2**
400 **4** *20* **Bonnell (IRE)**^{11} [3418] 7-10-5 **86** .... WayneHutchinson 64+
(K J Burke) *hld up towards rr: making sme hdwy whn stmbld bdly and lost position 6th: hung rt after: styd on past btn horses fr 2 out* **33/1**

664 **5** *1 ¾* **Come What Augustus**[52] 2681 4-10-5 **98**.......................... JamesDavies 57
(R M Stronge) *prom: led 6th: rdn after 3 out: narrowly hdd and hit 2 out: sn wknd* **8/1**

-314 **6** *1 ¾* **Coach Lane**[17] 3333 5-11-12 **107**.. SamThomas 76
(Miss Venetia Williams) *in tch: jnd ldrs and nt fluent 4th: rdn and ev ch after 3 out: hdd and hld whn stmbld last: wknd* **4/1**[3]

-0P0 **7** *11* **Star Galaxy (IRE)**[32] 2983 6-10-0 **81** oh1...................... TomScudamore 39
(Andrew Turnell) *trckd ldrs: rdn and ev ch after 3 out: wkng whn hit next* **25/1**

0440 **8** *23* **The Rip**[32] 2995 5-10-1 **82**..(t) JimCrowley 17
(R M Stronge) *mid div tl wknd appr 3 out* **14/1**

6-00 **9** *dist* **Tiger Island (USA)**[46] 2802 6-9-11 **83** oh3 ow2............. DerekLaverty[(5)] —
(A E Jones) *a towards rr: t.o after 6th* **100/1**

4342 **P** **Albert House (IRE)**[10] 3441 8-11-6 **101**........................ AndrewThornton —
(R H Alner) *led: nt fluent 3rd: being eased whn hdd and mstke 6th: sn p.u* **3/1**[1]

4m 49.6s (13.60) **Going Correction** +0.475s/f (Soft)
WFA 4 from 5yo+ 11lb **10** Ran SP% **115.7**
Speed ratings: **90,89,86,78,77 76,72,62,—,—** CSF £68.15 CT £321.65 TOTE £5.30: £1.10, £9.20, £2.20; EX 114.30 Place 6 £12.57, Place 5 £5.66.
Owner Brilliant By You! **Bred** Mme J Guingo **Trained** Ramsnest Common, Surrey

FOCUS
A moderate novices' handicap, run at a steady early pace, resulting in a moderate time. Weak form and a race that is unlikely to throw up many winners.

NOTEBOOK
Nobel Bleu De Kerpaul(FR), whose best previous effort was on the similarly tight Plumpton track, raced wide in search of better ground and travelled well. He went on at the second last but then had to battle to hold off the late challenge of the runner-up. He looks capable of further improvement with this under his belt. *(op 4-1 tchd 9-2)*
Hatteras(FR) has had plenty of chances, especially around here and Plumpton, but was given a good waiting ride and looked likely to win when delivering his challenge on the flat. He could not go past and may need headgear. *(op 25-1)*
Tamreen(IRE), making his handicap debut, had caught the eye on his previous run and, although stepping up in trip, looked as if even further would suit as he did not have the pace to deliver an effective challenge. *(op 3-1 tchd 5-1 in places)*
Bonnell(IRE), well beaten over fences on his last appearance, ran on after a bad stumble early on the final circuit had looked to end his chance. He was beaten some way, but can be given credit for *sticking to his task and may be acclimatising to his new surroundings. Official explanation: jockey said gelding hung badly right*
Come What Augustus, a keen sort, again showed promise but, as last time, did not look to get this longer trip. He may be worth trying at the minimum on good ground. *(op 9-1)*
Coach Lane, whose recent form has been on more testing ground, appeared to have every chance on the home turn but got very tired in the closing stages. *(op 5-1 tchd 11-2 in a place)*
Albert House(IRE), who stays further than this, again forced the pace but lost his action and was quickly pulled up after a mistake on the final circuit. He seemed sound afterwards so may just have suffered a knock, and can find a similar event soon if none the worse. *(tchd 10-3 in places)*
T/Plt: £33.00 to a £1 stake. Pool: £49,808.55. 1,100.60 winning tickets. T/Qpdt: £11.30 to a £1 stake. Pool: £3,543.40. 230.10 winning tickets. TM

3174 CHELTENHAM (L-H)
Saturday, January 28
3604 Meeting Abandoned - Frost

3477 CHEPSTOW (L-H)
Saturday, January 28

OFFICIAL GOING: Soft (heavy in places)
Wind: Moderate, behind Weather: Fine but cold

3611 LETHEBY & CHRISTOPHER MAIDEN HURDLE (11 hdls) 2m 4f
1:15 (1:18) (Class 4) 4-Y-O+ **£3,415** (£1,002; £501; £250)

Form RPR
4-23 **1** **Dream Alliance**[45] 2829 5-11-5 .... RichardJohnson 131+
(P J Hobbs) *chsd ldr: led 4 out: clr 2 out: easily* **10/11**[1]

4-52 **2** *7* **Principe Azzurro (FR)**[23] 3248 5-11-5 .... JoeTizzard 111
(H D Daly) *hld up: hdwy 6th: chsd wnr fr 4 out: no imp fr 2 out* **13/2**[2]

66/ **3** *14* **Carew Lad**[734] 10-11-5 .... BenjaminHitchcott 101+
(Mrs D A Hamer) *a.p: j.lft and nrly uns rdr 1st: wknd 2 out* **100/1**

04-0 **4** *24* **Montrolin**[66] 2427 6-11-5 .... RJGreene 73
(S C Burrough) *hld up: hdwy after 7th: sn rdn: wknd 4 out* **100/1**

3 **5** *shd* **Exceptionnel (FR)**[22] 3277 7-10-12 .... MrJNewbold[(7)] 73
(Lady Connell) *hld up: hdwy 6th: wknd 4 out* **10/1**

3-05 **6** *½* **Lunch Was My Idea (IRE)**[60] 2559 6-11-5 .... ChristianWilliams 72
(P F Nicholls) *hld up and bhd: short-lived effrt after 7th* **25/1**

4-F5 **7** *1 ½* **Back Among Friends**[18] 3328 7-11-5 .... JasonMaguire 71
(J A B Old) *j.lft: led to 4 out: sn wknd* **10/1**

3 **8** *9* **Dayoff (IRE)**[7] 3254 5-10-12 ....(p) AntonyEvans 55
(P D Evans) *bhd most of way* **25/1**

02 **9** *6* **Ocean Of Storms (IRE)**[21] 3283 11-10-9 .... MarkHunter[(10)] 56
(N I M Rossiter) *bhd: short-lived effrt after 7th* **66/1**

10 *10* **Red Echo (FR)** 5-11-5 .... TimmyMurphy 46
(M C Pipe) *a bhd: lost tch 5th* **14/1**

11 *17* **Tempsford (USA)**[105] 6-11-5 .... APMcCoy 29
(Jonjo O'Neill) *hld up: hdwy after 7th: wknd 4 out: j.lft 3 out* **7/1**[3]

F **U** **Justice Jones**[23] 3249 5-10-12 .... JamesWhite[(7)] —
(Mrs P Ford) *blnd and uns rdr 2nd* **100/1**

P **Sovietta (IRE)**[44] 5-10-12 .... BrianCrowley —
(A G Newcombe) *hld up: hdwy 6th: wknd and p.u bef 4 out* **33/1**

00/0 **P** **Blind Smart (IRE)**[43] 2866 8-10-12 .... CharliePoste[(7)] —
(M F Harris) *a bhd: lost tch 5th: t.o whn p.u after 2 out* **100/1**

5m 5.80s (3.10) **Going Correction** +0.25s/f (Yiel) **14** Ran SP% **119.2**
Speed ratings: **103,100,94,85,84 84,84,80,78,74 67,—,—,—** CSF £6.60 TOTE £1.80: £1.10, £2.30, £23.80; EX 9.40.
Owner The Alliance Partnership **Bred** Rewbell Syndicate **Trained** Withycombe, Somerset

FOCUS
Very comfortable for the odds-on favourite, who was value for 20 lengths, with the first two close to their marks setting the level.

NOTEBOOK
Dream Alliance had much the best form on offer and he ran out a very comfortable winner. Considered to be at his best on better ground, he hurdled particularly well and looks the type to make a nice chaser next season. *(op 6-5)*
Principe Azzurro(FR), runner-up in a similar event at Hereford, ran respectably again but was comfortably second best when diving through the final flight. *(op 9-1)*
Carew Lad, a winner between the flags, was having his first run since pulling up lame in a point two years ago. He ran well for a long way, especially as he was nearly out of the contest at the first, but it remains to be seen if he can reproduce this.
Montrolin was tailed off on his hurdling debut here two months ago and he did not achieve much this time, despite adding a numeral to his formline.
Exceptionnel(FR) ran well over three miles on his hurdling debut and this drop in trip was not what he wanted. *(op 9-1)*
Red Echo(FR) *Official explanation: jockey said gelding was never travelling (op 12-1)*
Tempsford(USA) won seven times on the Flat at up to 14 furlongs for Sir Mark Prescott. He showed little on this hurdles debut but gave the impression that he can improve for the experience, although he is going to have to. *(op 11-2)*
Sovietta(IRE) *Official explanation: jockey said mare had a breathing problem (op 40-1 tchd 50-1)*

3612 P & C MORRIS NOVICES' CHASE (18 fncs) 3m
1:45 (1:47) (Class 3) 5-Y-O+ **£7,700** (£2,405; £1,295)

Form RPR
U341 **1** **Bob Bob Bobbin**[8] 3480 7-11-9 .... JoeTizzard 139+
(C L Tizzard) *mde all: sltly reluctant paddock exit after 7th: mstke 9th: clr 3 out: comf* **2/5**[1]

-144 **2** *11* **Dancer Life (POL)**[38] 2938 7-11-9 122......................... ChristianWilliams 129+
(Evan Williams) *hld up: rdn to chse wnr appr 3 out: no imp* **8/1**[3]

U221 **3** *16* **He's The Guv'Nor (IRE)**[28] 3142 7-11-9 118............. BenjaminHitchcott 119+
(R H Buckler) *chsd wnr: mstke 9th: hit 5 out: wkng whn mstke 2 out* **7/2**[2]

P000 **P** **Chocolate Bombe (IRE)**[23] 3250 9-11-3 49...................... AntonyEvans —
(S Lycett) *a in rr: t.o whn p.u bef 8th* **100/1**

6m 25.3s (10.40) **Going Correction** +0.25s/f (Yiel) **4** Ran SP% **105.8**
Speed ratings: **92,88,83,—** CSF £3.81 TOTE £1.30; EX 3.10.
Owner Mrs Sarah Tizzard **Bred** M H Ings **Trained** Milborne Port, Dorset

FOCUS
An uncompetitive event, and a moderate winning time and the winner is now rated up to his hurdles form.

NOTEBOOK
Bob Bob Bobbin, off the mark over fences in a similar race over course and distance, won comfortably enough without being overly impressive. He put in a mixed round of jumping, but was generally safe, and will have another run before going for the Royal & SunAlliance, although he will miss Cheltenham if the ground is quick. *(tchd 4-9)*
Dancer Life(POL) put in another creditable effort but was always being comfortably held by the favourite. His turn will come at a lower level. *(tchd 17-2)*
He's The Guv'Nor(IRE), who scored in testing ground at Uttoxeter, was in second place when an error at the first fence in the home straight spelt the beginning of the end. *(op 3-1)*
Chocolate Bombe(IRE) *Official explanation: vet said gelding bled from the nose*

3613 BET365 CALL 08000 322 365 NOVICES' H'CAP HURDLE (12 hdls) 3m
2:20 (2:21) (Class 4) (0-110,110) 4-Y-O+ **£3,903** (£1,146; £573; £286)

Form RPR
2 **1** **Mayoun (IRE)**[22] 3279 9-9-8 **85**..(p) MrTJO'Brien[(7)] 100+
(Evan Williams) *hld up and bhd: hdwy 7th: led on bit 4 out: rdn and hung lft fr 2 out: drvn out* **9/2**[2]

42P2 **2** *1 ¼* **Brave Spirit (FR)**[9] 3469 8-10-8 **92**..(v) JoeTizzard 107+
(C L Tizzard) *hld up: hdwy whn hmpd and lost pl 6th: rallied appr 4 out: rdn and ev ch 2 out: nt qckn flat* **6/4**[1]

-3P1 **3** *19* **Bar Gayne (IRE)**[23] 3250 7-10-9 **93**.................................. JasonMaguire 87
(T R George) *a.p: rdn and ev ch 4 out: wknd appr 2 out* **5/1**[3]

3332 **4** *18* **Welsh Dane**[19] 3325 6-10-1 **88**...(p) OwynNelmes[(3)] 64
(M Sheppard) *chsd ldr appr 2nd: led 4th to 6th: led 8th: rdn and hdd 4 out: wknd appr 2 out* **11/1**

050 **5** *15* **Candlelight Valley (IRE)**[23] 3253 7-10-10 **94**.............. RichardJohnson 55
(P J Hobbs) *a bhd* **25/1**

3230 **6** *½* **Notanotherdonkey (IRE)**[33] 2994 6-10-5 **96**................ JohnKington[(7)] 56
(M Scudamore) *led 1st to 4th: wknd 7th* **20/1**

2333 **7** *28* **No Guarantees**[21] 3291 6-11-12 **110**................................... AntonyEvans 42
(N A Twiston-Davies) *t.k.h: bhd fr 6th: t.o* **8/1**

-653 **P** **Desertmore Chief (IRE)**[18] 3332 7-10-1 **90**............(v) StephenCraine[(5)] —
(B De Haan) *prom tl j.lft and bmpd 6th: sn rdn and struggling: t.o whn p.u bef 4 out* **25/1**

405 **P** **What'sonyourmind (IRE)**[14] 3393 6-11-2 **100**........................ APMcCoy —
(Jonjo O'Neill) *hld up: hdwy on ins to ld 6th: hdd 8th: rdn and ev ch 4 out: wknd 3 out: p.u bef last* **12/1**

6m 15.7s (-1.10) **Going Correction** +0.25s/f (Yiel) **9** Ran SP% **114.4**
Speed ratings: **111,110,104,98,93 93,83,—,—** CSF £11.61 CT £33.21 TOTE £5.40: £1.40, £1.10, £2.60; EX 12.50.
Owner D Tumman & R F Bloodstock **Bred** Jerry Keegan **Trained** Cowbridge, Vale Of Glamorgan

FOCUS
A moderate race and a decent winning time for the class. The first two pulled well clear from the second last and the winner is back to his Irish form.

NOTEBOOK
Mayoun(IRE), upped in trip for his second run for this yard, travelled best before showing ahead at the fourth from home. He had to assert on the long run between the last two flights but knuckled down well to hold off the favourite. He could well improve again now that he has finally won over hurdles, although he is reported to be quirky by his trainer. *(op 4-1 tchd 5-1)*
Brave Spirit(FR) was reverting to hurdles off no less than 30lb lower than his chase mark. Last of a group of five to have pulled a mile clear turning into the home straight, he responded to pressure to throw down a sustained challenge from the second last but could never quite get his head in front. *(op 13-8)*
Bar Gayne(IRE), winner of a weak classified hurdle last time, could only plug on at the same pace from the second last as the first two pulled well clear. There seems no reason to assume that he did not run his race. *(op 11-2 tchd 6-1)*
Welsh Dane has crept up the ratings without having managed to win and he was another 3lb higher here. He had his chance, but seems more effective on better ground. *(tchd 10-1 and 12-1)*
Candlelight Valley(IRE), well beaten in three novice events, appeared to have plenty of weight for this handicap debut and he was never a factor. *(tchd 33-1)*
What'sonyourmind(IRE) jumped better than he did at Wetherby and travelled well until coming *under pressure early in the home straight. Soon weakening, he did not stay this longer trip. (op 10-1)*

3614 BATHROOMEXPRESS.CO.UK H'CAP CHASE (22 fncs) 3m 2f 110y
2:55 (2:55) (Class 3) (0-125,122) 5-Y-O+ **£7,543** (£2,247; £1,373; £583; £305)

Form RPR
-463 **1** **Korelo (FR)**[14] 3389 8-11-10 **120**....................................... TimmyMurphy 140+
(M C Pipe) *hld up in rr: stdy hdwy 12th: mstke 17th: led after 2 out: styd on* **13/8**[1]

P45P **2** *nk* **Kittenkat**[14] 3390 12-10-3 **99**... SeanCurran 114
(N R Mitchell) *w ldr: led 3rd to 10th: led appr 12th tl after 2 out: hrd rdn and styd on flat* **50/1**

-0P2 **3** *20* **Earl's Kitchen**[8] [3481] 9-11-3 **113**..(t) JoeTizzard 108
(C L Tizzard) *led to 3rd: nt fluent 5th: led 10th tl appr 12th: wknd appr 4 out* **6/1**[2]

P-PP **4** *5* **Fox In The Box**[44] [2847] 9-11-5 **120**..............................(v[1]) DarylJacob[(5)] 113+
(R H Alner) *hld up: hdwy 8th: w ldr 17th: ev ch 4 out: hit 3 out: sn wknd* **20/1**

1-PR **5** *dist* **Coursing Run (IRE)**[42] [2875] 10-11-11 **121**...............(p) RichardJohnson —
(H D Daly) *prom: rdn after 11th: wknd 12th: t.o* **25/1**

5P12 **P** **Major Benefit (IRE)**[28] [3144] 9-11-0 **117**.................. RichardSpate[(7)] —
(Mrs K Waldron) *a bhd: t.o whn p.u bef 16th* **12/1**

224- **F** **King On The Run (IRE)**[325] [4254] 13-11-6 **119**.................. PaulO'Neill[(3)] —
(Miss Venetia Williams) *prom: 5th whn fell 10th* **22/1**

4F-5 **P** **Lets Go Dutch**[88] [1972] 10-10-2 **98**.. PJBrennan —
(K Bishop) *hld up towards rr: hmpd 10th: t.o whn p.u bef 5 out* **16/1**

50-5 **P** **Fasgo (IRE)**[78] [2162] 11-11-7 **117**.......................... ChristianWilliams —
(P F Nicholls) *hld up in tch: wknd 13th: t.o whn p.u bef 5 out* **6/1**[2]

-130 **P** **Snowy Ford (IRE)**[33] [3000] 9-11-8 **118**.................................. JamesDavies —
(N J Gifford) *bhd: nt fluent and reminders 8th: t.o 12th: p.u bef 16th* **25/1**

112 **P** **Gallik Dawn**[244] [572] 8-10-8 **111**.................................... MrTJO'Brien[(7)] —
(A Hollingsworth) *hld up and bhd: hdwy after 11th: wknd 15th: t.o whn p.u bef 5 out* **16/1**

5P-1 **P** **Lord Brock**[21] [3290] 7-11-12 **122**.. AntonyEvans —
(N A Twiston-Davies) *bhd: reminders after 4th: hdwy 7th: wknd qckly 5 out: p.u bef 3 out* **8/1**[3]

7m 16.8s (-0.30) **Going Correction** +0.25s/f (Yiel) **12** Ran SP% **116.0**
Speed ratings: **110,109,103,102,**— —,—,—,—,— CSF £93.47 CT £411.51 TOTE £2.70: £1.50, £5.70, £2.90; EX 86.10.

Owner D A Johnson **Bred** G Cherel **Trained** Nicholashayne, Devon

FOCUS

A fair handicap and a group of five pulled a long way clear on the home turn. The winner is value for further and the race has been rated positively.

NOTEBOOK

Korelo(FR) lost his way when tried over fences two seasons ago and has since proved himself a smart hurdler, with a current BHB rating of 155 in that sphere. Reverting to fences off a favourable mark, he looked in a spot of trouble on the home turn but, staying on the inner up the home straight, he got to the leader between the last two fences and was always pulling out sufficient. Murphy was not too hard on him and this should have done his confidence good. *(op 7-4)*

Kittenkat is well at home in testing ground and she ran a big race. In and out of the lead all the way, she was headed by the favourite after the second last but was renewing her effort on the run-in. *(op 33-1)*

Earl's Kitchen was 4lb higher than when scoring over three miles here earlier this month. He ran his race but could not go with the leaders over the last four fences. *(op 15-2)*

Fox In The Box has been pulled up on his last three runs, covering the past year, but he showed a bit more spark in the first-time visor. He likes it at Chepstow, having been unbeaten in two previous visits. *(op 18-1)*

Gallik Dawn should reap the benefits of this first run in eight months and he should pay his way in the spring when the ground dries out. *(op 14-1)*

Lord Brock was put up 12lb for landing a novice handicap on his chase debut. Upped in trip, he was among five left with a chance turning into the home straight but he was the first of them to crack and was eventually pulled up. *(op 14-1)*

3615 LETHEBY & CHRISTOPHER H'CAP HURDLE (8 hdls) 2m 110y

3:30 (3:30) (Class 2) (0-145,128) 4-Y-0+

£12,526 (£3,700; £1,850; £926; £462; £232)

Form RPR

1-51 **1** **Ursis (FR)**[92] [1912] 5-11-7 **123**.. APMcCoy 136+
(Jonjo O'Neill) *a gng wl: led on bit 2 out: easily* **3/1**[2]

2221 **2** *1 3/4* **Private Be**[29] [3130] 7-11-4 **120**................................ RichardJohnson 123
(P J Hobbs) *chsd ldr after 1st: led 3rd: rdn and hdd 2 out: kpt on flat: no ch w wnr* **11/4**[1]

6P-2 **3** *3 1/2* **Goldbrook**[9] [3467] 8-11-2 **125**.................................. JamesWhite[(7)] 125
(R J Hodges) *hld up: hdwy appr 4 out: rdn and one pce fr 2 out* **20/1**

2143 **4** *11* **Woody Valentine (USA)**[23] [3256] 5-11-1 **120**.................. PaulO'Neill[(3)] 109
(Miss Venetia Williams) *hld up: mstke 4th: hdwy appr 4 out: wknd 2 out* **7/1**[3]

1512 **5** *6* **Killing Me Softly**[14] [3397] 5-11-1 **120**..................(v) RobertStephens[(3)] 107+
(J Gallagher) *led to 3rd: sn rdn: wknd 3 out: blnd 2 out* **14/1**

-120 **6** *dist* **Not Left Yet (IRE)**[21] [3298] 5-11-6 **122**.......................... TimmyMurphy —
(M C Pipe) *prom tl wknd 4 out: t.o* **3/1**[2]

00PF **F** **Spring Pursuit**[14] [3397] 10-11-7 **128**.......................... StephenCraine[(5)] —
(E G Bevan) *hld up and bhd: last whn fell 4th* **10/1**

4m 12.7s (2.30) **Going Correction** +0.25s/f (Yiel) **7** Ran SP% **109.7**
Speed ratings: **104,103,101,96,93** —,— CSF £10.97 CT £120.80 TOTE £4.20: £2.50, £2.70; EX 11.50.

Owner C H McGhie **Bred** Serge Bernereau Sarl **Trained** Cheltenham, Gloucs

FOCUS

A fairly uncompetitive affair for the money on offer. The winner is value for five times the winning margin and the form looks solid enough with the placed horses close to their marks.

NOTEBOOK

Ursis(FR) was 6lb higher than when scoring on his most recent start at Wetherby three months ago. He made all that day, but reverted to hold-up tactics here and picked off Private Be at the second last for a very cosy victory. There should be more to come. *(op 7-2 tchd 4-1)*

Private Be, back on a left-handed track for this handicap debut, kept straight this time and ran a decent race, although he was no match for the favourite and is flattered to have been beaten under two lengths. He will be suited by a return to further. *(op 3-1 tchd 5-2)*

Goldbrook was racing off a career-high mark, having been raised 5lb for finishing second to subsequent winner Nippy Des Mottes at Taunton. He ran respectably but lacked the pace to go with the leaders from the second last. *(op 14-1)*

Woody Valentine(USA) threatened to be involved in the finish when challenging at the first in the home straight but was soon left toiling. *(op 11-2 tchd 8-1)*

Killing Me Softly has been much improved this winter but was another 3lb higher here, and the drop back in trip was another factor in this defeat. *(tchd 16-1)*

Not Left Yet(IRE) was down in grade after finishing in midfield behind stablemate Desert Air in the *Ladbroke at Sandown. He weakened tamely early in the straight and has questions to answer. (op 5-2)*

Spring Pursuit took a heavy fall. *(tchd 11-1)*

3616 LETHEBY & CHRISTOPHER CONDITIONAL JOCKEYS' NOVICES' H'CAP HURDLE (8 hdls) 2m 110y

4:00 (4:02) (Class 4) (0-110,102) 4-Y-0+ **£3,903** (£1,146; £573; £286)

Form RPR

042F **1** **Spike Jones (NZ)**[16] [3360] 8-11-10 **100**.................................. DerekLaverty 104+
(Mrs S M Johnson) *hld up: hdwy after 4th: led on bit 3 out: clr last: pushed out* **7/1**[3]

3-PP **2** *7* **L'Orphelin**[26] [3212] 11-10-3 **79**..............................(b) RobertStephens 75+
(C L Tizzard) *chsd ldr: led 3rd: j.lft fr 4 out: hdd 3 out: one pce* **8/1**

0511 **3** *14* **Golden Feather**[8] [3485] 4-10-5 **95**.............................. LiamTreadwell[(3)] 79+
(Miss Venetia Williams) *prom: ev ch whn blnd and rdr lost iron 3 out: nt rcvr* **6/5**[1]

41F0 **4** *2 1/2* **Random Quest**[18] [3333] 8-11-12 **102**..................(p) StephenCraine 80
(B J Llewellyn) *led to 3rd: rdn and wknd after 4th* **9/1**

2052 **5** *dist* **Tech Eagle (IRE)**[15] [3371] 6-11-0 **100**.......................... WayneBurton[(10)] —
(R Curtis) *plld hrd: sn prom: wknd appr 4 out: t.o* **4/1**[2]

06-P **6** *18* **New Diamond**[23] [3250] 7-9-12 **77**.................................... JamesWhite[(3)] —
(Mrs P Ford) *plld hrd early: a bhd: t.o* **100/1**

355U **F** **Dusty Dane (IRE)**[11] [3429] 4-10-4 **99**......................(t) RichardGordon[(8)] —
(W G M Turner) *hld up: hdwy 4th: w ldr whn fell 4 out* **16/1**

U306 **F** **Presenter (IRE)**[18] [3333] 6-11-2 **95**.................................. DarylJacob[(3)] 73
(M Sheppard) *hld up: hdwy 4th: wknd appr 4 out: no ch whn fell 2 out* **25/1**

64P0 **U** **Redlynch Spirit (IRE)**[29] [3127] 6-10-2 **78**.......................... OwynNelmes —
(C L Tizzard) *hld up: mstke 3rd: sme hdwy after 4th: 5th and wkng whn hmpd and uns rdr 4 out* **33/1**

4m 19.9s (9.50) **Going Correction** +0.25s/f (Yiel)
WFA 4 from 6yo+ 11lb **9** Ran SP% **112.7**
Speed ratings: **87,83,77,75,**— —,—,—,— CSF £58.01 CT £111.31 TOTE £8.50: £1.70, £1.70, £1.20; EX 94.40.

Owner G Button **Bred** D M Kerr **Trained** Lulham, H'fords

FOCUS

A moderate time, over seven seconds slower than the preceding contest. This probably did not take too much winning and the winner is the best guide based on recent efforts.

NOTEBOOK

Spike Jones(NZ), who has been knocking on the door recently, has changed stables since his last run. While the luck was with him to an extent this time, he scored comfortably and would probably have won even had the favourite not blundered away his chance. *(tchd 15-2)*

L'Orphelin, reverting to hurdles off no less than a 33lb lower mark, had only completed the course in one of his last seven starts and this was more encouraging. Jumping out to his left as the pressure was on up the home straight, he was probably third best on merit. *(tchd 9-1)*

Golden Feather, shooting for a hat-trick off a 12lb higher mark, looked in serious trouble when ridden along on the long home turn, but came back on the bridle in the straight. He was alongside the eventual winner when he lost his momentum, and his rider an iron, with a blunder at the third last. The chances are that he would have finished second. *(tchd Evens and 5-4)*

Random Quest, wearing cheekpieces for the first time, did not last much beyond halfway and only collected fourth prize due to casualties in front of him. *(op 11-1 tchd 12-1)*

Dusty Dane(IRE), debuting over hurdles, improved on the long home turn and was right in contention when coming down at the first flight in the home straight. He jumped the flight well enough but stumbled on landing. *(op 11-1 tchd 20-1)*

3617 WESTERN DAILY PRESS STANDARD OPEN NATIONAL HUNT FLAT RACE 2m 110y

4:35 (4:36) (Class 6) 4-6-Y-0 **£1,626** (£477; £238; £119)

Form RPR

4 **1** **Dark Corner**[27] [3181] 4-10-0.................................. StevenCrawford[(7)] 95+
(N A Twiston-Davies) *t.k.h: a.p: rdn and outpcd over 5f out: rallied to ld over 3f out: edgd rt over 2f out: r.o* **15/8**[1]

5 **2** *1 1/4* **Captain Marlon (IRE)**[33] [3001] 5-11-4.................................. JoeTizzard 102+
(C L Tizzard) *w ldr: ev ch over 3f out: kpt on ins fnl f* **8/1**

3 *12* **Master Eddy** 6-11-4.. AntonyEvans 90
(S Lycett) *bhd: rdn and hdwy over 5f out: styd on one pce fnl 2f* **33/1**

4 *3* **Sula's Legend** 5-10-13.. DarylJacob[(5)] 87
(D P Keane) *prom: led briefly over 5f out: wknd over 1f out* **33/1**

006 **5** *3* **Schindler's List**[32] [3024] 6-11-4.................................. PhilipHide 84
(C Roberts) *hld up and bhd: hdwy on ins 4f out: wknd 2f out* **33/1**

3 **6** *8* **Sky Mack (IRE)**[60] [2565] 5-11-1.................................. PaulO'Neill[(3)] 76
(Evan Williams) *hld up: sn mid-div: hdwy over 5f out: wknd over 2f out* **9/1**

7 *1 1/4* **Aymard Des Fieffes (FR)** 4-10-7.............................. JimmyMcCarthy 64
(R A Harris) *hld up in mid-div: hdwy 10f out: led over 5f out tl over 3f out: wknd over 2f out* **33/1**

8 *nk* **Ice Melted (IRE)** 5-10-11.. MrAJBerry[(7)] 74
(Jonjo O'Neill) *hld up: hdwy 8f out: rdn and wknd over 3f out* **3/1**[2]

9 *3 1/2* **Topamendip (IRE)** 6-11-4.................................. ChristianWilliams 71
(P F Nicholls) *hld up in mid-div: hdwy over 5f out: wknd 4f out* **9/2**[3]

40 **10** *dist* **Overamorous**[60] [2565] 5-10-6.................................. StephenCraine[(5)] —
(J L Needham) *led tl hdd & wknd over 5f out: t.o* **40/1**

0 **11** *7* **Auburn Grey**[17] [3346] 4-10-0.................................. LeeNewnes[(7)] —
(M D I Usher) *sn prom: rdn 10f out: wknd over 6f out: t.o* **66/1**

12 *dist* **Stockton Flyer** 5-11-4.. JamesDavies —
(Mrs D A Butler) *a bhd: t.o fnl 10f* **100/1**

4m 12.5s (2.30) **Going Correction** +0.25s/f (Yiel)
WFA 4 from 5yo 11lb 5 from 6yo 8lb **12** Ran SP% **115.8**
Speed ratings: **104,103,97,96,94 91,90,90,88,**— —,— CSF £16.52 TOTE £3.10: £1.10, £2.50, £5.80; EX 15.30 Place 6 £4.00, Place 5 £2.93..

Owner H R Mould **Bred** S Pike **Trained** Naunton, Gloucs

FOCUS

Just a fair bumper. The winner has been rated better than the bare result but below his Cheltenham figure.

NOTEBOOK

Dark Corner, upped in trip, was driven to lead with over three furongs to run and was always holding the persistent runner-up. He is a promising youngster who will be suited by the return to better ground, but it is optimistic to think of him as a Cheltenham Festival candidate. *(op 5-2)*

Captain Marlon(IRE) refused to go down without a fight and made the favourite work for his victory. This was a pleasing run from a horse whose future lies over fences. *(tchd 9-1)*

Master Eddy, whose dam is a half-sister to a winning hurdler, stayed on from off the pace to go third inside the final furlong. This was a reasonable start to his career.

Sula's Legend, out of a half-sister to winning chaser Fluff 'N' Puff, made a satisfactory debut and was only run out of third place inside the last. *(op 22-1)*

Schindler's List has been unplaced in four bumpers now but does have a bit of ability. He seemed to run his race and helps set the level of this form.

Ice Melted(IRE) is out of a sister to useful but ill-fated hurdler/chaser Ross Moff. He was the subject of on-course support but he found little when coming off the bridle early in the home straight. *(op 9-2 tchd 5-2)*

T/Plt: £7.80 to a £1 stake. Pool: £71,015.95. 6,632.45 winning tickets. T/Qpdt: £5.20 to a £1 stake. Pool: £3,409.70. 479.40 winning tickets. KH

[1275]SOUTHWELL (L-H)

Saturday, January 28

OFFICIAL GOING: Good to soft, good in places

Meeting transferred from Doncaster.

Wind: Virtually nil

3618 SKYBET PRESS RED TO BET ON ATR HBLB NOVICES' CHASE (13 fncs) 2m

1:20 (1:20) (Class 2) 5-Y-O+ **£13,012** (£3,820; £1,910; £954)

Form RPR

-421 **1** **Green Tango**[23] 3251 7-11-7 .... MarkBradburne 142+
(H D Daly) *trckd ldrs: smooth hdwy 4 out: led after next: comf* **5/6**[1]

3105 **2** *2 ½* **Feel The Pride (IRE)**[14] 3387 8-11-3 129..........(b) NoelFehily 131
(Jonjo O'Neill) *hld up in tch: hdwy 4 out: rdn 2 out: chsd wnr last: kpt on* **16/1**

-U21 **3** *3 ½* **Roman Ark**[25] 3236 8-11-7 .... AndrewThornton 133+
(J M Jefferson) *cl up: effrt 3 out and ev ch tl rdn and one pce next* **8/1**[3]

0-32 **4** *6* **Reel Missile**[40] 2924 7-11-2 .... AdamPogson 123+
(C T Pogson) *led: j. persistently rt: rdn along 4 out: mstke next and sn hdd: hit 2 out and sn wknd: hit last* **14/1**

44-F **5** *10* **Pole Star**[18] 3329 8-11-2 .... LeightonAspell 113+
(J R Fanshawe) *nt fluent: hld up: effrt and pushed along 4 out: rdn bef next and sn btn* **11/4**[2]

5P-P **P** **Astronomic**[37] 2943 6-11-2 .... GrahamLee —
(J Howard Johnson) *chsd ldrs: rdn along 5 out: sn wknd and p.u after next* **25/1**

4m 11.8s (-0.80) **Going Correction** +0.15s/f (Yiel) **6** Ran SP% **108.7**

Speed ratings: **108,106,105,102,97** — CSF £12.87 TOTE £1.60: £1.10, £3.30; EX 8.00.

Owner Mrs Strachan,Gabb,Lady Barlow & Harford **Bred** Southill Stud **Trained** Stanton Lacy, Shropshire

FOCUS

A good novice event, run at a fair gallop, and the form looks solid rated through the runner-up. The winner is progressive.

NOTEBOOK

Green Tango ◆, whose recent success over Don't Be Shy at Hereford was well advertised when that rival subsequently hosed up at Haydock, followed-up with a convincing success under a penalty and can be rated value for further. He would have ideally preferred a stronger pace, deserves credit for quickening as he did after being short of room turning for home, and again his jumping was assured. Given that he is probably at his best on genuinely good ground, it would be little surprise to see him turn up at the Cheltenham Festival, and the Grand Annual Handicap - which his trainer won with the novice Palarshan in 2003 - looks a viable target providing he is alloted an official mark under 140. *(op 10-11 tchd evens in places)*

Feel The Pride(IRE), reverting to novice company, was doing her best work from two out and looked to run near to her official rating in defeat. The first-time blinkers had a positive effect, and she can strike again over fences, but may have to revert to competing against her own sex in order to do so in the short-term. *(op 11-1)*

Roman Ark, off the mark as a chaser over further at Ayr last time, had every chance yet could not quicken with the winner when it mattered and was ultimately well held. He would have ideally preferred a deeper surface over this trip, however, and he continues to go the right way. *(op 6-1)*

Reel Missile did not help his cause by continually jumping to his right, and again made mistakes when under pressure, but still left the impression he can rate higher as a chaser when getting his act together. He should fare better when entering the handicap arena and will be suited by a return to further. *(tchd 12-1)*

Pole Star, who took a crashing fall on his recent chasing bow at Leicester, not all that surprisingly lacked confidence over his fences and ran well below expectations. This clear round should have helped his confidence, however, and it is far too early to be write him off. *(op 7-2)*

Astronomic has gone backwards and is one to avoid. *(op 22-1)*

3619 YOU'RE EITHER VEGAS OR YOU'RE NOT MANSION HOUSE H'CAP CHASE (13 fncs) 2m

1:50 (1:50) (Class 2) (0-140,137) 5-Y-O+ **£13,012** (£3,820; £1,910; £954)

Form RPR

2060 **1** **Almaydan**[16] 3357 8-11-4 129..........(b[1]) RobertThornton 142+
(R Lee) *led to 5th: cl up tl led again appr 3 out: rdn after next: styd on* **7/1**

3532 **2** *2 ½* **Bleu Superbe (FR)**[28] 3136 11-11-5 130.......... SamThomas 140+
(Miss Venetia Williams) *cl up: led 5th: pushed along and blnd 5 out: rdn and hdd appr 3 out: rallied u.p 2 out: mstke last: one pce* **10/3**[1]

U03P **3** *12* **Turgeonev (FR)**[33] 2993 11-11-0 125.......... RussGarritty 121
(T D Easterby) *chsd ldng pair: rdn along 5 out: drvn and one pce appr 3 out* **16/1**

4041 **4** *1 ¼* **Palua**[16] 3357 9-11-12 137.......... MarcusFoley 133+
(Miss E C Lavelle) *chsd ldrs: rdn along 5 out: chsd ldng pair next: sn one pce* **9/1**

1P21 **5** *3* **Royal Hector (GER)**[19] 3323 7-11-6 131.......... NoelFehily 126+
(Jonjo O'Neill) *midfield: rdn along whn blnd 8th: sn wknd* **5/1**[2]

-525 **6** *1 ¾* **Super Nomad**[49] 2768 11-10-10 124.......... MrTGreenall[(3)] 114
(M W Easterby) *in tch: rdn along 8th: sn wknd* **11/1**

1F10 **7** *11* **Oso Magic**[7] 3495 8-11-1 126.......... DavidO'Meara 110+
(Mrs S J Smith) *mstke 3rd: a rr* **5/1**[2]

P-20 **U** **Terre De Java (FR)**[244] 571 8-10-4 115.......... TomDoyle —
(Mrs H Dalton) *rr whn blnd and uns rdr 3rd* **12/1**

33P0 **P** **Log On Intersky (IRE)**[50] 2754 10-9-11 113 oh3 ow2..... MarkNicolls[(5)] —
(J R Cornwall) *a rr: bhd fr 1/2-way: p.u bef 4 out* **100/1**

P1P2 **P** **Nowator (POL)**[7] 3495 9-10-11 122.......... AndrewThornton —
(Robert Gray) *chsd ldrs: rdn along 1/2-way: sn wknd and bhd whn p.u bef 3 out* **13/2**[3]

5-00 **P** **Waterspray (AUS)**[46] 2813 8-10-6 117.......... HenryOliver —
(Ian Williams) *nt fluent: rr whn mstke 6th: sn rdn along and bhd: p.u bef 4 out* **40/1**

4m 11.9s (-0.70) **Going Correction** +0.15s/f (Yiel) **11** Ran SP% **117.6**

Speed ratings: **107,105,99,99,97 96,91,—,—,—** — CSF £31.64 CT £366.81 TOTE £6.50: £2.30, £1.10, £4.30; EX 27.80.

Owner George Brookes & Family **Bred** Shadwell Estate Company Limited **Trained** Byton, H'fords

FOCUS

A good handicap, run at a sound pace, and the first two came clear. The form, rated through the winner and the consistent runner-up, looks solid and could be rated higher.

NOTEBOOK

Almaydan, popular in the betting ring, bounced right back to his best with a hard-fought success and the first-time blinkers clearly had the desired effect. He was given a positive ride by Thornton, which suited, and he did well to keep responding in the home straight when under pressure. His future hopes probably rely on the headgear having the same effect in the future, but providing the Handicapper does not raise him too much for this, another crack at the Grand Annual at Cheltenham - in which he disappointed last season - appears realistic enough. *(op 10-1)*

Bleu Superbe(FR) turned in yet another valliant effort and his fate was only sealed after a blunder at the final fence. He is a model of consistency, and was well clear of the rest at the finish, but he has not won since 2003 and always seems to find one or two too good these days.

Turgeonev(FR), pulled up at Wetherby last time, finished his race well enough and showed his true colours in defeat. He is on a long losing run, but is on a fair mark as a result, and could be placed to find race when reverting to a more suitably longer trip.

Palua, winner of this event from a 9lb lower mark in 2004, was racing off a 6lb higher mark than when successful at Ludlow 16 days previously and was not disgraced under top weight. The Handicapper now looks firmly in charge, however. *(op 8-1)*

Royal Hector(GER), raised 3lb for his fortunate success at Tautnon last time, failed to sparkle over this shorter trip in hotter company. He may be best in smaller fields, and probably wants further, but still has to prove he is up to this new mark. *(op 6-1)*

Oso Magic lacked fluency over his fences and was disappointing. He has a fair deal to prove now.

Nowator(POL) ran below expectations and seemingly has two ways of running these days. *(op 8-1 tchd 9-1)*

3620 SKY BET CHASE (A H'CAP) (FORMERLY THE GREAT YORKSHIRE CHASE) (LISTED RACE) (19 fncs) 3m 110y

2:25 (2:25) (Class 1) (0-145,143) 5-Y-O+

£34,212 (£12,834; £6,426; £3,204; £1,608; £804)

Form RPR

14-0 **1** **A Glass In Thyne (IRE)**[77] 2176 8-10-12 128.......... AndrewThornton 140+
(B N Pollock) *midfield: hdwy to trck ldrs 1/2-way: effrt 3 out: rdn to ld and j.lft next: drvn last and styd on wl* **16/1**

0P25 **2** *2 ½* **Europa**[49] 2760 10-11-1 136.......... ThomasDreaper[(5)] 146+
(Ferdy Murphy) *hld up in rr: stdy hdwy appr 3th: trckd ldrs 4 out: ev ch next: rdn and sltly hmpd 2 out: kpt on same pce* **16/1**

011/ **3** *8* **Keltic Bard**[651] 4860 9-11-6 136.......... NoelFehily 140+
(C J Mann) *hld up and bhd: stdy hdwy 1/2-way: trckd ldrs 14th: effrt and ev ch 3 out: sltly hmpd next and no ex bef last* **14/1**

4/00 **4** *11* **Our Armageddon (NZ)**[14] 3385 9-10-11 130.......... LarryMcGrath[(3)] 122+
(R C Guest) *in tch: hdwy to trck ldrs 1/2-way: led 5 out: rdn along 3 out: hdd and hit next: sn wknd* **20/1**

-012 **5** *1 ½* **Too Forward (IRE)**[27] 3180 10-11-8 138.......... CarlLlewellyn 130+
(M Pitman) *hld up: gd hdwy to join ldrs 13th: pushed along and blnd 4 out: sn rdn and wknd bef next* **9/2**[1]

-253 **6** *5* **Aristoxene (FR)**[21] 3293 6-11-2 132.......... MickFitzgerald 119+
(N J Henderson) *mstkes: chsd ldrs: blnd 10th: rdn along 14th and plugged on same pce fr 4 out* **10/1**

06-P **7** *13* **Polar Red**[56] 2636 9-10-13 129..........(t) TomScudamore 104+
(M C Pipe) *hld up towards rr: hmpd 10th and a bhd after* **50/1**

0-6P **P** **Horus (IRE)**[21] 3296 11-11-5 138..........(p) TomMalone[(3)] —
(M C Pipe) *a rr: bhd whn p.u bef 3 out* **50/1**

-2UP **P** **Colourful Life (IRE)**[63] 2491 10-11-1 138.......... LiamHeard[(7)] —
(P F Nicholls) *towards rr whn blnd bdly 12th and sn p.u* **8/1**

-0P3 **P** **Jakari (FR)**[21] 3296 9-11-0 130.......... MarkBradburne —
(H D Daly) *chsd ldrs to 6th: lost pl and towards rr whn hmpd 10th: bhd whn p.u bef 3 out* **11/2**[2]

-010 **P** **Scots Grey**[49] 2760 11-11-7 137.......... MarcusFoley —
(N J Henderson) *led to 3rd: prom tl rdn along 1/2-way and grad wknd: bhd whn p.u bef 3 out* **33/1**

P22- **P** **Royal Emperor (IRE)**[357] 3707 10-11-10 140.......... DavidO'Meara —
(Mrs S J Smith) *towards rr: mstke 4th: rdn along 1/2-way and bhd whn p.u bef 3 out* **25/1**

P311 **P** **Sonevafushi (FR)**[9] 3469 8-11-12 142.......... SamThomas —
(Miss Venetia Williams) *cl up: led 5th: rdn along and hdd 5 out: wknd next and bhd whn p.u bef last* **13/2**[3]

2000 **P** **Mixsterthetrixster (USA)**[32] 3019 10-11-0 130.......... HenryOliver —
(Mrs Tracey Barfoot-Saunt) *chsd ldrs: mstke 11th: sn lost pl and bhd whn p.u bhd whn p.u bef 13th* **50/1**

1-4U **U** **King Harald (IRE)**[63] 2491 8-11-4 134.......... MatthewBatchelor 126
(M Bradstock) *cl up: led 3rd to 5th: rdn along 4 out: drvn whn hit next and sn wknd: 5th and wl hld whn blnd and uns rdr last* **9/2**[1]

6m 37.9s (-5.90) **Going Correction** +0.15s/f (Yiel) **15** Ran SP% **121.1**

Speed ratings: **115,114,111,108,107 106,101,—,—,— —,—,—,—,—** CSF £224.18 CT £3637.68 TOTE £18.30: £3.80, £4.10, £3.60; EX 348.80 Trifecta £2609.40 Pool £,3675.28 - 1winning unit..

Owner J B Dale **Bred** Mrs M Fox **Trained** Medbourne, Leics

FOCUS

A good handicap and the winning time was about as one would expect for a race of its stature and, despite some disappointing efforts, the form still appears decent enough rated through the second.

NOTEBOOK

A Glass In Thyne(IRE), who reportedly needed time to recover from the exertions of his seasonal bow when behind Innox at Cheltenham in November, put in a superb round of jumping and landed his first handicap success in ready fashion. He could have been called the winner after jumping three out and, despite looking to idle a touch on the run-in, was always holding sway over the runner-up. This his second success from just four outings over fences, and he has very few miles on the clock, so providing he comes out of this race in good heart, fully deserves to take his chance in one of the handicaps at the Cheltenham Festival in March.

Europa enjoyed the return to this longer trip, and ran a most solid race, finishing a clear second-best. He would have been closer, but for being hampered at the penultimate fence, and considering he is at best on faster ground, this has to rate a very pleasing effort. He really does deserve a change of luck and the Kim Muir at Cheltenham in March is reportedly his big target. *(op 25-1)*

Keltic Bard ◆, making his return from a 651-day layoff and searching for a third straight win over fences, posted a very promising comeback display. He had yet to be asked a serious question when moving into contention four out, but ultimately his lack of a recent race told when put under pressure, and he could not stay with the front pair. He should still look fairly treated should he go up in the weights for this and could be an ideal type for the Mildmay Of Flete in March. *(op 12-1)*

Our Armageddon(NZ), whose trainer sent out Tyneandthyneagain to win this event in 2004, showed much-improved form and only faded out of contention after jumping the penultimate fence. This trip stretched his stamina, but it was nevertheless a much more encouraging display, and he can build on this when reverting to shorter. *(op 16-1)*

Too Forward(IRE) looked like playing a part in the finish when moving up to join the leaders, but he failed to sustain his effort and was eventually well beaten. He boasted some decent form over shorter distances before coming into this and may show his true colours again when dropping back in trip. *(tchd 5-1)*

Colourful Life(IRE), who took this event last season from an 8lb lower mark, was starting to struggle prior to making a serious error and being pulled up. *(tchd 5-1)*

Jakari(FR), back to form at Sandown last time, ran no sort of race and proved most disappointing. He has it all to prove now. *(tchd 5-1)*

Sonevafushi(FR), bidding for a hat-trick from a career-high mark over fences, ultimately paid for helping set the decent early pace. He has had a fairly busy time of late, however, and is capable of better. *(tchd 5-1)*

King Harald(IRE), last seen unseating in the Hennessy, was starting to beat a retreat three out and was well beaten when unshipping his rider at the final fence. He has a fair amount to prove now, but is probably happier over shorter and is not one to write off just yet. *(tchd 5-1)*

3621 IT MATTERS MORE WHEN THERE'S MONEY ON IT MARES' ONLY H'CAP HURDLE (9 hdls) 2m

3:00 (3:05) (Class 2) 4-Y-0+ **£19,518** (£5,730; £2,865; £1,431)

Form				RPR
1	**1**		**Bold Fire**[7] 3511 4-9-13 **128** ow1 ... LiamHeard(7) (P F Nicholls) *in tch: hdwy to trck ldr 4th: led appr 2 out: clr bef last: shkn up and kpt on* **5/4**[1]	125+
-422	**2**	*4*	**Pay Attention**[21] 3295 5-10-13 **124** ... RussGarritty (T D Easterby) *trckd ldrs: hdwy and cl up 5th: rdn along 3 out: styng on u.p whn hit last: one pce flat* **11/2**[3]	125+
/UF2	**3**	*2*	**Perle De Puce (FR)**[22] 3278 7-11-5 **137** ...(v[1]) MrSWaley-Cohen(7) (N J Henderson) *prom: cl up 5th: rdn along appr 2 out: drvn and one pce appr last* **16/1**	135
1F14	**4**	*6*	**Heltornic (IRE)**[14] 3388 6-10-7 **118** ... TomScudamore (M Scudamore) *cl up: pushed along 1/2-way: rdn 3 out and outpcd bef next* **12/1**	110
0321	**5**	*½*	**De Blanc (IRE)**[22] 3278 6-10-12 **123** ... SamThomas (Miss Venetia Williams) *bhd: hdwy to chse ldrs 1/2-way: rdn along 4 out and sn outpcd* **14/1**	115
134	**6**	*2 ½*	**Miss Pebbles (IRE)**[21] 3295 6-10-2 **113** ... WayneHutchinson (R Dickin) *hld up in rr: hdwy to chse ldrs 3 out: sn rdn and wknd next* **10/1**	102
0453	**7**	*1 ¼*	**Emmasflora**[21] 3287 8-10-1 **117** oh8 ow6 ... AdamPogson(5) (C T Pogson) *led: rdn along 3 out: hdd and drvn bef next: sn wknd and bhd whn blnd last* **50/1**	109+
13-0	**F**		**Miss Academy (FR)**[21] 3298 5-11-0 **128** ... TomMalone(3) (M C Pipe) *in tch whn fell 2nd* **9/2**[2]	—
0-P3	**P**		**Dancing Pearl**[21] 3295 8-10-12 **123** ... MarkBradburne (C J Price) *trckd ldrs: blnd 3rd: sn rdn along and bhd whn p.u bef 3 out* **12/1**	—

4m 8.70s (1.50) **Going Correction** +0.30s/f (Yiel)
WFA 4 from 5yo+ 11lb **9** Ran SP% **117.0**
Speed ratings: **108,106,105,102,101 100,99,—,—** CSF £9.27 CT £75.32 TOTE £1.90: £1.10, £1.70, £5.30; EX 9.20.
Owner Mrs Sue Craven **Bred** Theakston Stud **Trained** Ditcheat, Somerset

FOCUS
A good mares-only handicap, run at a sound pace, and the field came home strung out. The form looks solid rated through the runner-up.

NOTEBOOK
Bold Fire, off the mark on her debut for connections at Wincanton a week previously, duly made it two wins from as many starts since switching from France and was full value for her winning margin. She has started handicap life on a good mark, and this was a much-improved display, but the Handicapper will likely make her life harder after this so she will need to keep progressing in order to land the hat-trick in this sphere. *(op 6-5 tchd 6-4)*
Pay Attention ran another solid race and would have been a touch closer but for making an error at the last flight. She is a decent benchmark for this form and really does deserve to find another race. *(op 13-2 tchd 7-1 and 9-2)*
Perle De Puce(FR), reverting to hurdles with a first-time visor replacing blinkers, could only muster the same pace under pressure yet was not disgraced under top weight and posted her best effort for some time. She needs all to fall right in her races and is in need of respite from the Handicapper in this sphere. *(op 10-1)*
Heltornic(IRE), making her handicap debut, not surprisingly found this an insufficient stamina test and did not perform badly in the circumstances. She has further prizes in her against her own sex when reverting to a suitably longer trip. *(op 14-1)*
De Blanc(IRE), off the mark as a chaser at Towcester last time, did not jump with any fluency on this return to hurdling and appeared to find things happening all too quickly. She needs further and is capable of better than this. *(op 20-1)*
Miss Academy(FR) took a crashing fall at the second flight and her confidence may well need restoring after this. *(op 5-1 tchd 11-2)*

3622 SKYBET.COM H'CAP HURDLE (11 hdls) 2m 4f 110y

3:35 (3:40) (Class 3) (0-135,135) 4-Y-0+ **£6,506** (£1,910; £955; £477)

Form				RPR
F21	**1**		**Hoh Viss**[28] 3139 6-10-11 **120** ... NoelFehily (C J Mann) *towards rr: j. slowly 5th and bhd: pushed along and hdwy after 7th: in tch 3 out: effrt next: rdn last: r.o to ld last 100* **5/2**[1]	132+
4101	**2**	*2*	**Euro American (GER)**[19] 3318 6-10-11 **120** ... AlanDempsey (E W Tuer) *hld up: stdy hdwy 7th: cl up 3 out: rdn to ld appr last: drvn flat: hdd and no ex last 100 yds* **15/2**	130+
-F41	**3**	*11*	**Go For Bust**[16] 3360 7-11-3 **126** ... MarcusFoley (N J Henderson) *hld up and bhd: stdy hdwy 7th: chsd ldrs 3 out: rdn and ch next: sn drvn and wknd* **7/1**[3]	124
4255	**4**	*shd*	**Le Royal (FR)**[33] 2975 7-9-5 **110** ... JamesReveley(10) (K G Reveley) *wl bhd tl hdwy 3 out: styd on wl fr next: nrst fin* **20/1**	108
UP-0	**5**	*1 ¾*	**Benbyas**[14] 3383 9-11-4 **132** ... JohnnyLevins(5) (D Carroll) *led to 7th: cl up: led again after 3 out: rdn and hdd next: sn drvn and grad wknd* **66/1**	128+
53P0	**6**	*16*	**Arrayou (FR)**[21] 3298 5-11-2 **125** ...(v) LeightonAspell (O Sherwood) *nvr bttr than midfield* **25/1**	105
2312	**7**	*1*	**Enhancer**[161] 1266 8-11-1 **124** ... JohnMcNamara (M J McGrath) *bhd fr 1/2-way* **28/1**	103
0-01	**8**	*1 ¼*	**Pretty Star (GER)**[33] 2999 6-11-11 **134** ... RobertThornton (A King) *chsd ldrs: rdn along bef 3 out and sn wknd* **9/1**	112
1221	**9**	*12*	**Sunday City (JPN)**[16] 3351 5-10-8 **122** ... TomGreenway(5) (P Bowen) *cl up: led 7th: rdn along 3 out and wknd qckly appr 2 out* **8/1**	88
PP40	**10**	*9*	**Powder Creek (IRE)**[63] 2498 9-10-6 **115** ... AndrewThornton (K G Reveley) *midfield: mstkes 7th and 8th: sn bhd* **100/1**	72
02-4	**11**	*3 ½*	**Papini (IRE)**[28] 3135 5-11-2 **125** ... MickFitzgerald (N J Henderson) *chsd ldrs: rdn along 7th: sn lost pl and bhd* **10/1**	78
U12F	**12**	*2*	**Direct Flight (IRE)**[19] 3323 8-10-6 **118** ... WilliamKennedy(3) (Noel T Chance) *in tch: blnd 7th: sn lost pl and bhd* **11/2**[2]	69
50P0	**13**	*3*	**Fontanesi (IRE)**[21] 3298 6-11-12 **135** ... TomScudamore (M C Pipe) *hld up: a rr* **66/1**	83
0510	**14**	*20*	**Smart Boy Prince (IRE)**[25] 2952 5-10-2 **116** ... MarkNicolls(5) (C Smith) *cl up: rdn along after 7th: sn wknd* **33/1**	44
440-	**F**		**Widemouth Bay (IRE)**[350] 3809 8-10-11 **120** ... SamThomas (Miss H C Knight) *midfield: hdwy 7th: led 2 out: sn rdn and hdd: 3rd and hld whn fell last* **33/1**	—

5m 23.8s (2.30) **Going Correction** +0.30s/f (Yiel) **15** Ran SP% **120.3**
Speed ratings: **107,106,102,102,101 95,94,94,89,86 85,84,83,75,—** CSF £19.73 CT £120.61 TOTE £3.50: £1.30, £2.90, £2.60; EX 30.10 Trifecta £216.60 Pool £1,220.50 - 4 winning units..
Owner D F Allport **Bred** D F Allport **Trained** Upper Lambourn, Berks

FOCUS
A fair and competitive handicap for the class, run at a decent pace, and the first pair came clear. Both appear to be progressing nicely and the form looks solid.

NOTEBOOK
Hoh Viss ◆, having his first outing in a handicap over timber, made his rider work hard in the home straight, but ultimately ran out a ready winner and followed-up his facile success at Uttoxeter in novice company 28 days previously. He is clearly fast-improving, and while the Handicapper will now have his say, a bold bid for the hat-trick looks assured. *(tchd 11-4)*
Euro American(GER), raised 10lb for winning at Newcastle last time, held every chance and turned in a personal-best in defeat. He is still improving and, considering he was well clear of the rest at the finish, can be placed to resume winning ways in the coming weeks. *(op 8-1)*
Go For Bust, back up in trip and racing off a 6lb higher mark than when winning at Ludlow 16 days previously, had his chance and only started to struggle from the penultimate flight. He did not see out the longer distance as may have been expected, but clearly remains in good form, and should continue to pay his way from this new mark. *(op 9-1)*
Le Royal(FR), returning to hurdles and very well backed, got going all too late under his inexperienced rider and was never a serious factor. Granted a more prominent ride in this sphere in the future, he really ought to get closer from his current mark. *(tchd 22-1)*
Benbyas fared best of those to help force the early gallop and posted much his best effort for some time. While he may need a little further respite from the Handicapper, this proves his engine is still very much intact, and he ought to come on again fitness-wise for the outing. A drop back to two miles will also be right up his street.
Arrayou(FR) *(op 22-1)*
Pretty Star(GER) *(op 8-1)*
Direct Flight(IRE), who had the race in the bag last time at Taunton before falling at the final fence, never looked happy at any stage and proved most disappointing. *(op 5-1)*
Widemouth Bay(IRE), who badly lost his way last season, was booked for third spot prior to taking a crashing fall at the final flight and has to rate unlucky. This was his first outing for 350 days, and it was full of promise, yet his confidence will have been dented and his next outing should reveal more.

3623 PLAY ELVIS 5 REEL SLOT - PRESS RED "JUNIOR" STANDARD OPEN NATIONAL HUNT FLAT RACE 2m

4:05 (4:12) (Class 6) 4-Y-0 **£2,055** (£599; £299)

Form				RPR
1	**1**		**Alfie Flits**[56] 2642 4-11-7 ... TomDoyle (G A Swinbank) *trckd ldrs: smooth hdwy to ld 2f out: sn clr: v easily* **10/11**[1]	115+
	2	*6*	**Ovide (FR)** 4-11-0 ... GrahamLee (J Howard Johnson) *led 2f: cl up tl led again over 4f out: rdn 3f out: hdd 2f out and sn one pce* **7/1**[3]	96
1	**3**	*¾*	**Jass**[81] 2105 4-11-0 ... PhilKinsella(7) (K G Reveley) *hld up in tch: hdwy to trck ldrs 6f out: effrt and ch 3f out sn rdn and kpt on same pce fnl 2f* **4/1**[2]	102
	4	*7*	**Sweet Medicine** 4-10-0 ... RichardKilloran(7) (P Howling) *a.p: rdn along over 4f out and sn one pce* **20/1**	81
	5	*11*	**Sea Cadet** 4-11-0 ... DavidO'Meara (T D Easterby) *pushed along and bhd 1/2-way: styd on fnl 4f: nrst fin* **33/1**	77
	6	*¾*	**Glinton** 4-11-0 ... PaulMoloney (Mrs P Sly) *midfield: hdwy and in tch 6f out: rdn along over 3f out and sn outpcd* **20/1**	76
	7	*¾*	**Tour Card (IRE)** 4-11-0 ... NoelFehily (Jonjo O'Neill) *bhd tl styd on fnl 4f* **12/1**	76
0	**8**	*15*	**Papswoodmoss**[45] 2830 4-10-7 ... AndrewThornton (Mrs A L M King) *a rr* **25/1**	54
5	**9**	*16*	**Aqua**[23] 3259 4-10-4 ... AnthonyCoyle(3) (P T Midgley) *bhd fr 1/2-way* **66/1**	38
0	**10**	*15*	**Jose Bove**[40] 2927 4-10-4 ... JosephStevenson(10) (R Dickin) *plld hrd: led after 2f tl hdd & wknd over 4f out* **100/1**	30
0	**11**	*5*	**Westgate (IRE)**[14] 3392 4-11-0 ... TomScudamore (S Gollings) *cl up: pushed along over 6f out and sn wknd* **100/1**	25
	12	*18*	**Webbow (IRE)** 4-11-0 ... RussGarritty (T D Easterby) *in tch: rdn along over 6f out and sn wknd* **20/1**	—
	13	*dist*	**Bodell (IRE)** 4-11-0 ... MarkBradburne (Mark Campion) *bhd fr 1/2-way* **100/1**	—
0	**14**	*dist*	**Montanah Jet**[27] 3188 4-10-9 ... TomGreenway(5) (C N Kellett) *a bhd: t.o fr 1/2-way* **125/1**	—

4m 12.2s (7.70) **Going Correction** +0.30s/f (Yiel) **14** Ran SP% **118.9**
Speed ratings: **92,89,88,85,79 79,78,71,63,55 53,44,—,—** CSF £6.61 TOTE £1.60: £1.10, £2.70, £1.50; EX 9.10 Place 6 £60.81, Place 5 £42.43..
Owner Dom Flit **Bred** Shadwell Estate Company Limited **Trained** Melsonby, N Yorks

FOCUS
Just an ordinary bumper, but it was hard not to be impressed with Alfie Flits who looks decent.

NOTEBOOK
Alfie Flits ◆, off the mark on his debut in a mile-six bumper at Warwick, defied his penalty to follow up pretty easily. He is held in high regard and connections will try and win twice more in bumpers before embarking on a Flat campaign. *(op Evens tchd 11-10 in a place)*
Ovide(FR), a 56,000gns full-brother to winning two-mile hurdler Emanic, had no chance with the very comfortable winner but offered promise in second. He has already held an entry over hurdles, and will probably be switched to obstacles sooner rather than later. *(tchd 15-2)*
Jass won what looked a reasonable enough bumper on his debut at Huntingsdon, but was put in his place this time. He can probably do better when faced with obstacles and stepped up in trip. *(op 9-2)*
Sweet Medicine, the first foal of a mare who showed ability in Irish bumpers, made a satisfactory debut for her in-form yard. *(op 14-1)*
Sea Cadet looked as though he would improve a fair bit for the experience.
T/Plt: £168.30 to a £1 stake. Pool: £85,441.85. 370.50 winning tickets. T/Qpdt: £42.60 to a £1 stake. Pool: £5,135.50. 89.20 winning tickets. JR

3624 - 3630a (Foreign Racing) - See Raceform Interactive

3246 HEREFORD (R-H)
Sunday, January 29

3631 Meeting Abandoned - Frost

3638 - (Foreign Racing) - See Raceform Interactive

3408 LEOPARDSTOWN (L-H)
Sunday, January 29

OFFICIAL GOING: Yielding to soft (yielding in places on chase course)

3639a BAILEYS ARKLE PERPETUAL CHALLENGE CUP NOVICE CHASE (GRADE 1) (11 fncs) 2m 1f
1:50 (1:51) 5-Y-0+ **£35,862** (£10,482; £4,965; £1,655)

RPR

1 **Missed That**[34] 3006 7-11-12 ..... DJCasey 156+
(W P Mullins, Ire) *hld up in tch: impr into mod 2nd after 4 out: 3rd 2 out: sn rdn: cl 2nd and chal bef last: led early run-in: styd on wl* **3/1**[3]

2 ¾ **Arteea (IRE)**[21] 3308 7-11-12 ..... AndrewJMcNamara 154
(Michael Hourigan, Ire) *hld up: prog into 3rd 3 out: chal and led after 2 out: strly pressed bef last: hdd early run-in: kpt on* **25/1**

3 9 **Justified (IRE)**[18] 3341 7-11-12 ..... APMcCoy 146
(E Sheehy, Ire) *cl up in 2nd: led fr 5th: edgd clr after 4 out: mstke 2 out: sn hdd: 3rd and no ex bef last* **5/2**[2]

4 10 **On The Net (IRE)**[34] 3012 8-11-12 123 ..... DNRussell 136
(Eoghan O'Grady, Ire) *hld up: reminders 2nd: prog into 4th bef 4 out: no ex u.p fr bef 2 out* **50/1**

5 14 **Augherskea (IRE)**[10] 3473 7-11-12 ..... PCarberry 122
(Noel Meade, Ire) *led: hdd 5th: remained prom tl slt mstke and wknd 3 out* **33/1**

6 25 **Mansony (FR)**[34] 3006 7-11-12 ..... BJGeraghty 96
(A L T Moore, Ire) *settled 3rd: mstke 4th: slt mstke next: dropped to rr and rdn 6 out: sn lost tch: t.o* **12/1**

P **Nickname (FR)**[14] 3409 7-11-12 ..... CO'Dwyer —
(Martin Brassil, Ire) *hld up in tch: mstke 4th: dropped to rr 4 out: p.u bef next* **11/8**[1]

4m 16.8s **Going Correction** -0.60s/f (Firm) **7** Ran SP% **112.1**
Speed ratings: **108,107,103,98,92 80,**— CSF £51.34 TOTE £3.40: £2.10, £4.00; DF 54.00.
Owner Mrs Violet O'Leary **Bred** Exors Of The Late T F M Corrie **Trained** Muine Beag, Co Carlow

FOCUS
A good-class renewal and, with the third, fourth and fifth all running to their marks, the form looks very solid.

NOTEBOOK
Missed That, whose atrocious jumping performance on his chasing debut seems a long time ago now, put up a sound performance to score in battling style. One can imagine him once again flying at the finish up the Cheltenham Hill come March, but whether he will have the pace to cope with the speedier former hurdlers is perhaps more open to question. He is currently 7-1 for the Arkle and that looks fair. *(op 11/4)*
Arteea(IRE) turned over Wild Passion last time and at one stage he looked likely to cause another upset, as he travelled well into the straight. In the end he was outbattled by Missed That but he lost little in defeat and connections have every right to take their chance with him in the Arkle at Cheltenham. *(op 20/1)*
Justified(IRE), who did not impress everyone when winning in workmanlike fashion at Newbury last time, found the competition here too hot. This effort appeared to suggest that he is just short of top class, and his Arkle odds were pushed out to 16-1, but it was later discovered that he was suffering from a viral infection, so it might be too early to write him off. *(op 9/4)*
On The Net(IRE), who looked out of his depth in this company, ran right up to his best and looks a good benchmark for the form.
Augherskea(IRE), rated 130 over hurdles, did not run too badly given that he was pushed in at the deep end on his chasing debut. *(op 25/1)*
Mansony(FR) was let down by his jumping.
Nickname(FR) made an early mistake and was never going thereafter. He had impressed in softer ground on his first two starts over fences and perhaps this ground was livelier than ideal, but he *was later found to have bled, so he had a valid excuse. Official explanation: jockey said gelding did not travel and jumped poorly; vet said gelding was found to have broken a blood vessel (op 6/4)*

3641a AIG EUROPE CHAMPION HURDLE (GRADE 1) (8 hdls) 2m
2:55 (2:55) 4-Y-0+ **£68,965** (£19,655; £9,310; £3,103)

RPR

1 **Brave Inca (IRE)**[31] 3109 8-11-10 166 ..... APMcCoy 164+
(C A Murphy, Ire) *cl up and disp ld: j.w: slt advantage 3 out: rdn and strly pressed fr 2 out: styd on wl u.p fr last* **6/5**[1]

2 1 **Macs Joy (IRE)**[31] 3109 7-11-10 162 ..... BJGeraghty 163+
(Mrs John Harrington, Ire) *settled 4th: 3rd bef 3 out: cl 2nd travelling best 2 out: rdn to chal last: briefly outpcd run-in: styd on wl cl home* **13/2**

3 4 **Golden Cross (IRE)**[56] 2669 7-11-10 161 .....(p) JMurtagh 159
(M Halford, Ire) *hld up in tch: 5th and rdn 3 out: 4th bef last: kpt on u.p* **6/1**[3]

4 2 **Sadlers Wings (IRE)**[609] 589 8-11-10 ..... DJCasey 157
(W P Mullins, Ire) *hld up in tch: 4th 3 out: 3rd and rdn after 2 out: no imp: kpt on same pce fr last* **33/1**

5 7 **The French Furze (IRE)**[28] 3177 12-11-10 ..... TonyDobbin 150
(N G Richards) *led and disp: hdd 4 out: sn lost pl: last appr 2 out: kpt on u.p st* **33/1**

6 1½ **Arch Rebel (USA)**[14] 3411 5-11-6 128 .....(b) PCarberry 145?
(Noel Meade, Ire) *hld up in rr: lost tch bef 4 out: prog 2 out: 5th and effrt appr last: sn no ex* **50/1**

7 25 **Hardy Eustace (IRE)**[29] 3154 9-11-10 167 ..... CO'Dwyer 124
(D T Hughes, Ire) *settled 3rd: reminder 4th: led briefly 4 out: cl 2nd next: rdn and wknd qckly 2 out: virtually p.u st* **9/4**[2]

4m 0.20s **Going Correction** -0.60s/f (Firm) **7** Ran SP% **111.7**
Speed ratings: **104,103,101,100,97 96,83** CSF £9.23 TOTE £2.20: £1.60, £3.10; DF 10.20.
Owner Novices Syndicate **Bred** D W Macauley **Trained** Gorey, Co Wexford

FOCUS
A top race on paper with last season's Champion Hurdle 1st, 3rd & 5th all lining up, but the below-par effort from Hardy Eustace detracted from it. Brave Inca is as tough as they come and picked up again once Macs Joy came to challenge. He is the one they will all have to beat come March. Sadlers Wings shaped extremely well, travelling strongy and doing more than enough to suggest he retains his ability.

NOTEBOOK
Brave Inca(IRE) has developed into Ireland's leading two-mile hurdler this season and again showed why he is the one to beat come March, picking up as Macs Joy came to him and ultimately winning with a bit in hand. A hugely reliable gelding, there are one of two potential 'dark horses' that could trouble him at the Festival, but there will be very few coming up the hill with the zest of this fellow. His excellent Cheltenham record (winner of the Supreme Novices' two seasons ago and close-up third in last year's Chamipon Hurdle) only enhances his claims and, with reigning champion Hardy Eustace running a long way below his best back in a distant seventh, the scene is set for the tough gelding to take centre stage on the big day. *(op 11/10)*
Macs Joy(IRE), as with many of his stable's runners this season, has been some way below his best, but this was more like it and he went down fighting in his bid to win this race for the second consecutive season. A strong traveller, he was going best of all as they turned into the straight, but the winner kept finding and chances of him reversing the form at the Festival look slim, with the faster ground and uphill finish set to suit Brave Inca better than most. *(op 6/1)*
Golden Cross(IRE), narrowly denied by Solerina on his return to hurdling at Fairyhouse in December, stepped up on that effort with a staying-on third and looks as good as ever. He is not far behind the best over two miles and it is not hard to see him running a big race in the Champion, but connections appear to be favouring a crack at the World Hurdle. *(op 6/1 tchd 13/2)*
Sadlers Wings(IRE), a smart novice two seasons back who has been sidelined through injury, could hardly have faced a stiffer reintroduction, but he acquited himself extremely well, jumping slickly throughout, and was travelling best of all with half a mile to run. As was to be expected however, he soon became tired as the long lay-off began to take its toll and he was passed by Golden Cross for third. The one negative to take from this was his awkward head carriage throughout, but he deserves the benefit of the doubt for the time being and with a faster gallop and better ground sure to suit at the Festival, there could be worse long shots.
The French Furze(IRE), a surprise yet deserved winner at Cheltenham on New Year's Day when slipping the field, found this much tougher and was aways struggling to muster the speed. He is a grand old performer and will find more realistic chances back in England.
Arch Rebel(USA), who found the competition of the Ladbroke Hurdle too hot to handle earlier in the month, was more at home in this smaller field, but the class of opposition was the problem on this occasion and he unsurprisingly failed to make an impact.
Hardy Eustace(IRE), a winner at the last three Cheltenham Festivals with victories in the Royal & SunAlliance Hurdle and back-to-back Champion Hurdles, made a satisfactory reappearance when winning at Punchestown last month and was expected to step up on that here. Things did not go according to plan however and, having received an early reminder, it was clear things were not right. He dropped right away from the turn-in and it subsequently transpired that his blood was *wrong, so he deserves to have the run ignored. Official explanation: jockey said gelding felt flat throughout and made mistakes (op 9/4 tchd 5/2)*

3642a P.J.WALLS GOLDEN CYGNET NOVICE HURDLE (GRADE 3) (10 hdls) 2m 4f
3:30 (3:30) 5-Y-0+ **£15,713** (£4,610; £2,196; £748)

RPR

1 **Nicanor (FR)**[22] 3301 5-10-12 ..... PCarberry 146+
(Noel Meade, Ire) *trckd ldrs on outer: impr into 3rd 4 out: led travelling easily appr 2 out: edgd clr bef last: nt extended* **10/11**[1]

2 11 **Travino (IRE)**[42] 2909 7-11-12 ..... JLCullen 144
(Ms Margaret Mullins, Ire) *settled 2nd: led fr 5th: rdn and hdd appr 2 out: no ex whn slt mstke last: no ch w wnr* **9/2**[3]

3 25 **Finger Onthe Pulse (IRE)**[34] 3003 5-10-12 ..... BJGeraghty 110
(T J Taaffe, Ire) *cl up in 3rd: 2nd bef 5 out: rdn 3 out: wknd bef next* **7/2**[2]

4 5 **Justpourit (IRE)**[15] 3400 7-11-2 .....(b[1]) APMcCoy 110
(D T Hughes, Ire) *trckd ldrs in 4th: rdn and no ex appr 3 out: trailing fr 2 out* **14/1**

5 12 **Knight Legend (IRE)**[8] 3512 7-11-2 ..... RMPower 100
(Mrs John Harrington, Ire) *hld up in tch: prog into 5th 4 out: rdn and no imp whn mstke next: trailing fr 2 out* **8/1**

6 11 **Oran Climate (IRE)**[73] 2306 6-11-2 107 ..... DNRussell 92
(John Paul Brennan, Ire) *hld up in tch: rdn and wknd fr 4 out* **50/1**

7 20 **Up Above (IRE)**[8] 3513 6-11-5 .....(p) AndrewJMcNamara 79
(S Donohoe, Ire) *sn led: hdd 5th: wknd after 5 out: trailing next: mstke 3 out: t.o* **33/1**

P **Liss Ard (IRE)**[27] 3224 5-10-12 ..... DJCasey —
(John Joseph Murphy, Ire) *a towards rr: trailing 4 out: p.u after 3 out* **33/1**

5m 6.40s **Going Correction** -0.60s/f (Firm) **8** Ran SP% **118.4**
Speed ratings: **81,76,66,64,59 55,47,**— CSF £5.81 TOTE £2.10: £1.10, £1.80, £1.40; DF 5.40.
Owner D P Sharkey **Bred** M Pierre Hayeau **Trained** Castletown, Co Meath

NOTEBOOK
Nicanor(FR) ◆, beaten at 1-6 in a slowly-run race at Navan on his previous start, got back on track with an easy success on this step up in class, and reversed placings with Travino from two starts back in the process. This was his best effort to date on RPRs and he goes for the Royal & SunAlliance progressing very nicely indeed. *(op 1/1)*
Travino(IRE) was not weighted to confirm recent Navan placings with Nicanor and duly found that one too good this time. Still, given he was conceding 14lb to that rival, this was a fine effort at the weights. *(op 7/2 tchd 5/1)*
Finger Onthe Pulse(IRE) would have found this tougher than the maiden hurdle he won over two miles two here on his previous start, but was not at his best in any case. *(op 4/1)*
Justpourit(IRE) could not produce his best in first-time blinkers.
Knight Legend(IRE) was well below the form he showed to win at Naas on his previous start. *(op 9/1 tchd 10/1)*

3643 - 3644a (Foreign Racing) - See Raceform Interactive

3456 LUDLOW (R-H)
Monday, January 30

OFFICIAL GOING: Good to firm (good in places)
Wind: Almost nil Weather: Overcast

3645 BULL RING JUVENILE NOVICES' HURDLE (9 hdls) 2m
1:30 (1:31) (Class 4) 4-Y-O **£4,228** (£1,241; £620; £310)

Form RPR

1 **Political Intrigue**[109] 4-10-12 ..... JimCrowley 111+
(T G Dascombe) *in tch: rdn to ld 3 out: r.o* **6/1**[2]

F4FF 2 1½ **Ellerslie Tom**[19] 3340 4-10-7 ..... LeeStephens(5) 110+
(P Bowen) *led: hdd after 4 out: sn regained ld: hdd 3 out: stl ev ch tl no ex towards fin* **12/1**

3 6 **Pearl King (IRE)**[115] 4-10-12 ..... APMcCoy 105+
(P J Hobbs) *midfield: hdwy appr 4 out: rdn to chal 3 out: one pce fr last* **4/6**[1]

4 7 **Devils River (IRE)**[182] 4-10-5 ..... MarcGoldstein(7) 96+
(N A Twiston-Davies) *midfield: hdwy appr 4 out: rdn bef next: wknd bef 2 out* **25/1**

5 2½ **Mac Federal (IRE)**[113] 4-10-2 ..... TimothyBailey(10) 94+
(M G Quinlan) *hld up: hdwy 4 out: rdn appr 3 out: 5th and hld whn blnd 2 out* **28/1**

0 **6** *24* **Kryena**[19] 3340 4-10-5 .... JimmyMcCarthy 62
(Mrs P Robeson) *cl up tl wknd after 4 out* **28/1**
7 *11* **Showtime Faye**[6] 4-10-2 .... AnthonyCoyle(3) 51
(A Bailey) *in rr: pushed along after 4th: nvr on terms* **150/1**
8 *1* **Edict**[40] 4-10-5 .... MarkBradburne 50
(C J Down) *towards rr: mstke 3rd: rdn after next: nvr on terms* **150/1**
06 **9** *4* **Love Beauty (USA)**[13] 3431 4-10-5 .... CharliePoste(7) 53
(M F Harris) *midfield: struggling 4 out: sn btn* **50/1**
10 *2* **Blackcomb Mountain (USA)**[470] 4-10-5 .... PJBrennan 44
(M F Harris) *midfield: mstke 2nd: j. slowly 5th: bhd after* **66/1**
P0 **11** *2* **Harry May**[21] 3324 4-10-12 .... JoeTizzard 49
(C L Tizzard) *racd keenly: midfield: struggling 4 out: sn btn* **66/1**
05U **12** *1 ¾* **Halcyon Express (IRE)**[13] 3431 4-10-12 .... RJGreene 47
(Mary Meek) *chsd ldrs tl wknd 4 out* **100/1**
13 *5* **Ceiriog Valley**[94] 4-10-5 .... TomDoyle 35
(P R Webber) *blnd 1st: a bhd* **12/1**
R0 **14** *4* **Lightening Fire (IRE)**[40] 2935 4-10-12 ....(b) OllieMcPhail 38
(B J Llewellyn) *chsd ldrs tl wknd 5th* **200/1**
50 **15** *1 ¼* **Ember Dancer**[42] 2927 4-10-12 .... NoelFehily 37
(Ian Williams) *a bhd* **66/1**
1P **F** **Baie Des Flamands (USA)**[42] 2921 4-11-4 110.................. HenryOliver 96
(Miss S J Wilton) *w ldr: led after 4 out: sn hdd: wknd 3 out: 6th and btn whn fell 2 out* **11/1**[3]

3m 44.2s (-8.10) **Going Correction** -0.325s/f (Good) **16** Ran SP% **118.0**
Speed ratings: **107,106,103,99,98 86,81,80,78,77 76,75,73,71,70** — CSF £67.43 TOTE £6.50: £1.50, £3.40, £1.20; EX 97.40.
Owner ONEWAY National Hunt Partnership **Bred** Juddmonte Farms **Trained** Lambourn, Berks

FOCUS
A fair juvenile hurdle which should produce a few winners.

NOTEBOOK
Political Intrigue, trained by Henry Cecil on the Flat, was put up to a mark of 95 after landing a twelve-furlong handicap in July but was well held in two subsequent starts. Making his hurdling debut, he took a narrow lead at the first flight in the home straight and stayed on well to score. He is well regarded and may go for the Victor Ludorum at Haydock now. *(op 13-2)*
Ellerslie Tompreviously had the unfortunate record of three falls in four runs over hurdles, but he confirmed that he possesses ability with a decent run. Fast ground looks best for him. *(op 10-1)*
Pearl King(IRE), rated 88 on the Flat, was sold out of Michael Jarvis's yard for 115,000gns. A threat at the third last, he soon could muster only the one pace but he is capable of better than this. *(op 5-6 tchd 10-11 in places)*
Devils River(IRE) ran just once on the Flat, showing a little promise in a Windsor maiden in August. He could not go with the two principals from the second last but ought to be up to winning over hurdles. *(op 22-1)*
Mac Federal(IRE) was narrowly beaten in a heavy-ground maiden in Italy at two on his only start on the Flat, when with this yard. He shaped with promise on this hurdles bow after a 14-month lay-off and the return to easier ground ought to suit him. *(op 25-1)*
Love Beauty(USA) *Official explanation: trainer said gelding bled from nose*
Halcyon Express(IRE) *Official explanation: trainer said vet removed tongue-strap at start as it was too tight (op 150-1)*
Baie Des Flamands(USA), the only previous hurdles winner on show, ran his race but was held when capsizing at the second last. *(op 8-1)*

3646 J. H. NEWTON MEMORIAL NOVICES' HURDLE (11 hdls) 2m 5f
2:00 (2:00) (Class 4) 5-Y-0+ **£3,903** (£1,146; £573; £286)

Form RPR
00 **1** **Secured (IRE)**[47] 2829 6-10-12 .... JimmyMcCarthy 105
(Ian Williams) *trckd ldrs: led after 4 out: rdn appr 2 out whn strly pressed: r.o* **100/1**
-04P **2** *shd* **Adventurist**[19] 3342 6-10-12 110.................. ChristianWilliams 105
(P Bowen) *midfield: hdwy appr 3 out: sn ev ch: rdn bef 2 out: edgd lft and jnd wnr run-in: r.o* **12/1**
11-1 **3** *7* **Square Mile (IRE)**[120] 1611 6-11-5 116.................. APMcCoy 105
(Jonjo O'Neill) *trckd ldrs: rdn to chal 3 out: one pce run-in* **4/6**[1]
-001 **4** *½* **Waterloo Son (IRE)**[35] 2968 6-11-5 114.................. RichardJohnson 105
(H D Daly) *midfield: mstke 3rd: hdwy appr 3 out: kpt on same pce fr last* **9/2**[2]
0-06 **5** *4* **Golden Crew**[53] 2720 6-10-9 .... ColinBolger(3) 95+
(Miss Suzy Smith) *in tch: ev ch appr 3 out: wknd bef 2 out: btn whn mstke last* **40/1**
0 **6** *3* **Darn Good**[19] 3342 5-10-12 ....(t) RobertThornton 91+
(A King) *hld up: j. slowly 6th: sn pushed along: nvr rchd ldrs* **25/1**
44F **7** *hd* **It's The Limit (USA)**[13] 3441 7-10-12 104..................(t) TonyDobbin 90
(W K Goldsworthy) *in tch: rdn appr 3 out: wknd bef 2 out* **15/2**[3]
4P60 **8** *nk* **Cresswell Willow (IRE)**[11] 3461 6-10-0 64..................(b[1]) LeeStephens(5) 84+
(W K Goldsworthy) *prom: led 7th: hdd after 4 out: wknd appr 3 out: btn whn mstke last* **100/1**
60 **9** *½* **Champion's Day (GER)**[9] 3496 5-10-12 .... NoelFehily 92+
(Jonjo O'Neill) *hld up: pushed along whn mstke 3 out: nvr rchd ldrs* **33/1**
50 **10** *½* **Grand Slam Hero (IRE)**[45] 2864 5-10-5 .... MrTJO'Brien(7) 91+
(P Bowen) *midfield: hdwy appr 7th: rdn and wkng whn blnd 3 out* **66/1**
P0P0 **11** *dist* **Walton Way**[31] 3127 6-10-12 .... HenryOliver —
(P W Hiatt) *led: hdd 7th: rdn and wknd after 4 out: t.o* **100/1**
00 **12** *2* **Dryliner**[40] 2941 6-10-9 .... OwynNelmes(3) —
(A E Price) *a bhd: t.o* **100/1**
-00P **13** *30* **Luscious (IRE)**[45] 2860 6-10-5 .... LeightonAspell —
(K C Bailey) *bhd fr 5th: n.d whn blnd last: t.o* **100/1**
0 **P** **Highland Games (IRE)**[18] 3354 6-10-12 ....(t) TomDoyle —
(P R Webber) *prom tl p.u after 2nd: dismntd* **18/1**
0- **P** **In No Hurry (IRE)**[317] 4465 5-10-12 .... JamesDavies —
(M G Quinlan) *hld up: sme hdwy after 4 out: sn wknd: bhd whn p.u bef 2 out* **100/1**

5m 11.4s (-6.90) **Going Correction** -0.325s/f (Good) **15** Ran SP% **119.5**
Speed ratings: **100,99,97,97,95 94,94,94,94,93** —,—,—,—,— CSF £1005.19 TOTE £146.10: £27.00, £4.10, £1.10; EX 2217.10.
Owner Favourites Racing VIII **Bred** Miss Mary And Miss Sarah Keane **Trained** Portway, Worcs

FOCUS
A shock outcome to this fair novice hurdle, rated through the runner-up.

NOTEBOOK
Secured(IRE)was a shock winner, having shown little in two previous appearances, one over hurdles. *Travelling well before taking a slim lead, he held on in a desperate finish.Official explanation: trainer said, regarding the improved form shown, gelding may have been suited by faster ground*
Adventurist held every chance from the third last and might even have edged ahead on the run-in, but missed out in the photo. He finished clear of the rest and his turn should come, perhaps in handicap company. *(tchd 11-1)*
Square Mile(IRE), absent for the best part of four months, suffered his first defeat. He never really seemed happy after an error down the far side and he could need a further step up in trip. *(op 10-11)*
Waterloo Son(IRE), who gained his Market Rasen win in softer conditions, was held under his penalty but was keeping on over this longer trip. *(op 3-1)*
Golden Crew ran a fair race on this hurdles debut but did not appear to see out the trip. *(tchd 50-1)*
Darn Good won three minor staying handicaps on the Flat. Having his second run over hurdles, and equipped with a tongue tie, he was staying on past beaten rivals at the end.
It's The Limit(USA) had ground conditions in his favour but this looks about as good as he is. *(op 8-1)*
Cresswell Willow(IRE) had previously shown very poor form but the first-time blinkers appeared to bring about an improvement.
Champion's Day(GER), a stablemate of the beaten favourite, ran a little better than his finishing position suggests and he looks one to keep an eye on now that he is qualified for handicaps. *(op 28-1)*
Highland Games(IRE) *Official explanation: vet said gelding was struck into on right hind-leg (op 20-1)*

3647 DINHAM BEGINNERS' CHASE (13 fncs) 2m
2:30 (2:30) (Class 4) 5-Y-0+ **£4,400** (£1,311; £663; £340; £177)

Form RPR
1-03 **1** **Norma Hill**[69] 2422 5-10-1 .... TomDoyle 100+
(R Hollinshead) *chsd ldr to 3rd: settled in tch after 5th (water): hdwy bef 4 out: blnd and lft in ld next: drvn out* **10/3**[3]
-033 **2** *1 ¼* **Marcel (FR)**[9] 3501 6-11-2 .... TimmyMurphy 114+
(M C Pipe) *hld up: hdwy appr 6th: ev ch 2 out: nt qckn* **5/4**[1]
P004 **3** *12* **Imperial Rocket (USA)**[11] 3457 9-10-11 94..................(t) LeeStephens(5) 104+
(W K Goldsworthy) *chsd ldr 3rd tl after 5th (water): remained prom: ev ch 2 out: wknd last* **80/1**
204 **4** *dist* **Solar At'Em (IRE)**[18] 3356 8-11-2 87..................(p) MarkBradburne 59
(M Sheppard) *hld up: pushed along appr 7th: sn btn: t.o* **40/1**
PF05 **5** *3 ½* **Let's Rock**[11] 3457 8-10-9 67.................. MrRHodges(7) 56
(Mrs A Price) *a bhd: lost tch 5th (water): t.o* **100/1**
30PP **P** **Ideal Jack (FR)**[11] 3465 10-11-2 79..................(v) RJGreene —
(G A Ham) *midfield: wknd 8th: t.o whn p.u bef last* **100/1**
P-P0 **F** **Don't Matter**[11] 3457 6-10-6 .... OwynNelmes(3) —
(A E Price) *a bhd: lost tch 5th (water): t.o whn fell 3 out* **100/1**
/PPP **P** **Neophyte (IRE)**[3] 3599 7-11-2 ....(b) JamesDavies —
(B De Haan) *plld hrd: led: blnd 3rd: hit 7th: hdd appr 8th: wknd 9th: t.o whn p.u bef 4 out* **80/1**
213F **F** **Phar Out Phavorite (IRE)**[20] 3329 7-11-2 130..................(v) NoelFehily —
(Miss E C Lavelle) *chsd ldrs: wnt 2nd after 5th (water): led appr 8th: fell 3 out: dead* **13/8**[2]

3m 53.5s (-10.60) **Going Correction** -0.425s/f (Good)
WFA 5 from 6yo+ 8lb **9** Ran SP% **113.5**
Speed ratings: **109,108,102,—,—** —,—,—,— CSF £8.23 TOTE £4.60: £1.60, £1.50, £4.70; EX 11.30.
Owner Geoff Lloyd **Bred** Mrs M E Hill **Trained** Upper Longdon, Staffs

FOCUS
This was run at a decent pace. Not an easy race to assess, it could have been rated a stone higher but the third limits the form.

NOTEBOOK
Norma Hill, who ran well behind two smart novices on her chasing debut, was receiving plenty of weight here and made it tell. Usually a front-runner, but ridden differently as Neophyte tore off in front, she was left with a narrow lead at the third last and had too much pace for Marcel from that point. *(op 4-1)*
Marcel(FR) had every chance but could not match the winner's turn of foot from the second last. He is well capable of winning races over fences, but his Arkle entry is starting to look pretty optimistic. *(op 7-4)*
Imperial Rocket(USA) ran his best race to date over fences and only cried enough after the second last. An ordinary novice chase on a sound surface should come his way. *(op 66-1)*
Neophyte(IRE), a keen type and a bit of a hairy ride, was responsible for setting a good pace and he eventually paid the price. *(op 66-1)*
Phar Out Phavorite(IRE) was still in front, but being strongly pressed, when he took a heavy fall at the last ditch and broke his shoulder. A sad end for a promising chaser. *(op 66-1)*

3648 STOKESAY MARES' ONLY H'CAP HURDLE (11 hdls) 2m 5f
3:00 (3:00) (Class 4) (0-115,114) 4-Y-0+ **£4,554** (£1,337; £668; £333)

Form RPR
-342 **1** **Zaffaran Express (IRE)**[35] 2977 7-11-6 **108**.................. TonyDobbin 114+
(N G Richards) *in tch: hdwy 4 out: mstke 3 out: led appr last: edgd lft run-in: r.o* **4/1**[2]
/6-4 **2** *2 ½* **Precious Mystery (IRE)**[25] 3247 6-11-3 **105**............(v[1]) RobertThornton 108+
(A King) *a.p: ev ch fr 3 out: mstke last: no ex run-in* **9/1**
3103 **3** *8* **Festive Chimes (IRE)**[39] 2952 5-11-6 **111**.................. OwynNelmes(3) 108+
(N B King) *in tch: led appr 3 out: hdd bef last: edgd rt and wknd run-in* **20/1**
0542 **4** *10* **My Rosie Ribbons (IRE)**[6] 3548 7-10-1 **96**.................. MrMWall(7) 80
(B W Duke) *prom: led appr 7th: hdd 4 out: sn wknd* **18/1**
012F **5** *½* **Miss Skippy**[80] 2166 7-10-13 **101**.................. BrianCrowley 84
(A G Newcombe) *hld up: rdn after 4 out: nvr on terms* **10/1**
-02P **6** *19* **Hopbine**[106] 1760 10-11-2 **104**..................(p) APMcCoy 75+
(J L Spearing) *hld up: hdwy 4 out: sn rdn: wknd appr next* **9/1**
U-5P **7** *3 ½* **Gordon Highlander**[75] 2271 7-10-10 **98**..................(t) JimmyMcCarthy 59
(Mrs P Robeson) *led: hdd appr 7th: wknd 4 out* **25/1**
306 **8** *2 ½* **Elegant Eskimo**[25] 3249 7-10-8 **96**.................. JoeTizzard 54
(S E H Sherwood) *t.k.h: in tch: losing pl whn blnd 6th: bhd after* **40/1**
3-00 **9** *12* **Manque Pas D'Air (FR)**[66] 2486 6-10-2 **90**.................. PJBrennan 36
(T R George) *prom: hit 5th: rdn after 4 out: sn wknd* **33/1**
0004 **10** *dist* **Ericas Charm**[54] 2704 6-10-5 **93**.................. ChristianWilliams —
(P Bowen) *trckd ldrs: led 4 out: hdd appr 3 out: sn wknd: t.o* **7/2**[1]
P-13 **P** **Pearly Bay**[31] 3130 8-10-12 **100**.................. JamieMoore —
(M G Rimell) *hld up: pushed along whn mstke 7th: t.o whn p.u bef 3 out* **7/1**
6445 **F** **Sardagna (FR)**[23] 3295 6-11-12 **114**.................. TimmyMurphy 114+
(M C Pipe) *hld up: hdwy after 4 out: cl up 4th and styng on whn fell 2 out* **5/1**[3]

5m 12.3s (-6.00) **Going Correction** -0.325s/f (Good) **12** Ran SP% **119.7**
Speed ratings: **98,97,94,90,90 82,81,80,75,—** —,— CSF £38.50 CT £653.64 TOTE £4.40: £1.30, £3.70, £8.00; EX 55.40.
Owner A Clark/W B Morris/J Dudgeon **Bred** A W Buller **Trained** Greystoke, Cumbria

FOCUS
Not a strong race but reasonably solid form, with the winner rated value for further.

NOTEBOOK
Zaffaran Express(IRE), another 4lb higher, came under pressure on the home turn and was then awkward at the first in the straight, but she came through between horses to lead before the last and won going away. She is on the upgrade. *(tchd 7-2)*
Precious Mystery(IRE) ran an improved race in the first-time visor and appeared to stay this longer trip, but she could not hold off the winner on the run to the final flight. *(op 8-1)*

Festive Chimes(IRE) showed in front at the head of the straight but was collared at the last before hanging on the run-in. She just looks high enough in the weights.
My Rosie Ribbons(IRE) dropped out of contention once headed at the last flight in the back straight, but she was keeping on again at the end and probably remains in form. *(op 16-1)*
Miss Skippy, having her first run since a fall in November, never reached a challenging position but was keeping on past beaten horses. *(op 9-1)*
Ericas Charm, making her handicap debut on ground that should have suited, went on at the last down the far side but was swallowed up approaching the straight. She was eased when beaten and this was probably not her running. *(op 10-3)*
Sardagna(FR), back up in trip, was staying on in fourth place when she slipped on landing over the second last and came down. She would have been involved in the shake-up. *(op 11-2 tchd 9-2)*
Pearly Bay *Official explanation: trainer said mare bled from nose (op 11-2 tchd 9-2)*

3649 HIS ROYAL HIGHNESS THE PRINCE OF WALES CHALLENGE TROPHY (AN AMATEUR RIDERS' H'CAP CHASE) (19 fncs) 3m

3:30 (3:30) (Class 4) (0-110,110) 5-Y-0+
£5,401 (£1,687; £843; £422; £210; £106)

Form RPR
32U3 **1** **Fin Bec (FR)**[6] 3547 13-10-9 **100**........(b) MrElmelov(7) 115+
(A P Jones) *led: hdd bef 2nd (water): chsd clr ldr: blnd 7th and rdr lost irons briefly: led bef 13th: clr after 15th: rdr lost* **15/2**
2260 **2** *8* **Tribal Dancer (IRE)**[26] 3241 12-10-2 **93**........ MrWBiddick(7) 99
(Miss Venetia Williams) *led appr 2nd (water): sn clr: hdd bef 13th: chsd wnr after: no imp fr 4 out* **6/1**
2143 **3** *11* **Channahrlie (IRE)**[41] 2931 12-9-13 **90**........(p) MrCHughes(7) 87+
(R Dickin) *hld up: lost pl appr 7th: wnt mod 3rd last: n.d* **9/1**
2113 **4** *6* **Miss Shakira (IRE)**[18] 3358 8-11-9 **110**........ MrGTumelty(3) 100+
(N A Twiston-Davies) *hld up: nt fluent 5th: hdwy appr 10th: wknd after 15th* **11/2**[3]
P-45 **5** *17* **Lord Seamus**[19] 3343 11-11-1 **102**........ MrJSnowden(3) 80+
(K C Bailey) *hld up: wkng whn mstke 12th* **13/2**
P-23 **6** *10* **Hever Road (IRE)**[4] 3578 7-11-2 **107**........(v[1]) MrRQuinn(7) 85+
(M C Pipe) *hld up: blnd 10th: struggling 14th: n.d* **11/2**[3]
3215 **F** **Ede'Iff**[21] 3326 9-11-7 **108**........ MrTJO'Brien(3) —
(W G M Turner) *hld up: hdwy appr 12th: 8 l 3rd whn fell 4 out* **9/2**[1]
2314 **P** **Good Outlook (IRE)**[7] 3533 7-11-4 **105**........ MrCMulhall(3) —
(R C Guest) *hld up: blnd 3rd: hdwy 13th: wknd after 15th: t.o whn p.u bef 4 out: dismntd* **5/1**[2]

6m 1.30s (-10.80) **Going Correction** -0.425s/f (Good) **8** Ran SP% **115.0**
Speed ratings: **101,98,94,92,87 83,—,—** CSF £51.76 CT £412.47 TOTE £6.90: £3.20, £1.90, £2.50; EX 64.60.
Owner P Newell **Bred** Haras De Saint-Voir **Trained** Lambourn, Berks
■ A first winner for Bulgarian amateur Emil Imelov, and possibly a last winner for Anthony Jones who is to hand in his licence.

FOCUS
A weak race, and suspect form which has been rated at face value.

NOTEBOOK
Fin Bec(FR) soon lost his lead and was content to chase the clear pacesetter, himself some way ahead of the bunch. In front with six to jump, he was never seriously threatened from then on. His inexperienced rider finished without irons, having lost them at the first in the home straight and, after regaining them, again at the second last. *(op 7-1)*
Tribal Dancer(IRE) went off too fast and was headed in the back straight on the final circuit, but he still managed to stick on for second which underlines the weak nature of this race. *(op 13-2 tchd 7-1)*
Channahrlie(IRE), usually a front-runner, was unable to assume that role and he merely stayed on when the race was effectively over. *(op 8-1)*
Miss Shakira(IRE), reverting to fences, was never within hailing distance of the leaders. She has yet to prove she stays this far under Rules. *(op 13-2 tchd 5-1)*
Hever Road(IRE) made a bad blunder at the last fence with a lap to go, Quinn doing well to stay aboard, and was never able to get involved. *(op 9-2)*
Ede'Iff, patiently ridden, had a bit to do, but was third and staying on, when she departed at the first fence in the home straight. *(op 6-1)*
Good Outlook(IRE) *Official explanation: vet said gelding was lame (op 6-1)*

3650 CHURCH STRETTON H'CAP HURDLE (9 hdls) 2m

4:00 (4:00) (Class 3) (0-120,120) 4-Y-0+ **£5,855** (£1,719; £859; £429)

Form RPR
2-24 **1** **Prairie Moonlight (GER)**[51] 2765 6-11-12 **120**........ NoelFehily 135+
(C J Mann) *hld up: hdwy appr 3 out: led on bit bef last: readily drew clr run-in* **9/2**[3]
216 **2** *5* **Predator (GER)**[35] 2991 5-10-10 **104**........ APMcCoy 109
(Jonjo O'Neill) *a.p: rdn and ev ch fr 3 out: nt qckn run-in* **11/4**[1]
440 **3** *2* **Herakles (GER)**[47] 2826 5-10-9 **103**........ MickFitzgerald 106+
(N J Henderson) *midfield: pushed along after 4 out: hdwy appr 2 out: styd on run-in* **11/2**
5262 **4** *5* **Billyandi (IRE)**[20] 3333 6-10-1 **102**........ MarcGoldstein(7) 101+
(N A Twiston-Davies) *led: hdd appr last and nt fluent: wknd run-in* **12/1**
42F1 **5** *nk* **Spike Jones (NZ)**[2] 3616 8-10-1 **100**........ DerekLaverty(5) 100+
(Mrs S M Johnson) *midfield: rdn appr 3 out: hdwy whn nt fluent 2 out: kpt on same pce* **7/2**[2]
2630 **6** *1 ½* **Red Moor (IRE)**[9] 3510 6-11-4 **112**........ RobertThornton 108
(Mrs D A Hamer) *in tch: effrt appr 2 out: one pce bef last* **25/1**
-PP5 **7** *4* **Broke Road (IRE)**[18] 3360 10-10-12 **113**........(t) MrTJO'Brien(7) 105
(Mrs H Dalton) *trckd ldrs tl rdn and wknd after 3 out* **20/1**
1566 **8** *3 ½* **General Smith**[128] 1553 7-10-0 **94** oh2........ PJBrennan 83
(H J Evans) *hld up: hdwy appr 2 out: no imp bef last* **66/1**
-020 **9** *1* **Wiscalitus (GER)**[198] 1010 7-11-8 **116**........ AlanO'Keeffe 104
(Miss Venetia Williams) *trckd ldrs: rdn and wkng whn hit 3 out* **14/1**
350 **10** *½* **Pseudonym (IRE)**[128] 1551 4-9-7 **105** oh7........ CharliePoste(7) 81
(M F Harris) *a bhd* **66/1**
2-36 **11** *3* **Master Mahogany**[9] 3510 5-11-2 **110**........ RichardJohnson 94
(R J Hodges) *prom tl rdn and wknd appr 3 out* **11/1**
000U **12** *7* **Sir Walter (IRE)**[15] 3456 13-10-0 **94**........ RJGreene 71
(D Burchell) *t.k.h: a in rr* **66/1**
0-P0 **13** *1 ½* **Atahuelpa**[18] 3360 6-11-12 **120**........(t) JosephByrne 96
(Jennie Candlish) *a bhd* **50/1**
0460 **P** **Margarets Wish**[24] 2940 6-9-11 **94** oh14........ OwynNelmes(3) —
(T Wall) *midfield tl wknd 4 out: t.o whn p.u bef 2 out* **100/1**

3m 45.4s (-6.90) **Going Correction** -0.325s/f (Good)
WFA 4 from 5yo+ 11lb **14** Ran SP% **121.2**
Speed ratings: **104,101,100,98,97 97,95,93,92,92 91,87,86,—** CSF £17.09 CT £71.76 TOTE £6.70: £2.50, £1.60, £2.20; EX 39.20.
Owner Celtic Bloodstock Ltd **Bred** Gestut Etzean **Trained** Upper Lambourn, Berks

FOCUS
The winner was rated value for double the official margin in this reasonable handicap and can do better still, while the second and third, both novices, are on the upgrade.

NOTEBOOK
Prairie Moonlight(GER) always travelled well and, once striking the front, only needed to be shaken up to come away after the last. Capable of better still, she must have decent ground and may be targeted at a mares' race at the Punchestown festival. *(tchd 5-1)*
Predator(GER), on his handicap debut, ran well on this faster ground but was no match for the progressive winner. *(tchd 5-2)*
Herakles(GER), making his handicap debut on only his fourth start, stayed on without troubling the first two. There are races to be won with him and a stiffer track should suit. *(op 4-1)*
Billyandi(IRE) adopted his regular tactics and was was only collared going to the final flight. He might benefit from a slightly longer trip. *(op 14-1 tchd 16-1)*
Spike Jones(NZ), without a penalty for his win in a conditionals' race at Chepstow two days earlier, ran respectably on this better ground but the race probably came a bit soon. He is going to be on a career-high mark when his new rating takes effect.
Red Moor(IRE) ran well here two runs back but disappointed next time. This was better, but he looks high enough in the weights.

3651 WEDDING RECEPTION AT LUDLOW "JUNIOR" STANDARD OPEN NATIONAL HUNT FLAT RACE 1m 6f

4:30 (4:30) (Class 5) 4-Y-0 **£2,277** (£501; £501; £166)

Form RPR
26 **1** **Tooting (IRE)**[29] 3181 4-11-0........ MickFitzgerald 94
(J Nicol) *in tch: rdn to ld 3f out: r.o* **15/8**[1]
4 **2** *1* **Sundarbob (IRE)**[42] 2927 4-11-0........ TomDoyle 93
(P R Webber) *midfield: pushed along and hdwy 3f out: ev ch fr 2f out: styd on* **9/2**[3]
2 *dht* **Tickford Abbey** 4-11-0........ JimmyMcCarthy 93
(Mrs P Robeson) *a.p: rdn and ev ch fr 3f out: styd on* **40/1**
4 *nk* **Basic Fact (IRE)** 4-11-0........ APMcCoy 92
(Jonjo O'Neill) *trckd ldrs: rdn and ev ch fr 2f out: no ex cl home* **6/1**
6 **5** *2 ½* **Don Castille (USA)**[23] 3292 4-11-0........ JamesDavies 89
(P R Webber) *hld up: hdwy 5f out: nt clr run over 2f out: sn rdn: styd on same pce* **16/1**
3 **6** *3* **Piper Paddy**[47] 2830 4-10-7........ RichardJohnson 79
(P R Chamings) *in tch: rdn over 3f out: one pce fnl f* **7/2**[2]
01 **7** *3 ½* **Insurgent (IRE)**[24] 3273 4-10-11........ JohnFlavin(10) 89
(R C Guest) *hld up: hdwy over 2f out: nvr trbld ldrs* **14/1**
8 *8* **Ladro Volante (IRE)** 4-10-7........ MrRHodges(7) 72
(S E H Sherwood) *plld hrd: prom: rdn and ev ch 3f out: wknd over 1f out* **20/1**
0 **9** *7* **Jamadast Roma**[47] 2830 4-10-0........ StevenCrawford(7) 57
(N A Twiston-Davies) *led: rdn and hdd 3f out: sn wknd* **28/1**
0 **10** *8* **Trooper Lee (IRE)**[19] 3346 4-11-0........ JimCrowley 54
(Mrs H Dalton) *hld up: rdn over 4f out: nvr on terms* **25/1**
0 **11** *7* **Midnight Fury**[88] 2013 4-10-7........ ChrisDavies(7) 46
(J G M O'Shea) *a bhd* **100/1**
12 *17* **Sun Of The Glen (IRE)** 4-10-7........ LeightonAspell 18
(B D Leavy) *a bhd* **66/1**

3m 22.1s **12** Ran SP% **119.0**
WIN: Tooting £3.60. PL: Tooting £1.50, Sundarbob £1.30, Tickford Abbey £7.70. EX: T/S £6.10, T/TA £57.80. CSF: T/S £4.82, T/TA £52.65. Place 6 £60.04, Place 5 £50.91.
Owner Miss Anita Farrell **Bred** Churchtown House Stud **Trained** Newmarket, Suffolk

FOCUS
The runners stayed where they were for a few seconds after the tapes went back and the race was run at a steady pace, turning into a three-furlong sprint. The form is suspect.

NOTEBOOK
Tooting(IRE) gave another boost to the form of the listed bumper won by Burnt Oak at Cheltenham. Striking for home with three furlongs to run, he had the stands' rail to race against and held off challenges from three rivals. *(op 11-4 tchd 3-1)*
Sundarbob(IRE) ran a fair race on his debut and this was another respectable effort. He was one of four in line at the furlong pole but just lacked the pace of the winner. *(op 7-1)*
Tickford Abbey, a half-brother to Mighty Surprise, who won at 2m 6f over hurdles, had every chance in the final sprint but was not helped by racing deepest on the track. This was a promising start. *(op 7-1)*
Basic Fact(IRE), a 65,000gns three-year-old whose dam is out of a half-sister to Champion Hurdle winners Granville Again and Morley Street, just lacked a turn of foot in the sprint to the line. He should be capable of better. *(op 3-1)*
Don Castille(USA), encountering better ground this time, was caught out when the pace finally lifted with three to run. *(op 12-1)*
Piper Paddy was another found wanting in the sprint to the line. *(tchd 4-1)*
Insurgent(IRE), penalised for his Musselburgh win, was held up in a slowly-run race and could never get into the action. *(op 11-1)*
T/Plt: £52.10 to a £1 stake. Pool: £47,040.30. 658.95 winning tickets. T/Qpdt: £31.10 to a £1 stake. Pool: £2,774.70. 65.90 winning tickets. DO

3618 SOUTHWELL (L-H)

Monday, January 30

OFFICIAL GOING: Good (good to soft in places)
Wind: Almost nil

3652 BETFRED NOVICES' H'CAP CHASE (16 fncs) 2m 4f 110y

1:50 (1:50) (Class 4) (0-100,99) 5-Y-0+ **£4,879** (£1,432; £716; £357)

Form RPR
-454 **1** **Roman Court (IRE)**[21] 3326 8-11-2 **89**........ AndrewThornton 97+
(R H Alner) *led 2nd tl hdd 11th: rdn whn lft 2nd 3 out: 6l down whn lft clr 2 out* **4/1**[1]
4056 **2** *5* **Opportunity Knocks**[23] 3285 6-9-7 **73** oh3........(p) KeiranBurke(7) 71
(N J Hawke) *in tch: rdn 11th: no ch whn lft 2nd 2 out* **25/1**
-540 **3** *½* **Protagonist**[30] 3146 8-11-5 **99**........ TomMessenger(7) 97
(B N Pollock) *in tch: rdn 12th and lost tch w front 3: lft 3rd 2 out* **14/1**
2400 **4** *7* **Mac Dargin (IRE)**[24] 3276 7-11-4 **91**........(b[1]) TomScudamore 85+
(N A Twiston-Davies) *mstke 6th and other errors: mid-div tl 11th* **15/2**[2]
336P **5** *5* **Jonny's Kick**[35] 2966 6-11-7 **94**........ RussGarritty 80
(T D Easterby) *trckd ldrs: rdn and wknd 11th* **17/2**
1-PU **6** *2 ½* **Jack Lynch**[35] 2982 10-11-1 **93**........ ThomasDreaper(5) 76
(Ferdy Murphy) *hld up: a bhd* **16/1**
-P44 **7** *3 ½* **Vanormix (FR)**[14] 3426 7-11-4 **98**........(v) BernieWharfe(7) 78
(C J Gray) *in tch early: rdn 1/2-way: sn bhd* **20/1**
-5P0 **8** *14* **Bobsourown (IRE)**[46] 2839 7-9-12 **76** ow1........ StephenCraine(5) 42
(D McCain) *led to 2nd: lost tch 1/2-way* **15/2**[2]
P06P **F** **Back De Bay (IRE)**[35] 2966 6-9-11 **73** oh8........ LeeVickers(3) —
(J R Cornwall) *a rr: bhd whn fell 12th* **66/1**
646- **P** **Salliemak**[396] 3101 8-10-3 **76**........(t) TomSiddall —
(A J Wilson) *hld up: t.o whn p.u bef 11th* **20/1**

P-PP **P** **Gamma-Delta (IRE)**[30] [3140] 11-10-12 **90**...................... AdamPogson(5) —
(C T Pogson) *blnd and nrly uns rdr 3rd: p.u bef next* **33/1**
P-53 **F** **Quatrain (IRE)**[31] [3126] 6-11-6 **93**..................................(t) JohnMcNamara —
(D R Gandolfo) *hld up: hdwy whn hit 11th: 2nd and 3l down whn fell 3 out* **8/1**[3]
FU22 **F** **Toon Trooper (IRE)**[23] [3290] 9-11-6 **98**........................ MarkNicolls(5) 114+
(R Lee) *mid-div: stdy hdwy to ld 11th: in command 3 out: 6l clr whn fell 2 out: broke nk: dead* **4/1**[1]
5m 35.1s (6.00) **Going Correction** -0.075s/f (Good) **13** Ran SP% **115.5**
Speed ratings: **85,83,82,80,78 77,76,70,—,—,— —,—,—** CSF £101.90 CT £1272.63 TOTE £5.60: £1.60, £7.00, £2.50; EX 85.70.
Owner Club Ten **Bred** Mrs Irene Appelbe **Trained** Droop, Dorset

FOCUS
A modest early pace and a moderate winning time, and these obstacles proved very stiff for these novices, especially with regard to what happened over the last three fences. The winner is rated value for further.

NOTEBOOK
Roman Court(IRE), down in trip, was always up with the pace but would probably only have finished third had it not been for the grief at the third-last and second-last fences. He probably prefers a stiffer test. *(op 10-3)*
Opportunity Knocks, disappointing in three outings since showing promise on his chasing debut, is grossly flattered to have finished second and should be considered fourth-best on merit.
Protagonist, who showed nothing in his only previous try over fences nearly 17 months ago, only grabbed third place thanks to the misfortune of others. This ground would have been quick enough for him. *(op 9-1)*
Mac Dargin(IRE) should have liked this ground, but his jumping was not up to scratch and he is flattered by his finishing position. *(op 9-1)*
Bobsourown(IRE) *Official explanation: trainer said gelding finished distressed (op 9-1)*
Toon Trooper(IRE), whose best form had come on much softer ground than this, jumped well in the main apart from a blunder at the seventh. He seemed to have the race in the bag when jumping too high at the second last and taking an X-rated and immediately fatal fall.
Quatrain(IRE), beaten a long way despite finishing third on his chasing debut, looked destined for second spot behind the ill-fated Toon Trooper when coming down at the third last

3653 BETFRED BEGINNERS' CHASE (19 fncs) 3m 110y
2:20 (2:20) (Class 4) 5-Y-0+ **£5,332** (£1,655; £891)

Form RPR
12R2 **1** **Shining Strand**[19] [3342] 7-11-5 120................................ AndrewTinkler 132+
(N J Henderson) *mde all: sn clr: unchal* **3/1**[2]
6P-6 **2** *dist* **Classic Rock**[69] [2419] 7-11-5 .... AndrewThornton 87
(J W Unett) *bhd: t.o 12th: styd on one pce fr 3 out to go remote 2nd post* **66/1**
-002 **3** *hd* **Great As Gold (IRE)**[16] [3380] 7-11-5 ....(b) WilsonRenwick 87
(B Ellison) *bhd: wnt poosr 2nd appr 3 out: rdn and wknd next: lost 2nd post* **9/2**[3]
P-00 **F** **Star Wonder**[53] [2721] 6-10-5 .... MrLRPayter(7) —
(G R I Smyly) *in tch tl wknd 6th: fell 8th* **100/1**
0- **F** **Billy Bush (IRE)**[308] [4633] 7-11-0................................ ThomasDreaper(5) —
(Ferdy Murphy) *chsd ldrs: disputing 2nd whn fell 12th* **8/1**
P **Echo Blu (IRE)**[310] 8-11-5 .... JasonMaguire —
(Miss Joanne Priest) *chsd clr ldr to 12th: sn wknd: t.o whn p.u bef 15th* **33/1**
0324 **P** **Very Optimistic (IRE)**[34] [3017] 8-11-5 .... RichardMcGrath —
(Jonjo O'Neill) *chsd wnr 12th tl wknd appr 3 out: p.u bef next* **1/1**[1]
/-0P **P** **Redhouse Chevalier**[30] [3148] 7-10-12 .... CharlieStudd(7) —
(B G Powell) *chsd ldrs to 5th: bhd whn blnd bdly 8th: p.u bef next* **50/1**
6m 32.7s (-11.10) **Going Correction** -0.075s/f (Good) **8** Ran SP% **111.7**
Speed ratings: **114,—,—,—,— —,—,—** CSF £121.10 TOTE £4.00: £1.60, £3.80, £1.10; EX 108.20.
Owner The Queen **Bred** Queen Elizabeth **Trained** Upper Lambourn, Berks

FOCUS
A very smart winning time for the type of race, 5.7 seconds quicker than the following handicap over the same trip. As in the first race, the fences took their toll on these novices. An uncompetitive contest was made even more so with the favourite running so badly, but the winner, rated value for 45l, could hardly have done any more.

NOTEBOOK
Shining Strand, making his chasing debut, was immediately sent into a decisive lead, handled these tricky fences really well, and nothing was ever able to get anywhere near him. With the favourite flopping so badly, the form probably amounts to little but the winning time was very good so it is probably worth giving him the benefit of the doubt. *(tchd 7-2)*
Classic Rock, having his second start following a long lay-off and also making his chasing debut, plodded on to just about win the separate race for second but probably did not achieve a great deal. *(op 100-1)*
Great As Gold(IRE), on much faster ground than when runner-up on his chasing debut, had nonetheless gained all three of his victories over hurdles on good ground so this has to go down as disappointing. *(op 11-2 tchd 4-1)*
Very Optimistic(IRE), sent in pursuit of the winner starting out on the final circuit, never got remotely close and stopped to nothing on the home bend. He was subsequently found to have bled. *Official explanation: vet said gelding bled internally (op 6-5 tchd 10-11 and 5-4 in places)*
Billy Bush(IRE), making his chasing debut on his first run in this country, and returning from a ten-month break, was amongst the group chasing the runaway winner when coming down at the *last fence on the penultimate circuit. He had run far enough to derive some benefit for the outing. (op 6-5 tchd 10-11 and 5-4 in places)*

3654 BETFRED H'CAP CHASE (19 fncs) 3m 110y
2:50 (2:50) (Class 4) (0-100,99) 5-Y-0+ **£4,879** (£1,432; £716; £357)

Form RPR
2552 **1** **Umbrella Man (IRE)**[17] [3368] 10-11-12 **99**.......................... MarcusFoley 118+
(Miss E C Lavelle) *hld up in mid-div: smooth hdwy 13th: led 3 out: sn clr* **11/2**[1]
1445 **2** *6* **Up The Pub (IRE)**[25] [3252] 8-10-8 **81**..............................(t) RobertWalford 90+
(R H Alner) *trckd ldrs: led 15th to 3 out: kpt on one pce* **7/1**[3]
4630 **3** *1 ½* **Southerndown (IRE)**[25] [3252] 13-10-4 **80**..................... WilliamKennedy(3) 87+
(R Lee) *hld up in rr: hdwy 13th: sstyd on: nvr nrr* **18/1**
3PP3 **4** *hd* **Supreme Sir (IRE)**[25] [3252] 8-10-3 **76**......................... MatthewBatchelor 82+
(P G Murphy) *led tl hdd 15th: rdn and one pce after* **11/2**[1]
33P0 **5** *30* **Tipp Top (IRE)**[17] [3368] 9-10-2 **80**...............................(t) StephenCraine(5) 55
(O Brennan) *hld up in mid-div: nvr on terms* **28/1**
-2P1 **6** *11* **Squantum (IRE)**[21] [3325] 9-11-3 **90**................................. JasonMaguire 54
(Miss Joanne Priest) *trckd ldrs tl wknd 4 out* **7/1**[3]
6255 **7** *dist* **Moscow Leader (IRE)**[39] [2955] 8-11-7 **97**..................(p) LarryMcGrath(3) —
(R C Guest) *hld up: hdwy appr 10th: wknd after 13th: t.o* **11/2**[1]
FP5- **P** **Johnyyouronlyjoken (IRE)**[25] [3260] 10-9-11 **73** oh10.(p) TomMalone(3) —
(N F Glynn, Ire) *a bhd: t.o 12th: p.u bef 4 out* **16/1**
P0P5 **U** **Oscar Performance (IRE)**[26] [3241] 11-10-1 **74**....(b) BenjaminHitchcott —
(R H Buckler) *trckd ldr tl blnd and uns rdr 9th* **20/1**

43PP **P** **Princesse Grec (FR)**[35] [2996] 8-11-3 **90**....................... TomScudamore —
(M Scudamore) *trckd ldrs tl wknd 15th: t.o whn p.u bef 3 out* **16/1**
P1-3 **P** **Frosty Run (IRE)**[21] [3326] 8-11-10 **97**.......................... AndrewTinkler —
(Mrs H Dalton) *trckd ldrs tl rdn appr 13th: t.o whn p.u bef 4 out* **6/1**[2]
-PPP **P** **Be Upstanding**[35] [2986] 11-10-7 **80**............................(p) RichardMcGrath —
(Ferdy Murphy) *hld up: reminders after 12th: t.o whn p.u bef 15th* **20/1**
6m 38.4s (-5.40) **Going Correction** -0.075s/f (Good) **12** Ran SP% **115.4**
Speed ratings: **105,103,102,102,92 89,—,—,—,— —,—** CSF £41.88 CT £647.75 TOTE £6.10: £2.60, £2.00, £7.30; EX 50.10.
Owner Mrs J Dollar & Mrs M Hall **Bred** Mrs A Berry **Trained** Wildhern, Hants
■ Stewards' Enquiry : Stephen Craine one-day ban: used whip when out of contention (Feb 10)

FOCUS
A modest early pace for this handicap and the winning time was 5.7 seconds slower than the preceding beginners' chase. The form is probably ordinary though the winner carried top weight and scored with a bit in hand, value for 10l. The second and third ran to their marks.

NOTEBOOK
Umbrella Man(IRE), despite top weight, was down to a mark 3lb lower than for his only previous win three years ago despite having run with credit several times since. He was always travelling extremely well and found plenty when asked to go and win his race, but it did appear as though this easy three miles was as far as he wanted. *(op 13-2)*
Up The Pub(IRE), tried in a tongue-strap, was always up with the pace and kept on going, though he had no answer whatsoever to the winner. His best previous form had come on softer ground.
Southerndown(IRE) would probably have preferred a stiffer test, but he likes a sound surface and that helped him plug on for third. *(tchd 20-1)*
Supreme Sir(IRE), pulled up in five of his previous seven races under Rules, made much of the running but was done for foot after losing the advantage. He finished about as far behind Up The Pub as he did when third behind him at Chepstow in November. *(op 6-1 tchd 5-1)*
Moscow Leader(IRE) would have preferred a stiffer track and softer ground, but even so this was disappointing. *(op 6-1)*
Frosty Run(IRE) on the face of it was disappointing, but he was an ideal candidate to bounce so it *may be worth forgiving him this. Official explanation: jockey said gelding was never travelling (op 9-2)*

3655 BETFRED MARES' ONLY H'CAP HURDLE (9 hdls) 2m
3:20 (3:21) (Class 4) (0-100,99) 4-Y-0+ **£3,773** (£1,107; £553; £276)

Form RPR
356 **1** **Proprioception (IRE)**[24] [3275] 4-10-8 **92**................... WayneHutchinson 89+
(A King) *trckd ldrs: rdn to ld sn after 2 out: mstke last: drvn out* **3/1**[1]
0332 **2** *1* **Flower Haven**[28] [3217] 4-10-0 **89** ow1........................... ChrisHonour(5) 84
(M J Gingell) *hld up: hdwy appr 3 out: rdn and styd on to chse wnr appr last* **11/2**[2]
022B **3** *3* **Think Quick (IRE)**[81] [2140] 6-10-1 **84**......................... AdamHawkins(10) 87
(R Hollinshead) *in tch: outpcd appr 2 out: styd on run-in* **10/1**
0544 **4** *3* **Honey's Gift**[13] [3439] 7-11-9 **99**................................ RobertStephens(3) 99
(G G Margarson) *in tch: led on bnd after 3 out: hdd sn after next: one pce after* **8/1**
6530 **5** *1 ½* **Calomeria**[35] [2981] 5-11-7 **99**.. StephenCraine(5) 97
(D McCain) *prom tl fdd fr 2 out* **15/2**
326- **6** *2 ½* **Cullian**[628] [312] 9-11-6 **93**.. AndrewThornton 89
(J G M O'Shea) *hld up: effrt 3 out: wknd next* **25/1**
0U1 **7** *3* **Nuzzle**[86] [2040] 6-10-3 **83**.. ScottMarshall(7) 77+
(N G Richards) *hld up in rr: hdwy appr 3 out: wknd next* **7/1**[3]
3400 **8** *10* **Half Inch**[30] [3146] 6-11-1 **95**.....................................(p) TomMessenger(7) 82+
(B I Case) *trckd ldr: wknd appr 2 out* **18/1**
62FF **9** *nk* **Bonnet's Pieces**[14] [3418] 7-11-5 **92**............................... PaulMoloney 80+
(Mrs P Sly) *led: nt a fluent: hdd on bnd after 3 out: wknd qckly* **12/1**
0F46 **10** *29* **Leap Year Lass**[12] [3442] 6-11-3 **90**............................. RichardMcGrath 43
(C Grant) *t.k.h: a bhd* **22/1**
045 **11** *8* **Clare Galway**[14] [3423] 5-10-7 **85**.................................. JohnnyLevins(5) 30
(B G Powell) *a bhd: lost tch after 5th* **9/1**
4m 7.30s (0.10) **Going Correction** +0.10s/f (Yiel)
WFA 4 from 5yo+ 11lb **11** Ran SP% **116.0**
Speed ratings: **103,102,101,99,98 97,96,91,90,76 72** CSF £19.89 CT £146.18 TOTE £3.60: £1.10, £4.20, £3.20; EX 22.50.
Owner Rupert Dubai Racing **Bred** Timothy Coughlan **Trained** Barbury Castle, Wilts

FOCUS
A moderate mares' handicap hurdle run at an ordinary early pace and there were still seven within a couple of lengths of each other at the second last. The first two home are both juveniles who showed improvement, as they were entitled to on their Flat form, and the form looks sound enough.

NOTEBOOK
Proprioception(IRE), making her handicap debut, was off the bridle in fifth place exiting the back straight and her prospects did not look great, but the further they went the better she was going and she was well in control before a sloppy jump at the last made things more difficult than they should have been. She may prefer a stiffer test than this. *(op 7-2)*
Flower Haven, dropped 2lb after finishing second of five in a very uncompetitive event of this type at Folkestone last time, stayed on over the last three flights and was given a chance by the winner's blunder at the last, but she could not take advantage. She may also prefer a stiffer test than this. *(tchd 6-1)*
Think Quick(IRE), suited by a flat track, ran her race, but she is totally exposed and has been beaten in sellers. *(tchd 12-1)*
Honey's Gift, down to a mark 1lb lower than for her last win, was given a positive ride over a trip short of her best but was still done for foot where it mattered. *(op 11-2)*
Calomeria seems a shadow of the horse that won three times as a juvenile and even a plunging handicap mark is not resulting in much improvement. *(op 8-1 tchd 7-1)*
Nuzzle, making her handicap debut after winning a seller last time, threatened to get involved rounding the home bend but her effort came to little. *(op 13-2 tchd 6-1)*

3656 BETFRED H'CAP HURDLE (13 hdls) 3m 110y
3:50 (3:50) (Class 5) (0-85,85) 4-Y-0+ **£2,740** (£798; £399)

Form RPR
4233 **1** **Perfect Balance (IRE)**[35] [2967] 5-11-6 **84**..................... PaddyMerrigan(5) 92+
(D W Thompson) *hld up in tch: hdwy to ld appr 2 out: sn clr* **11/2**[2]
0500 **2** *7* **Silver Gift**[30] [3146] 9-11-1 **74**.. GerrySupple 74
(G Fierro) *hld up in rr: styd on fr 3 out to chse wnr sn after 2 out* **20/1**
0P30 **3** *9* **Carroll's O'Tully (IRE)**[13] [3437] 6-10-9 **75**................... JustinMorgan(7) 68+
(L A Dace) *hld up in tch: hdwy to ld 4 out: rdn and hdd appr 2 out: wknd bef last* **20/1**
/1P **4** *6* **Mill Bank (IRE)**[85] [2073] 11-11-3 **76**...............................(p) PaulMoloney 61
(Evan Williams) *mid-div: styd on one pce after 3 out* **9/2**[1]
PP36 **5** *¾* **Kings Square**[7] [3540] 6-11-7 **83**.. MrTGreenall(3) 67
(M W Easterby) *in tch tl rdn and wknd after 3 out* **15/2**
6-10 **6** *6* **Southerncrosspatch**[72] [2341] 15-11-7 **80**............................ MarcusFoley 58
(Mrs Barbara Waring) *hld up: outpcd appr 9th: and nvr on terms after* **16/1**

The Form Book, Raceform Ltd, Compton, RG20 6NL

-P50 **7** *5* **Cleymor House (IRE)**[11] 3460 8-10-12 **74**......................(b) LeeVickers(3) 47
(John R Upson) *led tl hdd 4 out: wknd after next* **16/1**
4002 **8** *8* **Double Royal (IRE)**[60] 2582 7-11-2 **82**.............................. MrJETudor(7) 47
(Mrs T J Hill) *prom tl rdn and wknd on bnd after 3 out* **12/1**
5500 **P** **Missy Moscow (IRE)**[25] 3252 8-11-1 **74**...................... RichardHobson —
(H J Evans) *a bhd: p.u after 3 out* **50/1**
0040 **P** **Washington Pink (IRE)**[10] 3487 7-10-9 **75**................ MrBenHamilton(7) —
(C Grant) *bhd whn blnd 8th: p.u bef next* **18/1**
0-0P **P** **Charlie Castallan**[225] 782 6-10-7 **73**...................(p) BenOrde-Powlett(7) —
(D W Thompson) *a bhd: t.o whn p.u bef 9th* **80/1**
/0-2 **P** **Here Comes Harry**[238] 665 10-11-7 **80**.............................. PhilipHide —
(C J Down) *mid-div whn blnd 8th: bhd whn p.u after 3 out* **6/1**[3]
5000 **P** **Alchimiste (FR)**[10] 3483 5-10-11 **77**.............................. MrRLangley(7) —
(Mrs E Langley) *trckd ldrs tl wknd qckly and p.u after 3 out* **66/1**
P654 **P** **Gay Kindersley (IRE)**[12] 3443 8-10-10 **79**................ JamesReveley(10) —
(K G Reveley) *prom tl wknd after 9th: p.u after 3 out* **12/1**
PP53 **P** **Kyber**[24] 3271 5-11-12 **85**.. DominicElsworth —
(R F Fisher) *trckd ldr: mstke 5th: wknd appr 4 out: p.u after next* **6/1**[3]
00PP **P** **It's Official (IRE)**[35] 2956 7-11-6 **79**.......................(v[1]) MatthewBatchelor —
(Miss A M Newton-Smith) *in tch tl wknd 4 out: p.u after next* **66/1**

6m 38.9s (17.30) **Going Correction** +0.10s/f (Yiel) **16** Ran SP% **122.0**
Speed ratings: **76,73,70,68,68 66,65,62,—,— —,—,—,—,—,—** — CSF £117.55 CT £2070.44 TOTE £6.40: £1.50, £4.70, £6.40, £1.90; EX 199.70.
Owner Mrs Ann Davis **Bred** Lodge Park Stud **Trained** Bolam, Co Durham

FOCUS
A big field, but a moderate early pace that did not pick up until under a mile from home resulted in a pedestrian winning time. The form probably amounts to little.

NOTEBOOK
Perfect Balance(IRE), trying this trip for the first time, outstayed his rivals even though the moderate early pace did not make this the test of stamina it might have been. The slow winning time also raises serious questions over the merit of the form. *(op 9-2)*
Silver Gift, a proven stayer, kept on in the home straight without ever looking like getting in a blow at the winner. She is now 17lb lower than for her last win, but that was getting on for three years ago. *(op 33-1)*
Carroll's O'Tully(IRE), making her handicap debut, did not seem to quite see out this longer trip but this was still a big improvement on her latest effort and the better ground may have been the key. She only made her racecourse debut the previous month, so she may have some further improvement in her. *(tchd 25-1)*
Mill Bank(IRE), pulled up on his return to hurdling last month, seemed to run his race with no excuses. A 16lb rise for his victory over fences at Uttoxeter in October means that he is now a stone lower over hurdles than he is over the larger obstacles, so it will be interesting to see what connections do with him now. *(op 7-2)*
Kings Square seemed to have every chance, but had nothing more to give in the home straight. He gained his last victory under similar conditions so there is no reason to believe he did not run his race. *(op 8-1 tchd 7-1)*
Here Comes Harry, returning from a seven-month break, ran no sort of race but was found to have burst. *He has obviously not been easy to train. Official explanation: trainer's representative said gelding bled from the nose (op 8-1)*

3657 EXPERIENCE NOTTINGHAMSHIRE MAIDEN NATIONAL HUNT FLAT RACE (CONDITIONAL JOCKEYS AND AMATEUR RIDERS) 2m
4:20 (4:20) (Class 6) 5-6-Y-O **£2,055** (£599; £299)

Form RPR
1 **Nightfly (IRE)** 5-10-11 .... RobertLucey-Butler(5) 108+
(M Pitman) *hld up: hdwy 4f out: led over 1f out: r.o wl* **3/1**[2]
2 *2 ½* **Mr Shambles** 5-10-13 .... WilliamKennedy(3) 102
(S Gollings) *hld up: hdwy to trck ldrs 1/2-way: ev ch 2f out: kpt on wl* **14/1**
2 **3** *2* **Medic (IRE)**[18] 3353 5-10-9 .... DavidCullinane(7) 101+
(T J Fitzgerald) *t.k.h early: trckd ldr tl led 2f out: hdd over 1f out: no ex fnl f* **11/4**[1]
00 **4** *10* **Tuatara Bay (IRE)**[10] 3490 6-10-9 .... MrBMcHugh(7) 90
(R A Fahey) *led tl rdn and hdd 2f out: sn btn* **28/1**
00 **5** *3 ½* **Bartercard (USA)**[47] 2823 5-10-6 .... KevinTobin(10) 87
(C J Mann) *nvr bttr than mid-div* **15/2**[3]
04 **6** *1 ¼* **Romney Marsh**[29] 3188 5-9-13 .... WayneBurton(10) 79
(R Curtis) *hld up: hdwy 1/2-way: wknd 3f out* **20/1**
7 *hd* **Back In Vogue** 5-10-4 .... StephenCraine(5) 79
(J G Portman) *a towards rr* **10/1**
4 **8** *2 ½* **Mr Ironman**[75] 2268 5-10-13 .... RobertStephens(3) 83
(R C Guest) *in rr: effrt 1/2-way: nvr on terms* **12/1**
6 **9** *11* **Toothill Gunner**[275] 131 5-10-9 .... DavidBoland(7) 72
(J K Cresswell) *trckd ldrs tl wknd over 6f out* **66/1**
10 *17* **Another Penny** 6-10-2 .... JohnPritchard(7) 48
(R Dickin) *a wl bhd* **33/1**
0 **11** *dist* **On Tilt**[5] 3563 5-10-9 .... MrLWheatley(7) —
(M W Easterby) *trckd ldrs tl dropped out 1/2-way: t.o* **25/1**
/04 **12** *1 ¾* **Watercress**[24] 3273 6-10-4 ....(t) PaddyMerrigan(5) —
(Miss M E Rowland) *in tch tl wknd over 4f out: t.o* **12/1**
13 *16* **Cottam Eclipse** 5-10-9 .... MrOGreenall(7) —
(M W Easterby) *hld up: lost tch 6f out: t.o* **8/1**
P **Doyounoso** 6-10-9 .... MrRArmson(7) —
(R J Armson) *in rr: t.o whn p.u over 7f out* **100/1**

4m 3.70s (-0.80) **Going Correction** +0.10s/f (Yiel) **14** Ran SP% **123.2**
Speed ratings: **106,104,103,98,97 96,96,95,89,81** —,—,—,— CSF £42.69 TOTE £6.80: £4.20, £4.70, £1.40; EX 43.90 Place 6 £107.41, Place 5 £34.17 .
Owner Malcolm C Denmark **Bred** Thomas Steele **Trained** Upper Lambourn, Berks
■ Stewards' Enquiry : Mr B McHugh one-day ban: used whip with excessive frequency (Feb 10)

FOCUS
Probably a fair bumper for the track. The winning time was 3.6 seconds faster than the mares-only handicap hurdle, which is encouraging, and the winner looks a nice prospect.

NOTEBOOK
Nightfly(IRE), a 32,000euros gelding, is a full-brother to an Irish bumper winner out of a dam who is from the family of Harbour Pilot and Monty's Pass. From a stable that does so well in this type of race, he was always travelling supremely well off the pace and when asked to go and win his race, found enough despite running green. He looks sure to come on a good deal for this and looks a nice prospect. *(op 7-2)*
Mr Shambles, whose dam scored four times over hurdles, had every chance but probably came across an above-average rival for a race like this. He showed enough ability himself on this debut though, and looks to have a future.
Medic(IRE), with the benefit of previous experience having finished runner-up on his debut, had every chance but did not really improve much and it may be that this was a stronger bumper than the Catterick one. *(op 3-1 tchd 10-3 and 5-2)*
Tuatara Bay(IRE), given a much more positive ride than in his two previous outings, did not get *home and does not seem to be progressing. Now may be the time to switch him to hurdles. (op 25-1)*
Bartercard(USA) did not improve much on his two previous performances. *(op 17-2 tchd 9-1)*

T/Plt: £88.50 to a £1 stake. Pool: £46,780.50. 385.70 winning tickets. T/Qpdt: £7.10 to a £1 stake. Pool: £4,285.20. 445.80 winning tickets. JS

3429 FOLKESTONE (R-H)
Tuesday, January 31

OFFICIAL GOING: Chase course - good to soft (soft in places); hurdle course - soft (good to soft in places)
Wind: Light, against Weather: Overcast

3658 WESTENHANGER RAILWAY STATION NOVICES' HURDLE (DIV I) 2m 1f 110y
(9 hdls)
1:30 (1:31) (Class 4) 4-Y-O+ **£2,927** (£859; £429; £214)

Form RPR
1 **1** **Straw Bear (USA)**[21] 3328 5-11-11 .... APMcCoy 129+
(N J Gifford) *hld up in midfield: prog 5th: trckd ldr after 2 out: led bef last: sn jnd: hdd flat: shkn up to ld again last 100yds* **2/9**[1]
2- **2** *1 ¼* **Classic Role**[331] 4201 7-11-4 .... JamieMoore 116+
(L Wells) *t.k.h: hld up: prog 5th: effrt to join wnr bef last: led briefly flat: sn outpcd u.p* **14/1**[2]
0- **3** *3* **Tagula Blue (IRE)**[193] 2764 6-11-4 .... WayneHutchinson 113
(Ian Williams) *t.k.h: hld up towards rr: stdy prog 3 out: chsd ldng pair bef last: pushed along and kpt on wl: quite promising* **50/1**
4 *16* **White On Black (GER)**[121] 5-11-4 .... PhilipHide 99+
(G L Moore) *mstke 1st: prom: led 3 out: hdd & wknd bef last* **18/1**
-000 **5** *2 ½* **King Louis (FR)**[31] 3133 5-11-4 .... BrianCrowley 94
(R Rowe) *led to 3rd: led again 5th tl next: stl in tch after 2 out: wknd* **66/1**
200 **6** *5* **Haloo Baloo**[15] 3422 6-11-1 .... TJPhelan(3) 89
(Jonjo O'Neill) *hld up towards rr: outpcd bef 2 out: shkn up and nvr on terms after* **100/1**
53 **7** *nk* **Sarin**[240] 643 8-11-4 .... SamThomas 89
(Miss Venetia Williams) *t.k.h: hld up in midfield: outpcd 2 out: n.d after* **16/1**[3]
P/5- **8** *2 ½* **Newtown**[618] 478 7-10-11 .... CharliePoste(7) 87
(M F Harris) *stdd s: hld up in last trio: sme prog 3 out: nt on terms next: no hdwy after* **100/1**
05 **9** *½* **Harcourt (USA)**[15] 3422 6-10-13 .... RobertLucey-Butler(5) 86
(M Madgwick) *stdd s: hld up in last trio: lost tch whn nt fluent 3 out: nudged along after 2 out: styd on flat: do bttr* **50/1**
500 **10** *shd* **Street Life (IRE)**[21] 3328 8-11-4 .... LeightonAspell 94+
(W J Musson) *trckd ldrs: prog to chse ldr 3 out: terrible blunder next: nt rcvr: 6th and wl btn last: heavily eased flat* **40/1**
11 *15* **Tricky Venture**[17] 6-11-4 .... PJBrennan 71
(Mrs L C Jewell) *t.k.h: hld up towards rr: prog 3 out: nt on terms w ldrs 2 out: wkng rapidly whn blnd last* **100/1**
0 **12** *22* **Naja De Billeron (FR)**[48] 2826 5-11-4 .... TimmyMurphy 49
(M C Pipe) *hld up in rr: nt fluent 5th: lost tch next: pushed along and no prog 2 out: heavily eased wl bef last* **28/1**
P0 **13** *20* **Tigu (IRE)**[15] 3425 5-11-4 .... JimCrowley 29
(A Ennis) *prom to 3rd: sn lost pl: last after 5th: t.o* **150/1**
P-U0 **14** *1 ¼* **Premier Cheval (USA)**[24] 3283 7-11-4 64.......................... HenryOliver 28
(P R Hedger) *stdd s: hld up in last trio: wknd 3 out: t.o* **150/1**
FPP **P** **Little Gannet**[15] 3422 5-10-11 .... JamesDavies —
(T D McCarthy) *t.k.h: prog to ld 3rd: hdd & wknd 5th: t.o after 2 out: p.u bef last* **150/1**

4m 18.9s (-10.40) **Going Correction** -0.45s/f (Good) **15** Ran SP% **115.9**
Speed ratings: **105,104,103,96,94 92,92,91,91,91 84,74,65,65,—** CSF £3.61 TOTE £1.30: £1.10, £1.80, £5.60; EX 4.90.
Owner John P McManus **Bred** Cyril Humphris **Trained** Findon, W Sussex

FOCUS
The winning time was as you would expect for a race like this, despite being 3.7 seconds faster than the second division. Straw Bear is rated value for further with the second close to his mark, and the race should produce winners.

NOTEBOOK
Straw Bear(USA) made it two from two over hurdles although he was not as impressive as he had been at Leicester. Joined at the last, he was momentarily in trouble but quickened up to assume control in the last 100 yards. Value for a little further, he may go for the Supreme Novices' but fast ground would scupper that plan. *(op 1-4 tchd 1-3 and 2-7 in places)*
Classic Role had not run since finishing second on his hurdling debut last March. Improving on the long run between the last two flights, he led for a stride or two after the last but could not hold off the winner who appeared to have the greater appetite for a battle. This was a good comeback and he should not be long in winning over hurdles. *(op 10-1)*
Tagula Blue(IRE), a miler on the Flat, had looked a non-stayer on his only previous hurdles run over a year ago. Having his first outing since July, and first for this yard, he shaped with promise and had no problem with the trip. He could even get further as his half-brother Rhapsody In Blue stayed three miles.
White On Black(GER), formerly trained in Germany, was a winner in Belgium on his most recent start in October. He showed ability on this hurdles debut before fading on the long run to the last, and should come on for this. *(op 20-1 tchd 16-1)*
King Louis(FR), who has been sent off at big prices on all his starts to date, was up with the pace until weakening on the long run from two out.
Harcourt(USA) again caught the eye, albeit finishing well beaten, and is now eligible for a handicap mark.
Street Life(IRE), in second place when he blundered at the penultimate flight, splintering the *hurdle, was quickly beaten and ended up finishing lame. Official explanation: vet said gelding was lame*
Little Gannet *Official explanation: jockey said mare hung badly both ways (op 100-1)*

3659 WESTENHANGER RAILWAY STATION NOVICES' HURDLE (DIV II) 2m 1f 110y
(9 hdls)
2:00 (2:01) (Class 4) 4-Y-O+ **£2,927** (£859; £429; £214)

Form RPR
3 **1** **Tarlac (GER)**[22] 3324 5-11-4 .... APMcCoy 115+
(N J Henderson) *led after 2nd: mde rest: mstke 2 out: in command whn mstke last: rdn out* **5/6**[1]
2 *6* **Toparudi**[27] 5-11-4 .... LeightonAspell 108+
(M H Tompkins) *t.k.h: hld up in midfield: prog 5th: chsd wnr after 2 out: hld whn nt fluent last: eased nr fin* **12/1**
2300 **3** *7* **River Ripples (IRE)**[25] 3275 7-11-4 ....(t) JasonMaguire 99+
(T R George) *led to after 2nd: chsd wnr tl after 2 out: rdn and one pce* **22/1**
4 *5* **Mith Hill**[102] 5-11-4 .... WayneHutchinson 94+
(Ian Williams) *mstkes: wl in tch: outpcd 2 out: n.d after: plugged on* **10/1**[3]

2 **5** *1 1/2* **Noble Bily (FR)**[59] [2618] 5-10-11 .... AndrewGlassonbury(7) 91
(M C Pipe) *mstke 2nd: trckd ldrs: wl in tch after 3 out: outpcd after 2 out: plugged on* **14/1**

00 **6** *11* **El Corredor (IRE)**[19] [3355] 7-11-4 .... SamStronge 80
(M F Harris) *hld up wl in rr: mstke 5th: wl off the pce after: kpt on fr 2 out: no ch* **100/1**

60 **7** *1 3/4* **Future Legend**[78] [2249] 5-11-4 .... PJBrennan 78
(J A B Old) *w ldrs: rdn and outpcd bef 2 out: steadily fdd* **25/1**

60 **8** *1 1/4* **Trebello**[25] [3275] 5-10-13 .... StephenCraine(5) 77
(J R Boyle) *sltly hmpd 1st: mstke 2nd: hld up wl in rr: wl off the pce 3 out: no ch after* **50/1**

2 **9** *7* **Dark Parade (ARG)**[12] [3464] 5-11-4 .... JamieMoore 70
(G L Moore) *w ldrs: hit 2nd: u.p whn mstke 2 out: wknd rapidly: eased bef last* **3/1**[2]

0060 **10** *11* **Nelson Du Ronceray (FR)**[12] [3464] 5-11-4 .... TimmyMurphy 59
(M C Pipe) *t.k.h: hld up wl in rr: sme prog after 5th but nvr nr ldrs* **40/1**

P-00 **11** *10* **Cambo (FR)**[70] [2421] 5-10-11 .... MarcGoldstein(7) 49
(Miss Sheena West) *j.rt 1st: nvr beyond midfield: wl off the pce whn blnd 3 out: wknd next* **66/1**

0 **12** *2* **Zolash (IRE)**[14] [3429] 4-10-7 .... BenjaminHitchcott 36
(Mrs L C Jewell) *t.k.h: hld up in midfield: lost tch w ldng gp after 5th: wknd 2 out* **100/1**

P-U0 **13** *18* **Red Jester**[15] [3422] 5-10-13 .... DerekLaverty(5) 29
(A E Jones) *a wl in rr: mstke 3rd: t.o after 3 out* **100/1**

14 *dist* **Public Eye**[136] 5-10-11 .... JustinMorgan(7) —
(L A Dace) *hld up: a in last trio: t.o 3 out* **100/1**

P **Night Cap (IRE)**[363] 7-11-4 .... JamesDavies —
(T D McCarthy) *plld hrd: hld up: wknd 5th: t.o whn p.u bef last* **100/1**

4m 22.6s (-6.70) **Going Correction** -0.45s/f (Good)
WFA 4 from 5yo+ 11lb **15** Ran SP% **122.0**
Speed ratings: **96,93,90,88,87 82,81,81,78,73 68,67,59,—,—** CSF £12.72 TOTE £2.10: £1.20, £2.10, £3.90; EX 14.00.
Owner John P McManus **Bred** Gestut Olympia **Trained** Upper Lambourn, Berks

FOCUS
A modest winning time, 3.7 seconds slower than the first division. The winner is rated value for further and the form looks solid enough.

NOTEBOOK
Tarlac(GER), keen to go faster and in front before the third, made errors at the last two flights while being pressed but stayed on strongly. Like the winner of the first division, and in the same ownership, he could go to the Festival but he will need to improve a good deal on this if he is to make an impact at Cheltenham. *(op Evens)*
Toparudi, a winner over a mile on the Flat, shaped with promise on this hurdling debut, but after moving into second place on the home turn he could not get to the favourite. He was eased towards the finish and can step up on this before long. *(op 16-1)*
River Ripples(IRE), equipped with a tongue-tie, adopted different tactics and this was better, although he was beaten from the home turn. *(op 25-1)*
Mith Hill, four times a winner on the Flat for Ed Dunlop at up to twelve furlongs, was sold for 55,000gns in October. Not fluent on this initial try over hurdles, he was outpaced by the leaders at the second last but did stick on in his own time. *(op 9-1 tchd 11-1)*
Noble Bily(FR) is a limited performer, but there should be improvement to come from him over further, maybe in handicap company. *(op 11-1)*
Dark Parade(ARG) raced prominently until weakening on the long home turn. *Official explanation: jockey said horse was never travelling (tchd 10-3)*
Night Cap(IRE) *Official explanation: trainer said gelding finished distressed*

3660 THE LOOKOUT RESTAURANT MAIDEN CHASE (15 fncs) 2m 5f
2:30 (2:30) (Class 4) 5-Y-0+ **£3,903** (£1,146; £573; £286)

Form RPR

3-U2 **1** **The Outlier (IRE)**[15] [3426] 8-11-2 107 .... SamThomas 100+
(Miss Venetia Williams) *hld up in cl tch: led 11th and increased pce: mstke 3 out: clr fr 2 out: easily* **8/13**[1]

603U **2** *6* **Sett Aside**[14] [3430] 8-11-2 73 ....(p) BenjaminHitchcott 82
(Mrs L C Jewell) *nt a fluent: led 5th: mde most at stdy pce tl hdd 11th: chsd wnr after 3 out: no imp next* **12/1**

4-U3 **3** *3* **Twenty Degrees**[15] [3426] 8-11-2 95 ....(b) JamieMoore 81+
(G L Moore) *t.k.h: hld up in tch: blnd 2nd: nt fluent 9th: effrt 3 out: rdn to dispute 2nd 2 out and last: fnd nil* **5/1**[2]

4P **4** *dist* **Harrihawkan**[62] [2574] 8-11-2 .... PhilipHide —
(Mrs T J Hill) *nt a fluent: in tch tl wknd 12th: t.o: btn 56 l* **7/1**[3]

P5 **F** **Run To The King (IRE)**[4] [3601] 8-11-2 .... AndrewThornton —
(P C Ritchens) *trckd ldrs: cl 4th whn fell 10th* **20/1**

P **Buckland Bobby**[317] 8-10-11 .... RobertLucey-Butler(5) —
(M Madgwick) *plld hrd: led to 5th: last fr next: t.o whn p.u bef 9th* **66/1**

505 **P** **Bally Rainey (IRE)**[21] [3329] 7-11-2 .... LeightonAspell —
(Mrs L C Jewell) *nt fluent: t.k.h: w ldr 5th to 11th: w wnr 3 out: wknd rapidly: poor 4th whn mstke 2 out and p.u* **33/1**

5m 33.6s (9.20) **Going Correction** +0.025s/f (Yiel) **7** Ran SP% **108.0**
Speed ratings: **83,80,79,—,— —,—** CSF £7.45 TOTE £1.70: £1.40, £3.20; EX 9.00.
Owner P J Murphy **Bred** Mrs Joerg Vasicek **Trained** Kings Caple, H'fords

FOCUS
A very slow winning time. The winner was value for a much greater margin of victory in this weak event.

NOTEBOOK
The Outlier(IRE) jumped soundly bar a mistake at the third last, a ditch, and came home a very comfortable winner, value for a lot further. He had nothing to beat and it would have been a concern had he not won in the manner he did. *(op 4-6)*
Sett Aside, who would have been no less than 34lb better off with the winner in a handicap, predictably proved no match but did get the better of a tussle for second.
Twenty Degrees, a better horse over hurdles, finished a good deal closer to The Outlier than he had on his chasing debut but that is not saying a great deal. Not always fluent at his fences, he looked a less than straightforward ride. *(op 17-2)*
Bally Rainey(IRE), the Jewell second string, made his share of jumping errors but remained prominent until weakening quickly on the home turn. He did win a point-to-point in Ireland but has shown little in a variety of races under Rules. *(op 25-1)*

3661 WEATHERBYS BANK H'CAP HURDLE (9 hdls) 2m 1f 110y
3:00 (3:00) (Class 4) (0-110,107) 4-Y-0+ **£4,554** (£1,337; £668; £333)

Form RPR

3213 **1** **Honan (IRE)**[61] [2585] 7-11-2 **97** ....(v) APMcCoy 99+
(M C Pipe) *hld up in midfield: prog 4th: led between last 2: clr last: rdn out* **7/2**[1]

0200 **2** *6* **Jayed (IRE)**[41] [2940] 8-10-9 **90** .... WayneHutchinson 85+
(M Bradstock) *racd freely: led: rdn and hdd between last 2: sn outpcd: kpt on again flat to snatch 2nd on line* **12/1**

2341 **3** *shd* **Isam Top (FR)**[29] [3223] 10-10-5 **89** .... RobertStephens(3) 84+
(M J Hogan) *hld up in tch: effrt 2 out: chal between last 2: sn no ch w wnr: lost 2nd fnl stride* **9/1**

6200 **4** *nk* **Shaman**[30] [3185] 9-10-11 **92** .... JamieMoore 86
(G L Moore) *hld up in tch: effrt 2 out: rdn to dispute 2nd flat: one pce* **10/1**

-FP1 **5** *3/4* **Barton Gate**[31] [3141] 8-11-0 **100** ....(b) DarylJacob(5) 93
(D P Keane) *chsd ldr tl after 2 out: sn outpcd under presure: kpt on again flat* **14/1**

-001 **6** *4* **Ressource (FR)**[25] [451] 7-10-5 **93** ....(b) MrWRussell(7) 82
(G L Moore) *hld up in rr: urged along and nt keen 2 out: plugged on one pce* **25/1**

2533 **7** *2 1/2* **Monsal Dale (IRE)**[14] [3441] 7-10-1 **82** ....(tp) PJBrennan 68
(Mrs L C Jewell) *t.k.h: hld up in last pair: prog 5th: wl in tch 2 out: wknd bef last* **25/1**

/P40 **8** *3 1/2* **Instant Appeal**[29] [3211] 9-10-8 **89** .... PhilipHide 75+
(P Winkworth) *trckd ldrs: wl in tch 2 out: wknd bef last: eased flat* **13/2**[3]

11U0 **9** *3 1/2* **Zeloso**[25] [3279] 8-9-13 **87** ....(v) CharliePoste(7) 69+
(M F Harris) *lost pl and rdn bef 4th: bhd fr 3 out: no ch after: plugged on* **12/1**

516- **10** *7* **Up At Midnight**[332] [4192] 6-11-4 **99** .... MickFitzgerald 71
(R Rowe) *trckd ldrs: lost pl but wl in tch 2 out: wd bnd after and steadily wknd* **7/1**

4505 **11** *dist* **Just Beware**[14] [3431] 4-9-9 **92** oh7 ....(b1) RobertLucey-Butler(5) —
(Miss Z C Davison) *lost pl and drvn bef 4th: sn bhd: t.o bef 2 out: btn 84 l* **50/1**

11P4 **P** **Dangerousdanmagru (IRE)**[10] [3495] 10-11-12 **107** .... MarcusFoley —
(A E Jones) *hld up in last pair: rdn 3rd: nvr gng wl after: t.o 3 out: p.u bef last* **4/1**[2]

4m 23.6s (-5.70) **Going Correction** -0.45s/f (Good)
WFA 4 from 6yo+ 11lb **12** Ran SP% **118.9**
Speed ratings: **94,91,91,91,90 89,87,86,84,81 —,—** CSF £44.37 CT £355.41 TOTE £4.10: £2.00, £4.80, £2.60; EX 65.70 Trifecta £345.90 Pool: £535.98 - 1.10 winning tickets..
Owner Eminence Grise Partnership **Bred** Miss Ashling O'Connell **Trained** Nicholashayne, Devon

FOCUS
Not too much strength in depth to this ordinary handicap and the time was modest. The winner ran to his best.

NOTEBOOK
Honan(IRE), reunited with McCoy, was always travelling best and came away on the flat to gain his first hurdling win outside selling company. He is still nicely handicapped over hurdles but is a 10lb better horse over fences. *(op 9-2 tchd 5-1 in places)*
Jayed(IRE) ran the only way he knows, out in front. Headed by the winner between the last two flights, he was only fourth over the last but rallied to grab second. This was a good effort, and he can win off this mark, probably on better ground. *(op 14-1)*
Isam Top(FR) ran a solid race under the 7lb penalty for his recent course and distance win, but was no match for the winner in the straight and was pipped for second on the line. *(op 8-1)*
Shaman was one of three tussling for second place on the run-in behind the decisive winner. He continues to fall down the handicap and could add to his sole hurdling success to date. *(op 9-1)*
Barton Gate, successful in selling company last time, was in second place for much of the way and, having lost his pitch, was closing again on the placed horses at the end. *(op 12-1)*
Dangerousdanmagru(IRE) was never going well and the ground was probably not the sole reason *for this performance. Official explanation: trainer was unable to offer any explanation for poor form shown (tchd 7-2)*

3662 FEARLESS IMP H'CAP CHASE (18 fncs) 3m 1f
3:30 (3:30) (Class 5) (0-90,89) 5-Y-0+ **£3,578** (£1,050; £525; £262)

Form RPR

0054 **1** **Joseph Beuys (IRE)**[10] [3499] 7-11-0 **82** .... DarylJacob(5) 90+
(D P Keane) *hld up in rr: prog 12th: mstke next: trckd ldr 3 out: led next: drvn and styd on wl flat* **8/1**

41P2 **2** *1 1/2* **Cool Song**[19] [3359] 10-10-9 **75** .... ColinBolger(3) 81+
(Miss Suzy Smith) *in tch: n.m.r after 12th: sn rdn: effrt u.p after 3 out: chsd wnr bef and looked dangerous: nt qckn flat* **4/1**[2]

P0FF **3** *1 3/4* **Murphy's Magic (IRE)**[15] [3427] 8-11-5 **82** ....(p) AndrewThornton 85+
(Mrs T J Hill) *hld up in rr: blnd 4th: effrt and mstke 12th: rdn after: nt on terms 3 out: taken wd and styd on fr 2 out: nrst fin* **33/1**

1341 **4** *3 1/2* **Rosetown (IRE)**[12] [3460] 8-11-6 **83** ....(b) JasonMaguire 85+
(T R George) *prom: pckd bdly 6th: chsd ldr 11th to 3 out: sn u.p: one pce fr next* **11/4**[1]

U04P **5** *1 1/2* **Royale Acadou (FR)**[24] [3285] 8-11-12 **89** ....(p) LeightonAspell 86
(Mrs L J Mongan) *w ldr fr 3rd: led 7th: j.w in ld: hdd 2 out: fnd nil* **25/1**

43-3 **6** *shd* **Regal River (IRE)**[83] [2129] 9-9-11 **65** .... MarkNicolls(5) 62+
(John R Upson) *settled wl in rr: lost tch w ldrs 13th: stl wl off the pce 3 out: styd on fr next: no ch* **5/1**[3]

-3PP **7** *11* **Just Anvil (IRE)**[15] [3427] 8-10-10 **80** ....(p) JustinMorgan(7) 71+
(L Wells) *led to 7th: chsd ldr to 11th: wknd u.p 3 out* **11/1**

3026 **8** *20* **Alfred The Grey**[19] [3359] 9-10-13 **76** ....(p) BenjaminHitchcott 42
(Miss Suzy Smith) *nt fluent: w ldr to 2nd: pushed along 9th: lost tch 13th: sn t.o* **14/1**

P3-P **9** *1 3/4* **Pip Moss**[83] [2126] 11-10-5 **68** .... MarkBradburne 32
(J A B Old) *in tch: mstkes 10th and 12th: lost tch next: t.o* **11/1**

PR1- **P** **Gee Aker Malayo (IRE)**[286] [4934] 10-11-12 **89** .... JimmyMcCarthy —
(R T Phillips) *hld up: in tch tl wknd rapidly 13th: p.u bef next* **9/1**

6m 35.3s (1.90) **Going Correction** +0.025s/f (Yiel) **10** Ran SP% **114.6**
Speed ratings: **97,96,95,94,94 94,90,84,83,—** CSF £40.48 CT £1002.36 TOTE £11.10: £2.50, £1.80, £9.40; EX 58.20.
Owner The Don't Tell Daddy Racing Partnership **Bred** Daniel O'Mahony **Trained** North End, Dorset

FOCUS
A weak race, run in a modest time, which has been rated through the second.

NOTEBOOK
Joseph Beuys(IRE), running over fences for only the second time, produced an improved performance to get off the mark. In front at the second last, he pecked when diving right at the final fence but held on. Described as a 'headbanger' by Keane, he has not been easy to train but could add to his tally. *(tchd 9-1)*
Cool Song was hampered against the inside rail turning down the side of the course on to the last circuit. He needed plenty of driving from that point, but eventually recovered and stayed on in the straight to keep the winner up to his work. *(op 9-2 tchd 5-1 in a place)*
Murphy's Magic(IRE), who had cheekpieces back on in place of the blinkers, made a couple of errors when held up. Taken wide in the home straight, he stayed on steadily but had set himself too much to do. Still a maiden under Rules, he looks to need a severe test of stamina.
Rosetown(IRE), went up 9lb for winning at Ludlow and, although still 20lb lower than his chase mark, is not well handicapped on his chase form. An early mistake did not help his cause, but he *had his chance before being outpointed from the third last. (op 5-2 tchd 3-1, 10-3 in places and 7-2 in a place)*
Royale Acadou(FR), with the sheepskin back on, made much of the running to the second last, jumping soundly, but had no answers when headed. This looked too far for her.

3663 EASTWELL MANOR H'CAP CHASE (12 fncs) 2m
4:00 (4:00) (Class 4) (0-100,98) 5-Y-0+ £5,204 (£1,528; £764; £381)

Form RPR

-036 **1** **Adecco (IRE)**[41] 2940 7-11-5 **91** .... JamieMoore 102+
(G L Moore) *t.k.h: hld up off frntic pce: clsd 8th: rdn to ld sn after 2 out: in command last: styd on wl* **9/1**

/P54 **2** 3 1/2 **Inaki (FR)**[14] 3430 9-11-4 **90** .... (b) PhilipHide 100+
(P Winkworth) *trckd clr ldng pair fr 4th: clsng whn mstkes 7th, 9th and 3 out: nt qckn 2 out: styd on to take 2nd flat* **6/1**[3]

F/P2 **3** 1 1/2 **Victory Roll**[14] 3432 10-11-12 **98** .... MarcusFoley 104
(Miss E C Lavelle) *chsd ldr to 2nd: sn off the pce in midfield: effrt 8th: rdn to chal 2 out: one pce bef last* **5/1**[2]

1031 **4** 3/4 **Julies Boy (IRE)**[7] 3546 9-10-10 **89** .... (t) WillieMcCarthy[(7)] 95+
(T R George) *chsd frntic pce set by ldr fr 2nd and clr of rest fr 4th: rdn to ld bef 2 out: hdd sn after 2 out: wknd* **15/8**[1]

F00- **5** 17 **Sweet Minuet**[296] 4798 9-10-7 **84** .... RobertLucey-Butler[(5)] 72
(M Madgwick) *off the pce in midfield: tried to cl and jst in tch 8th: wknd 3 out* **50/1**

-060 **6** 1/2 **Beluga (IRE)**[21] 3328 7-11-4 **90** .... PaulMoloney 78
(M Pitman) *off the pce towards rr: nt on terms w ldng gp after 7th: no ch after* **20/1**

-14F **7** 6 **French Direction (IRE)**[36] 2960 7-11-5 **91** .... TimmyMurphy 77+
(R Rowe) *set off at furious gallop and sn clr w one rival: hdd bef 2 out: wknd rapidly* **5/1**[2]

00F0 **8** shd **Major Belle (FR)**[18] 3370 7-10-6 **78** .... HenryOliver 60
(John R Upson) *a struggling in last pair: wl bhd fr 8th* **50/1**

5560 **P** **Wee Anthony (IRE)**[21] 3328 7-11-8 **94** .... APMcCoy —
(Jonjo O'Neill) *nt fluent: a last: wl bhd fr 7th: t.o whn p.u bef 2 out* **7/1**

4m 4.40s (-2.40) **Going Correction** +0.025s/f (Yiel) 9 Ran SP% **113.6**
Speed ratings: **107,105,104,104,95 95,92,92,**— CSF £59.68 CT £299.24 TOTE £8.60: £1.70, £1.70, £2.30; EX 71.90.
Owner N J Jones **Bred** M J Halligan **Trained** Woodingdean, E Sussex

FOCUS
A fair handicap in which the winner improved to the level of his old hurdles form. It was run at a strong pace.

NOTEBOOK
Adecco(IRE), making his chasing debut, took it up between the last two fences and was soon in command, giving a flash or two of the tail as he cleared away on the run-in. He has to go right-handed and ideally wants better ground. *(op 10-1 tchd 12-1)*
Inaki(FR), back down in trip, made his share of errors and was only fourth over the last before staying on. This was his best run of the season and he is certainly well handicapped, currently 12lb lower than when gaining his latest win two years ago. *(op 13-2)*
Victory Roll, runner-up to subsequent winner Roznic off the same mark here last time, ran another sound race although he was unable to dominate as he likes. He improved off the home turn to deliver his challenge but could not quicken up from the final fence. *(op 9-2)*
Julies Boy(IRE) was unpenalised for his Leicester win a week earlier. After chasing the clear leader, he showed ahead briefly early in the home straight before his exertions told. *(op 7-4 tchd 2-1)*
French Direction(IRE), an unlucky last-fence faller on Boxing Day, was racing off an 8lb higher mark. Setting off at a rate of knots, he was reeled in on the home turn and not surprisingly had nothing more to give. *(op 9-2)*
Wee Anthony(IRE) failed to make the frame over hurdles and looked to have been given plenty of weight for this chasing debut. Not jumping at all well, he was quickly left behind. He is going to need a lot further. *(op 17-2 tchd 9-1)*

3664 STELLING MINNIS NOVICES' HURDLE (11 hdls) 2m 6f 110y
4:30 (4:30) (Class 4) 4-Y-0+ £3,253 (£955; £477; £238)

Form RPR

03 **1** **Doc Row (IRE)**[10] 3500 6-11-6 .... TimmyMurphy 105+
(M C Pipe) *reluctant ldr at slow pce to 4th: trckd ldr: led again 8th: kicked on after 3 out: mstke 2 out: kpt on wl u.p after* **9/4**[1]

12-0 **2** 1 3/4 **Bumper (FR)**[10] 3500 5-11-6 .... APMcCoy 100+
(M C Pipe) *nt fluent: t.k.h: hld up in rr: prog 8th: effrt after 2 out: kpt on to snatch 2nd nr fin* **10/1**

23 **3** shd **Fast Forward (NZ)**[36] 2988 6-11-6 .... SamThomas 101+
(Miss Venetia Williams) *trckd ldrs: mstke 3 out: effrt to chse wnr sn after 2 out: kpt on but no real imp after last* **10/3**[2]

0-0P **4** 22 **Chilly Milly**[25] 3277 5-10-13 .... PhilipHide 73+
(V Smith) *hld up wl in rr: outpcd after 8th: prog fr 3 out to chse ldrs after 2 out: pushed along and sn outpcd again* **100/1**

-60U **5** 8 **Orange Street**[49] 2809 6-11-6 .... JamieMoore 72+
(Mrs L J Mongan) *prom: rdn to chse wnr briefly 2 out: wknd between last 2* **66/1**

4223 **6** 4 **Corker**[49] 2803 4-10-7 104 .... JamesDavies 53
(D B Feek) *hld up wl in rr: outpcd after 8th: effrt and jst in tch whn mstke 2 out: sn btn* **7/2**[3]

042 **7** 1 1/4 **Ammunition (IRE)**[29] 3216 6-11-6 .... PaulMoloney 65
(M Pitman) *t.k.h: hld up wl in rr: prog to trck ldrs 3 out: wknd after 2 out* **8/1**

15/5 **8** 30 **Historic Place (USA)**[27] 3238 6-11-6 .... MarkBradburne 35
(J A Geake) *cl up: chsd wnr 3 out to 2 out: wknd rapidly: blnd last* **8/1**

51/P **9** hd **Marchensis (IRE)**[29] 3210 8-11-6 .... LeightonAspell 34
(O Sherwood) *t.k.h: cl up tl wknd bef 2 out: t.o* **33/1**

-000 **10** 28 **Lord Leonardo (IRE)**[42] 2928 6-10-13 .... JustinMorgan[(7)] 6
(L Wells) *in tch: rdn after 6th: wknd next: t.o* **100/1**

11 dist **Lochanee (IRE)**[241] 6-10-10 .... CraigMessenger[(10)] —
(Mrs L C Jewell) *in tch tl wknd rapidly 7th: sn wl t.o* **100/1**

60- **P** **Mortar**[361] 3689 7-11-6 .... (t) BrianCrowley —
(R Rowe) *t.k.h: led 4th to 8th: wknd rapidly: t.o whn p.u bef last* **50/1**

6m 1.60s (-7.50) **Going Correction** -0.45s/f (Good)
WFA 4 from 5yo+ 12lb 12 Ran SP% **116.7**
Speed ratings: **95,94,94,86,83 82,82,71,71,61** —,— CSF £25.29 TOTE £3.70: £1.10, £3.00, £2.50; EX 21.70 Place 6 £51.59, Place 5 £46.40.
Owner D A Johnson **Bred** Robert McLean **Trained** Nicholashayne, Devon

FOCUS
This was run at a very steady pace. Not an easy race to rate, with the winner better than the bare result and the second and third running to levels similar to their bumper form.

NOTEBOOK
Doc Row(IRE), upped in trip, set a slow pace over the early flights and was back in front again with four to jump. Introducing a bit of pace after the third last, he clouted the next flight but stayed on well. A likeable sort, he could add to this over hurdles but looks an embryonic chaser. *(op 7-2)*
Bumper(FR) travelled quite well in the pack and closed up the home straight, going second near the line. He finished a good deal closer to stablemate Doc Row than he did on his recent hurdles debut and is going the right way. *(op 15-2)*
Fast Forward(NZ) ran well in both his bumpers and this was a fair effort on his hurdles debut. He finished a long way clear of the rest and should have no problem winning a novice hurdle. *(op 5-2)*
Chilly Milly, who searched out the better ground out wide, made promising headway on the home turn but could not sustain the progress in the straight. This was her best run to date and she could be the type for low-grade handicaps.
Orange Street ran his best race so far over hurdles but faded on the home turn and might not have stayed.
T/Jkpt: £3,413.90 to a £1 stake. Pool: £33,658.50. 7.00 winning tickets. T/Plt: £40.40 to a £1 stake. Pool: £61,908.20. 1,116.25 winning tickets. T/Qpdt: £25.90 to a £1 stake. Pool: £3,988.20. 113.80 winning tickets. JN

3463 TAUNTON (R-H)
Tuesday, January 31
3665 Meeting Abandoned - Frost

3545 LEICESTER (R-H)
Wednesday, February 1

OFFICIAL GOING: Hurdle course - soft (good to soft in places); chase course - good (good to firm in places)
Wind: Almost nil Weather: Overcast & cloudy

3672 LADBROKES.COM MAIDEN CHASE (18 fncs) 2m 7f 110y
1:45 (1:45) (Class 4) 6-Y-0+ £4,436 (£1,310; £655; £327; £163)

Form RPR

/U22 **1** **Stavordale Lad (IRE)**[30] 3218 8-11-0 110 .... ChristianWilliams 108+
(P F Nicholls) *j. awkwardly at times: prom: led 10th: pushed clr 2 out: unchal* **2/5**[1]

005P **2** 12 **Joe McHugh (IRE)**[37] 2986 7-11-0 67 .... NoelFehily 93
(C J Mann) *hld up: hdwy 11th: wnt 2nd 13th: no imp fr 3 out* **18/1**

P426 **3** 18 **Fight The Feeling**[210] 913 8-11-0 .... JasonMaguire 75
(J W Unett) *bhd: lost tch 11th: sme hdwy to mod 3rd 15th: wknd and struggling next* **11/1**[3]

024U **4** 20 **Luckycharm (FR)**[206] 948 7-11-0 72 .... JamieMoore 55
(R Dickin) *chsd ldrs: rdn after 8th: lost tch completely fr 15th* **16/1**

-0PP **5** shd **Redhouse Chevalier**[2] 3653 7-10-7 .... (b[1]) CharlieStudd[(7)] 55
(B G Powell) *led tl 3rd: u.p 6th: rr 9th: blnd next: t.o and nt looking keen fr 14th* **50/1**

-3P0 **6** dist **House Warmer (IRE)**[71] 2424 7-11-0 66 .... (t) LeightonAspell —
(A Ennis) *last whn blnd 5th: t.o 12th: blnd 2 out* **25/1**

6P6 **P** **Diamond Merchant**[30] 3215 7-11-0 105 .... WayneHutchinson —
(Ian Williams) *led 3rd: j.lft 8th: hdd 10th: mstke 11th: wknd bdly 15th: t.o and p.u last* **8/1**[2]

5m 58.2s (-7.20) **Going Correction** -0.20s/f (Good) 7 Ran SP% **107.8**
Speed ratings: **104,100,94,87,87** —,— CSF £7.73 TOTE £1.30: £1.10, £5.80; EX 5.90.
Owner T G A Chappell & Paul K Barber **Bred** Stephen Cahill **Trained** Ditcheat, Somerset

FOCUS
An uncompetitive affair in which the odds-on winner did not have to run to anything like that rating to get off the mark over fences. A very difficult race to rate accurately.

NOTEBOOK
Stavordale Lad(IRE) stood out beforehand as the one to beat and did not have to run to anywhere near his rating of 110 to get off the mark in this moderate heat. The blinkers were left off this time but once again he failed to impress with his jumping, and he looks one to keep taking on if returned to handicap company.
Joe McHugh(IRE), an Irish point-to-point winner, was having his second start over fences under Rules following three outings over hurdles in the autumn. He was pulled up on his chasing debut but this was far more encouraging. He briefly threatened to make a race of it with the winner leaving the back straight, and were he able to race in a handicap off his current mark of 67 in the *near future he would not be without a chance. He was later reported to have bled from the nose. Official explanation: vet said gelding bled from nose (op 16-1 tchd 20-1)*
Fight The Feeling, who was returning from a 210-day absence, was only rated 87 over hurdles and merely stayed on past already beaten horses for third place on this chasing debut. *(op 12-1)*
Luckycharm(FR) was the most experienced chaser in the line-up but he is exposed as plating class.
Diamond Merchant has an official mark of 105 as a result of his exploits over hurdles but nothing he has done over fences so far suggests he can run to that sort of rating. *(op 13-2)*

3673 LADBROKES.COM NOVICES' CLAIMING HURDLE (9 hdls) 2m
2:15 (2:16) (Class 4) 4-Y-0+ £3,253 (£955; £477; £238)

Form RPR

1565 **1** **Rojabaa**[22] 3332 7-11-5 90 .... LiamHeard[(5)] 102+
(B D Leavy) *midfield tl prog gng wl 5th: lft 2nd after schemozzle ent st: led last: rdn clr* **6/1**

301P **2** 5 **Blackthorn**[43] 2930 7-11-1 92 .... RichardYoung[(3)] 89
(M Appleby) *led: drvn and hdd last: nt qckn* **12/1**

0P **3** 7 **Sistema**[50] 2809 5-11-5 .... OwynNelmes[(3)] 86
(A E Price) *cl up: ev ch 3 out: rdn and wknd bef last* **125/1**

051 **4** 6 **Barella (IRE)**[13] 3456 7-10-13 96 .... (p) CharlieStudd[(7)] 82+
(B G Powell) *prom: bdly hmpd ent st: rdn and fdd after 2 out* **7/2**[2]

00-P **5** 2 1/2 **Native Commander (IRE)**[25] 3283 11-11-1 97 ..... ChristopherMurray[(5)] 76
(Jim Best) *hld up and wl bhd: smooth prog bef 3 out: gng wl after rdn and fnd nil 2 out* **15/2**

P/ **6** 3 1/2 **Brunston Castle**[8] 3637 6-11-10 .... (t) WayneHutchinson 76
(A W Carroll) *j.big in midfield: drvn and no imp fr 3 out* **66/1**

5 **7** 4 **After Lent (IRE)**[20] 3355 5-11-8 .... TimmyMurphy 70
(M C Pipe) *hld up: hdwy bef 3 out: pressed ldrs after tl rdn and fdd tamely bef 2 out* **4/1**[3]

00 **8** 15 **Silverpro**[22] 3332 5-10-7 .... RyanCummings[(10)] 50
(D J Wintle) *in tch tl 5th: struggling bef next* **125/1**

063/ **9** 3/4 **Adventino**[269] 11-10-11 .... AdrianScholes[(7)] 50
(P R Johnson) *cl up tl rdn and wknd bef 3 out* **80/1**

P0 **10** 1 3/4 **Inch High**[41] 2942 8-11-3 .... MrGGoldie[(7)] 55
(J S Goldie) *j. slowly 3rd: cl up tl rdn and wknd qckly bef 2 out* **40/1**

062O **R** **It's My Party**[2] 3332 5-10-10 87 .... RichardGordon[(10)] —
(W G M Turner) *prom: virtually disputing ld whn tk wrong crse bef 3 out* **20/1**

-P0P **P** **Mostakbel (USA)**[62] 2584 7-11-1 .... (v[1]) LeeNewnes[(7)] —
(M D I Usher) *a wl bhd and nt fluent: t.o 5th: p.u next* **100/1**

P **P** **Osorno**[47] 2860 6-11-8 ...... AndrewTinkler —
(W M Brisbourne) *tubed: mstke 1st: keen and hld up wl bhd: t.o and p.u 3 out* **100/1**

056 **C** **Tinian**[12] 3488 8-11-1 89 ......(p) AnthonyCoyle(3) —
(Miss Tracy Waggott) *cl up: chal 5th: virtually disputing ld whn tk wrong crse bef 3 out* **25/1**

1001 **P** **Biscar Two (IRE)**[22] 3332 5-11-5 120 ......(b) DerekLaverty(5) —
(A E Jones) *drvn in rr all way: a gng bdly and hopeless task: t.o and p.u 3 out: dismntd: lame* **3/1**[1]

4m 0.70s (-6.90) **Going Correction** -0.60s/f (Firm) **15** Ran SP% **118.3**
Speed ratings: **93,90,87,84,82 81,79,71,71,70** —,—,—,—,— CSF £68.16 TOTE £5.20: £1.20, £4.60, £23.60; EX 81.10.
Owner Mrs Renee Farrington-Kirkham **Bred** The Lavington Stud **Trained** Forsbrook, Staffs
■ Stewards' Enquiry : Richard Gordon two-day ban: careless riding (12-13 Feb); 10-day ban: took wrong course (14-23 Feb)

FOCUS
An ordinary claimer and, with the clear ratings choice Biscar Two running no sort of race, it took even less winning.

NOTEBOOK
Rojabaa finished well behind Biscar Two here last time, but that was over half a mile further, and the drop back to the minimum distance appeared to suit him well. He travelled nicely throughout and, when asked to go on at the final flight, pulled readily clear. A fairly consistent performer, he should continue to go well at a modest level. *(tchd 5-1)*
Blackthorn, a winner of a seller here in December, likes to make the running and clearly goes well at this track. He ran a fair race in defeat. *(op 11-1)*
Sistema had shown little in his first two starts in better company and appreciated the drop into claiming grade. He will need to find some improvement to win a similar race, though. *(op 100-1 tchd 150-1)*
Barella(IRE) ran better than his finishing position suggests, as he was badly hampered in an incident on the home turn. *(op 10-3 tchd 4-1)*
Native Commander(IRE), who stopped quickly on his reappearance last month, once again promised more than he delivered, suggesting a problem. *(op 9-1 tchd 7-1)*
It's My Party was right up with the pace when his rider made the error of directing him on to the chase course on the entrance to the home straight. *(tchd 22-1)*
Tinian was unfortunate to be taken out of the race when It's My Party took the wrong course at the head of the straight. *(op 10-3 tchd 7-2)*
Biscar Two(IRE), who had today's winner behind when successful here last time, ran no sort of race but there appeared a valid reason. *Official explanation: jockey said gelding pulled up lame (op 10-3 tchd 7-2)*

3674 HELEN OF TROY LADY RIDERS' H'CAP HURDLE (9 hdls) 2m
2:45 (2:45) (Class 4) (0-100,96) 4-Y-0+**£3,802** (£1,123; £561; £280; £140)

Form RPR

2000 **1** **Imperial Royale (IRE)**[37] 2968 5-11-1 87 ...... MissSSharratt(7) 92
(P L Clinton) *pressed ldr tl led bef 3 out: drvn clr bef last: styd on wl* **11/1**

4453 **2** *6* **Upright Ima**[19] 3371 7-10-6 78 ...... MissLAllan(7) 77
(Mrs P Sly) *settled in rr: prog after 5th to chse wnr bef 3 out: rdn and wl hld fr appr last* **4/1**[3]

023/ **3** *15* **Robbie Can Can**[15] 4304 7-11-5 91 ...... MissCTizzard(7) 75
(A W Carroll) *last pair and sn wl off pce: rdn and lft mod 4th 3 out: tk poor 3rd at last* **15/8**[1]

0-00 **4** *6* **Fiddlers Creek (IRE)**[9] 3534 7-11-6 88 ......(tp) MissEJJones(3) 66
(R Allan) *pressed ldrs tl rdn and wknd 3 out: lost 3rd pl at last* **14/1**

P-PP **5** *25* **Comete Du Lac (FR)**[22] 3330 9-9-12 70 ......(p) AnnStokell(7) 23
(Mrs N Macauley) *led tl hdd bef 3 out: dropped out v rapidly: t.o* **40/1**

4410 **6** *18* **Wardash (GER)**[78] 2261 6-11-4 90 ......(b[1]) MissLGardner(7) 25
(M C Chapman) *midfield: c wd and urged along bef 3 out: fnd nil and sn wl btn: t.o* **22/1**

0000 **P** **Broughton Knows**[30] 9-9-11 69 ......(v) AngharadFrieze(7) —
(Mrs C J Ikin) *chsd ldrs tl lost pl and lost action and p.u after 5th* **100/1**

0044 **U** **Needwood Spirit**[14] 3446 11-9-11 69 ...... MissJRiding(7) —
(Mrs A M Naughton) *last pair tl hdwy after 5th: disputing 4th and in tch whn bdly hmpd and uns rdr 3 out* **12/1**

P541 **R** **Woodford Consult**[14] 3442 4-11-0 96 ...... MissJCoward(7) —
(M W Easterby) *hld up in midfield: hanging lft bef 3 out where ducked lft and crashed through wing whn disputing 4th* **3/1**[2]

3m 59.9s (-7.70) **Going Correction** -0.60s/f (Firm)
WFA 4 from 5yo+ 9lb **9** Ran SP% **110.3**
Speed ratings: **95,92,84,81,69 60**,—,—,— CSF £51.45 CT £112.99 TOTE £14.50: £3.40, £1.10, £1.10; EX 52.00.
Owner In The Clear Racing **Bred** Andrew Bradley **Trained** Doveridge, Derbys

FOCUS
A moderate handicap which is unlikely to be a source of future winners. It has been rated through the runner-up.

NOTEBOOK
Imperial Royale(IRE) showed the advantage of being dropped back to two miles having struggled to get home over further. This race did not take a lot of winning, though, so he would not appeal as a likely type to follow up. *(op 10-1 tchd 9-1)*
Upright Ima is fully exposed and is still a maiden. She will not find many weaker handicaps to get off the mark in and remains opposable. *(tchd 7-2)*
Robbie Can Can, fit from the Flat but not seen over hurdles for almost two years, never threatened the principals from off the pace. He is usually ridden this way but on this occasion the leaders did not come back to him. *(op 9-4)*
Fiddlers Creek(IRE) has still to get off the mark over timber and the re-fitting of cheekpieces failed to bring about an improved show. *(op 9-1)*
Woodford Consult, who won a weak mares' race last time out, had just been switched to come with her challenge when she took it into her head to run out at the third last. Crashing through the wing, she hampered Needwood Spirit in the process, causing his rider to be unseated. *(op 10-3 tchd 7-2)*

3675 LADBROKES.COM GOLDEN MILLER H'CAP HURDLE (12 hdls) 2m 4f 110y
3:15 (3:15) (Class 3) (0-120,116) 4-Y-0+
£7,515 (£2,220; £1,110; £555; £277; £139)

Form RPR

14-P **1** **Kilgowan (IRE)**[82] 2166 7-11-8 112 ...... WayneHutchinson 119+
(Ian Williams) *settled rr: prog gng wl in 2nd bef 3 out: jnd ldr next: rdn clr last: styd on* **7/1**[3]

2-45 **2** *1 3/4* **Heir To Be**[76] 2292 7-11-8 112 ...... LeightonAspell 116+
(Mrs L Wadham) *in tch: rdn and outpcd bef 3 out: 6th next: tk 3rd last: r.o but nt rch wnr* **9/2**[2]

3-36 **3** *3 1/2* **Idiome (FR)**[32] 3135 10-11-6 115 ...... LiamHeard(5) 115+
(Mrs L C Taylor) *keen and hld up: effrt bef 3 out where nt fluent: no imp after tl kpt on after last wout threatening* **16/1**

-604 **4** *nk* **Prince Of Persia**[74] 2347 6-11-9 113 ......(p) JohnMcNamara 111
(R S Brookhouse) *led: drvn and jnd 2 out: hdd last: sn wknd* **20/1**

P-F2 **5** *6* **Fred's In The Know**[23] 3318 11-11-3 110 ...... AnthonyCoyle(3) 102
(Miss Tracy Waggott) *hit 3rd: hld up in rr: rdn and effrt bef 3 out: sn finding little* **11/1**

3U03 **6** *nk* **Abzuson**[8] 3548 9-10-12 105 ...... LeeVickers(3) 97
(J R Norton) *pressed ldr tl hrd drvn and lost pl after 7th: plugged on* **40/1**

1534 **7** *25* **Devito (FR)**[13] 3467 5-11-3 114 ...... MrDEdwards(7) 98+
(G F Edwards) *settled in rr: effrt ins after 7th: rdn and btn 2 out: eased after last* **12/1**

-114 **8** *1 1/2* **Jaunty Times**[25] 3289 6-11-12 116 ...... RichardJohnson 91+
(H D Daly) *midfield: lost tch qckly bef 3 out: eased last* **9/4**[1]

2-PP **F** **Mazzareme (IRE)**[32] 3143 8-11-6 110 ...... SamThomas —
(Miss Venetia Williams) *stmbld and fell after 1st* **9/1**

0005 **P** **Flying Spur (IRE)**[27] 3248 5-10-10 100 ...... APMcCoy —
(M C Pipe) *prom on outer: nt fluent 5th: rdn whn mstke 3 out: wknd and p.u next* **7/1**[3]

150P **P** **Money Line (IRE)**[13] 3465 7-11-1 105 ...... NoelFehily —
(Jonjo O'Neill) *racd in last pl: lost tch and j. stickily 5th: toiled on tl t.o and p.u 3 out* **40/1**

5m 23.7s (-11.10) **Going Correction** -0.60s/f (Firm) **11** Ran SP% **115.5**
Speed ratings: **97,96,95,94,92 92,82,82**,—,— — CSF £37.74 CT £483.86 TOTE £10.40: £3.00, £1.90, £3.30; EX 46.00 Trifecta £360.00 Part won. Pool: £507.18 - 0.10 winning ticket..
Owner The Ferandlin Peaches **Bred** Thomas McParland **Trained** Portway, Worcs

FOCUS
A competitive handicap and sound enough form for the grade, though the time was modest, 4.2 seconds slower than the later novice hurdle over the same trip.

NOTEBOOK
Kilgowan(IRE) was disappointing at Cheltenham on his seasonal reappearance but came back wrong that day and physio work since appears to have done the trick. A winner here as a novice, this track clearly suits him well, and he would not be denied in the battle to the line. *(tchd 15-2)*
Heir To Be ran creditably in a better race than this at Market Rasen last time, and this soft ground was never going to pose him any problems. Still fairly lightly raced over timber, there could be a similar event in him off this sort of mark, perhaps over slightly further. *(tchd 5-1)*
Idiome(FR) is getting on a bit now but he retains his ability and is fairly consistent. His performance is probably a reasonable guide to the level of the form. *(op 18-1)*
Prince Of Persia, on whom different tactics were adopted, ran well considering the ground was softer than ideal. A similar front-running ride back on a decent surface could pay dividends. *(tchd 22-1)*
Fred's In The Know ran well when unfancied at Newcastle last month but failed to build on that promise. *(op 8-1)*
Jaunty Times was very disappointing, being beaten before the turn into the home straight. This was not his true running. *Official explanation: trainer was unable to offer any explanation for poor form shown (op 3-1)*
Flying Spur(IRE), a drifter in the market beforehand, did not look that keen under pressure and is probably one to leave alone. *(op 9-2)*

3676 LADBROKES.COM H'CAP CHASE (15 fncs) 2m 4f 110y
3:45 (3:52) (Class 4) (0-105,105) 5-Y-0+ **£4,554** (£1,337; £668; £333)

Form RPR

-654 **1** **Caribbean Cove (IRE)**[103] 1819 8-11-2 98 ...... PaulO'Neill(3) 103+
(Miss Venetia Williams) *hld up and wl in tch: rdn and sustained chal fr 3 out: fnlly edgd ahd nr fin* **5/4**[1]

4-05 **2** *1* **Parish Oak**[50] 2814 11-11-12 105 ...... WayneHutchinson 108
(Ian Williams) *wnt 2nd at 7th: led 11th: rdn and narrow advantage fr 2 out: hdd and no ex nr fin* **14/1**

060 **3** *8* **Lord Gunnerslake (IRE)**[8] 3549 6-10-7 89 ...... AnthonyCoyle(3) 87+
(Miss C J E Caroe) *hld up in tch: 2nd briefly bef 3 out: sn rdn: ev ch whn hit next: wkng whn hit last* **33/1**

-10F **4** *1/2* **Motcombe (IRE)**[28] 3241 8-11-6 99 ......(v) AndrewThornton 94
(R H Alner) *led but nvr looked v happy: hdd 11th: fdd tamely after 3 out* **7/2**[2]

5306 **5** *5* **Deliceo (IRE)**[13] 3459 13-11-6 99 ......(p) JimmyMcCarthy 89
(M Sheppard) *chsd ldr tl 7th: rdn 11th: wknd after 3 out* **20/1**

1/2U **F** **Afro Man**[37] 2960 8-11-9 102 ...... NoelFehily —
(C J Mann) *hld up: 7th and in tch whn fell 9th* **4/1**[3]

P **Life Begins (IRE)**[630] 316 7-10-10 89 ...... APMcCoy —
(Jonjo O'Neill) *j. slowly 1st: blnd 2nd: rarely fluent in last: t.o and p.u 8th* **10/1**

1/P- **U** **Looking Forward**[642] 93 10-11-4 97 ...... BarryKeniry —
(Mrs S A Watt) *uns and rn off bef s: hld up in rr: outpcd and mstke 8th: rallied 11th: cl 4th whn blnd and uns rdr 3 out* **25/1**

5m 16.3s (-7.30) **Going Correction** -0.20s/f (Good) **8** Ran SP% **114.0**
Speed ratings: **105,104,101,101,99** —,—,— CSF £17.47 CT £385.66 TOTE £2.40: £1.10, £3.10, £6.50; EX 16.40.
Owner Paul Beck **Bred** Mrs Joan Doran **Trained** Kings Caple, H'fords

FOCUS
A moderate event but interesting nonetheless, and it would not be a surprise to see one or two winners come out of it. The race has been rated through the runner-up.

NOTEBOOK
Caribbean Cove(IRE), whose trainer has a great record with her chasers at this track, having now won with 10 of her 29 starters over the last five seasons, provided owner Paul Beck with another winner from the bunch he switched to her stable from that of Richard Guest. Running off a mark 1lb higher than when last successful and missing his usual headgear, the grey found plenty for pressure, responding well in a driving finish. He is the type who needs to be held up until the last minute and should not go up much for this, so it would not be a surprise to see him placed to win again in the coming weeks. *(op 13-8 after early 7-4 in places)*
Parish Oak looked on a fairly stiff mark beforehand but he ran well in defeat, forcing the favourite to pull out all the stops. *(op 8-1)*
Lord Gunnerslake(IRE) had not shown anything recently, albeit in much better company the last twice, to suggest he could play a major part here, so this must go down as a decent effort on his part. *(op 22-1)*
Motcombe(IRE) did not seem to be helping her rider and is not progressing as one would have hoped. *(op 4-1 tchd 9-2)*
Looking Forward was last seen on a racecourse in April 2004 so one could forgive him for needing this reappearance outing. He got loose beforehand, too, but was allowed to take his chance, and he was in the process of running a blinder when all but falling at the first in the home straight and losing his rider. He is currently on the same mark as when last successful, and he will deserve respect in similar company next time. *(op 12-1)*
Afro Man was still going well enough, although there was a long way to go, when taking a clumsy fall on the far side. He subsequently had to be put down. *(op 12-1)*
Life Begins(IRE) *Official explanation: vet said gelding bled from nose (op 12-1)*

The Form Book, Raceform Ltd, Compton, RG20 6NL

3677 EUROPEAN BREEDERS FUND "NATIONAL HUNT" NOVICES' HURDLE (QUALIFIER) (12 hdls) 2m 4f 110y
4:15 (4:19) (Class 3) 4-7-Y-0

£6,263 (£1,850; £925; £463; £231; £116)

Form — RPR

0-42 **1** **Yaboya (IRE)**46 2873 7-11-4 ... APMcCoy 119+
(P J Hobbs) *hld up in rr: hdwy 7th: 3rd and drvn last: swtchd ins: kpt on wl to ld fnl 50 yds* **5/2**2

P-1 **2** *1 1/4* **Five Colours (IRE)**27 3248 6-11-9 ... RobertThornton 123+
(A King) *nt fluent 1st: trckd ldrs: led after 7th: rdn and hit 2 out: contested ld after tl hdd and no ex cl home* **9/2**3

4-12 **3** *hd* **Menchikov (FR)**54 2749 6-11-9 ... MickFitzgerald 122
(N J Henderson) *settled cl up: chal bef 3 out: w ldr whn hit next: drvn and duelled for advantage tl no ex fnl 50 yds* **9/4**1

2 **4** *1/2* **Taking My Cut**92 1975 6-11-4 ... RichardJohnson 116
(Jonjo O'Neill) *hld up and bhd: last after 4th: stdy prog bef 3 out: drvn and one pced next: 4l 4th at last: styd on stoutly nr fin* **8/1**

5-63 **5** *22* **Major Oak (IRE)**49 2823 5-11-4 ... BarryKeniry 94
(G M Moore) *hld up: effrt 7th: rdn and wknd 3 out* **20/1**

5-53 **6** *nk* **Geordie Peacock (IRE)**12 3477 7-11-4 ... SamThomas 94
(Miss Venetia Williams) *trckd ldrs: effrt ins to contest ld briefly after 7th: sn rdn: wknd next* **10/1**

46 **7** *dist* **Witness Run (IRE)**19 3369 6-11-4 ... LeightonAspell —
(N J Gifford) *hld up in midfield: rdn and lost tch tamely after 7th: btn 62l* **14/1**

2-63 **8** *19* **Campaign Charlie**27 3246 6-11-4 ... MarkBradburne —
(H D Daly) *midfield: blnd 6th: lost tch bef 3 out: btn 81l* **40/1**

0-6 **9** *1 1/2* **Incandescence (IRE)**19 3373 5-11-4 ... JimmyMcCarthy —
(Mrs P Robeson) *prom: nt fluent 1st and 5th: wknd after next: btn 82l* **100/1**

P **10** *14* **Benefit Fund (IRE)**26 3275 6-11-4 ... HenryOliver —
(D J Wintle) *hld up: prog after 5th: led briefly 7th: fdd rapidly bef next: btn 96l* **200/1**

0 **P** **Moritz (FR)**55 2720 6-11-4 ... RichardMcGrath —
(K G Reveley) *a wl bhd: t.o 7th: p.u next* **150/1**

000F **P** **Lordington Lad**19 3369 6-11-4 ... JamesDavies —
(B G Powell) *set mod pce: hdd after 7th: t.o and p.u 2 out* **25/1**

0- **P** **The Bees Knees**410 2905 6-11-1 ... RichardYoung(3) —
(M Appleby) *hdstr to post: plld v hrd to go 2nd fr 2nd tl wknd rapidly 5th: mstke next: t.o and p.u 7th* **150/1**

5m 19.5s (-15.30) **Going Correction** -0.60s/f (Firm) **13** Ran SP% **118.3**
Speed ratings: **105,104,104,104,95 95**,—,—,—,— —,—,— CSF £13.90 TOTE £4.50: £1.90, £1.10, £1.50; EX 14.90 Place 6 £66.72, Place 5 £53.62.
Owner John P McManus **Bred** T W Nicholson **Trained** Withycombe, Somerset

FOCUS
A decent novice hurdle run at a steady early pace, but it produced a thrilling finish and the time was 4.2 seconds quicker than the earlier handicap. It looks sure to produce winners.

NOTEBOOK
Yaboya(IRE) came out on top in the end under a strong ride from the Champion. He had shaped encouragingly behind a decent type at Haydock last time and appeared to appreciate the hold-up ride he got here. Bred for the Flat, he could improve again for a faster surface. *(tchd 11-4 in places)*
Five Colours(IRE), who has an entry in the Brit Insurance Novices' Hurdle at the Festival, was a shock winner last time out, but he confirmed the favourable impression of his Hereford success with a solid effort under his penalty. He is clearly no star on the gallops but his performances on the track suggest he has a fair amount of ability. *(tchd 11-2)*
Menchikov(FR), another penalised runner, was far from disgraced. A French-bred, he coped with this easier ground well. *(op 5-2)*
Taking My Cut, J P McManus' second string, did not look to be going anywhere fast early in the straight but he was finishing better than anything at the death, and a step up to three miles could see him off the mark. *(op 10-1)*
Major Oak(IRE) finished a fair way behind the principals but is entitled to come on for this hurdling debut. *(op 25-1)*
Geordie Peacock(IRE), who was weak in the market beforehand, has questions to answer now, as he looked to hold a chance turning into the straight but soon stopped to nothing. *(op 8-1)*
T/Jkpt: Not won. T/Plt: £98.20 to a £1 stake. Pool: £52,280.10. 388.50 winning tickets. T/Qpdt: £12.00 to a £1 stake. Pool: £6,137.50. 377.10 winning tickets. IM

3442 NEWCASTLE (L-H)
Wednesday, February 1
3678 Meeting Abandoned - Frost

3274 TOWCESTER (R-H)
Thursday, February 2

OFFICIAL GOING: Good to soft
Wind: Nil Weather: Dull and cold

3685 GG.COM NOVICES' HURDLE (10 hdls) 2m 3f 110y
1:40 (1:41) (Class 4) 4-Y-0+ **£3,903** (£1,146; £573; £286)

Form — RPR

5 **1** **Molostiep (FR)**81 2211 6-11-4 ... TomScudamore 101+
(Mrs Susan Nock) *a.p: led 6th: rdn appr last: r.o* **9/2**2

0/0 **2** *1 3/4* **Regal Term (IRE)**27 3275 8-10-8 ... JosephStevenson(10) 97
(R Dickin) *hld up and bhd: hdwy appr 7th: lft 2nd last: kpt on* **33/1**

64 **3** *29* **Coleraine (IRE)**29 3240 6-11-4 ... LeightonAspell 68
(O Sherwood) *hld up in tch: wknd appr 2 out: swvd rt last* **12/1**

42 **4** *3 1/2* **Panzer (GER)**32 3167 5-10-13 ... StephenCraine(5) 65
(D McCain) *hld up: hdwy 5th: rdn appr 3 out: wknd appr 2 out* **9/4**1

4 **5** *4* **Ridjit (FR)**17 3422 6-11-4 ... JamesDavies 61
(N J Gifford) *hld up: hdwy after 5th: rdn and wknd appr 2 out* **10/1**3

332 **6** *6* **Kobai (IRE)**38 2988 7-11-4 ... WayneHutchinson 59+
(A King) *prom: mstke 7th: sn rdn: wknd after 3 out: mstke 2 out* **9/4**1

55 **7** *1* **Parkinson (IRE)**12 3496 5-10-8 ... WayneJones(10) 54
(Jonjo O'Neill) *bhd fr 7th* **40/1**

0-P **8** *22* **Katy's Classic (IRE)**60 2663 6-11-4 ... (p) JohnMcNamara 32
(K C Bailey) *sn chsng ldr: wknd appr 3 out* **100/1**

0 **9** *dist* **Windyx (FR)**14 3463 5-11-4 ... TimmyMurphy —
(M C Pipe) *keen early: a bhd: t.o* **16/1**

0 **P** **Hi Blue**239 685 7-10-11 ... JohnPritchard(7) —
(R Dickin) *a bhd: t.o whn p.u bef 2 out* **150/1**

F6 **P** **Ben Tally Ho**47 2878 5-11-1 ... JoffretHuet(3) —
(Ian Williams) *a bhd: mstke 6th: t.o whn p.u bef 2 out* **33/1**

0 **P** **Wine River (IRE)**68 2507 7-11-1 ... LeeVickers(3) —
(John R Upson) *hld up: rdn after 4th: sn bhd: t.o whn p.u bef 2 out* **66/1**

00- **P** **Pintail**387 3307 6-11-4 ... JimmyMcCarthy —
(Mrs P Robeson) *led to 6th: wknd after 7th: t.o whn p.u bef 2 out* **100/1**

P **The Fast Frog (FR)** 5-10-11 ... MrJNewbold(7) —
(Lady Connell) *hld up and bhd: hdwy appr 6th: wknd 3 out: p.u bef 2 out* **100/1**

/0-P **P** **The Trojan Horse (IRE)**12 3505 6-11-4 ... SamThomas —
(Miss H C Knight) *keen early: a bhd: rdn appr 6th: t.o whn p.u bef 3 out* **66/1**

P **R** **Senor Set (GER)**27 3277 5-10-8 ... AngharadFrieze(10) 97
(P A Blockley) *hld up: hdwy appr 6th: chsd wnr whn mstke 3 out: 2l 2nd whn hung lft and rn out through wing last* **50/1**

5m 15.2s (-0.60) **Going Correction** +0.15s/f (Yiel) **16** Ran SP% **119.3**
Speed ratings: **107,106,94,93,91 89,88,80**,—,— —,—,—,—,— — CSF £138.83 TOTE £6.20: £2.30, £7.20, £3.10; EX 177.20.
Owner Camilla & Rosie Nock **Bred** M Contignon **Trained** Icomb, Gloucs

FOCUS
A moderate affair with the front two finishing 29 lengths clear of the third after Senor Set, who was in second at the time, ran out at the last. The second limits the form and the winner is rated well below his bumper mark.

NOTEBOOK
Molostiep(FR), a winning pointer who shaped particularly well when fifth in a decent bumper at the Paddy Power meeting back in November, looked to hold obvious claims in what was an ordinary affair and put up a strong galloping performance. His trainer is more than capable of housing the odd decent performer and, with a step up in trip unlikely to be a problem, this fine-looking animal appears to have a bright future. *(op 10-3)*
Regal Term(IRE), an eight-year-old having only his third racecourse outing, stepped up massively on his two previous pieces of form, staying on strongly up the straight to claim a clear second. Three miles should bring about further improvement, but it is unlikely he will be winning until contesting low-grade handicaps. *(op 20-1)*
Coleraine(IRE) travelled well into the straight, but was soon left toiling and in the end was quite disappointing. He is one whose best opportunities of winning are likely to come in handicaps. *(op 16-1)*
Panzer(GER), a modest sort on the Flat, was always likely to find this distance around a stiff track beyond him and he faded tamely in the straight. A sharp two miles on a sound surface, probably in handicaps, is going to prove his ideal conditions. *(op 11-4 tchd 3-1 in places)*
Ridjit(FR), who shaped as though this sort of distance would suit when a keeping-on fourth at Plumpton, was unable to build on that and failed to see out the trip. He may not be seen at his best until tackling fences. *(op 8-1)*
Kobai(IRE), a modest sort in bumpers, failed to improve for the switch to hurdles and was never jumping with any real fluency. He may be worth another chance. *(op 11-4 tchd 3-1)*
Senor Set(GER), a moderate Flat performer who showed little on his hurdling debut, was in the process of running a huge race and leaving that form way behind when running out at the last. It is hoped this does not affect confidence, but he cannot be relied upon to repeat it. *(op 50-1)*
Wine River(IRE) *Official explanation: jockey said gelding bled from the nose (op 50-1)*

3686 SIS H'CAP CHASE (12 fncs) 2m 110y
2:10 (2:10) (Class 5) (0-95,93) 5-Y-0+ **£3,253** (£955; £477; £238)

Form — RPR

6P00 **1** **Glen Thyne (IRE)**9 3547 6-10-0 **67** oh1 ... (b) TomScudamore 83
(K C Bailey) *a.p: rdn and outpcd 8th: rallied appr 2 out: led appr last: r.o wl* **28/1**

50-P **2** *5* **Razzamatazz**33 3146 8-11-12 **93** ... WayneHutchinson 104
(R Dickin) *hld up in mid-div: stmbld 6th: hdwy 7th: rdn to ld 2 out: hdd appr last: one pce* **25/1**

0633 **3** *5* **Spider Boy**16 3430 9-9-9 **67** oh2 ... (p) RobertLucey-Butler(5) 73
(Miss Z C Davison) *hld up and bhd: hdwy 7th: rdn 3 out: wknd last* **5/1**1

P1P1 **4** *1 1/4* **Yassar (IRE)**38 2984 11-11-11 **92** ... WarrenMarston 97
(D J Wintle) *a.p: mstke 8th: rdn and ev ch 2 out: wknd last* **6/1**3

U444 **5** *6* **Jour De Mee (FR)**7 3582 9-11-9 **90** ... JimCrowley 89
(Mrs H Dalton) *bhd: rdn appr 7th: styd on fr 2 out: n.d* **5/1**1

3U63 **6** *1/2* **Twist N Turn**27 3270 6-9-9 **67** ... StephenCraine(5) 66
(D McCain) *hld up in mid-div: hdwy appr 7th: wknd after 2 out: hit last* **11/2**2

/032 **7** *3 1/2* **Munadil**9 3546 8-10-8 **78** ... (t) TomMalone(3) 73
(A M Hales) *hld up and bhd: hdwy appr 7th: sltly hmpd 3 out: sn rdn and wknd* **11/2**2

0P00 **8** *18* **Tails I Win**17 3418 7-10-2 **72** oh6 ow5 ... AnthonyCoyle(3) 49
(Miss C J E Caroe) *prom: led 5th to 2 out: wkng whn mstke last* **16/1**

4P4P **9** *8* **Auditor**13 3482 7-10-5 **72** ... (v) MarkGrant 41
(S T Lewis) *j.rt: led to 5th: rdn appr 8th: wknd after 3 out* **8/1**

-450 **10** *dist* **Polish Pilot (IRE)**20 3370 11-10-8 **75** ... RichardHobson —
(J R Cornwall) *racd wd: hld up towards rr: hdwy 7th: hit 3 out: sn wknd: t.o* **11/1**

4PP- **P** **Shah (IRE)**462 1875 13-10-0 **67** oh10 ... HenryOliver —
(P Kelsall) *in tch: lost pl after 3rd: t.o whn p.u after 5th* **66/1**

POPP **P** **Shannon Quest (IRE)**34 3129 10-9-7 **67** oh2 ... (b) TomMessenger(7) —
(C L Popham) *prom tl rdn and wknd after 6th: sn lost tch: t.o whn p.u bef 3 out* **25/1**

4m 21.2s (1.90) **Going Correction** +0.15s/f (Yiel) **12** Ran SP% **116.3**
Speed ratings: **101,98,96,95,92 92,91,82,78**,— —,— CSF £523.10 CT £4037.94 TOTE £26.80: £4.80, £5.00, £1.30; EX 271.90.
Owner Dream Makers Partnership **Bred** J J Harding **Trained** Preston Capes, Northants

FOCUS
The went a sound gallop and Glen Thyne stayed on from a long way back to win going away from some very tired rivals. The third and fourth set the standard with the winner a big improver, but the time was reasonable.

NOTEBOOK
Glen Thyne(IRE), dropping markedly in distance having shown little in two previous attempts over fences, failed to improve for blinkers at Leicester last time. However, they had the desired affect on this occasion and, having looked in trouble with half a mile to run, he began to motor and galloped on relentlessly to win going away from some tired rivals. It is highly doubtful he will be able to cope with two miles on a tighter track, but may yet be open to further improvement at two and a half. *(op 25-1)*
Razzamatazz ◆ left his disappointing seasonal reappearance behind and did well to get so close considering his jumping was not all that. He looked the likeliest winner turning in, but the huge weight concession to the Glen Thyne told in the final furlong and he was unable to cope. This was a highly creditable effort and he can find a similar race if building on this. *(op 22-1)*
Spider Boy has been in decent form and recorded another respectable effort, but he has yet to win in 20 attempts and is one to continue to take on. *(tchd 13-2)*
Yassar(IRE) has a nasty habit of pulling up, but he had won his last two completed starts and was entitled to run well. He is likely to remain vulnerable off this sort of mark. *(op 9-2)*
Jour De Mee(FR) continues to struggle off this sort mark and he lacked the basic pace to get involved in the finish, plugging on again in the straight to claim a moderate fifth. *(op 9-2 tchd 4-1)*

Twist N Turn comes from a stable that has had a cracking time of it in recent weeks, but she has yet to add her name to the roll of honour and would probably have found this ground on the slow side.
Shah(IRE) *Official explanation: jockey said gelding bled from the nose (op 50-1)*

3687 LEVY BOARD H'CAP HURDLE (8 hdls) 2m

2:40 (2:41) (Class 4) (0-110,105) 4-Y-0+ **£3,903** (£1,146; £573; £286)

Form RPR

6-35 **1** **Ellway Prospect**^{32} [3185] 6-10-5 **84** JamieMoore 95+
(M G Rimell) *hld up in tch: hit 3 out: sn rdn: led appr last: r.o wl* **11/4**^{1}

FUPP **2** *6* **A Bit Of Fun**^{21} [3360] 5-11-12 **105** JohnMcNamara 108
(J T Stimpson) *chsd ldrs: led 4th: rdn and hdd appr last: one pce* **66/1**

0315 **3** *1 ¾* **Wenger (FR)**^{34} [3128] 6-11-6 **99** (bt) PhilipHide 100
(P Winkworth) *hld up: hdwy 4th: ev ch 2 out: sn rdn: one pce* **7/1**

3 **4** *¾* **Lets Try Again (IRE)**^{26} [3283] 9-10-2 **81** TomDoyle 82
(R A Farrant) *hld up in mid-div: hdwy 5th: rdn appr 2 out: one pce* **14/1**

3-60 **5** *12* **Andy Gin (FR)**^{51} [2813] 7-11-2 **100** MarkNicolls$^{(5)}$ 89
(Miss E M England) *hld up in tch: ev ch 3 out: sn rdn: wknd appr last* **22/1**

010 **6** *3* **Jug Of Punch (IRE)**^{51} [2816] 7-10-3 **89** PatrickCStringer$^{(7)}$ 75
(S T Lewis) *hld up and bhd: hdwy appr 3 out: rdn and wknd appr 2 out* **33/1**

P5-1 **7** *½* **Montecorvino (GER)**^{27} [3275] 5-11-11 **104** TomSiddall 89
(N A Twiston-Davies) *hld up in tch: rdn whn mstke 5th: wknd appr 3 out* **10/3**^{3}

532/ **8** *13* **Jamaican Flight (USA)**^{30} [1691] 13-11-4 **100** LeeVickers$^{(3)}$ 72
(Mrs S Lamyman) *led tl appr 2nd: prom: rdn after 4th: wknd appr 3 out* **50/1**

0P06 **9** *2 ½* **Migration**^{38} [2964] 10-11-12 **105** MarkBradburne 75
(Mrs S Lamyman) *hld up and bhd: short-lived effrt on outside appr 3 out* **25/1**

040 **10** *9* **Najca De Thaix (FR)**^{17} [3422] 5-11-9 **105** ColinBolger$^{(3)}$ 66
(Mrs L Wadham) *a bhd* **9/1**

PRPP **11** *24* **Mr Rhubarb (IRE)**^{64} [2578] 8-9-8 **80** TomMessenger$^{(7)}$ 17
(C J Drewe) *hld up in mid-div: hdwy 5th: sn rdn: wknd after 3 out* **100/1**

2-10 **12** *3* **Alessandro Severo**^{257} [451] 7-11-0 **93** BenjaminHitchcott 27
(Mrs D A Hamer) *hld up in tch: wknd appr 3 out* **25/1**

0-21 **F** **Make My Hay**^{20} [3371] 7-11-6 **99** (b) BrianCrowley —
(J Gallagher) *led appr 2nd to 4th: wkng whn fell 3 out* **3/1**^{2}

4m 11.9s (0.50) **Going Correction** +0.15s/f (Yiel) **13** Ran SP% **123.3**
Speed ratings: **104,101,100,99,93 92,92,85,84,79 67,66,—** CSF £187.27 CT £1209.64 TOTE £4.10: £1.30, £16.50, £2.40; EX 165.30.
Owner Mrs M L Luck **Bred** Ellway Breeding **Trained** Leafield, Oxon

FOCUS
They went a decent pace throughout and that suited Ellway Prospect, but those in the frame behind the winner suggest the for is reasonably solid.

NOTEBOOK
Ellway Prospect was well suited by the demands of this stiff track and came home strongly up the hill to win going away from outsider A Bit Of Fun. She has been running only reasonably, but the change in tactics clearly helped and she may yet be capable of better. *(op 3-1)*
A Bit Of Fun has been in desperate form, yet the Handicapper has failed to ease his burden and he certainly will not be doing so after an effort like this. He made a bold bid having taken it up after the fourth, but the 21lb concession to the winner proved beyond him and he was readily brushed aside in the final furlong. It is hoped he can go on from this.
Wenger(FR), whose best form has come on speed orientated tracks, was kept wide in search of the better ground and ran a better race, the re-applied tongue tie clearly helping.
Lets Try Again(IRE) has shown enough in two starts since arriving from Ireland to suggest he will find a small race off this sort of mark, but it is likely to be back at shorter. *(tchd 16-1)*
Andy Gin(FR) ◆, who looked a potentially smart juvenile several seasons back, continues to drop *in the weights and shaped reasonably well. He could be one to take a chance on next time. (op 20-1 tchd 25-1)*
Montecorvino(GER) made a winning reappearance at the course last month, but was unable to build on that and did not appear suited by the change in tactics. He is only five and likely to do better once chasing. *(op 3-1)*
Make My Hay had run his race and was held when falling at the third-last. *(op 6-1)*

3688 WEATHERBYS BANK H'CAP CHASE (18 fncs) 3m 110y

3:10 (3:10) (Class 4) (0-115,114) 6-Y-0+ **£5,070** (£1,497; £748; £374; £187)

Form RPR

4/P0 **1** **Lord Broadway (IRE)**^{9} [3547] 10-9-13 **90** TJPhelan$^{(3)}$ 103+
(N M Babbage) *hld up in rr: hdwy 13th: led 2 out: drvn out* **6/1**^{3}

0P54 **2** *1* **Follow The Flow (IRE)**^{52} [2800] 10-10-11 **102** (p) OwynNelmes$^{(3)}$ 113
(P A Pritchard) *a.p: led 12th: rdn and hdd 2 out: styd on flat* **4/1**^{2}

2665 **3** *6* **Runaway Bishop (USA)**^{23} [3333] 11-10-4 **92** ow1 RichardHobson 97
(J R Cornwall) *hld up: hdwy 11th: one pce fr 3 out* **6/1**^{3}

304F **4** *1 ¼* **Charlies Future**^{24} [3326] 8-11-10 **112** TomDoyle 116
(S C Burrough) *led to 3rd: led 7th to 12th: rdn and one pce fr 3 out* **8/1**

P-62 **5** *7* **Misty Future**^{24} [3326] 8-11-11 **113** SamThomas 111+
(Miss Venetia Williams) *hld up: hdwy after 11th: rdn appr 3 out: wknd 2 out* **7/2**^{1}

45P2 **F** **Kittenkat**^{5} [3614] 12-10-11 **99** TomScudamore —
(N R Mitchell) *prom: n.m.r 4th: wkng whn fell 4 out* **4/1**^{2}

PP30 **P** **Maybeseven**^{27} [3276] 12-9-7 **88** oh25 (b) JohnPritchard$^{(7)}$ —
(R Dickin) *racd wd: hld up in tch: wknd 13th: blnd 2 out: p.u bef last* **50/1**

3000 **P** **Valleymore (IRE)**^{14} [3460] 10-10-0 **88** oh1 TomSiddall —
(S A Brookshaw) *led 3rd: j.rt 4th: hdd 7th: hit 12th: bhd whn hit 14th: sltly hmpd 4 out: p.u bef 2 out* **12/1**

6m 43.5s (-3.10) **Going Correction** +0.15s/f (Yiel) **8** Ran SP% **111.6**
Speed ratings: **106,105,103,103,101 —,—,—** CSF £29.35 CT £146.16 TOTE £7.00: £2.30, £1.30, £1.80; EX 33.70.
Owner D G & D J Robinson **Bred** Robert Kenny Jnr **Trained** Brockhampton, Gloucs

FOCUS
Ordinary form but could be rated higher with the fourth setting the standard and the placed horses below recent efforts..

NOTEBOOK
Lord Broadway(IRE), who still looked in need of it at Leicester last time, was at an advantage here in shouldering a low weight and he galloped on too strongly for gallant runner-up Follow The Flow. His last win had come off a mark of 80, but there could be a bit more to come from him on this *evidence. Official explanation: trainer said, regarding the improved form shown, gelding was better suited by a return to Towcester (op 8-1)*
Follow The Flow(IRE), who has found a bit of form again since having the cheekpieces fitted, ran a bold race in defeat and kept galloping away once headed. He goes extremely well at this course and is capable of winning again now he is back down to a fair mark. *(op 9-2)*
Runaway Bishop(USA) plugged on best he could to claim third, but was not match for the front two and may need to drop a few pounds before winning again. *(tchd 5-1)*
Charlies Future disputing the lead when falling at the final fence at Taunton last time, showed no ill-effects of the spill and ran a decent race, his big weight proving too much in the end. *(op 11-2)*
Misty Future would have found this ground on the soft side and, with his stable's period of *invincibilty coming to an end in the past week or so, it was no surprise he failed to run to form. (op 10-3)*
Kittenkat ran her best race for a long time when running Korelo close at Chepstow at the weekend, but the worry was always going to be whether she found this coming too soon and that appeared to be the case, as she took a tired fall when beaten four out. *(tchd 9-2)*

3689 E.B.F./TATTERSALLS (IRELAND) MARES' ONLY NOVICES' CHASE (QUALIFIER) (16 fncs) 2m 6f

3:40 (3:40) (Class 4) 5-Y-0+ **£5,257** (£1,684; £936)

Form RPR

3215 **1** **De Blanc (IRE)**^{5} [3621] 6-11-6 118 SamThomas 126+
(Miss Venetia Williams) *mde all: clr 3 out: easily* **9/4**^{1}

-143 **2** *16* **Viciana**^{56} [2718] 7-11-0 LeightonAspell 100+
(Mrs L Wadham) *a.p: wnt 2nd 4 out: no ch w wnr* **7/2**^{3}

U **3** *dist* **Glenkill (IRE)**^{28} [3251] 8-11-0 MarkGrant —
(S M Jacobs) *hld up in rr: lost tch fr 12th* **100/1**

1005 **F** **Granny Shona (IRE)**^{13} [3484] 5-10-6 TomDoyle —
(P R Webber) *hld up: mstke 9th: hdwy 11th: 3l 4th whn fell 12th* **20/1**

FPFP **U** **The Sneakster (IRE)**^{14} [3461] 8-11-0 TomSiddall —
(S A Brookshaw) *prom: in tch whn tried to run out and uns rdr 7th* **100/1**

0-F2 **P** **Horcott Bay**^{49} [2846] 6-11-0 95 JamieMoore —
(M G Rimell) *prom: mstkes 4th and 10th: wkng whn sltly hmpd 12th: t.o whn p.u bef 3 out* **11/2**

-P23 **P** **Glenogue (IRE)**^{20} [3375] 8-11-0 94 (b) JohnMcNamara —
(K C Bailey) *in tch: reminders fr 5th: rdn appr 8th: bhd fr 11th: t.o whn p.u bef 3 out* **12/1**

2051 **U** **Elfkirk (IRE)**^{17} [3426] 7-11-6 115 BenjaminHitchcott —
(R H Buckler) *prom tl wknd 3 out: poor 3rd whn stmbld 2 out: exhausted whn landed on fence and uns rdr last* **5/2**^{2}

5m 56.6s (-9.40) **Going Correction** +0.15s/f (Yiel) **8** Ran SP% **111.4**
WFA 5 from 6yo+ 7lb
Speed ratings: **107,101,—,—,— —,—,—** CSF £10.25 TOTE £2.80: £1.10, £1.80, £7.50; EX 13.10.
Owner Jeremy Hancock **Bred** Pat Galavan **Trained** Kings Caple, H'fords

FOCUS
De Blanc showed her rivals little mercy, but the race ultimately look little winning with less than half of the eight runners successfully negotiating the course. The winner was value for more the official margin and could be rated a few pounds higher.

NOTEBOOK
De Blanc(IRE), unable to get competitive over hurdles at the weekend, appreciated the return to the larger obstacles and was able to dominate throughout in a race that ultimately took little winning, with less than half the field managing to negotiate the course. She will face stiffer tasks than this, but could do no more than win and is an obvious candidate for the Mares' Novice Chase Final at Uttoxeter in March. *(op 11-4 after 3-1 in places)*
Viciana, a modest, yet consistent hurdler, made an adequate start to her chasing career in a well-beaten second, but she is entitled to learn from the experience and remains open to a little further improvement. *(op 3-1 tchd 4-1)*
Glenkill(IRE) was the only other to complete and gets a mention for no other reason. *(tchd 80-1)*
Elfkirk(IRE) had run her race and was virtually walking on approach to the last, not having the legs to get over it and unshipping her rider. It was probably a good thing in hindsight as it would not have been pleasant to see her crawl up the hill, but it casts serious doubts over her future *prospects and she warrants a decent break after this.Official explanation: trainer said mare was found to be distressed post race (op 11-4 tchd 9-4)*
Granny Shona(IRE) was not out of things when coming down, but it remains to be seen how this affects confidence. *(op 11-4 tchd 9-4)*

3690 HAPPY BIRTHDAY AMY PHILLIPS MARES' ONLY NOVICES' HURDLE (8 hdls) 2m

4:10 (4:10) (Class 4) 4-Y-0+ **£3,253** (£955; £477; £238)

Form RPR

1 **Queen's Dancer**^{73} 4-10-5 MarcusFoley 92+
(N J Henderson) *prom: lost pl 4th: smooth hdwy appr 3 out: led appr 2 out: clr appr last: easily* **3/1**^{2}

5 **2** *10* **Wee Dinns (IRE)**^{14} [3463] 5-11-1 TimmyMurphy 92+
(M C Pipe) *hld up and bhd: hdwy on ins after 3 out: j.lft 2 out: no ch w wnr* **9/4**^{1}

3 *5* **Cois Na Tine Eile**^{129} 4-10-5 TomSiddall 73
(N A Twiston-Davies) *hld up: j.rt 1st: hdwy after 3 out: rdn appr last: one pce* **14/1**

-45 **4** *3* **Little Venus (IRE)**^{26} [3287] 6-11-1 MarkBradburne 80
(H D Daly) *hld up in mid-div: hdwy after 3 out: sn rdn: one pce fr 2 out* **7/2**^{3}

0/ **5** *½* **Diplomatic Daisy (IRE)**^{680} [4529] 7-11-1 TomDoyle 83+
(D R Gandolfo) *hld up towards rr: hdwy after 5th: led briefly after 3 out: wkng whn hit 2 out and last* **50/1**

3260 **6** *4* **Twist The Facts (IRE)**^{32} [3188] 6-11-1 NoelFehily 76
(N P Littmoden) *hld up and bhd: hdwy appr 3 out: rdn and wknd appr 2 out* **11/1**

0-16 **7** *5* **Ballymena**^{70} [2457] 5-11-1 JamieMoore 71
(C Roberts) *hld up in mid-div: hdwy appr 4th: rdn and ev ch whn hung lft and sltly hmpd 3 out: sn wknd* **14/1**

46 **8** *21* **Quotable**^{24} [3322] 5-11-1 LeightonAspell 50
(O Sherwood) *hld up in tch: hdwy appr 4th: wknd after 3 out* **10/1**

P0 **9** *dist* **Dargin's Lass (IRE)**^{9} [3550] 5-10-8 TomMessenger$^{(7)}$ —
(B N Pollock) *led to 5th: wknd after 3 out: t.o* **100/1**

0-00 **10** *2 ½* **Tanzanite Dawn**^{38} [2997] 5-11-1 JimCrowley —
(Andrew Turnell) *sn bhd: t.o fr 3rd* **50/1**

P **Miss Shontaine**^{59} 4-10-0 JohnnyLevins$^{(5)}$ —
(B G Powell) *plld hrd: a bhd: t.o whn p.u bef 2 out* **66/1**

P **Pragmatica**^{29} 5-11-1 WayneHutchinson —
(R M H Cowell) *sn prom: wknd after 3 out: p.u bef 2 out* **33/1**

P **P** **Cultured**^{24} [3322] 5-11-1 (b^{1}) AndrewTinkler —
(Mrs A J Bowlby) *w ldr tl mstke 5th: sn wknd: t.o whn p.u bef 3 out* **66/1**

0/6P **P** **Dutch Star**^{16} [3437] 7-10-5 JayPemberton$^{(10)}$ —
(G P Enright) *prom: hit 2nd: ev ch whn mstke 3 out: sn wknd: p.u bef 2 out* **50/1**

0F-P **P** **Panama Royale (IRE)**^{9} [3550] 8-10-10 AdamPogson$^{(5)}$ —
(J R Holt) *plld hrd in rr: hdwy 4th: led 5th tl after 3 out: wknd qckly: p.u bef 2 out* **125/1**

4m 18.9s (7.50) **Going Correction** +0.15s/f (Yiel)
WFA 4 from 5yo+ 9lb **15** Ran SP% **122.3**
Speed ratings: **87,82,79,78,77 75,73,62,—,— —,—,—,—,—** CSF £10.28 TOTE £5.40: £1.40, £2.00, £4.60; EX 14.70.

Owner Mrs Christian Marner **Bred** Kingwood Bloodstock **Trained** Upper Lambourn, Berks

FOCUS

A moderate winning time, seven seconds slower than the earlier handicap and, the winner apart, they look a poor bunch with the fourth the best guide to the level.

NOTEBOOK

Queen's Dancer, a moderate sort on the Flat, recovered from briefly losing her position to make rapid headway under a confident Foley, and she quickly settled the matter once going on two out. This was a decent display in conditions that were hard to quicken out of and, although no Cheltenham-class animal, she should be able to defy a penalty and provide connections with some fun. *(tchd 4-1)*

Wee Dinns(IRE) appeared to step up on her initial experience of hurdles to do did best of the rest, but that is not saying much and her future looks destined for low-grade handicaps. *(tchd 5-2)*

Cois Na Tine Eile, just about banded-class on the level, plugged on to claim a moderate third and *is likely to be helped by further, but she looks little better than selling-class on this evidence. (op 10-1)*

Little Venus(IRE) failed to build on her hurdling debut fifth and, even on a course that was riding particularly testing, she failed to cope with this significant drop in distance. *(op 9-2)*

Diplomatic Daisy(IRE) ran well to a point, but was ultimately found out by the conditions. *(op 40-1)*

Cultured *Official explanation: jockey said mare lost its action (op 50-1)*

Panama Royale(IRE) *Official explanation: trainer said that, on scoping after the race, mare was found to have blood in her lung (op 50-1)*

3691 GG.COM INTERMEDIATE OPEN NATIONAL HUNT FLAT RACE — 2m

4:40 (4:40) (Class 6) 4-7-Y-0 — **£1,626** (£477; £238; £119)

Form — RPR

4P **1** Top Ram (IRE)^{37} [3024] 6-11-4 .... MarkBradburne 101+
(J A B Old) *w ldr: led over 6f out: drvn out* **12/1**

110 **2** *1 1/4* **Sword Of Damascus (IRE)**^{32} [3181] 4-10-13 .... StephenCraine(5) 100
(D McCain) *hld up: hdwy 8f out: chsd wnr over 4f out: rdn over 2f out: kpt on ins fnl f* **11/4**[2]

3 *15* **Devils And Dust (IRE)** 5-11-4 .... TimmyMurphy 85
(D McCain) *hld up and bhd: hdwy over 3f out: rdn and wknd over 2f out* **20/1**

4 *1 3/4* **Celtic Society (IRE)** 5-10-13 .... LeeStephens(5) 83
(P C Ritchens) *prom: lost pl 8f out: rdn and rallied over 5f out: wknd over 2f out* **50/1**

1 **5** *3 1/2* **Victor Daly (IRE)**^{38} [2987] 5-11-4 .... ShaneWalsh(7) 88+
(Mrs H Dalton) *hld up: hdwy over 5f out: wknd over 2f out* **7/1**

425 **6** *3 1/2* **Sobers (IRE)**^{64} [2572] 5-11-1 .... PaulO'Neill(3) 78+
(R C Guest) *t.k.h in mid-div: hdwy after 6f: wknd over 2f out* **6/4**[1]

0 **7** *23* **Glorious Castlebar**^{19} [3392] 5-11-4 .... SeanFox 53
(J C Fox) *hld up and bhd: hdwy over 4f out: wknd over 3f out* **50/1**

3 **8** *8* **Rapallo (IRE)**^{38} [2987] 5-10-13 .... RobertLucey-Butler(5) 45
(M Pitman) *prom 8f* **4/1**[3]

060 **9** *6* **Lilian Alexander**^{28} [3259] 4-9-10 .... LiamTreadwell(5) 22
(J R Holt) *t.k.h in mid-div: hdwy over 4f out: sn bhd* **40/1**

00 **10** *2* **Rosemary's Fancy**^{38} [2987] 5-10-11 .... JosephByrne 30
(C N Kellett) *led: hdd over 6f out: rdn and wknd over 5f out* **100/1**

0-P **11** *dist* **Fashion Shoot**^{132} [1543] 5-10-11 .... HenryOliver —
(P Kelsall) *prom 5f: t.o fnl 8f* **66/1**

4m 9.50s (-2.40) **Going Correction** +0.15s/f (Yiel) — **11** Ran SP% **120.5**

WFA 4 from 5yo+ 9lb

Speed ratings: **95,94,86,86,84 82,71,67,64,63** — CSF £44.95 TOTE £10.00: £2.90, £1.10, £3.60; EX 61.90 Place 6 £242.82, Place 5 £47.48.

Owner W E Sturt **Bred** W E Sturt **Trained** Barbury Castle, Wilts

FOCUS

Not a bad bumper with two fair sorts pulling 15 lengths clear of the remainder. The second sets the standard and the form could rate higher.

NOTEBOOK

Top Ram(IRE), who was unable to build on the promise of his Warwick debut fourth when pulled up lame at Chepstow back in December, had been given time to recover and showed what he is capable of, grinding it out under a positive ride from Bradburne. A chaser in the making, he will *probably require two and a half miles over hurdles and looks one to keep on the right side of. (op 9-1 tchd 14-1)*

Sword Of Damascus(IRE) ◆ lost his unbeaten record in a Listed bumper at Cheltenham on New Year's day, but this first try at two miles saw him in a much better light and he stuck on to finish clear of the third. As his first two wins showed, he is very tough and looks the sort to take well to hurdles. *(tchd 9-4)*

Devils And Dust(IRE), a stablemate of the runner-up, was ultimately well-beaten in third and is probably more 'one for the future' but it would not be a total surprise to see him win a race in this sphere, with the experience certain to bring him on. *(op 12-1)*

Celtic Society(IRE) showed signs of inexperience, as was to be expected, but it is unlikely he will be up to winning in this sphere.

Victor Daly(IRE), a winner first time up at the course on Boxing Day, never really got into it and was unable to build on that win. He may be worthy of another chance. *(op 6-1 tchd 11-2 and 15-2)*

Sobers(IRE) is highly thought of, but he has yet to do it on the course and again failed to live up to expectations. The best of him is unlikely to be seen until tackling obstacles. *(op 7-4 tchd 2-1)*

T/Plt: £221.50 to a £1 stake. Pool: £51,949.40. 171.20 winning tickets. T/Qpdt: £13.00 to a £1 stake. Pool: £5,078.70. 288.40 winning tickets. KH

3505 WINCANTON (R-H)

Thursday, February 2

OFFICIAL GOING: Good

Wind: Nil

3692 JOHN SMITH'S/E.B.F. MARES' ONLY "NATIONAL HUNT" NOVICES' HURDLE (QUALIFIER) (11 hdls) — 2m 6f

1:00 (1:00) (Class 4) 4-Y-0+ — **£3,903** (£1,146; £573; £286)

Form — RPR

253- **1** **Hollywood**^{294} [4841] 5-11-1 .... AndrewThornton 82+
(V R A Dartnall) *led tl idled: hdd and lost pl after 6th: sn rcvrd:chal 2 out: slt ld last: hung lft u.p run-in: hld on wl* **20/1**[2]

1111 **2** *1* **Ben's Turn (IRE)**^{33} [3149] 5-11-7 .... RobertThornton 88+
(A King) *trckd ldrs: hit 5th: chal 7th tl slt ld 2 out: narrowly hdd last: carried lft and n.m.r fnl 100yds: one pce* **2/11**[1]

000F **3** *10* **The Laying Hen (IRE)**^{16} [3437] 6-10-10 .... DarylJacob(5) 71
(D P Keane) *bhd: hdwy 6th: chsd ldrs 3 out: ev ch appr 2 out: one pce sn after* **100/1**

3300 **4** *3/4* **Milanshan (IRE)**^{29} [3240] 6-10-8 .... WayneKavanagh(7) 70
(J W Mullins) *chsd ldrs: slt ld after 6th tl hdd appr 2 out: sn on pce* **100/1**

300 **5** *17* **Miss Chippy (IRE)**^{14} [3461] 6-11-1 .... JasonMaguire 53
(T R George) *bhd: hdwy 6th: chsd ldrs 4 out: rdn next: sn wknd* **28/1**

000 **6** *1/2* **Overjoyed**^{26} [3280] 5-10-12 .... WilliamKennedy(3) 53
(Miss Suzy Smith) *chsd ldrs: chal 7th to 3 out: sn wknd* **100/1**

05- **7** *6* **Primrose Park**^{568} [955] 7-11-1 .... PJBrennan 47
(K Bishop) *chsd ldrs: wknd 3 out: no ch whn rn v wide bnd appr 2 out* **66/1**

40-P **8** *1* **Kayleigh (IRE)**^{13} [3477] 8-10-8 90 .... KeiranBurke(7) 46
(P R Rodford) *rdn 5th: a in rr but mod hdwy u.p after 2 out* **40/1**

2000 **9** *1* **Kentford Lady**^{38} [2995] 5-10-12 88 .... RichardYoung(3) 45
(J W Mullins) *bhd: hdwy 6th: sn wknd* **33/1**

0 **10** *3* **Gulshique**^{33} [3149] 6-11-1 .... CarlLlewellyn 42
(N A Twiston-Davies) *chsd wnr to 5th: sn wknd* **25/1**[3]

5m 36.6s (11.50) **Going Correction** +0.125s/f (Yiel) — **10** Ran SP% **106.5**

Speed ratings: **84,83,80,79,73 73,71,70,70,69** CSF £23.40 TOTE £9.50: £1.60, £1.10, £8.00; EX 15.00.

Owner A Hordle **Bred** Woodditton Stud Ltd **Trained** Brayford, Devon

■ Stewards' Enquiry : Andrew Thornton two-day ban: careless riding (Feb 13-14)

FOCUS

Little strength in depth to this modest mares' event, which was run at an ordinary pace, and the first two came clear. The winner sets the standard.

NOTEBOOK

Hollywood, who had shown fair form in four previous bumper outings, made a winning return to action and got off the mark over timber at the first-time of asking with a battling display. Having settled in the lead early on, she then lost her position by cocking her jaw and appearing to almost pull herself up down the back straight, yet she recovered her momentum and displayed a decent attitude to get back to the lead and fend off the runner-up close home. This was a welcome boost for her stable and she ought to improve again for the experience. *(op 12-1)*

Ben's Turn(IRE), unbeaten in three bumpers and a mares' novice hurdle previously, failed to cope with the challenge of the winner on the run-in and, while she was not helped by that rival hanging into her inside the final 100 yards, she appeared held at the time. Considering she finished well clear of the rest, it should still rate a fair effort in defeat, and the return to softer ground and a stiffer track in the future can only be to her advantage. *(op 1-5)*

The Laying Hen(IRE) held every chance in the home straight and posted much her best effort to date. Her confidence should be restored now and a slight drop back in trip should help her get closer in this division.

Milanshan(IRE) was firmly put in her place after the third last flight, but improved for the return to a faster surface nevertheless. She is clearly modest, but should fare better when eligible for a handicap mark after her next outing.

3693 STEWART TORY MEMORIAL HUNTERS' CHASE (20 fncs 1 omitted) — 3m 1f 110y

1:30 (1:32) (Class 6) 6-Y-0+ — **£1,977** (£608; £304)

Form — RPR

1-41 **1** **Red Brook Lad**^{26} 11-12-4 107 .... MissCTizzard(3) 119+
(C St V Fox) *t.k.h: trckd ldrs: chal 4 out tl led 2 out: shkn up and kpt on strly run-in* **4/1**[2]

-113 **2** *2* **No Retreat (NZ)**^{257} [453] 13-12-0 111 .... MrWHill(7) 114
(J Groucott) *trckd ldr: chal 4 out: led 3 out: hdd next: sn one pce* **3/1**[1]

/P-1 **3** *8* **Trade Off (IRE)**^{26} 8-11-11 91 .... MrIChanin(7) 103
(Mrs S Alner) *led: hdd 3 out: wknd and hit next* **6/1**[3]

1-F1 **4** *9* **Coolefind (IRE)**^{26} 8-12-7 .... MrSMorris 97
(W J Warner) *nt fluent: chsd ldrs: hit 3rd: 7th and 12th: rdn 15th: wknd after 4 out* **3/1**[1]

1-PP **5** *15* **Mister Club Royal**^{235} 10-12-2 82 .... MrRWoollacott(5) 89+
(Miss Emma Oliver) *chsd ldrs: rdn 15th: wknd sn after* **50/1**

0605 **F** **Isard III (FR)**^{137} [1489] 10-12-4 117 .... MrTJO'Brien(3) —
(Mrs K Waldron) *bhd tl fell 6th* **10/1**

U **Mister Sher (IRE)**^{270} 7-12-0 .... MrACharles-Jones —
(Mrs L J Young) *mstke and uns rdr 1st* **25/1**

-P6P **F** **Good Bone (FR)**^{11} 9-12-4 82 .... MrAWintle(3) —
(S Flook) *bhd: hdwy to chse ldrs whn fell 15th* **50/1**

PPP/ **P** **Come On Boy**^{256} 12-11-7 .... (p) MrGDavies(7) —
(T G Williams) *a in rr: t.o whn p.u after 12th* **125/1**

-34P **U** **Mondial Jack (FR)**^{113} [1715] 7-12-0 130 .... (p) MrRQuinn(7) —
(Mrs K Waldron) *bhd tl hmpd and uns rdr 15th* **11/1**

3P4/ **U** **Soul King (IRE)**^{250} 11-11-7 .... (b1) MrRBliss(7) —
(Michael Blake) *hit 5th: in rr tl hmpd and uns rdr 6th* **66/1**

2-PP **P** **General O'Keeffe**^{19} 9-11-7 86 .... MrJBarnes(7) —
(Mrs Susie Old) *chsd ldrs to 12th: sn wknd: t.o whn p.u bef 3 out* **50/1**

6P1- **P** **General Tantrum (IRE)**^{319} [4480] 9-11-11 79 .... (p) MrTCollier(7) —
(Mrs Sue Popham) *bmpd 1st: bhd: hdwy 13th: wknd sn after: p.u after 4 out* **50/1**

6m 44.0s (4.10) **Going Correction** +0.125s/f (Yiel) — **13** Ran SP% **115.7**

Speed ratings: **98,97,94,92,87** —,—,—,—,— —,—,— CSF £15.92 TOTE £4.40: £1.80, £1.50, £1.80; EX 22.90.

Owner C St V Fox **Bred** T H Jagger **Trained** Gillingham, Dorset

FOCUS

A fair event of its type with the winner rated value for further. The form looks solid and should work out. First open ditch bypassed on second circuit.

NOTEBOOK

Red Brook Lad, who made a winning comeback at Larkhill 26 days previously, followed-up on this return to Rules with a convincing success under a fine ride from Tizzard. The ground was in his favour, he jumped particularly well throughout, and could have been called the winner from four out. He is a most consistent and likeable performer in this sphere. *(op 7-2)*

No Retreat(NZ), having his first run for 257 days, had every chance, but was always playing second fiddle to the winner. This still rates a pleasing comeback effort, however, and he looks sure to win another race in this sphere before too long. He will also be happier when reverting to a stiffer track. *(op 7-2)*

Trade Off(IRE), whose trainer sent out Kingscliff to win this event in 2003, had his chance from the front and posted a fair effort at the weights in defeat. He reversed his recent point form with Coolefind on 3lb better terms and may be able to get his head back in front under a slightly more patient ride in the future. *(op 8-1)*

Coolefind(IRE), who had the measure of Trade Off when winning his point 26 days previously, failed to reverse that form on 3lb worse terms and was well held. He would have been better off *with a more positive ride, but he still has to really convince with his jumping under Rules. (tchd 11-4)*

3694 HMG PAINTS "NATIONAL HUNT" NOVICES' HURDLE (11 hdls) — 2m 6f

2:00 (2:04) (Class 2) 5-Y-0+ — **£8,768** (£2,590; £1,295; £648; £323; £162)

Form — RPR

312 **1** **Gungadu**^{54} [2762] 6-11-5 135 .... ChristianWilliams 136+
(P F Nicholls) *mde all: c wl clr after 3 out: v easily* **1/5**[1]

P642 **2** *17* **Hill Forts Timmy**^{12} [3505] 6-11-0 109 .... RichardYoung 110+
(J W Mullins) *hdwy 5th: chsd wnr after 3 out but sn no ch: kpt on for clr 2nd* **12/1**[3]

220U **3** *7* **Malaga Boy (IRE)**[31] 3215 9-11-5 107 JoeTizzard 106
(C L Tizzard) *hdwy 5th: disp 2nd after 3 out but nvr any ch w wnr: sn wknd* **50/1**

00/P **4** *1 1/4* **See More Jock**[13] 3477 8-11-0 RobertWalford 100
(Dr J R J Naylor) *a in rr and nvr in contention* **125/1**

1-0P **5** *11* **Sommelier**[28] 3249 6-11-0 (t) CarlLlewellyn 89
(N A Twiston-Davies) *chsd ldr: lost pl 5th: rallied after next: disp 2nd u.p after 3 out: sn wknd* **66/1**

005- **6** *17* **Liberty Ben (IRE)**[367] 3621 6-11-0 AndrewThornton 79+
(R H Alner) *chsd wnr fr 3rd tl wknd qckly after 3 out* **50/1**

23 **P** **Art Virginia (FR)**[48] 2865 7-11-0 MickFitzgerald —
(N J Henderson) *chsd ldrs: j. slowly 6th: hit next and wknd qckly: t.o whn p.u bef 2 out* **10/1**[2]

5m 27.6s (2.50) **Going Correction** +0.125s/f (Yiel) **7** Ran SP% **106.3**
Speed ratings: **100,93,91,90,86 80,—** CSF £2.64 TOTE £1.20: £1.10, £2.50; EX 3.10.
Owner Paul K Barber & Mrs M Findlay **Bred** Mrs Hugh Maitland-Jones **Trained** Ditcheat, Somerset

FOCUS
A modest winning time for a race of its class and the field finished strung out behind the easy winner. The form is straightforward, rated through the first three, and should work out.

NOTEBOOK
Gungadu ran out an emphatic winner - as he was entitled to at these weights - despite not appearing too happy on the tight track back over this shorter trip. The ground would have also been against him, as he has looked much more at home on a deep surface previously, so he deserves extra credit and is fast developing into a very useful performer. While his real future lies back over fences, he is not far off the best staying novice hurdlers, and he is a possible for both the Royal & SunAlliance and the Brit Insurance novice hurdles at Cheltenham. If the ground were to come up soft in March, he would be a leading player in the latter event. *(op 2-9 tchd 1-4)*
Hill Forts Timmy turned in another sound effort and got home well enough over the longer distance. He is a decent benchmark for this form and will be better off when switching to handicaps in due course. *(tchd 10-1 and 14-1)*
Malaga Boy(IRE), who unseated early on his chasing bow last time, ran his race and this should have served as a confidence booster for a return to the bigger obstacles.
See More Jock, pulled up on his recent hurdling bow and return from a layoff at Chepstow last time, posted a more encouraging effort and can build on this. He should find his feet when qualifying for handicaps after his next outing and it would be little surprise to see him sent over fences before too long. *(op 100-1)*
Liberty Ben(IRE) *Official explanation: jockey said gelding hung left (tchd 40-1)*
Art Virginia(FR), up in trip, was disappointing and has it to prove after this. He has not really taken to hurdling all that well, but it would be unwise to assume he will not be capable of better when going chasing in due course. *Official explanation: jockey said gelding was lame (op 7-1)*

3695 DICK REYNOLDS NOVICES' H'CAP CHASE (13 fncs) 2m
2:30 (2:32) (Class 2) 5-Y-0+ **£12,641** (£3,815; £1,965; £1,041)

Form RPR

-113 **1** **Cerium (FR)**[61] 2634 5-11-2 139 PJBrennan 142+
(P F Nicholls) *prom: chsd ldr 6th: led appr 3 out and nt fluent: drvn out run-in* **10/11**[1]

0/13 **2** *1 1/2* **Hors La Loi III (FR)**[22] 3341 11-11-7 142 LiamHeard(5) 146
(P F Nicholls) *chsd ldrs: rdn after 4 out: styd on u.p to take 2nd cl home but nt rch wnr* **13/2**[3]

-F33 **3** *3/4* **Muhtenbar**[28] 3251 6-10-6 122 PaulMoloney 125
(Miss H C Knight) *led tl hdd appr 3 out: styd on u.p fr next: one pce run-in: lost 2nd cl home* **13/2**[3]

1052 **4** *dist* **Feel The Pride (IRE)**[5] 3618 8-10-13 129 (b) APMcCoy —
(Jonjo O'Neill) *j. slowly 3rd: nt fluent 5th (water): hdwy 7th: rdn: wknd and hit 4 out: wl bhd whn mstke 2 out: t.o* **6/1**[2]

3143 **P** **Serpentine Rock**[38] 2998 6-10-7 123 RichardJohnson —
(P J Hobbs) *chsd ldr to 5th: wknd 8th: t.o whn p.u bef 3 out* **7/1**

3m 58.8s (-3.10) **Going Correction** +0.125s/f (Yiel)
WFA 5 from 6yo+ 6lb **5** Ran SP% **105.8**
Speed ratings: **112,111,110,—,—** CSF £6.49 TOTE £1.80: £1.30, £2.00; EX 4.40.
Owner B Fulton, T Hayward, S Fisher, L Brady **Bred** Sarl Haras De Saint-Faust And Andre-Paul Larrieu **Trained** Ditcheat, Somerset

FOCUS
A decent novices' handicap, run at a generous pace, and the first three came clear. The form looks solid enough, with the third to mark and should work out.

NOTEBOOK
Cerium(FR) resumed winning ways over fences with a ready display, and should be rated value for a touch further, as he appeared to be idling in front on the run-in. While he looks just off the very top of the two-mile novice chasers this term, he has done nothing wrong over fences to date. He reportedly heads straight to the Arkle now, and deserves to take his chance, however the Maghull Novices' Chase at Aintree in April may be more his sort of race. *(op 11-10)*
Hors La Loi III(FR), third behind Justified at Newbury last time, got outpaced before staying on with purpose approaching the final fence and posted a solid effort under top weight. He now looks to be crying out for a stiffer test and the Jewson Novices' Handicap Chase at the Cheltenham Festival could be right up his street. However, he will receive no respite from the Handicapper with efforts like this, and will probably have to carry near top weight in that event. *(op 5-1)*
Muhtenbar ◆, third behind subsequent winners Green Tango and Don't Be Shy at Hereford previously, ensured a decent pace and turned in a personal-best in defeat. He handled the faster surface without fuss, continues to improve in the jumping department, and really does deserve to find an opening over fences. *(op 6-1 tchd 7-1)*
Feel The Pride(IRE), runner-up to Green Tango at Southwell five days previously, was just starting to look in trouble prior to making a serious error four from home and probably found this coming too soon. *(op 9-2)*
Serpentine Rock, facing his stiffest task to date, was never a serious factor and proved *disappointing. He probably wants softer ground. Official explanation: trainer said gelding bled from the nose (tchd 8-1)*

3696 BYOTROL H'CAP HURDLE (8 hdls) 2m
3:00 (3:00) (Class 3) (0-125,123) 4-Y-0+ **£6,506** (£1,910; £955; £477)

Form RPR

5-00 **1** **Noble Request (FR)**[12] 3510 5-11-7 118 RichardJohnson 135+
(P J Hobbs) *hld up in tch: stdy hdwy 3 out: led gng wl appr next: sn clr: v easily* **6/1**

320- **2** *8* **Lunar Crystal (IRE)**[299] 4768 8-11-12 123 APMcCoy 122
(M C Pipe) *led tl hdd appr 2 out: sn no ch w wnr but hld on wl u.p for 2nd run-in* **7/2**[3]

11P **3** *nk* **In Media Res (FR)**[33] 3143 5-11-5 123 CharlieStudd(7) 122
(N J Henderson) *chsd ldrs: rdn and outpcd 4 out: styd on u.p fr next: kpt on run-in to press for 2nd but nvr nr wnr* **12/1**

3312 **4** *2* **Armariver (FR)**[21] 3360 6-11-2 113 ChristianWilliams 110
(P F Nicholls) *chsd ldr: chal 3 out: rdn and btn appr 2 out* **5/2**[1]

-111 **5** *7* **The Hairy Lemon**[23] 3333 6-11-4 115 RobertThornton 105
(A King) *chsd ldrs: rdn and outpcd 4th: nvr in contention after* **3/1**[2]

6-45 **6** *1 1/4* **L'Oudon (FR)**[33] 3135 5-11-4 120 LiamHeard(5) 110+
(P F Nicholls) *hld up in rr: hdwy 3 out but nvr rchd ldrs: sn wknd* **7/1**

3m 47.0s (-2.10) **Going Correction** +0.125s/f (Yiel) **6** Ran SP% **110.3**
Speed ratings: **110,106,105,104,101 100** CSF £26.16 TOTE £5.50: £2.40, £2.60; EX 35.90.
Owner Mrs Karola Vann **Bred** P Chedeville And Antoinette Tamagni **Trained** Withycombe, Somerset

FOCUS
A fair handicap, run at a sound pace, and the winner should be rated value for more than double his winning margin. he placed horses give the form a solid look.

NOTEBOOK
Noble Request(FR), who had shown just fair form in two previous outings this term, bounced right back to his best with a facile success and justified support in the betting ring. He could have been called the winner turning for home, clearly enjoyed the better ground, and should be rated value for around double his winning margin. While the Handicapper will no doubt hike him back up in the weights now, he has learnt to settle much better in his races this term, and could have more to offer. *(op 8-1)*
Lunar Crystal(IRE), making his return from a 299-day absence, proved a sitting duck for the winner at the top of the straight, but stuck to his task when headed and still posted an encouraging comeback display. *(op 10-3)*
In Media Res(FR), pulled up on heavy ground in his quest for the hat-trick last time, improved as expected for the return to less taxing ground and was doing his best work towards the finish. He will appreciate the return to a stiffer track in the future. *(op 8-1)*
Armariver(FR), raised 5lb for his latest effort when a disqualified winner at Cheltenham, ultimately *paid for his early exertions and was found wanting at the top of the straight. He is capable of* better. *(tchd 9-4 and 11-4)*
The Hairy Lemon, bidding for his fourth consecutive handicap success, was beaten a long way from home and failed to give his true running on this much quicker ground. *(op 11-4 tchd 5-2)*
L'Oudon(FR) looked as though he may play a part in the finish when making ground coming out of the back straight, but failed to sustain his effort and dropped away tamely under pressure. He is a *frustrating performer and it would be little surprise to see him sent over fences before too long. (op 8-1)*

3697 HBLB COTSWOLD CHASE (GRADE 2) (21 fncs) 3m 1f 110y
3:30 (3:30) (Class 1) 6-Y-0+ **£23,076** (£8,824; £4,552; £2,404)

Form RPR

-450 **1** **See You Sometime**[32] 3180 11-11-5 138 AndrewThornton 146
(J W Mullins) *chsd ldr: led 11th to next: chal 15th to 16th: led 4 out: rdn fr 3 out: hld on all out* **18/1**

-515 **2** *1 1/4* **Royal Auclair (FR)**[38] 2972 9-11-6 161 (t) ChristianWilliams 150+
(P F Nicholls) *chsd ldrs: led 10th to next: led 13th tl mstke and hdd 4 out: ralled next: mstke 2 out: kpt on again run-in: no ex nr fin* **6/4**[1]

-106 **4** *25* **Ollie Magern**[38] 2972 8-11-10 154 CarlLlewellyn 108
(N A Twiston-Davies) *led to 10th: hit 13th and wknd: mstke 4 out: t.o* **11/2**[2]

/1-F **U** **One Knight (IRE)**[37] 3022 10-11-6 153 RichardJohnson —
(P J Hobbs) *mstke and uns rdr 2nd* **6/4**[1]

6m 38.7s (-1.20) **Going Correction** +0.125s/f (Yiel) **5** Ran SP% **108.3**
Speed ratings: **106,105,—,—,—** CSF £45.63 TOTE £20.20: £2.90, £1.50; EX 43.30.
Owner J A G Meaden **Bred** J A G And Mrs S R B Meaden **Trained** Wilsford-Cum-Lake, Wilts

FOCUS
A sub-standard renewal of this Grade Two event - best known as the Pillar Property Chase - which had been switched to this track after the recent abandoned meeting at Cheltenham, where it was to be run as the Letheby & Christopher. The form is highly suspect, and it cannot be considered a proper Gold Cup trial on such a differing type of track. It was also a moderate winning time for a race of its type.

NOTEBOOK
See You Sometime, officially the lowest rated performer in the race, gamely fended off the runner-up from three out to score his first success since December 2004. He did boast some decent form over fences as a novice, and really enjoyed himself tussling for the lead on this sharp track. While his task was greatly aided by the runner-up's crucial error four out, he deserves real credit for the manner in which he stuck to his task from the penultimate fence, and is clearly back in top form now. He is a possible for the Betfair Bowl at Aintree in April, a course he likes, as *advertised when finding only Like-A-Butterfly too good in the Mildmay Novices' Chase last season. (op 25-1 tchd 16-1)*
Royal Auclair(FR), fifth behind Kicking King in the King George last time, looked the most likely winner prior to making a terrible blunder four out and was always up against it from that point onwards and was eventually held by a rival officially rated 23lb his inferior. This must be considered a missed opportunity - with One Knight and Ollie Magern disappointing - but it could have been a different story had his jockey ridden him with more restraint. Although he is a previous course-and-distance winner, that came in 2004, and he is almost certainly more suited by a stiffer test these days. *(op 13-8 tchd 7-4)*
Ballycassidy(IRE) was never on terms and turned in a lifeless performance. He has it to prove after this. *(op 20-1 tchd 22-1)*
Ollie Magern never appeared happy at any stage and looked a shadow of the horse that staked his claim as a genuine Gold Cup contender when beating Kingscliff in the Charlie Hall at Wetherby back in October. Granted he is a happier horse on a right-handed and more galloping track, but he *cannot be backed with any confidence until showing more signs of his former self. Official explanation: trainer said gelding was distressed (op 10-3 tchd 6-1)*
One Knight(IRE) again had his jumping frailties exposed and disappointingly unshipped Johnson at the second fence. He promises so much, yet the fact remains he has now failed to complete in three of his last four outings, and really is a frustrating performer to follow. *(op 13-8 tchd 15-8)*

3698 CPM GROUP LTD (STEVEN HANNEY MEMORIAL) H'CAP CHASE (21 fncs) 3m 1f 110y
4:00 (4:02) (Class 4) (0-115,115) 5-Y-0+ **£4,554** (£1,337; £668; £333)

Form RPR

661F **1** **Florida Dream (IRE)**[28] 3258 7-11-12 115 (b) CarlLlewellyn 128+
(N A Twiston-Davies) *mde virtually all: drvn and styd on u.p fr 3 out: nt fluent last: kpt on wl* **20/1**

-324 **2** *3* **Treasulier (IRE)**[13] 3480 9-10-3 99 KeiranBurke(7) 106
(P R Rodford) *chsd ldrs: wnt 2nd 9th: rdn and lost 2nd appr 3 out: chsd wnr again sn after but no imp* **12/1**

P3 **3** *2* **Nykel (FR)**[29] 3241 5-10-4 104 RobertThornton 100+
(A King) *impr 9th: chsd ldrs 15th: hit 17th: chsd wnr appr 3 out and mstke: sn lost 2nd and one pce* **7/2**[2]

4-4P **4** *nk* **Bubble Boy (IRE)**[13] 3481 7-10-11 107 CharlieStudd(7) 112
(B G Powell) *mid-div: rdn 4 out: kpt on fr 3 out to press for 3rd run-in but nvr gng pce to rch wnr* **20/1**

0-46 **5** *4* **Walter's Destiny**[12] 3509 14-10-10 99 ChristianWilliams 100
(C W Mitchell) *wl bhd: stl plenty to do 3 out but kpt on wl fr next: fin wl but nt rch ldrs* **40/1**

3020 **6** *10* **Even More (IRE)**[14] 3469 11-11-5 108 AndrewThornton 109+
(R H Alner) *chsd ldrs: chal 6th: rdn and lost pl 13th: rallied 16th: blnd next: wknd 4 out* **9/1**

05F3 **7** *1 3/4* **Joe Deane (IRE)**[26] 3285 10-10-5 94 (p) RJGreene 83
(M J Coombe) *blnd 14th: a in rr* **9/1**

-230 **P** **Durlston Bay**[26] 3296 9-11-4 **107** MickFitzgerald —
(S Dow) *bhd: blnd 15th: p.u bef next* **18/1**

P-P1 **P** **Boundary House**[29] 3241 8-10-3 **92** JasonMaguire —
(J A B Old) *a bhd: t.o whn p.u bef 11th* **8/1**[3]

3-02 **P** **Boddidley (IRE)**[34] 3129 8-10-10 **104** LiamHeard(5) —
(P F Nicholls) *hit 2nd and 14th: a in rr: t.o whn p.u bef 2 out* **3/1**[1]

F2P0 **P** **Noble Baron**[31] 3212 10-11-5 **108** (tp) JoeTizzard —
(C G Cox) *chsd ldrs: rdn 12th: sn wknd: t.o whn p.u bef 3 out* **12/1**

/1P4 **F** **Bertiebanoo (IRE)**[63] 2596 8-11-10 **113** (t) APMcCoy —
(M C Pipe) *in tch: drvn to chse wnr: 2l down and styng on whn fell 4 out* **10/1**

P0-P **B** **Flying Trix (IRE)**[7] 3578 10-10-10 **99** (b[1]) RichardJohnson —
(P J Hobbs) *chsd ldrs: hit 15th and 17th: 4th and styng on whn b.d 4 out* **22/1**

6m 42.3s (2.40) **Going Correction** +0.125s/f (Yiel)
WFA 5 from 7yo+ 11lb **13** Ran SP% **124.4**
Speed ratings: **101,100,99,99,98 95,94,—,—,— —,—,—** CSF £236.39 CT £1058.12 TOTE £23.60: £4.60, £3.30, £1.70; EX 416.10 Trifecta £421.90 Part won. Pool: £594.32 - 0.60 winning tickets..
Owner D J & S A Goodman **Bred** Mrs Patricia Mackean **Trained** Naunton, Gloucs

FOCUS
An ordinary winning time for the grade, only 1.7 seconds faster than the hunter chase, and the form looks fairly straightforward, rated through the placed horses.

NOTEBOOK
Florida Dream(IRE) got his chasing career firmly back on track with a dour staying performance under top weight. He is versatile as regards underfoot conditions, seems to go on most types of track, and is clearly still capable of rating higher. *(op 16-1)*
Treasulier(IRE), the subject of on-course support in the betting, posted a game effort and looked to run above his rating in defeat. He remains a maiden, but clearly likes this venue, and really does deserve to go one better. *(op 20-1)*
Nykel(FR), very well backed, ran his race yet again did not look to get home over the trip. He needs to drop in trip and can get off the mark in this sphere when doing so. *(op 5-1)*
Bubble Boy(IRE) posted his best effort of the current campaign and has clearly slipped to a more realistic mark now. He may well prefer a drop back in trip in the future.
Walter's Destiny was doing his best work at the finish, having been set too much to do by his rider, and can be rated slightly better than the bare form. *(tchd 50-1)*
Flying Trix(IRE), in first-time blinkers, was in the process of running an improved race prior to being brought down with four to jump. *(tchd 4-1)*
Boundary House, raised 7lb for getting off the mark over course and distance last time, proved *most disappointing and is clearly a fragile performer.Official explanation: trainer said gelding bled from the nose (tchd 4-1)*
Boddidley(IRE) failed to build on the promise of his improved display on his chasing bow at Taunton last time and never looked happy at any stage. He is one to have definite reservations about. *Official explanation: trainer said gelding was unsuited by the good ground (tchd 4-1)*

3699 WINCANTON RACECOURSE STANDARD NATIONAL HUNT FLAT RACE (CONDITIONAL JOCKEYS AND AMATEUR RIDERS) 2m
4:30 (4:34) (Class 6) 4-6-Y-O **£2,055** (£599; £299)

Form RPR

1 **1** **Kicks For Free (IRE)**[29] 3244 5-11-6 LiamHeard(5) 124+
(P F Nicholls) *hld up in rr: smooth hday 5f out: led gng wl 2f out: won on bit* **2/9**[1]

2 1 ¾ **Stripe Me Blue** 4-10-8 ow3 GinoCarenza(3) 95
(P J Jones) *chsd ldrs: ev chance fr 3f out to 2f out: kpt on but nvr any ch w v easy wnr* **66/1**

3 ½ **West Ridge** 5-10-8 RichardKilloran(10) 102
(B G Powell) *chsd ldrs: lft in ld 9f out: rdn over 3f out: hdd 2f out: kpt on fnl f but no ch w v easy wnr* **40/1**

4 4 **It Happened Out (IRE)** 5-10-11 WayneKavanagh(7) 98
(J W Mullins) *bhd: hdwy 6f out: chsd ldrs and kpt on same pce fnl 3f* **100/1**

0 **5** ½ **Wednesday Country (IRE)**[24] 3327 5-10-11 MrFelixDeGiles(7) 97
(J A T De Giles) *in tch: chsd ldrs 5f out: styd on same pce fnl 3f* **100/1**

6 2 **Flight Leader (IRE)** 6-11-1 RobertStephens(3) 95
(C L Tizzard) *bhd: hdwy to chse ldrs 5f out: one pce fnl 2f* **40/1**

6 **7** 8 **Hazzard A Guess**[16] 3435 5-10-4 SimonElliott(7) 80
(J W Mullins) *bhd: rdn and styd on fnl 3f: nvr trbld ldrs* **150/1**

0 **8** 1 ½ **Triggernometry**[80] 2242 5-10-11 MissCTizzard(7) 86
(C L Tizzard) *chsd ldrs: chal 4f out: wknd ins fnl 3f* **66/1**

5- **9** ½ **Rathcannon Man (IRE)**[374] 3520 6-10-11 MrGTumelty(7) 85
(A King) *mid-div: rdn 6f out: sn outpcd and n.d* **28/1**

10 3 **Oscar Buck (IRE)**[264] 5-10-11 MrJJDoyle(7) 82
(V R A Dartnall) *chsd ldrs: rdn over 4f out: wknd fr 3f out* **25/1**[3]

0 **11** 2 ½ **Kyliemoss**[38] 3001 5-10-4 KeiranBurke(7) 73
(N R Mitchell) *chsd ldrs 12f* **150/1**

0 **12** dist **Reflector (IRE)**[38] 2961 5-10-13 DarylJacob(5) —
(Miss H C Knight) *chsd ldrs tl wknd 5f out: t.o* **33/1**

2 **13** 28 **Parish House (IRE)**[33] 3138 6-10-11 MrMWall(7) —
(B W Duke) *chsd ldrs tl wknd 6f out: t.o* **11/1**[2]

6 **P** **Le Burf (FR)**[99] 1882 5-10-11 AndrewGlassonbury(7) —
(G R I Smyly) *saddle slipped and p.u after 2f* **25/1**[3]

P **P** **Stingray (IRE)**[22] 3346 4-9-12 MarkHunter(10) —
(N I M Rossiter) *t.k.h: led 7f: hung bdly lft and sn p.u* **100/1**

3m 42.9s (-8.80) **Going Correction** +0.125s/f (Yiel)
WFA 4 from 5yo+ 9lb **15** Ran SP% **116.4**
Speed ratings: **106,105,104,102,102 101,97,96,96,95 93,—,—,—,—** CSF £34.03 TOTE £1.30: £1.02, £12.60, £6.50; EX 37.10 Place 6 £10.96, Place 5 £10.76.
Owner Mark Tincknell **Bred** Martin Cullinane **Trained** Ditcheat, Somerset
■ Stewards' Enquiry : Mr M Wall two-day ban: used whip without giving gelding time to respond and when out of contention (Feb 13-14)

FOCUS
A decent winning time for a bumper and the impressive winner is value for 15 lengths with the seventh and ninth the best guides to the form.

NOTEBOOK
Kicks For Free(IRE), a facile winner of a hotter event over course-and-distance on his debut 29 days previously, further enhanced his growing reputation with a smooth success under his 7lb penalty. This proved he is versatile as regards underfoot conditions, but whether this track is the ideal prep test for the Champion Bumper at Cheltenham - his next intended target - has to be considered a doubt, and his ability to handle that more undulating and stiffer track must be taken on trust. *(op 2-7)*
Stripe Me Blue, a half-sister to bumper winner Lady Bling Bling, posted a very encouraging debut effort even despite the fact he is greatly flattered by his proximity to the winner at the finish. He should come on for this experience and, considering his dam won over 2m 6f over timber, he can be expected to be suited by a stiffer test in due course. *(op 50-1 tchd 40-1)*
West Ridge ◆, a brother to Irish bumper winner Ridgewood Ploy, stuck to his task well under pressure when headed in the straight and registered a pleasing debut display. He can find a race in this division granted the normal improvement. *(op 25-1)*
It Happened Out(IRE), half-brother to winning hurdler/chaser Correct And Right, showed some hope for the future and looked to enjoy the good ground. He should improve as he becomes more streetwise.
Parish House(IRE) *Official explanation: trainer said gelding was found to have an elevated temperature (op 10-1)*
Le Burf(FR) *Official explanation: jockey said saddle slipped (op 14-1)*
Stingray(IRE) *Official explanation: jockey said colt made a noise (op 14-1)*
T/Jkpt: Not won. T/Plt: £16.80 to a £1 stake. Pool: £38,729.75. 1,682.05 winning tickets. T/Qpdt: £14.10 to a £1 stake. Pool: £2,567.60. 134.00 winning tickets. ST

3700 - 3706a (Foreign Racing) - See Raceform Interactive

3557 CATTERICK (L-H)
Friday, February 3

3707 Meeting Abandoned - Frost

3598 FONTWELL (L-H)
Friday, February 3

OFFICIAL GOING: Good (good to firm in places)
Fast ground which the jockeys described as 'rolled mud'. The ground appeared to get rougher as the afternoon progressed.
Wind: Virtually nil Weather: Mild

3714 DOCKER HUGHES MEMORIAL JUVENILE NOVICES' HURDLE (9 hdls) 2m 2f 110y
1:40 (1:40) (Class 4) 4-Y-O **£3,253** (£955; £477; £238)

Form RPR

1 **1** **Blazing Bailey**[17] 3436 4-11-5 RobertThornton 118+
(A King) *mid div: hdwy 5th to join ldrs: led 3 out: clr whn nt fluent last: easily* **9/4**[2]

140 **2** 12 **Flaming Weapon**[38] 3021 4-11-5 JamieMoore 103+
(G L Moore) *t.k.h: trckd ldrs: rdn to chse wnr after 3 out: kpt on but no ch w wnr fr next* **25/1**

3 **3** 2 ½ **Avalon**[22] 3355 4-10-12 APMcCoy 94+
(Jonjo O'Neill) *hld up towards rr: hdwy and mstke 6th: rdn and sltly outpcd after 3 out: styd on to go 3rd run-in* **7/2**[3]

U603 **4** shd **Before Time**[15] 3463 4-10-7 88 DerekLaverty(5) 94+
(Mrs A M Thorpe) *chsd ldrs: stmbld on bnd after 1st: lost pl briefly appr 6th: hit 3 out: sn rdn: 3rd and hld whn mstke last* **66/1**

5 ½ **Bayazid (IRE)**[130] 4-10-12 MickFitzgerald 92
(N J Henderson) *w ldr: led 5th tl 3 out: sn rdn: one pced whn hit next* **2/1**[1]

6 **6** ¾ **Cold Mountain (IRE)**[17] 3436 4-10-9 RichardYoung(3) 91
(J W Mullins) *hld up bhd: hit 3 out: hdwy next: kpt on same pce* **100/1**

5 **7** ¾ **Patronage**[79] 2274 4-10-12 NoelFehily 91
(Jonjo O'Neill) *hld up towards rr: hdwy after 3 out: sn rdn: blnd 2 out: kpt on same pce* **33/1**

06 **8** 3 ½ **Hereditary**[17] 3429 4-10-12 PJBrennan 89+
(Mrs L C Jewell) *hld up towards rr: blnd 3rd: hdwy after 5th: rdn after 3 out: sn wknd* **100/1**

U1B4 **9** 2 ½ **Prime Contender**[27] 3294 4-11-5 123 LeightonAspell 95+
(O Sherwood) *hld up towards rr: hdwy to trck ldrs after 5th: rdn after 3 out: wknd after next* **6/1**

332P **10** dist **Lord Of Adventure (IRE)**[17] 3431 4-10-12 103 ChristianWilliams —
(Mrs L C Jewell) *chsd ldrs tl 3 out: sn wl bhd* **66/1**

11 dist **The Chequered Lady**[214] 4-10-5 JamesDavies —
(T D McCarthy) *in tch: hit 5th: sn wl bhd* **100/1**

P **12** 1 ¾ **Liberty Run (IRE)**[22] 3354 4-10-7 JohnnyLevins(5) —
(Mrs A J Hamilton-Fairley) *led tl 5th: wknd after next: t.o* **100/1**

4m 32.0s (-4.00) **Going Correction** +0.025s/f (Yiel) **12** Ran SP% **114.3**
Speed ratings: **109,103,102,102,102 102,102,100,99,— —,—** CSF £51.63 TOTE £4.10: £1.10, £2.70, £1.40; EX 32.20.
Owner Three Line Whip **Bred** A M Tombs **Trained** Barbury Castle, Wilts

FOCUS
Probably the most interesting race on the card. The pace was decent and the winning time was 3.8 seconds faster than the novice hurdle for older horses later on the card, with the winner rated value for further. The form should work out.

NOTEBOOK
Blazing Bailey ◆ maintained his unbeaten record over hurdles with a very impressive success. A winner on much softer ground over course and distance on his hurdling debut, though he had winning form on fast ground on the Flat, he was sent to the front jumping the third-last flight and just pulled further and further clear. He is in a couple of races at Cheltenham and may have one more run beforehand, but he does look something of a stayer. *(tchd 5-2 in places)*
Flaming Weapon, who had faced a couple of stiff tasks since winning at Plumpton on his debut over timber, performed much better at this slightly more realistic level and finished a clear second best. There should be another race in him if not too highly tried. *(tchd 33-1)*
Avalon, given a patient ride, stayed on over the last half-mile but was always making hard work of it and he is still to really prove that this is his game. *(op 4-1 tchd 9-2)*
Before Time, who showed his first sign of ability last time out, ran with credit once again but he is only rated 88 and may be better off in handicaps.
Bayazid(IRE), a dual winner over middle distances in the French Provinces, came into this hurdling debut with expectations apparently high, but after showing up for about a mile and a half he then faded rather disappointingly. Perhaps the ground was not ideal, but he does have plenty of questions to answer now. *(tchd 85-40 in a place)*
Cold Mountain(IRE), beaten over 50 lengths by Blazing Bailey on his hurdling debut here, at least managed to halve that gap and does seem to possess a little ability.
Prime Contender was very disappointing and performed miles below his official mark. *(op 7-1)*
The Chequered Lady *Official explanation: trainer said filly finished distressed*

3715 3663 FIRST FOR FOOD SERVICE (S) HURDLE (11 hdls) 2m 6f 110y
2:10 (2:10) (Class 5) 5-Y-O+ **£2,081** (£611; £305; £152)

Form RPR

/-46 **1** **Mizinky**[27] 3283 6-9-7 75 RichardGordon(10) 85
(W G M Turner) *mid div: hdwy 5th: rdn after 7th: mstke next: outpcd after 3 out: hit 2 out: styd on u.str.p run-in: led fnl strides* **10/1**

44P6 **2** nk **Windy Spirit (IRE)**[38] 3017 11-10-10 ChristianWilliams 93+
(Evan Williams) *led: sn clr: rdn and hdd after 3 out: rallied to regain ld at the last: sn drifted lft: ct fnl strides* **7/2**[2]

5P04 **3** 2 **Smilingvalentine (IRE)**[15] 3461 9-10-3 98 JodieMogford 83
(D J Wintle) *chsd ldrs: rdn to ld appr 2 out: hdd last: no ex* **4/1**[3]

2-PP **4** 5 **Ilabon (FR)**[15] 3467 10-10-10 102 (v) APMcCoy 87+
(M C Pipe) *hld up: gd hdwy 8th: mstke 3 out: jnd ldr on bit sn after: w.w: ev ch appr last: fnd nil* **11/4**[1]

05P- **5** *22* **Ehab (IRE)**[350] [3920] 7-10-10 83 .... MatthewBatchelor 63
(Miss A M Newton-Smith) *chsd ldrs tl wknd after 7th* **25/1**

00/0 **6** *2* **Dirty Sanchez**[18] [3423] 8-10-7 .... ColinBolger(3) 61
(Miss A M Newton-Smith) *a bhd* **33/1**

3-53 **7** *12* **At The Double**[18] [3428] 10-11-10 90 ....(b) PhilipHide 73+
(P Winkworth) *mid div: hdwy 8th: rdn and wknd after 3 out* **6/1**

0-PP **8** *dist* **Duncanbil (IRE)**[15] [2632] 5-10-3 71 .... JamieGoldstein —
(J J Bridger) *in tch: rdn after 7th: sn wknd: t.o* **66/1**

P06/ **P** **Springer The Lad**[702] [4120] 9-10-5 80 .... RobertLucey-Butler(5) —
(Miss M P Bryant) *sn bhd: t.o and p.u bef 6th: b.b.v* **25/1**

2 **P** **Gotontheluckyone (IRE)**[25] [3321] 6-10-3 80 .... KeiranBurke(7) —
(P R Rodford) *chsd ldrs: mstke 7th: wknd appr 3 out: t.o and p.u bef 2 out: b.b.v* **8/1**

5m 43.2s (-1.60) **Going Correction** +0.025s/f (Yiel) **10** Ran SP% **115.5**
Speed ratings: **103,102,102,100,92 92,87,—,—,—** CSF £43.99 TOTE £10.30: £3.70, £1.50, £1.60; EX 53.90.There was no bid for the winner.
Owner Bob Chandler **Bred** P A Watts **Trained** Sigwells, Somerset
■ Stewards' Enquiry : Christian Williams one-day ban: used whip with excessive frequency (Feb 14)

FOCUS
A moderate seller which only concerned four horses from a very long way out. The form looks suspect and the ratings could be a fair amount out.

NOTEBOOK
Mizinky, who had shown that she still retained ability when reappearing from a very long break early last month, may well have 'bounced' when she ran again just five days later. There was no sign of fatigue here though as she needed all her stamina reserves to grab what had seemed an unlikely victory on the run-in. This was her first victory over hurdles at the tenth attempt. *(op 14-1)*
Windy Spirit(IRE), better known as a chaser these days and having his first run over hurdles since August 2000, was given a very positive ride. After looking sure to be swallowed up rounding the home bend, he managed to battle his way back to the front jumping the last but was just unable to withstand the winner's late flourish in the shadow of the post. *(tchd 4-1)*
Smilingvalentine(IRE), fourth in a Ludlow maiden hurdle last time, had every chance but did not seem to see out this slightly longer trip. *(tchd 5-1)*
Ilabon(FR), pulled up in his last two starts after reappearing from a long layoff, though he did have possible excuses, was taking a drop in class. He looked sure to win when cruising to the front turning for home, but did not find anything like as much off the bridle as had appeared likely and he looks one to treat with caution. *(op 3-1 tchd 10-3 in places)*
Ehab(IRE), making his debut for the yard, was entitled to need this after a year off.
At The Double may still just have needed this, though in truth he was up against it at the weights. *(op 5-1)*
Springer The Lad *Official explanation: jockey said gelding had bled from the nose (op 9-1)*
Gotontheluckyone(IRE) *Official explanation: trainer said gelding had bled from the nose (op 9-1)*

3716 LEIGHTON ASPELL FAN CLUB H'CAP CHASE (16 fncs) 2m 6f
2:40 (2:40) (Class 5) (0-90,85) 5-Y-0+ **£3,578** (£1,050; £525; £262)

Form RPR

PP3P **1** **Quizzling (IRE)**[30] [3239] 8-10-13 **75** .... OwynNelmes(3) 88+
(B J M Ryall) *chsd ldrs tl 7th: sn pushed along: hdwy to ld 11th: nt fluent 3 out: wnt lft 2 out and last: kpt on: rdn out* **7/2**[2]

30-2 **2** *2 ½* **Smart Guy**[27] [3285] 14-11-7 **80** ....(p) LeightonAspell 88+
(Mrs L C Jewell) *led: hit 8th: hdd 11th: rdn and ev ch 3 out: kpt on but hld by wnr fr next* **11/2**

PP4 **3** *7* **Aisjem (IRE)**[14] [3482] 7-10-5 **71** ....(p) MrRhysHughes(7) 74+
(Evan Williams) *w ldr tl 9th: chsd ldrs: rdn after 12th: blnd 3 out: kpt on same pce* **5/1**[3]

1530 **4** *6* **Taksina**[30] [3239] 7-11-5 **78** .... BenjaminHitchcott 72
(R H Buckler) *chsd ldrs tl outpcd 11th: nt a danger after* **7/2**[2]

1P-P **5** *17* **Twotensforafive**[17] [3430] 13-11-5 **85** .... KeiranBurke(7) 62
(P R Rodford) *chsd ldrs tl lost tch after 10th* **16/1**

63P2 **6** *6* **Sunshan**[120] [1650] 10-11-5 **85** .... JamesWhite(7) 66+
(R J Hodges) *chsd ldrs tl wknd after 4 out* **5/2**[1]

5m 41.7s (-2.10) **Going Correction** -0.10s/f (Good) **6** Ran SP% **110.9**
Speed ratings: **99,98,95,93,87 85** CSF £21.59 TOTE £4.50: £2.60, £1.50; EX 22.60.
Owner I & Mrs K G Fawcett **Bred** Basil Brindley **Trained** Rimpton, Somerset

FOCUS
A dire contest with the co-top weights rated just 85. The runner-up sets the level for the form.

NOTEBOOK
Quizzling(IRE) is something of an enigma as he had been pulled up in almost half of his 13 outings over fences, but he does possess ability and showed it here with a game victory. This faster *ground may be the key to him, but in reality the from probably amounts to little.Official explanation: trainer said, regarding the improved form shown, gelding was better suited by today's faster ground (op 4-1)*
Smart Guy, whose four career victories had all come here, was still 7lb above his highest winning mark. A drifter on the exchanges in the morning, he was given every chance under a positive ride *but he just lacked the pace of the winner over the last couple of fences. He has now been retired. (op 4-1)*
Aisjem(IRE) appears to have been helped by the application of cheekpieces and was still in with some sort of a chance when making an almighty blunder at the final ditch. *(op 7-1)*
Taksina never really got competitive and her best performance came when she was able to dominate from the off. *(op 4-1)*
Twotensforafive, lightly raced these days, again ran poorly and seems to have lost his way. *(op 11-1)*
Sunshan ran as though this first outing in four months was needed. *(op 11-4)*

3717 EUROPEAN BREEDERS FUND "NATIONAL HUNT" NOVICES' HURDLE (QUALIFIER) (9 hdls) 2m 2f 110y
3:10 (3:10) (Class 4) 4-7-Y-0 **£3,253** (£955; £477; £238)

Form RPR

30-1 **1** **Dusky Lord**[109] [1772] 7-11-10 .... LeightonAspell 118+
(N J Gifford) *mid div: smooth hdwy appr 3 out: jnd ldrs 2 out: led sn after last: r.o wl: rdn out* **11/4**[2]

6313 **2** *3* **Idris (GER)**[13] [3505] 5-11-10 115 .... PhilipHide 113+
(G L Moore) *prom: led 3rd tl after 5th: styd prom: led appr 2 out : hdd sn after last: no ex* **2/1**[1]

05 **3** *4* **Portland Bill (IRE)**[15] [3466] 6-11-4 .... TomScudamore 103
(R H Alner) *chsd ldrs: led after 5th: rdn and hdd appr 2 out: kpt on same pce* **33/1**

-054 **4** *1 ½* **Reach For The Top (IRE)**[29] [3248] 5-11-4 .... TimmyMurphy 103+
(Miss H C Knight) *mid div: pushed along after 5th: hdwy after next: rdn and effrt whn hit 2 out: sn hung lft: kpt on same pce* **11/1**

13 **5** *4* **College Ace (IRE)**[29] [3248] 5-11-10 120 .... RichardJohnson 105+
(P J Hobbs) *led tl 3rd: prom: rdn and ev ch appr 2 out: one pced whn hit last* **7/2**[3]

-045 **6** *2 ½* **Royal Stardust**[34] [3133] 5-11-4 105 .... JamieMoore 96+
(G L Moore) *in tch: tk clsr order after 5th: mstke 3 out: rdn and effrt whn hit 2 out: one pced after* **14/1**

0 **7** *12* **Posh Act**[21] [3369] 6-11-4 .... PaulMoloney 83
(Miss H C Knight) *hld up towards rr: sme hdwy appr 3 out: wknd 2 out* **100/1**

33 **8** *2* **It Would Appear (IRE)**[68] [2527] 7-11-4 .... APMcCoy 85+
(Jonjo O'Neill) *in tch: rdn after 3 out: wkng whn mstke 2 out* **9/1**

3U05 **9** *8* **Scalini'S (IRE)**[7] [3595] 6-11-4 .... MickFitzgerald 73
(Jonjo O'Neill) *trckd ldrs: jnd ldrs 3rd tl 5th: wknd appr 3 out* **33/1**

0F0 **10** *2 ½* **Lord Musgrave (IRE)**[15] [3466] 7-10-11 .... JustinMorgan(7) 71
(L Wells) *a bhd: lost tch fr 6th* **100/1**

0-UP **11** *18* **Allborn Lad (IRE)**[30] [3240] 6-11-4 .... NoelFehily 53
(C J Mann) *a bhd: lost tch fr 6th* **100/1**

00 **12** *9* **Popsleebobross (IRE)**[17] [3435] 5-10-6 .... RobertLucey-Butler(5) 37
(P Butler) *a bhd: lost tch fr 6th* **100/1**

4m 35.8s (-0.20) **Going Correction** +0.025s/f (Yiel) **12** Ran SP% **117.1**
Speed ratings: **101,99,98,97,95 94,89,88,85,84 76,73** CSF £8.67 TOTE £3.10: £1.20, £1.90, £7.10; EX 11.60.
Owner The American Dream **Bred** J K M Oliver **Trained** Findon, W Sussex

FOCUS
One of the more interesting races on the card, even though the winning time was 3.8 seconds slower than the juveniles in the opener. The winner is rated value for further, and along with the fourth and sixth sets the level.

NOTEBOOK
Dusky Lord travelled very well before showing a decent turn of foot on the run in to get the better of the favourite. This was certainly an improvement on the form of his Plumpton maiden hurdle victory and, as he had already shown that he goes particularly well fresh, the four-month layoff was never going to be a problem. He is likely to be aimed at the final of the series at Sandown next month. *(op 3-1 tchd 7-2)*
Idris(GER) ran right up to his best and had every chance, but could not match the winner's turn of speed after the final flight. This was his ninth outing over hurdles and he will remain vulnerable to progressive types in races like this, so may be worth trying in handicaps. *(tchd 9-4, 5-2 in a place)*
Portland Bill(IRE) ◆ is progressing with each outing and ran well over a trip possibly shorter than ideal. He looks a sure-fire winner over further.
Reach For The Top(IRE), another that probably needs a stiffer test, was far from disgraced but anything he achieves over hurdles is going to be a bonus. *(op 9-1)*
College Ace(IRE), another potential chaser, had every chance turning for home but was soon making hard work of it and this was a little bit disappointing. *(op 4-1 tchd 9-2)*
Royal Stardust showed up for a long way and emerged with credit. He might be interesting off his current mark in a novices' handicap.
It Would Appear(IRE) was close enough on the home bend, but found nothing at all off the bridle and does not seem to be progressing. *(op 6-1 tchd 11-2)*

3718 MALSAR KEST H'CAP CHASE (13 fncs) 2m 2f
3:40 (3:40) (Class 4) (0-105,104) 5-Y-0+
£6,263 (£1,850; £925; £463; £231; £116)

Form RPR

4201 **1** **He's The Gaffer (IRE)**[35] [3126] 6-11-1 **93** ....(b) RobertThornton 114+
(R H Buckler) *hld up but in tch: shkn up to take clsr order 8th: jnd ldr after 10th: led sn after 3 out: kpt on wl: rdn out* **5/2**[1]

6-43 **2** *9* **Matthew Muroto (IRE)**[15] [3465] 7-11-2 **99** .... DarylJacob(5) 112+
(R H Alner) *hit 1st: chsd ldng trio: rdn after 4 out: wnt 2nd after 2 out: hld whn nt fluent last* **5/1**[2]

1622 **3** *9* **Jupon Vert (FR)**[14] [3482] 9-11-3 **95** .... APMcCoy 101+
(R J Hodges) *led: nt fluent 10th: rdn and hdd sn after 3 out: one pced after* **5/2**[1]

020P **4** *14* **Acertack (IRE)**[33] [3187] 9-11-6 **98** .... TimmyMurphy 87
(R Rowe) *chsd ldrs: pckd 8th: rdn and wknd after 4 out* **12/1**

523P **5** *1 ¼* **Green Gamble**[57] [2719] 6-11-0 **92** ....(b[1]) JamesDavies 80
(D B Feek) *chsd ldrs: mstke 9th: sn wknd* **13/2**

25-1 **6** *dist* **Just A Touch**[21] [3370] 10-11-12 **104** .... LeightonAspell —
(P Winkworth) *a in rr: mstkes 3rd and 6th: lost tch fr 8th* **11/2**[3]

4m 30.2s (-4.90) **Going Correction** -0.10s/f (Good) **6** Ran SP% **110.2**
Speed ratings: **106,102,98,91,91** — CSF £14.60 TOTE £2.90: £2.30, £2.50; EX 12.60.
Owner M J Hallett **Bred** Pat O'Donovan **Trained** Melplash, Dorset

FOCUS
There was certainly no hanging about in this with Jupon Vert setting a very strong pace. The form could rate higher and should work out.

NOTEBOOK
He's The Gaffer(IRE), raised 8lb for his Taunton victory in December, certainly was not travelling like a winner at halfway, but the leaders had gone off fast enough and that enabled him to gradually pick them off on the final circuit. Once jumping to the front at the final ditch three out, the race was *his and, as this was only his third start over fences, he is entitled to carry on improving. (op 11-4 tchd 9-4, 3-1 in a place)*
Matthew Muroto(IRE) eventually emerged to chase the winner home, but was never able to get on terms with him. He almost certainly found this trip on a sound surface an inadequate test, but his new yard should be able to find an opportunity for him. *(op 7-1)*
Jupon Vert(FR) was responsible for the rapid early pace, but a sloppy jump four out cost him *momentum and he had little left when the winner headed him at the next. (op 11-4 tchd 10-3, 7-2 in a place)*
Acertack(IRE) dropped away tamely over the last half-mile and seems to reserve his best for Plumpton. *(op 8-1)*
Green Gamble did not improve for the first-time blinkers. *(tchd 6-1, 7-1 in a place)*
Just A Touch, 9lb higher than when successfully returning from a year off at Huntingdon last *month, hardly went a yard and was reportedly unsuited by the fast ground. Official explanation: jockey said gelding was unsuited by the fast ground (op 9-2 tchd 6-1 in a place)*

3719 BETFREDPOKER.COM H'CAP HURDLE (9 hdls) 2m 2f 110y
4:10 (4:10) (Class 4) (0-115,106) 4-Y-0+ **£3,903** (£1,146; £573; £286)

Form RPR

0621 **1** **Amanpuri (GER)**[17] [3441] 8-11-1 **95** .... ChristianWilliams 101
(Mrs A M Thorpe) *chsd ldrs: jnd ldr 5th: rdn to ld appr 2 out: kpt on: drvn out* **7/1**

0006 **2** *3* **Maclean**[15] [3467] 5-11-8 **102** ....(b) JamieMoore 105
(G L Moore) *mid div: hdwy 6th: rdn after 3 out: wnt 2nd and hung lft appr last: kpt on but no imp on wnr run-in* **11/2**[3]

50-0 **3** *2 ½* **Barclay Boy**[29] [3248] 7-11-10 **104** .... TomDoyle 104
(A J Lidderdale) *hld up: stdy hdwy fr 6th: rdn after 3 out: styd on to go 3rd sn after last* **8/1**

4F0 **4** *2* **It's The Limit (USA)**[4] [3646] 7-11-5 **104** ....(bt[1]) LeeStephens(5) 105+
(W K Goldsworthy) *led: rdn: edgd lft and hdd appr 2 out: hit next: disputing 3rd but hld whn hit last* **10/1**

0210 **5** *30* **Silistra**[33] [3185] 7-10-9 **89** ....(p) BenjaminHitchcott 57
(Mrs L C Jewell) *hld up: making hdwy whn stmbld on bnd after 5th: hit next: sn wknd* **16/1**

1F-P **6** *9* **Sesame Rambler (IRE)**[59] [2685] 7-11-12 **106** .... PhilipHide 65
(G L Moore) *chsd ldrs: drvn along after 5th: wknd next* **16/1**

The Form Book, Raceform Ltd, Compton, RG20 6NL

35P- **7** *16* **Kety Star (FR)**[365] 3664 8-11-1 **95** TimmyMurphy 38
(A W Carroll) *racd freely: hld up: hdwy to trck ldrs after 3rd: rdn after 3 out: sn wknd* **10/3**[1]

4203 **8** *12* **Cava Bien**[17] 3436 4-11-1 **106** RichardJohnson 26
(B J Llewellyn) *in tch: lost pl and dropped rr after 3rd: nvr a danger after* **7/2**[2]

020P **P** **Borehill Joker**[59] 2684 10-10-8 **95** MrJJDoyle(7) —
(V R A Dartnall) *mid div tl wknd 6th: t.o and p.u bef last* **9/1**

0/6- **P** **Major Speculation (IRE)**[15] 493 6-11-9 **103** SamThomas —
(J M Bradley) *hit 3rd: sn bhd: t.o and p.u bef 2 out: b.b.v* **50/1**

0/0- **P** **Mixed Marriage (IRE)**[365] 3664 8-11-8 **102** NoelFehily —
(Miss Victoria Roberts) *chsd ldrs tl wknd 6th: t.o and p.u bef 2 out* **66/1**

4m 34.3s (-1.70) **Going Correction** +0.025s/f (Yiel)
WFA 4 from 5yo+ 9lb **11** Ran SP% **118.6**
Speed ratings: **104,102,101,100,88 84,77,72,—,—** — CSF £46.32 CT £319.83 TOTE £8.30: £2.50, £1.10, £1.60; EX 31.90.
Owner Mrs A M Thorpe **Bred** H Von Finck **Trained** Bronwydd Arms, Carmarthens

FOCUS
The most competitive race on the card, but even these conditions seemed to find out the majority of the field and four had broken well clear coming to the second last.

NOTEBOOK
Amanpuri(GER), who broke his duck over hurdles at the tenth attempt here last time, was 5lb higher over this shorter trip but eventually won this in game style and his established stamina proved handy in the run to the line. Things will be tougher for his hat-trick bid once reassessed, but at least he is developing the winning habit. *(op 5-1)*
Maclean, whose last win came over course and distance last May, had been running poorly since the autumn but the return to this track resulted in a much-improved effort. A similar race could come his way off this sort of mark, if he could be relied on to repeat this, but he is not proving very consistent.
Barclay Boy ◆, making his handicap debut after finishing unplaced in all three starts over hurdles, had obviously benefited from his return from a nine-month break last month and this was much better. He is still relatively lightly raced and may have a bit more improvement left. *(op 12-1)*
It's The Limit(USA) made a bold bid to make every yard in the first-time blinkers, but did not quite get home. If the headgear works again he could be interesting with similar tactics back over two miles on a sound surface.
Silistra was left behind over the last half-mile and reserves his best for Plumpton. *(op 20-1)*
Kety Star(FR), not seen since pulling up on his return to hurdles exactly a year go, raced wide throughout but did himself few favours by taking a good grip and failed to see it out. He is worth another chance with this effort under his belt provided he can settle better. *(tchd 7-2)*
Cava Bien may have been taking on older horses for the first time, but this was still too bad to be true. *Official explanation: trainer had no explanation for the poor form shown (op 9-2)*
Major Speculation(IRE) *Official explanation: trainer's representative said gelding bled from the nose*

3720 HARDINGS BAR & CATERING SERVICES INTERMEDIATE NATIONAL HUNT FLAT RACE (CONDITIONAL/AMATEUR RIDERS) 2m 2f 110y

4:40 (4:40) (Class 6) 4-6-Y-O **£1,626** (£477; £238; £119)

Form RPR

1 **Notre Cyborg (FR)** 5-10-13 LiamHeard(5) 103+
(P F Nicholls) *a travelling wl: hld up:hdwy to join ldrs over 4f out: led 2f out: sn clr: easily* **4/11**[1]

2 *7* **Beths Choice** 5-10-11 ChrisDavies(7) 88
(J M Bradley) *trckd ldr: jnd ldrs 4f out: rdn 3f out: no ch w wnr fr over 1f out* **10/1**[3]

0 **3** *2 ½* **A Sea Commander (GER)**[33] 3181 4-10-0 WayneKavanagh(7) 74
(J W Mullins) *hld up: wnt 2nd 1/2-way: jnd ldr 5f out: led 3f out tl 2f out: lost 2nd over 1f out: one pced after* **4/1**[2]

00 **4** *8* **Just Poppytee**[15] 3468 4-9-11 WilliamKennedy(3) 59
(R H Alner) *led tl 3f out: one pced after* **25/1**

5 *dist* **Kelly Bidewell** 4-9-9 RobertLucey-Butler(5) —
(D B Feek) *chsd ldrs tl 6f out* **25/1**

4m 47.6s (8.30) **Going Correction** +0.025s/f (Yiel)
WFA 4 from 5yo 9lb **5** Ran SP% **110.1**
Speed ratings: **83,80,79,75,—** CSF £5.02 TOTE £1.40: £1.10, £5.00; EX 3.20 Place 6 £83.13, Place 5 £46.06.
Owner C G Roach **Bred** F Cottin **Trained** Ditcheat, Somerset

FOCUS
An uninformative bumper, run at a steady pace on what at this stage was bad ground and won in predictable style by the long odds-on favourite, who is value for further with the fourth setting the level.

NOTEBOOK
Notre Cyborg(FR) found this easy pickings, always travelling within himself and needing only to be shaken up to come clear in the straight. A 50,000gns half-brother to a Listed-hurdle winner in France, he was still noticeably green and will have gained valuable experience from this outing. *(op 4-6 tchd 8-11 in a place)*
Beths Choice, a half-brother to two winning hurdlers and a winning pointer, stuck on in pleasing fashion to secure second but in all likelihood is only moderate. He should get further when he switches to hurdles. *(tchd 11-1)*
A Sea Commander(GER) had his chance but failed to give another boost to the form of the Listed bumper at Cheltenham's New Year meeting in which he made his debut. That event was over only a mile and a half and he is a half-brother to four Flat winners on the continent, so his lack of stamina could have found him out. *(op 9-4)*
Just Poppytee made much of the running, but has now been well held in all three of her outings so far. *(op 14-1)*
T/Plt: £98.50 to a £1 stake. Pool: £65,862.75. 488.00 winning tickets. T/Qpdt: £22.40 to a £1 stake. Pool: £5,925.10. 195.30 winning tickets. TM

3294 SANDOWN (R-H)

Saturday, February 4

OFFICIAL GOING: Chase course - good to firm (good in places); hurdle course - good (good to soft in places)
Wind: Nil

3722 ANTHONY BAKER JUVENILE NOVICES' HURDLE (8 hdls) 2m 110y

12:25 (12:26) (Class 3) 4-Y-O **£5,204** (£1,528; £764; £381)

Form RPR

01 **1** **Detroit City (USA)**[24] 3340 4-11-3 RichardJohnson 135+
(P J Hobbs) *lw: prom: hdwy to trck ldrs 4th: led wl bef 2 out: c clr last: easily* **2/1**[2]

42 **2** *7* **Royals Darling (GER)**[24] 3340 4-11-3 MickFitzgerald 125+
(N J Henderson) *chsd ldrs: led 4th: narrowly hdd next: chal 3 out: tl appr next and mstke: no ch w wnr run-in: hld on for 2nd* **11/8**[1]

4 **3** *1 ½* **Linnet (GER)**[47] 2921 4-10-5 PCarberry 110+
(Ian Williams) *hld up rr but in tch: hdwy to trck ldrs 3 out: rdn appr next: disp 2nd last: sn one pce* **20/1**

4 *2 ½* **Ouste (FR)**[64] 4-10-12 ADuchene(5) 120+
(F Doumen, France) *leggy: hld up rr but in tch: hdwy to trck ldrs 3 out: rdn 2 out: sn one pce: wknd run-in* **12/1**

334 **5** *3 ½* **Cave Of The Giant (IRE)**[18] 3436 4-10-12 104 JimCrowley 110
(T D McCarthy) *chsd ldrs: rdn and outpcd after 3 out: styd on again run-in* **66/1**

3 **6** *7* **Brads House (IRE)**[14] 3498 4-10-12 CarlLlewellyn 104+
(J G M O'Shea) *leggy: rr but in tch: rdn after 3 out: nvr a danger* **11/1**

5510 **7** *20* **Quasimodo (IRE)**[18] 3436 4-11-3 118 GrahamLee 98+
(A W Carroll) *led tl hdd after 2nd: stl ev ch 3 out: sn rdn and wknd* **33/1**

4P21 **8** *6* **Desert Secrets (IRE)**[28] 3281 4-10-10 100 TimmyMurphy 91+
(J G Portman) *w ldr: led after 2nd: hdd 4th: led again next: rdn: hdd & wknd wl bef 2 out* **50/1**

11 **F** **Kalmini (USA)**[26] 3324 4-11-1 JamieGoldstein —
(Miss Sheena West) *neat: rr but in tch whn fell 4th* **8/1**[3]

3m 56.8s (-12.10) **Going Correction** -0.60s/f (Firm) **9** Ran SP% **113.7**
Speed ratings: **104,100,100,98,97 93,84,81,—** CSF £5.03 TOTE £3.10: £1.40, £1.50, £3.30; EX 5.80.
Owner Terry Warner **Bred** E J Kelly **Trained** Withycombe, Somerset
■ Stewards' Enquiry : Richard Johnson caution: careless riding

FOCUS
A decent little juvenile event which produced a very worthy candidate for the Triumph Hurdle in Detroit City, who has been rated value for 10 lengths. A race to treat positively.

NOTEBOOK
Detroit City(USA) ◆ had overcome being hampered early on when winning at Newbury last time and some took the view that his superiority over Royals Darling was probably greater than the margin of victory suggested. That opinion was vindicated here as he not only got the better of the Henderson runner again, despite being 7lb worse off, but he also beat him further. He travelled strongly on this good ground, jumped well, quickened away from the rest and was value for further than the official winning margin. The 10-1 generally available for the Triumph Hurdle looks decent value as he will enjoy the fast pace at the Festival and there is no doubt that he will be staying on strongly up the hill. He has plenty going for him. *(op 11-4)*
Royals Darling(GER) was expected by many to reverse Newbury form with Detroit City on 7lb better terms, especially as he was having his first outing for three and a half months that day, but he could not go with the winner when he quickened up from the second last. Perhaps this German-bred will need easier ground and/or a longer trip to be seen at his best. *(op 5-4)*
Linnet(GER) won a ten-furlong handicap on the Flat here last summer, and showed improved form against some decent types here. She likes genuinely fast ground and looks sure to find a race or two this spring.
Ouste(FR), an athletic type and a winner at Enghien last time out, held every chance going to the second last, but like the rest was left behind when the winner quickened. The majority of his form in France was naturally on very soft or heavy ground, and it remains to be seen if he needs those sort of conditions over here, too. *(tchd 14-1)*
Cave Of The Giant(IRE) ran on after getting outpaced and looks a real stayer in the making. *(op 100-1)*
Brads House(IRE) was hampered by the fall of Kalmini and struggled thereafter. *(op 10-1)*
Quasimodo(IRE) won what was an average affair here last month in testing conditions, and this tougher competition on quicker ground found him out.
Kalmini(USA), who is not the biggest, fell too far out to know whether she would have been involved in the finish. *(op 7-1)*

3723 H.B.L.B. CLEEVE HURDLE GRADE 2 (12 hdls) 3m

12:55 (12:59) (Class 1) 5-Y-O+
£22,808 (£8,556; £4,284; £2,136; £1,072; £536)

Form RPR

P222 **1** **Fire Dragon (IRE)**[40] 2999 5-11-0 145 (b) APMcCoy 150
(Jonjo O'Neill) *led 3rd: narrowly hdd 6th: styd chalng: led 8th: hdd appr 2 out: rallied to ld last: drvn out* **16/1**

-012 **2** *2* **Mighty Man (FR)**[34] 3177 6-11-4 156 RichardJohnson 157+
(H D Daly) *in tch: hdwy on rails to chse ldrs whn bdly hmpd bnd appr 2 out:switch lft after 2 out:r.o strly: nt rch wnr* **15/8**[1]

40P4 **3** *1 ½* **Westender (FR)**[34] 3177 10-11-4 151 (p) TimmyMurphy 151
(M C Pipe) *bhd: hdwy to chse ldrs 2 out: kpt on same pce run-in* **28/1**

F14- **4** *nk* **Patriarch Express**[343] 4063 9-11-8 158 DominicElsworth 155
(Mrs S J Smith) *chsd ldrs: led appr 2 out: hdd last: wknd nr fin* **14/1**

11-1 **5** *3 ½* **No Refuge (IRE)**[78] 2326 6-11-8 150 GrahamLee 153+
(J Howard Johnson) *in tch: hdwy 6th: chsd ldrs and mstke 2 out: wknd bef last* **11/2**[2]

4F0F **6** *5* **Sporazene (IRE)**[34] 3177 7-11-0 149 BJGeraghty 140+
(P F Nicholls) *lw: mstke 4th: rr but in tch: hdwy to chse ldrs 4 out: carried rt bnd appr 2 out: wknd sn after: blnd last* **16/1**

54/3 **7** *2 ½* **Starzaan (IRE)**[39] 3020 7-11-0 149 JimCrowley 137+
(H Morrison) *lw: rr but in tch: hdwy and blnd 4 out: n.d after* **16/1**

F064 **8** *5* **Redemption**[34] 3180 11-11-0 144 CarlLlewellyn 133+
(N A Twiston-Davies) *chsd ldrs to 3 out* **20/1**

12-0 **9** *4* **Mistanoora**[39] 3020 7-11-0 151 (b) TomScudamore 127
(N A Twiston-Davies) *led to 2nd: styd w ldr tl slt ld 6th: hdd 8th: wknd and edgd rt bnd appr 2 out* **28/1**

-011 **10** *3* **Attorney General (IRE)**[34] 3179 7-11-0 149 SamThomas 124
(J A B Old) *swtg: a bhd* **13/2**[3]

2-55 **11** *dist* **Brewster (IRE)**[39] 3020 9-11-4 150 MickFitzgerald —
(Ian Williams) *led 2nd to 3rd: chsd ldrs: wknd 3 out: t.o* **16/1**

P **Millenium Royal (FR)**[76] 2403 6-11-8 ADuchene 122
(F Doumen, France) *w'like: j. slowly 1st: hit 6th: a in rr: t.o whn p.u bef last* **10/1**

5m 54.2s **12** Ran SP% **114.4**
CSF £44.76 TOTE £17.90: £3.90, £1.30, £7.30; EX 49.80.
Owner Mrs Gay Smith **Bred** Juddmonte Farms **Trained** Cheltenham, Gloucs

FOCUS
Transferred from the previous week's abandoned Cheltenham card, this looked a competitive renewal, but the pace was not strong and the winner benefited from racing prominently throughout. The form might not be totally reliable.

NOTEBOOK
Fire Dragon(IRE), who had the blinkers back on, was given a good ride in a race lacking in early pace. Towards the fore throughout, he responded well to McCoy's urgings up the straight and saw off the attentions of Patriarch Express in good style. He has had wind problems in the past and this decent surface suited him well. Though still 25-1 in places for the World Hurdle, he represents an age-group which has never provided a winner of the stayers' championship race at the Festival.
Mighty Man(FR) ◆ can be considered an unlucky loser. Despite not having the race run to suit once again, and suffering interference (deemed to be accidental by the Stewards) on the home turn, he picked up strongly from the second last and was eating up the ground on the run-in. He shapes as though he will relish the uphill finish at Cheltenham and, with doubts about many of the other leading contenders, he looks sure to go to Cheltenham with a live chance in the World Hurdle. *(op 9-4)*

Westender(FR), wearing cheekpieces for a change, has done all his winning on good ground or good to firm, and this was the first time he had had his favoured racing surface since he finished fourth in the World Hurdle last year. He is a difficult horse to place these days and ran as well as one could have hoped for. *(op 25-1 tchd 33-1)*

Patriarch Express, who won this race last year when it was run at its proper home at Cheltenham, looked fit enough and shaped with plenty of promise on this first start for almost a year. However, he is a horse who has shown in the past that he goes well fresh, indeed he had won on his seasonal debut for the past three years, and so one wonders if he will build much on this next time. *(op 12-1)*

No Refuge(IRE), whose trainer had warned beforehand that he would need the run, was still in with every chance with two to run when making a costly error which knocked the stuffing out of him. His stamina for the World Hurdle might not be guaranteed and he might not be the most fluent hurdler around, but we know he likes the track at Cheltenham and decent ground will suit him, too, so it would be unwise to write him off. *(op 4-1)*

Sporazene(IRE), who enjoyed a valuable confidence-boosting outing, was still going well enough early in the straight, but then his stamina gave out. He remains difficult to place but he won the County Hurdle off a mark of 151 in 2004, and perhaps the hurly-burly of a big handicap will see him return to his best. He is in Newbury's totesport Trophy on a mark of 149, and might be in with a squeak. *(op 20-1)*

Starzaan(IRE), whose best form is at around two and a half miles, never got in a blow. He did not run badly on his return from a lengthy absence in the Long Walk Hurdle, but this was a step backwards. *(op 20-1)*

Redemption, given a clear view of his hurdles on the outside of the field, had a stiff task in this company but might have been seen to better effect off a faster gallop.

Mistanoora does not look as good as he was and his two efforts since returning from over a year on the sidelines suggest his current rating flatters him.

Attorney General(IRE) sweated up quite a lot beforehand and was beaten a long way from home. Presumably the ground was too quick for him. *(op 15-2 tchd 8-1)*

Millenium Royal(FR), who is slightly on the leg, was a Grade One winner on very soft ground in France but was never competitive on this much quicker going. *(tchd 11-1)*

3724 VICTOR CHANDLER H'CAP CHASE (GRADE 3) (13 fncs) 2m

1:30 (1:35) (Class 1) 5-Y-O+

£22,808 (£8,556; £4,284; £2,136; £1,072; £536)

Form	Pos	Dist	Horse / details	Jockey	SP	RPR
-413	**1**		**Tysou (FR)**[28] 3299 9-11-2 **140** (N J Henderson) *mid-div: hit 6th: hdwy appr 3 out: pressed ldr last: led sn after: drvn out*	MickFitzgerald	**10/1**	150+
13-1	**2**	*2*	**Dempsey (IRE)**[28] 3299 8-11-12 **150** (M Pitman) *lw: t.k.h: trckd ldrs: chal 4th: led next: rdn last: hdd sn after: one pce*	AndrewTinkler	**11/2**[2]	159+
F062	**3**	*3*	**Kalca Mome (FR)**[21] 3387 8-10-7 **131** (P J Hobbs) *rr: stl plenty to do after 4 out: hrd drvn and hdwy next: fin strly run-in to take 3rd cl home: nt rch ldrs*	RichardJohnson	**25/1**	136
3-10	**4**	*½*	**Bambi De L'Orme (FR)**[85] 2163 7-10-13 **137** (Ian Williams) *lw: hit 3rd: hld up in rr: hdwy 9th: wnt 3rd and rdn 3 out: chsd ldr next to last: wknd run-in*	PCarberry	**15/2**[3]	143+
121	**5**	*1½*	**Hoo La Baloo (FR)**[40] 2970 5-11-2 **147** (P F Nicholls) *led 2nd: j. slowly and hdd 5th: chsng ldr whn blnd 9th: wknd after 2 out*	BJGeraghty	**9/4**[1]	146+
10-6	**6**	*7*	**Locksmith**[63] 2635 6-11-9 **147** (M C Pipe) *hld up in rr: hdwy and hit 4 out: nvr gng pce to rch ldrs*	TimmyMurphy	**40/1**	144+
/03-	**7**	*5*	**Jurado Express (IRE)**[442] 2322 10-9-9 **124** oh2 (Miss Venetia Williams) *chsd ldrs: hit 6th and 9th: wknd 4 out*	LeeStephens(5)	**66/1**	115
F-62	**8**	*½*	**Old Flame (IRE)**[13] 3527 7-10-10 **134** (Paul Nolan, Ire) *w'like: led and stmbld 1st: sn hdd: bhd fr 6th*	JLCullen	**15/2**[3]	128+
6211	**9**	*1½*	**Town Crier (IRE)**[30] 3256 11-11-7 **145** (Mrs S J Smith) *chsd ldrs tl wknd after 4 out*	DominicElsworth	**15/2**[3]	134
61-2	**10**	*nk*	**Tikram**[28] 3299 9-11-8 **146** (G L Moore) *hit 3rd: mstke 6th: nvr travelling after and a bhd*	(b) APMcCoy	**11/2**[2]	137+

3m 49.9s (-12.60) **Going Correction** -0.50s/f (Good)
WFA 5 from 6yo+ 6lb **10** Ran SP% **113.7**
Speed ratings: **111,110,108,108,107 104,101,101,100,100** CSF £62.42 CT £1334.54 TOTE £12.20: £2.70, £2.40, £4.40; EX 59.90.

Owner W J Brown **Bred** Gilles Deroubaix **Trained** Upper Lambourn, Berks

FOCUS

Another race originally scheduled to take place at Cheltenham the previous week, although run for much less money now and with key runners racing off different marks. The addition of exciting novice Hoo La Baloo to the race when it was re-opened added extra spice to this traditionally competitive handicap. Although not the classiest of renewals, they went a strong gallop from the off and the form looks rock solid.

NOTEBOOK

Tysou(FR) was 8lb better off with Dempsey for a four and three-quarter length beating here last month, and the ground was more in his favour this time, too. The strong pace suited him and he came from off the pace to grab the top-weight on the run-in. He will take another hike in the weights for this, but he seems better than ever this season and, given his ground, will surely not be disgraced in the Grand Annual, as he tends to run well at Cheltenham. *(op 8-1)*

Dempsey(IRE), who looked very well, had to carry 4lb more in this re-scheduled race than he was due to carry at Cheltenham the previous week, but on the flip side he got to race right-handed again, which is thought correctly by connections to be a plus. He raced keenly and jumped well in front, but might have used up too much energy early on as he did not quite get home in the end. Improving all the time, he is fully entitled to take his chance in the Queen Mother Champion Chase, although he will be an outsider there. *(op 5-1 tchd 13-2)*

Kalca Mome(FR) prefers easier ground than this but the fast early pace which initially saw him struggle brought him into the race in the closing stages. He was disputing last place going to the Pond Fence but picked up well over the last two fences and charged up the run-in. While he could not be described as particularly well handicapped, he is at his best in fast-run handicaps, and it would not be a surprise to see him go well at a price in the Grand Annual.

Bambi De L'Orme(FR) is another who at best is only fairly handicapped at present, but he too goes well in these top two-mile handicaps, where the pace is fast and his hold-up style of racing is most effective. He ran a solid race. *(op 8-1 tchd 7-1)*

Hoo La Baloo(FR), the only novice in the field, was all the rage in the market, but he was denied by Dempsey of an easy time of it in front, and he made novicey mistakes along the way. To his credit he was still in there fighting for a place going to the last fence, but he weakened on the run-in. He had a hard race here and might need some time to get over it, but while he is unlikely to run in the Arkle as he prefers a right-handed track, there are good races to be won with him. Punchestown in the spring might suit him. *(op 5-2 tchd 2-1)*

Locksmith, who usually races freely in front, was ridden with great restraint this time. He never threatened to get competitive but this effort should not do his handicap mark any harm, and he is one to keep an eye on for the future. *(op 33-1 tchd 50-1)*

Jurado Express(IRE), having his first outing for 442 days, was pitched in at the deep end on his reappearance. This ex-Irish ten-year-old should find easier opportunities than this in future.

Old Flame(IRE), flattered to get within four lengths of Fota Island last time, had never raced over obstacles on ground as quick as this before and he found the pace too hot. He will be happier back on softer ground. *(op 8-1)*

Town Crier(IRE) is lightly raced for his age but he was put up 8lb for his win at Newbury in November on his last start over fences. Still in with a chance jumping the Pond Fence, he found nothing off the bridle and dropped out of it completely. Perhaps the Handicapper has him now. *(op 13-2)*

Tikram was 4lb better off with Dempsey for less than a length's beating here last time, but he was never going on this occasion, finding the combination of quick ground and a fast pace all too much. He probably needs a longer trip these days. *(op 7-1 tchd 15-2)*

3725 AGFA UK HURDLE (LISTED RACE) (8 hdls) 2m 110y

2:05 (2:08) (Class 1) 5-Y-O+

£17,106 (£6,417; £3,213; £1,602; £804; £402)

Form	Pos	Dist	Horse / details	Jockey	SP	RPR
2534	**1**		**Royal Shakespeare (FR)**[14] 3492 7-11-4 150 (S Gollings) *chsd ldrs: rdn 2 out: 3l down and styng on one pce whn lft disputing ld last: sn led: drvn out*	TomScudamore	**9/4**[1]	132
4131	**2**	*1¼*	**Alph**[34] 3185 9-11-0 117 (B R Johnson) *rr but in tch: hdwy and hit 3 out: one pce sn after: rallied to chse ldr 2 out: lft disputing ld last: kpt on: no ex cl hom*	MatthewBatchelor	**25/1**	128+
5412	**3**	*2*	**Mister McGoldrick**[14] 3492 9-11-0 150 (Mrs S J Smith) *in tch: rdn and outpcd 3 out: kpt on again whn hmpd last: fin wl*	DominicElsworth	**4/1**[3]	126+
-400	**4**	*½*	**Dalaram (IRE)**[28] 3298 6-11-0 137 (J Howard Johnson) *lw: chsd ldr: rdn and one pce fr 2 out*	(t) GrahamLee	**12/1**	125+
1-11	**5**	*hd*	**Rasharrow (IRE)**[90] 2062 7-11-0 127 (L Lungo) *rr whn stmbld after 2nd: gd hdwy after 3 out: j. slowly next: one pce whn sltly hmpd last*	TonyDobbin	**11/2**	128+
0420	**6**	*4*	**Self Defense**[28] 3298 9-11-8 152 (Miss E C Lavelle) *in tch: j. slowly and bhd 4 out: kpt on fr 2 out but nvr gng pce to rch ldrs*	MickFitzgerald	**5/2**[2]	128
06F5	**7**	*11*	**Milligan (FR)**[14] 3492 11-11-0 113 (Dr P Pritchard) *hit 1st: a bhd but sme prog after 2 out*	DrPPritchard	**200/1**	109
	F		**Fiepes Shuffle (GER)**[21] 6-11-0 (C Von Der Recke, Germany) *w'like: t.k.h early: led: hit 2 out: stl 3l clr and styng on whn fell last*	RobertThornton	**25/1**	132

3m 58.6s (-10.30) **Going Correction** -0.60s/f (Firm) **8** Ran SP% **110.6**
Speed ratings: **100,99,98,98,98 96,91,**— CSF £47.59 TOTE £3.60: £1.40, £2.70, £1.90; EX 72.50 Trifecta £301.00 Pool £1,145.02. 2.70 winning units.

Owner J B Webb **Bred** London Thoroughbred Services & Mme A Rothschild **Trained** Scamblesby, Lincs

FOCUS

No stars of the hurdling ranks on show here and a steady early pace produced a moderate time, a dodgy result, and nothing of interest for the Champion Hurdle. With Alph and Milligan too close for comfort, Royal Shakespeare has been rated more than 20lb off his best form. The third and fourth were also well off their best.

NOTEBOOK

Royal Shakespeare(FR) had conditions in his favour but the enterprisingly ridden Fiepes Shuffle looked to have his measure when crashing out at the final flight. A lucky winner on this day, he is nevertheless a consistent and smart two-mile hurdler, and while this race did not count for the Order Of Merit, he remains a big player in that contest.

Alph, an improving novice hurdler, ran way above expectations to finish second, two lengths clear of the rest. The way the race was run no doubt contributed to his prominent showing, but this was still antother much improved effort. He might find things difficult in handicap company once the Handicapper has had his say, but connections always have the option of returning to novice races.

Mister McGoldrick, whose connections chose to run him in this race rather than under top-weight in the Victor Chandler Chase earlier on the card, no doubt found the ground much too quick for his liking. Even so, it was strange, in the absence of a natural front-runner, that he was not ridden more positively. *(op 10-3)*

Dalaram(IRE) had the ground more in his favour this time and strictly at the weights ran well, but he is proving a difficult horse to place this season. *(op 11-1)*

Rasharrow(IRE), unimpressive when winning a novice hurdle at Ayr in November, had plenty to find in this company but the better ground was expected to suit him. He is highly regarded and, although he has so far failed to live up to the promise he showed in bumpers, he is lightly raced and surely capable of better in time. *(op 5-1 tchd 9-2)*

Self Defense, who won this race last year, normally runs well here. Indeed, he had finished in the first two in all but one of his previous eight visits to the track. He was below his best this time, though, looking beaten a long way out. *(op 7-2 tchd 4-1)*

Fiepes Shuffle(GER), an athletic sort who was a Group Three winner (six and a half furlongs) on the Flat and a winner of a hurdle and two chases in Germany, pulled himself to the front and soon built up a healthy advantage. In a race lacking early pace this proved very valuable. Given a breather down the far side, he kicked on again rounding the turn into the straight and looked to have the race in the bag when falling at the last. He is likely to struggle to get home at Cheltenham in the Champion Hurdle but might well be suited to Aintree or Ayr. *(op 20-1)*

3726 TOTESPORT.COM SCILLY ISLES NOVICES' CHASE GRADE 1 (17 fncs) 2m 4f 110y

2:35 (2:39) (Class 1) 5-Y-O+ **£28,510** (£10,695; £5,355; £2,670)

Form	Pos	Dist	Horse / details	Jockey	SP	RPR
12F2	**1**		**Napolitain (FR)**[34] 3178 5-10-12 139 (P F Nicholls) *led to 2nd: led 4th: rdn and nt fluent 3 out: hdd sn after next: lft w 2l advantage last: drvn and hld on all out*	APMcCoy	**3/1**[3]	134+
1-13	**2**	*nk*	**Turpin Green (IRE)**[62] 2654 7-11-6 (N G Richards) *lw: disp cl 3rd tl chsd wnr 3 out: chal next: sn led: 2l ahd whn tried to refuse and hdd last: rallied run-in: jst failed*	TonyDobbin	**9/4**[2]	149+
4230	**3**	*21*	**Stance**[28] 3299 7-11-6 128 (G L Moore) *led 2nd to 3rd: styd chsng wnr to 4 out: wknd and hit next*	(p) JamieMoore	**16/1**	120
3132	**4**	*4*	**Albuhera (IRE)**[39] 3039 8-11-6 144 (P F Nicholls) *lw: disp cl 3rd: hdwy and pushed along 13th: wknd 3 out*	(t) BJGeraghty	**6/5**[1]	116

5m 8.00s (-12.80) **Going Correction** -0.50s/f (Good)
WFA 5 from 7yo+ 7lb **4** Ran SP% **107.1**
Speed ratings: **104,103,95,94** CSF £9.80 TOTE £3.80; EX 9.50.

Owner The Stewart Family **Bred** Francois Cottin **Trained** Ditcheat, Somerset

■ Stewards' Enquiry : Tony Dobbin one-day ban: improper riding - struck gelding on horsewalk when returning to enclosure (Feb 15); caution: used whip with excessive frequency

FOCUS

Not the strongest renewal, but it was run at a good pace and the first two came clear of a fair yardstick in third. Turpin Green has been rated a seven-length winner and to the level of his hurdles form.

NOTEBOOK

Napolitain(FR) jumped well in front but he had ceded the advantage and looked held in second when Turpin Green almost refused at the last. Left in front on the run-in, he kept on just well enough to hang on for a fortunate victory. *(op 7-2 tchd 5-2)*

Turpin Green(IRE), who looked particularly well and moved well to post, was supported in the market and proved himself perfectly capable of handling this quicker surface. He had the race at his mercy when almost refusing at the final fence and the fact that he rallied so gamely on the run-in showed that he was an unlucky loser. This mishap can be put down to relative inexperience and the Royal & SunAlliance Chase, where the longer trip should suit, remains firmly on the agenda. *(op 11-4 tchd 3-1)*
Stance, who had the cheekpieces back on, ran close to form with Napolitain on their Wincanton *running earlier in the season and is exposed as below the class required to win at this level. (tchd 18-1)*
Albuhera(IRE) was weak in the market beforehand and proved very disappointing. The ground should have been to his liking and clearly he did not give his running. *(op 10-11 tchd 5-4)*

3727 TOTESCOOP6 SANDOWN H'CAP HURDLE GRADE 3 (11 hdls) 2m 6f

3:10 (3:13) (Class 1) 4-Y-0+

£28,510 (£10,695; £5,355; £2,670; £1,340; £670)

Form				RPR
1124	**1**		**Ungaro (FR)**[34] 3174 7-10-8 **128** ... JimCrowley (K G Reveley) *bhd: stdy hdwy fr 7th: led after 3 out: hrd drvn after 2 out: styd on strly run-in* **11/2**[2]	135+
5005	**2**	*2 ½*	**Sh Boom**[14] 3502 8-11-1 **140** ... LiamHeard[(5)] (S A Brookshaw) *bhd: hdwy and hit 8th: rdn and styd on fr 2 out: chsd wnr run-in but no imp* **25/1**	143
5/2-	**3**	*1 ¾*	**Material World**[474] 1763 8-9-11 **120** oh9 ... ColinBolger[(3)] (Miss Suzy Smith) *chsd ldrs: wnt 2nd 2 out: rdn and nt fluent last: kpt on same pce* **50/1**	122+
00-	**4**	*½*	**Danaw (FR)**[64] 5-11-7 **146** ... (t) ADuchene[(5)] (F Doumen, France) *hld up in rr: stdy hdwy fr 6th: chsd wnr appr 2 out: sn rdn: nt qckn run-in* **33/1**	149+
3032	**5**	*1*	**Fenix (GER)**[14] 3502 7-10-0 **130** ... (b) MattyRoe[(10)] (Mrs L Wadham) *in tch: chsd ldrs form 5th: rdn 2 out: kpt on run-in but nvr gng pce to chal* **12/1**	131+
1-01	**6**	*1 ¼*	**Rayshan (IRE)**[21] 3383 6-10-5 **132** ... MissRDavidson[(7)] (N G Richards) *chsd ldrs: pushed along and one pce 2 out: hit last: kpt on run-in but gng pce to chal* **10/1**[3]	131+
3/P0	**7**	*8*	**Special Rate (IRE)**[21] 3389 9-10-5 **125** ... RobertThornton (A King) *rr and reminder after 3rd: hit 6th: hrd drvn fr 4 out: stl plenty to do 2 out: styd on run-in: nvr nr ldrs* **50/1**	117+
11	**8**	*hd*	**Magnifico (FR)**[33] 3219 5-10-8 **135** ... AndrewGlassonbury[(7)] (M C Pipe) *chsd ldrs: rdn 2 out: sn btn* **14/1**	125
13-0	**9**	*1 ¼*	**Waltzing Beau**[83] 2207 5-9-13 **124** ... JohnnyLevins[(5)] (B G Powell) *chsd ldrs: hit 8th: rdn and effrt 2 out: wknd bef last* **66/1**	113
-P02	**10**	*13*	**Stormez (FR)**[34] 3179 9-11-1 **135** ... (t) TomScudamore (M C Pipe) *bhd and sn drvn along: sme hdwy fr 2 out* **33/1**	111
4366	**11**	*5*	**Hasty Prince**[21] 3389 8-11-10 **144** ... APMcCoy (Jonjo O'Neill) *hld up in rr: hdwy 7th: chsd ldrs 3 out: wknd next* **12/1**	121+
P026	**12**	*2 ½*	**Nonantais (FR)**[40] 2974 9-10-0 **127** ... PatrickCStringer[(7)] (M Bradstock) *led: sn clr: hdd after 3 out: wknd bef next* **66/1**	95
P434	**13**	*1*	**Dream Falcon**[21] 3389 6-10-2 **129** ... JamesWhite[(7)] (R J Hodges) *chsd ldrs to 3 out* **25/1**	96
6136	**14**	*3 ½*	**Alikat (IRE)**[77] 2336 5-10-13 **133** ... TimmyMurphy (M C Pipe) *hld up in rr: sme hdwy 3 out: sn wknd* **16/1**	97
-126	**15**	*1 ½*	**Mioche D'Estruval (FR)**[51] 2847 6-10-4 **124** ... RJGreene (M C Pipe) *hit 5th: a in rr* **33/1**	86
0422	**16**	*21*	**Openide**[20] 3408 5-9-7 **120** oh3 ... (b) MrMWall[(7)] (B W Duke) *chsd ldrs: t.k.h: blnd 4th: sn bhd* **20/1**	61
P-5P	**P**		**Lord Sam (IRE)**[57] 2744 10-11-9 **143** ... MickFitzgerald (V R A Dartnall) *bhd: sme hdwy 5th: rr whn mstke 7th: t.o whn p.u bef 2 out* **11/1**	—
-111	**P**		**Be Be King (IRE)**[21] 3388 7-11-0 **134** ... BJGeraghty (P F Nicholls) *lw: chsd ldrs: j. slowly 6th: sn rdn and wknd: t.o whn p.u bef 2 out* **9/4**[1]	—

5m 15.0s (-22.90) **Going Correction** -0.60s/f (Firm) **18** Ran SP% **119.7**
Speed ratings: **117,116,115,115,114 114,111,111,111,106 104,103,103,101,101 93,—,—** CSF £136.94 CT £6091.97 TOTE £6.50: £1.70, £4.80, £7.20, £6.20; EX 198.30 TRIFECTA Not won..
Owner Sir Robert Ogden **Bred** Neustrian Associates **Trained** Lingdale, Redcar & Cleveland

FOCUS
A big field, but two novices dominated the market, and one of them proved well up to beating a largely exposed bunch of rivals. The winning time was decent, even for such a competitive race, and the form should work out well enough.

NOTEBOOK
Ungaro(FR), fourth behind Denman at Cheltenham in a Grade One race for novices last time out, proved himself well handicapped on a mark of 128. He travelled well for much of the race and saw the trip out strongly, suggesting he should not have any trouble getting three miles in time. He will be sent over fences next season. *(op 6-1 tchd 13-2)*
Sh Boom ran his best race for some time and is finally back down to a mark which gives him some sort of a chance. He always did appreciate a decent surface and will surely take his chance in the Pertemps Final at the Festival.
Material World ran a blinder from 9lb out of the weights on her return from 474 days on the sidelines. It remains to be seen, however, whether she can build on this or whether she bounces next time.
Danaw(FR), last seen in this country when finishing down the field in the Triumph Hurdle, was saddled with top weight but might have finished closer had he not jumped the last two flights slowly. Most of his successes in France have come on very soft ground so this was a decent effort in the circumstances. *(op 25-1)*
Fenix(GER) seems to reserve his best for this track and is usually doing his best work at the finish. He ran well on his first attempt at this longer trip, and perhaps the distance helped offset the fact that the ground was quicker than he would ideally have liked.
Rayshan(IRE) had different ground conditions ths time and coped well enough. He appeared to get the longer trip fairly well and remains on the upgrade. *(tchd 11-1)*
Special Rate(IRE) was a useful novice back in 2004, but he has had his problems and been lightly raced in recent times. This was his best effort since returning to the track and hopefully a sign of better to come. *(op 66-1)*
Magnifico(FR) did not look favourably rated beforehand for his handicap debut and his performance appeared to confirm that impression. *(op 12-1)*
Waltzing Beau was given a sympathetic ride on his return from almost three months off, and he will be interesting when his handicap mark slips a bit further.
Hasty Prince is fairly handicapped on his best form and travelled well for a long way, but he did not get home. He will be more effective over a shorter trip. *(tchd 14-1 in places)*
Lord Sam(IRE), who has not made the grade over fences, has an entry in the World Hurdle, but this performance did not enhance his claims in that direction. *(op 2-1 tchd 5-2 in places)*
Be Be King(IRE), who looks a real chasing type, struggled to keep up when the pace picked up. *The ground can probably be blamed for that. Official explanation: trainer said gelding was unsuited by good, good to soft in places ground (op 2-1 tchd 5-2 in places)*

3728 AGFA DIAMOND H'CAP CHASE (22 fncs) 3m 110y

3:45 (3:48) (Class 2) (0-145,143) 5-Y-0+

£28,183 (£8,325; £4,162; £2,083; £1,039; £522)

Form				RPR
1F12	**1**		**Dunbrody Millar (IRE)**[14] 3509 8-10-0 **120** ... TomMalone[(3)] (P Bowen) *lw: mde all: hmpd by loose horse appr 9th: drvn and r.o strly run-in* **8/1**	135+
331F	**2**	*2*	**Ladalko (FR)**[28] 3296 7-11-2 **133** ... BJGeraghty (P F Nicholls) *lw: chsd ldrs: hit 4th: chsd wnr 3 out: sn hrd rdn: kpt on run-in but no imp nr fin* **7/4**[1]	145+
U1F4	**3**	*nk*	**Underwriter (USA)**[58] 2724 6-10-0 **117** oh6 ... GrahamLee (Ferdy Murphy) *hld up in rr: stdy hdwy fr 14th: chsd ldrs 3 out: kpt on u.p fr 2 out: nt pce to chal* **20/1**	129+
FP-5	**4**	*3 ½*	**Limerick Boy (GER)**[34] 3180 8-11-12 **143** ... SamThomas (Miss Venetia Williams) *lw: in tch: hdwy 12th: chsd ldrs fr 4 out: rdn next: one pce whn hit last* **14/1**	151+
5222	**5**	*3*	**Shalako (USA)**[28] 3296 8-10-1 **118** ... RichardJohnson (P J Hobbs) *chsd ldrs: hit 17th: lost pl next: rallied fr 2 out: kpt on again run-in* **11/2**[2]	123+
2242	**6**	*shd*	**The Kew Tour (IRE)**[30] 3258 10-10-0 **117** ... DominicElsworth (Mrs S J Smith) *disp 2nd to 4 out: sn rdn: wknd fr 2 out* **16/1**	121
0-1P	**7**	*6*	**Iris Bleu (FR)**[70] 2491 10-11-10 **141** ... TimmyMurphy (M C Pipe) *hld up in rr: hit 6th: hdwy 16th: chsd ldrs 4 out: sn rdn: wknd next* **7/1**[3]	141+
-104	**8**	*2 ½*	**Run For Paddy**[34] 3176 10-11-6 **137** ... CarlLlewellyn (M Pitman) *lw: bhd: j. slowly 12th: blnd 17th: sme prog fr 3 out* **7/1**[3]	134+
0510	**9**	*3 ½*	**Cassia Heights**[45] 2938 11-9-7 **117** oh6 ... (t) MrTJO'Brien[(7)] (S A Brookshaw) *disp 2nd to 18th: wknd qckly 3 out* **66/1**	109
4-4F	**10**	*27*	**Campaign Trail (IRE)**[63] 2637 8-10-3 **120** ... AndrewTinkler (Jonjo O'Neill) *swtg: hit 2nd: bhd: hdwy 12th: sn rdn: wknd 16th* **20/1**	85
2/60	**F**		**Iris Royal (FR)**[34] 3180 10-11-5 **136** ... MickFitzgerald (N J Henderson) *fell 1st* **16/1**	—

6m 12.6s (-18.90) **Going Correction** -0.50s/f (Good) **11** Ran SP% **117.3**
Speed ratings: **110,109,109,108,107 107,105,104,103,94** — CSF £22.85 CT £279.84 TOTE £8.20: £2.20, £1.50, £4.60; EX 29.80 Trifecta £1131.10 Part won. Pool £1,593.18. 0.70 winning units..
Owner Dundon Else Partnership **Bred** Lord Donegall **Trained** Little Newcastle, Pembrokes

FOCUS
A decent handicap and the finish was contested by the three improvers in the field. The form should work out.

NOTEBOOK
Dunbrody Millar(IRE) was allowed an uncontested lead and proved game in front, pulling out more when threatened by the eventual runner-up. He saw the trip out strongly, should get further in time, and could yet defy another rise in the weights for his stable, which has improved him so much (rated just 90 three months ago) since he arrived from Ireland. The Betfred Gold Cup might be a possible target. *(op 9-1)*
Ladalko(FR) looked to have a fine chance of making up for his unfortunate exit at the second last here last time out, and a 2lb higher mark should not have been a problem, but he just could not *claw back the leader over the last two fences. Perhaps the ground was quicker than ideal for him. (tchd 15-8 and 2-1 in places)*
Underwriter(USA) ◆, returning from a two-month break, came in for some interesting support at big prices and rewarded his backers with an each-way return, staying on really well up the straight. He was running from 6lb out of the handicap here so will take a hit from the Handicapper now, but he was the youngest horse in this field, the only novice, and is open to more improvement than most. *(op 50-1)*
Limerick Boy(GER) looks held by the Handicapper off his current chase mark and this stiff finish would not have been to his liking. He will be more effective back on a sharper track. *(op 11-1)*
Shalako(USA) had the ground in his favour, but he hit the last of the Railway fences second time around and was being pushed along going to the Pond Fence. He was keeping on well at the finish, but he has no secrets from the Handicapper these days. *(op 6-1 tchd 13-2 in a place)*
The Kew Tour(IRE) has not won a race for almost two years but his handicap rating has barely budged in the meantime. He is another about whom the Handicapper seemingly knows all. *(op 14-1)*
Iris Bleu(FR), last seen being pulled up in the Hennessy, should not have been inconvenienced by the quicker ground, but he is now on a mark 8lb higher than when successful at Wincanton on his seasonal reappearance. *(op 8-1 tchd 13-2)*
Run For Paddy, ridden patiently out the back, hit the second of the Railway fences on the final circuit and was struggling thereafter. *(op 9-1 tchd 10-1)*
Cassia Heights, the oldest runner in the field, had it to do from 6lb out of the weights and was left behind when the pace hotted up leaving the back straight for the final time. *(tchd 80-1)*

3729 MILWARD PRINTING NOVICES' H'CAP HURDLE (9 hdls) 2m 4f 110y

4:20 (4:24) (Class 3) (0-120,120) 4-Y-0+ **£5,204** (£1,528; £764; £381)

Form				RPR
1	**1**		**Temoin**[19] 3423 6-11-2 **110** ... MickFitzgerald (N J Henderson) *w'like: leggy: trckd ldrs: wnt 2nd gng wl appr 2 out: chal last: led on bit fnl half f: cleverly* **8/1**[3]	133+
-221	**2**	*1 ¾*	**Oscatello (USA)**[40] 2967 6-10-11 **105** ... PCarberry (Ian Williams) *str: slt ld to 4th: styd w ldr tl slt advantage 3 out: drvn whn chal 2 out: hdd last half f: sn outpcd* **5/2**[1]	113
2-21	**3**	*6*	**Brankley Boy**[19] 3428 8-11-7 **120** ... SamCurling[(5)] (N J Henderson) *chsd ldrs: rdn after 3 out: outpcd fr next* **8/1**[3]	122
360	**4**	*6*	**Absolutelythebest (IRE)**[39] 3023 5-9-12 **95** ... TomMalone[(3)] (J G M O'Shea) *bhd: hdwy 3 out: styd on fr 2 out but nvr nr ldrs* **14/1**	92+
024	**5**	*10*	**Here We Go (IRE)**[15] 3478 7-10-1 **100** ... LeeStephens[(5)] (W K Goldsworthy) *lw: chsd ldrs: rdn 4 out: wknd 2 out* **33/1**	86
0004	**6**	*¾*	**Nice Horse (FR)**[14] 3500 5-11-2 **110** ... TimmyMurphy (M C Pipe) *bhd: sme hdwy and rdn 3 out: n.d* **10/1**	95
2-34	**7**	*2*	**New Mischief (IRE)**[18] 3441 8-10-3 **100** ... WilliamKennedy[(3)] (Noel T Chance) *chsd ldrs: wknd after 3 out* **14/1**	83
-505	**8**	*6*	**High Altitude (IRE)**[11] 3548 5-10-11 **105** ... (v[1]) RichardJohnson (A King) *chsd ldrs: rdn 4 out: wknd after next* **20/1**	84+
0044	**9**	*2 ½*	**Peppershot**[18] 3433 6-9-7 **94** oh14 ... (t) JayPemberton[(7)] (R Gurney) *hit 2nd: bhd: mod prog fr 2 out* **100/1**	69
4331	**10**	*3 ½*	**Youlbesolucky (IRE)**[70] 2497 7-11-9 **117** ... APMcCoy (Jonjo O'Neill) *bmpd 1st: chsd ldrs tl wknd fr 3 out* **9/2**[2]	90+
0060	**11**	*8*	**Mokum (FR)**[23] 3358 5-10-4 **98** ... GrahamLee (A W Carroll) *a in rr* **25/1**	61
5100	**12**	*7*	**Smart Boy Prince (IRE)**[7] 3622 5-11-2 **115** ... MarkNicolls[(5)] (C Smith) *w ldr: led 4th tl narrowly hdd 3 out: sn wknd* **33/1**	71
6020	**13**	*8*	**Smileafact**[115] 1711 6-9-11 **94** oh5 ... (b[1]) TJPhelan[(3)] (Mrs Barbara Waring) *a in rr* **100/1**	42
613	**14**	*16*	**Shaka's Pearl**[29] 3275 6-10-11 **105** ... JamesDavies (N J Gifford) *a in rr* **8/1**[3]	37

5m 0.40s (-13.00) **Going Correction** -0.60s/f (Firm) **14** Ran SP% **119.0**
Speed ratings: **100,99,97,94,90 90,89,87,86,85 82,79,76,70** CSF £27.04 CT £170.34 TOTE £6.90: £3.10, £1.60, £3.80; EX 26.30 Place 6 £418.89, Place 5 £330.45.

Owner The Unemployables **Bred** Bloomsbury Stud **Trained** Upper Lambourn, Berks

FOCUS
An ordinary novice handicap in which the first four home were some of the least experienced in the field. They went quite steady in the first half of the race. The winner has been rated value for 15 lengths, and while that can only be guesswork his Flat form gave him every chance of aspiring to at least that level. The second, third and fourth also put up personal bests.

NOTEBOOK
Temoin won in desperate ground at Plumpton on his debut but he showed his versatility by coping with these much quicker conditions in good style, winning very cheekily indeed under a confident ride from Fitzgerald. The step up in trip suited and it is anyone's guess what he had in hand, but the Handicapper is sure to take drastic action and his best option in the short term might be to return to novice company where he can surely find another race under a penalty. *(op 5-1)*
Oscatello(USA) travelled nicely into the straight and presumably Carberry thought the race was his for the taking, only to find Fitzgerald cruising up to him on Temoin approaching the second last. He *finished nicely clear of the third and was unlucky to run into a handicap blot. (op 11-4 tchd 3-1 and 7-2 in a place)*
Brankley Boy, the Henderson second-string, kept on well enough for a clear third. He had won an ordinary event at Plumpton last time but had top-weight here, underlining the average quality of the field as a whole.
Absolutelythebest(IRE), making his debut in handicap company following the necessary three outings, came in for some shrewd each-way support at big prices, but he suffered the fate of all such bets by finishing fourth. *(op 33-1)*
Here We Go(IRE) shapes as though he needs further.
Nice Horse(FR), who almost refused to race last time, consented to jump away with the rest on this occasion, but he remains one to have reservations about. *(op 13-2 tchd 11-1)*
T/Jkpt: Not won. T/Plt: £334.80 to a £1 stake. Pool: £107,050.30. 233.40 winning tickets. T/Qpdt: £169.80 to a £1 stake. Pool: £6,542.90. 28.50 winning tickets. ST

3139 UTTOXETER (L-H)
Saturday, February 4

OFFICIAL GOING: Good to soft (soft in places) (meeting abandoned after race 4 due to lack of medical cover)
Ground was described as 'tacky and dead'. Final fence omitted all chases; final hurdle back straight omitted all hurdles.
Wind: Almost nil. Weather: Overcast and cool

3730 STRATSTONE JAGUAR DERBY MARES' ONLY NOVICES' HURDLE (9 hdls 1 omitted) 2m
1:35 (1:35) (Class 4) 4-Y-0+ **£2,927** (£859; £429; £214)

Form | | | | RPR
2426 **1** **Sweet Oona (FR)**[31] 3242 7-10-12 100 PaulO'Neill(3) 101+
(Miss Venetia Williams) *hld up: hdwy 6th: effrt appr 2 out: styd on to ld last 100yds* **9/4**[1]
2 **2** *4* **Rowlands Dream (IRE)**[18] 3435 6-11-1 RobertWalford 99+
(R H Alner) *sn trcking ldrs: chal 3 out: 3rd whn mstke last: styd on to take 2nd nr fin* **7/2**[2]
1 **3** *1* **Nevsky Bridge**[11] 3550 4-10-7 StephenCraine(5) 94+
(D McCain) *hld up: hdwy 6th: led appr 3 out: wknd and hdd last 100yds* **7/2**[2]
3314 **4** *7* **Sunisa (IRE)**[23] 3347 5-11-1 97 (t) PJBrennan 89+
(J Mackie) *hld up: hdwy 6th: chal 2 out: wknd run-in* **4/1**[3]
PP **5** *3* **Dandygrey Russett (IRE)**[50] 2860 5-11-1 JodieMogford 86
(B D Leavy) *t.k.h: led tl appr 3 out: wknd after 2 out* **33/1**
FP0 **6** *22* **Heathers Girl**[11] 3550 7-11-1 HenryOliver 64
(R Dickin) *nt fluent: in rr: sme hdwy 6th: sn wl outpcd* **66/1**
7 *1 1/4* **Imperialistic (IRE)**[91] 5-11-1 BarryKeniry 63
(K R Burke) *t.k.h: blnd and rdr lost iron briefly 1st: hdwy to chse ldrs 6th: wknd appr next* **11/1**
00P- **8** *dist* **Bourneagainkristen**[317] 4529 8-11-1 NoelFehily —
(C C Bealby) *mstkes: blnd and lost pl 5th: sn bhd: t.o: btn 32l* **100/1**
-PP5 **9** *7* **Pinkerton Mill**[49] 2873 6-11-1 BrianCrowley —
(J T Stimpson) *hld up: in rr whn sltly hmpd 5th: bhd fr 3 out: t.o* **25/1**
0 **10** *24* **Showtime Faye**[5] 3645 4-10-2 AnthonyCoyle(3) —
(A Bailey) *chsd ldrs: lost pl after 5th: sn bhd: wl t.o* **100/1**
000 **P** **Rashida**[44] 2954 4-10-2 (tp) RichardYoung(3) —
(M Appleby) *mid-div: sddle slipped after 2nd: sn p.u* **100/1**
P-0 **P** **Primeshade Promise**[26] 3324 5-11-1 OllieMcPhail —
(D Burchell) *chsd ldrs: rdn and lost pl after 5th: sn bhd: t.o whn p.u bef 3 out* **100/1**

4m 14.8s (14.40) **Going Correction** +0.925s/f (Soft)
WFA 4 from 5yo+ 9lb 12 Ran SP% **115.8**
Speed ratings: **101,99,98,95,93 82,81,—,—,— —,—** CSF £9.96 TOTE £2.60: £1.40, £2.00, £1.50; EX 12.90.
Owner The Leadenhall Partnership **Bred** Hubert Guy **Trained** Kings Caple, H'fords

FOCUS
A modest mares-only novices' hurdle but the form looks fairly reliable rated through the winner and the third.

NOTEBOOK
Sweet Oona(FR), runner-up no less than six times over hurdles previously, was ridden with a degree of patience and she had this won before she could change her mind. *(op 5-2)*
Rowlands Dream(IRE), who looks every inch a chaser, looked well held when clattering the last but in the end her superior stamina saw her claim second spot. *(tchd 4-1)*
Nevsky Bridge, who looked in top trim, went on travelling comfortably but, collared by the winner on the run-in, she was very tired near the line and lost second place.
Sunisa(IRE), in the thick of things two out, faded badly on the run-in.
Dandygrey Russett(IRE), a keen type, took them along but did not see it right out and may need less-testing conditions. *(op 40-1)*
Imperialistic(IRE) would not settle early and made a mess of the first flight. Travelling nicely on the heels of the leaders going to three out, it remains to be seen if her stamina truly lasts out two miles. *(op 9-1)*
Pinkerton Mill *Official explanation: jockey said mare had a breathing problem (op 28-1)*
Rashida *Official explanation: jockey said saddle slipped*

3731 PETER J DOUGLAS ENGINEERING (S) HURDLE (10 hdls 2 omitted) 2m 4f 110y
2:10 (2:10) (Class 5) 4-Y-0+ **£2,081** (£611; £305; £152)

Form | | | | RPR
020U **1** **Prairie Law (GER)**[11] 3546 6-10-11 89 TomMessenger(7) 103+
(B N Pollock) *trckd ldrs: led appr 6th: hdd brifely next: clr 2 out: eased towards fin* **7/1**[3]
6020 **2** *15* **The Wife's Sister**[25] 3335 5-10-6 85 (b) StephenCraine(5) 78
(D McCain) *hld up: hdwy to chse ldrs 5th: wnt 2nd 3 out: no ch w wnr* **8/1**
00-4 **3** *8* **The Last Mohican**[35] 3141 7-10-11 104 (p) RichardSpate(7) 77
(A G Juckes) *in rr: hdwy 6th: sn chsng ldrs: wnt 3rd 3 out: one pce* **5/1**[2]
-635 **4** *1 3/4* **Westernmost**[16] 3467 8-11-4 93 PJBrennan 75
(K Bishop) *wnt prom 6th: rdn and wknd appr 3 out* **10/3**[1]
5522 **5** *14* **Makandy**[25] 3330 7-10-11 84 MrRArmson(7) 70+
(R J Armson) *hld up in rr: hdwy to chse ldrs 5th: led briefly 7th: wknd appr next: poor 5th whn blnd last* **12/1**
F516 **6** *7* **Ask The Umpire (IRE)**[22] 3367 11-11-11 98 (b) MrGBarfoot-Saunt(5) 66
(N E Berry) *chsd ldrs: lost pl after 7th: sn bhd* **5/1**[2]
0030 **7** *8* **Pilca (FR)**[16] 3456 6-10-11 92 (b) WillieMcCarthy(7) 46
(R M Stronge) *trckd ldrs: rdn and lost pl appr 3 out* **12/1**
-660 **P** **Allez Mousson**[52] 2822 8-11-4 79 (p) AndrewThornton —
(A Bailey) *bhd and drvn along 4th: t.o 6th: p.u bef 3 out* **16/1**
0PP0 **U** **Turaath (IRE)**[16] 3458 10-11-11 108 StevenCrawford(5) —
(A J Deakin) *hld up: hdwy and prom whn blnd bdly and uns rdr 4th* **11/1**
/0-P **P** **Gwens Girl**[15] 3478 6-10-4 MrRHodges(7) —
(J Rudge) *t.k.h: led appr 2nd: hdd appr 6th: sn wknd: t.o whn p.u bef 3 out* **100/1**
-0PP **P** **Murotoevation (IRE)**[29] 3275 7-11-4 (v) AntonyEvans —
(D G Bridgwater) *w ldrs: reminders 5th: sn lost pl and bhd: t.o whn p.u bef next* **100/1**
2P **P** **Herons Cove (IRE)**[14] 3496 7-11-4 BrianCrowley —
(W M Brisbourne) *led tl appr 2nd: reminders and lost pl 4th: sn bhd: t.o whn p.u bef 3 out* **33/1**

5m 29.1s (17.00) **Going Correction** +0.925s/f (Soft) **12** Ran SP% **114.5**
Speed ratings: **104,98,95,94,89 86,83,—,—,— —,—** CSF £59.77 TOTE £8.10: £2.30, £2.30, £2.00; EX 67.20.The winner was bought in for 4,800gns.
Owner The Net Partnership **Bred** P Vischer **Trained** Medbourne, Leics

FOCUS
A truly-run seller with an improved effort by the winner and the second running to her mark.

NOTEBOOK
Prairie Law(GER), who likes it round here, was back over hurdles and though he had a bit to find on official ratings, he made this look very simple. It was his first success over jumps on his seventh start and clearly appreciated the extra distance. *(op 11-2)*
The Wife's Sister, a maiden after ten previous starts, put a poor effort at Sedgefield behind her, running close to the mark that saw her finish runner-up here on her previous visit. *(tchd 9-1)*
The Last Mohican, who had a stone in hand of the winner on official figures, was having his second outing in five weeks after a year on the sidelines. *(op 7-1)*
Westernmost, dropped in grade, has yet to prove he truly stays this far. *(op 7-2)*
Makandy, a maiden, would be better off competing at this level in handicaps.

3732 HYDROP NOVICES' H'CAP CHASE (14 fncs 2 omitted) 2m 5f
2:45 (2:45) (Class 4) (0-100,100) 5-Y-0+ **£4,228** (£1,241; £620; £310)

Form | | | | RPR
40F2 **1** **Malko De Beaumont (FR)**[18] 3430 6-11-7 95 JohnMcNamara 110+
(K C Bailey) *hld up: wnt prom 8th: led 3 out: hit next: styd on* **9/2**[2]
0412 **2** *5* **Rosses Point (IRE)**[14] 3499 7-11-3 94 (p) PaulO'Neill(3) 104+
(Evan Williams) *prom: blnd and rdr lost iron briefly 4th: chal 3 out: kpt on same pce* **4/1**[1]
034P **3** *1/2* **Point**[28] 3290 9-11-6 94 MarkBradburne 101
(W Jenks) *mstke 4th: hdwy to chse ldrs 8th: rdn 3 out: styd on run-in* **16/1**
2FP0 **4** *17* **Lady Lambrini**[175] 1203 6-9-9 74 oh3 DerekLaverty(5) 64
(Mrs L Williamson) *chsd ldrs: wknd 3 out* **50/1**
36P5 **5** *4* **Jonny's Kick**[5] 3652 6-11-1 94 (b) StephenCraine(5) 80
(T D Easterby) *hit 2nd: hdwy 8th: rdn 11th: btn appr next* **16/1**
0/1P **6** *11* **Martin Ossie**[22] 3372 9-11-12 100 WarrenMarston 75
(J M Bradley) *led 2nd to 3 out: sn wknd* **12/1**
4-40 **7** *15* **Darnayson (IRE)**[79] 2282 6-11-10 98 AntonyEvans 58
(N A Twiston-Davies) *chsd ldrs: wknd 3 out: 4th whn blnd next: clamboured over last: fin tired* **15/2**
442F **8** *30* **Assumetheposition (FR)**[22] 3368 6-11-2 90 (p) LarryMcGrath 20
(R C Guest) *nt fluent: in rr: sme hdwy whn blnd 8th: bhd fr 11th* **16/1**
PPP- **P** **Harry Harestone**[21] 11-10-8 85 (t) GinoCarenza(3) —
(P J Jones) *bhd fr 8th: t.o whn p.u bef 11th* **50/1**
4P56 **P** **Incorporation**[11] 3549 7-10-10 91 RichardSpate(7) —
(M Appleby) *blnd 2nd: bhd fr 7th: p.u bef 9th* **40/1**
1523 **P** **Avadi (IRE)**[21] 3398 8-10-11 85 AndrewThornton —
(P T Dalton) *sn in rr and drvn along: bhd fr 7th: p.u bef next* **6/1**[3]
63-6 **P** **Smurfit (IRE)**[29] 3274 7-10-3 84 TomMessenger(7) —
(C C Bealby) *led to 2nd: lost pl 9th: sn bhd: t.o whn p.u bef last* **14/1**
P554 **P** **Scarlet Fantasy**[40] 2982 6-11-4 95 OwynNelmes(3) —
(P A Pritchard) *j.rt in rr: bhd fr 9th: t.o whn p.u bef 3 out* **50/1**
4P53 **P** **Thyne Man (IRE)**[35] 3144 8-11-9 97 PJBrennan —
(J Mackie) *prom: reminders and lost pl after 7th: bhd whn p.u bef next* **8/1**

5m 39.1s (11.60) **Going Correction** +0.70s/f (Soft) **14** Ran SP% **115.7**
Speed ratings: **105,103,102,96,94 90,85,73,—,— —,—,—,—** CSF £22.15 CT £257.88 TOTE £4.70: £1.60, £2.50, £5.10; EX 13.90.
Owner Dream Makers Partnership **Bred** Mme Karine Colson **Trained** Preston Capes, Northants
■ Stewards' Enquiry : Warren Marston two-day ban: careless riding (15-16 Feb)

FOCUS
They went a sound gallop and the form looks sound enough rated through the third with both the first two on the up.

NOTEBOOK
Malko De Beaumont(FR), having just his third start over fences, took this in most decisive fashion and this ex-French horse may have even better in him. *(op 5-1)*
Rosses Point(IRE) almost came to grief at the fourth fence. He landed upsides three out but between the last two it was clear that second best was the most he could hope for. He is clearly in good form with himself. *(op 7-2)*
Point jumped better on the whole and the way he stuck to his task on the run-in suggests an even stiffer test will suit him.
Lady Lambrini, 3lb out of the handicap and absent since August, jumped better but her chance had slipped three out. *(op 40-1)*
Jonny's Kick, with the blinkers back on, was struggling early on the final circuit. *(op 14-1)*
Martin Ossie, a multiple point winner, was soon taking them along but the conditions took their toll and he had no more to give when headed three out. He has started life in handicap company from a stiff mark. *(op 9-1 thcd 16-1 in a place)*
Thyne Man(IRE) *Official explanation: jockey said gelding pulled up in a distressed state (op 9-1 tchd 10-1)*
Avadi(IRE) *Official explanation: jockey said gelding was never travelling (op 9-1 tchd 10-1)*

3733 WEATHERBYS INSURANCE H'CAP HURDLE (10 hdls 2 omitted) 2m 4f 110y
3:15 (3:15) (Class 4) (0-115,110) 4-Y-0+ **£5,204** (£1,528; £764; £381)

Form RPR
30P0 **1** **Old Feathers (IRE)**[16] 3458 9-11-4 **102**....(b) NoelFehily 108
(Jonjo O'Neill) *led to 5th: lft in ld 6th: hrd rdn and kpt on fr 3 out: clr between last 2: all out* **9/1**
0261 **2** *3 1/2* **Herecomestanley**[9] 3577 7-10-1 **92**.... CharliePoste(7) 94
(M F Harris) *in rr: hdwy 6th: sn chsng ldrs: wnt 2nd 3 out: kpt on run-in* **9/2**[1]
P-35 **3** *10* **Chamacco (FR)**[19] 3425 6-11-3 **101**.... WarrenMarston 93
(M F Harris) *chsd ldrs: one pce fr 3 out* **25/1**
1515 **4** *7* **Novacella (FR)**[30] 3247 5-11-4 **102**.... AndrewThornton 87
(R H Alner) *hdwy and prom 4th: wknd 3 out* **9/2**[1]
2662 **5** *2* **Eljutan (IRE)**[19] 3428 8-10-8 **99**....(p) ShaneWalsh(7) 82
(J Joseph) *hdwy and prom whn hmpd and lost pl 6th: no threat after* **16/1**
PP60 **6** *17* **Ashleybank House (IRE)**[11] 3548 9-10-10 **94**....(t) RichardHobson 60
(David Pearson) *in rr: reminders 5th: t.o 3 out* **66/1**
3202 **7** *1 1/4* **Haditovski**[17] 3445 10-11-5 **103**....(v) PJBrennan 68
(J Mackie) *chsd ldrs: hmpd 6th: wknd appr 3 out* **5/1**[2]
-044 **8** *17* **Salopian**[23] 3358 6-10-11 **95**.... MarkBradburne 43
(H D Daly) *chsd ldrs: outpcd whn hmpd 6th: bhd fr 3 out* **7/1**[3]
PP64 **B** **All Sonsilver (FR)**[35] 3140 9-10-4 **88**.... HenryOliver —
(P Kelsall) *w ldrs: b.d 6th* **28/1**
2P-3 **P** **Desert Tommy**[35] 3140 5-11-2 **100**.... AntonyEvans —
(Evan Williams) *in rr and drvn 5th: hmpd next: sn p.u* **14/1**
P001 **F** **Titian Flame (IRE)**[11] 3548 6-10-13 **100**....(p) RobertStephens(3) —
(D Burchell) *chsd ldr: led 5th: fell heavily next* **8/1**
P005 **P** **Mnason (FR)**[16] 3465 6-11-9 **107**.... JohnMcNamara —
(S J Gilmore) *bhd fr 6th: t.o whn j. bdly lft 2 out: sn p.u* **33/1**
-PPF **U** **Mazzareme (IRE)**[3] 3675 8-11-9 **110**.... PaulO'Neill(3) —
(Miss Venetia Williams) *wnt prom 3rd: bdly hmpd and uns rdr 6th* **11/1**

5m 32.7s (20.60) **Going Correction** +0.925s/f (Soft) **13** Ran SP% **119.3**
Speed ratings: **97,95,91,89,88 81,81,75,—,— —,—,—** CSF £48.48 CT £996.14 TOTE £11.20: £2.30, £1.60, £17.30; EX 28.20 Place 6 £22.23, Place 5 £17.92.
Owner John Connor **Bred** Roland H Alder **Trained** Cheltenham, Gloucs
■ The lack of adequate medical cover after Robert Stephens was taken to hospital led to the last two races being abandoned.

FOCUS
Not a strong pace and the runner-up looks the key to the value of the overall form.

NOTEBOOK
Old Feathers(IRE), rated a stone higher in his prime, was handed the advantage back and his rider left nothing at all to chance. At the line there was not an ounce left to spare.
Herecomestanley, improved since being fitted with blinkers, went in pursuit of the winner. Although he never gave up he was always going to come off second best. *(op 5-1)*
Chamacco(FR), on his handicap bow, was far from disgraced but he looks on a stiff mark.
Novacella(FR) was again below her best and a shorter trip on less-testing ground might prove the answer. *(op 4-1)*
Eljutan(IRE), in cheekpieces, was effectively put out of the contest in the melee at the sixth flight.
All Sonsilver(FR) was in the process of running a much better race when brought to the ground at the first flight on the final circuit. *(op 25-1)*
Titian Flame(IRE), 9lb higher, had just taken charge when she gave her young rider a horrible-looking fall at the first flight on the final circuit. Happily he was not as badly injured as first feared, but he faces a long road back. *(op 25-1)*
Desert Tommy *Official explanation: jockey said gelding was hampered by a faller and lost its action (op 25-1)*

3734 SHONE BUILDING LTD H'CAP CHASE 2m 6f 110y
() (Class 4) (0-115,) 5-Y-0+ £

3735 BETFAIR.COM STANDARD OPEN NATIONAL HUNT FLAT RACE 2m
() (Class 6) 4-6-Y-0 £

T/Plt: £20.10 to a £1 stake. Pool £55,231.80. 1996.90 winning units T/Qpdt: £5.80 to a £1 stake. Pool £3,653.70. 461.10 winning units WG

3539 WETHERBY (L-H)
Saturday, February 4

OFFICIAL GOING: Soft (good to soft in places)
Wind: Virtually nil Weather: Overcast

3736 WILMOT-SMITH MEMORIAL CUP (A HUNTERS' CHASE) (18 fncs) 3m 1f
1:10 (1:10) (Class 6) 6-Y-0+ **£1,977** (£608; £304)

Form RPR
15-P **1** **Denvale (IRE)**[28] 8-11-11.... MrRCope(3) 117+
(Mrs Caroline Bailey) *cl up: led 6th: rdn along 2 out: hit last: drvn out* **4/1**[2]
4/22 **2** *3* **Marrasit (IRE)**[260] 440 10-10-10.... MrSCharlton(7) 104+
(H E Thorpe) *trckd ldrs: hdwy to chse wnr after 5 out: rdn 2 out: blnd last: kpt on* **12/1**
/P0- **3** *2* **Red Striker**[441] 2344 12-11-5.... MissTJackson(5) 107
(Miss T Jackson) *keen: mstke 1st: hld up towards rr: hdwy 5 out: chsd ldrs next rdn appr 2 out and kpt on same pce* **22/1**
3PP- **4** *2 1/2* **Knife Edge (USA)**[324] 4409 11-11-5 140....(p) MrAJBerry(5) 107+
(Jonjo O'Neill) *trckd ldrs: effrt and mstke 5 out: rdn along after next and kpt on same pce* **5/1**[3]
03-1 **5** *10* **The Butterwick Kid**[275] 196 13-11-11 96....(b) MrRTATate(7) 105+
(T P Tate) *led to 6th: cl up tl rdn along 5 out and grad wknd fr next* **15/2**
30-6 **6** *dist* **Donnybrook (IRE)**[278] 151 13-11-13 92....(p) MrBWoodhouse(5) —
(R D E Woodhouse) *midfield: pushed along 1/2-way: rdn and wknd 6 out: sn bhd* **40/1**
U3-3 **F** **Gatsby (IRE)**[20] 10-11-11.... MrRHFowler(3) —
(J Groucott) *trckd ldrs tl fell 6th* **5/1**[3]
55P- **P** **Camp Hill**[425] 2676 12-11-11.... MrSWByrne(7) —
(J S Haldane) *a rr: bhd whn p.u bef 5 out* **66/1**
52-1 **U** **Raiseapearl**[266] 350 11-11-7.... MissTessaClark(7) —
(Patrick Thompson) *bhd tl blnd and uns rdr 6th* **40/1**
11-1 **P** **Mister Friday (IRE)**[283] 48 9-12-1 112....(v) MrCMulhall(3) —
(C A Mulhall) *rr whn hit 4th: pushed along and sme hdwy whn j. slowly 10th and next: sn lost tch and bhd whn p.u bef 4 out* **15/8**[1]

6m 39.2s (-0.80) **Going Correction** -0.20s/f (Good) **10** Ran SP% **118.3**
Speed ratings: **93,92,91,90,87 —,—,—,—,—** CSF £46.95 TOTE £4.70: £1.60, £2.50, £4.30; EX 57.70.
Owner A Hurn **Bred** R R Clarke **Trained** Holdenby, Northants

FOCUS
A decent hunter chase, with the winner back to the level of his Towcester victory last season.

NOTEBOOK
Denvale(IRE) ◆ looked a bright prospect when scoring at Towcester last March but failed to build on that in three subsequent tries, and this was more like it. Fitter for an outing in a point-to-point at Larkhill last month, he was in front after a mile and stayed on well, jumping soundly apart from hitting the final fence. He is one to keep on the right side. *(op 6-1)*
Marrasit(IRE), having her first run since May, chased the winner hard over the last five fences and a blunder at the last finally ended her challenge. She is still looking for her first win but a greater test of stamina should see her off the mark. *(op 14-1)*
Red Striker, formerly with Richard Guest, gained his last win in the Peter Marsh Chase at Haydock four years ago. Running for the first time since November 2004, he showed that there is still life in him at this lower level. *(op 16-1)*
Knife Edge(USA), last seen pulling up in the World Hurdle at Cheltenham, was equipped with cheekpieces on this hunter chase debut. A mistake five from home did not help, but he lacked anything in the way of a change of gear from that point. All his wins have come at around two miles but he probably stays this trip now. *(tchd 11-2)*
The Butterwick Kid paid his way last term and this was a satisfactory return to action against some useful opposition. *(op 13-2)*
Mister Friday(IRE) put in a number of sluggish jumps and was left behind on the final circuit. He was also pulled up on his seasonal reappearance in this event a year ago before stringing together *five wins, so is well worth another chance, especially on better ground. Official explanation: jockey said gelding had a breathing problem (tchd 9-4)*

3737 RICHARD WHITELEY MEMORIAL H'CAP HURDLE (9 hdls) 2m
1:45 (1:45) (Class 4) (0-115,115) 4-Y-0+ **£3,253** (£955; £477; £238)

Form RPR
2505 **1** **Flake**[40] 2994 6-10-6 **95**.... PadgeWhelan 101+
(Mrs S J Smith) *trckd ldng pair: hdwy 5th: led 4 out: pushed clr after next: rdn and slt ld whn lft clr last* **3/1**[2]
4102 **2** *5* **Eborarry (IRE)**[12] 3539 4-10-11 **110**.... RussGarritty 101
(T D Easterby) *hld up in tch: hdwy 4 out: ch 2 out: sn rdn and kpt on same pce appr last* **3/1**[2]
3F33 **3** *9* **Nerone (GER)**[22] 3378 5-11-2 **105**.... TomDoyle 98+
(P Monteith) *keen: hld up: hdwy after 4 out: chsd ldrs next: rdn after 2 out: sn hung lft and btn* **11/2**[3]
6F10 **4** *10* **Merryvale Man**[22] 3378 9-10-8 **97**.... AlanDempsey 79
(Miss Kariana Key) *led: rdn along 5th: hdd 4 out and wknd bef next* **11/1**
1-00 **5** *13* **Fair Spin**[39] 3040 6-11-5 **108**....(v) WilsonRenwick 77
(M D Hammond) *chsd ldrs: rdn along 1/2-way: sn wknd and bhd fr 4 out* **25/1**
15- **6** *10* **Hegarty (IRE)**[489] 1584 7-11-5 **115**.... MrAJBerry(7) 74
(Jonjo O'Neill) *cl up: rdn along 4 out: sn wknd and bhd fr next* **10/1**
-222 **U** **Turbo (IRE)**[110] 1772 7-11-3 **109**....(t) MrTGreenall(3) 112+
(M W Easterby) *hld up in rr: stdy hdwy on inner 3 out: effrt to chal and ev ch whn mstke and uns rdr last* **11/4**[1]

3m 57.3s (-2.10) **Going Correction** -0.20s/f (Good)
WFA 4 from 5yo+ 9lb **7** Ran SP% **113.3**
Speed ratings: **97,94,90,85,78 73,—** CSF £12.51 TOTE £3.90: £2.10, £2.20; EX 19.20.
Owner Keith Nicholson **Bred** Raffin Stud **Trained** High Eldwick, W Yorks

FOCUS
This was run at a fair pace and the form looks solid enough.

NOTEBOOK
Flake, back down to two miles, was in front leaving the far side and still going well enough, holding an advantage of perhaps half a length, when he was left clear at the last. He should still be well handicapped compared with his chase mark after he has been re-assessed. *(tchd 10-3)*
Eborarry(IRE), whose best performances this term have come in heavy ground, ran a respectable race but was third best on merit. *(op 4-1)*
Nerone(GER), once again rather keen, made his move in the straight but did not find very much and remains essentially frustrating. *(tchd 5-1)*
Merryvale Man, 7lb higher than when winning at Ayr last month, again tried to make all but the game was soon up once he was headed four from home. *(op 9-1 tchd 8-1)*
Hegarty(IRE), previously with Christy Roche, was without the usual tongue-strap for this first start since October 2004 and ran as if the race was needed after such a long absence. *(op 8-1)*
Turbo(IRE), having his first start for Easterby, was without the cheekpieces but had his tongue tied down. Patiently ridden, he gradually closed on the leaders in the home straight and was in second place, about half a length down, when stepping into the final flight and unshipping Greenall. How much he would have found under pressure is open to question and he remains a frustrating maiden over hurdles. *(op 3-1 tchd 10-3 in places)*

3738 BRIT INSURANCE NOVICES' HURDLE (REGISTERED AS THE RIVER DON NOVICES' HURDLE) GRADE 2 (12 hdls) 3m 1f
2:20 (2:20) (Class 1) 4-Y-0+ **£16,662** (£6,238; £3,116; £1,556)

Form RPR
1412 **1** **Neptune Collonges (FR)**[39] 3020 5-11-11 155.... ChristianWilliams 144+
(P F Nicholls) *mde all: pushed along & qcknd 3 out: rdn next: styd on wl* **2/5**[1]
1064 **2** *7* **Rimsky (IRE)**[40] 2956 5-11-11 125....(b) TomSiddall 136
(N A Twiston-Davies) *cl up: effrt 3 out and sn rdn: drvn and one pce after 2 out* **22/1**
/116 **3** *1 3/4* **Ask The Gatherer (IRE)**[34] 3174 8-11-9 122.... PaulMoloney 132
(M Pitman) *hld up in tch: pushed along 4 out: rdn and hdwy next: kpt on u.p appr last* **20/1**
-121 **4** *7* **L'Antartique (FR)**[57] 2755 6-11-9.... JasonMaguire 128+
(Ferdy Murphy) *trckd ldng pair: effrt appr 3 out: sn rdn and hit next: sn btn* **9/2**[2]
1021 **5** *9* **Supreme's Legacy (IRE)**[30] 3253 7-11-5.... RichardMcGrath 114+
(K G Reveley) *hld up in tch: pushed along 4 out: sn rdn and outpcd fr next* **12/1**[3]

6m 19.5s (5.00) **Going Correction** -0.20s/f (Good) **5** Ran SP% **106.4**
Speed ratings: **84,81,81,78,76** CSF £8.78 TOTE £1.40: £1.10, £6.00; EX 7.50.
Owner J Hales **Bred** Gaec Delorme Freres **Trained** Ditcheat, Somerset
■ This event is usually held at Doncaster.

FOCUS
A moderate winning time for a race of its stature. The winner was 12lb below his Chepstow form with the runner-up back to the level of his early-season form.

NOTEBOOK
Neptune Collonges(FR), runner-up in the re-arranged Long Walk Hurdle at Chepstow, gained his second win at this level. Setting only a steady pace, he had a fight on his hands as Rimsky ranged alongside early in the home straight but he kept galloping and pulled away over the last two flights. A thorough stayer, he looks an obvious contender for another the Cheltenham Festival version of the Brit Insurance Novices' Hurdle, although he would not want fast ground. *(tchd 4-9 in places)*
Rimsky(IRE) posed a real threat to the favourite when challenging on the home turn, if anything going the better, but he could not go with his rival from the second last. This was a creditable effort and a return to something like his form of the autumn. *(op 20-1 tchd 25-1)*
Ask The Gatherer(IRE), tackling his stiffest test to date, stayed on quite well late in the day to secure third place on the run-in but in truth was never a threat to the two principals.

L'Antartique(FR) raced in third place for much of the way, but could not go with the first two when the heat was on and was eventually caught for third on the flat as his stamina waned over this longer trip.
Supreme's Legacy(IRE), successful over a quarter of a mile less here a month ago, was found wanting in this company and was always at the rear of the field. *(op 10-1)*

3739 TOTESPORT 0800 221 221 H'CAP CHASE (15 fncs) 2m 4f 110y
2:50 (2:51) (Class 2) (0-150,138) 5-Y-0+
£12,526 (£3,700; £1,850; £926; £462; £232)

Form RPR
-043 **1** **Claymore (IRE)**[21] 3385 10-11-6 **132**.......... LeightonAspell 146+
(O Sherwood) *hld up in tch: hdwy 5 out: chal 3 out: led bef next: rdn last: styd on wl* **5/1**[3]
0202 **2** *1 1/2* **Better Days (IRE)**[21] 3385 10-11-0 **126**.......... RichardMcGrath 140+
(Mrs S J Smith) *in tch: hdwy 5 out: rdn along next: drvn and kpt on fr 2 out* **8/1**
0-43 **3** *3/4* **Non So (FR)**[35] 3136 8-11-11 **137**.......... MarcusFoley 149+
(N J Henderson) *hld up in rr: hdwy 5 out: trckd ldrs 3 out: effrt next: sn rdn and ch tl drvn and one pce flat* **9/2**[2]
-125 **4** *3/4* **Edmo Yewkay (IRE)**[21] 3385 6-11-3 **129**..........(b) RussGarritty 139
(T D Easterby) *a.p: led 8th: rdn along 4 out: hdd appr 2 out: sn drvn and no ex last* **10/1**
6251 **5** *14* **Wain Mountain**[14] 3503 10-11-2 **128**..........(b) JasonMaguire 126+
(J A B Old) *led to 4th: prom tl rdn along appr 4 out and grad wknd* **7/2**[1]
-141 **6** *13* **Schuh Shine (IRE)**[28] 3293 9-11-6 **132**.......... AlanO'Keeffe 123+
(Miss Venetia Williams) *cl up: hit 3rd: led next: hdd 8th: mstke 10th: cl up and rdn along 4 out: wkng whn blnd next* **5/1**[3]
-23F **7** *18* **Halexy (FR)**[76] 2368 11-10-11 **128**.......... PaddyMerrigan[(5)] 93
(Jonjo O'Neill) *in tch: pushed along 1/2-way: rdn 5 out and sn wknd* **10/1**
260P **8** *22* **Quazar (IRE)**[34] 3180 8-11-7 **133**..........(t) ChristianWilliams 76
(Jonjo O'Neill) *towards rr: rdn along 9th: bhd fr 5 out* **16/1**
200- **9** *1 1/2* **The Last Cast**[112] 4382 7-11-12 **138**.......... TomDoyle 80
(P R Webber) *nt fluent: a rr: bhd fr 5 out* **25/1**
5m 12.3s (-8.40) **Going Correction** -0.20s/f (Good) **9** Ran SP% **112.8**
Speed ratings: **108,107,107,106,101 96,89,81,80** CSF £42.99 CT £190.63 TOTE £5.80: £2.40, £2.40, £1.20; EX 47.30 Trifecta £119.60 Pool £556.20. 3.30 winning units..
Owner B T Stewart-Brown **Bred** Cyril O'Hara **Trained** Upper Lambourn, Berks

FOCUS
A decent handicap and a strongly-run event. The first four all ran very close to their marks, suggesting that the form should work out.

NOTEBOOK
Claymore(IRE) took advantage of a lenient mark to post his first victory since he scored over hurdles at this venue two years ago. The strong pace suited him and he was always finding enough once moving to the front, reversing Carlisle form with Better Days on this less testing ground. The valuable Vodafone Gold Cup at Newbury is his suggested target.
Better Days(IRE), 3lb higher, ran another solid race and stayed on to take second place after the last, but could not confirm Carlisle placings with today's winner on 4lb worse terms. *(op 9-1)*
Non So(FR), back up in trip, was steadily introduced into the picture but, having looked to be going well three out, once more found little when let down. He remains one to take on. *(op 4-1 tchd 5-1)*
Edmo Yewkay(IRE) ran another respectable race but looks to be high enough in the weights, 11lb above the mark off which he won over course and distance two months ago. *(op 9-1)*
Wain Mountain, put up 6lb for his win at Lingfield, was taken on for the lead this time and the blinkers did not have quite the same galvanising effect.
Schuh Shine(IRE), racing from a career-high mark, was unable to get his own way in front and, *following errors at the first two fences in the home straight, he came home well beaten.Official explanation: trainer's representative had no explanation for the poor form shown (op 11-2)*
The Last Cast, last of 34 in the Cesarewitch on his most recent start, has since left Hughie Morrison's yard. Saddled with a big weight for a small horse and not jumping well, he was always trailing and looks one to leave alone until he shows signs of a revival.

3740 TOTEPOOL TOWTON NOVICES' CHASE GRADE 2 (18 fncs) 3m 1f
3:25 (3:25) (Class 1) 5-Y-0+ **£18,460** (£7,059; £3,641; £1,923)

Form RPR
-F41 **1** **Halcon Genelardais (FR)**[21] 3391 6-11-10.......... WayneHutchinson 147+
(A King) *trckd ldrs: pushed along 1/2-way: hdwy and cl up 6 out: led appr 4 out: rdn clr next: blnd last* **5/6**[1]
11 **2** *15* **Preacher Boy**[40] 2996 7-11-8 120.......... ChristianWilliams 133+
(R J Hodges) *led tl hdd and hit 10th: mstkes next and 12th: sn rdn along and outpcd: blnd 4 out: styd on u.p to take 2nd nr line* **9/1**
1 **3** *3/4* **Mort De Rire (FR)**[25] 3331 6-11-8.......... DarylJacob 127+
(R H Alner) *trckd ldrs: hdwy to ld 5 out: rdn along and hdd bef next: sn drvn and outpcd fr 3 out: lost 2nd nr line* **8/1**[3]
F213 **4** *18* **Rebel Rhythm**[21] 3391 7-11-4.......... RussGarritty 112+
(Mrs S J Smith) *cl up: led 10th tl rdn along and hdd 5 out: sn wknd* **7/2**[2]
1-12 **F** **Julius Caesar**[63] 2643 6-11-4.......... RichardMcGrath —
(J Howard Johnson) *rr tl fell 11th* **8/1**[3]
6m 39.6s (-0.40) **Going Correction** -0.20s/f (Good) **5** Ran SP% **109.0**
Speed ratings: **92,87,86,81,—** CSF £8.21 TOTE £1.90: £1.10, £3.60; EX 10.80.
Owner Ian Payne & Kim Franklin **Bred** G Descours & Mlle Constance Descours **Trained** Barbury Castle, Wilts

FOCUS
A very moderate time for a Grade Two, slower even than the earlier hunter chase. The winner is rated to his Warwick mark.

NOTEBOOK
Halcon Genelardais(FR) confirmed the favourable impression he gave at Warwick with what was ultimately an authoritative victory. He did not travel all that well for the first circuit, but came back on the bridle to show ahead on the home turn. Soon pulling clear, he had the race seemingly in command when he belted the final fence. He is a high-class novice but his tendency to hit a flat spot could cost him in a more competitive event. *(tchd 11-10 in places)*
Preacher Boy, upped in grade, made a series of jumping errors, one at the fourth from home ending what chance he had. To his credit, he did rally bravely to take second on the run-in. Tackling this trip for the first time under Rules, he looks suited by a test of stamina and was happier going this way round. He is well handicapped at present. *(op 7-1 tchd 10-1)*
Mort De Rire(FR) was quickly elevated in grade after his winning debut in Britain which came on his 13th run over fences. He jumped soundly, but lacked the pace to go with the winner from the third last and was eventually run out of second spot. *(tchd 15-2)*
Rebel Rhythm was 11lb better off with Halcon Genelardais compared with their Warwick meeting but could not take advantage, racing up with the pace for a long way but eventually dropping out of contention in the straight. That is two lacklustre efforts in a row and he has something to prove now. *Official explanation: jockey said gelding had a breathing problem (tchd 4-1)*
Julius Caesar was in last place, and being niggled at, when he appeared distracted by a rival's mistake at the 11th and took a crashing fall. Although he appeared physically unhurt, he might need some time to get over the experience.

3741 TOTEEXACTA H'CAP HURDLE (12 hdls) 2m 7f
4:00 (4:00) (Class 3) (0-135,131) 4-Y-0+ **£6,506** (£1,910; £955; £477)

Form RPR
/5-0 **1** **Albany (IRE)**[30] 3256 6-10-9 **119**.......... BrianHughes[(5)] 124+
(J Howard Johnson) *trckd ldrs: hdwy and cl up 4 out: led appr next and sn rdn clr: styd on wl* **25/1**
4001 **2** *8* **Habitual Dancer**[33] 3208 5-11-1 **120**.......... AlanDempsey 117
(Jedd O'Keeffe) *a.p: effrt to chse wnr 3 out: rdn next and kpt on same pce appr last* **10/1**
0042 **3** *3* **Vicars Destiny**[28] 3289 8-10-11 **116**..........(p) TomSiddall 111+
(Mrs S Lamyman) *hld up: hdwy 1/2-way: chsd ldrs 3 out: sn rdn and mstke next: kpt on u.p fr last* **7/1**
-F44 **4** *nk* **Predicament**[14] 3510 7-10-1 **111**.......... PaddyMerrigan[(5)] 105
(Jonjo O'Neill) *hld up in rr: stdy hdwy 8th: chsd ldrs 3 out: rdn next: sn no imp* **5/1**[3]
5P23 **5** *3* **Totally Scottish**[40] 2990 10-10-2 **117**.......... JamesReveley[(10)] 108
(K G Reveley) *hld up towards rr: sme hdwy 4 out: sn rdn and nvr nr ldrs* **6/1**
-UR1 **6** *14* **Huka Lodge (IRE)**[28] 3289 9-11-0 **119**.......... RichardMcGrath 96
(Mrs K Walton) *led: rdn along 4 out: hdd bef next and sn wknd* **3/1**[1]
4-40 **7** *1 1/4* **Inching Closer**[33] 3208 9-11-9 **131**.......... PeterBuchanan[(3)] 106
(J Howard Johnson) *j.rt and racd wd: in tch tl lost pl and bhd fr 1/2-way* **10/1**
4153 **8** *8* **Tynedale (IRE)**[26] 3318 7-10-10 **120**.......... ThomasDreaper[(5)] 87
(Mrs A Hamilton) *rn in snatches: chsd ldrs: rdn along 4 out: drvn and wknd bef next* **7/2**[2]
5m 45.9s (42.90) **Going Correction** -0.20s/f (Good) **8** Ran SP% **112.7**
Speed ratings: **110,107,106,106,105 100,99,96** CSF £233.69 CT £1939.69 TOTE £33.90: £5.40, £1.60, £2.30; EX 202.50.
Owner Andrea & Graham Wylie **Bred** Jeremy Gompertz **Trained** Billy Row, Co Durham

FOCUS
This fair handicap has been rated through the second but there is a case for rating it higher.

NOTEBOOK
Albany(IRE), returning to a more suitable trip, went for home on the approach to the third last and was always in command from that point. He is well treated on his juvenile form and could be capable of further improvement.
Habitual Dancer, raised 5lb for his Ayr win, was beaten twice off this mark earlier in the season. *Tackling his longest trip to date, he could never get to the front but ran a solid race nonetheless. (op 8-1)*
Vicars Destiny kept on again close home to take third after the last. She could have done with a stronger gallop. *(op 15-2)*
Predicament, previously kept to two miles, was given plenty to do. He improved to threaten briefly *early in the straight, but the winner got first run and he soon faded. This was a bit far for him. (tchd 11-2)*
Totally Scottish has gone up the weights following a brace of respectable placed efforts and could never get into the action. *(op 9-2)*
Huka Lodge(IRE) was unable to dominate in the way that he did at Haydock and was also found *out by the considerably higher mark. Official explanation: trainer had no explanation for the poor form shown (tchd 11-4)*
Inching Closer has now twice failed to confirm the promise of his comeback run at Haydock. *(op 11-1 tchd 12-1)*
Tynedale(IRE) was under pressure a long way out and looked a difficult ride. *(op 9-2 tchd 5-1)*

3742 PHANTOM EUROPEAN STANDARD OPEN NATIONAL HUNT FLAT RACE 2m
4:30 (4:30) (Class 5) 4-6-Y-0 **£2,740** (£798; £399)

Form RPR
22 **1** **Kealshore Lad**[50] 2864 5-10-13.......... DougieCostello[(5)] 105+
(G M Moore) *cl up: led 1/2-way: rdn clr over 2f out: hdd ins last: drvn and rallied to ld nr fin* **4/1**[2]
2 *shd* **Mount Sandel (IRE)** 5-11-4.......... LeightonAspell 105+
(O Sherwood) *hld up: stdy hdwy over 4f out: str run to ld ins last: sn rdn and edgd lft: hdd and no ex towards fin* **10/1**[3]
3 **3** *11* **Classic Harry**[35] 3145 5-11-4.......... RussGarritty 94
(P Beaumont) *led to 1/2-way: cl up tl rdn along over 3f out and kpt on same pce* **14/1**
3 **4** *nk* **Lord Collingwood (IRE)**[21] 3399 5-11-4.......... NeilMulholland 94
(M D Hammond) *hld up towards rr: hdwy over 3f out: kpt on same pce fnl 2f* **12/1**
0 **5** *6* **Colonel Hayes (IRE)**[44] 2948 6-10-13.......... BrianHughes[(5)] 89+
(J I A Charlton) *hld up in tch: effrt over 4f out: sn rdn and no imp fnl 2f* **40/1**
5 **6** *6* **Mi Fa Sol Aulmes (FR)**[73] 2446 6-10-11.......... AlanDempsey 75
(W T Reed) *in tch: hdwy to chse ldrs 6f out: rdn along over 4f out and sn wknd* **50/1**
12 **7** *hd* **Hennessy (IRE)**[26] 3327 5-11-6.......... RobertLucey-Butler[(5)] 89
(M Pitman) *hld up in tch: pushed along 1/2-way: rdn 6f out and sn btn* **4/5**[1]
0 **8** *3* **Smart Street**[69] 2520 4-10-1.......... PhilKinsella[(7)] 69
(K G Reveley) *bhd tl sme late hdwy* **50/1**
9 *5* **Sparky Boy (IRE)** 5-11-1.......... MichalKohl[(3)] 74
(J I A Charlton) *midfield: hdwy to chse ldrs 1/2-way: rdn over 4f out and sn wknd* **33/1**
5 **10** *3* **Young Bobby**[21] 3399 6-11-4.......... AnthonyRoss 71
(P Beaumont) *prom tl rdn along over 5f out and sn wknd* **33/1**
11 *6* **Young Blade** 5-11-4.......... RichardMcGrath 65
(C Grant) *prom tl rdn along over 4f out and sn wknd* **28/1**
36 **12** *9* **Persian Prince (IRE)**[104] 1849 6-11-1.......... PaddyAspell[(3)] 56
(J Wade) *a rr: bhd fr 1/2-way* **40/1**
3m 57.2s (-7.20) **Going Correction** -0.20s/f (Good)
WFA 4 from 5yo+ 9lb **12** Ran SP% **117.1**
Speed ratings: **98,97,92,92,89 86,86,84,82,80 77,73** CSF £40.02 TOTE £5.40: £1.60, £2.70, £4.10; EX 26.90 Place 6 £208.72, Place 5 £50.05.
Owner J Pickavance **Bred** A K Smeaton **Trained** Middleham, N Yorks
■ Stewards' Enquiry : Michal Kohl caution: careless riding

FOCUS
Not many got into this bumper, which was run at no great pace. The form is fair, the first two looking reasonable prospects.

NOTEBOOK
Kealshore Lad, runner-up on his first two starts, looked as if he would have to settle for second again when he was collared with 100 yards to run but he rallied to snatch the race, his greater experience settling the issue. He should stay well when he goes over hurdles. *(tchd 9-2)*
Mount Sandel(IRE), whose dam was a sister to smart hurdler Mighty Mogul, is a brother to useful novice chase winner Court Leader. Coming from off the pace, he looked sure to win when cutting down the leader inside the last, only to run green in front and invite his rival in for another chance.
Classic Harry filled the same position on his debut at Uttoxeter but this was the better effort.

Lord Collingwood(IRE) ran to a similar level to that of his debut over a quarter of a mile shorter here and confirmed the impression that he is a staying type. *(op 20-1)*
Colonel Hayes(IRE) did not shape without promise on his Ayr debut and confirmed that he has ability.
Hennessy(IRE) was beaten a good way out and this was disappointing. A stronger pace would have suited him and he might not have handled the ground, but had an excuse as he was later reported to have scoped dirty. *Official explanation: jockey said gelding ran flat (tchd 5-6 in places)*
T/Plt: £448.10 to a £1 stake. Pool: £53,013.65. 86.35 winning tickets. T/Qpdt: £13.30 to a £1 stake. Pool: £4,476.70. 248.50 winning tickets. JR

3743 - 3749a (Foreign Racing) - See Raceform Interactive

3611 CHEPSTOW (L-H)
Sunday, February 5
3750 Meeting Abandoned - Frost

3484 MUSSELBURGH (R-H)
Sunday, February 5
OFFICIAL GOING: Good to firm (good in places)
Wind: Moderate, across

3757 JOHN SMITH'S NO NONSENSE H'CAP HURDLE (12 hdls) 2m 4f
1:10 (1:13) (Class 5) (0-95,95) 4-Y-0+ **£2,740** (£798; £399)

Form RPR
5601 **1** **Silver Seeker (USA)**[18] [3446] 6-10-9 **85**.................... PatrickMcDonald(7) 90
(A R Dicken) *hld up towards rr: hdwy to trck ldrs 3 out: rdn to chse ldr after 2 out: hit last: styd on to ld last 100 yds* **16/1**
6-45 **2** 1½ **I Got Rhythm**[30] [3271] 8-11-12 **95**.................................. RichardMcGrath 99
(K G Reveley) *hld up towards rr: gd hdwy on inner after 4 out: led next: hit 2 out: rdn last: hdd and no ex last 100 yds* **8/1**[3]
6400 **3** 1½ **Opal's Helmsman (USA)**[16] [3487] 7-10-13 **82**..........(v) DominicElsworth 84
(W S Colthered) *in tch: hdwy 3 out: rdn next: styd on appr last: nrst fin* **50/1**
0066 **4** 1½ **Silver Bow**[33] [3235] 5-11-2 **85**.................................. GrahamLee 86
(J M Jefferson) *in tch: hdwy to chse ldrs 3 out: rdn next and kpt on same pce* **25/1**
6PP0 **5** 3½ **Emerald Destiny (IRE)**[24] [3349] 4-10-12 **92**..................... AlanDempsey 78
(Jedd O'Keeffe) *midfield: hdwy to chse ldrs 4 out: rdn along next and kpt on same pce: fin 6th, 1½l, 1½l, 1½l, 1l & 2½l: plced 5th* **33/1**
6 3 **Ablastfromthepast (IRE)**[56] [2783] 6-11-5 **88**..................... TonyDobbin 82
(C F Swan, Ire) *hld up in tch: smooth hdwy to trck ldrs 4 out: shkn up next: rdn 2 out and sn wknd: fin 7th, plcd 6th* **10/1**
2P00 **7** 1¼ **Talarive (USA)**[24] [3351] 10-11-12 **95**................................(tp) JimCrowley 88
(P D Niven) *hld up rr: hdwy appr 3 out: kpt on: nvr a factor: plcd 7th* **25/1**
5664 **8** 6 **Drumossie (AUS)**[11] [3562] 6-11-1 **84**.............................(p) LarryMcGrath 73+
(R C Guest) *chsd ldrs: hdwy to ld after 4 out: rdn and hdd next: sn drvn and wknd 2 out: fin 9th, plcd 8th* **25/1**
0500 **9** 10 **Norminster**[23] [3376] 5-10-9 **85**.. GarethThomas(7) 62
(R Nixon) *a rr: fin 10th, plcd 9th* **66/1**
10 hd **Master Massini (IRE)**[41] [3013] 6-11-12 **95**...................(v[1]) MickFitzgerald 72
(P Hughes, Ire) *chsd ldrs: rdn along 4 out: sn wknd: fin 11th, plcd 10th* **16/1**
-056 **11** 15 **Killer Cat (FR)**[61] [2687] 5-11-10 **93**...............................(tp) TimmyMurphy 67+
(M C Pipe) *chsd ldrs: rdn along 1/2-way: effrt to chse ldrs 3 out: wknd next: fin 12th, plcd 11th* **13/2**[2]
434F **12** 3½ **Prince Adjal (IRE)**[24] [3348] 6-10-9 **81**.................................. MrCStorey(3) 39
(Miss S E Forster) *prom: led and hit 5th: mstke 7th: rdn 4 out: sn hdd & wknd: fin 13th, plcd 12th* **25/1**
61F0 **13** 5 **Scarrabus (IRE)**[16] [3489] 5-11-2 **90**............................. DeclanMcGann(5) 43
(A Crook) *chsd ldrs: hit 4th: mstke 7th: rdn and wknd next: plcd 13th* **50/1**
6P0P **D** **Brave Effect (IRE)**[26] [3338] 10-11-1 **91**........................ StevenGagan(7) —
(Mrs Dianne Sayer) *led tl tk wrong crse after 3rd: cont'd: fin 5th: disq* **33/1**
P **Commanche Tryer (IRE)**[14] [3522] 8-11-6 **89**........................ TomSiddall —
(C F Swan, Ire) *bhd: t.o whn blnd 7th and p.u after* **33/1**
2311 **U** **Bohemian Spirit (IRE)**[30] [3272] 8-11-5 **95**.................. MissRDavidson(7) —
(N G Richards) *trckd ldrs tl stmbld and uns rdr 2nd* **11/8**[1]
P **Pathughkenjo (IRE)**[99] [1932] 6-10-8 **82**...................... PaddyMerrigan(5) —
(S Donohoe, Ire) *prom: lft in ld after 3rd: hdd and hit 5th: wknd qckly after next: bhd whn p.u bef 8th* **20/1**
4m 51.5s (-3.00) **Going Correction** -0.10s/f (Good)
WFA 4 from 5yo+ 10lb 17 Ran SP% **121.8**
Speed ratings: **102,101,100,100,98 97,97,94,90,90 84,83,81,—,— —,—** CSF £121.19 CT £6186.68 TOTE £21.80: £2.80, £1.80, £6.10, £3.90; EX 128.40.
Owner A R Dicken **Bred** Darley Stud Management, L L C **Trained** West Barns, E Lothian
■ Stewards' Enquiry : Steven Gagan 24-day ban: took wrong course (10 days) and continued to race after doing so (14 days) (Feb 16-Mar 11)

FOCUS
A low-grade affair, but appears sound enough rated through the placed horses and the form should work out. The pace was sound and the principals came from the rear.

NOTEBOOK
Silver Seeker(USA) followed up his Ayr win off a 7lb higher mark. He had a bit of work to do leaving the back straight, but as at Ayr the strong pace suited him, and he knuckled down well to get on top after the last. He is versatile with regard to ground conditions.
I Got Rhythm, sharper for her recent run and down in trip, showed ahead at the first flight in the home straight and only gave best halfway up the run-in. *(tchd 10-1)*
Opal's Helmsman(USA), visored for the first time over hurdles, came home in good style but too late. This trip is a bit sharp for him. *(op 40-1)*
Silver Bow ran an improved race on this handicap debut and produced form in line with her first run in a bumper. *(op 20-1)*
Emerald Destiny(IRE) has yet to be placed over hurdles but the step up to two and a half miles did bring about an improved effort. *(tchd 50-1)*
Ablastfromthepast(IRE) had been well beaten on all five of his starts in Ireland, but all were on testing ground over two miles. After travelling strongly, he failed to produce much when let down. *(op 12-1)*
Brave Effect(IRE) was in front when taking the chase course at the intersection turning out of the end of the back straight. At first Gagan seemed to realise his mistake and to be about to pull his mount up, but when the rest of the runners appeared alongside him in the home straight he carried on, racing ahead of the field. He took the wrong course again at the same point on the second circuit, continued once more, and actually took the last flight in front and rode a finish before passing the post in fifth. Unsurprisingly the Stewards came down hard on him.
Bohemian Spirit(IRE) was bidding for a course hat-trick off no less than 27lb lower than his current chase mark. He made all for his two wins over fences, but was held up behind the leaders at the time of his slightly unfortunate early departure. *(op 6-4)*

3758 JOHN SMITH'S HUNTERS' CHASE (18 fncs) 3m
1:40 (1:40) (Class 6) 5-Y-0+ **£1,977** (£608; £304)

Form RPR
6/B- **1** **Albatros (FR)**[14] 9-11-7 .... MrRTrotter(7) 96+
(A R Trotter) *trckd ldrs: hdwy to ld after 5 out: rdn 2 out: styd on wl flat* **8/1**
2 2 **Gudasmum**[14] 8-11-4 .... MissRDavidson(3) 87
(J P Elliot) *hld up in tch: hdwy on inner 4 out: rdn to chal 2 out and ev ch tl one pce fr last* **3/1**[2]
-21P **3** 1¾ **Jupiter's Fancy**[14] 11-11-7 .... MrSWByrne(7) 92
(M V Coglan) *hld up: hdwy 5 out: chsd ldrs 3 out: rdn and ch 2 out: sn drvn and one pce last* **6/1**
435 **4** 20 **Starbuck**[14] 12-11-7 80.. MissTessaClark(7) 80+
(Miss J Fisher) *cl up: reminders 9th: rdn along after 5 out and wknd after next* **11/4**[1]
P44- **U** **Lisdante (IRE)**[14] 13-11-9 100......................................(p) MrTDavidson(5) —
(W G Young) *a rr: bhd whn blnd and uns rdr 6 out* **16/1**
-P45 **P** **Mydante (IRE)**[7] 11-11-11 79..(t) MrAWintle(3) —
(S Flook) *trckd ldrs: blnd and lost pl 10th: p.u after next* **10/3**[3]
P-66 **F** **Nisbet**[253] [555] 12-12-0 67.. MissJRiding(7) —
(Miss M Bremner) *led: hit 5th: rdn along and slt ld whn fell 5 out* **16/1**
6m 2.00s (-3.00) **Going Correction** -0.10s/f (Good) 7 Ran SP% **111.9**
Speed ratings: **101,100,99,93,— —,—** CSF £31.62 TOTE £9.10: £4.10, £1.60; EX 27.10.
Owner A R Trotter **Bred** Mrs Martine Van De Kerchove **Trained** Duns, Borders

FOCUS
A modest event of its type and the form is suspect, but the time was fair and it might work out.

NOTEBOOK
Albatros(FR), behind Jupiter's Fancy in point on his recent return from a lay-off, showed the clear benefit of that outing and ran out a ready winner on ground he loves. His task was aided by the fall of Nisbet five from home, but this proves he stays three miles on an easy track, and this one-time fair Irish performer can build on this now he has got his head back in front.
Gudasmum, having her first outing under Rules, held every chance, but found just the same pace when it really mattered on the run-in. She is consistent, may have found this ground a touch too quick, and has the ability to go one better in a similar race this year. *(op 15-8)*
Jupiter's Fancy, who had the winner behind her when fourth on her recent return between the flags a fortnight previously, failed to confirm that form on this quicker ground and looks in need of the return to a stiffer test. *(op 15-2 tchd 8-1 in places)*
Starbuck, well backed, turned in a tame effort by his own standards and was never a serious threat. He may benefit from the application of some headgear in the future. *(op 7-2 tchd 4-1 in places)*
Mydante(IRE) was quickly pulled up after a bad error at the tenth fence and disappointed. *(op 7-2)*
Nisbet was being ridden prior to falling five out, but was still in with a big chance of being placed at the least and has to rate a little unlucky. *(op 7-2)*

3759 JOHN SMITH'S SCOTTISH TRIUMPH HURDLE TRIAL (A JUVENILE NOVICES' HURDLE) (9 hdls) 2m 1f
2:15 (2:15) (Class 2) 4-Y-0 **£12,572** (£3,746; £1,896; £972; £508)

Form RPR
2 **1** **Premier Dane (IRE)**[30] [3267] 4-10-12 .... TonyDobbin 115+
(N G Richards) *hld up: nt fluent: smooth hdwy appr 3 out: shkn up next: rdn to chal last: drvn to ld flat: kpt on* **5/2**[1]
262 **2** hd **My Immortal**[9] [3594] 4-10-12 .... TimmyMurphy 115+
(M C Pipe) *set gd pce: pushed along and qcknd 3 out: rdn along next: jnd and hit last: drvn and hdd flat: kpt on gamely* **3/1**[2]
1 **3** ¾ **Dear Villez (FR)**[19] [3429] 4-11-3 .... LiamHeard 119+
(P F Nicholls) *trckd ldrs: pushed along and outpcd 4 out: hdwy after next: sn rdn and styd on wl flat* **7/2**[3]
21 **4** 22 **Gidam Gidam (IRE)**[48] [2921] 4-11-3 ....(p) TomSiddall 96
(J Mackie) *chsd ldng pair: mstke 3rd: hit next: rdn along and nt fluent: outpcd fr 4 out* **16/1**
5320 **5** hd **Best Game**[16] [3203] 4-10-12 105......................................(p) OwynNelmes 91
(D W Thompson) *chsd ldr: cl up and hit 4 out: sn rdn and wknd next* **100/1**
21 **P** **Ortolan Bleu (FR)**[40] [3038] 4-11-6 .... GrahamLee —
(J Howard Johnson) *trckd ldrs tl p.u lame after 3rd* **3/1**[2]
0U0P **F** **Annals**[9] [3594] 4-10-5 .... JohnFlavin —
(R C Guest) *a rr: bhd fr 1/2-way: t.o whn fell 2 out* **200/1**
4m 9.60s (3.90) 7 Ran SP% **108.2**
CSF £9.39 TOTE £3.50: £2.00, £2.10; EX 9.80.
Owner Jim Ennis **Bred** J F Tuthill **Trained** Greystoke, Cumbria

FOCUS
A fair juvenile hurdle in which three of the four principals in the market pulled clear. The third, fourth and fifth were close to their marks and the form should work out.

NOTEBOOK
Premier Dane(IRE), a useful sort on the Flat in Ireland, needed to step up significantly on his debut second at the course last month and did himself no favours with an untidy round of jumping. He still proved good enough however, making stylish headway into a challenging position before battling on gamely to hold the dogged My Immortal, who could not get back up. He will need to brush up his jumping for future assignments, but remains open to improvement and should be capable of defying a penalty. *(op 3-1)*
My Immortal second past the post in a controversial race at Fakenham towards the end of last month, was given a non-nonsense ride by Murphy and tried to stretch his field, but lacked the pace to get away from his rivals. He battled back gamely on the run-in, but was unable to get back up and the mistake he made at the last may have cost him. Ideally suited by a softer surface, it is a matter of time before he finds a race and he could be the type to run well under similar tactics in the juvenile handicap at the Festival. *(op 9-4)*
Dear Villez(FR), tried unsuccessfully in Listed hurdles in France, made a good start to his British career when winning at Folkestone, but this was a much better race on contrasting ground and he was unable to defy his penalty. The best horse in the race at the weights, a return to easier going will help and he remains a promising sort. *(op 11-4)*
Gidam Gidam(IRE) did it well at Doncaster under similar ground conditions, but this was an altogether better contest and he lacked the class to get involved. He will find easier opportunities and is likely to appreciate further in time. *(op 14-1)*
Ortolan Bleu(FR), experiencing quick ground for the first time, sadly broke a leg with under a circuit to go and had to be put down. *(op 4-1)*

3760 JOHN SMITH'S BEGINNERS' CHASE (18 fncs) 3m
2:50 (2:50) (Class 4) 5-Y-0+ **£3,903** (£1,146; £573; £286)

Form RPR
1536 **1** **Hot Weld**[54] [2812] 7-10-13 107...................................... ThomasDreaper(5) 110+
(Ferdy Murphy) *cl up: led 12th: rdn clr 4 out: styd on wl* **9/2**[3]
3-40 **2** 22 **Manx Royal (FR)**[29] [3289] 7-11-4 .... TimmyMurphy 98+
(M C Pipe) *hld up and bhd: mstke 10th: hit 12th: pushed along 5 out: rdn next styd on to chse wnr 3 out: sn drvn and no imp* **4/6**[1]

-1P3 **3** *5* **Bellaney Jewel (IRE)**[35] 3170 7-10-11 .... GrahamLee 77+
(J J Quinn) *cl up: led 3rd to 12th: rdn along after 5 out: drvn and wkng whn blnd 3 out* **7/2**[2]

5050 **4** *3 ½* **Derainey (IRE)**[27] 3317 7-11-4 .... KennyJohnson 80+
(R Johnson) *led to 3rd: prom tl mstke 13th and sn wknd* **50/1**

0066 **5** *7* **Hot Air (IRE)**[24] 3352 8-11-1 ....(t) MichalKohl[(3)] 74+
(J I A Charlton) *chsd ldrs: hit 8th: blnd 12th: sn rdn and wknd after 5 out* **33/1**

P00 **U** **Chanteuse**[49] 2901 6-10-4 .... PhilKinsella[(7)] —
(Mrs Marjorie Fife) *in tch tl blnd and uns rdr 11th* **25/1**

6m 3.30s (-1.70) **Going Correction** -0.10s/f (Good) **6** Ran SP% **109.1**
Speed ratings: **98,90,89,87,85** — CSF £7.99 TOTE £5.30: £1.80, £1.10; EX 11.50.
Owner S Hubbard Rodwell **Bred** Cartmel Bloodstock **Trained** West Witton, N Yorks

FOCUS
A modest event that took little winning, and the field came home strung out behind the easy winner. The form looks suspect.

NOTEBOOK
Hot Weld got off the mark over fences at the fourth attempt with a clear-cut display. While this race took little winning - with Manx Royal performing well below expectations - he could do no more than this win as he did. He has the scope to rate higher as a chaser and the faster ground was clearly much to his liking. *(op 5-2 tchd 5-1)*
Manx Royal(FR), rated 130 over hurdles, was ridden to get this trip, yet never appeared convincing over his fences and his fate was sealed a long way from home on this chasing bow. This was disappointing, but he is at least entitled to improve for the experience, and he should be happier when reverting to shorter. *(op 4-5)*
Bellaney Jewel(IRE) ran her race and was ultimately well beaten. She should fare better when sent handicapping and returning to a stiffer track in the future. *(op 4-1 tchd 5-1 in a place)*
Derainey(IRE) turned in his best effort to date and enjoyed the chance to race prominently. He eventually found this trip too far, but his jumping was better this time, and he should find his feet in low-grade handicaps in this sphere. *(op 33-1)*

3761 JOHN SMITH'S SCOTTISH COUNTY HURDLE (A H'CAP) (9 hdls) 2m
3:25 (3:25) (Class 2) (0-140,132) 4-Y-0+
£18,789 (£5,550; £2,775; £1,389; £693; £348)

Form RPR

134 **1** **Crow Wood**[86] 2161 7-11-4 **124** .... RussGarritty 135+
(J J Quinn) *trckd ldng pair gng wl: led 3 out: wandered and mstke next: rdn and qcknd clr flat* **9/2**[2]

6U11 **2** *7* **Saif Sareea**[49] 2904 6-10-4 **110** .... PadgeWhelan 111
(R A Fahey) *hld up in midfield: hdwy whn hit 4 out: cl up next: rdn and ev ch 2 out: kpt on* **15/2**[3]

2134 **3** *½* **Rising Generation (FR)**[23] 3378 9-10-9 **125** .... FearghalDavis[(10)] 126
(N G Richards) *cl up: rdn along 3 out: drvn next and kpt on same pce appr last* **66/1**

1145 **4** *¾* **High Day**[41] 2991 6-10-10 **123** .... PatrickMcDonald[(7)] 123
(Ferdy Murphy) *in tch: pushed along and sltly outpcd appr 3 out: rdn and kpt on fr next* **33/1**

113 **5** *¾* **Acambo (GER)**[26] 3328 5-11-9 **129** .... TimmyMurphy 130+
(M C Pipe) *hld up towards rr: hdwy on outer 4 out: chsd ldrs next: swtchd rt and rdn bef last: sn drvn and one pce* **2/1**[1]

P-21 **6** *3 ½* **Motive (FR)**[35] 3171 5-11-1 **121** .... GrahamLee 117
(J Howard Johnson) *hld up towards rr: hdwy 4 out: chsd ldrs next: sn rdn and one pce fr 2 out* **14/1**

0500 **7** *¾* **Border Tale**[48] 2925 6-9-9 **106** oh1 .... DougieCostello[(5)] 101
(James Moffatt) *bhd tl styd on fr 3 out: nrst fin* **100/1**

1F0- **8** *½* **Liberty Seeker (FR)**[167] 4860 7-11-6 **126** .... TonyDobbin 121+
(G A Swinbank) *hld up in tch: hdwy to chse ldrs appr 3 out: rdn and wknd next* **12/1**

0111 **9** *1 ¼* **Nippy Des Mottes (FR)**[15] 3510 5-11-7 **132** ....(t) LiamHeard[(5)] 125
(P F Nicholls) *in tch: rdn along appr 3 out: wknd fr next* **9/2**[2]

5201 **10** *nk* **Calatagan (IRE)**[26] 3329 7-11-0 **125** .... ThomasDreaper[(5)] 120+
(J M Jefferson) *mde most tl rdn along, mstke, and hdd 3 out: drvn and hit next: sn wknd* **25/1**

-422 **11** *¾* **Miss Kilkeel (IRE)**[182] 1172 8-9-7 **106** oh2 .... DavidCullinane[(7)] 98
(R T J Wilson, Ire) *hld up in rr: hdwy appr 3 out: sn rdn and nvr a factor* **200/1**

2U2P **12** *7* **Andre Chenier (IRE)**[22] 3383 5-10-11 **117** .... NeilMulholland 102
(P Monteith) *hld up in rr: hdwy and in tch 4 out: rdn along next and sn wknd* **50/1**

-600 **13** *2 ½* **Credit (IRE)**[23] 3378 5-10-5 **116** .... BrianHughes[(5)] 99
(J Howard Johnson) *midfield: rdn along appr 4 out and sn wknd* **50/1**

2P5F **14** *hd* **Gone Too Far**[23] 3378 8-10-11 **120** ....(v) PaddyAspell[(3)] 102
(P Monteith) *midfield: rdn along and wknd appr 4 out* **66/1**

0025 **15** *7* **Bodfari Signet**[16] 3487 10-10-0 **106** oh1 .... TomSiddall 81
(Mrs S C Bradburne) *chsd ldrs: pushed along 5th: sn lost pl and bhd* **66/1**

-134 **16** *nk* **Millagros (IRE)**[23] 2904 6-10-7 **113** .... JimCrowley 88
(I Semple) *hld up: a rr* **16/1**

2520 **17** *1 ½* **Sovereign State (IRE)**[45] 2952 9-10-5 **114** ....(p) OwynNelmes[(3)] 88
(D W Thompson) *midfield: mstke 4th: sn rdn along and bhd fr 4 out* **80/1**

3m 46.0s (-5.20) **Going Correction** -0.10s/f (Good) **17** Ran SP% **119.6**
Speed ratings: **109,105,105,104,104 102,102,102,101,101 100,97,96,96,92 92,91** CSF £35.96 CT £1973.80 TOTE £5.20: £1.80, £1.90, £7.90, £5.20; EX 32.10 TRIFECTA Not won..
Owner Mrs Marie Taylor **Bred** C Humphris **Trained** Settrington, N Yorks

FOCUS
A very competitive handicap, run at a decent pace, and personal bests from both of the first two, who still look capable of even better. The form looks solid.

NOTEBOOK
Crow Wood, making his handicap debut in this sphere and returning from an 86-day break, ran out a most convincing winner and clearly relished the return to a flatter track and faster ground. He did well to win as he did after awkward jumps over the final two flights and he will no doubt improve again for this experience. His next intended targets are reportedly the Winter Derby Trial at Lingfield and the Supreme Novices' Hurdle at Cheltenham, but he did not look totally at home on the latter track on his previous outing, and the Grade Two over two miles at Aintree would appeal as a better novice opportunity. Connections also have the handicap option still, and the John Smith's Extra Smooth Handicap at Aintree and the Swinton Hurdle at Haydock would be right up his street. *(op 4-1 tchd 5-1 in a place)*
Saif Sareea, bidding for the hat-trick from an 8lb higher mark, having won his last two outings over course and distance, was put in his place by the winner yet turned in a personal best in defeat. He had conditions very much to suit, and is progressive, but the Handicapper will no doubt raise him again after this. *(op 8-1)*
Rising Generation(FR) posted another rock-solid effort in defeat, on ground he would have found plenty quick enough, and clearly remains in decent heart at present. While he will get no respite from the Handicapper with efforts such as this, he is currently rated 9lb lower over fences, and would be well worth supporting if switched to that arena in the coming weeks.
High Day returned to form with a sound effort on this handicap debut. He did not appear totally suited by this sharp track, however, and is open to improvement from his current mark when reverting to a stiffer test.
Acambo(GER), reverting to a faster surface and making his handicap debut over hurdles, threatened to play a part at the top of the straight, but he failed to sustain his effort when it mattered and was ultimately well held. This was disappointing and he has it all to prove now. *(op 7-4 tchd 13-8 and 9-4 in a place)*
Motive(FR), raised 5lb for winning at Catterick last time, was not at all disgraced from this new mark, but the Handicapper looks to have him about right now. *(tchd 12-1)*
Nippy Des Mottes(FR), bidding for a four-timer, could offer no more when it mattered from the penultimate flight and most likely found the combination of this much sharper track and quicker ground against him. *(op 5-1 tchd 6-1)*
Millagros(IRE) *Official explanation: jockey said mare was never travelling (op 20-1)*

3762 JOHN SMITH'S H'CAP CHASE (18 fncs) 3m
3:55 (3:55) (Class 5) (0-95,93) 5-Y-0+ **£3,253** (£955; £477; £238)

Form RPR

-PF5 **1** **No Kidding**[16] 3486 12-10-3 **73** .... MichalKohl[(3)] 87+
(J I A Charlton) *in tch: hdwy 4 out: rdn along 2 out: led appr last: styd on wl* **25/1**

0054 **2** *1 ¼* **Renvyle (IRE)**[16] 3486 8-11-1 **92** ....(e) JohnFlavin[(10)] 105+
(R C Guest) *in tch: hdwy 4 out: rdn to chse ldrs 2 out: styd on u.p fr last* **12/1**

362 **3** *nk* **Gangsters R Us (IRE)**[16] 3486 10-11-5 **93** .... PhilKinsella[(7)] 105
(A Parker) *hld up in rr: stdy hdwy 6 out: led 3 out: riddemn and hdd appr last: one pce* **9/2**[3]

F4P1 **4** *2* **Another Club Royal**[16] 3486 7-11-2 **88** ....(bt) StephenCraine[(5)] 98
(D McCain) *trckd ldrs: pushed along 10th: reminders next: drvn along and lost pl after 5 out: styd on u.p fr 2 out* **7/2**[2]

0P60 **5** *3* **Benefit**[12] 3547 12-10-4 **71** .... TomSiddall 80+
(Miss L C Siddall) *cl up: led after 5 out: rdn and hdd 3 out: wknd after next* **13/2**

1-U0 **6** *10* **Gallion's Reach (IRE)**[41] 2957 11-10-1 **68** ow1..............(p) PaulMoloney 65
(M F Harris) *led: rdn along 6 out: hdd after next and sn wknd* **8/1**

0656 **7** *28* **Pornic (FR)**[18] 3446 12-9-12 **68** ....(b) OwynNelmes[(3)] 37
(A Crook) *trckd ldrs: hdwy and cl up 1/2-way: pushed along whn hit 5 out: rdn along and wknd next* **16/1**

40/0 **P** **Troysgreen (IRE)**[40] 3042 8-10-0 **67** oh4 .... JimCrowley —
(P D Niven) *a rr: bhd fr 1/2-way: p.u bef 4 out* **50/1**

0003 **P** **Bromley Abbey**[16] 3484 8-10-13 **85** ....(p) DougieCostello[(5)] —
(Miss S E Forster) *nt fluent: a rr: bhd fr ½-wy: p.u bef 4 out* **20/1**

4P22 **P** **Not A Trace (IRE)**[16] 3489 7-11-12 **93** .... WilsonRenwick —
(Mrs S C Bradburne) *chsd ldrs: rdn along 11th: wknd 6 out and bhd whn p.u bef 4 out* **5/2**[1]

5m 58.7s (-6.30) **Going Correction** -0.10s/f (Good) **10** Ran SP% **117.6**
Speed ratings: **106,105,105,104,103 100,91,—,—,—** CSF £281.25 CT £1610.23 TOTE £46.70: £6.00, £3.50, £2.10; EX 338.00.
Owner Miss J Palmer **Bred** Miss Joyce Palmer **Trained** Stocksfield, Northumberland

FOCUS
A surprise result with 25/1 No Kidding galloping on too strongly for all his rivals. The third and fourth were close to their marks and the form appears solid.

NOTEBOOK
No Kidding has down all his racing here since returning in November and, off a 10lb lower mark than for that first run back, he was able to win for the first time since October 2003. He is obviously getting no better at the age of 12, but was on a good mark and it will be interesting to see if he can hold his form. *Official explanation: trainer's representative had no explanation for the improved form shown (op 20-1)*
Renvyle(IRE) has long been a tricky customer, but he did little wrong in defeat and was simply not good enough on the day. He is back on a fair mark and it would not surprise to see him find a small race in the coming weeks. *(op 10-1 tchd 14-1)*
Gangsters R Us(IRE) is a tough, consistent gelding, but he has gone without a win since completing a hat-trick in February of 2004 and is likely to remain vulnerable. *(op 4-1 tchd 5-1)*
Another Club Royal, up 13lb for his course win last month, was unable to handle the rise, but is definitely going the right way and may yet be capable of improving further. *(op 3-1 tchd 4-1 in places)*
Benefit is back on a fair mark but needs to show more than he did here before he can be considered. *(op 7-1)*
Not A Trace(IRE) has been in decent form and was again expected to go well here, but he failed to run his race and something may well have been amiss. *Official explanation: trainer said gelding appeared to run ungenuine today and may benefit from blinkers next time (op 7-2)*

3763 JOHN SMITH'S INTERMEDIATE OPEN NATIONAL HUNT FLAT RACE 2m
4:30 (4:30) (Class 6) 4-6-Y-0 **£2,055** (£599; £299)

Form RPR

1 **New Dancer** 4-10-8 .... TonyDobbin 94+
(K A Ryan) *in tch: hdwy to trck ldrs 6f out: led over 3f out: rdn clr 2f out: styd on wl* **11/2**[3]

2 *7* **Gripit N Tipit (IRE)**[41] 3008 5-11-4 .... MickFitzgerald 94
(C F Swan, Ire) *hld up: hdwy over 4f out: rdn over 2f out: kpt on appr last* **9/2**[2]

4 **3** *3* **Duke Of Stradone (IRE)**[72] 2480 6-10-13 .... PaddyMerrigan[(5)] 91
(S Donohoe, Ire) *chsd clr ldr: rdn along 4f out: drvn and kpt on same pce fnl 2f* **25/1**

4 *3* **Wee Bertie (IRE)** 4-10-8 .... GrahamLee 78
(J Howard Johnson) *towards rr: hdwy 6f out: rdn along 3f out: kpt on fnl 2f* **25/1**

5 *3* **Farmer Brown (IRE)**[77] 2400 5-11-11 .... JamieSpencer 92
(P Hughes, Ire) *hld up: hdwy 6f out: effrt to chse wnr over 3f out: rdn 2f out and sn wknd* **1/1**[1]

6 *3 ½* **Tom's Toybox** 4-10-8 .... DominicElsworth 74+
(J M Jefferson) *hld up towards rr: hdwy over 4f: rdn and kpt on fnl 2f: nrst fin* **12/1**

2 **7** *2* **Mister Jungle (FR)**[30] 3273 4-10-5 .... PeterBuchanan[(3)] 70
(Mrs S C Bradburne) *in tch: rdn along 4f out: kpt on same pce fr over 2f out* **16/1**

14- **8** *6* **Harry Flashman**[295] 4865 5-11-6 .... StephenCraine[(5)] 81
(D W Whillans) *chsd ldrs: rdn along 4f out: wknd 3f out* **12/1**

9 *14* **William Bonney (IRE)**[161] 1355 6-11-4 .... MrBConnell[(7)] 67
(Anthony Mullins, Ire) *led and sn clr: rdn along 5f out: hdd over 3f out and sn wknd* **8/1**

0 **10** *10* **Blast The Past**[16] 3490 4-10-1 .... JimCrowley 33
(T D Walford) *a rr* **66/1**

0 **11** *21* **Bella Cosa (IRE)**[31] 3259 4-10-1 .... NeilMulholland 12
(Mrs L B Normile) *bhd fr 1/2-way* **150/1**

12 *dist* **Wellstream Blue** 5-11-1 .... OwynNelmes[(3)] —
(Mrs H O Graham) *chsd ldrs 6f: sn lost pl and bhd fnl 6f* **100/1**

0 **13** *9* **Domesday (UAE)**[49] 2906 5-10-13 .... BrianHughes[(5)] —
(W G Harrison) *bhd fr 1/2-way* **150/1**

14 *dist* **Bellaney Hall (IRE)**[274] 6-10-6 .... DougieCostello[(5)] —
(J J Quinn) *midfield: pushed along 1/2-way: sn lost pl and bhd fnl 4f* **66/1**

3m 44.0s (-7.30) **Going Correction** -0.10s/f (Good)
WFA 4 from 5yo+ 9lb **14** Ran SP% **128.9**
Speed ratings: **103,99,98,96,95 93,92,89,82,77 66,—,—,—** CSF £32.21 TOTE £7.30: £2.50, £2.20, £3.60; EX 31.00 Place 6 £384.33, Place 5 £74.73.
Owner Mrs R G Hillen **Bred** Hollington Stud **Trained** Hambleton, N Yorks

FOCUS
Ordinary bumper form at best, but an easy winner in New Dancer, who looks a potentially fair prospect, with the placed horses the best guide to the level.

NOTEBOOK
New Dancer, whose stable's only previous representative in this race was also victorious, created a strong impression on this racecourse debut, pulling right away under pressure. He admittedly beat little, but there was plenty to like about the performance and he looks one to keep on the right side. *(op 12-1)*
Gripit N Tipit(IRE) surprisingly did best of the Irish raiders and showed the benefit of his initial outing at Leopardstown. He is nothing special, but can find a race at the right level over hurdles. *(tchd 5-1)*
Duke Of Stradone(IRE) is steadily going the right way and kept on well enough for third. Connections have clearly been toying with the idea of sending him over fences, having been a non-runner in three chases already this season, and he is likely to improve for the larger obstacles.
Wee Bertie(IRE), whose stable are in mixed form at present, ran a pleasing race in a keeping-on fourth and may be capable of winning a race in this sphere if kept to a similarly modest level. He will stay further over hurdles.
Farmer Brown(IRE), a fair bumper in Ireland, had the assistance of Champion Flat jockey Jamie Spencer, but was underpriced as a result and he failed to reproduce his form on this fast surface. The weight concession may also have had an effect and he deserves another chance. *(tchd 11-10 and 6-5 in places)*
William Bonney(IRE), another Irish raider, was soon in a clear lead, but paid for it late on and faded badly in the straight. *(op 11-1)*
Bellaney Hall(IRE) *Official explanation: jockey said mare lost its action*
T/Jkpt: Not won. T/Plt: £180.70 to a £1 stake. Pool: £57,417.55. 231.90 winning tickets. T/Qpdt: £15.70 to a £1 stake. Pool: £6,096.60. 286.70 winning tickets. JR

3764 - 3771a (Foreign Racing) - See Raceform Interactive

3400 PUNCHESTOWN (R-H)
Sunday, February 5

OFFICIAL GOING: Yielding

3772a BYRNE GROUP PLC NOVICE HURDLE (GRADE 2) 2m
1:40 (1:40) 5-Y-O+ **£24,693** (£7,244; £3,451; £1,175)

RPR

1 **Mounthenry (IRE)**[24] 3363 6-11-5 .... AndrewJMcNamara 139+
(C Byrnes, Ire) *disp ld: led fr 5th: rdn and strly pressed after 2 out: nt fluent last: styd on wl* **3/1**[2]

2 *1 ½* **Iktitaf (IRE)**[63] 2667 5-11-7 136..(t) PCarberry 140
(Noel Meade, Ire) *trckd ldrs in 3rd: slt mstke 5th: impr into 2nd after 3 out: rdn to chal after next: no imp fr last: kpt on wl* **10/11**[1]

3 *13* **Tolpuddle (IRE)**[14] 3521 6-11-2 ....(t) WJLee 122
(T Stack, Ire) *hld up in rr: prog 1/2-way: 4th and rdn 2 out: kpt on same pce* **10/1**

4 *14* **Sublimity (FR)**[39] 3077 6-11-2 ....(t) PACarberry 116+
(John G Carr, Ire) *hld up in tch: 3rd and brief effrt 2 out: sn no ex* **5/1**[3]

5 *8* **Ceeawayhome**[22] 3400 7-11-2 .... JLCullen 100
(John E Kiely, Ire) *disp ld: hdd 5th: rdn and wknd 3 out* **16/1**

4m 12.5s **Going Correction** +0.525s/f (Soft) **5** Ran SP% **109.0**
Speed ratings: **102,101,94,87,83** CSF £6.28 TOTE £4.40: £1.20, £1.40; DF 7.50.
Owner Mrs Martha Reidy **Bred** Miss Ann Twomey **Trained** Ballingarry, Co Limerick

NOTEBOOK
Mounthenry(IRE) was not clever at the last but was always on top on the run-in. He is not a Cheltenham contender according to his trainer, but he would still rate highly enough amongst the Irish novices and would be of interest any time a decent pace could be guaranteed. *(op 7/2)*
Iktitaf(IRE) returned with a badly gashed near-fore which will rule him out of Cheltenham and possibly for the rest of the season. The injury was possibly sustained when he blundered five out. It says plenty for his ability and courage that he remained in contention until finding no extra from the last. *Official explanation: trainer said gelding received a bad gash on its near fore leg which required treatment (op 4/5 tchd 1/1)*
Tolpuddle(IRE), a narrow winner of an ordinary maiden at Cork last month, was restrained in the rear and, although making some progress before two out, was never a contender. *(op 7/1)*
Sublimity(FR) looked a smart enough recruit when winning at Leopardstown but the race has not worked out and he was done with quickly after two out. He scoped abnormally after this. *Official explanation: trainer said horse scoped abnormally post race (op 9/2)*

3774a BYRNE GROUP PLC TIED COTTAGE CHASE (GRADE 2) 2m
2:40 (2:40) 5-Y-O+ **£23,795** (£6,981; £3,326; £1,133)

RPR

1 **Central House**[14] 3527 9-11-12 159......................................(t) RLoughran 163
(D T Hughes, Ire) *mde all: rdn and jnd briefly after 3 out: styd on strly fr next* **11/4**[3]

2 *6* **Jim (FR)**[56] 2793 9-11-10 150.. RMPower 155+
(J T R Dreaper, Ire) *settled 2nd: rdn 4 out: 4th and outpcd next: kpt on fr last* **9/2**

3 *2* **Accordion Etoile (IRE)**[84] 2208 7-11-10 .... JLCullen 153
(Paul Nolan, Ire) *hld up in rr: 4th fr 5th: prog into 3rd and rdn after 3 out: 2nd after 2 out: kpt on: nt pce of wnr* **5/2**[2]

4 *hd* **Watson Lake (IRE)**[85] 2195 8-11-12 150..................................... PCarberry 155
(Noel Meade, Ire) *trckd ldrs in 3rd: impr into 2nd travelling wl 4 out: disp ld briefly after next: 3rd and rdn after 2 out: no ex whn mstke* **9/4**[1]

5 *dist* **Strike Back (IRE)**[14] 3527 8-11-4 131.................................... BJGeraghty —
(Mrs John Harrington, Ire) *3rd early: mstke and dropped to rr 5th: trailing fr 7th: t.o* **16/1**

4m 13.9s **Going Correction** +0.175s/f (Yiel) **5** Ran SP% **110.1**
Speed ratings: **116,113,112,111,—** CSF £14.71 TOTE £3.60: £2.30, £2.10; DF 15.00.
Owner John F Kenny **Bred** A J Ilsley **Trained** Osborne Lodge, Co. Kildare
■ The first winner since turning professional for Roger Loughran, on his first day back after his two-week ban.

NOTEBOOK
Central House turned in a contrasting performance here compared to his Fairyhouse effort a fortnight earlier. In front throughout, he was able to turn it on when challenged three out and took complete control between the last two. He still has a bit to find before he can be regarded a serious Champion Chase candidate. *(op 100/30)*
Jim(FR) is not a two-miler and the ground was not soft enough for him. He lost his place after four out and held out out no hope in fourth place going to the last, but he fairly motored on the run-in to finish a comfortable second. Two and a half miles at Aintree might suit. *(op 4/1)*
Accordion Etoile(IRE) had no easy task as a novice taking on more experienced rivals on what was his first run since November and only his third in all over fences. He blew up after the second last and will improve on this. He prefers better ground and is still probably the best of the Irish in the Arkle. *(op 9/4)*
Watson Lake(IRE) has had his problems with a foot injury and was having a good blow after the race. He was travelling well enough turning for home and looked a possibilty for a few strides but blew up after the second last. He has the Ryanair Chase option as well as the Champion Chase. *(op 7/4)*

3773 - 3778a (Foreign Racing) - See Raceform Interactive

3551 SEDGEFIELD (L-H)
Monday, February 6

OFFICIAL GOING: Soft (good to soft in places, heavy in places final 1 1/2f)
Third last fence omitted both chases.
Wind: Moderate, half-across

3779 GOSFORTH DECORATING AND BUILDING SERVICES NOVICES' HURDLE (DIV I) (10 hdls) 2m 5f 110y
1:30 (1:30) (Class 4) 4-Y-O+ **£2,927** (£859; £429; £214)

Form RPR

0212 **1** **Stagecoach Diamond**[207] 992 7-11-11 103............... DominicElsworth 120+
(Mrs S J Smith) *a.p: hit 3 out: effrt next: rdn last: led flat: styd on* **16/1**

322 **2** *1 ¼* **Character Building (IRE)**[34] 3237 6-11-4 .... RussGarritty 112+
(J J Quinn) *cl up: led 5th: rdn along after 2 out: drvn and hdd flat: kpt on* **7/2**[2]

32-2 **3** *13* **Love That Benny (USA)**[117] 1722 6-11-1 108................. PaddyAspell[(3)] 100+
(J Wade) *chsd ldrs: rdn along appr 2 out: kpt on same pce* **7/2**[2]

1 **4** *14* **Serbelloni**[64] 2652 6-11-11 110... TonyDobbin 99+
(M D Hammond) *hld up in tch: hdwy to trck ldrs 3 out: rdn along bef next: sn drvn and wknd* **4/1**[3]

P2 **5** *30* **Izzyizzenty**[52] 2859 7-10-13 .... ThomasDreaper[(5)] 55
(J M Jefferson) *a bhd: t.o fr 1/2-way* **11/1**

250 **6** *20* **Super Revo**[46] 2948 5-11-4 .... RichardMcGrath 35
(Mrs K Walton) *midfeild: hdwy on outer and in tch 4th: rdn along bef 6th: sn wknd and bhd* **50/1**

P0P **7** *23* **Whatcanyasay**[35] 3205 5-10-8 .... StevenGagan[(10)] 12
(Mrs E Slack) *nt fluent: a rr: mstke 7th and bhd after* **200/1**

P **Moneamon** 7-11-4 .... KennyJohnson —
(R Johnson) *a bhd: t.o whn p.u bef 6th* **100/1**

0155 **P** **Kerry's Blade (IRE)**[6] 2372 4-10-9 107......................... PaddyMerrigan[(5)] —
(P C Haslam) *a towards rr: bhd whn p.u bef 2 out* **33/1**

F **Golden Crest** 6-11-1 .... GaryBerridge[(3)] —
(W Amos) *chsd ldrs: effrt and ev ch whn stmbld and fell after jumping 3 out* **100/1**

2 **P** **Balyan (IRE)**[25] 3347 5-11-4 ....(p) GrahamLee —
(J Howard Johnson) *hld up: stdy hdwy to trck ldrs whn blnd 3 out and p.u after* **5/2**[1]

2U03 **P** **Step Perfect (USA)**[36] 3167 5-11-4 95.................................. BarryKeniry —
(G M Moore) *led to 5th: cl up tl rdn along and wknd qckly 3 out: p.u bef next* **33/1**

5m 28.4s (12.70) **Going Correction** +0.625s/f (Soft)
WFA 4 from 5yo+ 10lb **12** Ran SP% **117.6**
Speed ratings: **101,100,95,90,79 72,64,—,—,— —,—** CSF £71.19 TOTE £20.20: £4.60, £1.50, £1.60; EX 98.50.
Owner Mrs Jacqueline Conroy **Bred** R Russell **Trained** High Eldwick, W Yorks

FOCUS
A good time compared with the second division, and the form has been rated fairly positively.

NOTEBOOK
Stagecoach Diamond was proven over this sort of trip, but had not run since July and pretty much all his form had been on fast ground. Staying on strongly to lead on the flat, he won going away in the end. This was his best performance so far. *(op 14-1)*
Character Building(IRE), placed in each of his three bumpers, looked like making a winning hurdles debut at one stage but he was cut down on the run-in. He still looked green. *(op 4-1)*
Love That Benny(USA) was beaten a fair way by the two in front of him and did not quite stay this far in soft ground. *(op 9-2)*
Serbelloni was found wanting under a penalty, the five-furlong increase in trip being an obvious factor. *(op 7-2 tchd 9-2)*
Izzyizzenty did not build on an encouraging performance at Uttoxeter. *(op 10-1)*
Balyan(IRE) was tackling more than five furlongs further than he had on his debut and wore first-time cheekpieces. He was going well enough, but his stamina had yet to be seriously tested, when he blundered badly at the third from home and was pulled up. *(tchd 9-4, 11-4 in places after 3-1 early)*
Kerry's Blade(IRE) *Official explanation: jockey said gelding pulled up lame (tchd 9-4, 11-4 in places after 3-1 early)*
Golden Crest was right on the scene when he came down at the third last, stumbling on landing after jumping the flight well. This was an encouraging debut. *(tchd 9-4, 11-4 in places after 3-1 early)*

3780 GOSFORTH DECORATING AND BUILDING SERVICES NOVICES' HURDLE (DIV II) (10 hdls) 2m 5f 110y
2:00 (2:00) (Class 4) 4-Y-O+ **£2,927** (£859; £429; £214)

Form RPR

4642 **1** **Major Catch (IRE)**[13] 3545 7-10-13 110......................... AdamPogson[(5)] 107+
(C T Pogson) *trckd ldrs: hdwy 7th: led appr 2 out: rdn and hdd last rallied u.p to ld flat: r.o wl* **5/2**[2]

3212 **2** *1 ½* **Mr Mischief**[106] 1854 6-11-13 117................................. PaddyMerrigan[(5)] 120+
(P C Haslam) *in tch: hdwy to trck ldrs 7th: cl up 2 out: effrt to ld and slt mstke last: sn edgd lft: put hd in air: hdd and nt runon* **7/4**[1]

1 **3** *6* **Zeitgeist (IRE)**[36] 3167 5-11-11 .... GrahamLee 108+
(J Howard Johnson) *a.p: hit 7th: led next: rdn along and hdd appr 2 out: drvn appr last: one pce* **7/2**[3]

0-P **4** *29* **Oyster Pearl (IRE)**[32] 3246 7-11-4 .... RichardJohnson 70
(P Bowen) *keen: rapid hdwy and cl up 2nd: led 4th: pushed along and hdd 3 out: sn rdn and outpcd bef next* **6/1**

6-P0 **5** *7* **Platinum Point (IRE)**[17] 3488 7-11-4 .... AlanDempsey 63
(E W Tuer) *chsd ldrs: rdn along 3 out and sn outpcd* **100/1**

50P **6** *14* **Grand Daum (FR)**[32] 3253 5-11-4 .... JasonMaguire 49
(T P Tate) *led to 2nd: cl up: hit 7th: sn rdn and wknd bef 3 out* **50/1**

5P **7** *25* **Stoneriggs Merc (IRE)**[93] 2036 5-10-8 .... StevenGagan[(10)] 24
(Mrs E Slack) *a rr* **100/1**

0 **8** *2 ½* **Saw Doctor (IRE)**[14] 3534 6-10-11 ....(p) MrEMagee[(7)] 22
(J K Magee, Ire) *hld up: hit 1st: a rr* **100/1**

9 25 **Tartan Classic (IRE)** 5-10-13 BrianHughes(5) —
(J Howard Johnson) *a rr: b ehind fr 1/2-way* **40/1**

100 P **Moscow Blue**[12] [3559] 5-11-11 109 (t) AndrewThornton —
(Robert Gray) *in tch: hdwy to trck ldrs 4th: rdn along 6th and sn wknd: bhd whn p.u bef 3 out* **33/1**

5m 32.2s (16.50) **Going Correction** +0.625s/f (Soft) **10** Ran SP% **111.8**
Speed ratings: **95,94,92,81,79 74,65,64,55,—** CSF £7.04 TOTE £3.30: £1.10, £1.10, £1.40; EX 9.40.

Owner C T Pogson **Bred** Mrs Patricia A Byrne **Trained** Farnsfield, Notts

FOCUS
The winning time was 3.8 seconds slower than the first division, but the first two ran pretty much to their marks.

NOTEBOOK
Major Catch(IRE) is well at home when the mud is flying and he battled back well to regain the advantage early on the run-in. He should continue to pay his way. *(op 3-1)*
Mr Mischief was returning from a winter break. He showed narrowly ahead going to the last, but was awkward at the flight, relinquishing the lead, and then hung in behind his rival who was always holding him. He did not look straightforward on this occasion, but he is a consistent sort who *deserves the benefit of the doubt as he was lumping a big weight in bad ground. (op 2-1 tchd 13-8, 9-4 in a place)*
Zeitgeist(IRE) was not impressive when making a winning hurdles debut, and the form has since been let down by the next three home. He had his chance, but did not really see out this longer trip in worse ground, having been keen early on. *(op 2-1)*
Oyster Pearl(IRE), an Irish point winner having his second run for this yard, was collared three from home and ended up well beaten. He looks the type for three-mile chases. *(op 8-1)*
Moscow Blue, having his second run since being sold out of Evan Williams's yard for 6,000gns, was still in touch when he was eased before the third last and pulled up. *(op 25-1)*

3781 GOSFORTH DECORATING AND BUILDING SERVICES BEGINNERS' CHASE (14 fncs 2 omitted) 2m 5f
2:30 (2:30) (Class 4) 5-Y-0+ **£4,228** (£1,241; £620; £310)

Form RPR

1P44 **1** **Vicario**[23] [3397] 5-10-3 StephenCraine(5) 113
(D McCain) *a.p: led 8th: rdn along appr 2 out: drvn and jnd last: kpt on u.p flat* **10/3**[3]

530- **2** 2 **Henry's Pride (IRE)**[369] [3648] 6-10-11 PaddyMerrigan(5) 122+
(P C Haslam) *hld up in tch: hdwy to trck ldng pair 1/2-way: effrt appr 2 out: sn rdn: chal and ev ch whn pckd last: no ex* **12/1**

3P22 **3** ½ **Dark Ben (FR)**[25] [3352] 6-10-11 110 DougieCostello(5) 118
(Miss Kate Milligan) *led to 8th: cl up tl rdn along after 3 out: outpcd bef next: styd on u.p last* **9/4**[1]

33-P **4** dist **Mickey Croke**[99] [1939] 9-11-2 GrahamLee —
(M Todhunter) *prom tl pushed along 7th and sn outpcd: remote 4th fr 5 out* **8/1**

0B06 **5** 3½ **Fairy Skin Maker (IRE)**[42] [2975] 8-11-2 (p) RichardMcGrath —
(G A Harker) *hld up in rr: hit 1st: a bhd* **12/1**

-P0P **6** 25 **Viking Song**[27] [3338] 6-11-2 60 KennyJohnson —
(F Kirby) *chsd ldrs: mstke 7th: sn rdn along and outpcd fr next* **100/1**

P **P** **Germany Park (IRE)**[10] [3598] 8-10-13 GinoCarenza(3) —
(W B Stone) *a rr: mstke 7th and bhd whn p.u bef 10th* **100/1**

-045 **P** **Cragg Prince (IRE)**[13] [3554] 7-11-2 90 DominicElsworth —
(Mrs S J Smith) *nt jump wl: a bhd: t.o whn p.u bef 10th* **16/1**

0-F **P** **Billy Bush (IRE)**[7] [3653] 7-10-11 ThomasDreaper(5) —
(Ferdy Murphy) *prom: hit 3rd and next: rdn along and mstke 9th: sn bhd and p.u bef 4 out* **3/1**[2]

5m 34.3s (10.90) **Going Correction** +0.625s/f (Soft)
WFA 5 from 6yo+ 7lb **9** Ran SP% **113.2**
Speed ratings: **104,103,103,—,— —,—,—,—** CSF £40.40 TOTE £6.30: £1.50, £3.70, £1.10; EX 57.00.

Owner Jon Glews **Bred** Mrs A Yearley **Trained** Cholmondeley, Cheshire

FOCUS
A fair novice chase for the track and the form should work out. The runner-up has been rated the winner.

NOTEBOOK
Vicario, well suited by testing conditions over hurdles, made a winning chase bow. He jumped soundly and stayed on willingly after his nearest challenger had blundered at the last. Perhaps a little fortunate to collect, he will be vulnerable under a penalty. *(op 7-2 tchd 3-1)*
Henry's Pride(IRE), formerly with Heather Dalton, made a promising chase debut. He loomed up behind the leaders at halfway travelling easily, but came under pressure at the top of the hill. Challenging two from home, he was alongside the eventual winner when he went through the last, costing him momentum and quite probably a winning chance. *(op 10-1)*
Dark Ben(FR), back over a more suitable trip, looked well held by the first two at the second last but then stayed on to reduce the gap. His turn will come. *(op 2-1 tchd 5-2 and 11-4 in a place)*
Mickey Croke, having his second look at fences, achieved little in leading home the stragglers in fourth. *(op 10-1)*
Billy Bush(IRE) is well regarded by his trainer, but he jumped sketchily and was left behind on the *final circuit before being pulled up. Official explanation: jockey said gelding never travelled (tchd 10-3)*

3782 BET365 CALL 08000 322 365 NOVICES' H'CAP HURDLE (8 hdls) 2m 1f
3:00 (3:00) (Class 5) (0-90,88) 4-Y-0+ **£2,398** (£698; £349)

Form RPR

4545 **1** **West Hill (IRE)**[54] [2822] 5-10-4 71 (t) StephenCraine(5) 78+
(D McCain) *midfield: smooth hdwy to trck ldrs 4 out: led after 2 out: sn rdn: drvn flat and r.o* **5/1**[3]

P200 **2** 1¼ **That's Racing**[23] [3395] 6-10-9 74 PaddyAspell(3) 81+
(J Hetherton) *led: rdn and blnd 2 out: sn hdd: drvn and ev ch last: kpt on u.p flat* **14/1**

0- **3** 4 **Sarobar (IRE)**[32] [3260] 6-11-12 88 TomScudamore 89
(M Scudamore) *hld up towards rr: hdwy 3 out: rdn and styd on fr next: nrst fin* **7/2**[1]

400P **4** 5 **Mae Moss**[23] [3381] 5-11-2 78 DominicElsworth 74
(W S Coltherd) *bhd tl styd on appr 2 out: nrst fin* **33/1**

5032 **5** 7 **Munaawesh (USA)**[27] [3335] 5-11-5 81 NeilMulholland 70
(Mrs Marjorie Fife) *chsd ldr: rdn along after 3 out: drvn and one pce bef next* **4/1**[2]

0000 **6** 4 **Barney (IRE)**[25] [3347] 5-10-2 74 (t) StevenGagan(10) 59
(Mrs E Slack) *bhd: gd hdwy to chse ldr 5th: rdn along after 3 out and grad wknd* **33/1**

1050 **7** 5 **Acceleration (IRE)**[53] [2843] 6-11-9 85 (t) TonyDobbin 65
(R Allan) *trckd ldrs: hdwy 4th: hit next: rdn along 3 out and sn wknd* **9/1**

0040 **8** 7 **Filey Flyer**[32] [3253] 6-11-9 85 AnthonyRoss 58
(J R Turner) *a towards rr* **25/1**

6PP0 **9** 8 **Faraway Echo**[12] [3557] 5-10-1 73 MichaelMcAvoy(10) 38
(James Moffatt) *bhd fr 1/2-way* **16/1**

0/P0 **P** **First Grey**[62] [2693] 7-10-12 74 AlanDempsey —
(E W Tuer) *in tch: blnd 3rd: sn lost pl and bhd: p.u bef last* **33/1**

6000 **P** **Quarry Island (IRE)**[19] [3442] 5-11-2 85 PhilKinsella(7) —
(M Todhunter) *chsd ldrs: lost pl 1/2-way: sn bhd and p.u bef 2 out* **14/1**

6P-P **P** **Kituhwa (USA)**[36] [3173] 6-10-8 70 (t) WilsonRenwick —
(R Shiels) *chsd ldrs: rdn along 1/2-way: sn wknd and bhd whn p.u bef 2 out* **50/1**

406 **P** **Bohemian Brook (IRE)**[62] [2690] 5-11-6 82 GrahamLee —
(J Howard Johnson) *midfield: rdn along 1/2-way: sn lost pl and bhd whn p.u bef 3 out* **11/2**

4m 18.0s (11.50) **Going Correction** +0.625s/f (Soft) **13** Ran SP% **118.1**
Speed ratings: **97,96,94,92,88 87,84,81,77,— —,—,—** CSF £66.39 CT £278.86 TOTE £7.70: £2.60, £5.40, £1.40; EX 59.00.

Owner Essential Racing **Bred** Darley **Trained** Cholmondeley, Cheshire

FOCUS
A low-grade affair but the form should work out.

NOTEBOOK
West Hill(IRE), down in grade, was well ridden by Craine and steadily improved to track the *leaders before taking over between the last two flights. There was little left in the tank in the end. (op 4-1)*
That's Racing tried to make all of the running but a blunder at the second last and a slightly awkward jump at the final flight sealed his fate. This was a return to the sort of form he had shown at Kelso before Christmas. *(op 16-1)*
Sarobar(IRE), a maiden in Ireland, latterly for Dusty Sheehy, was reverting to hurdles on his debut for this yard. He was doing his best work at the end and the return to further should suit. *(op 6-1)*
Mae Moss looked like finishing well out the back on this hurdles debut but she stayed on well over the last two flights.
Munaawesh(USA) was 4lb higher than when runner-up in a seller on his latest start. *(op 9-2)*
Barney(IRE), tried in a tongue tie on this handicap bow, showed a bit more this time but again finished weakly. *Official explanation: jockey said gelding had a breathing problem (tchd 40-1)*
Bohemian Brook(IRE) *Official explanation: jockey said gelding never travelled (op 5-1)*

3783 RACECOURSE VIDEO SERVICES H'CAP HURDLE (7 hdls 1 omitted) 2m 1f
3:30 (3:30) (Class 4) (0-110,108) 4-Y-0+ **£3,578** (£1,050; £525; £262)

Form RPR

1P6 **1** **Etoile Russe (IRE)**[17] [3479] 4-9-5 93 (t) GaryBartley(10) 104+
(P C Haslam) *cl up: hit 4th: sn led and clr after next: unchal* **7/1**[3]

560F **2** dist **Bollin Thomas**[63] [2680] 8-11-1 97 TonyDobbin 85
(R Allan) *hld uip in midfield: hdwy to chse clr ldrs 5th: drvn along after next: plugged on same pce* **9/2**[2]

6534 **3** 10 **George Stubbs (USA)**[31] [3267] 8-11-4 100 WilsonRenwick 68
(B Ellison) *hld up: hdwy 1/2-way: ridden along to chse ldrs 5th: sn drvn and no imp* **8/1**

4-10 **4** 1½ **Charlie Tango (IRE)**[46] [2950] 5-11-0 101 PaddyMerrigan(5) 67
(D W Thompson) *set str pce: hit 4th and sn hdd: drvn along after next and grad wknd* **10/1**

0 **5** dist **Rock Back (IRE)**[15] [3529] 5-10-4 89 PeterBuchanan(3) —
(Miss Lucinda V Russell) *bhd fr 1/2-way* **16/1**

01/0 **F** **The Joker (IRE)**[24] [3378] 8-11-5 108 MrEMagee(7) —
(J K Magee, Ire) *chsd ldng pair whn fell 2nd* **9/2**[2]

3414 **B** **North Landing (IRE)**[46] [2952] 6-11-3 99 LarryMcGrath —
(R C Guest) *hld up in tch whn b.d 2nd* **3/1**[1]

3420 **P** **Templet (USA)**[24] [3378] 6-10-13 95 (b) JimmyMcCarthy —
(W G Harrison) *a rr: bhd fr 1/2-way: t.o whn p.u bef last* **7/1**[3]

4m 14.7s (8.20) **Going Correction** +0.625s/f (Soft)
WFA 4 from 5yo+ 9lb **8** Ran SP% **112.4**
Speed ratings: **105,—,—,—,— —,—,—** CSF £37.51 CT £255.71 TOTE £6.80: £2.00, £2.10, £1.80; EX 53.80.

Owner M C Mason **Bred** Roland H Alder **Trained** Middleham, N Yorks
■ Jockey Gary Bartley's first winner over jumps.

FOCUS
This turned into an uncompetitive event and a tricky one to assess, which could have been rated much higher. The second-last flight was bypassed on the final circuit to avoid an injured rider.

NOTEBOOK
Etoile Russe(IRE) went past the leader in the back straight and, keeping to the outer where the ground was less poached, soon built up a big lead which was never challenged. While this was a sizeable step up on his previous form, his featherweight obviously helped and he is likely to be hit hard by the handicapper for this.
Bollin Thomas moved into a distant second place passing the omitted penultimate flight but was never the slightest threat to the winner. *(op 13-2)*
George Stubbs(USA), whose best form has been on fast ground, achieved very little in plugging on for a remote third. *(op 7-1)*
Charlie Tango(IRE), making his handicap debut over hurdles, eventually paid for setting a good pace. *(op 8-1 tchd 15-2)*
Rock Back(IRE) was hampered in the melee at the second and always trailing thereafter. *(op 25-1)*
The Joker(IRE) took a bad fall at the second and it was pleasing to see him get up seemingly unhurt. *(op 11-4)*
North Landing(IRE) had nowhere to go when a rival fell in his path at the second. *(op 11-4)*
Templet(USA) *Official explanation: jockey said gelding bled from the nose (op 11-4)*

3784 TOUCHLINE EVENT MANAGEMENT H'CAP CHASE (11 fncs 2 omitted) 2m 110y
4:00 (4:00) (Class 4) (0-115,112) 5-Y-0+ **£4,879** (£1,432; £716; £357)

Form RPR

3033 **1** **Miss Pross**[27] [3339] 6-10-6 92 RobertWalford 105+
(T D Walford) *trckd ldrs: hdwy 3 out: cl up next: rdn to ld last: styd on wl* **7/1**[3]

5322 **2** 5 **Red Man (IRE)**[12] [3562] 9-10-9 105 (p) StevenGagan(10) 109+
(Mrs E Slack) *led to 3rd: cl up tl led 5th: rdn along after 3 out: hdd and pckd last: sn drvn and no ex* **7/1**[3]

0041 **3** 7 **Cedar Rapids (IRE)**[12] [3562] 6-10-8 94 DavidO'Meara 91+
(H P Hogarth) *trckd ldrs: hdwy to chse ldr 5th: ev ch tl rdn and one pce fr 2 out* **13/2**[2]

3152 **4** 8 **Amadeus (AUS)**[55] [2816] 9-10-8 94 TomScudamore 82
(M Scudamore) *hld up in tch: effrt 4 out: sn rdn along and no imp appr 2 out* **5/2**[1]

632F **5** 4 **Sands Rising**[24] [3379] 9-11-5 105 KennyJohnson 89
(R Johnson) *hld up: hdwy on outer 6th: chsd ldrs 3 out: sn rdn along and wknd 2 out* **7/1**[3]

P400 **6** 2½ **Powder Creek (IRE)**[9] [3622] 9-11-10 110 AndrewThornton 94+
(K G Reveley) *in tch: lost pl and hit 5th: pushed along and hdwy 7th: in tch next: sn drvn and btn* **10/1**

503 **7** 30 **College City (IRE)**[14] [3543] 7-10-13 109 (p) JohnFlavin(10) 61
(R C Guest) *a towards rr: bhd fr 1/2-way* **12/1**

0/P- **8** *6* **General Cloney (IRE)**[109] 1812 10-10-2 **95**..................(b) ShaneWalsh(7) 41
(S Donohoe, Ire) *keen: cl up tl led 3rd: hdd 5th: rdn along and wkng whn hit 3 out and sn bhd* **12/1**

5156 **P** **Kids Inheritance (IRE)**[16] 3495 8-11-7 **112**............... ThomasDreaper(5) —
(J M Jefferson) *chsd ldrs: blnd bdly 7th and p.u after* **8/1**

4m 23.7s (9.50) **Going Correction** +0.625s/f (Soft) **9** Ran SP% **115.0**
Speed ratings: **102,99,96,92,90 89,75,72,—** CSF £54.71 CT £334.38 TOTE £8.20: £2.90, £2.50, £3.20; EX 95.80.

Owner D Coates **Bred** A W J Perry **Trained** Sheriff Hutton, N Yorks

FOCUS
The winner did it well and is rated value for further. The principals all raced up with the pace.

NOTEBOOK
Miss Pross, making her chasing debut, was given a patient ride. Challenging from the second last, she came clear on the flat for a comfortable victory. She is going the right way and a return to further will not inconvenience her. *(tchd 15-2)*

Red Man(IRE), running in only his second chase, ran another good race but could not contain the mare after pecking at the final fence. *(op 8-1)*

Cedar Rapids(IRE), on his handicap debut, was always towards the fore but could find no extra between the last two fences. *(op 15-2)*

Amadeus(AUS), back over fences, could never get into the action in a race in which it paid to be prominent. He returned with a cut but it should not keep him out for long. *(op 7-2)*

Sands Rising, without the usual tongue tie, briefly looked like playing a role at the finish when closing on the leaders with three to jump but soon faded. *(op 8-1)*

3785 JOHN SMITH'S EXTRA SMOOTH MAIDEN NATIONAL HUNT FLAT RACE (CONDITIONAL JOCKEYS/AMATEUR RIDERS) 2m 1f

4:30 (4:32) (Class 6) 4-6-Y-0 **£1,713** (£499; £249)

Form RPR

40 **1** **Stagecoach Opal**[68] 2572 5-10-8 .... MichaelO'Connell(10) 100+
(Mrs S J Smith) *chsd ldrs: hdwy over 4f out: led 3f out: rn green: edgd rt and rdn over 1f out and ins last: styd on* **16/1**

2 *6* **Sams Lad (IRE)**[41] 3048 5-10-13 .... ThomasDreaper(5) 92
(S Donohoe, Ire) *hld up: stdy hdwy 6f out: rdn to chse wnr 2f out: drvn and kpt on fnl f* **10/1**

3 *6* **The Gleaner** 4-10-4 ow3.. MrOGreenall(7) 81+
(M W Easterby) *trcking ldrs: hdwy over 4f out: rdn along and ev ch 3f out: kpt on same pce fnl 2f* **25/1**

24 **4** *12* **Sydney Greenstreet (GER)**[42] 2988 5-11-1 .... MrTGreenall(3) 74
(C R Egerton) *led: rdn along 6f out: drvn and hdd 3f out: grad wknd* **9/4**[1]

3 **5** *7* **Sybarite Chief (IRE)**[49] 2927 4-10-1 .... MrBMcHugh(7) 65+
(R A Fahey) *bhd tl styd on fnl 6f: nrst fin* **5/1**[3]

6 *11* **King Daniel** 5-10-8 .... StevenGagan(10) 56
(Mrs E Slack) *hld up: gd hdwy and cl up 1/2-way: disp ld 6f out tl rdn and wknd over 3f out* **50/1**

7 *5* **Justwhateverulike (IRE)** 5-10-11 .... TomMessenger(7) 51
(Miss S E Forster) *midfield: rdn along over 4f out: sn no hdwy* **50/1**

3 **8** *1 1/4* **Top Dressing (IRE)**[17] 3490 5-10-13 .... BrianHughes(5) 50
(J Howard Johnson) *hld up: hdwy to trck ldrs: rdn along over 4f out and sn wknd* **5/2**[2]

9 *2 1/2* **Sales Flow** 4-9-8 .... MrLWheatley(7) 30
(M W Easterby) *chsd ldrs on outer: rdn along over 6f: wknd over 4f out* **16/1**

10 *3 1/2* **Zarbeau** 4-10-3 .... PaddyMerrigan(5) 34
(J M Jefferson) *a rr* **20/1**

3 **11** *1/2* **Still Solvent**[50] 2906 5-11-1 .... PaddyAspell(3) 43
(J R Turner) *unruly s: plld hrd: a rr* **11/1**

50 **12** *dist* **Larry The Tiger (IRE)**[68] 2572 6-10-11 .... MrMSollitt(7) —
(Mrs S J Smith) *chsd ldrs: rdn along over 6f out: sn wknd* **66/1**

0 **13** *9* **Roman Gypsy**[19] 3448 5-10-4 .... PhilKinsella(7) —
(Mrs K Walton) *a rr* **100/1**

4m 16.2s (9.30) **Going Correction** +0.625s/f (Soft)
WFA 4 from 5yo+ 9lb **13** Ran SP% **120.2**
Speed ratings: **101,98,95,89,86 81,78,78,77,75 75,—,—** CSF £159.16 TOTE £12.00: £3.10, £4.10, £15.10; EX 139.60 Place 6 £44.61, Place 5 £20.31.

Owner John Conroy Jaqueline Conroy **Bred** R A Hughes **Trained** High Eldwick, W Yorks
■ The first winner in Britain for jockey Michael O'Connell.

FOCUS
Not the strongest of bumpers.

NOTEBOOK
Stagecoach Opal completed a first and last-race double for connections. Less than two lengths behind subsequent winner Stolen Moments last time, he was in front with three furlongs to run and went on to win despite wanting to hang right in the latter stages. *(tchd 20-1)*

Sams Lad(IRE) failed to finish in two runs between the flags but was runner-up on his bumper debut at Down Royal. He briefly posed a threat to the eventual winner with two furlongs to run but could not find that extra kick. *(op 15-2)*

The Gleaner, out of a bumper winner, was always in the front rank and kept on without being able to procure a change of gear. This was a satisfactory debut. *(op 16-1)*

Sydney Greenstreet(GER) set a modest pace and did not offer a great deal when headed with three furlongs to run. He does not seem to be going the right way but it could have been that he did not handle this soft ground. *(op 5-2)*

Sybarite Chief(IRE) was upped half a mile in trip from his debut but this still looked an insufficient test. *(op 6-1 tchd 9-2)*

King Daniel, whose dam is from a good family on the Flat in Germany, showed a little promise before fading in the last three furlongs.

Top Dressing(IRE) made a promising debut on different ground at Musselburgh but was beaten half a mile out here. *(op 3-1 tchd 10-3 and 9-4)*

Still Solvent, third in an ordinary race on his debut, played up down at the start and it looked as if he might be withdrawn. He was allowed to take part but was soon trailing. *(op 8-1)*

T/Plt: £69.50 to a £1 stake. Pool: £57,554.50. 603.70 winning tickets. T/Qpdt: £53.30 to a £1 stake. Pool: £4,024.40. 55.80 winning tickets. JR

2962 MARKET RASEN (R-H)

Tuesday, February 7

OFFICIAL GOING: Good
There had been no rain since January 19th but the ground was still described as 'tacky'. The rails on the hurdle track were moved out by two metres.
Wind: Fresh, half-against Weather: Fine but cool

3786 JUSTIN BOUNDS' JUVENILE NOVICES' HURDLE (DIV I) (8 hdls) 2m 1f 110y

1:20 (1:21) (Class 4) 4-Y-0 **£4,228** (£1,241; £620; £310)

Form RPR

1 **Jack The Giant (IRE)**[140] 4-10-12 .... MickFitzgerald 99+
(N J Henderson) *w ldrs: hmpd 1st: led 3rd: hit next 2: hdd 2 out: chal and regained ld last: styd on* **4/1**[3]

03 **2** *3 1/2* **Maneki Neko (IRE)**[25] 3374 4-10-12 .... NeilMulholland 97+
(E W Tuer) *trckd ldrs: t.k.h early: wnt 2nd 6th: led next: blnd and hdd last: no ex* **14/1**

4 **3** *2* **Backbord (GER)**[21] 3431 4-10-12 .... LeightonAspell 92
(Mrs L Wadham) *chsd ldrs: hrd drvn after 5th: edgd rt and styd on run-in* **9/2**

33 **4** *4* **Copper Bay (IRE)**[42] 3038 4-10-12 .... RobertThornton 89+
(A King) *w ldrs: led appr 2nd: hdd 3rd: one pce fr 2 out* **7/2**[2]

0P **5** *6* **Trappeto (IRE)**[12] 3579 4-10-9 .... WilliamKennedy(3) 82
(C Smith) *in rr: hdwy 6th: nvr rchd ldrs* **200/1**

0UP **6** *1* **Commanche Sioux**[20] 3442 4-10-5 .... WilsonRenwick 74
(M W Easterby) *hld up in rr: hdwy 5th: nvr nr to chal* **250/1**

UP **7** *21* **Beaumont Girl (IRE)**[11] 3594 4-10-0 .... MarkNicolls(5) 53
(Miss M E Rowland) *in rr: bhd fr 6th* **200/1**

8 *1 1/4* **Sultan Fontenaille (FR)**[137] 4-10-12 .... PJBrennan 64+
(N J Hawke) *mstkes: mid-div: hdwy 4th: lost pl appr 2 out* **25/1**

P **9** *4* **C'Est La Vie**[42] 3038 4-10-5 .... PadgeWhelan 48
(Miss J E Foster) *chsd ldrs: lost pl after 6th* **100/1**

46 **10** *1* **Water Pistol**[22] 3415 4-10-12 .... KennyJohnson 54
(M C Chapman) *a in rr: bhd fr 6th* **100/1**

06 **11** *3 1/2* **Celtic Saloon (IRE)**[32] 3273 4-10-12 .... RichardMcGrath 50
(K G Reveley) *nt jump wl: in rr: bhd fr 5th* **50/1**

6F **12** *3 1/2* **Investment Wings (IRE)**[12] 3579 4-10-12 .... APMcCoy 47
(M C Pipe) *led: j. slowly 1st: hdd appr next: lost pl 5th: sn bhd* **3/1**[1]

00 **13** *1/2* **Tudor Oak (IRE)**[68] 2580 4-10-7 .... DerekLaverty(5) 46
(Mark Campion) *rr-div: hdwy 3rd: lost pl 5th: sn bhd* **200/1**

14 *3 1/2* **Kova Hall (IRE)**[163] 4-10-12 .... RichardJohnson 43
(P J Hobbs) *chsd ldrs: rdn and lost pl after 6th: sn bhd* **5/1**

4m 15.8s (-0.60) **Going Correction** +0.025s/f (Yiel) **14** Ran SP% **118.4**
Speed ratings: **102,100,99,97,95 94,85,84,83,82 81,79,79,77** CSF £54.98 TOTE £5.10: £2.70, £3.40, £1.40; EX 50.60.

Owner Hanbury Syndicate **Bred** Mrs F Schwarzenbach **Trained** Upper Lambourn, Berks

FOCUS
The winning time was over three seconds slower than the second division, due to the steady early gallop, and the field finished strung out. The form should be treated with a degree of caution.

NOTEBOOK
Jack The Giant(IRE), rated 72 on the Flat and who looked a picture of health ahead of this hurdling bow, took full advantage of the runner-up's final flight blunder and got his career over timber off to a perfect start. He was nearly taken out at the first flight, so deserves credit for recovering as positively as he did thereafter, and he jumped well in the main for a debutant. He must rate flattered by his winning margin, and he still has to prove his effectiveness over this trip in a strongly-run race, but he has joined a powerful yard and it will be interesting to see where he is pitched in next. *(op 7-2)*

Maneki Neko(IRE) has to rate unlucky as he was on top of the eventual winner before making an final flight error which proved decisive. This was his best effort to date in this sphere, he will be better in a more strongly-run race, and he now has the option of handicaps. *(op 11-1)*

Backbord(GER) was doing all of his best work at the finish and ran close to the level of his recent debut at Folkestone. He should fare better when eligible for handicaps after his next outing and ought to appreciate a stiffer test in the future. *(tchd 5-1)*

Copper Bay(IRE), who had two handlers in the paddock, was in an exciteable mood beforehand and ran freely through the early parts. He ultimately paid for those exertions when the race got serious turning for home and, while he now qualifies for handicaps, looks one to have reservations about at present. *(tchd 4-1)*

Investment Wings(IRE), who took a crashing fall at Warwick just 12 days previously, tried to refuse over the first flight - hampering the winner in the process - and not that surprisingly lacked any conviction over his hurdles. His fall at Warwick clearly dented his confidence, and he was beaten too far out for this to be his true running, so it would be unwise to write him off just yet now *that he is eligible for handicaps. Official explanation: jockey said gelding had lost its confidence after a heavy fall last time out (op 9-2)*

Kova Hall(IRE), rated 85 on the Flat when with Dermot Weld, ran no sort of race on this hurdling bow for new connections and something was presumably amiss. *(op 9-2 tchd 4-1)*

3787 JUSTIN BOUNDS' JUVENILE NOVICES' HURDLE (DIV II) (8 hdls) 2m 1f 110y

1:50 (1:50) (Class 4) 4-Y-0 **£4,228** (£1,241; £620; £310)

Form RPR

23 **1** **Slew Charm (FR)**[21] 3429 4-10-12 .... TomDoyle 110+
(Noel T Chance) *hdwy to chse ldrs 4th: led and hit last: edgd rt: rdn rt out* **5/1**[2]

F **2** *2 1/2* **Bureaucrat**[26] 3355 4-10-12 .... RichardJohnson 103+
(P J Hobbs) *w ldr: led appr 2nd: hdd last: no ex* **4/6**[1]

64 **3** *1 1/4* **Shannon Springs (IRE)**[29] 3324 4-10-12 .... PJBrennan 103+
(Andrew Turnell) *chsd ldrs: wnt 2nd 6th: cl up whn hit 2 out: nt qckn run-in* **11/2**[3]

45 **4** *18* **Monash Lad (IRE)**[11] 3594 4-10-12 .... LeightonAspell 84
(M H Tompkins) *chsd ldrs: drvn 6th: wknd appr next* **14/1**

0 **5** *1/2* **William Tell (IRE)**[36] 3203 4-10-12 .... GrahamLee 83
(M D Hammond) *in rr: sme hdwy 5th: lost pl appr 2 out* **50/1**

500 **6** *1 1/2* **Ember Dancer**[8] 3645 4-10-12 .... WayneHutchinson 82
(Ian Williams) *hdwy to chse ldrs 4th: hrd drvn and outpcd 6th: sn lost pl* **100/1**

7 *10* **Finnegans Rainbow**[26] 4-10-12 .... KennyJohnson 72
(M C Chapman) *in rr: bhd fr 5th* **200/1**

0 **8** *29* **Blackcomb Mountain (USA)**[8] 3645 4-9-12 .... CharliePoste(7) 36
(M F Harris) *a in rr: bhd fr 5th* **100/1**

P60 **9** *9* **With Honours**[60] 2753 4-10-5 .... PadgeWhelan 27
(T J Fitzgerald) *in rr: reminders after 3rd: sn bhd* **150/1**

P5 **10** *2 1/2* **The Iron Giant (IRE)**[26] 3354 4-10-12 .... SamThomas 31
(Miss H C Knight) *led tl appr 2nd: lost pl 5th: sn bhd* **33/1**

U **11** *dist* **Turn On The Style**[11] 3594 4-10-9 .... LeeVickers(3) —
(M J Polglase) *chsd ldrs: lost pl 5th: sn bhd: t.o: btn 62 l* **200/1**

00 **P** **Amadores**[33] [3259] 4-10-5 .... DominicElsworth —
(J Ryan) *in rr: bhd fr 5th: t.o whn p.u bef next* **125/1**

P **P** **Solarias Quest**[42] [3021] 4-10-12 .... RobertThornton —
(A King) *chsd ldrs: hit 5th: lost pl after next: bhd whn p.u bef last* **8/1**

4m 12.7s (-4.90) **Going Correction** +0.025s/f (Yiel) **13** Ran SP% **119.2**
Speed ratings: **109,107,107,99,99 98,94,81,77,76** —,—,— CSF £9.06 TOTE £9.60: £1.60, £1.10, £1.80; EX 15.20.
Owner Premier Chance Racing **Bred** J Biraben And Mme Jean Biraben **Trained** Upper Lambourn, Berks

FOCUS
A fair time for a race like this and over three seconds faster than the first division and the form looks solid with the first three coming clear. The winner can be rated value for further.

NOTEBOOK
Slew Charm(FR) got off the mark over hurdles at the third attempt with an authoritative success. He was always travelling kindly in behind the leaders, quickened without fuss when asked to hit the front, and should be rated value for further than his winning margin. He enjoyed this faster ground, and it will be interesting to see how the Handicapper reacts, as he could be a likely sort for the Fred Winter at Cheltenham next month. *(op 9-2 tchd 6-1)*
Bureaucrat, who had the race at his mercy when falling at the final flight on debut at Ludlow 26 days previously, was given every chance from the front and was simply beaten by a better horse on the day. Time may show there was no disgrace in this defeat, he may prefer sitting off a lead in the future, and does deserve to find a race in the coming weeks. *(tchd 8-11)*
Shannon Springs(IRE) looked a big player turning for home, but he failed to sustain his effort after a blunder at the penultimate flight and was ultimately well held. This must still rate a personal-best in this sphere, however, and he is now eligible for handicaps. *(op 7-1)*
Monash Lad(IRE) was firmly put in his place by the principals and again did enough to suggest he can find a race in due course. He now also qualifies for handicaps.
Solarias Quest, pulled up in the Grade One Finale Hurdle on his debut 42 days previously, proved easy in the market and ran no sort of race. He has it all to prove now. *(op 10-1)*

3788 ERIC & LUCY PAPWORTH H'CAP CHASE (12 fncs) 2m 1f 110y
2:20 (2:20) (Class 4) (0-115,115) 5-Y-0+ **£4,554** (£1,337; £668; £333)

Form RPR

U3 **1** **Madison Du Berlais (FR)**[24] [3387] 5-11-2 **112** .... APMcCoy 115+
(M C Pipe) *trckd ldrs: led 8th: shkn up appr 3 out: styd on: drvn rt out* **9/4**[1]

6/16 **2** *1* **Joey Tribbiani (IRE)**[26] [3357] 9-11-5 **108** .... WayneHutchinson 117
(T Keddy) *in rr: hdwy 7th: chsng ldrs 9th: kpt on same pce run-in* **10/1**

B-25 **3** *1 1/2* **Moment Of Madness (IRE)**[25] [3379] 8-11-4 **107** .... PadgeWhelan 116+
(T J Fitzgerald) *hld up: hdwy to trck ldrs 6th: chal 2 out: kpt on same pce* **14/1**

0150 **4** *13* **Roofing Spirit (IRE)**[17] [3507] 8-11-12 **115** .... MickFitzgerald 110
(D P Keane) *in rr: pushed along 5th: hdwy to chse ldrs 9th: outpcd appr next* **6/1**[3]

3645 **5** *1/2* **Argento**[25] [3378] 9-11-4 **107** .... BarryKeniry 101
(G M Moore) *chsd ldrs: lost pl appr 3 out* **8/1**

3P0P **6** *4* **Log On Intersky (IRE)**[10] [3619] 10-11-5 **108** .... RichardHobson 98
(J R Cornwall) *w ldrs: led 5th: hdd 8th: lost pl after next* **66/1**

5415 **7** *3* **Mexican (USA)**[35] [3233] 7-10-3 **92** .... (b) NeilMulholland 80+
(M D Hammond) *in rr: sme hdwy 8th: sn btn* **25/1**

05-2 **P** **Big Bone (FR)**[29] [3323] 6-11-9 **112** .... PJBrennan —
(P J Hobbs) *led to 5th: wknd rapidly 8th: t.o whn p.u after next* **3/1**[2]

20-P **P** **Downpour (USA)**[38] [3135] 8-11-7 **110** .... RobertThornton —
(Ian Williams) *prom: hit 7th: wknd qckly next: wl bhd whn p.u after 9th* **8/1**

635P **P** **Imaginaire (USA)**[24] [3398] 11-11-5 **108** .... (b[1]) SamThomas —
(Miss Venetia Williams) *w ldrs: hit 4th: wknd qckly after 8th: t.o whn p.u bef 3 out* **28/1**

4m 37.7s (6.60) **Going Correction** +0.60s/f (Soft)
WFA 5 from 6yo+ 6lb **10** Ran SP% **116.8**
Speed ratings: **109,108,107,102,101 100,98**,—,—,— CSF £24.60 CT £259.99 TOTE £3.60: £1.70, £3.20, £2.30; EX 40.30.
Owner Roger Stanley & Yvonne Reynolds II **Bred** Jean-Marc Lucas **Trained** Nicholashayne, Devon

FOCUS
A modest handicap, run at a generous gallop, and the form looks solid for the grade.

NOTEBOOK
Madison Du Berlais(FR), dropped 2lb despite finishing a fair third at Warwick last time, opened his account for connections at the third attempt under a typically strong ride from McCoy. He looked a sitting duck nearing two out, but he stuck gamely to his task under pressure, and was eventually full value for his winning margin. *(op 5-2 tchd 11-4)*
Joey Tribbiani(IRE) showed the benefit of a drop in class and ran above his mark in defeat. He is well suited by this sort of ground and could be placed to go one better in the coming weeks providing he fully recovers from these exertions. *(op 12-1)*
Moment Of Madness(IRE) put a dismal effort at Kelso last time behind him with a solid effort in defeat. This is much more like his true form and he will not mind the return to easier ground in the future. *(op 12-1)*
Roofing Spirit(IRE), very well backed, failed to improve for the drop in trip and class and was well beaten under top weight. He never really looked happy this time and is struggling for form at present. *(op 10-1)*
Argento could offer no more after jumping four from home and, despite falling in the weights, continues to perform below expectations. *(op 7-1)*
Big Bone(FR) proved very disappointing and has it to prove after this tame effort. *Official explanation: vet said gelding had bled from the nose (op 5-2)*

3789 EUROPEAN BREEDERS FUND "NATIONAL HUNT" NOVICES' HURDLE (QUALIFIER) (10 hdls) 2m 3f 110y
2:50 (2:51) (Class 3) 4-7-Y-0 **£5,204** (£1,528; £764; £381)

Form RPR

1-31 **1** **Bougoure (IRE)**[69] [2571] 7-11-10 .... DominicElsworth 123+
(Mrs S J Smith) *w ldrs: led 5th: styd on strly fr 2 out: readily* **15/8**[1]

3/20 **2** *7* **French Envoy (FR)**[86] [2212] 7-11-4 .... APMcCoy 107+
(Ian Williams) *trckd ldrs: wnt 2nd 7th: kpt on same pce between last 2* **5/2**[2]

/4- **3** *8* **Elverys (IRE)**[400] [3210] 7-11-4 .... AnthonyRoss 97+
(R A Fahey) *hld up in rr: hdwy to trck ldrs 6th: one pce fr 2 out* **33/1**

2 **4** *1 1/2* **Canada Street (IRE)**[91] [2106] 5-11-4 .... GrahamLee 95+
(J Howard Johnson) *w ldrs: 2nd whn blnd 7th: fdd appr 2 out* **6/1**

42-1 **5** *16* **Zanzibar Boy**[76] [2432] 7-11-4 .... JimCrowley 78
(H Morrison) *trckd ldrs: lost pl appr 2 out* **5/1**[3]

6 *4* **Inishturk (IRE)**[366] 7-11-4 .... RobertThornton 74
(A King) *in rr: hit 3rd: sme hdwy 6th: lost pl 8th* **25/1**

143- **7** *3/4* **Jeringa**[324] [4477] 7-11-1 .... PaddyAspell[(3)] 73
(J Wade) *in rr: sme hdwy 7th: sn lost pl* **50/1**

8 *1/2* **Honest Abe (IRE)** 5-11-4 .... AndrewThornton 73
(B N Pollock) *in rr: bhd fr 8th* **50/1**

0-15 **9** *3* **Not For Diamonds (IRE)**[24] [3392] 6-11-4 .... AndrewTinkler 70
(Mrs H Dalton) *chsd ldrs: drvn along 7th: lost pl next* **12/1**

0-30 **10** *hd* **Geraldine**[54] [2844] 5-10-8 .... LeeVickers[(3)] 63
(Mrs S Lamyman) *a in rr: wl bheind fr 8th* **66/1**

-0P4 **11** *14* **Cadtauri (FR)**[33] [3246] 5-11-4 .... PaulMoloney 56
(Miss H C Knight) *hld up in rr: sme hdwy 7th: sn lost pl* **50/1**

4 **12** *24* **Hollandia (IRE)**[19] [3462] 5-11-4 .... SamThomas 32
(Miss H C Knight) *t.k.h in rr: hdwy 7th: sn lost pl and bhd: t.o* **33/1**

0-0 **P** **Silver Hill Lad**[24] [3399] 5-11-4 .... NeilMulholland —
(C W Fairhurst) *chsd ldrs: lost pl after 6th: t.o 8th: sn p.u* **100/1**

040 **P** **Finsbury Fred (IRE)**[55] [2829] 5-11-4 .... CarlLlewellyn —
(N A Twiston-Davies) *led: hung bdly lft and hdd 5th: eased and sn p.u* **50/1**

4m 50.6s (0.60) **Going Correction** +0.025s/f (Yiel) **14** Ran SP% **122.1**
Speed ratings: **99,96,93,92,86 84,84,83,82,82 77,67**,—,— CSF £6.41 TOTE £3.00: £1.80, £2.00, £4.90; EX 9.00.
Owner Trevor Hemmings **Bred** John Meagher **Trained** High Eldwick, W Yorks

FOCUS
A fair novice event, run at a modest pace, and the form looks solid enough. The winner can rate higher.

NOTEBOOK
Bougoure(IRE) ◆, off the mark over hurdles at Catterick last time, duly followed up with an impressive display under his penalty. He could have been called the winner at the top of the home straight, looked better the further he went, and should be rated value for further. The final of this series at Sandown next month - in which his yard saddled Rebel Rhythm to finish third under top weight in 2005 - will surely be his target, as the longer trip in that event should play to his strengths, and he is clearly progressing fast. *(op 9-4 tchd 7-4)*
French Envoy(FR), most disappointing when favourite at Fontwell 86 days previously, showed his true colours with a fair effort in defeat and finished a clear second-best. He was firmly put in his place by the winner, but should be placed to go one better before the season's end. *(tchd 9-4 and 11-4)*
Elverys(IRE), who showed ability on his debut in a Wetherby bumper in 2005, was not given too hard a time on this hurdling bow and ran with credit. He travelled nicely until appearing to blow-up approaching the penultimate flight, and should improve a deal for the experience. *(op 25-1)*
Canada Street(IRE), runner-up to Chef De Cour on his hurdling bow 90 days previously, failed to see out his race and was ultimately well held. He is not the first horse from his yard to struggle to get home in the past fortnight, however, and it would be a surprise were he not to better this form in due course. *(tchd 7-1)*
Zanzibar Boy, last seen taking a Chepstow bumper in good style 76 days previously, failed to find anything when push came to shove and was allowed to come home pretty much in his own time. This was disappointing, but it is well worth noting that his bumper win in November was his stable's last success, and he has the scope to leave this form behind in due course. *(op 6-1)*
Finsbury Fred(IRE) *Official explanation: jockey said gelding hung violently left*

3790 EUROPEAN BREEDERS' FUND/TATTERSALLS (IRELAND) MARES' ONLY NOVICES' CHASE (QUALIFIER) (14 fncs) 2m 4f
3:20 (3:20) (Class 4) 5-Y-0+ **£6,506** (£1,910; £955; £477)

Form RPR

1432 **1** **Viciana**[5] [3689] 7-11-0 .... LeightonAspell 103+
(Mrs L Wadham) *led to 3rd: led 6th: hrd rdn run-in: all out* **4/5**[1]

324P **2** *3/4* **Lizzie Bathwick (IRE)**[34] [3239] 7-10-9 **94** .... StephenCraine[(5)] 103+
(J G Portman) *chsd ldrs: drvn along 8th: upsides 2 out: kpt on run-in: jst hld* **10/3**[2]

-30F **3** *11* **Simple Glory (IRE)**[33] [3247] 7-11-0 .... WayneHutchinson 91
(R Dickin) *chsd ldrs: blnd 7th: one pce fr 11th* **10/1**

313P **4** *25* **Sunny South East (IRE)**[11] [3593] 6-11-3 **97** .... WilliamKennedy[(3)] 72
(S Gollings) *led 3rd to 6th: lost pl 10th: sn bhd* **14/1**

00-P **5** *nk* **Top Gale (IRE)**[38] [3149] 7-11-0 .... HenryOliver 66
(R Dickin) *nt fluent: in tch to 10th: poor 5th whn blnd 3 out* **50/1**

/3-3 **6** *24* **Lady Harriet**[21] [3439] 7-11-0 .... JimmyMcCarthy 42
(C J Mann) *trckd ldrs: wknd appr 3 out: sn bhd: virtually p.u* **11/2**[3]

5m 20.1s (17.40) **Going Correction** +0.60s/f (Soft) **6** Ran SP% **111.7**
Speed ratings: **89,88,84,74,74 64** CSF £4.02 TOTE £1.80: £1.50, £1.40; EX 3.70.
Owner G W Paul **Bred** G W Paul **Trained** Newmarket, Suffolk
■ Stewards' Enquiry : Henry Oliver two-day ban: used whip with excessive force and frequency (Feb 19-20)

FOCUS
This produced a very moderate winning time for the class of contest and the first two came clear. The form is ordinary.

NOTEBOOK
Viciana, runner-up at Towcester on her chasing bow five days previously, had to pull out all the stops to land the spoils and open her account in this sphere. She should be rated better than the bare form, as she would have found this coming plenty quick enough, and remains open to a little more improvement as a chaser. *(op 8-11 tchd 5-6 and 10-11 in places)*
Lizzie Bathwick(IRE), making her debut for a new yard, gave the winner a real fight and showed her true colours in defeat. She was well clear of the rest at the finish and certainly has a race in her over fences when racing against her own sex. *(op 9-2 tchd 3-1 and 5-1 in a place)*
Simple Glory(IRE), rated 96 over hurdles, could not go with the front pair and was well beaten on this chasing bow. She is entitled to improve for the experience, however, and as a former winning pointer she may well need further over fences. *(op 9-1 tchd 8-1)*
Lady Harriet, who made a promising return from a layopff over hurdles last time, failed to stay the longer trip and probably found this coming too soon. She is capable of better than this, but has a little to prove now all the same. *(op 6-1 tchd 13-2)*

3791 BBC RADIO LINCOLNSHIRE MIKE MOLLOY MEMORIAL H'CAP CHASE (14 fncs) 2m 6f 110y
3:50 (3:51) (Class 4) (0-105,99) 5-Y-0+ **£3,773** (£1,107; £553; £276)

Form RPR

4504 **1** **King's Bounty**[68] [2588] 10-11-7 **99** .... (b) StephenCraine[(5)] 117+
(T D Easterby) *trckd ldrs: led 4 out: hit last: pushed out* **8/1**

0562 **2** *7* **Opportunity Knocks**[8] [3652] 6-9-7 **73** oh3 .... KeiranBurke[(7)] 80+
(N J Hawke) *w ldrs: lft in ld 6th: hdd 10th: chsd wnr fr 3 out: no imp* **14/1**

-3U4 **3** *12* **Calcot Flyer**[38] [3151] 8-11-9 **96** .... RobertThornton 95+
(A King) *w ldrs: led 10th: j.rt and slowly and hdd 4 out: wknd 2 out: v tired run-in* **11/2**[1]

/3PP **4** *8* **Roddy The Vet (IRE)**[14] [3547] 8-10-5 **78** .... JimCrowley 64
(A Ennis) *chse3d ldrs: upsides 8th: wknd 4 out* **14/1**

255 **5** *3* **Wee William**[37] [3170] 6-11-12 **99** .... RobertWalford 82
(T D Walford) *in rr: mstke 2nd: sme hdwy 4 out: hit next: nvr on terms* **20/1**

-656 **6** *2 1/2* **Levallois (IRE)**[21] [3434] 10-11-6 **93** .... PhilipHide 74
(P Winkworth) *in rr fr 8th: nvr a factor* **13/2**[2]

0F64 **7** *1 1/2* **Iloveturtle (IRE)**[11] [3593] 6-10-0 **73** oh2 .... (t) KennyJohnson 52
(M C Chapman) *a in rr: bhd fr 8th* **25/1**

6542 **8** *9* **Game On (IRE)**[43] [2984] 10-11-11 **98** .... AndrewThornton 68
(B N Pollock) *hit 1st and 8th: prom: outpcd 10th: 6th and wl btn whn blnd 2 out* **11/2**[1]

20PP **9** *4* **Meggie's Beau (IRE)**[21] 3434 10-11-9 **99** .... PaulO'Neill(3) 65
(Miss Venetia Williams) *chsd ldrs: drvn along 9th: sn lost pl and bhd* **14/1**

61/6 **U** **Longstone Loch (IRE)**[25] 3368 9-10-12 **85** .... PaulMoloney —
(C C Bealby) *led tl blnd bdly and uns rdr 6th* **14/1**

3-PF **P** **Dumadic**[26] 3350 9-11-3 **97** .... PhilKinsella(7) —
(R E Barr) *in rr: hdwy to chse ldrs 7th: lost pl 10th: bhd whn p.u bef 3 out* **7/1**[3]

P-24 **P** **Extra Cache (NZ)**[43] 2957 13-10-0 **73** oh1 .... JamieMoore —
(O Brennan) *hdwy and in tch 4th: drvn along 7th: sn lost pl: bhd whn p.u bef 3 out* **7/1**[3]

025P **P** **Hazel Bank Lass (IRE)**[31] 3285 10-11-3 **90** .... PJBrennan —
(Andrew Turnell) *in rr: hdwy and in tch whn stmbld landing 10th: sn lost pl: bhd whn p.u bef 3 out* **20/1**

(13.60) **Going Correction** +0.60s/f (Soft) **13** Ran SP% **120.3**
Speed ratings: **100,97,93,90,89 88,88,85,83,— —,—,—** CSF £109.49 CT £676.68 TOTE £10.10: £2.80, £4.90, £3.80; EX 150.20.
Owner C H Stevens **Bred** Mrs David Gordon Lennox **Trained** Great Habton, N Yorks

FOCUS
A moderate handicap which saw the field finish well strung out behind the facile winner.

NOTEBOOK
King's Bounty, backed on course, could have been called the winner before jumping to the front four from home and, despite a mistake at the final fence, ultimately came home to win as he pleased. Value for further, this was just about his best display to date, and he clearly appreciates good ground. A hike in the weights can now be expected, but he is at the right end of the handicap, and can defy a higher mark. *(op 11-1)*
Opportunity Knocks, with the cheekpieces left off, finished a clear second-best and posted a solid effort from 4lb out of the handicap. He has been improved since racing on a faster surface the last twice. *(op 12-1)*
Calcot Flyer, dropped in trip, failed to sustain his effort when headed by the winner and was legless at the finish. He once again failed to really convince over his fences and is a frustrating sort to follow. *(op 7-1)*
Roddy The Vet(IRE) found just the same pace under pressure and, while he at least completed this time, continues to look regressive.
Game On(IRE) proved mediocre in the jumping department and was beaten before his stamina for this longer trip became an issue. *(tchd 5-1 and 6-1)*

3792 GBM UK CONSTRUCTION NOVICES' H'CAP HURDLE (10 hdls) 2m 6f
4:20 (4:21) (Class 4) (0-110,107) 4-Y-0+ **£3,220** (£938; £469)

Form RPR

P6P- **1** **Wild Chimes (IRE)**[341] 4136 7-11-6 **101** .... (b) RichardJohnson 111+
(P J Hobbs) *wnt prom 5th: led last: hung lft: rdn rt out: all out* **14/1**

031 **2** *¾* **Franco (IRE)**[43] 2985 8-10-13 **101** .... MrRJBarrett(7) 110+
(Mrs A E Brooks) *sn led: hdd 7th: led after next to last: kpt on wl: jst hld towards fin* **12/1**

4530 **3** *4* **Emmasflora**[10] 3621 8-11-3 **103** .... AdamPogson(5) 108+
(C T Pogson) *in rr: hdwy appr 2 out: styd on wl run-in to take 3rd: nt rch 1st 2* **16/1**

F0F0 **4** *1 ¼* **Montevideo**[53] 2871 6-11-9 **104** .... APMcCoy 109+
(Jonjo O'Neill) *nt fluent: hld up in rr: hdwy to chse ldrs 6th: wnt 2nd 2 out: one pce appr last* **11/1**

4253 **5** *12* **Shady Baron (IRE)**[13] 3559 7-11-1 **99** .... PaddyAspell(3) 91
(J Wade) *chsd ldrs: hrd drvn 7th: sn wl outpcd* **40/1**

-2P3 **6** *shd* **Sir Pandy (IRE)**[34] 3238 6-11-12 **107** .... AndrewThornton 99+
(R H Alner) *hld up in rr: gd hdwy 7th: sn chsng ldrs: wknd between last 2* **14/1**

-6PP **7** *1* **Midnight Gold**[22] 3428 6-11-5 **100** .... RobertThornton 91
(A King) *chsd ldrs: rdn 7th: lost pl appr 2 out* **15/2**[3]

4603 **8** *4* **It's Bertie**[43] 2968 6-11-3 **98** .... DominicElsworth 85
(Mrs S J Smith) *trckd ldrs: led 7th: hdd after next: wknd 2 out* **10/1**

9 *dist* **Dev (IRE)**[334] 4292 6-11-2 **97** .... (t) PaulMoloney —
(M G Quinlan) *trckd ldrs: hit 3 out: sn lost pl and bhd: virtually p.u: t.o: btn 31 l* **3/1**[1]

-325 **10** *9* **Royal Coburg (IRE)**[32] 3277 6-11-9 **104** .... CarlLlewellyn —
(N A Twiston-Davies) *led eraly: drvnb and lost pl 5th: sn bhd: t.o 3 out* **8/1**

43P **P** **Megapac (IRE)**[22] 3426 8-11-2 **97** .... BrianCrowley —
(Noel T Chance) *bef 2 out: drvn along 4th: lost pl next: bhd whn p.u* **20/1**

4-UP **P** **Murat (FR)**[216] 916 6-11-4 **99** .... (v) TomScudamore —
(M C Pipe) *chsd ldrs: blnd 5th: lost pl and hit next: t.o whn p.u bef 3 out* **40/1**

-264 **P** **Extra Smooth**[63] 2690 5-11-3 **98** .... WayneHutchinson —
(C C Bealby) *in rr: sme hdwy 7th: lost pl after next: bhd whn p.u bef 2 out* **6/1**[2]

23-0 **P** **Lost Boy (IRE)**[33] 3253 7-11-5 **100** .... TonyDobbin —
(R Bastiman) *prom: reminders 3rd: lost pl next: sn bhd: t.o whn p.u bef 2 out* **16/1**

5m 24.3s (-4.00) **Going Correction** +0.025s/f (Yiel) **14** Ran SP% **122.0**
Speed ratings: **108,107,106,105,101 101,101,99,—,— —,—,—,—** CSF £170.45 CT £2717.13 TOTE £16.20: £4.80, £4.40, £5.50; EX 285.00 Place 6 £24.27, Place 5 £6.60.
Owner Mrs Susie Chown **Bred** Mrs Cancre-Devine Pascaline **Trained** Withycombe, Somerset

FOCUS
A decent handicap for the class, run at a generous pace, and the first two came clear on the run-in.

NOTEBOOK
Wild Chimes(IRE), having his first run for new connections, made a winning return from a 341-day layoff in dogged fashion under a strong ride from Johnson - who appears to be at the top of his game at present. He proved disappointing when with Paul Nicholls last term, and it is not difficult to see why he wears blinkers, but this was a personal-best effort over hurdles and the change of stable looks to have had a positive effect. His next outing will reveal whether he is ready to fulfil his potential and, as a former winning pointer, he could be sent over fences before too long. *(op 16-1)*
Franco(IRE), raised 6lb for winning at Towcester last time, had every chance and turned in a brave effort, but could not cope with the late challenge of the winner. He was nicely ahead of the rest at the finish and remains capable of further success from this sort of mark. *(op 8-1)*
Emmasflora was staying on stoutly from two out and posted a return to form. She is hard to win with, but is well worth riding more prominently over this trip in the future.
Montevideo spoilt his chance with some less-than-fluent jumping and was ultimately well held. This was a more encouraging effort, and he has an engine, but is never one to trust. *(op 14-1)*
Midnight Gold, well backed, found nothing when push came to shove and his fate was sealed before the turn for home. He at least completed this time, however, and may appreciate the return to a longer distance in the future. *(tchd 7-1)*
Dev(IRE), very well backed throughout the day ahead of this handicap debut, failed to sustain his effort after a serious error three out having looked most likely to have a say in the finish up to that point. *(op 7-2)*
T/Plt: £39.60 to a £1 stake. Pool: £50,735.15. 933.45 winning tickets. T/Qpdt: £11.30 to a £1 stake. Pool: £4,144.90. 269.60 winning tickets. WG

[3380]CARLISLE (R-H)
Wednesday, February 8

OFFICIAL GOING: Soft (heavy in places in back straight)
After 4mm of overnight rain the ground was described as 'very holding'. The running rail on the hurdle track was at its' tightest, right on the inner.
Wind: Light, half-behind Weather: Fine but cold

3793 ANDREW FLINTOFF BENEFIT IN AID OF LEIKAEMIA RESEARCH NOVICES' HURDLE (9 hdls) 2m 1f
1:10 (1:10) (Class 4) 4-Y-0+ **£3,083** (£898; £449)

Form RPR

-451 **1** **Regal Heights (IRE)**[16] 3534 5-11-5 115 .... StephenCraine(5) 119+
(D McCain) *trckd ldrs: led 3 out: styd on strly between last 2: readily* **16/1**

13 **2** *2 ½* **Two Miles West (IRE)**[89] 2161 5-11-10 .... APMcCoy 113
(Jonjo O'Neill) *hld up in mid-div: hdwy 6th: wnt 2nd between last 2: no imp* **8/13**[1]

502 **3** *4* **Boulders Beach (IRE)**[30] 3314 6-11-3 .... DominicElsworth 102
(Mrs S J Smith) *chsd ldrs: kpt on same pce fr 2 out* **14/1**[3]

2 **4** *7* **Nikola (FR)**[29] 3328 5-11-3 .... CarlLlewellyn 95
(N A Twiston-Davies) *chsd ldrs: wnt 2nd 3 out: wknd appr last* **10/3**[2]

5 *¾* **Secret Pact (IRE)**[474] 4-10-7 .... TonyDobbin 84
(I McMath) *mid-div: hdwy 6th: kpt on one pce fr 3 out* **50/1**

0-0 **6** *1 ¼* **Nile Moon (IRE)**[108] 1849 5-11-3 .... AlanDempsey 93
(J Howard Johnson) *hld up in rr: hdwy 5th: one pce fr 3 out* **200/1**

2064 **7** *½* **Rothbury**[19] 3490 6-11-0 .... MichalKohl(3) 94+
(J I A Charlton) *sn trcking ldrs: wkng whn blnd 2 out* **33/1**

0-00 **8** *8* **Easby Mandarin**[56] 2821 5-11-3 .... RussGarritty 84
(C W Thornton) *hld up in rr: hday 6th: edgd rt and lost pl appr 2 out* **100/1**

03 **9** *nk* **Silent Bay**[97] 2007 7-11-0 .... PaddyAspell(3) 84
(J Wade) *chsd ldrs: drvn along 5th: lost pl 3 out* **100/1**

1 **10** *4* **Red Poker**[84] 2268 6-11-3 .... RichardMcGrath 80
(G A Harker) *trckd ldrs: t.k.h: wknd qckly 2 out* **20/1**

0P0 **11** *6* **Bishop's Brig**[16] 3534 6-10-12 .... MichaelMcAlister(5) 74
(N W Alexander) *in tch: lost pl after 6th* **500/1**

0-1P **12** *6* **Suprendre Espere**[15] 3545 6-11-3 .... JosephByrne 68
(Jennie Candlish) *led to 3 out: sn lost pl* **125/1**

0-03 **13** *5* **Ebac (IRE)**[52] 2903 5-11-3 .... (t) GrahamLee 63
(J Howard Johnson) *a in rr* **40/1**

0-0 **14** *nk* **Dusky Dawn (IRE)**[81] 2340 5-10-12 .... ThomasDreaper(5) 62
(J M Jefferson) *in rr: sme hdwy 6th: wknd and j.rt last 2* **200/1**

-50 **15** *2 ½* **Sticky End**[30] 3319 5-10-10 .... BenOrde-Powlett(7) 60
(J B Walton) *in rr: hdwy 4th: sn chsng ldrs: lost pl after 6th* **200/1**

16 *14* **The Corby Glenn (IRE)**[289] 31 5-11-0 .... PaulO'Neill(3) 46
(Barry Potts, Ire) *prom: lost pl 6th: sn bhd* **200/1**

00/ **17** *8* **Glimpse Of Glory**[817] 2136 6-11-3 .... NeilMulholland 38
(C W Thornton) *in tch: blnd 6th: sn lost pl* **200/1**

0/0 **P** **Old Barns (IRE)**[77] 2444 6-10-12 .... DougieCostello(5) 9
(G A Swinbank) *in rr: bhd fr 5th: t.o whn p.u bef 3 out* **200/1**

4m 31.5s (5.80) **Going Correction** +0.275s/f (Yiel)
WFA 4 from 5yo+ 9lb **18** Ran SP% **115.6**
Speed ratings: **97,95,93,90,90 89,89,85,85,83 80,78,75,75,74 67,64,—** CSF £25.48 TOTE £15.60: £2.70, £1.10, £2.70; EX 28.10.
Owner Mrs Janet Heler **Bred** Mrs R Deane **Trained** Cholmondeley, Cheshire

FOCUS
A much improved effort from the winner but the suspicion was that the two market leaders were not at their very best. The winning time was almost six seconds faster than the later handicap, but still only modest for the grade.

NOTEBOOK
Regal Heights(IRE), who looked in tremendous condition, is going from strength to strength and took this in fine style. He will make an even better chaser in time. *(op 14-1)*
Two Miles West(IRE), given a patient ride, went in pursuit of the winner but was never going to finish anything but second best. His effort here seemed to lack any sparkle. *(op 4-5 tchd 5-6)*
Boulders Beach(IRE) is on the up and surely it is only a question of time before he gets off the mark.
Nikola(FR) was already making hard work of it when sent in pursuit of the winner and he called enough going to the final flight. He was not at his best for some reason here. *(op 5-2 tchd 7-2)*
Secret Pact(IRE), a winner twice at two, made a satisfctory hurdling bow after being absent for 16 months.
Nile Moon(IRE), unplaced in two bumper starts, showed a fair bit more on his first try over hurdles and he can improve further given a little more time.
Rothbury, after four outings in bumpers, went well on his hurdling bow but his goose was cooked when blundering two out.

3794 KIER NORTHERN NOVICES' H'CAP CHASE (16 fncs 2 omitted) 3m 110y
1:45 (1:46) (Class 3) (0-115,114) 5-Y-0+ **£6,506** (£1,910; £955; £477)

Form RPR

35U2 **1** **Pass Me By**[25] 3382 7-11-6 **111** .... (e) PaulO'Neill(3) 126+
(R C Guest) *j.rt: mde virtually all: clr 2 out: pushed out* **7/2**[2]

-3F3 **2** *9* **Kitski (FR)**[44] 2976 8-11-6 **113** .... ThomasDreaper(5) 115
(Ferdy Murphy) *in rr: hdwy 8th: wnt 3 out: no imp* **12/1**

6-13 **3** *2 ½* **Theatre Knight (IRE)**[37] 3204 8-11-4 **106** .... GrahamLee 106
(J Howard Johnson) *chsd ldrs: outpcd 10th: kpt on run-in to take 3rd nr fin* **11/2**[3]

5503 **4** *¾* **Bannister Lane**[16] 3541 6-10-4 **97** .... StephenCraine(5) 97+
(D McCain) *trckd ldrs: chal 11th: wknd fr 3 out: eased and lost 3rd nr line* **14/1**

3140 **5** *2 ½* **Dead Mans Dante (IRE)**[26] 3377 8-10-12 **107** .... PatrickMcDonald(7) 105+
(Ferdy Murphy) *hld up in rr: hdwy 9th: wknd 3 out* **20/1**

-22F **6** *8* **See You There (IRE)**[25] 3382 7-11-9 **114** .... PeterBuchanan(3) 105+
(Miss Lucinda V Russell) *chsd ldrs: reminders 8th: struggling whn hit 10th: sn no threat* **5/2**[1]

5310 **7** *6* **Nocatee (IRE)**[19] 3489 5-10-4 **108** .... PaddyMerrigan(5) 79
(P C Haslam) *hld up in rr: hit 9th: nvr on terms* **6/1**

1-00 **U** **Cha Cha Cha Dancer**[19] 3487 6-10-5 **98** .... DougieCostello(5) —
(G A Swinbank) *hld up: blnd and uns rdr 1st* **12/1**

-0UP **P** **Em's Royalty**[48] 2945 9-10-12 **100** .... AlanDempsey —
(A Parker) *chsd ldrs: drvn along 7th: lost pl after next: t.o 11th: p.u bef 2 out* **28/1**

6m 40.7s
WFA 5 from 6yo+ 11lb **9** Ran SP% **110.7**
CSF £40.49 CT £214.18 TOTE £4.00: £1.80, £3.10, £1.40; EX 54.90.

Owner Paul Beck **Bred** Miss Coreen McGregor **Trained** Brancepeth, Co Durham

■ Stewards' Enquiry : Stephen Craine seven-day ban: dropped hands and lost third place (Feb 19-25)

FOCUS

Pass Me By ground the opposition into the ground but with the favourite running poorly it was not a strong event. First fence in back straight omitted.

NOTEBOOK

Pass Me By, his confidence boosted by the fitting of eyeshields, jumped boldly but tended to go right at his fences. He kept up the gallop in relentless fashion and seems to just stay. *(op 3-1)*

Kitski(FR), having just his fourth start over fences, jumped better and kept on in vain pursuit of the winner. *(op 11-1)*

Theatre Knight(IRE), suited by the testing conditions, kept on after struggling to keep up to snatch a fortuitous third place. *(op 4-1)*

Bannister Lane took on the winner but he was reported to have a problem with his wind from three out. He was hanging on to third spot when prematurely eased near the line earning his rider a seven-day ban. The lesson will hopefully not be lost on him. *(op 12-1)*

Dead Mans Dante(IRE), a keen-type, moved up as if about to enter contention but he found little and seems better over two and a half miles.

See You There(IRE) did not impress with his jumping, laboured at times. Given some sharp reminders with a full circuit to go, his chance was already slim when he clouted the seventh-last fence hard. He was possibly remembering his fall here last time. *(op 11-4 tchd 3-1)*

3795 JOHN SMITH'S/E.B.F. MARES' ONLY "NATIONAL HUNT" NOVICES' HURDLE (QUALIFIER) (11 hdls) 2m 4f

2:20 (2:20) (Class 4) 4-Y-0+ **£3,903** (£1,146; £573; £286)

Form	Pos	Dist	Horse	RPR
4563	**1**		**Jontys'Lass**[16] 3540 5-10-12 88 .... MrTGreenall(3) (A Crook) *w ldrs: led 5th: kpt on run-in: jst hld on* **20/1**	91
15-F	**2**	½	**Funny Times**[94] 2062 5-11-1 .... TonyDobbin (N G Richards) *t.k.h: wnt prom 6th: hung lft appr last: j.rt: styd on wl towards fin: jst hld* **11/8**[1]	90+
-400	**3**	*nk*	**Treasured Memories**[21] 3442 6-11-1 88 .... AndrewThornton (Miss S E Forster) *wnt prom 6th: wandered between last 2: edgd lft and styd on wl run-in* **22/1**	91+
6122	**4**	*6*	**Cloudless Dawn**[32] 3287 6-11-7 115 .... RussGarritty (P Beaumont) *w ldrs: chal 3 out: fdd last 150yds* **13/8**[2]	90
-053	**5**	*7*	**Buffy**[21] 3442 6-11-1 90 .... NeilMulholland (B Mactaggart) *chsd ldrs: wknd appr last* **25/1**	77
043	**6**	*6*	**More Likely**[26] 3376 5-10-10 .... DougieCostello(5) (Mrs A F Tullie) *wnt prom 6th: one pce fr 3 out* **12/1**[3]	71
00	**7**	*10*	**Gulshique**[6] 3692 6-11-1 .... CarlLlewellyn (N A Twiston-Davies) *sn in rr and drvn along: sme hdwy 7th: nvr nr ldrs* **50/1**	61
04	**8**	*3*	**Monifieth**[21] 3448 6-10-12 .... PeterBuchanan(3) (D W Whillans) *in rr: sme hdwy 7th: lost pl appr 3 out* **50/1**	58
0440	**9**	*4*	**Political Pendant**[16] 3534 5-10-8 92 .... GarethThomas(7) (R Nixon) *hit 1st: hdwy and in tch 6th: lost pl after 8th* **33/1**	54
P45	**10**	½	**Another Jameson (IRE)**[65] 2674 6-10-10 .... ThomasDreaper(5) (J M Jefferson) *t.k.h: led to 2nd: led 4th to 5th: wknd appr 3 out* **50/1**	56+
F	**11**	*9*	**Hillary Harbour (IRE)**[55] 2856 7-10-10 .... PaddyMerrigan(5) (J G Cosgrave, Ire) *chsd ldrs: hung lft 8th: sn lost pl* **66/1**	45
0-4	**12**	*19*	**Losing Grip (IRE)**[15] 3551 7-11-1 .... DominicElsworth (Mrs S J Smith) *w ldrs: led 2nd to 4th: lost pl 8th: sn bhd* **25/1**	26
P462	**P**		**Roadworthy (IRE)**[15] 3552 9-11-1 65 .... WilsonRenwick (W G Young) *bhd fr 5th: p.u bef 8th* **200/1**	—
0-0	**P**		**Teen Lady**[14] 3563 7-11-1 .... KeithMercer (Ferdy Murphy) *in rr: bhd fr 5th: t.o whn p.u bef 9th* **200/1**	—

5m 20.4s (3.30) **Going Correction** +0.275s/f (Yiel) **14** Ran SP% **116.0**

Speed ratings: **104,103,103,101,98 96,92,90,89,89 85,77,—,—** CSF £45.44 TOTE £28.80: £3.20, £1.10, £4.00; EX 69.20.

Owner A Crook - T Oglesby - S Hollingsworth **Bred** Mrs E M Charlton **Trained** Harmby, N Yorks

FOCUS

Seemingly a much improved effort from the winner rated just 88. The second ought to have won, the third looks back on the rails after two below-par efforts.

NOTEBOOK

Jontys'Lass, dropping right back in trip, stole a march on her rivals and in the end the post came just in time. On the day she really looked only third best. *(op 22-1 tchd 25-1)*

Funny Times, a smart bumper mare, has been off for three months after crashing out at the final flight on her hurdling debut. Very keen, she gave her rider problems going to the last and jumped it right-handed. Getting her act together on the run-in, she would have made it in a few more strides. *She may be a bit funny but she has a good engine and the experience will not be lost on her. (op 11-10 tchd 6-4)*

Treasured Memories showed a return to form and really picked up on the run-in. She should improve again and find a similar event. *(op 25-1)*

Cloudless Dawn went with the winner up front but in the end the penalty on this ground proved too much. *(op 15-8 tchd 2-1 in places)*

Buffy again showed ability but this may be as good as she is.

More Likely could not match the leaders up the final hill and it transpired that she had spread a front plate. *Official explanation: trainer said mare spread a front plate*

3796 WEATHERBYS BANK NOVICES' CHASE (11 fncs 1 omitted) 2m

2:55 (2:56) (Class 3) 5-Y-0+ **£6,506** (£1,910; £955; £477)

Form	Pos	Dist	Horse	RPR
21-1	**1**		**Monet's Garden (IRE)**[94] 2065 8-11-10 .... TonyDobbin (N G Richards) *trckd ldr: chal 5th: led next: clr fr 8th: v easily: won by 40 l* **2/7**[1]	145+
/4P6	**2**	*dist*	**Been Here Before**[38] 3170 6-11-0 .... RichardMcGrath (G A Harker) *wnt poor 3rd 7th: 20 l bhd 3 out: 30 l down last: sn tk remote 2nd* **40/1**[3]	84+
/3U0	**3**	*1*	**More Flair**[44] 2975 9-10-0 .... BenOrde-Powlett(7) (J B Walton) *wnt poor 3rd 4th: struggling to keep up 7th: one pce* **100/1**	73
306P	**4**	*9*	**Silver Dagger**[14] 3557 8-10-9 80 .... (tp) MichaelMcAlister(5) (J C Haynes) *sn remote: poor 4th fr 7th* **150/1**	69
U-41	**5**	*2*	**Iron Man (FR)**[25] 3380 5-11-3 .... GrahamLee (J Howard Johnson) *led to 6th: chsd wnr: wknd rapidly sn after last* **7/2**[2]	70+
3	**6**	*8*	**Delaware Trail**[25] 3394 7-11-0 .... KennyJohnson (R Johnson) *stdd s: a detached in last: hit 5th* **100/1**	59

4m 13.8s (-3.30) **Going Correction** +0.125s/f (Yiel)

WFA 5 from 6yo+ 6lb **6** Ran SP% **105.1**

Speed ratings: **113,—,—,—,—** — CSF £8.41 TOTE £1.40: £1.10, £5.60; EX 9.50.

Owner David Wesley Yates **Bred** William Delahunty **Trained** Greystoke, Cumbria

FOCUS

They went a strong gallop and the winner could hardly have been more impressive. The winning time was decent when compared to the later handicap. First fence in back straight omitted.

NOTEBOOK

Monet's Garden(IRE) ◆, back after pulling a muscle, made short work of Iron Man and came home in glorious isolation. He will have another outing, possibly here, before his spring targets are outlined. *(op 1-4 tchd 3-10 in a place)*

Been Here Before, a point winner, kept on up the final hill to take a remote second spot soon after the last. He will have a much more realistic chance in novice handicaps.

More Flair, winner of three points, tries hard and much easier opportunities will occur in the spring.

Silver Dagger, reverting to fences, at least picked up some prize money by simply completing. *(op 100-1)*

Iron Man(FR), who needs to go right-handed, took them along at a strong gallop. Left for dead by the winner up the final hill, he was legless at the last and soon lost second place.

3797 ANDREW FLINTOFF BENEFIT SUPPORTING LEUKAEMIA RESEARCH H'CAP HURDLE (9 hdls) 2m 1f

3:30 (3:30) (Class 4) (0-105,105) 4-Y-0+ **£2,927** (£859; £429; £214)

Form	Pos	Dist	Horse	RPR
0504	**1**		**Front Rank (IRE)**[29] 3332 6-11-6 99 .... RichardMcGrath (Mrs Dianne Sayer) *led to 4th: led 3 out: clr last: eased towards fin* **13/2**[3]	113+
00	**2**	*13*	**Lagudin (IRE)**[17] 3523 8-11-9 102 .... (b) TonyDobbin (Paul John Gilligan, Ire) *trckd ldrs: wnt 2nd after 3 out: 6 l down and no imp whn hit last* **9/2**[1]	102+
0-FF	**3**	*5*	**Robert The Bruce**[101] 1940 11-11-6 102 .... GaryBerridge(3) (L Lungo) *hld up: hdwy 6th: sn chsng ldrs: kpt on to take mod 3rd last* **16/1**	96+
0604	**4**	*3*	**Fearless Foursome**[36] 3231 7-10-11 90 .... GrahamLee (N W Alexander) *chsd ldrs: one pce fr 3 out* **6/1**[2]	80
FP00	**5**	*1¼*	**Infini (FR)**[29] 3339 10-10-8 97 .... MichaelO'Connell(10) (Mrs S J Smith) *trckd ldrs: led and qcknd 4th: hdd 3 out: sn wknd* **20/1**	86
212U	**6**	*1¼*	**Comical Errors (USA)**[19] 3485 4-10-11 105 .... PaddyMerrigan(5) (P C Haslam) *hld up in rr: effrt 6th: nvr nr ldrs* **13/2**[3]	83
0514	**7**	*13*	**Star Trooper (IRE)**[15] 3552 10-9-8 80 .... (p) TomMessenger(7) (Miss S E Forster) *chsd ldrs: drvn along 5th: lost pl 3 out* **8/1**	55
0435	**8**	*5*	**Millennium Hall**[37] 3206 7-11-6 102 .... PeterBuchanan(3) (Miss Lucinda V Russell) *mid-div: hit 5th: sn btn* **7/1**	72
000-	**9**	*dist*	**Lampion Du Bost (FR)**[334] 4303 7-10-6 90 .... ThomasDreaper(5) (A Parker) *trckd ldrs: wknd 6th: sn bhd: t.o: btn 33 l* **11/1**	—
2010	**10**	*21*	**Good Investment**[94] 2064 4-9-6 91 .... (p) GaryBartley(10) (P C Haslam) *in rr fr 3rd: sn bhd: t.o 3 out* **8/1**	—
00P4	**11**	*1*	**The Rooken (IRE)**[234] 785 7-10-2 81 oh10 ow2 .... KennyJohnson (P Spottiswood) *trckd ldrs: wknd qckly 5th: t.o 3 out* **100/1**	—
41F0	**12**	½	**Peter's Imp (IRE)**[25] 3395 11-11-2 95 .... NeilMulholland (A Berry) *a in rr: bhd fr 4th: sn t.o* **40/1**	—

4m 37.4s (11.70) **Going Correction** +0.275s/f (Yiel)

WFA 4 from 6yo+ 9lb **12** Ran SP% **116.3**

Speed ratings: **83,76,74,73,72 71,65,63,—,— —,—** CSF £35.22 CT £451.74 TOTE £8.10: £2.10, £2.40, £5.00; EX 47.90.

Owner Andrew Sayer **Bred** Ballymacoll Stud Farm Ltd **Trained** Hackthorpe, Cumbria

FOCUS

A weak race and no gallop at all over the first three-quarters of a mile, resulting in a very slow winning time for a race like this, nearly six seconds slower than the earlier novice event.

NOTEBOOK

Front Rank(IRE), who has changed stables, was in the right place throughout and in the end prove much too determined for the runner-up. In this frame of mind he should continue to give a good account of himself at this level even when reassessed. *(op 17-2 tchd 9-1)*

Lagudin(IRE), very useful in his younger days on the level, is still a maiden over hurdles after 19 starts now. He went in pursuit of the winner but was finding next to nothing when he clouted the last. *(tchd 5-1)*

Robert The Bruce, who last tasted success over five years ago, is slipping to a lenient mark but time is definitely not on his side. *(tchd 20-1)*

Fearless Foursome again ran well but this may be as good as he is. *(op 8-1)*

Infini(FR), back in trip, went on and stepped up the pace, but when the real race began he was quickly put in his place. *(op 16-1)*

Comical Errors(USA), happy to sit at the back, had little chance of entering the argument the way the race was run. *(op 4-1)*

3798 JASON HODGSON & FRIENDS SUPPORTING LEUKAEMIA RESEARCH H'CAP CHASE (11 fncs 1 omitted) 2m

4:05 (4:05) (Class 4) (0-105,101) 5-Y-0+ **£3,578** (£1,050; £525; £262)

Form	Pos	Dist	Horse	RPR
3P00	**1**		**Alfy Rich**[19] 3487 10-11-12 101 .... (p) TonyDobbin (M Todhunter) *trckd ldrs: led 2 out: drvn out* **12/1**	118+
2500	**2**	*3½*	**The Miner**[26] 3379 8-10-6 88 .... (p) TomMessenger(7) (Miss S E Forster) *chsd ldrs: drvn along 6th: kpt on same pce run-in* **7/1**	100
0006	**3**	*3*	**Nifty Roy**[21] 3445 6-10-0 80 .... DougieCostello(5) (I McMath) *in rr: hdwy 7th: chsng ldrs next: kpt on same pce between last 2* **20/1**	89
3330	**4**	*4*	**The Frosty Ferret (IRE)**[19] 3486 8-11-1 90 .... GrahamLee (J M Jefferson) *chsd ldrs: led 4th tl 2 out: one pce* **11/2**[3]	95
630P	**5**	*9*	**Hollows Mill**[48] 2946 10-11-6 100 .... ThomasDreaper(5) (F P Murtagh) *stedied s: hdwy to chse ldrs 6th: wknd fr 2 out* **6/1**	96
/033	**6**	*11*	**Tagar (FR)**[21] 3447 9-11-1 93 .... MrTGreenall(3) (C Grant) *prom: outpcd 8th: sn wknd* **4/1**[1]	78
0/64	**7**	*23*	**Saxon Mill**[15] 3555 11-10-6 81 .... OllieMcPhail (T J Fitzgerald) *chsd ldrs: wknd 6th: sn bhd* **14/1**	43
31P/	**P**		**Icy River (IRE)**[775] 2951 9-11-3 92 .... RichardMcGrath (K G Reveley) *bhd fr 3rd: t.o 5th: p.u bef 8th* **8/1**	—
P2P	**P**		**Jballingall**[25] 3398 7-10-9 84 .... (b) WilsonRenwick (N Wilson) *set mod pce to 4th: wknd 6th: sn bhd: t.o whn p.u bef 3 out* **5/1**[2]	—
3P05	**P**		**Bernardon (GER)**[41] 3106 10-11-4 98 .... PaddyMerrigan(5) (Barry Potts, Ire) *prom: drvn 6th: sn lost pl: t.o whn p.u bef 3 out* **20/1**	—

4m 18.5s (1.40) **Going Correction** +0.125s/f (Yiel) **10** Ran SP% **113.8**

Speed ratings: **101,99,97,95,91 85,74,—,—,—** CSF £91.49 CT £1655.28 TOTE £15.00: £2.70, £2.70, £6.90; EX 145.50.

Owner The Carlisle Cavaliers **Bred** Paul M Rich **Trained** Orton, Cumbria

FOCUS

The winning time was close to par for the grade despite being 4.7 seconds slower than the earlier novice chase. Overall the form looks sound. First fence in back straight omitted.

NOTEBOOK

Alfy Rich, galvanised by first-time cheekpieces, stuck to his task in determined fashion under a strong ride. *(op 14-1)*

The Miner, with cheekpieces this time, was the first to come under pressure. He stuck on in pursuit of the winner but in truth was never going to get in a serious blow. His record of just one win from 27 starts now tells all. *(tchd 8-1)*

Nifty Roy, out of sorts over timber, was making his chasing debut over a trip that is his bare minimum. *(tchd 25-1)*

The Frosty Ferret(IRE), dropping back in trip, went on and stepped up the pace but in the end he simply proved much too slow. *(op 13-2 tchd 7-1)*
Hollows Mill, who took this a year ago from a 6lb lower mark, is not in anything like the same sort of form now. *(op 13-2 tchd 11-2)*
Tagar(FR), dropping back in trip, ran a very tame sort of race. *(op 9-2)*
Bernardon(GER) *Official explanation: jockey said gelding hung badly right-handed (tchd 25-1)*

3799 HBLB "JUNIOR" STANDARD OPEN NATIONAL HUNT FLAT RACE 1m 6f
4:35 (4:35) (Class 6) 4-Y-O **£2,055** (£599; £299)

Form	Pos	Dist	Horse	Jockey	RPR
11	1		**Alfie Flits**[11] [3623] 4-11-3	DougieCostello(5)	116+
			(G A Swinbank) *trckd ldrs: led on bit over 3f out: clr over 1f out: v easily* **8/11**[1]		
	2	7	**Starting Point** 4-10-12	WilsonRenwick	91
			(Miss Lucinda V Russell) *trckd ldrs: kpt on to go 2nd 1f out: no ch w wnr* **100/1**		
44	3	4	**Asrar**[34] [3259] 4-10-2	PeterBuchanan(3)	80
			(Miss Lucinda V Russell) *chsd ldrs: kpt on same pce fnl 3f* **40/1**		
	4	nk	**Action Strasse (IRE)** 4-10-12	GrahamLee	87
			(J Howard Johnson) *trckd ldrs: keen: one pce fnl 3f* **16/1**		
	5	3/4	**Triple Deal** 4-10-12	TonyDobbin	86
			(N G Richards) *mid-div: hdwy 6f out: wnt 2nd over 2f out: one pce fnl f* **13/2**[3]		
	6	1/2	**Hot Zone (IRE)** 4-10-12	APMcCoy	85
			(Jonjo O'Neill) *hld up in rr: hdwy 5f out: one pce fnl 3f* **5/1**[2]		
010	7	3	**Insurgent (IRE)**[9] [3651] 4-10-9	JohnFlavin(10)	89
			(R C Guest) *hld up: hdwy 5f out: sn chsng ldrs: wknd over 1f out* **33/1**		
2	8	9	**Ruby Joy**[34] [3259] 4-9-12	TomMessenger(7)	66
			(Mrs H O Graham) *led 3f: led 6f out tl over 3f out: lost pl over 1f out* **20/1**		
	9	3 1/2	**Cavers Glen** 4-10-5	EwanWhillans(7)	70
			(A C Whillans) *trckd ldrs: t.k.hm led after 3f: hdd 6f out: hung lft over 4f out: sn lost pl* **28/1**		
	10	10	**More Equity** 4-10-5	DominicElsworth	53
			(Mrs A F Tullie) *chsd ldrs: lost pl 7f out: sn bhd* **80/1**		
	11	1	**Billsgrey (IRE)** 4-10-12	NeilMulholland	59
			(J S Haldane) *in rr: bhd fnl 6f* **100/1**		
	12	7	**Pennybid (IRE)** 4-10-9	PaddyAspell(3)	52
			(C R Wilson) *t.k.h in rr: bhd fnl 7f* **100/1**		
	13	23	**Over The Odds** 4-10-0	(t) BrianHughes(5)	22
			(W Storey) *in rr: lost pl over 4f out: virtually p.u over 1f out: t.o* **100/1**		

3m 47.9s **13** Ran SP% **112.6**
CSF £150.21 TOTE £1.50: £1.10, £21.00, £4.20; EX 74.70 Place 6 £97.12, Place 5 £71.94.
Owner Dom Flit **Bred** Shadwell Estate Company Limited **Trained** Melsonby, N Yorks

FOCUS
The winner defied a double penalty and looks a smart prospect. They were on the whole big, backward types in the paddock and as usual the pace was very modest.

NOTEBOOK
Alfie Flits ♦, a class act, defied his double penalty in effortless style. He is clearly one of the better bumper horses and he should have no trouble making his mark on the Flat proper. *(tchd 4-6 and 4-5)*
Starting Point, a big type, stuck to his task to claim second spot but the winner was in a different league. *(op 80-1)*
Asrar put her poor effort at Wetherby behind her but basicailly she looks to lack much in the way of size and scope. *(op 50-1)*
Action Strasse(IRE), who stands over plenty of ground, could have done with a much stronger pace. The experience will not be lost on him. *(op 14-1)*
Triple Deal, a well-made newcomer, went in pursuit of the winner but in the end he was made to look very one paced. *(op 5-1 tchd 7-1)*
Hot Zone(IRE), a big, potential chaser, was happy to sit off the pace. He kept on in his own time up the final hill and looks essentially a stayer. *(tchd 9-2)*
Ruby Joy *Official explanation: jockey said filly had a breathing problem (op 16-1)*
T/Plt: £163.40 to a £1 stake. Pool: £37,794.65. 168.75 winning tickets. T/Qpdt: £72.40 to a £1 stake. Pool: £2,439.10. 24.90 winning tickets. WG

3645 LUDLOW (R-H)
Wednesday, February 8

OFFICIAL GOING: Good to firm (good in places)
The ground according to the jockeys was not as fast as the official description, some calling it 'tacky' and 'dead'.
Wind: Moderate, against Weather: Fine, clouding over later

3800 BROMFIELD "NATIONAL HUNT" MAIDEN HURDLE (9 hdls) 2m
1:30 (1:30) (Class 4) 4-Y-0+ **£4,228** (£1,241; £620; £310)

Form	Pos	Dist	Horse	Jockey	RPR
	1		**Paro (FR)**[84] 5-10-11 110	AndrewGlassonbury(7)	103+
			(M C Pipe) *sn chsng ldr: led 3rd: clr appr 3 out: hit last: comf* **8/1**[3]		
66	2	9	**Wenlocks Wonder**[27] [3354] 5-11-4	JohnMcNamara	88
			(K C Bailey) *hld up and bhd: hdwy after 6th: chsd wnr appr 3 out: no imp* **16/1**		
2202	3	3	**Arumun (IRE)**[23] [3417] 5-11-4	TomScudamore	85
			(M Scudamore) *t.k.h: led to 3rd: chsd wnr tl appr 3 out: one pce* **4/5**[1]		
0000	4	1	**Post It**[20] [3463] 5-10-11	JamieMoore	78+
			(R J Hodges) *hld up: hdwy 5th: rdn appr 3 out: one pce: hit last* **40/1**		
00	5	1	**Koral Bay (FR)**[20] [3461] 5-10-4 110	MrSWaley-Cohen(7)	76
			(R Waley-Cohen) *j.rt: hld up: hdwy 5th: rdn appr 3 out: one pce* **11/1**		
4P6	6	dist	**Templer (IRE)**[30] [3327] 5-11-4	RichardJohnson	—
			(P J Hobbs) *bhd fr 5th: t.o* **11/2**[2]		
000	7	1 3/4	**Fill The Bunker (IRE)**[33] [3275] 6-11-4	AntonyEvans	—
			(N A Twiston-Davies) *a bhd: t.o* **20/1**		
0-0	8	dist	**Percy Jay (NZ)**[49] [2941] 7-11-4	MarkBradburne	—
			(W Jenks) *stdd s: plld hrd in rr: nt fluent: t.o* **66/1**		
00-5	9	3/4	**Noviciate (IRE)**[95] [2050] 6-11-4	WarrenMarston	—
			(Simon Earle) *stdd s: plld hrd: a in rr: t.o* **50/1**		
00	10	dist	**Montanah Jet**[11] [3623] 4-10-3	TomGreenway(5)	—
			(C N Kellett) *mstke 2nd: a bhd: t.o* **100/1**		
-0U	P		**Green Collar**[19] [3478] 7-11-4	(t) WayneHutchinson	—
			(M Salaman) *bhd fr 5th: t.o whn p.u bef 3 out* **66/1**		
4500	P		**Butler Services (IRE)**[12] [3591] 6-11-4	MickFitzgerald	—
			(Jonjo O'Neill) *a bhd: t.o whn p.u bef 2 out* **20/1**		
200P	P		**Princess Yum Yum**[20] [3466] 6-10-6	JamesDiment(5)	—
			(J L Spearing) *chsd ldrs: j.rt 3rd: wknd 6th: t.o whn p.u bef 2 out* **100/1**		
0P0P	P		**Oui Exit (FR)**[90] [2142] 5-10-13	StevenCrawford(5)	—
			(N A Twiston-Davies) *chsd ldrs: carried rt 3rd: mstke 5th: rdn and wknd after 6th: t.o whn p.u bef 3 out* **50/1**		

3m 51.6s (-0.70) **Going Correction** -0.15s/f (Good)
WFA 4 from 5yo+ 9lb **14** Ran SP% **117.1**
Speed ratings: **95,90,89,88,88** —,—,—,—,— —,—,—,— CSF £106.16 TOTE £11.10: £2.70, £4.30, £1.02; EX 81.60.
Owner M C Pipe **Bred** M Lalanne **Trained** Nicholashayne, Devon

FOCUS
Riders involved in the first race did not feel that the ground was as fast as the official description suggested, calling it 'tacky' and 'dead'. This was by no stretch of the imagination a strong novice hurdle, and very few got into the action as the two leaders soon went clear. The winning time was just under a second slower than the seller and the winner probably did not need to improve on his French form.

NOTEBOOK
Paro(FR), anxious to get on with things, was ahead at the final flight with a circuit to run and was never seriously threatened thereafter. Bought out of a claimer after the last of his four runs in France, he had only met with testing conditions previously but this surface clearly suited him admirably and he won with a bit to spare, despite more than one ragged jump. He may well struggle under a penalty, but he stays a bit further than this which increases his options. *(tchd 10-1)*
Wenlocks Wonder, not disgraced in a better race of this type over course and distance on his hurdles debut, was given a patient ride before emerging from the pack to give chase. He never looked likely to reach the winner, who went away from him again over the last couple of flights, but his turn should come. *(tchd 20-1)*
Arumun(IRE), a keen-going sort who was walked to post some way minutes before the rest, was only able to lead to the third flight but settled well enough behind the leader, clear of the remainder. He weakened at the head of the straight but stuck on for third, and a return to a longer trip might not come amiss. *(op 10-11 tchd evens in places)*
Post It, a bumper winner, had not shown much in three novice hurdles and this was a little better, with the faster ground a likely factor.
Koral Bay(FR), who was placed over hurdles and fences in France, showed her first sign of ability in this country, stepping down in trip and without the headgear.
Templer(IRE) showed promise on his bumper debut but does not appear to be progressing.
Oui Exit(FR) *Official explanation: jockey said gelding lost its action*

3801 BITTERLEY BEGINNERS' CHASE (19 fncs) 3m
2:05 (2:05) (Class 4) 5-Y-0+
£4,697 (£1,387; £693; £347; £173; £87)

Form	Pos	Dist	Horse	Jockey	RPR
-232	1		**Martha's Kinsman (IRE)**[14] [3558] 7-11-4	RichardJohnson	120+
			(H D Daly) *a.p: rdn to ld 2 out: drvn out* **7/4**[1]		
14-2	2	1/2	**Dickensbury Lad (FR)**[27] [3356] 6-11-4 115	AntonyEvans	120+
			(J L Spearing) *led to 7th: chsd ldr: hit 14th: led 15th: hit 4 out: rdn and hdd 2 out: r.o flat* **3/1**[3]		
-4FP	3	3/4	**Portavo (IRE)**[50] [2934] 6-11-4 92	PaulMoloney	118+
			(Miss H C Knight) *hld up and bhd: hdwy 11th: rdn and ev ch last: nt qckn* **25/1**		
0200	4	9	**Penny Pictures (IRE)**[38] [3179] 7-11-4	TomScudamore	113+
			(M C Pipe) *sn prom: hit 10th and 3 out: rdn and wkng whn mstke 2 out* **11/4**[2]		
6UFP	5	24	**Jonanaud**[19] [3480] 7-11-4 112	(b[1]) SeanCurran	85
			(H J Manners) *hld up: hdwy appr 12th: blnd 13th: n.d after* **25/1**		
P/00	6	hd	**Lady Wurzel**[35] [3240] 7-10-8	MissPGundry(3)	78
			(J G Cann) *prom: lost pl 9th: bhd fr 14th* **50/1**		
560-	7	3/4	**Man From Highworth**[373] [3629] 7-10-11	MrJAJenkins(7)	84
			(H J Manners) *t.k.h: hdwy 4th: led 7th tl blnd 15th: wknd appr 4 out* **14/1**		
-3P0	8	21	**The Muratti**[34] [3251] 8-10-11	MissLHorner(7)	63
			(G Brown) *bhd fr 12th: t.o* **100/1**		
PP	P		**Havit**[19] [3477] 8-10-11	MissLBrooke(7)	—
			(Lady Susan Brooke) *bhd fr 9th: t.o 12th: p.u bef 4 out* **100/1**		
0PF0	P		**Sidcup's Gold (IRE)**[20] [3460] 6-11-4 71	(b[1]) JimmyMcCarthy	—
			(M Sheppard) *bhd fr 9th: t.o 12th: p.u bef 4 out* **100/1**		
	P		**Lincoln Leader (IRE)**[306] 8-10-6	LeeStephens(5)	—
			(Evan Williams) *hld up in mid-div: hit 9th: bhd fr 12th: t.o whn p.u bef 14th* **18/1**		
4P4	P		**Harrihawkan**[8] [3660] 8-11-4	RobertThornton	—
			(Mrs T J Hill) *chsd ldr to 6th: lost pl appr 7th: bhd whn blnd 12th: p.u bef 14th* **25/1**		

6m 0.90s (-11.20) **Going Correction** -0.45s/f (Good) **12** Ran SP% **116.4**
Speed ratings: **100,99,99,96,88 88,88,81**,—,— —,— CSF £6.92 TOTE £2.80: £1.10, £1.40, £6.20; EX 6.40.
Owner Barlow, Hartley and Brereton **Bred** Michael Ward-Thomas, Susan Lady Barlow And Richard **Trained** Stanton Lacy, Shropshire

FOCUS
Just a moderate beginners' chase, which produced a stirring three-way finish.

NOTEBOOK
Martha's Kinsman(IRE), upped in trip after two promising efforts over fences, was well at home over the three miles and after edging ahead at the second last he stayed on willingly to hold two challengers. His wins to date have come on flat, right-handed tracks, although on this occasion he did jump out to his left at times. *(op 15-8 tchd 13-8)*
Dickensbury Lad(FR), who made a promising chasing bow over half a mile less at this venue but stayed this trip over hurdles, jumped soundly throughout and went down fighting after being headed for a second time with two to jump. He should not be long in going one better. *(op 5-2 tchd 10-3 in places)*
Portavo(IRE) took a bad fall on his chasing debut at Taunton but a subsequent run over hurdles obviously had the right effect. He made steady progress on the final circuit to close down the leading quartet and was produced to win his race at the last, but could not find a change of gear. This was his best run so far and he can win a chase if improving from this.
Penny Pictures(IRE) was the best of these over hurdles but was not the most consistent and proved hard to place. He looked a threat when taking the first fence in the home straight in second spot, but his jumping let him down when the pressure was on. He might be happier over slightly shorter. *(op 10-3 tchd 7-2)*
Jonanaud showed no improvement for the blinkers but at least completed the course this time.
Man From Highworth, a fair hurdler who was making his chasing debut on this first start for a year, pulled himself to the front at the seventh but relinquished the lead when down on his nose at the last fence on the far side. He was quickly on the retreat but has the ability to win over fences if settling better.
Harrihawkan *Official explanation: trainer said gelding bled from nose*

3802 HENLEY HALL GOLD CUP MARES' ONLY H'CAP HURDLE (11 hdls) 2m 5f
2:40 (2:40) (Class 2) 4-Y-0+
£12,526 (£3,700; £1,850; £926; £462; £232)

Form	Pos	Dist	Horse	Jockey	RPR
1311	1		**She's Our Native (IRE)**[27] [3358] 8-11-4 120	MrNWilliams(5)	126+
			(Evan Williams) *hld up in tch: led appr 3 out: drvn out* **13/8**[1]		
-P3P	2	3	**Dancing Pearl**[11] [3621] 8-11-12 123	MarkBradburne	123
			(C J Price) *a.p: hit 7th: rdn and ev ch 3 out: one pce fr 2 out* **8/1**		

5431 **3** 2 ½ **Reem Two**[19] [3484] 5-10-3 **100** .... TimmyMurphy 98+
(D McCain) *w ldr to 2nd to 6th: outpcd 8th: rallied 3 out: one pce fr 2 out* **10/3**[2]

001F **4** 2 **Titian Flame (IRE)**[4] [3733] 6-10-0 **100** .... (p) WilliamKennedy(3) 95
(D Burchell) *hld up: hdwy appr 7th: led briefly after 8th: wknd 3 out* **14/1**

514P **5** 3 ½ **Ballyhoo (IRE)**[23] [3424] 6-9-7 **97** oh3........ WayneKavanagh(7) 90+
(J W Mullins) *hld up: pushed along appr 7th: no hdwy whn mstke 2 out* **25/1**

F144 **6** 7 **Heltornic (IRE)**[11] [3621] 6-11-7 **118** .... TomScudamore 106+
(M Scudamore) *led tl after 8th: eased whn btn appr 3 out* **9/2**[3]

6543 **P** **Latin Queen (IRE)**[43] [3017] 6-11-1 **112** .... RichardJohnson —
(J D Frost) *hld up: short-lived effrt 8th: eased and p.u bef 3 out* **11/1**

5m 13.9s (-4.40) **Going Correction** -0.15s/f (Good) **7** Ran SP% **109.3**
Speed ratings: **102,100,99,99,97 95,—** CSF £13.54 TOTE £3.00: £1.70, £2.20; EX 16.90.
Owner Ian Brice **Bred** J Mangan **Trained** Cowbridge, Vale Of Glamorgan

FOCUS
This mares' handicap was run at a sound pace, though the winning time was 2.4 seconds slower than the later novice hurdle and the winner probably did not need to improve on her recent course-and-distance win. There seems no reason why the form should not stand up.

NOTEBOOK
She's Our Native(IRE) defied a 12lb rise to gain her third course-and-distance victory of the winter, the first of which came off a mark no less than 29lb lower than she was racing off here. The handicapper might catch up with her over hurdles now, although a crack at the Coral Cup has been mooted, but she has the option to revert to fences off a favourable mark, currently 27lb lower than she is over hurdles. *(op 11-8 tchd 5-4 and 7-4 in places)*
Dancing Pearl delivered a strong challenge at the third from home but her stamina just let her down in the latter stages. This was more encouraging, and as she has won in March in each of the last three years there could be a race for her next month. *(op 14-1)*
Reem Two, a consistent mare reverting to handicap company, forfeited a prominent position towards the end of the back straight but was running on again at the finish. *(op 3-1)*
Titian Flame(IRE) showed no ill effects from a heavy fall at Uttoxeter on Saturday but the 9lb rise for her win at Leicester told over the final three flights. *(op 10-1)*
Ballyhoo(IRE) was found wanting for pace but this was a respectable effort from 3lb out of the weights. *(tchd 28-1)*
Heltornic(IRE) was taken on for the lead by Reem Two and eventually faded on the long run round *to the straight. Her wins this term have come in testing ground.Official explanation: jockey said mare hung badly left-handed (op 5-1 tchd 11-2)*

3803 ATTWOOD MEMORIAL TROPHY H'CAP CHASE (17 fncs) 2m 4f
3:15 (3:15) (Class 3) (0-130,124) 5-Y-0+

£7,515 (£2,220; £1,110; £555; £277; £139)

Form RPR

P131 **1** **Bob The Builder**[20] [3459] 7-11-6 **118** .... AntonyEvans 134+
(N A Twiston-Davies) *j.lft: mde all: j. bdly lft 2 out: mstke last: drvn out* **5/2**[1]

5504 **2** 1 **Spring Lover (FR)**[23] [3420] 7-11-9 **121** .... SamThomas 129
(Miss Venetia Williams) *hld up: hdwy appr 10th: rdn to chse wnr 4 out: hit last: nt qckn* **14/1**

3122 **3** ½ **Winsley**[62] [2725] 8-11-4 **116** .... (v[1]) LeightonAspell 124+
(O Sherwood) *hld up and bhd: hdwy 13th: rdn appr 4 out: r.o flat* **7/2**[2]

6404 **4** 6 **Saafend Rocket (IRE)**[20] [3459] 8-11-1 **113** .... RichardJohnson 114
(H D Daly) *hld up and bhd: sme hdwy 13th: styd on one pce fr 4 out* **8/1**

12-4 **5** 4 **Northern Deal (IRE)**[34] [3249] 11-11-7 **124** .... MrNWilliams(5) 123+
(Evan Williams) *t.k.h: chsd wnr tl rdn 4 out: wknd appr 2 out* **8/1**

2165 **6** 8 **Kind Sir**[20] [3459] 10-10-11 **109** .... WayneHutchinson 98
(A W Carroll) *hld up in mid-div: hdwy appr 10th: rdn appr 4 out: wknd 3 out* **33/1**

46 **7** 3 **Lord Archie (IRE)**[28] [3343] 8-10-8 **106** .... (tp) MarkBradburne 92
(M Sheppard) *nvr nr ldrs* **20/1**

-FU0 **8** 2 ½ **Farlington**[63] [2703] 9-11-4 **119** .... TomMalone(3) 103
(P Bowen) *hld up and bhd: hdwy 9th: wknd 11th* **28/1**

121U **9** 13 **Bishop's Bridge (IRE)**[30] [3323] 8-11-6 **118** .... PJBrennan 89
(Andrew Turnell) *hld up in mid-div: hdwy 7th: hit 13th: rdn appr 4 out: wknd appr 2 out* **9/1**

F055 **10** 18 **Let's Rock**[9] [3647] 8-10-0 **105** oh31 ow7........ MrRHodges(7) 58
(Mrs A Price) *hld up in tch: rdn 9th: sn struggling* **200/1**

0-P0 **P** **Talbot Lad**[272] [311] 10-11-2 **114** .... (t) JasonMaguire —
(Mrs H Dalton) *hld up in tch: wknd 11th: t.o whn p.u bef 4 out* **20/1**

0320 **P** **Benrajah (IRE)**[14] [3560] 9-11-2 **114** .... RobertThornton —
(M Todhunter) *prom: mstke 5th: wknd after 9th: t.o whn p.u bef 4 out* **7/1**[3]

4m 57.5s (-13.20) **Going Correction** -0.45s/f (Good) **12** Ran SP% **118.6**
Speed ratings: **108,107,107,105,103 100,99,98,92,85 —,—** CSF £33.57 CT £126.00 TOTE £2.60: £2.00, £3.80, £1.50; EX 31.20 Trifecta £140.20 Pool: £612.22 - 3.10 winning tickets..
Owner Mr & Mrs Peter Orton **Bred** Mrs Susan Orton **Trained** Naunton, Gloucs

FOCUS
Quite a well contested handicap chase, contested by any number of Ludlow regulars and run at a good pace. The winner was well in and probably just repeated his last effort.

NOTEBOOK
Bob The Builder, set a sound tempo throughout as he followed up his recent course win off a 12lb higher mark. He jumped to his left all the way - something he also does on left-handed tracks - and survived a bad blunder when diving left at the last to win with a bit up his sleeve in the end. He may go for the Fulke Walwyn Kim Muir at the Festival, and although his jumping would be tested to the full at Cheltenham he should be kept on the right side. *(op 11-4 tchd 3-1 in places)*
Spring Lover(FR) showed a liking for this track last spring and did nothing wrong, but after the winner's antics at the final fence had appeared to let him in, that rival found more once straightened up. This is his trip.
Winsley, tried in a visor for the first time but no stranger to headgear, was staying on strongly at *the death and has now run three solid races in handicaps since landing a beginners' chase. (op 10-3)*
Saafend Rocket(IRE), who was runner-up in this event a year ago, made late gains for fourth but in truth was never a factor. This trip looks more suitable than the minimum these days. *(op 7-1)*
Northern Deal(IRE) was sharper for his recent return to action over hurdles, but could not get to the front with Bob The Builder in opposition and had been seen off turning for home. *(op 6-1)*
Bishop's Bridge(IRE) was disputing second facing up to the last four fences but soon faded. *(op 14-1)*
Talbot Lad *Official explanation: jockey said gelding had a breathing problem (tchd 25-1)*

3804 RACECOURSE PLUMBER (S) HURDLE (9 hdls) 2m
3:50 (3:50) (Class 5) 4-Y-0+ **£2,602** (£764; £382; £190)

Form RPR

-334 **1** **Ambersong**[5] [2560] 8-11-13 95........ WayneHutchinson 104
(A W Carroll) *hld up and bhd: hdwy 6th: rdn appr 3 out: r.o to ld nr fin* **9/1**

02B3 **2** ½ **Elaala (USA)**[19] [3485] 4-9-7 95........ PhilKinsella(7) 76
(M Todhunter) *hld up and bhd: hdwy appr 5th: led after 2 out: hdd nr fin* **9/2**[1]

3030 **3** 6 **Jamaaron**[20] [3456] 4-9-11 92........ RichardGordon(10) 78+
(W G M Turner) *hld up and bhd: hdwy after 6th: led 3 out tl after 2 out: wknd flat* **8/1**

0514 **4** 5 **Barella (IRE)**[7] [3673] 7-11-4 96........ HowieEphgrave(5) 88
(L Corcoran) *hld up towards rr: hdwy 6th: no imp fr 2 out* **13/2**

P0FP **5** 1 ½ **Tunes Of Glory (IRE)**[20] [3459] 10-11-3 97........ (p) JasonMaguire 81
(D McCain) *chsd ldrs: rdn after 3 out: wknd 2 out* **16/1**

3604 **6** 12 **Brochrua (IRE)**[90] [2150] 6-10-11 93........ ChrisHonour(5) 68
(J D Frost) *mid-div: rdn and lost pl after 4th: n.d after* **6/1**[3]

0-P5 **7** 3 **Native Commander (IRE)**[7] [3673] 11-10-12 97.... ChristopherMurray(5) 66
(Jim Best) *chsd ldrs: led after 6th to 3 out: sn wknd* **16/1**

030 **8** 1 ¼ **Firebird Rising (USA)**[58] [1085] 5-10-10 69........ AntonyEvans 57
(R Brotherton) *hld up and bhd: hdwy on outside after 6th: sn rdn and wknd* **100/1**

50- **9** ¾ **Lahob**[3] [3307] 6-11-3 .... JamieMoore 64
(P Howling) *hld up: hdwy appr 5th: rdn and wknd appr 3 out* **33/1**

R00 **10** 3 ½ **Lightening Fire (IRE)**[9] [3645] 4-10-0 .... (b) WillieMcCarthy(7) 50
(B J Llewellyn) *w/ bhd fr 3rd* **100/1**

0405 **11** 6 **Weet Watchers**[20] [3456] 6-11-3 79........ JohnMcNamara 56+
(T Wall) *hld up and bhd: hdwy 6th: wknd qckly 3 out* **20/1**

6-PP **12** 3 ½ **Made In France (FR)**[67] [2626] 6-11-13 .... (p) TomScudamore 61
(M C Pipe) *prom: led appr 5th tl after 6th: wknd qckly* **5/1**[2]

50P0 **13** 12 **Simiola**[20] [3456] 7-10-10 73........ MarkGrant 32
(S T Lewis) *hld up in mid-div: hdwy appr 5th: wknd after 6th* **100/1**

0P **14** 1 ¼ **Viking Star (IRE)**[11] [2658] 5-11-0 .... (p) LeeVickers(3) 37
(A D Brown) *prom tl wknd after 6th* **100/1**

/6-P **15** 7 **Major Speculation (IRE)**[5] [3719] 6-11-3 103........ (b[1]) SamThomas 30
(J M Bradley) *led tl appr 5th: wknd after 6th* **66/1**

U06 **P** **Southern Shore (IRE)**[26] [1563] 4-10-4 90........ (bt) WilliamKennedy(3) —
(D Burchell) *bhd fr 5th: t.o whn p.u bef 3 out* **12/1**

P **Heartbeat**[25] 5-10-3 .... MissClaireMilne(7) —
(I A Wood) *mid-div: j.lft and lost pl 4th: t.o fr 5th: p.u bef 3 out* **100/1**

3m 50.7s (-1.60) **Going Correction** -0.15s/f (Good)
WFA 4 from 5yo+ 9lb **17** Ran SP% **117.2**
Speed ratings: **98,97,94,92,91 85,84,83,83,81 78,76,70,69,66 —,—** CSF £46.30 TOTE £11.80: £3.20, £2.60, £3.30; EX 64.50.There was no bid for the winner. Elaala was claimed by P. A. Blockley for £6,000. Jamaaron was claimed by J. Spearing for £6,000.
Owner Pursuit Media **Bred** Miss K Rausing **Trained** Cropthorne, Worcs

FOCUS
An ordinary seller in which the principals all came from off the pace as the leaders came back to them. The winning time was just under a second faster than the maiden hurdle, but still only ordinary for the grade.

NOTEBOOK
Ambersong still had plenty on his plate turning into the straight and was only third over the final flight, but he knuckled down well on the flat to force his head in front. Fit from a couple of runs on the sand, he has now gained all three of his hurdling wins over this track and trip. *(op 6-1)*
Elaala(USA), another who was ridden patiently, showed ahead going to the final flight but could not hold off the winner, from whom she was getting no less than 34lb. She can find a race in this grade for her new connections. *(op 11-2 tchd 6-1)*
Jamaaron was still travelling well when striking the front with three to jump, but lack of stamina is a persistent problem and he was collared before the last. *(tchd 9-1)*
Barella(IRE), a course-and-distance winner, was without the cheekpieces on his first outing since leaving the Brendan Powell yard and ran a sound race. *(op 15-2 tchd 6-1)*
Tunes Of Glory(IRE) has been out of form this term but showed more spark in the first-time cheekpieces. *(op 25-1)*
Brochrua(IRE) found this much too sharp on her first run for three months and merely passed beaten rivals at the end. *(op 11-2)*
Made In France(FR), equipped with cheekpieces for the first time, failed to take advantage of the drop in grade and weakened pretty quickly once headed leaving the back straight. *(op 11-2 tchd 6-1)*
Southern Shore(IRE) *Official explanation: trainer said gelding was scoped and found to have bled (op 14-1 tchd 11-1)*

3805 WEATHERBYS CHASE HUNTERS' CHASE (19 fncs) 3m
4:25 (4:25) (Class 5) 6-Y-0+

£2,700 (£843; £421; £211; £105; £53)

Form RPR

5-23 **1** **An Capall Dubh (IRE)**[277] [221] 10-11-10 .... MrRBurton 93+
(Mrs Edward Crow) *led 2nd: j.lft 8th: hit 9th: drvn out* **1/1**[1]

U34- **2** 1 ½ **Montebank (IRE)**[32] 10-11-3 .... MrGWalters(7) 91+
(Mrs O Bush) *hld up and bhd: hdwy 11th: wnt 2nd 4 out: rdn and ev ch last: nt qckn* **50/1**

-PP0 **3** 6 **Khaladjistan (IRE)**[37] 8-11-6 73 ow3........ (t) MrJHandley(7) 87
(Mrs S E Handley) *hld up: hdwy 4th: rdn 4 out: wknd 2 out* **25/1**

0PP/ **4** 3 ½ **Magicien (FR)**[10] 10-11-3 .... MissLBrooke(7) 81
(Steve Isaac) *hld up: pckd 10th: hdwy 15th: wknd 2 out* **9/1**

-36P **5** 12 **Guignol Du Cochet (FR)**[17] 12-11-7 95........ MrAWintle(3) 69
(S Flook) *led to 2nd: chsd wnr to 4 out: wknd 2 out* **4/1**[2]

/5-0 **6** 3 **Chief Mouse**[242] 13-11-3 65........ (p) MrRHodges(7) 66
(Steve Isaac) *hld up in tch: mstke 12th: rdn and wknd appr 4 out* **25/1**

4 **7** 1 ¼ **Catch The Bus (IRE)**[25] 9-11-10 .... MrSMorris 66+
(Mrs K Smyly) *hld up and bhd: hdwy 11th: wknd after 15th* **14/1**

60P/ **8** 4 **Zola (IRE)**[333] 10-11-3 .... MrPSheldrake(7) 60
(Mrs J Sidebottom) *bhd whn mstkes 12th and 15th* **18/1**

5-20 **P** **Lord Of The Hill (IRE)**[227] [840] 11-11-5 101........ MissLHorner(5) —
(G Brown) *prom tl wknd 13th: bhd whn p.u after 2 out* **15/2**[3]

0/P- **P** **Barton Bandit**[11] 10-11-3 .... MrJoshuaHarris(7) —
(Miss Sarah Kent) *bhd: nt fluent 11th (water): blnd 13th: t.o whn p.u bef 14th* **50/1**

6m 5.60s (-6.50) **Going Correction** -0.45s/f (Good) **10** Ran SP% **115.3**
Speed ratings: **92,91,89,88,84 83,82,81,—,—** CSF £67.66 TOTE £1.80: £1.30, £10.00, £7.10; EX 65.70.
Owner D Pugh **Bred** Thoroughbred Investments **Trained** Shrewsbury, Shropshire

FOCUS
An ordinary hunter chase in which the winner probably did not need to be at his best.

NOTEBOOK
An Capall Dubh(IRE), who was runner-up twice here last term, gained his first success under Rules in Britain. Making most of the running, he generally jumped soundly and, although he looked vulnerable at the final fence, he found plenty to see off the runner-up. *(op 11-10 tchd 11-8)*
Montebank(IRE), fit from a point-to-point run a month ago, improved in the straight to look a threat going to the final fence, but could not quicken up. This was a decent run but he remains a maiden.
Khaladjistan(IRE) lost his way under Rules but has now produced a couple of fair efforts since switching to hunt racing. He has yet to prove he wants this far, though.
Magicien(FR) is a decent ladies' horse between the flags but he has yet to show the same aptitude for regulation fences, although this was better. *(op 10-1 tchd 11-1 and 8-1)*
Guignol Du Cochet(FR), a course-and-distance winner who landed a point last month, chased the winner for much of the way before weakening once reaching the straight. *(op 5-1 tchd 7-2)*

The Form Book, Raceform Ltd, Compton, RG20 6NL

Lord Of The Hill(IRE), a fair handicapper having his first run since June, has shown his best form at up to two and a half miles and this was too far for him. *(op 6-1)*

3806 LUDLOW SPARKY NOVICES' HURDLE (11 hdls) 2m 5f
4:55 (4:55) (Class 4) 5-Y-0+ **£3,903** (£1,146; £573; £286)

Form RPR

04P2 **1** **Adventurist**[9] 3646 6-10-12 110 ....(p) MickFitzgerald 114+
(P Bowen) *hld up towards rr: hdwy after 8th: led 2 out: rdn and r.o wl flat* **4/1**[3]

4220 **2** *4* **Smart Mover**[73] 2530 7-10-12 104 .... TimmyMurphy 111+
(Miss H C Knight) *hld up in tch: led and j.rt 3 out: hdd 2 out: one pce* **7/2**[2]

2 **3** *5* **Master Wells (IRE)**[32] 3291 5-10-12 .... RichardJohnson 107+
(P J Hobbs) *hld up and bhd: hdwy appr 7th: carried rt 3 out: wknd appr last* **11/10**[1]

505 **4** *13* **Flirty Jill**[15] 3550 5-10-5 ....(t) TomDoyle 90+
(P R Webber) *hld up in tch: hdwy 7th: led after 8th: hdd and carried rt 3 out: wknd after 2 out* **28/1**

31P4 **5** *6* **Schumann**[44] 2967 5-10-12 .... AndrewTinkler 86
(M Pitman) *hld up in mid-div: rdn after 8th: no imp* **11/1**

0-6P **6** *5* **Red Granite**[58] 2799 6-10-12 .... JohnMcNamara 81
(K C Bailey) *hld up and bhd: hdwy 8th: wknd appr 3 out* **40/1**

2 **7** *15* **Dante's Promise (IRE)**[273] 299 10-10-5 .... MrTJO'Brien[(7)] 66
(C J Down) *prom: led after 6th to 7th: wkng whn mstke 3 out* **25/1**

0400 **8** *8* **Brave Jo (FR)**[34] 3248 5-10-5 .... KeiranBurke[(7)] 58
(N J Hawke) *chsd ldr: led 7th tl after 8th: sn wknd* **100/1**

06 **9** *6* **Darn Good**[9] 3646 5-10-12 ....(t) RobertThornton 52
(A King) *bhd whn mstke 5th: n.d after* **20/1**

430 **P** **Northern Endeavour**[66] 2665 7-10-12 .... WarrenMarston —
(Simon Earle) *bhd fr 8th: t.o whn p.u bef 3 out* **50/1**

PP **P** **Jacobin (USA)**[27] 3355 5-10-5 .... JohnKington[(7)] —
(M Scudamore) *t.k.h: led: clr to 6th: sn hdd & wknd: t.o whn p.u bef 3 out* **100/1**

-240 **P** **Dan's Man**[20] 3466 5-10-12 .... AntonyEvans —
(N A Twiston-Davies) *hld up in tch: rdn and wkng whn blnd 3 out: p.u bef 2 out* **20/1**

0-06 **F** **Sparklinspirit**[20] 3466 7-10-12 .... JamieMoore 95
(J L Spearing) *hld up and bhd: hdwy appr 8th: disputing 4th and btn whn fell last* **100/1**

5m 11.5s (-6.80) **Going Correction** -0.15s/f (Good) **13** Ran SP% **122.4**
Speed ratings: **106,104,102,97,95 93,87,84,82,—** —,—,— CSF £17.64 TOTE £6.30: £1.60, £1.40, £1.70; EX 18.50 Place 6 £12.44, Place 5 £9.36 .
Owner The Leonard Curtis Partnership **Bred** A L Penfold And H Lascelles **Trained** Little Newcastle, Pembrokes

FOCUS
An ordinary novice hurdle, though the winning time was 2.4 seconds faster than the earlier mares' handicap and the winner seems to be progressing.

NOTEBOOK
Adventurist, on whom Fitzgerald had been busy for some time, took advantage of shenanigans at the third last to move to the front and eventually scored with a degree of comfort. This victory was ample compensation for a narrow defeat over course and distance last month and the reapplication of cheekpieces, in which he had been successful on the Flat, also seemed to help. He seems to be getting the hang of things now and shaped here as though he would get a bit further. *(tchd 9-2)*
Smart Mover had travelled well up until jumping out to his right at the third-last, which may have been a sign of him getting tired. Although eventually well beaten by the winner, this was an improvement on his effort in a Newbury handicap last time and he had already shown enough before that to suggest there is a race like this in him. *(op 10-3 tchd 4-1)*
Master Wells(IRE) looked a big threat turning for home, but although getting squeezed out at the third last would not have helped him, he was eventually beaten too far to say that it cost him the race. He probably needs softer ground. *(op 11-8)*
Flirty Jillwas well held in the end, but was still in with some sort of a chance when getting hampered at the third last and she is not without hope. *(op 25-1)*
Schumann encountered his fastest surface to date but was never able to land a blow. *(op 14-1 tchd 10-1)*
Sparklinspirit was held in fourth when slipping on landing after the last, but this was still a big improvement on his previous efforts. *(op 16-1)*
Dan's Man *Official explanation: jockey said gelding lost its action (op 16-1)*
T/Jkpt: £2,566.20 to a £1 stake. Pool: £23,494.24. 6.50 winning tickets. T/Plt: £7.50 to a £1 stake. Pool: £47,028.10. 4,574.05 winning tickets. T/Qpdt: £5.90 to a £1 stake. Pool: £2,949.10. 366.20 winning tickets. KH

3807 - 3813a (Foreign Racing) - See Raceform Interactive

3367 HUNTINGDON (R-H)
Thursday, February 9

OFFICIAL GOING: Chase course - good (good to firm in places); hurdle course - good to firm
Wind: Light, behind Weather: Fine and sunny

3814 BETFREDPOKER H'CAP HURDLE (12 hdls) 3m 2f
1:40 (1:46) (Class 4) (0-110,110) 4-Y-0+ **£3,253** (£955; £477; £238)

Form RPR

B425 **1** **Knighton Lad (IRE)**[35] 3249 6-11-5 103 ....(v[1]) RobertThornton 107+
(A King) *a.p: hmpd 3 out: led last: drvn out* **14/1**

21 **2** *hd* **Mayoun (IRE)**[12] 3613 9-10-4 95 ....(p) MrTJO'Brien[(7)] 100+
(Evan Williams) *hld up: hdwy 8th: chal and mstke 2 out: styd on u.p* **7/2**[2]

2132 **3** *1 3/4* **The Gangerman (IRE)**[29] 3345 6-11-8 106 .... CarlLlewellyn 106
(N A Twiston-Davies) *chsd ldrs: lost pl after 4th: rallied appr 3 out: styd on u.p* **13/2**[3]

6-00 **4** *2 1/2* **Ballistigo (IRE)**[62] 2755 7-11-7 105 .... WayneHutchinson 103
(A King) *hld up: hdwy 5th: rdn after 7th: led 3 out: rdn and hdd last: no ex* **33/1**

2463 **5** *5* **Amazing Valour (IRE)**[31] 3325 4-10-9 105 ....(b) RichardJohnson 87+
(P Bowen) *chsd ldrs: rdn after 3 out: wknd flat* **10/1**

2554 **6** *3 1/2* **Le Royal (FR)**[12] 3622 7-11-1 109 .... JamesReveley[(10)] 98
(K G Reveley) *hld up and bhd: mstke 3rd: styd on fr 2 out: nvr nr to chal* **9/1**

0050 **7** *13* **Son Of Greek Myth (USA)**[49] 2952 5-11-2 100 ....(b) JamieMoore 76
(G L Moore) *hld up: effrt 9th: n.d* **14/1**

6430 **8** *7* **Standing Bloom**[27] 3368 10-10-12 96 .... PaulMoloney 65
(Mrs P Sly) *prom: rdn after 7th: wknd bef next* **66/1**

P-3P **9** *5* **Greek Star**[45] 2994 5-10-9 93 .... PJBrennan 57
(K A Morgan) *hld up: hdwy after 7th: rdn and wknd appr 3 out* **22/1**

00/ **10** *3* **Keepakicker (IRE)**[18] 3522 10-11-0 103 ....(p) BCByrnes[(5)] 64
(E McNamara, Ire) *hld up: rdn 5th: wknd 9th: bhd whn hmpd 3 out* **12/1**

-214 **U** **Present Glory (IRE)**[21] 3458 7-11-10 108 .... TomDoyle —
(C Tinkler) *led: rdn after 9th: tried to run out and uns rdr next* **3/1**[1]

F-04 **P** **Emphatic (IRE)**[31] 3325 11-10-8 97 ....(b) StephenCraine[(5)] —
(J G Portman) *w ldr to 5th: wknd appr 8th: bhd whn p.u bef 3 out* **20/1**

500P **P** **Good Call (IRE)**[24] 3426 7-11-2 100 ....(v[1]) APMcCoy —
(Jonjo O'Neill) *chsd ldrs: mstke 7th: rdn and wknd 9th: bhd whn p.u bef next* **40/1**

6m 20.4s (-2.00) **Going Correction** -0.05s/f (Good)
WFA 4 from 5yo+ 11lb **13** Ran SP% **116.7**
Speed ratings: **101,100,100,99,98 97,93,90,89,88** —,—,— CSF £59.22 CT £358.63 TOTE £15.00: £4.60, £1.90, £2.00; EX 90.90.
Owner Mrs M M Stobart **Bred** C Murphy **Trained** Barbury Castle, Wilts

FOCUS
A fairly competitive handicap for the class, run at a modest early gallop, and the form appears fair enough rated around the runner-up and could rate higher.

NOTEBOOK
Knighton Lad(IRE), equipped with a first-time visor for this handicap debut, got off the mark over timber at the fifth attempt with a battling display. Considering he was hampered soon after the third last flight he deserves extra credit and the return to a sound surface enabled him to finally show his true colours. His future hopes probably rest on the headgear having the same effect in the future, but at least connections can now be confident he stays this far, and he should prove even better when sent over fences in due course. *(tchd 16-1)*
Mayoun(IRE), raised 10lb for winning on testing ground at Chepstow last time, looked very likely to follow-up prior to pecking on landing after the penultimate flight and was ultimately just held by the winner. While he must rate unfortunate, this was another solid effort, and he proved his effectiveness as regards underfoot conditions. He is also currently rated 10lb lower over fences and it would not come as surprise to see him in that sphere before too long. *(op 11-4 tchd 5-2)*
The Gangerman(IRE), whose previous best form had been on soft ground, looked like dropping out under pressure at halfway, but he stuck dourly to his task and was coming back at the leaders on the run-in. He is a consistent stayer, and can build on this when returning to a suitably softer surface, but he had a hard race and will most likely need time to recover from this experience. *(op 6-1)*
Ballistigo(IRE), markedly up in trip for this handicap bow, had every chance and turned in his best effort to date. He probably wants slightly easier ground and is up to finding a race when reverting to around three miles. *(op 25-1)*
Amazing Valour(IRE) was handy throughout and only cried enough approaching the final flight. He looks capable of finding a race from his current mark, but is not one to overly trust. *(tchd 12-1)*
Le Royal(FR), upped in trip, was again set too much to do by his inexperienced rider and never threatened. *Official explanation: jockey said, regarding the running and riding, his orders were to drop gelding out and utilise its finishing speed, adding that gelding was reluctant to race any closer on the first circuit in spite of his urgings with the whip down the shoulder on its left side; vet said gelding finished lame on its near fore (tchd 10-1)*
Present Glory(IRE), very well backed, was still bang in contention before attempting to run out approaching the third-last flight, giving his rider no chance of maintaining their partnership. *(op 4-1 tchd 9-2)*

3815 BETFREDCASINO H'CAP CHASE (16 fncs) 2m 4f 110y
2:10 (2:18) (Class 4) (0-110,109) 5-Y-0+ **£3,903** (£1,146; £573; £286)

Form RPR

2160 **1** **Runner Bean**[21] 3459 12-11-6 103 .... RobertThornton 119+
(R Lee) *chsd ldrs: led 9th: clr last: eased flat* **33/1**

6P3U **2** *7* **Priscilla**[21] 3465 8-11-2 99 .... JohnMcNamara 103
(K Bishop) *hld up: hdwy 6th: styd on same pce fr 2 out* **11/1**

UF32 **3** *2* **Randolph O'Brien (IRE)**[21] 3465 6-10-10 93 .... CarlLlewellyn 95
(N A Twiston-Davies) *chsd ldrs: led 7th to 9th: rdn after 3 out: styd on same pce fr next* **8/1**[3]

2 **4** *nk* **Fieldsofclover (IRE)**[21] 3460 9-10-5 88 .... MarcusFoley 90
(Miss E C Lavelle) *hld up: hdwy 10th: rdn appr 2 out: styd on same pce* **4/1**[1]

F54 **5** *3/4* **Barton Hill**[70] 2594 9-10-11 99 ....(b) DarylJacob[(5)] 100
(D P Keane) *hld up: hdwy 10th: styd on same pce fr 2 out* **20/1**

3061 **6** *1* **Lubinas (IRE)**[27] 3368 7-11-4 101 .... AndrewThornton 105+
(F Jordan) *hld up: hdwy 11th: hit next: styd on same pce appr 2 out* **6/1**[2]

4113 **7** *9* **Clouding Over**[20] 3489 6-11-9 106 .... JimCrowley 98+
(K G Reveley) *hld up: mstke 1st: hit 2 out: nvr nr to chal* **12/1**

1P50 **8** *22* **Haafel (USA)**[29] 3344 9-11-12 109 .... PhilipHide 78
(G L Moore) *disp ld to 7th: wknd appr 3 out* **50/1**

-5PF **9** *nk* **Celtic Major (IRE)**[19] 3499 8-10-7 95 .... LeeStephens[(5)] 64
(P Bowen) *mid-div: lost pl after 5th: bhd fr 8th* **66/1**

3F4 **10** *1* **Kimono Royal (FR)**[21] 3460 8-10-12 98 .... GinoCarenza[(3)] 66
(A King) *hld up: mstkes 7th and 9th: a in rr* **8/1**[3]

0-2 **11** *6* **Roaringwater (IRE)**[93] 2109 7-11-2 99 .... RichardJohnson 61
(R T Phillips) *mstkes: a in rr* **10/1**

11-P **P** **Laurier D'Estruval (FR)**[29] 3344 7-11-9 106 .... TomDoyle —
(S E H Sherwood) *mde most to 7th: wknd and p.u bef last: dismntd* **50/1**

6133 **U** **Hiers De Brouage (FR)**[36] 3239 11-11-0 102 ....(tp) StephenCraine[(5)] —
(J G Portman) *chsd ldrs: wkng whn blnd and uns rdr 4 out* **12/1**

3/2- **P** **Amid The Chaos (IRE)**[134] 1573 6-11-11 108 .... JimmyMcCarthy —
(C J Mann) *hld up: hdwy 6th: wknd 9th: bhd whn p.u bef 2 out* **12/1**

-052 **P** **Parish Oak**[8] 3676 11-11-8 105 .... WayneHutchinson —
(Ian Williams) *hld up: hdwy 10th: mstke 13th: hit next: wknd and p.u bef 2 out* **20/1**

5m 9.10s (3.00) **Going Correction** -0.05s/f (Good) **15** Ran SP% **114.9**
Speed ratings: **92,89,88,88,88 87,84,75,75,75 73,—,—,—,—** CSF £327.56 CT £3179.42 TOTE £26.70: £7.10, £4.40, £3.20; EX 376.40.
Owner H F P Foods Limited **Bred** Helshaw Grange Farms Ltd **Trained** Byton, H'fords

FOCUS
This modest handicap chase was run at a fair gallop, which saw the field fairly strung out from an early stage, and the first were clear at the finish. However, it produced a moderate time for the grade, but nevertheless the form looks solid rated through those in the frame behind the winner.

NOTEBOOK
Runner Bean, whose stable took this event in 2005 with Woodenbridge Dream, hit the front full of running turning for home and ultimately came home to score as he pleased. He is not the easiest to predict these days, but his form figures as chaser at this track now read 1313211U1, and he is proven on this sort of ground. He will now face a hike back up in the weights, however, and he is *not one to rely on for a follow-up bid. Official explanation: trainer said, regarding the improved form shown, gelding was better suited by this track*
Priscilla, who unseated at the final fence with the race at her mercy last time at Taunton, ran a sound race off this 5lb higher mark yet proved no match for the winner. She helps set the standard of this form and deserves to find an opening. *(op 10-1 tchd 12-1)*
Randolph O'Brien(IRE), who would have finished behind Priscilla at Taunton last time had that rival not unseated, was given a positive ride and acquitted himself well enough. However, he again left the impression he will be better served by an even stiffer test. *(tchd 9-1)*
Fieldsofclover(IRE), raised 5lb after finishing second on his recent British debut, was set a fair bit to do from off the pace on this drop back in trip and was never a serious threat. He has begun life for his new connections in good heart and can get closer from this mark when reverting to a longer trip. *(op 7-2)*
Barton Hill failed to see out this trip all that well, but posted a fair effort all the same and is entitled to improve a touch for this outing.

Lubinas(IRE), up 9lb for scoring comfortably over course and distance 27 days previously, was well held and the Handicapper now appears to have his measure. *(op 9-2)*
Clouding Over *Official explanation: trainer's representative said mare was unsuited by the fast ground (tchd 11-1)*
Parish Oak *Official explanation: jockey said gelding was unsuited by the fast ground (tchd 14-1)*
Amid The Chaos(IRE) *Official explanation: jockey said gelding had a breathing problem (tchd 14-1)*
Laurier D'Estruval(FR) *Official explanation: jockey said gelding lost its action (tchd 14-1)*

3816 BETFRED "THE BONUS KING" NOVICES' H'CAP CHASE (19 fncs) 3m
2:40 (2:48) (Class 3) (0-125,125) 5-Y-0+ **£7,807** (£2,292; £1,146; £572)

Form				RPR
-41F	**1**		**Alderburn**[30] [3331] 7-11-7 **120** .... RichardJohnson (H D Daly) *hld up in tch: led 14th: styd on wl* **9/4**[1]	141+
1	**2**	*5*	**Compo (IRE)**[39] [3201] 8-9-13 **103** .... BCByrnes[(5)] (E McNamara, Ire) *hld up: hdwy 13th: chsd wnr appr 2 out: no ex last* **7/2**[2]	112
1545	**3**	*9*	**The Dark Lord (IRE)**[30] [3331] 9-11-11 **124** .... LeightonAspell (Mrs L Wadham) *hld up: j. slowly 3rd: mstke 12th: hdwy next: wkng whn j.rt last* **17/2**	127+
0146	**4**	*7*	**Va Vavoom (IRE)**[39] [3176] 8-11-8 **121** .... CarlLlewellyn (N A Twiston-Davies) *w ldr tl led 10th: hdd 13th: wknd 2 out* **8/1**	116+
3024	**5**	*dist*	**Bell Lane Lad (IRE)**[40] [3142] 9-10-6 **105** ....(b[1]) HenryOliver (D J Wintle) *chsd ldrs to 13th* **12/1**	—
0-P1	**6**	*30*	**Wenceslas (IRE)**[51] [2929] 6-10-7 **106** .... PaulMoloney (Miss H C Knight) *led: j. slowly 4th: hdd 10th: led 13th to next: wknd 4 out* **7/1**	—
261P	**P**		**First De La Brunie (FR)**[27] [3368] 5-10-0 **110** .... RobertThornton (A King) *prom: dropped rr whn hit 10th: bhd whn p.u bef 12th* **5/1**[3]	—

6m 4.50s (-7.80) **Going Correction** -0.05s/f (Good)
WFA 5 from 6yo+ 11lb **7** Ran SP% **111.5**
Speed ratings: **111,109,106,104,— —,—** CSF £10.37 CT £52.05 TOTE £3.50: £2.20, £2.50; EX 14.20.
Owner Mrs D P G Flory **Bred** Mrs D P G Flory **Trained** Stanton Lacy, Shropshire

FOCUS
This was a fair handicap - markedly weakened by the six late withdrawals - which was run at an average gallop and the field finished strung out behind. It was a fair winning time for the grade and the winner was value for more than double the official margin with the runner-up to his mark.

NOTEBOOK
Alderburn ◆ got his career firmly back on track with a commanding success on this handicap bow. His jumping was particularly assured considering his recent experience at Leicester, the longer trip proved right up his street, and he should be rated value for further than his winning margin. While a rise in the weights is now inevitable, he still remains relatively unexposed over fences, yet his entry in the Royal & SunAlliance at Cheltenham still looks slightly optimistic, and it could be that the Aintree Festival may provide his best chance of bagging a decent novice prize. *(op 2-1)*
Compo(IRE) had every chance on ground he would have found plenty quick enough, yet was unable to live with the winner after two out. He was nicely clear of the remainder at the finish and is capable of winning off this mark. *(op 3-1)*
The Dark Lord(IRE) was again none too convincing over his fences and never seriously threatened. This was a more encouraging display, however, and he enjoyed the faster ground. *(op 8-1 tchd 9-1)*
Va Vavoom(IRE) again left the impression he does not get home over this trip, but is a happier horse on a softer surface, and he could get closer once again when reverting to shorter. *(op 7-1)*
Wenceslas(IRE), off the mark in novice company last time, had no more to offer approaching four from home and looks one to have reservations about. *(op 8-1)*
First De La Brunie(FR), pulled up at this venue last time, made a mistake passing the stands for the first time and was never going thereafter. He has become disappointing and has it all to prove after this. *(op 4-1)*

3817 BETFRED CHATTERIS FEN JUVENILE NOVICES' HURDLE (8 hdls) 2m 110y
3:10 (3:15) (Class 2) 4-Y-O **£16,265** (£4,775; £2,387; £1,192)

Form				RPR
21	**1**		**Afsoun (FR)**[61] [2756] 4-11-6 .... MickFitzgerald (N J Henderson) *trckd ldrs: wnt 2nd after appr 4th: led on bit bef 3 out: clr last: r.o wl: eased nr fin* **4/11**[1]	140+
11F	**2**	*10*	**Kalmini (USA)**[5] [3722] 4-10-13 .... JamieGoldstein (Miss Sheena West) *mstke 1st: sn pushed along in rr: hdwy 5th: chsd wnr appr 2 out: no ex last* **14/1**[3]	115
41B1	**3**	*7*	**Prize Fighter (IRE)**[13] [3594] 4-11-3 .... APMcCoy (Jonjo O'Neill) *chsd ldrs: rdn appr 2 out: sn wknd* **4/1**[2]	113+
4FF2	**4**	*11*	**Ellerslie Tom**[10] [3645] 4-10-12 .... LeeStephens (P Bowen) *led: hit 2nd: hdd whn hit 3 out: sn wknd* **18/1**	102+
06	**5**	*11*	**Kryena**[10] [3645] 4-10-5 .... JimmyMcCarthy (Mrs P Robeson) *hld up: wknd 5th* **150/1**	78
0	**6**	*7*	**Mayadeen (IRE)**[57] [2824] 4-10-12 .... TomDoyle (J G M O'Shea) *a bhd* **150/1**	78
00PP	**7**	*dist*	**Ghabesh (USA)**[23] [3429] 4-10-12 .... OllieMcPhail (Evan Williams) *a bhd* **250/1**	—
0	**8**	*dist*	**Kirin**[13] [3594] 4-10-12 ....(t) LeightonAspell (D E Cantillon) *hit 2nd: a bhd* **100/1**	—
P4	**F**		**Power Glory**[11] [3349] 4-10-12 .... ChrisHonour (M J Gingell) *a bhd: fell last* **150/1**	78
FP00	**P**		**Champagne Rossini (IRE)**[39] [2753] 4-10-12 .... PatrickCStringer (M C Chapman) *racd keenly: chsd ldr: lost pl whn hit 4th: sn wknd: t.o whn p.u bef last* **250/1**	—

3m 49.5s (-6.20) **Going Correction** -0.05s/f (Good) **10** Ran SP% **109.0**
Speed ratings: **112,107,104,98,93 90,—,—,—,—** CSF £6.26 TOTE £1.20: £1.10, £1.20, £1.20; EX 5.10.
Owner Million In Mind Partnership **Bred** S A Aga Khan **Trained** Upper Lambourn, Berks

FOCUS
No strength in depth to this juvenile event, which saw a rather disappointing turnout for the prizemoney on offer, but the race was run at a decent pace and the form still looks solid nevertheless.

NOTEBOOK
Afsoun(FR) ◆ enhanced his credentials as a leading candidate for the Triumph Hurdle at Cheltenham in good style and was value for further than his already wide winning margin. Given a positive ride, he would have found this track plenty sharp enough, but the added experience will be to his advantage come March, and more importantly he has now fully proved his ability to handle most types of ground. He is evidently a tough customer, and should go very close in the Triumph, so it was no surprise that he was immediately trimmed to 6/1 for that event. *(op 2-5)*
Kalmini(USA), who fell early on at Sandown just five days previously, took time to warm to her task yet did so in tenacious fashion and stayed on to finish a clear second-best. This was a decent effort under her penalties considering her experience at Sandown previously and, as she has a deal to find with the top juveniles, the Fred Winter Handicap would a more realistic target than the Triumph. *(op 10-1)*
Prize Fighter(IRE), a controversially disqualified winner at Fakenham last time, ran his race in third but was ultimately put in his place by the first two. He may appreciate the return to slightly easier ground in the future.
Ellerslie Tom eventually paid for his exertions at the head of affairs and was not given too hard a time when his chance evaporated. He can find easier opportunities to get off the mark. *(op 14-1 tchd 20-1)*
Kryena, while never a threat to the first four, would have found this ground too fast for her liking and becomes eligible for a handicap mark now.

3818 BETFRED 560 SHOPS NATIONWIDE H'CAP HURDLE (10 hdls) 2m 4f 110y
3:40 (3:46) (Class 4) (0-100,100) 4-Y-0+ **£3,253** (£955; £477; £238)

Form				RPR
-500	**1**		**Coralbrook**[72] [2563] 6-11-1 **89** ....(b[1]) JimmyMcCarthy (Mrs P Robeson) *chsd ldrs: led 3 out: clr whn hit next: drvn out* **18/1**	100+
4	**2**	*2*	**Gold Flo (IRE)**[38] [3226] 9-10-13 **92** .... BCByrnes[(5)] (E McNamara, Ire) *hld up: rdn 5th: hdwy 7th: sn outpcd: rallied to chse wnr 2 out: styd on* **13/2**	98
14P4	**3**	*11*	**Thedublinpublican (IRE)**[52] [2925] 6-11-5 **100** .... TomMessenger[(7)] (C C Bealby) *led to 2nd: chsd ldr tl led 7th: hdd 3 out: wknd next* **7/2**[1]	95
3P-5	**4**	*2*	**Boing Boing (IRE)**[275] [275] 6-11-0 **95** .... RichardSpate[(7)] (Miss S J Wilton) *prom: racd keenly: rdn after 7th: wknd appr 2 out* **25/1**	88
0040	**5**	*6*	**Wally Wonder (IRE)**[28] [3351] 8-10-13 **97** ....(b) JamesReveley[(10)] (K G Reveley) *led 2nd: mstke 6th: hdd next: wknd after 3 out* **8/1**	84
540	**6**	*12*	**Grand Bay (USA)**[21] [3464] 5-11-8 **96** .... APMcCoy (Jonjo O'Neill) *trckd ldrs: rdn and wknd after 3 out* **6/1**[3]	71
6-0P	**7**	*19*	**Late Claim (USA)**[38] [3214] 6-10-11 **95** .... ShaunJohnson[(10)] (R T Phillips) *hld up: bhd fr 5th* **40/1**	51
P	**8**	*2½*	**Dorneys Well (IRE)**[116] [1753] 6-11-2 **90** .... PaulMoloney (Evan Williams) *mid-div: lost pl 4th: hdwy 6th: wknd appr 3 out* **8/1**	44
13	**9**	*20*	**Gaelic Roulette (IRE)**[17] [1322] 6-11-8 **96** .... LeightonAspell (J Jay) *bhd whn hit 3rd: no ch whn hmpd 3 out* **4/1**[2]	30
0014	**F**		**Uncle John**[28] [3351] 5-10-8 **89** ....(v) PhilKinsella[(7)] (M E Sowersby) *hld up: wknd qckly 7th: bhd whn fell 3 out* **8/1**	—

4m 55.5s (0.20) **Going Correction** -0.05s/f (Good) **10** Ran SP% **114.7**
Speed ratings: **97,96,92,91,89 84,77,76,68,—** CSF £128.87 CT £511.68 TOTE £24.30: £4.50, £2.30, £1.90; EX 312.60.
Owner Mrs P Robeson **Bred** Mrs T D Pilkington **Trained** Tyringham, Milton Keynes

FOCUS
A moderate affair, and another event weakened by withdrawals, which was run at a solid pace and the first two came clear, with the winner value for more than double the official margin.

NOTEBOOK
Coralbrook, who had no shown all that much enthusiasm in six previous hurdle outings, finally proved his worth. He has clearly benefited from a recent break, but it was more likely the combination of first-time blinkers and a switch to fast ground that worked the oracle, and he should be rated value for a bit further as he was markedly idling on the run-in. He probably has more to offer on this sort of ground over timber, but whether the headgear has the same effect next time remains to be seen. *(op 20-1)*
Gold Flo(IRE), racing off a 10b higher mark than when successful at Limerick in December, was under pressure a long way from home - looking uneasy on the quick surface - but stuck to her task in resolute fashion and was coming back at the idling winner on the run-in. She can do better from this mark when reverting to a suitably easier surface in the future. *(op 6-1)*
Thedublinpublican(IRE) was given a positive ride, but could not go with the winner when that rival asserted approaching the home turn and was well beaten. His only previous success came on a quick surface, so he can have no excuses on that front. *(op 9-2 tchd 5-1)*
Boing Boing(IRE), returning from a 275-day layoff, was not disgraced and should come on plenty for this outing. *(op 20-1)*
Wally Wonder(IRE) failed to really improve for the re-application of blinkers and dropped out of the lead when the race got serious after four out.
Grand Bay(USA), making his handicap debut, found nothing for pressure when it mattered and looks one to avoid on this evidence. *(op 7-2)*
Gaelic Roulette(IRE) made an error at the third flight and was never going thereafter. *(op 5-1)*

3819 BETFRED IN SHOP, ON-LINE & ON PHONE NOVICES' HUNTERS' CHASE (19 fncs) 3m
4:10 (4:16) (Class 6) 5-Y-0+ **£1,249** (£387; £193; £96)

Form				RPR
223/	**1**		**Drombeag (IRE)**[694] [4398] 8-12-0 .... MrJTMcNamara (Jonjo O'Neill) *trckd ldrs gng wl: nt asked for effrt tl chal and mstke 2 out: outpcd briefly: drvn and rallied to ld cl home* **13/8**[1]	109+
11P/	**2**	*nk*	**Bosham Mill**[789] [2722] 8-11-11 .... MrTJO'Brien[(3)] (P J Hobbs) *prom: nt fluent 15th: led after 3 out: hrd rdn and r.o flat: ct nr fin* **11/4**[2]	107+
-23P	**3**	*7*	**Beauchamp Oracle**[265] [440] 9-11-7 .... MrMWalford[(7)] (S Flook) *settled towards rr: effrt to go cl up 3 out: drvn bef next: 2nd and chalng whn blnd last: nt rcvr* **20/1**	101+
UP-	**4**	*nk*	**Kerstino Two**[26] 9-11-11 .... MrDAlers-Hankey[(3)] (Mrs Caroline Keevil) *nt a fluent: hld up towards rr: effrt 15th: rdn and outpcd 3 out: rallied briefly: btn whn blnd 2 out* **16/1**	98
P-24	**5**	*2*	**Wings Of Hope (IRE)**[18] 10-11-11 89 ....(p) MrDSJones[(3)] (James Richardson) *keen: pressed ldr tl lft in front 10th: hdd after 3 out: fdd after next* **28/1**	97+
P01/	**6**	*dist*	**Lightning Strikes (IRE)**[1025] [4691] 12-11-7 .... MrMatthewSmith[(7)] (Mrs L Wadham) *settled trcking ldrs: j. slowly 14th (water): mstke next: rdn and wknd 3 out: eased next: btn 46l* **33/1**	—
	7	*1*	**Killard Point (IRE)**[32] 7-11-11 .... MrRCope[(3)] (Mrs Caroline Bailey) *hld up towards rr: gng wl 15th: rdn and outpcd after 3 out: tired next: eased: btn 47l* **12/1**	—
2	**U**		**Which Pocket (IRE)**[18] 8-11-11 .... MrPCowley[(3)] (A D Peachey) *stmbld after 2nd and uns rdr* **50/1**	—
U-2F	**P**		**Blaze On**[26] 7-11-11 .... MrPYork[(3)] (R H York) *a bhd: last whn nt fluent 11th: lost tch 13th: t.o and p.u 2 out* **50/1**	—
612-	**U**		**Lady Misprint**[25] 10-11-4 .... MissSGaisford[(3)] (Mrs Rebecca Jordan) *racd up to ld 6th: dived at 8th and uns rdr* **8/1**[3]	—
P/P-	**U**		**Irilut (FR)**[26] 10-11-9 ....(p) MrSWaley-Cohen[(5)] (R Waley-Cohen) *wl in rr whn blnd 2nd and rdr eventually fell off bkwards* **9/1**	—
0FU/	**F**		**Tender Tangle**[277] 11-12-0 .... MrSMorris (Miss S A Loggin) *bad mstke 1st: keen in ld: hdd 6th: lft in front again 8th tl fell heavily 10th* **33/1**	—

6m 10.2s (-2.10) **Going Correction** -0.05s/f (Good) **12** Ran SP% **117.5**
Speed ratings: **101,100,98,98,97 —,—,—,—,— —,—** CSF £5.70 TOTE £2.80: £1.50, £2.20, £3.20; EX 7.00.

Owner John P McManus **Bred** Daniel J O'Keeffe **Trained** Cheltenham, Gloucs

FOCUS

This was a decent event of its type which was run at a sound gallop and, despite the early departure of prolific pointer Irilut early on, the form looks solid with the first two in the betting coming clear on the run-in and has been rated positively.

NOTEBOOK

Drombeag(IRE) ◆, last seen finishing third under today's rider in the National Hunt Chase at Cheltenham in 2004, got his career in the sphere off to a perfect start with a workmanlike success. He was full of running prior to a serious error at the penultimate fence, so deserves credit for recovering as he did, and then showing his class to get on top of the runner-up close home. The return to a softer surface in the future should prove to his advantage, and he must rate an above-average recruit to the hunter chase ranks. Providing his next intended assignment goes to according plan, he should head for the Foxhunters' Chases at Cheltenham and Aintree with a leading chance. *(op 9-4)*

Bosham Mill ◆, a former Listed winner on the Flat having his first-ever outing over fences, turned in a sterling effort on this return from a 789-day layoff and made the winner fight all the way to the line. He jumped well, enjoyed the quick ground, and was well clear of the rest at the finish. Like the *winner, he must rate a decent recruit in this sphere, and should soon be placed to go one better.* *(op 3-1 tchd 5-2)*

Beauchamp Oracle was still upsides the first two prior to losing any chance with a final fence blunder and posted a solid effort in defeat. He helps set the level of this form and should improve a touch for the outing. *(tchd 25-1)*

Kerstino Two was ridden with more restraint than has often been the case in the past, and may well have been better served by more positive tactics, as he stays well and found just the same pace when it really mattered. He can find easier opportunities. *(op 12-1)*

3820 DONCASTER BLOODSTOCK SALES/E.B.F. MARES' ONLY STANDARD OPEN NATIONAL HUNT FLAT RACE — 2m 110y

4:40 (4:45) (Class 6) 4-7-Y-0 — **£2,055** (£599; £299)

Form					RPR
1	**1**		**Apollo Lady**[45] [2961] 5-11-2 — MrGTumelty(7) (A King) *hld up in rr: urged 5f out: wnt 2nd over 3f out: drvn ahd over 1f out: rn green: kpt on* **9/4**[1]		99+
	2	*1 ½*	**True Dove** 4-10-6 — AnthonyRoss (R A Fahey) *midfield: rdn over 2f out: hrd drvn to go 2nd ins fnl f: no imp* **20/1**		77
21	**3**	*2 ½*	**Tihui Two (IRE)**[225] [866] 6-11-9 — MickFitzgerald (G R I Smyly) *awkward s: last away but sn plld her way to a clr ld: rdn and hdd over 1f out: nt qckn* **3/1**[2]		92
6	**4**	*2 ½*	**Itsy Bitsy**[74] [2521] 4-10-6 — PaulMoloney (W J Musson) *keen in rr: outpcd briefly 4f out: rn green but kpt on ins fnl f: n.d* **10/1**		72
0	**5**	*1 ¼*	**Ma Burls**[270] [375] 6-10-9 — ShaneWalsh(7) (K F Clutterbuck) *pressed clr ldr tl over 3f out: drvn and wknd ins fnl f* **66/1**		81
54	**6**	*3*	**Forest Emerald (IRE)**[29] [3346] 4-10-3 — RichardYoung(3) (J W Mullins) *midfield: urged along 3f out: sn outpcd* **8/1**		68
	7	*5*	**Circus Rose** 4-10-6 — WarrenMarston (Mrs P Sly) *cl up over 12f: sn btn* **17/2**		63
	8	*16*	**Premier Hope (IRE)** 5-11-2 — MarcusFoley (Miss E C Lavelle) *hld up in bunch tl wknd tamely 3f out: t.o* **5/1**[3]		57
	9	*9*	**Molly McGredy** 5-10-13 — TJPhelan(3) (G Haine) *last most of way: struggling fnl 4f: t.o* **40/1**		48
0	**10**	*2 ½*	**Kathleen Kennet**[40] [3138] 6-11-2 — JamesDavies (Mrs H Sweeting) *plld hrd: prom in bunch for 12f: dropped out qckly: t.o* **33/1**		45

3m 55.7s (-0.80) **Going Correction** -0.05s/f (Good)
WFA 4 from 5yo 9lb 5 from 6yo+ 6lb — **10** Ran SP% **114.8**
Speed ratings: **97,96,95,93,93 91,89,82,77,76** CSF £52.07 TOTE £3.20: £1.50, £5.30, £1.10; EX 37.50 Place 6 £56.35, Place 5 £17.22.

Owner Jerry Wright & Andy Longman **Bred** Mrs J M Bailey **Trained** Barbury Castle, Wilts

FOCUS

Devalued by withdrawals, this was just a fair race of its type. The pace was reasonable and the winner is value for more than the official margin with the fourth setting the level.

NOTEBOOK

Apollo Lady made a winning debut over course and distance on Boxing Day and followed up under her penalty. She momentarily looked in trouble when pushed along towards the end of the back straight, but soon came back on the bridle and, wearing down the leader with a furlong and a half to run, she went on to score a shade readily. She is a promising mare who should get further when going over hurdles, but she might be vulnerable if turned out under a double penalty in a bumper. \n\x\x \bTrue Dove\p, out of a winning hurdler, stayed on nicely to chase home the favourite. She ought to benefit from the run *(op 2-1 tchd 15-8 and 5-2)*

True Dove, out of a winning hurdler, stayed on nicely to chase home the favourite. She ought to benefit from the run and looks up to winning a similar race. *(op 12-1)*

Tihui Two(IRE) had not run since winning at Worcester last June, since when she has left Simon Earle. Again giving problems at the start, as she had at Worcester, she was nonetheless soon in front but she could not hold off her challengers in the straight. She has the size to go hurdling and her action hints that she will handle easier ground. *(tchd 11-4 and 7-2)*

Itsy Bitsy, upped in trip from her debut, lost her pitch with half a mile to run and was only seventh turning for home, but she stayed on quite nicely. *(op 8-1 tchd 12-1)*

Ma Burls was the reluctant early leader before tracking the eventual third. She looked in need of this first run since her inauspicious debut in May and her new yard will be pleased with the way she stuck on to finish fifth.

T/Jkpt: Not won. T/Plt: £35.80 to a £1 stake. Pool: £71,746.00. 1,461.15 winning tickets. T/Qpdt: £4.30 to a £1 stake. Pool: £5,919.70. 1,002.00 winning tickets. CR

[3374]KELSO (L-H)

Thursday, February 9

3821 Meeting Abandoned - Frost

3835 - (Foreign Racing) - See Raceform Interactive

[3532]AYR (L-H)

Friday, February 10

3836 Meeting Abandoned - Frost

[2817]BANGOR-ON-DEE (L-H)

Friday, February 10

OFFICIAL GOING: Chase course - good to soft; hurdle course - good

The meeting only went ahead following four inspections after temperatures had gone down to -6c overnight.

Wind: Nil Weather: Sunny

3842 EUROPEAN BREEDERS FUND "NATIONAL HUNT" NOVICES' HURDLE (QUALIFIER) (DIV I) (9 hdls) — 2m 1f

1:30 (1:31) (Class 4) 4-7-Y-0 — **£3,903** (£1,146; £573; £286)

Form				RPR
-532	**1**		**Call Oscar (IRE)**[29] [3354] 7-11-3 — TomScudamore (C Tinkler) *led to 2nd: led 4th: rdn appr last: drvn out* **85/40**[1]	112+
1411	**2**	*1 ½*	**Unjust Law (IRE)**[25] [3417] 5-11-6 — MrTGreenall(3) (N J Henderson) *hld up in tch: hit 4th: wnt 2nd after 3 out: ev ch whn blnd 2 out and hit last: nt qckn* **13/2**	119+
4-23	**3**	*5*	**Hibernian (IRE)**[69] [2631] 6-11-3 — LeightonAspell (O Sherwood) *a.p: hit 5th: wnt 2nd briefly 3 out: sn rdn: one pce* **9/4**[2]	106
2-02	**4**	*3 ½*	**Bumper (FR)**[10] [3664] 5-11-3 — APMcCoy (M C Pipe) *led 2nd to 4th: chsd wnr tl rdn 3 out: sn wknd* **4/1**[3]	102
-121	**5**	*18*	**Lindbergh Law (USA)**[231] [828] 6-11-3 — JimCrowley (Mrs H Dalton) *hld up and bhd: hit 6th: nvr nr ldrs* **16/1**	84
43	**6**	*5*	**Mohayer (IRE)**[29] [3353] 4-10-7 — GrahamLee (D McCain) *hld up towards rr: rdn and sme hdwy whn hit 3 out: wknd and eased appr 2 out* **16/1**	69
/3-5	**7**	*3*	**Ten Pressed Men (FR)**[20] [3511] 6-11-3 — MickFitzgerald (Jonjo O'Neill) *hld up in mid-div: bhd fr 6th* **25/1**	76
-060	**8**	*27*	**Clifford T Ward**[29] [3347] 6-11-3 — DominicElsworth (D McCain) *a bhd: t.o* **66/1**	49
	9	*21*	**Young Roscoe** 7-11-0 — AnthonyCoyle(3) (M Mullineaux) *a bhd: t.o* **100/1**	28

4m 6.80s (-4.10) **Going Correction** -0.10s/f (Good)
WFA 4 from 5yo+ 9lb — **9** Ran SP% **114.2**
Speed ratings: **105,104,101,100,91 89,88,75,65** CSF £16.35 TOTE £3.00: £1.10, £2.20, £1.50; EX 17.30.

Owner George Ward **Bred** Mrs E M Musgrave **Trained** Compton, Berks

FOCUS

Despite the steady pace, this was only fractionally slower than the weaker second division and the first four ran to their marks giving the form a solid appearance, and it should work out.

NOTEBOOK

Call Oscar(IRE) built on a couple of solid performances over hurdles and took advantage of the runner-up's sloppy jumping at the final two flights. *(op 5-2 tchd 2-1)*

Unjust Law(IRE) would have given the winner even more to think about had he not been let down by his hurdling at a critical stage. *(op 4-1)*

Hibernian(IRE) ◆, dropping back in distance, got beaten for speed on this good ground in a race where they went no pace. He is capable of winning when back up in trip. *(op 5-2)*

Bumper(FR) was another running over a shorter trip on better ground who would probably have preferred a stiffer test. *(op 11-2)*

Mohayer(IRE) *Official explanation: trainer said colt had a breathing problem*

Young Roscoe *Official explanation: trainer said gelding was lame when returning home*

3843 EUROPEAN BREEDERS FUND "NATIONAL HUNT" NOVICES' HURDLE (QUALIFIER) (DIV II) (9 hdls) — 2m 1f

2:00 (2:01) (Class 4) 4-7-Y-0 — **£3,903** (£1,146; £573; £286)

Form				RPR
4000	**1**		**Lord Ryeford (IRE)**[22] [3463] 6-11-3 — JasonMaguire (T R George) *mde virtually all: hit 5th: rdn after 2 out: hit last: drvn out* **8/1**	102+
40-0	**2**	*1*	**Freddie Ed**[36] [3248] 5-11-3 — WayneHutchinson (R N Bevis) *hld up: hdwy 6th: chsd wnr 2 out: sn rdn: kpt on flat* **50/1**	100
0-	**3**	*15*	**Nikolaiev (FR)**[297] [4922] 5-10-10 — CharlieStudd(7) (N J Henderson) *a.p: hit 6th: ev ch 3 out: sn rdn: wknd appr last* **11/4**[2]	86+
P0-0	**4**	*8*	**Griffens Brook**[85] [2295] 6-11-3 — WarrenMarston (Mrs P Sly) *w wnr tl rdn 3 out: wknd appr 2 out* **33/1**	77
330	**5**	*1 ½*	**It Would Appear (IRE)**[7] [3717] 7-11-3 — APMcCoy (Jonjo O'Neill) *hld up: hdwy 4th: rdn and wknd after 3 out* **15/8**[1]	78+
0-P0	**6**	*18*	**Sunny Daze**[106] [1890] 6-10-10 — MrDAFitzsimmons(7) (D McCain) *a bhd: lost tch 5th* **16/1**	57
0-34	**7**	*9*	**Itsdowntoben**[262] [484] 5-11-3 — DominicElsworth (D McCain) *hld up in tch: j.lft 2nd: rdn appr 6th: sn wknd: mstke 3 out* **9/2**[3]	48
	8	*dist*	**Dino's Dandy** 7-11-3 — AndrewThornton (B N Pollock) *a towards rr: t.o 5th* **11/1**	—
0P	**P**		**Casalani (IRE)**[51] [2937] 7-10-10 — AlanO'Keeffe (Jennie Candlish) *a bhd: t.o whn p.u bef 2 out* **25/1**	—

4m 6.60s (-4.30) **Going Correction** -0.10s/f (Good) — **9** Ran SP% **113.7**
Speed ratings: **106,105,98,94,94 85,81,—,—** CSF £298.76 TOTE £9.70: £1.90, £17.00, £1.30; EX 223.60.

Owner Five Valleys Racing Partnership **Bred** Joseph And Declan Maher **Trained** Slad, Gloucs

FOCUS

This looked much the weaker of the two divisions and the form is difficult to assess.

NOTEBOOK

Lord Ryeford(IRE) had finished a very respectable fourth on his bumper debut on similar ground at Hereford in November. Stepping up considerably on his two previous efforts over timber in the soft, it seems to be that good going is the key to him. *(op 7-1)*

Freddie Ed was another who had shown signs of ability on his bumper debut prior to being well beaten over hurdles. He did nothing wrong but the value of this form remains to be seen.

Nikolaiev(FR) had failed to get home up the Towcester hill on his bumper debut last April. Despite being well supported in the ring, he ran as if this may have been needed. *(op 11-2)*

Griffens Brook put up his best effort so far which is not saying a lot.
It Would Appear(IRE) seemed to have found a good opportunity but was again very disappointing. *(op 5-4)*

3844 GREDINGTON NOVICES' H'CAP CHASE (12 fncs) 2m 1f 110y

2:30 (2:30) (Class 4) (0-105,105) 5-Y-0+ **£3,773** (£1,107; £553; £276)

Form	Pos	Dist	Runner	Jockey	SP	RPR
05P-	**1**		**Haile Selassie**[477] 1791 6-10-10 **89** (W Jenks) *hld up: rdn and hdwy after 3 out: lft clr 2 out: rdn out*	MarkBradburne	**33/1**	97+
6033	**2**	*3 1/2*	**Brooklyn's Gold (USA)**[52] 2929 11-11-10 **103** (Ian Williams) *prom: lft 2nd 3rd: rdn and outpcd 4 out: hmpd 2 out: kpt on flat: nt trble wnr*	RichardJohnson	**11/2**[2]	104
U4P5	**3**	*2*	**Italiano**[27] 3380 7-11-12 **105** (P Beaumont) *hld up in mid-div: blnd and lost pl 2nd: bhd whn sltly hmpd 3rd: hdwy 3 out: wnt 2nd last: no ex*	(p) RussGarritty	**11/1**	107+
350	**4**	*5*	**Arctic Cherry (IRE)**[32] 3320 8-10-0 **79** oh2 (R Ford) *led to 8th: rdn 3 out: btn whn lft 2nd 2 out: wknd flat*	PJBrennan	**9/2**[1]	75+
00F3	**F**		**Moorlaw (IRE)**[63] 2751 5-11-2 **102** (D McCain) *chsd ldr: pckd 1st: fell 3rd*	GrahamLee	**13/2**[3]	—
02PP	**P**		**Flower Of Pitcur**[46] 2958 9-10-13 **92** (T R George) *a bhd: t.o whn p.u bef 2 out*	JasonMaguire	**8/1**	—
-PP4	**P**		**Ilabon (FR)**[7] 3715 10-11-9 **102** (M C Pipe) *hld up towards rr: hdwy 6th: mstke 3 out: sn wknd: p.u bef 2 out*	(v) APMcCoy	**7/1**	—
1464	**F**		**Donovan (NZ)**[29] 3348 7-10-11 **93** (R C Guest) *chsd ldrs: sltly hmpd 1st: led 8th: pressed whn fell 2 out*	(b[1]) PaulO'Neill[(3)]	**11/2**[2]	101+
-546	**P**		**Bel Ombre (FR)**[25] 3418 6-10-12 **91** (O Sherwood) *hld up: hmpd 3rd: bhd fr 6th: mstke 8th: t.o whn p.u bef 2 out*	LeightonAspell	**11/1**	—
2-50	**F**		**Fantastic Arts (FR)**[25] 3418 6-11-11 **104** (Miss Venetia Williams) *hld up and bhd: hdwy appr 7th: ev ch whn fell 2 out*	SamThomas	**12/1**	112+

4m 29.6s (3.20) **Going Correction** +0.425s/f (Soft)
WFA 5 from 6yo+ 6lb **10** Ran SP% **113.2**
Speed ratings: **109,107,106,104,**— —,—,—,—,— CSF £202.96 CT £2144.81 TOTE £63.80: £17.30, £2.40, £2.60; EX 347.00.
Owner W Jenks **Bred** George Joseph Hicks **Trained** Deuxhill, Shropshire

FOCUS
An eventful novices' handicap with the winner rated value for further and as having dead-heated with the two fallers. The third sets the standard and the form might work out.

NOTEBOOK
Haile Selassie was making his chasing debut having not been seen since October 2004. A close third when two fell in front of him at the penultimate fence, he was effectively presented the race.
Brooklyn's Gold(USA), dropped 2lb, rather surprisingly got tapped for toe at the fourth last. He eventually found a second wind but may have benefited from the misfortune of others. *(op 6-1)*
Italiano, not helped by an early blunder, ran easily his best race so far over fences. However, he could also have been a beneficiary of the grief of the second last. *(op 10-1)*
Arctic Cherry(IRE), 2lb out of the handicap, seemed to appreciate the better ground but was still well held in the end. *(op 5-1 tchd 11-2)*
Fantastic Arts(FR), improving considerably on his two previous outings over fences, had not appeared to have put a foot wrong when coming to grief two out. *(op 7-1)*
Donovan(NZ), tried in blinkers, had two rivals on his tail but had not been asked a real question when coming down at the second last. *(op 7-1)*

3845 CAZENOVE CAPITAL MANAGEMENT H'CAP CHASE (21 fncs) 3m 6f

3:05 (3:05) (Class 3) (0-120,116) 5-Y-0+ **£6,831** (£2,005; £1,002; £500)

Form	Pos	Dist	Runner	Jockey	SP	RPR
-533	**1**		**Calvic (IRE)**[40] 3186 8-11-8 **112** (T R George) *hld up and bhd: hdwy appr 3 out: hrd rdn appr 2 out: swtchd rt and mstke last: styd on gamely to ld cl home*	PaulMoloney	**5/1**[1]	121+
1231	**2**	*1/2*	**Precious Bane (IRE)**[21] 3481 8-11-2 **106** (M Sheppard) *led to 17th: rdn 3 out: led and mstke last: hdd cl home*	AndrewThornton	**6/1**[2]	114+
2231	**3**	*2*	**Finzi (IRE)**[15] 3578 8-10-7 **97** (M Scudamore) *a.p: rdn 16th: outpcd 4 out: rallied appr 2 out: n.m.r last: styd on one pce flat*	TomScudamore	**6/1**[2]	102
1225	**4**	*shd*	**Chabrimal Minster**[31] 3336 9-10-12 **102** (R Ford) *a.p: mstke 15th: led 17th: rdn appr 2 out: hung lft and hdd last: no ex*	PJBrennan	**9/1**	108+
-1PP	**5**	*7*	**Sir Frosty**[58] 2819 13-11-0 **104** (B J M Ryall) *prom: mstke 3rd: lost pl 12th: mstke 17th: styd on fr 2 out: n.d*	JoeTizzard	**14/1**	104+
4U4P	**6**	*21*	**Sungates (IRE)**[15] 3578 10-10-12 **102** (C Tinkler) *hld up: sn in tch: mstke 11th: rdn appr 13th: wknd 16th*	AndrewTinkler	**25/1**	79
1323	**7**	*2*	**Admiral Peary (IRE)**[30] 3343 10-11-10 **114** (C R Egerton) *hld up: hdwy 13th: wknd 4 out*	APMcCoy	**15/2**	96+
P356	**P**		**Lazy But Lively (IRE)**[32] 3315 10-10-12 **102** (R F Fisher) *a bhd: t.o whn p.u bef 4 out*	JimmyMcCarthy	**9/1**	—
P12P	**P**		**Major Benefit (IRE)**[13] 3614 9-11-5 **116** (Mrs K Waldron) *bhd fr 3rd: lost tch 9th: p.u bef 11th*	RichardSpate[(7)]	**20/1**	—
-4P0	**U**		**Bob's The Business (IRE)**[46] 2965 12-10-5 **95** (Ian Williams) *hld up towards rr: blnd and uns rdr 11th*	(b[1]) WayneHutchinson	**10/1**	—
4132	**P**		**Lost In Normandy (IRE)**[27] 3398 9-10-2 **92** (Mrs L Williamson) *hld up in mid-div: hdwy 13th: rdn 16th: wknd 4 out: bhd whn p.u bef 2 out*	(b) RichardJohnson	**13/2**[3]	—

7m 57.6s (-12.10) **Going Correction** +0.425s/f (Soft) **11** Ran SP% **114.7**
Speed ratings: **112,111,111,111,109 103,103,**—,—,— — CSF £34.88 CT £183.36 TOTE £5.30: £1.90, £3.00, £2.30; EX 33.80.
Owner The Alchabas Partnership **Bred** Kevin Neville **Trained** Slad, Gloucs

FOCUS
A decent winning time for this marathon event which proved to be just as competitive as the betting suggested. The winner and third were close to recent marks suggesting the form is reasonable.

NOTEBOOK
Calvic(IRE) took advantage of having come down a total of 8lb in the ratings and showed just how well he stays. He would not have minded softer ground and will now go straight to his long-term target which is the Midlands National at Uttoxeter next month. *(op 11-2 tchd 6-1)*
Precious Bane(IRE), raised 9lb, is another who likes plenty of give in the ground. This extended trip held no terrors for him and he hardly deserved to get beaten after fighting his way back into the lead at the final fence.
Finzi(IRE), up 6lb, was yet again in the prizemoney and the fourth did him no favours at the last. *(op 5-1)*
Chabrimal Minster, back to the same mark as when successful at Aintree in October, rather shot himself in the foot by going left at the final fence.
Sir Frosty, pulled up in a similar event here in December, was not beaten as far as seemed likely when he missed out at the fifth last. *(op 16-1)*

3846 JPCS NOVICES' HURDLE (12 hdls) 3m

3:35 (3:35) (Class 3) 4-Y-0+ **£6,831** (£2,005; £1,002; £500)

Form	Pos	Dist	Runner	Jockey	SP	RPR
111	**1**		**Denman (IRE)**[40] 3174 6-11-13 152 (P F Nicholls) *a gng wl: led appr 7th: clr 8th: hung rt appr 2 out: easily*	ChristianWilliams	**1/12**[1]	144+
	2	*17*	**One Sniff (IRE)**[679] 7-11-5 (N G Richards) *hld up in mid-div: hdwy appr 8th: wnt 2nd appr 3 out: no ch w wnr*	TonyDobbin	**12/1**[2]	116+
5-20	**3**	*16*	**Abraham Smith**[71] 2592 6-11-0 100 (B J Eckley) *led tl after 6th: wknd appr 2 out*	MarkNicolls[(5)]	**33/1**	96
1-5	**4**	*27*	**Fibre Optics (IRE)**[20] 3505 6-11-5 (Jonjo O'Neill) *chsd ldr: led briefly after 6th: wknd after 3 out*	APMcCoy	**20/1**[3]	70+
3-50	**5**	*15*	**Master Of The Ward (IRE)**[20] 3496 6-11-5 (D McCain) *a towards rr: lost tch 7th: t.o*	JasonMaguire	**50/1**	54
0-0	**6**	*dist*	**Cloud Venture**[58] 2821 6-11-5 (S E H Sherwood) *plld hrd early in rr: t.o fr 7th*	JoeTizzard	**66/1**	—
00P0	**P**		**Times Up Barney**[56] 2860 6-11-5 (C W Moore) *a bhd: t.o fr 7th: p.u bef 2 out*	JosephByrne	**100/1**	—

5m 48.9s (-7.90) **Going Correction** -0.10s/f (Good) **7** Ran SP% **112.2**
Speed ratings: **109,103,98,89,84** —,— CSF £1.68 TOTE £1.10: £1.10, £2.70; EX 3.30.
Owner Paul K Barber & Mrs M Findlay **Bred** Colman O'Flynn **Trained** Ditcheat, Somerset

FOCUS
Most of the interest in this event was lost with the morning withdrawal of Black Jack Ketchum. The race is rated through the third.

NOTEBOOK
Denman(IRE) was left with a straightforward task after his rival in the betting for the Royal & SunAlliance at Cheltenham was scratched. Still showing signs of inexperience, the 3/1 for the Festival seems plenty short enough, especially given that he will not run if the ground is faster than good. *(tchd 1-10 in a place)*
One Sniff(IRE) ◆ was having his first run since landing the second of his two points in Ireland in the spring of 2004. Although finding the winner in a different league, he showed plenty of promise for the future and is one to keep an eye on.
Abraham Smith did the donkey work until approaching halfway.
Fibre Optics(IRE) seemed to get found out by the big step up in distance.
Cloud Venture *Official explanation: jockey said gelding hung badly right-handed*

3847 GILBERT COTTON MEMORIAL HUNTERS' CHASE (15 fncs) 2m 4f 110y

4:10 (4:13) (Class 6) 6-Y-0+ **£2,142** (£659; £329)

Form	Pos	Dist	Runner	Jockey	SP	RPR
05-P	**1**		**Telemoss (IRE)**[104] 1925 12-12-4 (N G Richards) *hld up: hdwy 8th: led appr last: r.o wl*	MissRDavidson[(3)]	**5/2**[1]	125+
1U4-	**2**	*6*	**Gielgud**[540] 1218 9-12-0 (B G Powell) *a.p: led 10th: rdn and hdd appr last: one pce*	MrJMaxse[(7)]	**20/1**	113
22F-	**3**	*15*	**Foly Pleasant (FR)**[307] 4772 12-12-7 140 (Mrs K Waldron) *mstkes: hld up: hdwy 5th: rallied after 3 out: no imp fr 2 out*	(t) MrRBurton	**11/4**[2]	104+
UP-4	**4**	*10*	**Ivanoph (FR)**[268] 10-12-4 111 (S Flook) *hld up and bhd: hdwy 9th: wknd 2 out*	MrAWintle[(3)]	**16/1**	88
513P	**5**	*19*	**Silence Reigns**[156] 1435 12-12-0 104 (Mrs K Waldron) *hld up: bmpd 3rd: hdwy 10th: rdn 4 out: wknd appr 2 out*	(bt) MrRQuinn[(7)]	**12/1**[3]	69
4-00	**U**		**King's Travel (FR)**[26] 10-11-11 (Miss Sarah Robinson) *blnd and uns rdr 1st*	MissSarahRobinson[(7)]	**66/1**	—
	P		**Ferryport House (IRE)**[306] 9-11-7 (R J Hewitt) *bmpd 1st: hmpd 3rd: sn bhd: t.o whn p.u bef 3 out*	MrAWadlow[(7)]	**66/1**	—
P0-6	**P**		**River Pirate (IRE)**[292] 4 9-12-0 107 (David W Drinkwater) *led tl after 9th: sn wknd: t.o whn p.u bef 3 out*	MrJMahot[(7)]	**33/1**	—
F4-1	**P**		**Spring Margot (FR)**[12] 10-12-7 131 (David M Easterby) *bhd: mstke 3rd: hdwy appr 11th: wknd after 3 out: p.u bef last*	MrTGreenall	**5/2**[1]	—
	P		**Meentagh Loch**[319] 9-11-7 (Miss H Brookshaw) *hld up in mid-div: j.lft 1st and 3rd: j. slowly and lost pl 9th: t.o whn p.u bef 11th*	(t) MrJJarrett[(7)]	**100/1**	—
F-	**F**		**Wrapitup (IRE)**[120] 1733 8-12-0 (Mrs Joanne Brown) *t.k.h and hung lft: chsd ldr: led after 9th to 10th: wknd 11th: no ch whn fell 2 out*	MrsJoanneBrown[(7)]	**20/1**	—

5m 23.1s (10.60) **Going Correction** +0.425s/f (Soft) **11** Ran SP% **113.8**
Speed ratings: **96,93,88,84,76** —,—,—,—,— — CSF £50.89 TOTE £3.10: £1.10, £4.00, £1.70; EX 76.00.
Owner Mrs Alix Stevenson **Bred** M G Masterson **Trained** Greystoke, Cumbria

FOCUS
A potentially informative hunter chase but two of the three at the head of the market ran below par. The winner is value for double the official margin with the runner-up to his mark.

NOTEBOOK
Telemoss(IRE) is potentially a smart recruit to this division and took full advantage of his two market rivals failing to perform. *(tchd 11-4 and 3-1 in places)*
Gielgud ◆ was another making his hunter chase debut and will not always come up against one as useful as the winner.
Foly Pleasant(FR) was narrowly beaten in the Cheltenham Foxhunters' last March. He may have remembered his fall in the Grand National and did not jump very well. *(tchd 5-2 and 3-1)*
Ivanoph(FR), previously trained by Paul Nicholls, would not have minded softer ground on his seasonal reappearance. *(tchd 14-1)*
Silence Reigns could not repeat last year's victory in this event and was found to be lame on *routine post-race examination by the Veterinary Officer.Official explanation: vet said gelding returned lame (op 8-1)*
Spring Margot(FR), another former inmate of the Paul Nicholls stable, was something of a flop on his debut in this sphere. *(op 3-1 tchd 100-30 in places)*

3848 MIDDLETON & CO. SOLICITORS H'CAP HURDLE (9 hdls) 2m 1f

4:40 (4:41) (Class 4) (0-110,110) 4-Y-0+ **£3,773** (£1,107; £553; £276)

Form	Pos	Dist	Runner	Jockey	SP	RPR
0033	**1**		**Speed Venture**[41] 3152 9-10-2 **93** (J Mackie) *a.p: rdn appr 2 out: r.o to ld nr fin*	(vt) PhilKinsella[(7)]	**6/1**[2]	98
0641	**2**	*1/2*	**Kayceecee (IRE)**[27] 3386 5-11-10 **108** (H D Daly) *hld up in mid-div: hdwy 5th: led 3 out: rdn appr last: hdd nr fin*	RichardJohnson	**4/1**[1]	113+
222U	**3**	*1 1/4*	**Turbo (IRE)**[6] 3737 7-11-8 **109** (M W Easterby) *hld up and bhd: hdwy appr 2 out: hung lft appr last: r.o wl flat*	(t) MrTGreenall[(3)]	**6/1**[2]	112
4366	**4**	*shd*	**Xamborough (FR)**[36] 3257 5-11-7 **105** (B G Powell) *a.p: hit 4th: rdn and wnt 2nd appr 2 out: nt qckn flat*	MickFitzgerald	**16/1**	108
1-56	**5**	*hd*	**White Dove (FR)**[36] 3247 8-10-3 **90** (Ian Williams) *hld up in mid-div: hdwy 5th: rdn to chse wnr 2 out: hit last: nt qckn*	JoffretHuet[(3)]	**28/1**	93

The Form Book, Raceform Ltd, Compton, RG20 6NL

0055 **6** *4* **Flame Phoenix (USA)**^{62} [2766] 7-11-12 **110**........................(t) GrahamLee 110+
(D McCain) *hld up in mid-div: lost pl after 4th: hdwy fr 2 out: nvr nrr* **9/1**^{3}

3360 **7** *1/2* **Dr Cerullo**^{29} [3360] 5-11-10 **108**.. TomDoyle 107
(C Tinkler) *hld up in tch: no hdwy fr 3 out* **20/1**

306F **8** *3 1/2* **Presenter (IRE)**^{13} [3616] 6-10-9 **93**.. PaulMoloney 88
(M Sheppard) *hld up and bhd: hdwy 6th: hung lft appr last: wknd flat* **66/1**

641- **9** *3* **Dark Society**^{374} [3417] 8-11-0 **98**................................ WayneHutchinson 91+
(A W Carroll) *hld up and bhd: hdwy when nt clr run after 3 out: nd after* **9/1**^{3}

4-50 **10** *3/4* **Shady Anne**^{51} [2940] 8-10-4 **98**..............................(p) ThomasBurrows$^{(10)}$ 89
(F Jordan) *led to 3 out: wknd 2 out* **66/1**

P216 **11** *3* **First Fought (IRE)**^{82} [2367] 4-11-0 **108**.............................(t) JasonMaguire 86
(D McCain) *nvr trbld ldrs: b.b.v* **20/1**

42F **12** *1/2* **Lysander (GER)**^{14} [3597] 7-11-7 **105**.. PJBrennan 93
(M F Harris) *hld up and bhd: hdwy 6th: wknd after 3 out* **6/1**^{2}

63-5 **13** *2 1/2* **Lyon**^{279} [216] 6-11-7 **105**.. LeightonAspell 90
(O Sherwood) *a towards rr* **20/1**

-200 **14** *6* **Top Achiever (IRE)**^{145} [1488] 5-11-10 **108**.......................... JosephByrne 87
(C W Moore) *bhd fr 6th* **66/1**

1PF **15** *7* **Baie Des Flamands (USA)**^{11} [3645] 4-11-2 **110**..............(p) HenryOliver 72
(Miss S J Wilton) *chsd ldrs tl wknd 6th* **50/1**

/03- **16** *nk* **Major Blade (GER)**^{464} [1981] 8-10-2 **89**............................... TJPhelan$^{(3)}$ 61
(Mrs H Dalton) *prom tl wknd after 3 out* **28/1**

404P **P** **New Currency (USA)**^{64} [2734] 6-10-13 **97**.........................(vt^{1}) APMcCoy —
(M C Pipe) *chsd ldr tl appr 3 out: sn wknd: p.u bef 2 out* **12/1**

4m 7.70s (-3.20) **Going Correction** -0.10s/f (Good)
WFA 4 from 5yo+ 9lb **17** Ran SP% **124.1**
Speed ratings: **103,102,102,102,102 100,99,98,96,96 95,94,93,90,87 87,—** CSF £27.78 CT £154.81 TOTE £6.10: £1.50, £5.20, £1.40, £2.20; EX 23.30 Place 6 37.53, Place 5 £27.50.
Owner Wall Racing Partners **Bred** Woodsway Stud And Chao Racing And Bloodstock Ltd **Trained** Church Broughton , Derbys

FOCUS
Around two lengths covered the first five home in this competitive handicap, which looks solid enough with the winner, third fifth and eighth to their marks.

NOTEBOOK
Speed Venture has been running well since having the visor refitted and deserves full marks for the way he stuck to his task. *(op 11-2 tchd 13-2)*
Kayceecee(IRE), on the fastest ground he has encountered so far, was the last to come under pressure but the 9lb hike in the ratings proved just too much. *(op 5-1)*
Turbo(IRE) still only had a few behind him leaving the back straight. Hanging left when making ground, this character still finished with a flourish. *(op 13-2)*
Xamborough(FR) appreciated being back on some decent ground and gave a good account of himself on his handicap debut.
White Dove(FR) ran well for one who really wants softer ground and a bit further. *(op 25-1)*
Flame Phoenix(USA) found this trip on the short side, especially on a course as sharp as this. *(op 14-1)*
Dark Society could well have finished closer with a trouble-free run.
First Fought(IRE) *Official explanation: trainer's representative said gelding had bled from the nose (op 25-1)*
T/Plt: £88.30 to a £1 stake. Pool: £52,656.35. 435.00 winning tickets. T/Qpdt: £12.60 to a £1 stake. Pool: £5,411.60. 316.20 winning tickets. KH

^{3532}AYR (L-H)

Saturday, February 11

OFFICIAL GOING: Soft
First fence in home straight omitted.
Wind: Moderate, half-against

3849 LLOYDS TSB SCOTLAND H'CAP CHASE (15 fncs 2 omitted) 2m 4f
1:45 (1:45) (Class 4) (0-110,107) 5-Y-O+ **£3,903** (£1,146; £573; £286)

Form RPR

/215 **1** **Jimmy Bond**^{37} [3255] 7-10-12 **93**.. NeilMulholland 103+
(M D Hammond) *in tch: outpcd 9th: rallied bef 4 out: led next: edgd rt and styd on wl fr last* **9/2**^{2}

313P **2** *6* **Silver Jack (IRE)**^{51} [2945] 8-11-10 **105**...............................(p) GrahamLee 109+
(M Todhunter) *led to 2nd: cl up: led 10th to 3 out: rallying whn mstke and no ex last* **7/2**^{1}

0001 **3** *1 1/4* **Isellido (IRE)**^{29} [3375] 7-11-7 **107**.................................. DougieCostello$^{(5)}$ 109+
(R C Guest) *led 2nd to 10th: cl up: outpcd appr 3 out: kpt on fr last* **6/1**

P662 **4** *dist* **Jerom De Vindecy (FR)**^{19} [3543] 9-10-0 **84**............... PeterBuchanan$^{(3)}$ —
(Miss Lucinda V Russell) *s.v.s: hdwy and in tch 1/2-way: wknd fr 4 out* **12/1**

533 **P** **Grand Slam (IRE)**^{18} [3555] 11-10-0 **81** oh1.......................... BarryKeniry —
(A C Whillans) *a bhd: t.o whn p.u bef 11th* **12/1**

30F4 **P** **Kharak (FR)**^{40} [3204] 7-11-7 **102**.. WilsonRenwick —
(Mrs S C Bradburne) *in tch tl wknd 8th: p.u bef 11th* **11/2**

5P30 **P** **Bold Investor**^{51} [2955] 9-11-6 **101**.................................. RichardMcGrath —
(C Grant) *in tch tl lost pl 7th: t.o whn p.u bef 9th* **16/1**

31P2 **P** **Fountain Brig**^{19} [3533] 10-10-0 **86**........................... MichaelMcAlister$^{(5)}$ —
(N W Alexander) *chsd ldrs hit 4th: wknd 8th: t.o whn p.u bef 4 out* **5/1**^{3}

5m 39.0s (16.10) **Going Correction** +0.70s/f (Soft) **8** Ran SP% **108.0**
Speed ratings: **95,92,92,—,— —,—,—** CSF £18.87 CT £80.86 TOTE £6.50: £1.60, £1.40, £2.50; EX 22.40.
Owner M D Hammond **Bred** Mrs A J Findlay **Trained** Middleham, N Yorks

FOCUS
A fair gallop but a modest winning time, six seconds slower than the following novice chase over the same trip, and the form looks weak, rated through the third.

NOTEBOOK
Jimmy Bond ◆, back up in trip, put a disappointing run over two miles behind him (run may have come too quickly) to post a career-best effort over fences. He has the size and scope to improve again. *(op 5-1)*
Silver Jack(IRE) had been disappointing on his previous two starts but returned to something like his best in the first-time cheekpieces. He may be vulnerable to progressive or well handicapped sorts from this mark but remains capable of winning another race around this trip. *(tchd 3-1 and 4-1)*
Isellido(IRE) ran creditably back in handicap company, despite being taken on for the lead. She will be of more interest in ordinary company when it looks as though she will get an uncontested lead. *(op 4-1)*
Jerom De Vindecy(FR), who showed his first worthwhile form over fences on his handicap debut last time, did not get home over this longer trip but left the impression that he has one or two ideas of his own about the game.
Bold Investor, having his first run for a new stable, continues to disappoint. *(tchd 6-1)*
Fountain Brig looked to have plenty in his favour regarding ground, trip and current form but ran poorly and a hard race in bad ground here last time may have taken the edge off him. *(tchd 6-1)*
Kharak(FR), down in trip, ran a tame race and consistency does not look to be his strongest suit. *(tchd 6-1)*

3850 LLOYDS TSB SCOTLAND NOVICES' CHASE (15 fncs 2 omitted) 2m 4f
2:15 (2:16) (Class 3) 5-Y-O+ **£6,506** (£1,910; £955; £477)

Form RPR

1-12 **1** **Wild Cane Ridge (IRE)**^{77} [2496] 7-11-8 .... TonyDobbin 138+
(L Lungo) *hld up: hdwy 1/2-way: cl up whn lft 2nd 11th: j.rt next: led bef 3 out: sn clr* **8/13**^{1}

P2 **2** *23* **Junior Des Ormeaux (FR)**^{39} [3236] 9-11-2 .... WilsonRenwick 112+
(S H Shirley-Beavan) *led to bef 3 out: kpt on: no ch w wnr* **9/1**^{3}

/4BP **3** *14* **Jexel (FR)**^{39} [3234] 9-11-2 .... RichardMcGrath 88
(B Storey) *in tch: outpcd 8th: wnt remote 3rd bef 3 out: no imp* **66/1**

4-PP **4** *10* **Highland Brig**^{275} [322] 10-10-11 85........................... DougieCostello$^{(5)}$ 78
(T Butt) *chsd ldrs: hit 4th: outpcd whn lft 3rd 11th: n.d after* **125/1**

-3FF **5** *shd* **Moonlit Harbour**^{17} [3558] 7-10-11 118.................... ThomasDreaper$^{(5)}$ 78
(Ferdy Murphy) *bhd: rdn 1/2-way: sme hdwy 3 out: nvr on terms* **16/1**

0-0P **6** *15* **Brora Sutherland (IRE)**^{79} [2447] 7-10-13 78.............. PeterBuchanan$^{(3)}$ 63
(Miss Lucinda V Russell) *chsd ldrs tl outpcd fr 8th* **100/1**

006F **7** *5* **Political Cruise**^{18} [3555] 8-10-9 72................................ GarethThomas$^{(7)}$ 58
(R Nixon) *nt fluent: nvr on terms* **100/1**

0-55 **8** *30* **Try Catch Paddy (IRE)**^{79} [2458] 8-10-6 107................. DavidDaSilva$^{(10)}$ 28
(P Monteith) *bhd: shortlived effrt 8th: sn n.d* **33/1**

P-21 **U** **Kasthari (IRE)**^{54} [2924] 7-11-12 .... GrahamLee —
(J Howard Johnson) *cl up whn blnd bdly and uns rdr 11th* **5/2**^{2}

5m 33.0s (10.10) **Going Correction** +0.70s/f (Soft) **9** Ran SP% **113.6**
Speed ratings: **107,97,92,88,88 82,80,68,—** CSF £7.10 TOTE £1.70: £1.10, £1.60, £8.40; EX 7.10.
Owner Ashleybank Investments Limited **Bred** Greenville House Stud And M Morgan **Trained** Carrutherstown, D'fries & G'way

FOCUS
A novice contest with little strength in depth and the departure of Kasthari left the race at the mercy of Wild Cane Ridge, with the first two rated better than the bare result.

NOTEBOOK
Wild Cane Ridge(IRE) was left with little to beat once main market rival Kasthari came to grief before the race started in earnest. Although he is a capable sort who won with plenty in hand, his jumping is still not foot-perfect and he will find life tougher in handicaps or under a double penalty against the better novices. *(op 4-5 tchd 10-11 in places)*
Junior Des Ormeaux(FR) probably ran to a similar level as over course and distance on his previous start. He remains vulnerable to the better novices in this type of event but jumped soundly and looks capable of picking up a small race. *(op 10-1)*
Jexel(FR), a 98-rated hurdler who has only hinted at ability over hurdles after a lengthy break, was not totally disgraced on this chasing debut but is likely to be seen to better effect in ordinary *handicaps in this sphere in due course. Official explanation: jockey said gelding was unsuited by the soft ground (op 100-1)*
Highland Brig, a winning pointer in 2003 who showed ability in modest hunter chases last year, faced a stiff task at these weights and is another that will be seen to better effect in handicap company. *(op 100-1)*
Moonlit Harbour got round this time but did not show enough to suggest he will be of any interest in this grade next time or from his current mark in handicap company.
Brora Sutherland(IRE), a poor hurdler, was predictably well beaten on this chasing debut.
Kasthari(IRE), who has a good record at Doncaster, came to grief before the race began in earnest. Although he has form on soft ground, he is ideally suited by a sound surface and he is worth another chance in this sphere. *(op 7-4)*

3851 LLOYDS TSB SCOTLAND SCOTTISH RACING H'CAP CHASE (17 fncs 2 omitted) 3m 1f
2:50 (2:52) (Class 2) (0-145,137) 5-Y-O+
£12,526 (£3,700; £1,850; £926; £462; £232)

Form RPR

-POF **1** **The Bajan Bandit (IRE)**^{28} [3397] 11-11-10 **135**................(b) TonyDobbin 150+
(L Lungo) *hld up: hdwy 1/2-way: led 4 out: drew clr bef next: eased run in* **9/1**

22-P **2** *14* **Royal Emperor (IRE)**^{14} [3620] 10-11-11 **136**................ DominicElsworth 127+
(Mrs S J Smith) *prom: outpcd 6 out: rallied 2 out: wnt 2nd run in: styd on: no ch w wnr* **9/1**

412 **3** *1 1/4* **King Barry (FR)**^{40} [3207] 7-10-1 **112**................................ RichardMcGrath 103+
(Miss P Robson) *hld up: hdwy to chse ldrs 13th: wnt 2nd whn mstke 2 out: no ex last* **7/1**^{3}

413- **4** *3/4* **Another Rum (IRE)**^{13} [3643] 8-11-12 **137**............................ AnthonyRoss 124
(I A Duncan, Ire) *bhd: mstke and outpcd 10th: kpt on fr 3 out: n.d* **8/1**

13/4 **5** *3* **Big-And-Bold (IRE)**^{33} [3318] 10-10-9 **120**..........................(t) RussGarritty 106+
(N G Richards) *cl up: hit 10th: led 12th to 4 out: one pce fr 3 out* **6/1**^{2}

P2F0 **6** *28* **Strong Resolve (IRE)**^{46} [3022] 10-11-2 **130**............... PeterBuchanan$^{(3)}$ 86
(Miss Lucinda V Russell) *mde most to 7th: wknd fr 12th* **7/1**^{3}

P-6P **7** *20* **Hussard Collonges (FR)**^{37} [3258] 11-10-5 **116**.................. TomSiddall 52
(P Beaumont) *cl up: led 7th to 12th: sn lost pl* **50/1**

51-3 **P** **Rosie Redman (IRE)**^{69} [2656] 9-10-5 **116**............................ GrahamLee —
(J R Turner) *midfield: outpcd 10th: p.u 12th* **4/1**^{1}

3154 **P** **Leading Man (IRE)**^{28} [3391] 6-11-2 **132**..................... ThomasDreaper$^{(5)}$ —
(Ferdy Murphy) *sn bhd and struggling: p.u 6th* **10/1**

32P1 **P** **Interdit (FR)**^{29} [3377] 10-10-4 **115**...................................... WilsonRenwick —
(Mrs B K Thomson) *hld up: hdwy 1/2-way: rdn and wknd 13th: t.o whn p.u bef 3 out* **7/1**^{3}

6m 54.4s (8.70) **Going Correction** +0.70s/f (Soft) **10** Ran SP% **113.9**
Speed ratings: **114,109,109,108,107 98,92,—,—,—** CSF £84.25 CT £600.23 TOTE £10.10: £2.80, £2.90, £2.70; EX 84.00.
Owner Ashleybank Investments Limited **Bred** R J Whitford **Trained** Carrutherstown, D'fries & G'way

FOCUS
A fair handicap run at what appeared an ordinary gallop, but a decent winning time for a race of its class with the winner value for more than the official margin.

NOTEBOOK
The Bajan Bandit(IRE), back over fences for the first time in nearly three years, relished the conditions and showed he is just as good over the larger obstacles as over hurdles. However, as he will be hiked in the weights and, given his recent hurdle record has been very patchy, he would not be one to lump on at short odds next time. *(op 7-1)*
Royal Emperor(IRE) has not really progressed in the anticipated manner over fences since his last win (failed to complete on half of his previous eight starts) but has come down in the weights and was not disgraced by this bare form. He is suited by a good test of stamina but again did not look the easiest of rides. *(op 8-1)*
King Barry(FR), a progressive and lightly raced sort, seemed to get found out in the conditions over this longer trip but has not got many miles on the clock. He will be of more interest back over shorter or on a sounder surface at this trip. *(op 8-1)*
Another Rum(IRE), who has a good record at this course, shaped as though better than the bare form and, although he tends to make the odd mistake, will be of interest at decent odds in the Scottish National if the ground is less testing. *(op 15-2 tchd 10-1 in a place)*

Big-And-Bold(IRE) ◆, having his second start after a very lengthy break, again shaped as though retaining plenty of ability. He is only lightly raced and showed enough to suggest he can win a similar race before the season is out. *(op 5-1)*
Strong Resolve(IRE) has been most disappointing over fences since running poorly in last year's Grand National and he looks one to tread carefully with at present. *(op 8-1)*
Hussard Collonges(FR) continues to plummet in the weights but again offered little encouragement.
Rosie Redman(IRE), who shaped well on her reappearance run in December, is usually a consistent sort who had conditions to suit. She ran as though something was amiss and, given *she reportedly coughed after the race, is worth another chance.Official explanation: vet said mare was found to be coughing; jockey said mare was never travelling (tchd 5-1)*
Leading Man(IRE) *Official explanation: jockey said gelding lost its action (tchd 5-1)*

3852 LLOYDS TSB SCOTLAND AYR RACECOURSE H'CAP CHASE (11 fncs 1 omitted) 2m
3:20 (3:25) (Class 3) (0-135,135) 5-Y-0+ **£7,619** (£2,324; £1,214; £659)

Form				RPR
-F44	1		**Do L'Enfant D'Eau (FR)**[39] 3233 7-10-2 **111** .... RichardMcGrath	125+
			(B Storey) *cl up: led bef 3 out: styd on wl* **6/1**[3]	
3-0F	2	6	**Brave Thought (IRE)**[39] 3233 11-10-4 **113** .... DominicElsworth	121+
			(P Monteith) *hld up: hdwy 7th: outpcd after next: rallied to chse wnr between last two: one pce run in* **12/1**	
P311	3	9	**Oliverjohn (IRE)**[19] 3543 9-9-11 **109** oh2 .... PeterBuchanan(3)	107
			(Miss Lucinda V Russell) *mde most to bef 3 out: no ex* **6/1**[3]	
5256	4	21	**Super Nomad**[14] 3619 11-10-13 **122** .... RussGarritty	105+
			(M W Easterby) *in tch tl wknd bef 4 out* **8/1**	
2012	F		**Shares (IRE)**[33] 3317 6-9-12 **117** .... DavidDaSilva(10)	—
			(P Monteith) *hld up in tch: fell 6th* **11/4**[1]	
2-1F	P		**Island Faith (IRE)**[46] 3019 9-11-9 **132** .... GrahamLee	—
			(J Howard Johnson) *a bhd: struggling 5th: t.o whn p.u bef 3 out* **9/2**[2]	
5300	P		**St Pirran (IRE)**[29] 3378 11-11-7 **135** ....(p) DougieCostello(5)	—
			(R C Guest) *in tch: j. slowly 4th: wknd 7th: p.u bef 3 out* **33/1**	
03-0	P		**Jurado Express (IRE)**[7] 3724 10-10-13 **122** .... TonyDobbin	—
			(Miss Venetia Williams) *chsd ldrs: effrt and ev ch 3 out: mstke next: wknd qckly and p.u bef last* **6/1**[3]	

4m 16.4s (11.90) **Going Correction** +0.70s/f (Soft) **8** Ran SP% **109.5**
Speed ratings: **98,95,90,80,— —,—,—** CSF £63.64 CT £412.47 TOTE £6.90: £2.10, £3.40, £1.50; EX 43.50.
Owner W J E Scott & Mrs M A Scott **Bred** Earl Moulin **Trained** Kirklinton, Cumbria

FOCUS
An uncompetitive handicap in which the pace was fair and the placed horses to their marks set a solid standard.

NOTEBOOK
Do L'Enfant D'Eau(FR) extended his creditable run of form for his current stable with his best effort yet. He showed the right attitude in the closing stages and, although vulnerable to progressive types after reassessment, should continue to give a good account. *(op 11-2)*
Brave Thought(IRE) showed himself to be none the worse for his recent fall at this track, but he has little margin for error from his current mark and is likely to remain vulnerable to progressive or well handicapped types. *(op 10-1 tchd 14-1)*
Oliverjohn(IRE), who won uncompetitive races at this course and at Wetherby last month, did not really settle in the early stages but was beaten on merit and, on this evidence, will have to improve to win a similar race from this mark. *(op 11-2)*
Super Nomad was again well below his best form and, given he has not won for almost four years, remains one to tread carefully with. *(op 15-2)*
St Pirran(IRE) *Official explanation: jockey said gelding bled from the nose (op 25-1)*
Jurado Express(IRE) who missed last year, had shaped as though retaining ability on his reappearance but, although looking the likely winner turning for home, stopped very quickly at the *penultimate fence. His rider reported that he lost his action and he is worth another chanceOfficial explanation: jockey said gelding lost its action (op 25-1)*
Island Faith(IRE) has a good record fresh but otherwise his form is very patchy and he was beaten before the race began in earnest. Several from this stable have run below expectations in recent times and he remains one to tread carefully with. *(op 25-1)*
Shares(IRE) is looking a more reliable proposition over fences than he was over hurdles but he fell before the race began to unfold. He is worth another chance away from progressive sorts. *(op 25-1)*

3853 LLOYDS TSB SCOTLAND H'CAP HURDLE (9 hdls) 2m
3:50 (3:54) (Class 4) (0-115,114) 4-Y-0+ **£3,578** (£1,050; £525; £262)

Form				RPR
1214	1		**Birdwatch**[28] 3384 8-11-0 **102** ....(b) RichardMcGrath	110+
			(K G Reveley) *mde all: rdn and r.o strly fr 3 out* **3/1**[1]	
0P46	2	5	**Lethem Air**[19] 3534 8-10-9 **102** ....(p) DougieCostello(5)	103+
			(T Butt) *a.p: effrt and chsd wnr bef 3 out: kpt on fr last* **25/1**	
0205	3	8	**Time To Roam (IRE)**[24] 3445 6-10-9 **100** ....(p) PaddyAspell(3)	92
			(Miss Lucinda V Russell) *a cl up: effrt and ev ch 3 out: one pce next* **16/1**	
605F	4	1	**Brave Vision**[29] 3378 10-11-0 **109** .... EwanWhillans(7)	100
			(A C Whillans) *midfield: outpcd 1/2-way: rallied 3 out: no imp after next* **20/1**	
2146	5	6	**Farne Isle**[19] 3542 7-11-4 **111** ....(p) ThomasDreaper(5)	96
			(G A Harker) *hld up midfield: hdwy and prom 4 out: rdn and one pce fr 2 out* **12/1**	
F234	6	nk	**Hollywood Critic (USA)**[40] 3206 5-10-9 **107** .... DavidDaSilva(10)	95+
			(P Monteith) *bhd: hdwy whn hit 3 out: n.d* **25/1**	
206-	7	1 ½	**Diamond Mick**[297] 4926 6-10-9 **104** .... MissRDavidson(7)	87
			(Mrs R L Elliot) *cl up: hit 3rd: outpcd 4 out: no imp fr next* **6/1**[2]	
2002	8	5	**Timbuktu**[40] 3206 5-10-2 **90** .... BarryKeniry	68
			(B Storey) *cl up tl wknd after 3 out* **9/1**	
0P-P	9	4	**Captain's Leap (IRE)**[92] 2171 10-10-1 **92** ow4 .... GaryBerridge(3)	66
			(L Lungo) *j.lft in rr: nvr on terms* **50/1**	
F104	F		**Merryvale Man**[6] 3737 9-10-7 **95** .... GrahamLee	—
			(Miss Kariana Key) *chsd ldrs: fell 5th* **13/2**[3]	
336/	P		**Cita Verda (FR)**[784] 2848 8-11-12 **114** .... TonyDobbin	—
			(P Monteith) *towards rr: struggling 1/2-way: t.o whn p.u bef 3 out* **6/1**[2]	
-300	P		**Duke Orsino (IRE)**[87] 2262 6-10-1 **92** .... PeterBuchanan(3)	—
			(Miss Lucinda V Russell) *midfield: outpcd 4 out: t.o whn p.u bef last* **16/1**	
0663	P		**Tiger King (GER)**[41] 3168 5-11-3 **105** .... WilsonRenwick	—
			(P Monteith) *towards rr: struggling bef 4 out: t.o whn p.u bef next* **14/1**	

4m 10.9s (13.60) **Going Correction** +0.95s/f (Soft) **13** Ran SP% **117.4**
Speed ratings: **104,101,97,97,94 93,93,90,88,— —,—,—** CSF £82.36 CT £1045.30 TOTE £4.10: £1.60, £5.00, £5.50, £6.50; EX 122.60.
Owner Jeremy Mitchell And Janet Powney **Bred** W R Lewis **Trained** Lingdale, Redcar & Cleveland

FOCUS
An ordinary handicap in which the pace seemed sound but those racing prominently held the edge. The first two seem on the upgrade and the third sets the level for the form.

NOTEBOOK
Birdwatch, back in trip, had the run of the race and showed the right attitude to notch his third win of the winter. There was plenty to like about the manner of this win and he should continue to give a good account. *(op 7-2 tchd 4-1)*
Lethem Air, tried in cheekpieces, ran creditably in an ordinary event. On this evidence the return to further should suit but given his record is patchy, he would not be one to place too much faith in.
Time To Roam(IRE)'s form for his current stable has been very patchy since his Hereford win last March and, although running creditably this time, is not guaranteed to give it his best shot next time. *(op 20-1)*
Brave Vision fared the best of those that attempted to make ground from just off the pace and may be a bit better than the bare form. He seems more effective on a sound surface and remains one to keep an eye on.
Farne Isle is a capable sort on testing ground when in the mood but, although she had conditions to suit, she was again below her best and has little margin for error from her current mark. *(op 16-1)*
Hollywood Critic(USA) may be a little better than the bare form of this race given how things panned out, but he will have to improve a fair bit to win a handicap from his current mark. However, he is in good hands and is not one to write off yet. *(op 33-1)*
Cita Verda(FR) *Official explanation: jockey said mare was distressed (op 13-2 tchd 7-1 in places)*
Duke Orsino(IRE) *Official explanation: jockey said gelding lost a shoe (op 13-2 tchd 7-1 in places)*

3854 LLOYDS TSB SCOTLAND SCOTTISH RACING H'CAP HURDLE (12 hdls) 2m 6f
4:25 (4:25) (Class 4) (0-115,115) 4-Y-0+ **£3,578** (£1,050; £525; £262)

Form				RPR
/01-	1		**Fair Question (IRE)**[615] 653 8-11-1 **109** .... LiamTreadwell(5)	139+
			(Miss Venetia Williams) *keen early: mde all: rdn and r.o strly fr 3 out* **12/1**	
0362	2	21	**Imtihan (IRE)**[19] 3542 7-10-6 **95** .... DominicElsworth	95
			(Mrs S J Smith) *prom: effrt 4 out: chsd wnr run in: no imp* **7/2**[1]	
P542	3	5	**Kempski**[19] 3532 6-9-12 **94** oh2 ow5 ....(b) GarethThomas(7)	89
			(R Nixon) *keen early: chsd wnr: rdn 4 out: one pce 3 out: lost 2nd run in* **33/1**	
F/63	4	5	**Thosewerethedays**[40] 3208 13-11-7 **115** .... ThomasDreaper(5)	106+
			(Miss P Robson) *sn bhd: rdn 8th: hdwy whn mstke 2 out: n.d* **16/1**	
5121	5	nk	**Aston Lad**[47] 2994 5-11-12 **115** .... BarryKeniry	105
			(M D Hammond) *midfield: effrt and prom 4 out: one pce next* **5/1**[2]	
P223	6	½	**Notaproblem (IRE)**[24] 3443 7-11-2 **105** .... RichardMcGrath	94
			(G A Harker) *hld up midfield: effrt bef 4 out: one pce next* **11/2**[3]	
3110	7	16	**General Duroc (IRE)**[28] 3384 10-11-0 **110** ....(p) MrMSeston(7)	83
			(B Storey) *j.rt: chsd ldrs tl wknd fr 4 out* **20/1**	
5430	8	4	**Speed Kris (FR)**[22] 3487 7-10-1 **97** ....(v) DavidDaSilva(7)	66
			(Mrs S C Bradburne) *bhd: struggling 1/2-way: nvr on terms* **16/1**	
163P	9	3	**Thoutmosis (USA)**[28] 3383 7-11-9 **115** .... GaryBerridge(3)	81
			(L Lungo) *hld up: shortlived effrt on outside 8th: wknd next* **20/1**	
-520	10	hd	**Lord Jack (IRE)**[64] 2745 10-11-12 **115** .... TonyDobbin	81
			(N G Richards) *midfield: reminders 1/2-way: effrt 8th: wknd next* **13/2**	
2-PF	11	shd	**Minster Fair**[29] 3375 8-9-13 **95** ow4 .... EwanWhillans(7)	61
			(A C Whillans) *midfield tl wknd bef 4 out* **25/1**	
2461	12	18	**Caesar's Palace (GER)**[40] 3209 9-10-7 **99** ....(p) PeterBuchanan(3)	47
			(Miss Lucinda V Russell) *prom: lost pl bef 4th: no ch fr 1/2-way* **16/1**	
412-	13	dist	**Wainak (USA)**[546] 1184 8-10-0 **94** ....(p) DougieCostello(5)	—
			(Miss Lucinda V Russell) *prom to 1/2-way: sn lost pl* **33/1**	
2000	P		**Roobihoo (IRE)**[33] 3318 7-11-1 **104** .... AnthonyRoss	—
			(C Grant) *prom tl wknd bef 4 out: t.o whn p.u bef next* **14/1**	
4050	P		**Crackleando**[29] 3378 5-10-9 **105** .... PatrickMcDonald(7)	—
			(A R Dicken) *towards rr: reminders 4th: sn btn: t.o whn p.u bef 3 out* **33/1**	

6m 5.60s (24.00) **Going Correction** +0.95s/f (Soft) **15** Ran SP% **121.8**
Speed ratings: **94,86,84,82,82 82,76,75,74,74 73,67,—,—,—** CSF £50.37 CT £1369.97 TOTE £13.20: £4.80, £2.30, £9.50; EX 51.40.
Owner The MerseyClyde Partnership **Bred** Airlie Stud **Trained** Kings Caple, H'fords
■ Stewards' Enquiry : David Da Silva two-day ban: used whip whilst out of contention (Feb 22-23)

FOCUS
A modest winning time for a race of its type but an impressive win after a long absence from Fair Question, who was value for more than the official margin and remains capable of better.

NOTEBOOK
Fair Question(IRE) ◆, absent since winning on fast ground in June 2004, had been dropped 6lb since but turned in a career-best effort to rout an admittedly ordinary field. He will be up a fair bit in the weights but appeals as the type to win again if staying sound. *(op 14-1)*
Imtihan(IRE) has not won for nearly two years but lost nothing in defeat behind the proverbial tartar in Fair Question. He should have no problems staying three miles, is in good hands and is sure to win another race. *(tchd 4-1 in places)*
Kempski, an inconsistent maiden, was not disgraced in a race that suited those racing close to the pace with the blinkers on again but, given his record, would not be one to take too short a price about next time.
Thosewerethedays has not had much racing, despite his advancing years, and fared the best of those that made ground from off the pace. He will need more respite from the Handicapper if he is to return to winning ways, though. *(tchd 14-1 and 20-1)*
Aston Lad was found out from this higher mark over this longer trip and is likely to remain vulnerable to progressive or well handicapped sorts in this grade. *(tchd 11-2, 6-1 in places)*
Notaproblem(IRE) had been running creditably up to three miles on a soft surface but was below his best this time. He is mainly a consistent sort so is not one to write off just yet. *(tchd 6-1)*

3855 LLOYDS TSB SCOTLAND "NATIONAL HUNT" NOVICES' HURDLE (12 hdls) 3m 110y
4:55 (4:56) (Class 4) 5-Y-0+ **£3,253** (£955; £477; £238)

Form				RPR
1	1		**Money Trix (IRE)**[29] 3376 6-11-4 .... TonyDobbin	133+
			(N G Richards) *in tch: led 7th: hit 4 out: sn clr: v easily* **4/6**[1]	
5345	2	25	**Sotovik (IRE)**[29] 3376 5-10-5 103 .... EwanWhillans(7)	87+
			(A C Whillans) *hld up: hdwy 8th: chsd wnr bef 3 out: no imp* **9/1**	
-544	3	1 ½	**Kirkside Pleasure (IRE)**[40] 3205 5-10-12 101 .... WilsonRenwick	77
			(Mrs S C Bradburne) *prom: effrt 4 out: no imp whn hit next* **8/1**[3]	
0P	4	nk	**Native Coll**[39] 3232 6-10-5 .... TomMessenger(7)	76
			(N W Alexander) *hld up in tch: effrt 4 out: wknd bef next* **125/1**	
34-4	5	dist	**Wise Man (IRE)**[290] 62 11-10-12 100 .... RichardMcGrath	—
			(N W Alexander) *in tch tl wknd bef 8th: t.o* **14/1**	
0-0	P		**Birtley Boy**[272] 375 7-10-7 .... DeclanMcGann(5)	—
			(W Amos) *chsd ldrs to 7th: sn wknd: t.o whn p.u bef 4 out* **100/1**	
0-0	P		**Mountain Mix**[39] 3237 6-10-7 .... DesFlavin(5)	—
			(Mrs L B Normile) *in tch tl wknd 7th: t.o whn p.u bef 4 out* **100/1**	
00P4	P		**Lethem Present (IRE)**[19] 3532 6-10-0 75 .... DougieCostello(5)	—
			(T Butt) *led to 7th: sn wknd: t.o whn p.u bef 4 out* **100/1**	
-P00	P		**Bubba Boy (IRE)**[29] 3376 6-10-2 83 .... DavidDaSilva(10)	—
			(P Monteith) *hld up: effrt 8th: wknd next: t.o whn p.u after 2 out* **100/1**	
PP-0	P		**Goodandplenty**[40] 3205 8-10-9 64 .... PaddyAspell(3)	—
			(Mrs J C McGregor) *cl up to 6th: lost tch fr next: t.o whn p.u bef 4 out* **200/1**	
-425	P		**Winapenny (IRE)**[56] 2878 7-10-7 105 .... ThomasDreaper(5)	—
			(Ferdy Murphy) *hld up: rdn and hdwy to chse wnr after 7th: wknd qckly after 4 out: p.u next* **4/1**[2]	

6m 53.5s (21.70) **Going Correction** +0.95s/f (Soft) **11** Ran SP% **113.0**
Speed ratings: **103,95,94,94,**— —,—,—,—,— — CSF £7.60 TOTE £1.80: £1.10, £2.00, £2.10; EX 6.70 Place 6 £221.94, Place 5 £145.32.
Owner Craig Bennett **Bred** John R Cox **Trained** Greystoke, Cumbria

FOCUS
An ordinary pace and ordinary form behind the impressive winner, who was value for 40 lengths and looks a stayer to keep on the right side.

NOTEBOOK
Money Trix(IRE) ◆ duly improved for the step up to this trip and beat an ordinary field with any amount in hand. He has won two fairly uncompetitive events but appeals strongly as the type to do better in this sphere before going over fences. *(tchd 4-5)*
Sotovik(IRE) finished a similar distance behind the winner as he had done at Kelso over two miles and two on his previous start. He is likely to do better over hurdles in ordinary handicap company at up to this trip.
Kirkside Pleasure(IRE) again had his limitations exposed in this grade and is another that will be suited by the step into ordinary handicap company.
Native Coll bettered the form of his hurdle debut but is likely to remain vulnerable in this type of event.
Wise Man(IRE), a fair staying chaser on his day, was well beaten back over hurdles on this first start since April of last year.
Birtley Boy *Official explanation: vet said gelding had bled from the nose (op 9-2)*
Winapenny(IRE) was again a big disappointment and ran this time as though something was amiss. He has the ability to win a small race but remains one to tread carefully with at present. *(op 9-2)*
T/Plt: £137.20 to a £1 stake. Pool: £94,620.15. 503.10 winning tickets. T/Qpdt: £94.60 to a £1 stake. Pool: £7,177.10. 56.10 winning tickets. RY

3340 NEWBURY (L-H)
Saturday, February 11
3856 Meeting Abandoned - Frost

The meeting was only called off at 12.53 p.m. and many people felt it should have gone ahead.

3577 WARWICK (L-H)
Saturday, February 11
3863 Meeting Abandoned - Frost

3210 EXETER (R-H)
Sunday, February 12

OFFICIAL GOING: Good to soft
Flight on top corner of course omitted.
Wind: Mild, across

3876 TOTEPLACEPOT AMATEUR RIDERS' H'CAP HURDLE (10 hdls 1 omitted) 2m 6f 110y
2:00 (2:00) (Class 4) (0-105,104) 4-Y-0+ **£3,123** (£968; £484; £242)

Form	Pos	Dist	Horse	Rider	RPR
P-3P	1		**Desert Tommy**[8] 3733 5-11-8 **100**	MrNWilliams	113+
			(Evan Williams) *in tch: tk clsr order 6th: rdn appr 3 out: led after 2 out: styd on: drvn out*	**12/1**	
003P	2	4	**Abragante (IRE)**[77] 2530 5-11-3 **102**	(p) MrRQuinn(7)	109+
			(M C Pipe) *in tch: smooth hdwy to ld appr 3 out: rdn and hdd after 2 out: no ex*	**7/4**[1]	
6-4P	3	8	**El Hombre Del Rio (IRE)**[71] 2623 9-11-7 **102**	MrDEdwards(3)	102+
			(V G Greenway) *trckd ldrs: rdn after 6th: led after next: hdd appr 3 out : kpt on same pce*	**50/1**	
-P00	4	7	**Bak To Bill**[41] 3214 11-11-6 **103**	MissLGardner(5)	95
			(Mrs S Gardner) *in tch: rdn and effrt after 7th: one pced fr next*	**14/1**	
3441	5	8	**Aspra (FR)**[191] 1154 6-11-3 **102**	MrCHughes(7)	86
			(C J Down) *hld up towards rr: sme hdwy after 7th: no further imp fr 3 out*	**11/1**	
-040	6	½	**Dere Lyn**[47] 3018 8-11-4 **101**	(v) MrRWoollacott(5)	85
			(Mrs D A Hamer) *hld up and a towards rr*	**12/1**	
3566	7	nk	**Micky Cole (IRE)**[41] 3211 6-11-0 **99**	(b) MrHSkelton(7)	82
			(P F Nicholls) *mid div: rdn after 7th: sn wknd*	**8/1**[3]	
3135	8	24	**Baloo**[98] 2072 10-11-5 **104**	MrBMoorcroft(7)	63
			(J D Frost) *mid div: rdn after 6th: wknd after next*	**11/1**	
63P6	9	7	**Noble Calling (FR)**[34] 3325 9-11-8 **103**	MrJSnowden(3)	55
			(R J Hodges) *mid div tl 5th: sn bhd*	**6/1**[2]	
/00-	10	dist	**Capricorn**[14] 8-10-10 **95**	(b) MrCHolman(7)	—
			(Miss L Day) *a bhd*	**100/1**	
6360	P		**Alva Glen (USA)**[24] 3467 9-11-1 **100**	(t) MrRMcCarthy(7)	—
			(B J Llewellyn) *mid div tl 5th: t.o and p.u bef 3 out*	**33/1**	
106P	P		**Surfboard (IRE)**[23] 3477 5-11-3 **100**	MissFayeBramley(5)	—
			(P A Blockley) *led tl 7th: wknd qckly: p.u bef 3 out*	**20/1**	
4440	P		**Spring Junior (FR)**[41] 3210 5-11-8 **103**	MrTJO'Brien(3)	—
			(P J Hobbs) *chsd ldrs tl wknd 7th: bhd whn p.u bef 3 out*	**12/1**	

5m 54.1s (14.80) **Going Correction** +0.675s/f (Soft) **13** Ran SP% **118.8**
Speed ratings: **101,99,96,94,91 91,91,82,80,**— —,—,— CSF £33.16 CT £1068.81 TOTE £16.50: £3.90, £1.40, £9.40; EX 66.30.
Owner All Adda Winna Racing Club **Bred** Silfield Bloodstock **Trained** Cowbridge, Vale Of Glamorgan
■ Stewards' Enquiry : Mr N Williams one-day ban: used whip with excessive frequency and with arm above shoulder height (Feb 23)

FOCUS
A moderate start to the day on ground riding pretty much as described. The form sets the standard with the first two capable of better.

NOTEBOOK
Desert Tommy, who had excuses when pulling up at Uttoxeter last time, was on his form today and stayed on too strongly for the favourite once nosing ahead two out. He has a decent record when completing and may well have more to offer, being just a five-year-old. *(op 11-1)*
Abragante(IRE) has done better since being fitted with cheekpieces and appeared to hold strong claims in a modest contest. He travelled well, but was soon headed once taking it up and in the end was no match for the winner. This was a step back in the right direction having pulled up last time, but he will continue to be vulnerable unless improving. *(op 15-8 tchd 13-8, 2-1 in a place)*
El Hombre Del Rio(IRE), who is better known as a chaser, does little for the form, but this was his best run for around a year and he has slipped down to a fair mark. *Official explanation: jockey said gelding hung right-handed (op 66-1)*
Bak To Bill is without a hurdling win in over three years and, although not disgraced back in fourth, he makes little appeal with the future in mind. *(op 16-1)*
Aspra(FR) was making her handicap debut off a stiff-looking mark after winning at Worcester back in August and it was no surprise to see her struggle. *(op 12-1)*

3877 TOTEPOOL A BETTER WAY TO BET H'CAP CHASE (19 fncs) 3m 1f 110y
2:30 (2:31) (Class 3) (0-135,132) 5-Y-0+ **£9,759** (£2,865; £1,432; £715)

Form	Pos	Dist	Horse	Rider	RPR
-464	1		**Gunther McBride (IRE)**[18] 3560 11-11-8 **128**	RichardJohnson	140+
			(P J Hobbs) *led 2nd: mde rest: rdn appr 4: styd on gamely: drvn out*	**5/1**[2]	
-0FP	2	2	**Philson Run (IRE)**[47] 3022 10-11-3 **128**	LiamHeard(5)	136+
			(Nick Williams) *hld up towards rr: stdy hdwy fr 11th: chsd wnr after 15th: sn rdn: kpt on: hld whn nt fluent last*	**16/1**	
-05P	3	25	**World Wide Web (IRE)**[47] 3022 10-11-3 **123**	(b) MickFitzgerald	105
			(Jonjo O'Neill) *hld up towards rr: mstke 9th (water): sme hdwy after 14th: sn rdn: wnt 3rd appr 4 out: wknd 3 out*	**14/1**	
516P	4	3	**Victory Gunner (IRE)**[29] 3390 8-11-3 **123**	OllieMcPhail	102
			(C Roberts) *prom: rdn after 15th: sn wknd*	**40/1**	
-PP4	5	2	**Fox In The Box**[15] 3614 9-10-11 **117**	(v) AndrewThornton	94
			(R H Alner) *mid div tl lost pl 4th: towards rr: hdwy to chse ldrs 14th: sn rdn: wknd after 15th*	**14/1**	
411F	6	dist	**Dead-Eyed Dick (IRE)**[29] 3390 10-11-6 **126**	ChristianWilliams	—
			(Nick Williams) *hld up towards rr: sltly hmpd 10th: hdwy after 12th into mid div: rdn after 15th: sn wknd: virtually p.u run-in*	**5/1**[2]	
P-PP	F		**Supreme Catch (IRE)**[22] 3509 9-10-1 **114**	MrTJO'Brien(7)	—
			(Miss H C Knight) *mid div tl fell 10th*	**25/1**	
2-U1	P		**Lease Back (FR)**[262] 514 7-10-1 **114** ow2	JustinMorgan(7)	—
			(L Wells) *prom tl wknd qckly after 13th: p.u bef next*	**9/2**[1]	
B-F5	P		**Field Roller (IRE)**[81] 2430 6-10-6 **112**	TimmyMurphy	—
			(M C Pipe) *hld up towards rr: wknd qckly 14th: p.u bef next*	**12/1**	
P0-0	P		**Be My Royal (IRE)**[29] 3389 12-11-0 **120**	RobertWalford	—
			(R H Alner) *mid div: blnd 7th: nt rcvr and p.u after next*	**33/1**	
10-2	P		**Rosemauve (FR)**[16] 3600 6-11-5 **125**	(b) TomScudamore	—
			(M C Pipe) *chsd ldrs: rdn appr 12th: sn wknd: bhd and p.u after 14th*	**7/1**[3]	
1-4P	P		**Indalo (IRE)**[47] 3022 11-11-6 **126**	SamThomas	—
			(Miss Venetia Williams) *led tl 2nd: chsd ldrs: rdn appr 12th: sn wknd: p.u bef 4 out*	**5/1**[2]	

6m 44.8s (16.80) **Going Correction** +0.675s/f (Soft) **12** Ran SP% **116.8**
Speed ratings: **101,100,92,91,91** —,—,—,—,— —,— CSF £76.18 CT £1053.62 TOTE £6.30: £2.40, £6.00, £4.20; EX 116.00 Trifecta £394.70 Part won. Pool: £556.00 - 0.30 winning units..
Owner M J Tuckey **Bred** Michael F Condon **Trained** Withycombe, Somerset

FOCUS
A competitive staying chase on paper, but two emerged as being far superior on the day and they are rated as having run to their marks. The form should work out well enough.

NOTEBOOK
Gunther McBride(IRE), who has struggled off higher marks this season, had slipped down to a mark 6lb lower than when scoring at Doncaster last season and put up a cracking effort. Sent into the lead approaching the second fence, Johnson was seen at his best and he put in a fine round of jumping. He looked vulnerable down the straight, but kept finding for pressure and fully deserved the win. He will find life tougher back up in the weights, but should continue to pay his way. *(op 11-2)*
Philson Run(IRE) is a very useful staying handicap chaser on his day and returned to something like his best. Given a patient ride by Heard, he made good headway and it was clear from the turn-in it was between he and the winner. He gave his all and was held when making a slight mistake at the last, but looks to be hitting form at the right time with a bid for back-to-back Midlands Grand Nationals no doubt on the card. *(tchd 20-1)*
World Wide Web(IRE), pulled up in the Welsh National on his return to fences, ran better than his finishing position suggests and was not that far behind turning in, but tired badly in the final three furlongs. Some further help from the Handicapper may see him on a good enough mark to score again. *(tchd 12-1)*
Victory Gunner(IRE) is a strong stayer, but his current mark is too high and he will not be winning off it unless finding some improvement. *(op 50-1)*
Fox In The Box, although ultimately well-beaten here, has raced a bit more enthusiastically since having the visor fitted and is one to watch out for later in the season on his favoured sound surface.
Dead-Eyed Dick(IRE) may have had his confidence knocked by a fall last tiem, as this was not his form and it was worrying to see him finished so tired.
Lease Back(FR), who on a line through formerly smart chaser Massac looked to be running off a good mark, was well supported throughout the day and largely expected to go close on this debut over fences in Britain (twice a winner over them in France) but, having raced up on the outside and jumped well in the main, he stopped very quickly and will no doubt have left connections scratching their heads. He is evidently believed to be better than he has shown, hence a Gold Cup entry, but has a bit to prove after this. *Official explanation: jockey said gelding had a breathing problem (op 4-1 tchd 5-1)*

3878 TOTESPORT.COM NOVICES' HURDLE (LISTED RACE) (7 hdls 1 omitted) 2m 1f
3:00 (3:00) (Class 1) 4-Y-0+ **£11,902** (£4,456; £2,226; £1,112)

Form	Pos	Dist	Horse	Rider	RPR
-311	1		**Noland**[36] 3297 5-11-11 138	ChristianWilliams	137+
			(P F Nicholls) *in tch: hdwy to join ldr appr 3 out: led sn after 2 out: r.o: rdn out*	**6/5**[1]	
2141	2	2	**Mister Quasimodo**[41] 3210 6-11-9 120	JoeTizzard	130
			(C L Tizzard) *trckd ldr: led after 3rd: rdn and hdd sn after 2 out: kpt on but a hld by wnr*	**12/1**	
1113	3	15	**Boychuk (IRE)**[42] 3174 5-11-11	RichardJohnson	118+
			(P J Hobbs) *chsd ldrs: outpcd and dropped towards rr after 4th: styd on again fr 2 out: wnt 3rd run-in*	**7/2**[2]	
/15-	4	9	**Manners (IRE)**[441] 2518 8-11-3	MickFitzgerald	100
			(Jonjo O'Neill) *hld up towards rr: hdwy after 4th: rdn to dispute 3rd appr 3 out: kpt on same pce*	**7/1**	
2-2	5	2½	**Classic Role**[12] 3658 7-11-3	JustinMorgan	98
			(L Wells) *mid div: tk clsr order after 4th: rdn and effrt appr 3 out: one pced after*	**16/1**	
121	6	2½	**Siberian Highness (FR)**[24] 3464 5-11-2 119	WayneHutchinson	96+
			(A King) *in tch: hdwy to chse ldng pair after 4th: hit 3 out: sn rdn: wkng whn mstke last*	**6/1**[3]	
	7	5	**Miss Grace**[620] 6-10-10	JamesDavies	83
			(J D Frost) *towards rr: sme hdwy after 4th: no further imp*	**200/1**	
0	8	9	**Charmatic (IRE)**[36] 3281 5-10-10	(t) PhilipHide	74
			(Andrew Turnell) *a towards rr*	**100/1**	
5	9	1½	**Illuminati**[36] 3294 4-10-7	HowieEphgrave	70
			(L Corcoran) *a towards rr*	**100/1**	

00 **10** *27* **Mr Tambourine Man (IRE)**[24] [3463] 5-11-3 .... OllieMcPhail 53
(B J Llewellyn) *led tl after 3rd: wknd after next* **100/1**

U **Story Arms** 4-10-7 .... AngharadFrieze —
(D Burchell) *wnt lft and uns rdr 1st* **250/1**

4m 19.1s (9.90) **Going Correction** +0.675s/f (Soft)
WFA 4 from 5yo+ 9lb **11** Ran SP% **111.9**
Speed ratings: **103,102,95,90,89 88,86,81,81,68** — CSF £17.05 TOTE £2.50: £1.10, £2.80, £1.40; EX 18.80.

Owner J Hales **Bred** The Niarchos Family **Trained** Ditcheat, Somerset

FOCUS

A very good novices' hurdle for the track. The form looks strong, rated through the winner, and the race should produce its share of winners at a decent level.

NOTEBOOK

Noland, a fair bumper who looked nothing special when beaten on his hurdling debut at Wincanton, has made rapid progress since that defeat, winning stylishly at Cheltenham before taking the Grade One Tolworth Hurdle at Sandown. The latter event was weak by its standards, but he could do no more than win and was only running here as a result of the abandonment of Newbury the previous day. Asked to improve from well over half a mile out, he needed plenty of driving to get past the runner-up. It is no coincidence his improvement has come since encountering soft ground and this good-looking five-year-old looks certain to stay further in time. Two miles is his trip for the moment however, and the Supreme Novices, for which he is a best-priced 8/1, is the obvious target. He currently looks the best of the British challenge for that contest given sufficient cut in the ground. *(op 11-8 tchd 6-4 in places)*

Mister Quasimodo ◆ is a high-class chaser in the making and the fact he is able to show so much ability over hurdles must delight connections. Back on track when winning here last time, he had quite a bit to find with the likes of Noland and Boychuk on form, but under a positive ride from Tizzard he really stretched the winner and was doing his best to get back at him towards the finish. The form looks particularly good and this tall gelding handled the drop in trip remarkably well, travelling best of all into the straight. Soft ground at a galloping track is always going to suit well and in six starts at Chepstow and Exeter combined he has yet to finish outside the front two. Cheltenham and Aintree will presumably be off the agenda this term and it may be the valuable novices' handicap hurdle final at Sandown in March that is his main target. Either way he could have the world at his feet next season if staying sound and is definitely one to keep on the right side of. *(op 10-1)*

Boychuk(IRE) came into this looking the most obvious danger to the favourite, having finished a fair third behind Denman in the Grade One Challow Hurdle at Cheltenham last time, but he was unable to repeat the form and looked to run flat. It is also a possibility he now finds this trip too sharp and it is now likely he will end up in the Royal & SunAlliance Hurdle at the Festival. *(tchd 10-3, 4-1 in places)*

Manners(IRE), off since November 2004, has always been well thought of and showed enough on this reappearance to suggest he retains plenty of ability. Although ultimately well beaten, it is highly unlikely he would have been finely-tuned for this and improvement is to be expected. *(op 6-1)*

Classic Role was unable to build on his reappearance second to the smart Straw Bear at Folkestone, but would have struggled to match the front pair even if he had run to form. He has yet to win over hurdles and may need his sights lowering. *(op 14-1)*

Siberian Highness(FR) bounced back from a disappointing effort when winning at Taunton last time, but this was an altogether different test and she was simply not good enough. She is a useful mare nonetheless and will find further success against her own sex. *(op 5-1)*

Charmatic(IRE) *Official explanation: jockey said mare had a breathing problem*

3879 SOUTH-WEST RACING CLUB NOVICES' CHASE (15 fncs) 2m 3f 110y

3:30 (3:31) (Class 3) 5-Y-0+ **£7,807** (£2,292; £1,146; £572)

Form RPR

2-11 **1** **Racing Demon (IRE)**[71] [2634] 6-11-12 .... TimmyMurphy 162+
(Miss H C Knight) *a travelling wl: trckd ldr: lft in ld 7th: j.rt and brushed wing 4 out: j.rt thereafter: clr 3 out:r.o wl: easily* **2/7**[1]

2142 **2** *15* **Cornish Sett (IRE)**[32] [3341] 7-11-8 140 .... (b) ChristianWilliams 144+
(P F Nicholls) *trckd ldrs: chsd wnr fr 7th: rdn appr 4 out: no ch w wnr fr 3 out* **4/1**[2]

-24F **3** *19* **Back Nine (IRE)**[43] [3134] 9-11-2 120 .... AndrewThornton 122+
(R H Alner) *hld up: wnt 3rd appr 3 out: styd on but nvr trbld ldrs* **20/1**[3]

00U5 **4** *9* **Mythical King (IRE)**[19] [3549] 9-11-2 .... TomDoyle 107
(R Lee) *in tch: wnt 3rd after 9th tl 3 out: sn wknd* **40/1**

PP0 **5** *7* **Master Billyboy (IRE)**[34] [3326] 8-11-2 102 .... WayneHutchinson 102+
(Mrs S D Williams) *j.rt thrght: in tch: mstke 3rd: wknd after 11th* **100/1**

33-0 **6** *dist* **Lesdream**[59] [2848] 9-11-2 .... JamesDavies —
(J D Frost) *t.o fr 7th* **80/1**

366/ **F** **Only Wallis (IRE)**[695] [4445] 9-11-2 .... JoeTizzard —
(C L Tizzard) *led tl fell heavily 7th: dead* **100/1**

P-0F **U** **Powra**[24] [3457] 6-10-9 .... JamesWhite(7) —
(R J Hodges) *plld hrd: sn mid div: blnd and uns rdr 6th* **250/1**

U **La Source A Gold (IRE)**[644] 7-11-2 .... PhilipHide —
(Nick Williams) *hld up: bdly hmpd and uns rdr 7th* **150/1**

FP-P **P** **River Of Wishes**[36] [3280] 8-10-9 .... SeanCurran —
(C W Mitchell) *lost tch fr 7th: t.o and p.u bef 9th* **250/1**

(6.10) **Going Correction** +0.675s/f (Soft) **10** Ran SP% **109.6**
Speed ratings: **114,108,100,96,94** —,—,—,—,— CSF £1.52 TOTE £1.30: £1.02, £1.40, £1.50; EX 1.90.

Owner Mrs T P Radford **Bred** Con O'Keeffe **Trained** West Lockinge, Oxon

FOCUS

A straightforward success for hot favourite Racing Demon, who now heads to Cheltenham as the one to beat in the Arkle. The runner-up sets the level for the form.

NOTEBOOK

Racing Demon(IRE) ◆ has missed numerous engagements in recent weeks for one reason or another, but he had been found an ideal Cheltenham-prep here and Murphy wisely rode him prominently in a race where there was always likely to be trouble in behind. Barring a scare at the fourth-last where he brushed through the wing of the fence, it was plain sailing and he steadily drew clear to win impressively. He has yet to go left-handed over fences however, and the way he jumped right at the four fences in the straight would be a worry at the Festival, but there is no denying his outstanding Arkle claims and he goes there as the one to beat. *(tchd 1-4 and 1-3)*

Cornish Sett(IRE) is a talented individual, but he has his share of quirks and as expected, he proved no match for Racing Demon. A sound jumper, all bar one of his wins have come on good ground and it is reasonable to expect better back on a decent surface, but the Grand Annual rather than the Arkle seems the wisest Festival option. *(tchd 9-2)*

Back Nine(IRE) has not yet gone on from a promising chase-debut second at Lingfield, but he has faced several stiff tasks and fared as well as could have been expected. He will win races at the right level and would make some appeal in handicaps off this sort of mark. *(op 16-1 tchd 14-1)*

Mythical King(IRE) is not the biggest and will no doubt continue to find things tough over fences, but he ran well to a point and is another who will find life easier down in grade.

Master Billyboy(IRE) ◆ was the only other to get involved, disputing third until the turn-in, and running arguably his best race to date over fences. Off a mark of 102, he has to be backed once returning to handicaps.

River Of Wishes *Official explanation: jockey said mare bled from the nose (op 200-1)*

3880 TOTESPORT 0800 221 221 H'CAP HURDLE (7 hdls 1 omitted) 2m 1f

4:00 (4:00) (Class 3) (0-120,120) 4-Y-0+ **£5,204** (£1,528; £764; £381)

Form RPR

3-16 **1** **Gods Token**[48] [2969] 8-11-9 117 .... SamThomas 134+
(Miss Venetia Williams) *mde all: clr 2 out: easily* **4/1**[1]

-FFP **2** *8* **Mister Mustard (IRE)**[109] [1880] 9-11-10 118 .... WayneHutchinson 121+
(Ian Williams) *hld up: hdwy 2nd: chsd wnr appr 3 out: sn rdn: kpt on same pce* **16/1**

042 **3** *2* **Jockser (IRE)**[43] [3143] 5-10-7 108 .... WayneKavanagh(7) 108
(J W Mullins) *in tch: rdn appr 3 out: kpt on same pce* **9/1**[3]

2512 **4** *hd* **Inaro (IRE)**[22] [3500] 5-11-11 119 .... (t) RichardMcGrath 119
(Jonjo O'Neill) *in tch on outer: hdwy after 4th: sn rdn: kpt on same pce* **4/1**[1]

036 **5** *12* **Iffy**[80] [2455] 5-10-11 105 .... TomDoyle 100+
(R Lee) *towards rr: rdn and sme hdwy appr 3 out: no imp after* **10/1**

2P-2 **6** *1 ½* **Idaho D'Ox (FR)**[276] [315] 10-11-12 120 .... TomScudamore 106
(M C Pipe) *chsd ldrs: rdn appr 3 out: wknd 2 out* **12/1**

53/0 **7** *¾* **Pro Dancer (USA)**[53] [2939] 8-11-3 118 .... MrTJO'Brien(7) 104
(P Bowen) *mid div tl wknd 3 out* **20/1**

2114 **8** *7* **Rift Valley (IRE)**[169] [1341] 11-10-12 116 .... DarrenO'Dwyer(10) 95
(P J Hobbs) *w wnr tl wknd after 4th* **16/1**

2F15 **9** *19* **Spike Jones (NZ)**[13] [3650] 8-10-10 109 .... DerekLaverty(5) 69
(Mrs S M Johnson) *hld up and a towards rr* **14/1**

-223 **10** *8* **Magnesium (USA)**[29] [3386] 6-11-1 109 .... TimmyMurphy 61
(B G Powell) *a towards rr* **4/1**[1]

2P-P **11** *16* **Mambo (IRE)**[48] [2969] 8-11-8 116 .... MickFitzgerald 52
(N J Henderson) *mid div: lost position after 4th: hdwy 3 out: wknd next* **15/2**[2]

4m 20.0s (10.80) **Going Correction** +0.675s/f (Soft) **11** Ran SP% **121.7**
Speed ratings: **101,97,96,96,90 89,89,86,77,73 65** CSF £67.89 CT £558.00 TOTE £5.80: £2.00, £5.50, £3.40; EX 155.40.

Owner The Silver Cod Partnership **Bred** C I Ratcliffe **Trained** Kings Caple, H'fords

FOCUS

A fair handicap and a dominant display by Gods Token, who simply galloped his rivals into submission. The placed horses and the fifth were close to their marks which suggests the form should work out well enough.

NOTEBOOK

Gods Token, who failed to go on from a winning reappearance at the course when only sixth at Sandown on Boxing Day, was given a fine ride by Thomas and led throughout for an easy victory, galloping right away in the final quarter mile. This was his fifth win from 13 starts and the eight-year-old remains open to a little further improvement. *(op 11-2)*

Mister Mustard(IRE), who had failed to complete in his three most recent starts, twice falling, enjoyed a nice, confidence-boosting outing and it was only the relentless winner that foiled him. He travelled well for a long way and is attractively weighted on his best form. *(tchd 20-1)*

Jockser(IRE), who remains over a stone higher than when last successful, lacked the pace of the front two and again ran in a manner that suggests further is required. He is only five and has some improving to do.

Inaro(IRE), needed to find some improvement to win off this mark on his handicap debut, but he failed to do so, the first-time tongue tie doing little for him. As with Jockser, he is only five and shapes as though there will be better to come at two and a half miles. *(op 7-2 tchd 10-3, 9-2 in places and 5-1 in a place)*

Iffy, a modest sort on the Flat, has not shaped too badly since going hurdling, bt was unable to live with the principals and never really got involved. He may find life easier at a slightly lower level. *(op 9-1)*

Magnesium(USA) has been running consistently well, but this was not such a good effort and he *failed to progress beyond the rear. He gives the impression he will continue to be hard to win with. Official explanation: jockey said gelding had a breathing problem (op 11-2)*

Mambo(IRE), who is well-weighted over hurdles compared with his chase form, continues to show little and may need genuine quick ground to revive his form. *(op 6-1)*

3881 TOTEEXACTA "NATIONAL HUNT" NOVICES' HURDLE (DIV I) (9 hdls 1 omitted) 2m 3f

4:30 (4:31) (Class 4) 4-Y-0+ **£2,927** (£859; £429; £214)

Form RPR

31 **1** **Keenan's Future (IRE)**[29] [3393] 5-11-11 .... WayneHutchinson 119+
(Ian Williams) *in tch: tk clsr order 6th: rdn appr 3 out: led sn after 2 out: styd on: drvn out* **11/2**[3]

2 **2** *1 ¾* **Rare Gold (IRE)**[27] [3425] 6-11-4 .... AndrewThornton 109+
(R H Alner) *led tl 4th: w ldr: led briefly appr 3 out: sn rdn: hit 2 out: styd on run-in* **10/1**

5-03 **3** *2 ½* **Corals Laurel (IRE)**[29] [3393] 7-11-4 .... RichardJohnson 106
(R T Phillips) *hld up towards rr: gd hdwy after 6th: led 3 out: rdn and hdd sn after 2 out: no ex* **16/1**

1/ **4** *13* **Chelsea Bridge (IRE)**[1086] [3754] 8-11-4 .... TimmyMurphy 96+
(Miss H C Knight) *hld up towards rr: smooth prog on outer after 6th: trcking ldrs whn nt fluent next: sn wknd* **5/1**[2]

16 **5** *3* **Briscoe Place (IRE)**[91] [2211] 6-11-4 .... RichardMcGrath 90
(Jonjo O'Neill) *t.k.h: trckd ldrs: rdn and mstke 3 out: sn wknd* **14/1**

6 *½* **Merriott's Oscar (IRE)**[295] 6-10-11 .... MrJSnowden(7) 89
(N J Hawke) *trckd ldrs: outpcd appr 3 out: styd on past btn horses fr 2 out* **100/1**

54/P **7** *6* **Idbury (IRE)**[23] [3478] 8-11-4 .... OllieMcPhail 83
(V J Hughes) *w ldr: led 4th tl appr 3 out: sn wknd* **150/1**

2/P **8** *10* **How Is The Lord (IRE)**[29] [3388] 10-11-4 .... PhilipHide 73
(C J Down) *hld up and a towards rr* **66/1**

-112 **9** *30* **Craven (IRE)**[30] [3369] 6-11-11 .... MickFitzgerald 65+
(N J Henderson) *mid div: hdwy to trck ldrs 6th: rdn appr 3 out: wknd qckly* **8/11**[1]

00/3 **10** *6* **Sparkling Sabrina**[53] [2937] 6-10-11 .... ChristianWilliams 30
(P Bowen) *chsd ldrs tl wknd after 6th* **50/1**

P **Call Out (IRE)**[288] 6-10-11 .... MissLGardner(7) —
(Mrs S Gardner) *t.o fr 4th: p.u bef 3 out* **50/1**

0/0P **P** **Valderrama**[48] [3001] 6-10-11 .... TomMessenger(7) —
(L Waring) *a bhd: blnd 2nd: t.o fr 5th: p.u after 6th* **200/1**

4m 55.2s (14.30) **Going Correction** +0.675s/f (Soft) **12** Ran SP% **119.2**
Speed ratings: **96,95,94,88,87 87,84,80,67,65** —,— CSF £56.95 TOTE £6.80: £1.70, £3.00, £5.00; EX 34.00.

Owner Dsm Demolition Limited **Bred** Charles Micheal Gildea **Trained** Portway, Worcs

FOCUS

Despite the disappointment of favourite Craven, this looked a stronger race than the second division with the runner-up setting the level.

NOTEBOOK

Keenan's Future(IRE), a winning pointer who was impressive on his hurdles debut at Wetherby last month, benefited from the below-par performance of the favourite and ran out a ready winner, staying on well from two out. Evidently progressive, this five-year-old remains open to a fair amount of improvement and is the type to end up in the valuable EBF novices' handicap final at Sandown in March. *(op 5-1)*

Rare Gold(IRE) ◆, a winning pointer, was given a nice introduction when second on his hurdling debut at Plumpton, and stepped up on that effort under a more positive ride. Always travelling well in front, he became outpaced and lost momentum with a mistake two out, but was coming back at the winner after the last and shaped as though a step up to three miles will see further improvement. He is sure to make a better chaser in time. *(tchd 9-1)*

Corals Laurel(IRE) easily ran his best race thus far over hurdles, coming through to take a narrow lead three out before tiring in the final furlong or so. This was a fair race and he is sure to find better opportunities in handicaps.

Chelsea Bridge(IRE), whose bumper win back in February 2003 could not have worked out much better (Trabolgan, Dempsey and Distant Thunder next three home) had not run since. It was always likely he was going to need the run and, having travelled well to a point he soon became tired and was not given a hard time once beaten. Whilst this was undoubtedly promising and he is entitled to come on for the outing, it is debatable what he can achieve over hurdles and he is hardly one to follow given he is not going to be overraced and is clearly vulnerable injury wise. *(op 9-2 tchd 11-2)*

Briscoe Place(IRE) ran well to a point on this hurdles debut, but is unlikely to be seen at his best until tackling handicaps. *(op 20-1)*

Craven(IRE), who finally came unstuck last time having made hard work of winning his first two starts, flopped badly and was never moving/jumping with any fluency. Whilst this was clearly not his form, his lazy style of racing is offputting and he will need to raise his game once switched to fences. *Official explanation: trainer's representative had no explanation for the poor form shown (op 5-6 tchd 10-11)*

3882 TOTEEXACTA "NATIONAL HUNT" NOVICES' HURDLE (DIV II) (9 hdls 1 omitted) 2m 3f

5:00 (5:02) (Class 4) 4-Y-0+ **£2,927** (£859; £429; £214)

Form				RPR
-115	1		**Its A Dream (IRE)**[42] [3174] 6-11-11 ... MickFitzgerald (N J Henderson) *rn in snatches: mid div: lost pl 4th and pushed along: hdwy after 6th: rdn to ld 2 out: hit last: kpt on wl: drvn out* **8/13**[1]	127+
4-04	2	1	**Sharajan (IRE)**[27] [3425] 6-11-4 ... WayneHutchinson (A King) *mid div: hdwy to chse ldng pair appr 3 out: sn rdn: styng on and ev ch whn nt fluent last: no ex* **25/1**	112
25U2	3	5	**Commander Kev (IRE)**[16] [3595] 5-11-4 ... TomDoyle (Noel T Chance) *chsd ldrs: led appr 3 out: rdn and hdd 2 out: kpt on same pce* **9/2**[3]	108+
344	4	13	**Bring Me Sunshine (IRE)**[47] [3024] 5-11-4 ... JoeTizzard (C L Tizzard) *chsd ldrs tl outpcd appr 3 out: styd on again fr 2 out* **25/1**	94+
350	5	6	**So Long**[78] [2507] 6-10-11 ... RobertWalford (C L Popham) *mid div: rdn and one pced fr 3 out* **200/1**	82+
20-1	6	7	**Dunsfold Duke**[27] [3425] 6-11-11 120 ... PhilipHide (P Winkworth) *chsd ldrs: led 6th tl 3 out: sn wknd* **4/1**[2]	90+
66/3	7	1 3/4	**Carew Lad**[15] [3611] 10-11-4 ... BenjaminHitchcott (Mrs D A Hamer) *led tl 2nd: w ldr tl wknd after 6th* **66/1**	79
200-	8	26	**Irish Totty**[336] [4349] 7-10-11 ... JimmyMcCarthy (C J Down) *hld up towards rr: hdwy after 6th: wknd after 3 out* **150/1**	46
	P		**Los Suenos (IRE)** 5-11-4 ... ChristianWilliams (Nick Williams) *a in rr: t.o and p.u bef 2 out* **100/1**	—
40-	P		**Bayford Boy**[599] [812] 6-10-11 ... (t) JamesWhite[(7)] (K Bishop) *lost tch after 3rd: p.u bef next* **100/1**	—
	P		**Officer Cadet (IRE)**[365] 7-11-4 ... RichardJohnson (P J Hobbs) *racd keenly: led 2nd tl 6th: sn wknd: p.u bef 3 out* **50/1**	—

4m 50.4s (9.50) **Going Correction** +0.675s/f (Soft) **11** Ran SP% **114.4**

Speed ratings: **107,106,104,99,96 93,92,81,—,—** — CSF £20.23 TOTE £1.70: £1.10, £2.70, £1.80; EX 17.60 Place 6 £117.43, Place 5 £53.57.

Owner Mrs R Murdoch & David Murdoch **Bred** Mrs Esther Power **Trained** Upper Lambourn, Berks

FOCUS

What looked a simple opportunity for It's A Dream to record his second win over hurdles turned into quite a grind. The faster of the two divisions but fair enough form, with the winner and third to their marks.

NOTEBOOK

Its A Dream(IRE), whose stamina came to the fore when winning in heavy ground at Sandown on his hurdling debut, found things happening too quickly for him when upped in class for the Grade One Challow Hurdle behind Denman at Cheltenham, but this was a significantly easier race and he was expected to win easily. Things did not work out as planned however and, as with his stable companion in the previous race, he was never travelling with an real fluency. His superior staying power got him out of trouble in the end though, grinding it out under a spirited ride fom Fitzgerald, but he will need to up his game significantly in future and may be in need of three miles. *(op 4-6)*

Sharajan(IRE) is gradually heading the right way and he made the hot favourite work mightily hard, but a mistake at the last which cost him momentum handed the advantage to the winner and he was forced to settle for second. *(tchd 28-1)*

Commander Kev(IRE) has shown a fair level of form on each of his two completed starts over hurdles and there is a race for him at around this distance, probably on one of the lesser tracks. He will make a chaser in time, but is the type to do well in handicap hurdles beforehand. *(op 5-1 tchd 4-1)*

Bring Me Sunshine(IRE), a modest sort in bumpers, was helped by this extra distance, but will *ultimately require three miles and is sure to find easier opportunities.Official explanation: jockey said gelding hung left-handed round final bend (op 33-1)*

So Long failed to progress in bumpers, but this was a pleasing hurdles debut and she will find life easier against her own sex. *(op 150-1)*

Dunsfold Duke, a tidy winner on his hurdles debut at Plumpton and largely expected to provide the winner with most to do, led into the straight, but was readily brushed aside and ended up well beaten. This was not his form, but there appeared to be no obvious excuse for the defeat. *(tchd 7-2 and 9-2)*

T/Jkpt: £4,733.30 to a £1 stake. Pool: £10,000.00. 1.50 winning tickets. T/Plt: £201.40 to a £1 stake. Pool: £61,947.45. 224.45 winning tickets. T/Qpdt: £13.00 to a £1 stake. Pool: £3,854.10. 218.80 winning tickets. TM

3246 HEREFORD (R-H)

Sunday, February 12

OFFICIAL GOING: Good to soft

Wind: Light, across Weather: Overcast

3883 DENCO AT DOLPHIN HOUSE MAIDEN HURDLE (8 hdls) 2m 1f

1:40 (1:40) (Class 4) 4-Y-0+ **£3,578** (£1,050; £525; £262)

Form				RPR
4	1		**Mith Hill**[12] [3659] 5-11-4 ... JasonMaguire (Ian Williams) *chsd ldr: led 2 out: drvn out* **16/1**	115+
2	2	1 1/2	**Vaughan**[44] [3127] 5-11-4 ... MarkBradburne (H D Daly) *hld up in mid-div: hdwy appr 5th: hit 3 out: sn rdn: ev ch after 2 out: nt qckn flat* **11/4**[2]	114+
46	3	5	**Whistle Blowing (IRE)**[41] [3203] 4-10-5 ... StephenCraine[(3)] (D McCain) *a.p: rdn and kpt on same pce fr 2 out* **16/1**	100+
	4	4	**Kingham**[757] 6-11-4 ... CarlLlewellyn (Mrs Mary Hambro) *led: hit and hdd 2 out: sn wknd* **100/1**	106+
2	5	24	**Traprain (IRE)**[24] [3463] 4-10-8 ... PJBrennan (P J Hobbs) *t.k.h towards rr: hdwy appr 5th: hit 3 out: rdn and wknd 2 out: blnd last* **9/4**[1]	86+
	6	21	**Cirrious**[230] 5-10-8 ... TomMalone[(3)] (P J Hobbs) *plld hrd in rr: no ch whn blnd 2 out: t.o* **22/1**	59+
2	7	1 3/4	**Easy Laughter (IRE)**[16] [3591] 5-11-4 ... RobertThornton (A King) *hld up in mid-div: bhd fr 5th: t.o* **14/1**	58
	8	10	**Pagan Sky (IRE)**[85] 7-11-1 ... PaulO'Neill[(3)] (Miss Venetia Williams) *prom tl wknd 5th: no ch whn blnd 2 out: t.o* **6/1**	48
	9	19	**Macaroni Gold (IRE)**[14] 6-11-4 ... PaulMoloney (D J Daly) *nt fluent 1st: a bhd: t.o* **40/1**	29
	P		**Lord Of Methley**[544] 7-11-4 ... AntonyEvans (S Lycett) *bhd fr 5th: t.o whn p.u bef 2 out* **200/1**	—
20	U		**Dark Parade (ARG)**[12] [3659] 5-11-4 ... JamieMoore (G L Moore) *hld up in mid-div: mstke and uns rdr 3rd* **20/1**	—
	P		**Thenford Boy (IRE)**[308] 6-10-13 ... JamesDiment[(5)] (B L Lay) *a bhd: reminders appr 3rd: rdn after 4th: sn t.o: p.u bef 2 out* **200/1**	—
4	P		**Shamayoun (FR)**[26] [3429] 4-10-8 ... AndrewTinkler (C R Egerton) *hld up and bhd: mstke 2nd: hdwy 4th: sn rdn: wknd 5th: no ch whn blnd 2 out: t.o whn p.u bef last* **11/2**[3]	—

4m 4.20s (1.10) **Going Correction** +0.425s/f (Soft)

WFA 4 from 5yo+ 9lb **13** Ran SP% **119.1**

Speed ratings: **107,106,103,102,90 80,80,75,66,—** —,—,— CSF £59.31 TOTE £16.20: £4.10, £1.50, £4.00; EX 79.80.

Owner P J Vogt **Bred** Floors Farming, Hmh Management Ltd And John Warren **Trained** Portway, Worcs

FOCUS

A decent novice hurdle for the track, and the form should work out.

NOTEBOOK

Mith Hill, sharper for his recent hurdles debut, showed a commendably gutsy attitude to hold off his rival. This was a sizeable improvement on the form of his debut effort and there should be more to come from him over a longer trip. *(op 12-1)*

Vaughanmoved up going well but was unable to get past a determined rival. He certainly has the size to make a name for himself at this game and his turn should not be long delayed. *(op 7-2)*

Whistle Blowing(IRE), having his third look at hurdles, ran respectably but was held when diving at the final flight. *(op 12-1)*

Kingham won his sole start at two for John Gosden but ran just twice in each of the following two seasons for this yard. Making his hurdling debut, he raced freely in front and had no answers when headed at the second last, but this was a promising debut.

Traprain(IRE) was again keen, as he was on his hurdles debut at Taunton, and that refusal to settle cost him as he faded rather tamely from the second last. *(op 5-2 tchd 11-4)*

Pagan Sky(IRE) is a useful performer on the Flat at up to 12 furlongs, but he did not last much beyond halfway on this hurdles debut. *(op 8-1)*

Macaroni Gold(IRE) *Official explanation: vet said gelding finished lame*

Shamayoun(FR) was a tired sixth when he jumping the second last slowly and was soon pulled up. *(op 6-1)*

3884 JOHN SMITH'S/E.B.F. MARES' ONLY "NATIONAL HUNT" NOVICES' HURDLE (QUALIFIER) (10 hdls) 2m 3f 110y

2:10 (2:10) (Class 3) 4-Y-0+ **£5,855** (£1,719; £859; £429)

Form				RPR
-U13	1		**Senorita Rumbalita**[48] [2997] 5-11-6 ... RobertThornton (A King) *led appr 3 out: clr whn j.rt last: rdn out* **2/5**[1]	117+
-521	2	6	**Colline De Fleurs**[26] [3435] 6-11-0 ... JasonMaguire (J A B Old) *a.p: ev ch 2 out: sn rdn: one pce* **9/2**[2]	103
P600	3	13	**Cresswell Willow (IRE)**[13] [3646] 6-10-9 90 ... (b) LeeStephens[(5)] (W K Goldsworthy) *led: mstke 5th: hit 6th: hdd appr 3 out: wknd appr 2 out* **100/1**	91+
20	4	9	**Blackbriery Thyne (IRE)**[48] [2961] 7-11-0 ... MarkBradburne (H D Daly) *hld up in mid-div: hdwy appr 6th: rdn appr 7th: wknd after 3 out* **20/1**	84+
322P	5	12	**Martovic (IRE)**[93] [2166] 7-11-0 100 ... JohnMcNamara (K C Bailey) *hld up and bhd: hdwy appr 7th: wknd 3 out* **14/1**[3]	69
0	6	29	**Young Siouxsie**[81] [2446] 6-10-9 ... StevenCrawford[(5)] (N A Twiston-Davies) *hld up: hdwy 3rd: rdn 6th: wknd 7th* **100/1**	40
5	7	23	**Fleur Des Pres (FR)**[32] [3346] 4-9-10 ... CharlieStudd[(7)] (B G Powell) *hld up and bhd: hdwy 5th: wknd 7th: t.o* **25/1**	6
-P4P	8	8	**Roseville (IRE)**[37] [3275] 6-11-0 ... MarkGrant (S T Lewis) *prom to 4th: t.o* **150/1**	9
50	9	25	**Lansdowne Princess**[42] [3181] 4-9-12 ... EamonDehdashti[(5)] (G A Ham) *t.k.h: prom: nt fluent 2nd: hit 7th: sn wknd: t.o* **100/1**	—
0	F		**Another Penny**[13] [3657] 6-11-0 ... HenryOliver (R Dickin) *hld up towards rr: fell 4th* **200/1**	—
0	B		**Pyleigh Lady**[24] [3468] 5-10-11 ... TomMalone[(3)] (S C Burrough) *hld up and bhd: b.d 4th* **100/1**	—
004	P		**Loose Morals (IRE)**[22] [3511] 5-11-0 ... MarcusFoley (Miss E C Lavelle) *a towards rr: t.o whn p.u bef 2 out* **25/1**	—
0-PP	P		**Turnnocard (IRE)**[57] [2878] 7-11-0 ... PaulMoloney (Ian Williams) *hld up in tch: hit 6th: sn wknd: t.o whn p.u bef 2 out* **125/1**	—

4m 56.4s (8.50) **Going Correction** +0.425s/f (Soft)

WFA 4 from 5yo+ 9lb **13** Ran SP% **114.6**

Speed ratings: **100,97,92,88,84 72,63,60,50,—** —,—,— CSF £2.06 TOTE £1.50: £1.02, £1.20, £14.80; EX 3.00.

Owner Let's Get Ready To Rumble Partnership **Bred** Wothersome Grange Stud **Trained** Barbury Castle, Wilts

FOCUS

Not much strength in depth in this mares' event. The winner did not need to be at her best to score, while the runner-up ran to the level of her bumper form.

NOTEBOOK

Senorita Rumbalita, a disappointment when last in action on Boxing Day, atoned with a straightforward victory although she did run down the last when in command. Probably best over shorter, she may take her chance in the Supreme Novices' Hurdle, a race in which mares have a decent record. *(tchd 4-9 in places)*

Colline De Fleurs, a bumper winner in heavy ground, ran up to that form on this hurdles debut and there was no disgrace in going down to a useful rival. Her dam is a half-sister to Earth Summit and she had no problem with this longer trip. *(op 5-1 tchd 11-2)*

Cresswell Willow(IRE) was headed leaving the back straight and could only plug on in a fairly remote third from that point. The blinkers have clearly improved her but this drop in trip was not ideal. *(op 150-1)*

Blackbriery Thyne(IRE), making her hurdles debut, confirmed that she has ability but lacked the pace to go with the leaders from the third last. She was placed in point-to-points and might need further. *(op 33-1)*

Loose Morals(IRE) *Official explanation: trainer said mare never travelled*

3885 BET365 CALL 08000 322365 MAIDEN CLAIMING HURDLE (10 hdls) 2m 3f 110y

2:40 (2:40) (Class 5) 4-Y-O+ **£2,081** (£611; £305; £152)

Form				RPR
0063	1		**Sunley Future (IRE)**[16] 3592 7-10-13 92 .... CharliePoste(7) *(M F Harris) led 1st: clr whn hit last: r.o: dismntd after fin* **4/1**[1]	96+
6200	2	7	**It's My Party**[11] 3673 5-11-3 87 .... RobertLucey-Butler(5) *(W G M Turner) hld up and bhd: hdwy appr 7th: chsd wnr after 3 out: no imp* **4/1**[1]	90
00	3	23	**Knotty Ash Girl (IRE)**[67] 2704 7-10-11 .... WarrenMarston *(D J Wintle) hld up towards rr: hdwy 5th: wkng whn mstke 2 out* **5/1**[2]	59+
0	4	1	**Red Rocky**[94] 2139 5-10-1 .... AdamHawkins(10) *(R Hollinshead) hld up towards rr: hdwy 6th: sn pushed along: wknd 3 out* **22/1**	55
P/6	5	16	**Brunston Castle**[11] 3673 6-11-11 .... StephenCraine(3) *(A W Carroll) hld up in tch: chsd wnr appr 7th tl wknd after 3 out* **16/1**	56
0	6	10	**Giant's Rock (IRE)**[22] 1011 4-10-11 ....(t) PJBrennan *(B J Llewellyn) hld up and bhd: hdwy 6th: rdn appr 7th: mstke 3 out* **10/1**	29
P-	7	14	**Harps Hall (IRE)**[434] 2660 12-10-8 .... MarkHunter(10) *(N I M Rossiter) bhd fr 4th: t.o* **100/1**	22
0	8	20	**Stewarts Dream (IRE)**[101] 2007 5-11-8 .... JodieMogford *(B D Leavy) a bhd: t.o* **33/1**	6
0-PP	9	22	**Gwens Girl**[8] 3731 6-10-11 .... GerrySupple *(J Rudge) a bhd: t.o whn blnd last* **66/1**	—
0-U	P		**Gay Millenium**[22] 3511 6-11-7 .... MarkGrant *(N I M Rossiter) a bhd: t.o whn p.u bef 5th* **50/1**	—
0P	P		**Roussea (IRE)**[47] 3017 8-11-3 .... AdrianScholes(7) *(S G Griffiths) hld up in tch: t.o whn p.u bef 2 out* **7/1**[3]	—
PPP	P		**Havit**[4] 3801 8-10-11 ....(p) MissLBrooke(7) *(Lady Susan Brooke) chsd ldrs to 3rd: t.o whn p.u bef 2 out* **100/1**	—
	P		**Kalabell Prince**[308] 7-11-5 .... WilliamKennedy(3) *(R A Farrant) hld up in mid-div: short-lived effrt 6th: t.o whn p.u bef 2 out* **8/1**	—
	P		**Oktis Morilious (IRE)**[33] 5-10-13 .... RichardSpate(7) *(J A Danahar) prom: chsd wnr appr 5th tl rdn appr 7th: wknd qckly: p.u bef 3 out* **25/1**	—
U-PP	P		**There Goes Wally**[23] 3480 8-11-3 ....(b[1]) LeeStephens(5) *(A Ennis) led tl j.lft 1st: chsd wnr tl appr 5th: wknd appr 6th: t.o whn p.u bef 2 out* **25/1**	—

5m 1.50s (13.60) **Going Correction** +0.425s/f (Soft)
WFA 4 from 5yo+ 9lb **15** Ran SP% **115.7**
Speed ratings: **89,86,77,76,70 66,60,52,43,— —,—,—,—,—** CSF £17.25 TOTE £5.00: £1.80, £2.30, £2.40; EX 10.10.
Owner M Harris **Bred** John Foley **Trained** Edgcote, Northants

FOCUS

A dire race, rated through the first two.

NOTEBOOK

Sunley Future(IRE) is a keen sort but the hood and cotton wool in his ears used on his last two starts have had a calming effect. He made most of the running and, clear turning down the far side on the final circuit, kept up the gallop to score decisively. He was dismounted after the race and led back, but appeared to be sound. *(op 5-1)*

It's My Party went after the winner on the climb after three out but could make no real impression. He is not a straightforward ride but has it in him to win a seller. *(tchd 9-2)*

Knotty Ash Girl(IRE) won a selling handicap on the Flat back in 2003 and this was her best run over hurdles so far, although she was still beaten 30 lengths in this desperate affair. *(op 6-1)*

Red Rocky, a poor performer on the Flat having her second run over hurdles, might have plugged on for third place had she not made a mistake at the final flight. *(op 25-1)*

Brunston Castle was without the tongue tie. After jumping the last flight in the back straight in second place, he was quickly on the retreat.

Oktis Morilious(IRE), a banded-class runner on the level, did not stay on this hurdles debut.

3886 HEREFORDSHIRE H'CAP CHASE 3m 7f

3:10 (3:10) (Class 4) (0-110,106) 5-Y-O+ **£6,263** (£1,850; £925; £463; £231; £116)

Form				RPR
0324	1		**Charango Star**[16] 3598 8-11-3 102 ....(v) LeeStephens(5) *(W K Goldsworthy) a.p: rdn 17th: led appr 2 out: sn clr: eased flat* **7/1**	119+
524P	2	12	**Sir Cumference**[58] 2863 10-11-0 97 ....(b) PaulO'Neill(3) *(Miss Venetia Williams) hld up in tch: led after 4 out tl appr 2 out: sn btn* **6/1**[3]	100+
3006	3	3	**Paddy The Optimist (IRE)**[19] 3547 10-9-11 80 oh1. WilliamKennedy(3) *(D Burchell) hld up in mid-div: hit 7th: hdwy 14th: btn whn lft 3rd bef 2 out* **13/2**	78
6P05	4	17	**Auburn Spirit**[17] 3578 11-11-5 99 .... WarrenMarston *(M D I Usher) w ldr: led 4th to 13th: wknd after 4 out* **9/1**	82+
-12P	5	20	**King Of Gothland (IRE)**[66] 2717 7-11-6 100 .... JohnMcNamara *(K C Bailey) hld up and bhd: short-lived effrt 17th* **8/1**	61
P542	6	15	**Follow The Flow (IRE)**[10] 3688 10-11-9 106 ....(p) OwynNelmes(3) *(P A Pritchard) hld up in tch: rdn appr 18th: wknd appr 19th: t.o* **9/1**	52
-060	7	½	**Spanish Main (IRE)**[88] 2265 12-11-7 101 .... CarlLlewellyn *(N A Twiston-Davies) a bhd: lost tch 16th: t.o* **14/1**	47
/0-P	8	10	**June's River (IRE)**[42] 3175 13-10-4 89 .... DrPPritchard(5) *(Dr P Pritchard) a bhd: t.o fr 15th* **100/1**	25
4353	P		**Waterberg (IRE)**[48] 2965 11-11-4 98 ....(b) MarkBradburne *(H D Daly) mid-div: mstke and lost pl 12th: t.o fr 16th: p.u bef 3 out* **11/2**[2]	—
1-F6	P		**Pewter Light (IRE)**[38] 3252 9-10-0 80 oh1 ....(b) PJBrennan *(B J M Ryall) led to 4th: w ldr: led 13th tl after 4 out: wknd 3 out: tired 3rd whn p.u bef 2 out* **9/2**[1]	—

8m 17.5s **Going Correction** 0.0s/f (Good) **10** Ran SP% **112.5**
CSF £47.52 CT £284.10 TOTE £6.20: £1.70, £2.10, £2.80; EX 44.40.
Owner Cliff Johnson **Bred** Mrs Joanna Cross **Trained** Yerbeston, Pembrokes
■ The first race over this distance at Hereford.

FOCUS

Not a strong handicap. The winner was back to the level of his Stratford win while the second ran to his mark.

NOTEBOOK

Charango Star came under pressure with six to jump, but responded well and came right away from the second last to score in good style. He may go for the cross-country handicap at Cheltenham now. *(op 6-1)*

Sir Cumference showed ahead leaving the back straight but was left treading water when the winner passed him going to the second last. *(op 13-2 tchd 7-1)*

Paddy The Optimist(IRE) has never run over this far before but he seemed to stay, albeit in his own time. Slow but sure, he has now completed the course on his last 22 starts and has never fallen. *(op 9-1)*

Auburn Spirit stays all day, but after disputing the lead he had been dropped with four to jump. He has not been at his best this season. *(op 10-1 tchd 11-1)*

Pewter Light(IRE) had the blinkers on for the first time since he won over shorter here in February. Given a forcing ride, he was unable to fight back when headed after the last in the back straight but was still in with a chance of a place when he lost his action going to the second last and was pulled up. *Official explanation: jockey said gelding lost its action (op 5-1)*

3887 "ROMANCE AT THE RACES" H'CAP CHASE (12 fncs) 2m

3:40 (3:43) (Class 4) (0-100,94) 5-Y-O+ **£3,757** (£1,110; £555; £277; £138; £69)

Form				RPR
1444	1		**Before The Mast (IRE)**[26] 3432 9-10-7 82 .... CharliePoste(7) *(M F Harris) hld up and bhd: hdwy 6th: led last: r.o* **9/1**	93+
5-23	2	2½	**Very Special One (IRE)**[76] 2552 6-11-8 90 .... JohnMcNamara *(K C Bailey) hld up: hdwy 4th: led 3 out: rdn and hdd last: nt qckn* **3/1**[1]	99+
6223	3	14	**Jupon Vert (FR)**[9] 3718 9-11-12 94 .... JimCrowley *(R J Hodges) a.p: led 7th to 3 out: sn wknd* **7/2**[2]	88
/050	4	2½	**Corroboree (IRE)**[30] 3368 9-11-10 92 .... CarlLlewellyn *(N A Twiston-Davies) hld up in tch: hmpd and lost pl 6th: styd on fr 3 out: n.d* **8/1**[3]	83
P333	5	¾	**Wild Power (GER)**[66] 2719 8-11-5 90 ....(tp) OwynNelmes(3) *(Mrs H R J Nelmes) hld up: hdwy 5th: wknd appr 3 out* **12/1**	80
/606	6	6	**Prairie Minstrel (USA)**[55] 2926 12-11-2 84 ....(p) HenryOliver *(R Dickin) led: j.lft 1st: hdd 2nd: wknd 6th* **12/1**	68
6/P0	7	nk	**John Foley (IRE)**[77] 2522 8-10-12 85 ....(tp) DarylJacob(5) *(D P Keane) led 2nd to 7th: wknd appr 3 out* **14/1**	69
P4P0	8	½	**Auditor**[10] 3686 7-10-2 70 ....(b) MarkGrant *(S T Lewis) hld up and bhd: hdwy 7th: wknd after 4 out* **25/1**	53
6043	9	¾	**Blazing Batman**[23] 3482 13-10-2 75 .... DrPPritchard(5) *(Dr P Pritchard) a bhd* **22/1**	58
1000	10	10	**Young Tot (IRE)**[66] 2721 8-10-12 80 .... PJBrennan *(M Sheppard) prom whn n.m.r and lost pl 3rd: blnd 3rd: sn bhd: short-lived effrt 7th* **14/1**	53
6F56	P		**Goldseam (GER)**[16] 3602 7-9-11 68 oh6 ....(b[1]) TomMalone(3) *(S C Burrough) a bhd: mstke 5th: t.o whn p.u bef 2 out* **66/1**	—
-F2P	F		**Call Me Jack (IRE)**[67] 2705 10-10-4 77 ....(t) LeeStephens(5) *(M J M Evans) prom: cl 3rd whn fell 6th (water)* **10/1**	—

4m 7.60s (5.10) **Going Correction** +0.50s/f (Soft) **12** Ran SP% **115.8**
Speed ratings: **107,105,98,97,97 94,93,93,93,88 —,—** CSF £35.94 CT £114.73 TOTE £12.90: £3.10, £2.60, £2.10; EX 53.90.
Owner Walk The Plank Partnership **Bred** John McGuinness **Trained** Edgcote, Northants

FOCUS

A modest handicap run at a decent pace. The first two are unexposed and finished clear and the race could rate higher.

NOTEBOOK

Before The Mast(IRE), running for only the second time over fences, was suited by the sound pace, and, showing ahead at the last fence, which he brushed through, he scored decisively. He is better over fences than he is over hurdles but is unlikely to be well handicapped after this.

Very Special One(IRE), placed off this mark over hurdles last time, ran well on this chasing deut but could not contain the winner from the final fence. A winning pointer in Ireland, she really needs further than this. *(op 10-3)*

Jupon Vert(FR), who has been kept busy of late, ran his race once more but could not go with the first two from the third last. *(op 4-1 tchd 9-2 in places)*

Corroboree(IRE), 9lb lower, was hampered by a faller at the water jump and struggled to get back in touch thereafter, although he was running on after the last. This looked too sharp for him. *(op 10-1)*

Wild Power(GER), tried with a tongue-strap to go with the cheekpieces, had no excuses and remains difficult to win with. *(op 11-1)*

John Foley(IRE) *Official explanation: trainer said gelding had a breathing problem*

3888 JOIN THE AA NOVICES' H'CAP CHASE (14 fncs) 2m 3f

4:10 (4:12) (Class 4) (0-100,98) 5-Y-O+ **£4,384** (£1,295; £647; £324; £161; £81)

Form				RPR
0563	1		**Baron Blitzkrieg**[30] 3367 8-10-1 73 .... JodieMogford *(D J Wintle) hld up: hdwy appr 7th: led appr 3 out: clr appr last: eased flat* **11/2**[2]	85+
4552	2	4	**Lucky Sinna (IRE)**[41] 3221 10-10-9 88 ....(p) CharlieStudd(7) *(B G Powell) led after 1st tl appr 3 out: one pce fr 2 out* **13/2**	90
0361	3	1½	**Adecco (IRE)**[12] 3663 7-11-12 98 .... JamieMoore *(G L Moore) hld up and bhd: smooth hdwy 6th: rdn after 4 out: wnt 2nd briefly and blnd 2 out: nt rcvr* **4/1**[1]	102+
-F6P	4	1	**Dramatic Quest**[23] 3480 9-11-2 95 ....(v[1]) RichardSpate(7) *(A G Juckes) hld up in mid-div: mstke 6th: hdwy 8th: rdn 4 out: styd on same pce fr 2 out* **22/1**	94
U444	5	1	**Caper**[119] 1751 6-10-13 85 .... PaulMoloney *(R Hollinshead) hld up and bhd: hdwy 8th: styd on same pce fr 2 out* **12/1**	83
0U	6	1½	**Drive On Driver (IRE)**[23] 3480 9-10-3 82 .... MissLBrooke(7) *(Lady Susan Brooke) mid-div: struggling 4 out: styd on fr 2 out* **66/1**	79
0-05	7	10	**Dante's Back (IRE)**[102] 1988 8-11-8 94 .... CarlLlewellyn *(N A Twiston-Davies) prom tl hit 3rd: sn mid-div: blnd 7th: bhd fr 10th* **11/1**	81
0-3	8	½	**Sarobar (IRE)**[6] 3782 6-11-5 91 .... BrianCrowley *(M Scudamore) hld up towards rr: hdwy 7th: wknd after 4 out* **6/1**[3]	77
PU1P	9	25	**Erins Lass (IRE)**[112] 1852 9-11-2 88 .... HenryOliver *(R Dickin) a bhd: blnd 4th: t.o fr 9th* **20/1**	49
220P	F		**Prayerful**[43] 3140 7-10-12 87 .... OwynNelmes(3) *(J G M O'Shea) fell 2nd* **20/1**	—
2044	U		**Solar At'Em (IRE)**[13] 3647 8-10-12 84 ....(p) MarkBradburne *(M Sheppard) prom tl blnd and uns rdr 7th* **16/1**	—
25F6	F		**Look To The Future (IRE)**[17] 3582 12-10-3 75 .... PJBrennan *(M J M Evans) prom to 6th: t.o whn fell 4 out* **25/1**	—
60-P	P		**Baileys Prizze (USA)**[26] 3433 9-10-1 80 ....(b) KeiranBurke(7) *(P R Rodford) prom to 7th: t.o 9th: p.u bef last* **66/1**	—
/P23	P		**Victory Roll**[12] 3663 10-11-12 98 .... MarcusFoley *(Miss E C Lavelle) led tl after 1st: prom tl wknd after 4 out: blnd 3 out: p.u bef 2 out* **7/1**	—

5m 0.30s (13.70) **Going Correction** +0.50s/f (Soft) **14** Ran SP% **118.1**
Speed ratings: **91,89,88,88,87 87,83,82,72,— —,—,—,—** CSF £37.31 CT £159.40 TOTE £7.80: £2.90, £2.20, £1.10; EX 60.50.
Owner Mrs Ann Bish **Bred** T G And Mrs Bish **Trained** Naunton, Gloucs

FOCUS

A weak race in which the winner is rated value for ten lengths and is open to improvement.

NOTEBOOK

Baron Blitzkrieg, a maiden over hurdles making his chasing debut, was backed at 25/1 in the morning and landed the gamble in fluent style. He jumped well, bar a minor error at the first, and there could be more improvement in him. *(op 7-1)*

Lucky Sinna(IRE) has proved hard to win with and the cheekpieces were tried for the first time. He jumped soundly in front, but had no answers when the winner eased past him going to the third last and is probably better over further. *(op 11-2 tchd 7-1)*

Adecco(IRE), raised 7lb for his Folkestone win, was trying to close on the winner when he blundered at the second last, which probably cost him the runner-up spot.

Dramatic Quest, tried in a visor instead of cheekpieces, boxed on after coming under pressure following a mistake early on the final circuit. He stays further than this. *(op 20-1)*

Caper, who won a selling hurdle here last spring, had the cheekpieces left off for this chasing debut. Given that he has shown a preference for fast ground and that this trip was on the short side, he was not disgraced. *(tchd 14-1)*

Sarobar(IRE), back over fences after his recent debut for the yard over hurdles, could not get into contention following an error five from home. *(op 9-1)*

Victory Roll did not appear suited by this step up in trip and was already beaten when blundering three from home. *(op 11-2 tchd 15-2)*

3889 "VICTIM TO CUPIDS ARROW" H'CAP HURDLE (8 hdls) 2m 1f

4:40 (4:41) (Class 4) (0-110,110) 4-Y-0+ **£3,903** (£1,146; £573; £286)

Form				RPR
00F2	1		**Walsingham (IRE)**[29] 3386 8-10-12 **94** ... RobertThornton (R Lee) *chsd ldr: led appr last: hrd rdn flat: all out* **5/1**[2]	94
UPP2	2	nk	**A Bit Of Fun**[10] 3687 5-11-12 **108** ... JohnMcNamara (J T Stimpson) *chsd ldrs: rdn and outpcd 2 out: rallied appr last: r.o flat* **16/1**	108
31P2	3	¾	**Josear**[27] 3422 4-10-11 **110** ... ShaneWalsh(7) (C J Down) *a.p: led appr 5th: rdn appr 2 out: hdd appr last: kpt on flat* **9/1**	100+
2002	4	2½	**Jayed (IRE)**[12] 3661 8-10-1 **90** ... LeeNewnes(7) (M Bradstock) *led tl appr 5th: rdn and kpt on same pce fr 2 out* **8/1**	88+
2565	5	7	**Hunting Lodge (IRE)**[24] 3464 5-10-11 **100** ... MrJAJenkins(7) (H J Manners) *mid-div: hit 5th: styd on fr 2 out: nvr trbld ldrs* **12/1**	90
0000	6	7	**Marrel**[24] 3458 8-11-9 **105** ... (v) AntonyEvans (D Burchell) *hld up and bhd: hdwy appr 5th: rdn and wknd appr 2 out* **25/1**	88
13-P	7	2½	**Hoh Nelson**[119] 1751 5-11-2 **105** ... (p) MrRHodges(7) (Mrs A Price) *hld up and bhd: rdn and sme hdwy whn hit 5th: n.d after* **50/1**	85
00PP	8	9	**Nick's Choice**[24] 3458 10-11-2 **103** ... MarkNicolls(5) (D Burchell) *bhd fr 5th* **25/1**	74
/054	9	shd	**Pawn Broker**[29] 3386 9-11-3 **99** ... (b) JamieMoore (Miss J R Tooth) *hld up and bhd: hdwy after 4th: rdn after 3 out: wknd 2 out* **15/2**[3]	70
1034	10	½	**Desert Spa (USA)**[182] 1218 11-10-9 **98** ... CharliePoste(7) (G E Jones) *hdwy 3rd: rdn and wknd 3 out* **20/1**	69
PPOU	11	18	**Turaath (IRE)**[8] 3731 10-11-12 **108** ... PJBrennan (A J Deakin) *a bhd* **33/1**	61
-00P	12	dist	**Moving On Up**[19] 3549 12-11-7 **103** ... (b) RichardHobson (C N Kellett) *hld up in tch: rdn after 2nd: sn struggling: t.o fr 4th* **100/1**	—
PU/0	P		**Geri Roulette**[24] 3467 8-10-8 **95** ... DarylJacob(5) (S C Burrough) *a bhd: t.o whn p.u bef last* **66/1**	—
3514	P		**Ishka Baha (IRE)**[39] 3243 7-11-1 **97** ... JasonMaguire (T R George) *hld up in tch: rdn and wknd after 4th: t.o whn p.u bef 2 out* **15/8**[1]	—

4m 7.90s (4.80) **Going Correction** +0.425s/f (Soft)
WFA 4 from 5yo+ 9lb **14** Ran SP% **117.7**
Speed ratings: **98,97,97,96,93 89,88,84,84,84 75,—,—,—** CSF £72.13 CT £705.79 TOTE £6.40: £2.20, £2.60, £2.60; EX 79.80 Place 6 £26.42, Place 5 £6.17.
Owner Keith And Sue Lowry **Bred** William McCarthy **Trained** Byton, H'fords

FOCUS

An ordinary handicap run at a sound pace, and the principals were always to the fore. The form looks solid enough rated around the first four.

NOTEBOOK

Walsingham(IRE) was put up 4lb for finishing second at Towcester. Always in the first two, he showed ahead going to the last but really had to fight to retain his lead as the runner-up clawed him back. *(tchd 9-2 and 11-2)*

A Bit Of Fun, back up the weights again, was slightly outpaced by the leaders at the second last but really found his feet from the final flight and finished well. A return to two and a half miles will suit him. *(op 14-1)*

Josear gave away his lead when running wide on the home turn, but he rallied and was alongside the eventual winner when he was awkward at the final flight. He is in good heart at present. *(op 7-1)*

Jayed(IRE) did his usual thing out in front and, like at Folkestone, kept battling away once headed. *(tchd 15-2)*

Hunting Lodge(IRE) was in a similar position throughout, and in truth was never a factor. *(op 11-1)*

Ishka Baha(IRE), back over hurdles and 10lb higher than when successful at Wincanton, came under pressure at halfway and dropped away in disappointing fashion before being pulled up. *(op 5-2)*

T/Plt: £63.90 to a £1 stake. Pool: £49,643.75. 566.45 winning tickets. T/Qpdt: £19.70 to a £1 stake. Pool: £3,486.20. 130.70 winning tickets. KH

3638 LEOPARDSTOWN (L-H)

Sunday, February 12

OFFICIAL GOING: Yielding (yielding to soft in places)

3890a CASHMANS JUVENILE HURDLE (GRADE 2) (8 hdls) 2m

1:20 (1:20) 4-Y-0 **£24,693** (£7,244; £3,451; £1,175)

			RPR
1		**Mister Hight (FR)**[43] 3157 4-11-0 ... DJCasey (W P Mullins, Ire) *hld up in tch: 6th whn slt mstke 3 out: smooth hdwy after next: led whn slt mstke last: qcknd clr run-in: easily* **4/9**[1]	133+
2	4½	**Breathing Fire**[8] 3744 4-11-0 ... RMPower (Mrs John Harrington, Ire) *hld up towards rr: 6th 2 out: hdwy ent st: nt fluent last: 2nd early run-in: edgd lft u.p cl home* **66/1**	123
3	1	**First Row (IRE)**[17] 3584 4-11-0 ... RLoughran (D T Hughes, Ire) *cl up: led fr 4th: hdd 2 out: kpt on u.p: sltly hmpd cl home* **12/1**	122
4	hd	**Dreux (FR)**[29] 3401 4-11-0 ... BJGeraghty (Thomas Cooper, Ire) *settled 3rd: 2nd after 3 out: led next: rdn and hdd appr last: kpt on same pce* **11/1**[3]	122
5	3	**Marhaba Million (IRE)**[29] 3401 4-11-3 ... APMcCoy (E McNamara, Ire) *trckd ldrs in 4th: slt mstke 4 out: 3rd 2 out: sn rdn and no imp: 5th whn slt mstke last* **7/1**[2]	123+
6	dist	**Cogans Lake (IRE)**[38] 3262 4-11-0 ... JMAllen (Kieran Purcell, Ire) *trckd ldrs: 3rd after 3 out: wknd qckly next: eased fr last* **12/1**	—
7	20	**Noend (IRE)**[17] 3584 4-11-0 ... (t) CO'Dwyer (Ms F M Crowley, Ire) *chsd ldrs: reminders after 4th: wknd after 4 out: t.o fr 2 out* **40/1**	—
8	8	**Vox Populi (USA)**[47] 3049 4-11-0 107 ... PCarberry (S J Mahon, Ire) *led: hdd 4th: wknd qckly after 3 out: t.o fr next* **12/1**	—

3m 57.9s **Going Correction** -0.55s/f (Firm) **8** Ran SP% **117.1**
Speed ratings: **112,109,109,109,107 —,—,—** CSF £38.84 TOTE £1.60: £1.10, £4.50, £3.40; DF 28.10.
Owner Peter Garvey **Bred** M Francois Petit & M Jerome An **Trained** Muine Beag, Co Carlow

FOCUS

A decent juvenile contest in which the winner is value for more than double the official margin and the third, fourth and fifth set the standard.

NOTEBOOK

Mister Hight(FR), rated 103 on the Flat, made it two out of two over hurdles. He pulled hard but was settled in the rear and the mistake three out was not his own doing. He would like softer ground but his Cheltenham prospects are enhanced by the guarantee of a strong pace in the Triumph. *(op 4/9 tchd 1/2)*

Breathing Fire stayed on without ever threatening, edging left on the run-in.

First Row(IRE) was struggling after two out and was well held when hampered on the run-in. *(op 10/1)*

Dreux(FR) led two out but was readily outpaced by the winner when headed. *(op 10/1 tchd 12/1)*

Marhaba Million(IRE) finished second to the winner at Punchestown but was done with at the second last. He will have his share of weight in the four-year-old handicap at the Festival.

3892a DELOITTE NOVICE HURDLE (GRADE 1) (9 hdls) 2m 2f

2:20 (2:20) 5-Y-0+ **£44,827** (£13,103; £6,206; £2,068)

			RPR
1		**Mr Nosie (IRE)**[47] 3052 5-11-7 134 ... PCarberry (Noel Meade, Ire) *trckd ldrs: 2nd fr 5th: sltly hmpd 4 out: 3rd and rdn after 2 out: led bef last: slt mstke: styd on wl: eased cl home* **11/10**[1]	137+
2	3	**Royaldou (FR)**[47] 3050 5-11-7 ... BJGeraghty (A L T Moore, Ire) *hld up in tch: 4th 4 out: 3rd next: 2nd and chal after 2 out: no imp fr last: kpt on* **16/1**	130+
3	11	**Schindlers Hunt (IRE)**[14] 3638 6-11-10 ... RLoughran (D T Hughes, Ire) *chsd ldrs: 3rd whn hit 3rd: 4th and rdn bef 2 out: kpt on fr last to go mod 3rd cl home* **16/1**	122
4	¾	**Blueberry Boy (IRE)**[47] 3052 7-11-10 ... DFO'Regan (Paul Stafford, Ire) *led: strly pressed 2 out: hdd & wknd bef last* **4/1**[2]	121
5	20	**Mossbank (IRE)**[56] 2909 6-11-10 ... CO'Dwyer (Michael Hourigan, Ire) *hld up in tch: hmpd 4 out: 5th and rdn next: no imp whn slt mstke 2 out: eased st* **5/1**[3]	101+
6	20	**Alexander Taipan (IRE)**[35] 3309 6-11-10 ... DJCasey (W P Mullins, Ire) *a bhd: reminders 5th: trailing fr 4 out* **8/1**	81
U		**Glenfinn Captain (IRE)**[41] 3227 7-11-10 ... APMcCoy (T J Taaffe, Ire) *cl up in 2nd tl mstke and uns rdr 4th* **5/1**[3]	—

4m 32.8s **Going Correction** -0.30s/f (Good) **7** Ran SP% **123.8**
Speed ratings: **112,110,105,105,96 87,—** CSF £22.78 TOTE £2.20: £1.70, £3.30; DF 14.00.
Owner Mrs P Sloan **Bred** Miss Josephine O'Flynn **Trained** Castletown, Co Meath

FOCUS

A traditionally decent race and the winner was value for more than double the official margin.

NOTEBOOK

Mr Nosie(IRE) was hampered four out and looked in trouble after the second last, but he found plenty in the straight and was three lengths clear when making a slight mistake at the last. He beat two maidens very easily and will accompany the stable's Nicanour to Cheltenham for the SunAlliance Novices' Hurdle with Carberry left to make the decision. *(op 6/4)*

Royaldou(FR), second to the winner's stable companion Sweet Wake here at Christmas, probably ran to that level of form. Better than an average maiden, he will not be hard to place.

Schindlers Hunt(IRE), still a maiden, stayed on to take third place near the finish. *(op 14/1)*

Blueberry Boy(IRE) has some smart form but weakened quickly in the straight after making the running. *Official explanation: trainer said vet subsequently found gelding to have a blood disorder (op 7/2)*

Mossbank(IRE) was hampered four out but was not going to be a player when making a mistake at the second last. He was eased right down in the straight. *(op 6/1)*

3893a DR. P. J. MORIARTY NOVICE CHASE (GRADE 1) (14 fncs) 2m 5f

2:50 (2:50) 5-Y-0+ **£49,310** (£14,413; £6,827; £2,275)

			RPR
1		**The Railway Man (IRE)**[28] 3409 7-11-12 ... DNRussell (A L T Moore, Ire) *hld up: prog into 5th after 1/2-way: 4th 3 out: 2nd next: led travelling best appr last: kpt on wl u.p run-in* **16/1**	146
2	1½	**Father Matt (IRE)**[28] 3409 8-11-12 ... PCarberry (Noel Meade, Ire) *prom: led fr 6th: clr after 3 out: j.lft 2 out: sn strly pressed: hdd appr last: kpt on wl u.p* **8/1**	144
3	nk	**Our Ben**[21] 3528 7-11-12 ... DJCasey (W P Mullins, Ire) *hld up in tch: 4th 4 out: 5th next: hdwy u.p after 2 out: 3rd and styd on wl fr last* **10/3**[2]	144+
4	7	**Kill Devil Hill (IRE)**[48] 3006 6-11-12 ... JLCullen (Paul Nolan, Ire) *mid-div: prog into 4th 1/2-way: 3rd 5 out: effrt after 3 out: 3rd and no ex appr last* **7/1**[3]	137
5	1	**Southern Vic (IRE)**[22] 3514 7-11-12 147 ... CO'Dwyer (T M Walsh, Ire) *led: hdd 6th: remained prom: rdn and outpcd after 3 out: no ex after 2 out* **9/4**[1]	136
6	15	**Kerryhead Windfarm (IRE)**[28] 3409 8-11-12 ... AndrewJMcNamara (Michael Hourigan, Ire) *trckd ldrs: 6th 6 out: no ex fr 4 out* **33/1**	126+
7	11	**Sher Beau (IRE)**[17] 3588 7-11-12 ... BJGeraghty (Philip Fenton, Ire) *hld up: 7th 5 out: no imp fr next: slt mstke 3 out: sn eased* **10/3**[2]	110
8	25	**Lordofourown (IRE)**[64] 2776 8-11-12 ... RMPower (S Donohoe, Ire) *a in rr: trailing fr 6 out* **25/1**	85
9	11	**Major Vernon (IRE)**[28] 3409 7-11-12 128 ... DFO'Regan (W P Mullins, Ire) *plld hrd early: settled 2nd: slow and lost pl 7th: blnd next: wknd 4 out* **33/1**	74
P		**Baily Breeze (IRE)**[48] 3012 7-11-12 ... (p) MDarcy (M F Morris, Ire) *5th to 1/2-way: sn wknd: p.u bef 5 out* **20/1**	—

5m 36.2s **Going Correction** -0.45s/f (Good) **10** Ran SP% **120.9**
Speed ratings: **115,114,114,111,111 105,101,91,87,—** CSF £131.83 TOTE £20.90: £3.40, £1.80, £1.70; DF 95.80.
Owner Cathal M Ryan **Bred** Kenneth Parkhill **Trained** Naas, Co Kildare

FOCUS

A good novice event rated around the placed horses.

NOTEBOOK
The Railway Man(IRE), impressive on his chase debut at Navan in November, blundered his way out of it here last month behind Nickname. He jumped well this time and second turning for home, he led before the last and stayed on best. He will stay at home with the Powers Gold Cup at Fairyhouse his Easter target. *Official explanation: trainer said, regarding improved form shown, gelding was unable to show true form in previous race due to a bad mistake, and extremely testing ground resulting in him being pulled up; he added that today's better ground and improved jumping helped*
Father Matt(IRE) has been somewhat underestimated but his form is solid enough and he had every chance in front.
Our Ben is the Cheltenham candidate from the race. He kept in touch but still had four in front of him over the third last and little prospect of winning landing over the next. Wide into the straight, he stayed on strongly on the run-in to be nearest at the finish. This was a more than promising trial for the Royal & SunAlliance Chase which looks weak enough this year. *(op 5/2)*
Kill Devil Hill(IRE) had his chances from two out but had not the pace to take them.
Southern Vic(IRE), dropping in trip, could not dominate this time. He needs heavy ground and three miles, along with opportunistic handling.
Sher Beau(IRE) was well supported but never looked like taking a hand in the finish. *(op 3/1)*
Baily Breeze(IRE) *Official explanation: jockey said gelding went badly lame in running*

3894a T. C. MATTHEWS CARPETS H'CAP HURDLE (8 hdls) 2m
3:20 (3:22) (0-140,128) 4-Y-0+ £14,142 (£4,149; £1,976; £673)

			RPR
1		**Studmaster**[28] 3411 6-11-6 124 ... TPTreacy (Mrs John Harrington, Ire) *trckd ldrs in 5th: prog into 2nd 3 out: led appr next: drew clr after last: easily* **5/2**[1]	146+
2	5	**Freddie Foster (IRE)**[48] 3005 7-9-13 103 ... (b[1]) NPMadden (Noel Meade, Ire) *hld up: hdwy 3 out: 5th next: impr into 2nd whn bad mstke last: no ex* **20/1**	115
3	2	**Moore's Law (USA)**[590] 132 8-10-10 114 ... DFO'Regan (M J Grassick, Ire) *rr of mid-div: 9th 3 out: mod 5th bef last: kpt on wl* **25/1**	124
4	1	**Don't Be Bitin (IRE)**[71] 2650 5-11-10 128 ... BJGeraghty (Eoin Griffin, Ire) *trckd ldrs in 4th: 3rd 4 out: rdn after 2 out: kpt on same pce* **11/2**[3]	137
5	4	**City Of Sails (IRE)**[22] 3517 7-10-9 113 ... DNRussell (A J McNamara, Ire) *bhd: trailing 4 out: hdwy after 3 out: mod 8th after 2 out: kpt on* **14/1**	118
6	4	**Maxxium (IRE)**[45] 3107 5-10-10 121 ... (t) EMButterly[(7)] (M Halford, Ire) *trckd ldrs: 6th bef 1/2-way: 5th 3 out: impr into 2nd and rdn to chal after next: wknd bef last* **13/2**	122
7	6	**Lakil Princess (IRE)**[21] 3519 5-10-10 117 ... RMMoran[(3)] (Paul Nolan, Ire) *led: hdd & wknd appr 2 out* **12/1**	112
8	2	**Strike Back (IRE)**[7] 3774 8-11-3 128 ... ADLeigh[(7)] (Mrs John Harrington, Ire) *mid-div: 7th 3 out: mod 6th next: sn no ex* **20/1**	121
9	10	**La Mandragola**[57] 2898 9-10-1 105 ... PACarberry (R J Osborne, Ire) *rr of mid-div: mod 8th and effrt 2 out: sn no ex* **16/1**	88
10	7	**Macs Valley (IRE)**[45] 3107 9-10-9 116 ... MrPJCasey[(3)] (Miss A M Winters, Ire) *mid-div: 8th 3 out: sn no ex* **20/1**	92
11	12	**Champion Gold (IRE)**[24] 3470 7-9-9 104 ... NJO'Shea[(5)] (Charles Coakley, Ire) *chsd ldrs in 3rd: dropped to 6th 3 out: sn no ex* **14/1**	68
12	20	**Green Valley (IRE)**[17] 3586 6-9-10 100 ... WJLee (P F O'Donnell, Ire) *rr of mid-div: no ex fr 3 out: t.o* **16/1**	44
13	10	**King Carew (IRE)**[231] 722 8-10-12 123 ... SJHassett[(7)] (Michael Hourigan, Ire) *a bhd: t.o* **33/1**	57
14	4 ½	**Eye Candy (IRE)**[91] 2209 5-10-11 118 ... TGMRyan[(3)] (Mrs Sandra McCarthy, Ire) *chsd ldrs early: wknd fr 1/2-way: t.o* **16/1**	48
15	1 ½	**Almier (IRE)**[85] 2334 8-10-10 114 ... AndrewJMcNamara (Michael Hourigan, Ire) *cl up in 2nd: dropped to 4th 3 out: sn wknd: t.o* **14/1**	42
16	1 ½	**Silk Screen (IRE)**[17] 3586 6-11-0 125 ... RJKiely[(7)] (W P Mullins, Ire) *nvr a factor: t.o* **16/1**	52
17	dist	**No Sound (FR)**[17] 3586 5-10-1 105 ... (b) PCarberry (Noel Meade, Ire) *trckd ldrs: 6th appr 1/2-way: sn wknd: completely t.o* **5/1**[2]	—
F		**Calladine (IRE)**[388] 3450 10-11-2 120 ... APCrowe (C Roche, Ire) *hld up towards rr: fell 3 out* **20/1**	—
P		**High Reef (FR)**[28] 3411 8-10-1 105 ... DJCasey (C F Swan, Ire) *a bhd: trailing 1/2-way: p.u bef 3 out* **16/1**	—

3m 57.6s **Going Correction** -0.55s/f (Firm) 19 Ran SP% **156.9**
Speed ratings: **113,110,109,109,107 105,102,101,96,92 86,76,71,69,68 67,—,—,—** CSF £70.62 CT £1221.93 TOTE £3.20: £1.60, £4.80, £22.40, £2.10; DF 440.70.
Owner Mothership Racing Club **Bred** Martyn Arbib **Trained** Moone, Co Kildare
■ Stewards' Enquiry : D N Russell three-day ban: rode an ill-judged race (Feb 22-23,25)

NOTEBOOK
Studmaster ◆, who has yet to be out the three in eight attempts over hurdles, followed up his Pierse win in mightily impressive fashion and had little trouble shouldering the 10lb penalty. Never far off the pace in a race run at a proper gallop, he tanked along just off the pace and, having taken it up before the turn-in, responded well when asked to go clear, ultimately winning easily. Another rise will be imminent following this, but he seems to be progressing at a rate of knots, coinciding with his stable's return to form, and the Sandown's Imperial Cup is his next reported target. In the long-term it is not beyond the realms of possibility he could develop into a Champion Hurdler for 2007, with his stable having moulded both Spirit Leader and Macs Joy from handicapper to high-class two-miler in recent seasons. *(op 5/2 tchd 11/4)*
City Of Sails(IRE) *Official explanation: jockey said, regarding running and riding, trainer advised him to use his discretion, so he decided to settle gelding early as it was nervous and prone to run free last time out, adding that when he squeezed it up after first hurdle it came off bridle but he felt due to the strong pace the field might come back to him; he admitted that from two out gelding stayed on particularly well and he had misjudged his riding tactics; trainer said he was disappointed gelding was so far back early on*
High Reef(FR) *Official explanation: jockey said mare was never travelling (op 14/1)*

3895a HENNESSY COGNAC GOLD CUP CHASE (GRADE 1) (17 fncs) 3m
3:55 (3:55) 5-Y-0+
£75,724 (£23,869; £11,275; £3,827; £1,965; £724)

			RPR
1		**Beef Or Salmon (IRE)**[46] 3081 10-11-12 170 ... PCarberry (Michael Hourigan, Ire) *hld up in 6th: prog into 4th 6 out: bad mstke next: impr into 3rd 3 out: 2nd 2 out: led early st: drew clr fr last: easily* **2/5**[1]	171+
2	12	**Hedgehunter (IRE)**[46] 3081 10-11-12 160 ... DJCasey (W P Mullins, Ire) *attempted to make all: rdn and strly pressed after 2 out: hdd early st: kpt on wout troubling wnr* **10/3**[2]	159+
3	7	**Native Upmanship (IRE)**[24] 3472 13-11-12 144 ... (b[1]) CO'Dwyer (A L T Moore, Ire) *trckd ldrs on inner: 4th and rdn 4 out: mod 3rd after 2 out: kpt on same pce* **50/1**	150
4	5	**Nil Desperandum (IRE)**[42] 3176 9-11-12 137 ... TPTreacy (Ms F M Crowley, Ire) *trckd ldrs on outer: 3rd 6 out: 4th after 3 out: rdn and no imp fr next* **33/1**	145
5	2 ½	**Jack High (IRE)**[17] 3585 11-11-12 138 ... GCotter (T M Walsh, Ire) *hld up in rr: rdn and no imp fr 2 out* **25/1**	142
6	25	**Prince Of Tara (IRE)**[47] 3053 9-11-12 128 ... BJGeraghty (S J Mahon, Ire) *prom: 2nd whn mstke 8th: lft 2nd fr 13th: rdn after 3 out: wknd fr next* **25/1**	117
F		**Strong Project (IRE)**[24] 3472 10-11-12 144 ... JMAllen (Sean O O'Brien, Ire) *trckd ldrs in 3rd: 2nd fr 8th tl fell 13th* **20/1**[3]	—

6m 30.1s **Going Correction** +0.175s/f (Yiel) 7 Ran SP% **111.9**
Speed ratings: **115,111,108,107,106 97,—** CSF £1.85 TOTE £1.50: £1.30, £1.80; DF 2.10.
Owner B J Craig **Bred** John Murphy **Trained** Patrickswell, Co Limerick

FOCUS
An uncompetitive renewal of this top-class contest, rated through the third, fourth and fifth.

NOTEBOOK
Beef Or Salmon(IRE) logged his fifth Grade One over the course and distance and his second successive win in this event. He got away with a bad blunder five but was back on the bridle over the next, extending a length and a half advantage at the last to 12 lengths at the line. This just confirmed his current well being, and Cheltenham still remains his bete noir. *(op 4/11)*
Hedgehunter(IRE) ran along in front and only tired from the last. There is improvement in him and the temptation to run at Cheltenham before Aintree is considerable. *(op 3/1)*
Native Upmanship(IRE) stayed on without ever threatening for his share of the pot.
Nil Desperandum(IRE) remains a light of other days. *(op 25/1)*
Jack High(IRE) had a tender time of it, making no impression in the straight when he should have been staying on.

3891 - 3897a (Foreign Racing) - See Raceform Interactive

3422 PLUMPTON (L-H)
Monday, February 13

OFFICIAL GOING: Good to soft
Wind: Fine & mild Weather: Light against

3898 SPORTSGUIDE 25TH ANNIVERSARY JUVENILE NOVICES' HURDLE (9 hdls) 2m
2:00 (2:00) (Class 3) 4-Y-0 £5,204 (£1,528; £764; £381)

Form				RPR
12	1		**Heathcote**[23] 3498 4-11-5 ... JamieMoore (G L Moore) *t.k.h: pressed ldrs: disp ld 3 out: drvn bef next: upsides whn lft in ld last: kpt on u.p* **8/13**[1]	106+
	2	1 ½	**Ardglass (IRE)**[109] 4-10-12 ... MatthewBatchelor (Mrs P Townsley) *nt a fluent: t.k.h: wl in tch: effrt to dispute ld 3 out: cl 3rd whn mstke last and lft 2nd: nt qckn flat* **12/1**	97
33	3	3 ½	**Avalon**[10] 3714 4-10-12 ... APMcCoy (Jonjo O'Neill) *led at slow pce to 2nd: styd pressing ldrs: rdn after 3 out: one pce fr next* **7/2**[2]	94+
	4	15	**Jubilee Dream**[6] 4-10-12 ... LeightonAspell (Mrs L J Mongan) *hld up in tch: pushed along 5th: outpcd and rdn bef 3 out: n.d after* **28/1**	78
	5	½	**Bilkie (IRE)**[223] 4-10-12 ... AndrewTinkler (John Berry) *pressed ldrs: led 5th: j. slowly next: hdd 3 out: wknd bef next* **50/1**	80+
0U	6	17	**Greenacre Legend**[44] 3132 4-10-7 ...[1] RobertLucey-Butler[(5)] (D B Feek) *t.k.h: in tch: rdn bef 6th: wknd bef 3 out* **66/1**	61
0	7	10	**Cool Society**[43] 3188 4-10-12 ... RobertWalford (R H Alner) *t.k.h: led 2nd to 5th: wknd rapidly 3 out* **33/1**	51
	8	dist	**Cry Of The Wolf**[632] 4-10-12 ... JamesDavies (R M Stronge) *t.k.h: nt fluent: hld up in last pair: lost tch after 5th: wl t.o: btn 78l* **66/1**	—
	P		**Imperioli**[54] 4-10-12 ... AntonyEvans (P A Blockley) *t.k.h: in tch tl wknd after 6th: t.o whn p.u bef 2 out* **66/1**	—
5	F		**Mac Federal (IRE)**[14] 3645 4-10-2 ... TimothyBailey[(10)] (M G Quinlan) *t.k.h: cl up: disp ld 3 out: narrow ld next: jnd and fell last* **9/1**[3]	97
B	F		**Maya's Prince**[33] 3340 4-10-12 ... BenjaminHitchcott (M D I Usher) *plld hrd: nt jump wl: a in rr: wknd 5th: wl t.o whn fell 3 out* **66/1**	—

4m 14.5s (13.30) **Going Correction** +0.95s/f (Soft) 11 Ran SP% **116.2**
Speed ratings: **104,103,101,94,93 85,80,—,—,—** — CSF £9.15 TOTE £1.30: £1.02, £3.50, £1.30; EX 9.00.
Owner B Siddle & B D Haynes **Bred** Miss K Rausing **Trained** Woodingdean, E Sussex

FOCUS
An ordinary juvenile event in which the early pace was decidedly steady. The winner was rated below his mark witrh the runner-up setting the standard.

NOTEBOOK
Heathcote, unsuited by the steady pace, took quite a grip and would not settle in the early stages, but he stayed on strongly up the hill, and even had Mac Federal stayed on his feet it is unlikely that he would have been denied. This was a fair effort under his penalty and connections now plan to run him in the Fred Winter at the Festival. *(op 4-6 tchd 4-7 and 8-11 in a place)*
Ardglass(IRE) did not go unsupported in the market, which was understandable given that his connections had gone to the trouble of entering him for the Triumph and Royal & SunAlliance Hurdle. Only a modest maiden on the Flat, it looks as though he is going to be more successful over timber.
Avalon was pretty weak in the betting beforehand and ran no more than a modest race back in third. On the plus side, he is now eligible for a handicap mark, and perhaps he will spring into life in that sphere. *(op 3-1 tchd 4-1)*
Jubilee Dream, fit from the Flat where he proved only modest, was well held in fourth on his hurdling debut. *(op 33-1)*
Mac Federal(IRE) jumped the second-last just in front and was disputing the lead when crashing out at the last, but he just looked to be coming to the end of his tether at the time. He ran quite well on testing ground on the Flat in Italy and these conditions seemed to suit him. *(tchd 8-1)*

3899 RACING POST "HANDS AND HEELS" JUMPS SERIES H'CAP HURDLE (FOR CONDITIONAL JOCKEYS/AMATEUR RIDERS) (9 hdls) 2m
2:30 (2:30) (Class 5) (0-90,88) 4-Y-0+ £2,398 (£698; £349)

Form			RPR
0033	1	**Better Moment (IRE)**[42] 3222 9-11-7 88 ... (v) MrCWallis[(5)] (M C Pipe) *led to 5th: lost pl and pushed along bef next: rallied 3 out: led bef next: in command last: hanging lft and nt keen flat:* **7/2**[1]	92+

P530 **2** *2* **Sunset King (USA)**[25] 3456 6-10-10 **75** .... KeiranBurke(3) 76
(R J Hodges) *hld up wl off the pce: stdy prog fr 6th: effrt to chse wnr 2 out: pushed along and nt qckn flat* **4/1**[2]

5330 **3** *8* **Monsal Dale (IRE)**[13] 3661 7-10-13 **80** .... (tp) CraigMessenger(5) 73
(Mrs L C Jewell) *chsd ldrs: pushed along fr 1/2-way: cl up bef 3 out: sn lost pl: kpt on again bef last* **13/2**[3]

4-04 **4** *3* **Grand Prairie (SWE)**[11] 502 10-11-9 **88** .... (b) MrDHutchison(3) 79+
(G L Moore) *prom: led 6th: nt keen and hdd bef 2 out where mstke: fdd* **7/1**

665P **5** *11* **Tianyi (IRE)**[25] 3460 10-11-6 **82** .... (v) JohnKington 61
(M Scudamore) *pressed ldrs: pushed along after 5th: cl enough after 3 out: btn next: wknd bdly flat* **10/1**

-5PP **6** *1 ½* **Grandee Line**[25] 3465 11-10-12 **79** .... MrIChanin(5) 57
(R H Alner) *nvr on terms w ldng gp: no prog 6th: wl btn whn blnd 3 out: plugged on fr next* **16/1**

0-0P **7** *1 ½* **Alasil (USA)**[49] 2995 6-11-3 **79** .... (b) WayneKavanagh 55
(Mrs N Smith) *j.lft several flights: pressed ldrs: led 5th to 6th: wknd after 3 out* **16/1**

06 **8** *5* **Jug Of Punch (IRE)**[11] 3687 7-11-9 **88** .... MrNPearce(3) 59
(S T Lewis) *nvr on terms w ldrs: pushed along after 4th: wl btn bef 3 out: eased bef next* **12/1**

-54P **9** *7* **Canni Thinkaar (IRE)**[15] 2556 5-11-8 **87** .... (p) MrTCollier(3) 51
(P Butler) *chsd ldrs: pushed along and struggling after 4th: rallied briefly 6th: wl btn after 3 out* **14/1**

1/P0 **10** *dist* **Newsplayer (IRE)**[159] 1433 10-11-10 **86** .... (t) SeanQuinlan —
(R T Phillips) *stdd s: hld up wl bhd: nvr on terms: 20 l bhd wnr whn mstke 2 out: virtually p.u flat: btn 109l* **11/1**

06/P **11** *3* **Springer The Lad**[10] 3715 9-10-13 **80** .... (p) MissMBryant(5) —
(Miss M P Bryant) *hld up: sn wl bhd: wl t.o fr 5th: stl appr 2 out after rest had j. last: btn 112l* **33/1**

50P- **P** **Falmer For All (IRE)**[107] 4914 8-11-7 **88** .... MrJBurdon(5) —
(J Ryan) *hld up wl off the pce: struggling whn p.u bef 5th: lost action* **66/1**

4m 16.0s (14.80) **Going Correction** +0.95s/f (Soft) **12** Ran SP% **116.0**
Speed ratings: **101,100,96,94,89 88,87,85,81,— —,—** CSF £17.72 CT £86.77 TOTE £5.70: £1.90, £1.90, £2.20; EX 7.90.

Owner M C Pipe **Bred** Bernard Cooke **Trained** Nicholashayne, Devon

■ The first winner for Charlie Wallis.

FOCUS

A poor race contested by plating-class performers, and they were all being pushed along from some way out. The first two set the level for the form.

NOTEBOOK

Better Moment(IRE), the most prolific runner in the line-up with five previous wins over timber to his name, came out on top, his stamina seeing him through in the end, and rewarding those who supported him back into favouritism after seeing him drift in the morning. *(op 5-1)*

Sunset King(USA) ran poorly at Ludlow last time but his previous effort in soft ground at Wincanton gave him a chance in this company. He kept on fairly well, finishing clear of the rest, but this effort only went to emphasise why he is still a maiden after 25 starts on the Flat and over timber. *(op 3-1)*

Monsal Dale(IRE) likes a bit of cut in the ground so the rain that arrived earlier in the day will have suited him, but he is another who finds it very difficult to win. *(op 6-1 tchd 11-2)*

Grand Prairie(SWE) was having his first outing over hurdles since May but had had a spin on the All-Weather earlier this month so a lack of fitness should not have been a concern. *(op 8-1)*

Tianyi(IRE), back over hurdles after being pulled up over fences last time, prefers faster ground. *(op 9-1 tchd 11-1)*

Jug Of Punch(IRE) *Official explanation: jockey said, regarding the apparent tender ride, his orders were to jump off behind the leaders, let gelding find its feet and ride his race thereafter, adding that gelding was outpaced in the early stages, appeared unsuited by the good to soft ground and stayed on in the home straight, appearing to need a longer trip than today's 2m (op 11-1)*

Falmer For All(IRE) *Official explanation: jockey said gelding lost its action (op 50-1)*

3900 CHRIS POOLE AND GEORGE ENNOR CELEBRATION NOVICES' CHASE (18 fncs) 3m 2f

3:00 (3:00) (Class 3) 5-Y-0+ **£6,286** (£1,873; £948; £486; £254)

Form RPR

2151 **1** **De Blanc (IRE)**[11] 3689 6-10-11 120 .... SamThomas 126+
(Miss Venetia Williams) *trckd ldr: lft in ld 8th: mde rest: in command after 3 out: quite easily* **11/10**[1]

1260 **2** *3 ½* **Mioche D'Estruval (FR)**[9] 3727 6-11-4 120 .... (v) TomScudamore 121
(M C Pipe) *trckd ldrs fr 4th: chsd wnr 13th: only danger after next: no imp fr 3 out* **5/1**[3]

U1UP **3** *18* **Concert Pianist**[18] 3581 11-11-4 113 .... PhilipHide 106+
(P Winkworth) *nt fluent 3rd: in tch: chsd wnr 10th to 13th: outpcd after next: n.d after* **20/1**

3423 **4** *16* **Five Alley (IRE)**[28] 3427 9-11-4 88 .... BenjaminHitchcott 87
(R H Buckler) *mstke 4th and dropped to rr: rdn 12th: wl outpcd after next: no ch after* **20/1**

2-33 **5** *8* **Bohemian Boy (IRE)**[28] 3419 8-11-4 116 .... TimmyMurphy 82+
(M Pitman) *hld up: effrt 13th: no rspnse next: wl btn after: wknd 2 out* **7/2**[2]

PP42 **F** **Special Conquest**[18] 3578 8-11-1 108 .... RichardYoung(3) —
(J W Mullins) *led: drvn into fences fr 6th: fell 8th* **13/2**

7m 3.30s (9.30) **Going Correction** +0.425s/f (Soft) **6** Ran SP% **109.4**
Speed ratings: **102,100,95,90,88** — CSF £6.81 TOTE £1.70: £1.10, £2.20; EX 7.30.

Owner Jeremy Hancock **Bred** Pat Galavan **Trained** Kings Caple, H'fords

FOCUS

A fair novice event for stayers rated around the winner, who was value for further.

NOTEBOOK

De Blanc(IRE) was weak in the market beforehand despite hailing from an in-form yard and being 15lb clear on adjusted Racing Post Ratings, and perhaps that was due to the longer trip. However, she had shown plenty of stamina when winning over 2m6f at Towcester last time, and was always in control. She won with more in hand than the winning margin suggests and her main target next month is apparently the E.B.F. Mares' Novice Chase Final at Uttoxeter on the 18th. *(op 10-11 tchd 6-5 in places)*

Mioche D'Estruval(FR) was down the field in a valuable handicap hurdle at Sandown last time and had less to do on this return to chasing. Supported in the market, he did not run badly, given that in a handicap he would have been 7lb better off with the winner. *(op 8-1)*

Concert Pianist had failed to complete in five of his previous six starts so this should have done his confidence some good. *(tchd 25-1)*

Five Alley(IRE) had a lot to do in this grade and will be more effective back in modest handicap company.

Bohemian Boy(IRE) could perhaps do with a pair of blinkers being fitted to help him concentrate. *Official explanation: jockey had no explanation for the poor form shown (op 4-1 tchd 10-3)*

3901 EVENING STANDARD COMMEMORATES CHRIS POOLE H'CAP HURDLE (12 hdls) 2m 5f

3:30 (3:30) (Class 3) (0-120,120) 4-Y-0+ **£6,506** (£1,910; £955; £477)

Form RPR

-P01 **1** **Alright Now M'Lad (IRE)**[28] 3422 6-11-9 **117** .... APMcCoy 132+
(Jonjo O'Neill) *racd on outer: hld up: prog 9th: led 3 out: drvn clr 2 out: eased flat* **8/1**

6211 **2** *7* **Amanpuri (GER)**[10] 3719 8-10-8 **102** .... ChristianWilliams 105
(Mrs A M Thorpe) *mostly racd towards outer: prom: drvn and lost pl 3 out: rallied next: wnt 2nd last: no imp on wnr* **8/1**

-505 **3** *1 ¼* **King Georges (FR)**[44] 3143 8-10-6 **100** .... JodieMogford 103+
(J C Tuck) *racd on outer: hld up: mstke 3rd: hmpd 7th: gd prog 9th: chsd wnr 3 out: btn next: lost 2nd last* **33/1**

PP30 **4** *12* **Carly Bay**[43] 3185 8-10-5 **99** .... RichardJohnson 89
(G P Enright) *sltly hmpd 1st and lost tch: prog 8th: styd on inner after next: wl btn after 3 out* **25/1**

-P20 **5** *11* **Westmeath Flyer**[17] 3600 11-11-2 **120** .... (p) AngharadFrieze(10) 102+
(P A Blockley) *racd towards outer: hld up: prog to ld 9th: hdd 3 out: wknd bef next: blnd last* **66/1**

-003 **6** *6* **Maletton (FR)**[30] 3384 6-11-10 **118** .... SamThomas 93+
(Miss Venetia Williams) *racd on inner: led to 2nd: led again 8th to 9th: wknd 3 out* **14/1**

F351 **7** *5* **Nobel Bleu De Kerpaul (FR)**[17] 3603 5-10-4 **98** .... LeightonAspell 73+
(P Winkworth) *mstkes: racd mostly in middle of trck: in tch: effrt 3 out: wknd bef next* **8/1**

-433 **U** **Calusa Charlie (IRE)**[39] 3253 7-11-2 **110** .... TomDoyle —
(B G Powell) *jinked 1st and uns rdr* **11/2**[2]

-P2F **P** **Cockatoo Ridge**[23] 3508 9-10-6 **100** .... JoeTizzard 84
(N R Mitchell) *cl up: blnd bdly 7th: nt rcvr: t.o 9th: p.u bef 2 out* **20/1**

2612 **P** **Herecomestanley**[9] 3733 7-9-9 **96** .... CharliePoste(7) —
(M F Harris) *in tch: drvn and wknd rapidly 5th: t.o whn p.u bef 8th* **6/1**[3]

5014 **P** **Come Bye (IRE)**[28] 3428 10-11-7 **115** .... (bt) MatthewBatchelor —
(Miss A M Newton-Smith) *racd on inner: j.rt: led 2nd to 8th: wknd rapidly: t.o next: p.u bef 2 out* **33/1**

-F13 **P** **Sea The Light**[42] 3210 6-11-7 **115** .... RobertThornton —
(A King) *racd on inner: t.k.h early: trckd ldrs: mstke 8th and reminder: wknd 3 out: poor 8th whn p.u bef last* **9/4**[1]

5m 28.4s (3.60) **Going Correction** +0.95s/f (Soft) **12** Ran SP% **116.4**
Speed ratings: **107,104,103,99,95 92,90,—,—,— —,—** CSF £64.77 CT £1997.29 TOTE £8.30: £2.90, £2.40, £6.40; EX 35.70 Trifecta £880.80 Part won. Pool £1,240.67 - 0.68 winning units.

Owner John P McManus **Bred** John Fowler **Trained** Cheltenham, Gloucs

FOCUS

A fair handicap and sound form judged on the performance of the runner-up. The winner is value for nearly double the official margin with the placed horses setting the level. The form looks solid and should work out.

NOTEBOOK

Alright Now M'Lad(IRE) ◆ proved himself very favourably rated on a mark of 117 for his handicap debut. Unfancied when successful here last time in novice company, he followed up in good style, readily pulling clear from the bottom of the hill. The step up in trip suited this improving chasing sort, and he will be in with a big shout of completing a hat-trick even after being reassessed. *(op 15-2 tchd 7-1)*

Amanpuri(GER), whose performance gives the form a fairly solid look, has been in cracking form of late and was chasing a hat-trick off a 7lb higher mark than for the latest of his Fontwell successes. *(tchd 15-2)*

King Georges(FR) ran his best race of the season so far, but the Handicapper still appears to have his measure.

Carly Bay, the only mare in the race, is a regular around here. She ran much better than she did on New Year's Day, appearing to appreciate professional handling. *(op 33-1)*

Westmeath Flyer ran a bit better on his second start for his new stable, but will probably need to drop a few pounds before he is winning again. *(op 50-1)*

Sea The Light was weak in the market beforehand and proved disappointing, racing keenly in the early stages and looking out on his feet turning into the straight. His trainer reported that the gelding was unsuited by the good to soft ground. *Official explanation: trainer said gelding was unsuited by today's good to soft going (op 13-8)*

3902 CHRIS POOLE MEMORIAL EVENING STANDARD MARES' ONLY NOVICES' HURDLE (9 hdls) 2m

4:00 (4:00) (Class 4) 4-Y-0+ **£3,083** (£898; £449)

Form RPR

3 **1** **Trompette (USA)**[18] 3579 4-10-4 .... AndrewTinkler 96+
(N J Henderson) *cl up: effrt 3 out: led next: in command whn slowed into last: drvn to hold on flat* **9/2**[3]

2P4 **2** *½* **Blaeberry**[32] 3354 5-11-0 .... MarcusFoley 101
(Miss E C Lavelle) *led to 2 out: nt qckn w wnr: lft w ch after last: jst hld flat* **4/1**[2]

F412 **3** *3* **Methodical**[16] 3483 4-9-13 97 .... JohnnyLevins(5) 88
(B G Powell) *prom: lost pl 5th: 7th jumping 3 out but gng wl: stdy prog next: reminder bef last where wnt 3rd: rdn and kpt on flat* **8/1**

-523 **4** *½* **Makeabreak (IRE)**[25] 3461 7-10-4 100 .... KevinTobin(10) 98
(C J Mann) *racd on inner: pressed ldr: mstke 3 out: rdn and nt qckn bef next: keeping on whn mstke last* **11/2**

114- **5** *1 ½* **Giovanna**[312] 4753 5-11-0 .... WarrenMarston 96
(R T Phillips) *plld hrd: hld up on inner: stl taking t.k.h and wl in tch whn mstke 3 out: fnd nil bef next: one pce after* **7/1**

-351 **6** *shd* **Ellway Prospect**[11] 3687 6-11-7 94 .... JamieMoore 103
(M G Rimell) *sn midfield: pushed along fr 4th: struggling to stay in tch fr 6th: kpt on: nt pce to rch ldrs* **9/1**

055 **7** *18* **Falcon Beneficial (IRE)**[37] 3281 4-9-13 .... EamonDehdashti(5) 74+
(G L Moore) *racd awkwardly: prom: stl cl up 3 out: wkng whn blnd 2 out* **33/1**

4000 **8** *1* **Allez Melina**[81] 2457 5-11-0 .... PhilipHide 89+
(Mrs A J Hamilton-Fairley) *hld up: last 1/2-way: gng wl but outpcd 6th: stdy prog on bit after 3 out: nvr nr ldrs: eased flat: do bttr* **100/1**

2 **9** *1 ½* **Screen Test**[18] 3579 4-10-4 .... RobertThornton 65
(A King) *hld up: trckd ldrs fr 5th: rdn 3 out: sn wknd* **3/1**[1]

0-0 **10** *1* **Balloch**[281] 230 5-10-7 .... CharlieStudd(7) 74
(Mary Meek) *racd on inner: lost pl and in rr fr 4th: bhd fr 6th* **100/1**

P **11** *dist* **Redneck Girl (IRE)**[28] 3425 7-10-9 .... DerekLaverty(5) —
(A E Jones) *in tch to 4th: sn bhd: t.o 6th: stl appr last as rest fin* **100/1**

6 **P** **Dawn Wager**^{75} [2579] 5-11-0 .... JamesDavies —
(D B Feek) *in tch: effrt to chse ldrs bef 6th: sn wknd: t.o whn p.u bef 2 out* **100/1**

4m 12.7s (11.50) **Going Correction** +0.95s/f (Soft)
WFA 4 from 5yo+ 9lb **12** Ran SP% **119.1**
Speed ratings: **109,108,107,107,106 106,97,96,95,95** —,— CSF £23.35 TOTE £6.50: £1.70, £1.80, £2.30; EX 22.70.
Owner Elite Racing Club **Bred** Wertheimer & Frere **Trained** Upper Lambourn, Berks

FOCUS
A fair mares' novice hurdle with the winner value for further and those in the frame behind her close to their marks.

NOTEBOOK
Trompette(USA) enhanced her trainer's fine record with hurdlers at this venue. She was probably just showing signs of inexperience when veering left and jumping the final flight slowly as she *found extra when tackled by Blaeberry on the run-in, and there should be better to come. (op 10-3 tchd 3-1)*
Blaeberry had shown enough on her previous starts to warrant plenty of respect in this company, but the easier ground would not have been in her favour and it is to her credit that she fought back *on the run-in. This keen-going sort is worth another try on a decent surface around a sharp track. (op 7-2)*
Methodical, one of the most experienced hurdlers in the line-up, confirmed her improvement since winning a seller at Taunton last month with a solid effort in third. Two and a half miles should suit her better. *(op 16-1)*
Makeabreak(IRE) was under pressure from the turn out of the back straight but she gets further than this and kept plugging away. She too will be suited by returning to a longer trip. *(op 13-2)*
Giovanna could not replicate her decent bumper form on her hurdling debut but is entitled to come on for her seasonal reappearance. *(op 8-1)*
Screen Test failed to build on the promise of her Warwick debut, proving another disappointment for the Alan King stable on the card. *(op 7-2 tchd 4-1)*
Dawn Wager *Official explanation: jockey said mare hung right*

3903 TYSER INSURANCE LTD BEGINNERS' CHASE (12 fncs) 2m 1f
4:30 (4:31) (Class 3) 5-Y-0+ **£6,286** (£1,873; £948; £486; £254)

Form RPR

14-6 **1** **Idole First (IRE)**^{39} [3251] 7-11-2 .... AlanO'Keeffe 134+
(Miss Venetia Williams) *nt a fluent: trckd ldr to 4th: effrt to chse ldr again 4 out: squeezed through on inner to ld 2 out: r.o wl* **11/2**

13-5 **2** *4* **Nycteos (FR)**^{114} [1823] 5-10-9 .... ChristianWilliams 123
(P F Nicholls) *led at decent pce: nt fluent 7th and 4 out: narrowly hdd 2 out: nt qckn last* **5/4**^{1}

-P32 **3** *26* **Medison (FR)**^{17} [3599] 6-11-2 .... TimmyMurphy 120+
(M C Pipe) *hld up: prog 6th: cl 5th whn hmpd 8th: rapid prog to press ldng pair 3 out: nudged along & no rspnse next: eased to walk fl* **11/4**^{2}

56P3 **4** *16* **Corrib Drift (USA)**^{27} [3432] 6-10-13 85.................. ColinBolger$^{(3)}$ 88
(Jamie Poulton) *nt a fluent in midfield: rdn and nt on terms fr 1/2-way: wl bhd 4 out: t.o* **50/1**

5-00 **5** *dist* **Top Dog (IRE)**^{77} [2554] 7-10-9 .... JustinMorgan$^{(7)}$ —
(L Wells) *sn detached in last pair: t.o fr 7th: btn 117l* **100/1**

00 **F** **Spiritual Society (IRE)**^{30} [3386] 6-11-2 .... TomScudamore —
(M Scudamore) *plld hrd: chsd ldr 4th: disputing 2nd whn fell 8th* **25/1**

-06P **P** **Handy Money**^{37} [3298] 9-11-2 .... RobertThornton —
(A King) *nt a fluent: prom: chsd ldr 8th to 4 out: wkng whn j. bdly rt 3 out: poor 5th whn p.u bef 2 out* **5/1**^{3}

430- **U** **Grouse Moor (USA)**^{326} [4538] 7-11-2 .... LeightonAspell —
(P Winkworth) *detached in last pair fr 2nd: nvr on terms after: t.o in 5th whn blnd and uns rdr 2 out* **25/1**

4m 26.1s (2.00) **Going Correction** +0.425s/f (Soft)
WFA 5 from 6yo+ 6lb **8** Ran SP% **113.8**
Speed ratings: **112,110,97,90,**— —,—,— CSF £13.21 TOTE £6.40: £2.10, £1.50, £1.10; EX 18.10.
Owner Miss V M Williams **Bred** Ralph Alfandari **Trained** Kings Caple, H'fords

FOCUS
A decent contest for the course, and it unearthed a couple of useful sorts in the form of Idole First and Nycteos. The runner-up and the fourth are the best guides to the level of the form.

NOTEBOOK
Idole First(IRE) ◆, a 145-rated hurdler and winner of last season's Coral Cup, was disappointing when only sixth in a good race behind Green Tango and Don't Be Shy at Hereford on his chasing debut where the soft ground appeared to be the obvious excuse. Having won over two miles five at the Festival last season, he was always going to be doing his best work late, and he stayed on too strongly for Nycteos. A versatile sort with regards to trip and ground, there should be better to come, and he may make a quick reappearance in a novice chase at Fontwell at the weekend, but his long-term target is likely to be the Jewson Novices' Handicap Chase at Cheltenham, where the likely strong pace and uphill finish will again hold no fears. *(tchd 5-1 and 6-1)*
Nycteos(FR), officially rated 25lb inferior to the winner over hurdles, had shaped well on his debut for the yard in a handicap hurdle at Aintree back in October, but chasing was always likely to be his game and he was entitled to plenty of respect with the five-year-olds' allowance. Like many French-breds, he took to the fences with relish, his rider evidently keen to set a decent gallop, and he had them well strung out down the back straight. The winner proved just too strong in the end, but a repetition of this effort should see him find a race, and two and a half miles may well bring about some improvement. *(op 13-8 tchd 7-4)*
Medison(FR) looked far from enthusiastic in defeat at Fontwell and, having recovered from being hampered to track the front two approaching the turn-in, he found absolutely nothing. He is one to avoid. *Official explanation: jockey said gelding had no more to give (tchd 3-1 and 10-3 in places)*
Handy Money, a useful hurdler launching a chase career rather late in life, was never jumping with *any fluency and looked very tired when pulled up before the second-last. Official explanation: trainer said gelding was unsuited by the good to soft going (op 9-2 tchd 7-2)*

3904 EVENING STANDARD REMEMBERS CHRIS POOLE MAIDEN OPEN NATIONAL HUNT FLAT RACE 2m 2f
5:00 (5:00) (Class 6) 4-6-Y-0 **£1,713** (£499; £249)

Form RPR

1 **Cockspur (IRE)** 5-11-4 .... APMcCoy 107+
(Jonjo O'Neill) *racd wd for most of r: wl in tch: rdn in 5th 3f out: swtchd to inner and renewed effrt 2f out: led 1f out: r.o wl* **13/2**^{3}

6 **2** *1 ½* **Flight Leader (IRE)**^{11} [3699] 6-11-4 .... JoeTizzard 104
(C L Tizzard) *pressed ldr: led 7f out: rdn and hdd over 2f out: stl upsides 1f out: outpcd by wnr* **15/2**

3 *1 ¼* **Trigger The Light** 5-11-4 .... WayneHutchinson 103
(A King) *wl in tch: outpcd and rdn over 3f out: styd on again fnl 2f: gng on at fin* **20/1**

24 **4** *½* **Marshalls Run (IRE)**^{30} [3392] 6-11-4 .... RobertThornton 102
(A King) *cl up: effrt to ld narrowly over 2f out: hdd and one pce 1f out* **5/2**^{2}

5 *1 ¼* **Gaelic Gift (IRE)** 4-9-8 .... MrTJO'Brien$^{(7)}$ 84
(J G Cann) *hld up in rr but wl in tch: prog 7f out: chal 3f out: nt qckn 2f out: rn green but kpt on* **40/1**

4 **6** *1 ¾* **Classic Fantasy**^{35} [3327] 5-10-11 .... ChristianWilliams 93+
(P F Nicholls) *wl in tch: effrt to chal 3f out: upsides over 1f out: wknd fnl f* **5/4**^{1}

7 *16* **Arriman** 4-10-1 .... SimonElliott$^{(7)}$ 73
(J A Geake) *rn v green: in tch: outpcd 4f out: no ch after: plugged on* **33/1**

00 **8** *25* **At Loggerheads**^{35} [3327] 5-10-1 .... RichardKilloran$^{(10)}$ 51
(B G Powell) *in tch to 1/2-way: sn struggling in last: t.o* **100/1**

9 *5* **Golding Hop** 6-11-4 .... PhilipHide 53
(P Winkworth) *racd wd thrght: wl in tch tl wknd over 3f out: t.o* **25/1**

4/ **10** *¾* **Thebellinnbroadway**^{674} [4739] 6-10-11 .... TomDoyle 45
(S C Burrough) *led to 7f out: wknd 4f out: t.o* **50/1**

5P **11** *8* **April Showers**^{35} [3327] 6-10-11 .... JodieMogford 37
(J C Tuck) *trckd ldrs tl rdn and wknd 4f out: t.o* **100/1**

4m 48.8s (24.05) **Going Correction** +0.95s/f (Soft)
WFA 4 from 5yo+ 9lb **11** Ran SP% **116.0**
Speed ratings: **84,83,82,82,82 81,74,63,60,60 56** CSF £49.85 TOTE £5.90: £2.10, £1.70, £3.70; EX 34.20 Place 6 £30.36, Place 5 £27.14.
Owner John P McManus **Bred** Mrs L Eadie **Trained** Cheltenham, Gloucs

FOCUS
An ordinary bumper run at a steady early gallop, and they finished in something of a bunch. The fourth sets the standard.

NOTEBOOK
Cockspur(IRE) is a half-brother to a couple of bumper winners in No Shenanigans and Kingfisher Flyer, and he made a winning debut under a good ride from McCoy, who kept the son of Darazari wide for most of the way, seeking out the better ground, and got him running on the climb to the line. Defying a penalty will be harder, but he is entitled to improve. *(op 6-1 tchd 7-1)*
Flight Leader(IRE) was not disgraced behind exciting bumper performer Kicks For Free on his debut and this represented a weaker race. Up there all the way, he was always well positioned in a race run at a steady early pace prior to the sprint for home. *(op 9-1)*
Trigger The Light ◆, who is by Double Trigger out of a half-sister to Hurricane Lamp, was slightly outpaced running out of the back straight and still had work to do to catch the leaders inside the final two furlongs, but he stayed on really well. Had the pace been quicker in the early stages he might well have won, and he looks one to keep in mind when the emphasis is on stamina.
Marshalls Run(IRE) had every chance, but would also surely have fared better in a stronger-run race. He should get further when he is sent over hurdles. *(op 15-8)*
Gaelic Gift(IRE), a cheap purchase as a three-year-old, did not shape badly but there is a chance that she was flattered by the way the race was run. *(op 33-1)*
Classic Fantasy proved disappointing, as she was well placed turning into the straight but simply *failed to get home. Perhaps she needs better ground. Official explanation: jockey said mare was never travelling (op 7-4)*
T/Jkpt: £1,183.30 to a £1 stake. Pool: £10,000.00. 6.00 winning tickets. T/Plt: £17.90 to a £1 stake. Pool: £58,589.35. 2,379.70 winning tickets. T/Qpdt: £14.60 to a £1 stake. Pool: £3,046.20. 153.40 winning tickets. JN

3658 FOLKESTONE (R-H)
Tuesday, February 14

OFFICIAL GOING: Chase course - good to soft; hurdle course - soft
Wind: Light, behind Weather: Mostly fine

3905 DYMCHURCH H'CAP HURDLE (11 hdls) 2m 6f 110y
1:50 (1:50) (Class 5) (0-95,95) 4-Y-0+ **£2,927** (£859; £429; £214)

Form RPR

04-P **1** **Yes My Lord (IRE)**^{56} [2934] 7-11-10 93.................................. TimmyMurphy 102+
(M C Pipe) *trckd ldrs: j. slowly 7th: led 3 out: pressed bef last: drvn out flat* **7/2**^{2}

-0FP **2** *3 ½* **Buckland Gold (IRE)**^{64} [2802] 6-11-7 90.................................. JamesDavies 92
(D B Feek) *hld up in rr: stdy prog fr 7th: wl in tch 2 out: rdn to chse wnr bef last: no imp flat* **50/1**

0P/- **3** *1 ½* **Redwood Grove (USA)**^{1087} [3778] 10-10-11 87............(t) MrTJO'Brien$^{(7)}$ 87
(Miss Tor Sturgis) *prom: rdn to chse wnr 2 out tl bef last: kpt on same pce* **6/1**^{3}

6142 **4** *19* **English Jim (IRE)**^{29} [3424] 5-11-2 85.................................. MatthewBatchelor 66
(Miss A M Newton-Smith) *nt a fluent: hld up in midfield: outpcd bef 2 out: n.d after* **3/1**^{1}

0-56 **5** *7* **Black Collar**^{38} [3287] 7-11-2 85.................................. JohnMcNamara 59
(K C Bailey) *mstkes: t.k.h: trckd ldng pair: lft in ld after 5th: hdd 3 out: wknd on long run between last 2* **16/1**

UPPP **6** *17* **Geography (IRE)**^{29} [3428] 6-10-9 83..................(p) RobertLucey-Butler$^{(5)}$ 40
(P Butler) *hld up in rr: pushed along bef 7th: sn struggling: no ch fr 2 out* **66/1**

-530 **7** *2 ½* **At The Double**^{11} [3715] 10-11-7 90..................................(b) PhilipHide 45
(P Winkworth) *hld up in tch: prog to chse ldrs 8th: wknd after 3 out* **16/1**

2335 **8** *1 ¼* **Barranco (IRE)**^{28} [3433] 5-11-2 85..................................(b) JamieMoore 38
(G L Moore) *in tch: rdn bef 7th: struggling fr next: no ch bef 2 out* **6/1**^{3}

-U0P **P** **Jackie Boy (IRE)**^{75} [2592] 7-11-2 85.................................. AntonyEvans —
(N A Twiston-Davies) *led tl tk wrong crse after 5th: p.u* **16/1**

5425 **P** **Full On**^{38} [3285] 9-11-9 95.................................. WilliamKennedy$^{(3)}$ —
(A M Hales) *pressed ldr tl tk wrong crse after 5th: p.u* **10/1**

4500 **P** **Breezer**^{39} [3279] 6-10-6 82..................................(p) SimonElliott$^{(7)}$ —
(J A Geake) *struggling in last pair fr 4th: hit 6th: sn t.o: p.u bef 2 out* **16/1**

2P/P **P** **Cougar (IRE)**^{56} [2934] 6-11-0 88..................................(t) LiamTreadwell$^{(5)}$ —
(R Rowe) *a wl in rr: mstke 6th and rdn: wknd bef next: t.o whn p.u after 2 out* **33/1**

020 **P** **Ocean Of Storms (IRE)**^{17} [3611] 11-11-0 86.................. OwynNelmes$^{(3)}$ —
(N I M Rossiter) *nt fluent: in tch: wknd 3 out: disputing poor 8th whn p.u bef last* **25/1**

6m 11.3s (2.20) **Going Correction** +0.075s/f (Yiel) **13** Ran SP% **118.7**
Speed ratings: **99,97,97,90,88 82,81,81,**—,— —,—,— CSF £172.92 CT £1035.21 TOTE £4.30: £2.30, £16.10, £2.00; EX 300.10.
Owner D A Johnson **Bred** Owen Dermody **Trained** Nicholashayne, Devon
■ Stewards' Enquiry : William Kennedy ten-day ban: took wrong course (Feb 25-28, Mar 1-6)
Antony Evans ten-day ban: took wrong course (Feb 25-28, Mar 1-6)

FOCUS
An ordinary contest to open with, but if there was one horse in the field who was better than its form suggested, it was the winner and he did not let his supporters down.

NOTEBOOK
Yes My Lord(IRE) ◆, an eye-catcher on his third and final start last season, pulled up lame on his handicap debut at Fontwell back in December and had been off since, but the support for him in the market suggested he was over whatever caused his lameness. Always travelling strongly under a typically confident Murphy, he decided to take charge after the third-last, but was unable to shake off outsider Buckland Gold and Redwood Grove, in the end running out just a workmanlike winner. An attractive-looking son of Mister Lord, it is entirely possible better ground will suit and, with three *miles plus unlikely to prove a problem, he can win again before going on to fences. (op 11-4 tchd 5-2)*

Buckland Gold(IRE) had not looked the same since taking a fall at Fontwell in March of last year, and was understandably ranked amongst the outsiders having broken blood-vessels when last seen at Plumpton in December. However, he put up a significantly improved effort and it looked for much of the final half mile as though he was going to really push the winner. He was clear of the third and a similar effort at this level should see him winning, with a step up to three miles likely to help.

Redwood Grove(USA)would no doubt have delighted connections with this first run since February 2003 as he was still travelling well enough as they started to swing for home. It was only in the final quarter mile his absence began to tell, but he kept on well enough and can hopefully go the right way from this. *(op 5-1)*

English Jim(IRE) gave himself little chance with several sloppy errors and was always struggling to get involved. *(op 7-2 tchd 4-1)*

Black Collar ran well for a long way on this handicap debut, but it was disappointing she stopped so quickly once beaten.

Ocean Of Storms(IRE) *Official explanation: jockey said gelding made a noise (tchd 12-1)*

Full Onwas up with the leader when he took the wrong course before the turn into the straight with a circuit to go and was immediately pulled up. *(tchd 12-1)*

Jackie Boy(IRE) set the pace until he took the wrong course before the turn into the straight with a circuit to go and was immediately pulled up. *(tchd 12-1)*

3906 BARRY LOVES POSH BIRDS MAIDEN HURDLE (10 hdls) 2m 4f 110y

2:20 (2:20) (Class 4) 4-Y-0+ **£3,253** (£955; £477; £238)

Form				RPR
2	**1**		**Opera Mundi (FR)**36 [3324] 4-10-7 .... APMcCoy (P F Nicholls) *trckd ldrs: clsd 2 out: sn rdn: r.o to ld bef last: sn clr: eased last 100yds* **4/6**[1]	103+
23	**2**	*3 1/2*	**Palm Island (FR)**21 [3545] 5-11-4 .... TomDoyle (Noel T Chance) *hld up in midfield: wl in tch 2 out: outpcd between last 2: styd on to take 2nd flat: no imp on wnr* **7/1**[3]	105
620-	**3**	*1 1/2*	**Ceoperk (IRE)**332 [4465] 7-10-11 .... WarrenMarston (D J Wintle) *hld up in midfield: clsd 2 out: drvn and effrt between last 2: kpt on* **20/1**	97
5-12	**4**	*1/2*	**Major Miller**50 [2983] 5-11-4 .... MickFitzgerald (N J Henderson) *ldng trio: mstke 7th: led sn after next (3 out) hdd bef last: fdd flat* **11/2**[2]	105+
4	**5**	*7*	**Petitjean**50 [3001] 6-11-4 .... RichardJohnson (P J Hobbs) *nt a fluent: t.k.h in ldng trio: rdn to chal between last 2: wknd last* **20/1**	98+
34	**6**	*9*	**Count Boris**39 [3275] 5-11-4 .... JimmyMcCarthy (J A Geake) *trckd ldrs: wl in tch 2 out: steadily wknd sn after* **25/1**	88+
6	**7**	*10*	**Forest Miller**83 [2432] 7-11-4 .... WayneHutchinson (R T Phillips) *wl in rr: drvn after 5th: nvr on terms after: plugged on fr 2 out* **66/1**	77
2-45	**8**	*1 1/2*	**Sheriff Roscoe**24 [3500] 6-11-4 .... LeightonAspell (P Winkworth) *mstke 1st: hld up in midfield: outpcd after 3 out: sme prog fr 2 out: n.d: wknd and eased bef last* **12/1**	76
	9	*25*	**High Point (IRE)**16 8-11-4 .... RobertThornton (G P Enright) *nt jump wl: chsd ldrs to 7th: struggling after next: t.o* **20/1**	51
	10	*2 1/2*	**Dancing Bear**26 5-11-4 .... AntonyProcter (Lucinda Featherstone) *led at gd pce: hit 6th: hdd sn after 3 out: mstke 2 out: wknd rapidly: t.o* **100/1**	48
-6P6	**11**	*7*	**Red Granite**6 [3806] 6-11-4 .... JohnMcNamara (K C Bailey) *hld up towards rr: in tch whn nt fluent 6th: lost tch fr 3 out: t.o* **100/1**	41
	P		**Brooking (IRE)** 8-11-4 .... TomSiddall (R T Phillips) *hld up in last pair: rdn and wknd after 5th: t.o whn p.u bef 3 out* **66/1**	—
	P		**Froghole Flyer**652 7-11-4 .... PhilipHide (G L Moore) *mstke 1st: a wl in rr: wknd after 5th: t.o whn p.u bef 3 out* **66/1**	—
0	**P**		**Public Eye**14 [3659] 5-10-11 .... JustinMorgan(7) (L A Dace) *hld up in last pair: mstke 4th: wknd next: t.o 6th: p.u bef 2 out* **100/1**	—

5m 31.6s (-1.20) **Going Correction** +0.075s/f (Yiel)
WFA 4 from 5yo+ 10lb **14** Ran SP% **121.1**
Speed ratings: **105,103,103,102,100 96,93,92,82,81 79**,—,—,— CSF £5.18 TOTE £1.50: £1.10, £2.10, £6.60; EX 8.60.

Owner Sir Robert Ogden **Bred** F M Cottin **Trained** Ditcheat, Somerset

FOCUS

An ordinary maiden hurdle in which favourite Opera Mundi made hard enough work of winning. The placed horses were close to previous marks and the form should work out.

NOTEBOOK

Opera Mundi(FR), runner-up on his sole start over hurdles in France, filled the same position behind the useful Kalmini on his British debut at Taunton last month, a level of form that entitled him to win this well. However, despite having the race run to suit, he was tapped for toe from half a mile out and needed every yard of the trip to get on top, hitting top gear approaching the last and finally asserting. He is undoubtedly promising, but looks the sort to make a better chaser than hurdler. *(op 8-11 tchd 4-5 in places)*

Palm Island(FR) had shown himself to be nothing better than a modest performer in two previous attempts, but this was better and the way he was keeping on late suggests three miles will bring about further progress. *(tchd 15-2)*

Ceoperk(IRE), a winner on her bumper debut at the course last season, made a highly pleasing hurdles debut and, as with the runner-up, another rise is distance should see further improvement. Mares-only races are likely to provide her with easier opportunities.

Major Miller really served it up to the winner and went on taking the second-last, but ran out of gas in the final furlong and was hard done by to be run out of a place. He is nothing special, but may benefit from a return to two miles. *(op 5-1 tchd 6-1)*

Petitjean, as with Major Miller, ran better than his finishing position suggests and was arguably travelling best turning for home. Fourth at Wincanton behind Pepperoni Pete on his sole outing in bumpers, he still looks quite weak and should have little trouble finding races in time.

3907 FOLKESTONE-RACECOURSE.CO.UK BEGINNERS' CHASE (15 fncs) 2m 5f

2:50 (2:50) (Class 4) 5-Y-0+ **£4,554** (£1,337; £668; £333)

Form				RPR
6-22	**1**		**Reveillez**21 [3549] 7-11-2 .... APMcCoy (J R Fanshawe) *pckd 1st: settled in midfield: clsd 3 out: trckd ldr next: led last: cleverly* **30/100**[1]	136+
0-23	**2**	*2*	**Pardishar (IRE)**36 [3323] 8-11-2 119 .... JamieMoore (G L Moore) *sn trckd ldng pair: clsd 3 out: led bef next: rdn and hdd last: kpt on wl flat but no ch w wnr* **10/1**	124
/1-4	**3**	*14*	**Its Wallace Jnr**50 [2999] 7-11-2 114 ....(t) JamieGoldstein (Miss Sheena West) *chsd ldr tl after 3 out: sn drvn and outpcd* **8/1**[2]	110
1P	**4**	*15*	**Pedros Brief (IRE)**31 [3388] 8-11-2 .... RichardJohnson (R T Phillips) *led at gd pce and sn clr: hit 8th: hdd bef 2 out: wknd rapidly and clambered over last* **9/1**[3]	100+
0P10	**5**	*7*	**Big Quick (IRE)**145 [1525] 11-10-9 .... JustinMorgan(7) (L Wells) *mstkes in last pair: lost tch 9th: sn t.o: plugged on* **50/1**	88
00-5	**6**	*1 1/4*	**Sweet Minuet**14 [3663] 9-10-4 82 .... RobertLucey-Butler(5) (M Madgwick) *chsd ldrs: lost tch and mstke 10th: sn wl bhd* **66/1**	80
PU3-	**P**		**Zaffre D'Or (IRE)**323 [4619] 9-11-2 78 .... JohnMcNamara (M J McGrath) *in tch in rr tl wknd 9th: t.o whn p.u bef 12th* **66/1**	—

5m 21.7s (-2.70) **Going Correction** +0.075s/f (Yiel) **7** Ran SP% **112.1**
Speed ratings: **108,107,101,96,93 93**,— CSF £4.22 TOTE £1.20: £1.10, £1.90; EX 3.60.

Owner John P McManus **Bred** Mrs A Yearley **Trained** Newmarket, Suffolk

FOCUS

An uncompetitive affair won in convincing fashion by hot favourite Reveillez who was value for 12 lengths, and the runner-up sets the level.

NOTEBOOK

Reveillez put up a visually impressive performance, but his two previous attempts over fences when second to Montgermont and Billyvoddan entitled him to win as he did. The decent early gallop set by Richard Johnson on Pedros Brief played right into the ex-Flat racer's hands and he merely had to be shaken up to score. He will reportedly be kept to a sensible level for the time being, and will look for a novice event to defy a penalty, but it would come as no surprise to see him end up in one of the handicaps at Aintree's Grand National meeting. *(op 2-7)*

Pardishar(IRE) left a disappointing effort in handicap company at Taunton behind, but was a sitting duck the winner had little trouble picking off. Officially rated 119, he will ultimately end up back in handicaps, but it may be worth trying to seek out a similar race at one of the lesser tracks first.

Its Wallace Jnr made a nice transition to fences, jumping soundly, but lacked the class to challenge. Previously progressive over hurdles, he remains unexposed and can find races at the right level.

Pedros Brief(IRE) was unable to sustain the gallop and dropped right away in the final furlong or so, but there were plenty of positives to be taken from this and it is hoped the sizeable gelding, *who jumped boldly throughout, is ridden with a little more restraint in future.Official explanation: trainer said gelding bled from the nose (op 10-1)*

3908 BURMARSH NOVICES' HURDLE (9 hdls) 2m 1f 110y

3:20 (3:20) (Class 4) 4-Y-0+ **£3,253** (£955; £477; £238)

Form				RPR
53	**1**		**Topkat (IRE)**26 [3464] 5-11-3 .... APMcCoy (M C Pipe) *t.k.h: hld up wl in tch: gd prog after 2 out: led on outer bef last: sn clr* **4/1**[2]	117+
13	**2**	*5*	**Border Castle**61 [2849] 5-11-10 .... SamThomas (Miss Venetia Williams) *hit 1st: trckd ldrs: rdn after 2 out: chsd wnr last: wl outpcd flat* **3/1**[1]	116
2-3	**3**	*9*	**Wellbeing**33 [3354] 9-11-3 .... RichardJohnson (P J Hobbs) *pressed ldrs: led narrowly 3 out: hdd & wknd bef last* **7/1**	100
	4	*1 3/4*	**Onward To Glory (USA)**460 6-11-3 .... PJBrennan (P J Hobbs) *hld up in midfield: prog 3 out: chal after 2 out: wknd and mstke last* **40/1**	98
P2	**5**	*2 1/2*	**Spear Thistle**28 [3431] 4-10-7 .... MarcusFoley (Mrs N Smith) *mstkes: pressed ldr to 2 out: steadily fdd u.p* **11/2**[3]	88+
	6	*1 1/4*	**Saltrio**850 8-11-3 .... WayneHutchinson (A King) *hld up in rr: in tch at rr of ldng gp after 2 out: shkn up and styd on bef last: nvr nrr* **25/1**	95
351	**7**	*25*	**Sole Agent (IRE)**28 [3431] 4-11-0 115 .... PhilipHide (G L Moore) *led: hdd and hit 3 out: wknd between last 2: tired and eased to walk flat* **4/1**[2]	87+
02	**8**	*22*	**Glimmer Of Light (IRE)**29 [3423] 6-11-3 .... RobertThornton (A King) *chsd ldrs tl wknd 2 out: t.o whn j. bdly rt last* **11/1**	48
	9	*1/2*	**Wiggy Smith**144 7-11-3 .... LeightonAspell (O Sherwood) *j. bdly: in tch in rr: wknd 2 out: t.o* **10/1**	47
45	**10**	*3*	**Ridjit (FR)**12 [3685] 6-11-3 .... JamesDavies (N J Gifford) *prom tl wknd rapidly after 3 out: t.o* **33/1**	44
3P	**11**	*2*	**Outside Half (IRE)**41 [3238] 4-10-2 ....(t) HowieEphgrave(5) (L Corcoran) *in tch in rr tl wknd rapidly aned mstke 2 out: t.o* **100/1**	32
	12	*shd*	**Murrieta**47 4-9-11 .... OwynNelmes(3) (Miss J R Gibney) *stdd s: a in last pair: lost tch 5th: t.o* **100/1**	25
	13	*15*	**Esperance (IRE)**175 6-11-3 .... JimCrowley (J Akehurst) *stdd s: a in last pair: lost tch 5th: t.o* **100/1**	27

4m 36.7s (7.40) **Going Correction** +0.075s/f (Yiel)
WFA 4 from 5yo+ 9lb **13** Ran SP% **122.5**
Speed ratings: **86,83,79,79,77 77,66,56,56,54 54,53,47** CSF £16.82 TOTE £3.00: £1.70, £2.30, £1.70; EX 22.60.

Owner B A Kilpatrick **Bred** Kitty's Sister Syndicate **Trained** Nicholashayne, Devon

FOCUS

An intriguing contest with several interesting newcomers on show, but it was those with previous experience that came to the fore. The winner is value for more than the official margin and with the placed horses to their marks the form should prove reliable.

NOTEBOOK

Topkat(IRE), a useful sort with David Elsworth on the level, had finished behind a couple of decent sorts on his first two attempts, and proved too strong for the penalised Border Castle from before the last. He should have little trouble staying two and a half miles on a sound surface, but is fully effective at this distance and it would not surprise to see him progress again for switching to handicaps. *(tchd 7-2 and 9-2)*

Border Castle, although holding obviously strong claims, was always likely to be vulnerable under his 7lb penalty and he found Topkat too good in the end. His Exeter reverse came over a trip too far *and the son of Grand Lodge is another likely to do better once moving into handicaps. (op 7-2 tchd 9-2)*

Wellbeing, a formerly high-class Flat-racer, has trouble seeing out this sort of distance and, having led turning into the straight, he faded tamely in the final furlong. Faster ground may enable him to pick up a small race, but his potential is limited. *(op 6-1)*

Onward To Glory(USA) ◆, a 66-rated Flat performer for John Dunlop, had always looked the sort to appreciate a switch to hurdles and, despite racing keenly and failing to jump with any fluency in the early stages, he warmed to the task and came through to dispute it with Wellbeing before the turn into the straight. Considering this was his first outing since November 2004 it was always likely he was going to get tired and he had nothing left to give from well before the last. With the match-practice expected to bring him on appreciably, it will be most disappointing if he does not go close next time, and he rates as the one to take from the race.

Spear Thistle was up on the pace throughout and ran a little better than his finishing position suggests, but it is unlikely he will be seen at his best until tackling handicaps. *(op 6-1)*

Saltrio ◆ was rated 85 on the Flat and looked a fascinating contender on this hurdles debut, but market signals were negative and he was clearly not expected to feature prominently. He travelled well on this first start since October 2003 and briefly threatened to take a hand, but got tired in the end and had to make do with sixth. There were many positives to take from this and he is another worth watching out for in future. *(op 33-1)*

Wiggy Smith was the disappointment of the race, racing far too keenly and making several novicey mistakes, and it was no surprise to see him finish very tired. A useful handicapper on the Flat, it is hoped he learns from this and he is worth giving another chance.

3909 NUMBER ENGAGED H'CAP CHASE (18 fncs) 3m 1f

3:50 (3:50) (Class 5) (0-90,90) 5-Y-O+ **£3,578** (£1,050; £525; £262)

Form RPR

-451 **1** **Tallow Bay (IRE)**[29] 3427 11-10-2 **73**.............................. MrGTumelty(7) 91+
(Mrs S Wall) *in tch: prog and prom fr 10th: led 15th: drew clr fr next: in n.d after: rdn out* **8/1**

4452 **2** *7* **Up The Pub (IRE)**[15] 3654 8-11-4 **82**............................(t) RobertWalford 90
(R H Alner) *settled in midfield: effrt 14th: outpcd fr 3 out: styd on fr next to take 2nd last: no ch w wnr* **11/2**[2]

4035 **3** *4* **Kappelhoff (IRE)**[39] 3276 9-10-3 **67**.........................(b) MatthewBatchelor 73+
(Mrs L Richards) *hld up in rr: prog into midfield 12th: chsng ldrs 3 out: sn outpcd by wnr: mstke last: kpt on* **16/1**

P400 **4** *2* **Instant Appeal**[14] 3661 9-11-9 **87**.. PhilipHide 89
(P Winkworth) *hld up wl in rr: prog 10th: jnd ldrs 13th: outpcd by wnr 3 out: wnt 2nd bef 2 out tl wknd last* **25/1**

6353 **5** *1 3/4* **Dun Locha Castle (IRE)**[25] 3481 11-11-7 **85**................... TomScudamore 85
(N R Mitchell) *led to 11th: sn pushed along: effrt to ld again 13th to 15th: wknd bef 2 out* **12/1**

3P-3 **6** *3* **Hobbycyr (FR)**[28] 3434 11-11-0 **85**.................................... MrPMason(7) 82
(J A T De Giles) *in tch towards rr: bdly outpcd fr 14th: no ch after: kpt on fr 2 out* **8/1**

P555 **7** *7* **Deltic Arrow**[18] 3598 8-11-0 **85**....................................... MrJAJenkins(7) 75
(D L Williams) *w ldrs: cl up whn mstke 15th: sn outpcd and btn: wknd 2 out* **33/1**

5-53 **8** *12* **Alfa Sunrise**[18] 3600 9-11-5 **83**................................... BenjaminHitchcott 65+
(R H Buckler) *chsd ldrs: j.v.slowly 6th: lost pl: last at 12th and nvr gng wl after* **8/1**

12P2 **9** *1 3/4* **Ebony Jack (IRE)**[29] 3427 9-11-1 **79**.................................(p) JoeTizzard 56
(C L Tizzard) *prom: lost pl 10th: drvn in rr 12th: struggled on* **9/2**[1]

11U2 **10** *5* **Never Awol (IRE)**[39] 3276 9-11-5 **90**.......................(p) TomMessenger(7) 62
(B N Pollock) *chsd ldrs: rdn fr 10th: prog to chal and j. slowly 13th: btn fr 15th: wknd* **10/1**

343- **11** *2* **Eastern Point**[340] 4308 12-10-8 **79** ow6.............................. MrPYork(7) 49
(R H York) *hld up: prog into midfield 12th: j. slowly 13th: struggling whn mstke 3 out: wknd* **33/1**

PP5F **12** *19* **Peveril Pride**[33] 3359 8-11-5 **83**...............................(t) JimmyMcCarthy 34
(J A Geake) *a in rr and nt fluent: lost tch 14th: t.o* **100/1**

5-54 **P** **Dr Mann (IRE)**[29] 3427 8-11-1 **79**.. MarcusFoley —
(Miss Tor Sturgis) *terrible blunder 2nd: nvr rcvrd: t.o 4th: p.u bef 7th* **6/1**[3]

P **Il Penseroso (IRE)**[332] 4471 8-11-10 **88**............................... PJBrennan —
(P A Blockley) *plld hrd: sn prom: mstke 7th: led 11th to 13th: wknd rapidly and p.u bef 3 out* **25/1**

6m 32.4s (-1.00) **Going Correction** +0.075s/f (Yiel) **14 Ran SP% 118.4**
Speed ratings: **104,101,100,99,99 98,96,92,91,90 89,83,—,—** CSF £49.40 CT £697.44 TOTE £12.10: £2.70, £2.20, £5.40; EX 60.60.
Owner Mrs S Wall **Bred** Mrs S P H Oliver **Trained** Dallington, E Sussex

FOCUS
A modest handicap chase made up of largely exposed sorts and honours went the way of in-form 11-year-old Tallow Bay. The second sets the standard and the form appears reasonable.

NOTEBOOK
Tallow Bay(IRE) received a fine ride from Tumelty, who took the race by the scruff of the neck approaching the third-last and a mighty leap there gave him the momentum he needed to press clear. The 11lb rise he incurred for ending a three-year losing run at Plumpton proved to be no obstacle and, in this sort of form, it is impossible to rule out the completion of a hat-trick.
Up The Pub(IRE) emerged from the pack to finished second, but he was never anywhere near the winner and will continue to be vulnerable due to his lack of finishing kick. *(tchd 6-1)*
Kappelhoff(IRE) made good headway to boast a decent position with around half a mile to run but, like many, he was found out by the winner's injection of pace. He has found some consistency this season and is probably capable of winning off this sort of mark.
Instant Appeal, who had not shown a great deal over hurdles since returning from injury, clearly appreciated the challenge of jumping fences for the first time and ran with much credit back in fourth, despite racing wide throughout.
Dun Locha Castle(IRE) was disputing it right from the off, but was unable to sustain the gallop and ended up well held.
Hobbycyr(FR), although unable to improve on last month's course third, was putting in his best work late and may benefit from a more aggressive ride in future. *(op 9-1)*
Ebony Jack(IRE) *Official explanation: jockey said gelding was never travelling; vet said gelding had been struck into (op 4-1)*

3910 DIGWEED DECADE HUNTERS' CHASE (FOR THE R. E. SASSOON MEMORIAL TROPHY) (16 fncs 2 omitted) 3m 1f

4:20 (4:23) (Class 6) 5-Y-O+ **£1,648** (£507; £253)

Form RPR

32F- **1** **Swincombe (IRE)**[23] 11-11-9 **91**.................................... MrAHickman(5) 101+
(Mrs S J Hickman) *hld up in rr: prog bef 12th: led sn after 3 out and qckly drew 10l clr: nt fluent 2 out: rdn out flat* **12/1**

033- **2** *3/4* **Cracking Dawn (IRE)**[31] 11-11-11 **114**.......................... MrTJO'Brien(3) 102+
(Mrs S Alner) *settled in midfield: cl up 3 out: sn outpcd: wnt 2nd bef 2 out: clsd on wnr bef last: nvr quite able to chal* **4/1**[3]

12-1 **3** *6* **Paddy For Paddy (IRE)**[293] 49 12-12-4 .... MrAWintle(3) 101
(G L Landau) *settled in rr: prog to chse ldrs 3 out: sn bdly outpcd: kpt on fr 2 out: no ch* **2/1**[1]

2P-1 **4** *2 1/2* **Millenium Way (IRE)**[9] 12-12-0 .... MrsCLTaylor(7) 98
(Mrs C L Taylor) *nt fluent: hld up in last: stl last 4 out: gd prog on outer after 3 out: one pce after 2 out: no ch* **25/1**

5 *8* **Brer Bear**[31] 7-11-7 .... MrGWalters(7) 85+
(Mrs E Insley) *several positions: in tch: dropped to rr and bmpd along 4 out: kpt on again fr 2 out* **14/1**

12-2 **6** *10* **Yeoman Sailor (IRE)**[269] 453 12-12-7 .... MrNHarris 85+
(Miss Grace Muir) *w ldr: j. slowly 2nd and 8th: chal and upsides 3 out: sn outpcd by wnr: wknd bef 2 out* **11/4**[2]

P/40 **7** *6* **Father Jim**[30] 11-11-7 ....(b) MrFelixDeGiles(7) 67
(J A T De Giles) *t.k.h: w ldr 4th to 7th: lost pl fr 11th: wknd after 3 out* **33/1**

0 **8** *1/2* **Ichi Cavalo (IRE)**[9] 9-12-7 .... MrDEvatt 75+
(Ian Cobb) *mde most to 3 out: wknd bef next* **33/1**

542/ **9** *5* **Running Machine (IRE)**[725] 3926 9-11-11 .... MrDEdwards(3) 62
(L Corcoran) *in tch: rdn whn mstke 3 out: wkng whn mstke 2 out* **20/1**

412- **P** **Kingston-Banker**[30] 10-12-0 **115**... MrIChanin(7) —
(Mrs S Alner) *t.k.h: mstke 5th: prom tl wknd and mstke 4 out: wl bhd whn p.u bef 2 out* **25/1**

6P3/ **P** **Owen's Pet (IRE)**[352] 12-11-11 .... MrGTumelty(3) —
(Mrs S Wall) *stdd s: hld up in rr: prog and prom 9th: rdn 11th: wknd rapidly next: t.o whn p.u bef 2 out* **66/1**

6m 37.2s (3.80) **Going Correction** +0.075s/f (Yiel) **11 Ran SP% 114.2**
Speed ratings: **96,95,93,93,90 87,85,85,83,— —** CSF £54.26 TOTE £15.40: £3.60, £1.30, £1.40; EX 57.10.
Owner Mrs Kate Digweed **Bred** T J Whitley **Trained** Rye, E Sussex

FOCUS
A decent hunter chase likely to produce a few winners, although the time was ordinary. The fourth is the best guide to the level. Second fence on side of the course omitted.

NOTEBOOK
Swincombe(IRE), narrowly denied in a four-mile point at Dunthrop last month, got first run on the unfortunate runner-up and his stamina enabled him to hold on after the last. Although he may be found wanting in the class department, he deserves to take his place in the Foxhunters, as there will not be many finishing better. *(op 9-1)*
Cracking Dawn(IRE) ◆, highly thought-of in his younger days and at the time believed to be as good as Sir Rembrandt when with Robert Alner, got his career back on track when scoring on his point debut at Barbury last month, and looked the potential class act in the line up. However, having travelled well in the middle of the pack, his rider seemed happy not to make his move too soon and a mistake led to him getting outpaced and Swincombe stole many valuable lengths on him. Despite making rapid headway down the straight, he was unable to reel in the winner and a slow jump at the last lost him some valuable momentum. He is relatively unexposed for an 11-year-old and could be an interesting one for the Foxhunters' Chase at the Festival. *(tchd 10-3)*
Paddy For Paddy(IRE), twice a previous winner of this event, did little wrong in defeat, but this years renewal was simply stronger and he was unable to maintain his 100% course record. *(op 9-4 tchd 5-2, 11-4 in places)*
Millenium Way(IRE) made rapid headway from the rear to loom dangerously before the turn in, but he had nothing in reserve for the final push.
Brer Bear, who finished second to Cracking Dawn at Barbury, lost his position over half a mile out and was unable to get back into it. *(op 11-1)*
Yeoman Sailor(IRE) set a fair standard and was expected to take the beating on this seasonal reappearance, but he was readily tapped for toe as the pace quickened and faded disappointingly in the straight. He may well have needed it and as a result warrants another chance. *(op 5-2 tchd 9-4)*

3911 LEVY BOARD INTERMEDIATE OPEN NATIONAL HUNT FLAT RACE 2m 1f 110y

4:50 (4:50) (Class 6) 4-6-Y-O **£1,713** (£499; £249)

Form RPR

021 **1** **Pangbourne (FR)**[32] 3373 5-11-11 ....(be) RobertThornton 126+
(A King) *mde all: jnd 4f out: shkn up and drew rt away fr 3f out: rdn out: quite impressive* **5/1**[2]

2 *20* **Fredensborg (NZ)** 5-11-4 .... SamThomas 99
(Miss Venetia Williams) *trckd ldrs: jnd wnr 4f out and gng wl: rdn and wl outpcd fr 3f out: fin tired* **4/1**[1]

2-4 **3** *1 1/4* **Boston Strong Boy (IRE)**[41] 3244 6-11-4 .... AndrewTinkler 97
(C Tinkler) *hld up in tch: prog to dispute 2nd 5f out: wl outpcd over 3f out: plugged on* **6/1**[3]

63 **4** *1 1/4* **Lady Wilde (IRE)**[28] 3435 6-10-11 .... TomDoyle 89
(Noel T Chance) *hld up in rr: prog 6f out: wl outpcd over 3f out: n.d after* **8/1**

5 **5** *5* **Nougat De L'Isle (FR)**[19] 3583 5-11-4 .... JoeTizzard 91
(C L Tizzard) *in tch: drvn 5f out: sn wl outpcd and bhd: plugged on* **12/1**

5 **6** *10* **Team Leader (IRE)**[62] 2823 6-10-13 .... StevenCrawford(5) 81
(N A Twiston-Davies) *prom: rdn and lost pl 5f out: wl btn 4f out* **20/1**

4 **7** *8* **For All Mankind**[19] 3583 5-11-4 .... APMcCoy 73
(M Pitman) *hld up and racd wd: prog 1/2-way: disp 2nd and pushed along 5f out: wknd 4f out* **4/1**[1]

0 **8** *3 1/2* **Swift Half (IRE)**[36] 3327 4-10-1 .... WayneKavanagh(7) 60
(J W Mullins) *in tch: rdn 7f out: stl chsng ldrs 5f out: wknd 4f out* **40/1**

10 **9** *3* **Legal Glory (IRE)**[50] 3001 6-11-1 .... RichardKilloran(10) 74
(B G Powell) *in tch: struggling in last trio 7f out: brief effrt 5f out: sn wknd* **20/1**

0 **10** *3/4* **Double The Trouble**[111] 1882 5-10-8 .... PaulDavey(10) 66
(R H Buckler) *hld up wl in rr: prog over 5f out: sn rdn and btn* **100/1**

1 **11** *5* **Safari Adventures (IRE)**[44] 3188 4-11-1 .... PhilipHide 58
(P Winkworth) *hld up: in tch tl wl outpcd 5f out: eased fnl 2f* **13/2**

0 **12** *3 1/2* **Migigi**[28] 3435 6-10-11 .... JamieMoore 50
(M J Roberts) *prom to 1/2-way: t.o fnl 5f* **100/1**

4 **13** *13* **Two Shillings**[28] 3435 6-10-8 .... TomMalone(3) 37
(R Curtis) *prom to 1/2-way: t.o fnl 5f* **40/1**

4m 27.5s (-6.60) **Going Correction** +0.075s/f (Yiel)
WFA 4 from 5yo+ 9lb **13 Ran SP% 119.5**
Speed ratings: **109,100,99,99,96 92,88,87,85,85 83,81,76** CSF £23.81 TOTE £6.60: £3.60, £1.20, £2.60; EX 37.40 Place 6 £29.02, Place 5 £7.78.
Owner P E Atkinson **Bred** Haras De Reuilly And Gerard Ben Lassin **Trained** Barbury Castle, Wilts

FOCUS
A modest bumper in all truth, but a most impressive performance by Pangbourne, who put distance between himself and the remainder in the straight, sprniting clear in impressive fashion. The third, fourth and fifth were all close to their marks.

NOTEBOOK
Pangbourne(FR) ◆, a workmanlike winner at Huntingdon last time, he is clearly improving with racing and having held a narrow advantage over newcomer Fredensborg as they turned in, he fairly sprinted clear once Thornton gave him a smack with the whip, looking value for upwards of 25 lengths. He has looked quirky on occasions, but clearly stays well, has a change of gear and plenty of experience to boast, so there may be worse long-shots at the Festival if that is the chosen route. *(op 9-2)*
Fredensborg(NZ) comes from a stable always to be feared in this sphere, but he was no match for the winner from the turn in and ultimately finished tired. A little improvement should be enough to see him win a similar race.
Boston Strong Boy(IRE) lacks the potential of the front two, but did little wrong and was keeping on in the straight. He will appreciate further over hurdles and can pay his way at a modest level. *(tchd 13-2)*
Lady Wilde(IRE) made a little late headway, but never threatened to trouble the winner and may find life easier against her own sex. *(op 9-1)*
Nougat De L'Isle(FR) was unable to build on his promising debut and looked unsuited by the course. He is a nice, scopey sort and will not be seen at his best until tackling fences.
T/Plt: £47.70 to a £1 stake. Pool: £48,475.30. 740.75 winning tickets. T/Qpdt: £10.10 to a £1 stake. Pool: £4,185.70. 306.40 winning tickets. JN

[3442] NEWCASTLE (L-H)

Tuesday, February 14

OFFICIAL GOING: Soft
Wind: Moderate, against

3912 JOIN VIKING RACING CLUB FOR FREE NOVICES' HURDLE (9 hdls) 2m

1:40 (1:40) (Class 5) 4-Y-O+ **£2,602** (£764; £382; £190)

Form RPR

-421 **1** **Harmony Brig (IRE)**[42] 3231 7-11-10 **115**............................ TonyDobbin 118+
(N G Richards) *led: rdn along and hdd 2 out: drvn and rallied to chal last: led flat: hld on wl* **10/3**[2]

231 **2** ½ **First Look (FR)**[72] [2658] 6-11-0 DavidDaSilva(10) 116
(P Monteith) *a.p: effrt to chal 3 out: rdn to ld next: hdd flat: drvn and rallied wl towards fin: jst hld* **7/2**[3]

11 **3** 10 **Alfred The Great (IRE)**[32] [3374] 4-11-2 PaddyMerrigan(5) 105+
(P C Haslam) *nt fluent: trckd ldrs: pushed along whn mstke 6th: hdwy and rdn whn blnd next: sn drvn and btn* **11/8**[1]

-045 **4** 11 **Ring The Boss (IRE)**[44] [3167] 5-11-3 RichardMcGrath 88
(K G Reveley) *hld up and bhd: tl styd on fr 3 out: nrst fin* **50/1**

3400 **5** 8 **Phantom Major (FR)**[32] [3376] 5-10-10 MissRDavidson(7) 80
(Mrs R L Elliot) *midfield: rdn along and hdwy after 6th: no imp fr next* **200/1**

5 **6** 1¾ **Great Approach (IRE)**[54] [2947] 5-11-3 GrahamLee 80+
(N G Richards) *hld up towards rr: sme hdwy 6th: blnd next and sn no imp* **9/1**

2506 **7** ¾ **Super Revo**[8] [3779] 5-10-10 ColmSharkey(7) 78
(Mrs K Walton) *chsd ldrs: rdn along appr sixth and sn outpcd* **200/1**

-130 **8** hd **Planters Punch (IRE)**[40] [3257] 5-11-10 109 BarryKeniry 84
(G M Moore) *chsd ldrs: reminders after 3rd: rdn along 6th and wknd bef next* **20/1**

0 **9** 4 **Calculaite**[73] [2627] 5-11-3 AlanDempsey 73
(M Todhunter) *midfield: smooth hdwy to trck ldrs 4th: chsd wnr 6th: rdn along and wknd appr next* **66/1**

10 19 **Bobbing Cove** 7-10-12 DesFlavin(5) 54
(Mrs L B Normile) *chsd ldrs: mstkes 3rd and 4th: rdn along 6th and grad wknd* **200/1**

0 **11** 11 **Mr Attitude**[32] [3374] 6-11-3 DavidO'Meara 43
(W S Coltherd) *hld up: effrt and sme hdwy 4th: rdn along after next and sn wknd* **500/1**

066- **12** 1 **Belter**[372] [3744] 6-11-0 AnthonyCoyle(3) 42
(S P Griffiths) *a bhd* **200/1**

0 **13** 16 **Gala Sunday (USA)**[55] [2444] 6-11-0 (t) MrTGreenall(3) 26
(M W Easterby) *a rr* **100/1**

14 1 **Dispol Peto**[355] 6-11-3 KennyJohnson 25
(R Johnson) *keen: hld up and mstke 2nd: sn in rr and bhd fr 1/2-way* **200/1**

P **Saros (IRE)**[155] 5-11-0 GaryBerridge(3) —
(W Amos) *a rr: bhd whn p.u bef 2 out* **200/1**

0 **F** **Arctic Cove**[72] [2658] 5-11-3 WilsonRenwick —
(M D Hammond) *in tch whn stmbld and fell after 4th* **16/1**

P **P** **Deep Rising**[22] [3544] 8-10-3 MrJEClare(7) —
(S P Griffiths) *midfield: rdn along and wknd 5th: bhd whn p.u bef 3 out* **200/1**

0 **P** **Cabopino Lad (USA)**[33] [3349] 4-10-7 PadgeWhelan —
(Miss Tracy Waggott) *in tch: to 1/2-way: sn bhd and p.u bef 2 out* **500/1**

4m 12.6s (6.30) **Going Correction** +0.50s/f (Soft)
WFA 4 from 5yo+ 9lb **18** Ran SP% **116.4**
Speed ratings: **104,103,98,93,89 88,88,87,85,76 70,70,62,61,— —,—,—** CSF £14.83 TOTE £4.80: £1.70, £2.10, £1.10; EX 19.80.
Owner It's A Bargain Syndicate **Bred** Mrs O E Matthews **Trained** Greystoke, Cumbria

FOCUS
A fair novice for the track, with the first four running to their pre-race marks.

NOTEBOOK
Harmony Brig(IRE), making the running once more, was marginally collared two from home but got back to the front on the run-in. He did not appear to be putting it all in but produced sufficient to hold on. *(tchd 7-2)*
First Look(FR) looked the likely winner when showing narrowly ahead two from home but was run out of it on the flat. He finished clear of the rest and lost little in defeat.
Alfred The Great(IRE) relinquished his unbeaten hurdling record under his double penalty. He came under pressure leaving the back straight and had no chance with the first two after a blunder three from home. *(op 6-4 tchd 13-8)*
Ring The Boss(IRE), having his first run on soft ground, stayed on from the rear of the field. He is now qualified for handicaps and a step back up in trip will suit him. *(op 33-1)*
Phantom Major(FR) made late progress from out of the pack but was never near the leaders.
Great Approach(IRE), a stablemate of the winner, did not jump particularly well and was never a factor. A half-brother to quirky Whitbread winner Harwell Lad, out of a half-sister to Hennessy winner Approaching, he should improve with experience. *(op 12-1 tchd 8-1)*
Calculaite, a winner at up to ten furlongs on the Flat, was one of the few to actually get into the race but he did not appear to stay. A sharper track and quicker ground should suit him.

3913 CANTOR SPREADFAIR CHELTENHAM PREVIEW EVENINGS HUNTERS' CHASE (FOR THE N'THUMB'ND HUSSARS CHALL TPHY) (18 fncs) 3m
2:10 (2:10) (Class 6) 6-Y-0+ **£1,249** (£387; £193; £96)

Form RPR

3-15 **1** **The Butterwick Kid**[10] [3736] 13-11-6 96 (b) MrRTATate(7) 105+
(T P Tate) *led 2nd: mde rest: hit 13th: kpt on wl fr 4 out* **6/4**[1]

3S-2 **2** 1¼ **Reasonably Sure (IRE)**[16] 6-11-10 (b¹) MrTGreenall 98
(David M Easterby) *hld up: hdwy and prom 5th: outpcd 4 out: rallied bef last: kpt on wl to take 2nd nr fin* **7/1**[3]

/2-3 **3** nk **Lord O'All Seasons (IRE)**[268] 13-11-7 88 MissRDavidson(3) 97
(J P Elliot) *hld up: hdwy 1/2-way: chsd wnr 6 out: effrt and kpt on same pce bef last: lost 2nd cl home* **7/1**[3]

P-3P **4** 19 **Kilcaskin Gold (IRE)**[23] 11-11-3 MrAJFindlay(7) 80+
(R A Ross) *chsd ldrs: pushed along fr 1/2-way: wknd bef 4 out* **33/1**

2-1U **5** 9 **Raiseapearl**[10] [3736] 11-11-6 MissTessaClark(7) 72
(Patrick Thompson) *in tch to 5 out: rdn and wknd bef next* **20/1**

6-15 **6** dist **Red Rampage**[282] [240] 11-11-6 97 (bt) MrDGreenway(7) —
(P H Hogarth) *nt fluent: led to 2nd: chsd wnr to 13th: wknd after next* **7/1**[3]

1231 **P** **Imps Way**[262] [555] 11-11-3 MrCMulhall(3) —
(Mrs T Corrigan-Clark) *hld up: rdn 6 out: sn btn: t.o whn p.u bef 3 out* **10/3**[2]

UU-4 **P** **El Lute (IRE)**[3] 10-11-3 MrREGCollinson(7) —
(Mrs E M Collinson) *sn towards rr: struggling fr 1/2-way: t.o whn p.u bef 4 out* **66/1**

03P- **P** **Shining Tyne**[23] 12-11-10 59 (p) MrPJohnson —
(R Johnson) *hld up: hdwy and prom 8th: wknd qckly bef next: t.o whn p.u 6 out* **66/1**

6m 28.7s (3.90) **Going Correction** +0.05s/f (Yiel) **9** Ran SP% **111.3**
Speed ratings: **95,94,94,88,85 —,—,—,—** CSF £11.71 TOTE £2.50: £1.02, £1.90, £3.30; EX 12.30.
Owner R T A Tate **Bred** Scorrier Stud **Trained** Tadcaster, N Yorks

FOCUS
An ordinary hunter chase in which the winner is rated value for a bit further.

NOTEBOOK
The Butterwick Kid was in front at the second and kept up the gallop to score, value for slightly further. This was a measure of compensation for horse and rider who were disqualified after winning this last year for taking the wrong course. *(op 13-8 tchd 7-4 and 15-8 in a place)*
Reasonably Sure(IRE), a maiden point winner last month, was fitted with blinkers for this debut over regulation fences. After looking held in third place up the home straight, he produced a strong finish, and he should be capable of better still as he gains experience. *(op 9-1)*
Lord O'All Seasons(IRE) ran well on this first start since May, but having looked booked for second he was caught for that position near the line. *(op 8-1 tchd 9-1)*
Kilcaskin Gold(IRE), third in a confined race at Alnwick on his reappearance, lacked the pace to go with the leaders up the straight but ran close to form.
Imps Way *Official explanation: jockey said mare was unsuited by the soft ground (op 7-2)*

3914 VIKINGRACINGCLUB.COM MAIDEN HURDLE (13 hdls) 3m
2:40 (2:40) (Class 5) 4-Y-0+ **£2,602** (£764; £382; £190)

Form RPR

6323 **1** **Laertes**[73] [2638] 5-11-2 100 MrTGreenall(3) 108+
(C Grant) *hld up: stdy hdwy 8th: jnd ldrs 4 out: led next: rdn 2 out: drvn and styd on wl flat* **9/1**

-222 **2** 5 **My Final Bid (IRE)**[32] [3376] 7-11-2 PeterBuchanan(3) 104+
(Mrs A C Hamilton) *hld up in tch: hdwy 1/2-way: led 4 out: rdn and hdd next: ev ch tl drvn and one pce last* **15/8**[1]

6233 **3** dist **Nevada Red**[50] [2979] 5-11-2 101 StephenCraine(3) 50
(D McCain) *hld up: hdwy 8th: chsd ldrs 4 out: rdn and hit next: sn drvn and wknd* **7/1**

0 **4** 7 **High Five**[36] [3319] 6-11-5 KennyJohnson 39
(S G Waugh) *trckd ldrs on outer: hdwy and cl up 4 out: rdn along and wkng whn blnd next* **100/1**

422S **5** 11 **Bywell Beau (IRE)**[54] [2944] 7-11-2 102 (t) MichalKohl(3) —
(J I A Charlton) *led and sn clr: pushed along 9th: nt fluent and hdd next: sn drvn and wknd: blnd 3 out* **5/1**[2]

0 **6** 21 **Bafana Boy**[32] [3376] 6-10-9 FearghalDavis(10) —
(N G Richards) *hld up towards rr: hdwy 8th: rdn along to chse ldrs 4 out: drvn and wl hld whn mstke next* **50/1**

P52P **P** **Sportula**[42] [3235] 5-10-12 90 RichardMcGrath —
(C Grant) *a bhd: p.u bef 3 out* **50/1**

0F **P** **Callingwood (IRE)**[20] [3559] 6-11-5 KeithMercer —
(Ferdy Murphy) *a bhd: p.u bef 3 out* **66/1**

6P24 **P** **Verstone (IRE)**[22] [3544] 4-10-0 93 DominicElsworth —
(R F Fisher) *a rr: bhd whn p.u bef 3 out* **33/1**

35-0 **P** **Cash Bonanza (IRE)**[43] [3205] 6-11-5 TonyDobbin —
(N G Richards) *bhd fr 1/2-way: p.u bef 3 out* **10/1**

P **P** **Silver Chancelor (IRE)**[43] [3205] 5-11-5 GrahamLee —
(J Howard Johnson) *a rr: rdn along and t.o fr 7th: p.u bef 3 out* **33/1**

405 **P** **Witch Power**[31] [3381] 5-10-7 DeclanMcGann(5) —
(A M Crow) *in tch: rdn along 8th: sn wknd and bhd whn p.u bef 3 out* **100/1**

0030 **P** **Brundeanlaws**[54] [2947] 5-10-7 TomGreenway(5) —
(Mrs H O Graham) *prom tl rdn along 8th and sn wknd: bhd whn p.u bef 3 out* **80/1**

P **P** **Uncle Neil (IRE)**[270] [440] 9-11-5 (b) MarkBradburne —
(P Monteith) *prom: rdn along 8th: outpcd fr next and bhd whn p.u bef 3 out* **14/1**

P042 **P** **Pride Of Finewood (IRE)**[27] [3443] 8-11-5 100 AlanDempsey —
(E W Tuer) *chsd ldrs: rdn along 9th: sn wknd and bhd whn p.u bef 3 out* **13/2**[3]

00 **P** **Ad Murum (IRE)**[20] [3559] 7-11-5 BarryKeniry —
(G M Moore) *hld up towards rr: sme hdwy 8th: rdn along next and sn wknd bhd whn p.u bef 3 out* **80/1**

6m 18.7s (0.30) **Going Correction** +0.50s/f (Soft)
WFA 4 from 5yo+ 11lb **16** Ran SP% **118.8**
Speed ratings: **108,106,—,—,— —,—,—,—,— —,—,—,—,— —** CSF £25.40 TOTE £12.30: £2.40, £1.90, £2.60; EX 34.60.
Owner Panther Racing Ltd **Bred** S I Pittendrigh **Trained** Newton Bewley, Co Durham

FOCUS
A real stamina test and few got home. The race could be rated a lot higher, but the testing conditions suggest a cautious approach is advisable.

NOTEBOOK
Laertes, who has twice had the misfortune to come up against the progressive Nine De Sivola, got off the mark with a decisive victory. He had no problem with the slightly longer trip and stayed on strongly once collaring the favourite. *(op 8-1)*
My Final Bid(IRE) has now finished second on all five of his starts, but his appetite for a battle does not seem to be in question. His hurdling was not too fluent, but he handled the big step up in trip and was beaten on merit. *(op 2-1)*
Nevada Red, who stays further, plodded on up the home straight for a distant third, passing the post something like 14 seconds after the runner-up. *(op 6-1)*
High Five was runner-up in a maiden point last year but was well beaten in a bumper a month ago. He was not disgraced on this hurdles debut but was beaten a long way by the principals.
Bywell Beau(IRE), back over three miles, set a decent pace but was quickly beaten once headed with four to jump. *(op 6-1)*
Brundeanlaws *Official explanation: jockey said mare had a breathing problem (op 66-1)*

3915 ROBERT GRAY TRAINS FOR VIKING RACING CLUB H'CAP CHASE (16 fncs) 2m 4f
3:10 (3:12) (Class 4) (0-100,99) 5-Y-0+ **£3,903** (£1,146; £573; £286)

Form RPR

-043 **1** **Mr Prickle (IRE)**[27] [3444] 6-10-12 85 RussGarritty 112+
(P Beaumont) *cl up: led 5 out: drew clr bef next: eased run in* **6/1**[1]

2550 **2** 19 **Moscow Leader (IRE)**[15] [3654] 8-11-10 97 (p) LarryMcGrath 99+
(R C Guest) *led to 5 out: kpt on: no ch w wnr* **13/2**[2]

5344 **3** 6 **True Temper (IRE)**[50] [2977] 9-9-13 77 DeclanMcGann(5) 70
(A M Crow) *prom tl rdn and no ex after 5 out* **10/1**

P-R5 **4** 4 **Jimmys Duky (IRE)**[80] [2495] 8-9-9 73 oh6 DougieCostello(5) 62
(D M Forster) *in tch: mstke 2nd: effrt 5 out: no imp next* **12/1**

6654 **5** 15 **Rifleman (IRE)**[20] [3558] 6-11-2 89 (t) TonyDobbin 63
(Robert Gray) *prom tl rdn and wknd after 5 out* **25/1**

0336 **6** 1½ **Arctic Lagoon (IRE)**[39] [3268] 7-10-3 76 (t) MarkBradburne 49
(Mrs S C Bradburne) *midfield: blnd 8th: n.d after* **8/1**

0302 **7** 12 **Glenfarclas Boy (IRE)**[36] [3320] 10-11-0 90 (p) PeterBuchanan(3) 51
(Miss Lucinda V Russell) *prom: lost pl bef 7th: no ch after* **15/2**[3]

P-3P **8** 5 **Gaucho**[21] [3555] 9-9-12 78 (p) MissTJackson(7) 34
(Miss T Jackson) *hld up: effrt u.p 11th: wknd bef 5 out* **50/1**

-PU6 **9** 23 **Jack Lynch**[15] [3652] 10-10-10 88 ThomasDreaper(5) 21
(Ferdy Murphy) *a bhd* **8/1**

5201 **P** **Mikasa (IRE)**[27] [3447] 6-10-9 82 KeithMercer —
(R F Fisher) *a bhd: t.o whn p.u bef 4 out* **10/1**

5646 **P** **Goodbadindiferent (IRE)**[25] [3489] 10-10-3 79 PaddyAspell(3) —
(Mrs J C McGregor) *a bhd: t.o whn p.u bef 4 out* **25/1**

/P-U **P** **Looking Forward**[13] [3676] 10-11-10 97 BarryKeniry —
(Mrs S A Watt) *prom tl wknd 12th: t.o whn p.u bef 4 out* **12/1**

1P/P **P** **Icy River (IRE)**[6] 3798 9-11-5 **92** RichardMcGrath —
(K G Reveley) *a bhd: struggling 1/2-way: t.o whn p.u after 2 out* **33/1**
PF55 **P** **Nomadic Blaze**[21] 3555 9-10-3 **83** PhilKinsella(7) —
(P G Atkinson) *midfield: outpcd 10th: sn btn: t.o whn p.u bef 4 out* **20/1**
4P6U **P** **Lutin Du Moulin (FR)**[27] 3444 7-11-12 **99** (b) WilsonRenwick —
(L Lungo) *racd wd in midfield: rdn and wknd 6th: t.o whn p.u bef 9th* **16/1**

5m 29.2s (0.50) **Going Correction** +0.05s/f (Yiel) **15** Ran SP% **118.4**
Speed ratings: **101,93,91,89,83 82,78,76,66,**— —,—,—,— CSF £41.60 CT £388.76 TOTE £7.80: £3.70, £3.10, £3.40; EX 68.40 Trifecta £650.60 Pool: £1,026.00 - 1.12 winning units..
Owner Smith Bannister Bowring **Bred** Mrs J O Onions **Trained** Stearsby, N Yorks

FOCUS
A modest event which turned into a one-horse race, the winner rated value for 25l. The form seems reliable enough.

NOTEBOOK
Mr Prickle(IRE), dropped 5lb and stepping back in trip, ran out a very easy winner, drawing right away over the final four fences. He jumped particularly well and, as this was only his third chase, *there should be more improvement in him, although the Handicapper will certainly have his say. (op 5-1 ctdh 13-2 in a place)*
Moscow Leader(IRE), who has been running over further, adopted a change of tactics. When the winner eased past him with five to jump he had no answers whatsoever, but he kept going to hold second. *(op 7-1 tchd 15-2)*
True Temper(IRE), a maiden over hurdles, was making her debut over fences although she did contest three point-to-points in Ireland last year. She ran respectably but is exposed as very moderate. *(op 9-1)*
Jimmys Duky(IRE) was not disgraced from 6lb out of the handicap and seems to be getting his act together. *(op 16-1)*
Rifleman(IRE) *Official explanation: jockey said gelding had a breathing problem*

3916 WIN WITH BARRY THE VIKING (S) H'CAP HURDLE (9 hdls) 2m
3:40 (3:42) (Class 5) (0-95,95) 4-Y-0+ **£2,081** (£611; £305; £152)

Form RPR
PU00 **1** **Winds Supreme (IRE)**[54] 2944 7-10-2 **78** (t) MissAngelaBarnes(7) 87+
(M A Barnes) *hld up towards rr: stdy hdwy 1/2-way: cl up 4 out: effrt after 2 out: led run-in: styd on* **33/1**
0054 **2** *1 ½* **Lord Baskerville**[27] 3445 5-11-2 **85** NeilMulholland 90
(W Storey) *in tch: hdwy on inner and cl up 5th: effrt 3 out: rdn to ld appr next: drvn last: hdd and nt qckn flat* **7/1**[3]
462P **3** *8* **Roadworthy (IRE)**[6] 3795 9-10-0 **69** oh4 WilsonRenwick 66
(W G Young) *bhd: gd hdwy on inner 1/2-way: led appr 4 out: rdn along and jnd next: sn drvn and hdd: kpt on same pce appr last* **16/1**
-050 **4** *14* **Only Words (USA)**[31] 3395 9-11-0 **83** (b) GrahamLee 66
(A J Lockwood) *hld up towards rr: gd hdwy to chse ldrs 4 out: rdn along and hit next: sn btn* **10/1**
3U43 **5** *7* **Ideal Du Bois Beury (FR)**[25] 3486 10-11-2 **95** DavidDaSilva(10) 71
(P Monteith) *bhd tl styd on fr 3 out: nvr a factor* **12/1**
502P **6** *4* **Gospel Song**[21] 3552 14-10-11 **87** EwanWhillans(7) 59
(A C Whillans) *chsd ldrs: rdn along 5th: wknd bef next* **8/1**
0U62 **7** *2* **Named At Dinner**[27] 3446 5-10-12 **84** (b) PeterBuchanan(3) 54
(Miss Lucinda V Russell) *led and sn clr: pushed along 5th: sn hdd: drvn and wknd bef 3 out* **11/2**[1]
26PP **8** *19* **Samson Des Galas (FR)**[35] 3335 8-9-9 **69** oh3 TomGreenway(5) 20
(Robert Gray) *hld up: a towards rr* **12/1**
PP00 **9** *17* **Friedhelmo (GER)**[35] 3335 10-10-1 **73** (t) PaddyAspell(3) —
(S B Clark) *a rr* **33/1**
PP-0 **10** *4* **Magic Bengie**[35] 3334 7-10-0 **69** oh1 (t) KennyJohnson —
(F Kirby) *prom: mstke 1st: rdn along 4th: sn wknd* **50/1**
5203 **11** *13* **Armentieres**[20] 3557 5-10-11 **90** (v) StevenGagan(10) —
(Mrs E Slack) *prom: rdn along 5th: sn wknd* **7/1**[3]
056C **12** *½* **Tinian**[13] 3673 8-11-3 **89** (p) AnthonyCoyle(3) —
(Miss Tracy Waggott) *chsd ldrs: rdn along appr 3 out and sn wknd* **12/1**
P-PP **P** **Kituhwa (USA)**[8] 3782 6-10-1 **70** (b1) KeithMercer —
(R Shiels) *chsd ldrs: rdn along and wknd 5th: bhd whn p.u bef 3 out* **66/1**
0334 **P** **Siena Star (IRE)**[50] 2981 8-11-2 **85** TonyDobbin —
(Robert Gray) *midfield: rdn along 1/2-way and sn bhd: p.u bef 3 out* **13/2**[2]
00P0 **P** **New Wish (IRE)**[20] 3557 6-9-7 **69** oh3 ColmSharkey(7) —
(S B Clark) *hld up towards rr: rapid hdwy and cl up 3rd: rdn along and wknd 5th: bhd whn p.u bef 3 out* **40/1**

4m 18.5s (12.20) **Going Correction** +0.50s/f (Soft) **15** Ran SP% **114.7**
Speed ratings: **89,88,84,77,73 71,70,61,52,50 44,44,**—,—,— CSF £236.09 CT £3828.95 TOTE £91.80: £16.60, £2.10, £5.50; EX 571.60.The winner was sold to Niall Hannity for 3,000gns.
Owner M Barnes **Bred** William Neville **Trained** Farlam, Cumbria

FOCUS
A poor race as one would expect for the grade, rated through the runner-up.

NOTEBOOK
Winds Supreme(IRE), who has shown absolutely nothing for around two years, was given a decent ride by his inexperienced rider and came through late to win going away. He has dropped to a decent mark and should continue to pay his way at a similarly low level.
Lord Baskerville has yet to win since going hurdling, but he has run several good races in defeat and he again gave his all in second. He will find a race at this level if holding his form. *(op 13-2)*
Roadworthy(IRE) seemed to offer a bit more with this drop in trip, appreciating the positive ride and plugging on well enough once headed. She is not the most consistent however and makes little appeal with the future in mind.
Only Words(USA), who had the blinkers back on for the first-time since May 2002, shaped a little better, keeping on late, but he was beaten a long way and will remain vulnerable. *(tchd 11-1)*
Ideal Du Bois Beury(FR) plugged on late, but never posed a serious threat on this return to hurdles.
Named At Dinner, who ran well over two and a half miles latest, was given a positive ride on this drop in trip, but may have done a bit too much in a clear early lead and he failed to see out his race, finishing tired. He is better than this and deserves another chance. *(op 9-2)*
Tinian *Official explanation: jockey said gelding was unsuited by the soft ground*

3917 VIKING RACING CLUB H'CAP CHASE (18 fncs) 3m
4:10 (4:11) (Class 4) (0-110,110) 5-Y-0+
£3,757 (£1,110; £555; £277; £138; £69)

Form RPR
2506 **1** **Red Perk (IRE)**[32] 3377 9-10-4 **88** (p) LarryMcGrath 105+
(R C Guest) *hld up: hdwy 1/2-way: led 5 out: clr bef last: pushed out* **6/1**[2]
6343 **2** *7* **Harrovian**[32] 3377 9-11-7 **110** (p) DougieCostello(5) 117
(Miss P Robson) *prom: pushed along 1/2-way: outpcd 5 out: rallied 3 out: chsd wnr last: no imp* **5/1**[1]
3-5P **3** *1 ¾* **Devil's Run (IRE)**[40] 3258 10-11-8 **109** PaddyAspell(3) 115+
(J Wade) *cl up: led 11th to 5 out: drvn whn hit 2 out: kpt on same pce* **16/1**
6361 **4** *3 ½* **Sound Of Cheers**[31] 3398 9-11-10 **108** (t) KennyJohnson 110
(F Kirby) *hld up and bhd: hdwy and in tch 11th: rdn bef 4 out: one pce next* **12/1**
P520 **5** *½* **Heidi III (FR)**[50] 2965 11-11-12 **110** (p) GrahamLee 114+
(M D Hammond) *prom: rdn bef 4 ou: outpcd fr 2 out* **10/1**
F-0P **6** *15* **Mister Dave'S (IRE)**[50] 2965 11-10-11 **95** DavidO'Meara 81
(Mrs S J Smith) *mstkes in rr: hdwy u.p after 5 out: no imp fr next* **16/1**
05PU **7** *27* **Ta Ta For Now**[36] 3315 9-10-2 **86** MarkBradburne 45
(Mrs S C Bradburne) *sn wl bhd: no ch fr 1/2-way* **33/1**
42F1 **8** *10* **Green Ideal**[22] 3533 8-11-12 **110** (b) KeithMercer 59
(Ferdy Murphy) *prom: outpcd whn hit 4 out: sn btn* **5/1**[1]
4P56 **9** *6* **Diamond Cottage (IRE)**[21] 3554 11-10-0 **84** oh3 PadgeWhelan 27
(S B Bell) *bhd: struggling fr 1/2-way* **33/1**
P5 **10** *1* **Trovaio (IRE)**[43] 3204 9-9-11 **84** oh11 (p) PeterBuchanan(3) 26
(Miss Lucinda V Russell) *chsd ldrs to 1/2-way: sn lost pl* **66/1**
-P55 **P** **Hugo De Grez (FR)**[43] 3207 11-11-6 **104** RichardMcGrath —
(A Parker) *hld up: outpcd whn hit 12th: p.u next* **12/1**
P-12 **P** **Go Nomadic**[266] 481 12-9-8 **85** (tp) PhilKinsella(7) —
(P G Atkinson) *midfield: outpcd 11th: t.o whn p.u bef 4 out* **7/1**[3]
014P **P** **Almire Du Lia (FR)**[36] 3315 8-11-2 **100** TonyDobbin —
(Mrs S C Bradburne) *sn bhd and nvr gng wl: t.o whn p.u after 8th* **8/1**
P1-P **P** **Secret Drinker (IRE)**[35] 3336 10-10-0 **84** oh2 (b) WilsonRenwick —
(N P McCormack) *led to 11th: sn rdn: outpcd whn blnd 5 out: p.u next* **16/1**

6m 23.3s (-1.50) **Going Correction** +0.05s/f (Yiel) **14** Ran SP% **120.7**
Speed ratings: **104,101,101,99,99 94,85,82,80,80** —,—,—,— CSF £36.72 CT £467.20 TOTE £6.40: £1.70, £2.50, £7.00; EX 34.60.
Owner B Chorzelewski,P Davies & P Hodgkinson **Bred** Alex Heskin **Trained** Brancepeth, Co Durham

FOCUS
A cosy win in the end for the lowly weighted Red Perk who is value for more than the official margin and the race could be rated higher.

NOTEBOOK
Red Perk(IRE), back down to a winning mark after several moderate efforts, stays this trip well and he gradually forged clear in the straight to win comfortably. Consistency has never been his strong *point, but he is clearly alright on his day. Official explanation: trainer said, regarding the improved form shown, stable's runners had been out of form but now appear to be running more consistently (op 13-2)*
Harrovian continues to run well in defeat and kept on well in second. His consistency should see *him rewarded sooner rather than later, but he will continue to creep up the handicap. (op 9-2 tchd 11-2)*
Devil's Run(IRE) ran his best race in three attempts this season, keeping on in third, but he may need a little further assistance from the Handicapper before winning again.
Sound Of Cheers, a winner at Wetherby last month, was trying three miles for the first time and he saw it out well enough, but gave the impression he is better at two and a half. *(op 10-1 tchd 14-1)*
Heidi III(FR) is a strong stayer who was simply unable to go with the principals in the final half mile, his big weight holding him back. He is honest enough, but his lack of pace will continue to hold him back.
Green Ideal, up 5lb for winning at Ayr last month, was not as effective at this longer trip and a mistake four out ended his chance. *(op 11-2 tchd 6-1)*
Hugo De Grez(FR) *Official explanation: jockey said gelding was never travelling (op 14-1)*

3918 READ ALL ABOUT IT AT RACINGDIARY.CO.UK H'CAP HURDLE (11 hdls) 2m 4f
4:40 (4:42) (Class 4) (0-100,100) 4-Y-0+ **£3,253** (£955; £477; £238)

Form RPR
0022 **1** **Seymar Lad (IRE)**[31] 3393 6-11-8 **96** RussGarritty 104+
(P Beaumont) *prom: effrt 3 out: led bef last: styd on wl* **4/1**[1]
3554 **2** *5* **August Rose (IRE)**[27] 3442 6-10-13 **90** PeterBuchanan(3) 91+
(Miss Lucinda V Russell) *in tch: outpcd 4 out: rallied and ev ch 2 out: nt fluent last: kpt on run in* **22/1**
104F **3** *1 ¼* **Merryvale Man**[3] 3853 9-11-2 **95** BrianHughes(5) 94+
(Miss Kariana Key) *led: rdn 3 out: hdd bef last: one pce run in* **33/1**
UF00 **4** *18* **Kidithou (FR)**[39] 3271 8-11-2 **95** MichaelMcAlister(5) 75
(W T Reed) *bhd: hdwy u.p 7th: kpt on fr 3 out: nvr rchd ldrs* **100/1**
06F0 **5** *2* **Political Cruise**[3] 3850 8-9-13 **83** GarethThomas(7) 59+
(R Nixon) *midfield: drvn bef 4 out: no imp bef next* **66/1**
360P **6** *16* **Ireland's Eye (IRE)**[39] 3279 11-9-13 **80** MrSFMagee(7) 42
(J R Norton) *in tch: hit 2nd: nt fluent next two and sn dropped rr: sme late hdwy: nvr on terms* **33/1**
P-00 **7** *15* **Top The Bill (IRE)**[39] 3271 6-11-12 **100** KeithMercer 47
(Mrs S A Watt) *hld up: rdn 1/2-way: nvr on terms* **33/1**
U63P **8** *2 ½* **Nowa Huta (FR)**[50] 2977 5-10-9 **90** BenOrde-Powlett(7) 34
(Jedd O'Keeffe) *chsd ldrs tl rdn and wknd after 4 out* **28/1**
1P61 **9** *7* **Etoile Russe (IRE)**[8] 3783 4-10-5 **100** 7ex (t) GaryBartley(10) 26
(P C Haslam) *cl up to 4 out: sn rdn and btn* **11/2**[2]
0-12 **P** **Court One**[223] 913 8-11-3 **98** PhilKinsella(7) —
(R E Barr) *a bhd: t.o whn p.u bef 3 out* **33/1**
3033 **P** **Our Joycey**[21] 3551 5-10-11 **92** ColmSharkey(7) —
(Mrs K Walton) *a bhd: t.o whn p.u bef 3 out* **25/1**
4365 **P** **Truckle**[31] 3395 4-10-10 **95** BarryKeniry —
(C W Fairhurst) *a bhd: t.o whn p.u bef 3 out* **8/1**
414B **F** **North Landing (IRE)**[8] 3783 6-11-1 **99** JohnFlavin(10) —
(R C Guest) *hld up: rdn 6th: no imp: fell 4 out* **14/1**
000 **P** **Swahili Dancer (USA)**[50] 2991 5-10-7 **81** GrahamLee —
(M D Hammond) *hld up: rr bef 7th: nvr on terms: p.u bef 3 out* **25/1**
0P/6 **P** **Maradan (IRE)**[43] 3206 10-10-7 **86** DougieCostello(5) —
(Mrs J C McGregor) *midfield early: sn lost pl: bhd whn p.u after 5th* **100/1**
4-02 **P** **Northern Shadows**[32] 3367 7-10-13 **87** RichardMcGrath —
(K G Reveley) *in tch tl wknd after 7th: t.o whn p.u after 3 out* **6/1**[3]
4003 **P** **Opal's Helmsman (USA)**[9] 3757 7-10-8 **82** (v) DominicElsworth —
(W S Coltherd) *chsd ldrs tl wknd bef 6th: t.o whn p.u bef 3 out* **20/1**
P22F **P** **Sergio Coimbra (IRE)**[50] 2994 7-11-11 **99** TonyDobbin —
(N G Richards) *midfield on outside: outpcd 5th: t.o whn p.u bef 3 out* **6/1**[3]
42F0 **P** **Assumetheposition (FR)**[10] 3732 6-11-7 **95** (p) LarryMcGrath —
(R C Guest) *hld up wd: hdwy 5th: wknd after next: t.o whn p.u bef 3 out* **14/1**

5m 25.0s (9.20) **Going Correction** +0.50s/f (Soft)
WFA 4 from 5yo+ 10lb **19** Ran SP% **123.9**
Speed ratings: **101,99,98,91,90 84,78,77,74,**— —,—,—,—,— —,—,—,— CSF £94.83 CT £2592.60 TOTE £4.40: £1.30, £5.50, £5.60, £25.80; EX 142.70 Place 6 £50.97, Place 5 £45.27.
Owner Trevor Hemmings **Bred** Orlagh Nolan And Barry O'Neill **Trained** Stearsby, N Yorks

FOCUS
A good winner in Seymar Lad, who ran out a ready winner of what was a moderate race and is value for further in a race that could rate higher.

NOTEBOOK

Seymar Lad(IRE), who has got his act together in recent starts, finishing second at both Market Rasen and Wetherby, found enough improvement to make a winning handicap debut. Never far from the lead, he was asked to improve early in the straight and always had things under control once going to the front before the last. Evidently progressive, it will be surprising if he fails to win again this season, before going on to fences next term. *(op 9-2 tchd 5-1)*

August Rose(IRE) appreciated this step back up in distance, staying on well in second without being able to trouble the winner. There is a small race in her on this evidence. *(op 20-1)*

Merryvale Man has been kept very busy of late, but he seems to be taking it very well and showed no ill-affects of a fall last time. This was a fair effort and he finished clear of the fourth.

Kidithou(FR) plugged on through beaten rivals to claim a distant fourth and offered some hope for the future, the step back up to three miles likely to suit.

Political Cruise ran above market expectation, but will not be winning until dropped in grade.

Etoile Russe(IRE) raised 7lb for his win last time, found this more competitive. *(tchd 6-1)*

Maradan(IRE) *Official explanation: jockey said gelding lost its action (op 7-1 tchd 5-1)*

Northern Shadows *Official explanation: jockey said mare was unsuited by the soft ground (op 7-1 tchd 5-1)*

Sergio Coimbra(IRE) *Official explanation: jockey said gelding was unsuited by the soft ground (op 7-1 tchd 5-1)*

T/Jkpt: Not won. T/Plt: £152.60 to a £1 stake. Pool: £53,603.45. 256.35 winning tickets. T/Qpdt: £143.00 to a £1 stake. Pool: £3,266.00. 16.90 winning tickets. RY

3672 LEICESTER (R-H)

Wednesday, February 15

OFFICIAL GOING: Soft (good to soft in places, heavy on flat crossing)

An all-chase card.

Wind: Fresh behind Weather: Cloudy with sunny spells

3919 MICHAEL CANNON - A SURE-FIRE BET H'CAP CHASE (15 fncs) 2m 4f 110y

2:10 (2:10) (Class 4) (0-105,104) 5-Y-0+ **£4,554** (£1,337; £668; £333)

Form				RPR
6560	**1**		**Jack Fuller (IRE)**[22] 3547 9-10-9 **87**.....(b) LeightonAspell (P Winkworth) *hld up: hdwy 4th: chsd ldr 5 out: led after 2 out: mstke last: drvn out* **7/2**[2]	110+
12U5	**2**	7	**Bay Island (IRE)**[22] 3547 10-11-2 **94**.....(tp) PaulMoloney (M Pitman) *chsd ldr tl led 7th: rdn and hdd after 2 out: wknd flat* **11/4**[1]	108
3060	**3**	16	**Elegant Eskimo**[16] 3648 7-11-0 **92**..... JoeTizzard (S E H Sherwood) *led to 7th: wknd after 4 out* **16/1**	90
R1-P	**4**	13	**Gee Aker Malayo (IRE)**[15] 3662 10-10-8 **86**..... JimmyMcCarthy (R T Phillips) *hld up: mstkes 4th and 10th: wknd bef next* **9/1**	71
5403	**5**	1 3/4	**Protagonist**[16] 3652 8-10-11 **96**..... TomMessenger(7) (B N Pollock) *hld up: hdwy 6th: wkng whn blnd 4 out* **10/1**	79
43UP	**6**	dist	**Uncle Max (IRE)**[29] 3430 6-11-3 **95**..... TomScudamore (N A Twiston-Davies) *prom: wknd after 5 out: mstke next* **10/1**	—
0P15	**7**	5	**Scotch Corner (IRE)**[33] 3372 8-11-10 **102**..... AntonyEvans (N A Twiston-Davies) *hld up in tch: lost pl 5th: wknd 7th: bhd whn j.rt 10th* **8/1**[3]	—
06U0	**P**		**Kadito**[20] 3578 10-10-0 **78** oh4.....(b[1]) WayneHutchinson (R Dickin) *hld up: hit 3rd: p.u and dismntd after 5th* **28/1**	—
5/00	**P**		**Plantaganet (FR)**[64] 2816 8-10-9 **87**..... JimCrowley (Ian Williams) *hld up: hdwy 5 out: sn wknd: bhd whn p.u bef 2 out* **8/1**[3]	—
25PP	**P**		**Hazel Bank Lass (IRE)**[8] 3791 10-10-10 **91** ow1.....(b[1]) GinoCarenza(3) (Andrew Turnell) *chsd ldrs: rdn after 7th: wknd appr 10th: bhd whn p.u bef 3 out* **20/1**	—
PP4P	**P**		**Nephite (NZ)**[76] 2583 12-11-12 **104**.....(b) SamThomas (Miss Venetia Williams) *chsd ldrs: hit 3rd: lost pl and mstke 5th: bhd whn p.u bef 7th* **22/1**	—

5m 20.5s (-3.10) **Going Correction** 0.0s/f (Good) **11** Ran SP% **117.7**

Speed ratings: **105,102,96,91,90** —,—,—,—,— — CSF £13.74 CT £136.03 TOTE £4.80: £2.10, £1.30, £3.40; EX 13.40.

Owner The Brightling Club 1997 **Bred** Susan Doyle **Trained** Ramsnest Common, Surrey

FOCUS

A moderate contest and there were only two in it from the fourth last. The winner sets the standard and the time was fair for the grade.

NOTEBOOK

Jack Fuller(IRE) was having his first run for this yard, his previous trainer Peter Hedger having retired. The drop back in trip suited and he was able to reverse recent course form with the runner-up. *(tchd 10-3 and 4-1)*

Bay Island(IRE) was tried in cheekpieces for the first time and taking a drop in trip. Always in the first two, he was collared by the winner after the second last and could not counter. *(op 7-2)*

Elegant Eskimo, winner of her sole run between the flags, was not disgraced on this chasing debut although she was booked for third place over the final four fences. *(tchd 14-1)*

Gee Aker Malayo(IRE), just a pound higher than when succesful at Worcester in April, was having only his second run since.

Protagonist improved under pressure to get into contention but was already struggling to go with the leaders when blundering at the last ditch.

Scotch Corner(IRE) *Official explanation: trainer's representative said gelding did not act on ground (op 15-2)*

Kadito *Official explanation: jockey said gelding lost its action in straight (op 33-1)*

3920 BRIAN DUNN MAIDEN CHASE (12 fncs) 2m

2:40 (2:40) (Class 4) 5-Y-0+ **£4,753** (£1,404; £702; £351; £175)

Form				RPR
052	**1**		**Launde (IRE)**[50] 3017 7-11-2 113..... AndrewThornton (B N Pollock) *led: mstke 1st: hdd appr 4 out: led bef 2 out: clr last: eased flat* **1/1**[1]	114+
0	**2**	13	**Depth Perception (IRE)**[18] 3630 6-11-2..... PJBrennan (Paul John Gilligan, Ire) *chsd ldrs: led appr 4 out: hdd whn mstke 2 out: sn wknd* **25/1**	94+
00	**3**	6	**Castle Frome (IRE)**[64] 2803 7-11-2..... OllieMcPhail (A E Price) *hld up: styd on flat: nvr nr to chal* **66/1**	86
5F	**4**	7	**Hardybuck (IRE)**[41] 3246 5-10-10.....(t) AntonyEvans (N A Twiston-Davies) *prom to 4 out* **11/1**	73
5U-	**5**	10	**Risington**[364] 3883 8-11-2..... SamThomas (Miss Venetia Williams) *chsd ldr: mstke 6th: ev ch 4 out: wknd next* **11/2**[2]	73+
64	**F**		**Cottingham (IRE)**[19] 3597 5-10-10..... KennyJohnson (M C Chapman) *hld up: bhd whn fell 3 out* **25/1**	—
0F3F	**F**		**Moorlaw (IRE)**[5] 3844 5-10-10 102..... JasonMaguire (D McCain) *chsd ldrs: 5th and rdn whn fell 5 out* **7/1**	—
0PPP	**P**		**Ellie Moss**[36] 3329 8-10-2.....(t) MrGTumelty(7) (A W Carroll) *hld up: bhd fr 4th: t.o whn p.u bef 4 out* **100/1**	—
00/P	**P**		**Golden Tamesis**[46] 3146 9-11-2 66..... WayneHutchinson (R Dickin) *hld up: bhd fr 4th: t.o whn p.u bef 4 out* **125/1**	—
23P	**P**		**Jolejoker**[73] 2660 8-11-2 95..... RichardJohnson (R Lee) *hld up: mstke 3rd (water): sn wknd: t.o whn p.u bef 4 out* **13/2**[3]	—
P-P3	**P**		**Miss Colmesnil (FR)**[27] 3457 6-10-9.....(p) PaulMoloney (A E Jessop) *mid-div: hdwy 3rd: mstke 6th: sn wknd: bhd whn p.u bef last* **20/1**	—

4m 11.5s (3.90) **Going Correction** +0.35s/f (Yiel)

WFA 5 from 6yo+ 6lb **11** Ran SP% **115.3**

Speed ratings: **104,97,94,91,86** —,—,—,—,— — CSF £33.46 TOTE £1.80: £1.10, £7.90, £13.50; EX 41.00.

Owner Dave Mee **Bred** G W Turner **Trained** Medbourne, Leics

FOCUS

No strength in depth to this maiden chase with the winner value for 20 lengths, but the time was reasonable.

NOTEBOOK

Launde(IRE), who overjumped at the first, was kept wide by his rider, not for the better ground but in order to stay out of trouble. He was headed before the last ditch, but was soon back in front and ultimately scored comfortably. *(op 5-4 tchd 6-5 in places)*

Depth Perception(IRE) is a winning pointer in Ireland but had previously shown little over regulation fences. He briefly looked to have the favourite's measure, but that rival soon asserted again. *(op 28-1 tchd 33-1)*

Castle Frome(IRE), a winning pointer, showed nothing in two novice hurdles this term and merely stayed on from well behind on this chasing debut.

Hardybuck(IRE), equipped with a tongue-strap for this chasing debut, could not go with the leaders from the fourth last and needs to return to two and a half miles.

Risington, a winning pointer, had not been seen since unseating his rider in this event a year ago. He showed ability before getting tired and might come on for the run. *(op 13-2)*

Moorlaw(IRE) was in touch, but being ridden, when he took his third fall in his last four runs. *(op 9-2)*

3921 SMARTER INVESTOR BETS WITH MARTYN OF LEICESTER H'CAP CHASE (18 fncs) 2m 7f 110y

3:10 (3:10) (Class 3) (0-125,125) 5-Y-0+

£8,141 (£2,405; £1,202; £601; £300; £150)

Form				RPR
-113	**1**		**Harris Bay**[39] 3284 7-10-10 **109**.....(t) TimmyMurphy (Miss H C Knight) *hld up in tch: lost pl 6th: mstke 11th: hdwy 5 out: led flat: drvn out* **9/2**[2]	118
3P-6	**2**	3/4	**Dungarvans Choice (IRE)**[80] 2532 11-11-12 **125**..... MarcusFoley (N J Henderson) *trckd ldrs: led 13th: hdd 3 out: led last: sn rdn and hdd: styd on* **8/1**[3]	133
22U-	**3**	3 1/2	**Desailly**[414] 3049 12-11-12 **125**..... MarkBradburne (J A Geake) *hld up: hdwy 5 out: led 2 out: hdd last: styd on same pce* **16/1**	131+
56-1	**4**	1	**Rubberdubber**[35] 3344 6-11-9 **122**..... APMcCoy (C R Egerton) *hld up: hdwy 5 out: led 3 out: hdd next: rdn and ev ch last: no ex flat* **11/10**[1]	126+
-656	**5**	3 1/2	**The Merry Mason (IRE)**[62] 2841 10-10-13 **112**..... DominicElsworth (Mrs S J Smith) *chsd ldrs: reminders 8th: led next: hdd 12th: outpcd 3 out: styd on flat* **20/1**	114+
4344	**6**	25	**Keepthedreamalive**[22] 3549 8-11-7 **120**..... BenjaminHitchcott (R H Buckler) *led: j. slowly and hdd 9th (water): led 12th to next: wknd appr 2 out* **9/1**	100+
-4F0	**7**	11	**Campaign Trail (IRE)**[11] 3728 8-11-1 **114**..... RichardJohnson (Jonjo O'Neill) *hld up: mstke 6th: j. slowly next: hdwy appr 3 out: sn rdn and wknd* **14/1**	89+
41U3	**P**		**Balladeer (IRE)**[29] 3440 8-11-2 **115**..... AndrewThornton (Mrs T J Hill) *hld up in tch: hmpd 10th: blnd 13th: sn p.u* **12/1**	—
P/3-	**P**		**Carbury Cross (IRE)**[341] 4313 12-10-6 **112**..... MrAJBerry(7) (Jonjo O'Neill) *prom: lost pl 5th: rdn and wknd after 8th: bhd whn p.u after 10th* **50/1**	—
/0F-	**P**		**Broadstone Road (IRE)**[18] 3627 9-10-12 **111**..... PJBrennan (Paul John Gilligan, Ire) *chsd ldr to 8th: j.lft and lost pl 10th: wkng whn hit next: bhd whn p.u bef 4 out* **66/1**	—

6m 10.1s (4.70) **Going Correction** +0.35s/f (Yiel) **10** Ran SP% **115.4**

Speed ratings: **106,105,104,104,103 94,91**,—,—,— CSF £38.99 CT £527.77 TOTE £7.20: £1.80, £1.40, £4.90; EX 38.60 Trifecta £374.50 Pool: £580.25 - 1.10 winning tickets..

Owner Mrs G M Sturges & H Stephen Smith **Bred** R J Spencer **Trained** West Lockinge, Oxon

FOCUS

A fair, competitive handicap that saw four in the air together at the last. The form is not that solid but might produce winners.

NOTEBOOK

Harris Bay, tackling his longest trip to date, saved ground on the inside. He was only fourth at the second last, but showed ahead on the run-in and stayed on well to make it three wins from four starts since the tongue tie was applied. *(op 5-1)*

Dungarvans Choice(IRE) had underfoot conditions to suit and showed ahead briefly at the last before having to give best. There is a race in him from this mark. *(op 7-1)*

Desailly ran a cracker on his first start since unseating his rider in last season's Welsh National, but might have been in front sooner than was desirable and he was run out of it from the last. *(op 18-1)*

Rubberdubber was taking a sizeable step up in trip on this second run over fences, and was 10lb higher in the weights. After a mistake at the last ditch, he moved to the front at the next but could not hold on. Although he is bred for stamina, he did not quite get home. *(op 6-5)*

The Merry Mason(IRE) ran a much better race than on his reappearance, although the principals had the legs of him over the last three fences.

Keepthedreamalive had seemed likely to appreciate this longer trip, but he did not appear to see it out. *(op 10-1)*

Campaign Trail(IRE) could not take advantage of a 6lb ease in his handicap mark. He was given reminders before halfway, before eventually dropping out of contention from the third last. *(op 12-1)*

3922 GUS O'NEILL AND THE GIRLS H'CAP CHASE (12 fncs) 2m

3:40 (3:40) (Class 4) (0-115,115) 5-Y-0 **£4,753** (£1,404; £702; £351; £175)

Form				RPR
13-0	**1**		**Executive Decision (IRE)**[39] 3299 12-11-9 **112**.....(v) LeightonAspell (Mrs L Wadham) *hld up: hdwy appr 3 out: chalng whn lft last: drvn out* **14/1**	117+
4-2P	**2**	6	**Lamp's Return**[35] 3344 7-11-5 **108**..... RobertThornton (A King) *chsd ldrs: outpcd 7th: hdwy appr 3 out: styng on same pce whn lft 2nd last* **8/1**	106
0603	**3**	3/4	**Lord Gunnerslake (IRE)**[14] 3676 6-10-0 **92** oh1 ow3.. AnthonyCoyle(3) (Miss C J E Caroe) *hld up: styd on fr 2 out: sltly hmpd last: nrst fin* **20/1**	90+
203P	**4**	5	**Jericho III (FR)**[32] 3387 9-11-7 **113**.....(b) PaulO'Neill(3) (Miss Venetia Williams) *led: hdd 2 out: wkng whn lft 3rd last* **11/2**[3]	107+
10P0	**5**	20	**Encore Cadoudal (FR)**[25] 3495 8-11-5 **115**..... MrMSeston(7) (H P Hogarth) *prom: wknd appr 3 out: bhd whn blnd last* **25/1**	87
-20U	**6**	1 1/2	**Terre De Java (FR)**[18] 3619 8-11-12 **115**..... JodieMogford (Mrs H Dalton) *chsd ldr: ev ch appr 3 out: rdn and wknd bef next* **22/1**	86

-P6P **7** *dist* **Per Amore (IRE)**[51] 2993 8-11-7 **110**............................(b) RichardHobson —
(David Pearson) *sn bhd* **125/1**
4214 **F** **Nagano (FR)**[65] 2802 8-11-1 **104**.................... RichardJohnson —
(Ian Williams) *fell 1st* **2/1**[1]
4006 **P** **Powder Creek (IRE)**[9] 3784 9-11-7 **110**.................... JimCrowley —
(K G Reveley) *sn bhd: t.o whn p.u bef 2 out* **33/1**
-243 **P** **Simoun (IRE)**[22] 3549 8-11-12 **115**.................... AndrewThornton —
(B N Pollock) *mid-div: wknd 4th: t.o whn p.u bef 3 out* **8/1**
21-1 **U** **Moor Spirit**[33] 3379 9-11-10 **113**.................... RussGarritty 118+
(P Beaumont) *mid-div: hdwy 5th: led 2 out: slt ld whn blnd and uns rdr last* **4/1**[2]

4m 13.9s (6.30) **Going Correction** +0.45s/f (Soft) **11** Ran SP% **114.3**
Speed ratings: **102,99,98,96,86 85,—,—,—,—** — CSF £107.89 CT £2231.33 TOTE £17.80: £1.70, £2.20, £5.60; EX 68.50.
Owner Ms K J Austin **Bred** Pondsfield Stud **Trained** Newmarket, Suffolk

FOCUS
A modest handicap in which the leaders appeared to go off too fast. The winner and third set the standard but the form is not that solid.

NOTEBOOK
Executive Decision(IRE), who had been well held from out of the handicap in a better race on his reappearance, was very much at home on this soft ground. Steadily picking off the pace-setters, he was challenging the leader when left in command at the last. He would probably have prevailed in any case. *(op 16-1)*
Lamp's Return was unable to get to the front but settled well enough. She closed with three to jump, having been outpaced at halfway, but the effort soon flattened out. *(tchd 17-2)*
Lord Gunnerslake(IRE), who had ground and trip to suit, posted another decent effort but was getting going when it was too late.
Jericho III(FR) generally jumped well out in front, but he took off too soon at the final ditch, which cost him momentum, and eventually paid for his exertions. *(op 5-1)*
Terre De Java(FR) raced in second place until suddenly finding nothing after the third last. *(tchd 20-1)*
Nagano(FR), back over fences, was towards the rear when overjumping at the first and coming down. *(op 5-2)*
Moor Spirit, 8lb higher than at Kelso, was just about in front, but under pressure, when he gave his rider no chance of staying aboard at the last. Jumping is obviously a problem. *(op 5-2)*

3923 A & A RACING H'CAP CHASE (18 fncs) 2m 7f 110y
4:10 (4:12) (Class 5) (0-85,85) 5-Y-0+ **£3,578** (£1,050; £525; £262)

Form RPR
40P3 **1** **Jacarado (IRE)**[27] 3460 8-10-7 **73**............................(v) JohnPritchard[(7)] 88+
(R Dickin) *a.p: led 5 out: j.rt 2 out: hung lft appr last: drvn out* **14/1**
060F **2** *2* **Zimbabwe (FR)**[41] 3252 6-11-8 **81**............................(p) AndrewThornton 93
(N J Hawke) *led to 2nd: led 8th: mstke and hdd 5 out: rdn appr last: styd on same pce flat* **11/1**
P001 **3** *15* **Glen Thyne (IRE)**[13] 3686 6-11-2 **75**............................(b) TomScudamore 75+
(K C Bailey) *hld up in tch: j.rt 1st: mstke 5 out: wknd appr last* **6/1**[3]
5166 **4** *22* **Ask The Umpire (IRE)**[11] 3731 11-11-7 **80**....................(b) OllieMcPhail 55
(N E Berry) *hld up: bhd 7th: hdwy 11th: wknd 13th* **10/1**
PP03 **5** *16* **Penalty Clause (IRE)**[19] 3602 6-11-1 **74**.................... LeightonAspell 33
(Lucinda Featherstone) *mid-div: hdwy 7th: hit 4 out: wknd next* **14/1**
0532 **6** *dist* **Matmata De Tendron (FR)**[22] 3553 6-11-5 **78**............. MarkBradburne —
(A Crook) *mid-div: j.lft 3rd: hdwy 7th: j.lft 10th: wknd 12th* **4/1**[1]
5PU0 **F** **Buzybakson (IRE)**[73] 2662 9-11-6 **79**.................... RichardHobson —
(J R Cornwall) *hmpd and fell 1st* **20/1**
P-04 **P** **Son Of Man (IRE)**[95] 2188 7-11-2 **75**.................... JodieMogford —
(B D Leavy) *in rr whn blnd 5th: t.o whn p.u bef 9th* **66/1**
36-P **P** **Potoffairies (IRE)**[61] 2863 11-11-12 **85**............................(b) TomDoyle —
(Mrs S A Bramall, Ire) *hld up: a in rr: bhd whn p.u bef 12th* **18/1**
654P **P** **Gay Kindersley (IRE)**[16] 3656 8-11-6 **79**.................... JimCrowley —
(K G Reveley) *led 2nd to 8th: wknd 12th: bhd whn p.u bef 4 out* **12/1**
55P0 **P** **Kirby's Vic (IRE)**[33] 3367 6-11-7 **80**.................... AntonyEvans —
(N A Twiston-Davies) *hld up: hdwy after 8th: wknd 11th: bhd whn p.u bef 4 out* **12/1**
64-0 **P** **Jackem (IRE)**[61] 2863 12-11-12 **85**.................... RobertThornton —
(Ian Williams) *mid-div: hmpd 3rd: hit 6th: sn lost pl: bhd whn p.u bef 12th* **5/1**[2]
PP31 **P** **Heartache**[40] 3276 9-11-5 **78**............................(b) MatthewBatchelor —
(R Mathew) *chsd ldrs: hmpd bnd after 8th: wknd appr 3 out: bhd whn p.u bef next* **9/1**
5-4P **P** **Rohan**[27] 3460 10-11-10 **83**............................(p) JohnMcNamara —
(R F Johnson Houghton) *hld up: hit 8th: hdwy bef next: wknd 11th: bhd whn p.u bef 14th* **28/1**

6m 12.9s (7.50) **Going Correction** +0.45s/f (Soft) **14** Ran SP% **122.1**
Speed ratings: **105,104,99,92,86** —,—,—,—,— —,—,—,— CSF £158.30 CT £1039.76 TOTE £20.60: £4.70, £2.60, £2.90; EX 221.60.
Owner R G & R A Whitehead **Bred** Robert W Fletcher **Trained** Atherstone on Stour, Warwicks

FOCUS
A weak race rated through the runner-up, and although it could be rated higher is not a contest to be too positive about.

NOTEBOOK
Jacarado(IRE) confirmed the improvement shown on his latest start and was able to record his first victory. In front five from home, he was never going to be caught despite a couple of minor errors. He is on the upgrade. *(op 16-1)*
Zimbabwe(FR), always up with the pace, ran a better race and was keeping on after the last to confirm that he does stay this far. *(tchd 12-1)*
Glen Thyne(IRE), a winner over Towcester's stiff two miles last time, briefly looked a threat when disputing second with three to jump but could make no further impression. *(op 5-1 tchd 7-1)*
Ask The Umpire(IRE), 10lb lower than when successful over hurdles last month, was never able to get into the action. *(tchd 11-1)*
Penalty Clause(IRE) faded after a mistake at the final ditch and seems best over two and a half miles.
Matmata De Tendron(FR) , down in trip and minus the tongue tie, made a mistake at the ditch in *the back straight on the final circuit and could never get into the action thereafterOfficial explanation: jockey said gelding was never jumping fluently (tchd 7-2)*
Jackem(IRE) *Official explanation: trainer said gelding was unsuited by soft, good to soft in places ground (op 15-2)*
Heartache, effectively 8lb higher, raced with the leaders for a long way but weakened once into the home straight and was pulled up. *(op 15-2)*

3924 TRENDHORSES.CO.UK DICK SAUNDERS NOVICES' HUNTERS' CHASE (15 fncs) 2m 4f 110y
4:40 (4:40) (Class 5) 6-Y-0+ **£2,761** (£880; £453; £239)

Form RPR
F2F **1** **Raregem**[271] 440 8-11-7 .... MrWBiddick[(7)] 114+
(M Biddick) *hld up: hdwy 8th: led 3 out: clr last: eased flat* **2/1**[1]
P/ **2** *24* **Bill Haze**[648] 10-11-7 .... MrRhysHughes[(7)] 89
(P Dando) *led: hung lft appr 6th: hdd 3 out: wknd after next* **33/1**
3 *16* **Nailed On**[24] 7-11-9 .... MrAndrewMartin[(5)] 73
(Andrew J Martin) *chsd ldrs: j.lft: lost pl 4th: bhd fr 6th: blnd 10th: lft remote 3rd last* **14/1**
4 *dist* **Fizzical Fizz**[291] 7-11-2 .... MrPGHall[(5)] —
(Mrs D M Grissell) *hld up: hdwy 8th: wknd after 4 out* **8/1**
U **Midnight Arrival**[24] 6-11-1 ow1.................... MrlanHowe[(7)] —
(Ian Howe) *hld up: blnd and uns rdr 4th* **66/1**
00P/ **U** **Ikemba (IRE)**[318] 9-11-7 .... MrWHill[(7)] —
(J Groucott) *chsd ldr: hit 2nd: mstke and uns rdr 8th* **4/1**[2]
32-P **U** **The Vintage Dancer (IRE)**[24] 10-11-7 .... MrGKerr[(7)] —
(Mrs Nicola Pollock) *prom tl blnd and uns rdr 7th* **7/1**
F/34 **P** **River Dante (IRE)**[213] 1019 9-12-0 ....(t) MrNHarris —
(Miss L A Blackford) *prom to 10th: bhd whn p.u bef 3 out* **8/1**
F/F **R** **Cloudy Bay Boy**[38] 8-11-11 .... MrRCope[(3)] —
(Mrs Caroline Bailey) *hld up in tch: ev ch 3 out: wknd after next: mod 3rd whn ref last* **13/2**[3]

5m 30.0s (6.40) **Going Correction** +0.45s/f (Soft) **9** Ran SP% **112.5**
Speed ratings: **105,95,89,—,—,—,—,—,—** CSF £58.20 TOTE £3.50: £1.60, £6.90, £3.80; EX 107.30 Place 6 £623.32, Place 5 £357.05 .
Owner Mrs J Alford **Bred** R P And M Berrow **Trained** Bodmin, Cornwall

FOCUS
Plenty of incident in this moderate event, which saw an easy victory for the favourite. The winner sets the standard.

NOTEBOOK
Raregem had been a casualty on two of his three previous forays under Rules, but he jumped really well and ran out a very comfortable winner in the end. This was a pleasing seasonal return and he can win again. *(op 11-8)*
Bill Haze, off the track since May 2004, was without the customary cheekpieces for what was only his second run under Rules. A quirky sort, he ran a decent race but was no match for the winner.
Nailed On, winner of a maiden over this trip at Dunthrop last month, did not jump these bigger fences well and was fortunate to collect third prize. *(op 16-1)*
Fizzical Fizz, a lightly-raced mare, won a maiden point on her latest start in April last year. *(op 7-1 tchd 6-1)*
Cloudy Bay Boy, unsuited by the rain-softened ground, was nonetheless in with a chance until weakening up the straight. He eventually declined to jump the final fence, like he did on his latest run between the flags. *(op 6-1)*
T/Jkpt: Not won. T/Plt: £601.10 to a £1 stake. Pool: £58,015.10. 70.45 winning tickets. T/Qpdt: £362.70 to a £1 stake. Pool: £3,480.80. 7.10 winning tickets. CR

3757 MUSSELBURGH (R-H)
Wednesday, February 15

OFFICIAL GOING: Good (good to firm in places)
Wind: Moderate, half-across

3925 LAGOONS JUVENILE NOVICES' HURDLE (9 hdls) 2m
2:00 (2:00) (Class 4) 4-Y-O **£3,253** (£955; £477; £238)

Form RPR
P404 **1** **Lerida**[26] 3485 4-10-9 93.................... PeterBuchanan[(3)] 91
(Miss Lucinda V Russell) *led: rdn along and hdd 3 out: styd cl up: kpt on u.p to ld appr last: drvn out* **50/1**
032 **2** *4* **Maneki Neko (IRE)**[8] 3786 4-10-12 .... NeilMulholland 87
(E W Tuer) *trckd ldrs: cl up 4th: slt ld 3 out: rdn next: hdd appr last: sn drvn and one pce flat* **13/2**[2]
4 **3** *5* **Ophistrolie (IRE)**[91] 2263 4-10-7 .... DougieCostello[(5)] 82
(J R Weymes) *hld up: hdwy 3 out: rdn along next: styd on appr last: nrst fin* **50/1**
P **4** *nk* **Minnesinger**[26] 3484 4-10-5 .... GrahamLee 75
(M Todhunter) *in tch: hdwy after 4 out: rdn to chse ldng pair 2 out: drvn and one pce last* **33/1**
21 **5** *2 ½* **Premier Dane (IRE)**[10] 3759 4-11-8 .... BrianHarding 89
(N G Richards) *hld up in midfield: hdwy appr 4 out: chsd ldrs next: sn rdn and btn after 2 out* **1/5**[1]
6 *¾* **In Dream's (IRE)**[147] 4-10-5 ....(t) BenOrde-Powlett[(7)] 78
(M A Barnes) *hld up: outpcd and bhd fr 5th: hdwy after 3 out: styd on wl fr next: nrst fin* **66/1**
0P **7** *1 ½* **Singhalongtasveer**[96] 2167 4-10-12 ....(tp) AlanDempsey 77
(W Storey) *chsd ldrs: hit 4th: rdn along appr 3 out and grad wknd* **300/1**
00 **8** *1 ¾* **Turtle Bay**[44] 3203 4-10-5 .... RichardMcGrath 68
(B Storey) *midfield: hit 4th: rdn along after 4 out and grad wknd* **200/1**
00 **9** *11* **Mr Marucci (USA)**[23] 3539 4-10-12 .... WilsonRenwick 72+
(B Ellison) *prom: rdn along appr 3 out: wknd bef next* **250/1**
10 *7* **Frith (IRE)**[278] 4-10-7 .... DesFlavin[(5)] 57
(Mrs L B Normile) *a towards rr* **20/1**[3]
U **11** *2* **Mighty Fella**[44] 3203 4-10-2 .... StevenGagan[(10)] 55
(Mrs E Slack) *keen: chsd ldrs: rdn along appr 4 out and sn wknd* **250/1**
12 *2 ½* **Buldaan (FR)**[201] 4-10-7 .... DeclanMcGann[(5)] 53
(W Amos) *prom tl rdn along after 4 out and sn wknd* **150/1**
P00 **13** *dist* **Moment Of Clarity**[19] 3594 4-10-12 ....(e) LarryMcGrath —
(R C Guest) *towards rr: hit 3rd: bhd fr 1/2-way* **300/1**
P00P **14** *6* **Mercari**[44] 3203 4-10-5 .... KeithMercer —
(Mrs J C McGregor) *a bhd* **300/1**
F **Super Baby (FR)** 4-10-9 .... GaryBerridge[(3)] 75
(J P L Ewart) *midfield: sme hdwy 3 out: sn rdn and no imp: fell last* **50/1**

3m 49.4s (-1.80) **Going Correction** +0.025s/f (Yiel) **15** Ran SP% **114.7**
Speed ratings: **105,103,100,100,99 98,97,97,91,88 87,85,—,—,—** CSF £331.05 TOTE £39.00: £4.30, £1.10, £6.30; EX 100.70.
Owner D G Pryde **Bred** Worksop Manor Stud **Trained** Arlary, Perth & Kinross

FOCUS
With the odds-on favourite failing to run his race this form has a distinctly moderate look to it and the form appears suspect despite the reasonable time.

NOTEBOOK
Lerida, with the heavy odds-on favourite failing to run his race, took full advantage and got off the mark over timber at the fifth attempt. He would be impossible to fancy under a penalty so a switch *to handicap company looks the best option. Official explanation: trainer said, regarding the improved form shown, gelding had run of race and appreciated being able to dominate*
Maneki Neko(IRE), runner-up to a fair sort at Market Rasen last time, failed to take advantage of the disappointing performance of the odds-on favourite. He will not find many easier openings in this sort of grade, and handicaps are likely to offer better prospects now. *(op 11-2)*
Ophistrolie(IRE) did not run much better here than when a well-beaten fourth on his hurdling debut at Hexham. *(op 66-1)*
Minnesinger, a fair ten-furlong handicapper on the Flat for Ralph Beckett, was pulled up on her hurdling debut here last month. This was a step in the right direction. *(op 50-1)*

Premier Dane(IRE) was bitterly disappointing in a race which did not look like taking much winning beforehand. Once again far from fluent, he was to be one of three odds-on shots sent out by the stable on this card, and each was beaten. This was not his true form and he deserves *another chance. Official explanation: trainer said horse ran flat and that race may have come too soon* (op 2-9 tchd 1-4)

In Dream's(IRE), a plating-class maiden on the Flat sold cheaply out of Brian Gubby's yard, was tongue-tied for the first time and keeping on at the finish, shaping with modest promise.

3926 ANDERSON STRATHERN HUNTERS' CHASE (18 fncs) 3m

2:30 (2:30) (Class 6) 5-Y-0+ **£1,977** (£608; £304)

Form				RPR
21P3	1		**Jupiter's Fancy**10 [3758] 11-11-7 ..... MrSWByrne(7)	94+
			(M V Coglan) *led to 11th: led again after 5 out: rdn along 3 out: drvn last: kpt on gamely flat* **4/1**2	
2	2	¾	**Gudasmum**10 [3758] 8-11-4 ..... MissRDavidson(3)	87+
			(J P Elliot) *trckd ldrs on inner: blnd 13th: hdwy 4 out: chsd wnr 2 out: swtchd lft and rdn last: ev ch flat: no ex nr fin* **4/7**1	
4354	3	14	**Starbuck**10 [3758] 12-11-7 80 ..... MrJARichardson(7)	80+
			(Miss J Fisher) *cl up: led 11th: rdn along and hdd after 5 out: sn wknd* **7/1**3	
	4	14	**Boardsmill Rambler (IRE)**10 7-12-0 ..... MrMThompson	78+
			(V Thompson) *trckd ldrs: hdwy 6 out: cl up and evt ch whn blnd 4 out and next: sn btn* **25/1**	
P/6P	P		**Little Blackie**11 9-11-0 ..... MrRWGreen(7)	—
			(S J Marshall) *racd wd: chsd ldrs: lost pl and bhd fr 6 out: p.u bef 2 out* **33/1**	
	P		**Shirostran**10 8-11-7 ..... MrCDawson(7)	—
			(Paul Williamson) *hld up: hit 9th: rdn along and mstke 12th: sn lost tch and bhd whn p.u bef 2 out* **14/1**	

6m 8.00s (3.00) **Going Correction** +0.025s/f (Yiel) **6** Ran SP% **109.6**
Speed ratings: **96,95,91,86,—** — CSF £6.77 TOTE £4.50: £1.90, £1.10; EX 10.60.

Owner M V Coglan **Bred** Miss Julie Liddle **Trained** Crook, Co Durham

■ The first winner for young amateur Shane Byrne.

■ Stewards' Enquiry : Miss R Davidson one-day ban: used whip without giving time to respond (Feb 27)

Mr M Thompson caution: careless riding

FOCUS

A moderate hunter chase and largely a re-run of a similar event held here earlier in the month. The first two sets the standard.

NOTEBOOK

Jupiter's Fancy, who finished a length and three-quarters behind Gudasmum over the course and distance last time, knuckled down well when challenged by that rival on the run-in and reversed the form on the same terms. She likes a decent surface and probably would not want the ground any softer than this. (op 9-2 tchd 5-1 in places and 11-2 in a place)

Gudasmum had every chance but could not confirm recent course and distance form with Jupiter's Fancy, despite racing on the same terms. (tchd 8-13 in places)

Starbuck, well held by the first two in a similar heat here earlier in the month, ran close to that form. (op 9-1 tchd 13-2)

Boardsmill Rambler(IRE), a maiden in point-to-points, had a chance when making a bad blunder at the fourth last, but that mistake was followed by another at the third last, and his race was soon over. (op 20-1)

3927 EBF "NATIONAL HUNT" NOVICES' HURDLE (QUALIFIER) (12 hdls) 2m 4f

3:00 (3:01) (Class 3) 4-7-Y-0 **£5,204** (£1,528; £764; £381)

Form				RPR
4P0	1		**Top Brass (IRE)**59 [2901] 5-10-10 ..... PhilKinsella(7)	99+
			(K G Reveley) *trckd ldrs: hdwy 3 out: led next: rdn and hit last: styd on* **25/1**	
0-00	2	3 ½	**Arctic Moss (IRE)**28 [3442] 7-10-7 ..... PaddyAspell(3)	88+
			(E W Tuer) *hld up towards rr: smooth hdwy 4 out: chsd ldrs next: cl up and hit 2 out: sn rdn and ev ch: hit last: one pce flat* **10/1**	
P6	3	3 ½	**Cooldine Lad (IRE)**25 [3496] 6-10-12 ..... BrianHughes(5)	93+
			(J Howard Johnson) *a.p: mstke 8th: rdn along and hit 2 out: sn drvn and wknd appr last* **14/1**	
350	4	12	**Overnight**43 [3237] 6-10-10 ..... EwanWhillans(7)	81+
			(Mrs A C Hamilton) *keen: hdwy to chse ldrs 3rd: cl up 6th: hung lft: lost pl and mstke 7th: rdn along and kpt on fr 3 out* **80/1**	
0606	5	2 ½	**Fly Tipper**59 [2901] 6-11-3 ..... NeilMulholland	78+
			(W Storey) *led: hit 6th: mstke 9th: sn rdn along: hdd next and grad wknd* **80/1**	
F	6	hd	**Ley Preacher (IRE)**83 [2450] 5-11-3 ..... BarryKeniry	76
			(G M Moore) *cl up: rdn along and mstke 3 out: sn wknd* **33/1**	
0-PP	7	5	**Killwillie (IRE)**280 [301] 7-11-0 ..... MichalKohl(3)	71
			(J I A Charlton) *hld up: hdwy and in tch 3 out: sn rdn along and no imp* **100/1**	
5P0	8	3 ½	**Stoneriggs Merc (IRE)**9 [3780] 5-10-7 ..... StevenGagan(10)	68
			(Mrs E Slack) *midfield: pushed along bef 4 out and sn btn* **100/1**	
-P05	9	14	**Platinum Point (IRE)**9 [3780] 7-11-3 ..... AlanDempsey	54
			(E W Tuer) *a towards rr* **33/1**	
43	10	1 ½	**Duke Of Stradone (IRE)**10 [3763] 6-10-12 ..... ThomasDreaper(5)	52
			(S Donohoe, Ire) *chsd ldrs: rdn along appr 3 out: sn wknd* **6/1**2	
50	11	4	**Olmetta (FR)**28 [3442] 4-9-7 ..... ScottMarshall(7)	31
			(J P L Ewart) *in tch: j. slowly 1st: pushed along and lost pl 1/2-way: sn bhd* **20/1**	
500	P		**Talisker Rock (IRE)**26 [3490] 6-11-3 ..... WilsonRenwick	—
			(A Parker) *a bhd: t.o whn p.u bef 2 out* **80/1**	
2	P		**First Cry (IRE)**272 [424] 6-11-3 ..... BrianHarding	81+
			(N G Richards) *in tch on inner: hdwy to chse ldrs after 4 out: rdn along appr 2 out: sn btn and p.u bef last* **5/6**1	
0/6-	P		**Luthello (FR)**658 [55] 7-11-3 ..... GrahamLee	—
			(J Howard Johnson) *hld up towards rr: effrt and sme hdwy 7th: rdn along next: sn wknd and bhd whn p.u bef 2 out* **8/1**3	

4m 54.0s (-0.50) **Going Correction** +0.025s/f (Yiel)
WFA 4 from 5yo+ 10lb **14** Ran SP% **115.9**
Speed ratings: **102,100,99,94,93 93,91,89,84,83 82,—,—,—** CSF £232.63 TOTE £19.90: £5.00, £6.40, £3.00; EX 280.40.

Owner Sir Robert Ogden **Bred** Sir Robert Ogden **Trained** Lingdale, Redcar & Cleveland

FOCUS

A moderate novice hurdle and, with the favourite running poorly, the form looks ordinary, rated through the sixth.

NOTEBOOK

Top Brass(IRE) had not built on his bumper promise in his first two starts over hurdles but he had apparently had treatment for neck and shoulder problems since. Someone clearly expected him to show a bit more this time as he was nibbled in from 40-1. Pushed along leaving the back straight, *he kept responding to pressure, and on this evidence he will appreciate a step up to three miles. Official explanation: trainer said, regarding the improved form shown, gelding went back to its owner after its run at Musselburgh last time and was found to be suffering from a trapped nerve, which was treated by the owner's physio, but added that gelding had always been sound in his care and probably just won a weak, uncompetitive race here ridden by a jockey who has schooled it extensively at home and gets on well with it* (op 40-1)

Arctic Moss(IRE) is another who showed plenty of promise in bumpers but had up until now failed to translate that ability to hurdling. This was far more encouraging, though, and while she found the winner staying on too strongly for her despite having the rail to help in the straight, she should be able to build on this. (tchd 12-1)

Cooldine Lad(IRE), a point-to-point winner in Ireland, ran his best race over hurdles to date, seemingly appreciating the quicker ground. (op 12-1)

Overnight did not shape badly on his hurdling debut, but he is going to have to learn to settle if he is going to achieve anything at this game. (op 66-1)

Fly Tipper made the running and had every chance if good enough. He is now eligible for handicaps. (op 66-1)

Duke Of Stradone(IRE) was quite disappointing on his hurdling debut and perhaps chasing will suit him better. (op 8-1)

Talisker Rock(IRE) *Official explanation: jockey said gelding had breathing problem* (op Evens tchd 4-5 and 11-10 in a place)

First Cry(IRE), well supported to make a winning debut over timber, moved up menacingly turning out of the back straight but he was soon being pushed along and the response was limited. Pulled up before the last, it is probably fair to assume that this was not his true form, and he was not the *only one from his stable to run below expectations on this card. Official explanation: vet said gelding was lame on right hind* (op Evens tchd 4-5 and 11-10 in a place)

3928 ANDERSON STRATHERN CHALLENGE TROPHY NOVICES' H'CAP CHASE (18 fncs) 3m

3:30 (3:30) (Class 4) (0-110,106) 5-Y-0+ **£5,530** (£1,623; £811; £405)

Form				RPR
4P14	1		**Another Club Royal**10 [3762] 7-10-5 **88** ..... (bt) StephenCraine(3)	102+
			(D McCain) *trckd ldrs: hdwy to ld appr 4 out: rdn appr last: drvn and hld on wl flat* **4/1**2	
6/20	2	shd	**Frankie Dori (IRE)**24 [3530] 7-10-10 **97** ..... MrATDuff(7)	110+
			(S Donohoe, Ire) *in tch: hit 9th and lost pl: hdwy 6 out: chsd ldrs 4 out: rdn to chse wnr 2 out: drvn last: styd on wl flat* **7/2**1	
4-30	3	½	**Forever Eyesofblue**71 [2691] 9-10-9 **89** ..... AlanDempsey	101
			(A Parker) *in tch: hdwy and cl up 6th: rdn along after 5 out: styd on fr 3 out: drvn and ev ch last: kpt on flat* **8/1**	
P22P	4	18	**Not A Trace (IRE)**10 [3762] 7-10-13 **93** ..... (v1) WilsonRenwick	89+
			(Mrs S C Bradburne) *trckd ldr: led 7th: rdn along and hdd appr 4 out: drvn and wknd 2 out* **11/1**	
6446	5	3 ½	**Little Flora**22 [3555] 10-9-10 **81** ..... MichaelMcAlister(5)	71
			(S J Marshall) *hld up: hdwy and in tch 6th: chsd ldrs 1/2-way: rdn along 5 out and wknd next: hit 3 out* **25/1**	
-133	6	3	**Theatre Knight (IRE)**7 [3794] 8-11-12 **106** ..... GrahamLee	93
			(J Howard Johnson) *in tch: hdwy to chse ldrs 1/2-way: pushed along and hit 12th: rdn next and wknd fr 5 out* **6/1**3	
3PP4	7	9	**Cirrus (FR)**58 [2922] 7-10-4 **91** ..... (b) PhilKinsella(7)	69
			(K G Reveley) *in tch: pushed along 12th: sn rdn and bhd fr 5 out* **20/1**	
3222	F		**Red Man (IRE)**9 [3784] 9-11-1 **105** ..... (p) StevenGagan(10)	—
			(Mrs E Slack) *fell 1st* **9/1**	
3461	P		**Sconced (USA)**19 [3593] 11-10-7 **87** ..... (b) LarryMcGrath	—
			(R C Guest) *sn bhd and t.o whn p.u bef 11th* **10/1**	
F1PP	P		**One Five Eight**32 [3398] 7-11-5 **102** ..... (b1) MrTGreenall(3)	—
			(M W Easterby) *a rr: bhd whn p.u bef 5 out* **25/1**	
2P14	P		**Swallow Magic (IRE)**59 [2900] 8-10-6 **91** ..... (v) ThomasDreaper(5)	—
			(Ferdy Murphy) *led to 7th: rdn along and lost pl 9th: p.u bef 11th* **9/1**	
0-4P	P		**Profowens (IRE)**74 [2630] 8-11-7 **101** ..... AnthonyRoss	—
			(P Beaumont) *chsd ldrs: pushed along 1/2-way: mstke 11th: sn bhd and p.u bef 4 out* **25/1**	

6m 4.00s (-1.00) **Going Correction** +0.025s/f (Yiel) **12** Ran SP% **121.3**
Speed ratings: **102,101,101,95,94 93,90,—,—,— —,—** CSF £18.54 CT £104.84 TOTE £7.10: £2.80, £1.40, £4.00; EX 20.30.

Owner Halewood International Ltd **Bred** Halewood International Ltd **Trained** Cholmondeley, Cheshire

■ Stewards' Enquiry : Alan Dempsey one-day ban: used without giving gelding time to respond (Feb 26)

FOCUS

A moderate handicap for novices, but the first three pulled nicely clear and the form looks sound enough for the grade.

NOTEBOOK

Another Club Royal showed that the Handicapper has not got to him yet as he defied a 13lb higher mark than when last successful. He only just held off the late challenges of the placed horses but he might be value for a cosier success than that as those two came from off the pace. There could be more improvement to come. (tchd 5-1)

Frankie Dori(IRE), knocked back by a mistake at around halfway, stayed on strongly in the closing stages and was in front a few strides after the line. His record suggests he is a much better horse on a decent surface like this, and it will be a surprise if he is not winning again soon. (op 4-1 tchd 10-3)

Forever Eyesofblue, having his first outing over fences for over a year, shaped with promise, although perhaps this sharp track did not present a great enough test of stamina for him. (op 11-1)

Not A Trace(IRE), visored for the first time, ran well for a long way but got tired going to the fourth last. The Handicapper might just have his measure for the time being.

Little Flora, stepping up in trip from two miles, shaped like a blatant non-stayer. (op 33-1)

Theatre Knight(IRE) probably needs easier ground to be seen at his best. (tchd 13-2)

Swallow Magic(IRE) *Official explanation: trainer's representative said gelding finished distressed*

3929 HORSERACE BETTING LEVY BOARD H'CAP HURDLE (9 hdls) 2m

4:00 (4:02) (Class 3) (0-130,125) 4-Y-0+ **£7,807** (£2,292; £1,146; £572)

Form				RPR
2-44	1		**Sun King**21 [3561] 9-9-4 **99** oh3 ..... (t) JamesReveley(10)	109+
			(K G Reveley) *trckd ldrs: hdwy on inner to ld 3 out: rdn clr appr last: styd on* **12/1**	
U112	2	hd	**Saif Sareea**10 [3761] 6-10-11 **110** ..... PadgeWhelan	120+
			(R A Fahey) *hld up: smooth hdwy 3 out: cl up next: rdn last: drvn flat and styd on wl: jst failed* **11/4**2	
P5F0	3	14	**Gone Too Far**10 [3761] 8-11-7 **120** ..... (v) NeilMulholland	116
			(P Monteith) *led: rdn along and hdd 3 out: drvn next and grad wknd* **50/1**	
1343	4	2 ½	**Rising Generation (FR)**10 [3761] 9-11-2 **125** ..... FearghalDavis(10)	118
			(N G Richards) *prom: rdn along 3 out: grad wknd* **12/1**	

1340 **5** *3 1/2* **Millagros (IRE)**[10] 3761 6-10-11 **113** PaddyAspell[(3)] 105+
(I Semple) *hld up in tch: chsd ldrs 3 out: sn rdn and btn whn sltly hmpd next* **16/1**

5000 **6** *5* **Border Tale**[10] 3761 6-10-6 **105** JamesDavies 90
(James Moffatt) *hld up towards rr: hdwy 3 out: sn rdn and no imp* **20/1**

0643 **7** *1 3/4* **Ballyhurry (USA)**[40] 3267 9-10-5 **104** RichardMcGrath 87
(J S Goldie) *hld up in rr: hdwy 5th:rdn along 4 out and nvr nr ldrs* **20/1**

663P **8** *1 3/4* **Tiger King (GER)**[4] 3853 5-10-6 **105** WilsonRenwick 86
(P Monteith) *chsd ldrs: rdn along appr 4 out: sn wknd* **100/1**

-214 **9** *10* **Lennon (IRE)**[39] 3297 6-11-2 **115** GrahamLee 107+
(J Howard Johnson) *hld up: gd hdwy to chse ldrs 3 out: rdn and btn whn sltly hmpd next and eased* **9/4**[1]

6000 **10** *1 3/4* **Credit (IRE)**[10] 3761 5-10-12 **116** (b[1]) BrianHughes[(5)] 86
(J Howard Johnson) *in tch: rdn along 4 out and sn wknd* **33/1**

0250 **11** *13* **Bodfari Signet**[10] 3761 10-10-3 **105** OwynNelmes[(3)] 62
(Mrs S C Bradburne) *a rr* **50/1**

/P-0 **12** *23* **General Cloney (IRE)**[9] 3784 10-10-12 **118** (b) MrATDuff[(7)] 52
(S Donohoe, Ire) *a rr* **100/1**

12-0 **F** **Dont Call Me Derek**[67] 2765 5-11-5 **123** DougieCostello[(5)] 129+
(J J Quinn) *cl up: nt fluent: blnd 4th: cl 2nd whn fell 2 out* **9/2**[3]

320- **P** **Mr Meyer (IRE)**[275] 391 9-9-7 **99** (b) PhilKinsella[(7)] —
(S Donohoe, Ire) *chsd ldrs: rdn along and wknd 5th: bhd whn p.u bef 3 out* **40/1**

3m 47.4s (-3.80) **Going Correction** +0.025s/f (Yiel) **14** Ran SP% **117.7**
Speed ratings: **110,109,102,101,99 97,96,95,90,89 83,71,—,—** CSF £42.47 CT £1627.89 TOTE £14.80: £3.10, £1.50, £9.70; EX 46.30.
Owner Reveley Farms **Bred** Sir Robert Ogden **Trained** Lingdale, Redcar & Cleveland

FOCUS
A fair race for the track but the top weight was rated 5lb below the ceiling of 130 and this did not look to a very strong handicap hurdle for the grade, although the pace was decent.

NOTEBOOK
Sun King had been running creditably in defeat recently and stepped up on those efforts from 3lb out of the handicap to end a losing run stretching back to 2002 under a decent ride from his 16-year-old jockey. This could have provided him with a welcome confidence boost, but his overall record means he cannot be backed with much confidence to follow up. *(op 9-1)*
Saif Sareea has been in great form in three runs over this course and distance since returning to hurdling and, able to race off the same mark as when second in a decent handicap on his most recent start, was just held. He was well clear of the remainder and, while he will go up in the weights as a result, he clearly remains in great form and must be kept on the right side of. *(op 2-1)*
Gone Too Far has not been in much form lately and is winless over hurdles since 2003 but, given a positive ride, this was quite promising. He will be 2lb lower in future and it will have to be hoped he can build on this. *(tchd 66-1)*
Rising Generation(FR) was just half a length behind today's runner-up over this course and distance on his previous start, so it was perhaps a little disappointing he did not finish closer. *(op 10-1)*
Millagros(IRE) beat just one in a good handicap over this course and distance on her previous start, but she showed that running to be wrong with a better display this time. *(op 14-1)*
Lennon(IRE) ran a shocker and a lot of his stable's horses are not running very well at all. He won twice here in bumper company, including on similar ground, so the conditions cannot be blamed. *(op 7-2 tchd 4-1 in a place)*
Dont Call Me Derek, well beaten when returned to hurdles at Doncaster just over two months previously, was in the process of bettering that when falling two out. He might have gone very close had he stood up. *(op 7-1)*

3930 ANDERSON STRATHERN H'CAP CHASE (18 fncs) 3m
4:30 (4:30) (Class 5) (0-95,93) 5-Y-0+ **£3,253** (£955; £477; £238)

Form RPR

2UP0 **1** **Chancers Dante (IRE)**[22] 3554 10-9-7 **67** oh4 (b) PatrickMcDonald[(7)] 80+
(Ferdy Murphy) *prom: led 4th: rdn along 2 out: drvn last: styd on wl* **6/1**[3]

-0P2 **2** *3/4* **Cool Dessa Blues**[33] 3375 7-11-2 **83** AlanDempsey 92
(W Amos) *hld up in tch: hdwy 5 out: chsd wnr fr next: rdn and ev ch last: drvn and no ex flat* **12/1**

0PP6 **3** *3* **Jupsala (FR)**[26] 3486 9-9-9 **67** oh6 (p) TomGreenway[(5)] 73
(S B Bell) *bhd: hdwy 13th: rdn along 4 out: styd on fr next: nrst fin* **33/1**

00PU **4** *6* **Terramarique (IRE)**[26] 3486 7-10-5 **75** (p) GaryBerridge[(3)] 76+
(L Lungo) *trckd ldrs: blnd 12th: rdn along 4 out: drvn and one pce fr next* **7/1**

623 **5** *12* **Gangsters R Us (IRE)**[10] 3762 10-11-5 **93** PhilKinsella[(7)] 81
(A Parker) *hld up towards rr: hdwy 6 out: rdn along 4 out: sn no imp* **4/1**[2]

PF51 **6** *12* **No Kidding**[10] 3762 12-10-10 **80** 7ex MichalKohl[(3)] 56
(J I A Charlton) *in tch: rdn along 5 out: sn wknd* **9/1**

1342 **7** *5* **Celtic Flow**[28] 3444 8-10-3 **73** PaddyAspell[(3)] 44
(C R Wilson) *trckd ldrs: effrt 12th: rdn along next and wknd 5 out* **8/1**

0542 **8** *dist* **Renvyle (IRE)**[10] 3762 8-11-1 **92** (e) JohnFlavin[(10)] —
(R C Guest) *trckd ldrs: pushed along and sltly outpcd whn hmpd 5 out and no ch after* **3/1**[1]

-05P **P** **Minster Brig**[85] 2413 7-10-0 **67** oh7 (p) WilsonRenwick —
(A Parker) *a rr: bhd whn p.u bef 12th* **100/1**

5P0- **P** **Shays Lane (IRE)**[445] 2484 12-10-4 **71** KeithMercer —
(Ferdy Murphy) *a rr: bhd whn p.u after 12th* **22/1**

2UPP **U** **Pessimistic Dick**[26] 3486 13-10-3 **75** MichaelMcAlister[(5)] —
(Mrs J C McGregor) *led to 4th: prom tl blnd and uns rdr 5 out* **20/1**

6m 4.60s (-0.40) **Going Correction** +0.025s/f (Yiel) **11** Ran SP% **113.6**
Speed ratings: **101,100,99,97,93 89,88,—,—,—,—** CSF £66.88 CT £2160.91 TOTE £8.50: £1.80, £3.00, £5.00; EX 164.60.
Owner Mrs P B Symes **Bred** Patrick Moore **Trained** West Witton, N Yorks
■ Stewards' Enquiry : Alan Dempsey one-day ban: used whip without giving time to respond (Feb 26)

FOCUS
A moderate handicap chase with the winner value for more than the official margin, but fairly solid form.

NOTEBOOK
Chancers Dante(IRE) had failed to complete on seven of his previous 12 starts over fences, and was down the field over hurdles on his most recent outing. However, returned to fences with blinkers re-fitted, he proved good enough despite racing from 4lb out of the handicap. His overall record suggests he is not one to take a short price about following up. *(tchd 13-2)*
Cool Dessa Blues, second in a novice chase on her debut over fences at Kelso, confirmed that promise with another creditable effort. She has shown enough to suggest there is a moderate race or two in her. *(op 10-1)*
Jupsala(FR), a winning pointer last year, has not been in much form since returning to racing under Rules, but this was better from 6lb out of the handicap. He saw his race out well and could have even more to offer.
Terramarique(IRE), in the process of running a good race when unseating over this course and distance on his previous start, got round this time but was well held in fourth. *(op 11-2 tchd 8-1)*
Gangsters R Us(IRE) continues on quite a frustrating losing run. *(op 9-2 tchd 5-1 in a place)*
Renvyle(IRE) failed to build on the form of his recent course and distance effort but basically looked to lose his chance when hampered by Pessimistic Dick five out. *(op 4-1 tchd 9-2)*

3931 DONCASTER BLOODSTOCK SALES/E.B.F. MARES' ONLY STANDARD OPEN NATIONAL HUNT FLAT RACE (QUALIFIER) 2m
5:00 (5:00) (Class 6) 4-7-Y-0 **£2,055** (£599; £299)

Form RPR

U **1** **Eden Linty**[21] 3563 5-11-0 NeilMulholland 90
(W Storey) *hld up towards rr: hdwy over 4f out: swtchd rt and rdn to chse ldrs over 2f out: styd on wl to ld ins last: r.o* **100/1**

1-1 **2** *1* **Knockara Luck (IRE)**[66] 2796 5-11-10 BrianHarding 99
(N G Richards) *trckd ldrs on inner: smooth hdwy over 5f out: led over 2f out: rdn over 1f out: drvn and hdd ins last: no ex towards fin* **8/15**[1]

3 *1/2* **Misleain (IRE)** 6-11-0 GrahamLee 88
(J R Turner) *hld up: smooth hdwy 4f out: rdn to chal over 1f out and ev ch tl nt qckn ins last* **33/1**

0-1 **4** *hd* **Sparron Hawk (FR)**[22] 3556 6-11-0 ScottMarshall[(7)] 95
(N G Richards) *trckd ldrs on outer: hdwy 4f out: rdn along and outpcd 3f out: saitched rt and styd on appr last: nrst fin* **12/1**[3]

3 **5** *nk* **The Music Queen**[22] 3556 5-10-9 DougieCostello[(5)] 88
(G A Swinbank) *trckd ldng pair: hdwy 4f out: rdn along over 2f out and kpt on same pce* **3/1**[2]

03 **6** *12* **Heavenly Chorus**[21] 3563 4-9-9 JamesReveley[(10)] 69+
(K G Reveley) *hld up towards rr: smooth hdwy 1/2-way: led 4f out: rdn and hdd over 2f out: grad wknd* **16/1**

0 **7** *4* **Sales Flow**[9] 3785 4-10-5 WilsonRenwick 65+
(M W Easterby) *cl up: led 1/2-way: rdn along and hdd 4f out: wknd 3f out* **100/1**

00 **8** *1 1/2* **Bella Cosa (IRE)**[10] 3763 4-9-12 PatrickMcDonald[(7)] 61
(Mrs L B Normile) *chsd ldrs: rdn along over 4f out: sn wknd* **200/1**

1 **9** *22* **Agent Lois (IRE)**[82] 2480 5-11-0 MrATDuff[(7)] 55
(S Donohoe, Ire) *in tch: hdwy 5f out: rdn to chse ldrs 3f out: sn drvn and wknd* **16/1**

00 **10** *6* **Marton Jubilee**[34] 3353 4-10-2 (p) LeeVickers[(3)] 33
(A D Brown) *led to 1/2-way: sn rdn along and lost pl over 5f out* **200/1**

11 *7* **Givitago** 7-10-9 MichaelMcAlister[(5)] 35
(B Storey) *keen: chsd ldrs: rdn along over 3f out and sn wknd* **100/1**

0 **S** **Falcon's Tribute (IRE)**[26] 3490 4-10-5 AnthonyRoss 26
(P Beaumont) *slowly away: hld up in rr tl n.m.r: stmbld and fell 7f out* **80/1**

3m 50.8s (-0.50) **Going Correction** +0.025s/f (Yiel)
WFA 4 from 5yo+ 9lb **12** Ran SP% **117.8**
Speed ratings: **102,101,101,101,101 95,93,92,81,78 74,—** CSF £159.36 TOTE £140.60: £14.40, £1.02, £5.80; EX 706.40 Place 6 £1,460.01, Place 5 £193.01.
Owner Mrs Barbara Miller **Bred** The Samurai Partnership **Trained** Muggleswick, Co Durham

FOCUS
A fair mares' bumper, but the first five finished in a bunch, and the form looks ordinary rated through the fourth and fifth. However, it should still produce winners at a similar level.

NOTEBOOK
Eden Linty, 18/1 from 25/1 when unseating on her debut in a Catterick bumper, was unconsidered in the market this time but showed that earlier confidence was not totally misplaced with a decisive success. This was by no means a strong race, but it would be unwise to underestimate her.
Knockara Luck(IRE) looked a nice prospect in winning on her debut at Cheltenham last season and following up in a Punchestown bumper on her only start this year, so this has to be considered disappointing. Her RPR was 13lb lower than on her last start, so it safe to assume she is quite a bit better than this. *(op 1-2 tchd 8-13 and 4-6 in places)*
Misleain(IRE), a 24,000euros, half-sister to the useful two and a half mile chaser Schuh Shine, made a very pleasing debut in third. She looks to have a future.
Sparron Hawk(FR), a stablemate of the runner-up, was probably not that far off the form she showed to win a similar event at Sedgefield on her previous start. *(op 10-1)*
The Music Queen got closer to Sparron Hawk than when fifth on her debut a Sedgefield and emerges with credit. *(op 4-1)*
T/Plt: £2,408.50 to a £1 stake. Pool: £38,108.25. 11.55 winning tickets. T/Qpdt: £1,685.10 to a £1 stake. Pool: £3,871.20. 1.70 winning tickets. JR

3932 - 3937a (Foreign Racing) - See Raceform Interactive

3814 HUNTINGDON (R-H)
Thursday, February 16
OFFICIAL GOING: Good (good to soft in places on chase course)
Wind: Fresh, half-behind Weather: Sunshine giving way to cloud

3938 RACING UK AMATEUR RIDERS' H'CAP CHASE (18 fncs 1 omitted) 3m
2:00 (2:03) (Class 5) (0-90,88) 5-Y-0+ **£3,123** (£968; £484; £242)

Form RPR

P414 **1** **Boardroom Dancer (IRE)**[23] 3547 9-11-9 **88** MrTJO'Brien[(3)] 116+
(Miss Suzy Smith) *mde all: clr 11th: unchal* **85/40**[1]

513P **2** *22* **Lambrini Bianco (IRE)**[217] 989 8-10-7 **69** (p) MrTGreenall 72
(Mrs L Williamson) *chsd ldrs: wnt remote 2nd 4 out: no imp* **10/1**

3161 **3** *13* **Regal Vision (IRE)**[52] 2957 9-11-5 **86** MissCDyson[(5)] 79+
(Miss C Dyson) *mid-div: nt jump wl: hdwy 11th: no imp fr next* **7/1**[3]

4004 **4** *9* **Mac Dargin (IRE)**[17] 3652 7-11-6 **87** (b) MrDEngland[(5)] 68
(N A Twiston-Davies) *in rr whn hmpd 2nd: sn bhd: nvr nrr* **17/2**

0-P0 **5** *12* **Bronhallow**[34] 3367 13-9-9 **64** oh3 ow2 (bt) MrMWall[(7)] 33
(Mrs Barbara Waring) *chsd wnr 4th: hit 10th: outpcd fr 12th: wknd and lost 2nd 4 out* **66/1**

P500 **6** *11* **Cleymor House (IRE)**[17] 3656 8-9-11 **62** oh8 (b) MrGTumelty[(3)] 20
(John R Upson) *chsd ldrs to 10th* **8/1**

0PP5 **7** *dist* **Redhouse Chevalier**[15] 3672 7-9-10 **65** (b) MrTCollier[(7)] —
(B G Powell) *j.lft 1st: mid-div: lost pl 5th: bhd fr 8th* **33/1**

0-PP **8** *9* **Lantern Lad (IRE)**[37] 3338 10-11-0 **81** (p) MissSSharratt[(5)] —
(R Ford) *bhd fr 5th* **33/1**

-000 **F** **Manque Pas D'Air (FR)**[17] 3648 6-11-2 **85** MrRMcCarthy[(7)] —
(T R George) *fell 1st* **16/1**

P30P **U** **Maybeseven**[14] 3688 12-9-8 **63** (b) MrCHughes[(7)] —
(R Dickin) *hmpd and uns rdr 1st* **25/1**

0P30 **U** **Soroka (IRE)**[23] 3547 7-9-9 **64** oh6 ow2 (b) MrCKester[(7)] —
(C N Kellett) *prom: blnd and uns rdr 3rd* **66/1**

PP43 **U** **Aisjem (IRE)**[13] 3716 7-10-1 **70** (p) MrRhysHughes[(7)] —
(Evan Williams) *w wnr tl blnd and uns rdr 2nd* **6/1**[2]

60/ **P** **Kestle Mill (IRE)**[732] 10-9-8 **63** (t) MissRAGreen[(7)] —
(M J Coombe) *bhd fr 4th: t.o whn p.u bef 14th* **12/1**

6m 26.0s (13.70) **Going Correction** +0.675s/f (Soft) **13** Ran SP% **115.8**
Speed ratings: **104,96,92,89,85 81,—,—,—,— —,—,—** CSF £22.06 CT £126.79 TOTE £2.80: £1.50, £2.90, £2.00; EX 23.60.
Owner Dr D J Meecham Jones **Bred** Patrick Higgins **Trained** Lewes, E Sussex

FOCUS
A very weak handicap which saw the field finish well strung out behind the impressive winner. The runner-up is the best guide to the level of the form.

NOTEBOOK

Boardroom Dancer(IRE) got back to winning ways with a commanding display of front-running under top weight and clearly relished the return to this faster surface. He had his rivals in trouble from an early stage and, while he can now expect a hike in the weights, he is relatively lightly-raced for his age and really is in great heart at present. *(op 5-2)*

Lambrini Bianco(IRE), last seen pulling up at Cartmel 217 days previously, stayed on at his own pace and is entitled to improve a deal for this outing. *(op 9-1 tchd 17-2)*

Regal Vision(IRE), raised 4lb for winning over course and distance last time, failed to jump with any fluency and was never a serious threat. He can do better, but evidently has two ways of running. *(op 8-1 tchd 6-1)*

Mac Dargin(IRE), back up in trip, appeared to lose his confidence after being hampered at the second fence and proved disappointing. *(op 9-1)*

3939 CASH CONVERTERS LINCOLN JUVENILE NOVICES' HURDLE (8 hdls) 2m 110y

2:30 (2:32) (Class 4) 4-Y-O **£3,253** (£955; £477; £238)

Form RPR

43 **1** **Linnet (GER)**[12] 3722 4-10-3 GrahamLee 105+
(Ian Williams) *chsd ldrs: lft in ld 3 out: drvn out* **15/8**[2]

402 **2** *1* **Flaming Weapon**[13] 3714 4-11-1 108 PhilipHide 114
(G L Moore) *hld up in tch: chal 2 out: rdn flat: no ex nr fin* **12/1**[3]

3 **3** *15* **Rawaabet (IRE)**[19] 1955 4-10-10 JimmyMcCarthy 94
(P W Hiatt) *hld up: hdwy appr 3 out: rdn and wknd last* **22/1**

05 **4** *6* **Estate**[36] 3340 4-10-10 JohnMcNamara 88
(R S Brookhouse) *hld up: hdwy 3 out: mstke and wknd next* **18/1**

6 **5** *3 ½* **Ramsgill (USA)**[9] 1797 4-10-10 PaulMoloney 85
(N P Littmoden) *led to 3 out: wknd bef next* **22/1**

05 **6** *5* **Benedict Bay**[30] 3436 4-10-3 (v) SimonElliott(7) 80
(J A Geake) *mid-div: mstke 4th: wknd next* **80/1**

0 **7** *10* **The Chequered Lady**[13] 3714 4-10-3 JamesDavies 63
(T D McCarthy) *hld up in tch: plld hrd: wkng whn hmpd 3 out* **400/1**

8 *shd* **New Wave**[142] 4-10-10 TomDoyle 69
(R Lee) *hld up: hdwy appr 3 out: sn wknd* **40/1**

6P15 **9** *20* **Dishdasha (IRE)**[122] 1774 4-11-1 94 AndrewThornton 54
(C R Dore) *hld up: sme hdwy after 5th: sn wknd* **100/1**

00P **10** *5* **Top Man Tee**[30] 3431 4-10-3 (t) MrMatthewSmith(7) 44
(D J Daly) *mid-div: mstke 1st: bhd fr 5th* **150/1**

00P **11** *2* **Keresforth**[36] 2949 4-10-10 (p) LeightonAspell 42
(Mrs L C Jewell) *hld up: mstke and rdn 5th: a in rr* **200/1**

B0 **12** *9* **Son Of Bathwick (IRE)**[30] 3429 4-10-10 SeanCurran 33
(Mrs Norma Pook) *w ldr tl mstke 5th: wknd bef next* **250/1**

50 **B** **Patronage**[13] 3714 4-10-10 NoelFehily —
(Jonjo O'Neill) *hld up: in rr whn b.d 3 out* **28/1**

P **Polesworth**[11] 4-10-3 JosephByrne —
(C N Kellett) *hld up: a bhd: t.o whn p.u bef 2 out* **400/1**

P0 **P** **Akram (IRE)**[30] 3431 4-10-10 MickFitzgerald —
(Jonjo O'Neill) *prom to 4th: t.o whn p.u bef 2 out* **33/1**

5006 **P** **Ember Dancer**[9] 3787 4-10-7 PaulO'Neill(3) —
(Ian Williams) *plld hrd: sddle slipped and p.u after 1st* **100/1**

1 **F** **Princelet (IRE)**[28] 3463 4-11-1 APMcCoy —
(N J Henderson) *prom: j.rt 3rd: chsd ldr 5th: led and fell next* **11/10**[1]

P **Precious Sammi**[241] 4-10-10 AntonyProcter —
(Lucinda Featherstone) *hld up: mstke 3rd: a in rr: t.o whn p.u bef 2 out* **250/1**

4m 3.50s (7.80) **Going Correction** +0.675s/f (Soft) **18** Ran SP% **118.6**
Speed ratings: **108,107,100,97,96 93,88,88,79,77 76,71,—,—,— —,—,—** CSF £21.85 TOTE £3.20: £1.10, £3.60, £4.10; EX 30.10.
Owner Cockbury Court Partnership **Bred** Gestut Hof Ittlingen **Trained** Portway, Worcs

FOCUS

A modest juvenile hurdle, run at a fair pace, and the first two came clear. The third sets the level and the form should work out well enough.

NOTEBOOK

Linnet(GER) got off the mark at the third attempt over hurdles and must rate a fortunate winner. She was left in front after the departure of the favourite three from home - when that rival looked to have her measure - and had to then work hard to see off the eventual runner-up despite being in receipt of 12lb. That said, the balance of her form to date in this sphere is above average, and she remains open to further improvement. *(op 9-4)*

Flaming Weapon went down fighting and again emerges with credit in defeat. He is vulnerable under his penalty in this division, but has found his feet again now, and is a decent benchmark for this form. *(op 10-1 tchd 14-1)*

Rawaabet(IRE), third on his hurdling debut in October and fit from a recent spin on the Flat, could offer no more approaching the final flight and ultimately was well held. However, this must still rate another fair effort, and he should be of more interest over timber when eligible for handicaps after his next outing.

Estate, having his first run for new connections, tired approaching the penultimate flight, yet still *offered enough to suggest he can find a race in due course and now qualifies for handicaps. (op 20-1)*

Princelet(IRE), off the mark on his hurdling debut at Taunton 28 days previously, looked all over the winner prior to falling three from home and must rate unfortunate. He can make amends before too long. *(op Evens tchd 6-5 in a place)*

Precious Sammi *Official explanation: vet said gelding bled from the nose (op Evens tchd 6-5 in a place)*

Ember Dancer *Official explanation: jockey said saddle slipped (op Evens tchd 6-5 in a place)*

3940 HUNTINGDON-RACECOURSE.CO.UK NOVICES' H'CAP CHASE (16 fncs) 2m 4f 110y

3:00 (3:02) (Class 3) (0-115,115) 5-Y-O+ **£6,506** (£1,910; £955; £477)

Form RPR

5110 **1** **Magico (NZ)**[26] 3507 8-11-4 110 (b) PaulO'Neill(3) 124+
(Miss Venetia Williams) *chsd ldrs: led 11th: hit last: rdn out* **7/1**

P3U2 **2** *5* **Priscilla**[7] 3815 8-10-10 99 JohnMcNamara 103+
(K Bishop) *hld up: mstkes 6th and next: hdwy 10th: chsd wnr appr 2 out: sn rdn: styd on same pce last* **3/1**[1]

343U **3** *nk* **Cyborg De Sou (FR)**[38] 3317 8-11-6 109 RichardMcGrath 112
(G A Harker) *hld up: hdwy 3 out: rdn appr last: styd on same pce* **6/1**[2]

0/50 **4** *19* **Pin High (IRE)**[70] 2723 7-10-8 97 PaulMoloney 81
(Miss H C Knight) *hld up: wknd appr 3 out* **20/1**

-53F **5** *10* **Quatrain (IRE)**[17] 3652 6-10-4 93 (t) TomDoyle 77+
(D R Gandolfo) *hld up: wknd 3 out: bhd whn blnd last* **13/2**[3]

-2PP **6** *3* **Majestic Moonbeam (IRE)**[30] 3434 8-10-8 97 (b[1]) APMcCoy 68
(Jonjo O'Neill) *prom: chsd wnr 3 out: rdn and wknd bef next* **15/2**

4P24 **7** *10* **Kyper Disco (FR)**[28] 3465 8-11-1 104 (t) MickFitzgerald 65
(N J Henderson) *chsd ldr: j.lft 5th: mstke 9th: rdn 3 out: wknd bef next* **6/1**[2]

-135 **P** **King Coal (IRE)**[40] 3284 7-11-3 106 LeightonAspell —
(R Rowe) *led to 11th: wknd after next: t.o whn p.u bef 2 out* **13/2**[3]

2006 **P** **Haloo Baloo**[16] 3658 6-10-10 99 NoelFehily —
(Jonjo O'Neill) *mid-div: dropped rr 6th: bhd fr 8th: t.o whn p.u bef 12th* **25/1**

5m 22.4s (16.30) **Going Correction** +0.675s/f (Soft) **9** Ran SP% **113.1**
Speed ratings: **95,93,92,85,81 80,76,—,—** CSF £28.72 CT £133.13 TOTE £7.00: £2.50, £1.60, £2.30; EX 19.90.
Owner Paul Beck **Bred** Bardowie Stud Ltd **Trained** Kings Caple, H'fords

FOCUS

A modest novices' handicap, run at an average pace, and the first three came well clear. he winner is value for ten lengths with the placed horses to form.

NOTEBOOK

Magico(NZ), thwarted in his bid for the hat-trick from this mark last time, showed his true colours on this return to novice company and resumed winning ways with a decisive success. The average pace over this trip was much to his liking, but his jumping was assured bar the final fence, and he *proved a cut above this opposition. Official explanation: trainer's representative said, regarding improved form shown, gelding was suited by drop in class and had been slightly hampered on previous run (op 13-2 tchd 11-2)*

Priscilla is starting to become a little frustrating to follow now, but still posted another sound effort in defeat and shaped as though she really needs a longer trip to be seen at her best. *(op 7-2)*

Cyborg De Sou(FR) ◆ looked a threat to the winner when making ground from off the pace turning for home, yet he failed to sustain his effort from two out and did not see out this longer trip all that well. He is on a decent mark in relation to his hurdles rating and can resume winning ways if reverting to a shorter distance in the coming weeks. *(op 13-2 tchd 15-2)*

Pin High(IRE), making his chasing debut, failed to stay this distance and did enough to suggest he will be better off back over two miles. He is fragile, but has a race over fences within his compass from this sort of mark. *(op 14-1)*

Kyper Disco(FR) never looked happy after blundering at the ninth fence and again disappointed. He is one to avoid. *(op 11-2 tchd 13-2)*

3941 ADVANCE PLUMBING "NATIONAL HUNT" NOVICES' HURDLE (12 hdls) 3m 2f

3:30 (3:31) (Class 4) 5-Y-O+ **£3,903** (£1,146; £573; £286)

Form RPR

0612 **1** **Harrycone Lewis**[31] 3420 8-11-6 117 (b) PaulMoloney 118+
(Mrs P Sly) *chsd ldrs: led and mstke 9th: clr whn hit last* **7/2**[2]

3-54 **2** *5* **Original Thought (IRE)**[62] 2866 6-11-0 NoelFehily 102
(B De Haan) *led 2nd to 9th: ev ch 3 out: sn rdn: styd on same pce fr next* **12/1**

2226 **3** *16* **Love Of Classics**[27] 3477 6-11-0 115 (v) LeightonAspell 90+
(O Sherwood) *mid-div: hdwy 8th: wkng whn mstke 3 out* **7/2**[2]

-536 **4** *dist* **Geordie Peacock (IRE)**[15] 3677 7-10-11 PaulO'Neill(3) —
(Miss Venetia Williams) *prom: racd keenly: wknd appr 3 out* **17/2**[3]

40P **P** **Ballyowen (IRE)**[75] 2638 7-11-0 PJBrennan —
(Mrs P Sly) *hld up: a in rr: t.o whn p.u bef 9th* **66/1**

3200 **P** **Back With A Bang (IRE)**[62] 2864 7-11-0 JodieMogford —
(Mrs N S Evans) *bhd fr 5th: t.o whn p.u bef 8th* **66/1**

-P **P** **Pine Marten**[43] 3240 7-11-0 (v[1]) JimmyMcCarthy —
(J A Geake) *prom: mstke and lost pl 5th: t.o whn p.u bef 9th* **100/1**

0-06 **P** **Stark Raven**[106] 1990 6-11-0 MarcusFoley —
(Miss E C Lavelle) *chsd ldrs tl wknd appr 8th: t.o whn p.u bef next* **50/1**

P **It Plays Itself (IRE)** 7-11-0 APMcCoy —
(Jonjo O'Neill) *hld up: hdwy 8th: rdn and wknd after next: t.o whn p.u bef 2 out* **11/1**

000 **P** **Nigwell Forbees (IRE)**[34] 3376 5-11-0 GrahamLee —
(J Howard Johnson) *hld up: hdwy after 5th: wknd after 7th: p.u bef next* **80/1**

0-P0 **P** **Katy's Classic (IRE)**[14] 3685 6-11-0 (p) JamesDavies —
(K C Bailey) *in rr: rdn after 3rd: bhd fr 7th: t.o whn p.u bef 2 out* **100/1**

44F- **P** **Lord Atterbury (IRE)**[313] 4772 10-10-7 AndrewGlassonbury(7) —
(M C Pipe) *chsd ldrs: rdn after 7th: wknd bef next: t.o whn p.u bef 2 out* **15/8**[1]

05P **P** **Buffers Lane (IRE)**[27] 3478 7-10-7 MarcGoldstein(7) —
(N A Twiston-Davies) *chsd ldrs: mstke 3rd: j.lft 7th: wknd appr 3 out: p.u bef next* **28/1**

6m 37.9s (15.50) **Going Correction** +0.675s/f (Soft) **13** Ran SP% **117.4**
Speed ratings: **103,101,96,—,— —,—,—,—,— —,—,—** CSF £42.11 TOTE £5.60: £1.80, £3.60, £1.40; EX 43.40.
Owner The Craftsmen **Bred** Mrs P Sly **Trained** Thorney, Cambs

FOCUS

A modest novice event, which proved a real stamina test, and just four runners completed. The winner is value for twice the official margin with the runner-up improving but the third below form.

NOTEBOOK

Harrycone Lewis, with the blinkers back on, made a successful return to hurdling and should be rated value for further than his winning margin as he was idling on the run-in. He is clearly a dour stayer, has now won twice from as many starts over course and distance, and has developed into a very consistent novice hurdler now. *(op 4-1 after early 5-1 and 9-2 in places)*

Original Thought(IRE) was the only one to go with the winner approaching the home turn, but he was always playing second fiddle to that rival and was eventually firmly put in his place. However, he still finished a clear second-best and improved for the stiffer test, so ought to be placed to advantage in this sphere before too long. *(op 10-1)*

Love Of Classics turned in a below-par effort and failed to really improve for the return to this better ground. He is a tricky ride, but is probably a happier horse over a shorter trip. *(tchd 4-1)*

Geordie Peacock(IRE) ultimately paid for running too freely through the early parts and proved disappointing. He is not progressing as once appeared likely. *(op 8-1)*

Lord Atterbury(IRE) , last seen falling at the first fence in last season's Grand National, was injured while running loose at Aintree. Having his first ever outing over timber, he stopped very quickly when the race started to get serious and proved very disappointing. *(op 5-2)*

Back With A Bang(IRE) *Official explanation: trainer said gelding was unsuited by good (good to soft in places) ground (op 5-2)*

3942 WEATHERBYS PRINTING H'CAP CHASE (19 fncs) 3m

4:00 (4:02) (Class 3) (0-130,130) 5-Y-O+ **£6,665** (£2,069; £1,114)

Form RPR

621P **1** **Cruising River (IRE)**[45] 3213 7-11-0 118 PaulMoloney 117
(Miss H C Knight) *a.p: chsd clr ldr 3rd: lft in ld 12th: rdn and hung rt flat: all out* **25/1**

-PPP **2** *nk* **Distant Thunder (IRE)**[40] 3296 8-11-8 126 AndrewThornton 125
(R H Alner) *hld up: hdwy 8th: lft 3rd 12th: chsd wnr 14th to 4 out: wnt 2nd again 2 out: styd on u.p* **11/2**[3]

2430 **3** *18* **Pak Jack (FR)**[82] 2489 6-11-3 121 PJBrennan 102
(P J Hobbs) *hld up: hdwy 13th: wknd appr 2 out* **7/1**

-064 **F** **Jack Martin (IRE)**[20] 3596 9-10-10 114 JohnMcNamara —
(S Gollings) *pckd 1st: hld up: fell 9th* **33/1**

0001 **P** **Migwell (FR)**[52] 2959 6-11-5 123 JimmyMcCarthy —
(Mrs L Wadham) *hld up: a in rr: t.o whn p.u bef 15th* **8/1**

12P **P** **Gallik Dawn**[19] 3614 8-10-7 **111** .... MickFitzgerald —
(A Hollingsworth) *bhd fr 4tf: t.o whn p.u bef 11th* **16/1**

2R21 **U** **Shining Strand**[17] 3653 7-11-2 **120** .... AndrewTinkler —
(N J Henderson) *led: clr 3rd tl tried to run out and uns rdr appr 12th* **5/2**[1]

0F-P **C** **Broadstone Road (IRE)**[1] 3921 9-10-2 **111** .... JohnnyLevins(5) —
(Paul John Gilligan, Ire) *chsd ldrs to 5th: in rr whn carried out 10th* **150/1**

61P1 **P** **Glacial Delight (IRE)**[38] 3326 7-11-3 **121** .... MarcusFoley —
(Miss E C Lavelle) *hld up: hmpd 9th: hdwy 13th: wknd 15th: t.o whn p.u bef 2 out* **8/1**

216- **P** **Eric's Charm (FR)**[336] 4407 8-11-12 **130** .... LeightonAspell —
(O Sherwood) *mstkes: chsd ldr to 3rd: remained handy tl wknd and p.u bef 3 out* **9/2**[2]

031 **P** **Thistlecraft (IRE)**[31] 3419 7-11-7 **125** .... NoelFehily 106
(C C Bealby) *hld up: hdwy and hit 11th: chsd wnr 4 out: rdn and ev ch after next: wkng whn blnd 2 out: p.u bef last* **20/1**

6m 22.1s (9.80) **Going Correction** +0.675s/f (Soft) **11** Ran SP% **115.0**
Speed ratings: **110,109,103,—,— —,—,—,—,—** — CSF £152.33 CT £1083.25 TOTE £33.60: £7.20, £2.40, £2.20; EX 202.00 Trifecta £563.00 Part won. Pool: £793.00 - 0.30 winning tickets..
Owner Four Stablemates **Bred** John And Paul Cousins **Trained** West Lockinge, Oxon

FOCUS
A decent handicap for the class, run at a solid pace, and only three runners managed to complete. The winner is the best guide to the form but not a race to be confident about.

NOTEBOOK
Cruising River(IRE), pulled up in novice company last time, showed a decent attitude to hold off the persistent challenge of the runner-up and make a winning handicap debut. The return to a better surface was clearly much to his liking, his jumping was assured, and he does stay very well. Despite an inevitable rise in the weights, he should have more to offer in this sphere, and is a possible contender for the National Hunt Chase at Cheltenham next month. *(op 33-1)*
Distant Thunder(IRE), pulled up on his previous three outings, bounced back to form with a brave effort in defeat. He may well have won under a more positive ride, but his confidence will still have been done the world of good by this experience, and he could be an interesting contender for the William Hill Handicap at the Cheltenham Festival, as he is undeniably well-handicapped at present in relation to his novice form. *(tchd 6-1)*
Pak Jack(FR), stepping up from two miles, was running a decent race until his lack of stamina became apparent approaching the turn for home. He is struggling for an optimum trip at present, but he does have the talent to score from this mark, and is worth dropping back to around two and a half miles for his next assignment. *(op 8-1)*
Eric's Charm(FR), last seen finishing sixth in the Jewson Novices' Handicap at the Cheltenham Festival 336 days previously, stopped quickly when push came to shove and was disappointingly pulled up. He has a deal to prove now. *(tchd 5-1)*
Gallik Dawn *Official explanation: trainer said gelding was unsuited by good (good to soft in places) ground (tchd 5-1)*
Shining Strand, who made all in a beginners' chase at Southwell last time on his fencing bow, was still going strongly in front prior to trying to run out approaching the 12th fence and giving Tinkler no chance of maintaining their partnership. This was a stiff enough task considering it was only his second outing over fences, and he clearly has an engine, but his quirky nature dictates he can never be backed with any real confidence. *(tchd 5-1)*
Glacial Delight(IRE), raised 8lb for winning at Taunton last time, evidently does not possess the ability to run consecutive races alike. *(tchd 5-1)*

3943 KEECH COTTAGE CHILDREN'S HOSPICE NOVICES' H'CAP HURDLE (10 hdls) 2m 4f 110y
4:30 (4:35) (Class 4) (0-110,106) 4-Y-0+ **£3,253** (£955; £477; £238)

Form RPR

4403 **1** **Herakles (GER)**[17] 3650 5-11-9 **103** .... MickFitzgerald 118+
(N J Henderson) *hld up: hdwy 7th: led last: r.o wl* **9/4**[1]

4246 **2** *2 ½* **Water Taxi**[52] 2977 5-11-7 **101** .... KeithMercer 108+
(Ferdy Murphy) *hld up: hdwy after 5th: led 2 out: hdd and nt fluent last: sn outpcd* **15/2**[3]

6322 **3** *12* **Mistified (IRE)**[21] 3577 5-10-7 **90** .... RichardYoung(3) 83
(J W Mullins) *hld up: rdn 7th: styd on fr 2 out: n.d* **5/1**[2]

05-6 **4** *shd* **Liberty Ben (IRE)**[14] 3694 6-11-4 **98** .... AndrewThornton 92+
(R H Alner) *chsd ldrs: led after 7th: hdd 2 out: wknd last* **20/1**

364 **5** *3 ½* **Legally Fast (USA)**[28] 3464 4-11-1 **105** .... PJBrennan 86+
(S C Burrough) *hld up: plld hrd: hdwy 6th: ev ch 3 out: wknd last* **10/1**

5000 **6** *6* **Hialeah**[38] 3314 5-10-13 **96** .... MrTGreenall(3) 80
(M W Easterby) *hld up in tch: rdn and wknd appr 2 out: no ch whn blnd last* **33/1**

2236 **7** *8* **Corker**[16] 3664 4-11-0 **104** .... JamesDavies 70
(D B Feek) *hld up: mstkes 3rd and 5th: rdn bef next: wknd after 7th* **20/1**

5-P **8** *30* **Swazi Prince**[81] 2530 7-10-12 **99** .... BernieWharfe(7) 45
(N A Twiston-Davies) *chsd ldrs: led 4th: hdd whn mstke 3 out: wknd qckly* **33/1**

F-04 **R** **Movie King (IRE)**[46] 1607 7-10-10 **95** .... (t) AdamPogson(5) —
(S R Bowring) *ref to r* **40/1**

-555 **P** **Scotmail Too (IRE)**[52] 2979 5-11-1 **95** .... GrahamLee —
(J Howard Johnson) *prom: rdn 6th: sn wknd: t.o whn p.u bef 2 out* **10/1**

56-P **P** **Terminology**[100] 2099 8-11-1 **95** .... LeightonAspell —
(K C Bailey) *hld up: effrt 7th: sn wknd: t.o whn p.u bef 2 out* **25/1**

2/4P **P** **Loup Bleu (USA)**[78] 2574 8-11-9 **103** .... JodieMogford —
(Mrs A V Roberts) *led to 4th: wknd after 6th: t.o whn p.u bef 2 out* **100/1**

-353 **P** **Chamacco (FR)**[12] 3733 6-11-6 **100** .... PaulMoloney —
(M F Harris) *hld up: hdwy appr 6th: wknd bef 3 out: t.o whn p.u bef 2 out* **25/1**

-236 **P** **Hever Road (IRE)**[17] 3649 7-11-3 **104** .... (b[1]) AndrewGlassonbury(7) —
(M C Pipe) *hld up: hdwy 5th: wknd after 7th: t.o whn p.u bef 2 out* **14/1**

20U1 **P** **Prairie Law (GER)**[12] 3731 6-10-13 **100** .... TomMessenger(7) —
(B N Pollock) *s.i.s: reminders 1st: hdwy after next: ev ch after 7th: wknd 3 out: t.o whn p.u bef last* **10/1**

5m 11.2s (15.90) **Going Correction** +0.675s/f (Soft)
WFA 4 from 5yo+ 10lb **15** Ran SP% **119.7**
Speed ratings: **96,95,90,90,89 86,83,72,—,— —,—,—,—,—** CSF £16.93 CT £79.35 TOTE £2.80: £1.40, £2.70, £2.20; EX 21.90.
Owner Mrs Maureen Buckley & Mrs A M Halls **Bred** E Jahns **Trained** Upper Lambourn, Berks

FOCUS
A modest novices' handicap, run at an average pace, and the first two came clear. The winner is value for about eight lengths and the form should work out.

NOTEBOOK
Herakles(GER), very well backed, duly rewarded his supporters and readily got off the mark over timber at the fifth time of asking. He made smooth headway through the pack to join the pace turning for home, and could have been called the winner from two out, with this better ground *clearly much to his liking. He is at the right end of the handicap to progress further this term. (op 5-2 tchd 11-4 in places)*
Water Taxi had every chance and, while he was not aided by a mistake at the final flight, it made little difference to the overall result. This must rate a personal-best over timber, a decent surface is clearly key to him, and he can be placed to strike before too long on this evidence. *(op 8-1 tchd 7-1)*
Mistified(IRE) was doing his best work at the finish and is well worth riding more positively over this trip in the future. *(op 11-2 tchd 6-1)*
Liberty Ben(IRE) had his chance and posted a more encouraging effort. It would be no surprise to *see him sent over the larger obstacles before the end of the current campaignOfficial explanation: jockey said gelding hung left-handed (op 16-1)*
Legally Fast(USA), making his handicap debut, ultimately paid for running too freely under restraint and failed to see out the trip as a result. He is capable of better than this. *(op 8-1)*

3944 ENTERTAIN CLIENTS AT HUNTINGDON RACECOURSE H'CAP HURDLE (8 hdls) 2m 110y
5:00 (5:04) (Class 4) (0-115,110) 4-Y-0+ **£3,253** (£955; £477; £238)

Form RPR

-020 **1** **Candarli (IRE)**[26] 2716 10-11-5 **108** .... SamCurling(5) 112
(D R Gandolfo) *mde all: sn clr: rdn appr last: r.o* **33/1**

51 **2** *3* **Arry Dash**[34] 2950 6-11-7 **110** .... PaddyMerrigan(5) 112+
(M J Wallace) *mid-div: hdwy 3 out: chsd wnr next: blnd last: hung lft flat: styd on same pce* **5/1**

002 **3** *½* **Lagudin (IRE)**[8] 3797 8-11-4 **102** .... (b) PaulMoloney 102
(Paul John Gilligan, Ire) *hld up: hdwy 5th: rdn appr 2 out: styd on* **14/1**

600 **4** *7* **Majorca**[59] 2923 5-10-13 **97** .... GrahamLee 91+
(J Howard Johnson) *hld up: hdwy 3 out: styd on same pce fr next* **25/1**

6034 **5** *¾* **Before Time**[13] 3714 4-10-0 **93** .... (b[1]) PJBrennan 78+
(Mrs A M Thorpe) *chsd clr ldr: ev ch 3 out: wkng whn j.rt last* **9/2**[3]

P01P **6** *5* **Barton Park**[70] 2716 6-11-2 **100** .... NoelFehily 87
(D P Keane) *hld up: hdwy after 5th wknd appr 2 out* **14/1**

0062 **7** *22* **Maclean**[13] 3719 5-11-7 **105** .... (b) PhilipHide 85+
(G L Moore) *hld up: wknd after 3 out* **11/1**

2131 **8** *2* **Honan (IRE)**[16] 3661 7-11-7 **105** .... (v) APMcCoy 83+
(M C Pipe) *chsd ldrs: mstke 3 out: sn wknd* **7/2**[2]

0530 **9** *12* **Tytheknot**[72] 2685 5-10-3 **94** .... LukasSloup(7) 72+
(O Sherwood) *hld up: hdwy 4th: wknd 3 out* **50/1**

3445 **P** **Sabreur**[45] 3210 5-11-3 **101** .... MickFitzgerald —
(Ian Williams) *hld up: wknd 5th: t.o whn p.u bef 2 out* **3/1**[1]

4m 6.40s (10.70) **Going Correction** +0.675s/f (Soft)
WFA 4 from 5yo+ 9lb **10** Ran SP% **112.5**
Speed ratings: **101,99,99,96,95 93,83,82,76,—** CSF £184.82 CT £2434.71 TOTE £43.10: £6.60, £2.10, £3.40; EX 338.80 Place 6 £54.96, Place 5 £36.29.
Owner A E Frost **Bred** His Highness The Aga Khan's Studs S C **Trained** Wantage, Oxon
■ Stewards' Enquiry : Paddy Merrigan two-day ban: careless riding (Feb 27-28)

FOCUS
A moderate handicap, run at a fair gallop, and the form is worth treating with a degree of caution. The placed horses set the level for the form.

NOTEBOOK
Candarli(IRE), whose previous two outings had been in maiden company on the All-Weather, showed much-improved form on this return to hurdling and made all in determined fashion. This was his first success since going in at Newbury in 2004 from a 1lb lower mark, and he was full value for his winning margin, but it was not a strong event and he is far from certain to follow-up after a rise in the weights. *(op 40-1)*
Arry Dash was not helped by a final flight blunder, but was held by the winner at the time. This *must still rate a fair effort under top weight considering he most likely wants a faster surface. (op 7-2)*
Lagudin(IRE) ran his race, appreciating the better ground, and is a fair benchmark for this form.
Majorca, making his handicap debut in this sphere, was made to look very one paced when it mattred yet still turned in his best effort to date over hurdles. His fortunes should improve when his stable emerges from it's current lean spell. *(op 22-1)*
Before Time, making his handicap debut and equipped with first-time blinkers, had his chance yet was put in his place approaching the penultimate flight. *(op 5-1 tchd 4-1)*
Honan(IRE) ran well below the level of his most recent efforts and was very disappointing. *(tchd 4-1 in places)*
Sabreur, well backed for this handicap bow, ran no sort of race and has it all to prove after this. *Official explanation: jockey said gelding was unsuited by good (good to soft in places) ground (op 7-2 tchd 4-1)*

T/Jkpt: Part won. £10,455.80 to a £1 stake. Pool: £14,726.50. 0.50 winning tickets. T/Plt: £57.30 to a £1 stake. Pool: £53,904.35. 685.75 winning tickets. T/Qpdt: £18.60 to a £1 stake. Pool: £3,700.30. 146.95 winning tickets. CR

3463 TAUNTON (R-H)
Thursday, February 16

OFFICIAL GOING: Good to soft (soft in places)
Wind: Mild, across

3945 GREYHOUND INN AT STAPLE FITZPAINE (S) HURDLE (9 hdls) 2m 1f
2:10 (2:12) (Class 5) 4-7-Y-0 **£2,192** (£639; £319)

Form RPR

0631 **1** **Sunley Future (IRE)**[4] 3885 7-11-1 92 .... CharliePoste(7) 100+
(M F Harris) *led after 2nd: mde rest: nt fluent 2 out: kpt on: drvn out* **7/2**[2]

-F33 **2** *1 ½* **Lewis Island (IRE)**[8] 2754 7-11-2 115 .... JamieMoore 92+
(G L Moore) *hld up mid div: hdwy after 5th: rdn in 3rd after 3 out: kpt on same pce: wnt 2nd run-in* **6/4**[1]

2002 **3** *1* **It's My Party**[4] 3885 5-10-11 87 .... RobertLucey-Butler(5) 90
(W G M Turner) *in tch: chsd wnr 3 out: sn rdn: kpt on same pce: lost 2nd run -in* **17/2**

2P **4** *24* **Gotontheluckyone (IRE)**[13] 3715 6-10-9 80 .... KeiranBurke(7) 66
(P R Rodford) *chsd ldrs tl wknd 3 out* **33/1**

P405 **5** *3 ½* **Desert Moonbeam (IRE)**[27] 3479 4-10-0 76 .... TomScudamore 46
(R J Hodges) *nt fluent 2nd: a towards rr* **25/1**

P **6** *9* **Kalabell Prince**[4] 3885 7-10-13 .... (v[1]) WilliamKennedy(3) 53
(R A Farrant) *led tl after 2nd: chsd wnr: reminders after 4th: wknd bef 3 out* **66/1**

50 **7** *dist* **After Lent (IRE)**[15] 3673 5-11-2 .... TimmyMurphy —
(M C Pipe) *mid div: rdn after 6th: sn wknd* **9/1**

UP0P **8** *dist* **Huw The News**[20] 3602 7-11-2 85 .... RJGreene —
(S C Burrough) *mid div: hit 4th: lost tch fr next: t.o* **100/1**

00- **P** **Mr Strowger**[331] 4367 5-11-2 .... SeanFox —
(J C Fox) *a towards rr: t.o after 5th: p.u bef 3 out* **100/1**

P-02 **P** **Pop Gun**[86] 2419 7-10-9 84 .... RichardSpate(7) —
(Mrs K Waldron) *a towards rr: t.o 3 out: p.u bef 2 out* **11/1**

0-43 **P** **The Last Mohican**[12] 3731 7-10-13 99 .... (p) StephenCraine(3) —
(A G Juckes) *mid div: wknd after 6th: t.o and p.u bef 2 out* **5/1**[3]

4m 7.60s (-1.20) **Going Correction** +0.025s/f (Yiel)
WFA 4 from 5yo+ 9lb **11** Ran SP% **118.0**
Speed ratings: **103,102,101,90,88 84,—,—,—,—** — CSF £9.29 TOTE £4.50: £1.20, £1.60, £2.40; EX 9.10.The winner was bought in for 3,200gns.

Owner M Harris **Bred** John Foley **Trained** Edgcote, Northants

FOCUS

An uncompetitive selling hurdle in which only a handful could be given a realistic chance. The winner showed slight improvement and the time was reasonable for the grade.

NOTEBOOK

Sunley Future(IRE), worryingly dismounted after the finish when winning at Hereford four days previously, showed no signs of a problem here and having began to stretch the field at the first down the far side, he travelled smoothly into the straight before staying on too strongly for both Lewis Island and It's My Party. Evidently progressive, the application of a hood and deafeners has benefited him greatly and, with his effectiveness on both fast and soft proven, he may well be up to completing a hat-trick at this sort of level. *(tchd 4-1)*

Lewis Island(IRE) is best known for his quirks these days and had to be coaxed into the start. He did not travel quite as well as could have been expected, but found plenty under pressure and rallied past It's My Party for second on the run-in, not quite being able to get to the winner. He has the ability to win races at this level, but his attitude will continue to be a concern. *(op 2-1)*

It's My Party, second to Sunley Future at Hereford, was unable to reverse the form despite being weighted to get close and is clearly not as progressive as the winner. *(op 10-1 tchd 11-1)*

Gotontheluckyone(IRE) returned to something like his course form of last month, but remains below a winning level. *(op 28-1)*

Desert Moonbeam(IRE) plugged on from some way back having got a bit behind early. She looks in need of further now. *(op 20-1)*

3946 SOUTHWESTRACING.COM BEGINNERS' CHASE (17 fncs) 2m 7f 110y

2:40 (2:40) (Class 4) 5-Y-0+ **£5,530** (£1,623; £811; £405)

Form				RPR
115-	**1**		**Commercial Flyer (IRE)**[299] [4982] 7-11-4 ....(t) TimmyMurphy (M C Pipe) *j.w: sn trcking ldrs: wnt 2nd after 7th: j. into ld 12th: drew clr fr 3 out: readily* **1/2**[1]	130+
2F60	**2**	*4*	**Blue Business**[46] [3179] 8-10-13 133....................(b) MrCJSweeney(5) (P F Nicholls) *trckd ldrs: rdn after 12th: chsd wnr after 4 out: effrt 3 out : no ch w wnr fr next* **17/2**[3]	121+
0-4F	**3**	*21*	**Team Tassel (IRE)**[35] [3356] 8-11-4 ....(v) TomScudamore (M C Pipe) *led tl 12th: sn rdn: one pced in 3rd and hld whn pckd bdly 3 out* **12/1**	101+
03-0	**4**	*3 ½*	**Blushing Bull**[26] [3502] 7-11-4 .... ChristianWilliams (P F Nicholls) *j.lft thrght: hld up: mstke 5th: tk clsr order 11th: outpcd after 12th: nt a danger after* **5/1**[2]	97+
3P3-	**5**	*14*	**Smart Savannah**[459] [2220] 10-11-4 .... RobertThornton (C Tinkler) *hld up: hdwy 11th: nt fluent 13th: sn wknd* **25/1**	80
P-PP	**6**	*shd*	**A Pound Down (IRE)**[48] [3126] 9-10-13 68.................... MarkNicolls(5) (N G Ayliffe) *chsd ldrs tl 12th: sn wknd* **200/1**	80
44	**7**	*8*	**Beaufort County (IRE)**[37] [3329] 9-11-4 115.................... AntonyEvans (Evan Williams) *hld up bhd: sme hdwy 11th: wknd after next: tired whn mstke last* **50/1**	72
0PPP	**P**		**Shannon Quest (IRE)**[14] [3686] 10-11-4 62.................... RobertWalford (C L Popham) *w ldr tl 7th: sn wknd: bhd whn p.u after 10th* **200/1**	—

6m 9.70s (4.60) **Going Correction** +0.40s/f (Soft) 8 Ran SP% **108.4**

Speed ratings: **108,106,99,98,93 93,91,—** CSF £4.76 TOTE £1.50: £1.10, £1.80, £2.00; EX 7.30.

Owner D A Johnson **Bred** Col W B Mullins **Trained** Nicholashayne, Devon

FOCUS

This turned into a solo spin for Commercial Flyer, who put in a spectacular round of jumping for a novice and needed only to be pushed out to score cosily. The time was decent and the race should throw up winners.

NOTEBOOK

Commercial Flyer(IRE), a prolific scorer last season when winning five handicaps in less than a month, was taking up this engagement rather than the Grade One Reynoldstown at the weekend and ran out a most authoritative winner. He put in a spectacular round of jumping, and a stunning leap at the third-last quickly settled the issue. A significant mover in the Royal & SunAlliance Chase market during the morning, the support does not seem misplaced and, although lacking the experience usually required to take that race, it would not surprise to see connections squeeze in another outing before the Festival, where his ability to jump so accurately will obviously stand him in good stead. He gave the impression he does not like being in front for too long, flashing his tail and not looking too keen early in the straight, but there are not many better jockeys around than Murphy for executing waiting tactics and he goes to Cheltenham as a major player. *(op 4-7)*

Blue Business has not looked the same since falling when still in with a chance against Church Island and Celtic Son at Cheltenham in November, throwing in a couple of moody displays, but this was better and he could not have been expected to do any better against the classy winner. There is still room for some improvement in his jumping, but this half-brother to See More Business is a strong stayer and reportedly has the four-mile National Hunt Chase as his target. *(op 7-1 tchd 9-1)*

Team Tassel(IRE) has not taken to fences as well as expected, and remains some way below the best of his form from early last season. He took them along early here, but was readily brushed aside down the back and was well held when pecking badly at the third-last. *(op 10-1)*

Blushing Bull, the supposed Nicholls first string judging by the betting, was let down by his jumping on this chasing debut, looking slow over the first couple and jumping out to his left thereafter. A useful hurdler, he raced a little lazily here, but not many from his stable suffer jumping problems and it is reasonable to expect an improved showing next time. *(op 6-1)*

Smart Savannah briefly threatened to get involved, but in the end it all proved a little too hot for him. *(op 22-1)*

3947 ASPEN WAITE CHARTERED ACCOUNTANTS MAIDEN HURDLE (DIV I) (9 hdls) 2m 1f

3:10 (3:10) (Class 4) 4-Y-0+ **£4,554** (£1,337; £668; £333)

Form				RPR
	1		**Anemix (FR)**[104] 5-10-11 .... HowieEphgrave(5) (L Corcoran) *hld up bhd: smooth hdwy to trck ldrs 5th: qcknd up wl to ld appr 2 out: clr whn hit last: easily* **20/1**	112+
2-10	**2**	*12*	**Mars Rock (FR)**[95] [2211] 6-11-2 .... SamThomas (Miss Venetia Williams) *chsd ldrs: led briefly 5th: rdn and ev ch after 3 out: kpt on but nt pce of wnr* **7/2**[2]	97
4	**3**	*4*	**Megaton**[28] [3463] 5-11-2 .... ChristianWilliams (P Bowen) *chsd ldrs: led after 5th: hit 3 out: rdn and hdd appr 2 out: kpt on same pce* **4/1**[3]	95+
5	**4**	*6*	**Temple Place (IRE)**[34] [3374] 5-10-13 ....(t) StephenCraine(3) (D McCain) *mid div: hdwy 5th: ev ch after 3 out: sn rdn: one pced fr next* **5/1**	90+
0	**5**	*16*	**Bucks**[52] [2968] 9-11-2 .... WayneHutchinson (Ian Williams) *mid div: 5th whn mstke 3 out: sn wknd* **16/1**	71
	6	*4*	**Positano (IRE)** 6-11-2 .... TomScudamore (M Scudamore) *hld up and a towards rr* **33/1**	67
2040	**7**	*6*	**Thenameescapesme**[34] [3369] 6-11-2 .... JasonMaguire (T R George) *a bhd* **9/1**	61
0	**8**	*8*	**Sultan Fontenaille (FR)**[9] [3786] 4-10-7 .... JoeTizzard (N J Hawke) *in tch: mstke 6th: sn wknd* **25/1**	44
	9	*11*	**Ladino (FR)**[505] 6-11-2 .... RichardJohnson (P J Hobbs) *in tch tl wknd 3 out* **3/1**[1]	42
	10	*6*	**Honorary Citizen**[115] 4-10-4 .... WilliamKennedy(3) (Evan Williams) *mid div tl 5th: sn bhd* **40/1**	27
P	**11**	*1 ¾*	**Bombaybadboy (NZ)**[35] [3354] 7-11-2 ....(p) HenryOliver (Ian Williams) *led tl 5th: sn wknd* **100/1**	34
P	**P**		**Jigsaw Jumper (IRE)**[35] [3354] 6-10-9 .... JimCrowley (Andrew Turnell) *a bhd: t.o and p.u bef 6th* **100/1**	—
0	**P**		**Be Lucky Lady (GER)**[111] [1904] 4-9-7 .... KeiranBurke(7) (N J Dawe) *mstke 1st: chsd ldrs tl wknd rapidly 5th: p.u bef next* **100/1**	—

4m 6.40s (-2.40) **Going Correction** +0.025s/f (Yiel)

WFA 4 from 5yo+ 9lb 13 Ran SP% **116.7**

Speed ratings: **106,100,98,95,88 86,83,79,74,71 70,—,—** CSF £86.41 TOTE £28.20: £4.60, £1.70, £1.60; EX 125.10.

Owner M Ephgrave **Bred** Wertheimer & Frere **Trained** Kingsbridge, Devon

FOCUS

An impressive winner, who was value for more than the official margin, but this was probably the weaker of the two divisions, an impression comfirmed by the time which was over a second slower.

NOTEBOOK

Anemix(FR), a modest sort on the Flat in France, posted quite an impressive performance in beating the fancied runners, quickening clear in the final quarter-mile having cantered into the lead turning in. He has no fancy entries and connections are planning on keeping it low-key, so he should be up to defying a penalty in a novice event at a sensible level. *(tchd 22-1)*

Mars Rock(FR), who won on his second bumper start at Plumpton back in October, was unable to cope with the rise into Listed company when down the field at Cheltenham in November, but the switch to hurdles saw him produce an improved effort and he kept on well enough for second. Readily outpaced by the winner, he does give the impression he is in the need of two and a half miles and better can be expected at that trip. *(tchd 15-4 in a place)*

Megaton made a pleasing British debut when fourth behind Princelet at the course last month, but was unable to build on it and was another completely undone by the winner's burst. He may do better on a faster surface. *(op 7-2)*

Temple Place(IRE), who failed to get home at Kelso when fifth on his hurdling debut, should have fared much better on this more speed-reliant track, but he was simply not good enough on the day and could only manage fourth, again appearing not to last out. He has a bit to prove after this. *(op 7-2 tchd 11-2)*

Ladino(FR), who travelled well for the first 12-furlongs of the race, became readily outpaced after a slow jump down the back and dropped away tamely. It is hoped he can do better next time with the experience under his belt. *(op 4-1)*

3948 ASPEN WAITE CHARTERED ACCOUNTANTS MAIDEN HURDLE (DIV II) (9 hdls) 2m 1f

3:40 (3:40) (Class 4) 4-Y-0+ **£4,554** (£1,337; £668; £333)

Form				RPR
64	**1**		**Mystery Lot (IRE)**[20] [3594] 4-10-0 .... RobertThornton (A King) *mde all: qcknd clr after 3 out: nt fluent last: heavily eased* **7/2**[3]	110+
5	**2**	*16*	**Sakenos (POL)**[38] [3324] 6-11-2 ....(t) RichardJohnson (P J Hobbs) *chsd ldrs: wnt 2nd after 5th: rdn after 3 out: sn nt pce of wnr: hit last* **5/2**[2]	106+
43	**3**	*2*	**Cruise Director**[31] [3422] 6-11-2 .... WayneHutchinson (Ian Williams) *in tch: tk clsr order 5th: rdn to chse wnr after 3 out: kpt on same pce* **9/4**[1]	104+
	4	*18*	**Inchloch**[114] 4-10-7 .... SamThomas (Miss Venetia Williams) *hld up towards rr: gd hdwy to trck ldrs 5th: rdn after 3 out : wknd next* **4/1**	78+
0	**5**	*15*	**Kofi**[36] [3340] 4-10-7 .... BenjaminHitchcott (Miss K M George) *in tch: rdn and wknd after 6th* **66/1**	61
	6	*5*	**Lucky Shame (FR)**[370] 4-10-7 .... OllieMcPhail (A J Whitehead) *a bhd* **100/1**	56
0-0P	**7**	*1 ½*	**Red Raptor**[35] [3355] 5-11-2 ....(t) MarkBradburne (J A Geake) *hld up and a towards rr* **66/1**	64
P	**8**	*dist*	**Malibu (IRE)**[36] [2212] 5-11-2 .... JamieMoore (S Dow) *mid div tl wknd 6th* **28/1**	—
	9	*dist*	**Projectfiveonefive** 7-11-2 .... RJGreene (Mrs S D Williams) *chsd ldrs tl wknd 5th: sn wl bhd* **50/1**	—
00	**P**		**Dopey Bob**[85] [2432] 5-11-2 .... AntonyEvans (N A Twiston-Davies) *a bhd: t.o and p.u bef 6th* **40/1**	—
0-00	**P**		**Judy's Lad**[26] [3511] 7-10-13 .... OwynNelmes(3) (Mrs H R J Nelmes) *chsd ldrs tl 5th: sn wknd: bhd and p.u bef 3 out* **150/1**	—
0	**P**		**Oscar Royal (IRE)**[91] [2288] 5-10-11 .... DarylJacob(5) (Mrs S E Busby) *t.k.h in mid div: wknd after 5th: bhd and p.u bef 3 out* **150/1**	—
60/P	**P**		**Steel Warrior**[64] [2821] 9-10-11 .... RobertLucey-Butler(5) (J S Smith) *j.rt and nvr fluent: a bhd: t.o and p.u bef 6th* **100/1**	—

4m 5.30s (-3.50) **Going Correction** +0.025s/f (Yiel)

WFA 4 from 5yo+ 9lb 13 Ran SP% **115.7**

Speed ratings: **109,101,100,92,85 82,81,—,—,— —,—,—** CSF £12.30 TOTE £4.70: £1.40, £1.20, £1.50; EX 9.70.

Owner Four Mile Racing **Bred** E O'Leary **Trained** Barbury Castle, Wilts

FOCUS

A marginally better race than the first division, with an even more impressive winner in Mystery Lot, who was value for 20 lengths and also posted a quicker time. The form behind looks solid enough.

NOTEBOOK

Mystery Lot(IRE), subjected to a more aggressive ride on this occasion, really enjoyed herself out in the front and attacked her hurdles with great enthusiasm, having them all in trouble turning for home and bolting clear with the minimum of fuss. In receipt of 7lb upwards from her rivals, she will find life tougher in future, but has the option of switching to mares-only company and can surely be found a suitable opportunity to follow up. *(op 9-2)*

Sakenos(POL), fifth in a decent event at the course last month, held a good position throughout, but was unable to keep tabs on the winner and was made to look paceless back in second. He can probably win an ordinary novice event, but will not be seen at his best until contesting handicaps. *(tchd 11-4 and 3-1 in places)*

Cruise Director has displayed a similar level of ability in all three starts over hurdles and like the runner-up he will appeal more once handicapping. *(op 5-2 tchd 11-4)*

Inchloch, rated 77 on the Flat, appealed as the type to make a decent hurdler, but having raced keenly early on he was left trailing from half a mile out and failed to offer much encouragement for the future. It is entirely possible the run was needed however, and he warrants another chance, with better ground also likely to suit. *(op 7-2)*

3949 S.I.S. H'CAP CHASE (15 fncs 2 omitted) 2m 7f 110y
4:10 (4:10) (Class 4) (0-115,113) 5-Y-0+ £5,530 (£1,623; £811; £405)

Form RPR
0206 1 Even More (IRE)[14] 3698 11-11-6 107 RobertWalford 119+
(R H Alner) *mid div: rdn and hdwy after 10th: chsd ldr after 3 out: styd on strly to ld after last: drvn out* 16/1
U221 2 1 1/2 Stavordale Lad (IRE)[15] 3672 8-11-9 110 ChristianWilliams 119
(P F Nicholls) *led 3rd: rdn and hrd pressed fr 3 out: hdd after last: no ex* 11/2[1]
/554 3 5 Wild Oats[70] 2729 8-10-5 95 OwynNelmes[(3)] 100+
(B J M Ryall) *hld up towards rr: stdy prog fr 10th: chsd ldng pair after 3 out: rdn and effrt next: kpt on same pce* 16/1
3242 4 21 Treasulier (IRE)[14] 3698 9-10-7 101 KeiranBurke[(7)] 87+
(P R Rodford) *chsd ldrs: rdn appr 10th: outpcd 12th: nt a danger after* 15/2[3]
-33P 5 hd Message Recu (FR)[27] 3482 10-10-7 94 (b) JoeTizzard 77
(C L Tizzard) *chsd ldrs: rdn after 11th: mstke 3 out: sn wknd* 20/1
5-2P 6 25 Barren Lands[26] 3507 11-11-2 103 RJGreene 61
(K Bishop) *a bhd: lost tch fr 9th* 50/1
-F40 7 2 Tiger Tips Lad (IRE)[38] 3326 7-11-1 102 AntonyEvans 58
(N A Twiston-Davies) *towards rr: hdwy to trck ldrs 9th: rdn whn hit 11th and 12th: sn wknd* 8/1
U4-U F Miss Mailmit[27] 3481 9-10-9 96 MarkBradburne —
(J A B Old) *mid div: j. slowly 4th: fell next* 16/1
23-6 F Definite Approach (IRE)[90] 2327 8-11-1 102 (t) RichardJohnson —
(R T Phillips) *wnt bdly rt and fell 1st* 12/1
-432 U Matthew Muroto (IRE)[13] 3718 7-10-7 99 DarylJacob[(5)] —
(R H Alner) *chsng ldrs whn blnd bdly and uns rdr 3rd* 6/1[2]
15-0 P Kim Fontenail (FR)[26] 3507 6-11-10 111 TimmyMurphy —
(N J Hawke) *bdly hmpd 1st: nvr rcvrd and a t.o: p.u run-in* 20/1
-3P4 P Tradingup (IRE)[27] 3481 7-10-2 89 JimCrowley —
(Andrew Turnell) *led tl hit 3rd: chsd ldrs tl 6th: bhd whn p.u bef 10th* 6/1[2]
3P26 P Sunshan[13] 3716 10-9-7 87 oh3 JamesWhite[(7)] —
(R J Hodges) *chsd ldrs: hit 7th: wknd after 11th: t.o whn p.u bef 2 out* 33/1
-625 U Misty Future[14] 3688 8-11-12 113 SamThomas —
(Miss Venetia Williams) *in tch: blnd 9th and dropped rr: blnd and uns rdr 11th* 8/1

6m 10.6s (5.50) **Going Correction** +0.40s/f (Soft) 14 Ran SP% 117.7
Speed ratings: **106,105,103,96,96 88,87,—,—,— —,—,—,—** CSF £97.53 CT £1452.57 TOTE £16.10: £3.90, £1.70, £5.50; EX 130.50.
Owner G Keirle **Bred** Martin J Dibbs **Trained** Droop, Dorset

FOCUS
An ordinary but eventful handicap chase in which Even More recorded his fifth career success. Along with the third he sets the standard for the form. Last fence omitted.

NOTEBOOK
Even More(IRE), who was back down to a decent mark, ground out the result on the long run-in to record his fifth career success. Without a win in over a year coming into this, he was given a fine ride by Walford, who crept him into contention and got a sustained run out of him down the straight. He is not getting any better, but is clearly capable of winning at the right level when in the mood. *Official explanation: trainer said, regarding the improved form shown, gelding was better suited by the strong early pace*
Stavordale Lad(IRE) is not the quickest around and his lack of finishing speed was again evident, but he is usually on the scene and will always be a danger when the emphasis is on stamina. *(op 5-1)*
Wild Oats ◆, who was hunted around in rear before making a promising forward move early in the back straight, looked to be in with every chance turning for home, but the longer the contest went on the weaker he looked and he ended up having to settle for third. This was his first run since December and he would make some appeal back on a better surface. *(op 20-1)*
Treasulier(IRE) finished well adrift of the front three and has yet to win under Rules, but his previous efforts suggested finding a race off this sort of mark would not prove an impossibility. *(op 8-1)*
Message Recu(FR) travelled well, but was unable to go on when asked and continues to frustrate
Tiger Tips Lad(IRE) made too many mistakes and it was no surprise to see him fade out of it late on. *(op 12-1)*

3950 BACK AND LAY ON GGBET.COM H'CAP HURDLE (10 hdls) 2m 3f 110y
4:40 (4:40) (Class 4) (0-110,105) 4-Y-0+ £3,253 (£955; £477; £238)

Form RPR
0006 1 Marrel[4] 3889 8-11-12 105 (v) AntonyEvans 108+
(D Burchell) *chsd ldrs: led after 5th: rdn appr 2 out: all out* 16/1
006 2 3/4 El Corredor (IRE)[16] 3659 7-9-12 84 CharliePoste[(7)] 85+
(M F Harris) *towards rr: stdy prog fr 5th: pressed wnr fr 7th: rdn and ev ch 2 out: kpt on but no ex cl home* 17/2
6354 3 4 Westernmost[12] 3731 8-10-13 92 RJGreene 89+
(K Bishop) *led tl 2nd: chsd ldrs: outpcd after 3 out: styd on again fr 2 out* 9/1
446P 4 14 Hi Fi[77] 2594 8-11-2 105 DavidBoland[(10)] 91+
(Ian Williams) *mid div: nt fluent 4th: hdwy to join ldrs 6th: rdn after 3 out: one pced fr next* 33/1
66-P 5 1 1/2 Karoo[63] 2845 8-10-12 91 WayneHutchinson 72
(K Bishop) *hld up towards rr: hdwy 7th: rdn after 3 out: no further imp* 20/1
530 6 15 Sarin[16] 3658 8-11-6 99 SamThomas 65
(Miss Venetia Williams) *mid div: hdwy to trck ldrs 7th: sn rdn: wknd after 3 out* 7/2[1]
0135 7 1/2 Assoon[40] 3286 7-11-10 103 (b) JamieMoore 68
(G L Moore) *led 2nd tl after 5th: cl up: rdn after 3 out: sn btn* 13/2[3]
3042 8 5 Samandara (FR)[28] 3461 6-11-4 100 (v) GinoCarenza[(3)] 60
(A King) *blnd bdly 1st: towards rr: sme hdwy 7th: wknd 3 out* 11/2[2]
3PPP 9 8 Princesse Grec (FR)[17] 3654 8-11-4 97 TomScudamore 49
(M Scudamore) *chsd ldrs: mstke 6th and dropped rr: wknd after 3 out* 33/1
06 10 5 Idian Mix (FR)[45] 3214 5-11-12 105 (v[1]) TimmyMurphy 52
(M C Pipe) *in tch: tk clsr order 6th: wknd next* 7/1
004- P Dunshaughlin (IRE)[303] 4920 9-11-7 100 JasonMaguire —
(J A B Old) *a bhd: t.o and p.u bef 7th* 12/1
00-P P Montu[38] 3326 9-10-6 85 BenjaminHitchcott —
(Miss K M George) *mid div tl 5th: t.o and p.u bef 3 out* 66/1
0500 P Xila Fontenailles (FR)[52] 2995 5-10-2 88 KeiranBurke[(7)] —
(N J Hawke) *towards rr: lost tch after 6th: p.u bef 3 out* 20/1
0P0 P Open Range (IRE)[38] 3325 6-11-7 100 AlanO'Keeffe —
(Jennie Candlish) *mstke 5th: a towards rr: t.o and p.u bef 2 out* 100/1

4m 54.2s (8.20) **Going Correction** +0.025s/f (Yiel) 14 Ran SP% 115.4
Speed ratings: **84,83,82,76,75 69,69,67,64,62 —,—,—,—** CSF £130.45 CT £1307.17 TOTE £23.20: £5.80, £3.80, £2.50; EX 199.30.
Owner Don Gould **Bred** Hilborough Stud Farm Ltd **Trained** Briery Hill, Blaenau Gwent

FOCUS
Ordinary form and not that strong although the first two have rated higher in the past.

NOTEBOOK
Marrel, fourth at Hereford four days previously, was taken to the front with just under a circuit to go, but had plenty to worry about turning in, with El Corredor, Westernmost and Hi Fi all snapping at his heels, and mistakes at each of the last two hurdles did not boost his chance, but he galloped on resolutely and was always holding them after the last. It will be interesting to see if he is turned out quickly once more, in a bid to defy a penalty. *(op 14-1)*
El Corredor(IRE), a handicap debutant, excelled himself in second, confirming the promise of his recent Folkestone sixth behind Tarlac. He was given a confident ride by Poste and had made headway into second before the turn-in, but was unable to get the better of Marrel despite the hefty weight concession. He will find a race if going on from this, off what is a decent-looking mark. *(op 8-1 tchd 9-1)*
Westernmost was allowed to settle in behind the leaders having led in the very early stages, and he was there with every chance turning in, but was unable to go on from the third-last, only being able to find the one pace. *(op 15-2)*
Hi Fi offered a little more on this return to hurdles, but quickly back-tracked in the straight and remains below a winning level at present. *(op 22-1)*
Karoo often spoils his chance by racing keenly, but he was not too bad on this occasion and saw his race out well enough, looking outpaced from half a mile out. He may improve for a switch to fences. *(tchd 22-1)*
Sarin, making his handicap debut, travelled strongly, but found disappointingly little and looks one to be wary of in future *(op 11-2)*
Idian Mix(FR) continues to disappoint, the first-time visor failing to inject any life into him. *(op 13-2)*
Open Range(IRE) *Official explanation: jockey said gelding hung right-handed (op 66-1)*

3951 TRULL MARES' ONLY H'CAP HURDLE (12 hdls) 3m 110y
5:10 (5:10) (Class 5) (0-95,90) 4-Y-0+ £2,740 (£798; £399)

Form RPR
24P2 1 Lizzie Bathwick (IRE)[9] 3790 7-11-12 90 TimmyMurphy 93+
(J G Portman) *chsd ldrs: rdn to ld after 2 out: drifted lft fr last: styd on: drvn out* 3/1[1]
0-03 2 2 1/2 Royal Niece (IRE)[27] 3483 7-10-9 83 RyanCummings[(10)] 83
(D J Wintle) *in tch: sltly outpcd whn hmpd 9th: rdn and styd on again appr 2 out: wnt 2nd run-in* 7/2[2]
/655 3 5 Bosworth Gypsy (IRE)[23] 3545 8-10-9 80 ShaneWalsh[(7)] 76+
(Miss J S Davis) *led: mstke 5th: rdn and narrowly hdd whn hmpd last: no ex* 20/1
0136 4 1/2 Hilarious (IRE)[30] 3439 6-11-8 86 JamieGoldstein 81
(Dr J R J Naylor) *trckd ldrs: rdn and effrt after 3 out: kpt on same pce* 13/2[3]
6P06 5 2 1/2 Alderbrook Girl (IRE)[31] 3424 6-10-13 80 (v[1]) ColinBolger[(3)] 72
(R Curtis) *prom: rdn after 3 out: kpt on same pce* 50/1
6 6 1 3/4 Tinvane Rose (IRE)[27] 3483 7-10-8 79 ChrisDavies[(7)] 69
(J G M O'Shea) *hld up: hdwy after 7th: rdn and effrt after 3 out: one pced fr next* 25/1
-P00 7 1/2 Fortanis[26] 3505 7-10-8 75 WilliamKennedy[(3)] 65
(P C Ritchens) *mid div: tk clsr order 7th: rdn and effrt after 3 out: sn one pced* 100/1
0P0 8 3 They Grabbed Me (IRE)[42] 3250 5-11-4 82 (t) GerrySupple 69
(M C Pipe) *hld up towards rr: rdn after 8th: no further imp fr 3 out* 20/1
0-P0 9 3 1/2 Kayleigh (IRE)[14] 3692 8-11-1 86 (p) KeiranBurke[(7)] 69
(P R Rodford) *chsd ldrs tl 6th: wknd after 3 out* 25/1
-P13 F Balmoral Queen[33] 3395 6-10-10 77 StephenCraine[(3)] —
(D McCain) *in tch: cl up whn fell 9th* 7/2[2]
-461 P Mizinky[13] 3715 6-11-7 90 RobertLucey-Butler[(5)] —
(W G M Turner) *in tch tl 6th: lost tch 8th: p.u bef 3 out* 12/1
4510 B Penny's Crown[38] 3325 7-11-7 90 EamonDehdashti[(5)] —
(G A Ham) *hld up towards rr: stdy hdwy after 7th: in tch whn b.d 9th* 12/1

6m 13.8s (5.20) **Going Correction** +0.025s/f (Yiel) 12 Ran SP% 118.3
Speed ratings: **92,91,89,89,88 88,87,86,85,— —,—** CSF £12.90 CT £179.05 TOTE £3.80: £2.10, £1.40, £3.60; EX 23.70 Place 6 £68.46, Place 5 £49.49.
Owner W Clifford **Bred** James Barry **Trained** Compton, Berks

FOCUS
A typically weak mares-only hurdle with the placed horses the best guide to the level.

NOTEBOOK
Lizzie Bathwick(IRE) has largely been running well over fences, but it took a return to hurdles for her to score. Always travelling strongly under Murphy, who was intent on sticking to the rail, she went ahead after the second-last and stayed on too strongly for Royal Niece. She has yet to win over fences, but jumps soundly enough and remains open to a little further improvement when returning to the larger obstacles. *(op 10-3 tchd 7-2 and 4-1 in a place)*
Royal Niece(IRE) is beginning to put a decent string of efforts together and, although she has yet to score in 12 attempts, there is surely a race for her at a similarly lowly level. *(op 4-1)*
Bosworth Gypsy(IRE) towed them along until just before the last, where she was hampered, and she did well to hang on for third in the end. This was only her sixth career start and the likelihood is that there is more to come. *(op 25-1 tchd 28-1)*
Hilarious(IRE) came with a challenge in the straight, but did not see the three-mile trip out as strongly as the principals. *(op 9-2 tchd 7-1)*
Alderbrook Girl(IRE) raced sweetly in the first-time visor but, if anything, she may have raced a little too enthusiastically and in the end she was unable to stick with the leaders.
Tinvane Rose(IRE) was noted travelling strongly from some way out, but she did not find a great deal off the bridle *(op 28-1)*
Penny's Crown had not been asked for her effort when brought down by the fall of Balmoral Queen. This will hopefully not affect her confidence in future. *(op 9-2 tchd 5-1)*
Balmoral Queen was still going well and looked likely to get involved for her in-form stable, only to fall at the ninth. It is hoped this does not affect her confidence. *(op 9-2 tchd 5-1)*
T/Plt: £110.10 to a £1 stake. Pool: £50,977.30. 337.80 winning tickets. T/Qpdt: £55.90 to a £1 stake. Pool: £3,062.20. 40.50 winning tickets. TM

3952 - 3954a (Foreign Racing) - See Raceform Interactive

3591

FAKENHAM (L-H)
Friday, February 17

OFFICIAL GOING: Good to soft (soft in places) changing to soft (good to soft in places) after race 2 (2.20)
Wind: Nil Weather: Overcast

3955 "ONE YEAR ON AND HUNTING STILL CONTINUES" BEGINNERS' CHASE (18 fncs) 3m 110y
1:50 (1:50) (Class 4) 5-Y-0+ £4,098 (£1,203; £601; £300)

Form RPR
2333 1 Eskimo Pie (IRE)[27] 3494 7-11-4 118 (b[1]) NoelFehily 124+
(C C Bealby) *settled 3rd: mstkes 9th and 10th: wnt 2nd 15th: led u.p 2 out: drew clr* 15/8[2]

1/24 **2** *10* **Tufty Hopper**[25] [3541] 9-11-4 113 .... KeithMercer 112
(Ferdy Murphy) *trckd ldrs: rdn after 13th: chal and ev ch 2 out: sn outpcd* **9/1**

1552 **3** *1 ¾* **Jackson (FR)**[32] [3419] 9-11-4 .... RobertThornton 112+
(A King) *slt ld: rdn after 3 out: jnd and blnd next: sn btn* **13/8**[1]

-00P **4** *22* **Mobasher (IRE)**[53] [2990] 7-11-4 .... SamThomas 93+
(Miss Venetia Williams) *mstkes: towards rr: rdn 13th: struggling bdly after* **12/1**

0-PP **5** *6* **Beauchamp Prince (IRE)**[28] [3480] 5-10-7 113 .... RJGreene 71
(M Scudamore) *mstkes and landing steeply: bhd: rdn 11th: lost tch qckly after 13th* **25/1**

2-0P **6** *11* **Will Of The People (IRE)**[77] [2608] 11-11-4 123 ....(v) TomScudamore 71
(M C Pipe) *j. slowly 3rd: handy tl dropped rr and j. slowly 11th: nt keen after: t.o 15th* **13/2**[3]

PP6 **P** **The Rainbow Man**[32] [3417] 6-11-4 .... HenryOliver —
(J Ryan) *mstke 1st: a last: lost tch 9th: t.o and p.u after 13th* **200/1**

/0-5 **P** **Cupla Cairde**[48] [3164] 6-11-4 ....(b) JamieMoore —
(O Brennan) *cl 2nd tl jnd ldr 9th to 11th: mstke 14th and rdn: wknd and mstke next: remote whn clambered over 3 out and p.u* **25/1**

6m 43.0s (5.40) **Going Correction** +0.35s/f (Yiel)
WFA 5 from 6yo+ 11lb **8** Ran SP% **112.1**
Speed ratings: **105,101,101,94,92 88,—,—** CSF £17.66 TOTE £2.40: £1.10, £2.00, £1.10; EX 11.70.
Owner Irvin S Naylor **Bred** Patrick Moakley **Trained** Barrowby, Lincs

FOCUS
Not a bad beginners' chase, but it only really concerned three horses from some way out and Eskimo Pie confirmed earlier promise to win decisively. The ground looked to be riding worse than good to soft, and the official description was duly changed later on the card.

NOTEBOOK
Eskimo Pie(IRE) had been shaping as though set to make a nice chaser until disappointing when dropped back to two and a half miles behind a decent sort at Haydock on his previous start but, stepped back up in trip with blinkers on for the first time, he confirmed that earlier promise with a clear-cut success. He does not seem in the slightest bit ungenuine, but the headgear just appeared to get him travelling that bit better and it should continue to have a positive effect. He is well regarded by his connections, as his entries in the Royal & SunAlliance, the Jewson and the Kim Muir suggest, and the last-named race is said to be his most likely target at the Festival. *(op 9-4 tchd 5-2)*
Tufty Hopper, pretty disappointing at Wetherby on his previous start, was no match for the winner but kept on well enough for second. This was better, and equates to a similar level to his old hurdle form. *(op 10-1 tchd 17-2)*
Jackson(FR) seems at his best on good ground, so this was a respectable effort, and he would have finished closer had he not made a bit of a mess of the second last. He should not be long in winning over fences. *(tchd 7-4)*
Mobasher(IRE), a 112-rated hurdler who had the blinkers left off for his debut over fences, was beaten a long way out and did not help his chances by making mistakes. *(op 10-1 tchd 14-1)*
Beauchamp Prince(IRE), pulled up on both his previous starts this season, including on his debut over fences at Chepstow last time, completed this time but that was about all he managed.

3956 KEEP TAIL DOCKING FOR WORKING DOGS (S) H'CAP HURDLE (9 hdls) 2m
2:20 (2:20) (Class 5) (0-90,90) 4-Y-0+ **£2,535** (£738; £369)

Form RPR

044U **1** **Needwood Spirit**[16] [3674] 11-10-2 **72** ow3 .... ThomasBurrows(7) 74
(Mrs A M Naughton) *bhd: last bef 3 out: sn bdly outpcd: 8l 5th and drvn next: rapid burst to ld bef last: sn clr* **11/2**[2]

0600 **2** *2 ½* **Purr**[38] [3330] 5-9-8 **64** ....(p) MrSRees(7) 63
(M Wigham) *hld up and bhd: jnd ldrs after 5th: led bef 2 out: sn clr: wd st: hdd bef last: nt qckn* **17/2**[3]

P00P **3** *13* **Champagne Rossini (IRE)**[8] [3817] 4-10-2 **74** oh13 ow2 KennyJohnson 54+
(M C Chapman) *keen: led: mstke 4th: rdn and hdd bef 2 out: sn wl btn* **25/1**

F000 **4** *9* **Ray Mond**[32] [3417] 5-9-9 **63** oh4 .... DerekLaverty(5) 40
(M J Gingell) *plld v hrd: pressed ldr: ev ch 3 out: fdd qckly bef next* **25/1**

06-0 **5** *4* **Ethan Snowflake**[21] [3592] 7-11-9 **89** .... OwynNelmes(3) 62
(N B King) *hld up: prog and mstke 6th: 4th and rdn whn hit next: sn fnd nil* **4/1**[1]

00-P **6** *1 ¾* **Final Lap**[31] [3433] 10-9-12 **66** oh3 ow3 ....(p) MarkNicolls(5) 37
(H H G Owen) *keen early: chsd ldrs: rdn and wknd qckly bef 6th* **28/1**

0P00 **7** *1 ½* **Simiola**[9] [3804] 7-10-10 **73** .... MarkGrant 43
(S T Lewis) *cl up: rdn 5th: wknd bef 3 out* **14/1**

005 **8** *20* **Trackattack**[37] [2954] 4-11-4 **90** .... JamieMoore 31
(P Howling) *chsd ldrs: drvn 4th: labouring bdly 3 out* **4/1**[1]

P00 **P** **Dargin's Lass (IRE)**[15] [3690] 5-9-12 **68** .... TomMessenger(7) —
(B N Pollock) *reluctant: rr and rdn 2nd: sn t.o: eventually p.u 3 out* **14/1**

PP60 **P** **Approaching Land (IRE)**[23] [3557] 11-10-12 **78** .... MrTGreenall(3) —
(M W Easterby) *hld up in rr: rdn and mstke 6th: lost tch next: t.o and p.u 2 out* **4/1**[1]

4m 15.7s (6.80) **Going Correction** +0.35s/f (Yiel)
WFA 4 from 5yo+ 9lb **10** Ran SP% **110.4**
Speed ratings: **97,95,89,84,82 81,81,71,—,—** CSF £46.96 CT £1008.19 TOTE £4.50: £1.90, £2.50, £7.60; EX 47.10.There was no bid for the winner.
Owner Famous Five Racing **Bred** Needwood Stud **Trained** Richmond, N Yorks
■ A first winner for jockey Tom Burrows.

FOCUS
A very moderate race, even by selling stands, but the 11-year-old Needwood Spirit seemed to enjoy himself as he came from a hopeless-looking position to ultimately win well. As in the first race, the ground looked to be riding worse than good to soft.

NOTEBOOK
Needwood Spirit, winless since December 2001, looked set to continue on that losing run when seemingly going nowhere at the penultimate hurdle but, as those in front of him began to slow, he suddenly picked up, showing tremendous enthusiasm, and looked to have a little bit left in reserve as he pinged the last having made his way to the front. An 11-year-old, he seemed to thoroughly enjoy himself in the latter stages and it was a pleasure to watch, although he is obviously no sure thing to repeat this next time. *(op 5-1)*
Purr seemed to benefit from the fitting of cheekpieces and found only one too good. There could be a similar race in him if the headgear continues to have such a positive effect, although he may just want holding on to a little longer in future. *(op 15-2 tchd 7-1 and 9-1)*
Champagne Rossini(IRE), a very moderate maiden on the Flat and over hurdles, held on for third despite having raced keenly in front from no less than 13lb out of the handicap. His proximity makes the form look very weak indeed.
Ray Mond, 4lb out of the handicap on his return to selling company, travelled strongly for much of the way but slowed quickly when asked for an effort. *(op 33-1)*
Ethan Snowflake looked to have an obvious chance on this return to selling company, but was a long way below the pick of his form and proved disappointing. *(op 7-2)*
Trackattack, dropped into selling company on his return hurdling, ran abysmally. *(op 9-2)*
Approaching Land(IRE) has now completed in just four of his last nine starts. *(op 9-2 tchd 7-2)*

3957 "HUNTING WILL SURVIVE THE BAN" EBF "NATIONAL HUNT" NOVICES' HURDLE (QUALIFIER) (11 hdls) 2m 4f
2:50 (2:52) (Class 4) 4-7-Y-0 **£5,204** (£1,528; £764; £381)

Form RPR

4-14 **1** **Mr Pointment (IRE)**[65] [2829] 7-11-9 .... AndrewTinkler 125+
(C R Egerton) *chsd ldr: led 5th: drvn between last two: nt fluent last: styd on* **1/1**[1]

0-11 **2** *6* **Dusky Lord**[14] [3717] 7-11-13 .... LeightonAspell 125+
(N J Gifford) *settled in 3rd: wnt 2nd 7th: rdn and mstke 3 out: 4l down 2 out: no imp whn mstke last* **13/8**[2]

0030 **3** *dist* **The Langer (IRE)**[226] [912] 6-11-3 .... MarkGrant —
(S T Lewis) *4th and sn toiling: t.o fr 7th: btn 69l* **150/1**

540 **4** *21* **Stroom Bank (IRE)**[57] [2950] 6-11-3 .... PaulMoloney —
(C C Bealby) *labouring in last: t.o 7th: btn 90l* **100/1**

5216 **F** **Dearson (IRE)**[47] [3175] 5-11-9 112 .... NoelFehily —
(C J Mann) *led at modest pce: hdd 5th: 7l 3rd and tiring qckly whn fell 3 out* **9/2**[3]

5m 15.2s (3.00) **Going Correction** +0.35s/f (Yiel) **5** Ran SP% **107.9**
Speed ratings: **108,105,—,—,—** CSF £2.90 TOTE £1.90: £1.10, £1.20; EX 3.30.
Owner Stockton Heath Racing **Bred** Miss A Gibson Fleming and Mrs E Cooper **Trained** Chaddleworth, Berks

FOCUS
With Dearson already looking held before he fell, Mr Pointment only had Dusky Lord to beat and never looked in too much danger.

NOTEBOOK
Mr Pointment(IRE) would have found this much less competitive than the novice hurdle he finished fourth in at Newbury when last seen just over two months previously, but Dusky Lord offered reasonable enough competition and he had to be kept going all the way to the line to hold that one off. This was just a workmanlike display, but he is clearly going the right way and deserves his chance in better company. The EBF Final at Sandown and the Brit Insurance Novices' Hurdle at Cheltenham are apparently amongst his options. *(op 11-10 tchd 6-5 in places and 6-4 in a place)*
Dusky Lord, successful in ordinary novice company on both his previous starts over hurdles, had no easy task conceding 4lb to Mr Pointment and was held by that rival from a fair way out. For a brief moment going towards the last it looked as though he might pick up and pose a serious threat, but he made a mess of the hurdle and his challenge did not materialise. This was still a personal best, and he may be aimed at the EBF Final at Sandown. *(tchd 7-4)*
The Langer(IRE) had no chance whatsoever with the front two. *(op 80-1)*
Dearson(IRE) was beginning to struggle when he fell three out. This was a lacklustre effort. *(op 4-1 tchd 5-1)*

3958 HANDS OFF OUR HUNTING H'CAP CHASE (FOR THE PRINCE CARLTON CHALLENGE CUP) (18 fncs) 3m 110y
3:20 (3:20) (Class 4) (0-100,87) 5-Y-0+ **£4,033** (£1,184; £592; £295)

Form RPR

3P05 **1** **Tipp Top (IRE)**[18] [3654] 9-11-0 **75** ....(t) JohnMcNamara 84+
(O Brennan) *2nd tl led briefly 7th: j. slowly 10th: led again 11th: jnd briefly out 3 out: drvn 4l clr whn tired jump last: all out* **5/2**[1]

F640 **2** *nk* **Iloveturtle (IRE)**[10] [3791] 6-10-10 **71** ....(t) KennyJohnson 78+
(M C Chapman) *several slow jumps: bhd: rdn 12th: outpcd 14th: 6l 3rd and effrt whn mstke 2 out: styd on fr last: jst hld* **7/2**[3]

004 **3** *1* **Reach The Clouds (IRE)**[64] [2842] 14-11-7 **87** .... MarkNicolls(5) 91
(John R Upson) *settled rr: hdwy 12th: wnt 2nd after next: jnd wnr 3 out: rdn and outpcd bef last where lft w ch: onepced* **8/1**

0P0 **4** *29* **Thyne Spirit (IRE)**[29] [3457] 7-10-10 **71** .... MarkGrant 46
(S T Lewis) *trckd ldrs: reminders after 7th: blnd 11th: sn lost tch: mstke 13th: continued remote* **13/2**

10/U **5** *6* **Silent Snipe**[24] [3547] 13-10-9 **70** .... RJGreene 39
(Miss L C Siddall) *mde nrly all tl 11th: drvn and wknd bef 15th: blnd bdly next: sn t.o: blnd last* **10/1**

1/6U **F** **Longstone Loch (IRE)**[10] [3791] 9-11-10 **85** .... PaulMoloney —
(C C Bealby) *chsd ldrs: j. slowly 5th: mstke 9th: drvn 14th: disputing 2nd whn fell next* **11/4**[2]

6m 58.1s (20.50) **Going Correction** +0.875s/f (Soft) **6** Ran SP% **111.0**
Speed ratings: **102,101,101,92,90** — CSF £11.61 CT £55.56 TOTE £2.90: £2.10, £1.70; EX 9.30.
Owner T W R Bayley **Bred** Leslie Mellon **Trained** Worksop, Notts

FOCUS
Grim stuff, and it only concerned three horses from a fair way out.

NOTEBOOK
Tipp Top(IRE) had just a beginners' chase success to his name in 14 previous starts over fences, but that sole win came on soft ground at Towcester, suggesting he appreciates a proper stamina test. Racing off a career-low mark, he just did enough, although a slow jump at the last allowed his two closest pursuers every chance on the run-in. *(op 11-4)*
Iloveturtle(IRE), whose only success in 59 previous career starts came in a two-year-old maiden at Beverley in 2002, missed out on a big chance of ending his shocking losing run. Despite not jumping well, he began to stay on at the top of the straight and just failed to take advantage of Tipp Top's mistake at the last. He was due to be dropped 4lb. *(op 9-2)*
Reach The Clouds(IRE), back on a winning mark, ran well, albeit in a bad race. *(op 11-2)*
Thyne Spirit(IRE), twice a point winner in Ireland, has yet to inspire confidence under Rules. *(op 5-1 tchd 8-1)*
Longstone Loch(IRE) was making very hard work of it when falling at the 15th. *(op 10-3)*

3959 HUNTING ACT - "STILL UNWORKABLE LEGISLATION" - H'CAP HURDLE (13 hdls) 2m 7f 110y
3:50 (3:50) (Class 4) (0-115,102) 4-Y-0+ **£4,554** (£1,337; £668; £333)

Form RPR

2111 **1** **New Perk (IRE)**[32] [3416] 8-10-9 **90** .... ChrisHonour(5) 93
(M J Gingell) *prom: led 9th: hrd drvn and edgd rt flat: all out: v game* **2/1**[1]

5444 **2** *hd* **Honey's Gift**[18] [3655] 7-11-8 **98** .... JamieMoore 101
(G G Margarson) *hld up mid field: j. slowly 7th: drvn to go 2nd 3 out: ev ch next: sltly outpcd last: rallied and jst failed* **9/2**[2]

5356 **3** *15* **Oulton Broad**[48] [3141] 10-10-12 **91** ....(p) StephenCraine(3) 79
(R Ford) *hld up in rr: rdn and outpcd bef 3 out: mod 5th bef next where mstke and lft 4th: nvr on terms* **8/1**

015 **4** *16* **In The Hat (IRE)**[32] [3416] 10-10-11 **87** .... JodieMogford 59
(J R Jenkins) *hld up: rdn after 9th: brief effrt in 2nd bef 3 out: sn btn: wnt rt next: nt run on* **12/1**

12F5 **5** *5* **Miss Skippy**[18] [3648] 7-11-10 **100** .... AndrewThornton 67
(A G Newcombe) *prom: wnt 2nd 5th: led briefly bef 9th: rdn and wknd bef 3 out: t.o* **11/2**

2P16 **6** *17* **Squantum (IRE)**[18] [3654] 9-11-1 **91** ....(p) TomScudamore 41
(Miss Joanne Priest) *chsd ldr tl 5th: rdn 9th: lost tch u.p after next: t.o* **5/1**[3]

5P24 **P** **Alexander Sapphire (IRE)**[12] [3415] 5-10-12 **91**.........(t) OwynNelmes(3) —
(N B King) *hld up in rr: stopped to nil after 9th: p.u next* **20/1**

-P00 **P** **Long Shot**[36] [3351] 9-10-9 **85**.. RJGreene —
(Miss L C Siddall) *led: niggled 7th: hdd & wknd qckly after next: t.o and p.u 3 out* **50/1**

F000 **F** **Courant D'Air (IRE)**[21] [3600] 5-11-12 **102**........................ LeightonAspell —
(Lucinda Featherstone) *mid field: rdn and outpcd 3 out: disputing 10l 3rd whn bmpd and fell 2 out* **14/1**

6m 23.2s (16.80) **Going Correction** +0.875s/f (Soft) **9** Ran SP% **115.8**
Speed ratings: **107,106,101,96,94 89,—,—,—** CSF £11.90 CT £58.67 TOTE £3.40: £1.50, £1.40, £2.20; EX 12.90.
Owner A White **Bred** Tim Mulhare **Trained** North Runcton, Norfolk

FOCUS
The top weight was rated 13lb below the ceiling of 115 and this was a moderate handicap hurdle for the grade, but a fine effort from course-specialist New Perk, who completed a Fakenham four-timer in game fashion.

NOTEBOOK
New Perk(IRE), successful in two novices chases round here before winning a handicap hurdle over course and distance on his most recent start, defied an 8lb rise to complete the four-timer. He clearly loves Fakenham and should continue to go well there, especially as connections will have the option of sending him back over fences. *(op 7-4 tchd 9-4 in places)*
Honey's Gift was unproven over a trip this far, but got it well and made the in-form course specialist work very hard. Now she has proven her stamina, connections should have more options. *(op 5-1)*
Oulton Broad, back up in trip on his first run since returning to Richard Ford's stable, took just a moderate third. His last two wins over hurdles came in claiming company. *(op 9-1 tchd 10-1)*
In The Hat(IRE) again gave the impression he is high enough in the weights. He could do better if dropped back into selling company. *(tchd 14-1)*
Miss Skippy gained her last success in a seller and should do better at that level. *(op 5-1)*
Squantum(IRE), back over hurdles, did not improve for the fitting of cheekpieces but this ground was probably soft enough. *(op 8-1)*
Courant D'Air(IRE) was making hard work of it and a little way off the leader in third when falling two out. *(op 16-1 tchd 18-1)*
Alexander Sapphire(IRE) *Official explanation: jockey said mare had a breathing problem (op 16-1 tchd 18-1)*

3960 P.H. BETTS (HOLDINGS) LTD HUNTERS' CHASE (FOR THE WALTER WALES CUP) (16 fncs) 2m 5f 110y
4:20 (4:20) (Class 5) 5-Y-0+ **£3,296** (£1,014; £507)

Form RPR

2230 **1** **Galway Breeze (IRE)**[26] 11-11-7 107............................ MrMMackley(7) 114+
(Mrs Julie Read) *j.w: pressed ldr: drvn level 2 out: forged clr bef last* **5/1**[2]

230- **2** *6* **Cantarinho**[13] 8-11-9 .... MrDKemp(5) 109+
(D J Kemp) *j.w: led: rdn and jnd and bmpd 2 out: styd w wnr tl ent st: btn whn mstke last* **4/6**[1]

1354 **3** *13* **Moving Earth (IRE)**[183] [1248] 13-12-3 118.......................... MrCWard(7) 104
(C E Ward) *lost 15l s: sn jst in tch: last tl appr 12th: outpcd next: wnt mod 3rd bef last* **12/1**

P/0- **4** *½* **Perange (FR)**[365] [3903] 10-11-7 122................................ MrAMerriam(7) 94
(Mrs D M Grissell) *mid field: rdn 13th: 8l 3rd next: sn wknd* **12/1**

36P5 **5** *hd* **Guignol Du Cochet (FR)**[9] [3805] 12-11-11 95.................. MrAWintle(3) 93
(S Flook) *settled in rr: lost tch 13th* **7/1**[3]

3F0/ **P** **Bregogue (IRE)**[558] [1153] 12-11-7 .... MrRStearn(7) —
(Sean Regan) *j. slowly 1st: mid field tl rdn after 9th: wknd 11th: last whn plld 13th* **33/1**

3105 **P** **Get The Point**[134] [1659] 12-12-5 89................................ MrJOwen(5) —
(Perry Harding-Jones) *keen: settled 3rd: j.rt 9th: rdn 12th: 2nd briefly and slow next: sn wknd: t.o and p.u last* **20/1**

6m 2.50s (18.00) **Going Correction** +0.875s/f (Soft) **7** Ran SP% **112.2**
Speed ratings: **102,99,95,94,94** —,— CSF £8.94 TOTE £9.50: £2.90, £1.10; EX 19.90.
Owner Mrs E M Clarke **Bred** Frank Cruess-Callaghan **Trained** Newmarket, Suffolk

FOCUS
This was won in 2005 by the subsequent Cheltenham Fox Hunters and Aintree handicap winner Sleeping Night, but there was nothing approaching his calibre in the field this time. The winner has been rated to last spring's handicap form.

NOTEBOOK
Galway Breeze(IRE), rated 116 at his peak when trained by Kate Walton, had been well held in a couple of fast-ground points recently, but this surface would have suited much better and he made a successful hunter chase debut in good style. He could go for the big hunter chase at Aintree's National meeting. *(op 9-2 tchd 11-2)*
Cantarinho, returned to hunter chasing following two wins in point-to-point company recently, was ultimately no match for the winner. *(op 10-11 tchd evens in places)*
Moving Earth(IRE), fourth in a claiming hurdle on his last start six months previously, was up to his old tricks at the start and never really posed a serious threat in the race itself. He is a challenge for his new connections. *(op 7-1)*
Perange(FR) offered some hope off the back of a year-long absence. *(op 16-1 tchd 18-1)*
Guignol Du Cochet(FR) continues below his best, but looks better suited by good ground. *(op 6-1)*

3961 "GO HUNTING TOMORROW" DONCASTER BLOODSTOCK SALES/EBF MARES' INTERMEDIATE OPEN NH FLAT RACE QUALIFIER 2m
4:50 (4:50) (Class 6) 4-7-Y-0 **£2,192** (£639; £319)

Form RPR

2 **1** **Wyldello**[44] [3244] 5-11-2 .... RobertThornton 102+
(A King) *trckd ldrs in v slow race: drvn over 3f out: led over 1f out:r.o* **8/11**[1]

2 **2** *2½* **Tambourine Davis (FR)**[65] [2830] 4-10-7 .... OllieMcPhail 88
(N J Henderson) *settled cl up: led 4f out: sn rdn: hdd over 1f out: nt qckn* **5/2**[2]

1-10 **3** *14* **Rosita Bay**[82] [2534] 5-11-12 .... LeightonAspell 95+
(O Sherwood) *hld up: in tch: rdn 4f out: sn lft bhd* **13/2**[3]

3 **4** *14* **Nannys Gift (IRE)**[27] [3497] 7-10-13 .... LeeVickers(3) 69
(O Brennan) *in tch: rdn half way: lost tch 4f out* **33/1**

4 **5** *4* **Karrie**[32] [3421] 5-10-9 .... TomMessenger(7) 65
(C C Bealby) *cl 2nd in crawl tl led 1/2-way: hdd 4f out: immediately compounded* **100/1**

0 **6** *3½* **Follow My Leader (IRE)**[86] [2446] 6-10-13 .... StephenCraine(3) 62
(R Ford) *led at pedestrian pce tl 1/2-way: lost tch qckly 4f out* **33/1**

04/ **7** *dist* **Bonny Busona**[684] [4670] 6-10-9 .... ShaneWalsh(7) —
(K F Clutterbuck) *bhd: rdn 1/2-way: t.o 6f out: btn 84l* **80/1**

8 *dist* **Ellie Lou** 5-10-9 .... MattyRoe(7) —
(A E Jessop) *in tch on suffernce tl crawl lifted 1/2-way: sn hopelessly t.o: btn 152l* **150/1**

4m 18.9s (8.70) **Going Correction** +0.875s/f (Soft)
WFA 4 from 5yo+ 9lb **8** Ran SP% **108.6**
Speed ratings: **101,99,92,85,83 82,—,—** CSF £2.31 TOTE £2.00: £1.02, £1.20, £1.70; EX 3.00 Place 6 £12.67, Place 5 £10.38.
Owner Mickleton Racing Club **Bred** R Chugg **Trained** Barbury Castle, Wilts

FOCUS
The first three are all reasonable types and this was not a bad mares' bumper, although the early pace was predictably steady.

NOTEBOOK
Wyldello, a sister to the classy bumper and hurdles performer Marello and second behind a smart prospect on her debut at Wincanton, confirmed the promise she showed there to get off the mark. She took a while to pick up, but the slow pace would not have suited and she can do better again. *(tchd 4-5 in places)*
Tambourine Davis(FR), a promising second in an ordinary mile and a half bumper on her debut at Newbury just over two months earlier, was ultimately no match for the winner but finished clear of the remainder. She seems to be going the right way and really should find a similar race. *(op 9-4 tchd 11-4 in places)*
Rosita Bay, successful on her first two starts before running down the field in a good race at Newbury last time, had no easy task giving weight away all round and, with the steady pace totally against her, she proved no match for the front two. She is bred to stay and could be ready for a switch to obstacles. *(op 8-1)*
Nannys Gift(IRE) found this much tougher than the Haydock bumper she was third in on her debut. *(op 25-1)*
Karrie would have found this more competitive than the course and distance bumper she was fourth in on her debut. *(op 66-1)*
T/Plt: £8.80 to a £1 stake. Pool: £50,405.85. 4,177.70 winning tickets. T/Qpdt: £3.00 to a £1 stake. Pool: £3,381.30. 825.90 winning tickets. IM

[3786]MARKET RASEN (R-H)
Friday, February 17

OFFICIAL GOING: Hurdle course - good to soft; chase course - soft (good to soft in places in back straight)
The hurdle running rail had been moved 6' out and the bends brought in by 12'.
The ground was described as 'very tacky'.
Wind: Moderate, half-against Weather: Mainly fine but cold

3962 BETFREDCASINO.COM NOVICES' HURDLE (12 hdls) 3m
2:00 (2:00) (Class 3) 4-Y-0+ **£5,204** (£1,528; £764; £381)

Form RPR

01 **1** **Atlantic Jane**[29] [3461] 6-11-4 .... DominicElsworth 115+
(Mrs S J Smith) *led to 2nd: chsd ldr: styd on u.p fr 3 out: chal next: sn led: drew away run-in* **6/1**[3]

2321 **2** *6* **Ballyshan (IRE)**[28] [3477] 8-11-11 120.............................. AntonyEvans 118+
(N A Twiston-Davies) *led 2nd: qckned 6th: drvn along 9th: hdd after 2 out: a length down and hld whn hit last: no ex* **8/13**[1]

600 **3** *dist* **Champion's Day (GER)**[18] [3646] 5-11-4 .... APMcCoy 65
(Jonjo O'Neill) *chsd ldrs: outpcd whn hit 8th: tk mod 3rd 2 out: btn a total of 51 l* **14/1**

230 **4** *6* **Beau De Turgeon (FR)**[43] [3253] 5-11-4 114..................... RichardJohnson 59
(Ian Williams) *chsd ldrs: reminders 8th: lost pl 3 out: t.o next: kpt on run-in: beaten 57 l* **4/1**[2]

0 **5** *4* **Cayman Calypso (IRE)**[24] [3545] 5-11-4 .... WarrenMarston 59+
(Mrs P Sly) *t.k.h: wnt prom 5th: wknd appr 2 out: mod 4th whn blnd last: beaten 61 l* **20/1**

504 **6** *4* **Mange Tout (IRE)**[32] [3417] 7-11-4 .... SeanCurran —
(K J Burke) *t.k.h in last: sme hdwy 9th: lost pl after next: sn bhd: beaten 65 l* **100/1**

P **Curate (USA)**[616] 7-11-4 .... AlanDempsey —
(M E Sowersby) *tubed: in tch 4th: reminders 7th: wknd qckly next: sn t.o and p.u* **150/1**

6m 17.1s (10.30) **Going Correction** +0.525s/f (Soft) **7** Ran SP% **109.3**
Speed ratings: **103,101,—,—,— —,—** CSF £9.68 TOTE £6.70: £1.80, £1.30; EX 11.00.
Owner P J Hughes Developments Ltd **Bred** G G A Gregson **Trained** High Eldwick, W Yorks

FOCUS
They went no gallop at all for the first circuit but in the end it was a true test of stamina and the first two came a long way clear. The winner is progressing well.

NOTEBOOK
Atlantic Jane, who has changed stables, had to work hard to get to grips with the leader but ultimately ran out a most convincing winner, stepping up significantly on the form of her Ludlow win. All she seems to do is stay. *(tchd 5-1)*
Ballyshan(IRE) quickened it up after the first circuit. He was hard at work four out and in the end the weight concession to the winner proved beyond him. *(op 4-6)*
Champion's Day(GER) was struggling to keep in touch when hitting the first flight in the back straight on the final circuit and in the end finished a distant third. This type of ground is probably against him. *(op 11-1)*
Beau De Turgeon(FR), who looks every inch a chaser, dropped right away starting the final turn and for a while looked in danger of being pulled up. He took it in to his mind to stay on after the last and does not look entirely straight forward. *(op 7-2)*
Cayman Calypso(IRE), a free-going sort, emptied in a matter of strides and ought to be capable of a fair bit better on a much less testing surface. *(op 25-1)*

3963 BETFRED WE PAY DOUBLE RESULT MAIDEN HURDLE (8 hdls) 2m 1f 110y
2:30 (2:30) (Class 4) 4-Y-0+ **£3,578** (£1,050; £525; £262)

Form RPR

1 **Orcadian**[104] 5-11-4 .... MarkBradburne 126+
(J M P Eustace) *led after 1st: j. slowly and hdd next: led after 3 out: hdd next: styd on to ld 1f out: kpt on* **2/1**[1]

500/ **2** *1* **Ken's Dream**[566] [4460] 7-11-4 .... TomDoyle 120+
(Mrs L Wadham) *trckd ldrs: slt ld 2 out: hdd run-in: no ex* **3/1**[2]

63P5 **3** *dist* **Keen Warrior**[32] [3417] 6-11-1 .... LeeVickers(3) 88
(Mrs S Lamyman) *chsd ldrs: outpcd appr 2 out: hrd rdn and edgd lft run-in: btn a total of 33 l* **40/1**

4 *1½* **Olival (FR)**[137] 4-10-9 .... APMcCoy 78
(Jonjo O'Neill) *in tch: drvn along after 3 out: one pce* **11/2**[3]

000 **5** *1¼* **Wot Way Chief**[36] [3347] 5-10-13 .... ThomasDreaper(5) 86
(J M Jefferson) *t.k.h in rr: hdwy 5th: nvr nr ldrs* **33/1**

6 *8* **Time To Relax (IRE)**[168] 5-10-11 .... WayneHutchinson 71
(R Dickin) *mid-div: hdwy 5th: sn chsng ldrs: wkng whn blnd 2 out* **40/1**

The Form Book, Raceform Ltd, Compton, RG20 6NL

50 **7** *½* **Penny Park (IRE)**[87] 2421 7-11-4 .... PJBrennan 77
(P J Hobbs) *led tl after 1st: lft in ld next: hdd after 3 out: lost pl appr next* **9/1**

00 **8** *3 ½* **Windyx (FR)**[15] 3685 5-10-11 .... AndrewGlassonbury(7) 73
(M C Pipe) *hld up towards rr: stdy hdwy 5th: lost pl appr 2 out* **50/1**

0P **9** *½* **First Centurion**[44] 3238 5-11-1 .... PaulO'Neill(3) 72
(Ian Williams) *chsd ldrs: lost pl after 3 out* **33/1**

000 **10** *7* **Another Chat (IRE)**[29] 3466 6-10-11 .... SeanQuinlan(7) 65
(R T Phillips) *bhd fr 5th* **66/1**

0P0 **11** *2 ½* **Bally Abbie**[36] 3347 5-10-11 .... AnthonyRoss 55
(P Beaumont) *prom: wknd 3 out* **125/1**

00 **12** *2* **Naja De Billeron (FR)**[17] 3658 5-11-1 .... TomMalone(3) 60
(M C Pipe) *hld up: stdy hdwy on ins and n.m.r appr 3 out: lost pl bef 2 out* **25/1**

13 *11* **Corble (IRE)**[299] 6-11-4 .... RichardJohnson 49
(P J Hobbs) *w ldrs: hit 5th: wknd qckly appr 2 out* **11/1**

6000 **14** *10* **Lone Rider (IRE)**[21] 3597 5-11-4 .... RichardMcGrath 39
(Jonjo O'Neill) *a in rr: bhd fr 3 out* **100/1**

P **Song Of Vala**[156] 5-11-4 ....(t) JimmyMcCarthy —
(C J Mann) *mid-div: lost pl 5th: bhd whn p.u bef 2 out* **12/1**

5 **P** **Carnival Town**[53] 2961 5-11-4 .... MickFitzgerald —
(Jonjo O'Neill) *in rr: bhd fr 3 out: t.o whn p.u bef last* **22/1**

P **Mr Buddy (IRE)** 5-11-4 .... GrahamLee —
(J Howard Johnson) *j. poorly: sn in rr: bhd fr 4th: t.o whn p.u bef 2 out* **33/1**

00- **P** **Never Cried Wolf**[527] 1393 5-10-11 .... JohnPritchard(7) —
(R Dickin) *in rr: bhd fr 3 out: t.o whn p.u bef last* **125/1**

4m 21.3s (4.90) **Going Correction** +0.525s/f (Soft)
WFA 4 from 5yo+ 9lb **18** Ran SP% **127.7**
Speed ratings: **110,109,**—,—,— —,—,—,—,— —,—,—,—,— —,—,— CSF £7.36 TOTE £3.80: £1.60, £1.60, £6.00; EX 12.40.
Owner J C Smith **Bred** Littleton Stud **Trained** Newmarket, Suffolk

FOCUS
Good novice form, with Orcadian a former Group Three winner on the Flat and currently rated 102, and the runner-up very promising too. They went a good gallop and the form should stand up.

NOTEBOOK
Orcadian, a smart but wayward stayer on the level, jumped soundly on the whole apart from slowing up at the second. He put his head down and battled, and after this encouraging start his trainer will be keen to get another outing into him before deciding his Cheltenham target. *(tchd 9-4)*
Ken's Dream ◆, last seen on the Flat a year and a half ago, really took the eye in the paddock and came in for plenty of support. He travelled strongly and went a neck up, but in the end had to settle for second best. He richly deserves to go one better. *(op 9-2)*
Keen Warrior, who had two handlers in the paddock, was left for dead by the first two going to two out. Under severe pressure he went badly left on the run-in but did just enough to hang on to a remote third spot, running creditably behind two decent rivals.
Olival(FR), winner of a bumper in France, is a tall, weak-looking sort. He ran a satisfactory first race but hardy appeals as a likely winner in the short term. *(op 6-1 tchd 13-2)*
Wot Way Chief, who looks more of a chaser, seemed to be ridden with one eye on teaching him to settle. *(op 28-1)*
Carnival Town *Official explanation: jockey said gelding lost its action (op 25-1 tchd 20-1)*

3964 BETFRED "THE BONUS KING" H'CAP CHASE (12 fncs) 2m 1f 110y
3:00 (3:00) (Class 4) (0-110,108) 5-Y-0+
£4,070 (£1,202; £601; £300; £150; £75)

Form RPR
P0P6 **1** **Log On Intersky (IRE)**[10] 3788 10-11-12 **108** .... RichardHobson 118+
(J R Cornwall) *led 2nd: kpt on gamely fr 3 out: all out* **14/1**

0314 **2** *1 ¾* **Julies Boy (IRE)**[17] 3663 9-10-7 **96** ....(t) WillieMcCarthy(7) 102+
(T R George) *led to 2nd: chsd wnr: chal 3 out: kpt on same pce between last 2* **5/2**[2]

4441 **3** *2* **Before The Mast (IRE)**[5] 3887 9-10-0 **89** 7ex .... CharliePoste(7) 93+
(M F Harris) *in tch: hit 7th: jnd ldrs 9th: rdn next: kpt on same pce* **15/8**[1]

0105 **4** *11* **Honest Endeavour**[23] 3558 7-11-4 **105** .... ThomasDreaper(5) 99+
(J M Jefferson) *in tch: n.m.r bnd appr 6th: blnd bdly 7th: no threat after: tk mod 4th last* **9/1**

6560 **5** *3* **Pornic (FR)**[12] 3762 12-9-9 **82** oh14 ....(b) DeclanMcGann(5) 74+
(A Crook) *chsd ldrs: outpcd whn hit 9th: sn lost pl* **22/1**

0032 **6** *24* **Vulcan Lane (NZ)**[24] 3555 9-10-3 **85** ....(p) LarryMcGrath 65+
(R C Guest) *j. slowly and rt-handed: in tch: hit 7th: sn lost pl and bhd* **3/1**[3]

/0-P **U** **Pauntley Gofa**[12] 10-10-11 **100** .... JohnPritchard(7) —
(R C Harper) *t.k.h: trckd ldrs: wkng and mod 4th whn blnd and uns rdr 3 out* **33/1**

4m 49.9s (18.80) **Going Correction** +1.175s/f (Heav) **7** Ran SP% **112.3**
Speed ratings: **105,104,103,98,97 86,**— CSF £48.88 TOTE £11.40: £5.90, £1.60; EX 64.50.
Owner J R Cornwall **Bred** Mrs Maureen Mackey **Trained** Long Clawson, Leics
■ Richard Hobson's first winner for more than a year, including eight months out with a shoulder problem.

FOCUS
A modest contest, but it was run at a sound pace. The winner was well in on the best of his autumn form and the second and third ran to their marks.

NOTEBOOK
Log On Intersky(IRE), whose last success in 2003 came from a 21lb higher mark, rolled back the years. A sound jump at the last sealed it and gave his rider a welcome winner on his return to the saddle. *Official explanation: trainer had no explanation for the improved form shown other than the gelding enjoying being able to dominate (op 12-1)*
Julies Boy(IRE), who is fast climbing the ratings, landed upides three out but was booked for second spot after being outjumped at the last. *(op 9-4)*
Before The Mast(IRE), making a quick return to action, looked to be going marginally best on the turn in to three out but, soon under the whip, had no excuse. *(op 2-1 tchd 9-4 and 7-4, 5-2 in a place)*
Honest Endeavour almost demolished the open ditch down the back and did well to finish as close as he did. He remains capable of better over fences. *(op 8-1 tchd 10-1)*
Pornic(FR), a stone out of the handicap, had decided he had done enough for one day when he clouted the fourth last. *(tchd 20-1)*
Vulcan Lane(NZ) ran a stinker, jumping slowly and going right-handed throughout. *(op 10-3 tchd 7-2)*

3965 BETFREDPOKER.COM H'CAP CHASE (17 fncs) 3m 1f
3:30 (3:30) (Class 3) (0-120,118) 5-Y-0+ **£6,506** (£1,910; £955; £477)

Form RPR
P0P6 **1** **Naunton Brook**[29] 3469 7-11-12 **118** ....(t) AntonyEvans 135+
(N A Twiston-Davies) *led to 3rd: led 6th: blnd 13th: hit last: jst hld on* **12/1**

06P0 **2** *shd* **Hawk's Landing (IRE)**[65] 2818 9-10-8 **100** .... APMcCoy 114
(Jonjo O'Neill) *hld up in tch: smooth hdwy and prom 12th: chsd wnr fr 4 out: chal 2 out: hrd rdn run-in: jst hld* **9/1**

F-F2 **3** *dist* **Denada**[35] 3372 10-10-7 **104** .... StevenCrawford(5) —
(Mrs Susan Nock) *chsd ldrs: drvn along 1tth: rallied 4 out: lost pl appr next and lft mod 3rd: btn 63 l* **9/1**

0156 **4** *dist* **Strong Magic (IRE)**[32] 3420 14-10-4 **96** .... RichardHobson —
(J R Cornwall) *prom: reminders and lost pl 11th: sn bhd: t.o 4 out: btn a total of 130 l* **40/1**

2-3B **U** **Tom Fruit**[86] 2445 9-11-3 **109** .... RussGarritty —
(T D Easterby) *in last pl whn blnd and uns rdr 1st* **7/2**[1]

2FP4 **P** **Pardini (USA)**[22] 3578 7-10-0 **92** ....(v) PJBrennan —
(M F Harris) *prom: lost pl 10th: bhd next: p.u bef 12th* **16/1**

4233 **F** **Dante Citizen (IRE)**[27] 3509 8-11-0 **106** .... JasonMaguire 110
(T R George) *chsd ldrs: 3rd and wkng whn fell 3 out* **4/1**[2]

P-53 **P** **Cordilla (IRE)**[57] 2946 8-11-12 **118** .... TonyDobbin —
(N G Richards) *mstkes: prom: reminders 10th: lost pl 12th: p.u bef 4 out* **7/2**[1]

2224 **P** **Superrollercoaster**[34] 3382 6-10-7 **99** ....(v) JamesDavies —
(O Sherwood) *w ldrs: j.rt: led 3rd to 6th: lost pl 12th: sn bhd: t.o 6th whn p.u bef 3 out* **5/1**[3]

6m 44.4s (7.00) **Going Correction** +1.175s/f (Heav) **9** Ran SP% **117.1**
Speed ratings: **107,106,**—,—,— —,—,—,— CSF £112.98 CT £1026.41 TOTE £12.30: £2.90, £2.40, £2.80; EX 96.20.
Owner David Langdon **Bred** C W And Mrs Moore **Trained** Naunton, Gloucs

FOCUS
This was run at a sound gallop. The first two have been rated to the best of their previous form this season, but the race could be rated higher.

NOTEBOOK
Naunton Brook, in a tongue tie this time, did well to survive a blunder five out. In the end he really battled to hang on by a whisker. *(op 14-1 tchd 16-1)*
Hawk's Landing(IRE), who has slipped right down the weights, was hunted round. He came there upsides, travelling the better, but despite the champion throwing everything at him on the run-in he just missed out.
Denada, struggling early on the final circuit, worked his way on to the coat tails of the leaders on the final turn but the first two quickly left him for dead. At least he has now completed on two successive outings. *(op 17-2)*
Strong Magic(IRE) began to lose touch with a full circuit to go.
Tom Fruit parted company with his rider at the very first fence. *(op 5-1)*
Cordilla(IRE) tended to run in snatches and was let down by his jumping. *Official explanation: jockey said gelding was never travelling (op 5-1)*
Dante Citizen(IRE), whose three career wins have all been in March, looked to have reached the end of his tether when taking a crashing fall three out. *(op 5-1)*

3966 BETFRED.COM H'CAP HURDLE (10 hdls) 2m 6f
4:00 (4:01) (Class 3) (0-125,125) 4-Y-0+ **£6,506** (£1,910; £955; £477)

Form RPR
134P **1** **Day Of Claies (FR)**[29] 3458 5-10-10 **109** ....(b1) CarlLlewellyn 117+
(N A Twiston-Davies) *wnt prom 5th: hit next: led after 3 out: styd on wl fr 2 out: drvn out* **10/1**

1012 **2** *4* **Euro American (GER)**[20] 3622 6-11-12 **125** .... AlanDempsey 130+
(E W Tuer) *hld up in rr: wnt prom 6th: wnt 2nd after 3 out: nt qckn run-in* **7/4**[1]

0423 **3** *6* **Vicars Destiny**[13] 3741 8-11-2 **115** ....(p) TomSiddall 113
(Mrs S Lamyman) *rr-div: chsd ldrs 5th: outpcd 3 out: wnt mod 3rd next: kpt on same pce* **5/1**[3]

PPUP **4** *1 ¼* **Grattan Lodge (IRE)**[52] 3018 9-10-10 **109** .... GrahamLee 106
(J Howard Johnson) *w ldrs: drvn 5th: one pce fr 3 out* **20/1**

32/0 **5** *6* **Jamaican Flight (USA)**[15] 3687 13-9-7 **99** oh2 .... PhilKinsella(7) 90
(Mrs S Lamyman) *led tl after 3 out: sn wl outpcd* **40/1**

U4P5 **6** *9* **Cill Churnain (IRE)**[36] 3350 13-11-7 **120** .... DominicElsworth 102
(Mrs S J Smith) *chsd ldrs: rdn and outpcd after 7th: no threat after* **33/1**

F444 **7** *1* **Predicament**[13] 3741 7-10-12 **111** .... APMcCoy 92
(Jonjo O'Neill) *t.k.h in rr: stdy hdwy 7th: shkn up and fnd nthing bef 2 out* **7/2**[2]

3000 **8** *13* **Altitude Dancer (IRE)**[28] 3487 6-9-12 **102** .... DeclanMcGann(5) 70
(A Crook) *reminders 2nd: bhd and drvn 5th: out of tch whn mstke 7th* **20/1**

336P **9** *dist* **Ardashir (FR)**[53] 2957 7-11-12 **125** .... MarcusFoley —
(Mrs S J Humphrey) *w ldrs: drvn 6th: sn lost pl and bhd: t.o: btn total of 77 l* **66/1**

101P **P** **Sheer Guts (IRE)**[38] 3339 7-9-12 **102** ....(vt) TomGreenway(5) —
(Robert Gray) *prom: hit 4th: rdn and lost pl next: bhd fr 7th: t.o whn p.u bef 2 out* **25/1**

03-2 **P** **Crazy Horse (IRE)**[35] 3378 13-11-5 **121** .... GaryBerridge(3) 104
(L Lungo) *hld up in rr: stdy hdwy 7th: wnt handy 3rd after next: wkng whn j. slowly and lost pl 2out: 8th whn p.u run-in* **8/1**

5m 37.1s (8.80) **Going Correction** +0.70s/f (Soft) **11** Ran SP% **115.7**
Speed ratings: **112,110,108,107,105 102,102,97,**—,— — CSF £26.32 CT £101.51 TOTE £11.50: £2.50, £1.30, £1.90; EX 32.10 Trifecta £317.60 Pool: £671.00 - 1.50 winning tickets..
Owner Million In Mind Partnership **Bred** J P Chauvet And Mme Jean-Paul Chauvet **Trained** Naunton, Gloucs

FOCUS
A sound gallop, and the first-time blinkers worked the oracle on the winner, who showed improved form.

NOTEBOOK
Day Of Claies(FR), pulled up last time, was galvanised by blinkers and,under a determined ride, *did too much in the end for the runner-up.Official explanation: trainer's representative said, regarding the improved form shown, gelding was suited by the use of first time blinkers (op 12-1)*
Euro American(GER), creeping up the weights, looked to be travelling the better when sent in pursuit of the winner but in the end he did not see the extended trip out as well as him. *(op 13-8 tchd 6-4, 15-8 in places)*
Vicars Destiny, from a stable finding form, had her stablemate in to set the pace. She stuck on in her own time and is worth another try over three miles plus, as she is suited by extreme distances on the Flat. *(op 6-1)*
Grattan Lodge(IRE), slipping down the ratings, ran a lot better and may be ready for a return to fences.
Jamaican Flight(USA), a shadow of his former self, did his best to set up the race for stablemate Vicars Destiny and deserves credit for his pacemaking role.
Predicament, anchored at the back, was still on the steel starting the home turn but when asked a question the response was very much in the negative. *(op 4-1)*
Crazy Horse(IRE) looked a danger when moving on to the heels of the first two starting the final turn but he stopped as if something had gone wrong two out and was eventually pulled up and *dismounted on the run-in. A winner seven times, he must be nearing retirement now.Official explanation: jockey said gelding lost its action (op 7-1)*

3967 BETFRED 570 SHOPS NATIONWIDE H'CAP HURDLE (8 hdls) 2m 1f 110y

4:30 (4:30) (Class 4) (0-115,115) 4-Y-0+ **£5,204** (£1,528; £764; £381)

Form RPR

0646 **1** **Overstrand (IRE)**[27] 3492 7-11-12 **115**.................. TonyDobbin 121
(Robert Gray) *in tch: pushed along 3rd: wnt prom 5th: styd on fr 2 out: led last 150yds* **13/2**[3]

500 **2** *3* **Pseudonym (IRE)**[18] 3650 4-10-0 **98**.................. PJBrennan 92
(M F Harris) *hld up in rr: hdwy to chse ldrs 5th: led and mstke last: hdd and no ex* **33/1**

0-0U **3** *2* **Caraman (IRE)**[27] 2964 8-11-3 **111**.................. DougieCostello(5) 112+
(J J Quinn) *trckd ldrs: led 2 out: hdd last: no ex* **3/1**[1]

5051 **4** *3* **Flake**[13] 3737 6-10-12 **101**.................. PadgeWhelan 99
(Mrs S J Smith) *w ldrs: led 3 out: hdd next: fdd last* **4/1**[2]

5 **5** *shd* **Oscar D'Hyrome (FR)**[46] 3203 4-10-4 **102**.................. RichardMcGrath 91+
(C Grant) *in tch: hit 2nd: hdwy to chse ldrs 4th: outpcd 3 out: styd on wl appr last: fin wl* **16/1**

20P0 **6** *18* **Pont Neuf (IRE)**[30] 3442 6-10-3 **95**..................(t) PaddyAspell(3) 75
(A Crook) *chsd ldrs: lost pl after 5th: sn bhd* **50/1**

231- **7** *2 ½* **Miss Holly**[571] 1044 7-10-9 **98**.................. DominicElsworth 75
(Mrs S J Smith) *in tch: outpceed after 5th: lost pl appr 2 out* **4/1**[2]

5-30 **8** *3* **Iberus (GER)**[4] 1987 8-10-11 **103**..................(p) WilliamKennedy(3) 77
(S Gollings) *led: j.lft 3rd: hdd 3 out: lost pl appr next* **12/1**

P060 **9** *5* **Migration**[15] 3687 10-10-13 **102**.................. TomSiddall 71
(Mrs S Lamyman) *hld up in rr: sme hdwy 3 out: lost pl appr next* **20/1**

01 **10** *dist* **Muntami (IRE)**[21] 3591 5-10-12 **101**.................. RichardJohnson —
(John A Harris) *chsd ldrs: drvn 5th: sn lost pl: t.o 2 out: btn total of 94 l* **7/1**

0005 **P** **Vrisaki (IRE)**[28] 3488 5-10-6 **95**.................. AlanDempsey —
(M E Sowersby) *t.k.h: w ldrs: hmpd 3rd: lost pl 5th: sn wl bhd: t.o whn p.u bef 2 out* **33/1**

4m 28.5s (12.10) **Going Correction** +0.70s/f (Soft)
WFA 4 from 5yo+ 9lb **11 Ran SP% 117.0**
Speed ratings: **101,99,98,97,97 89,88,86,84,—** — CSF £194.05 CT £775.79 TOTE £6.40: £2.00, £7.30, £2.00; EX 156.20.

Owner Naughty Diesel Ltd **Bred** Airlie Stud **Trained** Malton, N Yorks

FOCUS
Just a steady pace. The winner has been rated to the best of this season's form, and the runner-up recorded a personal best.

NOTEBOOK
Overstrand(IRE), with Tony Dobbin back in the saddle, looked to be struggling with a full circuit to go but in the end his rider's perserverance paid off. *(op 11-2)*

Pseudonym(IRE), having his second outing in a handicap, blundered his way to the front at the final flight but in the end could not match the winner. This was much more encouraging.

Caraman(IRE), his confidence boosted by an All-Weather win, travelled strongly but in the end seemed to struggle to see it right out. *(op 7-2)*

Flake, 6lb higher, looked to be travelling best when going on three out but in the end he couldn't see it out. *(tchd 7-2)*

Oscar D'Hyrome(FR), having just his second outing here, finished best of all after getting outpaced and is well worth a try over further. *(op 14-1)*

Miss Holly, absent since July, never got competitive. *(op 5-1)*

3968 BETFRED IN SHOPS, ON THE PHONE AND ON-LINE HUNTERS' CHASE (14 fncs) 2m 4f

5:00 (5:00) (Class 6) 5-Y-0+ **£1,648** (£507; £253)

Form RPR

1 **Bedtime Boys**[19] 9-11-7.................. MrJDocker(7) 114
(Miss H Campbell) *chsd ldrs: led after 9th: styd on fr 3 out* **8/1**[3]

5-P1 **2** *3* **Telemoss (IRE)**[7] 3847 12-12-2.................. MissRDavidson(3) 116
(N G Richards) *hld up in rr: wnt prom 5th: reminders 11th: kpt on to go 2nd last: kpt on: nvr landed a blow* **4/11**[1]

06/0 **3** *11* **Danaeve (IRE)**[149] 1515 11-11-7.................. MrLHicks(7) 105+
(R Harvey) *trckd ldrs: mstke 7th: sn led: hdd after 9th: 3rd and struggling whn blnd 3 out: one pce* **33/1**

P4-4 **4** *3 ½* **Kjetil (USA)**[34] 6-12-2 117.................. MrRCope(3) 106+
(Mrs Caroline Bailey) *chsd ldrs: wnt 2nd after 11th: 3rd and one pce whn j.rt and hit last: sn wknd* **11/2**[2]

/4-4 **5** *dist* **Chaos Theory**[12] 11-11-7 86.................. MrDThomas(7) —
(John Cranage) *led: blnd 2nd: hdd after 7th: lost pl 9th: sn bhd: t.o: btn a total of 61 l* **20/1**

1PP/ **P** **Old Bean (IRE)**[676] 4790 10-11-7.................. MrMBriggs(7) —
(O R Dukes) *blnd 2nd: in rr whn blnd 4th: sn lost tch: p.u bef next* **33/1**

5m 31.2s (28.50) **Going Correction** +1.45s/f (Heav) **6 Ran SP% 110.5**
Speed ratings: **101,99,95,94,—** — CSF £11.97 TOTE £6.80: £1.90, £1.10; EX 15.60 Place 6 £105.54, Place 5 £79.14.

Owner Miss Mary Samworth **Bred** C And Mrs Wilson **Trained** Tilton On The Hill, Leics

FOCUS
The winner, a prolific scorer in points, met Telemoss on a bad day.

NOTEBOOK
Bedtime Boys, a winner of seven points, showed the benefit of his comeback outing two weeks earlier. Making his debut under Rules he travelled strongly and never really looked like being overhauled.

Telemoss(IRE), pulled out quickly in order to qualify for Cheltenham, never looked that happy. He took second spot at the last but was never going to get in a blow. This was probably too soon after Bangor, but his trainer's hands were tied. *(tchd 2-5 in places)*

Danaeve(IRE), a winner seven times under Rules in Ireland, has come to this late in life and essentially looks a school master.

Kjetil(USA), pulled up in a point a month earlier, continually swished his tail in the paddock and stopped to nothing after getting the last wrong. *(op 6-1 tchd 13-2 and 5-1)*

Old Bean(IRE) *Official explanation: jockey said gelding lost its action*

T/Jkpt: Not won. T/Plt: £103.30 to a £1 stake. Pool: £48,844.50. 345.10 winning tickets. T/Qpdt: £57.40 to a £1 stake. Pool: £3,126.10. 40.30 winning tickets. WG

3491 HAYDOCK (L-H)

Saturday, February 18

OFFICIAL GOING: Heavy
Wind: Almost nil Weather: Fine

3969 BRIT INSURANCE PRESTIGE NOVICES' HURDLE GRADE 2 (12 hdls) 2m 7f 110y

12:40 (12:40) (Class 1) 4-Y-0+

£17,106 (£6,417; £3,213; £1,602; £804; £402)

Form RPR

4121 **1** **Neptune Collonges (FR)**[14] 3738 5-11-11 152.................. ChristianWilliams 129+
(P F Nicholls) *cl up: led 2nd: mde rest: hit 2 out: drvn out* **2/11**[1]

P-12 **2** *1* **Five Colours (IRE)**[17] 3677 6-11-8 125.................. WayneHutchinson 123+
(A King) *in tch: nt fluent 5th: chsd wnr 2 out: ev ch last: hung lft and nt qckn run-in: styd on u.p but hld towards fin* **16/1**[2]

3021 **3** *5* **Rathowen (IRE)**[40] 3316 7-11-8 110.................. GrahamLee 117
(J I A Charlton) *prom: rdn appr 2 out: one pce* **25/1**[3]

52-4 **4** *nk* **Accordello (IRE)**[28] 3491 5-10-11.................. RichardMcGrath 106
(K G Reveley) *hld up in rr: j. slowly 6th: hdwy appr 2 out: styd on wl run-in* **50/1**

111P **5** *¾* **Jeremy Cuddle Duck (IRE)**[97] 2206 5-11-11.................. AntonyEvans 120+
(N A Twiston-Davies) *hld up: hdwy after 7th: pushed along appr 4 out: outpcd bef 2 out: no imp after* **16/1**[2]

2312 **6** *19* **Gritti Palace (IRE)**[43] 3277 6-11-8 120.................. MarkNicolls 97
(John R Upson) *led to 2nd: remained prom: pushed along appr 7th: wknd 8th: t.o* **33/1**

6m 8.40s (4.20) **Going Correction** +0.325s/f (Yiel) **6 Ran SP% 105.1**
Speed ratings: **106,105,104,103,103 97** CSF £3.00 TOTE £1.10: £1.10, £2.70; EX 3.70.

Owner J Hales **Bred** Gaec Delorme Freres **Trained** Ditcheat, Somerset

FOCUS
This looked easy pickings for Neptune Collonges, but they went a steady early pace in the very testing ground and he was far from impressive.

NOTEBOOK
Neptune Collonges(FR) made most of the running but was merely workmanlike when this should have been a cakewalk for him. Although he revels in this testing ground, jumps well and stays all day, this was nothing like his best form.He will go to Cheltenham, where the three-mile Brit Insurance Novices' Hurdle is the likeliest target, only if the ground is considered soft enough. *(op 1-5 tchd 1-6)*

Five Colours(IRE) is officially rated 27lb lower than Neptune Collonges, but with that one failing to run to his best, and the step up to three miles for the first time eliciting some improvement, he ran the hot favourite close. He jumped the last upsides, was only beaten on the run-in and looks a promising stayer in the making. In time he should make a decent staying chaser. *(op 14-1)*

Rathowen(IRE) appeared to be up against it in this company and the fact that he got so close probably has a lot to do with the steady gallop which was set in the early stages. *(op 20-1)*

Accordello(IRE), who was a touch keen, appreciated the step up from two miles, as one would expect of a daughter of high-class staying hurdler Marello. She can win in lesser company. *(op 33-1)*

Jeremy Cuddle Duck(IRE), who bled from the nose on his last start when pulled up at Cheltenham in November, was keen and did not jump that fluently. He was struggling from a fair way out but did at least keep going

3970 PERTEMPS H'CAP HURDLE (QUALIFIER) (12 hdls) 2m 7f 110y

1:10 (1:11) (Class 2) 5-Y-0+ **£13,012** (£3,820; £1,910; £954)

Form RPR

20-3 **1** **Olaso (GER)**[98] 2175 7-10-13 **129**.................. APMcCoy 140+
(Jonjo O'Neill) *hld up: hdwy 4 out: chsd ldr appr 2 out: styd on to ld run-in: drvn out towards fin* **9/2**[1]

0560 **2** *1 ¼* **Carlys Quest**[35] 3389 12-11-5 **135**..................(b) KeithMercer 142
(Ferdy Murphy) *in tch: lost pl 7th: rallied fr 3 out: r.o to take 2nd towards fin* **25/1**

01-1 **3** *nk* **Fair Question (IRE)**[7] 3854 8-10-9 **125**.................. AlanO'Keeffe 132+
(Miss Venetia Williams) *racd keenly: prom: led 5th: clr appr 3 out: rdn and hung lft after last: hdd run-in: no ex towards fin* **7/1**[2]

P6F2 **4** *9* **Jiver (IRE)**[23] 3581 7-9-9 **118**..................(v) JohnKington(7) 117+
(M Scudamore) *trckd ldrs: rdn appr 3 out: styd on same pce* **33/1**

-632 **5** *6* **Hidden Bounty (IRE)**[54] 2990 10-10-13 **129**.................. RichardMcGrath 121
(K G Reveley) *midfield: rdn and lost pl appr 4 out: kpt on fr last* **10/1**

2-00 **6** *3 ½* **Monolith**[90] 2369 8-11-0 **133**.................. GaryBerridge(3) 122+
(L Lungo) *hld up in rr: hdwy 3 out: kpt on run-in: nvr nr to chal* **40/1**

301P **7** *1 ¾* **Robbo**[24] 3560 12-9-5 **117**.................. JamesReveley(10) 103
(K G Reveley) *bhd: kpt on fr 2 out: nvr on terms* **33/1**

1- **8** *2 ½* **The Reverend (IRE)**[475] 1928 6-10-4 **120**.................. GrahamLee 105+
(J Howard Johnson) *midfield: hdwy whn hmpd 3 out: wknd appr next* **11/1**

1121 **9** *2* **Drumbeater (IRE)**[53] 3018 6-10-4 **120**.................. PJBrennan 102
(P J Hobbs) *midfield: hdwy 4 out: sn rdn: wknd appr 2 out* **8/1**[3]

-110 **10** *2 ½* **Rooftop Protest (IRE)**[98] 2175 9-11-2 **135**..................(t) DFO'Regan(3) 116+
(T Hogan, Ire) *in tch: chsd ldr after 4 out: lost 2nd u.p appr 2 out: wknd last* **20/1**

-P32 **11** *7* **Bengo (IRE)**[28] 3506 6-10-1 **120**.................. StephenCraine(3) 92
(B De Haan) *trckd ldrs: rdn whn nt fluent 8th: wknd 8th* **33/1**

1-30 **12** *14* **Sunset Light (IRE)**[23] 3581 8-10-3 **119**.................. TomDoyle 77
(C Tinkler) *in tch: mstke 7th: sn rdn: wknd next: eased after 2 out* **25/1**

P-26 **13** *8* **Idaho D'Ox (FR)**[6] 3880 10-9-13 **120**.................. PaddyMerrigan(5) 70
(M C Pipe) *in rr: rdn appr 4 out: nvr on terms* **33/1**

4-0P **14** *1 ¾* **Quick**[248] 759 6-11-5 **142**..................(v) MrRQuinn(7) 91
(M C Pipe) *mstkes: led: hdd 5th: wknd after 4 out* **50/1**

1/1- **15** *7* **Kivotos (USA)**[658] 110 8-10-10 **126**.................. JimCrowley 68
(M C Pipe) *midfield: hdwy appr 7th: rdn after 4 out: sn wknd* **11/1**

-400 **16** *3 ½* **Inching Closer**[14] 3741 9-10-9 **130**..................(b) BrianHughes(5) 68
(J Howard Johnson) *midfield: rdn after 4 out: sn wknd* **50/1**

110 **17** *25* **Magnifico (FR)**[14] 3727 5-10-11 **134**.................. AndrewGlassonbury(7) 47
(M C Pipe) *midfield: rdn appr 7th: wknd 8th* **25/1**

106- **18** *26* **Liberman (IRE)**[338] 4412 8-10-12 **128**.................. GerrySupple 15
(M C Pipe) *a bhd: t.o* **33/1**

3121 **P** **Nor'Nor'East (IRE)**[77] 2633 8-10-9 **125**.................. DJCasey —
(Jonjo O'Neill) *hld up: p.u after 3rd: dismntd* **8/1**[3]

6122 **P** **Wild Is The Wind (FR)**[35] 3384 5-10-7 **123**.................. BrianHarding —
(Jonjo O'Neill) *midfield: pushed along appr 7th: wknd next: t.o whn p.u bef 3 out* **14/1**

6m 2.80s (-1.40) **Going Correction** +0.325s/f (Yiel) **20 Ran SP% 122.7**
Speed ratings: **115,114,114,111,109 108,107,106,106,105 103,98,95,95,92 91,83,74,—,—**
CSF £119.38 CT £791.72 TOTE £4.60: £1.50, £5.20, £2.10, £6.40; EX 209.60 TRIFECTA Not won..

Owner John P McManus **Bred** M Beining **Trained** Cheltenham, Gloucs

■ Stewards' Enquiry : Gary Berridge 14-day ban: failed to take all reasonable and permissible measures to obtain best possible placing (Mar 1-14)

FOCUS

They went a good gallop in this qualifier for the Final at Cheltenham and the first two came from off the pace. The winning time was 5.6sec faster than the preceding Grade Two novice hurdle and Olaso provided the Jonjo O'Neill stable with its third win in the race from the last five years.

NOTEBOOK

Olaso(GER), who was a well-supported favourite, travelled well for most of the race and appreciated the good gallop. He appeared to score more comfortably than the winning margin suggests, although his rider was adamant that he was all out at the finish. This was only his fifth start over hurdles and he is open to further improvement, with the Final of the series clearly an ideal target. Better ground should not cause him any problems. *(op 7-1)*

Carlys Quest ◆, third in this race last year, was back on the same mark and went one place better, finishing with his customary late rattle. A good pace is essential to him and so it was to his credit that he managed to finish so well into fifth in the Final of this series last year off a muddling gallop. A better pace at Cheltenham this time around might see him go well at a price, despite his advancing years. *(op 28-1 tchd 33-1)*

Fair Question(IRE) deserves plenty of credit for his third place as he helped set a pretty strong gallop given the conditions. Racing off a 16lb higher mark than when successful at Ayr a week earlier, he only knows one way to race, and while these tactics might be difficult to pull off at Cheltenham, Aintree may well suit him. *(op 6-1)*

Jiver(IRE) ran with credit given that the Handicapper had raised him 8lb for his narrow defeat at Warwick last time.

Hidden Bounty(IRE) was raised 4lb for finishing runner-up at Wetherby on Boxing Day and the Handicapper appears to be keeping up with his steady improvement over hurdles. *(tchd 11-1)*

Monolith ◆, whose stable won this race last year, was not given a hard ride on his return from a three-month absence and the stewards took a dim view of his jockey's efforts, banning him for 14 days for not achieving his best possible placing. His trainer saddled Freetown to win the Final of this series in 2002, and it would not be a surprise to see this eight-year-old go close in the main event as he will be better suited by the likelier sounder surface at the Festival.

Robbo last won a race over hurdles over three years ago.

The Reverend(IRE), last seen winning on his hurdling debut back in October 2004, did not shape too badly given the absence and the fact that his stable is bang out of form. *(op 9-1)*

Drumbeater(IRE) was not beaten by his 6lb higher mark but rather by the very testing ground. He should not be dismissed back on a sounder surface.

Rooftop Protest(IRE) looked harshly treated here, as he was 5lb higher than when well held in seventh on his last start at Cheltenham in November. Olaso finished four places in front of him that day and yet, for some reason, was 1lb better off with him this time. *(op 16-1)*

Nor'Nor'East(IRE) *Official explanation: jockey said gelding lost its action (op 15-2 tchd 7-1)*

3971 RED SQUARE VODKA GOLD CUP CHASE (H'CAP) GRADE 3 (22 fncs) — 3m 4f 110y

1:40 (1:41) (Class 1) 5-Y-O+

£71,275 (£26,737; £13,387; £6,675; £3,350; £1,675)

Form				RPR
0613	**1**		**Ossmoses (IRE)**^{44} [3258] 9-10-0 **126** oh3 ... RichardMcGrath (D M Forster) *a.p: led after 2 out: rdn clr after last: styd on wl* **14/1**	148+
411P	**2**	*15*	**Model Son (IRE)**^{92} [2311] 8-10-2 **133** ... PaddyMerrigan(5) (P C Haslam) *led: hdd after 2 out: sn rdn: no ex run-in* **25/1**	143+
PPF2	**3**	*8*	**Sir Rembrandt (IRE)**^{35} [3390] 10-11-5 **145** ... WarrenMarston (R H Alner) *chsd ldrs: rdn 17th: wknd 3 out* **12/1**	143
PP/6	**4**	*27*	**Tyneandthyneagain**^{35} [3385] 11-10-8 **137** ...(p) PeterBuchanan(3) (J Howard Johnson) *in rr: struggling 11th: lft poor 4th last: nvr on terms* **50/1**	108
-641	**5**	*2 ½*	**L'Aventure (FR)**^{53} [3022] 7-11-0 **140** ...(bt) GrahamLee (P F Nicholls) *bhd: struggling 11th: nvr on terms* **9/1**	109
-3P3	**6**	*6*	**Truckers Tavern (IRE)**^{28} [3493] 11-10-12 **138** ... DavidO'Meara (Mrs S J Smith) *nt jump wl: midfield: wknd 16th* **40/1**	101
4F10	**7**	*25*	**Double Honour (FR)**^{35} [3390] 8-11-0 **140** ...(b) PJBrennan (P J Hobbs) *prom: sn pushed along: wknd 16th* **25/1**	78
01F1	**8**	*dist*	**Ebony Light (IRE)**^{28} [3493] 10-10-11 **140** ...(p) StephenCraine(3) (D McCain) *bhd: mstke 5th: struggling 11th: blnd 17th: t.o* **15/2**^{3}	—
0-P0	**P**		**Chives (IRE)**^{35} [3389] 11-11-6 **146** ... DominicElsworth (Mrs S J Smith) *bhd: struggling 11th: t.o whn p.u bef 17th* **25/1**	—
-5PU	**P**		**First Gold (FR)**^{84} [2492] 13-11-0 **140** ...(b) APMcCoy (F Doumen, France) *cl up: rdn 16th: sn wknd: t.o whn p.u bef last* **20/1**	—
-411	**P**		**Eurotrek (IRE)**^{35} [3390] 10-11-8 **148** ... ChristianWilliams (P F Nicholls) *bhd: pushed along 10th: t.o whn p.u bef 16th* **15/2**^{3}	—
24/	**P**		**What A Native (IRE)**^{34} [3410] 10-10-0 **126** oh1 ... DJCasey (C F Swan, Ire) *midfield: j. slowly 7th: wknd 16th: t.o whn p.u bef 2 out* **4/1**^{1}	—
-203	**R**		**A New Story (IRE)**^{23} [3587] 8-9-11 **126** oh2 ... DFO'Regan(3) (Michael Hourigan, Ire) *hld up: nt fluent 12th: hdwy 18th: wknd 3 out: mod 4th whn ref last* **15/2**^{3}	97
F-1B	**F**		**Joaaci (IRE)**^{35} [3390] 6-11-5 **152** ... AndrewGlassonbury(7) (M C Pipe) *midfield: hdwy 14th: rdn appr 4 out: wknd bef next: lft poor 4th whn fell last: winded* **11/2**^{2}	121

7m 19.8s (-12.90) **Going Correction** +0.325s/f (Yiel) **14** Ran SP% **115.7**

Speed ratings: **117,112,110,103,102 100,93,—,—,— —,—,—,—** CSF £314.15 CT £4253.85 TOTE £17.60: £4.40, £6.20, £2.90; EX 438.40 TRIFECTA Not won..

Owner D M Forster **Bred** Mrs Julia Foran **Trained** Redworth, Co Durham

FOCUS

A competitive handicap on paper, befitting the prize-money on offer, but they finished well strung out due to the testing conditions, and the form might not translate well elsewhere.

NOTEBOOK

Ossmoses(IRE), who stays all day and had no weight on his back, thrives in testing ground so had everything in his favour on this step up in class. A tough sort who just gallops, he was one of few who coped with conditions, and as a relatively lightly-raced nine-year-old he is clearly still improving. The Midlands Grand National looks an ideal target, as that often turns out to be a similar slog in the mud.

Model Son(IRE) ◆, who won a couple of novice chases in the autumn, had been given time off since being pulled up at Exeter the following month. Having his first outing for his new yard and versatile with regard to ground preference, he made a most encouraging return to action. Given that this was only his sixth start over fences, there should be better to come from him, and he could win a decent prize somewhere this season.

Sir Rembrandt(IRE) ◆ confirmed the promise of his last two starts and is clearly peaking at the right time with the spring Festivals in mind. He remains a tempting each-way price for the Gold Cup at 33-1 as he has shown in the past that the track and stamina test of the Blue Riband bring out the best in him.

Tyneandthyneagain inherited fourth when Joacci fell at the last and A New Story refused at the same fence. This was still an encouraging performance, though, from a gelding having only his second start back after being pulled up in the 2004 Scottish Grand National.

L'Aventure(FR) was never a danger, always struggling towards the rear, but she does stay forever and was keeping on at the finish. *(op 8-1)*

Truckers Tavern(IRE) was similarly never a threat to the principals and, not for the first time, was far from fluent.

Double Honour(FR) was hard work as usual and any jockey who rides him must be a three Shredded Wheat man.

Ebony Light(IRE) was racing from a 9lb lower mark than for his shock defeat of Kingscliff four weeks previously but hung right and did not jump as well as he did on that occasion, although he was never up at the head of affairs this time. *(op 10-1 tchd 7-1)*

What A Native(IRE), who had run up a four-timer in Ireland, had a 9lb higher mark to defy than for the latest of those successes. He did not take to these fences, though, and was never going like a 4-1 favourite. *Official explanation: jockey said gelding was never travelling (tchd 9-2)*

Eurotrek(IRE), who had a lot of weight to carry in this ground, was struggling a long way out and *proved disappointing off a mark 13lb higher than when he was successful at Warwick last month. Official explanation: jockey said gelding was unsuited by the heavy ground (tchd 9-2)*

A New Story(IRE), who had conditions to suit, was out on his feat but still in fourth place when refusing at the last. *(tchd 9-2)*

Joaaci(IRE), who briefly inherited fourth when A New Story refused at the last, was winded after falling at the same fence. He had a tough task lumping top weight around here in these gruelling conditions. *(tchd 9-2)*

3972 POLYFLOR VICTOR LUDORUM JUVENILE NOVICES' HURDLE (8 hdls) — 2m

2:15 (2:16) (Class 2) 4-Y-O **£13,012** (£3,820; £1,910; £954)

Form				RPR
	1		**Overlut (FR)**^{94} 4-11-8 ... DGallagher (F-M Cottin, France) *mde all: j.lft last 2: rdn out* **5/1**^{3}	135+
11	**2**	*4*	**Bold Fire**^{21} [3621] 4-11-1 134 ... ChristianWilliams (P F Nicholls) *chsd wnr thrght: nt fluent 4 out: j.rt fr 3 out: ev ch 2 out: one pce run-in* **1/1**^{1}	123+
1	**3**	*12*	**Onnix (FR)**^{28} [3498] 4-11-4 ... ADuchene (F Doumen, France) *hld up in rr: rdn and outpcd after 3 out: nvr able to chal* **11/4**^{2}	118+
64	**4**	*14*	**Ortega (FR)**^{23} [3579] 4-10-12 ... PJBrennan (P J Hobbs) *hld up: rdn appr 3 out: wknd bef next* **12/1**	98+
1	**5**	*20*	**Astronomical (IRE)**^{79} [2587] 4-11-4 115 ... GrahamLee (Miss S J Wilton) *chsd ldrs: nt fluent 4th: mstke 3 out: sn wknd: t.o* **12/1**	99+

4m 3.10s (4.00) **Going Correction** +0.325s/f (Yiel) **5** Ran SP% **108.7**

Speed ratings: **103,101,95,88,78** CSF £10.66 TOTE £6.60: £2.20, £1.30; EX 12.50.

Owner Paul Green **Bred** Dr Isabelle Claude-Meggs & Francois Cottin **Trained** France

FOCUS

A decent little event for juveniles, but it is not form to get too carried away with. The winner was granted an uncontested lead in testing ground and proved difficult to peg back.

NOTEBOOK

Overlut(FR), a winner on his last two starts in France, is a front-runner, and so poaching a three-length advantage at the start was a valuable bonus. Giving weight all round, he was granted an uncontested lead in this small field, and made every yard, finding extra when challenged by the eventual runner-up two from home. He is in the Triumph Hurdle and Supreme Novices' at Cheltenham, but is not a certain runner, and may well have to prove himself on quicker ground if he turns up at the Festival. *(op 9-2)*

Bold Fire, chasing a hat-trick, had more testing ground to cope with this time and tended to jump out to her right. She still had every chance two out but got tired in the ground and could not claw back the leader. Better ground might see her in a better light. *(op 10-11 tchd 6-5)*

Onnix(FR), a winner on his hurdling debut at Lingfield, was given a lot to do on a day when making up ground in these testing conditions proved difficult. *(op 10-3 tchd 5-2 and 7-2 in places)*

Ortega(FR) might like better ground and will find life easier in handicap company. *(op 16-1)*

Astronomical(IRE), who won on his hurdling debut in good to soft ground, liked a decent surface on the Flat, and it is probable that these conditions were too testing for him.

3973 SPORTING INDEX NOVICES' H'CAP CHASE (15 fncs) — 2m 4f

2:50 (2:50) (Class 2) 5-Y-O+ **£13,012** (£3,820; £1,910; £954)

Form				RPR
4P2	**1**		**No Full (FR)**^{35} [3391] 5-11-1 **120** ... TomDoyle (P R Webber) *hld up in tch: hdwy 4 out: led between last 2: drew clr and hung lft run-in: styd on wl* **12/1**	134+
1FF	**2**	*6*	**Lord Olympia (IRE)**^{28} [3509] 7-11-9 **121** ... AlanO'Keeffe (Miss Venetia Williams) *led: rdn and hdd between last 2: hit last: one pce run-in* **6/1**	132+
6-	**3**	*10*	**Just (IRE)**^{13} [3777] 7-10-10 **111** ...(p) DFO'Regan(3) (Michael Hourigan, Ire) *hld up: hdwy appr 3 out: rdn bef next: wknd bef last* **15/8**^{1}	111
-231	**4**	*1*	**My World (FR)**^{22} [3599] 6-11-4 **116** ... WarrenMarston (R H Alner) *prom: blnd 1st: rdn after 3 out: wknd appr last* **11/2**^{3}	115
1155	**5**	*6*	**Another Native (IRE)**^{28} [3507] 8-11-2 **114** ... PJBrennan (C J Mann) *hld up: hdwy after 4 out: ch next: wknd appr last* **11/2**^{3}	109+
P52F	**6**	*6*	**Itsuptoharry (IRE)**^{44} [3255] 7-10-13 **114** ... StephenCraine(3) (D McCain) *trckd ldrs: rdn whn blnd 3 out: sn wknd: btn whn mstke next* **4/1**^{2}	108+
00	**7**	*21*	**Lusaka De Pembo (FR)**^{28} [3495] 7-11-12 **124** ... AntonyEvans (N A Twiston-Davies) *hld up: rdn and btn 3 out* **25/1**	90

5m 22.0s (-2.20) **Going Correction** +0.325s/f (Yiel)

WFA 5 from 6yo+ 7lb **7** Ran SP% **111.4**

Speed ratings: **113,110,106,106,103 101,93** CSF £75.01 TOTE £10.70: £3.20, £3.00; EX 38.40.

Owner Patrick Delaney Jnr **Bred** F Cottin **Trained** Mollington, Oxon

FOCUS

A modest handicap chase, but the winner was value for 10 lengths or so as he drew clear for a comfortable win, and he looks capable of better.

NOTEBOOK

No Full(FR) proved suited by the drop back from three miles and turned out to be well handicapped on a mark of 120. He drew clear in decent style from the last, despite hanging over to the inside rail, and showed much improved form. He could run in the Jewson Novices' Handicap Chase at Cheltenham, although he may have to deal with quicker ground there. *(op 8-1)*

Lord Olympia(IRE), who made most of the running, jumped well in the main, although he fluffed the last when already headed. A faller on his previous two starts, this should have done his confidence the world of good. *(op 7-1)*

Just(IRE), an Irish raider who had won his last two starts but was 10lb higher than his last chase win, stayed on from off the pace but was never a real threat to the principals. He was rated just 85 when winning for the first time over fences in October, so he has come a long way in a short time, but perhaps the Handicapper has his measure now. *(op 7-4 tchd 2-1)*

My World(FR) did not seem to get home over this longer trip and will appreciate a drop back to distances around two miles. *(op 13-2 tchd 5-1)*

Another Native(IRE) had only been dropped 1lb since his last start and that proved insufficient. He continues to look held by the Handicapper. *(op 9-2 tchd 13-2)*

Itsuptoharry(IRE), who fell last time out, was struggling when blundering at the third last. He looks to be going the wrong way. *(op 9-2)*

3974 CASINO 36 CLASSIC H'CAP CHASE (12 fncs) 2m
3:25 (3:26) (Class 2) 5-Y-O+ £16,265 (£4,775; £2,387; £1,192)

Form RPR
0623 1 **Kalca Mome (FR)**[14] 3724 8-10-12 131 PJBrennan 143+
(P J Hobbs) *hld up: hdwy 7th: chsd ldr 4 out: led appr last: drvn out* **11/2**[2]
5322 2 2 1/2 **Bleu Superbe (FR)**[21] 3619 11-10-13 132 AlanO'Keeffe 140
(Miss Venetia Williams) *led: rdn and hdd appr last: no ex cl home* **11/2**[2]
2631 3 15 **Tanikos (FR)**[35] 3387 7-10-4 128 SamCurling(5) 124+
(N J Henderson) *in tch: effrt to chse ldrs appr 3 out: wknd last* **11/2**[2]
0601 4 3 **Almaydan**[21] 3619 8-11-2 135 (b) TomDoyle 125
(R Lee) *cl up: reminder after 3rd: lost pl 8th: n.d after* **14/1**
4105 5 1 1/4 **Sir Storm (IRE)**[28] 3495 10-10-0 119 oh2 (p) BarryKeniry 108
(G M Moore) *hld up: hdwy 8th: wknd after 4 out* **16/1**
-52P 6 dist **Mistral De La Cour (FR)**[47] 3207 6-9-11 119 oh4 (p) StephenCraine(3) —
(R Ford) *prom tl wknd after 4 out: t.o* **50/1**
P121 7 24 **Barton Nic**[28] 3495 13-10-0 122 (b) PeterBuchanan(3) —
(D P Keane) *a bhd: t.o* **8/1**[3]
U213 B **Roman Ark**[21] 3618 8-10-13 132 GrahamLee —
(J M Jefferson) *hld up: b.d 5th* **9/2**[1]
1P2P B **Nowator (POL)**[21] 3619 9-10-3 122 AlanDempsey —
(Robert Gray) *trckd ldrs tl b.d 5th: dead* **25/1**
2110 F **Town Crier (IRE)**[14] 3724 11-11-12 145 DominicElsworth —
(Mrs S J Smith) *prom tl fell 5th* **9/2**[1]

4m 6.70s (-0.30) **Going Correction** +0.325s/f (Yiel) **10** Ran SP% **112.0**
Speed ratings: **109,107,100,98,98** —,—,—,—,— CSF £35.00 CT £171.64 TOTE £7.70: £2.00, £1.90, £1.90; EX 38.80.
Owner Miss I D Du Pre **Bred** A R Deschere **Trained** Withycombe, Somerset

FOCUS
A decent and competitive handicap and sound enough form.

NOTEBOOK
Kalca Mome(FR) has been running well of late, especially in the Victor Chandler Chase earlier this month and, with the ground more in his favour this time, he defied a 2lb higher mark than for his last chase win in December 2004. He is now three from five at this track, and may now go for one of the handicaps at the Festival. *(op 5-1 tchd 6-1)*
Bleu Superbe(FR), who last won a race in November 2003 off this identical mark, enjoyed being in front on his own and put up another bold show. Yet to be out of the first three in five starts over fences at this track, he too revels in testing conditions. *(op 5-1)*
Tanikos(FR), who beat Kalca Mome by a length and a half at Warwick, was 3lb worse off at the weights this time and the ground was more in his rival's favour. *(tchd 5-1 and 6-1)*
Almaydan was racing off a career-high mark following his success in first-time blinkers at Southwell last month and prefers better ground than this.
Sir Storm(IRE) has looked held since winning at Wetherby on Boxing Day, and this effort was more of the same. *(op 14-1)*
Barton Nic was up in class again and racing from a 10lb higher mark than last time. *(op 10-1)*
Town Crier(IRE) took a crashing fall at the fifth fence and brought down Nowator and Roman Ark. He is likely to need plenty of time to get over this, and it would not be a surprise to see him turn out over hurdles when next on the racecourse. *(op 4-1)*

3975 RED SQUARE VODKA "FIXED BRUSH" NOVICES' HURDLE (10 hdls) 2m 4f
4:00 (4:00) (Class 4) 4-7-Y-O £4,554 (£1,337; £668; £333)

Form RPR
1F21 1 **Cloudy Lane**[42] 3291 6-11-6 115 StephenCraine(3) 118+
(D McCain) *hld up: hdwy appr 5th: rdn bef 3 out: led 2 out: j.rt last: styd on gamely towards fin* **11/4**[2]
1023 2 2 1/2 **Miko De Beauchene (FR)**[35] 3388 6-11-9 121 WarrenMarston 113
(R H Alner) *hld up: hdwy after 4th: led after 4 out: rdn and hdd 2 out: stl ev ch run-in: no ex towards fin* **11/10**[1]
0P0P 3 10 **Times Up Barney**[8] 3846 6-11-3 79 JosephByrne 97
(C W Moore) *prom: led 6th: hdd after 4 out: wknd appr 2 out* **100/1**
4 dist **Back For The Craic (IRE)** 7-10-12 SamCurling(5) 67
(N J Henderson) *hld up: hdwy appr 4 out: wknd bef 2 out* **9/2**[3]
5 7 **Hold The Bid (IRE)**[643] 6-11-3 DavidO'Meara 60
(Mrs S J Smith) *in tch: rdn after 4 out: sn wknd* **20/1**
05 6 22 **Sparkling Taff**[65] 2838 7-11-3 BarryKeniry 38
(Mrs S J Smith) *trckd ldrs tl wknd 6th: t.o* **12/1**
046 P **William Butler (IRE)**[28] 3504 6-11-3 AlanDempsey —
(S A Brookshaw) *a bhd: t.o whn p.u bef 3 out* **66/1**
4230 P **Jimmy Bedney (IRE)**[44] 3248 5-11-3 GrahamLee —
(M G Rimell) *led: hdd 6th: wknd appr 4 out: t.o whn p.u bef 3 out* **16/1**

5m 10.5s (1.30) **Going Correction** +0.325s/f (Yiel) **8** Ran SP% **113.3**
Speed ratings: **110,109,105**,—,—,—,—,— CSF £6.24 TOTE £3.60: £1.50, £1.10, £7.70; EX 6.80 Place 6 £1,021.65, Place 5 £955.32.
Owner Trevor Hemmings **Bred** Gleadhill House Stud Ltd **Trained** Cholmondeley, Cheshire
■ Stewards' Enquiry : Joseph Byrne two-day ban: using whip unnecessarily when clearly third (Mar 1-2)

FOCUS
A fair event over the brush hurdles, but the proximity of the 79-rated third does not do a lot for the value of the form.

NOTEBOOK
Cloudy Lane, who won over these obstacles last time, put that valuable experience to good use and followed up in gritty style, notching another success for his in-form stable. He likes this sort of ground, will get further than this and will obviously make a chaser in time. *(op 3-1 tchd 7-1 in a place)*
Miko De Beauchene(FR), officially rated 6lb better than Cloudy Lane, had the advantage of the rail to help him on the run-in, but in the end he was outbattled. He finished clear of the third, but that one's rating leaves a question mark over what the first two actually achieved. *(op 11-8 tchd 13-8)*
Times Up Barney, a seemingly exposed plating-class performer over timber, ran by far his best race to date on his first start over brush hurdles. It is anyone's guess as to whether this was a fluke or whether he has found improvement from somewhere, but for time being it would probably be wise to err on the side of caution. *(tchd 66-1)*
Back For The Craic(IRE), whose dam was a maiden in bumpers and over timber, looked a threat early in the straight but weakened pretty quickly thereafter. He is entitled to come on for this debut over obstacles. *Official explanation: jockey said gelding had a breathing problem (op 11-4)*
Hold The Bid(IRE), disqualified from fourth in a point-to-point after his rider failed to weigh in, did not make much of an impression on his hurdling debut. *(op 25-1 tchd 18-1)*
T/Jkpt: Not won. T/Plt: £458.10 to a £1 stake. Pool: £68,598.35. 109.30 winning tickets. T/Qpdt: £152.30 to a £1 stake. Pool: £3,077.00. 14.95 winning tickets. DO

3498 LINGFIELD (L-H)
Saturday, February 18

OFFICIAL GOING: Heavy (soft in places on chase course); all-weather - standard
Meeting switched from Ascot. The fourth fence (open ditch) was omitted in all chases on all circuits.
Wind: Almost nil Weather: Light rain after race two

3976 TOTEPOOL REYNOLDSTOWN NOVICES' CHASE GRADE 2 (16 fncs 2 omitted) 3m
12:55 (12:55) (Class 1) 5-Y-O+ £20,892 (£8,422; £4,684)

Form RPR
231 1 **Montgermont (FR)**[47] 3215 6-11-4 132 MarkBradburne 145+
(Mrs L C Taylor) *lw: several minor mstkes: hld up in last: prog to press ldr 12th: led 3 out: in command next: rdn out* **17/2**
3411 2 11 **Bob Bob Bobbin**[21] 3612 7-11-8 JoeTizzard 139+
(C L Tizzard) *lw: led: j. slowly 5th: hdd 7th: w ldr whn lft in ld 10th: rdn and hdd 3 out: btn whn blnd next* **6/1**
P-11 3 dist **Idle Talk (IRE)**[47] 3213 7-11-8 JasonMaguire 114
(T R George) *trckd ldng pair: lft chsng ldr 10th to 12th: mstke next and wknd: sn t.o: btn 59l* **5/1**[3]
-111 F **The Listener (IRE)**[48] 3178 7-11-10 AndrewThornton —
(R H Alner) *w ldr: led 7th tl crashing fall 10th* **5/4**[1]
14 P **Crozan (FR)**[54] 2973 6-11-10 MickFitzgerald —
(N J Henderson) *settled in 4th: wknd rapidly 10th: sn t.o: p.u bef 13th* **7/2**[2]

6m 19.0s (-4.70) **Going Correction** +0.15s/f (Yiel) **5** Ran SP% **108.1**
Speed ratings: **113,109**,—,—,— CSF £48.86 TOTE £13.00: £3.10, £1.70; EX 56.00.
Owner Mrs L C Taylor **Bred** D Allard **Trained** Upper Lambourn, Berks

FOCUS
With both Idle Talk and Crozan running well below form, and The Listener falling, this was a disappointing renewal of the Reynoldstown and it developed into a match from quite a way out. The time was decent and it has been rated through the second running to his mark

NOTEBOOK
Montgermont(FR) got his act together when winning a minor race at Exeter over two miles three on his previous start (Bradburne replaced Andrew Thornton that day) and continued his progression with a clear-cut success, upped significantly in grade and trip. His task was made much easier with three of his four rivals failing to give their running for one reason or another, but he still finished clear of a useful sort in Bob Bob Bobbin. He is not entered at the Cheltenham Festival, and will instead be given a break before heading to the Aintree and Ayr festivals towards the end of the season. *(op 10-1)*
Bob Bob Bobbin, chasing a hat-trick following two wins in minor company at Chepstow, had his ideal conditions and, as it turned out, only one horse to beat, but he floundered in the straight and never looked like going with the eventual winner. Although beaten by a horse who always promised to be very useful, this could be considered a little disappointing. *(op 9-1)*
Idle Talk(IRE), the winner of both his previous starts over fences, looked well worth his chance in this sort of company, but he made a bad mistake at the 13th fence and could not recover. He is much better than this and can be given another chance.
Crozan(FR) is held in high regard and looked a serious prospect when winning on his British debut at Cheltenham, but he disappointed when only fourth in the Feltham at Sandown on his last start *and this was even worse. Something is clearly not quite right and he has plenty to prove now. Official explanation: vet said gelding lost a front shoe (tchd 10-3)*
The Listener(IRE), a high-class novice chaser who was bidding for a four-timer following three straight wins since being switched to fences, made a rare mistake and crashed out before the race got serious. His jumping is usually so good but, as his trainer said afterwards, at least he fell in this race and not the Royal & SunAlliance, and he will still go to Cheltenham provided the ground is not fast. *(tchd 10-3)*

3977 ASCOT TOTESPORT CHASE GRADE 1 (14 fncs) 2m 4f 110y
1:25 (1:28) (Class 1) 5-Y-O+ £57,288 (£21,658; £10,978; £5,608; £2,948)

Form RPR
P-1P 1 **Our Vic (IRE)**[70] 2760 8-11-7 158 TimmyMurphy 166+
(M C Pipe) *lw: led to 2nd: led 7th: pestered by loose horse after: clr 3 out: styd on wl* **2/1**[1]
2023 2 6 **My Will (FR)**[54] 2992 6-11-7 147 JoeTizzard 158+
(P F Nicholls) *lw: trckd ldrs: mstke 7th: chsd wnr 8th to 9th: rdn in 4th after 4 out: kpt on to take 2nd again flat* **10/3**[2]
-4B1 3 2 **Fondmort (FR)**[48] 3180 10-11-7 157 MickFitzgerald 153
(N J Henderson) *lw: hld up in tch: prog to chse wnr 9th to 4 out and again 3 out: no imp: wknd and lost 2nd flat* **5/1**[3]
2-40 4 20 **It Takes Time (IRE)**[71] 2744 12-11-7 152 JamieMoore 143+
(M C Pipe) *hld up in last: prog to chse wnr 4 out to next: wknd after 2 out: tired and eased flat* **15/2**
F-30 5 dist **Supreme Prince (IRE)**[84] 2492 9-11-7 144 RichardJohnson —
(P J Hobbs) *in toch tl wknd 8th: sn t.o: btn 75l* **14/1**
5362 U **Take The Stand (IRE)**[54] 2992 10-11-7 156 TonyDobbin —
(P Bowen) *in tch tl blnd and uns rdr 5th* **6/1**
2U-4 F **Fundamentalist (IRE)**[53] 3039 8-11-7 154 (t) CarlLlewellyn —
(N A Twiston-Davies) *led 2nd to 7th: cl 2nd whn fell 8th* **20/1**

5m 17.7s (-1.30) **Going Correction** +0.375s/f (Yiel) **7** Ran SP% **110.6**
Speed ratings: **117,114,113,106**,— —,— CSF £8.61 TOTE £2.70: £1.70, £2.60; EX 12.60.
Owner D A Johnson **Bred** Col W B Mullins **Trained** Nicholashayne, Devon

FOCUS
A good renewal of this Grade One event and a high-class performance from the often frustrating Our Vic, who sets the standard. The form looks solid.

NOTEBOOK
Our Vic(IRE) ◆ does not have the consistency to match his talent, but to be fair his stable was not firing when he was pulled up in the Robin Cook Memorial Gold Cup at Cheltenham on his most recent outing. Although he was continually pestered by the loose Take The Stand, and could have been taken out of the race completely at the penultimate fence, he showed the right attitude to continue with his challenge and returned to the sort of form that saw him win the Paddy Power Gold Cup the time before. This should have set him up nicely for the Cheltenham Festival and, while he would have an obvious chance in the Ryanair Chase, connections have not ruled out a tilt at the Gold Cup. He did win over an extended three miles in good company as a novice, and with the Gold Cup looking less competitive than usual he is worth taking a chance on at the 28/1 still available after this race. *(op 9-4 tchd 5-2 and 11-4 in a place)*
My Will(FR), a little disappointing when a beaten favourite and only third in the Rowland Meyrick Chase at Wetherby on his previous start, ran much better this time. Although formerly a two-miler, his last success came over three miles and he seemed to find this trip on the sort side, staying on under a hard ride without threatening the winner. *(op 3-1 tchd 7-2 in places)*
Fondmort(FR) ran a game enough race in defeat but was not quite in the same sort of form that saw him win a Listed handicap off a mark of 152 at Cheltenham on his previous start, and he seems to reserve his best for that track. This ground would also have been soft enough. *(op 4-1)*

It Takes Time(IRE), last year's winner, looked set to pose a serious threat to his stablemate at one stage, but hung badly on the downhill turn into the straight and could not sustain a challenge. The track cannot be blamed for his waywardness, as he won over course and distance last season, but he stopped quickly when well beaten on his last start and something may not be quite right at the moment. *(op 9-1)*
Supreme Prince(IRE) was a touch out of his depth, but could still have been expected to have fared better. He has been far from convincing this season but, to be fair, the ground may not have suited this time.
Take The Stand(IRE), not for the first time and probably not the last time either, was let down by his jumping. These were not his conditions in any case, and last year's Gold Cup second will be suited by a return to a longer trip on better ground. *(op 16-1)*
Fundamentalist(IRE), disappointing on his return from injury in the Castleford Chase last time, fell before the race got serious. He has had a far from ideal season so far, and could not be backed with confidence if turning up at the Cheltenham Festival (he is entered in three races over a range of trips), but he is seriously talented when at his best and cannot be totally discounted. *(op 16-1)*

3978 LINGFIELD-RACECOURSE.CO.UK NOVICES' HURDLE (10 hdls) 2m 3f 110y
2:00 (2:01) (Class 4) 5-Y-0+ **£4,554** (£1,337; £668; £333)

Form RPR
-P31 **1** **Zipalong Lad (IRE)**^{48} [3184] 6-11-6 .... TonyDobbin 137+
(P Bowen) *lw: trckd ldrs: led wl bef 2 out: sn clr: comf* **4/1**^{2}
0-21 **2** *19* **Snakebite (IRE)**^{28} [3500] 6-11-6 .... CarlLlewellyn 119+
(M Pitman) *led tl hdd wl bef 2 out: btn whn hit 2 out: fin tired* **10/11**^{1}
3 *8* **Buster Collins (IRE)**^{307} 6-11-0 .... TimmyMurphy 101
(Miss E C Lavelle) *lengthy: str: chsd ldr to 3 out: shuffled along and outpcd bef 2 out: n.d after* **25/1**
0-16 **4** *2 1/2* **Dunsfold Duke**^{6} [3882] 6-11-6 120..................... MatthewBatchelor 106+
(P Winkworth) *lw: hld up: reminders and prog 5th: wnt 2nd 3 out: rdn to chal wl bef 2 out: sn wknd* **12/1**
0/3- **5** *12* **King's Mill (IRE)**^{437} [2705] 9-11-0 .... LeightonAspell 87
(Mrs L Wadham) *bkwd: hld up in rr: stdy prog fr 7th but nvr rchd ldrs: wknd 2 out* **11/1**
0063 **6** *dist* **Tamreen (IRE)**^{22} [3603] 5-11-0 105..................... JamieMoore —
(G L Moore) *lw: chsd ldrs: rdn after 5th: wknd wl bef 2 out: v tired and virtually p.u flat: btn 90l* **10/1**^{3}
0- **7** *5* **Alderman Rose**^{305} [4922] 6-11-0 .... RichardJohnson —
(R T Phillips) *t.k.h: trckd ldng pair tl lost pl bef 5th: wknd 6th: t.o after 3 out: btn 95l* **33/1**
0 **U** **Tricky Venture**^{18} [3658] 6-10-4 .... CraigMessenger$^{(10)}$ —
(Mrs L C Jewell) *in tch whn mstke 3rd and eventually uns rdr* **100/1**
02P **P** **Nagam (FR)**^{53} [3023] 5-11-0 .... SeanCurran —
(A Ennis) *chsd ldrs: rdn whn blnd 6th: wknd rapidly: t.o 3 out: p.u bef next* **33/1**
P **Yenaled**^{24} 9-11-0 .... JamesDavies —
(P S McEntee) *t.k.h: hld up in rr: lost tch fr 7th: t.o in 7th whn p.u bef 2 out* **66/1**
P41P **P** **Dare Too Dream**^{47} [3210] 7-11-6 .... MickFitzgerald —
(K Bishop) *in tch tl wknd after 6th: sn t.o: 9th whn p.u bef 2 out* **16/1**
120 **P** **Pan The Man (IRE)**^{33} [3425] 5-10-7 .... WayneKavanagh$^{(7)}$ —
(J W Mullins) *in tch tl wknd and mstke 5th: sn wl t.o: ms bhd whn blnd 2 out: p.u bef last* **50/1**

5m 10.7s (8.00) **Going Correction** +0.65s/f (Soft) **12** Ran SP% **117.6**
Speed ratings: **110,102,99,98,93** —,—,—,—,— —,— CSF £7.84 TOTE £4.70: £1.60, £1.10, £5.90; EX 9.00.
Owner A P Davies **Bred** James Larkin **Trained** Little Newcastle, Pembrokes

FOCUS
This looked like a reasonable novice hurdle. Zipalong Lad created a very good impression and is the type to rate higher, while the runner-up ran to his mark.

NOTEBOOK
Zipalong Lad(IRE) ◆, off the mark over two miles five at Plumpton on his previous start, followed up with a very impressive victory. Although he was dropping in trip, the heavy ground ensured this was enough of a stamina test and he produced a good galloping display. He is rightly held in high regard by his connections and could now go for the Royal & SunAlliance Novices' Hurdle. While he still has to prove his effectiveness on decent ground, he certainly deserves his chance in better company and looks a typical Peter Bowen improver. *(tchd 7-2)*
Snakebite(IRE), finally off the mark under similar conditions over course and distance on his previous start, proved no match whatsoever for the eventual winner in the straight. Time may show he was beaten by a very nice horse, but he could still have been expected to finish a little closer. *(op Evens tchd 11-10 in places)*
Buster Collins(IRE), successful in an Irish point 307 days previously, made a pleasing return to racing under Rules. Very much a chasing type, he looked as though he would come on for the run and should progress. *(op 20-1)*
Dunsfold Duke has not progressed as one might have hoped from his successful debut over hurdles at Plumpton. *(tchd 14-1 in a place)*
King's Mill(IRE), returning from a 437-day absence and having just his second start since 2003, finished up beaten quite a way but it was not without promise. Providing he stands training, he should do better. *(op 10-1 tchd 12-1)*
Dare Too Dream *Official explanation: jockey said gelding had a breathing problem (op 12-1)*
Nagam(FR) *Official explanation: trainer later reported he had no explanation for the poor form shown (op 12-1)*
Pan The Man(IRE) *Official explanation: trainer said gelding was unsuited by the heavy going (op 12-1)*

3979 GOLF & RACING AT LINGFIELD PARK MARES' ONLY NOVICES' HURDLE (8 hdls) 2m 110y
2:30 (2:32) (Class 4) 4-Y-0+ **£3,253** (£955; £477; £238)

Form RPR
2 **1** **Sonnengold (GER)**^{25} [3550] 5-11-2 .... LeightonAspell 106+
(Mrs L Wadham) *wl in tch: chal 3 out: led sn after 2 out: clr last: rdn out* **5/1**^{3}
005 **2** *7* **Koral Bay (FR)**^{10} [3800] 5-10-9 100..................... MrSWaley-Cohen$^{(7)}$ 98
(R Waley-Cohen) *trckd ldrs: chal 3 out: rdn bef 2 out: kpt on to go 2nd last: no imp on wnr* **33/1**
22 **3** *3/4* **Rowlands Dream (IRE)**^{14} [3730] 6-11-2 .... TimmyMurphy 99+
(R H Alner) *lw: racd wd: led to 2nd: w ldrs: led narrowly 3 out: mstke 2 out and sn hdd: one pce* **11/4**^{2}
1 **4** *3 1/2* **Queen's Dancer**^{16} [3690] 4-11-0 .... MickFitzgerald 92
(N J Henderson) *prom: rdn bef 2 out: kpt on tl no ex bef last* **2/1**^{1}
6-32 **5** *1 1/4* **Adlestrop**^{31} [3448] 6-11-2 .... RichardJohnson 93
(R T Phillips) *hld up in tch: prog to join ldng gp 3 out: shkn up bef 2 out: fdd bef last* **14/1**
1346 **6** *6* **Miss Pebbles (IRE)**^{21} [3621] 6-10-13 113..................... JosephStevenson$^{(10)}$ 97+
(R Dickin) *w ldrs: chal 3 out: btn after 2 out: tired and mstke last* **5/1**^{3}
3 **7** *dist* **Cois Na Tine Eile**^{16} [3690] 4-10-7 .... CarlLlewellyn —
(N A Twiston-Davies) *led 2nd to 3 out: sn wknd: btn 57l* **20/1**
0-00 **8** *dist* **She's No Muppet**^{42} [3281] 6-11-2 .... SeanCurran —
(N R Mitchell) *lw: in tch: mstke 4th: sn rdn and wknd: t.o: btn 95l* **66/1**
0/0 **9** *14* **My Big Sister**^{60} [2928] 7-10-9 .... WayneKavanagh$^{(7)}$ —
(J W Mullins) *a in rr: t.o last after 4th: plodded rnd: btn 109l* **100/1**
0 **P** **Miss Domino**^{36} [3373] 5-10-11 .... JamesDiment$^{(5)}$ —
(S J Gilmore) *hld up in rr: lost tch w ldng gp fr 5th: wl bhd in poor 10th whn p.u bef 2 out* **100/1**
/6PP **P** **Dutch Star**^{16} [3690] 7-10-6 .... JayPemberton$^{(10)}$ —
(G P Enright) *j.lft 1st: struggling in last trio after 3rd: t.o after next: p.u bef last* **100/1**
P **Aunty Lil (USA)**^{260} [626] 6-11-2 95..................... MatthewBatchelor —
(N J Gifford) *w'like: hld up in rr: lost tch w ldng gp 5th: wl bhd in 9th whn p.u bef 2 out* **40/1**
600 **P** **Molly's Spirit (IRE)**^{25} [3550] 5-11-2 .... JamesDavies —
(P R Webber) *drvn and struggling after 2nd: t.o and gng v slowly fr 5th: j. 2 out as wnr fin: p.u bef last* **100/1**
0/00 **P** **Barfleur (IRE)**^{86} [2457] 6-11-2 .... JamieMoore —
(P Bowen) *hld up in last trio: pushed along and lost tch after 4th: sn bhd: sme prog 3 out but stl wl bhd: 8th whn p.u bef 2 out* **66/1**

4m 19.7s (13.60) **Going Correction** +0.85s/f (Soft)
WFA 4 from 5yo+ 9lb **14** Ran SP% **117.1**
Speed ratings: **102,98,98,96,96 93**,—,—,—,— —,—,—,— CSF £147.35 TOTE £6.50: £2.30, £10.70, £1.50; EX 254.90.
Owner Sonnengold Partnership **Bred** J Schmidt **Trained** Newmarket, Suffolk

FOCUS
A moderate mares-only novice hurdle rated through the placed horses.

NOTEBOOK
Sonnengold(GER) confirmed the promise she showed when second on her hurdling debut to run out a ready winner. This was a pretty ordinary event, but she is clearly progressing and could defy a penalty in mares-only company. *(op 9-2 tchd 6-1)*
Koral Bay(FR)'s proximity casts real doubt over the strength of the form, but she offered some hope when fifth at Ludlow on her previous start and is clearly now going the right way. *(op 28-1)*
Rowlands Dream(IRE) did not shape badly when second on her hurdling debut at Uttoxeter and promised to be suited by these conditions, but she was well held in third and can be considered disappointing. *(op 7-2)*
Queen's Dancer ran below the form she showed to win a weak race on her hurdling debut at Towcester. She should not have minded the conditions and basically looks just moderate. *(tchd 9-4)*
Adlestrop offered plenty of promise in three runs in bumpers, but was well held on her hurdling debut. *(op 12-1 tchd 10-1)*
Miss Pebbles(IRE) was well below her official mark of 113 and the ground would not have suited at all. *(tchd 9-2 and 11-2 in places)*
My Big Sister *Official explanation: trainer said mare was unsuited by the heavy going*
Dutch Star *Official explanation: jockey said mare lost a front shoe*

3980 LEVY BOARD GAME SPIRIT CHASE GRADE 2 (11 fncs 1 omitted) 2m
3:05 (3:05) (Class 1) 5-Y-0+ **£22,808** (£8,556; £4,284; £2,136)

Form RPR
0021 **1** **Don't Be Shy (FR)**^{28} [3494] 5-10-11 .... TimmyMurphy 155+
(M C Pipe) *lw: hld up: trckd clr ldr 6th: clsd to ld 3 out: j.lft next: in command last: rdn and kpt on flat* **5/4**^{1}
-151 **2** *1 3/4* **Armaturk (FR)**^{49} [3136] 9-11-6 158..................... MickFitzgerald 159
(P F Nicholls) *chsd ldr tl j. slowly 5th: reminder next and nt gng wl: styd in tch: outpcd 3 out: rallied last: wnt 2nd nr fin* **13/8**^{2}
4123 **3** *1 1/2* **Mister McGoldrick**^{14} [3725] 9-11-10 160..................... RichardJohnson 163+
(Mrs S J Smith) *lw: led: clr fr 6th: tl hdd 3 out: sltly hmpd next: no ex flat: lost 2nd nr fin* **4/1**^{3}
0-66 **4** *dist* **Locksmith**^{14} [3724] 6-11-5 145..................... JamieMoore —
(M C Pipe) *plld hrd: chsd ldr 5th to 6th: sn wknd: t.o after 8th: btn 65l* **20/1**

4m 7.90s **Going Correction** +0.375s/f (Yiel)
WFA 5 from 6yo+ 6lb **4** Ran SP% **107.3**
Speed ratings: **115,114,113**,— CSF £3.73 TOTE £2.60; EX 3.70.
Owner D A Johnson **Bred** P Talvard, P Deshayes And J P Deshayes **Trained** Nicholashayne, Devon

FOCUS
A disappointing turnout for this re-scheduled contest, originally due to be run at Newbury, but still a decent effort from the novice Don't Be Shy to beat three smart sorts on just his third start over fences. The third sets the level and the form looks solid with the time good.

NOTEBOOK
Don't Be Shy(FR) created a good impression when getting off the mark over fences in a two and a half mile novice chase at Haydock on his previous start and confirmed that promise upped significantly in grade and dropped in trip. He took a while to get going, but his stamina and ability to cope with such testing ground came into play in the straight and he ultimately won quite well. The Arkle is now his aim but, while he clearly has the required class to go very close, he may be forced to race on good ground for the first time. Even if he handles a better surface, he could find things happening a touch too quickly for him, but his trainer's tremendous record in the race offers plenty of encouragement. *(op 13-8 tchd 7-4 in places)*
Armaturk(FR), the winner of his previous three starts over this course and distance, again showed his liking for the track with a good effort considering he was conceding 9lb to the winner. He looked in trouble some way out, but responded to pressure in the straight to take second on the run-in. *(op 6-4 tchd 7-4 in a place)*
Mister McGoldrick, back over fences after a couple of creditable efforts over hurdles recently, was given every chance under a positive ride but had no easy task giving weight away all round and was just found out. It is probably worth noting that he has not won away from Wetherby since April 2004. *(op 3-1 tchd 9-2 in a place)*
Locksmith, a stablemate of the winner, is best when able to dominate and, unable to do so, was too keen for his own good. *(op 16-1)*

3981 TOTEEXACTA H'CAP CHASE (16 fncs 2 omitted) 3m
3:40 (3:40) (Class 4) (0-110,110) 5-Y-0+ **£3,903** (£1,146; £573; £286)

Form RPR
500F **1** **Happy Shopper (IRE)**^{28} [3499] 6-10-9 **93**..................... RichardJohnson 110+
(M C Pipe) *lw: mde most: nt fluent 5th: clr fr 12th: rdn after 2 out: kpt on wl flat* **9/4**^{1}
10F4 **2** *5* **Motcombe (IRE)**^{17} [3676] 8-10-13 **97**.....................(p) MatthewBatchelor 106
(R H Alner) *lw: chsd ldng pair to 7th: lost pl and last 10th: wl bhd 12th: styd on again bef 3 out: wnt 2nd last: pushed along and styd* **9/2**^{3}
1F42 **3** *8* **Stormy Skye (IRE)**^{32} [3434] 10-11-1 **99**.....................(b) JamieMoore 100
(G L Moore) *w wnr to 11th: nt fluent next: rdn and one pce bef 3 out: wknd last* **5/1**
F1F1 **4** *1 1/2* **Trenance**^{28} [3499] 8-10-12 **96**..................... JasonMaguire 97+
(T R George) *settled in rr: effrt to chse wnr 12th: no imp 3 out: wknd and lost 2nd last* **5/2**^{2}

F-5P **P** **Lets Go Dutch**[21] 3614 10-10-9 **93**....................(t) CarlLlewellyn —
(K Bishop) *a in rr: reminder 11th: sn wknd and t.o: 6th whn p.u bef 3 out* **9/1**

/P0- **P** **Indian Chance**[402] 3322 12-11-12 **110**.................... LeightonAspell —
(O Sherwood) *lw: settled in rr: lost tch after 11th: sn t.o: 5th whn p.u bef 3 out* **14/1**

6m 42.0s (18.30) **Going Correction** +0.60s/f (Soft) **6** Ran SP% **110.9**
Speed ratings: **93,91,88,88,**— — CSF £12.47 TOTE £2.70: £1.70, £2.10; EX 17.50.
Owner Heli-Beds Racing **Bred** John Kelleher **Trained** Nicholashayne, Devon

FOCUS
An ordinary handicap chase won in good style, although the time was moderate and the unreliable runner-up is the best guide to the form.

NOTEBOOK
Happy Shopper(IRE), still in front and looking the likliest winner when falling three out here on his chasing debut, showed no ill-effects of the spill and put in a sound round of jumping, staying on strongly under Johnson to win with a fair amount in hand. He is evidently in the process of making better chaser than hurdler and, with further improvement likely to come from the six-year-old, he is *one to keep on the right side of. Official explanation: trainer's representative had no explanation for the improved form shown*
Motcombe(IRE), who is not the easiest of horses, gave an improved performance in the cheekpieces, staying on well down the straight without really threatening to topple the winner. She stays three miles well, but is hardly consistent and is likely to go back up a little in the weights following this. *(op 5-1)*
Stormy Skye(IRE) held every chance and appeared to run his race back in third. He finished tired in the end and will remain vulnerable off this mark. *(op 6-1)*
Trenance, who has had trouble with his jumping in the past, came into this having won his last two completed starts and again looked set to go well despite racing off a 6lb higher mark. Held up early, he was unable to go on with the winner from the turn-in and faded out of it disappointingly. He has a bit to prove after this. *(op 9-4)*
Indian Chance has not offered a great deal since returning from injury and is going to need some further help from the Handicapper. *(tchd 16-1)*
Lets Go Dutch failed to improve for the tongue tie and continues to regress. *(tchd 16-1)*

3982 TOTESPORT 0800 221 221 H'CAP HURDLE (12 hdls) 2m 7f
4:10 (4:12) (Class 4) (0-115,115) 4-Y-0+ **£4,554** (£1,337; £668; £333)

Form RPR

560P **1** **Wee Anthony (IRE)**[18] 3663 7-10-5 **94**.................... RichardJohnson 106+
(Jonjo O'Neill) *trckd ldrs: led bef 2 out: clr last: comf* **8/1**

-005 **2** *8* **Supreme Piper (IRE)**[28] 3508 8-11-0 **110**.................... MissCDyson[(7)] 112+
(Miss C Dyson) *mde most to 7th: led again 3 out: bmpd along and hdd bef next: sn outpcd: kpt on and mstke last: no ch w wnr* **33/1**

3003 **3** *4* **River Ripples (IRE)**[18] 3659 7-10-11 **100**.................... JasonMaguire 98+
(T R George) *hld up in tch: prog 3 out: chsd wnr 2 out: no imp: wknd last* **2/1**[1]

4-14 **4** *3* **Roman Rampage**[38] 3345 11-10-0 **89**....................(p) MatthewBatchelor 83
(Miss Z C Davison) *chsd ldrs: drvn after 3 out: sn outpcd: btn in 4th whn blnd 2 out: plugged on* **16/1**

124 **5** *12* **Best Profile (IRE)**[63] 2878 6-11-10 **113**.................... CarlLlewellyn 95
(N A Twiston-Davies) *hld up in rr: lost tch after 7th and rdn: rallied 3 out to chse ldrs bef next: sn no prog and btn* **5/1**[2]

4635 **6** *1* **Amazing Valour (IRE)**[9] 3814 4-10-5 **105**....................(b) SeanCurran 75
(P Bowen) *pressed ldr: led 7th to 3 out: hrd rdn and wknd 2 out* **11/2**[3]

6P05 **7** *17* **Jaloux D'Estruval (FR)**[33] 3428 9-11-8 **111**....................(t) JamieMoore 75
(Mrs L C Taylor) *t.k.h: hld up in rr: shkn up 8th: prog to chal 3 out : sn wknd* **9/1**

1-00 **8** *22* **Alagon (IRE)**[42] 3289 6-11-10 **113**.................... JamesDavies 55
(Ian Williams) *chsd ldrs: pushed along 7th: struggling bef 3 out: t.o next* **16/1**

51P0 **9** *19* **Moustique De L'Isle (FR)**[23] 3581 6-11-2 **105**....................(b) TimmyMurphy 28
(C C Bealby) *lw: in tch tl wknd 8th: t.o bef 3 out* **8/1**

5-30 **P** **Easibrook Jane**[93] 2297 8-11-12 **115**.................... MickFitzgerald —
(C L Tizzard) *lw: racd wd: wl in tch tl wknd bef 9th: t.o whn p.u bef 2 out* **25/1**

056- **P** **The Cad (IRE)**[302] 4954 6-10-6 **95**.................... LeightonAspell —
(R H Alner) *bit bkwd: hld up: prog 9th: cl up 3 out: sn wknd rapidly: t.o whn p.u bef 2 out* **25/1**

6m 24.0s (17.00) **Going Correction** +0.85s/f (Soft)
WFA 4 from 6yo+ 10lb **11** Ran SP% **120.0**
Speed ratings: **104,101,99,98,94 94,88,80,74,**— — CSF £236.49 CT £733.50 TOTE £11.20: £2.40, £6.70, £2.00; EX 1215.20.
Owner John P McManus **Bred** J Shefflin **Trained** Cheltenham, Gloucs

FOCUS
Just a modest handicap hurdle rated through the third and fourth, with the winner showing considerable improvement.

NOTEBOOK
Wee Anthony(IRE) ◆, pulled up on his chasing debut over two miles at Folkestone, was well suited by this significant step up in trip on his return to hurdling and gained his first-career success in decent style. He is at the right end of the handicap and should win again granted similar *conditions. Official explanation: trainer's representative had no explanation for the improved form shown other than that gelding may have benefited from the heavy ground* *(tchd 9-1 and 10-1 in places)*
Supreme Piper(IRE) did not shape badly at Wincanton on his previous start and stepped up on that effort to take a very creditable second. He has dropped to a fair mark and could find a similar race if able to repeat this form.
River Ripples(IRE), stepped up to his furthest trip to date, did not see out his race as one might *have hoped and is proving hard enough to win with. Official explanation: trainer said he was unable to fit the declared tongue-strap (op 9-4 tchd 11-4 in a place)*
Roman Rampage acquitted himself creditably given his last success came in a seller. *(op 14-1 tchd 20-1)*
Best Profile(IRE) had conditions to suit but is not progressing as one might have hoped and has to be considered disappointing. *(tchd 11-2)*
Amazing Valour(IRE) seems better suited by a decent surface.
Alagon(IRE) *Official explanation: trainer's representative said gelding made a noise*

3983 MARSH GREEN STANDARD OPEN NATIONAL HUNT FLAT RACE 2m
4:40 (4:52) (Class 6) 4-6-Y-0 **£1,713** (£499; £249)

Form RPR

1 **1** **Ringaroses**[59] 2941 5-11-8 .... PaulO'Neill[(3)] 106+
(Miss H C Knight) *lw: racd wd: hld up in rr: prog over 3f out: rdn wl over 2f out: hanging but r.o to ld jst ins fnl f: styd on wl* **13/8**[1]

42 **2** *¾* **Sundarbob (IRE)**[19] 3651 4-10-9 .... JamesDavies 86
(P R Webber) *trckd ldrs: effrt on inner 2f out: got through to chal 1f out: jst outpcd* **11/2**[3]

1 **3** *¾* **Dubai Sunday (JPN)**[28] 3504 5-11-11 .... JamieMoore 102
(P S McEntee) *hld up in tch: prog to trck ldrs over 2f out: drvn to chal 1f out: kpt on same pce* **5/2**[2]

36 **4** *½* **Piper Paddy**[19] 3651 4-10-2 .... RichardJohnson 78
(P R Chamings) *prom: cl up jst over 1f out: sn nt qckn: r.o again last 75yds* **16/1**

5 *½* **Go On Ahead (IRE)** 6-10-11 .... MrsMRoberts[(7)] 95+
(M J Coombe) *w'like: ldr: chal 2f out: upsides over 1f out: hld whn squeezed out nr fin* **25/1**

002 **6** *1 ½* **Persian Native (IRE)**[28] 3504 6-11-4 .... MickFitzgerald 92
(C C Bealby) *led at stdy pce: rdn 2f out: hdd & wknd jst ins fnl f* **14/1**

46 **7** *3* **Viennchee Run**[120] 1820 5-10-11 .... ShaneWalsh[(7)] 89
(K F Clutterbuck) *trckd ldrs: lost pl on inner 5f out: renewed effrt to chse ldrs over 2f out: outpcd over 1f out* **100/1**

0- **8** *1* **Bonny Jago**[465] 2129 5-11-4 .... LeightonAspell 88
(R Brotherton) *trckd ldrs: lost pl on inner ovedr 4f out: rallied to chse ldrs 2f out: no imp over 1f out* **33/1**

9 *3* **Gandy Dancer (IRE)** 6-10-11 .... JasonMaguire 78
(Miss E C Lavelle) *w'like: hld up: last 5f out: prog but outpcd over 3f out: shuffled along and kpt on: nvr nr ldrs* **33/1**

340 **10** *5* **Reveal (IRE)**[66] 2830 4-9-10 ow1.................... LukasSloup[(7)] 65
(H E Haynes) *hld up wl in rr: prog over 3f out: chsd ldrs but no on terms over 2f out: wknd over 1f out* **50/1**

11 *3 ½* **Napalm (IRE)** 5-10-8 .... JamesPeters[(10)] 77
(C C Bealby) *lengthy: scope: hld up: a in rr: outpcd over 3f out: no ch after* **40/1**

12 *4* **The Main Man** 5-11-4 .... TimmyMurphy 73
(M G Rimell) *gd sort: str: pressed ldrs: reminders 9f out: rdn over 4f out: sn lost pl and btn* **8/1**

13 *½* **Lady Jay Jay** 6-10-4 .... MissJKelly[(7)] 65
(Mrs Norma Pook) *unf: taken down early: rel to r and lft s: rcvrd after 5f: prog to dispute ld 7f out: wknd 5f out* **100/1**

14 *2 ½* **Valprimo** 4-10-9 .... MatthewBatchelor 61
(G L Moore) *str: scope: bkwd: in tch tl wknd over 3f out* **20/1**

3m 38.1s
WFA 4 from 5yo+ 9lb **14** Ran SP% **126.6**
CSF £10.94 TOTE £2.70: £1.70, £1.80, £1.70; EX 18.10 Place 6 £162.72, Place 5 £10.34.
Owner Mrs Nicholas Jones/Martin Broughton **Bred** Coln Valley Stud **Trained** West Lockinge, Oxon

FOCUS
Not a bad bumper, but a steady early pace compressed the beaten distances. The race is rated through the sixth to previous course form.

NOTEBOOK
Ringaroses, off the mark in a reasonable good-ground bumper at Ludlow on his previous start, coped well with the switch to Polytrack narrowly defied his penalty. The predictably steady pace compressed the beaten distances and he was probably value for more than the winning margin, although he did not exactly help his rider by hanging under pressure. He may now be aimed the Aintree Bumper. *(op 9-4 tchd 11-4 in places and 5-2 in places)*
Sundarbob(IRE), upped to two miles for the first time, confirmed the promise he showed on both his previous starts with a solid effort in second. *(op 9-1)*
Dubai Sunday(JPN), quite an impressive winner of a moderate course and distance bumper on his debut, was found under his penalty in this better company. *(op 9-4 tchd 11-4)*
Piper Paddy, upped in trip, was unsuited by the steady early pace and acquitted himself creditably in the circumstances. *(op 14-1)*
Go On Ahead(IRE), a 20,000euros half-brother to the smart middle-distance stayer Astrocharm, made a pleasing debut and can progress. *(tchd 33-1)*
The Main Man finished down the field but very much caught the eye in the paddock. Very much a long-term chasing type, he should come on a fair bit for the run. *(op 15-2)*
T/Plt: £164.90 to a £1 stake. Pool: £50,251.85. 222.45 winning tickets. T/Qpdt: £10.40 to a £1 stake. Pool: £3,664.20. 258.75 winning tickets. JN

3730 UTTOXETER (L-H)
Saturday, February 18

OFFICIAL GOING: Heavy (soft in places)
The inside running rail on the hurdle track was moved in three yards, providing fresh ground. The going was described as 'like a gluepot'.
Wind: Almost nil Weather: Fine and sunny

3984 TOTEPLACEPOT NOVICES' HURDLE (12 hdls) 2m 4f 110y
1:20 (1:20) (Class 3) 4-Y-0+ **£5,530** (£1,623; £811; £405)

Form RPR

33 **1** **Triple Mint (IRE)**[46] 3232 5-11-0 .... PaddyAspell[(3)] 108
(D McCain) *chsd ldrs: pushed along 7th: styd on fr 3 out: led last 100yds* **9/1**

6421 **2** *1 ½* **Major Catch (IRE)**[12] 3780 7-11-3 110.................... AdamPogson[(5)] 112+
(C T Pogson) *hld up: smooth hdwy 7th: wnt 2nd 9th: led next: hit last: hdd and no ex run-in* **7/4**[1]

4 **3** *1 ¾* **Clemax (IRE)**[111] 1938 5-10-10 .... PatrickMcDonald[(7)] 104
(Ferdy Murphy) *hld up in last: hdwy 8th: sn chsng ldrs: upsides last: kpt on same pce* **11/2**[3]

2303 **4** *dist* **Dillay Brook (IRE)**[32] 3437 6-10-3 .... WillieMcCarthy[(7)] 67
(T R George) *chsd ldrs: pushed along 6th: wknd after 3 out: btn total of 34l* **7/1**

P-52 **5** *¾* **Stoop To Conquer**[47] 3219 6-11-3 114....................(t) NoelFehily 73
(A W Carroll) *led after 1st: nt fluent and j.rt: hdd 3 out: sn wknd: bhd whn blnd last* **3/1**[2]

P45- **6** *21* **Real Definition**[302] 4954 7-11-3 .... OllieMcPhail 52
(M G Rimell) *led tl after 1st: chsd ldr to 9th: sn lost pl: t.o 2 out* **16/1**

P **Return Fire**[335] 7-11-3 .... PaulMoloney —
(Miss H C Knight) *t.k.h in rr: wknd 7th: t.o whn p.u bef next* **16/1**

5m 25.2s (13.10) **Going Correction** +1.00s/f (Soft) **7** Ran SP% **111.0**
Speed ratings: **103,102,101,**—,— — —,— CSF £24.50 TOTE £6.00: £2.20, £2.00; EX 24.90.
Owner Mrs Janet Heler **Bred** J O'Keeffe **Trained** Cholmondeley, Cheshire

FOCUS
Just a steady gallop but a true test in the end. The race could be rated higher through the third.

NOTEBOOK
Triple Mint(IRE), who stands over plenty of ground, was under pressure to keep up setting out on to the final circuit. He stuck to his task and his superior stamina carried the day late on. *(op 8-1)*
Major Catch(IRE) looked to be travelling easily best and looked nailed on when taking charge. He clouted the last and in the end did not see it out as well as the winner. *(op 15-8)*
Clemax(IRE), a winner over fences in bad ground in France, is a very narrow individual. Patiently ridden, he worked his way upsides at the final flight but could then pull out no more. *(tchd 6-1)*
Dillay Brook(IRE) was struggling to keep up with a circuit to go and in the end he was left toiling. *(op 8-1)*
Stoop To Conquer, fitted with a tongue strap, was keen to get on with it and his jumping let him down. Once collared he stopped to nothing and put in a very tired jump at the last. *(op 5-2)*

The Form Book, Raceform Ltd, Compton, RG20 6NL

3985 PETER J DOUGLAS ENGINEERING NOVICES' (S) HURDLE (10 hdls) 2m

1:50 (1:50) (Class 5) 4-Y-O+ **£2,081** (£611; £305; £152)

Form				RPR
0202	1		**The Wife's Sister**[14] 3731 5-10-6 83..............................(b) PaddyAspell(3) (D McCain) *chsd ldrs: rdn to ld appr 3 out: hit last: eased towards fin* **9/2**[1]	82+
-P50	2	8	**Native Commander (IRE)**[10] 3804 11-10-11 90... ChristopherMurray(5) (Jim Best) *in tch: hdwy to trck ldrs 6th: wnt 2nd after 3 out: rdn appr last: no imp* **25/1**	81
500P	3	7	**Mickey Pearce (IRE)**[29] 3479 4-10-2 80...............(v[1]) StevenCrawford(5) (J G M O'Shea) *trckd ldrs: one pce fr 3 out* **50/1**	65
01P2	4	7	**Blackthorn**[17] 3673 7-11-0 92.................................. TomMessenger(7) (M Appleby) *w ldrs: led 6th: hdd appr 3 out: wknd between last 2* **7/1**[3]	72
F460	5	10	**Leap Year Lass**[19] 3655 6-10-9 85.................................... AlanDempsey (C Grant) *in rr whn hmpd 3rd: sme hdwy 7th: nvr nr ldrs* **17/2**	50
0/5P	6	2 ½	**John's Treasure (IRE)**[28] 3496 6-10-9 ....(t) BenOrde-Powlett(7) (M A Barnes) *in rr whn hmpd 3rd: sn bhd and drvn along: sme hdwy 7th: nvr a factor* **25/1**	55
-005	7	½	**Bonjour Bond (IRE)**[81] 2560 5-10-13 80.....................(p) OwynNelmes(3) (J G M O'Shea) *prom: wknd 7th* **66/1**	54
0600	8	5	**Clifford T Ward**[8] 3842 6-10-9 .... MrDAFitzsimmons(7) (D McCain) *mid-div whn hmpd 3rd: hdwy 6th: wknd appr 3 out* **20/1**	49
4324	9	8	**Buz Kiri (USA)**[31] 3222 8-10-9 83...........................(t) ThomasBurrows(7) (P L Clinton) *in rr: drvn 5th: nvr a factor* **16/1**	41
P6P	10	dist	**Mist Opportunity (IRE)**[18] 3443 4-9-11 ....(vt) GaryBartley(10) (P C Haslam) *chsd ldrs: hit 4th: lost pl after 6th: sn bhd: t.o: btn total of 78l* **12/1**	—
5625	F		**Darko Karim**[23] 3577 4-10-0 90......................................(b) JamesWhite(7) (R J Hodges) *w ldrs: fell 3rd* **11/2**[2]	—
0064	B		**Little Villain (IRE)**[168] 1395 8-11-2 66..........................(p) RobertWalford (T Wall) *prom: b.d 3rd* **66/1**	—
6	P		**Al Alba (USA)**[25] 3550 4-9-7 .... PatrickMcDonald(7) (Mrs H Dalton) *rr-div: bhd fr 6th: t.o whn p.u bef 2 out* **7/1**[3]	—
/P-P	P		**Crazy Like A Fool (IRE)**[54] 2967 7-10-6 .... TimothyBailey(10) (M G Quinlan) *stdd s: bhd: t.o whn p.u bef 6th* **100/1**	—
63/0	P		**Adventino**[17] 3673 11-10-9 .... AdrianScholes(7) (P R Johnson) *chsd ldrs to 6th: sn wknd: bhd whn p.u bef 3 out* **66/1**	—
010	P		**Barking Mad (USA)**[12] 2261 8-11-7 100................................. NoelFehily (C R Dore) *j.rt: led to 6th: sn lost pl: bhd whn p.u bef 3 out* **8/1**	—
04	P		**Red Rocky**[6] 3885 5-9-13 .... AdamHawkins(10) (R Hollinshead) *in rr: sme hdwy 6th: wknd 3 out: bhd whn p.u bef next* **25/1**	—

4m 15.7s (15.30) **Going Correction** +1.00s/f (Soft)
WFA 4 from 5yo+ 9lb **17 Ran SP% 117.5**
Speed ratings: **101,97,93,90,85 83,83,81,77,—** —,—,—,—,— —,— CSF £118.65 TOTE £4.80: £2.00, £7.60, £19.40; EX 214.00.The winner was sold to Nick Shutts for 7,400gns
Owner Mrs D McCain **Bred** Wood Farm Stud **Trained** Cholmondeley, Cheshire
■ Stewards' Enquiry : Gary Bartley two-day ban: using whip when out of contention (Mar 1,23)

FOCUS
A very ordinary seller and very few got into it. The race could rate higher but has been treated cautiously.

NOTEBOOK
The Wife's Sister, who has run some of her best races here, broke her duck at the 12th attempt. She changed hands at the auction. *(op 11-2)*
Native Commander(IRE), no spring chicken, went in pursuit of the winner but was never really going to get in a telling blow.
Mickey Pearce(IRE), running in a seller for the first time, swapped cheekpieces for a visor.
Blackthorn went on but after losing out to the winner he tired badly going to the final flight. *(op 13-2)*

3986 TOTESCOOP6 H'CAP HURDLE (12 hdls) 2m 4f 110y

2:25 (2:26) (Class 2) (0-140,136) 4-Y-O+ **£18,591** (£5,520; £2,760; £1,377; £690; £348)

Form				RPR
2511	1		**Dom D'Orgeval (FR)**[28] 3502 6-11-12 136................. WayneHutchinson (Nick Williams) *hld up towards rr: hdwy 8th: styd on fr 3 out: led between last 2: all out* **17/2**[3]	145+
1B-0	2	1 ¼	**Victom's Chance (IRE)**[28] 3502 8-10-9 122............. WilliamKennedy(3) (Noel T Chance) *hld up towards rr: hdwy 7th: wnt 2nd and j.ft 3 out: j.lft last: hung lft and styd on: nt rch wnr* **14/1**	130+
1101	3	2	**Nous Voila (FR)**[28] 3491 5-11-6 133................................. TomMalone(3) (M C Pipe) *w ldrs: led appr 7th: hdd between last 2: kpt on same pce* **7/2**[2]	138+
5-32	4	dist	**Only Vintage (USA)**[54] 2974 6-11-12 136........................... PaulMoloney (Miss H C Knight) *in tch: hdwy 7th: chsng ldrs 9th: wknd fr 3 out: btn total of 41l* **16/1**	115
F211	5	13	**Hoh Viss**[21] 3622 6-11-3 127.. NoelFehily (C J Mann) *hld up in rr: stdy hdwy 9th: nvr on terms* **11/4**[1]	96
0325	6	1 ½	**Fenix (GER)**[14] 3727 7-10-10 130.......................................(b) MattyRoe(10) (Mrs L Wadham) *in tch: hdwy 7th: wknd 9th* **11/1**	98
1613	7	19	**Patman Du Charmil (FR)**[53] 3021 4-10-4 124...................... TomSiddall (N A Twiston-Davies) *mid-div: hdwy 7th: lost pl after 9th* **10/1**	—
0P00	8	10	**Fontanesi (IRE)**[21] 3622 6-11-8 132...................................... SamStronge (M C Pipe) *nvr a factor* **100/1**	—
1120	9	11	**Magot De Grugy (FR)**[49] 3135 6-10-8 118....................... RobertWalford (R H Alner) *a in rr* **16/1**	—
5125	10	14	**Killing Me Softly**[21] 3615 5-10-10 120...............................(v) MarcusFoley (J Gallagher) *a in rr: bhd fr 7th* **25/1**	—
0260	11	9	**Nonantais (FR)**[14] 3727 9-10-8 125........................... PatrickCStringer(7) (M Bradstock) *chsd ldrs: lost pl after 9th* **25/1**	—
4222	P		**Pay Attention**[21] 3621 5-11-0 124.. RussGarritty (T D Easterby) *in rr: bhd whn p.u bef 3 out* **12/1**	—
P-05	P		**Benbyas**[21] 3622 9-11-6 130... DNolan (D Carroll) *led tl appr 7th: lost pl 8th: t.o whn p.u bef 3 out* **40/1**	—
-013	P		**Torkinking (IRE)**[35] 3383 7-10-8 125......................(t) BenOrde-Powlett(7) (M A Barnes) *chsd ldr: sddle slipped 3rd: lost pl after 9th: modest 8th whn p.u bef next* **16/1**	—

5m 21.3s (9.20) **Going Correction** +1.00s/f (Soft)
WFA 4 from 5yo+ 10lb **14 Ran SP% 120.0**
Speed ratings: **110,109,108,—,—** —,—,—,—,— —,—,—,— CSF £116.08 CT £500.14 TOTE £11.60: £3.50, £3.30, £2.40; EX 175.10 Trifecta £743.80 Pool £31,745.95. 30.30 winning units.
Owner Mrs Jane Williams **Bred** Max De Minden **Trained** George Nympton, Devon
■ Stewards' Enquiry : D Nolan one-day ban: anticipating start (Mar 1)
Ben Orde-Powlett one-day ban: anticipating start (Mar 1)
Tom Malone one-day ban: anticipating start (Mar 1)

FOCUS
The early pace was strong and the overall time decent, but in the end only three figured. The race could rate much higher but the ground conditions count against it.

NOTEBOOK
Dom D'Orgeval(FR), happy to sit off a strong pace, took charge going to the last but at the line he looked a tired horse. He now heads for the Coral Cup. *(op 15-2)*
Victom's Chance(IRE) looked to have come on for his initial outing. He too sat off the strong pace but he went left at the last and then gave his rider problems hanging in behind the winner on the run-in.
Nous Voila(FR) ◆, keen to jump off first, took it up setting out on to the final circuit. He stuck on all the way to the line, the only one of the first three to race up with the pace and he deserves plenty of credit for this. *(op 3-1)*
Only Vintage(USA), weighted to reverse Newbury placings with the winner, did not handle the testing conditions anywhere near as well. *(op 18-1)*
Hoh Viss sat way off the pace and only making an effort four out, he never figured. This is best overlooked. *Official explanation: jockey said gelding was never travelling (op 3-1 tchd 10-3, 5-2 and 7-2 in a place)*
Fenix(GER), closely matched with the winner on Lingfield form, has not won for over two years now.
Torkinking(IRE), handicapped early on by a slipped saddle, did well to stay in contention until four out. *Official explanation: jockey said saddle slipped (op 20-1)*

3987 BETFRED POKER H'CAP HURDLE SERIES FINAL (14 hdls) 3m

2:55 (2:56) (Class 2) 4-Y-O+ **£12,526** (£3,700; £1,850; £926; £462; £232)

Form				RPR
0501	1		**Corlande (IRE)**[35] 3384 6-10-2 119......................... MichaelO'Connell(10) (Mrs S J Smith) *trckd ldrs: led 9th: styd on fr 3 out: hung lft run-in: hld on wl towards fin* **4/1**[2]	124+
4223	2	½	**Just Beth**[48] 3179 10-10-7 119... DerekLaverty(5) (G Fierro) *chsd ldrs: wnt 2nd 10th: upsides last: no ex towards fin* **7/1**	121
2435	3	24	**Mouseski**[54] 2974 12-10-6 116... TomMalone(3) (P F Nicholls) *in tch: outpcd 8th: kpt on fr 3 out: tk mod 3rd run-in* **13/2**	94
4340	4	15	**Dream Falcon**[14] 3727 6-11-1 129.................................... JamesWhite(7) (R J Hodges) *hld up in rr: sme hdwy 9th: mod 5th whn hit 11th: sn wknd* **16/1**	92
P111	5	1 ¼	**Nine De Sivola (FR)**[35] 3389 5-11-5 133.................. PatrickMcDonald(7) (Ferdy Murphy) *hld up in last pl: hdwy 8th: wnt 3rd 10th: rdn and wknd appr 2 out* **15/8**[1]	95+
0136	6	dist	**Jethro Tull (IRE)**[39] 3336 7-9-11 107 oh10..............(p) WilliamKennedy(3) (G A Harker) *hld up towards rr: hdwy and in tch 9th: lost pl 11th: btn total of 78l* **16/1**	—
P120	7	dist	**Irishkawa Bellevue (FR)**[35] 3389 8-10-11 123.............(b) MarkNicolls(5) (Jean-Rene Auvray) *chsd ldrs: drvn along 8th: wknd next: in rr whn hit 10th: sn t.o: btn total of 111l* **20/1**	—
2221	P		**Russian Sky**[54] 2990 7-10-2 116.................................... TomMessenger(7) (Mrs H O Graham) *led: hit 6th: hdd 9th: lost pl next: t.o 3 out: p.u bef next* **11/2**[3]	—
1000	P		**Nick The Silver**[43] 3271 5-9-9 107 oh7.......................(p) TomGreenway(5) (Robert Gray) *mid-div: hdwy 3rd: sn chsng ldrs: reminders 7th: lost pl 9th: t.o whn p.u bef 11th* **40/1**	—

6m 23.0s (18.00) **Going Correction** +1.00s/f (Soft) **9 Ran SP% 115.0**
Speed ratings: **110,109,101,96,96** —,—,—,— CSF £32.02 CT £177.65 TOTE £4.50: £1.50, £1.50, £2.40; EX 13.90.
Owner Crow Partnership **Bred** Dr Paschal Carmody **Trained** High Eldwick, W Yorks

FOCUS
Not a strong field for the money on offer and the race is rated through the first two to their marks.

NOTEBOOK
Corlande(IRE), 9lb higher, pressed on at the first flight on the final circuit. His young rider impressed changing his whip hand three times from the last and at the line there was a fraction more still to come. If he wins a race at the Cheltenham Festival he will pick up a £100,000 bonus, but he is unlikely to get the soft ground he needs there.
Just Beth, on a lengthy losing run, ran her heart out but in the end was not quite good enough.
Mouseski, struggling with a circuit to go, kept going in his own time to secure a remote third spot. *(op 5-1)*
Dream Falcon, put to sleep at the back, was making limited headway when an error four out finished him off altogether. *(op 20-1)*
Nine De Sivola(FR), happy to sit last, went in pursuit of the first two five out but he suddenly began to make hard work of it after three out and he soon dropped right away. This was not his true running. *(op 9-4 tchd 5-2 in places)*
Nick The Silver *Official explanation: jockey said gelding was unsuited by the heavy, soft in places going and had a breathing problem (op 5-1)*
Russian Sky *Official explanation: jockey said gelding ran flat (op 5-1)*

3988 SINGER & FRIEDLANDER (A H'CAP CHASE) (16 fncs) 2m 6f 110y

3:35 (3:35) (Class 2) 5-Y-O+ **£34,105** (£10,142; £5,082; £2,546; £1,287; £660)

Form				RPR
/004	1		**Our Armageddon (NZ)**[21] 3620 9-11-2 130...................... LarryMcGrath (R C Guest) *w ldrs: led appr 9th: styd on fr 4 out: drvn rt out* **11/1**	146+
2213	2	4	**He's The Guv'Nor (IRE)**[21] 3612 7-10-4 118............ BenjaminHitchcott (R H Buckler) *in rr: mstke 8th: hdwy 11th: wnt 2nd 4 out: upsides whn blnd 2 out: kpt on same pce run-in* **8/1**[3]	130+
2022	3	6	**Better Days (IRE)**[14] 3739 10-10-13 127....................... RichardMcGrath (Mrs S J Smith) *prom: lost pl after 4th: hdwy 2 out: styd on wl run-in* **8/1**[3]	129
FB12	4	6	**Be My Better Half (IRE)**[28] 3503 11-10-13 127......................... APMcCoy (Jonjo O'Neill) *trckd ldrs: blnd 8th: rdn 12th: fdd after 3 out* **7/2**[1]	123
5361	5	10	**Haut De Gamme (FR)**[35] 3397 11-11-9 137......................... KeithMercer (Ferdy Murphy) *in rr: hdwy 11th: chsng ldrs 12th: wknd appr next* **9/1**	123
-500	6	16	**Whereareyounow (IRE)**[48] 3180 9-10-8 122........................ TomSiddall (N A Twiston-Davies) *chsd ldrs: outpcd whn blnd 10th: wkng whn j.lft 12th* **11/1**	92
-P50	7	27	**Amberleigh House (IRE)**[90] 2370 14-11-2 133............. PaddyAspell(3) (D McCain) *lost pl4th: sn bhd: t.o fr 8th: eventually completed* **50/1**	76
4025	P		**Spring Grove (IRE)**[28] 3509 11-10-5 119......................... RobertWalford (R H Alner) *bhd and drvn 9th: bhd whn p.u bef 3 out* **18/1**	—
0P5F	P		**Kadount (FR)**[28] 3503 8-11-12 140.............................. WayneHutchinson (A King) *in rr: reminders 8th: bhd fr 10th: t.o whn p.u bef 4 out* **16/1**	—
1254	P		**Edmo Yewkay (IRE)**[14] 3739 6-11-0 128..........................(b) RussGarritty (T D Easterby) *prom: mstke 6th: lost pl 10th: bhd whn p.u bef 3 out* **14/1**	—

02-F **P** **Juveigneur (FR)**[90] 2370 9-11-11 **139** MarcusFoley —
(N J Henderson) *mstkes: in rr: hdwy 10th: chsng ldrs 4 out: sn wknd: p.u bef 2 out* **14/1**

-121 **P** **Bannow Strand (IRE)**[42] 3288 6-11-7 **138** TomMalone(3) —
(M C Pipe) *led: mstke 8th: hdd appr next: lost pl after 10th: bhd whn p.u bef 12th* **7/1**[2]

F351 **P** **Almost Broke**[28] 3509 9-11-6 **139** MrCJSweeney(5) —
(P F Nicholls) *in rr: hmpd 8th: hdwy 10th: wkng whn hmpd 12th: bhd whn p.u bef 3 out* **10/1**

6m 11.1s **Going Correction** +0.575s/f (Soft) **13** Ran SP% **119.1**
Speed ratings: **115,113,111,109,105 100,91,—,—,— —,—,—** CSF £96.96 CT £753.95 TOTE £15.00: £4.10, £3.60, £2.80; EX 137.10 TRIFECTA Not won..
Owner Leslie John Garrett **Bred** L W Bowater And C Marchant **Trained** Brancepeth, Co Durham

FOCUS
A decent handicap run at a strong gallop in the conditions and the winner bounced back after being in the wilderness since his 2004 Cathcart success. The first two are rated better than the bare form.

NOTEBOOK
Our Armageddon(NZ) went on with a circuit to go and even in the tacky ground his jumping was sound. He kept up the gallop all the way to the line and the Topham Trophy at Aintree is his main spring objective.
He's The Guv'Nor(IRE), who has gone up 8lb after his two most recent runs, would have given the winner even more to do but for getting the second last all wrong. This was only his fifth start over fences and there may be even better to come. *(op 9-1 tchd 10-1)*
Better Days(IRE), without a win for over two years, made up many lengths over the last two fences and finished best of all. He is well worth another try over three miles.
Be My Better Half(IRE), a confirmed heavy-ground specialist, was all the rage. He nearly went at the last with a circuit to go and, hard at work five out, did not see it out anywhere near as well as the first three. *(op 13-2 tchd 7-1 in a place)*
Haut De Gamme(FR), back over fences with the Grand National weights set in stone, was having his first outing for five weeks. *(op 10-1)*
Whereareyounow(IRE), who took this a year ago from a 4lb higher mark, is not in the same sort of form this time round. *(op 14-1)*
Amberleigh House(IRE) was soon struggling and completed very much in his own time. He will have one more outing before another crack at the Grand National then retirement. *(op 40-1)*
Bannow Strand(IRE), who looked magnificent, took them along at a strong gallop but a mistake at the last fence with a circuit to go seemed to sap his strength and once headed, he quickly dropped away. *(op 12-1)*
Juveigneur(FR) did not jump well in the ground but at least this will have put him right for Cheltenham, where he won the Kim Muir last time. *(op 12-1)*

3989 TOTESPORT.COM H'CAP CHASE (20 fncs) 3m 2f
4:05 (4:06) (Class 3) (0-125,121) 5-Y-0 **£6,286** (£1,873; £948; £486; £254)

Form RPR

411P **1** **Blunham Hill (IRE)**[38] 3343 8-10-1 **101** MarkNicolls(5) 108+
(John R Upson) *chsd ldrs: 2nd and hld whn lft in ld 2 out: j.lft last: hung lft run-in: hld on towards fin* **6/1**

3-F5 **2** *1 ½* **Glen Warrior**[35] 3390 10-11-12 **121** PaulMoloney 125
(J S Smith) *hld up: hdwy 10th: lft 2nd 2 out: chal last: no ex last 75yds* **7/1**

122R **3** *16* **Young Lorcan**[23] 3578 10-9-13 **101** RichardSpate(7) 93+
(Mrs K Waldron) *chsd ldrs: 3rd and one pce whn blnd 3 out: sn wknd* **5/1**[2]

-PR5 **4** *6* **Coursing Run (IRE)**[21] 3614 10-11-6 **115** (p) MarkBradburne 97
(H D Daly) *chsd ldrs: drvn and lost pl 13th: bhd fr 15th* **8/1**

P054 **5** *6* **Auburn Spirit**[6] 3886 11-10-4 **99** WayneHutchinson 75
(M D I Usher) *w ldr: wknd 15th* **11/2**[3]

1P30 **F** **Trust Fund (IRE)**[38] 3343 8-11-7 **116** RobertWalford 129+
(R H Alner) *mde most: 5l clr and styng on whn fell 2 out* **9/2**[1]

U4P6 **P** **You Owe Me (IRE)**[42] 3293 9-11-4 **113** TomSiddall —
(N A Twiston-Davies) *in tch: wkng whn mstke 16th: bhd whn blnd 2 out: p.u bef last* **11/1**

0541 **P** **Joseph Beuys (IRE)**[18] 3662 7-9-11 **95** oh4 WilliamKennedy(3) —
(D P Keane) *hld up in rr: sme hdwy 15th: lost pl appr 4 out: bhd whn p.u bef 2 out* **6/1**

7m 25.5s (20.30) **Going Correction** +0.575s/f (Soft) **8** Ran SP% **110.7**
Speed ratings: **91,90,85,83,81** —,—,— CSF £43.72 CT £214.37 TOTE £7.10: £2.00, £2.40, £1.80; EX 60.10.
Owner The Reserved Judgment Partnership **Bred** Oliver McDonnell **Trained** Maidford, Northants

FOCUS
A modest contest and almost certainly a lucky winner. The first two are rated to their marks.

NOTEBOOK
Blunham Hill(IRE), pulled up at Newbury, was handed the prize two out but in the end it was quite a struggle. *(op 13-2)*
Glen Warrior, fourth a year ago, showed he is back on song on this just his third outing this time. *(op 13-2)*
Young Lorcan, who gave no problems at the start this time, likes it round here but his chance had already slipped when he made a bad mistake three out. *(op 9-2)*
Coursing Run(IRE), whose last win almost a year ago came from a 2lb higher mark, seemed to lose all interest setting out on to the final circuit. *(op 7-1)*
Auburn Spirit, who has won at up to a mile six, is not at his best and stopped six out. *(op 5-1)*
Trust Fund(IRE) took them along at a sound gallop and looked to have it in the bag when taking a somewhat unlucky fall two out. He deserves compensation.

3990 KEVIN DEAN BENEFIT YEAR H'CAP HURDLE (10 hdls) 2m
4:35 (4:35) (Class 4) (0-105,105) 4-Y-0+ **£3,903** (£1,146; £573; £286)

Form RPR

0331 **1** **Speed Venture**[8] 3848 9-11-0 **98** (vt) PatrickMcDonald(7) 106
(J Mackie) *hld up: stdy hdwy 6th: prom next: led between last 2: rdn clr* **7/1**[2]

10-2 **2** *6* **Misbehaviour**[47] 3223 7-11-1 **97** ChristopherMurray(5) 99
(Jim Best) *hld up: stdy hdwy 6th: led appr 2 out: hdd between last 2: no ex* **7/1**[2]

01/ **3** *7* **Elegant Clutter (IRE)**[845] 1811 8-10-7 **84** WayneHutchinson 80+
(R N Bevis) *hld up: stdy hdwy 7th: chsng ldrs 3 out: one pce between last 2* **33/1**

3124 **4** *2 ½* **Lankawi**[26] 3539 4-11-5 **105** BrianHarding 89
(Jedd O'Keeffe) *w ldr: led 2nd to 7th: led next: hdd appr 2 out: wknd appr last* **3/1**[1]

-21F **5** *3 ½* **Make My Hay**[16] 3687 7-11-7 **98** (b) MarcusFoley 87
(J Gallagher) *led to 2nd: w ldr: led 7th to next: wknd appr 2 out* **8/1**[3]

0236 **6** *17* **Haunted House**[28] 3500 6-11-12 **103** MarkBradburne 80+
(H D Daly) *hdwy to chse ldrs 6th: ev ch 3 out: wknd appr next* **10/1**

0001 **7** *15* **Imperial Royale (IRE)**[17] 3674 5-10-9 **93** ThomasBurrows(7) 50
(P L Clinton) *chsd ldrs: hit 6th: wknd after 3 out* **12/1**

2020 **P** **Haditovski**[14] 3733 10-11-5 **103** (v) MrGTumelty(7) —
(J Mackie) *chsd ldrs: lost pl 7th: bhd whn p.u bef next* **7/1**[2]

FP15 **P** **Barton Gate**[18] 3661 8-11-8 **99** (b) NoelFehily —
(D P Keane) *chsd ldrs: lost pl 6th: t.o whn p.u bef 3 out* **7/1**[2]

0400 **P** **Najca De Thaix (FR)**[16] 3687 5-11-11 **102** RussGarritty —
(Mrs L Wadham) *in rr: bhd fr 5th: t.o whn p.u bef 3 out* **20/1**

-605 **P** **Andy Gin (FR)**[16] 3687 7-11-2 **98** MarkNicolls(5) —
(Miss E M England) *in rr: bhd whn hit 6th: sn t.o: t.o whn p.u bef 2 out* **20/1**

150 **P** **Polar Passion**[147] 1551 4-10-3 **99** AdamHawkins(10) —
(R Hollinshead) *chsd ldrs: lost pl and blnd 5th: bhd whn hit next: sn t.o: p.u bef 3 out* **25/1**

4m 16.3s (15.90) **Going Correction** +1.00s/f (Soft)
WFA 4 from 5yo+ 9lb **12** Ran SP% **119.2**
Speed ratings: **100,97,93,92,90 82,74,—,—,— —,—** CSF £52.98 CT £1528.58 TOTE £8.00: £2.40, £2.30, £5.90; EX 58.90 Place 6 £309.21, Place 5 £156.19.
Owner Wall Racing Partners **Bred** Woodsway Stud And Chao Racing And Bloodstock Ltd **Trained** Church Broughton , Derbys

FOCUS
A modest event run at an even tempo. The runner-up sets the level for the form.

NOTEBOOK
Speed Venture is not very big but is all heart and his rider's allowance came in handy. He defied a 5lb hike in the weights but another similar rise is on the cards.
Misbehaviour, having his second outing for his new yard after a break, travelled strongly but in the end simply found the winner too strong and determined. *(op 8-1)*
Elegant Clutter(IRE), absent since winning a novice hurdle in October 2003, gave a good account of himself, but will he bounce?
Lankawi, making his handicap debut, helped set a sound pace but in the end he did not truly see it out. *(op 7-2)*
Make My Hay, back after a fall, helped take them along but his chance had gone going to two out. *(op 7-1)*
Haditovski *Official explanation: jockey said gelding ran flat*
T/Plt: £307.20 to a £1 stake. Pool: £60,758.15. 144.35 winning tickets. T/Qpdt: £40.50 to a £1 stake. Pool: £4,673.00. 85.20 winning tickets. WG

3692 WINCANTON (R-H)
Saturday, February 18

OFFICIAL GOING: Chase course - soft; hurdle course - good to soft (soft in places)
Wind: Nil

3991 BLUE SQUARE CASINO NOVICES' CHASE (REGISTERED AS THE KINGMAKER NOVICES' CHASE) GRADE 2 (13 fncs) 2m
1:35 (1:35) (Class 1) 5-Y-0+ **£17,106** (£6,417; £3,213; £1,602)

Form RPR

-111 **1** **Voy Por Ustedes (FR)**[49] 3150 5-11-1 RobertThornton 153+
(A King) *trckd ldr: led 4 out: in command fr next: hit 2 out: readily* **10/11**[1]

1215 **2** *2 ½* **Hoo La Baloo (FR)**[14] 3724 5-11-4 147 SamThomas 147
(P F Nicholls) *led tl 4 out: sn rdn: kpt on but a hld by wnr fr next* **6/5**[2]

/30- **3** *dist* **Dictum (GER)**[441] 2626 8-11-3 TomScudamore 112+
(Mrs Susan Nock) *hld up bhd ldrs: lost tch 8th: blnd 9th: wnt distant 3rd 4 out* **25/1**

-1F2 **4** *hd* **Tighe Caster**[94] 2270 7-11-3 120 JohnMcNamara 110
(P R Webber) *chsd ldng pair tl lost tch 8th: chal for distant 3rd fr 4 out* **22/1**[3]

3m 59.5s (-2.40) **Going Correction** +0.325s/f (Yiel) **4** Ran SP% **106.0**
Speed ratings: **119,117,—,—** CSF £2.34 TOTE £1.90; EX 2.70.
Owner Sir Robert Ogden **Bred** Ecurie Macaire Guillaume, And Francis Picoulet **Trained** Barbury Castle, Wilts
■ This race was rescheduled after the loss of the Warwick fixture two weeks ago.

FOCUS
An improved showing from the winner, who confirmed himself a serious Arkle contender and has been rated value for 9 lengths.

NOTEBOOK
Voy Por Ustedes(FR) ◆ made it four straight wins over fences and showed much improved form in beating a classy rival decisively. Although untidy at both the last two fences, he jumped pretty well in the main and has to be taken seriously as an Arkle Trophy candidate now, even though this looks an above average year. *(tchd Evens)*
Hoo La Baloo(FR), back in novice company, could not go with his market rival from the home turn but did reduce the gap on the run-in. He was giving the winner 3lb, but although they will meet off levels in the Arkle he might struggle to reverse the form. *(op 5-4)*
Dictum(GER), making his chasing debut and appearing for the first time since December 2004, *was unsurprisingly no match for the big two but did get the better of a scrap for third place. (op 20-1)*
Tighe Caster was outpaced by the big guns in the back straight and just missed out in the duel for third. *(op 14-1 tchd 25-1)*

3992 BLUE SQUARE POKER H'CAP CHASE (17 fncs) 2m 5f
2:10 (2:10) (Class 3) (0-130,120) 5-Y-0+ **£9,759** (£2,865; £1,432; £715)

Form RPR

2003 **1** **Spectrometer**[92] 2312 9-11-6 **114** JohnMcNamara 125+
(Ian Williams) *prom: hit 8th: lost pl but in tch 12th: hdwy to ld and hit 3 out: narrowly hdd next: chalng whn hit last: led fnl stride* **17/2**

2202 **2** *nk* **Bee An Bee (IRE)**[38] 3343 9-11-12 **120** (b) RobertThornton 130+
(T R George) *trckd ldrs: rdn into narrow advantage 2 out: drifted rt and fnd little in front run-in: ct fnl stride* **11/2**

11P4 **3** *8* **Soeur Fontenail (FR)**[38] 3344 9-10-10 **111** KeiranBurke(7) 111
(N J Hawke) *led: rdn and hdd 3 out: kpt on same pce* **14/1**

35U1 **4** *20* **East Lawyer (FR)**[28] 3507 7-11-6 **119** LiamHeard(5) 99
(P F Nicholls) *hld up: rdn and no imp after 13th: lft poor 4th 2 out* **11/4**[2]

4-FP **P** **Gingerbread House (IRE)**[48] 3176 8-11-10 **118** JimmyMcCarthy —
(R T Phillips) *hld up: grad lost tch fr 10th: t.o and p.u bef 3 out* **28/1**

3324 **P** **Mark Equal**[54] 2998 10-11-5 **113** (vt) TomScudamore —
(M C Pipe) *hld up bhd ldrs: rdn and effrt after 13th: wknd after 4 out: p.u bef 2 out* **5/1**[3]

4331 **F** **Nice Try (IRE)**[23] 3582 7-11-5 **113** SamThomas 109
(Miss Venetia Williams) *hld up: mstke 10th: drvn to press ldr appr 4 out: 4th and hld whn fell 2 out* **9/4**[1]

5m 30.5s (7.40) **Going Correction** +0.325s/f (Yiel) **7** Ran SP% **110.1**
Speed ratings: **98,97,94,87,— —,—** CSF £49.47 TOTE £9.80: £3.00, £2.60; EX 49.30.
Owner Concertina Racing Too **Bred** Stanley Estate And Stud Co **Trained** Portway, Worcs

FOCUS
Not strong form.

NOTEBOOK

Spectrometer, currently rated 21lb lower over fences than he is over hurdles, was stepping back up in trip for this first run in three months. Upsides when clouting the last, he rallied to catch the reluctant leader on the run-in. *(op 12-1 tchd 8-1)*

Bee An Bee(IRE), who is normally campaigned over three miles, was seemingly left in charge when his challenger got the last fence wrong, but he proved reluctant to put it all in and was run out of it. He is too consistent for the handicapper to cut him much slack, but it is no coincidence that he has finished second on five of his last seven starts. *(op 6-1 tchd 13-2)*

Soeur Fontenail(FR) had no answers from the second last and has now been held three times from this sort of mark since her back-to-back wins before Christmas. *(tchd 12-1)*

East Lawyer(FR) had a 9lb rise for his course-and-distance win to contend with, but this was still a big disappointment. He has never been too reliable a proposition. *(op 3-1 tchd 4-1)*

Mark Equal was soon on the retreat after pecking at the cross fence four out. *(op 2-1 tchd 7-4)*

Nice Try(IRE), 8lb higher, got away with a couple of mistakes before succumbing at the second last when in fourth place and going nowhere. *(op 2-1 tchd 7-4)*

3993 BLUE SQUARE H'CAP HURDLE (11 hdls) 2m 6f

2:45 (2:46) (Class 3) (0-135,135) 4-Y-0+

£18,789 (£5,550; £2,775; £1,389; £693; £348)

Form			Horse / Trainer / Comment	Jockey	SP	RPR
/2-3	1		**Material World**[14] [3727] 8-10-9 **121** (Miss Suzy Smith) *chsd ldrs: sltly outpcd 7th: hdwy appr 2 out: led appr last: styd on: drvn out*	ColinBolger(3)	**12/1**	128
3121	2	1 ¾	**Gungadu**[16] [3694] 6-11-7 **135** (P F Nicholls) *chsd ldrs: rdn to hold pl after 8th: styd on fr 2 out: wnt 2nd run-in*	LiamHeard(5)	**9/4**[1]	141+
2020	3	7	**Double Dizzy**[48] [3174] 5-9-11 **109** oh3 (R H Buckler) *chsd ldr: led 3rd: clr after 3 out: rdn and hdd appr last: no ex*	TJPhelan(3)	**40/1**	110+
-P2P	4	5	**Tana River (IRE)**[54] [2974] 10-11-5 **128** (Miss E C Lavelle) *led tl 3rd: chsd ldrs: rdn after 3 out: kpt on same pce*	JohnMcNamara	**33/1**	121
4135	5	2	**Kings Castle (IRE)**[22] [3600] 11-9-7 **109** oh2 (R J Hodges) *towards rr: styd on fr 3 out: nvr trbld ldrs*	KeiranBurke(7)	**66/1**	100
1206	6	¾	**Not Left Yet (IRE)**[21] [3615] 5-10-12 **121** (M C Pipe) *mid div: hdwy after 6th: rdn after 3 out: kpt on same pce*	TomScudamore	**20/1**	112+
20U3	7	2 ½	**Malaga Boy (IRE)**[16] [3694] 9-9-11 **109** oh2 (C L Tizzard) *in tch: rdn after 3 out: sn one pced*	RichardYoung(3)	**100/1**	97
6113	8	½	**Businessmoney Jake**[42] [3286] 5-9-7 **109** (V R A Dartnall) *towards rr: drvn along after 8th: styd on past btn horses fr 2 out*	MrJJDoyle(7)	**10/1**[3]	96
4P21	9	7	**Adventurist**[10] [3806] 6-10-0 **114** (P Bowen) *chsd ldrs: rdn after 3 out: wknd next*	(p) LeeStephens(5)	**25/1**	94
2212	10	1 ¾	**Supreme Serenade (IRE)**[42] [3288] 7-11-5 **135** (P J Hobbs) *mid div: smooth hdwy appr 3 out: rdn appr 2 out: sn wknd*	MrTJO'Brien(7)	**12/1**	114
1121	11	2 ½	**Welcome To Unos**[37] [3352] 9-9-12 **114** (K G Reveley) *mid div tl lost pl 6th: nt a danger after*	PhilKinsella(7)	**12/1**	90
3-00	12	13	**Waltzing Beau**[14] [3727] 5-10-8 **122** (B G Powell) *in tch tl wknd 3 out*	JohnnyLevins(5)	**33/1**	85
0166	13	5	**Flying Enterprise (IRE)**[63] [2876] 6-11-12 **135** (Miss Venetia Williams) *mid div tl 7th*	SamThomas	**25/1**	93
F413	14	19	**Go For Bust**[21] [3622] 7-11-2 **125** (N J Henderson) *hld up towards rr: hdwy 8th: chsd ldrs after 3 out: wknd next*	AndrewTinkler	**16/1**	64
1-32	P		**Tensile (IRE)**[275] [425] 11-10-4 **113** (R J Hodges) *a towards rr: t.o and p.u bef last*	RJGreene	**100/1**	—
-452	P		**Heir To Be**[17] [3675] 7-10-7 **116** (Mrs L Wadham) *a towards rr: t.o and p.u bef 2 out*	(t) JimmyMcCarthy	**16/1**	—
0	P		**Naos De Mirande (FR)**[35] [3389] 5-11-1 **124** (T Doumen, France) *a towards rr: t.o and p.u bef 2 out*	RobertThornton	**6/1**[2]	—
6044	P		**Prince Of Persia**[17] [3675] 6-9-13 **113** (R S Brookhouse) *mid div tl wknd 3 out: p.u bef 2 out*	RobertLucey-Butler(5)	**50/1**	—
/10-	P		**Distant Prospect (IRE)**[126] [4397] 9-11-3 **129** (A M Balding) *chsd ldrs tl 6th: sn bhd: t.o and p.u bef 2 out*	MrTGreenall(3)	**12/1**	—
0050	P		**Salut Saint Cloud**[49] [3135] 5-11-0 **123** (G L Moore) *towards rr: hdwy into mid div 4th: wknd after 3 out: p.u bef last*	PhilipHide	**25/1**	—

5m 26.8s (1.70) **Going Correction** +0.425s/f (Soft) **20** Ran SP% **126.7**

Speed ratings: **113,112,109,108,107 107,106,105,103,102 101,97,95,88,— —,—,—,—,—** CSF £36.56 CT £1123.47 TOTE £14.80: £2.70, £1.60, £10.90, £9.90; EX 57.10 TRIFECTA Not won..

Owner Southern Bloodstock **Bred** Temple Farming **Trained** Lewes, E Sussex

FOCUS

The pace was sound and not many got into it. This is good handicap form, rated through the fifth.

NOTEBOOK

Material World ran a fine race on her return to action at Sandown and this was another improved effort. As she is missing her left eye she really needs to go right-handed, so Cheltenham is probably out and she will be aimed instead at the Punchestown Festival. *(op 11-1)*

Gungadu, a smart novice taking on handicappers for the first time, stayed on to chase the mare on the run-in but drifted left under pressure and could not get to her. This was a decent effort on a track that did not really suit him. *(tchd 2-1)*

Double Dizzy went clear on the home turn and looked set for a shock win, but he was untidy at the second last as he began to tire and he was soon worn down. This was another boost to the form of the Challow Hurdle, in which he was well beaten behind Denman.

Tana River(IRE), who is not the most consistent, plugged on again up the straight after the leaders had got away from him. *(tchd 40-1)*

Kings Castle(IRE) came home well without ever posing a threat. He is a little high in the weights and his last three wins have all come in conditions sellers.

Not Left Yet(IRE) has not gone on from his Cheltenham victory at the Open meeting, but this was more encouraging and he was fourth over the final flight before fading. *(op 22-1)*

Malaga Boy(IRE) ran a creditable race on this first run in a handicap but might appreciate a slightly shorter trip.

Businessmoney Jake, raised 2lb after a good run in defeat at Fontwell, was never really going but did stay on late in the day and could be worth a try at three miles. *(op 16-1)*

Adventurist, on his handicap bow, paid in the end for chasing the pace. *(op 20-1)*

Supreme Serenade(IRE), reverting to hurdles, travelled well but again produced less than she had promised. *(op 14-1)*

Tensile(IRE) *Official explanation: vet said gelding was lame (tchd 13-2)*

Heir To Be *Official explanation: jockey said gelding was never travelling (tchd 13-2)*

Naos De Mirande(FR), back down in trip and dropped 3lb despite an eye-catching run at Warwick, *could never get out of the rear-division. Official explanation: trainer said, regarding the poor form shown, gelding was outpaced and unable to get into the race (tchd 13-2)*

3994 BATHWICK TYRES KINGWELL HURDLE GRADE 2 (8 hdls) 2m

3:20 (3:22) (Class 1) 4-Y-0+

£39,914 (£14,973; £7,497; £3,738; £1,876; £938)

Form			Horse / Trainer / Comment	Jockey	SP	RPR
1-20	1		**Briareus**[42] [3298] 6-11-2 133 (A M Balding) *mde all: drew clr after 2 out: comf*	MrTGreenall	**14/1**	152+
5341	2	14	**Royal Shakespeare (FR)**[14] [3725] 7-11-10 150 (S Gollings) *trckd wnr: jnd wnr 3rd: rdn and effrt appr 2 out: kpt on but nt pce of wnr*	TomScudamore	**10/1**	146
5114	3	1 ½	**Natal (FR)**[54] [2971] 5-11-2 142 (P F Nicholls) *hld up in tch: trckd wnr after 3 out: effrt next: nt qckn*	(t) LiamHeard	**4/1**[3]	137
0-21	4	2 ½	**Desert Air (JPN)**[42] [3298] 7-11-6 142 (M C Pipe) *chsd ldrs: outpcd appr 3 out: styd on again fr 2 out*	(t) RJGreene	**8/1**	138
1412	5	3	**Whispered Promises (USA)**[42] [3297] 5-11-2 132 (R S Brookhouse) *hld up: hdwy after 3 out: sn rdn: one pced fr next*	JohnMcNamara	**25/1**	131
P-23	6	¾	**Goldbrook**[21] [3615] 8-11-2 125 (R J Hodges) *hld up: styd on appr 2 out: nvr trbld ldrs*	AndrewTinkler	**66/1**	130
1-34	7	18	**Penzance**[70] [2761] 5-11-6 145 (A King) *in tch: shkn up after 4th: short lived effrt appr 2 out: sn wknd*	RobertThornton	**9/4**[1]	119+
2-24	8	6	**Chief Yeoman**[42] [3298] 6-11-2 140 (Miss Venetia Williams) *chsd ldrs: hit 2nd and 3 out: sn wknd*	SamThomas	**7/2**[2]	106
3	9	1 ¾	**Tolpuddle (IRE)**[13] [3772] 6-11-2 (T Stack, Ire) *in tch tl after 3 out*	(t) WJLee	**14/1**	105

3m 44.8s (-4.30) **Going Correction** +0.425s/f (Soft) **9** Ran SP% **111.9**

Speed ratings: **117,110,109,108,106 106,97,94,93** CSF £136.19 TOTE £13.90: £2.80, £2.40, £2.00; EX 118.00.

Owner Miss E J Lambourne **Bred** N A Ovett **Trained** Kingsclere, Hants

FOCUS

Much improved form from the winner, but a race with limited value as a Champion Hurdle trial. The time was good and it could have been rated higher.

NOTEBOOK

Briareus, suited by this better ground, made every yard at a decent pace and drew clear between the last two flights to score in taking style. He is on the upgrade, and based on this he would have been a good thing for the abandoned Totesport Trophy off 10st. Connections are considering supplementing him for the Champion Hurdle at a cost of £17,000. *(tchd 12-1)*

Royal Shakespeare(FR) has been admirably consistent this season and this was another decent effort on ground that was too soft for him. *(op 8-1)*

Natal(FR), well backed for the abandoned Totesport Trophy at Newbury, ran with credit, especially as his rider was unable to draw his claim, but he lacked a turn of foot from the second last. He will go for the Supreme Novices' now, where faster ground would suit him. *(op 9-2)*

Desert Air(JPN), who was put up 10lb for his Ladbroke win at Sandown, looked set to finish well adrift when under strong pressure in the back straight, but he did stay on from the second last. *(op 9-1 tchd 15-2)*

Whispered Promises(USA), often a front runner but held up here, ran as well as he ever has against these smart opponents. *(tchd 33-1)*

Goldbrook, on a career-high mark in handicaps at the moment, ran up to his very best in this warm company.

Penzance, who had plenty of supporters for the abandoned Totesport Trophy, ran a lacklustre *race. He was subsequently reported to have a bad case of 'thumps', or horse hiccups. Official explanation: trainer said, regarding the poor form, gelding was distressed (tchd 5-2)*

Chief Yeoman, another to have been declared for the Totesport Trophy, was beaten with three to jump and has not gone on from an encouraging return to action this season.

Tolpuddle(IRE), a Champion Hurdle entry, had his limitations cruelly exposed. *(op 16-1)*

3995 COUNTRY GENTLEMEN'S ASSOCIATION CHASE (A LIMITED H'CAP) (LISTED RACE) (21 fncs) 3m 1f 110y

3:55 (3:55) (Class 1) 5-Y-0+ **£28,644** (£10,829; £5,489; £2,804; £1,474)

Form			Horse / Trainer / Comment	Jockey	SP	RPR
U152	1		**All In The Stars (IRE)**[71] [2744] 8-10-7 **132** (D P Keane) *hld up bhd: stdy hdwy fr 16th: wnt 3rd after 4 out: led sn after 2 out: styd on strly: rdn out*	DarylJacob(5)	**8/1**[3]	141+
1244	2	7	**Celtic Son (FR)**[38] [3341] 7-11-10 **144** (M C Pipe) *hld up: hit 15th: hdwy next: led after 4 out: sn rdn: hdd sn after 2 out: no ex*	(t) TomScudamore	**8/1**[3]	148+
6PP	3	4	**Horus (IRE)**[21] [3620] 11-10-12 **132** (M C Pipe) *led 3rd: rdn and hdd appr 3 out: kpt on same pce*	(v) RJGreene	**33/1**	130
4501	4	dist	**See You Sometime**[16] [3697] 11-11-10 **144** (J W Mullins) *chsd ldrs: hit 12th: wkng whn blnd 17th*	AndrewThornton	**14/1**	—
/60F	5	dist	**Iris Royal (FR)**[14] [3728] 10-11-2 **136** (N J Henderson) *in tch: wnt 2nd after 14th: blnd 17th: sn rdn: wknd after 4 out*	AndrewTinkler	**20/1**	—
2P-P	U		**Bathwick Annie**[28] [3509] 10-10-0 **127** (B G Powell) *hld up: blnd and uns rdr 6th*	CharlieStudd(7)	**16/1**	—
311P	P		**Sonevafushi (FR)**[21] [3620] 8-11-8 **142** (Miss Venetia Williams) *led tl 3rd: chsd ldr tl 14th: sn wknd: p.u bef 4 out*	SamThomas	**8/1**[3]	—
11-4	P		**Silver Birch (IRE)**[23] [3581] 9-11-8 **142** (P F Nicholls) *in tch: mstke 9th: dropped rr 12th: sn lost tch: p.u bef 16th*	JoeTizzard	**2/1**[1]	—
1322	P		**Black De Bessy (FR)**[28] [3507] 8-10-6 **126** (D R C Elsworth) *hld up: tk clsr order 12th: hit 15th: sn wknd: p.u bef 4 out*	RobertThornton	**5/2**[2]	—

6m 45.5s (5.60) **Going Correction** +0.45s/f (Soft) **9** Ran SP% **115.5**

Speed ratings: **109,106,105,—,— —,—,—,—** CSF £69.15 CT £1992.02 TOTE £9.90: £2.40, £2.50, £7.30; EX 82.00.

Owner Mrs H R Cross **Bred** Denis Paul Cremin **Trained** North End, Dorset

FOCUS

This was run at a sound pace and became something of a slog. The winner posted a slight personal best and the second was not far short of the impressive form he showed here on his chasing debut.

NOTEBOOK

All In The Stars(IRE), suited by the strong pace which rendered this a stamina test, came through to win going away in the end. His target is the Scottish National, and the longer trip and likely fast ground at Ayr ought to suit him. *(tchd 9-1)*

Celtic Son(FR), back up in trip, ran his best race since his impressive chasing debut at this course back in November. He looked the likeliest winner when moving to the front but was clawed back between the last two fences and didn't entirely convince as a stayer.

Horus(IRE), with the visor refitted, seemed to appreciate the positive ride but the game was up once his stablemate caught him turning for home. He is very well handicapped on his best form of last season. *(tchd 28-1)*

See You Sometime, who was put up 6lb for his win here in a substandard Grade 2, was already beaten when blundering at the last fence down the far side. *(op 12-1 tchd 16-1)*

Iris Royal(FR), who has yet to rediscover the form he showed in 2003/4, seemed to find this too far. *(op 14-1)*

Sonevafushi(FR) looked somewhat reluctant to continue exerting himself early on the final circuit and has now run two poor races from this career-high mark. *(tchd 7-4)*
Silver Birch(IRE), running over fences for the first time since last season's Welsh National win, put up a dire display which baffled his trainer. The return to a left-handed track could help and he may be given another run over hurdles now before heading for the John Smith's Grand National, in which he has been given 10-10. *Official explanation: trainer was unable to explain the poor run (tchd 7-4)*
Black De Bessy(FR) had hitherto been most consistent and this was most disappointing, *especially as he has shown a liking for this course. Official explanation: trainer said, regarding the poor form shown, gelding was unsuited by the soft ground (tchd 7-4)*

3996 BLUE SQUARE SPEED DIAL 64555 NOVICES' HURDLE (8 hdls) 2m
4:25 (4:28) (Class 4) 4-Y-0+ **£4,554** (£1,337; £668; £333)

Form / RPR

122 **1** **Turko (FR)**[53] [3021] 4-11-5 ....(t) SamThomas 124+
(P F Nicholls) *in tch: hdwy after 3 out to press ldr: sn rdn: narrow advantage last: styd on to assert fnl 50yds: drvn out* **4/6**[1]

2 **2** 1 3/4 **Pablo Du Charmil (FR)**[78] [2617] 5-12-0 .... RJGreene 131+
(M C Pipe) *led tl 5th: prom: led appr 2 out: sn rdn: narrowly hdd last: no ex* **7/1**[3]

3 **3** 4 **Vinando**[66] [2826] 5-11-2 .... AndrewTinkler 114+
(C R Egerton) *chsd ldrs: rdn after 3 out: kpt on to go 3rd run-in* **7/2**[2]

2P **4** 3/4 **Amour Multiple (IRE)**[35] [3383] 7-11-8 126 .... TomScudamore 120+
(S Lycett) *prom: led 5th tl appr 2 out: sn rdn: kpt on same pce* **20/1**

66 **5** 14 **Cold Mountain (IRE)**[15] [3714] 4-10-4 .... RichardYoung(3) 90
(J W Mullins) *hld up mid div: lost pl and dropped rr after 4th: styd on again fr 2 out* **50/1**

00 **6** 6 **Vengeance**[80] [2573] 6-11-2 .... JodieMogford 93
(S Dow) *hld up towards rr: hdwy after 3 out: no further imp fr next* **50/1**

-500 **7** 3 1/2 **Miller's Monarch**[37] [3354] 6-11-2 .... JimmyMcCarthy 90
(Andrew Turnell) *chsd ldrs: rdn after 3 out: wknd next* **66/1**

6 **8** 1 1/4 **Lordsbridge (USA)**[28] [3511] 4-10-2 .... DarylJacob(5) 79
(D P Keane) *hld up bhd: sme late hdwy: nvr a danger* **66/1**

050 **9** 1 **Harcourt (USA)**[18] [3658] 6-11-2 .... PhilipHide 87
(M Madgwick) *mid div tl wknd appr 2 out* **66/1**

50 **10** 1 1/4 **Mister Chatterbox (IRE)**[30] [3466] 5-10-9 .... MrTJO'Brien(7) 86
(P J Hobbs) *in tch tl wknd appr 3 out* **50/1**

6 **11** 27 **Wins Now**[35] [3388] 5-11-2 ....(t) AndrewThornton 59
(T Doumen, France) *chsd ldrs tl wknd after 3 out* **16/1**

006 **12** 3 1/2 **So Wise So Young**[45] [3244] 5-10-13 .... TJPhelan(3) 56
(R H Buckler) *mid div: nt fluent 4th: sn bhd* **100/1**

06 **13** dist **Sapient**[33] [3423] 5-10-9 .... MarcGoldstein(7) —
(M Scudamore) *a bhd* **100/1**

P **Steely Dan**[245] 7-10-9 .... CharliePoste(7) —
(J R Best) *a bhd: t.o and p.u after 3 out* **40/1**

0P05 **P** **Dream On Maggie**[42] [3280] 6-10-4 .... LeeStephens(5) —
(P Bowen) *mid div tl 5th: bhd whn p.u and dismntd after 2 out* **50/1**

0 **P** **Barjou (NZ)**[40] [3324] 5-11-2 .... RobertThornton —
(A King) *in tch: mstke 3rd: wknd appr 3 out: t.o and p.u bef 2 out* **33/1**

-234 **P** **Chunky Lad**[100] [2148] 6-10-11 .... RobertLucey-Butler(5) —
(W G M Turner) *hit 1st: mid div tl 5th: t.o and p.u bef 2 out* **50/1**

3m 51.6s (2.50) **Going Correction** +0.55s/f (Soft)
WFA 4 from 5yo+ 9lb **17** Ran SP% **127.0**
Speed ratings: **107,106,104,103,96 93,92,91,90,90 76,75,—,—,— —,—** CSF £5.93 TOTE £1.60: £1.20, £2.00, £1.40; EX 4.10.
Owner The Stewart Family **Bred** B Forges **Trained** Ditcheat, Somerset

FOCUS
The time was nearly seven seconds slower than the earlier Kingwell Hurdle over the same distance. The winner has been rated 18lb off his best mark, with the second and third both posting improved form.

NOTEBOOK
Turko(FR), off since finishing second in the Grade One Finale Hurdle at Christmas, had his tongue tied down for the first time. He had to work hard to prevail under a double penalty back in this ordinary company, but should not be ruled out of the Triumph Hurdle reckoning as the fast pace of that event will suit him. *(op 4-7 tchd 8-11)*
Pablo Du Charmil(FR), who holds entries in the two shorter novice hurdles at Cheltenham, ran well on this better ground and made the odds-on favourite work for his victory. *(op 8-1 tchd 9-1)*
Vinando, without the tongue tie and blinkers for this second run over hurdles, ran an improved race but is capable of still better based on his Flat form. A stiffer track should suit him. *(op 6-1 tchd 7-1)*
Amour Multiple(IRE), high enough in the weights and back in novice company, shared the lead until the entrance to the home straight, from which point the principals went away from him. *(op 25-1)*
Cold Mountain(IRE), well held in two races won by Blazing Bailey at Fontwell, is now qualified for handicaps. *(tchd 66-1)*
Vengeance, a useful middle-distance performer on the Flat, is now eligible for handicaps after this third run. *(op 33-1)*
Lordsbridge(USA) gave the impression that there could be better to come as he gains in experience.
Wins Now was equipped with a tongue tie but again faded tamely. *(tchd 14-1)*
Chunky Lad *Official explanation: jockey said gelding was unsuited by the good to soft, soft in places going*

3997 BLUE SQUARE 0800 587 0200 H'CAP HURDLE (11 hdls) 2m 6f
4:55 (4:57) (Class 4) (0-100,99) 4-Y-0+ **£3,253** (£955; £477; £238)

Form / RPR

P06P **1** **Pure Magic (FR)**[29] [3477] 5-10-1 81 .... CharliePoste(7) 92+
(Miss J S Davis) *chsd ldr: led after 3 out: sn clr: styd on strly* **50/1**

3223 **2** 9 **Mistified (IRE)**[2] [3943] 5-11-0 90 .... RichardYoung(3) 91+
(J W Mullins) *mid div: hdwy after 3 out: wnt 2nd at the next: kpt on but no further imp on wnr after* **11/2**[2]

P5-P **3** 5 **Bright Green**[38] [3345] 7-11-3 95 .... RobertLucey-Butler(5) 90
(C J Gray) *hld up towards rr: making hdwy whn hmpd 3 out: sn rdn: styd on: hung lft run-in* **100/1**

6024 **4** 3/4 **Ballybawn House**[32] [3437] 5-11-10 97 .... SeanFox 92+
(J C Fox) *mid div: hdwy 6th: rdn in 3rd after 3 out: kpt on same pce* **16/1**

6-66 **5** 9 **Syncopated Rhythm (IRE)**[101] [2126] 6-10-5 85 .... BernieWharfe(7) 70
(N A Twiston-Davies) *chsd ldrs: hit 2nd and lost pl: rdn after 3 out: one pced* **16/1**

60R6 **6** 3 **Business Traveller (IRE)**[30] [3458] 6-11-0 87 ....(bt) SamThomas 69
(R J Price) *bhd: hmpd 3 out: styd on past btn horses fr next* **11/1**[3]

P446 **7** 7 **Mandica (IRE)**[47] [3212] 8-11-10 97 ....(b[1]) AndrewTinkler 72
(T R George) *led: wnt lft 3 out: sn hdd and rdn: wknd 2 out* **12/1**

3466 **8** 11 **Coeur D'Alene**[29] [3478] 5-11-11 98 .... AndrewThornton 67+
(Dr J R J Naylor) *mid div: making hdwy whn hmpd 3 out: wknd appr next* **33/1**

00F3 **9** 2 **The Laying Hen (IRE)**[16] [3692] 6-10-12 90 .... DarylJacob(5) 52
(D P Keane) *hld up and a in rr* **20/1**

030P **10** 27 **Maximinus**[30] [3465] 6-11-10 97 .... PhilipHide 32
(M Madgwick) *chsd ldrs: hmpd 3 out: sn wknd* **16/1**

-2P0 **11** 7 **Optimistic Alfie**[28] [3500] 6-11-5 99 .... CharlieStudd(7) 27
(B G Powell) *chsd ldrs: wkng whn bdly hmpd 3 out* **25/1**

1664 **12** 3 1/2 **Ask The Umpire (IRE)**[3] [3923] 11-11-9 96 ....(b) HenryOliver 21
(N E Berry) *a towards rr* **18/1**

02-0 **F** **Armagh South (IRE)**[33] [3422] 7-11-1 88 .... JodieMogford —
(J C Tuck) *mid div whn fell 5th* **14/1**

0P00 **P** **Star Galaxy (IRE)**[22] [3603] 6-10-4 77 .... JimmyMcCarthy —
(Andrew Turnell) *a towards rr: t.o and p.u bef 2 out* **66/1**

360/ **P** **Peerless Motion (IRE)**[336] 11-11-5 95 .... MrTGreenall(3) —
(S Lycett) *chsd ldrs tl wknd after 7th: t.o and p.u bef 3 out* **50/1**

40P **P** **Call Me Edward (IRE)**[67] [2815] 5-11-3 97 .... MarcGoldstein(7) —
(N A Twiston-Davies) *mid div tl 7th: sn bhd: p.u after 3 out* **20/1**

-056 **P** **Lunch Was My Idea (IRE)**[21] [3611] 6-10-10 88 ....(t) LiamHeard(5) —
(P F Nicholls) *chsd ldrs: mstke 8th: sn wknd: p.u bef 2 out* **11/2**[2]

P635 **P** **Miss Midnight**[35] [3386] 5-11-4 91 .... RobertThornton —
(R J Hodges) *hld up towards rr: bdly hmpd 5th: nt rcvr and p.u bef 7th* **16/1**

0404 **F** **Argent Ou Or (FR)**[77] [2632] 5-11-9 96 .... TomScudamore —
(M C Pipe) *mi div: hdwy after 6th: cl 3rd and gng wl whn fell 3 out: dead* **7/2**[1]

5m 37.8s (12.70) **Going Correction** +0.55s/f (Soft) **19** Ran SP% **127.2**
Speed ratings: **98,94,92,92,89 88,85,81,81,71 68,67,—,—,— —,—,—,—** CSF £305.47 CT £24650.10 TOTE £45.30: £11.90, £2.10, £21.10, £4.20; EX 1025.00 Place 6 £489.72, Place 5 £254.04.
Owner West Country Racing - Winter Warmer **Bred** Recent A/S **Trained** Codrington, S Gloucs

FOCUS
A weak race on paper and a very difficult one to assess. It has been rated through the runner-up.

NOTEBOOK
Pure Magic(FR) was placed on the Flat in Denmark but had shown next to nothing over hurdles. Given an enterprising ride here on his handicap debut, he had compiled a clear lead leaving the back straight and never looked likely to be caught. He may well have been flattered.
Mistified(IRE) went after the winner at the penultimate flight but never looked like bridging the deficit. Still without a win to his name, he has now been placed on his last five starts. *(op 5-1 tchd 9-2)*
Bright Green, who returned to the track last month after 14 months on the sidelines, made late progress from out of the pack and might have been a little closer had he not been impeded at the third last.
Ballybawn House, upped in trip for this handicap debut, appeared to stay well enough but might have preferred genuine soft ground. *(op 18-1)*
Syncopated Rhythm(IRE) ran respectably switched back to hurdles for this first run in three months.
Mandica(IRE) showed more spark in the blinkers in this return to hurdles, setting the pace until fading once the eventual winner collared him on the approach to the home turn. *(op 11-1)*
Argent Ou Or(FR) had moved into third place, and seemed to be travelling easily, when he fell at the third from home and broke his neck. *(op 5-1)*
T/Plt: £467.00 to a £1 stake. Pool: £55,250.25. 86.35 winning tickets. T/Qpdt: £35.50 to a £1 stake. Pool: £4,472.55. 93.05 winning tickets. TM

3998 - (Foreign Racing) - See Raceform Interactive

3584 GOWRAN PARK (R-H)
Saturday, February 18

OFFICIAL GOING: Soft

3999a RED MILLS CHASE (GRADE 2) 2m 4f
2:45 (2:46) 5-Y-0+ **£22,448** (£6,586; £3,137; £1,068)

RPR

1 **Forget The Past**[52] [3081] 8-11-12 148 .... BJGeraghty 164+
(M J P O'Brien, Ire) *settled 2nd: impr to ld 3 out: clr fr next: eased cl home: comf* **9/4**[2]

2 2 1/2 **Jim (FR)**[13] [3774] 9-11-10 150 .... PCarberry 157
(J T R Dreaper, Ire) *led: rdn and hdd 3 out: no imp fr next: kpt on same pce u.p* **9/10**[1]

3 9 **Strong Project (IRE)**[6] [3895] 10-11-8 144 .... JMAllen 146
(Sean O O'Brien, Ire) *settled 3rd: bad mstke 8 out: rdn after 4 out: last next: kpt on same pce u.p* **8/1**

4 8 **Mariah Rollins (IRE)**[53] [3051] 8-11-7 143 .... JLCullen 142+
(P A Fahy, Ire) *hld up in rr: nt fluent early: prog into 3rd and drvn along bef 3 out: no ex after 2 out* **11/2**[3]

5m 8.40s **4** Ran SP% **109.9**
CSF £4.99 TOTE £4.30; DF 4.60.
Owner S Mulryan **Bred** M H Dare **Trained** Naas, Co Kildare

NOTEBOOK
Forget The Past, reported as having burst when third behind Beef Or Salmon and War Of Attrition at Leopardstown at Christmas, bounced back here for an easy win. He had finished behind Jim in the Durkan but this was a comprehensive success and he might yet be given his chance in the Gold Cup. A quick reappearance is envisaged. *(op 5/2 tchd 2/1)*
Jim(FR) ran to his best, but faded pretty tamely after the third last. *(op 4/5 tchd 1/1)*
Strong Project(IRE) could not handle this rise in class.
Mariah Rollins(IRE) weakened after the second last but might be interesting in another month or so. *(op 5/1)*

4000a RED MILLS TRIAL HURDLE (GRADE 2) 2m
3:15 (3:16) 4-Y-0+ **£26,937** (£7,903; £3,765; £1,282)

RPR

1 **Macs Joy (IRE)**[20] [3641] 7-11-11 164 .... BJGeraghty 155+
(Mrs John Harrington, Ire) *settled 3rd: impr to ld 3 out: clr after next: eased cl home: easily* **2/5**[1]

2 4 1/2 **Asian Maze (IRE)**[295] [116] 7-11-6 144 .... PCarberry 141+
(Thomas Mullins, Ire) *led: hdd and outpcd 3 out: last bef next: r.o wl fr last* **13/2**[3]

3 1 1/2 **Ground Ball (IRE)**[52] [3082] 9-11-6 133 .... CO'Dwyer 139
(C F Swan, Ire) *hld up in rr: hdwy 3 out: 2nd bef last: kpt on same pce* **25/1**

4 4 **Essex (IRE)**[51] [3109] 6-11-6 157 .... TGMRyan 135
(M J P O'Brien, Ire) *trckd ldr in 2nd: rdn appr 3 out: 3rd and no ex bef last: wknd run-in* **4/1**[2]

3m 55.8s **4** Ran SP% **108.6**
CSF £3.58 TOTE £1.50; DF 2.20.
Owner Mac's J Racing Syndicate **Bred** Northern Breeders Association **Trained** Moone, Co Kildare

The Form Book, Raceform Ltd, Compton, RG20 6NL

NOTEBOOK
Macs Joy(IRE) had an easy task and this was a straightforward win. This race has provided the stepping stone for Hardy Eustace before winning last two Champion Hurdles and, given the probability of better ground, he can certainly improve on last season's fifth placing. *(op 4/9)*
Asian Maze(IRE) ran well on her first appearance since last April. Readily outpaced after making the running to the third last, she stayed on with some purpose into second place on the run-in. She will take her chance in the World Hurdle after this most encouraging effort. *(op 11/2 tchd 7/1)*
Ground Ball(IRE) is better known as a chaser but was not disgraced. *(op 16/1)*
Essex(IRE) went with the winner from the third last but was a spent force between the last two flights. *(op 3/1)*

3714 FONTWELL (L-H)

Sunday, February 19

OFFICIAL GOING: Heavy
The two fences before the open ditch were omitted.
Wind: Moderate, across

4005 TOTEPOOL A BETTER WAY TO BET NOVICES' HURDLE (11 hdls) 2m 6f 110y
2:00 (2:00) (Class 4) 4-Y-0+ **£3,253** (£955; £477; £238)

Form				RPR
6302	1		**Saltango (GER)**[29] 3508 7-11-8 120 WilliamKennedy(3) — (A M Hales) *trckd ldrs: wnt 2nd sn after 3 out: led appr next: styd on wl* **4/7**[1]	111+
0P	2	10	**Heavy Weather (IRE)**[30] 3478 8-11-4 JasonMaguire — (Miss Joanne Priest) *led: hit 7th: hdd bef mstke 2 out: sn btn and fin tired* **33/1**	96+
1/P0	3	14	**Marchensis (IRE)**[19] 3664 8-11-4 LeightonAspell — (O Sherwood) *chsd ldrs to 8th: weakened 3 out* **33/1**	80
0/P4	4	1 1/4	**See More Jock**[17] 3694 8-10-11 WayneKavanagh(7) — (Dr J R J Naylor) *mid-div: hdwy 6th: wnt 2nd 4 out: tl wknd sn after next* **14/1**[3]	79
4/3	5	25	**Caged Tiger**[31] 3466 7-11-4 NoelFehily — (C J Mann) *a bhd: no ch whn blnd 2 out* **9/2**[2]	54
	6	4	**Angello (FR)**[170] 5-10-11 KeiranBurke(7) — (N J Hawke) *trckd ldrs: wkng whn mstke 3 out* **25/1**	50
0000	7	27	**Lord Leonardo (IRE)**[19] 3664 6-10-11 JustinMorgan(7) — (L Wells) *chsd ldrs tl rdn 6th: bhd whn blnd 4 out* **100/1**	23
00	8	2	**Once (FR)**[51] 3127 6-11-4 JamieMoore — (M G Rimell) *bhd whn mstke 7th: nvr on terms* **20/1**	21
0	9	dist	**Grenoli (FR)**[39] 3342 5-11-4 ChristianWilliams — (P F Nicholls) *hld up in rr: a bhd: t.o* **16/1**	—
0-60	10	dist	**Northern Link (IRE)**[46] 3238 7-11-4 MatthewBatchelor — (Miss Tor Sturgis) *a wl bhd: t.o* **100/1**	—
P	P		**Buckland Bobby**[19] 3660 8-10-13 RobertLucey-Butler(5) — (M Madgwick) *bhd whn p.u after 2nd* **100/1**	—
00	P		**Gwyn's Choice**[228] 917 5-11-4 PhilipHide — (R A Harris) *mstke 1st in rr: mstke 4th: t.o whn p.u bef 6th* **66/1**	—
040	P		**Bob's Finesse**[271] 487 6-10-8 RichardYoung(3) — (J W Mullins) *mid-div to 6th: wknd qckly: p.u bef next* **100/1**	—
0P	P		**Crystal Hollow**[29] 3511 6-11-4 SeanCurran — (N R Mitchell) *a bhd: rdn appr 6th: t.o whn p.u bef last* **100/1**	—
	P		**My Only Bid (IRE)**[293] 8-10-11 WillieMcCarthy(7) — (A J Whiting) *trckd ldr tl blnd 7th: sn bhd: t.o whn p.u bef 2 out* **100/1**	—

5m 58.5s (13.70) **Going Correction** +0.725s/f (Soft) **15** Ran SP% **116.3**
Speed ratings: **105,101,96,96,87 86,76,76,—,— —,—,—,—,—** CSF £31.28 TOTE £1.50: £1.10, £5.00, £5.20; EX 36.40.
Owner CohenClearyKaplanMinnsPayneWatsonWilson **Bred** Gestut Wittekindshof **Trained** Quainton, Bucks

FOCUS
A modest novice event, run in very testing ground, and the field finished well and truly strung out. The form is suspect.

NOTEBOOK
Saltango(GER) had to work hard to get to the front at the bottom of the home straight, but duly stuck to his task, and eventually outstayed his rivals to score readily under his penalty. He did not have to run near to his official mark to win this, but this proved his ability to handle most underfoot conditions, and he is a likeable performer. *(op 8-11 tchd 4-5 in places)*
Heavy Weather(IRE), pulled up at Chepstow last time after proving reluctant at the start, enjoyed dictating at the head of affairs and showed his best form over timber to date. He may need time to get over these exertions, as he was legless at the finish, but he has the ability to build on this. *(op 40-1)*
Marchensis(IRE) was eventually found out by the rising finish, but still posted a more encouraging effort and acted on the testing ground.
See More Jock did not appear all that happy on the deep surface and failed to sustain his effort when it mattered. *(op 12-1)*
Caged Tiger proved easy to back and never figured. He is capable of plenty better than this and will be eligible for handicaps after his next outing. *(op 7-2)*
Buckland Bobby *Official explanation: jockey said saddle slipped*

4006 CENKOS SECURITIES NOVICES' CHASE (11 fncs 4 omitted) 2m 4f
2:30 (2:30) (Class 3) 5-Y-0+ **£9,626** (£3,006; £1,619)

Form				RPR
1112	1		**Le Volfoni (FR)**[29] 3501 5-11-3 138 JoeTizzard — (P F Nicholls) *mde all: clr appr 3 out: hit last: eased run-in* **1/7**[1]	143+
3644	2	18	**Lago D'Oro**[29] 3494 6-10-7 93 JamesDavies — (Dr P Pritchard) *bhd: mstke 3rd: styd on to go poor 2nd appr last* **10/1**[2]	95
U	3	dist	**La Source A Gold (IRE)**[7] 3879 7-11-0 PJBrennan — (Nick Williams) *mstked 2nd: in tch: wnt 2nd appr 5th: blnd 7th and 8th: lost tch bef blnd 3 out: lost 2nd appr last: t.o* **16/1**[3]	87
0	P		**Lochanee (IRE)**[19] 3664 6-11-0 OllieMcPhail — (Mrs L C Jewell) *trckd wnr tl appr 5th: slipped on flat after 7th: sn t.o: p.u appr 3 out* **40/1**	—

5m 22.8s (14.90) **Going Correction** +0.725s/f (Soft)
WFA 5 from 6yo+ 7lb **4** Ran SP% **104.9**
Speed ratings: **99,91,—,—** CSF £2.10 TOTE £1.20; EX 2.10.
Owner Million In Mind Partnership **Bred** I Plessis And Bertrand Plessis **Trained** Ditcheat, Somerset

FOCUS
A stroll in the park for Le Volfoni, who faced an easy task after the withdrawl of all his creditable challengers and is value for much further, with the second to his mark.

NOTEBOOK
Le Volfoni(FR) was presented with the most simple of tasks after the withdrawal of all three of his credible challengers, and he had little trouble disposing of vastly inferior opposition to record his fourth victory since arriving in Britain. Sent straight into the lead by Tizzard, it was fairly straightforward and, barring a mistake at the last, there was never a moment's worry. A progressive five-year-old, he has more than paid his way already this season, but it is worth bearing in mind all his form is in testing conditions.
Lago D'Oro is exposed as moderate and she never got anywhere near the winner. A return to low-grade handicaps awaits. *(op 9-1)*
La Source A Gold(IRE), who unseated on his Rules debut, ran well for a long way and looked booked for second until getting very tired in the final quarter-mile or so. He is not yet a lost cause. *(op 14-1)*

4007 MORSON GROUP H'CAP CHASE (13 fncs 6 omitted) 3m 2f 110y
3:00 (3:00) (Class 4) (0-110,107) 5-Y-0+
£6,263 (£1,850; £925; £463; £231; £116)

Form				RPR
2P20	1		**Ebony Jack (IRE)**[5] 3909 9-9-11 81 oh2 (p) RichardYoung(3) — (C L Tizzard) *mde all: j.w: styd on stoutly* **11/2**[3]	96+
340	2	4	**Hazeljack**[60] 2938 11-10-5 93 WillieMcCarthy(7) — (A J Whiting) *trckd wnr tl appr 3 out: rallied to go 2nd again 2 out: styd on: no imp run-in* **10/1**	101
-4P4	3	7	**Bubble Boy (IRE)**[17] 3698 7-11-5 107 CharlieStudd(7) — (B G Powell) *trckd ldrs: mstke 10th: one pce fr 3 out* **5/1**[2]	112+
6566	4	5	**Levallois (IRE)**[12] 3791 10-10-8 89 (b[1]) PhilipHide — (P Winkworth) *a in tch: wnt 2nd appr 3 out: tl wknd next* **5/1**[2]	87+
244U	5	17	**Uncle Mick (IRE)**[115] 1893 11-11-10 105 (v) JoeTizzard — (C L Tizzard) *trckd ldrs tl wknd after 13th:* **12/1**	88+
605U	6	4	**Multi Talented (IRE)**[46] 3241 10-10-5 93 (p) JustinMorgan(7) — (L Wells) *a bhd and nvr gng wl* **14/1**	68
0430	7	dist	**Blazing Batman**[7] 3887 13-9-11 83 oh6 ow2 DrPPritchard(5) — (Dr P Pritchard) *sn struggling in rr: t.o whn mstke 12th* **33/1**	—
-02P	P		**Boddidley (IRE)**[17] 3698 8-11-4 104 LiamHeard(5) — (P F Nicholls) *a bhd: rdn after 9th: t.o whn p.u bef 13th* **8/1**	—
0203	P		**Flash Cummins (IRE)**[34] 3423 6-11-10 105 TimmyMurphy — (M C Pipe) *hld up in rr: blnd 14th: sn lost tch: t.o whn p.u bef 3 out* **5/2**[1]	—

7m 12.7s (11.60) **Going Correction** +0.725s/f (Soft) **9** Ran SP% **114.8**
Speed ratings: **111,109,107,106,101 100,—,—,—** CSF £56.99 CT £291.98 TOTE £7.90: £1.90, £2.40, £2.40; EX 23.80 Trifecta £186.70 Pool £684.04 - 2.60 winning units.
Owner K S B Bloodstock **Bred** Mrs Joerg Vasicek **Trained** Milborne Port, Dorset

FOCUS
A modest staying handicap, run at a sound gallop, and the field came home strung out. The winner recorded a personal-best and may rate higher, and the placed horses set the level for the form.

NOTEBOOK
Ebony Jack(IRE), disappointing at Folkestone five days previously, bounced back to his best with a dour success from the front under his light weight. He clearly likes this venue - his close second over course and distance to Dunbrody Miller in December looks all the better now with that rival subsequently winning the Sussex National and Afga Diamond Chase - and his ability to act on most surfaces is a clear positive. Providing he can maintain this mood he should still look feasibly treated despite an inevitable rise in the weights. *(op 8-1)*
Hazeljack could not get to the winner up the rising finish, try as he might, but improved for the return to this track and the more testing surface. He has now dropped to a fair mark and could well go one better if found a suitable opportunity on a similar surface in the coming weeks. *(op 12-1)*
Bubble Boy(IRE) could only manage the same pace when it mattered, but was far from disgraced in defeat under his big weight. He will appreciate the return to a shorter trip in the future and has clearly fallen to a fair mark now. *(tchd 11-2)*
Levallois(IRE), up in trip and in first-time blinkers, once again failed to find as much as appeared likely when off the bridle and was well held. *(op 13-2)*
Boddidley(IRE) *Official explanation: jockey said gelding was unsuited by the heavy going (op 2-1 tchd 15-8 and 11-4)*
Flash Cummins(IRE), making his chase debut under Rules, never appeared happy on the heavy surface and proved disappointing. He should not be written off on the back of this effort, but he does have a fair bit to prove now all the same. *(op 2-1 tchd 15-8 and 11-4)*

4008 TOTESPORT.COM NATIONAL SPIRIT HURDLE GRADE 2 (10 hdls) 2m 4f
3:30 (3:30) (Class 1) 4-Y-0+
£25,353 (£9,549; £4,779; £2,389; £1,197; £598)

Form				RPR
2-21	1		**My Way De Solzen (FR)**[54] 3020 6-11-11 157 RobertThornton — (A King) *mde all: wnt clr appr 2 out: edgd rt bef last: pushed out run-in* **10/11**[1]	158+
-U36	2	9	**Dancing Bay**[29] 3502 9-11-3 143 MickFitzgerald — (N J Henderson) *trckd wnr thrght: rdn appr 2 out: no ch whn wnt bdly lft last* **12/1**	142+
F0F6	3	9	**Sporazene (IRE)**[15] 3723 7-11-3 148 ChristianWilliams — (P F Nicholls) *racd wd thrght: hdwy 3 out: rdn and wkng whn hit 2 out* **12/1**	133+
0/23	4	4	**Mughas (IRE)**[36] 3397 7-11-3 143 WayneHutchinson — (A King) *t.k.h: rdn appr 4 out: wknd next* **5/1**[3]	128
2F43	5	24	**Turtle Soup (IRE)**[29] 3502 10-11-3 145 JasonMaguire — (T R George) *trckd ldrs rdn after 6th: wknd appr 3 out* **9/2**[2]	110+
5224	6	dist	**Nathos (GER)**[29] 3502 9-11-3 139 NoelFehily — (C J Mann) *hld up in rr: rdn 4 out: sn wl bhd: t.o* **14/1**	—

5m 9.80s (6.00) **Going Correction** +0.725s/f (Soft) **6** Ran SP% **109.3**
Speed ratings: **117,113,109,108,98** — CSF £11.75 TOTE £2.10: £1.10, £2.60; EX 13.00.
Owner B Winfield,A Longman,J Wright & C Fenton **Bred** C Ricous-Guerin & Jacques Guerin **Trained** Barbury Castle, Wilts

FOCUS
Just a fair renewal of this Grade Two event, but the winner made all in decent fashion under his penalty, and the form appears sound, with the runner-up the best guide.

NOTEBOOK
My Way De Solzen(FR) ◆, winner of the Long Walk Hurdle at Chepstow last time, once again advertised his clear liking for a testing surface and made all to run out an impressive winner over this shorter trip. He is clearly at the top of his game at present, and must now rate near the top of the tree in this division, with further improvement likely as he is still a six-year-old. He was rightly cut in the betting for the World Hurdle at Cheltenham, and in the unlikely event of soft ground at the Festival in March, he has the ability to secure that prize in an open-looking year for the division. However, it must be noted that he flopped on good ground in the Supreme Novices' in 2005 and the key to him is surely a deep surface. *(op 5-6 tchd Evens)*
Dancing Bay was firmly put in his place by the winner, but still ran close to his best in defeat, and was clear of the remainder at the finish. He is a smart performer on his day, but he has not scored over hurdles since 2004, and is never one for win-only purposes. *(op 9-1)*
Sporazene(IRE) failed to get home on this testing ground and was never a serious threat. He has still shown signs of improvement lately, however, and is worth another chance over this trip on a faster surface in the future. A tilt at the Coral Cup at Cheltenham in March looks realistic from his current rating. *(op 10-1)*

Mughas(IRE) proved hard to settle through the early parts and ultimately found little when it mattered approaching the turn for home. He is capable of better, and deserves another crack at the *Coral Cup at the Cheltenham Festival, in which he finished fourth in 2004 from a 1lb higher mark. (tchd 11-2)*

Turtle Soup(IRE), fourth in this event last season, ran well below his best on ground he has looked suited by in the past. He has it to prove now. *(op 6-1)*

4009 "EARTHMOVER" FOXHUNTERS TRIAL (A HUNTERS' CHASE) (13 fncs 6 omitted) 3m 2f 110y

4:00 (4:00) (Class 4) 5-Y-O+ **£3,834** (£1,464)

Form					RPR
3-3F	**1**		**Gatsby (IRE)**[15] 3736 10-12-0 .... MrJMPritchard (J Groucott) *mde all: hit 7th: in command fr 3 out though tired run-in*	**11/4**[2]	115+
-41F	**2**	*8*	**Vinnie Boy (IRE)**[275] 440 9-12-7 .... MissPGundry (Mrs O Bush) *rdn and lost pl after 5th: wnt 3rd after 9th: chsd wnr appr 3 out: no imp after*	**10/3**[3]	108
	P		**Noggler**[281] 7-12-0 .... MissSBrotherton (M J Brown) *bhd whn p.u after 9th*	**25/1**	—
	U		**Dolly Devious**[1044] 11-11-2 .... MrDavidTurner(5) (D I Turner) *bhd whn blnd and uns rdr 3rd*	**66/1**	—
/222	**U**		**Marrasit (IRE)**[15] 3736 10-11-0 .... MrSCharlton(7) (H E Thorpe) *j. slowly 2nd: blnd and fell 10th*	**5/2**[1]	—
U/10	**P**		**Merry Path (IRE)**[238] 842 12-12-4 115 .... MrJETudor(3) (Evan Williams) *chsd wnr tl appr 3 out: wkng whn blnd 2 out: p.u sn after*	**5/1**	—
40P/	**R**		**Altareek (USA)**[7] 9-11-7 .... (b) MrGGallagher(7) (K Tork) *prom whn hit 7th: bhd and v tired whn failed to clr 3 out and uns rdr: rmntd and refused*	**20/1**	—

7m 23.2s (22.10) **Going Correction** +0.725s/f (Soft) **7** Ran SP% **105.1**
Speed ratings: **96,93,—,—,—** —,— CSF £10.42 TOTE £3.00: £1.10, £2.20; EX 12.50.
Owner Mrs J K Powell **Bred** Donald Joseph King **Trained** Much Wenlock, Shropshire

FOCUS
Only two of the seven runners managed to complete in what was an average hunters' chase, rated through the runner-up.

NOTEBOOK
Gatsby(IRE), a proven performer in such conditions, slugged it out from the front and showed no ill-effects of a fall last time, coming away from Vinnie Boy before getting tired and running around on the climb to the line. He is a decent performer on his day and will continue to go well when the emphasis is on stamina. *(op 9-4)*
Vinnie Boy(IRE), held by the winner on their Cheltenham form, has a decent strike-rate and did nothing wrong here, simply being unable to cope with the 7lb concession to the winner. He is still unexposed for one of his age and likely to be capable of better still. *(op 9-2)*
Merry Path(IRE) offered little on this reappearance, but deserves another chance on account of the ground. *(op 7-2 tchd 11-2)*
Altareek(USA) was spent and had nothing left to offer when stopping before the third last through *tiredness. His rider then attempted to remount and complete for third, but he was too tired. (op 7-2 tchd 11-2)*
Marrasit(IRE), a consistent sort, has yet to win and was not going particularly well here, appearing to be struggling when falling at the tenth. *(op 7-2 tchd 11-2)*

4010 TOTESPORT 0800 221 221 H'CAP HURDLE (9 hdls) 2m 2f 110y

4:30 (4:30) (Class 5) (0-95,95) 4-Y-O+ **£2,602** (£764; £382; £190)

Form					RPR
-540	**1**		**Park City**[93] 2324 7-11-3 **90** .... ShaneWalsh(7) (J Joseph) *led tl hdd appr 4 out: led again after next: kpt on gamely run-in*	**33/1**	92+
5-P6	**2**	*1 ½*	**Lady Alderbrook (IRE)**[33] 3437 6-10-7 **80** .... AndrewGlassonbury(7) (C J Down) *trckd ldrs: wnt 2nd 2 out: hit lat: kpt on*	**12/1**	80+
P/55	**3**	*2*	**Stakeholder (IRE)**[48] 3211 8-9-11 **68** .... DarylJacob(5) (Mrs H E Rees) *chsd ldrs: outpcd 3 out: styd on fr next*	**8/1**[3]	65
0060	**4**	*4*	**Picot De Say**[8] 3577 4-10-2 **78** .... OllieMcPhail (C Roberts) *hld up: hdwy fr 6th: chsng ldng pair whn hit last*	**14/1**	62+
0004	**5**	*13*	**Denarius Secundus**[34] 3424 9-9-9 **68** .... (b) KeiranBurke(7) (N R Mitchell) *chsd ldrs: led appr 4 out: hdd after next: wknd*	**14/1**	50+
0016	**6**	*13*	**Ressource (FR)**[19] 3661 7-11-4 **91** .... (b) MrWRussell(7) (G L Moore) *chsd ldrs: ev ch 3 out: sn wknd*	**16/1**	58
5113	**7**	*4*	**Golden Feather**[22] 3616 4-11-2 **95** .... PaulO'Neill(3) (Miss Venetia Williams) *trckd wnr to 4 out: rdn next: sn btn*	**11/8**[1]	56+
3303	**8**	*3*	**Monsal Dale (IRE)**[6] 3899 7-11-0 **80** .... (tp) LeightonAspell (Mrs L C Jewell) *in tch tl wknd after 3 out*	**10/1**	40
0U55	**9**	*7*	**Firstflor**[68] 2816 7-9-12 **67** .... OwynNelmes(3) (F Jordan) *a bhd*	**11/1**	20
0-P0	**10**	*8*	**June's River (IRE)**[7] 3886 13-11-0 **85** .... DrPPritchard(5) (Dr P Pritchard) *a wl in rr*	**66/1**	30
	11	*9*	**Massini Expres (IRE)**[11] 3809 6-10-11 **77** .... JasonMaguire (Philip Fenton, Ire) *t.k.h on outside: rn wd on bnd after 3 out: sn btn*	**13/2**[2]	13
54P0	**P**		**Canni Thinkaar (IRE)**[6] 3899 5-11-2 **87** .... (p) RobertLucey-Butler(5) (P Butler) *a bhd: t.o whn p.u bef 2 out*	**33/1**	—

4m 57.5s (21.50) **Going Correction** +0.725s/f (Soft)
WFA 4 from 5yo+ 9lb **12** Ran SP% **118.3**
Speed ratings: **83,82,81,79,74 68,67,65,63,59 55,**— CSF £379.14 CT £3471.13 TOTE £46.80: £7.30, £3.30, £2.30; EX 418.20.
Owner Jack Joseph **Bred** Dunchurch Lodge Stud Co **Trained** Coleshill, Bucks

FOCUS
A race it paid to race prominently in and outsider Park City sprang something of a surprise. However, the form looks reasonable sound, but the level is low and not an obvious source of future winners.

NOTEBOOK
Park City was massively favoured in being ridden prominently on a day when it was hard to make ground and, having been outpaced coming down to the fourth last, he surged his way back to the front before staying on too strongly for Lady Alderbrook. A proven performer in testing conditions, he cannot be relied upon to repeat the effort and as a result is worth taking on next time. *(op 25-1)*
Lady Alderbrook(IRE), another to hold a prominent position throughout, ran her best race to date and kept on right the way to the line. She is clearly very modest, but looks open to a little further progress and there may be a race in her at this sort of level. *(op 14-1)*
Stakeholder(IRE), at an obvious advantage racing off a feather weight, kept on well for third, but was unable get to the front pair. He is nothing better than a selling plater and will stand more of a chance at the lowest level. *(op 11-1)*
Picot De Say ran an improved race despite not being obviously well suited by the ground conditions and is one to watch out for when faced with a less demanding test.
Denarius Secundus, dropping significantly in trip, went on before the fourth last, but found disappointingly little and was ultimately well held. He is another who may have found this company too hot. *(op 16-1)*
Golden Feather came into this with obviously strong claims on form, but he had something to prove on the surface and failed to get home having travelled well. He is better than this, but now has a bit to prove with his good spell seemingly over. *(tchd 6-4)*

4011 HARBEN'S EQUINE CARE CENTRE MAIDEN OPEN NATIONAL HUNT FLAT RACE 2m 2f 110y

5:00 (5:00) (Class 6) 4-6-Y-O **£1,626** (£477; £238; £119)

Form					RPR
	1		**Paix Eternelle (FR)** 5-10-12 .... MickFitzgerald (N J Henderson) *trckd ldrs: led 4f out: styd on wl fnl f*	**7/1**	99+
	2	*4*	**Chorizo (IRE)** 5-11-5 .... ChristianWilliams (P F Nicholls) *hld up: hdwy to go 2nd over 2f out: wnt bdly lft fnl f but kpt on*	**4/1**[2]	105+
52	**3**	*½*	**Captain Marlon (IRE)**[22] 3617 5-11-5 .... JoeTizzard (C L Tizzard) *t.k.h: a.p: chsd wnr over 3 out: ev ch over 1f out: wknd fnl f*	**5/2**[1]	102+
	4	*9*	**Lord Norman (IRE)** 5-11-5 .... LeightonAspell (L Wells) *bhd: rdn 7f out: styd on past btn horses fr over 2f out*	**25/1**	93
33	**5**	*2 ½*	**Graphex**[48] 3216 4-10-9 .... RobertThornton (A King) *hld up: hdwy over 4f out: rdn and wknd over 2f out*	**6/1**	80
	6	*dist*	**Mister Moonax (IRE)** 6-11-5 .... JamieMoore (M G Rimell) *chsd ldrs tl lost tch over 3f out: t.o*	**16/1**	—
03	**7**	*10*	**Kalamazoo (IRE)**[50] 3138 5-11-5 .... PJBrennan (Nick Williams) *chsd ldrs tl wknd qckly over 3f out: t.o*	**5/1**[3]	—
	8	*shd*	**Foxxtrot Oscar (IRE)** 5-11-5 .... WayneHutchinson (Nick Williams) *hld up: a bhd: t.o*	**33/1**	—
046	**9**	*14*	**Romney Marsh**[20] 3657 5-10-2 .... WayneBurton(10) (R Curtis) *plld hrd: mde most tl hdd 4f out: wknd over 2f out: t.o*	**33/1**	—
2	**10**	*8*	**Beths Choice**[16] 3720 5-10-12 .... ChrisDavies(7) (J M Bradley) *prom tl wknd over 4f out: t.o*	**25/1**	—
	11	*dist*	**Delcombe** 5-11-5 .... SeanCurran (N R Mitchell) *bhd: lost tch 1/2-way: t.o*	**50/1**	—
	12	*dist*	**My Mon Amour** 5-10-9 .... RichardYoung(3) (J W Mullins) *a bhd: t.o*	**33/1**	—

4m 52.8s (13.50) **Going Correction** +0.725s/f (Soft)
WFA 4 from 5yo+ 9lb **12** Ran SP% **116.4**
Speed ratings: **100,98,98,94,93** —,—,—,—,— —,— CSF £31.98 TOTE £5.90: £2.30, £1.50, £1.90; EX 46.80 Place 6 £71.17, Place 5 £47.74.
Owner Baydon Bloodstock **Bred** F Lagouche **Trained** Upper Lambourn, Berks

FOCUS
A good bumper for the course won tidily by the potentially smart Paix Eternelle. The third and fifth are the best guides to the level and the race should produce its share of winners.

NOTEBOOK
Paix Eternelle(FR) ◆, weak in the market beforehand, appeared to face a stiff task on this racecourse debut, racing mainly against geldings in the bog-like ground, but she showed her class with a strong galloping performance, coming clear in the final quarter mile. Although receiving weight, she was expected to need the outing, so the fact she was able to win first time up suggests she has a bright future and she looks an obvious contender for the Mares' Final at Cheltenham in April. *(op 13-2)*
Chorizo(IRE), who is well thought-of by connections, took a late walk in the market, presumably due to question marks hanging over his ability to handle the ground, but he got through it well enough and stayed on to get the better of favourite Captain Marlon for second, doing well considering it was hard to make up ground in the sloppy conditions. He was no match for the winner, but a sounder surface is likely to help and he should have little trouble finding a race in this sphere. *(op 11-4 tchd 5-2)*
Captain Marlon(IRE) set the standard having shown fair placed form in similar conditions at Chepstow last time, but he was unable to go with the winner as she went clear and tired up the hill, being claimed for second by Chorizo. He will appreciate more of a stamina test over hurdles and should make a chaser in time. *(op 9-4 tchd 11-4)*
Lord Norman(IRE), a half-brother to Sir Rembrandt, emerged best of the rest and will no doubt have delighted connections with this debut fourth, keeping on well having been behind. He is going to require further over hurdles and is a promising sort.
Graphex, the sole four-year-old in the line-up, appeared to get bogged down in the conditions and *failed to reproduce his previous placed efforts. He is better than this and deserves another chance. (op 8-1 tchd 11-2)*
Kalamazoo(IRE), a decent third in an All-Weather bumper at Lingfield, failed to handle the conditions and stopped very quickly under pressure. *(op 8-1)*
T/Jkpt: £14,399.70 to a £1 stake. Pool: £40,562.75. 2.00 winning tickets. T/Plt: £409.70 to a £1 stake. Pool: £65,675.60. 117.00 winning tickets. T/Qpdt: £204.10 to a £1 stake. Pool: £3,476.10. 12.60 winning tickets. JS

3685 TOWCESTER (R-H)

Sunday, February 19

OFFICIAL GOING: Soft (good to soft in places on chase course)
Wind: Fresh, across Weather: Overcast

4012 BRIAN GOODYEAR TELEBET 0808 108 1122 H'CAP HURDLE (12 hdls) 3m

2:20 (2:20) (Class 4) (0-105,107) 4-Y-O **£4,119** (£1,216; £608; £304; £152)

Form					RPR
-3P1	**1**		**Desert Tommy**[7] 3876 5-11-9 107 7ex .... MrNWilliams(5) (Evan Williams) *chsd ldrs: rdn after 9th: led 2 out: drvn out*	**8/1**[3]	113+
03-3	**2**	*7*	**Classic Sight**[27] 3544 6-11-0 **93** .... (b) JohnMcNamara (C C Bealby) *chsd ldrs: led appr 8th: mstke 3 out: hdd next: styd on same pce last*	**22/1**	92
0600	**3**	*8*	**Miss Fahrenheit (IRE)**[26] 3548 7-11-11 **104** .... SamStronge (C Roberts) *mid-div: hdwy 7th: wknd 2 out*	**33/1**	95
1-1U	**4**	*3*	**Graceful Dancer**[30] 3481 9-11-7 **105** .... JohnnyLevins(5) (B G Powell) *led to 2nd: chsd ldrs: rdn 9th: wknd next*	**11/2**[2]	93
0223	**5**	*5*	**Kyno (IRE)**[37] 3372 5-11-3 **96** .... (t) AndrewThornton (M G Quinlan) *hld up: hdwy 7th: wknd appr 2 out*	**12/1**	79
6546	**6**	*20*	**Pardon What**[24] 3581 10-11-11 **104** .... (b) KeithMercer (S Lycett) *hld up: hmpd 5th: hdwy 8th: rdn and wknd after 3 out*	**14/1**	72+
14P0	**7**	*14*	**The Pecker Dunn (IRE)**[45] 3250 12-10-8 **87** .... JodieMogford (Mrs N S Evans) *hld up: hdwy appr 8th: rdn and wknd appr 2 out*	**33/1**	36
/0-5	**P**		**Flexible Concience (IRE)**[55] 2985 11-10-5 **84** .... MarkBradburne (J A B Old) *a in rr: t.o whn p.u bef 3 out*	**25/1**	—
00P0	**P**		**Moving On Up**[7] 3889 12-11-3 **103** .... (b) MissSusannahWileman(7) (C N Kellett) *a bhd: t.o whn p.u bef 3 out*	**100/1**	—
P606	**P**		**Ashleybank House (IRE)**[15] 3733 9-10-11 **90** .... (t) RichardHobson (David Pearson) *a bhd: t.o whn p.u bef 3 out*	**66/1**	—
U036	**P**		**Abzuson**[18] 3675 9-11-7 **103** .... LeeVickers(3) (J R Norton) *prom: rdn 7th: wknd bef next: t.o whn p.u bef 3 out*	**14/1**	—
3661	**P**		**Strolling Vagabond (IRE)**[34] 3424 7-10-1 **80** .... JamieGoldstein (John R Upson) *prom: rdn 7th: wknd and p.u bef 2 out*	**5/1**[1]	—
F	**P**		**Georges Boy (IRE)**[34] 3426 8-11-1 **97** .... GinoCarenza(3) (P J Jones) *mid-div: j.rt 5th: wknd 8th: t.o whn p.u after 3 out*	**33/1**	—

0406 **P** **Dere Lyn**[7] [3876] 8-11-3 **101**..........(v) LeeStephens(5) — (Mrs D A Hamer) *sn pushed along in rr: bhd fr 6th: t.o whn p.u bef 2 out* **25/1**

3020 **P** **Good Potential (IRE)**[24] [3577] 10-10-11 **90**..........(t) WarrenMarston — (D J Wintle) *prom: rdn and lost pl 5th: bhd whn p.u after next* **22/1**

1F31 **P** **Twotiming Gent (IRE)**[27] [3540] 13-9-10 **82**.......... CraigLidster(7) — (P D Niven) *led 2nd: hdd appr 8th: rdn and wknd 3 out: bhd whn p.u bef last* **8/1**[3]

P4P5 **P** **Good Judgement (IRE)**[36] [3382] 8-11-12 **105**.......... RichardJohnson — (Jonjo O'Neill) *hld up in tch: mstke and wknd 9th: t.o whn p.u bef 2 out* **11/1**

5-10 **P** **Montecorvino (GER)**[17] [3687] 5-11-10 **103**.......... CarlLlewellyn — (N A Twiston-Davies) *in rr whn mstkes 1st and 2nd: sn drvn along: bhd fr 5th: t.o whn p.u bef 2 out* **8/1**[3]

6m 39.5s (8.50) **Going Correction** +0.50s/f (Soft) **18** Ran SP% **122.4**
Speed ratings: **105,102,100,99,97 90,86,—,—,— —,—,—,—,— —,—,—** CSF £176.70 CT £5433.30 TOTE £8.40: £1.80, £4.30, £6.10, £1.80; EX 254.80.
Owner All Adda Winna Racing Club **Bred** Silfield Bloodstock **Trained** Cowbridge, Vale Of Glamorgan

FOCUS
A moderate handicap, which saw only seven runners complete, and it proved a real slog in the conditions. The winner, however, is on the upgrade.

NOTEBOOK
Desert Tommy, back to winning ways at Exeter a week previously, duly followed-up with a decisive success under his 7lb penalty. He is clearly in the form of his life at present, this proves his versatility as regards underfoot conditions, and he saw out the stiff three miles without fuss. A bold bid for the hat-trick should be expected and he really does get on well with today's rider. *(op 7-1)*
Classic Sight, making her handicap debut, was given a positive ride over this longer trip and finished a clear second-best. An easier three miles will suit her better in the future and she does deserve to find an opening.
Miss Fahrenheit(IRE) again shaped as though this trip is beyond her, yet still posted a more encouraging effort in defeat. She is well suited by a deep surface and, considering she has now fallen to a more realistic official mark, could well build on this when reverting to a shorter trip.
Graceful Dancer, who unseated over fences last time, was not disgraced on this return to hurdling, yet she does appear held by the Handicapper at present in this sphere. *(op 6-1)*
Kyno(IRE) *Official explanation: trainer said gelding had choked (tchd 10-1)*
Abzuson *Official explanation: jockey said gelding was never travelling*
Strolling Vagabond(IRE), raised 8lb for breaking his duck at Plumpton last time, was very *disappointing as he is proven over the trip and on testing ground.Official explanation: trainer said gelding was unsuited by soft ground*

4013 BRIAN GOODYEAR'S NATIONAL ANTE-POST SERVICE (S) H'CAP HURDLE (8 hdls) 2m

2:50 (2:52) (Class 5) (0-90,90) 4-Y-0+ **£2,602** (£764; £382; £190)

Form				RPR
3F00	**1**		**Lady Maranzi**[30] [3483] 7-11-1 **79**.......... BenjaminHitchcott (Mrs D A Hamer) *a.p: led 5th: hdd after 3 out: rallied to ld and mstke next: clr whn hit last: drvn out* **9/1**	95+
P040	**2**	*13*	**Rockys Girl**[37] [3367] 4-10-2 **80**..........(b[1]) LeeStephens(5) (R Flint) *hld up: hdwy 5th: led after 3 out: rdn and hdd next: wknd last* **14/1**	75+
6000	**3**	*2½*	**Too Posh To Share**[50] [3147] 8-9-7 **67** ow1.......... RyanCummings(10) (D J Wintle) *hld up: hdwy 4th: rdn after 3 out: wknd next* **12/1**	67
4445	**4**	*4*	**Jour De Mee (FR)**[17] [3686] 9-11-0 **81**.......... TJPhelan(3) (Mrs H Dalton) *chsd ldrs: rdn appr 3 out: wknd next* **9/2**[1]	77
0044	**5**	*12*	**Darialann (IRE)**[37] [3367] 11-11-1 **86**..........(b) DarrenO'Dwyer(7) (O Brennan) *mid-div: effrt appr 4th: sn wknd* **8/1**	70
00U0	**6**	*3½*	**Sir Walter (IRE)**[20] [3650] 13-11-7 **90**.......... MrNWilliams(5) (D Burchell) *hld up: hdwy 4th: ev ch 3 out: wknd bef next* **20/1**	71
000	**P**		**Silverpro**[18] [3673] 5-10-8 **72**.......... WarrenMarston (D J Wintle) *hld up: bhd fr 3rd: t.o whn p.u bef 2 out* **22/1**	—
P0P0	**P**		**Huw The News**[3] [3945] 7-11-7 **85**..........(p) RJGreene (S C Burrough) *hld up: bhd fr 3rd: t.o whn p.u bef 2 out* **40/1**	—
000P	**P**		**My Retreat (USA)**[55] [2995] 9-10-0 **71**.......... TomMessenger(7) (R Fielder) *hld up: bhd fr 3rd: t.o whn p.u bef 2 out* **33/1**	—
-000	**P**		**Barcelona**[51] [3125] 9-10-13 **84**..........(t) MissLBrooke(7) (Lady Susan Brooke) *hld up: bhd fr 3rd: t.o whn p.u bef 2 out* **25/1**	—
3/	**P**		**General Hopkins (IRE)**[343] 11-10-2 **73**.......... MrGPewter(7) (G R Pewter) *led to 4th: wknd next: t.o whn p.u after 3 out* **100/1**	—
5225	**P**		**Makandy**[15] [3731] 7-10-12 **83**.......... MrRArmson(7) (R J Armson) *hld up: hdwy appr 4th: wknd 3 out: t.o whn p.u bef next* **7/1**[3]	—
61/	**P**		**Watermouse**[824] [2226] 6-10-8 **82**.......... JosephStevenson(10) (R Dickin) *hld up in tch: rdn and wknd after 3 out: t.o whn p.u bef next* **9/1**	—
-000	**P**		**Sullivan's Cascade (IRE)**[44] [3147] 8-10-9 **73**..........(t) TomDoyle (E G Bevan) *mid-div: hdwy 4th: wknd after next: t.o whn p.u bef 2 out* **28/1**	—
0604	**P**		**Winter Coral (FR)**[26] [3550] 4-10-12 **85**..........(p) JodieMogford (Mrs N S Evans) *chsd ldrs: mstke 2nd: wknd after 5th: t.o whn p.u bef 2 out* **11/2**[2]	—
0P00	**P**		**Walton Way**[20] [3646] 6-10-3 **67**.......... JimmyMcCarthy (P W Hiatt) *chsd ldrs tl led 4th: mstke and hdd next: stmbld and wknd 3 out: t.o whn p.u bef next* **20/1**	—

4m 22.2s (10.80) **Going Correction** +0.675s/f (Soft)
WFA 4 from 5yo+ 9lb **16** Ran SP% **119.1**
Speed ratings: **100,93,92,90,84 82,—,—,—,— —,—,—,—,— —** CSF £110.14 CT £1525.12 TOTE £10.40: £2.10, £3.00, £3.20, £1.90; EX 112.10.There was no bid for the winner.
Owner Mrs D A Hamer **Bred** D I Bare **Trained** Nantycaws, Carmarthens

FOCUS
A very weak affair, run at an ordinary gallop, and another race where more of the field were pulled up than managed to complete. The form, rated through the third, should be treated with caution.

NOTEBOOK
Lady Maranzi relished this drop back down in class and showed her true colours with a career-first success at the eighth attempt. She proved much easier to settle this time, which proved decisive, and the stiff test over this trip was clearly right up her street. A rise in the weights will make her life more difficult, but she has found her level now, and may have a bit more to offer. *(op 10-1 tchd 11-1)*
Rockys Girl, equipped with first-time blinkers, showed just about his best form over hurdles to date on this drop in trip/class. She was ultimately put in her place by the winner, but did more than enough to suggest she can open her account if kept to this grade. *(op 12-1)*
Too Posh To Share failed to rate a serious threat, but still posted an improved display and enjoyed the return to this stiff track. She has clearly now found her level. *(op 14-1)*
Jour De Mee(FR), reverting to hurdles, failed to see out the race all that well and finished tired. *(op 5-1)*
Makandy *Official explanation: jockey said gelding had a breathing problem (op 5-1)*
Winter Coral(FR) ran a tame race on this drop in class and something may well have been amiss. *Official explanation: jockey said filly had a breathing problem (op 5-1)*

4014 BRIAN GOODYEAR COMING SOON TO SKYTEXT H'CAP CHASE (14 fncs) 2m 3f 110y

3:20 (3:22) (Class 4) (0-115,115) 5-Y-0 **£6,338** (£1,872; £936; £468; £234)

Form				RPR
-U21	**1**		**The Outlier (IRE)**[19] [3660] 8-11-4 **107**.......... SamThomas (Miss Venetia Williams) *a.p: led last: hung lft flat: drvn out* **9/4**[1]	115+
5165	**2**	*5*	**Terivic**[24] [3580] 6-11-12 **115**.......... JohnMcNamara (K C Bailey) *chsd ldr: led 3rd to 6th: led 11th: rdn and hdd last: no ex flat* **14/1**	117+
4P32	**3**	*10*	**Pietro Vannucci (IRE)**[33] [3440] 10-11-7 **110**.......... RichardJohnson (Jonjo O'Neill) *hld up: drvn along 10th: nvr trbld ldrs* **7/2**[2]	104+
6653	**4**	*3*	**Runaway Bishop (USA)**[17] [3688] 11-10-2 **91**.......... RichardHobson (J R Cornwall) *prom: lost pl 2nd: sn bhd: hdwy 9th: outpcd next: styd on flat* **15/2**	86+
04F4	**5**	*¾*	**Charlies Future**[17] [3688] 8-11-8 **111**.......... TomDoyle (S C Burrough) *led to 3rd: led 6th to 11th: wknd 2 out* **8/1**	100+
0P00	**6**	*12*	**Monty Be Quick**[213] [1044] 10-9-8 **90** oh17 ow1.......... CharliePoste(7) (J M Castle) *hdwy 3rd: rdn and wknd appr 2 out* **40/1**	66
-4F0	**7**	*12*	**Kosmos Bleu (FR)**[39] [3344] 8-11-5 **108**.......... AndrewThornton (R H Alner) *hld up: hdwy 9th: wknd appr 2 out* **5/1**[3]	72
20P5	**P**		**Golly (IRE)**[60] [2939] 10-9-10 **92**.......... MrFelixDeGiles(7) (D L Williams) *mid-div: rdn 10th: wknd 3 out: t.o whn p.u bef next* **33/1**	—
0F00	**P**		**Major Belle (FR)**[19] [3663] 7-9-11 **89** oh13.......... LeeVickers(3) (John R Upson) *hld up: hdwy 7th: rdn 9th: wknd appr 3 out: t.o whn p.u bef next* **66/1**	—
243P	**P**		**Simoun (IRE)**[4] [3922] 8-11-5 **115**.......... TomMessenger(7) (B N Pollock) *chsd ldrs: j. slowly and lost pl 7th: hdwy appr 3 out: sn wknd: t.o whn p.u bef next* **16/1**	—

5m 29.4s (9.40) **Going Correction** +0.40s/f (Soft) **10** Ran SP% **112.0**
Speed ratings: **97,95,91,89,89 84,79,—,—,—** CSF £30.67 CT £105.73 TOTE £2.90: £1.80, £2.80, £1.80; EX 30.80.
Owner P J Murphy **Bred** Mrs Joerg Vasicek **Trained** Kings Caple, H'fords

FOCUS
A modest handicap, run at a fair gallop, and could be rated higher, but the third to fifth were well below their marks and limit the form.

NOTEBOOK
The Outlier(IRE), off the mark in a maiden chase at Folkestone last time, advertised his current rude health with another dour success on ground he clearly enjoys. He can expect to go up a fair amount in the weights now, but he may well have more to offer this season, and looks one to follow. *(tchd 2-1)*
Terivic ultimately just found the stiff finish over this longer trip stretch his stamina, but he was well clear of the remainder of his rivals at the finish, and turned in a sound effort under top weight. He is on a fair mark at present, likes this track, and can get back to winning ways when dropped back in trip. *(tchd 16-1)*
Pietro Vannucci(IRE), as has often been the case previously, ran in snatches and was doing all of his best work too late in the day. He is on a decent mark at present, but cannot be backed with any confidence. *(op 4-1)*
Runaway Bishop(USA) did not prove suited by the drop back to this trip, but still gives the form a fair look, and should get closer when reverting to a stiffer test. *(op 7-1 tchd 8-1)*
Charlies Future had his chance from the front, but was ultimately a sitting duck at the top of the straight and is another who did not appear suited by the drop back to this trip. *(tchd 7-1)*
Kosmos Bleu(FR) ran a tame race and is struggling for form at present. *(op 11-2)*

4015 B & G RACING NOVICES' HURDLE (8 hdls) 2m

3:50 (3:50) (Class 3) 4-Y-0+ **£6,889** (£2,035; £1,017; £509; £254; £127)

Form				RPR
6122	**1**		**Livingonaknifedge (IRE)**[29] [3491] 7-11-7 116.......... RichardJohnson (Ian Williams) *a.p: chsd ldr appr 4th: swtchd lft appr last: hung lft flat: styd on u.p to ld post* **6/4**[2]	105
1101	**2**	*shd*	**Gardasee (GER)**[27] [3539] 4-11-1.......... TonyDobbin (T P Tate) *led: nt jump wl: hit 2nd and 5th: blnd 3 out: sn rdn: hdd post* **8/11**[1]	102+
05-	**3**	*7*	**Felix Rex (GER)**[418] [3053] 6-10-9.......... MrMatthewSmith(7) (J Pearce) *hld up: styd on fr 3 out: nt trble ldrs* **100/1**	93
0	**4**	*2½*	**Cabrillo (IRE)**[31] [2950] 5-10-9.......... TomSiddall (John A Quinn, Ire) *hld up in tch: outpcd 3rd: hit next: styd on fr 3 out: nvr trbld ldrs* **66/1**	83
0-00	**5**	*24*	**Tuesday Club (IRE)**[66] [2849] 7-11-2.......... MarkBradburne (J A B Old) *hld up: j.rt 1st: bhd fr 3rd* **66/1**	66
00-P	**6**	*25*	**Pintail**[17] [3685] 6-11-2.......... JimmyMcCarthy (Mrs P Robeson) *chsd ldr to appr 4th: wknd next* **150/1**	41
UP	**7**	*dist*	**Nellie The Nod**[26] [3550] 7-10-2.......... MrJAJenkins(7) (M J Gingell) *hld up: bhd fr 3rd* **250/1**	—
	P		**Mr Mayfair (IRE)**[383] 4-10-7.......... PaulMoloney (Miss L Day) *sn bhd: t.o whn p.u bef 2 out* **100/1**	—
	P		**Mardonicdeclare**[574] 5-11-2.......... AntonyEvans (S Lycett) *bhd fr 3rd: t.o whn p.u bef 2 out* **100/1**	—
/040	**P**		**Minster Park**[31] [3466] 7-11-2.......... RJGreene (S C Burrough) *bhd fr 3rd: t.o whn p.u bef 2 out* **100/1**	—
	P		**Lyster (IRE)**[190] [1215] 7-10-11.......... JamesDiment(5) (D L Williams) *hld up: bhd fr 3rd: t.o whn p.u bef 2 out* **25/1**[3]	—
P	**P**		**Altenburg (FR)**[50] [3132] 4-10-7.......... MarcusFoley (Mrs N Smith) *chsd ldrs: blnd 3rd: wknd 5th: t.o whn p.u bef 2 out* **66/1**	—
U	**P**		**Story Arms**[7] [3878] 4-10-0.......... AngharadFrieze(7) (D Burchell) *mid-div: hmpd 1st: bhd fr 3rd: hung lft and p.u bef 3 out* **100/1**	—

4m 21.4s (10.00) **Going Correction** +0.675s/f (Soft)
WFA 4 from 5yo+ 9lb **13** Ran SP% **112.2**
Speed ratings: **102,101,98,97,85 72,—,—,—,— —,—,—** CSF £2.72 TOTE £2.60: £1.20, £1.10, £9.00; EX 4.20.
Owner Concertina Racing **Bred** Denis Ring **Trained** Portway, Worcs

FOCUS
No strength in depth to this novice event, but it saw the two market leaders fight out the finish. The first two are rated as having run well below their best marks.

NOTEBOOK
Livingonaknifedge(IRE), dropped in class, deservedly resumed winning ways with a hard-fought success under his penalty. He is not the most straightforward, but he has developed into more consistent performer all the same, and is right at home on this sort of testing ground. In the long term, this former winning pointer should reach greater heights next season as a novice chaser and now appears ready to tackle a longer trip once again. *(tchd 11-8)*

Gardasee(GER) made a terrible blunder three out - at which his rider did very well to maintain their partnership - and that ultimately proved costly as he was still only just denied at the finish by the most narrow of margins. This was the worst round of jumping he has put in to-date, and he will need to brush up in that department, but this still proves he has an engine and he can soon be placed to find compensation. *(tchd 4-5)*
Felix Rex(GER), returning from a 418-day layoff, stayed on well enough towards the finish and posted an encouraging effort. His next outing should reveal more and he will then be eligible for that all-important handicap mark. *(op 66-1)*
Cabrillo(IRE), who showed very little in her previous two outings on the All-Weather, was another doing her best work at the finish. She ought to find her feet in low-grade handicaps in due course.

4016 BUDGIE FLIES THE RAF NEST BEGINNERS' CHASE (18 fncs) 3m 110y
4:20 (4:20) (Class 4) 5-Y-0+ **£4,119** (£1,216; £608; £304; £152)

Form — RPR
36P2 **1** **Ardaghey (IRE)**[50] 3148 7-11-4 .... CarlLlewellyn 138+
(N A Twiston-Davies) *mde virtually all: j.lft 9th: clr 2 out: jinked lft flat: eased towards fin* **9/4**[2]
0023 **2** *9* **Great As Gold (IRE)**[20] 3653 7-11-4 ....(p) WilsonRenwick 122+
(B Ellison) *hld up: hdwy 8th: chsd wnr 15th: rdn appr 2 out: styd on same pce* **16/1**
11/2 **3** *13* **Supreme Toss (IRE)**[87] 2464 10-11-4 .... RichardJohnson 109+
(R T Phillips) *chsd ldrs: mstke 6th: outpcd 11th: rallied 14th: wknd appr 2 out* **2/1**[1]
35 **4** *nk* **Exceptionnel (FR)**[22] 3611 7-10-11 .... MrJNewbold(7) 108
(Lady Connell) *hld up: mstke 1st: hdwy 9th: rdn and wknd after 3 out* **16/1**
3243 **5** *½* **Woodlands Genpower (IRE)**[30] 3480 8-11-4 118.....(p) MarkBradburne 107
(P A Pritchard) *chsd wnr: pckd 11th: rdn 14th: rdn and wknd appr 2 out* **5/1**[3]
P5F **6** *dist* **Run To The King (IRE)**[19] 3660 8-11-4 .... AndrewThornton —
(P C Ritchens) *mid-div: bhd fr 6th* **100/1**
0P0/ **F** **Kings Avenue**[1119] 3315 9-11-4 .... TomDoyle —
(A J Chamberlain) *hld up: a in rr: fell 12th* **200/1**
PP **P** **Germany Park (IRE)**[13] 3781 8-10-11 ....(v[1]) MrNMoore(7) —
(W B Stone) *prom to 9th: t.o whn p.u bef 11th* **125/1**
P **Bold 'N' Brave**[323] 7-11-4 .... JohnMcNamara —
(C C Bealby) *prom: wknd after 8th: t.o whn p.u bef 14th* **33/1**
0U6 **P** **Drive On Driver (IRE)**[7] 3888 9-10-4 82.......... MissLBrooke(7) —
(Lady Susan Brooke) *hld up: a in rr: t.o whn p.u bef 3 out* **100/1**
UFP5 **P** **Jonanaud**[11] 3801 7-10-11 102.......... (b) MrJAJenkins(7) —
(H J Manners) *hld up: hdwy after 9th: wknd 11th: t.o whn p.u bef 3 out* **33/1**
P-62 **P** **Classic Rock**[20] 3653 7-11-4 .... WarrenMarston —
(J W Unett) *hld up: hdwy 8th: rdn and wknd 13th: t.o whn p.u bef 3 out* **50/1**
0-5P **P** **Drat**[79] 2610 7-11-4 88.......... RJGreene —
(R Mathew) *chsd ldrs: hit 3rd: lost pl 7th: bhd fr 9th: hit next: t.o whn p.u bef 11th* **125/1**
3230 **P** **Admiral Peary (IRE)**[9] 3845 10-11-4 112.......... AndrewTinkler —
(C R Egerton) *chsd ldrs: rdn 14th: wknd after 3 out: t.o whn p.u bef last* **7/1**

6m 47.1s (0.50) **Going Correction** +0.40s/f (Soft) 14 Ran SP% **116.9**
Speed ratings: **105,102,97,97,97** —,—,—,—,— —,—,—,— CSF £34.26 TOTE £3.30: £1.50, £2.50, £1.80; EX 47.50.
Owner D J & S A Goodman **Bred** Roy W Tector **Trained** Naunton, Gloucs
■ Stewards' Enquiry : Mr J Newbold four-day ban: used whip with excessive frequency and without allowing sufficient time to respond (Mar 2-5)

FOCUS
A modest beginners' chase, run at a sound pace, and the winner should be rated value for nearly double the winning margin.

NOTEBOOK
Ardaghey(IRE) ran out a facile winner to belatedly open his account as a chaser at the fifth time of asking. He has been much-improved since stepping up in trip, could hardly have won this any easier, and he appeared to relish the testing surface. Now that his confidence will be sky high, further improvement cannot be ruled out, and he deserves another crack at graded company before the season's end. *(tchd 5-2)*
Great As Gold(IRE), while flattered by his proximity to the winner, turned in his best effort to date as a chaser and was well clear of the rest at the finish. He enjoyed this softer ground and will surely be of more interest off his current mark when switched to a handicap over fences. *(op 12-1)*
Supreme Toss(IRE), a decent second on his return from a long absence at Uttoxeter last time, was none too fluent and found the stiff finish all too much on this return to three miles. He is capable of better than this, but has a deal to prove now all the same. *(op 5-2 after early 3-1 and 11-4 in places)*
Exceptionnel(FR), a former winning pointer having his first outing over fences under Rules, was not totally disgraced and is best kept to shorter trips on this evidence. He is one to consider when entering the handicap arena. *(tchd 20-1)*
Woodlands Genpower(IRE), tried in first-time cheekpieces, managed to improve a touch on his recent Chepstow effort yet still disappointed and has not progressed as looked likely from his chase debut back in December. *(op 4-1)*
Admiral Peary(IRE) *(op 11-2)*

4017 NAPS 1ST FOR INDEPENDENT BOOKMAKERS MARES' ONLY INTERMEDIATE OPEN NATIONAL HUNT FLAT RACE 2m
4:50 (4:51) (Class 5) 4-6-Y-0 **£2,602** (£764; £382; £190)

Form — RPR
1 **Amaretto Rose** 5-11-2 .... MarcusFoley 98+
(N J Henderson) *trckd ldrs: racd keenly: led over 6f out: hdd over 4f out: led over 2f out: styd on wl* **9/2**[2]
2 *5* **Les Baux Belle (IRE)** 6-11-2 .... WarrenMarston 90
(D J Wintle) *hld up: hdwy 10f out: rdn to chse wnr over 1f out: no ex ins fnl f* **6/1**[3]
44 **3** *3* **Maryscross (IRE)**[37] 3373 6-10-13 .... LeeVickers(3) 87
(O Brennan) *hld up: hdwy 6f out: rdn over 2f out: styd on* **14/1**
4 *½* **Ring Back (IRE)** 5-10-11 .... MarkNicolls(5) 87
(B I Case) *led 3f: chsd ldrs: led over 4f out: rdn and hdd over 2f out: wknd fnl f* **25/1**
5 *5* **Peppery Pamela** 5-10-9 .... MrTJO'Brien(7) 82
(V R A Dartnall) *hld up: hdwy 1/2-way: wknd over 1f out* **9/1**
6 *1½* **The Shirley Hunt** 6-11-2 .... RichardJohnson 80
(R T Phillips) *hld up: hdwy 1/2-way: wknd 2f out* **9/2**[2]
4 **7** *7* **Nefertari**[31] 3468 4-10-7 .... TomDoyle 66+
(P R Webber) *pulled hrd and prom: rdn over 3f out: wknd 2f out* **8/1**
8 *6* **Silent City** 6-10-11 .... LeeStephens(5) 67
(P D Williams) *prom: lost pl 10f out: hdwy 4f out: hung rt and wknd over 2f out* **66/1**
2 **9** *dist* **Riodan (IRE)**[26] 3556 4-10-2 .... DougieCostello(5) —
(J J Quinn) *pulled hrd and prom: lost pl over 6f out: sn wknd* **4/1**[1]
6 **10** *½* **Is There More**[26] 3556 5-10-11 .... TJDreaper(5) —
(J M Jefferson) *a in rr* **25/1**
0 **11** *hd* **Wiljen (IRE)**[32] 3448 6-11-2 .... AnthonyRoss —
(B S Rothwell) *hld up inn tch: rdn over 5f out: sn wknd* **100/1**
0 **12** *nk* **Shoestodiefor**[73] 2727 6-11-2 .... TomSiddall —
(S A Brookshaw) *chsd ldr: led 13f out: hdd over 6f out: wknd over 4f out* **50/1**
0 **13** *4* **Back In Vogue**[20] 3657 5-11-2 .... AndrewTinkler —
(J G Portman) *hld up in tch: rdn over 5f out: sn wknd* **28/1**
14 *28* **The Old Spinner** 4-10-7 .... RJGreene —
(P R Chamings) *hld up: effrt 1/2-way: sn wknd* **66/1**
P **Rosehill Lady** 6-10-13 .... AnthonyCoyle(3) —
(M J Polglase) *prom 6f: t.o whn p.u over 3f out* **50/1**
00 **P** **Winsome Wendy (IRE)**[73] 2720 6-10-11 ....(t) TomGreenway(5) —
(P A Pritchard) *prom 5f: t.o whn p.u bef over 5f out* **100/1**

4m 14.6s (2.70) **Going Correction** +0.675s/f (Soft)
WFA 4 from 5yo 9lb 5 from 6yo 6lb 16 Ran SP% **118.5**
Speed ratings: **108,105,104,103,101 100,97,94,**—,— —,—,—,—,— — CSF £28.55 TOTE £6.10: £2.00, £1.90, £4.30; EX 30.70 Place 6 £42.84, Place 5 £8.59.
Owner Weatherbys Racing Club **Bred** C F C Jackson **Trained** Upper Lambourn, Berks

FOCUS
A fair mares' bumper, run at a decent pace, and the field finished strung out behind the ready winner. The third and seventh set the level for the form.

NOTEBOOK
Amaretto Rose ◆, who hails from a stable that does so well in this sphere, got her career off to a perfect start with a convincing success. The deep surface was much to her liking, she clearly stays well, and can win again in this division before going hurdling. *(op 5-1)*
Les Baux Belle(IRE), whose half-sister Royal Niece finished third for this yard in the corresponding event in 2004 on her debut, was doing her best work at the finish and posted a pleasing debut effort. She looks a fair prospect for novice hurdling and she ought to be seen in a better light when faced with a longer trip in due course. *(op 11-2 tchd 5-1)*
Maryscross(IRE) turned in her best effort to date and proved she acts on this sort of testing ground. She now looks ready to tackle hurdles and is another who should appreciate further in due course. *(op 12-1)*
Ring Back(IRE), who cost 38,000 euros as a four-year-old and is related to a bumper/hurldes winner, showed up well from the front until tiring before two out. She may be better off with slightly more patient tactics next time and does have a future. *(op 20-1)*
The Shirley Hunt, half-sister to her yard's promising novice hurdler The Mick Weston, looked much in need of the experience and was well beaten. Better can be expected next time, however.
Riodan(IRE) ultimately paid for refusing to settle through the early parts and failed by some way to run up to the level of her recent Sedgefield debut. *(op 7-2)*
T/Plt: £65.50 to a £1 stake. Pool: £69,865.80. 777.70 winning tickets. T/Qpdt: £8.00 to a £1 stake. Pool: £4,245.00. 389.10 winning tickets. CR

3624 NAVAN (L-H)
Sunday, February 19
OFFICIAL GOING: Soft to heavy (heavy in back straight)

4018a LADBROKES.COM FLYINGBOLT NOVICE CHASE (GRADE 2) 2m
2:10 (2:10) 5-Y-0+ **£23,517** (£6,586; £3,137)

RPR
1 **Mansony (FR)**[21] 3639 7-11-4 .... CO'Dwyer 143+
(A L T Moore, Ire) *mde all: clr tl mstke 5 out: edgd clr again fr 2 out: comf* **2/1**[2]
2 *25* **Zum See (IRE)**[21] 3640 7-11-4 125.......... PCarberry 129
(Noel Meade, Ire) *hld up in tch: impr into 2nd bef 4 out: rdn and no imp bef 2 out: no ex whn mstke last* **15/8**[1]
3 *dist* **Logical Approach (IRE)**[456] 2353 9-11-4 .... DNRussell —
(Edward U Hales, Ire) *mod 2nd: clsr 3rd 5 out: no ex after mstke 4 out: p.u appr 3 out: later returned to complete crse and fin completely t.o* **25/1**
F **Court Leader (IRE)**[31] 3474 8-11-2 116.......... BJGeraghty —
(Thomas Mullins, Ire) *fell 1st* **6/1**
F **Monjoyau (FR)**[182] 1284 6-11-4 .... APMcCoy —
(E J O'Grady, Ire) *trckd ldrs: 3rd 4 out: sn rdn: no imp whn fell next* **7/2**[3]
U **Greenhall Rambler (IRE)**[15] 3745 7-10-13 106.......... APLane —
(P A Fahy, Ire) *hld up in tch: 4th whn mstke and uns rdr 7th* **25/1**

4m 20.0s 6 Ran SP% **112.3**
CSF £6.50 TOTE £3.00: £1.30, £1.90; DF 5.40.
Owner Michael Mulholland **Bred** M Hubert Bruckmann **Trained** Naas, Co Kildare

NOTEBOOK
Mansony(FR) put some ordinary efforts behind him with the return to front-running tactics. He was *not foot-perfect though, and the idea that he might go for the Arkle is an ambitious oneOfficial explanation: trainer said, regarding the improved form shown, gelding was going to be dropped in just behind the leaders last time but a strong gallop meant it ended up going a shade too quickly early on, adding that a bad mistake at fourth fence also took its toll that day (op 2/1 tchd 15/8)*
Zum See(IRE) is really only a handicapper with just one success, off 115, behind him. He just played second fiddle from four out. *(op 7/4 tchd 2/1)*
Monjoyau(FR) needs better ground to be competitive. *(op 100/30)*

4019a MCCABE BUILDERS LTD BOYNE HURDLE (GRADE 3) 2m 7f
2:40 (2:40) 5-Y-0+ **£22,448** (£6,586; £3,137; £1,068)

RPR
1 **Golden Cross (IRE)**[21] 3641 7-11-12 161..........(t) JMurtagh 149+
(M Halford, Ire) *mod 2nd: tk clsr order 1/2-way: rdn after 3 out: chal next: styd on wl after last to ld cl home* **8/15**[1]
2 *1½* **Florida Coast (IRE)**[29] 3513 11-11-5 128.......... DNRussell 137
(James Bowe, Ire) *attempted to make all: clr early: strly pressed 2 out: rdn after last: hdd cl home* **11/4**[2]
3 *11* **Holy Orders (IRE)**[24] 3585 9-11-12 133..........(b) DJCondon 133
(W P Mullins, Ire) *settled 3rd: 4th 5 out: rdn after 4 out: mod 3rd after 2 out: kpt on same pce* **8/1**[3]
4 *13* **Keepatem (IRE)**[35] 3413 10-11-8 128.......... CO'Dwyer 122+
(M F Morris, Ire) *hld up in 4th: drvn along briefly after 4th: prog into 3rd 5 out: rdn and no imp after 2 out: no ex fr 2 out* **16/1**
5 *25* **Im A Witness (IRE)**[10] 3835 6-11-2 ....(t) APLane 85
(David Martin Kelly, Ire) *a in rr: in tch appr 4 out: sn rdn and wknd* **150/1**

6m 4.80s 6 Ran SP% **109.6**
CSF £2.37 TOTE £1.50: £1.10, £1.90; DF 2.00.
Owner P Johnson **Bred** Mrs A Riddell Martin **Trained** the Curragh, Co Kildare

NOTEBOOK

Golden Cross(IRE) drifted alarmingly in the betting beforehand and was matched at 19-1 in running, but he got up in the last 30 yards or so to register his first success over flights since his 66-1 shock in a Leopardstown Grade One December 2003. He looked in trouble turning for home but stayed on dourly to lead near the finish. There was no brilliance in this performance, just a hard fought win over an inferior opponent, but he did not display any stamina deficiencies, and a pair of cheekpieces might help him at Cheltenham in the World Hurdle. He will only go there if there is give in the ground, though. *(op 1/3 tchd 4/7)*

Florida Coast(IRE), an encouraging runner-up to stablemate Solerina at Naas last time, put in a top performance. He tried to do it from the front and travelled best throughout, only giving best under pressure close home. At this stage of his career he might not be the most reliable yardstick, but he was well supported and ran above his mark. *(op 9/2)*

Holy Orders(IRE) was struggling a long way from home and this was not a going day for him.

Keepatem(IRE) made little impact on only his second outing since Cheltenham last year. *(op 14/1)*

4022a LADBROKES.COM TEN UP NOVICE CHASE (GRADE 2) 3m

4:10 (4:11) 5-Y-0+ **£23,795** (£6,981; £3,326; £1,133)

RPR

1 **Church Island (IRE)**[29] [3514] 7-11-8 .... AndrewJMcNamara 141+
(Michael Hourigan, Ire) *settled 2nd: j.w: led fr 5 out: clr after 4 out: styd on wl: nt extended* **7/2**[1]

2 *6* **American Jennie (IRE)**[31] [3474] 8-11-0 109........ DNRussell 125
(Michael Cullen, Ire) *trckd ldrs: 5th 1/2-way: prog into mod 3rd bef 3 out: 2nd 2 out: kpt on wout threatening wnr* **20/1**

3 *25* **Homer Wells (IRE)**[29] [3514] 8-11-5 127........ DJCasey 109
(W P Mullins, Ire) *settled 3rd: rdn after 5 out: mod 2nd bef 3 out: no ex after 2 out* **5/1**[3]

4 *12* **Macs Flamingo (IRE)**[24] [3588] 6-11-5 124........ APLane 93
(P A Fahy, Ire) *trckd ldrs: 4th 1/2-way: no ex after 4 out* **16/1**

5 *8* **Mr Babbage (IRE)**[22] [3630] 8-11-5 .... DJCondon 85
(W P Mullins, Ire) *hld up: slow 4th: 6th and rdn bef 5 out: no ex after next* **7/2**[1]

6 *12* **Coljon (IRE)**[24] [3587] 8-11-5 128........(p) JLCullen 73
(Paul Nolan, Ire) *led: bad mstke 7 out: slt mstke next: mstke and hdd 5 out: sn rdn: wknd 3 out: eased fr next* **4/1**[2]

7 *dist* **Coast To Coast (IRE)**[53] [3079] 7-11-5 ....(t) PWFlood —
(E J O'Grady, Ire) *hld up: 5th 5 out: wknd fr next: virtually p.u fr last* **12/1**

P **Augherskea (IRE)**[10] [3833] 7-11-5 .... PCarberry —
(Noel Meade, Ire) *hld up: racd wd: rdn and wknd 5 out: t.o whn p.u bef 4 out* **4/1**[2]

6m 38.1s 8 Ran SP% **119.4**
CSF £64.02 TOTE £5.00: £1.80, £3.10, £2.00; DF 99.00.
Owner B J Craig **Bred** J S Bolger **Trained** Patrickswell, Co Limerick

NOTEBOOK

Church Island(IRE) was entitled to win this and was not overburdened to do so after leading five out. He will take his chance in the Royal & SunAlliance Chase, and his successful experience over the Cheltenham fences will stand him in good stead. Better ground than this would also be in his favour. *(op 3/1)*

American Jennie(IRE) has been running consistently in mares' chases and won a valuable race at Cork in December but this was a marked improvement in her form, possibly brought about by the extra distance. *(op 16/1)*

Homer Wells(IRE) is quite devoid of anything in the way of a turn of foot. *(op 9/2)*

Macs Flamingo(IRE) was totally outclassed. *(op 14/1)*

Mr Babbage(IRE) was successful over the course and distance last time when gaining his first success over fences, but he had his limitations rather cruelly exposed here.

Coljon(IRE) made mistakes but he is really just a handicapper and somewhat flattered by his rating. *(op 7/2)*

4023 - 4024a (Foreign Racing) - See Raceform Interactive

3793 CARLISLE (R-H)

Monday, February 20

4025 Meeting Abandoned - Waterlogged

3876 EXETER (R-H)

Tuesday, February 21

OFFICIAL GOING: Soft

Wind: Fresh, against Weather: Wintry showers Flight past stands omitted

4032 "BOSUNS" MEMORIAL "NATIONAL HUNT" MAIDEN HURDLE (DIV I) (7 hdls 1 omitted) 2m 1f

2:00 (2:00) (Class 4) 4-Y-0+ **£2,740** (£798; £399)

Form RPR

110/ 1 **Flying Falcon**[689] [4649] 7-11-4 .... SamThomas 116+
(Miss Venetia Williams) *led: nt fluent 1st: sn hdd: a.p: led appr 3 out: rdn out* **8/1**

2 *1 1/4* **Nobody Tells Me (FR)** 5-11-4 .... TomScudamore 115
(M C Pipe) *hld up: hdwy 2nd: rdn and ev ch 2 out: nt qckn flat* **20/1**

3 *13* **Paulo Dancer (FR)**[252] 5-11-4 .... ChristianWilliams 103+
(P F Nicholls) *hld up: hdwy and hmpd 2nd: rdn appr 3 out: wknd 2 out* **7/2**[3]

6 4 *7* **Inishturk (IRE)**[14] [3789] 7-11-4 .... RobertThornton 95
(A King) *hld up: hdwy 2nd: lost pl 3rd: rallied after 4th: rdn appr 3 out: wknd 2 out* **40/1**

1- 5 *2* **Young Dude (IRE)**[317] [4801] 7-11-4 .... APMcCoy 95+
(Jonjo O'Neill) *lft in ld 2nd: rdn and hdd appr 3 out: wknd 2 out* **13/2**

500 6 *17* **Mister Chatterbox (IRE)**[3] [3996] 5-11-4 .... PJBrennan 79+
(P J Hobbs) *prom tl rdn and wknd appr 3 out* **25/1**

45 7 *7* **Petitjean**[7] [3906] 6-11-4 .... RichardJohnson 69
(P J Hobbs) *a bhd* **10/3**[2]

4-04 8 *22* **Montrolin**[24] [3611] 6-11-4 .... RJGreene 47
(S C Burrough) *prom: rdn appr 2nd: wkng whn blnd 3 out: no ch whn blnd last: t.o* **66/1**

300 9 *9* **Whatcanisay**[68] [2849] 7-10-13 .... ChrisHonour[(5)] 38
(J D Frost) *a bhd: lost tch fr 3rd: t.o* **100/1**

P 10 *23* **The Fast Frog (FR)**[19] [3685] 5-10-11 .... MrJNewbold[(7)] —
(Lady Connell) *a bhd: t.o fr 3rd* **100/1**

1- 11 *14* **Hop Fair**[667] [7] 7-10-11 .... AntonyEvans —
(J L Spearing) *a bhd: t.o fr 4th* **33/1**

21 U **Milan Deux Mille (FR)**[81] [2611] 4-10-2 .... AndrewGlassonbury[(7)] —
(M C Pipe) *led after 1st tl j. bdly lft and uns rdr 2nd* **2/1**[1]

000 P **Shinjiru (USA)**[56] [3024] 6-11-4 .... JasonMaguire —
(P A Blockley) *bhd fr 3rd: nt fluent 4th: t.o whn p.u bef 3 out* **100/1**

4m 26.9s (17.70) **Going Correction** +1.00s/f (Soft)
WFA 4 from 5yo+ 9lb 13 Ran SP% **121.5**
Speed ratings: **98,97,91,88,87 79,75,65,61,50 43,—,—** CSF £142.98 TOTE £8.40: £2.50, £4.00, £1.80; EX 115.10.
Owner Miss V M Williams **Bred** Dandy's Farm **Trained** Kings Caple, H'fords

FOCUS

A modest maiden event, run at an average gallop, which saw the first two come clear. It was the stronger of the two divisions and is best rated around the third and fourth.

NOTEBOOK

Flying Falcon, a dual bumper winner in 2004 returning from a 689-day layoff, made a winning return to action with a game success under a positive ride. His jumping improved the further he went, he acted well on the deep surface, did enough to suggest he should get a bit further in due course. While he clearly retains his ability - and remains open to further improvement - this may not have taken a great deal of winning and backers should be wary of the bounce factor ahead of his next assignment. *(op 10-1)*

Nobody Tells Me(FR), who cost 52,000 euros and is a half-brother to two winning jumpers in France, was seemingly unfancied for this debut, yet that did not stop him from running a very pleasing race in defeat, and he was clear of the rest at the finish. He will not be such a big price next time and looks sure to win races for his powerful stable. *(op 25-1)*

Paulo Dancer(FR), making his British debut, proved easy to back and never seriously threatened. A stiffer test in the future could see him in a better light and he appears very much a future chasing type. *(op 5-2 tchd 5-1)*

Inishturk(IRE) did not appear suited by the drop back to this trip, but still improved a touch on his recent hurdling debut and will be of more interest when qualifying for handicaps after his next assignment. *(op 33-1)*

Young Dude(IRE), a fast-ground bumper winner on his debut in April 2005, showed up well enough from the front until appearing to blow-up at the top of the straight. He is entitled to improve for the experience and should be capable of leaving this form behind in due course. *(op 9-2 tchd 7-1)*

Petitjean, popular in the betting ring, ran well below expectations and never figured on this drop back in trip. He has a deal to prove now, but should do better when reverting to further in due course. *(op 7-2)*

Milan Deux Mille(FR), strongly backed on course, gave his young rider little chance of staying aboard when jinking badly to his left approaching the second flight. He is not straightforward, but is clearly thought capable of winning a race or two in this division. *(op 4-1 tchd 9-2)*

4033 "BOSUNS" MEMORIAL "NATIONAL HUNT" MAIDEN HURDLE (DIV II) (7 hdls 1 omitted) 2m 1f

2:30 (2:30) (Class 4) 4-Y-0+ **£2,740** (£798; £399)

Form RPR

6234 1 **Mahogany Blaze (FR)**[52] [3132] 4-10-9 .... CarlLlewellyn 100+
(N A Twiston-Davies) *hld up: hdwy 2nd: led appr last: r.o wl* **5/2**[2]

233 2 *9* **Fast Forward (NZ)**[21] [3664] 6-11-4 .... SamThomas 101+
(Miss Venetia Williams) *a.p: led appr 3 out: rdn and hdd appr last: one pce* **5/6**[1]

4/P0 3 *9* **Idbury (IRE)**[9] [3881] 8-11-4 .... OllieMcPhail 89
(V J Hughes) *a.p: ev ch appr 3 out: wknd appr 2 out* **66/1**

P 4 *15* **Gimmeabreak (IRE)**[69] [2826] 6-11-4 .... MarcusFoley 74
(Miss E C Lavelle) *hld up and bhd: styd on fr 2 out: n.d* **20/1**

6-00 5 *shd* **Harrival**[48] [3238] 6-10-11 .... MrGTumelty[(7)] 74
(Miss M Bragg) *hld up in tch: rdn and wknd appr 3 out* **100/1**

2/P0 6 *6* **How Is The Lord (IRE)**[9] [3881] 10-11-4 .... PhilipHide 73+
(C J Down) *w ldr: led and hit 2nd: hdd appr 3 out: sn wknd: 4th and no ch whn mstke last* **66/1**

300 7 *3 1/2* **Willy The Slip**[35] [3429] 4-10-9 ....(t) AndrewThornton 55
(R H Alner) *a bhd* **25/1**

0 8 *1 1/2* **Red Echo (FR)**[24] [3611] 5-11-4 .... TomScudamore 63
(M C Pipe) *hld up in tch: hit 2nd: rdn after 3rd: wknd appr 3 out* **33/1**

-1P0 9 *5* **Suprendre Espere**[13] [3793] 6-11-4 .... JosephByrne 58
(Jennie Candlish) *led to 2nd: sn wknd* **50/1**

4P66 10 *1 1/2* **Templer (IRE)**[13] [3800] 5-11-4 .... RichardJohnson 56
(P J Hobbs) *hld up and bhd: short-lived effrt after 4th* **25/1**

1-54 11 *14* **Fibre Optics (IRE)**[11] [3846] 6-11-4 .... APMcCoy 42
(Jonjo O'Neill) *bhd fr 3rd* **8/1**[3]

4m 26.7s (17.50) **Going Correction** +1.00s/f (Soft)
WFA 4 from 5yo+ 9lb 11 Ran SP% **115.6**
Speed ratings: **98,93,89,82,82 79,77,77,74,74 67** CSF £4.65 TOTE £2.60: £1.60, £1.10, £9.70; EX 7.20.
Owner Mrs Lorna Berryman **Bred** Le Thenney S A **Trained** Naunton, Gloucs

FOCUS

This second division of the maiden was the weaker of the two, but it was run in a marginally quicker time, and the form looks sound with the two market leaders duly fighting out the finish and the fifth and sixth close to their marks.

NOTEBOOK

Mahogany Blaze(FR) got off the mark over timber at the third time of asking and ultimately came home to win as he pleased. He was suited by the stiff test over this trip and the soft ground, so could well go on from this and defy a penalty now his confidence will have been significantly boosted. However, he will have to improve plenty again in order to justify his entry in the Fred Winter at the Cheltenham Festival. *(op 2-1 tchd 3-1)*

Fast Forward(NZ), very well backed, had every chance yet could not go with the winner on the run-in and was made to look one paced. The drop back in trip did not play to his strengths, and he is starting to look exposed now, but still finished a clear-second best and certainly has a race of this nature within his compass this term. *(op 11-8)*

Idbury(IRE) turned in by far his best effort to date and was only put in his place from the penultimate flight. The return to a stiffer test in the future should prove to his advantage and he looks well worth switching to a handicap now. *(op 50-1)*

Gimmeabreak(IRE), pulled up on his debut at Newbury in December, was doing his best work at the finish and shaped better than the bare form suggests. On breeding, he ought to be seen in a much better light when faced with a longer trip in the future. *(tchd 16-1)*

Fibre Optics(IRE), very easy to back, turned in a shocking effort and never figured on this drop back in trip. He looked a fair recruit when landing a bumper on debut in 2005, is now eligible for handicaps, and is capable of plenty better than he showed this time. *(op 5-1)*

4034 WEATHERBYS BANK MARES' ONLY H'CAP HURDLE (9 hdls 1 omitted) 2m 3f

3:00 (3:00) (Class 3) (0-125,122) 4-Y-0+

£7,515 (£2,220; £1,110; £555; £277; £139)

Form RPR

4210 1 **Bally Bolshoi (IRE)**[26] [3577] 6-10-3 99........ RichardJohnson 106
(Mrs S D Williams) *hld up: stdy hdwy 5th: rdn to ld appr last: drvn out* **11/2**

1511 **2** 1 ¾ **De Blanc (IRE)**[8] 3900 6-11-10 **120** SamThomas 125
(Miss Venetia Williams) *hld up in tch: hdwy 4th: led appr 3 out: rdn and hdd appr last: nt qckn flat* **6/4**[1]

6-42 **3** 10 **Precious Mystery (IRE)**[22] 3648 6-10-13 **109** (v) RobertThornton 106+
(A King) *hld up: hdwy 4th: ev ch appr 3 out: wkng whn mstke 2 out* **4/1**[2]

23-0 **4** 30 **Longstone Lady (IRE)**[115] 1921 9-9-11 **98** oh6 ow2 ChrisHonour(5) 63
(J D Frost) *a bhd* **33/1**

U665 **5** 5 **Sword Lady**[35] 3439 8-11-5 **115** (b) PJBrennan 75
(Mrs S D Williams) *led: rdn and hdd appr 3 out: sn wknd* **15/2**

-44F **6** 21 **Darjeeling (IRE)**[96] 2297 7-10-12 **108** ChristianWilliams 47
(P F Nicholls) *hld up in tch: wknd 5th: t.o* **5/1**[3]

P **P** **Nostra (FR)**[31] 3495 5-11-12 **122** APMcCoy —
(M C Pipe) *chsd ldr tl rdn and wknd after 6th: p.u bef 3 out* **20/1**

4m 55.4s (14.50) **Going Correction** +1.00s/f (Soft) 7 Ran SP% 111.5
Speed ratings: **109,108,104,91,89 80,**— CSF £13.96 TOTE £8.20: £2.60, £1.60; EX 18.20.
Owner Mrs Rowena Cotton **Bred** Stephen Lanigan-O'Keeffe **Trained** Mariansleigh, Devon

FOCUS
A fair mares' handicap, run at a solid gallop, and the form appears solid with the placed horses running to their marks.

NOTEBOOK
Bally Bolshoi(IRE) resumed winning ways under a typically strong ride from Johnson and found the drop back in trip much to her liking. She is a progressive mare, loves soft ground, and should be able to defy another weight rise in this division. *(op 7-1 tchd 15-2)*

De Blanc(IRE), reverting to hurdles having been successful in her last two outings over fences, looked the most likely winner two out, but her stride shortened thereafter, and she proved powerless to resist the winner's late challenge. This must rate another solid effort, she is a very versatile mare and is probably happier given a stiffer test, so should be placed to go one better again before too long. *(op 13-8 tchd 15-8)*

Precious Mystery(IRE) was beaten prior to an error at the penultimate flight and failed to improve for the drop back in trip. She is more effective on a less-taxing surface. *(tchd 9-2)*

Sword Lady had her chance from the front, but proved a sitting duck nearing three out, and eventually paid for her early exertions. *(op 9-1 tchd 10-1 and 7-1)*

Darjeeling(IRE), who fell on her chasing bow when last seen 96 days previously, was beaten a long way from home and is out of sorts at present. *(tchd 11-2)*

4035 ELIZABETH FINN CARE NOVICES' CHASE (19 fncs) 3m 1f 110y
3:30 (3:30) (Class 3) 5-Y-0+ **£10,057** (£2,997; £1,517; £777; £406)

Form RPR

F411 **1** **Halcon Genelardais (FR)**[17] 3740 6-11-12 RobertThornton 147+
(A King) *prom: rdn 12th: hmpd 15th: sltly outpcd 4 out: rallied to ld last: all out* **11/8**[1]

-031 **2** ¾ **Basilea Star (IRE)**[52] 3148 9-11-8 (t) TimmyMurphy 142+
(M C Pipe) *hld up: pushed along after 11th: hit 14th: hdwy 15th: rdn appr 4 out: hit 2 out: ev ch last: styd on* **4/1**[2]

212P **3** 2 **Lord Killeshanra (IRE)**[50] 3213 7-11-12 130 JoeTizzard 143+
(C L Tizzard) *a.p: blnd 15th: led after 2 out: hdd last: nt qckn* **12/1**

2312 **4** 16 **Reflected Glory (IRE)**[50] 3213 7-11-12 134 ChristianWilliams 129+
(P F Nicholls) *prom: led and hit 12th: hdd 14th: lft in ld 15th: mstke 2 out: sn hdd & wknd* **5/1**[3]

P **5** dist **Mighty Moose (IRE)**[95] 2311 6-11-2 AndrewThornton —
(Nick Williams) *a bhd: mstke 6th: sn lost tch: t.o* **200/1**

-13P **P** **Red Georgie (IRE)**[80] 2643 8-11-8 131 CarlLlewellyn —
(N A Twiston-Davies) *led to 3rd: hit 5th: wknd 10th: p.u after 11th* **25/1**

/F22 **U** **Tighten Your Belt (IRE)**[29] 3541 9-11-2 SamThomas —
(Miss Venetia Williams) *w ldr: led 3rd to 12th: led 14th tl blnd and uns rdr 15th* **4/1**[2]

6m 48.0s (20.00) **Going Correction** +1.00s/f (Soft) 7 Ran SP% 110.8
Speed ratings: **109,108,108,103,**— —,— CSF £7.03 TOTE £2.40: £1.70, £2.70; EX 7.40.
Owner Ian Payne & Kim Franklin **Bred** G Descours & Mlle Constance Descours **Trained** Barbury Castle, Wilts

FOCUS
A decent novice event for the class, run at a sound pace, it saw four horses in with every chance jumping two out. The form looks solid with the first two to their marks.

NOTEBOOK
Halcon Genelardais(FR) landed the hat-trick over fences with a very hard-fought success. He looked held approaching the turn for home, but his stamina came into play, and he gamely got on top of his rivals on the run-in. This is his ground, and he clearly stays all day long, so it will be interesting to see where connections pitch him in next in an attempt to maintain his unbeaten record as a chaser. *(op 15-8 tchd 2-1 in a place)*

Basilea Star(IRE), off the mark on his chasing bow at Warwick 52 days previously, ran in snatches throughout and it was amazing that he was ultimately only denied in the final 50 yards. It would come as no surprise to see some headgear applied after this, and he clearly needs a proper stamina test to be seen at his best in this sphere, so the National Hunt Chase at Cheltenham could be his sort of race. *(op 11-4 tchd 5-2)*

Lord Killeshanra(IRE), pulled up over course and distance last time, showed his true colours with a solid effort in defeat. He just failed to see out the race as well as the front pair, but there was a lot to like about the manner in which he travelled until two out, and he is a very useful performer on his day. He appeals as a future National horse at this stage. *(op 14-1 tchd 16-1)*

Reflected Glory(IRE) would have been closer at the finish but for a bad error two from home. He has his limitations, but stays very well, and this was the first time he had finished out of the places in nine career outings. *(op 6-1 tchd 7-1)*

Tighten Your Belt(IRE) looked to be going as well as anything prior to unshipping Thomas and has to rate slightly unfortunate. *(op 7-2 tchd 10-3)*

Red Georgie(IRE) *Official explanation: jockey said gelding bled from the nose (op 7-2 tchd 10-3)*

4036 MAX DUNFORD NOVICES' H'CAP HURDLE (10 hdls 1 omitted) 2m 6f 110y
4:00 (4:00) (Class 3) (0-125,119) 4-Y-0+ **£7,543** (£2,247; £1,137; £583; £305)

Form RPR

-024 **1** **Bumper (FR)**[11] 3842 5-11-1 **108** APMcCoy 113
(M C Pipe) *hld up: hdwy 5th: rdn and outpcd 3 out: rallied to ld last: drvn out* **4/1**[2]

2322 **2** 2 **Seeador**[32] 3478 7-10-0 **100** WayneKavanagh(7) 103
(J W Mullins) *a.p: led 3 out: sn rdn and hung rt: hdd last: nt qckn* **11/2**[3]

4221 **3** 5 **The Luder (IRE)**[31] 3508 5-11-7 **119** LiamHeard(5) 122+
(P F Nicholls) *hld up in tch: rdn and outpcd appr 3 out: rallied appr last: styng on one pce whn hung bdly lft cl home* **6/4**[1]

2-13 **4** 5 **Ballyjohnboy Lord (IRE)**[25] 3598 7-11-10 **117** TomScudamore 111+
(M Scudamore) *chsd ldr: led appr 5th to 3 out: wknd last* **6/1**

/4-1 **5** dist **Beyondtherealm**[90] 2428 8-9-12 **96** ChrisHonour(5) —
(J D Frost) *hld up: hdwy 6th: wknd after 7th* **20/1**

2P4- **P** **Joizel (FR)**[369] 3909 9-9-9 **93** oh17 CharliePoste(5) —
(V G Greenway) *hld up: hdwy 5th: wknd 7th: t.o whn p.u bef 3 out* **80/1**

3604 **P** **Absolutelythebest (IRE)**[17] 3729 5-9-12 **94** TomMalone(3) —
(J G M O'Shea) *hld up in tch: wknd 5th: t.o whn p.u bef 3 out* **9/1**

P2FP **P** **Cockatoo Ridge**[8] 3901 9-10-7 **100** NoelFehily —
(N R Mitchell) *led tl appr 5th: sn wknd: mstke 7th: t.o whn p.u bef 3 out* **16/1**

6m 10.1s (30.80) **Going Correction** +1.40s/f (Heav) 8 Ran SP% 111.5
Speed ratings: **102,101,99,97,**— —,—,— CSF £25.03 CT £44.98 TOTE £3.30: £1.10, £2.80, £1.10; EX 30.90.
Owner A J White **Bred** Gaetan Gilles **Trained** Nicholashayne, Devon

FOCUS
A modest novices' handicap, run at an average gallop, and the form looks a little suspect, despite the fact the placed horses were close to their marks.

NOTEBOOK
Bumper(FR), back up in trip for this handicap debut, looked like playing a minor role jumping three from home, but he ultimately stuck to his task and outstayed his rivals to score. While he acted on the ground, he may well be happier on a faster surface, and should have more to offer now he has got his head in front. *(op 10-3 tchd 9-2)*

Seeador, popular in the betting ring, had every chance yet could offer no more when headed by the winner jumping the final flight. He really does deserve to go one better. *(op 6-1 tchd 13-2)*

The Luder(IRE), raised 8lb for winning on his handicap bow at Wincanton last time, was beaten from three out and proved disappointing. He may be ready to tackle three miles now, and his real *future lies back over fences, so he should not be written off on the back of this display. (op 13-8 tchd 7-4 in places)*

Ballyjohnboy Lord(IRE) found just the same pace when it mattered and was eventually well beaten. He should be capable of getting closer again when returning to a longer distance. *(op 9-2)*

4037 CHARLES STANLEY H'CAP CHASE (12 fncs) 2m 1f 110y
4:30 (4:30) (Class 3) (0-125,124) 5-Y-0+
£7,828 (£2,312; £1,156; £578; £288; £145)

Form RPR

U31 **1** **Madison Du Berlais (FR)**[14] 3788 5-11-0 **118** APMcCoy 131+
(M C Pipe) *hld up: hdwy 5th: nt fluent 6th: led appr 4 out: rdn appr last: drvn out* **3/1**[1]

-FU2 **2** 4 **Big Rob (IRE)**[96] 2296 7-11-9 **121** LeightonAspell 133
(B G Powell) *hld up: hdwy 7th: rdn 8th: outpcd 4 out: rallied and wnt 2nd last: no ex flat* **7/2**[2]

F502 **3** 2 **Key Phil (FR)**[41] 3344 8-11-4 **116** WarrenMarston 126
(D J Wintle) *chsd ldr: led after 8th: sn hdd: 3rd and hld whn mstke last* **7/2**[2]

1504 **4** 7 **Roofing Spirit (IRE)**[14] 3788 8-10-10 **113** (b[1]) DarylJacob(5) 118+
(D P Keane) *hld up and bhd: hdwy 5th: ev ch 4 out: sn rdn: wknd after 2 out* **7/1**

3-06 **5** 23 **Lesdream**[9] 3879 9-10-9 **112** ChrisHonour(5) 92
(J D Frost) *bhd fr 8th* **25/1**

20-4 **6** 11 **Jarro (FR)**[67] 2870 10-10-9 **117** CraigThompson(10) 86
(Miss Venetia Williams) *led: clr 2nd: hdd after 8th: sn wknd: blnd 4 out* **8/1**

5-16 **7** 1 ¾ **Just A Touch**[18] 3718 10-10-5 **103** PhilipHide 70
(P Winkworth) *a bhd* **16/1**

/11- **P** **Young Collier**[405] 3323 7-11-12 **124** JasonMaguire —
(J A B Old) *chsd ldr tl j. slowly 5th: sn wknd: t.o whn p.u bef 8th* **11/2**[3]

4m 35.0s (18.10) **Going Correction** +1.25s/f (Heav)
WFA 5 from 7yo+ 6lb 8 Ran SP% 118.2
Speed ratings: **109,107,106,103,93 88,87,**— CSF £15.03 CT £38.34 TOTE £4.10: £1.50, £1.70, £1.70; EX 18.10.
Owner Roger Stanley & Yvonne Reynolds II **Bred** Jean-Marc Lucas **Trained** Nicholashayne, Devon

FOCUS
A fair handicap for the class, run at a sound gallop, and the form looks straightforward and solid, rated through the second.

NOTEBOOK
Madison Du Berlais(FR), raised 6lb for winning at Market Rasen last time, followed up with a game success and was well on top at the finish. He basically saw out the trip better than his rivals *on this deep surface, and is clearly coming good now, so further improvement cannot be ruled* out. *(tchd 11-4 and 7-2)*

Big Rob(IRE), returning to chasing after a 96-day break, had every chance and turned in another sound effort. He is entitled to improve for the outing, may be happiest over back a longer trip in the future, and can build on this.

Key Phil(FR), well backed, found just the same pace from two out and was eventually well held. This must rate another improved effort, however, and he can find a race from this mark in the coming weeks on an easier track. *(op 9-2)*

Roofing Spirit(IRE), tried in first-time blinkers, did not find much when put under pressure and was firmly put in his place from the third last. This was a slightly more encouraging effort, however, and he helps set the level of this form. *(op 8-1 tchd 11-1)*

Young Collier, making his seasonal reappearance, was disappointing and has plenty to prove after this. *(op 5-1 tchd 9-2)*

4038 GG.COM "JUNIOR" STANDARD OPEN NATIONAL HUNT FLAT RACE 1m 5f
5:00 (5:00) (Class 5) 4-Y-0 **£2,261** (£659; £329)

Form RPR

1 **Sherwoods Folly** 4-10-12 RichardJohnson 95+
(H D Daly) *chsd ldrs: led 3f out: rdn clr over 1f out: r.o wl* **3/1**[2]

2 7 **Where's My Baby (IRE)** 4-10-12 NoelFehily 85
(M Pitman) *hld up: rdn 7f out: hdwy 4f out: sltly outpcd over 2f out: styd on ins fnl f: no ch w wnr* **9/1**

3 ¾ **Ganache (IRE)** 4-10-12 MickFitzgerald 85
(P R Chamings) *led: hdd 3f out: sn rdn: r.o one pce fnl f* **4/1**[3]

4 **4** ¾ **Basic Fact (IRE)**[22] 3651 4-10-12 APMcCoy 84
(Jonjo O'Neill) *hld up in tch: rdn over 2f out: chsd wnr over 1f out tl no ex ins fnl f* **7/4**[1]

6 **5** 1 ¼ **Handel With Care (IRE)**[41] 3346 4-10-5 MrTJO'Brien(7) 83
(R A Farrant) *hld up in tch: rdn over 2f out: one pce fnl f* **16/1**

6 2 ½ **William's Way** 4-10-12 JamieMoore 80
(I A Wood) *hld up and plld hrd: hdwy over 3f out: fdd ins fnl f* **16/1**

00 **7** 3 **Marlowe (IRE)**[50] 3216 4-10-12 TimmyMurphy 77
(R J Hodges) *hld up: rdn 6f out: no real prog fnl 3f* **20/1**

004 **8** 11 **Just Poppytee**[18] 3720 4-10-5 TomScudamore 59
(R H Alner) *w ldr tl over 5f out: rdn and wknd over 3f out* **20/1**

9 6 **Intra Vires (IRE)** 4-10-0 JamesDiment(5) 53
(J L Spearing) *hld up and bhd: hdwy on ins over 3f out: wknd over 2f out* **33/1**

0 **10** 27 **Inching West**[43] 3327 4-10-5 PhilipHide 26
(C J Down) *chsd ldrs: lost pl over 5f out: t.o* **50/1**

11 7 **Riolo (IRE)** 4-10-5 ShaneWalsh(7) 26
(K F Clutterbuck) *a bhd: t.o* **33/1**

U Global Party (IRE) 4-10-7 .... LiamHeard(5) —
(Miss C J Williams) *unruly and uns rdr sn after s* **28/1**

3m 26.3s **12** Ran SP% **123.9**

CSF £28.76 TOTE £4.60: £1.80, £3.20, £1.20; EX 28.60 Place 6 £9.66, Place 5 £2.34.

Owner E R Hanbury **Bred** E R Hanbury **Trained** Stanton Lacy, Shropshire

■ Stewards' Enquiry : Timmy Murphy two-day ban: used whip with excessive force and down the shoulder in the forehand position (Mar 4,5)

FOCUS

A modest junior bumper, and while the form is not easy to assess, with the eighth the best guide to the level, the winner did the job in impressive fashion.

NOTEBOOK

Sherwoods Folly, a half-brother to useful Irish hurdler Thaix, got his career off to a pefect start and should be rated value for further than his winning margin. He looked right at home on this deep surface, should improve when upped to around two miles, and rates a nice prospect for connections. *(op 11-4)*

Where's My Baby(IRE), a half-brother to a winning Irish pointer and whose dam was placed over hurdles, stayed on nicely in the final furlong and did enough to suggest he will be much happier when faced with a stiffer test. *(op 8-1 tchd 15-2 and 10-1)*

Ganache(IRE), whose dam was a useful miler on the Flat, failed to see out the race all that well and may have been better off with a more patient ride. He was very well backed on course and is presumably thought capable of better. *(op 8-1 tchd 10-1)*

Basic Fact(IRE) failed to improve on his recent debut at Ludlow and may have found this ground too soft for his liking. He also looks ready to tackle two miles now. *(tchd 2-1)*

Handel With Care(IRE), sixth at Newbury 41 days previously, improved a touch for this softer ground and helps set the level of this form. *(op 14-1)*

T/Jkpt: Not won. T/Plt: £9.30 to a £1 stake. Pool: £54,031.55. 4,198.70 winning tickets. T/Qpdt: £4.40 to a £1 stake. Pool: £4,179.90. 693.30 winning tickets. KH

3779 SEDGEFIELD (L-H)

Tuesday, February 21

OFFICIAL GOING: Heavy

Conditions were very testing. First flight past winning post omitted in all hurdles. Second fence in back st & last fence in home st omitted all chases.

Wind: Blustery, behind

4039 JOHN SMITH'S EXTRA SMOOTH NOVICES' HURDLE (DIV I) (7 hdls 1 omitted) 2m 1f

1:50 (1:50) (Class 4) 4-Y-0+ **£3,253** (£955; £477; £238)

Form RPR

22U3 **1** **Turbo (IRE)**[11] 3848 7-10-13 110 ....(t) MrTGreenall(3) 115+
(M W Easterby) *trckd ldrs: smooth hdwy 2 out: rdn to ld flat: styd on wl* **2/1**[1]

31 **2** *12* **Patxaran (IRE)**[102] 2167 4-10-2 ....(t) PaddyMerrigan(5) 98+
(P C Haslam) *a.p: effrt appr 2 out and sn ev ch: swtchd rt: rdn and hit last: drvn flat and no ex last 100 yds* **5/2**[2]

64U **3** *12* **John Forbes**[10] 3539 4-10-7 .... WilsonRenwick 84+
(B Ellison) *chsd ldrs: pushed along and sltly outpcd 3 out: n.m.r home bnd: sn rdn: hung lft last: lft 3rd nr fin* **16/1**

0-60 **4** *5* **The Right People (IRE)**[39] 3374 6-10-13 .... GaryBerridge(3) 86
(L Lungo) *nt fluent: j.lft and bhd tl hdwy 2 out: styd on appr last: nvr a factor* **28/1**

6 **5** *½* **In Dream's (IRE)**[6] 3925 4-10-0 ....(t) BenOrde-Powlett(7) 80+
(M A Barnes) *trckd ldrs: sddle slipped 2nd and cl up next: rdn along and hit 3 out: sn wknd* **28/1**

6 *14* **Neptune Joly (FR)**[159] 5-11-2 .... KeithMercer 72
(Ferdy Murphy) *racd wd: in tch: pushed along 3 out: rdn to chse ldrs next: wknd appr last* **6/1**

POUS **7** *dist* **Galahad (FR)**[29] 3534 5-11-2 .... BrianHarding —
(B Storey) *a rr: outpcd and bhd fr 1/2-way* **150/1**

2FF **P** **Unexplored (IRE)**[51] 3173 6-11-2 .... GrahamLee 107+
(J Howard Johnson) *led: pushed along appr 2 out: rdn last: hdd & wknd qckly flat: heavily eased: p.u and dismntd bef line* **7/2**[3]

4m 24.6s (18.10) **Going Correction** +1.20s/f (Heav)

WFA 4 from 5yo+ 9lb **8** Ran SP% **111.9**

Speed ratings: **105,99,93,91,91 84,—,—** CSF £7.06 TOTE £2.70: £1.10, £2.10, £3.20; EX 8.90.

Owner Mrs M E Curtis **Bred** Mrs F M Gordon **Trained** Sheriff Hutton, N Yorks

FOCUS

An ordinary event but solid form, with the winner to his best and the placed horses to their marks.

NOTEBOOK

Turbo(IRE) has had his connections and supporters pulling their hair out but finally got off the mark over hurdles. In the end he did it well, pulling nicely clear once shaken up on the flat. *(op 9-4 tchd 5-2)*

Patxaran(IRE), off the track for over three months, was encountering heavy ground for the first time. Attempting to get in a challenge when a little short of room on the approach to the last, having to be switched, she hit the flight and could produce no more on the run-in. *(op 9-4 tchd 2-1)*

John Forbes has had two runs on sand since his latest hurdles start. He was beaten at the top of the hill and each-way backers were fortunate to collect as he was presented with a remote third place close home. *(op 33-1)*

The Right People(IRE), having his third run over hurdles, was kept wide on the less-poached ground. Not producing a good round of hurdling, he was keeping on at the finish and looks a stayer. *(op 33-1)*

In Dream's(IRE) was unable to show his true form as the saddle slipped forward at an early stage. *(op 25-1)*

Neptune Joly(FR), a winning chaser in France, was making his debut for Murphy and running over hurdles for the first time. He probably needs further and better ground. *(op 11-2 tchd 5-1)*

Unexplored(IRE), attempting to make all, only gave best to the winner on the run-in and was still in second when his rider eased him on the run-in, dismounting and losing third near the line. He was found to have broken down. *Official explanation: jockey said gelding pulled up lame (tchd 4-1)*

4040 JOHN SMITH'S EXTRA SMOOTH NOVICES' HURDLE (DIV II) (7 hdls 1 omitted) 2m 1f

2:20 (2:20) (Class 4) 4-Y-0+ **£3,253** (£955; £477; £238)

Form RPR

-112 **1** **According To Pete**[68] 2844 5-11-2 .... GrahamLee 106+
(J M Jefferson) *trckd ldrs: hdwy and hit 3 out: chal and pckd next: rdn and sn led: drvn flat and styd on wl* **4/5**[1]

346 **2** *2½* **Third Empire**[40] 3347 5-11-2 103 .... RichardMcGrath 102+
(C Grant) *cl up: led after 3rd: hit 3 out and sn rdn: hdd after 2 out: drvn and blnd last: rallied flat: no ex last 100 yds* **5/2**[2]

500 **3** *9* **Boris The Spider**[57] 2991 5-11-2 .... WilsonRenwick 92
(M D Hammond) *chsd ldrs: rdn along 3 out: drvn and one pce fr next* **20/1**

4 *6* **Star Zero** 5-11-2 .... AlanDempsey 86
(J Howard Johnson) *hld up and bhd: stdy hdwy appr 3 out: chsd ldrs whn j.lft next: sn rdn and wknd* **20/1**

050 **5** *3½* **Futoo (IRE)**[35] 2947 5-11-2 94 .... RussGarritty 82
(G M Moore) *led tl after 3rd: cl up tl rdn along after 3 out and grad wknd appr next* **7/1**[3]

06SR **6** *3* **Teutonic (IRE)**[34] 3442 5-10-6 .... PeterBuchanan(3) 72
(R F Fisher) *plld hrd: in tch: hdwy to chse ldrs 3 out: sn rdn and wknd* **100/1**

4-60 **7** *24* **Top Tenor (IRE)**[79] 2657 6-10-11 75 .... MrMThompson(5) 55
(V Thompson) *chsd ldrs: hdwy and cl up 4th: sn rdn and wknd 3 out* **100/1**

500P **8** *dist* **Butler Services (IRE)**[13] 3800 6-11-2 .... MrJTMcNamara —
(Jonjo O'Neill) *a rr* **33/1**

4m 26.8s (20.30) **Going Correction** +1.20s/f (Heav)

WFA 4 from 5yo+ 9lb **8** Ran SP% **111.1**

Speed ratings: **100,98,94,91,90 88,77,—** CSF £2.74 TOTE £1.80: £1.20, £1.10, £3.40; EX 3.60.

Owner P Nelson **Bred** Peter Nelson **Trained** Norton, N Yorks

FOCUS

A moderate contest ultimately dominated by the market leaders The form is not easy to assess but makes sense on time.

NOTEBOOK

According To Pete, a dual bumper winner, made a winning start over hurdles. Surviving a peck at the second last, he was soon in front and found plenty on the run-in. While he handed the testing conditions, the return to better ground will suit him much more. *(op 10-11 early 11-10 places)*

Third Empire, collared between the last two, flattened the final flight but attempted to rally on the run-in. He seemed to appreciate the return to easier ground and a similar race should come his way. *(op 7-2)*

Boris The Spider ran his best race so far over hurdles but looks a modest performer, although a step up in trip should suit.

Star Zero, whose dam was a useful staying filly, is a half-brother to winning jumpers Stoney Valley and Advance East. He showed promise on this racecourse debut and the experience should stand him in good stead. *(op 16-1)*

Futoo(IRE), who had a run on sand last month, raced prominently until fading from the top of the hill. *(op 5-1)*

4041 E.B.F./TATTERSALLS (IRELAND) MARES' ONLY NOVICES' CHASE (QUALIFIER) (12 fncs 4 omitted) 2m 5f

2:50 (2:50) (Class 4) 5-Y-0+

£4,384 (£1,295; £647; £324; £161; £81)

Form RPR

U0P6 **1** **Sarahs Quay (IRE)**[25] 3601 7-10-7 78 ....(p) MrMatthewSmith(7) 103+
(K J Burke) *mde all: clr 1/2-way: rdn along 3 out: hit next: drvn and kpt on gamely fr last* **100/1**

U2U2 **2** *7* **Ornella Speed (FR)**[28] 3551 6-10-13 90 ....(t) PatrickMcDonald(7) 103+
(J R Weymes) *hld up in rr: stdy hdwy 1/2-way: trckd ldrs 4 out: rdn to chse wnr and mstke last: drvn flat and kpt on same pce* **7/1**

1P33 **3** *8* **Bellaney Jewel (IRE)**[16] 3760 7-11-0 .... GrahamLee 89+
(J J Quinn) *chsd wnr: rdn along 4 out and plugged on same pce fr next* **4/1**[2]

-430 **4** *3* **Scratch The Dove**[33] 3460 9-10-11 92 .... OwynNelmes(3) 85
(A E Price) *midfield: hdwy and in tch 4 out: sn rdn along and plugged on same pce fr next* **9/1**

0331 **5** *4* **Miss Pross**[15] 3784 6-11-3 101 .... PaulO'Neill(3) 89+
(T D Walford) *hld up in tch: smooth hdwy 4 out: chsd wnr next: rdn after 2 out and wknd last* **5/2**[1]

4F00 **6** *20* **Celtic Blaze (IRE)**[27] 3561 7-11-6 100 ....(t) AnthonyRoss 67
(B S Rothwell) *a rr: bhd fr 4 out* **25/1**

3U03 **U** **More Flair**[13] 3796 9-10-7 .... BenOrde-Powlett(7) —
(J B Walton) *midfield whn blnd and uns rdr 1st* **33/1**

-PF0 **P** **Minster Fair**[10] 3854 8-11-0 91 .... BarryKeniry —
(A C Whillans) *a bhd: t.o fr 4 out: p.u bef last* **33/1**

0-03 **U** **Seeking Shelter (IRE)**[50] 3209 7-11-0 67 .... BrianHarding —
(N G Richards) *towards rr whn blnd and uns rdr 6th* **14/1**

3443 **F** **True Temper (IRE)**[7] 3915 9-10-9 77 .... DeclanMcGann(5) —
(A M Crow) *chsd ldrs: 4th and rdn along whn fell 4 out* **14/1**

5305 **P** **Calomeria**[22] 3655 5-10-7 .... TonyDobbin —
(D McCain) *chsd ldrs tl rdn alonga nd lost pl hyalfway: bhd whn p.u bef 3 out* **9/2**[3]

5m 43.6s (20.20) **Going Correction** +1.10s/f (Heav)

WFA 5 from 6yo+ 7lb **11** Ran SP% **113.3**

Speed ratings: **105,102,99,98,96 89,—,—,—,— —** CSF £675.16 TOTE £80.40: £10.50, £2.10, £2.00; EX 600.50.

Owner K Burke **Bred** Sean McKeown **Trained** Bourton-on-the-Water, Gloucs

■ A shock winner, and a first training success under Rules for former amateur jockey Kahlil Burke.

FOCUS

A moderate event but the form appears reasonable with the placed horses close to their marks.

NOTEBOOK

Sarahs Quay(IRE), who wore cheekpieces rather than the blinkers she had on her two most recent starts, made all and kept galloping for an unlikely victory. A winning pointer on heavy ground in Ireland, she showed a little ability last summer but had been well beaten on her recent efforts. *(op 66-1)*

Ornella Speed(FR), back over fences, ran a decent race but, having given chase to the winner approaching the final fence, she could make no impression up the extended run-in. *(op 11-2 tchd 5-1)*

Bellaney Jewel(IRE), encountering very different ground, raced prominently until fading three from home, keeping going for a well beaten third. *(tchd 7-2, 9-2 in places)*

Scratch The Dove will be suited by a return to handicaps on less-testing ground. *(tchd 8-1 and 10-1)*

Miss Pross, a comfortable winner over an extended two miles on her chasing debut here, looked to be going best as she moved into second place three from home, but she weakened before the last and lost third on the run-in. *She just did not stay, in this ground at any rate. Official explanation: trainer said mare failed to stay 2m5f (op 7-2)*

True Temper(IRE) was still in touch, and might have made the frame, when coming down four from home. *(op 18-1)*

4042 RAMSIDE EVENT CATERING H'CAP CHASE (15 fncs 6 omitted) 3m 3f

3:20 (3:21) (Class 4) (0-110,103) 5-Y-0+

£4,384 (£1,295; £647; £324; £161; £81)

Form RPR

5326 **1** **Matmata De Tendron (FR)**[6] 3923 6-9-10 **78** .... DougieCostello(5) 93
(A Crook) *a.p: rdn along and outpcd 3 out: styd on u.p appr last: drvn flat: kpt on gamely to ld last 75 yds* **7/1**

5021 **2** *3* **Canavan (IRE)**[28] 3553 7-11-1 **97** TJDreaper(5) 110+
(Ferdy Murphy) *trckd ldrs: hdwy 10th: led after 4 out: clr 2 out: drvn flat: wknd and hdd last 75 yds* **11/4**[1]

-P4P **3** *15* **Recent Edition (IRE)**[34] 3444 8-9-11 **77** (b) PaddyAspell(3) 74
(J Wade) *bhd and sn rdn along: hdwy 11th: styd on fr 3 out: nrst fin* **20/1**

F116 **4** *12* **Bang And Blame (IRE)**[27] 3560 10-11-7 **103** MichaelMcAlister(5) 96+
(M W Easterby) *led: pushed along whn blnd 11th: rdn and hdd after 4 out: drvn next and sn wknd* **5/1**[2]

5061 **5** *6* **Red Perk (IRE)**[7] 3917 9-11-4 **95** 7ex (p) LarryMcGrath 74
(R C Guest) *racd wd: chsd ldrs: rdn along 12th and sn outpcd* **11/2**[3]

6P65 **6** *20* **Falchion**[43] 3315 11-10-10 **87** (bt[1]) WilsonRenwick 46
(J R Bewley) *towards rr: hdwy 1/2-way: hit 9th: rdn along 12th and sn no further prog* **14/1**

356P **7** *19* **Lazy But Lively (IRE)**[11] 3845 10-11-3 **94** KeithMercer 34
(R F Fisher) *a rr: wl bhd fr 1/2-way* **9/1**

-P63 **8** *dist* **The River Joker (IRE)**[46] 3276 10-9-13 **81** MarkNicolls(5) —
(John R Upson) *a rr: wl bhd fr 1/2-way* **16/1**

PFPF **P** **Missoudun (FR)**[51] 3170 6-9-7 **77** oh8 (b) MrSFMagee(7) —
(J R Weymes) *chsd ldrs: rdn along 10th: sn lost pl and bhd whn p.u bef 4 out* **150/1**

02F3 **P** **Gimme Shelter (IRE)**[28] 3554 12-10-12 **89** GrahamLee —
(S J Marshall) *prom tl rdn along and lost pl 8th: bhd whn p.u bef 10th* **16/1**

P560 **P** **Diamond Cottage (IRE)**[7] 3917 11-9-11 **81** TomMessenger(7) —
(S B Bell) *chsd ldrs: rdn along 10th: sn lost pl and bhd whn p.u after 12th* **33/1**

-52F **P** **Moon Mist**[34] 3444 8-10-6 **86** PeterBuchanan(3) —
(N W Alexander) *chsd ldrs: rdn along and 10th: sn lost pl and bhd whn p.u bef 2 out* **16/1**

7m 17.4s (10.60) **Going Correction** +1.10s/f (Heav) **12** Ran SP% **113.9**
Speed ratings: **105,104,99,96,94 88,82,—,—,— —,—** CSF £26.02 CT £367.52 TOTE £7.20: £2.00, £2.00, £5.30; EX 33.60.
Owner Lucky Catch Partnership **Bred** G Mercier **Trained** Harmby, N Yorks

FOCUS
A real slog in the conditions but the form appears reasonable.

NOTEBOOK
Matmata De Tendron(FR) reversed last month's course and distance form with Canavan on 19lb better terms. He was outpaced by the leading pair with three to jump, but had moved into second place before the last. Even halfway up the run-in he looked held by the favourite, but he then began to motor and he won going away in the end. All he does his stay and the return to this trip suited him, as well as the left-handed track. *(op 6-1)*
Canavan(IRE) took it up three from home, going strongly, and looked well in command halfway up the extended run-in, but once past the omitted final fence his stride shortened and he was cut down. He emerges with plenty of credit despite this defeat. *(tchd 5-2 and 3-1 in places)*
Recent Edition(IRE), 7lb lower, merely stayed on past toiling rivals over the last three fences, taking third spot on the run-in.
Bang And Blame(IRE), attempting to retain his unbeaten record over course and distance, tried to make all once more but had no answer when the winner swept past.
Red Perk(IRE), on a career-high mark under the penalty for his Newcastle win, has never been the most consistent and was well held. *(op 5-1)*

4043 RACECOURSE VIDEO SERVICES H'CAP HURDLE (11 hdls 2 omitted) 3m 3f 110y
3:50 (3:51) (Class 4) (0-110,108) 4-Y-0+ **£3,903** (£1,146; £573; £286)

Form RPR

1100 **1** **General Duroc (IRE)**[10] 3854 10-11-12 **108** (p) BrianHarding 118
(B Storey) *mde most: rdn clr 2 out: drvn and hdd flat: rallied to ld nr line* **16/1**

0/P3 **2** *shd* **Ocean Tide**[47] 3250 9-10-6 **88** (v) RichardMcGrath 98
(R Ford) *a.p: rdn along after 3 out: styd on u.p to chal flat: drvn to ld last 100 yds: hdd and no ex nr line* **12/1**

2201 **3** *15* **San Peire (FR)**[28] 3554 9-11-11 **107** GrahamLee 105+
(J Howard Johnson) *hld up towards rr: hdwy 4 out: rdn along to chse ldrs after next: drvn and one pce appr last* **7/2**[2]

2331 **4** *9* **Perfect Balance (IRE)**[22] 3656 5-10-9 **91** KeithMercer 77
(D W Thompson) *towards rr: rdn along 3 out: styd on appr last: nrst fin* **7/1**

1UUP **5** *2 1/2* **Dark Thunder (IRE)**[57] 2978 9-9-9 **84** (b) PatrickMcDonald(7) 67
(Ferdy Murphy) *hld up in rr: hdwy 4 out: rdn along next: styd on appr last: nrst fin* **11/2**[3]

0552 **6** *1 1/2* **Hidden Storm (IRE)**[93] 2378 7-9-7 **82** oh9 (b) TomMessenger(7) 64
(Mrs S J Humphrey) *midfield: hdwy to chse ldrs 7th: rdn along 3 out and grad wknd* **33/1**

1502 **7** *6* **Primitive Poppy**[42] 3339 7-10-1 **90** PhilKinsella(7) 66
(Mrs A Hamilton) *in tch: hdwy to chse ldrs 6th: rdn along 3 out and grad wknd* **8/1**

1-42 **8** *12* **Letitia's Loss (IRE)**[28] 3554 8-11-9 **105** TonyDobbin 89+
(N G Richards) *in tch: hdwy to chse wnr 3 out: rdn along next: wkng whn blnd last: eased* **3/1**[1]

0P3U **9** *22* **Harry Hooly**[28] 3554 11-10-11 **98** TomGreenway(5) 40
(Mrs H O Graham) *cl up: pushed along 7th: sn lost pl and mstke next: bhd after* **11/1**

4300 **10** *dist* **Speed Kris (FR)**[10] 3854 7-10-6 **95** (v) DavidDaSilva(7) —
(Mrs S C Bradburne) *chsd ldrs: nt fluent: rdn along whn blnd 5th: sn lost pl and bhd* **25/1**

7m 26.0s (22.10) **Going Correction** +1.20s/f (Heav) **10** Ran SP% **114.9**
Speed ratings: **103,102,98,96,95 94,93,89,83,—** CSF £186.04 CT £829.40 TOTE £13.90: £3.60, £3.70, £1.70; EX 218.20.
Owner F S Storey **Bred** Frank Burke **Trained** Kirklinton, Cumbria

FOCUS
A very modest event with the winner to his previous mark and the runner-up improving a stone.

NOTEBOOK
General Duroc(IRE) won twice before Christmas, including over this course and distance, but had been well held off higher marks on his last two starts. Well at home in the conditions, he made just about all and, although joined on the run-in, he fought back for a narrow success.
Ocean Tide had a couple of lengths to make up on the leader at the final flight, but he got his head momentarily in front on the run-in only to be touched off. He lost nothing in defeat and is well handicapped on some old form.
San Peire(FR) is well at home at this track in testing conditions, but the 9lb rise for his recent win here proved too much for him to overcome. *(op 9-2)*
Perfect Balance(IRE) went up 7lb for his victory at Southwell three weeks ago. Tackling an extra three furlongs, he was never a factor but survived a last-flight mistake to get the best of a tussle for fourth. *(op 9-2)*
Dark Thunder(IRE), handicapped up to his best for this return to hurdling, was never able to get in a challenge. *(op 15-2)*
Letitia's Loss(IRE), 4lb higher than when runner-up to San Peire here last time, went after the winner with three to jump but faded at the top of the hill. She was a tired fourth when blundering badly at the last and was allowed to come home in her own time. *(tchd 11-4)*

4044 SIS NOVICES' HUNTERS' CHASE (12 fncs 4 omitted) 2m 5f
4:20 (4:20) (Class 6) 5-Y-0+ **£999** (£309; £154; £77)

Form RPR

23/1 **1** **Drombeag (IRE)**[12] 3819 8-12-4 118 MrJTMcNamara 109+
(Jonjo O'Neill) *hld up in midfield: hmpd and blnd 7th: hdwy to chse ldrs 4 out: rdn last: styd on to ld flat* **1/3**[1]

5- **2** *16* **Solway Sunset**[290] 7-11-4 MrDJewett(3) 90+
(Ms Lisa Harrison) *racd wd: trckd ldrs: hdwy to ld 4 out: rdn and hdd flat: sn one pce* **20/1**[3]

3 *29* **Queenies Girl**[3] 10-11-0 MissJFoster(7) 53
(Paul Frank) *chsd ldrs: rdn along 4 out: drvn and wknd fr next* **25/1**

4 *1* **Moscowtastic (IRE)**[16] 8-11-10 ow3 MrSimonRobinson(7) 62
(S J Robinson) *t.k.h: led to 4th: prom tl rdn and wknd 4 out* **50/1**

5 *4* **Classic Echo**[16] 6-11-0 MrSCharlton(7) 48
(J J Davies) *in tch: hdwy 7th: rdn along 4 out and sn wknd* **25/1**

000- **6** *11* **Summer Stock (USA)**[10] 8-11-7 (t) MrCDawson(7) 44
(R A Mills) *rr whn mstke 5th: a bhd* **66/1**

P **Knock Davron (IRE)**[16] 7-12-0 MrMThompson —
(V Thompson) *blnd 3rd and sn bhd: p.u bef 7th* **33/1**

03/P **P** **Sea Knight (IRE)**[17] 9-11-7 MrAJFindlay(7) —
(Ms J M Findlay) *towards rr: bhd fr 1/2-way: p.u bef 3 out* **50/1**

3-46 **P** **High Expectations (IRE)**[285] 322 11-12-0 72 MrTGreenall —
(J S Haldane) *in tch to 5th: bhd fr 7th: p.u bef 3 out* **25/1**

P/ **P** **Mr Hawkeye (USA)**[682] 7-11-11 MrMSeston(3) —
(Mrs A Hamilton) *trckd ldrs: hdwy to ld 4th: hdd 9th: sn rdn and wknd: p.u bef 2 out* **9/1**[2]

P-PL **P** **Gunson Hight**[17] 9-11-7 65 (t) MrJThompson(7) —
(Miss Sarah E Gledson) *chsd ldrs: rdn along 7th and sn wknd: bhd whn p.u 4 out* **100/1**

5m 55.1s (31.70) **Going Correction** +1.55s/f (Heav) **11** Ran SP% **110.7**
Speed ratings: **101,94,83,83,81 77,—,—,—,— —** CSF £9.45 TOTE £1.40: £1.10, £2.80, £4.10; EX 7.30.
Owner John P McManus **Bred** Daniel J O'Keeffe **Trained** Cheltenham, Gloucs

FOCUS
An uncompetitive contest in which they went 20/1 bar-two, but the favourite made hard work of it in the conditions and the form is difficult to rate with any confidence.

NOTEBOOK
Drombeag(IRE) followed up his Huntingdon victory but had to work. Given reminders after a mistake at halfway, when a rival jumped across him, he got to the front early on the run-in and eventually pulled away, but the margin of victory does flatter him. He is now qualified for the Cheltenham Foxhunters'. *(op 4-11)*
Solway Sunset landed a maiden point when last seen back in May. She still held a slight lead over the final fence but the winner asserted on the extended run-in, and she was eased down when beaten towards the line. *(op 22-1)*
Queenies Girl, a consistent point-to-pointer, was pulled up on her recent return after a year's absence. Having her first run on a racecourse proper and faced with heavy ground for the first time, she was well beaten in the end but not disgraced. *(op 20-1)*
Moscowtastic(IRE), a winning pointer in Ireland, is a keen sort and made the early running, but was well beaten with four to jump. Almost down at the final fence, his rider making a good recovery, he was pretty tired on the long run-in as he attempted in vain to get up for third under some strong driving.
Mr Hawkeye(USA) won a fast-ground maiden point at Higham when last seen in April 2004. He showed ability after this long absence and should improve for the outing. *(op 8-1)*

4045 ST JAMES SECURITY CONDITIONAL JOCKEYS' H'CAP HURDLE (7 hdls 1 omitted) 2m 1f
4:50 (4:50) (Class 4) (0-110,106) 4-Y-0+ **£3,253** (£955; £477; £238)

Form RPR

-411 **1** **Polar Gunner**[38] 3395 9-11-7 **101** TJDreaper 116+
(J M Jefferson) *trckd ldrs: hdwy to ld after 3 out: hit next: clr last: wandered flat: rdn out* **6/4**[1]

34F0 **2** *5* **Prince Adjal (IRE)**[16] 3757 6-10-1 **81** DougieCostello 88
(Miss S E Forster) *racd wd: led tl after 3rd: cl up: rdn along appr 2 out: kpt on same pce appr last* **28/1**

1524 **3** *15* **Amadeus (AUS)**[15] 3784 9-9-6 **80** JohnKington(8) 72
(M Scudamore) *hld up: hdwy 3 out: rdn along whn lft poor 3rd 2 out: sn drvn and no imp* **7/2**[2]

053P **4** *8* **Countrywide Sun**[80] 2639 4-9-11 **91** EwanWhillans(5) 66
(A C Whillans) *bhd tl styd on appr 2 out: nvr a factor* **50/1**

66-6 **5** *2 1/2* **Baby Gee**[38] 3395 12-10-5 **95** GarryWhillans(10) 77
(D W Whillans) *midfield: rdn along bef 3 out and nvr a factor* **10/1**

0326 **6** *2 1/2* **Vulcan Lane (NZ)**[4] 3964 9-9-10 **86** oh2 ow6 (b) JohnWilley(10) 65
(R C Guest) *a towards rr* **8/1**[3]

5140 **7** *4* **Star Trooper (IRE)**[13] 3797 10-9-11 **80** oh1 (p) TomMessenger(3) 55
(Miss S E Forster) *a rr* **20/1**

B20P **8** *10* **Top Style (IRE)**[80] 2629 8-11-7 **106** MichaelO'Connell(5) 71
(G A Harker) *a rr* **20/1**

-104 **P** **Charlie Tango (IRE)**[15] 3783 5-11-4 **98** KeithMercer —
(D W Thompson) *chsd ldrs: rdn along appr 3 out and sn wknd: bhd whn p.u after 2 out* **14/1**

04F3 **U** **Merryvale Man**[7] 3918 9-11-1 **95** BrianHughes 97
(Miss Kariana Key) *cl up: led after 3rd: rdn 3 out: sn hdd and wkng in 3rd whn blnd and uns rdr 2 out* **8/1**[3]

4m 26.9s (20.40) **Going Correction** +1.20s/f (Heav)
WFA 4 from 5yo+ 9lb **10** Ran SP% **115.1**
Speed ratings: **100,97,90,86,85 84,82,77,—,—** CSF £48.15 CT £132.52 TOTE £2.20: £1.20, £7.10, £2.10; EX 58.10 Place 6 £41.32, Place 5 £27.54.
Owner Mrs M E Dixon **Bred** Mrs P Nicholson **Trained** Norton, N Yorks

FOCUS
The pace was sound for the conditions and not many got into the race. The winner was value for more than the official margin.

NOTEBOOK
Polar Gunner was raised 15lb for his win in a weak race at Wetherby, but was still a stone below his current chase mark. He completed the hat-trick in decisive fashion, although he was a little tired when jinking to his right halfway up the run-in. *(op 13-8 tchd 11-8, 7-4 in places)*
Prince Adjal(IRE), who steered a wide course throughout, was always up with the pace and, after a mistake at the second last, he was keeping on at the end. *(op 25-1)*
Amadeus(AUS), reverting to hurdles off a mark 12lb lower than he is currently rated over fences, could never get in a blow. *(tchd 4-1)*
Countrywide Sun, back down in trip, achieved little in plugging on for a remote fourth. *(op 40-1)*
Baby Gee, never near the leaders, was run out of a distant fourth place at the final flight. *(op 9-1)*

The Form Book, Raceform Ltd, Compton, RG20 6NL

Merryvale Man, following a slow start, could not get to the front until after the third flight. Headed at the top of the hill, he was held in third place when giving his rider no chance of staying aboard at the second last. *(op 7-1)*
T/Plt: £29.40 to a £1 stake. Pool: £43,469.35. 1,077.90 winning tickets. T/Qpdt: £17.10 to a £1 stake. Pool: £3,389.10. 146.20 winning tickets. JR

3800 LUDLOW (R-H)

Wednesday, February 22

OFFICIAL GOING: Good (good to firm in places)
Wind: Moderate, behind Weather: Showers

4046 CORVE NOVICES' (S) HURDLE (11 hdls) 2m 5f
2:00 (2:01) (Class 5) 4-7-Y-O **£2,602** (£764; £382; £190)

Form RPR
60 **1** **Jug Of Punch (IRE)**9 3899 7-11-2 88 PatrickCStringer(7) 86
(S T Lewis) *hld up and bhd: hdwy appr 7th: led after 8th to 3 out: btn whn lft clr last: dismntd after fin* **9/1**
6264 **2** *7* **Relative Hero (IRE)**140 1643 6-11-3 79 (p) NoelFehily 74+
(Miss S J Wilton) *a.p: led 7th to 8th: rdn appr 3 out: wknd appr 2 out* **9/1**
06 **3** *7* **Giant's Rock (IRE)**10 3885 4-10-7 (t) RichardJohnson 56
(B J Llewellyn) *hld up in tch: wknd appr 3 out: mstke 2 out* **7/1**3
0P-3 **4** *½* **Lavenoak Lad**36 3433 6-10-10 66 (p) KeiranBurke(7) 66
(P R Rodford) *hld up in tch: wknd after 8th* **20/1**
0FP0 **5** *dist* **Form And Beauty (IRE)**6 3579 4-10-7 OllieMcPhail —
(C Roberts) *hld up in mid-div: hdwy 7th: rdn 8th: sn wknd: t.o* **25/1**
001P **P** **Biscar Two (IRE)**21 3673 5-11-8 120 (p) DerekLaverty(5) —
(A E Jones) *a bhd: t.o whn p.u bef 8th* **5/1**2
PPP- **P** **Millie's Fortune**345 4369 5-10-10 AnthonyRoss —
(M Mullineaux) *rel to r: a t.o: p.u bef 3 out* **66/1**
F **Kuka**17 5-10-7 AdamHawkins(10) 46
(R Hollinshead) *hld up: hdwy 7th: wknd after 8th: no ch whn fell last* **16/1**
-02P **P** **Pop Gun**6 3945 7-10-10 84 RichardSpate(7) —
(Mrs K Waldron) *a bhd: blnd 7th: t.o whn p.u bef 3 out: lame* **10/1**
0F **P** **Desertmore King (IRE)**41 3356 6-11-3 VinceSlattery —
(J A Danahar) *j.lft: bhd fr 5th: t.o whn p.u bef 3 out* **66/1**
2B32 **F** **Elaala (USA)**14 3804 4-10-0 92 PJBrennan 74+
(P A Blockley) *hld up and bhd: hdwy after 8th: led 3 out: 8l clr whn fell last* **7/4**1
0 **P** **Quiteb'Chance (IRE)**85 2565 5-10-10 SeanCurran —
(Miss J S Davis) *led: j.lft 3rd: hdd after 6th: wknd 8th: t.o whn p.u bef 3 out* **66/1**
54P0 **P** **Nepal (IRE)**28 3557 4-10-0 78 (b1) AlanO'Keeffe —
(M Mullineaux) *chsd ldr: led after 6th to 7th: led 8th: sn hdd & wknd: bhd whn p.u bef 3 out* **16/1**

5m 18.4s (0.10) **Going Correction** -0.025s/f (Good)
WFA 4 from 5yo+ 10lb **13** Ran SP% **119.5**
Speed ratings: **98,95,92,92,**— —,—,—,—,— —,—,— CSF £83.49 TOTE £10.40: £3.50, £2.90, £2.00; EX 78.20.There was no bid for the winner. Elaala was claimed by Barry Leavy for £6,000.
Owner Simon T Lewis **Bred** T J Monaghan **Trained** Longdon, Worcs

FOCUS
Jug Of Punch was a most fortunate winner of this very moderate seller and is rated to the level of his previous win, with the faller rated an 11 length winner.

NOTEBOOK
Jug Of Punch(IRE), who put up an eyecatching display over two miles at Plumpton last time, was back over the course and distance where he gained his sole previous win. After moving up stylishly to lead, he was soon left in the favourite's wake only to be presented with the race at the final flight. *He was dismounted after the finish as he had lost a shoe. Official explanation: jockey said he felt gelding go lame before winning post and so he dismounted on pulling up; trainer said gelding lost a shoe (op 8-1)*
Relative Hero(IRE) ran a sound race on this first start since October but was only third best on merit. A slightly shorter trip is ideal. *(tchd 10-1)*
Giant's Rock(IRE), down in grade for this third run over hurdles, did not stay this longer trip and was well beaten in the end. *(op 8-1 tchd 17-2)*
Lavenoak Lad made the frame again but it is going to be a very bad race if he is ever to win.
Pop Gun *Official explanation: vet said gelding pulled up lame (op 9-2 tchd 7-1)*
Biscar Two(IRE) seems to have lost what enthusiasm he had for racing. *(op 9-2 tchd 7-1)*
Nepal(IRE), in first-time blinkers, shared the lead until her stamina for this longer trip began to wane. *(op 9-2 tchd 7-1)*
Elaala(USA) was claimed out of Martin Todhunter's yard after finishing second here last time. After coming clear with little effort, she seemed to have the race in the bag when knuckling over at the last and can be counted most unlucky. She stayed this longer trip and can gain compensation. *(op 9-2 tchd 7-1)*

4047 TEME CONDITIONAL JOCKEYS' H'CAP CHASE (19 fncs) 3m
2:30 (2:30) (Class 4) (0-105,101) 5-Y-0+
£4,697 (£1,387; £693; £347; £173; £87)

Form RPR
P3P1 **1** **Quizzling (IRE)**19 3716 8-10-4 **79** OwynNelmes 89+
(B J M Ryall) *hld up in mid-div: lost pl 11th: hdwy and hit 12th: hit 4 out and 2 out: rdn to ld flat: r.o* **7/1**
5F30 **2** *½* **Joe Deane (IRE)**20 3698 10-11-0 **94** (p) AndrewGlassonbury(5) 103
(M J Coombe) *hld up in tch: led 4 out: rdn 3 out: hdd flat: r.o* **14/1**
P43U **3** *1 ½* **Aisjem (IRE)**6 3938 7-9-11 **77** oh5 ow2 TimothyBailey(5) 85+
(Evan Williams) *hld up: hdwy 15th: styd on flat* **12/1**
2602 **4** *hd* **Tribal Dancer (IRE)**23 3649 12-11-1 **93** LiamTreadwell(3) 100
(Miss Venetia Williams) *a.p: led 15th: rdn and hdd 4 out: ev ch last: nt qckn* **4/1**1
34P3 **5** *1 ¼* **Point**18 3732 9-11-5 **94** RobertLucey-Butler 101+
(W Jenks) *hld up and bhd: mstke 7th: hdwy after 15th: rdn 3 out: one pce fr 2 out* **9/1**
S236 **6** *1* **Sissinghurst Storm (IRE)**48 3250 8-9-6 **75** JohnPritchard(8) 81+
(R Dickin) *prom: lost pl 6th: hit 9th: styd on flat: nt rch ldrs* **9/2**2
-54P **7** *5* **Dr Mann (IRE)**8 3909 8-10-4 **79** (b1) WilliamKennedy 80+
(Miss Tor Sturgis) *nvr trbld ldrs* **6/1**3
-0P6 **8** *½* **Celia's High (IRE)**34 3460 7-10-0 **75** oh13 (t) PaddyAspell 75
(D McCain) *prom: rdn appr 15th: wknd 4 out* **33/1**
-P50 **9** *2* **Lucky Luk (FR)**63 2936 7-10-3 **78** MarkNicolls 76
(K C Bailey) *hld up towards rr: hdwy 10th: wknd 15th* **10/1**
32/6 **10** *dist* **Jorodama King**54 3125 12-9-9 **75** oh11 KeiranBurke(5) —
(N J Hawke) *led to 15th: wknd 4 out: t.o* **66/1**
-F33 **P** **Lough Rynn (IRE)**46 3282 8-11-12 **101** LiamHeard —
(Miss H C Knight) *hld up and bhd: hdwy 10th: wknd 14th: t.o whn p.u bef 4 out* **10/1**

6m 6.20s (-5.90) **Going Correction** -0.125s/f (Good) **11** Ran SP% **111.9**
Speed ratings: **104,103,103,103,102 102,100,100,100,**— — CSF £92.69 CT £1141.18 TOTE £9.50: £2.70, £11.20, £3.30; EX 99.70.
Owner I & Mrs K G Fawcett **Bred** Basil Brindley **Trained** Rimpton, Somerset

FOCUS
A very moderate affair, but it was run at a sound pace and the form should stand up with the fourth and fifth to their marks.

NOTEBOOK
Quizzling(IRE) followed up his Fontwell win from a 4lb higher mark. Well ridden, he got away with a couple of sketchy jumps in the straight to show ahead early on the flat. He is obviously in good heart at present and will not go up much for this. *(tchd 15-2)*
Joe Deane(IRE) took a narrow lead at the first in the home straight but was just run out of it after the last. He has won just once over fences but is well enough handicapped to add to his tally. *(op 12-1)*
Aisjem(IRE) ◆, who was 5lb out of the weights, was without the cheekpieces she has been wearing recently. Staying on strongly after the last, she can find a small race over this trip on a stiffer track. *(op 14-1)*
Tribal Dancer(IRE) likes Ludlow and ran a decent race, but he is without a win since scoring here in May 2004 and is getting no younger. *(tchd 7-2)*
Point, returned to three miles, made a couple of errors but was still in with a shout between the last two fences before failing to muster any extra. *(op 8-1)*
Sissinghurst Storm(IRE), back over fences, was keeping on again at the end having been outpaced by the leaders at one stage. *(op 7-2)*

4048 J D & SUE ANNIVERSARY "NATIONAL HUNT" NOVICES' HURDLE (9 hdls) 2m
3:00 (3:00) (Class 4) 4-Y-O+ **£4,228** (£1,241; £620; £310)

Form RPR
214 **1** **Fier Normand (FR)**40 3369 7-11-9 115 APMcCoy 120+
(Jonjo O'Neill) *hld up in tch: wnt 2nd 6th: led appr 3 out: easily* **8/11**1
0 **2** *3* **Four For A Laugh (IRE)**97 2288 7-11-2 RobertThornton 104+
(A King) *hld up: hdwy 4th: mstke 3 out: wnt 2nd last: nt ch w wnr* **25/1**
1 **3** *2 ½* **Paro (FR)**14 3800 5-11-2 114 AndrewGlassonbury(7) 108+
(M C Pipe) *led: sn clr: rdn and hdd appr 3 out: 3rd and btn whn nt fluent last* **9/4**2
130 **4** *21* **Houlihans Free (IRE)**217 1037 7-11-2 (t) ChristianWilliams 81+
(P F Nicholls) *hld up: hdwy 4th: wkng whn mstke 2 out* **20/1**
0 **5** *½* **Lucent (IRE)**44 3327 5-11-2 PaulMoloney 78
(Miss H C Knight) *hld up and bhd: hdwy after 6th: wkng whn j.lft 3 out* **33/1**
00 **6** *3 ½* **Native Forest (IRE)**34 3462 5-11-2 MatthewBatchelor 75
(Miss H C Knight) *a bhd* **40/1**
6F-F **7** *¾* **Aber Gale**54 3130 7-10-9 RichardJohnson 67
(Mrs S M Johnson) *keen early: a bhd* **66/1**
0 **8** *11* **Tour Card (IRE)**25 3623 4-10-7 NoelFehily 54
(Jonjo O'Neill) *j. slowly 4th: a bhd* **33/1**
0-00 **P** **Percy Jay (NZ)**14 3800 7-11-2 MarkBradburne —
(W Jenks) *a bhd: nt fluent 2nd: t.o whn p.u bef 3 out* **66/1**
-10P **P** **Slick (FR)**78 2683 5-11-2 AndrewTinkler —
(N J Henderson) *chsd clr ldr to 6th: sn wknd: t.o whn p.u bef 2 out* **10/1**3
-340 **P** **Itsdowntoben**12 3843 5-11-2 JasonMaguire —
(D McCain) *hld up in tch: wkng whn j. slowly 5th: t.o whn p.u bef 3 out* **33/1**

3m 50.3s (-2.00) **Going Correction** -0.025s/f (Good)
WFA 4 from 5yo+ 9lb **11** Ran SP% **120.6**
Speed ratings: **104,102,101,90,90 88,88,82,**—,— — CSF £27.06 TOTE £1.80: £1.10, £4.40, £1.10; EX 19.40.
Owner John P McManus **Bred** Thierry Picard **Trained** Cheltenham, Gloucs

FOCUS
A fair novices' event with the winner value for 11 lengths and the fifth and sixth rated as close to their bumper marks.

NOTEBOOK
Fier Normand(FR) disappointed at Huntingdon but bounced back here with a fluent victory which should have done his confidence good. He will stay further. *(op 5-6)*
Four For A Laugh(IRE), beaten favourite for a bumper back in November, shaped with promise on this hurdles debut and is well capable of winning a similar race before going over fences. *(op 16-1)*
Paro(FR), successful over course and distance on his British debut, was found out under his penalty in this stronger company. Going off plenty fast enough, he was collared on the approach to the home straight and lost second when going out to his right at the final flight. *(op 5-2 tchd 2-1)*
Houlihans Free(IRE), who finished sore on his last start back in July, ran respectably but probably needs further. *(op 16-1)*
Lucent(IRE), well beaten in a bumper last month, ran pleasingly enough on this hurdles debut.
Aber Gale *Official explanation: jockey said, regarding running and riding, his orders were to finish as close as possible bearing in mind mare is inclined to run freely and had fallen on two previous hurdle runs; he added that the race was run at a fast pace which made the mare keen early on, and though she settled down the back straight she only latterly ran on past beaten horses and made no headway on leaders (op 50-1)*
Itsdowntoben *Official explanation: trainer said gelding bled from the nose (op 25-1)*

4049 ARROW H'CAP CHASE (13 fncs) 2m
3:30 (3:30) (Class 3) (0-120,114) 5-Y-£7,515 (£2,220; £1,110; £555; £277)

Form RPR
1415 **1** **Lindsay (FR)**42 3344 7-11-11 **111** MarkBradburne 116
(H D Daly) *chsd ldr: led appr 4 out: rdn and r.o wl flat* **15/8**2
2150 **2** *1 ¾* **Harry Potter (GER)**41 3357 7-11-8 **108** ChristianWilliams 111
(Evan Williams) *hld up: hdwy 9th: ev ch 3 out: rdn appr last: nt qckn flat* **10/1**
-514 **3** *2 ½* **Amarula Ridge (IRE)**48 3255 5-11-8 **114** APMcCoy 111+
(P J Hobbs) *hld up: hit 3rd: hdwy whn mstke 4 out: swtchd rt and rdn appr 2 out: no ex flat* **6/4**1
0043 **4** *16* **Imperial Rocket (USA)**23 3647 9-10-13 **104** (t) LeeStephens(5) 95+
(W K Goldsworthy) *led tl appr 4 out: wknd appr 2 out* **8/1**
113P **5** *27* **L'Oiseau (FR)**97 2300 7-11-12 **112** JoeTizzard 70
(J G Portman) *hld up in tch: pushed along appr 4 out: sn lost tch: t.o* **13/2**3

4m 1.60s (-2.50) **Going Correction** -0.125s/f (Good)
WFA 5 from 7yo+ 6lb **5** Ran SP% **108.3**
Speed ratings: **101,100,98,90,77** CSF £16.71 TOTE £3.40: £1.50, £2.10; EX 16.70.
Owner John R Wilson **Bred** Rene Ricous And Mrs Ricous **Trained** Stanton Lacy, Shropshire

FOCUS
A modest handicap and there was no change in the order until the field faced up to the final line of four fences. The winner sets the standard and the form could rate a little higher.

NOTEBOOK
Lindsay(FR), freshened up by a break since his last run, took it up at the first in the home straight and was always holding his pursuers. There was nothing wrong with his jumping this time and he is progressing steadily. *(op 10-3)*
Harry Potter(GER) made his chasing debut last month over course and distance in a much more competitive event than this. He ran a good race in defeat and a minor handicap could come his way on faster ground. *(op 9-1 tchd 11-1)*
Amarula Ridge(IRE), a close fourth when getting in too close to the first fence up the straight, was soon disputing second but was unable to get in a blow at the winner. He is the sort who needs things to fall just right. *(op 11-8 tchd 13-8)*
Imperial Rocket(USA) was put up 10lb for finishing third in a decent novice chase at this venue last month, and that told up the home straight. *(op 6-1)*
L'Oiseau(FR) showed no sparkle on this first run since November and, in last place throughout, was the first beaten. *Official explanation: trainer said gelding finished distressed (op 4-1)*

4050 IAN COOPER BIRTHDAY H'CAP HURDLE (9 hdls) 2m
4:00 (4:00) (Class 3) (0-120,119) 4-Y-0+ **£5,204** (£1,528; £764; £381)

Form RPR
-126 **1** **Andreas (FR)**[103] [2163] 6-11-7 **119**..........................(t) LiamHeard(5) 139+
(P F Nicholls) *hld up: hdwy 4th: led after 6th: clr 3 out: easily* **2/1**[2]
1122 **2** *10* **Saif Sareea**[7] [3929] 6-11-4 **111**.......................... PadgeWhelan 116
(R A Fahey) *hld up: hdwy appr 6th: wnt 2nd 3 out: sn rdn: no ch w wnr* **13/8**[1]
F04 **3** *4* **It's The Limit (USA)**[19] [3719] 7-10-5 **103**..................(bt) LeeStephens(5) 105+
(W K Goldsworthy) *led tl after 6th: wknd 3 out* **9/1**[3]
5655 **4** *3½* **Hunting Lodge (IRE)**[10] [3889] 5-10-0 **100**.............. MrJAJenkins(7) 98
(H J Manners) *hld up in tch: lost pl 4th: bhd 6th: styd on fr 3 out: n.d* **20/1**
2-12 **5** *2* **Allumee**[100] [2246] 7-11-7 **114**.......................... PJBrennan 111+
(P J Hobbs) *hld up in tch: wknd 3 out* **12/1**
6F50 **6** *14* **Milligan (FR)**[18] [3725] 11-11-3 **113**.......................... TJPhelan(3) 95
(Dr P Pritchard) *w ldr to 6th: sn wknd* **33/1**
3341 **7** *1* **Ambersong**[14] [3804] 8-11-3 **110**.......................... CarlLlewellyn 91
(A W Carroll) *prom tl wknd 5th* **16/1**
P-1F **8** *7* **Whaleef**[28] [3562] 8-11-6 **113**..........................(tp) ChristianWilliams 87
(B J Llewellyn) *bhd fr 6th* **22/1**
6140 **F** **Napoleon (IRE)**[28] [3561] 5-11-10 **117**..........................(b) RichardJohnson —
(P J Hobbs) *prom: fell 3rd: broke leg: dead* **12/1**
-P00 **P** **Atahuelpa**[23] [3650] 6-11-11 **118**..........................(t) AlanO'Keeffe —
(Jennie Candlish) *plld hrd early in rr: a bhd: t.o whn p.u bef 3 out* **66/1**

3m 47.3s (-5.00) **Going Correction** -0.025s/f (Good) **10** Ran SP% **116.2**
Speed ratings: **111,106,104,102,101 94,93,90,—,—** CSF £5.53 CT £21.65 TOTE £2.90: £1.50, £1.10, £2.20; EX 5.20 Trifecta £43.40 Pool: £618.62 - 10.10 winning tickets..
Owner Mark Tincknell **Bred** M Gosse And Mlle Noelle Bataille **Trained** Ditcheat, Somerset

FOCUS
A fair time for the class of contest with the winner value for 15 lengths. The form looks solid enough with those in the frame behind the winner running to their marks.

NOTEBOOK
Andreas(FR) has had a breathing operation since his last outing in November. Taking full advantage of a mark 25lb lower than his current chase rating, he was value for a good deal further and now goes to the Grand Annual Chase at Cheltenham with a live chance. *(op 9-4 tchd 5-2 in places)*
Saif Sareea, in fine form at Musselburgh this winter, ran his race on this similar track but had no chance with the well handicapped winner. *(tchd 7-4 in a place)*
It's The Limit(USA), twice withdrawn recently due to unsuitable ground, again tried front-running tactics but could not counter when the winner passed him at the end of the back straight. *(op 12-1)*
Hunting Lodge(IRE) ran his usual sort of race, staying on past beaten rivals when in sight of home.
Allumee was running for the first time since his chasing debut three months ago. He turned into the straight in fourth place, some way clear of the rest, but soon began to weaken. *(op 10-1 tchd 9-1)*
Ambersong was put up just over a stone for landing a seller here last time and is going to be vulnerable from this sort of mark.

4051 ONNY HUNTERS' CHASE (19 fncs) 3m
4:30 (4:37) (Class 5) 6-Y-0+ **£2,186** (£677; £338; £169)

Form RPR
-411 **1** **Red Brook Lad**[20] [3693] 11-12-0 107.......................... MissCTizzard(3) 119
(C St V Fox) *hld up: hdwy 7th: hit 8th: rdn appr last: led flat: r.o* **15/8**[2]
1P/2 **2** *shd* **Bosham Mill**[13] [3819] 8-11-7.......................... MrTJO'Brien(3) 112
(P J Hobbs) *a.p: led 15th: rdn appr last: hdd flat: r.o* **11/8**[1]
34PU **3** *13* **Mondial Jack (FR)**[20] [3693] 7-11-3 130..........................(p) MrRQuinn(7) 101+
(Mrs K Waldron) *hld up: hdwy 11th: rdn 4 out: j.rt 2 out: sn wknd* **16/1**
P6PF **4** *3½* **Good Bone (FR)**[20] [3693] 9-11-7 82.......................... MrAWintle(3) 95
(S Flook) *hld up and bhd: hdwy 15th: wknd 3 out* **25/1**
-231 **5** *½* **An Capall Dubh (IRE)**[14] [3805] 10-12-0.......................... MrRBurton 109+
(Mrs Edward Crow) *led to 15th: ev ch whn blnd and rdr lost reins 4 out: nt rcvr: hmpd and mstke 2 out* **7/1**[3]
34-2 **6** *1* **Montebank (IRE)**[14] [3805] 10-11-3.......................... MrGWalters(7) 94
(Mrs O Bush) *prom tl wknd after 3 out* **16/1**
PP/4 **7** *dist* **Magicien (FR)**[14] [3805] 10-11-3.......................... MissLBrooke(7) —
(Steve Isaac) *chsd ldrs: wkng whn hit 12th: t.o* **40/1**
011/ **U** **Arctic Sky (IRE)**[10] 9-11-7.......................... MrSJoynes(3) —
(T M Stephenson) *hmpd and uns rdr 2nd (water)* **25/1**
U/P- **F** **Chaparro Amargoso (IRE)**[328] [4672] 13-11-3 91.......................... MrLEdwards(7) —
(F L Matthews) *fell 2nd (water)* **66/1**
-1U5 **U** **Raiseapearl**[8] [3913] 11-11-7.......................... MissTessaClark(7) —
(Patrick Thompson) *uns rdr & rn loose bef s: bhd: hmpd 2nd (water): mstkes: t.o 5th: mstke and uns rdr 15th* **40/1**

6m 5.20s (-6.90) **Going Correction** -0.125s/f (Good) **10** Ran SP% **115.2**
Speed ratings: **106,105,101,100,100 99,—,—,—,—** CSF £4.75 TOTE £2.60: £1.80, £1.10, £2.80; EX 6.10.
Owner C St V Fox **Bred** T H Jagger **Trained** Gillingham, Dorset
■ Stewards' Enquiry : Mr T J O'Brien one-day ban: careless riding (Mar 5)

FOCUS
A decent winning time for a hunter chase and a second quicker than the earlier handicap chase over the same trip. The first two and the fourth were close to form and give the contest a sound appearance.

NOTEBOOK
Red Brook Lad kept on really strongly up the home straight to deny Bosham Mill close to the line. He is probably better on a sharp course over this kind of trip, which may rule him out of a serious challenge in the Cheltenham Foxhunters' if taking up that engagement. *(op 13-8 tchd 2-1 in a place)*
Bosham Mill did little wrong for the second race in a row, following a lengthy absence, but again found one too good close to the line. Formally a very useful stayer on the Flat, this effort means he is now qualified for the Foxhunters' at the Cheltenham Festival, in which he would be a very interesting outsider over a course and distance more suitable for his staying qualities. *(op 7-4)*
Mondial Jack(FR) was well beaten by the first two but kept galloping all the way to the line after being under pressure some way from home. He has an official rating of 130 from his days with Martin Pipe, but is clearly nowhere near that standard now. *(op 14-1)*
Good Bone(FR) was another who was under pressure a long way from home and never really figured with a serious chance. *(op 33-1)*
An Capall Dubh(IRE) still had every chance when a mistake four out cost his rider his reins, and the jockey did well just to finish the race with three fences still to jump. He can be counted slightly *unlucky not to have been involved at the business end of the race. Official explanation: jockey was unable to ride out for fourth place having lost his reins at the first fence in home straight (op 13-2)*
Raiseapearl *(tchd 50-1)*

4052 LUGG MAIDEN HURDLE (12 hdls) 3m
5:00 (5:02) (Class 4) 4-Y-0+ **£3,903** (£1,146; £573; £286)

Form RPR
2433 **1** **Aces Four (IRE)**[109] [2036] 7-11-4.......................... KeithMercer 111+
(Ferdy Murphy) *hld up in mid-div: hdwy after 7th: led 3 out: clr whn hit 2 out: easily* **6/1**
2 *7* **One Love (IRE)**[330] 8-10-11.......................... APMcCoy 89
(P J Rothwell, Ire) *led: rdn after 9th: hdd 3 out: one pce fr 2 out* **9/1**
500 **3** *6* **Grand Slam Hero (IRE)**[23] [3646] 5-10-11.......................... MrTJO'Brien(7) 91+
(P Bowen) *t.k.h in mid-div: hdwy appr 8th: rdn and wknd appr 3 out* **33/1**
2/P6 **4** *1¼* **Polyanthus Jones**[34] [3461] 7-10-11.......................... RichardJohnson 82
(H D Daly) *prom tl wknd appr 3 out* **20/1**
/4-3 **5** *hd* **Elverys (IRE)**[15] [3789] 7-11-4.......................... AnthonyRoss 90+
(R A Fahey) *hld up: hit 3rd: hdwy appr 8th: rdn 9th: wkng whn mstke 3 out* **5/1**[3]
0 **6** *10* **Keswick (IRE)**[70] [2829] 6-11-4.......................... MarcusFoley 79
(N J Henderson) *prom: mstke 9th: sn wknd* **3/1**[1]
FU **7** *dist* **Justice Jones**[25] [3611] 5-10-11.......................... WayneKavanagh(7) —
(Mrs P Ford) *mstke 6th: a bhd: t.o* **100/1**
06P **8** *dist* **Novack Du Beury (FR)**[87] [2527] 5-11-4.......................... AlanO'Keeffe —
(Ferdy Murphy) *mstke 1st: a bhd: t.o* **66/1**
0P **9** *4* **When Your Readyles (IRE)**[48] [3253] 6-11-1.......................... PaddyAspell(3) —
(M Todhunter) *rdn after 6th: a bhd: t.o* **100/1**
10 *dist* **Buckie Briar (IRE)**[233] [897] 6-10-8.......................... TJPhelan(3) —
(Mrs H Dalton) *a bhd: t.o* **66/1**
0- **P** **Red Alf**[309] [4922] 7-10-11.......................... MrRArmson(7) —
(Miss J Wormall) *a bhd: t.o whn p.u after 7th* **100/1**
U-0P **P** **General Grey (IRE)**[40] [3372] 6-11-4 104.......................... PaulMoloney —
(Miss H C Knight) *bhd fr 9th: t.o whn p.u bef 3 out* **12/1**
6F **P** **Supremely Smart (IRE)**[112] [1990] 6-11-4.......................... AntonyEvans —
(N A Twiston-Davies) *j. bdly: a bhd: t.o whn p.u bef 7th* **33/1**
5-33 **P** **Finely Tuned (IRE)**[37] [3417] 7-11-4 102.......................... CarlLlewellyn —
(M Pitman) *chsd ldr: cl 2nd whn p.u and dismntd bef 3 out* **9/2**[2]
0- **P** **Brunate**[477] [1979] 7-10-11.......................... MrPCallaghan(7) —
(J A Danahar) *t.k.h: prom: wknd 8th: mstke 9th: t.o whn p.u bef 3 out* **100/1**
0 **P** **Tight Corner (IRE)**[53] [3145] 7-11-4.......................... RobertThornton —
(Ian Williams) *hld up in mid-div: wkng whn mstke 8th: t.o whn p.u bef 3 out* **11/1**

5m 56.5s (1.90) **Going Correction** -0.025s/f (Good) **16** Ran SP% **117.7**
Speed ratings: **95,92,90,90,90 86,—,—,—,— —,—,—,—,—** — CSF £53.91 TOTE £9.60: £2.20, £2.40, £12.30; EX 47.20 Place 6 £75.25, Place 5 £21.97.
Owner The DPRP Aces Partnership **Bred** J R And Mrs S Cox **Trained** West Witton, N Yorks

FOCUS
A modest time for the class of contest and, although the winner is value for more than double the official margin, the form is unlikely to prove solid.

NOTEBOOK
Aces Four(IRE), having his first run for the Ferdy Murphy stable, won with plenty in hand after travelling smoothly for much of the race. He saw out the trip far better than anything else and his future lies in the hands of the Handicapper. *(op 15-2)*
One Love(IRE), who finished behind Standin Obligation in one of her races between the flags in Ireland, set off to make all but was collared three flights from home. It was a fine effort after a long break and she will be of interest next time, especially if racing against her own sex. *(tchd 8-1)*
Grand Slam Hero(IRE) showed more than he had done previously but not quite enough to suggest he will be winning next time. It was by far his best effort to date but the trip may have stretched him after he had travelled well in the early stages. *(op 40-1)*
Polyanthus Jones was always close up but raced apart from the rest of the field on the worst of the ground. It remains to be seen how much ability she truly possesses.
Elverys(IRE) never got to the leaders after being held up and may not have seen out the three-mile trip. He is worth another chance if dropped down in distance next time, given his previous form and the way he travelled in the early stages of the race. *(tchd 4-1)*
Keswick(IRE) was well fancied after showing some promise in a hot novice hurdle run at Newbury on his debut. A mistake at about halfway knocked him backwards and he never recovered after that. *(op 9-4)*
Finely Tuned(IRE) was still in contention when pulled up sharply on the home turn. He was found *to have suffered quite a serious tendon injury. Official explanation: trainer's representative said gelding pulled up lame (op 5-1 tchd 4-1)*
T/Jkpt: £8,097.10 to a £1 stake. Pool: £11,404.50. 1.00 winning ticket. T/Plt: £114.30 to a £1 stake. Pool: £43,343.40. 276.70 winning tickets. T/Qpdt: £3.80 to a £1 stake. Pool: £4,429.40. 842.90 winning tickets. KH

3652 SOUTHWELL (L-H)
Wednesday, February 22

OFFICIAL GOING: Soft
Wind: Virtually nil

4053 BETFRED NOVICES' H'CAP CHASE (16 fncs) 2m 4f 110y
1:50 (1:50) (Class 4) (0-105,105) 5-Y-0+ **£4,879** (£1,432; £716; £357)

Form RPR
-56P **1** **Lord Rodney (IRE)**[67] [2874] 7-11-10 **103**.......................... TomSiddall 132+
(P Beaumont) *a.p: led 5 out: clr after next: easily* **33/1**
-U33 **2** *dist* **Twenty Degrees**[22] [3660] 8-10-11 **90**..........................(b) JamieMoore 81
(G L Moore) *midfield: blnd 8th: hdwy 4 out: rdn along and kpt on fr next: tk 2nd flat: no ch w wnr* **14/1**
5631 **3** *1¼* **Baron Blitzkrieg**[10] [3888] 8-10-1 **80** 7ex.......................... JodieMogford 70
(D J Wintle) *hld up: hdwy to trck ldrs 1/2-way: pushed along 5 out: rdn next: drvn and btn 3 out* **7/2**[1]
4P62 **4** *2½* **Been Here Before**[14] [3796] 6-10-8 **87**.......................... RichardMcGrath 74
(G A Harker) *midfield: nt fluent: mstke 3rd: pushed along 10th: rdn bef 5 out: plugged on same pce* **7/1**[3]
0 **5** *2½* **Dev (IRE)**[15] [3792] 6-11-4 **97**..........................(t) AndrewThornton 82
(M G Quinlan) *led: hdd 9th: cl up tl rdn along 4 out and grad wknd* **15/2**

PU60 **F** **Jack Lynch**[8] [3915] 10-10-4 **88** .... TJDreaper(5) —
(Ferdy Murphy) *rr whn fell 4th* **33/1**

0PPP **P** **Konker**[29] [3549] 11-10-9 **88** .... RichardHobson —
(J R Cornwall) *a bhd: p.u bef 5 out* **80/1**

-00U **P** **Cha Cha Cha Dancer**[14] [3794] 6-11-0 **98** .... DougieCostello(5) —
(G A Swinbank) *a rr: bhd whn p.u bef 3 out* **22/1**

P-P0 **U** **Heatherlea Squire (NZ)**[133] [1717] 8-10-0 **79** oh6 .... HenryOliver —
(D J Wintle) *towards rr whn blnd and uns rdr 2nd* **66/1**

-03F **U** **Kingfisher Sunset**[43] [3336] 10-10-11 **90** .... DavidO'Meara —
(Mrs S J Smith) *chsd ldrs tl blnd and uns rdr 2nd* **11/2**[2]

0245 **P** **Moorland Monarch**[33] [3482] 8-9-13 **83** ow4 .... ChrisHonour(5) —
(J D Frost) *chsd ldrs to 1/2-way: sn lost pl and bhd whn p.u bef 5 out* **7/1**[3]

1120 **P** **Caesarean Hunter (USA)**[35] [3445] 7-11-12 **105** .... WarrenMarston —
(R T Phillips) *hld up in rr: pushed along 9th: bhd whn p.u bef 4 out* **14/1**

-064 **F** **Seeyaaj**[227] [937] 6-11-3 **99** .... (t) PeterBuchanan(3) —
(Miss Lucinda V Russell) *in tch: hdwy 5 out: rdn along next: styd on to chse wnr whn fell 3 out* **25/1**

111P **P** **Jolly Boy (FR)**[30] [3533] 7-11-10 **103** .... (b) SamThomas —
(Miss Venetia Williams) *cl up: led 9th: rdn along and hdd 5 out: wknd after next and bhd whn p.u bef 2 out* **8/1**

5m 38.6s (9.50) **Going Correction** +0.60s/f (Soft) **14** Ran SP% **115.6**
Speed ratings: **105**,—,—,—,— —,—,—,— —,—,—,— CSF £394.36 CT £2033.29 TOTE £37.60: £8.50, £2.20, £2.70; EX 644.80.
Owner Estio Racing **Bred** J K M Oliver **Trained** Stearsby, N Yorks

FOCUS
The ground and these stiff fences combined to take their toll on these novices with only five of the 14 runners completing. The winner is value for 38 lengths with the runner-up to his mark.

NOTEBOOK
Lord Rodney(IRE) probably needed the run on his chasing debut at Haydock and showed that effort to be all wrong. He was always close to the pace and already had the race in safe keeping when his nearest pursuer came down three out. There was no fluke about this and he should find other opportunities.
Twenty Degrees, often placed but without a win since making a successful debut in a bumper over two years ago, plodded around to complete but finished tired and only inherited second place due to the misfortune of others. *(op 18-1)*
Baron Blitzkrieg, carrying a 7lb penalty for his Hereford victory, had every chance but seemed to find these more testing conditions too much. *(tchd 10-3)*
Been Here Before had the distinction of finishing second to the ultra-smart Monet's Garden at Carlisle last time, but was well beaten and this performance is a better indicator of his true ability. The winner of a soft-ground point, he looks just a stayer. *(op 6-1)*
Dev(IRE), the winner of an Irish point making his chasing debut under Rules, made much of the running but did not get home in the conditions. *(op 13-2)*
Konker *Official explanation: trainer said gelding was sore on its off hind (op 6-1)*
Seeyaaj ◆, returning from a seven-month break, had moved into second place though still a long way behind the winner when capsizing three from home. It is reasonable to assume that he would have finished a clear second best and, considering all his best form has been on much faster ground, he deserves a fair amount of credit. The outing ought to have done him good and the ground should come more and more in his favour as spring approaches. *(op 6-1)*
Jolly Boy(FR) again dropped out very tamely after showing up prominently and looks a shadow of the horse that was in such sparkling form at the end of last year. He may have a problem. *(op 6-1)*

4054 DINE IN THE QUEEN MOTHER RESTAURANT BEGINNERS' CHASE (19 fncs) 3m 110y
2:20 (2:20) (Class 4) 5-Y-O+ **£5,204** (£1,528; £764; £381)

Form RPR

652 **1** **Squires Lane (IRE)**[33] [3480] 7-11-1 119 .... GinoCarenza(3) 96+
(Andrew Turnell) *cl up: led 4th: rdn 2 out: styd on wl* **5/2**[2]

4263 **2** *2 ½* **Fight The Feeling**[21] [3672] 8-11-4 .... TonyDobbin 88
(J W Unett) *trckd ldrs: hdwy 4 out: cl up next: rdn 2 out: ev ch last: kpt on same pce flat* **16/1**

43-1 **3** *1 ¼* **On Y Va (FR)**[91] [2430] 8-11-4 114 .... (t) WarrenMarston 90+
(R T Phillips) *trckd ldrs: nt fluent: pushed along 4 out: cl up next and ev ch tl rdn appr last: no ex flat* **10/3**[3]

304- **4** *dist* **Jamerosier (FR)**[373] [3853] 9-11-4 93 .... AndrewThornton —
(Mrs L C Taylor) *led to 4th: cl up: reminders 8th: mstke 10th: sn outpcd and bhd fr 5 out* **13/2**

0P-P **F** **Comte De Chambord**[299] [107] 10-11-4 .... MarkGrant —
(Mark Campion) *a rr: fell 4 out* **80/1**

30-2 **U** **Henry's Pride (IRE)**[16] [3781] 6-10-13 .... PaddyMerrigan(5) —
(P C Haslam) *trckd ldrs tl uns rdr 2nd* **13/8**[1]

7m 10.0s (26.20) **Going Correction** +0.60s/f (Soft) **6** Ran SP% **110.2**
Speed ratings: **82,81,80**,—,— — CSF £31.65 TOTE £3.60: £2.10, £5.50; EX 34.00.
Owner M Tedham **Bred** Sean O'Donovan **Trained** Broad Hinton, Wilts

FOCUS
A very poor race and they would have gone down to the start faster than on the first circuit. The winning time was very slow and the form looks moderate.

NOTEBOOK
Squires Lane(IRE), a confirmed stayer, was in the ideal place in a moderately run race and despite jumping right over the last three fences, always appeared to have enough in hand to keep his two pursuers at bay. This looked a poor race though, and he will probably need to improve again in order to follow up. *(op 10-3)*
Fight The Feeling was always close to the pace and had every chance, but could not deliver his confirmed Flat speed in this ground on the run-in. He looks moderate and may be better off in novice handicaps. *(op 20-1)*
On Y Va(FR), making his chasing debut, did not jump very well so the fact that he finished as close as he did rather sums up the merit of the form. These fences would have been a stiff test for another horse trying fences for the first time, so he is probably worth another chance at another venue. *(op 9-4 tchd 7-2)*
Jamerosier(FR) was off the bridle after a circuit which was a worry considering they went a pedestrian early pace and it eventually became all too much. He has plenty of experience over fences and looks just plain moderate. *(op 8-1)*
Comte De Chambord was well beaten when taking a pearler at the last in the back straight on the final circuit. *(op 2-1)*
Henry's Pride(IRE) only made it as far as the first ditch when his rider fell off. *(op 2-1)*

4055 BOOK TICKETS ON-LINE HUNTERS' CHASE (16 fncs) 2m 4f 110y
2:50 (2:50) (Class 6) 5-Y-O+ **£1,648** (£507; £253)

Form RPR

2P4- **1** **Abalvino (FR)**[51] 12-11-7 105 .... (t) MissJWickens(7) 95+
(Miss J Wickens) *mde all: rdn clr 5 out: styd on* **9/2**[3]

31P **2** *dist* **Viscount Bankes**[51] 8-11-11 .... MrJNewbold(7) —
(Mrs Rosemary Gasson) *a.p: chsd wnr fr 1/2-way: rdn along and outpcd fr 5 out* **14/1**

0-6P **3** *dist* **River Pirate (IRE)**[12] [3847] 9-12-1 103 .... (b) MrJMahot(7) —
(David W Drinkwater) *chsd ldrs: rdn along 5 out. sn outpcd* **25/1**

F-5P **4** *22* **Gue Au Loup (FR)**[278] [437] 12-11-7 78 .... MrWKinsey(7) —
(J Groucott) *in tch: rdn along and outpcd fr 5 out* **25/1**

2143 **F** **Emperor Ross (IRE)**[238] [857] 11-11-11 111 .... MrCJCallow(7) —
(N G Richards) *prom tl fell 4th* **6/4**[1]

6-40 **P** **Master Papa (IRE)**[298] [127] 7-11-7 106 .... MrDGreenway(7) —
(P H Hogarth) *mstke 1st: a rr: bhd whn p.u bef 10th* **10/3**[2]

U **Fifth Column (USA)**[11] 5-11-0 .... MrSWByrne(7) —
(M V Coglan) *keen: cl up: mstke and lost pl 3rd: sn bhd and uns rdr 7th* **9/1**

P **Student Night (IRE)**[382] 7-11-7 .... MrFBarr(7) —
(John E F Skelton) *blnd 1st: nt jump wl after and sn t.o: blnd bdly 8th and p.u after* **20/1**

6m 0.30s (31.20) **Going Correction** +0.60s/f (Soft)
WFA 5 from 7yo+ 7lb **8** Ran SP% **110.4**
Speed ratings: **64**,—,—,—,— —,—,— CSF £52.25 TOTE £5.40: £1.60, £2.90, £6.60; EX 65.80.
Owner Miss J Wickens **Bred** Mrs Martine Van De Kerchove **Trained** Lingfield, Surrey

FOCUS
Even for a hunter chase, this was dire and these horses seemed to find the fences and the conditions all too much. It also took an absolute age to run and the winning time was 21.7 seconds slower than the opening contest over the same trip. The contest should be readily dismissed for form purposes with the future in mind.

NOTEBOOK
Abalvino(FR), a useful two-mile handicap chaser for Paul Webber a few years ago, was given a positive ride and was kept noticeably wide in search of better ground. He patently did not stay this trip in the conditions and was very tired over the last three fences, so the fact that he still won by a distance should be ignored with the future in mind as it just sums up how bad the opposition was after the favourite departed. *(tchd 4-1)*
Viscount Bankes achieved absolutely nothing in finishing a very remote second and the only saving grace is that this ground would have been far too soft for him. *(op 12-1)*
River Pirate(IRE) showed up for a while, but eventually dropped right away and looks a shadow of the horse he was.
Gue Au Loup(FR) *Official explanation: jockey said gelding was unsuited by the soft ground (op 33-1)*
Emperor Ross(IRE), reappearing from an eight-month break, was amongst the group chasing the eventual winner when coming down at the fourth. *(op 25-1 tchd 16-1)*
Master Papa(IRE), reappearing from a ten-month break and making his hunter-chase debut, seemed to get unnerved after a mistake at the first and was eventually pulled up a mile from home. *(op 25-1 tchd 16-1)*
Student Night(IRE) *Official explanation: jockey said gelding was unsuited by the soft ground (op 25-1 tchd 16-1)*

4056 MORE JUMPING ON 3RD MARCH (S) HURDLE (9 hdls) 2m
3:20 (3:21) (Class 5) 4-6-Y-O **£2,398** (£698; £349)

Form RPR

P0 **1** **Benefit Fund (IRE)**[21] [3677] 6-11-2 .... WarrenMarston 79+
(D J Wintle) *racd wd: a.p: pushed along 2 out: sn rdn and led bef last: drvn out flat* **15/2**[3]

-PP0 **2** *2* **Made In France (FR)**[14] [3804] 6-12-0 105 .... (v[1]) TomScudamore 87
(M C Pipe) *hld up: hdwy on bit 4 out: cl up 2 out: sn led and hung bdly rt and lft: hdd appr last: drvn and one pce flat* **4/1**[1]

00 **3** *6* **Heversham (IRE)**[17] [2763] 5-11-2 .... GrahamLee 69
(J Hetherton) *in tch: rdn along and sltly outpcd 4 out: rdn next: styd on u.p fr 2 out* **4/1**[1]

00 **4** *1* **Karrnak**[16] [2949] 4-10-1 ow1 .... (p) MrMatthewSmith(7) 62+
(Miss J Feilden) *led: rdn along after 3 out: hdd after next and sn wknd* **12/1**

-P06 **5** *8* **Sunny Daze**[12] [3843] 6-10-9 71 .... MrDAFitzsimmons(7) 60
(D McCain) *chsd ldrs: rdn along 5th: wknd 3 out* **18/1**

6404 **6** *3 ½* **Theflyingscottie**[33] [3479] 4-10-2 81 .... ChrisHonour(5) 48
(J D Frost) *prom: pushed along and hit 4 out: sn rdn and wknd after next* **5/1**[2]

R0R- **7** *2* **Golden Fields (IRE)**[66] [1292] 6-10-9 .... RichardMcGrath 48
(G A Harker) *reluctant s: bhd tl sme hdwy 4 out: sn rdn and nvr a factor* **12/1**

2060 **8** *3 ½* **Another Misk**[33] [3485] 4-10-4 85 .... PeterBuchanan(3) 42
(M E Sowersby) *bhd fr 1/2-way* **17/2**

PP-P **P** **Barbilyrifle (IRE)**[37] [3415] 5-10-9 .... (b) TomMessenger(7) —
(H H G Owen) *a bhd: p.u bef 3 out* **100/1**

0P **P** **Cabopino Lad (USA)**[8] [3912] 4-10-4 .... AnthonyCoyle(3) —
(Miss Tracy Waggott) *in tch: rdn along and wknd 3 out: plld bef next* **66/1**

50P6 **P** **Barneys Reflection**[28] [3562] 6-11-7 97 .... (b) PatrickMcDonald(7) —
(A Crook) *chsd ldrs: rdn along 4 out and sn wknd: bhd whn p.u bef last* **15/2**[3]

4m 20.9s (13.70) **Going Correction** +0.60s/f (Soft)
WFA 4 from 5yo+ 9lb **11** Ran SP% **113.9**
Speed ratings: **89,88,85,84,80 78,77,76**,—,— — CSF £37.02 TOTE £8.50: £2.40, £1.50, £2.00; EX 33.80.There was no bid for the winner. Theflyingscottie was claimed by Roger Milward for £6,000.
Owner D J Wintle **Bred** Patrick Hennessy **Trained** Naunton, Gloucs
■ Stewards' Enquiry : Mr Matthew Smith three-day ban: used whip with excessive frequency and force (Mar 6-8)

FOCUS
This was a very poor race run in a modest time, even for a seller, and form amounts to very little.

NOTEBOOK
Benefit Fund(IRE), pulled up on his first start over hurdles and beaten nearly 100 lengths in the second, was taking a significant drop in class and the market clearly suggested a big improvement was expected. He seemed to be travelling much better than his rivals from some way out and though it took him some while to get on top, he got there in plenty of time and would have won by a bit further had it not been for a clumsy jump at the last. The form means little, but that may not *matter now that the gamble has been landed.Official explanation: trainer said, regarding the improved form shown, gelding was suited by drop in class and distance (op 12-1)*
Made In France(FR), visored for the first time, was close enough turning for home but this ground would have been softer than ideal and he seemed to get tired between the last two flights. The winner's slow jump at the last gave him another chance, but he lacked the resources to capitalise on it.
Heversham(IRE), well beaten in banded company on the Fibresand since a couple of outings in better company over hurdles in December, ran as though even this was an insufficient test but the form amounts to little in any case. *(tchd 9-2)*
Karrnak, another comfortably held in banded company on sand since his last outing over hurdles, had the cheekpieces on for the first time. Given a positive ride, he tended to jump very big over these brush hurdles early on and, though he was still in front at the second last, the distress signals were soon going out and he had nothing more to give. *(op 10-1 tchd 14-1)*
Sunny Daze has already been well beaten at this level and achieved nothing here. *(op 14-1 tchd 20-1)*
Theflyingscottie did not build on his Chepstow effort on this further drop in class. *(op 4-1)*

4057 SOUTHWELL-RACECOURSE.CO.UK JUVENILE NOVICES' HURDLE (9 hdls) 2m

3:50 (3:52) (Class 4) 4-Y-O **£3,253** (£955; £477; £238)

Form RPR

4P **1** **Shamayoun (FR)**[10] [3883] 4-10-12 ....(b[1]) SamThomas 123+
(C R Egerton) *led and sn clr: j. repeatedly lft: rdn after 3 out: styd on wl* **20/1**

21 **2** *16* **Tora Bora (GER)**[78] [2681] 4-11-5 110.............................. TimmyMurphy 111+
(B G Powell) *chsd ldrs: effrt 3 out: rdn bef next: kpt on same pce u.p: no ch w wnr* **10/3[2]**

323 **3** *3/4* **Victorias Groom (GER)**[42] [3340] 4-10-12 112................. LeightonAspell 103+
(Mrs L Wadham) *chsd wnr: rdn along after 3 out: drvn next and kpt on same pce* **11/10[1]**

2P55 **4** *1* **Dock Tower (IRE)**[30] [3539] 4-10-9 104.......................(t) PeterBuchanan(3) 101
(M E Sowersby) *in tch: hit 4th and sn lost pl: rdn along 4 out: styd on fr 2 out: nvr a factor* **25/1**

U044 **5** *15* **Inn For The Dancer**[37] [3423] 4-10-12 .... JosephByrne 86
(Mrs H Dalton) *chsd ldrs: rdn along and mstke 4 out: sn drvn and outpcd* **33/1**

514 **6** *dist* **Vocative (GER)**[91] [2442] 4-10-7 .... PaddyMerrigan(5) —
(P C Haslam) *hld up: a rr* **11/1**

7 *dist* **Cetshwayo**[126] 4-10-12 .... AndrewThornton —
(J M P Eustace) *a bhd* **40/1**

P **Orenay (USA)**[46] 4-10-5 .... TomMessenger(7) —
(W B Stone) *a rr: bhd whn p.u bef 2 out* **80/1**

20 **U** **Kickahead (USA)**[27] [3579] 4-10-12 .... GrahamLee —
(Ian Williams) *prom whn uns rdr 1st* **16/1**

6 **P** **Lucky Shame (FR)**[6] [3948] 4-10-12 .... JamesDavies —
(A J Whitehead) *a bhd: p.u after 4th* **100/1**

0P5 **P** **Trappeto (IRE)**[15] [3786] 4-10-12 93.............................. JamieMoore —
(C Smith) *towards rr: mstke 6th: sn bhd and p.u bef 2 out* **100/1**

12 **P** **Parsley's Return**[33] [3485] 4-11-5 112.............................. WayneHutchinson —
(M Wigham) *midfield: lost pl and bhd fr 1/2-way: p.u bef 2 out* **7/1[3]**

50 **P** **Sandysnowing (FR)**[75] [2753] 4-10-7 .... BrianHughes(5) —
(J Howard Johnson) *chsd ldrs: nt fluent: mstke 6th: sn lost pl and bhd whn p.u bef 2 out* **80/1**

4m 13.8s (6.60) **Going Correction** +0.60s/f (Soft) **13** Ran SP% **115.9**
Speed ratings: **107,99,98,98,90** —,—,—,—,— —,—,— CSF £82.63 TOTE £25.80: £4.50, £1.50, £1.10; EX 99.10.
Owner Ronald Brimacombe **Bred** S A Aga Khan **Trained** Chaddleworth, Berks

FOCUS
No messing about in this and the winning time was over seven seconds faster than the seller. The winner was very impressive, but also still looked quirky.

NOTEBOOK
Shamayoun(FR), blinkered for the first time, still looked very wayward, hanging all over the track and jumping alarmingly to his left at most flights, but he still managed to bolt up having been given a positive ride from the start. He obviously has plenty of ability, but is clearly quirky and backing him will always carry a risk. *Official explanation: trainer said, regarding the improved form shown, colt was suited by first time blinkers (op 22-1)*
Tora Bora(GER) was probably not helped by dropping back in trip and was making hard work of it from some way out. He probably came across a talented if enigmatic type in the winner in pretty difficult conditions, and should not be written off just yet. *(op 9-2 tchd 11-2)*
Victorias Groom(GER) could never get anywhere near the winner and even these testing conditions could not hide his lack of pace over this trip. He really needs further. *(op Evens tchd 6-5)*
Dock Tower(IRE) has not really built on early promise, but is another that looks to need a longer trip now. *(op 33-1)*
Inn For The Dancer was left behind from the home bend, but may prefer better ground.
Lucky Shame(FR) *Official explanation: jockey said saddle slipped*

4058 BETFRED H'CAP HURDLE (11 hdls) 2m 4f 110y

4:20 (4:20) (Class 3) (0-120,120) 4-Y-O+ **£5,204** (£1,528; £764; £381)

Form RPR

0-F5 **1** **Presumptuous**[65] [2925] 6-10-11 **105**.............................. DavidO'Meara 125+
(Mrs S J Smith) *a.p: effrt 3 out: led next: rdn clr appr last: styd on* **11/2[3]**

433U **2** *14* **Calusa Charlie (IRE)**[9] [3901] 7-11-2 **110**.............................. TomDoyle 112
(B G Powell) *cl up: led 6th: rdn along 3 out: hdd next: sn drvn and one pce* **15/2**

PP22 **3** *5* **A Bit Of Fun**[10] [3889] 5-11-0 **108**.............................. JohnMcNamara 105
(J T Stimpson) *hld up: hdwy to trck ldrs 1/2-way: effrt and cl up 3 out: sn rdn and one pce fr next* **11/1**

31-P **4** *4* **Blairgowrie (IRE)**[108] [2078] 7-11-9 **120**.............................. PeterBuchanan(3) 113
(J Howard Johnson) *led to 6th: j. slowly next: cl up tl rdn along 3 out and grad wknd* **33/1**

3362 **5** *8* **Ingres**[34] [3458] 6-10-12 **113**.............................. CharlieStudd(7) 98
(B G Powell) *hld up and bhd: hdwy 1/2-way: pushed along and in tch 3 out: sn drvn and no imp* **11/1**

-F25 **6** *22* **Fred's In The Know**[21] [3675] 11-10-13 **110**.................. AnthonyCoyle(3) 73
(Miss Tracy Waggott) *hld up: hdwy7th: rdn along in tch whn blnd 3 out and sn wknd* **33/1**

040P **7** *11* **Always Waining (IRE)**[53] [3143] 5-11-7 **115**.............................. SamStronge 67
(R M Stronge) *cl up: rdn along 4 out: wknd next* **16/1**

1434 **8** *10* **Woody Valentine (USA)**[25] [3615] 5-11-8 **116**.............................. SamThomas 58
(Miss Venetia Williams) *a rr: rdn along 3rd: nvr a factor* **3/1[1]**

-125 **9** *11* **Petwick (IRE)**[51] [3214] 7-11-5 **113**.............................. WayneHutchinson 44
(A King) *reminders in rr 2nd: a bhd* **5/1[2]**

-P01 **10** *27* **Supreme Leisure (IRE)**[30] [3542] 9-11-4 **117**.............................. BrianHughes(5) 21
(J Howard Johnson) *in tch: rdn along 7th: sn wknd and bhd bef 3 out* **16/1**

F/0- **P** **Red Sun**[20] [111] 9-11-3 **118**..............................(t) PatrickMcDonald(7) —
(J Mackie) *prom tl lost pl 5th: sn bhd and p.u bef 2 out* **20/1**

P-P0 **P** **Mambo (IRE)**[10] [3880] 8-11-8 **116**.............................. MickFitzgerald —
(N J Henderson) *chsd ldrs: rdn along and lost pl 7th: sn bhd and p.u bef 3 out* **22/1**

31P1 **U** **Topanberry (IRE)**[62] [2944] 7-11-1 **109**.............................. TonyDobbin —
(N G Richards) *in tch on inner: pushed along 7th: sn wknd and bhd whn p.u bef 2 out* **8/1**

5m 31.8s (10.30) **Going Correction** +0.60s/f (Soft) **13** Ran SP% **123.4**
Speed ratings: **104,98,96,95,92 83,79,75,71,61** —,—,— CSF £46.18 CT £447.05 TOTE £7.30: £2.20, £2.50, £3.30; EX 68.60.
Owner Sam Berry,C Bradford-Nutter,J Berry **Bred** J And Mrs Berry **Trained** High Eldwick, W Yorks

FOCUS
A modest handicap run in very soft conditions. The winner almost certainly handled conditions better than most and the form, rated through the second to his mark, should be treated with caution.

NOTEBOOK
Presumptuous had not been seen since breaking a blood-vessel back in December - a race that featured three subsequent winners in front of him. He handled the ground conditions really well, stretching further clear of his rivals all the way up the straight. The Handicapper is sure to have his say after such a clear success so things will not be so easy next time, unless he is turned out fairly quickly under similar conditions. *(op 7-1)*
Calusa Charlie(IRE), who unseated his jockey early last time, shaped nicely over the French-style hurdles and is viewed very much as a chaser in the making. He kept on well to the line but had no chance with the winner. *(op 8-1)*
A Bit Of Fun gave the impression he never got home in the ground. He can be given another chance over the trip when the going is less testing. *(op 9-1)*
Blairgowrie(IRE) did not run too badly but was failed to get home under his big weight.
Ingres never got into contention after being behind in the early stages. *(op 12-1)*
Woody Valentine(USA) failed to make any impression during the race and is probably much better suited by a less-demanding surface. *Official explanation: trainer had no explanation for the poor form shown (op 4-1)*

4059 BOOK HOSPITALITY HERE MARES' ONLY INTERMEDIATE OPEN NATIONAL HUNT FLAT RACE 2m

4:50 (4:51) (Class 6) 4-6-Y-O **£2,055** (£599; £299)

Form RPR

2 **1** **Karello Bay**[34] [3468] 5-11-2 .... MickFitzgerald 96+
(N J Henderson) *hld up: stdy hdwy on outer over 6f out: led wl over 2f out: pushed clr over 1f out: easily* **8/11[1]**

00 **2** *12* **Tuckers Bay**[41] [3353] 5-10-11 .... AdamPogson(5) 78
(J R Holt) *a.p: led over 6f out: rdn along over 3f out: hdd wl over 2f out: sn drvn and one pce* **66/1**

204 **3** *3/4* **Even Flo**[58] [2987] 5-11-2 .... JimmyMcCarthy 77
(Jean-Rene Auvray) *midfield: hdwy to trck ldrs 1/2-way: cl up over 4f out: rdn along 3f out: drvn and one pce fnl 2f* **25/1**

4 *8* **Parthian Shot** 6-11-2 .... WarrenMarston 69
(R T Phillips) *hld up: hdwy 6f out: styd on fnl 2f: nvr nr ldrs* **9/1[3]**

5 *2 1/2* **Elaeagnus** 4-10-7 .... RichardMcGrath 58
(C Grant) *trckd ldrs on inner: effrt 6f out: sn rdn along and wknd fnl 3f* **40/1**

6 *11* **So Chic** 4-10-7 .... WayneHutchinson 47
(A King) *in tch: rdn along 5f out: sn wknd* **5/1[2]**

P **7** *9* **Bannow Beach (IRE)**[41] [3353] 5-10-9 .... PatrickMcDonald(7) 47
(J Mackie) *led: hdd over 6f out: sn drvn and wknd 4f out* **9/1[3]**

8 *21* **True Tara** 4-10-2 .... JamesDiment(5) 17
(J L Spearing) *cl up: rdn along over 6f out and sn wknd* **40/1**

0 **9** *dist* **Molly McGredy**[13] [3820] 5-11-2 .... JamieMoore —
(G Haine) *in tch: rdn along over 6f out: sn wknd* **66/1**

10 *4* **Bee Vee Pea (IRE)** 6-10-6 .... MichaelO'Connell(10) —
(Mrs S J Smith) *chsd ldrs: rdn along 1/2-way: snw eakened* **25/1**

6 **11** *shd* **Falcon's Cliche**[35] [3448] 5-11-2 .... RussGarritty —
(P Beaumont) *chsd ldrs: rdn along over 6f out and sn wknd* **20/1**

12 *29* **Tofta Tilly** 6-11-2 .... KennyJohnson —
(L R James) *a rr: bhd fnl 4f* **66/1**

0 **13** *dist* **Scarlet Romance**[106] [2105] 4-10-7 .... WilsonRenwick —
(M W Easterby) *a rr: t.o fnl 4f* **40/1**

4m 15.2s (10.70) **Going Correction** +0.60s/f (Soft)
WFA 4 from 5yo 9lb 5 from 6yo 6lb **13** Ran SP% **118.8**
Speed ratings: **97,91,90,86,85 79,75,64,**—,— —,—,— CSF £97.20 TOTE £1.50: £1.02, £27.20, £5.00; EX 82.80 Place 6 £225.33, Place 5 £75.17.
Owner Turf Club 2004 **Bred** R D And Mrs J S Chugg **Trained** Upper Lambourn, Berks
■ Stewards' Enquiry : Jimmy McCarthy two-day ban: used whip with excessive force (Mar 5-6)

FOCUS
A very moderate bumper in which at least half of the field were tailed off by halfway. Apart from the winner, who was value for half as much again, the form looks very limited.

NOTEBOOK
Karello Bay, who had experience behind her, won really nicely but the form of the race will almost certainly amount to very little given the calibre of opposition she faced and the state of the ground. She clearly has ability but will need testing against better company before knowing exactly how good she is. *(op 4-6)*
Tuckers Bay, who had shown very little in two previous runs, claimed the runner-up spot but was not in the same league as the winner. The trainer does well with his small string but he will struggle to find an opening in the short term for his mare.
Even Flo kept on well but did not seem to appreciate the ease in the ground.
Parthian Shot, who is a half-sister to Senorita Rumbalita, stayed on readily enough in the final stages after being left behind rounding the home turn. She is one of only a very few in the race that can be given another chance next time. *(op 8-1)*
Elaeagnus stayed on well throughout the final stages but will probably need much further than two miles to be at her best. However, the effort was not without promise.
So Chic never featured at any stage and was very disappointing. She may not have appreciated the ground and can be given another chance in a similar grade. *(op 6-1)*
T/Plt: £412.00 to a £1 stake. Pool: £46,286.15. 82.00 winning tickets. T/Qpdt: £23.60 to a £1 stake. Pool: £3,515.60. 109.80 winning tickets. JR

3771 PUNCHESTOWN (R-H)

Wednesday, February 22

OFFICIAL GOING: Heavy

4060a BOOK YOUR FESTIVAL TICKETS HURDLE 2m 4f

2:15 (2:15) 5-Y-O **£6,671** (£1,554; £685; £395)

RPR

1 **Sir Overbury**[11] [3869] 5-11-12 .... DJCasey 118+
(Daniel O'Connell, Ire) *in tch: bdly hmpd and lost pl 4 out: mod 7th after 2 out: hdwy ent st: 3rd last: sn chal: led 100 yds out: kpt on wl u.p* **11/2[3]**

2 *1 1/2* **Prideoftheyankees (IRE)**[20] [3702] 5-11-12 .... PCarberry 115
(W J Burke, Ire) *cl up: led fr 3rd: rdn clr after 2 out: strly pressed after last: hdd 100 yds out: kpt on u.p* **9/4[1]**

3 *1* **Mercuric**[14] [3808] 5-11-12 .... TPTreacy 114
(Mrs John Harrington, Ire) *hld up in tch: 6th 3 out: 5th whn slt mstke and rdn next: hdwy on inner ent st: 2nd appr last: kpt on u.p* **5/2[2]**

4 *6* **Ballyfinney (IRE)**[46] [3303] 5-11-3 .... RLoughran(3) 102
(D T Hughes, Ire) *prom: 2nd fr 5th: rdn after 3 out: kpt on same pce u.p fr next* **25/1**

5 *2* **Patsy Bee (IRE)**[48] [3263] 5-11-12 .... PWFlood 106
(E J O'Grady, Ire) *trckd ldrs in 4th: 3rd after 4 out: 2nd and rdn after 2 out: hung lft ent st: no ex fr last* **12/1**

The Form Book, Raceform Ltd, Compton, RG20 6NL

6 3 ½ **Openide**[18] [3727] 5-11-5 ....(b) MrMWall(7) 102
(B W Duke) *led: hdd 3rd: drvn along bef 4 out: 4th u.p next: no ex fr 2 out* **12/1**

7 13 **Code Of Rules (IRE)**[31] [3525] 5-11-12 109.................... BJGeraghty 89
(T J Taaffe, Ire) *hld up in tch: slt mstke 2nd: prog into 4th 2 out: sn rdn: no ex last: eased run-in* **11/2**[3]

F **Reinedoff (IRE)**[32] [3517] 5-11-7 113.................... LJFleming(5) —
(Noel Lawlor, Ire) *settled 5th: cl up whn fell 4 out* **8/1**

P **Powerful Pearl (IRE)**[14] [3808] 5-10-8 .... JPFortune(7) —
(P J Rothwell, Ire) *a bhd: rdn and wknd after 5th: t.o whn p.u after 2 out* **100/1**

5m 23.7s **9** Ran SP% **121.4**
CSF £19.87 TOTE £6.90: £1.70, £1.90, £1.70; DF 32.60.
Owner Hannigans Bar Again Syndicate **Bred** Peter Parkinson **Trained** Bansha, Co Tipperary

NOTEBOOK
Sir Overbury overcame difficulties in running which saw him with no chance before two out, but he stayed on strongly, was able to challenge after the last and got up inside the last half furlong. It was a decent performance in the circumstances and he is clearly progressive. *(op 5/1 tchd 6/1)*
Prideoftheyankees(IRE) would be rated higher than the winner on previous form and looked like justifying favouritism until pegged back on the run-in. He may be better off reverting to more patient tactics in the future. *(op 9/4 tchd 5/2)*
Mercuric did not look particularly happy though the first half of the contest, but still emerged to have every chance at the last, before finding only the one pace. *(op 9/4)*
Ballyfinney(IRE) ran well although a bit out of his class. *(op 25/1 tchd 33/1)*
Openide had far too much on his plate in this company. *(op 12/1 tchd 14/1)*
Code Of Rules(IRE) flattened out in the home straight and proved disappointing. *(op 5/1 tchd 6/1)*
Powerful Pearl(IRE) *Official explanation: 60-day ban: uncompetitive performances; trainer said, regarding the poor form shown, mare has a soft palate problem and would benefit from better ground; jockey said mare made a noise in running (op 66/1)*

4064 - 4066a (Foreign Racing) - See Raceform Interactive

3969 HAYDOCK (L-H)
Thursday, February 23

OFFICIAL GOING: Heavy
Wind: Light, across Weather: Persistent showers

4067 COTEBROOK NOVICES' H'CAP HURDLE (8 hdls) 2m
1:50 (1:50) (Class 3) (0-120,112) 4-Y-0+ **£5,204** (£1,528; £764; £381)

Form RPR
2624 1 **Billyandi (IRE)**[24] [3650] 6-11-2 **102**.................... CarlLlewellyn 107+
(N A Twiston-Davies) *in tch: rdn 2 out: edgd lft and styd on to ld run-in: drvn out* **6/1**[3]

5651 2 1 ¼ **Rojabaa**[22] [3673] 7-10-11 **102**.................... LiamHeard(5) 105
(B D Leavy) *midfield: hdwy after 4th: chalng 2 out: styd on u.p towards fin* **16/1**

6P2 3 shd **Auenmoon (GER)**[31] [3534] 5-11-12 **112**.................... RichardJohnson 115
(P Monteith) *led: hdd briefly 3 out: rdn appr last: hdd run-in: kpt on u.p* **10/1**

6-31 4 4 **Fabulous Jet (FR)**[42] [3355] 6-11-5 **105**.................... SamThomas 105+
(Miss Venetia Williams) *racd keenly: chsd ldr: led briefly 3 out: rdn appr last: no ex run-in* **6/1**[3]

405P 5 7 **What'sonyourmind (IRE)**[26] [3613] 6-10-11 **97**.................... APMcCoy 89
(Jonjo O'Neill) *hld up: niggled along after 3rd: outpcd appr 2 out: nvr on terms* **13/2**

0456 6 ½ **Royal Stardust**[20] [3717] 5-11-0 **105**.................... EamonDehdashti(5) 97
(G L Moore) *chsd ldrs: rdn appr 2 out: wknd bef last* **14/1**

0600 7 16 **Mokum (FR)**[19] [3729] 5-10-9 **95**....................(v¹) GrahamLee 71
(A W Carroll) *a bhd* **14/1**

2141 8 3 ½ **Birdwatch**[12] [3853] 8-11-11 **111**....................(b) RichardMcGrath 83
(K G Reveley) *in tch: lost pl after 3rd: struggling after* **9/2**[1]

1022 9 2 ½ **Eborarry (IRE)**[19] [3737] 4-11-1 **110**.................... RussGarritty 71
(T D Easterby) *hld up: hdwy appr 3 out: rdn and wknd bef last* **11/2**[2]

0053 P **Network Oscar (IRE)**[58] [3042] 5-10-6 **95**.................... MrTGreenall(3) —
(M W Easterby) *midfield: junked rt 3rd: blnd 4th: wknd after 4 out: t.o whn p.u bef 2 out* **9/1**

4m 0.70s (1.60) **Going Correction** +0.275s/f (Yiel)
WFA 4 from 5yo+ 9lb **10** Ran SP% **113.8**
Speed ratings: **107,106,106,104,100 100,92,90,89,—** CSF £90.85 CT £938.01 TOTE £7.90: £2.50, £4.50, £3.30; EX 125.90 TRIFECTA Not won..
Owner Hamsard Ltd **Bred** Keith Watson **Trained** Naunton, Gloucs

FOCUS
This was a decent race of its type and the form looks sound enough. Improved form from the first three with the fourth setting the standard.

NOTEBOOK
Billyandi(IRE) usually makes the running, but with several confirmed front runners in opposition different tactics were applied, to good effect. This likeable sort acts on most types of ground and will stay further. *(tchd 13-2)*
Rojabaa was put up 12lb for his win in a Leicester claimer. After travelling well into the straight, he could not quicken from the penultimate flight but did snatch second near the line.
Auenmoon(GER), whose Ayr conqueror Regal Heights has franked the form, won the battle for the lead. He was shaded with three to run but fought back with the rail to race against until unable to pull out any extra on the run-in. *(op 8-1)*
Fabulous Jet(FR) was unable to make the running with Auenmoon in opposition, but briefly headed that opponent before having to give best going to the last. This was only his fourth run over hurdles and he has improvement in him. *(op 9-2)*
What'sonyourmind(IRE) is proven on heavy ground, having won a bumper in similar conditions, *but this drop in trip appeared to find him out and he could never reach a challenging position. (op 11-2)*
Birdwatch has been in fine form recently but he was never going here from this 9lb higher mark. *He probably needs to lead. Official explanation: trainer had no explanation for the poor form shown (tchd 5-1)*

4068 BEAR NOVICES' H'CAP CHASE (17 fncs) 2m 6f
2:20 (2:20) (Class 3) (0-130,120) 5-Y-0+ **£6,506** (£1,910; £955; £477)

Form RPR
5034 1 **Bannister Lane**[15] [3794] 6-10-3 **97**.................... DominicElsworth 118+
(D McCain) *led to 2nd: regained ld appr 5th: clr bef last: comf* **4/1**[1]

4341 2 14 **Simon**[33] [3506] 7-11-6 **114**.................... GrahamLee 124+
(J L Spearing) *j.lft: led 2nd: hdd appr 5th: w wnr tl pushed along bef 3 out: btn bef last* **4/1**[1]

P441 3 10 **Vicario**[17] [3781] 5-11-2 **120**.................... PaddyAspell(3) 110+
(D McCain) *hld up in tch: outpcd whn hit 12th: n.d after* **9/2**[2]

P-1P 4 8 **Lord Brock**[26] [3614] 7-11-12 **120**.................... CarlLlewellyn 111+
(N A Twiston-Davies) *bhd fr 3rd: blnd next: struggling after* **4/1**[1]

1254 5 27 **Avitta (IRE)**[37] [3440] 7-11-6 **114**.................... SamThomas 74
(Miss Venetia Williams) *hld up in tch: wknd 13th: t.o* **9/2**[2]

-431 6 dist **Master Sebastian**[52] [3207] 7-11-6 **117**.................... PeterBuchanan(3) —
(Miss Lucinda V Russell) *j.rt: trckd ldrs: lost pl 7th: n.d after: t.o* **8/1**[3]

5m 48.0s (-0.80) **Going Correction** +0.15s/f (Yiel)
WFA 5 from 6yo+ 7lb **6** Ran SP% **107.5**
Speed ratings: **107,101,98,95,85** — CSF £18.48 TOTE £5.60: £2.60, £2.20; EX 29.10.
Owner Shaw Hill Golf Club(Sage Cott Props Ltd) **Bred** Halewood International Ltd **Trained** Cholmondeley, Cheshire

FOCUS
The winner was nicely in on his Wetherby run and produced an improved showing, while the runner-up ran better than he did when a lucky winner last time.

NOTEBOOK
Bannister Lane was getting over a stone from all of his rivals and that helped in this testing ground. He jumped particularly well and the slightly shorter trip suited him, although he was certainly not stopping at the end. *(tchd 9-2)*
Simon was a lucky winner at Wincanton and the Handicapper actually dropped him a pound. Jumping out to his left all the way, he could not go with the winner from the home turn and was held when untidy at the second last. *(tchd 9-2, 5-1 in places)*
Vicario, a stablemate of the winner, ran respectably on only his second run over fences but would have been suited by an even stiffer test. *(tchd 5-1 in places)*
Lord Brock jumped stickily and was soon struggling in rear, although he did keep going to earn *some prize money. He has now flopped twice since his successful chase debut at this course. (tchd 7-2)*
Avitta(IRE) was a disappointment and there was no obvious excuse this time. *(tchd 5-1)*
Master Sebastian was 7lb higher than when landing a very ordinary race at Ayr. Again jumping out to his right, he was in trouble from an early stage. *(op 6-1)*

4069 RENDLESHAM HURDLE (GRADE 2) (12 hdls) 2m 7f 110y
2:50 (2:51) (Class 1) 4-Y-0+ **£22,915** (£8,663; £4,391; £2,243; £1,179)

Form RPR
2-P2 1 **Royal Emperor (IRE)**[12] [3851] 10-11-4 148.................... PadgeWhelan 150+
(Mrs S J Smith) *mde all: pushed along after 4 out: rdn appr 2 out: styd on to draw clr run-in* **10/1**

P 2 19 **Millenium Royal (FR)**[19] [3723] 6-11-12 .... ADuchene 143+
(F Doumen, France) *in tch: hit 8th: hdwy after 4 out: rdn whn lft cl 2nd last: sn wknd* **16/1**

4344 3 12 **Crystal D'Ainay (FR)**[40] [3390] 7-11-12 159....................(v) RobertThornton 131+
(A King) *trckd ldrs: hit 8th: rdn and wknd after 4 out* **5/2**[1]

0052 4 5 **Sh Boom**[19] [3727] 8-11-4 143.................... LiamHeard 116+
(S A Brookshaw) *racd keenly: hld up: mstke 4th: j.rt and hdwy 8th: wknd after 4 out* **7/1**

10-2 5 dist **Blue Canyon (FR)**[97] [2326] 8-11-12 .... APMcCoy —
(F Doumen, France) *hld up in rr: hit 4 out: sn struggling: nvr on terms: t.o* **3/1**[3]

14-4 F **Patriarch Express**[19] [3723] 9-11-12 158.................... DominicElsworth 153+
(Mrs S J Smith) *trckd ldr: rdn appr 2 out: cl 2nd whn stmbld and fell last* **11/4**[2]

6m 13.1s (8.90) **Going Correction** +0.525s/f (Soft) **6** Ran SP% **107.7**
Speed ratings: **106,99,95,94,—** — CSF £111.88 TOTE £11.70: £3.40, £3.90; EX 68.60.
Owner Widdop Wanderers **Bred** Mrs Eleanor Hadden **Trained** High Eldwick, W Yorks
■ Race switched from Kempton.

FOCUS
Not a strong pointer to the World Hurdle, with Royal Emperor the only runner not to be entered in the Cheltenham race. The form is difficult to assess, with the runner-up stepping up on his Sandown form, the third 31lb off his best hurdles form but running to a similar level as recent chase runs and the faller heading for a figure on a par with his recent chase runs. Royal Rosa, due to appear for the first time since last year's Rendlesham, missed the race with a stone bruise and will not run this season.

NOTEBOOK
Royal Emperor(IRE), well at home in the mud, made all the running and stayed on strongly after gradually winding up the pace on the second circuit, but fortune was perhaps on his side as he was left clear by his stablemate's fall at the last. He is not in the World Hurdle and his Cheltenham target is the Gold Cup, but he would need very testing conditions to have any sort of a chance.
Millenium Royal(FR), the Doumen second string, looked a possible threat between the last two flights but did not really go through with his effort. He may accompany Baracouda in the World Hurdle line-up but really needs soft ground. *(op 14-1)*
Crystal D'Ainay(FR), reverting to hurdles, is without a win since taking this event at Kempton a year ago. He was never really travelling after being hampered by Sh Boom at the fifth flight from home and was beaten a long way into third. His trainer hopes a spell of hunting will freshen him up for the World Hurdle. *(tchd 11-4)*
Sh Boom returned to form last time, but this was a step back up in both class and trip, and on different ground. *(op 8-1)*
Blue Canyon(FR) was having his first run over a trip this far, although that was probably not the sole reason for this lacklustre effort. *(tchd 10-3 in places)*
Patriarch Express was throwing down a challenge to his stable companion, and might well have gone on to win, when he stumbled and came down a stride or two after the final flight. He was injured in last year's renewal and the Rendlesham is just not his race. Better ground will help his World Hurdle chances. *(op 5-2 tchd 3-1 in a place)*

4070 KNUTSFORD H'CAP CHASE (18 fncs) 3m
3:20 (3:21) (Class 3) (0-130,128) 5-Y-0+ **£7,807** (£2,292; £1,146; £572)

Form RPR
-31F 1 **King Bee (IRE)**[34] [3481] 9-10-10 **112**.................... RichardJohnson 131+
(H D Daly) *hdwy 2nd: led 4th: mde rest: drvn out* **11/2**[2]

14-F 2 3 ½ **Moulin Riche (FR)**[75] [2758] 6-11-12 **128**.................... RobertThornton 143+
(F Doumen, France) *hld up: mstke 10th (water): hdwy appr 11th: swtchd lft bef 2 out: rdn bef last: one pce run-in* **2/1**[1]

-312 3 3 ½ **Undeniable**[81] [2656] 8-11-6 **122**.................... DominicElsworth 135+
(Mrs S J Smith) *bhd 3rd: hit 8th: hdwy 9th: mstke 10th (water): sn lost pl: hdwy 4 out: rdn appr 2 out: no ex towards fin* **11/2**[2]

2515 4 7 **Wain Mountain**[19] [3739] 10-11-12 **128**....................(b) APMcCoy 134+
(J A B Old) *in tch: hdwy appr 11th: hit 12th: ev ch 3 out: wknd after last* **6/1**[3]

2261 5 26 **Jungle Jinks (IRE)**[40] [3396] 11-10-12 **114**.................... BarryKeniry 91
(G M Moore) *cl up: reminder and lost pl appr 10th (water): clsd 11th: wknd 12th* **7/1**

2F06 6 ½ **Strong Resolve (IRE)**[12] [3851] 10-11-4 **123**.................... PeterBuchanan(3) 100
(Miss Lucinda V Russell) *led to 4th: pushed along after and lost pl after 10th (water): bhd after* **20/1**

-3BU P **Tom Fruit**[6] [3965] 9-10-7 **109**.................... DavidO'Meara —
(T D Easterby) *cl up tl mstke and wknd 14th: t.o whn p.u bef 3 out* **6/1**[3]

6m 29.0s (0.70) **Going Correction** +0.275s/f (Yiel) **7** Ran SP% **109.9**
Speed ratings: **109,107,106,104,95 95,—** CSF £16.31 TOTE £6.30: £2.80, £1.80; EX 25.00.

Owner Trevor Hemmings **Bred** Lawson Burriss **Trained** Stanton Lacy, Shropshire

FOCUS

Probably a decent race and the form has been rated positively, with the winner up 11lb on his previous best and the runner-up running close to the level of his hurdles form last season.

NOTEBOOK

King Bee(IRE) is a progressive chaser and he defied a mark 6lb higher than when he won at Warwick on New Year's Eve. He had the run of the race from the front and stayed on dourly to fend off his challengers. *(op 13-2)*

Moulin Riche(FR) had not run over fences since winning at Auteuil in November 2004. On ground that did not suit him he could never quite get to the winner, but this was a good trial for the William Hill Trophy Chase at Cheltenham, a race the stable won last year with Kelami. *(tchd 9-4, 5-2 in places)*

Undeniable, 6lb higher than when a short-head runner-up to subsequent Red Square Vodka Gold Cup winner Ossmoses at Kelso, was in there fighting from the second last but could never quite find that bit extra required. *(op 4-1)*

Wain Mountain, who disappointed last time, ran his race again back over three miles, only conceding defeat from the final fence.

Jungle Jinks(IRE), put up 2lb for winning a weak race at Wetherby, found this more competitive. *(op 8-1)*

Strong Resolve(IRE) has become well handicapped, currently 8lb lower than when runner-up in last season's Welsh National, but he remains bang out of form. *(op 16-1)*

4071 RED SQUARE VODKA "FIXED BRUSH" NOVICES' HURDLE (10 hdls) — 2m 4f

3:55 (3:55) (Class 4) 4-7-Y-0 — **£4,554** (£1,337; £668; £333)

Form			Horse	Jockey	RPR
-231	1		**Dream Alliance**[26] 3611 5-11-9 (P J Hobbs) *a cl up: led 2 out: drew clr run-in: v easily* **1/3**[1]	RichardJohnson	120+
-434	2	12	**Woodview (IRE)**[41] 3372 7-11-3 105 (K C Bailey) *in tch: rdn and hung lft whn outpcd appr 2 out: kpt on to take 2nd towards fin: no ch w wnr* **8/1**[2]	(p) JohnMcNamara	89
0PP	3	1	**Casalani (IRE)**[13] 3843 7-10-10 (Jennie Candlish) *led: hdd 2 out: rdn and hung lft appr last: wknd run-in* **100/1**	JosephByrne	81
046P	4	¾	**William Butler (IRE)**[5] 3975 6-10-12 (S A Brookshaw) *prom: w ldrs 3rd: ev ch 3 out: rdn and wkng whn hit last* **50/1**	LiamHeard[(5)]	87
0	5	2½	**Tempsford (USA)**[26] 3611 6-11-3 (Jonjo O'Neill) *hld up: pushed along and outpcd after 4 out: kpt on run-in: nvr able to chal* **10/1**[3]	APMcCoy	85
643	6	¾	**Coleraine (IRE)**[21] 3685 6-11-3 (O Sherwood) *hld up: rdn and outpcd after 4 out: kpt on run-in: no imp* **10/1**[3]	TonyDobbin	84
6P	7	6	**Mr Smithers Jones**[69] 2859 6-11-3 (Mrs S M Johnson) *hld up: hdwy 6th: wknd appr 2 out* **50/1**	JodieMogford	80+
0	8	dist	**Dino's Dandy**[13] 3843 7-10-10 (B N Pollock) *racd keenly: w ldr: wknd 5th: n.d whn hit 4 out: t.o* **66/1**	TomMessenger[(7)]	—

5m 17.2s (8.00) **Going Correction** +0.525s/f (Soft) **8 Ran SP% 110.7**

Speed ratings: **105,100,99,99,98 98,95,**— CSF £3.37 TOTE £1.20: £1.02, £1.50, £11.30; EX 3.70.

Owner The Alliance Partnership **Bred** Rewbell Syndicate **Trained** Withycombe, Somerset

■ Stewards' Enquiry : Joseph Byrne three-day ban: used whip with excessive force and frequency (Mar 6-8)

FOCUS

The odds-on favourite, who had very little to beat, has been rated value for 25l in running to his mark.

NOTEBOOK

Dream Alliance had no problem supplementing his Chepstow gains, but the opposition was negligible. He looks worth his place in the Royal & SunAlliance Hurdle line-up at Cheltenham, where better ground will suit him. *(tchd 4-11)*

Woodview(IRE), reverting to hurdles, is not straightforward which explains the fitting of cheekpieces. Staying on up the run-in after jumping the last of the brush flights in fourth place, he will be suited by a return to three miles. *(tchd 7-1 in places)*

Casalani(IRE), winner of a maiden Irish point in April 2004, showed a lot more than on her previous outings under Rules.

William Butler(IRE), well beaten on his recent hurdles debut, ran to the level of his bumper form. A chasing type, he has been placed in a point-to-point.

Tempsford(USA) did finish closer to Dream Alliance than he had at Chepstow, but has a lot to prove now after two distinctly modest attempts over hurdles *(tchd 9-1)*

4072 TARVIN STANDARD OPEN NATIONAL HUNT FLAT RACE — 2m

4:30 (4:30) (Class 6) 4-6-Y-0 — **£1,713** (£499; £249)

Form			Horse	Jockey	RPR
01	1		**Night Safe (IRE)**[77] 2720 5-11-4 (N A Twiston-Davies) *led: hdd after 2f: remained prom: led again 1/2-way: rdn and hdd over 3f out: regained ld 2f out: edgd lft over 1f out: sty* **25/1**	MarcGoldstein[(7)]	113+
11	2	2	**Heraldry (IRE)**[89] 2507 6-11-4 (P C Haslam) *always prom: rdn 4f out: ev ch 2f out: no ex cl home* **7/1**[3]	GaryBartley[(10)]	114+
1-23	3	¾	**Oakapple Express**[63] 2948 6-11-11 (G A Harker) *trckd ldrs: rdn and hung lft whn outpcd over 2f out: styd on towards fin* **10/1**	AlanDempsey	109
1	4	9	**Wolds Way**[88] 2520 4-11-2 (T D Easterby) *in tch: hdwy 1/2-way: rdn over 3f out: hung lft and wknd over 2f out* **22/1**	RussGarritty	91
	5	hd	**Little Rocker (IRE)** 5-11-4 (M Pitman) *midfield: hdwy 1/2-way: rdn and outpcd 5f out: no imp after* **16/1**	MarkGrant	93
	6	hd	**Whitewater Dash** 6-11-4 (J A B Old) *hld up: pushed along and hdwy 3f out: nvr rchd ldrs* **33/1**	CarlLlewellyn	93
	7	¾	**Dancewiththedevil (IRE)**[42] 3366 5-11-4 (Jonjo O'Neill) *trckd ldrs: led over 3f out: hdd 2f out: wknd 1f out* **2/1**[1]	APMcCoy	92
	8	6	**Ajay (IRE)** 5-10-11 (T D Walford) *midfield: rdn 5f out: sn wknd* **100/1**	MrMWalford[(7)]	86
	9	nk	**Mister Etek** 5-11-1 (T D Walford) *in tch: rdn and wknd 5f out* **100/1**	PeterBuchanan[(3)]	86
4	10	2	**Man Of Mine**[52] 3216 5-11-4 (Mrs H Dalton) *racd keenly: hld up: rdn 6f out: nvr on terms* **20/1**	JohnMcNamara	84
	11	1½	**Fingersthumbsngums (IRE)** 5-11-4 (Jennie Candlish) *trckd ldrs tl wknd 7f out* **33/1**	JosephByrne	82
0	12	1½	**Coorbawn Vic (IRE)**[35] 3462 5-10-13 (S A Brookshaw) *hld up: rdn 5f out: no imp* **100/1**	LiamHeard[(5)]	81
	13	2½	**Nodforms Victoria (IRE)** 5-11-4 (Karen McLintock) *in tch: wknd over 6f out* **33/1**	TonyDobbin	78
	14	1	**Cooldine Boy (IRE)**[277] 5-11-4 (P J Hobbs) *sweating: prom: led after 2f: hdd 1/2-way: ev ch over 3f out: wknd 2f out* **9/4**[2]	RichardJohnson	77
	15	7	**Electric Times (IRE)** 5-11-4 (D McCain) *midfield: rdn over 4f out: sn wknd* **25/1**	GrahamLee	70
	16	9	**Master Bury** 5-10-11 (Miss T Jackson) *a bhd* **100/1**	MissTJackson[(7)]	61
	17	1¾	**Irish Guard** 5-11-4 (J G O'Neill) *midfield: hdwy after 4f: wknd 4f out* **100/1**	SeanCurran	60
	18	20	**Bronze King** 6-11-4 (J A B Old) *a bhd* **66/1**	WarrenMarston	40
	19	12	**Kerne Bridge** 6-10-11 (Mrs S M Johnson) *a bhd* **100/1**	JodieMogford	21
	20	dist	**Jillanory** 4-9-11 (C W Moore) *midfield: bhd fr 1/2-way: t.o* **100/1**	LiamTreadwell[(5)]	—

4m 2.00s (5.60) **Going Correction** +0.525s/f (Soft)

WFA 4 from 5yo 9lb 5 from 6yo 6lb **20 Ran SP% 125.6**

Speed ratings: **107,106,105,101,101 100,100,97,97,96 95,94,93,93,89 85,84,74,68,**— CSF £179.22 TOTE £34.90: £7.30, £2.30, £2.30; EX 145.90.

Owner C B Sanderson **Bred** John Blake **Trained** Naunton, Gloucs

■ Stewards' Enquiry : Marc Goldstein caution: careless riding

FOCUS

The four previous winners filled the first four places and this was a decent bumper, rated through the second. The form should work out well enough.

NOTEBOOK

Night Safe(IRE), back in front early in the home straight, battled on well to the line and is clearly a stayer. *Already proven on better ground, he may go for the Champion Bumper at Cheltenham now. (op 20-1)*

Heraldry(IRE), who sweated up in the preliminaries, ran well in this hat-trick bid and confirmed *November form here with Oakapple Express. He is well at home in testing ground. (op 8-1 tchd 9-1, 10-1 in places)*

Oakapple Express put in another solid run under his penalty. He will be suited by two and a half miles when he goes over hurdles. *(op 16-1, 20-1 in places)*

Wolds Way, who had subsequent scorer Tooting behind when making a successful debut nearly *three months ago, ran respectably but this longer trip in testing ground told in the last quarter-mile. (op 20-1)*

Little Rocker(IRE), a 26,000gns half-brother to the yard's useful chaser Too Forward, did best of the newcomers and obviously has ability. *(op 11-1)*

Whitewater Dash, whose dam was only a plater, made pleasing late progress from the back of the field.

Dancewiththedevil(IRE), runner-up on heavy ground at Limerick on his debut last month, took up the running going best but began to flounder with two furlongs to run and did not get home. He looks to have stamina limitations, in testing conditions at any rate. *(op 7-4 tchd 9-4 in places)*

Cooldine Boy(IRE), remounted to win an Irish maiden point last May, was rather disappointing on this debut under Rules but could need better ground. *(op 11-4 tchd 3-1 and 2-1)*

4073 WALRUS HUNTERS' CHASE (17 fncs) — 2m 6f

5:00 (5:00) (Class 3) 5-Y-0+ — **£7,182** (£2,227; £1,113; £556)

Form			Horse	Jockey	RPR
1U-P	1		**Cobreces**[40] 8-12-2 116 (Mrs L Borradaile) *cl up: upsides 3 out: led last: kpt on u.p* **5/1**[3]	MrJSnowden[(3)]	123
	2	¾	**Mage D'Estruval (FR)**[270] 6-11-11 (H D Daly) *led to 3rd: remained prom: led again after 4 out: jnd next: hdd last: hung lft run-in: nt qckn cl home* **10/3**[2]	MrPCallaghan[(5)]	119
5-P1	3	dist	**Denvale (IRE)**[19] 3736 8-12-2 (Mrs Caroline Bailey) *prom: led 3rd: hdd after 4 out: wknd next* **6/4**[1]	MrRCope[(3)]	91
/36-	4	8	**Curly Spencer (IRE)**[334] 12-11-5 108 (R J Hewitt) *hld up: hdwy 4th: lost pl 7th: hdwy 10th: hit 13th: rdn appr 3 out: wkng whn hit 2 out* **17/2**	MrAWadlow[(7)]	79
-151	5	8	**The Butterwick Kid**[9] 3913 13-11-12 96 (T P Tate) *a bhd* **6/1**	(b) MrRTATate[(7)]	75
5P-P	6	dist	**Camp Hill**[19] 3736 12-12-0 84 (J S Haldane) *in tch: j. slowly 2nd: reminder and lost pl after 9th (water): rdn and wknd 11th: t.o* **66/1**	MrWLMorgan[(5)]	—
66P/	P		**On The Mend (IRE)**[12] 13-11-7 (Miss S Balshaw) *hld in tch: hdwy 8th: wknd 11th: t.o whn p.u bef 3 out* **33/1**	MrGBrewer[(5)]	—

5m 52.0s (3.20) **Going Correction** +0.375s/f (Yiel) **7 Ran SP% 109.0**

Speed ratings: **109,108,**—,—,— —,— CSF £20.40 TOTE £5.60: £2.50, £2.40; EX 28.50 Place 6 £2,177.14, Place 5 £438.99.

Owner Mr & Mrs D Borradaile **Bred** Bering S A **Trained** Beaminster, Dorset

FOCUS

Good hunter form, which could be rated a lot higher, but those outside the first two were below form.

NOTEBOOK

Cobreces, fit from a run in a point-to-point at Barbury last month, just got the better of a fine duel in which neither participant gave an inch. While the Cheltenham Foxhunters' might be flying a bit high, he should win plenty more races. *(tchd 6-1 in places)*

Mage D'Estruval(FR) ♦ had only run once in his life, when winning a chase over an extended 17 furlongs at Meslay du Maine in the French provinces last May. Jumping these fences like an old hand, he just missed out after battling with the winner from the third last. He looks a smart recruit to this sphere and should have no problem going one better. *(op 4-1)*

Denvale(IRE) was rather disappointing although he ideally needs further. Not allowed an uncontested lead, he was immediately beaten once headed although he did stay on for a remote third. *(tchd 7-4 in places)*

Curly Spencer(IRE) ran a respectable race on his first start since winning a point-to-point at Whittington 11 months ago. *(op 7-1)*

The Butterwick Kid , runner-up in this event last year, produced an uncharacteristically flat effort. *(tchd 7-1 in places)*

T/Jkpt: Not won. T/Plt: £3,231.10 to a £1 stake. Pool: £57,762.20. 13.05 winning tickets. T/Qpdt: £139.10 to a £1 stake. Pool: £4,493.20. 23.90 winning tickets. DO

3938 HUNTINGDON (R-H)

Thursday, February 23

OFFICIAL GOING: Good to soft changing to soft after race 2 (2.30)

Wind: Light, half-behind Weather: Raining

4074 BRAYBROOK RACING FIRST FOR CUSTOMER SERVICE MARES' ONLY MAIDEN HURDLE (8 hdls) — 2m 110y

2:00 (2:01) (Class 4) 4-Y-0+ — **£3,253** (£955; £477; £238)

Form			Horse	Jockey	RPR
3-24	1		**Tessanoora**[47] 3280 5-11-0 (N J Henderson) *chsd ldrs: led 5th: hdd bef next: led after 3 out: mstke next: drvn clr flat* **15/8**[1]	MickFitzgerald	101+

2606 **2** *7* **Twist The Facts (IRE)**[21] 3690 6-11-0 .... PaulMoloney 92+
(N P Littmoden) *hld up: hdwy 4th: rdn appr 2 out: styd on same pce* **33/1**
52 **3** *3 ½* **Wee Dinns (IRE)**[21] 3690 5-11-0 .... TimmyMurphy 95+
(M C Pipe) *hld up in tch: hmpd 4th: led and hit 3 out: sn hdd: j.lft and wknd last* **2/1**[2]
4 *2* **Simply St Lucia**[6] 4-10-0 .... DougieCostello[(5)] 78
(J R Weymes) *mid-div: hdwy 4th: rdn whn hit 2 out: styd on same pce* **20/1**
0- **5** *½* **Sister Grace**[388] 3633 6-11-0 .... JamesDavies 87+
(N J Gifford) *hld up: hdwy 5th: styd on same pce fr 2 out: mstke last* **33/1**
6 *hd* **Cashbar**[223] 5-11-0 .... PJBrennan 86
(J R Fanshawe) *hld up in tch: rdn after 2 out: wknd last* **15/2**[3]
0000 **7** *11* **Allez Melina**[10] 3902 5-11-0 .... PhilipHide 75
(Mrs A J Hamilton-Fairley) *hld up: effrt appr 3 out: nvr trbld ldrs* **33/1**
460 **8** *7* **Quotable**[21] 3690 5-11-0 .... LeightonAspell 68
(O Sherwood) *hld up: hmpd 4: hdwy next: wknd 3 out* **20/1**
P **9** *5* **Sovietta (IRE)**[26] 3611 5-11-0 .... AndrewThornton 63
(A G Newcombe) *hdwy 3rd: wknd 3 out* **25/1**
3005 **10** *1 ¼* **Miss Chippy (IRE)**[21] 3692 6-11-0 .... JasonMaguire 62
(T R George) *hld up: effrt after 5th: sn wknd* **40/1**
40 **11** *5* **Ausone**[93] 2425 4-10-2 .... OwynNelmes[(3)] 48
(Miss J R Gibney) *hld up: hdwy 5th: wknd bef next* **50/1**
12 *11* **Lujain Rose**[35] 4-10-2 .... TJPhelan[(3)] 37
(N M Babbage) *hld up: a in rr* **150/1**
0-0P **13** *3* **Gay Gladys**[33] 3496 6-10-7 .... BernieWharfe[(7)] 43
(T H Caldwell) *prom tl wknd after 5th* **18/1**
00 **14** *28* **Blackcomb Mountain (USA)**[16] 3787 4-10-0 ....(v[1]) CharliePoste[(5)] 6
(M F Harris) *chsd ldrs: lft in ld 4th: hdd next: wknd appr 3 out* **150/1**
4-P **15** *2 ½* **One Alone**[30] 3550 5-11-0 ....(b) DaveCrosse 12
(Jean-Rene Auvray) *hld up: hmpd 4th: sn wknd* **66/1**
16 *dist* **Shoof (USA)**[18] 7-10-9 .... DerekLaverty[(5)] —
(M J Gingell) *a bhd* **100/1**
PP **F** **Cultured**[21] 3690 5-11-0 ....(b) AndrewTinkler —
(Mrs A J Bowlby) *chsd ldrs tl fell 4th* **100/1**
P **Inmom (IRE)**[51] 5-10-9 .... AdamPogson[(5)] —
(S R Bowring) *led: blnd 4th: sn hdd & wknd: t.o whn p.u bef last* **100/1**

4m 4.80s (9.10) **Going Correction** +0.625s/f (Soft)
WFA 4 from 5yo+ 9lb **18** Ran SP% **117.5**
Speed ratings: **103,99,98,97,96 96,91,88,85,85 83,77,76,63,62** —,—,— CSF £69.39 TOTE £2.00: £1.20, £6.60, £1.10; EX 33.50.
Owner Miss Tessa Henderson **Bred** R D And Mrs J S Chugg **Trained** Upper Lambourn, Berks

FOCUS
A typically uncompetitive mares' only event in which favourite Tessanoora continued Nicky Henderson's fine recent run of form with his mares. The race has been rated through the winner.

NOTEBOOK
Tessanoora, whose stable is in cracking form at present, particularly with its mares, surged clear in the final quarter mile to win going away and deserved to get her head in front. It is worth remembering however that this was a weak contest, as most mares-only events are, and she will need to up her game if attempting to defy a penalty. *(tchd 2-1)*
Twist The Facts(IRE) stepped up significantly on her Towcester sixth and stayed on well past Wee Dinns to claim second. She is clearly on the up and, with a step up in trip expected to bring about further improvement, she should be capable of finding a race at this level.
Wee Dinns(IRE) held obvious claims on the form of her Towcester second, but a mistake at the third-last seemed to throw her rhythm and she jumped badly to her left at each of the last two flights. She has the ability to win a small race and would make some appeal in low-grade handicaps. *(op 5-2 tchd 11-4)*
Simply St Lucia, a moderate sort on the Flat, made a pleasing hurdling debut and was keeping on late under her featherweight. A more positive ride in future may help and there is surely a race for her in this sphere. *(op 22-1)*
Sister Grace, down the field in a Kempton bumper over a year ago, made a little late headway *despite not jumping with any real fluency and she can be expected to improve for the experience. (op 22-1)*
Cashbar, a fair sort on the Flat, lost her form towards the end of last season and had a bit to prove at this distance, but she ran well to a point. Although failing to prove she stays this far, her trainer knows the time of day with his hurdles and the mare deserves another chance. *(op 6-1 tchd 8-1)*

4075 BRAYBROOK RACING HUNTINGDON'S LOCAL BOOKMAKER H'CAP HURDLE (8 hdls) 2m 110y

2:30 (2:31) (Class 4) (0-105,99) 4-Y-0+ **£3,253** (£955; £477; £238)

Form RPR
0-22 **1** **Misbehaviour**[5] 3990 7-11-7 **97** .... ChristopherMurray[(5)] 109+
(Jim Best) *hld up: hdwy appr 2 out: led last: r.o wl: eased nr fin* **4/1**[1]
2004 **2** *4* **Shaman**[23] 3661 9-11-7 **92** .... JamieMoore 95
(G L Moore) *mid-div: hdwy and hit 3 out: rdn and ev ch last: no ex flat* **11/2**[2]
002 **3** *4* **Pseudonym (IRE)**[6] 3967 4-11-4 **98** .... SamStronge 88
(M F Harris) *hld up: hdwy after 5th: outpcd 3 out: sn rdn: hung rt flat: styd on same pce* **11/2**[2]
P022 **4** *½* **The Castilian (FR)**[27] 3592 4-10-12 **99** ....(v) AndrewGlassonbury[(7)] 90+
(M C Pipe) *prom: racd keenly: led 4th: mstke next: hdd 3 out: sn led again: hdd & wknd last* **4/1**[1]
-2F6 **5** *1 ¾* **Foxtrot Yankee (IRE)**[42] 3355 7-11-2 **87** .... PJBrennan 84
(Andrew Turnell) *hld up: hdwy after 5th: wknd last* **7/1**[3]
130 **6** *2 ½* **Gaelic Roulette (IRE)**[14] 3818 6-11-11 **96** .... LeightonAspell 90
(J Jay) *hld up in tch: plld hrd: wknd appr 2 out* **10/1**
330 **7** *¾* **Laconicos (IRE)**[63] 2954 4-11-0 **94** .... PhilipHide 79
(W B Stone) *prom: rdn appr 2 out: wknd appr last* **20/1**
4106 **8** *7* **Wardash (GER)**[22] 3674 6-11-3 **88** ....(bt) KennyJohnson 75
(M C Chapman) *disp ld tl led 3 out: sn hdd: wknd after next* **40/1**
00-0 **9** *3 ½* **Birchall (IRE)**[115] 1957 7-11-0 **85** ....(t) JasonMaguire 82+
(Ian Williams) *led to 4th: ev ch and nt fluent 2 out: wknd flat* **9/1**
236P **10** *13* **Moldavia (GER)**[222] 826 5-11-4 **92** .... OwynNelmes[(3)] 62
(N B King) *chsd ldrs: rdn after 5th: wknd bef next* **40/1**
00F0 **11** *26* **Orions Eclipse**[27] 3597 5-9-9 **71** oh4 .... DerekLaverty[(5)] 15
(M J Gingell) *hld up: rdn and wknd appr 3 out* **100/1**

4m 14.6s (18.90) **Going Correction** +1.125s/f (Heav)
WFA 4 from 5yo+ 9lb **11** Ran SP% **113.0**
Speed ratings: **100,98,96,96,95 94,93,90,88,82 70** CSF £24.63 CT £119.37 TOTE £4.40: £1.90, £2.50, £2.20; EX 27.70.
Owner The Bad Boys **Bred** Mrs R Pease **Trained** Lewes, E Sussex
■ A first winner from his new base for Jim Best.

FOCUS
Suspect form due to the slow time, but the second, third and fourth all ran to their marks. Although a moderate event, it should produce the odd winner at a similar level.

NOTEBOOK
Misbehaviour, 13lb higher than when winning in March of last year, appreciates this sort of ground and cleared away after the last to win comfortably. He is progressive and, although a further rise will follow, there is nothing to say he will not prove up to winning again. *(op 7-2 tchd 9-2)*
Shaman is without a win in over two years, but he has dropped to a decent mark as a result and this run suggested he may soon be able to capitalise on it. *(op 8-1)*
Pseudonym(IRE) showed significantly improved form when going close at Market Rasen last week and confirmed it to be no fluke with another sound placed effort. There is a similar race in him off this sort of mark. *(op 6-1 tchd 5-1)*
The Castilian(FR) has been in decent form, twice finishing second, but he was up 4lb here and failed to see out his race having travelled a little too enthusiastically in the early stages. He continues to frustrate. *(op 9-2 tchd 5-1 in places)*
Foxtrot Yankee(IRE) ran well on this handicap debut, but still looks in need of a little more time. *(op 8-1)*
Birchall(IRE) *Official explanation: jockey said gelding made a noise (op 6-1)*

4076 DAVID BRAYBROOK MEMORIAL HBLB NOVICES' CHASE (12 fncs) 2m 110y

3:00 (3:01) (Class 3) 5-Y-0+ **£6,506** (£1,910; £955; £477)

Form RPR
6442 **1** **Sharp Rigging (IRE)**[53] 3183 6-11-0 121 .... JimmyMcCarthy 140+
(A M Hales) *a.p: chsd ldr 9th: j.lft 2 out: led flat: drvn out* **4/1**[2]
51P5 **2** *3 ½* **Nyrche (FR)**[82] 2634 6-11-10 139 .... WayneHutchinson 147
(A King) *led: rdn and hdd flat: no ex* **9/2**[3]
31BF **3** *25* **Crossbow Creek**[59] 2970 8-11-6 137 .... JamieMoore 128+
(M G Rimell) *sn prom: lft 3rd 3 out: sn rdn: wknd next: eased flat* **11/4**[1]
4-61 **4** *15* **Idole First (IRE)**[10] 3903 7-11-10 .... AlanO'Keeffe 107
(Miss Venetia Williams) *hld up in tch: dropped rr 3rd: bhd fr 6th* **11/4**[1]
5 *10* **Neptune D'Anzy (FR)**[109] 2084 5-11-4 .... NoelFehily 96+
(Jonjo O'Neill) *chsd ldrs to 9th: wkng whn hmpd next* **12/1**
323- **6** *21* **Mr Boo (IRE)**[330] 4664 7-11-0 .... PhilipHide 66
(G L Moore) *hld up: bhd fr 6th* **40/1**
5334 **7** *17* **Kercabellec (FR)**[30] 3546 8-11-0 79 .... RichardHobson 49
(J R Cornwall) *hld up: bhd fr 6th* **250/1**
3441 **F** **Aleron (IRE)**[17] 3558 8-11-6 130 ....(p) PJBrennan —
(J J Quinn) *chsd ldr to 9th: cl 3rd whn fell 3 out* **10/1**

4m 10.2s (0.90) **Going Correction** +0.25s/f (Yiel)
WFA 5 from 6yo+ 6lb **8** Ran SP% **111.1**
Speed ratings: **107,105,93,86,81 71,63,**— CSF £21.47 TOTE £6.40: £1.90, £2.50, £1.10; EX 38.80.
Owner The Sharpshooters **Bred** Anamoine Ltd **Trained** Quainton, Bucks

FOCUS
A good novice chase in which six of the eight runners looked to hold a chance, but two drew clear after the fall of Aleron and Sharp Rigging simply had too much speed for Nyrche after the last. The form has been rated positively.

NOTEBOOK
Sharp Rigging(IRE), who had shown a decent level of form in defeat on all three previous attempts over fences, handled the ground conditions better than many of his rivals and simply had too much pace for the gallant runner-up, going clear on the run-in. Potentially on a good mark with handicaps in mind, the Grand Annual could be a possible target as connections will no doubt be keen to atone *for last year's mishap when falling at the second-last in the Coral Cup (still going well at the time). (op 11-2)*
Nyrche(FR), a bold-jumping front-runner, did his best to give the weight to the winner, but simply lacked his pace and had to settle for second. He has plenty of form on a sound surface and will be more at home in handicaps, the two-mile Red Rum Chase at the Grand National meeting looking a possible target. *(op 5-1)*
Crossbow Creek, a very useful hurdler, was in the process of finishing a good second to Hoo La Baloo in the Wayward Lad Novices' Chase at Sandown on Boxing Day only to fall at the second last, and held obvious form claims against this lesser opposition, but he has always been at his best on a sound surface and was simply unable to cope with the ground. He is better than this and it would not surprise to see him bounce back on better going in the spring. *(tchd 7-2)*
Idole First(IRE), who did not jump particularly well when winning at Plumpton last time, faced a stiff enough task under joint top weight and was another who appeared to struggle in the ground. He has form in soft, but all his best efforts over hurdles were on a sound surface and he too *deserves another chance, with a step up in distance likely to help in future. (tchd 3-1 and 10-3 in places)*
Neptune D'Anzy(FR), a smart sort in France who finished fourth in a Grade One at Auteuil on his most recent outing back in November, was left trailing down the back straight and offered little encouragement with the future in mind. He is not the first smart recruit from either the Flat or France to disappoint for his stable this season. *(op 8-1 tchd 14-1)*
Aleron(IRE), who ran as though something was amiss on the Flat earlier in the month, had previously got off the mark over fences at Catterick and had the hurdles form to play a hand here, but having travelled nicely he came down at the third-last when still going well and it remains to be seen how this affects his confidence. *(op 15-2 tchd 7-1)*

4077 BRAYBROOK RACING SIDNEY BANKS MEMORIAL NOVICES' HURDLE (10 hdls) 2m 4f 110y

3:30 (3:31) (Class 2) 4-Y-0+ **£13,012** (£3,820; £1,910; £954)

Form RPR
1111 **1** **Refinement (IRE)**[47] 3295 7-11-0 130 .... NoelFehily 131+
(Jonjo O'Neill) *hld up: hdwy after 5th: led on bit last: shkn up and styd on strly* **4/6**[1]
1 **2** *13* **Raffaello (FR)**[33] 3505 5-11-7 .... ChristianWilliams 119
(P F Nicholls) *trckd ldrs: led 5th: rdn and hdd last: wknd flat* **7/2**[2]
41 **3** *shd* **Mith Hill**[11] 3883 5-11-3 .... JasonMaguire 115+
(Ian Williams) *led to 5th: chsd ldr: ev ch fr 2 out tl wknd flat* **8/1**
1/0 **4** *10* **Something Gold (FR)**[59] 2983 6-11-3 .... MatthewBatchelor 105+
(M Bradstock) *prom: rdn appr 6th: wknd next: bhd whn hit 3 out* **40/1**
32-4 **5** *9* **Patrixprial**[124] 1827 5-11-3 123 .... LeightonAspell 101+
(M H Tompkins) *hld up: hdwy 7th: wknd 3 out* **15/2**[3]
460 **6** *dist* **Water Pistol**[16] 3786 4-10-7 .... KennyJohnson —
(M C Chapman) *chsd ldrs to 6th* **300/1**
0 **7** *dist* **Mylord Collonges (FR)**[50] 3240 6-11-3 .... TomScudamore —
(Mrs Susan Nock) *chsd ldr to 5th: wknd after next* **50/1**
0 **8** *11* **Finnegans Rainbow**[16] 3787 4-10-7 .... JamieGoldstein —
(M C Chapman) *hld up: plld hrd: wknd after 5th* **300/1**

5m 17.2s (21.90) **Going Correction** +1.125s/f (Heav)
WFA 4 from 5yo+ 10lb **8** Ran SP% **110.2**
Speed ratings: **103,98,98,94,90** —,—,— CSF £3.05 TOTE £1.60: £1.02, £1.60, £1.50; EX 3.60.

Owner Michael Tabor **Bred** M Tabor **Trained** Cheltenham, Gloucs

FOCUS
A useful novices' hurdle won in impressive fashion by Refinement who is now Festival-bound. She was rated value for 20l, with the second and third pretty much to form.

NOTEBOOK

Refinement(IRE), a useful bumper performer, maintained her 100% record over hurdles with this fifth win of the season and the manner of her victory suggests she is still improving. Given a confident ride by Fehily, she cantered into the lead and powered clear once asked to put the result beyond doubt, winning with plenty to spare over a couple of fair prospects. A strong traveller, she seemed to relish this new distance and she deserves her place at the Festival in either the Royal & SunAlliance Hurdle or the Coral Cup, with the latter making the more appeal of the two. *(op 10-11)*

Raffaello(FR), a workmanlike winner from some modest opposition on his British debut at Wincanton last month, faced a stiffer task here in attempting to concede 7lb to the winner and he was not up to it, being readily brushed aside at the last. This trip in the ground may have proved beyond him at this stage of his career and the five-year-old, who is sure to make a chaser next season, deserves another chance. *(op 5-2)*

Mith Hill, who did it well on his second attempt over hurdles at Hereford earlier in the month, faced a much stiffer task and failed to see out the distance as strongly as the winner, just losing out on second. Better ground is likely to suit the son of Daylami in future and he looks capable of further improvement back at two miles. *(op 13-2)*

Something Gold(FR), a winner on his bumper debut at Ascot back in March 2004, ran well to a point on his first start since at Towcester in December and stepped up on that effort with a reasonable fourth. He will find easier opportunities than this and is one to keep an eye on. *(op 28-1)*

Patrixprial was simply outclassed and will be better off in handicaps. *(op 8-1 tchd 10-1)*

4078 BRAYBROOK RACING JOHN BIGG OXO H'CAP CHASE (19 fncs) 3m
4:05 (4:06) (Class 4) (0-115,114) 5-Y-O+ **£3,903** (£1,146; £573; £286)

Form				RPR
P33	1		**Nykel (FR)**21 [3698] 5-10-5 **104** ... WayneHutchinson (A King) *chsd ldrs: led 11th to next: led 14th to next: led 16th: drvn out* **4/1**1	107+
PPF	2	6	**Supreme Catch (IRE)**11 [3877] 9-11-5 **114** ... MrTJO'Brien(7) (Miss H C Knight) *hld up: hdwy 6th: rdn after 3 out: styd on same pce fr 2 out* **9/1**	121
2-45	3	3 1/2	**Menphis Beury (FR)**38 [3420] 6-10-13 **101** ... MarkBradburne (H D Daly) *hld up: hdwy 13th: mstke and outpcd 3 out: hmpd next: styd on flat* **6/1**	110+
/055	4	7	**Patriarch (IRE)**41 [3368] 10-10-5 **93** ... PaulMoloney (P Bowen) *hld up: hit 8th: hmpd 2 out: n.d* **5/1**2	92+
/45-	5	2	**Would You Believe**326 [4726] 10-10-7 **95** ... PJBrennan (P J Hobbs) *chsd ldrs: mstke 8th: led 10th to next: led 12th to 14th: led 15th to next: wkng whn hmpd 2 out* **11/2**3	95+
6534	6	22	**Runaway Bishop (USA)**4 [4014] 11-10-3 **91** ... RichardHobson (J R Cornwall) *hld up: rdn and lost tch 12th* **11/1**	64
P42F	7	30	**Special Conquest**10 [3900] 8-11-6 **108** ... AndrewThornton (J W Mullins) *led to 2nd: chsd ldrs: j. slowly 4th: wknd 3 out* **9/1**	51
35PP	8	dist	**Imaginaire (USA)**16 [3788] 11-10-13 **106** ...(b) LeeStephens(5) (Miss Venetia Williams) *prom to 15th* **33/1**	—
2-P5	F		**Cinnamon Line**34 [3481] 10-10-10 **98** ... TomDoyle (R Lee) *hld up: hdwy 11th: rdn to dispute 3 l 2nd whn fell 2 out* **8/1**	103
PP-6	P		**Native Performance (IRE)**47 [3284] 11-11-6 **108** ... JimCrowley (N J Gifford) *led 2nd: hdd and hit 10th: sn wknd: t.o whn p.u bef 13th* **50/1**	—

6m 28.4s (16.10) **Going Correction** +0.75s/f (Soft)
WFA 5 from 6yo+ 11lb **10** Ran SP% **110.7**
Speed ratings: **103,101,99,97,96 89,79,—,—,—** CSF £37.29 CT £201.61 TOTE £3.90: £1.70, £3.60, £2.30; EX 50.30.

Owner The Unlucky For Some Partnership **Bred** Marc Trinquet & Bernard Trinquet **Trained** Barbury Castle, Wilts

FOCUS

A modest yet competitive race won in good style by five-year-old Nykel, who is steadily progressive.

NOTEBOOK

Nykel(FR), whose placed efforts from Wincanton earlier in the year entitled him to go close, put in a decent round of jumping under a positive ride and stayed on too strongly for Supreme Catch, from whom he was receiving 14lb. This was a good effort from a horse who has not long been five, and it will be surprising if he cannot better this in future, with further improvement anticipated. *(op 7-2)*

Supreme Catch(IRE), well handicapped on the best of his form from a couple of seasons back, was completing for the first time since returning, but was unable to get to grips with the winner and may benefit from a more positive ride in future. *(op 15-2)*

Menphis Beury(FR) continues to slip back down the handicap, but this mark of 101 is still a little higher than he would like and it is unlikely he will be winning until dropping into the 90s. *(op 8-1)*

Patriarch(IRE) was the disappointment of the race, failing to get into it having been held up and plugging on late to suggest he would have appreciated a more aggressive ride. He is attractively weighted if connections can find the key. *(op 6-1)*

Would You Believe, who is still a maiden, was a little disappointing on this seasonal return and remains one to avoid despite an ever-declining mark. *(op 9-2)*

Cinnamon Line, racing off a good mark, was in the process of running a big race and held every chance when falling at the second-last. It is hoped this does not affect confidence. *(op 9-1 tchd 10-1 and 15-2)*

4079 BRAYBROOK WE SUPPORT SPORT HUNTERS' CHASE (19 fncs) 3m
4:40 (4:40) (Class 6) 5-Y-O+ **£1,977** (£608; £304)

Form				RPR
1132	1		**No Retreat (NZ)**21 [3693] 13-12-0 106 ... MrWHill(7) (J Groucott) *led to 2nd: j. slowly next: sn lost pl: hdwy 11th: chsd ldr 4 out: 3 l 2nd and rdn whn lft clr 2 out* **10/11**1	117+
0P-F	2	9	**Lucky Bay (IRE)**18 10-11-7 120 ... MrsHKemp(7) (Mrs H M Kemp) *chsd ldrs: hit 10th: outpcd 13th: hdwy and lft 2nd 2 out: no ch w wnr* **7/2**2	98
-245	3	2 1/2	**Wings Of Hope (IRE)**14 [3819] 10-12-0 89 ...(p) MrSMorris (James Richardson) *chsd ldrs: rdn 3 out: styng on same pce whn lft 3rd 2 out* **9/1**	96
2P-P	4	14	**Mr Banker**46 11-11-7 76 ... MrJBarnes(7) (N Bush) *hld up: hit 2nd: hdwy 5th: mstke and wknd 5 out: bhd whn j.rt last* **80/1**	82
P-44	5	15	**Ivanoph (FR)**13 [3847] 10-11-11 105 ... MrAWintle(3) (S Flook) *hld up: hdwy 15th: wknd appr 2 out* **16/1**	67
-P31	6	30	**Maggies Brother**281 [403] 13-12-5 ... MrJMPritchard (R Shail) *hld up: bhd fr 8th* **16/1**	42
212/	F		**Full Minty**52 11-11-7 ... MrGDisney(7) (Mrs Sarah Stafford) *led 2nd: 3 l ahd whn fell 2 out* **6/1**3	113+

6m 36.0s (23.70) **Going Correction** +1.025s/f (Soft) **7** Ran SP% **111.9**
Speed ratings: **101,98,97,92,87 77,—** CSF £4.44 TOTE £2.00: £1.40, £2.50; EX 5.50.

Owner M W & A N Harris **Bred** B G Francis, J S Mee And J R Watts **Trained** Much Wenlock, Shropshire

FOCUS

The outcome of this changed quickly in the straight with Full Minty, who was around three lengths up going best, falling at the second last and leaving the way clear for No Retreat. The winner has been rated to the level of last season's best form, the faller as the 4l winner.

NOTEBOOK

No Retreat(NZ) has developed into a consistent performer in these events and, despite looking a fortunate winner on this occasion, it is hard to begrudge the 13-year-old another victory. On the pace from the off, he looked in trouble as Full Minty held a three-length advantage, but luck was on his side and he should continue to pay his way. *(op 11-8 after early 6-4)*

Lucky Bay(IRE), a decent performer on his day, would not have necessarily been suited by the soft ground, but ran well nonetheless and plugged on for a fortunate second. He still has the potential to do better in this sphere. *(op 11-2 tchd 6-1)*

Wings Of Hope(IRE) has not won a race since 2002 and, although not disgraced here, he is likely to continue to struggle. *(op 8-1)*

Mr Banker, a multiple winning pointer, has been disappointing since hunter-chasing and he was out of his depth here. *(op 66-1)*

Ivanoph(FR) is not the force of old and has now disappointed on both starts since winning at point in May. *(op 20-1)*

Maggies Brother faced a stiff task under top weight, but could have been expected to show a little more. *(op 10-1)*

Full Minty was disputing it from an early stage and looked to have No Retreat held when falling at the second-last. He is a consistent sort who should continue to pay his way if unaffected by this incident. *(op 11-4)*

4080 VILLA-SEABREEZE.COM H'CAP HURDLE (10 hdls) 2m 4f 110y
5:10 (5:13) (Class 5) (0-95,95) 4-Y-O+ **£2,740** (£798; £399)

Form				RPR
-P43	1		**Colophony (USA)**59 [2958] 6-10-10 **86** ... PatrickMcDonald(7) (K A Morgan) *hld up in tch: led 2 out: rdn out* **8/1**	94+
0405	2	4	**Wally Wonder (IRE)**14 [3818] 8-11-2 **95** ...(b) JamesReveley(10) (K G Reveley) *led: hdd 2 out: mstke last: no ex flat* **22/1**	99+
600	3	11	**Trebello**23 [3659] 5-11-7 **90** ... LeightonAspell (J R Boyle) *hld up: hdwy 7th: rdn appr 2 out: sn wknd* **7/1**3	82
2660	4	1 1/2	**Amalfi Storm**59 [2991] 5-10-13 **82** ... WilsonRenwick (M W Easterby) *chsd ldrs: rdn appr 3 out: wknd bef next* **25/1**	72
3243	5	2	**He's A Rascal (IRE)**28 [3577] 8-11-4 **87** ...(tp) TomDoyle (A J Lidderdale) *hld up: hdwy 7th: rdn and wknd bef next* **7/1**3	75
U0PP	6	1 1/4	**Jackie Boy (IRE)**9 [3905] 7-11-2 **85** ... AntonyEvans (N A Twiston-Davies) *prom: rdn after 7th: wknd bef next* **20/1**	72
R30-	7	shd	**Homer (IRE)**437 [2813] 9-10-10 **82** ... TJPhelan(3) (N M Babbage) *bhd: nvr nrr* **50/1**	69
425P	8	1/2	**Full On**9 [3905] 9-11-9 **95** ... WilliamKennedy(3) (A M Hales) *hld up: rdn after 5th: wknd next* **20/1**	81
2145	9	10	**Dont Ask Me (IRE)**105 [2150] 5-11-1 **91** ...(vt1) AndrewGlassonbury(7) (M C Pipe) *mid-div: mstke 5th: hdwy next: wknd appr 2 out* **6/1**2	67
0-30	10	1	**Sarobar (IRE)**11 [3888] 6-11-6 **89** ...(p) TomScudamore (M Scudamore) *hld up: hdwy 6th: rdn and wknd appr 3 out* **16/1**	64
0062	11	15	**El Corredor (IRE)**7 [3950] 7-11-1 **84** ... PJBrennan (M F Harris) *hld up: rdn after 5th: blnd and wknd 7th* **11/2**1	44
0664	12	dist	**Silver Bow**18 [3757] 5-10-12 **86** ... TJDreaper(5) (J M Jefferson) *prom to 7th* **16/1**	—
P466	P		**Pearly Star**42 [3358] 5-11-4 **94** ... MrGTumelty(7) (A King) *prom to 6th: t.o whn p.u bef 2 out* **11/1**	—
P03P	P		**Mooresini (IRE)**38 [3424] 6-11-6 **89** ...(tp) AndrewThornton (N J Gifford) *hld up: wknd 6th: bhd whn p.u bef next* **10/1**	—
4000	P		**Carnt Spell**72 [2816] 5-11-0 **83** ... JimCrowley (J T Stimpson) *chsd ldrs tl wknd appr 3 out: t.o whn p.u bef 2 out* **66/1**	—
/640	P		**Saxon Mill**15 [3798] 11-11-1 **84** ... OllieMcPhail (T J Fitzgerald) *prom: rdn 7th: wknd bef next: t.o whn p.u bef 2 out* **33/1**	—

5m 15.2s (19.90) **Going Correction** +1.125s/f (Heav) **16** Ran SP% **119.1**
Speed ratings: **107,105,101,100,99 99,99,99,95,95 89,—,—,—,—** — CSF £171.88 CT £1298.83 TOTE £11.10: £3.30, £4.20, £2.40, £4.70; EX 214.10 Place 6 £4.50, Place 5 £3.56.

Owner H A Blenkhorn & Miss C J Blenkhorn **Bred** Juddmonte Farms Inc **Trained** Waltham on the Wolds, Leics

FOCUS

A modest handicap hurdle that is unlikely to work out.

NOTEBOOK

Colophony(USA), who was always going well, was finally able to get off the mark over hurdles and did so with a little to spare. He has improved for the step up in distance and may yet be capable of better off this sort of mark. *(tchd 15-2)*

Wally Wonder(IRE) is back on a decent mark and ran a game race in second, keeping on once headed and pulling clear of the third. He will remain vulnerable to something less exposed however. *(op 28-1)*

Trebello made a little late headway from the rear, but he was hardly finishing with a purpose and is likely to continue to struggle. *(op 9-1)*

Amalfi Storm has thus far been disappointing over hurdles, following placed form in bumpers, but this was a better effort on her handicap debut and she is not one to give up on just yet. *(op 20-1)*

He's A Rascal(IRE) remains a maiden and makes little appeal with the future in mind. *(op 5-1)*

Jackie Boy(IRE) may now be ready for a return to fences as he is going to continue to struggle over hurdles. *(op 22-1)*

Dont Ask Me(IRE), refitted with the visor, failed to run to form and remains a little high in the handicap. *(tchd 13-2)*

El Corredor(IRE), who ran a blinder on his handicap debut at Taunton last week, appeared to hold outstanding claims, but never got involved and was unable to build on last weeks effort. *(op 6-1 tchd 13-2)*

T/Plt: £7.00 to a £1 stake. Pool: £40,483.20. 4,189.75 winning tickets. T/Qpdt: £4.80 to a £1 stake. Pool: £3,120.40. 478.60 winning tickets. CR

4081 - 4087a (Foreign Racing) - See Raceform Interactive

3722 SANDOWN (R-H)
Friday, February 24

OFFICIAL GOING: Chase course - soft (heavy in places); hurdle course - heavy

4088 DEVINE IAC "NATIONAL HUNT" NOVICES' HURDLE (8 hdls) 2m 110y
2:00 (2:00) (Class 3) 5-Y-O+ **£5,204** (£1,528; £764; £381)

Form				RPR
15-4	1		**Manners (IRE)**12 [3878] 8-11-0 ... APMcCoy (Jonjo O'Neill) *hld up rr: hdwy to trck ldrs 3 out: c stands side and chal 2 out: sn led: drvn out* **8/11**1	111+
3132	2	4	**Idris (GER)**21 [3717] 5-11-4 118 ... PhilipHide (G L Moore) *lw: chsd ldrs: chal fr 3 out: c stands side: chal and hit 2 out: kpt on same pce u.p appr last* **15/8**2	111+

0005 **3** *1 ¼* **King Louis (FR)**[24] [3658] 5-11-0 .... LeightonAspell 104
(R Rowe) *lw: chsd ldrs: slt ld and nt fluent 3 out: hit 2 out and sn hdd: kpt on same pce sn after* **20/1**[3]

000 **4** *11* **Royal Hilarity (IRE)**[51] [3240] 6-11-0 .... PaulMoloney 94+
(Ian Williams) *pressed ldrs: slt ld 4th to 3 out: ev ch whn hit 2 out: wknd and hit last* **66/1**

0-50 **5** *½* **Krismas Cracker**[55] [3133] 5-11-0 ....(t) MarcusFoley 93
(N J Henderson) *scope: bhd: sme hdwy 3 out: sn rdn: n.d* **20/1**[3]

P **6** *15* **Froghole Flyer**[10] [3906] 7-11-0 .... WayneHutchinson 78
(G L Moore) *str: bhd: hdwy to chse ldrs 3 out: wknd sn after* **100/1**

102- **7** *25* **Arctic Spirit**[381] [3746] 11-11-0 .... BenjaminHitchcott 53
(R Dickin) *led tl narrowly hdd 4th: styd prom tl wknd after 3 out* **33/1**

0F **8** *15* **Another Penny**[12] [3884] 6-10-0 .... JohnPritchard[(7)] 31
(R Dickin) *a bhd* **100/1**

0P **9** *23* **Hi Blue**[22] [3685] 7-10-4 .... JosephStevenson[(10)] 15
(R Dickin) *in tch to 4 out* **100/1**

00 **10** *dist* **The Piker (IRE)**[34] [3511] 5-11-0 .... JohnMcNamara —
(T R George) *blnd 1st: rdr lost iron: a bhd and nt fluent after: virtually p.u nr fin: t.o* **50/1**

4m 19.9s (11.00) **Going Correction** +0.525s/f (Soft) **10** Ran SP% **111.6**
Speed ratings: **89,87,86,81,81 74,62,55,44,—** CSF £2.00 TOTE £1.90: £1.10, £1.10, £1.90; EX 2.60.
Owner Michael Tabor **Bred** M Tabor **Trained** Cheltenham, Gloucs
■ Stewards' Enquiry : Philip Hide two-day ban: used whip with excessive frequency and without allowing sufficient time for response (Mar 7-8)

FOCUS
A modest novice event, run at a sedate early gallop in a time 8.5 seconds slower than the later handicap, and the first three came clear. The form - assesed through the third and fourth - is weak, and the first two have both been rated below their best.

NOTEBOOK
Manners(IRE) showed the clear benefit of his recent seasonal comeback at Exeter and belatedly opened his account over timber at the third time of asking. He acted without fuss on the deep surface, put in by far his best round of jumping to date, and had the race in the bag when hitting the front two from home. That said, he has yet to translate his decent bumper form in this sphere, and while he may be open to further improvement, on this form he is a long way short of Cheltenham class. *(op 4-5 tchd 4-6)*
Idris(GER) turned in another sound effort under his penalty, but was readily put in his place by the winner from two out. While he will remain vulnerable in this division under his penalty, he is consistent and has the scope to improve further when sent over fences in due course. A return to a less taxing surface should also prove to his benefit. *(tchd 2-1)*
King Louis(FR) posted his best effort to date and would have been closer had his jumping not deteriorated late on. This stiffer track proved to his liking, he is going the right way, and should come into his own when sent over fences next season. *(op 16-1)*
Royal Hilarity(IRE) was let down by his jumping from three out, and is probably flattered by his proximity at the finish, but this was a bit more encouraging and he now qualifies for a handicap mark. *(op 50-1)*
Krismas Cracker, equipped with a first-time tongue tie, turned in a laboured effort and never figured. He probably requires a stiffer test and is another who may fare better now he is eligible for a handicap mark. *(op 12-1)*

4089 ALLIED IRISH BANK GB PRIVATE BANKING H'CAP CHASE (FOR THE ALANBROOKE CHALLENGE CUP) (13 fncs) 2m
2:35 (2:35) (Class 3) (0-135,130) 5-Y-0+ **£9,394** (£2,775; £1,387; £694)

Form RPR

P422 **1** **Jacks Craic (IRE)**[36] [3457] 7-11-2 **120** .... GrahamLee 132+
(J L Spearing) *lw: keen early: hld up and trckd ldrs: slt ld 3 out: narrowly hdd last: rallied gamely run-in to ld cl home* **7/4**[1]

-134 **2** *hd* **Without A Doubt**[48] [3288] 7-11-12 **130** .... PaulMoloney 141
(M Pitman) *led: kpt slt advantage tl narrowly hdd 9th: led again 4 out: hdd 3 out: hit 2 out:led last: kpt on u.p: ct cl home* **15/8**[2]

/162 **3** *6* **Joey Tribbiani (IRE)**[17] [3788] 9-10-7 **111** .... WayneHutchinson 116
(T Keddy) *trckd ldrs: rdn fr 4 out: styd on same pce fr 3 out* **7/2**[3]

3-0P **4** *½* **Jurado Express (IRE)**[13] [3852] 10-10-13 **122** .... LeeStephens[(5)] 126
(Miss Venetia Williams) *pressed ldr fr 3rd: j. slowly 6th: slt ld 9th: hdd 4 out: wknd 2 out* **11/2**

4m 7.10s (4.60) **Going Correction** +0.525s/f (Soft) **4** Ran SP% **108.8**
Speed ratings: **109,108,105,105** CSF £5.54 TOTE £2.30; EX 4.50.
Owner Bbb Computer Services **Bred** Michael Murphy **Trained** Kinnersley, Worcs
■ Stewards' Enquiry : Paul Moloney caution: used whip in an incorrect place

FOCUS
A fair handicap, run at a solid pace despite the small field, and the first two came clear.

NOTEBOOK
Jacks Craic(IRE) just did enough to come out on top of a thrilling battle from the last and win his first race over fences at the fifth attempt. The rising finish was much to his liking, he went through the testing ground without fuss. Connections are keen to have a crack at the Grand Annual, where the track and likely ground would suit, but he is far from certain to get a run in that event despite an inevitable rise in the weights. *(tchd 2-1)*
Without A Doubt posted a brave effort under top weight and this must rate a personal-best over fences. He deserves credit for battling on as he did despite hitting two out, and the stiff two miles at this track is clearly right up his street. *(op 5-2)*
Joey Tribbiani(IRE) lacked fluency over his fences and proved unsuited by the testing surface. He kept to his task throughout, however, and can get closer from his current mark on better ground. *(op 10-3 tchd 3-1)*
Jurado Express(IRE), easy to back, failed to find anything when push came to shove and was ultimately well beaten. He looks one to have reservations about on recent evidence. *(op 4-1 tchd 13-2)*

4090 ROYAL ARTILLERY GOLD CUP CHASE (22 fncs) 3m 110y
3:10 (3:10) (Class 3) 5-Y-0+ **£6,246** (£1,937; £968; £484)

Form RPR

5615 **1** **Inca Trail (IRE)**[77] [2745] 10-12-7 139 ....(b) MrJSnowden[(3)] 123+
(P F Nicholls) *lw: hld up in tch: disp 2nd fr 13th: bmpd 2 out: disp ld sn after: qcknd to ld under hand driving sn after last: kpt on wl* **11/8**[2]

24F3 **2** *hd* **Back Nine (IRE)**[12] [3879] 9-11-7 120 ....(t) MrDAlers-Hankey[(3)] 109+
(R H Alner) *lw: trckd ldrs: disp 2nd fr 13th tl slt ld after 2 out: hrd drvn and hdd sn after last: nt pce of wnr cl home* **11/10**[1]

-P3P **3** *15* **Mercato (FR)**[66] [2931] 10-11-12 98 .... CaptAMichael[(7)] 103
(J R Best) *blnd 6th: wl bhd 12th: hdwy 17th: chsd ldrs 4 out: outpcd fr next* **12/1**[3]

4/P- **4** *3* **Lord Kilpatrick (IRE)**[33] 12-11-3 .... CaptTWCEdwards[(7)] 91
(Mrs H J Houghton) *led tl hdd after 2 out: sn btn* **20/1**

3F32 **5** *4* **Cedar Chief**[40] 9-11-3 71 ....(b) LtHWallace[(7)] 87
(K Tork) *blnd bdly 1st:hit 2nd: chsd ldrs and mstke 9th: wknd fr 17th* **40/1**

515/ **6** *shd* **Double Account (FR)**[12] 11-11-7 .... MajorBeverleyTunley[(7)] 91
(Gareth Cheshire) *chsd ldrs: chsd ldr 10th: blnd 11th: lost 2nd 13th: wknd 4 out* **25/1**

3UP/ **7** *dist* **River Paradise (IRE)**[333] 10-11-3 .... L/BdrCHaigh[(7)] —
(Jamie Broom) *racd wd: chsd ldr: hit 5th: wknd qckly after 11th: t.o* **66/1**

6m 47.2s (15.70) **Going Correction** +0.525s/f (Soft) **7** Ran SP% **110.0**
Speed ratings: **95,94,90,89,87 87,—** CSF £3.07 TOTE £2.20: £1.30, £1.80; EX 3.50.
Owner Major A M J Shaw **Bred** Ballysheehan Stud **Trained** Ditcheat, Somerset

FOCUS
An average renewal of this event, run at a modest pace. The form has been rated through the third, with both of the first two well off their best.

NOTEBOOK
Inca Trail(IRE) resumed winning ways under a fine ride by Snowden, who kept a firm hold of him until after the last. He has always been quirky and one never knows what he will find when asked for maximum effort, but he does have plenty of talent. He is likely to follow a similar path to the stable's 2005 winner Whitenzo, who went on to land the Grand Military Gold Cup over the same course and distance in March. *(op 13-8 tchd 15-8)*
Back Nine(IRE), third to Racing Demon in novice company last time and sporting a first-time tongue tie, had every chance yet was always being held from the last. He may be better over a sharper three miles in the future and should get off the mark over fences before too long. *(tchd 10-11)*
Mercato(FR), runner-up in this event in 2004 and third last season, stayed on at the finish after being set a fair amount to do. This must rate one of his better recent efforts, and he is on a fair handicap mark at present, but he has become difficult to predict. *(op 11-1)*
Lord Kilpatrick(IRE) showed up well enough from the front, but was a sitting duck nearing two out, and was eventually put firmly in his place by the principals. *(tchd 16-1)*
River Paradise(IRE) *Official explanation: trainer said he was unable to fit the declared tongue-strap (op 50-1)*

4091 DURKAN GROUP H'CAP HURDLE (8 hdls) 2m 110y
3:45 (3:45) (Class 3) (0-130,125) 4-Y-0+
£9,394 (£2,775; £1,387; £694; £346; £174)

Form RPR

31 **1** **Tarlac (GER)**[24] [3659] 5-11-2 **115** .... APMcCoy 127+
(N J Henderson) *in tch: stdy hdwy 4 out:hit next: trckd ldr gng wl appr 2 out: led wl bef last and mstke: drvn out run-in* **5/6**[1]

20-2 **2** *¾* **Lunar Crystal (IRE)**[22] [3696] 8-11-9 **122** .... TomScudamore 131
(M C Pipe) *led: hrd drvn appr 2 out: hdd wl bef last: rallied u.p to press wnr run-in: no ex nr fin* **9/2**[2]

411- **3** *22* **Lord Henry (IRE)**[464] [2275] 7-11-5 **125** .... MrTJO'Brien[(7)] 112
(P J Hobbs) *b.bkwd: t.k.h early: chsd ldr: rdn appr 2 out and sn wknd* **10/1**

3120 **4** *nk* **Enhancer**[27] [3622] 8-11-11 **124** .... LeightonAspell 111
(M J McGrath) *chsd ldrs: rdn and hit 3 out: wknd bef next* **33/1**

2003 **5** *9* **Guru**[28] [3599] 8-11-2 **115** ....(p) PhilipHide 93
(G L Moore) *lw: chsd ldrs: hit 3rd: mstke and rdn 3 out: sn btn* **9/1**

-0P3 **6** *11* **Aldiruos (IRE)**[32] [3542] 6-10-6 **105** .... WayneHutchinson 72
(A W Carroll) *in tch 3rd: rdn 3 out: wknd sn after* **6/1**[3]

4m 11.4s (2.50) **Going Correction** +0.525s/f (Soft) **6** Ran SP% **109.1**
Speed ratings: **109,108,98,98,93 88** CSF £4.90 TOTE £1.90: £1.20, £2.30; EX 4.50.
Owner John P McManus **Bred** Gestut Olympia **Trained** Upper Lambourn, Berks
■ Stewards' Enquiry : Tom Scudamore two-day ban: used whip with excessive frequency (Mar 7-8)

FOCUS
A fair handicap, run at a sound pace, and the first two came well clear. The winner was probably value for a bit further and the runner-up was back to his best.

NOTEBOOK
Tarlac(GER), off the mark in a moderate maiden last time, made a winning handicap debut in only workmanlike fashion. He failed to really convince over his hurdles - probably on account of the testing ground - but there was a fair amount to like about the manner in which he made up his ground to join the leader two out and once in front he was always holding on. He promises to be even better when racing off a genuinely strong pace and he appeals at the type to defy a weight rise in this sphere. In the long term, his trainer believes he will make a nice novice chaser. *(op 8-11 tchd 10-11)*
Lunar Crystal(IRE), runner-up on his recent return to action on good ground at Wincanton, posted another solid effort from the front and stuck to his task most gamely when headed. He will always be vulnerable to anything progressive, but he is a very likeable performer, and really does deserve to go one better. *(op 5-1)*
Lord Henry(IRE), returning from a 464-day layoff and having his first outing in a handicap, ultimately paid for refusing to settle through the early parts. This must rate an encouraging comeback effort, however, and a return to better ground and a longer trip should see him in a better light. *(op 11-2)*
Enhancer was not disgraced on ground he would have found too soft. He probably also needs further. *(op 25-1)*
Guru *(op 11-1 tchd 8-1)*

4092 ALLIED IRISH BANK GB HUNTERS' CHASE (FOR THE "UBIQUE" CHALLENGE CUP) (17 fncs) 2m 4f 110y
4:20 (4:20) (Class 6) 6-Y-0+ **£1,873** (£581; £290; £145)

Form RPR

06-0 **1** **First Love**[300] [127] 10-11-7 114 .... MrJSnowden[(3)] 117
(N J Henderson) *mde virtually all: hung bdly lft u.p run-in: all out* **3/1**[2]

33-2 **2** *1* **Cracking Dawn (IRE)**[10] [3910] 11-11-7 114 .... MrMGMiller[(3)] 116
(Mrs S Alner) *lw: bhd: hit 6th: drvn and stl plenty to do 4 out: chsd wnr bef 3 out: styd on appr last: gng on cl home but nt get up* **6/5**[1]

P-35 **3** *dist* **Newick Park**[47] 11-11-10 91 .... MrPGHall[(5)] 90
(Mrs D M Grissell) *in tch: hit 3rd: rdn 7th: sn no ch: hit 10th: t.o* **12/1**

5P-P **4** *6* **El Bandito (IRE)**[19] 12-11-11 113 .... MrSPHanson[(7)] 84
(M J Footer) *a bhd: t.o* **33/1**

13P/ **U** **Scotmail Boy (IRE)**[671] [4965] 13-11-12 .... MrTJO'Brien[(3)] —
(S Garrott) *b.bkwd: chsd wnr to 5th: wknd: mstke and uns rdr 8th* **4/1**[3]

400- **P** **Venn Ottery**[323] [4750] 11-12-4 145 .... MrTGreenall —
(Miss L A Blackford) *b.bkwd: hit 1st: chsd wnr 6th: chal 9th to next: wknd 4 out: lost 2nd and p.u bef 3 out* **12/1**

5m 33.5s (12.70) **Going Correction** +0.525s/f (Soft) **6** Ran SP% **108.8**
Speed ratings: **96,95,—,—,— —** CSF £6.92 TOTE £4.10: £1.50, £1.30; EX 7.50.
Owner The Queen **Bred** Queen Elizabeth **Trained** Upper Lambourn, Berks

FOCUS
Difficult form to assess, and it could have been rated a fair bit higher, as the first two are both capable of much better.

NOTEBOOK
First Love, making his debut in this sphere after a 300-day layoff, got back to winning ways under another fine ride by Snowden - who has now ridden eight winners from 17 rides at this venue. A recent spell of hunting looks to have worked the oracle and he was clever with his jumping this time, but this looks about as far as he wants to go. *(op 11-4 tchd 7-2)*
Cracking Dawn(IRE) was set a lot to do by his rider and did well to close the gap on the winner from the home turn, but he lacked the speed to go mow down that rival on the run-in. He is capable of better when reverting to further. *(tchd evens)*

Newick Park, a course and distance winner in 2001, did not appear overly suited by this deep surface yet still ran respectably. *(op 11-1)*
Scotmail Boy(IRE) was going as well as any prior to unshipping his rider. *(op 6-1)*
Venn Ottery showed there is still life in him, but eventually got very tired in this taxing ground and was legless when pulled up. *Official explanation: vet said gelding was distressed (op 6-1)*

4093 FOUNDATION DEVELOPMENTS LTD CONDITIONAL JOCKEYS' H'CAP HURDLE (8 hdls) 2m 110y

4:55 (4:55) (Class 4) (0-115,112) 4-Y-0+ **£3,903** (£1,146; £573; £286)

Form				RPR
2500	**1**		**Danse Macabre (IRE)**[31] 3548 7-10-7 **98**.................. WillieMcCarthy(5) (A W Carroll) *lw: hld up in rr: hdwy 3 out: led last: hung rt u.p sn after: edgd lft cl home: all out* **10/3**[1]	100+
F000	**2**	½	**Visibility (FR)**[36] 3467 7-11-4 **112**..........(v) AndrewGlassonbury(8) (M C Pipe) *wnt 2nd 3rd: hit 4th: chal 3 out: rdn and outpcd 2 out: rallied and hit last: styd on strly cl home: nt quite get up* **11/2**[3]	112+
41-0	**3**	½	**Sir Brastias**[43] 3360 7-11-8 **108**.................................. MarkNicolls (K C Bailey) *led: nt fluent 3rd: hdd appr 2 out: kpt on u.p run-in: styng on whn swtchd rt nr fin* **6/1**	108+
3664	**4**	2 ½	**Xamborough (FR)**[14] 3848 5-11-3 **106**.......................... JohnnyLevins(3) (B G Powell) *chsd ldr to 3rd: led appr 2 out: hdd last: kpt on same pce u.p* **9/2**[2]	103+
01	**5**	2 ½	**Huckster (ZIM)**[76] 2763 7-11-9 **112**............................ LiamTreadwell(3) (Miss Venetia Williams) *chsd ldrs: rdn appr 2 out: one pce appr last* **10/3**[1]	106
15-6	**6**	2 ½	**Hegarty (IRE)**[20] 3737 7-11-9 **112**..............................(t) ShaneWalsh(3) (Jonjo O'Neill) *lw: stdd s: hld up in rr: hday appr 2 out: sn rdn: nt ex wl bef last* **6/1**	103

4m 18.7s (9.80) **Going Correction** +0.525s/f (Soft) **6** Ran SP% **108.3**
Speed ratings: **91,90,90,89,88 87** CSF £19.69 TOTE £4.80: £2.00, £3.20; EX 22.40 Place 6 £4.39, Place 5 £4.21.
Owner Miss V M Brown **Bred** Mrs D A Merry **Trained** Cropthorne, Worcs

FOCUS
A modest handicap in which there were doubts about several runners handling the ground. It was run at an ordinary pace, and the form should be treated with caution.

NOTEBOOK
Danse Macabre(IRE) won his first race since switching from Ireland in 2005 under a well-judged ride from McCarthy. He had been below-par of late, but had previously run his best races for *connections on this track, and looked well suited by the soft ground this time.Official explanation: trainer said, regarding the improved form shown, at the time of gelding's previous run some of his horses had been under the weather, adding that gelding had run well at Sandown in the past (op 7-2)*
Visibility(FR), very well backed, looked to be on a going day until sticking his head in the air when the race became serious nearing two out and losing ground. He was flying at the finish, however, and may well have got on top in another 100 yards. While he may improve when returning to a longer trip, he is never one to rely on. *(op 9-1 tchd 10-1)*
Sir Brastias showed the benefit of his recent seasonal bow at Ludlow and ran right up to his mark in defeat. This proved he is versatile as regards underfoot conditions and he can get back to winning ways from this mark when reverting to further in due course. *(op 11-2 tchd 7-1)*
Xamborough(FR) had his chance, but he was not really happy on the ground, and he is capable of better when reverting to a faster surface in the future. *(op 7-2)*
Huckster(ZIM), making his handicap debut under top weight, failed to really convince on this ground. He is another who ideally needs a faster surface, and is not one to write off. *(op 11-4)*
Hegarty(IRE), with the tongue tie back on, failed to get into the thick of things from off the pace and again disappointed. *(op 11-2 tchd 13-2)*
T/Plt: £31.10 to a £1 stake. Pool: £54,715.10. 1,282.40 winning tickets. T/Qpdt: £8.70 to a £1 stake. Pool: £3,004.70. 254.90 winning tickets. ST

3577 WARWICK (L-H)

Friday, February 24

OFFICIAL GOING: Chase course - soft (heavy in places); hurdle course - heavy
Wind: Light against Weather: Fine

4094 EUROPEAN BREEDERS FUND "NATIONAL HUNT" NOVICES' HURDLE (QUALIFIER) (9 hdls) 2m 3f

1:40 (1:41) (Class 4) 4-7-Y-0 **£4,228** (£1,241; £620; £310)

Form				RPR
-522	**1**		**Principe Azzurro (FR)**[27] 3611 5-11-3 .... RichardJohnson (H D Daly) *hld up in tch: rdn to ld 2 out: drvn out* **15/8**[2]	111+
2-21	**2**	nk	**Wogan**[44] 3342 6-11-9 .... MickFitzgerald (N J Henderson) *a.p: led 3 out: hdd and nt fluent 2 out: sn rdn: r.o flat* **8/11**[1]	118+
0-06	**3**	16	**Alf's Spinney**[50] 3248 6-11-3 .... JasonMaguire (Ian Williams) *a.p: ev ch appr 2 out: sn rdn: wknd appr last* **66/1**	95
0	**4**	½	**Ice Melted (IRE)**[27] 3617 5-11-3 .... NoelFehily (Jonjo O'Neill) *hld up and bhd: hdwy 5th: ev ch appr 2 out: sn rdn and wknd* **33/1**	94
53	**5**	11	**Le Briar Soul (IRE)**[70] 2864 6-11-3 .... PJBrennan (V R A Dartnall) *t.k.h: led tl after 1st: chsd ldr: j.rt and hit 3rd: led appr 5th to 3 out: wknd appr 2 out* **14/1**[3]	84+
4-50	**6**	30	**Thenford Star (IRE)**[38] 3437 5-10-10 ....(t) MarkBradburne (D J S Ffrench Davis) *bhd fr 5th: t.o* **66/1**	46
200	**7**	hd	**Deep Moon (IRE)**[36] 3466 6-11-3 .... WarrenMarston (Miss H C Knight) *hld up: reminder after 4th: rdn 5th: sn struggling: t.o* **66/1**	53
0-	**8**	1 ¾	**Red Dawn (IRE)**[654] 284 7-11-3 .... TimmyMurphy (Miss H C Knight) *a in rr: t.o* **33/1**	51
	P		**Double Date (FR)** 5-11-3 .... JimmyMcCarthy (C P Morlock) *hld up: mstke 3rd: bhd fr 5th: t.o whn p.u bef 2 out* **80/1**	—
00	**P**		**Posh Act**[21] 3717 6-11-3 .... MatthewBatchelor (Miss H C Knight) *plld hrd: hung rt: hdwy to ld after 1st: hit 2nd: clr after 3rd: hdd appr 5th: sn wknd: t.o whn p.u befor* **100/1**	—

4m 42.7s (-1.30) **Going Correction** +0.40s/f (Soft) **10** Ran SP% **111.9**
Speed ratings: **103,102,96,95,91 78,78,77,—,—** CSF £3.43 TOTE £3.10: £1.10, £1.10, £9.60; EX 4.60.
Owner W J Tolhurst **Bred** F Di Mino **Trained** Stanton Lacy, Shropshire

FOCUS
The two main protagonists came clear, and this is fair novice form which should work out.

NOTEBOOK
Principe Azzurro(FR) may well have come up against a decent type in Dream Alliance at Chepstow last time and showed the right sort of attitude on the run-in. *(tchd 7-4)*
Wogan may not have won a great event by Newbury standards last time but this was a sound effort on softer ground under his penalty. *(op 5-6 tchd 10-11 in places)*
Alf's Spinney produced his best performance so far over hurdles and should do better back at two miles particularly when the ground is this demanding.
Ice Melted(IRE) had also failed to deliver when the chips were down in a bumper on his debut in similar ground at Chepstow.
Le Briar Soul(IRE) again ran too freely on this graduation from bumpers. *(op 12-1)*

4095 ROSCOE HARVEY MEMORIAL NOVICES' CHASE (20 fncs) 3m 2f

2:15 (2:15) (Class 4) 5-Y-0+ **£3,903** (£1,146; £573; £286)

Form				RPR
2254	**1**		**Chabrimal Minster**[14] 3845 9-11-4 102.................................. PJBrennan (R Ford) *hld up: hdwy after 10th: led 14th: clr last: comf* **2/1**[1]	116+
003P	**2**	15	**Ironside (IRE)**[34] 3499 7-11-4 92.................................. RichardJohnson (H D Daly) *sn prom: chsd wnr fr 15th: rdn 3 out: wknd appr last* **4/1**[2]	103+
3100	**3**	10	**Nocatee (IRE)**[16] 3794 5-10-2 104............................(p) PaddyMerrigan(5) (P C Haslam) *a.p: lost pl and reminders appr 9th: bhd 11th: styd on fr 3 out: n.d* **5/1**[3]	84+
-003	**4**	13	**Tank Buster**[43] 3356 6-11-4 88.. VinceSlattery (Mrs E Langley) *hld up and bhd: hit 2nd: mstke 7th: hdwy 11th: lost pl 12th: rallied 15th: nt fluent 16th: wknd 3 out* **33/1**	77
/1P6	**5**	27	**Martin Ossie**[20] 3732 9-11-4 100.. WarrenMarston (J M Bradley) *hld up: mstkes 6th and 9th: hdwy 14th: wknd 4 out* **9/1**	65+
3-6F	**P**		**Definite Approach (IRE)**[8] 3949 8-11-4 102..............(t) JimmyMcCarthy (R T Phillips) *hld up: hit 2nd: hdwy 6th: wknd after 10th: t.o whn p.u bef 13th* **9/1**	—
0/1-	**P**		**Red Square Lad (IRE)**[350] 4305 10-11-4 102.......................... RJGreene (Mrs L Williamson) *hung and j.rt: led to 7th: led after 10th to 4 out: hit 15th: sn wknd: p.u bef 4 out* **8/1**	—
F2P	**P**		**Horcott Bay**[22] 3689 6-10-11 95.. JamieMoore (M G Rimell) *chsd ldr: reminders after 1st: led 7th: hdd and rdn after 10th: wknd appr 14th: t.o whn p.u bef 4 out* **11/1**	—

6m 57.1s (-6.90) **Going Correction** +0.20s/f (Yiel)
WFA 5 from 6yo+ 11lb **8** Ran SP% **112.4**
Speed ratings: **102,97,94,90,82 —,—,—** CSF £10.14 TOTE £3.00: £1.20, £1.40, £2.40; EX 13.90.
Owner B Mills, C Roberts, M & M Burrows **Bred** A Eubank **Trained** Cotebrook, Cheshire

FOCUS
This was not a great renewal and the winner probably didn't need to be at his best to win easily.

NOTEBOOK
Chabrimal Minster, back down in distance, had much less to do than when a close fourth in a competitive handicap at Bangor. *(op 9-4 tchd 5-2)*
Ironside(IRE), disappointing at Lingfield last time, bounced back to the sort of form he had shown on his chasing debut. However, it was obvious between the last two fences that this was one case he was not going to solve. *(op 5-1)*
Nocatee(IRE) had been without cheekpieces since prior to beating today's winner by a length and a quarter on 2lb better terms over three miles at Newcastle in December. *(op 4-1)*
Definite Approach(IRE) *Official explanation: trainer said gelding finished distressed (op 7-1)*
Red Square Lad(IRE) had not been seen since landing a maiden hunter chase at Leicester almost a year ago. He wants a right-handed course on this evidence. *(op 7-1)*

4096 RACING UK JUVENILE NOVICES' HURDLE (8 hdls) 2m

2:50 (2:50) (Class 3) 4-Y-0 **£5,204** (£1,528; £764; £381)

Form				RPR
1	**1**		**Opera De Coeur (FR)**[29] 3579 4-11-4 .... RichardJohnson (H D Daly) *mde all: rdn appr last: r.o wl* **2/1**[2]	116+
231	**2**	3	**Slew Charm (FR)**[17] 3787 4-11-1 115.......................(t) WilliamKennedy(3) (Noel T Chance) *chsd ldrs: rdn appr 2 out: j.lft last: one pce* **11/4**[3]	110+
32	**3**	4	**Ostrogoth (FR)**[48] 3294 4-10-12 .... MickFitzgerald (N J Henderson) *a.p: ev ch 2 out: rdn and swtchd lft appr last: wknd flat* **15/8**[1]	99
6F0	**4**	7	**Investment Wings (IRE)**[17] 3786 4-10-12 .... TimmyMurphy (M C Pipe) *prom: outpcd 5th: 4th and btn whn mstke last* **16/1**	94+
	5	4	**Four Schools (IRE)**[143] 4-11-8 124.. NoelFehily (Jonjo O'Neill) *hld up in mid-div: btn appr 2 out* **20/1**	100+
006P	**6**	nk	**Ember Dancer**[8] 3939 4-10-12 .... RJGreene (Ian Williams) *w.r.s: hdwy appr 3rd: hit 4th: wknd 2 out* **100/1**	88
20U	**7**	6	**Kickahead (USA)**[2] 4057 4-10-12 .... JasonMaguire (Ian Williams) *hld up and bhd: hdwy 4th: wkng whn hit 2 out* **25/1**	85+
33	**8**	½	**Rawaabet (IRE)**[8] 3939 4-10-12 .... JimmyMcCarthy (P W Hiatt) *t.k.h in tch: hit 2nd: short-lived effrt appr 2 out* **25/1**	81
06	**9**	25	**Mayadeen (IRE)**[15] 3817 4-10-12 ....(t) TomDoyle (J G M O'Shea) *a bhd: lost tch fr 5th: t.o* **100/1**	56

4m 1.50s (3.20) **Going Correction** +0.40s/f (Soft) **9** Ran SP% **115.1**
Speed ratings: **93,91,89,86,84 83,80,80,68** CSF £7.70 TOTE £3.40: £1.20, £1.60, £1.10; EX 8.30.
Owner The Hon Mrs A E Heber-Percy **Bred** N Burlot, Olivier Burlot,& Michel Le Bris **Trained** Stanton Lacy, Shropshire

FOCUS
They went 16/1 bar the first three home in this interesting juvenile contest. The winner is improving and the race has been rated through the second.

NOTEBOOK
Opera De Coeur(FR) continues to progress and followed up his course and distance victory last month with a decisive win. His trainer thinks that soft ground is not essential to him although he would not want it too fast. He is now likely to be stepped up in class. *(op 11-4)*
Slew Charm(FR), tried in a tongue strap, looked to be getting the worse of the argument against a decent type when going left at the final flight. *(op 10-3)*
Ostrogoth(FR) was a shade disappointing but may have come up against a couple of above-average sorts. *(op 13-8 tchd 9-4)*
Investment Wings(IRE) seemed to have lost his confidence at Market Rasen last time following his fall at the last when just behind Opera De Coeur here on his previous outing. He could never really get back into it after getting caught flat-footed and looked leg-weary when missing out at the last. *(op 14-1)*
Four Schools(IRE) was a dual winner on soft ground over hurdles in the French Provinces when *trained by Guillaume Macaire. Easy to back, he found this company too hot under his penalties. (op 14-1)*

4097 JOHN WATSON SERVICES H'CAP HURDLE (8 hdls) 2m

3:25 (3:25) (Class 2) 4-Y-0+ **£11,710** (£3,438; £1,719; £858)

Form				RPR
-161	**1**		**Gods Token**[12] 3880 8-11-2 **124** 7ex.. SamThomas (Miss Venetia Williams) *led to 3rd: chsd ldr: led after 5th: rdn and hdd after 3 out: led after 2 out: r.o* **2/1**[2]	134+
1	**2**	8	**Neveesou (FR)**[56] 3127 5-11-6 **128**.................................... TimmyMurphy (M C Pipe) *hld up: hdwy after 5th: hit 3 out: sn led: rdn and hdd after 2 out: eased whn btn flat* **5/4**[1]	133+
4-60	**3**	5	**Hawadeth**[48] 3289 11-11-12 **134**... JimCrowley (V R A Dartnall) *chsd ldr: led 3rd tl after 5th: sn rdn: wknd appr 2 out* **12/1**	131+

036- **4** *21* **Monte Cinto (FR)**[343] 4438 6-11-5 **127** ChristianWilliams 108+
(P F Nicholls) *hld up: hdwy 4th: wknd 5th* **7/2**[3]
F44- **5** *26* **Porak (IRE)**[414] 3233 9-9-9 **108** oh1 DerekLaverty(5) 57
(W Davies) *bhd fr 4th: t.o* **50/1**
3m 53.2s (-5.10) **Going Correction** +0.40s/f (Soft) **5** Ran SP% **109.7**
Speed ratings: **113,109,106,96,83** CSF £5.04 TOTE £2.70: £1.30, £2.00; EX 4.20.
Owner The Silver Cod Partnership **Bred** C I Ratcliffe **Trained** Kings Caple, H'fords

FOCUS
A poor turnout for some good prize money, but the time was good when compared to the preceding novice hurdle. The winner is rated to the level of his Exeter victory, with a big step up from the second. The third is well handicapped at present.

NOTEBOOK
Gods Token, described by his trainer as gutsy, would have had another 6lb to carry had his new *mark been in force. The softest ground he has encountered so far held no terrors for him. (op 9-4 tchd 15-8)*
Neveesou(FR), against a rival 6lb well in, had more than his fair share of weight based on what he actually achieved at Taunton. *(op 11-8 tchd 6-4)*
Hawadeth, who attempted just short of three miles last time, ran much better than on his two previous outings this season. *(op 10-1 tchd 14-1)*
Monte Cinto(FR) was having his first outing since being struck into in the County Hurdle at the *Cheltenham Festival last year. He had not run on ground this bad since he came over from France. (tchd 4-1)*

4098 STRADFORM H'CAP CHASE (22 fncs) 3m 5f
3:55 (3:55) (Class 3) (0-135,135) 5-Y-0+ **£6,506** (£1,910; £955; £477)

Form RPR
0142 **1** **Moorlands Again**[41] 3396 11-10-5 **114** (t) MarkBradburne 125
(M Sheppard) *led 2nd: rdn 17th: styd on wl flat* **9/4**[1]
1040 **2** *3* **Run For Paddy**[20] 3728 10-11-12 **135** NoelFehily 143
(M Pitman) *hld up in rr: hdwy appr 16th: ev ch last: rdn and nt qckn* **11/1**
16P4 **3** *7* **Victory Gunner (IRE)**[12] 3877 8-11-0 **123** ChristianWilliams 125+
(C Roberts) *prom: rdn after 18th: sltly outpcd 3 out: edgd lft and wknd appr last* **7/1**
-311 **4** *3* **Mrs Be (IRE)**[33] 10-10-6 **118** MissPGundry(3) 116
(J G Cann) *led to 2nd: lost pl 12th: bhd 15th: styd on appr 2 out: n.d* **9/2**[3]
631P **5** *25* **Willie John Daly (IRE)**[54] 3176 9-11-7 **130** (b[1]) RichardJohnson 103
(P J Hobbs) *prom: jnd wnr 15th: hit 4 out: wknd appr 2 out* **13/2**
1-13 **P** **Native Ivy (IRE)**[69] 2875 8-11-2 **125** TomDoyle —
(C Tinkler) *hld up: hdwy after 12th: rdn and wknd 16th: t.o whn p.u bef 18th* **5/2**[2]
7m 40.1s (-8.80) **Going Correction** +0.20s/f (Yiel) **6** Ran SP% **111.7**
Speed ratings: **104,103,101,100,93** — CSF £23.40 TOTE £2.90: £1.60, £2.90; EX 23.10.
Owner W J Odell **Bred** R Williams **Trained** Eastnor, H'fords

FOCUS
A reasonable pace for the testing conditions put the emphasis on stamina. The winner did not need to show the same form as when successful here in December, and the second, third and fourth all ran to their pre-race marks.

NOTEBOOK
Moorlands Again appeared to find more after the runner-up had looked a big danger in the short home straight. *(op 2-1 tchd 11-4)*
Run For Paddy seemed all set to pick off the winner under his big weight until getting outstayed from the final fence. He has never scored on ground this testing. *(op 9-1 tchd 12-1)*
Victory Gunner(IRE) was already set to drop 2lb having struggled since being raised for his win at Market Rasen on Boxing Day. *(op 12-1)*
Mrs Be(IRE) won a point-to-point at Dunthrop last month. On her first start under Rules since winning the race formerly called the Horse And Hound Cup at Stratford last May, she was off the same mark as when third in the cross-country event at last year's Cheltenham Festival. *(tchd 4-1)*
Willie John Daly(IRE) was tried in blinkers after his disappointing run last time. *(op 8-1)*
Native Ivy(IRE) *Official explanation: trainer said gelding was never travelling (op 9-4)*

4099 DRIVE VAUXHALL LEAMINGTON AND VAUXHALL COMBO NOVICES' HURDLE (12 hdls) 3m 1f
4:30 (4:30) (Class 3) 4-Y-0+ **£6,506** (£1,910; £955; £477)

Form RPR
4262 **1** **Kildonnan**[35] 3477 7-11-4 115 JasonMaguire 110+
(J A B Old) *hld up: hdwy after 3 out: led 2 out: rdn clr flat: eased towards fin* **5/2**[2]
2 *6* **Ballyboley (IRE)** 8-11-4 JimmyMcCarthy 99
(R T Phillips) *hld up: rdn and hdwy 3 out: wnt 2nd last: no ch w wnr* **33/1**
040P **3** *6* **Finsbury Fred (IRE)**[17] 3789 5-11-4 CarlLlewellyn 94+
(N A Twiston-Davies) *hld up and bhd: hdwy 7th: mstke 8th: rdn appr 3 out: wkng whn wnt lft last* **25/1**
PU0 **4** *1 1/4* **Irish Raptor (IRE)**[44] 3342 7-11-4 AntonyEvans 94+
(N A Twiston-Davies) *led 2nd: nt fluent 8th: blnd 3 out: rdn and hdd 2 out: wknd last* **16/1**
0411 **5** *10* **Alfasonic**[28] 3598 6-11-12 115 RobertThornton 92+
(A King) *hld up in tch: rdn appr 8th: wknd 3 out* **11/8**[1]
12F4 **6** *6* **Baron Romeo (IRE)**[31] 3545 6-11-4 RichardJohnson 77+
(R T Phillips) *led: mstke 1st: hdd 2nd: prom tl wknd appr 2 out* **6/1**[3]
2-61 **7** *4* **Kings Rock**[71] 2845 5-11-9 108 PJBrennan 77
(P A Blockley) *t.k.h: prom: rdn appr 8th: wknd 3 out* **8/1**
05-F **F** **Mrs Fizziwig**[44] 3342 7-10-11 WarrenMarston —
(R T Phillips) *hld up in rr: fell 6th* **33/1**
6m 38.0s (7.70) **Going Correction** +0.65s/f (Soft) **8** Ran SP% **111.7**
Speed ratings: **98,96,94,93,90 88,87,—** CSF £70.09 TOTE £4.10: £1.80, £8.30, £3.60; EX 149.90.
Owner W E Sturt **Bred** J S Wright **Trained** Barbury Castle, Wilts

FOCUS
The slow time reflected the pedestrian gallop. Not a race to assess confidently, but the winner has been rated value for eleven lengths.

NOTEBOOK
Kildonnan seems to have benefitted from more patient tactics and looks capable of defying a penalty. *(op 9-4)*
Ballyboley(IRE) ◆, a half-brother to an Irish bumper winner, fell in his only point in Ireland three years ago. This was a most satisfactory start to his career under Rules.
Finsbury Fred(IRE) showed improvement on this step up in trip but was well held in the end.
Irish Raptor(IRE) was another who ran better over a longer distance until eventually getting tired. *(op 14-1 tchd 18-1)*
Alfasonic was disappointing even taking into account that he had a double penalty. *(op 15-8 tchd 2-1 in places)*

4100 WILLOUGHBY DE BROKE HUNTERS' CHASE (18 fncs) 3m 110y
5:05 (5:05) (Class 6) 5-Y-0+ **£1,318** (£405; £202)

Form RPR
2F-3 **1** **Foly Pleasant (FR)**[14] 3847 12-12-0 132 (t) MrRBurton 117+
(Mrs K Waldron) *hld up: hit 10th: hdwy 3 out: led on bit after 2 out: j.lft last: rdn out* **8/15**[1]
/P-U **2** *6* **Irilut (FR)**[15] 3819 10-11-9 (p) MrSWaley-Cohen(5) 107+
(R Waley-Cohen) *hld up: hdwy appr 10th: led 3 out: rdn and hdd after 2 out: one pce* **7/2**[2]
U2PU **3** *18* **Ikdam Melody (IRE)**[13] 10-12-0 85 (p) MissJFoster(7) 95
(P Foster) *prom: hit 5th: wknd 14th* **16/1**
U4P/ **4** *1* **Dalcassian Buck (IRE)**[679] 4855 12-11-11 MrDEdwards(3) 88+
(Mrs L J Young) *hld up: hit 6th: hdwy 10th: led 13th: rdn and hdd 3 out: wknd 2 out* **40/1**
1U5U **5** *4* **Raiseapearl**[2] 4051 11-11-11 MrSRoss(7) 87
(Patrick Thompson) *prom: hit 5th: wknd 12th: bhd whn mstke 14th* **25/1**
-325 **6** *10* **Teeton Priceless**[20] 11-11-4 MrNPearce(7) 73+
(Mrs Joan Tice) *led to 13th: wknd after 3 out* **11/1**[3]
6m 39.7s (17.40) **Going Correction** +0.45s/f (Soft) **6** Ran SP% **108.0**
Speed ratings: **101,99,93,93,91 88** CSF £2.64 TOTE £1.50: £1.30, £1.40; EX 2.60 Place 6 £8.95, Place 5 £8.33.
Owner Nick Shutts **Bred** Adrien Landes **Trained** Stoke Bliss, Worcs

FOCUS
An uncompetitive contest. The winner, value for 10l, was 33lb of his mark when second in last year's Cheltenham Foxhunters'.

NOTEBOOK
Foly Pleasant(FR) came through to land the odds in convincing style. He jumped better than at Bangor but there is still some room for improvement. *(op 4-6)*
Irilut(FR) has a fine record in points. Completing for the first time under Rules, he eventually proved no match for the winner. *(op 2-1)*
Ikdam Melody(IRE) had shown he could handle this sort of ground when pipped on the post at Cartmel last May. *(op 20-1 tchd 25-1)*
Dalcassian Buck(IRE) was making his Hunter Chase debut having been off course since April 2004.
T/Jkpt: £707.80 to a £1 stake. Pool: £13,957.00. 14.00 winning tickets. T/Plt: £10.60 to a £1 stake. Pool: £45,068.90. 3,098.70 winning tickets. T/Qpdt: £6.70 to a £1 stake. Pool: £2,528.70. 277.80 winning tickets. KH

[3611] CHEPSTOW (L-H)
Saturday, February 25

OFFICIAL GOING: Soft (heavy in places)
The going was sticky, placing the emphasis on stamina. The second-last flight was omitted in all hurdle races, leaving a very long run to the last.
Wind: Strong, across Weather: Sunny, cold wind

4101 LETHEBY & CHRISTOPHER CONDITIONAL JOCKEYS' (S) H'CAP HURDLE (7 hdls 1 omitted) 2m 110y
2:05 (2:05) (Class 5) (0-90,90) 4-Y-0+ **£2,081** (£611; £305; £152)

Form RPR
F001 **1** **Lady Maranzi**[6] 4013 7-11-8 **86** 7ex LiamHeard 96+
(Mrs D A Hamer) *led 1st: rdn clr appr last: r.o wl* **15/8**[1]
-500 **2** *9* **Shalati Princess**[36] 3483 5-10-6 **75** RichardGordon(5) 75
(D Burchell) *t.k.h in tch: chsd wnr 4th tl appr 2 out: wnt 2nd again last: no ch w wnr* **14/1**
-044 **3** *2 1/2* **Grand Prairie (SWE)**[12] 3899 10-11-3 **87** (b) EamonDehdashti(6) 88+
(G L Moore) *hld up: hdwy 4th: rdn to chse wnr whn hit 2 out: one pce* **11/1**
00P3 **4** *2 1/2* **Mickey Pearce (IRE)**[7] 3985 4-10-7 **80** (v) OwynNelmes 66
(J G M O'Shea) *hld up in tch: lost pl 3rd: rallied appr 3 out: styd on fr 2 out* **8/1**
0PP/ **5** *5* **Without Pretense (USA)**[678] 4897 8-10-3 **67** MarkNicolls 57
(N G Ayliffe) *hld up in tch: wknd appr 3 out* **40/1**
064B **6** *1* **Little Villain (IRE)**[7] 3985 8-9-13 **66** (p) ShaneWalsh(3) 55
(T Wall) *led to 1st: prom tl wknd 4th* **16/1**
0-P6 **7** *6* **Final Lap**[8] 3956 10-9-11 **64** oh4 (v) TomMessenger(3) 47
(H H G Owen) *prom tl wknd appr 3 out* **50/1**
3001 **8** *3* **Irish Blessing (USA)**[46] 3330 9-11-4 **90** (tp) ThomasBurrows(8) 70
(F Jordan) *hmpd 2nd: a bhd* **9/2**[2]
050 **9** *17* **Bonjour Bond (IRE)**[7] 3985 5-10-8 **80** (b) ChrisDavies(8) 43
(J G M O'Shea) *bhd: j.lft 2nd: rdn appr 4th: t.o 3 out* **20/1**
0402 **U** **Rockys Girl**[6] 4013 4-10-7 **80** (b) PaddyMerrigan —
(R Flint) *stmbld and uns rdr 1st* **11/2**[3]
05PP **P** **Exclusive Air (USA)**[40] 3415 7-10-0 **64** oh7 DarylJacob —
(H H G Owen) *bhd: hmpd 2nd: t.o whn p.u bef last* **80/1**
4m 16.4s (6.00) **Going Correction** +0.525s/f (Soft)
WFA 4 from 5yo+ 9lb **11** Ran SP% **110.7**
Speed ratings: **98,93,92,91,89 88,85,84,76,—** — CSF £25.26 CT £214.54 TOTE £2.10: £1.40, £2.70, £3.70; EX 32.90.There was no bid for the winner.
Owner Mrs D A Hamer **Bred** D I Bare **Trained** Nantycaws, Carmarthens

FOCUS
Very moderate fare. Improved form from the winner, with the next two running pretty much to their marks.

NOTEBOOK
Lady Maranzi, who got off the mark six days earlier, had no problem following up under a penalty. The key seems to be allowing her to do her own thing in front. *(op 7-4)*
Shalati Princess, still a maiden, was back in the right grade and ran respectably, but the winner was much too good. *(tchd 16-1)*
Grand Prairie(SWE), back in selling grade, was run out of second place at the final flight. He is not the heartiest. *(tchd 12-1)*
Mickey Pearce(IRE), on his handicap bow, shaped as if he really needs further. *(op 7-1)*

4102 DENTS ORIGINAL FINE ART GALLERY CHEPSTOW RACECOURSE BEGINNERS' CHASE (16 fncs) 2m 3f 110y
2:40 (2:40) (Class 4) 5-Y-0+ **£3,903** (£1,146; £573; £286)

Form RPR
3-52 **1** **Nycteos (FR)**[12] 3903 5-10-5 124 LiamHeard(5) 128+
(P F Nicholls) *t.k.h: hdwy 4th: led on bit 3 out: easily* **5/4**[1]
432U **2** *5* **Matthew Muroto (IRE)**[9] 3949 7-10-12 99 DarylJacob(5) 117
(R H Alner) *hld up in tch: led 4 out to 3 out: no ch w wnr flat* **18/1**
06-3 **3** *16* **Shuhood (USA)**[116] 1971 6-11-3 TomDoyle 104+
(P R Webber) *a.p: ev ch 5 out: sn rdn: wknd 4 out: lft 3rd and hmpd 3 out* **9/2**[2]

120/ **4** 2½ **Chopneyev (FR)**[1082] [4102] 8-11-3 127 .... WarrenMarston 99
(R T Phillips) *hld up and bhd: hdwy 11th: no further prog fr 5 out* **8/1**

0U54 **5** dist **Mythical King (IRE)**[13] [3879] 9-11-3 .... AlanO'Keeffe —
(R Lee) *hld up towards rr: lost tch fr 8th: t.o* **15/2**

P440 **6** ¾ **Vanormix (FR)**[26] [3652] 7-10-10 93 .... (v) BernieWharfe(7) —
(C J Gray) *led to 5th: prom tl wknd appr 5 out: t.o* **40/1**

543U **U** **Give Me Love (FR)**[60] [3017] 6-10-12 119 .... (t) PaddyMerrigan(5) —
(P F Nicholls) *hmpd and uns rdr 1st* **7/1**[3]

-0FU **P** **Powra**[13] [3879] 6-10-12 .... JayHarris(5) —
(R J Hodges) *stdd s: plld hrd in rr: j. bdly rt: mstke 1st: t.o whn p.u after 8th* **100/1**

U3 **P** **Glenkill (IRE)**[23] [3689] 8-10-7 .... RichardYoung(3) —
(S M Jacobs) *plld hrd: prom: mstke 11th: wknd appr 5 out: t.o whn p.u bef 3 out* **100/1**

100 **F** **Alessandro Severo**[23] [3687] 7-11-3 .... BenjaminHitchcott —
(Mrs D A Hamer) *w ldr: led 5th to 4 out: cl 3rd whn fell 3 out: dead* **50/1**

5m 14.8s (3.50) **Going Correction** +0.30s/f (Yiel)
WFA 5 from 6yo+ 6lb **10** Ran SP% **109.6**
Speed ratings: **97,95,88,87,— —,—,—,—,—** CSF £22.35 TOTE £1.70: £1.30, £2.50, £1.60; EX 25.80.
Owner The Stewart Family **Bred** C Lacorie **Trained** Ditcheat, Somerset

FOCUS
The easy winner was rated value for 18l and should be capable of better. The runner-up ran to the upgraded level of his Fontwell second.

NOTEBOOK
Nycteos(FR), who only had to repeat the form of his chasing debut to land this, moved to the front three from home and was laughing at his rivals from then on. This longer trip was not a problem, certainly in this company. *(tchd 11-10)*
Matthew Muroto(IRE) is a consistent sort and he ran his race, but the winner proved far too good. *(op 20-1 tchd 22-1 and 16-1)*
Shuhood(USA) was left behind from the final ditch in ground which was probably too soft for him. *(op 4-1 tchd 5-1)*
Chopneyev(FR), off the track since finishing down the field in the Pertemps Final at the 2003 Cheltenham Festival, was well beaten on this chasing bow but is entitled to come on for the outing. *(op 7-1 tchd 9-1)*
Alessandro Severo ran well on this chasing debut but sadly took a fatal fall at the third last.

4103 EARTH SUMMIT "NATIONAL HERO" H'CAP CHASE (22 fncs) 3m 2f 110y
3:15 (3:15) (Class 3) (0-125,122) 5-Y-0+ **£6,349** (£1,936; £1,011; £549)

Form RPR

PP45 **1** **Fox In The Box**[13] [3877] 9-10-11 112 .... (v) DarylJacob(5) 131+
(R H Alner) *a.p: led 4 out: sn clr: easily* **13/2**

2313 **2** 12 **Finzi (IRE)**[15] [3845] 8-9-8 97 .... JohnKington(7) 102
(M Scudamore) *prom: sltly outpcd 16th: rallied after 17th: rdn and wkng whn lft 3rd 4 out: tk 2nd after 2 out: no ch w wnr* **4/1**[2]

116P **3** 14 **Kausse De Thaix (FR)**[55] [3186] 8-11-2 112 .... LeightonAspell 107+
(O Sherwood) *chsd ldr: led 5th: reminders 7th: hdd 4 out: wknd 2 out* **11/2**[3]

/P01 **4** 25 **Lord Broadway (IRE)**[23] [3688] 10-9-12 97 .... TJPhelan(3) 63
(N M Babbage) *hit 12th: a bhd* **12/1**

0P23 **P** **Earl's Kitchen**[28] [3614] 9-11-0 113 .... (t) RichardYoung(3) —
(C L Tizzard) *a bhd: hit 6th: mstke 14th: p.u bef 16th* **7/2**[1]

5P2F **P** **Kittenkat**[23] [3688] 12-10-9 105 .... SeanCurran —
(N R Mitchell) *prom: lost pl 8th: hit 11th: sn struggling: p.u bef 12th* **9/1**

-043 **P** **Cowboyboots (IRE)**[37] [3469] 8-11-5 122 .... JustinMorgan(7) —
(L Wells) *hld up: hit 8th: short-lived effrt 11th: bhd whn p.u bef 15th* **10/1**

1-16 **F** **Cherry Gold**[261] [694] 12-9-13 102 .... MrTJO'Brien(7) —
(Evan Williams) *led to 5th: chsd ldr: mstke 12th: nt fluent 13th: 3l 3rd whn fell 4 out: dead* **6/1**

7m 14.2s (-2.90) **Going Correction** +0.30s/f (Yiel) **8** Ran SP% **112.0**
Speed ratings: **108,104,100,92,— —,—,—** CSF £31.98 CT £150.76 TOTE £8.30: £1.90, £1.50, £3.20; EX 33.20.
Owner Peter Bonner **Bred** S Hadley **Trained** Droop, Dorset

FOCUS
The winner was back to something near his best, and this form looks solid enough with the second running to his mark.

NOTEBOOK
Fox In The Box came clear from the fourth last for a very comfortable victory, slightly awkward *jumps at the last two fences not affecting his momentum. He has a good record at Chepstow. (op 9-1 tchd 10-1)*
Finzi(IRE) ran his race but if anything found this an insufficient test of stamina. *(op 7-2 tchd 10-3 and 9-2)*
Kausse De Thaix(FR) ran a better race on this return from a short break but was well held in the end. *(op 7-1)*
Lord Broadway(IRE) *Official explanation: jockey said gelding was unsuited by track (op 8-1)*
Cherry Gold, Williams's first winner with a full licence and a prolific scorer for the yard, was sadly killed in a fall at the final ditch. *(op 8-1)*
Earl's Kitchen won last year's running of this event off an 8lb lower mark but was soon trailing this time. *Official explanation: jockey said gelding was never travelling (op 8-1)*

4104 VISIT DENTS GALLERY AT THE FESTIVAL NOVICES' H'CAP HURDLE (7 hdls 1 omitted) 2m 110y
3:50 (3:53) (Class 4) (0-110,113) 4-Y-0+ **£3,253** (£955; £477; £238)

Form RPR

P0 **1** **Dorneys Well (IRE)**[16] [3818] 6-10-9 90 .... (t) PaulMoloney 89
(Evan Williams) *hld up and bhd: smooth hdwy appr 2 out: led sn after last: hung lft: drvn out* **16/1**

24F- **2** ½ **Northaw Lad (IRE)**[381] [3764] 8-11-12 107 .... TomDoyle 105
(C Tinkler) *plld hrd early in tch: ev ch 2 out: rdn appr last: r.o flat* **33/1**

3146 **3** hd **Coach Lane**[29] [3603] 5-11-9 107 .... PaulO'Neill(3) 106+
(Miss Venetia Williams) *led to 3 out: hrd rdn to ld appr last: hdd sn after last: kpt on* **9/1**

333 **4** 13 **Original Fly (FR)**[39] [3431] 4-10-11 106 .... (b[1]) LiamHeard(5) 86+
(P F Nicholls) *hld up in tch: wknd 2 out: bdly hmpd last* **7/2**[2]

40F3 **5** ½ **David's Symphony (IRE)**[36] [3479] 4-10-6 96 .... LeightonAspell 71
(A W Carroll) *chsd ldr: wknd appr 3 out* **14/1**

31 **6** nk **Trompette (USA)**[12] [3902] 4-11-1 105 .... AndrewTinkler 82+
(N J Henderson) *hld up towards rr: hdwy 4th: ev ch 2 out: rdn and wkng whn hmpd last* **11/8**[1]

240F **7** 11 **Tom Bell (IRE)**[115] [1982] 6-11-10 105 .... DaveCrosse 78
(J G M O'Shea) *hld up and bhd: hdwy 4th: rdn and wknd 3 out: no ch whn hmpd last* **22/1**

0P3 **8** 1¼ **Sistema**[24] [3673] 5-10-5 89 .... OwynNelmes(3) 61
(A E Price) *hld up in tch: j. slowly and lost pl 2nd: sn bhd: rallied after 4th: wknd appr 3 out* **50/1**

-033 **F** **Corals Laurel (IRE)**[13] [3881] 7-11-8 103 .... WarrenMarston 99
(R T Phillips) *t.k.h: a.p: led 3 out tl appr last: 2l 4th and wkng whn fell last* **4/1**[3]

4m 23.7s (13.30) **Going Correction** +0.525s/f (Soft)
WFA 4 from 5yo+ 9lb **9** Ran SP% **116.1**
Speed ratings: **81,80,80,74,74 74,69,68,—** CSF £389.15 CT £4948.22 TOTE £19.40: £3.60, £9.10, £3.30; EX 382.20.
Owner R E R Williams **Bred** A McCarren **Trained** Cowbridge, Vale Of Glamorgan

FOCUS
The pace was pretty pedestrian until it picked up once into the home straight, and the form looks very suspect. The winning time was 7.3 seconds slower than the opener.

NOTEBOOK
Dorneys Well(IRE), having his second run for the yard, had never previously been placed in ten career starts, although he was an unlucky last-flight faller at Thurles last March. The drop in trip, fitting of a tongue tie and return to soft ground combined to do the trick as he took it up early on *the run-in and hung on despite drifting to his left.Official explanation: trainer said, regarding the improved form shown, gelding may have benefited from the fitting of a tongue strap on this occasion (op 9-1)*
Northaw Lad(IRE), returning after a year's absence, was slightly outpaced by the leaders in fifth place on the long run between the last two flights, but jumped the last in third and finished strongly. He could have done with a stronger pace. *(op 50-1)*
Coach Lanerallied to lead going to the final flight but had to give best on the short run-in. Winner of a maiden hurdle over course and distance, he looks held by the Handicapper. *(op 14-1)*
Original Fly(FR), blinkered for his handicap debut, was held when hampered by a faller at the final flight. The lack of pace did not suit him as he seems to need more of a stamina test. *(op 11-4)*
Trompette(USA), having only her third run over hurdles, was right there at the second last but did not find a great deal when let down. *(op 6-4 tchd 13-8 and 7-4 in places)*
Corals Laurel(IRE) was dropping in trip for his handicap debut. In front three from home, he was eventually collared on the approach to the final flight, where he came down. *(op 5-1)*

4105 DAVID DENT H'CAP HURDLE (10 hdls 2 omitted) 3m
4:20 (4:22) (Class 3) (0-125,116) 4-Y-0+ **£5,204** (£1,528; £764; £381)

Form RPR

2515 **1** **Kilty Storm (IRE)**[37] [3458] 7-10-13 110 .... AndrewGlassonbury(7) 126+
(M C Pipe) *hld up: hdwy 5th: led on bit appr 3 out: sn clr: easily* **8/1**

3120 **2** 12 **Keepers Mead (IRE)**[30] [3581] 8-11-7 116 .... DarylJacob(5) 116+
(R H Alner) *led tl appr 7th: outpcd appr 3 out: wnt 2nd after 2 out: no ch w wnr* **20/1**

6003 **3** 13 **Miss Fahrenheit (IRE)**[6] [4012] 7-11-0 104 .... SamStronge 89
(C Roberts) *a.p: led appr 7th: rdn and hdd appr 3 out: wknd after 2 out* **12/1**

1-11 **4** 1¾ **Passenger Omar (IRE)**[30] [3581] 8-11-2 111 .... (t) DougieCostello(5) 94
(Noel T Chance) *hld up in mid-div: rdn after 4th: sn struggling: styd on fr 2 out: n.d* **4/1**[3]

3U46 **5** 22 **Bunkum**[60] [3018] 8-11-2 106 .... TomDoyle 67
(R Lee) *prom tl rdn and wknd 5th* **8/1**

212 **6** dist **Mayoun (IRE)**[16] [3814] 9-10-4 101 .... (p) MrTJO'Brien(7) —
(Evan Williams) *a bhd: t.o* **7/2**[2]

4-UF **7** 9 **Miss Mailmit**[9] [3949] 9-10-8 98 .... MarkBradburne —
(J A B Old) *bhd fr 5th: t.o* **18/1**

0PP0 **8** 7 **Nick's Choice**[13] [3889] 10-10-7 102 .... MarkNicolls(5) —
(D Burchell) *t.k.h: w ldr: wknd appr 7th: t.o* **33/1**

10-P **P** **Litzinsky**[132] [1751] 8-9-11 90 .... OwynNelmes(3) —
(J G M O'Shea) *a bhd: t.o whn p.u bef 6th* **40/1**

1-4P **P** **Silver Birch (IRE)**[7] [3995] 9-11-4 113 .... (b[1]) LiamHeard(5) —
(P F Nicholls) *prom tl wknd after 7th: t.o whn p.u bef last* **3/1**[1]

6m 18.1s (1.30) **Going Correction** +0.525s/f (Soft) **10** Ran SP% **112.5**
Speed ratings: **110,106,101,101,93 —,—,—,—,—** CSF £139.06 CT £1886.14 TOTE £9.30: £2.00, £4.10, £2.20; EX 89.90.
Owner Sean Lucey **Bred** Denis O'Donnell **Trained** Nicholashayne, Devon

FOCUS
This was run at a sound pace and not many got into it. The winner improved 15lb on his Newbury win and the race has been rated through the runner-up.

NOTEBOOK
Kilty Storm(IRE), racing from a 6lb higher mark, took up the running going to the third last and quickly pulled right away. Eased down on the run-in with the race in safe keeping, he could be capable of better still. *(op 15-2 tchd 9-1)*
Keepers Mead(IRE) set a fair pace and plugged on to recapture second place on the long run between the last two flights.
Miss Fahrenheit(IRE) had no chance with the winner from the third last and was caught for second before the final flight. She does not quite stay this far. *(op 14-1)*
Passenger Omar(IRE), 10lb higher on his bid for a four-timer, was beaten before halfway but he did struggle past toiling rivals when it was too late. *(op 9-2)*
Silver Birch(IRE), making a quick reappearance after his poor run at Wincanton the previous weekend, was blinkered for the first time on this return to hurdling. Losing touch with the leaders at the end of the back straight and eventually pulled up, he has not been ruled out of the Grand National yet but his trainer suspects he might have a breathing problem.

4106 STRATSTONE JAGUAR CARDIFF MAIDEN HURDLE (9 hdls 2 omitted) 2m 4f
4:55 (4:58) (Class 4) 4-Y-0+ **£3,578** (£1,050; £525; £262)

Form RPR

24 **1** **Taking My Cut**[24] [3677] 6-11-3 .... APMcCoy 114
(Jonjo O'Neill) *hld up: stdy hdwy 4th: rdn appr 3 out: styd on u.p to ld cl home* **8/13**[1]

36 **2** 1 **Brads House (IRE)**[21] [3722] 4-10-7 .... DaveCrosse 103
(J G M O'Shea) *t.k.h: a.p: led appr 3 out: clr 2 out: sn rdn: hdd cl home* **7/2**[2]

053 **3** 10 **Portland Bill (IRE)**[22] [3717] 6-10-12 .... DarylJacob(5) 103
(R H Alner) *t.k.h: a.p: rdn after 3 out: wknd appr last* **7/1**[3]

035 **4** 1½ **Blue Splash (FR)**[36] [3478] 6-11-3 .... PaulMoloney 102
(Evan Williams) *led tl appr 3 out: wknd 2 out* **18/1**

0/02 **5** 5 **Regal Term (IRE)**[23] [3685] 8-10-7 .... JosephStevenson(10) 97
(R Dickin) *hld up in tch: wknd appr 3 out* **20/1**

0 **6** dist **Palamedes**[36] [3488] 7-11-3 .... TomDoyle —
(B J Llewellyn) *hld up towards rr: short-lived effrt after 6th: t.o* **50/1**

55-P **7** 27 **Baranook (IRE)**[84] [2618] 5-11-3 100 .... OllieMcPhail —
(B J Llewellyn) *hld up in tch: rdn 5th: wknd appr 3 out: t.o* **50/1**

0 **8** 6 **Honorary Citizen**[9] [3947] 4-10-4 .... PaulO'Neill(3) —
(Evan Williams) *a bhd: t.o* **100/1**

P **9** 6 **Ganymede**[10] [1680] 5-11-0 .... OwynNelmes(3) —
(J G M O'Shea) *hld up: hdwy 4th: wknd appr 3 out: t.o* **66/1**

P-00 **10** dist **Hayley's Pearl**[268] [613] 7-10-3 64 .... WayneKavanagh(7) —
(Mrs P Ford) *a bhd: t.o* **150/1**

P0 **11** dist **Bombaybadboy (NZ)**[9] [3947] 7-11-3 .... HenryOliver —
(Ian Williams) *chsd ldr tl lost pl after 3rd: t.o* **150/1**

500- **U** **Pipers Legend**[486] [1858] 7-10-12 .... MarkNicolls(5) —
(D Burchell) *j. bdly rt and uns rdr 1st* **150/1**

P **Cool Linnett** 5-11-3 .... MarkBradburne —
(P A Blockley) *a bhd: mstke 4th: t.o whn hung rt 5th: p.u bef last* **100/1**

33/6 **P** **Pertemps Timmy**[32] [3545] 8-10-10 .... SeanQuinlan(7) —
(R T Phillips) *prom tl wknd 5th: t.o whn blnd last: p.u flat* **25/1**

5m 12.2s (9.50) **Going Correction** +0.725s/f (Soft)
WFA 4 from 5yo+ 10lb **14** Ran SP% **119.9**
Speed ratings: **102,101,97,97,95** —,—,—,—,— —,—,—,— CSF £2.77 TOTE £1.50: £1.10, £1.30, £2.30; EX 4.20.
Owner John P McManus **Bred** Mrs Mercy Rimell **Trained** Cheltenham, Gloucs

FOCUS
A modest event containing a lot of dead wood and run at a pretty steady pace, but the form looks solid enough.

NOTEBOOK
Taking My Cut came under pressure on the approach to the third last and still had a lot of ground to make up on the leader when moving into second place two from home. However McCoy, who had travelled from Sandown for this one ride, made his journey worthwhile by forcing him up near the line. A stronger gallop will suit him and he should stay further. *(op 4-7 tchd 4-6 in places)*
Brads House(IRE) looked to have made a race-winning move when kicking clear on the approach to the second last, but despite doing nothing wrong he eventually succumbed near the finish. His turn should come. *(op 9-2 tchd 5-1)*
Portland Bill(IRE), tackling his longest trip so far, ran his race but was made to look rather one-paced from the second last. He looks the type for handicaps. *(op 8-1 tchd 9-1)*
Blue Splash(FR) showed a bit more on this drop in trip and needs one more run for a handicap mark. There are races to be won with him. *(tchd 16-1 and 20-1)*
Regal Term(IRE) probably showed a similar level of form as when runner-up at Towcester on his previous start. *(op 16-1)*

4107 BRIAN RAYNER TRANSPORT HUNTERS' CHASE (22 fncs) 3m 2f 110y
5:25 (5:25) (Class 6) 5-Y-0+ **£1,124** (£348; £174; £87)

Form RPR

1F- **1** **Camden Carrig (IRE)**[42] 11-11-10 .... MrNPhillips(7) 90+
(Simon Bloss) *mde all: drew wl clr fr 5 out: eased considerably flat* **7/4**[1]

033/ **2** *21* **Hades De Sienne (FR)**[299] 11-11-7 .... (t) MrABrown(7) 49+
(Miss Tracey Watkins) *a.p: hit 2nd: wnt 2nd 11th: w wnr after 17th: rdn appr 4 out: btn whn hit 3 out* **8/1**

/6-4 **3** *19* **Lucky Master (IRE)**[41] 14-11-7 .... MissGSwan(7) 24
(Miss G Swan) *hld up: no ch fr 10th* **13/2**

0P/0 **4** *¾* **Zola (IRE)**[7] 10-11-7 .... MrPSheldrake(7) 23
(Mrs J Sidebottom) *chsd wnr to 11th: wknd 14th* **4/1**[3]

356- **5** *dist* **Supreme Silence (IRE)**[307] 9-11-10 80 .... MrNickKent(7) —
(Nick Kent) *wl bhd fr 10th* **3/1**[2]

P2/P **P** **Castle Arrow (IRE)**[48] 13-11-7 .... MissRosemaryWilliams(7) —
(Miss R Williams) *a in rr: blnd 8th: sn lost tch: t.o whn p.u bef 16th* **50/1**

7m 38.1s (21.00) **Going Correction** +0.50s/f (Soft) **6** Ran SP% **107.8**
Speed ratings: **80,73,68,67**,— — CSF £14.19 TOTE £3.30: £1.10, £2.10; EX 20.30 Place 6 £380.80, Place 5 £186.93.
Owner J G Phillips **Bred** Mrs Joan Buckley **Trained** Bibury, Gloucs

FOCUS
An uncompetitive race and a slow time even for a hunter chase, around 24 seconds slower than the earlier handicap over the same trip. The winner was value for 38l.

NOTEBOOK
Camden Carrig(IRE) was pulled up in a decent open point-to-point won by Irilut at Barbury last month. He jumped nicely throughout and, enjoying being able to dominate, burnt off his sole challenger up the home straight. *(op 9-4)*
Hades De Sienne(FR), having his first run since May and without the regular cheekpieces, did not jump these regulation fences all that fluently. He momentarily constituted a threat on the long home turn but was soon left well behind. *(op 15-2 tchd 9-1)*
Lucky Master(IRE), well held in two ladies' opens so far this year, was never a factor but did snatch third place near the line. Slow but sure, he has completed the course on his last 25 starts, including points, and has never fallen. *(op 8-1)*
Zola(IRE) finished alone in a two-horse members' race at Erw Lon a week earlier. He struggled to keep in touch with the first two down the far side on the final circuit and was eventually caught for third place close home. *(op 11-4)*
Supreme Silence(IRE) was always in the rear division on this first run for ten months. *(tchd 7-2)*
T/Plt: £514.60 to a £1 stake. Pool: £55,587.05. 78.85 winning tickets. T/Qpdt: £99.30 to a £1 stake. Pool: £3,169.80. 23.60 winning tickets. KH

3912 NEWCASTLE (L-H)
Saturday, February 25

OFFICIAL GOING: Heavy (soft in places)
First flight after winning post and last flight in back straight omitted all hurdles.
Penultimate fence in back straight omitted all chases.
Wind: Fairly strong, half-against

4108 TOTEPLACEPOT NOVICES' H'CAP HURDLE (8 hdls 3 omitted) 2m 4f
1:50 (1:50) (Class 2) 4-Y-0+
£9,394 (£2,775; £1,387; £694; £346; £174)

Form RPR

0122 **1** **Euro American (GER)**[8] [3966] 6-11-12 **129** .... AlanDempsey 135+
(E W Tuer) *keen: hld up in tch: smooth hdwy whn mstke 3 out: led between last two: pushed out* **5/1**[3]

6122 **2** *1 ½* **You Do The Math (IRE)**[53] [3234] 6-10-2 **105** .... TimmyMurphy 107
(L Lungo) *hld up: drvn and outpcd 6th: rallied 3 out: kpt on wl to go 2nd cl home: no ch w wnr* **3/1**[2]

2121 **3** *nk* **Stagecoach Diamond**[19] [3779] 7-10-12 **115** .... DominicElsworth 119+
(Mrs S J Smith) *chsd ldrs: rdn 4 out: ev ch whn blnd 2 out: edgd lft and one pce run in* **6/1**

60F2 **4** *9* **Bollin Thomas**[19] [3783] 8-9-11 **103** oh8 .... PaddyAspell(3) 97+
(R Allan) *in tch: effrt bef 3 out: sn one pce: lft 4th last* **33/1**

0221 **5** *13* **Seymar Lad (IRE)**[11] [3918] 6-10-1 **104** .... GrahamLee 84
(P Beaumont) *chsd ldrs: drvn 4 out: outpcd after next* **5/2**[1]

323P **6** *8* **Posh Stick**[42] [3385] 9-10-0 **103** oh2 .... BrianHarding 75
(J B Walton) *in tch: outpcd 6th: n.d after* **33/1**

1626 **7** *dist* **Chef De Cour (FR)**[43] [3378] 5-11-3 **120** .... TonyDobbin —
(L Lungo) *hld up: shortlived effrt after 4 out: hit next and sn wknd* **5/1**[3]

5631 **F** **Jontys'Lass**[17] [3795] 5-9-11 **103** oh3 .... PeterBuchanan(3) 102
(A Crook) *led to between last two: 4l down and hld whn fell last* **18/1**

5m 21.1s (5.30) **Going Correction** +0.175s/f (Yiel) **8** Ran SP% **113.0**
Speed ratings: **96,95,95,91,86 83**,—,— CSF £20.35 CT £89.78 TOTE £7.00: £1.90, £2.00, £1.60; EX 26.90.
Owner Shore Property **Bred** Euro-American Bet Verm Gmbh **Trained** Great Smeaton, N Yorks

FOCUS
A fair event run at just an ordinary gallop in the testing conditions. The winner was value for slightly further and the form seems sound enough.

NOTEBOOK
Euro American(GER) did not find much off the bridle over two and three-quarter miles last time but appreciated the drop back to this trip and turned in his best effort. Given the way he travels he should prove effective over shorter and he may be capable of further success. *(op 13-2)*
You Do The Math(IRE) ◆ extended his run of creditable efforts, and on this evidence will be very well suited by the return to three miles on this sort of ground. He appeals strongly as the type to win another race at around this trip. *(op 7-2)*
Stagecoach Diamond, up 12lb for winning an ordinary novice event at Sedgefield last time, ran arguably his best race over hurdles. He is in good hands, should stay three miles and may well be capable of further success in ordinary company. *(tchd 5-1)*
Bollin Thomas ran creditably from 8lb out of the handicap returned to this longer trip but, given his inconsistency and the fact that he has yet to win over hurdles, he would be no good thing from his proper mark next time. *(op 25-1)*
Seymar Lad(IRE), who turned in an improved effort when winning over course and distance on his previous start, was disappointing, despite going up in the weights and in grade. However given he *is only lightly raced and has plenty of scope, he is well worth another chance. Official explanation: jockey said today's race may have come too quickly after gelding's previous run on Feb 14th* *(op 9-4 tchd 3-1)*
Posh Stick was soundly beaten returned to hurdles and, although on a fair mark in this sphere, will have to show more before she is worth a bet. *(op 25-1)*
Chef De Cour(FR), who disappointed when a short-priced favourite at Kelso last time, was beaten in a matter of strides before stamina over this longer trip became an issue. He is one to tread *carefully with at present. Official explanation: jockey said gelding failed to stay 2m4f on heavy, soft in places going*
Jontys'Lass, who showed improved form to win a novices' event last time, had been raised 15lb for that success and was held when coming to grief after enjoying an uncontested lead. She is going to have to progress again to win from this mark. *(op 20-1)*

4109 TOTESCOOP6 H'CAP CHASE (12 fncs 1 omitted) 2m 110y
2:25 (2:25) (Class 3) (0-130,128) 5-Y-0+ **£6,349** (£1,936; £1,011; £549)

Form RPR

-0F2 **1** **Brave Thought (IRE)**[14] [3852] 11-10-11 **113** .... TimmyMurphy 125+
(P Monteith) *hld up in tch: stdy hdwy bef 4 out: 2l down whn blnd 2 out: hung lft: led run in: styd on* **7/2**[2]

P043 **2** *½* **Flight Command**[35] [3495] 8-11-2 **118** .... (p) RussGarritty 129+
(P Beaumont) *prom: led after 5 out: rdn 3 out: hdd run in: kpt on* **7/2**[2]

32F5 **3** *22* **Sands Rising**[19] [3784] 9-10-2 **104** .... (t) KennyJohnson 96+
(R Johnson) *hld up: mstke 2nd: hdwy and in tch bef 5 out: wknd next: lft poor 3rd last* **11/2**[3]

0P05 **4** *14* **Encore Cadoudal (FR)**[10] [3922] 8-10-11 **113** .... (tp) DavidO'Meara 93+
(H P Hogarth) *prom: hdwy to ld 6th: hdd after 5 out: wknd next* **9/1**

F441 **P** **Do L'Enfant D'Eau (FR)**[14] [3852] 7-11-2 **118** .... RichardMcGrath —
(B Storey) *cl up tl lost pl 4th: wknd bef 5 out: p.u lame bef 3 out* **11/4**[1]

4-63 **F** **Through The Rye**[54] [3207] 10-11-12 **128** .... JohnMcNamara 137+
(E W Tuer) *led to 6th: cl up: outpcd 4 out: rallied after next: ev ch whn fell last* **6/1**

4m 20.6s (-2.60) **Going Correction** +0.025s/f (Yiel) **6** Ran SP% **110.8**
Speed ratings: **107,106,96,89**,— — CSF £15.84 TOTE £3.60: £1.50, £3.10; EX 13.30.
Owner Hamilton House Limited **Bred** Michael Purcell **Trained** Rosewell, Midlothian
■ Stewards' Enquiry : John McNamara caution: used whip down the shoulder in the forehand position

FOCUS
An ordinary handicap in which the pace was just fair. The first two were nicely in on their best form and ran to their marks.

NOTEBOOK
Brave Thought(IRE) has gained his last two wins over this course and distance in the hands of Timmy Murphy and he showed more resolution than the runner-up in the closing stages. However he looked high enough in the weights going into this race so will find life tougher after reassessment, especially against progressive sorts. *(op 9-2)*
Flight Command, down in the weights again, had the run of the race in the first-time cheekpieces and ran his best race for some time. However he is likely to continue to look vulnerable in more competitive company after reassessment. *(tchd 4-1 in places)*
Sands Rising was again below the form of his course-and-distance second in December and, given he has only won once since November 2003, remains one to tread carefully with. *(op 9-2)*
Encore Cadoudal(FR), back on the same mark as when last successful in November over this trip, was again disappointing and remains one to watch for now. *(op 14-1)*
Through The Rye, down in trip, was in the process of running up to his best when coming to grief but he is another of the principals from this race that is likely to struggle in a more competitive handicap from his current mark. *(tchd 3-1)*
Do L'Enfant D'Eau(FR), who beat today's winner at Ayr last time, was a long way below that level and, although it transpired that he was lame, he is going to struggle to win a competitive handicap from his current mark. *Official explanation: vet said gelding was lame (tchd 3-1)*

4110 TOTESPORT.COM H'CAP HURDLE (7 hdls 2 omitted) 2m
3:00 (3:01) (Class 3) (0-135,127) 4-Y-0+
£5,323 (£1,572; £786; £393; £196; £98)

Form RPR

013P **1** **Torkinking (IRE)**[7] [3986] 7-11-2 **124** .... (t) BenOrde-Powlett(7) 135+
(M A Barnes) *chsd ldr: led bef 3rd: reminders after 4 out: edgd lft and kpt on gamely fr 2 out* **3/1**[1]

2-0F **2** *1 ½* **Dont Call Me Derek**[10] [3929] 5-11-10 **125** .... GrahamLee 133+
(J J Quinn) *prom: chsd wnr after 4 out: effrt and ev ch 2 out: one pce run in* **7/2**[2]

U2P0 **3** *8* **Andre Chenier (IRE)**[20] [3761] 5-11-0 **115** .... TimmyMurphy 115+
(P Monteith) *hld up: hdwy bef 3 out: one pce next: hld whn j.rt last* **16/1**

0415 **4** *nk* **Culcabock (IRE)**[33] [3542] 6-10-9 **113** .... PeterBuchanan(3) 112
(Miss Lucinda V Russell) *prom: rdn bef 3 out: kpt on fr last: no imp* **33/1**

F22 **5** *3 ½* **Double Vodka (IRE)**[36] [3488] 5-10-10 **111** .... RichardMcGrath 107
(C Grant) *hld up: rdn and effrt 3 out: no imp fr next* **5/1**[3]

5250 **6** *3 ½* **Uptown Lad (IRE)**[43] [3378] 7-10-0 **101** oh1 .... (p) KennyJohnson 93
(R Johnson) *bhd: rdn 1/2-way: sme hdwy after 3 out: n.d* **7/1**

1361 **7** *2 ½* **Texas Holdem (IRE)**[31] [3561] 7-11-5 **125** .... MichaelMcAlister(5) 115
(M Smith) *chsd ldrs: lost pl 4 out: n.d after* **7/1**

-05P **8** *½* **Benbyas**[7] [3986] 9-11-7 **127** .... JohnnyLevins(5) 116
(D Carroll) *led to bef 3rd: rdn and wknd appr 3 out* **20/1**

6461 **9** *hd* **Overstrand (IRE)**[8] [3967] 7-11-9 **124** .... (b) TonyDobbin 113
(Robert Gray) *prom tl rdn and wknd bef 3 out* **14/1**

36/P **10** *23* **Cita Verda (FR)**[14] [3853] 8-10-13 **114** .... WilsonRenwick 80
(P Monteith) *a bhd: rdn and wknd fr 4 out* **33/1**

4m 5.30s (-1.00) **Going Correction** +0.175s/f (Yiel) **10** Ran SP% **112.1**
Speed ratings: **109,108,104,104,102 100,99,99,99,87** CSF £13.29 CT £137.42 TOTE £4.30: £1.70, £1.10, £4.80; EX 10.10.

Owner J G Graham, Scott Lowther **Bred** James Browne **Trained** Farlam, Cumbria
■ Stewards' Enquiry : Ben Orde-Powlett caution: careless riding

FOCUS
Another fair handicap but, although the pace seemed fair in the conditions, those racing prominently held the edge. This is rock-solid handicap form, with improved form from the first two, and the next three close to their marks.

NOTEBOOK
Torkinking(IRE), a really tough sort whose previous run over two and a half miles last week can be ignored (slipped saddle), showed a splendid attitude to maintain his unbeaten record over course and distance. A further rise in the weights will make life tougher in a more competitive event but he is the sort to continue giving it his best shot. *(op 9-2 tchd 5-1 and 11-4)*
Dont Call Me Derek showed himself none the worse for a recent fall but did not find as much off the bridle as seemed likely and failed to overturn last March's course and distance placings (much better terms) with the gritty winner. He was clear of the remainder though, and is capable of winning again after reassessment away from progressive sorts. *(op 2-1)*
Andre Chenier(IRE) has little margin for error from his current mark but may be a bit better than the bare form as he fared the best of those that was held up. He may have to come down a few pounds before regaining the winning thread. *(op 12-1)*
Culcabock(IRE) ran better than at Wetherby last time but left the impression that a stiffer test of stamina would have been more to his liking. His overall record suggests he is not one to place maximum faith in. *(tchd 40-1)*
Double Vodka(IRE), making his handicap debut, looked in good shape and was not disgraced given this race favoured those racing prominently. He handles better ground and is worth another chance in ordinary company, especially when a better gallop looks likely. *(op 9-2 tchd 11-2 in places)*
Uptown Lad(IRE) has been below his best since running creditably over course and distance on heavy ground in December and the fact that he has not won for over two years means he remains one to tread carefully with. *(op 9-1)*

4111 TOTESPORT EIDER (A H'CAP CHASE) (22 fncs 3 omitted) 4m 1f
3:35 (3:37) (Class 2) (0-150,137) 5-Y-0+
£46,477 (£13,800; £6,900; £3,442; £1,725; £870)

Form — RPR

0FP2 **1** **Philson Run (IRE)**[13] 3877 10-11-6 **131** .... GrahamLee 143+
(Nick Williams) *hld up: hdwy 1/2-way: led 3 out: sn hrd pressed: drvn out run in* **10/1**[3]

-323 **2** *1 ¼* **High Cotton (IRE)**[31] 3560 11-9-4 **111** oh9 .... JamesReveley(10) 120
(K G Reveley) *hld up: hdwy 17th: effrt bef 3 out: chsd wnr next: kpt on* **12/1**

4631 **3** *½* **Korelo (FR)**[28] 3614 8-11-4 **129** .... TimmyMurphy 140+
(M C Pipe) *hld up bhd: stdy hdwy fr 15th: effrt bef 3 out: sltly outpcd next: kpt on fr last* **7/2**[1]

16-P **4** *1 ¼* **Baron Windrush**[61] 2992 8-11-12 **137** .... CarlLlewellyn 146+
(N A Twiston-Davies) *hld up: hdwy and ev ch whn blnd 17th: led 4 out to next: no ex fr last* **16/1**

F121 **5** *dist* **Dunbrody Millar (IRE)**[21] 3728 8-11-0 **128** .... TomMalone(3) —
(P Bowen) *mde most to 4 out: wknd appr next* **5/1**[2]

-521 **6** *13* **Kerry Lads (IRE)**[51] 3258 11-11-0 **128** .... (p) PeterBuchanan(3) —
(Miss Lucinda V Russell) *w ldrs: blnd 18th: wknd after 4 out* **12/1**

01P0 **7** *5* **Robbo**[7] 3970 12-10-4 **122** .... MissRDavidson(7) —
(K G Reveley) *sn wl bhd: nvr on terms* **25/1**

1242 **8** *27* **Miss Mattie Ross**[43] 3377 10-9-9 **111** oh1 .... MichaelMcAlister(5) —
(S J Marshall) *prom: rdn 1/2-way: wknd fr 17th* **20/1**

-5P3 **U** **Devil's Run (IRE)**[11] 3917 10-9-11 **111** oh3 .... PaddyAspell(3) —
(J Wade) *midfield: blnd and uns rdr 9th* **16/1**

2P22 **P** **Brave Spirit (FR)**[28] 3613 8-10-11 **122** .... (v) TonyDobbin —
(C L Tizzard) *in tch tl wknd and p.u bef 17th* **10/1**[3]

-3P4 **U** **Malek (IRE)**[51] 3258 10-10-13 **124** .... (b[1]) RichardMcGrath —
(K G Reveley) *in tch whn blnd and uns rdr 11th: dead* **12/1**

-P0P **P** **Chives (IRE)**[7] 3971 11-11-12 **137** .... DavidO'Meara —
(Mrs S J Smith) *w ldrs tl wknd fr 17th: t.o whn p.u bef 4 out* **66/1**

P-PU **P** **Bathwick Annie**[7] 3995 10-11-2 **127** .... JohnMcNamara —
(B G Powell) *midfield on outside: wknd 13th: p.u bef 15th* **50/1**

4214 **P** **D J Flippance (IRE)**[32] 3554 11-10-0 **111** oh8 .... WilsonRenwick —
(A Parker) *in tch to 1/2-way: sn lost pl: t.o whn p.u bef 4 out* **50/1**

P14U **P** **Supreme Breeze (IRE)**[31] 3560 11-10-5 **116** .... DominicElsworth —
(Mrs S J Smith) *chsd ldrs tl wknd 15th: t.o whn p.u bef 4 out* **16/1**

-P00 **P** **Your A Gassman (IRE)**[78] 2747 8-11-0 **125** .... (b) KeithMercer —
(Ferdy Murphy) *midfield: drvn and outpcd 17th: n.d after: t.o whn p.u bef last* **33/1**

-12P **U** **Datito (IRE)**[36] 3481 11-10-0 **111** oh6 .... JimmyMcCarthy —
(R T Phillips) *hld up: hdwy u.p 18th: wknd after next: no ch whn blnd and uns rdr last* **33/1**

9m 3.80s **17** Ran SP% **117.7**
CSF £111.48 CT £508.11 TOTE £12.10: £2.90, £2.20, £1.60, £3.50; EX 181.10 Trifecta £1275.60 Pool: £1,976.30 - 1.10 winning tickets..
Owner Gale Force One **Bred** Martin Hoste **Trained** George Nympton, Devon

FOCUS
Only a few progressive sorts for this slog in the mud but, although the runner-up was out of the handicap and has yet to win a race, this was a fair performance by the winner, who is all stamina. He has been rated a bit better than the bare result.

NOTEBOOK
Philson Run(IRE), who shaped much better over an extended three miles last time, returned to winning ways back over this marathon trip and in ground he likes. Although he looks ungainly under pressure he did nothing wrong and is the sort to continue to go well in this type of event when the emphasis is firmly on stamina. *(tchd 11-1)*
High Cotton(IRE), whose forte is stamina, kept trying and ran as well as he ever has done from 9lb out of the handicap. However,as he has yet to win from 30 career starts, he would not be one to lump on at short odds next time. *(op 16-1)*
Korelo(FR) ◆, 9lb higher than when successful in lesser company at Chepstow, ran a blinder. There was no problem with stamina, his jumping seemed fairly sound and given he is nearly two stones lower over fences than over hurdles, he remains one to keep on the right side. *(tchd 10-3 and 4-1)*
Baron Windrush has not had much racing in recent times but showed he retains plenty of ability and ran his best race since winning over three miles and five at Warwick last January. He is capable of winning again but has little margin for error from his current mark. *(op 14-1)*
Dunbrody Millar(IRE) had gone up in the weights for his gutsy win at Sandown but, although his effort petered out fairly tamely this time, he may well be better in less testing ground and he is not one to write off just yet. *(op 9-2)*
Kerry Lads(IRE) struggles to last home over this trip when the ground is on top so was always likely to be up against it in these conditions. His best form over fences has been over shorter when able to boss less-competitive fields.
Brave Spirit(FR) *Official explanation: jockey said gelding lost its action (tchd 11-1)*

4112 TOTESPORT 0800 221 221 NOVICES' CHASE (16 fncs 2 omitted) 3m
4:05 (4:11) (Class 2) 5-Y-0+ **£19,464**

Form — RPR

-F16 **1** **King Killone (IRE)**[55] 3178 6-11-12 125 .... DavidO'Meara 138
(H P Hogarth) *cl up: chal 11th: led 4 out: 1l in front and keeping on wl whn lft alone last* **9/1**[3]

-441 **F** **Olney Lad**[33] 3541 7-11-9 131 .... RussGarritty —
(Mrs P Robeson) *led to 4 out: cl 2nd whn fell next* **7/4**[2]

PP **P** **Uncle Neil (IRE)**[11] 3914 9-11-4 .... (b) TJDreaper —
(P Monteith) *cl up: blnd 4th: blnd and wknd 10th: t.o whn p.u bef 4 out* **50/1**

P/PP **P** **Moonzie Laird (IRE)**[106] 2169 8-11-4 .... PeterBuchanan —
(Miss Lucinda V Russell) *prom tl wknd 10th: t.o whn p.u bef 4 out* **150/1**

-121 **F** **Wild Cane Ridge (IRE)**[14] 3850 7-11-12 130 .... TonyDobbin 138
(L Lungo) *in tch: mstke 4th: blnd 6th: hdwy 1/2-way: outpcd bef 4 out: rallied and lft 2nd next: keeping on and 1l down whn fell last* **4/6**[1]

6m 34.6s (9.80) **Going Correction** +0.375s/f (Yiel) **5** Ran SP% **109.0**
Speed ratings: **98**,—,—,—,— CSF £10.00 TOTE £11.40: £4.70; EX 7.50.
Owner Hogarth Racing **Bred** Sylvester Barrett **Trained** Stillington, N Yorks

FOCUS
An eventful race in which the winner was left alone at the final fence. He has been rated as dead-heating with last-fence faller Wild Cane Ridge.

NOTEBOOK
King Killone(IRE)won this as his jumping stood up in the closing stages as those around him came to grief or pulled up. He is a gutsy sort but will find life tougher against anything progressive under a double penalty in this type of race or from his current mark of 125 in handicaps. *(tchd 11-1)*
Olney Lad, a winner at Wetherby in testing ground on his previous start, was in the process of running creditably and was far from a spent force when coming to grief. He looks capable of better in this sphere if his jumping holds up. *(op 100-1)*
Moonzie Laird(IRE) was predictably outclassed on this chasing debut. *(op 100-1)*
Uncle Neil(IRE) faced an impossible task on these terms. *(op 100-1)*
Wild Cane Ridge(IRE)has jumped sketchily even in victory and he was again found out by lack of fluency, eventually coming to grief after making hard work of mounting a challenge. There is no certainty he would have won this even if he had not fallen, and he will have to jump much better than this if he is to defy his 130 mark in handicaps. *(op 100-1)*

4113 TOTEEXACTA CONDITIONAL JOCKEYS' H'CAP HURDLE (10 hdls 3 omitted) 3m
4:35 (4:37) (Class 5) (0-95,95) 4-Y-0+ **£2,277** (£668; £334; £166)

Form — RPR

P40P **1** **Cody**[61] 2975 7-10-4 **76** .... (bt) MichaelMcAvoy(3) 79+
(James Moffatt) *hld up: hdwy after 4 out: led 2 out: mstke last: all out* **16/1**

P-6P **2** *½* **The Masareti Kid (IRE)**[180] 1361 9-10-8 **80** .... MichaelO'Connell(3) 81
(I McMath) *prom: led briefly bef 2 out: kpt on fr last* **33/1**

F004 **3** *3 ½* **Kidithou (FR)**[11] 3918 8-11-10 **93** .... EwanWhillans 90
(W T Reed) *early ldr: dropped rr 3rd: hdwy after 4 out: outpcd next: kpt on fr last* **9/1**

1532 **4** *5* **Villago (GER)**[36] 3487 6-11-12 **95** .... WillieMcCarthy 88+
(E W Tuer) *prom: drvn and outpcd bef 3 out: n.d after* **11/8**[1]

0005 **5** *8* **Cloudmor (IRE)**[47] 3314 5-11-6 **92** .... DavidBoland(3) 80+
(L Lungo) *keen: hld up in tch: hdwy to ld 6th: hdd bef 2 out: wknd* **3/1**[2]

UUP5 **6** *dist* **Dark Thunder (IRE)**[4] 4043 9-11-1 **84** .... (b) ScottMarshall —
(Ferdy Murphy) *chsd ldrs tl wknd bef 3 out* **6/1**[3]

PP0P **7** *dist* **Fifteen Reds**[32] 3552 11-9-12 **70** .... (p) JohnFlavin(3) —
(J C Haynes) *s.s: sn rcvrd and led: hit and hdd 6th: sn wknd* **50/1**

-05F **P** **Team Resdev (IRE)**[38] 3446 6-10-5 **77** .... (p) FearghalDavis(3) —
(F P Murtagh) *a bhd: t.o whn p.u bef 3 out* **16/1**

0-0P **P** **Lady Past Times**[46] 3339 6-10-6 **80** .... GarryWhillans(5) —
(D W Whillans) *towards rr: lost tch and p.u bef 6th* **16/1**

6m 40.8s (22.40) **Going Correction** +0.525s/f (Soft) **9** Ran SP% **113.9**
Speed ratings: **83,82,81,80,77** —,—,—,— CSF £367.32 CT £4938.33 TOTE £13.70: £4.10, £4.60, £2.20; EX 92.00.
Owner The Vilprano Partnership **Bred** Miss K Rausing **Trained** Cartmel, Cumbria

FOCUS
A very ordinary handicap indeed which the pace was fair. The race has been rated though the winner.

NOTEBOOK
Cody, returned to hurdles and back up in trip, put his best foot forward with the tongue-tie and blinkers back on to get off the mark for the first time in 46 career starts. His record suggests he is not one for short odds next time. *(op 14-1)*
The Masareti Kid(IRE) returned to something like his best on this second start for the yard but, given his inconsistency, his losing run and the fact this race took little winning, would not really be one to be interested in at shortish odds next time.
Kidithou(FR), back over three miles, shaped as though an even stiffer test of stamina over this trip would have suited. He is capable of winning from this mark but is another that is rarely one for maximum faith.
Villago(GER) looked to have decent claims in this company but proved a disappointment. He may be better in less testing ground, though, and is worth another chance in similar company. *(op 13-8 tchd 7-4 in places)*
Cloudmor(IRE) ◆, upped markedly in trip, failed to get home in the conditions having travelled powerfully for much of the way. He is in very good hands and, although this was not much of a race, will be much more of interest back over shorter, especially if there is any market support for him. *(tchd 11-4 and 10-3 in places)*
Dark Thunder(IRE), an inconsistent sort who stays well and has form in testing ground, was again well below his best and he remains one to tread carefully with at present.

4114 TOTESPORTCASINO.COM NOVICES' HURDLE (7 hdls 2 omitted) 2m
5:05 (5:06) (Class 4) 4-Y-0+ **£3,253** (£955; £477; £238)

Form — RPR

24 **1** **Nikola (FR)**[17] 3793 5-11-2 .... CarlLlewellyn 111+
(N A Twiston-Davies) *cl up: led bef 3rd: mde rest: styd on strly fr 2 out* **8/13**[1]

50F2 **2** *5* **Kilmackilloge**[53] 3231 7-11-2 100 .... GrahamLee 103
(M Todhunter) *hld up: stdy hdwy bef 3 out: chsd wnr next: rdn and hung lft: kpt on same pce last* **7/2**[2]

030 **3** *10* **Silent Bay**[17] 3793 7-10-13 .... PaddyAspell(3) 93
(J Wade) *chsd ldrs: outpcd bef 3 out: kpt on fr last: no imp* **20/1**

1300 **4** *1 ¾* **Planters Punch (IRE)**[11] 3912 5-11-9 107 .... BarryKeniry 99+
(G M Moore) *chsd ldrs tl rdn and wknd fr 2 out* **10/1**[3]

040 **5** *14* **Monifieth**[17] 3795 6-10-9 .... DominicElsworth 70
(D W Whillans) *lost pl after 2nd: sn struggling: sme hdwy 3 out: nvr on terms* **33/1**

P0 **6** *17* **Colonel James (IRE)**[47] 3314 5-11-2 .... KennyJohnson 60
(R Johnson) *prom tl lost pl 3rd: n.d after* **50/1**

0-00 **7** *25* **Dusky Dawn (IRE)**[17] [3793] 5-10-11 .... TJDreaper[(5)] 35
(J M Jefferson) *hld up: rdn after 4 out: wknd bef next* **66/1**

36 **F** **Hush Tiger**[43] [3374] 5-10-9 .... GarethThomas[(7)] —
(R Nixon) *plld hrd: in tch: rdn bef 3 out: btn whn fell last* **16/1**

4m 15.2s (8.90) **Going Correction** +0.525s/f (Soft) **8** Ran SP% **110.3**
Speed ratings: **98,95,90,89,82 74,61,—** CSF £2.67 TOTE £1.50: £1.02, £2.00, £2.90; EX 3.50 Place 6 £2,211.11, Place 5 £1,139.38.
Owner Graham And Alison Jelley **Bred** D Laupretre **Trained** Naunton, Gloucs

FOCUS
Ordinary form from the placings downwards but the winner looks the type to improve again. The form might work out.

NOTEBOOK
Nikola(FR) ◆ did not have to improve to win an ordinary event but there was plenty to like about the manner of the victory. He should stay further and, given he is open to further progress, is the type to win more races. *(op 1-2 tchd 4-6)*
Kilmackilloge ran creditably despite edging off a true line but he is likely to remain vulnerable to the more progressive novices in this type of event and will be of more interest in ordinary handicaps in due course. *(op 9-2)*
Silent Bay, having only his second outing over hurdles, left the impression that the step up to two *and a half miles plus and the step into ordinary handicap company would suit in due course. (op 25-1)*
Planters Punch(IRE) has been disappointing since winning at Carlisle in November and is likely to remain vulnerable under a penalty in this type of event. *(op 8-1)*
Monifieth shaped as though a thorough test of stamina and low-grade handicaps are going to suit once assessed.
Colonel James(IRE) faced a very stiff task at the weights and was not surprisingly well beaten on *this third run for a handicap mark. Official explanation: jockey said gelding hung right-handed in straight (op 100-1)*
T/Jkpt: Not won. T/Plt: £1,034.40 to a £1 stake. Pool: £75,740.20. 53.45 winning tickets. T/Qpdt: £332.70 to a £1 stake. Pool: £4,496.50. 10.00 winning tickets. RY

4088 SANDOWN (R-H)

Saturday, February 25

OFFICIAL GOING: Chase course - soft (good to soft in places); hurdles course - soft (heavy in places)
Meeting switched from Kempton Park.
Wind: Strong, behind

4115 ANGLO IRISH BANK COMMERCIAL PROPERTY LENDING NOVICES' HURDLE (REGISTERED AS DOVECOTE NOVICES' HDLE) (8 hdls) 2m 110y
1:35 (1:36) (Class 1) 4-Y-0+ **£15,965** (£5,989; £2,998; £1,495; £750)

Form RPR

U131 **1** **Senorita Rumbalita**[13] [3884] 5-11-2 .... RobertThornton 124
(A King) *hld up bhd ldrs: tk clsr order appr 2 out: swtchd lft in cl 3rd appr last: r.o wl to ld cl home: rdn out* **11/2**[3]

1412 **2** *1 1/4* **Mister Quasimodo**[13] [3878] 6-11-6 120 .... JoeTizzard 127
(C L Tizzard) *trckd ldrs: pressed ldr appr 2 out: rdn into narrow advantage last: kpt on but no ex whn hdd cl home* **5/4**[1]

4511 **3** *1/2* **Regal Heights (IRE)**[17] [3793] 5-11-6 133 .... JasonMaguire 126
(D McCain) *lw: led: rdn sn after 2 out: narrowly hdd last: kpt on* **13/2**

33 **4** *9* **Vinando**[7] [3996] 5-11-2 .... (b) APMcCoy 114+
(C R Egerton) *lw: trckd ldrs: rdn and effrt appr 2 out: kpt on same pce* **7/2**[2]

F1 **5** *3/4* **Blu Teen (FR)**[56] [3133] 6-11-6 .... (t) ChristianWilliams 117
(P F Nicholls) *str: trckd ldr: ev ch appr 2 out: sn rdn: one pce after* **8/1**

4m 15.0s (6.10) **Going Correction** +0.225s/f (Yiel) **5** Ran SP% **106.5**
Speed ratings: **90,89,89,84,84** CSF £12.46 TOTE £5.30: £2.40, £1.60; EX 10.00.
Owner Let's Get Ready To Rumble Partnership **Bred** Wothersome Grange Stud **Trained** Barbury Castle, Wilts

FOCUS
An unsatisfactory result, with Regal Heights setting just a steady gallop and playing directly into the hands of smart bumper performer Senorita Rumbalita, who has speed to burn. Mister Quasimodo set a strong standard on the form of his Exeter second, but he was unsuited by the pace and it was a little surprising Tizzard did not strike for home earlier. Suspect form.

NOTEBOOK
Senorita Rumbalita, a smart bumper performer who has taken well enough to hurdles without looking a star in the making, posted an improved performance here in beating Mister Quasimodo, but in truth, the race panned out ideally for the speedy mare and she was always going to outpace the runner-up, who is a future three-mile chaser, after the last. She is evidently one of, if not the, best mare around over hurdles and is entitled to take her chance at Cheltenham, but this effort flatters her and the 33/1 still on offer represents her chance of landing the Festival curtain-raiser, so maybe Aintree in the wiser option. *(op 9-2)*
Mister Quasimodo ◆, an attractive gelding who stamped himself as a very useful novice when pushing Noland all the way at Exeter earlier in the month, made the running that day in order to make it a true test at the distance (first run at two miles over hurdles) but for whatever reason connections decided against pressing on from the front on this occasion and despite picking up well to come through and lead approaching the last, he had no answer to the winner's burst on the run-in. He would probably have won had he been ridden more positively, but this future three-mile *chaser is merely passing time over hurdles and he remains an exciting prospect for next season. (op 11-8 tchd 6-4 in places)*
Regal Heights(IRE), in search of a hat-trick following wins at Ayr and Carlisle, appeared to hold sound claims, whilst looking vulnerable to a classier type at the same time, and he ran a cracking race for his bang in-form stable. At an advantage in being able to lead at his own steady gallop, he kept responding to Maguire's urgings but, as was the case with Mister Quasimodo, he found himself a sitting duck to the winner. He is a decent type who should have little trouble finding another race in the North before going on to fences next season. *(op 7-1)*
Vinando, unsuccessful in two previous attempts over hurdles, was expected to raise his game with the blinkers back on, but he was readily outpaced as the principals went on. He will find easier opportunities, and an additional half-mile is likely to help. *(op 5-1)*
Blu Teen(FR), just a workmanlike winner at Lingfield, may still have been feeling the affects of his previous fall at Chepstow there (hacking clear on bridle at time). The drift in the market beforehand evidently told the story, and the first-time tongue tie hinted at a possible problem with his breathing, but either way he has a bit to prove now. *(op 11-2 tchd 5-1)*

4116 RACING POST 20 YEARS OF SERVICE PENDIL NOVICES' CHASE GRADE 2 (17 fncs) 2m 4f 110y
2:10 (2:10) (Class 1) 5-Y-0+ **£18,460** (£7,059; £3,641; £1,923)

Form RPR

2F21 **1** **Napolitain (FR)**[21] [3726] 5-11-3 139 .... ChristianWilliams 134
(P F Nicholls) *lw: j.w: mde all: kpt on wl to assert appr last: rdn out* **2/1**[2]

-11 **2** *5* **Gallant Approach (IRE)**[73] [2825] 7-11-7 132 .... APMcCoy 136+
(C R Egerton) *lw: trckd wnr: disputing whn blnd 11th: ev ch 2 out: sn rdn: no ex and sn hld* **4/5**[1]

6442 **3** *30* **Lago D'Oro**[6] [4006] 6-10-10 93 .... JamesDavies 92
(Dr P Pritchard) *j.lft thrght: hld up in 4th: losing tch whn lft 3rd at the 8th* **66/1**

-144 **4** *6* **Roman Rampage**[7] [3982] 11-11-3 .... (p) RobertLucey-Butler 93
(Miss Z C Davison) *a towards rr: lost tch fr 8th* **100/1**

0-13 **F** **Big Moment**[75] [2798] 8-11-3 .... JimCrowley —
(Mrs A J Perrett) *chsd ldng pair: cl up whn fell 8th* **5/1**[3]

5m 22.3s (1.50) **Going Correction** +0.225s/f (Yiel)
WFA 5 from 6yo+ 7lb **5** Ran SP% **108.0**
Speed ratings: **97,95,83,81,—** CSF £4.03 TOTE £3.00: £1.40, £1.30; EX 4.60.
Owner The Stewart Family **Bred** Francois Cottin **Trained** Ditcheat, Somerset

FOCUS
The winner has been rated to the level of his upgraded course and distance win and the runner-up a few pounds below his Newbury success. As it stands however, the form falls short of the standard required to win at the Festival. The winning time also modest.

NOTEBOOK
Napolitain(FR) ◆, down and out when Turpin Green tried to refuse at the last and gifted him the Grade One Scilly Isles over course and distance last time, set a clear standard with likely favourite Bold Bishop absent and was allowed to go off at surprisingly generous odds. Ridden positively by Williams, he jumped with tremendous accuracy and enthusiasm and picked up again to go clear from two out. Equally effective on a sound surface, he should have no trouble staying three miles and on the form of his Cheltenham second to The Listener on New Year's Day, the 33/1 still available for the Royal & SunAlliance Chase (often won by a tough, experienced sort) makes plenty of appeal, even though he is only a five-year-old. *(op 15-8 tchd 9-4 in a place)*
Gallant Approach(IRE) is undoubtedly promising, but how he was allowed to go off at such short odds is hard to fathom. Giving weight to a horse with Grade One course and distance winning form, it was no surprise to see him beaten, although in fairness it was only his second outing over fences and a bad blunder through inexperience at the first of the railway fences did him no favours, though he did not lose much ground at it and was soon back on the bridle. The winner simply had too much for him in the end though and he was held well before the last. A return to three miles will help and he can find a decent race before the season is out. *(op 11-10)*
Lago D'Oro got the better of Roman Rampage in their own private battle for third and acheived her objective in picking up some place money. *(tchd 80-1 and 100-1 in a place)*
Roman Rampage jumped reasonably enough on this chasing debut, and although he was always losing the battle with Lago D'Oro for third this was arguably improved form. *(op 66-1)*
Big Moment, whose two previous chasing efforts yielded a win and good third behind Voy Por Ustedes at Plumpton, had something to find with the winner, but had not been asked a question when he failed to get very high at the eighth. He is not the biggest, but has a future over fences at the right level. *(op 7-2 tchd 11-2 in a place)*

4117 RPSPORT NO 1 FOR SPORTS BETTING ADONIS JUVENILE NOVICES' HURDLE GRADE 2 (8 hdls) 2m 110y
2:45 (2:45) (Class 1) 4-Y-0 **£15,965** (£5,989; £2,998; £1,495; £750; £375)

Form RPR

33 **1** **Kasbah Bliss (FR)**[92] 4-11-5 .... ADuchene 145
(F Doumen, France) *lw: in tch: pushed along appr 3rd: hdwy after 3 out: narrow advantage 2 out: sn edgd rt: styd on wl: rdn out* **2/1**[1]

11 **2** *1 1/2* **Blazing Bailey**[22] [3714] 4-11-2 .... RobertThornton 141
(A King) *chsd ldrs: wnt prom 3rd: led after 3 out: narrowly hdd next: sn rdn and swtchd lft appr last: kpt on* **5/2**[2]

615 **3** *dist* **Twist Magic (FR)**[60] [3021] 4-11-5 132 .... (t) ChristianWilliams 100
(P F Nicholls) *hld up but in tch: rdn to go distant 3rd appr 2 out: wknd appr last: btn 46 l* **11/2**[3]

3510 **4** *8* **Sole Agent (IRE)**[11] [3908] 4-11-2 115 .... PhilipHide 89
(G L Moore) *towards rr: reminders on bnd after 2nd: rdn after 5th: outpcd after 3 out: wnt mod 4th after 2 out: btn 54 l* **50/1**

5 *4* **Osako D'Airy (FR)**[39] 4-10-12 .... TomScudamore 81
(S Gollings) *chsd ldrs: wnt prom 3rd: travelling wl 3 out: sn rdn and wknd: btn 58 l* **12/1**

1 **6** *7* **Political Intrigue**[26] [3645] 4-11-2 .... JimCrowley 78
(T G Dascombe) *w ldr: led 3rd: hit next: hdd after 3 out: sn wknd: btn 65 l* **12/1**

0 **7** *1 3/4* **Love Angel (USA)**[49] [3294] 4-10-12 .... SamThomas 72
(J J Bridger) *led tl 3rd: grad fdd: t.o: btn 66 3/4 l* **66/1**

P **Rustler**[129] 4-10-12 .... MickFitzgerald —
(N J Henderson) *scope: hld up in tch: hit 5th: wknd 3 out: t.o and p.u bef 2 out* **7/1**

4m 5.10s (-3.80) **Going Correction** +0.225s/f (Yiel) **8** Ran SP% **108.6**
Speed ratings: **113,112,—,—,— —,—,—** CSF £6.54 TOTE £3.10: £1.40, £1.40, £2.40; EX 8.30.
Owner Henri De Pracomtal **Bred** Haras D'Ecouves Et H De Pracomtal **Trained** Bouce, France

FOCUS
Hardly a vintage renewal of this key Triumph Hurdle trial, but Kasbah Bliss and Blazing Bailey were well clear of the remainder in a race that developed into a real test of stamina, and both deserve their chance at the Festival.

NOTEBOOK
Kasbah Bliss(FR) came into this boasting several useful pieces of placed form to his name, notably a third behind smart pair Fair Along and Afoun at Cheltenham back in November, and he posted a decent effort in beating hat-trick seeking Blazing Bailey, running on well after the last to win going away. He now heads for the Triumph, with his trainer believing he will be suited by a better surface, but it was not a particularly strong renewal of this prestigious Cheltenham trial and the 12/1 widely available seems about right. *(op 5-2)*
Blazing Bailey has quickly developed into a useful juvenile and, having twice won at Fontwell, this gallant second represented another step in the right direction. He took it up soon after the third-last, his rider eager to press on and make full use of his stamina, but Kasbah Bliss always looked to be going too well for him and he was unable to repel the French raider. He may be capable of better in a fast-run Triumph hurdle and, although he would be 3lb worse off the winner there, that race *makes more appeal than connections' intended target for him, the Royal & SunAlliance Hurdle. (op 15-8 tchd 11-4 in a place)*
Twist Magic(FR), last seen finishing fifth in the Grade One Junior Finale hurdle at Chepstow over Christmas, had a tongue tie on here for the first time, but it clearly failed to have the desired effect and he trailed in a remote third. He is not up to Triumph class and it is unlikely he will be seen at his best until tackling fences next season. *(op 5-1 tchd 6-1)*
Sole Agent(IRE) had any amount to find with the principals and fourth was about the best he could have hoped for. He was well held and will appreciate a return to something easier.
Osako D'Airy(FR) ◆, an athletic sort, is the interesting one to take from the race. Unbeaten in two starts at Pau for previous connections, one on the Flat and one over fences, this was a tough race in which to make his hurdling debut, but there were few going better as they turned for home and he looked sure to play a role in the finish. He ultimately faded out of contention, but his stable know what to do with a good horse, as demonstrated with Royal Shakespeare, and he should have little trouble finding an ordinary juvenile event. *(op 14-1)*

Political Intrigue, a tidy winner on his hurdling debut at Ludlow, faced contrasting ground conditions here and was unable to build on his initial effort. He deserves another chance on better ground. *(op 9-1)*
Love Angel(USA) took them along early, but as was to be expected, he was unable to live with the principals.
Rustler was potentially the most interesting runner on show, having won his last two outings on the Flat and been talked of as a smart sort by connections, but the testing ground was always likely to cause the son of Green Desert problems and he failed to make an impact. He ought to be capable of considerably better, but the reported breathing problem is a concern and it's worth *bearing in mind he acquired visors on the Flat.. Official explanation: jockey said gelding had a breathing problem (op 9-1)*

4118 RACING POST CHASE (H'CAP) GRADE 3 (22 fncs) 3m 110y

3:20 (3:21) (Class 1) 5-Y-O+

£57,020 (£21,390; £10,710; £5,340; £2,680; £1,340)

Form					SP	RPR
10-1	**1**		**Innox (FR)**[105] 2176 10-11-0 **143** (F Doumen, France) *chsd ldrs: led after 13th: j.lft fr 17th: hdd 4 out: led next: sn hrd rdn: styd on gamely: drvn out*	(b) APMcCoy	**8/1**	154+
3-24	**2**	*2 1/2*	**L'Ami (FR)**[61] 2972 7-11-7 **155** (F Doumen, France) *lw: hld up towards rr: stdy hdwy fr 16th: chsd ldrs appr 3 out: sn rdn: styd on to go 2nd run-in*	ADuchene(5)	**8/1**	163
0232	**3**	*1/2*	**My Will (FR)**[7] 3977 6-11-4 **147** (P F Nicholls) *chsd ldrs: outpcd after 4 out: styd on again fr 2 out: mstke last: wnt 3rd cl home*	JoeTizzard	**8/1**	156+
31F2	**4**	*3/4*	**Ladalko (FR)**[21] 3728 7-10-7 **136** (P F Nicholls) *chsd ldrs: rdn and effrt after 4 out: nt fluent next: styd on*	ChristianWilliams	**11/2**[1]	145+
0503	**5**	*3/4*	**Ballycassidy (IRE)**[23] 3697 10-10-10 **139** (P Bowen) *led 3rd tl 13th: led 4 out: rdn and hdd next: kpt on but no ex run-in*	JasonMaguire	**100/1**	146+
U-21	**6**	*29*	**Graphic Approach (IRE)**[49] 3296 8-10-11 **140** (C R Egerton) *mid div: smooth hdwy to trck ldrs 16th: rdn after 3 out: wknd last*	PJBrennan	**8/1**	126+
6134	**7**	*17*	**Lacdoudal (FR)**[55] 3179 7-11-6 **149** (P J Hobbs) *mid div: hdwy after 11th: rdn after 4 out: wknd after 3 out*	RichardJohnson	**13/2**[2]	109
-1P0	**F**		**Iris Bleu (FR)**[21] 3728 10-10-10 **139** (M C Pipe) *lw: hld up towards rr: fell 11th*	TomScudamore	**14/1**	—
23F0	**P**		**Halexy (FR)**[21] 3739 11-10-0 **129** oh2 (Jonjo O'Neill) *nvr travelling and a in rr: t.o and p.u bef 16th*	JimCrowley	**100/1**	—
/2P-	**P**		**Calling Brave (IRE)**[426] 2943 10-11-3 **146** (N J Henderson) *mid div tl 12th: sn bhd: t.o and p.u bef 16th*	MickFitzgerald	**14/1**	—
/3-P	**P**		**Irish Hussar (IRE)**[61] 2972 10-11-8 **151** (N J Henderson) *mid div: hit 11th and 12th: sn dropped rr: t.o and p.u bef 3 out*	MarcusFoley	**33/1**	—
1416	**P**		**Schuh Shine (IRE)**[21] 3739 9-10-3 **132** (Miss Venetia Williams) *led tl 3rd: prom: rdn and wknd after 4 out: t.o and p.u bef last*	SamThomas	**28/1**	—
1/33	**P**		**Fork Lightning (IRE)**[55] 3176 10-10-9 **138** (A King) *lw: in tch: lost pl after 12th: wkng whn mstke 15th: t.o and p.u bef 3 out*	RobertThornton	**7/1**[3]	—
PPP2	**F**		**Distant Thunder (IRE)**[9] 3942 8-10-3 **132** oh3 ow3 (R H Alner) *facing wrong way whn tapes rose: bhd: making sme hdwy whn stmbld and fell 17th*	AndrewThornton	**8/1**	—
P62S	**R**		**Risk Accessor (IRE)**[77] 2760 11-10-7 **136** (Jonjo O'Neill) *hld up towards rr: stdy hdwy after 4 out: rdn after 3 out: styng on and chalng for cl 3rd whn rn out last*	NoelFehily	**33/1**	137

6m 19.8s (-11.70) **Going Correction** +0.225s/f (Yiel) **15** Ran SP% **121.4**
Speed ratings: **118,117,117,116,116 107,101,**—,—,— —,—,—,—,— CSF £69.36 CT £538.36 TOTE £7.50: £2.70, £2.90, £2.40; EX 42.70 Trifecta £704.70 Pool: £21,139.03 - 21.90 winning tickets..
Owner John P McManus **Bred** Bernard Trinquet And Marc Trinquet **Trained** Bouce, France
■ A 1-2 for Chantilly trainer Francois Doumen.
■ Stewards' Enquiry : Jason Maguire one-day ban: disobeyed starter's orders (Mar 8)
Joe Tizzard one-day ban: disobeyed starter's orders (Mar 8)

FOCUS

A decent time for this quality renewal, with King George fourth and Gold Cup contender L'Ami finding only his improved stable companion Innox too good on the day. The prominent placing of the highly consistent My Will gives the form a solid look and the race is likely to have a bearing on races such as the William Hill Trophy Chase, Gold Cup and Grand National. High-class handicap form, as it was entitled to be.

NOTEBOOK

Innox(FR), fresh into this having last been seen winning at Cheltenham's Paddy Power meeting, is a strong stayer who may have struggled had this been staged at Kempton. Prominent from an early stage, his jumping was not perfect down the back and he jumped out to his left taking the Pond Fence, but he relished every yard of the stamina test and stayed on strongly up the hill. He now heads straight to the Grand National, as he is best fresh, and although only seventh in it last year off a mark of 135, he looks an improved performer. French-breds traditionally struggle there, but he has already negotiated the course safely and goes there with a good chance. *(op 9-1)*
L'Ami(FR), who boasts a prominent position in the Gold Cup lists thanks to good efforts in the Hennessy and King George, needed to run a big race here off this mark if he were to keep the Cheltenham dream alive, and he did just that, staying on well in the straight to make it a one-two for his trainer, having looked to be going nowhere turning in. He has not won for over 13-months now, but there is no doubting his resolution and, in a wide-open year, it is not hard to see him going close in March.
My Will(FR) is a versatile sort with regards to trip and he ran yet another good race in defeat, getting going all too late after hitting the last. He takes his racing well and is now likely to take his chance in the William Hill Handicap Chase at the Festival. *(op 12-1)*
Ladalko(FR) has done little wrong this season since returning to fences and ran his third good race at the course since January, keeping on well after the last without quite being able to reach a place. He is still only seven and hopefully has quite a bit of improvement left in him. *(op 6-1)*
Ballycassidy(IRE) ◆, who ran a lifeless race when last of three to finish in the rescheduled Letheby & Christopher Chase at Wincanton earlier in the month, has always been considered to be at his best on a sound surface, but he handled the going well and seemed to appreciate being ridden positively. Rated around 10lb higher this time last year, there is a decent race in him if able to build on this.
Graphic Approach(IRE), a progressive and unexposed chaser, faced a stiff task off a mark 8lb higher than when a fortunate winner at the course on less testing ground last time. He moved up threateningly towards the end of the back straight, but didn't get home. He scoped clear afterwards, and the only explanation his trainer could offer was that he did not stay in the tacky ground. Cheltenham - probably the shorter Racing Post Plate - remains on the agenda. *(op 7-1)*
Lacdoudal(FR), bidding to maintain his trainer's dominance of this race in recent years, was 6lb higher than when winning over course and distance back in December and had a rare off day on this return to fences, labouring from over a fair way out. He may be in the grip of the Handicapper - *his rider's belief that the ground did not suit does not really wash - but he is a lot better than this. (op 6-1 tchd 7-1 and 15-2 in a place)*
Risk Accessor(IRE), a talented yet quirky individual, was in the process of running his best race for a long time and he was still battling it out for the places when running through the wing of the last fence. He is most capable on his day and showed here he is well handicapped, but simply cannot be relied upon. *(op 12-1)*
Calling Brave(IRE), a horse who has traditionally been at his best on good ground, failed to make an impact on this return from injury, but better can be expected in the spring. *(op 12-1)*
Irish Hussar(IRE), who like stable companion Calling Brave was returning from a lay-off, failed to shine and dropped away tamely before being pulled up. He is capable of smart form on his day, but this delicate gelding can never be backed with confidence. *(op 12-1)*
Fork Lightning(IRE), a useful staying chaser who has returned from injury in good form this season, was encountering this sort of ground for the first time in a long time and he recorded a *laboured effort. Official explanation: jockey said gelding was unsuited by the soft (good to soft in places) ground (op 12-1)*
Distant Thunder(IRE), extremely well-weighted on his Lingfield novice form with L'Ami, returned to form when going close at Huntingdon last week (first time he has completed this season, would have won had his rider got serious) and he was still travelling okay here when falling in the back straight. A more positive ride will suit in future, but in fairness his rider had little choice but to hold him up here after he was caught facing the wrong way as the tapes went up. It remains to be seen how this affects his confidence. *(op 12-1)*
Schuh Shine(IRE), progressive at a lower level, ran well to a point before pulling up and will find easier opportunities. *(op 12-1)*

4119 CORAL BACKING THE NSPCC H'CAP HURDLE (9 hdls) 2m 4f 110y

3:55 (3:59) (Class 3) (0-130,127) 4-Y-O+

£12,526 (£3,700; £1,850; £926; £462; £232)

Form					SP	RPR
-P05	**1**		**New Entic (FR)**[61] 2969 5-11-0 **115** (G L Moore) *lw: a travelling wl and racd wd: trckd ldrs: led on bit appr 2 out: sn clr: heavily eased run-in*	(p) JamieMoore	**4/1**[2]	129+
3310	**2**	*4*	**Youlbesolucky (IRE)**[21] 3729 7-11-2 **117** (Jonjo O'Neill) *lw: trckd ldrs: ev ch after 3 out: sn rdn: kpt on to go 2nd appr last: no ch w wnr*	NoelFehily	**7/1**[3]	116
4-P1	**3**	*4*	**Kilgowan (IRE)**[24] 3675 7-11-3 **118** (Ian Williams) *hld up: tk clsr order 6th: rdn to chse wnr appr 2 out: lost 2nd appr last: kpt on same pce*	WayneHutchinson	**11/4**[1]	113
P205	**4**	*1/2*	**Westmeath Flyer**[12] 3901 11-11-2 **117** (P A Blockley) *hld up: hdwy and swtchd rt appr 2 out: sn rdn: kpt on run-in*	(p) PJBrennan	**12/1**	112
030-	**5**	*3 1/2*	**Chicago Bulls (IRE)**[420] 3151 8-11-5 **127** (A King) *b.bkwd: chsd ldrs: slow jump 5th: rdn and effrt after 3 out: one pce fr next*	MrGTumelty(7)	**10/1**	118
0061	**6**	*3 1/2*	**Marrel**[9] 3950 8-10-12 **113** (D Burchell) *j.lft thrght: trckd ldr: led 3 out: rdn and hdd appr next: one pce after*	(v) RichardJohnson	**7/1**[3]	101
363	**7**	*1 3/4*	**Idiome (FR)**[24] 3675 10-11-0 **115** (Mrs L C Taylor) *hld up: rdn and effrt appr 2 out: one pce after*	AndrewThornton	**4/1**[2]	101
1140	**8**	*17*	**Rift Valley (IRE)**[13] 3880 11-10-5 **116** (P J Hobbs) *j.rt thrght: led tl 3 out: sn wknd: eased fr next*	DarrenO'Dwyer(10)	**20/1**	92+

5m 17.0s (3.60) **Going Correction** +0.225s/f (Yiel) **8** Ran SP% **113.2**
Speed ratings: **98,96,94,94,93 92,91,84** CSF £31.10 CT £88.03 TOTE £4.60: £1.10, £2.80, £1.60; EX 36.40.
Owner H R Hunt **Bred** M L Bloodstock Limited **Trained** Woodingdean, E Sussex

FOCUS

Not a strong race for the money and the well-treated New Entic destroyed the modest opposition. The runner-up was back to his Newcastle mark, and there's a case for rating the form even higher.

NOTEBOOK

New Entic(FR) ◆, down to a decent mark and in need of this step up in distance, raced sweetly in the first-time cheekpieces and came clear in stylish fashion under a confident Jamie Moore, winning heavily eased, value for 15 lengths. A useful juvenile last season, the rise in distance is *going to be the making of him and there will be plenty of worse long-shots for the Coral Cup. (op 6-1)*
Youlbesolucky(IRE) was unfortunate to bump into the tranformed winner, keeping on well and *doing his best in second. His potential is limited, but he can find another race at the right level. (op 5-1 tchd 9-2)*
Kilgowan(IRE), up 6lb for winning at Leicester earlier in the month, travelled into contention, but was left for dead by New Entic and was unable to stay on as strongly as the runner-up. This was not a bad effort, but he will need to improve to defy this mark. *(op 9-4 tchd 3-1 in places)*
Westmeath Flyer is back down to a winning mark, but the 11-year-old was totally outclassed by the winner and will find easier opportunities. *(op 14-1 tchd 16-1)*
Chicago Bulls(IRE) was not discredited on this return from a lay-off, plugging on over a trip significantly short of his best, and could be of interest next time. *(op 9-1 tchd 12-1)*
Marrel was unable to build on his recent Taunton success, the 8lb higher mark finding him out, and he is best kept to the lesser tracks. *(op 8-1)*
Idiome(FR) has gone without a win over hurdles for four years and he did little here to suggest he is about to end that run. *(op 9-2)*

4120 RPSPORT - READ, WATCH, WIN H'CAP CHASE (17 fncs) 2m 4f 110y

4:30 (4:30) (Class 3) (0-125,117) 5-Y-O+ **£6,506** (£1,910; £955; £477)

Form					SP	RPR
-F11	**1**		**Roznic (FR)**[30] 3580 8-11-6 **111** (P Winkworth) *hld up in tch: trckd ldrs 6th: hit 13th: led 3 out: kpt on wl fr last: readily*	PhilipHide	**5/2**[1]	122+
110/	**2**	*5*	**Indian Gunner**[1058] 4472 13-11-3 **108** (Dr J R J Naylor) *trckd ldrs: nt fluent 11th: rdn after 3 out: wnt 2nd appr last: kpt on but a hld by wnr*	AndrewThornton	**12/1**	107
1/6P	**3**	*1 3/4*	**Biliverdin (IRE)**[35] 3507 12-11-12 **117** (J A Geake) *led: blnd 6th: hdd 10th: w ldr: mstke 4 out: rdn after 3 out: 3rd and hld whn hit last*	MarcusFoley	**10/1**	117+
20P4	**4**	*17*	**Acertack (IRE)**[22] 3718 9-10-5 **96** (R Rowe) *trckd ldrs: led 10th: nt fluent 11th (water): hdd 3 out: wknd after next: lft 4th at the last*	PJBrennan	**11/1**	83+
121P	**5**	*20*	**Walcot Lad (IRE)**[29] 3596 10-10-5 **99** (A Ennis) *chsd ldr tl 9th: in tch: wknd appr 3 out*	(p) ColinBolger(3)	**10/1**	59
P-51	**S**		**Cyborsun (FR)**[46] 3338 9-10-0 **96** (M F Harris) *hld up but in tch tl stmbld and fell on bnd appr 7th: broke leg: dead*	CharliePoste(5)	**11/4**[2]	—
3334	**U**		**Myson (IRE)**[67] 2931 7-10-9 **100** (D B Feek) *lw: hld up but in tch: mstke 6th: rdn after 4 out: 4th and hld whn blnd and uns rdr last*	JamesDavies	**7/2**[3]	90

5m 26.8s (6.00) **Going Correction** +0.225s/f (Yiel) **7** Ran SP% **111.7**
Speed ratings: **88,86,85,78,71** —,— CSF £28.03 TOTE £2.90: £1.70, £5.20; EX 42.40 Place 6 £18.31, Place 5 £11.88.
Owner Etoile Racing **Bred** Francis Faure **Trained** Ramsnest Common, Surrey

FOCUS

This turned out to be a pretty uncompetitive handicap chase and the in-form Roznic cleared away to win cosily, value for around 12 lengths. The time was moderate for a race of its class, and neither the second nor the third have been rated anywhere near their old form.

NOTEBOOK
Roznic(FR), in search of a hat-trick, having won at both Folkestone and Warwick, had an extra half a mile to contend with here, but he saw it out well and simply had too much in hand for old-timers Indian Chance and Biliverdin. He has really got his act together of late and deserves to take his chance at a higher level now. *(op 3-1)*
Indian Gunner appeared fit for this first outing since April 2003 and stayed on well to claim second, having chased the early leaders. The veteran, who has had a tendon problem, was not given an overly hard race by Thornton and it is hoped he can go the right way from this. *(tchd 11-1)*
Biliverdin(IRE) is still relatively unexposed for a horse of his age and he has dropped to a decent mark, having previously shown little since returning from yet another injury. He made too many mistakes to win the race, but it was a decent effort nonetheless. If his jumping can be brushed up, there may yet be another race or two in him on better ground. *(op 12-1)*
Acertack(IRE) helped to force the early pace, but he was readily brushed aside after the Pond Fence and ended up well beaten. *(op 9-1)*
Walcot Lad(IRE) was the only other to finish, but he was well held and would have found this a bit too hot. *(tchd 8-1)*
Cyborsun(FR) tragically came down taking the bend before the seventh fence and broke a leg. *(op 9-2)*
Myson(IRE), a tough and consistent sort, had run his race and was held when unseating Davies at the last. *(op 9-2)*
T/Plt: £22.90 to a £1 stake. Pool: £97,199.15. 3,093.25 winning tickets. T/Qpdt: £15.40 to a £1 stake. Pool: £4,437.80. 212.30 winning tickets. TM

4121 - (Foreign Racing) - See Raceform Interactive

[3932]FAIRYHOUSE (R-H)
Saturday, February 25

OFFICIAL GOING: Soft to heavy

4122a OSMOSIS IRELAND LIMITED WINNING FAIR JUVENILE HURDLE (GRADE 3) (9 hdls) 2m
2:50 (2:50) 4-Y-0 **£16,836** (£4,939; £2,353; £801)

Form	Pos	Dist	Horse	RPR
	1		**First Row (IRE)**[13] [3890] 4-10-8 RLoughran(3) (D T Hughes, Ire) *cl up in 2nd: led after 3 out: sn rdn and strly pressed: slt mstke whn lft clr 2 out: styd on wl u.p* **2/1**[2]	124
	2	*15*	**Bobs Pride (IRE)**[27] [3638] 4-10-11 BJGeraghty (D K Weld, Ire) *trckd ldrs in 5th: 4th 4 out: 3rd and effrt after 3 out: no imp whn lft 2nd 2 out: sn no ex* **13/8**[1]	109
	3	*7*	**Count Kearney (IRE)**[17] [3807] 4-10-8 TGMRyan(3) (S J Mahon, Ire) *led: hdd after 3 out: sn no ex: lft mod 3rd fr next* **12/1**	102
	4	*5*	**Vox Populi (USA)**[13] [3890] 4-10-11 107 PCarberry (S J Mahon, Ire) *mid-div: 6th 1/2-way: mod 5th after 3 out: lft 4th and no ex fr next* **12/1**	97
	5	*7*	**Zaccheus (IRE)**[197] 4-10-11 GCotter (Mrs Seamus Hayes, Ire) *in rr early: prog into 7th 4 out: no imp fr next* **50/1**	90
	6	*7*	**Packie Tam (IRE)**[17] [3807] 4-10-8 90 (t) SMMcGovern(3) (Patrick O Brady, Ire) *chsd ldrs: 4th 1/2-way: wknd 3 out* **25/1**	83
	7	*7*	**Astalanda (FR)**[17] [3807] 4-9-13 97 SGCarey(7) (Garvan Donnelly, Ire) *mid-div early: lost pl 1/2-way: no ex fr 4 out* **10/1**[3]	71
	8	*hd*	**Jubilant Note (IRE)**[60] [3049] 4-10-11 (t) KWhelan (Michael David Murphy, Ire) *hld up: 9th and effrt after 4 out: sn no ex* **14/1**	76
	9	*dist*	**Arafan (IRE)**[14] [3869] 4-10-11 AndrewJMcNamara (Michael Hourigan, Ire) *a bhd: t.o* **16/1**	—
	F		**Cogans Lake (IRE)**[13] [3890] 4-11-1 JMAllen (Kieran Purcell, Ire) *trckd ldrs in 3rd: impr into cl 2nd after 3 out: chalng travelling best whn fell 2 out* **10/1**[3]	124+

4m 5.90s **Going Correction** +0.45s/f (Soft) **11** Ran SP% **123.4**
Speed ratings: **110,102,99,96,93 89,86,85,—,—** CSF £6.27 TOTE £2.20: £1.70, £1.70, £4.40; DF 5.00.
Owner Busted Sofa Syndicate **Bred** Killeen Castle Stud **Trained** Osborne Lodge, Co. Kildare

NOTEBOOK
First Row(IRE) might just have been a bit fortunate to benefit from the fall of Cogans Lake at the second last. Left clear, he won unchallenged. Prior to this he might have been interesting in the juvenile handicap at Cheltenham, but connections feel he's earned a tilt at the Triumph. *(op 2/1 tchd 7/4)*
Bobs Pride(IRE) wasn't going anywhere when left second after two out. He will be more effective on better ground in the future. *(op 6/4 tchd 2/1)*
Count Kearney(IRE) made the running as usual, but again his effort petered out quickly.
Vox Populi(USA) seems to be going the wrong way on the evidence of this performance.
Cogans Lake(IRE) appeared to be going just the best when falling two from home. His confidence will need restoring after this.

4123a OSMOSIS IRELAND LIMITED BOBBYJO CHASE (GRADE 2) (20 fncs) 3m 1f
3:20 (3:20) 5-Y-0+ **£22,448** (£6,586; £3,137; £1,068)

Form	Pos	Dist	Horse	RPR
	1		**Forget The Past**[7] [3999] 8-11-10 155 BJGeraghty (M J P O'Brien, Ire) *in tch: 4th after 1/2-way: impr into 2nd 6 out: led next: clr after 4 out: easily* **4/9**[1]	165+
	2	*8*	**Garvivonnian (IRE)**[55] [3199] 11-11-6 137 MJFerris (Edward P Mitchell, Ire) *prom: led briefly 8 out: 3rd and drvn along 5 out: mod 2nd after 3 out: kpt on same pce* **9/1**[3]	141
	3	*13*	**Marcus Du Berlais (FR)**[30] [3587] 9-11-3 134 (p) DJCasey (A L T Moore, Ire) *hld up: slt mstke 3rd: mod 7th 4 out: kpt on u.p to go remote 3rd fr last* **16/1**	125
	4	*6*	**Rince Ri (IRE)**[27] [3643] 13-11-10 (b) AndrewJMcNamara (T M Walsh, Ire) *led and disp: hdd 11th: 4th 6 out: rdn and no imp fr next* **20/1**	126
	5	*6*	**Cane Brake (IRE)**[30] [3587] 7-11-8 129 (b[1]) KWhelan (David Wachman, Ire) *cl up and disp: led 7 out: hdd and rdn 5 out: outpcd after next: slt mstke 3 out: sn wknd* **25/1**	118
	6	*14*	**Kymandjen (IRE)**[30] [3587] 9-11-6 134 RMMoran (Paul Nolan, Ire) *hld up: prog into 6th after 1/2-way: rdn 6 out: 4th briefly 5 out: wknd and eased 3 out* **7/1**[2]	102
	7	*3 1/2*	**Alcapone (IRE)**[37] [3472] 12-11-10 130 MDarcy (M F Morris, Ire) *trckd ldrs in 5th: pushed along 7 out: wknd fr 5 out* **33/1**	103
	P		**Rand (NZ)**[577] [1063] 12-11-3 PCarberry (Noel Meade, Ire) *a towards rr: trailing whn p.u bef 4 out* **25/1**	—
	P		**Prince Of Tara (IRE)**[13] [3895] 9-11-3 128 CO'Dwyer (S J Mahon, Ire) *in tch: 5th 1/2-way: wknd 8 out: p.u bef 4 out* **12/1**	—

7m 4.00s **Going Correction** +0.70s/f (Soft) **9** Ran SP% **120.7**
Speed ratings: **112,109,105,103,101 96,95,—,—** CSF £5.56 TOTE £1.50: £1.10, £2.00, £2.80; DF 6.60.
Owner S Mulryan **Bred** M H Dare **Trained** Naas, Co Kildare

NOTEBOOK
Forget The Past had an easy task on figures and followed up his Gowran win with a facile success. It was by no means a stamina test and he won without being extended. The idea is that he'll take his chance in the Gold Cup, and while plenty more than this will be needed, his jumping is pretty sound and he is a better horse on a less taxing surface. *(op 1/2)*
Garvivonnian(IRE) ran as sound a trial for the Aintree National as you could possibly wish for and still represents some value for that contest. *(op 8/1)*
Marcus Du Berlais(FR) just gave a glimpse of a return to form, staying on from way back. *(op 14/1)*
Rince Ri(IRE) might have a race in him yet judged on this showing.

[4005]FONTWELL (L-H)
Sunday, February 26

OFFICIAL GOING: Heavy
The ground was better than at the last meeting but still extremely testing, with grass on the thin side.
Wind: Slight, across

4128 BAY STUDIO SIGNS LITTLEHAMPTON 01903 717227 MAIDEN HURDLE (9 hdls) 2m 2f 110y
2:10 (2:10) (Class 5) 4-Y-0+ **£2,927** (£859; £429; £214)

Form	Pos	Dist	Horse	RPR
02	1		**Grasp**[40] [3429] 4-10-9 (bt) JamieMoore (G L Moore) *racd wd: led 2nd: c clr 2 out: blnd last: sn rcvrd: pushed out: readily* **1/1**[1]	111+
0/3-	2	*5*	**Beare Necessities (IRE)**[659] [232] 7-11-5 LeightonAspell (M J Hogan) *bhd: hdwy fr 4 out: mstke next:styd on wl fr 2 out to take 2nd run-in but nvr any ch w wnr* **20/1**	109+
2220	3	*3/4*	**Kanpai (IRE)**[61] [3021] 4-10-9 107 TomDoyle (J G M O'Shea) *chsd ldrs: wnt 2nd 3 out but nvr any ch w wnr: one pce u.p and lost 2nd run-in* **5/1**[3]	97
4/06	4	*3*	**Return Ticket**[47] [3328] 7-11-5 RichardJohnson (R T Phillips) *bhd: hdwy 5th: chsng ldrs but nvr in contention whn stmbld 2 out: wknd bef last* **10/1**	106+
060	5	*dist*	**Love Beauty (USA)**[27] [3645] 4-10-4 CharliePoste(5) (M F Harris) *chsd ldrs tl wknd 4 out: no ch whn blnd last: t.o* **66/1**	—
5	6	*12*	**Bayazid (IRE)**[23] [3714] 4-10-9 (b[1]) MarcusFoley (N J Henderson) *wnt bdly lft 1st: mstke next: chsd ldr tl wknd 4 out: no ch whn mstke 2 out: t.o* **7/2**[2]	—
1P45	7	*3/4*	**Schumann**[18] [3806] 5-11-5 AndrewTinkler (M Pitman) *a bhd: t.o* **25/1**	—
400-	8	*5*	**See Me**[353] [4283] 7-11-2 GinoCarenza(3) (Andrew Turnell) *chsd ldrs to 4th: wknd next: t.o* **66/1**	—
RPP0	9	*3 1/2*	**Mr Rhubarb (IRE)**[24] [3687] 8-10-12 74 TomMessenger(7) (C J Drewe) *in ouch tl wknd and mstke 5th: t.o* **100/1**	—
60-P	10	*21*	**Mortar**[26] [3664] 7-11-5 JimCrowley (R Rowe) *led to 2nd: wknd 5th: t.o* **100/1**	—
0-0	11	*4*	**Cartier Opera**[57] [3133] 6-11-5 AlanO'Keeffe (Miss Venetia Williams) *in tch: hdwy 5th: wknd 4 out* **50/1**	—
PP	12	*13*	**Time To Succeed**[170] [1440] 4-10-9 ChristianWilliams (Mrs A M Thorpe) *a wl bhd: t.o* **100/1**	—
0-30	13	*dist*	**Jeepers Creepers**[132] [1777] 6-11-0 DerekLaverty(5) (Mrs A M Thorpe) *hit 3rd: prom to 5th: t.o* **100/1**	—

4m 47.1s (11.10) **Going Correction** +0.725s/f (Soft)
WFA 4 from 5yo+ 9lb **13** Ran SP% **115.5**
Speed ratings: **105,102,102,101,— —,—,—,—,— —,—,—** CSF £24.56 TOTE £1.90: £1.20, £2.70, £1.60; EX 28.00.
Owner R A Green **Bred** A D G Oldrey **Trained** Woodingdean, E Sussex

FOCUS
A weak juvenile event, run at a fair pace in the testing ground, and the winner was value for 12l. The form is believable.

NOTEBOOK
Grasp, runner-up in a fair juvenile event at Folkestone last time, had the race in the bag prior to a final-flight error and duly got off the mark over timber at the third time of asking. He is well suited by a testing surface, the recent application of blinkers has clearly had a positive effect, and it is unlikely that we have seen the best of him yet. The Fred Winter at Cheltenham is reportedly a possible future target, but he is unlikely to get his ground in that event. *(op 5-4)*
Beare Necessities(IRE), having his first outing for 659 days and making his debut for new connections, stayed on well after jumping two out and turned in an encouraging return to action. He is entitled to improve a fair deal for this experience, acted well on the testing surface, and now qualifies for handicaps. *(op 33-1)*
Kanpai(IRE), firmly put in his place in Grade One company at Chepstow last time, tired markedly up the rising finish and will be suited by the return to a sharper test in the future. With an official mark of 107 he puts this form into perspective. *(tchd 11-2)*
Return Ticket failed to seriously get involved and did not improve on the form of his hurdling debut behind the promising Straw Bear at Leicester. He ought to be of more interest when qualified for a handicap mark after his next outing. *(tchd 11-1)*
Bayazid(IRE), an expensive failure on his hurdling debut at this venue 29 days previously, failed improve for the application of first-time blinkers and did not convince over his hurdles. He may prove better back on faster ground in the future, and when switching to handicaps in due course, but he appears one to have reservations about all the same. *(op 5-2)*

4129 BETBROKERS "BETTING JUST GOT BETTER" MARES' ONLY NOVICES' HURDLE (10 hdls) 2m 4f
2:40 (2:42) (Class 4) 4-Y-0+ **£5,204** (£1,528; £764; £381)

Form	Pos	Dist	Horse	RPR
0/1-	1		**Philomena**[655] [308] 7-11-3 PJBrennan (V R A Dartnall) *led to 2nd: chsd ldrs: chal 3 out: led appr 2 out: rdn and mstke last: hld on all out* **12/1**	100+
	2	*1 1/4*	**Cemgraft**[6] 5-11-3 (t) MarkBradburne (A J Lidderdale) *bhd: hdwy 4 out: chsd wnr 2 out: drvn to chal last: dged lft u.p run-in: no ex nr fin* **25/1**	97
4261	3	*8*	**Sweet Oona (FR)**[22] [3730] 7-11-9 104 SamThomas (Miss Venetia Williams) *chsd ldrs: rdn and ev ch appr 2 out: wknd sn after* **3/1**[2]	97+

5 **4** *8* **Fuss**[88] 2573 5-11-3 .... RichardJohnson 83+
(P J Hobbs) *led 2nd: hit 5th: hdd after 3 out: wknd next: no ch whn blnd last* **7/1**[3]

5234 **5** *4* **Makeabreak (IRE)**[13] 3902 7-11-3 100.......... NoelFehily 77
(C J Mann) *in tch to 4 out: wknd after next* **11/4**[1]

3/0- **P** **Poggenip**[658] 253 7-10-10 .... CharlieStudd(7) —
(B G Powell) *in tch to 5th: t.o whn p.u bef last* **28/1**

UP0 **P** **Nellie The Nod**[7] 4015 7-10-10 .... MrJAJenkins(7) —
(M J Gingell) *a bhd: t.o whn p.u after 2 out* **100/1**

0-00 **P** **Balloch**[13] 3902 5-11-3 .... JimmyMcCarthy —
(Mary Meek) *racd on ins: in tch to 5th: t.o whn p.u run-in* **100/1**

0550 **P** **Falcon Beneficial (IRE)**[13] 3902 4-10-7 .... JamieMoore —
(G L Moore) *racd on ins: bhd fr 4th: t.o whn p.u bef 4 out* **14/1**

4123 **F** **Methodical**[13] 3902 4-10-2 97.......... JohnnyLevins(5) 63
(B G Powell) *racd on ins: hdwy to chse ldrs 6th: squeezed through for slt ld on rails after 3 out:sn hdd:6th and no ch whn fell last* **11/4**[1]

5m 19.5s (15.70) **Going Correction** +0.725s/f (Soft)
WFA 4 from 5yo+ 10lb **10** Ran SP% **114.5**
Speed ratings: **97,96,93,90,88** —,—,—,—,— CSF £233.70 TOTE £15.10: £3.20, £4.40, £1.20; EX 206.30.
Owner Dorset Racing **Bred** And Mrs Peter Forbes **Trained** Brayford, Devon

FOCUS
A modest mares' only novice event, run at a sound pace, and the first two came clear. Probably not good form.

NOTEBOOK
Philomena, last seen winning a bumper at the second time of asking 655 days previously, got her hurdling career off to a perfect start with a battling display on this belated return to action. Given a positive ride, she saw out this longer trip with aplomb, and could be rated value for a touch further as she looked to be idling up the run-in. One will have to be wary of the bounce factor on her next outing, but she ought to have more to offer in this division. *(op 9-1)*
Cemgraft, rated 45 on the Flat and runner-up over 12 furlongs at Lingfield in first-time cheekpieces four days previously, made a pleasing debut and was the only one to go with the winner from two out. She clearly has a future in this sphere and saw out the trip well.
Sweet Oona(FR), finally off the mark at Uttoxeter, had every chance under her penalty yet ultimately failed to see out the longer trip on this testing surface. *(op 11-4 tchd 7-2)*
Fuss, fifth on her debut at Plumpton 88 days previously, could offer no more when headed three from home and most probably found this ground too taxing. *(op 8-1)*
Makeabreak(IRE) ran well below her previous best and was beaten before the turn for home. This was disappointing, but she may show her true colours back on a better surface in the future. *(op 5-2 tchd 3-1)*
Methodical, well backed, was beating a retreat prior to falling at the final flight and may need time to recover from this experience. *(op 10-3)*

4130 EAU DE COLOGNE NOVICES' H'CAP CHASE (19 fncs) 3m 2f 110y
3:10 (3:11) (Class 3) (0-125,121) 5-Y-0+ **£9,626** (£3,006; £1,619)

Form RPR

1FF2 **1** **Lord Olympia (IRE)**[8] 3973 7-11-12 **121**.......... SamThomas 130+
(Miss Venetia Williams) *chsd ldr: mstke 5th and rdr lost iron:wnt 2nd 15th: led 4 out: gng wl whn mstke 2 out: easily* **8/15**[1]

/454 **2** *14* **Fisherman Jack**[55] 3221 11-10-0 **95** oh26..........(p) JodieMogford 79
(G J Smith) *led to 3rd: chal fr 6th tl led 10th: hit 15th: hdd and hit 4 out: sn no ch wnr: veered rt after last: hld on for 2nd run-in* **14/1**

2014 **3** *3/4* **Party Games (IRE)**[36] 3509 9-11-5 **114**..........(p) PhilipHide 97
(G L Moore) *chsd ldrs: jumed slowly 9th: chal 15th: wknd 3 out:* **3/1**[2]

P31P **P** **Heartache**[11] 3923 9-10-0 **95** oh17..........(b) WayneHutchinson —
(R Mathew) *led 3rd to 10th: rdn 14th: sn wknd: t.o whn p.u bef 3 out* **9/1**[3]

7m 23.0s (21.90) **Going Correction** +1.05s/f (Soft) **4** Ran SP% **106.9**
Speed ratings: **109,104,104**,— CSF £6.72 TOTE £1.60; EX 9.50.
Owner Mrs Sally-Anne Ryan **Bred** G Merrigan **Trained** Kings Caple, H'fords

FOCUS
A very weak event, which saw the field trail home behind the odds-on favourite, who is value for 25l. The race has been rated through the second.

NOTEBOOK
Lord Olympia(IRE) relished the step back up in trip and ran out a facile winner, being value for further than his already wide winning margin. He was entitled to win this as he did, and at times was again less than fluent, but nevertheless it proved he is happy over this sort of trip and does enjoy a deep surface. Of his three entries at the Cheltenham Festival, the Kim Muir would appeal as the most viable target, and he has won on good ground in the past. *(op 1-2)*
Fisherman Jack, nearly two stone out of the handicap, ran as well as could have been expected and looked to give his all in defeat. He can find much easier opportunities and the return to slightly better ground in the future ought to prove to his liking. *(tchd 16-1)*
Party Games(IRE) found this too gruelling a test and finished tired. He is capable of better, but may be a little flattered by his current official mark. *(op 7-2 tchd 4-1)*
Heartache, 17lb out of the handicap, has now been pulled up on his last two outings. *(op 6-1)*

4131 WEATHERBYS BANK H'CAP HURDLE (9 hdls) 2m 2f 110y
3:40 (3:41) (Class 3) (0-120,117) 4-Y-0+
£8,141 (£2,405; £1,202; £601; £300; £150)

Form RPR

2112 **1** **Amanpuri (GER)**[13] 3901 8-10-11 **102**.......... ChristianWilliams 105+
(Mrs A M Thorpe) *led 2nd: hrd drvn after 2 out: hld on gamely run-in* **9/4**[1]

F332 **2** *1* **Lewis Island (IRE)**[10] 3945 7-11-5 **110**.......... JamieMoore 113+
(G L Moore) *reluctant to s and lost 12l: sn rcvrd: stdy hdwy to trck ldrs 3 out: chal and mstke 2 out: chsd wnr run-in: no ex* **10/1**

1115 **3** *6* **The Hairy Lemon**[24] 3696 6-11-1 **113**.......... MrGTumelty(7) 109+
(A King) *in tch: hdwy 4 out: trckd ldrs next: chal 2 out: sn one pce u.p* **10/3**[2]

01F4 **4** *6* **Titian Flame (IRE)**[18] 3802 6-10-2 **100**..........(p) MrTJO'Brien(7) 89
(D Burchell) *led to 2nd: chsd ldrs tl rdn and wknd 4 out* **9/2**[3]

/5-0 **5** *2 1/2* **Newtown**[26] 3658 7-9-13 **95**.......... CharliePoste(5) 82
(M F Harris) *chsd ldrs: rdn 4 out: wknd after next* **12/1**

FP5P **6** *3/4* **Jonanaud**[7] 4016 7-11-5 **117**..........(b) MrJAJenkins(7) 103
(H J Manners) *chsd ldrs: rdn 5th: sn wknd* **25/1**

41-0 **7** *dist* **Dark Society**[16] 3848 8-10-7 **98**.......... WayneHutchinson —
(A W Carroll) *bhd fr 1/2-way: t.o* **11/2**

4m 50.8s (14.80) **Going Correction** +0.725s/f (Soft) **7** Ran SP% **108.0**
Speed ratings: **97,96,94,91,90 90**,— CSF £21.08 CT £62.76 TOTE £2.90: £1.80, £3.20; EX 17.80.
Owner Mrs A M Thorpe **Bred** H Von Finck **Trained** Bronwydd Arms, Carmarthens

FOCUS
A modest handicap, run at an average pace, and the form looks sound enough.

NOTEBOOK
Amanpuri(GER), thwarted in his bid for the hat-trick when runner-up from this mark at Plumpton last time, was well backed to resume winning ways and duly rewarded his supporters with a battling display. He has now been successful three times from as many starts at this track - indeed they are his only career wins in this sphere to date - and he is clearly versatile as regards underfoot conditions. *(op 5-2)*
Lewis Island(IRE), beaten in a seller last time, has to rate as unfortunate after losing so much ground at the start and then making a crucial error two from home. He is well up to winning off this sort of mark, but has not been in the winner's enclosure since 2004, and always seems to find a way of getting beaten these days. *(op 9-1)*
The Hairy Lemon, easy to back, was put in his place nearing the final flight and appears held by the Handicapper now. *(op 5-2)*
Titian Flame(IRE) failed to improve for the return to this much softer ground and ran close to her recent level. *(op 6-1)*
Dark Society was a notable drifter in the betting ring and never figured. He may need a few more runs to bring him to his peak and is capable of plenty better on his day. *(op 9-2)*

4132 BETBROKERS "OPEN AN ACCOUNT ON 0844 855 2111" NOVICES' H'CAP CHASE (13 fncs) 2m 2f
4:10 (4:11) (Class 5) (0-95,90) 5-Y-0+ **£3,665** (£1,137; £612)

Form RPR

4344 **1** **Foxmeade Dancer**[31] 3577 8-10-4 **68** oh1 ow4.......... AndrewThornton 77+
(P C Ritchens) *trckd ldrs: wnt 2nd 9th: chal 3 out tl led after next: pushed out run-in* **9/4**[1]

0045 **2** *6* **Denarius Secundus**[7] 4010 9-10-4 **68**..........(b) DaveCrosse 70+
(N R Mitchell) *chsd ldr 2nd: hit 3rd: led and hit 9th: rdn 3 out: hdd after next: sn one pce* **15/2**

4004 **3** *11* **Instant Appeal**[12] 3909 9-11-8 **86**.......... PhilipHide 82+
(P Winkworth) *rr but in tch: hday to press ldrs whn blnd 8th: nt rcvr but effrt after 4 out: but nvr any ch* **11/4**[2]

6P64 **R** **Kinkeel (IRE)**[34] 3543 7-10-13 **77**..........(bt[1]) WayneHutchinson —
(A W Carroll) *led to 9th: sn rdn: wknd 4 out: t.o whn ref last* **12/1**

6320 **P** **Flying Patriarch**[44] 3368 5-11-6 **90**..........(bt) JamieMoore —
(G L Moore) *prom early: dropped rr 4th: reluctant fr next: t.o whn p.u after 7th* **3/1**[3]

P0OP **U** **Star Galaxy (IRE)**[8] 3997 6-10-8 **72**.......... GerrySupple 66
(Andrew Turnell) *in tch: chsd ldrs and hit 8th: rdn 4 out: disputing 3l 3rd and no ch w ldrs whn blnd and uns rdr 2 out* **16/1**

4m 59.9s (24.80) **Going Correction** +1.05s/f (Soft)
WFA 5 from 6yo+ 6lb **6** Ran SP% **107.8**
Speed ratings: **86,83,78**,—,—,— CSF £16.78 CT £39.92 TOTE £3.10: £1.60, £3.40; EX 15.20.
Owner Ian Fraser & Hughie Taylor **Bred** Mrs A E Morton **Trained** Shipton Bellinger, Hants

FOCUS
A very poor handicap, run at an ordinary gallop, and only three completed. The winner is value for further and the race has been rated through the second.

NOTEBOOK
Foxmeade Dancer, racing from a pound out of the handicap and whose jockey put up 4lb overweight, ran out a comfortable winner on this return to chasing and should be rated value for around double his winning margin. He jumped particularly well and would be of obvious interest if found a suitable opportunity under a penalty. *(op 2-1)*
Denarius Secundus, making his chase debut, did not jump with any real fluency, but stuck to his task well enough when headed by the winner and finished a clear second-best. He is capable of going one better in this sphere providing he improves his jumping. *(op 7-1 tchd 8-1)*
Instant Appeal lost any chance with a terrible blunder at the eighth fence and stayed on well enough in the circumstances. He is capable of a deal better. *(op 7-2)*
Flying Patriarch, equipped with a first-time tongue tie, turned in a mulish effort and is one to avoid. *(tchd 11-4)*

4133 DENIS CASEY 70TH BIRTHDAY CELEBRATION H'CAP HURDLE (11 hdls) 2m 6f 110y
4:40 (4:40) (Class 5) (0-85,86) 4-Y-0+ **£2,927** (£859; £429; £214)

Form RPR

P000 **1** **Silverio (GER)**[76] 2799 5-11-5 **78**.......... JamieMoore 85
(G L Moore) *hld up in rr: hdwy 6th: chsd ldr 2 out: drvn to chal last: rdn out* **5/1**[2]

1U00 **2** *4* **Zeloso**[26] 3661 8-11-7 **85**..........(v) CharliePoste(5) 88
(M F Harris) *hld up in rr: hdwy 7th: trckd ldrs 4 out: led bnd appr 2 out: sn rdn: jnd last: one pce u.p run-in* **10/1**

0P-0 **3** *18* **Scarface**[277] 506 9-11-2 **75**.......... PJBrennan 60
(J L Spearing) *chsd ldr: chal 7th: led 4 out: hdd bnd appr 2 out: sn wknd* **10/1**

5526 **4** *26* **Hidden Storm (IRE)**[5] 4043 7-10-7 **73**..........(b) MrMatthewSmith(7) 32
(Mrs S J Humphrey) *in tch: hdwy 7th: wknd 3 out* **13/2**[3]

05PP **5** *18* **Impero**[51] 3279 8-10-2 **66**..........(b) EamonDehdashti(5) 7
(G F Bridgwater) *led tl hdd 4 out: sn wknd* **40/1**

0502 **6** *5* **Gunship (IRE)**[55] 3211 5-11-5 **78**.......... RichardJohnson 14
(P J Hobbs) *chsd ldrs: rdn 7th: wknd 4 out: no ch whn mstke next* **9/4**[1]

66 **7** *1 1/4* **Tinvane Rose (IRE)**[10] 3951 7-10-10 **76**.......... ChrisDavies(7) 11
(J G M O'Shea) *rdn 7th: a in rr* **15/2**

04/P **P** **Probus Lady**[37] 3483 9-10-5 **64**.......... JimmyMcCarthy —
(C J Down) *a bhd: t.o whn p.u bef 4 out* **40/1**

0564 **P** **Little Word**[67] 2937 7-10-5 **69**.......... LeeStephens(5) —
(P D Williams) *chsd ldrs to 6th: t.o whn p.u bef 2 out* **16/1**

6/P0 **P** **Springer The Lad**[13] 3899 9-11-2 **80**..........(v[1]) RobertLucey-Butler(5) —
(Miss M P Bryant) *a bhd: t.o whn p.u bef 6th* **50/1**

P303 **P** **Carroll's O'Tully (IRE)**[27] 3656 6-10-9 **75**..........(t) JustinMorgan(7) —
(L A Dace) *chsd ldrs: rdn and wknd 7th: t.o whn p.u bef 2 out* **8/1**

0PP/ **P** **Grove Lodge**[1069] 3822 9-9-11 **63**.......... CharlieStudd(7) —
(L A Dace) *keen early: in tch: hit 4th and 5th: sn wknd: t.o whn p.u bef 7th* **66/1**

5m 58.7s (13.90) **Going Correction** +0.725s/f (Soft) **12** Ran SP% **116.0**
Speed ratings: **104,102,96,87,81 79,78**,—,— —,— CSF £51.57 CT £482.77 TOTE £5.70: £1.80, £3.30, £4.60; EX 60.60 Trifecta £410.50 Place 6 £91.96, Place 5 £64.95.
Owner G L Moore **Bred** Gestut Hof Ittlingen **Trained** Woodingdean, E Sussex

FOCUS
A seller in disguise. The field finished strung out and the form should be treated with caution.

NOTEBOOK
Silverio(GER), popular in the betting ring, ground out his first success to date under a strong ride from Moore on this handicap debut. He saw out this trip well in the heavy ground and, considering he is entitled to improve again for the outing, could have more to offer from a higher future mark. *(op 8-1 tchd 9-2)*
Zeloso only gave way to the winner up the run-in and showed his true colours in defeat. He has never won in this sphere outside of selling company, however, and he helps to put this form into perspective. *(op 13-2)*
Scarface showed up well under a prominent ride on this return from a nine-month layoff and should come on a fair bit fitness-wise for the outing. *(op 8-1)*
Hidden Storm(IRE), unplaced over further at Sedgefield six days previously, ran to a similar level on this drop back in trip and finished tired. *(op 7-1)*
Gunship(IRE) was being ridden from the halfway stage and ran below expectations. While he may have been unsuited by the deep surface, this was disappointing, and it would be little surprise to see some headgear applied in the future. *(tchd 5-2)*
T/Jkpt: Not won. T/Plt: £305.30 to a £1 stake. Pool: £77,180.65. 184.50 winning tickets. T/Qpdt: £66.50 to a £1 stake. Pool: £5,281.80. 58.70 winning tickets. ST

The Form Book, Raceform Ltd, Compton, RG20 6NL

4134 - 4135a (Foreign Racing) - See Raceform Interactive

[3869]NAAS (L-H)

Sunday, February 26

OFFICIAL GOING: Soft to heavy (heavy in places)

4136a ANGLO IRISH BANK NAS NA RIOGH NOVICE CHASE (GRADE 2) 2m 4f
3:20 (3:20) 5-Y-0+ **£22,448** (£6,586; £3,137; £1,068)

RPR

1 **Lordofourown (IRE)**[14] 3893 8-11-5 .... AndrewJMcNamara 125+
(S Donohoe, Ire) *hld up in 4th: lft 2nd 6 out: 3rd next: led bef 2 out: clr fr last: comf* **12/1**[3]

2 9 **Chetwind Music (IRE)**[29] 3628 8-11-5 .... RLoughran 113
(William Coleman O'Brien, Ire) *led: j.w: hdd appr 7th: lft in ld 6 out: hdd bef 2 out: kpt on u.p wout troubling wnr* **20/1**

3 25 **Kill Devil Hill (IRE)**[14] 3893 6-11-12 .... CO'Dwyer 95
(Paul Nolan, Ire) *settled 3rd: sltly hmpd 6 out: 2nd next: slow 4 out: rdn and no imp after 3 out: no ex bef last* **7/4**[2]

4 dist **Sound Witness (IRE)**[266] 662 8-11-5 112 .... BMCash —
(Robert Tyner, Ire) *hld up in rr: mod 4th whn fell 3 out* **33/1**

U **Father Matt (IRE)**[14] 3893 8-11-5 .... PCarberry —
(Noel Meade, Ire) *slow 1st: settled 2nd: led appr 7th: blnd and uns rdr 6 out* **8/11**[1]

5m 36.0s **7** Ran SP% **109.7**
CSF £112.36 TOTE £11.10: £2.80, £3.60; DF 135.50.
Owner G M Bourke **Bred** Aubrey Bourke **Trained** Cootehill Road, Co. Cavan

NOTEBOOK
Lordofourown(IRE), runner-up to Arkle-bound Missed That at Navan in December, was supported at long odds here and put a below-par run at Leopardstown behind him. He had everything under control when going left at the last, but might find it more difficult if plans to encompass Aintree and *Ayr materialise. Official explanation: trainer's representative said, regarding the improved form shown, gelding made a mistake at the first at Leopardstown last time out and appeared to sulk thereafter (op 10/1)*
Chetwind Music(IRE) was readily outpaced from two out, but stuck to his task in game fashion all the same.
Kill Devil Hill(IRE) ran like a sick horse and is reportedly finished for the season. *Official explanation: vet said gelding was found to have a respiratory tract infection (op 7/4 tchd 13/8)*
Father Matt(IRE) took it up at the seventh before blundering badly at the next, leaving Carberry to make a spectacular exit. *(op 4/6)*

4137a BAR-ONE RACING JOHNSTOWN NOVICE HURDLE (GRADE 2) 2m 4f
3:50 (3:51) 4-Y-0+ **£22,448** (£6,586; £3,137; £1,068)

RPR

1 **Merdeka (IRE)**[49] 3309 6-11-5 .... BJGeraghty 133+
(T J Taaffe, Ire) *mde all: sn clr: rdn and styd on wl fr 2 out* **7/2**[2]

2 2½ **Back To Bid (IRE)**[42] 3408 6-11-5 .... PCarberry 131
(Noel Meade, Ire) *settled 4th: lost pl 5 out: rdn bef next: hdwy into 2nd after 3 out: hit 2 out: kpt on u.p* **5/1**[3]

3 3½ **Stoneville (IRE)**[24] 3702 6-11-5 130 .... APMcCoy 127
(E McNamara, Ire) *hld up: 6th after 4 out: prog after next: 4th bef 2 out: 3rd u.p bef last: kpt on same pce* **6/4**[1]

4 4 **Patsy Hall (IRE)**[42] 3413 6-11-5 126 .... TimmyMurphy 123
(Michael Cunningham, Ire) *hld up early: prog into 3rd after 1/2-way: 2nd after 4 out: 3rd and rdn after next: 4th and no imp after 2 out* **13/2**

5 3½ **Wanango (GER)**[61] 3052 5-11-2 128 .... WJLee 117
(T Stack, Ire) *hld up in rr: prog on outer after 3 out: slt mstke next: sn no ex* **7/1**

6 6 **Justpourit (IRE)**[28] 3642 7-11-5 .... RLoughran 114
(D T Hughes, Ire) *sn 3rd: 2nd 1/2-way: 4th and rdn 3 out: sn no ex* **25/1**

7 8 **Sir Frederick (IRE)**[8] 4002 6-11-5 121 .... DNRussell 106
(W J Burke, Ire) *mod 2nd: 3rd 1/2-way: 4th and pushed along bef 4 out: wknd fr next* **10/1**

4m 58.5s **Going Correction** +0.05s/f (Yiel)
WFA 4 from 5yo+ 10lb **9** Ran SP% **117.7**
Speed ratings: **106,105,103,102,100 98,95** CSF £22.27 TOTE £4.20: £2.30, £3.50; DF 23.30.
Owner Maurice Clifford **Bred** Brian Moore **Trained** Straffan, Co Kildare

NOTEBOOK
Merdeka(IRE) was given a more enterprising ride this time and was never headed. Highly regarded by his trainer, he has now been put away until starting his career over fences next season. *(op 3/1)*
Back To Bid(IRE) wasn't particularly fluent and was making little impression on the winner when clouting the second last. Still, this rates an improved performance, and he is a consistent performer. *(op 5/1 tchd 6/1)*
Stoneville(IRE), up in class, was toiling early in the straight and although staying on over the last flights was never on challenging terms. *(op 7/4 tchd 11/8)*
Patsy Hall(IRE) is a handicapper and ran near to his mark in defeat. *(op 6/1 tchd 7/1)*
Wanango(GER) extended the poor record of his age group in this race and ran below his best. *(op 5/1)*

4138a TOTE "ONLINE BETTING FOR CHELTENHAM" NEWLANDS CHASE (GRADE 2) 2m
4:20 (4:20) 5-Y-0+ **£26,937** (£7,903; £3,765; £1,282)

RPR

1 **Sir Oj (IRE)**[78] 2760 9-11-10 138 ....(b) PCarberry 151+
(Noel Meade, Ire) *settled 2nd: led 4 out: rdn and hdd 2 out: rallied u.p last: led again early run-in: styd on wl u.p* **5/1**[3]

2 1½ **Nickname (FR)**[28] 3639 7-11-10 .... CO'Dwyer 149
(Martin Brassil, Ire) *sn led: slt mstke and hdd 4 out: regained ld 2 out: strly pressed last: hdd early run-in: kpt on wl u.p: no ex cl home* **6/4**[1]

3 15 **Green Belt Flyer (IRE)**[28] 3640 8-11-7 139 ....(b) TPTreacy 132
(Mrs John Harrington, Ire) *hld up: prog 5 out: 3rd 3 out: sn rdn and no imp: kpt on same pce* **7/2**[2]

4 nk **Steel Band**[42] 3411 8-11-4 130 .... GTHutchinson 128
(Paul A Roche, Ire) *hld up: slow 5th: 7th 5 out: prog into mod 4th 2 out: kpt on same pce* **33/1**

5 20 **Colnel Rayburn (IRE)**[31] 3587 10-11-7 136 ....(p) RMMoran 111
(Paul Nolan, Ire) *hld up: prog into 3rd 1/2-way: 4th and no ex after 3 out: wknd next* **7/1**

6 ¾ **Commonchero (IRE)**[62] 3007 9-11-4 132 .... TGMRyan 107
(M J P O'Brien, Ire) *mid-div: lost tch 5 out: no imp fr next* **16/1**

7 12 **Golden Row (IRE)**[17] 3830 12-11-7 120 .... AndrewJMcNamara 98
(Miss Mary Louise Hallahan, Ire) *3rd early: wknd fr 5 out* **33/1**

8 2 **John James (IRE)**[56] 3199 10-11-7 131 .... DJCasey 96
(J H Scott, Ire) *prom: 3rd appr 1/2-way: wknd after 5 out* **33/1**

P **Balapour (IRE)**[267] 641 8-11-4 109 ....(t) SMMcGovern —
(Patrick O Brady, Ire) *a bhd: slow 4th: lost tch bef 1/2-way: completely t.o whn p.u after 2 out* **66/1**

4m 15.8s **Going Correction** -0.125s/f (Good) **9** Ran SP% **107.6**
Speed ratings: **113,112,104,104,94 94,88,87,—** CSF £11.90 TOTE £5.80: £2.10, £1.10, £1.60; DF 14.90.
Owner Brian Keenan **Bred** Gareth Metcalfe **Trained** Castletown, Co Meath

NOTEBOOK
Sir Oj(IRE) proved he is a very tough chaser and gave plenty to assert for a second time close home. He boasts decent course form at Cheltenham, and has multiple engagements there, including the Ryanair Chase. *(op 4/1)*
Nickname(FR), obviously recovered from what ailed him at Leopardstown when pulled up behind Missed That, was unable to build his customary long lead but stuck on gamely over the last two. The winner, much more experienced over fences, was just too strong in the closing stages. He is unlikely to take up his Arkle engagement and may be at his very best over a bit further. *(op 11/10)*
Green Belt Flyer(IRE), rated a pound above the winner, ran below form but could still go to Cheltenham, possibly for the Racing Post Plate (the old Mildmay of Flete). *(op 3/1)*
Steel Band stayed on late without making much impression.
Colnel Rayburn(IRE) ran well enough to keep his Aintree dream alive, weakening after three out over this inadequate trip. *(op 8/1)*

4139 - 4140a (Foreign Racing) - See Raceform Interactive

[3849]AYR (L-H)

Monday, February 27

OFFICIAL GOING: Soft (good to soft in home straight)

First fence in home straight omitted.
Wind: Light, half-against

4141 WEDDINGS AT WESTERN HOUSE MAIDEN HURDLE (11 hdls) 2m 4f
2:00 (2:01) (Class 4) 4-Y-0+ **£3,253** (£955; £477; £238)

Form RPR

2-23 1 **Love That Benny (USA)**[21] 3779 6-11-0 108 .... PaddyAspell(3) 112+
(J Wade) *a.p: rdn to ld 3 out: styd on wl* **7/1**[3]

300P 2 4 **Duke Orsino (IRE)**[16] 3853 6-11-0 92 .... PeterBuchanan(3) 107
(Miss Lucinda V Russell) *hld up: hdwy 7th: chsng ldrs and rdn whn mstke 2 out: chsd wnr last: kpt on* **50/1**

P462 3 5 **Lethem Air**[16] 3853 8-10-12 103 ....(p) DougieCostello(5) 103+
(T Butt) *led to 3 out: kpt on same pce after next* **13/2**[2]

3222 4 3 **Character Building (IRE)**[21] 3779 6-11-3 .... RussGarritty 99
(J J Quinn) *keen: cl up: rdn and edgd lft fr 3 out: sn outpcd* **4/5**[1]

263 5 6 **Orang Outan (FR)**[38] 3488 4-10-4 108 ....(t) GaryBerridge(3) 83
(J P L Ewart) *hld up: hdwy and in tch 7th: rdn and no imp bef 3 out* **12/1**

5423 6 8 **Kempski**[16] 3854 6-10-10 90 ....(b) GarethThomas(7) 85
(R Nixon) *nt fluent: in tch: rdn 4 out: outpcd whn mstke next* **33/1**

7 ½ **Glen Harley (IRE)**[16] 6-10-10 ....(t) TomSiddall 78
(R T J Wilson, Ire) *bhd: rdn 7th: hdwy u.p bef 3 out: n.d* **33/1**

0/02 8 3½ **Le Millenaire (FR)**[55] 3232 7-11-3 .... TonyDobbin 81
(S H Shirley-Beavan) *chsd ldrs: rdn whn j. slowly 4 out: sn btn* **10/1**

5060 9 1¾ **Super Revo**[13] 3912 5-10-10 .... ColmSharkey(7) 79
(Mrs K Walton) *hld up: pushed along 7th: sn btn* **50/1**

-600 10 15 **Top Tenor (IRE)**[6] 4040 6-10-12 75 .... MrMThompson(5) 64
(V Thompson) *in tch tl wknd fr 7th* **200/1**

3/PP 11 2 **Rainha**[84] 2674 9-10-10 .... BarryKeniry 55
(A C Whillans) *towards rr: rdn 6th: nvr on terms* **66/1**

-0PF 12 2½ **Romanov Rambler (IRE)**[67] 2947 6-11-3 .... MarkBradburne 60
(Mrs S C Bradburne) *a bhd: no ch fr 7th* **200/1**

0P4 13 29 **Native Coll**[16] 3855 6-10-12 .... DesFlavin(5) 31
(N W Alexander) *a towards rr* **200/1**

14 1¾ **Speedy Tactics (IRE)**[51] 3306 7-10-3 .... MMMcNiff(7) 22
(Lindsay Woods, Ire) *hld up outside: rdn 6th: sn btn* **20/1**

-000 U **Rab Cee**[55] 3237 6-11-3 .... WilsonRenwick —
(W G Young) *bhd whn wnt bdly lft and uns rdr 3rd* **200/1**

0 P **Givitago**[12] 3931 7-10-5 .... MichaelMcAlister(5) —
(B Storey) *prom tl wknd qckly 6th: t.o whn p.u bef 4 out* **200/1**

-000 P **Cashema (IRE)**[38] 3488 5-10-5 69 .... DeclanMcGann(5) —
(D R MacLeod) *in tch to 7th: sn wknd: t.o whn p.u bef 3 out* **200/1**

5m 9.20s (-3.50) **Going Correction** 0.0s/f (Good)
WFA 4 from 5yo+ 10lb **17** Ran SP% **117.2**
Speed ratings: **107,105,103,102,99 96,96,95,94,88 87,86,74,74,— —,—** CSF £291.91 TOTE £10.40: £1.80, £14.30, £3.10; EX 208.90.
Owner John Wade **Bred** Cynthia Knight **Trained** Mordon, Co Durham

FOCUS
There appeared to be a lot of sand on the track and as a result the ground may not have been as soft as the official description would suggest. This looked to be an ordinary novice hurdle run at an even pace and those that raced handily seemed to hold an advantage. The form appears pretty solid rated through the winner and third.

NOTEBOOK
Love That Benny(USA), suited by the slight drop in trip, may also have been helped by the sand on the track making this less of a test of stamina than it might have been. He was never far off the *pace and saw it out well, but probably did not do much more than his official rating entitled him to. (op 6-1)*
Duke Orsino(IRE), who had shown nothing in three outings since reappearing in the autumn, was the only one to make any real impression from off the pace and stayed on well without ever threatening the winner. His proximity may appear to hold the form down, but he had given the impression in the past that he would be suited by a step up in trip and so it proved.
Lethem Air tried to make every yard on this step back up in trip, but looked short of speed over the last couple of flights. He was not beaten because he did not stay and this looks to be about as good as he is. *(op 8-1)*
Character Building(IRE) seemed to hold every chance, but did not pick up as had seemed likely and was disappointing. Perhaps this rather strange ground did not suit him and he is worth another chance back on genuinely soft ground with no sand on it. *(op Evens tchd 11-10 in a place)*
Orang Outan(FR) was not disgraced against his elders, but did not seem to improve for the step up in trip and did not run up to his official mark. *(op 14-1)*
Cashema(IRE) *Official explanation: jockey said mare had breathing problem*

4142 CENTRAL HEATING ADVISORY SERVICE UK NOVICES' H'CAP CHASE (11 fncs 1 omitted) 2m
2:35 (2:35) (Class 4) (0-100,98) 5-Y-0+ **£3,903** (£1,146; £573; £286)

Form RPR

0063 1 **Nifty Roy**[19] 3798 6-10-3 80 .... DougieCostello(5) 95+
(I McMath) *keen: hld up: smooth hdwy 4 out: led gng wl appr last: shkn up and r.o strly* **9/2**[1]

632U **2** *6* **Albertino Lad**[40] [3447] 9-11-5 **94**.................................. PeterBuchanan(3) 102+
(Miss Lucinda V Russell) *set decent pce: rdn 3 out: hdd appr last: kpt on same pce* **5/1**[2]

U435 **3** *½* **Ideal Du Bois Beury (FR)**[13] [3916] 10-10-0 **75**.............. PaddyAspell(3) 82
(P Monteith) *hld up: pushed along 7th: no imp tl kpt on fr 2 out: nrst fin* **5/1**[2]

3304 **4** *1* **The Frosty Ferret (IRE)**[19] [3798] 8-11-3 **89**......................(p) GrahamLee 96+
(J M Jefferson) *chsd ldrs: wnt 2nd 6th: rdn whn blnd 3 out: one pce after next* **5/1**[2]

4442 **5** *12* **Dance Party (IRE)**[48] [3334] 6-11-8 **97**.............................. MrTGreenall(3) 91
(M W Easterby) *hld up: rdn 5th: no imp fr 4 out* **6/1**[3]

-3P0 **6** *21* **Gaucho**[13] [3915] 9-9-11 **76**..(b[1]) MissTJackson(7) 49
(Miss T Jackson) *chsd ldr to 6th: wknd after next* **16/1**

4BP3 **7** *dist* **Jexel (FR)**[16] [3850] 9-11-12 **98**... RichardMcGrath —
(B Storey) *a bhd: no ch fr 1/2-way* **10/1**

0006 **P** **Barney (IRE)**[21] [3782] 5-9-9 **78** oh4........................... MichaelMcAlister(5) —
(Mrs E Slack) *bhd: outpcd whn blnd 7th: t.o whn p.u bef 3 out* **25/1**

6044 **P** **Fearless Foursome**[19] [3797] 7-11-3 **89**.............................. BrianHarding —
(N W Alexander) *towards rr: struggling fr 1/2-way: t.o whn p.u bef 3 out* **8/1**

4m 3.90s (-0.60) **Going Correction** -0.10s/f (Good)
WFA 5 from 6yo+ 6lb **9** Ran SP% **112.4**
Speed ratings: **97,94,93,93,87 76,—,—,—** CSF £26.89 CT £114.47 TOTE £5.60: £1.80, £1.50, £2.00; EX 24.10.
Owner Mrs A J McMath **Bred** Mrs Norma Peebles **Trained** Cumwhinton, Cumbria

FOCUS
A moderate race with the top weight rated just 98, although the form looks solid enough rated through the placed horses. They went a fierce early pace, but were not able to maintain it and the race was rather set up for the favourite.

NOTEBOOK
Nifty Roy ideally needs further than this so the rapid pace proved ideal. At the same time as the front-runners started to wilt in the home straight he could be seen gradually picking them off on the bridle and in the end he won going away. This was not a great race but he is entitled to improve, especially over further. *(op 4-1 tchd 5-1 in a place)*
Albertino Lad, back over probably his best trip, tried to run his rivals into the ground but there was nothing he could do once the favourite arrived on the scene and in the end he barely held on to second. He could be difficult to catch if adopting these tactics on a sharper track. *(op 9-2)*
Ideal Du Bois Beury(FR) would have found this trip far too sharp and the strong early pace enabled him to plug on and finish as close as he did. The fact that he is still a novice at his age, despite plenty of experience over fences, does rather tell its own story. *(op 11-2 tchd 6-1)*
The Frosty Ferret(IRE), tried in cheekpieces, was never too far away but was already making hard work of trying to get on terms with the runaway leader when awkward at the third last. His best trip is yet to be identified, but he looks nothing special in any case. *(tchd 11-2 in places)*
Dance Party(IRE) never got involved and did not step up on her chasing debut. *(op 7-1)*

4143 WEATHERBYS BANK NOVICES' HURDLE (9 hdls) 2m
3:05 (3:06) (Class 4) 4-Y-0+ **£4,554** (£1,337; £668; £333)

Form RPR

F333 **1** **Nerone (GER)**[23] [3737] 5-11-2 104... GrahamLee 103+
(P Monteith) *keen: chsd ldrs: led 5th: hrd pressed between last two: styd on wl* **9/4**[1]

1-32 **2** *1½* **Blue Buster**[63] [2968] 6-10-13 .... MrTGreenall(3) 100
(M W Easterby) *prom: effrt bef 3 out: disp ld after last: no ex run in* **5/2**[2]

4013 **3** *1½* **Calfraz**[35] [3539] 4-11-0 105.. NeilMulholland 98+
(M D Hammond) *midfield: hdwy bef 4 out: outpcd bef next: rallied 2 out: kpt on run in* **4/1**[3]

00 **4** *8* **Calculaite**[13] [3912] 5-11-2 .... RussGarritty 91
(M Todhunter) *hld up: hdwy bef 3 out: outpcd fr next* **25/1**

4400 **5** *¾* **Political Pendant**[19] [3795] 5-10-2 90.......................... GarethThomas(7) 83
(R Nixon) *cl up: j. slowly 5th: outpcd 4 out: rallied after next: no imp* **50/1**

032- **6** *7* **Reseda (IRE)**[422] [3146] 9-10-9 101...........................(t) BenOrde-Powlett(7) 83
(M A Barnes) *led to 5th: wknd bef 3 out* **12/1**

P00 **7** *¾* **Inch High**[26] [3673] 8-11-2 .... DominicElsworth 82
(J S Goldie) *chsd ldrs tl wknd bef 4 out* **100/1**

0 **8** *1¾* **The Last Viking**[67] [2948] 6-11-2 .... AlanDempsey 80
(A Parker) *nt fluent: a bhd* **50/1**

0-0F **9** *7* **Kiwijimbo (IRE)**[45] [3374] 6-11-2 .... BarryKeniry 73
(A C Whillans) *keen: hld up: hdwy and prom 4th: wknd bef 3 out* **40/1**

2/5- **10** *7* **Flame Of Zara**[459] [2435] 7-10-6 .... GaryBerridge(3) 59
(L Lungo) *towards rr: rdn bef 4 out: sn btn* **12/1**

0-60 **P** **Endless Power (IRE)**[113] [2062] 6-11-2 .... TonyDobbin —
(J Barclay) *a bhd: t.o whn p.u bef 3 out* **33/1**

P **Insubordinate**[248] 5-11-2 .... RichardMcGrath —
(J S Goldie) *bhd: struggling 1/2-way: t.o whn p.u bef 3 out* **66/1**

50 **P** **Sparky Rocket**[52] [3273] 5-10-9 .... BrianHarding —
(B Storey) *in tch tl lost pl bef 4th: n.d after: p.u bef 3 out* **100/1**

4m 2.30s (5.00) **Going Correction** +0.40s/f (Soft)
WFA 4 from 5yo+ 9lb **13** Ran SP% **111.3**
Speed ratings: **103,102,101,97,97 93,93,92,88,85 —,—,—** CSF £7.08 TOTE £2.70: £1.80, £1.60, £1.40; EX 8.00.
Owner D A Johnson **Bred** A Pereira **Trained** Rosewell, Midlothian

FOCUS
There may have been 13 runners, but this was a three-horse race according to the market and so it proved. The first three and fifth all ran close to their marks suggesting the form is reasonable. The ground looked to have been cut up by the runners in the first race.

NOTEBOOK
Nerone(GER), who has kept on finding one or two to beat him in recent outings, finally managed to get off the mark. After taking over at halfway, he kicked clear starting up the home straight but the runner-up eventually ranged alongside him and it looked as though he was going to miss out again. However, he found a little bit extra under pressure and managed to keep him at bay. Despite this victory, he still does not strike as the type to wade in on next time. *(op 5-2 tchd 2-1)*
Blue Buster, reverting to the minimum trip, looked a big danger to the favourite coming to the last flight, but just lacked a turn of foot where it mattered. He ideally needs further. *(op 11-4 tchd 10-3)*
Calfraz, given a patient ride, rather ran in snatches but stayed on to finish a respectable third and could be interesting if stepped up in trip. *(op 3-1)*
Calculaite was very much best of the rest and could be of interest in a novices' handicap. Most of his best Flat form came on fast ground.
Political Pendant is only moderate, but this trip would have been much too short. *(op 66-1)*

4144 RECTANGLE GROUP H'CAP CHASE (17 fncs 2 omitted) 3m 1f
3:40 (3:40) (Class 4) (0-110,110) 5-Y-0+ **£3,903** (£1,146; £573; £286)

Form RPR

F45P **1** **Skenfrith**[44] [3382] 7-10-0 **84** oh1... NeilMulholland 108+
(Miss S E Forster) *trckd ldrs: led 12th: clr 3 out: r.o strly* **8/1**

3432 **2** *8* **Harrovian**[13] [3917] 9-11-7 **110**......................................(p) DougieCostello(5) 122
(Miss P Robson) *rn in snatches: in tch: outpcd 1/2-way: rallied bef 3 out: wnt 2nd run in: no ch w wnr* **4/1**[1]

3 *1* **Holey Moley (IRE)**[62] [3043] 9-10-11 **95**................................... TomSiddall 106
(R T J Wilson, Ire) *hld up midfield: hdwy 10th: outpcd bef 3 out: rallied to chse wnr briefly last: one pce* **33/1**

14PP **4** *1* **Almire Du Lia (FR)**[13] [3917] 8-11-0 **98**..........................(v) MarkBradburne 108
(Mrs S C Bradburne) *cl up: lft in ld 10th: hdd 12th: rdn and one pce fr 3 out* **33/1**

/ **5** *10* **Lovely Native (IRE)**[296] 10-10-4 **91**.............................. GaryBerridge(3) 91
(L Lungo) *keen: hld up: smooth hdwy 11th: effrt and chsd wnr bef 3 out: wknd after next* **12/1**

3020 **6** *2½* **Glenfarclas Boy (IRE)**[13] [3915] 10-10-1 **88**.............(p) PeterBuchanan(3) 86
(Miss Lucinda V Russell) *towards rr: struggling 1/2-way: rallied bef 3 out: outpcd fr next* **12/1**

63PP **P** **Behavingbadly (IRE)**[48] [3336] 11-10-0 **84** oh1................. AlanDempsey —
(A Parker) *a bhd: t.o whn p.u bef 3 out* **20/1**

-PP4 **P** **Highland Brig**[16] [3850] 10-10-1 **85**.................................... KeithMercer —
(T Butt) *mstkes: a wl bhd: t.o whn p.u bef 12th* **33/1**

P55P **P** **Hugo De Grez (FR)**[13] [3917] 11-10-13 **97**........................(p) TonyDobbin —
(A Parker) *led to 3rd: cl up tl wknd fr 10th: p.u 12th* **20/1**

1P2P **P** **Fountain Brig**[16] [3849] 10-10-1 **85**......................................(p) BrianHarding —
(N W Alexander) *towards rr: struggling and p.u after 9th* **12/1**

5205 **P** **Heidi III (FR)**[13] [3917] 11-11-10 **108**....................................(p) GrahamLee —
(M D Hammond) *in tch: outpcd 6th: struggling whn p.u bef 10th* **8/1**

-423 **P** **Trisons Star (IRE)**[55] [3236] 8-11-3 **106**................................ DesFlavin(5) —
(Mrs L B Normile) *midfield: outpcd 1/2-way: t.o whn p.u bef 3 out* **5/1**[2]

FP61 **P** **Briar's Mist (IRE)**[49] [3315] 9-10-10 **94**........................(b) RichardMcGrath —
(C Grant) *nvr gng wl: sn towards rr: t.o whn p.u bef 12th* **7/1**[3]

P656 **P** **Falchion**[6] [4042] 11-10-3 **87**..(bt) WilsonRenwick —
(J R Bewley) *led 3rd: hit 9th: blnd and hdd next: wknd 12th: t.o whn p.u bef 3 out* **14/1**

6m 37.3s (-8.40) **Going Correction** -0.10s/f (Good) **14** Ran SP% **119.5**
Speed ratings: **109,106,106,105,102 101,—,—,—,— —,—,—,—** CSF £38.18 CT £998.33 TOTE £10.70: £3.30, £1.60, £2.90; EX 72.60 TRIFECTA Not won..
Owner J M & Miss H M Crichton, Miss S Forster **Bred** Frazer S F Hines And Mrs Heather Moreno **Trained** Kirk Yetholm, Borders

FOCUS
A decent pace for this staying handicap chase and it took its toll with eight of the 14 runners pulling up. The form looks sensible enough with the placed horses close to their marks.

NOTEBOOK
Skenfrith, disappointing over fences to date, may have been 1lb out of the handicap but was still two stone below his hurdles mark. He made no mistake this time either, and once he was sent for home rounding the final bend he never looked like being caught. Now that he has finally got his act together over fences, it might be wise to run him fairly quickly under a penalty as the Handicapper *seems likely hit him for this. Official explanation: trainer said, regarding improved form shown, gelding's jumping was much improved having been ridden more prominently (op 9-1)*
Harrovian, not for the first time, was inclined to run in snatches before staying on to snatch the runner-up prize at a respectful distance. He keeps on finding one or two to beat him at the moment and may be worth a try over a marathon trip. *(op 5-1 tchd 11-2 in a place)*
Holey Moley(IRE), a former Irish winning pointer making his debut in this country, stayed on well to make the frame and obviously retains his ability. He should find an opportunity at some stage.
Almire Du Lia(FR), pulled up in his last two starts and with the visor back on, was always close to the pace and kept on though he could not go with the winner over the last four fences. This was better. *(op 25-1)*
Lovely Native(IRE), winner of three points and a hunter chase in Ireland, was making her debut in this country. Given a patient ride, she travelled really well and looked a real danger when moving up to track the leaders on the home bend, but then went from one to extreme to the other. As this was her first run in nine months, there is every chance she blew up and she should be capable of better if given a little time to get over this.
Heidi III(FR) *Official explanation: jockey said gelding was never travelling (tchd 11-2)*
Falchion, given a very positive ride, made a mistake at the ninth but was still a couple of lengths clear when a more serious one at the next ended his chance. *(tchd 11-2)*
Briar's Mist(IRE) probably needs an even greater test of stamina than this, but even so he never *looked happy and this was too bad to be true. Official explanation: jockey said gelding was never travelling (tchd 11-2)*
Trisons Star(IRE) should have had no problem with the trip or ground yet ran a shocker. *Official explanation: jockey said gelding was unsuited by going - soft in back straight, good to soft in home straight (tchd 11-2)*

4145 RACING POST "HANDS AND HEELS" JUMP SERIES H'CAP HURDLE (CONDITIONAL JOCKEYS/AMATEUR RIDERS) (11 hdls) 2m 4f
4:15 (4:15) (Class 5) (0-90,90) 4-Y-0+ **£2,927** (£859; £429; £214)

Form RPR

P424 **1** **Oscar The Boxer (IRE)**[38] [3487] 7-11-5 **86**.................... MrOWilliams(3) 89+
(J M Jefferson) *cl up: led 7th: mde rest: blnd last: kpt on wl* **9/2**[2]

6P-0 **2** *1* **Another Superman (IRE)**[92] [2545] 7-11-6 **87**..............(p) MMMcNiff(3) 86
(Lindsay Woods, Ire) *hld up: hdwy to press wnr appr 3 out: rdn and edgd lft: one pce last* **20/1**

00P4 **3** *3½* **Mae Moss**[21] [3782] 5-11-1 **79** ow1.. MrMSeston 76+
(W S Coltherd) *led to 2nd: cl up: ev ch bef 3 out: one pce next* **14/1**

P00U **4** *1¼* **Leonia's Rose (IRE)**[56] [3209] 7-10-5 **74**......................... MrDOakden(5) 68
(Miss Lucinda V Russell) *bhd tl gd hdwy bef 2 out: kpt on: n.d* **16/1**

0360 **5** *1¾* **Green 'N' Gold**[103] [2267] 6-11-5 **88**..................................... CWilliams(5) 80
(M D Hammond) *keen in rr: hdwy and prom 7th: rdn and no ex bef 2 out* **16/1**

62P3 **6** *10* **Roadworthy (IRE)**[13] [3916] 9-10-0 **67**............................... JohnFlavin(3) 49
(W G Young) *hld up: hdwy and prom 4 out: wknd next* **10/1**

1400 **7** *10* **Star Trooper (IRE)**[6] [4045] 10-10-10 **79**...................(p) MissCarlyFrater(5) 51
(Miss S E Forster) *cl up: led 2nd to 7th: wknd after 4 out* **25/1**

44P5 **8** *nk* **Bramble Princess (IRE)**[34] [3553] 7-11-4 **85**.................... RyanCummings(3) 57
(Miss Lucinda V Russell) *prom tl lost pl 7th: n.d after* **33/1**

0-P0 **9** *½* **Paperchaser**[62] [3042] 6-10-1 **68**.. MrCJCallow(3) 39
(F P Murtagh) *chsd ldrs tl wknd fr 4 out* **33/1**

10 *½* **Shanteen Lass (IRE)**[61] [3087] 6-11-5 **86**......................... MrSWByrne(3) 57
(Ferdy Murphy) *in tch: rdn 7th: btn after next* **16/1**

U0-0 **11** *nk* **Browneyes Blue (IRE)**[85] [2657] 8-10-10 **74**...................... DavidCullinane 45
(D R MacLeod) *midfield: wknd 4 out* **33/1**

0PP0 **12** *2½* **Inmate (IRE)**[63] [2979] 5-10-0 **64**...................................... ScottMarshall 32
(Mrs E Slack) *bhd: rdn 7th: nvr on terms* **14/1**

41-3 **13** *¾* **Inn From The Cold (IRE)**[40] [3445] 10-11-5 **86**.......... MrGWilloughby(3) 53
(L Lungo) *prom to 4 out: sn rdn and wknd* **3/1**[1]

5P-0 **14** *nk* **Blackout (IRE)**[55] [3236] 11-10-5 **72**.................................. MrHHaynes(3) 39
(J Barclay) *chsd ldrs to 7th: sn wknd* **66/1**

P001 **15** *7* **Alfy Rich**[19] [3798] 10-11-9 **90**..(p) FearghalDavis(3) 50
(M Todhunter) *midfield: rdn 7th: sn btn* **15/2**[3]

00-0 **16** *3* **Baby Sister**[63] 2977 7-11-2 **85** GarryWhillans(5) 42
(D W Whillans) *a bhd* **33/1**

F6/0 **F** **Caymans Gift**[13] 2169 6-10-11 **75** EwanWhillans —
(A C Whillans) *in tch: effrt after 4 out: 5l down and hld whn fell next* **16/1**

5m 17.9s (5.20) **Going Correction** +0.40s/f (Soft) **17** Ran SP% **122.8**
Speed ratings: **105,104,103,102,102 98,94,93,93,93 93,92,92,91,89 87,—** CSF £96.40 CT £1193.41 TOTE £6.20: £2.10, £3.60, £3.00, £5.50; EX 134.40.
Owner Boundary Garage (Bury) Limited **Bred** Susan M Hogan **Trained** Norton, N Yorks
■ Stewards' Enquiry : M M McNiff seven-day ban: using whip in a "hands and heels" race (Mar 10,12,16-18,20,22)

FOCUS
A moderate contest though quite competitive and sound enough form. The winning time was 6.7 seconds slower than the opener, but the ground did appear to have deteriorated a bit in the meantime.

NOTEBOOK
Oscar The Boxer(IRE), back to probably his best trip, was always up with the pace and even making a mess of the last could not stop him from winning his first race with a degree of comfort. The form of these contests always has to be treated with some caution, but considering his best previous form had been on faster ground he may well find another opportunity before too long.
Another Superman(IRE), like the winner a maiden coming into this, was given a very patient ride early. Gradually creeping into it rounding the home turn, he could never quite get to the winner and could not take advantage of his rival's untidy jump at the last. *(op 16-1)*
Mae Moss, given a positive ride on this step back up in trip, hung in there the whole way but could not find anything more over the last couple of flights. This does seem to be her right distance and a small race should be found. *(op 12-1)*
Leonia's Rose(IRE), no closer than ninth in seven previous tries over hurdles, was doing all her best work late and looks a stayer.
Green 'N' Gold may just have needed this and was not totally disgraced. *(op 14-1)*
Inn From The Cold(IRE) dropped away very tamely from the home bend and this looked a classic case of the bounce factor. *(op 4-1 tchd 9-2 in places)*

4146 CONFERENCES AT AYR RACECOURSE HUNTERS' CHASE (17 fncs 2 omitted) 3m 1f
4:45 (4:46) (Class 6) 6-Y-0+ **£1,648** (£507; £253)

Form RPR

P0-3 **1** **Red Striker**[23] 3736 12-11-9 **116** MissTJackson(5) 87+
(Miss T Jackson) *sn led: blnd and hdd 10th: led bef 3 out: hrd pressed after next: styd on wl run in* **4/9**[1]

4 **2** *1* **Boardsmill Rambler (IRE)**[12] 3926 7-12-0 MrMThompson 82
(V Thompson) *cl up: effrt bef 3 out: ev ch after next: kpt on run in* **10/1**

6/ **3** *dist* **Wraparound You (IRE)**[8] 9-11-9 MrPCallaghan(5) —
(Norman Sanderson) *bhd: struggling 12th: lft poor 3rd 3 out* **25/1**

P **U** **Noggler**[8] 4009 7-12-0 MissSBrotherton —
(M J Brown) *prom: led 10th to bef 3 out: 7l 3rd and wkng whn blnd and uns rdr 3 out* **7/1**[3]

PUP- **U** **Primitive Rites**[323] 9-11-7 MissCBrown(7) —
(M J Brown) *keen: chsd ldrs tl wknd 4 out: last and wl btn whn uns rdr after next* **6/1**[2]

7m 5.60s (19.90) **Going Correction** -0.10s/f (Good) **5** Ran SP% **109.0**
Speed ratings: **64,63,—,—,—** CSF £5.44 TOTE £1.30: £1.10, £3.20; EX 2.50.
Owner H L Thompson **Bred** Mrs D Jenks **Trained** Loftus, Cleveland

FOCUS
A dire contest in which nothing wanted to lead early and the winning time was over 28 seconds slower than the earlier handicap over the same trip.

NOTEBOOK
Red Striker was soon sent to the front when it became clear that nothing else wanted to lead, but looked to have blown it when making an almighty blunder just after halfway. He was given time to recover and eventually regained the advantage, but had to fight hard to keep the runner-up at bay. To be fair, he was entitled to bounce from his return performance at Wetherby and is now at the veteran stage, so should not be condemned too much for making harder work of this than might have been expected. *(tchd 1-2 and 8-15 in a place tchd 2-5 in places)*
Boardsmill Rambler(IRE) did not jump all that well, but still managed to get himself into a challenging position and made sure the favourite had to pull out all the stops. In reality the winner was probably not at his best, in which case the form may be flattering.
Wraparound You(IRE) is a bad pointer and only inherited third place due to the misfortune of others.
Primitive Rites had dropped away to last place when his rider fell off several yards after the third-last fence. *(op 8-1)*
Noggler showed up for a long way, but was losing touch with the front pair when blundering away his rider three out. *(op 8-1)*

4147 RACING UK STANDARD OPEN NATIONAL HUNT FLAT RACE 2m
5:15 (5:18) (Class 6) 4-6-Y-0 **£1,713** (£499; £249)

Form RPR

1 **The Pious Prince (IRE)** 5-11-3 TonyDobbin 115+
(L Lungo) *hld up: smooth hdwy to ld 3f out: shkn up and drew clr over 1f out* **5/1**[2]

542 **2** *13* **Nevertika (FR)**[49] 3319 5-11-3 RichardMcGrath 100
(Mrs K Walton) *prom on outside: effrt and disp ld 3f out: one pce fr 2f out* **11/4**[1]

03 **3** *shd* **Scarlet Cloak (USA)**[55] 3237 5-11-3 KeithMercer 100
(Mrs L B Normile) *towards rr: hdwy over 5f out: rdn and kpt on same pce fr 3f out* **8/1**[3]

4 *10* **Sea Senor** 4-10-5 MrTGreenall(3) 81
(M W Easterby) *keen in midfield: stdy hdwy over 4f out: pushed along 3f out: one pce* **12/1**

5 *8* **Hiddenfortune (IRE)**[128] 6-11-0 PeterBuchanan(3) 82
(Miss Lucinda V Russell) *cl up: led briefly over 3f out: wknd 2f out* **20/1**

0 **6** *½* **Justwhateverulike (IRE)**[21] 3785 5-11-3 NeilMulholland 81
(Miss S E Forster) *prom: effrt over 3f out: wknd 2f out* **66/1**

7 *shd* **Contendo** 5-11-3 MarkBradburne 81
(N W Alexander) *in tch: outpcd over 5f out: n.d after* **66/1**

8 *½* **Thatlldoforme** 4-10-1 EwanWhillans(7) 72
(A C Whillans) *bhd: rdn 1/2-way: rallied 3f out: n.d* **33/1**

4 **9** *¾* **Open De L'Isle (FR)**[55] 3237 4-10-5 GaryBerridge(3) 71
(J P L Ewart) *led to over 3f out: sn lost pl* **12/1**

10 *7* **Striking Silver** 5-10-13 ow3 MrDJewett(7) 76
(I McMath) *towards rr: rdn and hdwy over 5f out: hung lft and wknd fr 3f out* **40/1**

5 **11** *6* **Unfair Dismissal (IRE)**[49] 3319 5-11-3 GrahamLee 67
(M D Hammond) *prom tl rdn and wknd fr over 2f out* **10/1**

0 **12** *½* **Young Blade**[23] 3742 5-11-3 (t) DominicElsworth 67
(C Grant) *a bhd* **33/1**

13 *21* **Indian Wind** 4-10-1 BenOrde-Powlett(7) 37
(M A Barnes) *towards rr on ins: rdn 1/2-way: nvr on terms* **25/1**

422- **14** *8* **General Hardi**[390] 3653 5-11-0 PaddyAspell(3) 38
(J Wade) *prom tl rdn and wknd fr 4f out* **5/1**[2]

00 **15** *dist* **Over'n Out**[261] 720 5-10-10 BrianHarding —
(A R Dicken) *in tch to 1/2-way: sn rdn and wknd* **100/1**

16 *2* **Popinpeat** 4-10-8 WilsonRenwick —
(W G Young) *bhd: no ch fr 1/2-way* **100/1**

3m 54.0s (-5.20) **Going Correction** +0.40s/f (Soft)
WFA 4 from 5yo+ 9lb **16** Ran SP% **117.5**
Speed ratings: **111,104,104,99,95 95,95,94,94,91 88,87,77,73,—** — CSF £16.79 TOTE £6.10: £2.60, £1.80, £3.30; EX 18.10 Place 6 £57.83, Place 5 £12.48.
Owner Len Lungo Racing Limited **Bred** John Bourke **Trained** Carrutherstown, D'fries & G'way

FOCUS
Unusually for a bumper, this was run at a good pace and the winning time was 8.3 seconds faster than the earlier handicap hurdle over the same trip. The winner was very impressive and looks above average with the placed horses setting the level.

NOTEBOOK
The Pious Prince(IRE) ◆, who fetched 37,000euros as a three-year-old, is out of a half-sister to the dual Whitbread Gold Cup-winner Topsham Bay. Held up early, he travelled extremely well the whole way and once he cruised to the front against the stands' rail soon after turning in there was only going to be one winner. He looks a very useful recruit and can go on to much better things. *(op 10-3)*
Nevertika(FR) had every chance and was just unfortunate to again bump into a useful prospect. He has the ability to win a race like this, but now that he has run in four bumpers and will have to switch to hurdles unless he contests one of the championship races. *(op 3-1 tchd 7-2)*
Scarlet Cloak(USA) stayed on well up the home straight and almost got up for second. Although beaten out of sight by the winner like all the others, this was probably his best effort yet and he looks to have a future.
Sea Senor, out of a multiple winner over hurdles and fences, fetched just 2,000gns as a foal but there was encouragement in this debut effort and he is likely to come on for it. *(op 14-1)*
Hiddenfortune(IRE), winner of an Irish point when last seen four months earlier, ran well for a long way and is likely to come into his own when faced with a greater test of stamina.
General Hardi should have been suited by conditions, but dropped away very tamely over the last half-mile and this was far too bad to be true. *(op 8-1)*
T/Jkpt: Not won. T/Plt: £76.60 to a £1 stake. Pool: £47,265.70. 450.40 winning tickets. T/Qpdt: £10.90 to a £1 stake. Pool: £3,969.30. 269.30 winning tickets. RY

3898 PLUMPTON (L-H)
Monday, February 27

OFFICIAL GOING: Soft (heavy in places)
Wind: Almost nil Weather: Overcast

4148 WEATHERBYS PRINTING NOVICES' HURDLE (12 hdls) 2m 5f
2:10 (2:10) (Class 4) 4-Y-0+ **£4,554** (£1,337; £668; £333)

Form RPR

3444 **1** **Bring Me Sunshine (IRE)**[15] 3882 5-11-3 JoeTizzard 109+
(C L Tizzard) *hld up in cl tch: rdn bef 3 out: styd on to ld 2 out: clr last: drvn out* **6/1**[3]

232 **2** *4* **Palm Island (FR)**[13] 3906 5-11-3 **109** TomDoyle 105+
(Noel T Chance) *hld up in last: pushed along 8th: outpcd after next: styd on bef 2 out: wnt 2nd last: kpt on* **6/4**[1]

3000 **3** *14* **Willy The Slip**[6] 4033 4-10-7 (v[1]) AndrewThornton 84+
(R H Alner) *nt fluent: led at slow pce to 3rd: led 6th tl bef 3 out: drvn and upsides 2 out: wknd last* **33/1**

-314 **4** *7* **Just A Splash (IRE)**[56] 3218 6-11-9 AndrewTinkler 89
(N J Gifford) *w ldr: led 3rd and maintained slow pce: hdd 7th: outpcd bef 3 out: fdd* **8/1**

23 **5** *4* **Quartier Latin (USA)**[46] 3347 5-11-3 APMcCoy 91+
(C Von Der Recke, Germany) *t.k.h: trckd ldrs: led bef 3 out and kicked on: jnd whn blnd 2 out: wknd rapidly* **7/4**[2]

P **6** *18* **It Plays Itself (IRE)**[11] 3941 7-11-3 NoelFehily 61
(Jonjo O'Neill) *trckd ldrs tl wknd bef 3 out: t.o whn mstke last* **33/1**

5m 45.2s (20.40) **Going Correction** +0.70s/f (Soft)
WFA 4 from 5yo+ 10lb **6** Ran SP% **107.6**
Speed ratings: **89,87,82,79,77 71** CSF £14.69 TOTE £8.20: £3.70, £1.90; EX 20.50.
Owner R G Tizzard **Bred** James Robinson **Trained** Milborne Port, Dorset

FOCUS
A moderate winning time, nearly 11 seconds slower than the later handicap, as a result of the steady gallop, and the form is suspect.

NOTEBOOK
Bring Me Sunshine(IRE), a consistent sort in bumpers, shaped well when a staying-on fourth on his hurdling debut at Exeter and this step up in distance enabled the gelding to get off the mark, grinding clear in the straight to win with a bit in hand. A future three-mile chaser, he remains open to further improvement and may be capable of defying a penalty if placed well. *(op 5-1 tchd 9-2)*
Palm Island(FR) has yet to finish out the three in four starts over hurdles, but he is finding winning hard and could only keep on at the one pace for second, having been held up early. He will find a race eventually and may be better off in handicaps. *(op 7-4 tchd 2-1)*
Willy The Slip ran an improved race in the first-time visor, despite not jumping that well, but may have been flattered in dominating at a slow tempo and it will be interesting to see if he can repeat the effort. A move into handicaps may help.
Just A Splash(IRE), who failed to shine on his chasing debut at Folkestone last month, looked vulnerable under his penalty and struggled to get involved. *(op 9-1 tchd 13-2)*
Quartier Latin(USA), placed on each of his two previous ventures over hurdles, was expected to improve for this step up in distance but, having been sent on taking three out, he folded tamely after a mistake at the second-last (already beaten) and clearly failed to see out the distance. *(op 13-8 tchd 6-4)*
It Plays Itself(IRE) was never involved and will no doubt turn up in a handicap at one of the gaff tracks next season when ready to win.

4149 WELLS EXPRESS MAIDEN HURDLE (9 hdls) 2m
2:45 (2:46) (Class 5) 4-Y-0+ **£2,740** (£798; £399)

Form RPR

4 **1** **White On Black (GER)**[27] 3658 5-11-2 PhilipHide 107+
(G L Moore) *racd wd: cl up: gng easily 3 out: pressed ldr next: led last: rdn and kpt on wl flat* **8/1**[2]

1-22 **2** *¾* **Liathroidisneachta (IRE)**[37] 3496 6-11-2 APMcCoy 107+
(Jonjo O'Neill) *trckd ldrs: led after 6th: pressed 2 out: hanging lft and hdd last : hung lft flat: nt qckn u.p* **2/5**[1]

0052 **3** *6* **Koral Bay (FR)**[9] 3979 5-10-2 **104** MrSWaley-Cohen(7) 93
(R Waley-Cohen) *cl up: trckd ldr bef 3 out tl 2 out: one pce after* **8/1**[2]

P **4** *3* **Yenaled**[9] 3978 9-11-2 JamieMoore 99+
(P S McEntee) *t.k.h: hld up: prog after 6th: effrt on outer 2 out: disputing 3rd whn blnd last: fdd flat* **25/1**

P0P **5** *20* **Akram (IRE)**[11] 3939 4-10-7 NoelFehily 68
(Jonjo O'Neill) *disp ld tl after 6th: sn wknd* **25/1**

450 **6** *1* **Ridjit (FR)**[13] 3908 6-11-2 .... LeightonAspell 76
(N J Gifford) *hld up in tch: rdn and wknd bef 3 out* **20/1**[3]

0U **7** *2 ½* **Tricky Venture**[9] 3978 6-11-2 .... BenjaminHitchcott 74
(Mrs L C Jewell) *t.k.h: hld up in tch: stl chsng ldrs after 3 out: sn wknd rapidly* **100/1**

P **Maddox (POL)**[21] 4-10-4 .... ColinBolger(3) —
(Mrs P Townsley) *disp ld tl 6th: wknd rapidly: t.o whn p.u bef 2 out* **80/1**

P **P** **On The Fairway (IRE)**[51] 3281 7-10-4 .... RobertLucey-Butler(5) —
(Miss M P Bryant) *hld up in last: lost tch 5th: sn wl t.o: p.u bef 2 out* **200/1**

4m 10.0s (8.80) **Going Correction** +0.70s/f (Soft)
WFA 4 from 5yo+ 9lb **9** Ran SP% **108.8**
Speed ratings: **106,105,102,101,91 90,89,—,—** CSF £11.20 TOTE £7.10: £1.50, £1.02, £1.30; EX 15.50.
Owner Bryan Pennick **Bred** M Ommer **Trained** Woodingdean, E Sussex

FOCUS
A minor shock, but the favourite did look vulnerable and it was the speedy White On Black that took the honours. The race could rate higher.

NOTEBOOK
White On Black(GER), a winner on the Flat in Germany who shaped well when fourth on his hurdling debut at Folkestone, had clearly learnt from that outing and caused quite a surprise, staying on too well for the hot favourite. This was a decent performance and he particularly impressed with the way he travelled. He could defy a penalty, but it is likely to best of him will not be seen until he is contesting decent two-mile handicap hurdles next season. *(op 7-1)*
Liathroidisneachta(IRE) looked vulnerable dropping back half a mile in distance, but he was made a short-priced favourite due to the supposed lack of creditable opposition. He led them in to the straight, but it was clear the winner was going better and he looked suspect under pressure, hanging out to his left and making it tough for McCoy to get stuck into him. The step back up in distance will suit, but he may be one to have reservations about. *(tchd 4-9)*
Koral Bay(FR) is well exposed and she was again not good enough despite receiving 14lb from each of the front two. Either a return to fences or move into handicaps is required. *(op 13-2)*
Yenaled, never involved on his hurdling debut at Lingfield, travelled well to a point here and threatened to get involved, but found it too much of a test in the end and gradually weakened in the straight. He may do better in handicaps, but it is also possible he lacks the resolution for hurdles. *(tchd 33-1)*
Akram(IRE) is unlikely to be seen at his best until tackling handicaps next season. *(op 33-1)*
On The Fairway(IRE) *Official explanation: jockey said mare hung badly right (op 100-1)*

4150 JOHN SMITH'S NOVICES' H'CAP CHASE (14 fncs) 2m 4f
3:15 (3:15) (Class 4) (0-110,105) 5-Y-O **£5,028** (£1,498; £758; £388; £203)

Form RPR

U332 **1** **Twenty Degrees**[5] 4053 8-10-11 **90** .... (b) JamieMoore 102+
(G L Moore) *trckd ldrs: led 4 out to next: sn drvn to ld again: jnd bef last: gained upper hand nr fin: all out* **8/1**[3]

1222 **2** *½* **Mystical Star (FR)**[57] 3187 9-10-13 **92** .... LeightonAspell 101
(M J Hogan) *trckd ldrs: chal 4 out: led briefly next: sn rdn: upsides wnr bef last: no ex nr fin* **11/8**[1]

0-P4 **3** *7* **Ri Na Realta (IRE)**[281] 465 11-10-11 **90** .... AndrewThornton 92
(J W Mullins) *settled in last pair: lost tch fr 8th: wl off the pce 4 out: styd on steadily bef 2 out: nudged along flat: nvr nrr* **25/1**

5550 **4** *nk* **Deltic Arrow**[13] 3909 8-10-0 **86** ow7 .... MrJAJenkins(7) 89+
(D L Williams) *led: str reminders after 6th and on several occasions after: mstke 9th: hdd next: sn outpcd: plugged on* **11/1**

4-F3 **5** *dist* **Prato (GER)**[46] 3352 6-11-10 **103** .... (b) TomScudamore —
(C Von Der Recke, Germany) *trckd ldr tl after 9th: wknd 4 out: no ch whn mstke 2 out: eased: btn 63l* **12/1**

00-F **P** **Geton (IRE)**[105] 2243 6-11-12 **105** .... TimmyMurphy —
(M C Pipe) *in tch: reminder after 8th and no rspnse: wknd and p.u after 9th* **5/2**[2]

/3F- **P** **Peterson's Cay (IRE)**[488] 1853 8-11-1 **94** .... (p) JoeTizzard —
(C L Tizzard) *settled in last pair: blnd 7th and 8th: sn t.o: p.u bef 10th* **14/1**

5m 19.4s (0.95) **Going Correction** +0.60s/f (Soft) **7** Ran SP% **108.3**
Speed ratings: **107,106,104,103,— —,—** CSF £18.38 TOTE £7.10: £3.00, £1.60; EX 11.50.
Owner W E Baird **Bred** W E Baird **Trained** Woodingdean, E Sussex

FOCUS
A good finish to what was a modest contest with the form rated through the runner-up to his mark.

NOTEBOOK
Twenty Degrees, who has been running well in defeat in similar races, was never far off the pace and went to the front four from home, but Mystical Star was soon on his tail, travelling strongly. That rival was unable to get by however, as Moore extracted extra from him after the last, sticking his neck out gamely. This was only his fifth start over fences and with a such a determined attitude he looks set for further success at a similar level. *(op 7-1)*
Mystical Star(FR) has taken really well to fences, winning on his chasing debut at the course back in October, but he has finished second on each of his four subsequent attempts and was unable to match the winner's determination here. He seems genuine enough, but is likely to go up again for this and winning is becoming increasingly harder. *(tchd 6-4)*
Ri Na Realta(IRE) ran easily his best race to date since going chasing, keeping on under a conservative ride by Thornton to claim third from the tiring Deltic Arrow. He could be interesting off this sort of mark next time. *(op 20-1)*
Deltic Arrow had to be encouraged to go faster with a circuit to go, and he showed up well until becoming outpaced down the back, this drop in distance seemingly not doing him any good. His jumping was a little sketchy, but there is a race in him at three miles if that can be sorted out. *(op 14-1 tchd 10-1)*
Prato(GER) was already well held when blundering at the second-last and he was allowed to come home in his own time. *(op 14-1 tchd 16-1)*
Geton(IRE), in the process of running a big race on his chasing debut at Leicester in November when falling four from home, was having his first outing since and again failed to complete, this time pulling up after losing a front shoe. He is potentially well handicapped and his trainer will get it right with him eventually. *Official explanation: vet said gelding had sensitive left fore leg having lost a shoe (tchd 2-1 and 11-4 in a place)*

4151 JOHN SMITH'S MARES' ONLY H'CAP HURDLE (12 hdls) 2m 5f
3:50 (3:50) (Class 4) (0-105,98) 4-Y-O+ **£3,253** (£955; £477; £238)

Form RPR

16-0 **1** **Up At Midnight**[27] 3661 6-11-11 **97** .... LeightonAspell 101+
(R Rowe) *disp ld tl def advantage fr 8th: mde rest: rdn 2 out: styd on wl flat* **10/3**[2]

P304 **2** *6* **Carly Bay**[14] 3901 8-11-12 **98** .... RichardJohnson 99+
(G P Enright) *racd wd: cl up: mstke 8th: effrt next: chsd wnr 3 out: cl up whn slipped bnd bef next: sn rdn: no imp last: fdd* **7/2**[3]

510B **3** *13* **Penny's Crown**[11] 3951 7-10-13 **90** .... EamonDehdashti(5) 75
(G A Ham) *racd wd: cl up: pushed along 8th: chsd wnr next to 3 out: wknd bef 2 out* **17/2**

-P5P **4** *13* **Dancing Shirley**[56] 3222 8-10-3 **75** .... MatthewBatchelor 47
(Miss A M Newton-Smith) *disp ld to 8th: u.p and lost pl bef next: sn wl bhd: plugged on again fr 2 out* **16/1**

5 **P** **Orbys Girl (IRE)**[91] 2553 6-11-1 **87** .... (bt[1]) PaulMoloney —
(M Pitman) *prom to 6th: rdn and struggling in rr 8th: sn t.o: p.u bef 2 out* **9/2**

-P62 **P** **Lady Alderbrook (IRE)**[8] 4010 6-10-1 **80** .... AndrewGlassonbury(7) —
(C J Down) *j. bdly rt 1st: in tch: rdn and struggling 7th: wknd next: p.u after 9th* **9/4**[1]

5m 34.4s (9.60) **Going Correction** +0.70s/f (Soft) **6** Ran SP% **110.7**
Speed ratings: **109,106,101,96,— —** CSF £15.02 TOTE £3.50: £2.20, £2.90; EX 11.70.
Owner D R L Evans **Bred** Mrs D J Evans **Trained** Sullington, W Sussex

FOCUS
A fair winning time for the class, almost 11 seconds faster than the opening novice hurdle, and the form looks sound enough.

NOTEBOOK
Up At Midnight ◆, winner of a fair race at Kempton last season, had not gone on from that in three starts since, but with her reappearance outing under her belt she was able to find her winning form again, excelling under a positive ride and really attacking her hurdles before staying on strongly up the straight. Clearly effective in testing conditions, she gives the impression three miles will be within her stamina range and this unexposed mare can win off a higher mark before tackling fences next season. *(op 11-4 tchd 5-2)*
Carly Bay has largely been out of form, but she showed a little more when fourth last time and she raced with plenty of zest here, travelling well until slipping before the bend turning in. She was unable to get near the winner in the straight, but it is hoped she can build on this and find a small race. *(tchd 5-1)*
Penny's Crown ran well to a point, holding her own with the front two until being dropped after the third-last. She has largely struggled since winning at Taunton in December and needs a little help from the Handicapper. *(op 8-1 tchd 10-1)*
Dancing Shirley kept going in her own time, but was beaten a long way and she remains winless. *(op 20-1)*
Lady Alderbrook(IRE), who ran well when second in bottomless conditions when second at Fontwell, may still have been feeling the effects of that as she had a hard enough race and was *never travelling. She is better than this, but now has a little to prove.Official explanation: jockey said mare made mistake at first and was never travelling thereafter (op 6-1)*
Orbys Girl(IRE), reverting to hurdles, ran well to halfway in the first-time blinkers, but was soon dropped and recorded a tame effort. *(op 6-1)*

4152 THB BRITISH EQUESTRIAN AMATEUR RIDERS' H'CAP CHASE (FOR THE GAY KINDERSLEY SALVER) (18 fncs) 3m 2f
4:25 (4:25) (Class 4) (0-115,111) 5-Y-O **£3,615** (£1,139; £576; £295; £154)

Form RPR

4511 **1** **Tallow Bay (IRE)**[13] 3909 11-9-11 **85** oh2 .... MrGTumelty(3) 96
(Mrs S Wall) *wl in rr: reminders after 12th: lft in 3rd 14th: sn pressed ldr: looked btn 2 out: rallied flat to ld last stride* **4/1**[3]

025P **2** *shd* **Spring Grove (IRE)**[9] 3988 11-11-5 **111** .... MrlChanin(7) 123+
(R H Alner) *settled in rr: outpcd 13th: lft cl up next: sn led: drew 5l clr 2 out: bmpd along flat: hdd last stride* **8/1**

3535 **3** *16* **Dun Locha Castle (IRE)**[13] 3909 11-10-0 **85** oh2 .... MissPGundry 80
(N R Mitchell) *led to 4th: w ldr to 9th: outpcd 13th: lft in tch next: sn no ch: plugged on to take modest 3rd flat* **8/1**

P201 **4** *¾* **Ebony Jack (IRE)**[8] 4007 9-9-12 **86** 7ex .... (p) MissCTizzard(3) 80
(C L Tizzard) *w ldr: led 4th to 9th: pressed ldr tl stmbld 13th and lost pl: lft in ld next: sn hdd: wknd 3 out* **3/1**[1]

1/U5 **5** *dist* **Mcsnappy**[58] 3140 9-10-0 **92** .... MissRAGreen(7) —
(J W Mullins) *mstke 5th: a in last pair: outpcd 13th: no ch after: t.o: btn 49l* **25/1**

4-3P **R** **Surefast**[93] 2502 11-10-3 **91** .... MrTJO'Brien(3) —
(K Bishop) *last fr 3rd and gng bdly: lost tch 5th: t.o whn ref and uns rdr 8th* **9/1**

0P61 **F** **Sarahs Quay (IRE)**[6] 4041 7-10-0 **90** 7ex ow5 .... (p) MrMatthewSmith(5) —
(K J Burke) *trckd ldrs: mstke 7th: led 9th: mstke 11th: clr w one rival whn fell 14th* **10/1**

00F1 **U** **Happy Shopper (IRE)**[9] 3981 6-11-0 **102** .... MrDEdwards(3) —
(M C Pipe) *trckd ldrs: mstke 8th: wnt 2nd after 13th: clr of rest whn blnd bdly and uns rdr next* **7/2**[2]

7m 7.50s (13.50) **Going Correction** +0.60s/f (Soft) **8** Ran SP% **112.4**
Speed ratings: **103,102,98,97,— —,—,—** CSF £33.82 CT £240.56 TOTE £6.10: £1.70, £2.20, £1.60; EX 40.80.
Owner Mrs S Wall **Bred** Mrs S P H Oliver **Trained** Dallington, E Sussex

FOCUS
A moderate event but an interesting race and a close finish. The form looks reasonable with the winner improving and the runner-up to his mark.

NOTEBOOK
Tallow Bay(IRE), who has been in cracking form, winning his last two starts and shooting from a mark of 62 to 85, looked to be struggling from some way out, but he responded well to pressure and was a clear second turning in. Spring Grove looked to have things under control jumping the last, but Tumelty conjured a strong run out of him and in the end it was the jockeys that made the difference. He will go up again for this and may struggle to defy a further rise, but there is the possibility of further improvement back under more positive tactics.
Spring Grove(IRE), extremely well handicapped on his old form, shot clear rounding for home and looked to have the race secure, but he received little assistance from the saddle and was unable to repel the determined challenge of Tallow Bay. He probably deserved to win, but a victory should not be too far off if he is able to repeat the effort off this sort of mark. *(tchd 9-1)*
Dun Locha Castle(IRE) again ran his race, taking them along early before becoming outpaced. He tries hard enough, but finds winning difficult and may need some assistance from the Handicapper. *(op 10-1)*
Ebony Jack(IRE), who had a hard race in winning at Fontwell recently, may still have been feeling the effects of that effort and failed to see out his race as strongly as could have been expected. *(op 10-3 tchd 7-2 and 11-4)*
Mcsnappy again offered little and has yet to prove he retains all his ability since returning from injury.
Surefast is capable on his day, but he has thrown in a couple of moody displays thus far this season and was working hard when pulling the plug at the eighth. *(op 11-4 tchd 4-1)*
Sarahs Quay(IRE), bidding to follow-up her recent Sedgefield success, was still going nicely under her 7lb penalty when coming down at the fourth-last. It is hoped this does not affect her confidence. *(op 11-4 tchd 4-1)*
Happy Shopper(IRE) was going nicely enough and had Spring Grove in his sights when blundering badly and unseating his rider at the fifth from the finish. He may well have been unbeaten over fences had his jumping been a little slicker, having fallen at Lingfield when still in front, and he should remain capable of winning off this sort of mark. *(op 11-4 tchd 4-1)*

4153 WEATHERBYS MESSAGING SERVICE H'CAP HURDLE (9 hdls) 2m
4:55 (4:55) (Class 4) (0-115,113) 4-Y-0+ £4,554 (£1,337; £668; £333)

Form RPR
-221 1 **Misbehaviour**[4] 4075 7-10-12 104 7ex ChristopherMurray(5) 109+
(Jim Best) *racd wd: hld up in last: outpcd after 5th: stdy prog bef 3 out: poised to chal whn lft in ld 2 out: drvn out flat* **2/1**[1]
0543 2 6 **Anna Panna**[34] 3550 5-10-5 92 AndrewThornton 94+
(R H Alner) *racd wd: trckd ldr: led after 3 out gng strly: pressed whn blnd 2 out and hdd: nt rcvr* **11/4**[2]
1P23 3 9 **Josear**[15] 3889 4-10-12 113 ShaneWalsh(5) 96+
(C J Down) *racd wd: led: hdd and outpcd after 3 out* **4/1**[3]
2105 4 2 **Silistra**[24] 3719 7-10-1 88 (p) BenjaminHitchcott 76
(Mrs L C Jewell) *racd on inner: in tch tl outpcd bef 6th: n.d after: plugged on* **10/1**
5340 5 24 **Devito (FR)**[26] 3675 5-11-5 113 MrDEdwards(7) 77
(G F Edwards) *racd on inner: cl up: outpcd after 6th: no ch after 3 out: wknd* **10/1**
6130 6 22 **Shaka's Pearl**[23] 3729 6-11-4 105 JamesDavies 47
(N J Gifford) *racd on outer: cl up: rdn after 5th: outpcd fr next: sn struggling: t.o* **7/1**
41-0 P **Fireside Legend (IRE)**[278] 502 7-9-9 87 oh10(v) RobertLucey-Butler(5) —
(Miss M P Bryant) *racd towards inner: in tch to 5th: sn wknd and t.o: p.u bef 2 out* **50/1**

4m 11.0s (9.80) **Going Correction** +0.70s/f (Soft)
WFA 4 from 5yo+ 9lb 7 Ran SP% **112.6**
Speed ratings: **103,100,95,94,82 71**,— CSF £7.95 TOTE £2.20: £2.30, £1.70; EX 8.30 Place 6 £22.09, Place 5 £11.80 .
Owner The Bad Boys **Bred** Mrs R Pease **Trained** Lewes, E Sussex

FOCUS
An uncompetitive contest in which the front two drew clear. The winner ran to the level of his previous win and the runner-up is rated as having finished closer and having run to his mark.

NOTEBOOK
Misbehaviour, a recent winner at Huntingdon, had just about joined Anna Panna when that one hit the second-last, leaving her clear to win cosily. She is evidently in cracking form at present and it will be interesting to see how much she is raised before assessing her chances of completing the hat-trick. *(tchd 9-4)*
Anna Panna has slowly been progressing in ordinary novice hurdles, and this switch to handicaps brought about improved effort. She still had every chance when blundering at the second-last and there is surely a mares-only handicap in her. *(op 7-2 tchd 5-2)*
Josear, a tough and consistent juvenile, took them along for most of the way, but was readily outpaced after the third-last and could only plug on at the one pace. He will continue to pay his way and may be ready for a rise in distance. *(op 3-1)*
Silistra was kept on what was probably the worse ground of all on the inside and unsurprisingly he failed to figure. *(op 14-1)*
Shaka's Pearl has gone the wrong way from her Towcester win in December and has a bit to prove at present. *(op 9-1)*
T/Plt: £18.00 to a £1 stake. Pool: £52,078.20. 2,108.75 winning tickets. T/Qpdt: £10.30 to a £1 stake. Pool: £3,117.40. 222.40 winning tickets. JN

4154 - (Foreign Racing) - See Raceform Interactive

3557 CATTERICK (L-H)
Tuesday, February 28

4155 Meeting Abandoned - Frost

3919 LEICESTER (R-H)
Tuesday, February 28

OFFICIAL GOING: Soft (heavy in places)
Wind: Fresh, behind Weather: Sunny but cold

4162 GG.COM BEGINNERS' CHASE (12 fncs) 2m
2:20 (2:20) (Class 4) 5-Y-0+ £6,320 (£1,907; £982; £520)

Form RPR
3143 1 **The Local**[33] 3580 6-11-0 117 (p) APMcCoy 123
(C R Egerton) *led: hit 6th: rdn and hdd appr 2 out: styd on u.p to ld last 50 yds* **1/2**[1]
43UU 2 hd **Give Me Love (FR)**[3] 4102 6-10-9 119 (bt) LiamHeard(5) 124+
(P F Nicholls) *trckd wnr: racd keenly: led appr 2 out: rdn whn mstke last: hdd fnl 50 yds: styd on* **11/4**[2]
3340 3 dist **Kercabellec (FR)**[5] 4076 8-11-0 79 RichardHobson —
(J R Cornwall) *chsd ldrs to 3 out* **50/1**
5U-5 4 dist **Risington**[13] 3920 8-11-0 SamThomas —
(Miss Venetia Williams) *hld up in tch: mstke 7th: wkng whn hit 3 out* **14/1**
0-P2 P **Razzamatazz**[26] 3686 8-11-0 95 WayneHutchinson —
(R Dickin) *prom: dropped rr 3rd: bhd whn blnd 5th: t.o whn p.u bef 4 out* **12/1**[3]

4m 10.9s (3.30) **Going Correction** +0.20s/f (Yiel) 5 Ran SP% **109.7**
Speed ratings: **99,98**,—,—,— CSF £2.37 TOTE £1.10: £1.10, £1.40; EX 2.50.
Owner Barry Marsden **Bred** Chippenham Lodge Stud And Rathbarry Stud **Trained** Chaddleworth, Berks

FOCUS
No strength in depth to this beginners' chase but the form looks reasonable as the early pace was fair and the two market leaders ran to their marks in playing out the finish.

NOTEBOOK
The Local, equipped with first-time cheekpieces, eventually required all of McCoy's strength to prevail in his battle with the runner-up and register his first success over fences at the third attempt. He clearly likes this venue, as he has now been successful over hurdles and fences from just two outings at the track, and a soft surface is also important to him. However, he will probably need to improve to defy a penalty in better company. *(tchd 4-7)*
Give Me Love(FR), despite taking a pull through the early parts, looked booked for success when hitting the front at the penultimate fence, but he did not find much, and could offer no more when rechallenged by the winner close home. He was well clear of the remainder, and this was his best display for some time, but he is clearly a tricky customer. *(op 3-1)*
Kercabellec(FR) faced a very stiff task at the weights and was not totally disgraced in the circumstances.
Risington never seriously figured and failed to improve on the form of his recent return to action. His one success between the flags came on a quick surface, so he may be capable of showing his true colours when reverting to better ground in the future. *(tchd 16-1)*

4163 SHERWOOD RANGERS YEOMANRY H'CAP CHASE (18 fncs) 2m 7f 110y
2:50 (2:50) (Class 4) (0-115,112) 5-Y-0 £6,338 (£1,872; £936; £468; £234)

Form RPR
4-P1 1 **Yes My Lord (IRE)**[14] 3905 7-11-0 100 TimmyMurphy 116+
(M C Pipe) *trckd ldrs: led 10th to 12th: led 2 out: drvn out* **7/2**[1]
6P02 2 1 **Hawk's Landing (IRE)**[11] 3965 9-11-6 106 APMcCoy 119
(Jonjo O'Neill) *hld up in tch: ev ch fr 3 out: rdn flat: nt qckn nr fin* **5/1**[3]
4240 3 20 **Elvis Returns**[47] 3352 8-11-5 110 TJDreaper(5) 103
(J M Jefferson) *chsd ldrs: mstke 12th: n.m.r 4 out: rdn and wknd next : no ch whn hit 2 out* **28/1**
0113 4 2 **Merry Storm (IRE)**[47] 3359 7-10-1 94 RichardSpate(7) 85+
(Mrs K Waldron) *hld up: hdwy 13th: led appr 3 out: rdn and hdd next: wknd qckly bef last* **4/1**[2]
1601 5 10 **Monger Lane**[35] 3547 10-10-8 94 PJBrennan 77+
(K Bishop) *chsd ldrs: rdn after 10th: wknd 4 out* **7/2**[1]
PU0F 6 dist **Buzybakson (IRE)**[13] 3923 9-10-1 87 oh7 ow1 RichardHobson —
(J R Cornwall) *hld up: rdn after 6th: bhd fr 9th* **80/1**
1433 7 20 **Channahrlie (IRE)**[29] 3649 12-10-3 89 (p) WayneHutchinson —
(R Dickin) *led to 10th: led 13th: hdd & wknd appr 3 out* **10/1**
-30P 8 28 **General Gossip (IRE)**[52] 3293 10-11-12 112 WarrenMarston —
(R T Phillips) *hld up: hdwy 8th: wknd 11th* **28/1**
4556 U **Highland Chief (IRE)**[54] 3246 6-10-7 93 SamThomas —
(Miss H C Knight) *hld up in tch: lost pl after 6th: last whn mstke and uns rdr 8th* **15/2**

6m 8.10s (2.70) **Going Correction** +0.20s/f (Yiel) 9 Ran SP% **110.1**
Speed ratings: **103,102,96,95,92** —,—,—,— CSF £19.97 CT £383.46 TOTE £4.50: £2.40, £2.30, £4.80; EX 23.60.
Owner D A Johnson **Bred** Owen Dermody **Trained** Nicholashayne, Devon

FOCUS
A modest handicap, run at a fair gallop, and the first two came well clear. The form looks sound rated through the third.

NOTEBOOK
Yes My Lord(IRE), off the mark over timber at Fontwell a fortnight previously, followed-up in good style to make a winning chase debut from a 7lb higher mark. He had no trouble with the extra furlong and, while another rise in the weights is inevitable, he remains unexposed and should go close in his quest for the hat-trick. *(op 4-1 tchd 9-2)*
Hawk's Landing(IRE), narrowly denied at Market Rasen last time and racing off a 6lb higher mark, posted another improved effort and finished well clear of the rest. He was not all that suited by this drop back in trip, however, and is certainly capable of winning from this mark when reverting to around three miles.
Elvis Returns was put in his place from three out and again was not all that fluent over his fences. He has not progressed as looked likely at the start of the current campaign, but this was still an improved effort, and he should do better as he gains further experience over fences. *(op 33-1)*
Merry Storm(IRE) failed to improve for this return to his favoured soft ground and faded rather tamely having moved well until jumping three out. He has a bit to prove now. *(tchd 7-2)*
Monger Lane, raised 8lb for winning on her return to chasing over course and distance 35 days previously, turned in a moody-looking effort and was beaten a long way out. She is capable of better, but seemingly has two ways of running. *(op 10-3 tchd 3-1 and 6-1)*

4164 DAN FROST MEMORIAL NOVICES' H'CAP CHASE (15 fncs) 2m 4f 110y
3:20 (3:22) (Class 5) (0-90,90) 5-Y-0+ £3,578 (£1,050; £525; £262)

Form RPR
550 1 **Parkinson (IRE)**[26] 3685 5-9-10 72 ShaneWalsh(5) 87+
(Jonjo O'Neill) *hld up: hdwy 5th: led appr 3 out: clr next* **12/1**
6402 2 12 **Iloveturtle (IRE)**[11] 3958 6-10-7 71 (t) KennyJohnson 78
(M C Chapman) *hld up: hdwy 10th: ev ch appr 3 out: styd on same pce fr next* **20/1**
4/U4 3 1 1/4 **Spinaround**[46] 3368 8-11-2 80 TomDoyle 86
(P R Webber) *hld up: hdwy 7th: styd on same pce fr 2 out* **4/1**[2]
0PP0 4 20 **Be Telling (IRE)**[46] 3367 7-11-7 85 PaulMoloney 71
(B J Curley) *hld up: effrt after 4 out: sn wknd* **20/1**
3441 5 10 **Foxmeade Dancer**[2] 4132 8-10-6 70 7ex AndrewThornton 61+
(P C Ritchens) *prom: hmpd and lost pl 7th: hdwy appr 3 out: sn wknd: bhd whn blnd last* **7/2**[1]
3-6P 6 9 **Smurfit (IRE)**[24] 3732 7-11-0 78 (p) NoelFehily 45
(C C Bealby) *prom tl wknd after 4 out* **25/1**
/023 7 17 **Carl's Boy**[278] 519 10-9-11 68 MrPSheldrake(7) 18
(D A Rees) *hld up: mstke 4th: hmpd 5 out: effrt after next: sn wknd* **10/1**
00B- P **Its A Cracker (IRE)**[483] 1968 7-10-0 64 oh1 TimmyMurphy —
(M C Pipe) *hld up: bhd whn p.u after 7th* **8/1**
00-P U **Logger Rhythm (USA)**[23] 73 6-10-0 64 WayneHutchinson —
(R Dickin) *mstke 1st: blnd and uns rdr next* **40/1**
6-PP F **Terminology**[12] 3943 8-11-12 90 JohnMcNamara —
(K C Bailey) *hld up in tch: mstke 10th: cl 6th whn fell 5 out* **66/1**
4445 P **Caper**[16] 3888 6-11-5 83 TomScudamore —
(R Hollinshead) *hld up: a in rr: bhd whn hmpd 3 out: t.o whn p.u bef last* **16/1**
000P P **Miniperse (FR)**[59] 3147 6-10-10 81 MrLRPayter(7) —
(G R I Smyly) *mid-div: racd keenly: wkng whn hit 10th: bhd whn p.u bef 4 out* **150/1**
6PP- F **Gloster Gunner**[510] 1607 7-10-0 64 PJBrennan —
(T R George) *chsd ldrs: led 3rd to next: led 9th: hdd and wkng whn fell 3 out* **7/1**[3]
06PF C **Back De Bay (IRE)**[29] 3652 6-9-12 65 LeeVickers(3) —
(J R Cornwall) *mid-div: hdwy 4th: rdn after 8th: wknd 10th: bhd whn p.u bef 4 out* **100/1**
003 F **Castle Frome (IRE)**[13] 3920 7-11-9 87 (v[1]) OllieMcPhail —
(A E Price) *trckd ldrs: plld hrd: led 3rd to next: led and blnd 5th: hdd next: cl up whn fell 7th* **28/1**
24U4 B **Luckycharm (FR)**[27] 3672 7-10-1 65 (v) JamieMoore —
(R Dickin) *led to 3rd: led 4th to next: led 6th: hmpd by loose horse appr 8th: hdd next: wkng whn b.d 3 out* **20/1**

5m 26.8s (3.20) **Going Correction** +0.20s/f (Yiel)
WFA 5 from 6yo+ 7lb 16 Ran SP% **115.7**
Speed ratings: **101,96,95,88,84 81,74**,—,—,—,—,—,—,—,—,— — CSF £219.19 CT £1131.66 TOTE £14.50: £4.10, £2.70, £1.60, £9.00; EX 213.60.
Owner Trevor Hemmings **Bred** E J O'Sullivan **Trained** Cheltenham, Gloucs
■ Stewards' Enquiry : Mr L R Payter two-day ban: careless riding (Mar 12-13)

FOCUS
A weak handicap, run at a decent early gallop, and the field came home strung out. The winner is value for further with the modest runner-up setting the level.

NOTEBOOK

Parkinson(IRE), who showed little in three previous outings over hurdles this term, finally showed his true colours and ran out a clear-cut winner on this handicap and chase debut under Rules. While this was a weak affair, he could not have done the job much easier, and jumped with aplomb throughout. A hike in the weights is likely after this, but he is at the right end of the handicap to *progress further as a chaser. Official explanation: trainer said, regarding the improved form shown, gelding was having its first run over fences (op 14-1)*

Iloveturtle(IRE) held every chance, but was firmly put in his place by the winner, and the drop back in trip proved against him. He is slowly going the right way in this sphere, has dropped to a fair mark now, and can be placed to get off the mark when reverting to further in due course. *(op 16-1)*

Spinaround had his chance, yet could offer no more from two out and was readily held at the finish. He is up to winning from this current mark, but ideally wants better ground. *(op 9-2)*

Be Telling(IRE), making his chase debut, showed a little improvement despite being well beaten. He is probably better over further. *(op 18-1)*

Foxmeade Dancer, a comfortable winner at Fontwell two days previously, got badly hampered at the seventh fence and that proved costly. He is worth another chance to prove his worth. *(op 3-1)*

Its A Cracker(IRE), making his chase and handicap debut after 483-day layoff, proved disappointing yet may well have needed the outing and is surely capable of better in this sphere from his current lowly mark. *(op 7-1)*

4165 LEICESTERSHIRE AND DERBYSHIRE YEOMANRY H'CAP CHASE (AMATEUR RIDERS) (15 fncs) 2m 4f 110y

3:50 (3:50) (Class 4) (0-105,102) 5-Y-0+ **£4,909** (£1,565; £806; £426)

Form — RPR

F323 **1** **Randolph O'Brien (IRE)**[19] [3815] 6-10-12 **93** MrDEngland(5) 115+
(N A Twiston-Davies) *chsd ldrs: led 5th: clr 2 out* **5/4**[1]

-PPO **2** *dist* **Red Alert Man (IRE)**[43] [3427] 10-9-11 **76** oh13 (b) MrGTumelty(3) —
(Mrs L Williamson) *led: j.lft 3rd: hdd next: rdn whn hit 7th: sn wknd: tk remote 2nd towards fin* **10/1**

4500 **3** *3 1/2* **Polish Pilot (IRE)**[26] [3686] 11-9-7 **76** oh6 MissUMoore(7) —
(J R Cornwall) *bhd fr 5th: lft remote 2nd last: lost runner-up spot towards fin* **20/1**

P6PO **4** *23* **Per Amore (IRE)**[13] [3922] 8-11-5 **102** (b) MrWKinsey(7) —
(David Pearson) *bhd fr 5th* **40/1**

/4FP **U** **Predestine (FR)**[42] [3434] 6-11-4 **97** MrJSnowden(3) —
(K C Bailey) *w ldr: led 4th to next: wknd 9th: blnd and uns rdr 4 out* **10/3**[3]

4454 **F** **Jour De Mee (FR)**[9] [4013] 9-10-8 **87** MrTJO'Brien(3) 79
(Mrs H Dalton) *prom: chsd wnr 7th: rdn and ev ch 3 out: wknd next: clr 2nd whn fell last* **3/1**[2]

5m 24.0s (0.40) **Going Correction** +0.20s/f (Yiel) **6** Ran SP% **108.8**
Speed ratings: **107**,—,—,—,— — CSF £12.48 TOTE £2.40: £1.30, £2.70; EX 10.10.
Owner Geoffrey & Donna Keeys **Bred** Miss Alison And David Laverty **Trained** Naunton, Gloucs

FOCUS

A poor handicap that saw an easy winner in a decent time but the form should be treated with caution.

NOTEBOOK

Randolph O'Brien(IRE) gained a deserved career-first success with a most convincing display. He acted on the testing surface without fuss, and put in his best round of jumping to date, but while his confidence should be sky high now, he may well struggle in the future if the Handicapper takes this form literally. *(op 11-8)*

Red Alert Man(IRE) is flattered by his finishing position and looked very slow. This was still a slightly-improved display, however. *(op 8-1)*

Polish Pilot(IRE) saw booked for second spot, but his rider took it too easy on the run-in and he was eventually denied the runner-up spot. *(op 16-1)*

Jour De Mee(FR), reverting to fences, was clear in second prior to taking a tired fall at the final fence and looks in need of a break.

4166 RUTLAND WATER NOVICES' CHASE (18 fncs) 2m 7f 110y

4:20 (4:20) (Class 3) 5-Y-0+ **£9,799** (£3,180; £1,792)

Form — RPR

P11F **1** **Millenaire (FR)**[68] [2953] 7-12-0 126 APMcCoy 136+
(Jonjo O'Neill) *hld up: hdwy 9th: hung rt and lft fr 3 out: led next: drvn clr flat* **4/1**[3]

3124 **2** *10* **Reflected Glory (IRE)**[7] [4035] 7-12-0 134 ChristianWilliams 131+
(P F Nicholls) *chsd ldrs: mstke 7th: led 10th: hdd 2 out: 2l 2nd and rdn whn blnd last: wknd flat* **5/6**[1]

OFF3 **3** *dist* **Murphy's Magic (IRE)**[28] [3662] 8-11-4 85 (p) AndrewThornton —
(Mrs T J Hill) *hld up: effrt 13th: wknd 4 out: lft remote 3rd 2 out* **20/1**

PP-P **F** **Kim Buck (FR)**[146] [1644] 8-10-12 ow1 MrSPeltell(7) —
(K A Morgan) *hld up: bhd fr 7th: fell 10th* **100/1**

606P **F** **Ashleybank House (IRE)**[9] [4012] 9-11-4 94 (tp) RichardHobson —
(David Pearson) *led to 2nd: led 6th tl after 8th: rdn and wkng whn fell 11th* **100/1**

112- **F** **Hunting Yuppie (IRE)**[507] [1652] 9-11-4 CarlLlewellyn 106
(N A Twiston-Davies) *led 2nd to 6th: led after 8th to 10th: hung lft after 3 out: 3rd and wkng whn fell next* **5/2**[2]

6m 15.4s (10.00) **Going Correction** +0.40s/f (Soft) **6** Ran SP% **109.9**
Speed ratings: **99,95**,—,—,— — CSF £7.89 TOTE £4.50: £1.80, £1.20; EX 8.60.
Owner The Risky Partnership **Bred** Pierre J Delage **Trained** Cheltenham, Gloucs

FOCUS

A fair novice event that saw the field finish strung out in the conditions, and the form is not that solid and should be treated with a degree of caution.

NOTEBOOK

Millenaire(FR), easy to back, found the race run to suit and got back to winning ways in ready fashion. He hs now been successful on both his starts over course and distance, this represented a career-best effort, and it proved his versatility as regards underfoot conditions. *(op 7-2)*

Reflected Glory(IRE) had his chance, but could not live with the winner from the penultimate fence and was eventually well held. He would have most likely found this coming soon enough after his latest outing a week previously at Exeter and would likely benefit from a break now. *(op 10-11 tchd evens in a place)*

Murphy's Magic(IRE) kept to his task and was not disgraced at the weights. He ideally wants better ground and should be capable of winning a handicap from his current mark granted a stiffer test in due course. *(tchd 22-1)*

Hunting Yuppie(IRE) was well backed on this return from a 507-day layoff, but he was treading water from the final bend, and took a tired fall two out. He may need time to recover from this experience. *(op 3-1)*

4167 QUEENS ROYAL LANCERS MAIDEN HUNTERS' CHASE (18 fncs) 2m 7f 110y

4:50 (4:50) (Class 5) 6-Y-0+ **£2,430** (£759; £379; £189; £94)

Form — RPR

P/2 **1** **Bill Haze**[13] [3924] 10-11-10 MrPSheldrake(7) 102+
(P Dando) *plld hrd and prom: led 2 out: flashed tail run-in: drvn out* **20/1**

200/ **2** *1 1/4* **Ramirez (IRE)**[359] 8-11-10 MrNickKent(7) 100
(Nick Kent) *hld up: hdwy 8th: chsd wnr appr last: styd on* **5/1**[3]

S-22 **3** *17* **Reasonably Sure (IRE)**[14] [3913] 6-12-3 (b) MrTGreenall 86+
(David M Easterby) *hld up: hdwy 4 out: hit 2 out: sn wknd* **9/4**[1]

0U6/ **4** *8* **Bonny Boy (IRE)**[10] 11-11-10 (vt) MrJoshuaHarris(7) 81+
(D A Rees) *prom: racd keenly: led 9th: hdd 2 out: blnd and wknd last* **40/1**

5 *11* **Talioso (IRE)**[408] 9-11-12 MissSSharratt(5) 64
(R Hollinshead) *led and nt a fluent: hdd 9th: hit 12th and 14th: wknd after 4 out* **6/1**

6 *21* **Solar King**[10] 10-11-10 (p) MrPMann(7) 43
(Mrs J M Mann) *mid-div: rdn 6th: wknd 10th* **66/1**

4F0- **7** *8* **Lady Baronette**[31] 9-11-5 MrAndrewMartin(5) 28
(Ian Howe) *chsd ldrs: lost pl 4th: wknd 9th* **18/1**

PUU- **F** **Wyle Post (IRE)**[283] 7-11-10 MrWBiddick(7) —
(Mrs K Waldron) *hld up: hdwy 8th: fell 12th* **10/1**

P **Our Bill**[30] 8-11-10 MrWKinsey(7) —
(David Pearson) *hld up: j.lft 6th: lost tch 8th: t.o whn p.u bef 12th* **100/1**

P **Lord Of The Bog (IRE)**[51] 7-11-10 MrPMason(7) —
(B Tulloch) *chsd ldrs: hit 8th: wknd 4 out: t.o whn p.u bef 2 out* **3/1**[2]

P **Pollerton Run (IRE)**[10] 8-11-10 MrGDavies(7) —
(T G Williams) *in rr whn hit 5th: bhd fr 7th: t.o whn p.u after next: b.b.v* **100/1**

2PP/ **P** **Green Smoke**[993] [622] 10-11-10 (p) MrNPearce(7) —
(Miss M J Benson) *prom: mstke 1st: hit 7th: sn rdn: wknd 9th: t.o whn p.u bef 11th* **20/1**

6m 15.0s (9.60) **Going Correction** +0.40s/f (Soft) **12** Ran SP% **116.5**
Speed ratings: **100,99,93,91,87 80,77**,—,—,— —,— CSF £113.03 TOTE £31.10: £4.30, £2.10, £1.10; EX 115.10 Place 6 £22.07, Place 5 £19.91.
Owner P Dando **Bred** Mrs K M Dando **Trained** Cardiff

■ Stewards' Enquiry : Mr Nick Kent two-day ban: used whip with excessive frequency, without giving gelding time to respond and in the wrong place (Mar 12-13)

FOCUS

A moderate hunter chase that saw the first two come clear on the run-in. The form might work out but it could be too high.

NOTEBOOK

Bill Haze, despite showing temperament under pressure when in front on the run-in, was always holding sway over the runner-up and ran out a deserved winner. He is value for further and clearly likes this venue.

Ramirez(IRE) ◆, last seen winning between the flags 359 days previously, posted a solid return to action and was closing on the idling winner at the finish. The return to three miles and a less-taxing surface in the future should see back in the winner's enclosure. *(op 11-2 tchd 6-1)*

Reasonably Sure(IRE) was not helped by a mistake two from home, but was always being held by the front pair and this must rate a below-par effort. *(tchd 5-2)*

Bonny Boy(IRE) proved a sitting duck nearing the penultimate fence and was treading water when blundering over the last. *(op 50-1)*

Talioso(IRE), a notable drifter in the betting ring, did not convince at his fences and was beaten at the top of the straight. He probably hated this taxing surface, however, and is capable of improving when returning to quicker ground. *(op 10-3)*

Pollerton Run(IRE) *Official explanation: vet said gelding bled from nose (op 4-1 tchd 9-2)*

Lord Of The Bog(IRE) was well backed, yet looked unhappy on the ground and was disappointingly pulled up. *(op 4-1 tchd 9-2)*

T/Plt: £22.20 to a £1 stake. Pool: £66,503.45. 2,181.50 winning tickets. T/Qpdt: £9.80 to a £1 stake. Pool: £5,040.50. 380.40 winning tickets. CR

3905 FOLKESTONE (R-H)

Wednesday, March 1

4168 Meeting Abandoned - Frost

3736 WETHERBY (L-H)

Wednesday, March 1

4175 Meeting Abandoned - Frost

4046 LUDLOW (R-H)

Thursday, March 2

4189 Meeting Abandoned - Frost

3945 TAUNTON (R-H)

Thursday, March 2

4196 Meeting Abandoned - Frost

4203 - 4209a (Foreign Racing) - See Raceform Interactive

3340 NEWBURY (L-H)

Friday, March 3

OFFICIAL GOING: Good (good to soft in places) changing to good after race 2 (2.00)

The meeting went ahead after the entire track was covered with the material used to protect crops from frost.

Wind: Virtually nil

4210 STAN JAMES CONDITIONAL JOCKEYS' NOVICES' H'CAP HURDLE (11 hdls) 2m 3f

1:30 (1:30) (Class 4) (0-105,105) 4-Y-0+ **£3,220** (£938; £469)

Form — RPR

-340 **1** **New Mischief (IRE)**[27] [3729] 8-11-5 **98** (t) JohnKington 101+
(Noel T Chance) *trckd ldrs: chal 2 out: led sn after: nt fluent last: drvn run-in: jst hld on* **14/1**

34P5 **2** *shd* **Zouave (IRE)**[46] [3415] 5-10-4 **91** (b) KevinTobin(8) 92
(C J Mann) *mid div: hit 3rd: hdwy 3 out: styd on str run-in: fin strly: jst failed* **50/1**

4P01 **3** *1* **Top Brass (IRE)**[16] [3927] 5-10-12 **97** .... JamesReveley(6) 98+
(K G Reveley) *lw: led: t.k.h early: rdn and hit 2 out: hdd sn after: hung lft u.p and no ex nr fin* **7/1**[2]

0224 **4** *nk* **The Castilian (FR)**[8] [4075] 4-10-8 **99** ....(v) AndrewGlassonbury(3) 90
(M C Pipe) *hld up in rr: stdy hdwy appr 3 out: qcknd to chal run-in: shkn up: fnd nthing and sn btn* **9/1**

500 **5** *4* **Penny Park (IRE)**[14] [3963] 7-10-5 **90** .... DarrenO'Dwyer(6) 87+
(P J Hobbs) *lw: chsd ldrs: rdn 2 out: wknd last* **13/2**[1]

0-03 **6** *3 ½* **Barclay Boy**[28] [3719] 7-11-12 **105** .... DavidCullinane 98
(A J Lidderdale) *bhd: hdwy appr 3 out: styd on same pce fr next* **10/1**

5054 **7** *1 ¼* **Flirty Jill**[23] [3806] 5-10-8 **90** ....(t) KeiranBurke(3) 81
(P R Webber) *chsd ldrs: hit 3 out: sn outpcd* **10/1**

0001 **8** *2* **Silverio (GER)**[5] [4133] 5-10-3 **85** 7ex .... JayPemberton(3) 74
(G L Moore) *bhd: hdwy and wd after 4 out: nvr gng pce to trble ldrs* **9/1**

424 **9** *2* **Panzer (GER)**[29] [3685] 5-11-5 **98** .... EwanWhillans 85
(D McCain) *bhd: hdwy 4 out: rdn and mstke 3 out: sn wknd* **15/2**[3]

P210 **10** *½* **Desert Secrets (IRE)**[6] [3722] 4-10-9 **100** .... DavidBoland(3) 78
(J G Portman) *chsd ldrs: wnt 2nd 3 out: rdn sn after: wknd after next* **11/1**

-00F **11** *½* **Avesomeofthat (IRE)**[197] [753] 5-10-13 **95** .... WayneKavanagh(3) 81
(J W Mullins) *bhd: hdwy 5th: chsd ldrs appr 3 out: wknd next* **33/1**

0F00 **12** *1 ¼* **Thievery**[77] [2859] 5-10-5 **89** .... CraigThompson(5) 74
(H D Daly) *lw: bhd: sme hdwy and wd after 4 out: n.d* **20/1**

2F04 **13** *1* **Murphy's Nails (IRE)**[67] [2958] 9-10-8 **95** ....(p) NathanSmith(8) 79
(K C Bailey) *chsd ldrs to 4 out: wknd bef next* **20/1**

240P **14** *6* **Dan's Man**[23] [3806] 5-11-2 **98** .... BernieWharfe(3) 76
(N A Twiston-Davies) *chsd ldr: chal 4th: rdn 3 out: sn wknd* **20/1**

4660 **15** *nk* **Coeur D'Alene**[13] [3997] 5-10-13 **95** .... RyanCummings(3) 73
(Dr J R J Naylor) *a in rr* **66/1**

-060 **P** **Lannigans Lock**[46] [3425] 5-10-9 **91** .... RichardGordon(3) —
(R Rowe) *prom early: wknd 5th: t.o 6th: p.u bef 3 out* **14/1**

4m 36.2s (-10.60) **Going Correction** -0.525s/f (Firm)
WFA 4 from 5yo+ 7lb **16** Ran SP% **118.1**
Speed ratings: **101,100,100,100,98 97,96,95,95,94 94,94,93,91,91** — CSF £593.40 CT £5217.41 TOTE £17.10: £2.90, £8.80, £1.70, £1.90; EX 589.20.
Owner R W And J R Fidler **Bred** A Malone **Trained** Upper Lambourn, Berks

FOCUS
A moderate event for the track, not run at a great pace. Although this was a slight personal best for the winner, and the second was also stepping up, there was not much of interest for the future.

NOTEBOOK
New Mischief(IRE) ◆, who had some fair form in bumpers in the distant past on similarly quick going, showed real battling qualities to just defy the late challenge of Zouave. Off the bridle some way from the line, he stuck on really well, after hitting the last, and should be competitive next time even when reassessed given his lowly rating. *(op 12-1)*
Zouave(IRE), who was a fair sort of the Flat and was making his handicap debut over hurdles, only got going late in the day and never quite got to the winner. He has become unpredictable over timber but clearly has the ability to win a race off a similar mark.
Top Brass(IRE), making his handicap debut, made a lot of the early running and kept on respectably when headed. His form has improved since he was treated for a trapped nerve in his back, prior to his win last time. *(op 5-1)*
The Castilian(FR) is fully entitled to any rude names given to him, as despite his jockey's best efforts, he once again found absolutely nothing when asked to quicken, this after looking to be going very easily halfway up the run in. He has become an in-running exchange layer's dream. *(tchd 10-1)*
Penny Park(IRE) did not shape without promise on his handicap debut but gave the impression that he did not quite get home. The jury is still out as to his preferred distance over hurdles. *(op 7-1 tchd 15-2)*
Barclay Boy ran fairly well under his big weight but appears to have little in hand of the Handicapper at this early stage of his career.
Lannigans Lock *Official explanation: vet said gelding bled from the nose (op 12-1)*

4211 KARCHER JUVENILE NOVICES' HURDLE (8 hdls) 2m 110y
2:00 (2:02) (Class 4) 4-Y-O **£3,253** (£955; £477; £238)

Form RPR

F2 **1** **Bureaucrat**[24] [3787] 4-10-12 .... RichardJohnson 115+
(P J Hobbs) *lw: mde all: keen early: c clr after 2 out: pushed out run-in: readily* **3/1**[2]

43 **2** *5* **Backbord (GER)**[24] [3786] 4-10-12 .... LeightonAspell 107
(Mrs L Wadham) *chsd ldrs: wnt 2nd and rdn 2 out: sn no ch w wnr but styd on wl for clr 2nd* **14/1**

2341 **3** *6* **Mahogany Blaze (FR)**[10] [4033] 4-11-5 .... CarlLlewellyn 109+
(N A Twiston-Davies) *bhd: j.big 3 out and rdn: hdwy and nt fluent 2 out: kpt on to take 3rd run-in but nvr gng pce to rch ldrs* **11/1**

6 **4** *7* **Daraybad (FR)**[35] [3594] 4-10-12 .... MickFitzgerald 96+
(N J Henderson) *ken hold early: chsd ldrs: rdn after 3 out: wknd after next* **8/1**[3]

5 *3* **Sea Wall**[197] 4-10-12 .... APMcCoy 92+
(Jonjo O'Neill) *lw: str: hld up mid-div: hdwy after 4 out: chsd ldrs and rdn 2 out: sn wknd* **11/4**[1]

F14 **6** *4* **Le Corvee (IRE)**[111] [2178] 4-11-5 .... RobertThornton 94
(A King) *in tch: lost position after 4 out: rdn and sme hdwy whn hit 3 out: n.d after* **11/4**[1]

50B **7** *1 ¼* **Patronage**[15] [3939] 4-10-12 .... NoelFehily 86
(Jonjo O'Neill) *bhd: pushed along appr 3 out: n.d* **50/1**

0 **8** *9* **Krasivi's Boy (USA)**[123] [1948] 4-10-12 .... PhilipHide 77
(G L Moore) *chsd ldrs: rdn and hit 3 out: sn wknd* **100/1**

4 **9** *shd* **Jubilee Dream**[18] [3898] 4-10-12 .... JamieMoore 77
(Mrs L J Mongan) *in tch: rdn and hdwy to chse ldrs appr 3 out: sn btn* **100/1**

10 *20* **Carpet Ride**[16] 4-10-7 .... JohnnyLevins(5) 57
(B G Powell) *w'like: str: t.o 4th: nvr in contention* **100/1**

5100 **11** *3 ½* **Quasimodo (IRE)**[27] [3722] 4-11-5 113 .... WayneHutchinson 88+
(A W Carroll) *chsd ldrs: rdn and hit 3 out: sn wknd* **33/1**

12 *26* **Suivez Moi (IRE)**[135] 4-10-12 .... PJBrennan 27
(M F Harris) *a in rr* **66/1**

5F **F** **Mac Federal (IRE)**[18] [3898] 4-10-2 .... TimothyBailey(10) 97
(M G Quinlan) *bhd: hdwy app 3 out: chsng ldrs whn nt fluent 2 out: disputing 5th and no ch whn hmpd and fell last* **25/1**

3m 51.9s (-11.70) **Going Correction** -0.525s/f (Firm) **13** Ran SP% **117.7**
Speed ratings: **106,103,100,97,96 94,93,89,89,79 78,66,—** CSF £40.96 TOTE £4.30: £1.50, £3.30, £2.70; EX 50.00.
Owner Peter Luff **Bred** Newgate Stud Co **Trained** Withycombe, Somerset

FOCUS
A solid-looking juvenile hurdle, run at a strong pace, in which the first two both improved for the better ground. The time was very good and the race should work out.

NOTEBOOK
Bureaucrat ◆ had shaped as if two miles stretched his stamina in his two previous races over timber, but ran out a ready winner on this quicker ground after leading at a brisk pace. Now those stamina fears seem to have been allayed, he looks like having a bright future over hurdles, and a decent race at Aintree, where his speed and aggressive style of running will be potent weapons, could be within his compass. The only negative to take form his performance was that he continually jumped out to the left over the hurdles. *(op 10-3 tchd 7-2)*
Backbord(GER) ◆ continues to shape well over hurdles and was one of a few in the race who gave the impression they would be suited by a step up in trip. He will now be handicapped and would be of some interest in that sphere given a realistic mark. *(op 12-1 tchd 16-1)*
Mahogany Blaze(FR), carrying a penalty, has always looked as though he needs a stiffer test at two miles, and he failed to land a blow after being held up off the pace. *(op 14-1 tchd 10-1)*
Daraybad(FR) ran with slightly more promise than he had done on his first run over timber, and may benefit from further in time. *(tchd 9-1)*
Sea Wall moved nicely for much of the race but simply failed to get involved. He will surely need further in time given his form on the Flat. *(op 7-2)*
Le Corvee(IRE), not seen since running in a hot juvenile event at Cheltenham in November, lost his position at the top of the straight and never got back into things after hitting the third last. This was a disappointing effort. *(op 9-4)*
Patronage finished sore according to his jockey. *Official explanation: jockey said gelding pulled up sore (tchd 40-1)*
Carpet Ride *Official explanation: jockey said gelding jumped poorly back straight*
Mac Federal(IRE) was staying on - albeit well held - when taking another heavy fall at the last. It remains to seen what affect this has on his confidence. *(op 20-1)*

4212 ARKELL'S 3B BITTER "NATIONAL HUNT" NOVICES' HURDLE (11 hdls) 2m 5f
2:30 (2:34) (Class 4) 5-Y-O+ **£4,554** (£1,337; £668; £333)

Form RPR

60U5 **1** **Orange Street**[31] [3664] 6-10-12 .... LeightonAspell 108+
(Mrs L J Mongan) *in tch: hdwy 6th: trcking ldrs whn blnd 3 out: cl 2nd and styng on wl whn lft in ld 2 out: pushed clr run-in* **20/1**

3 **2** *7* **Buster Collins (IRE)**[13] [3978] 6-10-12 .... TimmyMurphy 101+
(Miss E C Lavelle) *lw: led: hdd and hit 2 out: styd chsng wnr but sn no ch* **5/1**[3]

1/10 **3** *10* **Here's Johnny (IRE)**[57] [3248] 7-10-12 .... JimCrowley 92+
(V R A Dartnall) *t.k.h early: chsd ldrs: wnt 2nd 6th: ev ch 3 out: lft disputing ld whn bumped 2 out: wknd bef last* **15/8**[2]

-06F **4** *20* **Sparklinspirit**[23] [3806] 7-10-12 .... PhilipHide 70
(J L Spearing) *bhd: hdwy and mstke 3 out: nvr a danger* **28/1**

5 *2* **Sir Bathwick (IRE)** 7-10-12 .... NoelFehily 68
(B G Powell) *w'like: b.bkwd: nt fluent in rr: mod hdwy appr 3 out: nvr in contention* **25/1**

6/ **6** *24* **Christon Cane**[698] [4670] 8-10-12 .... AndrewThornton 44
(Dr J R J Naylor) *hit 6th: a bhd* **40/1**

0- **7** *¾* **All For A Reason (IRE)**[450] [2708] 7-10-9 .... OwynNelmes(3) 43
(Miss J R Gibney) *in tch: rdn and wknd 4 out* **66/1**

P **8** *2 ½* **Lyster (IRE)**[12] [4015] 7-10-7 .... JamesDiment(5) 41
(D L Williams) *chsd ldrs tl rdn 6th: sn wknd* **40/1**

0 **P** **Icomb (IRE)**[79] [2829] 6-10-12 .... PJBrennan —
(Mrs Susan Nock) *in tch: hit 4th: wknd 6th: p.u bef 3 out* **100/1**

1-13 **F** **Square Mile (IRE)**[32] [3646] 6-11-4 115 ....(t) APMcCoy 112
(Jonjo O'Neill) *lw: chsd ldr to 6th: drvn to take narrow ld whn fell 2 out* **11/8**[1]

05 **P** **Wednesday Country (IRE)**[29] [3699] 5-10-12 .... BenjaminHitchcott —
(J A T De Giles) *chsd ldrs tl mstke 4th: wknd 6th: t.o whn p.u bef 2 out* **40/1**

5m 1.90s (-11.10) **Going Correction** -0.525s/f (Firm) **11** Ran SP% **115.4**
Speed ratings: **100,97,93,85,85 76,75,74,—,—** — CSF £108.55 TOTE £28.60: £3.00, £1.80, £1.40; EX 167.50.
Owner Mrs P J Sheen **Bred** Miss M Gledhill **Trained** Epsom, Surrey

FOCUS
A very modest event by the course's standards. The time was 4.7 seconds slower than the later handicap and the form does not look anything special.

NOTEBOOK
Orange Street survived a blunder three out to win in good style, and the further he went the better he looked. He had only shown the odd glimmer of ability in the past - significantly though, on fast ground - and his victory must rate as something of a shock, so it remains to be seen how he progresses from the race. However, his trainer believes that he is improving mentally all the time. *(op 33-1)*
Buster Collins(IRE) set a decent pace in the early stages but became weary in the home straight. He stays at least three miles, having won a soft ground point-to-point in Ireland, so the tempo he set may have been a bit too quick. *(op 7-2)*
Here's Johnny(IRE) did not impress with his jumping technique in the early stages but still had every chance two out. From that point, he did not seem to get home, and he has yet to translate his considerable bumper promise to hurdling. *(tchd 2-1)*
Sparklinspirit had not shown a great deal in the past and was beaten a long way. *(op 25-1)*
Sir Bathwick(IRE), who is nicely bred for jumping, jumped poorly in the early stages and only showed a modicum of ability, staying on from the rear when the race was effectively over. Clearly he has had his problems getting to the course, and he may still need more time.
Square Mile(IRE), wearing a tongue tie for the first time, was still just in front when he took a crashing fall at the second last. He wasn't going quite as well as the eventual winner and this must rate as a slightly disappointing effort, given the modest opposition. *(op 15-8)*
Icomb(IRE) *Official explanation: jockey said gelding lost its action (op 15-8)*

4213 SECURON H'CAP CHASE (FOR THE GEOFFREY GILBEY TROPHY) (13 fncs) 2m 1f
3:05 (3:05) (Class 3) (0-135,129) 5-Y-O+ **£7,807** (£2,292; £1,146; £572)

Form RPR

U311 **1** **Madison Du Berlais (FR)**[10] [4037] 5-11-3 **125** 7ex .... APMcCoy 141+
(M C Pipe) *chsd ldrs: rdn 9th: wnt 2nd 3 out: chal next: sn led: drvn clr run-in* **6/4**[1]

-5PP **2** *6* **Bonus Bridge (IRE)**[97] [2489] 11-11-12 **129** .... MarkBradburne 141+
(H D Daly) *chsd ldrs: rdn and lost pl after 8th: mstke next: blnd 4 out: styd on wl fr next: tk 2nd run-in: nt trble winner* **14/1**

6024 **3** *5* **Master Rex**[50] [3357] 11-11-11 **128** ....(b[1]) NoelFehily 136+
(B De Haan) *t.k.h: led: rdn 3 out: hdd after next: wknd run-in* **7/1**

-5PF **4** *1* **Gazump (FR)**[97] [2489] 8-11-2 **119** .... CarlLlewellyn 125+
(N A Twiston-Davies) *bhd: j. slowly 5th: rdn and hit 9th: blnd 4 out: styd on after 2 out: kpt on run-in: nt trble ldrs* **9/1**

1P12 **5** *¾* **Glengarra (IRE)**[36] [3580] 9-11-0 **117** .... TomDoyle 122+
(D R Gandolfo) *led to 3rd: chsd ldr: blnd 9th: wknd 2 out* **11/2**[3]

2153 **6** *8* **Lorient Express (FR)**[50] [3357] 7-11-7 **124** .... SamThomas 121+
(Miss Venetia Williams) *bhd: hdwy 7th: rdn and blnd 9th: nvr gng pce to trble ldrs after* **5/1**[2]

6005 **7** *1* **Day Du Roy (FR)**[35] [3596] 8-10-0 **103** oh4 TomSiddall 99+
(Miss L C Siddall) *bhd: hdwy to chse ldrs 8th: hit 4 out and sn wknd* **20/1**

4150 **8** *1 1/4* **Romany Dream**[48] [3387] 8-10-0 **103** (b) WayneHutchinson 96
(R Dickin) *in tch: wknd 9th* **20/1**

4m 1.10s (-8.30) **Going Correction** -0.35s/f (Good)
WFA 5 from 7yo+ 4lb **8** Ran SP% **110.7**
Speed ratings: **105,102,99,99,99 95,94,94** CSF £20.48 CT £107.16 TOTE £2.00: £1.20, £3.20, £2.10; EX 23.10.
Owner Roger Stanley & Yvonne Reynolds II **Bred** Jean-Marc Lucas **Trained** Nicholashayne, Devon

FOCUS
Adecent handicap, run in a good time. The winner is an improving sort, while the placed horses are nicely handicapped. The form should work out.

NOTEBOOK
Madison Du Berlais(FR) ◆ looked to be going nowhere jumping the cross fence, but under a typically determined McCoy ride, he stayed on really strongly to win with plenty in hand crossing the line. A step up in trip should suit him and he would be of some interest for one of the handicaps at Cheltenham if he got in, which, at this stage, looks most unlikely. *(tchd 11-8)*
Bonus Bridge(IRE) made a couple of mistakes and did well to stay on and finish as close as he *did. He is nicely handicapped at present, but will need to jump better if he is to take advantage. (op 20-1)*
Master Rex, wearing blinkers for the first time at the age of eleven, travelled like a dream for most of the race and looked like winning easily entering the home straight. However, his stride shortened noticeably after the third last and he eventually finished well beaten. If ridden with more restraint, given that he has often not found a lot off the bridle, he would be of some interest off his current mark. *(op 9-1)*
Gazump(FR) was another who made too many mistakes to be a factor at the business end. He has suffered with jumping problems in the past, so is one to treat with caution until showing more fluency. *(op 7-1 tchd 10-1)*
Glengarra(IRE) moved with ominous ease throughout the race until a blunder ended his interest. He has risen plenty in the weights for his recent success and may have reached his level. *(op 5-1)*
Lorient Express(FR) shaped with some promise on his return to action after just over a month off, *but looked very much in the grip of the Handicapper after his successful spell earlier in the season. (tchd 11-2)*

4214 ARKELL'S BREWERY NOVICES' H'CAP CHASE (17 fncs) 2m 6f 110y
3:40 (3:40) (Class 3) (0-125,120) 5-Y-0+ **£7,807** (£2,292; £1,146; £572)

Form RPR

162F **1** **Von Origny (FR)**[41] [3506] 5-11-0 **118** RichardJohnson 128+
(H D Daly) *prom: dropped rr 10th: hdwy 13th: styng on whn mstke 3 out: chsd ldr 2 out: rdn to ld after last: drvn out* **11/2**[2]

R21U **2** *2* **Shining Strand**[15] [3942] 7-11-12 **120** AndrewTinkler 137+
(N J Henderson) *lw: led: reminders bnd after 7th: wnt lft and mstke last: hdd sn after: one pce u.p* **4/1**[1]

5334 **3** *13* **Lord Dundaniel (IRE)**[84] [2748] 9-10-11 **105** NoelFehily 109+
(B De Haan) *chsd ldrs: hit 5th: dropped rr 11th: hdwy and wnt lft 2 out: nt rch ldrs and one pce fr next* **6/1**[3]

0616 **4** *nk* **Lubinas (IRE)**[22] [3815] 7-10-7 **101** TomDoyle 106+
(F Jordan) *j.lft: chsd ldr to 3 out: wknd after next: mstke last* **16/1**

3-P2 **5** *1 1/2* **Quid Pro Quo (FR)**[85] [2729] 7-11-5 **113** ChristianWilliams 116+
(P F Nicholls) *in tch: blnd 4th: rdn and hit 13th: wknd after 3 out* **9/1**

40-0 **6** *8* **Wakeup Smiling (IRE)**[51] [3344] 8-10-7 **101** MarcusFoley 94
(Miss E C Lavelle) *chsd ldrs early: bhd fr 8th* **14/1**

4420 **7** *5* **Papillon De Iena (FR)**[90] [2636] 6-11-4 **112** (p) APMcCoy 101+
(M C Pipe) *bhd most of way* **6/1**[3]

U211 **8** *12* **The Outlier (IRE)**[12] [4014] 8-11-6 **114** 7ex SamThomas 98+
(Miss Venetia Williams) *in tch: sme hdwy 8th: rdn 12th: sn wknd* **9/1**

30F3 **P** **Simple Glory (IRE)**[24] [3790] 7-10-2 **96** WayneHutchinson —
(R Dickin) *bhd tl p.u bef 8th* **66/1**

1U3P **P** **Balladeer (IRE)**[16] [3921] 8-11-7 **115** AndrewThornton —
(Mrs T J Hill) *a in rr: mstke 8th: t.o whn p.u bef 12th* **33/1**

2011 **U** **He's The Gaffer (IRE)**[28] [3718] 6-10-9 **103** (b) RobertThornton —
(R H Buckler) *bhd: hdwy 13th: nt rch ldrs and sn rdn: wkng whn blnd and uns rdr 3 out* **7/1**

5m 35.5s (-12.20) **Going Correction** -0.35s/f (Good) course record
WFA 5 from 6yo+ 5lb **11** Ran SP% **113.4**
Speed ratings: **107,106,101,101,101 98,96,92,—,— —** CSF £27.58 CT £135.25 TOTE £6.00: £2.40, £1.90, £2.00; EX 24.60 Trifecta £274.20 Pool: £849.80 - 2.20 winning units.
Owner E R Hanbury **Bred** Bruno Matt **Trained** Stanton Lacy, Shropshire

FOCUS
A fair novices' handicap, although it was run in a moderate time. The first two could prove to be better than their current marks.

NOTEBOOK
Von Origny(FR) ◆ has been making quiet progress over fences and finished strongly to collar the long-time leader from well off the pace. He saw the trip out really well, after taking his time to get to the leaders, and will surely be suited by three miles in time. His trainer does so well with this type of horse, and it would be surprising if there is not plenty more improvement to come. *(op 4-1)*
Shining Strand looks far from trustworthy at any paddockturn, but his jockey was alive to the danger this time, and with the aid of a few cracks with the whip made sure he went off on his final circuit. To be fair, he did not do much wrong this time, and he was collared only on the run-in, giving plenty of weight to the winner. He would be even more interesting if he would settle off the pace rather than tear off in front. *(tchd 9-2)*
Lord Dundaniel(IRE) probably ran up to his best and had little chance with the first two home, given their progressive profiles. He has plenty of placed form over fences but struggles to get his head in front. *(op 11-1 tchd 12-1)*
Lubinas(IRE) is fairly moderate over fences and ran as well as he was entitled to. *(op 12-1)*
Quid Pro Quo(FR), returning from a break, made an early mistake and never really got into contention. *(op 10-1 tchd 17-2)*
Papillon De Iena(FR) is going right off the boil after showing some form over hurdles and fences in the past. He is one to avoid until showing better form. *(op 13-2 tchd 11-2)*
The Outlier(IRE) found the quick ground a world away from the war of attrition in which he prevailed at Towcester the time before. *(op 7-1)*
Simple Glory(IRE) *Official explanation: jockey said mare moved poorly throughout (op 50-1)*

4215 LING DESIGN H'CAP HURDLE (IN AID OF WEST BERKSHIRE MENCAP) (11 hdls) 2m 5f
4:15 (4:15) (Class 3) (0-125,125) 4-Y-0+ **£5,204** (£1,528; £764; £381)

Form RPR

11 **1** **Temoin**[27] [3729] 6-11-12 **125** MickFitzgerald 144+
(N J Henderson) *hld up mid-div: smooth hdwy fr 4 out: trckd ldrs 2 out: chal last: sn led and nvr c off bit* **7/2**[1]

1140 **2** *1/2* **Jaunty Times**[30] [3675] 6-11-2 **115** RichardJohnson 122
(H D Daly) *lw: chsd ldrs: chal 5th: slt ld 3 out: rdn whn strly chal after 2 out: kpt on but no ch w v easy wnr run-in* **20/1**

11P3 **3** *6* **In Media Res (FR)**[29] [3696] 5-11-1 **121** CharlieStudd[(7)] 122
(N J Henderson) *prom: rdn and kpt on fr 3 out: nvr gng pce to rch ldrs* **20/1**

2162 **4** *8* **Predator (GER)**[32] [3650] 5-10-7 **106** (p) APMcCoy 100+
(Jonjo O'Neill) *lw: led 3rd: rdn and narrowly hdd 3 out: wknd next* **5/1**[2]

P320 **5** *1/2* **Bengo (IRE)**[13] [3970] 6-11-5 **118** (b[1]) NoelFehily 112+
(B De Haan) *bhd: sme hdwy and nt fluent 3 out: styd on fr next: nt trble ldrs* **20/1**

U-10 **6** *2* **October Mist (IRE)**[53] [3318] 12-10-5 **114** JamesReveley[(10)] 105
(K G Reveley) *led to 3rd: wknd 3 out* **50/1**

0035 **7** *3* **Anatar (IRE)**[67] [2999] 8-10-13 **112** (v) TomScudamore 100
(M C Pipe) *chsd ldrs: lost pl after 4 out: kpt on again fr 2 out* **20/1**

2501 **8** *hd* **Screenplay**[16] [2530] 5-11-5 **118** JamieGoldstein 105
(Miss Sheena West) *bhd: rdn and hdwy appr 3 out: sn one pce: wknd after 2 out* **8/1**

2-40 **9** *10* **Papini (IRE)**[34] [3622] 5-11-5 **123** SamCurling[(5)] 100
(N J Henderson) *in tch: rdn to chse ldrs appr 3 out: wknd after next* **33/1**

-P00 **10** *16* **Etendard Indien (FR)**[50] [3360] 5-10-11 **110** AndrewTinkler 71
(N J Henderson) *bhd: hdwy to press ldrs 4th: wknd after 3 out* **33/1**

46P4 **11** *7* **Hi Fi**[15] [3950] 8-10-6 **105** PJBrennan 59
(Ian Williams) *prom early: dropped rr 4th: n.d after* **66/1**

/10- **12** *shd* **Regents Walk (IRE)**[352] [4394] 8-11-3 **116** TimmyMurphy 70
(B De Haan) *bhd most of way* **14/1**

40-F **13** *5* **Widemouth Bay (IRE)**[34] [3622] 8-11-7 **120** SamThomas 69
(Miss H C Knight) *j. slowly 4th and bhd: n.d after* **20/1**

1114 **P** **Ostfanni (IRE)**[98] [2483] 6-11-7 **120** GrahamLee —
(M Todhunter) *a bhd: tailed of whn p.u bef 2 out* **14/1**

P051 **P** **New Entic (FR)**[6] [4119] 5-11-9 **122** 7ex (p) JamieMoore —
(G L Moore) *in tch: rdn 3 out: sn wknd: t.o whn p.u bef last* **11/2**[3]

34P1 **P** **Day Of Claies (FR)**[14] [3966] 5-11-4 **117** (b) CarlLlewellyn —
(N A Twiston-Davies) *rdn and bhd 5th: t.o whn p.u bef last* **12/1**

FFP2 **P** **Mister Mustard (IRE)**[19] [3880] 9-11-5 **118** WayneHutchinson —
(Ian Williams) *bhd: sme hdwy 7th: wknd 3 out: p.u bef last* **20/1**

4m 57.2s (-55.80) **Going Correction** -0.525s/f (Firm) **17** Ran SP% **124.3**
Speed ratings: **109,108,106,103,103 102,101,101,97,91 88,88,86,—,— —,—** CSF £76.35 CT £1268.52 TOTE £4.10: £1.90, £6.30, £5.40, £2.10; EX 106.60.
Owner The Unemployables **Bred** Bloomsbury Stud **Trained** Upper Lambourn, Berks

FOCUS
A competitive handicap won in facile style. The time was very good and the form is likely to stand up. Temoin has been rated a 12 length winner, although it is impossible to know.

NOTEBOOK
Temoin ◆was visually very impressive, travelling on the bridle from start to finish and winning with an incalculable amount in hand. He is clearly a very smart novice, but his only engagement at Cheltenham is at two miles, so he is likely to wait for Aintree. It remains to be seen what he will find off the bridle in a better race, but he is a most exciting prospect and one to keep on the right side of wherever he turns up next. *(op 3-1)*
Jaunty Times ◆ bumped into a real tartar and had no chance of winning once Temoin cruised up to his girths approaching the last. That said, he set a new personal best in beating the rest in clear style and is another indicator that the stable in returning to top form. The only worry is that the Handicapper raises him plenty for finishing so close to the winner.
In Media Res(FR) ◆, a stable-mate of the winner, appreciated the ground and may still have another race in him during the spring.
Predator(GER) helped to set the pace in his first-time cheekpieces, but he may have been a bit keen and didn't get home. He is worth another chance over a shorter trip. *(op 11-2)*
Bengo(IRE), a winner on the corresponding card in 2005, showed more sparkle than of late in the first-time blinkers and might be coming back into form. He would be of some interest in a novices' handicap chase if returned to that discipline.
Screenplay came into the race with plenty of positives but never got involved at any stage. The Handiacpper may have his measure for now. *(op 10-1)*
New Entic(FR) *Official explanation: jockey said gelding was unsteerable (tchd 5-1 and 6-1)*

4216 JACQUELINE JARDINE'S 21ST BIRTHDAY HUNTERS' CHASE (IN AID OF WEST BERKSHIRE MENCAP) (17 fncs) 2m 6f 110y
4:45 (4:50) (Class 6) 6-Y-0+ **£1,648** (£507; £253)

Form RPR

4- **1** **Christy Beamish (IRE)**[12] 9-11-9 MrGHanmer[(3)] 113+
(P Jones) *hld up in rr: stdy hdwy fr 12th: led wl bef last: pushed clr run-in* **6/1**

PP-4 **2** *4* **Knife Edge (USA)**[27] [3736] 11-11-7 132 (p) MrAJBerry[(5)] 110+
(Jonjo O'Neill) *chsd ldrs: led 6th: blnd 11th: kpt slt advantage tl hdd wl bef last and mstke: sn one pce* **4/1**[3]

23-2 **3** *5* **Minella Silver (IRE)**[310] [47] 13-11-12 MrRBurton 103
(G L Landau) *trckd ldr: chal fr 12th: stl upsides 3 out: one pce fr next* **10/3**[1]

01/6 **4** *12* **Lightning Strikes (IRE)**[22] [3819] 12-11-7 MrMatthewSmith[(5)] 93+
(Mrs L Wadham) *nt fluent: chsd ldrs and hit 4th and 9th: wknd 3 out* **16/1**

45-P **5** *3/4* **Coral Island**[40] 12-11-12 77 MissPGundry 90
(Mrs Bernice Stronge) *led to 6th: styd w ldr to 10th: wknd fr 4 out* **22/1**

3-15 **6** *1 1/2* **Be My Dream (IRE)**[286] [453] 11-11-12 MrMWilesmith[(7)] 96
(Mrs C Wilesmith) *in tch: no ch fr 13th* **12/1**

7 *dist* **To The Top**[12] 8-11-9 MrJETudor[(3)] —
(Alan Hill) *in tch: j. slowly 9th: rdn 11th: wknd next: t.o* **7/1**

/P-0 **R** **Eskimo Jack (IRE)**[125] [1931] 10-11-7 MrWLMorgan[(5)] —
(Mrs H J Houghton) *ref to r* **7/2**[2]

U-06 **P** **Sporting Chance**[27] 14-11-10 83 MrMMunrowd[(7)] —
(Mrs Jo Sleep) *a bhd: mstke 8th: t.o whn p.u bef 3 out* **100/1**

-545 **P** **Hot Plunge**[12] 10-11-12 MrJOwen[(5)] —
(Mrs J P Lomax) *bhd: sme hdwy 12th: rdn: blnd and wknd 4 out:t.o whn p.u bef 2 out* **50/1**

5m 40.2s (-7.50) **Going Correction** -0.35s/f (Good) **10** Ran SP% **113.0**
Speed ratings: **99,97,95,91,91 90,—,—,—,—** CSF £29.74 TOTE £6.10: £1.80, £1.90, £1.50; EX 33.00 Place 6 £115.55, Place 5 £31.44.
Owner M Mann **Bred** C Beamish **Trained** Burnhill Green, Staffs

FOCUS
A competitive hunter chase, but a very moderate time.

NOTEBOOK
Christy Beamish(IRE), who reportedly returned sick after his last venture in hunter company, won in good style after passing Knife Edge going to the last. This was a massive step up on his previous form under Rules, but his overall record is very impressive - six wins and two fourths from only eight runs - and there is no reason to doubt the form. With no Cheltenham aspirations this season his main target is the John Corbet at Stratford in May, but it would be no surprise to see him win again before then. *(op 11-4)*
Knife Edge(USA), once rated 151 over fences, is a shadow of the horse he once was and may need a drop in trip to be more competitive, even in this grade. *(op 5-1)*
Minella Silver(IRE), returning after a 310-day layoff, ran well despite his advancing years and may need slightly further now under Rules. *(op 4-1 tchd 3-1)*
Lightning Strikes(IRE) has not had much racing in recent years and is entitled to improve again for the run. *(tchd 20-1)*
To The Top was a massive disappointment given his recent form in points. He usually likes to make the pace and may have sulked when not having things all his own way.

Eskimo Jack(IRE) did not make any new friends on his English debut when refusing to race. He is one to treat with caution. *(op 9-2)*
T/Jkpt: Not won. T/Plt: £111.30 to a £1 stake. Pool: £84,335.10. 552.75 winning tickets. T/Qpdt: £15.10 to a £1 stake. Pool: £7,975.80. 390.35 winning tickets. ST

4053 SOUTHWELL (L-H)
Friday, March 3
4217 Meeting Abandoned - Frost

4067 HAYDOCK (L-H)
Saturday, March 4
4223 Meeting Abandoned - Frost

3374 KELSO (L-H)
Saturday, March 4
4230 Meeting Abandoned - Frost

3976 LINGFIELD (L-H)
Saturday, March 4

OFFICIAL GOING: Standard
Wind: Light, against Weather: Sunny, cold

4237 MARSH GREEN STANDARD NATIONAL HUNT FLAT RACE (CONDITIONAL JOCKEYS AND AMATEUR RIDERS) 2m
5:10 (5:10) (Class 6) 4-6-Y-O **£1,713** (£499; £249) **Stalls** Low

Form				RPR
	1		**Ballykelly (IRE)**[385] 5-10-11 .... SeanQuinlan(7) (R T Phillips) *gd sort: strong: rangy: lw: wl in tch: prog to ld 3f out: clr wl over 1f out: pushed out* **10/1**	104+
	2	4	**Strawberry (IRE)** 5-10-4 .... WayneKavanagh(7) (J W Mullins) *in tch: pushed along 4f out: sn outpcd: rdn and r.o fr over 1f out: wnt 2nd last 100yds: fin wl* **16/1**	90
422	3	4	**Sundarbob (IRE)**[14] [3983] 4-10-5 .... MarkNicolls(5) (P R Webber) *led: set v stdy pce to 6f out: hdd 3f out: no ch w wnr fr 2f out: lost 2nd last 100yds* **5/2**[1]	85
0	4	1 ¾	**Valprimo**[14] [3983] 4-10-5 .... EamonDehdashti(5) (G L Moore) *trckd ldrs: rdn and in tch 3f out: sn outpcd: no imp over 1f out* **25/1**	83
	5	hd	**Seal Harbour (FR)** 6-11-1 ....(t) GinoCarenza(3) (A King) *prom: rdn and in tch 3f out: sn outpcd: one pce after* **10/1**	91
	6	2	**Best Deal** 5-10-11 .... TomMessenger(7) (B I Case) *hld up in last: stdy prog over 4f out: nvr rchd ldrs: outpcd over 2f out* **16/1**	89
2	7	1 ¼	**Tickford Abbey**[33] [3651] 4-10-3 .... MrSPJones(7) (Mrs P Robeson) *prom: rdn over 3f out: outpcd and btn over 2f out* **4/1**[3]	80
	8	1 ½	**Bach Beauty (IRE)** 4-9-12 .... SamCurling(5) (N J Henderson) *t.k.h: prom: n.m.r 5f out: sn pushed along: wd and outpcd over 2f out: one pce after* **11/4**[2]	71
	9	13	**Safeguard (IRE)** 5-10-13 .... JamesDiment(5) (S J Gilmore) *in tch: pushed along 6f out: sn struggling: wl bhd fr 3f out* **50/1**	73
0	10	¾	**Nar Valley**[86] [2720] 5-10-11 .... MrGTumelty(7) (A King) *prom: lost pl over 5f out: sn rdn and struggling: wl bhd 3f out* **16/1**	73
	11	hd	**Commanche Dawn** 4-9-7 .... JayPemberton(10) (G P Enright) *a towards rr: lost tch w ldng gp over 4f out: bhd fnl 3f* **50/1**	57
	12	dist	**Oursweetsurprise** 5-11-1 .... ColinBolger(3) (A Ennis) *chsd ldrs tl wknd rapidly 5f out: t.o* **20/1**	—
0	13	12	**Gessecapade**[58] [3259] 4-10-0 .... OwynNelmes(3) (P S McEntee) *prom tl wknd rapidly 6f out: t.o* **66/1**	—

3m 35.1s
WFA 4 from 5yo+ 7lb **13** Ran SP% **125.1**
CSF £158.23 TOTE £14.80: £3.30, £8.00, £1.60; EX 128.70 Place 6 £17.67, Place 5 £11.25..
Owner Nut Club Partnership **Bred** David Bamber **Trained** Adlestrop, Gloucs
■ The remainder of the jumps meeting of which this was a part was abandoned and replaced by an All-Weather Flat meeting.
■ Stewards' Enquiry : Eamon Dehdashti one-day ban: careless riding (Mar 18)

FOCUS
In all probability an ordinary event but the winner won with a good deal of authority and may well be capable of better.

NOTEBOOK
Ballykelly(IRE), a winning Irish pointer on his sole previous start in February of last year, created a most favourable impression on this debut under Rules. He will be suited by further, is the type physically to take to obstacles and very much has a future. *(op 7-1)*
Strawberry(IRE), a half-sister to a hurdle/chase winner in Ireland, showed more than enough on this racecourse debut to suggest a similar event can be found. *(op 14-1)*
Sundarbob(IRE), the most experienced in this field, had the run of the race and looks a good guide to the worth of this form. He looks sure to win a modest race when sent over obstacles. *(op 9-4 tchd 11-4)*
Valprimo fared better than on his debut, despite showing a tendency to hang to his left in the closing stages. He appeals as the type to do better once handicapped over obstacles. *(op 33-1)*
Seal Harbour(FR), who cost 13,000gns and is related to a winning chaser, was relatively easy to back but showed ability on this racecourse debut. He is in good hands and is entitled to come on for the experience. *(tchd 11-1)*
Best Deal, the second foal of a poor maiden pointer, left the impression that he was possessed with more in the way of stamina than speed on this racecourse debut.
Tickford Abbey, who dead-heated for second place with Sundarbob on his racecourse debut, was below that level this time. He may be capable of better in due course. *(op 7-1)*
Bach Beauty(IRE), the second foal of a dual bumper winner and useful staying hurdler, is from a stable that does well in this type of event but she did not show enough on this racecourse debut to suggest she will be of much interest next time. *(op 3-1)*
Commanche Dawn *Official explanation: jockey said filly hung left*
T/Plt: £13.20 to a £1 stake. Pool: £61,643.35. 3,384.80 winning tickets. T/Qpdt: £5.30 to a £1 stake. Pool: £4,284.50. 587.30 winning tickets. JN

4210 NEWBURY (L-H)
Saturday, March 4

OFFICIAL GOING: Good to firm
The meeting went ahead after the entire track was covered with the material used to protect crops from frost.
Wind: Light, half behind

4238 VODAFONE "NATIONAL HUNT" NOVICES' HURDLE (13 hdls) 3m 110y
1:35 (1:35) (Class 3) 4-Y-0+ **£5,855** (£1,719; £859; £429)

Form				RPR
2202	1		**Smart Mover**[24] [3806] 7-11-3 110 .... SamThomas (Miss H C Knight) *rr but in tch: hit 4th: hdwy after 4 out:chsd ldrs 3 out:edgd lft u.p after 3 out: chal last:led fnl 100yds: all out* **9/4**[1]	111+
-542	2	nk	**Original Thought (IRE)**[16] [3941] 6-11-3 108 .... NoelFehily (B De Haan) *lw: led: kpt narrow advantage: rdn 3 out: hit 2 out and hdd: sn slt ld again: hdd u.p fnl 100yds: no ex nr fin* **9/4**[1]	111+
-334	3	8	**Autumn Red (IRE)**[36] [3595] 6-11-3 100 .... TomDoyle (P R Webber) *lw: trckd ldrs: chal 3 out: slt ld and rdn 2 out: sn hdd: wknd last* **13/2**[2]	103+
4F-P	4	3 ½	**Lord Atterbury (IRE)**[16] [3941] 10-10-10 ....(p) AndrewGlassonbury(7) (M C Pipe) *lw: chsd ldr: chal 7th to 4 out: rdn bef next: wknd 2 out* **10/1**	99
06	5	20	**Keswick (IRE)**[10] [4052] 6-11-3 .... MickFitzgerald (N J Henderson) *hld up rr but in tch: hit 4th: rdn and blnd 3 out: sn wknd* **7/1**[3]	79
2-15	6	½	**Zanzibar Boy**[25] [3789] 7-11-3 .... JimCrowley (H Morrison) *lw: rr but in tch: hdwy 5th: j. slowly 7th: rdn and nt fluent 3 out: wknd qckly* **10/1**	78
-000	7	13	**Tanzanite Dawn**[30] [3690] 5-10-10 .... PJBrennan (Andrew Turnell) *str: chsd ldrs tl rdn and wknd qckly appr 3 out* **100/1**	58
0/30	8	26	**Sparkling Sabrina**[20] [3881] 6-10-10 .... ChristianWilliams (P Bowen) *a bhd: lost tch fr 6th* **66/1**	32
	P		**Talk The Talk**[370] 6-10-10 .... APMcCoy (Jonjo O'Neill) *w'like: w ldr 2nd: prom to 7th: sn wknd: t.o whn p.u bef 3 out* **16/1**	—

5m 54.4s (-7.70) **Going Correction** -0.35s/f (Good) **9** Ran SP% **113.9**
Speed ratings: **98,97,95,94,87 87,83,75,—** CSF £6.93 TOTE £3.20: £1.30, £1.40, £2.40; EX 7.40.
Owner Rendezvous Racing **Bred** Richard Chugg **Trained** West Lockinge, Oxon

FOCUS
A pretty modest contest by Newbury standards, run at a slow tempo. The form is slightly questionable but could rate a little higher.

NOTEBOOK
Smart Mover looked a bit ungenuine and was inclined to waver under pressure, but once straightened out again after the final flight he fought back strongly. His future is probably as a chaser. *(tchd 2-1)*
Original Thought(IRE) responded well to strong driving and almost landed the spoils through his bravery. He appears to relish a test of stamina but has still to get his head in front. *(op 3-1)*
Autumn Red(IRE), a chasing type, moved quite nicely during the race but did not get home as well as the front two. He will probably be better suited by a bit shorter in future, but we are unlikely to see the best of him until he goes over fences. *(op 8-1 tchd 6-1)*
Lord Atterbury(IRE) showed more than he had done at Huntingdon last time but was put firmly in his place. This didn't look the performance of a horse likely to go close again in the Grand National. *(tchd 14-1)*
Keswick(IRE), a chasing type, has not really gone on from his debut but at least he will now be handicapped. *(op 11-2 tchd 15-2)*
Zanzibar Boy moved well for a lot of the race but simply did not get home after making some mistakes. He has plenty of talent but looks a non stayer over this sort of trip and is another who is probably more of a chaser. *(op 9-1)*
Talk The Talk, who unseated his rider in both of his starts in the point-to-point sphere, took a grip in the early stages of the race and was pulled up in the home straight. He would appear to be one of the lesser lights in the stable. *(op 12-1)*

4239 VODAFONE NOVICES' H'CAP CHASE (FOR THE JACKY UPTON TROPHY) (15 fncs) 2m 2f 110y
2:10 (2:12) (Class 3) (0-125,122) 5-Y-0+ **£7,807** (£2,292; £1,146; £572)

Form				RPR
6-14	1		**Rubberdubber**[17] [3921] 6-11-12 122 .... APMcCoy (C R Egerton) *lw: hld up in tch: trckd ldrs 5th: led 4 out: in command fr 2 out: pushed out: comf* **6/5**[1]	138+
2P02	2	2	**Lord On The Run (IRE)**[47] [3418] 7-10-6 105 .... RichardYoung(3) (J W Mullins) *trckd ldrs: hit 2nd: chsd wnr appr 3 out: wnt lft and mstke 2 out: wnt lft again last: no imp run-in* **9/1**	117+
22-2	3	19	**Ryders Storm (USA)**[68] [2976] 7-10-12 108 .... NoelFehily (T R George) *hld up: mstke 7th: styd on one pce fr 4 out* **5/1**[2]	100
000	4	2 ½	**Lusaka De Pembo (FR)**[14] [3973] 7-11-7 117 ....(t) CarlLlewellyn (N A Twiston-Davies) *trckd ldr: led 4th to 5 out: wknd 2 out: hit last* **16/1**	108+
1101	5	8	**Magico (NZ)**[16] [3940] 8-11-5 118 ....(b) PaulO'Neill(3) (Miss Venetia Williams) *led to 4th: led 5 out: rdn and hdd next: sn wknd* **6/1**[3]	100
05-P	6	9	**Royal Katidoki (FR)**[98] [2488] 6-11-5 115 ....(t) MickFitzgerald (N J Henderson) *hit 2nd: in tch: tl rdn appr 10th: sn bhd* **9/1**	88
21U0	7	1 ½	**Bishop's Bridge (IRE)**[24] [3803] 8-11-5 118 .... GinoCarenza(3) (Andrew Turnell) *a bhd: lost tch 10th* **22/1**	89
2230	P		**Magnesium (USA)**[20] [3880] 6-10-13 109 ....(t) RobertThornton (B G Powell) *a bhd: rdn 8th: rdn and blnd 4 out: p.u bef next* **16/1**	—

4m 31.9s (-9.50) **Going Correction** -0.35s/f (Good) **8** Ran SP% **112.5**
Speed ratings: **106,105,97,96,92 88,88,—** CSF £12.41 CT £39.90 TOTE £2.00: £1.20, £2.00, £1.50; EX 10.90 Trifecta £59.00 Pool £673.12 - 8.10 winning units..
Owner Mr & Mrs Peter Orton **Bred** Mrs Susan Orton **Trained** Chaddleworth, Berks

FOCUS
This was run at a good gallop. The winner is a progressive type and was value for a bit more than the official winning margin. The race could rate a little higher, but there was not much strength in depth.

NOTEBOOK
Rubberdubber, who probably did not stay last time, seemed much better suited by the shorter trip and stronger pace to win with a little bit in hand. He is not qualified for any of his entries at Cheltenham but he should be seen again as long as he comes out of the race well. The trainer voiced slight concerns that the ground may have been too quick for the horse, and hopes that it will not have affected him. *(op 5-4 tchd 11-10)*
Lord On The Run(IRE) was Rubberdubber's closest pursuer over the last two fences but had made the odd mistake and never really threatened to break his duck. It was still a decent performance and he ought to pick up a similar race provided the Handicapper is not too harsh on him for this. *(op 8-1)*

Ryders Storm(USA) has a consistent profile but has yet to win over fences. He could never get *anywhere near the front, which he usually does, and was basically outpaced at the trip. (op 6-1 tchd 13-2 in places)*
Lusaka De Pembo(FR), wearing a tongue tie for the first time, set a really good pace but, not for the first time, failed to get home. He seems to be too keen for his own good at the moment.
Magico(NZ) raced close to the pace but was in the process of being collared when a mistake four out ended his chance. The Handicapper seems to have caught up with him. *(op 7-1)*
Royal Katidoki(FR) showed up early until being completely outpaced down the far straight. He is not progressing. *(op 8-1 tchd 10-1 in places)*
Magnesium(USA) *Official explanation: jockey said gelding had a breathing problem*

4240 VODAFONE H'CAP CHASE (18 fncs) 3m
2:40 (2:41) (Class 3) (0-130,130) 5-Y-0+

£15,657 (£4,625; £2,312; £1,157; £577; £290)

Form | | | | RPR
2111 **1** **Presenting Express (IRE)**[46] [3434] 7-10-7 **111**................. MarcusFoley 130+
(Miss E C Lavelle) *lw: blnd 2nd: rr: hdwy 10th: mstke 12th and 14th: trckd ldr 4 out: led 3 out: clear sn after: comf* **9/2**[2]
5-0P **2** *7* **Parsons Legacy (IRE)**[42] [3509] 8-11-6 **124**.......................... PJBrennan 131
(P J Hobbs) *lw: hit 3rd: chsd ldrs: led 9th: rdn appr 4 out: hdd 3 out: kpt on but no ch w wnr fr 2 out* **20/1**
0P3P **3** *1 3/4* **Jakari (FR)**[35] [3620] 9-11-12 **130**....................................... MarkBradburne 136+
(H D Daly) *chsd ldrs tl outpcd 3 out: drvn and kpt on again appr last: styd on run-in* **7/1**
0-P0 **4** *2 1/2* **Bounce Back (USA)**[99] [2483] 10-11-5 **123**..........................(p) APMcCoy 126
(M C Pipe) *lw: chsd ldrs: blnd 12th: rdn after 14th: one pce u.p fr 3 out* **14/1**
14P/ **5** *nk* **Rodalko (FR)**[686] [4861] 8-11-2 **120**.................................... LeightonAspell 123+
(O Sherwood) *chsd ldrs: lft in ld 5th: hdd 9th: styd trcking ldrs: hit 12th: chal 4 out: drvn and one pce fr next* **8/1**
1P-P **6** *4* **Mamideos (IRE)**[113] [2162] 9-10-7 **111**.............................(t) JasonMaguire 110+
(T R George) *bhd: hit 7th: sme hdwy 13th: rdn and mstke 14th: wknd fr 4 out* **40/1**
2225 **F** **Shalako (USA)**[28] [3728] 8-10-12 **116**............................. RichardJohnson —
(P J Hobbs) *chsd ldrs tl fell 9th: dead* **4/1**[1]
61F1 **U** **Florida Dream (IRE)**[30] [3698] 7-11-4 **122**..................(b) TomScudamore —
(N A Twiston-Davies) *led tl mstke and uns rdr 5th* **15/2**
6121 **P** **Harrycone Lewis**[16] [3941] 8-11-2 **120**.............................(b) PaulMoloney —
(Mrs P Sly) *blunder 1st: bhd tl t.o and p.u bef 14th* **11/2**[3]
341P **P** **Le Jaguar (FR)**[62] [3186] 6-11-0 **123**................................(bt) LiamHeard(5) —
(P F Nicholls) *chsd ldrs early: rr 8th: blnd 10th: t.o whn p.u bef 3 out* **12/1**
0P10 **P** **Lord Maizey (IRE)**[49] [3385] 9-11-11 **129**........................... CarlLlewellyn —
(N A Twiston-Davies) *rr: hit 5th: mstke next: sn lost tch: t.o whn p.u bef 9th* **16/1**

5m 51.9s (-13.10) **Going Correction** -0.35s/f (Good) **11** Ran SP% **116.4**
Speed ratings: **107,104,104,103,103 101,—,—,—,—** — CSF £83.84 CT £624.37 TOTE £4.20: £2.10, £7.30, £2.80; EX 207.30 Trifecta £707.10 Part won. Pool £996.00 - 0.70 winning units..
Owner N Mustoe **Bred** Patrick O'Dwyer **Trained** Wildhern, Hants

FOCUS
A solid handicap run at a frenetic pace. The winner is rated value for 12 lengths, the form should be sound and the race can produce a few winners. Holy Joe w/d Rule 4 deduct 5p in £.

NOTEBOOK
Presenting Express(IRE) ◆, stepping up in class and already 31lb higher in the handicap than for his first win over fences, won in the style of a rapidly improving chaser despite making a shocking mistake at the second. He was slightly niggled along entering the home straight but kept on really strongly to win easily. The trainer made a conscious decision to spare him the hurly-burly of Cheltenham and will give him time to develop as a chaser, but he could go to Aintree. He might even be worth a speculative entry in the BetFred Gold Cup at Sandown. *(new market op 5-1 tchd 11-2)*
Parsons Legacy(IRE) ◆ helped to cut out the strong pace but was readily left behind in the closing stages. He is back to a fair mark and would be of some interest if taking up his engagement in the Kim Muir again at Cheltenham, a race in which he finished third in last year. *(new market tchd 25-1)*
Jakari(FR), from a stable back in form, could not get to the lead early - as he likes to - and never really got into the race with a winning chance. However, he is nicely handicapped now and can be found a race in the spring. *(new market op 9-1)*
Bounce Back(USA) finished well beaten, but showed a little more of his old sparkle. He is really well handicapped on his last piece of winning form, in the 2002 Attheraces Gold Cup, so it would be no surprise to see him pop up again soon, possibly in the Kim Muir at Cheltenham. *(new market)*
Rodalko(FR) ◆, returning after a lengthy absence, raced very keenly towards the head of affairs and failed to see out the trip. He gave every indication that he retains plenty of his ability, and it was a highly satisfactory return to action. The Scottish National might be the right type of race for *him and he will have plenty of time to get over this and avoid the bounce factor. (new market tchd 15-2)*
Mamideos(IRE), returning after a break, showed some promise for the future but was ultimately outclassed. *(new market tchd 33-1)*
Shalako(USA) was close up when taking a fatal fall at the first in the back straight. *(new market)*
Harrycone Lewis, returning to fences after landing a novice hurdle last time, showed his mulish *side again, declining to take an interest from an early stage.Official explanation: jockey said gelding was unsuited by the good to firm ground (new market)*
Florida Dream(IRE) was already taking liberties with his fences when losing his jockey at the fifth. *(new market)*
Le Jaguar(FR), who is reportedly being aimed at the cross-country race at the Cheltenham Festival, never got competitive behind the really strong pace. *(new market)*

4241 VODAFONE GOLD CUP H'CAP CHASE (LISTED RACE) (16 fncs) 2m 4f
3:15 (3:15) (Class 1) 5-Y-0+

£39,205 (£39,205; £10,710; £5,340; £2,680; £1,340)

Form | | | | RPR
6PP3 **1** **Horus (IRE)**[14] [3995] 11-10-9 **131**.......................................(v) JamieMoore 141
(M C Pipe) *led 2nd to 6th: led again 9th: rdn and hdd 50yds out: rallied to force dead-heat line* **22/1**
1422 **1** *dht* **Cornish Sett (IRE)**[20] [3879] 7-11-4 **140**.......................................(b) RWalsh 150
(P F Nicholls) *a in tch: wnt 2nd 2 out: rdn to ld fnl 50yds: jnd post* **5/1**[1]
-3F1 **3** *6* **Windsor Boy (IRE)**[36] [3596] 9-10-1 **130**.............. AndrewGlassonbury(7) 134
(M C Pipe) *trckd ldrs: lost pl after 6th: styng on whn hit 4 out: kpt on but no ch w dead-heaters run-in* **9/1**
1324 **4** *shd* **Albuhera (IRE)**[28] [3726] 8-11-8 **144**......................................(t) JoeTizzard 149+
(P F Nicholls) *in tch tl lost pl 9th: hit 3 out and bhd tl styd on run-in* **12/1**
0431 **5** *4* **Claymore (IRE)**[28] [3739] 10-11-1 **137**............................... LeightonAspell 137
(O Sherwood) *mid-div: hdwy to trck ldrs 8th: chsd ldr 3 out tl wknd next* **8/1**[3]
0332 **6** *1 1/4* **Marcel (FR)**[33] [3647] 6-10-9 **131**.. APMcCoy 131+
(M C Pipe) *lw: mid-div whn hit 12th: hdwy appr 4 out: rdn and wkng whn hit 2 out* **15/2**[2]
60P0 **7** *2 1/2* **Quazar (IRE)**[28] [3739] 8-10-3 **125**...(tp) NoelFehily 121
(Jonjo O'Neill) *lw: in rr: styd on fr 3 out: nvr nr to chal* **20/1**
F1P6 **8** *1* **Full House (IRE)**[56] [3299] 7-10-13 **135**.................................... TomDoyle 130
(P R Webber) *mid-div: hdwy 8th: hit 4 out and 3 out: sn btn* **10/1**
/132 **9** *1/2* **Hors La Loi III (FR)**[30] [3695] 11-11-2 **143**......................... LiamHeard(5) 138
(P F Nicholls) *lw: hmpd 1st: a bhd* **14/1**
3253 **10** *8* **Made In Japan (JPN)**[62] [3180] 6-11-3 **139**............................ PJBrennan 127+
(P J Hobbs) *lw: trckd ldrs: blnd 8th: wnt 2nd 5 out: wknd after next* **8/1**[3]
200- **11** *4* **Iznogoud (FR)**[329] [4772] 10-11-2 **138**............................. TomScudamore 121
(M C Pipe) *chsd ldrs tl rdn and wknd appr 4 out* **66/1**
-305 **12** *dist* **Supreme Prince (IRE)**[14] [3977] 9-11-8 **144**.................. RichardJohnson —
(P J Hobbs) *led to 2nd: led again 6th to 9th: rdn appr 5 out: sn wknd: t.o* **22/1**
U0P0 **13** *9* **Seebald (GER)**[77] [2876] 11-11-4 **143**.............................(p) TomMalone(3) —
(M C Pipe) *j. slowly 8th: t.o fr 5 out* **66/1**
P252 **P** **Europa**[35] [3620] 10-11-4 **140**...(t) JasonMaguire —
(Ferdy Murphy) *in tch on outside whn blnd 11th: hit next: wknd and p.u bef 3 out* **14/1**
0640 **U** **Redemption**[28] [3723] 11-10-12 **134**.. CarlLlewellyn —
(N A Twiston-Davies) *bhd: sme hdwy whn blnd 5 out: blnd again and uns rdr 3 out* **10/1**

4m 54.2s (-12.20) **Going Correction** -0.35s/f (Good) **15** Ran SP% **116.3**
Speed ratings: **110,110,107,107,105 105,104,104,103,100 99,—,—,—,—**WIN: CS 2.90, H 12.20 Pl: CS £2.00, H £6.10 WS £3.60 Exacta: CS/H £122.80, H/CS £88.90. CSF: CS/H £56.25, H/CS £60.94. T'cst: CS/H/WB £479.94, H/CS/WB £539.90. T'fecta CS/H/WB £2,080.50. Pool £8,204.80-1.40 w/u, H/CS/WB £1,456.30. Pool £2,080.50 - 2 w/u
Owner B A Kilpatrick, **Bred** B A Kilpatrick, **Trained** Nicholashayne, Devon.
Owner Peter Hart **Bred** J F C Maxwell **Trained** Ditcheat, Somerset

FOCUS
A really competitive renewal of the race and an exciting finish. The pace was fast early, probably too quick,and not many got into contention. The third, fourth and sixth set the level for the form.

NOTEBOOK
Horus(IRE) ◆, off an 8lb lower mark than when second in the corresponding race in 2005, helped set a really strong pace and had most of his rivals in trouble entering thestraight. He kept on really strongly considering the pace he had gone, and he showed plenty of courage to get back up on the line to share the prize. He has several options at Cheltenham and must be of serious interest wherever he lines up. *(op 11-2 tchd 6-1 in places)*
Cornish Sett(IRE) took a long time to get to the front and had to share the spoils after being rejoined on the line by Horus, who he had headed after the final fence. He may have the odd quirk, but he can hardly be faulted this solid effort which paid a big compliment to Racing Demon, current favourite for the Arkle Chase with some bookmakers. He has two heads for Cheltenham, and he will *have an obvious chance in the Jewson Novices' Chase with just a 4lb penalty. (op 11-2 tchd 6-1 in places)*
Windsor Boy(IRE) ran a nice race despite blighting his chance with a mistake at the fourth last. He has an entry in the Racing Post Plate at the Cheltenham Festival and would be of some interest in that if his jumping held up. *(op 8-1)*
Albuhera(IRE) faced a stiff task from the top of the handicap as a novice in this company, and could not get involved until staying on strongly in the final stages. It was a really good effort under the weight and he should have plenty of options in the future, given that he is effective over a range of trips.
Claymore(IRE), who was laid out for the race all season, never managed to get competitive on ground that may have been plenty fast enough for him. He is now quite high in the weights on all of his winning form. *(op 7-1)*
Marcel(FR) moved nicely for much of the race but failed to get home after making a mistake two out. He really does not seem to be enjoying himself over fences, even allowing for the competitive nature of the race, but he is probably better at shorter and his current handicap mark still gives him *possibilities if he can recapture the enthusiasm he was showing over hurdles last season. (op 17-2 tchd 9-1 in places)*
Quazar(IRE) is really well handicapped after a disappointing season and showed a glimmer of promise for the short-term. He could be an interesting outsider for the Racing Post Plate at Cheltenham off his current mark, while he acts around the Mildmay track at Aintree and one of the handicaps there might suit. *(tchd 22-1)*
Hors La Loi III(FR) was always thought to need a step up in trip over fences but failed to landed a blow at any stage. He is better than this effort indicates. *(op 11-1)*
Made In Japan(JPN) made errors down the far straight that halted any chance he had. *(op 7-1)*
Iznogoud(FR), having his first run since the 2005 Grand National, was close up in the chasing bunch for much of the race, but weakened right out of contention. No firm conclusions can be drawn from this.
Supreme Prince(IRE), the winner of the race last year off a 2lb lower mark, helped to set a really strong pace but was spent force at cross fence. He definitely went off too quickly in front. *(op 20-1)*
Seebald(GER), in first-time cheekpieces, was settled in rear early and never got into the race. The Handicapper has given him a chance recently, but he looks on a downward curve at the age of 11.
Redemptionagain ruined his chance with some sloppy jumping once put into the race. *(op 12-1)*
Europa, in a first-time tongue tie, was running well until a couple of jumping errors ruined any chance he had. He is a bit too high in the weights to have an obvious winning chance in similarly strong company. *(op 12-1)*

4242 VODAFONE H'CAP HURDLE (8 hdls) 2m 110y
3:45 (3:47) (Class 3) (0-130,127) 4-Y-0+

£9,394 (£2,775; £1,387; £694; £346; £174)

Form | | | | RPR
U113 **1** **Desert Quest (IRE)**[78] [2871] 6-11-7 **127**..........................(b) LiamHeard(5) 140+
(P F Nicholls) *hld up rr: stdy hdwy appr 3 out: trcking ldr: travelling wl and 2nd whn lft in ld last: pushed out run-in* **4/1**[2]
2162 **2** *1 3/4* **Pirate Flagship (FR)**[62] [3175] 7-11-7 **122**.................................. RWalsh 128
(P F Nicholls) *in tch: drvn and outpcd appr 3 out: kpt on again fr 2 out: r.o to go 2nd run-in: kpt on u.p but nt pce of wnr* **11/2**[3]
2561 **3** *9* **Anticipating**[94] [2573] 6-10-9 **110**.. PhilipHide 109+
(G L Moore) *hld up mid-div: hit 4 out: hdwy appr next: chsd ldrs 2 out: styng on one pce whn mstke last* **8/1**
1211 **4** *nk* **Tokala**[36] [3595] 5-11-7 **122**... APMcCoy 119+
(B G Powell) *lw: bhd: drvn and stl plenty to do 3 out: kpt on fr next: r.o u.p run-in but nvr gng pce to rch ldrs* **6/1**
163- **5** *5* **Greenhope (IRE)**[323] [4846] 8-11-9 **124**............................... MickFitzgerald 117+
(N J Henderson) *slt ld to 4th: styd disputing ld tl drvn into slt advantage 2 out: sn hdd: wknd last* **12/1**
2P4 **6** *1 3/4* **Amour Multiple (IRE)**[14] [3996] 7-11-10 **125**.................. RobertThornton 115
(S Lycett) *pressed ldr tl slt advantage fr 4th: rdn 3 out: narrowly hdd 2 out: sn wknd* **100/1**
-236 **7** *6* **Goldbrook**[14] [3994] 8-11-3 **125**... JamesWhite(7) 109
(R J Hodges) *lw: chsd ldrs to 3 out: wknd next* **33/1**
-125 **8** *3* **Allumee**[10] [4050] 7-10-12 **113**... RichardJohnson 94
(P J Hobbs) *chsd ldrs tl lost pl 4 out: sme hdwy and rdn and mstke 3 out: n.d after* **25/1**
4440 **9** *6* **Predicament**[15] [3966] 7-10-10 **111**......................................(t) PJBrennan 86
(Jonjo O'Neill) *lw: chsd ldrs tl wknd appr 3 out* **40/1**

The Form Book, Raceform Ltd, Compton, RG20 6NL

PP50 **10** 3 1/2 **Broke Road (IRE)**[33] 3650 10-10-11 **112** ....(t) JimCrowley 83
(Mrs H Dalton) *chsd ldrs tl wknd and mstke 3 out* **100/1**

2-25 **11** 14 **Classic Role**[20] 3878 7-11-7 **122** .... JamieMoore 79
(L Wells) *bhd: hit 4 out: mod prog whn mstke and wknd 3 out* **16/1**

531 **F** **Topkat (IRE)**[18] 3908 5-11-0 **118** .... TomMalone(3) —
(M C Pipe) *rr whn fell 3rd: dead* **7/2**[1]

24U0 **U** **Kawagino (IRE)**[42] 3510 6-10-4 **108** .... RichardYoung(3) —
(J W Mullins) *towards rr whn uns rdr 4th* **20/1**

1332 **F** **Fandani (GER)**[98] 2487 6-11-7 **122** .... NoelFehily 132+
(C J Mann) *hld up rr: stdy hdwy after 4 out: trckd ldrs 3 out: led gng wl after 2 out: 1/2l ahd and travelling ok whn fell last* **12/1**

3m 52.3s (-11.30) **Going Correction** -0.35s/f (Good) **14** Ran SP% **120.2**
Speed ratings: **112,111,106,106,104 103,100,99,96,94 88,—,—,—** CSF £25.12 CT £171.10 TOTE £5.60: £2.20, £2.00, £3.70; EX 32.80 Trifecta £238.80 Pool £1,446.30 - 4.30 winning units..
Owner Mrs M Findlay **Bred** Ballygallon Stud **Trained** Ditcheat, Somerset

FOCUS
A race that featured a number of progressive hurdlers. The pace was very sound and it should produce winners.

NOTEBOOK
Desert Quest(IRE) ◆, who beat live Champion Hurdle outsider Briareus earlier in the season, is still not a horse to have the mortgage on but he is improving at a rate of knots since having the blinkers fitted and was full of running all the way up the straight. At his best when held up off a strong pace, he will have a major chance in Cheltenham's County Hurdle with just a 4lb penalty. *(op 9-2)*
Pirate Flagship(FR) looked well beaten at one stage coming down the straight but stayed on surprisingly well for pressure. He is sure to make a fine chaser next season but will probably take in the EBF Novices' Final at Sandown next, as long as the ground stays on the quick side. *(op 6-1)*
Anticipating, who has been waiting for quicker ground, shaped nicely for the future and ran above his current rating. He is the sort who may well appreciate Aintree's sharp track if the ground was on the fast side. *(tchd 15-2)*
Tokala, under a change of riding tactics, was set quite a lot to do from off the pace, but stayed on stoutly after the leaders had gone beyond recall. Remaining a decent prospect, he will probably *appreciate a step up in trip and more ease in the ground in the future.Official explanation: trainer said gelding was unsuited by the good to firm ground (tchd 7-1)*
Greenhope(IRE) made a highly satisfactory return to the racecourse, and his main target remains the Grand Annual at Cheltenham. *(tchd 14-1)*
Topkat(IRE) was in the rear when taking a fatal fall at the third. *(tchd 4-1 in places)*
Fandani(GER) ◆ travelled really well and was in the process of giving Desert Quest plenty to think about when coming down heavily at the final hurdle. It was cruel luck for connections, but he clearly has a race like this in him when he recovers. *(tchd 4-1 in places)*

4243 VODAFONE NOVICES' H'CAP HURDLE (8 hdls) 2m 110y
4:20 (4:20) (Class 3) (0-115,115) 4-Y-0+ **£6,506** (£1,910; £955; £477)

Form RPR

2-33 **1** **Wellbeing**[18] 3908 9-11-2 **103** .... RichardJohnson 123+
(P J Hobbs) *hld up in rr: hdwy fr 5th: wnt 2nd 2 out: hrd rdn to ld fnl 50yds: all out* **10/3**[2]

1 **2** shd **Jack The Giant (IRE)**[25] 3786 4-10-13 **108** .... MickFitzgerald 120+
(N J Henderson) *lw: plld hrd early: led appr 3rd: hung rt u.p run-in and hdd fnl 50yds* **2/1**[1]

0525 **3** 6 **Tech Eagle (IRE)**[35] 3616 6-10-12 **99** .... TomDoyle 112
(R Curtis) *hld up in rr: hdwy fr 5th: chsd ldng pair fr 2 out* **20/1**

006 **4** 6 **Vengeance**[14] 3996 6-10-12 **99** .... LeightonAspell 106
(S Dow) *in rr: hdwy whn mstke 3 out: nvr nr to chal* **14/1**

445P **5** 5 **Sabreur**[16] 3944 5-11-0 **101** .... WayneHutchinson 103
(Ian Williams) *led 1st: hdd appr 3rd: prom tl rdn and wknd 3 out* **11/1**

0-40 **6** 6 **Quarrymount**[104] 2372 5-10-10 **97** .... JasonMaguire 94+
(J A B Old) *prom: wkng whn mstke 2 out* **16/1**

020P **7** 1 1/4 **Amnesty**[19] 3371 7-10-7 **94** ....(b) JamieMoore 89
(G L Moore) *hld up in rr: rdn 3 out: nvr on terms* **40/1**

5-F3 **8** 14 **Liberia (FR)**[61] 3220 7-11-4 **105** .... AndrewTinkler 92+
(N J Henderson) *in tch: wkng whn bdly hmpd 3 out* **33/1**

06PP **9** 24 **Surfboard (IRE)**[20] 3876 5-10-8 **95** .... MarkBradburne 52
(P A Blockley) *led to 1st: lost pl 5th: sn wl bhd* **50/1**

512 **P** **Arry Dash**[16] 3944 6-11-11 **112** .... PJBrennan —
(M J Wallace) *in tch tl wknd qckly and p.u bef 3 out* **14/1**

03-0 **P** **Major Blade (GER)**[22] 3848 8-9-13 **89** .... TJPhelan(3) —
(Mrs H Dalton) *a bhd: rdn 5th: t.o whn p.u bef 3 out* **100/1**

6003 **F** **Champion's Day (GER)**[15] 3962 5-11-1 **102** ....(b[1]) APMcCoy —
(Jonjo O'Neill) *trckd ldrs: rdn and hld whn fell 3 out: dead* **12/1**

643 **P** **Shannon Springs (IRE)**[25] 3787 4-11-6 **115** .... PaulMoloney —
(Andrew Turnell) *mid-div: wknd 5th: t.o whn p.u bef 3 out* **5/1**[3]

-360 **P** **Master Mahogany**[33] 3650 5-11-7 **108** .... TomScudamore —
(R J Hodges) *a bhd: brief effrt after 5th: t.o whn p.u bef last* **33/1**

3m 53.0s (-10.60) **Going Correction** -0.35s/f (Good)
WFA 4 from 5yo+ 7lb **14** Ran SP% **124.4**
Speed ratings: **110,109,107,104,101 99,98,91,80,— —,—,—,—** CSF £10.47 CT £121.43 TOTE £4.80: £1.80, £1.50, £5.00; EX 10.50.
Owner Gillian, Lady Howard De Walden **Bred** Lord Howard De Walden **Trained** Withycombe, Somerset

FOCUS
A finish dominated by two horses who had looked potentially well in. The first four all look improving types and the race is one to treat positively.

NOTEBOOK
Wellbeing ◆, who once held a Champion Hurdle entry, finally showed some of his old Flat ability on his handicap debut over timber. He took his time to get to the lead and may benefit from a little bit further now, although if continuing his progress he could make up into a Swinton Hurdle type, where the pace is always strong. *(op 5-1)*
Jack The Giant(IRE) clearly has plenty of talent but might have a few quirks. He will probably be at his best from the front, as he can take a strong pull in behind horses, but he failed to convince under pressure, hanging in both directions in the final stages. Although he holds an entry in the Triumph Hurdle, Aintree would seem the better option given that he shows plenty of natural pace. *(tchd 9-4)*
Tech Eagle(IRE) has shown plenty of form at a low level to suggest he will be winning soon. There must be little doubt he bumped into two potential blots on the handicap, and he would be very unfortunate to run into similar types next time. *(op 25-1)*
Vengeance ◆, making his handicap debut, is on a very fair mark over hurdles and is one to have on your side next time, especially if stepped up in trip. He handled quick ground on the Flat, where he was a very useful sort, so the spring weather should see him have his favoured conditions. *(op 16-1)*
Arry Dash had excuses for his below-par effort. *Official explanation: jockey said gelding lost its action (op 11-2)*
Master Mahogany dropped out quickly after threatening briefly. *Official explanation: jockey said gelding lost its action (op 11-2)*
Shannon Springs(IRE) looked a very interesting contender on his first start in handicap company, but he failed to land a blow. This could not have been his true running given his earlier efforts over hurdles. *Official explanation: jockey said gelding lost its action (op 11-2)*
Champion's Day(GER) was starting to back-pedal when taking a crashing fall at the third last. *(op 11-2)*

4244 VODAFONE INTERMEDIATE OPEN NATIONAL HUNT FLAT RACE 2m 110y
4:55 (4:55) (Class 6) 4-6-Y-0 **£2,192** (£639; £319)

Form RPR

1 **1** **Wichita Lineman (IRE)**[97] 2534 5-11-4 .... MrJPMagnier(5) 115+
(Jonjo O'Neill) *hld up in rr: smooth hdwy fr 6f out to take slt ld ins fnl 3f: shkn up and hld on wl fnl f* **9/4**[2]

23 **2** 1 1/4 **Kimi (IRE)**[59] 3244 5-11-2 .... TomDoyle 105
(Noel T Chance) *hld up in rr: hdwy 5f out: drvn and carried lft ins fnl 3f: styd on wl to chse wnr ins last but no imp* **14/1**

1 **3** 3/4 **Pepporoni Pete (IRE)**[68] 3001 5-11-9 .... RWalsh 111+
(P F Nicholls) *hld up in rr: stdy hdwy 6f out: chal gng wl 3f out: hrd drvn over 1f out: one pce ins last* **8/11**[1]

2 **4** 4 **Mount Sandel (IRE)**[28] 3742 5-11-2 .... LeightonAspell 100
(O Sherwood) *str: lw: chsd ldr: rdn and ev ch 3f out: one pce fnl 2f* **12/1**[3]

4 **5** 2 1/2 **It Happened Out (IRE)**[30] 3699 5-10-13 .... RichardYoung(3) 98
(J W Mullins) *lengthy: chsd ldrs: rdn 3f out: one pce fnl 2f* **50/1**

6 **6** 1/2 **Sexy Rexy (IRE)**[49] 3392 5-10-11 .... StevenCrawford(5) 97
(N A Twiston-Davies) *lw: sn led and set modest pce: rdn: hung lft and hdd ins fnl 3f: wknd over 1f out* **33/1**

3 **7** 2 1/2 **Master Eddy**[35] 3617 6-11-2 .... JasonMaguire 95
(S Lycett) *chsd ldrs: hrd drvn over 3f out: wknd ins fnl 2f* **66/1**

8 1 1/2 **Navy Lark** 4-10-8 .... PJBrennan 85
(M C Pipe) *w'like: leggy: chsd ldrs: rdn and one pce whn pushed lft ins fnl 3f: wknd ins fnl 2f* **25/1**

1 **9** 7 **One More Step**[147] 1688 5-11-2 .... MrTJO'Brien(7) 100+
(R A Farrant) *chsd ldrs: slipped 6f out: wknd fr 3f out* **20/1**

10 12 **Grey Tornado** 5-11-2 .... MarkBradburne 74
(C G Cox) *w'like: mid-div: drvn and hdwy to chse ldrs 4f out: wknd ins fnl 3f* **66/1**

0 **11** hd **Sky By Night**[59] 3244 5-10-9 .... JoeTizzard 67
(B J M Ryall) *in tch 10f* **100/1**

4m 3.40s (0.10) **Going Correction** -0.35s/f (Good)
WFA 4 from 5yo+ 7lb **11** Ran SP% **120.5**
Speed ratings: **85,84,84,82,81 80,79,78,75,69 69** CSF £31.64 TOTE £3.40: £1.50, £2.40, £1.10; EX 35.80 Place 6 £43.32, Place 5 £34.75..
Owner Mrs John Magnier **Bred** Pat Tobin **Trained** Cheltenham, Gloucs

FOCUS
A strong field for a bumper so close to the Cheltenham Festival, but it was run at a muddling pace and the proximity of so many beaten horses holds the form down, although the first three are sure to make up into very nice types. The race time should be ignored as they did not start for about ten seconds after the tapes went up.

NOTEBOOK
Wichita Lineman(IRE) probably won with a bit more in hand than was evident, as it was a muddling affair and his amateur jockey was up against two good professionals in the finish. The opposition looked particularly strong, and although Aintree rather than Cheltenham may be the target, he should not be ignored if turning up at the latter course, where his half-brother Rhinestone Cowboy was beaten so controversially. *(op 2-1)*
Kimi(IRE) has run into a potential star every time he has made it to the track. He did absolutely nothing wrong and deserves better luck. *(tchd 16-1)*
Pepporoni Pete(IRE), who looks a chasing type, was all the rage before the race but came up short, giving weight away, when the chips were down. Ruby Walsh reported after the race he was unsuited by the way the race was run, and he will almost certainly head to Aintree next for their Championship bumper. *(op 10-11 tchd evens in places)*
Mount Sandel(IRE) was always close to the pace and shaped nicely on much faster ground than he had encountered on his first run. He is the sort to progress with more time. *(tchd 14-1)*
It Happened Out(IRE), a chasing type, continues to show promise but is not in the class of the principals. *(tchd 66-1)*
Sexy Rexy(IRE) seems to be well regarded - he made debut in a Listed bumper - but has limitations on the evidence available so far *(tchd 50-1)*
Master Eddy is very much a chasing type.
One More Step *Official explanation: jockey said saddle slipped (op 25-1)*
T/Jkpt: £1,186.50 to a £1 stake. Pool: £13,369.50. 8.00 winning tickets. T/Plt: £24.90 to a £1 stake. Pool: £151,072.20. 4,414.95 winning tickets. T/Qpdt: £21.60 to a £1 stake. Pool: £7,856.30. 268.00 winning tickets. ST

3842 BANGOR-ON-DEE (L-H)
Sunday, March 5
4245 Meeting Abandoned - Frost & Snow

4074 HUNTINGDON (R-H)
Sunday, March 5
4252 Meeting Abandoned - Frost

4259 - 4276a (Foreign Racing) - See Raceform Interactive

3883 HEREFORD (R-H)
Monday, March 6

OFFICIAL GOING: Good (good to soft in places)
First flight in back straight omitted all hurdle races.
Wind: Light, across Weather: Fine

4277 HEREFORD TRUCK SHOW NOVICES' H'CAP HURDLE (11 hdls 2 omitted) 3m 2f
2:10 (2:10) (Class 5) (0-95,95) 4-Y-0+ **£2,927** (£859; £429; £214)

Form RPR

0 **1** **The Small Farmer (IRE)**[59] 3279 9-10-0 **74** .... JamesDiment(5) 82+
(Mrs A E Brooks) *led 2nd tl after 3rd: prom: led 7th: rdn after 2 out: styd on* **18/1**

3P13 **2** 1 1/2 **Bar Gayne (IRE)**[37] 3613 7-11-3 **93** .... WillieMcCarthy(7) 98
(T R George) *a.p: rdn appr 2 out: styd on same pce flat* **7/2**[1]

-032 **3** 1 **Royal Niece (IRE)**[18] 3951 7-10-6 **85** .... RyanCummings(10) 90+
(D J Wintle) *a.p: rdn after 2 out: one pce flat* **6/1**

6-0P **4** *dist* **Star Time (IRE)**[60] 3252 7-10-10 **79**..............................(v) TomScudamore 52
(M Scudamore) *prom: lost pl 6th: bhd fr 8th: t.o* **33/1**
6P0P **5** *2* **Safe To Blush**[52] 3367 8-10-0 **74**.................................. TomGreenway(5) 45
(P A Pritchard) *hld up in mid-div: hdwy 8th: wknd 3 out* **50/1**
6553 **6** *dist* **Bosworth Gypsy (IRE)**[18] 3951 8-10-4 **80**..................... MarcGoldstein(7) —
(Miss J S Davis) *led to 2nd: prom: rdn appr 7th: wknd appr 3 out: t.o* **14/1**
6-P6 **7** *dist* **New Diamond**[37] 3616 7-9-11 **73**.............................. WayneKavanagh(7) —
(Mrs P Ford) *a bhd: t.o fr 3 out* **100/1**
/P03 **P** **Marchensis (IRE)**[15] 4005 8-11-7 **90**.............................. LeightonAspell —
(O Sherwood) *a bhd: t.o whn p.u bef 3 out* **14/1**
3-P0 **P** **Pip Moss**[34] 3662 11-10-5 **74**.. JasonMaguire —
(J A B Old) *bhd most of way: t.o whn p.u bef last* **33/1**
-565 **P** **Black Collar**[20] 3905 7-11-2 **85**.. JohnMcNamara —
(K C Bailey) *t.k.h in tch: wkng: t.o whn p.u bef 3 out* **20/1**
3314 **P** **Perfect Balance (IRE)**[13] 4043 5-11-3 **91**.......................... LiamHeard(5) —
(D W Thompson) *prom tl wknd 5th: t.o whn p.u bef last* **9/2**[3]
06P0 **P** **Novack Du Beury (FR)**[12] 4052 5-11-5 **88**......................... KeithMercer —
(Ferdy Murphy) *a bhd: lost tch 6th: t.o whn p.u bef 3 out* **50/1**
P0 **P** **Swazi Prince**[18] 3943 7-11-12 **95**................................. CarlLlewellyn —
(N A Twiston-Davies) *a bhd: j.rt 2nd: t.o whn p.u bef last* **28/1**
46-P **P** **Salliemak**[35] 3652 8-10-7 **76**..(t) TomSiddall —
(A J Wilson) *in tch: j. slowly and lost pl 3rd: t.o whn p.u bef 7th* **40/1**
433F **P** **Hard N Sharp**[108] 2310 6-11-10 **93**.............................. ChristianWilliams —
(Evan Williams) *hld up and bhd: rdn and hdwy after 8th: wknd 3 out: t.o whn p.u bef last* **4/1**[2]
0P00 **U** **They Grabbed Me (IRE)**[18] 3951 5-10-9 **78**..................(vt[1]) GerrySupple —
(M C Pipe) *mid-div: mstke 1st: hdwy to ld after 3rd: rdn and hdd 7th: blnd and uns rdr 8th* **28/1**

6m 34.5s (6.50) **Going Correction** +0.35s/f (Yiel) **16** Ran SP% **118.2**
Speed ratings: **104,103,103,—,—** —,—,—,—,— —,—,—,—,— — CSF £72.91 CT £438.11 TOTE £22.40: £4.90, £1.40, £1.30, £9.60; EX 199.40.
Owner T L Brooks **Bred** S R McKee **Trained** Towcester, Northamptonshire

FOCUS
This was a very modest event but the pace was sound and the race concerned only three from a long way out. The placed horses represent the best guide to the level of the form.

NOTEBOOK
The Small Farmer(IRE), a winning pointer in 2005, was a never-nearer seventh on his return to hurdling at Towcester two months ago but proved good enough to break his duck under Rules, the longer trip and better ground evidently the deciding factors. Always up with the pace, he had two rivals snapping at his heels from the third last but was always holding them at bay. He was dismounted after the finish but there did not appear anything too seriously wrong. *(op 14-1)*
Bar Gayne(IRE) was in the van all the way but was just unable to get past the winner. Winner of a classified hurdle over course and distance in January, he clearly stays very well and had no problem with this faster ground. *(op 9-2)*
Royal Niece(IRE), who was fifth in this event a year ago, ran her race again but once more was forced to settle for place money. She is honest enough but lacks a change of pace. *(op 11-2)*
Star Time(IRE), back over hurdles for this first run for two months, was under pressure with well over a circuit to run but plugged on to claim a remote fourth.
Safe To Blush was without the cheekpieces or tongue strap she wore last time. *(op 40-1)*
Pip Moss *Official explanation: trainer said gelding had a breathing problem (op 4-1 tchd 5-1)*
Perfect Balance(IRE) *Official explanation: trainer said gelding was unsuited by the good, good to soft in places ground (op 4-1 tchd 5-1)*

4278 WEATHERBYS PRINTING NOVICES' (S) HURDLE (7 hdls 1 omitted) 2m 1f
2:40 (2:47) (Class 5) 4-Y-0+ **£2,081** (£611; £305; £152)

Form RPR
0P30 **1** **Sistema**[9] 4104 5-10-12 87... OwynNelmes(3) 89+
(A E Price) *hld up and bhd: hdwy appr 3 out: rdn to ld appr last: r.o wl* **13/2**
PP **2** *3 ½* **Bold Trump**[8] 1158 5-11-1 .... JodieMogford 83
(Mrs N S Evans) *led: clr most of way: rdn appr 2 out: hdd appr last: one pce flat* **50/1**
P502 **3** *1 ½* **Native Commander (IRE)**[16] 3985 11-10-10 90(b[1]) ChristopherMurray(5) 81
(Jim Best) *hld up in tch: rdn appr 3 out: one pce flat* **9/2**[3]
500 **4** *2 ½* **After Lent (IRE)**[18] 3945 5-11-1 87.................................... TimmyMurphy 79
(M C Pipe) *plld hrd: chsd ldr: j.lft 1st: one pce fr 2 out* **7/2**[2]
2021 **5** *5* **The Wife's Sister**[16] 3985 5-10-7 90................................(b) RichardSpate(7) 73
(Mrs K Waldron) *mid-div: rdn and no real prog fr 3 out* **5/2**[1]
040F **6** *10* **Griffin's Legacy**[56] 3321 7-10-10 90.............................. MarkNicolls(5) 64
(N G Ayliffe) *mid-div: mstke 2nd: n.d after* **16/1**
P64R **7** *2 ½* **Kinkeel (IRE)**[8] 4132 7-10-12 87................................... StephenCraine(3) 61
(A W Carroll) *mid-div: wknd appr 2 out* **18/1**
0PP **8** *5* **Roussea (IRE)**[22] 3885 8-10-8 .... AdrianScholes(7) 56
(S G Griffiths) *prom: wkng whn bdly hmpd 3 out* **18/1**
PPPP **9** *5* **Neophyte (IRE)**[35] 3647 7-10-10 .... JamesDiment(5) 51
(M J M Evans) *a bhd* **66/1**
P **10** *8* **Oktis Morilious (IRE)**[22] 3885 5-10-8 .... MrTCollier(7) 43
(J A Danahar) *a bhd* **50/1**
00-U **11** *dist* **Pipers Legend**[9] 4106 7-11-1 .... OllieMcPhail —
(D Burchell) *a bhd: t.o fr 3rd* **50/1**
00- **F** **King Of Scots**[446] 2817 5-11-1 .... MarcusFoley —
(R J Price) *bhd whn fell 4th* **40/1**
P **Wilson Blyth**[385] 8-11-1 .... PJBrennan —
(R Ford) *bhd: bmpd 3 out: t.o whn p.u bef 2 out* **50/1**
00-6 **F** **Honest Injun**[18] 1302 5-10-8 80..............................(vt[1]) TomMessenger(7) —
(A G Juckes) *mid-div: struggling whn fell 3 out* **16/1**
U **Pearl Island (USA)**[22] 5-10-5 ....(p) RyanCummings(10) —
(D J Wintle) *prom: disputing 3rd whn blnd and uns rdr 3 out* **12/1**
P **Nebraska City**[42] 5-10-8 .... BenOrde-Powlett(7) —
(D W Thompson) *plld hrd: sn prom: wkng whn bdly hmpd 3 out: p.u bef 2 out* **33/1**

4m 11.5s (8.40) **Going Correction** +0.35s/f (Yiel) **16** Ran SP% **127.0**
Speed ratings: **94,92,91,90,88 83,82,79,77,73** —,—,—,—,— — CSF £304.69 TOTE £10.00: £2.80, £10.50, £1.60; EX 656.00.The winner was bought in for 5,250gns.
Owner Mrs H L Price **Bred** Azienda Agricola Patrizia **Trained** Leominster, H'fords

FOCUS
A modest winning time, even for a seller. A desperate affair and the form is going to be worth very little although the third and fourth ran to their marks.

NOTEBOOK
Sistema, who had run well in a claimer two outings ago and was found wanting in a falsely-run handicap on his latest start, came from some way back to claim the leader and scored cosily enough in the end. He might stay a bit further. *(op 8-1)*
Bold Trump was pulled up on his two previous ventures over hurdles and has been beaten in banded races on the sand this winter. Given an enterprising ride, he was clear at the flight in the back straight, three from the finish, but was worn down on the home turn. He has a sprinting pedigree and his stamina is limited.
Native Commander(IRE) was still travelling well approaching the second last but, not for the first time, he failed to find much when let down. *(op 4-1)*
After Lent(IRE) was very keen from the start and it says something about the standard of this race that he was only seen off from the second last. *(op 15-2)*
The Wife's Sister, who accounted for today's third when scoring at Uttoxeter, was below that form on her first run for new connections. The faster ground appeared against her and she could never reach a challenging position, although she was keeping on at the end. *(tchd 3-1)*
Pearl Island(USA), a mile winner on Fibresand, was in with a chance on this hurdles debut when blundering away his rider at the third last.

4279 WEATHERBYS CHELTENHAM FESTIVAL BETTING GUIDE BEGINNERS' CHASE (19 fncs) 3m 1f 110y
3:10 (3:10) (Class 4) 5-Y-0+ **£4,714** (£1,404; £711; £364; £190)

Form RPR
1234 **1** **Amicelli (GER)**[63] 3213 7-11-3 .... RichardJohnson 129+
(P J Hobbs) *hld up: hit 1st: bmpd 2nd: hdwy appr 5th: hit 14th: led 3 out: sn clr: rdn out* **4/11**[1]
1P-P **2** *8* **Monteforte**[69] 3018 8-11-3 .... JasonMaguire 117+
(J A B Old) *led to 3 out: sn btn* **11/1**[3]
2PP **3** *3 ½* **Horcott Bay**[10] 4095 6-10-10 95...(b[1]) JamieMoore 104
(M G Rimell) *chsd ldr: rdn appr 12th: one pce fr 4 out* **33/1**
00P4 **4** *12* **Mobasher (IRE)**[17] 3955 7-11-3 .... SamThomas 101+
(Miss Venetia Williams) *hld up in tch: rdn and wkng whn mstke 4 out* **14/1**
PPPP **5** *dist* **Ellie Moss**[19] 3920 8-10-3 ....(v[1]) WillieMcCarthy(7) —
(A W Carroll) *t.k.h: j.rt 2nd: bhd fr 5th: lost tch 11th: t.o* **200/1**
0U6P **P** **Drive On Driver (IRE)**[15] 4016 9-10-3 78...................... MissLBrooke(7) —
(Lady Susan Brooke) *a bhd: lost tch 10th: t.o whn p.u bef 3 out* **150/1**
3F32 **P** **Kitski (FR)**[26] 3794 8-11-3 113.. KeithMercer —
(Ferdy Murphy) *a bhd: hit 6th: mstkes 8th and 10th: t.o whn p.u bef 2 out* **11/2**[2]
/P0P **P** **Stars'N'Stripes (IRE)**[69] 3017 8-11-3 .... PaulMoloney —
(W W Dennis) *hld up: hdwy and pckd 3rd: hit 11th: sn wknd: t.o whn p.u bef 3 out* **66/1**

6m 38.1s (3.90) **Going Correction** +0.35s/f (Yiel) **8** Ran SP% **109.3**
Speed ratings: **108,105,104,100,—** —,—,— CSF £4.74 TOTE £1.10: £1.02, £2.30, £2.70; EX 6.00.
Owner Jack Joseph **Bred** Gestut Brummerhof **Trained** Withycombe, Somerset

FOCUS
A reasonable beginners' chase for the track with the winner value for more than the official margin and the placed horses close to their marks.

NOTEBOOK
Amicelli(GER), fourth in a warm little race at Exeter in January on his chase debut, got off the mark over fences. Surviving a couple of early scares, he showed ahead three from home before scoring in workmanlike fashion. He likes this ground and will probably be kept on the go through the summer. *(op 4-9)*
Monteforte, sent off favourite on his last two starts in handicap hurdles but pulled up with breathing problems both times, made a satisfactory chasing debut, but was inclined to jump to his left at times and was unable to counter when collared by the favourite. He collapsed in the unsaddling enclosure after the race but recovered and was able to walk away. *(op 7-1)*
Horcott Bay, blinkered for the first time, again looked a hard ride and was beaten with four to jump, but this was a bit more encouraging.
Mobasher(IRE) was again not exactly fluent and did not achieve a great deal in finishing fourth. *(op 28-1)*
Kitski(FR) had made a reasonable start to his chasing career but he did not jump well and was in trouble with a circuit to run. *(op 5-1)*

4280 WEATHERBYS INSURANCE NOVICES' HURDLE (9 hdls 1 omitted) 2m 3f 110y
3:40 (3:43) (Class 4) 4-Y-0+ **£3,578** (£1,050; £525; £262)

Form RPR
2212 **1** **Oscatello (USA)**[30] 3729 6-11-9 110........................... WayneHutchinson 124+
(Ian Williams) *hld up in tch: rdn to ld after 2 out: sn clr* **5/4**[1]
0014 **2** *13* **Waterloo Son (IRE)**[35] 3646 6-11-9 115.......................... MarkBradburne 112+
(H D Daly) *a.p: ev ch 2 out: sn rdn: btn whn hit last* **15/2**[3]
14-5 **3** *5* **Giovanna**[21] 3902 5-10-9 .... WarrenMarston 91
(R T Phillips) *hld up and bhd: hdwy appr 3 out: wknd after 2 out* **10/1**
52 **4** *3 ½* **Sakenos (POL)**[18] 3948 6-11-2 ....(t) RichardJohnson 96+
(P J Hobbs) *led: rdn and hdd after 2 out: wknd appr last* **9/2**[2]
5 *1 ¾* **Airgusta (IRE)**[61] 5-11-2 .... TomDoyle 93
(C P Morlock) *hld up towards rr: hdwy 3 out: wknd after 2 out* **100/1**
50 **6** *nk* **Illuminati**[22] 3878 4-10-2 .... HowieEphgrave(5) 83
(L Corcoran) *hld up in tch: rdn 3 out: wknd 2 out* **16/1**
0 **7** *4* **Pagan Sky (IRE)**[22] 3883 7-11-2 .... SamThomas 88
(Miss Venetia Williams) *mid-div: lost pl 5th: n.d after* **28/1**
0 **8** *nk* **Corble (IRE)**[17] 3963 6-11-2 .... PJBrennan 88
(P J Hobbs) *hld up towards rr: hdwy after 5th: wknd appr 2 out* **100/1**
F150 **9** *3* **Spike Jones (NZ)**[22] 3880 8-10-11 108.......................... DerekLaverty(5) 85
(Mrs S M Johnson) *prom tl wknd 3 out* **20/1**
3326 **10** *1 ¾* **Kobai (IRE)**[32] 3685 7-11-2 .... RobertThornton 83
(A King) *w ldr tl rdn and wknd after 3 out* **14/1**
6-06 **11** *6* **A Few Kind Words (IRE)**[114] 2185 5-10-9 .... RichardSpate(7) 77
(Mrs K Waldron) *a bhd* **100/1**
P **Hot Rod (IRE)**[60] 6-11-2 .... APMcCoy —
(Jonjo O'Neill) *mid-div: wknd 5th: t.o whn p.u bef 3 out* **8/1**
0- **P** **Silk Appeal**[424] 3238 6-9-13 .... RyanCummings(10) —
(D J Wintle) *a bhd: t.o whn p.u bef 3 out* **100/1**
5P **P** **Carnival Town**[17] 3963 5-11-2 .... MickFitzgerald —
(Jonjo O'Neill) *mid-div: bhd fr 5th: t.o whn p.u bef 3 out* **66/1**

4m 54.4s (6.50) **Going Correction** +0.35s/f (Yiel)
WFA 4 from 5yo+ 7lb **14** Ran SP% **120.8**
Speed ratings: **101,95,93,92,91 91,89,89,88,87 85,—,—,—** CSF £10.95 TOTE £2.10: £1.60, £2.20, £2.20; EX 9.20.
Owner Rye Braune **Bred** Highland Farms Inc **Trained** Portway, Worcs

FOCUS
An interesting novice hurdle and the form looks as if it ought to stand up with the runner-up setting the level.

NOTEBOOK
Oscatello(USA) had been unfortunate to come up against the progressive Temoin at Sandown but made no mistake and won in decent style. He will not meet his engagement at Cheltenham but should continue to give a good account. *(op 7-4)*
Waterloo Son(IRE), the pick on official figures, had every chance but could not match the winner from the second last. He will come into his own when he goes over fences. *(op 7-1)*
Giovanna looked a threat when improving down the back straight but had again failed to settle in the early stages and she did not get home over this longer trip. *(tchd 11-1)*

Sakenos(POL) tried to make all and was only seen off after the second last. He is now eligible for a handicap mark. *(tchd 11-2)*
Airgusta(IRE) is a very limited performer at staying trips on the Flat but this was a pleasing hurdles debut. *Official explanation: vet said gelding was found to be sore*
Illuminatiran a fair race and is now eligible for handicaps. *(op 12-1)*
Pagan Sky(IRE) showed a bit more than he had over shorter on his recent hurdles debut at this venue. *(op 33-1)*
Corble(IRE) showed definite signs of ability on this second run over hurdles and will be qualified for handicaps after one more run.

4281 BETFAIR.COM H'CAP CHASE (12 fncs) 2m

4:10 (4:11) (Class 4) (0-105,104) 5-Y-0+

£4,697 (£1,387; £693; £347; £173; £87)

Form				RPR
3335	**1**		**Wild Power (GER)**[22] [3887] 8-10-7 **88** ... OwynNelmes(3) (Mrs H R J Nelmes) *hld up: hdwy 7th: led 3 out: rdn and r.o flat* **7/1**	98+
2233	**2**	*½*	**Jupon Vert (FR)**[22] [3887] 9-11-1 **93** ... TomScudamore (R J Hodges) *prom: led 3rd to 3 out: rdn and ev ch last: r.o* **13/2**	101+
-1F0	**3**	*1 ½*	**Whaleef**[12] [4050] 8-11-10 **102** ... (t) ChristianWilliams (B J Llewellyn) *hld up in tch: reminder after 5th: rdn and ev ch 3 out: kpt on flat* **16/1**	108
0-PU	**4**	*6*	**Pauntley Gofa**[17] [3964] 10-11-0 **97** ... MarkNicolls(5) (R C Harper) *mid-div: hdwy 6th: rdn 8th: one pce fr 4 out* **66/1**	97
214F	**5**	*2 ½*	**Nagano (FR)**[19] [3922] 8-11-12 **104** ... RobertThornton (Ian Williams) *hld up: hdwy 7th: wknd 3 out* **7/2**[1]	102+
044U	**6**	*7*	**Solar At'Em (IRE)**[22] [3888] 8-10-6 **84** ... (p) MarkBradburne (M Sheppard) *a.p: ev ch 3 out: sn wknd* **20/1**	76+
2306	**7**	*5*	**Notanotherdonkey (IRE)**[37] [3613] 6-10-13 **98** ... JohnKington(7) (M Scudamore) *nvr nr ldrs* **12/1**	83
F2PF	**8**	*nk*	**Call Me Jack (IRE)**[22] [3887] 10-9-11 **78** oh1 ... (t) StephenCraine(3) (M J M Evans) *led to 3rd: rdn 7th: wknd 4 out* **12/1**	63
-153	**9**	*4*	**Madison De Vonnas (FR)**[52] [3370] 6-11-12 **104** ... (t) BarryFenton (Miss E C Lavelle) *j.rt 4th: a bhd* **9/2**[2]	87+
P150	**10**	*17*	**Scotch Corner (IRE)**[19] [3919] 8-11-7 **99** ... (t) CarlLlewellyn (N A Twiston-Davies) *prom tl wknd 5th* **6/1**[3]	63
0550	**11**	*hd*	**Let's Rock**[26] [3803] 8-9-7 **78** oh11 ... MrRhysHughes(7) (Mrs A Price) *a bhd* **66/1**	42
3505	**R**		**Humid Climate**[40] [3562] 6-10-12 **90** ... WayneHutchinson (M Sheppard) *ref to r: tk no part* **33/1**	—
U1P0	**P**		**Bobsbest (IRE)**[213] [1152] 10-11-0 **92** ... MarcusFoley (R J Price) *a bhd: t.o whn p.u bef 3 out* **25/1**	—

4m 9.10s (6.60) **Going Correction** +0.35s/f (Yiel) **13** Ran SP% **116.3**
Speed ratings: **97,96,96,93,91 88,85,85,83,75 75,—,—** CSF £48.70 CT £702.42 TOTE £7.20: £2.00, £1.70, £6.70; EX 54.10.
Owner K A Nelmes **Bred** M Ommer **Trained** Warmwell, Dorset
■ A first winner for trainer Helen Nelmes, whose son Owyn was in the saddle.

FOCUS
A moderate but reasonably competitive handicap and the form appears solid, rated through the placed horses.

NOTEBOOK
Wild Power(GER) took full advantage of the chance given to him by the Handicapper and gained his first win since November 2004, with the exception of a recent charity Flat race at a point-to-point. He has not always found much when the pressure has been on, but his attitude *could not be faulted this time. Official explanation: trainer's representative said, regarding the improved form shown, gelding is inconsistent (op 8-1)*
Jupon Vert(FR) is laudably consistent but just found one too good. He has won off a 6lb higher mark and his turn should come round again. *(op 6-1 tchd 7-1)*
Whaleef ran a sound race after his recent confidence booster over hurdles but lacked a change of pace from the third last. *(tchd 20-1)*
Pauntley Gofa had pulled up four times in a row, three of them in points, before unseating his rider last time. He put that series of non-completions behind him with a better run, but merely plugged on in the latter stages.
Nagano(FR) could not make any impression from the fourth last and looks high enough in the weights over fences. *(op 5-1 tchd 10-3)*
Solar At'Em(IRE) ran well for a long way but faded from the second last. *(op 18-1 tchd 16-1)*
Madison De Vonnas(FR) should have finished close to Jupon Vert based on their meeting at Huntingdon in January but was always struggling after a mistake at the fourth. *(op 3-1 tchd 5-1)*

4282 WEATHERBYS BANK H'CAP HURDLE (9 hdls 1 omitted) 2m 3f 110y

4:40 (4:41) (Class 4) (0-110,110) 4-Y-0+ **£3,903** (£1,146; £573; £286)

Form				RPR
-203	**1**		**Abraham Smith**[24] [3846] 6-10-11 **100** ... MarkNicolls(5) (B J Eckley) *mde all: mstke 5th: pushed along whn lft clr last* **33/1**	112+
3561	**2**	*14*	**Proprioception (IRE)**[35] [3655] 4-10-5 **98** ... RobertThornton (A King) *hld up in mid-div: hdwy 4th: rdn appr 3 out: btn whn lft clr last* **11/2**[3]	89+
06F0	**3**	*3 ½*	**Presenter (IRE)**[24] [3848] 6-9-13 **90** ... MrLRPayter(7) (M Sheppard) *hld up and bhd: hdwy appr 3 out: wknd 2 out* **33/1**	85+
3-P0	**4**	*7*	**Hoh Nelson**[22] [3889] 5-10-13 **104** ... (p) MrRHodges(7) (Mrs A Price) *mid-div: rdn after 5th: no real prog fr 3 out* **100/1**	94+
P0-1	**5**	*8*	**Prestbury Knight**[66] [3131] 6-11-9 **107** ... CarlLlewellyn (N A Twiston-Davies) *prom tl wknd appr 3 out* **12/1**	86
44-5	**6**	*shd*	**Porak (IRE)**[10] [4097] 9-11-1 **104** ... DerekLaverty(5) (W Davies) *prom tl rdn and wknd appr 3 out* **100/1**	82
466P	**7**	*nk*	**Pearly Star**[11] [4080] 5-10-8 **92** ... (v[1]) WayneHutchinson (A King) *prom tl rdn and wknd after 3 out* **16/1**	70
60P6	**8**	*1 ½*	**Ol' Man River (IRE)**[39] [3577] 6-10-3 **87** ... MarkBradburne (H D Daly) *a bhd* **14/1**	64
PP00	**9**	*8*	**Nick's Choice**[9] [4105] 10-10-4 **95** ... MrTJO'Brien(7) (D Burchell) *mid-div: bhd fr 3 out* **28/1**	64
0-4P	**10**	*dist*	**Jesper (FR)**[292] [416] 9-10-10 **101** ... (t) SeanQuinlan(7) (R T Phillips) *a bhd: t.o* **50/1**	—
PPFU	**11**	*8*	**Mazzareme (IRE)**[30] [3733] 8-11-12 **110** ... SamThomas (Miss Venetia Williams) *hld up in tch: rdn and wknd 4th: t.o* **10/1**	—
-112	**12**	*8*	**Return Home**[40] [3561] 7-11-2 **100** ... PaulMoloney (J S Smith) *hld up in tch: wknd 5th: t.o* **4/1**[1]	—
05P5	**P**		**What'sonyourmind (IRE)**[11] [4067] 6-10-10 **94** ... APMcCoy (Jonjo O'Neill) *bhd tl p.u bef last* **5/1**[2]	—
261-	**P**		**Chef Tartare (FR)**[318] [4966] 6-11-5 **110** ... (t) RichardSpate(7) (Mrs K Waldron) *hld up: hdwy 4th: wknd 3 out: p.u bef 2 out* **16/1**	—
-500	**P**		**Shady Anne**[24] [3848] 8-10-11 **95** ... (p) LeightonAspell (F Jordan) *prom: rdn appr 3 out: sn wknd: bhd whn p.u after 2 out* **33/1**	—
1	**U**		**Anemix (FR)**[18] [3947] 5-11-7 **110** ... HowieEphgrave(5) (L Corcoran) *hld up and bhd: hdwy after 5th: rdn after 2 out: 3l 2nd and hld whn stmbld and uns rdr last* **6/1**	117+

4m 51.5s (3.60) **Going Correction** +0.35s/f (Yiel)
WFA 4 from 5yo+ 7lb **16** Ran SP% **117.8**
Speed ratings: **106,100,99,96,93 92,92,92,89,— —,—,—,—,— —** CSF £198.10 CT £5998.36 TOTE £38.10: £4.50, £1.50, £6.30, £35.60; EX 304.60.
Owner Brian Eckley **Bred** B J Eckley **Trained** Llanspyddid, Powys

FOCUS
An ordinary handicap, in which the winner set a fair pace and sound enough form with those in the frame behind the winner close to their marks.

NOTEBOOK
Abraham Smith, not disgraced behind Denman at Bangor last time, made every yard. He made more than one jumping error, but stayed on dourly and was in command when his nearest pursuer departed at the final flight. *(op 25-1)*
Proprioception(IRE), 6lb higher than when scoring at Southwell but officially a pound well in, did not really stay this longer trip but was left in second at the final flight. *(op 7-1)*
Presenter(IRE) kept on to notch only his second placing in nine attempts over hurdles. The Handicapper has given him a chance and this longer trip helped.
Hoh Nelson ran his best race since joining this yard from Charlie Mann but never looked like getting to the leaders. *(op 66-1)*
Prestbury Knight, a winner in novice company in December, ran respectably but probably found this trip on the short side. He was due to race in a tongue strap, but it was removed at the start as *he was resenting it, and Llewellyn said that this adversely affected the gelding's performance. Official explanation: jockey said tongue strap was removed at start as gelding was resenting it and this adversely affected its performance*
Pearly Star ran a fair race in the first-time visor but faded on the approach to the second last. *(tchd 14-1)*
Return Home , who was never able to get in the hunt, was no less than 19lb higher than when gaining his first win on New Year's Eve. *(op 5-1 tchd 11-2)*
Anemix(FR), winner of his only previous run over hurdles and saddled with top weight, looked sure to win when cruising into second place, but when coming off the bridle on the home turn he did not find a great deal and he was held when stumbling and ejecting his rider at the last. He is still unexposed and there could be more improvement in him. *(op 4-1)*
What'sonyourmind(IRE) was the subject of support in the morning but was struggling with a circuit to run and eventually pulled up. *(op 4-1)*

4283 JULIAN GRAVES NOVICES' HUNTERS' CHASE (14 fncs) 2m 3f

5:10 (5:11) (Class 6) 6-Y-0+ **£1,249** (£387; £193; £96)

Form				RPR
0F5/	**1**		**Abbey Days (IRE)**[8] 9-11-11 ... MrAWintle(3) (S Flook) *hld up in mid-div: hdwy whn mstke 5th: mstke 7th: led 4 out: clr 2 out: easily* **10/3**[3]	98+
0/P-	**2**	*20*	**Jac An Ree (IRE)**[310] 10-11-9 ... MrPGHall(5) (Mrs D M Grissell) *bhd: rdn 8th: hdwy appr 3 out: wnt 2nd appr last: no ch w wnr* **3/1**[2]	78
3	**3**	*3*	**Nailed On**[19] [3924] 7-11-9 ... MrAndrewMartin(5) (Andrew J Martin) *j. bdly lft: hld up: hdwy 6th: chsd wnr 2 out tl appr last: one pce* **9/2**	80+
0P/	**4**	*dist*	**Gunsmoke**[16] 8-11-7 ... MrJMahot(7) (Ms Caroline Walker) *led to 9th: wknd 4 out: t.o* **33/1**	—
	5	*2 ½*	**Bristol Bridge**[16] 9-11-7 ... MissIsabelTompsett(7) (Ms M L Byrom) *chsd ldrs tl wknd after 4 out: t.o* **66/1**	—
00/	**P**		**Tuff Joint (IRE)**[317] 8-11-7 ... (t) MrRHodges(7) (Mrs A Price) *t.o fr 3rd: p.u bef 9th* **33/1**	—
5P6P	**P**		**Lost Treasure (IRE)**[135] [1832] 9-11-7 63 ... MrRhysHughes(7) (Mrs M Evans) *t.o fr 3rd: p.u bef 9th* **9/1**	—
PFP-	**F**		**Itsallupintheair**[16] 10-11-9 ... MrsLucyRowsell(5) (Miss A Meakins) *a bhd: t.o whn fell 4 out* **20/1**	—
PP/P	**P**		**Come On Boy**[16] 12-11-7 ... (b) MrRMcCarthy(7) (T G Williams) *chsd ldr tl after 5th: wknd qckly 6th: p.u bef 8th* **66/1**	—
/P-P	**P**		**Barton Bandit**[26] [3805] 10-11-7 ... (p) MrJoshuaHarris(7) (Miss Sarah Kent) *prom: rdn 6th: wkng whn mstke 7th: p.u bef 9th* **66/1**	—
/00-	**P**		**Classi Maureen**[23] 6-11-2 ... MrRWoollacott(5) (S A Hughes) *prom: mstke 4th: led 9th tl mstke 4 out: wknd after 2 out: p.u bef last* **11/4**[1]	—

4m 55.8s (9.20) **Going Correction** +0.35s/f (Yiel) **11** Ran SP% **118.0**
Speed ratings: **94,85,84,—,— —,—,—,—,— —** CSF £13.62 TOTE £3.20: £2.30, £3.30, £1.40; EX 20.20 Place 6 £215.24, Place 5 £99.10.
Owner S Flook **Bred** Denis Horgan **Trained** Leominster, Herefordshire

FOCUS
A poor hunter chase in which few of the runners could boast any form under Rules.

NOTEBOOK
Abbey Days(IRE), winner of consecutive point-to-points in January prior to a couple of defeats, proved much too good for his rivals, jumping well and coming clear from the third last. The fast pace suited him on this drop in trip. *(op 11-4)*
Jac An Ree(IRE), fairly consistent at a low level between the flags, was having his first run since April. He moved into a remote second on the home turn but needs further than this. *(op 9-2)*
Nailed On jumped alarmingly out to his left at times, forfeiting a lot of ground. He has finished third in his last two hunter chases but is a very risky proposition.
Classi Maureen, runner-up in an intermediate point-to-point last month on her return to action, lost her lead when blundering at the final ditch and was well beaten in fourth when pulling up before the last. *Official explanation: jockey said mare was exhausted (op 5-2 tchd 7-2)*
T/Plt: £213.90 to a £1 stake. Pool: £52,451.60. 179.00 winning tickets. T/Qpdt: £38.70 to a £1 stake. Pool: £4,478.10. 85.50 winning tickets. KH

4032 EXETER (R-H)

Tuesday, March 7

OFFICIAL GOING: Heavy
Bottomless ground and it was especially hard to come from off the pace, particularly on the hurdles course.
Wind: Light, across Weather: Light rain

4284 GREGORY DISTRIBUTION NOVICES' HURDLE (DIV I) (10 hdls 3 omitted) 3m 110y

2:20 (2:25) (Class 4) 4-Y-0+ **£2,927** (£859; £429; £214)

Form				RPR
-415	**1**		**In Accord**[71] [2956] 7-11-9 115 ... RichardJohnson (H D Daly) *hld up and bhd: hdwy 7th: rdn appr last: styd on to ld last strides* **10/11**[1]	117
-4P3	**2**	*nk*	**El Hombre Del Rio (IRE)**[23] [3876] 9-11-3 102 ... JoeTizzard (V G Greenway) *a.p: led 7th: j.rt last: hrd rdn flat: ct last strides* **8/1**	111
2	**3**	*30*	**Just For Men (IRE)**[62] [3240] 6-11-3 ... ChristianWilliams (P F Nicholls) *hld up in mid-div: hdwy after 5th: wknd appr 2 out* **6/1**[3]	81

60 **4** *hd* **Forest Miller**[21] 3906 7-11-3 .... WarrenMarston 81
(R T Phillips) *hld up: sltly hmpd 5th: hdwy appr 6th: wkng whn mstke 2 out* **66/1**

5 *6* **Captain Windsor (IRE)**[317] 5-11-3 .... APMcCoy 80+
(P F Nicholls) *hld up and bhd: hdwy 7th: ev ch appr 2 out: sn rdn and wknd: fin tired* **11/4**[2]

- **P** **Monzon (FR)**[111] 6-10-12 .... JohnnyLevins(5) —
(B G Powell) *chsd ldr: wknd qckly and p.u bef 2 out* **40/1**

-300 **F** **Jeepers Creepers**[9] 4128 6-10-12 .... DerekLaverty(5) —
(Mrs A M Thorpe) *hld up in tch: 3l 4th whn fell 5th* **250/1**

60 **P** **Cleverality (IRE)**[42] 3545 6-11-3 .... PaulMoloney —
(Evan Williams) *led to 7th: wknd qckly: t.o whn p.u bef 2 out* **100/1**

6m 48.8s (35.50) **Going Correction** +1.35s/f (Heav) **8** Ran SP% **109.8**
Speed ratings: **97,96,87,87,85** —,—,— CSF £8.37 TOTE £1.10: £1.10, £1.80, £1.90; EX 7.40.
Owner T F F Nixon **Bred** T F F Nixon **Trained** Stanton Lacy, Shropshire

FOCUS
An ordinary novices' hurdle on paper and the form looks suspect to say the least. The winner is rated to his mark but the 102-rated runner-up finished 30-lengths clear of the third. Richard Johnson deserves much credit for his winning ride. Flight past stands and middle flight in straight omitted.

NOTEBOOK
In Accord, last seen when disappointing on good ground at Huntingdon back in December, has clearly benefited from a break and handled the heavy ground, which he won on at Chepstow earlier in the season, perfectly well. He looked held jumping the last, but rallied bravely under a strong ride from Johnson to get up close home. His trainer's horses are back in fine form now and this future three-mile chaser may now be ready for a move into handicaps. *(op 11-8)*
El Hombre Del Rio(IRE) is best known as a chaser, but he ran well in a moderate handicap hurdle here last month and the extra quarter-mile suited him well. He came through to take it up a fair way out and looked to have done enough, but tired a little on the run-in and was mown down close home. He does little for the form, but is clearly in good heart and can find a race back in handicaps. *(op 12-1 tchd 7-1)*
Just For Men(IRE), runner-up at Wincanton on his Rules debut, was expected to be suited by this sterner test of stamina but, having jumped less than fluently, he began to struggle over half a mile out and finished very tired. He deserves another chance under slightly less taxing circumstances, but does not look one of his powerful yard's brighter prospects. *(op 5-1 tchd 9-2)*
Forest Miller kept going well to just miss out on third, recording his best effort thus far. By dour Flat-stayer Classic Cliche, stamina is clearly his strong suit and he may be open to a little improvement in low-grade handicaps. *(op 40-1)*
Captain Windsor(IRE), the supposed Nicholls first-string, was undoubtedly the most interesting runner in the line-up, and the booking of McCoy took the eye. Withdrawn because of the fast ground at Newbury the previous weekend, he did not jump particularly fluently, but still came through to have every chance turning in, only to fade disappointingly. He finished so tired McCoy had to dismount after the line and it remains to be seen what he is capable of. *(tchd 10-3 in a place)*
Monzon(FR), ex-Francois Doumen-trained, showed little on this first start for Brendan Powell, but it *is entirely possible this ground proved too much for him and he may be worthy of another chance. (op 28-1)*

4285 GREGORY DISTRIBUTION NOVICES' HURDLE (DIV II) (10 hdls 3 omitted) 3m 110y
2:50 (2:57) (Class 4) 4-Y-0+ **£2,927** (£859; £429; £214)

Form RPR

0/12 **1** **Before Dark (IRE)**[39] 3598 8-11-9 110 .... RichardJohnson 110+
(Mrs H Dalton) *hld up: hdwy to ld appr 4th: j.rt 2 out and last: drvn out* **9/2**[2]

4234 **2** *1* **Five Alley (IRE)**[22] 3900 9-11-3 100 .... BenjaminHitchcott 101
(R H Buckler) *w ldrs: ev ch 2 out: sn rdn: nt qckn flat* **20/1**[3]

3/04 **3** *2* **The Wooden Spoon (IRE)**[46] 3477 8-11-3 .... LeightonAspell 99
(L Wells) *led tl appr 4th: a.p: rdn appr 2 out: styd on one pce flat* **25/1**

0-62 **4** *nk* **Heros Collonges (FR)**[70] 3022 11-11-3 .... JohnMcNamara 100+
(P F Nicholls) *hld up and bhd: hdwy 5th: rdn after 2 out: one pce flat* **2/5**[1]

00 **5** *dist* **Red Echo (FR)**[14] 4033 5-11-0 .... TomMalone(3) —
(M C Pipe) *prom tl wknd 8th: t.o* **50/1**

P-0 **6** *30* **Harps Hall (IRE)**[23] 3885 12-10-7 .... MarkHunter(10) —
(N I M Rossiter) *hld up: lost tch fr 6th: t.o* **250/1**

P **7** *nk* **Call Out (IRE)**[23] 3881 6-10-10 .... MissLGardner(7) —
(Mrs S Gardner) *plld hrd: prom tl wknd 7th: sn t.o* **100/1**

P **P** **Brooking (IRE)**[21] 3906 8-11-3 .... WarrenMarston —
(R T Phillips) *bhd fr 7th: t.o whn p.u after 8th* **100/1**

P **Darkest Peru (IRE)** 6-10-10 .... JamesWhite(7) —
(A S T Holdsworth) *plld hrd in rr: hit 7th: sn t.o: p.u bef 2 out* **100/1**

-00P **P** **Judy's Lad**[19] 3948 7-11-0 .... OwynNelmes(3) —
(Mrs H R J Nelmes) *a bhd: nt fluent 5th: t.o whn p.u after 2 out* **250/1**

6m 55.7s (42.40) **Going Correction** +1.35s/f (Heav) **10** Ran SP% **103.9**
Speed ratings: **86,85,85,84,**— —,—,—,—,— CSF £50.86 TOTE £5.30: £1.10, £2.00, £2.30; EX 13.70.
Owner C B Compton **Bred** Mrs D R Lonergan **Trained** Norton, Shropshire

FOCUS
The weaker of the two divisions on paper, despite the presence of smart staying-chaser Heros Collonges with the first two giving the best guide to the level of the form. Flight past stands and middle flight in straight omitted.

NOTEBOOK
Before Dark(IRE) came through to lead having been in rear early, a wise move considering it was hard to make ground, and he ground it out down the straight to hold on well from the persistent challenge of Five Alley. Previously successful over three-miles two-furlongs, stamina was never going to be a problem and connections must now be tempted to try their hand handicapping with him. *(op 4-1)*
Five Alley(IRE) has never found winning easy, but he was one of the more obvious ones under these conditions and he was at an advantage in racing prominently. He led turning in, but the winner proved too strong in the end. *(op 14-1)*
The Wooden Spoon(IRE) is gradually heading the right way, and he is now qualified to contest handicaps. *(op 20-1)*
Heros Collonges(FR), a good thing on his chasing form, failed to live up to expectations on this return to hurdles and looked particularly slow back in fourth. His trainer was inclined to blame the ground, which is a reasonable enough excuse, but for such a strong-stayer it was disappointing he was not made more use of on a day when it seemed hard to make ground. This was hardly an ideal Grand National prep, but he ran well in the race last year, finished second in this season's *Welsh version, and could go well at Aintree again with the better ground likely to suit. (tchd 4-11 and 4-9)*
Red Echo(FR) will be capable of better once handicapping. *(op 33-1)*

4286 JOHN SMITH'S/E.B.F. MARES' ONLY "NATIONAL HUNT" NOVICES' HURDLE (QUALIFIER) (7 hdls 3 omitted) 2m 3f
3:20 (3:26) (Class 4) 4-Y-0+ **£4,554** (£1,337; £668; £333)

Form RPR

66-5 **1** **Miss Doublet**[141] 1776 5-10-11 82 .... RichardYoung(3) 82+
(J W Mullins) *a.p: led after 5th: hit 2 out: drvn out* **16/1**[3]

2101 **2** *1 1/4* **Bally Bolshoi (IRE)**[14] 4034 6-11-12 107 .... RichardJohnson 92
(Mrs S D Williams) *hld up: hdwy and hit 4th: ev ch 2 out: sn rdn: nt qckn flat* **4/6**[1]

06 **3** *1/2* **Young Siouxsie**[23] 3884 6-10-9 .... StevenCrawford(5) 79
(N A Twiston-Davies) *a.p: hrd rdn and ev ch appr last: nt qckn flat* **33/1**

0/ **4** *2 1/2* **Emma's Dream**[696] 4739 7-11-0 .... ChristianWilliams 77
(P F Nicholls) *hld up in tch: rdn and one pce fr 2 out* **16/1**[3]

/6 **5** *2 1/2* **Madam Fleet (IRE)**[123] 2021 7-10-7 .... MrsMRoberts(7) 74
(M J Coombe) *prom tl wknd appr last* **100/1**

123P **6** *nk* **Bonchester Bridge**[89] 2718 5-11-0 .... MickFitzgerald 74
(N J Henderson) *hld up: hdwy appr 5th: ev ch 2 out: sn rdn: wknd flat* **7/2**[2]

7 *17* **Miss Flossy (IRE)** 5-11-0 .... WayneHutchinson 57
(Mrs S D Williams) *hld up in tch: wknd 2 out: mstke last* **25/1**

0060 **8** *1* **She's Our Daisy (IRE)**[71] 2997 6-11-0 70 .... RJGreene 56
(R H Buckler) *hld up towards rr: mstke 3rd: hdwy 5th: j.rt 2 out: sn wknd: j.rt and mstke last* **16/1**[3]

-000 **9** *dist* **She's No Muppet**[17] 3979 6-11-0 67 .... SeanCurran —
(N R Mitchell) *t.k.h: led tl after 5th: sn rdn and wknd: t.o* **100/1**

0B **10** *4* **Pyleigh Lady**[23] 3884 5-10-11 .... TomMalone(3) —
(S C Burrough) *a bhd: t.o fr 3rd* **66/1**

00-0 **P** **Irish Totty**[23] 3882 7-11-0 .... JimmyMcCarthy —
(C J Down) *plld hrd towards rr: short-lived effrt 5th: t.o whn p.u bef 2 out* **66/1**

5m 18.7s (37.80) **Going Correction** +1.35s/f (Heav) **11** Ran SP% **111.6**
Speed ratings: **74,73,73,72,71 71,63,63,**—,— — CSF £26.64 TOTE £26.80: £4.00, £1.10, £5.10; EX 46.10.
Owner Sir Nicholas Bowden **Bred** N R Bowden **Trained** Wilsford-Cum-Lake, Wilts
■ Stewards' Enquiry : Tom Malone seven-day ban: failed to take all reasonable and permissible measures to obtain best possible placing (Mar 18-24)

FOCUS
A very slow pace and it was again an advantage to race prominently. The form looks very suspect. Flight past stands and middle flight in straight omitted.

NOTEBOOK
Miss Doublet ◆, who was up there from an early stage, stayed on too strongly for the penalised favourite Bally Bolshoi under pressure. Well beaten in all previous tries over hurdles, she was never jumping when tried in a novices' handicap chase at Plumpton back in October, but she had been given a break since and has clearly improved. Being a product of high-class Flat-stayer Double Trigger, stamina was never going to be a problem and it was more a case of whether or not she would be able to handle the ground, which she did admirably. Last year's winner of this Pennyrose Bay went on to collect the Listed Mares' Final at Newbury, and there could be worse long-shots if taking her chance. *(op 14-1)*
Bally Bolshoi(IRE) was bidding to provide Johnson with the first three winners on the card, but her double-penalty proved too much in the end and she was unable to get on top of the winner, keeping on at just the one pace in second. She too deserves her chance in the Mares' Final at Newbury. *(op 4-5 tchd 5-6)*
Young Siouxsie left her previous efforts behind faced with a proper test at the distance, staying on dourly down the straight under a strong ride from Crawford. This was only her third start and it is safe to assume there is more to come. *(op 20-1)*
Emma's Dream, returning from a lengthy absence, did remarkably well considering and it is hoped she can go on from this. *(op 11-1)*
Madam Fleet(IRE) ran way above expectations on this hurdles debut, but is probably not up to winning until competing at a lowly level in handicaps. *(op 66-1)*
Bonchester Bridge, whose previous form had come on a sounder surface, was unable to handle the testing conditions, floundering once asked for maximum effort. This is two poor efforts in a row now, but she may be able to leave this form behind back on faster ground. *(tchd 10-3)*
Pyleigh Lady *Official explanation: vet said mare was lame on second examination (op 50-1)*

4287 SPORTING INDEX DEVON NATIONAL H'CAP CHASE (17 fncs 4 omitted) 3m 6f 110y
3:50 (3:56) (Class 3) (0-125,125) 5-Y-0+
£12,526 (£3,700; £1,850; £926; £462; £232)

Form RPR

P23P **1** **Earl's Kitchen**[10] 4103 9-10-12 111 .... (p) JoeTizzard 121+
(C L Tizzard) *a.p: led 2 out: all out* **9/1**

230P **2** *1/2* **Admiral Peary (IRE)**[16] 4016 10-10-13 112 .... APMcCoy 121+
(C R Egerton) *a.p: led 8th: j.rt after: hdd 2 out: ev ch last: hrd rdn: styd on* **9/1**

0P61 **3** *12* **Naunton Brook**[18] 3965 7-11-12 125 .... (t) CarlLlewellyn 124+
(N A Twiston-Davies) *hdwy after 4th: wkng whn lft 3rd 2 out* **16/1**

P2FP **4** *7* **Kittenkat**[10] 4103 12-10-4 103 .... MatthewBatchelor 92
(N R Mitchell) *hld up in mid-div: mstke 7th: lost pl 8th: styd on fr 4 out: n.d* **16/1**

6400 **5** *21* **Twisted Logic (IRE)**[64] 3212 13-10-9 108 .... RobertWalford 76
(R H Alner) *hld up: hdwy appr 10th: hit 4 out: sn wknd* **22/1**

2435 **6** *13* **Woodlands Genpower (IRE)**[16] 4016 8-11-5 118 .....(p) MarkBradburne 73
(P A Pritchard) *prom: rdn and lost pl 6th: bhd fr 13th* **6/1**[2]

0F1U **P** **Happy Shopper (IRE)**[8] 4152 6-10-3 102 .... RichardJohnson —
(M C Pipe) *prom tl wknd 13th: bhd whn p.u bef 4 out* **5/2**[1]

2U31 **P** **Fin Bec (FR)**[36] 3649 13-10-10 109 .... (b) TomDoyle —
(R Curtis) *led to 8th: wknd appr 10th: t.o whn p.u bef 13th* **33/1**

4F45 **P** **Charlies Future**[16] 4014 8-10-10 109 .... PJBrennan —
(S C Burrough) *a bhd: rdn appr 10th: t.o whn p.u bef 13th* **25/1**

1PP5 **P** **Sir Frosty**[25] 3845 13-10-3 102 .... TimmyMurphy 91
(B J M Ryall) *hld up and bhd: hdwy 12th: wkng whn sltly hmpd 2 out: p.u flat* **13/2**[3]

2061 **F** **Even More (IRE)**[19] 3949 11-11-1 114 .... AndrewThornton 118
(R H Alner) *hld up: lost pl 5th: hdwy 11th: rdn appr 4 out: 3 l 3rd whn fell 2 out* **20/1**

1UP3 **P** **Concert Pianist**[22] 3900 11-11-0 113 .... LeightonAspell —
(P Winkworth) *a bhd: mstke 7th: rdn and struggling after 9th: t.o whn p.u bef 13th* **14/1**

8m 22.7s **12** Ran SP% **110.5**
CSF £76.55 CT £1210.56 TOTE £10.00: £3.50, £2.80, £5.00; EX 85.20.
Owner Mrs J E Purdie **Bred** Mrs J E Purdie **Trained** Milborne Port, Dorset

FOCUS
A race for only the most hardcore of stayers and a severe test. The form looks pretty solid with the first two close to their marks. First two fences past stands omitted.

NOTEBOOK
Earl's Kitchen, whose two solid placed efforts at Chepstow in January would have seen him a leading contender for this, was reportedly never travelling when pulled up at the Welsh track late last month and as a result had a bit to prove. However, he was able to return to his best in the first-time cheekpieces, slogging it out down the straight, and connections are now eyeing a crack at the Midlands Grand National. *(op 8-1)*

Admiral Peary(IRE) bounced back from a couple of poor efforts to take second, pushing the winner right the way to the line despite jumping out to his right in the straight. This ground suits the son of Lord Americo well however, and he is unlikely to get much more of it at this time of year. *(op 10-1 tchd 8-1)*

Naunton Brook, a recent winner at Market Rasen, deserves much credit for lumping 11st-12lb around under these conditions, and he kept going well enough back in third. He has found his form again. *(op 12-1)*

Kittenkat, believe it or not, had her ideal conditions and she was doing her best work late. A more positive ride would have seen her go close for third. *(op 14-1)*

Twisted Logic(IRE), a course specialist, ran well for a long way, third turning in, but in the end the heavy ground took its toll and he faded out of it. *(op 25-1)*

Woodlands Genpower(IRE) has not lived up to early expectation and this severe test, which should really have suited, failed to revive this fortunes. *(op 7-1 tchd 15-2)*

Sir Frosty, although traditionally a hold-up performer, today may have been the day to try something different as making ground was particularly hard. He travelled sweeter than he has for a while, but was simply unable to make headway. *Official explanation: jockey said gelding had no more to give (op 11-4 tchd 3-1 and 10-3 in a place)*

Even More(IRE), who recently scored at Taunton, has never won off a mark this high, but he was keeping on in third and not out of it when falling at the second-last. It is hoped this does not affect his confidence. *(op 11-4 tchd 3-1 and 10-3 in a place)*

Happy Shopper(IRE), who may have been unbeaten coming into this with a little more luck. He held a prominent early position, but it all proved too much for the inexperienced seven-year-old in the end and he was pulled in before the fourth last. *(op 11-4 tchd 3-1 and 10-3 in a place)*

4288 WEATHERBYS CHELTENHAM FESTIVAL BETTING GUIDE NOVICES' CHASE (13 fncs 2 omitted) 2m 3f 110y

4:20 (4:27) (Class 4) 5-Y-0+ **£4,228** (£1,241; £620; £310)

Form					RPR
-000	**1**		**Cousin Nicky**^{45} 3508 5-10-8 105 ... RichardJohnson (P J Hobbs) *led to 3rd: w ldr: led 7th: nt fluent 3 out: rdn clr appr last: eased flat*	**5/1**^{3}	115+
-065	**2**	*24*	**Lesdream**^{14} 4037 9-10-9 105 ... ChrisHonour(5) (J D Frost) *hld up in tch: chsd wnr fr 8th: blnd 9th: rdn whn mstkes 3 out and 2 out: eased whn btn flat*	**9/1**	111+
5221	**3**	*dist*	**Wizard Of Edge**^{47} 3465 6-11-0 100 ... (b) ChristianWilliams (R J Hodges) *hld up: hdwy and hit 8th: wknd after 9th: t.o*	**2/1**^{1}	—
56-P	**4**	*dist*	**The Cad (IRE)**^{17} 3982 6-10-9 90 ... DarylJacob(5) (R H Alner) *hld up in tch: wknd after 8th: t.o*	**16/1**	—
P05	**F**		**Master Billyboy (IRE)**^{23} 3879 8-11-0 102 ... WayneHutchinson (Mrs S D Williams) *3rd whn fell 3rd*	**4/1**^{2}	—
2305	**P**		**Missyl (FR)**^{91} 2683 6-11-0 105 ... AndrewThornton (R H Alner) *bhd fr 6th: t.o whn p.u bef 4 out*	**13/2**	—
000F	**P**		**Manque Pas D'Air (FR)**^{19} 3938 6-10-7 85 ... JasonMaguire (T R George) *w ldr: led 3rd to 7th: 3rd and wkng whn hit 9th: sn p.u*	**33/1**	—
120P	**P**		**Caesarean Hunter (USA)**^{13} 4053 7-10-7 102 ... SeanQuinlan(7) (R T Phillips) *a bhd: hmpd 3rd: rdn appr 6th: t.o whn p.u bef 4 out*	**11/1**	—

5m 11.3s (17.40) **Going Correction** +1.00s/f (Soft)

WFA 5 from 6yo+ 4lb **8** Ran SP% **110.5**

Speed ratings: **105,95,**—,—,— —,—,— CSF £44.11 TOTE £5.10: £2.30, £2.10, £1.10; EX 45.80.

Owner Patrick Beach **Bred** Andrew Jenkins **Trained** Withycombe, Somerset

FOCUS

An uncompetitive race in which chasing debutant Cousin Nicky ran out an easy winner with the second rated as beaten ten lengths. First two fences past stands omitted.

NOTEBOOK

Cousin Nicky, who had lost his form completely over hurdles, was revitalised by this switch to fences and Johnson had a fairly straightforward ride. Disputing it with outsider Manque Pas D'Air from an early stage, he had all bar Lesdream dead and buried turning in and he came well clear after the last. He has been allotted a mark of 105 and is an interesting prospect for handicaps, but will no doubt go up a fair bit for this and will need to progress. *(tchd 9-2)*

Lesdream gradually fell further behind in the straight, being eased off once beaten, but he was the only one who could live with the winner and for that deserves some credit. *(op 12-1)*

Wizard Of Edge, a fortunate winner at Taunton, was unable to operate under such severe conditions and it was no surprise to see him trail in a well-beaten third. He deserves another chance back on better ground. *Official explanation: jockey said gelding was unsuited by the heavy ground (op 13-8 tchd 6-4 and 9-4 in a place)*

The Cad(IRE), making his chasing debut, seemed to find the heavy going getting the better of him and is worthy of another chance back on better ground. *(op 25-1)*

Caesarean Hunter(USA) continues to go the wrong way, while Master Billyboy got no further than the third. *(op 7-1 tchd 6-1)*

Master Billyboy(IRE) looked to hold obvious claims on his recent course effort, but got no further than the third. *(op 7-1 tchd 6-1)*

Missyl(FR), who was kept wide in search of slightly better ground, but was struggling a long way out before being pulled-up. *(op 7-1 tchd 6-1)*

4289 SYDNEY JOHN DART H'CAP HURDLE (7 hdls 3 omitted) 2m 3f

4:50 (4:56) (Class 4) (0-115,115) 4-Y-0+ **£4,554** (£1,337; £668; £333)

Form					RPR
P004	**1**		**Bak To Bill**^{23} 3876 11-10-4 **100** ... MissLGardner(7) (Mrs S Gardner) *a.p: led appr 2 out: continually hmpd by loose horse: hit last: rdn out*	**12/1**	112+
4-1F	**2**	*1 1/2*	**Il'Athou (FR)**^{107} 2368 10-11-1 **104** ... JoeTizzard (S E H Sherwood) *led tl after 5th: rdn 2 out: kpt on flat*	**7/2**^{2}	111
0002	**3**	*15*	**Visibility (FR)**^{11} 4093 7-11-4 **114** ... (v) AndrewGlassonbury(7) (M C Pipe) *a.p: led 5th: rdn and hdd appr 2 out: wknd appr last*	**5/1**^{3}	107+
-40U	**4**	*3 1/2*	**Le Rochelais (FR)**^{50} 3426 7-11-2 **105** ... AndrewThornton (R H Alner) *hld up in mid-div: lost pl 4th: sme hdwy appr 2 out: no further prog*	**10/1**	93
1355	**5**	*2 1/2*	**Kings Castle (IRE)**^{17} 3993 11-10-11 **107** ... JamesWhite(7) (R J Hodges) *hld up: hdwy 3rd: wknd appr 2 out*	**9/1**	93
020	**6**	*28*	**Glimmer Of Light (IRE)**^{21} 3908 6-11-2 **105** ... RobertThornton (A King) *racd wd: hld up and bhd: hdwy appr 3rd: wknd after 2 out*	**16/1**	63
1400	**7**	*11*	**Rift Valley (IRE)**^{10} 4119 11-11-12 **115** ... RichardJohnson (P J Hobbs) *prom: lost pl after 2nd: sn bhd*	**33/1**	62
060	**P**		**Idian Mix (FR)**^{19} 3950 5-10-10 **102** ... TomMalone(3) (M C Pipe) *a bhd: t.o whn p.u bef 2 out*	**33/1**	—
2F55	**P**		**Miss Skippy**^{18} 3959 7-10-9 **98** ... JamesDavies (A G Newcombe) *prom tl wknd 3rd: t.o whn p.u bef 2 out*	**28/1**	—
006P	**R**		**Haloo Baloo**^{19} 3940 6-10-8 **97** ... APMcCoy (Jonjo O'Neill) *hld up and bhd: sme hdwy whn rn out and uns rdr 4th*	**12/1**	—
212	**P**		**Tora Bora (GER)**^{13} 4057 4-11-1 **113** ... TimmyMurphy (B G Powell) *hld up in mid-div: lost pl appr 3rd: hdwy 5th: sn rdn and wknd: p.u after 2 out*	**2/1**^{1}	—

5m 3.80s (22.90) **Going Correction** +1.35s/f (Heav)

WFA 4 from 5yo+ 7lb **11** Ran SP% **121.9**

Speed ratings: **105,104,98,96,95 83,79,**—,—,— — CSF £56.12 CT £245.54 TOTE £14.30: £3.10, £2.70, £1.90; EX 48.80.

Owner D V Gardner **Bred** D V Gardner **Trained** Longdown, Devon

FOCUS

A quite competitive handicap hurdle, but with the ground being as it was and favourite Tora Bora disappointing, the form needs treating with caution. The race is best rated through the first two on their chase form. Flight past stands and middle flight in straight omitted.

NOTEBOOK

Bak To Bill, without a win in over a year coming into it, travelled sweetly for his lady rider and went on taking before two-out. She stuck on well down the straight, towards the near-side rail, and was always holding the runner-up, who arguably should have won. He was racing off a decent mark and it will be interesting to see how he fares under a penalty.

Il'Athou(FR), rated 25lb lower over hurdles than fences, appeared to have an obvious chance, especially with usual front-running tactics employed, but Tizzard allowed him to drop off the lead turning in and forfeited both ground and momentum. Judging by the way he was making ground on the winner as they raced towards the line, one is entitled to believe he should have won, but either way this will have set him straight for a possible return to fences. *(op 4-1)*

Visibility(FR) is finding some form again and followed a solid second at Sandown with another decent effort in defeat. He led turning in, but was unable to see his race out as well as the front two. *(op 9-1)*

Le Rochelais(FR) made a little late headway on this return to hurdles, but was never in a challenging position. Good ground a return to fences should see him winning at long last. *(op 16-1)*

Kings Castle(IRE) has not won a handicap for four years and it is likely to take a drop back down in grade before he wins again. *(tchd 17-2)*

Glimmer Of Light(IRE), who could be given a big chance on the form of his Plumpton second to the potentially smart Temoin, was just another who failed to cope with the ground. *(op 11-1)*

Rift Valley(IRE) was the only other to complete, but on ground that he would not have liked, it was no surprise to see him trail in well beaten. *(op 20-1)*

Tora Bora(GER) failed to meet expectations and a trip to Cheltenham is now well and truly out of the question for the juvenile. *Official explanation: trainer said gelding was unsuited by the heavy ground (op 9-4 tchd 5-2)*

4290 DEVON AIR AMBULANCE TRUST AMATEUR RIDERS' H'CAP HURDLE (6 hdls 2 omitted) 2m 1f

5:20 (5:25) (Class 5) (0-95,95) 4-Y-0+ **£2,307** (£709; £354)

Form					RPR
0PP0	**1**		**Ghabesh (USA)**^{26} 3817 4-9-13 **83** ... (p) MrRhysHughes(7) (Evan Williams) *a.p: rdn to ld 2 out: hit last: all out*	**16/1**	79+
5PP6	**2**	*2*	**Grandee Line**^{22} 3899 11-10-3 **79** ... MrIChanin(7) (R H Alner) *led: rdn and hdd whn hit 2 out: kpt on flat*	**22/1**	78
/P06	**3**	*3/4*	**How Is The Lord (IRE)**^{14} 4033 10-10-6 **80** ... MrSWaley-Cohen(5) (C J Down) *hld up in mid-div: hdwy 4th: kpt on flat*	**8/1**	78
FP	**4**	*6*	**Georges Boy (IRE)**^{16} 4012 8-11-7 **95** ... (v1) MrDavidTurner(5) (P J Jones) *t.k.h: chsd ldr: rdn and wknd appr 2 out*	**28/1**	87
-005	**5**	*1*	**Harrival**^{14} 4033 6-10-10 **82** ... MrGTumelty(3) (Miss M Bragg) *hld up and bhd: hdwy after 4th: styd on fr 2 out: nvr trbld ldrs*	**10/1**	73
34	**6**	*4*	**Lets Try Again (IRE)**^{33} 3687 9-10-7 **81** ... MrJJDoyle(5) (R A Farrant) *prom tl wknd appr 2 out*	**11/2**^{2}	68
0F4/	**7**	*18*	**Kaluga (IRE)**^{705} 4631 8-10-0 **76** ... MrPHockley(7) (S C Burrough) *nvr nr ldrs*	**66/1**	45
6046	**8**	*4*	**Brochrua (IRE)**^{27} 3804 6-11-2 **92** ... MrDMcKenna(7) (J D Frost) *a bhd*	**25/1**	57
0P06	**9**	*3/4*	**Faddad (USA)**^{110} 2282 10-11-2 **90** ... (t) MrsLucyRowsell(5) (Mrs A M Thorpe) *hld up in tch: lost pl appr 2nd: sn bhd*	**40/1**	54
000	**10**	*8*	**Windyx (FR)**^{18} 3963 5-10-10 **86** ... MrDPick(7) (M C Pipe) *prom tl wknd appr 2 out*	**9/1**	42
5302	**11**	*10*	**Sunset King (USA)**^{22} 3899 6-10-8 **80** ... MrJSnowden(3) (R J Hodges) *a bhd*	**5/1**^{1}	26
-000	**12**	*27*	**Damarisco (FR)**^{64} 3214 6-11-5 **91** ... MrTJO'Brien(3) (P J Hobbs) *hld up in tch: hit 2nd: wknd appr 2 out: t.o*	**11/2**^{2}	10
6P00	**P**		**Life Estates**^{47} 3456 6-9-10 **72** ... MrBMoorcroft(7) (J D Frost) *bhd fr 3rd: t.o whn p.u bef 2 out*	**33/1**	—
4064	**F**		**Joli Classical (IRE)**^{46} 3483 4-10-5 **85** ... MissCTizzard(3) (R J Hodges) *a bhd: mstke 2 out: no ch whn fell last*	**6/1**^{3}	—

4m 41.3s (32.10) **Going Correction** +1.35s/f (Heav)

WFA 4 from 5yo+ 7lb **14** Ran SP% **116.3**

Speed ratings: **78,77,76,73,73 71,63,61,60,57 52,39,**—,— CSF £321.08 CT £3003.74 TOTE £18.50: £3.00, £4.80, £3.10; EX 434.40 Place 6 £119.13, Place 5 £87.52.

Owner M J Haines **Bred** Shadwell Farm Inc **Trained** Cowbridge, Vale Of Glamorgan

■ Ghabesh gave Rhys Hughes his first win under Rules.

FOCUS

A poor contest in which it again paid to race prominently and the third sets the level for the form. Flight past stands and middle flight in straight omitted.

NOTEBOOK

Ghabesh(USA), who had previously shown little, raced prominently throughout and got the better of long-time leader Grandee Line approaching the second-last, staying on well to provide his rider with his first winner under Rules. He had previously shown little, but the first-time cheekpieces and step into handicaps did the trick, and it will be interesting to see if the four-year-old can find any further improvement. *(op 14-1)*

Grandee Line held a clear early lead, but came back to his field, only to race on again with the winner. He stuck on well to hold How Is The Lord for second, but the 11-year-old will continue to find winning hard. *(op 33-1)*

How Is The Lord(IRE) travelled particularly well, but his rider failed to make enough use of him and he got going all too late. He is relatively unexposed and there could be a small race in him. *(op 12-1)*

Georges Boy(IRE) ran well under his big weight and kept plugging away to claim fourth. *(op 33-1 tchd 25-1)*

Harrival offered a little more on this handicap debut. *(op 11-1)*

Lets Try Again(IRE), whose only previous win had come on fast going, looked to struggle in the bottomless ground. *(op 5-1)*

Brochrua(IRE) *Official explanation: trainer said mare was unsuited by heavy going (op 16-1)*

Windyx(FR) continues to disappoint, this time failing to get home having raced keenly. Connections have yet to find the key. *(op 10-1 tchd 11-1)*

T/Plt: £68.80 to a £1 stake. Pool: £72,650.00. 770.15 winning tickets. T/Qpdt: £25.30 to a £1 stake. Pool: £5,495.30. 160.10 winning tickets. KH

4108 NEWCASTLE (L-H)
Tuesday, March 7
4291 Meeting Abandoned - Frost

ENGHIEN (L-H)
Tuesday, March 7
OFFICIAL GOING: Very soft

4298a PRIX D'ESSAI DES POULAINS (HURDLE) (MAIDEN) (C&G) 1m 7f
2:50 (2:59) 3-Y-O £15,890 (£7,945; £4,634; £3,145; £1,490)

RPR
1 **Mildon (FR)**[301] 3-10-6 LChaveroux —
(J-L Pelletan, France)
2 6 **Count Your Change (FR)** 3-10-3 ow2 CPieux —
(Y Fouin, France)
3 2 ½ **Pingus (FR)** 3-10-1 SBeaumard —
(C Scandella, France)
4 4 **Pecheur D'Islande (FR)** 3-10-1 BGicquel —
(G Macaire, France)
5 2 ½ **Lou Flight (FR)**[290] 3-10-1 EChazelle —
(G Cherel, France)
6 nk **Bonheur Du Rheu (FR)** 3-10-1 CGombeau —
(P Rago, France)
7 3 **Mixmen (FR)** 3-10-1 FLagarde —
(F Nicolle, France)
8 5 **Ecos De L'Orme (FR)**[213] 3-10-6 ELequesne —
(Ron Caget, France)
P **Piton (FR)** 3-10-1 SLeloup —
(F-M Cottin, France)
P **Luckos (FR)** 3-10-1 MDelmares —
(T Trapenard, France)
P **Willou (FR)** 3-10-1 AAcker —
(E Lemartinel, France)
P **Idolaire (FR)**[133] 3-10-1 J-LBeaunez —
(P Rago, France)
P **Du Kerroch (FR)**[105] 3-10-1 EMichel —
(G Brillet, France)
P **Chivitanova (FR)** 3-10-1 SDupuis —
(T Trapenard, France)
P **Sir Guillaume (FR)** 3-10-1 AKondrat —
(T Trapenard, France)
P **Russe D'Ouilly (FR)**[88] 3-10-6 CSanterne —
(Ron Caget, France)
P **Prince Bere (FR)**[135] 3-10-6 AAdelinedeBoisbrunet —
(J Bertran De Balanda, France)
P **Carlton Scroop (FR)**[125] 3-10-1 RO'Brien —
(J Jay) *close up when jumped very slowly and lost place 1st, continued to jump badly, behind when pulled up before 6th*

3m 54.0s 18 Ran
PARI-MUTUEL (including one euro stakes): WIN 61.20; PL 8.40, 1.80, 2.50; DF 57.80.
Owner R Temam **Bred** Raymond Bietola **Trained** France

3557 CATTERICK (L-H)
Wednesday, March 8
OFFICIAL GOING: Good to soft
The ground soon turned soft. The riders reckoned it was the softest they have ever known at this track yet the official version was never altered.
Wind: Almost nil Weather: Persistent rain.

4299 RACING POST - THE HORSES MOUTH (S) HURDLE (8 hdls) 2m
2:00 (2:01) (Class 5) 4-Y-0+ £2,740 (£798; £399)

Form RPR
/4-1 1 **Beau Torero (FR)**[40] [3592] 8-10-9 96 TomMessenger(7) 96+
(B N Pollock) *led to after 1st: cl up tl led again after 3 out: clr next: rdn last: drvn and wknd flat: jst hld on* **9/4**[1]
2 shd **Toulouse Express (IRE)**[237] [994] 7-10-9 81 MrTCollier(7) 93
(R Johnson) *hld up in tch: hdwy after 3 out: hit 2 out: rdn to chse wnr last: drvn and styd on wl flat: jst failed* **25/1**
0505 3 ¾ **Futoo (IRE)**[15] [4040] 5-11-2 92 (p) RussGarritty 92
(G M Moore) *hld up in midfield: hdwy and in tch 4th: effrt to chse wnr appr 2 out: rdn bef last: styd on wl u.p flat* **5/1**[2]
4605 4 3 **Leap Year Lass**[18] [3985] 6-10-9 83 RichardMcGrath 82
(C Grant) *hld up: hdwy 3 out: rdn along and styd on fr next: nrst fin* **7/1**[3]
2030 5 1 ¼ **Armentieres**[22] [3916] 5-11-2 89 (v) GrahamLee 88
(Mrs E Slack) *bhd and sn rdn along: hdwy after 3 out: drvn along and styd on fr 2 out: nvr a factor* **5/1**[2]
0R-0 6 5 **Golden Fields (IRE)**[14] [4056] 6-10-9 80 (p) AlanDempsey 76
(G A Harker) *s.s and bhd: hdwy 1/2-way: rdn along to chse ldrs appr 2 out: sn drvn and kpt on same pce* **33/1**
5605 7 6 **Pornic (FR)**[19] [3964] 12-10-11 80 (v) DeclanMcGann(5) 77
(A Crook) *prom: rdn along 3 out: drvn and wknd next* **20/1**
3266 8 ½ **Vulcan Lane (NZ)**[15] [4045] 9-10-6 78 (b) JohnWilley(10) 77
(R C Guest) *in tch: mstke 4th: sn rdn along: wknd after 3 out* **8/1**
P-00 9 24 **Magic Bengie**[22] [3916] 7-11-2 64 (t) KennyJohnson 60+
(F Kirby) *led after 1st: hit 4th: pushed along and hit next: hdd after 3 out: wknd appr next* **50/1**
0P40 10 14 **The Rooken (IRE)**[28] [3797] 7-10-11 69 StevenCrawford(5) 39
(P Spottiswood) *a bhd* **66/1**
03-0 11 4 **Milan King (IRE)**[66] [3169] 13-11-2 71 TonyDobbin 35
(A J Lockwood) *a rr: bhd fr 1/2-way* **50/1**
F **Orlando Blue** 6-10-11 MichaelMcAlister(5) —
(B Storey) *midfield whn fell 1st* **80/1**
0PFP P **Whitsun**[42] [3559] 6-10-11 DougieCostello(5) —
(Miss Kate Milligan) *a bhd: p.u bef 2 out* **150/1**
0P56 P **Pucks Court**[83] [2843] 9-11-2 73 AndrewTinkler —
(I A Brown) *bhd fr 1/2-way: p.u bef last* **20/1**
P **Turftanzer (GER)**[371] 7-10-9 MrMWalford(7) —
(Lady Susan Watson) *in tch: rdn along 5th: sn wknd and bhd whn p.u bef 2 out* **80/1**
5-PP P **Gaelic Jig**[117] [2169] 7-10-13 (b[1]) MichalKohl(3) —
(J I A Charlton) *towards rr whn blnd bdly 2nd: sn bhd and p.u bef 2 out* **125/1**
0F P **Fourswainby (IRE)**[62] [3257] 5-11-2 (b[1]) WilsonRenwick —
(B Ellison) *keen: chsd ldrs to 4th: sn lost pl and bhd whn p.u bef 2 out* **66/1**

3m 56.5s (0.20) **Going Correction** +0.05s/f (Yiel) **17 Ran SP% 114.9**
Speed ratings: **101,100,100,99,98 95,92,92,80,73 71,—,—,—,— —,—** CSF £63.47 TOTE £2.50: £1.80, £8.30, £2.60; EX 91.10.There was no bid for the winner. Futoo was claimed by David W. Chapman for £6,000.
Owner Mrs K Lloyd Mrs L Pollock L Stilwell **Bred** Armand Khaida **Trained** Medbourne, Leics

FOCUS
The ground had not been opened up for this first contest and the riders said they were getting through it well enough, but the rain soon had an effect. The form looks okay, with the winner back to his old level, and the runner-up improving 10lb or so on his Irish level.

NOTEBOOK
Beau Torero(FR), clear best on official figures, looked to have it safely in the bag but he became very leg weary on the run-in and in the end the line came in the nick of time. He is obviously fragile but useful in this class especially on less-testing ground. *(op 2-1)*
Toulouse Express(IRE), ex-Irish, had a stone to find with the winner on official ratings. Unplaced in eight previous starts and with the blinkers left off, he only just failed to get up. *(tchd 33-1)*
Futoo(IRE), who had just 4lb to find with the winner, wore cheekpieces on his first venture into selling company. Just found lacking, David Chapman stepped in and claimed him. *(op 9-2)*
Leap Year Lass, a maiden after 17 previous starts, probably ran up to her mark. *(op 8-1)*
Armentieres, hit and miss, consented to stay on late in the day. A stiffer test is in her favour when in the right mood. *(op 4-1)*
Golden Fields(IRE), in first-time cheekpieces, is a dodgy proposition at the start and she looked in two minds whether to jump off or not.

4300 ALAN THOMPSON 75TH BIRTHDAY NOVICES' H'CAP CHASE (19 fncs) 3m 1f 110y
2:30 (2:30) (Class 4) (0-100,98) 5-Y-O+ £3,903 (£1,146; £573; £286)

Form RPR
430/ 1 **Move Over (IRE)**[45] [3522] 11-10-10 92 JohnFlavin(10) 113+
(R C Guest) *trckd ldrs: led 6th: 20l clr last: heavily eased* **14/1**
-4PP 2 5 **Profowens (IRE)**[21] [3928] 8-11-10 96 (b[1]) RussGarritty 99
(P Beaumont) *chsd ldrs: outpcd 12th: styd on fr 2 out: tk 2nd last 100yds* **25/1**
P141 3 8 **Another Club Royal**[21] [3928] 7-11-8 97 (bt) StephenCraine(3) 95+
(D McCain) *chsd ldrs: drvn whn hit 12th: lft 2nd and hmpd 3 out: one pce* **9/1**
6444 4 3 **Barrons Pike**[43] [3553] 7-11-2 93 (p) MichaelMcAlister(5) 88+
(B Storey) *led 2nd to 4th: chsd ldrs: one pce fr 4 out: blnd 2 out* **20/1**
0P60 5 8 **Celia's High (IRE)**[14] [4047] 7-9-11 72 oh4 (t) PaddyAspell(3) 56
(D McCain) *chsd ldrs: outpcd fr 15th* **14/1**
443F 6 10 **True Temper (IRE)**[15] [4041] 9-9-12 75 DeclanMcGann(5) 53+
(A M Crow) *mstkes: chsd ldrs to 11th: sn lost pl* **15/2**
2555 7 23 **Wee William**[29] [3791] 6-11-2 91 (p) PeterBuchanan(3) 42
(T D Walford) *in tch: mstke 10th: lost pl after next* **16/1**
U60F P **Jack Lynch**[14] [4053] 10-10-7 86 PatrickMcDonald(7) —
(Ferdy Murphy) *in rr: bhd whn p.u bef 3 out* **40/1**
6PP0 P **Simlet**[27] [2840] 11-11-12 98 (bt) AlanDempsey —
(E W Tuer) *in rr and drvn 11th: t.o whn p.u bef next* **33/1**
0504 F **Derainey (IRE)**[31] [3760] 7-9-10 75 MrTCollier(7) —
(R Johnson) *led to 2nd: led 4th to 6th: 4l 2nd whn fell 15th* **12/1**
P/PP P **Icy River (IRE)**[22] [3915] 9-10-10 82 RichardMcGrath —
(K G Reveley) *mstkes in rr: bhd fr 12th: t.o whn p.u bef 4 out* **28/1**
0554 P **Patriarch (IRE)**[13] [4078] 10-11-3 89 TonyDobbin —
(P Bowen) *trckd ldrs: drvn and lost pl 7th: sn bhd: t.o whn p.u bef 9th* **9/2**[2]
2-23 P **Blackergreen**[53] [3382] 7-11-12 98 DavidO'Meara —
(Mrs S J Smith) *nt fluent in rr: hrd drvn 11th: sn bhd: p.u after 4 out* **4/1**[1]
P624 F **Been Here Before**[14] [4053] 6-10-6 85 PhilKinsella(7) —
(G A Harker) *in rr: hdwy b11th: wnt 2nd 4 out: 4l down and rdn whn fell 3 out* **7/1**[3]

6m 49.3s (0.90) **Going Correction** +0.05s/f (Yiel) **14 Ran SP% 116.8**
Speed ratings: **100,98,96,95,92 89,82,—,—,— —,—,—,—** CSF £314.96 CT £3293.31 TOTE £16.60: £5.80, £9.80, £2.60; EX 477.00.
Owner Mrs F A Lockwood **Bred** Tony Mullins **Trained** Brancepeth, Co Durham

FOCUS
A sound gallop and a true test in the deteriorating conditions, with the winner much improved and value for considerably further. The next three look solid enough for one to be positive about the winner.

NOTEBOOK
Move Over(IRE), a winner of a bumper and two hurdle races in Ireland, is not that big but he has a good leap in him. He enjoyed himself once in front and was value for around four times the winning margin. His new handler will be keen to get him out under a penalty. *(tchd 16-1)*
Profowens(IRE), pulled up on his last two starts, kept on to snatch second spot but he was probably only fourth best on the day.
Another Club Royal, 9lb higher, looked to have no more to give when impeded three out. The ground had turned against him.
Barrons Pike, with the cheekpieces back on, at least kept straight at his fences but he was at the end of his tether when hardly rising at the final ditch, two out. *(op 28-1)*
Celia's High(IRE), 4lb out of the handicap, keeps threatening something better but the mud here was probably not in his favour. *(op 16-1)*
True Temper(IRE) made far too many jumping errors to get competitive. *(op 7-1)*
Patriarch(IRE), keen to get on with it early on, dropped everything before halfway and, soon detached, his rider wisely called it a day. *Official explanation: trainer had no explanation for the poor form shown (tchd 14-1)*
Blackergreen, 4lb higher than Market Rasen, hardly jumped a fence out of this ground. *Official explanation: trainer had no explanation for the poor form shown (tchd 14-1)*
Been Here Before, who did not go unbacked, was flat out in pursuit of the winner when taking a crashing fall three out. He would surely have finished in the runner-up spot. *(tchd 14-1)*
Derainey(IRE), unplaced in eight previous tries, was in the process of running a much better race when departing five out. *(tchd 14-1)*

4301 RACING POST - OFFICIAL CHELTENHAM PAPER NOVICES' HURDLE (8 hdls) 2m

3:00 (3:00) (Class 4) 4-Y-0+ **£3,253** (£955; £477; £238)

Form RPR

-361 **1** **The Duke's Speech (IRE)**[64] 3232 5-11-9 119........... DominicElsworth 118+
(T P Tate) *led to after 1st: prom tl hdwy to ld appr 2 out: sn rdn: drvn last and kpt on wl flat* **1/1**[1]

-040 **2** ½ **Silver Dollars (FR)**[76] 2942 5-11-2 .... AlanDempsey 110
(J Howard Johnson) *cl up: led 4th: rdn along and hdd appr 2 out: drvn last: kpt on wl flat* **66/1**

54 **3** 3½ **Temple Place (IRE)**[20] 3947 5-10-13 ....(t) StephenCraine(3) 106
(D McCain) *hld up: smooth hdwy after 3 out: cl up whn hit next: swtchd lft and sn rdn: drvn last and no ex flat* **11/1**

214 **4** 6 **Gidam Gidam (IRE)**[31] 3759 4-11-1 114...........................(p) TomSiddall 99
(J Mackie) *led after 1st to 4th: prom tl rdn along appr 2 out and kpt on same pce* **11/1**

13 **5** 1 **Zeitgeist (IRE)**[30] 3780 5-11-9 ....(v) GrahamLee 108+
(J Howard Johnson) *chsd ldrs: j. bdly lft 4th: nt fluent after: rdn along after 3 out and wknd bef next* **5/1**[2]

3004 **6** 11 **Planters Punch (IRE)**[11] 4114 5-11-4 105.................. DougieCostello(5) 95
(G M Moore) *hld up in midfield: effrt and sme hdwy 3 out: sn rdn along and no imp fr next* **25/1**

FU5F **7** 2½ **Dubonai (IRE)**[42] 3561 6-11-9 102......................................(t) BarryKeniry 93
(G M Moore) *nvr nr ldrs* **20/1**

0-00 **8** 15 **Boxclever**[103] 2480 5-10-11 .... TJDreaper(5) 71
(J M Jefferson) *mstke 1st: a rr* **100/1**

0220 **9** 16 **Eborarry (IRE)**[13] 4067 4-11-1 109...................................... RussGarritty 54
(T D Easterby) *in tch: gd hdwy to chse ldrs after 3 out: rdn next and wknd qckly: blnd last* **9/1**[3]

43 **10** 5 **Megaton**[20] 3947 5-11-2 .... TonyDobbin 50
(P Bowen) *in tch: rdn along bef 3 out and sn wknd* **14/1**

30 **11** dist **Hurricane Francis**[279] 616 6-10-13 .... PeterBuchanan(3) —
(T D Walford) *a bhd* **100/1**

12 2½ **Countrywide Dancer (IRE)**[191] 6-10-6 .... PaddyAspell(3) —
(K W Hogg) *a bhd* **250/1**

P **Lion's Domane**[361] 9-11-2 .... LarryMcGrath —
(K W Hogg) *a bhd: t.o whn p.u after 3 out* **250/1**

P4 **P** **Minnesinger**[21] 3925 4-9-8 .... PhilKinsella(7) —
(M Todhunter) *a towards rr: bhd whn p.u bef last* **33/1**

F **Kyathos (GER)**[60] 5-11-4 ow2... SamStronge —
(M F Harris) *in tch: rdn along and wknd bef 3 out: bhd whn fell bef 2 out* **50/1**

3m 56.3s **Going Correction** +0.05s/f (Yiel)
WFA 4 from 5yo+ 7lb **15** Ran SP% **117.8**
Speed ratings: **102,101,100,97,96 91,89,82,74,71** —,—,—,—,— CSF £113.08 TOTE £2.00: £1.30, £11.50, £4.40; EX 103.10.
Owner The Ivy Syndicate **Bred** Eamonn Delaney **Trained** Tadcaster, N Yorks

FOCUS
A fair novice for the track, run at a strong gallop in the ground. It should work out.

NOTEBOOK
The Duke's Speech(IRE), happy to be given a lead, jumped much better but in the end had to dig deep. *A potential chaser, he does not appreciate the ground as deep as it had now become. (op 11-8 tchd 6-4 in a place)*
Silver Dollars(FR) ◆, the stable's second string, showed much improved form and made the winner fight hard in the end. This was much more like his true self, and with the yard returning to some sort of form, he deserves to go one better. *(op 80-1)*
Temple Place(IRE), with his tongue tied down again, came there on the bridle but after flattening two out, he found very little. His stamina is suspect, but this was improved form and on less testing ground he can surely find an opening this spring. *(op 10-1)*
Gidam Gidam(IRE), against his seniors, found this simply too tough under his penalty. *(op 8-1)*
Zeitgeist(IRE), with the visor on this time, was let down by his jumping. He will be seriously leniently treated when he gets the better ground he seems to need. *(op 9-2)*
Lion's Domane *Official explanation: jockey said gelding had a breathing problem*

4302 RACING POST - THE HORSES MOUTH H'CAP HURDLE (10 hdls) 2m 3f

3:30 (3:30) (Class 5) (0-95,95) 4-Y-0+ **£2,740** (£798; £399)

Form RPR

4F3U **1** **Merryvale Man**[15] 4045 9-11-7 95.................................. BrianHughes(5) 98
(Miss Kariana Key) *mde all: styd on fr 2 out: hld on towards fin* **10/1**

644- **2** 1¼ **Leadaway**[364] 4261 7-10-6 75... RichardMcGrath 77
(Miss P Robson) *trckd ldrs: outpcd after 3 out: styd on to go 2nd sn after last: no ex last 100yds* **9/2**[2]

003P **3** nk **Bromley Abbey**[31] 3762 8-10-9 85...........................(p) TomMessenger(7) 87
(Miss S E Forster) *chsd ldrs: wnt 2nd 6th: kpt on same pce run-in* **33/1**

1F00 **4** 15 **Scarrabus (IRE)**[31] 3757 5-10-13 87.......................... DeclanMcGann(5) 74
(A Crook) *in rr: hdwy 6th: sn chsng ldrs: wknd after 2 out* **33/1**

5P00 **5** 6 **Stoneriggs Merc (IRE)**[21] 3927 5-10-5 74........................ BrianHarding 55
(Mrs E Slack) *chsd ldrs: wknd 2 out* **40/1**

P060 **6** nk **Mad Max Too**[53] 3393 7-11-7 93...............................(p) PeterBuchanan(3) 73
(N Wilson) *bhd: sme hdwy 3 out: nvr on terms* **66/1**

0504 **7** ¾ **Only Words (USA)**[22] 3916 9-10-12 81.................................. GrahamLee 61
(A J Lockwood) *in rr: reminders after 5th: nvr on terms* **12/1**

4031 **8** 1¼ **Moyne Pleasure (IRE)**[43] 3552 8-11-2 85....................... KennyJohnson 63
(R Johnson) *hld up in rr: sme hdwy 3 out: nvr a factor* **9/1**

4P50 **9** ¾ **Jallastep (FR)**[80] 2900 9-11-3 93... MrGGoldie(7) 71
(J S Goldie) *chsd ldrs: lost pl appr 2 out* **28/1**

P050 **10** 4 **Platinum Point (IRE)**[21] 3927 7-10-5 74........................... AlanDempsey 48
(E W Tuer) *in rr: hdwy 7th: sn rdn: lost pl appr 2 out* **16/1**

10P6 **11** 26 **Miss Jessica (IRE)**[199] 1275 6-10-13 82.......................... JodieMogford 30
(Miss M E Rowland) *chsd ldrs: lost pl 7th* **22/1**

5/6P **12** nk **Batto**[72] 2994 6-10-11 80.. BarryKeniry 27
(G M Moore) *in rr: reminders 5th: nvr a factor* **40/1**

6000 **13** 5 **Tiger Talk**[42] 3557 10-10-11 80.......................................(b) LarryMcGrath 22
(R C Guest) *chsd ldrs: lost pl after 6th: bhd whn hmpd 3 out* **20/1**

030P **F** **Brundeanlaws**[22] 3914 5-10-10 84............................... TomGreenway(5) —
(Mrs H O Graham) *chsd ldrs: lost pl 6th: bhd whn fell 3 out* **33/1**

-002 **P** **Arctic Moss (IRE)**[21] 3927 7-11-0 86................................. PaddyAspell(3) —
(E W Tuer) *t.k.h in last: bhd fr 6th: sn t.o: p.u bef 2 out* **4/1**[1]

24-5 **P** **Destino**[226] 1066 7-11-2 85.. DominicElsworth —
(Mrs S J Smith) *prom: reminders 4th: lost pl 7th: bhd whn p.u bef 2 out* **7/1**[3]

P0P5 **P** **Brave Effect (IRE)**[31] 3757 10-11-3 91..................... MichaelMcAlister(5) —
(Mrs Dianne Sayer) *in tch: lost pl 6th: t.o 2 out: p.u bef last* **25/1**

0325 **P** **Munaawesh (USA)**[30] 3782 5-10-4 80.............................. PhilKinsella(7) —
(Mrs Marjorie Fife) *chsd ldrs: lost pl 6th: blnd next: t.o whn p.u bef 2 out* **8/1**

4m 55.1s (4.60) **Going Correction** +0.225s/f (Yiel) **18** Ran SP% **126.1**
Speed ratings: **99,98,98,92,89 89,89,88,88,86 75,75,73,—,—** —,—,— CSF £50.74 CT £1485.07 TOTE £14.30: £2.60, £1.70, £5.20, £15.70; EX 93.00.
Owner Miss Kariana Key **Bred** Arthur Symons Key **Trained** Knaresborough, N Yorks
■ Stewards' Enquiry : Brian Hughes two-day ban: used whip with excessive frequency (Mar 19-20)

FOCUS
Not much of a race, but the winner made it a true test and both horse and rider deserve full marks. The first three all ran close to form.

NOTEBOOK
Merryvale Man, 5lb higher than his last success, made every yard and never flinched. *(tchd 9-1)*
Leadaway, fourth in this last year, has changed stables and was well supported. Tapped for toe starting the final bend, he worked hard to secure second spot on the run-in but was never finding quite enough. An extra half mile will be in his favour. *(op 13-2)*
Bromley Abbey, hoisted a stone after Musselburgh, was back over hurdles and seemed to run out of her skin. She has yet to break her duck though after 15 attempts now.
Scarrabus(IRE), already winner of a chase, is trying hurdling again for his new connections. He is best suited by quick ground which he definitely did not encounter here. *(tchd 40-1)*
Stoneriggs Merc(IRE), on just his fifth start and on his handicap debut, offered connections a glimmer of hope. *(tchd 50-1)*
Mad Max Too, on his handicap debut, looked to have been given a very stiff mark.
Miss Jessica(IRE) *Official explanation: jockey said mare was unsuited by the good to soft ground (tchd 25-1)*
Munaawesh(USA) *Official explanation: jockey said gelding blundered and lost its action back straight (op 7-2 tchd 9-2 and 5-1 in a place)*
Arctic Moss(IRE), very keen early on her handicap debut, ran no race at all and connections *blamed the ground. That is remained good to soft all day was simply ridiculous. Official explanation: jockey said mare was unsuited by the good to soft ground (op 7-2 tchd 9-2 and 5-1 in a place)*

4303 RACING POST SELECT A STABLE MAIDEN CHASE (12 fncs) 2m

4:00 (4:00) (Class 4) 5-Y-0+ **£6,506** (£1,910; £955; £477)

Form RPR

5263 **1** **Persian Point**[42] 3562 10-10-13 82...................................... MrCStorey(3) 95+
(Miss S E Forster) *trckd ldrs: hdwy after 4 out: led next: sn rdn clr: styd on* **11/2**[3]

32P- **2** 8 **Minouchka (FR)**[368] 4181 6-10-2 105............................. MissKBryson(7) 79
(S H Shirley-Beavan) *chsd ldr: rdn: sltly hmpd and outpcd 3 out: styd on to chse wnr fr next: no imp* **5/1**[2]

3023 **3** 12 **Brave Rebellion**[66] 3173 7-11-2 .... RichardMcGrath 79+
(K G Reveley) *hld up in rr: mstke 3rd: hdwy 7th: effrt and cl up 3 out: sn rdn: nt fluent next and sn wknd: j. bdly lft last* **6/5**[1]

4 9 **Neuro (FR)**[111] 5-10-4 .... BenOrde-Powlett(7) 65+
(Jedd O'Keeffe) *led: rdn along 4 out: mstke and hdd next: sn drvn and wknd* **12/1**

U636 **5** 29 **Twist N Turn**[34] 3686 6-10-6 64..................................... StephenCraine(3) 29
(D McCain) *chsd ldrs: blnd 6th: sn rdn along and bhd bef 4 out* **12/1**

3P06 **6** 4 **Gaucho**[9] 4142 9-10-9 76...(b) MissTJackson(7) 32
(Miss T Jackson) *a rr: bhd fr 1/2-way* **28/1**

2026 **7** dist **Upswing**[54] 3370 9-11-2 85... LarryMcGrath —
(R C Guest) *hld up in rr: hmpd 2nd: j. slowly next: mstkes after and t.o fr 1/2-way* **7/1**

P0P6 **F** **Viking Song**[30] 3781 6-11-2 60.....................................(p) KennyJohnson —
(F Kirby) *chsd ldrs whn fell 2nd* **100/1**

0-00 **U** **Nicozetto (FR)**[20] 3488 6-11-2 .... WilsonRenwick —
(N Wilson) *keen: hld up in tch tl blnd and uns rdr 7th* **50/1**

4m 5.60s (2.60) **Going Correction** +0.225s/f (Yiel)
WFA 5 from 6yo+ 4lb **9** Ran SP% **111.8**
Speed ratings: **102,98,92,87,73 71,—,—,—** CSF £31.90 TOTE £5.40: £2.00, £1.80, £1.10; EX 31.60.
Owner C Storey **Bred** Theakston Stud **Trained** Kirk Yetholm, Borders

FOCUS
A very modest maiden chase in which the winner's proven stamina carried the day in the end.

NOTEBOOK
Persian Point, a former winning pointer, in the end ran out a decisive winner. This was seemingly a personal best, as he went into this rated just 82, which tells all. *(op 7-1 tchd 5-1)*
Minouchka(FR), having her first outing for a year, had 30lb in hand of the winner on official ratings. She kept on to chase him home, but would have given him more to do with a stronger rider in the saddle. *(op 9-2)*
Brave Rebellion, rated 37lb better than the winner over hurdles, is a bridle horse. He looked a big threat when landing upsides three out but he was out on his feet when going badly left-handed at the last. He does not want conditions as testing as they had become. *(op 5-4 tchd 6-4)*
Neuro(FR), who showed little in three starts in France the latest in November, took them along at a sound gallop but he looked at the end of his tether when getting the third last wrong. *(op 14-1)*
Upswing looked to lose his confidence altogether after being hampered at just the second fence. *(op 8-1)*

4304 RACING POST MARES' ONLY STANDARD NATIONAL HUNT FLAT RACE (CONDITIONAL JOCKEYS'/AMATEUR RIDERS' RACE) 2m

4:30 (4:30) (Class 6) 4-6-Y-0 **£2,055** (£599; £299)

Form RPR

1 **Westgrove Berry (IRE)** 6-10-9 .... EwanWhillans(7) 88+
(N G Richards) *hld up in rr: hdwy 5f out: led and hung lft 2f out: styd on wl* **3/1**[1]

2 3 **Wensleydale Web** 4-10-3 .... BrianHughes(5) 75
(M E Sowersby) *in rr: hdwy to trck ldrs 6f out: kpt on same pce appr fnl f* **50/1**

3 2½ **Morning Roses** 4-10-1 .... PhilKinsella(7) 72
(K G Reveley) *trckd ldrs: led over 3f out: hung rt and hdd 2f out: kpt on same pce* **8/1**

036 **4** 3 **Heavenly Chorus**[21] 3931 4-9-12 .... JamesReveley(10) 69
(K G Reveley) *hld up wl in rr: hdwy over 4f out: one pce fnl 2f* **5/1**[2]

0 **5** 8 **Ansa The Question**[64] 3237 5-11-2 .... KeithMercer 69
(A H Mactaggart) *chsd ldrs: outpcd over 3f out: no threat after* **50/1**

6 1 **Crimond (IRE)** 4-10-1 .... MrGTumelty(7) 60
(G A Harker) *chsd ldrs: lost pl 3f out* **11/2**[3]

7 1½ **Mollyalice** 4-10-5 .... StephenCraine(3) 59
(T D Easterby) *chsd ldrs: jnd ldrs 9f out: drvn over 4f out: lost pl over 3f out* **13/2**

20 **8** 6 **Ruby Joy**[28] 3799 4-10-1 .... TomMessenger(7) 53
(Mrs H O Graham) *w ldr: led after 4f tl over 3f out: wknd 3f out* **8/1**

9 13 **Emski** 5-10-11 .... TJDreaper(5) 48
(P Beaumont) *in rr: bhd fnl 5f* **12/1**

10 4 **Gale Dancer** 4-10-1 .... MrCWhillans(7) 36
(D W Whillans) *mid-div: lost pl 6f out: sn bhd* **28/1**

0 11 2 1/2 **Bee Vee Pea (IRE)**[14] 4059 6-10-9 .... MrMSollitt(7) 41
(Mrs S J Smith) *in tch: lost pl over 4f out: sn bhd* **33/1**

0S 12 1/2 **Falcon's Tribute (IRE)**[21] 3931 4-10-5 .... PaddyAspell(3) 33
(P Beaumont) *hld up in rr: hdwy 9f out: chsng ldrs 5f out: lost pl over 3f out* **28/1**

13 5 **Franceschiella (ITY)** 5-10-9 .... MrMWalford(7) 36
(Lady Susan Watson) *in rr: hdwy 9f out: sn chsng ldrs: lost pl over 3f out* **100/1**

0 14 dist **Fairfield**[43] 3556 5-10-11 .... MichaelMcAlister(5) —
(B Storey) *led 4f: lost pl over 4f out: sn bhd: t.o: btn total of 84l* **80/1**

15 23 **Bahama Boom** 4-10-3 .... DougieCostello(5) —
(C W Thornton) *in rr: drvn along 9f out: sn t.o: virtually p.u over 4f out* **25/1**

4m 2.00s (6.70) **Going Correction** +0.475s/f (Soft)
WFA 4 from 5yo+ 7lb **15** Ran SP% **120.1**
Speed ratings: **102,100,99,97,93 93,92,89,83,81 79,79,77,—,—** CSF £190.55 TOTE £3.60: £1.50, £10.00, £3.00; EX 140.30.
Owner West Coast Fiddlers **Bred** Miss E Hamilton **Trained** Greystoke, Cumbria

FOCUS
Just a steady gallop to past halfway in this mares only bumper, but the winner has some potential.

NOTEBOOK
Westgrove Berry(IRE), a big, well-made mare, was heavily supported to make a winning debut. In no hurry to join issue, her inexperience showed when taking charge. She looks essentially a stayer and should go on from here. *(op 11-2)*
Wensleydale Web, a narrow type, is out of a bumper winner and she made a satisfactory debut. Whether she will improve for it remains to be seen.
Morning Roses, a medium-sized newcomer, is out of a bumper winner. She looked very inexperienced when challenged by the winner and might do better on less testing ground. *(op 12-1)*
Heavenly Chorus, put to sleep at the back, elected to stick to the inner once in line for home. She never really threatened and might do better over hurdles. *(op 7-1)*
Ansa The Question, though well beaten in the end, showed a bit more than she had done on her debut two months earlier. *(op 40-1)*
Crimond(IRE), noisy and very fit, was in trouble turning in. *(op 7-2)*
Mollyalice, a decent sort and a good walker, can be expected to do a fair bit better on less-testing ground. *(op 7-1)*

4305 JOHN WADE SKIP HIRE NOVICES' HUNTERS' CHASE (19 fncs) 3m 1f 110y

5:00 (5:00) (Class 6) 5-Y-0+ **£1,561** (£484; £242; £121)

Form RPR

U 1 **Skew Whip**[10] 8-11-7 .... MrRWakeham(7) 94+
(C Brader) *chsd ldrs: blnd 14th: led 2 out: styd on u.p* **13/2**[2]

0P/U 2 2 **Ikemba (IRE)**[21] 3924 9-12-0 .... MrJMPritchard 89
(J Groucott) *led hit 12th: hdd 2 out: kpt on wl run-in* **8/1**[3]

0/U3 3 1 1/4 **Wilfie Wild**[18] 10-11-7 .... MrsLWard(7) 89+
(Mrs Lynne Ward) *hld up detached in last: stdy hdwy 12th: styd on to go 3rd 2 out: styd on run-in: nt rch 1st 2* **8/1**[3]

4 5 **Rebel Army (IRE)**[38] 7-12-0 .... MrRBurton 83
(Mrs C J Robinson) *chsd ldrs: outpcd 15th: kpt on fr 2 out* **11/4**[1]

3 5 1 3/4 **Queenies Girl**[15] 4044 10-11-0 .... MissJFoster(7) 75+
(Paul Frank) *chsd ldrs: blnd 1st: one pce fr 4 out* **40/1**

FU 6 8 **Bobby Buttons**[18] 9-11-9 .... MissTJackson(5) 76+
(Mrs J Jones) *in rr: mstkes 6th and 8th: hdwy and promient 10th: outpcd fr 4 out* **12/1**

-46P 7 18 **High Expectations (IRE)**[15] 4044 11-11-9 69 .... MrTDavidson(5) 58+
(J S Haldane) *chsd ldrs: mstke 9th: outpcd 13th: sn lost pl* **80/1**

PP/4 8 3/4 **Scenic Storm (IRE)**[10] 11-12-0 .... MrNTutty 55
(Miss Lucinda Broad) *chsd ldrs: hit 4th: weakend appr 3 out* **20/1**

4/4- P **Gayble**[553] 1347 8-11-9 .... MrNFSmith(5) —
(Nigel Smith) *j.rt: bhd: t.o whn p.u bef 12th* **100/1**

23P3 P **Beauchamp Oracle**[27] 3819 9-11-7 .... MrMWalford(7) —
(S Flook) *rn in snatches: in rr: hdwy 7th: outpcd 12th: sn lost pl: t.o whn p.u bef 2 out* **11/4**[1]

42 P **Boardsmill Rambler (IRE)**[9] 4146 7-12-0 .... MrMThompson —
(V Thompson) *mstkes: in rr: hdwy and in tch 11th: blnd and lost pl 13th: sn bhd: t.o whn p.u bef 2 out* **12/1**

7m 1.10s (12.70) **Going Correction** +0.475s/f (Soft) **11** Ran SP% **113.7**
Speed ratings: **99,98,98,96,95 93,87,87,—,—,—** CSF £53.81 TOTE £8.40: £2.80, £2.00, £2.00; EX 68.90 Place 6 £188.72, Place 5 £110.78.
Owner R G Brader **Bred** R Brader **Trained** Melton Mowbray, Leics

FOCUS
Although this novices' hunter chase appeared to be run at a sound clip, the time was very slow and not form to be confident about. A first winner under Rules for Charles Brader/Richard Wakeham.

NOTEBOOK
Skew Whip, a winner of four points, had failed to get round on his one previous outing under Rules. Surving one bad mistake, he was always doing just enough. *(op 9-2 tchd 7-1)*
Ikemba(IRE), with the champion point rider in the saddle, this point winner took them along at a good gallop and never gave up fighting. He deserves to win a maiden hunters' chase. *(op 11-1)*
Wilfie Wild, a winner of six points, was happy to give them all start. In pursuit of the first two at the penultime fence, he stayed on all the way to the line but his rider looked weak against the two men. *(op 9-1)*
Rebel Army(IRE), winner of four of his five start in points, looks essentially a stayer and he will be better suited by further. *(op 3-1 tchd 9-4)*
Queenies Girl, a dual point winner, may appreciate less testing and cut up ground than she was asked to race on here. *(op 33-1)*
Scenic Storm(IRE) *Official explanation: jockey said gelding had no more to give (tchd 16-1 and 22-1)*
Beauchamp Oracle, on and off the bridle, called it a day with a circuit to go and the ground had turned right against him. The official 'good to soft' was by now a figment of the clerk of the course's imagination! *(op 3-1 tchd 5-2)*
T/Plt: £135.10 to a £1 stake. Pool: £61,538.70. 332.40 winning tickets. T/Qpdt: £15.20 to a £1 stake. Pool: £5,126.90. 248.40 winning tickets. WG

4128 FONTWELL (L-H)

Wednesday, March 8

4306 Meeting Abandoned - Waterlogged

3793 CARLISLE (R-H)

Thursday, March 9

OFFICIAL GOING: Heavy (soft in places)

The two fences after the post were omitted all circuits in the chases. The flight after the post and the third-last flight were omitted all circuits in the hurdles.
Wind: Light, half-against Weather: Overcast, rain

4313 BETFREDPOKER NOVICES' HURDLE (8 hdls 3 omitted) 2m 4f

2:10 (2:10) (Class 4) 4-Y-0+ **£3,083** (£898; £449)

Form RPR

-510 1 **Some Touch (IRE)**[55] 3376 6-11-10 .... GrahamLee 118+
(J Howard Johnson) *mde all: rdn bef 2 out: styd on wl* **3/1**[2]

5 2 4 **Secret Pact (IRE)**[29] 3793 4-10-8 .... BrianHarding 95
(I McMath) *hld up: hdwy 1/2-way: effrt and chsd wnr 2 out: one pce last* **12/1**

12 3 2 1/2 **Numero Un De Solzen (FR)**[54] 3381 5-11-5 .... TJDreaper(5) 109
(J P L Ewart) *chsd ldrs: outpcd bef 2 out: kpt on fr last: no imp* **7/4**[1]

3-33 4 8 **Windy Hills**[77] 2947 6-11-3 .... TonyDobbin 98+
(N G Richards) *keen early: cl up tl rdn and wknd between last two* **3/1**[2]

1005 5 18 **Zaffie Parson (IRE)**[44] 3551 5-10-10 .... RichardMcGrath 69
(G A Harker) *in tch: rdn 5th: sn outpcd: n.d after* **50/1**

4005 6 13 **Phantom Major (FR)**[23] 3912 5-10-10 .... MissRDavidson(7) 63
(Mrs R L Elliot) *hld up: outpcd 5th: n.d after* **100/1**

7 hd **Neutrino**[183] 4-10-3 .... PaddyMerrigan(5) 53
(P C Haslam) *in tch tl rdn and wknd after 3 out* **16/1**

55 R **Oscar D'Hyrome (FR)**[20] 3967 4-10-5 101 .... MrTGreenall(3) —
(C Grant) *ref to r* **9/1**[3]

P P **Tigger Too**[94] 2678 8-10-12 .... MichaelMcAlister(5) —
(B Storey) *nt fluent 1st: cl up: blnd 4th: lost tch and p.u bef next* **200/1**

5m 25.0s (7.90) **Going Correction** +0.55s/f (Soft)
WFA 4 from 5yo+ 8lb **9** Ran SP% **113.4**
Speed ratings: **106,104,103,100,93 87,87,—,—** CSF £36.23 TOTE £3.80: £1.50, £3.40, £1.10; EX 37.80.
Owner Andrea & Graham Wylie **Bred** Walter Fennell **Trained** Billy Row, Co Durham

FOCUS
Not a bad novices' hurdle for the track. The winner has been rated value for a bit further but was still a bit below the level of his best bumper form.

NOTEBOOK
Some Touch(IRE), who had not been seen since his saddle slipped at Musselburgh in January, was prominent throughout and stayed on strongly on this return to two and a half miles to win comfortably and provide Howard Johnson with his first winner in around five weeks. He will struggle to defy a double penalty, but is open to a little further improvement and could be the type to do well in handicaps. *(op 4-1)*
Secret Pact(IRE), an 86-rated Flat performer, shaped well when fifth at the course on his debut and stepped up on that with a gallant effort in second, keeping on without proving a match for the winner. There is surely a race in him at a similar level. *(op 8-1)*
Numero Un De Solzen(FR) is a strong stayer who would have been suited by conditions, but he was unable to muster the speed to pose a threat to the winner and had to settle for a slightly disappointing third. He will remain vulnerable under his penalty, but is lightly-raced and may yet be capable of a little improvement. *(op 5-2)*
Windy Hills looked a major player on the best of his form, but having raced keenly, he failed to see out his race and the ground appeared to get the better of him. He will not be at his best until tackling fences. *(op 5-2)*

4314 BETFRED MILLION BEGINNERS' CHASE (14 fncs 2 omitted) 2m 4f

2:40 (2:40) (Class 4) 5-Y-0+ **£4,554** (£1,337; £668; £333)

Form RPR

0232 1 **Great As Gold (IRE)**[18] 4016 7-11-2 115 .... (p) WilsonRenwick 122+
(B Ellison) *chsd ldrs: blnd and rdr lost iron briefly 9th: rallied to ld 2 out: drvn out* **15/8**[1]

0-2U 2 1 **Henry's Pride (IRE)**[15] 4054 6-10-11 .... PaddyMerrigan(5) 118+
(P C Haslam) *cl up: led 5th to 9th: led bef 3 out to next: kpt on u.p fr last* **5/2**[2]

22-P 3 17 **Sports Express**[59] 3316 8-10-6 .... (p) PeterBuchanan(3) 94
(Miss Lucinda V Russell) *cl up tl rdn and one pce fr 3 out* **12/1**

-U65 4 hd **Sharp Jack (IRE)**[61] 3289 8-11-2 112 .... JimmyMcCarthy 102+
(R T Phillips) *led to 5th: led 9th to bef 3 out: wknd next* **7/2**[3]

PF34 5 27 **Wild About Harry**[50] 3444 9-11-2 65 .... KeithMercer 74
(A R Dicken) *hld up: outpcd 8th: sn btn* **33/1**

6F05 6 20 **Political Cruise**[23] 3918 8-10-9 72 .... GarethThomas(7) 54
(R Nixon) *towards rr: rdn 8th: sn btn* **100/1**

2506 7 16 **Uptown Lad (IRE)**[12] 4110 7-11-2 .... KennyJohnson 38
(R Johnson) *bhd: hdwy and prom 1/2-way: wknd 10th* **9/1**

/PPP F **Moonzie Laird (IRE)**[12] 4112 8-10-11 .... DeclanMcGann(5) —
(Miss Lucinda V Russell) *prom: outpcd whn hit 8th: t.o whn fell 10th* **100/1**

5m 32.7s (12.80) **Going Correction** +0.775s/f (Soft) **8** Ran SP% **108.2**
Speed ratings: **105,104,97,97,86 78,72,—** CSF £6.31 TOTE £2.40: £1.50, £1.90, £2.40; EX 4.50.
Owner Keith Middleton **Bred** Rathasker Stud **Trained** Norton, N Yorks

FOCUS
A reasonable beginners' chase in which the front two pulled well clear.

NOTEBOOK
Great As Gold(IRE) would ideally have prefered a longer trip, but his guaranteed stamina came to the fore in the latter part of the race and he stayed on dourly having taken it up after the second last. His jumping is hardly perfect, but he will continue to be a threat when stamina is at a premium. *(op 13-8 tchd 6-4 and 2-1)*
Henry's Pride(IRE), a slightly unfortunate loser on his fencing debut at Sedgefield, unseated early when bidding for compensation at Southwell last time, and he again found one too good. Having looked the winner for much of the way, jumping soundly, he was brushed aside by Great As Gold after the second last, before staying on right the way to the line. There is a similarly modest race in him, and a return to three miles will help. *(op 9-4 tchd 11-4 in places)*
Sports Express is effective under such conditions and she will no doubt have delighted connections with this switch to fences, battling on well to take third from the weary Smart Jack. She will find life easier against her own sex. *(tchd 14-1)*

Sharp Jack(IRE) had a bit to prove on this return to fences, but he jumped soundly on the heels of early leader Henry's Pride and took it up again leaving the back straight. However, his stamina ran out on the long slog for home and was run out of third on the line. *(op 11-2)*

Uptown Lad(IRE) was the only other who ever looked likely to get involved, but he was unable to race on with the front quartet and ultimately faded tamely. *(op 10-1 tchd 8-1)*

4315 BETFRED CASINO "NATIONAL HUNT" NOVICES' HURDLE (8 hdls 4 omitted) 3m 1f

3:15 (3:15) (Class 4) 4-Y-0+ **£3,083** (£898; £449)

Form					RPR
11	**1**		**According To John (IRE)**^{66} [3205] 6-12-1	TonyDobbin	120+
			(N G Richards) *prom: led bef 2 out: rdn and edgd lft between last 2: styd on strly*	**11/8**^{1}	
1350	**2**	*1*	**Capybara (IRE)**^{43} [3560] 8-11-3 105	DavidO'Meara	106+
			(H P Hogarth) *keen: led to bef 2 out: rallied: kpt on fr last*	**3/1**^{2}	
2	**3**	*½*	**Ballyboley (IRE)**^{13} [4099] 8-11-3	JimmyMcCarthy	105
			(R T Phillips) *hld up in tch: hdwy 5th: outpcd bef 2 out: kpt on fr last*	**10/1**	
	4	*9*	**Dinnie Flanagan (IRE)** 6-10-12	PaddyMerrigan$^{(5)}$	98+
			(P C Haslam) *hld up in tch: hdwy 1/2-way: ev ch bef 2 out: sn outpcd*	**50/1**	
3231	**5**	*7*	**Laertes**^{23} [3914] 5-11-6 115	MrTGreenall$^{(3)}$	95
			(C Grant) *prom tl rdn and wknd bef 2 out*	**7/2**^{3}	
05-	**6**	*22*	**Fastaffaran (IRE)**^{327} [4865] 5-11-3	BrianHarding	67
			(I McMath) *hld up: rdn after 3 out: wknd bef next*	**66/1**	
2333	**7**	*2 ½*	**Nevada Red**^{23} [3914] 5-11-3 101	DominicElsworth	64
			(D McCain) *chsd ldrs tl rdn and wknd bef 2 out*	**10/1**	
00-	**P**		**Bobby Icata**^{383} [3953] 5-11-3	LarryMcGrath	—
			(K W Hogg) *nt jump wl: sn t.o: p.u after 5th*	**200/1**	
0-0P	**P**		**Silver Hill Lad**^{30} [3789] 5-11-3	NeilMulholland	—
			(C W Fairhurst) *a bhd: t.o whn p.u bef 5th*	**200/1**	
0P	**P**		**Givitago**^{10} [4141] 7-10-5	(p) MichaelMcAlister$^{(5)}$	—
			(B Storey) *cl up to 1/2-way: qckly lost pl: p.u bef 3 out*	**200/1**	

6m 45.7s **10** Ran SP% **112.5**
CSF £5.58 TOTE £2.60: £1.60, £1.40, £2.30; EX 9.50.
Owner Sir Robert Ogden **Bred** John P Kiely **Trained** Greystoke, Cumbria
■ Stewards' Enquiry : David O'Meara caution: used whip with excessive frequency
Tony Dobbin caution: used whip with excessive frequency and in the incorrect place

FOCUS
An ordinary contest, but the potentially useful According To John defied 12st1lb in gritty fashion and rates an exciting chasing prospect. The runner-up ran to his hurdles mark.

NOTEBOOK
According To John(IRE), who was only workmanlike in winning last time, did not have an easy task with 12st1lb on his back, but he showed the right sort of attitude and battled on gamely under strong pressure to hold the second and third after the last. Briefly ridden with half a mile to run, he soon came back on the bridle and this fine physical specimen looks an above average sort. He will make a smart chaser in time and is one to keep on the right side. *(op 6-4 tchd 13-8)*

Capybara(IRE), runner-up in this contest last season, is better known as a chaser now, but he was well supported on this return to hurdles and went close to rewarding his supporters, rallying well to hassle the winner from after the last. He clearly stays well and can pick up a similar contest before returning to fences. *(op 5-1)*

Ballyboley(IRE), seemingly a surprise second at Warwick on his debut, is bred for this sort of test being by Roselier, and he showed stamina to be his strong suit with a fair effort in third, staying on well in the final quarter mile. He is lightly-raced for an eight-year-old, which suggests he has had problems, but he clearly has the ability to win races. *(op 8-1 tchd 11-1)*

Dinnie Flanagan(IRE) made little appeal on this racecourse debut, but shaped surprisingly well, making stealthy headway to come through and dispute it three out before tiring under pressure. He is entitled to benefit from the experience and slightly less-taxing conditions in future are likely to help. *(op 33-1)*

Laertes looked the obvious danger to the favourite, having won well in similar conditions at Newcastle, but he ran rather flat and was never really going like a winner, ending up well held. *(op 9-4)*

Nevada Red is usually a consistent sort, but he was below par and dropped away some way from the finish. *(op 12-1 tchd 14-1)*

4316 ELITE RACING CLUB H'CAP CHASE (16 fncs 4 omitted) 3m 2f

3:50 (3:50) (Class 4) (0-110,94) 5-Y-0+ **£3,903** (£1,146; £573; £286)

Form					RPR
P4P3	**1**		**Recent Edition (IRE)**^{16} [4042] 8-10-5 76	(b) PaddyAspell$^{(3)}$	93+
			(J Wade) *mde all: rdn and styd on wl fr 3 out*	**5/1**^{3}	
3261	**2**	*4*	**Matmata De Tendron (FR)**^{16} [4042] 6-11-0 87	DougieCostello$^{(5)}$	96
			(A Crook) *rn in snatches: prom: chsd wnr after 8th: outpcd 5 out: rallied and cl up after next: one pce appr last*	**9/2**^{2}	
56P0	**3**	*11*	**Lazy But Lively (IRE)**^{16} [4042] 10-11-3 85	KeithMercer	83
			(R F Fisher) *hld up: stdy hdwy 1/2-way: ouptaced 10th: rallied and prom 4 out: no ex next*	**5/1**^{3}	
13P2	**4**	*13*	**Lambrini Bianco (IRE)**^{21} [3938] 8-9-10 69	(p) DerekLaverty$^{(5)}$	55+
			(Mrs L Williamson) *chsd ldrs: sn drvn along: wknd fr 4 out*	**4/1**^{1}	
/612	**P**		**Dickie Lewis**^{45} [3540] 8-11-3 85	DominicElsworth	—
			(D McCain) *hld up: stdy hdwy 1/2-way: wknd 10th: p.u bef 4 out*	**4/1**^{1}	
P/1-	**P**		**Running Moss**^{340} [4712] 14-11-5 90	MrCStorey$^{(3)}$	—
			(A H Mactaggart) *in tch tl wknd 8th: t.o whn p.u bef next: dead*	**14/1**	
P61P	**P**		**Briar's Mist (IRE)**^{10} [4144] 9-11-12 94	(b) RichardMcGrath	—
			(C Grant) *cl up tl lost pl qckly after 8th: t.o whn p.u bef 10th*	**11/1**	
2F3P	**P**		**Gimme Shelter (IRE)**^{16} [4042] 12-10-11 84	MichaelMcAlister$^{(5)}$	—
			(S J Marshall) *chsd ldrs tl wknd bef 9th: t.o whn p.u bef 3 out*	**16/1**	

7m 22.4s (14.20) **Going Correction** +0.775s/f (Soft) **8** Ran SP% **112.4**
Speed ratings: **109,107,104,100,**— —,—,— CSF £27.23 CT £116.31 TOTE £7.20: £1.90, £1.90, £1.90; EX 31.00.
Owner John Wade **Bred** J J O'Neill **Trained** Mordon, Co Durham
■ Stewards' Enquiry : Derek Laverty five-day ban: used whip with excessive frequency (Mar 20-24)

FOCUS
Only half of the eight runners finished and Recent Edition was able to reverse recent Sedgefield form with Matmata De Tendron. Both ran to their marks, and the form makes sense.

NOTEBOOK
Recent Edition(IRE) could never be called consistent, but he is a capable performer at the right level on his day and was able to reverse recent Sedgefield form with the runner-up, benefiting from a more positive ride on this occasion. He was joined taking the fourth last, but quickly asserted again and stayed on dourly in the final quarter-mile. *(op 7-1)*

Matmata De Tendron(FR), 9lb higher than when winning at Sedgefield, was unable to confirm form with Recent Edition, the 10lb pull making the difference, but he gave his all and kept on right the way to the line. He is only six and may yet be capable of a little further improvement. *(op 5-1 tchd 11-2)*

Lazy But Lively(IRE) is a frustrating character who finds winning particularly hard and, although showing more than when behind the front two last time, his losing run continues. *(op 11-2 tchd 9-2)*

Lambrini Bianco(IRE) was still in with a chance approaching the fourth last, but he had been under pressure for some time and was quickly dropped. He was a pleasing second on his return from a long break at Huntingdon last month, but this was a step in the wrong direction. *(op 11-2)*

Briar's Mist(IRE) was up there early, but threw in the towel and began to struggle a long way out. His inconsistency continues to make him an unattractive betting proposition. *(op 8-1)*

Dickie Lewis, who has found some form over hurdles, was potentially interesting on this return to fences, but he was tired when going out to his left at the fifth-last fence and was pulled up soon after. He simply seems happier over hurdles. *(op 8-1)*

4317 BETFRED.COM CONDITIONAL JOCKEYS' H'CAP HURDLE (8 hdls 3 omitted) 2m 4f

4:25 (4:25) (Class 4) (0-110,101) 4-Y-0+ **£3,083** (£898; £449)

Form					RPR
5-4P	**1**		**Silken Pearls**^{77} [2944] 10-11-11 100	MichaelMcAlister	105
			(L Lungo) *cl up: led 3 out: hrd pressed last: hld on gamely*	**9/1**	
000P	**2**	*nk*	**Roobihoo (IRE)**^{26} [3854] 7-11-12 101	(t) PaddyAspell	106
			(C Grant) *prom: effrt after 3 out: ev ch last: edgd rt run in: kpt on: jst hld*	**9/2**^{2}	
4236	**3**	*17*	**Kempski**^{10} [4141] 6-11-1 90	(b) KeithMercer	80+
			(R Nixon) *prom: outpcd after 4th: rallied bef 2 out: no ch w first two*	**9/2**^{2}	
6011	**4**	*24*	**Silver Seeker (USA)**^{32} [3757] 6-10-13 91	PatrickMcDonald$^{(3)}$	55
			(A R Dicken) *hld up: rdn whn hit 3 out: outpcd bef next*	**9/2**^{2}	
5020	**5**	*dist*	**Primitive Poppy**^{16} [4043] 7-10-12 87	BrianHughes	—
			(Mrs A Hamilton) *chsd ldrs tl outpcd 5th: n.d after*	**11/2**^{3}	
02P6	**P**		**Gospel Song**^{23} [3916] 14-10-6 86	EwanWhillans$^{(5)}$	—
			(A C Whillans) *chsd ldrs: outpcd 5th: t.o whn p.u bef 2 out*	**14/1**	
11-2	**P**		**Nolife (IRE)**^{138} [1838] 10-11-10 99	DougieCostello	—
			(Miss Lucinda V Russell) *led to 3 out: rallied: wknd qckly and p.u next*	**3/1**^{1}	

5m 26.4s (9.30) **Going Correction** +0.55s/f (Soft) **7** Ran SP% **111.6**
Speed ratings: **103,102,96,86,**— —,— CSF £46.49 TOTE £8.00: £3.80, £2.00; EX 57.30.
Owner P E Truscott **Bred** Mrs A G Martin And Cobhall Court Stud **Trained** Carrutherstown, D'fries & G'way

FOCUS
An ordinary handicap, but they went a fair pace. The first two were the pick of the weights.

NOTEBOOK
Silken Pearls had been off the track since a poor effort over the Christmas period. Well at home in these conditions, she was locked together with the runner-up from the second last and just got the verdict. *(op 8-1)*

Roobihoo(IRE) has been out of form this term but the application of a tongue strap brought about a better performance. He threw down a strong challenge from the second last and, after edging over to the far rail on the run-in, just missed out.

Kempski, who looked set to finish right out the back at one stage, began to stay on once meeting the rising ground but could make no further impression between the last two flights. *(op 7-1)*

Silver Seeker(USA), gunning for the hat-trick off a 6lb higher mark, could never get within striking distance of the leaders. His last win came on a sound surface and, although he has won on soft, these conditions were too much for him. *(op 7-2)*

Nolife(IRE), 3lb higher for this first run since October, was always being harried for the lead. He was narrowly headed three from home and, dropping away quickly on the approach to the next, was pulled up. He should not be written off back on better ground. *(op 7-2 tchd 4-1)*

4318 BETFRED "THE BONUS KING" H'CAP CHASE (10 fncs 2 omitted) 2m

5:00 (5:00) (Class 4) (0-105,101) 5-Y-0+ **£3,578** (£1,050; £525; £262)

Form					RPR
30P5	**1**		**Hollows Mill**^{29} [3798] 10-11-4 98	TJDreaper$^{(5)}$	112+
			(F P Murtagh) *hld up: hdwy 3rd. led gng wl 3 out: rdn clr bef last: styd on*	**5/1**^{2}	
5002	**2**	*20*	**The Miner**^{29} [3798] 8-10-13 91	(p) MrCStorey$^{(3)}$	85
			(Miss S E Forster) *cl up: led 5th: mstke next: hdd 3 out: outpcd after next: fin tired*	**11/4**^{1}	
4300	**3**	*5*	**Ambition Royal (FR)**^{66} [3205] 6-11-3 95	PeterBuchanan$^{(3)}$	84
			(Miss Lucinda V Russell) *prom: outpcd 5th: kpt on fr 2 out: no ch w first two*	**13/2**^{3}	
2041	**4**	*7*	**Flaming Heck**^{44} [3555] 9-11-2 96	DesFlavin$^{(5)}$	78
			(Mrs L B Normile) *led to 5th: cl up tl wknd fr 3 out*	**5/1**^{2}	
201P	**5**	*dist*	**Mikasa (IRE)**^{23} [3915] 6-10-7 82	RichardMcGrath	—
			(R F Fisher) *bhd: outpcd whn j.lft 5th: nvr on terms*	**13/2**^{3}	
1B3P	**F**		**Longdale**^{43} [3562] 8-11-12 101	(p) AlanDempsey	—
			(M Todhunter) *hld up in tch: hdwy 1/2-way: 3l down and gng wl whn fell 3 out*	**9/1**	
0206	**P**		**Glenfarclas Boy (IRE)**^{10} [4144] 10-10-13 88	(p) GrahamLee	—
			(Miss Lucinda V Russell) *cl up tl reminders and lost pl bef 4th: sn btn: t.o whn p.u bef 4 out*	**5/1**^{2}	

4m 31.2s (14.10) **Going Correction** +0.775s/f (Soft) **7** Ran SP% **113.3**
Speed ratings: **95,85,82,79,**— —,— CSF £19.42 TOTE £7.80: £3.40, £2.00; EX 16.60.
Owner The Great Expectations Sporting Club **Bred** Catridge Farm Stud Ltd **Trained** Low Braithwaite, Cumbria

FOCUS
A slow-motion finish to a modest event. The winner was well in and has been rated to the level of his win in the same race last year.

NOTEBOOK
Hollows Mill was last successful in the corresponding event a year ago, when off the same mark as he was here. Under a patient ride, he showed ahead three from home and pulled clear of his pursuers. *(op 4-1)*

The Miner was 3lb higher than when runner-up over course and distance a month ago, form that has been boosted by the subsequent win of third home Nifty Roy, and was weighted to confirm the form with Hollows Mill. Racing prominently but not always fluent at his fences, he eventually dropped away from the second last. *(op 4-1)*

Ambition Royal(FR), on his chasing debut and without the visor, was struggling by halfway but did plug on to take a remote third place on the run-in. *(op 8-1)*

Flaming Heck, raised 6lb for his win at Sedgefield and on a career-high mark as a result, raced up with the pace until fading from the third last. He jumped the final fence in third place but was down almost to a walk on the run-in.

Longdale, equipped with cheekpieces for the first time, was close behind the leading trio and travelling strongly when coming down at the third last. How much he would have found when pressure was applied is open to question. *(op 7-1)*

4319 BETFRED ON 0800 731 1210 INTERMEDIATE OPEN NATIONAL HUNT FLAT RACE 2m 1f

5:30 (5:33) (Class 6) 4-6-Y-0 **£1,713** (£499; £249)

Form					RPR
	1		**Jack The Blaster** 6-11-4	GrahamLee	87
			(J Howard Johnson) *hld up in tch: smooth hdwy to ld over 2f out: rdn and kpt on wl fnl f*	**7/2**^{1}	

0 **2** 2 1/2 **Cavers Glen**[29] [3799] 4-10-3 .... EwanWhillans(7) 76
(A C Whillans) *keen: led to over 2f out: rdn and rallied: kpt on ins last* **10/1**

3 6 **High Moor** 4-10-10 .... DominicElsworth 70
(J D Bethell) *hld up: smooth hdwy to chse ldrs over 3f out: rdn over 2f out: one pce fnl f* **9/2**[2]

6 **4** 2 **Young Smokey (IRE)**[54] [3399] 5-11-4 .... RussGarritty 76
(P Beaumont) *keen: cl up: effrt and ev ch over 2f out: outpcd over 1f out* **6/1**[3]

5 **5** 7 **Stormont Dawn (IRE)**[44] [3556] 5-10-6 .... DesFlavin(5) 62
(Mrs L B Normile) *chsd ldrs tl rdn and wknd wl over 1f out* **12/1**

6 2 **Darazari Bay (IRE)** 5-11-4 .... RichardMcGrath 67
(K G Reveley) *hld up: rdn over 4f out: nvr rchd ldrs* **7/2**[1]

0 **7** 7 **Maylee (IRE)**[63] [3259] 4-10-3 .... KeithMercer 45
(Mrs H O Graham) *prom tl wknd over 3f out* **9/1**

8 dist **Nocloix (FR)** 5-11-4 .... PadgeWhelan —
(S B Bell) *prom: lost pl 7f out: no ch after* **16/1**

9 11 **Always Waiting (IRE)** 5-11-4 .... BrianHarding —
(Mrs Dianne Sayer) *sn towards rr: struggling fr 1/2-way* **50/1**

10 dist **Billy Row** 5-10-8 .... MichaelMcAvoy(10) —
(James Moffatt) *sn prom: rdn and wknd over 4f out* **33/1**

4m 58.1s (28.80) **Going Correction** +0.55s/f (Soft)
WFA 4 from 5yo+ 7lb **10** Ran SP% **114.5**
Speed ratings: **54,52,50,49,45 44,41,—,—,—** CSF £38.86 TOTE £3.90: £1.60, £2.70, £2.30; EX 48.80 Place 6 £45.17, Place 5 £29.76.
Owner R J Partnership and J Howard Johnson **Bred** N B Mason **Trained** Billy Row, Co Durham
■ The first winner under Rules for Charles Brader and Richard Wakeham.

FOCUS
A weak affair run at a particularly steady pace in the testing conditions.

NOTEBOOK
Jack The Blaster, whose dam was a winning hurdler, travelled well just off the very steady pace. *Taking a narrow lead with around a quarter of a mile to run, he was well on top inside the last.* *(op 3-1)*
Cavers Glen, well beaten in a similar event here a month ago, showed more on this occasion. Keen to get on with things and carrying his head low as he set a very sedate pace, he was taken on by the winner with over two furlongs to run but knuckled down well and was only put in his place inside the last. *(op 14-1)*
High Moor, whose dam showed nothing in two bumpers, travelled quite well but was unable to find a change of gear when let down. *(op 10-3)*
Young Smokey(IRE), still not the finished article, was found out when the tempo quickened but ran a thoroughly satisfactory race. *(op 9-1)*
Stormont Dawn(IRE) filled the same position as she had on her debut but this was the more encouraging effort. *(op 14-1 tchd 16-1)*
Darazari Bay(IRE), a half-brother to Commanche Quest who was a winning staying chaser for the Reveley yard, could never get into the action. *(op 4-1)*
T/Plt: £52.10 to a £1 stake. Pool: £37,207.00. 521.10 winning tickets. T/Qpdt: £21.30 to a £1 stake. Pool: £2,910.20. 100.70 winning tickets. RY

4012 TOWCESTER (R-H)
Thursday, March 9

OFFICIAL GOING: Heavy
Conditions were suited to pond life and, leaving aside the bumper, of the 61 runners that set out in the other six races, only 26 managed to complete.
Wind: Almost nil, becoming moderate across Weather: Showers

4320 LIBRAN COMPENSATION SERVICES CONDITIONAL JOCKEYS' H'CAP HURDLE (10 hdls) 2m 3f 110y
2:00 (2:02) (Class 5) (0-95,95) 4-Y-0+ **£2,999** (£931; £501)

Form RPR

6640 **1** **Ask The Umpire (IRE)**[19] [3997] 11-11-10 **93** .... (p) TomMalone 95+
(N E Berry) *hld up and bhd: nt fluent 1st: hdwy appr 6th: led after 3 out: clr appr last: r.o* **12/1**

5-05 **2** 14 **Newtown**[11] [4131] 7-11-9 **95** .... CharliePoste(3) 87+
(M F Harris) *hld up: hdwy 5th: ev ch 3 out: rdn 2 out: 6 l 2nd and btn whn blnd last* **20/1**

3 dist **Phareight Dei (IRE)**[266] [770] 8-10-4 **81** .... DavidBoland(8) —
(Ian Williams) *hld up in mid-div: wknd appr 6th: lft poor 3rd last* **20/1**

30-0 **P** **Homer (IRE)**[14] [4080] 9-10-13 **82** .... TJPhelan —
(N M Babbage) *a bhd: t.o 3rd: p.u bef 3 out* **25/1**

60P6 **P** **Ireland's Eye (IRE)**[23] [3918] 11-10-2 **76** .... DarrenO'Dwyer(5) —
(J R Norton) *a bhd: t.o whn p.u after 4th* **8/1**

P13F **P** **Balmoral Queen**[21] [3951] 6-10-5 **77** .... StephenCraine(3) —
(D McCain) *prom tl wknd after 7th: t.o whn p.u bef 2 out* **4/1**[1]

3024 **P** **Avanti Tiger (IRE)**[45] [3540] 7-9-8 **71** .... (v[1]) JamesPeters(8) —
(C C Bealby) *prom tl rdn and wknd 3rd: t.o whn p.u bef 2 out* **6/1**[2]

00-P **P** **Never Cried Wolf**[20] [3963] 5-10-2 **79** .... JohnPritchard(8) —
(R Dickin) *led to 2nd: prom tl wknd 7th: t.o whn p.u bef 3 out* **66/1**

0-04 **P** **Griffens Brook**[27] [3843] 6-10-6 **75** .... (b[1]) RobertLucey-Butler —
(Mrs P Sly) *t.k.h: prom tl wknd appr 6th: t.o whn p.u bef 7th* **12/1**

3F3/ **P** **John The Greek (IRE)**[1638] [1388] 10-10-4 **73** .... WilliamKennedy —
(A M Hales) *hld up: hdwy after 4th: wknd 5th: t.o whn p.u bef 6th* **33/1**

P-5 **P** **Ehab (IRE)**[34] [3715] 7-11-0 **83** .... ColinBolger —
(Miss A M Newton-Smith) *prom: led 2nd tl after 4th: wknd 7th: t.o whn p.u bef 3 out* **33/1**

P00P **P** **Walton Way**[18] [4013] 6-10-0 **69** oh2 .... (b[1]) JamesDiment —
(P W Hiatt) *sn prom: led 6th: mstke 3 out: sn hdd: 3rd and wkng whn p.u bef 2 out* **40/1**

0U1P **R** **Prairie Law (GER)**[21] [3943] 6-11-6 **95** .... TomMessenger(6) —
(B N Pollock) *prom: led after 4th to 6th: wknd appr 3 out: no ch whn ref 2 out* **15/2**[3]

0PP6 **P** **Jackie Boy (IRE)**[14] [4080] 7-10-8 **83** .... MarcGoldstein(6) —
(N A Twiston-Davies) *hld up: hdwy after 5th: wknd 7th: t.o whn p.u before 2 out* **15/2**[3]

P0FP **P** **Soleil D'Hiver**[48] [3483] 5-9-13 **73** .... AndrewGlassonbury(5) —
(C J Drewe) *bhd: rdn and hdwy 7th: wknd appr 3 out: t.o whn p.u bef 2 out* **33/1**

44U1 **R** **Needwood Spirit**[20] [3956] 11-10-4 **78** .... ThomasBurrows(5) —
(Mrs A M Naughton) *hld up in tch: rdn after 4th: wknd 7th: poor 3rd whn ref last* **12/1**

040P **P** **Secret Jewel (FR)**[58] [3332] 6-10-3 **77** .... DavidCullinane(5) —
(Miss C J E Caroe) *hld up towards rr: rdn and hdwy appr 6th: wknd 7th: t.o whn p.u bef 3 out* **100/1**

5m 46.4s (30.60) **Going Correction** +1.45s/f (Heav) **17** Ran SP% **119.1**
Speed ratings: **96,90,—,—,— —,—,—,— —,—,—,— —,—,—,—** CSF £229.18 CT £4687.40 TOTE £13.90: £3.40, £8.90, £6.70; EX 445.60.
Owner Craig Davies **Bred** Michael Conroy **Trained** Llanishen, Monmouths

FOCUS
They did not seem to go that quick, but even so the conditions proved far too much for most of these, with 12 horses pulling up and another two refusing. This form should basically be ignored and those that failed to complete should be given the benefit of the doubt.

NOTEBOOK
Ask The Umpire(IRE), a course-and-distance winner in soft ground back in January, obviously enjoys a slog, but these conditions were something else. He was kept wide when getting into the race approaching the uphill climb to the third last and that probably helped him as those that raced more towards the inner dropped like flies. Despite winning very easily in the end, he finished legless and will take some time to get over this. *(op 14-1)*
Newtown, unplaced in all five of his starts over hurdles in this country since arriving from France, was kept wide in search of better ground and that almost certainly helped him complete, though it was all he could do to clamber over the last. Given the melee of this contest however, his performance should be taken with a very large pinch of salt.
Phareight Dei(IRE), an Irish import making his debut in this country and racing for the first time in nine months, only inherited a very distant third due to the misfortune of others and we learned nothing about him. *(tchd 22-1)*
Needwood Spirit, raised 6lb for his Fakenham win, would have finished a bad third had he not decided that jumping the last flight was just too tall an order. *(op 7-1)*
Balmoral Queen showed up for a long way before finding it all too much. She was far from alone *there though, thanks to the conditions, and this performance should not be held against her.* *(op 7-1)*
Griffens Brook pulled too hard in the first-time blinkers and in these conditions that was the last thing he needed. *(op 7-1)*
Prairie Law(GER) showed up for a long way until becoming one of many to give up starting the final climb. He should be forgiven this. *(op 7-1)*
Walton Way, unplaced in three bumpers and four hurdles to date, had the blinkers on for the first time and showed up prominently until stopping to nothing on the run to the second last when still in third place. *(op 7-1)*

4321 STOP ENDOWMENT MORTGAGES TIME-BARRING H'CAP CHASE (14 fncs 4 omitted) 3m 110y
2:30 (2:32) (Class 5) (0-95,95) 5-Y-0+ **£3,578** (£1,050; £525; £262)

Form RPR

F **1** **Shrove Tuesday (IRE)**[62] [3276] 7-9-11 **71** .... RCColgan(5) 87+
(A J Martin, Ire) *hld up and bhd: j. slowly 3rd: hdwy 4 out: stmbld 2 out: rdn to ld towards fin* **11/2**[1]

124- **2** 1 **Another Conquest**[333] [4790] 7-11-8 **94** .... RichardYoung(3) 109+
(J W Mullins) *a.p: rdn to ld appr last: hdd and no ex towards fin* **16/1**

4542 **3** 3 1/2 **Fisherman Jack**[11] [4130] 11-10-0 **69** .... JodieMogford 79
(G J Smith) *led to 1st: a.p: rdn after 3 out: one pce flat* **11/2**[1]

5346 **4** 3/4 **Runaway Bishop (USA)**[14] [4078] 11-11-7 **90** .... RichardHobson 99
(J R Cornwall) *racd wd: mid-div: hdwy after 8th: led 10th to 11th: rdn appr 2 out: one pce* **10/1**

5353 **5** 1 3/4 **Dun Locha Castle (IRE)**[10] [4152] 11-11-0 **83** .... DaveCrosse 90
(N R Mitchell) *a.p: led 9th to 10th: rdn appr 2 out: no ex flat* **11/1**

FF33 **6** 14 **Murphy's Magic (IRE)**[9] [4166] 8-11-2 **85** .... (p) PhilipHide 80+
(Mrs T J Hill) *hld up: hdwy 6th: wkng whn mstke 3 out* **12/1**

P630 **7** 3 **The River Joker (IRE)**[16] [4042] 10-10-7 **81** .... MarkNicolls(5) 71
(John R Upson) *led 2nd to 4th: mstke 8th: wknd 3 out* **16/1**

U3-P **P** **Zaffre D'Or (IRE)**[23] [3907] 9-10-10 **79** ow1 .... (v[1]) JohnMcNamara —
(M J McGrath) *a bhd: t.o whn p.u bef 3 out* **66/1**

6024 **P** **Tribal Dancer (IRE)**[15] [4047] 12-11-10 **93** .... SamThomas —
(Miss Venetia Williams) *prom to 7th: t.o whn p.u bef 4 out* **7/1**[2]

-500 **P** **Dalus Park (IRE)**[62] [3276] 11-10-11 **85** .... MrSMorris(5) —
(C C Bealby) *prom: lost pl and rdn 6th: t.o whn p.u bef 3 out* **10/1**

0/ **P** **Watershed (IRE)**[47] [3516] 11-11-1 **84** .... PaulMoloney —
(Seamus G O'Donnell, Ire) *hld up in tch: wknd 9th: bhd whn p.u bef last* **9/1**

P-50 **P** **Shuffling Pals (IRE)**[56] [3359] 9-10-0 **69** oh4 .... (b) AlanO'Keeffe —
(S E H Sherwood) *hld up in mid-div: mstke 3 out: bhd whn blnd 2 out: sn p.u* **25/1**

05U6 **P** **Multi Talented (IRE)**[18] [4007] 10-10-13 **89** .... (b) JustinMorgan(7) —
(L Wells) *mid-div: rdn appr 6th: bhd fr 8th: t.o whn hit 3 out: p.u bef 2 out* **40/1**

1U20 **P** **Never Awol (IRE)**[23] [3909] 9-11-0 **90** .... (p) TomMessenger(7) —
(B N Pollock) *led 1st to 2nd: led 4th to 9th: led 10th: hdd and j. slowly 11th: sn wknd: p.u after 3 out* **8/1**[3]

7m 8.90s (22.30) **Going Correction** +0.975s/f (Soft) **14** Ran SP% **118.1**
Speed ratings: **103,102,101,101,100 96,95,—,—,— —,—,—,—** CSF £85.57 CT £511.18 TOTE £6.30: £2.20, £6.20, £1.90; EX 119.50.
Owner Mrs Kay Owens **Bred** Mrs Kay Owens **Trained** Summerhill, Co. Meath

FOCUS
Not the jumping test it might have been, with four fences omitted. Again the conditions took their toll, with half the field pulling up, but they had gone a sensible pace and there were still five in with every chance jumping the last. With the third to fifth all close to their marks it is worth being positive about the first two. Third fence after stands and third fence in back straight omitted.

NOTEBOOK
Shrove Tuesday(IRE), a faller here last time, made the long journey over from Ireland worthwhile on this occasion. Given a very sensible ride in the conditions, she gradually picked off her rivals over the final mile and showed great courage in the dour battle to the line. She looks an *out-and-out stayer. Official explanation: trainer said, regarding the improved form shown, mare had benefited from the heavy ground* *(old market op 5-1)*
Another Conquest, who has already proved her worth in testing ground here, was always up with the pace and had every chance but made a mistake at the second last just when she did not need it and found the winner just too strong on the run-in. This was a cracking effort after 11 months off, given the conditions. *(old market op 18-1)*
Fisherman Jack, still relatively unexposed over regulation fences, ran another fine race having been up with the pace from the off. He handles these conditions well, but he won a couple of points on good ground so may be capable of maintaining his consistent run of form even when the ground firms up. *(old market op 13-2 new market op 5-1)*
Runaway Bishop(USA), a consistent performer and proven on soft ground here, was kept wide in *search of the best ground and had every chance. He is a reliable yardstick for the form.* *(old market tchd 14-1)*
Dun Locha Castle(IRE) stays all day and had every chance, but even in these conditions his lack of pace was evident over the last couple of fences. *(old market op 11-1 new market tchd 10-1)*
The River Joker(IRE) *Official explanation: trainer said gelding bled from nose* *(new market op 20-1)*
Never Awol(IRE), in fine form here this winter, is on a stiff mark now and after showing up with the *leaders for a long way even he seemed to find these conditions all too much.* *(old market op 10-1 new market op 9-1)*

 The Form Book, Raceform Ltd, Compton, RG20 6NL

4322 "GAMBLE WITH BOOKIES NOT BANKS" H'CAP HURDLE (8 hdls) 2m

3:05 (3:05) (Class 4) (0-110,106) 4-Y-0+ **£4,477** (£1,351; £696; £368)

Form RPR

605P **1** **Andy Gin (FR)**[19] 3990 7-10-8 **93** ..... CharliePoste(5) 102+
(Miss E M England) *hld up in tch: led appr 2 out: clr appr last: r.o wl* **8/1**

P01 **2** *14* **Dorneys Well (IRE)**[12] 4104 6-11-0 **94** ..... (t) PaulMoloney 92+
(Evan Williams) *hld up and bhd: hdwy 4th: ev ch appr 2 out: sn rdn and btn* **4/1**[3]

3336 **3** *13* **Signature Tune (IRE)**[44] 3548 7-11-4 **98** ..... PhilipHide 80
(P Winkworth) *chsd ldr: led 5th tl appr 2 out: sn rdn and wknd* **3/1**[1]

6554 **4** *¾* **Hunting Lodge (IRE)**[15] 4050 5-10-12 **99** ..... MrJAJenkins(7) 80
(H J Manners) *hld up and bhd: hdwy 5th: wknd appr 2 out* **9/1**

005P **P** **Mnason (FR)**[33] 3733 6-11-6 **105** ..... JamesDiment(5) —
(S J Gilmore) *a bhd: t.o whn p.u bef 2 out* **25/1**

3311 **U** **Speed Venture**[19] 3990 9-11-4 **105** ..... (vt) PhilKinsella(7) —
(J Mackie) *blnd bdly and uns rdr 1st* **7/2**[2]

1P24 **P** **Blackthorn**[19] 3985 7-10-7 **90** ..... RichardYoung(3) —
(M Appleby) *led to 5th: wknd 3 out: t.o whn p.u bef 2 out* **10/1**

0U30 **P** **Malaga Boy (IRE)**[19] 3993 9-11-12 **106** ..... TomScudamore —
(C L Tizzard) *t.k.h in tch: chalng whn hit 3 out: sn wknd: p.u bef last* **13/2**

4m 33.4s (22.00) **Going Correction** +1.45s/f (Heav) **8** Ran SP% **114.6**
Speed ratings: **103,96,89,89,**— —,—,— CSF £40.61 CT £118.38 TOTE £10.20: £3.00, £2.10, £1.60; EX 74.60.
Owner Miss E M V England **Bred** M Latty-Vanvolsem **Trained** Priors Hardwick, Warwicks

FOCUS
They understandably went steadily in the early stages of this race. Again it seemed to be an advantage to race wide in search of the 'better' ground.

NOTEBOOK
Andy Gin(FR), who has fallen dramatically in the weights, was very well backed and made no mistake. He relished these conditions and racing widest of all probably made a big difference. He *was the day's fastest finish and has been rated back to the level of his best form.Official explanation: trainer had no explanation for the improved form shown (op 12-1 tchd 14-1)*
Dorneys Well(IRE), raised 4lb for his Chepstow victory and with the tongue tie retained, was given a patient ride before making progress starting the final climb and was only a length or so off the winner at the second last, but he then fell to pieces in the conditions. *(op 10-3)*
Signature Tune(IRE) was another to be kept wide and had every chance, but even the half-mile drop in trip did not enable him to get home in these conditions. *(op 7-2 tchd 11-4)*
Hunting Lodge(IRE) was given a patient ride, but never really got involved. His Flat wins all came on a fast surface so this ground was almost certainly not what he needed. *(op 8-1)*
Speed Venture crumpled on landing at the first and his rider can consider himself unlucky to have an unseated next to his name. *(op 10-3 tchd 5-1)*
Blackthorn went off in front and though he did not appear to go mad, the conditions still well and truly found him out. *(op 10-3 tchd 5-1)*

4323 ENDOWMENT MORTGAGES-CLEARING OBSTACLES NOVICES' CHASE (12 fncs 2 omitted) 2m 3f 110y

3:40 (3:42) (Class 3) 5-Y-0+ **£6,263** (£1,850; £925; £463; £231)

Form RPR

-000 **1** **Waltzing Beau**[19] 3993 5-10-3 ..... JohnnyLevins(5) 120+
(B G Powell) *racd wd: hld up: hdwy after 3 out: swtchd rt 2 out: sn led on bit and clr: easily* **7/1**

1652 **2** *16* **Terivic**[18] 4014 6-11-6 118 ..... JohnMcNamara 112
(K C Bailey) *led tl after 3 out: rdn to ld 2 out: sn hdd: no ch w wnr* **5/1**[3]

FF21 **3** *shd* **Lord Olympia (IRE)**[11] 4130 7-11-10 121 ..... SamThomas 117+
(Miss Venetia Williams) *chsd ldr: hit 5th and 3 out: sn led: hit 2 out and hdd: one pce* **8/11**[1]

4413 **4** *dist* **Vicario**[14] 4068 5-10-11 116 ..... StephenCraine(3) —
(D McCain) *prom: mstkes 1st and 4 out: wknd after 3 out: t.o* **7/2**[2]

P006 **5** *1 ½* **Monty Be Quick**[18] 4014 10-11-1 72 ..... CharliePoste(5) —
(J M Castle) *a bhd: lost tch fr 8th: t.o* **40/1**

5m 50.9s (30.90) **Going Correction** +1.375s/f (Heav)
WFA 5 from 6yo+ 4lb **5** Ran SP% **111.7**
Speed ratings: **93,86,86,**—,— CSF £38.06 TOTE £6.60: £2.70, £2.00; EX 54.00.
Owner David Cliff And Philippa Clunes **Bred** Christopher Shankland **Trained** Morestead, Hants

FOCUS
A moderate pace for this novice chase and in the end it came down to tactics, with the winner racing wide of the others for most of the contest. As a result the form may not be reliable. Third fence after stands and third fence in back straight omitted.

NOTEBOOK
Waltzing Beau, making his chasing debut, was kept very wide throughout, so wide that he raced close to the outside rail. He still seemed to have plenty to do coming to the third last, but was still on the bridle and eventually picked up his wilting rivals without turning a hair. The way the race was run makes the form looks very unreliable, but even so his young rider deserves plaudits for this superb piece of riding. *(op 10-1)*
Terivic was given a positive ride but, not for the first time, found this trip on a stiff track too much in the conditions especially as he took more of an inside route, where the ground looked more testing, compared with the enterprisingly-ridden winner. *(op 4-1)*
Lord Olympia(IRE), a winner over nearly a mile further in heavy ground last time, should have relished these conditions but he was kept to the inside of the track and the evidence is that was not *the place to be. Once the winner ranged alongside at the second last, he was totally swamped. (op 10-11)*
Vicario likes soft ground, but after showing up for much of the way he fell in a heap up the final climb. *(op 3-1)*

4324 "BET ON HORSES NOT HOUSES" MARES' ONLY "NATIONAL HUNT" NOVICES' HURDLE (11 hdls) 2m 5f

4:15 (4:15) (Class 4) 5-Y-0+ **£3,999** (£1,241; £668)

Form RPR

5212 **1** **Colline De Fleurs**[25] 3884 6-10-10 ..... MarkBradburne 110+
(J A B Old) *hld up in tch: wnt 2nd after 7th: led appr 2 out: sn clr* **10/11**[1]

20-3 **2** *dist* **Ceoperk (IRE)**[23] 3906 7-10-10 ..... WarrenMarston 80
(D J Wintle) *plld hrd in tch: hit 5th: led 7th tl appr 2 out: sn btn: 20 l 2nd whn mstke last* **9/2**[3]

43-0 **3** *dist* **Eastern Point**[23] 3909 12-10-6 ow3 ..... MrPYork(7) —
(R H York) *led to 4th: w ldr: hit 6th: rdn after 7th: wknd 8th* **66/1**

0 **P** **Another Burden**[91] 2727 5-10-10 ..... SamThomas —
(H D Daly) *a bhd: t.o whn p.u after 7th* **20/1**

5 **P** **Peppery Pamela**[18] 4017 5-10-3 ..... MrTJO'Brien(7) —
(V R A Dartnall) *bhd fr 7th: t.o whn p.u bef 2 out* **14/1**

3004 **P** **Milanshan (IRE)**[35] 3692 6-10-3 ..... WayneKavanagh(7) —
(J W Mullins) *plld hrd: a bhd: t.o whn p.u bef 8th* **25/1**

0F0 **P** **Another Penny**[13] 4088 6-10-3 ..... JohnPritchard(7) —
(R Dickin) *prom tl wknd after 5th: t.o whn p.u bef 8th* **100/1**

/1-1 **R** **Philomena**[11] 4129 7-10-10 ..... MrJJDoyle(7) —
(V R A Dartnall) *prom: rdn and wkng whn mstke 7th: poor 4th whn ref 2 out* **3/1**[2]

5-FF **F** **Mrs Fizziwig**[13] 4099 7-10-3 ..... SeanQuinlan(7) —
(R T Phillips) *chsd ldr: led 4th to 7th: 15 l 4th and wkng whn fell 3 out* **28/1**

6m 19.4s (38.20) **Going Correction** +1.95s/f (Heav) **9** Ran SP% **116.8**
Speed ratings: **105,**—,—,—,— —,—,—,— CSF £5.32 TOTE £1.70: £1.10, £1.40, £12.90; EX 8.60.
Owner The Wheels Have Come Off **Bred** J A B Old **Trained** Barbury Castle, Wilts

FOCUS
A dour test of stamina in the conditions and yet again the route the jockeys took played a big part in the outcome. By this stage the ground looked extremely poached.

NOTEBOOK
Colline De Fleurs ◆, whose bumper victory came on heavy ground, was given a fine tactical ride in that she was kept wide for most of the way and was switched to the untouched ground tight against the inside rail in the home straight. On reaching the run-in she was the only one still able to put one hoof in front of the other, and she remains a mare of some potential. *(op 11-10 tchd 6-5)*
Ceoperk(IRE) was keen enough and in this ground that was fatal. She was still in front starting the *turn for home, but then emptied completely and it was all she could do to reach the winning post. (op 7-2 tchd 5-1)*
Eastern Point, a multiple winning pointer/hunter chaser having her first start over hurdles, was given a positive ride but eventually found these conditions all too much. Her wins have all come on a sound surface. *(op 50-1)*
Philomena gave the inside away to no-one which was far from ideal, but she was a prime *candidate to bounce and these conditions would have made that scenario much more likely. Official explanation: trainer said mare was unsuited by the heavy ground (tchd 5-2)*
Mrs Fizziwig raced prominently for a long way, but was already fading right out of it when coming down three out. She has now fallen in all three of her starts over hurdles. *(tchd 5-2)*
Peppery Pamela *Official explanation: trainer said mare was distressed after race (tchd 5-2)*

4325 LIBRAN-COMPENSATION.CO.UK HUNTERS' CHASE (14 fncs 4 omitted) 3m 110y

4:50 (4:50) (Class 6) 6-Y-0+ **£1,873** (£581; £290; £145)

Form RPR

2-13 **1** **Paddy For Paddy (IRE)**[23] 3910 12-12-6 ..... MrRBurton 115+
(G L Landau) *hld up: hdwy 6th: 3 lengths 2nd whn lft clr 3 out: eased considerably flat* **5/4**[1]

33/2 **2** *dist* **Hades De Sienne (FR)**[12] 4107 11-11-5 ..... (t) MrSGray(7) 51
(Miss Tracey Watkins) *prom: j.lft 5th: lost pl 9th: styd on to go 2nd flat: no ch w wnr* **12/1**

56-5 **3** *7* **Supreme Silence (IRE)**[12] 4107 9-11-9 80 ..... MrNickKent(7) 48
(Nick Kent) *rn in snatches: no ch fr 4 out* **33/1**

44U5 **4** *10* **Uncle Mick (IRE)**[18] 4007 11-12-3 104 ..... (p) MrJSnowden(3) 42
(C L Tizzard) *hld up in tch: mstke 7th: struggling after 4 out: lft 2nd 3 out: wknd flat* **7/1**[3]

/400 **U** **Father Jim**[11] 11-11-5 ..... MrFelixDeGiles(7) —
(J A T De Giles) *bmpd 1st: mstke and uns rdr 3rd* **16/1**

-P13 **U** **Denvale (IRE)**[14] 4073 8-12-3 ..... MrRCope(3) —
(Mrs Caroline Bailey) *led: 3 l clr whn mstke and uns rdr 3 out* **15/8**[2]

P4/U **P** **Soul King (IRE)**[32] 11-11-5 81 ..... (b) MrRBliss(7) —
(Michael Blake) *a bhd: mstke 4th: lost tch 6th: t.o whn p.u bef 10th* **25/1**

/P-4 **P** **Galen (IRE)**[11] 15-11-7 67 ..... MissSSharratt(5) —
(Miss J Froggatt) *prom: j.rt 1st: lost pl 6th: t.o whn mstke 8th: p.u bef last* **50/1**

7m 18.7s (32.10) **Going Correction** +1.375s/f (Heav) **8** Ran SP% **114.0**
Speed ratings: **103,**—,—,—,— —,—,— CSF £16.32 TOTE £2.10: £1.40, £2.20, £5.00; EX 14.40.
Owner Mrs Jane Thornton **Bred** Mrs Louise Cooper-Joyce **Trained** Frome, Somerset

FOCUS
A very sensible pace in the conditions and they all raced wide in search of better ground. Third fence after stands and third fence in back straight omitted.

NOTEBOOK
Paddy For Paddy(IRE) has won over a mile further than this, so stamina was never going to be an issue. Patiently ridden, he was travelling as well as the leader when that rival departed at the third last and his only problem from then on was to avoid the unwanted attentions of two loose horses. He was value for at least 50 lengths. *(tchd 6-4)*
Hades De Sienne(FR) looks very slow and only finished a remote second due to the misfortune of others. *(tchd 14-1)*
Supreme Silence(IRE) never looked happy and although he has won on soft ground, he does not want the ground as bad as this. His finishing position is flattering. *(op 25-1)*
Uncle Mick(IRE) seemed to fins these conditions all too much. He did win on heavy ground over *hurdles in his younger days, but none of his chase victories has come on ground softer than good. (op 5-1)*
Denvale(IRE) made the running and was still in front and travelling as well as the favourite when his rider asked him to go long at the third last, but he ended up banking it and, although his pilot valiantly tried to stay aboard, gravity eventually won the day. *(op 9-4)*

4326 LIBRAN COMPENSATION CHARITY LAUNCH STANDARD OPEN NATIONAL HUNT FLAT RACE 2m

5:20 (5:20) (Class 5) 4-6-Y-0 **£2,602** (£764; £382; £190)

Form RPR

1 **Solid As A Rock**[320] 6-10-11 ..... MrTJO'Brien(7) 105
(J G Cann) *racd wd: hld up: hdwy over 5f out: rdn to ld ins fnl f: r.o* **16/1**

2 *¾* **Ordre De Bataille (FR)** 4-10-10 ..... MarkBradburne 96
(H D Daly) *hld up: hdwy after 6f: led over 2f out: rdn and hdd ins fnl f: nt qckn* **7/2**[2]

3 *21* **Victor George** 6-10-13 ..... StevenCrawford(5) 86+
(N A Twiston-Davies) *bhd: rdn and hdwy over 5f out: wknd over 1f out* **8/1**

4P1 **4** *17* **Top Ram (IRE)**[35] 3691 6-11-11 ..... CarlLlewellyn 73
(J A B Old) *led after 2f: hung lft 3f out: sn hdd: wknd wl over 1f out* **5/2**[1]

02 **5** *4* **Jobsworth (IRE)**[61] 3292 6-11-4 ..... ChristianWilliams 62
(Evan Williams) *prom: rdn and wknd over 2f out* **7/2**[2]

6 *5* **Opare (FR)** 4-10-3 ..... MrPCallaghan(7) 49
(H D Daly) *t.k.h in rr: hdwy after 6f: rdn 3f out: sn wknd* **20/1**

60 **7** *dist* **Hazzard A Guess**[35] 3699 5-10-4 ..... WayneKavanagh(7) —
(J W Mullins) *led 2f: prom: rdn over 5f out: wknd over 3f out: t.o* **28/1**

4 **8** *26* **Lord Norman (IRE)**[18] 4011 5-10-11 ..... JustinMorgan(7) —
(L Wells) *prom: pushed along after 4f: wknd 8f out: t.o* **15/2**[3]

0 **9** *18* **Irish Guard**[14] 4072 5-11-4 ..... SeanCurran —
(J G O'Neill) *bhd: short-lived effrt over 5f out: t.o* **80/1**

10 *dist* **Raki Rose** 4-10-10 ..... TomScudamore —
(M Scudamore) *bhd fnl 8f: t.o* **33/1**

11 *dist* **Wenrus Lady** 5-10-11 .... PaulMoloney —
(A W Carroll) *hld up: hdwy 8f out: wknd over 4f out: t.o* **40/1**

4m 28.6s (16.70) **Going Correction** +1.95s/f (Heav)
WFA 4 from 5yo 7lb 5 from 6yo 4lb **11** Ran SP% **116.6**
Speed ratings: **101,100,90,81,79 77,—,—,—,— —** CSF £67.86 TOTE £16.20: £4.20, £1.90, £3.70; EX 118.20 TRIFECTA Placce 6 £353.92, Place 5 £45.58.
Owner M H D Barlow **Bred** M J Spore **Trained** Cullompton, Devon.

FOCUS
A fair pace for this bumper in the conditions and, as was the case the whole afternoon, those that raced wide enjoyed a massive advantage. None of the form horses performed, so impossible to rate with any confidence.

NOTEBOOK
Solid As A Rock, a half-brother to a winning hurdler out of a winning stayer in the Flat, was the winner of one of his two points last spring and a faller in the other when still in with every chance. He was taken very wide throughout on this occasion and almost raced on the chase course. The ploy paid off too, and despite rather zig-zagging throughout the last furlong he just managed to get on top after a protracted duel with the runner-up. The form is a little suspect, but he is the sort that will relish a test of stamina when put back over obstacles. *(op 10-1)*
Ordre De Bataille(FR), who fetched 25,000gns as a three-year-old, raced wide and went to the front turning for home, but the winner was right on his shoulder and found that little bit more where it mattered. He should win his bumper.
Victor George, a 20,000gns yearling re-sold for only 6,500gns as a two-year-old, is out of a half-sister to Barathea and Gossamer. His breeding did not suggest he would appreciate such *testing conditions and that is the way it looked, even though he managed to make the frame.* *(op 7-1)*
Top Ram(IRE), carrying a penalty for his course-and-distance victory last month, made much of the running, but he stuck to the inside the whole way and that cannot have helped him. It was therefore no surprise to see him fold completely from the home bend. *(op 3-1 after 4-1 in a place)*
Jobsworth(IRE), runner-up in a soft-ground Haydock bumper last time, ran as though finding this even slower ground and more demanding track too much.
Opare(FR), out of a winning hurdler/cross-country chaser, pulled too hard on this debut to give him much chance of lasting home.
T/Plt: £414.00 to a £1 stake. Pool: £50,085.05. 88.30 winning tickets. T/Qpdt: £15.50 to a £1 stake. Pool: £4,830.60. 229.60 winning tickets. KH

[3991] WINCANTON (R-H)
Thursday, March 9

OFFICIAL GOING: Soft
Wind: Fairly strong behind

4327 ELITE MAIDEN HURDLE (8 hdls) 2m
1:50 (1:51) (Class 4) 4-Y-0+ **£3,426** (£998; £499)

Form RPR
5-10 **1** **Gentleman Jimmy**[83] 2866 6-11-2 .... JimCrowley 107+
(H Morrison) *trckd ldrs: shkn up to chse ldr appr 2 out: led last: r.o wl: readily* **25/1**
0 **2** *4* **Rapscallion (GER)**[3] 3133 7-11-2 .... AndrewTinkler 100+
(Mrs H Dalton) *led: clr 3rd: rdn after 2 out: hdd last: kpt on but nt pce of wnr* **16/1**
64 **3** *5* **Inishturk (IRE)**[16] 4032 7-11-2 .... RobertThornton 95
(A King) *hld up in tch: rdn to chse ldng pair appr 2 out: kpt on bot no further imp* **20/1**
04 **4** *1* **Ice Melted (IRE)**[13] 4094 5-11-2 .... RichardJohnson 94
(Jonjo O'Neill) *hld up towards rr: hdwy appr 3 out: rdn appr 2 out: kpt on same pce* **9/1**
44 **5** *13* **Great Memories**[47] 3505 7-10-11 .... ShaneWalsh(5) 84+
(Jonjo O'Neill) *hld up towards rr: hdwy into 5th after 3 out: sn rdn: one pce fr next* **16/1**
6 *8* **Marghub (IRE)**[967] 7-10-9 .... MissCDyson(7) 73
(Miss C Dyson) *racd wd: hld up towards rr: stdy hdwy after 3 out: styd on: nvr trbld ldrs* **150/1**
6 **7** *nk* **Positano (IRE)**[21] 3947 6-10-9 .... JohnKington(7) 73
(M Scudamore) *chsd ldrs: rdn after 3 out: wknd next* **66/1**
0060 **8** *dist* **So Wise So Young**[19] 3996 5-11-2 .... BenjaminHitchcott —
(R H Buckler) *j. slowly 2nd: a towards rr* **100/1**
2 **9** *3 1/2* **Ardglass (IRE)**[24] 3898 4-10-8 .... MatthewBatchelor —
(Mrs P Townsley) *mid div whn blnd bdly 2nd: bhd whn j.lft next: nvr a danger after* **6/1**[3]
10 *hd* **Montenda** 5-11-2 .... JasonMaguire —
(S C Burrough) *a bhd* **150/1**
00 **11** *4* **Mightymuller (IRE)**[41] 3594 4-10-8 .... TomDoyle —
(D R Gandolfo) *mstke 1st: a bhd* **66/1**
4 **12** *18* **Lunar Sovereign (USA)**[99] 2573 7-11-2 .... TimmyMurphy —
(M C Pipe) *mid div tl wknd qckly 2 out: eased run-in* **5/1**[2]
/4-0 **13** *8* **Dodger McCartney**[69] 3130 8-11-2 .... (t) RJGreene —
(K Bishop) *chsd ldrs: rdn after 3 out: sn wknd* **100/1**
14 *dist* **Roche Ecossaise (FR)**[358] 7-10-9 .... AndrewThornton —
(R H Alner) *mid div tl wknd appr 3 out: t.o* **66/1**
P **Major League (USA)**[121] 4-10-8 .... PJBrennan —
(K Bishop) *mid div tl wknd appr 3 out: t.o and p.u bef 2 out* **20/1**
500 **P** **Lansdowne Princess**[25] 3884 4-9-10 .... EamonDehdashti(5) —
(G A Ham) *hit 1st: mid div tl wknd appr 3 out: t.o and p.u bef 2 out* **100/1**
P **Promotion**[226] 6-11-2 .... MickFitzgerald —
(N J Henderson) *in tch: tk clsr order on bridle sn after 3 out: wknd qckly and p.u bef next* **11/8**[1]
0 **U** **Carpet Ride**[6] 4211 4-10-1 .... CharlieStudd(7) —
(B G Powell) *chsd ldrs: wnt 2nd at the 4th: rdn and wknd appr 2 out: bundered bdly whn uns rdr last* **100/1**

4m 1.30s (12.20) **Going Correction** +0.85s/f (Soft)
WFA 4 from 5yo+ 7lb **18** Ran SP% **118.0**
Speed ratings: **103,101,98,98,91 87,87,—,—,— —,—,—,—,— —,—,—** CSF £341.92 TOTE £19.70: £6.80, £5.40, £5.50; EX 432.10.
Owner Burridge,Burridge,Pilkington & Rutland **Bred** J G St Paul Burridge **Trained** East Ilsley, Berks
■ Stewards' Enquiry : John Kington one-day ban: used whip when out of contention (Mar 20)

FOCUS
Little strength in depth to this opening maiden hurdle, but it was run at a fair gallop and the field finished well strung out.

NOTEBOOK
Gentleman Jimmy, winner of a fast ground Taunton bumper in November, showed his true colours and got off the mark at the second time of asking over hurdles, looking value for around 7 lengths. Handy throughout, the drop back to this trip clearly played to his strengths, and his jumping was assured. His dam is a half-sister to Desert Orchid, so he can be expected to jump a fence in due course, and should improve again for this experience. *(op 20-1)*
Rapscallion(GER), third in an All-Weather claimer over an extended mile just three days previously, ran freely at the head of affairs and only gave way to the winner on the run-in. He is clearly on good terms with himself at present, proved he gets the trip, and ought to become of greater interest when eligible for handicaps after his next outing. Faster ground could help too.
Inishturk(IRE) was doing all of his best work at the finish and posted another improved effort. He is now eligible for handicaps and can find a race when upped to a suitably longer trip. *(tchd 22-1)*
Ice Melted(IRE) did not look overly suited by the drop in trip on this speed track, but he kept to his task well enough from two out, and is another who will obviously be of more interest when qualified for handicaps after his next assignment. In the long term, he looks very much a future staying chaser. *(op 8-1)*
Great Memories was not given too hard a time when push came to shove and should be rated slightly better than the bare form. He cost 47,000gns and should improve when faced with a stiffer *test in due course. Official explanation: jockey said gelding was unsuited by the soft ground (op 14-1)*
Marghub(IRE) finished her race well enough, having been set plenty to do, and can be rated better than the bare form. *(op 100-1)*
Ardglass(IRE) was never travelling with any fluency after an early mistake and posted a tame effort. *(op 4-1)*
Lunar Sovereign(USA) hugged the inside rail for most of the race, but had nothing to offer when the race became serious down the back straight, and this must rate a tame effort. While it would be unwise to assume he may not better this when eligible for handicaps, and when encountering a fast surface, his stamina for hurdling is still far from certain. *(op 11-2 tchd 6-1)*
Promotion, rated 100 on the Flat, proved bitterly disappointing on this hurdling bow. Having jumped neatly and moved well enough, he was quickly pulled up when the pace increased as though something might well have been amiss. This would have been the softest ground he has encountered on a racecourse to date but, as a half-brother to Border Castle - who was also formerly owned by The Queen and scored on his hurdling bow for Venetia Williams on testing ground this term - and being by Sadler's Wells, there were reasonable grounds to believe he should *act on this type of surface. He was later found to have burst a blood-vessel. Official explanation: vet said gelding bled from the nose (op 7-4)*

4328 KINGWELL LODGE B&B NOVICES' H'CAP CHASE (21 fncs) 3m 1f 110y
2:20 (2:20) (Class 4) (0-110,102) 5-Y-0+ **£5,204** (£1,528; £764; £381)

Form RPR
0F42 **1** **Motcombe (IRE)**[19] 3981 8-11-7 **97** .... (p) AndrewThornton 107+
(R H Alner) *w ldr tl 11th: sn drvn along in tch: rallied appr 3 out: led sn after last: styd on strly* **5/1**[2]
541P **2** *6* **Joseph Beuys (IRE)**[19] 3989 7-10-10 **91** .... DarylJacob(5) 96+
(D P Keane) *hld up: hit 9th:tk clsr order 14th:led after 17th:rdn and narrowly hdd 3 out: led next: hdd sn after last: no ex* **14/1**
2424 **3** *1 3/4* **Treasulier (IRE)**[21] 3949 9-11-2 **99** .... KeiranBurke(7) 101
(P R Rodford) *chsd ldrs: jnd ldr 11th: led 13th tl after 17th: sn rdn: kpt on same pce fr 3 out* **11/2**[3]
2541 **4** *2 1/2* **Chabrimal Minster**[13] 4095 9-11-12 **102** .... PJBrennan 106+
(R Ford) *in tch: wnt 3rd after 13th: jnd ldr 16th: rdn after 4 out: narrow advantage and wnt lft 3 out: blnd and hdd next: wknd* **6/4**[1]
4304 **5** *12* **Scratch The Dove**[16] 4041 9-10-10 **89** .... OwynNelmes(3) 81+
(A E Price) *in tch: blnd 1st: chsd ldrs 13th: rdn after 4 out: one pce fr next* **25/1**
60F2 **P** **Zimbabwe (FR)**[22] 3923 6-10-5 **81** .... (p) JoeTizzard —
(N J Hawke) *led tl 13th: grad fdd: bhd whn p.u bef 17th* **11/2**[3]
-P1P **P** **Boundary House**[35] 3698 8-11-2 **92** .... JasonMaguire —
(J A B Old) *hld up: wknd 16th: bhd and p.u bef 4 out* **11/1**
3P4P **P** **Tradingup (IRE)**[21] 3949 7-10-12 **91** ow4 .... (b[1]) GinoCarenza(3) —
(Andrew Turnell) *chsd ldrs tl lost pl after 12th: hdwy 15th: wknd after 17 : p.u bef next* **16/1**

7m 6.40s (26.50) **Going Correction** +1.10s/f (Heav) **8** Ran SP% **112.2**
Speed ratings: **103,101,100,99,96 —,—,—** CSF £62.69 CT £393.89 TOTE £5.30: £1.80, £3.60, £2.40; EX 58.10.
Owner Lady Cobham **Bred** Lady Cobham **Trained** Droop, Dorset

FOCUS
Not the strongest event for the class. It was run at a moderate early gallop, but the form looks fair enough.

NOTEBOOK
Motcombe(IRE) hit her usual flat spot when the tempo increased around five from home, before picking up strongly in the home straight to mow down her rivals and ultimately score with a bit up her sleeve. She is a tricky ride, and never one to overly trust, but she clearly enjoys this venue and the recent application of cheekpieces has certainly had the desired effect. Her next assignment is *likely to be in the EBF Mares' Final at Uttoxeter later this month before beginning a career at stud. (op 11-2)*
Joseph Beuys(IRE) appeared most likely to score when in front two out, but he could only find the same pace when pressed by the winner and was ultimately well held at the finish. This was a much more encouraging effort, however, and he still finished a clear second-best. *(tchd 16-1)*
Treasulier(IRE) ran his race in defeat and helps set the level of this form. He remains a maiden after 14 outings under Rules. *(op 13-2)*
Chabrimal Minster, successful in novice company over further last time, was being ridden prior to *a blunder at the penultimate fence which ended any chance he may have had of winning. (op 11-8 tchd 13-8)*
Scratch The Dove shaped as though she would have preferred a stronger early gallop on this step back up in trip. *(op 20-1)*
Zimbabwe(FR) *Official explanation: jockey said he dropped whip in back straight (op 5-1 tchd 6-1)*

4329 STEVEN & ROY HANNEY MEMORIAL H'CAP HURDLE (8 hdls) 2m
2:55 (2:55) (Class 3) (0-125,120) 4-Y-0+ **£6,506** (£1,910; £955; £477)

Form RPR
4U0U **1** **Kawagino (IRE)**[5] 4242 6-11-0 **108** .... JamieMoore 121+
(J W Mullins) *hld up bhd: smooth prog after 3 out: led sn after 2 out: wnt lft at the last: comf* **8/1**
42F0 **2** *7* **Lysander (GER)**[27] 3848 7-10-11 **105** .... PJBrennan 108+
(M F Harris) *hld up towards rr: rdn and hdwy after 3 out: ev ch whn mstke 2 out: kpt on same pce* **12/1**
120P **3** *6* **Purple Patch**[51] 3439 8-10-11 **105** .... RobertWalford 101
(C L Popham) *in tch: outpcd after 3 out: styd on strly fr last: tk 3rd cl home* **40/1**
0F21 **4** *2* **Walsingham (IRE)**[25] 3889 8-10-5 **99** .... RobertThornton 94+
(R Lee) *led: rdn after 3 out: hdd sn after 2 out: no ex: ct for 3rd cl home* **11/2**[3]
6412 **5** *2* **Kayceecee (IRE)**[27] 3848 5-11-5 **113** .... RichardJohnson 105
(H D Daly) *hld up in tch: tk clsr order 3 out: rdn and short lived effrt appr 2 out: wknd* **11/8**[1]
2211 **6** *13* **Misbehaviour**[10] 4153 7-10-13 **112** 7ex .... ChristopherMurray(5) 96+
(Jim Best) *hld up: short lived effrt after 3 out: one pced fr next* **7/2**[2]
0-05 **7** *6* **Its Crucial (IRE)**[133] 1891 6-11-9 **117** .... AntonyEvans 93+
(N A Twiston-Davies) *chsd ldr: nt fluent 1st: rdn after 3 out: sn wknd: hit 2 out and last* **22/1**

160- **P** **Clear Thinking**[145] [4371] 6-11-9 **120** ...... PaulO'Neill(3) —
(Miss Venetia Williams) *chsd ldr tl wknd qckly after 3 out: p.u bef next* **9/1**

3m 58.7s (9.60) **Going Correction** +0.85s/f (Soft)
WFA 4 from 5yo+ 7lb **8** Ran SP% **115.3**
Speed ratings: **110,106,103,102,101 95,92,**— CSF £93.23 CT £3566.97 TOTE £11.80: £2.50, £3.00, £5.30; EX 64.70 Trifecta £311.30 Part won. Pool £438.56 - 0.10 winning units.
Owner K J Pike **Bred** Neville O'Byrne **Trained** Wilsford-Cum-Lake, Wilts

FOCUS
A fair handicap, run at a sound gallop, and the field came home fairly strung out behind the clear-cut winner, who was well in on old form. The second to fourth were all close to their marks and the form should work out.

NOTEBOOK
Kawagino(IRE) ran out an easy winner. He was popular in the betting when unseating early on at Newbury five days previously and was again supported on course this time. The decent early pace played into his hands and he proved well suited by the sharp nature of this track. He also had no trouble with the softer ground, but while he ought to be high on confidence now, consistency has never been a strong suit and he may struggle if the Handicapper takes this form literally. *(op 10-1)*
Lysander(GER) hit a flat spot just after halfway, but responded to his rider's urgings and, whilst ultimately put firmly in his place by the winner, finished nicely clear of the remainder. He can build on this. *(op 14-1)*
Purple Patch looked held turning for home, but sprouted wings jumping the penultimate flight and eventually motored home to bag third place. She looks to have benefited from a recent break and will be of more interest when reverting to a stiffer test. *(tchd 50-1)*
Walsingham(IRE), raised 5lb for winning at Hereford last time, ultimately paid for his exertions at the head of affairs and finished tired. He now may benefit for the return to further on this evidence. *(op 7-1 tchd 15-2 and 5-1)*
Kayceecee(IRE), up 5lb for finishing second at Bangor last time and very well backed, found very little when push came to shove at the top of the straight and proved most disappointing. *(op 13-8)*
Misbehaviour, bidding for the hat-trick, failed to make any impression from off the pace and was well beaten under her penalty. *(tchd 4-1, 9-2 in a place)*

4330 DICK WOODHOUSE HUNTERS' CHASE (17 fncs) 2m 5f
3:30 (3:30) (Class 6) 5-Y-O+ **£1,977** (£608; £304)

Form RPR
F2F1 **1** **Raregem**[22] [3924] 8-12-0 ...... MrWBiddick(7) 117+
(M Biddick) *j.w: hld up bhd ldrs: jnd ldrs 13th: led 4 out: a in command after: canter* **4/5**[1]
4/ **2** *4* **The Kings Fling**[19] 10-11-9 ...... MrRWoollacott(5) 95
(Miss E Thompson) *hld up bhd ldrs: pckd 3rd: jnd ldrs 12th: rdn to chse wnr in vain fr 4 out* **8/1**[3]
P-13 **3** *21* **Trade Off (IRE)**[18] 8-12-0 94 ...... MrIChanin(7) 81
(Mrs S Alner) *w ldr: led 7th: nt fluent 8th: rdn and hdd 4 out: wknd* **9/4**[2]
1P2 **P** **Viscount Bankes**[15] [4055] 8-12-2 ...... MrSWaley-Cohen(5) —
(Mrs Rosemary Gasson) *chsd ldrs: jnd ldr 10th: wknd qckly after 4 out: p.u bef next* **18/1**
120/ **P** **Gudlage (USA)**[39] 10-11-7 ...... MissVShaw(7) —
(Mrs P J Shaw) *t.k.h: led: hit 2nd: hdd 7th: w ldr tl mstke 10th: sn lost tch: t.o and p.u bef 3 out* **16/1**

5m 42.3s (19.20) **Going Correction** +1.10s/f (Heav) **5** Ran SP% **108.6**
Speed ratings: **107,105,97,**—,— CSF £7.28 TOTE £1.60: £1.10, £3.30; EX 9.20.
Owner Mrs J Alford **Bred** R P And M Berrow **Trained** Bodmin, Cornwall

FOCUS
A modest event of its type, run at an average pace. The winner, whose Leicester win is working out better than expected, should be rated for at least treble his winning margin.

NOTEBOOK
Raregem followed up his recent facile success at Leicester in grand fashion under a confident ride by his trainer/rider. Ridden to get the slightly longer trip, he put in a fine round of jumping, and should be rated value for at least treble his winning margin. Still only an eight-year-old, he is progressing well. The Foxhunters' at Cheltenham may come a touch too soon, and Aintree looks a more viable target. *(op 8-15)*
The Kings Fling, a winner between the flags 19 days previously, posted a solid return to regulation fences on ground he would have found plenty soft enough. He jumped well, bar an error three out, and is capable of finding a similar race in the coming weeks. *(op 9-1 tchd 7-1)*
Trade Off(IRE), well backed, once again displayed a disliking for a testing surface and was made to look very one paced. He is worth another chance over this trip, but must have decent ground. *(op 4-1)*
Gudlage(USA) ran too keen early on and lacked any fluency over his fences. *(op 10-1)*
Viscount Bankes ran a touch freely and was not at all suited by the deep surface. *(op 10-1)*

4331 ROBERTA JOAN STOREY H'CAP HURDLE (11 hdls) 2m 6f
4:05 (4:05) (Class 5) (0-95,95) 4-Y-O+ **£2,740** (£798; £399)

Form RPR
50P- **1** **Festival Flyer**[389] [3831] 11-10-13 **82** ...... DavidDennis 89+
(Miss M Bragg) *chsd ldrs: jnd ldr 3 out: led 2 out: sn rdn: hit last: drvn out* **66/1**
5-P3 **2** *3* **Bright Green**[19] [3997] 7-11-5 **95** ...... BernieWharfe(7) 99+
(C J Gray) *chsd ldrs: lost position 8th:hit 3 out: hdwy next: chsd wnr appr last: styd on but wandered u.p run-in* **12/1**
0004 **3** *18* **From Dawn To Dusk**[47] [3496] 7-11-2 **85** ...... RichardJohnson 70+
(P J Hobbs) *led 2nd: rdn and hdd appr 2 out: wknd appr last* **5/1**[1]
44UR **4** *1 1/2* **Hill Forts Henry**[52] [3427] 8-9-11 **73** ...... SimonElliott(7) 57
(J W Mullins) *mid div: rdn after 3 out: sn one pced: nvr trbld ldrs* **16/1**
1364 **5** *18* **Hilarious (IRE)**[21] [3951] 6-11-2 **85** ...... AndrewThornton 51
(Dr J R J Naylor) *led tl 2nd: styd prom tl wknd 8th: t.o* **11/2**[2]
10B3 **6** *1 3/4* **Penny's Crown**[10] [4151] 7-11-2 **90** ...... EamonDehdashti(5) 54
(G A Ham) *mid div tl outpcd after 7th: nvr on terms after* **12/1**
040P **7** *14* **Minster Park**[18] [4015] 7-11-3 **86** ......(t) RJGreene 36
(S C Burrough) *mid div: hdwy after 7th: rdn to chse ldng pair after 3 out: wknd next: t.o* **100/1**
6-P0 **8** *dist* **Big Max**[49] [3458] 11-11-6 **89** ...... BenjaminHitchcott —
(Miss K M George) *chsd ldrs tl wknd 8th: t.o* **33/1**
26-6 **P** **Cullian**[38] [3655] 9-11-10 **93** ...... TomDoyle —
(J G M O'Shea) *a bhd: t.o and p.u bef 2 out* **14/1**
2FP- **P** **Follow The Bear**[326] [4889] 8-11-12 **95** ......(v1) LeightonAspell —
(D R Gandolfo) *sn wl bhd: p.u bef 4th* **28/1**
6-P5 **P** **Karoo**[21] [3950] 8-11-7 **90** ...... PJBrennan —
(K Bishop) *chsd ldrs tl wknd 7th: t.o and p.u bef 2 out* **25/1**
00P0 **P** **Top Man Tee**[21] [3939] 4-10-6 **84** ......(t) VinceSlattery —
(D J Daly) *hit 1st: a bhd: t.o and p.u bef 8th* **66/1**
0FP2 **P** **Buckland Gold (IRE)**[23] [3905] 6-11-9 **92** ...... JamesDavies —
(D B Feek) *a towards rr: t.o and p.u bef last* **10/1**[3]
540- **P** **Field Master (IRE)**[354] [4484] 9-10-5 **81** ...... RyanCummings(7) —
(C J Gray) *a towards rr: lost tch 6th: p.u bef 3 out* **33/1**
0B-P **P** **Its A Cracker (IRE)**[9] [4164] 7-10-0 **69** oh6 ...... TimmyMurphy —
(M C Pipe) *chsd ldrs tl 5th: sn bhd: t.o and p.u bef 3 out* **20/1**
-U10 **P** **Over Bridge**[273] [697] 8-11-4 **87** ...... RobertThornton —
(Mrs S M Johnson) *mid div tl wknd after 7th: bhd and p.u bef 3 out* **16/1**
0P40 **P** **Cadtauri (FR)**[30] [3789] 5-10-4 **76** ...... PaulO'Neill(3) —
(Miss H C Knight) *hld up towards rr: hdwy 7th: rdn and wknd after 3 out: p.u bef last* **14/1**
612P **P** **Paddy Boy (IRE)**[62] [3279] 5-11-0 **83** ...... JamieMoore —
(J R Boyle) *chsd ldrs: rdn into 3rd briefly after 3 out: sn wknd: bhd and p.u bef last* **11/2**[2]

5m 49.6s (24.50) **Going Correction** +0.85s/f (Soft)
WFA 4 from 5yo+ 8lb **18** Ran SP% **118.9**
Speed ratings: **89,87,81,80,74 73,68,**—,—,— —,—,—,—,— —,—,— CSF £681.34 CT £4658.62 TOTE £91.80: £11.10, £3.00, £1.60, £3.50; EX 1024.80.
Owner W H Whitley **Bred** Red House Stud **Trained** Buckfastleigh, Devon

FOCUS
An open-looking contest for the class, featuring mainly exposed performers, which was run at a modest pace. The winner was better than this at his best.

NOTEBOOK
Festival Flyer made a winning return from a 389-day layoff and did the job in good style on ground he would have found plenty soft enough. His rider's decision to kick for home at the top of the home straight paid dividends and he was always holding sway over the runner-up from the final flight. He has often been at his best fresh, so one will have to be wary of the bounce factor ahead of his next assignment, but he should still look feasibly treated on his previous best efforts.
Bright Green, third over course and distance last time, fared the best of those attempting to come from off the pace and was well clear of the rest at the finish. He helps set the standard of this form, and can go one better at this level in the coming weeks. *(op 14-1)*
From Dawn To Dusk, making his handicap debut, was still seemingly full of running turning for home, yet found nothing when pressed by the eventual winner, and ultimately paid for running freely at the head of affairs. A headstrong character, he is one to avoid on this evidence. *(tchd 6-1)*
Hill Forts Henry, popular at long odds in the betting ring ahead of this return to hurdling, kept on at his own pace from three out and was well beaten. He remains winless after 22 outings now. *(op 33-1)*
Paddy Boy(IRE), returning from a 62-day break, looked to be found out by the testing ground over this trip and was again disappointingly pulled up. *(tchd 5-1)*

4332 WINCANTON GOLF COURSE H'CAP CHASE (17 fncs) 2m 5f
4:40 (4:40) (Class 3) (0-125,123) 5-Y-O+ **£7,807** (£2,292; £1,146; £572)

Form RPR
/346 **1** **No Visibility (IRE)**[54] [3387] 11-11-4 **115** ...... AndrewThornton 131+
(R H Alner) *racd wd: prom tl 8th: chsd ldr: led 13th: nt fluent 2 out: in command whn lft wl clr last* **11/2**[2]
1601 **2** *29* **Runner Bean**[28] [3815] 12-11-1 **112** ...... RobertThornton 96
(R Lee) *hld up bit in tch: hdwy to trck ldrs 5th: ev ch 5 out: sn rdn: wknd after 4 out: lft distant 2nd at the last* **12/1**
-2P6 **3** *2 1/2* **Barren Lands**[21] [3949] 11-10-2 **99** ...... PJBrennan 81
(K Bishop) *chsd ldrs: ev ch 5 out: sn rdn: wknd after 4 out: lft distant 3rd whn sltly hmpd at the last* **11/1**
10/2 **4** *25* **Indian Gunner**[12] [4120] 13-10-11 **108** ...... RobertWalford 65
(Dr J R J Naylor) *led tl 4th: chsd ldr: led 11th: hdd after 13th: sn rdn: wknd after 4 out: lft remote 4th at the last* **6/1**[3]
5-0P **F** **Kim Fontenail (FR)**[21] [3949] 6-10-6 **110** ...... KeiranBurke(7) —
(N J Hawke) *in tch tl j. slowly 10th: sn bhd: t.o whn fell last* **22/1**
/6P3 **P** **Biliverdin (IRE)**[12] [4120] 12-11-6 **117** ...... MarcusFoley —
(J A Geake) *prom: pckd 1st: blnd 3rd: bhd and nvr a danger after: p.u before 4 out* **9/1**
133U **F** **Hiers De Brouage (FR)**[28] [3815] 11-10-5 **102** ......(tp) AndrewTinkler —
(J G Portman) *prom: led 4th tl 11th: rdn after 12th: cl 6th but wkng whn fell 4 out* **13/2**
0P43 **F** **Christopher**[47] [3507] 9-11-6 **117** ...... RichardJohnson 129
(P J Hobbs) *j. slowly 1st: bhd: gd hdwy to chse wnr after 13th: rdn appr 3 out: ev ch 2 out: 1 1/4 l down whn fell last* **7/4**[1]

5m 40.0s (16.90) **Going Correction** +1.10s/f (Heav) **8** Ran SP% **109.7**
Speed ratings: **111,99,99,89,**— —,—,— CSF £58.90 CT £646.04 TOTE £8.40: £2.20, £2.10, £2.80; EX 74.80.
Owner David O Moon **Bred** John Browne **Trained** Droop, Dorset

FOCUS
A fair handicap, weakened by the late withdrawal of top weight Big Rob. It was run at just an average pace and the form should be treated with a degree of caution.

NOTEBOOK
No Visibility(IRE), back up in trip, registered his first success since winning as a novice in 2003 and landed a gamble in the process. Given a positive ride, he was left to come home as he pleased when his only serious rival Christopher crashed out at the final fence, but he was running all over that rival at the time and it made no difference to the result. He loves this sort of ground, will be high on confidence now, and should continue to pay his way despite an inevitable rise back up in the weights. *(op 15-2 tchd 5-1)*
Runner Bean, raised 9lb for winning on a very quick surface at his favoured Huntingdon last month, appeared to be found out by the more taxing ground and is flattered by his finishing position. However, he still did enough to suggest he can get closer from this mark when returned to fast ground in due course. *(op 10-1)*
Barren Lands, supported at long odds in the betting ring, was made to look very one paced and was beaten before the turn for home. He can find easier assignments from this career-low mark, however. *(op 20-1)*
Indian Gunner, racing from the same mark as when successful in this event in 2003, failed to build on his decent comeback effort at Sandown 12 days previously and may well have bounced. *(op 15-2)*
Biliverdin(IRE) appeared to lose confidence after an early mistake and ran well below expectations. *(op 8-1 tchd 7-1 and 10-1)*
Christopher tended to run in snatches after a slow leap over the first flight, and raced wide for most of the contest, but kept to his task gamely enough and would have been a clear second but for falling at the final fence. His confidence is going to need restoring now and he is one to have reservations about. *(op 8-1 tchd 7-1 and 10-1)*

4333 THE BEST IN THE WEST MAIDEN OPEN NATIONAL HUNT FLAT RACE 2m
5:10 (5:10) (Class 6) 4-6-Y-O **£1,713** (£499; £249)

Form RPR
1 **Barbers Shop** 4-10-10 ...... MickFitzgerald 106
(N J Henderson) *hld up mid div: stdy hdwy fr 5f out: rdn to ld jst ins fnl f: sn drifted lft: all out* **7/2**[2]
2 *shd* **Silverburn (IRE)** 5-10-13 ...... LiamHeard(5) 114
(P F Nicholls) *racd wd: hld up towards rr: smooth prog fr 1/2-way: led 2f out: sn rdn: narrowly hdd jst ins fnl f: kpt on wl* **9/4**[1]
55 **3** *7* **Nougat De L'Isle (FR)**[23] [3911] 5-11-4 ...... RJGreene 107
(C L Tizzard) *chsd ldrs: led over 5f out: rdn and hdd 2f out: kpt on same pce* **18/1**

	4	½	**Miss Mitch (IRE)**[46] 5-10-11 .... AndrewThornton (R H Alner) *mid div: gd hdwy over 4f out: ev ch over 2f out: kpt on same pce* **12/1**	100
62	5	7	**Flight Leader (IRE)**[24] [3904] 6-11-4 .... JoeTizzard (C L Tizzard) *racd keenly w ldr: rdn and ev ch 3f out: kpt on same pce* **13/2**	100
	6	shd	**Niver Bai (FR)** 5-11-4 .... TimmyMurphy (Miss H C Knight) *hld up towards rr: styd on steadily fr 3f out: nvr trbld ldrs* **20/1**	100
42	7	1 ¾	**Old Benny**[54] [3399] 5-11-4 .... RobertThornton (A King) *mid div: hdwy 5f out: rdn and effrt 3f out: one pce fnl f* **6/1**[3]	98
3	8	½	**Trigger The Light**[24] [3904] 5-11-4 .... WayneHutchinson (A King) *mid div: hdwy to chse ldrs 4f out: wknd over 1f out* **12/1**	98
	9	15	**Sea Eagle (IRE)** 4-10-10 .... RichardJohnson (H D Daly) *a towards rr* **16/1**	75
00	10	9	**Triggernometry**[35] [3699] 5-11-1 .... OwynNelmes(3) (C L Tizzard) *a towards rr* **100/1**	74
0	11	15	**Bronze King**[14] [4072] 6-11-4 .... LeightonAspell (J A B Old) *a towards rr* **100/1**	59
0	12	½	**My Little Molly (IRE)**[47] [3504] 4-9-10 .... KeiranBurke(7) (J W Mullins) *chsd ldrs tl 5f out* **66/1**	43
U	13	shd	**Worth A Glance**[42] [3583] 5-11-4 .... AndrewTinkler (H D Daly) *chsd ldrs tl wknd 4f out* **100/1**	58
	14	1 ½	**Armoury House** 5-11-4 .... JasonMaguire (T R George) *chsd ldrs: rdn 3f out: sn wknd* **50/1**	56
65	15	1	**Handel With Care (IRE)**[16] [4038] 4-10-10 .... TomDoyle (R A Farrant) *chsd ldrs tl wknd 4f out* **100/1**	47
0	16	dist	**Tanners Grove**[78] [2941] 5-10-11 .... MissCDyson(7) (Miss C Dyson) *led tl over 5f out: sn wknd: t.o fnl 3f* **150/1**	—
U	17	dist	**Global Party (IRE)**[16] [4038] 4-10-3 .... JamesWhite(7) (Miss C J Williams) *bhd fr 1/2-way: virtually p.u 4f out* **125/1**	—

3m 57.4s (5.70) **Going Correction** +0.85s/f (Soft)
WFA 4 from 5yo+ 7lb **17 Ran SP% 120.8**
Speed ratings: **101,100,97,97,93 93,92,92,85,80 73,72,72,71,71** —,— CSF £11.19 TOTE £5.20: £2.40, £1.40, £8.80; EX 15.90 Place 6 £9,561.87, Place 5 £453.79.
Owner The Queen **Bred** Queen Elizabeth **Trained** Upper Lambourn, Berks

FOCUS
A fair bumper, run at a reasonable gallop for an event of its type, and the first two came clear. The form has been rated through the seventh.

NOTEBOOK
Barbers Shop, from a yard with an enviable strike-rate in such events this term, dug deep under a strong ride from Fitzgerald and just did enough to get his career off to a perfect start. The ground was in his favour and he looks a nice prospect for his leading connections.
Silverburn(IRE) ◆, a brother to his stable's leading Royal & SunAlliance Hurdle candidate Denman, only just failed to make a winning debut and posted a very pleasing effort in defeat. Having been given time to find his stride, he made up ground nicely before running green under pressure, and looked suited by the deep surface. He clearly has a future, will improve for the experience and, while he is ultimately a staying chaser in the making, looks a good thing for a similar event before the season's end. *(op 2-1)*
Nougat De L'Isle(FR) ran another sound race in defeat, if anything posing his best effort to date, and helps set the level of this form. He now looks ready to tackle hurdles and a stiffer test. *(op 16-1)*
Miss Mitch(IRE), an impressive winner of a mares; maiden point-to-point in Ireland 46 days previously, *shaped with plenty of promise on this racecourse debut and clearly has a future.* *(op 10-1)*
Flight Leader(IRE) was popular in the betting, but his fate was sealed around two furlongs from home, and ran slightly below the level of his recent effort at Plumpton. *(op 10-1)*
Niver Bai(FR), half-brother to numerous winners on both the Flat and over jumps in France, stayed on nicely for pressure in the home straight and left the definite impression he ought to come on a deal for this debut experience. *(tchd 25-1)*
Old Benny failed to improve for the return to this trip and was made to look very one paced. *(op 11-2 tchd 7-1)*
T/Jkpt: Not won. T/Plt: £15,765.90 to a £1 stake. Pool: £48,593.80. 2.25 winning tickets. T/Qpdt: £365.00 to a £1 stake. Pool: £5,327.90. 10.80 winning tickets. TM

4334 - 4335a (Foreign Racing) - See Raceform Interactive

4081 THURLES (R-H)
Thursday, March 9

OFFICIAL GOING: Soft

4336a MICHAEL PURCELL MEMORIAL NOVICE HURDLE (GRADE 2) 2m 4f
3:40 (3:40) 5-Y-0+ **£33,672** (£9,879; £4,706; £1,603)

				RPR
1		**Mounthenry (IRE)**[32] [3772] 6-11-8 .... AndrewJMcNamara (C Byrnes, Ire) *trckd ldrs in 4th: impr ins to 3rd 3 out: led after 2 out: led bef last: kpt on wl: comf* **11/10**[1]	132+
2	2	**Tengo Ambro**[110] [2356] 7-11-3 .... PWFlood (E J O'Grady, Ire) *hld up in tch: 5th and drvn along 4 out: hdwy after next: led u.p 2 out: hdd bef last: kpt on* **16/1**	123
3	5	**One Cool Cookie (IRE)**[98] [2602] 5-11-1 113 .... DJCasey (C F Swan, Ire) *prom: 2nd fr 5th: lost pl bef 3 out: 5th bef next: kpt on u.p* **16/1**	116
4	hd	**Oscar's Advance (IRE)**[71] [3086] 7-11-3 .... APMcCoy (C Roche, Ire) *hld up in tch: 6th 3 out: rdn and outpcd next: kpt on fr last* **5/1**[3]	118
5	4	**County Final (IRE)**[29] [3809] 7-11-3 120 .... PCarberry (Noel Meade, Ire) *hld up early: prog into 5th 1/2-way: cl 2nd and chal 3 out: no ex fr next* **10/1**	114
6	2 ½	**Knight Legend (IRE)**[39] [3642] 7-11-3 .... BJGeraghty (Mrs John Harrington, Ire) *led: clr 1/2-way: reduced advantage whn slt mstke 5 out: strly pressed 3 out: hdd next: sn wknd* **8/1**	111
7	dist	**Mercuric**[15] [4060] 5-11-1 .... TPTreacy (Mrs John Harrington, Ire) *trckd ldrs in 5th: slt mstke 7th: wknd fr 4 out: t.o* **9/1**	—
F		**Sir Overbury**[15] [4060] 5-11-1 .... DNRussell (Daniel O'Connell, Ire) *2nd early: 3rd 1/2-way: cl up whn fell 5 out* **9/2**[2]	—
P		**Dancing Water**[29] [3810] 7-11-3 84 .... DFO'Regan (Patrick O Brady, Ire) *hld up in tch: rdn and wknd fr 4 out: t.o whn p.u bef 2 out* **66/1**	—

5m 17.6s **10 Ran SP% 125.9**
CSF £24.70 TOTE £1.70: £1.10, £5.10, £4.80; DF 48.50.
Owner Mrs Martha Reidy **Bred** Miss Ann Twomey **Trained** Ballingarry, Co Limerick
■ Stewards' Enquiry : P W Flood caution: careless riding
Andrew J McNamara caution: careless riding

NOTEBOOK
Mounthenry(IRE) made it five wins from eight starts over hurdles and stayed the trip with plenty to spare. He will go to Punchestown next if the ground does not dry up by then. *(op 5/4)*
Tengo Ambro had an absence since November to overcome and this was a career-best performance. In front over the second last, he was comfortably held when the winner eased past him on the inner on the run between the last two.
One Cool Cookie(IRE) appeared outpaced before the third last but stayed on again in the straight.
Oscar's Advance(IRE) was hampered by the faller five out but had his chance before two out and just lacked pace from there on. *(op 9/2)*
County Final(IRE), a length behind Tengo Ambro in a maiden in November, has not made the same progress.
Knight Legend(IRE) tried to make all but was weakening when slightly hampered by the winner on the approach to the second last. *(op 7/1 tchd 9/1)*
Mercuric did not run to the level of his Punchestown effort. *(op 8/1)*

4337 - 4340a (Foreign Racing) - See Raceform Interactive

4141 AYR (L-H)
Friday, March 10

OFFICIAL GOING: Soft (heavy on bottom bend)
First fence in home straight omitted in all chases.
Wind: Light, half-behind

4341 MASERATI CHAUFFEUR DRIVE LTD CONDITIONAL JOCKEYS' H'CAP HURDLE (12 hdls) 3m 110y
2:00 (2:00) (Class 5) (0-95,93) 4-Y-0+ **£2,398** (£698; £349)

Form				RPR
4F02	1		**Prince Adjal (IRE)**[17] [4045] 6-11-1 **82** .... DougieCostello (Miss S E Forster) *mde all: sn wl clr: kpt on wl fr 3 out: unchal* **8/1**	100+
-6P2	2	27	**The Masareti Kid (IRE)**[13] [4113] 9-11-2 **83** .... PaddyMerrigan (I McMath) *hld up: hdwy 4 out: wnt 2nd between last two: no ch w wnr* **8/1**	73
0	3	4	**Shanteen Lass (IRE)**[11] [4145] 6-11-2 **86** .... KeithMercer(3) (Ferdy Murphy) *chsd wnr to 1/2-way: sn outpcd: rallied bef 3 out: kpt on: no imp* **40/1**	72
0P43	4	7	**Mae Moss**[11] [4145] 5-10-11 **78** .... PaddyAspell (W S Coltherd) *prom chsng gp: chsd clr ldr 1/2-way: no ex and lost 2nd between last two* **10/1**	57
00U4	5	3 ½	**Leonia's Rose (IRE)**[11] [4145] 7-10-7 **74** .... DeclanMcGann (Miss Lucinda V Russell) *bhd: hdwy u.p after 4 out: no imp fr next* **6/1**[2]	50
2P36	6	5	**Roadworthy (IRE)**[11] [4145] 9-9-9 **67** .... JohnFlavin(5) (W G Young) *bhd: drvn 4 out: effrt u.p appr next: n.d* **18/1**	38
L520	7	3	**Joe Malone (IRE)**[51] [3446] 7-10-6 **81** .... FearghalDavis(8) (N G Richards) *in tch: effrt 8th: wknd bef 3 out* **14/1**	49
0055	P		**Cloudmor (IRE)**[13] [4113] 5-11-11 **92** .... MichaelMcAlister (L Lungo) *a bhd: t.o whn p.u bef 4 out* **13/2**[3]	—
060P	P		**Zaffiera (IRE)**[45] [3553] 5-9-6 **69** .... (t) CWilliams(10) (M D Hammond) *nt fluent: sn towards rr: t.o whn p.u bef 3 out* **80/1**	—
0P00	P		**Bishop's Brig**[30] [3793] 6-11-6 **90** .... TomMessenger(3) (N W Alexander) *prom chsng gp tl wknd bef 4 out: p.u next* **100/1**	—
0043	U		**Kidithou (FR)**[13] [4113] 8-11-7 **93** .... EwanWhillans(5) (W T Reed) *hld up in tch: hdwy and cl up chsng gp whn blnd and uns rdr 8th* **5/1**[1]	—
5006	P		**Thorn Of The Rose (IRE)**[64] [3254] 5-10-5 **80** .... MichaelMcAvoy(8) (James Moffatt) *nt fluent in rr: blnd 5th: nvr on terms: t.o whn p.u bef 2 out* **10/1**	—
	P		**Pomfisch Lad (IRE)**[23] [3936] 8-11-9 **90** .... (b) AndrewJMcNamara (S Donohoe, Ire) *midfield: effrt whn hit and rdr lost iron briefly 4 out: sn btn: p.u after next* **15/2**	—

6m 40.2s (8.40) **Going Correction** +0.375s/f (Yiel) **13 Ran SP% 113.0**
Speed ratings: **101,92,91,88,87 86,85**,—,—,— —,—,— CSF £66.87 CT £2380.62 TOTE £11.90: £3.60, £2.20, £8.80; EX 62.20.
Owner C Storey **Bred** Adjalisa Syndicate **Trained** Kirk Yetholm, Borders

FOCUS
A weak event but one in which the winner never looked likely to be pegged back after quickly opening up a commanding advantage. This bare form could be rated higher but does not look reliable with the placed horses below their marks.

NOTEBOOK
Prince Adjal(IRE) has not been noted for his consistency but turned in an improved effort upped markedly in trip. He may have been flattered given he was allowed so much rope in front but, in any case, he will find things much tougher after reassessment. *(op 7-1)*
The Masareti Kid(IRE) who signalled a return to form at Newcastle, was not disgraced but had little chance of reeling in the easy winner given how things panned out. He looks capable of winning a small event. *(op 7-1)*
Shanteen Lass(IRE), who has shown precious little over hurdles, was not totally disgraced on her first run over three miles and left the impression that a thorough test of stamina would suit but this is not a race to be taking too many positives from. *(op 33-1)*
Mae Moss, back up to this trip, was not totally disgraced but may be better suited by less of a test of stamina at this stage. *(tchd 11-1)*
Leonia's Rose(IRE), who shaped as though the return to this trip would suit on her last run, again looked less than an easy ride and remains one to have reservations about. *(op 5-1 tchd 9-2)*
Roadworthy(IRE) is a poor and inconsistent maiden who remains one to have little faith in. *(op 20-1)*
Kidithou(FR) looked sure to be suited by the demands of this race but was again found out by his shoddy jumping and he remains one to tread carefully with. *(op 11-2 tchd 6-1)*
Bishop's Brig *Official explanation: jockey said gelding had a breathing problem (op 11-2 tchd 6-1)*
Thorn Of The Rose(IRE) *Official explanation: trainer said mare was found to have mucus on her lungs (op 11-2 tchd 6-1)*

4342 KIDZPLAY "NATIONAL HUNT" MAIDEN HURDLE (9 hdls) 2m
2:30 (2:31) (Class 5) 4-Y-0+ **£2,740** (£798; £399)

Form				RPR
0436	1		**More Likely**[30] [3795] 5-10-4 .... DougieCostello(5) (Mrs A F Tullie) *in tch: rdn 5th: rallied 3 out: led last: styd on wl* **9/2**[2]	94
34	2	7	**Lord Collingwood (IRE)**[34] [3742] 5-11-2 .... NeilMulholland (M D Hammond) *hld up in tch: hdwy to ld appr 3 out: hdd last: no ex* **10/1**	94
36F	3	5	**Hush Tiger**[13] [4114] 5-10-9 .... GarethThomas(7) (R Nixon) *nt fluent: led to appr 3 out: 7l down and one pce whn lft 3rd last* **25/1**	91+
4256	4	8	**Sobers (IRE)**[36] [3691] 5-10-13 .... PaulO'Neill(3) (R C Guest) *nt fluent: hld up: hdwy 4 out: kpt on fr next: nvr nr ldrs* **5/1**[3]	87+
	5	4	**Something Silver** 5-10-13 .... PaddyAspell(3) (J S Goldie) *bhd tl hdwy bef 3 out: no imp fr next* **66/1**	77
3504	6	10	**Overnight**[23] [3927] 6-10-9 .... EwanWhillans(7) (Mrs A C Hamilton) *hld up: sme hdwy bef 3 out: n.d* **33/1**	67

5 **7** 2½ **Benny The Piler (IRE)**[66] [3237] 6-11-2 .... TonyDobbin 65
(N G Richards) *prom to 4 out: sn wknd* **4/1**[1]

5 **8** 1¼ **Hiddenfortune (IRE)**[11] [4147] 6-10-13 .... PeterBuchanan[(3)] 63
(Miss Lucinda V Russell) *towards rr: rdn 1/2-way: nvr on terms* **33/1**

P **P** **Merits Pride**[45] [3551] 6-10-4 .... MichaelMcAlister[(5)] —
(B Storey) *a bhd: t.o whn p.u bef 3 out* **200/1**

00P **P** **It's No Easy (IRE)**[46] [3534] 5-11-2 .... BrianHarding —
(N G Richards) *a bhd: t.o whn p.u bef 3 out* **22/1**

00 **P** **Mr Attitude**[24] [3912] 6-11-2 .... DavidO'Meara —
(W S Coltherd) *in tch tl wknd bef 4 out: p.u bef next* **100/1**

P **It's A Roofer (IRE)** 6-11-2 .... RichardMcGrath —
(Mrs K Walton) *racd wd in midfield: wknd 5th: t.o whn p.u bef 2 out* **33/1**

-60P **P** **Endless Power (IRE)**[11] [4143] 6-11-2 .... GrahamLee —
(J Barclay) *towards rr: drvn 5th: sn btn: t.o whn p.u bef 3 out* **25/1**

P **Shootforthemoon (IRE)**[13] 6-11-2 .... AndrewJMcNamara —
(S Donohoe, Ire) *mstkes: keen: chsd ldrs tl wknd 5th: t.o whn p.u bef 3 out* **14/1**

205/ **U** **Milliesome**[728] [4292] 8-10-6 .... MichalKohl[(3)] —
(J I A Charlton) *midfield: rdn bef 4 out: 6l down and no imp whn hit and uns rdr next* **100/1**

14-0 **F** **Harry Flashman**[33] [3763] 5-11-2 .... WilsonRenwick 89
(D W Whillans) *keen: cl up: ev ch appr 3 out: blnd next: 7l down and hld whn fell last* **8/1**

033 **F** **Scarlet Cloak (USA)**[11] [4147] 5-11-2 .... KeithMercer 91
(Mrs L B Normile) *in tch: smooth hdwy and ev ch bef 3 out: 3l down and one pce whn fell last* **10/1**

4m 11.3s (14.00) **Going Correction** +0.875s/f (Soft) **17** Ran SP% **115.6**
Speed ratings: **100,96,94,90,88 83,81,81,—,— —,—,—,—,— —,—** CSF £41.89 TOTE £4.20: £1.50, £2.80, £8.10; EX 68.80.

Owner Mrs A F Tullie **Bred** Mrs A F Tullie **Trained** Whitemire, Borders

■ Aillie Tullie's first winner since renewing her permit after a long spell abroad.

■ Stewards' Enquiry : Paul O'Neill 21-day ban: failed to take all reasonable and permissible measures to obtain best possible placing (Mar 21-Apr 11). Guest fined £3,000 horse banned 40 days

FOCUS

An ordinary gallop to a race lacking anything in the way of strength and rated through the winner to her previous mark.

NOTEBOOK

More Likely, who had an excuse for a below-par run last time, turned in her best effort to win an ordinary event. She showed the right attitude and left the impression that the return to two and a half miles would suit even better. *(tchd 5-1)*

Lord Collingwood(IRE), who showed ability in testing ground in bumpers, showed enough on this hurdle debut to suggest that he is capable of winning a similar event.

Hush Tiger ran his best race on this third run over hurdles but needs to brush up in the jumping department. He may do better over further when stepped into modest handicap company. *(op 20-1)*

Sobers(IRE), who showed ability in bumpers, very much caught the eye under a considerate ride on this hurdle debut, despite jumping stickily early on. Despite connections reporting that the gelding choked in the race, the Stewards banned the horse, fined the trainer and suspended the rider under the non-triers rule. *On this evidence he looks sure to win an ordinary event.Official explanation: 40-day ban: (Mar 13-Apr 21) (op 6-1 tchd 13-2)*

Something Silver, a half-brother to a winning pointed, was not disgraced on this racecourse debut and looks the sort to do better over further in modest handicaps in due course.

Overnight shaped as though a stiffer test of stamina would suit but he looks more of a long-term prospect. *(op 28-1)*

Benny The Piler(IRE), who showed ability on his racecourse debut at this track in January, proved disappointing on this hurdle debut but, given his physique and the fact he is in good hands, is not one to write off just yet. *(tchd 9-2 in places)*

Harry Flashman was in the process of running creditably on this hurdle debut and first run in testing ground when coming to grief. He is the type to improve if none-the-worse for this experience. *(op 9-1)*

Scarlet Cloak(USA) looked held but was in the process of running creditably when coming to grief on this hurdle debut. He should stay two and a half miles and looks capable of winning a similar event. *(op 9-1)*

4343 ROYAL HIGHLAND FUSILIERS BEGINNERS' CHASE (17 fncs 2 omitted) 3m 1f

3:00 (3:00) (Class 4) 5-Y-O+ **£3,708** (£1,088; £544; £271)

Form RPR

-133 **1** **Ever Present (IRE)**[60] [3317] 8-11-3 .... TonyDobbin 123+
(N G Richards) *prom: led 5th: mde rest: hld on wl fr 3 out* **10/11**[1]

22F6 **2** ¾ **See You There (IRE)**[30] [3794] 7-11-0 114 .... PeterBuchanan[(3)] 124+
(Miss Lucinda V Russell) *chsd ldrs: clr w wnr fr 11th: effrt bef 3 out: nt fluent last: kpt on towards fin* **15/8**[2]

-0P4 **3** dist **No Picnic (IRE)**[96] [2654] 8-11-0 110 .... OwynNelmes[(3)] —
(Mrs S C Bradburne) *prom: outpcd 11th: no ch w first two thereafter* **14/1**

4 25 **Drumintine (IRE)**[19] 5-9-9 .... RJMolloy[(5)] —
(Liam Lennon, Ire) *led to 5th: prom: outpcd fr 11th* **10/1**[3]

P-00 **P** **Blackout (IRE)**[11] [4145] 11-11-3 53 .... BrianHarding —
(J Barclay) *cl up to 5th: sn lost pl: tailing off whn p.u 10th* **200/1**

12-0 **P** **Wainak (USA)**[27] [3854] 8-10-12 94 .... (p) DougieCostello[(5)] —
(Miss Lucinda V Russell) *towards rr: struggling 10th: t.o whn p.u bef 4 out* **40/1**

6m 52.0s (6.30) **Going Correction** +0.35s/f (Yiel)
WFA 5 from 7yo+ 10lb **6** Ran SP% **105.9**
Speed ratings: **103,102,—,—,— —** CSF £2.65 TOTE £1.80: £1.10, £2.10; EX 3.40.

Owner Ramsay Donald Brown **Bred** Martin Cullinane **Trained** Greystoke, Cumbria

FOCUS

An uncompetitive event in which the form horses pulled well clear in on the final circuit. The pace was sound and the runner-up would have won if he had jumped better.

NOTEBOOK

Ever Present(IRE), back over a more suitable trip, showed the right attitude to win an uncompetitive event. His jumping was sound and he is likely to win more races in this sphere when the emphasis is on stamina. *(op Evens)*

See You There(IRE) ran as well as he ever has and would have gone even closer had he been as fluent over the last three fences as the winner. A good test of stamina suits and he looks capable of winning an ordinary event. *(op 7-4)*

No Picnic(IRE), an inconsistent hurdler, was soundly beaten on this second start over fences. He is an infrequent winner whose form over fences falls short of his hurdle efforts and he remains one to tread carefully with. *(op 16-1)*

Drumintine(IRE), off the mark in a point last time, had his limitations exposed on this first run under Rules. *(op 8-1)*

Wainak(USA), who missed last year and showed nothing on his reappearance over hurdles last time, offered no immediate promise on this chasing debut. *(op 100-1)*

Blackout(IRE), a poor maiden, was predictably outclassed. *(op 100-1)*

4344 SCOTTISH MEDIA SERVICES H'CAP HURDLE (FOR THE JAMES BARCLAY CHALLENGE TROPHY) (12 hdls) 2m 6f

3:35 (3:35) (Class 4) (0-110,110) 4-Y-O+ **£3,578** (£1,050; £525; £262)

Form RPR

3421 **1** **Morgan Be**[46] [3532] 6-11-9 107 .... RichardMcGrath 121+
(Mrs K Walton) *hld up: hdwy 1/2-way: ev ch whn nt fluent 3 out: sn led: easily* **13/8**[1]

00-0 **2** 8 **Lampion Du Bost (FR)**[30] [3797] 7-10-3 87 .... AlanDempsey 79
(A Parker) *hld up in tch: outpcd 4 out: kpt on fr 2 out: no ch w wnr* **66/1**

P6UP **3** hd **Lutin Du Moulin (FR)**[24] [3915] 7-11-0 98 .... (b) TonyDobbin 90
(L Lungo) *chsd ldrs: led after 3 out to appr next: sn rdn: kpt on u.p fr last* **16/1**

4610 **4** nk **Caesar's Palace (GER)**[27] [3854] 9-10-12 99 .... (p) PeterBuchanan[(3)] 91
(Miss Lucinda V Russell) *led to 3rd: lost pl 5th: kpt on strly fr 2 out: no imp* **14/1**

-550 **5** 2 **Try Catch Paddy (IRE)**[27] [3850] 8-11-2 110 .... DavidDaSilva[(10)] 100
(P Monteith) *cl up: disp ld 4 out: led appr next to bef 2 out: flashed tail and no ex run in* **66/1**

0F4P **6** 7 **Kharak (FR)**[27] [3849] 7-11-11 109 .... WilsonRenwick 92
(Mrs S C Bradburne) *led 3rd to after 4 out: rdn and wknd bef next* **14/1**

5136 **7** 8 **Tobesure (IRE)**[49] [3487] 12-11-0 101 .... MichalKohl[(3)] 76
(J I A Charlton) *in tch tl wknd fr 8th* **10/1**[3]

0020 **P** **Timbuktu**[27] [3853] 5-10-5 89 .... GrahamLee —
(B Storey) *in tch tl wknd 8th: t.o whn p.u bef 3 out* **10/1**[3]

1-PF **P** **Aberdare**[66] [3234] 7-11-1 104 .... DougieCostello[(5)] —
(J R Bewley) *a bhd: rdn 1/2-way: t.o whn p.u bef 3 out* **14/1**

P **Yammy Wilson (IRE)**[61] [3311] 5-11-0 98 .... AndrewJMcNamara —
(S Donohoe, Ire) *hld up: struggling 8th: t.o whn p.u 4 out* **25/1**

P431 **P** **Colophony (USA)**[15] [4080] 6-10-3 94 .... PatrickMcDonald[(7)] —
(K A Morgan) *keen: chsd ldrs tl wknd 4 out: p.u after next* **7/2**[2]

6m 7.30s (25.70) **Going Correction** +0.875s/f (Soft) **11** Ran SP% **111.2**
Speed ratings: **88,85,85,84,84 81,78,—,—,— —** CSF £105.64 CT £1234.46 TOTE £2.40: £1.20, £11.10, £4.50; EX 83.30.

Owner S Breakspeare **Bred** Martin Blandford **Trained** Middleham, N Yorks

FOCUS

An ordinary event in which the gallop was fair but an improved effort from the winner, who may be capable of better still, with the runner-up setting the standard.

NOTEBOOK

Morgan Be ◆ turned in his best effort yet on this handicap debut and, given the way he travelled throughout the race, it will be a bit of a surprise if he is not capable of better still after reassessment. *(op 15-8 tchd 2-1 in places)*

Lampion Du Bost(FR) has been disappointing since his first run for connections but ran creditably this time and left the impression that the step up to three miles would be in his favour. He may be capable of picking up a small event.

Lutin Du Moulin(FR) has not been very consistent but ran creditably back over hurdles. He is back on a fair mark and can be placed to best advantage this spring. *(op 14-1)*

Caesar's Palace(GER) ran a typical race but, given he is not an easy ride and the fact that he is an infrequent winner, remains one to tread carefully with. *(op 12-1)*

Try Catch Paddy(IRE), back over hurdles on only this second start for his new stable, shaped with a bit more promise, despite flashing his tail. He is the type his trainer does well with but will almost certainly have to come down in the weights before regaining the winning thread. *(op 50-1)*

Kharak(FR) had the run of the race but folded tamely returned to hurdles and he will have to show more before he is worth a bet. *(op 16-1)*

Colophony(USA) failed to settle in the conditions and is worth another chance back on a sounder surface. *Official explanation: trainer said gelding had a breathing problem (op 11-4)*

Aberdare *Official explanation: jockey said mare was never travelling (op 11-4)*

4345 "BOOK FOR THE SCOTTISH GRAND NATIONAL" H'CAP CHASE (FOR THE ARTHUR CHALLENGE CUP) (17 fncs 2 omitted) 3m 1f

4:10 (4:10) (Class 3) (0-125,125) 5-Y-O+ **£7,807** (£2,292; £1,146; £572)

Form RPR

45P1 **1** **Skenfrith**[11] [4144] 7-10-0 99 7ex oh2 .... NeilMulholland 118+
(Miss S E Forster) *cl up: led 9th: mde rest: styd on wl fr 3 out* **7/2**[2]

/202 **2** 9 **Frankie Dori (IRE)**[9] [4185] 7-10-6 105 .... AndrewJMcNamara 116+
(S Donohoe, Ire) *prom: chsd wnr 5 out: effrt 3 out: kpt on same pce last* **8/1**[3]

F066 **3** 30 **Strong Resolve (IRE)**[15] [4070] 10-11-3 119 .... PeterBuchanan[(3)] 101+
(Miss Lucinda V Russell) *led to 9th: cl up: outpcd 13th: n.d after* **8/1**[3]

4 28 **Huncheon Paddy (IRE)**[9] [4185] 9-10-2 106 .... RJMolloy[(5)] 55
(I R Ferguson, Ire) *keen: prom: effrt 4 out: wknd next* **10/1**

5U21 **P** **Pass Me By**[30] [3794] 7-11-4 120 .... (e) PaulO'Neill[(3)] —
(R C Guest) *prom tl wknd 11th: p.u after next* **11/4**[1]

UR16 **P** **Huka Lodge (IRE)**[34] [3741] 9-11-4 117 .... RichardMcGrath —
(Mrs K Walton) *bhd: outpcd 10th: t.o whn p.u bef 4 out* **9/1**

2P1P **P** **Interdit (FR)**[27] [3851] 10-11-0 113 .... WilsonRenwick —
(Mrs B K Thomson) *in tch tl rdn fr 13th: t.o whn p.u bef 2 out* **9/1**

/634 **P** **Thosewerethedays**[27] [3854] 13-11-7 125 .... TJDreaper[(5)] —
(Miss P Robson) *nt fluent in rr: struggling whn p.u bef 12th* **20/1**

4-45 **P** **Wise Man (IRE)**[27] [3855] 11-11-9 122 .... GrahamLee —
(N W Alexander) *hld up in tch: hdwy 4 out: rdn and wknd bef next: p.u after 2 out* **9/1**

6m 49.9s (4.20) **Going Correction** +0.35s/f (Yiel) **9** Ran SP% **115.0**
Speed ratings: **107,104,94,85,— —,—,—,—** CSF £31.36 CT £208.63 TOTE £4.40: £1.50, £2.90, £2.70; EX 41.80.

Owner J M & Miss H M Crichton, Miss S Forster **Bred** Frazer S F Hines And Mrs Heather Moreno **Trained** Kirk Yetholm, Borders

FOCUS

An ordinary handicap but the pace was sound and it has been rated positively through the third.

NOTEBOOK

Skenfrith, from an in-form stable, had conditions to suit and followed up his recent course and distance win in workmanlike fashion. Testing ground suits him admirably but a further rise will make life tougher. *(tchd 10-3 and 4-1 in a place)*

Frankie Dori(IRE), an inconsistent chaser, was well beaten over three and a half miles last time but ran creditably, especially as his best form has been on better ground. However given his record, he would not be sure to put it all in next time.

Strong Resolve(IRE) had conditions to suit and had the run of the race but was again a long way below his best. He is best watched for now. *(op 15-2 tchd 10-1 in a place)*

Huncheon Paddy(IRE) ran a bit better than the distance beaten implies and left the impression that less of a test of stamina over this trip would have suited better. *(op 16-1)*

Interdit(FR) has now been pulled up on three of his last four starts and does seem a better animal when allowed to dominate at Kelso. *(tchd 10-1)*

Pass Me By had been running creditably over this trip in testing conditions but ran poorly and *reportedly choked. He is worth another chance. Official explanation: trainer said gelding finished distressed (tchd 10-1)*

4346 WESTERN HOUSE HOTEL NOVICES' H'CAP HURDLE (8 hdls 1 omitted) 2m
4:45 (4:48) (Class 4) (0-105,100) 4-Y-0+ **£4,554** (£1,337; £668; £333)

Form RPR
5003 **1** **Boris The Spider**[17] 4040 5-11-7 **95** WilsonRenwick 98+
(M D Hammond) *hld up: hdwy 3 out: led last: drvn out* **4/1**[2]
0F24 **2** *¾* **Bollin Thomas**[13] 4108 8-11-12 **100** TonyDobbin 101+
(R Allan) *chsd ldrs: led bef 2 out: hdd last: kpt on u.p* **5/2**[1]
5000 **3** *3* **Norminster**[33] 3757 5-9-13 **80** GarethThomas(7) 77
(R Nixon) *chsd ldrs: led bef 3 out: hdd bef next: sn outpcd: kpt on fr last* **20/1**
63P0 **4** *21* **Tiger King (GER)**[23] 3929 5-11-11 **99** GrahamLee 75
(P Monteith) *hld up: rdn 3 out: wknd bef next* **10/1**
0535 **5** *7* **Buffy**[30] 3795 6-11-2 **90** NeilMulholland 59
(B Mactaggart) *hld up in tch: hdwy bef 3 out: wknd bef next* **9/2**[3]
003 **6** *29* **Heversham (IRE)**[16] 4056 5-11-1 **92** (p) PaddyAspell(3) 32
(J Hetherton) *prom: effrt and ev ch after 3 out: wknd bef next* **12/1**
0005 **P** **Datbandito (IRE)**[46] 3540 7-10-1 **75** BrianHarding —
(L Lungo) *prom tl wknd 5th: t.o whn p.u bef 2 out* **5/1**
P **P** **Pathughkenjo (IRE)**[33] 3757 6-10-8 **82** AndrewJMcNamara —
(S Donohoe, Ire) *plld hrd: led and clr: wknd and hdd bef 3 out: p.u bef next* **25/1**

4m 10.7s (13.40) **Going Correction** +0.875s/f (Soft) **8** Ran SP% **108.8**
Speed ratings: **101,100,99,88,85 70**,—,— CSF £13.35 CT £152.21 TOTE £6.10: £1.60, £1.20, £4.90; EX 12.50.
Owner The Adbrokes Partnership **Bred** David Smeaton **Trained** Middleham, N Yorks

FOCUS
A low-grade event in which the pace was fair. The form could rate little higher.

NOTEBOOK
Boris The Spider confirmed recent Sedgefield promise and did enough to get off the mark over hurdles. However, he is not the most consistent around and would not be an obvious one for a follow-up at shortish odds next time. *(op 11-2)*
Bollin Thomas, back in trip, ran creditably in terms of form and is capable of winning a similar event. He did not do much wrong on this occasion but, as he has yet to win over hurdles, may not be one for short odds next time. *(op 3-1 tchd 10-3)*
Norminster showed his first worthwhile form over hurdles and, on this evidence, looks well worth another try over two and a half miles. *(op 16-1)*
Tiger King(GER) was again soundly beaten in testing ground but may do better back on a sound surface and he is not one to write off just yet. *(op 11-2)*
Buffy, who has form in testing ground, was disappointing on this handicap debut and may be one to tread carefully with at present. *(op 5-1)*
Datbandito(IRE), a modest maiden hurdler, dropped out in a matter of strides over this much shorter trip and has plenty to prove at present. *(op 4-1)*

4347 RACING TOMORROW HUNTERS' CHASE (FOR THE AYRSHIRE AGRICULTURAL ASSOCIATION CHALLENGE CUP) (16 fncs 2 omitted) 2m 5f 110y
5:20 (5:20) (Class 6) 6-Y-0+ **£1,648** (£507; £253)

Form RPR
P-4U **1** **Barryscourt Lad (IRE)**[33] 12-12-0 103 MrBWoodhouse(5) 92
(R D E Woodhouse) *prom: wnt 2nd 10th: led bef 3 out: clr whn hit last: easily* **6/4**[1]
P-P6 **2** *7* **Camp Hill**[15] 4073 12-12-0 77 MrTDavidson(5) 85
(J S Haldane) *cl up: led 5th to bef 3 out: no ch w wnr* **25/1**
P15- **3** *¾* **Jacksonville (FR)**[19] 9-11-12 92 (p) MissVickySimpson(7) 84
(Miss Vicky Simpson) *prom: outpcd 5 out: kpt on fr 2 out: no imp* **7/2**[2]
1P31 **4** *dist* **Jupiter's Fancy**[23] 3926 11-11-2 MrTCollier(7) —
(M V Coglan) *mstkes: led to 5th: wknd fr 11th* **13/2**
04-3 **5** *23* **Adolphus (IRE)**[12] 9-12-5 MrCStorey —
(C Storey) *mstkes: hld up: rdn 11th: sn btn* **4/1**[3]
U/0- **P** **Hadeqa**[307] 10-11-5 MrSCharlton(7) —
(M J Brown) *bhd: wknd and p.u 9th* **14/1**
6/3 **P** **Wraparound You (IRE)**[11] 4146 9-11-7 MrPCallaghan(5) —
(Norman Sanderson) *prom early: wknd and p.u bef 7th* **40/1**

6m 5.50s (11.80) **Going Correction** +0.35s/f (Yiel) **7** Ran SP% **108.5**
Speed ratings: **92,89,89**,—,— —,— CSF £29.68 TOTE £2.50: £1.80, £4.20; EX 25.90 Place 6 £128.65, Place 5 £24.57.
Owner R D E Woodhouse **Bred** W O'Brien **Trained** Welburn, N Yorks

FOCUS
An uncompetitive event in which the pace was fair.

NOTEBOOK
Barryscourt Lad(IRE) ◆ did not have to improve to win a weak race with plenty in hand but he appeals as the type to win more races in this sphere. *(op 5-4 tchd 13-8)*
Camp Hill had plenty to find with the winner in terms of official ratings but ran creditably and may be able to pick up a weak event in this sphere. *(tchd 28-1)*
Jacksonville(FR) is not the most reliable but left the impression that the return to three miles would be in his favour. *(op 9-2)*
Jupiter's Fancy was well beaten but, given his best form is on a sound surface, he is best not judged too harshly on this below-par effort. *(op 5-1 tchd 7-1, 13-2 in a place)*
Adolphus(IRE), who has a fair strike-rate in points, but was soundly beaten back over regulation fences and will have to jump with more fluency than he did here to win a similar event. *(op 5-1)*
T/Plt: £160.50 to a £1 stake. Pool: £48,456.55. 220.30 winning tickets. T/Qpdt: £8.80 to a £1 stake. Pool: £3,729.80. 313.20 winning tickets. RY

4162 LEICESTER (R-H)
Friday, March 10

OFFICIAL GOING: Heavy (soft in places)
An all-chase card. Fourth-last and final fences omitted.
Wind: Fresh, behind Weather: Overcast

4348 LADBROKESCASINO.COM H'CAP CHASE (11 fncs 4 omitted) 2m 4f 110y
2:20 (2:20) (Class 4) (0-110,106) 5-Y-0 **£5,070** (£1,497; £748; £374; £187)

Form RPR
22R3 **1** **Young Lorcan**[20] 3989 10-10-13 **100** RichardSpate(7) 112+
(Mrs K Waldron) *hld up: hdwy and hmpd 6th: chsd ldr 8th: led next: rdn after 2 out: all out* **9/1**
2U52 **2** *shd* **Bay Island (IRE)**[23] 3919 10-11-2 **96** (tp) PaulMoloney 108+
(M Pitman) *led: hit 3rd: hdd 9th: ev ch fr 2 out: sn rdn: styd on* **7/2**[3]
P022 **3** *13* **Hawk's Landing (IRE)**[10] 4163 9-11-12 **106** RichardJohnson 108+
(Jonjo O'Neill) *prom: j.rt: chsd ldr 5th to 8th: rdn whn hit last: sn wknd* **2/1**[1]
5601 **4** *8* **Jack Fuller (IRE)**[23] 3919 9-11-2 **96** (b) PhilipHide 94+
(P Winkworth) *hld up: hdwy and hmpd 6th: mstke next: hit 9th: rdn and wknd after 2 out* **85/40**[2]
4PU3 **5** *dist* **Mondial Jack (FR)**[16] 4051 7-11-4 **105** (p) MrRQuinn(7) —
(Mrs K Waldron) *chsd ldrs: hit 5th: wknd 9th* **14/1**
1P14 **6** *dist* **Yassar (IRE)**[36] 3686 11-10-12 **92** WarrenMarston —
(D J Wintle) *j.rt: chsd ldr: hit 2nd: wknd 5th* **16/1**

5m 31.0s (7.40) **Going Correction** +0.55s/f (Soft) **6** Ran SP% **110.1**
Speed ratings: **107,106,102,98**,— — CSF £38.73 TOTE £9.70: £3.30, £2.60; EX 42.30.
Owner Nick Shutts **Bred** Mrs Norma Dyer **Trained** Stoke Bliss, Worcs

FOCUS
A moderate handicap chase but run at a decent gallop and the form looks sound enough rated around the first two.

NOTEBOOK
Young Lorcan had conditions to suit and ran out the narrowest of winners under a fine ride from his 7lb claimer, who could not really be distinguished from the fully-fledged jockey in the closing stages. This is the highest mark her has ever won off, but he should not go up much for this and can remain competitive. *(op 10-1 tchd 8-1)*
Bay Island(IRE), 2lb higher than when second over course and distance on his previous start, handled the testing ground well and was just denied. He deserves to find a similar race and, upwards of 13 lengths clear of the remainder, looks capable of doing so. *(op 4-1)*
Hawk's Landing(IRE), without a win since landing a novice event in February 2004, failed to build on the promise of his recent efforts despite racing off a mark 5lb lower than in future and may not have been suited by this drop back in trip. *(op 7-4 tchd 9-4 and 5-2 in a place)*
Jack Fuller(IRE), 9lb higher than when winning over course and distance on his previous start, did not jump that well and could not confirm form with Bay Island. It could be argued the ground was softer than he would have liked, but he should still have run better. *(op 5-2 tchd 2-1)*
Mondial Jack(FR), a stablemate of the winner, would probably not have appreciated ground this testing. *(op 10-1)*

4349 THRUSTERS HUNTERS' CHASE (9 fncs 3 omitted) 2m
2:50 (2:50) (Class 5) 6-Y-0+ **£2,498** (£774; £387; £193)

Form RPR
P/21 **1** **Bill Haze**[10] 4167 10-11-9 MrPSheldrake(7) 102+
(P Dando) *plld hrd: led tl after 1st: chsd ldrs: led 2 out: flashed tail run-in: drvn out* **7/2**[3]
F/FR **2** *3* **Cloudy Bay Boy**[23] 3924 8-11-9 (b[1]) MrRCope(3) 93
(Mrs Caroline Bailey) *chsd ldr 2nd: ev ch 2 out: sn rdn: styd on same pce flat* **11/1**
UU-F **3** *19* **Wyle Post (IRE)**[10] 4167 7-11-5 MrWBiddick(7) 74
(Mrs K Waldron) *hld up: rdn appr 2 out: n.d* **25/1**
545P **4** *hd* **Hot Plunge**[7] 4216 10-11-11 (p) MrJOwen(5) 78
(Mrs J P Lomax) *s.s: hdwy 2nd: hit 5th: wknd next* **12/1**
2-22 **5** *1 ¾* **Coole Glen (IRE)**[294] 437 10-11-12 MrSMorris 72
(W J Warner) *chsd ldrs tl wknd appr 2 out* **5/2**[2]
3-10 **P** **Let's Fly (FR)**[19] 11-12-2 MissPGundry —
(Ross Oliver) *chsd ldrs: lost pl after 2nd: bhd fr 7th: t.o whn p.u bef last* **15/8**[1]
-40P **F** **Master Papa (IRE)**[16] 4055 7-11-5 98 MrDGreenway(7) —
(P H Hogarth) *racd keenly: led after 1st: hdd 2 out: 4l 3rd and rdn whn fell last* **14/1**

4m 17.9s (10.30) **Going Correction** +0.55s/f (Soft) **7** Ran SP% **112.1**
Speed ratings: **96,94,85,84,84** —,— CSF £36.09 TOTE £6.60: £2.80, £4.80; EX 38.10.
Owner P Dando **Bred** Mrs K M Dando **Trained** Cardiff

FOCUS
A pretty ordinary hunter chase rated around the winner to his recent course success.

NOTEBOOK
Bill Haze, successful in a similar event over just short over three miles here last time, had sufficient speed to cope with the drop back in trip and ran out a clear-cut winner. He flashed his tail under pressure, but still looked more determined than the runner-up and always looked like prevailing on the long run-in. He is clearly versatile and is one to keep on the right side of in similar company. *(op 10-3)*
Cloudy Bay Boy, who refused at the final fence when a moderate third in a similar event over two and a half miles here on his previous start, seemed to take well enough to first-time blinkers but still did not look as resolute as the eventual winner on the long run-in. To be fair, the ground would have been testing enough, and he can be given another chance back on a decent surface. *(op 12-1)*
Wyle Post(IRE), having just his fifth-career start under Rules, did not achieve a great deal in third and a return to further should suit.
Hot Plunge, with cheekpieces re-fitted, would not have appreciated ground this soft and did not look that keen to jump off.
Coole Glen(IRE) had never previously raced on ground this testing and it did not seem to suit. *(op 11-4)*
Let's Fly(FR), returned to Rules following three consecutive seconds in point-to-points, ran no sort of race and proved very disappointing. He won twice on heavy ground earlier in his career, so the *testing conditions cannot really be blamed. Official explanation: trainer said gelding was never travelling (op 12-1)*
Master Papa(IRE), pulled up at Southwell on his most recent start, would probably have been a moderate third had he not taken a horrible fall at the last. *(op 12-1)*

4350 LADBROKES.COM NOVICES' CHASE (11 fncs 4 omitted) 2m 4f 110y
3:25 (3:25) (Class 4) 5-Y-0+ **£5,070** (£1,497; £748; £374; £187)

Form RPR
61PP **1** **First De La Brunie (FR)**[29] 3816 5-10-10 103 (v[1]) RobertThornton 103
(A King) *trckd ldr to 6th: wnt 2nd again and mstke 8th: rdn 2 out: led over 1f out: drvn clr* **13/8**[2]
1134 **2** *23* **Merry Storm (IRE)**[10] 4163 7-10-9 94 RichardSpate(7) 86
(Mrs K Waldron) *hld up: hdwy 3rd: hit rails after 3 out: rdn and wknd next* **6/4**[1]
6311 **3** *5* **Sunley Future (IRE)**[22] 3945 7-10-11 98 CharliePoste(5) 84+
(M F Harris) *j.lft: led: clr 2nd: hit next: mstke last: sn hdd & wknd* **6/1**[3]
06PF **4** *dist* **Ashleybank House (IRE)**[10] 4166 9-11-2 94 (tp) RichardHobson —
(David Pearson) *prom: lost pl and mstke 3rd: bhd fr next* **25/1**
P000 **5** *11* **Tails I Win**[36] 3686 7-10-13 61 AnthonyCoyle(3) —
(Miss C J E Caroe) *bhd fr 4th* **50/1**
0300 **6** *11* **Pilca (FR)**[34] 3731 6-11-2 90 SamStronge —
(R M Stronge) *prom: mstke 3rd: chsd ldr 6th to 8th: wknd after next* **12/1**

5m 35.7s (12.10) **Going Correction** +0.55s/f (Soft)
WFA 5 from 6yo+ 5lb **6** Ran SP% **105.9**
Speed ratings: **98,89,87**,—,— — CSF £4.09 TOTE £2.50: £1.60, £1.40; EX 6.40.
Owner Mr & Mrs F C Welch **Bred** J Crouzillac Et Al **Trained** Barbury Castle, Wilts

FOCUS
A moderate novice chase in which First De La Brunie looks flattered by his winning margin, as Merry Storm did not pick up as one might have hoped, and Sunley Future emptied very quickly. The winner however, sets the standard.

NOTEBOOK
First De La Brunie(FR), pulled up on both his starts after winning a handicap chase at Wincanton, returned to form with a visor fitted for the first time but is flattered by the margin of victory. Having looked as though he was half thinking about whether or not to go through with his effort, Sunley Future emptied quickly and, with Merry Storm going nowhere quickly, he was left to win convincingly. He could be a false price next time and looks worth taking on. *(tchd 6-4)*
Merry Storm(IRE) looked to have the ground in his favour, but he made very hard work of this and never really looked comfortable under pressure. He basically only got second because Sunley Future stopped so quickly and this has to be considered a little disappointing. *(op 7-4 tchd 11-8)*
Sunley Future(IRE), chasing the hat-trick on his return to chasing following two wins over hurdles in maiden claiming and selling company respectively, went off predictably quickly but was facing a better quality of horse than on his last couple of starts, as well as testing ground, and could not sustain his effort. *(op 4-1)*
Ashleybank House(IRE) completed for just the second time over fences but was beaten a mile. *(op 20-1)*
Pilca(FR) *Official explanation: jockey said gelding had no more to give*

4351 MALLARD PAWNBROKERS HUNTERS' CHASE (14 fncs 4 omitted) 2m 7f 110y

4:00 (4:00) (Class 3) 6-Y-0+
£6,002 (£1,875; £937; £469; £234; £118)

Form				RPR
P5-5	**1**		**Another Raleagh (IRE)**[19] 12-11-5 114 MrLRPayter(7) (Graeme P McPherson) *chsd ldrs: led 3 out: clr whn hit last: styd on wl* **5/1**	120+
05-P	**2**	*20*	**Sea Ferry (IRE)**[12] 10-11-5 81 MrMBriggs(7) (Mrs Antonia Bealby) *mstkes: chsd ldr: rdn whn hit 2 out: wknd flat* **9/2**[3]	102+
61-P	**3**	*27*	**Chef Tartare (FR)**[4] 4282 6-11-13 120 (t) MrRQuinn(7) (Mrs K Waldron) *hld up: hit 1st: hdwy after 3 out: hit next: wknd last* **9/1**	90+
36-4	**4**	*1 ¾*	**Curly Spencer (IRE)**[15] 4073 12-11-5 103 MrAWadlow(7) (R J Hewitt) *hld up: hdwy 7th: wknd appr last* **9/1**	68
2301	**5**	*2 ½*	**Galway Breeze (IRE)**[21] 3960 11-11-9 107 MrMMackley(7) (Mrs Julie Read) *hld up: hit 3rd: hdwy 7th: wknd 11th* **4/1**[2]	70
P4-1	**6**	*dist*	**Abalvino (FR)**[16] 4055 12-11-9 105 (t) MissJWickens(7) (Miss J Wickens) *led and sn clr: hdd 3 out: wknd next* **9/1**	—
-156	**7**	*19*	**Red Rampage**[24] 3913 11-11-13 97 (bt) MrDGreenway(7) (P H Hogarth) *chsd ldrs: rdn 7th: hit 9th: wknd 11th* **25/1**	—
4-45	**P**		**Chaos Theory**[21] 3968 11-11-5 82 MrDThomas(7) (John Cranage) *sn bhd: t.o whn p.u after 8th* **66/1**	—
/0-4	**P**		**Perange (FR)**[21] 3960 10-11-5 114 MrAMerriam(7) (Mrs D M Grissell) *hld up: a in rr: hit 10th: t.o whn p.u bef 2 out* **33/1**	—
120-	**P**		**The Lyme Volunteer (IRE)**[19] 9-11-13 108 MrTGreenall (David M Easterby) *hld up: hdwy 7th: rdn 11th: wknd appr 2 out: t.o whn p.u bef last* **7/2**[1]	—

6m 12.0s (6.60) **Going Correction** +0.55s/f (Soft) **10** Ran SP% **115.4**
Speed ratings: **111,104,95,94,93** —,—,—,—,— CSF £27.74 TOTE £6.50: £2.60, £1.20, £5.10; EX 24.10.
Owner Mrs S M McPherson **Bred** Churchland Stud **Trained** Stow-on-the-Wold, Gloucs
■ The first winner under Rules for both Graeme McPherson and Liam Payter.

FOCUS
Quite a good hunter chase and rated positively as the winning time was 5.9 seconds faster than the later handicap over the same trip.

NOTEBOOK
Another Raleagh(IRE) ◆, second to useful sorts on his last two starts in point-to-points, ran out an impressive winner on his return to Rules. He is clearly talented and is a hunter chaser well worth keeping on the right side of. *(op 6-1)*
Sea Ferry(IRE), successful in a couple of point-to-points since he was last seen under Rules, did not jump that well on occasions, most notably when hitting the penultimate fence, and was ultimately no match for the winner. *(op 7-2)*
Chef Tartare(FR), back over fences having been pulled up over hurdles on his reappearance, travelled noticeably well for much of the way and his rider seemed full of confidence, but he was unproven over a trip this far and found little when asked. He can be expected to come on again for the run. *(op 8-1)*
Curly Spencer(IRE) found little under pressure and did not really build on the form he showed when fourth on his reappearance at Haydock two weeks previously. *(op 8-1)*
Galway Breeze(IRE) created quite a good impression when winning under similar conditions at Fakenham on his previous start, but he was quite a way below form, even allowing for this being a much tougher race. *(tchd 9-2)*
Abalvino(FR), upped to his furthest trip to date and faced with very testing ground, would have found this much more competitive than the race he won at Southwell on his previous start, and unsurprisingly failed to last home. *(op 11-1)*
Chaos Theory *Official explanation: jockey said gelding hung badly and did not jump well (op 9-2 tchd 10-3)*
The Lyme Volunteer(IRE), second in a point-to-point on her return from a break, failed to build on that on her return to Rules racing and was very disappointing. This ground may have been too testing for her. *Official explanation: jockey said mare was never travelling (op 9-2 tchd 10-3)*

4352 LADBROKES.COM PYTCHLEY MAIDEN CHASE (9 fncs 3 omitted) 2m

4:35 (4:35) (Class 4) 5-Y-0+ **£3,999** (£1,241; £668)

Form				RPR
-402	**1**		**Sargasso Sea**[65] 3239 9-11-5 105 PJBrennan (J A B Old) *mde all: sn clr: mstke last: unchal* **4/9**[1]	114+
2P4-	**2**	*21*	**Blank Canvas (IRE)**[476] 2321 8-11-5 89 JohnMcNamara (K C Bailey) *trckd ldrs: lft 2nd 3rd: rdn and wknd appr 2 out* **6/1**[3]	84
6PFC	**3**	*dist*	**Back De Bay (IRE)**[10] 4164 6-11-5 65 RichardHobson (J R Cornwall) *sn bhd: lft remote 3rd 3rd: sn t.o: hmpd by loose horse 2 out* **50/1**	—
5F4	**U**		**Hardybuck (IRE)**[23] 3920 5-11-0 (t) AntonyEvans (N A Twiston-Davies) *trckd wnr tl blnd and uns rdr 3rd* **10/3**[2]	—

4m 18.3s (10.70) **Going Correction** +0.55s/f (Soft)
WFA 5 from 6yo+ 4lb **4** Ran SP% **108.6**
Speed ratings: **95,84**,—,— CSF £3.64 TOTE £1.30; EX 2.90.
Owner W E Sturt **Bred** Sarah Blumberg **Trained** Barbury Castle, Wilts

FOCUS
A very uncompetitive maiden chase in which Sargasso Sea was never threatened and was value for 30 lengths and to his mark.

NOTEBOOK
Sargasso Sea, a promising second on his return to chasing over two miles five at Wincanton, confirmed that promise under a positive ride on this drop back in trip. This was a very weak race and he will face much stiffer competition in future, but is at least going the right way. *(op 4-11 tchd 1-2)*
Blank Canvas(IRE), an 89-rated hurdler, was no match whatsoever for the winner on his chasing debut. He should find easier opportunities in handicaps. *(op 15-2 tchd 8-1)*
Back De Bay(IRE) had it all to do at the weights and was never seen with a chance.
Hardybuck(IRE), fourth in a similar event over course and distance on his previous start, got rid of his rider too early to say how he might have fared. *(op 4-1)*

4353 LADBROKES.COM H'CAP CHASE (14 fncs 4 omitted) 2m 7f 110y

5:10 (5:11) (Class 5) (0-85,85) 5-Y-0+ **£3,578** (£1,050; £525; £262)

Form				RPR
5501	**1**		**Parkinson (IRE)**[10] 4164 5-10-5 79 7ex ShaneWalsh(5) (Jonjo O'Neill) *hld up: hdwy 8th: mstke next: outpcd appr 2 out: rallied and mstke last: rdn to ld over 1f out: styd on wl* **1/1**[1]	90+
0P31	**2**	*6*	**Jacarado (IRE)**[23] 3923 8-10-11 77 (v) JohnPritchard(7) (R Dickin) *mid-div: hdwy 5th: j.rt 9th: chalng whn j.rt 2 out: rdn to ld wl over 1f out: sn hung lft and hdd: one pce* **7/1**[3]	88+
PP02	**3**	*2*	**Red Alert Man (IRE)**[10] 4165 10-9-13 63 (b) DerekLaverty(5) (Mrs L Williamson) *w ldr tl led 5th: rdn and hdd wl over 1f out: no ex* **25/1**	70
U6/4	**4**	*7*	**Bonny Boy (IRE)**[10] 4167 11-10-0 59 oh8 (vt) RJGreene (D A Rees) *chsd ldrs: rdn 12th: mstke and wknd last* **15/2**	61+
0013	**5**	*17*	**Glen Thyne (IRE)**[23] 3923 6-11-2 75 (b) TomScudamore (K C Bailey) *hld up: hdwy 10th: wknd 2 out* **14/1**	60+
1-P4	**6**	*28*	**Gee Aker Malayo (IRE)**[23] 3919 10-11-12 85 WarrenMarston (R T Phillips) *hld up: hdwy 7th: j. slowly and lost pl next: hdwy and hit 10th: wknd appr 2 out* **25/1**	40
3-36	**7**	*9*	**Regal River (IRE)**[38] 3662 9-10-0 64 MarkNicolls(5) (John R Upson) *chsd ldrs tl wknd appr 2 out* **11/2**[2]	10
P5F0	**8**	*11*	**Peveril Pride**[24] 3909 8-10-13 72 (t) JimmyMcCarthy (J A Geake) *hld up: mstke 7th: sn lost tch* **100/1**	7
U0F6	**9**	*dist*	**Buzybakson (IRE)**[10] 4163 9-11-6 79 (t) RichardHobson (J R Cornwall) *hld up: mstke and rdn 5th: sn wl bhd* **40/1**	—
-530	**P**		**Alfa Sunrise**[24] 3909 9-11-0 73 RobertThornton (R H Buckler) *prom to 5th: bhd whn p.u bef 7th* **7/1**[3]	—
PP50	**P**		**Redhouse Chevalier**[22] 3938 7-9-7 59 oh7 (b) CharlieStudd(7) (B G Powell) *rdn to ld 1st: mstke 3rd: hdd 5th: j.lft 10th: wknd after 3 out: t.o whn p.u bef next* **50/1**	—

6m 17.9s (12.50) **Going Correction** +0.55s/f (Soft)
WFA 5 from 6yo+ 7lb **11** Ran SP% **121.9**
Speed ratings: **101,99,98,96,90 81,78,74**,—,— — CSF £9.07 CT £119.52 TOTE £2.10: £1.40, £2.80, £7.40; EX 12.40 Place 6 £175.10, Place 5 £32.94.
Owner Trevor Hemmings **Bred** E J O'Sullivan **Trained** Cheltenham, Gloucs

FOCUS
A moderate handicap chase in which the favourite Parkinson made hard enough work of following up his recent course success from a 9lb lower mark than in future. The race could rate a bit higher but the time suggests otherwise.

NOTEBOOK
Parkinson(IRE), 9lb lower than in future under the 7lb penalty he picked up for his success over two and a half miles round here on his previous start, made hard enough work of this but was well on top in the end. He will find things a little harder off his new mark, but is unlikely to be raised much beyond that given the manner of this victory and, clearly progressing, could have more to offer. *(op 11-8 after early 6-4 in places)*
Jacarado(IRE), 4lb higher than when winning under similar conditions over course and distance on his previous start, ran well in defeat and found only the progressive winner too good. *(tchd 8-1)*
Red Alert Man(IRE) was due to be dropped 3lb but he was still racing off the same mark than when gaining his last success in a course and distance handicap just over a year previously, and ran well in defeat under a positive ride. *(op 16-1)*
Bonny Boy(IRE), four times a point winner, has never scored under Rules but this was a creditable effort from 8lb out of the handicap. *(op 8-1)*
Glen Thyne(IRE) may not have been ideally suited by such a severe test of stamina.
Regal River(IRE) continues on a losing run stretching back to January 2003. *(tchd 13-2)*
Alfa Sunrise *Official explanation: jokcey said gelding was unsuited by ground - heavy with soft patches (op 9-1 tchd 6-1)*
T/Plt: £88.50 to a £1 stake. Pool: £48,867.85. 402.80 winning tickets. T/Qpdt: £8.80 to a £1 stake. Pool: £4,086.40. 340.90 winning tickets. CR

[4115] SANDOWN (R-H)

Friday, March 10

OFFICIAL GOING: Soft (good to soft in places on chase course; heavy in places on hurdle course)
Wind: Moderate, against Weather: Overcast with showers

4354 BARCLAYS AMATEUR RIDERS' H'CAP HURDLE (8 hdls) 2m 110y

2:10 (2:10) (Class 4) (0-115,111) 4-Y-0+ **£4,996** (£1,549; £774; £387)

Form				RPR
5001	**1**		**Danse Macabre (IRE)**[14] 4093 7-11-2 102 MrJSnowden(3) (A W Carroll) *lw: hld up off the pce: prog to trck ldng pair 5th: led 2 out: in command last: shkn up and hanging lft flat: kpt on* **15/8**[1]	111+
06-0	**2**	*6*	**Diamond Mick**[27] 3853 6-11-2 102 MrDAlers-Hankey(3) (Mrs R L Elliot) *lw: led 2nd and maintained gd pce: rdn and hdd 2 out: one pce* **11/2**[3]	103
023	**3**	*24*	**Pseudonym (IRE)**[15] 4075 4-10-3 101 MrJSole(7) (M F Harris) *hld up off the pce: clsd fr 5th: chsd ldng pair next: hanging rt and rdn bef 2 out: sn btn: wkng whn blnd last* **6/1**	76+
-300	**4**	*3*	**Iberus (GER)**[21] 3967 8-10-10 100 (tp) MajorHNorton(7) (S Gollings) *chsd ldng pair to 5th: sn lost pl and struggling: wl bhd after 3 out* **9/1**	74
0P5P	**5**	*6*	**Golly (IRE)**[19] 4014 10-10-6 94 MissLHorner(5) (D L Williams) *led to 2nd: chsd ldr tl after 5th: wknd sn after 3 out* **40/1**	62
6040	**P**		**Transit**[7] 2636 7-11-6 110 (p) CaptTWCEdwards(7) (B Ellison) *lw: hld up wl off the pce: clsd fr 4th: outpcd and struggling 3 out: sn wl bhd: p.u bef last* **9/4**[2]	—

4m 8.80s (-0.10) **Going Correction** +0.125s/f (Yiel)
WFA 4 from 6yo+ 7lb **6** Ran SP% **107.7**
Speed ratings: **105,102,90,89,86** — CSF £11.38 TOTE £2.50: £1.50, £2.10; EX 12.70.
Owner Miss V M Brown **Bred** Mrs D A Merry **Trained** Cropthorne, Worcs

FOCUS
By no means strong form, but a comfortable win for Danse Macabre, who looks to be on the upgrade and appeared to improve around 11lb on his recent course win.

NOTEBOOK
Danse Macabre(IRE) was at a massive advantage in having secured the services of Jamie Snowden and looked the obvious selection to follow up his win at the last meeting. Having travelled well into the straight, he went on and quickly settled the issue, winning comfortably. He likes testing going and has obvious claims of completing the hat-trick, despite having another rise to contend with. *(op 7-4 tchd 2-1)*
Diamond Mick, who did not shape badly on his seasonal return at Ayr last month, was able to build on that with a clear second to favourite Danse Macabre, keeping on well without proving a match. He scored twice at Kelso last season, and can win more races on this evidence. *(op 6-1)*
Pseudonym(IRE), a non-runner the last twice on account of unsuitable ground (good to firm & soft!), was allowed to take his chance here, but never got competitive, having been held up off the pace. He has been running reasonably well, but is clearly not up to much. *(op 5-1 tchd 13-2 in a place)*

Iberus(GER) showed up well early, but he was struggling a long way from the finish. The first-time tongue tie clearly made little difference and he remains out of form. *(tchd 11-1 in a place)*
Golly(IRE) is best known as a chaser and had little chance here.
Transit, who has been running okay on the Flat, hacked up in this race last season and was expected to go close off just a 3lb higher mark, but most of his best form is on decent ground and *he never looked happy under these testing conditions.Official explanation: trainer said gelding was unsuited by the soft, heavy in places ground (tchd 2-1)*

4355 THALES NOVICES' H'CAP CHASE (17 fncs) 2m 4f 110y
2:40 (2:41) (Class 3) (0-115,115) 5-Y-0+ **£6,506** (£1,910; £955; £477)

Form | | | | RPR
331F **1** **Nice Try (IRE)**[20] 3992 7-11-10 **113** .... SamThomas 127+
(Miss Venetia Williams) *lw: wl plcd: pressed ldr 11th: led 3 out: blnd next: drvn and kpt on wl fr last* **7/1**[3]
04P5 **2** *2 ½* **Royale Acadou (FR)**[38] 3662 8-10-0 **89** oh1 .... (p) JamieMoore 97
(Mrs L J Mongan) *pressed ldr: led 11th to 3 out: sn rdn: carried hd to one side and nt qckn flat* **8/1**
0251 **3** *24* **Alphabetical (IRE)**[62] 3284 7-11-12 **115** .... DaveCrosse 99
(C J Mann) *nt fluent: in tch: mstke 12th: outpcd 14th: lft modest 3rd and j.lft 2 out: j.lft last* **3/1**[2]
0341 **4** *15* **Bannister Lane**[15] 4068 6-11-0 **106** .... StephenCraine(3) 80+
(D McCain) *tended to jump lft: led: nt fluent 9th: hdd 11th: sn struggling: wl bhd after 14th* **7/4**[1]
660 **5** *1 ¾* **Salhood**[74] 2964 7-11-6 **112** .... WilliamKennedy(3) 79
(S Gollings) *in tch tl wknd after 14th: fin v tired* **25/1**
135P **P** **King Coal (IRE)**[22] 3940 7-11-2 **105** .... LeightonAspell —
(R Rowe) *lw: lost pl 4th: last after 6th and sn lost tch: t.o 11th: p.u bef 3 out* **12/1**
6000 **U** **Mokum (FR)**[15] 4067 5-10-0 **95** oh5 .... WayneHutchinson 87
(A W Carroll) *rn in snatches: mstke 3rd: lost pl 7th: rallied to press ldrs 12th to 3 out: 3rd and hld whn mstke 2 out and eventually uns* **15/2**

5m 24.4s (3.60) **Going Correction** +0.35s/f (Yiel)
WFA 5 from 6yo+ 5lb **7 Ran SP% 108.3**
Speed ratings: **107,106,96,91,90** —,— CSF £51.81 TOTE £6.10: £2.70, £3.90; EX 50.80.
Owner The Juggins Partnership **Bred** Gregory And Margaret Rossiter **Trained** Kings Caple, H'fords

FOCUS
With neither Alphabetical nor Bannister Lane running to par, this form may be suspect, especially as the runner-up has won only once in 41 attempts. However, the winner has provisionally been given the benefit of doubt.

NOTEBOOK
Nice Try(IRE), who was held when falling at Wincanton last time, took advantage of below-par performances from his main rivals and had them all in trouble taking the Pond Fence. A bad blunder at the second-last was unable to stop him and he stayed on well up the hill, always holding runner-up Royale Acadou. He has plenty of scope and remains open to further improvement, but will need to progress if he is to defy a higher mark. *(op 11-2)*
Royale Acadou(FR) ran well over a trip too far at Folkestone in January and she was better suited to this test. The fact remains, however, that she has now won just one of her 41 outings, and it was not hard to see why, looking at her suspect head carriage after the last. *(tchd 15-2 and 9-1)*
Alphabetical(IRE), shouldering top weight as a result of a harsh 17lb rise for winning a Fontwell handicap back in January, looked exposed off his new mark and trailed in a well-beaten third, never jumping with any real fluency. He is likely to continue to struggle. *(op 7-2)*
Bannister Lane, up 9lb for a comfortable win at Haydock, tended to jump left and lacked fluency. He was readily brushed aside by Nice Try and apparently struggled off this new mark, although it could be a different story when he goes left-handed again. *(op 15-8 tchd 13-8)*
Salhood has not shown a great deal since returning from injury, but this switch to fences seemed to help and he ran better than his finishing position suggests. *(op 16-1)*
King Coal(IRE), a huge gelding, continues to go the wrong way and, judging by his last two efforts, there may well be a problem. *(op 10-1)*
Mokum(FR) was in the process of making a pleasing switch to fences, looking booked for third, when unshipping his jockey after the second last. He is still only five and may yet be open to a little improvement. *(op 10-1)*

4356 GRAND MILITARY GOLD CUP (CHASE FOR AMATEUR RIDERS) (SPONSORED BY BAE SYSTEMS) (22 fncs) 3m 110y
3:15 (3:15) (Class 3) 6-Y-0+ **£7,495** (£2,324; £1,161; £580)

Form | | | | RPR
6151 **1** **Inca Trail (IRE)**[14] 4090 10-12-2 139 .... (b) MrJSnowden(3) 113+
(P F Nicholls) *hld up in last quartet: prog 15th: chsd clr ldr 3 out: clsd next: upsides last: hrd rdn and fnd little flat: jst prevailed* **5/6**[1]
0U40 **2** *shd* **Happy Hussar (IRE)**[91] 2745 13-11-7 90 .... MrJSole(7) 105
(Dr P Pritchard) *trckd clr ldrs: prog 12th: led 16th: clear 18th: jnd last: kpt on u.str.p flat: jst pipped* **100/1**
4F32 **3** *10* **Back Nine (IRE)**[14] 4090 9-11-11 120 .... (t) MrDAlers-Hankey(3) 98+
(R H Alner) *settled in last quartet: sme prog whn blnd 18th: nt on terms after: kpt on fr 2 out to take 3rd flat: n.d* **9/4**[2]
205- **4** *2 ½* **Burwood Breeze (IRE)**[370] 4189 10-11-7 115 .... CaptTWCEdwards(7) 93
(T R George) *wl plcd: chsd ldng pair after 3 out: no imp next: wknd flat* **16/1**
205P **5** *15* **Heidi III (FR)**[11] 4144 11-11-12 108 .... (p) CaptWBRamsay(7) 89+
(M D Hammond) *led to 2nd: led 7th to 8th: hit 10th: led 13th to 16th: wknd 3 out* **33/1**
F325 **6** *3 ½* **Cedar Chief**[14] 4090 9-11-7 71 .... (b) LtHWallace(7) 74
(K Tork) *lw: pressed ldrs: wl in tch 16th: wknd fr 19th* **100/1**
130P **7** *2* **Snowy Ford (IRE)**[41] 3614 9-11-12 117 .... (p) CaptAMichael(7) 77
(N J Gifford) *hld up in last quartet: sme prog whn mstke 12th: no imp on ldrs fr 16th: wl btn bef 3 out* **25/1**
4300 **8** *1 ½* **Blazing Batman**[19] 4007 13-11-7 70 .... MajorGWheeler(7) 71
(Dr P Pritchard) *nvr beyond midfield: struggling whn mstke 16th: wl btn fr 19th* **100/1**
15/6 **9** *8* **Double Account (FR)**[14] 4090 11-11-7 .... (v[1]) MajorBeverleyTunley(7) 63
(D L Williams) *racd freely: led 2nd to 7th and 8th to 13th: wkng whn mstke 19th: sn bhd* **100/1**
P3P3 **10** *dist* **Mercato (FR)**[14] 4090 10-11-7 98 .... MajorHNorton(7) —
(J R Best) *nt fluent: hld up in last quartet: mstke 13th: no prog 16th: no ch after: v tired flat: btn 84 l* **20/1**
1164 **11** *shd* **Bang And Blame (IRE)**[17] 4042 10-11-7 101 .... MajGThompson(7) —
(M W Easterby) *chsd ldrs but nvr on terms: wknd 16th: t.o after 19th: btn 84 l* **14/1**[3]
UP/0 **12** *21* **River Paradise (IRE)**[14] 4090 10-11-7 .... (t) L/BdrCHaigh(7) —
(Jamie Broom) *lw: wl in rr: rushed up to press ldrs after 11th: wknd after next: sn t.o: btn 105 l* **200/1**

6m 35.8s (4.30) **Going Correction** +0.35s/f (Yiel) **12 Ran SP% 113.9**
Speed ratings: **107,106,103,102,98 97,96,95,93,**— —,— CSF £123.75 TOTE £1.90: £1.30, £12.70, £1.30; EX 116.90.
Owner Major A M J Shaw **Bred** Ballysheehan Stud **Trained** Ditcheat, Somerset
■ Inca Trail was completing the same military double as stable-mate Whitenzo, also ridden by Jamie Snowden, had in 2005.

FOCUS
Inca Trail has been rated 30l off his best, but he only just does enough, and it would be unwise to read too much into the fact he only just scraped home from a veteran rated 49lb his inferior.

NOTEBOOK
Inca Trail(IRE), given a fine ride to land the Royal Artillery Gold Cup here last month, seemingly had only Back Nine to beat once again, but it was veteran outsider Happy Hussar who pushed him all the way, despite being rated 49lb his inferior. Although he jumped the last travelling as strongly as one would have expected, his rider really had to go for him on the run-in and he only just prevailed. This was nothing like his form, and connections blamed the ground, reasoning it was much more testing than at the Royal Artillery meeting. He goes to the sales now, with a Grand National entry. *(op 4-5 tchd 8-11)*
Happy Hussar(IRE), whose best effort this term came in the first of two early-season Cross Country races at Cheltenham, took several lengths out of the field down the back and was clear turning in, but in doing so was vulnerable to the winner's finishing burst. The burst never materialised however, and the 13-year-old forced Jamie Snowden on board the hot favourite to pull out all the stops. This was a gallant effort, but he is not getting any younger and needs a thorough test, so he will continue to find winning hard.
Back Nine(IRE), who went down narrowly to the favourite last time, attempted to track him through on this occasion, but a bad blunder at the last of the Railway fences cost him ground and momentum and he was unable to recover in time, only coming through late for third. He is a fair bit better than this, but remains winless over fences. *(tchd 11-4, 3-1 in a place)*
Burwood Breeze(IRE), who has gone well fresh in the past, looked fit enough and ran well for a *long way before getting weary. He used to be highly consistent and may yet recover his best form. (tchd 20-1)*
Heidi III(FR) is a shadow of the horse he once was, but he raced prominently for much of the way, despite throwing in several sloppy errors, and was not totally discredited back in fifth.

4357 SARAH PASK MEMORIAL H'CAP HURDLE (11 hdls) 2m 6f
3:50 (3:52) (Class 3) (0-120,118) 4-Y-0+ **£5,204** (£1,528; £764; £381)

Form | | | | RPR
1 **1** **Kipsigis (IRE)**[117] 2212 5-11-4 **110** .... LeightonAspell 114+
(Lady Herries) *hld up in tch: prog 6th: chsd ldr and blnd 3 out: led next: hrd pressed whn blnd and lft clr last: kpt on* **5/1**[2]
0/P4 **2** *8* **Heron's Ghyll (IRE)**[42] 3600 9-10-12 **104** .... SamThomas 101+
(Miss Venetia Williams) *pressed ldr: led 4th to 2 out: 4th and btn whn lft 2nd last* **14/1**
P050 **3** *19* **Jaloux D'Estruval (FR)**[20] 3982 9-11-2 **108** .... AndrewTinkler 83
(Mrs L C Taylor) *wl in rr: last and struggling whn mstke 8th: sn bhd: plugged on bef 2 out: lft remote 3rd last* **50/1**
/F4- **4** *2* **Rum Pointer (IRE)**[489] 2041 10-11-9 **115** .... BenjaminHitchcott 88
(R H Buckler) *nvr beyond midfield: lost tch w ldrs fr 3 out: no ch after* **20/1**
06-4 **5** *18* **Mesmeric (IRE)**[23] 1116 8-11-12 **118** .... MickFitzgerald 73
(B G Powell) *hld up in last: stdy prog fr 6th: trckd ldrs after 3 out: nudged along and wknd bef 2 out: eased* **25/1**
342P **6** *4* **Albert House (IRE)**[42] 3603 8-10-13 **105** .... RobertWalford 56
(R H Alner) *towards rr: u.p and struggling after 8th: sn no ch* **10/1**
1121 **7** *dist* **Amanpuri (GER)**[12] 4131 8-11-3 **109** 7ex .... ChristianWilliams —
(Mrs A M Thorpe) *trckd ldrs: drvn and wknd rapidly 3 out: t.o: btn 82 l* **10/1**
4353 **U** **Mouseski**[20] 3987 12-11-4 **115** .... LiamHeard(5) —
(P F Nicholls) *blnd and uns rdr 2nd* **7/1**[3]
-PP0 **B** **Alpha Gamble (IRE)**[84] 2868 6-10-5 **97** .... JimCrowley —
(R Rowe) *settled in midfield: prog into 4th and gng strly whn b.d 7th* **16/1**
0052 **F** **Supreme Piper (IRE)**[20] 3982 8-10-12 **111** .... MissCDyson(7) —
(Miss C Dyson) *led to 4th: lost pl: renewed effrt to chal whn fell 7th* **20/1**
2266 **P** **Salute (IRE)**[40] 1598 7-10-11 **110** .... MrJQuintin(7) —
(P G Murphy) *prom: pushed along whn hmpd 7th: sn rdn and wknd: t.o after 3 out: p.u bef next* **66/1**
F-P6 **F** **Sesame Rambler (IRE)**[35] 3719 7-10-13 **105** .... JamieMoore 107
(G L Moore) *hld up in rr: stdy prog fr 7th: rdn to cl 2 out: hrd rdn to chal and upsides whn fell last: winded* **33/1**
60P1 **F** **Wee Anthony (IRE)**[20] 3982 7-10-11 **103** .... APMcCoy 108+
(Jonjo O'Neill) *lw: hld up wl in rr: prog 7th: rdn 3 out: u.p but clsng to chal and upsides whn fell heavily last: winded* **13/8**[1]

5m 34.15s (-3.75) **Going Correction** +0.125s/f (Yiel) **13 Ran SP% 117.8**
Speed ratings: **111,108,101,100,93 92,**—,—,—,— —,—,— CSF £62.92 CT £3114.10 TOTE £5.90: £2.10, £3.80, £9.70; EX 102.80 TRIFECTA Not won..
Owner Lady Sarah Clutton **Bred** Angmering Park Stud **Trained** Patching, W Sussex

FOCUS
A particularly eventful contest, and Kipsigis had luck on his side when left clear at the last after Sesame Rambler and Wee Anthony had taken off upsides. Wee Anthony has been rated the narrow winner, with Sesame Rambler to his Taunton form and the winner improving slightly.

NOTEBOOK
Kipsigis(IRE), a surprise winner on his hurdling debut at Fontwell back in November, had not been seen since, but was evidently straight enough and was fighting it out with Sesame Rambler and Wee Anthony when that pair came down independently at the last. It would be unfair to say he would not have won, but the other's had just joined him and the likelihood is that he would have had to settle for a place. He could be worth taking on next time, even though he remains open to further improvement. *(op 7-2)*
Heron's Ghyll(IRE) failed to shine on his reappearance/chasing debut, but he shaped better when fourth over hurdles at Fontwell in January and this was a further step in the right direction. He was obviously a fortunate second, but there is surely a race in him off this sort of mark.
Jaloux D'Estruval(FR) was behind from an early stage, but plugged on through beaten rivals for a *remote third. He is back down to a winning mark and could be of interest in a lesser race next* time.
Rum Pointer(IRE), who has developed into a useful chaser over the past couple of seasons, looked as though he had done plenty of work but should still benefit from this first run in 489 days. This will no doubt have delighted connections. *(op 25-1)*
Mesmeric(IRE) appeared to face a pretty stiff task under top weight and was behind, not going particularly well early, but he made good headway to sit fifth turning in, only for his effort in making ground to take its toll. There were positives to be taken from this and he could be of interest next time. *(tchd 28-1)*
Supreme Piper(IRE) was still prominent, but looking vulnerable, when falling at the seventh. *(tchd 18-1)*
Sesame Rambler(IRE), who had shown little in two starts at Fontwell since returning, had responded well to pressure and was level taking the last, poised to go close, when falling. He looked particularly unlucky and it is hoped this does not affect his confidence, as he lay winded for a while. *(tchd 18-1)*
Alpha Gamble(IRE), a springer in the morning markets, was travelling well and in the process of *running his best race for some time when brought down down by the fall of Supreme Piper. (tchd 18-1)*

Wee Anthony(IRE), an easy winner on his handicap debut over hurdles at Lingfield last month, had been niggled at on and off for a circuit, but still came through under pressure to be upsides when falling, along with Sesame Rambler, at the last. It remains to be seen how long it takes for him to get over this. *(tchd 18-1)*

4358 QUEEN ELIZABETH THE QUEEN MOTHER MEMORIAL HUNTERS' CHASE (22 fncs) 3m 110y

4:25 (4:26) (Class 4) 6-Y-0+ **£4,372** (£1,355; £677; £338)

Form				RPR
6-01	1		**First Love**[14] 4092 10-12-3 114 MrJSnowden(3)	125
			(N J Henderson) *lw: mde all: drew clr fr 3 out: rdn out flat* **15/8**[1]	
34C-	2	*dist*	**Oracle Des Mottes (FR)**[13] 7-11-7 CaptTWCEdwards(7)	94
			(R Barber) *plld hrd: hld up in tch: chsd wnr 15th: blnd 18th: cl up bef 3 out: sn bmpd along and wknd: btn 32 l* **15/8**[1]	
P0-P	3	*dist*	**Indian Chance**[20] 3981 12-11-7 105 LtHWallace(7)	—
			(O Sherwood) *chsd ldrs to 12th: sn lost tch: t.o 19th: lft poor 3rd last: btn 77 l* **12/1**	
F61/	4	*dist*	**Rob Mine (IRE)**[34] 14-11-7 CaptAMichael(7)	—
			(C Sporborg) *nt fluent and nvr gng wl: a last: lost tch 11th: wl t.o fina circ: btn 130 l* **13/2**[2]	
20P/	R		**Haut Cercy (FR)**[47] 11-11-11 MrDAlers-Hankey(3)	—
			(G C Evans) *trckd wnr 8th to 15th: mstke 19th: wknd: wl btn whn mstke 2 out: poor 3rd whn ref last* **7/1**[3]	
P4F5	P		**Thieves'Glen**[187] 1406 8-11-13 100 MajorHNorton(7)	—
			(H Morrison) *plld hrd and racd wd: mostly chsd ldr to 8th: wknd 13th: t.o in 5th whn p.u bef 3 out* **16/1**	

6m 40.95s (9.45) **Going Correction** +0.35s/f (Yiel) **6** Ran SP% **109.0**
Speed ratings: **98**,—,—,—,— — CSF £5.51 TOTE £2.30: £1.60, £1.70; EX 4.70.
Owner The Queen **Bred** Queen Elizabeth **Trained** Upper Lambourn, Berks

■ A treble for Jamie Snowden, making it 11 from 20 at Sandown, and five successive wins here since his fourth in the Betfred.

FOCUS

An uncompetitive hunter chase in which only two could be given a serious chance. First Love is not a three-miler, but got the trip better than Oracle des Mottes

NOTEBOOK

First Love, a winner in this sphere at the course last time, had a bit to prove over the extra half a mile, but he settled better and saw it out well, certainly better than his main challenger Oracle Des Mottes, coming away to win easily. He will find life a lot tougher up in grade, but is at least heading in the right direction. *(op 13-8 tchd 2-1 in a place, 6-4 in places)*

Oracle Des Mottes(FR), a winner over three miles in a point last month, looked fit enough beforehand but pulled too hard for his own good and, having tracked the winner into the straight, got very tired. He may find life easier on faster ground. *(op 7-4 tchd 2-1)*

Indian Chance shaped a little better than when pulled up on his reappearance, but was struggling a long way from the finish and came home in his own time. *(op 14-1)*

Rob Mine(IRE), who has been running reasonably well in points, was struggling from an early stage, failing to jump with any real fluency. *(op 8-1 tchd 6-1)*

Haut Cercy(FR), a formerly useful staying chaser, had run his race and was tired when deciding enough was enough approaching the last. He has the ability to make an impact at this level, but has seldom convinced with his attitude. *(op 8-1 tchd 15-2 in a place)*

4359 BETFAIR.COM "NATIONAL HUNT" NOVICES' HURDLE (8 hdls) 2m 110y

5:00 (5:01) (Class 4) 4-Y-0+ **£5,204** (£1,528; £764; £381)

Form				RPR
3426	1		**Aztec Warrior (IRE)**[67] 3210 5-11-2 TimmyMurphy	119
			(Miss H C Knight) *mstke 1st: trckd ldrs: effrt and rdn bef 2 out: led sn after last: styd on wl* **11/2**[3]	
-123	2	*2 ½*	**Menchikov (FR)**[37] 3677 6-11-7 125 MickFitzgerald	122+
			(N J Henderson) *trckd ldrs: rdn wl bef 2 out: effrt to chal last: kpt on same pce flat* **15/8**[2]	
5113	3	*1 ¼*	**Regal Heights (IRE)**[13] 4115 5-11-9 132 StephenCraine(3)	126+
			(D McCain) *lw: pressed ldr: led wl bef 2 out: mstke 2 out and rdn: hdd sn after last: fdd* **13/8**[1]	
4-	4	*1 ½*	**Pass It On (IRE)**[462] 2604 7-11-2 APMcCoy	114
			(Jonjo O'Neill) *lw: hld up in last pair: prog 3 out: pushed along and nt on terms w ldng trio 2 out: kpt on steadily* **7/1**	
3	5	*23*	**Otantique (FR)**[58] 3346 4-10-8 BarryFenton	88+
			(Miss E C Lavelle) *lw: racd freely: led: hdd wl bef 2 out: wkng whn mstke 2 out: eased* **25/1**	
50-	6	*17*	**Acacia Avenue (IRE)**[349] 4552 6-11-2 DavidDennis	74
			(Ian Williams) *prom: rdn 3 out: wknd sn after* **33/1**	
P6	7	*10*	**Froghole Flyer**[14] 4088 7-11-2 LeightonAspell	64
			(G L Moore) *in tch to 5th: struggling fr next: sn wl bhd* **66/1**	
0	P		**Swift Water (IRE)**[254] 866 6-11-2 JasonMaguire	—
			(T R George) *a in rr: wknd bef 3 out: t.o whn p.u bef 2 out* **100/1**	
5/	P		**Mid Sussex Spirit**[767] 3650 7-11-2 JamieMoore	—
			(G L Moore) *in tch: mstkes 4th and 5th: sn wknd: t.o whn p.u bef 2 out* **33/1**	

4m 12.6s (3.70) **Going Correction** +0.125s/f (Yiel)
WFA 4 from 5yo+ 7lb **9** Ran SP% **113.0**
Speed ratings: **96,94,94,93,82 74,70**,—,— CSF £15.89 TOTE £6.50: £2.00, £1.40, £1.10; EX 16.30 Place 6 £62.23, Place 5 £37.66.
Owner Mrs T P Radford **Bred** R Guiry **Trained** West Lockinge, Oxon

FOCUS

An ordinary novices' hurdle in which the front four pulled clear. The form has been rated through the second and third, and this was a big step up from the winner.

NOTEBOOK

Aztec Warrior(IRE), who until now had not built on his promising Aintree bumper debut, came with a well-timed run under Murphy, taking it up just after the last and staying on dourly to win a shade comfortably. Sporting the same colours as leading Arkle contender Racing Demon, he will stay further in time and, with his liking for soft ground, connections can look forward to sending him chasing early next season. *(tchd 6-1)*

Menchikov(FR), favourite on all three previous outings over hurdles, was ridden prominently on this drop in trip and held every chance, but his 5lb penalty ultimately made the difference. A return to further will help and he too will jump fences next season. *(tchd 2-1)*

Regal Heights(IRE) set a fair standard, having finished a close third behind Senorita Rumbalita and Mister Quasimodo at the course last time. He went on before two out, travelling well, but his double penalty took its toll and faded on the climb to the line. He is a tough, consistent gelding who has a fine future over fences ahead of him. *(tchd 15-8)*

Pass It On(IRE), a promising fourth on his hurdling debut back in December 2004, looked fit enough for this reappearance and plugged on to finish a never-nearer fourth. Two and a half miles is likely to suit and there should be a small race in him. *(tchd 6-1)*

Otantique(FR), who shaped well in a juvenile bumper at Newbury on debut, was expected to be suited by this step up in distance on his hurdling debut and travelled best of all into the straight. However, he had raced keenly early on and that soon began to tell. Although ultimately well held, there was sufficient promise in his performance and he can be expected to improve with time. *(op 33-1)*

Acacia Avenue(IRE) looked fit enough for his first run in 349 days.

T/Jkpt: £2,496.50 to a £1 stake. Pool: £26,372.50. 7.50 winning tickets. T/Plt: £50.90 to a £1 stake. Pool: £62,920.45. 901.90 winning tickets. T/Qpdt: £4.80 to a £1 stake. Pool: £4,569.00. 695.70 winning tickets. JN

4341 AYR (L-H)

Saturday, March 11

OFFICIAL GOING: Soft (heavy in places)

Last fence in back straight, first fence in home straight and last hurdle in the back straight omitted all circuits.

Wind: Almost nil Weather: Overcast

4360 FERGUSON MEDIA JUVENILE NOVICES' H'CAP HURDLE (8 hdls 1 omitted) 2m

2:15 (2:15) (Class 4) (0-105,107) 4-Y-0 **£2,927** (£859; £429; £214)

Form				RPR
312	1		**Patxaran (IRE)**[18] 4039 4-11-5 103 (t) PaddyMerrigan(5)	106+
			(P C Haslam) *mde all: drew clr fr 2 out* **15/8**[1]	
0133	2	*10*	**Calfraz**[12] 4143 4-11-9 107 DougieCostello(5)	100
			(M D Hammond) *prom: drvn and outpcd 4 out: rallied bef next: wnt 2nd 2 out: no ch w wnr* **11/4**[2]	
53P4	3	*8*	**Countrywide Sun**[18] 4045 4-10-4 90 EwanWhillans(7)	76+
			(A C Whillans) *keen: cl up: ev ch whn mstke 3 out: outpcd next* **7/1**	
5410	4	*2 ½*	**Woodford Consult**[38] 3674 4-11-0 96 MrTGreenall(3)	79
			(M W Easterby) *hld up in tch: effrt bef 3 out: wknd next* **9/2**[3]	
	5	*6*	**Adalari (IRE)**[17] 4062 4-11-1 101 MrATDuff(7)	78
			(W J Codd, Ire) *chsd ldrs tl wknd bef 3 out* **10/1**	
0P5	6	*nk*	**Double Ells**[92] 2753 4-10-4 83 DavidO'Meara	60+
			(J M Jefferson) *keen: cl up tl lost pl 4 out: struggling fr next* **14/1**	

4m 11.1s (13.80) **Going Correction** +0.825s/f (Soft) **6** Ran SP% **107.9**
Speed ratings: **98,93,89,87,84 84** CSF £7.01 TOTE £2.90: £1.40, £1.80; EX 3.30.
Owner David H Morgan **Bred** Eddie O'Leary **Trained** Middleham, N Yorks

FOCUS

Not a competitive handicap and only a fair pace but a wide-margin winner, who looks on the upgrade and the form looks reasonable with the placed horses running to their marks.

NOTEBOOK

Patxaran(IRE) has improved with every outing over hurdles and, although this was not a competitive event, turned in her best effort yet. Life will be tougher after reassessment, but she may well be capable of better. *(op 7-4 tchd 13-8 and 2-1)*

Calfraz again tended to go in snatches but seemed to run his race and looks a good guide to this form. On the evidence so far he is certainly worth a try over two and a half miles.

Countrywide Sun ran well for a long way and may be capable of better under less-testing conditions but his inconsistency and the fact that he has yet to win in 16 career starts means he is not one to place too much faith in. *(op 9-1 tchd 10-1)*

Woodford Consult did not repeat the antics of last time when running out but underlined her inconsistency with a below-par effort and she does not look one to place too much faith in. *(tchd 5-1)*

Adalari(IRE) was again well beaten in handicap company on testing ground and will have to show more before he is worth a bet. *(op 12-1)*

Double Ells, who finished in front of Calfraz on her debut at Doncaster yet had a big pull in the weights with that rival, was soundly beaten on this handicap debut and she may appreciate less-testing conditions. *(op 12-1 tchd 16-1)*

4361 DAWN HOMES H'CAP CHASE (FOR THE JOHN BROWN MEMORIAL TROPHY) (18 fncs 6 omitted) 3m 5f

2:50 (2:50) (Class 4) (0-110,109) 5-Y-0+ **£4,554** (£1,337; £668; £333)

Form				RPR
4PP4	1		**Almire Du Lia (FR)**[12] 4144 8-11-0 97 (v) WilsonRenwick	108+
			(Mrs S C Bradburne) *w ldrs: led 5th: hld on wl u.p fr 3 out* **10/1**	
54-	2	*3 ½*	**Best China (IRE)**[31] 3811 6-9-9 83 oh6 RJMolloy(5)	92+
			(Liam Lennon, Ire) *hld up in tch: blnd 13th: effrt 4 out: ev ch whn nt fluent 3 out: outpcd next: kpt on fr last* **10/1**	
5P3U	3	*8*	**Devil's Run (IRE)**[14] 4111 10-11-8 108 PaddyAspell(3)	108+
			(J Wade) *keen early: cl up: outpcd bef 3 out: no imp fr next* **3/1**[2]	
5PU0	4	*11*	**Ta Ta For Now**[25] 3917 9-9-11 83 oh2 OwynNelmes(3)	70
			(Mrs S C Bradburne) *rn in snatches: prom: lost pl 6th: effrt bef 12th: outpcd fr 5 out* **14/1**	
P50	5	*24*	**Trovaio (IRE)**[25] 3917 9-9-11 83 oh10 (p) PeterBuchanan(3)	46
			(Miss Lucinda V Russell) *hld up: shortlived effrt bef 4 out: sn btn* **66/1**	
4P02	P		**Harlov (FR)**[45] 3560 11-11-12 109 (v) RichardMcGrath	—
			(A Parker) *prom: rdn bef 12th: sn outpcd: p.u after 4 out* **6/1**[3]	
3-P4	P		**Mickey Croke**[33] 3781 9-10-12 100 (p) TJDreaper(5)	—
			(M Todhunter) *in tch: rdn and outpcd whn blnd 12th: sn p.u* **20/1**	
121P	P		**Brandy Wine (IRE)**[56] 3382 8-11-12 109 (b) TonyDobbin	—
			(L Lungo) *cl up: blnd 1st: hit 3rd: wknd 13th: p.u after 4 out* **5/2**[1]	
52FP	P		**Moon Mist**[18] 4042 8-9-7 83 oh2 TomMessenger(7)	—
			(N W Alexander) *led to 5th: cl up tl wknd fr 14th: t.o whn p.u bef 2 out* **7/1**	

8m 44.7s **9** Ran SP% **111.5**
CSF £96.91 CT £366.20 TOTE £11.50: £1.90, £2.20, £2.10; EX 90.80.
Owner Hardie, Cochrane, Paterson & Steel **Bred** Alain Trepeu, And Valerie Dasque **Trained** Cunnoquhie, Fife

FOCUS

An uncompetitive event that did not take as much winning as seemed likely beforehand with three of the four market leaders disappointing. The winner's recent success and the placed horses suggest this form is solid.

NOTEBOOK

Almire Du Lia(FR), who shaped better last time, won an uncompetitive race back over this longer trip in gutsy style but his inconsistency coupled with the fact that this race did not take much winning means he would be no good thing to follow up next time.

Best China(IRE), a winning Irish pointer, turned in his best effort over regulation fences from 6lb out of the handicap but, although capable of winning a similar event, will have to brush up his jumping if he is to progress in this sphere. *(tchd 9-1)*

Devil's Run(IRE), from a stable among the winners, had plenty in his favour but, although failing to settle early on, seemed beaten on merit and may have to drop further in the handicap before regaining the winning thread. *(op 11-4 tchd 10-3 in places)*

Ta Ta For Now is a law unto himself and, although running better than he has done of late on ground that would have been plenty testing enough, remains a very risky betting proposition. *(op 20-1)*

Harlov(FR)'s form since his last win over three miles and six on soft ground at Bangor last January has been very patchy and he was well beaten for no apparent reason. He is another from this race to be wary of at shortish odds. *(tchd 3-1)*

Moon Mist has been very disappointing over fences since his win over three miles and one furlong just over a year ago and, although she had conditions to suit, was again soundly beaten and is best watched at present. *(tchd 3-1)*

Brandy Wine(IRE) looked to have plenty in his favour but was most disappointing once again, *even allowing for a couple of early mistakes and he is one to tread carefully with at present.Official explanation: trainer had no explanation for the poor form shown (tchd 3-1)*

4362 HORSERACINGBREAKS.COM NOVICES' H'CAP HURDLE (10 hdls 2 omitted) 3m 110y

3:25 (3:25) (Class 4) (0-110,103) 4-Y-0+ **£4,228** (£1,241; £620; £310)

Form				RPR
5443	**1**		**Kirkside Pleasure (IRE)**[28] 3855 5-11-10 **101**.............. WilsonRenwick (Mrs S C Bradburne) *chsd ldr: effrt bef 3 out: led run in: styd on wl* **13/2**	105+
0F43	**2**	2	**Roschal (IRE)**[51] 3459 8-10-11 **91**............................(p) PeterBuchanan(3) (Miss Lucinda V Russell) *led: rdn bef 3 out: hdd run in: no ex* **7/2**[2]	94+
3452	**3**	28	**Sotovik (IRE)**[28] 3855 5-11-5 **103**.................................. EwanWhillans(7) (A C Whillans) *in tch: effrt after 4 out: wkng whn hit next* **9/2**[3]	85+
5146	**4**	dist	**Vocative (GER)**[17] 4057 4-10-8 **100**............................ PaddyMerrigan(5) (P C Haslam) *hld up: outpcd 1/2-way: n.d after* **6/1**	—
053P	**P**		**Network Oscar (IRE)**[16] 4067 5-11-1 **95**....................... MrTGreenall(3) (M W Easterby) *chsd ldrs tl wknd 4 out: t.o whn p.u bef next* **8/1**	—
-040	**P**		**Reap The Reward (IRE)**[87] 2821 6-11-6 **97**....................... TonyDobbin (L Lungo) *in tch: stdy hdwy after 4 out: rdn and wknd bef next: t.o whn p.u after 2 out* **2/1**[1]	—

6m 46.6s (14.80) **Going Correction** +0.825s/f (Soft)
WFA 4 from 5yo+ 9lb **6** Ran SP% **112.5**
Speed ratings: **105,104,95,—,—** — CSF £29.39 TOTE £7.00: £2.90, £2.40; EX 25.20.
Owner Hardie, Cochrane, Yeaman & Mitchell **Bred** Mrs Mary O'Donoghue **Trained** Cunnoquhie, Fife

FOCUS
Little strength in depth and a race in which the market leader disappointed. The third is the best guide to the level.

NOTEBOOK
Kirkside Pleasure(IRE) has not been overly consistent over hurdles but turned in his best effort and showed the right attitude in the closing stages. A good test of stamina obviously suits and he may be capable of further improvement. *(op 7-1)*
Roschal(IRE), whose form over fences for Philip Hobbs was patchy since his last win, was tried in cheekpieces on this first run for his new stable and ran creditably back over hurdles. Less testing *ground over this trip may suit better and he looks capable of winning an ordinary event. (op 4-1 tchd 5-1 in places)*
Sotovik(IRE) had plenty in his favour regarding ground, trip and current form so his performance on this handicap debut has to go down as disappointing. He is not one to write off just yet but will have to show more before he is worth a bet. *(op 5-1 tchd 4-1 in places)*
Vocative(GER), who disappointed at Southwell last time, was again well beaten and looks one to tread carefully with at present. *(op 5-1)*
Reap The Reward(IRE), who hinted at ability in novice events, proved a disappointment on this handicap debut upped to this trip for the first time. Less of a test of stamina may suit though and, *given he is in very good hands, looks well worth another chance. Official explanation: trainer had no explanation for the poor form shown (tchd 9-4)*
Network Oscar(IRE), who ran his best race over three miles and one furlong on soft ground on his penultimate start, was again most disappointing and is another to watch for now. *(tchd 9-4)*

4363 EVENT MASTER H'CAP CHASE (FOR THE HAMILTON CAMPBELL TROPHY) (13 fncs 4 omitted) 2m 4f

4:00 (4:00) (Class 3) (0-120,120) 5-Y-0+ **£7,807** (£2,292; £1,146; £572)

Form				RPR
2F10	**1**		**Green Ideal**[25] 3917 8-10-11 **110**....................................(b) TJDreaper(5) (Ferdy Murphy) *w ldrs: led 6th: mde rest: styd on strly fr 3 out* **9/2**[3]	120+
2	15	**Dans Dealer (IRE)**[142] 1811 11-10-5 **106** ow1.................... MrATDuff(7) (S Donohoe, Ire) *chsd ldrs: effrt bef 3 out: one pce next* **8/1**	97
0432	**3**	1 1/4	**Flight Command**[14] 4109 8-11-10 **118**..............................(p) RussGarritty (P Beaumont) *prom: hit 9th: outpcd next: kpt on fr 2 out: no imp run in* **3/1**[2]	110+
3/45	**4**	12	**Big-And-Bold (IRE)**[28] 3851 10-11-9 **117**........................... TonyDobbin (N G Richards) *led to 6th: cl up tl wknd bef 3 out* **2/1**[1]	99+
4316	**5**	17	**Master Sebastian**[16] 4068 7-11-6 **117**......................... PeterBuchanan(3) (Miss Lucinda V Russell) *prom: rdn 4 out: sn btn* **16/1**	78
0F21	**P**		**Brave Thought (IRE)**[14] 4109 11-11-8 **116**..................... RichardMcGrath (P Monteith) *mstkes: hld up: hit 9th: sn rdn and btn: p.u bef 3 out* **6/1**	—

5m 47.0s (24.10) **Going Correction** +1.25s/f (Heav) **6** Ran SP% **107.8**
Speed ratings: **101,95,94,89,82** — CSF £33.27 CT £106.84 TOTE £5.40: £2.40, £1.70; EX 38.80.
Owner Mrs J Morgan **Bred** Juddmonte Farms **Trained** West Witton, N Yorks

FOCUS
An ordinary event in which the early pace was only fair at best. The form could rate much higher but better assessed through the winner to his previous best chasing form.

NOTEBOOK
Green Ideal proved well suited by the return to this trip and turned in his best effort yet. Although *he looks much more reliable these days, he will find life much tougher after reassessment. (tchd 5-1)*
Dans Dealer(IRE) does not have the best of completion records over fences but, given that his best form is over further and on better ground, was far from disgraced over this trip in testing ground and is the type to win another race or two. *(op 10-1)*
Flight Command, again sporting the cheekpieces, did not look the easiest of rides back over this longer trip and, although not totally disgraced, is likely to continue to look vulnerable from his current mark. *(op 11-4 tchd 10-3, 7-2 in places)*
Big-And-Bold(IRE) should have been spot on after two outings following a lengthy break but disappointed back over the distance of his last win. He may have been found out by these conditions but is proving expensive to follow. *(op 9-4 tchd 5-2 in places)*
Master Sebastian, a course and distance winner on his penultimate start, was again soundly beaten and he looks best watched in the short-term future. *(op 14-1)*
Brave Thought(IRE) did not jump with much fluency and was well beaten back over this longer trip. Although two miles seems to suit better, he is likely to remain vulnerable from his current mark. *Official explanation: jockey said gelding was never jumping with any fluency (op 5-1)*

4364 BULL H'CAP HURDLE (FOR THE AYRSHIRE YEOMANRY CUP) (9 hdls 2 omitted) 2m 4f

4:35 (4:35) (Class 3) (0-125,122) 4-Y-0+ **£5,204** (£1,528; £764; £381)

Form				RPR
2312	**1**		**First Look (FR)**[25] 3912 6-11-0 **120**............................. DavidDaSilva(10) (P Monteith) *cl up: led after 4 out: clr fr next: mstke last: pushed out* **3/1**[2]	127+
1215	**2**	5	**Aston Lad**[28] 3854 5-11-5 **115**... BarryKeniry (M D Hammond) *hld up: hdwy bef 3 out: kpt on fr last: nt rch wnr* **11/2**[3]	112
050P	**3**	3 1/2	**Crackleando**[28] 3854 5-9-11 **100**............................. TomMessenger(7) (A R Dicken) *led to after 4 out: drvn and outpcd next: kpt on fr 2 out: lft 3rd last: no imp* **33/1**	95+
2053	**4**	12	**Time To Roam (IRE)**[28] 3853 6-10-1 **100**.................(p) PeterBuchanan(3) (Miss Lucinda V Russell) *chsd ldrs tl outpcd fr bef 3 out: no imp whn lft 4th last* **9/1**	84+
2U31	**5**	18	**Turbo (IRE)**[18] 4039 7-11-0 **113**..(t) MrTGreenall(3) (M W Easterby) *hld up: rdn bef 3 out: sn btn* **9/4**[1]	77
4325	**6**	1 3/4	**Carapuce (FR)**[56] 3384 7-11-12 **122**.. TonyDobbin (L Lungo) *keen: chsd ldrs: rdn after 4 out: wknd bef next* **8/1**	84
2-3P	**P**		**Greenfield (IRE)**[75] 2974 8-11-7 **117**.................................(b) RussGarritty (R T Phillips) *prom tl wknd 5th: t.o whn p.u bef 3 out* **10/1**	—
5041	**P**		**Front Rank (IRE)**[31] 3797 6-11-5 **115**........................... RichardMcGrath (Mrs Dianne Sayer) *cl up tl wknd after 4 out: t.o whn p.u bef 2 out* **20/1**	—
-10B	**F**		**Muckle Flugga (IRE)**[67] 3234 7-9-11 **100**.......................... ScottMarshall(7) (N G Richards) *hld up: hdwy and cl up 4 out: rdn and no ex next: 12l 3rd whn fell last* **20/1**	96+

5m 27.7s (15.00) **Going Correction** +0.825s/f (Soft) **9** Ran SP% **113.8**
Speed ratings: **103,101,99,94,87 86,—,—,—** CSF £19.17 CT £444.38 TOTE £3.50: £2.60, £2.40, £6.30; EX 22.70.
Owner D A Johnson **Bred** Gestut Ittlingen **Trained** Rosewell, Midlothian

FOCUS
The favourite disappointed but still a fair effort from First Look, who had the run of the race, is value for twice the official margin, and appeals as the type to win again.

NOTEBOOK
First Look(FR) ◆ turned in his best effort upped to this trip for the first time and looked value for a bit more than the winning margin suggests. He is only lightly raced in this sphere and appeals as the type to win more races. *(op 7-2 tchd 4-1)*
Aston Lad, who was a bit disappointing over two miles and six at this course on his previous start, fared better this time and, although both his wins have been over two and a half miles, he looks worth another try over further. *(op 7-1)*
Crackleando had the run of the race and ran creditably but his overall record since his sole win over hurdles a year ago means he is not really one to place maximum faith in.
Time To Roam(IRE)'s form over hurdles for this stable has been very patchy and, although not *disgraced with the cheekpieces on again back up in trip, is not one to be placing much faith in. (op 7-1 tchd 10-1)*
Turbo(IRE), a quirky sort who broke a losing run and notched his first win over hurdles on his third start for this yard last time, found precious little for pressure over this longer trip and he remains one to tread carefully with. *(op 11-4)*
Carapuce(FR) is essentially a disappointing type who raced too freely to give himself much chance of lasting home. Although much better than this, he is another from this race to tread carefully with.
Muckle Flugga(IRE) looked held but nevertheless was in the process of running creditably on ground that may have been plenty soft enough when coming to grief. She will be of more interest back over three miles on a sound surface. *(op 16-1)*

4365 AYRSHIRE POST H'CAP CHASE (FOR THE HUGH BARCLAY CHALLENGE TROPHY) (10 fncs 2 omitted) 2m

5:05 (5:05) (Class 4) (0-105,103) 5-Y-0+ **£4,554** (£1,337; £668; £333)

Form				RPR
0232	**1**		**Polyphon (FR)**[86] 2842 8-11-12 **103**.............................. WilsonRenwick (P Monteith) *cl up: led 4 out: clr next: kpt on* **3/1**[2]	117+
034F	**2**	13	**Ton-Chee**[45] 3562 7-11-8 **99**... TonyDobbin (F P Murtagh) *prom: hdwy to chse wnr bef 3 out: one pce fr next* **4/1**[3]	105+
P-00	**3**	21	**General Cloney (IRE)**[24] 3929 10-10-8 **92**......................(b) MrATDuff(7) (S Donohoe, Ire) *chsd ldrs: outpcd bef 4 out: lft 4th next: no imp* **13/2**	72
4150	**4**	5	**Mexican (USA)**[32] 3788 7-10-13 **90**.................................(b) NeilMulholland (M D Hammond) *hld up in tch: hdwy and prom after 4 out: outpcd whn lft 3rd next: sn btn* **7/1**	65
32U2	**F**		**Albertino Lad**[12] 4142 9-11-0 **94**..................................... PeterBuchanan(3) (Miss Lucinda V Russell) *led: blnd bdly 6th: hdd next: 5l 3rd and outpcd whn fell 3 out: dead* **7/4**[1]	—

4m 22.4s (17.90) **Going Correction** +1.25s/f (Heav) **5** Ran SP% **107.2**
Speed ratings: **105,98,88,85,—** CSF £14.02 TOTE £3.60: £1.60, £1.70; EX 9.90.
Owner Mr & Mrs Raymond Anderson Green **Bred** A Levallois And Didier Marion **Trained** Rosewell, Midlothian

FOCUS
An ordinary handicap in which the pace seemed sound and the winner rated as value for eight lengths and to his mark.

NOTEBOOK
Polyphon(FR) has not always proved reliable but did more than enough to notch his third win from his last nine starts over fences. Whether this will be reproduced next time, remains to be seen, though. *(op 11-4 tchd 10-3, 7-2 in places)*
Ton-Chee travelled well for a long way but did not find as much as expected in these testing conditions. He does not have the best of strike-rates but will be of more interest in similar company on a sound surface. *(tchd 9-2)*
General Cloney(IRE), an inconsistent performer over fences, was again well beaten back over the *larger obstacles and his losing run of over six years means he is rarely one to be lumping on. (op 7-1)*
Mexican(USA), who beat the winner at Catterick in December, was soundly beaten for the third consecutive time since then. Better ground may suit but his inconsistency means he remains one to place little faith in. *(op 13-2 tchd 6-1)*
Albertino Lad, a consistent sort over fences, was in the process of running creditably when coming to grief but sadly had to be destroyed. *(op 2-1 tchd 9-4 in places)*

4366 SERENDIPITY INTERACTIVE STANDARD OPEN NATIONAL HUNT FLAT RACE 2m

5:35 (5:36) (Class 6) 4-6-Y-0 **£1,713** (£499; £249)

Form				RPR
1		**Gunner Jack** 5-11-4 .... TonyDobbin (N G Richards) *chsd ldrs: led 3f out: styd on wl* **2/1**[2]	99+
01	**2**	3	**Stolen Moments (FR)**[67] 3237 5-11-8 .... MrTGreenall(3) (P D Niven) *keen: in tch: effrt over 2f out: chsd wnr 1f out: one pce* **13/2**	100
33	**3**	4	**Classic Harry**[35] 3742 5-11-4 .... RussGarritty (P Beaumont) *set slow pce: hdd 3f out: one pce over 1f out* **6/1**[3]	90+
4	4	**Campli (IRE)** 4-10-10 .... NeilMulholland (M D Hammond) *hld up last: hdwy over 2f out: hung lft: no ex over 1f out* **12/1**	77
5	6	**Neutron (FR)** 5-11-4 .... WilsonRenwick (L Lungo) *prom: outpcd over 3f out: no imp after* **6/4**[1]	80+
6	2	**Askham Lad (IRE)** 5-10-13 .... TJDreaper(5) (M Todhunter) *in tch tl outpcd over 4f out: n.d after* **50/1**	77

4m 35.8s (36.60) **Going Correction** +0.825s/f (Soft)
WFA 4 from 5yo 7lb **6** Ran SP% **110.6**
Speed ratings: **41,39,37,35,32 31** CSF £14.62 TOTE £2.80: £1.80, £2.80; EX 8.10 Place 6 £205.38, Place 5 £164.35.
Owner Trevor Hemmings **Bred** Design And Planning Consultants Ltd **Trained** Greystoke, Cumbria

FOCUS
A couple of interesting newcomers on paper but a very slow pace means this bare form, rated around the placed horses, may not prove reliable.

NOTEBOOK

Gunner Jack ◆, the first foal of a winning hurdler/chaser and pointer, travelled strongly and created a favourable impression on this racecourse debut. He is in very good hands and, although this bare form may not be reliable, appeals strongly as the type to win more races. *(op 7-4 tchd 9-4)*

Stolen Moments(FR), a course and distance winner on his previous start, ran well under a penalty despite failing to settle and hanging under pressure. He may be vulnerable to the better sorts in this type of race but should continue to run well. *(op 6-1 tchd 7-1)*

Classic Harry was not disgraced, despite being allowed his own way in front, but he is likely to continue to look vulnerable in this type of event and will need a stiffer test than the one he got here when going over hurdles. *(op 7-1)*

Campli(IRE), related to winners on the Flat, took the eye in the preliminaries and was not disgraced on this racecourse debut, despite his apparent inexperience. Less testing ground and time will show him in a better light. *(op 8-1)*

Neutron(FR), reportedly well regarded by a yard that do well in this type of event, was well supported but proved a disappointment on this racecourse debut. However, it is far too soon to write him off yet. *(op 7-4)*

Askham Lad(IRE) was easy to back and was well beaten on this racecourse debut. A much stiffer test of stamina will suit when he goes over obstacles. *(op 33-1)*

T/Plt: £386.10 to a £1 stake. Pool: £47,156.50. 89.15 winning tickets. T/Qpdt: £98.50 to a £1 stake. Pool: £2,789.10. 20.95 winning tickets. RY

4101 CHEPSTOW (L-H)

Saturday, March 11

OFFICIAL GOING: Heavy

The third last hurdle was omitted.

Wind: Light, across. Weather: Fine

4367 GUINNESS DRAUGHT NOVICES' HURDLE (10 hdls 2 omitted) 3m

2:30 (2:30) (Class 4) 4-Y-0+ **£2,927** (£859; £429; £214)

Form	Pos	Dist	Horse	RPR
1	1		**Geeveem (IRE)**[66] 3238 6-11-9 **122** ChristianWilliams (P F Nicholls) *a.p: led 3 out: rdn clr appr last: styd on wl* **1/4**[1]	117+
43	2	6	**Clemax (IRE)**[21] 3984 5-10-10 PatrickMcDonald(7) (Ferdy Murphy) *hld up in mid-div: hdwy after 7th: chsd wnr fr 3 out: sn rdn: swtchd lft after 2 out: sn btn* **11/1**[2]	102
0354	3	13	**Blue Splash (FR)**[14] 4106 6-11-3 AntonyEvans (Evan Williams) *j.rt: led to 3rd: w ldr: led 7th to 3 out: sn hung lft and wknd* **14/1**[3]	94+
02PP	4	20	**Nagam (FR)**[21] 3978 5-11-3 JimCrowley (A Ennis) *w ldr: led 3rd to 7th: sn wknd* **18/1**	69
-5PP	5	17	**Drat**[20] 4016 7-11-3 **93** (b[1]) WayneHutchinson (R Mathew) *t.k.h: sn mid-div: wknd after 7th: fin lame* **100/1**	52
0	6	dist	**Projectfiveonefive**[23] 3948 7-11-3 RJGreene (Mrs S D Williams) *a bhd: lost tch fr 6th: t.o* **100/1**	—
06	7	18	**Palamedes**[14] 4106 7-11-3 VinceSlattery (B J Llewellyn) *a bhd: lost tch fr 6th: t.o* **100/1**	—
P0	P		**Redneck Girl (IRE)**[26] 3902 7-10-5 DerekLaverty(5) (A E Jones) *a bhd: lost tch 6th: t.o whn p.u bef 3 out* **80/1**	—
P06	F		**Financial Future**[51] 3463 6-11-3 SamStronge (C Roberts) *hld up in tch: wknd appr 3 out: no ch whn fell 2 out* **20/1**	—

6m 17.2s (0.40) **Going Correction** +0.05s/f (Yiel) **9** Ran SP% **109.2**

Speed ratings: **101,99,94,88,82** —,—,—,— CSF £3.07 TOTE £1.10: £1.02, £1.30, £2.20; EX 2.20.

Owner Paul Barber,Colin Lewis,Malcolm Calvert **Bred** James Barry **Trained** Ditcheat, Somerset

FOCUS

An uncompetitive event with the winner value for half as much again as the official margin, and the first two rated to their marks.

NOTEBOOK

Geeveem(IRE) had less to do than when scoring at Wincanton and made it look fairly straightforward. *(op 3-10 tchd 1-3 in a place)*

Clemax(IRE) was friendless in the market on this step up to three miles and eventually proved no match for the winner. *(op 6-1)*

Blue Splash(FR), returning to three miles, did not help his cause by jumping right-handed. *(op 12-1 tchd 16-1)*

Drat *Official explanation: trainer said gelding finished lame (tchd 150-1)*

4368 32RED.COM (S) H'CAP HURDLE (9 hdls 2 omitted) 2m 4f

3:05 (3:05) (Class 5) (0-90,90) 4-Y-0+ **£2,081** (£611; £305; £152)

Form	Pos	Dist	Horse	RPR
00-5	1		**Knockrigg (IRE)**[70] 3141 12-11-7 **87** DrPPritchard(5) (Dr P Pritchard) *hld up and bhd: gd hdwy appr 4th: led 2 out: r.o wl* **20/1**	90+
625F	2	3 ½	**Darko Karim**[21] 3985 4-11-6 **90** (b) JimCrowley (R J Hodges) *hld up towards rr: hdwy after 6th: sn rdn: ev ch 2 out: one pce* **10/1**	80+
0030	3	13	**John Jorrocks (FR)**[51] 3456 7-10-6 **67** (p) JodieMogford (J C Tuck) *led: rdn and hdd whn blnd 2 out: sn btn* **14/1**	57+
0003	4	1	**Too Posh To Share**[20] 4013 8-9-9 **66** RyanCummings(10) (D J Wintle) *t.k.h towards rr: hdwy 5th: wknd 2 out: 3rd and btn whn hit last* **4/1**[2]	51+
0P34	5	14	**Mickey Pearce (IRE)**[14] 4101 4-10-4 **79** (b[1]) StevenCrawford(5) (J G M O'Shea) *t.k.h: prom tl rdn and wknd appr 3 out* **5/1**[3]	40
6002	6	¾	**Purr**[22] 3956 5-9-13 **67** (p) MrSRees(7) (M Wigham) *prom tl wknd appr 3 out* **12/1**	36
0006	7	½	**Kaid (IRE)**[64] 3279 11-10-1 **69** MrTCollier(7) (R Lee) *prom tl wknd appr 3 out* **14/1**	37
64B6	8	3	**Little Villain (IRE)**[14] 4101 8-10-1 **62** (p) JamesDavies (T Wall) *prom tl wknd appr 3 out* **8/1**	27
P/-3	9	nk	**Redwood Grove (USA)**[25] 3905 10-11-7 **87** (t) LiamHeard(5) (Miss Tor Sturgis) *prom tl wknd 6th* **10/3**[1]	52
0U06	10	12	**Sir Walter (IRE)**[20] 4013 13-11-12 **87** RJGreene (D Burchell) *plld hrd early: a in rr* **25/1**	40
-00P	11	7	**Balloch**[13] 4129 5-10-7 **73** LiamTreadwell(5) (Mary Meek) *rdn after 6th: a bhd* **100/1**	19
2P4	P		**Gotontheluckyone (IRE)**[23] 3945 6-10-12 **80** KeiranBurke(7) (P R Rodford) *t.k.h: prom tl wknd 6th: t.o whn p.u bef last* **20/1**	—

5m 9.40s (6.70) **Going Correction** +0.05s/f (Yiel)

WFA 4 from 5yo+ 8lb **12** Ran SP% **115.3**

Speed ratings: **88,86,81,81,75 75,74,73,73,68 65**,— CSF £193.68 CT £2882.98 TOTE £24.80: £7.80, £3.40, £4.10; EX 199.90.There was no bid for the winner.

Owner Timber Pond Racing Club **Bred** Thomas McParland **Trained** Purton, Gloucs

FOCUS

A poor seller and a slow time, even for a race like this, with the placed horses achieving personal bests.

NOTEBOOK

Knockrigg(IRE), whose last victory came over fences five years ago, found the combination of two and a half miles and testing ground to his liking. *(op 14-1)*

Darko Karim had no excuses with ground conditions in his favour. *(op 8-1)*

John Jorrocks(FR), without the visor this time, was being strongly pressed when a bad mistake at the penultimate hurdle proved the final nail in the coffin.

Too Posh To Share needs to settle better if she is going to be effective at this sort of trip. *(op 11-2)*

Redwood Grove(USA) was very disappointing and his trainer could offer no explanation. *Official explanation: trainer had no explanation for the poor form shown (op 11-4 tchd 7-2)*

4369 32REDPOKER.COM BEGINNERS' CHASE (18 fncs) 3m

3:40 (3:40) (Class 4) 5-Y-0+ **£3,809** (£1,162; £607; £329)

Form	Pos	Dist	Horse	RPR
-PP5	1		**Beauchamp Prince (IRE)**[22] 3955 5-10-8 **108** RJGreene (M Scudamore) *a.p: mstke 2nd: led 4 out: clr fr 3 out: unchal* **12/1**[3]	105+
P/	2	14	**Royal Scandal**[309] 10-11-1 RichardYoung(3) (C J Down) *t.k.h: j.rt: led tl after 2nd: led 4th to 4 out: sn btn* **9/2**[2]	100
1/23	3	30	**Supreme Toss (IRE)**[20] 4016 10-11-4 **125** WarrenMarston (R T Phillips) *nt fluent: led after 2nd to 4th: rdn 11th: wknd appr 4 out* **2/5**[1]	80+
P-5P	4	dist	**Uncle Ada (IRE)**[113] 2313 11-11-4 **70** VinceSlattery (D J Minty) *mstke 2nd: bhd fr 7th: t.o* **100/1**	—
45/	P		**Opal Ridge**[737] 4146 9-11-4 SamStronge (C Roberts) *t.k.h in tch: wknd appr 5 out: bhd whn p.u bef 2 out: b.b.v* **20/1**	—
0	P		**Rioja Rally (IRE)**[49] 3500 6-10-11 SeanQuinlan(7) (R T Phillips) *hld up in rr: mstkes 9th and 13th: sn struggling: t.o whn p.u bef 3 out* **25/1**	—

6m 40.4s (25.50) **Going Correction** +0.275s/f (Yiel)

WFA 5 from 6yo+ 10lb **6** Ran SP% **106.9**

Speed ratings: **68,63,53**,—,— — CSF £54.31 TOTE £13.30: £2.60, £2.20; EX 57.80.

Owner The Yes - No - Wait Sorries **Bred** A W Buller **Trained** Bromsash, Herefordshire

FOCUS

A weak affair with the odds-on favourite let down by his jumping. The winning time was pedestrian but the first two were close to their marks.

NOTEBOOK

Beauchamp Prince(IRE), a fair juvenile hurdler on this sort of ground, jumped better this time but did not have much to beat. *(tchd 14-1)*

Royal Scandal had not been seen since winning a point in Ireland in heavy ground last May. Supported in the ring, this 9,500 gns purchase proved no match for the winner after jumping a shade right-handed. *(op 10-1)*

Supreme Toss(IRE) was again sluggish over several fences and the writing was on the wall early in the long home straight. *Official explanation: jockey said gelding was never travelling (op 2-7)*

Opal Ridge *Official explanation: jockey said gelding had bled from the nose (op 10-1)*

4370 32RED ONLINE CASINO H'CAP CHASE (22 fncs) 3m 2f 110y

4:15 (4:15) (Class 4) (0-100,93) 5-Y-0+ **£3,903** (£1,146; £573; £286)

Form	Pos	Dist	Horse	RPR
-655	1		**River Of Light (IRE)**[54] 3427 6-10-11 **83** DarylJacob(5) (D P Keane) *hld up: hdwy 15th: led appr 3 out: rdn and hdd last: led flat: drvn out* **17/2**	102+
0545	2	1 ¾	**Auburn Spirit**[21] 3989 11-11-12 **93** (b[1]) DaveCrosse (M D I Usher) *a.p: rdn 4 out: led last: hdd and no ex flat* **10/1**	110+
6303	3	10	**Southerndown (IRE)**[40] 3654 13-10-10 **80** WilliamKennedy(3) (R Lee) *hld up in tch: rdn and outpcd 5 out: styd on flat* **9/1**	85
-050	4	1 ¼	**Dante's Back (IRE)**[27] 3888 8-11-11 **92** AntonyEvans (N A Twiston-Davies) *hld up: mstke 13th: hdwy after 17th: wknd 2 out* **8/1**	96
2014	5	½	**Ebony Jack (IRE)**[12] 4152 9-11-6 **87** (p) JoeTizzard (C L Tizzard) *led: mstke 13th: hdd appr 3 out: wknd 2 out* **3/1**[1]	90
3414	6	dist	**Rosetown (IRE)**[39] 3662 8-11-2 **83** (b) JasonMaguire (T R George) *prom: ev ch whn mstke 4 out: wknd appr 2 out: eased whn no ch flat: t.o* **7/2**[2]	—
0063	P		**Paddy The Optimist (IRE)**[27] 3886 10-10-7 **79** LiamHeard(5) (D Burchell) *hld up in tch: lost pl and hit 16th: t.o whn p.u bef 3 out* **4/1**[3]	—
/U55	P		**Mcsnappy**[12] 4152 9-10-13 **87** WayneKavanagh(7) (J W Mullins) *hld up and bhd: rdn 12th: sn struggling: t.o whn p.u bef 16th: b.b.v* **25/1**	—

7m 22.1s (5.00) **Going Correction** +0.275s/f (Yiel) **8** Ran SP% **111.8**

Speed ratings: **103,102,99,99,99** —,—,— CSF £80.85 CT £773.79 TOTE £9.80: £2.10, £3.20, £2.30; EX 103.90.

Owner Wincanton Race Club **Bred** Mrs Jane Roche **Trained** North End, Dorset

FOCUS

The emphasis was on stamina in this modest handicap with the third and fourth setting the standard.

NOTEBOOK

River Of Light(IRE), the least exposed in the field, justified support in the ring with a game victory. *Official explanation: trainer said, regarding the improved form shown, gelding had benefited from being sent chasing and had acted well round Chepstow (op 10-1 tchd 11-1)*

Auburn Spirit, who has tumbled down the ratings, bounced back to form in the first-time blinkers. He seemed set to score when touching down ahead at the last but the weight concession proved too much. *(op 9-1)*

Southerndown(IRE) has yet to win on ground this soft but it helped that it put the emphasis on stamina. *(op 7-1)*

Dante's Back(IRE), back up in distance, had never previously encountered conditions this demanding. *(op 9-1 tchd 11-1)*

Ebony Jack(IRE) was 6lb higher than when successful over this trip at Fontwell last month. *(tchd 7-2)*

Mcsnappy *Official explanation: jockey said gelding had bled from the nose (op 18-1)*

4371 GUINNESS BREWED IN DUBLIN H'CAP CHASE (16 fncs) 2m 3f 110y

4:50 (4:50) (Class 3) (0-125,124) 5-Y-0+ **£6,320** (£1,907; £982; £520)

Form	Pos	Dist	Horse	RPR
-521	1		**Nycteos (FR)**[14] 4102 5-11-7 **124** LiamHeard(5) (P F Nicholls) *hld up: hdwy 6th: wnt 2nd 7th: hit 4 out: led after 3 out: rdn after 2 out: hung rt and hdd towards fin: sn led again: r.o* **4/5**[1]	133+
0521	2	1	**Launde (IRE)**[24] 3920 7-11-9 **115** AndrewThornton (B N Pollock) *led: hdd after 3 out: rallied to ld briefly towards fin: no ex* **7/2**[2]	125
2425	3	25	**Macmar (FR)**[53] 3440 6-11-0 **111** DarylJacob(5) (R H Alner) *hld up: sn bhd: hdwy appr 6th: rdn 9th: mstke 11th: wknd 5 out* **14/1**	96
21P5	4	9	**Walcot Lad (IRE)**[14] 4120 10-10-2 **97** (p) ColinBolger(3) (A Ennis) *chsd ldr: hit 3rd: lost 2nd 6th: wknd 8th* **20/1**	73
5023	P		**Key Phil (FR)**[18] 4037 8-11-10 **116** WarrenMarston (D J Wintle) *sn prom: wknd 8th: t.o whn p.u bef 2 out* **5/1**[3]	—

5m 13.7s (2.40) **Going Correction** +0.275s/f (Yiel)

WFA 5 from 6yo+ 4lb **5** Ran SP% **105.9**

Speed ratings: **106,105,95,92**,— CSF £3.79 TOTE £1.70: £1.10, £2.50; EX 3.90.

Owner The Stewart Family **Bred** C Lacorie **Trained** Ditcheat, Somerset

FOCUS

A poor turnout for some reasonable prizemoney with the winner value for more than the official margin.

NOTEBOOK

Nycteos(FR) managed to pull out more after he appeared to try and throw it away on the run-in. *(op 5-6 tchd 10-11)*

Launde(IRE) could not quite take full advantage of the winner's antics in the closing stages. *(tchd 10-3)*

Macmar(FR) was reported to have been unsuited by the course when disappointing in a visor last time. *(tchd 12-1 and 16-1)*

4372 PLAY CASINO GAMES AT 32RED H'CAP HURDLE (10 hdls 2 omitted) 3m

5:25 (5:26) (Class 4) (0-115,115) 4-Y-0+ **£3,253** (£955; £477; £238)

Form				RPR
6/30	**1**		**Carew Lad**[27] [3882] 10-11-2 **105**........ ChristianWilliams (Mrs D A Hamer) *mde all: clr 2 out: comf* **40/1**	112+
P11	**2**	*3 ½*	**Desert Tommy**[20] [4012] 5-11-7 **115**........ MrNWilliams(5) (Evan Williams) *a chsng wnr: pckd 3 out: sn rdn: no imp whn hit last* **13/2**[3]	120+
-114	**3**	*3*	**Passenger Omar (IRE)**[14] [4105] 8-11-5 **111**........(t) WilliamKennedy(3) (Noel T Chance) *prom: lost pl and rdn after 4th: styd on fr 2 out* **10/1**	109
P23P	**4**	*½*	**Kingsbay**[44] [3581] 7-11-2 **105**........ JimCrowley (H Morrison) *a.p: rdn 6th: one pce fr 2 out* **16/1**	102
1323	**5**	*1 ¾*	**The Gangerman (IRE)**[30] [3814] 6-11-1 **109**........ StevenCrawford(5) (N A Twiston-Davies) *hld up: bhd 4th: hdwy on ins after 7th: one pce fr 2 out* **10/3**[2]	104
0212	**6**	*24*	**Canavan (IRE)**[18] [4042] 7-9-8 **90**........(p) PatrickMcDonald(7) (Ferdy Murphy) *prom: rdn 6th: wknd after 7th* **7/4**[1]	61
041P	**7**	*3*	**Nero West (FR)**[53] [3441] 5-10-8 **102**........ DarylJacob(5) (Miss Lucy Bridges) *hld up and bhd: hdwy 6th: wknd 3 out* **50/1**	70
FU64	**8**	*28*	**Moscow Whisper (IRE)**[68] [3212] 9-11-0 **113**........ DarrenO'Dwyer(10) (P J Hobbs) *hld up in tch: rdn and wknd after 7th: t.o* **20/1**	53
-4P0	**9**	*dist*	**Star Angler (IRE)**[44] [3581] 8-11-8 **111**........ AndrewThornton (H D Daly) *hld up: rdn and hdwy 5th: wknd appr 3 out: t.o* **20/1**	—
0033	**P**		**Miss Fahrenheit (IRE)**[14] [4105] 7-11-1 **104** ow3........ SamStronge (C Roberts) *hld up towards rr: rdn 6th: t.o after 7th: p.u bef 2 out* **9/1**	—
-30P	**P**		**Easibrook Jane**[21] [3982] 8-11-7 **110**........(p) JoeTizzard (C L Tizzard) *hld up and bhd: rdn 7th: sn struggling: t.o whn p.u bef 3 out* **40/1**	—
01PP	**P**		**Biscar Two (IRE)**[17] [4046] 5-11-7 **115**........(p) DerekLaverty(5) (A E Jones) *hld up and bhd: hdwy 4th: sn rdn and lost pl: t.o 3 out: p.u bef last* **33/1**	—

6m 12.3s (-4.50) **Going Correction** +0.05s/f (Yiel) 12 Ran SP% **117.1**

Speed ratings: **109,107,106,106,106 98,97,87,—,— —,—** CSF £265.20 CT £2828.37 TOTE £54.10: £10.00, £2.10, £3.10; EX 302.40 Place 6 £1,052.22, Place 5 £993.05.

Owner Mrs Mandy Hinchliffe **Bred** Viscount Portman **Trained** Nantycaws, Carmarthens

FOCUS

An ordinary handicap with the first two rated better than the bare result but the third to fifth were all to their marks and the form should work out well enough.

NOTEBOOK

Carew Lad was suited by the longer distance on this switch to handicaps. *(op 33-1)*

Desert Tommy was trying to complete a hat-trick having gone up a total of 15lb. He always seemed to be fighting a losing battle after nodding on landing at the first in the straight. *(op 6-1 tchd 7-1)*

Passenger Omar(IRE) may only have won on sharp courses so far but again gave the impression he would be suited by somewhere like Towcester. *(op 7-1)*

Kingsbay was 13lb better off than when beaten two and a half lengths by Passenger Omar at Warwick on New Year's Eve. *(op 20-1 tchd 22-1)*

The Gangerman(IRE) was 13lb higher than when landing a similar contest here in December. *(op 7-2 tchd 4-1 and 3-1)*

Canavan(IRE) was struggling at the end of the back straight off a mark 12lb lower than his current chase rating. *(tchd 15-8)*

T/Plt: £818.20 to a £1 stake. Pool: £47,638.00. 42.50 winning tickets. T/Qpdt: £72.90 to a £1 stake. Pool: £3,075.50. 31.20 winning tickets. KH

4354 SANDOWN (R-H)

Saturday, March 11

OFFICIAL GOING: Soft (heavy in places on hurdle course; good to soft in places on chase course)

Wind: Virtually nil

4373 EUROPEAN BREEDERS FUND SUNDERLANDS "NATIONAL HUNT" NOVICES' H'CAP HURDLE FINAL GRADE 3 (9 hdls) 2m 4f 110y

2:10 (2:12) (Class 1) 4-7-Y-0

£34,212 (£12,834; £6,426; £3,204; £1,608; £804)

Form				RPR
F13	**1**		**Killaghy Castle (IRE)**[74] [3023] 6-11-7 **120**........ LeightonAspell (N J Gifford) *t.k.h early: hld up: hdwy to trck ldrs 4th: chal 2 out: sn led: nt fluent last and hung lft run-in: styd on wl* **15/2**[3]	132+
-042	**2**	*3*	**Sharajan (IRE)**[27] [3882] 6-11-7 **120**........ RobertThornton (A King) *chsd ldrs: rdn appr 2 out: styd on wl u.p run-in to take 2nd cl home but no imp on wnr* **20/1**	125+
-421	**3**	*¾*	**Yaboya (IRE)**[38] [3677] 7-11-9 **122**........ RichardJohnson (P J Hobbs) *lw: behind: hdwy 3 out: rdn to chse ldrs 2 out: kpt on u.p run-in: gng on cl home* **9/1**	128+
-212	**4**	*½*	**Snakebite (IRE)**[21] [3978] 6-11-7 **120**........ PaulMoloney (M Pitman) *mde most tl chal 2 out and sn hdd: kpt on u.p: one pce and lost 2nd cl home* **20/1**	124
-212	**5**	*1*	**Wogan**[15] [4094] 6-11-6 **119**........ MickFitzgerald (N J Henderson) *mid-div: hdwy 3 out: rdn wl bef 2 out: kpt on u.p run-in but nvr gng pce to rch ldrs* **7/1**[2]	123+
-233	**6**	*hd*	**Hibernian (IRE)**[29] [3842] 6-10-10 **109**........ GrahamLee (O Sherwood) *lw: bhd: hdwy 4 out: chsd ldrs after 3 out: sn rdn: kpt on run-in but nt a danger* **12/1**	113+
0046	**7**	*11*	**Nice Horse (FR)**[35] [3729] 5-10-11 **110**........ TimmyMurphy (M C Pipe) *bhd: hdwy 3 out: hdwy and styd far side appr 2 out: kpt on run-in but nvr gng pce to rch ldrs* **14/1**	102
3102	**8**	*1 ½*	**Youlbesolucky (IRE)**[14] [4119] 7-11-7 **120**........ BrianHarding (Jonjo O'Neill) *chsd ldrs: rdn wl bef 2 out: sn btn* **40/1**	111
0533	**9**	*shd*	**Portland Bill (IRE)**[14] [4106] 6-10-9 **108**........ TomScudamore (R H Alner) *chsd ldrs: rdn appr 2 out: sn wknd: no ch whn hit last* **33/1**	99+
5221	**10**	*2*	**Principe Azzurro (FR)**[15] [4094] 5-11-2 **115**........ MarkBradburne (H D Daly) *chsd ldrs: rdn bef 2 out: sn wknd: no ch whn hit last* **10/1**	104+
2-U3	**11**	*12*	**Easter Present (IRE)**[57] [3369] 7-10-7 **106**........ SamThomas (Miss H C Knight) *mid-div: mstke and rr 4th: hdwy after 3 out: nvr gng pce to trble ldrs: sn wknd* **33/1**	82
-311	**12**	*dist*	**Bougoure (IRE)**[32] [3789] 7-11-12 **125**........ DominicElsworth (Mrs S J Smith) *lw: chsd ldrs: chal 3 out tl stay far side bnd appr 2 out and sn wknd: t.o* **10/1**	—
6241	**13**	*19*	**Billyandi (IRE)**[16] [4067] 6-10-8 **107**........ CarlLlewellyn (N A Twiston-Davies) *pressed ldr tl after 3 out: wknd bef next: t.o* **14/1**	—
2114	**P**		**Tokala**[7] [4242] 5-11-9 **122**........ APMcCoy (B G Powell) *lw: bhd tl p.u bef 4th: broke leg: dead* **9/2**[1]	—
/202	**P**		**French Envoy (FR)**[32] [3789] 7-11-2 **115**........ PJBrennan (Ian Williams) *prom early: bhd fr 6th: t.o whn p.u bef 2 out* **25/1**	—
P013	**P**		**Top Brass (IRE)**[8] [4210] 5-9-4 **99**........ JamesReveley(10) (K G Reveley) *chsd ldrs tl pushed wd and wknd bnd after 3 out: t.o whn p.u bef next* **20/1**	—
-164	**P**		**Dunsfold Duke**[21] [3978] 6-11-1 **117**........ TomMalone(3) (P Winkworth) *bhd: hit 1st: j. slowly 2nd: sme hdwy and pushed wd bnd after 3 out: sn wknd: p.u bef next* **50/1**	—

5m 7.67s (-5.40) **Going Correction** -0.125s/f (Good) 17 Ran SP% **120.1**

Speed ratings: **105,103,103,103,103 102,98,98,98,97 92,—,—,—,— —,—** CSF £150.25 CT £1379.52 TOTE £8.40: £2.00, £4.70, £2.60, £3.80; EX 163.50 TRIFECTA Not won..

Owner Mrs S N J Embiricos **Bred** Gabriel White **Trained** Findon, W Sussex

■ Stewards' Enquiry : Leighton Aspell caution: used whip in an incorrect place

FOCUS

Not the highest quality renewal of this race, with the top-weight Bougoure rated just 125, but a race to be positive about nevertheless. There were plenty of potential chasers on show, and imppressive winner Killaghy Castle looks a particularly bright prospect. The race has been rated around the fifth and sixth, with the first four all showing improved form.

NOTEBOOK

Killaghy Castle(IRE) ◆, whose disappointment at Chepstow in December was put down to a splint problem, appeared to hold obvious claims on this handicap debut and, despite his trainer's recent barren spell, proved far too good off a mark of 120. Having travelled up smoothly, he took it up after the second-last and began to come clear, staying on well up the hill despite edging out to his left under pressure. He was probably value for around five lengths and this embyonic chaser looks to have a bright future, with next season's Royal & SunAlliance Chase reportedly the long-term aim. *(op 9-1)*

Sharajan(IRE) has been progressing with experience, but he still came into this without a win to his name and so his hard-fought second was a very decent effort. He will stay further in time, but is fully effective at this distance and can find an ordinary novice.

Yaboya(IRE) made hard enough work of winning at Leicester last time, but he gives the impression he is the sort who is never going to win by far and he too recorded a fine effort in third, keeping on up the hill without proving a match for the winner. Three miles over fences is going to suit in the long term, but he can win races over this distance if ridden more positively. *(op 8-1)*

Snakebite(IRE), beaten by Killaghy Castle at Folkestone earlier in the season, was entitled to go well again at the weights and he did just that, leading for most of the way and keeping on once headed. He is a three-mile chaser in the making, but can probably find another novice event this term.

Wogan looked in trouble a long way from home, being niggled to hold his position, but he did respond to Fitzgerald's urgings and began to make headway before two out. In the end he could only plod on, seeming to find this an inadequate test, but he is an attractive gelding and connections should have little trouble finding him another winning opportunity before going chasing next season. *(tchd 13-2 and 15-2)*

Hibernian(IRE) remains winless in six attempts, but he shaped with significant promise on this handicap debut and looked to be going particularly well on the long run to the second last. In the final quarter-mile he just lacked the speed of his rivals, but he is a scopey gelding and will find easier opportunities. His long-term future looks to be over fences.

Nice Horse(FR) was going on at the end of his race, but is not progressing and remains winless over hurdles.

Portland Bill(IRE), a future staying-chaser, found things happening a little too quickly on what was only the fifth start of his career. *(op 40-1)*

Principe Azzurro(FR), who beat Wogan at Warwick last time, looked one of the more likely winners, with his stable in good form, but he offered little once coming under pressure and dropped away disappointingly.

Bougoure(IRE), bidding for a hat-trick following two wins at lesser tracks, faced no easy task under top weight and, having been taken to race up the far rail he stopped quickly once coming under pressure. He is better than this, but now has a bit to prove. *(tchd 11-1)*

Dunsfold Duke was again below form, but is a chaser in the making. *(tchd 5-1)*

Tokala, well supported throughout the morning, was pulled up at an early stage. It transpired he had broken a leg. *(tchd 5-1)*

4374 SUNDERLANDS BOOKMAKERS H'CAP CHASE (22 fncs) 3m 110y

2:45 (2:47) (Class 3) (0-135,128) 5-Y-0+ **£7,807** (£2,292; £1,146; £572)

Form				RPR
16-P	**1**		**Eric's Charm (FR)**[23] [3942] 8-11-12 **128**........ LeightonAspell (O Sherwood) *lw: trckd ldr: slt advantage whn lft in ld 13th: sn clr and nvr in danger after: easily* **12/1**	150+
PPF2	**2**	*21*	**Supreme Catch (IRE)**[16] [4078] 9-10-5 **114**........ MrTJO'Brien(7) (Miss H C Knight) *mid-div: blnd 12th: hdwy 4 out: chsd wnr after 3 out: kpt on but no ch* **5/1**[1]	114+
P2P4	**3**	*6*	**Tana River (IRE)**[21] [3993] 10-11-11 **127**........ BarryFenton (Miss E C Lavelle) *chsd ldrs: wnt 2nd 4 out but nvr nr ultimate wnr: lost 2nd after 3 out and one pce* **8/1**	120
-46P	**4**	*nk*	**Supreme Developer (IRE)**[87] [2828] 9-11-11 **127**........ KeithMercer (Ferdy Murphy) *bhd: mstke 13th: sme hdwy whn blnd 19th: kpt on fr 3 out but nvr in contention* **20/1**	122+
31P5	**5**	*4*	**Willie John Daly (IRE)**[15] [4098] 9-11-12 **128**........ RichardJohnson (P J Hobbs) *rr: mstke 2nd and 8th: rdn after 4 out: kpt on fr 3 out: styd on run-in but nvr in contention* **15/2**[3]	117
-4PP	**6**	*shd*	**Indalo (IRE)**[27] [3877] 11-11-4 **123**........ PaulO'Neill(3) (Miss Venetia Williams) *chsd ldrs: blnd 4 out and sn wknd* **12/1**	114+
/1P-	**7**	*20*	**Elenas River (IRE)**[622] [828] 10-10-13 **115**........ PJBrennan (P J Hobbs) *nt fluent chsd ldrs: hit 12th and 18th: blnd next: wknd bef 3 out* **20/1**	84
3310	**8**	*3 ½*	**Latimer's Place**[63] [3296] 10-11-10 **126**........ JimmyMcCarthy (J A Geake) *bhd: hdwy to chse ldrs fr 18th: wknd after 3 out: no ch whn hit last* **7/1**[2]	91
001P	**9**	*hd*	**Migwell (FR)**[23] [3942] 6-11-5 **121**........ JohnMcNamara (Mrs L Wadham) *in tch: rdn 18th: wknd 4 out* **16/1**	86
0-FU	**10**	*9*	**Celioso (IRE)**[45] [3560] 9-10-12 **114**........ DominicElsworth (Mrs S J Smith) *sn wl bhd: hit 6th: blnd 15th* **12/1**	70
0-0P	**P**		**Be My Royal (IRE)**[27] [3877] 12-11-4 **120**........ PhilipHide (R H Alner) *p.u bef 2nd* **33/1**	—

The Form Book, Raceform Ltd, Compton, RG20 6NL

41F3 **P** **Mount Clerigo (IRE)**[60] 3331 8-11-12 **128** .... AndrewThornton —
(V R A Dartnall) *lw: a in rr: t.o whn p.u bef 3 out* **5/1**[1]

-PUP **U** **Bathwick Annie**[14] 4111 10-11-7 **123** ....(b[1]) TimmyMurphy —
(B G Powell) *led: narrowly hdd whn mstke and uns rdr 13th* **20/1**

6m 21.87s (-9.63) **Going Correction** +0.075s/f (Yiel) **13** Ran SP% **114.9**
Speed ratings: **118,111,109,109,107 107,101,100,100,97** —,—,— CSF £66.04 CT £515.08 TOTE £13.40: £4.40, £2.20, £3.10; EX 91.70 Trifecta £656.70 Part won. Pool: £925.02 - 0.20 winning tickets..

Owner M St Quinton & P Deal **Bred** Dominique Faugeras **Trained** Upper Lambourn, Berks

FOCUS

A fast gallop thanks to Bathwick Annie, and nothing could get anywhere near the strong-galloping Eric's Charm, who had pressed her from the start. Although the form overall looks a bit shakey, with question marks over many of the runners beforehand, this still looks a career-best effort from the winner.

NOTEBOOK

Eric's Charm(FR), showed himself to be quite capable over fences last season without reaching his old hurdles level, but he jumped moderately and offered little encouragement on his belated return at Huntingdon. It looked tough for him here with joint top-weight of 11st12lb, but Aspell gave him a peach of a ride and soon had him in a good rhythm, jumping superbly. Left clear when Bathwick Annie came down at the 13th, he galloped on resolutely and extended his advantage to win by a handsome margin. On hurdles form he would be capable of performing off a higher mark and the Betfred Gold Cup back here in April looks the obvious target for the 8yo, who must go *right-handed. Official explanation: trainer said, regarding the improved form shown, gelding had jumped poorly on previous run, its first for 11 months (op 11-1)*

Supreme Catch(IRE) has finally found his form again and he stayed on well in the straight for second. He was racing off a favourable mark here and can find a small race if able to repeat the effort. *(op 11-2)*

Tana River(IRE) has never convinced as a three-miler, but had to be respected on this return to fences. He travelled strongly, as was to be expected, but began to struggle taking the Pond Fence and was outstayed by Supreme Catch for second.

Supreme Developer(IRE) ◆ was one of the more interesting contenders if he could refind his best form and, despite the ground not being in his favour, he kept on nicely from the rear to just miss out on third. His time of year is apporaching, and he has a nice prize in him on a sound surface, possibly at Aintree.

Willie John Daly(IRE) has not quite looked the same horse since his bizarre win here in December, the blinkers failing to help last time. He could only plod on from the rear. *(op 7-1 tchd 8-1)*

Indalo(IRE) is back down to a fair mark and ran well for quite a way, but a blunder at the fourth-last was enough to halt him. *(op 14-1 tchd 16-1)*

Elenas River(IRE) ◆ did not look at his very best beforehand and was ultimately well beaten, but some sloppy jumps didn't help and he ran well for a long way. He may be one to watch out for next time. *(op 16-1)*

Latimer's Place ought to have run much better. *(op 8-1 tchd 13-2)*

Be My Royal(IRE) *Official explanation: jockey said gelding was lame (op 9-2 tchd 4-1)*

Bathwick Annie gave the winner a nice tow and was still going reasonably well herself in the first-time blinkers when unseating at the 13th. *(op 9-2 tchd 4-1)*

Mount Clerigo(IRE) has not gone on from a winning debut over fences and failed to shine on this *handicap debut, being unable to handle the fast tempo. His stable have had a disappointing year. Official explanation: trainer said gelding was unsuited by the soft, good to soft in places ground (op 9-2 tchd 4-1)*

4375 SUNDERLANDS IMPERIAL CUP H'CAP HURDLE (LISTED RACE) (8 hdls) 2m 110y

3:20 (3:24) (Class 1) (0-150,137) 4-Y-0+

£34,212 (£12,834; £6,426; £3,204; £1,608; £804)

Form RPR

0-3P **1** **Victram (IRE)**[55] 3411 6-9-12 **114** .... AELynch[(5)] 121+
(Adrian McGuinness, Ire) *hld up in rr: hit 4 out: hdwy on bit to trck ldrs and hit 2 out: slt ld and hit last: rdn run-in: hld on all out* **8/1**

2-00 **2** *nk* **Dusky Warbler**[49] 3502 7-11-10 **135** ....(p) JamieMoore 141
(G L Moore) *bhd: hdwy appr 2 out: hrd drvn appr last: styd on u.p run-in: gng on cl home* **20/1**

0110 **3** *½* **Verasi**[63] 3298 5-11-7 **132** ....(b) PhilipHide 138
(G L Moore) *lw: rdn and lost position 4 out: kpt on again after 2 out: fin wl: gng on cl home* **33/1**

0-22 **4** *1 ¼* **Lunar Crystal (IRE)**[15] 4091 8-11-2 **127** .... TomScudamore 131
(M C Pipe) *w ldr: led 4th: rdn appr 2 out: hdd last: styd on wl u.p run-in* **20/1**

311 **5** *1 ¼* **Tarlac (GER)**[15] 4091 5-10-12 **123** .... APMcCoy 127+
(N J Henderson) *trckd ldrs: wnt 2nd and rdn 2 out: one pce u.p run-in* **9/2**[1]

36-4 **6** *3 ½* **Monte Cinto (FR)**[15] 4097 6-11-0 **125** .... RWalsh 125
(P F Nicholls) *hld up in rr: hdwy appr 2 out: kpt on run-in but nvr gng pce to rch ldrs* **20/1**

P460 **7** *shd* **Cloudy Grey (IRE)**[63] 3298 9-11-8 **133** .... BarryFenton 132
(Miss E C Lavelle) *hld up in rr: hdwy 2 out: kpt on run-in but nvr gng pce to rch ldrs* **50/1**

11-1 **8** *¾* **United (GER)**[317] 88 5-11-12 **137** .... LeightonAspell 136
(Mrs L Wadham) *bit bkwd: hld up in rr: hdwy and hit 4 out: chsd ldrs and styd far side appr 2 out: one pce* **16/1**

1611 **9** *4* **Gods Token**[15] 4097 8-11-5 **130** .... SamThomas 126+
(Miss Venetia Williams) *led to 4th: rdn 3 out: wknd after 2 out* **14/1**

1312 **10** *3 ½* **Alph**[35] 3725 9-11-10 **135** .... MatthewBatchelor 126
(B R Johnson) *lw: trckd ldrs: rdn 2 out: wknd sn after* **33/1**

10-P **11** *3 ½* **Distant Prospect (IRE)**[21] 3993 9-11-3 **128** .... MarkBradburne 117+
(A M Balding) *chsd ldrs: rdn appr 2 out: wknd sn after* **50/1**

205- **12** *¾* **Bongo Fury (FR)**[330] 4847 7-11-0 **132** ....(v) AndrewGlassonbury[(7)] 119
(M C Pipe) *chsd ldrs: rdn 3 out: wknd next* **33/1**

UF23 **13** *3* **Perle De Puce (FR)**[42] 3621 7-11-3 **135** .... MrSWaley-Cohen[(7)] 120+
(N J Henderson) *in tch: rdn 3 out: wknd next: no ch whn mstke last* **40/1**

-046 **14** *2* **Escrea (IRE)**[55] 3411 7-11-1 **131** .... RMMoran[(5)] 113
(Paul Nolan, Ire) *w'like: hit 2nd: a in rr* **20/1**

11-2 **15** *3* **Silencio (IRE)**[49] 3510 5-11-1 **126** .... RobertThornton 105
(A King) *nvr bttr than mid-div* **20/1**

3256 **16** *1 ¾* **Fenix (GER)**[21] 3986 7-10-8 **129** ....(b) MattyRoe[(10)] 106
(Mrs L Wadham) *bhd most of way* **25/1**

1013 **17** *3 ½* **Nous Voila (FR)**[21] 3986 5-11-12 **137** .... TimmyMurphy 111
(M C Pipe) *lw: mid-div: drvn and hdwy to chse ldrs after 3 out: wknd next* **5/1**[2]

-134 **18** *13* **Ballyjohnboy Lord (IRE)**[18] 4036 7-9-13 **117** .... JohnKington[(7)] 78
(M Scudamore) *chsd ldrs: hit 2nd: wknd 3 out* **50/1**

-511 **P** **Ursis (FR)**[42] 3615 5-11-8 **133** .... MickFitzgerald —
(Jonjo O'Neill) *prom to 4th: t.o whn p.u bef last* **13/2**[3]

1221 **P** **Euro American (GER)**[14] 4108 6-11-11 **136** .... AlanDempsey —
(E W Tuer) *sn bhd: t.o whn p.u bef 2 out* **25/1**

-0F2 **P** **Dont Call Me Derek**[14] 4110 5-11-3 **128** .... GrahamLee —
(J J Quinn) *nvr bttr than mid-div: t.o whn p.u bef 2 out* **14/1**

3m 59.57s (-8.60) **Going Correction** -0.125s/f (Good) **21** Ran SP% **127.2**
Speed ratings: 116,115,115,115,114 112,112,112,110,108 107,106,105,104,103 102,100,94,—,— — CSF £157.18 CT £4961.60 TOTE £10.30: £2.80, £4.60, £7.10, £4.10; EX 392.10 Trifecta £6750.20 Part won. Pool: £9,507.33 - 0.30 winning tickets..

Owner Pinheads Pizza Syndicate **Bred** Thomas Kevin **Trained** Lusk, Co Dublin

■ This was Adrian Lynch's first ride back after ten weeks out with a broken arm.

■ Stewards' Enquiry : Jamie Moore caution: used whip with excessive frequency

FOCUS

A good, if not vintage, renewal of this prestigious race, and it went the way of Irish raider Victram, who travelled well and found more than many expected under pressure. Rock solid handicap form.

NOTEBOOK

Victram(IRE) was entitled to go well on his William Hill third here back in December and had excuses for a recent flop in the Pierse Hurdle. Having travelled as strongly as ever, he came through to sit on the tails of the leaders approaching two out and a blunder there was not enough to halt his progress. Whereas in the William Hill he found nothing off the bridle, this time he just pulled out what was required under pressure from the last. He now reverts to the Flat for the Irish Lincolnshire, which he won last year, but will be very interesting if returning for Aintree, Ayr or Haydock, all tracks where his speed will be a bigger asset.

Dusky Warbler, a smart novice who placed in the Supreme Novices', has been a bitter disappointment since returning this season, but the first-time cheekpieces brought him back to life and he flew up the hill to just miss out, having been behind early. He has a nice race in him, but whether or not the County Hurdle will come too quickly is open to debate, as he had a harder race than the winner here. *(op 16-1)*

Verasi, 8lb higher than when taking the William Hill, was bidding for his third course and distance win of the season and had the blinkers back on (replacing cheekpieces). He came home strongly again, having lost his place leaving the back straight, but he couldn't quite get there in time and it seems he needs genuinely heavy ground. A personal best nevertheless. *(op 40-1)*

Lunar Crystal(IRE), who pushed the favourite for this, Tarlac, close at the course last time, was 3lb better off here, yet around four times the price. He was prominent throughout under Scudamore, but while he reversed placings with Tarlac and stuck on gamely, he was outpaced by the winner from the last. *(op 22-1)*

Tarlac(GER), up 8lb for his recent course win, has now started favourite on all four appearances in this country, but he had no excuse here and simply failed to see his race out as strongly as those *around him. He still has improvement in him, and will make a chaser in time. (tchd 5-1and 11-2 in a place)*

Monte Cinto(FR) seems to save his best for this course and distance these days and he was going on at the end of his race. He has not dropped much in the handicap and could probably do with some respite from the Handicapper.

Cloudy Grey(IRE), who ran a blinder in the William Hill back in December, was subject to a change in tactics this time and attempted to come from behind. He made good headway early in the straight, but was unable to go through with it and could only plug on at the one pace.

United(GER), winner of a suspect Grade One at Punchestown towards the end of last season, looked to face a stiff task on this belated reappearance, but she was noted making some late headway and actually performed better than many expected. She could go to Aintree before a return visit to Punchestown.

Gods Token went about his business in his usual fashion, but was always going to be vulnerable in the latter stages.

Alph, raised 18lb for finishing a shock second to Royal Sheakspeare in the Agfa, came through to have a chance turning in, but his big weight soon told. He is likely to continue to struggle.

Bongo Fury(FR) looked fit enough for her first start in 330 days and did not run badly.

Nous Voila(FR), nominated by Pipe as the best of his three, failed to run his race despite the good support beforehand. He stopped very quickly under pressure from quarter of a mile out and may have a problem. *(op 7-1)*

Ursis(FR), a progressive gelding bidding for a hat-trick, had a 10lb higher mark to contest with, but should still gave done an awful lot better. He clearly failed to run his race. *(op 6-1 tchd 7-1 in a place)*

4376 DONCASTER BLOODSTOCK SALES/EBF MARES' ONLY STANDARD OPEN NATIONAL HUNT FLAT RACE FINAL (LISTED RACE) 2m 110y

3:55 (3:59) (Class 1) 4-7-Y-0

£14,255 (£5,347; £2,677; £1,335; £670; £335)

Form RPR

21 **1** **Karello Bay**[17] 4059 5-11-4 .... MickFitzgerald 109
(N J Henderson) *w'like: lengthy: lw: in tch: hdwy and drvn 3 out: led ins fnl f: hld on all out* **5/1**[3]

21 **2** *nk* **Wyldello**[22] 3961 5-11-4 .... RobertThornton 109
(A King) *w'like: lw: mid-div: hdwy over 2f out: styd on strly u.p fnl f: fin wl: jst failed* **4/1**[1]

11 **3** *1 ¼* **Apollo Lady**[30] 3820 5-11-0 .... MrGTumelty[(7)] 111
(A King) *unf: lengthy: chsd ldrs: rdn over 2f out: swtchd rt appr fnl f and sn slt ld: hdd ins last: one pce* **25/1**

20-0 **4** *2 ½* **Hiho Silver Lining**[93] 2727 5-10-7 .... MrSWaley-Cohen[(7)] 101
(H Morrison) *w'like: leggy: chsd ldrs: rdn to go 2nd 3f out: no imp: styd on same pce fr over 1f out* **100/1**

1 **5** *2* **Scarvagh Diamond (IRE)**[52] 3448 5-10-11 .... MissRDavidson[(7)] 103
(Mrs R L Elliot) *w'like: cl cpld: lw: w ldrs early: styd prom: drvn along over 3f out: kpt on fnl f but nvr a danger* **33/1**

12 **6** *2 ½* **Saratogane (FR)**[109] 2425 4-10-10 .... TomScudamore 93
(M C Pipe) *narrow: unf: chsd ldrs: led 5f out: hrd rdn over 3f out: hdd appr fnl f: wknd ins last* **9/1**

1-12 **7** *5* **Knockara Luck (IRE)**[24] 3931 5-11-7 .... BrianHarding 99
(N G Richards) *bhd: hdwy 5f out: chsd ldrs over 3f out: sn wknd* **11/2**

1 **8** *1 ¼* **Sovietica (FR)**[131] 1961 5-11-4 .... RichardJohnson 95
(S Pike) *led after 3f: hdd 6f out: wknd fr 3f out* **33/1**

22 **9** *5* **Tambourine Davis (FR)**[22] 3961 4-10-6 .... OllieMcPhail 78
(N J Henderson) *bhd: hdwy 5f out: wknd u.p 3f out* **18/1**

-103 **10** *16* **Rosita Bay**[22] 3961 5-11-7 .... LeightonAspell 77
(O Sherwood) *bhd: sme hdwy 5f out: nvr rchd ldrs and sn wknd* **33/1**

44 **11** *3 ½* **Solent Sunbeam**[49] 3497 6-10-9 .... MarkNicolls[(5)] 66
(K C Bailey) *str: a in rr* **100/1**

613 **12** *10* **Senora Snoopy (IRE)**[52] 3448 5-11-4 .... KeithMercer 60
(Ferdy Murphy) *bhd: sme hdwy 5f out: sn wknd* **22/1**

1 **13** *½* **Larkbarrow**[49] 3497 5-11-4 .... CarlLlewellyn 60
(N A Twiston-Davies) *leggy: rr and reminders after 4f: nvr in contention* **25/1**

0-14 **14** *5* **Sparron Hawk (FR)**[24] 3931 6-11-4 .... GrahamLee 55
(N G Richards) *w'like: leggy: bhd most of way* **25/1**

15 *3* **Heron Marsh (IRE)**[48] 3524 5-11-1 .... PaulO'Neill[(3)] 52
(Miss Venetia Williams) *angular: unf: in tch: chsd ldrs 5f out: sn wknd* **9/2**[2]

5-22 **16** *2* **Cloudina**[49] 3497 5-11-0 .... TomDoyle 46
(P T Dalton) *swtg: in tch: rdn 5f out: sn wknd* **100/1**

516 **17** *17* **She's The Lady**[93] [2727] 6-11-4 .... JohnMcNamara 33
(R S Brookhouse) *sn led: hdd after 3f: led again 6f out: hdd 5f out: sn wknd* **66/1**

0-01 **18** *dist* **Lady Bling Bling**[93] [2727] 5-11-1 .... GinoCarenza(3) —
(P J Jones) *chsd ldrs 10f: t.o* **33/1**

4m 3.12s (-6.75) **Going Correction** -0.125s/f (Good)
WFA 4 from 5yo+ 7lb **18** Ran SP% **117.6**
Speed ratings: **111,110,110,109,108 106,104,104,101,94 92,87,87,85,83 82,74,**— CSF £20.67 TOTE £5.20: £2.40, £2.00, £5.80; EX 28.00 Trifecta £390.80 Pool: £1,045.90 - 1.90 winning tickets..

Owner Turf Club 2004 **Bred** R D And Mrs J S Chugg **Trained** Upper Lambourn, Berks

FOCUS
There were 14 previous winners on show, and it was close relatives Karello Bay and Wyldello who fought out the finish. The form has been rated through the second and fifth, with the winner, third and fourth all improving.

NOTEBOOK
Karello Bay, off the mark at Southwell last month, comes from a stable with a strong hand of bumper mares and it was no surprise to see her improve on previous efforts to land the valuable prize. She took her time to get on top, and was just holding on from Wyldello as they approached the line. It is now mission accomplished in terms of getting black-type, and this relative of Marello will now go over hurdles. She will stay further. *(op 9-2 tchd 11-2 in places)*
Wyldello, a relative of the winner and full-sister to Marello, came into this with similar credentials to Karello Bay and was arguably an unlucky loser, not getting going in time and just failing to get there. This was a fine effort and she is going to improve over further when she goes hurdling. In the longer term, she should make a nice chaser. *(op 7-2)*
Apollo Lady seemed a big price considering she came into this unbeaten in two attempts and had a decent claimer on board. She held a prominent position throughout and kept on well, without being able to repel the front two, suggesting further will help over hurdles.
Hiho Silver Lining showed improved form for a change of tactics and, although she has yet to win in four attempts, the daughter of Silver Patriarch should make a hurdler. *(op 80-1)*
Scarvagh Diamond(IRE), a winner on her debut at Newcastle, kept on well having raced prominently throughout. This half-sister to staying chaser Toulouse-Lautrec is going to improve for further over hurdles.
Saratogane(FR), one of only two four-year-olds in the line-up, ran a bold race and held a clear advantage in the straight, but she was unable to maintain the gallop. *(op 8-1)*
Knockara Luck(IRE) faced her stiffest task to date and did not seem up to it. *(op 13-2 tchd 7-1 in a place)*
Heron Marsh(IRE), a winner at Cork in Janaury, was unable to build on that effort and put up a pretty tame show. *(op 4-1 tchd 5-1 in places)*
She's The Lady *Official explanation: trainer said mare had a breathing problem (op 100-1)*
Lady Bling Bling *Official explanation: trainer said mare was in season*

4377 SUNDERLANDS BOOKMAKERS NOVICES' CHASE (FOR THE BURNT OAK AND SPECIAL CARGO CHALLENGE CUP) (13 fncs) 2m

4:25 (4:28) (Class 3) 5-Y-0+ **£6,506** (£1,910; £955; £477)

Form RPR
2152 **1** **Hoo La Baloo (FR)**[21] [3991] 5-11-5 147 .... RWalsh 143+
(P F Nicholls) *hld up in 3rd: hdwy 7th: qcknd to ld on ins after 3 out: clr whn edgd rt appr last: drvn out run-in* **4/11**[1]

F333 **2** *8* **Muhtenbar**[37] [3695] 6-11-0 122 .... PaulMoloney 130+
(Miss H C Knight) *t.k.h: trckd ldr: led after 3rd: hdd 9th: led again 3 out: hdd sn after: sn one pce and no ch w wnr* **8/1**[3]

-10F **3** *12* **Priors Dale**[69] [3183] 6-11-0 .... BarryFenton 120+
(Miss E C Lavelle) *led tl after 3rd: nt fluent 5th: led 9th: hdd 3 out: sn wknd: no ch whn mstke 2 out* **5/1**[2]

6 **4** *14* **Neptune Joly (FR)**[18] [4039] 5-10-9 .... KeithMercer 98
(Ferdy Murphy) *a last: blundered 7th (water): sn lost tch* **25/1**

4m 3.95s (2.10) **Going Correction** +0.075s/f (Yiel) **4** Ran SP% **104.9**
Speed ratings: **99,95,89,82** CSF £3.45 TOTE £1.30; EX 2.80.

Owner The Stewart Family **Bred** N P Bloodstock **Trained** Ditcheat, Somerset

FOCUS
A simple task for smart novice Hoo La Baloo, who recorded his second course win of the season. Not the most solid of form however.

NOTEBOOK
Hoo La Baloo(FR) had run well in good company since his Grade Two win over course and distance back in December. This course suits him well and in what was a weak race, he had little trouble returning to winning form. Though usually ridden prominently, he was held up with a view to going further next season, and he quickened up to stamp his authority after the Pond Fence. He is a smart novice and is now likely to head to Wincanton again before a trip to Punchestown, where he could go well. *(tchd 2-5 in places)*
Muhtenbar has displayed a decent level of ability over fences against smart opponents, despite not winning, but he proved no match for the winner here, being readily brushed aside. He will find a race before long. *(op 7-1)*
Priors Dale, still in with a chance when falling at Plumpton on his chasing debut but off the track *since, was prominent throughout, but was readily brushed aside from the turn in and finished* tired.
Neptune Joly(FR), a winning chaser in France, did not shape with any real encouragement when sixth over hurdles on his British debut at Sedgefield, and was always struggling to lay up here. He will find easier opportunities.

4378 SUNDERLANDS H'CAP CHASE (13 fncs) 2m

4:55 (4:57) (Class 3) (0-125,124) 5-Y-0+ **£6,506** (£1,910; £955; £477)

Form RPR
03P4 **1** **Jericho III (FR)**[24] [3922] 9-10-12 **112** .... (b) PaulO'Neill(3) 128+
(Miss Venetia Williams) *mde all: rdn and 4l clr last: hld on all out* **8/1**

4221 **2** *½* **Jacks Craic (IRE)**[15] [4089] 7-11-12 **123** .... GrahamLee 137
(J L Spearing) *lw: keen early: rr but in tch: hdwy fr 4 out: styd on to go 2nd after 2 out: kpt on strly run-in: nt quite get up* **11/4**[2]

-0P4 **3** *12* **Jurado Express (IRE)**[15] [4089] 10-11-9 **120** .... SamThomas 122
(Miss Venetia Williams) *prom: chsd wnr 6th: hit 9th: mstke 4 out: rdn and no imp sn after: wknd and lost 2nd after 2 out* **12/1**

4303 **4** *1* **Pak Jack (FR)**[23] [3942] 6-11-10 **121** .... RichardJohnson 122
(P J Hobbs) *rr but in tch: hdwy 8th: chsd ldrs and rdn after 4 out: wknd next* **9/4**[1]

2564 **5** *5* **Super Nomad**[28] [3852] 11-11-8 **119** .... MickFitzgerald 115
(M W Easterby) *chsd ldrs: nt fluent 4th: nt fluent and wknd 9th* **6/1**

3-01 **6** *5* **Executive Decision (IRE)**[24] [3922] 12-11-6 **117** .... (v) LeightonAspell 108
(Mrs L Wadham) *lw: in tch tl wknd 9th* **5/1**[3]

02-0 **7** *30* **Arctic Spirit**[15] [4088] 11-10-6 **103** .... BenjaminHitchcott 64
(R Dickin) *chsd wnr to 6th: wknd 9th* **20/1**

4m 3.26s (1.00) **Going Correction** +0.075s/f (Yiel)
WFA 5 from 6yo+ 4lb **7** Ran SP% **112.0**
Speed ratings: **101,100,94,94,91 89,74** CSF £29.87 CT £261.29 TOTE £9.60: £3.60, £1.90; EX 38.60 Place 6 £290.74, Place 5 £83.02.

Owner Paul Beck **Bred** J Cypres And Laurent Couetil **Trained** Kings Caple, H'fords

FOCUS
An ordinary handicap in which the front two drew clear. The winner was well in on his best form, but the runner-up improved significantly.

NOTEBOOK
Jericho III(FR) has been struggling to see out his races of late, but he was allowed to dominate here and, although his advantage was gradually being whittled down, he just held on. He was back down to a reasonable mark here, but will not always be able to dominate and is likely to struggle to follow up off a higher mark. *(tchd 10-1)*
Jacks Craic(IRE) has progressed into a useful novice and looked to hold strong claims in an open event. He travelled strongly under Lee, but his rider may have been a little over confident and he couldn't quite get there in time. He is still improving and the fact he pulled 12 lengths clear of the third was encouraging. *(tchd 5-2 and 3-1 in a place)*
Jurado Express(IRE), a stablemate of the winner, is beginning to recover his form again and, although ultimately well held, a little further assistance from the Handicapper may see him winning again.
Pak Jack(FR), third over three miles at Huntingdon latest, had every chance on this drop in distance, but he was never really going and finished a disappointing fourth. He looks tripless at present. *(op 5-2 tchd 11-4 in places)*
Super Nomad, runner-up in the last two runnings of this, was below par on this occasion and made too many mistakes. *(op 11-2)*
Executive Decision(IRE), up 5lb for winning at Leicester last month, was unable to defy the rise and trailed in a well-beaten sixth. This was disappointing and he is not getting any better at the age of 12. *(op 6-1)*
T/Jkpt: Not won. T/Plt: £955.40 to a £1 stake. Pool: £142,465.66. 108.85 winning tickets. T/Qpdt: £75.60 to a £1 stake. Pool: £8,357.20. 81.75 winning tickets. ST

4383 - 4385a (Foreign Racing) - See Raceform Interactive

3962 MARKET RASEN (R-H)

Sunday, March 12

OFFICIAL GOING: Heavy (soft, good to soft in places in back straight)
With the chase track unraceable the card was made up of six hurdle races on ground described as 'very testing'.
Wind: Fresh, across Weather: Light snow showers

4386 THE SPORTSMAN OUT MARCH 22 CONDITIONAL JOCKEYS' "NATIONAL HUNT" NOVICES' HURDLE (DIV I) (10 hdls) 2m 3f 110y

2:15 (2:16) (Class 4) 5-Y-0+ **£2,740** (£798; £399)

Form RPR
2121 **1** **Oscatello (USA)**[6] [4280] 6-11-4 110 .... DavidBoland(8) 122+
(Ian Williams) *chsd ldrs: lft 2nd 4th: rdn after 3 out: led flat: styd on* **1/3**[1]

-630 **2** *½* **Campaign Charlie**[39] [3677] 6-10-12 .... PaddyMerrigan 106
(H D Daly) *hld up: hdwy 4th: chsd ldr 7th: rdn to ld appr 2 out: hdd flat: styd on u.p* **11/1**[3]

P61F **3** *9* **Sarahs Quay (IRE)**[13] [4152] 7-10-5 .... (p) TJPhelan 91+
(K J Burke) *led: lft clr 4th: rdn and hdd appr 2 out: styng on same pce whn mstke last* **9/1**[2]

00-P **P** **Bobby Icata**[3] [4315] 5-10-12 .... PaddyAspell —
(K W Hogg) *sn bhd: t.o whn p.u bef 7th* **150/1**

5 **U** **Hold The Bid (IRE)**[22] [3975] 6-10-4 .... MichaelO'Connell(8) —
(Mrs S J Smith) *w ldr tl mstke and uns rdr 4th* **20/1**

3-50 **P** **Lyon**[30] [3848] 6-10-12 103 .... TomMalone —
(O Sherwood) *chsd ldrs: mstkes 2nd and next: lost pl bef 4th: t.o whn p.u after 6th* **9/1**[2]

5m 6.70s (16.70) **Going Correction** +0.875s/f (Soft) **6** Ran SP% **108.8**
Speed ratings: **101,100,97,—,—** — CSF £4.65 TOTE £1.20: £1.10, £4.10; EX 4.60.

Owner Rye Braune **Bred** Highland Farms Inc **Trained** Portway, Worcs

■ Stewards' Enquiry : Paddy Merrigan two-day ban: used whip with excessive force (Mar 24-25)

FOCUS
The winning time was 11.4 seconds faster than the second division though the runners in this race probably had the best of the ground. The race is rated positively around the first two.

NOTEBOOK
Oscatello(USA) looked to have been found a simple opportunity but he made very heavy weather of it in the testing conditions and in the end did only just enough. He is surely better than he showed here. *(op 2-5)*
Campaign Charlie had first run on the winner and to his credit fought back hard all the way to the line. This seemed to mark a big improvement. *(op 10-1)*
Sarahs Quay(IRE), back over hurdles and with a mountain to climb, travelled better than the first two much of the way but her chance had gone when she met the last wrong. *(op 8-1)*
Lyon *Official explanation: vet said gelding had sustained a cut to its leg*

4387 THE SPORTSMAN OUT MARCH 22 CONDITIONAL JOCKEYS' "NATIONAL HUNT" NOVICES' HURDLE (DIV II) (10 hdls) 2m 3f 110y

2:45 (2:46) (Class 4) 5-Y-0+ **£2,740** (£798; £399)

Form RPR
5-13 **1** **Custom Design**[87] [2844] 5-10-12 .... WilliamKennedy 92+
(G A Harker) *hld up: mstkes 4th and 7th: sn rdn: hdwy next: led last: hung lft: drvn out* **4/7**[1]

-000 **2** *1 ½* **Willies Way**[83] [2923] 6-10-4 .... MichaelO'Connell(8) 86
(Mrs S J Smith) *chsd ldrs: led after 3rd: hdd next: rdn appr 6th: outpcd 3 out: r.o flat* **7/2**[2]

0 **3** *3 ½* **Honest Abe (IRE)**[33] [3789] 5-10-6 .... TomMessenger(6) 83
(B N Pollock) *hung lft thrght: chsd ldr: led 4th: rdn and hdd after 2 out : styd on same pce last* **12/1**

4 *3* **Wondersobright (IRE)**[69] [3228] 7-10-12 .... (p) PaddyMerrigan 83+
(K J Burke) *led and sn clr: mstkes 1st: 2nd and 3rd: sn hdd: remained handy: chsd ldr 7th: led after 2 out: hdd last: wknd last 50 yds* **7/1**[3]

05 **5** *14* **Floral Rhapsody**[46] [3563] 5-10-5 .... PaddyAspell 59
(P Beaumont) *bhd and j. slowly 1st: mstke next: hdwy appr 6th: wknd after next* **25/1**

5m 18.1s (28.10) **Going Correction** +1.40s/f (Heav) **5** Ran SP% **109.9**
Speed ratings: **99,98,97,95,90** CSF £2.99 TOTE £1.10: £1.10, £1.80; EX 3.60.

Owner A S Ward & A Cooper **Bred** D A Taylor And Mrs A B Collins **Trained** Thirkleby, N Yorks

■ Geoff Harker's first winner from his new yard near Thirsk.
■ Stewards' Enquiry : William Kennedy caution: used whip in an incorrect place

FOCUS
Much the slower of the two divisions and almost certainly much the weaker, rated through the runner-up, though the winner may be capable of better.

NOTEBOOK
Custom Design, faced with weak opposition on his hurdling bow, ran lazily and his jumping rather let him down. Flat out early on the final circuit, he worked his way to the front at the final flight but even then did not look entirely straightforward. *(op 8-11 tchd 4-5 in a place)*
Willies Way, absent for 12 weeks, was left for dead starting the final turn but he stayed on in gallant fashion on the run-in and would have troubled the errant winner with a bit further to go. He looks to just stay. *(tchd 4-1)*

Honest Abe(IRE) did well considering his rider was on one rein throughout. He will surely be better suited going the other way round. *(op 11-1 tchd 14-1)*
Wondersobright(IRE) stole a march at the start. He was wrong at each of the first three flights but after regaining the lead turning in he was very leg-weary in the closing stages.
Floral Rhapsody, making her hurdling debut, has plenty to learn but at least she settled better this time. *(op 14-1)*

4388 THE SPORTSMAN OUT MARCH 22 NOVICES' HURDLE (DIV I) (8 hdls) 2m 1f 110y

3:15 (3:16) (Class 4) 4-Y-0+ **£2,740** (£798; £399)

Form				RPR
P4	**1**		**Yenaled**[13] [4149] 9-11-2 .... RobertThornton (P S McEntee) *hld up: hdwy 5th: led on bit 2 out: comf* **9/4**[1]	89+
	2	*9*	**Pearl Fisher (IRE)**[14] [2777] 5-10-9 .... AlanDempsey (D Carroll) *led: hdd after 1st: chsd clr ldr: led after 3 out: hdd next: hit last: no ex* **14/1**	72+
60	**3**	*5*	**Positano (IRE)**[3] [4327] 6-10-9 .... JohnKington[(7)] (M Scudamore) *hld up: hdwy after 3 out: styd on same pce fr next* **5/1**[2]	73
0-0	**4**	*1 ¾*	**Quest On Air**[44] [3591] 7-11-2 .... (b[1]) GrahamLee (J R Jenkins) *chsd ldrs: rdn appr 2 out: styd on same pce* **16/1**	71
04	**5**	*16*	**Cabrillo (IRE)**[21] [4015] 5-10-9 .... TomSiddall (John A Quinn, Ire) *hld up in tch: rdn and wknd 5th* **9/4**[1]	52+
0	**6**	*12*	**Sinjaree**[4] [696] 8-10-13 .... (v) LeeVickers[(3)] (Mrs S Lamyman) *a bhd* **66/1**	43
P	**7**	*25*	**Lion's Domane**[4] [4301] 9-10-13 .... PaddyAspell[(3)] (K W Hogg) *plld hrd: led after 1st: sn clr: wknd and hdd after 3 out* **100/1**	18
00	**U**		**Sales Flow**[25] [3931] 4-10-1 .... WilsonRenwick (M W Easterby) *mstke and uns rdr 1st* **20/1**	—
0	**P**		**Overdrawn (IRE)**[99] [2627] 5-11-2 .... DominicElsworth (Mrs S J Smith) *chsd ldr tl hrd rdn and wknd after 4th: t.o whn p.u bef 2 out* **11/2**[3]	—

4m 41.3s (24.90) **Going Correction** +1.40s/f (Heav)
WFA 4 from 5yo+ 7lb **9** Ran SP% **113.4**
Speed ratings: **100,96,93,93,85 80,69,—,—** CSF £35.20 TOTE £2.60: £1.20, £2.40, £1.50; EX 23.50.
Owner Kevin Pattinson **Bred** R S A Urquhart **Trained** Newmarket, Suffolk

FOCUS
A very weak race taken in facile fashion by the nine-year-old Yenaled adding to his 13 wins on the level. The third provides the best guide to the level of the form

NOTEBOOK
Yenaled, having just his third try over hurdles, travelled strongly in a weak event and led home by a loose horse never came off the bridle. He will find things a lot tougher under his penalty. *(op 2-1)*
Pearl Fisher(IRE), fit from the All-Weather, regained the lead starting the final turn but it was soon very evident that she was no match whatsoever for the winner. *(op 16-1)*
Positano(IRE), having his second outing in just four days, is at least now qualified for a handicap mark. *(op 6-1)*
Quest On Air, in blinkers this time, at least jumped better and totally different ground would be in his favour. *(op 20-1)*
Cabrillo(IRE) was in trouble at the middle flight in the back straight. *(op 2-1 tchd 11-4 and 3-1 in a place)*
Overdrawn(IRE) was on the retreat at the halfway mark and has a lot to prove now. *(op 7-1)*

4389 THE SPORTSMAN OUT MARCH 22 NOVICES' HURDLE (DIV II) (8 hdls) 2m 1f 110y

3:45 (3:46) (Class 4) 4-Y-0+ **£2,740** (£798; £399)

Form				RPR
0UP6	**1**		**Commanche Sioux**[33] [3786] 4-10-1 .... WilsonRenwick (M W Easterby) *hld up: outpcd 5th: hdwy appr 2 out: led 100 yds out: r.o wl* **40/1**	78+
	2	*5*	**Mungo Jerry (GER)**[34] 5-11-2 .... AndrewThornton (B N Pollock) *chsd ldrs: mstke 3 out: sn led: hdd last 100 yds: sn outpcd* **11/1**	87
4	**3**	*2 ½*	**Olival (FR)**[23] [3963] 4-10-8 .... APMcCoy (Jonjo O'Neill) *chsd ldrs: rdn appr 2 out: ev ch whn wnt rt and almost uns rdr on landing over last: wknd towards fin* **4/1**[3]	80+
502	**4**	*shd*	**Magic Amigo**[55] [3415] 5-11-2 105 .... GrahamLee (J R Jenkins) *hld up: hit 4th: hdwy next: rdn after 2 out: styd on same pce* **3/1**[2]	85+
05	**5**	*12*	**Cayman Calypso (IRE)**[23] [3962] 5-11-2 .... PaulMoloney (Mrs P Sly) *hld up in tch: rdn whn hit last: sn wknd* **14/1**	72
-325	**6**	*7*	**Adlestrop**[22] [3979] 6-10-9 .... JimmyMcCarthy (R T Phillips) *hld up: hdwy 3 out: rdn and wknd bef next* **7/4**[1]	58
05	**7**	*19*	**Bucks**[24] [3947] 9-11-2 .... DavidDennis (Ian Williams) *led 2nd to 5th: ev ch 3 out: sn rdn and wknd* **10/1**	55+
0	**8**	*dist*	**Countrywide Dancer (IRE)**[4] [4301] 6-10-6 .... PaddyAspell[(3)] (K W Hogg) *hld up: a bhd* **100/1**	—
3P53	**P**		**Keen Warrior**[23] [3963] 6-10-13 .... LeeVickers[(3)] (Mrs S Lamyman) *led to 2nd: led 5th: hit 3 out: sn hdd: wkng whn hit next: sn p.u* **14/1**	—

4m 39.7s (23.30) **Going Correction** +1.40s/f (Heav)
WFA 4 from 5yo+ 7lb **9** Ran SP% **115.6**
Speed ratings: **104,101,100,100,95 92,83,—,—** CSF £410.49 TOTE £37.80: £6.80, £3.30, £1.70; EX 532.10.
Owner Mrs M E Curtis **Bred** I P Crane **Trained** Sheriff Hutton, N Yorks

FOCUS
The quicker of the two divisions and the winner looks to just stay with the third setting the standard.

NOTEBOOK
Commanche Sioux looked out of it starting the home turn but her stamina carried her to the front late on and in the end she won going right away. *(op 33-1)*
Mungo Jerry(GER) travelled best but after taking charge starting the final turn he was going up and down on the two furlong run-in and in the end the winner left him for dead. *(op 10-1 tchd 12-1)*
Olival(FR), a French bumper winner, showed a lot more than on his first try over hurdles but after almost unseating the champ when almost upsides at the last, he tired noticeably in the closing stages.
Magic Amigo, absent for eight weeks, has shown he can handle testing condition on the level but this was a very tame effort here. *(op 11-4)*
Adlestrop, flat out to make ground starting the home turn, was on the retreat before reaching two out. *This was too bad to be true. Official explanation: jockey said mare failed to travel in the latter stages of the race*

4390 THE SPORTSMAN OUT MARCH 22 H'CAP HURDLE (12 hdls) 3m

4:15 (4:17) (Class 4) (0-115,114) 4-Y-0+ **£5,204** (£1,528; £764; £381)

Form				RPR
C-53	**1**		**Clan Royal (FR)**[45] [3581] 11-11-7 109 .... APMcCoy (Jonjo O'Neill) *hld up: plld hrd: hdwy 7th: led 2 out: hit last: drvn out* **7/4**[1]	118+
064F	**2**	*2*	**Jack Martin (IRE)**[24] [3942] 9-11-5 110 .... (p) WilliamKennedy[(3)] (S Gollings) *chsd ldrs: rdn and ev ch 2 out: styd on* **16/1**	114
2236	**3**	*4*	**Notaproblem (IRE)**[29] [3854] 7-11-2 104 .... AlanDempsey (G A Harker) *hld up: hdwy appr 2 out: styd on* **8/1**	104
5546	**4**	*½*	**Le Royal (FR)**[31] [3814] 7-10-11 109 .... JamesReveley[(10)] (K G Reveley) *led: hdd 2 out: wknd flat* **5/1**[2]	109
4233	**5**	*1 ½*	**Vicars Destiny**[23] [3966] 8-11-12 114 .... (p) TomSiddall (Mrs S Lamyman) *hld up: hdwy 3 out: sn outpcd: styd on flat* **11/2**[3]	112
3-32	**6**	*10*	**Classic Sight**[21] [4012] 6-10-7 95 .... (b) PaulMoloney (C C Bealby) *prom: hit 3 out: rdn and wknd bef next* **7/1**	83
0000	**7**	*dist*	**Altitude Dancer (IRE)**[23] [3966] 6-10-4 97 .... DeclanMcGann[(5)] (A Crook) *bhd and pushed along 3rd: t.o* **25/1**	—
P455	**8**	*17*	**Chanticlier**[45] [3581] 9-11-2 104 .... (tp) RobertThornton (R T Phillips) *chsd ldrs tl rdn and wknd after 3 out: t.o* **12/1**	—
3P-P	**P**		**Kaparolo (USA)**[76] [2964] 7-10-12 100 .... AndrewThornton (John A Harris) *prom: chsd ldr 6th: rdn: wknd and p.u bef 2 out* **25/1**	—

6m 35.9s (29.10) **Going Correction** +1.40s/f (Heav) **9** Ran SP% **113.3**
Speed ratings: **107,106,105,104,104 101,—,—,—** CSF £28.58 CT £176.87 TOTE £2.20: £1.10, £6.10, £2.60; EX 47.30.
Owner John P McManus **Bred** Ctsse Bertrand De Tarragon **Trained** Cheltenham, Gloucs

FOCUS
An interesting race because of the favourite, who probably ran a personal best over hurdles though still a long way off his chase mark. The form looks reasonable with those in the frame behind the winner close to their marks.

NOTEBOOK
Clan Royal(FR), completing his Grand National preparation, was full of himself and very keen to get on with it. He took time to exert his superiority but was firmly in command at the line. Both the champ and Jonjo will be keeping their fingers crossed that he makes it third time lucky at Aintree and he has all the right credentials. *(op 2-1 tchd 9-4 in places)*
Jack Martin(IRE), back over hurdles and with the cheekpieces on, gave the winner a good tussle but he was very much second best at the line. *(op 14-1)*
Notaproblem(IRE), happy to sit off the pace, stayed on best of all on the extended run-in. *(op 13-2)*
Le Royal(FR) took them along at a sensible gallop but his response was a shade disapointing when asked to raise his game. *(op 7-1)*
Vicars Destiny, tapped for toe starting the final turn, kept on in her own time. She is rated to the limit but a slightly stronger pace would have been in her favour. *(op 9-2)*

4391 THE SPORTSMAN OUT MARCH 22 MARES' ONLY H'CAP HURDLE (10 hdls) 2m 3f 110y

4:45 (4:48) (Class 4) (0-105,102) 4-Y-0+ **£3,253** (£955; £477; £238)

Form				RPR
0-02	**1**		**Rude Health**[118] [2244] 6-9-7 76 .... KeiranBurke[(7)] (N J Hawke) *hld up in tch: led appr 2 out: clr last* **3/1**[1]	90+
-452	**2**	*12*	**I Got Rhythm**[35] [3757] 8-10-13 99 .... JamesReveley[(10)] (K G Reveley) *chsd ldrs: mstke 8th: styd on same pce fr 2 out* **11/2**	99
631F	**3**	*3*	**Jontys'Lass**[15] [4108] 5-11-9 102 .... MrTGreenall[(3)] (A Crook) *led to appr 6th: led 7th: wknd and hit last* **9/2**[2]	99
31-0	**4**	*2*	**Miss Holly**[23] [3967] 7-11-8 98 .... DominicElsworth (Mrs S J Smith) *hld up: hdwy appr 2 out: sn rdn: wkng whn hit last* **3/1**[1]	93
1306	**5**	*7*	**Gaelic Roulette (IRE)**[17] [4075] 6-11-5 95 .... RobertThornton (J Jay) *hld up in tch: ev ch appr 2 out: wknd bef last* **5/1**[3]	83
P065	**P**		**Alderbrook Girl (IRE)**[24] [3951] 6-9-13 78 .... (v) TomMalone[(3)] (R Curtis) *chsd ldr tl led appr 6th: hdd next: rdn and wknd after 3 out: t.o whn p.u bef next* **7/1**	—

5m 19.2s (29.20) **Going Correction** +1.40s/f (Heav) **6** Ran SP% **112.7**
Speed ratings: **97,92,91,90,87** — CSF £19.40 TOTE £5.00: £2.10, £2.20; EX 14.80 Place 6 £29.85, Place 5 £23.68.
Owner D R Mead **Bred** Cleaboy Farms Co **Trained** Hewish, Somerset

FOCUS
A moderate mares-only handicap hurdle run at just a steady pace but an easy and eased winner, value at least 20 lengths and the form might work out.

NOTEBOOK
Rude Health, improved in her new quarters, was dropping back in trip. She travelled easily best and had this won in a matter of strides when asked to stretch out. Eased in the end, she lived up to her name but will shoot up the ratings as a result. *(tchd 11-4 and 7-2)*
I Got Rhythm, 4lb higher, was in real trouble starting the turn for home but to her credit kept chipping away and her reward was a modest second place on the run-in. She prefers less-testing conditions but is an infrequent winner. *(op 6-1 tchd 9-2)*
Jontys'Lass, out of luck at Southwell, took them along much of the way but lost out on second spot after hitting the last. *(tchd 5-1)*
Miss Holly, happy to sit just off the pace, was in third and keeping on when she flattened the last. She should be cherry-ripe next time. *(tchd 11-4 and 7-2)*
Gaelic Roulette(IRE) moved into contention turning for home but she was leg weary between the last two. She does not want conditions as testing as this. *(tchd 9-2)*
T/Plt: £67.00 to a £1 stake. Pool: £43,371.40. 471.90 winning tickets. T/Qpdt: £69.20 to a £1 stake. Pool: £2,395.10. 25.60 winning tickets. CR

4094 WARWICK (L-H)

Sunday, March 12

OFFICIAL GOING: Heavy (soft in places on chase course)
Wind: Light across Weather: Overcast

4392 WARWICKSHIRE AND NORTHAMPTONSHIRE AIR AMBULANCE CONDITIONAL JOCKEYS' H'CAP HURDLE (8 hdls) 2m

2:00 (2:01) (Class 4) (0-100,98) 4-Y-0+ **£3,253** (£955; £477; £238)

Form				RPR
1/3	**1**		**Elegant Clutter (IRE)**[22] [3990] 8-11-1 84 .... StephenCraine (R N Bevis) *hld up: hdwy 4th: led after 3 out: clr 2 out: easily* **5/1**[1]	98+
402U	**2**	*6*	**Rockys Girl**[15] [4101] 4-9-12 80 .... (b) AndrewGlassonbury[(5)] (R Flint) *hld up: hdwy after 3rd: rdn and wnt 2nd 2 out: no ch w wnr* **11/2**[2]	75
5023	**3**	*5*	**Native Commander (IRE)**[6] [4278] 11-11-7 90 .... (b) RobertLucey-Butler (Jim Best) *hld up and bhd: hdwy 4th: rdn appr 2 out: one pce* **8/1**	89+
0P0	**4**	*3*	**First Centurion**[23] [3963] 5-11-2 85 .... (b[1]) DarylJacob (Ian Williams) *led: hdd after 3 out: sn rdn: 4th and wkng whn mstke last* **13/2**	81+
1-05	**5**	*shd*	**La Marette**[71] [3152] 8-11-12 95 .... MarkNicolls (John Allen) *hld up and bhd: rdn after 3rd: hdwy appr 2 out: styd on flat* **9/1**	90
3543	**6**	*½*	**Westernmost**[24] [3950] 8-11-10 93 .... LiamHeard (K Bishop) *hld up in tch: hdwy 4th: ev ch 3 out: rdn and wknd appr 2 out* **6/1**[3]	88
5-PP	**7**	*1*	**In Good Faith (USA)**[151] [1717] 5-11-2 88 .... SamCurling[(3)] (N J Henderson) *prom: rdn 3 out: wknd appr 2 out* **11/1**	84+

F040 **8** *1 ¼* **Able Charlie (GER)**[67] 3242 4-11-7 **98** OwynNelmes 82
(Mrs Tracey Barfoot-Saunt) *hld up towards rr: hdwy appr 4th: ev ch after 3 out: sn rdn and wknd* **33/1**

0010 **9** *18* **Irish Blessing (USA)**[15] 4101 9-10-13 **90** (tp) ThomasBurrows(8) 64
(F Jordan) *prom: lost pl after 3rd: sn rdn and bhd* **12/1**

0/06 **10** *2 ½* **Dirty Sanchez**[37] 3715 8-10-10 **79** ColinBolger 51
(Miss A M Newton-Smith) *rdn after 4th: a bhd* **16/1**

PPF4 **11** *½* **Fantasmic**[76] 2960 10-11-12 **95** JamesDiment 66
(M J M Evans) *chsd ldrs: lost pl after 3rd: n.d after* **25/1**

5PP5 **12** *15* **Impero**[14] 4133 8-9-11 **69** oh5 (b) EamonDehdashti(3) 25
(G F Bridgwater) *w ldr: rdn appr 4th: sn wknd* **66/1**

61/P **P** **Watermouse**[21] 4013 6-10-5 **82** JosephStevenson(8) —
(R Dickin) *prom to 4th: t.o whn p.u bef 2 out* **33/1**

-P0U **U** **Heatherlea Squire (NZ)**[18] 4053 8-9-10 **73** RyanCummings(8) —
(D J Wintle) *hld up in mid-div: blnd and uns rdr 5th* **33/1**

3m 56.5s (-1.80) **Going Correction** +0.075s/f (Yiel)
WFA 4 from 5yo+ 7lb **14** Ran SP% **116.9**
Speed ratings: **107,104,101,100,99 99,99,98,89,88 88,80,—,—** CSF £30.27 CT £218.22 TOTE £6.10: £1.80, £1.90, £3.70; EX 30.30.
Owner Kelvin Briggs **Bred** Limestone Stud **Trained** Threapwood, Cheshire

FOCUS
A weak handicap, run at a strong gallop, and the winner can be rated value for nearly double his winning margin. The form looks solid rated around the runner-up, fourth and fifth.

NOTEBOOK
Elegant Clutter(IRE), third from this mark on his return from a layoff at Uttoxeter 22 days previously, showed the benefit of that outing and ultimately came home to score as he pleased. He relished the deep surface, should be rated value for at least double his winning margin, and really has resumed this season in grand form. *(op 6-1)*
Rockys Girl, who unseated in a seller at Chepstow last time, kept on dourly from the penultimate flight and is flattered by her proximity to the winner. She is a tricky ride and remains winless after 24 career outings. *(op 9-2)*
Native Commander(IRE), third in a seller at Hereford six days previously, turned in another fair effort, yet was found wanting from two out and may have found this coming too soon. *(op 9-1)*
First Centurion, equipped with first-time blinkers, eventually paid for his early exertions at the head of affairs and was not at all disgraced in this circumstances. *(op 8-1)*
La Marette would have benefited from a more positive ride over this trip and ideally needs a stiffer test. *(op 12-1)*
Able Charlie(GER) *Official explanation: jockey said, regarding the apparent tender handling in the closing stages, his orders were to settle gelding early, as it tends to run free, and make sure it finished, adding that gelding pulled very hard over the first two but was given a breather down the hill, then found nothing when asked to quicken at the end of the back straight; trainer added that she was concerned that today's going might stretch gelding's stamina (tchd 40-1)*

4393 IANWILLIAMSRACING.COM NOVICES' HURDLE (12 hdls) 3m 1f
2:30 (2:32) (Class 4) 4-Y-0+ **£3,903** (£1,146; £573; £286)

Form RPR

2621 **1** **Kildonnan**[16] 4099 7-11-9 115 JasonMaguire 119+
(J A B Old) *a.p: led 9th: pushed clr 2 out: easily* **6/4[1]**

3/6P **2** *7* **Pertemps Timmy**[15] 4106 8-10-10 SeanQuinlan(7) 101
(R T Phillips) *hld up and bhd: hdwy after 7th: rdn and hung rt bnd after 3 out: wnt 2nd 2 out: no ch w wnr* **50/1**

2322 **3** *2* **Palm Island (FR)**[13] 4148 5-11-3 109 TomDoyle 100+
(Noel T Chance) *prom: pckd 1st: lost pl after 7th: rallied 9th: rdn appr 2 out: one pce* **7/2[3]**

4212 **4** *4* **Major Catch (IRE)**[22] 3984 7-11-4 112 AdamPogson(5) 102+
(C T Pogson) *t.k.h: prom: led 8th to 9th: rdn after 3 out: wknd 2 out* **15/2**

3240 **5** *15* **Buz Kiri (USA)**[22] 3985 8-10-10 82 ThomasBurrows(7) 80
(P L Clinton) *led to 6th: wknd appr 9th* **100/1**

6 *10* **Arc Of Stone (IRE)**[301] 6-11-3 WarrenMarston 70
(D J Wintle) *hld up towards rr: hdwy appr 5th: mstke 6th: rdn and wknd after 7th* **40/1**

7 *20* **My Vic (IRE)**[133] 6-11-3 LeightonAspell 50
(D R Gandolfo) *hld up: hdwy after 7th: wknd appr 9th* **18/1**

P00 **P** **Fair View (GER)**[47] 3550 5-10-10 TomScudamore —
(Dr P Pritchard) *hdwy 3rd: led 6th to 8th: wknd appr 9th: t.o whn p.u bef 2 out* **66/1**

311 **U** **Keenan's Future (IRE)**[28] 3881 5-11-10 LiamHeard(5) 102
(Ian Williams) *hld up in mid-div: hit 6th: hdwy after 7th: 5th and wkng whn blnd and uns rdr 2 out* **11/4[2]**

6m 37.9s (7.60) **Going Correction** +0.075s/f (Yiel) **9** Ran SP% **112.8**
Speed ratings: **90,87,87,85,81 77,71,—,—** CSF £72.68 TOTE £2.30: £1.20, £5.40, £1.40; EX 55.10.
Owner W E Sturt **Bred** J S Wright **Trained** Barbury Castle, Wilts

FOCUS
A moderate winning time, due to the sedate early gallop, and the form, rated through the modest fifth, should be treated with a degree of caution. However, the winner can still be rated value for further.

NOTEBOOK
Kildonnan, comfortably off the mark over course and distance 16 days previously, followed-up with another clear-cut display and should be rated value for further. The type of surface looks key to him, he is clearly progressing nicely, and does stay very well. *(op 7-4 tchd 15-8)*
Pertemps Timmy, up in trip, finished his race well enough and recorded a personal best in defeat. While his proximity at the finish does hold down this form, he showed ability in bumpers in 2002 *and he could be an improving performer, so it may be unwise to assume this was a fluke. Official explanation: trainer said gelding ran without tongie-strap*
Palm Island(FR) failed to really improve as expected for the step-up to this trip and again appeared tricky. He would look better off in handicaps from his current rating and, while he has only run on soft ground over hurdles to date, the evidence of his previous Flat form in France would suggest he may be happiest on a less-taxing surface. *(tchd 4-1)*
Major Catch(IRE) did not help his cause by refusing to settle early on and had no more to offer from the top of the home straight. He is capable of better when reverting to slightly shorter. *(op 6-1)*
Keenan's Future(IRE) rated a threat until the race got serious turning out of the back straight, but he failed to find an extra gear when it mattered, and was treading water prior to unshipping his rider two from home. This was not his true form. *(tchd 5-2, 3-1 in a place)*

4394 THE SPORTSMAN OUT MARCH 22 NOVICES' H'CAP CHASE (18 fncs) 3m 110y
3:00 (3:00) (Class 4) (0-105,105) 5-Y-0+ **£4,554** (£1,337; £668; £333)

Form RPR

05P2 **1** **Joe McHugh (IRE)**[39] 3672 7-10-0 **79** oh5 DaveCrosse 95+
(C J Mann) *hung rt: sn prom: led 14th: rdn and idled fr 2 out: drvn out* **11/2**

1F14 **2** *1 ¼* **Trenance**[22] 3981 8-11-3 **96** JasonMaguire 104+
(T R George) *hld up: hdwy after 7th: outpcd 3 out: rallied last: hrd rdn and edgd lft flat: kpt on* **7/1**

PP34 **3** *nk* **Supreme Sir (IRE)**[41] 3654 8-9-11 **79** oh3 ColinBolger(3) 86
(P G Murphy) *led after 1st to 4th: led 7th to 9th: rdn 13th: outpcd 3 out: styd on flat* **5/1[3]**

03P2 **4** *nk* **Ironside (IRE)**[16] 4095 7-10-13 **92** RichardJohnson 100+
(H D Daly) *nt fluent: hld up: hdwy 12th: outpcd appr 3 out: styd on flat* **3/1[1]**

354 **5** *nk* **Exceptionnel (FR)**[21] 4016 7-11-5 **98** JohnMcNamara 106+
(Lady Connell) *hld up: hdwy 7th: led appr 12th to 14th: rdn and ev ch after 3 out: hit 2 out: nt qckn flat* **7/2[2]**

-2P5 **6** *15* **Onyourheadbeit (IRE)**[48] 3541 8-11-7 **105** MarkNicolls(5) 96
(K C Bailey) *prom tl rdn and wknd appr 12th* **18/1**

U4P6 **7** *dist* **Sungates (IRE)**[30] 3845 10-11-1 **94** AndrewTinkler 70
(C Tinkler) *prom: led 4th to 7th: led 9th tl appr 12th: hit 14th: sn wknd: t.o* **15/2**

00-0 **P** **Capricorn**[28] 3876 8-10-11 **90** (b) AntonyEvans —
(Miss L Day) *a bhd: reminders after 7th: t.o whn p.u bef 12th* **66/1**

4U4B **P** **Luckycharm (FR)**[12] 4164 7-9-7 **79** oh19 (v) JohnPritchard(7) —
(R Dickin) *led tl after 1st: mstke and lost pl 5th: mstke 6th: bhd whn reminders after 7th: t.o whn p.u bef 12th* **40/1**

6m 26.4s (4.10) **Going Correction** -0.025s/f (Good) **9** Ran SP% **112.7**
Speed ratings: **92,91,91,91,91 86,—,—,—** CSF £42.46 CT £202.64 TOTE £6.30: £2.00, £2.20, £1.50; EX 42.50.
Owner Sally Morgan & Richard Prince **Bred** John Fowler **Trained** Upper Lambourn, Berks

FOCUS
A moderate affair, but the form looks fair for the class and solid enough. The winner is value for slightly further.

NOTEBOOK
Joe McHugh(IRE) ♦, who reportedly bled from the nose when runner-up at Leicester last time, showed his true colours and got off the mark under Rules at the sixth time of asking despite racing from 5lb out of the handicap. He idled in front late on, so can be rated value for further, and should have even more to offer when reverting to better ground in the future.
Trenance was coming back at the idling winner on the run-in, after hitting a flat spot nearing three from home, and posted a solid effort. His jumping was more assured this time and he remains capable of winning from his current handicap mark. *(op 6-1)*
Supreme Sir(IRE) posted a brave effort under a positive ride, and was another coming back at the finish, having been outpaced around three from home. He is a hard horse to actually win with, but helps set the level of this form nevertheless. *(op 11-2 tchd 9-2)*
Ironside(IRE), easy to back on course, spoilt his chances with some messy jumping and was never a serious threat to the winner. He has a deal to prove now, but is capable of better. *(op 5-2)*
Exceptionnel(FR) ♦, making his handicap debut, held every chance and only gave sway on the run-in. He will appreciate less-taxing ground in the future and is certainly capable of finding a race from his current mark. *(op 9-2)*

4395 THE SPORTSMAN OUT MARCH 22 H'CAP CHASE (FOR THE CRUDWELL CUP) (22 fncs) 3m 5f
3:30 (3:30) (Class 3) (0-125,121) 5-Y-0+ **£6,506** (£1,910; £955; £477)

Form RPR

PR54 **1** **Coursing Run (IRE)**[22] 3989 10-11-2 **111** (p) RichardJohnson 122+
(H D Daly) *a.p: led 13th: rdn appr 2 out: drvn out* **3/1[2]**

3132 **2** *2 ½* **Finzi (IRE)**[15] 4103 8-10-2 **97** TomScudamore 103
(M Scudamore) *led: nt fluent 5th: hdd 13th: rdn and ev ch appr 2 out: no ex flat* **11/4[1]**

-1U4 **3** *3 ½* **Graceful Dancer**[21] 4012 9-10-8 **103** JamesDavies 106
(B G Powell) *prom: lost pl appr 6th: rdn and hdwy 16th: styd on flat* **9/1**

11P1 **4** *8* **Blunham Hill (IRE)**[22] 3989 8-10-8 **108** MarkNicolls(5) 106+
(John R Upson) *hld up: hdwy 12th: wknd appr 2 out* **8/1[3]**

5426 **5** *dist* **Follow The Flow (IRE)**[28] 3886 10-10-8 **106** (p) OwynNelmes(3) —
(P A Pritchard) *w ldr: lost pl 15th: sn rdn: t.o fr 16th* **12/1**

-UF0 **6** *22* **Miss Mailmit**[15] 4105 9-10-1 **96** MarkBradburne —
(J A B Old) *hld up: hdwy 7th: j. slowly 8th: wkng whn mstke 17th* **20/1**

P451 **P** **Fox In The Box**[15] 4103 9-11-7 **121** (v) DarylJacob(5) —
(R H Alner) *bhd: mstke 7th: sn struggling: bhd whn p.u after 12th* **11/4[1]**

7m 39.9s (-9.00) **Going Correction** -0.025s/f (Good) **7** Ran SP% **111.9**
Speed ratings: **111,110,109,107,— —,—** CSF £11.60 CT £62.52 TOTE £4.30: £2.40, £1.90; EX 13.00.
Owner The Hon Mrs A E Heber-Percy **Bred** Denis O'Sullivan **Trained** Stanton Lacy, Shropshire

FOCUS
A real test at the distance and Coursing Run emerged best off a decent mark compared with his victory in this race last year. Those in the frame behind the winner give the form a solid appearance.

NOTEBOOK
Coursing Run(IRE), who has slipped to a decent mark, is at his best when stamina is at a premium and he ground it out under a positive ride from Johnson. Consistency has never been his strong point however, and there must be some doubt as to whether he will be capable of repeating the form next time. *(op 7-2)*
Finzi(IRE) gave the winner most to do but was unable to see his race out as strongly, despite the weight concession. He is a highly-consistent sort who should continue to go well in similar events. *(op 3-1)*
Graceful Dancer, 18lb higher than when winning at Towcester on Boxing Day, was up there from the off and held every chance, but she was unable to make any impression on the front two in the straight. *(op 11-2)*
Blunham Hill(IRE) had nothing left to give from the turn-in and was a little disappointing.
Follow The Flow(IRE) dropped away like an out-of-form horse and probably needs to drop a few pounds before winning again. *(tchd 11-1)*
Fox In The Box has never been at his best in heavy ground and he struggled off this 9lb higher mark. He deserves another chance on better ground. *(op 3-1 tchd 10-3, 7-2 in places)*

4396 THE SPORTSMAN OUT MARCH 22 H'CAP HURDLE (11 hdls) 2m 5f
4:00 (4:01) (Class 4) (0-110,108) 4-Y-0+ **£4,111** (£1,198; £599)

Form RPR

/PPP **1** **Be My Destiny (IRE)**[62] 3326 9-11-12 **108** TimmyMurphy 115+
(M Pitman) *racd wd: prom: lost pl after 6th: hrd rdn after 8th: rallied on ins to ld appr 2 out: sn edgd lft: r.o* **14/1**

2-0F **2** *1 ¾* **Durante (IRE)**[47] 3548 8-11-6 **102** PJBrennan 106+
(J A B Old) *hld up and bhd: hdwy appr 7th: led briefly appr 2 out: nt qckn flat* **10/3[2]**

4460 **3** *3* **Mandica (IRE)**[22] 3997 8-10-6 **95** (b) WillieMcCarthy(7) 95
(T R George) *t.k.h: prom: rdn and ev ch 3 out: hung lft appr 2 out: one pce* **6/1[3]**

4442 **4** *1 ¼* **Honey's Gift**[12] 3959 7-11-2 **103** LiamHeard(5) 102
(G G Margarson) *hld up in mid-div: hdwy appr 7th: rdn 3 out: outpcd 2 out: styd on flat* **3/1[1]**

0400 **5** *6* **Thenameescapesme**[24] 3947 6-11-4 **100** JasonMaguire 94+
(T R George) *hld up and bhd: hit 6th: hdwy 8th: wknd 2 out* **22/1**

PU04 **6** *4* **Irish Raptor (IRE)**[16] 4099 7-11-3 **99** AntonyEvans 88
(N A Twiston-Davies) *j.rt: led: hdd after 3 out: wknd 2 out* **7/1**

P043 **7** *8* **Smilingvalentine (IRE)**[37] 3715 9-11-2 98 JodieMogford 79
(D J Wintle) *racd wd: hld up and bhd: hit 5th: hdwy appr 7th: ev ch after 3 out: wknd 2 out* **50/1**

612P **8** *20* **Herecomestanley**[27] 3901 7-10-9 96 CharliePoste(5) 57
(M F Harris) *hld up and bhd: hdwy appr 7th: wknd 8th: mstke 3 out* **7/1**

3PP **P** **Megapac (IRE)**[33] 3792 8-10-13 95 (b[1]) TomDoyle —
(Noel T Chance) *hld up in mid-div: rdn appr 6th: t.o 7th: p.u bef 3 out* **20/1**

1306 **P** **Shaka's Pearl**[13] 4153 6-11-7 103 LeightonAspell —
(N J Gifford) *prom tl rdn and wknd appr 3 out: t.o whn p.u bef 2 out* **16/1**

0523 **P** **Koral Bay (FR)**[13] 4149 5-11-1 104 MrSWaley-Cohen(7) —
(R Waley-Cohen) *hld up in mid-div: nt fluent and wknd 7th: t.o whn p.u bef 2 out* **14/1**

5m 20.9s (4.80) **Going Correction** +0.075s/f (Yiel) **11** Ran SP% **117.7**
Speed ratings: **93,92,91,90,88 86,83,76,—,—** — CSF £60.47 CT £320.33 TOTE £12.30: £4.10, £1.70, £2.40; EX 67.50 Trifecta £365.90 Part won. Pool £515.48 - 0.30 winning units..
Owner Mrs Elizabeth Pearce **Bred** Glenn Turley **Trained** Upper Lambourn, Berks

FOCUS
A modest handicap hurdle which went the way of top weight Be My Destiny who looked well in at the weights. The third, fourth and fifth were close to their marks suggesting the form is sound.

NOTEBOOK
Be My Destiny(IRE), who has offered very little over fences since returning this season, pulling up on all three occasions, seemed helped by the combination of reverting to hurdles and being ridden more prominently and he battled on doggedly to defy top weight in good style. He is potentially well-handicapped over hurdles and may be capable of defying a higher mark. *(op 16-1)*
Durante(IRE) showed no ill-effects of a recent fall and came through to nose ahead two out, but the gallant winner had too much for him and he was outstayed in the testing conditions. There is definitely a race in him off this sort of mark. *(op 4-1 tchd 3-1)*
Mandica(IRE) shaped a little better in the binkers on this occasion, but he still raced a shade more keenly than his rider would have liked was unable to see his race out as strongly as the front two. *(op 15-2)*
Honey's Gift has been in reasonable form, but was racing off a 5lb higher mark than when second at Fakenham last month and she was unable to get competitive. A more positive ride in future may help, but she is hardly a frequent winner. *(op 10-3 tchd 7-2 in places)*
Thenameescapesme came into this as one of the less exposed, and he was able to step up on his previous efforts on this handicap debut. He will not be at his best until tackling fences. *(op 20-1)*
Irish Raptor(IRE), a fair fourth at the course last time, was unable to build on a decent effort over further and continually lost ground in jumping out to the right. This was disappointing, but he is another who will not be at his best until going back chasing. *(tchd 13-2)*

4397 THE SPORTSMAN OUT MARCH 22 HUNTERS' CHASE (FOR THE AIR WEDDING TROPHY) (20 fncs) 3m 2f
4:30 (4:30) (Class 6) 5-Y-0+ **£1,977** (£608; £304)

Form RPR

P-42 **1** **Knife Edge (USA)**[9] 4216 11-11-9 132 (p) MrAJBerry(5) 105+
(Jonjo O'Neill) *hld up and bhd: hdwy after 13th: led appr last: drvn clr flat* **5/6**[1]

-PP5 **2** *12* **Mister Club Royal**[38] 3693 10-11-13 82 MrRWoollacott(5) 94
(Miss Emma Oliver) *led 2nd to 5th: led 6th tl appr 9th: 15th to 16th: rdn and ev ch 2 out: one pce* **13/2**[3]

2-PU **3** *shd* **The Vintage Dancer (IRE)**[14] 10-11-7 MrGKerr(7) 90
(Mrs Nicola Pollock) *hld up: pckd 4th: hdwy after 10th: nt fluent 14th: led 16th: rdn appr 2 out: edgd rt and hdd appr last: one pce* **8/1**

P-0P **4** *28* **Jabiru (IRE)**[35] 13-12-4 96 (b) MrTJO'Brien(3) 69
(Mrs K M Sanderson) *led to 2nd: led 5th to 6th: led appr 9th: pckd 14th: hdd 15th: wknd 4 out* **9/2**[2]

6-43 **5** *5* **Lucky Master (IRE)**[15] 4107 14-11-7 MissGSwan(7) 57
(Miss G Swan) *chsd ldrs tl wknd 12th* **10/1**

UP-U **P** **Primitive Rites**[13] 4146 9-11-7 MissCBrown(7) —
(M J Brown) *bhd fr 10th: t.o whn p.u bef 17th* **20/1**

/P-F **R** **Chaparro Amargoso (IRE)**[18] 4051 13-11-7 91 MrGLoader(7) —
(F L Matthews) *hld up: lost pl 5th: bhd 10th: t.o whn blnd 15th: ref 16th* **66/1**

6m 59.9s (-4.10) **Going Correction** -0.025s/f (Good) **7** Ran SP% **112.5**
Speed ratings: **105,101,101,92,91** —,— CSF £6.88 TOTE £2.00: £1.20, £2.00; EX 12.80.
Owner John P McManus **Bred** John R Gaines Thoroughbreds Llc & John G Sikura **Trained** Cheltenham, Gloucs

FOCUS
Knife Edge appreciated the strong gallop and came through before the last to win well, clearing right away. The placed horses set the level for the form.

NOTEBOOK
Knife Edge(USA), a very useful chaser, was getting off the mark at the third attempt in this sphere and came right away under pressure to win comfortably. Stamina is his strong point these days and he can win again in this sphere. *(op 8-11 tchd 11-10, 6-5 in a place)*
Mister Club Royal faced a stiff task in attempting to concede 4lb to the winner and shaped as well as could have been expected, just grabbing second. He will find easier opportunities. *(op 9-1)*
The Vintage Dancer(IRE), a multiple point winner, was let down by his jumping and proved to be no match for the winner, being readily brushed aside before the last and just missing out on second. *(op 9-1 tchd 15-2)*
Jabiru(IRE), bidding to follow-up his recent point success, is not getting any younger and the way he dropped away suggests he is not up to it in these contests anymore. *(tchd 7-2)*

4398 THE SPORTSMAN OUT MARCH 22 MARES' ONLY MAIDEN OPEN NH FLAT RACE (FOR KEN BRIDGWATER MEM. TROPHY) 2m
5:00 (5:02) (Class 6) 4-6-Y-0 **£2,055** (£599; £299)

Form RPR

4 **1** **Ring Back (IRE)**[21] 4017 5-10-11 MarkNicolls(5) 92+
(B I Case) *a.p: led on bit over 3f out: rdn and hung rt ins fnl f: r.o* **10/1**

634 **2** *2* **Lady Wilde (IRE)**[26] 3911 6-11-2 TomDoyle 89
(Noel T Chance) *hld up in mid-div: hdwy over 6f out: rdn and ev ch over 2f out: edgd rt over 1f out: nt qckn* **3/1**[1]

40 **3** *nk* **Supreme Cara**[109] 2432 6-10-11 ChrisHonour(5) 89
(C J Down) *chsd ldr over 6f out tl over 3f out: nt qckn fnl f* **66/1**

0 **4** *18* **Premier Hope (IRE)**[31] 3820 5-11-2 BarryFenton 71
(Miss E C Lavelle) *prom: ev ch 4f out: sn rdn and wknd* **25/1**

5 *nk* **Linn Of Dee (IRE)** 5-11-2 AndrewTinkler 70
(N J Henderson) *hld up in mid-div: rdn over 7f out: sn struggling* **7/2**[2]

4 **6** *1 1/4* **Parthian Shot**[18] 4059 6-11-2 WarrenMarston 69
(R T Phillips) *led: hdd over 6f out: n.m.r and wknd 5f out* **9/1**

0 **7** *8* **Lucky Third Time**[50] 3497 4-10-8 TomScudamore 53
(M Scudamore) *nvr nr ldrs* **33/1**

8 *7* **Bredon Hill**[315] 6-10-6 ShaunJohnson(10) 54
(R T Phillips) *plld hrd early in rr: hdwy 8f out: wknd over 5f out* **50/1**

9 *1/2* **Slade Supreme (IRE)** 4-10-3 LeeStephens(5) 46
(D A Rees) *prom: rdn over 4f out: sn wknd* **66/1**

10 *3/4* **Silk Rope (IRE)** 6-11-2 RichardJohnson 53
(R T Phillips) *t.k.h towards rr: hdwy 8f out: wknd 5f out* **5/1**[3]

11 *21* **Two T'Three Weeks** 5-11-2 JamieMoore 32
(M G Rimell) *prom tl wknd 6f out: t.o* **7/1**

0-0 **12** *4* **Marys Moment**[45] 3583 6-10-11 TomGreenway(5) 28
(P A Pritchard) *bhd: rdn and short-lived effrt 6f out: t.o* **50/1**

6 **R** **The Shirley Hunt**[21] 4017 6-10-9 SeanQuinlan(7) —
(R T Phillips) *unruly and w.r.s: tk no part* **12/1**

P **Dunnicks Betsie** 6-10-9 SimonElliott(7) —
(F G Tucker) *a bhd: t.o whn p.u and dismntd 1f out* **100/1**

3m 56.2s (-2.60) **Going Correction** +0.075s/f (Yiel)
WFA 4 from 5yo 7lb 5 from 6yo 4lb **14** Ran SP% **117.9**
Speed ratings: **109,108,107,98,98 98,94,90,90,89 79,77,—,—** CSF £37.97 TOTE £11.50: £3.10, £2.00, £16.10; EX 40.50 Place 6 £37.32, Place 5 £19.09.
Owner D Allen **Bred** Nightingale Bloodstock **Trained** Edgcote, Northants

FOCUS
A modest bumper rated through the runner-up, but it should still produce the odd winner in mares-only events.

NOTEBOOK
Ring Back(IRE), a pleasing fourth on her debut at Towcester, was again ridden prominently and was travelling best of all racing into the final three furlongs. She found what was required under pressure, despite hanging to the right, and the five-year-old looks to have a bright future over hurdles.
Lady Wilde(IRE) set the standard on the basis of her three previous efforts, but she lacked the pace of the winner and only just claimed second. She will not be winning until sent hurdling. *(op 7-2 tchd 4-1)*
Supreme Cara recorded her best effort to date, but she is unlikely to prove good enough to win a bumper and will appreciate further over hurdles. *(op 100-1)*
Premier Hope(IRE) stepped up on her initial effort and should progress again, with more of a stamina test over hurdles likely to help. *(op 33-1)*
Linn Of Dee(IRE), whose stable traditionally does well in these events, failed to meet expectations and was struggling some way from the finish. She is likely to benefit from the experience. *(tchd 4-1)*
Silk Rope(IRE) was prominent in the market, but never made any impression and clearly failed to meet with expectations. *(op 9-2)*
T/Jkpt: Not won. T/Plt: £105.40 to a £1 stake. Pool: £61,027.45. 422.45 winning tickets. T/Qpdt: £32.90 to a £1 stake. Pool: £3,109.90. 69.80 winning tickets. KH

4399 - 4406a (Foreign Racing) - See Raceform Interactive

4148 PLUMPTON (L-H)
Monday, March 13
4409 Meeting Abandoned - Frost

1890 STRATFORD (L-H)
Monday, March 13
OFFICIAL GOING: Good to soft (good in places)
Wind: Fresh across Weather: Cloudy

4416 BETFAIRPOKER.COM JUVENILE NOVICES' HURDLE (9 hdls) 2m 110y
2:10 (2:10) (Class 3) 4-Y-O
£7,515 (£2,220; £1,110; £555; £277; £139)

Form RPR

11 **1** **Opera De Coeur (FR)**[17] 4096 4-11-8 RichardJohnson 122+
(H D Daly) *hld up in mid-div: hdwy 4th: led 5th: drvn out* **1/2**[1]

2 *1 3/4* **Orpen Wide (IRE)**[25] 4-10-11 LeeVickers(3) 109
(M C Chapman) *hld up in mid-div: hdwy appr 6th: ev ch whn hit last: nt qckn* **125/1**

21U **3** *7* **Milan Deux Mille (FR)**[20] 4032 4-10-7 AndrewGlassonbury(7) 104+
(M C Pipe) *t.k.h: a.p: 3rd and btn whn hit 2 out* **16/1**[3]

1B13 **4** *23* **Prize Fighter (IRE)**[32] 3817 4-11-5 APMcCoy 84
(Jonjo O'Neill) *led to 5th: wknd 3 out* **7/2**[2]

5 *2 1/2* **Paddys Tern**[46] 4-11-0 JamesDavies 77
(N M Babbage) *w ldr: j. slowly 1st: wknd appr 6th* **200/1**

0U **6** *5* **Carpet Ride**[4] 4327 4-10-9 JohnnyLevins(5) 72
(B G Powell) *hld up in tch: wknd after 5th* **125/1**

4606 **7** *11* **Water Pistol**[18] 4077 4-11-0 KennyJohnson 61
(M C Chapman) *prom to 5th* **100/1**

0 **8** *1 3/4* **New Wave**[25] 3939 4-11-0 TomDoyle 59
(R Lee) *hld up towards rr: short-lived effrt after 5th* **66/1**

6P **9** *11* **Lucky Shame (FR)**[19] 4057 4-10-7 AdrianScholes(7) 48
(A J Whitehead) *a bhd: mstkes 1st and 6th: no ch whn mstke last* **250/1**

10 *dist* **Taylor Maid**[53] 4-10-2 EamonDehdashti(5) —
(G A Ham) *hld up and bhd: mstke 1st: short-lived effrt after 4th: t.o* **400/1**

F **Sands Point (FR)**[148] 4-11-0 TomScudamore —
(M Scudamore) *bhd tl fell 4th* **28/1**

P **Doughty**[5] 4-10-4 RyanCummings(10) —
(D J Wintle) *a bhd: hmpd 4th: sn t.o: p.u bef last* **400/1**

P **P** **Mr Mayfair (IRE)**[22] 4015 4-11-0 PaulMoloney —
(Miss L Day) *a bhd: t.o fr 4th: p.u bef 3 out* **500/1**

P **Berkhamsted (IRE)**[31] 4-10-9 CharliePoste(5) —
(M F Harris) *nt jump wl: bhd fr 5th: t.o whn p.u after 3 out* **18/1**

3m 58.5s (0.10) **Going Correction** +0.25s/f (Yiel) **14** Ran SP% **109.1**
Speed ratings: **109,108,104,94,92 90,85,84,79,— —,—,—,—** CSF £108.14 TOTE £1.50: £1.10, £8.40, £2.20; EX 42.80.
Owner The Hon Mrs A E Heber-Percy **Bred** N Burlot, Olivier Burlot,& Michel Le Bris **Trained** Stanton Lacy, Shropshire

FOCUS
Plenty of dead wood in this event with some huge prices on offer, but the time was decent. The winner is value for further and should rate higher and the form, rated through the third, should work out.

NOTEBOOK
Opera De Coeur(FR) retained his unbeaten record on the fastest ground he has encountered to date. Under his double penalty, he had to work hard for his victory but showed the right attitude. He could go to Aintree, but not if underfoot conditions are too fast. *(op 8-13 tchd 4-6 in places)*
Orpen Wide(IRE) won five times for this yard on the Flat at up to a mile. Making his hurdling debut, he looked a big threat when moving into second place on the home turn but could not get past the determined winner. Stamina might be a problem on a stiffer track than this. *(op 100-1)*
Milan Deux Mille(FR) was out of the race at an early stage on his hurdles debut. This was better, but having been quite keen in the first part of the race he was held when rapping the penultimate flight. *(op 9-1)*
Prize Fighter(IRE), the most experienced in the line-up, did not put up much resistance when headed. *(op 3-1)*

Paddys Tern, a moderate maiden on the Flat, raced freely on this hurdles debut and did not get home. *(op 100-1)*

4417 IANWILLIAMSRACING.COM BEGINNERS' CHASE (15 fncs) 2m 4f
2:40 (2:42) (Class 3) 5-Y-0+ £7,543 (£2,247; £1,137; £583; £305)

Form RPR

P3-5 1 **Smart Savannah**[25] [3946] 10-11-0 115 TomDoyle 116+
(C Tinkler) *bhd: reminders after 1st: hdwy whn j. slowly 7th: rdn to ld appr last: r.o* **12/1**

1104 2 1 1/4 **Penneyrose Bay**[93] [2758] 7-10-7 JimmyMcCarthy 107+
(J A Geake) *led tl blnd 2nd: hit 4th: sltly outpcd 11th: rdn appr 2 out: kpt on flat* **85/40**[1]

6 3 1 1/2 **Merriott's Oscar (IRE)**[29] [3881] 6-10-7 MrJSnowden(7) 114+
(N J Hawke) *hld up in mid-div: hdwy appr 11th: cl 3rd whn mstke 2 out: no ex flat* **18/1**

-324 4 1 3/4 **Reel Missile**[44] [3618] 7-10-9 118 AdamPogson(5) 111+
(C T Pogson) *led appr 3rd: clr 7th: hdd appr last: one pce* **9/4**[2]

-402 5 15 **Manx Royal (FR)**[36] [3760] 7-10-7 AndrewGlassonbury(7) 98+
(M C Pipe) *hld up in tch: rdn 9th: wknd after 4 out: blnd 2 out* **5/1**[3]

F **Dan Ryan (IRE)**[44] [3626] 6-10-11 TGMRyan(3) —
(T G McCourt, Ire) *bhd: mstke 2nd: fell 6th* **40/1**

P0/F P **Kings Avenue**[22] [4016] 9-11-0 VinceSlattery —
(A J Chamberlain) *bhd: mstke 3rd: t.o fr 6th: p.u bef 4 out* **250/1**

U **The Well Lad (IRE)**[288] 7-11-0 MarcusFoley —
(A M Balding) *led 2nd: sn hdd: lost pl 6th: bhd whn blnd and uns rdr 8th* **16/1**

4F44 F **She's My Girl (IRE)**[52] [3489] 11-10-7 JamesDavies —
(John G Carr, Ire) *hld up in tch: mstke and lost pl 4th: bhd whn fell 6th* **20/1**

02 P **Depth Perception (IRE)**[26] [3920] 6-10-9 AELynch(5) —
(Paul John Gilligan, Ire) *hld up in tch: chsd ldr 8th tl mstke 3 out: nt rcvr: 6th and wkng whn p.u bef 2 out* **12/1**

5m 12.4s (12.40) **Going Correction** +0.80s/f (Soft) **10** Ran SP% **113.6**
Speed ratings: **107,106,105,105,99** —,—,—,—,— CSF £38.08 TOTE £12.80: £2.60, £1.40, £4.20; EX 40.20.
Owner George Ward **Bred** Pegasus Racing Ltd **Trained** Compton, Berks

FOCUS
A fair event of its type that could be rated higher but a race devalued by some poor jumping.

NOTEBOOK
Smart Savannah, sharper for his reappearance, responded to some early liveners and jumped soundly. Steadily put into the race, he asserted on the run to the final fence. The drop back in trip and drying ground suited him. *(op 8-1)*
Penneyrose Bay, on her chasing debut, breasted the first ditch and was slightly hesitant in her jumping afterwards. After appearing comfortably held, she came home strongly and she will benefit from this experience. *(op 5-2 tchd 2-1)*
Merriott's Oscar(IRE), making his chase debut after just one look at hurdles, was runner-up on his only outing in point-to-points. He was right in the action when blundering at the notoriously tricky penultimate fence, but for which he would have gone close. *(op 22-1 tchd 25-1)*
Reel Missile, who did not jump fluently in front on the final circuit, was collared between the final two fences and demoted two places on the run-in. *(tchd 5-2)*
Manx Royal(FR), back down in trip, dropped out of contention down the far side on the last circuit and has a good deal to prove now. *(op 6-1)*
Depth Perception(IRE), back up in trip, travelled quite well until clouting the third from home. That knocked the stuffing out of him and he was pulled up before the next. *(op 10-1 tchd 9-1)*

4418 BETFAIR UK TELBET 0870 9080121 (S) HURDLE (10 hdls) 2m 3f
3:10 (3:10) (Class 4) 4-6-Y-0 £3,903 (£1,146; £573; £286)

Form RPR

1 **Urowells (IRE)**[58] [3402] 6-11-5 TGMRyan(3) 97+
(S J Mahon, Ire) *w ldr: led 3 out: rdn clr 2 out: r.o wl* **9/4**[2]

000 2 8 **Theatre Belle**[94] [2749] 5-10-9 80 AntonyEvans 74
(Ms Deborah J Evans) *hld up and bhd: hdwy appr 7th: ev ch 3 out: sn rdn: one pce* **12/1**

00PP 3 11 **Walton Way**[4] [4320] 6-10-11 67 (b) JamesDiment(5) 70
(P W Hiatt) *nt fluent: chsd ldrs: lost pl 3rd: bhd whn mstke 7th: styd on fr 2 out: n.d* **50/1**

P301 4 1 1/2 **Sistema**[7] [4278] 5-11-5 87 OwynNelmes(3) 75
(A E Price) *hld up: rdn and short-lived effrt appr 3 out* **6/1**

23-0 5 1 1/2 **Soviet Joy (IRE)**[317] [136] 5-11-2 105 RussGarritty 68+
(J J Quinn) *led to 3 out: sn wknd* **15/8**[1]

0 P **Musicalish**[95] [2720] 5-11-2 WayneHutchinson —
(R Mathew) *sn chsng ldrs: wknd 7th: t.o whn p.u bef 2 out* **100/1**

PP02 P **Made In France (FR)**[19] [4056] 6-12-0 105 (v) APMcCoy —
(M C Pipe) *t.k.h: stdy hdwy 4th: rdn and wknd appr 3 out: t.o whn p.u bef 2 out* **9/2**[3]

4m 46.5s (11.20) **Going Correction** +0.25s/f (Yiel) **7** Ran SP% **108.7**
Speed ratings: **86,82,78,77,76** —,— CSF £24.49 TOTE £3.80: £2.20, £4.10; EX 39.00.The winner was bought in for 6,000gns.
Owner James Gough **Bred** Premier Bloodstock **Trained** Stamullen, Co Meath

FOCUS
A weak contest and a moderate time, even for a seller.

NOTEBOOK
Urowells(IRE), down in grade, took full advantage with a clear-cut victory. He was eased in the final 100 yards and was value for an even wider margin. *(op 5-2 tchd 11-4)*
Theatre Belle, well beaten at big prices in three novice hurdles this winter, ran creditably in this more suitable grade but was no match for the Irish challenger from the second last. *(tchd 14-1)*
Walton Way was struggling after a mistake four from home but stayed on in the latter stages. This was his best run so far and the blinkers seem to have made a difference. *(tchd 66-1)*
Sistema, tackling a slightly longer trip, was caught out when the race hotted up down the far side. *Official explanation: jockey said gelding hung left throughout (tchd 11-2)*
Soviet Joy(IRE), formerly with Declan Caroll, had not run for more than ten months. Making the running but harried by the eventual winner, he did not last long when headed but was still in third place over the final flight. *(op 2-1)*
Made In France(FR), on the downgrade and a tricky ride, was left behind in the back straight on *the second circuit and eventually pulled up. Official explanation: trainer's representative had no explanation for the poor form shown (op 4-1)*

4419 BETFAIR.COM IRISH DAY H'CAP CHASE (FOR THE GARRICK JUBILEE CHALLENGE CUP) (18 fncs) 3m
3:40 (3:40) (Class 3) (0-120,120) 5-Y-0+ £12,526 (£3,700; £1,850; £926; £462; £232)

Form RPR

5521 1 **Umbrella Man (IRE)**[42] [3654] 10-11-2 110 MarcusFoley 134+
(Miss E C Lavelle) *hld up and bhd: hdwy 13th: led after 3 out: sn clr: easily* **6/1**[2]

4-22 2 14 **Dickensbury Lad (FR)**[33] [3801] 6-11-7 115 AntonyEvans 120+
(J L Spearing) *w ldr: led 3rd: blnd 4 out: sn hdd: one pce fr 3 out* **10/1**

2602 3 1 1/4 **Mioche D'Estruval (FR)**[28] [3900] 6-11-12 120 (v) RJGreene 122+
(M C Pipe) *mid-div: mstkes 3rd and 4th: sn rdn: hdwy 10th: led after 4 out tl after 3 out: sn no ch w wnr* **16/1**

P0P 4 2 **Lulumar (FR)**[71] [3186] 7-11-4 112 (t) LeightonAspell 111
(O Sherwood) *hld up and bhd: stdy hdwy 13th: one pce fr 3 out* **33/1**

P331 5 11 **Nykel (FR)**[18] [4078] 5-10-8 112 RobertThornton 90
(A King) *prom: hit 10th: rdn appr 14th: sn wknd* **7/2**[1]

3630 6 1 1/2 **Idiome (FR)**[16] [4119] 10-11-9 117 AndrewThornton 104
(Mrs L C Taylor) *hld up: hit 9th: hdwy 10th: rdn 4 out: wknd after 3 out* **50/1**

-F23 7 4 **Denada**[24] [3965] 10-10-8 102 TomScudamore 85
(Mrs Susan Nock) *prom to 9th* **16/1**

4FP3 8 1 **Portavo (IRE)**[33] [3801] 6-11-6 114 PaulMoloney 96
(Miss H C Knight) *hit 10th: a bhd* **20/1**

1564 9 dist **Strong Magic (IRE)**[24] [3965] 14-10-0 94 oh1 RichardHobson —
(J R Cornwall) *led to 3rd: prom tl wkng whn hit 12th: t.o* **100/1**

334U P **Myson (IRE)**[16] [4120] 7-10-5 99 (p) JamesDavies —
(D B Feek) *prom to 7th: t.o whn p.u bef 3 out* **16/1**

P323 P **Pietro Vannucci (IRE)**[22] [4014] 10-11-1 109 (v[1]) APMcCoy —
(Jonjo O'Neill) *bhd fr 11th: t.o whn p.u bef 4 out* **8/1**

2PP P **Gallik Dawn**[25] [3942] 8-10-13 110 MissPGundry(3) —
(A Hollingsworth) *a bhd: rdn 11th: t.o whn p.u bef 3 out* **33/1**

1210 P **Welcome To Unos**[23] [3993] 9-11-6 114 RichardMcGrath —
(K G Reveley) *hdwy 5th: wknd 13th: t.o whn p.u bef 3 out* **20/1**

P-16 P **Nas Na Riogh (IRE)**[51] [3507] 7-11-8 116 (t) MickFitzgerald —
(N J Henderson) *prom tl wknd 13th: t.o whn p.u bef 3 out* **13/2**[3]

1-1U P **Moor Spirit**[26] [3922] 9-11-7 115 RussGarritty —
(P Beaumont) *hld up and bhd: sme hdwy 12th: sn rdn and struggling: t.o whn p.u bef 3 out* **8/1**

6m 14.6s (12.40) **Going Correction** +0.80s/f (Soft)
WFA 5 from 6yo+ 10lb **15** Ran SP% **117.2**
Speed ratings: **111,106,105,105,101 101,99,99**,—,— —,—,—,—,— CSF £57.70 CT £916.34 TOTE £6.20: £2.30, £3.00, £5.30; EX 59.60 Trifecta £518.30 Pool: £730.07 - 0.55 winning units.
Owner Mrs J Dollar & Mrs M Hall **Bred** Mrs A Berry **Trained** Wildhern, Hants

FOCUS
A decent winning time for the grade of contest and the field came home strung out behind the facile winner, who is value for more than the official margin. The form looks solid with the others ibn the frame close to their marks.

NOTEBOOK
Umbrella Man(IRE), raised 11lb for resuming winning ways at Southwell 42 days previously, made a mockery of his new higher mark and followed-up with a facile success. He is clearly back in top form now, stayed this trip very well, and really ought to be high on confidence after this. However, another hike in the weights is now inevitable. *(op 5-1)*
Dickensbury Lad(FR) turned in another sound effort, but was found wanting for pace when it really mattered, and looks high enough in the weights on this evidence. That said, he has time on his side and probably needs slightly better ground to be seen at his best. *(op 14-1)*
Mioche D'Estruval(FR) was firmly put in his place by the winner on the turn for home, and looked a non-stayer over this trip, but was still not disgraced under top weight. He is not the most fluent of jumpers, but can better this when reverting to slightly shorter. *(tchd 18-1)*
Lulumar(FR) turned in his best effort since joining connections from France and has clearly now dropped to a more realistic mark. He is another who is a happier horse over shorter, however. *(op 40-1)*
Nykel(FR), up 8lb for scoring at Huntingdon last time, appeared held by this higher mark and still left the impression he may benefit from a drop back in trip.
Nas Na Riogh(IRE) *Official explanation: jockey said mare had a breathing problem (op 8-1)*
Moor Spirit *Official explanation: jockey said gelding was unsuited by the ground - good to soft, good in places (op 8-1)*

4420 BETFAIRGAMES.COM H'CAP HURDLE (9 hdls) 2m 110y
4:10 (4:10) (Class 3) (0-125,124) 4-Y-0+ £10,020 (£2,960; £1,480; £740; £369; £185)

Form RPR

6512 1 **Rojabaa**[18] [4067] 7-10-6 104 RichardHobson 108
(B D Leavy) *hld up and bhd: hdwy appr 6th: led sn after 2 out: rdn out* **20/1**

-0U3 2 nk **Caraman (IRE)**[24] [3967] 8-10-9 112 DougieCostello(5) 116
(J J Quinn) *hld up in mid-div: hdwy 6th: rdn appr 2 out: ev ch last: r.o* **12/1**

2F02 3 2 1/2 **Lysander (GER)**[4] [4329] 7-10-2 105 CharliePoste(5) 108+
(M F Harris) *a.p: led and hit 3 out: hit 2 out: sn hdd: no ex flat* **14/1**

132 4 6 **Border Castle**[27] [3908] 5-11-6 118 SamThomas 115+
(Miss Venetia Williams) *hld up and bhd: hdwy after 5th: hit 3 out: 4th and btn whn hit last* **4/1**[2]

2P46 5 1 3/4 **Amour Multiple (IRE)**[9] [4242] 7-11-12 124 RobertThornton 117
(S Lycett) *chsd ldr: led after 5th: mstke 6th: hdd 3 out: wknd appr 2 out* **28/1**

2141 6 9 **Fier Normand (FR)**[19] [4048] 7-11-6 118 APMcCoy 104+
(Jonjo O'Neill) *hld up in mid-div: hdwy on ins appr 6th: rdn and wknd appr 3 out* **11/8**[1]

135 7 3 **College Ace (IRE)**[38] [3717] 5-11-3 115 RichardJohnson 96
(P J Hobbs) *nvr nr ldrs* **8/1**[3]

0603 8 nk **Bonny Grey**[51] [3510] 8-10-4 105 WilliamKennedy(3) 90+
(D Burchell) *bhd: blnd 6th: n.d* **14/1**

116R 9 2 **Lord Lington (FR)**[46] [3580] 7-11-1 113 WarrenMarston 92
(D J Wintle) *mstke 3 out: a bhd* **66/1**

061- 10 3 1/2 **Archie Babe (IRE)**[314] [4279] 10-11-3 115 RussGarritty 90
(J J Quinn) *a bhd* **40/1**

P223 11 hd **A Bit Of Fun**[19] [4058] 5-11-0 112 TomSiddall 87
(J T Stimpson) *prom: lost pl 4th: bhd fr 6th* **33/1**

13 12 dist **Paro (FR)**[19] [4048] 5-11-0 112 RJGreene —
(M C Pipe) *prom: hit 5th: sn rdn and wknd: t.o* **20/1**

5-66 P **Hegarty (IRE)**[17] [4093] 7-10-12 110 (t) RichardMcGrath —
(Jonjo O'Neill) *led tl after 5th: sn wknd: t.o whn p.u bef 2 out* **33/1**

3m 58.5s (0.10) **Going Correction** +0.25s/f (Yiel) **13** Ran SP% **117.0**
Speed ratings: **109,108,107,104,104 99,98,98,97,95 95**,—,— CSF £218.48 CT £3451.01 TOTE £25.70: £6.00, £3.60, £3.30; EX 479.70.
Owner Mrs Renee Farrington-Kirkham **Bred** The Lavington Stud **Trained** Forsbrook, Staffs

FOCUS
A modest handicap, run at a sound pace, but it produced a surprising result. The third, fourth and fifth are the best guides to the level of the form.

NOTEBOOK

Rojabaa dug deep to repel the runner-up from the penultimate flight and record a surprise success. He had previously shown his best form in plating company, and his latest success came from a mark of just 90, so this clearly has to rate as a career-best. This is his ground, and it will be interesting to see whether he is capable of further progression, as he should have plenty of options if kept going through the summer months.

Caraman(IRE) ◆ held every chance and went down with all guns blazing. He should soon be placed to go one better on this evidence. *(op 16-1)*

Lysander(GER) was not helped by some sloppy jumps when in front from three out and was eventually well held by the front pair. He still finished nicely clear of the rest, however, and is a fair benchmark for this form.

Border Castle, making his handicap debut in this sphere, ran below his mark in defeat and shaped as though he would prefer the return to a stiffer test in the future. *(op 5-1)*

Fier Normand(FR), very well backed for this handicap bow, performed below expectations and never seriously figured. He has it all to prove now. *(op 7-4)*

4421 MIDRANGE DIRECT NOVICES' HUNTERS' CHASE (FOR THE CREDIT CALL CUP) (16 fncs 2 omitted) 3m

4:40 (4:40) (Class 5) 5-Y-O+ **£3,038** (£949; £474; £237; £118)

Form				RPR
5	**1**		**Brer Bear**[27] [3910] 7-12-3 ... MrJMPritchard (Mrs E Insley) *hld up: stdy hdwy 8th: outpcd 2 out: rallied appr last: rdn to ld flat: r.o wl* **15/2**[2]	113+
4-1	**2**	*6*	**Christy Beamish (IRE)**[10] [4216] 9-12-3 ... MrGHanmer[(3)] (P Jones) *hld up and bhd: hdwy 10th: led on bit 2 out: sn clr: rdn and hdd flat: fnd nil* **4/7**[1]	114+
	3	*14*	**Magnus Veritas (IRE)**[15] 8-11-10 ... MrStuartRobinson[(7)] (Miss Gina Weare) *prom: mstke 3rd: led and hmpd by loose horse 12th: hdd 2 out: wknd appr last* **28/1**	93
2-P0	**4**	*3/4*	**Mollycarrs Gambul**[287] [594] 7-11-3 ... MissSarahRobinson[(7)] (Miss Sarah Robinson) *t.k.h: sn prom: led appr 10th to 12th: wknd after 2 out* **25/1**	86+
5-	**5**	*7*	**Wendys Dynamo**[9] 9-11-10 ... MrMMunrowd[(7)] (Mrs Jo Sleep) *hld up and bhd: j.lft 4th: hdwy 9th: wknd appr 2 out* **50/1**	85
	6	*dist*	**The Noble Roman**[23] 8-11-10 ... MrPMann[(7)] (T Ellis) *a bhd: t.o* **11/1**[3]	—
	P		**Draconian**[29] 7-11-10 ... MrMMackley[(7)] (Mrs L Pomfret) *sn t.o: p.u bef 12th* **150/1**	—
	U		**May Be Possible (IRE)**[23] 7-11-12 ... MrDavidTurner[(5)] (R Bryan) *blnd and uns rdr 1st* **25/1**	—
5	**F**		**Talioso (IRE)**[13] [4167] 9-11-12 ... MissSSharratt[(5)] (R Hollinshead) *prom: blnd 7th: fell 9th: dead* **16/1**	—
	U		**Agua Ardente**[15] 9-12-0 ... MrRCope[(3)] (Mrs Caroline Bailey) *hld up: hdwy 7th: blnd and uns rdr 9th* **16/1**	—
2R/	**P**		**Black Optimist (IRE)**[688] 12-12-3 ... MissPGundry (Mrs S J Maiden) *bhd fr 9th: t.o whn p.u after 12th* **28/1**	—
6P00	**P**		**La Folichonne (FR)**[23] 7-11-3 ... MrLJohnson[(7)] (C G Johnson) *led tl appr 10th: sn wknd: t.o whn p.u bef 2 out* **66/1**	—
P	**F**		**Student Night (IRE)**[19] [4055] 7-11-10 ... MrFBarr[(7)] (John E F Skelton) *nt jump wl: bhd: j.lft and mstke 3rd: fell 7th* **200/1**	—
	P		**Who's Eddie (IRE)**[15] 9-11-12 ... MrMHarris[(5)] (H W Wheeler) *prom: mstkes 7th and 8th: wknd 13th: mstke 14th: t.o whn p.u bef last* **66/1**	—

6m 21.3s (19.10) **Going Correction** +0.80s/f (Soft) 14 Ran SP% **116.2**

Speed ratings: **100,98,93,93,90** —,—,—,—,— —,—,—,— CSF £11.68 TOTE £7.90: £2.50, £1.10, £5.30; EX 26.10.

Owner C E P Insley **Bred** John Duckworth **Trained** Watlington, Oxfordshire

■ Stewards' Enquiry : Mr Stuart Robinson seven-day ban: improper riding - struck a riderless horse with his whip on final circuit (Mar 24-28, Apr 2-3, 5-6,8)

FOCUS

A modest hunter chase and the form looks sound enough with the third setting the standard. The fourth last and second last fences were bypassed on the final circuit.

NOTEBOOK

Brer Bear, fifth on his debut under Rules last time, responded to maximum pressure turning out of the back straight to mow down the runner-up after the last fence and win going away. This was a fine ride by his very capable pilot, and he has further improvement in him this year, especially when reverting to faster ground. *(op 7-1)*

Christy Beamish(IRE), bidding for the hat-trick, looked the winner when hitting the front full of running, but he eventually proved powerless to resist the winner's late challenge. This can be deemed as disappointing, but he ideally needs producing as late as possible in his races, and should not be written off on the back of this display. *(op 8-13, 4-6 in places)*

Magnus Veritas(IRE), making his debut under Rules, had his limitations exposed yet posted a fair effort in defeat. *(tchd 33-1)*

Mollycarrs Gambul, returning from a 287-day layoff, did not help her cause by running too freely through the early stages, yet stuck to her task well enough and can build on this. *(op 20-1)*

4422 BETFAIR.COM MAIDEN OPEN NATIONAL HUNT FLAT RACE 2m 110y

5:10 (5:10) (Class 4) 4-6-Y-O **£3,253** (£955; £477; £238)

Form				RPR
65	**1**		**Don Castille (USA)**[42] [3651] 4-11-0 ... TomDoyle (P R Webber) *a.p: rdn and swtchd rt wl over 1f out: rn green: r.o to ld cl home* **50/1**	84+
6P	**2**	*3/4*	**Le Burf (FR)**[39] [3699] 5-11-1 ... AndrewGlassonbury[(7)] (G R I Smyly) *hld up and bhd: hdwy over 5f out: led jst ins fnl f: hrd rdn and hung lft: hdd cl home* **25/1**	90
0	**3**	*1 1/4*	**Single Player (IRE)**[77] [3001] 6-11-5 ... WilliamKennedy[(3)] (Noel T Chance) *led: hdd 9f out: led over 4f out: rdn 2f out: hdd jst ins fnl f: nt qckn* **8/1**	89
00	**4**	*1/2*	**Tisfreetdream (IRE)**[77] [2988] 5-11-5 ... OwynNelmes[(3)] (P A Pritchard) *hld up in mid-div: hdwy after 6f: rdn and ev ch over 1f out: hmpd and swtchd rt wl ins fnl f: nt rcvr* **150/1**	90+
6	**5**	*shd*	**Hot Zone (IRE)**[33] [3799] 4-11-0 ... APMcCoy (Jonjo O'Neill) *hld up in mid-div: lost pl 4f out: swtchd rt and hdwy over 2f out: rdn over 1f out: swtchd rt and kpt on ins fnl f* **12/1**	80
2	**6**	*1/2*	**Fredensborg (NZ)**[27] [3911] 5-11-8 ... SamThomas (Miss Venetia Williams) *a.p: rdn 2f out: one pce fnl f* **15/8**[1]	88
0	**7**	*1/2*	**Cooldine Boy (IRE)**[18] [4072] 5-11-8 ... RichardJohnson (P J Hobbs) *hld up and bhd: hdwy 5f out: rdn over 1f out: one pce* **6/1**	87
0	**8**	*2*	**Ebony Queen**[53] [3468] 5-11-1 ... (t) PaulMoloney (Miss H C Knight) *hld up and bhd: hdwy over 1f out: nvr trbld ldrs* **66/1**	78
5	**9**	*2 1/2*	**Sea Cadet**[44] [3623] 4-11-0 ... RussGarritty (T D Easterby) *chsd ldr: led 9f out tl over 4f out: rdn and wknd wl over 1f out* **22/1**	75
5	**10**	*1 1/4*	**La Dame Brune (FR)**[84] [2927] 4-10-7 ... MickFitzgerald (N J Henderson) *prom: rdn over 4f out: wknd over 2f out* **5/1**[3]	67
6	**11**	*1 1/4*	**Whitewater Dash**[18] [4072] 6-11-8 ... WayneHutchinson (J A B Old) *hld up in mid-div: rdn and wknd over 4f out* **9/2**[2]	80
0	**12**	*1 1/2*	**Arriman**[28] [3904] 4-10-7 ... SimonElliott[(7)] (J A Geake) *bhd fnl 5f* **125/1**	71
0-5	**13**	*5*	**Saddlers' Harmony (IRE)**[256] [876] 5-11-8 ... RichardMcGrath (K G Reveley) *hld up in mid-div: hdwy over 5f out: wknd 3f out* **50/1**	74
00	**14**	*24*	**Perfectly Posh**[53] [3462] 5-10-8 ... DavidBoland[(7)] (J K Cresswell) *a bhd: t.o* **200/1**	43

4m 9.50s (2.80) **Going Correction** +0.25s/f (Yiel)

WFA 4 from 5yo 7lb 5 from 6yo 4lb 14 Ran SP% **118.3**

Speed ratings: **83,82,82,81,81 81,81,80,79,78 78,77,74,63** CSF £951.43 TOTE £28.50: £4.50, £4.20, £2.40; EX 698.60 Place 6 £287.59, Place 5 £211.35.

Owner D P Barrie & M J Rees **Bred** Blue Diamond Farm **Trained** Mollington, Oxon

■ Stewards' Enquiry : Andrew Glassonbury one-day ban: careless riding (Mar 24)

FOCUS

A rather messy affair due to a very modest early pace and the contest developed into something of a sprint. The winning time was therefore moderate, even for a bumper. Surprisingly though, the first five all ran close to their marks.

NOTEBOOK

Don Castille(USA) had finished unplaced in two previous bumpers, but to be fair he probably found the ground too soft first time and was undone by the drop in trip in the second. The pace was not ideal here either, but the return to two miles helped and he timed his effort just right. He still does not look the finished article and a good pace and proper test of stamina should see him in an even better light.

Le Burf(FR), undone by a slipping saddle last time, confirmed the promise he had shown on his debut. He looked like winning a furlong out, but then hung left through greenness and that gave the winner his chance. He still seems to be learning. *(op 28-1)*

Single Player(IRE) was in the ideal position throughout in a moderately-run race and it is very possible that has enabled him to hang in there for as long as he did.

Tisfreetdream(IRE) was still battling for a place when squeezed out between the second and third horses inside the last furlong. However, his two previous efforts plus the winning time suggest this effort may flatter him.

Hot Zone(IRE), up two furlongs from his debut and on better ground, would not have been suited by the pace and he probably did as much as he could in the circumstances. It will not be until he goes over fences that he will realise his potential. *(op 8-1)*

Fredensborg(NZ), runner-up on much softer ground on his debut, was tucked away on the inside for much of the way and did not see a great deal of daylight, but he lacked the pace to get himself out of it. *(op 2-1)*

Cooldine Boy(IRE) was on better ground this time and had every chance, but the way the race was run would not have helped him and he was done for finishing speed. He will show his true ability in a truly-run race and when faced with a proper test of stamina. *(tchd 7-1)*

T/Jkpt: Not won. T/Plt: £978.40 to a £1 stake. Pool: £68,355.85. 51.00 winning tickets. T/Qpdt: £141.30 to a £1 stake. Pool: £4,812.80. 25.20 winning tickets. KH

3945 TAUNTON (R-H)

Monday, March 13

OFFICIAL GOING: Good to soft (soft in places)

There was quite a strong wind and, with the ground drying out all the time, some of the jockeys reported the course as riding more like 'good'.

Wind: Strong across

4423 LANDLORD'S DAY (S) HURDLE (9 hdls) 2m 1f

2:20 (2:25) (Class 5) 4-6-Y-O **£2,192** (£639; £319)

Form				RPR
3350	**1**		**Barranco (IRE)**[27] [3905] 5-11-2 82 ... (b) JamieMoore (G L Moore) *led tl after 2nd: styd chsng ldr: led after 5th: rdn and edgd lft after 2 out: narrowly hdd last: hung lft and led run-in:* **4/1**[1]	88+
5002	**2**	*1*	**Shalati Princess**[16] [4101] 5-10-2 75 ... MrRhysHughes[(7)] (D Burchell) *chsd ldrs: wnt 2nd 3 out: chal 2 out: bmpd sn after: slt ld last: carried lft and hdd run-in: no ex cl home* **11/2**[2]	80+
	3	*1 3/4*	**All Square (IRE)**[523] [1120] 6-11-2 ... JimCrowley (R A Farrant) *bhd: hdwy 5th: chsd ldrs and rdn 3 out: wnt rt 2 out: and again last: kpt on same pce u.p run-in* **25/1**	84
0460	**4**	*hd*	**Brochrua (IRE)**[6] [4290] 6-10-11 92 ... ChrisHonour[(5)] (J D Frost) *bhd: hdwy 5th: hit 3 out: kpt on fr 2 out: r.o run-in but nvr gng pce to rch ldrs* **7/1**	85+
-000	**5**	*28*	**Will She Spin**[65] [3283] 5-10-2 ... WayneKavanagh[(7)] (J W Mullins) *bhd: sme hdwy fr 5th: wknd 3 out* **33/1**	49
4P0P	**6**	*1*	**Nepal (IRE)**[19] [4046] 4-9-10 78 ... (b) LiamTreadwell[(5)] (M Mullineaux) *chsd ldrs to 3 out: sn wknd* **20/1**	40
0040	**7**	*shd*	**Garhoud**[52] [3479] 4-10-5 75 ... (p) MissEJJones[(3)] (Miss K M George) *chsd ldrs: rdn 5th: sn wknd* **13/2**[3]	47
	8	*3 1/2*	**Must Be So**[336] 5-10-9 ... JasonMaguire (Mrs L J Young) *hit 1st: bhd: sme hdwy 4 out: sn rdn and wknd* **100/1**	44
2-34	**9**	*13*	**Pedler's Profiles**[95] [2728] 6-11-2 73 ... BenjaminHitchcott (Miss K M George) *a in rr* **15/2**	38
	10	*22*	**Fayr Firenze (IRE)**[26] 5-11-2 ... MarkGrant (M F Harris) *rdn 4 out: a in rr* **40/1**	16
	11	*hd*	**Marque Deposee (FR)**[358] 6-10-2 ... CharlieStudd[(7)] (B G Powell) *led after 2nd: t.k.h: hdd after 5th and sn wknd* **4/1**[1]	—
/0PP	**P**		**Valderrama**[29] [3881] 6-11-2 ... MarkBradburne (L Waring) *in tch: hit 4th: wknd 5th: t.o whn p.u bef 4 out* **66/1**	—
60P	**U**		**Whatsinitforme (IRE)**[52] [3479] 4-10-3 ... (b[1]) LeeStephens[(5)] (W K Goldsworthy) *mstke 2nd: in tch whn j. bdly rt and uns rdr 3rd* **25/1**	—

4m 14.6s (5.80) **Going Correction** +0.45s/f (Soft)

WFA 4 from 5yo+ 7lb 13 Ran SP% **113.3**

Speed ratings: **104,103,102,102,89 88,88,87,81,70 70**,—,— CSF £22.70 TOTE £4.70: £1.70, £2.00, £8.50; EX 20.60.There was no bid for the winner.

Owner G L Moore **Bred** Barronstown And Orpendale **Trained** Woodingdean, E Sussex

■ Stewards' Enquiry : Jamie Moore four-day ban: careless riding (Mar 24-27)

FOCUS

A typically weak selling hurdle, but they went a good pace pretty much from the start and the form looks reliable enough for the level, rated through the winner.

NOTEBOOK

Barranco(IRE), dropping back in both trip and grade, found himself in front much sooner than was probably ideal, but he had the right man on board and kept finding just enough under pressure to hold on. He wandered around badly after the last, doing the eventual runner-up few favours in the process, but Moore made his mind up for him. This was his first success since winning on the Flat in France back in May 2004 and, while he looks up to finding further success at this sort of level, he may not be one to take too short a price about. *(op 7-2)*

Shalati Princess showed she was in good form when second in a similar event at Chepstow on her previous start and ran well in second. She was done no favours by the eventual winner when that one wandered around, but was not an unlucky loser. *(op 9-2)*

All Square(IRE), a moderate maiden on the Flat and over hurdles in Ireland when last seen in 2004, ran well on his debut for new connections. There could be a similar race in him if he goes the right way from this. *(op 12-1)*
Brochrua(IRE) was the best off at the weights of those with official ratings, but took a while to get going and could not take advantage. *(op 5-1)*
Garhoud attracted market support, but his rider never really looked happy. *(op 16-1)*
Pedler's Profiles *Official explanation: jockey said gelding was never travelling (op 8-1)*
Marque Deposee(FR) was well backed on her British debut and looked to be happy setting a strong pace in front, but this was her first start in nearly a year, and her first outing over obstacles in 575 days, and she emptied very quickly, suggesting she needed the race quite badly. *(op 13-2)*

4424 WINE VAULTS OF YEOVIL BEGINNERS' CHASE (12 fncs) 2m 110y
2:50 (2:55) (Class 4) 5-Y-0+ **£5,204** (£1,528; £764; £381)

Form RPR
-232 **1** **Pardishar (IRE)**[27] [3907] 8-11-2 119 JamieMoore 124+
(G L Moore) *prom: chsd ldr 6th: chal fr next tl led sn after 4 out: sn hrd drvn: kpt on whn strly chal fr 2 out: all out* **7/4**[2]
3UU2 **2** *nk* **Give Me Love (FR)**[13] [4162] 6-10-11 119 (bt) LiamHeard(5) 124+
(P F Nicholls) *keen early: hld up in tch: trckd ldr 3 out: chal gng wl fr 2 out: rdn and stl upsides run-in: fnd little u.p* **6/5**[1]
60-0 **3** *30* **Man From Highworth**[33] [3801] 7-10-9 118 MrJAJenkins(7) 94
(H J Manners) *t.k.h: led to 2nd: led 4th: hdd after 4 out: sn wknd* **8/1**[3]
0023 **4** *hd* **It's My Party**[25] [3945] 5-10-6 RobertLucey-Butler(5) 89
(W G M Turner) *a in rr: rdn 7th: lost tch fr 8th* **16/1**
0FUP **R** **Powra**[16] [4102] 6-10-9 JamesWhite(7) —
(R J Hodges) *t.k.h: led 2nd: hdd 4th: wknd 7th: bhd 4 out: t.o whn ref 3 out* **200/1**
30-U **F** **Grouse Moor (USA)**[28] [3903] 7-11-2 MarkBradburne 90
(P Winkworth) *bhd: hit 7th: no ch whn hit 4 out: poor 4th whn fell last* **22/1**
U3 **F** **La Source A Gold (IRE)**[22] [4006] 7-10-13 RichardYoung(3) 87
(Nick Williams) *hit 3rd: bhd: sme hdwy 6th: sn wknd 5th and no ch whn fell last* **40/1**

4m 11.4s (-4.10) **Going Correction** -0.05s/f (Good)
WFA 5 from 6yo+ 4lb **7** Ran SP% **106.1**
Speed ratings: **107,106,92,92,**— —,— CSF £3.72 TOTE £2.20: £1.70, £1.50; EX 5.70.
Owner D R Hunnisett **Bred** His Highness The Aga Khan's Studs S C **Trained** Woodingdean, E Sussex

FOCUS
As is to be expected for the time of year, just an ordinary beginners' chase, but the front two, both officially rated 119, finished well clear and the form looks solid enough. The pace was good early on, but steadied at halfway.

NOTEBOOK
Pardishar(IRE) had no chance against the Cheltenham Festival-bound Reveillez when second at Folkestone on his previous start, but had nothing of that one's class to contend with and just proved good enough. He was hard at work from a little way out while Give Me Love was seemingly still on the bridle, but Moore was again seen to good effect in conjuring just enough out of his mount after the last once his rival came under serious pressure. His three previous runs over fences had come at around two and a half miles and he may just be better back over a little further. *(op 15-8)*
Give Me Love(FR) travelled best of all over the three fences in the home straight, but failed to pick up sufficiently after the last - just like at Leicester on his previous start. His conditional rider dropped his whip on the run-in, which cannot have helped, but he is probably not one to be making excuses for. *(op 11-10 tchd 5-4 in places)*
Man From Highworth did not have very much to find at all with the front two on hurdles ratings, but he was left behind when it mattered despite having had the run of the race. *(op 13-2 tchd 17-2)*
It's My Party had plenty to find on hurdles ratings on his chasing debut and was well held. *(tchd 20-1)*
Grouse Moor(USA) was well held when falling. *(op 33-1 tchd 50-1)*
La Source A Gold(IRE) was also well beaten when falling. *(op 33-1 tchd 50-1)*

4425 LICENSED VICTUALLERS MARES' ONLY MAIDEN HURDLE (10 hdls) 2m 3f 110y
3:20 (3:25) (Class 4) 4-Y-0+ **£3,903** (£1,146; £573; £286)

Form RPR
223 **1** **Rowlands Dream (IRE)**[23] [3979] 6-11-2 TimmyMurphy 97+
(R H Alner) *mde all: rdn 2 out: nt fluent last: drvn out* **8/13**[1]
-454 **2** *1 ½* **Little Venus (IRE)**[39] [3690] 6-11-2 MarkBradburne 94
(H D Daly) *prom: chsd wnr 2 out: rdn and effrt last: rdr dropped whip sn after: kpt on but no ex nr fin* **11/1**[3]
0B0 **3** *6* **Pyleigh Lady**[6] [4286] 5-10-11 ChrisHonour(5) 89+
(S C Burrough) *chsd ldrs: rdn 3 out: kpt on same pce fr 3 out* **150/1**
2 **4** *1 ½* **Cemgraft**[15] [4129] 5-10-11 (t) LiamHeard(5) 88+
(A J Lidderdale) *rr: hdwy 6th: chsd ldrs 3 out: rdn and hit 2 out: wknd last* **4/1**[2]
P0 **5** *15* **Four In Hand**[68] [3240] 8-10-11 MrTJO'Brien(5) 72
(Mrs K M Sanderson) *in tch: hdwy 6th: rdn 3 out: sn wknd* **50/1**
54 **6** *2* **Fuss**[15] [4129] 5-11-2 PJBrennan 70
(P J Hobbs) *chsd ldr: chal fr 4th to 7th: wknd after 3 out* **12/1**
0 **7** *4* **Miss Grace**[29] [3878] 6-11-2 JoeTizzard 66
(J D Frost) *chsd ldrs to 3 out: sn wknd* **20/1**
65 **8** *7* **Bobble**[257] [866] 6-10-9 MrGTumelty(7) 59
(R N Bevis) *bhd fr 5th* **33/1**
00 **9** *30* **Lagan Legend**[53] [3468] 5-11-2 BenjaminHitchcott 29
(Dr J R J Naylor) *chsd ldrs: rdn 4 out: wknd and hmpd 3 out* **66/1**
10 *1* **Belledesaro (IRE)** 6-10-13 TJPhelan(3) 28
(Mrs H Dalton) *j. slowly 1st: a bhd* **80/1**
05-0 **11** *1 ¾* **Primrose Park**[39] [3692] 7-10-9 DarrenO'Dwyer(7) 26
(K Bishop) *hit 3rd: a bhd* **66/1**
P **Nearly A Bay** 9-10-9 MrPYork(7) —
(R Fielder) *a in rr: t.o whn p.u bef 3 out* **200/1**
P **Tough Queen (USA)**[196] 5-10-9 KeiranBurke(7) —
(N J Hawke) *sn bhd: t.o whn p.u bef 3 out* **200/1**
30 **U** **Cois Na Tine Eile**[23] [3979] 4-10-7 CarlLlewellyn —
(N A Twiston-Davies) *j. slowly 1st: bhd: hdwy and hit 6th: styng on and disputing 4l 6th whn blnd and uns rdr 3 out* **33/1**

5m 1.50s (15.50) **Going Correction** +0.45s/f (Soft)
WFA 4 from 5yo+ 7lb **14** Ran SP% **116.4**
Speed ratings: **87,86,84,83,77 76,75,72,60,59 59,**—,—,— CSF £7.88 TOTE £1.90: £1.10, £1.90, £21.70; EX 10.20.
Owner D Brennan **Bred** Miss A Gibson Fleming and Mrs E Cooper **Trained** Droop, Dorset

FOCUS
The form looks pretty moderate, but that is probably to be expected for a mares-only maiden hurdle run in the middle of March. They went just an ordinary pace for much of the race, resulting in a moderate winning time, and the field were still well bunched at the fourth last before eventually being sorted out when the pace increased.

NOTEBOOK
Rowlands Dream(IRE), upped slightly in trip, confirmed the promise she showed in two runs in bumpers and a couple of novice hurdles to get off the mark at the fifth attempt. She did not have much in hand and will not find it easy to follow up, although she is obviously now eligible for a handicap and, in the longer term, can probably do better when sent over fences. *(op 5-6 tchd 10-11)*
Little Venus(IRE) appreciated the step back up in trip and finished to good effect to take a close second. She has now qualified for a handicap mark and that should give connections more options. *(op 17-2)*
Pyleigh Lady had shown very little on her two previous starts over hurdles, but caught the attention of the Stewards when well beaten at Exeter on her previous start when they considered that her rider had 'failed to take all reasonable and permissible measures'. She had also shown ability on her debut in a bumper, so this effort may not have been a total fluke, and she has now qualified for a handicap mark.
Cemgraft did not run badly but failed to really build on the promise she showed when second on her hurdling debut at Fontwell. *(op 6-1)*
Four In Hand was well beaten but is now eligible for a handicap mark. *(op 66-1)*
Bobble *Official explanation: trainer said mare had bled from the nose (tchd 50-1)*
Nearly A Bay *Official explanation: jockey said mare had bled from the nose (op 150-1)*

4426 MAKE MINE A FOAMING PINT H'CAP CHASE (14 fncs) 2m 3f
3:50 (3:55) (Class 4) (0-100,97) 5-Y-0+ **£3,578** (£1,050; £525; £262)

Form RPR
P322 **1** **Sitting Duck**[45] [3602] 7-10-4 82 CharlieStudd(7) 97+
(B G Powell) *led 3rd: drvn and hit 3 out: kpt on strly run-in* **6/1**[2]
2332 **2** *4* **Jupon Vert (FR)**[7] [4281] 9-11-8 93 JimCrowley 101
(R J Hodges) *chsd wnr and hit 5th: rdn and no imp fr 3 out* **7/1**
3623 **3** *1 ¼* **Woodenbridge Dream (IRE)**[59] [3368] 9-11-0 85 JohnMcNamara 93+
(R Lee) *chsd ldrs: disp 2nd 4 out: mstke 3 out: sn one pce: no imp whn mstke last* **6/1**[2]
/22- **4** *9* **Italian Counsel (IRE)**[554] [1372] 9-11-1 86 PJBrennan 84
(P J Hobbs) *in tch: chsd ldrs fr 5th: wknd after 4 out* **4/1**[1]
F302 **5** *nk* **Joe Deane (IRE)**[19] [4047] 10-11-4 96 (p) MrGTumelty(7) 93
(M J Coombe) *rr and blnd 4th: sn drvn along: nvr in contention but styd on u.p fr 2 out* **9/1**
45-6 **6** *6* **Real Definition**[23] [3984] 7-10-6 77 JamieMoore 71+
(M G Rimell) *nt jump wl: rr: mstkes 1st: 6th and 7th: hdwy and hit next: hit 10th: wknd 4 out* **13/2**[3]
3142 **7** *12* **Julies Boy (IRE)**[24] [3964] 9-11-5 97 (t) WillieMcCarthy(7) 76
(T R George) *chsd ldrs tl wknd 9th* **8/1**
33P5 **8** *6* **Message Recu (FR)**[25] [3949] 10-11-7 92 (bt) JoeTizzard 65
(C L Tizzard) *mstke 4th: a bhd* **7/1**
4406 **P** **Vanormix (FR)**[16] [4102] 7-11-8 93 (v) JasonMaguire —
(C J Gray) *led to 3rd: wknd 8th: t.o whn p.u then uns rdr 3 out* **33/1**

4m 57.5s (4.70) **Going Correction** -0.05s/f (Good) **9** Ran SP% **111.0**
Speed ratings: **88,86,85,82,81 79,74,71,**— CSF £44.72 CT £251.69 TOTE £6.30: £2.20, £1.50, £2.10; EX 37.20.
Owner M Powers **Bred** W Smith **Trained** Morestead, Hants

FOCUS
Just a moderate handicap chase and the winning time was ordinary. The placed horses set the standard and the form looks solid enough at a low level.

NOTEBOOK
Sitting Duck gained his first career success at the 14th attempt. He had been running well in defeat under similarly positive tactics in recent starts and confirmed the promise of those efforts to win without ever being seriously challenged. He is clearly progressing along the right lines and should continue to go well in similar company. *(op 5-1)*
Jupon Vert(FR) is not that easy to win with but usually gives his running and ran his usual sort of race in second. *(op 5-1)*
Woodenbridge Dream(IRE) is in good form at the moment and this was another reasonable performance, although his jumping could have been better in the straight. *(op 8-1)*
Italian Counsel(IRE), back over fences off a mark 31lb lower than that of his hurdles rating on his return from a 554-day absence, finished up well held but is entitled to come on quite a bit for the run. *(op 11-4)*
Joe Deane(IRE) appeared unsuited by the drop back from three miles and, having been struggling from some way out, got going all too late. *(op 11-1)*
Real Definition was faced with some pretty experience rivals on his chase debut and did not jump well enough. *(op 14-1 tchd 16-1)*
Julies Boy(IRE) has been in good form lately under this particular conditional rider, but posted a rare below-par effort with no obvious excuse. *(op 6-1)*

4427 FULL MEASURE NOVICES' H'CAP HURDLE (9 hdls) 2m 1f
4:20 (4:27) (Class 4) (0-100,95) 4-Y-0+ **£3,903** (£1,146; £573; £286)

Form RPR
0604 **1** **Picot De Say**[22] [4010] 4-10-1 78 OllieMcPhail 78+
(C Roberts) *hld up in rr: hdwy 4 out: slt ld and hit 2 out: hit last: pushed clr run-in: readily* **15/2**[3]
4050 **2** *10* **Manolo (FR)**[131] [1987] 6-11-10 93 JodieMogford 89+
(Mrs H Dalton) *chsd ldrs: led appr 5th: narrowly hdd 3 out: lft in slt ld appr next: sn: hdd: ev ch last: sn outpcd* **20/1**
4413 **3** *nk* **Before The Mast (IRE)**[24] [3964] 9-11-1 84 JohnMcNamara 80+
(M F Harris) *bhd: rdn after 4 out: hit 2 out: styd on u.p and hit last: r.o run-in and fin wl but no ch w wnr* **9/1**
0633 **4** *shd* **Laharna**[83] [2934] 6-11-10 93 BarryFenton 88
(Miss E C Lavelle) *slt ld tl hdd appr 5th: styd chsng ldrs: pushed along 2 out: kpt on run-in* **7/2**[1]
600 **5** *1 ½* **Future Legend**[41] [3659] 5-11-9 92 JasonMaguire 85+
(J A B Old) *chsd ldrs: pushed along 4 out: styd on fr 2 out but nvr in contention* **20/1**
-506 **6** *5* **Thenford Star (IRE)**[17] [4094] 5-10-9 78 (t) MarkBradburne 66
(D J S Ffrench Davis) *in tch: chsd ldrs and rdn 4 out: wknd appr 2 out* **33/1**
20P0 **7** *¾* **Amnesty**[9] [4243] 7-11-9 92 (b) JamieMoore 79
(G L Moore) *chsd ldrs to 3 out: sn wknd* **14/1**
5144 **8** *12* **Barella (IRE)**[33] [3804] 7-11-7 95 HowieEphgrave(5) 70
(L Corcoran) *chsd ldrs to 3 out: sn wknd* **33/1**
060 **9** *14* **Sapient**[23] [3996] 5-11-0 90 MrJMahot(7) 51
(M Scudamore) *hit 3rd: bhd most of way* **150/1**
0P-6 **10** *10* **La Professoressa (IRE)**[116] [2298] 5-11-0 90 (t) DarrenO'Dwyer(7) 41
(Mrs P N Dutfield) *nt fluent 1st: in tch 5th: wknd 4 out* **100/1**
0 **P** **In The Morning (IRE)**[50] [3528] 7-10-12 81 TimmyMurphy —
(A J Martin, Ire) *rr whn p.u and dismntd bef 3rd* **7/2**[1]
1005 **P** **Silver City**[68] [3242] 6-11-12 95 PJBrennan 91
(P J Hobbs) *w ldr tl led 3 out: gng wl whn p.u and dismntd bef next* **14/1**

1130 **P** **Golden Feather**[22] 4010 4-11-1 **95** PaulO'Neill(3) 80+
(Miss Venetia Williams) *in tch: rdn 5th: hdwy 4 out: wknd after next: p.u bef 2 out: dismntd* **4/1**[2]

4m 15.1s (6.30) **Going Correction** +0.45s/f (Soft)
WFA 4 from 5yo+ 7lb **13** Ran SP% **116.6**
Speed ratings: **103,98,98,98,97 95,94,89,82,77** —,—,— CSF £145.43 CT £1368.93 TOTE £9.10: £2.90, £10.00, £1.40; EX 150.80.
Owner Dr Simon Clarke **Bred** Henry And Mrs Rosemary Moszkowicz **Trained** Newport, Newport

FOCUS
The ground continued to dry out as the afternoon progressed, a view backed up by some of the jockeys and, while that cannot be blamed, three fancied horses in Golden Feather, In The Morning and Silver City all pulled up. A moderate handicap hurdle restricted to novices with the winner value for more than the official margin and the runner-up to his mark.

NOTEBOOK
Picot De Say had his chance made easier with some of the fancied horses pulling up, but this was still a much-improved effort from the bottom-weight. He had been well held in all of his runs since winning an 11-furlong claimer on the Flat last year, but was always travelling strongly and showed himself much better than his current mark by pulling well clear when seriously asked after the last to get off the mark over hurdles at the sixth attempt, despite hitting the last two flights. He will find things much tougher when reassessed as he will be raised significantly, but his chance would be obvious under a penalty. *(op 12-1)*
Manolo(FR) ran well off the back of a 131-day break, but was no match for the clearly well-handicapped winner. *(op 14-1 tchd 12-1)*
Before The Mast(IRE) has been in good form over fences recently and ran with credit on his return to hurdling. *(op 10-1)*
Laharna, a beaten favourite when last seen nearly three months previously, ran creditably enough on his return to action and could eventually find a moderate race. *(op 4-1 tchd 3-1)*
Future Legend ◆ ran well for a long way on his handicap debut and could well be worth taking from the race as he looks up to exploiting his current sort of mark if building on this. *(op 16-1)*
Silver City ◆ looked the most likely winner when kicking clear off the final bend, but lost his action under pressure and was pulled up before the second last. The drying ground would have suited and he is one to keep in mind this spring. *Official explanation: vet said gelding was lame behind (op 5-2)*
In The Morning(IRE) was pulled up after the second hurdle and was reported to be lame behind. *Official explanation: vet said gelding was lame (op 5-2)*
Golden Feather was pulled up before two out and his rider thought the gelding had gone lame, but *he was later found to be sound. Official explanation: jockey said he thought gelding had gone lame but it subsequently returned sound (op 5-2)*

4428 SAME AGAIN LANDLORD CLASSIFIED CHASE (17 fncs) 2m 7f 110y
4:50 (4:55) (Class 5) 5-Y-0+ **£3,083** (£898; £449)

Form				RPR
P4-P	**1**		**Joizel (FR)**[20] 4036 9-10-10 76 JamesWhite(7)	99+
			(V G Greenway) *rr: hdwy 8th: chsd ldrs 11th: chal 4 out: pushed along and slt ld whn lft wl clr 3 out: easily* **66/1**	
5522	**2**	*16*	**Lucky Sinna (IRE)**[29] 3888 10-10-10 88 (b[1]) CharlieStudd(7)	83+
			(B G Powell) *chsd ldrs: led 9th tl blnd 12th and sn narrowly hdd: wknd 4 out: lft mod 2nd 3 out* **9/2**[2]	
-PP6	**3**	*5*	**A Pound Down (IRE)**[25] 3946 9-11-3 68 DaveCrosse	76+
			(N G Ayliffe) *rr but in tch: efort 12th: nvr rchd ldrs: wknd 4 out: no ch whn lft poor 3rd 3 out: blnd last* **50/1**	
0P5U	**4**	*dist*	**Oscar Performance (IRE)**[42] 3654 11-11-3 74 (b) BenjaminHitchcott	—
			(R H Buckler) *chsd ldrs to 12th: t.o* **16/1**	
FP4P	**P**		**Pardini (USA)**[24] 3965 7-11-3 84 PJBrennan	—
			(M F Harris) *hit 9th: a bhd: t.o whn p.u bef 3 out* **8/1**[3]	
2/60	**P**		**Jorodama King**[19] 4047 12-10-10 59 KeiranBurke(7)	—
			(N J Hawke) *led tl after 3rd: wknd 11th: t.o whn p.u bef 4 out* **100/1**	
P24P	**P**		**Minat Boy**[55] 3430 10-11-3 71 JoeTizzard	—
			(C L Tizzard) *led after 3rd: hdd 9th: wknd 11th: t.o whn p.u bef 3 out* **12/1**	
05/	**U**		**Noble Buck (IRE)**[302] 10-11-3 81 JohnMcNamara	93
			(Mrs L J Young) *rr: hit 6th: hdwy 10th: chsd ldrs 4 out: 3l 3rd and styng on whn hmpd and uns rdr 3 out* **25/1**	
P132	**F**		**Bar Gayne (IRE)**[7] 4277 7-11-3 90 JasonMaguire	99
			(T R George) *chsd ldrs: reminders 8th: chsd ldrs 10th: wnt 2nd 11th: slt ld after 12th: hdd: pushed along but upsides whn fell 3 out* **4/6**[1]	

6m 15.2s (10.10) **Going Correction** -0.05s/f (Good) **9** Ran SP% **111.1**
Speed ratings: **81,75,74**,—,— —,—,—,— CSF £330.06 TOTE £79.60: £10.30, £1.10, £7.40; EX 140.50.
Owner V G Greenway **Bred** Dominique Chesneau, Marie-Odile Medard, Charlotte **Trained** Fitzhead, Somerset

FOCUS
As seemed to be the theme for the meeting, a moderate classified chase restricted to horses rated 90 or lower. The winning time was very slow.

NOTEBOOK
Joizel(FR) was a maiden over hurdles after 12 starts going into this and had not exactly shaped like a future winner when pulled up at 80/1 on his most recent start at Exeter, but he was always going well on his debut over fences and may just have been getting the favourite's measure when that one fell. He will go up significantly in the weights for this, so would be of obvious interest if turned out under a penalty, but he is clearly better suited by chasing and must be respected even after being reassessed. *(op 40-1)*
Lucky Sinna(IRE), with blinkers replacing cheekpieces and back up in trip, is flattered by his finishing position. *(op 4-1 tchd 7-2 and 5-1)*
A Pound Down(IRE) had quite a bit to find at the weights and is another flattered by his finishing position. *(op 25-1 tchd 66-1)*
Noble Buck(IRE), ex-Irish, had not been seen under Rules for the best part of two years, and was last seen finishing third in a point-to-point 302 days previously, but he was in the process of running a creditable race when unseating. He was left in second when Bar Gayne fell, but could not get out of the way of that one in time to avoid a collision. *(op 10-11 tchd Evens, 11-10 in a place)*
Bar Gayne(IRE), although upsides the eventual winner when falling three out, was making very hard work of it and was no sure thing to win had he stood up. This has to be considered disappointing given that he was the best off at the weights and had 14lb in hand of Joizel. *(op 10-11 tchd Evens, 11-10 in a place)*

4429 LAST ORDERS H'CAP HURDLE (10 hdls) 2m 3f 110y
5:20 (5:25) (Class 4) (0-105,105) 4-Y-0+ **£3,903** (£1,146; £573; £286)

Form				RPR
2P42	**1**		**Blaeberry**[28] 3902 5-11-7 **100** BarryFenton	106+
			(Miss E C Lavelle) *hld up in rr: hdwy 6th: w ldrs whn carried lft 4 out: drvn to chal last: led fnl 100yds: edgd lft: all out* **9/2**[2]	
-2PP	**2**	*nk*	**Manawanui**[51] 3508 8-10-11 **90** TimmyMurphy	95+
			(R H Alner) *chsd ldrs: rdn 3 out: styd on u.p fr next: r.o run-in: fin strly: nt quite get up* **5/1**[3]	
2112	**3**	*1 ¾*	**Magical Legend**[67] 3247 5-11-7 **105** HowieEphgrave(5)	109+
			(L Corcoran) *chsd ldrs: slt ld 3 out: carried lft by loose horse appr 2 out: sn rdn: hdd fnl 100yds: wknd nr fin* **3/1**[1]	
0P2	**4**	*17*	**Heavy Weather (IRE)**[22] 4005 8-11-9 **102** JasonMaguire	90+
			(Miss Joanne Priest) *led: carried rt by loose horse appr 3 out and sn narrowly hdd: rdn and wknd bef next* **28/1**	
000F	**5**	*6*	**Courant D'Air (IRE)**[24] 3959 5-11-7 **100** JohnMcNamara	79
			(Lucinda Featherstone) *bhd: sme hdwy 6th: rdn 4 out: wknd next* **25/1**	
0-P4	**6**	*3*	**Oyster Pearl (IRE)**[35] 3780 7-11-4 **100** TomMalone(3)	76
			(P Bowen) *chsd ldr to 6th: wknd 3 out* **11/1**	
5006	**7**	*dist*	**Mister Chatterbox (IRE)**[20] 4032 5-11-0 **93** PJBrennan	—
			(P J Hobbs) *in tch to 4 out: t.o* **9/1**	
4100	**8**	*1 ¾*	**Shingle Street (IRE)**[139] 1873 4-10-11 **99** AlanO'Keeffe	—
			(Miss Venetia Williams) *bhd: sme hdwy 6th: sn btn: t.o* **10/1**	
0244	**U**		**Ballybawn House**[23] 3997 5-11-3 **96** SeanFox	—
			(J C Fox) *uns rdr 1st* **11/1**	
6003	**U**		**Cresswell Willow (IRE)**[29] 3884 6-11-2 **95** (b) CarlLlewellyn	—
			(W K Goldsworthy) *uns rdr 1st* **33/1**	
0620	**P**		**Maclean**[25] 3944 5-11-11 **104** (b) JamieMoore	—
			(G L Moore) *bhd most of way: no ch whn p.u bef 2 out* **8/1**	
4-56	**F**		**Porak (IRE)**[7] 4282 9-11-6 **104** DerekLaverty(5)	—
			(W Davies) *in tch: hday to chse ldrs 6th: stl disputing 4l 5th whn fell 3 out* **50/1**	

4m 55.2s (9.20) **Going Correction** +0.45s/f (Soft)
WFA 4 from 5yo+ 7lb **12** Ran SP% **118.9**
Speed ratings: **99,98,98,91,88 87**,—,—,—,— —,— CSF £26.86 CT £79.03 TOTE £4.80: £3.30, £2.20, £2.20; EX 46.10 Place 6 £187.03, Place 5 £87.95.
Owner Lady Bland **Bred** Lady Bland **Trained** Wildhern, Hants

FOCUS
This did not look like a bad handicap hurdle for the grade, but they finished quite well strung out behind the front three and two loose horses continually interfered with the principals. The placed horses set the level for the form.

NOTEBOOK
Blaeberry ◆ had shaped with plenty of promise in novice company and took advantage of a very fair mark on her handicap debut. The drying ground was in her favour and she found just enough under pressure when asked, despite being pestered by a loose horse as she was attempting to get into top gear. She looks well up to defying a rise in the weights and is one to keep on the right side of. *(op 4-1 tchd 13-2)*
Manawanui had been pulled up on his last two starts but ran well off the back of a 51-day absence. He is another for whom the drying ground would not have posed a problem. *(op 9-2 tchd 11-2)*
Magical Legend travelled strongly throughout and looked the most likely winner when hitting the front, but she was hassled by a loose horse at a crucial stage and that cannot have done her chances any good. *(op 4-1 tchd 11-4)*
Heavy Weather(IRE) ◆ was another continually pestered by loose horses and his rider had to snatch up to avoid one of them approaching a hurdle just as the race was getting serious, so he can be rated better than the bare form and should be given another chance. *(op 25-1)*
Courant D'Air(IRE) has struggled since winning a novice hurdle in November 2004, but this was not that bad an effort. *(op 20-1)*
T/Plt: £44.30 to a £1 stake. Pool: £56,612.20. 932.25 winning tickets. T/Qpdt: £16.70 to a £1 stake. Pool: £4,086.90. 180.40 winning tickets. ST

3174
CHELTENHAM (Old Course) (L-H)
Tuesday, March 14

OFFICIAL GOING: Good (good to soft in places on cross-country course)
Wind: Light across Weather: Overcast. Light rain for two hours before racing

4430 ANGLO IRISH BANK SUPREME NOVICES' HURDLE GRADE 1 (8 hdls) 2m 110y
2:00 (2:02) (Class 1) 4-Y-0+
£57,020 (£21,390; £10,710; £5,340; £2,680; £1,340)

Form				RPR
3111	**1**		**Noland**[30] 3878 5-11-7 138 RWalsh	144+
			(P F Nicholls) *lw: in tch: pushed along 4 out: sn lost pl: nt fluent next: 5l down 2 out: 7l down and u.p last: str run run-in: led last strides* **6/1**[2]	
11	**2**	*nk*	**Straw Bear (USA)**[42] 3658 5-11-7 APMcCoy	145+
			(N J Gifford) *in touch: trckd ldrs 3 out: slt ld 2 out: 3l clr whn nt fluent last: styd on gamely whn chal run-in: hdd last strides* **11/1**	
1123	**3**	*1 ¼*	**Buena Vista (IRE)**[95] 2742 5-11-7 135 (p) TimmyMurphy	141
			(M C Pipe) *led: rdn fr 3 out: narrowly hdd next: rallied and ev ch run-in: outpcd nr fin* **14/1**	
4	**4**	*2*	**Sublimity (FR)**[37] 3772 6-11-7 (t) PACarberry	142+
			(John G Carr, Ire) *cmpt: str: bhd: hdwy whn hmpd by loose horse bnd appr 3 out: styd on fr 2 out: kpt on run-in but nt rch ldrs* **16/1**	
1	**5**	*hd*	**Sweet Wake (GER)**[52] 3515 5-11-7 PCarberry	139
			(Noel Meade, Ire) *str: hit 2nd: bhd: hdwy appr 3 out: styd on u.p and ev chance run-in: no ex nr fin* **5/2**[1]	
1143	**6**	*1 ¼*	**Natal (FR)**[24] 3994 5-11-7 142 (t) ChristianWilliams	140+
			(P F Nicholls) *lw: chsd ldrs: rdn whn n.m.r 3 out: styng on one pce whn hit last: kpt on again cl home* **16/1**	
	7	*nk*	**Jazz Messenger (FR)**[20] 4061 6-11-7 NPMadden	140+
			(Noel Meade, Ire) *w'like: hit 2nd: hmpd 3rd: nt fluent 4th: hdwy after 3 out: kpt on run-in but nt pce to trble ldrs* **22/1**	
4125	**8**	*shd*	**Whispered Promises (USA)**[24] 3994 5-11-7 132 JohnMcNamara	138
			(R S Brookhouse) *bhd: hdwy 3 out: kpt on appr last and styd on run-in: nvr gng pce to trble ldrs* **100/1**	
-115	**9**	*5*	**Rasharrow (IRE)**[38] 3725 7-11-7 132 TonyDobbin	134+
			(L Lungo) *bhd: rdn 3 out: sme hdwy next but nvr gng pce to rch ldrs* **14/1**	
12	**10**	*3*	**O'Muircheartaigh (IRE)**[100] 2667 6-11-7 BJGeraghty	132+
			(E J O'Grady, Ire) *leggy: lw: mid-div: hdwy 4 out: chsng ldrs whn n.m.r 3 out: wknd after 2 out* **14/1**	
	11	*3*	**Quatre Heures (FR)**[38] 3744 4-10-13 DJCasey	120+
			(W P Mullins, Ire) *lt-f: swtg: bhd: hdwy appr 3 out: rdn 2 out: wknd bef last* **10/1**[3]	
1341	**12**	*1*	**Crow Wood**[17] 3761 7-11-7 134 RussGarritty	126
			(J J Quinn) *chsd ldrs: rdn 3 out: wknd fr next* **16/1**	
1	**13**	*2 ½*	**Orcadian**[25] 3963 5-11-7 MarkBradburne	123
			(J M P Eustace) *lw: chsd ldrs: rdn and blnd 3 out: sn wknd* **25/1**	
2-45	**14**	*12*	**Patrixprial**[19] 4077 5-11-7 123 LeightonAspell	111
			(M H Tompkins) *bhd most of way* **200/1**	
24	**15**	*¾*	**Blueberry Boy (IRE)**[30] 3892 7-11-7 DFO'Regan	110
			(Paul Stafford, Ire) *tall: lengthy: hit 3rd: in tch: wknd fr 3 out* **40/1**	
	16	*2 ½*	**Kalderon (GER)**[8] 4267 6-11-7 CO'Dwyer	108
			(T Hogan, Ire) *tall: bhd: sme hdwy appr 3 out: sn wknd* **40/1**	
010	**17**	*shd*	**Muntami (IRE)**[25] 3967 5-11-7 100 AndrewTinkler	108
			(John A Harris) *a in rr* **200/1**	

211 **18** *16* **Masafi (IRE)**[53] 3488 5-11-7 .... GLee 92
(J Howard Johnson) *chsd ldr to 4th: rdn 4 out: sn wknd* **25/1**

241 **19** *2 ½* **Nikola (FR)**[17] 4114 5-11-7 ....(t) CarlLlewellyn 89
(N A Twiston-Davies) *prom: chsd ldr 4th tl after 3 out: sn wknd* **100/1**

22 **U** **Pablo Du Charmil (FR)**[24] 3996 5-11-7 .... RJGreene —
(M C Pipe) *in tch whn blnd and uns rdr 3rd* **33/1**

3m 54.5s (-4.70) **Going Correction** 0.0s/f (Good)
WFA 4 from 5yo+ 7lb **20** Ran SP% **120.8**
Speed ratings: **111,110,110,109,109 108,108,108,106,104 103,102,101,95,95** 94,94,86,85,— CSF £63.45 CT £897.82 TOTE £6.30: £2.60, £3.20, £4.40; EX 63.10 Trifecta £832.20 Pool: £7,619.36 - 6.50 winning units.

Owner J Hales **Bred** The Niarchos Family **Trained** Ditcheat, Somerset

FOCUS
Just a fair renewal of this event and the winner, though steadily progressive and improving yet again, has been rated 5lb below the 10-year average and 16lb behind Back In Front in 2003. The early gallop was not all that strong, and the winning time was only average for a race of its nature, 4.5 seconds slower than the Champion Hurdle.

NOTEBOOK
Noland was being ridden from an early stage and looked to have a near-impossible task approaching the penultimate flight, but his stamina eventually came to his rescue and he dug deep to produce a magnificent late surge which got him up near the line. This was his fourth consecutive success as a hurdler, and he has now won both of the Grade One novice events this season over the distance. Again he shaped as if he would relish the chance to race over a longer trip in the future, but while further progression in this sphere is entirely possible, he is very much a chaser in the making. He reportedly won't run again over hurdles and has next season's Arkle as his likely target. *(op 13-2 tchd 7-1)*

Straw Bear(USA) ◆, winner of both his previous outings over hurdles since switching from the Flat and having his first run in graded company, ran a huge race in defeat. Ideally positioned throughout, he looked all over the winner when surging to the front under McCoy turning for home, but he lost vital momentum when meeting the final flight wrong and, while he did extremely well to recover as he did up the run-in, it ultimately proved the difference between winning and losing. He is clearly developing into a high-class novice and, like the winner, he would have ideally preferred a stronger early gallop and a deeper surface. He would be entitled to go very close if turning out for the Champion Novice Hurdle at Punchestown next month. *(op 10-1)*

Buena Vista(IRE), last seen finishing third, giving 10lb to Noland, over course and distance 95 days previously, posted a very game effort in defeat and the application of cheekpieces certainly had a positive effect. He was unable to dictate as he prefers, and the easing of the ground was not in his favour, but this must rate a career-best display and he may be able to find more improvement when upped to a longer trip in due course. *(op 16-1)*

Sublimity(FR) ◆, who scoped badly after running below-par in Grade Two at Punchestown on his second outing over hurdles last time, stepped-up massively on that form and has to rate as unfortunate, as he was carried wide by the loose horse on the bend nearing three from home, losing ground at a crucial stage. He picked up in taking style after a fine leap two out, and still had every chance at the final flight, but he had no more to offer up the run-in. A return to a flat track in the future may be more to his advantage and, given that he is rated 108 on the Flat, further improvement in this sphere looks assured. *(op 18-1 tchd 20-1, 22-1 in a place)*

Sweet Wake(GER) came into this with a big reputation, having won both his outings over hurdles since joining connections from Germany. He travelled strongly for most of the race, yet found little off the bridle and was eventually well held. This could be deemed disappointing, but it was his first outing in graded company, and he may do better when reverting to a flat track in the future, so is not one to write off on the back of this effort. *(op 11-4 tchd 3-1 in places)*

Natal(FR), officially the highest rated British-trained runner in the race and who had run with credit in the face of stiff tasks the last twice, ran close to his best on this return to novice company and should be rated slightly better than the bare form as he was tight for room when the race became serious and was not fluent over the final flight. Like his winning stablemate, he too rates as a top prospect for novice chasing next season. *(tchd 14-1, 20-1 in places)*

Jazz Messenger(FR), formerly a very useful handicapper on the Flat and who had not done a great deal wrong in his four previous hurdle outings, was staying on up the rising finish and recorded a personal best in defeat. He is not the most fluent of hurdlers, but was not beaten far at the finish, and deserves extra credit as he was badly hampered at the third flight. *(op 25-1)*

Whispered Promises(USA), behind both Noland and Natal the last twice, turned in a blinding effort and was not beaten far. He travelled sweetly for most of the race, jumping with fluency, and only lacked the speed to get involved up the rising finish. He is clearly a very useful hurdler in the making, and is versatile as regards underfoot conditions, but he is not going to prove easy to place next season.

Rasharrow(IRE), reverting to novice company, having finished fifth in the Listed Afga Hurdle at Sandown last time, posted his best effort to date without rating a threat. He shaped as though he *may now want further and, as a seven-year-old, he will surely be sent over fences before too long. (tchd 16-1 in places)*

O'Muircheartaigh(IRE), who lost his unbeaten record over hurdles when runner-up in the Grade One Royal Bond at Fairyhouse when last seen 100 days previously, proved very easy to back and accordingly ran below his best. His lack of a recent run was a certain negative, however, and it would be unwise to assume this good-looking horse will not be capable of better in the future. He may also need further now.

Quatre Heures(FR), the sole four-year-old in the line-up, who had created a decent impression when winning on his previous two outings and looked a player when making ground to join the leaders three from home, yet he failed to sustain his effort and was ultimately well beaten. He did not appear to really enjoy this much stiffer track, and may need softer ground, but still has plenty of time to prove his worth as a hurdler. *(op 8-1)*

Crow Wood, who had an unorthodox preparation race for this when running in the Winter Derby Trial at Lingfield on the Polytrack 17 days previously, was given a prominent ride. However, as had been the case on his only previous outing over course and distance in November, he was again found out by the stiff nature of this track. He is capable of much better and would be well worth another chance if lining up at Aintree next month.

Orcadian, off the mark on his debut in this sphere at Market Rasen 25 days previously, appeared to run with the choke out through the first half of the contest and not suprisingly faded when asked for maximum effort. It is too soon to be writing him off as a hurdler and he may well need a longer trip to be seen at best. *(tchd 28-1)*

Masafi(IRE) *Official explanation: jockey said gelding had a breathing problem*

4431 IRISH INDEPENDENT ARKLE CHALLENGE TROPHY CHASE
GRADE 1 (12 fncs) **2m**
2:35 (2:38) (Class 1) 5-Y-0+

£79,828 (£29,946; £14,994; £7,476; £3,752; £1,876)

Form RPR

1111 **1** **Voy Por Ustedes (FR)**[24] 3991 5-11-2 .... RobertThornton 162+
(A King) *lw: prom: chsd ldr bef 3 out: drvn and narrow ld bef last: styd on wl flat* **15/2**

1-11 **2** *1 ¼* **Monet's Garden (IRE)**[34] 3796 8-11-7 .... TonyDobbin 165+
(N G Richards) *lw: mde most fr 2nd tl drvn and narrowly hdd bef last: kpt on wl flat but no imp wnr nr fin* **8/1**

22-1 **3** *5* **Foreman (GER)**[52] 3501 8-11-7 .... APMcCoy 160
(T Doumen, France) *lw: tended to jump lft: settled in last pair: prog fr 8th: outpcd by ldrs 3 out: styd on fr next to take 3rd last: nvr nrr* **5/1**[2]

-122 **4** *2* **Wild Passion (GER)**[65] 3308 6-11-7 .... PCarberry 159+
(Noel Meade, Ire) *led to 2nd: chsd ldr tl bef 3 out: 3rd and hld whn hit 2 out: one pce after* **20/1**

0211 **5** *3* **Don't Be Shy (FR)**[24] 3980 5-11-2 .... TimmyMurphy 150
(M C Pipe) *settled in midfield: pushed along fr 6th: bdly outpcd and struggling bef 3 out: styd on fr next: nrst fin* **8/1**

-411 **6** *6* **Missed That**[44] 3639 7-11-7 .... RWalsh 152+
(W P Mullins, Ire) *nt a fluent towards rr: outpcd fr 9th: keeping on but no ch whn n.m.r on inner bnd bef last: n.d* **6/1**[3]

111 **7** *¾* **Racing Demon (IRE)**[30] 3879 6-11-7 .... SamThomas 149+
(Miss H C Knight) *lw: racd wd: chsd ldrs: j.rt 3rd: outpcd 3 out: one pce and no prog after* **9/2**[1]

1442 **8** *1* **Arteea (IRE)**[44] 3639 7-11-7 .... AndrewJMcNamara 148+
(Michael Hourigan, Ire) *rangy: str: lw: chsd ldrs: rdn and losing pl whn j.rt 3 out: no ch after* **33/1**

-251 **9** *shd* **Tamarinbleu (FR)**[54] 3457 6-11-7 147 .... TomScudamore 149+
(M C Pipe) *mstke 1st: chsd ldrs: outpcd 3 out: one pce and n.d after* **33/1**

1131 **10** *11* **Cerium (FR)**[40] 3695 5-11-2 144 ....(b[1]) PJBrennan 133+
(P F Nicholls) *chsd ldng pair to 8th: u.p whn mstke and bmpd 3 out: wknd next* **50/1**

-1F1 **11** *18* **Coat Of Honour (USA)**[78] 2989 6-11-7 .... GLee 118
(J Howard Johnson) *racd wd and tended to jump rt: a in rr: t.o after 9th* **33/1**

12 *shd* **Mid Dancer (FR)**[100] 5-11-2 .... CO'Dwyer 113
(A Chaille-Chaille, France) *neat: racd wd: in tch: losing pl whn mstke 9th: wknd and eased: t.o* **14/1**

6213 **F** **Accordion Etoile (IRE)**[37] 3774 7-11-7 .... BJGeraghty —
(Paul Nolan, Ire) *in tch in midfield tl heavy fall 8th* **7/1**

1BF3 **P** **Crossbow Creek**[19] 4076 8-11-7 .... JamieMoore —
(M G Rimell) *blnd 2nd: nvr gng wl in last pair after: hmpd 8th: t.o whn p.u bef 3 out* **100/1**

3m 52.3s (-7.00) **Going Correction** 0.0s/f (Good)
WFA 5 from 6yo+ 4lb **14** Ran SP% **118.8**
Speed ratings: **117,116,113,112,111 108,108,107,107,101 92,92,—,—** CSF £61.61 CT £333.50 TOTE £8.90: £2.80, £2.70, £2.50; EX 62.30 Trifecta £492.80 Pool: £7,843.86 - 11.30 winning units.

Owner Sir Robert Ogden **Bred** Ecurie Macaire Guillaume, And Francis Picoulet **Trained** Barbury Castle, Wilts

FOCUS
The pace was strong and the winning time was well up to standard for a contest like this in the conditions. This was a cracking renewal and very sound form. The winner has been rated 2lb better than the ten-year average for this race and the runner-up, who was conceding 5lb, has been assessed as the season's top novice at this stage.

NOTEBOOK
Voy Por Ustedes(FR) ◆ maintained his perfect record over fences with a fine display. Always well placed and jumping superbly, he edged ahead before the final fence, where he took off a fraction too soon, before finding plenty up the hill. The fourth five-year-old to prevail in the last eight runnings of the Arkle, he looks sure to make up into a leading Champion Chase candidate next season. *(op 7-1 tchd 15-2 and 8-1 in places)*

Monet's Garden(IRE) ◆, soon in front, jumped and travelled really well and had all bar the winner on the stretch a long way out. Headed going to the final fence, at which he nodded slightly on landing, he could not match Voy Por Ustedes for pace on the flat but went down fighting. He lost nothing in defeat on ground slightly faster than he would have preferred, and as he is proven over three miles he looks the sort for the King George next season. *(tchd 7-1 in places)*

Foreman(GER) did best of those to come from off the pace. After improving in the back straight he could not go with the leading pair from the top of the hill, but stayed on well to claim third place at the last. Softer ground would have helped him. *(op 6-1)*

Wild Passion(GER), without the blinkers this time, ran a fine race on ground that was a little faster than ideal but was held in third when pecking at the second last.

Don't Be Shy(FR) has gained all his wins in very testing conditions and lacked the pace to be effective on faster ground over this trip. He could not go with the leaders from the top of the hill but did stay on well once switched around toiling rivals on the home turn. *(tchd 17-2 and 9-1 in places)*

Missed That did not put in a convincing round of jumping and in truth was never a factor, well held when hampered on the inside turning into the straight. *(op 13-2 tchd 7-1 in places)*

Racing Demon(IRE), partnered by Thomas for the first time, was kept wide, but with the French runner on his outer. Although jumping well, showing no signs of going out to his right, he lacked the pace to get in a blow and his trainer admitted that it was a mistake to run him here rather than *in the Royal & SunAlliance. He remains a class act and could be a Gold Cup horse next year. (tchd 5-1 in places)*

Arteea(IRE), whose best form has been on soft ground, gradually lost a prominent pitch and was beaten when jumping right and giving a bump to Tamarinbleu at the third last. *(tchd 25-1 in places)*

Tamarinbleu(FR) ran respectably, but did not fence fluently after an error at the first and was held when jumped into at the third from home. *(op 25-1)*

Cerium(FR) , blinkered for the first time, chased the pace but a mistake at the third from home quickly had him on the retreat.

Coat Of Honour(USA), appearing for the first time since Christmas, did not prove up to this class and was in rear throughout, showing a tendency to jump out to his right. *(tchd 40-1)*

Mid Dancer(FR) came into this unbeaten in nine races in France, three of them over fences, but his limitations were ruthlessly exposed on this first start for over three months. Kept wide, he was beginning to lose his pitch when making a slight mistake at the final ditch, four from home, and defeat was quickly accepted. He needs softer ground and a longer trip. *(op 16-1)*

Crossbow Creek seemed to unnerve himself with an early blunder and struggled in rear thereafter until eventually pulled up. *(tchd 15-2)*

Accordion Etoile(IRE) was just beginning to pick up the leaders when coming down at the eighth. He was fortunately none the worse. *(tchd 15-2)*

4432 SMURFIT KAPPA CHAMPION HURDLE CHALLENGE TROPHY
GRADE 1 (8 hdls) **2m 110y**
3:15 (3:21) (Class 1) 4-Y-0+

£202,683 (£76,032; £38,069; £18,981; £9,526; £4,763)

Form RPR

1311 **1** **Brave Inca (IRE)**[44] 3641 8-11-10 .... APMcCoy 173+
(C A Murphy, Ire) *lw: prom: pushed along 3rd: reminders after 4th: upsides 3 out: slt ld 2 out: hrd drvn run-in: styd on strly* **7/4**[1]

5421 **2** *1* **Macs Joy (IRE)**[24] 4000 7-11-10 .... BJGeraghty 172+
(Mrs John Harrington, Ire) *in tch: hdwy 4 out: trckd ldrs 2 out: drvn to chse wnr sn after last: kpt on wl but no imp nr fin* **13/2**[3]

1-10 **3** *3 ½* **Hardy Eustace (IRE)**[44] 3641 9-11-10 ....(v[1]) CO'Dwyer 168
(D T Hughes, Ire) *chsd ldrs: slt ld after 4th: narrowly hdd 2 out: styd pressing wnr u.p tl lost 2nd run-in: wknd nr fin* **11/2**[2]

01-1 **4** *6* **Al Eile (IRE)**[52] 3492 6-11-10 .... TimmyMurphy 162
(John Queally, Ire) *chsd ldrs: wnt 3rd 3 out: sn rdn: wknd after next* **8/1**

1-1P **5** *¾* **Arcalis**[52] 3492 6-11-10 159 .... GLee 163+
(J Howard Johnson) *hld up in rr: hdwy and hit 4 out: chsd ldrs and rdn next: wknd after 2 out* **9/1**

-201 **6** *9* **Briareus**[24] 3994 6-11-10 150 .... MrTGreenall 154+
(A M Balding) *lw: chsd ldrs: rdn and hit 4 out: btn next but kpt on again run-in* **20/1**

U0U1 **7** *shd* **Kawagino (IRE)**[5] 4329 6-11-10 108 .... JamieMoore 154+
(J W Mullins) *lw: bhd: hdwy 4 out: rdn and in tch 3 out: nvr rchd ldrs: no ch whn bdly hmpd last* **500/1**

-233 **8** *3/4* **Faasel (IRE)**[52] 3492 5-11-10 154 .... (b) TonyDobbin 153+
(N G Richards) *bhd: hdwy 4 out: drvn to chse ldrs 3 out: no imp and btn 2 out* **16/1**

-315 **9** *shd* **The French Furze (IRE)**[44] 3641 12-11-10 149 .... BrianHarding 151
(N G Richards) *bhd: kpt on fr 2 out: n.d* **150/1**

3412 **10** *8* **Royal Shakespeare (FR)**[24] 3994 7-11-10 150 .... TomScudamore 147+
(S Gollings) *rr whn hmpd 4th: nvr in contention after* **100/1**

2P20 **11** *6* **Intersky Falcon**[78] 2971 9-11-10 157 .... (bt) MickFitzgerald 145+
(Jonjo O'Neill) *chsng ldrs whn bdly hmpd 4th: n.d after* **66/1**

1100 **12** *15* **Admiral (IRE)**[66] 3298 5-11-10 147 .... PaulO'Neill 122
(R C Guest) *lw: chsd ldrs to 4th: rdn 4 out: wknd bef next* **150/1**

00P- **13** *dist* **Astonville (FR)**[58] 12-11-10 .... (t) BenjaminHitchcott —
(P Cottin, France) *sn bhd: t.o* **500/1**

F **14** *dist* **Fiepes Shuffle (GER)**[38] 3725 6-11-10 .... PCarberry —
(C Von Der Recke, Germany) *led tl hdd 4th: sn wknd: t.o* **50/1**

1-12 **F** **Asian Maze (IRE)**[24] 4000 7-11-3 .... RWalsh —
(Thomas Mullins, Ire) *chsd ldrs tl fell 4th* **12/1**

0P0- **P** **Turnium (FR)**[46] 11-11-10 .... (bt) JamesDavies —
(P Cottin, France) *a bhd: t.o whn p.u bef last* **500/1**

-340 **F** **Penzance**[24] 3994 5-11-10 145 .... RobertThornton 154
(A King) *in tch: rdn and hit 4 out: wknd 2 out: 6th and no ch whn fell last* **40/1**

F35 **P** **Leo's Luckyman (USA)**[52] 3491 7-11-10 .... JohnMcNamara —
(R S Brookhouse) *rr whn bdly hmpd 4th: n.d after: t.o whn p.u bef 2 out* **500/1**

3m 50.0s (-9.20) **Going Correction** 0.0s/f (Good) course record **18** Ran SP% **113.5**
Speed ratings: **121,120,118,116,115 111,111,111,111,107 104,97,—,—,— —,—,—** CSF £11.48 CT £50.89 TOTE £2.70: £1.30, £2.50, £2.40; EX 12.00 Trifecta £27.40 Pool: £12,297.98 - 318.58 winning units.

Owner Novices Syndicate **Bred** D W Macauley **Trained** Gorey, Co Wexford

■ Irish runners filled the first four places.

FOCUS

A strong line-up, even without the injured Harchibald and Feathard Lady, or Lingo who was put down on the gallops in February. This was a very good Champion Hurdle and Brave Inca has been rated 2lb above the ten-year average and just a pound below Istabraq (1998) and Alderbrook. It was a personal best too for Macs Joy, while Hardy Eustace has been rated to last season's winning mark. Al Eile has been rated to his mark, and Arcalis and Briareus both slight personal bests. The winning time was decent, even for the Champion Hurdle, 4.5 seconds quicker than the Supreme Novices' and 7.2 seconds quicker than the Fred Winter.

NOTEBOOK

Brave Inca(IRE) ◆, beaten two necks when third last year, always held a good position, but was already being niggled at by McCoy as the field headed away from the stands with a circuit to run. Challenging the reigning champion at the third last, he showed narrowly ahead on the turn and, although Macs Joy came at him on the run-in, he found plenty to hold him. As hard as nails, he has the class to match his constitution but his lazy way of running means he never makes it look easy. *(tchd 13-8, 15-8 in places)*

Macs Joy(IRE) moved into third place at the top of the hill and was still travelling well on the approach to the final flight, but after being switched to chase the winner soon after touching down over the obstacle he could not get past that gutsy opponent. He is a high-class hurdler and beat Brave Inca three times last season, but the only time he has done so in six meetings since last year's Champion was when Brave Inca fell at Aintree. *(op 6-1 tchd 7-1 in places)*

Hardy Eustace(IRE), bidding to become the sixth triple winner of this race, had headgear on for the first time since last year's Champion but it was a visor rather than blinkers. Unable to get to the front until around halfway, he fought valiantly when headed by the eventual winner but had no more to give on the run-in, forfeiting second place. This was a fine effort after a troubled preparation *(tchd 6-1)*

Al Eile(IRE), seventh last year, ran a solid race but was outpaced by the principals from the second last. He is at his best on softer ground, especially over this trip. *(op 9-1 tchd 7-1 in places)*

Arcalis, held up towards the back of the field, made up his ground smoothly but could could never get closer than disputing fourth place as the principals pulled away from him. Last year's Supreme Novices' Hurdle winner, he did best of the British but the ground was slower than ideal for him and his yard has not been in the best of form. *(op 7-1)*

Briareus a supplementary entry after his all-the-way Wincanton victory, was never able to get to the front and was in trouble after rapping the fourth last, but he did keep on late in the day to snatch sixth prize on the line. He has the build to make a classy chaser next season.

Kawagino(IRE), winner of a handicap off 108 last week, showed vastly improved form and was only just caught for sixth place after being hampered by the fall of Penzance at the final flight. His rating will take a hit but he will be going back over fences next season. *(op 300-1)*

Faasel(IRE), with blinkers replacing the visor, improved from the rear of the field at the fifth but his eventual finishing position was about as close as he could get. The last five-year-old to win the Champion Hurdle was See You Then back in 1985, since when no fewer than 70 have tried and failed. *(tchd 18-1 and 20-1 in a place)*

The French Furze(IRE) is often a front-runner but he was always trailing here prior to passing beaten rivals late on and almost catching his much younger stablemate.

Royal Shakespeare(FR) was never in the hunt after being hampered by a faller at the fourth but retains a healthy lead at the top of the BHB's Order Of Merit.

Intersky Falcon, who did best of the British runners when finishing sixth last year, could not recover after being hampered at the fourth. *(op 50-1)*

Admiral(IRE) was close up until weakening rapidly on reaching the top of the hill. *(op 100-1)*

Astonville(FR), who ran in this race last year as well as the Gold Cup and Grand National, has no pretensions to this class any more and his participation, along with that of stablemate Turnium, was rightly criticised.

Fiepes Shuffle(GER), somewhat keen, went off too fast and back-pedalled rapidly once headed by Hardy Eustace at the fourth. *(op 40-1)*

Penzance, a head in front of Faasel when landing the Triumph Hurdle here a year ago, ran a reasonable race in the face of a stiff task against his elders but was a beaten sixth when taking quite a nasty fall at the final flight. *(tchd 14-1)*

Asian Maze(IRE) ◆, runner-up to Macs Joy on her belated return to action, endured a bit of a kicking when coming down at the fourth and plans to pull her out again in the World Hurdle were wisely abandoned. She remains relatively unexposed over this trip. *(tchd 14-1)*

4433 WILLIAM HILL TROPHY H'CAP CHASE GRADE 3 (18 fncs 1 omitted) 3m 110y

4:00 (4:02) (Class 1) 5-Y-0+

£45,616 (£17,112; £8,568; £4,272; £2,144; £1,072)

Form RPR

111 **1** **Dun Doire (IRE)**[47] 3587 7-10-9 129 .... RWalsh 139+
(A J Martin, Ire) *lw: settled wl in rr: no prog and modest 14th after 16th: drvn and rapid prog bypassing 2 out: str run to ld last 100yds: sn clr* **7/1**[2]

2-FP **2** *2* **Juveigneur (FR)**[24] 3988 9-11-5 139 .... MickFitzgerald 147
(N J Henderson) *lw: trckd ldrs: effrt after 16th: chsd ldr bef last: styd on and upsides flat: outpcd by wnr last 100yds* **16/1**

3-PP **3** *1 1/4* **Irish Hussar (IRE)**[17] 4118 10-11-12 146 .... MarcusFoley 154+
(N J Henderson) *trckd ldr: led 12th: kicked on after 16th: drvn 4l clr bnd bef last: tired and hdd last 100yds* **66/1**

11P2 **4** *1 1/2* **Model Son (IRE)**[24] 3971 8-10-8 133 .... PaddyMerrigan[5] 140+
(P C Haslam) *nt fluent: trckd ldrs: lost pl 15th: 9th after next and struggling : styd on wl again bef last: nt pce to chal* **14/1**

1311 **5** *4* **Bob The Builder**[34] 3803 7-10-6 126 .... AntonyEvans 128+
(N A Twiston-Davies) *mde most tl hdd and mstke 12th: chsd ldr after: drvn to chal 3 out: no imp bypassing next: wknd and mstke last* **20/1**

/33P **6** *1 1/2* **Fork Lightning (IRE)**[17] 4118 10-11-2 136 .... RobertThornton 138+
(A King) *j.rt: wl in tch: chsd ldng pair 15th: cl enough 3 out: fdd bef last* **16/1**

41F1 **7** *3 1/2* **Alderburn**[33] 3816 7-10-10 130 .... RichardJohnson 128+
(H D Daly) *lw: settled in midfield: blnd 11th: effrt whn hit 16th: nt on terms w ldrs after* **8/1**

2U-3 **8** *3/4* **Desailly**[27] 3921 12-10-5 125 .... MarkBradburne 121
(J A Geake) *swtg: settled wl in rr: sme prog fr 13th: nt on terms w ldrs fr 16th: kpt on: n.d* **50/1**

0P00 **9** *nk* **Seebald (GER)**[10] 4241 11-11-9 143 .... (t) TomScudamore 139+
(M C Pipe) *lw: nt a fluent: trckd ldrs: lost pl 15th: effrt again bef 3 out but nt on terms: wknd and mstke last* **100/1**

000P **10** *2* **Mixsterthetrixster (USA)**[45] 3620 10-10-6 126 .... JoeTizzard 120+
(Mrs Tracey Barfoot-Saunt) *trckd ldrs: stl chsng after 16th: wknd bypassing 2 out* **100/1**

322P **11** *1/2* **Black De Bessy (FR)**[24] 3995 8-10-6 126 .... RobertWalford 119
(D R C Elsworth) *j.rt: nvr on terms w ldrs: no prog and wl btn after 16th* **33/1**

1464 **12** *1* **Va Vavoom (IRE)**[33] 3816 8-10-1 121 .... (t) TomSiddall 113
(N A Twiston-Davies) *trckd ldrs: stl wl in tch after 16th: wknd sn after 3 out* **100/1**

2530 **13** *1* **Made In Japan (JPN)**[10] 4241 6-11-5 139 .... (b) PJBrennan 132+
(P J Hobbs) *several mstkes: chsd ldrs tl wknd fr 16th* **33/1**

5-1 **14** *18* **No Half Session (IRE)**[37] 3771 9-10-6 126 .... PCarberry 99
(Noel Meade, Ire) *w'like: set off last: blnd 3rd: nt fluent and nvr a factor after: t.o* **8/1**

0/PP **15** *1* **Shardam (IRE)**[59] 3390 9-10-9 129 .... (t) CarlLlewellyn 101
(N A Twiston-Davies) *nvr on terms w ldrs: u.p in rr 12th: sn no ch: t.o* **33/1**

3213 **16** *17* **Classic Capers**[82] 2953 7-10-7 127 .... GLee 82
(J M Jefferson) *a towards rr: wkng whn mstke 15th: sn wl t.o* **50/1**

4-01 **F** **A Glass In Thyne (IRE)**[45] 3620 8-11-3 137 .... AndrewThornton —
(B N Pollock) *trckd ldrs tl fell 9th* **16/1**

252P **P** **Europa**[10] 4241 10-11-6 140 .... JasonMaguire —
(Ferdy Murphy) *a wl in rr: sltly hmpd 9th: mstke 12th: sn wknd: t.o whn p.u bef 3 out* **66/1**

1215 **P** **Dunbrody Millar (IRE)**[17] 4111 8-10-5 128 .... TomMalone[3] —
(P Bowen) *lw: prom: mstke 12th and lost pl: mstkes after and sn struggling: t.o whn p.u bef 3 out* **25/1**

6313 **P** **Korelo (FR)**[17] 4111 8-10-12 132 .... TimmyMurphy —
(M C Pipe) *nt fluent and nvr gng wl: struggling in last pair after 11th: sn wl bhd: t.o last whn p.u after 16th* **15/2**[3]

4-F2 **P** **Moulin Riche (FR)**[19] 4070 6-10-12 132 .... APMcCoy —
(F Doumen, France) *settled midfield: hmpd 9th: effrt and in tch whn mstke 15th and rdn: wknd bef 3 out: wl bhd whn p.u bef last* **10/3**[1]

6m 12.1s (-10.80) **Going Correction** 0.0s/f (Good) **21** Ran SP% **121.2**
Speed ratings: **137,116,115,115,114 113,112,112,112,111 111,111,110,105,104** 99,—,—,—,— — CSF £98.03 CT £6670.18 TOTE £6.70: £1.80, £3.90, £16.70, £2.80; EX 240.40 Trifecta £3102.80 Pool: £9,177.48 - 2.10 winning units.

Owner Dunderry Racing Syndicate **Bred** Mrs Sarah Martin **Trained** Summerhill, Co. Meath

■ The second last fence had to be bypassed.

FOCUS

Not an especially strong renewal of this race, but the form looks solid. The progressive winner has been raised another 5lb, and the runner-up also recorded a personal best.

NOTEBOOK

Dun Doire(IRE) ◆, hugely progressive over fences this term and off a mark 50lb higher here than when he began his winning sequence at Wetherby in November, came from out of the clouds to win this going away under a magnificent ride from Walsh. He was dropped right out through the early stages, and looked to be struggling at halfway, but he responded most gamely to his rider's urgings from three out, and clearly stays all day long. He again left the impression he has not yet reached his peak, and another hike in the weights may not be enough to stop him winning. He holds an entry in the Grand National next month, but with an allotted weight of 9-11 he is most unlikely to make the cut. However, he really does appeal strongly as an ideal type for that event and, considering he is rated just 97 over hurdles, it should come as little suprise to see him campaigned specifically for a crack at the 2007 equivalent. *(op 8-1 tchd 9-1)*

Juveigneur(FR) ◆, winner of the Kim Muir last year from an 11lb lower mark, had failed to complete in his previous outings this term, but bounced right back and showed his true colours with a personal best in defeat. The better ground was clearly much to his liking, as was the return to this course and distance, and this must rate a most encouraging trial for next month's Grand National.

Irish Hussar(IRE), runner-up in this event last season from a 6lb lower mark, turned in a brave effort under top weight and only gave way to the first two up the run-in. He has not won since his novice days in 2003, and is difficult to keep sound, but really is a smart chaser on his day. *(op 50-1)*

Model Son(IRE) ◆, runner-up from this mark in the Red Square Vodka Gold Cup at Haydock on heavy ground last time, was coming back at the principals up the run-in and produced another taking effort. He spoilt his chances with some messy jumping at crucial stages, and arguably would have been better served by a more aggressive ride over this shorter trip, but he has time on his side and it is most unlikely we have seen the best of him yet. It would be no surprise to see him come back for another crack at this next season and is another that appeals as a likely 2007 Grand National candidate.

Bob The Builder, bidding for the hat-trick, having been successful at Ludlow the last twice, showed up really well from the front but found the longer trep stretching his stamina. He proved well suited by this return to a left-handed track, enjoyed the good ground, and remains in very good form.

Fork Lightning(IRE), racing from the same mark as when successful in this event in 2003, left a disappointing effort in the Racing Post Chase at Sandown last time behind him and posted a sound effort in defeat. He did tend to jump right at his fences, however, and looks held by the Handicapper at present on this evidence. *(op 14-1)*

Alderburn, raised 10lb after an impressive success on fast ground at Huntingdon last time, was found out in the jumping department against these seasoned handicappers and was well held. He still has the option of novice events this term and is still young enough to progress to a higher level as a chaser.

No Half Session(IRE), reverting to fences, was never in the race and proved most disappointing. *He is capable of better and should leave this behind when returning to softer ground in due course.* *(tchd 17-2 in places)*

Europa *Official explanation: jockey said gelding pulled up lame (tchd 8-1)*

Korelo(FR), who had a very hard race when fourth in the Eider Chase over an extended four miles last time, was too slow over his fences and his fate was sealed from an early stage. He is better than this, but looks in need of a break now. *(tchd 8-1)*

Moulin Riche(FR), winner of the inaugural running of the Brit Insurance Novices' Hurdle at last year's Festival and very well backed for this, got badly hampered by the fall of A Glass In Thyne at the ninth fence and seemed to lose confidence thereafter. This was bitterly disappointing, but he is more than capable of taking a decent prize off this mark when things go his way and so is worth another chance. *Official explanation: jockey said gelding had been hampered by a faller (tchd 8-1)*

4434 SPORTING INDEX H'CAP CHASE (A CROSS COUNTRY CHASE) (32 fncs) 3m 7f

4:40 (4:40) (Class 2) 5-Y-O+

£25,052 (£7,400; £3,700; £1,852; £924; £464)

Form				RPR
P5P-	**1**		**Native Jack (IRE)**[37] 3776 12-10-8 **126**.................................. DNRussell (P J Rothwell, Ire) *lengthy: lw: hld up in rr: stdy hdwy fr 26th: chal last: hrd drvn to ld run-in: kpt on gamely* **7/2**[1]	134+
0-10	**2**	*2*	**Spot Thedifference (IRE)**[37] 3776 13-11-12 **144**.....(p) MrJTMcNamara (E Bolger, Ire) *hld up in rr: hdwy 20th: chal 2 out: slt ld appr last: hdd run-in: outpcd nr fin* **12/1**	147+
/45-	**3**	*5*	**Buailtes And Fadas (IRE)**[37] 3776 11-9-11 **118** oh2. MissNCarberry(3) (E Bolger, Ire) *str: lw: bhd: hdwy 20th: chsd ldrs 3 out: kpt on run in but nvr gng pce to chal* **6/1**[2]	116
0-50	**4**	*5*	**Il De Boitron (FR)**[37] 3776 8-10-6 **124**..................... AndrewJMcNamara (Thomas Gerard O'Leary, Ire) *in tch: chsd ldrs fr 24th: wknd fr 2 out* **100/1**	117
3405	**5**	*½*	**Koquelicot (FR)**[54] 3469 8-10-5 **123**............................. RichardJohnson (P J Hobbs) *led 4th to 23rd: led again 25th to 26th: styd chsng ldrs tl wknd last* **16/1**	116
1P3	**6**	*6*	**Good Step (IRE)**[20] 4061 8-10-12 **130**...................................... PCarberry (E Bolger, Ire) *lw: in tch: chsd ldrs 26th: blnd 3 out: sn btn* **7/2**[1]	120+
F/F-	**7**	*½*	**Never Compromise (IRE)**[37] 3776 11-9-11 **120**.............. MsKWalsh(5) (T M Walsh, Ire) *chsd ldrs: led 26th: hdd & wknd appr last* **16/1**	107+
5110	**8**	*3*	**Comanche War Paint (IRE)**[95] 2745 9-10-9 **127**................. JoeTizzard (P F Nicholls) *rr: hdwy 18th: mstke 27th: sme hdwy 4 out: sn wknd* **10/1**[3]	110
3114	**9**	*3*	**Mrs Be (IRE)**[18] 4098 10-9-11 **118** oh2.................. MissPGundry(3) (J G Cann) *mid-div: sme hdwy 27th: wknd 3 out* **14/1**	98
0P36	**10**	*10*	**Just In Debt (IRE)**[95] 2745 10-10-13 **131**......................... AlanDempsey (M Todhunter) *bhd: sme hdwy 23rd: nvr trbld ldrs* **33/1**	101
5200	**11**	*16*	**Lord Jack (IRE)**[31] 3854 10-11-5 **137**............................... BrianHarding (N G Richards) *led to 4th: styd chalng tl led 23rd: hdd 25th: wknd 28th* **25/1**	91
PP2R	**12**	*4*	**Tribal Venture (FR)**[72] 3176 8-10-12 **130**.......................(b) AlanO'Keeffe (Ferdy Murphy) *bhd most of way* **16/1**	80
5006	**13**	*28*	**Whereareyounow (IRE)**[24] 3988 9-10-0 **118**.................(t) CarlLlewellyn (N A Twiston-Davies) *j. slowly and rr 11th: blnd 16th: nvr in contention after* **33/1**	40
-300	**U**		**What Odds (IRE)**[37] 3775 10-10-1 **119**.................................... RGeraghty (T K Geraghty, Ire) *in rr tl mstke and uns rdr 15th* **20/1**	—
105F	**U**		**I Hear Thunder (IRE)**[78] 3000 8-10-7 **125**................ BenjaminHitchcott (R H Buckler) *chsd ldrs tl stmbld and uns rdr after 14th* **40/1**	—
2UPP	**P**		**Colourful Life (IRE)**[45] 3620 10-11-2 **134**.................... ChristianWilliams (P F Nicholls) *in tch: hit 2nd: rr whn blnd 21 and 22: p.u bef next* **40/1**	—

8m 30.1s (-13.20) **Going Correction** -0.10s/f (Good) **43** Ran SP% **120.2**

Speed ratings: **113,112,111,109,109 108,108,107,106,103 99,98,91,—,—** — CSF £41.29 CT £250.47 TOTE £3.80: £1.80, £2.90, £1.90, £21.50; EX 66.90 Trifecta £657.60 Pool: £6,020.32 - 6.50 winning units.

Owner G Burke/R J Bagnall/N O'Farrell/K Sexton **Bred** Billy Carroll **Trained** Tinahely, Co. Wicklow

■ A first Festival success for County Wicklow trainer Philip Rothwell.

FOCUS

An event which from a form point of view is relevant only to a handful of other races. It has been given a token rating through the runner-up, who has been assessed as having run to last season's winning mark. They took it very steadily for much of the way and it turned into a relative sprint at the end.

NOTEBOOK

Native Jack(IRE) has been in fine form this season, having won both his point-to-points before Christmas and a race over Punchestown's banks course last time. Only creeping into the race in the latter stages, he challenged at the last and ran on strongly up the hill to outpace his year-older rival. He will now have a shot at the 50,000euro bonus put up by sponsors Blue Square in the La Touche Cup at Punchestown next month, where he would meet Spot Thedifference on much worse terms. *(op 9-2)*

Spot Thedifference(IRE), the inaugural winner of this event a year ago when a pound lower, had been unplaced twice at Punchestown, once over hurdles, since losing his unbeaten record over this course in November. Travelling well in the cheekpieces, he struck the front going to the last but *could not match the winner for pace in a sprint up the hill. On this evidence he is as good as ever.* *(op 10-1)*

Buailtes And Fadas(IRE), one of three runners from the Bolger yard, was given a really patient ride, his unproven stamina in mind, and was only let down off the home turn. He stayed on to take third but had been left with a bit to do and was unable to get to the first two. *(op 13-2)*

Il De Boitron(FR), an inconsistent sort who went without the headgear this time, ran a solid race and kept on again up the hill to claim fourth.

Koquelicot(FR), who made much of the running, jumped these obstacles with aplomb and only faded going to the last. He was the only British runner to finish in the first seven.

Good Step(IRE) had been kept to hurdles over inadequate trips since his third over course-and-distance in December. The shortest-priced of the Bolger trio, he was chasing the leaders but being ridden when he blundered at the third last. Carberry did well to sit tight, but the mistake ended his chances. *(tchd 4-1 in places)*

Never Compromise(IRE), runner-up to Native Jack at Punchestown last month and 11lb better off, moved to the front seven from home but was collared on the home turn and was a tired horse up the final hill.

Mrs Be(IRE), racing off the same mark as when third in this a year ago, could never get into the action.

Just In Debt(IRE) ran respectably, but never got to the leaders and faded after turning into the short home straight in seventh place.

Lord Jack(IRE), proven over these fences, disputed the lead with Koquelicot until weakening with five to jump.

4435 FRED WINTER JUVENILE NOVICES' H'CAP HURDLE (LISTED RACE) (8 hdls) 2m 110y

5:20 (5:21) (Class 1) 4-Y-O

£42,765 (£16,042; £8,032; £4,005; £2,010; £1,005)

Form				RPR
4P1	**1**		**Shamayoun (FR)**[20] 4057 4-11-3 **124**.................................(b) PJBrennan (C R Egerton) *lw: pressed ldr 3rd: led 5th: clr 3 out: drvn bef last: styd on wl flat* **40/1**	129+
25	**2**	*2½*	**Artist's Muse (IRE)**[59] 3401 4-10-13 **120**..................................... RWalsh (T M Walsh, Ire) *lengthy: lw: hld up towards rr: stdy prog after 5th: chsd wnr 2 out: clsd and looked dangerous whn mstke last: one pce flat* **12/1**	122+
6130	**3**	*2½*	**Patman Du Charmil (FR)**[24] 3986 4-11-3 **124**................(t) CarlLlewellyn (N A Twiston-Davies) *detached in last pair 2nd: wl bhd tl sme prog u.p after 5th: r.o strly bef last: gaining at fin* **40/1**	123
1012	**4**	*2½*	**Gardasee (GER)**[23] 4015 4-11-3 **124**.................................. JasonMaguire (T P Tate) *mstkes: prom: drvn and struggling bef 3 out: kpt on again after 2 out* **33/1**	121+
	5	*¾*	**Proper Article (IRE)**[23] 4020 4-10-11 **118**.................. RichardJohnson (D K Weld, Ire) *hld up wl in rr: prog 5th: chsng ldrs but nt on terms 3 out: kpt on fr 2 out: nt rch ldrs* **16/1**	113
2622	**6**	*1¼*	**My Immortal**[37] 3759 4-11-5 **126**....................................... TimmyMurphy (M C Pipe) *trckd ldrs: effrt 3f out: drvn to dispute 2nd 2 out: 3rd and btn last: wknd flat* **10/1**	121+
112	**7**	*6*	**Bold Fire**[24] 3972 4-11-7 **133**... LiamHeard(5) (P F Nicholls) *wl in tch: prog to trck ldng pair after 5th: wknd after 2 out* **25/1**	121
324	**8**	*nk*	**Dreux (FR)**[30] 3890 4-11-7 **128**... DNRussell (Thomas Cooper, Ire) *settled midfield: prog into chsng gp bef 3 out: kpt on after 2 out: nt rch ldrs: wknd flat* **25/1**	116
15	**9**	*1¾*	**Marhaba Million (IRE)**[30] 3890 4-11-3 **129**........................ BCByrnes(5) (E McNamara, Ire) *chsd ldrs: mstke 3rd: drvn after 5th: stl chsng 2 out: wkng whn blnd last* **25/1**	117+
11F2	**10**	*7*	**Kalmini (USA)**[33] 3817 4-11-2 **123**................................... JamieGoldstein (Miss Sheena West) *wl in rr whn mstke 2nd: prog bef 5th: chsng ldrs bef 3 out: wknd sn after 2 out* **20/1**	102
641	**11**	*3*	**Mystery Lot (IRE)**[26] 3948 4-10-11 **118**........................ RobertThornton (A King) *lw: racd freely and hanging rt: led to 5th: chsd wnr tl mstke 2 out and wknd* **14/1**	96+
3	**12**	*6*	**Count Kearney (IRE)**[17] 4122 4-10-8 **118**......................... TGMRyan(3) (S J Mahon, Ire) *lt-f: pressed ldr to 3rd: styd prom tl wknd rapidly after 3 out* **50/1**	88
14	**13**	*2½*	**Clear Riposte (IRE)**[59] 3401 4-11-4 **125**.................................. DJCasey (W P Mullins, Ire) *neat: a towards rr: sltly hmpd 4th: off the pce and no ch after next* **20/1**	92
121P	**14**	*7*	**Dan's Heir**[50] 3539 4-10-13 **125**..................................... PaddyMerrigan(5) (P C Haslam) *detached in last pair 2nd: nvr a factor: wl off the pce after 5th* **100/1**	85
422	**15**	*½*	**Royals Darling (GER)**[38] 3722 4-11-5 **126**...................... MickFitzgerald (N J Henderson) *lw: towards rr: rdn whn mstke 4th: sn struggling: wl off the pce after next* **9/2**[1]	87+
113	**16**	*4*	**Alfred The Great (IRE)**[28] 3912 4-10-5 **117**.................... MrTJO'Brien(5) (P C Haslam) *lw: swtg: nvr on terms w ldrs: wl off the pce after 5th: bhd 3 out* **20/1**	73
021	**P**		**Grasp**[16] 4128 4-11-7 **128**...(bt) JamieMoore (G L Moore) *prom: rdn after 4th: sn wknd: tailing off whn p.u bef 2 out* **25/1**	—
213	**F**		**Bayard (USA)**[46] 3594 4-10-12 **119**.................................... LeightonAspell (J R Fanshawe) *towards rr: no ch after 5th: stmbld on landing and fell 3 out: dead* **25/1**	—
4	**P**		**Ouste (FR)**[38] 3722 4-11-1 **122**.. APMcCoy (F Doumen, France) *hld up: prog and mstke 5th: chsd ldrs bef next: sn wknd: wl bhd whn p.u bef last* **5/1**[2]	—
F146	**P**		**Le Corvee (IRE)**[11] 4211 4-11-1 **122**........................(v[1]) WayneHutchinson (A King) *nvr beyond midfield: wl off the pce after 5th: wl bhd whn p.u bef 3 out* **66/1**	—
304	**P**		**Vox Populi (USA)**[17] 4122 4-11-0 **121**................................... BJGeraghty (S J Mahon, Ire) *small: settled in rr: terrible blunder 4th: nt rcvr: t.o whn p.u bef 3 out* **40/1**	—
221	**P**		**Rosecliff**[61] 3354 4-11-1 **122**.. BarryFenton (A M Balding) *wl in rr whnb mstke 3rd: nvr on terms after: wl off the pce 5th : t.o whn p.u bef last* **15/2**[3]	—
	P		**Brandon Mountain (IRE)**[89] 2851 4-10-13 **120**.................... DFO'Regan (Gordon Elliott, Ire) *small: mstke 1st in rr: prog and prom 2nd: wknd next: bhd whn p.u bef 4th* **100/1**	—
21	**U**		**Opera Mundi (FR)**[28] 3906 4-11-2 **123**........................ ChristianWilliams (P F Nicholls) *nvr beyond midfield: wl off the pce after 5th: wl bhd whn bdly hmpd and uns rdr 3 out* **20/1**	—

3m 57.2s (-2.00) **Going Correction** 0.0s/f (Good) **87** Ran SP% **129.9**

Speed ratings: **104,102,101,100,100 99,96,96,95,92 91,88,87,83,83 81,—,—,—,— —,—,—,—** CSF £401.77 CT £17718.44 TOTE £61.90: £8.90, £2.50, £15.90, £6.60; EX 1259.50 TRIFECTA Not won. Place 6 £1,022.49, Place 5 £287.49.

Owner Ronald Brimacombe **Bred** S A Aga Khan **Trained** Chaddleworth, Berks

■ Paddy Brennan's first Cheltenham Festival winner.

FOCUS

This was run at a strong early pace, but winning time was ordinary for a race of its class, 2.7 seconds slower than the Supreme Novices' and 7.2 seconds slower than the Champion Hurdle. The form is hard to assess.

NOTEBOOK

Shamayoun(FR), emphatically off the mark at Southwell when equipped with first-time blinkers last time, followed up with another powerful display under a very positive ride from Brennan. His rider's decision to kick for home approaching the climb paid dividends, and he stuck to his task gamely when in front, which had not been the case even when successful previously. Formerly a useful middle-distance winner on the Flat in France, he is clearly progressing now connections have found the key to him, and should stay further in due course. However, a likely hike in the weights will make his life a lot tougher in handicaps, and he may be better off going for the four-year-old hurdle at Aintree next month in his quest for the hat-trick.

Artist's Muse(IRE), popular in the betting ring ahead of this handicap bow and with the blinkers left off, would have been closer with a better leap at the final flight yet it made little difference to the overall result. This was by far her best effort to date, she enjoyed this faster surface, and finished nicely clear of the rest.

Patman Du Charmil(FR), sporting a first-time tongue tie and dropping back in trip, ran an amazing race to bag third place and ran right up to his mark in defeat. He was detached at the back of the pack through the early stages, and even his jockey appeared to give up hope at halfway, but he found an extraordinary burst and motored up the rising finish. The ground was most probably too fast for his liking and he is well worth chancing again over further again on this evidence when returning to an easy surface. *(op 33-1)*

Gardasee(GER) ◆ was again none too fluent, but displayed his battling qualities with another brave effort. He is one to take from the race with the future in mind and looks a nice prospect for novice chasing next season.
Proper Article(IRE), making his handicap bow, was given plenty to do from off the pace, yet still emerged to have a chance approaching the climb for home before finding just the same pace when it really mattered. He has scope and can be rated slightly better than the bare form. *(op 14-1)*
My Immortal ran his race and was not disgraced considering he chased the strong early gallop. He is a tough sort and appeals as the type to improve with further racing. *(op 11-1 tchd 8-1 in places)*
Bold Fire, who has done little wrong since joining connections from France, posted a fair effort under top weight yet still ran below her official mark on this less testing ground. *(op 20-1)*
Royals Darling(GER), runner-up to leading Triumph Hurdle candidate Detroit City the last twice, *ran below expectations. He may need it softer, but this was disappointing nevertheless. (op 11-2 tchd 6-1 in places)*
Alfred The Great(IRE) sweated markedly before the race and got found out by the strong early gallop. Sadly he had to be put down a few days later. *(op 16-1)*
Rosecliff failed to pick up after an early error and ran a tame race. *(tchd 11-2)*
Ouste(FR), very well backed, did not appear that suited by this faster surface and mistakes down the back straight put paid to any chance he may have had. *(tchd 11-2)*
T/Jkpt: £35,500.00 to a £1 stake. Pool: £100,000.00. 2.00 winning tickets. T/Plt: £1,564.00 to a £1 stake. Pool: £652,063.88. 304.35 winning tickets. T/Qpdt: £164.80 to a £1 stake. Pool: £32,786.65. 147.20 winning tickets. ST

4039 SEDGEFIELD (L-H)
Tuesday, March 14

4436 Meeting Abandoned - Frost

4430 CHELTENHAM (Old Course) (L-H)
Wednesday, March 15

OFFICIAL GOING: Good (good to soft in places)
Race times suggest the ground was a bit faster than for the first day.
Wind: Half across Weather: Fine

4443 ROYAL & SUNALLIANCE NOVICES' HURDLE GRADE 1 (10 hdls) 2m 5f
2:00 (2:00) (Class 1) 4-Y-0+

£57,020 (£21,390; £10,710; £5,340; £2,680; £1,340)

Form | | | | RPR
3F21 **1** **Nicanor (FR)**^{45} [3642] 5-11-7 PCarberry 155+
(Noel Meade, Ire) *str: scope: hld up in rr: stdy hdwy fr 4 out: trckd ldrs next: wnt 2nd gng wl after 2 out:chal last:sn led:drvn and kpt on* **17/2**
1111 **2** *2 ½* **Denman (IRE)**^{33} [3846] 6-11-7 155 RWalsh 151+
(P F Nicholls) *chsd ldrs: stmbld after 6th: hit 3 out: slt ld 2 out: sn hrd rdn: hdd sn after last: styd on same pce* **11/10**^{1}
1111 **3** *6* **Refinement (IRE)**^{20} [4077] 7-11-0 130 APMcCoy 138+
(Jonjo O'Neill) *bhd: hit 5th: hdwy next: rdn to chse ldrs appr 3 out: kpt on same pce after* **11/2**^{2}
11 **4** *2 ½* **Mr Nosie (IRE)**^{31} [3892] 5-11-7 DFO'Regan 142
(Noel Meade, Ire) *w'like: lw: led tl after 2nd: led again 5th: narrowly hdd 3 out: styd on same pce u.p fr next* **9/1**
-141 **5** *¾* **Mr Pointment (IRE)**^{26} [3957] 7-11-7 125 PJBrennan 141
(C R Egerton) *str: lw: chsd ldrs: wnt 2nd 4 out: led and mstke next: narrowly hdd 2 out: sn outpcd* **50/1**
0642 **6** *4* **Rimsky (IRE)**^{39} [3738] 5-11-7 129 (b) CarlLlewellyn 138+
(N A Twiston-Davies) *j. poorly in rr: styd on fr 2 out: kpt on run-in: nvr in contention* **66/1**
3311 **7** *nk* **Glasker Mill (IRE)**^{53} [3496] 6-11-7 121 TimmyMurphy 139+
(Miss H C Knight) *in tch: hmpd bnd after 4th and rr: sme hdwy fr 4 out: rdn 3 out and n.d* **40/1**
04 **8** *3 ½* **Letterman (IRE)**^{35} [3809] 6-11-7 PWFlood 133
(E J O'Grady, Ire) *w'like: mid-div: drvn and effrt after 4 out: styd on same pce fr next* **100/1**
9 *nk* **Zaiyad (IRE)**^{74} 5-11-7 (t) BJGeraghty 133
(A Chaille-Chaille, France) *lengthy: sn in tch: chsd ldrs fr 4 out: rdn next: wknd after 2 out* **6/1**^{3}
3645 **10** *18* **Legally Fast (USA)**^{27} [3943] 4-10-12 105 AndrewThornton 106
(S C Burrough) *lw: bhd: rdn after 4 out: nvr rchd ldrs* **250/1**
1446 **11** *10* **Heltornic (IRE)**^{35} [3802] 6-11-0 118 TomScudamore 98
(M Scudamore) *led after 2nd: hdd 5th: wknd 3 out* **150/1**
U-15 **12** *½* **The Mick Weston**^{73} [3175] 7-11-7 118 RobertThornton 105
(R T Phillips) *lw: in tch: lost position after 4th: hdwy 6th: rdn 4 out: wknd next* **50/1**
3111 **13** *4* **She's Our Native (IRE)**^{35} [3802] 8-11-0 125 ChristianWilliams 94
(Evan Williams) *bhd fr 1/2-way* **66/1**
14 **Le Comte Est Bon (USA)**^{10} [4273] 5-11-7 (b) MickFitzgerald 101
(F Doumen, France) *str: chsd ldrs to 4 out: t.o* **33/1**
1/04 **15** **Something Gold (FR)**^{20} [4077] 6-11-7 (b^{1}) MatthewBatchelor 101
(M Bradstock) *chsd ldrs tl wknd qckly appr 4 out: t.o* **150/1**
6F04 **16** **Investment Wings (IRE)**^{19} [4096] 4-10-12 (vt^{1}) RJGreene 92
(M C Pipe) *lw: hit 5th and bhd: t.o* **200/1**
411 **P** **Turnstile**^{73} [3168] 5-11-7 GLee —
(J Howard Johnson) *lw: in tch: chsd ldrs 5th: sn pushed along: wknd appr 4 out: t.o whn p.u bef 3 out* **40/1**

5m 1.00s (-12.60) **Going Correction** -0.175s/f (Good)
WFA 4 from 5yo+ 8lb **17** Ran SP% **115.8**
Speed ratings: **117,116,113,112,112 111,110,109,109,102 98,98,97,97,97 97,—** CSF £17.27 CT £58.66 TOTE £10.20: £2.70, £1.30, £1.70; EX 23.10 Trifecta £64.80 Pool: £9,013.18 - 98.70 winning units.
Owner D P Sharkey **Bred** M Pierre Hayeau **Trained** Castletown, Co Meath
■ Nicanor was providing trainer Noel Meade with only his second-ever Festival winner.

FOCUS
No future Istabraqs or Hardy Eustaces on show here, with most of the runners looking future chasers. Denman, who had always given the impression he might struggle in a good renewal of this race, was around 6lb below his Challow form and lacked the pace of Nicanor. The pair are expected to make top staying chasers in time. The third to eighth have all been rated improvers.

NOTEBOOK
Nicanor(FR), whose form in Ireland, though good, did not really entitle him to take a race of this calibre, found the better ground in his favour and had too much speed for a rival that many rated one of the meeting's bankers. There are few better hold-up jockeys than Carberry, and he was oozing confidence on touching down after the second-last before deciding to go for home at the final flight, readily outpacing the favourite up the hill. He has the potential to be very good and is now likely to head to Punchestown, although connections are very much looking forward to sending him fencing next season, with the chasing version of this likely to be the aim. *(op 15-2)*
Denman(IRE), who looked dull in his coat, has quickly developed into a high-class novice this season, going from winning a couple of novice hurdles at Wincanton to taking the re-routed Challow in emphatic style at this course in January. He raced a tad free early on and a blunder at the third-last did him no favours, but he was in front taking the next and turned into the straight to have every chance. Although the winner's superior finishing kick told against this galloper, he is one of the best chasing prospects around and, with a return to three miles certain to suit, the 14/1 available for the 2007 Royal & SunAlliance Chase is not unappealing. *(op 11-8)*
Refinement(IRE), a fine mare who had won nine of her 12 starts in bumpers and hurdles coming into this, appeared to improve for the step up to this sort of distance when winning at Huntingdon last time and she recorded a personal best, keeping on well, having been off the pace early. She seems to be getting better all the time and, with a further rise in distance likely to suit next season, she remains one to keep on side. *(op 6-1 tchd 13-2 in places)*
Mr Nosie(IRE) ◆, a stablemate of the winner and second-string on riding arrangements, had been workmanlike in winning his races in Ireland, but still had the right sort of profile for this race (lots of wins next to his name) and he raced on the pace throughout. He was still in front heading down to two out, but soon became outpaced. He too rates as a fine chasing prospect, although it's hard to say at this stage what his distance will be. *(op 10-1)*
Mr Pointment(IRE), whose stable took the Fred Winter the previous day, ran a cracker on this sharp rise in grade, still fighting it out coming down to the second-last and keeping on well enough in the straight. He will not be seen at his best until tackling fences, and connections look to have another fine prospect on their hands.
Rimsky(IRE), a weak Grade Two winner early in the season, returned to form when finishing a fine second to Neptune Collonges at Wetherby latest, but he looked to face no realistic chance here and was never jumping. His stamina saw him run on late through some tiring rivals, and he too will make a staying chaser next term.
Glasker Mill(IRE) had got his act together in recent starts, winning at Fontwell and Haydock, but this represented an altogether different test and he was not up to it. There was no disgrace in his performance, as he lost his position after being hampered, and three miles over fences next season could be the making of him. *(tchd 50-1)*
Letterman(IRE) had been exposed in graded company in Ireland and, although still well beaten, he probably ran a little better than expected. *(op 66-1 tchd 150-1 in a place)*
Zaiyad(IRE) was the only major disappointment of the race. Running here as a result of an administrative error that ruled him out of the Supreme Novices', it was not easy to weigh up his French form, but he is highly regarded by connections and should really have done better. The *likelihood is that he did not stay and as a result he deserves another chance back at two miles. (op 5-1 tchd 13-2 in places)*
Turnstile, whose stable took this with No Refuge last season, looked one of the more interesting outsiders having won his last two races, albeit in weak contests up north, but he was simply not good enough and was pulled up.

4444 ROYAL & SUNALLIANCE CHASE GRADE 1 (19 fncs) 3m 110y
2:35 (2:38) (Class 1) 5-Y-0+

£79,828 (£29,946; £14,994; £7,476; £3,752; £1,876)

Form | | | | RPR
1231 **1** **Star De Mohaison (FR)**^{47} [3601] 5-10-8 143 (t) BJGeraghty 147+
(P F Nicholls) *a cl up: led 4 out: lft clr after 2 out: drvn out* **14/1**
113 **2** *6* **Idle Talk (IRE)**^{25} [3976] 7-11-4 JasonMaguire 149
(T R George) *led: j.rt 1st: hdd 4 out: rdn appr 3 out: lft 2nd after 2 out: one pce run-in* **33/1**
2111 **3** *11* **Darkness**^{79} [2973] 7-11-4 154 PJBrennan 143+
(C R Egerton) *lw: nt jump wl: in rr: 21l down and plenty to do 2 out: tk mod 3rd clsng stages: nvr on terms* **11/2**^{2}
12P3 **4** *4* **Lord Killeshanra (IRE)**^{22} [4035] 7-11-4 130 JoeTizzard 136+
(C L Tizzard) *midfield: hdwy 12th: blnd 4 out: sn rdn and wknd* **66/1**
4122 **5** *4* **Zabenz (NZ)**^{79} [2973] 9-11-4 (b) RichardJohnson 132+
(P J Hobbs) *w ldr: bmpd 1st: lost pl after 12th: struggling after* **12/1**
-123 **6** *6* **Bewleys Berry (IRE)**^{79} [2973] 8-11-4 GLee 132+
(J Howard Johnson) *prom: 3 l down and rdn disputing 3rd whn blnd 2 out: wknd qckly* **11/1**
52P1 **7** *10* **The Railway Man (IRE)**^{31} [3893] 7-11-4 DNRussell 114
(A L T Moore, Ire) *racd keenly: hld up: sme hdwy 13th (water): mstke next: bhd after* **12/1**
-P13 **U** **Our Ben**^{31} [3893] 7-11-4 RWalsh —
(W P Mullins, Ire) *lw: in tch: blnd and uns rdr 3rd* **7/1**
6P21 **U** **Ardaghey (IRE)**^{24} [4016] 7-11-4 CarlLlewellyn —
(N A Twiston-Davies) *hld up: mstke 1st: blnd and uns rdr 9th* **33/1**
20/4 **P** **Chopneyev (FR)**^{18} [4102] 8-11-4 127 TonyDobbin —
(R T Phillips) *bhd: rdn 8th: hamperd next: t.o whn p.u after 11th* **100/1**
15-1 **P** **Commercial Flyer (IRE)**^{27} [3946] 7-11-4 (t) TimmyMurphy —
(M C Pipe) *lw: hld up: mstke 3rd: hdwy 11th: lost pl after 15th: p.u bef 4 out: dismntd* **9/2**^{1}
2F13 **P** **Lough Derg (FR)**^{72} [3213] 6-11-4 146 TomScudamore —
(M C Pipe) *in tch: mstke 2nd: reminders appr 11th: wkng whn mstke 12th: t.o whn p.u bef 4 out* **33/1**
211 **U** **Bold Bishop (IRE)**^{109} [2492] 9-11-4 146 APMcCoy 147+
(Jonjo O'Neill) *hld up: rdn and outpcd after 4 out: nrly 8 l down and styng on whn hmpd: swvd rt and uns rdr 2 out* **12/1**
0-24 **U** **Back In Front (IRE)**^{79} [3014] 9-11-4 PWFlood 149
(E J O'Grady, Ire) *lw: midfield: blnd 6th: hdwy 10th: ev ch 3 out: 2nd and 2 l down whn sprawled on landing and uns rdr 2 out* **11/1**
111F **F** **The Listener (IRE)**^{25} [3976] 7-11-4 AndrewThornton 140
(R H Alner) *midfield: hit 1st: j. slowly 7th and lost pl: hdwy 15th: wl outpcd bef 3 out: 9 lenghts down and no imp whn fell 2 out* **6/1**^{3}

6m 9.20s (-13.70) **Going Correction** -0.175s/f (Good)
WFA 5 from 6yo+ 10lb **15** Ran SP% **118.1**
Speed ratings: **114,112,108,107,106 104,100,—,—,— —,—,—,—,—** CSF £395.26 CT £2835.38 TOTE £19.00: £4.30, £11.40, £2.20; EX 723.80 Trifecta £5943.10 Part won. Pool: £8,370.58 - 0.60 winning units..
Owner Sir Robert Ogden **Bred** J Veau **Trained** Ditcheat, Somerset

FOCUS
Not a strong renewal, and the winner has provisionally been rated 13lb below the 10-year-average, although he could be higher and, as a five-year-old, is open to more improvement. As is so often the case in this race, jumping proved to be the key, and leading contenders such as Darkness, Bewleys Berry, Back In Front, Bold Bishop, Our Ben and The Listener all failed in that department. That obviously made Star De Mohaison's task easier and he took advantage to run out an emphatic winner from Idle Talk, who helped set a fair enough pace.

NOTEBOOK

Star De Mohaison(FR) was held by The Listener on two bits of form this season, but both of those runs came on ground with soft in the description and this genuinely decent surface brought with it significant improvement. He was fitted with a tongue-tie for the first time when running out a ready winner at Fontwell on his previous start, and that aid has clearly done him no harm. He was unproven over a trip this far, but put in a better round of jumping than some of his principal rivals, and he ultimately saw his race out very well to win emphatically. Although he has won on a testing surface in his native France, good ground is clearly the key and he should develop into a high-class chaser on his favoured surface next season. *(op 12-1)*

Idle Talk(IRE), well below form when beaten a distance into third on heavy ground in the Reynoldstown Chase at Lingfield on his previous start, clearly appreciated the return to a decent surface and ran a huge race. He could not match the speed of the winner when that one committed for home, but he stayed on gamely for pressure and his effort is all the more creditable given he was constantly hassled up front by Zabenz. This was much improved form and his trainer thinks he will be a Grand National horse one day. *(tchd 40-1)*

Darkness, whose only defeat in his previous five runs over fences came when second over two miles to subsequent Arkle runner-up Monet's Garden, came here off the back of success in the Grade One Feltham at Sandown and was arguably the one to beat on chase form alone. However, he didnt jump at all well and dropped a very long way off the pace before finally consenting to run on when it was all too late. Given how far back he was when the race got serious he did remarkably well to manage third, although he was helped in that respect by all of the trouble at the second last. He is much better than he showed and has the natural ability to develop into a leading Gold Cup contender at some stage, but his jumping is far from ideal and the way he carries his tail *suggests all may not be well with his back, so one cannot place too much faith in him as a result. (op 6-1 tchd 7-1 in places)*

Lord Killeshanra(IRE) ran a good race without ever looking like playing a serious hand in the finish. He benefited from all the trouble at the second last fence to take fourth.

Zabenz(NZ), held by Darkness on his last two bits of form, raced alongside Idle Talk for much of the way and can have few excuses. *(tchd 14-1)*

Bewleys Berry(IRE) ◆, who did not look great beforehand, was third behind Darkness and Zabenz in the Feltham at Sandown on his previous start and is much better than his finishing position suggests. He was staying on quite nicely in third when making a mistake at the second last before being hampered by the unseating Back In Front. But for the trouble he encountered there he would surely have been third at the very worst and is a fine staying prospect. *(tchd 10-1 and 12-1 in places)*

The Railway Man(IRE), surprise winner of a Grade One chase at Leopardstown on his previous *start, could not repeat that level of form upped to three miles for the first time on better ground. (op 14-1 tchd 16-1 in places)*

Back In Front(IRE) ◆, a high-class hurdler at up to two and a half miles, easily won a two-mile beginners' chase at Limerick last time, but that was his only experience of chasing in public and he hardly looked a typical 'SunAlliance' horse. However, racing over three miles for the first time, he was a very close second and in the process of running a huge race until slipping on landing and unseating his rider at the penultimate fence. The eventual winner may just have been getting his measure at the time, and there is no way of knowing how he would have fared up the hill over this trip, but he clearly retains plenty of the ability that saw him win the 2004 Supreme Novices' Hurdle, and what's more he is obviously capable of running to a very smart level over fences. Connections *will have plenty of options in future and it will be fascinating to see how they campaign him. (op 12-1)*

Bold Bishop(IRE)'s two previous wins over fences came over two miles and two and half miles respectively, and he had never previously run over a trip this far, but he was staying on well for pressure until hampered and unseating two out and would probably not have been beaten too far had he avoided the trouble. *(op 12-1)*

Commercial Flyer(IRE), successful on his only previous start over fences in a beginners' chase at Taunton less than a month previously, was in serious trouble when losing his action and pulling up before four out. It emerged he lost a front shoe, so at least he had a valid excuse, and he may well *bounce back when his stable is in better form. Official explanation: jockey said he pulled gelding up after it made two mistakes; vet said gelding had lost a front shoe (op 12-1)*

Our Ben, third in the hurdle version of this race last year, had taken well to chasing this season but unseated too early to know how he might have fared. *(op 12-1)*

The Listener(IRE), a faller in the Reynoldstown Chase at Lingfield on his previous start, got outpaced at a crucial stage on ground that was quicker than he would have liked and was only staying on to perhaps battle for minor honours before taking another fall two out. *(op 12-1)*

4445 QUEEN MOTHER CHAMPION CHASE GRADE 1 (12 fncs) 2m

3:15 (3:22) (Class 1) 5-Y-O+

£165,358 (£62,031; £31,059; £15,486; £7,772; £3,886)

Form				RPR
5431	**1**		**Newmill (IRE)**[55] [3472] 8-11-10 .... AndrewJMcNamara (John Joseph Murphy, Ire) *t.k.h: pckd 1st: mde virtually all: hit 2 out: drvn clr appr last: kpt on strly run-in* **16/1**	172+
-U21	**2**	*9*	**Fota Island (IRE)**[52] [3527] 10-11-10 .... APMcCoy (M F Morris, Ire) *lw: in tch: hdwy 7th: chsd ldrs 3 out: sn one pce: kpt on u.p fr 2 out to take 2nd nr fin but no ch w wnr* **4/1**[2]	162
1233	**3**	*1 1/2*	**Mister McGoldrick**[25] [3980] 9-11-10 160........ DominicElsworth (Mrs S J Smith) *prom: chsd wnr fr 7th: rdn and effrt after 2 out: sn no ch w wnr: nt fluent last: wknd and lost 2nd cl home* **50/1**	162+
1341	**4**	*1/2*	**Central House**[38] [3774] 9-11-10 ....(t) RLoughran (D T Hughes, Ire) *chsd wnr to 7th: styd pressing ldrs: rdn and one pce 3 out: kpt on again run-in to press for 3rd but no ch w wnr* **7/1**	162+
-224	**5**	*1/2*	**Moscow Flyer (IRE)**[78] [3051] 12-11-10 .... BJGeraghty (Mrs John Harrington, Ire) *hmpd 3rd: bhd: hdwy 8th: chsd ldrs 4 out: rdn and outpcd next: kpt on again run-in: gng on cl home but no ch w wnr* **5/1**[3]	163+
2114	**6**	*18*	**Watson Lake (IRE)**[38] [3774] 8-11-10 ....(t) PCarberry (Noel Meade, Ire) *hmpd 3rd: a bhd* **18/1**	145+
2-21	**F**		**Kauto Star (FR)**[102] [2635] 6-11-10 167........(t) RWalsh (P F Nicholls) *trcking ldrs whn fell 3rd* **2/1**[1]	—
	U		**Kario De Sormain (FR)**[23] 8-11-3 ....(t) TMajorcryk (J-P Gallorini, France) *mstke 1st: uns rdr sn after* **20/1**	—
3-12	**B**		**Dempsey (IRE)**[39] [3724] 8-11-10 154........ AndrewTinkler (M Pitman) *lw: hld up in rr but in tch whn bdly hmpd and b.d 3rd* **14/1**	—
4-33	**U**		**Oneway (IRE)**[78] [3039] 9-11-10 157........ GLee (M G Rimell) *in rr: sme hdwy 7th: 8th but in tch whn blnd and uns rdr 4 out* **40/1**	—
36-2	**U**		**River City (IRE)**[12] [219] 9-11-10 147........ TomDoyle (Noel T Chance) *in rr: hdwy 8th: styng on and cl 6th whn blnd and uns rdr 4 out* **33/1**	—
U-4F	**F**		**Fundamentalist (IRE)**[25] [3977] 8-11-10 154........(t) CarlLlewellyn (N A Twiston-Davies) *lw: chsd ldrs: rdn 8th: wknd 3 out: 6th and btn whn fell 2 out* **16/1**	153+

3m 51.5s (-7.80) **Going Correction** -0.175s/f (Good) **12** Ran SP% **118.3**

Speed ratings: **112,107,106,106,106 97,—,—,—,— —,—** CSF £78.76 CT £3171.98 TOTE £22.90: £4.20, £2.00, £9.60; EX 131.30 Trifecta £8257.50 Part won. Pool: £11,630.33 - 0.40 winning units..

Owner Mrs Mary T Hayes **Bred** Mrs Veronica O'Farrell **Trained** Upton, Co. Cork

■ A first Festival winner for both trainer and jockey.

■ Stewards' Enquiry : Dominic Elsworth one-day ban: used whip with excessive force (Mar 26)

FOCUS

This looked no more than an average renewal on paper and the result did little to alter the view. The absence of Well Chief, Azertyuiop and Ashley Brook clearly devalued it, and with reigning champion Moscow Flyer looking nothing like the force of old the race took little winning once Kauto Star came down at the third. Only half of the 12 runners managed to complete, and the time was nothing spectacular - still nearly seven seconds outside Edredon Bleu's course record.

NOTEBOOK

Newmill(IRE) has looked a happier horse this season, twice running well behind Brave Inca over hurdles and enjoying a comfy success over Mossy Green at Thurles in January as a prep for this. He still looked to have masses to find on his chasing form, but he received a fine ride from McNamara, who made good use of the stamina he has shown over further by setting a good pace and keeping him well out of trouble before leaving Mister McGoldrick, the only real danger, trailing in the straight. He has a long way to go before he can be mentioned in the same breath as some previous winners of this race, but there was no apparent fluke about his massive improvement. He is now likely to have a break before heading to Punchestown.

Fota Island(IRE) ◆, cosy winner of last season's Grand Annual, has raised his game this season and made a highly pleasing reappearance when running High Cloy close in a contraversial contest at Leopardstown over Christmas. Considering he is a good ground horse, his recent winning effort at Fairyhouse in testing conditions was an ideal prep for this and he was the one expected to profit once Kauto Star came down. However, having travelled well into contention, he was outpaced by the front two and it was clear from two out he was not going to be winning, although he ultimately stayed on up the hill to claim Mister McGoldrick for second. This was slightly disappointing, but it still represented career-best from this lightly-raced ten-year-old, who is still open to further *improvement on genuine good, fast ground and now has the option of Aintree or Punchestown. (tchd 9-2 in places)*

Mister McGoldrick, a tough and versatile sort who has been running well at graded level over both hurdles and fences this term, ran way above expectations on ground that was expected to be too quick for him and he looked the only danger to the winner after the second-last. He soon became outpaced however and was tired when claimed by Fota Island for second up the hill, but that was more a case of him suffering from racing up on the gallop. Connections are now eyeing the two and a half mile Melling Chase at Aintree. *(op 40-1)*

Central House, who ran well for a long way in this last season, has really improved this term, winning three times and still being in front when his rider mistook the winning line at Leopardstown over Christmas. His best form has always been in soft or heavy ground, but he handled this faster surface well enough and kept on to challenge again for third up the hill. He was always near the leaders and this was another fine effort, so connections should be more than hopeful the *nine-year-old can score again at the top level before too long. (op 15-2 tchd 8-1 in places and 13-2 in places)*

Moscow Flyer(IRE) went three and a half years and 19 races unbeaten in his completed starts over fences, winning this race in both 2003 and 2005, plus two Melling Chases at Aintree, a Tingle Creek, and many more. However, a first defeat over fences at Punchestown last April, then two more, suggested age might at last have caught up with him, although the stable's lack of form clouded the issue. Here he recovered from being hampered early on, but looked in trouble at the top of the hill and, though keeping on late, lacked his customary zest. It was no surprise when connections announced his retirement, for he is clearly past his best and it would be wrong to allow his truly magnificent record to be tarnished any further. *(tchd 11-2 in places and 6-1 in a place)*

Watson Lake(IRE) lost his chance early on, being badly hampered at the third, and he was always trailing thereafter. He was entitled to run well on the best of his form, and it would be no surprise to see him line-up in the Melling Chase at Aintree. *(op 20-1 tchd 16-1)*

River City(IRE) ◆ enjoyed an unorthodox preparation for this when finishing third on the All-Weather at Wolverhampton the other day, but his third in last year's Arkle showed he had the class to take a hand if at his best and he was in the process of running a cracker, still going well, when unseating his rider four out. There was still some way to go, but connections must be left wondering what might have been. *(tchd 9-4 in places and 15-8 in places)*

Dempsey(IRE), a progressive handicapper who looked one of the more interesting outsiders, was unfortunate enough to be brought down at third. *(tchd 9-4 in places and 15-8 in places)*

Oneway(IRE), a fine fourth in this last year, was not out of it, although he was only going to be playing for places, when blundering and unseating Lee at the fourth-last. He falls just short of top-class. *(tchd 9-4 in places and 15-8 in places)*

Kauto Star(FR) had enjoyed a good comeback season, finishing a fine second on his reappearance in the Haldon Gold Cup on his reappearance and then beating Ashley Brook with a little in hand in the Tingle Creek, but his luck was out on the big day and he came down at the third, taking Dempsey down with him. It is hoped this does not affect confidence and he remains a top-class prospect. *(tchd 9-4 in places and 15-8 in places)*

Fundamentalist(IRE), a high-class novice hurdler whose first season over fences was cut short through injury, was beaten out of sight on his return in the Castleford, where the heavy ground would not have suited, but a fall most recently at Lingfield was hardly the ideal prep for such a big race and he could not be backed with confidence. He had run a decent race, but was well held, when taking a heavy fall at the second-last and it remains to be seen how this second successive tumble affects his confidence. *(tchd 9-4 in places and 15-8 in places)*

Kario De Sormain(FR), an athletic type, was a fascinating French raider and the only mare in the contest. She got no further than the first fence, though, where her jockey was unable to hold on *after a mistake. It would have been interesting to see how she would have fared. (tchd 9-4 in places and 15-8 in places)*

4446 CORAL CUP (A H'CAP HURDLE) GRADE 3 (10 hdls) 2m 5f

4:00 (4:02) (Class 1) 5-Y-O+

£42,765 (£16,042; £8,032; £4,005; £2,010; £1,005)

Form				RPR
-502	**1**		**Sky's The Limit (FR)**[102] [2646] 5-11-12 **144**........(v1) BJGeraghty (E J O'Grady, Ire) *w'like: midfield: hdwy 4 out: wnt 2nd appr 2 out: led bef last: shkn up to draw clr run-in: easily* **11/1**[3]	155+
2132	**2**	*4*	**Strangely Brown (IRE)**[48] [3585] 5-11-3 **140**........ BCByrnes(5) (E McNamara, Ire) *lw: midfield: hdwy appr 4 out: rdn between last 2: wnt 2nd after last: no ch w wnr* **25/1**	143
5111	**3**	*3/4*	**Dom D'Orgeval (FR)**[25] [3986] 6-11-12 **144**........ RichardJohnson (Nick Williams) *midfield: pckd 4 out: rdn and hdwy appr 2 out: r.o run-in* **20/1**	147+
-346	**4**	*nk*	**Phar Bleu (FR)**[95] [2761] 5-11-6 **138**........(t) RWalsh (P F Nicholls) *hld up: slipped on bnd after 4th: hdwy appr 2 out: r.o run-in* **10/1**[2]	141+
1103	**5**	*3/4*	**Verasi**[4] [4375] 5-11-0 **132**........(b) PhilipHide (G L Moore) *midfield: hdwy 6th: hung lft and styd on run-in* **25/1**	133
1241	**6**	*4*	**Ungaro (FR)**[39] [3727] 7-11-3 **135**........ JimCrowley (K G Reveley) *lw: hld up: hdwy appr 3 out: styd on wl towards fin: nvr nrr* **14/1**	132
2-0F	**7**	*shd*	**Inch Pride (IRE)**[115] [2369] 7-10-11 **129**........ TimmyMurphy (M C Pipe) *lw: prom: led appr 6th: rdn and hdd bef last: wknd run-in* **25/1**	127+
/234	**8**	*1 1/4*	**Mughas (IRE)**[24] [4008] 7-11-10 **142**........ WayneHutchinson (A King) *lw: trckd ldrs: rdn and outpcd appr 2 out: no imp after* **16/1**	138
U015	**9**	*1 3/4*	**Valley Ride (IRE)**[60] [3389] 6-11-6 **138**........ TomDoyle (C Tinkler) *towards rr: hdwy 2 out: kpt on run-in: nt trble ldrs* **66/1**	133+
-514	**10**	*2*	**Manorson (IRE)**[89] [2871] 7-11-0 **132**........ LeightonAspell (O Sherwood) *led to 1st: remained prom: led 5th: hdd appr next: hit 3 out: wknd last* **28/1**	124

The Form Book, Raceform Ltd, Compton, RG20 6NL

-214 **11** *3½* **Desert Air (JPN)**[25] 3994 7-11-9 **141**......(t) TomScudamore 130
(M C Pipe) *in tch: lost pl after 3rd: n.d after* **25/1**

3030 **12** *1¼* **Fait Le Jojo (FR)**[67] 3298 9-11-0 **137**...... HowieEphgrave(5) 124
(L Corcoran) *midfield: hdwy appr 4 out: rdn and wknd bef 3 out* **100/1**

U362 **13** *¾* **Dancing Bay**[24] 4008 9-11-11 **143**...... AndrewTinkler 130
(N J Henderson) *hld up: rdn and hdwy appr 3 out: one pce run-in* **33/1**

4-F5 **14** *½* **Pole Star**[46] 3618 8-11-6 **143**...... LiamHeard(5) 129
(J R Fanshawe) *lw: hld up: blnd 2nd: hdwy whn mstke 2 out: nvr rchd ldrs* **33/1**

F435 **15** *hd* **Turtle Soup (IRE)**[24] 4008 10-11-4 **143**...... WillieMcCarthy(7) 129
(T R George) *led 1st: hdd 4th: remained handy: rdn and wknd appr 2 out* **100/1**

2246 **16** *4* **Nathos (GER)**[24] 4008 9-11-7 **139**...... PJBrennan 121
(C J Mann) *hld up: rdn appr 3 out: nvr on terms* **50/1**

1-13 **17** *nk* **Fair Question (IRE)**[25] 3970 8-10-12 **130**...... SamThomas 113+
(Miss Venetia Williams) *in tch: wknd after 4 out* **12/1**

635 **18** *4* **Royal Paradise (FR)**[101] 2669 6-11-5 **137**...... CO'Dwyer 115
(Thomas Foley, Ire) *prom: led 4th to 5th: wkng appr 3 out* **20/1**

1-36 **19** *8* **Prins Willem (IRE)**[28] 3177 7-11-8 **140**......(t) CarlLlewellyn 112+
(J R Fanshawe) *a bhd* **16/1**

-2F6 **20** *5* **Il Duce (IRE)**[73] 3179 6-11-5 **137**...... RobertThornton 102
(A King) *in tch: rdn and wknd appr 3 out* **20/1**

4122 **21** *10* **Mister Quasimodo**[18] 4115 6-11-1 **133**...... JoeTizzard 98+
(C L Tizzard) *in tch: wknd appr 3 out: n.d whn hmpd last* **16/1**

3-66 **22** *2* **Paddy The Piper (IRE)**[115] 2369 9-11-3 **135**...... TonyDobbin 88
(L Lungo) *in tch: wknd after 6th* **66/1**

-324 **23** *11* **Only Vintage (USA)**[25] 3986 6-11-4 **136**...... PaulMoloney 78
(Miss H C Knight) *lw: midfield: j. slowly 6th: bhd after* **40/1**

4510 **24** *8* **Afrad (FR)**[67] 3298 5-11-6 **138**...... MickFitzgerald 72
(N J Henderson) *in tch: mstke 6th: wknd after 4 out* **25/1**

3U55 **25** *1¼* **Akilak (IRE)**[60] 3383 5-11-5 **137**...... GLee 69
(J Howard Johnson) *mstke 5th: a bhd* **28/1**

32 **F** **No Where To Hyde (IRE)**[46] 3625 6-11-1 **133**...... APMcCoy 129
(C Roche, Ire) *lw: hld up: hdwy 4 out: no imp whn fell last: dead* **5/1**[1]

0 **P** **Good Thyne Jack (IRE)**[18] 4126 8-11-2 **134**...... PCarberry —
(E McNamara, Ire) *lw: stmbld 1st: sn wl bhd: t.o whn p.u bef 2 out* **10/1**[2]

2004 **B** **Penny Pictures (IRE)**[35] 3801 7-10-11 **136**...... AndrewGlassonbury(7) 123
(M C Pipe) *hld up: rdn and hdwy appr 3 out: no imp whn b.d last* **50/1**

2150 **R** **All Star (GER)**[67] 3298 6-10-12 **130**...... MarcusFoley 127+
(N J Henderson) *midfield: hdwy appr 3 out: styng on in cl 4th whn rn out 2 out* **28/1**

132 **U** **Two Miles West (IRE)**[35] 3793 5-11-0 **132**...... DJCasey 114
(Jonjo O'Neill) *in tch: niggled along and lost pl after 5th: n.d whn hmpd and uns rdr last* **16/1**

5m 2.50s (-11.10) **Going Correction** -0.175s/f (Good) **150** Ran SP% **142.1**
Speed ratings: 114,112,112,112,111 110,110,109,109,108 106,106,106,106,105 104,104,102,99,97 94,93,89,86,85 CSF £270.21 CT £5442.78 TOTE £11.60: £3.70, £5.00, £7.20, £3.50; EX 421.10 Trifecta £2064.80 Pool: £11,923.68 - 4.10 winning units.
Owner Raymond J Rooney **Bred** Mme Danielle Merian, Earl Hara **Trained** Ballynonty, Co Tipperary

FOCUS
Only 15lb separated the 30 runners at the weights in what looked a good renewal and Sky's The Limit made light of joint top-weight to win easily. He has been rated value for 8 lengths and is clearly high class. The sort of winning time you would expect for a race like this, 1.5 seconds slower than the opening novice hurdle, and rock solid form.

NOTEBOOK
Sky's The Limit(FR) ◆, a progressive sort sporting a first-time visor, appeared to face no easy task but turned this into something of a procession, scooting clear on the run-in to win impressively. He has been wearing blinkers, but connections opted for a change here and if this effort is anything to go by, the five-year-old may be worth his place in the Aintree Hurdle. He could come back here for a crack at the World Hurdle next season if continuing to improve. *(op 10-1 tchd 12-1 in places)*
Strangely Brown(IRE), a Grade One winner in France last summer, gives the form a strong look in second and connections can feel a little unlucky to have bumped into what is clearly a very smart performer. He made good headway from half a mile out and took second after the last, suggesting a return to three miles may be in order. He is another progressive five-year-old, capable of better. *(tchd 20-1 in places)*
Dom D'Orgeval(FR), a tough, progressive gelding who has had a good time of it this winter, shouldered joint top-weight bravely into third, keeping on up the hill, but he was unable to get going in time on this faster ground. With the going likely to continue to firm up from now on, he may have a trip to Auteuil before the season is out.
Phar Bleu(FR), who has struggled off this mark this season, showed improved form for the step up in distance and may have challenged for second had he not slipped on the bend after the fourth flight. He got going late and, although this mark will continue to make life tough for him, he should stay three miles and can make a decent chaser next season. *(tchd 11-1 in places and 9-1 in places)*
Verasi, a winner of two decent Sandown two-mile handicaps this season, has shown all his best form in heavy ground, but he came into this in good form, having finished a running-on third in the Imperial Cup at the weekend, and he appreciated the step up in distance, running on despite hanging away to his left. He does all his running in the latter part of races and will stay further in time. *(op 20-1)*
Ungaro(FR) ◆, up 7lb for his Sandown win in February, got going all too late, finishing strongly along with Verasi, but being unable to get near the places. He is another who will stay three miles and there may yet be more to come. *(op 12-1)*
Inch Pride(IRE) ◆ ran a bold race, kicking on at the top of the hill and trying to stretch her field, but she was unable maintain the gallop and was run out of the places up the hill. This was her first start since November and she could be the type to do well during the spring, before going chasing next season.
Mughas(IRE), a fine fourth in a cracking renewal of this two seasons back, was racing off a 2lb lower mark here and was expected to be suited by the better ground. He was never far off the pace, but was unable to race on with Inch Pride and could only plod on at the one pace. It may take a further drop in the weights before he is winning again, and it will be interesting if connections decide to send him chasign next season. *(tchd 20-1 in places)*
Valley Ride(IRE), a progressive enough gelding, made a little late headway, but never threatened to play a hand. *(tchd 100-1)*
Manorson(IRE) was partly responsible for the pace, but as expected he failed to see the trip out. *Official explanation: vet said gelding finished distressed (tchd 33-1)*
Royal Paradise(FR), joint favourite for last seasons Royal & SunAlliance Hurdle, not for the first *time failed to live up to expectations and he was struggling with half a mile to run.Official explanation: trainer said gelding bled from the nose (op 16-1)*
Good Thyne Jack(IRE) was never going after stumbling at the first. This can be ignored. *(op 12-1 tchd 14- 1in places)*
All Star(GER) was in the process of running a cracking race, keeping on in fourth and holding every chance, when running out at the second last. He would have been fighting it out for the places had he stayed in the race and connections have every right to feel hard done by. *(op 12-1 tchd 14- 1in places)*
No Where To Hyde(IRE), a bright prospect who had been running well in defeat against some decent types in Ireland, was beaten when taking a fatal fall at the last, bring down Penny Pictures in the process. *(op 12-1 tchd 14- 1in places)*

4447 FULKE WALWYN KIM MUIR CHALLENGE CUP H'CAP CHASE (AMATEUR RIDERS) (19 fncs) 3m 110y

4:40 (4:45) (Class 2) (0-140,139) 5-Y-0+

£30,010 (£9,375; £4,685; £2,345; £1,170; £590)

Form RPR

621P **1** **You're Special (USA)**[58] 3420 9-10-12 **125**......(t) MrROHarding 146+
(Ferdy Murphy) *lw: chsd ldr: led 15th: drvn and kpt on wl fr 2 out* **33/1**

1211 **2** *3½* **Mon Mome (FR)**[57] 3438 6-10-5 **125**...... MrWBiddick(7) 143+
(Miss Venetia Williams) *prom: chsd wnr after 3 out: kpt on u.p run-in but no imp on wnr* **11/1**

3123 **3** *8* **Undeniable**[20] 4070 8-10-9 **122**...... MissNCarberry 130
(Mrs S J Smith) *chsd ldrs: rdn 3 out: styd on same pce fr next* **16/1**

2022 **4** *1½* **Bee An Bee (IRE)**[25] 3992 9-10-3 **123**......(v) MrRMcCarthy(7) 132+
(T R George) *bhd: hdwy 14th: chsd ldrs 2 out: 3rd and wkng whn mstke last* **25/1**

62S0 **5** *shd* **Risk Accessor (IRE)**[18] 4118 11-11-10 **137**...... MrJTMcNamara 143
(Jonjo O'Neill) *hit 3rd: bhd: hdwy 10th: chsd ldrs 4 out: one pce fr next* **16/1**

00-1 **6** *1¼* **Black Apalachi (IRE)**[59] 3410 7-10-13 **126**...... MrJJCodd 133+
(P J Rothwell, Ire) *hmpd bnd after 1st and rr: hdwy 8th: nt fluent 4 out: styd on same pce fr next* **8/1**[2]

1P0F **7** *1¾* **Iris Bleu (FR)**[18] 4118 10-11-5 **139**...... MrRQuinn(7) 144+
(M C Pipe) *lw: hmpd bnd after 1st and rr: sme hdwy 15th but n.d: wknd after 3 out* **25/1**

-0U5 **8** *2½* **Liberthine (FR)**[67] 3296 7-11-0 **132**...... MrSWaley-Cohen(5) 132
(N J Henderson) *bhd: rdn 4 out: mod prog 3 out but nvr in contention* **7/1**[1]

-0P2 **9** *1* **Parsons Legacy (IRE)**[11] 4240 8-10-11 **124**...... MrTJO'Brien 126+
(P J Hobbs) *lw: chsd ldrs to 4 out: sn wknd* **7/1**[1]

2234 **10** *3* **Lou Du Moulin Mas (FR)**[67] 3296 7-11-1 **128**......(bt) MrCJSweeney 124
(P F Nicholls) *chsd ldrs: hit 14th: n.d after* **10/1**

1F1U **11** *½* **Florida Dream (IRE)**[11] 4240 7-10-4 **122**......(b) MrDEngland(5) 119+
(N A Twiston-Davies) *led to 15th: styd pressing ldrs to 3 out: sn wknd* **40/1**

1F43 **12** *nk* **Underwriter (USA)**[39] 3728 6-10-7 **120**...... MrTGreenall 116
(Ferdy Murphy) *mstkes 1st and 2nd: sme hday 14th: wknd 4 out* **9/1**[3]

-421 **13** *10* **Briery Fox (IRE)**[83] 2953 8-10-10 **130**...... MrJDocker(7) 116
(H D Daly) *lw: nt jump wl: chsd ldrs: blnd 14th: wknd 4 out* **14/1**

-044 **P** **Adarma (IRE)**[59] 3410 8-10-12 **125**...... MrKEPower —
(C Roche, Ire) *hit 5th: bhd: t.o whn p.u bef 12th* **16/1**

0-PP **P** **Zeta's River (IRE)**[67] 3296 8-11-4 **134**...... MrDEdwards(3) —
(M C Pipe) *bhd most of way tl t.o and p.u bef last* **25/1**

1P1P **P** **Glacial Delight (IRE)**[27] 3942 7-10-3 **119**...... MrCMotherway(3) —
(Miss E C Lavelle) *a bhd: t.o whn p.u bef last* **66/1**

5523 **P** **Jackson (FR)**[26] 3955 9-10-2 **118**...... MrGTumelty(3) —
(A King) *chsd ldrs early: bhd fr 8th: t.o whn p.u bef 13th* **25/1**

13-4 **P** **Another Rum (IRE)**[32] 3851 8-11-5 **137**...... MrMJO'Hare(5) —
(I A Duncan, Ire) *bhd most of way tl t.o and p.u bef 3 out* **16/1**

010P **P** **Scots Grey**[46] 3620 11-11-10 **137**...... MrAFitzgerald —
(N J Henderson) *chsd ldrs to 8th: wknd 10th: t.o whn p.u bef 4 out* **40/1**

21P1 **P** **Cruising River (IRE)**[27] 3942 7-10-13 **126**...... MrDMurphy —
(Miss H C Knight) *lw: chsd ldrs to 10th: wknd and puled up after 14th* **25/1**

2536 **U** **Aristoxene (FR)**[46] 3620 6-11-2 **132**......(b[1]) MrJSnowden(3) —
(N J Henderson) *hmpd bnd after 1st: j.slowly 4th: mid-div: blnd 7th: blnd and uns rdr next* **20/1**

6m 10.3s (-12.60) **Going Correction** -0.175s/f (Good) **21** Ran SP% **127.0**
Speed ratings**13,111,109,108,108 108,107,107,106,105 105,105,102,—,—** —,—,—,—,— — CSF £339.00 CT £5971.53 TOTE £38.90: £6.50, £2.70, £3.00, £6.50; EX 554.20 Trifecta £2916.20 Pool: £6,571.94 - 1.60 winning units.
Owner Mrs Diane O'Rourke **Bred** Ralph C Wilson Jnr Trust Agreement **Trained** West Witton, N Yorks

■ A first Festival win for Irish-based amateur Richard Harding.
■ Stewards' Enquiry : Mr D England one-day ban: careless riding (Mar 28)

FOCUS
A typically competitive renewal of the Kim Muir, but the bare form looks nothing special for a race of this class. The pace looked pretty strong and the time very acceptable, yet the first three home were in the first three throughout.

NOTEBOOK
You're Special(USA) was a beaten favourite and very disappointing when pulled up at Fakenham on his last start nearly two months previously, but Ferdy Murphy's horses are in good form at the moment and he produced a career-best performance to win decisively. He will apparently now be considered for the Irish National and Betfred Gold Cup.
Mon Mome(FR) ◆, still a novice, ran a fine race against some far more experienced chasers and was a clear second. His three previous wins came on testing ground, but he handled this much better surface well and was beaten fair and square. He should keep progressing. *(op 12-1 tchd 14-1 in places)*
Undeniable did not look on a particularly attractive mark beforehand but he usually gives his running and posted a very creditable effort in third.
Bee An Bee(IRE), winless since March 2004, had a visor replacing blinkers and finished a very respectable fourth, in the process faring best of those to race from off the pace.
Risk Accessor(IRE), challenging for third before running out in the Racing Post Chase at Sandown on his previous start, is not an easy horse to win with and could never pose a serious threat.
Black Apalachi(IRE) ◆ could never get involved after being hampered soon after the first, but did keep on and this has to be considered a very respectable effort given the ground would have been a little quicker than he might have liked. *(tchd 9-1 in places)*
Iris Bleu(FR) was another hampered soon after the first and never really got involved thereafter.
Liberthine(FR), last year's Mildmay of Flete winner, never got involved and, given there was no obvious excuse for the slightly below-par effort, this has to be considered disappointing. *(op 11-2 tchd 15-2)*
Parsons Legacy(IRE) had conditions to suit but failed to run up to his best and was another to disappoint. *(op 10-1 tchd 12-1 in a place)*
Underwriter(USA), still a novice, did not jump well enough early on off a career-high mark. *(op 12-1 tchd 14-1 in places)*
Adarma(IRE) *Official explanation: jockey said mare was lame (op 14-1)*

4448 WEATHERBYS CHAMPION BUMPER (A STANDARD OPEN NATIONAL HUNT FLAT RACE) GRADE 1 2m 110y

5:20 (5:27) (Class 1) 4-6-Y-O

£22,808 (£8,556; £4,284; £2,136; £1,072; £536)

Form RPR

1 **Hairy Molly (IRE)**[17] 4140 6-11-5 ...... PCarberry 133
(Joseph Crowley, Ire) *w'like: scope: lw: a.p: led over 3f out: rdn over 2f out: all out cl home* **33/1**

1 **2** *hd* **Pressgang**[63] 3346 4-10-11 .... TomDoyle 125+
(P R Webber) *in tch: clsd 3f out: wnt 2nd over 2f out: rdn and hung rt over 1f out: r.o cl home* **20/1**

11 **3** *1 3/4* **Kicks For Free (IRE)**[41] 3699 5-11-5 .... MickFitzgerald 131
(P F Nicholls) *w'like: hld up: hdwy over 4f out: rdn and disputing 2nd over 2f out: nt qckn towards fin* **5/1**[2]

4 *1/2* **Perce Rock**[59] 3414 4-10-11 .... APMcCoy 122
(T Stack, Ire) *w'like: hld up: hdwy over 5f out: rdn 3f out: styd on ins fnl f* **12/1**

5 *2* **Dancing Hero (IRE)**[76] 3111 5-11-5 .... DNRussell 128
(Thomas Foley, Ire) *str: midfield: hdwy 4f out: rdn over 3f out: edgd rt ins fnl f: kpt on* **20/1**

6 *1* **Lord Over**[32] 3875 5-11-5 .... BJGeraghty 127
(Patrick J Flynn, Ire) *leggy: midfield: pushed along 5f out: hdwy over 3f out: one pce wl ins fnl f* **25/1**

7 *1/2* **Female (IRE)**[87] 2913 5-10-12 .... MrPRoche 120
(C Roche, Ire) *scope: lw: hld up: rdn and hdwy over 3f out: swtchd lft whn nt clr run ins fnl f: styd on wl* **40/1**

11 **8** *2* **Wind Instrument (IRE)**[60] 3399 5-11-5 .... TimmyMurphy 125
(T R George) *scope: in tch: pushed along 6f out: rdn 2f out: kpt on same pce* **50/1**

0211 **9** *hd* **Pangbourne (FR)**[29] 3911 5-11-5 ....(ve[1]) RobertThornton 125
(A King) *lw: prom: rdn over 3f out: hung lft whn no ex 1f out* **33/1**

11 **10** *3 1/2* **Wichita Lineman (IRE)**[11] 4244 5-11-5 .... MrJPMagnier 122+
(Jonjo O'Neill) *scope: hld up: hdwy 4f out: no imp fr over 2f out* **8/1**[3]

311 **11** *1 3/4* **Burnt Oak (UAE)**[73] 3181 4-10-11 .... BarryKeniry 111
(C W Fairhurst) *cmpt: in rr: rdn and hdwy 3f out: styd on ins fnl f* **20/1**

12 *1* **Equus Maximus (IRE)**[45] 3644 6-11-5 .... RWalsh 118
(W P Mullins, Ire) *w'like: midfield: hdwy over 5f out: rdn and btn over 2f out* **5/2**[1]

13 *1* **Ballytrim (IRE)**[34] 3835 5-11-5 .... JMurtagh 117
(W P Mullins, Ire) *str: prom tl rdn and wknd over 2f out* **8/1**[3]

1 **14** *2* **Nightfly (IRE)**[44] 3657 5-11-5 .... CarlLlewellyn 115
(M Pitman) *w'like: midfield: lost pl after 4f: bhd and outpcd over 4f out: kpt on fr over 1f out* **66/1**

11 **15** *nk* **Albertas Run (IRE)**[67] 3292 5-11-5 .... TonyDobbin 115
(Jonjo O'Neill) *w'like: prom tl niggled along and wknd 6f out* **40/1**

16 *1/2* **Freds Benefit (IRE)**[21] 4066 5-11-5 .... MsKWalsh 114
(W P Mullins, Ire) *str: in rr: rdn over 3f out: nvr rchd ldrs* **20/1**

41 **17** *3 1/2* **Dark Corner**[46] 3617 4-10-11 .... StevenCrawford 103
(N A Twiston-Davies) *leggy: in rr: niggled along after 6f: nvr on terms* **200/1**

11 **18** *1 1/2* **Leading Contender (IRE)**[122] 2211 5-11-5 .... RichardJohnson 109
(P J Hobbs) *lw: midfield: hdwy 1/2-way: rdn and wknd over 4f out* **12/1**

1 **19** *hd* **Mumbles Head (IRE)**[49] 3563 5-11-5 .... ChristianWilliams 109
(P Bowen) *str: in tch: rdn over 4f out: sn wknd* **200/1**

20 *1/2* **Shady Willow (IRE)**[38] 3778 4-10-11 .... DJCasey 101
(W P Mullins, Ire) *tall: hld up: rdn and carried hd high over 3f out: nvr on terms* **33/1**

21 *7* **Flowonlovelyriver (IRE)**[24] 4024 5-11-5 .... GLee 102
(Patrick J Flynn, Ire) *w'like: scope: led: rdn and hdd over 3f out: sn wknd* **16/1**

12 **22** *1/2* **Spartacus Bay (IRE)**[60] 3392 5-11-5 .... SamThomas 101
(Miss Venetia Williams) *w'like: trckd ldrs tl rdn and wknd 4f out* **100/1**

23 *dist* **First Author (IRE)**[88] 2899 5-11-5 .... KJManning —
(Gerard O'Leary, Ire) *w'like: scope: midfield: sltly hmpd 1/2-way: wknd over 6f out: t.o* **16/1**

3m 46.7s (-10.50) **Going Correction** -0.175s/f (Good)
WFA 4 from 5yo+ 7lb **23** Ran SP% **136.6**
Speed ratings: 117,116,116,115,114 114,114,113,113,111 110,110,109,108,108 108,106,106,105,105 102,102,— CSF £601.22 CT £3868.80 TOTE £27.00: £5.50, £7.10, £2.80; EX 1586.70 Trifecta £4627.00 Part won. Pool: £6,516.96 - 0.10 winning units. Place 6 £2,762.92, Place 5 £2,161.77.
Owner F T B Syndicate **Bred** T O'Malley **Trained** Piltown, Co. Kilkenny
■ Stewards' Enquiry : K J Manning one-day ban: careless riding (Mar 26)

FOCUS
With all four of the Willie Mullins horses running below expectations, and the likes of Wichita Lineman and Leading Contender failing to confirm earlier promise, the bare form is below the usual standard for this race. However, there were still some very nice horses on show, including some of those who failed to fire on the day, and it should still produce some classy winners.

NOTEBOOK
Hairy Molly(IRE) ◆, whose two wins from his four previous starts both came over two miles three at Naas, put his proven stamina to good use when committing for home about three furlongs out and just proved good enough. His task was made easier with some of the fancied horses running below form, but he is obviously very useful and should do well over hurdles next season.
Pressgang ◆, the winner of a mile and a half bumper at Newbury on his only previous start, was representing the same stable that produced De Soto to finish second in this race last year, and he too was only just denied. This was a fine effort for one so young and inexperienced, and he looks a really good prospect.
Kicks For Free(IRE) ◆, the easy winner of two bumpers at Wincanton, would have found this a very different test and ran a fine race in defeat. He could go a long way. *(op 6-1)*
Perce Rock ◆, a mightily impressive winner of a Leopardstown bumper on his debut and subsequently bought by J P McManus, did not get a clear run when McCoy was originally looking to make his move and ran on well up the hill when in the clear. It is an obvious thing to say about a horse close-up in a race of this nature, but he really is a high-class prospect.
Dancing Hero(IRE), the winner of his last two starts in minor bumper company in Ireland, ran a fine race upped significantly in class. He finished quite strongly up the hill and should do well over obstacles next season, possibly over a little further. *(tchd 25-1)*
Lord Over had today's winner behind in third when second at Naas on his previous start but could not confirm form and that one looks to have progressed past him for the time being. *(op 22-1)*
Female(IRE), successful in a Navan bumper on her only previous start nearly three months ago, *was the only mare in the line-up and ran well, especially considering she did not get a clear run. (op 33-1)*
Wind Instrument(IRE), the winner of both his previous starts, would have found this a lot tougher but ran with credit. *(tchd 66-1)*
Pangbourne(FR), with a visor replacing blinkers, did not help his chance by hanging left under pressure, but by no means ran badly. He possess plenty of ability and should eventually make a nice chaser if his connections can keep him sweet. *(op 28-1 tchd 25-1)*
Wichita Lineman(IRE), successful in Newbury bumpers on both his previous starts, never got involved and has to be considered a little disappointing. *(tchd 9-1 in places)*
Burnt Oak(UAE), the winner of a Listed bumper over a mile and a half here on his previous start, could not cope with some of he older horses upped to two miles for the first time. Still, he really took the eye beforehand and should develop into a very useful sort in time.
Equus Maximus(IRE) ◆ looked a fine prospect when winning a Leopardstown bumper that has already worked out well on his only previous start, and represented a trainer who had won his race five times in the last nine years, so this was very disappointing. He is better than this and must be given another chance. *(op 10-3 tchd 7-2 and 4-1 in places)*
Ballytrim(IRE) ◆ did not beat much when winning on his debut at Thurles, but still created a very good impression and looked set for a big run representing the same owner/trainer combination as last year's winner Missed That. However, he was quite keen and, after starting properly racing a little earlier than was ideal, his effort soon petered out. He is much better than this and can be followed when stepped up in trip and sent over obstacles. *(tchd 17-2 and 10-1 in places)*
Freds Benefit(IRE), an impressive winner of a heavy-ground bumper at Punchestown, failed to confirm that promise and probably found the ground too fast.
Leading Contender(IRE) was well below the form he showed to win a course and distance Listed bumper on his previous start and has to be considered very disappointing. *(tchd 14-1)*
First Author(IRE) *Official explanation: vet said gelding finished distressed*
T/Jkpt: Not won. T/Plt: £2,062.30 to a £1 stake. Pool: £637,491.25. 225.65 winning tickets. T/Qpdt: £379.30 to a £1 stake. Pool: £32,555.80. 63.50 winning tickets. ST

4074 HUNTINGDON (R-H)

Wednesday, March 15

OFFICIAL GOING: Good (good to soft in places)
Wind: Light, across Weather: Cloudy with sunny spells

4449 BETFRED MILLION (S) H'CAP HURDLE (10 hdls) 2m 5f 110y
1:50 (1:52) (Class 5) (0-90,89) 4-Y-0+ **£2,740** (£798; £399)

Form RPR

3563 **1** **Oulton Broad**[26] 3959 10-11-12 **89** ....(p) RichardMcGrath 96
(R Ford) *hld up: hdwy 6th: led flat: drvn out* **6/1**[3]

P-34 **2** *1/2* **Lavenoak Lad**[21] 4046 6-10-0 **70** ....(p) KeiranBurke[(7)] 77
(P R Rodford) *a.p: led 3 out: hdd next: led and j.rt last: hdd flat: styd on* **13/2**

P-03 **3** *3 1/2* **Scarface**[17] 4133 9-10-12 **75** .... JamieMoore 78
(J L Spearing) *chsd ldrs: led 2 out: hdd last: styd on same pce* **4/1**[1]

002 **4** *2 1/2* **Zeloso**[17] 4133 8-11-5 **87** ....(v) CharliePoste[(5)] 88
(M F Harris) *hld up: hdwy appr 6th: sn outpcd: rallied 3 out: styd on same pce fr next* **11/2**[2]

530U **5** *8* **Road King (IRE)**[51] 3540 12-10-9 **79** ....(p) MrMatthewSmith[(7)] 72
(Miss J Feilden) *chsd ldrs: led appr 6th: hdd 3 out: wknd appr last* **11/1**

063 **6** *24* **Giant's Rock (IRE)**[21] 4046 4-10-1 **73** ....(t) OllieMcPhail 33
(B J Llewellyn) *mid-div: wknd 6th* **6/1**[3]

-106 **7** *10* **Southerncrosspatch**[44] 3656 15-10-9 **79** .... MrMWall[(7)] 38
(Mrs Barbara Waring) *chsd ldrs: rdn after 5th: wknd 7th* **20/1**

0/50 **8** *24* **Phar The Best (IRE)**[274] 745 9-11-8 **85** ....(p) JohnMcNamara 20
(Mrs A L M King) *chsd ldrs: rdn appr 6th: sn wknd* **25/1**

4P00 **P** **The Pecker Dunn (IRE)**[24] 4012 12-11-8 **85** .... JodieMogford —
(Mrs N S Evans) *bhd fr 4th: p.u after next* **18/1**

1-0P **P** **Fireside Legend (IRE)**[16] 4153 7-10-9 **77** ....(p) RobertLucey-Butler[(5)] —
(Miss M P Bryant) *bhd fr 4th: t.o whn p.u bef 6th* **50/1**

006 **P** **Misters Sister**[83] 2954 4-10-11 **83** ....(b) JamesDavies —
(C A Dwyer) *prom: rdn and wknd appr 6th: t.o whn p.u bef 2 out* **20/1**

FP-4 **P** **Gilded Ally**[98] 2702 6-10-13 **76** .... RussGarritty —
(M Wigham) *hld up: plld hrd: bhd fr 4th: p.u after next: dismntd* **33/1**

000P **P** **Swahili Dancer (USA)**[29] 3918 5-10-13 **76** .... NeilMulholland —
(M D Hammond) *hld up: hdwy 6th: rdn and wknd next: t.o whn p.u after 3 out* **22/1**

P0OP **P** **Dargin's Lass (IRE)**[26] 3956 5-9-7 **63** ....(p) TomMessenger[(7)] —
(B N Pollock) *led: rdn and hdd appr 6th: rdn and wknd next: t.o whn p.u bef 2 out* **100/1**

5m 22.4s (11.60) **Going Correction** +0.425s/f (Soft)
WFA 4 from 5yo+ 8lb **14** Ran SP% **114.5**
Speed ratings: **95,94,93,92,89 81,77,68,—,— —,—,—,—** CSF £39.02 CT £174.23 TOTE £7.20: £2.20, £3.20, £2.50; EX 65.60.There was no bid for the winner.
Owner D W Watson **Bred** Fares Stables Ltd **Trained** Cotebrook, Cheshire

FOCUS
Very moderate form, with the runner-up the best guide to the level.

NOTEBOOK
Oulton Broad, having his second start for his new stable and dropping in grade, came on and off the bridle but he kept on resolutely enough to hang on from the rallying Lavenoak Lad. This was his first success over hurdles in almost two years and the competition was poor, so he would not be one to rely on to follow up.
Lavenoak Lad ran to a similar level as when fourth in a similarly poor event last time. *(op 7-1)*
Scarface has now been placed on five of his 15 starts over hurdles but is struggling to get his head in front. The drop into selling company for the first time did not prove the answer. *(tchd 5-1)*
Zeloso kept on under pressure but never really threatened. He could have been expected to have *done better back in this company but was racing off an 8lb higher mark than when last* successful. *(op 4-1)*
Road King(IRE), a veteran who remains a maiden, looked an unlikely stayer over this trip. *(op 10-1)*
The Pecker Dunn(IRE) *Official explanation: jockey said gelding was never travelling (tchd 16-1)*

4450 BETFRED MILLION MARES' ONLY MAIDEN HURDLE (8 hdls) 2m 110y
2:25 (2:26) (Class 4) 4-Y-0+ **£3,253** (£955; £477; £238)

Form RPR

632 **1** **Saraba (FR)**[67] 3280 5-11-0 100 .... JamieMoore 101+
(Mrs L J Mongan) *chsd ldrs: led 5th: clr 2 out: styd on* **9/4**[1]

2352 **2** *2* **Nobodys Perfect (IRE)**[56] 3442 6-10-7 93 .... PatrickMcDonald[(7)] 96
(Ferdy Murphy) *chsd ldrs: ev ch 3 out: styd on* **7/1**

6062 **3** *2* **Twist The Facts (IRE)**[20] 4074 6-10-7 .... MarcGoldstein[(7)] 94
(N P Littmoden) *chsd ldrs: rdn appr last: styd on same pce* **7/2**[3]

4 *3/4* **Beautiful Night (FR)**[112] 4-10-6 .... NeilMulholland 85
(M D Hammond) *hld up: hdwy 5th: styng on same pce whn mstke last* **14/1**

06-F **5** *1* **Floragalore**[67] 3281 5-10-11 .... OwynNelmes[(3)] 92
(O Sherwood) *hld up: hdwy appr 3 out: styd on same pce fr next* **25/1**

/0-P **6** *9* **Poggenip**[17] 4129 7-10-4 .... RichardKilloran[(10)] 83
(B G Powell) *hld up in tch: rdn appr 3 out: wknd next* **50/1**

5432 **7** *3* **Anna Panna**[16] 4153 5-11-0 93 .... RobertWalford 80
(R H Alner) *led to 5th: wknd appr 2 out* **11/4**[2]

30U **8** *1* **Cois Na Tine Eile**[2] 4425 4-10-6 .... AntonyEvans 71
(N A Twiston-Davies) *hld up: effrt after 3 out: n.d* **16/1**

0/00 **9** *nk* **My Big Sister**[25] 3979 7-10-7 .... WayneKavanagh[(7)] 79
(J W Mullins) *hld up: hdwy 5th: wknd 3 out* **100/1**

6P **10** *2* **Dawn Wager**[30] 3902 5-11-0 .... JamesDavies 77
(D B Feek) *chsd ldrs: rdn 3 out: sn wknd* **66/1**

11 *3/4* **La Gessa**[44] 4-10-4 ow5 .... MrMatthewSmith[(7)] 73
(John Berry) *plld hrd and prom: wknd after 3 out* **66/1**

0-00 **12** *5* **Bamby (IRE)**[122] 2211 6-11-0 .... RichardMcGrath 71
(R Ford) *hld up: sme hdwy after 5th: sn wknd* **40/1**

50 **13** *9* **Fleur Des Pres (FR)**[31] 3884 4-9-13 .... CharlieStudd[(7)] 54
(B G Powell) *hld up: bhd fr 5th* **40/1**

0-00 **14** *3* **Miss Sirius**[65] [3322] 6-10-9 .... MarkNicolls(5) 59
(John R Upson) *plld hrd and prom: hit 5th: wknd next: bhd whn blnd last* **66/1**
15 *6* **Trip To The Stars (IRE)** 6-10-9 .... DarylJacob(5) 53
(D P Keane) *hld up: a in rr* **33/1**
00 **16** *18* **Silver Seline**[57] [3437] 5-10-7 .... TomMessenger(7) 35
(B N Pollock) *hld up: plld hrd: wknd after 5th: bhd whn j.rt last 2 flights* **66/1**
0 **P** **Haenertsburg (IRE)**[45] [1011] 4-10-6 .... OllieMcPhail —
(A L Forbes) *hld up: bhd fr 4th: t.o whn p.u bef 2 out* **100/1**
PP **P** **On The Fairway (IRE)**[16] [4149] 7-10-9 .... RobertLucey-Butler(5) —
(Miss M P Bryant) *plld hrd and prom: wknd after 4th: t.o whn p.u bef 2 out* **100/1**

4m 6.30s (10.60) **Going Correction** +0.425s/f (Soft)
WFA 4 from 5yo+ 7lb **18** Ran SP% **127.3**
Speed ratings: **92,91,90,89,89 85,83,83,83,82 81,79,75,73,70 62,—,—** CSF £18.60 TOTE £2.80: £1.50, £2.20, £2.10; EX 21.70.
Owner Mrs P J Sheen **Bred** S A Aga Khan **Trained** Epsom, Surrey

FOCUS
A big field for this mares' race but few could be seriously fancied. The race, run in a slow time, has been rated around the first three.

NOTEBOOK
Saraba(FR), who has improved with every run, only needed to reproduce the form of her latest effort to win this modest affair. She will find things harder in handicap company. *(op 10-3)*
Nobodys Perfect(IRE) has had a number of chances but she is a fairly consistent performer and clearly ran close to her best, making the form easy to rate. The quicker ground proved no problem. *(op 6-1)*
Twist The Facts(IRE) was expected to appreciate the quicker conditions being a daughter of Un Desperado, but she was a touch disappointing, having her chance but failing to improve on her effort here last month. *(op 13-2)*
Beautiful Night(FR), unplaced in four starts (three over fences, one over hurdles) in France, made a satisfactory start to her career in this country and should come on for this first run since November. *(op 12-1)*
Floragalore should have benefited confidence-wise from completing this time having had an unfortunate experience on her hurdling debut.
Anna Panna, who has struggled to get home in her races, was not given an easy time of it in front and ended up running below her best. *(op 5-2)*
Bamby(IRE) *Official explanation: jockey said mare hung left (op 28-1)*

4451 "WEST HAM FOR EUROPE" H'CAP CHASE (19 fncs) 3m
3:00 (3:01) (Class 4) (0-100,99) 5-Y-0+ **£3,578** (£1,050; £525; £262)

Form RPR
0PP0 **1** **Meggie's Beau (IRE)**[36] [3791] 10-11-7 **97** ....(b[1]) PaulO'Neill(3) 110+
(Miss Venetia Williams) *chsd ldr: led 6th to 14th: led next: lft clr 2 out: mstke last* **8/1**
-62P **2** *9* **Classic Rock**[24] [4016] 7-10-8 **81** .... WarrenMarston 87+
(J W Unett) *hld up: plld hrd: mstke 3rd: hdwy and hit 9th: led 14th: hdd and blnd next: styng on same pce whn lft 2nd 2 out: hit last* **8/1**
33P0 **3** *nk* **Wayward Melody**[78] [3018] 6-11-4 **91** ....(p) JamieMoore 94
(G L Moore) *led to 6th: rdn 12th: outpcd fr 4 out: lft 3rd 2 out* **8/1**
4541 **4** *28* **Roman Court (IRE)**[44] [3652] 8-11-8 **95** .... RobertWalford 70
(R H Alner) *mid-div: nt fluent: wknd 15th* **4/1**[1]
03U2 **5** *8* **Sett Aside**[43] [3660] 8-10-4 **77** ....(p) BenjaminHitchcott 44
(Mrs L C Jewell) *hld up: n.d* **7/1**[3]
4035 **6** *½* **Protagonist**[28] [3919] 8-11-1 **95** ....(p) TomMessenger(7) 61
(B N Pollock) *hld up: bhd fr 11th* **12/1**
5622 **7** *14* **Opportunity Knocks**[36] [3791] 6-9-7 **73** .... KeiranBurke(7) 25
(N J Hawke) *chsd ldrs to 13th* **5/1**[2]
-P05 **8** *2 ½* **Bronhallow**[27] [3938] 13-10-0 **80** oh20 ow7........(bt) MrMWall(7) 30
(Mrs Barbara Waring) *chsd ldrs to 12th* **80/1**
3UP6 **9** *dist* **Uncle Max (IRE)**[28] [3919] 6-11-7 **94** ....(b) AntonyEvans —
(N A Twiston-Davies) *hld up: j. slowly 4th: hdwy appr 9th: rdn and wknd 11th* **12/1**
003- **F** **Kiftsgate**[481] [2319] 9-10-10 **83** .... JimmyMcCarthy 95+
(Mrs P Robeson) *chsd ldrs: cl 2nd whn fell 2 out* **16/1**
PPPP **P** **Over The Storm (IRE)**[64] [3336] 9-11-12 **99** .... DavidO'Meara —
(H P Hogarth) *mid-div: wknd 10th: t.o whn p.u bef 3 out* **10/1**

6m 13.5s (1.20) **Going Correction** +0.30s/f (Yiel) **11** Ran SP% **114.1**
Speed ratings: **110,107,106,97,94 94,90,89,—,—** — CSF £68.69 CT £528.71 TOTE £8.80: £2.90, £3.00, £2.90; EX 117.10.
Owner T England **Bred** Dan Mangan **Trained** Kings Caple, H'fords

FOCUS
A moderate handicap but the time was decent for the grade. The winner is rated to his best with the runner-up to recent mark.

NOTEBOOK
Meggie's Beau(IRE), blinkered for the first time, went well throughout and appeared to have things under control when Kiftsgate fell at the second last. Providing the headgear continues to have a positive effect, he could well follow up, as he was rated much higher than this last spring. *Official explanation: trainer's representative said, regarding the improved form shown, gelding was wearing first-time blinkers (op 15-2)*
Classic Rock did not settle and did not jump with much fluency either, almost unseating at the fifth last in fact, and in the circumstances he did quite well to finish second. He is probably on a mark he can win off if his jumping can be improved. *(op 9-1)*
Wayward Melody, returning to chasing following a break since her last run over hurdles in December, was well held turning for home but stayed on in the straight. She likes decent ground but is slow, and is the type who would ideally be suited by being held up hoping that the leaders go too quick and hit the wall. *(op 10-1)*
Roman Court(IRE), a fortunate winner last time out, was 6lb higher and had a longer trip to deal with, but it was his poor jumping which got him beaten not the extra weight or trip. *(op 11-2)*
Sett Aside, flattered by his last effort, was put in his place back in this handicap. *(op 6-1)*
Kiftsgate, making his chasing debut following three outings over hurdles back in 2004, looked assured of second place when crashing out at the second last. He should be able to make amends off this sort of mark providing the tumble has not dented his confidence.

4452 HELEN OF TROY LADY RIDERS' H'CAP HURDLE (8 hdls) 2m 110y
3:45 (3:46) (Class 4) (0-100,98) 4-Y-0+ **£3,903** (£1,146; £573; £286)

Form RPR
6041 **1** **Picot De Say**[2] [4427] 4-10-2 **85** 7ex........ MissEJJones(3) 89+
(C Roberts) *hld up: plld hrd: hdwy 5th: led last: rdn out* **1/1**[1]
4532 **2** *1 ¾* **Upright Ima**[42] [3674] 7-9-13 **78** .... MissLAllan(7) 86
(Mrs P Sly) *hld up: hdwy to chse ldr 4th: led appr 3 out: hdd last: styd on same pce* **9/2**[2]
0443 **3** *14* **Grand Prairie (SWE)**[18] [4101] 10-10-8 **87** ....(b) MissHGrissell(7) 83+
(G L Moore) *chsd ldr: hit 5th: wknd appr 2 out* **16/1**
42F **4** *9* **Rainbow Tree**[120] [2259] 6-11-2 **95** .... MissLGardner(7) 80
(C C Bealby) *chsd ldrs tl wknd appr 3 out* **10/1**
PP-4 **5** *1 ¼* **Who Cares Wins**[259] [863] 10-10-11 **90** ....(v) MissJCoward(7) 74
(J R Jenkins) *chsd ldrs to 5th* **40/1**
22B3 **6** *9* **Think Quick (IRE)**[44] [3655] 6-10-5 **84** .... MissSSharratt(7) 59
(R Hollinshead) *chsd ldrs to 3 out: bhd whn hit next* **7/1**[3]
-20P **7** *8* **Lord Of The Hill (IRE)**[35] [3805] 11-10-11 **90** .... MissLHorner(7) 57
(G Brown) *led: hdd appr 3 out: sn wknd* **33/1**
1-00 **8** *¾* **Dark Society**[17] [4131] 8-11-2 **95** .... MissRDavidson(7) 61
(A W Carroll) *hld up: hit 5th: a bhd* **12/1**
4PP **U** **Loup Bleu (USA)**[27] [3943] 8-11-5 **98** .... MissJKelly(7) —
(Mrs A V Roberts) *stmbld and uns rdr 2nd* **100/1**

4m 1.50s (-161.7) **Going Correction** +0.425s/f (Soft)
WFA 4 from 6yo+ 7lb **9** Ran SP% **109.7**
Speed ratings: **103,102,95,91,90 86,82,82,—** CSF £5.59 CT £36.22 TOTE £1.70: £1.20, £1.60, £2.80; EX 5.70.
Owner Dr Simon Clarke **Bred** Henry And Mrs Rosemary Moszkowicz **Trained** Newport, Newport
■ Emily Jones will now stick to riding on the Flat after partnering this winner.

FOCUS
Not a strong race, but the time was four seconds faster than the earlier mares' maiden over the same trip and the first two set the standard.

NOTEBOOK
Picot De Say, penalised for an easy win at Taunton two days earlier, followed up under a confident ride without being overly impressive. The ground was probably faster than ideal. *(op 5-6 tchd 8-11)*
Upright Ima tried to get away from her pursuers on the home turn but was collared at the last and there was no way back. Lacking a turn of foot, she has yet to win a race in 20 attempts but has made the frame 13 times. *(op 5-1)*
Grand Prairie(SWE) lost second place on the home turn but plugged on for third. He is running well enough this term but does not seem over-keen to get his head in front. *(tchd 18-1)*
Rainbow Tree was back over hurdles after taking quite a heavy fall on his chasing debut four months ago. *(op 9-1)*
Who Cares Wins had not run under Rules since June but reportedly won a charity Flat race at Fakenham recently. *(op 28-1)*
Think Quick(IRE) raced prominently until fading quickly on the home turn. *(op 9-1 tchd 11-1)*
Dark Society *Official explanation: jockey said gelding hung left on the final circuit (op 10-1)*

4453 WEATHERBYS PRINTING H'CAP HURDLE (12 hdls) 3m 2f
4:25 (4:25) (Class 4) (0-110,103) 4-Y-0+ **£3,253** (£955; £477; £238)

Form RPR
/P32 **1** **Ocean Tide**[22] [4043] 9-11-3 **94** ....(v) RichardMcGrath 101+
(R Ford) *hld up: hdwy 8th: mstke next: led after 2 out: edgd rt: rdn out* **9/2**[1]
R66 **2** *1 ½* **Business Traveller (IRE)**[25] [3997] 6-10-4 **86** ....(bt) MarkNicolls(5) 89
(R J Price) *bhd 4th: hmpd appr 3 out: hdwy bef next: hung rt flat: styd on: nt rch wnr* **10/1**
1P00 **3** *1 ¼* **Moustique De L'Isle (FR)**[25] [3982] 6-11-4 **102**......(v[1]) TomMessenger(7) 106+
(C C Bealby) *led: hdd after 2nd: led 5th: rdn after 3 out: pckd and hdd after 2 out: no ex last* **25/1**
25P0 **4** *3 ½* **Full On**[20] [4080] 9-10-12 **92** .... WilliamKennedy(3) 91+
(A M Hales) *hld up: hdwy 8th: mstke 2 out: styd on same pce* **14/1**
4424 **5** *10* **Honey's Gift**[3] [4396] 7-11-7 **103** .... PaddyMerrigan(5) 93+
(G G Margarson) *hld up: hdwy 9th: ev ch 3 out: wknd last* **13/2**[3]
5001 **6** *20* **Coralbrook**[34] [3818] 6-11-5 **96** ....(b) JimmyMcCarthy 64
(Mrs P Robeson) *mid-div: hdwy 4th: wknd appr 3 out* **7/1**
0500 **7** *¾* **Son Of Greek Myth (USA)**[18] [3814] 5-11-7 **98** ....(b) JamieMoore 66
(G L Moore) *hld up: hdwy 8th: wknd next* **20/1**
P2P0 **8** *14* **Putup Or Shutup (IRE)**[55] [3458] 10-11-4 **100** .... ChrisHonour(5) 54
(K C Bailey) *chsd ldrs: rdn after 7th: wkng whn hit 3 out* **14/1**
2-0F **9** *21* **Armagh South (IRE)**[25] [3997] 7-10-11 **88** .... JodieMogford 21
(J C Tuck) *hld up: j.lft and hit 5th: mstke next: lost tch 8th* **13/2**[3]
0044 **10** *hd* **Mac Dargin (IRE)**[27] [3938] 7-10-12 **96** ....(b) MarcGoldstein(7) 28
(N A Twiston-Davies) *drvn along thrght: led after 2nd: j. slowly next: hdd 5th: wknd after 8th* **20/1**
2126 **P** **Canavan (IRE)**[4] [4372] 7-10-8 **90** ....(b[1]) TJDreaper(5) —
(Ferdy Murphy) *chsd ldrs tl p.u bnd after 2nd: dead* **6/1**[2]
3250 **P** **Royal Coburg (IRE)**[36] [3792] 6-11-11 **102** ....(t) AntonyEvans —
(N A Twiston-Davies) *chsd ldrs to 9th: p.u bef next* **12/1**
/0-P **P** **Mixed Marriage (IRE)**[40] [3719] 8-11-9 **100** .... WarrenMarston —
(Miss Victoria Roberts) *chsd ldrs: rdn and wknd after 7th: bhd whn p.u bef next* **66/1**

6m 36.4s (14.00) **Going Correction** +0.425s/f (Soft) **13** Ran SP% **116.6**
Speed ratings: **95,94,94,93,90 83,83,79,72,72 —,—,—** CSF £45.45 CT £1012.82 TOTE £4.50: £1.80, £2.90, £5.70; EX 69.50.
Owner A Eyres & D F Price **Bred** Grundy Bloodstock Ltd **Trained** Cotebrook, Cheshire

FOCUS
A low-grade handicap that looks solid enough rated around those in the frame behind the winner.

NOTEBOOK
Ocean Tide, 6lb higher than when pipped at Sedgefield, was always going best. He got to the front between the last two flights and, although not fluent over the final flight, he stayed on well enough. *(op 7-1)*
Business Traveller(IRE) appeared set to finish out the back until beginning to pass rivals on the home turn. He was closing the gap on the winner at the end, despite hanging and looking a tricky ride. *(tchd 9-1)*
Moustique De L'Isle(FR), whose three wins so far have all been in heavy ground, was equipped with a visor in place of the blinkers. He lost his lead following a mistake at the second last and was demoted to third on the run-in. *(op 20-1)*
Full On, still a maiden, ran respectably and was keeping on without ever looking likely to win.
Honey's Gift, having her second run in four days, made good headway at the end of the back straight but had perhaps made up her ground too quickly and the run soon flattened out. *(op 5-1)*
Coralbrook, bidding to follow up his recent course win off a 7lb higher mark, was found out by this considerably longer trip. *(op 8-1)*
Armagh South(IRE) *Official explanation: jockey said gelding hung badly left (op 7-1 tchd 5-1)*
Mac Dargin(IRE), reverting to hurdles, looked less than enthusiastic and eventually gave up the ghost at the fifth last.
Canavan(IRE) sadly broke a foreleg on the Flat and had to be put down. *(op 4-1)*
Royal Coburg(IRE) *Official explanation: jockey said gelding was never travelling (op 4-1)*

4454 SIKA.CO.UK SIKAFLEX AND SIKABOND ADVANCED TECHNOLOGY NOVICES' CHASE (16 fncs) 2m 4f 110y
5:05 (5:05) (Class 4) 5-Y-0+ **£3,665** (£1,137; £612)

Form RPR
1130 **1** **Clouding Over**[34] [3815] 6-10-7 **104** .... RichardMcGrath 112+
(K G Reveley) *hld up: hdwy to chse ldr 10th: led 12th: clr next: j.lft 2 out: eased flat* **2/1**[2]
F6P4 **2** *16* **Dramatic Quest**[31] [3888] 9-10-7 **93** ....(v) RichardSpate(7) 94
(A G Juckes) *led: hdd after 5th: chsd ldr tl j.rt 9th: sn rdn: wknd 4 out* **25/1**

3613 **3** *8* **Adecco (IRE)**[31] [3888] 7-11-0 98 JamieMoore 89+
(G L Moore) *hld up: hit 5th and 8th: hdwy next: rdn 11th: wknd 4 out* **11/8**[1]

-50F **F** **Fantastic Arts (FR)**[33] [3844] 6-10-11 104 PaulO'Neill(3) —
(Miss Venetia Williams) *hld up: hdwy: hmpd and fell 9th* **9/2**[3]

0413 **P** **Cedar Rapids (IRE)**[37] [3784] 6-11-0 94 DavidO'Meara —
(H P Hogarth) *chsd ldr: hung lft: led after 5th: j.lft and hdd 12th: sn wknd: bhd whn p.u after 3 out* **9/1**

5m 14.7s (8.60) **Going Correction** +0.30s/f (Yiel) **5** Ran SP% **107.5**
Speed ratings: **95,88,85,—,—** CSF £28.06 TOTE £2.60: £1.70, £2.80; EX 35.00.
Owner W D Hockenhull **Bred** Shade Oak Stud **Trained** Lingdale, Redcar & Cleveland

FOCUS
An uncompetitive race in which the winner was value for 25 lengths but the form looks suspect.

NOTEBOOK
Clouding Over, back in novice company, came well clear from the fourth last for an easy victory. She went out to her left at the second last and was awkward at the final fence, but otherwise jumped pretty well. *(tchd 15-8)*

Dramatic Quest, the early leader, moved back into second place on the home turn but by that stage had only a distant rear view of the winner. *(op 12-1)*

Adecco(IRE) did not jump fluently and was in trouble early on the final circuit. He did move into second place at the fourth last but the winner pulled clear from that point and he was back in third turning from home. *(op 6-4)*

Fantastic Arts(FR) came down for the second consecutive race although in his defence he was unsighted a little going into the obstacle. *(op 4-1 tchd 5-1)*

Cedar Rapids(IRE), keen to get on with things and in front after the fifth, lost his lead when jumping badly out to his left at the 12th and, dropping away, was soon pulled up. He is a difficult ride. *Official explanation: jockey said gelding hung left (op 4-1 tchd 5-1)*

4455 SPEEDY HIRE STANDARD OPEN NATIONAL HUNT FLAT RACE 2m 110y
5:40 (5:41) (Class 6) 4-6-Y-0 **£1,713** (£499; £249)

Form RPR

1 **1** **Sir Jimmy Shand (IRE)**[55] [3462] 5-10-13 SamCurling(5) 112+
(N J Henderson) *chsd ldrs: led over 2f out: hung rt ins fnl f: rdn out* **5/6**[1]

2 *3* **Marine Life** 4-10-10 JamesDavies 99
(P R Webber) *a.p: rdn over 2f out: styd on* **7/2**[2]

3 **3** *3 1/2* **Ellerslie George (IRE)**[97] [2720] 6-11-4 JohnMcNamara 104+
(T P Tate) *led: rdn and hdd over 2f out: wknd ins fnl f* **8/1**[3]

4 *1/2* **Pantalaimon** 5-10-11 MrPCallaghan(7) 103
(H D Daly) *hld up: hdwy 1/2-way: rdn over 2f out: styd on same pce* **50/1**

5 *3* **Kedgeree** 4-10-10 MarkBradburne 92+
(H D Daly) *hld up: hdwy over 6f out: rdn over 2f out: wknd fnl f* **14/1**

6 *2 1/2* **Topless (IRE)** 5-10-6 DarylJacob(5) 90
(D P Keane) *hld up: styd on fnl 2f: nvr nrr* **100/1**

7 *3/4* **Thenford Flyer (IRE)** 6-11-1 OwynNelmes(3) 96
(D J S Ffrench Davis) *hld up: hdwy 1/2-way: wknd over 2f out* **100/1**

8 *1/2* **Southern Classic** 6-11-4 SamStronge 96
(R M Stronge) *hld up: hdwy 7f out: wknd over 3f out* **100/1**

45 **9** *1* **It Happened Out (IRE)**[11] [4244] 5-10-11 WayneKavanagh(7) 95
(J W Mullins) *chsd ldrs over 12f* **20/1**

10 *16* **Saddlers' Son (IRE)** 5-11-1 TJPhelan(3) 79
(Mrs H Dalton) *chsd ldrs: wknd 3f out: eased over 1f out* **66/1**

11 *1 1/2* **Bringewood Fox** 4-10-10 DavidDennis 69
(J L Needham) *chsd ldrs over 11f* **100/1**

12 *15* **Ringo Cody (IRE)**[129] 5-11-1 WilliamKennedy(3) 62
(D R Gandolfo) *a in rr* **100/1**

13 *15* **Doctor Supremo (IRE)** 5-10-13 RobertLucey-Butler(5) 47
(D B Feek) *hld up: hdwy 1/2-way: wknd over 6f out* **100/1**

14 *6* **I'm Posh** 6-11-4 RussGarritty 41
(P Beaumont) *hld up: a in rr* **80/1**

15 *4* **Northern Stars (IRE)** 5-11-4 DavidO'Meara 37
(H P Hogarth) *mid-div: hdwy 10f out: wknd 1/2-way* **100/1**

13 **16** *4* **Dubai Sunday (JPN)**[25] [3983] 5-11-11 JamieMoore 40
(P S McEntee) *hld up: hdwy 1/2-way: rdn and wknd over 4f out* **10/1**

17 *dist* **Grey Kite** 4-10-10 TomSiddall —
(A E Jessop) *a bhd* **125/1**

(3.50) **Going Correction** +0.425s/f (Soft)
WFA 4 from 5yo+ 7lb **17** Ran SP% **120.8**
Speed ratings: **108,106,104,104,103 102,101,101,101,93 92,85,78,75,74 72,—** CSF £3.39 TOTE £1.80: £1.10, £1.70, £2.10; EX 5.10 Place £99.46, Place 5 £53.19.
Owner W H Ponsonby **Bred** C Morgan **Trained** Upper Lambourn, Berks

FOCUS
Probably a decent race of its type, this was run in a fair time for a bumper with the third the best guide to the level.

NOTEBOOK
Sir Jimmy Shand(IRE) ◆, unpenalised for his impressive debut victory in a 'hands and heels' race at Ludlow, followed up in taking style despite wandering around in front, apparently through greenness. He should be kept on the right side *(op 11-10)*

Marine Life, a Khalid Abdulla cast-off for 30,000gns, is a half-brother to smart middle-distance filly Marani out of a mare who won the Cheshire Oaks. A stablemate of Pressgang, who was runner-up in the Champion Bumper 20 minutes earlier, he was never far away and stayed on to go second inside the final furlong, if no match for the easy winner. *(op 10-3 tchd 3-1)*

Ellerslie George(IRE) was a close third to subsequent winner Night Safe on his debut over course and distance in December, since when he has left Owen Brennan's yard. Attempting to make all, he *was outpaced by the winner in the straight and was run out of second spot inside the final furlong. (tchd 9-1)*

Pantalaimon ◆ is out of a mare who won a bumper and has already produced the yard's useful chaser Alderburn. Bred for stamina, he was staying on nicely at the end and should come on for this promising debut. *(op 40-1)*

Kedgeree is out of a winning stayer on the Flat and over hurdles. The shorter-priced of his trainer's pair, he showed ability and should benefit from the experience. *(op 9-1)*

Topless(IRE), out of a poor performer in this type of race, stayed on well in the latter stages and looks to possess plenty of stamina.

Thenford Flyer(IRE), a half-brother to three winners, notably useful Irish jumper Native-Darrig, showed ability on this debut.

Saddlers' Son(IRE), whose dam was an Irish bumper winner, shaped with more promise than his eventual position would imply.

Dubai Sunday(JPN), under a penalty for his Polytrack victory, was well held on this turf debut. *(op 8-1)*

Grey Kite *Official explanation: trainer said gelding scoped dirty after race (op 100-1)*

T/Plt: £492.00 to a £1 stake. Pool: £32,997.45. 48.95 winning tickets. T/Qpdt: £171.20 to a £1 stake. Pool: £2,939.60. 12.70 winning tickets. CR

4443
CHELTENHAM (New Course) (L-H)
Thursday, March 16

OFFICIAL GOING: Good (good to soft in places)
Wind: Moderate, half across. Weather: Overcast, cold.

4456 JEWSON NOVICES' H'CAP CHASE (LISTED RACE) (17 fncs) 2m 5f
2:00 (2:00) (Class 1) 5-Y-0+
£45,616 (£17,112; £8,568; £4,272; £2,144; £1,072)

Form RPR

-221 **1** **Reveillez**[30] [3907] 7-10-11 133 APMcCoy 150+
(J R Fanshawe) *lw: trckd ldrs: chal and hit 3 out: sn led: drvn and kpt on strly run-in: readily* **9/2**[1]

-121 **2** *1 1/4* **Copsale Lad**[75] [3134] 9-11-0 136 MickFitzgerald 149
(N J Henderson) *lw: rr: hdwy 12th: styd on to chse ldrs 3 out: chsd wnr next: kpt on wl u.p run-in but a hld* **8/1**[3]

3-03 **3** *9* **Tumbling Dice (IRE)**[42] [3704] 7-11-1 137 (p) BJGeraghty 142+
(T J Taaffe, Ire) *chsd ldrs: hit 8th and 11th: rdn 4 out: hit 3 out: sn chsng wnr: no imp: wknd appr last* **14/1**

12F0 **4** *shd* **Direct Flight (IRE)**[47] [3622] 8-10-4 126 oh1 (t) PCarberry 130
(Noel T Chance) *bhd: hdwy 13th: rdn 4 out: chsd ldrs next: kpt on same pce fr 2 out* **25/1**

-132 **5** *7* **Turpin Green (IRE)**[40] [3726] 7-11-7 143 TonyDobbin 142+
(N G Richards) *lw: in tch: hit 4th: blnd 10th: hit 11th: styng on whn hit 4 out: wknd after next* **5/1**[2]

1320 **6** *1 3/4* **Hors La Loi III (FR)**[12] [4241] 11-11-7 143 PJBrennan 139+
(P F Nicholls) *bhd: hdwy 4 out: rdn and effrt next: nvr rchd ldrs* **40/1**

4221 **7** *1* **Cornish Sett (IRE)**[12] [4241] 7-11-8 144 4ex (b) RWalsh 142+
(P F Nicholls) *bhd: sme hdwy whn blnd 4 out: nvr gng pce to rch ldrs: no ch whn hmpd 2 out* **9/1**

-21U **8** *shd* **Kasthari (IRE)**[33] [3850] 7-11-1 137 GLee 133+
(J Howard Johnson) *chsd ldrs: chal 10th and nt fluent: upsides next: hit 13th: styd front rnk tl mstke 3 out: sn btn* **33/1**

4P21 **9** *15* **No Full (FR)**[26] [3973] 5-10-4 131 oh1 TomDoyle 105
(P R Webber) *in tch to 12th* **14/1**

1214 **10** *1/2* **Whispered Secret (GER)**[109] [2531] 7-11-6 142 RJGreene 121
(M C Pipe) *nvr gng pce to rch ldrs* **50/1**

-614 **11** *18* **Idole First (IRE)**[21] [4076] 7-10-9 131 AlanO'Keeffe 92
(Miss Venetia Williams) *chsd ldrs to 9th: wknd next* **16/1**

125F **12** *3 1/2* **Chilling Place (IRE)**[87] [2924] 7-11-5 141 RichardJohnson 98
(P J Hobbs) *bhd: drvn fr 10th: nvr in contention* **20/1**

/245 **13** *29* **Garde Champetre (FR)**[111] [2482] 7-10-13 135 DJCasey 63
(Jonjo O'Neill) *nvr bttr than mid-div: bhd fr 12th* **20/1**

2442 **14** *4* **Celtic Son (FR)**[26] [3995] 7-11-10 146 (tp) TimmyMurphy 70
(M C Pipe) *lw: nt fluent 7th: a bhd* **14/1**

2303 **P** **Stance**[10] [3726] 7-10-6 128 (p) JamieMoore —
(G L Moore) *mstke 9th (water): a bhd: t.o whn p.u bef 4 out* **25/1**

1121 **F** **Le Volfoni (FR)**[25] [4006] 5-10-9 141 LiamHeard(5) —
(P F Nicholls) *hld up mid-div: hdwy fr 13th: clsng on ldrs and 2l down whn fell 3 out* **16/1**

112 **F** **Preacher Boy**[40] [3740] 7-10-9 131 JimCrowley —
(R J Hodges) *chsd ldr: hit 6th: mstke 9th (water): wknd next: no ch whn fell 4 out* **33/1**

-231 **F** **Demi Beau**[85] [2939] 8-10-13 135 ChristianWilliams 131
(Evan Williams) *lw: led: hit 5th and 16th: blnd 3 out and sn hdd: no ch whn fell 2 out* **14/1**

5m 5.00s (-21.70) **Going Correction** -0.70s/f (Firm) course record
WFA 5 from 7yo+ 5lb **18** Ran SP% **121.9**
Speed ratings: **113,112,109,109,106 105,105,105,99,99 92,91,80,78,— —,—,—** CSF £35.90 CT £478.93 TOTE £5.20: £2.10, £2.00, £2.30, £4.90; EX 43.40 Trifecta £809.60 Pool £6,842.46, 6.00 w/u.
Owner John P McManus **Bred** Mrs A Yearley **Trained** Newmarket, Suffolk
■ Tony McCoy's first Festival winner in the colours of his employer JP McManus.

FOCUS
A truly-run event and the form looks really solid. Reveillez confirmed himself the decent novice his Flat and hurdles form entitled him to be, and both the second and third showed improved form too

NOTEBOOK
Reveillez ◆ looked potentially well treated and travelled nicely in third or fourth as the two leaders set a strong pace, before easing into a narrow lead on the home turn. The runner-up looked a threat at the final fence, but he pulled out plenty to hold him with something to spare. Capable of further improvement over fences, he looks just the type for races such as the Paddy Power Gold Cup next season. *(op 5-1 tchd 6-1 and 4-1)*

Copsale Lad ◆, brought down in this event a year ago, ran a fine race, but despite giving his all and pulling clear of the remainder he could not get past the favourite on the run-in. He is a *consistent individual who can win a nice prize granted good ground on a left-handed track. (op 9-1 tchd 10-1 in a place and 12-1 in a place)*

Tumbling Dice(IRE), the sole Irish challenger and wearing cheekpieces for the first time, came here on the back of a win at Clonmel. Always prominent despite getting too close to a few fences, he had every chance on the home turn but weakened before the last and appeared to be hanging a little on the run-in. His trainer is reportedly thinking of running him in the Irish National over Easter but stamina would be an issue at Fairyhouse.

Direct Flight(IRE), a casualty on two of his three previous runs over fences, had the tongue tie refitted. He ran a sound race but just lacked the pace to go with the leaders over the last two fences.

Turpin Green(IRE) was not disgraced, but a series of errors hardly helped his chance. He gave the impression that another try over three miles might be merited. *(op 11-2 tchd 6-1)*

Hors La Loi III(FR), twice a winner at previous Festivals, including in the Champion Hurdle four years ago, could never get into the action and looks held off this mark.

Cornish Sett(IRE), under a penalty for dead-heating in the Vodafone Gold Cup at Newbury, was never able to get into the hunt and an error at the fourth from home was the last straw. *(op 8-1)*

Kasthari(IRE) helped push the pace until fading from the third last, where he made a mistake and was slightly hampered. *(tchd 40-1 in places)*

Idole First(IRE), successful in last season's Coral Cup, ought to have been suited by the step up to this trip but ran a lacklustre race.

Celtic Son(FR) was touted as a leading Royal & SunAlliance Chase contender after his impressive chasing debut at Wincanton, but he has largely disappointed since and the application of cheekpieces failed to bring about an improvement. His yard had a Cheltenham to forget. *(tchd 16-1)*

Demi Beau went up a stone after an impressive success at Ludlow before Christmas. Over this longer trip, he enjoyed himself out in front, getting away with a couple of errors, but appeared tired and was dropping back through the field when he took a heavy fall at the second last. He does not stay this trip, but provided this fall does not leave any lasting effects he can land a nice handicap over two miles. *(tchd 12-1)*

Le Volfoni(FR) ◆, who has been in good form in less competitive events on softer ground, was just behind the leaders when coming down at the third last. He was travelling well, with all to play for, at the time. *(tchd 12-1)*

4457 RYANAIR CHASE (REGISTERED AS THE FESTIVAL TROPHY) GRADE 2 (17 fncs) 2m 5f

2:35 (2:37) (Class 1) 5-Y-0+

£85,530 (£32,085; £16,065; £8,010; £4,020; £2,010)

Form RPR

4B13 **1** **Fondmort (FR)**[26] [3977] 10-11-0 157.................................. MickFitzgerald 164+
(N J Henderson) *trckd ldrs: mstke 12th: pressed ldr 4 out: rdn to ld 2 out: 4l clr last: tired flat: all out fin* **10/3**[1]

1340 **2** *1 ¼* **Lacdoudal (FR)**[19] [4118] 7-11-0 149.................................. RichardJohnson 160
(P J Hobbs) *lost pl and towards rr 3rd: effrt 10th: outpcd and struggling 4 out: styd on bef 2 out: clsd fr last: tk 2nd fnl strides* **20/1**

2113 **3** *hd* **Impek (FR)**[80] [2972] 10-11-3 164.................................. APMcCoy 166+
(Miss H C Knight) *lw: led 3rd to 5th and fr 7th: hdd and mstke 2 out: sn outpcd by wnr: styd on again flat but lost 2nd fnl strides* **10/3**[1]

2323 **4** *9* **My Will (FR)**[19] [4118] 6-11-3 149..................................(t) RWalsh 156+
(P F Nicholls) *nt fluent towards rr: lost tch w main gp 11th: wl bhd 4 out: styd on fr 2 out: n.d* **14/1**

3-45 **5** *1 ¼* **Hand Inn Hand**[103] [2635] 10-11-0 150.................................. RobertThornton 151+
(H D Daly) *hld up towards rr: prog 10th: trcking ldrs whn mstke 12th: outpcd fr 4 out: no imp after* **16/1**

3114 **6** *2 ½* **Hi Cloy (IRE)**[56] [3472] 9-11-5.................................. AndrewJMcNamara 153+
(Michael Hourigan, Ire) *lw: settled in rr: prog fr 10th but nt on terms w ldrs fr 12th: one pce fr 3 out* **8/1**[3]

2P-P **7** *17* **Calling Brave (IRE)**[19] [4118] 10-11-0 146..................................(t) MarcusFoley 130
(N J Henderson) *detached in last fr 4th: mstke next: nvr on terms after: t.o 4 out: r.o flat* **50/1**

5014 **8** *2 ½* **See You Sometime**[26] [3995] 11-11-3 138.................................. AndrewThornton 131
(J W Mullins) *pressed ldrs tl wknd after 13th: no ch 3 out* **66/1**

-1P1 **9** *dist* **Our Vic (IRE)**[26] [3977] 8-11-5 158.................................. TimmyMurphy 140
(M C Pipe) *led to 3rd and fr 5th to 7th: pressed ldr to 4 out: wknd rapidly next: j.v.slowly last and virtually p.u flat* **11/2**[2]

1512 **P** **Armaturk (FR)**[26] [3980] 9-11-0 158.................................. ChristianWilliams —
(P F Nicholls) *nt fluent 3rd: a in rr: lost tch 10th: t.o whn p.u bef 4 out* **14/1**

-611 **F** **Sir Oj (IRE)**[18] [4138] 9-11-3..................................(b) PCarberry —
(Noel Meade, Ire) *lw: chsd ldrs: pushed along 10th: disputing 7th and struggling whn fell 4 out* **8/1**[3]

5m 3.00s (-23.70) **Going Correction** -0.70s/f (Firm) course record **11** Ran SP% **111.2**
Speed ratings: **117,116,116,113,112 111,105,104,—,—** — CSF £62.28 CT £229.06 TOTE £3.90: £1.80, £5.30, £1.80; EX 91.10 Trifecta £280.80 Pool £7,830.90, 19.80 w/u.
Owner W J Brown **Bred** Hubert Carion **Trained** Upper Lambourn, Berks
■ New sponsors for the second running of this event.

FOCUS
A strongly-run renewal of this race, and the fastest of the three chases over the trip on the day by 2sec. The form looks very solid.

NOTEBOOK
Fondmort(FR) has been something of a standing dish at around this trip over the last few years, but was without a previous win at the Festival, despite having been placed in each of the last three seasons. He put up a fine performance to gain compensation for his narrow defeat in this contest last term, always travelling strongly, quickly asserting off the home turn, and having enough in hand to resist the challenges on the run-in. He is in the Grand National, but looks a very doubtful stayer so surely the Melling Chase is a better option if he goes to Aintree, with the Mira Showers Trophy at Cheltenham's April meeting another possibility. *(op 3-1 tchd 7-2 in places)*
Lacdoudal(FR), another who has some decent form on this track, was dropping back from three miles. He could not lay up with the early pace, but came through well from the bottom of the hill and was closing down the winner at the line. He could well be punished by the Handicapper for this effort and may have to continue to compete in this grade now. *(tchd 33-1 in a place)*
Impek(FR) ◆, who had to be led in and was later reported by connections as not being ready when the tapes went up, soon got to the front and, jumping fluently, helped set the pace. He was travelling well turning in but the winner got past him before the second last and he looked beaten. However, he rallied well up the hill when the second came at him and deserves plenty of credit for this effort. It would be no surprise to see him take his chance in the Melling Chase at Aintree in search of a well-deserved Grade One victory. *(op 3-1)*
My Will(FR), who has been running consistently well in defeat on much softer ground this season, found this pace too hot and his jumping suffered, but was keeping on at the end and a return to three miles will be in his favour. *(op 16-1)*
Hand Inn Hand has been below his best of late, indicated by the fact that his official rating has dropped 10lb since January 2005, but he travelled really well for a long way before fading on the downhill run. Having had a wind operation, this was his first outing for over three months. He may come on for it.
Hi Cloy(IRE), who has had a fine season in Ireland and is generally consistent, was settled at the back of the field and found this strong pace on this faster going not playing to his strengths. He is in the Grand National but there are better opportunities for him at Punchestown, where he should get easier ground. *(op 9-1)*
Calling Brave(IRE) has had his prblems but was noted putting in good work when the race was all over, having been unable to go the pace. He is a possible for the National.
Our Vic(IRE), who beat My Will and Fondmort at Lingfield last time, got into a battle for the lead with Impek and was the first to crack. He is far from consistent, but this below-par effort was echoed by many from his stable during the Festival and he was conspicuously uneasy in the market. *(op 5-1 tchd 6-1 in places)*
Armaturk(FR) *Official explanation: vet said gelding had bled from the nose (op 10-1)*
Sir Oj(IRE), another who came into this race on a roll, was beginning to feel the pinch when departing at the tricky fourth-last fence. This was not the ideal preparation with the Grand National next on the agenda, but easier conditions there will suit providing his confidence is not unduly affected. *(op 10-1)*

4458 LADBROKES WORLD HURDLE GRADE 1 (12 hdls) 3m

3:15 (3:19) (Class 1) 4-Y-0+

£131,146 (£49,197; £24,633; £12,282; £6,164; £3,082)

Form RPR

-211 **1** **My Way De Solzen (FR)**[25] [4008] 6-11-10 157.............. RobertThornton 166+
(A King) *trckd ldrs: chal appr 2 out tl drvn to ld wl bef last and edgd lft: hung rt u.p fnl 75yds: all out* **8/1**

/231 **2** *hd* **Golden Cross (IRE)**[25] [4019] 7-11-10..................................(tp) JMurtagh 166+
(M Halford, Ire) *lw: hld up in rr:hdwy 4 out:chsd ldrs and n.m.r appr last: styng on wl whn carried rt fnl 75yds: rallied: jst failed* **5/1**[3]

0122 **3** *4* **Mighty Man (FR)**[40] [3723] 6-11-10 156.................................. RichardJohnson 161
(H D Daly) *lw: chsd ldrs: pushed along 3 out: hrd drvn after next: swtchd lft last: kpt on u.p but no imp run-in* **4/1**[1]

2221 **4** *3* **Fire Dragon (IRE)**[40] [3723] 5-11-10 151..................................(b) TonyDobbin 158
(Jonjo O'Neill) *chsd ldrs: ev ch 2 out: stl gng wl whn n.m.r appr last: sn outpcd* **33/1**

12-2 **5** *2 ½* **Baracouda (FR)**[110] [2490] 11-11-10.................................. APMcCoy 156+
(F Doumen, France) *hld up in mid-div: hday 3 out: chsd ldrs next: ev ch and rdn wl bef last: wknd run-in* **9/2**[2]

4221 **6** *1 ¼* **Emotional Moment (IRE)**[49] [3585] 9-11-10.................................. RWalsh 154
(T J Taaffe, Ire) *bhd: hdwy 3 out: drvn and kpt on appr last: nvr gng pce to rch ldrs* **22/1**

4/30 **7** *7* **Starzaan (IRE)**[40] [3723] 7-11-10 145.................................. PCarberry 150+
(H Morrison) *lw: chsd ldrs: blnd 2 out and sn wknd* **100/1**

4-4F **8** *5* **Patriarch Express**[21] [4069] 9-11-10 158.................................. DominicElsworth 143+
(Mrs S J Smith) *chsd ldrs: chal 3 out: hrd drvn and slt ld 2 out:hdd wl bef last: wkng whn n.m.r sn after* **12/1**

1- **9** *5* **Ambobo (USA)**[17] [4154] 6-11-10..................................(t) BJGeraghty 137
(A Chaille-Chaille, France) *chsd ldrs: rdn 3 out: ev ch next: wknd bef last* **17/2**

12-0 **10** *1 ¾* **It's Just Harry**[110] [2493] 9-11-10 140.................................. PJBrennan 135
(C R Egerton) *bhd: rdn and sme hdwy 3 out: nvr in contention* **33/1**

0P43 **11** *shd* **Westender (FR)**[40] [3723] 10-11-10 151..................................(p) TimmyMurphy 135
(M C Pipe) *bhd: hmpd 5th: sme hdwy fr 2 out: nvr in contention* **25/1**

3443 **12** *7* **Crystal D'Ainay (FR)**[21] [4069] 7-11-10 159..................................(v) WayneHutchinson 128
(A King) *chsd ldr: chal 6th tl led 8th: narrowly hdd but stl upsides 2 out: sn wknd* **33/1**

1-15 **13** *2 ½* **No Refuge (IRE)**[40] [3723] 6-11-10 151.................................. GLee 126
(J Howard Johnson) *hit 7th: a bhd* **14/1**

0110 **14** *dist* **Attorney General (IRE)**[40] [3723] 7-11-10 149.................................. JasonMaguire 119
(J A B Old) *a in rr: t.o* **25/1**

P-35 **15** *3* **Davenport Milenium (IRE)**[88] [2910] 10-11-10..................................(t) DJCasey —
(W P Mullins, Ire) *bhd most of way: t.o* **200/1**

0-25 **16** *3* **Blue Canyon (FR)**[21] [4069] 8-11-10.................................. CO'Dwyer —
(F Doumen, France) *lw: led to 8th: sn wknd: t.o* **80/1**

2-00 **17** *12* **Mistanoora**[40] [3723] 7-11-10 148..................................(b) CarlLlewellyn —
(N A Twiston-Davies) *chsd ldrs to 6th: t.o* **100/1**

0524 **U** **Sh Boom**[21] [4069] 8-11-10 143.................................. LiamHeard —
(S A Brookshaw) *rr but in tch whn mstke and uns rdr 5th* **66/1**

P2 **P** **Millenium Royal (FR)**[21] [4069] 6-11-10.................................. MickFitzgerald —
(F Doumen, France) *bhd form 1/2-way: t.o whn p.u bef 2 out* **33/1**

0543 **P** **Holy Orders (IRE)**[25] [4019] 9-11-10..................................(b) DJCondon —
(W P Mullins, Ire) *a bhd: t.o whn j.v.slowly 3 out and p.u sn after: dead* **150/1**

5m 38.2s (-20.70) **Going Correction** -0.325s/f (Good) **20** Ran SP% **120.5**
Speed ratings: **121,120,119,118,117 117,115,113,111,111 111,108,107,—,—** —,—,—,—,— CSF £42.43 CT £188.48 TOTE £8.20: £3.00, £2.10, £2.20; EX 30.10 Trifecta £107.00 Pool £11,213.82, 74.40 w/u.
Owner B Winfield,A Longman,J Wright & C Fenton **Bred** C Ricous-Guerin & Jacques Guerin **Trained** Barbury Castle, Wilts

FOCUS
A big field, but not a vintage renewal, with last year's winner Inglis Driver, who was ruled out for the season in January, a notable absentee. The pace was sound and the time compared well with the later handicap.

NOTEBOOK
My Way De Solzen(FR) is well at home in testing ground but had no problem with these faster conditions. Getting to the front after the second last, he intimidated his main challenger when idling and drifting to his right on the run-in and the line came just in time. He gave the impression that he had more in hand than the narrow margin suggests and is most progressive. *(tchd 9-1, 10-1 in a place)*
Golden Cross(IRE) almost provided top Flat jockey Johnny Murtagh with a Cheltenham Festival winner. Sent in pursuit of My Way De Solzen going to the final flight and carried right as that opponent drifted over on the run-in, he ran on strongly in the dying stages but needed a couple more strides. A classy and versatile performer, he reportedly incurred an overreach but it was not thought to be too serious. *(tchd 11-2, 6-1 in a place)*
Mighty Man(FR) came under pressure some way out but responded to Johnson's efforts and kept staying on, if lacking the pace to get to the front two. A tough individual, he has bags of stamina and there should be more to come from him next season. *(tchd 9-2 in places)*
Fire Dragon(IRE) travelled strongly and only came under pressure on the lengthy run towards the final flight, when he was slightly short of room. Five-year-olds have a poor record in this event and this was a fine run.
Baracouda(FR) won this event in 2002 and 2003 when it was run as the Stayers', and he was runner-up in the most recent two runnings, but his abilities are finally on the wane. That said, this was still a commendable effort, but after coming back on the bridle turning for home he could not quite go with his younger rivals on the approach to the final flight. This was the first time since his hurdling debut six years ago that he has finished out of the first two. He has been retired. *(tchd 5-1)*
Emotional Moment(IRE), patiently ridden, ran well on ground that was too fast for him, but he was never quite able to get to the leaders. *(op 25-1)*
Starzaan(IRE) ran well for a long way but was held when blundering at the second last. He does not quite stay this far. *(tchd 66-1)*
Patriarch Express, in with every chance when diving at the second last, weakened on the long run to the final flight. *(op 10-1)*
Ambobo(USA), winner of a Grade 2 novices' hurdle here last January, was then off for nearly a year and has not been in quite the same form since returning, although he did win a little race at Marseilles Borely last month. He was right in the mix at the second last but in the end his stamina was found wanting. *(op 8-1 tchd 9-1 in places)*
Crystal D'Ainay(FR), a stablemate of the winner, helped force the pace and only faded out of contention after jumping to his right over the second-last flight. *(tchd 40-1 in a place)*
No Refuge(IRE) landed last year's Royal & SunAlliance Hurdle but his yard is not in the same form this time round. He was beaten too far out for stamina to have been the sole factor. *(op 12-1 tchd 16-1 in a place)*
Holy Orders(IRE), a smart performer both on the Flat and over hurdles, suffered a fractured hind leg and had to be put down. *(op 100-1)*
Sh Boom sadly developed a thrombosis the night after the race and had to be put down. *(op 100-1)*

4459 RACING POST PLATE (A H'CAP CHASE) (FORMERLY THE MILDMAY OF FLETE) GRADE 3 (17 fncs) 2m 5f

4:00 (4:01) (Class 1) 5-Y-0+

£42,765 (£16,042; £8,032; £4,005; £2,010; £1,005)

Form RPR

-433 **1** **Non So (FR)**[40] [3739] 8-11-3 **137**.................................. MickFitzgerald 155+
(N J Henderson) *lw: trckd ldrs: gng easily 4 out: wnt 2nd next: led 2 out: sn clr* **14/1**

51U0 **2** *9* **Kelrev (FR)**[61] [3385] 8-11-1 **135**.................................. SamThomas 141
(Miss Venetia Williams) *settled in midfield on inner: prog 11th: chsd ldrs 4 out: styd on fr 3 out to go 2nd last: no ch w wnr* **50/1**

-216 **3** *7* **Graphic Approach (IRE)**[19] [4118] 8-11-6 **140**.................................. APMcCoy 140+
(C R Egerton) *prom: chsd ldr and mstke 12th: drvn and lost 2nd 3 out: sn outpcd* **11/1**[3]

213B **4** *hd* **Roman Ark**[26] [3974] 8-10-12 **132**.................................. GLee 131
(J M Jefferson) *settled in midfield: prog 11th: chsd ldng gp but nt on terms fr 4 out: kpt on: n.d* **33/1**

3F13 **5** *½* **Windsor Boy (IRE)**[12] [4241] 9-10-3 **130**.............. AndrewGlassonbury[(7)] 130+
(M C Pipe) *chsd ldr fr 4th tl mstke 12th: sn drvn and lost pl rapidly: styd on again bef 2 out* **12/1**

044F **6** *1 ¼* **East Tycoon (IRE)**[124] 2177 7-10-9 **129**................................ BrianHarding 126
(Jonjo O'Neill) *towards rr: jst in tch at bk of main gp 13th: outpcd next: kpt on one pce fr 3 out* **33/1**

4426 **7** *2* **Le Passing (FR)**[74] 3180 7-11-12 **146**..........................(b) JoeTizzard 141
(P F Nicholls) *towards rr: struggling bdly 12th: virtually t.o 3 out: r.o fr next: fin wl* **33/1**

3P-6 **8** *nk* **Chauvinist (IRE)**[110] 2492 11-11-2 **136**................................ MarcusFoley 132+
(N J Henderson) *pressed ldrs: mstke 4 out: steadily wknd fr next* **33/1**

1341 **9** *6* **Billyvoddan (IRE)**[51] 3549 7-11-7 **141**.......................... RichardJohnson 130
(H D Daly) *chsd ldr to 4th: w ldng gp tl wknd fr 13th* **13/2**[2]

1513 **10** *1* **Tamango (FR)**[141] 1881 9-11-0 **134**.. PJBrennan 122
(P J Hobbs) *nvr beyond midfield: in tch at bk of main bunch 13th: no prog: wknd bef 3 out* **33/1**

6000 **11** *1 ½* **Tango Royal (FR)**[96] 2760 10-11-1 **135**................................(t) RJGreene 121
(M C Pipe) *u.p and wl in rr after 7th: hmpd next: t.o 13th: plugged on fr 3 out* **25/1**

0464 **12** *2 ½* **Bronzesmith**[141] 1881 10-10-4 **127**................................ OwynNelmes(3) 111
(B J M Ryall) *wl in rr: sme prog fr 10th: jst in tch at bk of main gp 12th: sn outpcd and struggling* **66/1**

F211 **13** *nk* **Napolitain (FR)**[19] 4116 5-11-1 **140**... RWalsh 118
(P F Nicholls) *chsd ldrs: struggling whn mstke 13th: no ch after: wknd 3 out* **13/2**[2]

2250 **14** *2* **Vandas Choice (IRE)**[61] 3385 8-10-12 **135**................ PeterBuchanan(3) 116
(Miss Lucinda V Russell) *a towards rr: rdn 9th: no prog: t.o fr 13th* **66/1**

00/2 **15** *3 ½* **Camden Tanner (IRE)**[42] 3704 10-10-9 **129**......................... DNRussell 107
(Robert Tyner, Ire) *j. bdly in last pair: t.o fr 12th* **25/1**

-664 **16** *16* **Locksmith**[26] 3980 6-11-11 **145**... JamieMoore 107
(M C Pipe) *mstkes: plld hrd: hld up in last pair: brief prog 12th: wknd after 4 out: t.o* **50/1**

640U **17** *13* **Redemption**[12] 4241 11-11-0 **134**....................................(t) CarlLlewellyn 83
(N A Twiston-Davies) *mstkes: racd wd: hld up wl in rr: prog and in tch 12th: sn wknd: t.o* **16/1**

62P3 **18** *2* **Green Belt Flyer (IRE)**[18] 4138 8-11-6 **140**..........................(b) TPTreacy 87
(Mrs John Harrington, Ire) *lw: mstke 3rd: chsd ldrs: wkng whn blnd 12th: t.o* **50/1**

41F3 **F** **Euro Leader (IRE)**[124] 2195 8-11-8 **142**.. DJCasey —
(W P Mullins, Ire) *towards rr whn fell 8th* **20/1**

-P03 **F** **Ross River**[60] 3410 10-10-10 **130**... PCarberry —
(A J Martin, Ire) *towards rr whn bmpd and fell 8th* **5/1**[1]

P215 **P** **Royal Hector (GER)**[47] 3619 7-10-11 **131**...................... RobertThornton —
(Jonjo O'Neill) *mstkes: wl in rr: hmpd 8th: nt gng wl after: p.u bef 12th* **50/1**

-214 **F** **Saintsaire (FR)**[54] 3503 7-10-10 **130**............................(b[1]) AndrewTinkler 143+
(N J Henderson) *led: drew 5l clr 13th: hdd 2 out: 3rd and btn whn fell last: winded* **25/1**

121P **P** **Bannow Strand (IRE)**[26] 3988 6-11-4 **138**...................... TimmyMurphy —
(M C Pipe) *lw: w ldrs tl wknd rapidly 10th: eased and t.o in last fr 12th: p.u bef 2 out* **14/1**

0125 **U** **Too Forward (IRE)**[47] 3620 10-11-4 **138**............................ TonyDobbin —
(M Pitman) *lw: in tch: prog to chse ldrs 10th: 6th and outpcd whn blnd 3 out: swvd and uns rdr after* **16/1**

5m 5.20s (-21.50) **Going Correction** -0.70s/f (Firm) course record
WFA 5 from 6yo+ 5lb **108** Ran SP% **126.3**
Speed ratings: 112,108,105,105,105 105,104,104,102,101 101,100,99,99,97 91,86,86,—,— —,—,—,**EM** CSF £587.50 CT £7750.84 TOTE £16.50: £3.30, £18.90, £2.90, £11.10; EX 848.50 Trifecta £5742.10 Part won. Pool £8,087.56 - 0.10 winning units.
Owner Roa Dawn Run Partnership **Bred** Ecurie Di Tullio **Trained** Upper Lambourn, Berks
■ The first running of this contest, formerly the Mildmay Of Flete, under its present title.

FOCUS
A decent, competitive handicap chase, but run two seconds slower than the earlier Grade Two contest. The winner was well in, but this was still improved form.

NOTEBOOK
Non So(FR) who has looked a somewhat weak finisher in recent runs on soft ground, proved that this sort of surface plays more to his strengths and, travelling well throughout, swept to the front off the turn and the issue was never in doubt from that point. The stable has hit form at just the right time and this was his first success since winning as a novice in January 2004. He will go up a fair amount for this, but his confidence will be high. *(op 12-1)*
Kelrev(FR), fourth in this race two seasons ago when the good ground helped him see out the trip, bounced back from a couple of below-par efforts helped by similar conditions. He does not look especially well handicapped, but having bounced back to form there could be a decent handicap in him before the season's end.
Graphic Approach(IRE), dropping back from three miles, was given a positive ride but could not stay with the winner from the bottom of the hill. He looks high enough in the handicap now. *(op 10-1 tchd 12-1 in a place)*
Roman Ark ◆, whose best form is on testing ground, ran really well on this faster surface. He was clearly none the worse for having been brought down last time, and as a novice, looks the ideal sort for the novice contests at Aintree and Ayr.
Windsor Boy(IRE), from a yard that has not had a good Festival, came into this on the back of a good effort in a similar valuable event at Newbury. He looked well beaten at one point, but then ran on again up the hill. He is probably a few pounds too high in the handicap at present. *(tchd 14-1 in a place)*
East Tycoon(IRE), last seen when falling in the Paddy Power Gold Cup at the November meeting, is well suited by a sound surface and ran a fair race for a stable that is not firing at present.
Le Passing(FR), runner-up in the Robin Cook Memorial over course and distance before Christmas, handles this ground but has looked much more effective in testing conditions. He was never in contention, but stayed on very strongly past beaten rivals.
Chauvinist(IRE), who had not run since November, showed up for a long way for his in-form yard. He is relatively lightly raced over fences and he may still have a nice prize in him despite his advancing years.
Billyvoddan(IRE), who gave 10lb and a beating to the winner of the opening race, Reveillez, at Leicester last time, could not get to the front and was struggling some way from home. This was disappointing, as the ground should not have been a problem, and he has shown in the past that he acts on the track. Twice a winner right-handed this season, he could be the sort for a race at the Punchestown Festival once he is freshened up. *(tchd 7-1 in places)*
Napolitain(FR) was another novice to disappoint, but as four of his five wins have been right handed and the other was on a figure of eight track, he may bounce back to form at Sandown's end-of-season meeting, a track where he is unbeaten in two outings. *(tchd 7-1 in a place)*
Camden Tanner(IRE) *Official explanation: jockey said gelding was unsuited by the ground (op 33-1)*
Redemption made his usual jumping errors but was in the firing line at the top of the hill before fading.
Too Forward(IRE) was still in contention when making a mistake and then swerving and losing his rider at the third from home. *(op 6-1 tchd 13-2 in a place)*
Saintsaire(FR), a novice stable companion of the winner, was lit up by the first-time blinkers and led the field a merry dance. He was clear at the bottom of the hill, but it was soon clear the winner was stalking him and once headed he got very tired. He may well have held onto a place though had he not come down at the last, but he lay winded for a while and may take some time to get over this race. However, headgear looks worth trying again, and he will be better suited by a flat track. *(op 6-1 tchd 13-2 in a place)*
Ross River, a well-backed favourite, departed at an early stage after being hampered. *(op 6-1 tchd 13-2 in a place)*
Royal Hector(GER) *Official explanation: jockey said gelding was never travelling (op 6-1 tchd 13-2 in a place)*

4460 LETHEBY & CHRISTOPHER NATIONAL HUNT CHASE CHALLENGE CUP (AMATEUR RIDERS' NOVICES' CHASE) (27 fncs) 4m 1f

4:40 (4:43) (Class 2) 5-Y-0+

£30,010 (£9,375; £4,685; £2,345; £1,170; £590)

Form RPR

5361 **1** **Hot Weld**[39] 3760 7-11-11 120.. MrROHarding 132+
(Ferdy Murphy) *led 2nd: hit 4 out and hdd: led again next: hrd drvn and hld on gamely run-in* **33/1**

2 *nk* **Beantown (IRE)**[32] 3896 8-11-7 .... MrPTobin 127+
(Sean Aherne, Ire) *str: lw: chsd ldrs: hit 3rd: one pce after 3 out: styd on u.p fr next: fin strly: nt quite get up* **40/1**

3 *1* **Far From Trouble (IRE)**[105] 2599 7-11-11 .... MrJTMcNamara 129+
(C Roche, Ire) *lw: hld up in rr: hdwy 22nd: j. slowly 3 out: kpt on wl fr 2 out: gng on cl home* **7/2**[1]

4 *3 ½* **Wolf Creek (IRE)**[11] 4264 6-11-11 .... MissNCarberry 126+
(E J O'Grady, Ire) *chsd ldrs: wnt 2nd 21st: chal 23rd: led 4 out: hdd next: one pce run-in* **10/1**[3]

1342 **5** *6* **Without A Doubt**[20] 4089 7-11-11 132.................................. MrTJO'Brien 125+
(M Pitman) *bdly hmpd 5th and bhd: hdwy 4 out: styd on wl fr 3 out: kpt on run-in but nvr gng pce to rch ldrs* **20/1**

1336 **6** *6* **Theatre Knight (IRE)**[29] 3928 8-11-11 104......................... MrMJO'Hare 113
(J Howard Johnson) *chsd ldrs to 4 out: wknd bef 2 out* **100/1**

40-0 **7** *1* **Brigadier Brown (IRE)**[39] 3775 9-11-7 .... MrMDHickey 108
(John Joseph Murphy, Ire) *hit 8th: bhd: kpt on fr 3 out: nvr rchd ldrs* **50/1**

3 **8** *1 ¾* **Holey Moley (IRE)**[17] 4144 9-11-7 .... MrWGRankin 106
(R T J Wilson, Ire) *w'like: rr: hit 8th and 13th: hmpd 3 out: kpt on but nvr a danger* **100/1**

1442 **9** *6* **Dancer Life (POL)**[47] 3612 7-11-11 122.............................. MrNWilliams 104
(Evan Williams) *chsd ldrs to 4 out: wknd after next* **16/1**

3232 **10** *½* **High Cotton (IRE)**[19] 4111 11-11-7 114................................ MrDThomas 100
(K G Reveley) *chsd ldrs tl wknd 20th* **16/1**

F602 **11** *7* **Blue Business**[28] 3946 8-11-7 132...................................(b) MrCJSweeney 93
(P F Nicholls) *chsd ldrs: hit 4th: blnd 4th: styd prom: wknd 4 out* **10/1**[3]

232 **12** *½* **Steppes Of Gold (IRE)**[48] 3601 9-11-7 128.......................... MrRWidger 92
(Jonjo O'Neill) *nvr bttr than mid-div* **12/1**

4423 **13** *10* **Lago D'Oro**[19] 4116 6-11-0 93.. DrPPritchard 75
(Dr P Pritchard) *blundered 18th: a bhd* **200/1**

11F1 **F** **Millenaire (FR)**[16] 4166 7-12-0 135.....................................(p) MrKEPower —
(Jonjo O'Neill) *in tch whn fell 5th: dead* **14/1**

4022 **P** **Iloveturtle (IRE)**[16] 4164 6-11-7 71..................................(t) MrDHDunsdon —
(M C Chapman) *a bhd: t.o whn p.u bef 23rd* **250/1**

2 **P** **Mage D'Estruval (FR)**[21] 4073 6-11-11 .... MrPCallaghan —
(H D Daly) *lw: bhd fr 1/2-way: t.o whn p.u bef 22nd* **14/1**

0312 **F** **Basilea Star (IRE)**[23] 4035 9-11-11 ....(t) MrRQuinn —
(M C Pipe) *hld up in rr: stdy hdwy 21st: clsng on ldrs whn fell 4 out: dead* **5/1**[2]

04F5 **U** **Mr Babbage (IRE)**[25] 4022 8-11-11 .... MrJJCodd —
(W P Mullins, Ire) *hld up in rr: hdwy 16th: styng on whn mstke and uns rdr 22nd: dead* **10/1**[3]

2-41 **P** **Dolmur (IRE)**[87] 2922 6-11-11 116.. MrTGreenall —
(Ferdy Murphy) *led to 2nd: hit 3rd: dropped rr 9th: hit 21st: t.o whn p.u bef 3 out* **25/1**

0065 **P** **Monty Be Quick**[7] 4323 10-11-11 72.. MrNPearce —
(J M Castle) *chsd wnr fr 4th: hit 7th: blnd 17th: hit 23rd and wknd: t.o whn p.u bef 3 out* **200/1**

P **Hazelhall Princess (IRE)**[39] 3775 7-11-7 .... MrCMotherway —
(John Paul Brennan, Ire) *cmpt: str: in tch whn hit 5th and 12th: sn wknd: t.o whn p.u bef 4 out* **66/1**

P21U **F** **Ardaghey (IRE)**[1] 4444 7-11-11 134..................................(t) MrDEngland —
(N A Twiston-Davies) *t.k.h early: chsd ldrs fr 8th: hit 19th: 3l down and stl travelling ok whn fell 3 out* **20/1**

8m 33.2s (-22.60) **Going Correction** -0.70s/f (Firm) course record **22** Ran SP% **124.5**
Speed ratings: **99,98,98,97,96 94,94,94,92,92 90,90,88,**—,— —,—,—,—,— —,— CSF £973.30 CT £5698.38 TOTE £34.70: £8.30, £9.20, £2.20; EX 735.30.
Owner S Hubbard Rodwell **Bred** Cartmel Bloodstock **Trained** West Witton, N Yorks

FOCUS
This was run at a slow pace, set by the eventual winner, and the form is not easy to rate. The race was marred by three fatalities.

NOTEBOOK
Hot Weld, able to dictate the pace and make virtually all the running, stayed on bravely to hold off two strong challenges on the run-in. He is on the upgrade and this fastish ground suited him well.
Beantown(IRE), a winning pointer, was having only his fourth start under Rules. Outpaced by the leading duo on the home turn and not fluent at the second last, he jumped the final fence in fourth place before staying on strongly and only just failing to catch the winner. *(op 50-1)*
Far From Trouble(IRE) has now started favourite in the last seven outings of an eight-race career. Having his first run since early December and apparently laid out for this, he was switched off towards the rear before steadily picking his way through the field. Closing on the two leaders once into the home straight, his rider appeared confident that he would make up the leeway, even taking a pull between the last two fences, but although he ran on up the hill he could not get to the winner and the runner-up also went past him. *(tchd 3-1, 9-2 in places and 4-1 in places)*
Wolf Creek(IRE), never far away and travelling strongly, looked the likely winner when challenging Hot Weld at the fourth from home. The pair pulled clear on the home turn but he was the first of them to crack and he lost two places on the run-in. *(op 16-1)*
Without A Doubt, whose best efforts over fences have been at two miles, stayed this marathon trip, albeit in a steadily-run event. In rear after being badly hampered at the fifth, he steadily crept closer in the latter stages without reaching the leading quartet.
Theatre Knight(IRE), whose best form has come on softer ground, ran well on this livelier surface but ultimately failed to see out the trip.
Brigadier Brown(IRE), a maiden over fences, merely stayed on without being able to get involved.
Dancer Life(POL) ran well until his stamina ebbed away from the third last.
High Cotton(IRE) was fourth to Sudden Shock in this event three years ago yet still hasn't won a race of any description.
Blue Business, whose rider made a good recovery at the fourth, travelled well behind the leaders but was another found out by this trip. *(op 8-1 tchd 11-1)*
Basilea Star(IRE), a promising chaser, was by no means out of contention when he took a heavy and fatal fall at the fourth last. *(tchd 11-1, 12-1 in places)*

Mr Babbage(IRE) was starting to close on the leaders when he blundered his way through the final ditch, breaking his leg and ejecting the rider. *(tchd 11-1, 12-1 in places)*
Millenaire(FR), winner of all of his completed starts over fences, unfortunately broke his back in an early fall. *(tchd 11-1, 12-1 in places)*
Ardaghey(IRE), a casualty in the previous day's Royal & SunAlliance Chase, had his tongue tied down here. Reluctant to go to post and keen in the early parts, he steadily worked his way into the picture but came down three from home when disputing third. *(tchd 11-1, 12-1 in places)*
Mage D'Estruval(FR) shaped with considerable promise in a hunter chase on his British debut but did not jump here and was towards the rear of the field until pulling up. *(tchd 11-1, 12-1 in places)*

4461 PERTEMPS FINAL (A H'CAP HURDLE) (LISTED RACE) (12 hdls) 3m
5:20 (5:23) (Class 1) 5-Y-O+

£34,212 (£12,834; £6,426; £3,204; £1,608; £804)

Form	Pos	Btn	Horse	RPR
0-20	1		**Kadoun (IRE)**39 [3771] 9-11-7 **142** ... TGMRyan(3) (M J P O'Brien, Ire) *lw: trckd ldrs: effrt to ld 2 out and kicked on: mstke last: drvn and styd on wl* **50/1**	148+
P-01	2	1 1/2	**Hordago (IRE)**60 [3413] 6-10-2 **125** ... (p) BCByrnes(5) (E McNamara, Ire) *hld up towards rr: prog 9th: n.m.r after 3 out: cl up 2 out: chsd wnr bef last: styd on but readily hld flat* **10/1**	128
-423	3	3 1/2	**Oodachee**97 [2747] 7-11-5 **137** ... (p) DJCasey (C F Swan, Ire) *lw: wl in tch: trckd ldrs 3 out: effrt after 2 out: r.o same pce bef last* **10/1**	137
06-0	4	1 1/4	**Liberman (IRE)**26 [3970] 8-10-8 **126** ... JamieMoore (M C Pipe) *hld up in rr: prog on wd outside bef 2 out: styd on: nt pce to rch ldrs* **20/1**	124
0P03	5	3/4	**Freetown (IRE)**68 [3289] 10-10-9 **127** ... (b) TonyDobbin (L Lungo) *prom: lost pl sltly after 3 out: renewed effrt next: styd on same pce* **33/1**	125
4000	6	3	**Inching Closer**26 [3970] 9-10-7 **125** ... GLee (J Howard Johnson) *hld up on inner: effrt after 3 out: chsng ldrs 2 out: styd on one pce* **50/1**	120
1360	7	3/4	**Alikat (IRE)**40 [3727] 5-11-0 **132** ... (p) BJGeraghty (M C Pipe) *t.k.h: hld up wl in rr: sme prog fr 2 out: r.o wl flat: nvr nrr* **40/1**	126
-F46	8	2	**Oulart**19 [4121] 7-10-11 **129** ... PCarberry (D T Hughes, Ire) *lw: plld hrd: w ldrs: upsides 2 out: wknd jst bef last* **4/1**1	122+
3663	9	nk	**Cool Roxy**75 [3135] 9-10-4 **127** ... ChrisHonour(5) (A G Blackmore) *w ldrs tl drvn and outpcd after 3 out: kpt on again bef last: one pce flat* **50/1**	118
215/	10	1 1/2	**Don Fernando**617 [4427] 7-10-2 **127** ... AndrewGlassonbury(7) (M C Pipe) *hld up wl in rr: prog and mstke 9th: nvr on terms w ldrs fr 2 out* **40/1**	117
4F00	11	1 3/4	**Campaign Trail (IRE)**29 [3921] 8-11-0 **132** ... (b1) RichardJohnson (Jonjo O'Neill) *cl up: chal 2 out: wknd wl bef last* **25/1**	120
1100	12	1 1/4	**Rooftop Protest (IRE)**26 [3970] 9-11-3 **135** ... (tp) RWalsh (T Hogan, Ire) *hld up towards rr: prog on outer 9th: chsd ldrs after 3 out: wknd bef last* **10/1**	122
-500	13	6	**Le Roi Miguel (FR)**80 [2999] 8-10-3 **126** ... (t) LiamHeard(5) (P F Nicholls) *settled in rr: outpcd after 3 out: sn wl adrift: kpt on flat* **28/1**	107
3660	14	1/2	**Hasty Prince**40 [3727] 8-11-8 **140** ... CO'Dwyer (Jonjo O'Neill) *hld up in last trio: stl at bk of field but gng easily 3 out: sme prog and mstke 2 out: shkn up and mstke last: nvr nr ldrs* **33/1**	120
5602	15	hd	**Carlys Quest**26 [3970] 12-11-8 **140** ... (b) KeithMercer (Ferdy Murphy) *in tch: dropped to rr u.p 1/2-way: wl bhd after 3 out: plugged on* **16/1**	120
	16	1	**According To Billy (IRE)**26 [4002] 7-10-7 **128** ... PWFlood(3) (E J O'Grady, Ire) *lw: wl in tch tl wknd u.p after 3 out* **12/1**	107
111P	17	hd	**Standin Obligation (IRE)**117 [2336] 7-11-12 **144** ... TimmyMurphy (M C Pipe) *hld up wl in rr: brief effrt on inner after 3 out: no imp on ldrs next: fdd* **9/1**3	123
-010	18	1	**Pretty Star (GER)**47 [3622] 6-11-2 **134** ... RobertThornton (A King) *lw: pressed ldrs: upsides 3 out: ev ch next: wknd rapidly* **25/1**	112
1115	19	4	**Nine De Sivola (FR)**26 [3987] 5-10-8 **133** ... PatrickMcDonald(7) (Ferdy Murphy) *settled midfield: prog 9th: jnd ldrs 3 out: sn drvn and wknd* **16/1**	107
-0P0	20	14	**Quick**26 [3970] 6-11-5 **140** ... (v) TomMalone(3) (M C Pipe) *led to 7th: wknd after 9th* **66/1**	100
12-4	21	3/4	**Glacial Sunset (IRE)**97 [2747] 11-11-1 **133** ... TomDoyle (C Tinkler) *t.k.h: w ldrs: led 7th to 2 out: wknd rapidly* **25/1**	92
5120	22	6	**Mikado**61 [3389] 5-10-7 **125** ... MickFitzgerald (Jonjo O'Neill) *wl in tch tl wknd 3 out* **28/1**	78
1100	23	11	**Magnifico (FR)**26 [3970] 5-11-0 **132** ... TomScudamore (M C Pipe) *prom to 5th: styd wl in tch tl wknd after 9th* **100/1**	74
0-31	P		**Olaso (GER)**26 [3970] 7-11-7 **139** ... APMcCoy (Jonjo O'Neill) *hld up: blnd 3rd: p.u after 5th: dead* **6/1**2	—

5m 46.9s (-12.00) **Going Correction** -0.325s/f (Good) **24** Ran SP% **133.3**
Speed ratings: 107,106,105,104,104 103,103,102,102,102 101,101,99,98,98 98,98,98,96,92 91,89,86,— CSF £465.50 CT £5405.68 TOTE £62.50: £9.30, £3.00, £3.20, £6.20; EX 727.20 Place 6 £600.81, Place 5 £210.02.
Owner John P McManus **Bred** Forenaghts Stud **Trained** Naas, Co Kildare
■ A one, two, three for the Irish, despite protests that their hurdlers were being treated unfairly by the Handicapper.

FOCUS
An ordinary gallop to this competitive handicap and the time was slow, but the form makes sense. It paid to be close to the pace at the top of the hill.

NOTEBOOK
Kadoun(IRE), who had been struggling for form since finishing runner-up in a Grade One at Punchestown last season, had won twice on fast ground in the distant past and appeared to appreciate it. Always travelling well in the bunch behind the leaders, he made a decisive move after jumping two out and always looked like holding on from that point. He did not look especially well handicapped and is sure to be raised for this, but can race over fences and hurdles so should have plenty of options. *(tchd 66-1 in places)*
Hordago(IRE), who had won both his previous starts on this track, had the cheekpieces re-fitted and travelled well enough but, going in pursuit of the winner before the last, could never reduce the margin enough to trouble that rival. He seemed to stay the trip well enough, but may be most effective back at shorter. *(tchd 11-1)*
Oodachee, placed on his last two visits here, was fitted with cheekpieces for the first time and again made the frame. He had a tough task off his mark and was unable to pick up on the run to the last, so could do with being dropped a few pounds. *(op 9-1)*
Liberman(IRE) ◆, who finished sixth in this last season, had been seen just once since when tailed off in a qualifier at Haydock. This track and trip suits him well and he was doing his best work at the finish. On this evidence there is a decent staying handicap to be won with him.
Freetown(IRE), winner of this race in 2002, has not won over hurdles since. Now 11lb lower in the handicap, he ran a terrific race, only fading in the final quarter mile, and a repeat of this could see him ending that long losing run. *(tchd 50-1, 66-1 in a place)*
Inching Closer, winner of this race in 2003, like the 2002 winner Freetown has not won over hurdles since. He moved into contention at the top of the hill, but like most from his stable at the Festival, lacked that extra sparkle in the closing stages. *(op 40-1)*
Alikat(IRE) ◆, who likes really fast ground, had her conditions and ran well as a result. Her wins though have all been on sharp, right-handed tracks and she is one to keep in mind for a race on that sort of course. *(op 33-1)*
Oulart, winner of this contest last season, had not scored since but had signalled his well-being in two outings in February and was heavily backed to complete the double. However, he was much too free in the early stages and left himself with nothing in reserve for the final climb. A stronger pace would have helped. *(op 5-1 tchd 11-2 in a place)*
Cool Roxy is an admirable performer who likes a sound surface and he showed up for a long way. However, he looks best at shorter trips than this.
Rooftop Protest(IRE) had the ground in his favour but, as in his last two races, he gave the impression he did not stay. He is one to bear in mind for races over shorter trips and, later in the year, the Galway Hurdle in July could be on the agenda. *(op 12-1)*
Hasty Prince ◆, in the same ownership as the winner and two others, travelled well for a long way and shaped much better than the bare facts suggest. He is one to keep an eye out for at Aintree, where the easier track would play to his strengths.
Carlys Quest stayed on when the race was over, as he had done in 2005.
Pretty Star(GER), stepping up in distance, showed up for a long way but did not appear to stay this extended trip. *(op 20-1)*
Olaso(GER) made a couple of early mistakes and was in the rear when stumbling on the home turn on the first circuit and sustaining a fatal injury. *(tchd 13-2, 7-1 in a place)*
T/Jkpt: Not won. T/Plt: £919.60 to a £1 stake. Pool: £613,048.38. 486.60 winning tickets. T/Qpdt: £226.20 to a £1 stake. Pool: £31,735.50. 103.80 winning tickets. ST

2262 HEXHAM (L-H)
Thursday, March 16

4462 Meeting Abandoned - Waterlogged

4456 CHELTENHAM (New Course) (L-H)
Friday, March 17

OFFICIAL GOING: Good
Wind: Light across Weather: Overcast & cold

4468 JCB TRIUMPH HURDLE GRADE 1 (8 hdls) 2m 1f
2:00 (2:05) (Class 1) 4-Y-O

£57,020 (£21,390; £10,710; £5,340; £2,680; £1,340)

Form	Pos	Btn	Horse	RPR
011	1		**Detroit City (USA)**41 [3722] 4-11-0 ... (v) RichardJohnson (P J Hobbs) *trckd ldrs: pushed along 4th: chsd ldr after 3 out: drvn appr 2 out: slt ld u.p last: rdn out* **7/2**1	150+
1134	2	5	**Fair Along (GER)**80 [3021] 4-11-0 138 ... PJBrennan (P J Hobbs) *led after 1st: rdn 2 out: narrowly hdd last: kpt on but outstyd by wnr* **25/1**	144
112	3	1	**Blazing Bailey**20 [4117] 4-11-0 ... RobertThornton (A King) *lw: in tch: chsd ldrs 4 out: sn rdn: 4th and styng on same pce whn lft 3rd last* **14/1**	143
1321	4	3 1/2	**Pace Shot (IRE)**30 [3182] 4-11-0 122 ... JamieMoore (G L Moore) *hit 1st: bhd: hdwy 4th: chsd ldrs 3 out: blnd 2 out: kpt on again but nvr gng pce to rch ldrs: lft 4th last* **100/1**	141+
211	5	4	**Afsoun (FR)**36 [3817] 4-11-0 ... MickFitzgerald (N J Henderson) *edgy: chsd ldrs: wnt 2nd briefly 3 out: sn rdn: blnd 2 out: btn sn after: no ch whn hmpd last* **5/1**3	138+
1221	6	1	**Turko (FR)**27 [3996] 4-11-0 143 ... (t) ChristianWilliams (P F Nicholls) *led tl after 1st: chsd ldrs tl outpcd appr 2 out: kpt on again run-in* **8/1**	135
3413	7	1 1/2	**Mahogany Blaze (FR)**14 [4211] 4-11-0 ... CarlLlewellyn (N A Twiston-Davies) *bhd: stl plenty to do after 2 out: kpt on appr last: fin strly but nvr in contention* **100/1**	133
1	8	1	**Mister Hight (FR)**33 [3890] 4-11-0 ... RWalsh (W P Mullins, Ire) *w'like: tended to jump rt thrght: hit 1st: j. slowly 3rd: sme hdwy 3 out: no further progres su.p after next* **4/1**2	133+
5331	9	8	**First Row (IRE)**20 [4122] 4-11-0 ... PCarberry (D T Hughes, Ire) *lw: chsd ldrs early: dropped rr 4th: sn rdn: n.d after* **12/1**	124
2	10	2	**Oh Calin (FR)**132 [2060] 4-11-0 ... (t) BJGeraghty (A Chaille-Chaille, France) *leggy: in tch: rdn to chse ldrs 3 out: wknd next* **33/1**	122
	11	2 1/2	**Restoration (FR)**47 [3638] 4-11-0 ... DNRussell (Noel Meade, Ire) *w'like: bhd: hdwy 4 out: chsd ldrs and rdn next: sn wknd* **150/1**	120
431	12	11	**Linnet (GER)**29 [3939] 4-10-7 112 ... GLee (Ian Williams) *in tch: chsd ldrs 4 out: wknd after next* **66/1**	102
00	13	6	**Love Angel (USA)**20 [4117] 4-11-0 ... RJGreene (J J Bridger) *hmpd 4th: a bhd* **200/1**	104+
1	14	8	**Night Bridge (IRE)**61 [3408] 4-11-0 ... AndrewJMcNamara (John Joseph Murphy, Ire) *w'like: leggy: chsd ldrs to 4 out* **66/1**	95
1	15	22	**Overlut (FR)**27 [3972] 4-11-0 ... DJCasey (F-M Cottin, France) *charged s: t.k.h: chsd ldr tl appr 3 out: sn wknd* **20/1**	73
331	F		**Kasbah Bliss (FR)**20 [4117] 4-11-0 ... APMcCoy (F Doumen, France) *lw: in tch whn fell 4th* **7/1**	—
2	F		**Breathing Fire**33 [3890] 4-11-0 ... DFO'Regan (Mrs John Harrington, Ire) *rr: hdwy 4th: styd on fr 3 out: sn rdn: clsng on ldrs: 4l 3rd and styng on whn fell last* **25/1**	143

3m 51.2s (-21.00) **Going Correction** -0.825s/f (Firm) course record **17** Ran SP% **118.4**
Speed ratings: **116,113,113,111,109 109,108,108,104,103 102,96,94,90,80** —,— CSF £92.09 CT £1106.36 TOTE £4.20: £1.50, £5.20, £2.10, £12.80; EX 113.30 Trifecta £1635.90 Pool: £10,368.84 - 4.50 winning units.
Owner Terry Warner **Bred** E J Kelly **Trained** Withycombe, Somerset
■ A triumph in the true sense of the word for Philip Hobbs, who saddled the first two home.

FOCUS
A strong turn out for Tuesday's Fred Winter resulted in a much smaller field than used to be the norm for the Triumph, but the gallop was as furious as ever and the winning time was a course record, a second and a half quicker than the County Hurdle. It was also a race in which it was an advantage to race up with the pace. The form has been rated very positively, and it looks as if this season's juveniles are a strong crop.

NOTEBOOK

Detroit City(USA) ◆ was equipped for the first time over hurdles with a visor, which had brought about an improvement in him on the Flat. Having, raced up with the pace in the early stages, the signs did not look good when he came off the bridle at halfway and threatened to lose his place. However, the further they went the better he was going and he eventually found enough to collar his stable-companion at the final flight before forging clear up the hill. This was the performance of a stayer, as befits a horse who won over 14 furlongs on the Flat, so it seems likely that he will need another half mile at least over hurdles next season. Unfortunately, second-season hurdlers have tended not to set the world alight in recent years, so with his stamina guaranteed it might be interesting to see if his trainer considers aiming him at a few of the top staying handicaps on the Flat in the meantime. After all, the stable landed the 2003 Northumberland Plate with Unleash, and he was a four-year-old. *(op 4-1)*

Fair Along(GER) soon established his usual position out in front and set a merry gallop. He did absolutely nothing wrong, but having already done so much he just found the climb from the final flight finding him out and his stable-companion saw it out that much better. Considering he was getting beaten in a Polytrack seller at Wolverhampton a year and a day earlier, his achievements over hurdles in the meantime have been staggering, but this may be as good as it gets. However, there can be little doubt that Aintree, where he has already won, is going to suit him.

Blazing Bailey ◆ has always looked a potential stayer and this performance tended to confirm that. Never that far away, like the winner he seemed to get better as the race progressed and he stayed on really well up the hill. He seems very versatile when it comes to ground and is still relatively unexposed over hurdles, so there will be more to come from him when faced with a stiffer test of stamina. He will also look well trreated if tried again on the Flat. *(op 16-1)*

Pace Shot(IRE), a disappointing favourite in a Polytrack maiden since winning his last start over hurdles on New Year's Day, was the revelation of the race and stepped up considerably on his previous form, running well above himself despite a blunder two out. His next outing should tell us much more.

Afsoun(FR), whose participation had been in doubt after he failed to eat up the previous weekend, was allowed to take his chance. He seemed to get himself into a bit of a state down at the start, but nonetheless showed up prominently until coming off the bridle and finding little on the long run between the last two flights. It is impossible to be sure whether he was at his very best here or not, *but he had looked a talented animal before this so he should be given the benefit of the doubt. Official explanation: jockey said gelding boiled over at start*

Turko(FR) was always handy, but there was always the danger that he would find himself outpaced at a vital stage on this ground and that is what happened. The way he stayed on up the hill showed that stamina is not a problem though and there should be better to come from him back on a softer surface. *(op 9-1 tchd 10-1 in places)*

Mahogany Blaze(FR) ◆, who failed to make the cut in the Fred Winter, raced at the rear and was still amongst the toiling backmarkers jumping the second last, but his stamina then came into play and he ran on past beaten rivals to finish a never-nearer seventh. This ground would have been all wrong for him, leaving aside the stiff task he faced on official ratings, so he emerges with plenty of credit.

Mister Hight(FR) seemed to be ridden with plenty of confidence off the pace, but his jumping left a lot to be desired and when he was finally asked for his effort the response was disappointing. His two wins over hurdles, and all his best form on the Flat, has been when there has been plenty of cut in the ground, which gives him a ready-made excuse for this. *(tchd 9-2, 5-1 in places)*

First Row(IRE) was among the very best of these on the Flat and had won twice over hurdles, but he was soon struggling on this better ground. *(tchd 14-1 in places)*

Oh Calin(FR), already a winner over fences in France, as well as in two hurdles, was struggling coming down the hill.

Overlut(FR) gave himself little chance of getting home.

Kasbah Bliss(FR)had the form to be very much involved in the finish but had questions to answer on this ground. He fell too far out to predict how he would have fared. *(op 13-2)*

Breathing Fire ◆, a winner on the Flat for Willie Musson last year, had chased home Mister Hight on his second outing over hurdles at Leopardstown last time. He would have turned that form around here as he was staying on well from off the pace and had just moved into third, though still with plenty of ground to make up on the first two, when crumpling on landing at the last. Provided this does not leave its mark, he certainly has a future at this game. *(op 13-2)*

4469 BRIT INSURANCE NOVICES' HURDLE (REGISTERED AS THE SPA NOVICES' HURDLE) GRADE 2 (12 hdls) 3m

2:35 (2:39) (Class 1) 4-Y-O+

£42,765 (£16,042; £8,032; £4,005; £2,010; £1,005)

Form RPR

-111 **1** **Black Jack Ketchum (IRE)**^{97} [2762] 7-11-7 145 .... APMcCoy 157+
(Jonjo O'Neill) *trckd ldrs: smooth effrt to ld sn after 2 out: rdn clr flat: r.o strly: impressive* **1/1**^{1}

214 **2** *9* **Powerstation (IRE)**^{89} [2909] 6-11-7 .... DNRussell 141
(C Byrnes, Ire) *settled wl in rr: stdy prog fr 7th: chsd clr ldng trio bef 2 out: drvn to chse wnr bef last: kpt on but no ch* **9/1**^{3}

212 **3** *3* **Travino (IRE)**^{47} [3642] 7-11-7 .... BJGeraghty 139+
(Ms Margaret Mullins, Ire) *w'like: str: lw: prom: trckd ldr 6th: hit 9th: sn led: hdd u.p sn after 2 out: hld whn hit last: one pce* **6/1**^{2}

132 **4** *1* **Back To Bid (IRE)**^{19} [4137] 6-11-7 .... DFO'Regan 138+
(Noel Meade, Ire) *tall: str: in tch in midfield: drvn on outer and struggling wl bef 2 out: sn outpcd: styd on again bef last* **33/1**

5 *1 1/4* **Shouette (IRE)**^{15} [4205] 6-11-0 .... AndrewJMcNamara 129
(John Joseph Murphy, Ire) *settled wl in rr: stdy prog 8th: hit 3 out: nt on terms w ldrs 2 out: hanging bef last: kpt on* **100/1**

2311 **6** *3* **Dream Alliance**^{22} [4071] 5-11-7 .... RichardJohnson 134+
(P J Hobbs) *lw: mstkes: chsd ldrs: bdly outpcd after 3 out: no ch after: styd on again flat* **16/1**

221P **7** *1 1/2* **Karanja**^{71} [3249] 7-11-7 ....(t) PJBrennan 133+
(V R A Dartnall) *s.s: in tch: pushed along and prog 8th: jnd ldrs 3 out: upsides 2 out: btn whn hit last: wknd* **33/1**

P311 **8** *1 1/2* **Zipalong Lad (IRE)**^{27} [3978] 6-11-7 .... TonyDobbin 130
(P Bowen) *chasing type: chsd ldrs tl outpcd u.p after 3 out: steadily wknd* **25/1**

1122 **9** *2 1/2* **Oscar Park (IRE)**^{62} [3388] 7-11-7 130 .... TomDoyle 127
(C Tinkler) *in tch in midfield: hit 8th: rdn and wknd wl bef 2 out* **16/1**

11P5 **10** *9* **Jeremy Cuddle Duck (IRE)**^{27} [3969] 5-11-7 125 .... CarlLlewellyn 119+
(N A Twiston-Davies) *settled towards rr: prog bef 7th: drvn and losing pl whn mstke 3 out: wknd* **66/1**

-122 **11** *11* **Five Colours (IRE)**^{27} [3969] 6-11-7 125 .... RobertThornton 107
(A King) *mstke 2nd: chsd ldrs tl wknd rapidly after 3 out* **33/1**

-226 **12** *9* **Mister Top Notch (IRE)**^{12} [4266] 7-11-7 .... CO'Dwyer 98
(D E Fitzgerald, Ire) *w'like: lengthy: pressed ldrs: led 5th: hdd after 9th: sn wknd* **28/1**

1151 **13** *3 1/2* **Its A Dream (IRE)**^{33} [3882] 6-11-7 135 .... MickFitzgerald 95
(N J Henderson) *dull in coat: in tch: mstke 9th: wknd next* **16/1**

5010 **14** *1/2* **Screenplay**^{14} [4215] 5-11-7 118 .... JamieGoldstein 94
(Miss Sheena West) *lw: wl in tch tl wknd sn after 3 out* **100/1**

043 **15** *dist* **It's The Limit (USA)**^{23} [4050] 7-11-7 103 ....(bt) LeeStephens —
(W K Goldsworthy) *chasing type: a wl in rr: lost tch whn bmpd 7th: t.o btn 115l* **100/1**

1163 **16** *5* **Ask The Gatherer (IRE)**^{41} [3738] 8-11-7 125 .... PaulMoloney —
(M Pitman) *mstke 4th: a in rr: wkng whn j.rt 7th: t.o: btn 121 l* **100/1**

1 **17** *7* **Toofarback (IRE)**^{68} [3309] 6-11-7 .... PCarberry —
(Noel Meade, Ire) *w'like: nt jump wl: a in rr: bhd fr 8th: t.o: btn 127l* **11/1**

13P **P** **Super Lord (IRE)**^{56} [3480] 8-11-7 .... JasonMaguire —
(J A B Old) *led to 5th: wknd and mstkes fr 8th: t.o whn p.u bef 2 out* **100/1**

0200 **P** **Smileafact**^{41} [3729] 6-11-7 89 ....(p) BenjaminHitchcott —
(Mrs Barbara Waring) *prom to 4th: wknde rapidly next: sn t.o: p.u bef 3 out* **100/1**

5m 38.3s (-20.60) **Going Correction** -0.825s/f (Firm) **19** Ran SP% **123.8**
Speed ratings: **101,98,97,96,96 95,94,94,93,90 86,83,82,82,— —,—,—,—** CSF £9.44 CT £40.16 TOTE £2.00: £1.40, £3.20, £1.80; EX 17.30 Trifecta £70.60 Pool: £7,687.08 - 77.20 winning units.

Owner Mrs Gay Smith **Bred** E Morrissey **Trained** Cheltenham, Gloucs

FOCUS

The second running of this race. Despite the pace not looking at all strong, it still proved too severe a test of stamina for a large number of these. The winner, who was value for further, looks a very exciting prospect and won very much as the betting suggested he should. The form should work out.

NOTEBOOK

Black Jack Ketchum(IRE) ◆, a chasing type who had not been seen since winning over course and distance in December after connections declined to take on Denman at Bangor last month, was considered the banker of the meeting for many and was backed accordingly. His supporters never had a moment's worry either, as he was in the ideal position throughout and he could hardly have wished for a smoother passage. The only question was how much he would find of the bridle, and the answer was plenty as he stormed clear up the hill to become probably the most impressive winner at the entire meeting. It will be fascinating to see where he goes from here. He was immediately quoted as short as 4-1 for the 2007 World Hurdle, but he is a year older than this season's winner My Way De Solzen and if connections are considering putting him over fences they may not want to wait another year. *(op 11-10 tchd 5-4 and 6-5 in places)*

Powerstation(IRE) ◆, like the winner not seen since December, was given a much more patient ride than the pair either side of him. He was closely matched with Travino on recent form and managed to reverse the form from their last meeting after staying on well from off the pace to win the separate race for second, but he was still beaten further by Black Jack Ketchum than when they met over a shorter trip here in November. This was the longest trip he has encountered to date *and by far the fastest ground, so he can still be considered to have performed with a lot of credit. (tchd 10-1 in places)*

Travino(IRE) ◆is a nice, chasing type who travelled well up with the pace and for a long way looked the one the favourite had to beat. However, he did not appear to see out this longer trip as well as the front pair and the fast ground would not have helped him either. As talented as he is over hurdles, the consensus is that he will be even better as a chaser. *(tchd 7-1 in places)*

Back To Bid(IRE) ◆, not considered the best the Irish had to offer in this contest, ran well nonetheless and the way he stayed on up the hill suggested his stamina for this longer trip was not *a problem, though the faster ground may have been. He looks a staying chaser in the making. (op 28-1)*

Shouette(IRE), winner of just one of her 13 starts over hurdles to date and that over two miles on heavy ground, ran way above herself. She never looked like winning though, and it may be that she possessed the necessary stamina to get home whereas many of her rivals did not. It may therefore be unwise to get too carried away.

Dream Alliance, trying a longer trip on unsuitably quick ground, was exposed for lack of foot on the downhill run to the second last, but still plodded on to fare second best of the British-trained *hurdlers in this contest. He still has scope and can do much better back on a softer surface. (op 14-1)*

Karanja ◆, who had excuses for his Hereford flop, was back to something like his best this time on ground that would not have suited and ran well for a very long way. There should be more to come from him back in the right grade.

Zipalong Lad(IRE) enjoys much softer ground and was not disgraced in the circumstances.

Oscar Park(IRE), who looked a decent prospect earlier in the season, could have been expected to have performed a bit better than this.

Five Colours(IRE) ◆ looked as if he might get involved when still travelling quite well at the top of the hill, but he soon stopped to nothing. The ground was almost certainly to blame and he should not be written off.

Mister Top Notch(IRE) *Official explanation: trainer said gelding was lame (op 25-1)*

Toofarback(IRE), whose previous outings have all been on soft ground, did not jump well enough on this quicker surface. *Official explanation: jockey said gelding was lame (op 10-1)*

4470 TOTESPORT CHELTENHAM GOLD CUP CHASE GRADE 1 (21 fncs 1 omitted) 3m 2f 110y

3:15 (3:21) (Class 1) 5-Y-O+

£228,080 (£85,560; £42,840; £21,360; £10,720; £5,360)

Form RPR

1152 **1** **War Of Attrition (IRE)**^{79} [3081] 7-11-10 .... CO'Dwyer 173+
(M F Morris, Ire) *lw: in tch and racd on outside: trckd ldr 18th: led at bypassed 3rd last: rdn next: styd on strly run-in* **15/2**^{3}

1-42 **2** *2 1/2* **Hedgehunter (IRE)**^{33} [3895] 10-11-10 .... RWalsh 170+
(W P Mullins, Ire) *hld up in rr: hdwy 16th: chsd ldrs at bypassed 3rd last: chsd wnr 2 out: kpt on run-in but no imp nr fin* **16/1**

3311 **3** *7* **Forget The Past**^{20} [4123] 8-11-10 .... BJGeraghty 165+
(M J P O'Brien, Ire) *tall: lengthy: in tch: hdwy 9th: hit 13th: led 15th: hit 16th and 4 out: hdd at bypassed 3rd last: one pce whn hit 2 out an* **9/1**

-242 **4** *3/4* **L'Ami (FR)**^{20} [4118] 7-11-10 .... MickFitzgerald 163
(F Doumen, France) *lw: trckd ldrs: rdn 4 out: outpcd at bypassed 3rd last: kpt on again run-in but nt a danger* **10/1**

362U **5** *1/2* **Take The Stand (IRE)**^{27} [3977] 10-11-10 156 .... TonyDobbin 165+
(P Bowen) *rr: mstke 2nd: hit next: blnd 13th: hdwy 16th: styng on whn hit 2 out: kpt on again run-in* **20/1**

2242 **6** *1/2* **Monkerhostin (FR)**^{81} [2972] 9-11-10 166 .... RichardJohnson 164+
(P J Hobbs) *rr whn blnd bdly 5th: hit next: rdn and hdwy 16th: hrd drvn and kpt on fr bypassed 3rd last: r.o run-in: nt rch ldrs* **13/2**^{2}

PF23 **7** *1 1/2* **Sir Rembrandt (IRE)**^{27} [3971] 10-11-10 144 .... AndrewThornton 161+
(R H Alner) *edgy: in tch: mstke 14th: lost pl and dropped rr 18th: kpt on again fr 2 out: fin wl* **25/1**

-P21 **8** *3* **Royal Emperor (IRE)**^{22} [4069] 10-11-10 135 .... DominicElsworth 161+
(Mrs S J Smith) *chsd ldrs: blnd 13th and rr: blnd 15th: plenty to do at bypassed 3rd last: kpt on wl fr 2 out: gng on nr fin* **40/1**

5152 **9** *nk* **Royal Auclair (FR)**^{43} [3697] 9-11-10 160 ....(t) ChristianWilliams 157
(P F Nicholls) *chsd ldrs tl lost pl 14th: kpt on again fr bypassed 3rd last: kpt on run-in but nvr a danger* **20/1**

21P2 **10** *2* **Kingscliff (IRE)**^{55} [3493] 9-11-10 169 ....(v^{1}) RobertWalford 156+
(R H Alner) *lw: in tch: blnd 13th and rr: hit 17th: kpt on fr bypassed 3rd but nvr in contention* **12/1**

-211 **11** *3/4* **Beef Or Salmon (IRE)**[33] 3895 10-11-10 .... PCarberry 155+
(Michael Hourigan, Ire) *nt fluent 2nd: bhd: hit 10th: sme hdwy 13th: rdn and no imp on ldrs fr 18th: sn btn* **4/1**[1]

1-20 **12** *17* **Tikram**[41] 3724 9-11-10 146...(b) JamieMoore 137
(G L Moore) *hit 1st: mid-div: hdwy and in tch 13th: rdn after 18th: sn wknd* **100/1**

U044 **13** *1 1/2* **Joes Edge (IRE)**[81] 2992 9-11-10 140.................................. KeithMercer 135
(Ferdy Murphy) *bhd fr 7th* **100/1**

5035 **14** *7* **Ballycassidy (IRE)**[20] 4118 10-11-10 139....................................... GLee 128
(P Bowen) *rr and hit 13th: rdn next: nvr in contention* **100/1**

00-0 **15** *5* **Iznogoud (FR)**[13] 4241 10-11-10 138.............................. TomScudamore 123
(M C Pipe) *bhd most of way* **200/1**

2-33 **16** *1/2* **Cornish Rebel (IRE)**[80] 3022 9-11-10 153.........................(b[1]) JoeTizzard 143+
(P F Nicholls) *edgy: blnd 1st: hit 11th: in tch: chsd ldrs 15th: stl wl there whn blnd 3 out* **16/1**

1064 **17** *10* **Ollie Magern**[43] 3697 8-11-10 151....................................... CarlLlewellyn 113
(N A Twiston-Davies) *led to 8th: led again 13th to 15th: blnd and wknd 18th* **33/1**

-P02 **18** *5* **Lord Of Illusion (IRE)**[75] 3176 9-11-10 141..................... JasonMaguire 118+
(T R George) *dull in coat: chsd ldr: led 8th to 13th: wknd 16th* **33/1**

130- **U** **Celestial Gold (IRE)**[364] 4435 8-11-10 160...................... TimmyMurphy —
(M C Pipe) *hld up in rr tl blnd and uns rdr 10th* **16/1**

112F **P** **Iris's Gift**[62] 3391 9-11-10 147.. APMcCoy —
(Jonjo O'Neill) *lw: chsd ldrs: hit 2nd and 4th: wknd 15th: t.o whn p.u bef 18th* **16/1**

P-54 **P** **Limerick Boy (GER)**[41] 3728 8-11-10 143........................... SamThomas —
(Miss Venetia Williams) *a bhd: hit 5th: blnd 11th and 13th: t.o whn p.u bef 2 out* **150/1**

1-FU **P** **One Knight (IRE)**[43] 3697 10-11-10 153................................. PJBrennan —
(P J Hobbs) *in tch: hit 10th: blnd 12th: blnd and wknd 16th: mstke 18th: t.o whn p.u bef 2 out* **20/1**

6m 31.7s (-25.40) **Going Correction** -0.45s/f (Good) **22** Ran SP% **126.0**
Speed ratings: 119,118,116,115,115 115,115,114,114,113 113,108,107,105,104 104,101,99,—,— —,— CSF £107.31 CT £1120.37 TOTE £7.50: £2.80, £4.00, £2.70; EX 218.10 Trifecta £869.90 Pool: £19,971.74 - 16.30 winning units.

Owner Gigginstown House Stud **Bred** Miss B A Murphy **Trained** Fethard, Co Tipperary

■ As with the Champion Hurdle, the first three home were all Irish trained, a feat unprecedented in the Gold Cup.

FOCUS

With several notable absentees, notably Kicking King, Trabolgan and the sadly departed Best Mate, this was an open-looking Gold Cup, but it produced a good race, run at a sound gallop, with few hard-luck stories. With the exception of the runner-up, the finish was dominated by relatively unexposed second-season chasers, and although War Of Attrition's RPR falls just short of the 10-year-average, he can go on to rate higher. The third-last fence was bypassed.

NOTEBOOK

War Of Attrition(IRE) ◆ came into this as a progressive young chaser, having taken the scalp of Kicking King on similar ground earlier in the campaign, but he was trying his longest trip to date. Allowed plenty of daylight on the outside, he travelled well and after moving smoothly into contention at the top of the hill and taking it up at the bypassed third last he battled on well in the straight to hold off the runner-up, who is a dour stayer. He settled the issue with prodigious leaps at the last two fences and pricked his ears on the run-in as if there was more in the tank. Still comparatively young, it would be no surprise to see him successfully defend his crown next season, when hopefully Kicking King will be back to take him on. Interestingly the last three horses to win the Gold Cup had all previously been runner-up in the Supreme Novices' Hurdle in their first season over hurdles. *(op 7-1)*

Hedgehunter(IRE) ◆, who did not look at his best in his coat, has had a light campaign since winning last year's National and had been well beaten twice by Beef Or Salmon. Nevertheless, he looked to be running into form last time and proved it with this career-best second to a younger, less exposed rival who just had a bit too much speed for him from the home turn. He has three weeks to recover before bidding for a repeat win at Aintree, where a 12lb higher mark than in 2005 may not be enough to stop him completing the double and emulating Rough Quest, who finished second in this before his greatest victory. *(op 14-1 tchd 20-1 in places)*

Forget The Past finished 11 lengths behind today's winner in the Lexus Chase at Leopardstown over Christmas and slightly improved on that effort, although errors though tiredness at the last two fences suggest this trip stretched his stamina to the limit. He has really blossomed in the last month or so and looks one to keep in mind for one of the big chases at Punchestown next month, *when hopefully he will get his favoured soft ground and will avoid War Of Attrition.* *(op 10-1 tchd 12-1 and 11-1 in places)*

L'Ami(FR) ◆, fourth in the Royal & SunAlliance Chase last season and runner-up in the Hennessy on similar ground, has really not had much luck in that respect, for he looks most effective on much softer going. After holding every chance he was once again outpaced in the closing stages, but he still gives the impression that there is a big chase to be won with him in this country if he gets his preferred conditions. He may go to Aintree for the Betfair Bowl. *(op 9-1)*

Take The Stand(IRE), runner-up in this last season, has not had the ground in his favour over fences this term until now and once again put up a fine performance, albeit one marred again by the odd mistake. He failed to complete in the National and Scottish National after running here last season, but will not go to Aintree which should give him more time to recover. Ayr in five weeks, or the Betfred Gold Cup the week after, represent more suitable targets. *(op 16-1)*

Monkerhostin(FR) has been the epitome of consistency in the last couple of seasons and tried his best again. However, over his longest trip to date, he did not help his chance with a couple of early errors and never reached a challenging position, although he did stay on. He is reportedly going to Aintree for the Betfair Bowl, but next season it will be no surprise if connections make the King George, in which he was narrowly beaten this year, his principal target. *(tchd 7-1, 15-2 in places)*

Sir Rembrandt(IRE), placed in the last two Gold Cups, ran his best race since. However, he has been generally below-par since this race last year and has not won since December 2003, so is not one to get too involved with for betting purposes.

Royal Emperor(IRE), runner-up in both the Pertemps Final and Royal & SunAlliance Chase at this meeting in the past, has returned from almost a year off in much better form and this represented a performance within a few pounds of his best over fences. He is no longer in the National, but is well suited by a flat, left-handed track and can switch back to hurdles for the long-distance hurdle at Aintree. Connections may also be tempted by the Scottish National at Ayr. *(op 50-1)*

Royal Auclair(FR), fourth in this last year before finishing second to Hedgehunter at Aintree, has been relatively lightly campaigned this season but this was disappointing. He will presumably go for the National next, in which he carries the same weight as last season, but one would have liked to have seen a little more sparkle.

Kingscliff(IRE) finally made the line-up after being forced to miss the race when well touted in previous seasons. Fitted with a first-time visor, he was never travelling that well and failed to get *involved. The ground may well have been a factor, but he has questions to answer now. Official explanation: jockey said gelding never travelled* *(tchd 14-1 in places)*

Beef Or Salmon(IRE), who had beaten both of the first two in Ireland this season, was sent off favourite but was on his toes beforehand. Beaten in three previous attempts to win this contest, he prefers a flat track and much softer ground, so it was no great surprise to see him struggling from *some way out. He may bounce back in the Heineken Gold Cup at Punchestown. Official explanation: jockey said gelding never travelled* *(op 5-1 tchd 11-2 in places)*

Tikram ran a fair race but did not look to stay the trip. Another crack at the Grade Two chase over two miles five here next month looks on the cards before turning out at Sandown's end-of-season meeting.

Cornish Rebel(IRE) ◆, fitted with blinkers for the first time after a few near misses in recent races, was on his toes. He made several mistakes but still looked to be travelling strongly when slipping on landing at the tricky fence at the top of the hill, which ended his chance. He is still in the National and, providing he is none the worse for this, could be very interesting if he handles the fences, as he is currently available at around 25/1.

One Knight(IRE), lightly raced of late, has also had jumping problems and it was no surprise that *he again made mistakes and put himself out of contention. Official explanation: jockey said gelding lost its action*

Iris's Gift, still a novice and not the best of jumpers on previous evidence, not surprisingly made mistakes and his rider sensibly drew stumps before the last ditch.

4471 CHRISTIE'S FOXHUNTER CHASE CHALLENGE CUP (21 fncs 1 omitted) 3m 2f 110y

4:00 (4:03) (Class 2) 5-Y-O+

£24,008 (£7,500; £3,748; £1,876; £936; £472)

Form RPR

1 **Whyso Mayo (IRE)**[33] 3896 9-12-0 .... MrDMurphy 126+
(Raymond Hurley, Ire) *trckd ldrs on outer: nt fluent 9th: blnd next: jnd issue 5 out: led next: j.rt 3 out: hrd pressed last: styd on wl flat* **20/1**

U- **2** *1* **First Down Jets (IRE)**[20] 4124 9-12-0 .... MrCJSweeney 126+
(W J Burke, Ire) *mstke and hmpd 1st: hld up wl in rr: plenty to do whn mstke 5 out: gd prog after 3 out: r.o to press wnr flat: a hld* **66/1**

/14- **3** *1 1/4* **Joe Blake (IRE)**[34] 11-12-0 .... MrMJO'Hare 125+
(I R Ferguson, Ire) *lw: t.k.h: trckd ldrs: upsides gng wl whn mstke and hmpd 3 out: rallied to chal 2 out: nt qckn: styd on flat* **14/1**

4 *3 1/2* **Bothar Na (IRE)**[298] 477 7-12-0 .... MrKEPower 120
(W P Mullins, Ire) *w'like: lw: settled towards rr: stdy prog fr 13th: trckd ldrs 4 out: effrt to chal gng wl 2 out: wknd last* **14/1**

5- **5** *3/4* **Savati (FR)**[20] 6-12-0 .... MrWGRankin 120
(R T J Wilson, Ire) *hld up wl in rr: plenty to do at bk of main gp 3 out: gd prog next: bmpd along bef last: kpt on: no ch* **25/1**

-P12 **6** *1/2* **Telemoss (IRE)**[28] 3968 12-12-0 .... MissRDavidson 121+
(N G Richards) *settled wl in rr: stl at bk of huge main gp 3 out: n.m.r bnd after: styd on fr 2 out: nvr rchd ldrs* **14/1**

2F11 **7** *1/2* **Raregem**[8] 4330 8-12-0 .... MrWBiddick 120+
(M Biddick) *t.k.h: pressed ldrs: mstke 11th: stl pressing 4 out: urged along and one pce fr 2 out* **14/1**

-3F1 **8** *1/2* **Gatsby (IRE)**[26] 4009 10-12-0 .... MrJMPritchard 120+
(J Groucott) *prog to press ldr 7th: led 12th: mstke 5 out: hdd next: outpcd 2 out: styd on flat* **50/1**

3/11 **9** *2 1/2* **Drombeag (IRE)**[24] 4044 8-12-0 114............................(b[1]) MrJTMcNamara 119+
(Jonjo O'Neill) *lw; bdly hmpd 1st: stdy prog and prom 10th: mstke 5 out and 3 out: wknd after 2 out* **11/2**[2]

P/22 **10** *1 1/4* **Bosham Mill**[23] 4051 8-12-0 .... MrTJO'Brien 115+
(P J Hobbs) *lw: pressed ldrs: mstke 4 out: stl chalng whn mstke 3 out: wknd next* **20/1**

1 **11** *nk* **Bedtime Boys**[28] 3968 9-12-0 .... MrJDocker 114
(Miss H Campbell) *hld up midfield: mstke 11th: wl in tch 4 out: sn rdn: wknd and mstke 3 out* **33/1**

U-P1 **12** *5* **Cobreces**[22] 4073 8-12-0 116.. MrJSnowden 111+
(Mrs L Borradaile) *hmpd 1st in rr: stdy prog and prom whn mstke 9th: losing pl whn mstke 4 out: n.d after next* **11/1**

1321 **13** *1 1/4* **No Retreat (NZ)**[22] 4079 13-12-0 109.. MrWHill 108
(J Groucott) *nvr beyond midfield: lost tch w main gp fr 4 out* **40/1**

211/ **14** *2* **Kestick**[19] 11-12-0 .... MissTCave 106
(Mrs R Kennen) *wl plcd: stl cl up 4 out: rdn and one pce after next: wknd 2 out* **80/1**

F-31 **15** *hd* **Foly Pleasant (FR)**[21] 4100 12-12-0 132.................................(t) MrRBurton 106
(Mrs K Waldron) *lw: nt a fluent: settled wl in rr: stl at bk of main gp 4 out: effrt on outer bef 2 out: sn wknd* **8/1**[3]

41F2 **16** *3/4* **Vinnie Boy (IRE)**[26] 4009 9-12-0 .... MissPGundry 105
(Mrs O Bush) *a wl in rr: lost tch w main gp 16th: wl bhd 3 out: plugged on* **100/1**

P-U2 **17** *1/2* **Irilut (FR)**[21] 4100 10-12-0 ....(p) MrSWaley-Cohen 104
(R Waley-Cohen) *settled in midfield: effrt 4 out: rdn and stl in tch at rr of main gp bef 2 out: wknd* **80/1**

1F-1 **18** *6* **Camden Carrig (IRE)**[20] 4107 11-12-0 .... MrNPhillips 98
(Simon Bloss) *nt a fluent: led to 12th: wknd fr 16th* **100/1**

15P2 **19** *5* **Caught At Dawn (IRE)**[12] 12-12-0 120.................................. MrTWeston 93
(M H Weston) *dull in coat: nvr out of rr gp: lost tch fr 16th: steadily wknd 2 out* **40/1**

/02- **F** **Boneyarrow (IRE)**[19] 10-12-0 .... MrJJCodd —
(Eoin Griffin, Ire) *lw: fell 1st* **25/1**

3-2 **P** **Double Ange (FR)**[12] 8-12-0 .... MrRHFowler —
(Mrs Katie Baimbridge) *nvr on terms w ldrs: mstke 10th: wknd 12th: t.o whn p.u bef 4 out* **150/1**

3-22 **P** **Cracking Dawn (IRE)**[21] 4092 11-12-0 112....................(v[1]) MrMGMiller —
(Mrs S Alner) *blnd 2nd: a in rr: last and tailing off whn terrible mstke 15th: p.u bef next* **25/1**

2F-1 **P** **Swincombe (IRE)**[31] 3910 11-12-0 91.................................... MrAHickman —
(Mrs S J Hickman) *set off in detached last: nvr remotely involved: wknd 16th: t.o whn p.u bef 3 out* **80/1**

24P- **P** **Harbour Pilot (IRE)**[33] 3896 11-12-0 ....(b) MissNCarberry —
(Noel Meade, Ire) *pressed ldrs: terrible mstke 7th and great rcvry by rdr: mstkes fr 12th and sn wknd: t.o whn p.u bef 3 out* **11/4**[1]

6m 42.7s (-14.40) **Going Correction** -0.45s/f (Good) **24** Ran SP% **126.8**
Speed ratings: **103,102,102,101,101 100,100,100,99,99 99,97,97,96,96 96,96,94,93,—** —,—,—,— CSF £931.20 CT £17397.40 TOTE £31.10: £6.90, £21.30, £5.20; EX 1227.20 Trifecta £3841.80 Pool: £5,952.12 - 1.10 winning units.

Owner Mrs Kathleen O'Driscoll **Bred** Edward O'Driscoll **Trained** Clonakilty, Co Cork

■ The first five were Irish-trained, all bar the third in the Republic. The tenth Irish winner at the Festival, a new record.

■ Stewards' Enquiry : Mr D Murphy one-day ban: used whip in an incorrect place (Mar 28)

FOCUS

Not a strong renewal of the amateurs' Gold Cup, and it was run 11sec slower than the real thing. The form is hard to pin down, but the race produced a good finish and it should yield plenty more winners before the hunter chase season is out. First fence in home straight bypassed final circuit.

NOTEBOOK

Whyso Mayo(IRE), a prolific winner in Irish points and hunter chases despite not always being the most reliable of jumpers, handled these stiff fences fairly well and, given a positive ride, battled on up the hill to resist a series of challenges. He handles all types of ground and it would be no surprise to see him turn out at Punchestown.

First Down Jets(IRE) ◆, who unseated in this race last year, was given a waiting ride and made a couple of errors before finishing strongly up the hill. He appeared to have every chance and this race should have set him up for another crack at the big hunter chase at Fairyhouse, which he won last season. *(op 50-1)*

Joe Blake(IRE), fourth in this back in 2002, has returned in fine form for his new trainer this season after a long absence. He travelled strongly throughout and looked a big threat when making a mistake at the third last, but then rallied well up the hill. He is in the Grand National but needs plenty to come out before he can get a run, and the Fox Hunters' at that meeting looks the obvious alternative.

Bothar Na(IRE) ◆, who completed a four-timer in points and hunter chases in the spring of last year, was having his first run for ten months. He ran well before fading up the hill and, with this outing under his belt, will be well fancied for the big hunter chases at Fairyhouse and Punchestown this spring.

Savati(FR), the best of whose form has been on much softer ground, ran on from the back and was as close at the finish as he had ever been, he will appreciate a return to an easier surface.

Telemoss(IRE) did best of the home contingent, running on well up the hill. He had previously looked better suited by trips short of three miles and looks just the sort for the Aintree Fox Hunters'. *(op 12-1 tchd 20-1 in places)*

Raregem has sorted out his jumping this season and had looked progressive in his two wins on soft ground. He was quite keen but ran very well until fading up the hill and probably just found this trip beyond him. There are more good hunter chases to be won with him before the season is out. *(op 16-1)*

Gatsby(IRE), fifth in this last year, finished a lot closer to the winner this time despite finishing eighth. He only faded up the hill and it would be no surprise to see him return here for the hunter chase evening meeting early in May. *(op 40-1)*

Drombeag(IRE), with blinkers on for the first time, was lucky not to have been brought down at the first and was stopped in his tracks. However, he was in contention before halfway and only faded after a couple of errors in the closing stages. He can be forgiven this effort and can bounce back on an easier surface. *(op 5-1)*

Bosham Mill ran close to Huntingdon form with Drombeag, having been ridden close to the pace from the start. He seems well suited by flat tracks, preferably right-handed, and may find an opportunity to get off the mark in this sphere at one of the west country courses.

Cobreces moved into contention on the second circuit but was soon on the retreat once the top of the hill was reached. *(tchd 12-1 in places)*

Foly Pleasant(FR), runner-up in this race last season, came into this renewal off the back of a win at Warwick last month but never really fired. *(op 10-1)*

Harbour Pilot(IRE), twice third behind Best Mate in the Gold Cup, was favourite to show the benefit of racing in this easier grade. However, he has always been prone to jumping errors and did his best to decant his rider early on, from which she made a remarkable recovery. From that point however, he was always struggling and further errors saw him drop out of contention on the second circuit. He did win a point in January, but his last win under Rules was more than four years ago and he may be better off enjoying himself over the less demanding point-to-point fences. *Official explanation: jockey said gelding bled from the nose (op 3-1 tchd 10-3, 7-2 in places)*

4472 JOHNNY HENDERSON GRAND ANNUAL CHASE CHALLENGE CUP (H'CAP) GRADE 3 (14 fncs) 2m 110y

4:40 (4:45) (Class 1) 5-Y-O+

£42,765 (£16,042; £8,032; £4,005; £2,010; £1,005)

Form — RPR

63-5 **1** **Greenhope (IRE)**[13] 4242 8-10-11 **132** .... AndrewTinkler 144+
(N J Henderson) *led 4th: hdd 8th: styd pressing ldr: led and hit 4 out: hdd next: sn led again: drvn and styd on wl fr 2 out* **20/1**

0-22 **2** *2* **Tiger Cry (IRE)**[34] 3870 8-10-13 **134** .... DJCasey 143
(A L T Moore, Ire) *str: lengthy: chsd ldrs: led 8th to 4 out: led again 3 out: sn hdd: kpt on u.p but no imp on wnr run-in* **6/1**[2]

3111 **3** *1* **Madison Du Berlais (FR)**[14] 4213 5-10-4 **129** 3ex .... TomScudamore 138+
(M C Pipe) *hmpd 3rd: prom 5th: blnd 3 out & lost pl: styd on strly fr next: fin wl but nt rch ldrs* **11/1**

1P52 **4** *1 ¼* **Nyrche (FR)**[22] 4076 6-11-2 **137** .... RobertThornton 144
(A King) *chsd ldrs: rdn and kpt on wl fr three out: one pce run-in* **20/1**

0/04 **5** *¾* **Davenport Democrat (IRE)**[124] 2208 8-11-7 **142** .... BJGeraghty 150+
(W P Mullins, Ire) *lw: in tch: hit 6th and lost position: hdwy fr 3 out: kpt on fr next but nt rch ldrs* **50/1**

4043 **6** *½* **Ground Ball (IRE)**[27] 4000 9-11-8 **143** .... APMcCoy 150+
(C F Swan, Ire) *in tch: pushed along and hdwy to chse ldrs fr 4 out: one pce fr 2 out* **11/1**

4211 **7** *1* **Green Tango**[48] 3618 7-11-4 **139** .... RichardJohnson 147+
(H D Daly) *hmpd 3rd: rr: blnd 9th: hit 10th: plenty to do 3 out: r.o fr 2 out: mstke last: fin wl but nt a danger* **6/1**[2]

0105 **8** *1* **Caracciola (GER)**[97] 2765 9-11-7 **142** .... MarcusFoley 148+
(N J Henderson) *hmpd 4th: bhd: stl plenty to do 3 out: kpt on fr 2 out: nt rch ldrs* **16/1**

-062 **9** *1 ¼* **Zum See (IRE)**[26] 4018 7-10-5 **126** .... (b[1]) PCarberry 129+
(Noel Meade, Ire) *lw: led to 4th: styd chsng ldrs: hit 4 out: blnd 3 out: sn one pce* **20/1**

-104 **10** *¾* **Bambi De L'Orme (FR)**[41] 3724 7-11-2 **137** .... GLee 140+
(Ian Williams) *hit 1st: t.k.h: blnd 3rd: in tch to 4 out* **16/1**

6313 **11** *10* **Tanikos (FR)**[27] 3974 7-10-2 **128** .... SamCurling(5) 124+
(N J Henderson) *bhd: sme hdwy whn blnd 10th: sn wknd* **50/1**

0316 **12** *8* **Duke Of Buckingham (IRE)**[139] 1918 10-11-5 **140** .... TomDoyle 124
(P R Webber) *lw: hit 1st: a bhd* **80/1**

3326 **13** *1 ¼* **Marcel (FR)**[13] 4241 6-10-10 **131** .... RJGreene 116+
(M C Pipe) *lw: hit 5th: chsd ldrs: mstke 5th: wknd 4 out: blnd next* **33/1**

6231 **14** *4* **Kalca Mome (FR)**[27] 3974 8-11-1 **136** .... PJBrennan 118+
(P J Hobbs) *a in rr: no ch whn hmpd 4 out* **50/1**

1261 **F** **Andreas (FR)**[23] 4050 6-11-9 **144** .... (t) RWalsh —
(P F Nicholls) *rr but in tch whn fell 4th* **4/1**[1]

216F **F** **Flying Spirit (IRE)**[15] 2970 7-11-1 **136** .... (b) JamieMoore —
(G L Moore) *mid-div whn fell 3rd* **50/1**

F0-0 **P** **Liberty Seeker (FR)**[40] 3761 7-10-8 **129** .... DNRussell —
(G A Swinbank) *lw: hmpd 3rd: sn wl bhd: t.o whn p.u bef 9th* **100/1**

3350 **P** **Strike Back (IRE)**[33] 3894 8-10-10 **131** .... NPMadden —
(Mrs John Harrington, Ire) *w'like: lw: a in rr: t.o whn p.u bef 4 out* **25/1**

4131 **P** **Tysou (FR)**[41] 3724 9-11-12 **147** .... MickFitzgerald —
(N J Henderson) *lw: hmpd 3rd: hdwy 8th: sn wknd: t.o whn p.u bef 2 out* **14/1**

B020 **P** **Tribal Dispute**[69] 3299 9-10-6 **127** .... DavidO'Meara —
(T D Easterby) *lw: rr: hmpd 4 out and next: t.o whn p.u bef 2 out* **40/1**

4133 **P** **Portavadie**[62] 3380 7-10-7 **128** .... TonyDobbin —
(J M Jefferson) *chsd ldrs: hit 7th and next: sn wknd: t.o whn p.u bef 3 out* **50/1**

4421 **F** **Sharp Rigging (IRE)**[22] 4076 6-10-9 **130** .... JimmyMcCarthy —
(A M Hales) *in tch: chsd ldrs 10th: rdn and stl in tch whn fell 3 out* **9/1**[3]

3222 **F** **Bleu Superbe (FR)**[27] 3974 11-10-11 **132** .... SamThomas —
(Miss Venetia Williams) *in tch: hdwy 10th: trcking ldrs and gng wl whn fell 4 out* **40/1**

3m 55.9s (-11.60) **Going Correction** -0.45s/f (Good) course record
WFA 5 from 6yo+ 4lb **23** Ran SP% **131.6**
Speed ratings: **109,108,107,107,106 106,105,105,104,104 99,96,95,93,— —,—,—,—,— —,—,E** CSF £130.85 CT £1443.26 TOTE £30.70: £6.00, £1.90, £2.30, £4.60; EX 213.60 Trifecta £3822.60 Pool: £9,152.74 - 1.70 winning units.

Owner Lynn Wilson Giles Wilson Martin Landau **Bred** Gay O'Callaghan **Trained** Upper Lambourn, Berks

■ An emotional victory for trainer Nicky Henderson in the race commemorating his father.

FOCUS

A typically strong renewal of this good handicap chase and contest where the first two were up with the pace from the start.

NOTEBOOK

Greenhope(IRE) ◆, who ran well in this race last year when still a novice, looked to have been laid out for it again having had just one outing, when fifth behind subsequent County Hurdle winner Desert Quest at Newbury at the beginning of the month. He jumped and travelled really well up with the pace and battled on really strongly to record an emotional victory for connections. The two-mile handicap at Aintree looks a suitable next objective, although he would also run well if switched back to hurdles. *(tchd 18-1)*

Tiger Cry(IRE) ◆ is a really useful novice chaser and handles fast ground pretty well. He did nothing wrong in finishing second and deserves to pick up a decent race. He has a good record at Fairyhouse and will be interesting if he takes his chance at the Easter meeting there, be it in a handicap or novice company. *(op 15-2 tchd 8-1 in places)*

Madison Du Berlais(FR) ◆ has been progressive over fences in the last couple of months and ran really well off a mark 17lb higher than for his first win over fences in this country. He ran on well up the hill to provide one of the few highlights in a well below-par week for the master trainer and, despite his rise in the weights, looks more than capable of winning again before long. *(op 12-1)*

Nyrche(FR) ◆, whose first season over fences has been a little mixed, appreciates good or easy ground and ran really well on this handicap debut. He could be the sort for the two-mile handicap or novice chase at Aintree, where he was in the process of winning a race in the autumn when his rider took the wrong course.

Davenport Democrat(IRE) ◆, who completed a hat-trick over fences in ireland in the autumn, had not run since finishing fourth in a Grade Two here in November. He ran a fine race for a novice after his break and presumably will have a spring campaign, taking in Aintree and Punchestown.

Ground Ball(IRE), who had been campaigned over hurdles since running over course and distance at the December meeting, had been runner-up in 2004 and was right up with the pace when falling in this race last year. Now 7lb higher, he travelled well but weakened from the turn in. He may well try to repeat last season's win in the Dan Moore Memorial at Fairyhouse now. *(op 12-1 tchd 14-1 in a place)*

Green Tango ◆, whose novice chases have been working out pretty well, looked to have a sound chance but did not look that great in his coat and hampered himself with some less than fluent jumping. In the circumstances he did well to finish as close as he did and, well suited by flat and sharp tracks, he could yet gain compensation if re-opposing some of these at Aintree. *Official explanation: trainer said gelding did not jump fluently (tchd 13-2, 7-1 in places)*

Caracciola(GER), a stable companion of the winner, has been struggling a little of late over fences and, having his first outing for three months, may be better back over hurdles when he can race off a lower mark.

Zum See(IRE), fitted with first-time blinkers, went off in front but was strugglinhg from the top of the hill. His best form is on softer ground. *(tchd 25-1)*

Bambi De L'Orme(FR), runner-up in this last year, was very keen and made a couple of early mistakes. He is likely to re-oppose a number of these in the Red Rum Chase at Aintree, but looks a few pounds too high in the handicap at present.

Bleu Superbe(FR) is a regular in these hot two-mile handicaps and was on the heels of the leaders when falling victim to the tricky fourth-last fence. He has not won since 2003 and deserves another success, but time is not on his side. *(tchd 33-1)*

Sharp Rigging(IRE), who beat today's fourth at Huntingdon last time, was still in contention when coming down and judged on Nyrche's effort would have been fighting for a place had he remained upright. *(tchd 33-1)*

Andreas(FR) started favourite having won over hurdles last month on his comeback from a break. However, he got no further than the third and plenty will be hoping for compensation if he turns out in the handicap at Aintree. *(tchd 33-1)*

4473 VINCENT O'BRIEN COUNTY H'CAP HURDLE GRADE 3 (8 hdls) 2m 1f

5:20 (5:23) (Class 1) 5-Y-O+

£37,063 (£13,903; £6,961; £3,471; £1,742; £871)

Form — RPR

1131 **1** **Desert Quest (IRE)**[13] 4242 6-10-10 **131** 4ex .... (b) RWalsh 148+
(P F Nicholls) *hld up in midfield: blnd 5th: stdy prog on inner after 3 out: delayed chal tl led sn after last: drew clr: impressive* **4/1**[1]

-001 **2** *2 ½* **Noble Request (FR)**[43] 3696 5-10-11 **132** .... RichardJohnson 143
(P J Hobbs) *hld up wl in rr: effrt on outer and j.rt 2 out: gd prog after to join ldr last: chsd wnr flat: outpcd* **25/1**

4-40 **3** *3 ½* **Adamant Approach (IRE)**[61] 3411 12-10-6 **134** .... RJKiely(7) 141
(W P Mullins, Ire) *chsd ldng gp: pushed along and prog after 3 out: sustained effrt to ld bef last: hdd sn after: outpcd* **50/1**

1622 **4** *1* **Pirate Flagship (FR)**[13] 4242 7-10-1 **122** .... PJBrennan 128
(P F Nicholls) *chsd ldng gp: effrt 2 out: sn rdn: hanging lft but styd on bef last: nt pce to rch ldrs* **10/1**[2]

340/ **5** *1 ¼* **Khetaam (IRE)**[12] 4269 8-10-4 **125** 4ex .... PCarberry 130
(Noel Meade, Ire) *wl in rr: stl plenty to do bef 2 out: gd prog bef last: styd on flat: nvr nrr* **10/1**[2]

4066 **6** *nk* **Borora**[69] 3298 7-10-6 **127** .... TomDoyle 131
(R Lee) *wl in rr: rdn and plenty to do bef 2 out: styd on gamely after: nrst fin* **66/1**

11-3 **7** *1 ¼* **Lord Henry (IRE)**[21] 4091 7-9-13 **125** .... MrTJO'Brien(5) 128
(P J Hobbs) *chsd furious pce set be ldr: mstke 3 out: led next: hdd bef last: fdd* **50/1**

5-01 **8** *½* **Bob Justice (IRE)**[104] 2641 10-10-9 **130** .... TonyDobbin 133
(J Howard Johnson) *led at furious pce: hdd 2 out: wknd last* **66/1**

/40- **9** *2 ½* **Grande Jete (SAF)**[342] 4768 9-10-9 **130** .... MickFitzgerald 130
(N J Henderson) *settled in midfield on inner: effrt 2 out: no prog and btn bef last* **11/1**[3]

1-11 **10** *nk* **Studmaster**[33] 3894 6-11-8 **143** .... TPTreacy 143
(Mrs John Harrington, Ire) *prom bhd ldrs: effrt to chal and upsides 2 out: wknd bef last* **4/1**[1]

1454 **11** *1 ¼* **High Day**[40] 3761 6-10-2 **123** .... KeithMercer 123+
(Ferdy Murphy) *chsd ldrs: blnd 3 out and lost pl: struggling after: kpt on flat* **40/1**

-240 **12** *hd* **Chief Yeoman**[27] 3994 6-11-0 **140** .... LeeStephens(5) 138
(Miss Venetia Williams) *wl in rr: struggling fr 2 out: no ch whn hit last: styd on flat* **33/1**

05-0 **13** *½* **Power Elite (IRE)**[124] 2209 6-11-5 **140** .... NPMadden 138
(Noel Meade, Ire) *hld up wl in rr: effrt on wd outside 2 out: sme prog bef last: carried hd high and reluctant* **25/1**

-002 **14** *nk* **Dusky Warbler**[6] 4375 7-11-0 **135** .... (p) JamieMoore 136
(G L Moore) *chsng ldrs whn bmpd 4th and rdr nrly uns: nvr rcvrd: struggling 2 out* **14/1**

3-06 **15** *hd* **Arch Rebel (USA)**[47] 3641 5-10-11 **132**....(bt) DFO'Regan 129
(Noel Meade, Ire) *chsd ldrs tl wknd fr 2 out* **20/1**

-255 **16** *1 ½* **Howle Hill (IRE)**[62] 3177 6-11-3 **138**.... WayneHutchinson 134
(A King) *nvr beyond midfield: dropped to last trio and wl btn 3 out: styd on again bef last* **33/1**

-224 **17** *1* **Lunar Crystal (IRE)**[6] 4375 8-10-6 **127**.... TomScudamore 122
(M C Pipe) *prom tl wknd 2 out* **40/1**

F230 **18** *½* **Perle De Puce (FR)**[6] 4375 7-10-7 **135**....(p) MrSWaley-Cohen[(7)] 129
(N J Henderson) *prom: chalng u.p whn mstke 2 out: wknd* **100/1**

3-0F **19** *shd* **Miss Academy (FR)**[48] 3621 5-10-0 **128**.... AndrewGlassonbury[(7)] 122
(M C Pipe) *chsd ldrs tl wknd fr 2 out* **66/1**

P000 **20** *hd* **Fontanesi (IRE)**[27] 3986 6-10-8 **129**.... RJGreene 123
(M C Pipe) *hld up wl in rr: no prog and btn whn hmpd 2 out* **25/1**

0F63 **21** *nk* **Sporazene (IRE)**[26] 4008 7-11-12 **147**.... ChristianWilliams 141
(P F Nicholls) *wl in rr: no ch whn hmpd 2 out* **40/1**

-603 **22** *2 ½* **Hawadeth**[21] 4097 11-10-4 **132**....(p) MrJJDoyle[(7)] 123
(V R A Dartnall) *chsd ldrs: terrible blunder 3rd: nvr gng after: wl bhd after 3 out* **40/1**

1135 **23** *3* **Acambo (GER)**[40] 3761 5-10-7 **128**....(v[1]) BJGeraghty 116
(M C Pipe) *chsd ldrs tl wknd bef 2 out* **20/1**

-2P0 **24** *10* **Adopted Hero (IRE)**[71] 3256 6-9-13 **125**.... BrianHughes[(5)] 103
(J Howard Johnson) *a wl in rr: rdn and no prog bef 2 out* **66/1**

1204 **25** *4* **Enhancer**[21] 4091 8-10-3 **124**.... DJCasey 98
(M J McGrath) *in tch to 5th: wl bhd after 3 out* **100/1**

0-65 **26** *4* **Publican (IRE)**[47] 3640 6-10-11 **132**.... APMcCoy 102
(P A Fahy, Ire) *nt jump wl: a bhd* **16/1**

1000 **27** *19* **Admiral (IRE)**[3] 4432 5-11-2 **147**.... JohnFlavin[(10)] 98
(R C Guest) *hmpd 2nd: effrt on outer to chse ldrs 5th: sn wknd* **80/1**

4-11 **F** **Buck Whaley (IRE)**[62] 3383 6-10-3 **124** ow1.... DNRussell —
(Jonjo O'Neill) *nvr on terms w ldrs: wl in rr whn fell 2 out: dead* **16/1**

4004 **P** **Dalaram (IRE)**[41] 3725 6-10-13 **134**....(t) GLee —
(J Howard Johnson) *towards rr whn blnd bdly 2nd: nt rcvr: p.u bef next* **40/1**

3m 52.7s (-19.50) **Going Correction** -0.825s/f (Firm) **129** Ran SP% **137.2**
Speed ratings: 112,110,109,108,108 107,107,107,105,105 105,105,104,104,104 103,103,103,103,103 102,101,100,95 CSF £112.31 CT £4548.96 TOTE £5.00: £2.40, £6.30, £11.10, £2.80; EX 117.60 TRIFECTA Not won. Place 6 £2,122.90, Place 5 £653.68.

Owner Mrs M Findlay **Bred** Ballygallon Stud **Trained** Ditcheat, Somerset

FOCUS
The Festival's usual closing cavalry charge. The pace was solid, without being too fast, and the winning time was 1.5 seconds slower than the Triumph Hurdle. There did not appear to be too many hard-luck stories and there were personal bests from both the first two, with the winner in particular looking the sort that could go on to even greater things. Sound form, as usual.

NOTEBOOK
Desert Quest(IRE) ◆ was carrying just a 4lb penalty for his easy Newbury victory and the ground had come absolutely perfect for him. Given the most patient of rides, he crept closer as the race progressed but was not asked to hit the front until after jumping the last, from which point he demonstrated a smart turn of foot to seal victory. He has maintained a smart level of form for the whole season and still appears to be progressing. Some very high-class hurdlers have either won or run well in this in recent seasons, notably Rooster Booster and Harchibald, and there seems no reason why he should not continue to thrive in a similar way. *(op 9-2 tchd 5-1 in places)*

Noble Request(FR) ◆ ran a blinder considering he was racing off a stone higher mark than for his Wincanton romp. He looked like winning at one stage too as he timed his effort just right, but the winner was arriving on the opposite side of the track at the same time and found the better turn of foot up the hill. This performance shows that he will remain a potent force off his new inflated mark and, given his liking for good ground, there should be further opportunities for him this spring.

Adamant Approach(IRE) has not enjoyed much luck in his visits to the Festival before, including when looking the likely winner of the Supreme Novices' four years ago until falling at the last. He hit the front before the final flight but found his two nearest rivals, both of them around half his age, much too speedy on the run-in. This was a cracking effort, but obviously at his age he does not possess the necessary scope to capitalise on it. *(op 40-1)*

Pirate Flagship(FR) ◆ ran a similar race to Newbury last time, getting outpaced at a vital stage before staying on up the hill, but the way he hung in the closing stages suggests this ground was just a bit too quick for him. A return to further would also not come amiss, whilst a switch to fences is also a possibility. He is certainly bred for the job. *(tchd 12-1 and 11-1 in places)*

Khetaam(IRE) was doing all his best work late under his penalty and, as he already has proven form on fast ground, there is every reason to believe he ran his race. *(op 11-1 tchd 12-1 in places)*

Borora, third at odds of 200/1 in this last year, put up a similar effort this time in coming from miles off the pace to reach his final position. Obviously races like this bring out the best in him, but he has not managed to win since July 2004 and it must be galling for connections that he cannot reproduce this sort of performance elsewhere.

Lord Henry(IRE) ◆ faced a stiff task considering his inexperience and that fact that he only reappeared from a very long layoff last month. He was always up with the pace and managed to hang in there for longer than might have been expected, but he does like a decent surface so it will be a surprise if he cannot build on this during the spring. *(op 40-1)*

Bob Justice(IRE) from a yard going through a quiet spell, needs softer ground but he nonetheless put up a very creditable performance in trying to make all the running and was not completely beaten off until coming to the last.

Grande Jete(SAF) who threw away a winning chance with a mistake at the last when fourth here a *year ago, was again making his seasonal reappearance, though not by design. (op 10-1 tchd 12-1 in places)*

Studmaster, panned by the Handicapper for his recent victories, was still in the thick of the action at the second last but could not raise his game and eventually had to concede defeat. He would have preferred easier ground, but even so he may be forced to contest conditions events now *rather than handicaps off this sort of mark. Official explanation: jockey said gelding was unsuited by the good ground (op 5-1 tchd 7-2, 11-2 in places)*

Power Elite(IRE) had every chance turning for home, but even though this ground would have been faster than ideal he did not impress at all with his head carriage approaching the last. *(op 20-1)*

Dusky Warbler, making a quick return after his fine second in the Imperial Cup six days earlier, should not be condemned too much for this as he prefers softer ground and his rider was nearly knocked out of the saddle at the fourth. *(op 16-1)*

Publican(IRE), over hurdles for the first time in almost a year after a spell of chasing, did not respect these smaller obstacles. Perhaps the quicker ground was to blame. *(op 14-1)*

T/Jkpt: Not won. T/Plt: £2,738.50 to a £1 stake. Pool: £664,183.25. 177.05 winning tickets. T/Qpdt: £609.20 to a £1 stake. Pool: £33,264.30. 40.40 winning tickets. ST

[3955]FAKENHAM (L-H)
Friday, March 17

OFFICIAL GOING: Good
Wind: Straight behind Weather: Very cold & overcast

4474 GG.COM BEGINNERS' CHASE (18 fncs) 3m 110y
2:15 (2:15) (Class 4) 5-Y-0+ **£4,798** (£1,489; £802)

Form RPR
-640 **1** **Fullards**[69] 3289 8-11-3 106....(t) WarrenMarston 100
(Mrs P Sly) *chsd ldr fr 6th: hrd rdn and outj. fr 13th: outpcd 15th: 15l down 2 out: 6l bhd and plugging on whn lft virtually solo last* **15/8**[1]

60F0 **2** *dist* **Unusual Suspect**[99] 2717 7-11-3 93....(b) PhilipHide —
(G L Moore) *last and u.p 8th: t.o whn clambered 13th: v reluctant after: lft 2nd at last: btn 71l* **10/1**

FP04 **3** *dist* **Lady Lambrini**[41] 3732 6-10-5 69.... DerekLaverty[(5)] —
(Mrs L Williamson) *mostly 2nd tl 6th: j. slowly 9th and sn lost pl: t.o 14th: lft 3rd last: knocked over helper and grnd to halt: continued* **16/1**

0P44 **F** **Mobasher (IRE)**[11] 4279 7-11-0.... PaulO'Neill[(3)] —
(Miss Venetia Williams) *j. slowly 1st: cl 3rd whn fell 10th* **9/4**[2]

40P **F** **Saddlers Cloth (IRE)**[74] 3218 6-10-10.... MarkBradburne 97+
(J A Geake) *j. best: led: drew clr 15th: 15l ahd 2 out: 6l ahd and looked tired whn fell last* **11/4**[3]

6m 31.6s (-6.00) **Going Correction** -0.45s/f (Good) **5** Ran SP% **107.2**
Speed ratings: **91**,—,—,—,— CSF £16.51 TOTE £2.50: £1.40, £2.60; EX 14.40.
Owner Michael H Sly **Bred** Mrs P Sly **Trained** Thorney, Cambs

FOCUS
A moderate winning time for the class of contest. This was not much of a race and the lucky winner has been rated 12lb off his best.

NOTEBOOK
Fullards was fitted with a tongue tie for this return to fences. Looking very hard work for Marston and steadily left behind by the leader, he was reducing the gap, but would not have won, when he was luckily handed victory at the final fence. *(op 13-8 tchd 2-1)*

Unusual Suspect was struggling and reluctant before halfway, but kept going for a remote second place. *Official explanation: jockey said gelding finished distressed*

Lady Lambrini, a very limited performer, eventually completed for third but not before she had knocked over a spectator who had run on the course to help pull Bradburne from underneath his fallen mount. *Official explanation: jockey said gelding finished distressed (tchd 14-1)*

Saddlers Cloth(IRE) looked sure to win after drawing clear of the favourite, but she was awkward at the second last and her stride was shortening when she came down at the final fence. She was an unlucky loser but will do well to find a similarly weak event. *(op 10-3 tchd 7-2)*

4475 NORTH NORFOLK RADIO (S) H'CAP HURDLE (9 hdls) 2m
2:50 (2:52) (Class 5) (0-90,89) 4-Y-0+ **£2,192** (£639; £319)

Form RPR
6-05 **1** **Ethan Snowflake**[28] 3956 7-11-7 **87**....(b[1]) OwynNelmes[(3)] 90+
(N B King) *chsd ldr 2nd: led after 5th: pckd 3 out: 3l clr last: hrd rdn and jst hld on* **13/2**[3]

P200 **2** *shd* **Aleemdar (IRE)**[66] 3330 9-10-13 **81**....(p) DerekLaverty[(5)] 82
(A E Jones) *settled midfield: wnt 3rd bef 3 out: rdn next: no imp tl styd on after last: jst failed* **9/2**[1]

0000 **3** *3 ½* **Protocol (IRE)**[66] 3330 12-11-2 **82**....(tp) LeeVickers[(3)] 80
(Mrs S Lamyman) *led tl after 5th: sn lost pl: plugged on again appr last: nt rch ldrs* **10/1**

6645 **4** *1 ½* **Power And Demand**[51] 3557 9-10-6 **72**....(p) DougieCostello[(3)] 68
(C W Thornton) *t.k.h: towards rr: mstke 4th: outpcd after 6th: kpt on u.p bef last: unable to chal* **9/2**[1]

4446 **5** *nk* **Chariot (IRE)**[57] 3456 5-11-0 **77**....(t) SeanCurran 73
(M R Bosley) *hld up: wnt 2nd after 5th: drvn bef 3 out: outpcd bef next* **9/2**[1]

0004 **6** *12* **Ray Mond**[28] 3956 5-9-7 **63** oh4.... PatrickCStringer[(7)] 47
(M J Gingell) *stdd s: plld hrd in last: effrt 6th: sn chsng ldng trio in vain: btn bef 2 out* **14/1**

-0PP **7** *6* **Charlie Castallan**[46] 3656 6-10-3 **73**.... TomMessenger[(7)] 51
(D W Thompson) *mid field: cajoled along after 6th: no reponse and sn wl btn* **28/1**

00/0 **8** *19* **Glimpse Of Glory**[37] 3793 6-10-5 **68**.... NeilMulholland 27
(C W Thornton) *hld up bhd: j. slowly 5th: sn rdn and struggling* **28/1**

0P30 **P** **Macreater**[92] 2843 8-10-5 **73**....(p) ShaneWalsh[(5)] —
(K A Morgan) *chsd ldr tl 2nd: last after 6th: t.o and p.u 2 out* **11/2**[2]

F55- **P** **Arkholme**[228] 2240 5-11-5 **89**....(b) JustinMorgan[(7)] —
(N A Dunger) *bhd: u.p 4th: lost tch rapidly next: t.o and p.u 6th* **8/1**

4m 7.90s (119.10) **Going Correction** -0.225s/f (Good) **10** Ran SP% **117.0**
Speed ratings: **93,92,91,90,90 84,81,71**,—,— CSF £36.60 CT £289.06 TOTE £6.70: £2.20, £2.60, £1.70; EX 37.30.There was no bid for the winner.
Owner St Gatien Racing Club **Bred** R And Mrs S Edwards **Trained** Newmarket, Suffolk

FOCUS
A modest time, even for a seller, and the slowest of the three hurdle races over the trip at the meeting. The form makes sense rated around the runner-up and fifth.

NOTEBOOK
Ethan Snowflake, whose only previous victory came over this course and distance, wore blinkers for the first time. In the process of going clear when pecking at the third last, he was all out to hold on in the end. *(op 8-1)*

Aleemdar(IRE), suited by this better ground, stayed on well on the run-in but needed another couple of strides. *(op 7-2)*

Protocol(IRE), bidding to win this for the third year running and 5lb lower than he was 12 months ago, was staying on again in the latter stages after losing his pitch. *(op 9-1)*

Power And Demand, back in the cheekpieces, stayed on late in the day without constituting a threat. *(op 7-2)*

Chariot(IRE) had his chance, but lacked the pace of the principals from the third last and was run out of third place on the run-in. *(op 11-2)*

Ray Mond travelled quite well in rear, if taking quite a tug, but after closing into fourth place at one stage he did not get home. *(op 12-1)*

Macreater *Official explanation: trainer's rep said mare coughed after race (op 7-1 tchd 9-1)*

Arkholme *Official explanation: jockey said gelding was unsuited by track (op 7-1 tchd 9-1)*

4476 TIM BARCLAY MEMORIAL H'CAP CHASE (16 fncs) 2m 5f 110y
3:30 (3:35) (Class 4) (0-115,115) 5-Y-0+ **£5,855** (£1,719; £859; £429)

Form RPR
1111 **1** **New Perk (IRE)**[28] 3959 8-9-13 **93** ow1.... ChrisHonour[(5)] 103+
(M J Gingell) *w ldr tl 7th: dropped bk last 11th: rallied and wnt 2nd bef 3 out: rdn to ld last: drew clr: v game* **11/4**[1]

1-32 **2** *2½* **Jaffa**[57] [3459] 14-11-5 **115** MrRArmson(7) 124+
(Miss J Wormall) *t.k.h in last: prog gng wl 11th: led bef 13th: sn 4l clr: rdn and hdd last: nt qckn* **9/2**[2]

413P **3** *19* **Eau Pure (FR)**[87] [2931] 9-10-7 **96** (bt) PhilipHide 85
(G L Moore) *hld up: in tch: rdn and dropped bk last after 12th: no ch after: snatched poor 3rd nr fin* **14/1**

2342 **4** *½* **Rookery Lad**[49] [3593] 8-10-9 **98** DaveCrosse 86
(C N Kellett) *t.k.h: cl up tl pce qcknd after 12th: struggling after* **7/1**

6541 **5** *5* **Caribbean Cove (IRE)**[44] [3676] 8-11-0 **106** PaulO'Neill(3) 89
(Miss Venetia Williams) *cl up: nt fluent 11th: outpcd bef 13th: blnd next* **11/4**[1]

052P **6** *dist* **Parish Oak**[36] [3815] 11-11-7 **110** DavidDennis —
(Ian Williams) *mde most tl 9th: wkng whn hit 12th: btn 65l* **25/1**

4P6P **P** **You Owe Me (IRE)**[27] [3989] 9-11-4 **107** (t) AntonyEvans —
(N A Twiston-Davies) *wnt 2nd 7th: led 9th: hdd after 12th: p.u and dismntd bef next* **5/1**[3]

5m 32.2s (-12.30) **Going Correction** -0.45s/f (Good) **7** Ran SP% **111.2**
Speed ratings: **104,103,96,96,94** —,— CSF £14.88 TOTE £2.30: £2.20, £2.10; EX 14.40.
Owner A White **Bred** Tim Mulhare **Trained** North Runcton, Norfolk

FOCUS
This moderate handicap was run at a reasonable pace. This was another step up from the winner and he could do a bit better yet.

NOTEBOOK
New Perk(IRE) found himself in last place with a circuit to run, albeit not far from the leaders, but he rallied from the third last and ground down the leader at the final fence to win going away. This was his fifth win on the bounce at the Norfolk track, three over fences and two over hurdles, and there could be more to come. *(op 5-2 tchd 3-1)*
Jaffa raced off the same mark as when second at Ludlow to Bob The Builder, who has franked the form. He looked set to score when moving to the front four out, but was worn down at the final fence. *(op 4-1)*
Eau Pure(FR) had the blinkers/tongue tie combination back on, but it had no great effect and she was well beaten. She has now been held three times from this mark after winning off 6lb lower in November. *(op 11-1)*
Rookery Lad, dropped back to what appears a more suitable trip, ran his race with no obvious excuses. *(op 13-2 tchd 8-1)*
Caribbean Cove(IRE) was found out by the 8lb rise for his defeat of Parish Oak at Leicester. *(op 3-1)*
You Owe Me(IRE) *Official explanation: vet said gelding had been struck into (op 11-2)*

4477 WILLIAM BULWER-LONG MEMORIAL NOVICES' FOX HUNTERS' CHASE (16 fncs) 2m 5f 110y
4:15 (4:18) (Class 6) 5-Y-0+ **£1,873** (£581; £290; £145)

Form RPR

UOF/ **1** **Rhythm King**[40] 11-11-6 MrGMaundrell(3) 112+
(G C Maundrell) *hld up: pressed ldrs fr 6th: cl 3rd bef 13th: let ldng pair go clr next: 8l 3rd 2 out: nt rdn but clsd to ld last: sn clr* **13/8**[1]

1/64 **2** *3* **Lightning Strikes (IRE)**[14] [4216] 12-11-4 MrMatthewSmith(5) 109+
(Mrs L Wadham) *nt a fluent: led bef 7th tl bef 10th: led again 12th: wavering bef last where hdd: immediately outpcd* **7/2**[2]

P/5- **3** *6* **Peachy (IRE)**[68] 11-11-2 MissLAllan(7) 106+
(S R Andrews) *keen: prom in 2nd or 3rd: rdn and ev ch whn blnd 2 out: wknd bef last* **6/1**

0 **4** *19* **Killard Point (IRE)**[36] [3819] 7-11-6 MrRCope(3) 86+
(Mrs Caroline Bailey) *mid field: effrt to trck ldrs 10th: wknd after 12th: dismntd sn after fin* **9/2**[3]

-2FP **5** *9* **Blaze On**[26] 7-11-6 MrPYork(3) 75+
(R H York) *keen in midfield: clsd to ld bef 10th: hdd and hit 12th: wknd qckly* **28/1**

P- **6** *22* **Shoveontommy (IRE)**[19] 11-11-4 ow2 (t) MrStuartRobinson(7) 54
(Miss Gina Weare) *keen: led tl bef 7th: lost pl 9th: wkng whn hit 11th: t.o* **50/1**

PU **P** **Noggler**[18] [4146] 7-11-2 MrSCharlton(7) —
(M J Brown) *hld up bhd: lost tch bef 10th: t.o and p.u 13th* **28/1**

P **Gumlayloy**[19] 7-11-9 MrAWintle —
(S Flook) *hld up last pair: lost tch 9th: tailed and p.u 12th: dismntd* **16/1**

P **Bewleys Newlands**[33] 9-11-4 MrJOwen(5) —
(Perry Harding-Jones) *several positions: rdn and wkng bef 10th: t.o and p.u 13th* **40/1**

P5-0 **P** **Ballykettrail (IRE)**[266] [824] 10-11-2 MrNPearce(7) —
(Mrs Julie Read) *last pair: nt fluent 3rd: struggling whn hit 5th: t.o and p.u 9th* **12/1**

02/ **P** **Tupgill Turbo**[27] 8-11-2 MrAMerriam(7) —
(W J Tolhurst) *keen: trckd ldrs: mstke 8th: rdn bef 10th: sn struggling: t.o and p.u 13th* **22/1**

5m 33.7s (-10.80) **Going Correction** -0.45s/f (Good) **11** Ran SP% **122.0**
Speed ratings: **101,99,97,90,87 79**,—,—,—,— — CSF £7.58 TOTE £2.20: £1.40, £2.20, £2.10; EX 10.50.
Owner G C Maundrell **Bred** Shade Oak Stud **Trained** Marlbrough, Wilts.

FOCUS
Probably a race worth taking a positive view about. The pace was strong and the placed horses are close to previous marks so it could work out.

NOTEBOOK
Rhythm King is a prolific winner in points, winner of his last 14 completed starts including a hat-trick this season. Under his veteran owner/trainer, he looked held in third place three from home but, despite Maundrell doing very little on him, he had no problem sweeping through to lead at the final fence. *(op 7-4 tchd 15-8)*
Lightning Strikes(IRE), who made more than one jumping error, got the better of a tussle with the eventual third but was put in his place by the winner from the final fence. *(op 4-1 tchd 9-2)*
Peachy(IRE), a bumper winner, made a successful point-to-point debut under this rider at Higham in January. Rather keen, he was duelling for the lead when blundering at the second last and soon faded. *(op 13-2 tchd 7-1)*
Killard Point(IRE), a decent pointer, was dropping down in trip after failing to get home over three *miles on his recent hunter-chase debut. Official explanation: jockey said gelding finished lame (op 6-1)*

4478 TOTEPOOL FAKENHAM SILVER CUP (A H'CAP HURDLE) (9 hdls) 2m
4:55 (4:56) (Class 3) (0-125,115) 4-Y-0+ **£6,766** (£1,986; £993; £496)

Form RPR

-220 **1** **Dhehdaah**[71] [3256] 5-11-7 **110** WarrenMarston 120+
(Mrs P Sly) *hld up: effrt 5th: trckd ldr gng wl 3 out: led bef last: nt fluent: drvn out* **6/1**[2]

1222 **2** *1* **Saif Sareea**[23] [4050] 6-11-5 **115** PhilKinsella(7) 123
(R A Fahey) *hld up: effrt 5th: led 3 out: hrd pressed tl hdd bef last: nt qckn* **85/40**[1]

3-04 **3** *21* **Hue**[11] [3534] 5-10-13 **102** (v[1]) WilsonRenwick 89
(B Ellison) *hld up: wnt cl up 5th tl and racd awkwardly 3 out: sn no ch* **8/1**[3]

4-1P **4** *11* **Lawaaheb (IRE)**[14] [456] 5-10-1 **95** (v) DerekLaverty(5) 71
(M J Gingell) *led at brisk pce and 5l clr: drvn and hdd 3 out: immediately btn* **18/1**

F604 **5** *6* **All Bleevable**[49] [3592] 9-10-2 **94** (p) LeeVickers(3) 64
(Mrs S Lamyman) *chsd clr ldr to 3rd: lost pl 5th: wl bhd bef 3 out* **18/1**

/41- **6** *20* **Flaming Cheek**[664] [466] 8-10-6 **100** ChrisHonour(5) 50
(A G Blackmore) *taken down early: prom: blnd 4th: wknd qckly next: t.o 3 out* **11/1**

C10P **P** **Vigoureux (FR)**[50] [3580] 7-10-7 **99** (p) WilliamKennedy(3) —
(S Gollings) *immediately struggling: t.o and p.u 6th* **33/1**

5200 **P** **Sovereign State (IRE)**[40] [3761] 9-11-6 **112** (p) OwynNelmes(3) —
(D W Thompson) *rr and nvr gng: lost tch u.p 3rd: t.o and p.u 6th* **25/1**

6421 **P** **Dance World**[49] [3597] 6-11-0 **110** MrMatthewSmith(7) —
(Miss J Feilden) *chsd ldrs tl effrt 5th: lost tch qckly after next: t.o and p.u after 3 out* **85/40**[1]

4m 0.88s (-8.02) **Going Correction** -0.225s/f (Good) **9** Ran SP% **115.0**
Speed ratings: **111,110,100,94,91 81**,—,—,— CSF £19.63 CT £103.02 TOTE £7.80: £2.40, £1.10, £2.10; EX 14.00.
Owner D Bayliss, T Davies, G Libson & P Sly **Bred** Wickfield Farm Partnership **Trained** Thorney, Cambs

FOCUS
A decent winning time for the grade and by far the fastest of the three two-mile hurdles on the card. It ended up as a duel, the rest well beaten, and the form should work out.

NOTEBOOK
Dhehdaah, suited by the strong pace, got to the front between the last two flights. He dived at the final obstacle but battled on well to hold off his rival. This was his first win over hurdles and he should be capable of further improvement. *(tchd 13-2)*
Saif Sareea finished second for the fourth time in a row but did nothing wrong and finished a mile clear of the rest. While he should continue to run well, he is now 13lb higher than when recording his latest win before Christmas. *(op 5-2)*
Hue, who has run twice on the sand since his last start over hurdles, was tried in a visor for the first time. Left behind by the first two over the last three flights, he does not look a straightforward conveyance. *(op 15-2)*
Lawaaheb(IRE), fit from the All-Weather, was responsible for the strong pace but had no answers when headed three out. *(op 14-1)*
Flaming Cheek was having his first run since landing a Stratford handicap off 5lb lower in May 2004. *(op 8-1)*
Dance World dominated when landing a novice event here last time but was never able to get to *the front on this handicap debut and was eventually pulled up, reportedly lame.Official explanation: jockey said gelding pulled up lame; vet said gelding lost both hind shoes (op 11-4 tchd 3-1 in a place)*

4479 EASCO CONDITIONAL JOCKEYS' MAIDEN HURDLE (9 hdls) 2m
5:30 (5:30) (Class 4) 4-Y-0+ **£3,448** (£1,012; £506; £252)

Form RPR

2 **1** **Toparudi**[45] [3659] 5-11-2 ColinBolger 102+
(M H Tompkins) *trckd ldrs: led bef 2 out: sn clr: unchal* **4/1**[2]

F- **2** *11* **Dunaskin (IRE)**[14] [4084] 6-11-2 DougieCostello 87
(Karen McLintock) *trckd clr ldr: led 6th: sn 5l clr: hdd bef 2 out: kpt on but no ch w wnr* **5/1**[3]

3 *hd* **Akash (IRE)**[196] 6-11-2 OwynNelmes 87
(Miss J Feilden) *hld up and bhd: impr qckly bef 3 out: rdn and outpcd bef next: 4th at last: styd on and nrly snatched 2nd* **22/1**

0636 **4** *2½* **Tamreen (IRE)**[27] [3978] 5-10-10 105 (p) EamonDehdashti(6) 85
(G L Moore) *plld hrd early: lost pl and drvn after 3rd: nt look keen: remote 3 out: r.o strly flat* **14/1**

00/2 **5** *¾* **Ken's Dream**[28] [3963] 7-10-6 117 MattyRoe(10) 87+
(Mrs L Wadham) *hld up midfield: rdn and bdly outpcd 3 out: poor 3rd after next: lost two pls flat* **4/5**[1]

3322 **6** *shd* **Flower Haven**[46] [3655] 4-10-2 92 DerekLaverty 70
(M J Gingell) *nvr bttr than midfield: rdn and btn after 3 out* **16/1**

7 *shd* **Otago (IRE)**[170] 5-10-6 KevinTobin(10) 84
(C J Mann) *hld up and bhd: rdn and outpcd 6th: kpt on bef last* **16/1**

P422 **8** *¾* **Seraph**[51] [3557] 6-10-11 83 DarrenO'Dwyer(5) 83
(O Brennan) *prom: mstke 4th: lost tch bef 3 out* **25/1**

P **Hello Tiger**[11] 5-11-2 ShaneWalsh —
(J A Supple) *stdd s: j. appallingly: t.o tl p.u after 3rd* **66/1**

P **King's Thought**[200] 7-11-2 WilliamKennedy —
(S Gollings) *led and clr tl hdd 6th: sn t.o: p.u 2 out* **20/1**

P **P** **Nebraska City**[11] [4278] 5-10-13 TomMessenger(3) —
(D W Thompson) *a bhd: lost tch after 5th: t.o and p.u 2 out* **100/1**

4m 6.40s (-2.50) **Going Correction** -0.225s/f (Good)
WFA 4 from 5yo+ 7lb **11** Ran SP% **126.1**
Speed ratings: **97,91,91,90,89 89,89,89**,—,— — CSF £25.24 TOTE £6.60: £1.60, £1.60, £6.60; EX 39.40 Place 6 £47.02, Place 5 £20.31.
Owner M P Bowring **Bred** M P Bowring **Trained** Newmarket, Suffolk

■ Stewards' Enquiry : Matty Roe four-day ban: failed to ride out for fourth place (Mar 28-31)

FOCUS
A moderate maiden hurdle that could be rated at least 8lb higher but the time was slow.

NOTEBOOK
Toparudi, who had made a promising hurdles debut when runner-up to subsequent scorer Tarlac at Folkestone, had no problem going one better. Showing ahead on the run to to the second last, he soon came clear for a ready win. *(op 9-2 tchd 5-1)*
Dunaskin(IRE), a faller on his only previous run over hurdles over a year ago, was runner-up on Polytrack earlier this month on his first start since September. Moving to the front with four to jump, he tried to get clear but was cut down by the winner before the second last, and only just held on for second as he tired on the run-in. *(op 9-2 tchd 11-2)*
Akash(IRE), a fair performer on the Flat for Mark Johnston, made a pleasing hurdles debut on a track that did not really suit him. He should be capable of better. *(tchd 28-1)*
Tamreen(IRE) was tried in cheekpieces for the first time. He looked less than enthusiastic from a relatively early stage and looked set to finish right out the back, but he flew on the run-in.
Ken's Dream never really got in a blow, and although improving from the second last he was beaten on the run-in. *(op Evens)*
King's Thought, a useful handicapper on the Flat at around ten furlongs, blazed the trail as usual on this hurdles debut. Headed at the sixth and stumbling soon after, he was quickly trailing and pulled up. He might have stamina limitations. *(op 16-1)*

T/Plt: £51.90 to a £1 stake. Pool: £38,544.20 - 541.30 winning units T/Qpdt: £9.80 to a £1 stake. Pool: £3,344.50 - 251.30 winning units IM

4480 - 4482a (Foreign Racing) - See Raceform Interactive

3807 DOWN ROYAL (R-H)

Friday, March 17

OFFICIAL GOING: Heavy (soft in places)

4483a TENNENT'S NO.1 CHASE 3m 2f

4:00 (4:05) 5-Y-0+ **£9,544** (£2,634; £1,255)

RPR

1 **Jack High (IRE)**[33] [3895] 11-11-2 137 GCotter 138
(T M Walsh, Ire) *hld up: mod 4th and no imp after 4 out: kpt on same pce: lft in ld 2 out: strly pressed after last: all out* **2/1**[1]

2 2 ½ **Nil Desperandum (IRE)**[33] [3895] 9-11-2 137 TGMRyan 136
(Ms F M Crowley, Ire) *trckd ldrs in 4th: 3rd bef 5 out: rdn and no imp after next: 2nd after 2 out: chal last: ev ch: jst failed* **9/4**[2]

3 dist **What A Native (IRE)**[27] [3971] 10-10-13 125 MDarcy(3) 113
(C F Swan, Ire) *trckd ldrs in 3rd: cl 2nd after 1/2-way: chal after 4 out: no ex after 3 out: wknd fr 2 out* **9/4**[2]

P **Ardlea Star (IRE)**[5] [4399] 8-10-6 TJDreaper(5) —
(Patrick O Brady, Ire) *hld up in rr: bad mstke 8 out: p.u bef next* **25/1**

P **Logical Approach (IRE)**[12] [4264] 9-10-9 100 MrAMO'Brien(7) —
(Edward U Hales, Ire) *cl up and disp ld to 1/2-way: wknd bef 6 out:* **16/1**

F **Romaha (IRE)**[48] [3630] 10-11-2 (t) BMCash 142+
(S J Mahon, Ire) *led and disp: strly pressed after 4 out: clr after next: 20l advantage whn fell 2 out* **14/1**[3]

7m 58.6s **6** Ran SP% **111.3**
CSF £7.07.
Owner Miss Brenda Ross **Bred** Michael Steinberg **Trained** Kill, Co Kildare

NOTEBOOK
Jack High(IRE) was not going to play any part in the finish from four out, but seized the opportunity presented at the second last and held on dourly on the run-in. This form is not all that far from what he showed when winning the Betfred at Sandown last season and the Grand National, for which he is currently weighted on 10-5, is a likely future option.
Nil Desperandum(IRE) a 20-length winner of this race last year, was not a contender until left *disputing the lead after the second last. He had every chance on the run-in, but does not quicken. (op 7/4)*
What A Native(IRE), four lengths down over the third last, was soon well in arrears and his progressive curve looks to have reached its peak.
Romaha(IRE) was given a positive ride, and went clear after the third last, holding a near 20-length advantage when crashing at the next. He loves this ground and was heading for a personal best prior to falling.

4484 - 4486a (Foreign Racing) - See Raceform Interactive

4108 NEWCASTLE (L-H)

Saturday, March 18

OFFICIAL GOING: Heavy (soft in places)
The cross hurdle after the winning post was omitted in all hurdle races. The penultimate fence in the back straight was omitted on all circuits of all chases.
Wind: Virtually nil

4487 THOMPKINS & THOMPKINS NOVICES' H'CAP HURDLE (10 hdls 1 omitted) 2m 4f

2:30 (2:30) (Class 5) (0-95,95) 4-Y-0+ **£2,277** (£668; £334; £166)

Form RPR

1 **Fox Point (USA)**[35] [3873] 6-11-7 95 PaddyMerrigan(5) 100+
(P C Haslam) *hld up in tch: hdwy to ld bef 2 out: kpt on wl fr last* **7/1**[3]

0600 2 3 ½ **Nelson Du Ronceray (FR)**[46] [3659] 5-10-13 92 DavidDaSilva(10) 91
(P Monteith) *hld up: hdwy bef 3 out: ev ch next: one pce run in* **7/2**[1]

5542 3 8 **August Rose (IRE)**[32] [3918] 6-11-5 91 DougieCostello(3) 82
(Miss Lucinda V Russell) *cl up: ev ch 4 out tl after next: sn no ex* **11/2**[2]

0500 4 4 **Platinum Point (IRE)**[10] [4302] 7-10-1 70 AlanDempsey 58+
(E W Tuer) *chsd ldrs: led 4 out to bef 2 out: sn outpcd* **28/1**

-006 5 hd **Top Dawn (IRE)**[75] [3209] 6-10-0 72 ow2 GaryBerridge(3) 58
(L Lungo) *hld up: hdwy and prom 4 out: rdn whn j.lft next: hung lft and sn outpcd* **7/2**[1]

0310 6 3 ½ **Moyne Pleasure (IRE)**[10] [4302] 8-11-2 85 KennyJohnson 72+
(R Johnson) *racd wd: hld up: hdwy 4 out: rdn and no imp fr next* **14/1**

2 7 14 **Toulouse Express (IRE)**[10] [4299] 7-11-3 93 MrTCollier(7) 64+
(R Johnson) *midfield: rdn 4 out: wknd fr next* **25/1**

/P0P 8 7 **First Grey**[40] [3782] 7-9-8 70 PatrickMcDonald(7) 32
(E W Tuer) *hld up: rdn 4 out: btn after next* **66/1**

0541 9 15 **Lazy Lena (IRE)**[121] [2290] 7-10-11 80 GLee 27
(Miss L C Siddall) *prom: ev ch 4 out: rdn and wknd appr next* **9/1**

01P5 10 12 **Mikasa (IRE)**[9] [4318] 6-10-10 79 KeithMercer 14
(R F Fisher) *midfield: rdn after 6th: sn btn* **25/1**

0UPP 11 10 **Casas (IRE)**[77] [3147] 9-9-13 71 oh2 ow2 (t) LeeVickers(3) —
(J R Norton) *blnd 1st: a bhd* **100/1**

006P P **Barney (IRE)**[19] [4142] 5-10-5 74 BrianHarding —
(Mrs E Slack) *cl up tl wknd 3 out: t.o whn p.u bef last* **50/1**

PPP P **Port Natal (IRE)**[134] [2025] 8-10-8 80 (p) PaddyAspell(3) —
(J Wade) *led to 4 out: sn rdn and wknd: p.u next* **150/1**

P434 P **Mae Moss**[8] [4341] 5-10-2 78 (p) PhilKinsella(7) —
(W S Coltherd) *prom tl rdn and wknd bef 3 out: t.o whn p.u bef last* **8/1**

5m 29.5s (13.70) **Going Correction** +0.30s/f (Yiel) **14** Ran SP% **116.4**
Speed ratings: **84,82,79,77,77 76,70,67,61,57 53,—,—,—** CSF £29.89 CT £146.46 TOTE £8.50: £2.70, £2.00, £2.80; EX 46.10.
Owner John P McManus **Bred** Mereworth Farm **Trained** Middleham, N Yorks

FOCUS
An ordinary event in which the pace was only fair and the winning time seven seconds slower than the following contest, but the first two pulled clear in the last quarter-mile and both may do better for their new stables.

NOTEBOOK
Fox Point(USA), down in grade and back in testing ground on this first run for Patrick Haslam, returned to something like the pick of his Irish form. He looks worth a try over three miles and can progress again for this stable. *(op 5-1 tchd 8-1)*
Nelson Du Ronceray(FR) ◆, who did not progress in novice events for Martin Pipe, attracted support and showed more than enough on this handicap debut and first run for Peter Monteith to suggest that a similar event can be found. *(op 6-1)*
August Rose(IRE), who ran creditably on her handicap debut over this course and distance last time, looked to give it her best shot and she looks a good guide to the worth of this form. She may be capable of winning an uncompetitive event. *(op 13-2 tchd 7-1)*
Platinum Point(IRE) was not disgraced on only this second outing in handicap company. Less testing ground may suit better and, although his proximity confirm the form of this race is ordinary, he may be capable of a bit better. *(op 25-1 tchd 33-1)*
Top Dawn(IRE) had shown little worthwhile form previously but was well supported and, although failing to justify the market confidence, ran his best race yet, despite hanging. He must have been showing something at home and is not one to write off yet. *(tchd 3-1)*
Moyne Pleasure(IRE), an inconsistent hurdler, was again below the form of his Sedgefield soft ground win and he remains one to tread carefully with.
Barney(IRE) *Official explanation: jockey said gelding had a breathing problem*

4488 ST JAMES SECURITY H'CAP HURDLE (10 hdls 1 omitted) 2m 4f

3:00 (3:00) (Class 4) (0-110,108) 4-Y-0+ **£3,253** (£955; £477; £238)

Form RPR

0015 1 **Silver Sedge (IRE)**[54] [3543] 7-10-1 86 PaddyAspell(3) 110+
(Mrs A Hamilton) *hld up: smooth hdwy bef 4 out: led next: kpt on strly to go clr fr next* **6/1**[2]

-P64 2 17 **Stormy Lord (IRE)**[54] [3542] 10-11-12 108 BrianHarding 112+
(J Wade) *led to 3 out: sn no ex* **20/1**

411F 3 2 **Ross Comm**[112] [2491] 10-11-3 99 PadgeWhelan 99
(Mrs S J Smith) *chsd ldrs: rdn after 4 out: one pce fr next* **4/5**[1]

2363 4 5 **Kempski**[9] [4317] 6-10-0 89 GarethThomas(7) 84
(R Nixon) *hld up: hdwy u.p 4 out: outpcd fr next* **14/1**

50P3 5 1 ½ **Crackleando**[7] [4364] 5-10-9 98 TomMessenger(7) 92
(A R Dicken) *cl up: rdn 5th: lost pl next* **16/1**

1F44 6 12 **Titian Flame (IRE)**[20] [4131] 6-10-12 99 (p) MrTJO'Brien(5) 81
(D Burchell) *in tch: drvn 6th: btn after next* **14/1**

0031 P **Boris The Spider**[8] [4346] 5-11-6 102 GLee —
(M D Hammond) *hld up: hit 5th: hdwy next: wknd after 4 out: p.u 3 out* **7/1**[3]

043U P **Kidithou (FR)**[8] [4341] 8-10-11 93 AlanDempsey —
(W T Reed) *chsd ldrs: early reminders: wknd 6th: t.o whn p.u bef 3 out* **16/1**

5m 22.5s (6.70) **Going Correction** +0.30s/f (Yiel) **8** Ran SP% **112.2**
Speed ratings: **98,91,90,88,83 87,—,—** CSF £98.53 CT £191.64 TOTE £8.40: £1.50, £5.70, £1.10; EX 210.70.
Owner Ian Hamilton **Bred** David Mooney **Trained** Great Bavington, Northumbland

FOCUS
Ordinary fare and the gallop was on the steady side in the first half of the race. The winner is value for more than the official margin and sets the standard.

NOTEBOOK
Silver Sedge(IRE) seems to go well at this course and he won an ordinary event with plenty in hand. However, the Handicapper is unlikely to look on this too favourably and he will find things much tougher after reassessment. *(tchd 13-2)*
Stormy Lord(IRE), who had not been in much form over hurdles or fences since his last win just over a year ago, was not totally disgraced but he had the run of the race and was readily brushed aside by a rival who had previously seemed fully exposed. He will have to show more before he is worth a bet.
Ross Comm was the big disappointment as he looked to have outstanding claims despite the drop in trip from this much lower hurdle rating if his latest chase improvement could be translated to the smaller obstacles. He may do better in this sphere back over three miles. *(op 5-6)*
Kempski is an inconsistent and fully exposed maiden hurdler who would have preferred a stiffer test of stamina over this trip but is not really one to place too much faith in.
Crackleando, who shaped well at Ayr on his previous start, failed to confirm that bit of promise. Consistency is not his strong suit and he remains one to tread carefully with. *(op 14-1)*
Titian Flame(IRE) had conditions to suit but proved a bit of a disappointment and will have to show more before she is worth a bet once again. *(op 12-1)*
Boris The Spider, off the mark over hurdles at Ayr the previous week, proved a disappointment and was beaten before stamina over this longer trip became an issue. He is rarely one for maximum faith. *Official explanation: jockey said gelding had a breathing problem*

4489 ERNIE TURNER FROM DEBMAT IS 60 H'CAP CHASE (12 fncs 1 omitted) 2m 110y

3:35 (3:35) (Class 4) (0-105,107) 5-Y-0 **£3,757** (£1,110; £555; £277; £138)

Form RPR

0414 1 **Flaming Heck**[9] [4318] 9-10-12 96 DesFlavin(5) 100
(Mrs L B Normile) *led to 5th: led 4 out: rdn next: kpt on u.p fr last: all out* **5/1**[3]

3315 2 hd **Miss Pross**[25] [4041] 6-11-1 101 MrMWalford(7) 105
(T D Walford) *prom: stdy hdwy 5 out: outpcd 3 out: kpt on wl fr last: jst hld* **11/4**[1]

4512 3 ¾ **Bob's Buster**[59] [3447] 10-11-2 95 KennyJohnson 99+
(R Johnson) *racd wd: hld up: hdwy to chse ldrs bef 4 out: 2l down whn hit 2 out: kpt on u.p fr last* **3/1**[2]

0P51 4 2 **Hollows Mill**[9] [4318] 10-12-0 107 GLee 109+
(F P Murtagh) *cl up: led 5th to 4 out: rallied: no ex run in* **11/4**[1]

6624 5 15 **Jerom De Vindecy (FR)**[35] [3849] 9-10-1 83 (b) PaddyAspell(3) 69
(Miss Lucinda V Russell) *chsd ldrs tl wknd fr 4 out* **8/1**

4m 28.6s (5.40) **Going Correction** +0.40s/f (Soft) **5** Ran SP% **106.1**
Speed ratings: **103,102,102,101,94** CSF £17.66 TOTE £6.30: £1.80, £2.20; EX 22.00.
Owner D A Whitaker **Bred** R L Green **Trained** Duncrievie, Perth & Kinross

FOCUS
No progressive sorts in this ordinary event, but the pace was fair and the first three were pretty much to their marks.

NOTEBOOK
Flaming Heck beaten over 30 lengths behind Hollows Mill at Carlisle last time, reversed that form in no uncertain terms and maintained his unbeaten record at this course. However, his record is *one of inconsistency and he would not be one to lump on at short odds next time.Official explanation: trainer's representative said, regarding the improved form shown, gelding is an inconsistent type who was allowed to dominate today (op 9-2 tchd 4-1)*
Miss Pross, an inconsistent hurdler, bettered the form of her previous start over fences and left the impression that a stronger overall gallop would have been in her favour. She is capable of winning another race but may not be one for maximum faith. *(op 5-2)*
Bob's Buster, a quirky sort, ran creditably back over this trip, especially as a stronger pace would have suited and he made a mistake at a crucial stage. He is capable of winning again away from progressive sorts when things drop right. *(op 11-4)*
Hollows Mill, whose three chase wins have been at Carlisle, ran creditably from this 9lb higher *mark and he will be of interest in similar company returned to his favourite course. (tchd 3-1 and 7-2 in places)*
Jerom De Vindecy(FR) is an unreliable chaser who ran poorly and he remains one to tread carefully with. *(op 11-1 tchd 15-2)*

4490 SPIKE RAWLINGS H'CAP HURDLE (8 hdls 1 omitted) 2m

4:10 (4:10) (Class 3) (0-130,130) 4-Y-0+ **£5,204** (£1,528; £764; £381)

Form RPR

P000 1 **Nick's Choice**[12] [4282] 10-9-9 104 oh10 MrTJO'Brien(5) 111+
(D Burchell) *cl up: led bef 2 out: rdn and r.o strly* **14/1**

222P **2** *6* **Pay Attention**[28] 3986 5-10-13 **124** ...... PhilKinsella(7) 125
(T D Easterby) *midfield: rdn 1/2-way: hdwy 3 out: styd on to go 2nd towards fin: no ch w wnr* **5/1**[2]

4154 **3** *2* **Culcabock (IRE)**[21] 4110 6-10-8 **112** ...... GLee 112+
(Miss Lucinda V Russell) *chsd ldrs: rdn bef 3 out: one pce after next* **11/2**[3]

2P03 **4** *7* **Andre Chenier (IRE)**[21] 4110 5-10-1 **115** ...... DavidDaSilva(10) 108+
(P Monteith) *hld up: smooth hdwy to ld 3 out: hdd bef next: sn rdn and btn* **11/2**[3]

13P1 **5** *5* **Torkinking (IRE)**[21] 4110 7-11-4 **129** ......(t) BenOrde-Powlett(7) 116
(M A Barnes) *led to 3 out: rdn and wknd next* **7/4**[1]

6/P0 **6** *nk* **Cita Verda (FR)**[21] 4110 8-10-10 **114** ...... AlanDempsey 101
(P Monteith) *hld up: rdn bef 4 out: nvr rchd ldrs* **33/1**

-63F **7** *20* **Through The Rye**[21] 4109 10-11-9 **130** ...... PaddyAspell(3) 97
(E W Tuer) *cl up: j. slowly 3rd: effrt bef 4 out: sn btn* **12/1**

104- **8** *23* **Middlethorpe**[406] 3708 9-11-12 **130** ......(b) KeithMercer 74
(M W Easterby) *hld up: hit and outpcd 3rd: sn btn* **14/1**

3434 **9** *1 1/4* **Rising Generation (FR)**[31] 3929 9-11-5 **123** ...... BrianHarding 65
(N G Richards) *in tch: hdwy 5th: wknd next* **14/1**

4m 7.20s (0.90) **Going Correction** +0.30s/f (Yiel) **9** Ran SP% **114.4**
Speed ratings: **109,106,105,101,99 98,88,77,76** CSF £82.42 CT £437.86 TOTE £20.70: £3.30, £1.60, £1.70; EX 122.60.
Owner Don Gould **Bred** John Brookman **Trained** Briery Hill, Blaenau Gwent

FOCUS
An ordinary event in which the pace was sound and the form looks solid rated through the placed horses.

NOTEBOOK
Nick's Choice ◆ seems to come to hand at this time of year and left some modest efforts well behind with an improved effort from 10lb out of the handicap back over this shorter trip. He goes on better ground and, given the manner of this win, would be very much of interest if turned out at *Warwick before reassessment. Official explanation: trainer said, regarding improved form shown, he had no explanation for poor run previous time, but added that gelding appears to be much improved in spring (op 16-1)*
Pay Attention, pulled up in a competitive event over two and a half miles last time, seemed to run her race back over this trip. She is vulnerable to well handicapped or progressive sorts but is a good guide to the level of this form. *(op 11-2)*
Culcabock(IRE) is not the most consistent but seemed to run creditably back at this course. However, he too looks high enough in the weights at present and will remain vulnerable to progressive or well handicapped types. *(op 8-1)*
Andre Chenier(IRE) not for the first time did not find anywhere near as much off the bridle as seemed likely and, although not totally disgraced in terms of form, remains one to have reservations about at shortish odds. *(op 6-1)*
Torkinking(IRE) lost his unbeaten record at this course and was a bit disappointing in the process - offering less resistance than is usually the case. He is not very big and may have been feeling the *effects of some tough races of late but may continue to look vulnerable in this sort of company. (op 6-4 tchd 2-1)*
Cita Verda(FR) ran her best race since her lengthy absence but left the impression that she would have to drop further in the weights before regaining the winning thread. *(tchd 40-1)*
Rising Generation(FR) *Official explanation: jockey said gelding was unsuited by the heavy (soft last 3f) ground (op 12-1)*

4491 BETFAIR.COM H'CAP HURDLE (12 hdls 1 omitted) 3m
4:40 (4:40) (Class 3) (0-125,124) 4-Y-0+ **£5,204** (£1,528; £764; £381)

Form RPR

0012 **1** **Habitual Dancer**[42] 3741 5-11-8 **120** ...... BrianHarding 135+
(Jedd O'Keeffe) *mde all: drew clr fr 3 out* **4/1**[2]

042P **2** *17* **Pride Of Finewood (IRE)**[32] 3914 8-10-1 **99** ...... AlanDempsey 90+
(E W Tuer) *chsd ldrs: effrt bef 3 out: hung lft and sn one pce* **12/1**

-PFP **3** *6* **Aberdare**[8] 4344 7-10-4 **102** ......(p) KeithMercer 85
(J R Bewley) *chsd ldrs: outpcd 1/2-way: kpt on fr 2 out: no ch w first two* **33/1**

052F **4** *3* **Supreme Piper (IRE)**[8] 4357 8-10-6 **111** ...... MissCDyson(7) 91
(Miss C Dyson) *cl up: hit 7th: wknd after 4 out* **10/1**

P235 **5** *1 3/4* **Totally Scottish**[42] 3741 10-10-12 **117** ...... PhilKinsella(7) 95
(K G Reveley) *hld up in tch: rdn 8th: wknd after next* **11/2**

6104 **F** **Caesar's Palace (GER)**[8] 4344 9-9-10 **99** ......(p) DeclanMcGann(5) —
(Miss Lucinda V Russell) *hmpd and fell 1st* **8/1**

4003 **P** **Treasured Memories**[38] 3795 6-10-3 **101** ...... NeilMulholland —
(Miss S E Forster) *bdly hmpd and p.u after 1st* **9/2**[3]

1001 **P** **General Duroc (IRE)**[25] 4043 10-11-3 **115** ......(p) GLee —
(B Storey) *wnt rt 1st: sn prom: drvn and lost pl 5th: p.u after next* **10/3**[1]

1/00 **P** **Corbie Lynn**[82] 2990 9-10-0 **105** ...... PatrickMcDonald(7) —
(W S Coltherd) *chsd ldrs tl wknd bef 4 out: t.o whn p.u bef next* **25/1**

6m 20.8s (2.40) **Going Correction** +0.30s/f (Yiel) **9** Ran SP% **111.3**
Speed ratings: **108,102,100,99,98 —,—,—,—** CSF £46.92 CT £1330.29 TOTE £4.50: £1.80, £4.10, £6.20; EX 46.80.
Owner The Country Stayers **Bred** Mrs A Yearley **Trained** Coverham, N Yorks

FOCUS
More ordinary fare but an improved effort from Habitual Dancer, who relished these conditions and is value for more than the official margin.

NOTEBOOK
Habitual Dancer confirmed previous promise to win an ordinary handicap with plenty in hand. However, as his market rivals disappointed this did not take as much winning as seemed likely and life will be much tougher after reassessment. *(op 7-2)*
Pride Of Finewood(IRE), an inconsistent hurdler, was not totally disgraced but once again looked a less than easy ride and had his limitations exposed from this mark on this handicap debut. He may be one to tread carefully with. *(op 16-1)*
Aberdare had failed to get round on his three previous starts but, although not totally disgraced in the first-time cheekpieces, looked anything but an easy ride and is another to go carefully with in the near future. *(op 25-1)*
Supreme Piper(IRE), who ran well in heavy ground on his penultimate start, was disappointing in this ordinary event and conditions did not look to be his strongest suit. *(op 8-1)*
Totally Scottish, an unreliable hurdler who has only won once since 2002, was disappointing and is not really one to be taking single-figure odds about. *(op 13-2 tchd 7-1)*
General Duroc(IRE) looked to have plenty in his favour regarding conditions, trip and a recent win, but showed the other side of his nature to record his third well beaten run from his last four starts. *He is a law unto himself. Official explanation: trainer had no explanation for the poor form shown (op 4-1 tchd 3-1)*
Treasured Memories, from an in-form stable, was badly hampered by the faller at the first flight *but is well worth another chance. Official explanation: jockey said mare was badly hampered first flight (op 4-1 tchd 3-1)*

4492 GUINNESS ST PATRICK'S DAY H'CAP CHASE (16 fncs 2 omitted) 3m
5:10 (5:10) (Class 4) (0-110,106) 5-Y-0+ **£3,850** (£1,202; £647)

Form RPR

6P03 **1** **Lazy But Lively (IRE)**[9] 4316 10-10-0 **80** oh1 ...... GLee 90
(R F Fisher) *chsd ldr to 4 out: lft 2l 2nd next: styd on wl fr last to ld cl home* **13/8**[1]

1405 **2** *1/2* **Dead Mans Dante (IRE)**[38] 3794 8-11-10 **104** ...... KeithMercer 115+
(Ferdy Murphy) *keen: prom: hdwy to chse ldr 4 out: hung lft: 3l down whn lft 2l up next: kpt on: hdd towards fin* **7/2**[3]

1003 **3** *dist* **Nocatee (IRE)**[22] 4095 5-10-7 **102** ......(t) PaddyMerrigan(5) —
(P C Haslam) *mstkes: chsd ldrs tl wknd 8th: t.o whn blnd and uns rdr 4 out: rmntd* **7/2**[3]

2PU1 **F** **Farington Lodge (IRE)**[59] 3444 8-11-0 **94** ...... PadgeWhelan 104+
(J M Saville) *set stdy pce: led: rdn bef 4 out: 3l up whn fell next* **3/1**[2]

6m 41.6s (16.80) **Going Correction** +0.40s/f (Soft)
WFA 5 from 8yo+ 10lb **4** Ran SP% **107.5**
Speed ratings: **88,87,—,—** CSF £7.25 TOTE £2.10; EX 4.10.
Owner S P Marsh **Bred** S P Marsh And R F Fisher **Trained** Ulverston, Cumbria

FOCUS
An uncompetitive race and a slow pace resulted in a moderate winning time, even allowing for the ground. The complexion of the race changed dramatically in the closing stages with the runner-up the best guide to the form.

NOTEBOOK
Lazy But Lively(IRE), an inconsistent chaser, looked held coming to the third last but things panned out in his favour and he did more than the runner-up to land the spoils in the closing stages. He would be one to field against at short odds next time. *(op 6-4 tchd 11-8)*
Dead Mans Dante(IRE), an inconsistent chaser, appeared to be handed the race when Farington Lodge came to grief but looked to throw it away by continually hanging to his left. He is anything but straightforward (also pulled) and remains one to tread carefully with. *(op 11-2)*
Nocatee(IRE), a course and distance winner in November, has been well below that level since and once again offered no immediate promise. *(tchd 10-3)*
Farington Lodge(IRE), who got off the mark over course and distance on his previous start, had the run of the race and looked in control when coming to grief. He can win a similar race if none-the-worse for this experience. *(op 11-4 tchd 5-2)*

4493 JAMES FLETCHER MARQUEE AND PAVILION HIRE NOVICES' HURDLE (8 hdls 1 omitted) 2m
5:40 (5:42) (Class 4) 4-Y-0+ **£2,927** (£859; £429; £214)

Form RPR

4323 **1** **Tous Chez (IRE)**[68] 3314 7-11-0 ...... PadgeWhelan 109+
(Mrs S J Smith) *chsd ldrs: led 4th: clr 2 out: styd on strly* **2/1**[1]

4623 **2** *13* **Lethem Air**[19] 4141 8-10-7 103 ......(p) PhilKinsella(7) 94
(T Butt) *cl up: effrt bef 3 out: one pce fr next* **10/3**[3]

54-4 **3** *3* **Lady Speaker**[308] 349 5-10-7 ...... NeilMulholland 84
(T D Easterby) *prom: effrt bef 3 out: kpt on same pce fr next* **25/1**

0F22 **4** *10* **Kilmackilloge**[21] 4114 7-11-0 107 ...... GLee 83+
(M Todhunter) *plld hrd: prom: effrt bef 3 out: btn next* **9/4**[2]

43-0 **5** *3 1/2* **Jeringa**[39] 3789 7-10-11 ...... PaddyAspell(3) 78
(J Wade) *prom tl rdn and wknd bef 3 out* **14/1**

6 *8* **Ben Nelly (IRE)** 5-11-0 ...... AlanDempsey 70
(M Todhunter) *bhd tl styd on fr 2 out: nvr on terms* **50/1**

056 **7** *shd* **Sparkling Taff**[28] 3975 7-11-0 ...... BrianHarding 69
(Mrs S J Smith) *in tch tl rdn and wknd fr 4 out* **25/1**

0 **8** *7* **Dispol Peto**[32] 3912 6-11-0 ...... KennyJohnson 62
(R Johnson) *keen: hld up bhd: nvr on terms* **100/1**

32-6 **9** *1/2* **Reseda (IRE)**[19] 4143 9-10-7 98 ......(t) BenOrde-Powlett(7) 62
(M A Barnes) *midfield to 1/2-way: sn btn* **20/1**

6 **10** *7* **Marghub (IRE)**[9] 4327 7-10-7 ...... MissCDyson(7) 55
(Miss C Dyson) *bhd: struggling 1/2-way: nvr on terms* **25/1**

F0F **P** **Classic Lease**[115] 2444 5-10-9 ...... PaddyMerrigan(5) —
(P C Haslam) *s.s: bhd: p.u after 2nd* **40/1**

F **P** **Orlando Blue**[10] 4299 6-11-0 ...... KeithMercer —
(B Storey) *led to 4th: sn wknd: t.o whn p.u bef 3 out* **100/1**

4m 12.6s (6.30) **Going Correction** +0.30s/f (Yiel) **12** Ran SP% **116.5**
Speed ratings: **96,89,88,83,81 77,77,73,73,69 —,—** CSF £8.18 TOTE £3.20: £1.90, £1.50, £4.00; EX 10.00 Place 6 £110.82, Place 5 £64.74.
Owner Keith Nicholson **Bred** Kevin Cullen **Trained** High Eldwick, W Yorks

FOCUS
An ordinary event with very little strength. The pace seemed sound but it is debatable whether the form will work out.

NOTEBOOK
Tous Chez(IRE) ◆ looked to have a good chance in this company on the pick of his bumper and hurdle form and he won this ordinary race with plenty to spare. He should stay two and a half miles and appeals as the type to win again. *(op 5-2)*
Lethem Air had been running creditably and looks a good guide to the worth of this form. He is likely to remain vulnerable over this trip and in this grade and the return to two and a half miles in handicap company should suit. *(tchd 3-1)*
Lady Speaker, who showed ability in bumpers, was not disgraced on this hurdle debut but left the strong impression that the step up to two and a half miles would be in her favour. She looks capable of winning a minor event.
Kilmackilloge looked to have fair claims in this company but pulled far too hard to give himself any chance of lasting home in these conditions. He has had a few chances now and does not look one to be lumping on at short odds. *(op 2-1 tchd 5-2)*
Jeringa has the physique to do better over obstacles and, although he had his limitations exposed once again, may do better in modest events once handicapped. *(op 16-1)*
Ben Nelly(IRE) hinted at ability on this racecourse debut and left the impression that a much stiffer test of stamina would be in his favour. He may be the type to do better in handicaps. *(op 40-1)*
T/Plt: £446.80 to a £1 stake. Pool: £58,576.95. 95.70 winning tickets. T/Qpdt: £172.90 to a £1 stake. Pool: £2,921.70. 12.50 winning tickets. RY

3984 UTTOXETER (L-H)
Saturday, March 18

OFFICIAL GOING: Heavy (soft in places)
Wind: Light, behind Weather: Overcast

4494 PETER J DOUGLAS ENGINEERING NOVICES' HURDLE (12 hdls) 2m 4f 110y
1:50 (1:50) (Class 4) 4-Y-0+ **£4,879** (£1,432; £716; £357)

Form RPR

-213 **1** **Brankley Boy**[42] 3729 8-11-8 124 ...... MickFitzgerald 126+
(N J Henderson) *trckd ldrs: shkn up after 4 out: led next: rdn clr appr last: eased nr fin* **5/2**[1]

5303 **2** *6* **Emmasflora**[39] 3792 8-10-10 104 ...... AdamPogson(5) 112
(C T Pogson) *a.p: rdn appr 2 out: wnt 2nd and no imp last* **33/1**

244 **3** 2 ½ **Marshalls Run (IRE)**[33] 3904 6-11-1 .... RobertThornton 110
(A King) *trckd ldrs: ev ch 3 out: styd on same pce appr last* **14/1**

F15 **4** 15 **Blu Teen (FR)**[21] 4115 6-11-8 127 ....(t) RWalsh 104+
(P F Nicholls) *disp ld tl hmpd 4th: led 8th to 3 out: wkng whn hit next* **11/4**[2]

-112 **5** nk **What A Vintage (IRE)**[76] 3184 6-11-1 .... WarrenMarston 94
(R T Phillips) *hld up: hdwy 8th: rdn and wknd 3 out* **13/2**

4441 **6** 5 **Bring Me Sunshine (IRE)**[19] 4148 5-11-8 113 .... JoeTizzard 96
(C L Tizzard) *hld up: hit 7th and next: rdn and wknd appr 3 out* **10/1**

3/1- **7** 7 **Chapel Times (IRE)**[686] 130 7-11-1 .... RichardJohnson 84+
(H D Daly) *disp ld tl led and j.rt 4th: hit 6th: hdd 8th: wknd 3 out* **22/1**

0- **8** 15 **Go Harvey Go (IRE)**[392] 3946 7-11-1 .... JimmyMcCarthy 67
(R T Phillips) *hld up: hit 3rd: effrt and mstke 4 out: sn wknd* **66/1**

21 **9** dist **Sonnengold (GER)**[28] 3979 5-11-1 112 .... LeightonAspell —
(Mrs L Wadham) *chsd ldrs tl wknd after 4 out* **7/2**[3]

P0 **10** dist **Call Out (IRE)**[11] 4285 6-10-8 .... MissLGardner(7) —
(Mrs S Gardner) *plld hrd and prom: lost pl after 3rd: bhd fr 6th* **150/1**

5m 21.5s (9.40) **Going Correction** +0.10s/f (Yiel) **10** Ran SP% **116.0**
Speed ratings: **86,83,82,77,76 75,72,66,—,—** CSF £81.43 TOTE £3.30: £1.80, £5.30, £3.50; EX 98.30.
Owner Gary Stewart **Bred** C D Harrison **Trained** Upper Lambourn, Berks

FOCUS
Just a fair novices' hurdle run at a very steady pace that did not pick up until inside the final mile, but the winner scored in good style and looks capable of going on to better things, while the second ran to her mark.

NOTEBOOK
Brankley Boy ◆, the form of whose third at Sandown has worked out well with the first two both winning since, settled well off the pace and came through to lead three out. Once in front the result was never in doubt and he handled the ground really well. He should make up into a decent novice chaser next season. *(op 2-1)*

Emmasflora, who until this had looked best on good ground, ran on past tiring rivals without ever looking likely to trouble the winner. Her proximity somewhat limits the form, but she is running well at present and may be able to pick up a similar contest, especially against her own sex. *(op 25-1)*

Marshalls Run(IRE), making his hurdling debut, had shown ability in bumpers giving the impression that this sort of trip would suit him. He was in the firing line turning for home, but could not produce extra pace once the winner went on. He still looks immature and is likely to improve considerably with another summer behind him. *(tchd 16-1)*

Blu Teen(FR) has not really gone on from an impressive debut at Chepstow, when he fell at the last having gone well clear, despite winning next time. He dropped away rather tamely as if not getting this longer trip. *(op 9-4)*

What A Vintage(IRE) was settled out the back and never reached a challenging position. On the face of it this was a disappointing effort, but it may be that it was not easy to get into contention from a long way off the pace on the day. *(op 8-1 tchd 6-1)*

Bring Me Sunshine(IRE), a soft-ground winner last time, was always out the back. *(op 12-1)*

Chapel Times(IRE), a bumper winner here in May 2004, had not been seen since. He led until the last on the far side and then not surprisingly dropped out. The main thing will be that he is in one piece after this. *(op 25-1)*

Sonnengold(GER), both of whose efforts over hurdles have been on similar ground, ran no sort of race. *It is likely an explanation for this poor performance will be forthcoming in due course.Official explanation: jockey said mare was never travelling (op 9-2)*

4495 EBF/TATTERSALLS (IRELAND) MARES' ONLY NOVICES' CHASE FINAL (A H'CAP) (LISTED RACE) (16 fncs) 2m 5f

2:20 (2:22) (Class 1) 5-Y-0+ **£17,041** (£6,505; £3,325; £1,732; £937)

Form RPR

61F3 **1** **Sarahs Quay (IRE)**[6] 4386 7-9-12 **100** oh9 ow1 ....(p) ColinBolger(3) 114+
(K J Burke) *chsd ldr 3rd: led 8th: rdn clr 2 out: hung lft flat: drvn out* **14/1**

4P21 **2** 10 **Lizzie Bathwick (IRE)**[30] 3951 7-9-11 **99** oh4 .... StephenCraine(3) 103
(J G Portman) *a.p: rdn appr 4 out: hmpd next: sn chsng wnr: no imp* **4/1**[2]

5112 **3** 8 **De Blanc (IRE)**[25] 4034 6-11-12 **125** .... APMcCoy 124+
(Miss Venetia Williams) *prom: chsd wnr and hit 10th: rdn: j.lft and hit 3 out: wknd next: hit last* **3/1**[1]

F421 **4** 7 **Motcombe (IRE)**[9] 4328 8-10-6 **105** ....(p) AndrewThornton 100+
(R H Alner) *chsd ldrs: hit 2nd: lost pl after 4th: n.d after* **4/1**[2]

2120 **5** 12 **Supreme Serenade (IRE)**[28] 3993 7-11-12 **125** .... RichardJohnson 102
(P J Hobbs) *hld up: mstke 2nd: hdwy 8th: hit 3 out: sn wknd* **4/1**[2]

051U **P** **Elfkirk (IRE)**[44] 3689 7-11-2 **115** .... SamHitchcott —
(R H Buckler) *hit 2nd: bhd fr 7th: t.o whn p.u after 9th* **20/1**

13P4 **P** **Sunny South East (IRE)**[39] 3790 6-9-11 **99** oh4...(p) WilliamKennedy(3) —
(S Gollings) *hld up: hit 9th: a in rr: t.o whn p.u bef 3 out* **50/1**

0013 **P** **Isellido (IRE)**[35] 3849 7-10-8 **107** .... PCarberry —
(R C Guest) *led and sn clr: hdd 8th: wknd 10th: hit next: t.o whn p.u bef 5 out* **11/2**[3]

5m 47.3s (19.80) **Going Correction** +1.00s/f (Soft) **8** Ran SP% **113.8**
Speed ratings: **102,98,95,92,87 —,—,—** CSF £69.67 CT £216.08 TOTE £18.80: £2.50, £1.60, £1.30; EX 48.60 Trifecta £190.80 wu.
Owner K Burke **Bred** Sean McKeown **Trained** Bourton-on-the-Water, Gloucs

FOCUS
Not a particularly strong renewal of this final race in the series and a somewhat surprise result. The winning time was ordinary for the grade but the form looks reasonable rated around the runner-up with the next two home not far off their marks.

NOTEBOOK
Sarahs Quay(IRE) has been transformed by the application of cheekpieces and relishes testing conditions. Despite being 9lb out of the handicap before the jockey's allowance, she got a lead for the first circuit then once in front was always travelling strongly and galloped on far too resolutely for her rivals. The form is only moderate but she has secured her paddock value and looks to have more races in her when the ground is testing. *(op 16-1)*

Lizzie Bathwick(IRE), who won her maiden hurdle on heavy ground here, has shown most of her recent form in less-testing conditions. She had every chance but the winner galloped on too strongly for her. *(op 3-1)*

De Blanc(IRE) has had a successful winter in similar races but as a result was giving a lot of weight away to the first two. She got into contention at the top of the straight but was soon struggling and appeared to find this ground too testing. *(op 10-3)*

Motcombe(IRE) had a good chance at the weights on her early-season running and had been performing better since the cheekpieces were applied. However, she never got into contention following an early error.

Supreme Serenade(IRE) has shown all her best form on good or easy ground and, held up as usual, seemed unable to operate on this heavy going. She is capable of a lot better and can be forgiven this. *(op 5-1)*

Elfkirk(IRE) *Official explanation: jockey said mare bled from nose (op 16-1)*

4496 JOHN SMITH'S MIDLANDS GRAND NATIONAL CHASE (H'CAP) (LISTED RACE) (24 fncs) 4m 1f 110y

2:55 (2:57) (Class 1) 5-Y-0+
£62,027 (£23,395; £11,735; £5,894; £2,979; £1,516)

Form RPR

-0P5 **1** **G V A Ireland (IRE)**[62] 3410 8-10-3 **122** .... RWalsh 140+
(F Flood, Ire) *chsd ldrs: led 3rd to 5th: led appr 4 out: drvn out* **5/1**[1]

6131 **2** 4 **Ossmoses (IRE)**[28] 3971 9-11-5 **138** .... RichardMcGrath 153+
(D M Forster) *led to 3rd: chsd ldrs: led 19th: hdd appr 4 out: sn rdn : no ex flat* **9/1**

6415 **3** 14 **L'Aventure (FR)**[28] 3971 7-11-2 **140** ....(bt) LiamHeard(5) 140
(P F Nicholls) *chsd ldrs: outpcd 17th: rallied 19th: wknd appr 4 out* **16/1**

6P43 **4** 6 **Victory Gunner (IRE)**[22] 4098 8-10-3 **122** ow1 .... ChristianWilliams 116
(C Roberts) *prom: hit 9th: rdn after 12th: lost pl 18th: rallied 5 out: wknd next* **25/1**

P30F **5** 17 **Trust Fund (IRE)**[28] 3989 8-10-1 **120** .... RobertWalford 99+
(R H Alner) *hld up: hit 2nd and 6th: hmpd 19th: n.d* **8/1**[3]

1P00 **6** 2 ½ **Robbo**[21] 4111 12-9-6 **121** .... JamesReveley(10) 96
(K G Reveley) *nt jump wl: sn wl bhd* **50/1**

30U3 **7** 1 ½ **Control Man (IRE)**[63] 3390 8-10-11 **130** ....(v) APMcCoy 103+
(M C Pipe) *chsd ldrs: led 5th to 19th: wknd appr 3 out* **20/1**

6-P0 **U** **Polar Red**[49] 3620 9-10-7 **126** ....(t) TomScudamore —
(M C Pipe) *mstke and uns rdr 2nd* **100/1**

FP21 **P** **Philson Run (IRE)**[21] 4111 10-11-5 **138** .... PCarberry —
(Nick Williams) *hld up: hit 18th: a in rr: bhd whn p.u bef 4 out* **7/1**[2]

1P55 **P** **Willie John Daly (IRE)**[7] 4374 9-10-8 **127** .... RichardJohnson —
(P J Hobbs) *hld up: rdn after 12th: bhd whn p.u bef 19th* **40/1**

P0F1 **P** **The Bajan Bandit (IRE)**[35] 3851 11-11-12 **145** ....(b) TonyDobbin —
(L Lungo) *prom: rdn and wkng whn j.lft 19th: p.u bef next* **18/1**

P020 **P** **Stormez (FR)**[42] 3727 9-11-8 **141** ....(t) RJGreene —
(M C Pipe) *sn pushed along in rr: mstkes: bhd whn j. slowly 17th: sn p.u* **50/1**

31F1 **P** **King Bee (IRE)**[23] 4070 9-10-2 **121** .... MarkBradburne —
(H D Daly) *prom: rdn 15th: lost pl and hit next: bhd whn p.u bef 19th* **7/1**[2]

P22P **P** **Brave Spirit (FR)**[21] 4111 8-10-2 **121** ....(bt[1]) JoeTizzard —
(C L Tizzard) *prom: hit 2nd: wknd after 16th: bhd whn p.u bef 18th* **25/1**

3331 **P** **Eskimo Pie (IRE)**[29] 3955 7-10-5 **124** ....(b) PJBrennan —
(C C Bealby) *prom: mstkes 15th and 17th: sn wknd: bhd whn p.u bef 19th* **12/1**

00P3 **P** **Marcus Du Berlais (FR)**[21] 4123 9-11-1 **134** ....(p) DJCasey —
(A L T Moore, Ire) *hld up: hdwy 16th: wknd 19th: bhd whn p.u bef 3 out* **10/1**

6-P4 **P** **Baron Windrush**[21] 4111 8-11-6 **139** .... CarlLlewellyn —
(N A Twiston-Davies) *hld up: hdwy 17th: wknd 4 out: bhd whn p.u bef 2 out* **11/1**

05P3 **P** **World Wide Web (IRE)**[34] 3877 10-10-1 **120** ....(p) RobertThornton —
(Jonjo O'Neill) *hld up: hdwy 10th: rdn 13th: wknd 16th: bhd whn p.u bef 19th* **20/1**

9m 30.6s **Going Correction** +1.00s/f (Soft) **18** Ran SP% **123.6**
Speed ratings: **112,111,107,106,102 101,101,—,—,— —,—,—,—,— —,—,—** CSF £45.57 CT £689.91 TOTE £6.30: £2.30, £3.10, £3.60, £5.10; EX 74.80 Trifecta £1910.70 wu.
Owner Exors of the late Donal O'Buachalla **Bred** Mrs Anne Kerr **Trained** Grange Con, Co Wicklow

FOCUS
A typically open renewal of this good staying handicap where despite the conditions it appeared best to race up with the pace. The first two both improved with the third a good way off her Welsh National mark.

NOTEBOOK
G V A Ireland(IRE) ◆, who handles most ground, had winning form on this sort of surface and was well supported to complete a good week for Irish-trained runners in this country. He was up with the pace from the start and galloped on resolutely to get the better of another dour stayer. He will head for the Irish National next and, as this was only his second run since Christmas, will go there a relatively fresh horse. *(op 4-1)*

Ossmoses(IRE) is a dour galloper and kept the winner company all the way. He was just worn down from the second last but lost little in defeat conceding 16lb. He may not run again this season, as the Scottish National is his only real option and the ground tends to be faster than he prefers, but he looks the sort for all the big long-distance handicaps next season. *(op 10-1 tchd 11-1)*

L'Aventure(FR), fourth in this last season and winner of the Welsh National this term, raced much closer to the pace than she usually does but could never land a blow in the last mile. She is not in the National this year, but it would be no surprise to see her take her chance in the Scottish National or Betfred Gold Cup next month. *(op 18-1)*

Victory Gunner(IRE) is a tough old stayer and a hard ride but went well until fading in the straight. It looked as though this trip stretched him and three miles five suits him better. *(op 20-1)*

Trust Fund(IRE), unlucky to fall when in front here last time, galloped on without getting into contention. He does seem to go well on this track but better ground and a shorter trip might suit him better.

Robbo was soon detached and merely galloped round in his own time. *(op 66-1)*

Control Man(IRE) raced prominently for much of the way but dropped away before the straight. He does not appear to get this trip in such testing ground. *(op 18-1)*

World Wide Web(IRE) *Official explanation: jockey said mare bled from nose (op 16-1)*

Marcus Du Berlais(FR), placed in two Irish Nationals, had the right credentials for this and should have handled the ground, but was in trouble some way from home. *(op 16-1)*

King Bee(IRE) showed up early but was trying a trip over a mile further than he had previously encountered and was well behind when pulled up. *(op 16-1)*

Philson Run(IRE), winner of this in 2005, seemed to travel well enough off the pace but did not pick up and was well behind when his rider drew stumps. It is possible that his hard race in the Eider on similar going had taken the edge off him. *(op 16-1)*

4497 TOTESCOOP6 H'CAP HURDLE (12 hdls) 2m 6f 110y

3:30 (3:30) (Class 2) (0-140,133) 4-Y-0+
£11,464 (£3,404; £1,702; £849; £425; £214)

Form RPR

452P **1** **Heir To Be**[28] 3993 7-10-8 **115** .... LeightonAspell 124+
(Mrs L Wadham) *a.p: rdn to chse wnr and hit 2 out: chalng whn hit last and lft clr* **14/1**

5466 **2** 9 **Pardon What**[27] 4012 10-9-11 **107** oh4 ....(b) StephenCraine(3) 106
(S Lycett) *hld up: hdwy appr 3 out: styd on flat* **25/1**

2232 **3** 1 **Just Beth**[28] 3987 10-10-10 **122** .... DerekLaverty(5) 121+
(G Fierro) *chsd ldrs: rdn 8th: styd on same pce fr 2 out* **9/1**

B-02 **4** 1 ½ **Victom's Chance (IRE)**[28] 3986 8-11-4 **128** .... WilliamKennedy(3) 125
(Noel T Chance) *hld up: mstke 5th: hdwy 9th: sn rdn: hung lft appr last: styd on same pce* **7/2**[2]

U545 **5** 2 ½ **Mythical King (IRE)**[21] 4102 9-11-5 **126** .... RichardJohnson 120
(R Lee) *hld up: hdwy appr 8th: outpcd bef 3 out: n.d after* **18/1**

P011 **6** *1 1/4* **Alright Now M'Lad (IRE)**[33] 3901 6-11-7 **128**........................ APMcCoy 121
(Jonjo O'Neill) *hld up: hdwy 6th: chsd ldr 8th: wknd 2 out* **11/4**[1]
40P0 **7** *14* **Always Waining (IRE)**[24] 4058 5-10-6 **113**........................ BarryFenton 92
(R M Stronge) *hld up: a in rr* **50/1**
0041 **8** *16* **Bak To Bill**[11] 4289 11-9-9 **109**........................ MissLGardner(7) 72
(Mrs S Gardner) *chsd ldrs tl wknd appr 3 out* **8/1**[3]
353U **P** **Mouseski**[8] 4357 12-10-8 **115**........................ RWalsh —
(P F Nicholls) *prom to 7th: bhd whn p.u bef 3 out* **9/1**
-300 **F** **Sunset Light (IRE)**[28] 3970 8-10-10 **117**........................ TomDoyle 124+
(C Tinkler) *led: rdn after 2 out: chal whn fell last: dead* **33/1**
-006 **P** **Monolith**[28] 3970 8-11-12 **133**........................ TonyDobbin —
(L Lungo) *hld up: hdwy 7th: wknd appr 9th: bhd whn p.u bef 3 out* **20/1**
/P00 **P** **Special Rate (IRE)**[42] 3727 9-11-2 **123**........................ RobertThornton —
(A King) *prom: riden 8th: wknd bef next: bhd whn p.u bef last* **12/1**
30-5 **P** **Chicago Bulls (IRE)**[21] 4119 8-10-11 **125**........................ MrGTumelty(7) —
(A King) *prom: mstke 5th: rdn and wknd 7th: bhd whn p.u bef 9th* **33/1**

5m 41.7s (-3.00) **Going Correction** +0.10s/f (Yiel) **13** Ran SP% **116.1**
Speed ratings: **109,105,105,105,104 103,98,93,—,— —,—,—** CSF £314.26 CT £3290.51 TOTE £13.30: £4.00, £7.90, £2.20; EX 341.50 Trifecta £652.30 wu.
Owner R B Holt **Bred** I Stewart-Brown And M Meacock **Trained** Newmarket, Suffolk

FOCUS
Just a fair staying handicap but run at a reasonable gallop although marred by the fatal fall of the leader at the last flight. The placed horses and the faller were close to their marks and the form looks pretty solid.

NOTEBOOK
Heir To Be ◆ had never encountered ground this testing over hurdles but did win over two miles on heavy on the Flat as a three-year-old. He proved well suited to the test and had drawn upsides and looked the most likely winner when the leader departed at the final flight, leaving him to come home without having been stretched. Presumably the Handicapper will not punish him too severley despite the official margin, and he could be capable of following up if he gets similar condtions next time. *(op 12-1)*
Pardon What has been struggling of late and his wins have been on a much less-testing surface, but he was running on well late and the fact that he was racing from 4lb out of the handicap will not aid his cause with the Handicapper.
Just Beth does not win very often, but usually runs her race and is the best guide to the level of the form but just lacks a change of gear. It may be worth trying her in cheekpieces as they have had a positive effect on a couple of mares that ran here earlier in the afternoon. *(op 10-1 tchd 17-2)*
Victom's Chance(IRE), runner-up to the progressive Dom D'Orgeval here last month in similar ground, was never travelling that well this time but did keep over the last couple of flights. He again hung left in the closing stages, but it is interesting that both his wins have been on right-handed tracks. *(op 11-4)*
Mythical King(IRE) has been racing in good company over fences of late and seemed happier back over hurdles. Still 6lb higher than for his last win 13 months ago, he could do with a drop in the handicap, but could be one to watch out for if contesting early-season staying handicaps on the Flat. *(op 20-1)*
Alright Now M'Lad(IRE), still a novice but successful in a handicap last time from a subsequent winner, was unsurprisingly made favourite despite being raised 11lb. However, like many of his stable companions of late, he ran a somewhat flat race. *(tchd 3-1)*
Bak To Bill, raised 9lb for his win at Exeter in similar ground, dropped out tamely having raced up with the pace. *(tchd 9-1 in places)*
Chicago Bulls(IRE) *Official explanation: trainer said gelding finished lame behind*
Special Rate(IRE) *Official explanation: trainer said mare was struck into*
Sunset Light(IRE) set off in front and looked to have stolen a decisive advantage early in the straight. However, he began to tire from the second-last flight and the winner had drawn alongside and looked to have his measure when he dived at the at the last hurdle and took a crashing, and sadly fatal, fall.

4498 TOTESPORT.COM NOVICES' H'CAP CHASE (18 fncs) 3m

4:00 (4:00) (Class 2) 5-Y-0+ **£12,610** (£3,896; £2,056; £1,134)

Form RPR
3412 **1** **Simon**[23] 4068 7-10-4 **114**........................ LeightonAspell 127+
(J L Spearing) *chsd ldrs: hit 10th: blnd 12th: sn outpcd: rallied appr last: led flat: drvn out* **14/1**
1F3P **2** *3* **Mount Clerigo (IRE)**[7] 4374 8-11-3 **127**........................ PJBrennan 134
(V R A Dartnall) *chsd ldrs: led 11th: hit next: rdn appr last: hung lft: wknd and hdd flat* **12/1**
2312 **3** *6* **Precious Bane (IRE)**[36] 3845 8-10-0 **110** oh2........................ RichardJohnson 114+
(M Sheppard) *led: hit 5th: hdd 11th: j.lft and hit 13th: sn rdn: styd on same pce fr 3 out* **9/2**[1]
33/0 **4** *12* **Lost Time (IRE)**[48] 3640 9-11-0 **124**........................ APMcCoy 117+
(C Roche, Ire) *hld up: hdwy 5 out: ev ch 2 out: wknd bef last* **11/2**[2]
F542 **P** **Rowley Hill**[63] 3394 8-10-0 **110** oh2........................ RobertThornton —
(A King) *mstkes: bhd and rdn 6th: p.u bef 10th* **7/1**
56P1 **P** **Lord Rodney (IRE)**[24] 4053 7-10-9 **119**........................ TomSiddall —
(P Beaumont) *prom: mstke 8th: hit 11th: sn wknd: bhd whn p.u bef 4 out* **9/1**
4112 **P** **Bob Bob Bobbin**[28] 3976 7-11-12 **136**........................ JoeTizzard —
(C L Tizzard) *chsd ldrs: hung lft fnl circ: wknd 4 out: p.u bef next* **9/2**[1]
2132 **F** **He's The Guv'Nor (IRE)**[28] 3988 7-10-10 **120**........................ BenjaminHitchcott 127+
(R H Buckler) *hld up: hdwy 7th: hit 4 out: ev ch whn fell 2 out* **6/1**[3]
F213 **P** **Lord Olympia (IRE)**[9] 4323 7-10-13 **126**........................ PaulO'Neill(3) —
(Miss Venetia Williams) *nt jump wl: reminders 5th: bhd and hit next: p.u after 10th* **10/1**

6m 50.8s (18.30) **Going Correction** +1.00s/f (Soft) **9** Ran SP% **112.0**
Speed ratings: **109,108,106,102,— —,—,—,—** CSF £154.46 CT £875.88 TOTE £18.00: £3.60, £3.90, £1.90; EX 183.60.
Owner Mrs Mercy Rimell **Bred** Mrs Mercy Rimell **Trained** Kinnersley, Worcs

FOCUS
A fair novices' handicap with a decent prize and reasonable line-up, but the conditions took their toll in the closing stages. The first three were close to their marks and the form looks solid.

NOTEBOOK
Simon, whose win at Wincanton was due to the misfortune of others, had been beaten over 33 lengths by the runner-up here earlier in the season and was only 13lb better off. However, this step up to three miles played to his strengths and, five lengths down at the second last, he really picked up and in the end scored going away. He looks a resolute stayer and should win more handicaps next season.
Mount Clerigo(IRE), unbeaten in three previous visits to the track, raced up with the pace from the start and looked to hold a decisive advantage going to the last. However, he began to tire and the winner came home much the better. It looks as if two miles six is his maximum trip at present. *(op 11-1)*
Precious Bane(IRE), a confirmed front-runner, set the pace again but was taken on for the lead by He's The Guv'nor and the runner-up. He looked beaten early in the straight but was keeping on again towards the finish. He has already proved he stays three miles six well and it would be no surprise to see him back at this meeting next year contesting the Midlands National.
Lost Time(IRE), an Irish raider, travelled well off the pace and moved into contention turning for home looking a big danger. However, he stopped very quickly going to the final fence as if he did not stay in the conditions. *(op 9-2)*
Bob Bob Bobbin raced up with the pace for over a circuit but was struggling when his rider called it a day. *(op 13-2)*
He's The Guv'Nor(IRE), a course and distance winner who ran very well in a valuable handicap here last month, over-pitched at several obstacles but moved into contention on the second circuit and was upsides the runner-up when coming down at the penultimate fence. He would certainly have been placed but whether he would have held the winner remains open to question. *(op 13-2)*

4499 ANTHONY FARMER MEMORIAL H'CAP CHASE (16 fncs) 2m 5f

4:30 (4:30) (Class 4) (0-105,104) 5-Y-0+
£4,384 (£1,295; £647; £324; £161; £81)

Form RPR
2R31 **1** **Young Lorcan**[8] 4348 10-11-5 **104**........................ RichardSpate(7) 113
(Mrs K Waldron) *hld up: hdwy to chse ldr and hit 11th: led after 5 out: rdn appr last: all out* **7/2**[2]
F00P **2** *hd* **Major Belle (FR)**[27] 4014 7-10-0 **78** oh2........................ HenryOliver 87
(John R Upson) *hld up in tch: hit 5th: outpcd 10th: mstke 4 out: rallied 2 out: hung lft flat: styd on wl* **20/1**
P4PP **3** *4* **Pardini (USA)**[5] 4428 7-10-1 **84**........................(v) CharliePoste(5) 90+
(M F Harris) *chsd ldr tl hit 2nd: rdn 10th: outpcd 12th: r.o flat* **10/1**
0F21 **4** *1 1/4* **Malko De Beaumont (FR)**[42] 3732 6-11-9 **101**........................ JohnMcNamara 110+
(K C Bailey) *hld up: hdwy 9th: hit 4 out: sn chsng wnr: blnd next: hit 2 out: wknd bef last* **11/8**[1]
132P **5** *11* **Lost In Normandy (IRE)**[36] 3845 9-11-0 **92**........................(b) DaveCrosse 85
(Mrs L Williamson) *chsd ldrs tl wknd appr 4 out* **7/1**[3]
P30U **6** *6* **Soroka (IRE)**[30] 3938 7-9-7 **78** oh22........................(b) CharlieStudd(7) 65
(C N Kellett) *sn wl bhd* **33/1**
261- **7** *2 1/2* **Native Eire (IRE)**[507] 1864 12-10-12 **90**........................ DNolan 74
(N Wilson) *hld up: hdwy 9th: jnd ldrs 5 out: wknd appr 2 out* **9/1**
-PP0 **8** *18* **Lantern Lad (IRE)**[30] 3938 10-10-0 **78** oh5........................(p) PJBrennan 44
(R Ford) *led and clr to 8th: hdd after 5 out: wkng whn blnd 3 out* **8/1**

6m 0.70s (33.20) **Going Correction** +1.00s/f (Soft) **8** Ran SP% **114.7**
Speed ratings: **76,75,74,73,69 67,66,59** CSF £60.16 CT £639.42 TOTE £4.60: £1.70, £4.20, £2.80; EX 78.50.
Owner Nick Shutts **Bred** Mrs Norma Dyer **Trained** Stoke Bliss, Worcs
■ Stewards' Enquiry : Henry Oliver caution: used whip without giving mare time to respond

FOCUS
A very moderate handicap run at a slow gallop with the placed horses close to their marks.

NOTEBOOK
Young Lorcan has been in fine form this season and gained his fourth win in eight starts in conditions that suit him well. He travelled nicely off the pace and after taking the lead at the last on the far side looked to have established a winning advantage two out. However, the runner-up was closing him down all the way to the line and he only just held on. At least he should not go up more than a pound or two for this as he is already 10lb higher than when scoring here in November. *(op 5-2)*
Major Belle(FR) had shown next to nothing since her debut over fences in this country 12 starts and 18 months ago. She was struggling mid-way down the back straight, but then started to run on in the straight and finished to such effect that she forced a photo-finish. Whether she will repeat this remains to be seen, but this was her first encounter with such testing ground over here and, as a winner on similar going in France, that appears to be what she needs.
Pardini(USA), another who appreciates the heavy ground, like the runner-up stayed on in the straight having been struggling, but not nearly to such good effect. *(op 9-1)*
Malko De Beaumont(FR), a course and distance winner on easy ground last time, took quite a keen hold under restraint and a combination of that and the softer ground appeared to find him out *in the closing stages. He is still a novice and remains open to further improvement.Official explanation: jockey said gelding lost his action after last (op 13-8 tchd 2-1)*
Lost In Normandy(IRE) raced up with the early pace but was in trouble as soon as the race began in earnest. *(op 6-1)*
Native Eire(IRE), having his first outing for 17 months, moved up to pose a threat early in the straight but then stopped quickly and probably blew up. *(op 12-1)*

4500 WEATHERBYS INSURANCE STANDARD OPEN NATIONAL HUNT FLAT RACE 2m

5:05 (5:05) (Class 6) 4-6-Y-0 **£1,626** (£477; £238; £119)

Form RPR
1 **Chaim (IRE)** 4-10-11........................ LeightonAspell 109+
(Mrs L Wadham) *hld up: hdwy over 5f out: led on bit over 2f out: rdn clr fnl f: eased nr fin* **25/1**
30 **2** *9* **Master Eddy**[14] 4244 6-11-4........................ AntonyEvans 101
(S Lycett) *prom: chsd ldr over 5f out: rdn and ev ch over 2f out: hung lft and wknd over 1f out* **12/1**
3 *1 1/2* **Natoumba (FR)** 5-10-11........................ MrPCallaghan(7) 100+
(H D Daly) *hld up: hdwy 5f out: outpcd over 3f out: styd on ins fnl f* **66/1**
4 *1 1/4* **Turnberry Bay (FR)** 5-11-4........................ TomScudamore 99
(M C Pipe) *chsd ldrs: rdn and ev ch over 2f out: wknd over 1f out* **14/1**
3 **5** *3 1/2* **Hopkins (IRE)**[51] 3583 5-11-4........................ RichardJohnson 95
(H D Daly) *hld up in tch: plld hrd: rdn and ev ch over 2f out: wknd over 1f out* **5/2**[2]
6 *1 3/4* **Jacksons Pier (IRE)**[153] 6-10-11........................ JohnKington(7) 94+
(M Scudamore) *led: rdn and hdd over 2f out: sn wknd* **25/1**
7 *1 3/4* **Obaki De Grissay (FR)** 4-10-11........................ MarkBradburne 85
(H D Daly) *hld up: pushed along 10f out: n.d* **33/1**
8 *6* **Go Johnny (IRE)** 6-11-4........................ JimCrowley 86
(V R A Dartnall) *prom: rdn over 6f out: wknd over 4f out* **8/1**[3]
9 *6* **The Entomologist (IRE)**[356] 5-11-4........................ APMcCoy 80
(C R Egerton) *hld up: hdwy 10f out: rdn and wknd over 2f out* **9/4**[1]
10 *23* **Perky Peaks (IRE)** 5-10-13........................ StevenCrawford(5) 57
(N A Twiston-Davies) *hld up: plld hrd: bhd fr 1/2-way* **16/1**
6R **11** *3 1/2* **The Shirley Hunt**[6] 4398 6-10-11........................ RobertThornton 46
(R T Phillips) *hld up: hdwy 9f out: wknd over 4f out* **33/1**
6 **12** *8* **Mister Moonax (IRE)**[27] 4011 6-11-4........................ OllieMcPhail 45
(M G Rimell) *prom: rdn and lost pl 11f out: sn bhd* **50/1**
0 **13** *2 1/2* **Fingersthumbsngums (IRE)**[23] 4072 5-11-4........................ AlanO'Keeffe 43
(Jennie Candlish) *chsd ldr over 10f: wknd over 3f out* **40/1**
14 *1 3/4* **Kevinsky Blue** 4-10-11........................ JohnMcNamara 34
(M J McGrath) *hld up: hdwy 10f out: wknd over 4f out* **50/1**
15 *27* **Nacho Des Uncheres (FR)** 5-10-13........................ TomGreenway(5) 14
(D G Bridgwater) *hld up: a in rr* **66/1**
3 **16** *16* **Devils And Dust (IRE)**[44] 3691 5-11-1........................ StephenCraine(3) —
(D McCain) *hld up: hdwy 1/2-way: wknd over 6f out* **12/1**
17 *3* **Rood Report** 6-11-4........................ PJBrennan —
(Andrew Turnell) *hld up: wknd 7f out* **50/1**

3m 59.1s (-0.70) **Going Correction** +0.10s/f (Yiel)
WFA 4 from 5yo 7lb 5 from 6yo 4lb **17** Ran SP% **123.3**
Speed ratings: **105,100,99,99,97 96,95,92,89,78 76,72,71,70,56 48,47** CSF £287.32 TOTE £37.30: £9.40, £2.70, £18.20; EX 454.90 Place 6 £1,437.01, Place 5 £472.44.
Owner Old Pals Partnership **Bred** Mrs Brid Doyle **Trained** Newmarket, Suffolk
■ Chaim completed a double for trainer Lucy Wadham and a treble for jockey Leighton Aspell.

FOCUS
An ordinary bumper but a most decisive winner who was value for 15 lengths and the second and fifth set the standard.
NOTEBOOK
Chaim(IRE) ◆, a half-brother to the chasers Over The Furze and Over The Glen, both of whom were suited by soft ground, settled off the pace in the early stages. He moved up at the end of the back straight travelling noticeably well and, once asked for an effort, came right away to score in good style. What he beat is open to question, but it was an impressive debut and he should have a future once tackling obstacles in due course. *(op 20-1)*
Master Eddy, well beaten in a hot-looking bumper on fast ground last time, had previously run well on his debut on a much softer surface. He was prominent all the way and stuck to his task despite having no chance with the winner. He should be up to winning races over hurdles.
Natoumba(FR) ◆, a half-brother to a chase winner in France, caught the eye staying on late in the day having looked to be struggling turning in. He fared best of the Daly trio despite being the least fancied on jockey bookings, and should come on a fair amount for the experience.
Turnberry Bay(FR), a half-brother to Royal Auclair and Canadiane amongst others, ran a fine race on this debut but, after coming through to challenge with the winner, faded in the closing stages. He can be expected to do better in time. *(op 16-1)*
Hopkins(IRE), a half-brother to Billyvoddan, did not really build on his debut performance but was *quite keen early on and that appeared to leave him with nothing in reserve for the closing stages. (op 9-4 tchd 11-4)*
Jacksons Pier(IRE), an Irish point winner on a sound surface, sensibly set the pace but a combination of the shorter trip and heavy ground left him unable to pick up at the business end. Connections will probably not waste much time before putting him over obstacles and stepping him up in trip.
Obaki De Grissay(FR), like his stable companion in third, was noted doing his best work at the finish. A half-brother to the chaser Jaquouille, he should improve with this under his belt.
Go Johnny(IRE), a half-brother to an Irish hurdles winner from the family of Blue Charm, was struggling from some way out on this racecourse debut. *(op 6-1)*
The Entomologist(IRE), who cost £90,000 as a four-year-old and is from the family of Cool Ground, had been an impressive winner of his sole Irish point. Sent off favourite, he seemed to find *the testing ground against him and could not pick up after being well placed turning for home. (op 2-1 tchd 5-2)*
T/Jkpt: Not won. T/Plt: £1,193.60 to a £1 stake. Pool: £134,082.20. 82.00 winning tickets. T/Qpdt: £127.20 to a £1 stake. Pool: £7,959.80. 46.30 winning tickets. CR

3736 WETHERBY (L-H)
Saturday, March 18

OFFICIAL GOING: Heavy
The ground was described as 'testing, very sticky'.
Wind: moderate 1/2 against Weather: fine but overcast and cold

4501 GUINNESS PADDOCK MARQUEE CONDITIONAL JOCKEYS' MAIDEN HURDLE (12 hdls) 3m 1f
2:15 (2:15) (Class 5) 4-Y-0+ **£3,083** (£898; £449)

Form RPR
1-3 **1** **Pontiff (IRE)**[56] 3496 6-11-1 RobertLucey-Butler(3) 101
(M Pitman) *trckd ldrs: chal 3 out: led next: hdd appr last: styd on to ld nr fin* **4/1**[2]
404 **2** *nk* **Hambaphambili**[76] 3184 6-11-1 OwynNelmes(3) 101
(O Sherwood) *j.rt: led: jnd 3 out: hdd next: led appr last: wknd and hdd nr fin* **14/1**
5364 **3** *1/2* **Geordie Peacock (IRE)**[30] 3941 7-11-1 105 LiamTreadwell(3) 100
(Miss Venetia Williams) *trckd ldrs: drvn and outpcd after 9th: hdwy between last 2: 5l down last: styd on strly fnl 75yds: fin wl* **13/2**[3]
-222 **4** *30* **Liathroidisneachta (IRE)**[19] 4149 6-11-4 115 ShaneWalsh 75+
(Jonjo O'Neill) *trckd ldrs: rdn appr 3 out: hung lft and sn btn: fin tired* **8/13**[1]
5264 **5** *23* **Hidden Storm (IRE)**[20] 4133 7-10-6 72 (b) AndrewGlassonbury(5) 40
(Mrs S J Humphrey) *chsd ldrs: rdn along 9th: sn lost pl and bhd* **25/1**
P **P** **Curate (USA)**[29] 3962 7-11-4 BrianHughes —
(M E Sowersby) *hld up in rr: wknd after 6th: bhd whn blnd 8th: sn p.u* **100/1**
00- **P** **Eileens Comet**[342] 4788 6-10-11 TJDreaper —
(M E Sowersby) *hld up in rr: wkng whn hit 6th: t.o whn p.u bef next* **100/1**
PPP/ **P** **Breezy Warrior (IRE)**[307] 7-10-13 MichaelO'Connell(5) —
(J M Saville) *t.k.h: sn trcking ldrs: lost pl after 8th: bhd whn p.u bef next* **40/1**
6m 39.2s (24.70) **Going Correction** +0.575s/f (Soft) 8 Ran SP% **110.2**
Speed ratings: **83,82,82,73,65** —,—,— CSF £44.38 TOTE £4.20: £1.10, £2.90, £2.10; EX 43.60.
Owner Malcolm C Denmark **Bred** J R Weston **Trained** Upper Lambourn, Berks
FOCUS
A very steady gallop resulting in a very slow winning time, even allowing for the ground. The form is doubtful and has been rated through the third.
NOTEBOOK
Pontiff(IRE), a different proposition this time, went on but looked booked for second spot at the last. With the leader tying up, he snatched the prize near the line. He should make an even better chaser next time round.
Hambaphambili continually gave away ground jumping to his right. He looked nailed on and was matched at 1.01 at the final flight, but he became very leg-weary indeed on the run-in and just failed to last home.
Geordie Peacock(IRE), tapped for toe starting the final turn, made ground hand over fist on the run-in and would have made it with a bit further to go. *(op 6-1 tchd 7-1)*
Liathroidisneachta(IRE) suddenly came under pressure on the long run round to three out. He wanted to do nothing but hang into the rail and in the end struggled to get across the finishing line. *He was later found to be lame. Official explanation: vet said gelding returned lame (tchd 4-6 in places)*

4502 CONSTANT SECURITY SERVICES NOVICES' CHASE (12 fncs) 2m
2:50 (2:51) (Class 3) 5-Y-0+ **£9,429** (£2,809; £1,422; £729; £381)

Form RPR
1555 **1** **Another Native (IRE)**[28] 3973 8-11-12 112 DaveCrosse 127
(C J Mann) *trckd ldng pair gng wl: jnd issue 6th: led on bit after 4 out: rdn clr run-in* **7/2**[3]
0431 **2** *16* **Mr Prickle (IRE)**[32] 3915 6-11-8 104 RussGarritty 107
(P Beaumont) *trckd ldr: led appr 4 out: sn hdd: wknd appr last: tired bdly run-in* **10/3**[2]
6605 **3** *1 3/4* **Salhood**[8] 4355 7-11-2 109 MarcusFoley 99
(S Gollings) *trckd ldrs: outpcd 4th: hit 7th: blnd next: kpt on to take modest 3rd sn after last* **12/1**
4425 **4** *2* **Dance Party (IRE)**[19] 4142 6-10-6 95 MrTGreenall(3) 90
(M W Easterby) *in rr fr 4th: kpt on fr 4 out: tk modest 4th run-in* **9/1**
1431 **5** *19* **The Local**[18] 4162 6-11-8 120 (p) AndrewTinkler 93+
(C R Egerton) *led: hdd appr 4 out: wknd next: lost modest 3rd sn after last: fin v tired* **1/1**[1]
P60 **P** **The Associate (IRE)**[63] 3380 9-10-13 PeterBuchanan(3) —
(Miss Lucinda V Russell) *in rr fr 4th: t.o 4 out: p.u bef 2 out* **50/1**
4m 13.5s (6.90) **Going Correction** +0.575s/f (Soft) 6 Ran SP% **115.0**
Speed ratings: **105,97,96,95,85** — CSF £16.28 TOTE £4.20: £2.00, £1.80; EX 17.10.
Owner The Sport of Kings Partnership **Bred** Mrs Brid McCrea **Trained** Upper Lambourn, Berks
FOCUS
A strong pace and the winner's stamina was a factor in his wide-margin success. The form looks solid enough.
NOTEBOOK
Another Native(IRE) travelled supremely well and came right away on the run-in. If there is give underfoot he may head for the Topham at Aintree. His rating will shoot up however as a result of this wide margin success. *(op 4-1 tchd 9-2 and 10-3)*
Mr Prickle(IRE) harried the leader. He went on turning in but was legless on the run-in. *(op 5-1)*
Salhood looked to sulk slightly not being in front. After two mistakes he kept on and would have snatched second spot with a bit further to go. *(op 16-1)*
Dance Party(IRE) was rather let down by her jumping and, keeping on in her own time over the last four, she is rather flattered by this. *(tchd 8-1)*
The Local did not enjoy an uncontested lead and after being headed looked exhausted. *Connections blamed the holding underfoot conditions.Official explanation: trainer's rep said gelding was unable to pick up off the holding ground (op 4-5 tchd 11-10, 5-4 in places)*

4503 IAN HUTCHINSON MEMORIAL CHALLENGE CUP (A H'CAP HURDLE) (9 hdls) 2m
3:20 (3:20) (Class 4) (0-115,110) 4-Y-0+ **£5,204** (£1,528; £764; £381)

Form RPR
4111 **1** **Polar Gunner**[25] 4045 9-11-7 110 TJDreaper(5) 120+
(J M Jefferson) *trckd ldng pair: led on bit appr 3 out: hit 2 out: drvn and styd on run-in* **8/11**[1]
020P **2** *4* **Haditovski**[28] 3990 10-11-0 101 (v) PeterBuchanan(3) 106
(J Mackie) *w ldr: kpt on fr 2 out: no real imp* **8/1**[3]
F3U1 **3** *9* **Merryvale Man**[10] 4302 9-10-12 101 BrianHughes(5) 98+
(Miss Kariana Key) *led: rdn and hdd appr 3 out: wknd fr next* **10/1**
433 **4** *5* **Cruise Director**[30] 3948 6-11-5 103 WayneHutchinson 94
(Ian Williams) *t.k.h: trckd ldrs: effrt appr 3 out: sn btn* **3/1**[2]
-005 **5** *dist* **Fair Spin**[42] 3737 6-11-5 103 (v) BarryKeniry —
(M D Hammond) *j. violently rt: wl in tch in last: reminders after 3rd: lost pl 5th: nrly rn off trck next: t.o: btn total of 94l* **20/1**
4m 5.90s (6.50) **Going Correction** +0.575s/f (Soft) 5 Ran SP% **107.9**
Speed ratings: **106,104,99,97**,— CSF £6.56 TOTE £1.40: £1.40, £3.10; EX 8.40.
Owner Mrs M E Dixon **Bred** Mrs P Nicholson **Trained** Norton, N Yorks
■ Stewards' Enquiry : Brian Hughes three-day ban: used whip with excessive frequency (Mar 29-31)
FOCUS
A sound gallop despite the small field and a ready winner. The form has a solid look about it.
NOTEBOOK
Polar Gunner, still lower rated over hurdles than fences, loves soft ground and travelled easily best but in the end he had to be kept right up to his work. *(op 4-5)*
Haditovski, who has not won for over two years, deserves credit for the way he stuck to his task but in truth he was never going to finish anything but second best. *(op 9-1 tchd 10-1)*
Merryvale Man, 6lb higher, had his own way in front but the winner went past him still on the bridle and despite his rider's encouragement, he had nothing left to give.
Cruise Director, on his handicap bow, would not settle and gave himself no chance of lasting home in this ground. *(op 5-2 tchd 7-2 in a place)*
Fair Spin jumped violently right and was well in arrears when almost running off the track four out. After this he has a lot to prove.

4504 GUY SALMON LANDROVER LEEDS H'CAP HURDLE (10 hdls) 2m 4f 110y
3:55 (3:55) (Class 3) (0-130,122) 4-Y-0+ **£7,605** (£2,246; £1,123; £561; £280)

Form RPR
2152 **1** **Aston Lad**[7] 4364 5-11-5 115 BarryKeniry 118+
(M D Hammond) *hld up: wnt prom 5th: wnt cl 2nd 3 out: led appr last: drvn out* **3/1**[1]
P010 **2** *1 1/2* **Supreme Leisure (IRE)**[24] 4058 9-11-1 116 BrianHughes(5) 117+
(J Howard Johnson) *trckd ldrs: jnd issue 5th: led appr 3 out: hdd and blnd last: kpt on wl* **10/1**
0011 **3** *10* **Danse Macabre (IRE)**[8] 4354 7-10-8 111 WillieMcCarthy(7) 101
(A W Carroll) *hld up in rr: hdwy appr 3 out: wnt modest 3rd last: nvr a real threat* **10/3**[2]
1210 **4** *5* **Amanpuri (GER)**[8] 4357 8-10-12 108 WayneHutchinson 94+
(Mrs A M Thorpe) *trckd ldrs: led 7th: hdd appr next: wknd 2 out* **6/1**
4P56 **5** *12* **Cill Churnain (IRE)**[29] 3966 13-10-9 115 MichaelO'Connell(10) 88
(Mrs S J Smith) *w ldr: slt ld 4th: hdd 7th: lost pl appr next* **25/1**
24P3 **6** *dist* **Kentucky Blue (IRE)**[52] 3561 6-11-10 120 RussGarritty —
(T D Easterby) *wnt prom 5th: wknd appr 3 out: bhd whn eased run-in: t.o: btn total of 68l* **8/1**
122P **P** **Wild Is The Wind (FR)**[28] 3970 5-11-7 122 (p) ShaneWalsh(5) —
(Jonjo O'Neill) *in rr: drvn along after 4th: sn lost tch: t.o whn p.u bef 7th* **5/1**[3]
3F0P **P** **Halexy (FR)**[21] 4118 11-11-5 115 (b[1]) MarcusFoley —
(Jonjo O'Neill) *led: racd w hd high: hdd 4th: lost pl after 7th: bhd whn blnd next: sn p.u* **10/1**
5m 17.2s (8.30) **Going Correction** +0.575s/f (Soft) 8 Ran SP% **112.2**
Speed ratings: **107,106,102,100,96** —,—,— CSF £30.74 CT £103.11 TOTE £3.30: £1.50, £3.60, £1.60; EX 36.60.
Owner S T Brankin **Bred** Micky Hammond Racing Ltd And S Branklin **Trained** Middleham, N Yorks
■ Stewards' Enquiry : Brian Hughes three-day ban: used whip with excessive frequency (Apr 1-2, 20)
FOCUS
A fair handicap and the winner is progressing nicely. The pace was sound and through the runner-up the form has a sound look about it.
NOTEBOOK
Aston Lad made this look very straightforward. His trainer is tempted to give him another season over hurdles after this. *(op 7-2)*
Supreme Leisure(IRE), 5lb higher than for his win here in January, was just getting the worst of the argument when he clattered through the last. His rider did not spare the stick and to his credit he stuck on in game fashion all the way to the line. *(op 17-2 tchd 14-1)*
Danse Macabre(IRE), 9lb higher, was quite happy to sit off the pace. He was given plenty to do *and never threatened to get near the first two. He might just be happier going right-handed. (op 11-4)*
Amanpuri(GER), back in trip, went on travelling comfortably but he fell in a heap two out. He is 6lb higher than for his two wins. *(op 7-1)*
Cill Churnain(IRE) basically continues out of sorts. *(op 20-1)*

Kentucky Blue(IRE) stopped too far out for stamina to be an issue at that point. *(op 7-1 tchd 9-1)*

4505 ROCOM H'CAP CHASE (18 fncs) 3m 1f

4:25 (4:25) (Class 3) (0-135,128) 5-Y-0+

£12,526 (£3,700; £1,850; £926; £462; £232)

Form RPR

5216 **1** **Kerry Lads (IRE)**[21] 4111 11-11-9 **128**........................(p) PeterBuchanan(3) 139+
(Miss Lucinda V Russell) *led to 5th: led 8th to 11th: led after 14th: j.lft last: hld on gamely* **7/1**

5003 **2** *3/4* **Wildfield Rufo (IRE)**[68] 3315 11-9-13 **108**........................(p) ColmSharkey(7) 117+
(Mrs K Walton) *hdwy to chse ldrs 9th: led 11th tl after 14th: hit 2 out: styd on wl towards fin* **12/1**

F161 **3** *1/2* **King Killone (IRE)**[21] 4112 6-11-9 **125**........................ DavidO'Meara 133
(H P Hogarth) *wnt prom 6th: effrt 13th: outpcd 4 out: styd on wl appr last: styd on strly towards fin* **4/1**[1]

0-31 **4** *3 1/2* **Red Striker**[19] 4146 12-10-7 **116**........................ MissTJackson(7) 123+
(Miss T Jackson) *mstke 5th: jnd ldrs 8th: blnd 14th: one pce fr 2 out* **25/1**

1124 **5** *27* **Sharp Belline (IRE)**[63] 3396 9-10-9 **111**........................ DominicElsworth 88
(Mrs S J Smith) *w ldrs: led 5th to 8th: lost pl 13th: n.d after* **9/2**[2]

2321 **6** *3 1/2* **Great As Gold (IRE)**[9] 4314 7-10-13 **115**........................(v[1]) WilsonRenwick 89
(B Ellison) *wnt prom 6th: lost pl appr 4 out: j. bdly rt 3 out* **11/2**[3]

2420 **7** *5* **Miss Mattie Ross**[21] 4111 10-10-3 **110**........................ MichaelMcAlister(5) 79
(S J Marshall) *chsd ldrs: drvn along 6th: lost pl after 12th: sn bhd* **14/1**

16P3 **F** **Kausse De Thaix (FR)**[21] 4103 8-10-7 **112**........................(b[1]) OwynNelmes(3) —
(O Sherwood) *trckd ldrs: fell 4th* **11/2**[3]

2615 **P** **Jungle Jinks (IRE)**[23] 4070 11-10-11 **113**........................ BarryKeniry —
(G M Moore) *chsd ldrs: reminders 3rd: outpcd 9th: lost pl 12th: t.o 14th: p.u bef 2 out* **6/1**

6m 42.4s (2.40) **Going Correction** +0.575s/f (Soft) **9 Ran SP% 113.9**

Speed ratings: **111,110,110,109,100 99,98,—,—** CSF £81.67 CT £380.38 TOTE £8.00: £2.10, £3.90, £2.00; EX 67.60.

Owner Mrs C G Greig **Bred** S O'Donoghue **Trained** Arlary, Perth & Kinross

FOCUS

A fair handicap and a true test in the conditions, rated around the first two.

NOTEBOOK

Kerry Lads(IRE), happy to force the pace, really put his head down and battled but in the end there was nothing at all to spare. He will now have his sights set on a fourth crack at the Scottish National. *(op 8-1 tchd 7-1 in places)*

Wildfield Rufo(IRE) took this a year ago from a 3lb lower mark. Absent for over two months, he would not give in and was closing the gap at the line. *(op 11-1)*

King Killone(IRE), on his handicap bow, was tapped for toe six out. He stayed on in really determined fashion going to the last and with him the stiffer the track the better.

Red Striker ran out of his skin but sadly collapsed and died on the walk back to the unsaddling area. *(tchd 33-1)*

Sharp Belline(IRE), absent since January, looked very ring rusty. *(op 4-1)*

Great As Gold(IRE), tried in a visor this time, was out of contention when jumping badly right three out. He has started life in handicap company from a stiffish sort of mark. *(op 5-1 tchd 13-2)*

4506 PARKINSON'S DISEASE SOCIETY (LEEDS) - KELLY & CO JUVENILE NOVICES' HURDLE (9 hdls) 2m

5:00 (5:00) (Class 4) 4-Y-0 **£5,204** (£1,528; £764; £381)

Form RPR

43 **1** **Olival (FR)**[6] 4389 4-10-7........................ ShaneWalsh(5) 93+
(Jonjo O'Neill) *trckd ldrs: led appr 3 out: styd on run-in* **7/2**[3]

2635 **2** *2 1/2* **Orang Outan (FR)**[19] 4141 4-10-9 108........................(t) GaryBerridge(3) 89
(J P L Ewart) *in tch: jnd ldrs 4th: chal 3 out: kpt on same pce run-in* **11/4**[2]

55R **3** *1 3/4* **Oscar D'Hyrome (FR)**[9] 4313 4-10-9 101........................ MrTGreenall(3) 87
(C Grant) *led 3rd tl appr 3 out: sn outpcd: styd on wl run-in* **12/1**

65 **4** *3 1/2* **In Dream's (IRE)**[25] 4039 4-10-12........................(t) DominicElsworth 85+
(M A Barnes) *wnt prom 4th: one pce fr 3 out* **16/1**

0F35 **5** *6* **David's Symphony (IRE)**[21] 4104 4-10-12 94........................ WayneHutchinson 78
(A W Carroll) *chsd ldrs: drvn along 4th: sn outpcd: kpt on fr 2 out* **8/1**

P554 **6** *1 1/4* **Dock Tower (IRE)**[24] 4057 4-10-9 104........................(t) PeterBuchanan(3) 81+
(M E Sowersby) *chsd ldrs: outpcd appr 3 out: 4th and wl btn whn hit last* **2/1**[1]

05 **7** *17* **William Tell (IRE)**[12] 3787 4-10-12........................ BarryKeniry 60
(M D Hammond) *chsd ldrs to 5th: wknd next* **14/1**

00U **8** *3* **Sales Flow**[6] 4388 4-10-5........................ WilsonRenwick 50
(M W Easterby) *a in rr: bhd fr 6th* **50/1**

PP0 **P** **Time To Succeed**[20] 4128 4-10-5........................ WillieMcCarthy(7) —
(Mrs A M Thorpe) *led to 3rd: reminders 5th: sn lost pl: t.o whn p.u bef 3 out* **100/1**

4m 9.70s (10.30) **Going Correction** +0.575s/f (Soft) **9 Ran SP% 116.5**

Speed ratings: **97,95,94,93,90 89,81,79,—** CSF £14.10 TOTE £3.80: £1.40, £1.50, £2.80; EX 15.10.

Owner John P McManus **Bred** Y Madiot **Trained** Cheltenham, Gloucs

FOCUS

A modest event run at just a steady pace and rated through the runner-up. The race took little winning but the winner is progressing at a rate of knots.

NOTEBOOK

Olival(FR), making a quick return, went on and despite his rider looking untidy he really knuckled down and in the end won going away. *(op 10-3 tchd 4-1, 5-1 in places)*

Orang Outan(FR), back in trip, threw down the gauntlet three out but in the end was very much second best. *(op 5-1)*

Oscar D'Hyrome(FR), who gave no problems at the start this time, stayed on strongly on the run-in after being left behind three out. *(op 10-1)*

In Dream's(IRE), handicpped by a slipping saddle last time, shaped nicely and was by no means knocked about. He is at least now qualified for a handicap mark. *(op 14-1 tchd 18-1)*

David's Symphony(IRE) is starting to look fully exposed. *(op 7-1)*

Dock Tower(IRE), tending to run in snatches, was well held when flattening the last. He looks anything but straightforward. *(op 7-4 tchd 9-4, 5-2 in places)*

4507 WETHERBY RACES FAMILY SUNDAY 30TH APRIL STANDARD OPEN NATIONAL HUNT FLAT RACE 2m

5:30 (5:31) (Class 5) 4-6-Y-0 **£2,398** (£698; £349)

Form RPR

1 **Scribano Eile (IRE)**[126] 5-10-11........................ MarcGoldstein(7) 120+
(N A Twiston-Davies) *mde all: styd on fnl 3f: jst hld on* **8/1**[3]

2 *1/2* **Tidal Bay (IRE)** 5-11-1........................ MichalKohl(3) 117
(J I A Charlton) *mid-div: hdwy to trck ldrs 6f out: wnt 2nd 2f out: hung lft: styd on wl towards fin* **40/1**

1 **3** *13* **Barton Belle**[72] 3259 4-10-8........................ DougieCostello(3) 97
(G A Swinbank) *trckd ldrs: wnt 2nd 4f out: one pce fnl 2f* **7/4**[1]

46 **4** *5* **Aldea (FR)**[68] 3319 5-11-4........................ DominicElsworth 99
(Mrs S J Smith) *trckd ldrs: one pce fnl 3f* **14/1**

5 *1 1/4* **Ever So Slightly (IRE)** 5-10-8........................ MichaelO'Connell(10) 98
(Mrs S J Smith) *prom: wl outpcd and lost pl 6f out: styd on wl fnl 2f* **25/1**

1 **6** *6* **Spitfire Sortie (IRE)**[68] 3319 5-11-8........................ MrTGreenall(3) 99
(M W Easterby) *rr div: pushed along and hdwy 7f out: wknd 3f out* **2/1**[2]

14 **7** *10* **Wolds Way**[23] 4072 4-11-4........................ RussGarritty 82
(T D Easterby) *chsd ldrs: wknd over 2f out* **12/1**

8 *8* **Dr Hellier (IRE)** 6-10-11........................ ColmSharkey(7) 74
(J R Turner) *trckd ldrs: hung rt and wknd over 2f out: eased* **80/1**

9 *11* **Panama At Once** 6-11-4........................ BarryKeniry 63
(J M Saville) *in rr: sme hdwy 6f out: lost pl over 3f out* **100/1**

10 *12* **Ellerslie Jackie** 6-10-8........................ LeeVickers(3) 44
(O Brennan) *a in rr: bhd fnl 6f* **40/1**

11 *10* **Pencil House (IRE)** 6-11-4........................ JamieMoore 41
(M G Rimell) *mid-div: hdwy 8f out: sn rdn and lost pl: t.o 5f out* **12/1**

20-5 **12** *3/4* **Kerrs Whin**[93] 2844 6-11-4........................ LarryMcGrath 40
(P G Atkinson) *mid-div: drvn along 8f out: sn lost pl: t.o 5f out* **25/1**

13 *5* **Monica Rose** 5-10-11........................ WilsonRenwick 28
(K G Reveley) *prom: lost pl 6f out: sn bhd* **25/1**

60 **14** *9* **Falcon's Cliche**[24] 4059 5-10-8........................ GaryBerridge(3) 19
(P Beaumont) *prom: lost pl 6f out: sn bhd* **80/1**

3m 57.8s (-6.60) **Going Correction** +0.575s/f (Soft)

WFA 4 from 5yo+ 7lb **14 Ran SP% 122.7**

Speed ratings: **112,111,105,102,102 99,94,90,84,78 73,73,70,66** CSF £302.78 TOTE £8.70: £2.20, £9.90, £1.40; EX 199.50 Place 6 £82.81, Place 5 £32.18.

Owner H R Mould **Bred** Mrs Brid Doyle **Trained** Naunton, Gloucs

FOCUS

A very smart winning time indeed when compared with the two hurdle races over the same trip. The first two look decent and the fourth sets the standard.

NOTEBOOK

Scribano Eile(IRE), related to the Gold Cup winner Bregawn, won a point in Ireland in April. He set a strong pace and in the end did just enough. He looks essentially a stayer. *(op 9-1 tchd 15-2)*

Tidal Bay(IRE) ◆, a strong, chasing-type, went in pursuit of the winner. Both his own and his rider's inexperience showed and he was closing the gap at the line. He looked the best horse on the day and deserves to go one better.

Barton Belle went in pursuit of the winner once in line for home but under her penalty could never find enough to seriously threaten. *(tchd 2-1, 9-4 in places)*

Aldea(FR), a tall individual, he may need more time before he is ready to prove his true worth over hurdles. *(op 12-1)*

Ever So Slightly(IRE), badly outpaced, stayed on grimly and looks to have a lot more stamina than speed.

Spitfire Sortie(IRE) ran very flat and never really travelled. *Official explanation: jockey said gelding never travelled (op 9-4)*

T/Plt: £102.80 to a £1 stake. Pool: £45,062.90. 319.85 winning tickets. T/Qpdt: £13.00 to a £1 stake. Pool: £2,611.90. 147.60 winning tickets. WG

4508 - 4514a (Foreign Racing) - See Raceform Interactive

4313

CARLISLE (R-H)

Sunday, March 19

OFFICIAL GOING: Soft (heavy in places)

The meeting had to survive an inspection the previous day after being waterlogged after heavy rain on Tuesday and conditions were very testing.

Wind: Light, half-behind Weather: Overcast and cold, light rain last two races.

4515 NEWS AND STAR NOVICES' H'CAP HURDLE (10 hdls 2 omitted) 3m 1f

2:00 (2:00) (Class 4) (0-105,105) 4-Y-0+ **£3,083** (£898; £449)

Form RPR

-23P **1** **Blackergreen**[11] 4300 7-11-1 **94**........................ DavidO'Meara 110+
(Mrs S J Smith) *trckd ldr: led appr 3 out: clr whn hit last* **5/2**[1]

5P5P **2** *15* **What'sonyourmind (IRE)**[13] 4282 6-10-11 **90**........................ APMcCoy 92+
(Jonjo O'Neill) *wnt mod 3rd 5th: wnt 2nd 3 out: kpt on same pce: no threat to wnr* **7/2**[3]

0UPP **3** *18* **Em's Royalty**[39] 3794 9-11-5 **105**........................ PhilKinsella(7) 87
(A Parker) *outpcd and lost pl 6th: t.o 3 out: styd on to take remote 3rd run-in* **16/1**

F432 **4** *10* **Roschal (IRE)**[8] 4362 8-11-2 **95**........................(p) RichardJohnson 67
(Miss Lucinda V Russell) *led tl appr 3 out: hung rt and wknd qckly between last 2* **3/1**[2]

-505 **5** *1 1/4* **Master Of The Ward (IRE)**[37] 3846 6-10-4 **86**........................ StephenCraine(3) 57
(D McCain) *hdwy 7th: sn chsng ldrs: rdn and wknd 3 out* **5/1**

P0P3 **P** **Times Up Barney**[29] 3975 6-11-2 **95**........................ JosephByrne —
(C W Moore) *rdn and lost pl 6th: t.o whn p.u bef 3 out* **9/1**

6m 38.2s **6 Ran SP% 108.3**

CSF £10.93 TOTE £3.20: £1.60, £1.80; EX 16.80.

Owner P England **Bred** Miss Leona Robertson **Trained** High Eldwick, W Yorks

FOCUS

A poor race run at a steady pace to halfway but the first two were close to previous marks and the form looks believable. Flight going away from the stands omitted.

NOTEBOOK

Blackergreen, back over hurdles, made the most of an easy opportunity. *(op 3-1)*

What'sonyourmind(IRE) was making hard work of it once sent in pursuit of the winner. He looked to be saving a bit for himself and never threatened to close the gap. *(op 11-4)*

Em's Royalty, a big type, struggled hopelessly to keep up. Remote at the at the foot of the final hill, he kept on to take a distant third place on the extended run-in *(op 14-1)*

Roschal(IRE), 4lb higher, took them along in his own time. Considering he was dropping back in trip, it was worrying the way he folded completely between the last two. *(op 5-2)*

Master Of The Ward(IRE) stopped to nothing at the third last flight. *(op 7-1)*

4516 VIACOM OUTDOOR BEGINNERS' CHASE (14 fncs 2 omitted) 2m 4f

2:35 (2:35) (Class 4) 5-Y-0+ **£5,204** (£1,528; £764; £381)

Form RPR

3-13 **1** **On Y Va (FR)**[25] 4054 8-11-2 114........................(t) RichardJohnson 114+
(R T Phillips) *hld up in tch: wnt 2nd 2 out: styd on u.p to ld last 150yds* **15/8**[1]

423P **2** *3/4* **Trisons Star (IRE)**[20] 4144 8-10-11 106........................ DesFlavin(5) 112
(Mrs L B Normile) *sn chsng ldr: led 8th: hdd and no ex last 150yds* **15/8**[1]

2R4P **3** *15* **Iris's Prince**[83] 2976 7-11-2 105........................ DavidO'Meara 100+
(A Crook) *chsd ldrs: wnt 2nd 9th: wknd 2 out* **9/1**[3]

2-P3 **4** *14* **Sports Express**[10] 4314 8-10-9 95........................(p) JimmyMcCarthy 76
(Miss Lucinda V Russell) *led to 8th: wknd after 4 out* **7/2**[2]

The Form Book, Raceform Ltd, Compton, RG20 6NL

P Aristocratic Yank (IRE)[70] 7-10-13 ....(p) LeeVickers(3) —
(S G Chadwick) *nt jump wl: lost pl 3rd: sn t.o: p.u bef 8th* **20/1**

5m 30.8s (10.90) **Going Correction** +0.725s/f (Soft) 5 Ran SP% **106.5**
Speed ratings: **107,106,100,95,—** CSF £5.54 TOTE £2.20: £1.10, £1.70; EX 5.20.
Owner ROA Red Alligator Partnership **Bred** M Van De Kerchove And Herve Bezobry **Trained** Adlestrop, Gloucs

FOCUS
A modest beginners' chas run at a sound gallop, but a close call in the end and rated through the runner-up to his best chase form. The two fences going away from the stands were omitted.

NOTEBOOK
On Y Va(FR) took an age to gain the upper hand and there was precious little to spare at the line. Three miles and less-testing ground may see him in a more favourable light. *(op 5-4 tchd 6-5 and 2-1)*
Trisons Star(IRE), pulled up last time, bounced back and went down fighting. He deserves to go one better. *(op 9-4 tchd 5-2)*
Iris's Prince, pulled up on his most recent start, is a big type. He tired badly over the last two fences and does not appreciate conditions as testing as he encountered here. *(op 10-1 tchd 12-1)*
Sports Express, well backed, took them along at a sound gallop but he stopped to nothing at the foot of the final hill. *(op 4-1 tchd 3-1)*

4517 DOBIES H'CAP HURDLE (10 hdls 1 omitted) 2m 4f
3:10 (3:10) (Class 4) (0-110,105) 4-Y-0+ **£3,083** (£898; £449)

Form				RPR
3622	1		**Imtihan (IRE)**[36] [3854] 7-11-2 **95** .... DominicElsworth *(Mrs S J Smith) chsd ldrs: wnt 2nd 6th: slt ld 2 out: hld on towards fin* **5/4**[1]	101+
00P2	2	½	**Roobihoo (IRE)**[10] [4317] 7-11-12 **105** ....(t) AnthonyRoss *(C Grant) chsd ldrs: led appr 3 out: hdd 2 out: kpt on gamely: no ex towards fin* **9/4**[2]	109
0305	3	21	**Armentieres**[11] [4299] 5-10-0 **89** ....(v) StevenGagan(10) *(Mrs E Slack) led tl appr 3 out: sn lost pl* **8/1**[3]	72
-0PP	4	5	**Lady Past Times**[22] [4113] 6-9-7 **79** oh1 .... PatrickMcDonald(7) *(D W Whillans) shkn up 2nd: reminders 5th: wnt mod 4th 3 out: nvr a threat* **14/1**	57
P3U0	5	dist	**Harry Hooly**[26] [4043] 11-10-12 **94** .... LeeVickers(3) *(Mrs H O Graham) chsd ldrs: lost pl 7th: sn bhd: t.o: btn total 66l* **10/1**	—
1F00	6	25	**Peter's Imp (IRE)**[39] [3797] 11-11-0 **93** .... LarryMcGrath *(A Berry) in rr: sme hdwy 6th: lost pl next: t.o whn blnd 2 out* **33/1**	—
0P0P	P		**Open Range (IRE)**[31] [3950] 6-11-7 **100** ....(p) AlanO'Keeffe *(Jennie Candlish) t.k.h: trckd ldrs: hit 5th: lost pl after 6th: bhd whn p.u bef 3 out* **50/1**	—

5m 24.9s (7.80) **Going Correction** +0.625s/f (Soft) 7 Ran SP% **107.0**
Speed ratings: **109,108,100,98,— —,—** CSF £3.95 CT £9.96 TOTE £2.20: £1.30, £1.90; EX 3.50.
Owner Keith Nicholson **Bred** Shadwell Estate Company Limited **Trained** High Eldwick, W Yorks

FOCUS
A sound gallop and a true test in the conditions. It was nip and tuck all the way to the line and the runner-up sets the standard, although the winner is capable of better on his old form. Flight going away from the stands omitted.

NOTEBOOK
Imtihan(IRE), whose last success two years ago came from a stone higher mark, had to battle hard but he never flinched. The pair will rise in the ratings as a result. *(op 6-4)*
Roobihoo(IRE), 4lb higher, again had his tongue tied down. He went down fighting and deserves credit for this but will most likely have to race from a higher mark next time. *(op 2-1)*
Armentieres, hit and miss, made this a true test but her stamina seemed to give out on the long climb up the final hill from three out. *(op 6-1)*
Lady Past Times, pulled up on her two most recent starts, recorded her one success in equally bad ground but she ran in snatches and never threatened to take a hand. *(tchd 16-1)*

4518 COLIN TITTERINGTON 40TH BIRTHDAY NOVICES' H'CAP CHASE (14 fncs 4 omitted) 3m 110y
3:45 (3:45) (Class 3) (0-115,115) 5-Y-0+ **£6,506** (£1,910; £955; £477)

Form				RPR
P333	1		**Bellaney Jewel (IRE)**[26] [4041] 7-10-0 **92** .... StephenCraine(3) *(J J Quinn) trckd ldrs: led 8th: clr 3 out: eased last 75 yds* **10/3**[2]	110+
2403	2	16	**Elvis Returns**[19] [4163] 8-11-5 **108** .... DominicElsworth *(J M Jefferson) chsd ldrs: wnt 2nd 4 out: sn no ch w wnr* **8/1**	103
03U	3	9	**More Flair**[26] [4041] 9-10-0 **89** oh14 .... LarryMcGrath *(J B Walton) sn chsng ldrs: hit 4 out: one pce* **33/1**	81+
5414	4	23	**Chabrimal Minster**[10] [4328] 9-10-13 **102** .... PJBrennan *(R Ford) nt fluent: prom: lost pl 9th: poor 4th whn blnd 4 out: sn t.o* **11/4**[1]	70+
3502	P		**Capybara (IRE)**[10] [4315] 8-11-12 **115** .... DavidO'Meara *(H P Hogarth) led to 1st: lost pl 6th: sn bhd: t.o whn p.u after next* **9/2**	—
30/1	P		**Move Over (IRE)**[11] [4300] 11-10-6 **105** .... JohnFlavin(10) *(R C Guest) t.k.h: led 1st to 8th: lost pl 10th: last whn p.u after 3 out* **7/2**[3]	—
036P	U		**Abzuson**[28] [4012] 9-10-13 **105** .... LeeVickers(3) *(J R Norton) prom: drvn along 8th: lost pl next: mod 4th whn mstke and uns rdr last* **25/1**	73

6m 47.4s 7 Ran SP% **108.0**
CSF £25.52 TOTE £3.80: £1.90, £3.00; EX 21.60.
Owner J W Rosbotham **Bred** J W Rosbotham **Trained** Settrington, N Yorks

FOCUS
A sound gallop and a wide margin, eased winner who is capable of even better. The form is best rated through the second. The two fences going away from the stands were omitted.

NOTEBOOK
Bellaney Jewel(IRE), whose form has been well advertised, came good in a big way and was *value for at least 25 lengths. Even from her revised mark she will still be of serious interest. (op 9-2 tchd 5-1)*
Elvis Returns, 2lb lower, kept on to finish clear second best but the winner trounced him. *(tchd 7-1 and 9-1)*
More Flair, a winner of three points, was running from a stone out of the handicap. *(op 25-1)*
Chabrimal Minster was again badly let down by his jumping and his chance had gone when making a nonsense of the fourth last. *(op 15-8)*
Move Over(IRE), friendless on the morning line, would not settle in front. Running from a 13lb higher mark, he stopped to nothing five out before calling it a day. *(op 5-1 tchd 11-2)*
Capybara(IRE) suddenly lost his place with just over a circuit to go and he was soon pulled up *looking in some distress. Official explanation: jockey said gelding finished distressed (op 5-1 tchd 11-2)*

4519 SEP EVENTS INTERMEDIATE OPEN NATIONAL HUNT FLAT RACE 2m 1f
4:20 (4:20) (Class 6) 4-6-Y-0 **£1,713** (£499; £249)

Form				RPR
	1		**Harbour Breeze (IRE)**[42] [3778] 4-10-11 .... AlanO'Keeffe *(Jennie Candlish) t.k.h on outer: hdwy to trck ldrs 6f out: chal 2f out: styd on to ld last 150yds* **9/1**	94
2	2	½	**Starting Point**[39] [3799] 4-10-11 .... RichardJohnson *(Miss Lucinda V Russell) reluctant ldr: qcknd 10f out: hdd and no ex ins last* **9/2**[2]	94
	3	2½	**Al Falcon** 4-10-4 .... PatrickMcDonald(7) *(M W Easterby) hld up detached in last: hdwy over 3f out: sn rdn: styd on wl: nt rch 1st 2: too much too do* **8/1**[3]	91
112	4	nk	**Heraldry (IRE)**[24] [4072] 6-12-0 .... APMcCoy *(P C Haslam) trckd ldrs: effrt 3f out: edgd rt over 1f out: kpt on same pce* **4/6**[1]	108
	5	dist	**Cash Man (IRE)** 5-10-8 .... StevenGagan(10) *(Mrs E Slack) hld up in rr: hdwy 10f out: chal over 4f out: wknd over 2f out: t.o: btn total 34l* **50/1**	—
0	6	2½	**Windygate (IRE)**[75] [3237] 6-11-1 .... StephenCraine(3) *(A Parker) chsd ldrs: lost pl over 3f out: sn bhd: t.o* **100/1**	—
	7	9	**Red Square Run** 4-10-11 .... PJBrennan *(M W Easterby) chsd ldr: lost pl over 4f out: sn bhd: t.o* **25/1**	—
	8	1¾	**Floral Future** 6-10-11 .... DominicElsworth *(A C Whillans) prom: lost pl over 4f out: sn bhd: t.o* **22/1**	—
0	P		**Ardent Number**[178] [1532] 6-11-4 .... DerekMcGaffin *(D A Nolan) chsd ldrs: lost pl 8f out: sn hopelessly t.o: p.u over 2f out* **100/1**	—

4m 41.6s (12.30) **Going Correction** +0.625s/f (Soft)
WFA 4 from 5yo 7lb 5 from 6yo 4lb 9 Ran SP% **111.4**
Speed ratings: **96,95,94,94,— —,—,—,—** CSF £45.07 TOTE £7.60: £2.00, £2.10, £1.40; EX 30.40.
Owner P and Mrs G A Clarke **Bred** Gainsborough Stud Management Ltd **Trained** Basford Green, Staffs
■ Stewards' Enquiry : Patrick McDonald eight-day ban: riding ill-judged race (Mar 30-Apr 3, Apr 5-7)

FOCUS
A moderate bumper in which they stood still for ten seconds when the tape was released and the gallop was funereal for the first three quarters of a mile. The winner could be rated higher having run well at Punchestown previously.

NOTEBOOK
Harbour Breeze(IRE), runner-up in a Punchestown bumper last month, dug deep and gained the upper hand near the line. *(op 6-1)*
Starting Point, who found himself in front, wound up the gallop from the halfway mark and in the end was just edged out. *(op 11-4)*
Al Falcon ◆, a big, rangy newcomer, was anchored rather detached in last place. Only called on for an effort at the foot of the hill three furlongs out, he came home best of all and should probably have won. The Stewards handed his inexperienced jockey an eight-day ban for riding an injudicious race. *(op 20-1)*
Heraldry(IRE) looked exceptionally well. He kept tabs on the leader but, flat out at the foot of the hill, never really looked like landing the odds. *(op 10-11 tchd Evens in places)*

4520 AZURE SUPPORT SERVICES H'CAP CHASE (14 fncs 2 omitted) 2m 4f
4:55 (4:55) (Class 4) (0-110,109) 5-Y-0+ **£3,665** (£1,137; £612)

Form				RPR
2151	1		**Jimmy Bond**[36] [3849] 7-11-2 **99** .... RichardMcGrath *(Mrs K Walton) chsd ldrs: led appr 2 out: 7 l clr last: idled: styd on towards fin* **6/4**[1]	110+
23P6	2	1¾	**Posh Stick**[22] [4108] 9-11-8 **105** .... DominicElsworth *(J B Walton) a handy: styd on fr 4 out: wnt 2nd appr last: styd on: hld nr line* **10/3**[2]	109
0010	3	22	**Alfy Rich**[20] [4145] 10-11-12 **109** ....(p) AlanDempsey *(M Todhunter) w ldrs: led 4th to 10th: 3rd and hld whn hit 3 out: sn wknd: lft mod 3rd last* **10/1**	101+
P2PP	P		**Jballingall**[39] [3798] 7-10-0 **83** oh2 ....(p) DNolan *(N Wilson) led to 3rd: drvn along 8th: wknd 10th: t.o 5th whn p.u bef 2 out* **6/1**	—
-0P6	P		**Brora Sutherland (IRE)**[36] [3850] 7-10-0 **83** oh5 .... JimmyMcCarthy *(Miss Lucinda V Russell) a last: wnt prom 8th: lost pl after next: sn t.o: p.u bef 2 out* **25/1**	—
222F	U		**Red Man (IRE)**[32] [3928] 9-11-0 **107** ....(p) StevenGagan(10) *(Mrs E Slack) nt fluent: w ldrs: led 3rd: hdd next: mstke 7th: led 10th: hdd appr 2 out: btn 3rd whn mstke and uns rdr last* **9/2**[3]	99

5m 30.7s (10.80) **Going Correction** +0.725s/f (Soft) 6 Ran SP% **108.5**
Speed ratings: **107,106,97,—,— —** CSF £6.66 TOTE £2.20: £1.40, £2.10; EX 6.80 Place 6 £24.66, Place 5 £13.58.
Owner P Chapman and Mrs J Higgins **Bred** Mrs A J Findlay **Trained** Middleham, N Yorks
■ Stewards' Enquiry : Dominic Elsworth caution: used whip with excessive frequency

FOCUS
Just a steady gallop. The winner is value for a lot more than the official margin. The two fences going away from the stands were omitted.

NOTEBOOK
Jimmy Bond, who has changed stables, was running from a 6lb higher mark. He had it in the bag at the last but idled on the run-in and had to be kept up to his work near the line. He should continue to give a good account of himself. *(op 15-8)*
Posh Stick, who took this a year ago from a 13lb lower mark, closed the gap on the run-in but the margin of defeat greatly flatters her. *(op 4-1)*
Alfy Rich, friendless in the market, was running from a career-high mark and his chance had slipped when he clouted the third last. *(op 9-2 tchd 11-1)*
Red Man(IRE), let down by his jumping on just his fourth start over fences, had run out of stamina when a mistake at the last severed the partnership. *(tchd 33-1)*
Brora Sutherland(IRE) *Official explanation: jockey said gelding hung badly left-handed home straight (tchd 33-1)*
T/Plt: £49.80 to a £1 stake. Pool: £33,815.90. 495.10 winning tickets. T/Qpdt: £19.40 to a £1 stake. Pool: £2,196.10. 83.40 winning tickets. WG

4128 FONTWELL (L-H)
Sunday, March 19

OFFICIAL GOING: Good to firm (good in places)
Wind: Moderate, across

4521 P&C MORRIS CATERING GROUP "NATIONAL HUNT" NOVICES' HURDLE (9 hdls) 2m 2f 110y
2:10 (2:10) (Class 4) 4-Y-0+ **£3,253** (£955; £477; £238)

Form				RPR
/6-P	1		**Maljimar (IRE)**[320] [178] 6-11-1 .... PaulMoloney *(Miss H C Knight) a travelling wl bhd ldrs: shkn up to ld sn after 2 out: r.o wl: comf* **12/1**[3]	93+
000	2	4	**Mightymuller (IRE)**[10] [4327] 4-10-2 .... SamCurling(5) *(D R Gandolfo) w ldr: led after 3rd tl 3 out: sn rdn: kpt on* **25/1**	80

1322 **3** *2 ½* **Idris (GER)**[23] 4088 5-11-8 118 PhilipHide 93+
(G L Moore) *trckd ldrs: led 3 out: rdn and hdd sn after 2 out: 3rd and hld whn hit last* **30/100**[1]

60 **4** *8* **That Man Fox**[51] 3591 5-11-1 AntonyProcter 78+
(Lucinda Featherstone) *mid div: hdwy 6th: rdn and effrt appr 2 out: kpt on same pce* **33/1**

6 **5** *1 ¾* **Buy Onling (IRE)**[64] 3393 5-11-1 DaveCrosse 75
(C J Mann) *hld up towards rr: sme late hdwy: nvr a danger: bbv* **14/1**

0-0P **6** *10* **Creinch**[66] 3354 5-11-1 LeightonAspell 65
(O Sherwood) *hld up towards rr and nvr trbld ldrs* **11/1**[2]

6-P0 **7** *dist* **Fort Royal (IRE)**[51] 3597 7-10-8 (p) MrGPewter(7) —
(G R Pewter) *t.k.h trcking ldrs: wknd after 6th* **100/1**

400 **8** *17* **Cape Guard**[52] 3579 4-10-7 HenryOliver —
(F Jordan) *lost tch fr 4th* **66/1**

0PP **9** *shd* **Crystal Hollow**[28] 4005 6-11-1 SeanCurran —
(N R Mitchell) *led tl after 3rd: styd prom tl wknd after 6th* **100/1**

P **10** *9* **My Only Bid (IRE)**[28] 4005 8-10-8 WillieMcCarthy(7) —
(A J Whiting) *mid div tl wknd after 6th* **66/1**

0U6 **P** **Greenacre Legend**[34] 3898 4-10-2 RobertLucey-Butler(5) —
(D B Feek) *mid div: pushed along after 3rd: wknd 6th: t.o and p.u bef last* **50/1**

4m 37.3s (1.30) **Going Correction** +0.15s/f (Yiel)
WFA 4 from 5yo+ 7lb **11 Ran SP% 113.3**
Speed ratings: **103,101,100,96,96 91,—,—,—,— —** CSF £214.26 TOTE £11.70: £2.60, £3.60, £1.02; EX 153.00.

Owner Jim Lewis **Bred** Robert B Hodgins **Trained** West Lockinge, Oxon

FOCUS
A modest affair to say the least and the disappointment of hot favourite Idris further devalues the form.

NOTEBOOK
Maljimar(IRE), whose stable had a disappointing week at Cheltenham, was clearly in good order for this return and he appeared to bounce off the fast ground, travelling strongly into contention before galloping away up the hill. With hot favourite Idris clearly under performing, it is questionable what the form is worth, but he will make a chaser and is likely to be kept on the go with ground conditions in his favour. *(op 14-1)*
Mightymuller(IRE) stepped up significantly on previous efforts, racing prominently before staying on well up the hill off his feather weight. The faster ground clearly suited him well and he may yet be capable of some further improvement. *(op 33-1)*
Idris(GER), who looked a stand-out on form, has had a good season and has hardly run a bad race, but he was never travelling like a 'good thing' should and was really brushed aside in third. Nearly all his form has been on good or softer, and perhaps this fast surface did not suit. *(op 2-7)*
That Man Fox stepped on his previous form, plugging on at the one pace to claim fourth, but he needs to do an awful lot better before he is winning. *(op 25-1)*
Buy Onling(IRE) offered a little more encouragement, although it was worrying that he broke a blood vessel. *Official explanation: jockey said gelding bled from the nose (op 20-1)*
Creinch continues to disappoint and he has not gone on from his Newbury debut win last season.

4522 NEWLY MARRIED ALISON AND PAUL GROS BEGINNERS' CHASE (16 fncs) 2m 6f
2:45 (2:45) (Class 4) 5-Y-0+ **£6,665** (£2,069; £1,114)

Form RPR

23-6 **1** **Mr Boo (IRE)**[24] 4076 7-11-0 105 PhilipHide 96+
(G L Moore) *trckd ldrs: wnt 2nd at the 10th: chalng whn sltly hmpd by loose horse 3 out: sn swtchd lft: led last: r.o wl* **11/8**[1]

45-P **2** *1 ½* **El Viejo (IRE)**[97] 2800 9-10-7 96 (b[1]) JustinMorgan(7) 92
(L Wells) *led at stdy pce: j.rt 12th: stl travelling wl whn chal 3 out: hdd last: nt qckn* **3/1**[3]

0/ **3** *dist* **Carricklee Boy (IRE)**[82] 3044 9-11-0 BenjaminHitchcott —
(Mrs L C Jewell) *disp ld tl nt fluent 8th: chsd ldrs tl wknd 4 out* **12/1**

U30P **U** **Malaga Boy (IRE)**[10] 4322 9-11-0 107 JoeTizzard —
(C L Tizzard) *hld up in cl 4th tl blnd and uns rdr 2nd* **2/1**[2]

6m 2.40s (18.60) **Going Correction** +0.15s/f (Yiel) **4 Ran SP% 108.1**
Speed ratings: **72,71,—,—** CSF £5.78 TOTE £1.70; EX 3.70.

Owner The Hon Mrs C Cameron **Bred** Mrs Eleanor Hadden **Trained** Woodingdean, E Sussex

FOCUS
A slowly-run race with a sprint finish, so dubious form.

NOTEBOOK
Mr Boo(IRE), a modest hurdler, faced a much simpler task than when down the field in a decent race on his chasing debut at Huntingdon and, although interfered with by Malaga Boy, who was running loose, he proved too strong for El Viejo in a sprint finish. He jumped well in the main and connections will now look for a novices' handicap in which to follow up. *(op 6-4 tchd 5-4)*
El Viejo(IRE) bounced back to a bit of form in the first-time blinkers, although he was able to dominate at a steady gallop and was receiving 7lb from the winner. It remains to be seen if he can repeat the effort. *(op 10-3 tchd 7-2)*
Carricklee Boy(IRE), an ex-Irish performer who has been running in hunter chases, was no match for the front two. *(op 10-1)*
Malaga Boy(IRE) held obvious claims on the best of his hurdling form but, as on his chasing debut at Exeter back in January, he unshipped his rider at an early stage. *(op 6-4 tchd 5-2)*

4523 PICNIC & HAMPER CO H'CAP HURDLE (9 hdls) 2m 2f 110y
3:20 (3:20) (Class 4) (0-110,108) 4-Y-0+ **£2,927** (£859; £429; £214)

Form RPR

0064 **1** **Vengeance**[15] 4243 6-11-2 98 LeightonAspell 114+
(S Dow) *hld up in tch: led 3 out: drew clr fr next: readily* **7/4**[1]

5401 **2** *14* **Park City**[28] 4010 7-10-9 96 ShaneWalsh(5) 94+
(J Joseph) *led tl 2nd: chsd ldrs: rdn after 3 out: kpt on same pce but no ch w wnr fr 2 out* **11/1**

0042 **3** *1 ¾* **Shaman**[24] 4075 9-10-11 93 JamieMoore 88
(G L Moore) *hld up in tch: rdn and effrt appr 2 out: kpt on same pce* **6/1**[3]

3153 **4** *shd* **Wenger (FR)**[45] 3687 6-11-4 100 (bt) PhilipHide 96+
(P Winkworth) *hld up towards rr: hdwy after 5th: w wnr and gng wl after 3 out: rdn after 2 out: wknd run-in* **7/2**[2]

30P0 **5** *17* **Maximinus**[29] 3997 6-10-12 94 ChristianWilliams 72
(M Madgwick) *trckd ldr: led 2nd tl 4th: led next tl 3 out: sn rn wd and wknd* **16/1**

S655 **6** *2* **Private Benjamin**[53] 2685 6-10-12 94 MatthewBatchelor 70
(M R Hoad) *hld up towards rr: hit 2nd: mstke 6th and 3 out: sn wknd* **12/1**

P62P **7** *¾* **Lady Alderbrook (IRE)**[20] 4151 6-9-12 83 OwynNelmes(3) 58
(C J Down) *chsd ldrs tl lost pl after 3rd: sn niggled along: lost tch after 6th* **17/2**

PP/P **8** *dist* **Grove Lodge**[21] 4133 9-9-13 88 oh19 ow6 JustinMorgan(7) —
(L A Dace) *in tch: hdwy to ld 4th: hdd next: wknd after 6th* **100/1**

4562 **P** **Hatteras (FR)**[51] 3603 7-11-4 105 RobertLucey-Butler(5) —
(Miss M P Bryant) *chsd ldrs tl 4th: bhd fr 6th: t.o and p.u bef 2 out* **16/1**

0166 **U** **Ressource (FR)**[28] 4010 7-10-0 89 (b) MrWRussell(7) 81
(G L Moore) *hit 1st: hld up towards rr: hit 3rd: mstke 6th: hdwy next: sn rdn: 5th and hld whn blnd and uns rdr last* **20/1**

4m 34.3s (-1.70) **Going Correction** +0.15s/f (Yiel) **10 Ran SP% 116.9**
Speed ratings: **109,103,102,102,95 94,94,—,—,—** CSF £22.01 CT £98.30 TOTE £2.70: £1.50, £2.70, £1.60; EX 41.30 Trifecta £190.00 Pool £1,333.23. - 4.98 winning units.

Owner T Staplehurst **Bred** T Staplehurst **Trained** Epsom, Surrey

FOCUS
A dominant display by favourite Vengeance, who has really come into his own since he qualified for handicaps and could be rated a fair bit higher. The runner-up ran to his mark and the form should work out.

NOTEBOOK
Vengeance ◆, who showed improved form to finish fourth on his recent handicap debut at Newbury, faced lesser opposition on this occasion and he came clear with the minimum of fuss, having taken it up before the turn into the straight. A useful handicapper on the Flat, he is clearly at home on this fast ground and looks one to keep on the right side of in the summer. *(op 2-1 tchd 9-4)*
Park City, a game winner in heavy ground at the course last month, faced a completely different test on this contrasting going, but he performed well under a 6lb rise and plugged on to hold second without proving a match for the winner. He is capable of better back on soft ground. *(op 10-1)*
Shaman is back in a bit of form and he kept on well enough in third without proving a threat to the winner. He does not win very often, but is always worth bearing in mind at this course. *(op 3-1)*
Wenger(FR), 5lb higher than when winning at the course back in December, looked to be going nicely with Vengeance after touching down at the third-last, but he found very little in the straight and was run out of a place close home. *(op 4-1)*
Maximinus finished well adrift of the principals and continues to gradually regress. *(tchd 14-1)*
Lady Alderbrook(IRE) *Official explanation: jockey said mare was unsuited by the good to firm (good in places) ground (op 18-1)*

4524 UNA HUMPHREY BIRTHDAY H'CAP CHASE (21 fncs) 3m 4f
3:55 (3:55) (Class 4) (0-105,103) 5-Y-0+ **£4,554** (£1,337; £668; £333)

Form RPR

1P54 **1** **Walcot Lad (IRE)**[8] 4371 10-11-2 96 (p) WilliamKennedy(3) 113+
(A Ennis) *mde virtually all: clr 3 out: styd on wl: comf* **12/1**

3535 **2** *5* **Dun Locha Castle (IRE)**[10] 4321 11-10-4 81 TomScudamore 90
(N R Mitchell) *chsd wnr thrght: rdn after 4 out: kpt on but no imp on wnr fr next* **6/1**

5664 **3** *7* **Levallois (IRE)**[28] 4007 10-10-4 81 (b) PhilipHide 84+
(P Winkworth) *in tch: hdwy after 4 out: rdn: kpt on same pce* **4/1**[2]

0260 **4** *2 ½* **Alfred The Grey**[47] 3662 9-9-11 77 oh3 (p) ColinBolger(3) 78+
(Miss Suzy Smith) *chsd ldrs: mstke 7th: rdn after 4 out: kpt on same pce* **7/1**

4U54 **5** *½* **Uncle Mick (IRE)**[10] 4325 11-11-6 97 JoeTizzard 97+
(C L Tizzard) *hld up bhd ldrs: tk clsr order after 15th: sn drvn along: hit next and 17th: sn btn* **6/1**

5452 **6** *7* **Auburn Spirit**[8] 4370 11-11-5 96 (b) DaveCrosse 94+
(M D I Usher) *hld up: hit 5th and 10th: reminders after 11th: rdn and no imp fr 17th: dismntd* **10/3**[1]

F423 **P** **Stormy Skye (IRE)**[29] 3981 10-11-7 98 (b) JamieMoore —
(G L Moore) *reminders in rr sn after s: rdn after 14th: sn bhd: t.o and p.u bef 3 out* **5/1**[3]

7m 29.1s (-3.70) **Going Correction** +0.15s/f (Yiel) course record **7 Ran SP% 108.5**
Speed ratings: **111,109,107,106,106 104,—** CSF £71.44 CT £306.23 TOTE £14.80: £4.80, £3.10; EX 82.30.

Owner Camis Burke Middleton Heaps **Bred** Jim Ruane **Trained** Beare Green, Surrey

FOCUS
A decent winning time for a race of its class and a new personal best for the winner over this longer trip.

NOTEBOOK
Walcot Lad(IRE), who is fully effective from two and a quarter miles to three, scored over the former distance at the course in January, but this was a new test and he showed improved form, seeing out every yard of it under a positive ride. All ground comes alike to this Fontwell specialist and his versatility will continue to stand him in good stead. *(op 10-1)*
Dun Locha Castle(IRE) is a consistent sort who gives his all in races, but he finds winning hard and again found one too good. *(op 11-2)*
Levallois(IRE) caught the eye going well before the turn into the straight, but his stamina appeared to give way and he was unable to see the race out as strongly as the front two. *(op 7-2)*
Alfred The Grey, who has been given a short break, did not fare too badly from out of the weights, but he continues to find winning hard. *(op 9-1)*
Uncle Mick(IRE), tried unsuccessfully in a hunter chase earlier in the month, continues out of form and was beaten some way from the finish. *(op 8-1)*
Auburn Spirit never got into it, but the fact he was dismounted after the finish suggests he may have finished lame. *Official explanation: vet said gelding had injured a stifle (tchd 4-1)*
Stormy Skye(IRE) was not on a going day and the only surprise was that he was not pulled up sooner. *(op 4-1)*

4525 BET365.COM H'CAP CHASE (13 fncs) 2m 2f
4:30 (4:30) (Class 5) (0-90,88) 5-Y-0+ **£3,253** (£955; £477; £238)

Form RPR

0P0 **1** **River Amora (IRE)**[226] 1156 11-10-11 69 (p) JamieMoore 88+
(Jim Best) *racd keenly: mde all: drew clr appr 3 out: easily* **10/1**

5660 **2** *8* **Stopwatch (IRE)**[83] 2958 11-10-0 58 oh1 (p) BenjaminHitchcott 67+
(Mrs L C Jewell) *w wnr: rdn after 4 out: kpt on but no ch w wnr fr next* **16/1**

4415 **3** *5* **Foxmeade Dancer**[19] 4164 8-11-3 75 AndrewThornton 77
(P C Ritchens) *chsd ldrs: rdn after 9th: lft 3rd 3 out: kpt on same pce* **3/1**[1]

0234 **4** *¾* **It's My Party**[6] 4424 5-11-7 88 (p) RobertLucey-Butler(5) 85
(W G M Turner) *bhd: styd on fr 2 out: wnt 4th run-in: nvr trbld ldrs* **15/2**

0452 **5** *2 ½* **Denarius Secundus**[21] 4132 9-10-10 68 (b) DaveCrosse 67
(N R Mitchell) *bhd: nudged along fr 5th: styd on fr 3 out: nvr trbld ldrs* **7/1**[3]

F56F **6** *15* **Barnards Green (IRE)**[22] 8-11-2 74 (p) JamieGoldstein 58
(M Madgwick) *in tch: mstke 2nd: rdn after 9th: wkng whn lft 4th 3 out* **20/1**

5PP5 **7** *dist* **Our Jolly Swagman**[52] 3582 11-11-1 80 (p) WayneKavanagh(7) —
(J W Mullins) *mid div: rdn after 9th: sn wknd* **10/1**

00FP **F** **Lordington Lad**[46] 3677 6-11-9 81 JamesDavies —
(B G Powell) *in tch tl fell 8th* **11/2**[2]

P5PP **P** **Rutland (IRE)**[61] 3432 7-10-1 66 TomMessenger(7) —
(C J Drewe) *chsd ldrs: wkng whn mstke 9th: t.o and p.u bef last* **33/1**

320P **F** **Flying Patriarch**[11] 4132 5-11-11 87 PhilipHide —
(G L Moore) *chsd ldrs tl lost pl appr 5th: towards rr whn fell 8th* **10/1**

 The Form Book, Raceform Ltd, Compton, RG20 6NL

0005 **U** **Tails I Win**[9] 4350 7-9-10 **61** .... DavidCullinane(7) —
(Miss C J E Caroe) *mid div: hdwy into 3rd after 8th: hit next: rdn after 4 out: chalng for 2nd whn blnd and uns rdr 3 out* **8/1**

4m 38.7s (3.60) **Going Correction** +0.15s/f (Yiel) **11** Ran SP% **116.6**
Speed ratings: **98,94,92,91,90 84,—,—,—,—** — CSF £149.78 CT £599.76 TOTE £11.70: £3.30, £4.10, £1.80; EX 115.90.

Owner Leon Best **Bred** Donal Sheahan **Trained** Lewes, E Sussex

FOCUS
A poor handicap chase won in good style by River Amora, who was back to his best on this return from a nice break.

NOTEBOOK
River Amora(IRE), returning from a lengthy break and reverting to fences, raced a bit too keenly for his rider's liking, but it did not make any difference and the 11-year-old and came clear having been given a fine front-running ride by Moore. This is his time of year and he is worth bearing in mind in future, with the ground in his favour.

Stopwatch(IRE), who is without a win in over four years, was never far from the winner, but could not go on when River Amora quickened it up and had to make do with second. He is likely to continue to struggle.

Foxmeade Dancer is generally a consistent sort, but this faster ground would not necessarily have been in his favour and he was unable to quicken. A return to a softer surface will help. *(op 10-3 tchd 7-2)*

It's My Party has shaped reasonably well in two starts since going chasing and the cheekpieces did no harm. He was going on at the end of his race and remains open to improvement at the age of five. *(op 9-1)*

Denarius Secundus was unable to build on a recent course second (chasing debut) and the faster surface may well have been his undoing. *(op 5-1)*

Tails I Win was in the process of running a big race and was fighting it out for the placings when unshipping his rider at the third-last. *(tchd 7-1)*

Lordington Lad was one of the more interesting contenders on this chasing debut, but he came down too early to determine how he would have fared and it remains to be seen how this affects his confidence. *(tchd 7-1)*

4526 RACING POST "HANDS & HEELS" JUMP SERIES H'CAP HURDLE (CONDITIONAL JOCKEYS AND AMATEUR RIDERS) (11 hdls) 2m 6f 110y

5:05 (5:05) (Class 5) (0-95,100) 4-Y-0+ **£2,277** (£668; £334; £166)

Form RPR

PPP6 **1** **Geography (IRE)**[33] 3905 6-10-4 **76** ....(p) RichardGordon(3) 80
(P Butler) *mid div: hdwy 7th: led after 3 out: hrd pressed fr next: slt advantage last: pushed out* **16/1**

4UR4 **2** *½* **Hill Forts Henry**[10] 4331 8-10-2 **71** ....(p) SimonElliott 75
(J W Mullins) *hld up towards rr: hdwy fr 8th: wnt 3rd after 3 out: ev ch last: kpt on but no ex cl home* **7/1**[3]

3030 **3** *3 ½* **Monsal Dale (IRE)**[28] 4010 7-10-4 **78** ....(tp) CraigMessenger(5) 79+
(Mrs L C Jewell) *t.k.h: mid div: hdwy 4th: led after 7th: hdd after 3 out: kpt pressing wnr: ev ch last: no ex* **11/1**

0-2P **4** *10* **Here Comes Harry**[48] 3656 10-10-11 **80** .... AndrewGlassonbury 70
(C J Down) *t.k.h in tch: outpcd appr 8th: styd on again fr 2 out* **5/1**[1]

40PP **5** *5* **Secret Jewel (FR)**[10] 4320 6-10-5 **74** .... DavidCullinane 59
(Miss C J E Caroe) *towards rr: hdwy into 5th after 3 out: no further imp* **33/1**

-0PP **6** *½* **Fireside Legend (IRE)**[4] 4449 7-10-3 **77** .... MissMBryant(5) 62
(Miss M P Bryant) *hld up towards rr: stdy prog fr 8th: kpt on same pce fr 2 out* **20/1**

-052 **7** *2* **Newtown**[10] 4320 7-11-12 **95** .... JohnKington 78
(M F Harris) *a towards rr* **8/1**

5300 **8** *2* **At The Double**[33] 3905 10-11-3 **89** ....(b) MrDHutchison(3) 71+
(P Winkworth) *hit 1st: mid div: tk clsr order 7th: hmpd 8th: sn rdn: wknd appr 2 out* **11/1**

4435 **9** *1 ¾* **Ashgan (IRE)**[71] 3283 13-10-8 **77** .... KeiranBurke 56
(Dr P Pritchard) *chsd ldrs tl dropped rr 5th: nvr a danger after* **11/2**[2]

0PPP **10** *2* **It's Official (IRE)**[48] 3656 7-10-3 **75** ....(v) RyanCummings(3) 55+
(Miss A M Newton-Smith) *chsd ldrs: rdn whn pckd bdly 8th: wknd after next* **14/1**

P105 **11** *5* **Big Quick (IRE)**[33] 3907 11-11-6 **92** .... MrRQuinn(3) 67+
(L Wells) *in tch tl wknd after 8th* **12/1**

0-0P **P** **Capricorn**[7] 4394 8-11-2 **90** ....(p) MrCHolman(5) —
(Miss L Day) *lost tch 4th: t.o and p.u bef 6th* **25/1**

3/P **U** **General Hopkins (IRE)**[28] 4013 11-10-1 **73** .... MrGPewter(3) —
(G R Pewter) *t.k.h: led after 1st: hit 4th: hdd after 7th: bdly hmpd uns rdr next* **50/1**

FP-P **S** **Follow The Bear**[10] 4331 8-11-12 **95** ....(b) MrGTumelty —
(D R Gandolfo) *led tl after 1st: chsd ldrs: cl up whn clipped heels: stumbled and uns rdr on bnd appr 8th* **12/1**

5m 46.9s (2.10) **Going Correction** +0.15s/f (Yiel) **14** Ran SP% **113.8**
Speed ratings: **102,101,100,97,95 95,94,93,93,92 90,—,—,—** CSF £113.75 CT £1290.28 TOTE £14.50: £5.20, £2.10, £3.60; EX 148.60 Place 6 £280.96, Place 5 £244.01.

Owner Homewoodgate Racing Club **Bred** Yeomanstown Stud **Trained** East Chiltington, E Sussex

FOCUS
Another desperate contest won by Geography who had been bang out of form. Both he and the runner-up were better than this last season.

NOTEBOOK
Geography(IRE), who has been out of form, at least managed to complete at Folkestone last time and he got on top in the final furlong for a workmanlike win. The form is worth little and it will be interesting to see if he can go on from this. *(op 25-1)*

Hill Forts Henry seems to have been helped by returning to hurdles and he made gradual headway through the field to challenge in the straight, but the winner was simply too strong. *(op 8-1)*

Monsal Dale(IRE) is without a win since December 2003 and, although keeping on to finish clear of the fourth, he makes little future appeal. *(op 10-1)*

Here Comes Harry shaped an awful lot better than when pulling up at Southwell, but the quick ground proved his undoing and he could only muster the one pace. *(op 9-2)*

Secret Jewel(FR) remains a maiden under both codes and she could make only a little headway. *(op 40-1)*

T/Jkpt: Not won. T/Plt: £201.90 to a £1 stake. Pool: £83,529.95. 302.00 winning tickets. T/Qpdt: £94.60 to a £1 stake. Pool: £3,569.30. 27.90 winning tickets. TM

3374 KELSO (L-H)

Sunday, March 19

OFFICIAL GOING: Good to soft (soft in places)
Wind: Breezy, half-behind

4527 TOTEPOOL "A BETTER WAY TO BET" MAIDEN HURDLE (DIV I) (8 hdls) 2m 110y

2:20 (2:20) (Class 4) 4-Y-0+ **£3,083** (£898; £449)

Form RPR

6P23 **1** **Auenmoon (GER)**[24] 4067 5-11-4 114 .... MarkBradburne 122+
(P Monteith) *mde all: rdn and r.o strly fr 2 out* **5/4**[1]

F225 **2** *10* **Double Vodka (IRE)**[22] 4110 5-11-4 109 .... RichardMcGrath 109+
(C Grant) *in tch: effrt and chsd wnr bef 2 out: no imp whn mstke last: kpt on* **7/2**[3]

2222 **3** *4* **My Final Bid (IRE)**[33] 3914 7-11-1 .... PeterBuchanan(3) 104
(Mrs A C Hamilton) *nt fluent: prom: rdn 3 out: kpt on fr next: no imp* **3/1**[2]

56 **4** *9* **Great Approach (IRE)**[33] 3912 5-11-4 .... TonyDobbin 96+
(N G Richards) *nt fluent in midfield: effrt and in tch whn mstke 3 out: no imp whn j.rt last* **14/1**

/6-P **5** *¾* **Luthello (FR)**[32] 3927 7-11-4 .... GLee 94
(J Howard Johnson) *hld up: pushed along bef 3 out: kpt on fr next: nvr rchd ldrs* **33/1**

32-2 **6** *2 ½* **Dawn Devoy (IRE)**[312] 301 7-11-1 105 .... DougieCostello(3) 92
(G A Swinbank) *hld up: shkn up 2 out: hmpd last: nvr nrr* **14/1**

0400 **7** *½* **Filey Flyer**[41] 3782 6-10-4 85 .... ColmSharkey(7) 84
(J R Turner) *cl up: effrt 3 out: wknd next* **100/1**

00 **8** *5* **The Last Viking**[20] 4143 6-11-4 .... AlanDempsey 86
(A Parker) *bhd: rdn 3 out: n.d* **100/1**

P **9** *15* **It's A Roofer (IRE)**[9] 4342 6-11-4 .... BrianHarding 71
(Mrs K Walton) *a bhd* **100/1**

0P00 **10** *16* **Bally Abbie**[30] 3963 5-10-6 72 .... TJDreaper(5) 48
(P Beaumont) *midfield: rdn 4 out: sn btn* **200/1**

0PF0 **11** *3* **Romanov Rambler (IRE)**[20] 4141 6-11-4 .... WilsonRenwick 52
(Mrs S C Bradburne) *sn bhd: no ch fr 1/2-way* **200/1**

12 *26* **Glen Oscar (IRE)**[323] 7-11-4 .... NeilMulholland 26
(Miss S E Forster) *bhd: short-lived effrt after 4 out: wknd next: eased run in* **100/1**

0-00 **13** *1 ¼* **Just Libbi**[116] 2446 6-10-11 .... KeithMercer 18
(Ferdy Murphy) *a bhd* **50/1**

14 *13* **Kalishka (IRE)**[21] 5-11-1 .... PaddyAspell(3) 12
(R Allan) *bhd: struggling fr 1/2-way* **100/1**

0 **15** *24* **Buldaan (FR)**[32] 3925 4-10-8 .... GaryBerridge(3) —
(W Amos) *prom tl wknd fr 3 out* **200/1**

0 **P** **Wellstream Blue**[42] 3763 5-10-13 ....(t) TomGreenway(5) —
(Mrs H O Graham) *pressed wnr to 1/2-way: sn wknd: t.o whn p.u bef 2 out* **200/1**

4m 6.70s (3.00) **Going Correction** +0.275s/f (Yiel)
WFA 4 from 5yo+ 7lb **16** Ran SP% **116.8**
Speed ratings: **103,98,96,92,91 90,90,88,81,73 72,59,59,53,41** — CSF £5.56 TOTE £2.20: £1.90, £1.60, £1.10; EX 7.20.

Owner I Bell **Bred** Gestut Auenquelle **Trained** Rosewell, Midlothian

FOCUS
The winning time was close to par for the grade, despite being 6.6 seconds faster than the second division, and the form appears solid, with the next four behind the winner close to their marks, and should work out.

NOTEBOOK
Auenmoon(GER), very well backed, ran out a clear-cut winner under an aggressive ride and deservedly got off the mark over timber at the fifth time of asking. He had the race sewn up when skipping clear at the top of the straight, once again advertising his liking for a deep surface, and should be high on confidence now. His current official mark looks very fair and it could be that a switch to handicaps is now his best option. *(op 11-8 tchd 11-10, 6-4 in places)*

Double Vodka(IRE) was put firmly in his place the winner, but improved a touch for this return to slightly better ground, and finished nicely clear of the rest. His turn should come before too long at this sort of level. *(tchd 4-1)*

My Final Bid(IRE), dropping back from three miles, again spoilt his chances with some messy jumping and his fate was sealed a fair way out. He is capable of much better, and should enjoy the return to further in due course, but he needs to improve his jumping in order to progress in this division. *(op 7-2)*

Great Approach(IRE) did not impress over his hurdles and lacked the pace to get involved. He now qualifies for handicaps, however, and really ought to better this when reverting to further in that sphere. *(op 12-1)*

Dawn Devoy(IRE) *Official explanation: jockey said gelding finished lame (tchd 16-1)*

4528 TOTESPORT 0800 221 221 BEGINNERS' CHASE (19 fncs) 3m 1f

2:50 (2:50) (Class 4) 5-Y-0+ **£5,204** (£1,528; £764; £381)

Form RPR

P223 **1** **Dark Ben (FR)**[41] 3781 6-11-1 110 .... DougieCostello(3) 109
(Miss Kate Milligan) *j.w: led to 15th: led 3 out to last: styd on wl to ld last 50yds* **3/1**[2]

0P22 **2** *2* **Cool Dessa Blues**[32] 3930 7-10-11 86 .... AlanDempsey 100
(W Amos) *hld up in tch: stdy hdwy whn hit 3 out: led last: sn rdn: hdd and no ex last 50yds* **10/1**

2F62 **3** *8* **See You There (IRE)**[9] 4343 7-11-1 114 .... PeterBuchanan(3) 102+
(Miss Lucinda V Russell) *nt fluent: chsd ldrs: rdn and effrt after 3 out: outpcd between last two* **13/8**[1]

221P **4** *16* **Russian Sky**[29] 3987 7-11-4 .... MarkBradburne 87+
(Mrs H O Graham) *cl up: led 15th to 3 out: wknd after next* **9/2**[3]

0P43 **5** *dist* **No Picnic (IRE)**[9] 4343 8-11-1 105 ....(p) PaddyAspell(3) —
(Mrs S C Bradburne) *in tch to 12th: wknd fr next* **12/1**

-03U **F** **Seeking Shelter (IRE)**[26] 4041 7-10-11 70 .... BrianHarding —
(N G Richards) *bhd whn fell 6th* **20/1**

-4P0 **F** **Kimbambo (FR)**[65] 3378 8-11-1 ....(p) GaryBerridge(3) —
(J P L Ewart) *chsng ldrs whn fell 10th* **16/1**

F0PP **P** **Roman Rebel**[83] 2978 7-11-4 84 .... RichardMcGrath —
(Mrs K Walton) *bhd: hit 8th: wknd 13th: t.o whn p.u bef 3 out* **50/1**

6m 30.3s (0.70) **Going Correction** +0.15s/f (Yiel) **8** Ran SP% **110.7**
Speed ratings: **104,103,100,95,— —,—,—** CSF £29.63 TOTE £2.70: £1.10, £1.60, £1.90; EX 23.50.

Owner J D Gordon **Bred** N Pharaon **Trained** Middleham, N Yorks

FOCUS
A moderate affair that saw the first two come clear and they set the level for the form.

NOTEBOOK

Dark Ben(FR) dug deep to repel the runner-up and score a first success over fences at the fourth attempt. He put in by far his best round of jumping to date and the step-up to this longer trip was clearly to his liking. This was his stable's first success since June 2005. *(op 7-2)*

Cool Dessa Blues, just touched off at Musselburgh last time, had every chance yet could not cope with the renewed challenge of the winner on the run-in. She has now found one too good on all of her three outings in this sphere to date, but continues to go the right way, and she would have to be of interest if switched to a handicap from her current mark.

See You There(IRE) lacked fluency over his fences and could not go with the front two from the penultimate fence. He may have found this coming a touch too soon after his effort in testing ground at Ayr nine days previously. *(op 11-10)*

Russian Sky, making his chasing debut, failed to see out the distance yet still left the impression he could improve in this sphere with further experience. *(op 13-2 tchd 7-1)*

4529 TOTEQUADPOT NOVICES' H'CAP HURDLE (10 hdls) 2m 2f
3:25 (3:25) (Class 3) (0-125,130) 4-Y-0+ **£6,506** (£1,910; £955; £477)

Form RPR

4211 **1** **Harmony Brig (IRE)**[33] 3912 7-11-9 122 .... TonyDobbin 132+
(N G Richards) *led to 4th: led after next: mde rest: clr bef last: rdr dropped whip run in: pushed out* **7/4**[1]

F242 **2** *9* **Bollin Thomas**[9] 4346 8-10-3 105 .... PaddyAspell(3) 106+
(R Allan) *in tch: effrt after 3 out: chsd wnr between last two: no ex run in* **10/1**

-411 **3** *10* **Scotmail (IRE)**[103] 2690 5-11-3 116 .... GLee 106
(J Howard Johnson) *chsd ldrs: outpcd bef 2 out: kpt on fr last: no ch w first two* **7/1**[3]

-513 **4** *1/2* **Air Of Affection**[102] 2704 5-9-11 103 .... ColmSharkey(7) 94+
(J R Turner) *cl up: led 4th to after next: cl up tl outpcd after 2 out: wknd run in* **20/1**

3121 **5** *2* **First Look (FR)**[8] 4364 6-11-7 130 .... DavidDaSilva(10) 119+
(P Monteith) *hld up: outpcd bef 4 out: rallied and prom next: wknd 2 out* **11/4**[2]

2215 **6** *10* **Seymar Lad (IRE)**[22] 4108 6-10-5 104 .... MarkBradburne 82
(P Beaumont) *nt fluent: sn dropped rr: no ch fr 1/2-way* **7/1**[3]

4361 **7** *2* **More Likely**[9] 4342 5-9-13 101 .... DougieCostello(3) 77
(Mrs A F Tullie) *prom: reminders bef 6th: wknd fr 4 out* **14/1**

5355 **8** *2 1/2* **Buffy**[9] 4346 6-10-0 99 oh9 .... NeilMulholland 72
(B Mactaggart) *hld up: rdn bef 6th: sn btn* **50/1**

-260 **P** **Witch Wind**[76] 3205 6-10-4 108 .... DeclanMcGann(5) —
(A M Crow) *chsd ldrs to 1/2-way: sn wknd: t.o whn p.u bef 2 out* **20/1**

4m 40.9s (1.00) **Going Correction** +0.275s/f (Yiel) **9** Ran SP% **115.3**
Speed ratings: **108,104,99,99,98 94,93,92,—** CSF £18.99 CT £100.31 TOTE £2.40: £1.20, £2.70, £2.20; EX 22.50.
Owner It's A Bargain Syndicate **Bred** Mrs O E Matthews **Trained** Greystoke, Cumbria

FOCUS

A modest handicap, run at a sound pace, and the progressive winner is value for further. The runner-up and fourth were close to their marks and the form looks reasonable.

NOTEBOOK

Harmony Brig(IRE), making his handicap debut, ran out a comfortable winner and landed the hat-trick in the process. He could have been called the winner at halfway, his jumping improves with every outing, and he is clearly developing into a very useful novice. The two-and-a-half-mile novice hurdle at Aintree is reportedly under consideration for his next outing and it should be noted that his trainer saddled Monet's Garden to finish second in that event in 2004. *(tchd 2-1, 9-4 in a place)*

Bollin Thomas, raised 5lb for finishing runner-up at Ayr nine days previously, had no chance with the winner yet turned in another improved effort and finished well clear of the rest. He saw out the longer trip well enough, but is yet to win a race over timber and another rise in the weights now looks inevitable. *(op 9-1)*

Scotmail(IRE), bidding for a hat-trick, did not prove suited by this drop back in trip and was not disgraced in the circumstances. The return to a deeper surface and longer trip should see him in a much better light. *(op 8-1)*

Air Of Affection, having her first outing in a handicap and returning from a 103-day break, had no more to offer nearing the final flight and shaped as though the race was needed.

First Look(FR), up 10lb for an impressive success at Ayr eight days previously, ran well below expectations and never threatened to reverse his Newcastle form with the winner. He probably wants further, but has plenty to prove now all the same. *(op 7-2)*

Seymar Lad(IRE) spoilt his chances with some messy jumping and posted a tame effort. *(op 11-2)*

More Likely *Official explanation: jockey said gelding lost its action*

Witch Wind *Official explanation: jockey said gelding bled from the nose*

4530 TOTESPORT.COM NOVICES' HURDLE (11 hdls) 2m 6f 110y
4:00 (4:01) (Class 4) 4-Y-0+ **£3,426** (£998; £499)

Form RPR

11 **1** **Money Trix (IRE)**[36] 3855 6-12-2 .... TonyDobbin 131+
(N G Richards) *in tch: hdwy to ld 7th: nt fluent next: clr fr 3 out: easily* **4/11**[1]

54- **2** *10* **Ally Shrimp**[358] 4552 5-11-2 .... BrianHarding 101+
(T P Tate) *prom: lost pl 2nd: rallied u.p 4 out: kpt on to go 2nd nr fin: no ch w wnr* **25/1**

1224 **3** *1/2* **Cloudless Dawn**[39] 3795 6-11-2 114 .... RussGarritty 99
(P Beaumont) *led to 2nd: led briefly bef 7th: chsd wnr tl one pce fr bef 2 out: lost 2nd nr fin* **9/1**[3]

55-3 **4** *17* **Springaway**[131] 2106 7-10-13 81 .... DougieCostello(3) 86+
(Miss Kate Milligan) *midfield: hit 4th: effrt whn mstke 3 out: sn outpcd* **66/1**

14 **5** *9* **Serbelloni**[41] 3779 6-11-9 110 .... GLee 80
(M D Hammond) *hld up: hdwy and prom 1/2-way: rdn and outpcd fr after 3 out* **8/1**[2]

06 **6** *dist* **Bafana Boy**[33] 3914 6-10-6 .... FearghalDavis(10) —
(N G Richards) *bhd: drvn 1/2-way: nvr on terms* **100/1**

0 **P** **Hooky's Quest**[54] 3556 4-9-9 .... TomGreenway(5) —
(Mrs H O Graham) *a bhd: t.o whn p.u bef 3 out* **100/1**

-PP0 **P** **Killwillie (IRE)**[32] 3927 7-10-13 .... PeterBuchanan(3) —
(J I A Charlton) *a bhd: t.o whn p.u bef 2 out* **200/1**

003P **P** **Scamp**[252] 941 7-10-9 75 .... KeithMercer —
(R Shiels) *cl up to 5th: sn lost pl: t.o whn p.u bef 2 out* **200/1**

F **P** **Golden Crest**[41] 3779 6-10-13 .... GaryBerridge(3) —
(W Amos) *prom tl wknd bef 7th: sn btn: t.o whn p.u bef 3 out* **25/1**

030 **P** **Ballynure (IRE)**[105] 2653 8-11-2 88 .... NeilMulholland —
(Mrs L B Normile) *chsd ldrs to 1/2-way: sn btn: t.o whn p.u bef 2 out* **100/1**

300 **P** **Hurricane Francis**[11] 4301 6-11-2 .... RobertWalford —
(T D Walford) *chsd ldrs to 6th: sn struggling: t.o whn p.u bef 2 out* **200/1**

22S5 **P** **Bywell Beau (IRE)**[33] 3914 7-10-13 102 .... MichalKohl(3) —
(J I A Charlton) *plld hrd in rr: hdwy to ld 2nd: hdd bef 7th: sn btn: t.o whn p.u bef 2 out* **20/1**

5m 49.6s (11.90) **Going Correction** +0.275s/f (Yiel)
WFA 4 from 5yo+ 8lb **13** Ran SP% **112.8**
Speed ratings: **90,86,86,80,77 —,—,—,—,— —,—,—** CSF £14.89 TOTE £1.40: £1.10, £2.70, £1.40; EX 14.40.
Owner Craig Bennett **Bred** John R Cox **Trained** Greystoke, Cumbria

FOCUS

A modest winning time, due to the sedate early gallop, and only six completed. The winner can rate plenty higher in due course and the runner-up and fourth help give the form substance.

NOTEBOOK

Money Trix(IRE) ◆ maintained his unbeaten status since joining connections from Ireland with a facile success under his double penalty. He has improved with each outing to date, the drop back to this trip proved no problem, and he has the scope to make a very nice novice chaser next season. In the immediate future, however, the three-mile novice hurdle at Aintree next month could well be on his agenda providing the ground is not fast, and he certainly deserves a shot in graded company. *(op 4-9 tchd 1-2 in places)*

Ally Shrimp, making his debut over timber and returning from a 358-day layoff, shaped as though this race would bring him on a deal fitness-wise and got the trip well. He should be placed to advantage in this sphere before too long. *(tchd 28-1)*

Cloudless Dawn ran her usual game race and helps to set the level of this form. A drop back in trip should be to her advantage and she would also appreciate the chance to race against her own sex. *(op 11-2)*

Springaway was stopped by an error three from home and is entitled to improve with this outing under his belt. *(tchd 100-1)*

Serbelloni was disappointing and did not last home over this trip. He was a fair stayer on the Flat, but a drop back in trip in this sphere now looks on the cards. *(tchd 10-1)*

4531 TOTEEXACTA H'CAP CHASE (12 fncs) 2m 1f
4:35 (4:37) (Class 3) (0-120,120) 5-Y-0+ **£6,506** (£1,910; £955; £477)

Form RPR

064F **1** **Seeyaaj**[25] 4053 6-10-2 99 .... (t) PeterBuchanan(3) 107+
(Miss Lucinda V Russell) *chsd ldrs: rdn whn checked bnd after 2 out: rallied and led last 50yds: kpt on* **12/1**

5645 **2** *1/2* **Super Nomad**[8] 4378 11-11-4 115 .... MrTGreenall(3) 121+
(M W Easterby) *led to 3rd: cl up: led 2 out: rdn and wandered run in: hdd last 50yds: no ex* **7/1**

3614 **3** *3 1/2* **Sound Of Cheers**[33] 3917 9-11-0 108 .... (t) KennyJohnson 110
(F Kirby) *chsd ldrs: led 4 out to 2 out: outpcd bef last: kpt on same pce run in* **9/1**

4-2 **4** *1 1/2* **Reivers Moon**[65] 3379 7-10-13 110 .... GaryBerridge(3) 110
(W Amos) *prom: effrt after 2 out: one pce run in* **11/2**[3]

156P **5** *shd* **Kids Inheritance (IRE)**[41] 3784 8-10-13 112 .... TJDreaper(5) 113+
(J M Jefferson) *hld up: rdn 4 out: kpt on run in: nvr rchd ldrs* **25/1**

P22 **6** *17* **Junior Des Ormeaux (FR)**[36] 3850 9-11-5 113 .... WilsonRenwick 103+
(S H Shirley-Beavan) *led 3rd to 4 out: wknd fr 2 out* **9/1**

4124 **7** *20* **South Bronx (IRE)**[76] 3207 7-11-12 120 .... (t) MarkBradburne 83
(Mrs S C Bradburne) *prom: outpcd 7th: n.d after* **15/2**

012F **F** **Shares (IRE)**[36] 3852 6-10-13 117 .... DavidDaSilva(10) —
(P Monteith) *hld up: stdy hdwy and in tch whn fell 7th* **9/2**[2]

0631 **U** **Nifty Roy**[20] 4142 6-9-11 94 oh2 .... DougieCostello(3) —
(I McMath) *keen: hld up in tch: blnd and uns rdr 1st* **4/1**[1]

54-0 **U** **Pillaging Pict**[77] 3172 11-11-1 109 .... GLee —
(J B Walton) *a bhd: no ch whn mstke 3 out: blnd bdly and uns rdr next* **20/1**

4m 21.1s (-2.10) **Going Correction** +0.15s/f (Yiel) **10** Ran SP% **114.1**
Speed ratings: **110,109,108,107,107 99,89,—,—,—** CSF £91.72 CT £795.64 TOTE £11.60: £3.00, £2.20, £2.70; EX 106.20.
Owner Brahms & Liszt **Bred** Milton Park Stud Partnership **Trained** Arlary, Perth & Kinross
■ Stewards' Enquiry : Mr T Greenall four-day ban: used whip with excessive frequency (Apr 2-3,5-6)

FOCUS

Quite a competitive handicap but fairly modest form, although solid enough rated around the third and fourth.

NOTEBOOK

Seeyaaj was entitled to win a race over fences off this sort of mark having been rated 13lb higher over hurdles at his best. He ground down Super Nomad in the closing stages and looks capable of improving for a faster surface, which he prefers, but the bare form of this race is nothing to write home about. *(op 11-1)*

Super Nomad, who had been dropped 7lb for his last two runs, made a bold bid but he is never one to be that confident about in a finish, and once again he had to settle for the runner-up spot. It is now over four years since he last won. *(op 8-1)*

Sound Of Cheers appears to need further than this these days, at least when the ground is anything other than very testing. *(tchd 10-1)*

Reivers Moon had every chance jumping the final fence but weakened on the run-in, just like on her seasonal reappearance here in January. *(op 5-1)*

Kids Inheritance(IRE) kept on from off the pace but was never a threat. When he has won he has not been given so much to do.

Shares(IRE), like most of the others at the time, was going well within himself when departing. *(op 5-1)*

4532 TOTEPOOL "A BETTER WAY TO BET" MAIDEN HURDLE (DIV II) (8 hdls) 2m 110y
5:10 (5:11) (Class 4) 4-Y-0+ **£3,083** (£898; £449)

Form RPR

2462 **1** **Water Taxi**[31] 3943 5-11-4 104 .... KeithMercer 107+
(Ferdy Murphy) *in tch: smooth hdwy and led 2 out: rdn out fr last* **5/2**[2]

130- **2** *2 1/2* **Arctic Echo**[333] 4935 7-11-1 .... DougieCostello(3) 103
(G A Swinbank) *prom: effrt and ev ch 2 out: kpt on fr last: nt rch wnr* **16/1**

3 *1/2* **Glingerbank (IRE)** 6-11-4 .... BrianHarding 106+
(N G Richards) *nt fluent: reminders in rr after 3rd: gd hdwy 3 out: effrt after next: kpt on u.p run in* **12/1**

52 **4** *4* **Secret Pact (IRE)**[10] 4313 4-10-11 .... TonyDobbin 92
(I McMath) *prom: effrt bef 2 out: no ex bef last* **13/8**[1]

-000 **5** *1 1/2* **Easby Mandarin**[39] 3793 5-11-4 .... RussGarritty 100+
(C W Thornton) *midfield: effrt bef 2 out: blnd last: no imp* **66/1**

3462 **6** *8* **Third Empire**[26] 4040 5-10-11 103 .... PhilKinsella(7) 90+
(C Grant) *w ldr: led 4 out: hdd 2 out: wknd last* **8/1**

-0F0 **7** *10* **Kiwijimbo (IRE)**[20] 4143 6-11-4 .... BarryKeniry 81+
(A C Whillans) *hld up: hdwy and prom 3 out: rdn and wknd next* **66/1**

0640 **8** *8* **Rothbury**[39] 3793 6-11-1 .... MichalKohl(3) 71
(J I A Charlton) *hld up: hdwy bef 3 out: rdn and wknd bef next* **7/1**[3]

0005 **9** *22* **Wot Way Chief**[30] 3963 5-10-13 .... TJDreaper(5) 49
(J M Jefferson) *keen in rr: struggling fr 4 out* **40/1**

The Form Book, Raceform Ltd, Compton, RG20 6NL

0 **10** *11* **Dantor**[168] 1601 4-10-4 ....(t) BenOrde-Powlett[(7)] 31
(M A Barnes) *midfield: rdn 4 out: sn btn* **200/1**
P **11** *13* **Moneamon**[41] 3779 7-11-4 ....(p) KennyJohnson 25
(R Johnson) *a bhd: struggling fr 1/2-way* **200/1**
06 **12** *10* **Justwhateverulike (IRE)**[20] 4147 5-11-4 .... NeilMulholland 15
(Miss S E Forster) *midfield: rdn 4 out: sn btn* **50/1**
13 *6* **Miss Iverley**[269] 4-9-11 .... DavidDaSilva[(7)] —
(J M Dun) *keen: led to 4 out: sn btn* **200/1**
0-26 **F** **Divex (IRE)**[113] 2497 5-11-4 .... GLee —
(M D Hammond) *hld up: fell 2nd* **16/1**
30 **P** **Debris (IRE)**[83] 2956 7-10-13 .... TomGreenway[(5)] —
(S B Bell) *in tch to 4 out: sn wknd: t.o whn p.u and dismntd bef 2 out* **50/1**

4m 13.3s (9.60) **Going Correction** +0.275s/f (Yiel)
WFA 4 from 5yo+ 7lb **62** Ran SP% **120.6**
Speed ratings: **88,86,86,84,84 80,75,71,61,56 50,45,42,—,—** CSF £40.55 TOTE £4.10: £2.00, £3.10, £3.30; EX 45.20.
Owner GWilson,RWheeler,Holmes,King,McHugh,Wade **Bred** Juddmonte Farms **Trained** West Witton, N Yorks
■ Stewards' Enquiry : Keith Mercer one-day ban: used whip with excessive frequency (Mar 30)

FOCUS
A modest maiden hurdle and run in a moderate time, 6.6 seconds slower than the first division. However, with most of the first five close to their marks the form should work out well enough.

NOTEBOOK
Water Taxi, who posted a personal best last time out and whose stable is enjoying a good time of it, did not find the drop back in distance inconveniencing him and, having travelled well for much of the race, drew a couple of lengths clear on the run-in. The time was slow in comparison with the first division, though, so the form is hardly solid. *(tchd 11-4 in a place)*
Arctic Echo, a dual bumper winner, made a satisfactory hurdling debut on his first outing in 11 months. His stable tends to get them fit at home, so whether he will find much improvement for this reappearance is open to question.
Glingerbank(IRE) ◆, who showed signs of inexperience throughout the race, came through to look a big danger going to the final flight, but was then outpaced. His dam is from the family of high-class staying chaser Run and Skip and he should come on a bundle for this outing. *(op 16-1)*
Secret Pact(IRE) was under pressure going to the second last and the drop back in trip did not appear to suit. He is now eligible for handicaps, which should give connections more options. *(op 9-4 tchd 5-2)*
Easby Mandarin made a bad blunder at the final flight when tracking the leader. He was under pressure at the time but would have finished closer without that mistake.
Third Empire may have been happier had he been granted an uncontested lead. *(op 11-2)*

4533 TOTECOURSE TO COURSE MAIDEN OPEN NATIONAL HUNT FLAT RACE 2m 110y

5:40 (5:42) (Class 6) 4-6-Y-O **£1,713** (£499; £249)

Form RPR
3 **1** **The Gleaner**[41] 3785 4-10-8 .... MrTGreenall[(3)] 88+
(M W Easterby) *hld up: hdwy 4f out: led over 1f out: edgd rt: drvn out* **13/2**[3]
00 **2** *3 ½* **Lily Tara**[106] 2642 4-9-13 .... DeclanMcGann[(5)] 78
(A M Crow) *hld up: hdwy 4f out: chsd wnr ins fnl f: r.o* **100/1**
0 **3** *5* **Ajay (IRE)**[24] 4072 5-11-4 .... RobertWalford 88+
(T D Walford) *mde most tl over 1f out: edgd lft and sn no ex* **10/1**
56 **4** *¾* **Mi Fa Sol Aulmes (FR)**[43] 3742 6-10-11 .... GLee 79
(W T Reed) *hld up midfield: hdwy and ev ch 3f out: one pce over 1f out* **8/1**
20 **5** *1 ¼* **Mister Jungle (FR)**[42] 3763 4-10-11 .... MarkBradburne 78
(Mrs S C Bradburne) *chsd ldrs tl rdn and no ex over 1f out* **9/1**
05 **6** *1* **Colonel Hayes (IRE)**[43] 3742 6-11-1 .... MichalKohl[(3)] 84
(J I A Charlton) *keen in tch: rdn over 3f out: one pce fr 2f out* **12/1**
5 **7** *3 ½* **Triple Deal**[39] 3799 4-10-11 .... TonyDobbin 73+
(N G Richards) *plld hrd: hld up: hdwy and in tch over 3f out: rdn and no ex fr 2f out* **5/2**[1]
6 **8** *9* **Madam Killeshandra**[53] 3563 6-10-4 .... PhilKinsella[(7)] 64
(A Parker) *bhd: drvn over 4f out: nvr rchd ldrs* **14/1**
0 **9** *hd* **More Equity**[39] 3799 4-10-1 .... DougieCostello[(3)] 57
(Mrs A F Tullie) *midfield: rdn 4f out: sn btn* **66/1**
2 **10** *shd* **Dundock**[58] 3490 5-11-4 .... BrianHarding 71
(A C Whillans) *hld up: hdwy over 4f out: wknd over 2f out* **4/1**[2]
4 **11** *2 ½* **The Saltire Tiger**[53] 3563 5-10-13 .... DesFlavin[(5)] 69
(Mrs L B Normile) *prom: effrt 3f out: wknd 2f out* **20/1**
0 **12** *2 ½* **Lowsha Green**[64] 3399 5-11-4 .... KennyJohnson 66
(R Johnson) *racd wd in midfield: rdn and wknd fr 4f out* **40/1**
0 **13** *5* **Thatlldoforme**[20] 4147 4-10-4 .... EwanWhillans[(7)] 54
(A C Whillans) *chsd ldrs tl rdn and wknd over 3f out* **25/1**
0 **14** *dist* **Indian Wind**[20] 4147 4-10-4 .... MissAngelaBarnes[(7)] —
(M A Barnes) *cl up tl lost pl qckly 5f out: t.o* **66/1**
00 **15** *13* **Cold Call**[90] 2927 4-10-11 .... NeilMulholland —
(C W Thornton) *midfield: lost pl over 6f out: t.o* **50/1**

4m 13.9s
WFA 4 from 5yo+ 7lb **15** Ran SP% **123.4**
CSF £574.61 TOTE £8.90: £3.20, £17.60, £6.90; EX 588.00 Place 6 £42.75, Place 5 £38.91.
Owner J W P Curtis **Bred** S I Pittendrigh **Trained** Sheriff Hutton, N Yorks

FOCUS
Modest bumper form but notable for a one-two for the sire Kayf Tara.

NOTEBOOK
The Gleaner, who posted a fair effort on his debut at Sedgefield, improved sufficiently for that to take this modest heat. A half-brother to Laertes, who won a three-mile maiden hurdle last month, he too should stay well when sent over timber. *(tchd 8-1)*
Lily Tara, a half-sister to Come Home Alone, who has won over an extended two miles five over timber, was ridden differently this time and finished well from off the pace. She is another who is likely to stay well once sent over hurdles.
Ajay(IRE), who made the running, was being pushed along with half a mile to run but to his credit he kept on well. *(op 14-1 tchd 16-1)*
Mi Fa Sol Aulmes(FR) kept on fairly well and looks the type to do much better when sent over obstacles. *(op 16-1)*
Mister Jungle(FR), a half-sister to Purgeon, who won over hurdles in France at up to two and a half miles, is another likely to be seen to better effect when faced with a flight of hurdles. *(op 8-1)*
Colonel Hayes(IRE) is a half-brother to Iceberge, who has won three times to date over three miles plus, both over hurdles and fences. *(op 25-1)*
Triple Deal looked a danger at the top of the straight but he had pulled hard in the early stages and those efforts told in the latter part of the race. *(op 9-4 tchd 15-8)*
Dundock *Official explanation: jockey said gelding finished lame (op 7-2 tchd 9-2)*
T/Plt: £24.00 to a £1 stake. Pool: £48,374.35. 1,468.85 winning tickets. T/Qpdt: £25.70 to a £1 stake. Pool: £2,549.20. 73.20 winning tickets. RY

4537 - 4541a (Foreign Racing) - See Raceform Interactive

4203 LIMERICK (R-H)
Sunday, March 19

OFFICIAL GOING: Soft (heavy in places)

4542a BANK OF IRELAND EUROPEAN BREEDERS FUND MARES NOVICE CHASE (GRADE 3) 2m 6f

3:30 (3:30) 5-Y-0+ **£22,448** (£6,586; £3,137; £1,068)

RPR
1 **American Jennie (IRE)**[28] 4022 8-10-11 124 .... DNRussell 119+
(Michael Cullen, Ire) *mde all: j.w: clr after 3 out: sltly reduced ld appr st: sn rdn clr: easily* **5/4**[1]
2 *15* **Sunami Storm (IRE)**[43] 3743 8-10-11 111 .... RWalsh 97
(W P Mullins, Ire) *trckd ldrs: pckd sltly 8th: wnt 2nd sn after 3 out: rdn bef st: sn no imp: kpt on same pce* **9/4**[2]
3 *nk* **Countess Trifaldi (IRE)**[22] 4124 6-10-11 102 .... DFO'Regan 97
(Michael John Phillips, Ire) *towards rr: rdn in mod 5th bef st: sn no imp: kpt on wout threatening into 3rd run-in* **25/1**
4 *nk* **Kilfinny Cross (IRE)**[17] 4204 7-10-11 .... AndrewJMcNamara 96
(Michael Hourigan, Ire) *trckd ldr in 2nd: rdn and dropped to 3rd appr st: sn no imp u.p: kpt on one pce* **8/1**
5 *½* **Jay Lo (IRE)**[24] 4085 8-10-6 109 ....(t) MJFerris[(5)] 96
(James G Sheehan, Ire) *towards rr: rdn in mod 4th appr st: sn no imp* **10/1**
F **Wont Leave An Oat (IRE)**[24] 4085 7-10-11 .... KTColeman —
(William P Murphy, Ire) *trckd ldrs in 3rd tl fell 6th* **6/1**[3]

6m 34.2s **9** Ran SP% **113.5**
CSF £4.75 TOTE £2.20: £1.40, £1.40; DF 3.00.
Owner L Murray **Bred** Tom Hodnett **Trained** New Ross, Co. Wexford

NOTEBOOK
American Jennie(IRE)set off in front and made all for a facile success. She is very athletic at her fences, should be rated value for plenty further, and a crack at Irish National next month was not ruled out by connections. *(op 11/10 tchd 11/8)*
Sunami Storm(IRE) made smooth headway in second place after three out but, not for the first time, began to resent the pressure applied turning for home and produced nothing thereafter. *(op 2/1)*
Countess Trifaldi(IRE) stayed on in the straight from an impossible position.
Kilfinny Cross(IRE) faced a very difficult task on her chase debut, but ran second for a long way before weakening on the approach to the straight. *(op 6/1)*

4543 - 4547a (Foreign Racing) - See Raceform Interactive

4407 AUTEUIL (L-H)
Sunday, March 19

OFFICIAL GOING: Very soft

4548a PRIX JACQUES D'INDY (HURDLE) (GRADE 3) 2m 2f

2:50 (2:53) 4-Y-0 **£39,527** (£19,724; £11,655; £8,069; £4,483; £3,138)

RPR
1 **Card'Son (FR)**[133] 2085 4-10-8 .... CPieux —
(B Secly, France)
2 *½* **Vitray (FR)**[7] 4407 4-9-13 .... BChameraud —
(J Bertran De Balanda, France)
3 *6* **Refutation (FR)**[344] 4-10-1 .... AKondrat —
(J J Napoli, France)
4 *nk* **Biens Nanti (IRE)**[329] 4-10-1 .... TGomme —
(M Cheno, France)
5 *1 ½* **Tidal Fury (IRE)**[133] 2085 4-10-10 .... SLeloup —
(J Jay) *led to 6th, led again 2 out, pushed along approaching last, headed 100 yards out, no extra SP 3-5F* **3/5**[1]
6 *2 ½* **Rose Du Bourg (FR)**[114] 4-10-1 .... DJolibert —
(P Demercastel, France)
7 *4* **Don Preuil (FR)**[44] 4-10-3 .... FDehez —
(P Boisgontier, France)
8 *5* **Orthence (FR)**[105] 4-9-13 .... RegisSchmidlin —
(M Rolland, France)
P **Lesoquera (FR)**[134] 2060 4-9-11 .... EChazelle —
(G Cherel, France)

4m 26.0s **9** Ran SP% **62.5**
PARI-MUTUEL: WIN 4.10; PL 1.90, 5.50, 5.60; DF 51.40.
Owner P Goral **Bred** Mme Joelle Morruzzi **Trained** France

NOTEBOOK
Tidal Fury(IRE) turned in his poorest effort to date in France, but he is expected to improve considerably after this first run of the year, and there was no disgrace in this defeat as he only tired close home. He is reportedly due to continue with a French campaign.

4277 HEREFORD (R-H)
Monday, March 20

OFFICIAL GOING: Good
Wind: Light, across Weather: Overcast

4549 FOWNHOPE CONDITIONAL JOCKEYS' H'CAP HURDLE (13 hdls) 3m 2f

2:10 (2:10) (Class 4) (0-110,110) 4-Y-0+ **£3,253** (£955; £477; £238)

Form RPR
600P **1** **Witness Time (IRE)**[79] 3148 10-11-2 **103** ....(b[1]) TomMessenger[(3)] 110+
(B J Eckley) *mde all: hit 2 out: sn rdn: clr whn hit last: rdn out* **14/1**
/P42 **2** *10* **Heron's Ghyll (IRE)**[10] 4357 9-11-3 **104** .... LiamTreadwell[(3)] 101
(Miss Venetia Williams) *hld up in tch: rdn after 3 out: chsd wnr fr 2 out: sn no imp* **5/1**[2]
3324 **3** *4* **Welsh Dane**[51] 3613 6-10-4 **88** ....(v[1]) OwynNelmes 82+
(M Sheppard) *chsd wnr: hit 6th: rdn after 9th: lost 2nd 2 out: 3rd and wkng whn nt fluent last* **10/3**[1]
52-0 **4** *7* **Metal Detector (IRE)**[60] 3458 9-11-11 **109** ....(p) MarkNicolls 95
(K C Bailey) *prom tl rdn and wknd 3 out* **50/1**
5/6 **5** *1 ½* **Carthago (IRE)**[128] 2182 9-10-9 **98** .... AndrewGlassonbury[(5)] 83
(Miss T McCurrich) *hld up in tch: rdn appr 9th: wknd 3 out* **50/1**

U1P0 **6** *5* **Erins Lass (IRE)**[36] [3888] 9-9-11 **89** JosephStevenson(8) 69
(R Dickin) *bhd tl styd on fr 2 out: nvr nr ldrs* **80/1**
601 **7** *shd* **Jug Of Punch (IRE)**[26] [4046] 7-10-5 **89** ColinBolger 68
(S T Lewis) *bhd: pushed along 7th: hdwy on ins 9th: sn rdn: wknd 3 out* **22/1**
565P **8** *1 ½* **The Flyer (IRE)**[55] [3548] 9-10-13 **100** (t) RichardSpate(3) 78
(Miss S J Wilton) *a bhd* **9/1**
0B36 **9** *8* **Penny's Crown**[11] [4331] 7-10-1 **88** EamonDehdashti(3) 60+
(G A Ham) *a towards rr* **20/1**
0-15 **10** *3 ½* **Prestbury Knight**[14] [4282] 6-11-1 **105** (t) MarcGoldstein(6) 71
(N A Twiston-Davies) *hld up in mid-div: hit 7th: hdwy 8th: hit 10th: wknd 3 out* **7/1**[3]
3220 **11** *2 ½* **Knight Of Silver**[123] [2296] 9-9-13 **88** DarrenO'Dwyer(5) 52
(S C Burrough) *hld up in tch: pushed along after 3rd: wknd 9th* **16/1**
000F **12** *½* **Society Buck (IRE)**[68] [3345] 9-11-7 **105** CharliePoste 68
(John Allen) *a bhd* **80/1**
P500 **13** *5* **Amberleigh House (IRE)**[30] [3988] 14-11-9 **110** StephenCraine(3) 68
(D McCain) *chsd ldrs: rdn after 7th: wknd 9th* **22/1**
-0PU **P** **Cosi Celeste (FR)**[79] [3146] 9-10-9 **93** JamesDiment —
(John Allen) *a bhd: t.o whn p.u bef 3 out* **150/1**
015- **P** **Cristophe**[635] [810] 8-11-3 **101** WilliamKennedy —
(P Bowen) *hld up in mid-div: wknd after 9th: t.o whn plld bef 3 out* **15/2**
0606 **P** **Beluga (IRE)**[48] [3663] 7-10-3 **90** RobertLucey-Butler(3) —
(M Pitman) *hld up in mid-div: wknd after 9th: t.o whn p.u bef last* **14/1**
-0P5 **P** **Sommelier**[46] [3694] 6-10-7 **99** BernieWharfe(8) —
(N A Twiston-Davies) *hld up in mid-div: nt fluent 9th: sn wknd: t.o whn p.u after 2 out* **25/1**

6m 32.9s (4.90) **Going Correction** +0.275s/f (Yiel) **17** Ran SP% **117.6**
Speed ratings: **103,99,98,96,96 94,94,94,91,90 89,89,88,—,— —,—** CSF £73.59 CT £294.57 TOTE £20.00: £4.10, £1.20, £1.90, £10.40; EX 119.70.
Owner Brian Eckley **Bred** Mrs James Hannon **Trained** Llanspyddid, Powys

FOCUS
Not many played a significant role in this very modest handicap. The winner set a decent pace and sets the standard for the form.

NOTEBOOK
Witness Time(IRE) was able to make all the running at a decent pace, staying on well when challenged from the second last. Runner-up in this event 12 months ago, he had been well beaten in a couple of chases this winter and appreciated the return to hurdles, while the blinkers clearly sharpened him up.
Heron's Ghyll(IRE), down in grade, gave chase to the winner two from home but could soon make no impression. This trip might just have stretched him. *(op 9-2 tchd 11-2)*
Welsh Dane, on whom a visor replaced the cheekpieces, made the frame yet again but his consistency is earning him no favours from the Handicapper. *(op 9-2)*
Metal Detector(IRE) travelled well in the cheekpieces but did not find a lot from the approach to the third last. *(op 33-1)*
Carthago(IRE) has been lightly raced since winning a members' point in April 2004 and this was a respectable effort on his first start since November. *(op 40-1)*
Erins Lass(IRE), in a race in which nothing got involved from behind, did come home quite well and seemed to stay this longer trip. *(op 66-1)*
Amberleigh House(IRE), the 2004 Grand National winner, was having his final warm-up for this year's event. Rated much lower over hurdles, he chased the pace until five from home before dropping away to finish last and, while not too much should be read into this performance, surely an honourable clear round is the most to be expected of him in the big one next month. *(op 16-1)*

4550 HOLME LACEY NOVICES' (S) HURDLE (10 hdls) 2m 3f 110y
2:40 (2:44) (Class 5) 4-6-Y-O **£2,081** (£611; £305; £152)

Form RPR
P345 **1** **Mickey Pearce (IRE)**[9] [4368] 4-10-2 78 (v) StevenCrawford(5) 75+
(J G M O'Shea) *bhd: hdwy after 3 out: chsd ldr after next: chal last: veered bdly rt u.p and collided w 2nd cl home: kpt on* **10/3**[1]
0215 **2** *1 ½* **The Wife's Sister**[14] [4278] 5-10-7 90 (b) RichardSpate(7) 82+
(Mrs K Waldron) *chsd ldrs: led appr 4 out: rdn after 2 out: wnt rt last: hung lft u.p run-in: hdd whn bdly bmpd cl home* **7/2**[2]
00P **3** *17* **Silverpro**[29] [4013] 5-9-12 68 RyanCummings(10) 57
(D J Wintle) *chsd ldrs tl rdn and dropped rr 6th: sn lost tch: drvn and styd on again fr 2 out to take 3rd run-in but nt a danger* **25/1**
P0 **4** *¾* **Oktis Morilious (IRE)**[14] [4278] 5-10-8 MrTCollier(7) 64+
(J A Danahar) *chsd ldrs: rdn 3 out: chsd ldr briefly 2 out but no ch: sn wknd* **66/1**
2P4P **5** *½* **Gotontheluckyone (IRE)**[9] [4368] 6-10-8 77 KeiranBurke(7) 67+
(P R Rodford) *w ldrs: led 3rd to 4th: tried to run out next: styd pressing ldrs to 4 out: wknd 2 out* **6/1**
R000 **6** *1 ½* **Lightening Fire (IRE)**[40] [3804] 4-10-7 72 (b) OllieMcPhail 53
(B J Llewellyn) *rr: hdwy and j. slowly 6th: wknd 3 out* **40/1**
0 **7** *16* **Marque Deposee (FR)**[7] [4423] 6-10-1 CharlieStudd(7) 38
(B G Powell) *rr: hdwy 4th: chsd ldr 4 out tl appr 2 out: wknd qckly* **16/1**
PP **8** *14* **Mr Mayfair (IRE)**[7] [4416] 4-10-7 BenjaminHitchcott 23
(Miss L Day) *chsd ldrs to 4 out* **100/1**
9 *21* **Mount Butler (IRE)**[516] 4-10-7 ChristianWilliams —
(J W Tudor) *prom to 5th: wknd after next* **25/1**
6000 **10** *26* **Clifford T Ward**[30] [3985] 6-10-12 83 StephenCraine(3) —
(D McCain) *in tch: chsd ldrs 6th: hit 4 out and wknd qckly* **5/1**[3]
00P6 **11** *11* **Irish Playwright (IRE)**[218] [1222] 6-10-10 (tp) TomGreenway(5) —
(D G Bridgwater) *led to 3rd: led again 4th to 5th: wknd 4 out* **16/1**
60PU **P** **Whatsinitforme (IRE)**[7] [4423] 4-10-2 (v[1]) LeeStephens(5) —
(W K Goldsworthy) *a in rr: t.o whn p.u bef 6th* **40/1**
P **P** **Orenay (USA)**[26] [4057] 4-10-0 (t) TomMessenger(7) —
(W B Stone) *chsd ldrs: led 5th tl appr 4 out: sn wknd: t.o whn p.u bef last* **25/1**

4m 58.1s (10.20) **Going Correction** +0.275s/f (Yiel)
WFA 4 from 5yo+ 7lb **13** Ran SP% **106.9**
Speed ratings: **90,89,82,82,82 81,75,69,61,50 46,—,—** CSF £12.00 TOTE £5.20: £2.10, £1.20, £14.50; EX 11.70.The winner was bought in for 5,500gns.
Owner The Lovely Jubbly's **Bred** John Hutchinson **Trained** Elton, Gloucs
■ Miniperse (11/1) was withdrawn (unruly at start). R4 applies, deduct 5p in the £.
■ Stewards' Enquiry : Steven Crawford four-day ban: careless riding (Mar 31-Apr 3)

FOCUS
A modest winning time, even for a seller. A desperate affair but the form ought to stand up in similar rock-bottom events. There was a controversial finish as the first two collided near the line, but the result stood.

NOTEBOOK
Mickey Pearce(IRE), given a patient ride, went after the leader on the home turn and looked for a moment as if he would not go through with his challenge, but he seized his opportunity as the mare hung right on the run-in. He drifted right when in front, his rider using the stick in his left hand, but his rival was hanging in the other direction and the pair came together close home. The incident happened too late for the result to be affected and he kept the race, but his rider was deemed to be the more culpable of the two. *(op 3-1 tchd 7-2)*
The Wife's Sister had the measure of Mickey Pearce on last month's Uttoxeter running, but that was on heavy ground. She looked the likeliest winner approaching the last, but hung right after the flight, forfeiting the lead, before drifting in the opposite direction under pressure and collecting a bump from the winner near the line. She was just held at the time. *(op 5-2 tchd 4-1)*
Silverpro came under pressure as early as the fifth and was still a remote seventh jumping the second last, but she stayed on for pressure. The longer trip brought about this slightly more encouraging effort.
Oktis Morilious(IRE) went into second place with two to jump but failed to get home. *(op 50-1)*
Gotontheluckyone(IRE)jinked going into the fifth and looked for a moment as if he would run out through the wing. *(op 8-1)*
Marque Deposee(FR) was ridden differently on this step up in trip, but again failed to see out her race after travelling well enough up to a point. *(op 14-1)*

4551 LUGWARDINE JUVENILE NOVICES' HURDLE (8 hdls) 2m 1f
3:10 (3:13) (Class 4) 4-Y-O **£3,903** (£1,146; £573; £286)

Form RPR
F21 **1** **Bureaucrat**[17] [4211] 4-11-3 118 RichardJohnson 132+
(P J Hobbs) *a gng wl: led appr 3rd: clr fr 2 out: easily* **4/9**[1]
463 **2** *20* **Whistle Blowing (IRE)**[36] [3883] 4-10-7 103 StephenCraine(3) 100+
(D McCain) *a.p: rdn 4th: hit 2 out: wnt 2nd appr last: no ch w wnr* **10/1**[3]
P233 **3** *11* **Josear**[21] [4153] 4-10-12 112 ShaneWalsh(5) 97+
(C J Down) *a.p: chsd wnr 5th: rdn after 3 out: wknd appr last* **20/1**
400 **4** *3 ½* **Ausone**[25] [4074] 4-10-0 OwynNelmes(3) 78
(Miss J R Gibney) *hld up and bhd: hdwy appr 4th: rdn 5th: wknd 3 out* **250/1**
15 **5** *½* **Astronomical (IRE)**[30] [3972] 4-10-10 115 RichardSpate(7) 92+
(Miss S J Wilton) *hld up in mid-div: hdwy appr 4th: wknd after 3 out* **22/1**
FF24 **6** *½* **Ellerslie Tom**[39] [3817] 4-10-5 110 LeeStephens(5) 84
(P Bowen) *chsd ldr: led appr 2nd tl appr 3rd: wknd 2 out* **11/2**[2]
00 **7** *1 ½* **Sultan Fontenaille (FR)**[32] [3947] 4-10-10 AndrewThornton 82
(N J Hawke) *hld up towards rr: mstke 3 out: stdy hdwy fr 2 out: n.d* **100/1**
203P **8** *18* **Knightsbridge Hill (IRE)**[65] [3386] 4-10-10 109 RobertThornton 64
(A King) *prom: rdn 3rd: hit 5th: wknd after 3 out* **20/1**
UP0 **9** *shd* **Beaumont Girl (IRE)**[31] [3786] 4-10-0 ow2 MarkNicolls(5) 59
(Miss M E Rowland) *rdn 3rd: a bhd* **250/1**
0 **10** *3 ½* **Kova Hall (IRE)**[41] [3786] 4-10-10 PJBrennan 60
(P J Hobbs) *rdn appr 3rd: bhd most of way* **50/1**
0 **11** *dist* **Cetshwayo**[26] [4057] 4-10-10 MarkBradburne —
(J M P Eustace) *a towards rr: t.o whn mstke last: virtually p.u flat* **200/1**
0 **P** **Raffish**[91] [2921] 4-10-10 TomScudamore —
(M Scudamore) *a in rr: t.o whn p.u bef last* **200/1**
P06 **P** **Cloonavery (IRE)**[140] [1955] 4-10-7 80 TJPhelan(3) —
(B Llewellyn) *a bhd: t.o whn p.u bef 2 out* **125/1**
P **P** **Opera Villevert (FR)**[62] [3436] 4-10-5 HowieEphgrave(5) —
(L Corcoran) *hld up in tch: rdn and wknd 5th: t.o whn p.u bef last* **200/1**
P **P** **Hannah's Tribe (IRE)**[143] [1904] 4-10-3 JosephByrne —
(C W Moore) *led tl appr 2nd: rdn and wknd appr 4th: t.o whn p.u bef 5th* **200/1**
P **P** **Doughty**[7] [4416] 4-10-10 WarrenMarston —
(D J Wintle) *bhd: sme hdwy 4th: wknd appr 5th: mstke 3 out: t.o whn p.u bef 2 out* **250/1**

4m 3.40s (0.30) **Going Correction** +0.275s/f (Yiel) **16** Ran SP% **114.5**
Speed ratings: **110,100,95,93,93 93,92,84,84,82 —,—,—,—,— —** CSF £4.72 TOTE £1.40: £1.20, £2.10, £2.30; EX 7.30.
Owner Peter Luff **Bred** Newgate Stud Co **Trained** Withycombe, Somerset

FOCUS
A fair juvenile event that was turned into a one-horse show, with the winner value for 25 lengths and a creditable winning time for a race of its class. The second and third ran to their marks.

NOTEBOOK
Bureaucrat ◆, in front before the third, dictated thereafter and pulled clear to win to win as he liked. Following up his initial hurdles success at Newbury, he gained more valuable experience here and looks a useful youngster. The valuable Anniversary Hurdle at Aintree is next on his schedule and the track should suit him. *(tchd 1-2)*
Whistle Blowing(IRE) found the winner in a different league but stayed on to go second on the home turn. Improving with racing, he shapes as if he would appreciate a step up in trip.
Josear is fully exposed - this was his 14th run of the season - and he helps set the level of the form. *(op 16-1)*
Ausone, having only her second look at hurdles, stayed on quite well to claim a fairly remote fourth.
Astronomical(IRE) had no excuses on account of the ground this time but did not always jump fluently. *(op 16-1)*
Ellerslie Tom, unable to get his own way in front, faded somewhat tamely from the second last. *(op 9-1)*
Sultan Fontenaille(FR), having his third run over hurdles, stayed on nicely in the latter stages and is not without hope. *(op 80-1)*

4552 WEATHERBYS MESSAGING SERVICE NOVICES' H'CAP CHASE (12 fncs) 2m
3:40 (3:40) (Class 4) (0-110,109) 5-Y-O+
£4,384 (£1,295; £647; £324; £161; £81)

Form RPR
5210 **1** **Nazimabad (IRE)**[130] [2149] 7-11-2 **99** (t) ChristianWilliams 110
(Evan Williams) *led tl hdd 4 out: styd cl 2nd: rallied to chal last: led run-in: hld on all out* **4/1**[2]
-PFF **2** *shd* **Misty Dancer**[114] [2488] 7-11-9 **109** PaulO'Neill(3) 121+
(Miss Venetia Williams) *hld up in rr: hdwy 7th: led 4 out: rdn and hdd run-in: rallied cl home: jst failed* **5/1**[3]
3060 **3** *12* **Notanotherdonkey (IRE)**[14] [4281] 6-10-12 **95** TomScudamore 94
(M Scudamore) *bhd: hit 5th: pushed along 8th: styd on after 2 out to take 3rd run-in but nvr gng pce to trble ldrs* **7/1**
P36P **4** *5* **Rash Moment (FR)**[84] [2982] 7-10-9 **99** RichardSpate(7) 93
(Mrs K Waldron) *rr: hit 4th: riden along fr 6th: nvr nr ldrs but mod prog to take 4th run-in* **20/1**
1F03 **5** *nk* **Whaleef**[14] [4281] 8-11-6 **103** (t) RichardJohnson 97
(B J Llewellyn) *chsd ldrs: wnt 2nd 5th: nt fluent 6th (water): hit next: wknd after 4 out: no ch whn hit last* **5/2**[1]
0434 **6** *1 ½* **Imperial Rocket (USA)**[26] [4049] 9-10-12 **100** (t) LeeStephens(5) 92
(W K Goldsworthy) *chsd wnr to 5th: wknd 4 out: no ch whn blnd last* **9/1**
4 **7** *1 ½* **Wondersobright (IRE)**[8] [4387] 7-10-1 **89** (p) PaddyMerrigan(5) 81+
(K J Burke) *t.k.h: rr: hit hit 1st: 4th and 7th: sme hdwy whn blnd 8th: sn wknd: no ch whn mstke 2 out* **6/1**
U6PP **P** **Drive On Driver (IRE)**[14] [4279] 9-9-9 **83** oh5 TomGreenway(5) —
(Lady Susan Brooke) *hit 5th: a bhd: t.o whn p.u bef 3 out* **66/1**

4m 8.60s (6.10) **Going Correction** +0.525s/f (Soft) **8** Ran SP% **108.3**
Speed ratings: **105,104,98,96,96 95,94,—** CSF £21.99 CT £116.89 TOTE £6.50: £1.70, £2.30, £2.60; EX 27.50.

Owner Fox And Hounds Racing **Bred** His Highness The Aga Khan's Studs S C **Trained** Cowbridge, Vale Of Glamorgan

FOCUS
A cracking finish to this novice handicap, in which the winner set a strong pace, and the race could rate higher.

NOTEBOOK
Nazimabad(IRE) bowled along in front, setting a good pace. The game looked to be up when he was collared at the fourth last, but he fought back to lead on the run-in and just held on as the runner-up rallied. He appreciated the drop back to the minimum trip and had been freshened up for a spring campaign since a disappointing run in November. *(op 3-1)*
Misty Dancer ◆ was having his first run since November, having taken two falls in as many starts over fences. Jumping really well this time, he showed ahead four from home but was unable to get clear and was collared after the last. Rallying, he just failed to get back up on the nod. He did nothing wrong at all and can find compensation. *(op 11-2 tchd 6-1)*
Notanotherdonkey(IRE) found this too sharp a test but stuck on to go third on the run-in. *(op 9-1 tchd 13-2)*
Rash Moment(FR), who needs much further than this and softer ground, was only getting going after the final fence. *(op 14-1)*
Whaleef eventually paid the price for chasing the pace and ran below par. *(op 3-1)*
Imperial Rocket(USA) , dropped 4lb, was beaten with four to jump but was only run out of third from the final fence. *(op 7-1)*

4553 BARTESTREE H'CAP CHASE (19 fncs) 3m 1f 110y
4:10 (4:10) (Class 5) (0-90,90) 5-Y-O+ **£3,253** (£955; £477; £238)

Form RPR
25P4 **1** **Valley Warrior**[67] 3359 9-9-8 **65** MrGTumelty(7) 79
(J S Smith) *hld up towards rr: hdwy 11th: rdn appr 4 out: n.m.r on ins after 3 out: led after 2 out: styd on wl* **6/1**[2]
43U3 **2** *5* **Aisjem (IRE)**[26] 4047 7-10-13 **77** (p) ChristianWilliams 86
(Evan Williams) *w ldr: led 14th: rdn appr 4 out: j.rt 3 out: sn edgd lft: hdd 2 out: no ex flat* **7/1**
063P **3** *7* **Paddy The Optimist (IRE)**[9] 4370 10-10-8 **77** MrTJO'Brien(5) 79
(D Burchell) *hld up in mid-div: hdwy 9th: rdn to ld and hit 2 out: sn hdd & wknd* **6/1**[2]
0F2P **4** *26* **Zimbabwe (FR)**[11] 4328 6-11-3 **81** (b[1]) AndrewThornton 57
(N J Hawke) *prom tl rdn and wknd 13th* **11/1**
1/PP **5** *6* **Designer Label (IRE)**[62] 3430 10-11-10 **88** (p) PaulMoloney 58
(M Pitman) *led to 14th: rdn and wknd 4 out* **25/1**
5-P6 **6** *hd* **Arceye**[60] 3457 9-9-8 **65** TomMessenger(7) 35
(W Davies) *mstkes 4th (water) and 11th: a bhd* **20/1**
43/0 **7** *14* **Isotop (FR)**[69] 3331 10-11-3 **86** MarkNicolls(5) 42
(John Allen) *mstke 10th: a bhd* **33/1**
P605 **8** *dist* **Celia's High (IRE)**[12] 4300 7-10-1 **68** (t) StephenCraine(3) —
(D McCain) *prom tl blnd bdly and lost pl 11th: bhd whn hit 12th: t.o* **11/1**
/006 **P** **Lady Wurzel**[40] 3801 7-10-7 **71** AndrewTinkler —
(J G Cann) *a bhd: t.o whn p.u bef 10th* **14/1**
-P00 **P** **Kayleigh (IRE)**[32] 3951 8-10-10 **81** (p) KeiranBurke(7) —
(P R Rodford) *a bhd: t.o 7th: p.u bef 15th* **80/1**
P5F6 **P** **Run To The King (IRE)**[29] 4016 8-10-13 **82** LeeStephens(5) —
(P C Ritchens) *a bhd: t.o 8th: p.u bef 12th* **66/1**
-000 **F** **Eveon (IRE)**[79] 3149 6-10-7 **71** DavidDennis —
(Ian Williams) *mid-div: hdwy 14th: 7l 5th and rdn whn fell 4 out* **16/1**
2366 **U** **Sissinghurst Storm (IRE)**[26] 4047 8-10-11 **75** WayneHutchinson —
(R Dickin) *mid-div: 7l down whn blnd and uns rdr 14th* **11/2**[1]
-PPF **P** **Terminology**[20] 4164 8-11-12 **90** JohnMcNamara —
(K C Bailey) *hld up in tch: wkng whn mstke and pckd bdly 14th: p.u bef 15th* **50/1**
-F6P **P** **Pewter Light (IRE)**[36] 3886 9-11-1 **79** (b) PJBrennan —
(B J M Ryall) *hld up in tch: rdn appr 5th: wknd 12th: bhd whn p.u after 13th* **13/2**[3]

6m 43.9s (9.70) **Going Correction** +0.525s/f (Soft) **15** Ran SP% **115.2**
Speed ratings: **106,104,102,94,92 92,88,—,—,— —,—,—,—,—** CSF £43.01 CT £263.33 TOTE £6.70: £1.80, £2.20, £2.00; EX 39.60.
Owner Mrs J A Benson **Bred** Mrs W Smith **Trained** Tirley, Gloucs
■ Stewards' Enquiry : Christian Williams caution: careless riding

FOCUS
Very few came into this low-grade handicap in any sort of form. The first three had it between them from the third last.

NOTEBOOK
Valley Warrior squeezed through to challenge going to the second last and, able to secure the shortest route around the home turn, stayed on well enough to break his duck. He had been runner-up off 12lb higher on his chase debut at Worcester in October but ran off a mere 65 here, with his rider taking off a handy 7lb. *(tchd 13-2)*
Aisjem(IRE) was always prominent with the cheekpieces back on but could not hold the lead on the home turn, from which point she was second best. She looks up to winning a little race somewhere. *(op 13-2)*
Paddy The Optimist(IRE), last year's winner, has become well handicapped, 11lb lower than when gaining his lastest victory over this course and distance 11 months ago, but he could not counter after blundering two from home when in with every chance. *(op 11-2 tchd 13-2)*
Zimbabwe(FR) ran well off this mark at Leicester two runs back but has been found wanting since, the blinkers having no great beneficial effect. He really needs softer ground.
Designer Label(IRE) was off the track a long time after winning at this venue in September 2003 and had been pulled up in two runs back. He showed a bit more in the cheekpieces but faded from the fourth last. *(tchd 28-1)*
Celia's High(IRE) *Official explanation: vet said gelding bled from nose (op 14-1)*
Sissinghurst Storm(IRE), whose two wins have been gained at this venue, was still in touch when departing. *(tchd 6-1)*
Lady Wurzel *Official explanation: jockey said mare was never travelling (tchd 6-1)*
Eveon(IRE), making her chasing debut after failing to trouble the judge in bumpers or novice hurdles, was in fifth place and not out of it when taking a heavy fall at the fourth last. *(tchd 6-1)*

4554 MARSTOW MAIDEN OPEN NATIONAL HUNT FLAT RACE 1m 5f
4:40 (4:41) (Class 6) 4-6-Y-O **£1,626** (£477; £238; £119)

Form RPR
0 **1** **Dancewiththedevil (IRE)**[25] 4072 5-11-4 APMcCoy 103+
(Jonjo O'Neill) *in tch: hdwy 5f out: trckd ldrs gng wl 3f out: slt ld 2f out: drvn out fnl f* **5/4**[1]
2 *1 ½* **Mocho (IRE)** 5-11-4 WayneHutchinson 101
(Ian Williams) *prom: chsd wnr ins fnl 2f: sn hrd drvn: one pce whn swtchd lft wl ins last* **12/1**
2 **3** *1 ¾* **Brinkmanship (USA)**[153] 1785 4-10-11 RichardJohnson 92
(Mrs H Dalton) *in tch: chsd ldrs fr 3f out: kpt on u.p fnl 2f but nvr gng pce to chal* **7/2**[2]
0 **4** *7* **Young Guns (IRE)**[138] 1985 5-11-4 DaveCrosse 92
(J G M O'Shea) *bhd: hdwy 6f out: drvn and hdwy to chse ldrs 3f out: kpt on same pce fr over 1f out* **66/1**
5 *¾* **Luccombe Bay** 6-10-11 JamieMoore 84
(M G Rimell) *t.k.h in rr: drvn along fr 1/2-way: hdwy fr 3f out: kpt on fr over 1f out but nvr gng pce to rch ldrs* **18/1**
3 **6** *5* **Ganache (IRE)**[27] 4038 4-10-11 MickFitzgerald 79
(P R Chamings) *chsd ldrs: slt ld over 3f out: hdd 2f out: sn wknd* **7/1**[3]
0 **7** *3 ½* **Intra Vires (IRE)**[27] 4038 4-9-13 JamesDiment(5) 69
(J L Spearing) *chsd ldrs: rdn 4f out: wknd fr 3f out* **66/1**
00 **8** *2* **Hakumatata**[68] 3346 4-10-6 RobertLucey-Butler(5) 74
(Miss Z C Davison) *bhd: hdwy to trck ldrs 5f out: sn rdn: wknd 3f out* **25/1**
06 **9** *1 ¾* **Follow My Leader (IRE)**[31] 3961 6-10-11 PJBrennan 72
(R Ford) *led tl hdd over 3f out: sn wknd* **11/1**
4 **10** *1 ¾* **Celtic Society (IRE)**[46] 3691 5-11-4 AndrewThornton 77
(P C Ritchens) *nvr bttr than mid-div* **20/1**
0 **11** *3 ½* **True Tara**[26] 4059 4-10-5 ow1 AntonyEvans 61
(J L Spearing) *plld hrd: bhd most of way* **50/1**
00 **12** *19* **Miss Millfield**[83] 3024 5-10-11 OllieMcPhail 48
(V J Hughes) *mid-div: rdn 1/2-way: sn bhd* **150/1**
00 **13** *5* **Dark Rosalina**[134] 2075 5-10-11 JosephByrne 43
(C W Moore) *a in rr* **150/1**
U0 **14** *12* **Global Party (IRE)**[11] 4333 4-10-4 JamesWhite(7) 31
(Miss C J Williams) *rr whn hmpd after 4f: a bhd* **150/1**
0 **15** *13* **Jillanory**[25] 4072 4-10-4 BenjaminHitchcott 11
(C W Moore) *chsd ldrs a m: sn wknd* **200/1**
P **16** *dist* **Tudor Rose (IRE)**[102] 2727 5-10-11 (t) JodieMogford —
(Mrs N S Evans) *chsd ldrs a m: t.o* **66/1**

3m 22.1s **16** Ran SP% **118.0**
CSF £17.09 TOTE £1.90: £1.40, £2.40, £1.50; EX 28.20.
Owner The Four Exiles **Bred** William J O'Brien **Trained** Cheltenham, Gloucs

FOCUS
Just an ordinary bumper rated around the third and ninth, but at least it was run at a true pace and the winner can rate higher.

NOTEBOOK
Dancewiththedevil(IRE) made steady progress before taking up the running going well, but McCoy had to get serious with him in the closing stages as he idled in front. The drop in trip and better ground did the trick after he had twice failed to get home over two miles in heavy conditions. *(op 11-8 tchd 6-4)*
Mocho(IRE), whose dam won a bumper on fast ground first time out, was being given reminders at an early stage but he responded to pressure to make the winner work for his victory. He is some way from the finished article and should come on for the experience. *(tchd 14-1)*
Brinkmanship(USA), runner-up to subsequent scorer Sword Of Damascus over this trip at Exeter in October, had his chance but appeared to run green when the pressure was on. *(tchd 4-1)*
Young Guns(IRE), runner-up in an Irish point but well held on his bumper debut, confirmed that he has ability without being able to land a blow. *(op 50-1)*
Luccombe Bay stayed on as if in need of further, as befits a daughter of a mare who was placed in three-mile chases. *(op 20-1)*
Ganache(IRE) showed in front at the end of the back straight but was soon headed by the winner and failed to get home. He would appear to have stamina limitations. *(op 9-2)*
Tudor Rose(IRE) *Official explanation: trainer said mare had breathing problem (op 50-1)*

4555 JULIAN GRAVES HUNTERS' CHASE (13 fncs 1 omitted) 2m 3f
5:10 (5:11) (Class 6) 5-Y-O+ **£1,249** (£387; £193; £96)

Form RPR
/211 **1** **Bill Haze**[10] 4349 10-12-0 MrRhysHughes(7) 106+
(P Dando) *led 2nd to 4th: led 9th: rdn and flashed tail appr last: hung bdly lft flat: r.o* **13/2**[2]
-000 **2** *3* **Dun An Doras (IRE)**[23] 10-11-7 106 MrDMcKenna(7) 94
(Mrs N Frost) *hld up in mid-div: hdwy appr 4 out: chsd wnr fr 3 out: one pce flat* **12/1**
4F5P **3** *6* **Thieves'Glen**[10] 4358 8-12-7 100 MrTJO'Brien 96+
(H Morrison) *hld up in tch: bmpd 9th: outpcd 4 out: styd fr 2 out* **16/1**
1P2P **4** *1 ¼* **Viscount Bankes**[11] 4330 8-12-0 MrSWaley-Cohen(5) 92
(Mrs Rosemary Gasson) *prom tl wknd 2 out* **33/1**
1-P3 **5** *1 ½* **Chef Tartare (FR)**[10] 4351 6-12-0 113 (t) MrRQuinn(7) 95+
(Mrs K Waldron) *hld up and bhd: blnd 6th and 7th: hdwy 4 out: wknd 2 out* **7/2**[1]
P5F/ **6** *shd* **Elgar**[707] 4782 9-11-7 (t) MrTCollier(7) 85
(M Hammond) *hld up and bhd: hdwy appr 3 out: wknd 2 out* **25/1**
163/ **7** *9* **Toscanini (GER)**[22] 10-11-7 MrSGray(7) 76
(Mark Doyle) *nvr nr ldrs* **33/1**
45P4 **8** *¾* **Hot Plunge**[10] 4349 10-12-0 MrJOwen(5) 81
(Mrs J P Lomax) *rel to r: hdwy 5th: rdn after 8th: wknd 4 out* **14/1**
1-24 **9** *3 ½* **Cornish Gale (IRE)**[22] 12-11-12 MrDAFitzsimmons(7) 79+
(D McCain Jnr) *prom: lost pl 4th: bhd fr 9th: no ch whn blnd 3 out* **7/2**[1]
-445 **10** *14* **Ivanoph (FR)**[25] 4079 10-12-0 96 MrAWintle 58
(S Flook) *hld up in tch: led 8th to 9th: wkng whn mstke 2 out* **14/1**
-6P3 **11** *5* **River Pirate (IRE)**[26] 4055 9-11-7 93 (b) MrJMahot(7) 53
(David W Drinkwater) *rdn 8th: a bhd* **66/1**
P-PP **12** *12* **Barton Bandit**[14] 4283 10-11-7 (p) MrJSole(7) 41
(Miss Sarah Kent) *prom: led 4th to 8th: wknd appr 4 out* **150/1**
4-P0 **13** *2 ½* **Joris De Vonnas (FR)**[15] 9-12-0 89 (t) MrRHodges(7) 46
(Rob Hodges) *mstke 1st: rdn appr 6th: a bhd* **100/1**
-10P **U** **Let's Fly (FR)**[10] 4349 11-11-12 MrWBiddick(7) —
(Ross Oliver) *led tl blnd and uns rdr 1st* **7/1**[3]
-00U **P** **King's Travel (FR)**[23] 10-11-9 MrRWoollacott(5) —
(Miss Sarah Robinson) *mid-div: blnd 7th: sn bhd: t.o whn p.u bef 4 out* **66/1**
12-0 **P** **Lincoln Place (IRE)**[23] 11-11-9 111 MrWLMorgan(5) —
(Mrs Marilyn Scudamore) *lft in ld 1st: hdd 2nd: wknd 8th: t.o whn p.u bef 2 out* **25/1**

5m 1.00s (14.40) **Going Correction** +0.525s/f (Soft) **16** Ran SP% **115.4**
Speed ratings: **90,88,86,85,85 85,81,80,79,73 71,66,65,—,—** — CSF £71.95 TOTE £8.10: £2.70, £3.70, £4.40; EX 110.40 Place 6 £22.18, Place 5 £9.61.
Owner P Dando **Bred** Mrs K M Dando **Trained** Cardiff

FOCUS
An ordinary hunter chase rated through the fourth with the placed horses also close to their marks. The middle fence in the back straight was bypassed on the final circuit.

NOTEBOOK
Bill Haze completed the hat-trick after a brace of victories at Leicester. Back in front at the ninth, he gave a trademark flash of the tail before the final fence before hanging right the way over to the stands' fence on the run-in, but was always going to hold on. Despite the idiosyncrasies, he does look something of a reformed character and he is a versatile sort with regards to the trip. *(op 9-2)*
Dun An Doras(IRE), sharpened up by a recent spin in a point, appreciated the drop to this more suitable trip but despite keeping on he could not trouble the winner. *(op 14-1)*
Thieves'Glen, having his second run in this sphere, stayed on in the latter stages after being outpaced leaving the back straight. *(op 14-1)*
Viscount Bankes is less than consistent and this was one of his better efforts. *(op 40-1)*

Chef Tartare(FR) survived some notable errors which left him with plenty to do. He made ground travelling quite well, but found little when let down from the second last.
Elgar, a one-time fair novice with Michael Scudamore, ran an encouraging race over an inadequate trip on this first start for nearly two years.
Hot Plunge, who won a similar race over two miles on this card a year ago, has now proved a bit reluctant to race on his last two starts. *(op 16-1)*
Cornish Gale(IRE) made a winning return to action in a men's open point last month and this was disappointing.
T/Jkpt: £10,152.80 to a £1 stake. Pool: £1,501,478.00. 105.00 winning tickets. T/Plt: £14.70 to a £1 stake. Pool: £113,269.05. 5,595.45 winning tickets. T/Qpdt: £6.80 to a £1 stake. Pool: £4,920.20. 533.20 winning tickets. KH

4284 EXETER (R-H)

Tuesday, March 21

OFFICIAL GOING: Good to soft (good in places)

Flight in front of stands and flight after the stands omitted all hurdle races. Last two fences in back straight omitted all chases.
Wind: Moderate, against Weather: Cloudy, cold

4556 PUNCH TAVERNS NOVICES' (S) HURDLE (5 hdls 3 omitted) 2m 1f
2:20 (2:21) (Class 5) 4-Y-0+ **£2,740** (£798; £399)

Form				RPR
3-04	1		**Longstone Lady (IRE)**[28] [4034] 9-10-2 90 ChrisHonour(5) (J D Frost) *led 1st: rdn 2 out: r.o wl* **5/1**[3]	84
0233	2	5	**Native Commander (IRE)**[9] [4392] 11-10-9 90 (b) ChristopherMurray(5) (Jim Best) *hld up and bhd: hdwy 1st: rdn 2 out: wnt 2nd last: one pce* **9/2**[2]	86
66P0	3	6	**Pearly Star**[15] [4282] 5-11-0 90 (v) WayneHutchinson (A King) *hld up in tch: chsd wnr appr 2 out to last: wknd flat* **7/2**[1]	80
40F6	4	7	**Griffin's Legacy**[15] [4278] 7-10-7 85 JamesWhite(7) (N G Ayliffe) *hld up in mid-div: btn whn lft 4th and hmpd 2 out* **16/1**	75+
FP4	5	hd	**Georges Boy (IRE)**[14] [4290] 8-10-11 95 (v) GinoCarenza(3) (P J Jones) *prom: reminders 1st: lost pl 2nd: n.d after* **9/2**[2]	73
0636	6	14	**Giant's Rock (IRE)**[6] [4449] 4-10-7 73 (bt) RichardJohnson (B J Llewellyn) *led to 1st: prom tl rdn and wknd appr 2 out* **9/1**	52
	7	5	**Ewar Finch (FR)**[82] 4-10-0 RobertWalford (C L Popham) *hld up and bhd: short-lived effrt appr 2 out* **100/1**	40
-6R6	8	dist	**Aruba Dam (IRE)**[202] [1383] 8-10-7 78 ChristianWilliams (A E Jones) *a bhd: t.o* **40/1**	—
	P		**Bewhatyouwanttobe** 5-10-0 MissSGaisford(7) (J D Frost) *t.o fr 1st: p.u bef 2 out* **100/1**	—
	P		**Penerak**[1203] 6-11-0 (t) RJGreene (Mrs L J Young) *plld hrd: a towards rr: mstke 3rd: t.o whn p.u bef 2 out* **100/1**	—
5004	F		**After Lent (IRE)**[15] [4278] 5-10-7 87 AndrewGlassonbury(7) (M C Pipe) *plld hrd early: in tch: 4th and btn whn fell 2 out* **10/1**	75
	U		**Lieuday**[219] 7-10-11 RichardYoung(3) (C L Tizzard) *hld up: hdwy 2nd: mstke 3rd: wknd appr 2 out: no ch whn blnd and uns rdr last* **20/1**	—

4m 21.7s (12.50) **Going Correction** +0.775s/f (Soft)
WFA 4 from 5yo+ 7lb **12 Ran SP% 110.4**
Speed ratings: **101,98,95,92,92 85,83,—,—,— —,—** CSF £25.40 TOTE £5.10: £2.10, £1.20, £2.10; EX 28.30.There was no bid for the winner
Owner Mrs J R Bastard **Bred** M Berry **Trained** Scorriton, Devon

FOCUS
A long run-in, with the last being omitted throughout the afternoon, but Longstone Lass galloped on resolutely and sets the standard for the form.

NOTEBOOK
Longstone Lady(IRE), taking a drop in grade, never had a moment's worry and she galloped on relentlessly to record her first win, ending her trainer's lengthy losing run in the process. Lightly-raced for her age, it was amazing she was allowed to go off at such a big price considering how well in she was at the weights. She held a three or four-length advantage over the runner-up taking the last and saw the trip out well, suggesting there are more races in her at around this distance. *(op 4-1 tchd 6-1)*
Native Commander(IRE), a three-time winner over fences in Ireland, has yet to race over fences in Britain, but he has been performing well in similarly low-grade contests over hurdles and produced another sound effort, possibly being given too much to do by his rider. *(tchd 11-2)*
Pearly Star had to be respected on this drop in grade, with his stable riding on such a high after a big-race double at the Festival last week. However, having come through to have every chance turning in, he failed to see his race out as strongly as the front two. There is a small race in him, but he is hardly one to make a habit of backing.
Griffin's Legacy has not gone on at all from his Chepstow bumper win back in 2004, but he battled on to just get fourth. *(op 20-1)*
Georges Boy(IRE) failed to build on a recent good effort at the course and the headgear clearly failed to have the same effect. *(tchd 4-1)*
Giant's Rock(IRE) continues to disappoint and he dropped away quickly before the turn-in. *(op 8-1)*
After Lent(IRE) was in the process of running a sound race when falling at the second last, but he is another who has failed to progress. *(op 9-1)*

4557 SIS NOVICES' H'CAP HURDLE (9 hdls 2 omitted) 2m 6f 110y
2:50 (2:50) (Class 4) (0-105,105) 4-Y-0+ **£3,903** (£1,146; £573; £286)

Form				RPR
06P0	1		**Haloo Baloo**[14] [4289] 6-11-0 93 MickFitzgerald (Jonjo O'Neill) *hld up and bhd: hdwy 4th: styd on to ld flat: drvn out* **14/1**	97+
6PP0	2	8	**Midnight Gold**[42] [3792] 6-11-4 97 WayneHutchinson (A King) *hld up in mid-div: hdwy appr 4th: rdn to ld appr 2 out: hdd and no ex flat* **16/1**	93
P063	3	9	**How Is The Lord (IRE)**[14] [4290] 10-10-0 82 OwynNelmes(3) (C J Down) *hld up towards rr: hdwy 5th: rdn and ev ch 2 out: hit last: wknd flat* **12/1**	71+
5-64	4	11	**Liberty Ben (IRE)**[33] [3943] 6-11-5 98 RobertWalford (R H Alner) *hld up and bhd: sme hdwy 6th: styd on fr 2 out: n.d* **16/1**	74
0001	5	3 ½	**Lord Ryeford (IRE)**[39] [3843] 6-11-5 98 JasonMaguire (T R George) *hld up in tch: led 5th: rdn and hdd appr 2 out: wknd appr last* **9/1**	76+
06P1	6	18	**Pure Magic (FR)**[31] [3997] 5-10-5 89 CharliePoste(5) (Miss J S Davis) *led tl after 1st: prom: rdn 3rd: wknd appr 2 out* **15/2**[3]	44
-036	7	7	**Barclay Boy**[18] [4210] 7-11-6 104 LiamHeard(5) (A J Lidderdale) *hld up in tch: wknd appr 2 out* **13/2**[2]	52
1424	8	dist	**English Jim (IRE)**[35] [3905] 5-10-6 85 MatthewBatchelor (Miss A M Newton-Smith) *hld up in mid-div: hdwy 4th: rdn 5th: wknd appr 2 out: t.o* **15/2**[3]	—
661P	9	dist	**Strolling Vagabond (IRE)**[30] [4012] 7-9-8 80 MarcGoldstein(7) (John R Upson) *prom: rdn after 3rd: sn struggling: t.o* **11/1**	—
4/PP	P		**Probus Lady**[23] [4133] 9-9-9 79 oh15 StevenCrawford(5) (C J Down) *a bhd: rdn 5th: blnd 6th: sn p.u* **100/1**	—
001P	P		**Sandmartin (IRE)**[71] [3325] 6-11-7 100 (b) RichardJohnson (P J Hobbs) *led after 1st: hdd 5th: wknd and p.u bef 2 out* **8/1**	—
1000	P		**Shingle Street (IRE)**[8] [4429] 4-10-11 99 (b) AlanO'Keeffe (Miss Venetia Williams) *prom to 5th: t.o whn p.u bef 2 out* **50/1**	—
03P2	P		**Abragante (IRE)**[37] [3876] 5-11-12 105 (p) TimmyMurphy (M C Pipe) *hld up and bhd: short-lived effrt after 6th: p.u bef 2 out* **4/1**[1]	—
P-P6	P		**Jollyshau (IRE)**[53] [3598] 8-10-1 85 ShaneWalsh(5) (Miss A M Newton-Smith) *hld up: short-lived effrt appr 4th: t.o whn p.u bef 6th* **100/1**	—
-10P	P		**Montecorvino (GER)**[30] [4012] 5-11-8 101 (t) AntonyEvans (N A Twiston-Davies) *nt fluent: prom: rdn after 3rd: sn struggling: t.o whn p.u bef 4th* **33/1**	—

5m 56.7s (17.40) **Going Correction** +0.775s/f (Soft)
WFA 4 from 5yo+ 8lb **15 Ran SP% 119.3**
Speed ratings: **100,97,94,90,89 82,80,—,—,— —,—,—,—,—** CSF £211.67 CT £2758.62 TOTE £14.10: £2.90, £5.00, £5.30; EX 219.50.
Owner Mrs Gay Smith **Bred** Miss F A Evans **Trained** Cheltenham, Gloucs

FOCUS
A modest contest ultimately that could be rated higher but the form does not look strong.

NOTEBOOK
Haloo Baloo, who was in the process of running well when running out at the course last time, was on his best behaviour on this occasion and, having moved into a challenging position mid-way down the back straight, he began to edge his way nearer the lead. He nosed ahead after the last before pulling clear in the final 100 yards, ultimately winning comfortably. Stamina is clearly his strong suit and, although he clearly has a quirk, there should be more to come from him as he was winning here off just a mark of 93. *(op 16-1)*
Midnight Gold has been out of sorts this season, but he offered a little more last time and came through to hold a narrow advantage at the end of the back straight. Despite jumping the last two well, he was unable to hold off the winner and ended up being well held. He can find a race if building on this. *(tchd 20-1)*
How Is The Lord(IRE) ran well when coming from a fair way back at the course earlier in the month, but he was up 2lb here and simply failed to see out the trip. He has clearly had problems, *this being only his sixth start at the age of ten, but there is a race in him at the right levelOfficial explanation: jockey said gelding hung left in closing stages*
Liberty Ben(IRE), a chaser in the making, got going all too late and looked rather pace less back in *fourth. He was being ridden some way from the finish and a step up to three miles looks required. (op 12-1)*
Lord Ryeford(IRE), a winner on his handicap debut at Bangor in February, stopped very quickly after the last and his stable's poor recent run of form continues. *(op 8-1)*
Barclay Boy has been shaping as though this rise in distance would suit, but he failed to get home having still been in striking distance turning in. *(tchd 7-1)*
Abragante(IRE), who was on and off the bit throughout, further demonstrated his inability to run two races alike and continued his stable's poor run of results. *(op 9-2 tchd 5-1)*
Sandmartin(IRE), a shock winner in the first-time blinkers at the course back in January, was reportedly 'wrong behind' when disappointing seven days later and the benefit of a nice break clearly failed to do anything for him as, having showed up well early, folded disappointingly under pressure. *(op 9-2 tchd 5-1)*

4558 TOZERS SOLICITORS NOVICES' H'CAP CHASE (13 fncs 4 omitted) 2m 7f 110y
3:20 (3:21) (Class 4) (0-110,108) 5-Y-0+ **£5,204** (£1,528; £764; £381)

Form				RPR
5543	1		**Wild Oats**[33] [3949] 8-10-10 95 OwynNelmes(3) (B J M Ryall) *hld up: hdwy 8th: rdn to ld 2 out: idled flat: r.o* **4/1**[1]	105+
0603	2	1 ½	**Elegant Eskimo**[34] [3919] 7-10-10 92 ChristianWilliams (S E H Sherwood) *led: rdn and hdd 2 out: kpt on flat* **14/1**	97
236P	3	13	**Hever Road (IRE)**[33] [3943] 7-11-3 106 (b) AndrewGlassonbury(7) (M C Pipe) *hld up and bhd: blnd 4th: rdn and hdwy appr 4 out: btn whn j.lft 2 out* **18/1**	104+
-11P	4	15	**Stack The Pack (IRE)**[139] [1988] 9-11-7 103 JasonMaguire (T R George) *prom tl rdn and wknd qckly 4 out* **4/1**[1]	80
42P6	5	20	**Albert House (IRE)**[11] [4357] 8-11-6 102 WarrenMarston (R H Alner) *hld up and bhd: rdn after 9th: no ch fr 4 out* **7/1**[3]	59
12PU	P		**Petolinski**[68] [3359] 8-10-0 82 oh3 (p) RobertWalford (C L Popham) *bhd fr 4th: t.o fr 7th: p.u bef 4 out* **12/1**	—
440P	P		**Spring Junior (FR)**[37] [3876] 5-10-6 98 RichardJohnson (P J Hobbs) *hld up: wknd qckly 8th: blnd 9th: t.o whn p.u bef 4 out* **9/2**[2]	—
4-P1	P		**Joizel (FR)**[8] [4428] 9-9-8 83 7ex JamesWhite(7) (V G Greenway) *hld up and bhd: hdwy 8th: rdn and wknd appr 4 out: mstke 3 out: p.u bef 2 out* **9/2**[2]	—

6m 8.50s (9.90) **Going Correction** +0.60s/f (Soft)
WFA 5 from 7yo+ 5lb **8 Ran SP% 108.5**
Speed ratings: **107,106,102,97,90 —,—,—** CSF £47.77 CT £794.22 TOTE £4.40: £1.60, £4.10, £3.30; EX 41.60.
Owner J & B Gibbs & Sons Ltd **Bred** Paul Matthews **Trained** Rimpton, Somerset

FOCUS
Not a great contest, but Wild Oats was scoring a deserved first success over fences and is rated value for further with the second to his hurdle mark.

NOTEBOOK
Wild Oats, outstayed at Taunton last time, sat quiet for the early part of the race, but came through to challenge Elegant Eskimo in the straight and he touched down in front after the second last. He got tired on the run-in and started to wander around, but had done enough and deserved this first victory over fences. He is lightly-raced and there may yet be a little improvement to come. *(tchd 9-2)*
Elegant Eskimo was well held off this mark on her chasing debut at Leicester last month, but the better ground enabled her to show improved form and she led them from the start. She was doing her best to get back at the winner and, with the ground now beginning to come in he favour, she should find plenty of opportunities. *(op 7-1)*
Hever Road(IRE) is not the most consistent, but he ran well considering he made a bad early *blunder. He remains a maiden however and cannot be backed with confidence in future. (op 16-1 tchd 20-1)*
Stack The Pack(IRE) showed good form in the summer, winning twice, but he was disappointing when bidding for a hat-trick at Huntingdon in November and again failed to meet with expectations on this first start since. His stable is not in the greatest of form and maybe he deserves another chance. *(op 6-1 tchd 13-2)*
Albert House(IRE), whose only previous start over fences yielded a decent second at Huntingdon back in October 2004, was one of the more interesting ones, but he was never really travelling and had nothing left from the turn-in. *(tchd 8-1)*
Joizel(FR) won what looked a modest contest on his chasing debut in a classified event at Taunton last week, and the 7lb penalty appeared to find him out, although it is possible the race came too soon. *Official explanation: trainer said race may have come too soon for gelding (op 4-1)*
Spring Junior(FR), a five-year-old making his chasing debut, was due to race off a 5lb higher mark in future and he was solid enough in the market, but he was unable to make an impact and *dropped away tamely down the back straight. He is beginning to look a lost cause.Official explanation: jockey said gelding finished distressed (op 4-1)*

The Form Book, Raceform Ltd, Compton, RG20 6NL

4559 CANADATRAVELCENTRE.CO.UK NOVICES' CHASE (13 fncs 2 omitted) 2m 3f 110y

3:50 (3:50) (Class 3) 5-Y-0+ **£6,506** (£1,910; £955; £477)

Form				RPR
0001	1		**Cousin Nicky**[14] [4288] 5-10-9 118 .... RichardJohnson (P J Hobbs) *led to 3rd: led after 4th: mstke 4 out: clr appr 2 out: eased towards fin* **11/10**[1]	122+
2321	2	11	**Pardishar (IRE)**[8] [4424] 8-11-7 119 .... TimmyMurphy (G L Moore) *hld up: rdn and wnt 2nd 4 out: no ch w wnr fr 2 out* **6/4**[2]	118+
1202	3	6	**Keepers Mead (IRE)**[24] [4105] 8-11-0 116 .... RobertWalford (R H Alner) *j.rt: prom: wnt 2nd briefly appr 4 out: wknd 3 out* **9/2**[3]	104+
4P-0	4	dist	**Champagne Sundae (IRE)**[309] [389] 8-11-0 73 .... (t) RJGreene (Mrs S D Williams) *prom: led 3rd tl after 4th: wknd 4 out: 3rd and no ch whn fell last: rmntd* **50/1**	103

5m 0.80s (6.90) **Going Correction** +0.60s/f (Soft)
WFA 5 from 8yo 4lb **4** Ran SP% **107.8**
Speed ratings: **110,105,103,—** CSF £3.22 TOTE £1.70; EX 3.80.
Owner Patrick Beach **Bred** Andrew Jenkins **Trained** Withycombe, Somerset

FOCUS
A dodgy round of jumping from all participants, but recent course scorer Cousin Nicky ended up winning with plenty in hand and the form is rated around the first two.

NOTEBOOK
Cousin Nicky, a recent course scorer, was receiving the handy weight-for-age allowance and he gradually came clear down the straight, ultimately winning with plenty in hand. The drier conditions he had to contend with here did not affect his performance and Johnson again adopted front-running tactics to ensure it was a good test. He guessed at a couple of the fences in the straight and is going to find life tougher in future, especially with the chances of soft ground lessening by the day, but there is no denying he is a progressive sort. *(tchd 11-8)*
Pardishar(IRE) set a fair standard having run subsequent Cheltenham winner Reveillez close at Folkestone on his penultimate outing, and a win at the start of last week would have done him no harm at all, but he did not travel as well as one could have expected and proved no match for the winner in straight. *(tchd 11-8)*
Keepers Mead(IRE), a fair staying hurdler, was always likely to find this an inadequate test and it was no surprise to see him readily outpaced in the final half mile. His jumping was sketchy at times and it would not surprise to see him return to hurdles as to preserve his novice status for next season. *(op 11-2 tchd 4-1)*
Champagne Sundae(IRE) looked to just be making up the numbers, but the first-time tongue tie brought about an improved performance and he was challenging for third when falling at the last. It remains to be seen what this does to his confidence. *(op 33-1)*

4560 ROBERT WEBB TRAVEL OPEN HUNTERS' CHASE (15 fncs 4 omitted) 3m 1f 110y

4:20 (4:22) (Class 5) 5-Y-0+ **£2,498** (£774; £387; £193)

Form				RPR
	1		**Deep Pockets (IRE)**[31] 7-11-9 .... MrJSnowden(3) (Mrs Caroline Keevil) *a.p: led and j.rt 4 out: hit 3 out: j.rt 2 out: sn rdn clr: styd on wl* **3/1**[1]	105+
PP52	2	14	**Mister Club Royal**[9] [4397] 10-11-9 82 .... MrMMunrowd(7) (Miss Emma Oliver) *led 2nd: rdn and hdd 4 out: one pce fr 3 out* **40/1**	96+
230/	3	10	**Handyman (IRE)**[30] 12-11-9 .... MrDEdwards(3) (Michael M Watson) *hld up in mid-div: hdwy 9th: lft 3rd 11th: rdn 4 out: no imp* **6/1**[3]	84+
300/	4	1 1/2	**Murt's Man (IRE)**[23] 12-11-5 .... MrCHeard(7) (Mrs A Holland) *led to 2nd: prom: lost pl 8th: styd on fr 3 out: n.d* **66/1**	78
-421	5	hd	**Knife Edge (USA)**[9] [4397] 11-11-11 120 .... (p) MrAJBerry(5) (Jonjo O'Neill) *hld up and bhd: stdy hdwy appr 10th: wknd 4 out* **4/1**[2]	81
P35/	6	3	**The Phair Crier (IRE)**[10] 11-11-7 .... MrRWoollacott(5) (S A Hughes) *j.rt: prom: lost pl 8th: short-lived effrt appr 4 out* **28/1**	74
12P	7	1 1/4	**Chasing The Bride**[52] 13-11-13 .... MissAGoschen(3) (Miss A Goschen) *mstke 3rd: a in rr* **20/1**	77
U00/	U		**Montezuma**[24] 13-10-12 .... MrJSole(7) (Ms Kim Holmes) *bhd tl blnd and uns rdr 8th* **150/1**	—
	U		**The Quarry Man**[44] 8-11-5 .... MissJCongdon(7) (A W Congdon) *hld up in tch: blnd and uns rdr 8th* **66/1**	—
10P/	P		**Quickswood (IRE)**[31] 13-11-9 .... MrGMaundrell(3) (G C Maundrell) *in tch to 4th: t.o whn p.u bef 4 out* **33/1**	—
P-P4	P		**Mr Banker**[26] [4079] 11-11-5 76 .... (p) MrJBarnes(7) (N Bush) *bhd fr 3rd: rdn 5th: t.o whn p.u after 11th* **100/1**	—
12-P	U		**Kingston-Banker**[30] 10-11-5 110 .... MrDDrake(7) (Mrs S Alner) *sn prom: cl 3rd whn blnd and uns rdr 11th* **16/1**	—
P/2	P		**Royal Scandal**[10] [4369] 10-11-12 .... MrTJO'Brien (C J Down) *prom tl wknd after 11th: bhd whn p.u bef 4 out* **14/1**	—
1	P		**Virgos Bambino (IRE)**[10] 9-11-6 .... MissSGaisford(3) (Miss V J Nicholls) *hld up: hdwy 11th: wknd appr 4 out: bhd whn p.u bef 2 out* **10/1**	—
P13U	P		**Denvale (IRE)**[12] [4325] 8-12-2 .... MrRCope(3) (Mrs Caroline Bailey) *hld up and bhd: sme hdwy 6th: hrd rdn appr 10th: wknd after 11th: t.o whn p.u bef 4 out* **4/1**[2]	—

6m 42.4s (14.40) **Going Correction** +0.60s/f (Soft) **15** Ran SP% **119.2**
Speed ratings: **101,96,93,93,93 92,91,—,—,— —,—,—,—,—** CSF £130.40 TOTE £4.40: £1.60, £10.00, £3.00; EX 180.90.
Owner The Deep Pockets Partnership **Bred** L N Sloan **Trained** Blagdon, Somerset

FOCUS
A decent hunter chase with a big field, but the absence of likely favourite Paddy For Paddy made things a little easier and it was Deep Pockets who ran out an authoritative winner and can rate higher with the second setting the level.

NOTEBOOK
Deep Pockets(IRE) ◆, a useful pointer who has won four of his last six starts in that field, emerged a clear winner, pulling away stylishly under pressure for the bang in-form Snowden, who always had him ideally positioned. Evidently a strong stayer, his pointing form, which includes a defeat of useful hunter Gatsby and a recent second at Barbury to formerly smart hunter chaser County Derry, is sound and it is likely the seven-year-old can develop into a leading hunter for years to come. *(op 7-2 tchd 4-1)*
Mister Club Royal led from the second fence onwards and fought his way back to the front before the fourth last, having momentarily surrendered it turning in, but he was unable to go on with the winner. He has found some form again and may have a similar contest in him. *(op 33-1)*
Handyman(IRE), a formerly useful handicap chaser with Philip Hobbs, made a winning return in a mens' open last month, and it looked for much of the way as though he was going to supplement that success, but he did not find as much under pressure as had looked likely and it is possible this trip stretched him. He is another worth bearing in mind for something similar. *(op 11-2)*
Murt's Man(IRE), who has hardly set the world alight in a couple of points, was a capable performer on his day and he made some late gains to claim fourth. *(op 50-1)*
Knife Edge(USA) failed to build on his first win in over four years at Warwick last time and was basically disappointing, failing to confirm form with Mister Club Royal.
Chasing The Bride never got into it after an early blunder.
Virgos Bambino(IRE) made a little headway at the end of the back straight, but was unable to make any further impression. *(op 9-2 tchd 5-1)*
Denvale(IRE) was struggling a long way from the finish. *(op 9-2 tchd 5-1)*

4561 PUNCH TAVERNS "RETAILER" H'CAP HURDLE (5 hdls 3 omitted) 2m 1f

4:50 (4:52) (Class 4) (0-115,115) 4-Y-0+ **£3,903** (£1,146; £573; £286)

Form				RPR
-331	1		**Wellbeing**[17] [4243] 9-11-7 110 .... RichardJohnson (P J Hobbs) *hld up and bhd: stdy hdwy 2nd: rdn to ld flat: r.o* **8/11**[1]	127+
060P	2	3	**Idian Mix (FR)**[14] [4289] 5-10-2 98 .... (t) AndrewGlassonbury(7) (M C Pipe) *hld up in mid-div: hdwy 1st: led 3rd: hrd rdn and hdd flat: nt qckn* **66/1**	107
2FPP	3	11	**Cockatoo Ridge**[28] [4036] 9-10-6 98 .... OwynNelmes(3) (N R Mitchell) *led to 1st: rdn and ev ch appr 2 out: one pce* **50/1**	96
3213	4	7	**Take A Mile (IRE)**[79] [3182] 4-11-0 115 .... JohnnyLevins(5) (B G Powell) *hld up towards rr: hdwy whn hit 2 out: wknd flat* **13/2**[2]	100+
202-	5	nk	**Complete Outsider**[414] [3621] 8-10-13 102 .... MarcusFoley (Nick Williams) *hld up and bhd: hdwy appr 2 out: swtchd lft appr last: sn wknd* **25/1**	93
-56F	6	6	**Porak (IRE)**[8] [4429] 9-10-13 102 .... JasonMaguire (W Davies) *hld up in tch: lost pl after 3rd: n.d after* **80/1**	87
1350	7	11	**Baloo**[37] [3876] 10-10-9 103 .... ChrisHonour(5) (J D Frost) *led 1st to 3rd: wknd appr 2 out* **66/1**	77
	8	3/4	**Sha Bihan (FR)**[377] 5-11-8 111 .... WayneHutchinson (A King) *hld up: hdwy 2nd: wknd appr 2 out* **8/1**[3]	84
014P	9	3/4	**Come Bye (IRE)**[36] [3901] 10-11-6 114 .... (bt) MrTJO'Brien(5) (Miss A M Newton-Smith) *prom tl wknd appr 2 out* **100/1**	86
1-PF	10	2	**Grey Brother**[71] [3323] 8-11-12 115 .... ChristianWilliams (Nick Williams) *prom: mstke and lost pl 1st: bhd fr 3rd* **33/1**	88+
-314	11	22	**Fabulous Jet (FR)**[26] [4067] 6-11-2 105 .... AlanO'Keeffe (Miss Venetia Williams) *a towards rr: mstke last: t.o* **9/1**	53
1320	12	16	**Polished**[70] [3333] 7-11-5 108 .... (b) MickFitzgerald (V R A Dartnall) *bhd most of way: rdn after 2nd: t.o* **12/1**	40
4000	13	3	**Rift Valley (IRE)**[14] [4289] 11-11-2 115 .... (v) DarrenO'Dwyer(10) (P J Hobbs) *bhd fr 2nd: t.o* **100/1**	44
/P03	P		**Idbury (IRE)**[28] [4033] 8-10-6 95 .... OllieMcPhail (V J Hughes) *prom tl rdn and wknd 2nd: t.o whn p.u bef 2 out* **50/1**	—

4m 17.2s (8.00) **Going Correction** +0.775s/f (Soft)
WFA 4 from 5yo+ 7lb **14** Ran SP% **116.9**
Speed ratings: **112,110,105,102,101 99,93,93,93,92 81,74,73,—** CSF £72.29 CT £1435.92 TOTE £1.30: £1.10, £11.80, £16.10; EX 75.30 Place 6 £265.27, Place 5 £172.12.
Owner Gillian, Lady Howard De Walden **Bred** Lord Howard De Walden **Trained** Withycombe, Somerset

FOCUS
A modest handicap but a decent winning time, 4.5 seconds faster than the seller. The winner was value for further and could be rated higher.

NOTEBOOK
Wellbeing, who battled hard to win on his handicap debut at Newbury, travelled with his usual gusto at the rear of the field and readily made ground when Johnson asked him. However, he was a bit caught out when the runner-up took several lengths out of him going down towards the last and it looked as though he was cooked, but the missing final flight meant there was plenty of time for his Flat speed to kick in and he eventually got there. He is heading the right way, but will need to raise his game if he is to complete the hat-trick. *(op 5-6)*
Idian Mix(FR) had dropped 15lb in a disappointing spell since arriving in Britain, but the application of a first-time tongue tie was expected to bring about an improved performance and he ran a blinder, kicking on early in the straight and very nearly causing an upset. It may have been a different story had the last been in place as the winner would not have had as long to reach his top stride, but connections can look forward to the five-year-old gaining compensation sooner rather than later, as long as this proves to be no fluke. *(op 100-1)*
Cockatoo Ridge, Rooster Booster's brother, had lost his form after a fall at Wincanton in January, but an earlier second in a course handicap suggested he could take a hand at his best and he stuck on well enough in third. He remains winless in 15 attempts over hurdles, but there is definitely a race in him off this sort of mark. *(op 66-1)*
Take A Mile(IRE), whose most recent outing saw him finish third to subsequent Triumph fourth Pace Shot, made a pleasing-enough return from a break and can be expected to improve for the outing, possibly back on a more speed-reliant track. *(tchd 7-1)*
Complete Outsider was having his first start in over a year and ran well considering the ground would have been slower than he likes. He is one to watch out for in the summer months. *(op 20-1)*
Sha Bihan(FR) made only an average start to his British career, making headway having been held up, only to tire badly in the straight. It is safe to assume he is capable of better. *(op 11-2)*
Grey Brother, reverting to hurdles on his first start for Nick Williams, held a good position on the long run down to the first, but he gave it an almighty whack and his race ended there and then. This trip would have proved on the short side anyhow and he is one to watch out for next time. *(tchd 40-1)*
T/Jkpt: Part won. £7,100.00 to a £1 stake. Pool: £10,000.00. 0.50 winning tickets. T/Plt: £786.90 to a £1 stake. Pool: £56,164.20. 52.10 winning tickets. T/Qpdt: £18.10 to a £1 stake. Pool: £4,899.80. 199.80 winning tickets. KH

4392 WARWICK (L-H)

Tuesday, March 21

OFFICIAL GOING: Good to firm
The meeting was decimated by a total of 38 non-runners on account of ground decribed variously as 'bare' and 'rough'.
Wind: Slight ahead

4562 ENTERTAIN CLIENTS AT WARWICK RACECOURSE MAIDEN HURDLE (11 hdls) 2m 5f

2:10 (2:10) (Class 4) 4-Y-0+ **£3,253** (£955; £477; £238)

Form				RPR
22	1		**Rare Gold (IRE)**[37] [3881] 6-11-2 .... AndrewThornton (R H Alner) *led after 1st: hdd after 5th: led again after 6th: clr after 3 out: wnt lft last: v easily* **1/4**[1]	109+
0P6	2	7	**Lookafterme (IRE)**[55] [3558] 6-11-2 .... MarkBradburne (A W Carroll) *prom: chsd wnr 4 out: drvn and no ch fr 3 out* **16/1**[3]	84
	3	2	**Silber Mond**[501] 4-10-8 .... JamieGoldstein (Miss Sheena West) *chsd ldrs: rdn and blnd 3 out: sn rcvrd and styd on same pce u.p* **7/1**[2]	76+
	4	dist	**Sterling Heights (NZ)** 7-11-2 .... HenryOliver (Mrs Tracey Barfoot-Saunt) *led tl after 1st:chal fr 4th tl led after next: hdd after 6th: blnd 7th and sn wknd: t.o* **20/1**	—
	5	1 1/4	**Future To Future (IRE)**[566] 6-11-2 .... BarryFenton (Miss E C Lavelle) *nt fluent: a in rr: t.o fr 4 out* **16/1**[3]	—

0-P F **Brunate**[27] 4052 7-10-9 .... MrPCallaghan(7) 72
(J A Danahar) *bhd: hdwy to get in tch after 6th: wknd after 4 out: poor 4th whn fell last* **50/1**

5m 7.30s (-8.80) **Going Correction** -0.95s/f (Hard)
WFA 4 from 5yo+ 8lb **6** Ran SP% **111.0**
Speed ratings: **78,75,74,—,—** — CSF £5.74 TOTE £1.30: £1.20, £2.90; EX 5.30.
Owner P M De Wilde **Bred** Miss D And P Keating **Trained** Droop, Dorset

FOCUS
A race particularly hard hit by no less than 12 non-runners. The favourite faced an easy task as a result and made no mistake, being value for 22 lengths, but the time was particularly slow given the ground and the form may not mean a lot.

NOTEBOOK
Rare Gold(IRE), winner of an Irish point on good ground, merely has to reproduce the form of his two previous outings in this country to score with ease. He did run markedly down the final flight and finished up on the chase course, but that would be ultra-critical and it was understandable on this ground. The form means very little, however. *(op 2-7 tchd 3-10)*
Lookafterme(IRE), trying hurdles for the first time having run in two chases, two points and bumper, managed to win the separate race for second but what he actually achieved is anyone's guess. This effort may mean that he starts a shorter price next time than he should. *(op 20-1 tchd 25-1 and 28-1 in places)*
Silber Mond, not seen since finishing well beaten in two outings on the Flat in the autumn of 2004, made a very bad mistake three out that may eventually have cost him second, but the form probably does not add up to much. *(op 11-2 tchd 8-1)*
Sterling Heights(NZ), a New Zealand-bred, matched strides with the favourite for much of the way and was kept wide presumably in search of less rough ground, but a sloppy jump five from home finished him off. At least he should be fitter after this. *(op 25-1)*
Future To Future(IRE), making his hurdling debut and racing for the first time since September 2004, *is yet to show any signs of ability. Official explanation: jockey said gelding was unsuited by good to firm ground (op 11-1)*
Brunate would have finished a remote fourth had he not come down at the last. *(op 33-1)*

4563 WARWICK H'CAP CHASE (17 fncs) 2m 4f 110y
2:40 (2:40) (Class 4) (0-110,110) 5-Y-0+ **£3,903** (£1,146; £573; £286)

Form RPR
3343 **1** **Lord Dundaniel (IRE)**[18] 4214 9-11-5 **103**..........................(p) APMcCoy 117+
(B De Haan) *mde all: nt fluent 4th and 11th: drvn clr fr 12th: unchal* **1/1**[1]
1500 **2** *6* **Romany Dream**[18] 4213 8-11-3 **101**............................(b) RobertThornton 107
(R Dickin) *trckd ldrs in 3rd: chsd wnr appr 12th: sn no ch* **6/1**
3321 **3** *12* **Twenty Degrees**[22] 4150 8-10-11 **95**............................(b) JamieMoore 92+
(G L Moore) *nt fluent 1st: rdn fr 9th: sme hdwy and j. slowly 11th: nvr nr ldrs and nvr in contention* **7/2**[2]
-P16 **4** *dist* **Wenceslas (IRE)**[40] 3816 6-11-7 **105**.................................. PaulMoloney —
(Miss H C Knight) *chsd wnr tl appr 11th: sn wknd: t.o* **4/1**[3]

5m 11.0s (-14.50) **Going Correction** -0.95s/f (Hard) **4** Ran SP% **106.5**
Speed ratings: **89,86,82,—** CSF £6.51 TOTE £1.90; EX 6.40.
Owner Willsford Racing Incorporated **Bred** Joseph And Declan Maher **Trained** Lambourn, Berks

FOCUS
Another race hit by three non-runners, two on account of the ground, and the pace was moderate until well past halfway. The first two set the level for the form but it looks suspect.

NOTEBOOK
Lord Dundaniel(IRE), with the cheekpieces on, was found a decent opportunity and made no mistake. Being set alight a mile from home was the key, as he took several lengths out of his rivals and, with his jumping proving a real asset from then on, he never looked like losing his advantage. He is consistent and seems to appreciate a sound surface, so with his confidence restored he may be able to find another opportunity this spring. *(op 5-4 tchd 11-8 in places)*
Romany Dream, proven on this sort of ground, got completely outpaced when the favourite went for home a mile out and despite her best efforts she never looked like reducing the deficit. *(op 11-2)*
Twenty Degrees, raised 5lb for his Plumpton win, came off the bridle before halfway and was *always fighting a losing battle from thereon in. All his best form has been on soft ground.Official explanation: jockey said gelding suffered a cut hind leg (op 9-4)*
Wenceslas(IRE), on ground that was neither deep nor even, suddenly stopped to nothing at halfway and something must surely have been amiss. *(op 5-1)*

4564 BANBURY NOVICES' HURDLE (8 hdls) 2m
3:10 (3:10) (Class 4) 4-Y-0+ **£3,253** (£955; £477; £238)

Form RPR
1 **Welcome Stranger**[186] 6-11-0 .... JamieMoore 102+
(G L Moore) *hld up rr but in tch: hdwy 4 out: chal fr 2 out tl slt ld sn after last: drvn and kpt on strly cl home* **11/8**[2]
22 **2** *½* **Vaughan**[37] 3883 5-11-0 .... MarkBradburne 98
(H D Daly) *hld up rr but in tch: hdwy to chsd ldrs 3 out: drvn to chllenge 2 out: slt advantage last: sn hdd: no ex nr fin* **6/5**[1]
-000 **3** *2* **Cambo (FR)**[49] 3659 5-11-0 .... JamieGoldstein 96
(Miss Sheena West) *led: sn clr: rdn appr 2 out: hdd last: sn one pce* **50/1**
165 **4** *11* **Briscoe Place (IRE)**[37] 3881 6-11-0 .... APMcCoy 86+
(Jonjo O'Neill) *hit 3rd: chsd ldrs: wnt 2nd 4th: rdn: nt fluent and wknd 2 out* **7/1**[3]
-P60 **5** *11* **New Diamond**[15] 4277 7-10-7 68............................... WayneKavanagh(7) 74
(Mrs P Ford) *t.k.h early: nt fluent 2nd: chsd ldrs: rdn and wknd 3 out* **100/1**
P **6** *5* **Lord Of Methley**[37] 3883 7-11-0 ....(t) KeithMercer 69
(S Lycett) *a in rr* **100/1**
P00 **7** *13* **Bombaybadboy (NZ)**[24] 4106 7-11-0 ....(p) HenryOliver 59+
(Ian Williams) *chsd ldr intil wknd qckly 4th* **100/1**
00 **8** *21* **Nemetan (FR)**[56] 3545 5-11-0 .... AndrewThornton 35
(R H Alner) *sn bhd: no ch whn hit 4 out* **33/1**
9 *1¼* **Rambo Blue**[42] 6-11-0 .... JodieMogford 34
(G J Smith) *in tch to 5th* **100/1**

3m 48.8s (-9.50) **Going Correction** -0.95s/f (Hard)
WFA 4 from 5yo+ 7lb **9** Ran SP% **108.9**
Speed ratings: **85,84,83,78,72 70,63,53,52** CSF £3.09 TOTE £2.50: £1.30, £1.10, £4.40; EX 3.80.
Owner Mike Charlton And Rodger Sargent **Bred** Henry And Mrs Rosemary Moszkowicz **Trained** Woodingdean, E Sussex

FOCUS
A race weakened by seven non-runners, but still a couple of interesting sorts in this and the pair dominated the market. There was no pace on early, however, and the winning time was eight seconds slower than the later handicap. The winner can rate higher with the second some way off his best.

NOTEBOOK
Welcome Stranger, a Listed-race winner on the Flat, was given a patient ride on this hurdling debut but travelled well and arrived there on the bridle in the home straight. When it came down to a turn of foot on the run-in, he had the legs of the favourite who was more of a stayer on the level, and the modest pace would have helped him in that respect. A truer pace will test his stamina properly, but this was still an encouraging start. *(tchd 6-5 and 6-4 in a place)*
Vaughan had the edge in hurdling experience over his main rival, but he was rated 15lb inferior to him on the Flat and was more of a stayer, so the pace of the race would not have been in his favour and he was just outspeeded on the run-in. He is not doing much wrong and can break his duck over timber given a truer pace. *(op 11-8 tchd 6-4)*
Cambo(FR), rated 49lb behind the winner on the level, has shown precisely nothing in four outings over hurdles so far. He was soon sent into a clear lead and his rivals were happy to let him do it, knowing he would come back to them, but he hung on for much longer than seemed likely. The way the race was run places serious doubts against the value of this effort and it would be unwise to get carried away. *(op 33-1)*
Briscoe Place(IRE), whose bumper win came on fast ground, tried to stay with the big two as they crept closer but had been beaten off on reaching the home straight. The fact that he could not even make any impression on Cambo rather puts this effort into perspective. *(op 9-2)*

4565 SPONSOR AT WARWICK NOVICES' CHASE (18 fncs) 3m 110y
3:40 (3:43) (Class 3) 5-Y-0+ **£6,506** (£1,910)

Form RPR
1-43 **1** **Its Wallace Jnr**[35] 3907 7-11-3 114...............................(t) JamieGoldstein 116+
(Miss Sheena West) *led 3rd: j.rt thrght: cme clr fr 3 out: easily* **8/11**[1]
42F0 **2** *13* **Special Conquest**[26] 4078 8-11-9 108.......................(p) AndrewThornton 106
(J W Mullins) *led: pckd 2nd: hdd 3rd: hdd 3rd: reminders appr 12th and wnt wd: effrt 4 out: wknd after 3 out* **13/8**[2]

6m 26.1s (3.80) **Going Correction** -0.95s/f (Hard)
WFA 5 from 7yo+ 10lb **2** Ran SP% **96.0**
Speed ratings: **55,50** TOTE £1.40.
Owner Michael Moriarty **Bred** G West **Trained** Falmer, E Sussex

FOCUS
A race reduced to a match after two horses were withdrawn on account of the ground, and the other was withdrawn at the start after refusing to line up. Not surprisingly this became a game of cat and mouse and the winning time was pedestrian given the conditions.

NOTEBOOK
Its Wallace Jnr, trying this trip for the first time, made the majority of the running and his advantage was only threatened very briefly on the home turn. The only problem was that he jumped to his right at almost every fence, sometimes markedly so, and must therefore have travelled a good bit further than his only rival. Also the way this race was run did not test his stamina properly so there are still some questions to answer. *(op 10-11)*
Special Conquest was soon content to get a lead from his rival and was also taken out wide in search of more consistent ground. He tried to close the gap on the final bend, but his effort came to little and he was allowed to come home in his own time. His stamina was more proven than that of the winner, so the shape of this race would not have been in his favour at all. *(op 6-4 tchd 7-4)*

4566 HELEN OF TROY LADY RIDERS' H'CAP HURDLE (8 hdls) 2m
4:10 (4:11) (Class 4) (0-100,100) 4-Y-0+ **£3,903** (£1,146; £573; £286)

Form RPR
5322 **1** **Upright Ima**[6] 4452 7-9-13 **78**... MissLAllan(7) 86+
(Mrs P Sly) *hld up: hdwy 4th: trckd ldr 4 out: led appr next: c clr appr 2 out: readily* **3/1**[2]
0001 **2** *4* **Nick's Choice**[3] 4490 10-11-7 **100** 6ex................. MissIsabelTompsett(7) 104+
(D Burchell) *prom: chsd wnr 3 out: sn rdn and no imp but kpt on wl for clr 2nd* **11/4**[1]
U0P- **3** *9* **Autumn Rain (USA)**[414] 3628 9-10-11 **90**....................... MissLHorner(7) 85
(G Brown) *bhd: hdwy 3 out: styng on whn barged through on rail bnd appr 2 out: kpt on for 3rd but nvr nr ldrs* **33/1**
5451 **4** *1* **West Hill (IRE)**[43] 3782 5-10-1 **80**...................................(t) MissEALalor(7) 74
(D McCain) *in tch: rdn and effrt 3 out: nt rch ldrs and sn one pce* **5/1**[3]
04-P **5** *2½* **Mcqueen (IRE)**[141] 1957 6-11-5 **98**............................ MissJCWilliams(7) 90
(Mrs H Dalton) *chsd ldrs: rdn 4 out: wknd after next* **14/1**
P0OP **6** *1* **Fair View (GER)**[9] 4393 5-9-7 **72**.................................. MissHMLewis(7) 63
(Dr P Pritchard) *sn slt ld: def advantage 3rd: nt fluent next: hdd appr 3 out: wknd sn after* **12/1**
3004 **7** *1¾* **Iberus (GER)**[11] 4354 8-11-4 **97**...................................(tp) MissLGardner(7) 86
(S Gollings) *w ldr to 3rd: styd prom: rdn 4 out: wknd after next* **8/1**
PPU **8** *1¼* **Loup Bleu (USA)**[6] 4452 8-11-5 **98**....................................... MissJKelly(7) 86
(Mrs A V Roberts) *pressed ldrs to 3rd: rdn 4th: wknd 3 out* **66/1**
5544 **9** *1¼* **Hunting Lodge (IRE)**[12] 4322 5-11-4 **97**.......................... MissABush(7) 83
(H J Manners) *a in rr* **15/2**
-000 **10** *3½* **Hayley's Pearl**[24] 4106 7-9-7 **72** oh8..................... MissCarolineHurley(7) 55
(Mrs P Ford) *chsd ldrs: rdn 4th: wknd 3 out: no ch whn bdly bmpd bnd appr 2 out* **100/1**
4433 **11** *20* **Grand Prairie (SWE)**[6] 4452 10-10-8 **87**....................(b) MissHGrissell(7) 50
(G L Moore) *hit nd: in tch: rdn 4th: wknd 4 out* **9/1**

3m 40.8s (-17.50) **Going Correction** -0.95s/f (Hard) **11** Ran SP% **121.0**
Speed ratings: **105,103,98,98,96 96,95,94,94,92 82** CSF £12.38 CT £231.66 TOTE £3.90: £1.40, £1.70, £12.30; EX 15.50.
Owner Mrs P M Sly **Bred** Mrs P Sly **Trained** Thorney, Cambs

FOCUS
Only one non-runner due to the ground, which left this by far the most competitive race on the card. The pace was solid as well, resulting in a time eight seconds quicker than the earlier novice hurdle and the race could rate a few pouns higher.

NOTEBOOK
Upright Ima ◆, unlucky not to have broken her duck before now, travelled incredibly well and still seemed to be pulling when taking over in front three out. Quickly sent into a clear lead, she was never in any danger after that and recorded her first win at the 21st attempt. She bounces off this ground and with conditions likely to be in her favour in the coming weeks, it seems unlikely to be her last. *(tchd 11-4)*
Nick's Choice, having won from 10lb out of the handicap on totally contrasting ground at Newcastle three days earlier, was actually able to race from a 4lb lower mark here even under his penalty. He did little wrong and beat the rest comfortably enough, but he could not match the winner for pace over the last couple of flights and this trip on the ground was probably an insufficient test of stamina. *(op 4-1 tchd 9-2)*
Autumn Rain(USA), who appears to have been hard to train in recent years, was trying to overcome another long layoff and merely plugged on to finish a remote third. To be fair this trip would have been much too sharp, especially on this ground. *(op 28-1)*
West Hill(IRE), raised a whopping 9lb for his Sedgefield victory on soft ground, was made to look very one paced over the last three flights on this ground. *(tchd 6-1)*
Mcqueen(IRE) has shown his best form on soft ground throughout his life and was also entitled to need this after a five-month break, so he should not be judged too harshly. *(tchd 12-1)*

4567 FLAT SEASON NEXT H'CAP CHASE (22 fncs) 3m 5f
4:40 (4:41) (Class 4) (0-100,93) 5-Y-0+ **£3,999** (£1,241; £668)

Form RPR
3P24 **1** **Lambrini Bianco (IRE)**[12] 4316 8-10-1 **68**................(b[1]) TomScudamore 82
(Mrs L Williamson) *led tl after 2nd: led 4th: hdd 17th: rdn and j.rt next: rallied and hit 2 out: chal last: led fnl 100yds: gamely* **5/2**[2]
P500 **2** *1* **Lucky Luk (FR)**[27] 4047 7-10-1 **73**....................................... MarkNicolls(5) 87+
(K C Bailey) *trckd wnr fr 8th: hit 11th: led 17th: blnd and rdn 2 out: hdd and no ex fnl 100yds* **3/1**[3]

0600 **3** *dist* **Spanish Main (IRE)**[37] [3886] 12-11-5 **93**........................(b) MrDEngland(7) 72
(N A Twiston-Davies) *led after 2nd to 4th: styd chsing ldrs: j. slowly 7th: hit 11th: rdn next: wknd 15th: t.o* **6/1**

P050 **R** **Bronhallow**[6] [4451] 13-9-11 **71** oh14 ow4...........................(bt) MrMWall(7) —
(Mrs Barbara Waring) *chsd ldrs: hit 4th and 11th: hit 14th and wknd: t.o whn j.v.slowly 4 out: ref next* **33/1**

024P **R** **Tribal Dancer (IRE)**[12] [4321] 12-11-5 **93**........................... MrWBiddick(7) —
(Miss Venetia Williams) *reluctant to r: t.o and j. slowly in rr tl hdwy to get in tch 8th: drvn whn ref and uns rdr 13th* **15/8**[1]

7m 17.5s (-31.40) **Going Correction** -0.95s/f (Hard) 5 Ran SP% **105.6**
Speed ratings: **105,104,—,—,—** CSF £9.56 TOTE £2.80: £1.40, £2.20; EX 11.40.
Owner Halewood International Ltd **Bred** John Brophy **Trained** Saighton, Cheshire

FOCUS
An eventful if dire contest, quite apart from four non-runners on account of the ground, with the favourite running no sort of race. This became virtually a match over the final mile and is rated around the first two to their marks.

NOTEBOOK
Lambrini Bianco(IRE), wearing blinkers for the first time rather than the usual cheekpieces, has shown that he can handle good ground before. Up there from the start, he seemed to be getting the worse of his duel Lucky Luk for most of the final mile, but his rider never gave up and he utilised the gelding's stamina to pull the race out of the fire. This was a very bad race, however. *(op 7-4)*
Lucky Luk(FR), whose stamina for this was open to doubt, took over a mile from home and seemed to have Lambrini Bianco covered, but he could never get away and his rival saw his race out that much better. He likes this sort of ground and he did not appear to be beaten because he did not stay. *(op 7-2)*
Spanish Main(IRE), with the blinkers back on for the first time in five years, is a proven stayer but *he is also on the decline and started to lose touch with the front pair well over a mile from home. (op 11-2 tchd 5-1 and 7-1)*
Tribal Dancer(IRE) did not want to know. After giving away 30 lengths at the start, he managed to get in touch with the other quartet after a circuit, but was starting to lose touch again when swerving and crashing through the wing of the first fence on the final lap. He looks one to avoid now. *(op 2-1 after early 9-4)*

4568 RACING UK MARES' ONLY H'CAP HURDLE (11 hdls) 2m 5f
5:10 (5:10) (Class 4) (0-115,113) 4-Y-0+ **£3,253** (£955; £477; £238)

Form RPR

5154 **1** **Novacella (FR)**[45] [3733] 5-10-13 **100**.............................. AndrewThornton 105+
(R H Alner) *bhd: hdwy 7th: mstke and dropped rr 4 out: plenty to do appr 2 out: styd on strly last: led fnl 50yds: drvn out* **9/4**[1]

4224 **2** *1 ½* **Di's Dilemma**[85] [2968] 8-10-5 **92**.................................. PaulMoloney 93
(C C Bealby) *rr but in tch: hdwy to chal 4 out: slt ld next: rdn 2 out: hdd and no ex fnl 50yds* **7/1**

1314 **3** *2 ½* **Chickapeakray**[64] [3416] 5-9-11 **87** oh1.......................... StephenCraine(3) 87+
(D McCain) *chsd ldrs: led 4 out: narrowly hdd next: rdn and ev ch whn blnd 2 out: sn one pce* **4/1**[3]

065 **4** *5* **Kryena**[40] [3817] 4-9-8 **96** oh5 ow1..................................... RichardSpate(7) 81
(Mrs P Robeson) *rr but in tch: hit 5th: j. slowly next: hdwy 7th: chal 4 out to next: wknd 2 out* **7/1**

1134 **5** *8* **Miss Shakira (IRE)**[50] [3649] 8-10-13 **100**........................... CarlLlewellyn 87+
(N A Twiston-Davies) *chsd ldrs: led appr 4th: hdd 7th: sn wknd* **5/2**[2]

1645 **6** *18* **Miss Merenda**[132] [2125] 5-10-7 **94**.. PJBrennan 61
(J F Panvert) *slt ld tl appr 4th: led again 7th: hdd 4 out: sn wknd* **20/1**

5m 2.30s (-13.80) **Going Correction** -0.95s/f (Hard)
WFA 4 from 5yo+ 8lb 6 Ran SP% **109.1**
Speed ratings: **88,87,86,84,81 74** CSF £16.50 CT £52.06 TOTE £2.90: £1.70, £2.40; EX 17.90 Place 6 £8.27, Place 5 £6.96.
Owner Mrs Norma Kelly **Bred** F Cottin And Mme Gilberte Chaignon **Trained** Droop, Dorset

FOCUS
This race was especially weakened by the nine non-runners on account of the ground. The early pace was also very modest , and even though the winning time was five seconds faster than the opener, it was still slow. However, the first four were close to their marks and the winner can rate higher.

NOTEBOOK
Novacella(FR) would have preferred a stronger pace and her prospects of winning looked to be zero when she made a mistake and dropped back to last four from home. However, with the leaders doing little in front, her stamina kicked in and she swept through on the run-in to gain an unlikely victory. *(op 7-4)*
Di's Dilemma, taking another step up in trip, looked to have only Chickapeakray to beat rounding the home bend and she eventually won that particular duel, but the winner swept by the pair of them which merely extended her frustrating run of placings. *(op 9-1)*
Chickapeakray, 7lb higher than for her Sedgefield victory, still had a chance when diving through *the second last and then had no more to offer. The Handicapper looks to have hold of her now. (op 13-2)*
Kryena, making her handicap debut and 6lb wrong taking into account her rider's 1lb overweight, did not see out the extra five furlongs against her elders. *(tchd 8-1)*
Miss Shakira(IRE), back over hurdles off a 10lb lower mark than over fences, dropped away very tamely over the last half-mile. She is better than this. *(op 9-4 tchd 2-1)*
Miss Merenda should have had no problem with the trip or ground and showed up for a long way *before dropping away over the last half-mile. She may have just needed this after four months off. (op 14-1)*
T/Plt: £12.50 to a £1 stake. Pool: £54,908.10. 3,192.40 winning tickets. T/Qpdt: £4.30 to a £1 stake. Pool: £2,906.40. 495.50 winning tickets. ST

4367 CHEPSTOW (L-H)
Wednesday, March 22

OFFICIAL GOING: Good to soft (good in places) changing to good (good to soft in places) after race 2 (2.40)
Wind: Light across Weather: Fine

4569 THE SPORTSMAN OUT TODAY NOVICES' HURDLE (8 hdls) 2m 110y
2:10 (2:10) (Class 4) 4-Y-0+ **£2,927** (£859; £429; £214)

Form RPR

3363 **1** **Chiaro (FR)**[136] [2085] 4-11-7 139..................................(b) RichardJohnson 139+
(P J Hobbs) *a.p: led appr 4 out: rdn clr appr last: easily* **5/4**[1]

1U **2** *18* **Anemix (FR)**[16] [4282] 5-11-2 115.................................. HowieEphgrave(5) 124+
(L Corcoran) *hld up in tch: ev ch 4 out: rdn 3 out: no ch w wnr fr 2 out* **5/2**[2]

41 **3** *13* **White On Black (GER)**[23] [4149] 5-11-7 117........................ JamieMoore 107+
(G L Moore) *hld up in mid-div: hdwy 3rd: wknd appr 3 out* **8/1**

6 **4** *2 ½* **Angello (FR)**[31] [4005] 5-10-7 .... KeiranBurke(7) 95
(N J Hawke) *hld up in mid-div: hit 3rd: styd on fr 2 out: n.d* **150/1**

64 **5** *10* **Daraybad (FR)**[19] [4211] 4-10-7 .... APMcCoy 82+
(N J Henderson) *nt fluent 1st: sn prom: wknd 4 out* **7/1**[3]

3505 **6** *2* **So Long**[38] [3882] 6-10-7 .... RobertWalford 76
(C L Popham) *nvr bttr than mid-div* **66/1**

60 **7** *½* **Lordsbridge (USA)**[32] [3996] 4-10-2 .... DarylJacob(5) 75
(D P Keane) *nvr nr ldrs* **66/1**

F214 **8** *½* **Walsingham (IRE)**[13] [4329] 8-11-7 99.............................. RobertThornton 89
(R Lee) *led tl appr 4 out: sn wknd* **16/1**

6 **9** *8* **Arc Of Stone (IRE)**[10] [4393] 6-11-0 .... WarrenMarston 74
(D J Wintle) *rdn 2nd: a towards rr* **100/1**

0 **10** *shd* **Montenda**[13] [4327] 5-10-9 .... ChrisHonour(5) 73
(S C Burrough) *prom tl wknd 4th* **200/1**

05 **11** *18* **Kofi**[34] [3948] 4-10-7 .... BenjaminHitchcott 48
(Miss K M George) *a bhd* **150/1**

PP/0 **12** *22* **Hurricane Coast**[7] [2627] 7-10-9 .... JohnnyLevins(5) 33
(K McAuliffe) *mstke 4th: a bhd: t.o* **150/1**

6P0 **13** *4* **Mr Smithers Jones**[27] [4071] 6-11-0 .... JodieMogford 29
(Mrs S M Johnson) *mid-div: hit 4th: sn struggling: t.o* **150/1**

14 *dist* **Scania Classic** 5-11-0 .... TomDoyle —
(R Lee) *a towards rr: t.o* **125/1**

0P-P **F** **Kingtobee (IRE)**[109] [2618] 8-11-0 .... JasonMaguire —
(J A B Old) *a bhd: no ch whn fell last* **125/1**

20 **P** **Beths Choice**[31] [4011] 5-10-7 .... ChrisDavies(7) —
(J M Bradley) *mid-div: rdn 3rd: struggling whn hit 4th: t.o whn p.u bef 2 out* **150/1**

3m 57.3s (-13.10) **Going Correction** -0.65s/f (Firm)
WFA 4 from 5yo+ 7lb 16 Ran SP% **111.9**
Speed ratings: **104,95,89,88,83 82,82,82,78,78 69,59,57,—,— —** CSF £3.97 TOTE £2.60: £1.10, £1.50, £2.20; EX 6.50.
Owner Andrew L Cohen **Bred** Hans Peter Sorg **Trained** Withycombe, Somerset

FOCUS
Despite the numbers few could be fancied and it proved a pretty uncompetitive affair, but the form looks solid enough rated through the third.

NOTEBOOK
Chiaro(FR), twice a winner of Listed hurdles in France, had been given an official rating of 139 and looked sure to take the beating against what was only fair opposition on his debut in this country. He won easily and could well be up to running a big race in the novice hurdle over two and a half miles at the Grand National meeting. *(op 13-8)*
Anemix(FR) had a tough task on his plate against the winner, who is officialy rated 24lb higher *than him, and was far from disgraced. He seemed to appreciate the drop back in trip. (op 3-1 tchd 9-4)*
White On Black(GER), a winner at Plumpton on his last start, ran a fairly solid race and his performance is probably a decent guide to the level of the form. *(op 7-1 tchd 13-2)*
Angello(FR) was not inconvenienced by the drop back in trip and ran a better race on his second start in this country. He might be more of a handicap type. *(op 100-1)*
Daraybad(FR) needed this third run for a mark and he was not knocked about. There was a big word for him prior to his hurdling debut at Fakenham and the chances are there is better to come from him in handicap company. *(op 9-2)*

4570 THE SPORTSMAN OUT TODAY (S) HURDLE (8 hdls) 2m 110y
2:40 (2:41) (Class 5) 4-7-Y-0 **£2,081** (£611; £305; £152)

Form RPR

-0P0 **1** **Can Can Flyer (IRE)**[65] [3423] 5-11-0 84........................... JodieMogford 88+
(J C Tuck) *mde all: shkn up appr last: r.o wl* **25/1**

P-PP **2** *¾* **Montesino**[70] [3345] 7-10-9 102...................................(p) EamonDehdashti(5) 85
(M Madgwick) *hld up in tch: wnt 2nd after 3rd: ev ch 2 out: nt qckn flat* **8/1**[2]

1350 **3** *17* **Assoon**[34] [3950] 7-11-5 103..(b) JamieMoore 75+
(G L Moore) *hld up in mid-div: hdwy 3rd: rdn after 4th: hung lft fr 3 out: nt run on* **4/7**[1]

F-P6 **4** *8* **Thespian Lady**[274] [804] 5-10-7 .... TomDoyle 53
(P R Chamings) *hld up and bhd: hdwy 3rd: no imp fr 4 out* **25/1**

P065 **5** *3 ½* **Sunny Daze**[28] [4056] 6-10-11 78.................................. StephenCraine(3) 57
(D McCain) *chsd wnr tl after 3rd: rdn appr 4 out: wknd 3 out* **12/1**[3]

0-U0 **6** *dist* **Pipers Legend**[16] [4278] 7-11-0 ....(p) OllieMcPhail —
(D Burchell) *t.k.h: sn prom: sltly hmpd 3rd: sn wknd: t.o* **40/1**

0300 **P** **Firebird Rising (USA)**[42] [3804] 5-10-7 69.......................... AntonyEvans —
(R Brotherton) *a bhd: t.o whn p.u bef 2 out* **18/1**

40P **U** **Little Rort (IRE)**[139] [2008] 7-11-0 87.................................. MarkNicolls(5) —
(S T Lewis) *hld up in tch: 4th whn blnd and uns rdr 3rd* **14/1**

0-P **P** **Silk Appeal**[16] [4280] 6-10-7 .... WarrenMarston —
(D J Wintle) *hld up and bhd: hmpd 3rd: t.o whn p.u bef 3 out* **50/1**

0 **P** **Graig Hill Cracker (IRE)**[165] [1681] 7-10-9 .... LiamTreadwell(5) —
(R L Brown) *plld hrd: hdwy after 1st: j. slowly and lost pl 2nd: sn bhd: t.o whn p.u bef 3 out* **50/1**

4m 4.70s (-5.70) **Going Correction** -0.65s/f (Firm) 10 Ran SP% **108.4**
Speed ratings: **87,86,78,74,73 —,—,—,—,—** CSF £187.40 TOTE £17.00: £6.40, £2.00, £1.02; EX 175.70.There was no bid for the winner.
Owner J C Tuck **Bred** I Robinson & A W Robinson **Trained** Oldbury on the Hill, Gloucs

FOCUS
A poor seller in which 84-rated Can Can Flyer proved too strong for horses officially rated much higher.

NOTEBOOK
Can Can Flyer(IRE), dropping into a seller for the first time, went well in front and knuckled down in good style when challenged in the latter stages. While he ran to his best, the same could not be said of the opposition, however, and the form looks very moderate. *(op 22-1)*
Montesino, pulled up on his last three starts, is not up to running to his current mark of 102 if this performance is any guide. He had every chance but found the 84-rated winner just too strong in the closing stages. *(tchd 9-1)*
Assoon was very disappointing, being under pressure a long way out and running a moody race. He does not look one to trust on this evidence. *(op 8-13)*
Thespian Lady, another being dropped into selling company for the first time, arguably ran her best race to date, although that is not saying much. *(op 40-1)*
Sunny Daze again showed himself to be a very poor performer.

4571 THE SPORTSMAN OUT TODAY H'CAP CHASE (18 fncs) 3m
3:15 (3:15) (Class 4) (0-100,96) 5-Y-0+ **£3,903** (£1,146; £573; £286)

Form RPR

5011 **1** **Parkinson (IRE)**[12] [4353] 5-10-8 **88**.. APMcCoy 97+
(Jonjo O'Neill) *hld up: hdwy 7th: wnt 2nd after 13th: hit 5 out: rdn to ld 2 out: clr flat: eased towards fin* **1/1**[1]

0-06 **2** *9* **Wakeup Smiling (IRE)**[19] [4214] 8-11-12 **96**......................... BarryFenton 105+
(Miss E C Lavelle) *led tl after 2nd: led 4th: hit 13th: rdn appr 3 out: hdd and hit 2 out: sn swtchd rt: one pce* **10/1**

5026 **3** *12* **Gunship (IRE)**[24] [4133] 5-10-0 **80** oh2.............................. RichardJohnson 64+
(P J Hobbs) *hld up and bhd: hdwy appr 8th: wnt 3rd 3 out: no imp whn j.rt 2 out and last* **6/1**[2]

50P **4** *10* **Honor And Glory**[129] 2213 6-9-11 **70**.......................... StephenCraine(3) 52+
(Nick Williams) *chsd ldrs: j.rt and reminders 3rd: wnt 2nd appr 8th: rdn after 13th: wknd 3 out* **16/1**

043 **5** *½* **Reach The Clouds (IRE)**[33] 3958 14-10-12 **87**.............. MarkNicolls(5) 67
(John R Upson) *hld up and bhd: hdwy after 7th: wknd after 13th* **50/1**

-5PP **6** *dist* **Apple Joe**[118] 2465 10-9-8 **71**..........................(p) JamesWhite(7) —
(A J Whiting) *a bhd: t.o fr 11th* **20/1**

P1PP **P** **Boundary House**[13] 4328 8-11-8 **92**.......................... JasonMaguire —
(J A B Old) *a bhd: t.o whn p.u bef 3 out* **40/1**

1444 **P** **Roman Rampage**[25] 4116 11-10-13 **88**............(p) RobertLucey-Butler(5) —
(Miss Z C Davison) *a bhd: t.o 11th: p.u bef 3 out* **28/1**

3P11 **P** **Quizzling (IRE)**[28] 4047 8-11-0 **84**.......................... JoeTizzard —
(B J M Ryall) *j.rt: hld up: hdwy after 7th: wknd 11th: t.o whn p.u bef 3 out* **8/1**[3]

5P3P **P** **Lucky Leader (IRE)**[61] 3481 11-11-2 **89**..................(v1) RichardYoung(3) —
(N R Mitchell) *hld up: sme hdwy 8th: wknd 11th: t.o whn p.u bef 4 out* **8/1**[3]

-UPP **P** **Banaluso (IRE)**[60] 3499 6-9-7 **70** oh5.......................... MrSPJones(7) —
(B G Powell) *w ldr: led after 2nd to 4th: mstke 5th: wknd 8th: t.o whn p.u bef 4 out* **80/1**

-400 **P** **Darnayson (IRE)**[46] 3732 6-11-9 **93**.......................... CarlLlewellyn —
(N A Twiston-Davies) *hld up: reminders and hdwy appr 8th: wknd 9th: t.o whn p.u bef 3 out* **33/1**

6m 14.3s (-0.60) **Going Correction** -0.40s/f (Good)
WFA 5 from 6yo+ 10lb **12** Ran SP% **118.3**
Speed ratings: **85,82,78,74,74** —,—,—,—,— —,— CSF £10.90 CT £44.47 TOTE £2.40: £1.10, £2.80, £2.50; EX 14.70.
Owner Trevor Hemmings **Bred** E J O'Sullivan **Trained** Cheltenham, Gloucs

FOCUS
A modest handicap chase but the winner looks progressive and a four-timer is clearly a possibility.

NOTEBOOK
Parkinson(IRE), who is by Presenting, the sire of Gold Cup winner War Of Attrition, does not do an awful lot in front but he completed a hat-trick here and is clearly progressing well. The Handicapper is struggling to keep up with his improvement and a four-timer is definitely on the cards, with his ability to handle a quicker surface as well as soft ground now proven. *(op 10-11 tchd 5-4)*
Wakeup Smiling(IRE) ran his best race to date over fences and was unfortunate to run into a well-handicapped and progressive rival. He looks capable of winning off this mark. *(op 8-1)*
Gunship(IRE), making his chasing debut, ran a satisfactory race and is entitled to improve for the experience. *(op 8-1)*
Honor And Glory, who was having his first run since November, won a maiden point last year but has yet to translate that promise to races under Rules. *(op 25-1 tchd 28-1)*
Reach The Clouds(IRE), successful in only two of his last 48 starts, has done his winning over trips around two miles and struggles to get home over this type of distance. *(op 40-1)*
Boundary House *Official explanation: jockey said gelding bled from nose (tchd 50-1)*

4572 THE SPORTSMAN OUT TODAY NOVICES' H'CAP CHASE (16 fncs) 2m 3f 110y
3:50 (3:50) (Class 4) (0-110,105) 5-Y-0+ **£4,554** (£1,337; £668; £333)

Form RPR

32U2 **1** **Matthew Muroto (IRE)**[25] 4102 7-11-4 **102**...................... DarylJacob(5) 117+
(R H Alner) *hld up: hdwy 7th: led 4 out: lft clr 2 out* **7/4**[2]

05F **2** *10* **Master Billyboy (IRE)**[15] 4288 8-11-5 **103** ow1................. MrNHarris(5) 103+
(Mrs S D Williams) *hld up in rr: hdwy 10th: nt fluent 11th: blnd 2 out: r.o to take 2nd post: no ch w wnr* **10/1**[3]

1P65 **3** *hd* **Martin Ossie**[26] 4095 9-11-7 **100**.......................... WarrenMarston 102+
(J M Bradley) *chsd ldr: led appr 3rd: j.rt 7th: blnd and hdd 4 out: wkng whn lft 2nd 2 out* **10/1**[3]

-400 **4** *dist* **River Indus**[57] 3548 6-10-13 **92**.......................... BenjaminHitchcott —
(R H Buckler) *a bhd: lost tch 9th: t.o* **10/1**[3]

430/ **F** **Eljay's Boy**[271] 8-10-6 **85**.......................... JoeTizzard 90+
(C L Tizzard) *hld up: hit 5th: hdwy 8th: 3l 2nd whn fell 2 out* **16/1**

4021 **P** **Sargasso Sea**[12] 4352 9-11-12 **105**.......................... JasonMaguire —
(J A B Old) *led: blnd 2nd: sn hdd: nt fluent 5th: wknd 5 out: p.u bef 4 out* **6/4**[1]

5m 7.40s (-3.90) **Going Correction** -0.40s/f (Good) **6** Ran SP% **109.5**
Speed ratings: **91,87,86**,—,— — CSF £16.92 TOTE £2.80: £1.30, £3.50; EX 17.90.
Owner Alvin Trowbridge **Bred** Patrick Gahan **Trained** Droop, Dorset

FOCUS
A moderate handicap chase for novices rated around the placed horses to their marks.

NOTEBOOK
Matthew Muroto(IRE) was still a maiden after 14 attempts going into this, but he has taken quite well to chasing and got off the mark with a comfortable success. His task was made easier with Eljay's Boy falling two out, but he may just have been holding that rival at the time and he is progressing along the right lines. *(tchd 13-8 and 2-1)*
Master Billyboy(IRE), a faller at Exeter on his previous start, got round this time but could take only a moderate second. *(op 9-1)*
Martin Ossie, dropped back nearly a mile in trip, raced too freely early on and did not jump well enough when challenged. *(op 11-1 tchd 14-1)*
River Indus, a moderate maiden hurdler, was never a threat on his chasing debut. *(op 12-1 tchd 14-1 and 9-1)*
Sargasso Sea, off the mark in a very uncompetitive four-runner beginners' chase at Leicester on his previous start, was taken on for the lead after making a bad mistake at the second fence and never looked happy. *Official explanation: trainer said gelding was wrong behind (tchd 11-8 and 7-4)*
Eljay's Boy, a winner over hurdles in Jersey when he was last seen 271 days previously, was making his chasing debut and was still in contention when he fell two from home. It is unclear whether he would have found enough under pressure to actually go on and win, especially given he was returning from an absence, but there was still enough in this effort to suggest he can exploit his current mark over fences. *(tchd 11-8 and 7-4)*

4573 NORLAND MANAGED SERVICES H'CAP HURDLE (11 hdls) 2m 4f
4:25 (4:25) (Class 3) (0-125,122) 4-Y-0+ **£5,530** (£1,623; £811; £405)

Form RPR

3P04 **1** **Kandjar D'Allier (FR)**[60] 3493 8-10-12 **108**.................. RobertThornton 119+
(A King) *hld up: hdwy 4th: led 2 out: sn rdn: r.o wl* **6/5**[1]

-560 **2** *4* **Rainbows Aglitter**[62] 3459 9-11-5 **115**.......................... TomDoyle 116
(D R Gandolfo) *plld hrd in rr: hdwy on ins 4 out: r.o one pce fr 2 out* **20/1**

/2P- **3** *1* **Grand Finale (IRE)**[451] 2977 9-11-7 **122**.................. LiamTreadwell(5) 122
(Miss Venetia Williams) *hld up: hdwy appr 7th: r.o one pce fr 2 out* **14/1**

F506 **4** *1 ¾* **Milligan (FR)**[28] 4050 11-11-1 **111**.......................... JoeTizzard 109
(Dr P Pritchard) *led: rdn and hdd 2 out: wknd last* **50/1**

-P6F **5** *6* **Sesame Rambler (IRE)**[12] 4357 7-10-13 **109**.................. JamieMoore 102+
(G L Moore) *hld up: hdwy appr 4 out: wknd 3 out* **9/2**[2]

5053 **6** *15* **King Georges (FR)**[37] 3901 8-10-4 **100**.................. JodieMogford 77
(J C Tuck) *hld up in rr: nt fluent 1st and 2nd: short-lived effrt appr 4 out* **7/1**

130 **P** **Sasso**[62] 3467 4-10-12 **116**.......................... APMcCoy —
(Jonjo O'Neill) *hld up in tch: p.u bef 4 out* **13/2**[3]

112/ **P** **Lazerito (IRE)**[738] 4340 8-11-2 **112**.......................... AlanO'Keeffe —
(Miss Venetia Williams) *chsd ldr to 4 out: sn wknd: bhd whn p.u bef last* **11/1**

4m 56.6s (-6.10) **Going Correction** -0.65s/f (Firm)
WFA 4 from 7yo+ 8lb **8** Ran SP% **111.2**
Speed ratings: **86,84,84,83,80 74**,—,— CSF £22.82 CT £219.72 TOTE £2.00: £1.10, £5.70, £3.70; EX 28.50.
Owner Let's Live Racing **Bred** Y Maupoil And Suc Edmond Maupoil **Trained** Barbury Castle, Wilts

FOCUS
An ordinary handicap hurdle for the grade and the form wants treating with caution, as the pace was steady for most of the way and did not increase noticeably until after the fourth last, which the remaining seven runners (Sasso had pulled up by this point) jumped almost in a line.

NOTEBOOK
Kandjar D'Allier(FR) had never previously won over hurdles, but he was 28lb lower than over fences as a result and took advantage to run out a clear-cut winner. The steady pace did not inconvenience him and he should be competitive when reassessed. *(op 11-8 tchd 13-8)*
Rainbows Aglitter, returned to hurdles, travelled well but proved no match for the reasonably-handicapped winner. *(op 12-1)*
Grand Finale(IRE) may well have appreciated the steady pace given this was his first outing in 451 days and ran with credit. *(op 12-1)*
Milligan(FR) had the run of the race and may be flattered by his finishing position. *(op 28-1)*
Sesame Rambler(IRE) had a nasty-looking fall less than two weeks previously at Sandown and was below form this time. *(op 5-1)*
Sasso *Official explanation: trainer said gelding hung badly right going down hill (op 9-2 tchd 4-1)*

4574 THE SPORTSMAN OUT TODAY INTERMEDIATE OPEN NATIONAL HUNT FLAT RACE 2m 110y
5:00 (5:02) (Class 6) 4-6-Y-O **£1,626** (£477; £238; £119)

Form RPR

1 **Sound Accord (IRE)** 5-11-4 .... TomDoyle 108+
(C Tinkler) *hld up towards rr: hdwy on ins over 4f out: rdn over 3f out: led wl ins fnl f: r.o* **9/1**

2 *1 ½* **Lappeenranta (IRE)** 5-11-4 .... JamieMoore 104
(V R A Dartnall) *chsd ldr tl over 6f out: rdn and wnt 2nd again over 3f out: led ins fnl f: sn hdd: nt qckn* **25/1**

3 **3** *3* **Goscar Rock (IRE)**[85] 3024 5-11-4 .... RichardJohnson 102+
(P J Hobbs) *led: clr over 3f out: hdd and no ex ins fnl f* **2/1**[1]

4 *3* **Nictos De Bersy (FR)** 5-11-4 .... JimmyMcCarthy 98
(C P Morlock) *hld up in mid-div: hdwy over 6f out: rdn over 4f out: wknd over 1f out* **66/1**

10 **5** *3 ½* **The Big Canadian (IRE)**[115] 2534 5-11-11 .... RobertThornton 101
(A King) *hld up and bhd: hdwy on ins 5f out: wknd wl over 1f out* **10/1**

6 *14* **Apatura Dik** 5-11-4 .... SeanCurran 80
(N R Mitchell) *hld up and bhd: hdwy after 4f: wknd 3f out* **100/1**

7 *1 ½* **Extra Bold** 4-10-8 .... WilliamKennedy(3) 72
(R Lee) *hld up and bhd: hdwy over 5f out: wknd 4f out* **33/1**

8 *1 ½* **Maori Legend** 5-10-6 .... DarylJacob(5) 70
(D P Keane) *prom tl wknd over 4f out* **25/1**

523 **9** *8* **Captain Marlon (IRE)**[31] 4011 5-11-4 .... JoeTizzard 80+
(C L Tizzard) *t.k.h in mid-div: hdwy 10f out: wnt 2nd over 6f out: ev ch over 4f out: eased whn btn over 2f out* **11/4**[2]

10 *5* **Marcus** 5-11-4 .... BarryFenton 64
(Miss E C Lavelle) *hld up and bhd: hdwy after 4f: wknd over 5f out* **50/1**

1 **11** *23* **Notre Cyborg (FR)**[47] 3720 5-11-6 .... LiamHeard(5) 48
(P F Nicholls) *hld up and bhd: short-lived effrt and c wd st: t.o* **4/1**[3]

0- **12** *dist* **Mr Freeze (IRE)**[683] 226 6-10-11 .... KeiranBurke(7) —
(J T Stimpson) *t.k.h in tch: wknd 9f out: t.o* **100/1**

13 *dist* **Bin Farmin** 6-11-1 .... RichardYoung(3) —
(N R Mitchell) *t.k.h in rr: rdn 8f out: t.o* **100/1**

3m 57.7s (-12.50) **Going Correction** -0.65s/f (Firm)
WFA 4 from 5yo+ 7lb **13** Ran SP% **116.1**
Speed ratings: **103,102,100,99,97 91,90,89,86,83 72**,—,— CSF £193.25 TOTE £10.50: £2.70, £6.50, £1.20; EX 64.60.
Owner George Ward **Bred** Greenville House Stud And M Morgan **Trained** Compton, Berks

FOCUS
A reasonable bumper, although perhaps not that much strength in depth.

NOTEBOOK
Sound Accord(IRE) ◆, an IR34,000 half-brother to the smart two-mile chaser River City, overcame his inexperience to make successful racecourse debut. He had quite a bit to do on the turn into the straight, but gradually got the hang of things and stayed on strongly to ultimately win going away. He looks a very nice prospect. *(old market op 12-1, new market op 8-1)*
Lappeenranta(IRE), a half-brother to a successful hurdler and chaser at up to three miles, belied his big odds with a promising second on his racecourse debut. He worked hard to reel in the long-time leader Goscar Rock and had nothing left when challenged late on by the eventual winner. It will be disappointing if he cannot find a similar race before going hurdling. *(new market)*
Goscar Rock(IRE) ◆, a promising third in a course and distance bumper on his debut nearly three months previously, got the run of the race and looked set to improve on that effort when clear in the straight for much of the way, but he seemingly got tired late on. He is obviously just needing a little bit of time and should do better. *(old market op 7-2, new market op 5-2)*
Nictos De Bersy(FR) represents a small stable and was sent off at 66/1 for this racecourse debut, but he was an 18,000gns purchase, out of a winning hurdler in France, and should not be used to hold the form down. There could be improvement to come. *(new market op 50-1)*
The Big Canadian(IRE), a winner on his debut at Haydock before being found out by better opposition at Newbury, was supported at big odds and gives the form a solid look. *(old market op 33-1, new market op 16-1)*
Captain Marlon(IRE) is probably going to better suited by a stiffer test of stamina and easier ground when sent over obstacles. *(old market op 8-1, new market op 5-1)*
Notre Cyborg(FR) looked a nice prospect when winning on his debut at Fontwell 47 days previously, but ran no sort of race this time and presumably something was amiss. *(old market op 9-2, new market op 11-4 tchd 6-1)*

4575 LETHEBY & CHRISTOPHER CONDITIONAL JOCKEYS' H'CAP CHASE (12 fncs) 2m 110y
5:30 (5:30) (Class 5) (0-90,90) 5-Y-0+ **£2,602** (£764; £382; £190)

Form RPR

0331 **1** **Better Moment (IRE)**[37] 3899 9-11-4 **90**..........(v) AndrewGlassonbury(8) 104+
(M C Pipe) *hld up: hdwy appr 2nd: led appr 5 out: sn clr: eased considerably flat* **5/1**[2]

0-56 **2** *3 ½* **Sweet Minuet**[36] 3907 9-11-4 **82**.......................... RobertLucey-Butler 85
(M Madgwick) *a.p: rdn after 7th: wnt 2nd 3 out: kpt on flat: no ch w wnr* **16/1**

U-54 **3** *1 ½* **Risington**[22] 4162 8-10-10 **77**.......................... LiamTreadwell(3) 81+
(Miss Venetia Williams) *j.rt: hld up and bhd: hdwy 4th: r.o one pce fr 2 out* **9/2**[1]

5304 **4** 2 ½ **Taksina**[47] 3716 7-10-5 **77** .... PaulDavey(8) 79+
(R H Buckler) *chsd ldr to 7th: rdn appr 5 out: one pce fr 3 out* **9/2**[1]
3000 **5** 6 **Blazing Batman**[12] 4356 13-10-6 **70** .... WilliamKennedy 64+
(Dr P Pritchard) *prom: lost pl 1st: n.d after* **6/1**
64R0 **6** 2 ½ **Kinkeel (IRE)**[16] 4278 7-10-6 **73** .... (b) WillieMcCarthy(3) 64
(A W Carroll) *led tl appr 5 out: wknd after 2 out* **20/1**
P26P **7** 1 ½ **Sunshan**[34] 3949 10-11-0 **84** .... JamesWhite(6) 74+
(R J Hodges) *sn bhd* **6/1**
6365 **8** 3 ½ **Twist N Turn**[14] 4303 6-9-11 **64** .... (b[1]) StephenCraine(3) 50
(D McCain) *hld up: nt fluent 2nd: hdwy appr 7th: rdn and wknd appr 5 out* **11/2**[3]
0/PP **F** **Golden Tamesis**[35] 3920 9-9-8 **66** .... JohnPritchard(8) —
(R Dickin) *fell 3rd* **66/1**

4m 14.0s (-8.90) **Going Correction** -0.40s/f (Good) **9** Ran SP% **109.1**
Speed ratings: **104,102,101,100,97 96,95,94,—** CSF £68.39 CT £348.35 TOTE £4.10: £1.40, £4.80, £2.60; EX 75.40 Place 6 £10.82, Place 5 £9.10.
Owner M C Pipe **Bred** Bernard Cooke **Trained** Nicholashayne, Devon
■ Better Moment ended a run of 67 losers over 18 days for Martin Pipe.

FOCUS
A moderate handicap chase restricted to conditional riders. Winner value for 10l.

NOTEBOOK
Better Moment(IRE) was a beaten favourite on his only previous start over fences back in 2002 but, in good form following a recent success in a similar event to this over hurdles on his previous start, he took well to the return to chasing and followed up in emphatic fashion. He should continue to go well both over hurdles and fences at a lowly level. *(op 9-2)*
Sweet Minuet, still a maiden over fences, looked to run her race in second but was no match for the winner. *(op 10-1)*
Risington would have appreciated the return to better ground but he was well held third and looks very limited. *(op 5-1)*
Taksina seems better when able to dominate over a longer trip. *(op 5-1)*
Blazing Batman is not really a horse to be following. *(op 11-2 tchd 5-1)*
Twist N Turn may not have taken to the first-time blinkers. *(op 9-2 tchd 6-1)*
T/Plt: £11.90 to a £1 stake. Pool: £47,578.90. 2,914.65 winning tickets. T/Qpdt: £7.00 to a £1 stake. Pool: £2,988.20. 315.10 winning tickets. KH

4320 TOWCESTER (R-H)
Wednesday, March 22

OFFICIAL GOING: Good
Wind: Almost nil Weather: Bright & cold.

4576 WAYSIDE AUDI H'CAP CHASE (18 fncs) 3m 110y
2:20 (2:21) (Class 4) (0-110,106) 5-Y-0+ **£4,436** (£1,310; £655; £327; £163)

Form RPR
45-5 **1** **Would You Believe**[27] 4078 10-10-11 **91** .... PJBrennan 107+
(P J Hobbs) *2nd or 3rd tl led 13th: drvn 2 out: styd on wl flat: all out* **9/2**[2]
P014 **2** 1 ½ **Lord Broadway (IRE)**[25] 4103 10-10-12 **95** .... TJPhelan(3) 111+
(N M Babbage) *rr early: stdy prog 9th: rdn after 3 out: chsd wnr fr next: styd on cl home but a hld* **6/1**
PP01 **3** 11 **Meggie's Beau (IRE)**[7] 4451 10-11-3 **104** 7ex .... (b) MrWBiddick(7) 109+
(Miss Venetia Williams) *trckd ldrs: wnt 2nd 15th: gng wl tl rdn and fnd nil bef 2 out: blnd last* **4/1**[1]
2160 **4** 5 **Midnight Gunner**[56] 3560 12-11-8 **102** .... TimmyMurphy 100
(A E Price) *towards rr: pushed along 8th: sme prog 12th: drvn and wknd bef 3 out* **15/2**
4342 **5** ½ **Woodview (IRE)**[27] 4071 7-11-6 **100** .... JohnMcNamara 97
(K C Bailey) *chsd ldrs: rdn bef 3 out: sn struggling* **9/1**
0353 **6** 3 **Kappelhoff (IRE)**[36] 3909 9-10-0 **80** oh14 .... (v) MatthewBatchelor 74
(Mrs L Richards) *rr div: rdn and sme hdwy whn hit 13th: btn whn pckd 15th* **12/1**
0P04 **7** dist **Thyne Spirit (IRE)**[33] 3958 7-10-0 **80** oh19 .... RJGreene —
(S T Lewis) *mstkes in rr: v bad blunder 4th: rdn 6th: struggling 10th: t.o 14th: btn 59l* **80/1**
0-P3 **8** 8 **Indian Chance**[12] 4358 12-10-12 **92** .... LeightonAspell —
(O Sherwood) *cl up: led 8th and mde virtually all tl 14th: fdd bef 3 out: j.rt 2 out and eased: j.rt last: btn 67l* **12/1**
5640 **9** 6 **Strong Magic (IRE)**[9] 4419 14-10-13 **93** .... RichardHobson —
(J R Cornwall) *rr and nt a fluent: lost tch 9th: t.o 12th: btn 73l* **66/1**
6300 **P** **The River Joker (IRE)**[13] 4321 10-10-0 **80** .... JamieGoldstein —
(John R Upson) *sn pushed along: lost tch 9th: t.o and p.u 11th* **11/2**[3]
U31P **P** **Fin Bec (FR)**[15] 4287 13-11-12 **106** .... (b) AndrewThornton —
(R Curtis) *led tl 8th: hit 10th: rejnd ldr after 11th tl 13th: hit next: wknd and nt fluent 15th: p.u 3 out* **9/1**

6m 25.4s (-21.20) **Going Correction** -0.575s/f (Firm) **11** Ran SP% **117.7**
Speed ratings: **110,109,106,104,104 103,—,—,—,— —** CSF £32.43 CT £117.84 TOTE £4.30: £1.80, £2.70, £1.90; EX 40.50.
Owner D Allen **Bred** Shade Oak Stud **Trained** Withycombe, Somerset

FOCUS
A strong gallop thanks to Fin Bec and the front two came clear on the stiff uphill climb. The form looks solid enough rated through the sixth.

NOTEBOOK
Would You Believe, who may have been in need of the outing on his reappearance at Huntingdon last month, always held a prominent position under Brennan and he saw it out best, running on strongly from the persistent runner-up. He has dropped to a very decent mark, but is going to find things tougher back up in the weights. *(tchd 5-1)*
Lord Broadway(IRE), a course and distance winner back in February, ran a sound race off what was a 5lb higher mark, but he was never getting to the winner. Slightly softer conditions would probably have suited and he is always worth bearing in mind here. *(op 15-2)*
Meggie's Beau(IRE) was unable to add to his stable's formidable record at the course, finding the combination of a 7lb rise for last weeks Huntingdon success and the stiff climb in the straight beyond him. He also wore first-time blinkers at Huntingdon and it is entirely possible they did not have quite the same effect. *(tchd 5-1)*
Midnight Gunner has struggled since winning at Warwick in October and he needs a little further respite from the Handicapper. *(op 7-1 tchd 9-1)*
Woodview(IRE) has yet to make any significant impact in two starts over fences, this move into handicaps failing to help. *(op 11-1)*
Indian Chance *Official explanation: trainer said gelding had lost a front shoe in running (op 14-1)*
Fin Bec(FR) was responsible for the strong early gallop, but he was unable to maintain it and stopped quickly. *(op 13-2)*
The River Joker(IRE) was struggling from an early stage and his winless run continues. *Official explanation: trainer said gelding found the good ground too fast (op 13-2)*

4577 XPRESS RELOCATION 10 YEAR (S) HURDLE (10 hdls) 2m 3f 110y
2:50 (2:51) (Class 5) 4-Y-0+ **£2,602** (£764; £382; £190)

Form RPR
6-6P **1** **Cullian**[13] 4331 9-10-8 **90** .... (p) AndrewThornton 81+
(J G M O'Shea) *settled rr: stdy prog 6th: led bef 2 out: sn clr: unchal* **9/4**[1]
1/PP **2** 9 **Watermouse**[10] 4392 6-11-1 **82** .... HenryOliver 76
(R Dickin) *hld up: midfield whn nt fluent 6th and rdn: effrt 3 out: wnt 2nd between last two: no ch w wnr* **20/1**
0005 **3** 3 **Will She Spin**[9] 4423 5-10-1 .... WayneKavanagh(7) 66
(J W Mullins) *settled rr: effrt 7th: 4l 8th 3 out: rdn and btn bef next* **22/1**
0PP3 **4** 3 **Walton Way**[9] 4418 6-10-10 **67** .... JamesDiment(5) 70
(P W Hiatt) *wnt 2nd bef 5th: led next: drvn and hdd bef 2 out: sn fdd* **12/1**
2-P4 **5** 2 **Adalie**[140] 1981 12-10-3 **82** .... ShaneWalsh(5) 62+
(J Joseph) *bhd: clsd on outside bef 3 out where cl up: rdn and fnd nil bef next* **13/2**[2]
0/FP **6** 3 ½ **Kings Avenue**[9] 4417 9-11-1 .... (b[1]) MarcusFoley 65
(A J Chamberlain) *prom: nt fluent 7th: stl cl up 3 out: fdd bef next: mstke last* **66/1**
0P-0 **7** 1 **Bourneagainkristen**[46] 3730 8-10-1 **64** .... TomMessenger(7) 57
(C C Bealby) *racd awkwardly: led tl 6th: stl cl up 3 out: wknd bef next* **66/1**
60P0 **8** 5 **Judy The Drinker**[113] 2559 7-10-8 .... (v[1]) DaveCrosse 52
(J G M O'Shea) *midfield: rdn 7th: little rspnse but stl cl up 3 out: struggling bef next* **14/1**
2PP6 **9** dist **Majestic Moonbeam (IRE)**[34] 3940 8-11-1 **93** .... (b) MickFitzgerald —
(Jonjo O'Neill) *cl up tl 5th: sn lost interest and bhd: rdn and lost tch bef 3 out: eased bef next: btn 73l* **9/4**[1]
3000 **10** 14 **At The Double**[3] 4526 10-11-8 **89** .... (b) PaddyMerrigan(5) —
(P Winkworth) *rdn 4th: last and nt keen u.p bef 6th: t.o next: btn 87l* **8/1**[3]

5m 9.60s (-6.20) **Going Correction** -0.55s/f (Firm) **10** Ran SP% **112.4**
Speed ratings: **90,86,85,84,83 81,81,79,—,—** CSF £49.27 TOTE £2.80: £1.10, £3.70, £5.30; EX 53.60.There was no bid for the winner.
Owner KJB Investments Ltd **Bred** C C Bromley And Son **Trained** Elton, Gloucs

FOCUS
A modest seller on the whole, but the front two may be capable of making their mark in low-grade handicaps. The remainder make no appeal with the future in mind.

NOTEBOOK
Cullian, whose last win came over three years ago, was still having to race off a 2lb higher mark, but the first-time cheekpieces helped her and the return to hold-up tactics enabled her to come through and win going away. She may be capable of getting competitive in low-grade handicaps *this summer. Official explanation: trainer's representative said, regarding improved form shown, mare benefited from the refitting of sheepskin cheekpieces (op 2-1 tchd 15-8)*
Watermouse ◆ had shown little in two starts since returning from a lengthy layoff, but this drop in grade enabled him to run a better race and, although proving no match for the winner, he should have little trouble finding a similar event. *(op 22-1 tchd 25-1)*
Will She Spin did best of the rest, but she was comfortably held and remains below a winning level. *(op 18-1 tchd 25-1)*
Walton Way is a poor performer who will continue to struggle. *(op 10-1)*
Adalie is getting no younger and she was unable to make an impact on this return to hurdles, finding little off the bridle. *(op 6-1)*
Majestic Moonbeam(IRE) was bitterly disappointing on this return to hurdles, showing a poor attitude and trailing in last but one. He has no future. *(op 7-2)*

4578 THE SPORTSMAN OUT TODAY BEGINNERS' CHASE (16 fncs) 2m 6f
3:25 (3:26) (Class 4) 5-Y-0+ **£3,903** (£1,146; £573; £286)

Form RPR
U654 **1** **Sharp Jack (IRE)**[13] 4314 8-11-2 **111** .... WayneHutchinson 115
(R T Phillips) *wnt 2nd at 7th: led 3 out: drvn to forge clr after last* **9/4**[1]
F32P **2** 2 **Kitski (FR)**[16] 4279 8-11-2 **113** .... KeithMercer 115+
(Ferdy Murphy) *nt fluent: hld up in tch: effrt 3 out: sn drvn: wnt 2nd and ch last: nt qckn* **3/1**[2]
3144 **3** 1 ½ **Just A Splash (IRE)**[23] 4148 6-11-2 **105** .... AndrewTinkler 113+
(N J Gifford) *settled on heels of ldrs: drvn to 2nd after 3 out: ev ch bef last: wknd flat* **10/3**[3]
2P56 **4** 14 **Onyourheadbeit (IRE)**[10] 4394 8-11-2 **105** .... TomScudamore 98
(K C Bailey) *led tl hdd 3 out: sn last and plodding on* **3/1**[2]
040P **F** **Bob's Finesse**[31] 4005 6-10-2 .... WayneKavanagh(7) —
(J W Mullins) *j. deliberately early: rdn 7th: last tl next: 4l 5th whn fell 9th* **40/1**
PPP **U** **Germany Park (IRE)**[31] 4016 8-11-2 .... (v) MarkGrant —
(W B Stone) *2nd tl 7th: lost pl and mstke next: last whn hit 9th and bdly hmpd and uns rdr 9th* **100/1**

5m 50.2s (-15.80) **Going Correction** -0.575s/f (Firm) **6** Ran SP% **107.3**
Speed ratings: **105,104,103,98,—** — CSF £8.77 TOTE £3.80: £2.00, £1.60; EX 12.30.
Owner Bellflower Racing Ltd **Bred** James Sheridan **Trained** Adlestrop, Gloucs

FOCUS
A modest beginners' chase, not the most solid piece of form and unlikely to produce many winners.

NOTEBOOK
Sharp Jack(IRE) did not run too badly on his second start over fences at Carlisle earlier in the month, and he was able to improve on that with a hard-fought win. He is only modest, but can make his mark at the right level in handicaps. *(tchd 2-1)*
Kitski(FR) is consistent, but he has yet to win over fences and he again found one too good, not looking that easy to handle. He will find a race eventually, but is clearly not one to make a habit of backing. *(op 9-4 tchd 7-2)*
Just A Splash(IRE), who failed to get home on his previous try over fences, three miles one at Folkestone, held every chance as they rounded for home, but he again failed to see his race out as one would have liked. A drop to two and a half miles may be required. *(op 7-2 tchd 11-4)*
Onyourheadbeit(IRE) is not progressing and he was readily brushed aside before folding tamely. *(op 4-1)*
Bob's Finesse was not out of it, although it is unlikely she would have won, when coming down at the ninth.

4579 THE SPORTSMAN OUT TODAY H'CAP HURDLE (12 hdls) 3m
4:00 (4:00) (Class 3) (0-120,120) 4-Y-0 **£5,070** (£1,497; £748; £374; £187)

Form RPR
/4-F **1** **Ranelagh Gray (IRE)**[92] 2929 9-10-6 **105** .... LeeStephens(5) 109+
(Miss Venetia Williams) *mde all: pushed along bef 2 out: flattened last: r.o gamely: rdn out* **33/1**
1210 **2** 2 **Drumbeater (IRE)**[32] 3970 6-11-12 **120** .... PJBrennan 122+
(P J Hobbs) *hld up towards rr: prog 6th: last of three gng clr after 3 out: mstke next: wnt 2nd bef last: no imp u.p* **9/2**[1]
23P4 **3** 1 ¾ **Kingsbay**[11] 4372 7-10-10 **104** .... (p) JimCrowley 102
(H Morrison) *settled 3rd: let ldng pair go clr 4th: clsd 7th: wnt 2nd and reminders next: ch and drvn bef 2 out: one pce bef last* **10/1**

6F24 **4** *14* **Jiver (IRE)**[32] [3970] 7-11-10 **118**....................................(v) TomScudamore 102
(M Scudamore) *trckd ldrs: effrt 7th: drvn and wknd after 3 out* **9/1**

4356 **5** *7* **Woodlands Genpower (IRE)**[15] [4287] 8-11-10 **118**...(p) MarkBradburne 99+
(P A Pritchard) *j. slowly or mstkes: mstke and u.p 6th: rr next: lost tch 8th: styng on again fr 2 out: no ch* **16/1**

30-1 **6** *7* **Golden Bay**[54] [3600] 7-11-2 **113**.. ColinBolger(3) 83
(Miss Suzy Smith) *midfield: pressed ldrs fr 8th tl rdn 3 out: sn wknd* **11/2**[2]

3625 **7** *4* **Ingres**[28] [4058] 6-10-12 **113**... CharlieStudd(7) 79
(B G Powell) *settled rr: effrt 9th: rdn and wknd 3 out* **12/1**

6655 **8** *8* **Sword Lady**[29] [4034] 8-11-4 **112**.......................................(b) RJGreene 77+
(Mrs S D Williams) *sn pressing ldr: drvn along fr 4th: lost 2nd 8th: sn fdd: mstke 3 out* **20/1**

2335 **F** **Vicars Destiny**[10] [4390] 8-11-6 **114**.....................................(p) TomSiddall —
(Mrs S Lamyman) *hld up and bhd: mstke 5th: 8l 7th and outpcd whn fell 3 out* **15/2**

6-45 **P** **Mesmeric (IRE)**[12] [4357] 8-11-7 **115**............................... JohnMcNamara —
(B G Powell) *hld up last pair: bried effrt on outside 8th: fdd rapidly 3 out: p.u next* **7/1**[3]

241 **P** **Taking My Cut**[25] [4106] 6-11-12 **120**.................................. MickFitzgerald —
(Jonjo O'Neill) *towards rr: rdn after 6th: sn labouring: last 7th: t.o and p.u after next* **9/2**[1]

6m 10.9s (-20.10) **Going Correction** -0.55s/f (Firm) **11** Ran SP% **116.4**
Speed ratings: **111,110,109,105,102 100,99,96,—,— —** CSF £177.44 CT £1629.59 TOTE £30.00: £5.70, £2.00, £3.60; EX 163.40.
Owner Christopher Drury **Bred** Cyril Naughton **Trained** Kings Caple, H'fords

FOCUS
A good gallop set by Ranelagh Gray, and the outsider kept it going on the stiff climb to the line to record quite a surprise. The form looks solid enough, rated through the third.

NOTEBOOK
Ranelagh Gray(IRE), whose stable has an admirable record at the course, had not been seen since falling on his chase debut at Fontwell in December, but he was entitled to plenty of respect on the best of his form from last season and it was some what surprising he was allowed to be sent off at such huge odds. Soon in the lead, only Drumbeater looked to be going better turning in, but the grey ground it out on the climb to the line and, despite walking through the last, he proved too strong. Testing ground suits ideally, so it is unlikely he will be kept on the go much longer, but he could do well returned to fences next season, despite his advancing years. *(tchd 40-1)*
Drumbeater(IRE), whose fine run of form came to an abrupt end at Haydock in February, was able to bounce back and it looked turning in as though he was the one to beat, travelling strongly. He was unable to get by the grey however, but there is no reason why he cannot improve further. *(op 5-1)*
Kingsbay ran a good race in the first-time cheekpieces, holding every chance throughout the final quarter mile, but she was unable to get past and is clearly not the most willing. *(op 12-1)*
Jiver(IRE) was well adrift of the front three and would have preferred a softer surface.
Woodlands Genpower(IRE), who has lost his form and looked bored of the game over fences, again went about his race with a lack of urgency and could only stay on through beaten rivals. He continues to disappoint.
Golden Bay found the combination of a 9lb higher mark and step up to three miles against her and she was unable to make any impression in the final three furlongs or so. *(op 15-2)*
Mesmeric(IRE) failed to build on a good recent effort at Sandown and the way he stopped suggested there may have been a problem. *(op 8-1)*
Taking My Cut, expected to be suited by the step up in distance, ran a laboured race and continued *his stable's run of indifferent form. Official explanation: trainer's representative was unable to offer any explanation for poor form shown (op 8-1)*

4580 BUCKINGHAM GROUP CONTRACTING H'CAP CHASE (14 fncs) 2m 3f 110y
4:35 (4:35) (Class 5) (0-90,88) 5-Y-0+ **£3,578** (£1,050; £525; £262)

Form RPR

P051 **1** **Tipp Top (IRE)**[33] [3958] 9-11-3 **79**................................(t) JohnMcNamara 90+
(O Brennan) *mde all: rdn bef 2 out: 4l clr but idling last: drvn and all out* **10/3**[2]

P106 **2** *1 ½* **New Leader (IRE)**[79] [3221] 9-10-7 **69**......................... MatthewBatchelor 73+
(Mrs L Richards) *hld up: j. slowly 7th: cl up fr 9th: drvn into 2nd after 3 out: wnt rt whn outpcd next: nt qckn* **3/1**[1]

3045 **3** *1 ¾* **Scratch The Dove**[13] [4328] 9-11-8 **84**......................... WayneHutchinson 85
(A E Price) *hld up in tch: drvn and outpcd 10th: btn after 3 out: styd on after last* **3/1**[1]

54P **4** *1 ¾* **Scarlet Fantasy**[46] [3732] 6-11-7 **88**................................ JamesDiment(5) 87
(P A Pritchard) *prom: 2nd and rdn 3 out: plugging on same pce whn j.rt next: lost 3rd after last* **14/1**

4P00 **5** *16* **Auditor**[38] [3887] 7-10-6 **68**.. RJGreene 57+
(S T Lewis) *cl up: blnd 10th and rdr dropped whip: hanging and racing awkwardly after: lost tch bef 3 out: j.rt fnl two* **7/1**[3]

0-P5 **P** **Top Gale (IRE)**[43] [3790] 7-11-5 **81**....................................... HenryOliver —
(R Dickin) *plld hrd in rr: mstke 6th: rdn 9th: sn wknd: t.o and p.u 2 out* **20/1**

-5P4 **P** **Uncle Ada (IRE)**[11] [4369] 11-10-2 **64** ow1.........................(b) DaveCrosse —
(D J Minty) *bhd: u.p 3rd and reluctant thrght: lost tch 9th: t.o and p.u 11th* **25/1**

5003 **P** **Polish Pilot (IRE)**[22] [4165] 11-10-5 **67**............................ RichardHobson —
(J R Cornwall) *racd in 2nd or 3rd: blnd 8th: jnd wnr briefly 10th: sn cajoled along: lost tch bef 3 out: t.o and p.u last* **10/1**

5m 24.4s (4.40) **Going Correction** -0.575s/f (Firm) **8** Ran SP% **109.9**
Speed ratings: **68,67,66,66,59 —,—,—** CSF £13.16 CT £29.16 TOTE £3.90: £1.10, £1.50, £1.80; EX 11.10.
Owner T W R Bayley **Bred** Leslie Mellon **Trained** Worksop, Notts

FOCUS
A moderate contest rated through the third, but the fancied runners came to the fore and Tipp Top's superior stamina won him the day.

NOTEBOOK
Tipp Top(IRE), back to winning ways at Fakenham last month, was made plenty of use of on this drop in trip and, although he idled in front both before and after the last, he always looked to be doing enough. It is possible he won with a little more in hand than it looked, and he may well be able to complete the hat-trick. *(op 4-1)*
New Leader(IRE), still 5lb higher than when winning at Folkestone in November, came through to chase the winner and momentarily looked in with a squeak, but his effort flattened out and he could only plod on. *(op 7-2)*
Scratch The Dove found this drop in trip against her, being outpaced before plugging on again. A softer surface suits ideally but her chances of getting that are lessening by the day. *(op 11-4)*
Scarlet Fantasy ran his best race to date over fences, but he got a little tired on the climb to the line and a return to two miles may be in order. *(op 12-1)*
Auditor seemed to sense Greene had dropped his whip as he soon began to misbehave and was eventually pulled up. *(op 15-2)*
Top Gale(IRE) *Official explanation: trainer said mare lost her action (op 16-1)*

4581 FREE LIVE COMMENTARY @ GG.COM "NATIONAL HUNT" NOVICES' HURDLE (8 hdls) 2m
5:10 (5:10) (Class 4) 4-Y-0+ **£3,802** (£1,123; £561; £280; £140)

Form RPR

460 **1** **Witness Run (IRE)**[49] [3677] 6-11-0 102................................ LeightonAspell 103+
(N J Gifford) *settled 2nd or 3rd: led gng wl after 3 out: drew clr after hitting next: flattened last: readily* **10/1**[3]

2366 **2** *5* **Haunted House**[32] [3990] 6-11-0 101.................................. MarkBradburne 96
(H D Daly) *hld up towards rr: 5th and prog 3 out: rdn to go 2nd whn j.rt through flattened hurdle last: no ch w wnr* **12/1**

14-5 **3** *6* **Classic Quart (IRE)**[161] [1711] 5-10-7 .... TomScudamore 83
(M Scudamore) *plld hrd in rr: nt fluent 3rd: effrt 5th: rdn and outpcd after next: lft mod 3rd at last* **25/1**

00P **4** *4* **Posh Act**[26] [4094] 6-11-0 .... PaulMoloney 86
(Miss H C Knight) *keen in rr: outpcd 3 out: kpt on fr next but n.d* **100/1**

-156 **5** *1 ¾* **Zanzibar Boy**[18] [4238] 7-11-0 .... JimCrowley 86+
(H Morrison) *led tl 3rd: w ldr tl rdn after 3 out: fdd next* **14/1**

4112 **6** *hd* **Unjust Law (IRE)**[40] [3842] 5-11-4 120.............................. MrTGreenall(3) 97+
(N J Henderson) *hld up: prog in 3rd 3 out: rdn next: relegated 7l 4th whn bdly hmpd last* **4/6**[1]

0-5 **7** *3 ½* **Sister Grace**[27] [4074] 6-10-7 .... JamesDavies 74
(N J Gifford) *cl up: rdn bef 3 out: one pce and sn btn* **25/1**

00 **8** *2* **Reflector (IRE)**[48] [3699] 5-11-0 .... TimmyMurphy 79
(Miss H C Knight) *j. slowly 3rd: hld up and nvr bttr than midfield: btn bef 2 out* **50/1**

0/00 **9** *7* **Gullivers Travels**[86] [2983] 7-11-0 .... PJBrennan 72
(N J Gifford) *nt fluent 3rd: bhd after: rdn and lost tch bef 3 out* **100/1**

0-0 **P** **Hazel Mere**[85] [3024] 6-10-7 .... JamieGoldstein —
(R Curtis) *keen briefly: a last: lost tch bef 4th: hopelessly t.o whn p.u 2 out* **100/1**

P **P** **Hot Rod (IRE)**[16] [4280] 6-11-0 .... MickFitzgerald —
(Jonjo O'Neill) *pressed ldrs tl drvn after 5th: stopped to nil after next: t.o and p.u 2 out* **50/1**

-102 **B** **Mars Rock (FR)**[34] [3947] 6-10-9 .... LeeStephens(5) 94+
(Miss Venetia Williams) *sn pulling hrd: led 3rd: mstke 5th: hdd after 3 out: rdn and jnd for 6l 2nd whn decked by rival jumping rt at last* **7/2**[2]

4m 6.60s (-4.80) **Going Correction** -0.55s/f (Firm) **12** Ran SP% **120.2**
Speed ratings: **90,87,84,82,81 81,79,78,75,— —,—** CSF £113.50 TOTE £13.40: £2.30, £4.30, £3.80; EX 139.10 Place 6 £121.47, Place 5 £70.58.
Owner Thurloe KTH **Bred** Michael Long **Trained** Findon, W Sussex

FOCUS
Not a bad novice event and Witness Run appreciated the combination off dropping back to two miles and a sound surface. The next four behind the winner were close to their marks and the form should work out.

NOTEBOOK
Witness Run(IRE), a winning pointer who until now had failed to meet expectations over hurdles, seems to have benefited from a break and he settled much better on this drop back to two miles. Evidently suited by the good ground, he was never far off the pace and came through to lead, travelling best, before the turn in. He quickly settled the issue and was too far clear for mistakes, which he made at both the last two hurdles, to make any difference. He is a promising sort and would make plenty of appeal in handicaps before going chasing next season. *(op 17-2 tchd 11-1 in a place)*
Haunted House, racing on this sort of ground for the first time - all previous outings on soft/heavy - emerged a clear second after being responsible for bringing down Mars Rock at the last, but was never anywhere near the winner. The going evidently helped and he can pick up a race in the summer. *(op 14-1)*
Classic Quart(IRE), a useful bumper, appreciated this drop in diatance, but still pulled hard and may have been closer had she settled. She should find a small race against her own sex. *(op 20-1)*
Posh Act stepped up on his previous efforts, running on late, and this future chaser looks sure to appreciate a step back up in distance.
Zanzibar Boy has not really gone on as expected over hurdles and, having taken them along early, he dropped away in disappointing fashion. His future is likely to lay over fences. *(op 16-1 tchd 20-1)*
Unjust Law(IRE) set a fair standard and looked sure to run his race, but he failed to meet with expectations and was already held when getting badly hampered at the last. He may be worthy of another chance, but it is likely any future success is going to be gained in handicaps. *(op 8-11 tchd 4-5)*
Reflector(IRE) is unlikely to be seen at his best until tackling handicap chases in a year or two. *(op 40-1)*
Hazel Mere *Official explanation: jockey said mare found good ground too fast (tchd 66-1)*
Mars Rock(FR) disputed the early lead and was still fighting away for second when knocked into by the runner-up and hitting the deck. *(tchd 66-1)*
Hot Rod(IRE) *Official explanation: jockey said gelding stopped very quickly (tchd 66-1)*
T/Plt: £557.50 to a £1 stake. Pool: £50,180.00. 65.70 winning tickets. T/Qpdt: £102.60 to a £1 stake. Pool: £3,607.50. 26.00 winning tickets. IM

4360 AYR (L-H)
Thursday, March 23

OFFICIAL GOING: Good (good to soft in places in back straight, good to firm in places in home straight)
The ground was described as 'patchy, a bit of everything and quick up the home straight.' The inside running rail had been moved out.
Wind: Almost nil Weather: Fine and sunny

4582 ALEXANDER MORTON HOMES "NATIONAL HUNT" NOVICES' HURDLE (11 hdls) 2m 4f
2:10 (2:11) (Class 4) 4-Y-0+ **£3,253** (£955; £477; £238)

Form RPR

4331 **1** **Aces Four (IRE)**[29] [4052] 7-11-8 107.................................. KeithMercer 125+
(Ferdy Murphy) *mde all: wnt clr appr 3 out: easily* **1/1**[1]

24 **2** *14* **Canada Street (IRE)**[44] [3789] 5-11-1 .... GLee 100+
(J Howard Johnson) *chsd ldrs: effrt and wnt 2nd appr 3 out: kpt on: no ch w wnr* **3/1**[2]

00P2 **3** *11* **Duke Orsino (IRE)**[24] [4141] 6-10-12 108...................... PeterBuchanan(3) 91+
(Miss Lucinda V Russell) *chsd ldrs: one pce fr 3 out* **5/1**[3]

/020 **4** *7* **Le Millenaire (FR)**[24] [4141] 7-10-8 106.............................. MissKBryson(7) 81
(S H Shirley-Beavan) *chsd ldrs: outpcd 8th: sn btn* **20/1**

-006 **5** *dist* **Bint Sesaro (IRE)**[76] [3267] 5-10-8 .... MarkBradburne —
(Mrs L B Normile) *in rr: t.o fr 8th* **100/1**

0405 **P** **Monifieth**[26] [4114] 6-10-1 .... EwanWhillans(7) —
(D W Whillans) *prom: lost pl 7th: t.o 5th whn p.u bef 3 out* **33/1**

0-0P **P** **Mountain Mix**[40] [3855] 6-10-10 .... DesFlavin(5) —
(Mrs L B Normile) *in rr: bhd fr 5th: t.o whn p.u bef 8th* **100/1**

UP61 **P** **Commanche Sioux**[11] [4389] 4-10-4 .... MrTGreenall(3) —
(M W Easterby) *in rr: drvn along and sme hdwy 6th: sn lost pl: t.o 8th: p.u bef next* **12/1**

4m 59.2s (-13.50) **Going Correction** -0.575s/f (Firm)
WFA 4 from 5yo+ 8lb **8** Ran SP% **109.0**
Speed ratings: **104,98,94,91,— —,—,—** CSF £3.72 TOTE £1.60: £1.10, £1.10, £1.60; EX 4.40.

Owner The DPRP Aces Partnership **Bred** J R And Mrs S Cox **Trained** West Witton, N Yorks

FOCUS
A moderate novice event, run at an average pace, and the impressive winner is value for further.

NOTEBOOK
Aces Four(IRE), off the mark on his recent debut for connections, duly followed-up by making all for a very straightforward success. The decision to set the pace over this shorter trip paid dividends, he can be rated value for further than his already wide winning margin, and is clearly best suited by a sound surface. He is reportedly due to return to this venue next month for a valuable novices' handicap on Scottish Grand National day. *(op 5-4 tchd 11-8 in places)*
Canada Street(IRE) appeared very one paced and, while he stuck to his task to finish a clear second-best, the winner was simply in a different league. He is now eligible for a handicap mark and may be open to improvement when upped to around three miles in the future. *(tchd 11-4)*
Duke Orsino(IRE) was put in his place nearing the third last and performed below the level of his recent improved effort over course and distance. He probably needs easier ground. *(op 7-2)*
Le Millenaire(FR) shaped as though he wants further and will be better off in low-grade handicaps in due course.

4583 ALEXANDER MORTON HOMES BEGINNERS' CHASE (17 fncs) 2m 4f
2:45 (2:45) (Class 4) 5-Y-0+ **£4,554** (£1,337; £668; £333)

Form RPR
1-P4 **1** **Blairgowrie (IRE)**[29] [4058] 7-10-13 120 .... PeterBuchanan(3) 121+
(J Howard Johnson) *mde all: clr 2 out: readily* **4/1**[2]
4255 **2** *10* **Tandava (IRE)**[73] [3318] 8-11-2 .... MarkBradburne 108+
(Mrs S C Bradburne) *in tch: wnt prom 12th: wnt 2nd 2 out: no imp* **4/1**[2]
3FF5 **3** *3/4* **Moonlit Harbour**[40] [3850] 7-10-11 115 .... TJDreaper(5) 106+
(Ferdy Murphy) *j.rt: chsd ldrs: wnt 2nd appr 4 out: one pce fr 2 out* **3/1**[1]
3530 **4** *12* **Marsh Run**[58] [3548] 7-10-6 .... MrTGreenall(3) 90+
(M W Easterby) *chsd ldrs: outpcd 12th: wknd appr 4 out: mstke last* **3/1**[1]
5505 **5** *3* **Try Catch Paddy (IRE)**[13] [4344] 8-11-2 100 .... GLee 91+
(P Monteith) *trckd ldrs: wnt cl 2nd 9th: wknd appr 4 out* **13/2**[3]
04 **6** *18* **High Five**[37] [3914] 6-11-2 .... KennyJohnson 76+
(S G Waugh) *chsd wnr: lost pl 11th: sn bhd: blnd last* **25/1**
00-P **U** **Tandawizi**[297] [591] 9-10-9 .... NeilMulholland —
(Mrs L B Normile) *racd in last: bhd whn j.rt 7th: t.o whn tried refuse and uns rdr 11th* **100/1**

5m 12.2s (-10.70) **Going Correction** -0.575s/f (Firm) **7** Ran SP% **108.2**
Speed ratings: **98,94,93,88,87 80,—** CSF £18.40 TOTE £5.40: £2.50, £2.20; EX 15.30.
Owner Andrea & Graham Wylie **Bred** Mrs M O'Driscoll **Trained** Billy Row, Co Durham

FOCUS
A modest beginners' chase, run at a fair gallop, and the field trailed home behind the clear-cut winner.

NOTEBOOK
Blairgowrie(IRE), pulled up on his chasing bow in November, made amends with a comfortable success from the front and provided a very welcome winner for his yard. He jumping was much-improved, he is versatile as regards underfoot conditions, and shaped as though he may have more to offer when faced with a stiffer test. *(op 7-2)*
Tandava(IRE), returning from a 73-day break, shaped well enough on this chasing bow without rating a threat to the winner. He is entitled to improve for the experience and can find a small race over fences in due course. *(tchd 9-2)*
Moonlit Harbour did himself few favours by jumping to his right and his fate was sealed a fair way from home. He is evidently going the wrong way and is flattered by his official rating. *(op 7-2)*
Marsh Run, making her chasing debut, posted no more than an average effort and may need further in this sphere. *(op 5-2)*
Try Catch Paddy(IRE) dropped out tamely when it mattered on this return to the larger obstacles and is one to avoid. *(op 8-1 tchd 9-1)*

4584 ALEXANDER MORTON HOMES NOVICES' H'CAP HURDLE (12 hdls) 3m 110y
3:15 (3:15) (Class 4) (0-110,108) 4-Y-0+ **£4,554** (£1,337; £668; £333)

Form RPR
4362 **1** **Powerlove (FR)**[62] [3484] 5-11-1 97 .... MarkBradburne 102+
(Mrs S C Bradburne) *trckd ldrs: led last: styd on wl* **5/1**[3]
03P3 **2** *1 3/4* **Bromley Abbey**[15] [4302] 8-9-12 87 .... (p) TomMessenger(7) 87
(Miss S E Forster) *led to 3rd: led 7th to 3 out: kpt on same pce run-in* **8/1**
405P **3** *1 1/2* **Hapthor**[80] [3209] 7-9-9 82 oh11 .... BrianHughes(5) 81
(F Jestin) *trckd ldrs: led 3 out to last: kpt on one pce* **50/1**
0-02 **4** *9* **Lampion Du Bost (FR)**[13] [4344] 7-10-5 87 .... AlanDempsey 78+
(A Parker) *trckd ldrs: outpcd 9th: kpt on fr 2 out* **14/1**
6531 **5** *6* **Nobel (FR)**[76] [3269] 5-11-5 108 .... MissRDavidson(7) 94+
(N G Richards) *hld up: hdwy and prom 8th: lost pl appr 3 out* **9/4**[1]
6UP3 **6** *9* **Lutin Du Moulin (FR)**[13] [4344] 7-11-2 98 .... (b) TonyDobbin 73
(L Lungo) *hld up in tch: effrt 9th: sn btn* **9/2**[2]
44P0 **7** *1 1/4* **King's Envoy (USA)**[46] [3488] 7-9-11 82 oh1 .... PaddyAspell(3) 55
(Mrs J C McGregor) *in rr: sme hewday 8th: outpcd fr next* **20/1**
2005 **8** *6* **Dalawan**[95] [2901] 7-10-5 92 ow2 .... TJDreaper(5) 59
(Mrs J C McGregor) *in rr: drvn 7th: sme hdwy 9th: sn btn* **14/1**
0U45 **9** *6* **Leonia's Rose (IRE)**[13] [4341] 7-9-11 82 oh10 .... PeterBuchanan(3) 43
(Miss Lucinda V Russell) *sn trcking ldrs: lost pl 8th* **8/1**
42PP **10** *3/4* **The Yellow Earl (IRE)**[110] [2639] 6-9-7 82 oh12 .... PhilKinsella(7) 43
(J M Jefferson) *led 3rd: hdd 7th: lost pl after 9th: sn in rr* **50/1**

6m 16.2s (-15.60) **Going Correction** -0.575s/f (Firm) **10** Ran SP% **109.9**
Speed ratings: **101,100,99,97,95 92,91,89,88,87** CSF £40.75 CT £1636.16 TOTE £8.00: £2.70, £2.80, £10.00; EX 30.90.
Owner Mark Fleming & Jane Cameron **Bred** B Rheinbold And Jean Pfersdorff **Trained** Cunnoquhie, Fife

FOCUS
A moderate handicap, run at an average gallop, and the form should be treated with a degree of caution.

NOTEBOOK
Powerlove(FR) dug deep to get on top of her rivals nearing the final flight and score a first success since April 2005. The step-up to this distance was much to her liking, she had no trouble with the faster surface, and should not be raised too much by the Handicapper for this. She ought to be capable of further improvement over this trip. *(op 9-2)*
Bromley Abbey could muster only the same pace from two out, but stuck gamely to her task and posted another sound effort. Her yard are in good form at present and she could be placed go one better in the coming weeks, especially if reverting to a slightly shorter trip. *(op 9-1)*
Hapthor, last seen pulling up over course and distance 80 days previously, was given a positive ride and showed her best form to date in defeat. She was racing from 11lb out of the handicap, however, so her proximity at the finish must cast a doubt over the strength of this form.
Lampion Du Bost(FR) did not look overly suited by this much quicker surface, so was not disgraced in the circumstances over this longer trip. *(op 12-1)*
Nobel(FR), raised 8lb for winning on a similar surface at Musselburgh last time, failed to get home over this longer trip and was most disappointing. His jumping was not fluent and it may have been that something was amiss, so it could be too soon to be writing him off just yet. *(op 2-1)*
Lutin Du Moulin(FR), popular in the betting ring, turned in a moody effort and was beaten a long way from home. He is one to avoid. *(op 6-1)*

4585 ALEXANDER MORTON HOMES AT IRVINE H'CAP HURDLE (9 hdls) 2m
3:50 (3:50) (Class 4) (0-105,102) 4-Y-0+ **£3,253** (£955; £477; £238)

Form RPR
311U **1** **Bohemian Spirit (IRE)**[46] [3757] 8-11-0 97 .... MissRDavidson(7) 113+
(N G Richards) *led to 1st: t.k.h: trckd ldrs: led appr 3 out: wnt clr run-in: v comf* **6/5**[1]
U001 **2** *6* **Winds Supreme (IRE)**[37] [3916] 7-10-10 86 .... (t) KeithMercer 90
(Ferdy Murphy) *hld up in rr: hdwy 5th: sn chsng ldrs: wnt 2nd last: no ch w wnr* **16/1**
0534 **3** *6* **Time To Roam (IRE)**[12] [4364] 6-11-5 98 .... (p) PeterBuchanan(3) 98+
(Miss Lucinda V Russell) *led 1st: hdd appr 3 out: 3rd and one pce whn hit last* **8/1**[3]
-544 **4** *6* **Caulkleys Bank**[68] [3393] 6-11-4 97 .... MrTGreenall(3) 90+
(M W Easterby) *trckd ldrs: outpcd appr 3 out: kpt on run-in* **4/1**[2]
P500 **5** *1* **Jallastep (FR)**[15] [4302] 9-11-0 90 .... GLee 82+
(J S Goldie) *in rr: hdwy 6th: one pce* **33/1**
0003 **6** *14* **Norminster**[13] [4346] 5-9-13 82 .... GarethThomas(7) 59
(R Nixon) *prom: drvn along 5th: lost pl after next* **14/1**
0500 **7** *2* **Acceleration (IRE)**[37] [3782] 6-10-8 84 .... (t) TonyDobbin 59
(R Allan) *prom: hit 5th: lost pl after next* **14/1**
0-00 **8** *1* **Baby Sister**[24] [4145] 7-10-0 83 .... EwanWhillans(7) 57
(D W Whillans) *in rr: wnt promient 4th: drvn and lost pl 6th* **50/1**
630 **9** *dist* **Circumspect (IRE)**[140] [2001] 4-11-5 102 .... BarryKeniry —
(P C Haslam) *t.k.h in rr: lost pl 6th: t.o whn j.lft last two: btn total 59 l* **10/1**

3m 52.0s (-5.30) **Going Correction** -0.575s/f (Firm)
WFA 4 from 5yo+ 7lb **9** Ran SP% **109.8**
Speed ratings: **90,87,84,81,80 73,72,72,—** CSF £19.03 CT £98.83 TOTE £1.70: £1.30, £2.50, £2.20; EX 16.90.
Owner Mr & Mrs Duncan Davidson **Bred** Patrick J Connolly **Trained** Greystoke, Cumbria

FOCUS
A modest handicap, run at a sound pace, and the field came home strung out. The winner should win again.

NOTEBOOK
Bohemian Spirit(IRE), despite refusing to settle throught the early parts, skipped away from his rivals from three out and ultimately ran out an easy winner. This was actually his first success over hurdles to date - despite being most prolific over fences - and the drop back to this trip proved no problem. He should not be too treated too harshly by the Handicapper for this and, condsidering he is currently rated 25lb higher as a chaser, further success looks likely in this sphere. *(op 5-4 tchd 11-10)*
Winds Supreme(IRE), up 8lb for winning a seller last time, had no chance with the winner yet still emerged to finish a clear second-best. This must rate a pleasing debut for his new connections, he is versatile as regards underfoot conditions, and has been improved by the recent application of a tongue-tie. However, he now faces another rise in the weights.
Time To Roam(IRE) was made to look very one paced when the winner swept past him three out and did not appear that suited by the drop back to this trip. However, he still ran close to his mark in defeat. *(tchd 9-1)*
Caulkleys Bank enjoyed this faster ground, but was done for speed when the winner kicked for home. On this evidence, he needs to revert to a longer trip if he is to get off the mark in this sphere. *(tchd 5-1)*

4586 ALEXANDER MORTON HOMES H'CAP CHASE (12 fncs) 2m
4:20 (4:20) (Class 4) (0-115,112) 5-Y-0+ **£5,204** (£1,528; £764; £381)

Form RPR
2321 **1** **Polyphon (FR)**[12] [4365] 8-11-10 110 .... GLee 120+
(P Monteith) *trckd ldr: led and qcknd 4th: wnt clr 4 out: pushed rt out* **7/2**[2]
-442 **2** *5* **Show Me The River**[87] [2989] 7-11-12 112 .... KeithMercer 116+
(Ferdy Murphy) *set mod pce: hdd 4th: kpt on same pce fr 4 out: no imp* **11/4**[1]
631U **3** *1* **Nifty Roy**[4] [4531] 6-10-3 92 .... DougieCostello(3) 96+
(I McMath) *hld up: hdwy and prom 5th: kpt on run-in* **5/1**
2110 **4** *11* **The Names Bond**[80] [3206] 8-10-10 103 .... MissRDavidson(7) 96+
(N G Richards) *j.rt: t.k.h: trckd ldrs: lost pl 7th: no threat after* **6/1**
2F53 **5** *8* **Sands Rising**[26] [4109] 9-11-2 102 .... (t) KennyJohnson 86
(R Johnson) *a last: racd wd in bk st: bhd fr 8th* **20/1**
43U3 **P** **Cyborg De Sou (FR)**[35] [3940] 8-11-7 110 .... WilliamKennedy(3) —
(G A Harker) *hld up: hit 4th and 5th: p.u bef 6th* **4/1**[3]

3m 56.4s (-8.10) **Going Correction** -0.575s/f (Firm) **6** Ran SP% **104.6**
Speed ratings: **97,94,94,88,84** — CSF £11.98 TOTE £3.90: £2.20, £2.60; EX 10.10.
Owner Mr & Mrs Raymond Anderson Green **Bred** A Levallois And Didier Marion **Trained** Rosewell, Midlothian

FOCUS
A modest handicap, run at an ordinary gallop, and the form looks fair for the class.

NOTEBOOK
Polyphon(FR), back to winning ways over course and distance 12 days previously, advertised his current rude health and followed-up in ready fashion despite racing from a 7lb higher mark. He has often frustrated, but this must rate a career-best effort and it could be that he is finally about to come good. *(op 10-3)*
Show Me The River, returning from an 87-day absence, shaped as though he would come on for the outing and will benefit for a return to slightly further on this evidence. *(op 3-1)*
Nifty Roy was doing his best work at the finish and ran above his official rating in defeat. He is on an upward curve as a chaser and the return to softer ground in the future will see him in a better light. *(op 11-2 tchd 9-2 and 6-1 in places)*
The Names Bond is yet to really convince as a chaser and looks in need of respite from the Handicapper in this sphere. *(op 7-2)*
Cyborg De Sou(FR) was quickly pulled up as though something was amiss. *(op 5-1)*

4587 ALEXANDER MORTON HOMES AT SYMINGTON H'CAP CHASE (18 fncs) 2m 5f 110y
4:55 (4:55) (Class 4) (0-105,95) 5-Y-0+ **£3,903** (£1,146; £573; £286)

Form RPR
/5 **1** **Lovely Native (IRE)**[24] [4144] 10-11-3 89 .... GaryBerridge(3) 108+
(L Lungo) *mde all: hit 4 out: 7 l clr whn blnd last: drvn rt out* **4/1**[1]
BP30 **2** *2 1/2* **Jexel (FR)**[24] [4142] 9-11-12 95 .... RichardMcGrath 106+
(B Storey) *chsd wnr: kpt on fr 4 out: styd on run-in: no imp* **16/1**
F345 **3** *5* **Wild About Harry**[14] [4314] 9-10-0 69 .... KeithMercer 74
(A R Dicken) *chsd ldrs: mstke 12th: one pce fr 14th* **8/1**

2631 **4** *5* **Persian Point**^{15} [4303] 10-11-5 **91** ... MrCStorey(3) 91
(Miss S E Forster) *hit 2nd: jnd ldrs 12th: outpcd fr 14th* **9/2**^{2}

4353 **5** *3/4* **Ideal Du Bois Beury (FR)**^{24} [4142] 10-10-3 **75** ... PaddyAspell(3) 77+
(P Monteith) *chsd ldrs: hrd drvn 13th: sn outpcd* **11/2**^{3}

3044 **6** *11* **The Frosty Ferret (IRE)**^{24} [4142] 8-11-5 **88** ... GLee 82+
(J M Jefferson) *hld up: hdwy 10th: reminders 12th: lost pl after next: bhd whn blnd 3 out* **4/1**^{1}

206P **7** *1 1/4* **Glenfarclas Boy (IRE)**^{14} [4318] 10-10-13 **85** ... PeterBuchanan(3) 72
(Miss Lucinda V Russell) *in tch: lost pl 13th: sn bhd* **12/1**

624F **P** **Been Here Before**^{15} [4300] 6-10-9 **85** ... PhilKinsella(7) —
(G A Harker) *in rr: hit 9th: sn lost pl: t.o 14th: p.u bef next* **10/1**

5m 37.8s (-15.90) **Going Correction** -0.575s/f (Firm) **8** Ran SP% **107.3**
Speed ratings: **105,104,102,100,100 96,95,—** CSF £51.51 CT £415.26 TOTE £5.50: £2.00, £3.70, £1.60; EX 99.40.
Owner John Turner **Bred** William Curtin **Trained** Carrutherstown, D'fries & G'way

FOCUS
A weak handicap, run at a sound gallop, and the form should work out.

NOTEBOOK
Lovely Native(IRE) ran out a gutsy winner under a strong ride and would have won by plenty further but for an error at the final fence. She has been improved since joining her new yard, looked well suited by making the running over this shorter trip, and should have more to offer in the short term. *(op 9-2)*
Jexel(FR) lacked the pace to trouble the winner and is flattered by his proximity to that rival at the finish. This was still one of his better efforts, however, and he was nicely clear of the rest. *(tchd 20-1)*
Wild About Harry ran his race and helps set the level of this form. He remains winless after 21 career outings, however. *(op 10-1)*
Persian Point, up 9lb for winning at Catterick last time, suprisingly lacked the necessary toe over this longer trip and looked very one paced. He still ran close to his new mark in defeat, however. *(op 4-1)*
The Frosty Ferret(IRE) was beaten before his stamina for this longer trip became an issue and was disappointing. *(tchd 9-2)*

4588 ALEXANDER MORTON HOMES STANDARD NATIONAL HUNT FLAT RACE (CONDITIONAL /AMATEUR RIDERS) 2m
5:25 (5:25) (Class 6) 4-6-Y-0 **£1,713** (£499; £249)

Form RPR

1 **Gold Thread (IRE)** 5-10-9 ... BrianHughes(5) 110+
(J Howard Johnson) *trckd ldrs: outpcd over 5f out: hdwy to chse ldrs 2f out: led jst ins last: kpt on strly* **16/1**

23 **2** *5* **Modicum (USA)**^{81} [3181] 4-10-0 ... MissRDavidson(7) 97+
(N G Richards) *hld up in mid-field: hdwy to ld 4f out: hdd jst ins last: fdd* **13/8**^{1}

3 *1/2* **Top Cloud (IRE)** 5-11-0 ... KeithMercer 103+
(Ferdy Murphy) *in rr: outpcd over 4f out: hdwy over 2f out: styd on wl ins last* **20/1**

4 *1/2* **Amhairghin (IRE)** 6-10-11 ... WilliamKennedy(3) 102
(G A Harker) *t.k.h in rr: hdwy 6f out: sn chsng ldrs: one pce fnl 2f* **20/1**

2 **5** *3/4* **Cheer Us On**^{116} [2521] 4-10-4 ... MrTGreenall(3) 94
(M W Easterby) *chsd ldrs: wnt 2nd over 3f out: fdd over 1f out* **5/1**^{3}

6 *6* **My Arch** 4-10-4 ... PaddyAspell(3) 88
(K A Ryan) *trckd ldrs: effrt over 3f out: wknd over 1f out* **9/4**^{2}

7 *4* **Well Disguised (IRE)** 4-9-4 ... GarryWhillans(10) 77
(D W Whillans) *chsd ldrs: lost pl over 3f out* **100/1**

8 *1 3/4* **Gunadoir (IRE)** 4-9-7 ... MrCJCallow(7) 76
(N G Richards) *in rr: lost pl over 5f out* **40/1**

02 **9** *3* **Cavers Glen**^{14} [4319] 4-10-0 ... EwanWhillans(7) 80
(A C Whillans) *set str pce: clr after 4f: jnd 6f out: hdd 4f out: hung lft and sn lost pl* **50/1**

P **Needwood** 5-10-11 ... DougieCostello(3) —
(G A Swinbank) *mid-div: drvn and lost pl 10f out: sn t.o: p.u 6f out* **33/1**

6 **P** **Askham Lad (IRE)**^{12} [4366] 5-10-9 ... TJDreaper(5) —
(M Todhunter) *t.k.h towards rr: lost pl after 5f: sn bhd: p.u 9f out* **100/1**

3m 47.4s (-11.80) **Going Correction** -0.575s/f (Firm)
WFA 4 from 5yo+ 7lb **11** Ran SP% **110.3**
Speed ratings: **106,103,103,103,102 99,97,96,95,—** — CSF £37.99 TOTE £13.80: £3.20, £1.10, £3.30; EX 60.30 Place 6 £56.76, Place 5 £52.54.
Owner Andrea & Graham Wylie **Bred** Mrs Carole Adams **Trained** Billy Row, Co Durham

FOCUS
A decent bumper for the track, run at a fair pace, and it should produce it's share of future winners.

NOTEBOOK
Gold Thread(IRE), out of an Irish point winner, got his career off to a perfect start with a ready success. There was plenty to like about the manner of this success, he looked better the further he went and, considering his yard are not noted for first-time winners in this sphere, he looks a nice prospect for novice hurdling.
Modicum(USA), whose previous two placed efforts in this sphere gave him an obvious chance in this, had his chance yet proved powerless to the winner's late challenge. He has done little wrong to date and is a decent benchmark for this form. *(op 7-4)*
Top Cloud(IRE), related to staying chasers, ran distinctly green yet came home nicely when the penny dropped and looks sure to improve plenty for this debut experience. *(op 16-1)*
Amhairghin(IRE), from a yard who do well in this sphere, ultimately paid for running too keenly through the early parts. However, he still shaped with promise and should be sharper next time.
Cheer Us On, runner-up on his debut at Doncaster 115 days previously, had his chance yet ultimately failed to see out this longer trip. He is entitled to come on for this outing, however. *(op 10-3 tchd 11-2)*
My Arch, very well backed, is a half-brother to his stable's smart Flat handicapper My Paris - best over a mile to ten furlong - and appeared a non-stayer over this distance. *(op 11-4 tchd 2-1)*
T/Plt: £98.10 to a £1 stake. Pool: £42,831.60. 318.50 winning tickets. T/Qpdt: £37.90 to a £1 stake. Pool: £3,237.10. 63.10 winning tickets. WG

4046 LUDLOW (R-H)
Thursday, March 23

OFFICIAL GOING: Good (good to firm in places)
Wind: Slight, behind Weather: Overcast

4589 SHIRLEY FOX SPECIAL BIRTHDAY NOVICES' HURDLE (12 hdls) 3m
2:00 (2:00) (Class 4) 4-Y-0+ **£4,554** (£1,337; £668; £333)

Form RPR

210P **1** **Lyes Green**^{76} [3277] 5-11-8 107 ... LeightonAspell 116+
(O Sherwood) *hld up: hdwy 4 out: led 3 out: rdn out* **11/2**

060 **2** *4* **Darn Good**^{43} [3806] 5-11-2 103 ... RobertThornton 105
(A King) *prom: rdn and ev ch 3 out: nt qckn appr next: styd on to take 2nd nr fin* **25/1**

P210 **3** *nk* **Adventurist**^{33} [3993] 6-11-8 113 ... (p) MickFitzgerald 114+
(P Bowen) *nt fluent: in rr: hdwy after 4 out: rdn and n.m.r 3 out: wnt 2nd 2 out: no imp on wnr run-in: lost 2nd nr fin* **7/2**^{2}

-04P **4** *9* **Beau Supreme (IRE)**^{99} [2828] 9-11-2 114 ... RichardJohnson 98+
(C J Down) *led: rdn whn j.lft and hdd 3 out: j.lft again last 2: wknd run-in* **4/1**^{3}

001 **5** *19* **Secured (IRE)**^{52} [3646] 6-11-8 ... JimmyMcCarthy 83
(Ian Williams) *cl up: rdn to chal after 4 out: wknd next* **8/1**

46P4 **6** *7* **William Butler (IRE)**^{28} [4071] 6-10-11 ... LiamHeard(5) 70
(S A Brookshaw) *midfield: hdwy 5th: rdn after 4 out: wknd bef next* **66/1**

0303 **7** *6* **The Langer (IRE)**^{34} [3957] 6-11-2 ... MarkGrant 64
(S T Lewis) *hld up in rr: rdr lost iron briefly 4th: brief effrt after 4 out: sn wl btn* **100/1**

5003 **8** *2 1/2* **Grand Slam Hero (IRE)**^{29} [4052] 5-11-2 ... ChristianWilliams 61
(P Bowen) *cl up: nt fluent 4 out: sn rdn and wknd: eased 2 out* **25/1**

4P0 **P** **Roseville (IRE)**^{39} [3884] 6-10-6 ... ColinBolger(3) —
(S T Lewis) *in tch: wknd after 6th: lost tch bef next: t.o whn p.u bef 3 out* **200/1**

1020 **P** **Youlbesolucky (IRE)**^{12} [4373] 7-11-8 120 ... APMcCoy —
(Jonjo O'Neill) *midfield: rdn and losing pl whn n.m.r after 4 out: wknd qckly: t.o whn p.u bef 3 out* **2/1**^{1}

5m 47.4s (-7.20) **Going Correction** -0.40s/f (Good) **10** Ran SP% **112.7**
Speed ratings: **95,93,93,90,84 81,79,79,—,—** CSF £112.21 TOTE £6.60: £2.00, £5.30, £1.30; EX 135.00.
Owner Absolute Solvents Ltd **Bred** P K Gardner **Trained** Upper Lambourn, Berks

FOCUS
Overnight frost meant that the card needed two inspections before being handed the go-ahead. The ground was 'very quick' according to riders in the first, a routine novices' hurdle in which the pace was pretty sedate. The race has been rated through the winner and the form is probably not that strong.

NOTEBOOK
Lyes Green gained his previous victory in very contrasting underfoot conditions, but he has some decent form on a sound surface notably a good second to Denman at Wincanton in October, although that effort flatters him. Under a patient ride, he showed narrowly ahead at the third from home and soon asserted. *(tchd 5-1)*
Darn Good, a fair stayer on the level, ran his best race so far over obstacles. One of four with a chance at the first flight in the straight, he was staying on again over this longer trip to secure second close home.
Adventurist appeared reluctant to have a cut at several flights and looked set to drop right away down the back, but was able to close on the long run to the home straight. He was one of four battling for supremacy at the third last but could not go with the winner from that point. *(op 9-2)*
Beau Supreme(IRE), a winner twice here over fences last term, ran a fair race on his first run over hurdles for nearly two years but could not produce a change of gear in the straight. *(op 11-2)*
Secured(IRE) should have finished close to Adventurist on their form at this track in January, but that was over three furlongs less and he did not appear to stay here. *(op 6-1)*
Youlbesolucky(IRE) was already beginning to retreat when he was short of room shortly after turning out of the back straight. Soon pulled up, this was not his running and the ground might have been to blame. *Official explanation: jockey said gelding was never travelling (op 6-4)*

4590 EDDIE MAPP MEMORIAL BEGINNERS' CHASE (13 fncs) 2m
2:35 (2:36) (Class 4) 5-Y-0+
£6,263 (£1,850; £925; £463; £231; £116)

Form RPR

0422 **1** **Cossack Dancer (IRE)**^{72} [3329] 8-11-2 114 ... (p) MatthewBatchelor 113+
(M Bradstock) *mde all: j.lft fr 6th: r.o wl after last* **4/7**^{1}

/U43 **2** *3 1/2* **Spinaround**^{23} [4164] 8-11-2 79 ... (v^{1}) TomDoyle 106+
(P R Webber) *in tch: chsd ldng pair appr 4 out: nt fluent 2 out: wnt 2nd towards fin: no imp on wnr* **7/1**^{3}

4400 **3** *3/4* **Predicament**^{19} [4242] 7-11-2 ... APMcCoy 107+
(Jonjo O'Neill) *midfield: hdwy 5th (water): ev ch fr 4 out tl intimidated 2 out: hit last: no ex run-in: lost 2nd towards fin* **5/1**^{2}

5F4U **4** *20* **Hardybuck (IRE)**^{13} [4352] 5-10-12 ... (t) AntonyEvans 82+
(N A Twiston-Davies) *chsd wnr: mstke 2nd: lost 2nd appr 4 out: sn wknd* **33/1**

P000 **5** *shd* **Simiola**^{34} [3956] 7-10-6 ... ColinBolger(3) 77
(S T Lewis) *hld up: lost tch w ldrs after 9th: n.d after* **50/1**

5500 **6** *6* **Let's Rock**^{17} [4281] 8-10-9 67 ... MrRHodges(7) 80+
(Mrs A Price) *midfield: hdwy 6th: wknd appr 4 out* **100/1**

U3P **7** *17* **Glenkill (IRE)**^{26} [4102] 8-10-9 ... MarkGrant —
(S M Jacobs) *hld up: lost tch w ldrs after 9th: sn wl btn* **100/1**

P **8** *24* **Lincoln Leader (IRE)**^{43} [3801] 8-10-9 ... ChristianWilliams —
(Evan Williams) *blnd 2nd: a bhd: t.o* **14/1**

PPPP **P** **Havit**^{39} [3885] 8-10-9 ... (p) MissLBrooke(7) —
(Lady Susan Brooke) *j.lft: a bhd: t.o whn p.u bef 4 out* **100/1**

2- **P** **The Glen Road (IRE)**^{509} [1910] 9-11-2 ... WayneHutchinson —
(A W Carroll) *chsd ldrs to 5th (water): bhd fr 6th: t.o whn p.u bef 4 out* **25/1**

3m 53.6s (-10.50) **Going Correction** -0.70s/f (Firm)
WFA 5 from 7yo+ 4lb **10** Ran SP% **111.2**
Speed ratings: **98,96,95,85,85 82,74,62,—,—** CSF £4.60 TOTE £1.40: £1.20, £1.10, £1.70; EX 4.20.
Owner The United Front Partnership **Bred** Noel O'Brien **Trained** Letcombe Bassett, Oxon

FOCUS
In contrast to the opener, this was run at a good clip. The winner was a stone off his best in a race rated around the form and fifth.

NOTEBOOK
Cossack Dancer(IRE) was found a good opportunity and made all the running at a decent pace. Tending to jump out to his left in the latter stages, most markedly at the second last, he won decisively enough but nowhere near as easily as he should have considering he had 35lb in hand on official figures. He may not prove too easy to place now that he has got off the mark over fences. *(op 4-6 tchd 8-11 in places)*
Spinaround, visored for the first time and at home on a sound surface, found the drop to the minimum trip on this sharp track against him but stayed on quite nicely to secure second spot on the run-in. *(op 6-1)*
Predicament, making his chasing debut, was keen to get on with things as he was anchored behind the leaders. He looked a threat when closing before the fourth last but he was intimidated into going out to his left as the winner went across him two from home and was held when clouting the final fence. He is not the sort to find a great deal when the pressure is on. *(op 7-2)*
Hardybuck(IRE) guessed at several fences in the early stages as he chased the eventual winner and he was beaten before the straight.
Simiola, a plating-class maiden over hurdles, was well beaten on this chasing debut but did come home quite well and almost snatched fourth. *(op 40-1)*
Glenkill(IRE) was always amongst the rear group and her running caught the attention of the Stewards. *Official explanation: jockey said, regarding the apparent tender ride, his orders were to drop mare in, settle her and get her jumping, but she was really outpaced throughout; trainer said mare did not settle at Chepstow last time and had a bad experience, having made a mistake, adding that today's trip of 2m was too short on this sharp track (op 66-1)*

4591 MID WALES WELDING CLAIMING HURDLE (9 hdls) 2m
3:05 (3:05) (Class 5) 4-Y-0+ **£2,927** (£859; £429; £214)

Form RPR
P500 **1** **Broke Road (IRE)**[19] 4242 10-11-6 110.............................(t) JimCrowley 93+
(Mrs H Dalton) *mde all: hit last whn hrd pressed: drvn out* **7/4**[1]
4050 **2** *1* **Weet Watchers**[34] 3804 6-11-0 78.................................... JohnMcNamara 85
(T Wall) *hld up: hit 5th: hdwy appr 3 out: rdn and ev ch fr 2 out: nt qckn towards fin* **25/1**
P02P **3** *3 1/2* **Made In France (FR)**[10] 4418 6-11-2 105............................(v) APMcCoy 84
(M C Pipe) *hld up: hdwy appr 3 out: chalng 2 out: fnd nil and edgd rt run-in* **8/1**
0340 **4** *6* **Desert Spa (USA)**[39] 3889 11-10-7 96................. MissIsabelTompsett(7) 78+
(G E Jones) *prom: rdn appr 3 out: wknd last* **11/1**
000P **5** *5* **Barcelona**[32] 4013 9-10-7 80...(t) MissLBrooke(7) 71
(Lady Susan Brooke) *hld up: rdn appr 2 out: no imp* **50/1**
3410 **6** *7* **Ambersong**[29] 4050 8-11-4 108.................................... WayneHutchinson 71+
(A W Carroll) *prom: rdn and wknd appr 3 out: no ch whn mstke last* **10/3**[2]
04P **7** *1/2* **Red Rocky**[33] 3985 5-9-11 .... AdamHawkins(10) 56
(R Hollinshead) *hld up: rdn appr 3 out: nvr on terms* **50/1**
505R **8** *21* **Humid Climate**[17] 4281 6-10-11 102.................................. MrLRPayter(7) 46
(M Sheppard) *midfield: rdn and wknd after 4 out* **25/1**
0 **9** *3* **Look No More**[9] 1 5-10-6 ....(p) RichardGordon(10) 41
(W G M Turner) *in tch: j.rt 1st 3: j. slowly 5th: wknd after 4 out* **66/1**
P0P6 **P** **Nepal (IRE)**[10] 4423 4-10-2 78..(b) AlanO'Keeffe —
(M Mullineaux) *in tch: rdn and wknd after 4 out: t.o whn p.u bef 3 out: b.b.v* **33/1**
/00- **F** **Remington (IRE)**[163] 4890 8-11-6 90............................ RichardJohnson 79+
(Mrs A M Thorpe) *in tch: nt fluent 4 out: j.rt 3 out: 3 l 5th whn fell 2 out* **9/2**[3]

3m 46.3s (-6.00) **Going Correction** -0.40s/f (Good)
WFA 4 from 5yo+ 7lb **11** Ran SP% **113.1**
Speed ratings: **98,97,95,92,90 86,86,76,74,—** — CSF £50.44 TOTE £2.10: £1.20, £4.30, £2.10; EX 56.50.
Owner Stephen Appelbee **Bred** J K Beckitt And Son **Trained** Norton, Shropshire

FOCUS
An ordinary claimer in which the winner set a decent gallop. Probably not strong form, limited by the runner-up.

NOTEBOOK
Broke Road(IRE) , taking a considerable drop in grade - he was tenth to subsequent County Hurdle winner Desert Quest in a decent handicap at Newbury last time - made every yard. He fought on well to repel his pursuers, but he is not as good as he was and might struggle back in handicaps. *(tchd 13-8)*
Weet Watchers was the last to show his hand but, despite trying hard, he could not get his head in front. His stamina has been questioned at times but he got home here.
Made In France(FR) came there cruising but there was no response when he was let down. He has ample ability but for some reason he will not put it in and he remains one to oppose. *(op 13-2)*
Desert Spa(USA) ran an honest race and there could still be a selling handicap in this veteran. \n\x\x \n *(op 10-1)*
Barcelona has not shown much since returning to hurdling this winter, but this was a shade more encouraging.
Ambersong, whose three hurdling successes have all been registered here, dropped away somewhat tamely approaching the home straight.
Remington(IRE), a winner on the Flat since his last outing over hurdles nearly a year ago, was in fifth place when taking what looked a heavy fall at the second last. *(op 11-2)*
Nepal(IRE) *Official explanation: trainer said filly bled from the nose (op 11-2)*

4592 SIDNEY PHILLIPS H'CAP CHASE (17 fncs) 2m 4f
3:40 (3:41) (Class 4) (0-115,113) 5-Y-0+
£6,263 (£1,850; £925; £463; £231; £116)

Form RPR
1030 **1** **Toulouse (IRE)**[71] 3344 9-11-12 113..............................(t) RobertWalford 125+
(R H Alner) *a.p: j.rt 13th: led 4 out: rdn out* **12/1**
4044 **2** *3 1/2* **Saafend Rocket (IRE)**[43] 3803 8-11-10 111................. RichardJohnson 121+
(H D Daly) *hld up: mstke 5th: hdwy appr 13th: wnt 2nd 3 out: hit 2 out: rdn after last: one pce towards fin* **3/1**[1]
215F **3** *7* **Ede'Iff**[52] 3649 9-11-2 108... RobertLucey-Butler(5) 109
(W G M Turner) *midfield: mstke 6th: outpcd appr 13th: styd on fr 4 out: no imp on ldng pair* **10/1**
52F3 **4** *9* **Alcopop**[55] 3596 7-11-3 111... MrWBiddick(7) 105+
(Miss Venetia Williams) *prom: mstke 13th: sn led: hdd 4 out: wknd appr last* **4/1**[2]
1656 **5** *9* **Kind Sir**[43] 3803 10-11-5 106... WayneHutchinson 89
(A W Carroll) *led: hdd after 13th: wknd appr 3 out* **14/1**
P-33 **6** *10* **Meehan (IRE)**[58] 3546 6-10-7 94.. SeanCurran 71+
(Miss J S Davis) *midfield: mstke 10th: wknd after 13th: n.d whn blnd 2 out: b.b.v* **12/1**
5-2P **7** *18* **Big Bone (FR)**[44] 3788 6-11-11 112................................ AndrewThornton 67
(B N Pollock) *nt fluent 9th (water): a bhd* **12/1**
-PU4 **8** *2 1/2* **Pauntley Gofa**[17] 4281 10-10-3 95..................................... MarkNicolls(5) 48
(R C Harper) *hld up: hdwy appr 5th: wknd after 13th* **33/1**
011U **P** **He's The Gaffer (IRE)**[20] 4214 6-11-2 103.................(b) RobertThornton —
(R H Buckler) *a bhd: rdn after 10th: t.o whn p.u bef 4 out* **9/2**[3]
P5P5 **P** **Golly (IRE)**[13] 4354 10-9-8 88.. CharlieStudd(7) —
(D L Williams) *midfield: lost pl after 9th (water): sn bhd: blnd 13th: t.o whn p.u bef 4 out* **12/1**

4m 53.7s (-17.00) **Going Correction** -0.70s/f (Firm) course record **10** Ran SP% **112.6**
Speed ratings: **106,104,101,98,94 90,83,82,—,—** CSF £48.10 CT £377.77 TOTE £13.00: £4.90, £1.70, £2.80; EX 65.40.
Owner Pell-Mell Partners **Bred** D J Fitzpatrick **Trained** Droop, Dorset

FOCUS
A reasonably competitive handicap in which all the principals had run well at this track before. The form is solid enough for the grade.

NOTEBOOK
Toulouse(IRE), third to a couple of progressive types over two miles here on his penultimate run, has been freshened up by a break since January and was wearing a tongue tie for the first time. Jumping ahead at the fourth last, he maintained the gallop to score but gave the impression this trip is as far as he wants to go. He likes this type of ground and will be kept on the go through the spring. *(op 16-1)*
Saafend Rocket(IRE) has been edging down the weights and this was his best run for some time, but his jumping was not the best and a mistake at the second last effectively ended his hopes. *(op 7-2)*
Ede'Iff comes alive at the Shropshire track, but her best form these days is over further and she could merely keep on without landing a blow.
Alcopop won this event a year ago but was 10lb higher this time round, although still fairly handicapped. After showing ahead on the home turn he was outjumped by the winner at the fourth last before fading steadily, not looking as if he fancied a battle. *(op 7-2)*
Kind Sir, who landed the equivalent event two years ago, has become difficult to win with and he soon gave up the ghost once headed on the approach to the home straight. *(op 20-1)*
Meehan(IRE) *Official explanation: trainer said gelding bled from the nose (op 7-1)*
He's The Gaffer(IRE)was never a factor and has now been well held twice from this mark since landing back-to-back handicaps at Taunton and Fontwell. *(op 4-1 tchd 5-1)*

4593 SUNDAY RACEDAY ON 30TH APRIL H'CAP HURDLE (11 hdls) 2m 5f
4:10 (4:11) (Class 4) (0-115,115) 4-Y-0+ **£5,204** (£1,528; £764; £381)

Form RPR
P5P0 **1** **Gan Eagla (IRE)**[97] 2868 7-11-1 104...................................(b) SamThomas 112+
(Miss Venetia Williams) *mde all: j.lft 3 out: sn rdn: hrd pressed whn lft clr last: eased run-in* **14/1**
3/00 **2** *8* **Pro Dancer (USA)**[39] 3880 8-11-7 115..........................(p) MrTJO'Brien(5) 108
(P Bowen) *sn settled in midfield: hdwy 6th: rdn and outpcd after 4 out: lft mod 2nd last: no ch w wnr* **20/1**
1500 **3** *6* **Spike Jones (NZ)**[17] 4280 8-11-2 105........................... RichardJohnson 95+
(Mrs S M Johnson) *hld up: hdwy after 4 out: rdn and no imp bef next* **16/1**
P000 **4** *3* **Etendard Indien (FR)**[20] 4215 5-11-5 108....................... MickFitzgerald 92
(N J Henderson) *hld up: hdwy 7th: rdn and wknd appr 3 out* **11/1**
4052 **5** *5* **Wally Wonder (IRE)**[28] 4080 8-10-10 99...........................(v) JimCrowley 78
(K G Reveley) *prom: j.lft 3rd: 4th and 5th: rdn after 4 out: sn wknd* **6/1**[2]
F15- **6** *6* **Lowe Go**[415] 3639 6-10-6 95.. SeanCurran 68
(Miss J S Davis) *trckd ldrs: nt fluent 4 out: sn rdn and wknd* **33/1**
3014 **B** **Sistema**[10] 4418 5-10-6 98... OwynNelmes(3) —
(A E Price) *hld up: mstke 1st: b.d 2nd* **66/1**
0420 **P** **Samandara (FR)**[35] 3950 6-10-8 100...........................(v) GinoCarenza(3) —
(A King) *a bhd: t.o whn p.u bef 3 out* **10/1**
6555 **F** **Wembury Point (IRE)**[82] 2756 4-11-4 115.................... RobertThornton —
(B G Powell) *midfield: fell 2nd* **7/1**
F **French Lieutenant (FR)**[361] 7-10-10 104.................. HowieEphgrave(5) —
(L Corcoran) *chsd ldrs to 6th: sn bhd: t.o whn fell 4 out* **66/1**
0P01 **P** **Old Feathers (IRE)**[47] 3733 9-11-7 110...............................(b) APMcCoy —
(Jonjo O'Neill) *midfield: niggled along after 3rd: lost pl after 5th: t.o whn p.u bef 3 out* **13/2**[3]
6121 **F** **Piran (IRE)**[63] 3458 4-11-4 115... PaulMoloney 115+
(Evan Williams) *hld up: hdwy 7th: chsd wnr appr 3 out: swtchd rt bef 2 out: rdn and upsides whn fell last* **2/1**[1]

5m 5.20s (-13.10) **Going Correction** -0.40s/f (Good)
WFA 4 from 5yo+ 8lb **12** Ran SP% **114.1**
Speed ratings: **107,103,101,100,98 96,—,—,—,— —,—** CSF £244.80 CT £4431.17 TOTE £16.10: £2.80, £6.30, £4.00; EX 183.30.
Owner T Hywel Jones **Bred** J S Bolger **Trained** Kings Caple, H'fords

FOCUS
Just a fair handicap, with not much strength in depth. The winner and the last-flight faller have been rated as dead-heating.

NOTEBOOK
Gan Eagla(IRE) became the third winner of the afternoon to make all the running, although luck was on his side. Returning from a three-month break, he came under pressure on the approach to the home straight and was being strongly tackled when left clear at the final flight. He was only a pound higher than when gaining his most recent victory over course and distance a year ago and can be hard to peg back when on song.
Pro Dancer(USA), a dual Listed winner when trained in Ireland, ran his best race since joining this yard but was fortunate to collect second prize. Wearing cheekpieces for the first time, he shaped as if this trip stretched his stamina a little. *(op 25-1)*
Spike Jones(NZ) has been held since scoring on his first run for this yard at Chepstow in January, but shaped as if worth another try at this sort of trip. *(op 25-1)*
Etendard Indien(FR) continues to fall in the handicap, but does not give the impression he is about to end his barren spell. *(op 12-1)*
Wally Wonder(IRE), in a visor rather than blinkers, was another to drop away on the long run to the third last and looks high enough in the weights now. *(op 5-1 tchd 9-2)*
Piran(IRE), raised 8lb for his win over three miles here last time, steadily closed on Gan Eagla and was alongside, just about appearing the likelier scorer, when he stepped into the last and took an ugly fall. He appeared physically unhurt but this experience might leave mental scars. *(op 9-4 tchd 15-8)*

4594 MAGNUS-ALLCROFT MEMORIAL TROPHY HUNTERS' CHASE (17 fncs) 2m 4f
4:45 (4:47) (Class 5) 5-Y-0+
£2,400 (£750; £374; £187; £93; £47)

Form RPR
4111 **1** **Red Brook Lad**[29] 4051 11-12-0 107.............................. MissCTizzard(3) 116+
(C St V Fox) *hld up: hdwy 11th: chsd ldr appr 3 out: led last: drvn out* **10/11**[1]
2 *1 1/4* **Lord Nellerie (FR)**[180] 7-11-10 115............................. MrGOpperman(7) 113+
(B G Powell) *prom: hit 1st: led 4th: hit 13th and 4 out: hdd last: nt qckn towards fin* **10/1**[3]
3 *16* **Alexander Fourball (IRE)**[25] 12-11-3 .... MrRJagger(7) 89
(R Teague) *prom: rdn appr 3 out: wknd bef 2 out* **100/1**
2315 **4** *1/2* **An Capall Dubh (IRE)**[29] 4051 10-12-0 .... MrRBurton 93
(Mrs Edward Crow) *midfield: hdwy appr 4 out: rdn bef next: sn no imp* **10/3**[2]
11P- **5** *9* **Redskin Raider (IRE)**[4] 10-11-7 106.............................. MrGHanmer(3) 80
(Miss S Sharratt) *midfield: hdwy 11th: rdn and wknd after 3 out* **40/1**
6 *2* **Another Client (IRE)**[99] 2836 10-11-3 .... MissTessaClark(7) 80+
(Mrs A R Hewitt) *hmpd s: hld up: rdn after 12th: kpt on steadily fr 3 out: n.d* **100/1**
F-F **7** *7* **Wrapitup (IRE)**[41] 3847 8-11-3 .... MrsJoanneBrown(7) 71
(Mrs Joanne Brown) *prom: hmpd 2nd: mstke 10th: wknd 4 out* **40/1**
/0-P **8** *3 1/2* **Hadeqa**[13] 4347 10-11-3 .... MrSCharlton(7) 67
(M J Brown) *hld up: struggling 13th: n.d* **50/1**
40PF **9** *8* **Master Papa (IRE)**[13] 4349 7-11-3 98.............................. MrDGreenway(7) 59
(P H Hogarth) *racd keenly: prom: j.rt 1st: led 3rd to 4th: handy tl wknd after 11th* **33/1**
/34P **10** *6* **River Dante (IRE)**[36] 3924 9-11-10 ....(t) MrNHarris 53
(Miss L A Blackford) *chsd ldrs: rdn appr 13th: mstke 4 out: sn rdn and wknd* **66/1**
643P **11** *1 1/4* **Fear Siuil (IRE)**[168] 1650 13-11-3 93...................................(t) MrRBliss(7) 52
(Michael Blake) *a wl bhd* **33/1**
0/ **U** **Golden Rivet**[369] 9-11-7 .... MrMGMiller(3) —
(Miss Lisa Bebbington) *hmpd and uns rdr s* **33/1**
553F **U** **Knight's Emperor (IRE)**[147] 1897 9-12-0 95...................... MrSJoynes(3) —
(Miss Alexandra Lindner) *blnd and uns rdr 1st* **40/1**

-5P4 **P** **Gue Au Loup (FR)**[29] 4055 12-11-3 73 .... MrWKinsey(7) —
(J Groucott) *midfield: wknd 10th: t.o whn p.u bef 4 out* **50/1**

P **Euro Craft (IRE)**[60] 9-11-3 .... MrAWadlow(7) —
(Mrs C J Robinson) *a bhd: struggling whn mstke 11th: t.o whn p.u bef 4 out* **50/1**

-2PP **P** **Solve It Sober (IRE)**[25] 12-11-7 77 ....(b) MissIsabelTompsett(7) —
(S G Griffiths) *blnd 1st: a bhd: t.o whn p.u bef 2 out* **100/1**

-230 **P** **Enitsag (FR)**[307] 437 7-11-10 94 .... MrAWintle —
(S Flook) *blnd 1st and rdr lost iron briefly: a wl bhd: t.o whn p.u bef 9th (water)* **25/1**

P24P **P** **Montifault (FR)**[46] 11-12-3 113 .... MrNWilliams —
(Andy Carter) *led: j.lft 1st and 2nd: hdd 3rd: lost pl 5th: sn bhd: t.o whn p.u bef 10th* **12/1**

4m 57.3s (-13.40) **Going Correction** -0.70s/f (Firm) **18** Ran SP% **122.6**
Speed ratings: **98,97,91,90,87 86,83,82,79,76 76,—,—,—,— —,—,—** CSF £9.90 TOTE £1.80: £1.10, £3.80, £18.70; EX 9.30.

Owner C St V Fox **Bred** T H Jagger **Trained** Gillingham, Dorset

FOCUS
Quite an interesting hunter chase. The first two are decent in this grade but the third limits the form.

NOTEBOOK
Red Brook Lad, an admirable performer, notched his seventh win in his last eight starts, including one point-to-point. The sound pace suited him and he came through to assert at the final fence. *While he was perhaps not at his best here, he should continue to run well in this type of event. (op 5-6 tchd evens in places)*

Lord Nellerie(FR) was successful on his most recent start, a chase over this trip at Le Pertre in September, his fourth victory in the French provinces. In front by the fourth and only cut down at the final fence, he looks an interesting recruit to this sphere although he could be the sort to benefit from stronger handling. *(op 7-1 tchd 11-1)*

Alexander Fourball(IRE), twice a winner for Arthur Moore in Ireland, has not been making waves in points since joining his current yard and this was an encouraging effort, although he was beaten a fair way by the first two in the end. *(tchd 125-1)*

An Capall Dubh(IRE) was a little below-par. He could not go with the leaders from the end of the back straight, but was keeping on at the end without landing a blow. *(op 5-1)*

Redskin Raider(IRE), a dual winning chaser for Tom George in 2004, had failed to complete in two point-to-points this year but this run proved he retains ability.

Another Client(IRE), a moderate performer when trained in Ireland, made a pleasing start for his new yard.

Montifault(FR), third of five on his recent debut between the flags, looks a shadow of his former self.

Enitsag(FR) *Official explanation: jockey said he lost his irons and gelding never got back into the race after a mistake at the first fence*

4595 LUDLOW POINT TO POINT - BITTERLEY SATURDAY 15TH APRIL STANDARD OPEN NATIONAL HUNT FLAT RACE 2m

5:15 (5:16) (Class 5) 4-6-Y-0 **£2,602** (£764; £382; £190)

Form RPR

1 **Risk Challenge (USA)** 4-10-11 .... WayneHutchinson 110+
(C J Price) *t.k.h: hdwy to ld after 2f: mde rest: qcknd clr 3f out: r.o wl* **33/1**

23 **2** *10* **Presentandcorrect (IRE)**[73] 3327 5-11-4 .... RichardJohnson 110+
(P J Hobbs) *t.k.h: in tch: wnt 2nd 7f out: rdn and hung bdly lft 3f out: no ch w wnr* **8/11**[1]

3 *2* **King Cyrus (IRE)** 4-10-11 .... ChristianWilliams 98
(Evan Williams) *hld up: hdwy 6f out: rdn 3f out: one pce* **14/1**

10 **4** *5* **One More Step**[19] 4244 5-11-11 .... APMcCoy 108+
(R A Farrant) *hld up: hdwy 1/2-way: rdn and wknd 3f out* **4/1**[2]

5 *1* **Sawpit Sunset** 5-10-6 .... JamesDiment(5) 92
(J L Spearing) *hld up: rdn and hdwy 3f out: kpt on fnl 2f: nvr rchd ldrs* **66/1**

0 **6** *7* **Kaddasan**[94] 2927 4-10-11 .... PaulMoloney 85
(D E Cantillon) *midfield: hdwy 1/2-way: wknd 4f out* **40/1**

00 **7** *3/4* **Coorbawn Vic (IRE)**[28] 4072 5-10-13 .... LiamHeard(5) 91
(S A Brookshaw) *hld up: hdwy 6f out: rdn and wknd over 4f out* **20/1**

8 *2 1/2* **Duke Of Kentford** 4-10-11 .... TomDoyle 82
(P R Webber) *rn green: in rr: pushed along 6f out: nvr on terms* **8/1**[3]

9 *2* **Mr Postman** 5-11-4 .... TomScudamore 87
(M Scudamore) *in tch: hung lft after 4f: wknd over 6f out* **50/1**

10 *10* **True Grit (FR)** 4-10-6 .... HowieEphgrave(5) 70
(L Corcoran) *in tch: rdn 4f out: sn wknd* **50/1**

11 *1 3/4* **Final Over** 6-10-6 .... MrTJO'Brien(5) 68
(W K Goldsworthy) *prom: lost pl after 5f: bhd after* **66/1**

0 **12** *dist* **Kerne Bridge**[28] 4072 6-10-11 .... JamesDavies —
(Mrs S M Johnson) *led for 2f: remained cl up tl wknd 9f out: t.o* **100/1**

00 **13** *5* **Simplyirresistible (IRE)**[291] 656 6-10-6 .... MarkNicolls(5) —
(S T Lewis) *chsd ldrs tl wknd 6f out: t.o* **100/1**

3m 37.2s (-15.00) **Going Correction** -0.40s/f (Good)
WFA 4 from 5yo+ 7lb **13** Ran SP% **114.7**
Speed ratings: **109,104,103,100,100 96,96,94,93,88 88,—,—** CSF £54.66 TOTE £52.40: £10.20, £1.10, £3.90; EX 172.70 Place 6 £213.26, Place 5 £48.12 .

Owner John and David Heymans **Bred** Juddmonte Farms Inc **Trained** Pudleston, H'fords

FOCUS
Probably a decent bumper, and a well above-average winner. The second and fourth have decent form but it is doubtful if either ran to their mark.

NOTEBOOK
Risk Challenge(USA), allowed to lead after a quarter of a mile, quickened away from his rivals with three furlongs to run and kept up the gallop to score in impressive fashion. Bred for the Flat, being a half-brother to smart six-and-seven-furlong performer Demonstrate who was a Royal Ascot scorer four years ago, he may take his chance in a maiden on the Flat proper. *(op 40-1)*

Presentandcorrect(IRE) hung quite badly over to the stands' rail in the home straight but it made no difference to the outcome. He collected place money for the third time in as many starts but gave the impression that he is going the wrong way. *(tchd 4-5 in places)*

King Cyrus(IRE), a brother to an Irish bumper winner, was keeping on at the end and this was a pleasing start to his career. *(op 12-1)*

One More Step, a Hexham winner for his previous yard, was held under his penalty but is probably better than this. *(tchd 9-2)*

Sawpit Sunset, out of a mare who was a fair staying hurdler for the Spearing yard, shaped with a bit of promise.

Kaddasan, a half-brother to smart two-mile chaser Kadarann and useful staying hurdler Kadara, showed a bit more promise on this second run. *(tchd 33-1)*

T/Plt: £255.80 to a £1 stake. Pool: £40,828.35. 116.50 winning tickets. T/Qpdt: £90.30 to a £1 stake. Pool: £3,466.00. 28.40 winning tickets. DO

4602 - (Foreign Racing) - See Raceform Interactive

4238 NEWBURY (L-H)

Friday, March 24

OFFICIAL GOING: Good
Wind: Slight, across

4603 STANJAMESUK.COM NOVICES' HURDLE (13 hdls) 3m 110y

2:00 (2:00) (Class 4) 4-Y-0+ **£3,903** (£1,146; £573; £286)

Form RPR

33U2 **1** **Calusa Charlie (IRE)**[30] 4058 7-11-2 110 .... TomDoyle 120+
(B G Powell) *prom: nt fluent 1st and 2nd: chsd ldr 5th to next: outpcd after 3 out: styd on fr next: pressed ldr last: led fnl 100yds: drvn out* **17/2**

5151 **2** *3/4* **Kilty Storm (IRE)**[27] 4105 7-11-8 124 .... APMcCoy 126+
(M C Pipe) *hld up mid-div: hdwy 7th: led app 3 out: c stand side sn after: hrd drvn fr 2 out: hung lft run-in: hdd and no ex fnl 100yd* **11/8**[1]

5422 **3** *9* **Original Thought (IRE)**[20] 4238 6-11-2 108 .... DaveCrosse 111+
(B De Haan) *led after 2nd:hit 3rd: hdd appr 3 out: wknd after 2 out* **10/3**[2]

2342 **4** *19* **Five Alley (IRE)**[17] 4285 9-10-9 100 .... MissCTizzard(7) 91
(R H Buckler) *chsd ldrs: nt fluent early: wknd 7th* **33/1**

5 **5** *1/2* **Sir Bathwick (IRE)**[21] 4212 7-11-2 .... LeightonAspell 91
(B G Powell) *mid-div: sme hdwy 8th: sn wknd* **33/1**

P0 **6** *20* **Lyster (IRE)**[21] 4212 7-10-11 .... JamesDiment(5) 71
(D L Williams) *a in rr* **100/1**

3P **7** *4* **Offemont (FR)**[119] 2482 5-11-2 106 .... MarkBradburne 71+
(Mrs L C Taylor) *prom: chsd ldr 7th: chal 4 out: riden and wknd rapidly appr 3 out* **25/1**

3212 **8** *15* **Ballyshan (IRE)**[35] 3962 8-11-8 120 .... CarlLlewellyn 58
(N A Twiston-Davies) *in tch: rdn after 5th: wknd 4 out* **9/2**[3]

0 **P** **Trip To The Stars (IRE)**[9] 4450 6-10-4 .... DarylJacob(5) —
(D P Keane) *a in rr: t.o whn p.u bef 3 out* **100/1**

000 **P** **The Piker (IRE)**[28] 4088 5-11-2 .... JasonMaguire —
(T R George) *bhd: lost tch 6th: t.o whn p.u bef 8th* **100/1**

00-0 **P** **Fine Enough (IRE)**[140] 2020 7-11-2 .... PJBrennan —
(R Rowe) *hit 4th: j. slowly 6th: a in rr: t.o whn p.u bef 8th* **100/1**

P **Considine (USA)**[160] 5-11-2 .... MickFitzgerald —
(C J Mann) *chsd ldrs early: mstke7th: blnd and no ch fr next: t.o whn p.u bef 2 out* **20/1**

-FFF **P** **Mrs Fizziwig**[15] 4324 7-10-9 .... RichardJohnson —
(R T Phillips) *led tl after 2nd: chsd ldr to 6th: wknd qckly 4 out: j.v.slowly and t.o 2 out: p.u bef next* **66/1**

5m 57.2s (-4.90) **Going Correction** -0.175s/f (Good) **13** Ran SP% **113.8**
Speed ratings: **100,99,96,90,90 84,82,78,—,— —,—,—** CSF £19.28 TOTE £8.40: £2.10, £1.50, £1.20; EX 20.20.

Owner Peter Luff **Bred** Martin Ryan **Trained** Morestead, Hants

FOCUS
No strength in depth to this novice event, which was run at an average pace, and the first two came clear. The race has been rated through the second and third.

NOTEBOOK
Calusa Charlie(IRE) got off the mark over hurdles at the sixth attempt with a hard-fought success on this first attempt at three miles. The better ground was in his favour and, while he is not the most fluent of hurdlers, he is open to further improvement over this sort of trip. *(op 8-1 tchd 9-1)*

Kilty Storm(IRE) looked all over the winner when hitting the front full of running at the top of the home straight, but he failed to sustain his momentum and was ultimately outstayed by the winner after the final flight. While he may have been better served by a more patient ride, and probably *needs softer ground to be at his best, on this evidence he is flattered by his official rating. (op 13-8 tchd 7-4 in places)*

Original Thought(IRE), runner-up on fast ground over course and distance last time, was made to look pedestrian when passed by Kilty Storm turning for home, yet he stuck to his task and helps to set the level of this form. *(tchd 7-2)*

Five Alley(IRE) failed to raise his game on this quicker surface and was never a serious threat. He is capable of slightly better. *(op 25-1)*

Ballyshan(IRE) was never a serious factor and proved very disappointing. He needs a deeper surface, but really ought to have finished much closer. *(op 4-1 tchd 5-1 in places)*

The Piker(IRE) *Official explanation: jockey said gelding had a breathing problem*

Trip To The Stars(IRE) *Official explanation: jockey said mare had a breathing problem*

4604 SABIN DU LOIR MEMORIAL MAIDEN HURDLE (11 hdls) 2m 5f

2:35 (2:36) (Class 3) 4-Y-0+

£7,515 (£2,220; £1,110; £555; £277; £139)

Form RPR

2 **1** **Nobody Tells Me (FR)**[31] 4032 5-11-2 .... APMcCoy 115+
(M C Pipe) *trckd ldrs: chal 3 out: sn led: nt fluent next: drvn and styd on strly run-in* **7/4**[1]

5/50 **2** *4* **Historic Place (USA)**[52] 3664 6-11-2 .... MarkBradburne 107
(J A Geake) *in tch: outpcd 6th: hdwy after 4 out: chsd wnr fr 2 out: kpt on run-in but no imp* **16/1**

4/35 **3** *2 1/2* **Caged Tiger**[33] 4005 7-11-2 .... DaveCrosse 105
(C J Mann) *bhd: hdwy 6th: chsd ldrs after 4 out: challnged next: sn rdn: kpt on same pce fr 2 out* **20/1**

4-0F **4** *6* **Double Law**[128] 2269 6-11-2 .... MarcusFoley 99
(Miss E C Lavelle) *in tch: chsd ldrs after 4 out: kpt on same pce after 3 out* **66/1**

05-3 **5** *1/2* **Felix Rex (GER)**[33] 4015 6-11-2 .... TimmyMurphy 99+
(J Pearce) *bhd: sme hdwy on rails after 4 out: j. slowly and outpcd 3 out: styng on whn blnd last: kpt on again cl home* **8/1**[3]

22- **6** *shd* **San Hernando**[426] 2770 6-11-2 .... BarryFenton 98
(Miss E C Lavelle) *bhd: j. slowly 4th: hdwy and hrd rdn after 3 out: kpt on run-in but nt rch ldrs* **14/1**

63 **7** *7* **Glen Omen (IRE)**[70] 3373 6-11-2 .... AlanO'Keeffe 91
(Jennie Candlish) *nt fluent in rr: hdwy fr 3 out: kpt on run-in but nvr in contention* **80/1**

304 **8** *7* **Beau De Turgeon (FR)**[35] 3962 5-11-2 112 ....(b[1]) GLee 84
(Ian Williams) *chsd ldrs: rdn 5th: hit next: wknd after 3 out* **16/1**

450 **9** *1* **Petitjean**[31] 4032 6-11-2 .... RichardJohnson 83
(P J Hobbs) *hit 2nd: bhd: hdwy to chse ldrs after 4 out: wknd fr 3 out* **16/1**

00 **10** *1 1/2* **Mylord Collonges (FR)**[29] 4077 6-11-2 .... PJBrennan 81
(Mrs Susan Nock) *led and hit 1st: hdd next: styd pressing ldr: led again 5th: hdd sn after 3 out and wknd qckly* **80/1**

0-0 **11** *8* **Alderman Rose**[34] 3978 6-11-2 .... WarrenMarston 73
(R T Phillips) *j. poorly in rr: rdn after 4 out: kpt on fr 2 out but nvr in contention* **66/1**

56 **12** *4* **Bayazid (IRE)**[26] 4128 4-10-8 .... MickFitzgerald 61
(N J Henderson) *hit 1st: nt fluent: bhd most of way* **14/1**

The Form Book, Raceform Ltd, Compton, RG20 6NL

5 **13** *3* **Sea Wall**[21] 4211 4-10-3 .... ShaneWalsh(5) 58
(Jonjo O'Neill) *chsd ldrs tl wknd 3 out* **11/1**
0P **14** *25* **Highland Games (IRE)**[53] 3646 6-11-2 ....(vt[1]) TomDoyle 41
(P R Webber) *chsd ldrs: chal 4 out: sn rdn: wknd after 3 out* **40/1**
0/05 **P** **Alf Lauren**[79] 3240 8-10-9 .... MrGTumelty(7) —
(A King) *j. slowly 6th: a bhd: t.o whn p.u bef 2 out* **40/1**
120P **P** **Pan The Man (IRE)**[34] 3978 5-11-2 99.................. AndrewThornton —
(J W Mullins) *hit 1st: mid-div to 3rd: wknd and p.u bef 5th* **33/1**
6 **P** **Saltrio**[38] 3908 8-11-2 .... WayneHutchinson —
(A King) *in tch: chsd ldrs 5th: wknd after 4 out: no ch whn p.u 2 out* **11/2**[2]
0600 **P** **So Wise So Young**[15] 4327 5-11-2 .... BenjaminHitchcott —
(R H Buckler) *w ldr tl wknd 4 out: t.o whn p.u bef 2 out* **100/1**
0 **P** **La Cuenta (IRE)**[88] 3001 6-10-11 .... LiamTreadwell(5) —
(Miss Venetia Williams) *mid-div: sme hdwy 4th: wknd 4 out: t.o whn p.u after 2 out* **33/1**
2023 **P** **Arumun (IRE)**[44] 3800 5-11-2 108.................. TomScudamore —
(M Scudamore) *led and hit 2nd: hdd 5th: wknd after 4 out: t.o whn p.u bef 2 out* **16/1**

5m 5.30s (-7.70) **Going Correction** -0.175s/f (Good)
WFA 4 from 5yo+ 8lb **20** Ran SP% **130.0**
Speed ratings: **107,105,104,102,102 102,99,96,96,95 92,91,90,80,— —,—,—,—,—** CSF £32.26 TOTE £3.10: £1.50, £5.80, £6.30; EX 73.00.
Owner B A Kilpatrick **Bred** D Pigouchet & Catherine Doucet **Trained** Nicholashayne, Devon
■ The race was sponsored by winning owner Brian Kilpatrick to commemorate his fine jumper Sabin Du Loir.

FOCUS
A reasonable novice event, run at a fair gallop, and the field finished strung out. The winner has been rated value for further with the second and third running to their marks. The race should throw up a few winners.

NOTEBOOK
Nobody Tells Me(FR), runner-up on his debut at Exeter last time, duly went one better with a ready display and was full value for his winning margin. This was a most welcome winner for his yard and, while his future ultimately lies over fences, he remains open to more improvement over timber and is a likeable sort. *(op 9-4)*
Historic Place(USA) was doing all of his best work at the finish and posted a much more encouraging effort. His yard appear to be coming out of a lean spell now and the way he finished suggests he is well worth chancing when upped to around three miles. He also now qualifies for handicaps.
Caged Tiger put a tame effort at Fontwell well behind him with a much-improved effort in defeat. This better ground was in his favour and he should fare better when switching to handicaps.
Double Law, making his debut for a new yard, failed to find all that much when it mattered, yet still posted a fairly encouraging return from his 128-day break. *(tchd 80-1 in a place)*
Felix Rex(GER) got going all too late in the day and failed to build on his latest improved effort at Towcester. *(op 5-1 tchd 17-2)*
Saltrio looked a big player turning for home, yet he stopped very quickly when asked for his effort, and something was clearly amiss. *(op 7-1 tchd 15-2)*
Pan The Man(IRE) *Official explanation: jockey said gelding had never been travelling (op 7-1 tchd 15-2)*

4605 MONTPELIER RE NOVICES' H'CAP CHASE (FOR THE BROWN CHAMBERLIN TROPHY) (17 fncs) 2m 6f 110y
3:10 (3:10) (Class 3) (0-120,120) 5-Y-O+ **£6,506** (£1,910; £955; £477)

Form RPR
2212 **1** **Stavordale Lad (IRE)**[36] 3949 8-11-7 **115**.................. ChristianWilliams 122+
(P F Nicholls) *led to 4th: led again6th: drvn nd nt fluent 3 out: 2l clr last: hld on all out* **13/2**
PP51 **2** *shd* **Beauchamp Prince (IRE)**[13] 4369 5-10-9 **113**.................. TomScudamore 108
(M Scudamore) *wnt lft 1st: hdwy 10th: hit 12th: plenty to do fr 4 out:styng on and wnt lft 2 out: 2l down and nt fluent last: str run:jst* **14/1**
21U2 **4** *2 ½* **Shining Strand**[21] 4214 7-11-12 **120**.................. AndrewTinkler 113+
(N J Henderson) *led 4th to 6th: styd chsng wnr: rdn 4 out and no imp: wknd and wnt lft 2 out* **2/1**[1]
2-23 **5** *13* **Ryders Storm (USA)**[20] 4239 7-10-13 **107**.................. JasonMaguire 91+
(T R George) *in tch: hdwy 9th: styng on whn blnd 13th: no ch w ldrs after* **12/1**
0-1P **6** *16* **Nawow**[13] 672 6-10-11 **105**.................. AndrewThornton 74+
(P D Cundell) *in tch: hdwy 9th: chsd ldrs 13th: wknd after 4 out* **33/1**
1223 **7** *13* **Winsley**[44] 3803 8-11-8 **116**.................. LeightonAspell 65
(O Sherwood) *chsd ldrs: chal 5th to 6th: wknd 10th* **5/1**[3]
0004 **8** *1 ½* **Lusaka De Pembo (FR)**[20] 4239 7-11-5 **113**..................(t) CarlLlewellyn 61
(N A Twiston-Davies) *bdly bmpd 1st: bhd most of way* **25/1**
1131 **P** **Harris Bay**[37] 3921 7-11-8 **116**..................(t) TimmyMurphy —
(Miss H C Knight) *rr and bdly bmpd 1st: in tch to 8th: wknd 12th: taild off whn p.u bef 3 out* **9/2**[2]
5-5P **P** **In Contrast (IRE)**[128] 2270 10-11-7 **115**.................. RichardJohnson —
(P J Hobbs) *chsd ldrs: hit 3rd: j. slowly 8th: wknd and hit 13th: t.o whn p.u bef 2 out* **25/1**

5m 41.7s (-6.00) **Going Correction** 0.0s/f (Good)
WFA 5 from 6yo+ 5lb **10** Ran SP% **114.8**
Speed ratings: **110,109,106,105,100 95,90,90,—,—** CSF £83.77 CT £981.27 TOTE £8.90: £2.50, £3.10, £3.40; EX 136.40.
Owner T G A Chappell & Paul K Barber **Bred** Stephen Cahill **Trained** Ditcheat, Somerset

FOCUS
A fair handicap, run at a solid pace, and the first two came well clear. The race could be rated a fair bit higher but with the favourite disappointing the form is a little suspect.

NOTEBOOK
Stavordale Lad(IRE) just did enough to resume winning ways under a very positive ride by Williams. He jumped really well, bar an error three from home, and enjoyed the return to slightly faster ground. While he is one of his powerful yard's lesser lights, he really has developed into a consistent chaser, and may be able to defy a higher mark in the coming weeks. *(tchd 6-1 and 7-1)*
Beauchamp Prince(IRE), off the mark in a beginners' chase last time, flew home on the run-in and only failed to reel in the winner by the smallest of margins. With a more positive ride, on this evidence he would most likely have prevailed, and he is clearly progressing now. *(op 20-1)*
Supreme Tadgh(IRE) posted a more encouraging effort, but was put in his place from the penultimate fence. On this evidence, the return to three miles will be more to his advantage. *(op 18-1 tchd 20-1)*
Shining Strand was surprisingly given a more patient ride than has often been the case in the past and performed well below his recent level. *(op 9-4 tchd 5-2 in places)*
Nawow *Official explanation: jockey said gelding had been unsuited by the good, good to soft in places ground (op 25-1)*
Winsley faded disappointingly when the race became serious and this is the first time he has failed to reach the frame over fences to date. *(op 4-1)*
Harris Bay turned in a lifeless effort and something was surely amiss. *Official explanation: jockey said gelding had been hanging right-handed (op 11-2)*

4606 RACING POST "HANDS AND HEELS" JUMPS SERIES FINALE NOVICES' H'CAP HURDLE (CONDITIONALS/AMATEURS) (11 hdls) 2m 3f
3:45 (3:46) (Class 3) (0-115,113) 4-Y-O+ **£6,506** (£1,910; £955; £477)

Form RPR
5425 **1** **Astyanax (IRE)**[71] 3358 6-10-9 **101**.................. MrCRNelson(5) 109+
(N J Henderson) *chsd ldrs tl outpcd 5th: hdwy 3 out: chsd ldr and drvn last: kpt on wl to ld cl home* **13/2**[2]
0114 **2** *½* **Down's Folly (IRE)**[62] 3508 6-11-8 **112**.................. MrPCallaghan(3) 119+
(H D Daly) *hit 1st: hld up in tch: led gng wl last: shkn up run-in: ct cl home* **7/1**[3]
3401 **3** *6* **New Mischief (IRE)**[21] 4210 8-11-1 **102**..................(t) JohnKington 102+
(Noel T Chance) *mid-div: hdwy 5th: led and hit 3 out: nt fluent 2 out: narrowly hdd last: sn outpcd* **6/1**[1]
2031 **4** *shd* **Abraham Smith**[18] 4282 6-11-9 **110**.................. TomMessenger 110+
(B J Eckley) *slt ld: hit 1st: hdd 3rd: styd prssing ldrs: ev ch fr 4 out to next: one pce appr last* **14/1**
0203 **5** *½* **Double Dizzy**[34] 3993 5-11-7 **108**.................. KeiranBurke 106+
(R H Buckler) *bhd: hit 4 out: hdwy fr next: styd on run-in but nvr gng pce to rch ldrs* **7/1**[3]
-101 **6** *½* **Gentleman Jimmy**[15] 4327 6-11-12 **113**.................. MrSWaley-Cohen 111
(H Morrison) *hld up in rr: hdwy 5th: trckd ldrs after 4 out: drvn after next: one pce appr last* **9/1**
015 **7** *¾* **Huckster (ZIM)**[28] 4093 7-11-6 **110**.................. MrWBiddick(3) 107
(Miss Venetia Williams) *chsd ldrs: rdn appr 3 out: rallied and ev ch 2 out: one pce appr last* **12/1**
346 **8** *½* **Count Boris**[38] 3906 5-11-3 **104**.................. SimonElliott 101
(J A Geake) *bhd: hdwy appr 3 out: kpt on fr 2 out but nvr nr ldrs* **14/1**
-233 **9** *7* **Thomo (IRE)**[276] 802 8-10-3 **95**..................(p) CraigThompson(5) 86+
(N E Berry) *chsd ldrs: mstke 2nd: blnd 4 out: wknd 2 out* **100/1**
033F **10** *7* **Corals Laurel (IRE)**[27] 4104 7-11-2 **103**.................. SeanQuinlan 86
(R T Phillips) *bhd: sme hdwy fr 3 out but nvr in contention* **14/1**
40P3 **11** *4* **Finsbury Fred (IRE)**[28] 4099 5-10-13 **100**.................. BernieWharfe 79
(N A Twiston-Davies) *led 3rd: rdn after 4 out: hdd 3 out: wknd next* **50/1**
422P **12** *12* **Dictator (IRE)**[18] 3243 5-10-6 **93**..................(t) MrGTumelty 60
(D R Gandolfo) *bhd most of way* **14/1**
5P-0 **13** *15* **Kety Star (FR)**[49] 3719 8-10-5 **95**.................. DarrenO'Dwyer(3) 47
(A W Carroll) *chsd ldrs to 4 out* **33/1**
000 **F** **Naja De Billeron (FR)**[35] 3963 5-11-3 **107**..................(t) MrRQuinn(3) —
(M C Pipe) *in rr whn fell 4th* **25/1**
566 **P** **Royal Stardust**[29] 4067 5-10-12 **102**.................. MrDHutchison(3) —
(G L Moore) *a bhd: t.o whn p.u bef 4 out* **20/1**
110 **P** **Lucky Do (IRE)**[132] 2173 9-11-4 **105**.................. MrsLucyRowsell —
(V J Hughes) *chsd ldrs to 6th: t.o whn p.u bef 2 out* **33/1**
-063 **P** **Alf's Spinney**[28] 4094 6-10-10 **97**.................. WillieMcCarthy —
(Ian Williams) *chsd ldrs tl wknd 4 out: t.o whn p.u bef 2 out* **16/1**

4m 41.5s (-5.30) **Going Correction** -0.175s/f (Good) **17** Ran SP% **120.3**
Speed ratings: **104,103,101,101,101 100,100,100,97,94 92,87,81,—,— —,—** CSF £47.54 CT £292.91 TOTE £8.40: £2.10, £2.50, £2.00, £3.70; EX 64.30.
Owner A Taylor **Bred** P D Player **Trained** Upper Lambourn, Berks
■ A winner on his first ride for Chris Nelson. John Kington is the Racing Post 'Hands and Heels' series winner.
■ Stewards' Enquiry : Darren O'Dwyer seven-day ban: improper riding; used whip in hands and heels race (Apr 5-6,9,16,23,26,28)

FOCUS
A fair event of its type, run at an average gallop, and the first two came clear. The third and fourth ran pretty much to their marks.

NOTEBOOK
Astyanax(IRE), a beaten favourite the last twice at Ludlow over further, showed a decent attitude to resume winning ways on this drop back in trip. He enjoys a decent surface and, while consistency is not his strong suit, it is unlikely we have yet seen to see the best of him in this sphere. *(op 7-1)*
Down's Folly(IRE) looked all over the winner when easing to the front nearing the final flight, but while he looked to do little wrong when asked to win his race on the run-in, he had no answer to the winner's late challenge. The drop back to this trip was to his liking and, considering he still finished nicely clear of the rest, he is well up to making amends from his current mark. *(tchd 15-2)*
New Mischief(IRE), raised 5lb for winning under today's rider over course and distance last time, had every chance yet was put in his place by the first two after the final flight. This is his ground and he should continue to pay his way if kept going through the summer months. *(tchd 11-2)*
Abraham Smith was none too fluent, but still turned in another improved effort from his 10lb higher mark and clearly remains in decent form at present. *(op 16-1)*
Double Dizzy, dropping in trip, would have been much better served by a more positive ride and should be rated better than the bare form. Granted stronger handling next time, he looks one to side with from his current mark. *(op 8-1)*
Gentleman Jimmy, off the mark at Wincanton last time, did not look overly suited by this faster surface and was never a serious threat under top weight. He is capable of better than this.

4607 MONTPELIER RE HUNTERS' CHASE (18 fncs) 3m
4:20 (4:20) (Class 6) 6-Y-O+ **£1,648** (£507; £253)

Form RPR
00/2 **1** **Ramirez (IRE)**[24] 4167 8-11-5 .... MrNickKent(7) 102
(Nick Kent) *chsd ldrs: wnt 2nd after 4 out: hit 2 out: wnt lft run-in and n.m.r 75 yds out: sn led: all out* **7/1**
P-F2 **2** *hd* **Montys Tag (IRE)**[27] 13-11-9 .... MrNBloom(3) 102
(S R Andrews) *led: narrowly hdd 14th: led again next: hit 2 out: wnt lft u.p run-in: hdd and no ex fnl 75yds* **20/1**
2-26 **3** *1 ¼* **Yeoman Sailor (IRE)**[38] 3910 12-12-2 .... MrNHarris 105
(Miss Grace Muir) *prom: rdn 14th: one pce fr 4 out: rallied fr next: kpt on run-in but nt pce to rch ldrs* **7/2**[1]
U4-2 **4** *19* **Gielgud**[42] 3847 9-11-9 105.................. MrJMaxse(7) 86
(B G Powell) *hld up in rr: sme hdwy 14th: no imp on ldrs fr 3 out* **9/2**[2]
P-14 **5** *1 ¼* **Millenium Way (IRE)**[5] 12-11-9 .... MrsCLTaylor(7) 85
(Mrs C L Taylor) *bhd: hdwy 14th: effrt 3 out: nt trble ldrs and sn btn* **11/1**
/0F- **6** *6* **The Granby (IRE)**[356] 12-11-5 ....(p) MrsHKemp(7) 75
(Mrs H M Kemp) *pressed ldrs: slt ld 14th: hdd next: sn wknd* **50/1**
3P3P **7** *22* **Beauchamp Oracle**[16] 4305 9-11-5 .... MrTCollier(7) 53
(S Flook) *in tch to 13th* **25/1**
206- **F** **Whatashock**[27] 11-11-9 .... MissETory(7) —
(Mrs H M Tory) *fell 1st* **40/1**
6P55 **P** **Guignol Du Cochet (FR)**[35] 3960 12-12-5 95.................. MrAWintle —
(S Flook) *a bhd: t.o: p.u bef last* **66/1**
222U **P** **Marrasit (IRE)**[33] 4009 10-10-12 .... MrSCharlton(7) —
(H E Thorpe) *bhd fr 10th: t.o whn p.u bef 3 out: dismntd* **8/1**
P **Palmers Peak (IRE)**[33] 7-11-12 .... MrRBurton —
(M Keighley) *in tch: hit 6th and 10th: sn wknd: t.o whn p.u bef last* **20/1**
0010 **P** **Corkan (IRE)**[144] 1960 12-11-5 69.................. MrSPJones(7) —
(Mrs F Kehoe) *prom early: rdn and bhd 7th: t.o whn p.u bef 13th* **100/1**

P3/P **P** **Owen's Pet (IRE)**[38] 3910 12-11-9 .... MrGTumelty(3) —
(Mrs S Wall) *in tch early: hit 7th: sn bhd: t.o whn p.u bef 12th* **100/1**

5-P5 **P** **Coral Island**[21] 4216 12-11-12 77 .... MrJMPritchard —
(Mrs Bernice Stronge) *chsd ldrs to 12th: t.o whn plld up bef last* **40/1**

2-PU **P** **Kingston-Banker**[3] 4560 10-11-12 110 .... MrIChanin(7) —
(Mrs S Alner) *chsd ldrs tl blnd bdly 11th: no ch after: t.o whn p.u bef last* **20/1**

12/F **U** **Full Minty**[29] 4079 11-11-5 .... MrGDisney(7) —
(Mrs Sarah Stafford) *trckd ldrs: blnd 5th:qckned to chal and styng on whn blnd and uns rdr 4 out* **11/2**[3]

6m 4.50s (-0.50) **Going Correction** 0.0s/f (Good) **16** Ran SP% **116.2**
Speed ratings: **100,99,99,93,92 90,83,—,—,— —,—,—,—,— —** CSF £129.53 TOTE £8.00: £2.50, £4.60, £1.90; EX 132.80.
Owner C Cottingham **Bred** Rathbarry Stud **Trained** Brigg, Lincs
■ Stewards' Enquiry : Mr N Bloom caution: used whip without giving gelding time to respond

FOCUS
A fair hunter chase, run at a sound pace, and few managed to get into the race from off the gallop. The first three came well clear.

NOTEBOOK
Ramirez(IRE), who shaped as thought the return to this trip would play to his strengths on his comeback at Leicester last time, dug deep when it mattered and resumed winning ways with a gritty success. He got outpaced at halfway, so his rider deserves credit for sticking to his task as he did, and it is likely we have yet to see the best of this talented performer just yet. *(tchd 13-2)*
Montys Tag(IRE) posted a very game effort from the front and only gave way to the winner in the closing stages. This is his ground and he really does deserve to go one better under Rules. *(op 25-1)*
Yeoman Sailor(IRE) hit a flat spot turning for home, yet he was flying at this finish and might well have got up in another 100 yards. He should be rated slightly better than the bare form and was a long way ahead of the rest at the finish. *(op 3-1)*
Gielgud failed to sustain his effort when it really mattered and was readily held from the third last. *(op 6-1)*
Millenium Way(IRE)
Full Minty had yet to be asked a serious question prior to unseating and is worth another chance on this evidence. *(op 4-1 tchd 6-1)*

4608 SPORTING INDEX H'CAP HURDLE (8 hdls) 2m 110y
4:50 (4:52) (Class 3) (0-135,133) 4-Y-0+ **£6,506** (£1,910; £955; £477)

Form RPR

111F **1** **Motorway (IRE)**[88] 2969 5-10-12 **119** .... RichardJohnson 127
(P J Hobbs) *trckd ldrs: nt fluent 2nd: chal 3 out: slt ld next: narrowly hdd last and 1l down: rallied u.p to ld cl home* **4/6**[1]

3UF- **2** *hd* **Bound**[429] 3416 8-11-1 **122** .... (t) LeightonAspell 130
(Mrs L Wadham) *chsd ldrs: chal 3 out tl slt ld last: drive and 1l up: hdd and no ex cl home* **25/1**

/333 **3** *8* **Pepe Galvez (SWE)**[88] 2974 9-11-0 **121** .... APMcCoy 121
(Mrs L C Taylor) *chsd ldrs: rdn 3 out: one pce fr 2 out* **11/2**[2]

15P/ **4** *2 ½* **Dumaran (IRE)**[20] 3282 8-10-0 **107** oh2 .... PaulMoloney 105
(W J Musson) *held up in rr: hdwy to trck ldrs 3 out: kpt on fr next but nvr gng pce to chal* **50/1**

2206 **5** *3 ½* **Silver Prophet (IRE)**[71] 3360 7-10-5 **112** .... SeanCurran 106
(M R Bosley) *led tl hdd 2 out: sn wknd* **40/1**

3P06 **6** *1* **Arrayou (FR)**[55] 3622 5-11-1 **122** .... (v) PJBrennan 115
(O Sherwood) *chsd ldrs: rdn appr 3 out: wknd next* **16/1**

-441 **7** *3* **Sun King**[37] 3929 9-9-4 **107** oh2 .... (t) JamesReveley(10) 97
(K G Reveley) *hld up mid-div: sme hdwy appr 3 out: nvr rchd ldrs: wknd 2 out* **14/1**

-130 **8** *7* **Black Hills**[81] 3210 7-10-13 **120** .... JimmyMcCarthy 103
(J A Geake) *blnd 1st: sn bhd: no ch w ldrs whn hit 3 out* **25/1**

4600 **9** *3* **Cloudy Grey (IRE)**[13] 4375 9-11-12 **133** .... BarryFenton 113
(Miss E C Lavelle) *a in rr* **11/1**[3]

2-23 **10** *15* **Silver Charmer**[181] 1548 7-11-0 **121** .... TimmyMurphy 86
(H S Howe) *racd wd: rr: sme hdwy 4 out: sn wknd* **20/1**

0-0P **11** *5* **Gift Voucher (IRE)**[71] 3351 5-10-0 **107** .... (t) TomDoyle 67
(P R Webber) *w ldr to 4 out: rdn: hit 3 out and wknd qckly* **66/1**

3m 58.5s (-5.10) **Going Correction** -0.175s/f (Good) **11** Ran SP% **114.6**
Speed ratings: **105,104,101,99,98 97,96,93,91,84 82** CSF £25.42 CT £59.44 TOTE £1.60: £1.10, £5.40, £1.90; EX 32.40 Place 6 £62.19, Place 5 £48.36.
Owner D Allen **Bred** Epona Bloodstock Ltd **Trained** Withycombe, Somerset

FOCUS
A decent handicap, which saw the first two come clear, and the form looks sound. The winner remains on an upwards curve.

NOTEBOOK
Motorway(IRE) ◆, last seen falling at Sandown on Boxing Day, showed a great attitude to get on top of his battle with the runner-up on the run-in and register his fourth success from his last five outings. He lacked confidence over his hurdles through the first half of the race - surely due to his previous Sandown experience - but he loves good ground and is clearly still an improving young hurdler. The likely rise in the weights he will now receive should be enough to ensure he gets a run in the valuable two-mile handicap at Aintree next month and, considering he should get his ground in that event, he ought to have every chance of maintaining his prolific profile. *(tchd 8-11)*
Bound, returning from a 429-day lay-off, ran a blinder in defeat and only just lost out. One will have to be wary of the potential bounce factor ahead of his next outing, but a reproduction of this effort ought to see him go one better before long. *(op 22-1)*
Pepe Galvez(SWE) was put in his place nearing the penultimate flight and helps set the level of this form. He may just prefer a stiffer test on this evidence. *(op 7-1)*
Dumaran(IRE), having his first outing over hurdles since 2003, shaped with some promise and can find much easier assignments in this sphere from his current rating. He is one to note when the market speaks more in his favour. *(tchd 66-1)*
Silver Prophet(IRE) showed up nicely from the front until not that surprisingly tiring after the penultimate hurdle. She is entitled to improve for the outing. *(tchd 50-1 in a place)*
T/Jkpt: Not won. T/Plt: £90.00 to a £1 stake. Pool: £74,529.95. 604.25 winning tickets. T/Qpdt: £38.30 to a £1 stake. Pool: £5,311.40. 102.40 winning tickets. ST

3842 BANGOR-ON-DEE (L-H)
Saturday, March 25

OFFICIAL GOING: Chase course - soft; hurdle course - good to soft (soft in places)
Wind: Light, across Weather: Rain after race 4

4609 COUNTRYSIDE DAY MARES' ONLY CLAIMING HURDLE (9 hdls) 2m 1f
2:05 (2:05) (Class 5) 4-Y-0+ **£2,877** (£838; £419)

Form RPR

2P0/ **1** **Mezereon**[33] 4625 6-10-13 .... WilliamKennedy(3) 101+
(D Carroll) *mde all: clr appr last: pushed out* **14/1**

1464 **2** *3* **Vocative (GER)**[14] 4362 4-10-1 99 .... (b[1]) MrTJO'Brien(5) 88
(P C Haslam) *hld up in tch: chsd wnr fr 6th: rdn and no imp fr 2 out* **7/2**[2]

6P1 **3** *20* **Cullian**[3] 4577 9-11-2 90 .... (p) AndrewThornton 78
(J G M O'Shea) *hld up in mid-div: lost pl 4th: styd on fr appr 2 out: tk 3rd post* **8/1**

0263 **4** *nk* **So Cloudy**[65] 3456 5-10-10 72 .... StephenCraine(3) 75
(D McCain) *t.k.h in rr: hdwy whn mstke 5th: rdn and wknd appr 2 out* **14/1**

0430 **5** *½* **Smilingvalentine (IRE)**[13] 4396 9-10-0 95 .... (b[1]) RyanCummings(10) 73+
(D J Wintle) *prom tl rdn and wknd appr 2 out: 3rd and wl btn whn blnd last* **11/2**[3]

5612 **6** *2* **Proprioception (IRE)**[19] 4282 4-10-9 98 .... WayneHutchinson 68
(A King) *chsd ldrs: rdn appr 4th: wknd after 6th* **6/4**[1]

0-40 **7** *4* **Losing Grip (IRE)**[45] 3795 7-11-2 .... DominicElsworth 71
(Mrs S J Smith) *prom tl wknd after 6th* **33/1**

50 **P** **Mrs Higham (IRE)**[67] 3435 5-10-3 .... JohnKington(7) —
(M Scudamore) *bhd fr 5th: t.o whn p.u bef 2 out* **50/1**

00U0 **P** **Sales Flow**[7] 4506 4-11-7 .... WilsonRenwick —
(M W Easterby) *a bhd: mstke 1st: t.o fr 4th: p.u bef 3 out* **66/1**

0400 **P** **Flashy Filly**[213] 1308 6-10-2 61 .... MichaelMcAlister(5) —
(J C Haynes) *hld up: rdn and bhd fr 5th: t.o whn p.u bef 2 out* **125/1**

PP00 **P** **Faraway Echo**[47] 3782 5-10-10 71 .... (v) TonyDobbin —
(James Moffatt) *hld up in mid-div: bhd fr 5th: t.o whn p.u bef 2 out* **25/1**

4m 14.8s (3.90) **Going Correction** +0.375s/f (Yiel) **11** Ran SP% **113.1**
Speed ratings: **105,103,94,94,93 92,90,—,—,— —** CSF £59.88 TOTE £15.50: £2.50, £1.80, £2.60; EX 49.60.So Cloudy was subject to a friendly claim.
Owner Diamond Racing Ltd **Bred** G And Mrs Middlebrook **Trained** Warthill, N Yorks

FOCUS
This did not take much winning with the favourite disappointing. The winner was well in on her Wetherby second to Howle Hill in November 2003 and has been rated to that level.

NOTEBOOK
Mezereon, who had been off for almost two years with leg trouble, had a pipe-opener on the sand last month. Nibbled at in the ring, she dictated matters from the front and appeared to score with a fair bit in hand. *(op 20-1)*
Vocative(GER), who presumably found three miles too far last time, could not cope with the winner in the first-time blinkers. She returned with a nasty-looking cut to the back of her off-side fore. *(op 4-1 tchd 9-2)*
Cullian found this an insufficient test of stamina having won a seller over two and a half furlongs further at Towcester three days earlier. *(op 9-2)*
So Cloudy had plenty to do at the weights and ran too freely on ground softer than she prefers. *(op 16-1)*
Smilingvalentine(IRE) may have held on for third had she not made a hash of the last. *(op 13-2)*
Proprioception(IRE), back down in distance, could have found that the ground was too soft for her liking. *Official explanation: jockey said filly was never travelling (tchd 11-8 and 13-8 in places)*
Sales Flow *Official explanation: trainer's representative said gelding was unsuited by good to soft, soft in places ground; trainer said mare was found to have a high temperature on returning to the yard (op 50-1)*

4610 TOMMY'S DARTS BEGINNERS' CHASE (18 fncs) 3m 110y
2:35 (2:36) (Class 4) 5-Y-0+ **£4,132** (£1,282; £690)

Form RPR

5423 **1** **Fisherman Jack**[16] 4321 11-11-3 69 .... (p) JodieMogford 81
(G J Smith) *chsd ldr to 8th: rdn 9th: outpcd 11th: 10 l 3rd whn lft in ld sn after last: drvn out* **15/2**[3]

/2-P **2** *1 ½* **Icare D'Oudairies (FR)**[121] 2466 10-11-3 .... OllieMcPhail 80
(A L Forbes) *hld up: pushed along after 9th: sn struggling: 12 l 4th whn lft 2nd sn after last: nt qckn* **18/1**

-2U2 **3** *3* **Henry's Pride (IRE)**[16] 4314 6-11-3 .... AndrewThornton 91+
(P C Haslam) *led: mstke and sddle slipped 4 out: j.rt 2 out: sn hdd: 2 l 2nd whn bdly hmpd and lft in ld last: sn hdd: nt recover* **10/11**[1]

0P **P** **Rioja Rally (IRE)**[14] 4369 6-10-10 .... SeanQuinlan(7) —
(R T Phillips) *hld up: hit 3rd: blnd 6th: lost pl 10th: t.o whn p.u after 14th* **25/1**

P-P2 **F** **Monteforte**[19] 4279 8-11-3 115 .... JasonMaguire 92+
(J A B Old) *j.lft: a.p: wnt 2nd 8th: j. slowly 12th and 14th: hrd rdn to ld after 2 out: 2 l clr whn fell last* **2/1**[2]

6m 52.7s (29.50) **Going Correction** +1.325s/f (Heav) **5** Ran SP% **106.6**
Speed ratings: **105,104,103,—,—** CSF £75.61 TOTE £4.50: £1.60, £3.70; EX 36.10.
Owner Graham Smith **Bred** Mrs H A Lynch **Trained** Six Hills, Leics

FOCUS
An eventful contest with the picture changing dramatically after a melee at the final fence. A tricky race to assess which could have been rated 10lb higher, it has been rated through the winner.

NOTEBOOK
Fisherman Jack was a very lucky winner and was only booked for third when the leader fell at the last, bringing Henry's Pride almost to a standstill. *(op 8-1)*
Icare D'Oudairies(FR) was another to benefit from the misfortune of others at the final fence. *(op 16-1)*
Henry's Pride(IRE) dragged his hind legs through the last ditch, after which his rider had to contend with a slipping saddle. His measure had been taken when he was stopped to a walk by the fall of Monteforte at the final fence. *(op Evens)*
Monteforte was inclined to jump a shade left-handed but seemed to have it in the bag when exiting at the last. *(tchd 15-8)*

4611 BANGORONDEERACES.CO.UK H'CAP CHASE (15 fncs) 2m 4f 110y
3:10 (3:10) (Class 3) (0-135,135) 5-Y-0+ **£10,409** (£3,056; £1,528; £763)

Form RPR

11F3 **1** **Ross Comm**[7] 4488 10-11-12 **135** .... DominicElsworth 151+
(Mrs S J Smith) *hld up: hdwy 7th: wnt 2nd 10th: led appr 2 out: rdn clr appr last: eased towards fin* **4/1**[2]

-10P **2** *12* **Noiseltine (FR)**[63] 3503 8-11-12 **135** .... (t) AlanO'Keeffe 137
(Miss Venetia Williams) *led: rdn and hdd appr 2 out: sn btn* **8/1**

254P **3** *4* **Edmo Yewkay (IRE)**[35] 3988 6-11-5 **128** .... (b) RussGarritty 126
(T D Easterby) *hld up in tch: reminders after 9th: wknd 3 out* **9/2**[3]

3461 **4** *dist* **No Visibility (IRE)**[16] 4332 11-10-13 **122** .... AndrewThornton —
(R H Alner) *prom: chsd ldr 6th to 10th: wknd 11th: 4th and no ch whn mstke 3 out: t.o* **7/2**[1]

52P6 **P** **Mistral De La Cour (FR)**[35] 3974 6-10-3 **115** .... (p) PeterBuchanan(3) —
(R Ford) *w ldr to 5th: wknd 6th: t.o whn p.u bef 11th* **28/1**

5042 **P** **Spring Lover (FR)**[45] 3803 7-10-13 **122** .... TonyDobbin —
(Miss Venetia Williams) *a bhd: hit 3rd: reminders after 4th: t.o whn p.u bef 3 out* **7/2**[1]

124- **P** **Family Venture (IRE)**[432] 3394 9-10-3 **112** .... KeithMercer —
(Ferdy Murphy) *hld up in rr: lost tch 10th: 5th and no ch whn mstke 11th: sn p.u lame: dead* **11/2**

5m 33.8s (21.30) **Going Correction** +1.325s/f (Heav) **7** Ran SP% **112.6**
Speed ratings: **112,107,105,—,— —,—** CSF £32.86 TOTE £6.20: £2.60, £4.50; EX 31.50.

Owner Kevin G Treanor **Bred** A Dawson **Trained** High Eldwick, W Yorks

FOCUS

This was nowhere near as competitive as the betting suggested. The winner's Carlisle victory could be rated this high. The race has been rated through the runner-up.

NOTEBOOK

Ross Comm, given a break after still being in the mix when falling six from home in the Hennessy, had disappointed when apparently well handicapped over hurdles a week ago. Running out a convincing winner over a trip short of his best, this live outsider for the Grand National needs ten horses to come out at Aintree. *(op 5-1)*

Noiseitine(FR) adopted her favourite tactics but was readily brushed aside in the home straight. *(op 9-1)*

Edmo Yewkay(IRE) could not keep tabs on the runner-up let alone the winner from the third last. *(op 3-1)*

No Visibility(IRE), raised 7lb, has run well but has yet to win going left-handed. *(tchd 10-3)*

Spring Lover(FR) has never won on ground this soft since coming over from France. *Official explanation: trainer's representative had no explanation for poor form shown (op 9-2)*

4612 TOMMY SHONE H'CAP HURDLE (12 hdls) 3m

3:45 (3:45) (Class 3) (0-135,133) 4-Y-0+ **£10,409** (£3,056; £1,528; £763)

Form RPR

3112 **1** **Ile Maurice (FR)**[61] [3544] 6-10-2 **116** PatrickMcDonald(7) 121+
(Ferdy Murphy) *mde all: clr appr 2 out: rdn out* **6/1**[3]

F211 **2** *2* **Cloudy Lane**[35] [3975] 6-10-12 **122** StephenCraine(3) 123
(D McCain) *hld up in mid-div: hdwy on ins appr 9th: sn rdn: wnt 2nd appr last: styd on flat: nt trble wnr* **4/1**[2]

2323 **3** *1 1/2* **Just Beth**[7] [4497] 10-10-10 **122** DerekLaverty(5) 121
(G Fierro) *a.p: rdn 8th: chsd wnr appr 3 out tl appr last: one pce* **6/1**[3]

-000 **4** *17* **Alagon (IRE)**[35] [3982] 6-10-3 **110** (b) DominicElsworth 94+
(Ian Williams) *hld up in tch: rdn appr 3 out: wknd 2 out* **18/1**

4130 **5** *5* **Go For Bust**[35] [3993] 7-11-3 **124** AndrewTinkler 101
(N J Henderson) *hld up in rr: hdwy 9th: rdn and wknd appr 2 out* **9/1**

3120 **6** *5* **Spring Breeze**[59] [3561] 5-10-10 **117** KeithMercer 89
(Ferdy Murphy) *a bhd* **12/1**

P-PP **7** *26* **Columbus (IRE)**[276] [814] 9-11-2 **123** (b) AlanO'Keeffe 69
(Jennie Candlish) *hld up in rr: lost tch 7th: t.o* **100/1**

121F **8** *24* **Wild Cane Ridge (IRE)**[28] [4112] 7-11-9 **130** TonyDobbin 52
(L Lungo) *hld up in mid-div: bhd fr 7th: t.o* **3/1**[1]

542P **9** *4* **Rowley Hill**[7] [4498] 8-11-12 **133** WayneHutchinson 51
(A King) *chsd wnr tl appr 3 out: sn wknd* **14/1**

P-50 **P** **Loup Charter (FR)**[100] [2848] 7-11-6 **127** (t) PaulMoloney —
(Miss H C Knight) *hld up in tch: rdn 8th: wknd after 3 out: t.o whn p.u bef last* **12/1**

1660 **P** **Flying Enterprise (IRE)**[35] [3993] 6-11-6 **132** LiamTreadwell(5) —
(Miss Venetia Williams) *t.k.h in tch: rdn after 7th: wknd 9th: t.o whn p.u bef last* **16/1**

6m 5.40s (8.60) **Going Correction** +0.375s/f (Yiel) **11** Ran SP% **117.8**
Speed ratings: **100,99,98,93,91 89,81,73,71,—** — CSF £30.87 CT £152.52 TOTE £6.80: £2.20, £2.00, £2.00; EX 33.60.

Owner N Iveson & F Murphy **Bred** Haras De Reuilly **Trained** West Witton, N Yorks

FOCUS

The finish concerned a couple of progressive horses with the winner enjoying a soft lead. The very consistent third ran to her mark.

NOTEBOOK

Ile Maurice(FR) goes well for her young rider and dictated matters on this step up in distance for her handicap debut. *(op 9-2)*

Cloudy Lane ◆ had a similar profile to the winner in that he was attempting three miles for the first time on this switch to handicaps. He gave the impression he would have preferred a stronger gallop and there was no disgrace in this. *(op 11-2 tchd 6-1)*

Just Beth is another who would not have minded a stronger pace. *(op 15-2)*

Alagon(IRE) had suffered with breathing difficulties on his two previous outings. *(op 16-1)*

Go For Bust needs better ground to be effective at this sort of distance. *(op 11-1)*

Wild Cane Ridge(IRE) ran a stinker on this return to hurdles. *(op 7-2 tchd 11-4)*

4613 LESLEY COURTNEY MEMORIAL NOVICES' HURDLE (9 hdls) 2m 1f

4:20 (4:20) (Class 4) 4-Y-0+ **£3,578** (£1,050; £525; £262)

Form RPR

543 **1** **Temple Place (IRE)**[17] [4301] 5-10-11 109 (t) StephenCraine(3) 123+
(D McCain) *a gng wl: led on bit appr 2 out: sn clr: j.rt and hit last: easily* **8/1**

PP5 **2** *13* **Dandygrey Russett (IRE)**[49] [3730] 5-10-7 JodieMogford 96+
(B D Leavy) *led: rdn and hdd appr 2 out: no ch w wnr* **33/1**

4-35 **3** *5* **Elverys (IRE)**[31] [4052] 7-11-0 AnthonyRoss 97
(R A Fahey) *hld up in mid-div: hdwy 6th: one pce fr 3 out* **14/1**

1324 **4** *hd* **Border Castle**[12] [4420] 5-11-7 118 AlanO'Keeffe 109+
(Miss Venetia Williams) *a.p: wnt 2nd after 6th: mstke 3 out: sn rdn and btn* **11/10**[1]

334 **5** *22* **Copper Bay (IRE)**[46] [3786] 4-10-7 105 WayneHutchinson 72+
(A King) *chsd ldrs: hit and pckd 6th: sn wknd* **4/1**[2]

F3FF **6** *14* **Moorlaw (IRE)**[38] [3920] 5-10-11 107 PaddyAspell(3) 61
(D McCain) *prom: mstke 2nd: lost pl 3rd: no ch fr 6th* **33/1**

4-52 **7** *nk* **Whosethatfor (IRE)**[113] [2606] 6-11-0 JasonMaguire 61
(J A B Old) *chsd ldr tl after 6th: wknd appr 3 out* **15/2**[3]

8 *dist* **Callituits (IRE)**[168] [1689] 4-10-7 JosephByrne —
(Jennie Candlish) *a bhd: t.o* **100/1**

0 **P** **Imlaak**[61] [3534] 4-10-7 (t) KeithMercer —
(James Moffatt) *a bhd: t.o whn p.u bef 2 out* **100/1**

-000 **P** **Just Ruby**[107] [2727] 5-10-4 OwynNelmes(3) —
(F Jordan) *a bhd: rdn after 3rd: t.o whn p.u bef 2 out* **100/1**

0-02 **P** **Freddie Ed**[43] [3843] 5-11-0 DominicElsworth —
(R N Bevis) *prom: rdn after 5th: sn wknd: t.o whn p.u bef 2 out* **16/1**

00- **P** **Earnest (IRE)**[352] [4760] 6-11-0 PaulMoloney —
(Ian Williams) *hld up and bhd: sltly hmpd 2nd: t.o whn p.u bef 2 out* **50/1**

P **P** **Habanero**[40] [3354] 5-10-7 RichardSpate(7) —
(Miss S J Wilton) *bhd: blnd 2nd: rdn 4th: mstke 5th: t.o whn p.u bef 2 out* **66/1**

60 **P** **Toothill Gunner**[54] [3657] 5-10-7 ThomasBurrows(7) —
(J K Cresswell) *prom: mstke 1st: rdn and struggling after 3rd: bhd whn j.rt and blnd 4th: t.o whn p.u bef 2 out* **125/1**

4m 16.8s (5.90) **Going Correction** +0.375s/f (Yiel)
WFA 4 from 5yo+ 7lb **14** Ran SP% **116.4**
Speed ratings: **101,94,92,92,82 75,75,—,—,— —,—,—,—** CSF £221.13 TOTE £11.80: £3.40, £6.00, £3.10; EX 349.10.

Owner Brendan Richardson and Jon Glews **Bred** Swettenham Stud **Trained** Cholmondeley, Cheshire

FOCUS

They went a reasonable pace in this ordinary event. A big step up on previous hurdling form from the winner who is rated value for 20l and is capable of much better on his best Flat form. The second also showed improved form while the race has been rated therough the third who ran to his mark.

NOTEBOOK

Temple Place(IRE), who was formerly Motivator's lead horse, proved a cut above this opposition *and did not have to break sweat. He now heads to Aintree where things will be a lot tougher. (op 9-1)*

Dandygrey Russett(IRE) had no answer once taken on by the easy winner.

Elverys(IRE), back on softer ground, seems to be struggling to find the right distance.

Border Castle does not appear to be progressing and found a mistake at the third last the beginning of the end. *(op Evens tchd 6-5)*

Freddie Ed *Official explanation: jockey said gelding bled from nose (op 20-1)*

4614 TOMMY'S DARTS H'CAP CHASE (12 fncs) 2m 1f 110y

4:50 (4:50) (Class 4) (0-105,102) 5-Y-0+ **£4,228** (£1,241; £620; £310)

Form RPR

546P **1** **Bel Ombre (FR)**[43] [3844] 6-10-8 **87** OwynNelmes(3) 99+
(O Sherwood) *hld up: hdwy on ins to chse ldr 6th: outpcd 4 out: rallied to ld appr 2 out: clr whn hung lft sn after last: rdn out* **8/1**

14F5 **2** *6* **Nagano (FR)**[19] [4281] 8-11-12 **102** WayneHutchinson 109+
(Ian Williams) *hld up: hmpd 2nd: hdwy to chse ldr 7th: rdn and ev ch appr 2 out: one pce* **7/2**[2]

PF40 **3** *7* **Fantasmic**[13] [4392] 10-11-6 **96** OllieMcPhail 96+
(M J M Evans) *prom: led 3rd tl appr 2 out: sn wknd* **14/1**

5243 **4** *10* **Amadeus (AUS)**[32] [4045] 9-10-9 **92** JohnKington(7) 80
(M Scudamore) *prom tl wknd after 6th* **4/1**[3]

4141 **P** **Flaming Heck**[7] [4489] 9-11-3 **98** DesFlavin(5) —
(Mrs L B Normile) *led to 3rd: wknd 7th: bhd whn p.u after 2 out* **4/1**[3]

P33P **P** **Ready To Rumble (NZ)**[135] [2141] 9-10-4 **83** (p) ColinBolger(3) —
(Miss Suzy Smith) *prom: rdn 5th: wknd 6th: mstke 7th: p.u bef 3 out* **5/2**[1]

06P4 **P** **Silver Dagger**[45] [3796] 8-9-9 **76** oh3 (tp) MichaelMcAlister(5) —
(J C Haynes) *nvr gng wl: bhd most of way: lost tch 7th: t.o whn p.u bef 2 out* **33/1**

4m 51.5s (25.10) **Going Correction** +1.325s/f (Heav) **7** Ran SP% **111.5**
Speed ratings: **97,94,91,86,— —,—** CSF £34.85 TOTE £11.00: £3.20, £2.30; EX 34.50.

Owner P Deal, J Tyndall, M St Quinton **Bred** Mrs Martine Van De Kerchove **Trained** Upper Lambourn, Berks

FOCUS

An uncompetitive handicap with two of the market leaders pulled up. The winner was back to the level of his Folkestone form and the runner-up ran to the level of his best form of the last 12 months.

NOTEBOOK

Bel Ombre(FR), who had dropped a total of 9lb, bounced back to the sort of form he was showing *when blundering away his chance at Folkestone early in January. Official explanation: trainer's representative said, regarding improved form shown, gelding's jumping had improved and it had regained his confidence (op 9-1)*

Nagano(FR) was unable to cope with the winner at these weights. *(op 3-1 tchd 4-1)*

Fantasmic, previously a stable companion of the winner, was having his first run over fences for his new yard. *(op 16-1)*

Amadeus(AUS) did not find a return to fences the answer.

Ready To Rumble(NZ) was already struggling when missing out at the seventh. *Official explanation: trainer's representative said gelding pulled up lame (op 3-1)*

4615 BERWYN HILLS MAIDEN NATIONAL HUNT FLAT RACE (CONDITIONAL JOCKEYS' AND AMATEUR RIDERS' RACE) 2m 1f

5:25 (5:29) (Class 6) 4-6-Y-0 **£1,884** (£549; £274)

Form RPR

1 **Closed Shop (IRE)**[83] 5-11-0 MrTJO'Brien(5) 106+
(P J Hobbs) *hld up in tch: led over 3f out: rdn clr 1f out: drvn out* **7/4**[1]

2 *5* **Just Supposin** 4-10-5 AndrewGlassonbury(7) 94
(M C Pipe) *hld up: sn in tch: led briefly over 3f out: sn rdn: one pce* **9/2**[2]

3 *5* **Devil's Disguise** 4-10-12 KeithMercer 89
(Ferdy Murphy) *hld up and bhd: hdwy 4f out: styd on fnl 2f* **16/1**

4 *1 3/4* **Man Overboard** 4-10-7 TomGreenway(5) 87
(T P Tate) *t.k.h in mid-div: hdwy and carried wd bnd 8f out: rdn over 4f out: wknd over 3f out* **7/1**

3 **5** *3* **Dance The Mambo**[79] [3259] 4-10-2 PaddyAspell(3) 77
(M W Easterby) *led 2f: led after 4f: rdn and hdd over 3f out: sn rdn: wknd over 2f out* **10/1**

5 **6** *11* **Little Rocker (IRE)**[30] [4072] 5-11-0 RobertLucey-Butler(5) 80
(M Pitman) *prom tl wknd over 4f out* **6/1**[3]

7 *1* **See My Soul (IRE)** 4-9-9 AdamHawkins(10) 65
(R Hollinshead) *nvr nr ldrs* **66/1**

8 *7* **Risky Patricia** 5-10-5 DavidCullinane(7) 65
(T J Fitzgerald) *plld hrd: prom tl wknd 4f out* **50/1**

00 **9** *13* **Burn Brook**[247] [1048] 6-10-5 MrRArmson(7) 52
(R J Armson) *a bhd* **66/1**

0 **10** *nk* **Electric Times (IRE)**[30] [4072] 5-11-2 StephenCraine(3) 59
(D McCain) *prom: rdn over 5f out: wknd over 4f out* **25/1**

11 *5* **Singing Wizard** 4-10-2 DarrenO'Dwyer(10) 47
(P J Hobbs) *bhd fnl 8f* **25/1**

12 *3* **Minster Lane**[349] 6-10-9 AndrewAdams(10) 51
(J M Saville) *hld up and bhd: hdwy whn carried wd bnd 8f out: wknd 4f out* **66/1**

0 **13** *dist* **I'm Posh**[10] [4455] 6-11-0 TJDreaper(5) —
(P Beaumont) *a towards rr: t.o* **50/1**

14 *10* **Shekel (IRE)** 4-10-5 MrGTumelty(7) —
(Miss H C Knight) *uns rdr and bolted bef s: hld up in mid-div: hdwy 8f out: wknd 4f out: t.o* **8/1**

15 *dist* **Dottie West** 6-10-5 MissMHugo(7) —
(Ms N M Hugo) *rrd and uns rdr at s: plld hrd: led after 2f to after 4f: hung rt and rn wd bnd 8f out: wknd qckly: t.o* **66/1**

4m 17.1s (6.00) **Going Correction** +0.375s/f (Yiel)
WFA 4 from 5yo+ 7lb **15** Ran SP% **125.0**
Speed ratings: **100,97,95,94,93 87,87,84,78,77 75,74,—,—,—** CSF £8.93 TOTE £2.70: £1.90, £1.90, £5.50; EX 11.90 Place 6 £5,629.09, Place 5 £2,019.01.

Owner Castlemore Securities Limited **Bred** Mrs Jacinta O'Regan **Trained** Withycombe, Somerset

FOCUS

A moderate bumper, but the winner looks above average. The race has been rated through the fifth.

NOTEBOOK

Closed Shop(IRE) ◆ had shown he could handle testing ground when winning his only Irish point on New Year's Day. He scored in decisive fashion and can go on from here. *(tchd 2-1)*

Just Supposin made a satisfactory debut and is certainly bred for the jumping game. *(op 6-1)*

Devil's Disguise showed some promise for the future and did not look short of stamina.
Man Overboard, a half-brother to Europa, was hardly thrown in at the deep end on his debut. *(op 13-2)*
Dance The Mambo had far more use made of her this time. *(op 11-1)*
T/Plt: £2,124.30 to a £1 stake. Pool: £40,013.95. 13.75 winning tickets. T/Qpdt: £192.40 to a £1 stake. Pool: £3,276.00. 12.60 winning tickets. KH

4603 NEWBURY (L-H)
Saturday, March 25

OFFICIAL GOING: Good to soft
Wind: Slight, across

4616 FREDDIE DUNCAN JUVENILE NOVICES' H'CAP HURDLE (11 hdls) 2m 3f
1:50 (1:50) (Class 3) (0-115,115) 4-Y-O **£5,204** (£1,528; £764; £381)

Form | | | | RPR
233 **1** **Pseudonym (IRE)**[15] [4354] 4-10-11 **100** PJBrennan 102+
(M F Harris) *hld up: smooth hdwy after 4 out: led after 2 out: pushed clr* **20/1**
2030 **2** *6* **Cava Bien**[50] [3719] 4-10-8 **104** WillieMcCarthy[(7)] 100+
(B J Llewellyn) *lw: led: hit 6th: hdd after 2 out: kpt on same pce* **20/1**
3345 **3** *½* **Cave Of The Giant (IRE)**[49] [3722] 4-11-5 **108** JimCrowley 103+
(T D McCarthy) *pressed ldr: outpcd after 3 out: kpt on fr last: no imp* **5/1**[2]
32P0 **4** *8* **Lord Of Adventure (IRE)**[25] [3714] 4-11-0 **103** LeightonAspell 90
(Mrs L C Jewell) *midfield: outpcd after 4 out: kpt on fr 2 out: no imp* **66/1**
056 **5** *8* **Benedict Bay**[37] [3939] 4-9-10 **92** oh2 ow3 (v) SimonElliott[(7)] 71
(J A Geake) *prom tl rdn and wknd appr 3 out* **20/1**
2244 **6** *1* **The Castilian (FR)**[22] [4210] 4-10-11 **100** (v) TomScudamore 78
(M C Pipe) *hld up and bhd: smooth hdwy to chse ldrs 3 out: rdn next: sn no ex* **14/1**
0400 **7** *1¾* **Able Charlie (GER)**[13] [4392] 4-10-2 **98** TomMessenger[(7)] 74
(Mrs Tracey Barfoot-Saunt) *midfield: effrt bef 3 out: wknd next* **50/1**
0003 **8** *14* **Willy The Slip**[26] [4148] 4-10-6 **100** DarylJacob[(5)] 62
(R H Alner) *nt fluent 1st: cl up to 6th: sn lost pl* **33/1**
3121 **9** *1¾* **Patxaran (IRE)**[14] [4360] 4-11-0 **113** (t) GaryBartley[(10)] 73
(P C Haslam) *chsd ldrs tl wknd bef 3 out* **6/1**[3]
10 *13* **Olazuro Du Mou (FR)**[33] 4-11-3 **106** APMcCoy 53
(T Doumen, France) *w'like: hld up: rdn after 4 out: nvr on terms* **9/2**[1]
PP01 **11** *6* **Ghabesh (USA)**[18] [4290] 4-10-1 **90** (p) ChristianWilliams 31
(Evan Williams) *midfield: hit 2nd: hdwy 5th: blnd 4 out: sn btn* **16/1**
14 **12** *1½* **Queen's Dancer**[35] [3979] 4-11-7 **110** MickFitzgerald 50
(N J Henderson) *midfield: rdn after 4 out: no imp whn blnd next* **7/1**
555F **13** *½* **Wembury Point (IRE)**[2] [4593] 4-11-5 **115** CharlieStudd[(7)] 54
(B G Powell) *bhd: rdn 4 out: sn btn* **25/1**
F355 **14** *nk* **David's Symphony (IRE)**[7] [4506] 4-10-5 **94** (v) MarkBradburne 33
(A W Carroll) *lw: chsd ldrs tl wknd fr 6th* **20/1**
644 **15** *hd* **Ortega (FR)**[35] [3972] 4-11-7 **110** RichardJohnson 49
(P J Hobbs) *lw: hld up: drvn after 4 out: btn next* **8/1**

4m 36.9s (-9.90) **Going Correction** -0.15s/f (Good) **15 Ran SP% 114.6**
Speed ratings: **107,104,100,97 97,96,90,89,84 81,81,80,80,80** CSF £325.51 CT £2301.59 TOTE £22.60: £5.30, £7.10, £1.80; EX 797.50.
Owner Mrs D J Brown **Bred** Ballymacoll Stud Farm Ltd **Trained** Edgcote, Northants

FOCUS
This was run at a strong pace and not many were able to get involved. Only a moderate juvenile handicap, rated around the second and fourth and probably not strong form.

NOTEBOOK
Pseudonym(IRE), upped in trip, travelled well before challenging at the second last and soon came clear to win nicely. He should prove better still on a sound surface.
Cava Bien tried to make all but was collared shortly after the second last and that was that. Just holding on to second, he is largely a consistent sort who is best on even softer ground. *(op 25-1)*
Cave Of The Giant(IRE), got warm beforehand and even with this return to a longer trip, ran a similar sort of race as when fifth to Detroit City at Sandown, staying on well at the end after becoming outpaced. *(op 9-2 tchd 11-2 in places)*
Lord Of Adventure(IRE), 4lb higher than when last in a handicap, has had a run on Polytrack since his last outing over hurdles. *(op 50-1)*
Benedict Bay, off his low weight, ran his best race so far over hurdles but has still to make the frame.
The Castilian(FR) once again made ground going nicely, but as soon as pressure was applied he did not want to know.
Willy The Slip will eventually make a chaser.
Olazuro Du Mou(FR), a French raider making his handicap debut, was always towards the rear of the field. *Official explanation: vet said gelding was dehydrated*
Queen's Dancer *Official explanation: jockey said filly was never travelling*

4617 STAN JAMES H'CAP CHASE (18 fncs) 3m
2:25 (2:26) (Class 3) (0-135,135) 5-Y-O+
£12,526 (£3,700; £1,850; £926; £462; £232)

Form | | | | RPR
/P14 **1** **Yardbird (IRE)**[65] [3469] 7-10-9 **118** PJBrennan 134+
(A King) *lw: bhd: hdwy 13th: blnd 14th: nt fluent 4 out:chsd ldr 2 out: styd on last: rdr dropped whip sn after: kpt on to ld last s* **8/1**[3]
4P/5 **2** *hd* **Rodalko (FR)**[21] [4240] 8-10-9 **118** LeightonAspell 134+
(O Sherwood) *lw: led to 2nd: led 3rd: 5l clr 9th: stl 3l ahd 3 out and drvn: kpt on gamely run-in: ct last strides* **7/1**[2]
5453 **3** *11* **The Dark Lord (IRE)**[44] [3816] 9-10-11 **120** JohnMcNamara 127+
(Mrs L Wadham) *chsd ldrs: rdn 4 out: wknd after 2 out: blnd last* **14/1**
4641 **4** *4* **Gunther McBride (IRE)**[41] [3877] 11-11-12 **135** RichardJohnson 138+
(P J Hobbs) *lw: led 2nd to next: chsd ldr: hit 4th: rdn 14th: wknd 2 out: no ch w ldrs whn blnd last* **17/2**
-PP0 **5** *2* **The Bandit (IRE)**[161] [1735] 9-10-13 **122** BarryFenton 120
(Miss E C Lavelle) *hld up in rr: hdwy 9th: mstke next: sme hdwy 14th: kpt on fr 2 out: gng on run-in but nt trble ldrs* **22/1**
P5P **6** *½* **Holy Joe (FR)**[77] [3296] 9-11-1 **124** SamThomas 122
(Miss Venetia Williams) *chsd ldrs:j. slowly 3rd: rdn and lost pl 12th: kpt on u.p fr 3 out: nt a danger* **22/1**
05FU **7** *2½* **I Hear Thunder (IRE)**[11] [4434] 8-11-2 **125** BenjaminHitchcott 120
(R H Buckler) *chsd ldrs: wnt 2nd briefly 3 out: sn wknd u.p* **50/1**
14-P **8** *3* **Whitenzo (FR)**[128] [2299] 10-11-5 **135** (t) MrJSnowden[(7)] 127
(P F Nicholls) *chsd ldrs: wknd 14th: no ch whn hit 3 out* **20/1**
5100 **9** *27* **Cassia Heights**[49] [3728] 11-9-13 **113** ow2 (t) LiamHeard[(5)] 78
(S A Brookshaw) *hit 12th: bhd most of way* **50/1**
0-55 **10** *11* **The Villager (IRE)**[77] [3293] 10-10-3 **112** TimmyMurphy 66
(T R George) *sn bhd* **16/1**
-22P **P** **Manbow (IRE)**[89] [2993] 8-10-3 **112** GLee —
(M D Hammond) *sn bhd: t.o whn p.u bef 4 out* **14/1**
-13P **P** **Native Ivy (IRE)**[29] [4098] 8-11-1 **124** TomDoyle —
(C Tinkler) *prom early: rdn and wknd 8th: t.o whn p.u bef 4 out* **16/1**
0/24 **P** **Indian Gunner**[16] [4332] 13-10-0 **109** oh2 RobertWalford —
(Dr J R J Naylor) *rr tl blnd 10th: t.o whn p.u bef 2 out* **100/1**
1111 **U** **Presenting Express (IRE)**[21] [4240] 7-11-2 **125** MarcusFoley —
(Miss E C Lavelle) *lw: hld up in rr tl mstke and uns rdr 5th* **3/1**[1]
-222 **P** **Dickensbury Lad (FR)**[12] [4419] 6-10-6 **115** AntonyEvans —
(J L Spearing) *bhd: pushed along 7th: sn wknd: t.o whn p.u bef 14th* **9/1**
30-0 **P** **Ballyvaddy (IRE)**[317] [311] 10-10-7 **116** (p) JimmyMcCarthy —
(J A Geake) *hit 4th: bhd: blnd 9th: sn wknd: t.o whn p.u bef 4 out* **33/1**
1421 **U** **Moorlands Again**[29] [4098] 11-10-9 **118** (t) MarkBradburne —
(M Sheppard) *chsd ldrs: mstkes 2nd and 4th: wknd 13th: mstke and uns rdr next* **14/1**

5m 59.0s (-6.00) **Going Correction** +0.025s/f (Yiel) **17 Ran SP% 122.2**
Speed ratings: **111,110,107,105,105 105,104,103,94,90** —,—,—,—,— —,— CSF £59.49 CT £789.25 TOTE £10.40: £1.90, £2.20, £3.20, £2.90; EX 39.20 Trifecta £342.10 Part won. Pool: £481.90 - 0.60 winning units..
Owner Gilco **Bred** T Horgan **Trained** Barbury Castle, Wilts

FOCUS
This was run at a strong pace and not many were able to get into it. Fair form, despite the early departure of the favourite, and the race should produce winners.

NOTEBOOK
Yardbird(IRE) was back down in trip but in the end it was stamina that won him the day. Only sixth when not fluent at the cross fence, he went after the long-time leader at the second last and got to him close home despite Brennan dropping his stick early on the run-in.
Rodalko(FR) ◆, jumping well in front and given a breather in the back straight, made just about all the running but was touched off after giving his all. The rain-softened surface was against him and he can find a race on faster ground this spring. *(op 9-1)*
The Dark Lord(IRE) ran well against these seasoned handicappers and his only serious mistake came at the final fence when he was held. Currently 15lb lower than he is over hurdles, he is well handicapped over fences and he had no problem with this easier ground. *(op 16-1 tchd 18-1)*
Gunther McBride(IRE), raised 7lb for his Exeter win, soon lost his lead to the eventual runner-up but ran a brave race and stuck on to finish in the frame. *(op 8-1 tchd 9-1)*
The Bandit(IRE), a stablemate of the beaten favourite, ran a nice race on this first start since October and passed three rivals on the run-in. *(op 20-1)*
Holy Joe(FR) could merely plug on in the latter stages without getting in a blow. *(op 20-1)*
I Hear Thunder(IRE) still looked a threat at the third last but then began to tire.
Presenting Express(IRE), attempting to defy a further rise of a stone on this bid for a five-timer, was in last place when parting company at the first ditch. *(op 10-3 tchd 7-2 in places)*

4618 THE SPORTSMAN H'CAP CHASE (13 fncs) 2m 1f
2:55 (2:59) (Class 3) (0-125,125) 5-Y-O+ **£6,506** (£1,910; £955; £477)

Form | | | | RPR
2212 **1** **Jacks Craic (IRE)**[14] [4378] 7-11-12 **125** AntonyEvans 141+
(J L Spearing) *lw: hld up: smooth hdwy bef 4 out: led 2 out: rdn and r.o strly* **4/1**[2]
0P43 **2** *8* **Jurado Express (IRE)**[14] [4378] 10-11-5 **118** SamThomas 125+
(Miss Venetia Williams) *trckd ldrs: led 4 out to 2 out: kpt on same pce* **14/1**
03P3 **3** *5* **Turgeonev (FR)**[56] [3619] 11-11-11 **124** GLee 125
(T D Easterby) *trckd ldrs: outpcd 4 out: rallied between last 2: kpt on run in* **8/1**
5044 **4** *1* **Roofing Spirit (IRE)**[32] [4037] 8-10-8 **112** (b) DarylJacob[(5)] 114+
(D P Keane) *hld up ins: hdwy and in tch whn checked 4 out: rdn 2 out: sn no ex* **8/1**
0243 **5** *1¼* **Master Rex**[22] [4213] 11-11-12 **125** (b) APMcCoy 127+
(B De Haan) *keen: led to 4th: led 8th to 4 out: no ex after 2 out* **10/3**[1]
1565 **6** *1¾* **O'Toole (IRE)**[72] [3357] 7-10-13 **112** RichardJohnson 111+
(P J Hobbs) *lw: hld up in tch: blnd 7th: sn rdn: n.d after* **13/2**[3]
000P **7** *19* **Batswing**[89] [2969] 11-11-10 **123** PhilipHide 101
(G L Moore) *hld up: rdn 7th: nvr on terms* **80/1**
40F3 **8** *7* **One Cornetto (IRE)**[57] [3601] 7-11-4 **124** JustinMorgan[(7)] 95
(L Wells) *chsd ldrs: rdn 8th: wknd fr next* **16/1**
-333 **F** **Neltina**[99] [2870] 10-11-1 **114** LeightonAspell —
(Mrs J E Scrase) *hld up: mstke 2nd: fell next (water)* **7/1**
00F **P** **Spiritual Society (IRE)**[40] [3903] 6-10-9 **108** TomScudamore —
(M Scudamore) *plld hrd: cl up: led 4th to 8th: wknd appr 3 out: p.u bef last* **25/1**
0P61 **P** **Log On Intersky (IRE)**[36] [3964] 10-10-13 **112** RichardHobson —
(J R Cornwall) *chsng ldrs whn blnd and lost pl 5th: sn btn: t.o whn p.u bef 4 out* **25/1**

4m 9.40s **Going Correction** +0.175s/f (Yiel) **11 Ran SP% 112.6**
Speed ratings: **107,103,100,100,99 99,90,86,**—,— — CSF £53.02 CT £422.99 TOTE £3.10: £1.70, £3.80, £2.50; EX 41.10.
Owner Bbb Computer Services **Bred** Michael Murphy **Trained** Kinnersley, Worcs

FOCUS
This was run at a rapid pace. The winner produced another step up in form while the second ran up to his best.

NOTEBOOK
Jacks Craic(IRE) is a progressive novice and the 2lb rise was nowhere near enough to stop him. Held up off the gallop before closing from the cross fence, he came away from the second last to win with a bit to spare. *(op 3-1 tchd 9-2 in places)*
Jurado Express(IRE) finished 12 lengths adrift of Jacks Craic at Sandown and was only 4lb better off here. Racing apart from the other runners at times, he showed in front four from home but was put in his place by his rival from the second last. *(op 16-1)*
Turgeonev(FR) has life in him yet and he was staying on again towards the finish after losing his pitch. A return to further might prove beneficial. *(op 10-1)*
Roofing Spirit(IRE), settled well towards the rear, was beginning to edge closer when he was short of room at the fourth last, from which point he was soon in trouble. *(op 9-1)*
Master Rex ran well for a long way but finally cried enough from the second last. He has become well treated and there could still be a race in him, possibly on better ground. *(op 7-2 tchd 3-1)*
O'Toole(IRE) got away with a serious error in the back straight and was keeping on past beaten rivals at the end. *(op 8-1)*
Spiritual Society(IRE), a faller on his recent chase debut, is a keen sort who eventually paid for helping set a strong pace. *(tchd 28-1)*

4619 JOHN SMITH'S/E.B.F. MARES' ONLY "NATIONAL HUNT" NOVICES' HURDLE FINAL (A LIMITED H'CAP) (LISTED) (11 hdls) 2m 5f
3:30 (3:34) (Class 1) 4-Y-O+
£28,510 (£10,695; £5,355; £2,670; £1,340; £670)

Form | | | | RPR
5211 **1** **Harringay**[75] [3322] 6-11-1 **109** (t) TimmyMurphy 116+
(Miss H C Knight) *hld up in rr: stdy hdwy after 4 out: sn drvn: styd alone far side: led appr last: drvn out* **13/2**[2]

31F3 **2** 2 ½ **Jontys'Lass**[13] [4391] 5-10-5 **102** .... MrTGreenall[(3)] 107
(A Crook) *led 2nd to 4th: styd chsng ldrs: rdn 3 out: chal next: chsd wnr last but no imp* **40/1**

3213 **3** 1 ¼ **Vertical Bloom**[57] [3595] 5-11-5 **113** .... WarrenMarston 117
(Mrs P Sly) *prom: drvn along after 4 out: kpt on u.p and styd on run-in but nt pce to trble ldrs* **11/1**

20P3 **4** 4 **Purple Patch**[16] [4329] 8-10-11 **105** .... RobertWalford 105
(C L Popham) *bhd: pushed along fr 4 out: styd on wl fr 2 out and kpt on run-in: nt rch ldrs* **28/1**

3011 **5** shd **Treaty Flyer (IRE)**[67] [3437] 5-10-6 **100** .... SamThomas 101+
(P G Murphy) *lw: racd under stands rail 1st to 3rd: hdwy 4th: trckd ldrs 6th: led appr 2 out: hdd sn after: outpcd run-in* **11/2**[1]

4460 **6** 2 ½ **Heltornic (IRE)**[10] [4443] 6-11-10 **118** .... TomScudamore 115
(M Scudamore) *lw: prom tl dropped rr 6th: plenty to do 3 out and u.p: kpt on wl after 2 out but nt rch ldrs* **18/1**

14P5 **7** 2 ½ **Ballyhoo (IRE)**[45] [3802] 6-9-11 **98** oh4 ....(v[1]) WayneKavanagh[(7)] 94+
(J W Mullins) *chsd ldrs: rdn appr 3 out: kpt on fr 2 out but n.d* **25/1**

23P6 **8** 6 **Bonchester Bridge**[18] [4286] 5-10-4 **98** oh4 .... MarcusFoley 89+
(N J Henderson) *chsd ldrs: j. slowly 4 out: wkg whn nt fluent next* **14/1**

5424 **9** 1 ¾ **My Rosie Ribbons (IRE)**[54] [3648] 7-9-11 **98** oh2 .... MrMWall[(7)] 85
(B W Duke) *chsd ldrs: rdn 5th: nvr in contention after* **80/1**

1012 **10** 6 **Bally Bolshoi (IRE)**[18] [4286] 6-10-12 **106** .... RJGreene 87
(Mrs S D Williams) *rr: mstke 4 out: nvr in contention* **25/1**

244U **11** dist **Ballybawn House**[12] [4429] 5-9-13 **98** oh2 .... SamCurling[(5)] 59
(J C Fox) *bhd most of way: t.o* **28/1**

3511 **12** ¾ **Sunley Shines**[67] [3439] 6-11-1 **114** .... JohnnyLevins[(5)] 80
(B G Powell) *lw: w ldrs: led 4th: hdd appr 2 out and mstke: sn wknd: t.o* **7/1**[3]

4221 **13** nk **Diklers Rose (IRE)**[61] [3544] 7-10-11 **105** .... RichardMcGrath 71
(K G Reveley) *chsd ldrs: rdn 4 out: wknd next: t.o* **17/2**

-321 **P** **Cash And New (IRE)**[66] [3443] 7-11-2 **110** .... RichardJohnson —
(R T Phillips) *blnd 2nd: bhd tl t.o and p.u bef 6th* **8/1**

0600 **P** **She's Our Daisy (IRE)**[18] [4286] 6-10-4 **98** oh28 .... TomDoyle —
(R H Buckler) *blnd 2nd: a in rr: t.o whn p.u bef 4 out* **150/1**

6-51 **P** **Miss Doublet**[18] [4286] 5-10-1 **98** oh3 .... RichardYoung[(3)] —
(J W Mullins) *j. slowly 1st: a bhd: t.o whn p.u bef 3 out: dismntd* **25/1**

003U **P** **Cresswell Willow (IRE)**[12] [4429] 6-10-4 **98** oh3 ....(b) CarlLlewellyn —
(W K Goldsworthy) *chsd ldrs to 5th: bhd whn bmpd 4 out: t.o whn p.u bef last* **50/1**

2211 **P** **Sabreflight**[60] [3551] 6-11-2 **110** .... GLee —
(J Howard Johnson) *mid-div: hdwy to trck ldrs 5th: rdn and hit 4 out: sn wknd: t.o whn p.u bef 2 out* **13/2**[2]

5m 5.00s (-8.00) **Going Correction** -0.05s/f (Good) **18** Ran SP% **121.2**
Speed ratings: **113,112,111,110,110 109,108,105,105,102** —,—,—,— —,—,— CSF £252.63 CT £2817.52 TOTE £6.80: £2.10, £7.60, £3.50, £5.70; EX 417.10 TRIFECTA Not won..
Owner Mrs R Vaughan **Bred** Mrs R I Vaughan **Trained** West Lockinge, Oxon

FOCUS
Not a strong renewal of this event, with the topweight only rated 118, but the pace was sound and this is solid handicap form.

NOTEBOOK
Harringay was only eighth to Penneyrose Bay in this a year ago but has improved this term. In fine form since being fitted with a tongue tie following a controversial reappearance at Towcester, she stayed on the inside of the course in the home straight in search of the best ground and, showing in front between the last two flights, battled on to complete the hat-trick. She will eventually make a chaser. *(tchd 7-1)*
Jontys'Lass, well at home in testing ground, was always prominent. Staying on the stands' side in the straight, she had every chance at the second last but could not contain the winner on the other side of the track.
Vertical Bloom beat today's winner at Huntingdon in December but was 4lb worse off here. She was always to the fore but lacked the pace of the first two when it mattered. *(op 12-1)*
Purple Patch, who had today's winner and third behind when runner-up at Towcester in November, was suited by this return to a more suitable trip and was doing her best work at the finish. *(op 25-1)*
Treaty Flyer(IRE), making her handicap debut, was close up when blundering at the fourth from home. She narrowly showed ahead in the straight, but could not hold on and was caught for fourth on the line. *(op 5-1)*
Heltornic(IRE) was unable to adopt her favoured front-running role and dropped to the rear at halfway, but to give her credit she was coming back for more at the end. *(op 20-1 tchd 22-1 in a place)*
Ballyhoo(IRE), tried in a visor for the first time, ran a solid race with no apparent excuses.
Ballybawn House *Official explanation: jockey said mare hung badly left-handed (op 25-1)*
Sunley Shines, bidding for a hat-trick off a 10lb higher mark, helped force the pace until her exertions told from the second last. *(op 13-2)*
Miss Doublet *Official explanation: jockey said mare lost her action (op 9-1 tchd 7-1, 10-1 in a place)*
Cash And New(IRE) *Official explanation: jockey said mare was never travelling (op 9-1 tchd 7-1, 10-1 in a place)*

4620 STANJAMESUK.COM NOVICES' H'CAP CHASE (15 fncs) 2m 2f 110y
4:05 (4:11) (Class 4) (0-110,109) 5-Y-0+ **£4,554** (£1,337; £668; £333)

Form RPR

P022 **1** **Lord On The Run (IRE)**[21] [4239] 7-11-5 **109** .... WillieMcCarthy[(7)] 124+
(J W Mullins) *chsd ldrs: lft 2nd 3rd: led 4 out: wnt lft next: 5l clr whn wnt lft and blnd last: r.o strly* **2/1**[1]

6164 **2** 11 **Lubinas (IRE)**[22] [4214] 7-11-4 **101** .... TomDoyle 106+
(F Jordan) *keen: lft in clr ld 3rd: hdd 4 out: 5l down and hld whn mstke last* **10/3**[3]

1530 **3** dist **Madison De Vonnas (FR)**[19] [4281] 6-11-6 **103** ....(t) BarryFenton —
(Miss E C Lavelle) *hld up chsng gp: hdwy to chse ldrs 9th: nt fluent and outpcd 11th: n.d after* **8/1**

P04P **4** 2 ½ **Cloudy Blues (IRE)**[79] [3252] 8-10-0 **83** oh9 .... BenjaminHitchcott —
(R H Buckler) *chsd ldrs: lost pl whn hit 8th: no ch after* **22/1**

3113 **R** **Sunley Future (IRE)**[15] [4350] 7-10-10 **98** .... CharliePoste[(5)] —
(M F Harris) *led: keen: sddle slipped early: rn out 3rd* **10/1**

3U22 **P** **Priscilla**[37] [3940] 8-11-4 **101** .... JohnMcNamara —
(K Bishop) *in tch: hdwy 9th: effrt bef 4 out: wkng whn j. slowly next: p.u bef 2 out* **5/2**[2]

4m 43.8s (2.40) **Going Correction** +0.175s/f (Yiel) **6** Ran SP% **109.5**
Speed ratings: **101,96**,—,—,— — CSF £8.87 TOTE £2.00: £1.60, £2.30; EX 11.10.
Owner Mrs Alurie O'Sullivan **Bred** William R Devereux **Trained** Wilsford-Cum-Lake, Wilts

FOCUS
A suspect race form-wise and the winner probably did not have to improve on his recent course second.

NOTEBOOK
Lord On The Run(IRE), not winning out of turn, scored decisively after reeling in the eventual runner-up, but he was pretty weary towards the end and survived a bad blunder at the final fence. *(tchd 15-8 and 9-4)*
Lubinas(IRE), left in front at the third, was soon clear of his pursuers but he was headed at the first in the home straight and could not counter. He is more at home on a sound surface and is capbale of better, possibly when reverting to hold-up tactics. *(op 3-1)*
Madison De Vonnas(FR) put in a couple of slow jumps and ended up well beaten. He is not progressing. *(op 6-1 tchd 17-2)*
Cloudy Blues(IRE), a plating-class performer who was 9lb out of the handicap, was the first beaten. *(tchd 20-1)*
Priscilla, dropped in trip, was beaten in third place when clambering over the third last and soon pulled up. *(op 4-1)*

4621 JOHNNY HAINE MEMORIAL NOVICES' HURDLE (8 hdls) 2m 110y
4:40 (4:46) (Class 4) 4-Y-0+ **£3,903** (£1,146; £573; £286)

Form RPR

1 **Midas Way**[197] 6-11-0 .... PJBrennan 118+
(P R Chamings) *w ldr tl led after 4 out: nt fluent 2 out whn lft w def advantage: drvn out run-in* **9/1**

-250 **2** 3 **Classic Role**[21] [4242] 7-11-0 118 .... GLee 114
(L Wells) *chsd ldrs: effrt 3 out: cl up whn lft chsng wnr next: kpt on run-in but no imp* **4/1**[3]

41-1 **3** 7 **Industrial Star (IRE)**[72] [3347] 5-11-7 109 .... NeilMulholland 114
(M D Hammond) *lw: blnd 1st: chsd ldrs: stl wl there whn sltly hmpd 2 out: kpt on same pce run-in* **10/1**

4 shd **Moon Over Miami (GER)**[202] 5-11-0 .... DaveCrosse 107
(C J Mann) *leggy: bhd: hdwy 3 out: kpt on wl fr 2 out and styd on cl home: nt rch ldrs* **12/1**

4 **5** 15 **Jack Rolfe**[73] [3340] 4-10-7 .... PhilipHide 95+
(G L Moore) *lw: chsd ldrs: rdn 3 out: wknd sn after* **5/2**[1]

00 **6** 18 **Krasivi's Boy (USA)**[22] [4211] 4-10-7 .... BenjaminHitchcott 67
(G L Moore) *hit 2nd: bhd: kpt on fr 3 out but nvr in contention* **50/1**

003P **7** 2 **No Way Back (IRE)**[80] [3242] 6-11-0 105 .... BarryFenton 72
(Miss E C Lavelle) *hld up in rr and racd on outside: nvr in contention* **20/1**

6P0 **8** nk **Dawn Wager**[10] [4450] 5-10-7 .... JamesDavies 65
(D B Feek) *mid-div: drvn and effrt after 4 out: nvr in contention* **100/1**

40 **9** 9 **Lunar Sovereign (USA)**[16] [4327] 7-11-0 ....(t) TimmyMurphy 63
(M C Pipe) *hld up in rr: nt fluent 2 out: nvr in contention* **25/1**

P **10** shd **Song Of Vala**[36] [3963] 5-11-0 .... MatthewBatchelor 63
(C J Mann) *j. modly in rr: a bhd* **66/1**

11 5 **Onslow Road (IRE)**[48] [3766] 6-11-0 .... TomDoyle 58
(Miss Venetia Williams) *in tch whn hit 4 out: wkng whn mstke next* **40/1**

12 ¾ **Glitter Ice**[181] 5-10-4 .... TJPhelan[(3)] 50
(G Haine) *led tl hdd after 4 out: wknd next* **66/1**

6 **13** 4 **Cirrious**[41] [3883] 5-10-7 .... RichardJohnson 46
(P J Hobbs) *blnd 4 out: a bhd* **20/1**

60P **14** 11 **Cleverality (IRE)**[18] [4284] 6-11-0 .... TomScudamore 42
(Evan Williams) *a in rr* **66/1**

36 **15** 2 ½ **Sky Mack (IRE)**[56] [3617] 5-11-0 .... ChristianWilliams 39
(Evan Williams) *hit 2nd: a in rr* **50/1**

00 **16** 1 ¼ **Glorious Castlebar**[51] [3691] 5-11-0 .... SeanFox 38
(J C Fox) *a in rr* **100/1**

4 **17** 4 **Lik Wood Power (NZ)**[315] [360] 9-11-0 104 .... HenryOliver 34
(D J Wintle) *blnd 1st: j. modly after and a in rr* **33/1**

51 **F** **Warningcamp (GER)**[102] [2803] 5-11-7 115 .... LeightonAspell 121
(Lady Herries) *lw: mstke 1st: chsd ldrs: hit 4th: drvn to chal and styng on whn fell 2 out* **10/3**[2]

4m 4.30s (0.70) **Going Correction** +0.05s/f (Yiel)
WFA 4 from 5yo+ 7lb **18** Ran SP% **127.6**
Speed ratings: **100,98,95,95,88 79,78,78,74,74 72,71,69,64,63 62,60**,— CSF £43.23 TOTE £11.20: £2.70, £1.80, £2.60; EX 66.40.
Owner Mrs Alexandra J Chandris **Bred** Mrs J Chandris **Trained** Baughurst, Hants

FOCUS
Quite a competitive event which should produce winners, and decent novice form.

NOTEBOOK
Midas Way, who looked very fit, was a very useful middle-distance stayer on the Flat, albeit not easy to place. Always in the first two, he showed ahead early in the home straight and was left in command at the second last to make a winning hurdles debut. He is the type to do better. *(op 10-1)*
Classic Role, back in more suitable company, showed a return to the sort of form he showed when runner-up to Straw Bear at Folkestone but gave the impression he would be happiest on genuine soft ground. *(op 5-1)*
Industrial Star(IRE), penalised for his win at Catterick in January, ran respectably in ground that had gone against him. *(op 12-1)*
Moon Over Miami(GER) ◆, a Listed winner over a mile in Germany, stayed on strongly from out of the pack and would have been third in another stride. He should be up to winning in ordinary company. *(op 8-1)*
Jack Rolfe was up with the pace thoughout and only capitulated from the second last. *(op 7-2)*
Krasivi's Boy(USA), having his third look at hurdles, was never in the hunt but did keep on past toiling opponents. *(op 40-1 tchd 66-1)*
No Way Back(IRE) gave the impression he might be capable of a bit better than this back over further. *(op 16-1)*
Lunar Sovereign(USA) *Official explanation: jockey said gelding had a breathing problem*
Warningcamp(GER), whose Folkestone win has worked out quite well, was in second place and very much in contention when coming down at the penultimate flight. *(op 11-4 tchd 7-2)*

4622 WEST BERKSHIRE RACING CLUB STANDARD OPEN NATIONAL HUNT FLAT RACE (DIV I) 2m 110y
5:10 (5:14) (Class 5) 4-6-Y-0 **£2,055** (£599; £299)

Form RPR

0 **1** **Joyryder**[140] [2049] 5-11-4 .... CarlLlewellyn 116+
(M Pitman) *cl up gng wl: led over 2f out: kpt on strly* **33/1**

2 3 **Ship's Hill (IRE)** 5-11-4 .... MarcusFoley 109
(N J Henderson) *angular: hld up: hdwy over 6f out: rdn 4f out: rallied over 2f out: chsd wnr ins fnl f: r.o* **7/1**[3]

6 **3** 3 ½ **Glinton**[56] [3623] 4-10-11 .... WarrenMarston 99+
(Mrs P Sly) *leggy: led to over 2f out: kpt on same pce* **40/1**

4 4 **Cathedral Rock (IRE)** 4-10-11 .... LeightonAspell 95+
(N J Gifford) *w'like: medium-sized: hld up: stdy hdwy over 3f out: nvr nrr* **25/1**

34 **5** 1 ¼ **Warlord**[63] [3504] 5-11-4 .... BenjaminHitchcott 100
(R H Buckler) *cl up: rdn over 3f out: sn outpcd* **12/1**

6 5 **Crashtown Hall (IRE)** 5-11-4 .... TomDoyle 97+
(C Tinkler) *w'like: bit bkwd: keen in midfield: shkn up 3f out: edgd lft and sn outpcd* **11/1**

7 5 **Lincoln's Inn (IRE)** 4-10-11 .... RichardJohnson 85+
(P J Hobbs) *leggy: athletic: prom tl rdn and wknd over 2f out* **12/1**

8 6 **Chase The Dawn** 4-10-11 .... DaveCrosse 77
(C J Mann) *w'like: str: bit bkwd: prom tl rdn and wknd fr 4f out* **33/1**

9 *16* **Zaffarsson (IRE)** 5-10-13 ShaneWalsh(5) 68
(J S Moore) *w'like: str: bit bkwd: hld up: rdn over 4f out: nvr on terms* **66/1**

10 *12* **Wantage Road (IRE)** 4-10-11 MickFitzgerald 49
(N J Henderson) *w'like: hld up: hdwy over 6f out: rdn and wknd over 4f out* **1/1**[1]

11 *17* **Benbridge** 5-11-4 JamesDavies 39
(Mrs S M Johnson) *w'like: hld up towards ins: rdn and wknd over 4f out* **100/1**

12 *26* **Ornoir (FR)** 4-10-11 APMcCoy 6
(T Doumen, France) *w'like: plld v hrd: racd wd first 6f: midfield tl wknd fr 6f out* **5/1**[2]

4m 1.80s (-1.50) **Going Correction** +0.05s/f (Yiel)
WFA 4 from 5yo+ 7lb **12** Ran SP% **117.5**
Speed ratings: **105,103,101,100,99 97,94,91,84,78 70,58** CSF £239.73 TOTE £33.80: £5.50, £2.00, £9.30; EX 282.90.
Owner Malcolm C Denmark **Bred** Downfield Cottage Stud **Trained** Upper Lambourn, Berks

FOCUS
Probably a weak bumper, with Joyryder value for 7l in the end. The first two look decent in a race which has been rated around the fifth.

NOTEBOOK
Joyryder was last of eight on his debut back in November, but had learnt from the experience and was able to run out a comfortable winner. He ran green early in the home straight but soon came back on the bridle and was value for around double the margin of victory at the end. *(tchd 40-1)*
Ship's Hill(IRE) ◆, the stable's second string, was under strong pressure early in the home straight but kept staying on and took second place inside the last. This was a promising debut and, out of a half-sister to a staying chaser, he will be suited by further in time. *(op 9-1)*
Glinton, a half-brother to the yard's useful hurdler Harley, was well beaten on the Southwell Fibresand on his bumper debut two months ago. After making the running, he stuck on quite well when headed, suggesting he will get further than this when he goes hurdling. *(op 25-1 tchd 50-1)*
Cathedral Rock(IRE), whose unraced dam is a half-sister to a winning hurdler over two and a half miles, made pleasing late progress. *(op 20-1 tchd 28-1)*
Warlord ran another reasonable race but just got tired in the final two furlongs. *(op 14-1)*
Crashtown Hall(IRE), whose dam is a sister to Jodami, is a half-brother to a couple of bumper winners and winning chaser Jodante. He should be capable of better with this experience behind him. *(op 10-1 tchd 12-1)*
Lincoln's Inn(IRE) *(op 11-1)*
Wantage Road(IRE), a good-bodied gelding out of a winning hurdler who was a half-sister to 1976 Irish Derby winner Malacate, cost 100,000gns as a three-year-old. He has reportedly worked very well and has been ready to run for some time, but he came under pressure before the straight had been reached and was soon on the retreat. He may be worth another chance. *(tchd 5-4, 11-8 in a place and 10-11 in places)*
Ornoir(FR) unshipped McCoy down at the start then gave him any number of problems in the early stages of the race, taking a keen tug and fly-jumping, then looking briefly as he would run out through the rail as he came right over to the stands' side before the first bend. McCoy eventually got him settled in the pack, but he was one of the first beaten. *(tchd 9-2)*

4623 WEST BERKSHIRE RACING CLUB STANDARD OPEN NATIONAL HUNT FLAT RACE (DIV II) 2m 110y
5:35 (5:45) (Class 5) 4-6-Y-O **£2,055** (£599; £299)

Form				RPR
	1		**Jean Le Poisson (FR)** 4-10-11 MarcusFoley (N J Henderson) *athletic: hld up rr: stdy hdwy 1/2-way: trckd ldr 4 out: chal 3f out: led wl over 2f out: drvn clr fnl f: readily* **16/1**	104+
232	**2**	*5*	**Kimi (IRE)**[21] 4244 5-11-4 TomDoyle (Noel T Chance) *led: rdn whn chal fr 3f out: hdd wl over 2f out: kpt on fnl f but no ch w wnr* **10/11**[1]	105+
	3	*5*	**Treasury Counsel (IRE)** 4-10-11 MickFitzgerald (N J Henderson) *tall: angular: mid-div: hdwy 6f out: drvn 3f out: kpt on fnl 2f to take 3rd fnl f but nvr gng pce to rch ldrs* **8/1**[3]	92
	4	*hd*	**Three Guesses (IRE)** 5-11-4 CarlLlewellyn (M Pitman) *w'like: prom: rdn and one pce 6f out: rdn and kpt on fnl 3f but nvr gng pce to rch ldrs* **8/1**[3]	99
	5	*6*	**Chez Bleu**[342] 5-11-4 RichardJohnson (P J Hobbs) *w'like: leggy: chsd ldr tl over 4f out: wknd over 2f out* **5/1**[2]	96+
	6	*18*	**Marlion (FR)** 4-10-11 MatthewBatchelor (B R Johnson) *leggy: t.k.h: hld up in rr: hdwy 5f out: n.d and sn wknd* **66/1**	73+
	7	*10*	**Mister Pink** 6-11-4 BarryFenton (R Rowe) *w'like: hdwy to chse ldrs 1/2-way: wknd over 4f out* **66/1**	65
	8	*½*	**Sukey Tawdray (IRE)** 5-11-4 WarrenMarston (D J Wintle) *leggy: a in rr* **50/1**	64
	9	*30*	**Headley (IRE)** 5-11-4 DaveCrosse (J S Moore) *str: bit bkwd: bhd: sme hdwy 6f out: sn wknd* **66/1**	34
	10	*shd*	**Volaire** 4-10-4 MarkBradburne (A J Lidderdale) *w'like: leggy: bhd: sme hdwy 6f out: sn wknd* **33/1**	20
	11	*1 ¾*	**High Minster (IRE)** 4-10-11 RJGreene (S C Burrough) *leggy: chsd ldrs 10f* **80/1**	25
5	**12**	*dist*	**Seal Harbour (FR)**[21] 4237 6-11-4 (t) PJBrennan (A King) *bhd fr 1/2-way: t.o* **12/1**	—
	13	*9*	**Big Palooka** 4-10-4 SimonElliott(7) (J A Geake) *leggy: bhd: sme hdwy 6f out: sn wknd: t.o* **66/1**	—
0	**14**	*dist*	**My Mon Amour**[34] 4011 5-10-8 RichardYoung(3) (J W Mullins) *w'like: in tch to 1/2-way: t.o and virtually p.u fnl 2f* **100/1**	—

4m 2.10s (-1.20) **Going Correction** +0.05s/f (Yiel)
WFA 4 from 5yo 7lb 5 from 6yo 4lb **14** Ran SP% **117.9**
Speed ratings: **104,101,99,99,96 87,83,82,68,68 67,—,—,—** CSF £30.03 TOTE £15.90: £2.90, £1.30, £3.00; EX 37.90 Place 6 £460.16, Place 5 £132.09.
Owner The Fourth Pheasant Inn Partnership **Bred** Sc Ecurie Des Chartreux **Trained** Upper Lambourn, Berks

FOCUS
Probably the weaker of the divisions, this has been rated around the runner-up who ran to his mark.

NOTEBOOK
Jean Le Poisson(FR), the longer-priced of the Henderson duo but quite a nice type, is a half-brother to a ten-furlong winner in France. After travelling well, he came nicely clear once striking the front. *(op 14-1)*
Kimi(IRE) had to settle for a place for the fourth time in as many runs. Attempting to make all but no match for the winner in the straight, he did not do much wrong other than hanging briefly on the home turn. *(tchd 8-11 and Evens in places)*
Treasury Counsel(IRE), a stablemate of the winner, was reportedly a little green going to post. He was outpaced at one stage but stayed on resolutely in the latter stages. *(op 7-1 tchd 9-1)*
Three Guesses(IRE), whose stablemate won the first division, is a half-brother to Grand Annual Chase winner St Pirran and staying hurdler No Forecast. He looks a staying type on the evidence of this debut.
Chez Bleu, third on his only previous racecourse appearance in an Irish point nearly a year ago, ran well for a long way and was still in third place entering the final furlong. *(op 7-1)*

T/Plt: £866.30 to a £1 stake. Pool: £89,246.05. 75.20 winning tickets. T/Qpdt: £146.00 to a £1 stake. Pool: £5,446.80. 27.60 winning tickets. ST

4379 NAVAN (L-H)
Saturday, March 25
OFFICIAL GOING: Soft to heavy (heavy in places)

4625a AN UAIMH CHASE (GRADE 3) 2m 4f
3:00 (3:00) 5-Y-0+ **£14,366** (£4,215; £2,008; £684)

			RPR
1		**Watson Lake (IRE)**[10] 4445 8-11-12 150 PCarberry (Noel Meade, Ire) *trckd ldr in 2nd: cl up travelling wl appr 3 out: rdn to ld last: styd on wl* **5/2**[3]	159+
2	*8*	**Nickname (FR)**[27] 4138 7-11-10 CO'Dwyer (Martin Brassil, Ire) *attempted to make all: slt mstke 8th: strly pressed 3 out: rdn and hdd last: no ex* **1/1**[1]	149
3	*2 ½*	**Hi Cloy (IRE)**[9] 4457 9-11-12 158 AndrewJMcNamara (Michael Hourigan, Ire) *hld up in tch: 3rd and rdn bef 2 out: sn no ex: one pce* **9/4**[2]	149
4	*dist*	**Native Beat (IRE)**[48] 3776 11-11-1 109 MrPDuggan(7) (J R H Fowler, Ire) *a in rr: wknd 1/2-way: completely t.o* **100/1**	—

5m 43.5s **4** Ran SP% **110.3**
CSF £5.77 TOTE £3.40; DF 4.90.
Owner John Corr **Bred** Thomas F O'Brien **Trained** Castletown, Co Meath

NOTEBOOK
Watson Lake(IRE) showed no ill effects from his Cheltenham effort behind Newmill and this was much more like his form. Always travelling well, he picked off Nickname as they took off at the last and showed his turn of foot on the run-in. He needs soft ground and there is no reason why he should not stay further than this. *(op 9/4 tchd 11/4)*
Nickname(FR) went off in front but clipped the eighth and was not great over the next. He still travelled well on the run round to the straight but proved vulnerable to the winner's bit speed from the last. *(op Evens tchd 11/10)*
Hi Cloy(IRE) was close enough over the third last but his effort began to peter out and he was beaten after the next. *(op 2/1 tchd 5/2)*

4626 - 4630a (Foreign Racing) - See Raceform Interactive

4386 MARKET RASEN (R-H)
Sunday, March 26
OFFICIAL GOING: Soft (good to soft in places back straight; heavy in places home straight)
The ground was described as 'very testing, bottomless in the home straight'.
Wind: Moderate; half behind Weather: Overcast, rain last three races

4631 WILLINGHAM WOODS JUVENILE NOVICES' HURDLE (8 hdls) 2m 1f 110y
2:10 (2:10) (Class 4) 4-Y-O **£3,253** (£955; £477; £238)

Form				RPR
3233	**1**		**Victorias Groom (GER)**[32] 4057 4-10-10 106 LeightonAspell (Mrs L Wadham) *trckd ldrs: led 3rd: clr appr 2 out: blnd last: drvn out* **5/4**[1]	116+
2144	**2**	*6*	**Gidam Gidam (IRE)**[18] 4301 4-10-9 114 (p) PatrickMcDonald(7) (J Mackie) *chsd ldrs: drvn and outpcd 4th: styd on to chse wnr after 2 out: kpt on run-in* **5/1**[2]	112
0322	**3**	*24*	**Maneki Neko (IRE)**[39] 3925 4-10-10 103 NeilMulholland (E W Tuer) *hld up in mid-div: hdwy to chse ldrs 4th: hit next: wnt 2nd appr 2 out: 3rd and wkng whn blnd last* **6/1**	86+
26	**4**	*6*	**Daldini**[62] 3539 4-10-10 PadgeWhelan (Mrs S J Smith) *trckd ldrs: wnt 2nd 4th: wknd appr 2 out* **12/1**	76
0	**5**	*6*	**City Of Manchester (IRE)**[54] 2521 4-10-5 PaddyMerrigan(5) (P C Haslam) *hld up in rr: sme hdwy 5th: nvr nr ldrs* **33/1**	70
2	**6**	*5*	**Orpen Wide (IRE)**[13] 4416 4-10-7 LeeVickers(3) (M C Chapman) *hld up: sme hdwy whn hit 4th: nvr nr ldrs* **11/2**[3]	67+
6060	**7**	*24*	**Water Pistol**[13] 4416 4-10-10 78 KennyJohnson (M C Chapman) *bhd and drvn 3rd* **200/1**	41
	8	*dist*	**Son Of Sophie**[18] 4-10-3 CharlieStudd(7) (C N Kellett) *in rr fr 4th: t.o 3 out: btn total of 103 l* **200/1**	—
	9	*dist*	**Neardown Bishop**[300] 4-10-3 MrSRees(7) (M Wigham) *s.i.s: t.o 3rd: btn total of 183 l* **150/1**	—
	U		**Kirkhammerton (IRE)**[20] 4-10-10 (v) AnthonyCoyle (M J Polglase) *in rr whn blnd and uns rdr 1st* **100/1**	
654	**P**		**In Dream's (IRE)**[8] 4506 4-10-5 98 ow2 (t) BenOrde-Powlett(7) (M A Barnes) *sddle sn slipped: p.u bef 2nd* **20/1**	—
6	**P**		**Ngauruhoe (IRE)**[131] 2258 4-9-12 TomGreenway(5) (John Berry) *mid-div: lost pl 4th: t.o whn p.u bef 2 out* **66/1**	—
5	**P**		**Bilkie (IRE)**[41] 3898 4-10-10 AndrewTinkler (John Berry) *prom to 3rd: bhd whn blnd 3 out: t.o whn p.u bef next* **66/1**	—
P	**P**		**Berkhamsted (IRE)**[13] 4416 4-10-10 WayneHutchinson (M F Harris) *led to 3rd: hit next: lost pl and j. slowly next: sn t.o: p.u bef 2 out* **28/1**	—

4m 28.5s (12.10) **Going Correction** +0.75s/f (Soft) **14** Ran SP% **115.3**
Speed ratings: **103,100,89,87,84 82,71,—,—,— —,—,—,—** CSF £6.80 TOTE £2.20: £1.30, £1.70, £2.00; EX 15.10.
Owner P H Betts (holdings) Ltd **Bred** P Ardsimba **Trained** Newmarket, Suffolk

FOCUS
They finished well string out in the testing ground. The winner was value for 10l while the runner-up improved a stone.

NOTEBOOK
Victorias Groom(GER), a decent sort who will make a chaser in time, took this modest event by the scruff of the neck and had them well strung out turning in. In the bad ground he had to be kept up to his work all the way to the line. *(tchd 11-8, 6-4 in places)*
Gidam Gidam(IRE), under his penalty, stayed on to chase home the winner and to his credit never gave up the battle. He may now be worth a try over a bit further. *(op 8-1)*
Maneki Neko(IRE), a keen type, went in pursuit of the winner turning in but he didn't see it out in the conditions. He will appreciate much better ground. *(tchd 11-2)*
Daldini went in pursuit of the winner at the halfway mark but he had nothing more to give going to two out. A free-running sort, he doesn't want conditions as testing as they were here. At least he is now qualified for a handicap mark. *(op 11-1)*
City Of Manchester(IRE), on his hurdling debut, kept on in his own time after being put to sleep at the back. He looks a stayer but may need more time yet. *(tchd 40-1)*
Orpen Wide(IRE), full of himself in the paddock, wouldn't want conditions as testing as they were here. *(op 9-2)*
Bilkie(IRE) *Official explanation: trainer said gelding was unsuited by the heavy ground (op 50-1)*

In Dream's(IRE) *Official explanation: jockey said saddle slipped (op 50-1)*
Ngauruhoe(IRE) *Official explanation: trainer said filly was unsuited by the heavy ground (op 50-1)*

4632 LEGSBY ROAD H'CAP HURDLE (8 hdls) 2m 1f 110y

2:40 (2:40) (Class 5) (0-90,90) 4-Y-0+ **£2,602** (£764; £382; £190)

Form				RPR
-063	**1**		**Theatre Tinka (IRE)**[34] 2940 7-10-13 **86**.................... AdamHawkins(10) (R Hollinshead) *prom: hit 2nd: wnt 2nd and swtchd rt appr 2 out: led last: styd on* **4/1**[2]	93
60P	**2**	*3*	**Fixateur**[68] 3431 4-11-5 **89**.................... WayneHutchinson (C C Bealby) *trckd ldrs: led after 3 out: edgd rt and hdd last: no ex* **6/1**[3]	86
4133	**3**	*6*	**Before The Mast (IRE)**[13] 4427 9-11-2 **84**.................... CharliePoste(5) (M F Harris) *rr-div: wnt promient 4th: styd on same pce fr 2 out* **10/3**[1]	82
0003	**4**	*8*	**Protocol (IRE)**[9] 4475 12-11-2 **82**....................(tp) LeeVickers(3) (Mrs S Lamyman) *w ldrs: mstke 3rd: outpcd appr 2 out* **11/1**	73+
0036	**5**	*¾*	**Heversham (IRE)**[16] 4346 5-11-10 **87**....................(p) GLee (J Hetherton) *mid-div: hdwy to chse ldrs 5th: outpcd after next* **16/1**	76
6SR6	**6**	*15*	**Teutonic (IRE)**[33] 4040 5-11-5 **82**.................... KeithMercer (R F Fisher) *rr-div: sme hewady 5th: nvr nr ldrs* **33/1**	66+
325P	**7**	*14*	**Munaawesh (USA)**[18] 4302 5-11-3 **80**.................... NeilMulholland (Mrs Marjorie Fife) *w ldr: led appr 5th: hdd after 3 out: wknd appr 2 out* **11/1**	40
-00P	**8**	*14*	**Dormy Two (IRE)**[89] 3042 6-11-5 **85**....................(p) PaddyAspell(3) (J S Wainwright) *a in rr* **28/1**	31
P035	**9**	*22*	**Penalty Clause (IRE)**[39] 3923 6-11-6 **83**.................... AntonyProcter (Lucinda Featherstone) *chsd ldrs: hrd drvn 5th: sn lost pl* **18/1**	7
0100	**10**	*12*	**Good Investment**[46] 3797 4-11-1 **90**....................(p) PaddyMerrigan(5) (P C Haslam) *chsd ldrs: hrd drvn 3rd: sn lost pl: t.o 3 out* **14/1**	—
P000	**11**	*9*	**Inch High**[27] 4143 8-11-5 **89**.................... MrGGoldie(7) (J S Goldie) *s.i.s: in rr and drvn along: t.o 3 out* **40/1**	—
1060	**F**		**Wardash (GER)**[31] 4075 6-11-10 **87**....................(bt) KennyJohnson (M C Chapman) *led: hdd and fell 5th* **40/1**	—
50-0	**P**		**Minstrel's Double**[325] 197 5-10-12 **80**.................... TJDreaper(5) (F P Murtagh) *in rr: t.o 3 out: p.u bef next* **50/1**	—
P0P5	**P**		**Akram (IRE)**[27] 4149 4-11-2 **86**.................... APMcCoy (Jonjo O'Neill) *hld up in rr: lost pl 5th: t.o next: p.u bef 2 out* **13/2**	—
/05-	**P**		**African Sunset (IRE)**[608] 1046 6-11-6 **83**.................... AlanDempsey (A Parker) *chsd ldrs: wknd qckly 3 out: t.o whn p.u bef 2 out* **20/1**	—

4m 36.7s (20.30) **Going Correction** +1.10s/f (Heav)
WFA 4 from 5yo+ 7lb **15** Ran SP% **123.2**
Speed ratings: **98,96,94,90,90 83,77,71,61,55 51,—,—,—,—** CSF £27.16 CT £91.65 TOTE £5.40: £2.30, £2.60, £1.80; EX 51.00.
Owner Tim Leadbeater **Bred** Ballylinch Stud **Trained** Upper Longdon, Staffs

FOCUS
Just a low-grade handicap but the first two went into this relatively unexposed. The winner ran to his mark.

NOTEBOOK
Theatre Tinka(IRE), a winner three times on the level, was having just his fifth start over hurdles. He stayed on the better on the run-in and there should be further improvement in him. *(tchd 7-2)*
Fixateur, a winner four times on the Flat in France, has been gelded since his last run. Having just his fourth start over hurdles and on his handicap bow, he did not go unbacked. After taking it up travelling strongly, he came off a straight line under pressure and was very much second best at the line. He has the ability to make his mark. *(op 8-1)*
Before The Mast(IRE), who had the ground to suit, was unable to get to grips with two relatively unexposed types. *(op 7-2 tchd 4-1)*
Protocol(IRE), who generally contests sellers these days, hung right-handed and was left behind on the run round to two out. *Official explanation: jockey said gelding hung right-handed*
Heversham(IRE), 5lb lower, still looks on a harsh sort of mark. *(tchd 18-1)*
Akram(IRE), useful on the Flat in Ireland, seems to have lost the plot altogether. The one hope might be totally different ground. *(op 11-2 tchd 5-1)*

4633 SPRIDLINGTON BEGINNERS' CHASE (14 fncs) 2m 4f

3:10 (3:11) (Class 4) 5-Y-0+ **£5,139** (£1,497; £749)

Form				RPR
403	**1**		**Kercabellec (FR)**[26] 4162 8-11-2 79.................... RichardHobson (J R Cornwall) *mde all: wnt wl clr bef 8th: hit last: eased towards fin* **25/1**	102+
R4P3	**2**	*19*	**Iris's Prince**[7] 4516 7-11-2 105.................... DavidO'Meara (A Crook) *chsd ldrs to 7th: hit 11th: kpt on to take remote 2nd run-in* **8/1**	77
00F5	**3**	*1*	**Courant D'Air (IRE)**[13] 4429 5-10-4 98.................... AdrianScholes(7) (Lucinda Featherstone) *j.lft: chsd ldrs: wnt 2nd 6th: hit 3 out and last: lost 2nd towards fin* **9/1**	73+
P44F	**4**	*10*	**Mobasher (IRE)**[9] 4474 7-11-2.................... SamThomas (Miss Venetia Williams) *nt fluent: in rr fr 8th: no threat after* **4/1**[2]	66
0PP	**P**		**Dannymolone (IRE)**[82] 3236 7-11-2.................... BarryKeniry (M D Hammond) *in last pl: bhd fr 8th: t.o whn p.u bef 10th* **40/1**	—
0-5P	**P**		**Cupla Cairde**[37] 3955 6-11-2 75.................... TomSiddall (O Brennan) *j.rt: chsd ldrs: lost pl 7th: bhd whn p.u bef 11th* **20/1**	—
325/	**P**		**Noble Hymn**[740] 4392 13-11-2....................(t) LarryMcGrath (C A Mulhall) *in tch: hmpd 5th and 7th: sn lost pl: t.o fr 8th: p.u bef 3 out* **80/1**	—
43PP	**U**		**Simoun (IRE)**[35] 4014 8-11-2 115.................... AndrewThornton (B N Pollock) *in tch to 7th: lost pl 10th: t.o whn tried refuse and uns rdr 3 out* **9/2**[3]	—
4-2P	**P**		**The Rising Moon (IRE)**[129] 2291 7-11-2.................... APMcCoy (Jonjo O'Neill) *hld up in raer: hit 6th: hdwy 9th: 4th and wkng qckly whn p.u bef 3 out* **9/4**[1]	—
6P42	**P**		**Dramatic Quest**[11] 4454 9-11-2 93....................(v) WayneHutchinson (A G Juckes) *in tch: reminders 7th: sn lost pl: bhd whn blnd 10th: t.o whn p.u bef 3 out* **6/1**	—

5m 35.1s (32.40) **Going Correction** +1.425s/f (Heav)
WFA 5 from 6yo+ 5lb **10** Ran SP% **116.6**
Speed ratings: **92,84,84,80,— —,—,—,—,—** CSF £202.76 TOTE £20.30: £5.00, £2.30, £3.40; EX 100.60.
Owner J R Cornwall **Bred** Loic Malivet And Roger-Yves Simon **Trained** Long Clawson, Leics

FOCUS
The winner, rated 110 over hurdles, was opening his account with a wide-margin success on his 24th start over fences, value for 25l. Suspect form and tricky to rate.

NOTEBOOK
Kercabellec(FR), seemingly fully exposed over fences, turned this into a procession but he was probably the only one in the line-up who truly handled the testing conditions. *(op 22-1 tchd 20-1)*
Iris's Prince stuck on in his own time to snatch a remote second place. The ground was against him.
Courant D'Air(IRE), making his chasing bow, continually jumped left-handed and, clumsy over the final three fences, lost out on second prize near the line. *(op 8-1)*
Mobasher(IRE) finds jumping fences tricky and he never figured. *(op 6-1)*
The Rising Moon(IRE), like so many from this yard, seems to have become lost in the wilderness and he emptied in a matter of strides before the champion wisely called it a day. *Official explanation: trainer was unable to offer any explanation for poor form shown (op 5-2 tchd 11-4)*

4634 PAUL TESTO'S 50TH BIRTHDAY NOVICES' H'CAP HURDLE (10 hdls) 2m 6f

3:40 (3:40) (Class 3) (0-130,119) 4-Y-0+ **£11,060** (£3,247; £1,623; £810)

Form				RPR
264P	**1**		**Extra Smooth**[47] 3792 5-10-5 **98**.................... WayneHutchinson (C C Bealby) *chsd ldrs: led after 7th: j.lft last: rdn rt out* **16/1**	104+
11	**2**	*7*	**Brumous (IRE)**[61] 3545 6-11-12 **119**.................... LeightonAspell (O Sherwood) *trckd ldrs: wnt 2nd 3 out: kpt on same pce run-in* **9/4**[1]	117
2F4	**3**	*19*	**Rainbow Tree**[11] 4452 6-9-7 **93**....................(b) TomMessenger(7) (C C Bealby) *hld up: hdwy 6th: wnt modest 3rd appr 2 out* **14/1**	72
011	**4**	*7*	**Atlantic Jane**[37] 3962 6-11-2 **119**.................... MichaelO'Connell(10) (Mrs S J Smith) *trckd ldrs: outpcd 6th: sn lost pl: kpt on run-in* **3/1**[2]	91
1410	**5**	*15*	**Birdwatch**[31] 4067 8-11-4 **111**....................(b) RichardMcGrath (K G Reveley) *j. slowly: led to 4th: lost pl after 6th: sn bhd* **11/1**	68
P	**P**		**Balasari (IRE)**[131] 2186 6-10-11 **104**.................... NeilMulholland (M D Hammond) *hld up in last: drvn along and lost pl after 5th: sn t.o: p.u bef 7th* **66/1**	—
0033	**P**		**River Ripples (IRE)**[36] 3982 7-10-7 **100**.................... JasonMaguire (T R George) *hld up: hdwy and promient 4th: rdn and lost pl appr 8th: t.o whn p.u bef next* **7/2**[3]	—
4P1P	**P**		**Day Of Claies (FR)**[23] 4215 5-11-10 **117**....................(b) CarlLlewellyn (N A Twiston-Davies) *trckd ldrs: led 4th: hit 7th: sn hdd & wknd: remote 4th whn p.u appr 2 out* **13/2**	—

5m 48.0s (19.70) **Going Correction** +1.10s/f (Heav) **8** Ran SP% **113.7**
Speed ratings: **108,105,98,96,90 —,—,—** CSF £53.08 CT £531.55 TOTE £21.10: £3.30, £1.50, £2.40; EX 84.70.
Owner C Martin **Bred** N Shutts **Trained** Barrowby, Lincs

FOCUS
Just a two-horse race from the third-last flight. A big step up from the winner, but the second ran to his mark and there is no reason to think it was a fluke.

NOTEBOOK
Extra Smooth, suited by the give underfoot, broke his duck over hurdles at the seventh attempt. He *should make a better chaser next time. Official explanation: trainer said, regarding the improved form shown, gelding could not go the pace last time out on quicker ground, but was suited by today's softer going (op 14-1)*
Brumous(IRE), making his handicap debut, went in pursuit of the winner but had to give best on the run-in. He too should make a better chaser than hurdler. *(op 2-1 tchd 5-2)*
Rainbow Tree, with the blinkers back on, did not see the trip out anywhere near as well as the first two. *(op 12-1)*
Atlantic Jane, making her handicap debut, was quite keen at first but she dropped everything going out into the country for the final time. *(op 4-1 tchd 11-4)*
Birdwatch would not have a cut at his hurdles and once headed he soon lost interest. *(op 9-1)*
River Ripples(IRE), dropping back in trip, stopped to nothing three out and is struggling to see his races out at present. *(op 4-1)*

4635 RASE VETERINARY CENTRE H'CAP CHASE (14 fncs) 2m 6f 110y

4:10 (4:11) (Class 3) (0-135,130) 5-Y-0+ **£14,313** (£4,202; £2,101; £1,049)

Form				RPR
1635	**1**		**Little Big Horse (IRE)**[106] 2767 10-11-8 **126**.................... DavidO'Meara (Mrs S J Smith) *chsd ldrs: shkn up 7th: wnt 2nd next: chalng whn hit 3 out: slt ld last: styd on u.p* **15/8**[1]	140+
FU22	**2**	*1¾*	**Big Rob (IRE)**[33] 4037 7-11-5 **123**.................... LeightonAspell (B G Powell) *j.rt: led 2nd: qcknd 8th: hdd last: no ex* **11/4**[2]	133
3114	**3**	*24*	**Silver Knight**[99] 2875 8-11-9 **127**.................... RussGarritty (T D Easterby) *trckd ldrs: cl 2nd whn mstke 8th: wknd 11th* **4/1**[3]	117+
3100	**4**	*9*	**Latimer's Place**[15] 4374 10-11-4 **122**.................... JimmyMcCarthy (J A Geake) *wnt prom 5th: lost pl 8th: sn bhd* **4/1**[3]	99
11P3	**F**		**Kid'Z'Play (IRE)**[143] 1531 10-11-12 **130**.................... RichardMcGrath (J S Goldie) *led to 2nd: chsng ldrs whn fell 6th* **20/1**	—

6m 14.9s (28.50) **Going Correction** +1.425s/f (Heav) **5** Ran SP% **106.2**
Speed ratings: **107,106,98,94,—** CSF £7.02 TOTE £3.30: £1.30, £1.90; EX 7.40.
Owner Paul J Dixon **Bred** A D C Cathers **Trained** High Eldwick, W Yorks

FOCUS
A poor turnout for a guaranteed prize of £22,000. In the end course specialist Little Big Horse, who looked well in, saw it out just the better than the progressive runner-up.

NOTEBOOK
Little Big Horse(IRE) loves it round here and recorded his fifth course win. He knows exactly where the winning line is and as soon as he crossed it he pulled himself up. *(op 9-4 tchd 7-4)*
Big Rob(IRE) continually gave away ground jumping to his right. He travelled the better in front but did not see the trip out quite as well as the winner. His two career wins have been on left-handed tracks. *(op 15-8)*
Silver Knight, absent since December, really needs further but ran here as if in need of the outing. *(op 9-2 tchd 5-1 and 7-2)*
Latimer's Place, still 5lb higher than when winning at Sandown in December, continues to struggle. *Official explanation: trainer said gelding scoped dirty after the race (op 5-1)*

4636 MACMILLAN CANCER RELIEF H'CAP CHASE (19 fncs) 3m 4f 110y

4:40 (4:41) (Class 4) (0-115,114) 5-Y-0+ **£6,506** (£1,910; £955; £477)

Form				RPR
1640	**1**		**Bang And Blame (IRE)**[16] 4356 10-10-5 **98**.......... MichaelMcAlister(5) (M W Easterby) *led 3rd: wnt clr 4 out: hrd rdn run-in: jst hld on* **13/2**[3]	115+
P031	**2**	*½*	**Lazy But Lively (IRE)**[8] 4492 10-10-0 **88** oh6.................... KeithMercer (R F Fisher) *in rr: hdwy to chse ldrs 14th: wnt 2nd 4 out: hit next: styd on run-in: jst hld* **7/1**	103
3464	**3**	*13*	**Runaway Bishop (USA)**[17] 4321 11-10-1 **89**.................... RichardHobson (J R Cornwall) *in rr: hdwy and promient 12th: one pce fr 4 out* **10/1**	92+
214P	**4**	*dist*	**D J Flippance (IRE)**[29] 4111 11-11-1 **103**....................(p) RichardMcGrath (A Parker) *in rr: reminders 10th: lost pl 15th: lft distant 4th 2 out: btn total of 72 l* **14/1**	—
05P5	**P**		**Heidi III (FR)**[16] 4356 11-11-2 **104**....................(p) GLee (M D Hammond) *wnt prom 6th: lost pl 9th: t.o whn p.u after 12th* **9/1**	—
61PP	**P**		**Briar's Mist (IRE)**[17] 4316 9-10-3 **94**....................(bt) StephenCraine(3) (C Grant) *w ldrs: lost pl 4th: t.o whn p.u bef 2 out* **17/2**	—
-FU0	**P**		**Celioso (IRE)**[15] 4374 9-11-8 **110**.................... DavidO'Meara (Mrs S J Smith) *chsd ldrs: mstkes: bhd fr 11th: t.o whn p.u after next* **14/1**	—
1U43	**P**		**Graceful Dancer**[14] 4395 9-10-13 **101**.................... JamesDavies (B G Powell) *chsd ldrs: j. slowly and lost pl 14th: t.o whn p.u bef 3 out* **4/1**[1]	—

0223 **P** **Hawk's Landing (IRE)**[16] [4348] 9-11-8 **110**............................ APMcCoy —
(Jonjo O'Neill) *hld up: wnt prom 7th: wnt 2nd 14th: wknd 4 out: bhd whn p.u bef 2 out* **9/2**[2]

P1PP **P** **Interdit (FR)**[16] [4345] 10-11-9 **111**.................................... WilsonRenwick —
(Mrs B K Thomson) *led to 3rd: reminders 12th: lost pl 14th: t.o whn p.u bef 3 out* **20/1**

64F2 **F** **Jack Martin (IRE)**[14] [4390] 9-11-9 **114**....................(p) WilliamKennedy(3) —
(S Gollings) *wnt prom 7th: blnd 10th: j. slowly and lost pl 14th: poor 5th whn fell 2 out* **16/1**

8m 10.6s (32.60) **Going Correction** +1.425s/f (Heav) **11** Ran SP% **117.6**
Speed ratings: **107,106,103,—,—** —,—,—,—,— — CSF £52.10 CT £455.78 TOTE £7.40: £1.70, £3.10, £3.60; EX 76.00.
Owner Edward C Wilkin **Bred** Miss Sandra Hunter **Trained** Sheriff Hutton, N Yorks

FOCUS
A true test in the conditions. The winner was back to his best and the second ran his best race since his Bangor third in December.

NOTEBOOK
Bang And Blame(IRE), two stone higher than the first of his three Sedgefield wins, made this a true test. He forged clear starting the final turn but in the end it was a close call. *(op 6-1)*
Lazy But Lively(IRE), out of the handicap and in effect 8lb higher, was soon making hard work of it. He went in pursuit of the winner and in the end was only just held at bay. *(op 13-2 tchd 15-2)*
Runaway Bishop(USA) plodded round and in the end that was sufficient to secure third prize.
D J Flippance(IRE), tried in cheekpieces, eventually completed.
Graceful Dancer, back in action two weeks after her punishing race at Warwick, dropped out with *a slow jump a mile from home and eventually gave up the cause. Official explanation: trainer was unable to offer any explanation for poor form shown (op 11-2)*
Hawk's Landing(IRE) went in pursuit of the winner but his stamina seemed to give out completely and he looked a tired horse when throwing in the towel. *(op 11-2)*

4637 SCUNTHORPE STANDARD OPEN NATIONAL HUNT FLAT RACE 2m 1f 110y
5:10 (5:11) (Class 6) 4-6-Y-0 **£1,850** (£539; £269)

Form				RPR
2	**1**		**Ovide (FR)**[57] [3623] 4-10-7 .... GLee (J Howard Johnson) *trckd ldrs: led over 3f out: clr over 1f out: readily* **11/8**[1]	100+
002	**2**	*8*	**Tuckers Bay**[32] [4059] 5-10-2 .... AdamPogson(5) (J R Holt) *chsd ldrs: kpt on fnl 2f: tk 2nd pl ins last: no ch w wnr* **25/1**	88
	3	*½*	**Sir Boreas Hawk** 4-10-4 .... DougieCostello(3) (G A Swinbank) *hld up in mid-div: hdwy 7f out: wnt 2nd over 2f out: kpt on same pce* **11/1**	88+
1	**4**	*3 ½*	**Golden Parachute (IRE)**[69] [3421] 5-11-0 .... TomMessenger(7) (C C Bealby) *led tl over 3f out: one pce* **5/1**[3]	98
	5	*5*	**Lord Gee (IRE)** 5-11-0 .... LeightonAspell (O Sherwood) *hld up in rr: hdwy 7f out: one pce fnl 3f: eased towards fin* **7/2**[2]	88+
	6	*6*	**Scarecrow (IRE)** 5-10-11 .... StephenCraine(3) (Mrs P Sly) *chsd ldrs: outpcd 7f out: no threat after* **20/1**	80
0-20	**7**	*15*	**Cardinal Sinn (UAE)**[117] [2565] 5-11-0 .... CarlLlewellyn (M Pitman) *racd wd in mid-field: lost pl 6f out* **11/1**	65
	8	*5*	**George The Grey** 5-10-11 .... WilliamKennedy(3) (S Gollings) *mid-div: lost pl 6f* **33/1**	60
	9	*7*	**Gemini Storm** 6-10-11 .... LeeVickers(3) (O Brennan) *in raer: bhd fnl 6f* **33/1**	53
	10	*26*	**The Hero Sullivan (IRE)** 5-11-0 .... WayneHutchinson (C C Bealby) *prom: lost pl over 4f out: eased and bhd fnl 2f* **33/1**	27
	11	*19*	**Booster Divin (FR)** 4-9-11 .... CareyWilliamson(10) (M J Gingell) *in raer: rdn and lost pl 9f out: t.o 5f out* **66/1**	1
	12	*18*	**Royal Factor** 6-11-0 .... AndrewTinkler (C Smith) *mid-div: lost pl 9f out: t.o 5f out* **40/1**	—

4m 36.8s (20.30) **Going Correction** +1.10s/f (Heav)
WFA 4 from 5yo 7lb 5 from 6yo 4lb **12** Ran SP% **119.0**
Speed ratings: **98,94,94,92,90 87,81,78,75,64 55,47** CSF £48.47 TOTE £2.20: £1.20, £4.80, £2.30; EX 44.30 Place 6 £145.88, Place 5 £112.62.
Owner Andrea & Graham Wylie **Bred** F Rimaud **Trained** Billy Row, Co Durham

FOCUS
A sound pace and a ready winner, rated value for 12l. The runner-up improved 10lb on his recent second but this is probably not form to get carried away with.

NOTEBOOK
Ovide(FR) travelled strongly and took this with the minimum of fuss. He seemed to relish the soft ground. *(op 13-8)*
Tuckers Bay, having her fourth start, showed her improved Southwell effort was no fluke.
Sir Boreas Hawk, who has size and scope, looked booked for second spot until tiring in the closing stages. *(op 7-1)*
Golden Parachute(IRE), under his penalty, was racing on much softer ground and deserves credit for taking them along until the winner took over the baton. *(tchd 11-2)*
Lord Gee(IRE), who looks a potential chaser, gave the leaders start but then proved too slow to pick them up. He is bred for stamina not speed. *(op 9-2)*
T/Jkpt: Not won. T/Plt: £136.40 to a £1 stake. Pool: £48,783.80. 260.95 winning tickets. T/Qpdt: £57.60 to a £1 stake. Pool: £2,812.90. 36.10 winning tickets. WG

[1974]WORCESTER (L-H)
Sunday, March 26

OFFICIAL GOING: Good (good to soft in places)
The jockeys thought that the going was slower than the official description and there was further rain during the afternoon.
Wind: Moderate across Weather: Rain after race two

4638 NEW TOP FLOOR GRANDSTAND HOSPITALITY BOXES MAIDEN HURDLE (DIV I) (12 hdls) 3m
2:20 (2:20) (Class 5) 4-Y-0+ **£2,398** (£698; £349)

Form				RPR
/064	**1**		**Return Ticket**[28] [4128] 7-11-2 .... RichardJohnson (R T Phillips) *hld up and bhd: hdwy appr 8th: hit 9th: rdn to ld after 2 out: hit last: drvn out* **6/4**[1]	103+
1-5	**2**	*3*	**Young Dude (IRE)**[33] [4032] 7-11-2 .... MickFitzgerald (Jonjo O'Neill) *hld up in tch: bmpd and rdr lost iron briefly first: hit 9th: led appr 3 out: rdn and hdd after 2 out: stdy on same pce fla* **11/4**[2]	99+
U-F3	**3**	*10*	**Wyle Post (IRE)**[16] [4349] 7-10-9 .... RichardSpate(7) (Mrs K Waldron) *hld up and bhd: hdwy 9th: wknd 2 out* **12/1**	88
554P	**4**	*dist*	**Riffles**[65] [3478] 6-10-4 ....(t) ShaneWalsh(5) (Mrs A J Bowlby) *hld up in mid-div: hdwy 6th: wknd appr 3 out* **14/1**	—
4-00	**5**	*13*	**Dodger McCartney**[17] [4327] 8-11-2 ....(t) RJGreene (K Bishop) *a bhd: j.rt 6th: t.o fr 7th* **40/1**	—
B00	**6**	*1*	**Desperate Dex (IRE)**[127] [2340] 6-11-2 .... JodieMogford (G J Smith) *led to 7th: sn rdn: led 8th tl appr 3 out: sn wknd: t.o* **66/1**	—
6060	**7**	*30*	**Bradders**[59] [3579] 4-10-7 .... TomScudamore (J R Jenkins) *hld up in tch: j.lft 1st: wknd appr 3 out: t.o* **40/1**	—
	8	*28*	**Kings Leader (IRE)**[806] [3296] 9-11-2 .... ChristianWilliams (Evan Williams) *a bhd: t.o fr 8th* **4/1**[3]	—
	P		**Mr Fast (ARG)**[25] 9-10-13 .... ColinBolger(3) (J Gallagher) *hld up in mid-div: j. slowly 7th: sn bhd: t.o 9th: p.u bef 2 out* **40/1**	—
00-F	**P**		**King Of Scots**[20] [4278] 5-10-11 .... MarkNicolls(5) (R J Price) *hld up towards rr: reminders after 6th: sn rdn: t.o fr 8th: t.o bef last* **66/1**	—
000P	**P**		**Shinjiru (USA)**[33] [4032] 6-10-9 .... MissFayeBramley(7) (P A Blockley) *chsd ldr: led 7th to 8th: wknd after 9th: pckd 3 out: t.o whn p.u bef 2 out* **100/1**	—

6m 24.7s (35.50) **Going Correction** +1.175s/f (Heav)
WFA 4 from 5yo+ 9lb **11** Ran SP% **112.3**
Speed ratings: **87,86,82,—,—** —,—,—,—,— — CSF £5.29 TOTE £2.70: £1.10, £1.50, £2.60; EX 5.10.
Owner Mr & Mrs F C Welch **Bred** Mrs S C Welch **Trained** Adlestrop, Gloucs

FOCUS
A modest maiden hurdle, rated by splitting the difference between the first two.

NOTEBOOK
Return Ticket ◆, a half-brother to the staying hurdler His Nibs, was certainly not inconvenienced by a big step up in distance. He can defy a penalty in this sort of company. *(tchd 11-8)*
Young Dude(IRE) ◆ was another trying a much longer trip. He made sure the winner did not have things his own way on ground that may have been on the soft side for him. He is capable of going one better. *(op 2-1 tchd 15-8)*
Wyle Post(IRE), pulled up on his only previous start over hurdles in June 2004, had finished third *in a two-mile hunter chase last time. He ran well over a distance that could be beyond his best. (tchd 14-1)*
Dodger McCartney *Official explanation: jockey said gelding was unsuited by good, good to soft in places ground*

4639 ENJOY THE NEWLY REFURBISHED GRANDSTAND H'CAP CHASE (15 fncs) 2m 4f 110y
2:50 (2:50) (Class 4) (0-100,100) 5-Y-0+ **£5,204** (£1,528; £764; £381)

Form				RPR
23PP	**1**		**Jolejoker**[39] [3920] 8-11-7 **95** .... RichardJohnson (R Lee) *hld up and bhd: hdwy 9th: led 2 out: r.o wl* **12/1**	110+
5P-1	**2**	*7*	**Haile Selassie**[44] [3844] 6-11-8 **96** .... MarkBradburne (W Jenks) *hld up: hdwy 7th: led after 3 out to 2 out: one pce* **9/1**	103
6014	**3**	*4*	**Jack Fuller (IRE)**[16] [4348] 9-11-8 **96** ....(b) PhilipHide (P Winkworth) *hld up in tch: sltly hmpd 8th: 5 l 3rd and hld whn mstke last* **5/1**[3]	101+
2P63	**4**	*15*	**Barren Lands**[17] [4332] 11-11-5 **93** .... PJBrennan (K Bishop) *a.p: lft in ld 8th: rdn and hdd after 3 out: wknd 2 out* **6/1**	81
3P50	**5**	*2 ½*	**Message Recu (FR)**[13] [4426] 10-11-2 **90** ....(v) JoeTizzard (C L Tizzard) *chsd ldr tl appr 3rd: rdn and wknd after 6th: sn bhd: no ch whn blnd 3 out* **12/1**	78+
F400	**6**	*dist*	**Tiger Tips Lad (IRE)**[38] [3949] 7-11-12 **100** ....(t) AntonyEvans (N A Twiston-Davies) *j.rt: hld up in mid-div: struggling whn mstke 4 out: t.o* **9/2**[2]	—
3424	**7**	*2*	**Rookery Lad**[9] [4476] 8-11-8 **96** .... DaveCrosse (C N Kellett) *prom: hit 5th: rdn 11th: wknd 4 out: t.o* **8/1**	—
-232	**F**		**Very Special One (IRE)**[42] [3887] 6-11-8 **96** .... TomScudamore (K C Bailey) *fell 2nd* **7/2**[1]	—
1440	**F**		**Barella (IRE)**[13] [4427] 7-11-2 **95** ....(b[1]) HowieEphgrave(5) (L Corcoran) *led tl fell 8th* **25/1**	—
/PP-	**P**		**Red Socialite (IRE)**[375] [4405] 9-11-12 **100** .... TomDoyle (D R Gandolfo) *j. bdly rt: a in rr: t.o whn p.u bef 4 out* **40/1**	—

5m 26.5s (19.00) **Going Correction** +1.175s/f (Heav) **10** Ran SP% **114.1**
Speed ratings: **110,107,105,100,99** —,—,—,—,— CSF £111.37 CT £613.17 TOTE £12.90: £3.80, £3.10, £2.40; EX 167.50.
Owner D E Edwards **Bred** R Burton **Trained** Byton, H'fords

FOCUS
A moderate contest but probably one to be positive about with the winner taking a big step up on form.

NOTEBOOK
Jolejoker came back to form on this first venture into handicaps. His trainer took the blame for *running him over the wrong trips when he was pulled up on his previous two outings. Official explanation: trainer said, regarding the improved form shown, gelding was better suited by today's trip (2m 4 1/2f) (op 10-1)*
Haile Selassie, trying a longer distance, was clearly second best having gone up 7lb for what had looked a fortunate win at Bangor. *(tchd 8-1)*
Jack Fuller(IRE) is usually campaigned over right-handed courses and already looked booked for third when missing out at the last. *(op 9-2)*
Barren Lands could not take advantage of having been dropped another 6lb. *(op 13-2)*
Message Recu(FR) did not find a switch back to a visor instead of blinkers doing the trick. *(op 16-1)*
Rookery Lad *Official explanation: jockey said gelding had breathing problem (op 15-2)*
Red Socialite(IRE) *Official explanation: jockey said gelding hung violently right-handed (op 22-1)*

4640 MISS WORCESTERSHIRE COMPETITION RACE NIGHT 6TH MAY NOVICES' H'CAP HURDLE (10 hdls) 2m 4f
3:20 (3:20) (Class 5) (0-85,87) 4-Y-0+ **£2,398** (£698; £349)

Form				RPR
3-00	**1**		**Le Forezien (FR)**[90] [2994] 7-11-2 **82** ....(t) BernieWharfe(7) (C J Gray) *hld up in tch: led after 7th: clr appr 2 out: drvn out flat* **16/1**	93+
6005	**2**	*4*	**Elle Roseador**[68] [3437] 7-11-9 **82** ....(p) JamieGoldstein (M Madgwick) *a.p: rdn after 7th: styd on flat: nt trble wnr* **7/1**[3]	86
65P/	**3**	*7*	**Yaiyna Tango (FR)**[358] 11-11-10 **83** .... PaulMoloney (Miss L Day) *a.p: chsd wnr fr 3 out tl wknd flat* **40/1**	81+
4220	**4**	*1 ¾*	**Seraph**[9] [4479] 6-11-3 **83** .... DarrenO'Dwyer(7) (O Brennan) *hld up in tch: nt fluent 5th: outpcd after 7th: rallied 2 out: wknd flat* **4/1**[1]	79+
2P0P	**5**	*1*	**Deo Gratias (POL)**[72] [3367] 6-11-7 **85** ....(t) RobertLucey-Butler(5) (M Pitman) *chsd ldr to 7th: sn rdn: wknd appr 3 out* **4/1**[1]	79
/500	**6**	*20*	**Phar The Best (IRE)**[11] [4449] 9-11-12 **85** ....(p) JohnMcNamara (Mrs A L M King) *a bhd* **9/1**	59
000P	**7**	*dist*	**Carnt Spell**[31] [4080] 5-11-8 **81** .... JimCrowley (J T Stimpson) *led tl after 7th: sn rdn: wknd appr 2 out: t.o* **25/1**	—
653P	**P**		**Desertmore Chief (IRE)**[57] [3613] 7-11-12 **85** .... JodieMogford (G J Smith) *a bhd: t.o 6th: p.u bef 3 out* **8/1**	—
P06F	**P**		**Financial Future**[15] [4367] 6-11-12 **85** .... OllieMcPhail (C Roberts) *a bhd: rdn after 6th: sn t.o: p.u bef 3 out* **5/1**[2]	—

45P6 **P** **Pick Of The Crop**[6] [3597] 5-11-11 **84**........................(b[1]) TomScudamore —
(J R Jenkins) *a bhd: hit 4th: mstke 6th: t.o whn p.u bef 3 out* **12/1**

5m 19.8s (31.80) **Going Correction** +1.175s/f (Heav) **10** Ran SP% **110.1**
Speed ratings: **83,81,78,77,77 69**,—,—,—,— CSF £115.70 CT £4104.85 TOTE £17.10: £4.70, £1.70, £17.50; EX 147.20.

Owner S C Botham **Bred** P Coyne-Bodin And Paul Coyne **Trained** Moorland, Somerset

FOCUS
Plating-class form, rated through the second.

NOTEBOOK
Le Forezien(FR) finally justified connections' faith in him after suffering from chipped bones and undergoing a wind operation since coming over from France. It seems that the fitting of a tongue tie may have done the trick but the form does not amount to much. *(op 14-1)*

Elle Roseador again ran well in the cheekpieces off a mark 12lb higher than when she was in a handicap two outings ago. *(op 15-2)*

Yaiyna Tango(FR), last seen when pulled up in a point almost a year ago, looks a shadow of his former self. *(op 33-1)*

Seraph did not find a return to a longer trip the answer. *(op 7-2)*

Deo Gratias(POL) would not have been helped by the rain that had got into the ground. *(op 9-2)*

4641 ARENA LEISURE PLC MARES' ONLY H'CAP HURDLE (8 hdls) 2m
3:50 (3:50) (Class 3) (0-125,123) 4-Y-0+ **£7,807** (£2,292; £1,146; £572)

Form RPR
241 **1** **Tessanoora**[31] [4074] 5-10-10 **107**.. MickFitzgerald 120+
(N J Henderson) *hld up towards rr: hdwy and hit 3 out: led last: drvn out* **4/1**[2]

-223 **2** *4* **Barton Flower**[119] [2515] 5-9-10 **98**.. DarylJacob[(5)] 104
(D P Keane) *led: rdn and hdd last: no ex* **5/1**[3]

6030 **3** *12* **Bonny Grey**[13] [4420] 8-10-7 **104**.. OllieMcPhail 98
(D Burchell) *a.p: rdn appr 3 out: wknd appr last* **9/1**

1123 **4** *2 ½* **Magical Legend**[13] [4429] 5-10-6 **108**........................... HowieEphgrave[(5)] 102+
(L Corcoran) *prom: n.m.r and lost pl after 2nd: rdn after 5th: mstke 2 out: styd on: n.d* **10/3**[1]

565 **5** *9* **White Dove (FR)**[44] [3848] 8-9-11 **97** oh6............................ JoffretHuet[(3)] 80
(Ian Williams) *prom: rdr dropped whip sn after 5th: wknd appr 2 out* **16/1**

PP0 **6** *nk* **Princesse Grec (FR)**[38] [3950] 8-10-0 **97** oh2............(v[1]) TomScudamore 79
(M Scudamore) *w ldr tl rdn after 5th: sn wknd* **50/1**

30-2 **7** *7* **Zalda**[169] [1677] 5-11-11 **122**.. RichardJohnson 97
(P J Hobbs) *hld up and bhd: hdwy 3 out: sn rdn: wknd after 2 out* **10/3**[1]

3466 **8** *10* **Miss Pebbles (IRE)**[36] [3979] 6-10-6 **113**................ JosephStevenson[(10)] 78
(R Dickin) *hld up and bhd: hdwy appr 3 out: wknd 2 out* **14/1**

523P **9** *19* **Koral Bay (FR)**[14] [4396] 5-9-13 **103** ow1.................. MrSWaley-Cohen[(7)] 49
(R Waley-Cohen) *prom to 5th: no ch whn j.rt 2 out* **25/1**

4m 3.30s (14.90) **Going Correction** +1.175s/f (Heav) **9** Ran SP% **111.2**
Speed ratings: **109,107,101,99,95 95,91,86,77** CSF £23.29 CT £161.19 TOTE £3.50: £1.60, £1.60, £2.20; EX 27.30.

Owner Miss Tessa Henderson **Bred** R D And Mrs J S Chugg **Trained** Upper Lambourn, Berks

FOCUS
This did not turn out to be as competitive as expected, but was still the best race on the card. The winner was value for 7l.

NOTEBOOK
Tessanoora, kept to mares-only company on this switch to handicaps, only had to be kept up to her work to make sure of it on the long run-in. *(op 7-2)*

Barton Flower could not hold the winner on ground that was on the soft side for her. She does not look harshly treated and can soon get off the mark. *(op 6-1)*

Bonny Grey is fully exposed and the Handicapper does seem to have her measure. *(tchd 8-1 and 10-1)*

Magical Legend, reverting to a shorter distance, has gone up a total of 10lb since switching to handicaps without actually winning. *(op 7-2 tchd 3-1)*

Zalda was 6lb higher than when runner-up on her previous outing in the race formerly known as the Free Handicap at Chepstow last October. She ran as if this outing may have been needed. *(op 3-1 tchd 11-4)*

4642 NEW TOP FLOOR GRANDSTAND HOSPITALITY BOXES MAIDEN HURDLE (DIV II) (12 hdls) 3m
4:20 (4:20) (Class 5) 4-Y-0+ **£2,398** (£698; £349)

Form RPR
214 **1** **Hot 'N' Holy**[66] [3466] 7-11-2.. RWalsh 100+
(P F Nicholls) *hld up: hdwy and nt fluent 8th: led last: drvn out* **4/9**[1]

604 **2** *1 ½* **Forest Miller**[19] [4284] 7-11-2.. RichardJohnson 97+
(R T Phillips) *a.p: led 8th: mstke 9th: rdn and hdd last: nt qckn towards fin* **17/2**[3]

3 *20* **Go For One (IRE)**[364] 7-11-2.. WarrenMarston 79+
(D J Wintle) *hld up: hdwy 8th: ev ch after 9th: hit 3 out: wknd 2 out* **7/1**[2]

40 **4** *13* **Man Of Mine**[31] [4072] 5-11-2.. MickFitzgerald 63
(Mrs H Dalton) *prom tl wknd after 9th* **9/1**

3030 **5** *5* **The Langer (IRE)**[3] [4589] 6-10-13.. ColinBolger[(3)] 58
(S T Lewis) *led to 8th: wknd appr 3 out* **100/1**

50P **6** *dist* **Oakfield Legend**[136] [2144] 5-11-2.. OllieMcPhail —
(P S Payne) *a bhd: mstke 4th: lost tch fr 7th: t.o* **150/1**

7 *dist* **Celtic Starlight** 7-10-9.. HenryOliver —
(R Dickin) *plld hrd: sn in tch: j. slowly 7th: wknd after 8th: t.o* **50/1**

P **Regal Fantasy (IRE)**[104] 6-10-9.. PJBrennan —
(P A Blockley) *prom tl wknd appr 8th: t.o whn p.u bef 3 out* **50/1**

P **P** **Echo Blu (IRE)**[55] [3653] 8-11-2.. PaulMoloney —
(Miss Joanne Priest) *hld up: blnd 8th: sn bhd: t.o whn p.u bef 2 out* **50/1**

6m 25.1s (35.90) **Going Correction** +1.175s/f (Heav) **9** Ran SP% **109.8**
Speed ratings: **87,86,79,75,73** —,—,—,— CSF £4.35 TOTE £1.40: £1.10, £2.10, £1.80; EX 3.60.

Owner Paul K Barber & C G Roach **Bred** R Chugg **Trained** Ditcheat, Somerset

FOCUS
An uncompetitive maiden hurdle. The winner ran to the level of his Taunton hurdle debut.

NOTEBOOK
Hot 'N' Holy made pretty hard work of landing the odds on this step up to three miles. Like most from his stable, his future will eventually lie over fences. *(op 8-13 tchd 2-5)*

Forest Miller ◆ gave the supporters of the odds-on favourite plenty of anxious moments. He appears to be going the right way and can find a suitable opportunity. *(op 6-1)*

Go For One(IRE) had not been seen since the second of his back-to-back wins in Irish points almost exactly a year ago. This was a reasonable debut under Rules. *(op 8-1)*

Man Of Mine at least seemed to settle better than he had done in his two bumpers. *(op 8-1)*

4643 TRY THE NEWLY REFURBISHED RESTAURANT H'CAP CHASE (18 fncs) 2m 7f 110y
4:50 (4:50) (Class 5) (0-95,95) 5-Y-0+ **£3,253** (£955; £477; £238)

Form RPR
4PP3 **1** **Pardini (USA)**[8] [4499] 7-10-13 **82**..(v) JohnMcNamara 99+
(M F Harris) *hld up: hdwy after 9th: led 11th: rdn appr 2 out: hung lft appr last: drvn out* **4/1**[1]

1200 **2** *6* **Irishkawa Bellevue (FR)**[36] [3987] 8-11-2 **85**....................(b) DaveCrosse 96
(Jean-Rene Auvray) *prom: mstke and lost pl 2nd: hld up in mid-div: rdn appr 10th: sn outpcd: rallied appr 4 out: wnt 2nd last:* **4/1**[1]

/1P4 **3** *8* **Mill Bank (IRE)**[55] [3656] 11-11-7 **90**.. PaulMoloney 95+
(Evan Williams) *prom: hit 8th: led appr 10th to 11th: mstke 12th: rdn after 14th: wknd last* **6/1**[2]

0043 **4** *2 ½* **Instant Appeal**[28] [4132] 9-11-2 **85**.. PhilipHide 86
(P Winkworth) *hld up: hdwy 14th: wknd 4 out* **4/1**[1]

0F3P **5** *dist* **Simple Glory (IRE)**[23] [4214] 7-11-3 **86**.. HenryOliver —
(R Dickin) *hld up in tch: wknd 12th* **10/1**

PPFP **P** **Terminology**[6] [4553] 8-11-2 **90**..(p) MarkNicolls[(5)] —
(K C Bailey) *hld up in tch: wknd 14th: t.o whn p.u bef 4 out* **28/1**

P4-2 **P** **Blank Canvas (IRE)**[16] [4352] 8-11-6 **89**.. TomScudamore —
(K C Bailey) *a bhd: mstke 1st: pckd 4th: t.o whn p.u bef 12th* **9/1**

-0PP **P** **Capricorn**[7] [4526] 8-11-2 **85**..(b) BenjaminHitchcott —
(Miss L Day) *w ldr: j.rt 2nd: mstke 7th: wknd 10th: t.o whn p.u after 13th* **50/1**

/PP- **P** **Pontius**[533] [1654] 9-11-12 **95**.. AntonyEvans —
(N A Twiston-Davies) *led: j. slowly 1st: hdd appr 10th: rdn and wknd appr 4 out: p.u bef 3 out* **17/2**[3]

6m 26.8s (31.90) **Going Correction** +1.175s/f (Heav) **9** Ran SP% **109.3**
Speed ratings: **93,91,88,87**,— —,—,—,— CSF £19.14 CT £84.27 TOTE £3.90: £1.10, £1.90, £2.20; EX 66.30.

Owner Prevention & Detection (Holdings) Ltd **Bred** Almagro De Actividades Commerciales S A **Trained** Edgcote, Northants

FOCUS
A weak handicap. The winner was well in on the form of his Haydock second in December and ran to that level here. The second ran to his chase mark.

NOTEBOOK
Pardini(USA) justified market support on this return to a longer trip despite lugging towards the far rail between the last two fences. *(op 6-1 tchd 7-2)*

Irishkawa Bellevue(FR) was reverting to fences off a mark no less than 35lb lower than his hurdles rating. He may not have been helped by a rival jumping across him when missing out at the first ditch. *(op 9-2 tchd 5-1)*

Mill Bank(IRE) has won on this sort of going but seems better suited to the top of the ground. *(op 7-2 tchd 13-2)*

Instant Appeal appears to be struggling to find the right trip. *(tchd 9-2)*

4644 COME RACING AT WORCESTER - SUNDAY 9TH APRIL STANDARD OPEN NATIONAL HUNT FLAT RACE 2m
5:20 (5:20) (Class 6) 4-6-Y-0 **£1,713** (£499; £249)

Form RPR
40 **1** **She's Humble (IRE)**[80] [3259] 4-10-4 ow1.. AntonyEvans 98+
(P D Evans) *t.k.h: led 3f: w ldr: led 9f out: clr over 2f out: hung rt over 1f out: rdn out* **33/1**

2 **2** *9* **Chorizo (IRE)**[35] [4011] 5-11-3.. RWalsh 101
(P F Nicholls) *hld up and bhd: rdn and hdwy over 4f out: chsd wnr over 2f out: no imp* **5/6**[1]

1 **3** *6* **Ballykelly (IRE)**[22] [4237] 5-11-10.. RichardJohnson 102
(R T Phillips) *plld hrd: led after 3f to 9f out: lost pl 3f out: styd on to take 3rd nr fin* **5/2**[2]

443 **4** *½* **Maryscross (IRE)**[35] [4017] 6-10-10.. TomDoyle 87
(O Brennan) *prom: rdn and outpcd over 4f out: n.d after* **25/1**

5 *9* **Whistle Dixie** 5-11-3.. JohnMcNamara 85
(K Bishop) *a bhd* **50/1**

6 *2* **Seize** 4-10-10.. TimmyMurphy 76
(Ian Williams) *hld up in mid-div: hdwy 9f out: wknd over 2f out* **14/1**[3]

025 **7** *11* **Jobsworth (IRE)**[17] [4326] 6-10-10.. MrJETudor[(7)] 72
(Evan Williams) *rdn 7f out: a bhd* **20/1**

8 *16* **Muckshifter** 5-11-3.. PJBrennan 56
(P A Blockley) *hld up in mid-div: hdwy 8f out: rdn over 4f out: wknd over 3f out* **14/1**[3]

03 **P** **A Sea Commander (GER)**[51] [3720] 4-10-7................ RichardYoung[(3)] —
(J W Mullins) *hld up in mid-div: rdn 7f out: sn struggling: t.o whn p.u over 1f out* **40/1**

4m 8.30s (20.50) **Going Correction** +1.175s/f (Heav)
WFA 4 from 5yo+ 7lb **9** Ran SP% **112.4**
Speed ratings: **95,90,87,87,82 81,76,68**,— CSF £58.40 TOTE £18.20: £3.60, £1.10, £1.50; EX 213.70 Place 6 £140.70, Place 5 £106.02.

Owner John P Jones **Bred** Pat Jones **Trained** Pandy, Abergavenny

FOCUS
The form of this bumper may be reasonable despite the small field. The winner showed a big improvement in form, but with the next three home all running their races there is no reason to regard this as a fluke.

NOTEBOOK
She's Humble(IRE) had no problem with the longer trip and, despite hanging towards the saddling boxes, turned over the odds-on favourite in no uncertain manner.

Chorizo(IRE) proved no match for the winner despite having a hard race. *(tchd 10-11 and Evens in places)*

Ballykelly(IRE) stayed on again to snatch the minor berth after pulling too hard under his penalty. *(op 3-1)*

Maryscross(IRE) does seem to have been blessed with stamina rather than speed.

T/Plt: £140.10 to a £1 stake. Pool: £49,117.70. 255.75 winning tickets. T/Qpdt: £38.70 to a £1 stake. Pool: £4,095.90. 78.20 winning tickets. KH

4645 - 4647a (Foreign Racing) - See Raceform Interactive

4148 PLUMPTON (L-H)
Monday, March 27

OFFICIAL GOING: Soft (heavy in places)
Wind: Strong, against Weather: Overcast

4648 PLANT MOVEMENTS JUVENILE NOVICES' HURDLE (9 hdls) 2m
2:20 (2:21) (Class 4) 4-Y-0 **£3,903** (£1,146; £573; £286)

Form RPR
316 **1** **Trompette (USA)**[30] [4104] 4-10-12 103.. MickFitzgerald 116+
(N J Henderson) *hld up in tch: effrt gng easily after 3 out: led 2 out: sn clr: eased nr fin* **5/2**[2]

	2	6	**Almavara (USA)**[211] 4-10-12 .... JimmyMcCarthy (C P Morlock) *disp ld: slt advantage 3 out: rdn and hdd next: kpt on but no ch w wnr* **50/1**	104
022	3	5	**Flaming Weapon**[39] 3939 4-11-5 112 .... PhilipHide (G L Moore) *trckd ldrs: cl up 3 out: rdn and nt qckn bef 2 out: one pce after* **10/11**[1]	106
	4	1	**Rosenblatt (GER)**[134] 4-10-12 .... JodieMogford (J C Tuck) *t.k.h: pressed ldrs: lost pl and mstke 6th: effrt to chal 3 out: no ex after 2 out* **8/1**[3]	99+
20	5	8	**Ardglass (IRE)**[18] 4327 4-10-12 .... MatthewBatchelor (Mrs P Townsley) *cl up: mstke 2nd: reminder 4th: mstke next: effrt to chal u.p 3 out: wknd next* **12/1**	93+
5450	6	18	**Ghaill Force**[85] 3182 4-10-7 93 .... (t) RobertLucey-Butler(5) (P Butler) *hld up in last pair: mstke 3rd: in tch 6th: wknd next* **66/1**	80+
0	P		**La Gessa**[12] 4450 4-10-5 .... MarcusFoley (John Berry) *nt fluent: hld up in last: wknd 6th: t.o whn p.u bef 3 out* **66/1**	—
4	P		**Inchloch**[39] 3948 4-10-12 .... SamThomas (Miss Venetia Williams) *disp ld tl wknd rapidly jst bef 3 out: wl bhd whn p.u bef last* **9/1**	—
PP	P		**Altenburg (FR)**[36] 4015 4-10-12 .... LeightonAspell (Mrs N Smith) *mstke 2nd: in tch: wkng whn mstke 3 out: wl bhd whn p.u bef last* **66/1**	—

4m 16.7s (15.50) **Going Correction** +1.25s/f (Heav) **9** Ran SP% **116.2**
Speed ratings: **111,108,105,105,101 92,—,—,—** CSF £96.32 TOTE £3.20: £1.10, £9.20, £1.10; EX 116.80.
Owner Elite Racing Club **Bred** Wertheimer & Frere **Trained** Upper Lambourn, Berks

FOCUS
A decent time for a race like this given the conditions. There had been two inches of rain in the last five days, including plenty in the morning, and the ground was very wet indeed. The winner was rated value for double the winning margin.

NOTEBOOK
Trompette(USA), one of two runners carrying a winner's penalty, revelled in the conditions and won easily under a patient ride. She could make a quick reappearance under a penalty in a valuable juvenile handicap at Uttoxeter on Saturday, and if conditions are similar she will merit the utmost respect. *(tchd 2-1)*
Almavara(USA), who has a most unlikely pedigree for hurdling, won on sand but was sold very cheaply at the end of last season. New connections, who gelded him, had winning a seller in mind, but on this evidence he will win something a bit better than that. *(op 33-1)*
Flaming Weapon had no obvious excuse other than perhaps the conditions, for the race he won on softish ground was a weak affair, and his better more recent form has been on good going. *(op Evens tchd 6-5 and 5-4 in a place)*
Rosenblatt(GER), who was nicely backed, showed promise on this hurdles debut. A German-trained winner of Derbys in both Slovakia and Hungary, he showed up all of the way. He may have been at a disadvantage sticking to the inner, which is usually the worst ground when it's soft, though the running of Captain's Legacy later in the day casts some doubt on the validity of that theory on this occasion. In any case, connections will find the right opportunity for him in due course. *(op 12-1 tchd 14-1)*
Inchloch was probably the best of these on the Flat but he isn't getting the trip so far over hurdles. *(op 10-1 tchd 11-1)*
La Gessa *Official explanation: trainer said filly was unsuited by the heavy ground (op 10-1 tchd 11-1)*

4649 LASTMINUTEBET JOE THE CAP FROM CARSHALTON MEMORIAL NOVICES' HURDLE (12 hdls) 2m 5f
2:50 (2:50) (Class 4) 4-Y-0+ **£3,083** (£898; £449)

Form				RPR
/3-2	1		**Beare Necessities (IRE)**[29] 4128 7-11-4 .... LeightonAspell (M J Hogan) *trckd ldrs: led 7th: hrd rdn whn hdd and mstke 2 out: sn led again: jnd flat: jst hld on* **7/4**[1]	101+
P	2	hd	**Captain's Legacy**[84] 3219 5-11-4 .... JamesDavies (D B Feek) *racd on inner: prom: chsd wnr 8th to 3 out: sn outpcd: rallied 2 out: jnd wnr flat: jst pipped* **33/1**	98
4F-2	3	7	**Northaw Lad (IRE)**[30] 4104 8-11-4 109 .... AndrewTinkler (C Tinkler) *hld up in rr: stdy prog 9th: chsd wnr 3 out: led and mstke 2 out: sn hdd: mstke last: wknd* **2/1**[2]	94+
	4	8	**Mister Completely (IRE)**[33] 5-11-4 .... JamieGoldstein (Miss Sheena West) *wl in tch: effrt 9th: outpcd sn after: rallied 2 out: wknd last* **8/1**	83
3-03	5	nk	**Eastern Point**[18] 4324 12-10-7 71 ow3 .... MrPYork(7) (R H York) *w ldrs: drvn 7th: sn lost pl and struggling: wl bhd after 9th: kpt on again fr 2 out* **66/1**	79
0-0	6	dist	**Red Dawn (IRE)**[31] 4094 7-11-4 .... PaulMoloney (Miss H C Knight) *hld up: lost tch w ldrs 9th: shuffled along and no imp 3 out: wknd: btn 62 l* **25/1**	—
P6	7	7	**The Hardy Boy**[117] 2574 6-11-4 .... MatthewBatchelor (Miss A M Newton-Smith) *led to 7th: wknd u.p next: j. slowly 9th: btn 69 l* **33/1**	—
0-UP	P		**Gay Millenium**[43] 3885 6-10-4 .... JustinMorgan(7) (L A Dace) *lost tch bef 4th: t.o whn p.u bef 7th* **100/1**	—
02	P		**Four For A Laugh (IRE)**[33] 4048 7-11-4 .... RobertThornton (A King) *trckd ldrs: blnd bdly 6th: nt rcvr: p.u bef 8th: lame* **9/2**[3]	—

5m 48.5s (23.70) **Going Correction** +1.25s/f (Heav)
WFA 4 from 5yo+ 8lb **9** Ran SP% **111.2**
Speed ratings: **104,103,101,98,98 —,—,—,—** CSF £55.70 TOTE £3.00: £1.60, £5.00, £1.40; EX 88.30.
Owner Mrs Barbara Hogan **Bred** Mrs M Quinn **Trained** North End, W Sussex

FOCUS
A gruelling affair and a slow-motion finish - form that one would only want to rely upon in similarly testing conditions. The time was almost a minute slower than standard - the equivalent of around half a mile.

NOTEBOOK
Beare Necessities(IRE) , a gift horse who has had serious problems, gained this gutsy win following an encouraging debut for the stable after 659 days off the track. He looked beaten when headed two out, but he was back in front at the last and then held on grimly. *(tchd 6-4 and 15-8)*
Captain's Legacy, pulled up in similar ground on his only previous start, stuck to the inner, which is usually a disadvantage but might not be any more as the outside is getting so cut up. He was only third jumping the last but rallied well and only just failed.
Northaw Lad(IRE), who had run well when returning from a long absence on his previous start, was given a patient ride until moving smoothly into contention starting down the far side. He looked the likely winner when stalking the leader into the straight but jumped awkwardly when taking it up two out and then made another mistake when headed at the last. He is worth another chance in less extreme conditions. *(op 9-4 tchd 5-2)*
Mister Completely(IRE), a multiple staying winner on the Flat for John Best, ran respectably on this hurdles debut and only faded at the final flight. *(tchd 9-1)*
Four For A Laugh(IRE) *Official explanation: jockey said gelding was lame behind (op 4-1)*

4650 WHIPPERS DELIGHT H'CAP CHASE (FOR THE HIGHFIELDS FARM CHALLENGE TROPHY) (15 fncs 3 omitted) 3m 2f
3:20 (3:21) (Class 4) (0-105,96) 5-Y-0+**£4,400** (£1,311; £663; £340; £177)

Form				RPR
02	1		**Hazeljack**[36] 4007 11-11-2 93 .... WillieMcCarthy(7) (A J Whiting) *pressed ldr: led 6th: mde most after: clr bef 2 out: styd on steadily* **7/1**[3]	110+
6333	2	9	**Spider Boy**[53] 3686 9-9-9 70 oh5 .... (p) RobertLucey-Butler(5) (Miss Z C Davison) *hld up in rr: prog 11th: trckd wnr 3 out: sn rdn and no imp: all out to hold on for 2nd* **16/1**	76
2145	3	1	**Tommy Carson**[69] 3434 11-11-9 96 .... ColinBolger(3) (Jamie Poulton) *chsd ldrs: drvn fr 6th: effrt u.p to chal 4 out: sn btn: plugged on fr 2 out* **11/1**	101
4522	4	1 1/4	**Up The Pub (IRE)**[41] 3909 8-10-13 83 .... (t) RobertWalford (R H Alner) *hld up in rr: effrt to chse ldrs bef 4 out: no imp and btn next: plugged on* **7/2**[2]	88+
5111	5	dist	**Tallow Bay (IRE)**[28] 4152 11-11-0 91 .... MrGTumelty(7) (Mrs S Wall) *trckd ldrs: drvn and chsd wnr briefly after 11th: sn btn: wl bhd whn j. slowly 2 out: btn 62 l* **10/1**	—
065P	P		**Monty Be Quick**[11] 4460 10-9-11 72 .... CharliePoste(5) (J M Castle) *chsd ldrs: rdn 8th: wknd and mstke 11th: sn p.u* **50/1**	—
5PP6	P		**Apple Joe**[5] 4571 10-9-8 71 .... (p) JamesWhite(7) (A J Whiting) *in tch in rr: mstkes 9th and 10th: wknd: p.u after next* **16/1**	—
5P21	P		**Joe McHugh (IRE)**[15] 4394 7-10-13 83 .... DaveCrosse (C J Mann) *settled in midfield: mstke 10th: sn rdn and no rspnse: tailing off whn p.u after 11th: b.b.v* **15/8**[1]	—
5352	U		**Dun Locha Castle (IRE)**[8] 4524 11-10-11 81 .... TomScudamore (N R Mitchell) *nt a fluent: led to 6th: led briefly 9th: 4th and wkng whn stmbld and uns rdr 3 out* **7/1**[3]	—
P5U4	P		**Oscar Performance (IRE)**[14] 4428 11-10-1 71 ..... (b) BenjaminHitchcott (R H Buckler) *hld up in tch: effrt to chse ldrs after 11th: wknd on long run to 4 out: t.o whn p.u bef 3 out* **66/1**	—

7m 24.2s (30.20) **Going Correction** +1.25s/f (Heav) **10** Ran SP% **114.6**
Speed ratings: **103,100,99,99,— —,—,—,—,—** CSF £103.78 CT £1214.40 TOTE £7.90: £2.20, £3.60, £2.90; EX 203.90.
Owner A J Whiting **Bred** Miss Sarah Marie Nicholls **Trained** North Nibley, Gloucs

FOCUS
Testing conditions rendered this a stiff test of stamina. Low-level form but solid enough. First fence in back straight omitted.

NOTEBOOK
Hazeljack was in his element. Always in the first two, he handled conditions better than any and was always jumping well out of the ground. He had it in the bag from three out, barring accidents, and came home nicely clear. He lacks pace and his only previous wins were both in soft and heavy ground, but he always does his best and has just come to himself again after a viral problem. His trainer hopes he goes up enough to make the cut in the Topham at Aintree, where he ought to have no problem at all with the big fences. *(op 13-2)*
Spider Boy has been running well lately and did well again from 5lb out of the proper handicap. Having been held up at the back, he moved into contention looking a danger down the far side for the last time, but the winner was too strong for him.
Tommy Carson can be very hard work and his rider really earned his fee here. To his credit, the 11-year-old kept plugging away. *(op 12-1 tchd 14-1)*
Up The Pub(IRE) should have enjoyed the ground, but he was never going well enough. *(op 4-1 tchd 10-3)*
Apple Joe *Official explanation: trainer said gelding was distressed (op 7-4 tchd 2-1)*
Joe McHugh(IRE), 4lb higher than at Warwick, was the only unexposed runner in the field, but he bled, as he has done on occasions before. *Official explanation: jockey said gelding bled from nose (op 7-4 tchd 2-1)*

4651 WEATHERBYS PRINTING (S) H'CAP HURDLE (9 hdls) 2m
3:50 (3:51) (Class 5) (0-90,89) 4-Y-0+ **£2,740** (£798; £399)

Form				RPR
P60	1		**Froghole Flyer**[17] 4359 7-11-12 89 .... PhilipHide (G L Moore) *led to 3rd: lft in ld next: clr fr 6th: blnd last: easily* **7/1**	101+
/060	2	13	**Dirty Sanchez**[15] 4392 8-10-10 76 .... ColinBolger(3) (Miss A M Newton-Smith) *prom: chsd wnr 4th to 6th: lft 2nd again 3 out: no imp: fin tired* **16/1**	73
500P	3	12	**Breezer**[41] 3905 6-10-12 75 .... (p) MarkBradburne (J A Geake) *in tch: rdn and outpcd fr 6th: n.d after: tk modest 3rd nr fin* **7/2**[2]	60
3020	4	3/4	**Sunset King (USA)**[20] 4290 6-11-2 79 .... JimCrowley (R J Hodges) *in tch: chsd ldrs 5th: rdn next: wl btn 3 out: lost modest 3rd nr fin* **4/1**[3]	63
02U2	5	4	**Rockys Girl**[15] 4392 4-10-5 82 .... (b) AndrewGlassonbury(7) (R Flint) *hld up: effrt bef 6th: sn rdn: disp modest 3rd and wl btn after 3 out: wknd bef last* **11/4**[1]	55
POUU	R		**Heatherlea Squire (NZ)**[15] 4392 8-10-10 73 .... WarrenMarston (D J Wintle) *w wnr: led 3rd tl rn out next* **7/1**	—
	P		**Thaticouldntsayno (IRE)**[722] 4680 8-10-11 74 .... RJGreene (A E Jones) *t.k.h: prom tl wknd rapidly 5th: t.o whn p.u bef 2 out* **14/1**	—
P00	U		**Crystal Ka (FR)**[72] 3182 4-10-9 70 .... TomScudamore (M R Hoad) *hld up: prog 5th: chsd wnr next: 5 l down whn blnd and uns rdr 3 out* **28/1**	—
60P	P		**Gameset'N'Match**[104] 2804 5-10-12 80 .... RobertLucey-Butler(5) (Miss M P Bryant) *hld up: outpcd 6th: wknd 3 out: wl bhd in 6th whn p.u bef 2 out* **40/1**	—

4m 23.4s (22.20) **Going Correction** +1.25s/f (Heav)
WFA 4 from 5yo+ 7lb **9** Ran SP% **112.3**
Speed ratings: **94,87,81,81,79 —,—,—,—** CSF £101.53 CT £454.14 TOTE £5.90: £1.80, £3.80, £1.90; EX 77.60.There was no bid for the winner.
Owner No Dramas Partnership **Bred** Dr D B A Silk **Trained** Woodingdean, E Sussex

FOCUS
A modest time even for a seller, 6.7 seconds slower than the opener. A desperate affair, but a massive step up in form from the winner, who has been rated value for 15l.

NOTEBOOK
Froghole Flyer, upon whom different tactics were applied on this handicap debut, ran out a stylish winner. He had shown next to nothing in novice company, but this was a big drop in class and he was off a mark of only 89 despite top weight. In front most of the way, he had the race won a fair way out and survived a bad mistake at the last to win easily. Connections, who were lucky to retain him without a bid, reckon that while he handled the conditions well enough he will be suited by better ground. He is plenty big enough to make a chaser next season. *(op 11-2)*
Dirty Sanchez, who returned to the track in January after three and a half years off, was gaining his first placing, although he was perhaps fortunate to finish second. *(op 14-1)*
Breezer won a seller last season but has been mainly out of form this term. *(op 11-4)*
Sunset King(USA) was running in his first seller but could not cash in. *(op 6-1)*
Crystal Ka(FR), dropped in class, was in second place, and appeared held, when parting company three from home. *(op 20-1)*

4652 WEATHERBYS INSURANCE CONDITIONAL JOCKEYS' H'CAP HURDLE (12 hdls) 2m 5f

4:20 (4:20) (Class 4) (0-105,105) 4-Y-0+ **£3,903** (£1,146; £573; £286)

Form RPR

0 **1** **Brendar (IRE)**[285] 762 9-11-6 **99** WilliamKennedy 101
(Jim Best) *hmpd 1st: hld up in last pair but wl in tch: prog to trck ldng trio 3 out: led bef next: kpt on wl flat* **14/1**

34UP **2** *2* **Myson (IRE)**[14] 4419 7-10-6 **85** (b[1]) RobertLucey-Butler 85
(D B Feek) *hld up in tch: effrt 3 out: chal next: chsd wnr after: kpt on but a hld* **7/1**

PP61 **3** *3/4* **Geography (IRE)**[8] 4526 6-9-13 **83** 7ex (p) RichardGordon(5) 82
(P Butler) *hld up in tch: prog 9th: led bef 3 out tl bef next: styd on same pce* **10/1**

-P32 **4** *5* **Bright Green**[18] 4331 7-11-2 **100** (p) BernieWharfe(5) 98+
(C J Gray) *t.k.h: wl in tch: mstke 4th: mstke 9th and lost pl: renewed effrt to chal after 3 out: wknd after 2 out* **11/2**[2]

024 **5** *14* **Zeloso**[12] 4449 8-10-5 **87** (v) CharliePoste(3) 67
(M F Harris) *pressed ldr: chal bef 3 out: nt run on u.p bef next* **5/1**[1]

3042 **6** *1/2* **Carly Bay**[28] 4151 8-11-5 **98** ColinBolger 80+
(G P Enright) *hld up in rr: losing tch whn mstke 3 out: plugged on again fr 2 out* **11/2**[2]

6625 **7** *13* **Eljutan (IRE)**[51] 3733 8-11-6 **99** (b[1]) ShaneWalsh 66
(J Joseph) *w ldrs: upsides bef 3 out: wknd rapidly bef 2 out* **20/1**

2345 **8** *3* **Makeabreak (IRE)**[29] 4129 7-10-10 **99** KevinTobin(10) 63
(C J Mann) *trckd ldrs tl wknd 3 out* **6/1**[3]

0503 **F** **Jaloux D'Estruval (FR)**[17] 4357 9-11-12 **105** LiamHeard —
(Mrs L C Taylor) *fell 1st* **7/1**

1F04 **P** **Random Quest**[58] 3616 8-11-4 **100** WillieMcCarthy(3) —
(B J Llewellyn) *mde most tl hdd & wknd rapidly bef 3 out: p.u bef last* **14/1**

5m 47.5s (22.70) **Going Correction** +1.25s/f (Heavy) **10** Ran SP% **113.9**
Speed ratings: **106,105,104,103,97 97,92,91,—,—** CSF £106.22 CT £1029.08 TOTE £16.50: £5.50, £4.40, £3.80; EX 220.90.
Owner Leon Best **Bred** J C Lett **Trained** Lewes, E Sussex

FOCUS
A moderate handicap run at a steady pace, which contributed to a winning time around nine seconds slower than the earlier novice over the same trip. They were all tightly grouped starting the final circuit. The form looks solid enough.

NOTEBOOK
Brendar(IRE), an ex-Irish gelding, was having his first race in more than nine months but he had apparently been in very good form and was well fancied. Having been patiently ridden after a horse fell in his path at the first, he slipped through a narrow gap approaching the straight and was driven out for a narrow, but decisive enough, success. He has been schooled over fences, and that is an option if the handicapper gets hold of him. *(op 18-1)*
Myson(IRE), over hurdles for the first time since November 2003, seemed to respond to the first-time blinkers and ran better than of late. *(tchd 15-2)*
Geography(IRE) carried a 7lb penalty for a win on much quicker ground at Fontwell last week. It proved too much for him and he was beaten fair and square after going to the front three out. *(op 15-2)*
Bright Greenwore cheekpieces for the first time. He came here in good form but was 5lb higher and was not helped by mistakes at the first down the far side on both circuits. *(op 7-2)*
Zeloso gained his two wins this term in sellers. He was starting to struggle when tightened up a bit and dropping out quickly. *(op 6-1)*
Carly Bay was beaten when she made a bad mistake at the third-last. *(op 15-2)*

4653 WEATHERBYS BANK NOVICES' H'CAP CHASE (12 fncs 2 omitted) 2m 4f

4:50 (4:50) (Class 4) (0-100,95) 5-Y-0+
£5,010 (£1,480; £740; £370; £184; £92)

Form RPR

-4P0 **1** **Kirov King (IRE)**[29] 6-10-13 **89** MrGGallagher(7) 108+
(R H York) *trckd ldrs: mstkes 1st and 6th: led and bmpd 4 out: clr next: in n.d after: eased flat* **33/1**

4525 **2** *14* **Denarius Secundus**[8] 4525 9-10-0 **69** oh1 (b) DaveCrosse 67+
(N R Mitchell) *pressed ldr: led 7th: hdd and bmpd 4 out: no ch w wnr fr next* **6/1**

3U25 **3** *5* **Sett Aside**[12] 4451 8-10-8 **77** (p) BenjaminHitchcott 69
(Mrs L C Jewell) *prom: trckd ldr briefly 8th: outpcd 4 out: wl hld whn mstke 2 out* **9/2**[2]

3213 **4** *17* **Twenty Degrees**[6] 4563 8-11-12 **95** (b) PhilipHide 70
(G L Moore) *hld up in rr: rdn after 5th: lost tch fr 7th: sn t.o: plugged on to take remote 4th nr fin* **15/2**

2222 **5** *nk* **Mystical Star (FR)**[28] 4150 9-11-12 **95** LeightonAspell 70
(M J Hogan) *trckd ldrs: mstke 5th: outpcd after 8th: no ch whn blnd 3 out* **10/3**[1]

-P43 **6** *5* **Ri Na Realta (IRE)**[28] 4150 11-11-7 **90** AndrewThornton 60
(J W Mullins) *hld up in tch: outpcd fr 8th: no ch after: t.o 4 out* **11/2**[3]

FP2P **7** *13* **Buckland Gold (IRE)**[18] 4331 6-11-9 **92** JamesDavies 49
(D B Feek) *hld up: pushed along and struggling in last pair bef 5th: wl bhd after 8th: t.o whn blnd 4 out* **12/1**

5F6P **P** **Run To The King (IRE)**[7] 4553 8-10-13 **82** JoeTizzard —
(P C Ritchens) *led to 7th: wknd rapidly next: t.o whn p.u bef 4 out* **33/1**

6313 **P** **Baron Blitzkrieg**[33] 4053 8-10-12 **81** JodieMogford —
(D J Wintle) *racd wd: hld up: pushed along and struggling bef 5th: t.o whn p.u after 8th* **11/2**[3]

5m 40.3s (21.85) **Going Correction** +1.25s/f (Heavy) **9** Ran SP% **111.7**
Speed ratings: **106,100,98,91,91 89,84,—,—** CSF £210.89 CT £1063.56 TOTE £36.60: £7.50, £3.40, £2.40; EX 291.20.
Owner K Tork **Bred** Mrs T V Ryan **Trained** Martyr's Green, Surrey

FOCUS
A weak novices' handicap chase. The winner was stepping up on all known form but it did not look a fluke. First fence in back straight omitted.

NOTEBOOK
Kirov King(IRE) was a shock winner, but it looked no fluke. He has been blazing off and failing to get home in point-to-points, but he had a severe bit on here and settled much better over this shorter trip behind a reasonable pace. Running off a mark of just 89, he made mistakes at the first in the straight on the first two circuits and collided with front-runner Denarius Secundus as he came to take it up four out, but it didn't put him off and he was soon in complete command, winning pretty much as he liked. Getting him to switch off was evidently the key, and he could win again now. *(op 25-1)*
Denarius Secundus, who was headed and bumped by the eventual winner at the fourth last, kept going well enough to finish clear of the rest. *(tchd 11-2 in places)*
Sett Aside was always prominent but could not go with the first two over the last four fences. *(op 6-1)*
Mystical Star(FR) has been in good form but was 20lb higher than when successful in October and was in trouble as they bypassed the fifth-last. *(op 4-1)*
Baron Blitzkrieg never looked happy. *Official explanation: jockey said gelding was unsuited by soft (heavy in places) going. (op 5-1 tchd 6-1)*

4654 WEATHERBYS MESSAGING SERVICE MAIDEN OPEN NATIONAL HUNT FLAT RACE 2m 2f

5:20 (5:20) (Class 6) 4-6-Y-0 **£1,713** (£499; £249)

Form RPR

1 **Classic Fiddle** 4-10-3 MarcusFoley 89+
(N J Henderson) *trckd ldrs: narrow ld over 2f out: rdn and styd on wl fnl f* **6/4**[1]

5 **2** *3* **Gaelic Gift (IRE)**[42] 3904 4-9-12 MrTJO'Brien(5) 84
(J G Cann) *trckd ldrs: gng wl 3 out: pressed wnr over 2f out: rdn and styd on same pce* **10/1**

3 *10* **Push The Port (IRE)** 4-10-10 LeightonAspell 81
(N J Gifford) *in tch: pushed along 6f out: effrt over 3f out: sn outpcd: kpt on fr over 1f out to take 3rd nr fin* **9/1**

4 *2* **Red Bells** 5-11-3 WarrenMarston 86
(D J Wintle) *s.s: racd on inner: hld up in tch: trckd ldrs over 2f out: wknd over 1f out* **28/1**

5 *nk* **Spartan Encore** 4-10-7 ColinBolger(3) 79
(Miss Suzy Smith) *racd on inner: plld hrd early: w ldrs: led 3f out to over 2f out: wknd over 1f out* **18/1**

00 **6** *11* **Double The Trouble**[41] 3911 5-11-3 AndrewThornton 76+
(R H Buckler) *in tch: chsd ldrs 3f out: wknd 2f out* **50/1**

7 *dist* **Anty Wren** 4-10-10 RJGreene —
(Mary Meek) *racd on inner: wl in tch: shkn up 7f out: wknd 5f out: t.o: btn 61 l* **66/1**

8 *dist* **Pharly Green** 4-9-7 JayPemberton(10) —
(G P Enright) *prom: led 11f out to 9f out: wknd rapidly 7f out: t.o: btn 176 l* **40/1**

64 **9** *19* **Itsy Bitsy**[46] 3820 4-10-3 (v[1]) TimmyMurphy —
(W J Musson) *pressed ldrs: led 9f out to 3f out: wknd rapidly and allowed to walk in fr over 1f out* **15/2**[3]

26 **P** **Fredensborg (NZ)**[14] 4422 5-11-3 SamThomas —
(Miss Venetia Williams) *led to 11f out: wknd rapidly: p.u 1/2-way* **5/2**[2]

4m 51.5s (26.75) **Going Correction** +1.25s/f (Heavy)
WFA 4 from 5yo 7lb **10** Ran SP% **114.0**
Speed ratings: **90,88,84,83,83 78,—,—,—,—** CSF £17.07 TOTE £2.60: £1.30, £1.80, £2.40; EX 18.50 Place 6 £439.06, Place 5 £346.49.
Owner Mrs E Roberts **Bred** Mrs E C Roberts **Trained** Upper Lambourn, Berks

FOCUS
A moderate winning time, even for a bumper. The extra two furlongs on testing ground made this a stiff test for inexperienced horses. Not much form to go on, but it could turn out to be better than it has been rated.

NOTEBOOK
Classic Fiddle is the first foal of the former smart staying chaser Fiddling The Facts, who revelled in the mud. She had her task made easier when her market rival was pulled up with a circuit to go, but she was still given a race by the runner-up. Her trainer reckons she doesn't necessarily need this ground, but it clearly doesn't hurt. *(tchd 7-4 in a place)*
Gaelic Gift(IRE) had run quite well here on her debut and she gave the favourite a race, if held in the final furlong. *(op 12-1)*
Push The Port(IRE), a half-brother to winning hurdler Hidden Genius, was pushed along a fair way out but plugged on for a modest third. *(op 5-1)*
Red Bells, whose dam won over hurdles and fences, played up in the paddock but did not run badly. *(op 25-1)*
Spartan Encore, a market springer, spoilt his chance by pulling hard. *(op 33-1)*
Pharly Green *Official explanation: trainer said filly scoped dirty following the race (op 33-1)*
Fredensborg(NZ) was pulled up with a circuit to go, having lost his action (he trotted sound afterwards). *Official explanation: jockey said gelding lost its action (tchd 3-1)*
T/Plt: £896.20 to a £1 stake. Pool: £60,831.80. 49.55 winning tickets. T/Qpdt: £413.30 to a £1 stake. Pool: £4,245.00. 7.60 winning tickets. JN

4039 SEDGEFIELD (L-H)

Tuesday, March 28

OFFICIAL GOING: Heavy
Last fence omitted all chases.
Wind: Moderate, half-behind

4655 GOSFORTH DECORATING AND BUILDING SERVICES BEGINNERS' CHASE (13 fncs) 2m 110y

2:00 (2:00) (Class 4) 5-Y-0+
£4,384 (£1,295; £647; £324; £161; £81)

Form RPR

22FU **1** **Red Man (IRE)**[9] 4520 9-10-6 107 (p) StevenGagan(10) 106+
(Mrs E Slack) *trckd ldr: hdwy to ld after 4 out: clr 2 out: styd on wl* **13/8**[1]

-R54 **2** *24* **Jimmys Duky (IRE)**[42] 3915 8-10-13 67 (p) DougieCostello(3) 76+
(D M Forster) *chsd ldrs: pushed along and outpcd after 5 out: rdn along 3 out: styd on appr last* **8/1**

FPFP **3** *2* **Missoudun (FR)**[35] 4042 6-10-9 61 (p) MrSFMagee(7) 72
(J R Weymes) *hld up towards rr: hdwy 1/2-way: rdn along to chse wnr after 2 out: drvn appr last and kpt on same pce* **66/1**

4 **4** *22* **Neuro (FR)**[20] 4303 5-10-5 BenOrde-Powlett(7) 56+
(Jedd O'Keeffe) *led: blnd 4 out: sn hdd and rdn: ten l down in 2nd whn blnd 2 out: sn drvn and wknd* **4/1**[2]

4000 **5** *8* **Star Trooper (IRE)**[29] 4145 10-10-13 79 (p) MrCStorey(3) 42
(Miss S E Forster) *a rr: bhd fr 1/2-way* **11/1**

0006 **6** *9* **Hialeah**[40] 3943 5-10-9 MrTGreenall(3) 29
(M W Easterby) *in tch: pushed along 7th: rdn 4 out: sn outpcd & bhd* **5/1**[3]

043- **F** **Lunar Dram**[378] 4393 8-11-2 RichardMcGrath —
(M Dods) *chsd ldng pair tl fell 5th* **9/1**

0P **P** **Made In Bruere (FR)**[140] 2099 6-11-2 KeithMercer —
(Ferdy Murphy) *a rr: bhd whn p.u bef 8th* **25/1**

-500 **P** **Firion King (IRE)**[30] 6-11-2 AlanDempsey —
(W S Coltherd) *midfield: pushed along and bhd fr 1/2-way: t.o whn p.u bef last* **66/1**

4m 32.1s (17.90) **Going Correction** +1.20s/f (Heavy)
WFA 5 from 6yo+ 4lb **9** Ran SP% **111.0**
Speed ratings: **105,93,92,82,78 74,—,—,—** CSF £14.43 TOTE £1.90: £1.70, £1.60, £13.10; EX 15.60.
Owner A Slack **Bred** Patrick Stamp **Trained** Hilton, Cumbria

FOCUS
A weak race in which the winner was value for 20l. The first three ran pretty much to their pre-race marks.

NOTEBOOK

Red Man(IRE) had failed to complete on his two most recent runs but he jumped pretty well here. In front after the fourth last, he went on to score with the minimum of fuss, but this was a weak race. *(op 7-4 tchd 15-8 and 6-4)*

Jimmys Duky(IRE), who wore cheekpieces for the first time, was bandaged on his near hind but it worked loose before the fourth last. Over a trip shorter than he had ever tackled before, he did not look an easy ride and was well beaten by the winner, but he did get the better of a tussle for second. *(op 17-2 tchd 9-1 and 15-2)*

Missoudun(FR), down in trip and sporting sheepskin instead of blinkers, completed the course for the first time in six runs but was run out of a remote second on the long run-in. *(op 50-1)*

Neuro(FR) travelled quite well, but lost his lead shortly after blundering four from home and, after mistakes at the last two fences, he was caught for second on the extended run-in. He may do better when handicapped. *(op 9-2 tchd 5-1 and 7-2)*

Hialeah, on his chasing debut, went into third place early on the final circuit but he did not get home in the conditions. *(op 7-1 tchd 9-2)*

4656 JOHN WADE FOR EQUINE FIBRE AND RUBBER (S) H'CAP HURDLE (QUALIFIER) — 2m 4f

2:30 (2:30) (Class 5) (0-95,95) 4-Y-O+ **£2,081** (£611; £305; £152)

Form — RPR

F056 **1** **Political Cruise**[19] 4314 8-10-1 **77** .... GarethThomas(7) — 79
(R Nixon) *a.p: rdn along after 3 out: styd on to ld last: drvn and kpt on wl flat* **10/1**

/00- **2** *shd* **Lago**[671] 504 8-10-5 **84** ....(p) MichaelMcAvoy(10) — 87+
(James Moffatt) *hld up in midfield: stdy hdwy appr 3 out: cl up next: ev ch whn rdn and hung bdly rt flat: kpt on towards fin* **7/1**[3]

5000 **3** *1* **Flemingstone (IRE)**[77] 3337 6-9-13 **75** .... MrSFMagee(7) — 76
(J R Norton) *trckd ldrs: effrt to ld after 3 out: rdn: jmpd rt and hdd last: drvn and kpt on flat* **16/1**

3605 **4** *nk* **Green 'N' Gold**[29] 4145 6-11-4 **87** .... NeilMulholland — 88
(M D Hammond) *hld up towards rr: stdy hdwy appr 3 out: rdn and styd on appr last: nrst fin* **9/2**[1]

0030 **5** *1 ½* **Welsh Dream**[75] 3351 9-11-7 **93** .... MrCStorey(3) — 92
(Miss S E Forster) *hld up in rr: hdwy after 3 out: rdn along bef next: kpt on flat: nrst fin* **15/2**

0-05 **6** *1 ¼* **Savannah River (IRE)**[69] 3446 5-10-6 **75** ....(p) PeterBuchanan — 73
(Miss Kate Milligan) *prom: rdn along and outpcd 3 out: kpt on u.p fr next* **22/1**

03PP **7** *2* **Scamp**[9] 4530 7-10-6 **75** .... KeithMercer — 72+
(R Shiels) *led: rdn along and hdd after 4 out: drvn and kpt on same pce appr 2 out* **25/1**

3053 **8** *8* **Armentieres**[9] 4517 5-10-10 **89** ....(v) StevenGagan(10) — 78+
(Mrs E Slack) *a towards rr* **6/1**[2]

0/00 **9** *5* **Glimpse Of Glory**[11] 4475 6-9-11 **69** oh7 .... DougieCostello(3) — 52
(C W Thornton) *racd wd: prom: effrt to ld after 4 out: rdn next: sn hdd & wknd after 2 out* **50/1**

P366 **10** *6* **Roadworthy (IRE)**[18] 4341 9-10-0 **69** oh3 .... WilsonRenwick — 50+
(W G Young) *midfield: hdwy and in tch 6th: rdn along and wknd fr 3 out* **7/1**[3]

0050 **11** *3* **Kicking Bear (IRE)**[63] 3552 8-9-7 **69** oh5 ....(p) RyanCummings(7) — 43
(J K Hunter) *a rr* **25/1**

-040 **12** *5* **Frankincense (IRE)**[282] 781 10-10-4 **80** ....(p) PhilKinsella(7) — 49
(A J Lockwood) *prom: rdn along appr 3 out and sn wknd* **8/1**

P6P0 **13** *dist* **Mist Opportunity (IRE)**[38] 3985 4-10-0 **77** oh2 .... BarryKeniry — —
(P C Haslam) *a rr: bhd fr 1/2-way* **16/1**

5m 28.2s (35.60) **Going Correction** +1.40s/f (Heav)
WFA 4 from 5yo+ 8lb — **13** Ran SP% **115.2**
Speed ratings: **84,83,83,83,82 82,81,78,76,73 72,70,—** CSF £72.83 CT £1114.22 TOTE £12.90: £3.30, £3.60, £3.70; EX 121.40.There was no bid for the winner. Flemingstone was claimed by M. J. Gingell for £5,000.
Owner Rayson & Susan Nixon **Bred** G R S And Mrs Nixon **Trained** Ettrickbridge, Borders

FOCUS
A good finish to this weak race, but suspect form. The time was very moderate, even for a seller, 8.2 seconds slower than the following novice hurdle over the same trip.

NOTEBOOK

Political Cruise, reverting to hurdles, held on in a desperate finish. He had been beaten 16 times since recording his only previous win, in similar conditions at Hexham in November 2004. *(op 12-1)*

Lago, having his first run since May 2004, was an unlucky loser. Surviving an error at the fourth from home, he was challenging at the last when the eventual third crowded him, then hung badly over to the stands' rail on the flat. Rallying, he needed another stride. *(op 9-2)*

Flemingstone(IRE), eased in grade for this handicap debut, wandered going into the final flight where she lost her lead but was keeping on up the run-in. She should remain competitive in this company. *(op 20-1)*

Green 'N' Gold, held up and kept wide on the better ground, came under pressure with three to jump and despite staying on could not quite land a blow.

Welsh Dream, trying to come from off the pace, was closing the gap on the leaders up the run-in. *(op 13-2)*

Savannah River(IRE) could not go with the leaders from the third last but was plugging on again at the end. *(op 20-1)*

Scamp, having her second run after a break, was headed after the fourth last but was keeping on at the finish. *(op 22-1)*

4657 JOHN SMITH'S EXTRA SMOOTH NOVICES' HURDLE — 2m 4f

3:00 (3:00) (Class 4) 4-Y-O+ **£3,578** (£1,050; £525; £262)

Form — RPR

3032 **1** **Emmasflora**[10] 4494 8-10-10 110 .... AdamPogson(5) — 114+
(C T Pogson) *led to after 1st: cl up tl led again 4 out: clr next: rdn appr last and styd on wl* **7/4**[1]

4621 **2** *14* **Water Taxi**[9] 4532 5-11-8 104 .... KeithMercer — 108+
(Ferdy Murphy) *in tch: hdwy on inner to chse wnr 3 out: rdn next: kpt on same pce* **3/1**[3]

1332 **3** *1 ¾* **Calfraz**[17] 4360 4-10-11 107 .... DougieCostello(3) — 98+
(M D Hammond) *hld up: hdwy to chse ldrs appr 3 out: rdn along bef next: no imp whn mstke last* **11/4**[2]

0 **4** *dist* **Tartan Classic (IRE)**[50] 3780 5-10-10 .... BrianHughes(5) — —
(J Howard Johnson) *chsd ldrs to 1/2-way: sn lost pl and t.o 4 out* **66/1**

P-PF **5** *18* **Comte De Chambord**[34] 4054 10-10-10 74 .... DerekLaverty(5) — —
(Mark Campion) *prom to 3rd: sn lost pl and bhd: t.o fr 1/2-way* **200/1**

PP **P** **Deep Rising**[42] 3912 8-10-8 .... AnthonyRoss — —
(S P Griffiths) *a bhd: p.u bef 3 out* **200/1**

0/ **P** **Sharp Exit (IRE)**[913] 1450 7-10-12 .... PaddyAspell(3) — —
(J Wade) *a rr: bhd fr 1/2-way: t.o whn p.u bef 3 out* **66/1**

P **P** **Conemara Breeze**[69] 3443 8-11-1 .... TomSiddall — —
(Miss L C Siddall) *bhd fr 1/2-way: t.o whn p.u bef 3 out* **100/1**

P **Miss Nosey** 4-10-0 .... BrianHarding — —
(Mrs E Slack) *hld up in rr: hdwy 1/2-way: in tch 6th: rdn along and wknd next: p.u bef 3 out* **25/1**

P **P** **Mr Buddy (IRE)**[39] 3963 5-11-1 .... AlanDempsey — —
(J Howard Johnson) *hld up: hdwy into midfield 1/2-way: lost pl 4 out: bhd and p.u bef next* **40/1**

4 **P** **Star Zero**[35] 4040 5-11-1 .... GLee — —
(J Howard Johnson) *plld hrd and rapid hdwy to ld after 1st: hdd 4 out: wknd qckly and bhd whn p.u bef 2 out* **8/1**

5m 20.0s (27.40) **Going Correction** +1.40s/f (Heav)
WFA 4 from 5yo+ 8lb — **11** Ran SP% **110.4**
Speed ratings: **101,95,94,—,— —,—,—,—,— —** CSF £6.70 TOTE £2.00: £1.10, £1.60, £1.20; EX 6.60.
Owner C T Pogson **Bred** Mrs J D Goodfellow **Trained** Farnsfield, Notts

FOCUS
A moderate event but a step up from the winner, with the next two running close to their marks.

NOTEBOOK

Emmasflora, who has been performing well in defeat, was found a weak race in which to record *her second victory. Staying on to score unchallenged, she is a consistent and versatile mare. (tchd 13-8 and 15-8)*

Water Taxi, back up in trip, went after the mare three from home but, in this bad ground, could make no inroads. *(op 7-2)*

Calfraz, upped in trip, could never get to the front two, but after a mistake at the last he was closing the gap to the runner-up at the line. *(op 3-1)*

Tartan Classic(IRE) struggled across the line for fourth prize when the first three were already boxed up and on the journey home.

Star Zero pulled his way to the front and eventually paid for not settling. Headed four from home, *he was exhausted in fourth when jumping slowly at the next and was quickly pulled up. (op 13-2 tchd 9-1)*

4658 HAPPY MOTHERS DAY ANGELA COWLEY H'CAP HURDLE (13 hdls) — 3m 3f 110y

3:30 (3:30) (Class 4) (0-110,107) 4-Y-O+ **£3,903** (£1,146; £573; £286)

Form — RPR

P003 **1** **Moustique De L'Isle (FR)**[13] 4453 6-11-3 **105** ....(v) TomMessenger(7) — 106
(C C Bealby) *led: rdn along appr 2 out: drvn and hdd last: rallied flat: led last 50 yds* **7/2**[1]

P321 **2** *½* **Ocean Tide**[13] 4453 9-11-5 **100** ....(v) RichardMcGrath — 101+
(R Ford) *trckd ldrs gng wl: hdwy and hit 3 out: effrt next: rdn to ld last: drvn flat: hdd and no ex last 50 yds* **7/2**[1]

033P **3** *5* **Our Joycey**[42] 3918 5-10-2 **90** .... ColmSharkey(7) — 85
(Mrs K Walton) *chsd ldrs: rdn along and outpcd 3 out: styd on appr last* **11/1**

40P1 **4** *2* **Cody**[31] 4113 7-9-6 **83** oh1 ow2 ....(bt) MichaelMcAvoy(10) — 76
(James Moffatt) *hld up: hdwy to chse ldrs 3 out: rdn along and n.m.r next: sn one pce* **7/1**[3]

2013 **5** *hd* **San Peire (FR)**[35] 4043 9-11-12 **107** .... GLee — 101+
(J Howard Johnson) *hld up in tch: hdwy on inner 3 out: cl up next: sn rdn and ev ch: hit last: drvn flat: wknd last 100 yds* **7/2**[1]

0000 **6** *30* **Altitude Dancer (IRE)**[16] 4390 6-10-7 **93** .... DeclanMcGann(5) — 56
(A Crook) *chsd ldng pair: reminders 4th: rdn along 7th: wknd 3 out* **20/1**

UP56 **7** *13* **Dark Thunder (IRE)**[31] 4113 9-9-7 **81** oh1 ....(b) PatrickMcDonald(7) — 31
(Ferdy Murphy) *racd wd: in tch: effrt and ev ch 3 out: sn rdn and wknd* **4/1**[2]

7m 37.7s (33.80) **Going Correction** +1.40s/f (Heav) — **7** Ran SP% **112.3**
Speed ratings: **103,102,101,100,100 92,88** CSF £15.82 CT £117.70 TOTE £3.80: £2.90, £1.70; EX 27.00.
Owner Michael Hill **Bred** Philippe Sayet **Trained** Barrowby, Lincs
■ Stewards' Enquiry : Richard McGrath two-day ban: careless riding (Apr 9, 11)
Michael McAvoy one-day ban: used whip with excessive frequency and without giving his mount time to respond (Apr 9)

FOCUS
Quite a competitive little race in which the winner did not need to match the form of his last victory. The second and third ran to their marks.

NOTEBOOK

Moustique De L'Isle(FR) had ground conditions to suit. Setting a fair pace, he was headed going to the last and got away from the flight in third place, but he rallied willingly to deny Ocean Tide, *with whom he was 3lb better off for two and three-quarter lengths on their Huntingdon meeting. (tchd 9-2)*

Ocean Tide was put up a further 6lb for his Huntingdon victory. Getting to the front at the final flight, he did nothing wrong but was run out of it close home. *(op 4-1)*

Our Joycey, slightly outpaced at the third last, was still only fifth over the final flight but she stayed on dourly. She was taking a sizeable step up in trip and handled it well. *(op 12-1 tchd 9-1)*

Cody was 7lb higher than when landing a weak race at Newcastle and that was enough to put him back in the grip of the handicapper. *(op 6-1)*

San Peire(FR), who has a good record here, rather ran in snatches. In with every chance when clipping the final flight, he tired badly on the run-in.

Altitude Dancer(IRE) looked a hard ride, coming under pressure at an early stage, and it is a credit to McGann's fitness that he only dropped away going to the second last.

Dark Thunder(IRE), whose two career wins have both come here, improved to challenge at the third last but the effort soon told and he dropped back through the field. *(op 9-2)*

4659 SALTWELL SIGNS H'CAP CHASE (16 fncs) — 2m 5f

4:00 (4:00) (Class 5) (0-95,94) 5-Y-O+ **£3,578** (£1,050; £525; £262)

Form — RPR

2443 **1** **Uneven Line**[63] 3553 10-10-5 **76** ....(p) MrCStorey(3) — 84+
(Miss S E Forster) *hld up: stdy hdwy 9th: chsd ldr after 2 out: 6l down and mstke last: styd on u.p flat to ld nr fin* **9/2**[1]

00P2 **2** *1 ½* **Major Belle (FR)**[10] 4499 7-10-12 **80** .... HenryOliver — 87+
(John R Upson) *trckd ldrs: hdwy to ld 3 out: 6l clr last: sn rdn: wknd last 100 yds: hdd and no ex nr fin* **8/1**

6050 **3** *3 ½* **Pornic (FR)**[20] 4299 12-9-9 **68** oh3 ....(v) DeclanMcGann(5) — 70
(A Crook) *chsd ldrs: rdn along after 3 out: plugged on same pce* **9/1**

0P64 **4** *5* **Scotmail Lad (IRE)**[69] 3447 12-11-1 **90** ow3 ....(p) MrCMulhall(7) — 87
(C A Mulhall) *chsd ldr: led 4th tl after next: prom tl rdn along and plugged on same pce fr 3 out* **12/1**

61-0 **5** *11* **Native Eire (IRE)**[10] 4499 12-11-5 **87** .... DNolan — 79+
(N Wilson) *midfield: effrt and sme hdwy 9th: rdn along and no imp fr 3 out* **7/1**[3]

PP3 **6** *dist* **Casalani (IRE)**[33] 4071 7-11-5 **87** .... JosephByrne — —
(Jennie Candlish) *a rr: bhd fr 1/2-way* **12/1**

P0-P **P** **Shays Lane (IRE)**[41] 3930 12-10-0 **68** oh2 .... KeithMercer — —
(Ferdy Murphy) *a rr: bhd whn p.u after 10th* **20/1**

-PP4 **P** **Jumbo's Dream**[77] 3338 15-9-7 **68** ....(p) RyanCummings(7) — —
(J E Dixon) *chsd ldrs tl lost pl 1/2-way: bhd whn p.u bef 2 out* **16/1**

PP63 **P** **Jupsala (FR)**^{41} 3930 9-9-9 **68** oh1 ....(p) TomGreenway$^{(5)}$ —
(S B Bell) *hld up in rr: sme hdwy 8th: in tch whn blnd 4 out: sn wknd and p.u bef last* **7/1**^{3}

6P1- **P** **Peterhouse**^{442} 3299 7-10-3 **71** .... BrianHarding —
(Mrs E Slack) *midfield: hdwy and in tch halfway: rdn along and wknd bef 4 out: bhd whn p.u bef 2 out* **6/1**^{2}

F55P **P** **Nomadic Blaze**^{42} 3915 9-10-8 **76** .... LarryMcGrath —
(P G Atkinson) *led to 4th: led again after 5th: rdn and hdd 3 out: wkng whn blnd next: p.u bef last* **15/2**

6m 2.50s (39.10) **Going Correction** +1.95s/f (Heav) **11** Ran SP% **116.4**
Speed ratings: **103,102,101,99,95** —,—,—,—,— — CSF £40.33 CT £312.15 TOTE £6.30: £1.80, £2.60, £3.80; EX 34.30.
Owner C Storey **Bred** North Farm Stud **Trained** Kirk Yetholm, Borders

FOCUS
A weak handicap, the topweight off just 90, but the form appears to make sense.

NOTEBOOK
Uneven Line gave chase to the clear leader between the last two fences but an error at the final obstacle - normally the penultimate fence - seemed to end her hopes. To her credit, and that of her rider, she wore down the flagging leader to snatch an unlikely victory close home. This was her first victory under Rules. *(tchd 5-1)*
Major Belle(FR) went on at the third last and soon came away, the race apparently hers, but she began to flag in the final 100 yards of this punishing run-in and she was claimed close home. The moral winner, she is well at home in testing ground. *(tchd 11-1)*
Pornic(FR), 3lb out of the handicap for this return to fences, ran creditably but extended his winless streak to 25 races. *(op 7-1)*
Scotmail Lad(IRE), a winning pointer a year or so ago, ran his best race since reverting to handicaps but is a very ordinary performer these days.
Native Eire(IRE), having his second run after a lengthy absence, should have no excuses on grounds of fitness next time. *(op 13-2)*
Casalani(IRE) *Official explanation: jockey said, regarding the apparent tender ride, his orders were to drop mare in and ride her to get home on the heavy ground, adding that she had schooled novicey over fences at home and he wanted to give her confidence over her fences; he further added that he kept mare going from second-last as the runners in front appeared to be tiring; trainer said mare is unsuited by heavy ground and she had considered withdrawing her today but the owners wished to run her (tchd 11-1)*
Nomadic Blaze, who made much of the running, was still in second over the penultimate fence but then tired badly. *(op 8-1)*
Peterhouse was entitled to need this first run since scoring at Newcastle in January last year. *(op 8-1)*

4660 STANLEY THOMPSON MEMORIAL OPEN HUNTERS' CHASE (16 fncs) 2m 5f
4:30 (4:30) (Class 6) 5-Y-0+ **£1,249** (£387; £193; £96)

Form RPR

2-33 **1** **Lord O'All Seasons (IRE)**^{3} 13-12-0 **88** .... MissRDavidson$^{(3)}$ 97+
(J P Elliot) *trckd ldr: led 8th: rdn 2 out: drvn flat: hld on gamely* **1/1**^{1}

60-0 **2** ½ **Polish Cloud (FR)**^{37} 9-11-10 **109** .... MrsHKemp$^{(7)}$ 96+
(Mrs H M Kemp) *nt fluent early in rr: hdwy to chse wnr 4 out: ev ch last: rdn and edgd rt flat: styd on wl towards fin* **11/2**^{3}

53P/ **3** 15 **Gollinger**^{9} 10-11-10 .... MrRTierney$^{(7)}$ 84+
(R H R Tierney) *mde most to 8th: rdn along after 3 out: ch last: drvn flat: hung rt and wknd last 200 yds* **7/1**

0-66 **4** 3 ½ **Donnybrook (IRE)**^{3} 13-11-12 **87** ....(p) MrBWoodhouse$^{(5)}$ 80+
(R D E Woodhouse) *trckd ldrs: mstke 8th: blnd next: sn rdn along and btn 4 out* **4/1**^{2}

1F0/ **U** **Just A Diamond**^{310} 13-11-3 .... MrCGillon$^{(7)}$ —
(Mrs D Walton) *hld up in tch tl blnd and uns rdr 8th* **20/1**

4 **F** **Moscowtastic (IRE)**^{35} 4044 8-11-10 .... MrSimonRobinson$^{(7)}$ —
(S J Robinson) *plld hrd: chsd ldrs: mstke 4th: hdwy to chse wnr whn fell 10th* **16/1**

6m 10.9s (47.50) **Going Correction** +2.30s/f (Heav) **6** Ran SP% **108.5**
Speed ratings: **101,100,95,93**,— — CSF £6.58 TOTE £1.90: £1.10, £2.80; EX 6.90 Place 6 £43.40, Place 5 £21.51.
Owner Mr & Mrs Duncan Davidson **Bred** Michael Cormack **Trained** Kelso, Borders

FOCUS
Not strong form, this has been rated through the winner.

NOTEBOOK
Lord O'All Seasons(IRE) was making a quick reappearance, having been beaten by a smart opponent in a two-horse ladies' point at the weekend. She just got the better of a dour battle up the extended run-in to land this uncompetitive event. *(op 10-11 tchd 5-6, 11-10 in places)*
Polish Cloud(FR) is a moderate pointer and the fact that he nearly won this does nothing for the form. He did not jump at all fluently but was still in with every chance up the long run-in, just losing out after a good tussle. *(tchd 5-1 and 6-1)*
Gollinger made all to land a maiden point this month on his first run in nearly two years. Still going well enough in third at the final fence, he found less than his rider seemed to expect him to when coming under pressure on the long run-in. *(op 9-1 tchd 10-1)*
Donnybrook(IRE), who came here off the back of a win in a heavy-ground confined point-to-point three days earlier, was struggling after a couple of errors. *(tchd 7-2 and 9-2 in a place)*
Moscowtastic(IRE), again far too keen, had just moved into second when coming down. He has a bit of ability but he will not fulfil it unless he can settle. *(op 20-1 tchd 22-1)*
T/Jkpt: £2,207.20 to a £1 stake. Pool: £296,887.75. 95.50 winning tickets. T/Plt: £145.70 to a £1 stake. Pool: £66,784.65. 334.40 winning tickets. T/Qpdt: £4.70 to a £1 stake. Pool: £5,654.40. 878.30 winning tickets. JR

4423 TAUNTON (R-H)
Wednesday, March 29

OFFICIAL GOING: Good to soft (soft in places)
Wind: Mild, across

4661 SOUTHWESTRACING.COM NOVICES' HURDLE (12 hdls) 3m 110y
2:10 (2:10) (Class 4) 4-Y-0+ **£5,204** (£1,528; £764; £381)

Form RPR

0 **1** **Twofan (USA)**^{86} 3224 5-11-3 ....(p) DNRussell 97
(C Byrnes, Ire) *hld up towards rr: hdwy after 8th to trck ldrs 3 out: rdn to ld appr 2 out: drifted lft run-in: all out* **5/2**^{2}

2066 **2** nk **Not Left Yet (IRE)**^{39} 3993 5-11-9 **118** ....(v^{1}) TimmyMurphy 104+
(M C Pipe) *hld up bhd: hdwy after 8th: chsd ldrs and rdn after 3 out: 3rd whn mstke last: swtchd rt run-in: styd on u.p* **6/4**^{1}

4042 **3** 5 **Hambaphambili**^{11} 4501 6-11-3 **105** .... LeightonAspell 92
(O Sherwood) *led: rdn and hdd appr 2 out: kpt on same pce* **15/2**

-342 **4** 4 **Lavenoak Lad**^{14} 4449 6-10-10 **75** ....(p) KeiranBurke$^{(7)}$ 88
(P R Rodford) *chsd ldrs: rdn after 9th: kpt on same pce fr 2 out* **50/1**

005 **5** 6 **Red Echo (FR)**^{22} 4285 5-11-0 .... TomMalone$^{(3)}$ 82
(M C Pipe) *mid div: tk clsr order 6th: mstke 7th: ev ch 3 out: sn rdn: wknd bef next* **50/1**

6-1 **6** 3 **Key To The Kingdom (IRE)**^{172} 1687 6-11-8 ....(p) MPButler$^{(7)}$ 91
(Eoin Doyle, Ire) *chsd ldrs tl wknd 3 out* **12/1**

/043 **7** 23 **The Wooden Spoon (IRE)**^{22} 4285 8-11-3 **98** .... MickFitzgerald 56
(L Wells) *prom tl wknd appr 3 out: sn t.o* **7/1**^{3}

P-06 **8** 19 **Harps Hall (IRE)**^{22} 4285 12-10-7 .... MarkHunter$^{(10)}$ 37
(N I M Rossiter) *prom tl 3rd: sn drvn along fr next towards rr: lost tch fr 8th: t.o* **250/1**

0000 **9** 8 **Allez Melina**^{34} 4074 5-10-10 .... PhilipHide 22
(Mrs A J Hamilton-Fairley) *hld up towards rr: hdwy after 8th: wknd 3 out: sn t.o* **66/1**

0-06 **P** **Blue Nun**^{297} 651 5-10-10 **75** .... RobertWalford —
(C L Popham) *a bhd: t.o fr 8th: p.u after 3 out* **200/1**

50 **P** **Double Spread**^{93} 2987 7-11-3 .... MarkBradburne —
(M Mullineaux) *mid div tl 8th: sn t.o: p.u bef 2 out* **150/1**

6m 12.6s (4.00) **Going Correction** +0.35s/f (Yiel) **11** Ran SP% **107.5**
Speed ratings: **107,106,105,104,102 101,93,87,85**,— — CSF £5.94 TOTE £4.80: £1.40, £1.10, £2.00; EX 12.50.
Owner Nay Syndicate **Bred** A Lakin And Sons **Trained** Ballingarry, Co Limerick
■ Stewards' Enquiry : D N Russell one-day ban: careless riding (Apr 19); further caution: used whip with excessive frequency

FOCUS
This was a modest opening novices' hurdle, run at an average gallop until halfway, and it lacked any real strength in depth. The race could have been rated a fair bit higher but the fourth and fifth limit the form.

NOTEBOOK
Twofan(USA), very well backed, dug deep in the first-time cheekpieces to break his duck over timber at the ninth attempt. Having shown just moderate form over hurdles before this, the step up to this trip was something of an unknown, but he did show his best form on the Flat over staying distances, and it was clearly much to his liking *(op 4-1)*
Not Left Yet(IRE), sporting a first-time visor for this first outing over three miles, rather spoilt his chance with some less than fluent hurdling yet still had every chance if good enough in the home straight. He did not appear that suited by this sharper track, and still finished a clear second-best, but his ability to stay this trip when returning to a more conventional circuit must still be taken on trust and he does appear flattered by his official mark at present. *(op 11-10)*
Hambaphambili posted another sound effort and, while he was ultimately put in his place by the first two, he fared by far the best of those to race handily. He should fare better when switching to handicaps from his current mark. *(op 7-1 tchd 8-1)*
Lavenoak Lad, beaten in selling company on his previous three outings, was ridden to get this longer trip and posted an improved effort without seriously threatening. He is going the right way, but his proximity at the finish does put this form into perspective. *(op 40-1)*
Red Echo(FR) ran freely and did not impress with his jumping, yet still posted his best effort to date in defeat. *(op 66-1 tchd 80-1)*
Key To The Kingdom(IRE), last seen winning at Hexham in October, failed to find much for *pressure and did not appear suited by this easier surface. He is capable of slightly better.Official explanation: , last seen winning at Hexham in October, failed to find much for pressure and did not appear suited by this easier surface. He is capable of slightly better.*
The Wooden Spoon(IRE) failed to raise his game and ran as though something may have been amiss. *(op 6-1 tchd 15-2)*

4662 JOE DINHAM MEMORIAL NOVICES' H'CAP CHASE (17 fncs) 2m 7f 110y
2:40 (2:40) (Class 4) (0-105,102) 5-Y-0+ **£6,396** (£1,930; £994; £526)

Form RPR

1342 **1** **Merry Storm (IRE)**^{19} 4350 7-10-8 **91** ....(t) RichardSpate$^{(7)}$ 100+
(Mrs K Waldron) *chsd ldrs: led after 4 out: in command fr next: readily* **10/3**^{2}

5P **2** 7 **Ehab (IRE)**^{20} 4320 7-10-1 **80** .... ColinBolger$^{(3)}$ 78
(Miss A M Newton-Smith) *sn led: rdn and hdd after 4 out: kpt on but no ch w wnr fr next* **25/1**

3PP4 **3** 1 ½ **Roddy The Vet (IRE)**^{50} 3791 8-10-0 **76** oh6 ....(b^{1}) JimCrowley 73
(A Ennis) *chsd ldrs: reminder after 4th: jnd ldr next tl 12th: one pce fr next* **8/1**

2632 **4** dist **Fight The Feeling**^{35} 4054 8-11-11 **101** .... CarlLlewellyn —
(J W Unett) *hld up towards rr: hdwy to chse ldrs after 10th: wknd after 13th: t.o* **14/1**

006P **P** **Lady Wurzel**^{9} 4553 7-10-0 **79** oh5 ow3 .... MissPGundry$^{(3)}$ —
(J G Cann) *mid div tl dropped rr 5th: sn t.o: p.u bef 8th* **14/1**

6-P4 **P** **The Cad (IRE)**^{22} 4288 6-11-0 **90** .... AndrewThornton —
(R H Alner) *chsd ldr: hit 11th: sn wknd: t.o and p.u bef 13th* **12/1**

P0P **P** **Swazi Prince**^{23} 4277 7-11-0 **90** ....(t) AntonyEvans —
(N A Twiston-Davies) *a towards rr: lost tch 10th: p.u bef next* **16/1**

02PP **P** **Boddidley (IRE)**^{38} 4007 8-11-7 **102** .... LiamHeard$^{(5)}$ —
(P F Nicholls) *in tch: drvn along after 10th: sn lost tch: p.u bef 4 out* **7/1**^{3}

551- **P** **Espresso Forte (IRE)**^{387} 4233 7-11-10 **100** .... TimmyMurphy —
(Miss H C Knight) *hld up bhd: sme hdwy 11th: wknd after 13th: t.o and p.u bef 3 out* **11/4**^{1}

033P **P** **Miss Fahrenheit (IRE)**^{18} 4372 7-11-11 **101** .... SamStronge —
(C Roberts) *chsd ldrs: hit 5th: sn dropped rr: nt fluent next: blnd 7th: t.o and p.u bef next* **12/1**

6m 14.4s (9.30) **Going Correction** +0.35s/f (Yiel) **10** Ran SP% **111.8**
Speed ratings: **98,95,95**,—,— —,—,—,—,— CSF £70.96 CT £606.31 TOTE £3.50: £1.90, £10.90, £1.90; EX 114.40.
Owner Nick Shutts **Bred** Jim Healy **Trained** Stoke Bliss, Worcs

FOCUS
A moderate handicap, run at a fair pace, which saw the field strung out from an early stage and only four runners managed to complete. The winner was value for 11l.

NOTEBOOK
Merry Storm(IRE), sporting a first-time tongue tie, found the race very much run to suit and deservedly resumed winning ways in ready fashion. He jumped with aplomb throughout and, while he did not have to improve on the form of his recent efforts to score, this consistent chaser should be rated value for further than his already wide winning margin. *(op 7-2)*
Ehab(IRE), pulled up over hurdles last time, posted a brave effort from the front on this return to the bigger obstacles and it must rate his best effort to date for current connections. *(tchd 28-1)*
Roddy The Vet(IRE), racing from 6lb out of the handicap and equipped with first-time blinkers, ran to his recent level in defeat and never seriously threatened. *(op 12-1)*
Miss Fahrenheit(IRE) *Official explanation: jockey said mare jumped poorly (op 3-1)*
Boddidley(IRE) never looked happy at any stage and was pulled up for the third consecutive occasion. *(op 3-1)*
Espresso Forte(IRE), last seen winning from a 10lb lower mark over hurdles 387 days previously, was in trouble before halfway and proved most disappointing on this chase debut. *(op 3-1)*

4663 SUMMER TIME H'CAP HURDLE (10 hdls) 2m 3f 110y
3:10 (3:10) (Class 3) (0-130,130) 4-Y-0+ **£12,676** (£3,744; £1,872; £936; £468)

Form RPR

5U10 **1** **Mcbain (USA)**[155] [1872] 7-11-10 **128**............................. RichardJohnson 134
(P J Hobbs) *hld up mid div: rdn and hdwy after 3 out: led last: hrd pressed run-in: all out* **12/1**

142U **2** *nk* **Nanga Parbat (FR)**[79] [3323] 5-10-13 **117**................................(t) RWalsh 124+
(P F Nicholls) *hld up towards rr: rdn and hdwy after 3 out: pressed ldrs next: ev ch fr last: no ex cl home* **5/1**[2]

P421 **3** *5* **Blaeberry**[16] [4429] 5-10-3 **107**.. BarryFenton 108
(Miss E C Lavelle) *hld up bhd: hdwy 7th: rdn to chse ldrs whn nt fluent 2 out: styd on run-in: tk 3rd cl home* **12/1**

1-20 **4** *hd* **Silencio (IRE)**[18] [4375] 5-11-7 **125**............................... RobertThornton 126
(A King) *t.k.h: led: rdn and hrd pressed after 3 out: narrowly hdd last: no ex: lost 3rd cl home* **14/1**

051P **5** *1 1/4* **New Entic (FR)**[26] [4215] 5-11-7 **125**..................................(p) JamieMoore 125
(G L Moore) *chsd ldrs: rdn and ev ch 2 out: kpt on same pce* **20/1**

121F **6** *1 1/2* **Le Volfoni (FR)**[13] [4456] 5-11-7 **130**.................................... LiamHeard(5) 128
(P F Nicholls) *mid div: rdn and hdwy appr 2 out: kpt on same pce* **3/1**[1]

0423 **7** *1 1/4* **Jockser (IRE)**[45] [3880] 5-9-10 **107**............................ WayneKavanagh(7) 104
(J W Mullins) *mid div: drvn along to hold position fr 5th: kpt on same pce fr 2 out* **17/2**

05-0 **8** *3/4* **Bongo Fury (FR)**[18] [4375] 7-11-12 **130**..............................(v) APMcCoy 127+
(M C Pipe) *mid div: lost pl briefly after 6th: trckd ldrs 3 out: rdn and ev ch 2 out: one pce after* **8/1**[3]

3405 **9** *shd* **Devito (FR)**[30] [4153] 5-10-3 **112**.. MrTJO'Brien(5) 108
(G F Edwards) *chsd ldrs: rdn after 3 out: one pce after* **28/1**

4340 **10** *8* **Woody Valentine (USA)**[35] [4058] 5-10-11 **115**................. SamThomas 103
(Miss Venetia Williams) *chsd ldrs: ev ch 3 out: sn rdn: wknd next* **20/1**

0616 **11** *shd* **Marrel**[32] [4119] 8-10-7 **111**...(v) AntonyEvans 99
(D Burchell) *prom: ev ch 3 out: sn rdn and wknd* **40/1**

0-P0 **12** *3 1/2* **Distant Prospect (IRE)**[18] [4375] 9-11-8 **126**................... MarkBradburne 110
(A M Balding) *chsd ldrs tl wknd 3 out* **16/1**

2360 **13** *3/4* **Goldbrook**[25] [4242] 8-11-5 **123**... TimmyMurphy 107
(R J Hodges) *a in rr* **11/1**

0P36 **14** *8* **Aldiruos (IRE)**[33] [4091] 6-10-0 **104** oh1...................... WayneHutchinson 80
(A W Carroll) *mid div tl wknd 3 out* **50/1**

F400 **P** **Forzacurity**[212] [1366] 7-9-11 **104** oh5.......................... WilliamKennedy(3) —
(D Burchell) *a bhd: t.o and p.u bef 6th* **200/1**

4m 49.6s (3.60) **Going Correction** +0.35s/f (Yiel) **15** Ran SP% **117.4**
Speed ratings: **106,105,103,103,103 102,102,101,101,98 98,97,96,93,—** CSF £65.34 CT £748.64 TOTE £12.90: £3.70, £2.20, £2.60; EX 86.00.
Owner Hill, Trembath, Bryan and Outhart **Bred** Lazy Lane Stables Inc **Trained** Withycombe, Somerset

FOCUS
A decent handicap for the prize money on offer and it was run at a solid pace. The first two came clear on the run-in and the form appears sound.

NOTEBOOK
Mcbain(USA), well backed on this return from a five-month break, dug deep under a typically strong ride from Johnson to repel the runner-up and score. While the ground had dried out somewhat, it would still have been plenty soft enough for his liking, so he deserves plenty of credit on that score. His form figures at this venue now read 1311. *(op 16-1 tchd 20-1)*
Nanga Parbat(FR), who unseated at this track on his chasing bow when last seen in early January, emerged to have every chance in the home straight and only just missed out. He was nicely clear of the rest at the finish. *(tchd 4-1)*
Blaeberry, off the mark on her handicap bow last time over course and distance, hit a flat spot at the top of the straight, yet was staying on again at the finish and was far from disgraced off her 7lb higher mark. *(op 8-1)*
Silencio(IRE) posted a solid effort and fared the best of those to help force the early gallop. This was much more like his true form and the return to genuinely good ground in the future can see him back in the winner's enclosure.
New Entic(FR) showed his true colours and did little wrong in defeat. He ideally needs a stiffer track, but still looks weighted to his best at present. *(op 16-1)*
Le Volfoni(FR), who would have likely filled a place behind Reveillez in the Jewson Novices' Handicap at Cheltenham but for coming to grief three out last time, was not disgraced under top weight on this return to hurdling, and his confidence should be restored now. *(tchd 7-2)*
Jockser(IRE) ran his race and helps set the level of this form. *(op 12-1)*
Bongo Fury(FR) looked a player turning for home, but her effort petered out and she was ultimately well held. This was an improvement on her recent comeback in the Imperial Cup. *(tchd 7-1)*
Distant Prospect(IRE) failed to improve for this longer trip and looks one to avoid at present.

4664 MARGARET IZABY-WHITE 60TH BIRTHDAY NOVICES' LIMITED H'CAP CHASE (12 fncs) 2m 110y
3:40 (3:40) (Class 3) (0-135,128) 5-Y-0+ **£12,676** (£3,744; £1,872; £936; £468)

Form RPR

PFF2 **1** **Misty Dancer**[9] [4552] 7-10-5 **109**... SamThomas 121+
(Miss Venetia Williams) *hld up but in tch: tk clsr order 6th: led appr 3 out: rdn after 2 out: jst hld on* **7/2**[3]

P323 **2** *shd* **Medison (FR)**[44] [3903] 6-11-4 **122**...................................... TimmyMurphy 135+
(M C Pipe) *hld up but in tch: tk clsr order 6th: hit 7th:rdn to chse wnr after 2 out: kpt on u.str.p fr last: jst failed* **5/1**

F111 **3** *5* **Roznic (FR)**[32] [4120] 8-11-3 **121**.. LeightonAspell 129+
(P Winkworth) *chsd ldrs: wnt 2nd at the 6th: ev ch whn blnd 2 out: sn rdn: no ex* **3/1**[2]

UU22 **4** *1* **Give Me Love (FR)**[16] [4424] 6-11-1 **119**................................(bt) RWalsh 124
(P F Nicholls) *chsd ldr tl 6th: rdn to dispute 2nd 4 out: kpt on same pce fr next* **5/2**[1]

10F3 **5** *8* **Priors Dale**[18] [4377] 6-11-10 **128**.. BarryFenton 128+
(Miss E C Lavelle) *led at decent pce: rdn and hdd appr 3 out: wkng whn hit 2 out* **5/1**

16R0 **P** **Lord Lington (FR)**[16] [4420] 7-11-2 **120**............................ WarrenMarston —
(D J Wintle) *hld up: lost tch after 6th: p.u bef 8th* **33/1**

4m 10.1s (-5.40) **Going Correction** +0.35s/f (Yiel) **6** Ran SP% **112.1**
Speed ratings: **111,110,108,108,104 —** CSF £20.65 TOTE £5.10: £2.20, £2.80; EX 16.20.
Owner Miss V M Williams **Bred** Mrs D O Joly **Trained** Kings Caple, H'fords

FOCUS
A slightly disappointing turnout for the prize money available but still a decent handicap. The winner ran to the upgraded level of his Hereford second.

NOTEBOOK
Misty Dancer, who just lost out at Hereford nine days previously, this time got the better of a cracking finish to make amends. The drying ground proved much to his advantage, he jumped neatly throughout, and he clearly likes this venue having won on his only previous outing over the course as a hurdler back in 2004. He looks progressive and is developing into a likeable performer. *(op 4-1)*
Medison(FR), a course and distance winner over hurdles and making his handicap debut in this sphere, was only just denied and was actually in front yards after passing the post. This has to rate his best effort to date over fences, but he again made mistakes when under pressure, and he really does appear reluctant when asked for maximum effort in his races. He is certainly capable of winning a chase from this sort of mark, however, and it will come as no surprise to see the application of some form of headgear ahead of his next assignment. *(op 4-1 tchd 11-2)*
Roznic(FR), bidding for a four-timer, was still yet to be asked a serious question prior to walking through the penultimate fence and effectively losing all chance. He remains progressive and may not be weighted out of winning yet. *(op 7-2 tchd 4-1)*
Give Me Love(FR) found nothing when asked for maximum effort and has to rate as disappointing. He is one to avoid. *(op 11-4)*
Priors Dale ultimately appeared to pay for setting the generous early pace. *(tchd 4-1)*

4665 CHERRY BLOSSOM MAIDEN HURDLE (9 hdls) 2m 1f
4:10 (4:11) (Class 5) 4-Y-0+ **£3,083** (£898; £449)

Form RPR

4 **1** **Kingham**[45] [3883] 6-11-5 .... CarlLlewellyn 123+
(Mrs Mary Hambro) *mde all: sn clr: unchal* **11/4**[2]

-060 **2** *19* **A Few Kind Words (IRE)**[23] [4280] 5-10-12 .... RichardSpate(7) 93
(Mrs K Waldron) *hld up towards rr: stdy hdwy fr 5th: rdn after 3 out: wnt distant 2nd appr 2 out: nvr any ch w wnr* **100/1**

3 *3/4* **So Brash (IRE)**[137] [2199] 6-11-5 .... AndrewThornton 92
(P C Ritchens) *mid div: stdy hdwy fr 5th: chal for distant 2nd fr 3 out* **25/1**

4 *14* **Cash On (IRE)**[171] 4-10-12 .... RWalsh 75+
(P F Nicholls) *chsd ldrs: hit 2nd: wknd 3 out* **11/8**[1]

00 **5** *16* **Miss Grace**[16] [4425] 6-10-12 .... JoeTizzard 55
(J D Frost) *a towards rr: t.o fr 3 out* **12/1**

50 **6** *3 1/2* **Sturbury**[81] [3280] 4-10-2 .... RichardYoung(3) 45
(J W Mullins) *mid div tl wknd 6th: sn t.o* **40/1**

05 **7** *4* **Lucent (IRE)**[35] [4048] 5-11-5 .... PaulMoloney 55
(Miss H C Knight) *mid div tl wknd appr 6th: sn t.o* **28/1**

P4 **8** *2* **Gimmeabreak (IRE)**[36] [4033] 6-11-5 .... BarryFenton 53
(Miss E C Lavelle) *a bhd: t.o fr 5th* **14/1**

3P-P **9** *15* **Shernatra (IRE)**[116] [2624] 7-11-5 .... JasonMaguire 38
(J A B Old) *a bhd: t.o fr 5th* **14/1**

0-3 **10** *1* **Nikolaiev (FR)**[47] [3843] 5-10-12 .... CharlieStudd(7) 37
(N J Henderson) *chsd ldrs: wnt 2nd after 4th: wknd qckly after 3 out* **6/1**[3]

P **Napapijri (FR)**[23] 4-9-9 .... RichardGordon(10) —
(W G M Turner) *mid div tl 4th: sn wknd: t.o and p.u bef 2 out* **150/1**

PP **P** **Opera Villevert (FR)**[9] [4551] 4-10-7 ....(b[1]) HowieEphgrave(5) —
(L Corcoran) *chsd ldrs tl wknd 6th: sn t.o: p.u bef 2 out* **200/1**

4m 12.7s (3.90) **Going Correction** +0.35s/f (Yiel)
WFA 4 from 5yo+ 7lb **12** Ran SP% **116.0**
Speed ratings: **104,95,94,88,80 78,77,76,69,68 —,—** CSF £257.38 TOTE £3.10: £1.20, £11.60, £7.00; EX 257.90.
Owner Richard Hambro **Bred** London Thoroughbred Services Ltd **Trained** Bourton-on-the-Hill, Gloucs

FOCUS
A very weak maiden which saw the field trail home behind the easy winner, who was value for 30l. Both he and the second showed improvement of around a stone.

NOTEBOOK
Kingham confirmed the promise of his hurdling bow at Hereford last time and ran his rivals ragged from the front to get off the mark at the second time of asking. He still looked in need of this experience, so is entitled to improve again, and could hardly have done the job any easier. *(op 9-4 tchd 10-3)*
A Few Kind Words(IRE) stayed on best of all from off the pace and posted a more encouraging effort. *(op 66-1)*
So Brash(IRE), fourth in a fair bumper on his debut under Rules at Naas when last seen in November, was not disgraced on this British debut for new connections. He shaped as though the race would bring him on, ought to fare better when eligible for handicaps in due course, and looks the one to take from the race with a view to the future. *(op 20-1)*
Cash On(IRE), a 12-furlong Polytrack maiden winner on the Flat, was very well backed on course for this hurdling debut yet proved most disappointing. He was in trouble from halfway and has it all to prove after this. *(op 5-2)*
Nikolaiev(FR) ran as though something was amiss. *Official explanation: jockey said gelding finished distressed (op 9-2 tchd 4-1)*

4666 GET DAILY RACING NEWS ON GG.COM H'CAP CHASE (14 fncs) 2m 3f
4:40 (4:41) (Class 5) (0-85,84) 5-Y-0+ **£3,768** (£1,098; £549)

Form RPR

24U0 **1** **Sailor A'Hoy**[98] [2936] 10-11-7 **79**.......................................(p) AlanO'Keeffe 94+
(M Mullineaux) *bhd: drvn along after 7th: hmpd 4 out: styd on u.p fr next: wnt 2nd approaching 2 out: led sn after last* **8/1**

0645 **2** *3 1/2* **Ingenu (FR)**[99] [2933] 10-11-4 **76**..(p) SeanCurran 87+
(P Wegmann) *chsd ldrs: lost pl appr 5th: led after 4 out: sn rdn: narrow advantage whn blnd last: no ex* **25/1**

6220 **3** *7* **Opportunity Knocks**[14] [4451] 6-11-1 **73**...........................(p) PJBrennan 76
(N J Hawke) *chsd ldrs: rdn after 9th: kpt on same pce fr 4 out* **9/1**

6643 **4** *7* **Levallois (IRE)**[10] [4524] 10-11-9 **81**................................(b) LeightonAspell 81+
(P Winkworth) *mid div: rdn after 10th: hmpd next: no imp after* **4/1**[1]

24PP **5** *1 1/2* **Minat Boy**[16] [4428] 10-10-13 **71**.. JoeTizzard 66
(C L Tizzard) *mid div tl lost pl 8th* **16/1**

P01 **6** *3/4* **River Amora (IRE)**[10] [4525] 11-11-4 **76** 7ex.......................(p) JamieMoore 70
(Jim Best) *w ldr: led 3rd tl blnd and hdd 5th: led after 7th: rdn and hdd after 4 out: wknd* **4/1**[1]

PP63 **7** *11* **A Pound Down (IRE)**[16] [4428] 9-11-3 **75**............................... DaveCrosse 58
(N G Ayliffe) *hld up bhd: hdwy after 7th: rdn and lft 4th 4 out: sn wknd* **12/1**

26P0 **P** **Sunshan**[7] [4575] 10-11-5 **84**.. JamesWhite(7) —
(R J Hodges) *mid div whn p.u bef 6th* **20/1**

3U-F **U** **Jacks Jewel (IRE)**[287] [759] 9-11-5 **80**............................. RichardYoung(3) —
(C J Down) *hld up: making hdwy whn blnd and uns rdr 9th* **11/1**

/60P **P** **Jorodama King**[16] [4428] 12-9-7 **58** oh4................................... KeiranBurke(7) —
(N J Hawke) *chsd ldrs tl wknd appr 9th: t.o and p.u bef 4 out* **40/1**

6/44 **U** **Bonny Boy (IRE)**[19] [4353] 11-9-11 **58** oh3.............(vt) WilliamKennedy(3) —
(D A Rees) *hld up: making gd prog whn blnd and uns rdr 9th* **11/2**[2]

-543 **F** **Risington**[7] [4575] 8-11-5 **77**... SamThomas —
(Miss Venetia Williams) *led tl 3rd: w ldr: led sn after 5th: hdd 7th: rdn in 4th whn fell heavily 4 out* **13/2**[3]

5m 0.60s (7.80) **Going Correction** +0.35s/f (Yiel) **12** Ran SP% **122.8**
Speed ratings: **97,95,92,89,89 88,84,—,—,— —,—** CSF £185.69 CT £1852.06 TOTE £12.00: £3.60, £6.50, £1.70; EX 203.10.
Owner R Williamson **Bred** Viscount Leverhulme **Trained** Alpraham, Cheshire

FOCUS
An open-looking contest for the class, run at a sound pace, and the field finished strung out. The winner was well in on the best of his form last year.

NOTEBOOK

Sailor A'Hoy sprouted wings at the top of the home straight to mow down his rivals and ultimately score a first success over fences with a little up his sleeve. He has clearly benefited from a recent break, enjoyed the ground, and should still appear feasibly treated in relation to his hurdling form despite a rise in the weights for this. *(op 11-1)*

Ingenu(FR) looked the most likely winner when kicking for home, but his stride began to shorten after the penultimate fence, and he looked held by the winner prior to a final-flight error. He has not won since 2002, but this did rate a pleasing return from his 99-day break. *(tchd 28-1)*

Opportunity Knocks ran in snatches on this drop back in trip, but kept to his task under pressure and should better this effort when returning to a suitably stiffer test. *(op 12-1)*

Levallois(IRE), dropping markedly in trip, was well backed yet never seriously threatened. He kept on as though the return to further would be more to his liking, but he remains one to have reservations about. *(op 7-1)*

River Amora(IRE), under a penalty for making all at Fontwell ten days previously, was not suited by being taken on for the lead and was in trouble with four to jump. *(op 9-2 tchd 11-2)*

Sunshan *Official explanation: jockey said gelding was lame (op 16-1)*

4667 SOMERSET MAIDEN OPEN NATIONAL HUNT FLAT RACE 2m 1f

5:10 (5:12) (Class 6) 4-6-Y-O **£1,850** (£539; £269)

Form RPR

6 **1** **Delena**[69] 3468 5-11-0 RWalsh 97+
(P F Nicholls) *mid div: rdn and hdwy 4f out: led jst over 1f out: r.o wl* **7/2**[2]

2 *7* **Gurteenoona (IRE)** 4-11-0 WayneHutchinson 90
(Ian Williams) *mid div: hdwy 6f out: rdn to ld over 2f out: hdd over 1f out: kpt on same pce* **16/1**

3 *1 ½* **Vintage Fabric (USA)** 4-10-7 KeiranBurke[(7)] 89
(N J Hawke) *hld up towards rr: stdy prog fr 7f out: rdn to chal 3f out: kpt on same pce* **50/1**

4 *1 ¾* **Kelv** 5-11-7 MarkBradburne 94
(J A B Old) *hld up towards rr: gd hdwy fr 5f out: rdn and effrt 3f out: sn edgd lft: kpt on same pce* **5/1**[3]

5 *8* **Sooky** 6-11-0 JoeTizzard 79
(J D Frost) *chsd ldrs: rdn over 3f out: sn one pce* **25/1**

6 *½* **Cash Back** 6-11-4 ChrisHonour[(3)] 85
(J D Frost) *led: rdn and hdd over 2f out: wknd over 1f out* **25/1**

6 **7** *3* **Niver Bai (FR)**[20] 4333 5-11-7 TimmyMurphy 82
(Miss H C Knight) *mid div: drvn along to hold pl 7f out: wknd over 2f out* **5/4**[1]

60- **8** *2* **Blakeney Run**[384] 4290 6-11-0 MrGTumelty[(7)] 80
(Miss M Bragg) *chsd ldrs tl wknd over 2f out* **33/1**

9 *3 ½* **Keyneema** 4-11-0 AndrewThornton 70
(Miss K M George) *a towards rr* **14/1**

10 *6* **Running Hotter** 5-11-0 PJBrennan 64
(N J Hawke) *a towards rr* **40/1**

11 *17* **Calver's Conquest** 4-10-9 MrJMead[(5)] 47
(J A B Old) *hld up towards rr: hdwy to chse ldrs on outer 9f out: wknd 5f out: t.o* **40/1**

12 *29* **Bonnykino** 4-10-7 TomDoyle 11
(S C Burrough) *chsd ldrs tl 7f out: sn bhd* **33/1**

13 *20* **Porty Fox** 5-11-7 TomScudamore 5
(N R Mitchell) *in tch tl 5f out* **40/1**

14 *dist* **Thorn** 4-11-0 JohnMcNamara —
(P W Hiatt) *in tch tl 8f out: sn wl bhd* **14/1**

4m 11.4s (2.80) **Going Correction** +0.35s/f (Yiel)
WFA 4 from 5yo+ 7lb **14** Ran SP% **125.4**
Speed ratings: **107,103,103,102,98 98,96,95,94,91 83,69,60,—** CSF £55.33 TOTE £7.30: £1.50, £4.10, £13.20; EX 66.90 Place 6 £660.26, Place 5 £543.69.
Owner Mrs A E Goodwin **Bred** Crandon Park Stud **Trained** Ditcheat, Somerset

FOCUS

An ordinary bumper run at a fair gallop for an event of its type, and the field came home strung out. Not much to go on, with the favourite disappointing, but a big step up from the winner.

NOTEBOOK

Delena, sixth on her debut over course and distance in January, took time to warm to her task, but ultimately ran out an easy winner and looked better the further she went. She is bred to make her mark over jumps, and really ought to appreciate a stiffer test, so rates a nice prospect for mares-only events next season. *(tchd 4-1)*

Gurteenoona(IRE), a half-brother to a winning pointer, kicked for home three out, but found just the same pace when it mattered and was readily held by the winner at the finish. He did little wrong in defeat and, like the winner, ought to improve for a longer trip when sent over hurdles in due course. *(op 14-1)*

Vintage Fabric(USA), whose dam was a mile winner in the US, showed up well on this debut and ought to come on a deal for the experience. He looked suited by this sharp track. *(op 40-1)*

Kelv, bred to be useful over jumps, was done for speed in the home straight yet still offered hope for the future. *(op 15-2 tchd 9-2)*

Niver Bai(FR), a promising sixth on his recent Wincanton debut, proved most disappointing and was beaten a long way from home. *(op 6-4)*

T/Plt: £984.50 to a £1 stake. Pool: £60,556.10. 44.90 winning tickets. T/Qpdt: £468.10 to a £1 stake. Pool: £4,428.40. 7.00 winning tickets. TM

4569 CHEPSTOW (L-H)

Thursday, March 30

4668 Meeting Abandoned - Waterlogged

4327 WINCANTON (R-H)

Thursday, March 30

OFFICIAL GOING: Soft

Wind: Strong, against

4674 WINCANTONRACECOURSE.CO.UK H'CAP HURDLE (8 hdls) 2m

2:10 (2:10) (Class 4) (0-115,112) 4-Y-O **£3,578** (£1,050; £525; £262)

Form RPR

0411 **1** **Picot De Say**[15] 4452 4-10-6 **92** OllieMcPhail 101+
(C Roberts) *hld up bhd ldrs: trckd ldng pair after 3 out: led last: r.o wl: pushed out* **2/1**[1]

3334 **2** *5* **Original Fly (FR)**[33] 4104 4-11-4 **104** (b) RWalsh 103
(P F Nicholls) *w ldr: led after 3 out: sn rdn: hdd last: kpt on same pce* **9/2**[3]

16 **3** *shd* **Shiny Thing (USA)**[78] 3340 4-11-3 **103** RobertThornton 103+
(A King) *hld up bhd ldrs: jnd ldr after 3 out: rdn and ev ch after 2 out: hit last: sn edgd rt: kpt on same pce* **4/1**[2]

5104 **4** *dist* **Sole Agent (IRE)**[33] 4117 4-11-12 **112** JamieMoore —
(G L Moore) *trckd ldrs: wknd appr 2 out* **6/1**

2100 **5** *7* **Desert Secrets (IRE)**[27] 4210 4-10-9 **98** StephenCraine[(3)] —
(J G Portman) *led tl after 3 out: wknd bef next* **11/1**

6450 **P** **Legally Fast (USA)**[15] 4443 4-11-5 **105** (b) AndrewThornton —
(S C Burrough) *nvr travelling and a in rr: p.u bef 3 out* **11/2**

3m 54.6s (5.50) **Going Correction** +0.425s/f (Soft) **6** Ran SP% **109.5**
Speed ratings: **103,100,100,—,—** — CSF £10.86 CT £28.42 TOTE £2.50: £1.60, £1.90; EX 10.70.
Owner Dr Simon Clarke **Bred** Henry And Mrs Rosemary Moszkowicz **Trained** Newport, Newport

FOCUS

The front three finished a distance clear of the remainder in what was an ordinary handicap hurdle. The progressive winner was value for 10l and the form looks sound enough.

NOTEBOOK

Picot De Say has really shown improved form since going handicapping, winning at Taunton and Huntingdon, and completing the hat-trick here in fine style. It would be unwise to get carried away with the form, but this strong traveller may yet have more to offer and it will be interesting to see how the Handicapper reacts. *(op 15-8 tchd 9-4)*

Original Fly(FR), Listed-placed in France last year, has not progressed as connections would have hoped and he had every chance back in second. The blinkers have not done anything for him, so he may be worth a try at two and a half miles. *(op 4-1)*

Shiny Thing(USA) ran well in ground that would not have suited, arguably travelling best into the straight, but being unable to go on after a blunder at he last. She may be capable of winning again during the summer on better ground.

Sole Agent(IRE) found himself outclassed in a graded event at Sandown last month, but this was *easier and he should have done an awful lot better than he did, trailing in a distant fourth. (op 13-2 tchd 7-1)*

Desert Secrets(IRE) took them along in the early strides, but she is basically a moderate performer who found herself outclassed. *(op 12-1 tchd 9-1)*

Legally Fast(USA) was struggling from a very early stage and it would not surprise to learn there was something amiss. *(op 8-1)*

4675 WINCANTON GOLF COURSE NOVICES' H'CAP CHASE (13 fncs) 2m

2:45 (2:45) (Class 4) (0-100,106) 5-Y-O+ **£6,506** (£1,910; £955; £477)

Form RPR

2213 **1** **Wizard Of Edge**[23] 4288 6-11-12 **100** (b) ChristianWilliams 103+
(R J Hodges) *trckd ldrs: wnt 2nd after 8th: narrow advantage whn pckd 3 out: kpt on: drvn out* **11/4**[1]

4R06 **2** *2* **Kinkeel (IRE)**[8] 4575 7-9-11 **74** oh1 (b) StephenCraine[(3)] 74
(A W Carroll) *led: racd wd up home st: narrowly hdd 3 out: sn rdn: kpt on but no ex fr last* **16/1**[3]

1333 **3** *1 ¾* **Before The Mast (IRE)**[4] 4632 9-10-13 **92** CharliePoste[(5)] 90
(M F Harris) *hld up bhd ldrs: tk clsr order after 9th: rdn and effrt appr 3 out: kpt on same pce* **11/4**[1]

344U **4** *8* **Terrible Tenant**[90] 3126 7-11-1 **89** AndrewThornton 80+
(J W Mullins) *trckd ldr tl 8th: chsd ldrs: pckd 4 out: sn rdn: wknd after next* **3/1**[2]

0320 **P** **Munadil**[56] 3686 8-10-3 **77** (t) RobertThornton —
(A M Hales) *hld up bhd ldrs: reminders after 7th: rdn and wknd qckly after 4 out: p.u bef next* **11/4**[1]

4m 13.7s (11.80) **Going Correction** +0.425s/f (Soft) **5** Ran SP% **110.9**
Speed ratings: **87,86,85,81,—** CSF £31.05 TOTE £2.80: £1.40, £4.30; EX 44.70.
Owner Mrs C Taylor & K Small **Bred** R G Percival And R Kent **Trained** Charlton Adam, Somerset

FOCUS

A weak race but a tight heat with three 11/4 co-favourites and Terrible Tenant at 3s. It was top weight Wizard Of Edge that came out on top, seeing his race out well under a strong ride from Williams. However, the winning time was very slow.

NOTEBOOK

Wizard Of Edge, who found the heavy ground against him at Exeter last time, again would have prefered a faster surface, but he still proved good enough and found plenty under a strong ride from Williams. The blinkers have definitely helped the six-year-old and he remains capable of better on a quicker surface in the coming months. *(op 5-2 tchd 3-1)*

Kinkeel(IRE), the only runner to be dismissed in the betting, enjoyed himself out in front and kept on well once headed to hold second. He has yet to win, but evidently has a small race in him off this sort of mark. *(op 14-1)*

Before The Mast(IRE) tends to mix hurdles and chasing, and he ran another fair race in defeat without doing enough to suggest he is ready to score off this mark. *(tchd 3-1)*

Terrible Tenant has largely been below his best this season and this was another modest effort, but his two wins last term both came on a fast surface and he could be one to look out for in the summer. *(op 4-1)*

Munadil is hardly the most consistent and it was no surprise to see him turn in a poor effort, *stopping quickly under pressure and possibly not enjoying the soft ground.Official explanation: jockey said gelding was unsuited by soft ground (tchd 3-1)*

4676 3 COUNTIES PLANT & TOOL HIRE NOVICES' HURDLE (11 hdls) 2m 6f

3:15 (3:15) (Class 4) 5-Y-O+ **£3,253** (£955; £477; £238)

Form RPR

2213 **1** **The Luder (IRE)**[37] 4036 5-11-5 119 (b[1]) RWalsh 127+
(P F Nicholls) *mde all: drew clr after after 3 out: shkn up after 2 out: styd on: comf* **1/1**[1]

35 **2** *8* **Surface To Air**[107] 2815 5-10-5 AngharadFrieze[(7)] 105+
(Mrs P N Dutfield) *hld up bhd: sme hdwy 6th: lot to do 3 out: hdwy appr 2 out: styd on to go 2nd at the last: nvr any ch w wnr* **14/1**

5330 **3** *7* **Portland Bill (IRE)**[19] 4373 6-10-12 108 RobertThornton 98
(R H Alner) *chsd ldrs: rdn after 3 out: kpt on same pce* **6/1**[3]

535 **4** *hd* **Le Briar Soul (IRE)**[34] 4094 6-10-12 MickFitzgerald 98
(V R A Dartnall) *hld up towards rr: stdy prog after 6th: rdn after 3 out: kpt on same pce* **12/1**

4253 **5** *9* **Macmar (FR)**[19] 4371 6-10-12 AndrewThornton 89
(R H Alner) *mid div: hdwy 6th to chse wnr: rdn after 8th: one pce after* **20/1**

0B03 **6** *3 ½* **Pyleigh Lady**[17] 4425 5-10-2 ChrisHonour[(3)] 81+
(S C Burrough) *mid div: hdwy 8th: rdn to chse wnr after 3 out: wknd bef 2 out* **40/1**

3223 **7** *1 ¾* **Palm Island (FR)**[18] 4393 5-10-9 109 WilliamKennedy[(3)] 84
(Noel T Chance) *mid div: rdn and hdwy appr 8th: one pce fr 3 out* **7/2**[2]

000 **P** **Lagan Legend**[17] 4425 5-10-5 RobertWalford —
(Dr J R J Naylor) *in tch tl 7th: t.o and p.u bef 2 out* **150/1**

0- **P** **Island Of Memories (IRE)**[456] 3080 6-10-0 (p) DarylJacob[(5)] —
(D P Keane) *a bhd: blnd 8th: t.o and p.u bef 2 out* **100/1**

P P **Double Date (FR)**[34] [4094] 5-10-12 .... JimmyMcCarthy —
(C P Morlock) *chsd ldrs: wkng whn j. bdly lft 6th: p.u bef next* **150/1**

P **Billy Bray**[347] 6-10-12 .... SamThomas —
(Miss Venetia Williams) *w wnr tl 6th: grad fdd: t.o and p.u bef 2 out* **100/1**

5 P **Picts Hill**[80] [3327] 6-10-12 .... ChristianWilliams —
(P F Nicholls) *a towards rr: mstke 5th: t.o and p.u bef 2 out* **40/1**

0P P **Oddington (IRE)**[107] [2815] 6-10-12 .... TomScudamore —
(Mrs Susan Nock) *chsd ldrs: hit 1st: wknd appr 8th: t.o and p.u bef last* **100/1**

PP-F P **Jasper Rooney**[87] [3215] 7-10-5 .... KeiranBurke(7) —
(C W Mitchell) *mid div: reminders after 4th: bhd whn hmpd 6th: p.u bef next* **200/1**

215 P **Lindbergh Law (USA)**[48] [3842] 6-10-9 .... DougieCostello(3) —
(Mrs H Dalton) *hld up towards rr: hdwy 4th: rdn to chse ldrs after 3 out: wknd qckly and p.u bef next* **33/1**

5m 31.0s (5.90) **Going Correction** +0.425s/f (Soft) **15** Ran SP% **118.2**
Speed ratings: **106,103,100,100,97 95,95,—,—,— —,—,—,—,—** CSF £16.80 TOTE £2.30: £1.10, £4.10, £2.60; EX 22.70.

Owner Derek Millard **Bred** T Lynch **Trained** Ditcheat, Somerset

FOCUS
An uncompetitive race in which only three could be given a chance. The winner is rated value for 15l and this is pretty solid form.

NOTEBOOK
The Luder(IRE), a disappointment when bidding to make it back-to-back handicap wins at Exeter last month, raced sweetly in the first-time blinkers and simply galloped his inferior rivals into the ground on this return to novice company. Soon in the lead, it was clear from over half a mile out he was going to win and he looked value for double the winning margin. A fine chasing prospect, he could not be in better hands and is one to keep on side. *(op 6-5 tchd 5-4)*
Surface To Air did not quite last out over 3m 1f at Warwick on his most recent outing, but this time he did not get going in time, coming through late to claim a never-nearer second. A more positive ride may help in future and he could be an interesting one for handicaps. *(op 16-1 tchd 12-1)*
Portland Bill(IRE) is all over a chaser and, to coin a phrase, 'anything he does over hurdles is a bonus'. He has not done a lot so far, but he has yet to tackle three miles and there is surely a race in him off this lowly mark. *(op 7-1)*
Le Briar Soul(IRE) comes from a stable who have had a poor year compared with previous seasons, and he did not shape too badly back in fourth. He may find a small race before going chasing. *(op 11-1 tchd 9-1)*
Macmar(FR) has largely been disappointing since arriving from France, and this debut over hurdles was not much better. He may still be in need of more time. *(op 16-1)*
Pyleigh Lady ran well for a long way and she would be of interest against her own sex in handicaps.
Palm Island(FR) has performed consistently in defeat since going hurdling, but this was not such a good effort and he now has a bit to prove. *(tchd 4-1)*

4677 CARLING H'CAP CHASE (17 fncs) 2m 5f
3:50 (3:50) (Class 3) (0-130,129) 5-Y-0+ **£8,889** (£2,711; £1,416; £769)

Form RPR

-011 1 **First Love**[20] [4358] 10-10-4 **114** .... MrJSnowden(7) 125
(N J Henderson) *led: hrd pressed appr 3 out: rdn and narrowly hdd last: rallied gamely to ld cl home* **5/2**[1]

1623 2 *shd* **Joey Tribbiani (IRE)**[34] [4089] 9-10-8 **111** .... WayneHutchinson 122
(T Keddy) *chsd ldrs: drvn along after 12th: chal 3 out: narrow advantage last: drifted lft u.p run-in: hdd cl home* **12/1**

P43F 3 *12* **Christopher**[21] [4332] 9-11-0 **117** .... PJBrennan 121+
(P J Hobbs) *chsd ldrs: racd wd up home st: wnt 2nd after 12th: chal 3 out: ev ch whn blnd 2 out: wknd* **3/1**[2]

1P43 4 *dist* **Soeur Fontenail (FR)**[40] [3992] 9-10-7 **110** .... AndrewThornton —
(N J Hawke) *w wnr tl after 12th: wknd after next: t.o* **4/1**[3]

165 P **Ghadames (FR)**[117] [2625] 12-11-12 **129** .... SamThomas —
(Miss Venetia Williams) *hld up: racd wd up home st: lost tch qckly after 8th: p.u bef next* **8/1**

324P P **Mark Equal**[40] [3992] 10-10-1 **111** .... AndrewGlassonbury(7) —
(M C Pipe) *sn trcking ldrs: rdn and effrt after 13th: 4th and wkng whn p.u bef 3 out* **15/2**

-4F3 P **Team Tassel (IRE)**[42] [3946] 8-11-7 **124** ....(p) TomScudamore —
(M C Pipe) *nvr fluent: chsd ldrs: reminders after 4th: dropped rr 6th: bhd whn p.u bef 9th* **14/1**

5m 27.2s (4.10) **Going Correction** +0.425s/f (Soft) **7** Ran SP% **110.8**
Speed ratings: **109,108,104,—,— —,—** CSF £27.59 CT £87.97 TOTE £2.80: £1.50, £3.90; EX 30.10.

Owner The Queen **Bred** Queen Elizabeth **Trained** Upper Lambourn, Berks

FOCUS
A fair event of its type and there was little between the first three home going to the second last. The winner has been rated as having run to the mark of his latest Sandown success.

NOTEBOOK
First Love has struck up a good relationship with Jamie Snowden and completed a hat-trick under his amateur rider on this return to handicap company. He jumped well for the most part and connections suggested that he may go back into the hunter chase division if the Handicapper puts him up too much. *(op 2-1 tchd 11-4 in a place)*
Joey Tribbiani(IRE), successful four times at around two miles, had his stamina to prove over this longer trip, but he saw it out really well and was only narrowly denied. This performance, a personal best on RPRs, opens up new opportunities for him. *(op 11-1)*
Christopher, who rarely runs a bad race when sent around a right-handed track, is on a winning mark at present and would have finished closer but for a mistake at the second last. *(tchd 5-2)*
Soeur Fontenail(FR), last of the four finishers, remains on a mark 4lb higher than for her last success and continues to look vulnerable. *(op 5-1)*
Ghadames(FR) *Official explanation: vet said gelding was lame behind (op 6-1 tchd 5-1)*

4678 KINGWELL LODGE B&B NOVICES' H'CAP HURDLE (11 hdls) 2m 6f
4:25 (4:25) (Class 3) (0-135,121) 4-Y-0+
£8,141 (£2,405; £1,202; £601; £300; £150)

Form RPR

3021 1 **Saltango (GER)**[39] [4005] 7-11-8 **120** .... WilliamKennedy(3) 132+
(A M Hales) *trckd ldrs: led 3 out: clr next: readily* **7/2**[2]

1245 2 *11* **Best Profile (IRE)**[40] [3982] 6-11-3 **112** ....(t) CarlLlewellyn 114+
(N A Twiston-Davies) *chsd ldrs: rdn to chal after 3 out: kpt on but no ch w wnr fr next* **16/1**

0232 3 *11* **Miko De Beauchene (FR)**[40] [3975] 6-11-12 **121** .... AndrewThornton 107
(R H Alner) *hld up: hdwy on inner appr 6th to trck ldrs: outpcd after 3 out: j.lft 2 out and last: styd on to go 3rd cl home* **5/1**[3]

6-01 4 *3/4* **Kaldouas (FR)**[104] [2866] 5-11-5 **114** .... RWalsh 103+
(P F Nicholls) *in tch: lost pl appr 6th: mstke 7th: hdwy 3 out: sn rdn: wknd 2 out: nt fluent last: lost 3rd cl home* **7/2**[2]

2336 5 *27* **Hibernian (IRE)**[19] [4373] 6-11-2 **111** .... LeightonAspell 69
(O Sherwood) *led tl 3 out: sn wknd: t.o* **2/1**[1]

5-P0 6 *dist* **Baranook (IRE)**[33] [4106] 5-10-5 **100** ....(t) RichardJohnson —
(B J Llewellyn) *a towards rr: nt fluent 5th: mstke 8th: wknd 3 out: t.o* **50/1**

/P44 7 *25* **See More Jock**[39] [4005] 8-10-5 **100** .... RobertWalford —
(Dr J R J Naylor) *chsd ldrs tl 3 out: sn wknd: t.o* **25/1**

0-10 P **Mikado Melody (IRE)**[88] [3175] 7-11-3 **112** .... RobertThornton —
(A King) *hld up: lost tch appr 3 out: t.o and p.u bef 2 out* **16/1**

5m 34.4s (9.30) **Going Correction** +0.425s/f (Soft) **8** Ran SP% **112.0**
Speed ratings: **100,96,92,91,81 —,—,—** CSF £50.71 CT £275.37 TOTE £4.10: £1.70, £2.80, £1.70; EX 42.90.

Owner CohenClearyKaplanMinnsPayneWatsonWilson **Bred** Gestut Wittekindshof **Trained** Quainton, Bucks

FOCUS
Run in a time 3.4sec slower than The Luder took to win the novice hurdle earlier on the card, this does not represent the strongest form around for this grade of contest.

NOTEBOOK
Saltango(GER), runner-up to The Luder over this course and distance in January, saw that form given a boost when his conqueror won the novice hurdle earlier on the card. Backed in from 9-2 on the strength of that, he saw off his rivals from the turn into the straight and saw the trip out strongly. He is suited by soft ground and a sharp track, but will have to find further improvement to defy a higher mark. *(op 9-2 tchd 3-1)*
Best Profile(IRE) ran a better race in the first-time tongue tie and is the type who should pay his way over fences next season providing any breathing problems can be sorted out. *(op 12-1)*
Miko De Beauchene(FR) has paid for his consistency with the Handicapper and is now on a mark 12lb higher than when successful on his seasonal debut in November. He had conditions to suit, though, and appeared to run his race once again. *(op 11-2)*
Kaldouas(FR), a winner at Windsor on his last start back in December, appeared to find these conditions too testing, and he will be worth another chance on a faster surface. *(tchd 9-2)*
Hibernian(IRE) looked sure to be suited by this longer trip but he dropped away quite tamely after being headed. He is a chaser in the making, however, and should be of more interest next season when presumably he will be sent over fences. *(op 15-8 tchd 9-4)*

4679 WESSEX WASTE NOVICES' CHASE (17 fncs) 2m 5f
4:55 (4:55) (Class 3) 5-Y-0+ **£6,506** (£1,910; £955; £477)

Form RPR

-1U1 1 **Taranis (FR)**[77] [3356] 5-11-3 136 ....(t) RWalsh 136+
(P F Nicholls) *j.w: trckd ldr: led on bit appr 3 out: qcknd clr after 2 out: readily* **4/9**[1]

06PP 2 *9* **Handy Money**[45] [3903] 9-10-12 130 .... RobertThornton 124+
(A King) *hld up bhd ldng pair: nt fluent 1st and 7th: mstke 12th: jnd wnr and ev ch 3 out: nt pce of wnr fr next* **4/1**[2]

4P52 3 *22* **Royale Acadou (FR)**[20] [4355] 8-10-5 89 ....(p) LeightonAspell 97+
(Mrs L J Mongan) *led: rdn and hdd appr 3 out: sn no ch* **9/1**[3]

/21- 4 *dist* **Waimea Bay**[669] [575] 7-10-0 97 .... DarylJacob(5) —
(D P Keane) *hld up: hit 4th: mstke 10th: sn lost tch: t.o* **11/1**

5m 31.1s (8.00) **Going Correction** +0.425s/f (Soft)
WFA 5 from 7yo+ 5lb **4** Ran SP% **107.6**
Speed ratings: **101,97,89,—** CSF £2.70 TOTE £1.40; EX 2.50.

Owner Foster Yeoman Limited **Bred** P De Maleissye Melun **Trained** Ditcheat, Somerset

FOCUS
A small field but the useful winner impressed with his jumping and can take higher rank. However, the race was steadily-run and as a result the form is questionable.

NOTEBOOK
Taranis(FR), off the track for 77 days, during which time he had undergone a breathing operation, returned to action with a very pleasing display, jumping well and picking up in good style when asked to quicken in the latter stages. He deserves a chance to prove himself in better grade, and he handles quicker ground than this. Aintree or Ayr might provide a suitable opportunity. *(op 2-5 tchd 1-2)*
Handy Money was disappointing on his chasing debut when pulled up at Plumpton, but he has always gone better on a right-handed track, indeed he was two from two here over hurdles, and this was far more encouraging. He will be more at home on a sounder surface. *(tchd 7-2)*
Royale Acadou(FR) was out of her depth against the first two but ran a solid race from the front. *(op 10-1 tchd 11-1)*
Waimea Bay, another up against it in this company, was returning from 22 months on the sidelines. *(op 14-1 tchd 10-1)*

4680 SPONSOR HERE AND BE A WINNER MAIDEN OPEN NATIONAL HUNT FLAT RACE 2m
5:25 (5:25) (Class 6) 4-6-Y-O **£1,713** (£499; £249)

Form RPR

2 1 **Silverburn (IRE)**[21] [4333] 5-11-4 .... RWalsh 99+
(P F Nicholls) *racd wd in mid divsion: smooth hdwy 5f out: led over 2f out: sn rdn: kpt on: drvn out* **4/6**[1]

2 *3/4* **High Calibre (IRE)** 5-11-4 .... APMcCoy 98+
(Jonjo O'Neill) *hld up towards rr: racd wd: smooth hdwy 5f out:rdn to chal wnr 2f out: kpt on but no ex ins fnl f* **2/1**[2]

3 *6* **Fixed Interest (IRE)** 4-10-11 .... MarkBradburne 85+
(H D Daly) *mid div: hdwy 5f out: rdn over 3f out: styd on to go 3rd ins fnl f* **33/1**

00 4 *1 1/4* **Cooldine Boy (IRE)**[17] [4422] 5-11-4 .... RichardJohnson 91
(P J Hobbs) *plld hrd towards rr: hdwy to trck ldrs after 5f: led over 3f out: hdd over 2f out: kpt on same pce* **25/1**[3]

5 *1 1/2* **I'm Supreme (IRE)** 4-10-11 .... RJGreene 82
(C J Down) *trckd ldrs: rdn and ev ch 3f out: kpt on same pce* **100/1**

56 6 *6* **Devonia Plains (IRE)**[142] [2105] 4-10-4 .... AngharadFrieze(7) 76
(Mrs P N Dutfield) *hld up bhd: styd on fr 2f out: n.d* **150/1**

7 *3* **Ballinabearna (IRE)**[32] 6-10-11 .... MPButler(7) 80
(Eoin Doyle, Ire) *led tl over 5f out: chsd ldrs: rdn over 3f out: wknd fnl f* **25/1**[3]

0 8 *1/2* **Fine Edge**[70] [3468] 5-10-11 .... DaveCrosse 73
(H E Haynes) *chsd ldr: led over 5f out: rdn and hdd over 3f out: sn wknd* **200/1**

9 *2* **I'm Free** 4-10-11 .... TomScudamore 71
(M C Pipe) *chsd ldrs tl 3f out* **33/1**

10 *2* **Primitive Academy** 4-10-8 .... TJPhelan(3) 69
(Mrs H Dalton) *in tch tl 3f out* **66/1**

0-0 11 *dist* **York Dancer**[310] [490] 5-10-11 .... LeightonAspell —
(A D Smith) *plld hrd in tch tl wknd 7f out: sn t.o* **200/1**

P **Boomerang Boy (IRE)** 5-10-11 .... MrTWeston(7) —
(M H Weston) *mid div: wkng whn rn wd on bnd 5f out and p.u* **200/1**

600 P **Hazzard A Guess**[21] [4326] 5-10-11 .... AndrewThornton —
(J W Mullins) *a towards rr: racd wd: t.o and p.u 2f out* **80/1**

3m 57.6s (5.90) **Going Correction** +0.425s/f (Soft)
WFA 4 from 5yo+ 7lb **13** Ran SP% **112.8**
Speed ratings: **102,101,98,98,97 94,92,92,91,90 —,—,—** CSF £1.73 TOTE £1.50: £1.10, £1.50, £4.90; EX 3.00 Place 6 £44.71, Place 5 £26.57.

Owner Paul Green **Bred** Colman O'Flynn **Trained** Ditcheat, Somerset

FOCUS
Perhaps not the most competitive bumper ever staged at the track, but the first two look promising types. It was steadily run and has been rated around the fourth and sixth.

NOTEBOOK
Silverburn(IRE) had shaped with plenty of promise on his debut over the course and distance three weeks earlier and made the most of that previous experience to get the better of a well-fancied newcomer from the Jonjo O'Neill stable. Given his breeding and performances to date, he will clearly be of interest when he is sent over timber next season. *(op Evens)*
High Calibre(IRE) ◆, who made 49,000gns as a three-year-old, lost nothing in defeat to the more experienced favourite. He pulled nicely clear of the third and looks a useful prospect for novice hurdles next season. *(op 7-4)*
Fixed Interest(IRE), whose dam was a winning two and a half-mile hurdler in Ireland, kept on under pressure and will be suited by a stiffer test once he is sent over hurdles. *(op 28-1)*
Cooldine Boy(IRE) was again found out by a steadily-run race. A stronger pace will help him settle better. *(op 20-1)*
I'm Supreme(IRE), a half-brother to a winning Irish pointer, did not shape too badly given that he was a cheap purchase and disregarded in the market.
Boomerang Boy(IRE) *Official explanation: jockey said saddle slipped (op 100-1)*
T/Plt: £17.40 to a £1 stake. Pool: £68,800.45. 2,870.55 winning tickets. T/Qpdt: £8.40 to a £1 stake. Pool: £5,021.10. 438.55 winning tickets. TM

4487 NEWCASTLE (L-H)
Friday, March 31

4683 Meeting Abandoned - Waterlogged

4521 FONTWELL (L-H)
Saturday, April 1

OFFICIAL GOING: Soft
Wind: Fresh, half-behind

4689 TOTEPLACEPOT MAIDEN HURDLE (11 hdls) 2m 6f 110y
2:20 (2:20) (Class 4) 5-Y-0+ **£3,332** (£1,034; £557)

Form				RPR
2263	1		**Love Of Classics**[44] 3941 6-11-2 113 (v) LeightonAspell (O Sherwood) *mid-div: hdwy to go 2nd appr 7th: led sn after 3 out: lft clr next: easily* **2/1**[1]	113+
/65	2	*dist*	**Madam Fleet (IRE)**[25] 4286 7-10-2 (t) MrsMRoberts(7) (M J Coombe) *t.o after 5th: lft remote 2nd 2 out: wnt 2nd cl home* **25/1**	—
P5P4	3	½	**Dancing Shirley**[33] 4151 8-10-6 70 ColinBolger(3) (Miss A M Newton-Smith) *j.rt 1st: racd wd in mid-div: rdn and wknd after 5th.lft poor 2nd after 2 out: lost 2nd cl home: t.o* **40/1**	—
2PP4	P		**Nagam (FR)**[21] 4367 5-11-2 103 (v1) JimCrowley (A Ennis) *prom tl rdn appr 7th: t.o whn p.u bef 2 out* **8/1**	—
5	P		**Future To Future (IRE)**[11] 4562 6-11-2 BarryFenton (Miss E C Lavelle) *a bhd: t.o whn p.u bef 4 out* **20/1**	—
00PP	P		**Judy's Lad**[25] 4285 7-10-13 OwynNelmes(3) (Mrs H R J Nelmes) *led tl after 1st: wknd after 7th: p.u bef next* **100/1**	—
/P-	P		**Hidden Weapon**[545] 1569 9-10-9 JustinMorgan(7) (L Wells) *bhd tl hdwy 5th: wknd qckly appr 3 out: t.o whn p.u bef next* **16/1**	—
	F		**Oscar Jack (FR)**[88] 5-11-2 SamThomas (Miss Venetia Williams) *led after 1st: hdd after 3 out: lft poor 2nd 2 out: fell last* **11/4**[2]	—
6235	P		**Boberelle (IRE)**[72] 3461 6-10-9 103 TomDoyle (C Tinkler) *hld up: hdwy to chse wnr after 3 out: hld whn p.u lame sn after 2 out* **3/1**[3]	—

5m 48.4s (3.60) **Going Correction** +0.25s/f (Yiel) 9 Ran SP% **114.0**
Speed ratings: **103**,—,—,—,— —,—,—,— CSF £52.16 TOTE £2.50: £1.10, £3.00, £5.70; EX 46.70.
Owner N C Byrne **Bred** Crandon Park Stud **Trained** Upper Lambourn, Berks

FOCUS
Not a strong race with neither Boberelle nor Oscar Jack managing to complete, and it was Love Of Classics who finally proved good enough to get off the mark. It has been rated through the winner.

NOTEBOOK
Love Of Classics has been in decent enough form in similar contests and, with neither of his two main rivals managing to complete, the path was left clear for him to finally get his head in front. The form is poor and it will be mightily surprising if he manages to defy a penalty in a novice event. *(op 5-2 tchd 11-4)*
Madam Fleet(IRE), although finishing second, was well beaten and achieved very little. She may find life easier against her own sex.
Dancing Shirley was presented with second after taking two out, but she was unable to hold on from Madam Fleet and had to make do with third. As with the runner-up she achieved next to nothing.
Oscar Jack(FR), a fair sort in France who raced mainly over fences, looked to hold obvious claims on this British debut, but he was weak in the market and had run his race when falling at the last. He has a bit to prove following this. *(op 9-4 tchd 10-3 and 7-2 in places)*
Boberelle(IRE), whose previous hurdles efforts entitled her to respect in a moderate contest, was pulled up before the second last and it emerged she had finished lame. The effort has to be ignored. *Official explanation: jockey said mare pulled up lame (op 9-4 tchd 10-3 and 7-2 in places)*

4690 TOTESPORT.COM SOUTHERN NATIONAL H'CAP CHASE (21 fncs) 3m 4f
2:55 (3:05) (Class 3) (0-135,125) 5-Y-0+
£15,492 (£4,600; £2,300; £1,147; £575; £290)

Form				RPR
021	1		**Hazeljack**[5] 4650 11-9-10 102 7ex ow2 WillieMcCarthy(7) (A J Whiting) *a.p: led appr 4 out: clr next: styd on wl* **6/1**[3]	110+
2P43	2	3	**Tana River (IRE)**[21] 4374 10-11-12 125 BarryFenton (Miss E C Lavelle) *trckd ldrs: chsd wnr after 4 out: kpt on one pce fr next* **20/1**	125
444P	3	*shd*	**Roman Rampage**[10] 4571 11-9-9 99 oh15 (p) RobertLucey-Butler(5) (Miss Z C Davison) *in rr tl hdwy to chal for 2f fr 3 out: styd on* **100/1**	99
043P	4	13	**Cowboyboots (IRE)**[35] 4103 8-11-0 120 JustinMorgan(7) (L Wells) *hld up: mstke 14th: blundered 6 out: kpt on but nvr on terms after* **16/1**	113+
2FP4	5	9	**Kittenkat**[25] 4287 12-10-3 102 TomScudamore (N R Mitchell) *trckd ldr tl led 15th: hdd appr 4 out: wknd sn after* **33/1**	82+
3241	6	10	**Charango Star**[48] 3886 8-11-2 115 (v) RichardJohnson (W K Goldsworthy) *mid-div: rdn after 9th: wknd after 5 out* **12/1**	83
3123	7	6	**Precious Bane (IRE)**[14] 4498 8-10-9 108 (p) AndrewThornton (M Sheppard) *led tl hdd 15th: wknd after next* **11/2**[2]	70
30P0	8	*dist*	**Snowy Ford (IRE)**[22] 4356 9-11-2 115 (p) SamThomas (N J Gifford) *mid-div tl wknd appr 6 out: t.o* **25/1**	—
F4-4	9	*dist*	**Rum Pointer (IRE)**[22] 4357 10-11-2 115 BenjaminHitchcott (R H Buckler) *hdlup in mid-div: stmbld bdly on landing 4 out: nt rcvr: t.o* **20/1**	—
5331	F		**Calvic (IRE)**[50] 3845 8-11-4 117 (b1) PaulMoloney (T R George) *in rr whn fell 4th* **8/1**	—
4P43	P		**Bubble Boy (IRE)**[41] 4007 7-10-0 106 CharlieStudd(7) (B G Powell) *a in rr: lost tch 16th: t.o whn p.u appr 3 out* **7/1**	—
6P3F	P		**Kausse De Thaix (FR)**[14] 4505 8-10-13 112 (p) LeightonAspell (O Sherwood) *chsd ldrs tl wknd 5 out: p.u bef 3 out* **12/1**	—
23P1	P		**Earl's Kitchen**[25] 4287 9-11-6 119 (p) JoeTizzard (C L Tizzard) *in tch: reminders after 7th: t.o whn p.u after 15th* **16/1**	—
-P11	P		**Yes My Lord (IRE)**[32] 4163 7-10-10 109 TimmyMurphy (M C Pipe) *hld up in rr and nvr gng wl: hit 10th: t.o whn p.u after 15th* **7/2**[1]	—

7m 27.3s (-5.50) **Going Correction** +0.05s/f (Yiel) course record 14 Ran SP% **120.0**
Speed ratings: **109,108,108,104,101 98,97**,—,—,— —,—,—,— CSF £121.74 CT £10428.81 TOTE £7.90: £2.10, £4.90, £15.70; EX 179.50 Trifecta £17638.20 Pool £84,464.61. - 3.40 winning units..
Owner A J Whiting **Bred** Miss Sarah Marie Nicholls **Trained** North Nibley, Gloucs

FOCUS
A competitive event on paper but with many of the leading players failing to run to form, Hazeljack was left with only a couple of the outsiders to beat. He was rated value for 8l, while the second ran to a similar level to his Sandown effort.

NOTEBOOK
Hazeljack, shouldering a 7lb penalty for his recent Plumpton success, received a fine ride from McCarthy and went on going to the fourth last, travelling extremely well. It was clear from the turn-in that the bold-jumping gelding was going to win barring a mishap and he was probably value for five or six lengths. He seems to be improving at a late stage in life and may well go on to complete the hat-trick if he can be found a suitable opportunity. *(op 8-1)*
Tana River(IRE), whose stamina for such a test looked in question, ran well for a long way behind Eric's Charm at Sandown and he again ran a blinder, keeping on surprisingly well under his big weight to reclaim second close home. He has a race in him over fences off this sort of mark, but connections are still searching for his ideal trip. *(op 16-1)*
Roman Rampage, having only his third start over fences, ran a massive race from out of the weights and only just missed out on second. He has been set some stiff tasks thus far over fences and he is likely to appreciate being set a more realistic task.
Cowboyboots(IRE) left behind a poor effort at Chepstow in February and plugged on for fourth, albeit he was well held. He may need some further assistance from the Handicapper before being able to win again. *(op 14-1)*
Kittenkat is a game old mare, but she has not been at her best of late and she faded in the straight. *(op 28-1)*
Precious Bane(IRE), a most progressive gelding this season, going from a mark of 71 to 110 last time, may have had one too many hard races and he is surely in line for a rest now. *(op 6-1 tchd 5-1)*
Earl's Kitchen *Official explanation: jockey said gelding bled from the nose (op 10-1)*
Bubble Boy(IRE) was well supported throughout the day, but he never made a show and was eventually pulled up. *Official explanation: jockey said gelding was unsuited by the soft ground (op 10-1)*
Yes My Lord(IRE), who made a successful switch to fences at Leicester in February, comes from a stable who have had many disappointments of late and he was struggling from an early stage. *He is better than this and may be capable of further improvement next season.Official explanation: jockey said gelding never travelled (op 10-1)*

4691 TOTESPORT 0800 221 221 NOVICES' HURDLE (9 hdls) 2m 2f 110y
3:25 (3:33) (Class 4) 4-Y-0+ **£3,903** (£1,146; £573; £286)

Form				RPR
212P	1		**Tora Bora (GER)**[25] 4289 4-10-13 113 (b) TimmyMurphy (B G Powell) *trckd ldrs: rdn to ld 3 out: hit next but in command after* **13/2**[3]	115+
6-F5	2	7	**Floragalore**[17] 4450 5-10-7 LeightonAspell (O Sherwood) *hld up in rr: rdn & hdwy to chse wnr appr 2 out: no imp* **25/1**	104+
164P	3	16	**Dunsfold Duke**[21] 4373 6-11-6 115 BenjaminHitchcott (P Winkworth) *chsd ldrs tl wknd after 3 out* **9/1**	98+
21P	4	4	**Grasp**[18] 4435 4-10-13 125 (bt) JamieMoore (G L Moore) *led tl rdn and hdd 3 out: wknd and lost 2nd bef next* **10/11**[1]	91+
21U3	5	5	**Milan Deux Mille (FR)**[19] 4416 4-10-7 APMcCoy (M C Pipe) *t.k.h: trckd ldrs 2nd: wknd 3 out* **9/2**[2]	76
-F30	6	7	**Liberia (FR)**[28] 4243 7-11-0 100 AndrewTinkler (N J Henderson) *chsd ldrs tl wknd after 3 out* **16/1**	76
2	7	*dist*	**Mungo Jerry (GER)**[20] 4389 5-11-0 AndrewThornton (B N Pollock) *hld up in tch:: effrt appr 4 out: sn wknd: t.o* **10/1**	—
0065	8	19	**Schindler's List**[63] 3617 6-11-0 OllieMcPhail (C Roberts) *a bhd: t.o 1/2-way* **50/1**	—
P	P		**Belshazzar (USA)**[91] 3133 5-11-0 MatthewBatchelor (D C O'Brien) *a in rr: t.o whn p.u bef 6th* **100/1**	—
0PP0	P		**Crystal Hollow**[13] 4521 6-11-0 SeanCurran (N R Mitchell) *trckd ldr to 3rd: sn bhd: t.o whn p.u bef 6th* **100/1**	—

4m 40.9s (4.90) **Going Correction** +0.35s/f (Yiel)
WFA 4 from 5yo+ 5lb 10 Ran SP% **116.7**
Speed ratings: **103,100,93,91,89 86**,—,—,—,— CSF £130.17 TOTE £8.10: £1.10, £4.20, £3.60; EX 101.70.
Owner D A Johnson **Bred** H Schroer-Dreesmann **Trained** Morestead, Hants

FOCUS
An ordinary contest and the poor showing of Grasp left Tora Bora with little to beat. Improved form from the first two.

NOTEBOOK
Tora Bora(GER), who ran a shocker in heavy ground at Exeter last month, had the blinkers on for the first time over hurdles and he was able to bounce back, forging clear to win comfortably. Only a four-year-old, he could develop into a useful handicapper next season. *(op 5-1 tchd 7-1 in places)*
Floragalore, the only mare in the line-up, ran undoubtedly her best race thus far over hurdles and, although proving no match for the winner, she can surely be found a race against her own sex.
Dunsfold Duke has not built on his Plumpton win and he looked vulnerable under his penalty, being left behind in the straight. A return to handicaps is likely to help, but he is one to be against at present. *(op 10-1)*
Grasp, a useful juvenile, never got competitive in the Fred Winter at the Festival and he may still have been feeling the effects of that outing judging by this effort as, having led for most of the way, he failed to respond to pressure and dropped away. He deserves another chance and will be capable of better next season. *(op 11-8)*
Milan Deux Mille(FR) had a bit to find with a couple of these and, like so many from his stable over the past few weeks, he folded under pressure. He had already shown himself to be better than this and deserves another chance. *(op 4-1)*
Liberia(FR) does not appear to be progressing and this was another poor effort. *(op 14-1)*

4692 OAKTREEHORSEBOXESSOUTHERNLTD.CO.UK BEGINNERS' CHASE (15 fncs) 2m 4f
4:00 (4:00) (Class 3) 5-Y-0+ £6,263 (£1,850; £925; £463; £231)

Form				RPR
3322	1		**Lewis Island (IRE)**[26] 4131 7-11-0 117 JamieMoore (G L Moore) *t.k.h: hld up tl hdwy to trck ldrs 4th: led 2 out: kpt up to work but in command run-in* **5/6**[1]	112+
5-P2	2	8	**El Viejo (IRE)**[13] 4522 9-10-7 96 (b) JustinMorgan(7) (L Wells) *j.w: led tl rdn and hdd 3 out: rallied to regain 2nd sn after last but no ch w wnr* **5/1**[3]	92
30PU	3	3	**Malaga Boy (IRE)**[13] 4522 9-11-0 105 JoeTizzard (C L Tizzard) *trckd ldr to 9th: led 3 out: hdd next: hld whn stmbld on landing last: sn lost 2nd and no ex* **5/2**[2]	92+
40PF	4	dist	**Bob's Finesse**[10] 4578 6-10-0 WayneKavanagh(7) (J W Mullins) *hld up: lost tch 4th: t.o* **16/1**	—
5PPP	5	hd	**Rutland (IRE)**[13] 4525 7-10-9 66 RobertLucey-Butler(5) (C J Drewe) *in tch to 4th: t.o fr 9th* **20/1**	—

5m 16.0s (8.10) **Going Correction** +0.45s/f (Soft) 5 Ran SP% **110.4**
Speed ratings: **101,97,96,—,—** CSF £5.62 TOTE £1.40: £1.20, £2.00; EX 3.30.
Owner Ashley Carr **Bred** Emmet Beston **Trained** Woodingdean, E Sussex

FOCUS
A weak race in which the winner was value for 20l but was still below his best.

NOTEBOOK
Lewis Island(IRE) is as quirky as they come and, having got him to jump off, Moore's next task was to settle him, which he did admirably. He jumped boldly throughout in his search for his first victory in over two years and, although not doing much under pressure, found what was required *to win comfortably. He will find things tougher when trying to defy a penalty. (op 10-11 tchd 4-5 and Evens in places)*
El Viejo(IRE) had a lot to find with the winner at the weights and, having took them along jumping well, he was readily brushed aside. He stuck on pluckily to claim second from the unfortunate Malaga Boy, but his best chances of winning are likely to come in handicaps. *(op 9-2 tchd 6-1)*
Malaga Boy(IRE) had failed to get far on his two previous outings over fences, but he jumped well enough here until unluckily stumbling after the last and handing second to El Viejo. *(op 3-1)*
Bob's Finesse, a faller on her chasing debut when still in with a chance at Towcester, was never going here and may have needed this to restore some confidence. *(op 20-1)*
Rutland(IRE) narrowly lost out in his own private battle with Bob's Finesse for fourth and will continue to struggle. *Official explanation: jockey said gelding was unsuited by the soft ground*

4693 FULLER'S LONDON PRIDE H'CAP HURDLE (11 hdls) 2m 6f 110y
4:30 (4:35) (Class 3) (0-130,120) 4-Y-0+
£7,515 (£2,220; £1,110; £555; £277; £139)

Form				RPR
P6F5	1		**Sesame Rambler (IRE)**[10] 4573 7-11-1 **109** JamieMoore (G L Moore) *hld up in tch: hdwy after 7th to trck ldrs: sddle slipped sn after: led appr last: kpt on wl despite rdr's difficulties* **3/1**[1]	114+
401/	2	1 3/4	**Pipssalio (SPA)**[538] 4664 9-11-5 **113** MatthewBatchelor (Jamie Poulton) *a in tch: rdn appr 2 out: kpt on run-in* **16/1**	111
2104	3	nk	**Amanpuri (GER)**[14] 4504 8-10-13 **107** RichardJohnson (Mrs A M Thorpe) *led tl rdn and hdd appr last: lost 2nd run-in* **3/1**[1]	105
530P	4	dist	**Alfa Sunrise**[22] 4353 9-10-11 **105** BenjaminHitchcott (R H Buckler) *trckd ldr to 5th: stmbld on landing 7th: wknd next: t.o* **8/1**	—
FP2P	5	1	**Mister Mustard (IRE)**[29] 4215 9-11-10 **118** WayneHutchinson (Ian Williams) *in tch tl rdn and wknd after 3 out: t.o* **11/2**[3]	—
21U-	6	3	**A Toi A Moi (FR)**[474] 2811 6-11-1 **109** AlanO'Keeffe (Miss Venetia Williams) *t.k.h: trckd ldrs rdn appr 3 out: sn wknd: t.o* **7/2**[2]	—
2UP	P		**Ballez (FR)**[70] 3506 5-11-7 **120** LiamHeard(5) (P F Nicholls) *hld up: struggling 6th: sn lost tch: t.o whn p.u bef 2 out* **9/1**	—

5m 54.4s (9.60) **Going Correction** +0.50s/f (Soft) 7 Ran SP% **114.6**
Speed ratings: **103,102,102,—,— —,—** CSF £43.54 TOTE £4.40: £2.00, £5.50; EX 85.70.
Owner Gillespie Brothers **Bred** R Jenks **Trained** Woodingdean, E Sussex

FOCUS
A good performance by both winning horse and jockey, with the saddle slipping nearly a circuit from the finish. The winner was value for further but the form is a little suspect.

NOTEBOOK
Sesame Rambler(IRE), who unluckily fell when disputing it at the last at Sandown on his penultimate outing, may have needed his most recent run to restore confidence and he won with a fair bit to spare here, his rider doing extremely well after the gelding's saddle had slipped with nearly a circuit left. He has more to offer and is one to keep on the right side. *(op 7-2)*
Pipssalio(SPA), whose last outing came on the Flat back in October 2004, was clearly straight for this return and he ran a cracker in second, staying on right to the way to the line to claim second from the ultra game Amanpuri. It is hoped he goes the right way from this. *(op 12-1 tchd 18-1)*
Amanpuri(GER), bidding to maintain his 100% record at the course, three from three coming into it, was ridden from the front by Johnson, but he proved no match for the winner and was run out of second on the claim to the line. *(op 7-2)*
Alfa Sunrise finished well adrift of the front three on this return to hurdling and remains out of form. *(op 12-1 tchd 14-1 in a place)*
Mister Mustard(IRE) is probably at his best on a sounder surface and this generally disappointing sort continues to frustrate. *(op 4-1)*
A Toi A Moi(FR), a promising novice, comes from a stable who know how to get one straight and therefore it was disappointing he did not do better on this belated seasonal return. *(op 3-1)*
Ballez(FR) continues to frustrate and, although just a five-year-old, it is unlikely connections will persevere for much longer. *(op 14-1)*

4694 3663 FIRST FOR FOODSERVICE H'CAP CHASE (13 fncs) 2m 2f
5:05 (5:06) (Class 4) (0-110,110) 5-Y-0+ £5,204 (£1,528; £764; £381)

Form				RPR
P541	1		**Walcot Lad (IRE)**[13] 4524 10-11-4 **105** (p) WilliamKennedy(3) (A Ennis) *mde all: j.w: fnd ex whn chal 3 out: drew clr appr last* **13/2**	120+
3214	2	13	**Smart Cavalier**[65] 3580 7-11-12 **110** (t) ChristianWilliams (P F Nicholls) *hld up in rr: hdwy 7th: kpt on one pce to go 2nd cl home* **11/2**[3]	110
3351	3	hd	**Wild Power (GER)**[26] 4281 8-10-6 **93** OwynNelmes(3) (Mrs H R J Nelmes) *hld up: hdwy 7th: chal appr 3 out: wknd rapidly run-in and lost 2nd cl home* **6/1**	93
P542	4	14	**Inaki (FR)**[60] 3663 9-10-8 **92** (b) BenjaminHitchcott (P Winkworth) *in tch but nt fluent: wknd appr 3 out* **7/2**[1]	80+
3044	5	11	**Taksina**[10] 4575 7-9-9 **84** oh9 MrTJO'Brien(5) (R H Buckler) *trckd ldrs to 1/2-way: sn bhd* **10/1**	59
0P44	P		**Acertack (IRE)**[35] 4120 9-10-9 **93** TimmyMurphy (R Rowe) *t.k.h: hld up on outside: wknd and p.u after 7th* **15/2**	—
4200	P		**Papillon De Iena (FR)**[29] 4214 6-11-9 **107** (v) APMcCoy (M C Pipe) *hld up: struggling fr 7th: t.o whn p.u bef 4 out* **4/1**[2]	—
P500	P		**Haafel (USA)**[51] 3815 9-11-7 **105** (b) JamieMoore (G L Moore) *trckd wnr to 6th: sn rdn and bhd: t.o whn p.u bef 3 out* **14/1**	—

4m 47.5s (79.30) **Going Correction** +0.875s/f (Soft) 8 Ran SP% **112.7**
Speed ratings: **107,101,101,94,90 —,—,—** CSF £40.89 CT £224.08 TOTE £4.00: £1.30, £2.40, £2.10; EX 21.50.
Owner Camis Burke Middleton Heaps **Bred** Jim Ruane **Trained** Beare Green, Surrey

FOCUS
A cracking display by the versatile Walcot Lad, who galloped his rivals into the ground to record a personal best mark. The second and third were below their best.

NOTEBOOK
Walcot Lad(IRE), a winner over three and half miles at this course last month, had already proved his versatility with regards to the distance and he was ridden aggressively here by Kennedy, jumping boldly and running his rivals ragged. This was his fourth win of the season and he continues to flourish. *(op 11-2)*
Smart Cavalier, a slight disappointment on his handicap debut last time, gave the winner too much rope, but he battled on to snatch second close home from Wild Power. A more positive ride in future is likely to help. *(op 4-1)*
Wild Power(GER), up 5lb for his Hereford win, stopped as if shot after the last and was found out by the hill. He may do better when the emphasis is more on speed. *(op 7-1 tchd 15-2)*
Inaki(FR), 10lb lower than when last successful, did not jump with any real fluency and had nothing left as they turned into the straight. This was disappointing. *(op 4-1)*
Papillon De Iena(FR) was yet another Pipe inmate to disappoint on the card and he has hardly *relished the return to fencing. Official explanation: jockey said gelding never travelled (op 9-2 tchd 5-1 in places and 11-2 in a place)*

4695 ANGELA & NOEL'S WEDDING DAY MARES' ONLY STANDARD OPEN NATIONAL HUNT FLAT RACE 2m 2f 110y
5:35 (5:35) (Class 6) 4-6-Y-0 £1,626 (£477; £238; £119)

Form				RPR
403	1		**Supreme Cara**[20] 4398 6-10-9 ChrisHonour(3) (C J Down) *led for 1f: led again 7f out: rdn 2f out: styd on wl fnl f* **4/1**	93+
	2	4	**Valley Hall (IRE)** 5-10-12 NoelFehily (C J Mann) *hld up on outside: hdwy over 6f out: wnt 2nd over 2f out: kpt on but no imp* **3/1**[1]	89+
50	3	7	**La Dame Brune (FR)**[19] 4422 4-10-5 AndrewTinkler (N J Henderson) *led after 1f: hdd 7f out: rdn and wknd 2f out* **10/3**[2]	75
	4	9	**Iron Maid** 5-10-12 LeightonAspell (O Sherwood) *hld up in tch: hdwy to chse ldrs 1/2-way: rdn and wknd over 2f out* **7/2**[3]	73
	5	dist	**Llys Y Fran** 4-10-5 ChristianWilliams (W K Goldsworthy) *trckd ldrs to 6f out: sn bhd: t.o* **14/1**	—
	6	4	**Gunner Getya** 5-10-12 HenryOliver (R Dickin) *a bhd: t.o* **12/1**	—
0	7	dist	**West Bay Mist**[124] 2558 5-10-9 OwynNelmes(3) (Mrs H R J Nelmes) *in tch tl wknd 1/2-way: t.o* **50/1**	—
	8	3/4	**Sharp Storm**[371] 6-10-5 CharlieStudd(7) (B G Powell) *in tch to 1/2-way: t.o* **16/1**	—

4m 39.4s (0.10) **Going Correction** +0.65s/f (Soft)
WFA 4 from 5yo+ 5lb 8 Ran SP% **112.5**
Speed ratings: **103,101,98,94,— —,—,—** CSF £15.86 TOTE £5.00: £1.50, £1.50, £1.20; EX 16.80 Place 6 £646.59, Place 5 £223.49.
Owner Christine And Aubrey Loze **Bred** Miss M Sherrington **Trained** Mutterton, Devon

FOCUS
A very weak mares' bumper, rated by splitting the difference between the first and third's pre-race marks.

NOTEBOOK
Supreme Cara, mildly progressive in similar events, put her experience to good use and was always on the pace, in the end staying on too strongly for the newcomer in second. She is only modest, but should make a hurdler. *(tchd 9-2)*
Valley Hall(IRE) will no doubt have pleased connections with this debut effort and she can probably find a similar race in the coming weeks. *(op 4-1)*
La Dame Brune(FR) is evidently one of her connections' lesser lights and she was unable to stay *on as well as either of the front two having disputed it with the winner early. (tchd 3-1 and 11-4 in a place)*
Iron Maid did not look devoid of ability, but she will need to raise her game if she is to be winning anytime soon. *(op 10-3)*
T/Plt: £1,048.50 to a £1 stake. Pool: £86,538.25. 60.25 winning tickets. T/Qpdt: £62.50 to a £1 stake. Pool: £5,940.20. 70.30 winning tickets. JS

4494 UTTOXETER (L-H)
Saturday, April 1
4696 Meeting Abandoned - Waterlogged

2262 HEXHAM (L-H)
Sunday, April 2
4703 Meeting Abandoned - Waterlogged

1380 NEWTON ABBOT (L-H)
Sunday, April 2
4710 Meeting Abandoned - Waterlogged

4646 AUTEUIL (L-H)
Sunday, April 2

OFFICIAL GOING: Heavy

4717a PRIX HYPOTHESE (GRADE 3) (HURDLE) 2m 3f 110y
3:50 (3:58) 5-Y-0+
£39,527 (£19,724; £11,655; £8,069; £4,483; £3,138)

			RPR
1		**Royale Athenia (FR)**[28] 4275 5-10-1 (b) CGombeau (B Barbier, France)	—
2	1	**River Charm (FR)**[28] 4275 6-10-3 PMarsac (G Cherel, France)	—

3	3	**Sunspot**[148] 2061 6-10-5 .... CPieux (A Chaille-Chaille, France)	—
4	1	**Lycaon De Vauzelle (FR)**[133] 2403 7-11-1 .... (J Bertran De Balanda, France)	—
5	8	**Royale Cazoumaille (FR)**[28] 4275 7-10-1 .... (B Barbier, France)	—
6	6	**Phonidal (FR)**[28] 4275 10-10-3 ....(b) (M Rolland, France)	—
7	20	**Kadabelle (FR)**[11] 5-9-9 .... (Mme L Audon, France)	—
P		**United (GER)**[22] 4375 5-10-0 ow3.......... LeightonAspell (Mrs L Wadham) *disp 5th, wnt cl 4th at 4th (of 12 hrdls), 6th & in tch whn mstke 7th, sn bhd, mstke 3 out, plld up bef next (10/1)* **10/1**[1]	—

8 Ran SP% **9.1**

PARI-MUTUEL: WIN 2.10 (coupled with Royale Cazoumaille); PL 1.10, 1.30, 1.40; DF 3.50.
Owner Mme G Gallot **Bred** Mme G Gallot **Trained** France

NOTEBOOK
United(GER) is a fast but low jumper and these more solid hurdles were always going to be a worry. She jumped perfectly adequately in the early stages but, at the worst possible moment, just as the tempo was increasing, she hit the sixth last and pitched on landing. This affected her confidence and, having got in close to the next two, she was already ten lengths detached from the field when making a complete horlicks of the third last. A return to the more flimsy British and Irish hurdles will suit.

ARGENTAN (R-H)
Sunday, April 2

OFFICIAL GOING: Good

4718a PRIX DE NECY (CROSS-COUNTRY CHASE) 2m 6f 110y
3:30 (12:00) 5-Y-0+ **£3,972** (£1,986; £1,159; £786; £372)

			RPR
1		**Indiana Jaune (FR)**[1973] 10-10-3 .... DDelorme (P Cottin, France)	—
2	8	**Kirless (FR)**[280] 845 8-10-6 .... ALeCourtois(4) (P Quinton, France)	—
3	2 ½	**Fleur D'Oudon (FR)** 9-10-1 .... GRichard(4) (D Cadot, France)	—
4	½	**Hanybald (FR)**[350] 11-10-6 .... (4) (P Cormier-Martin, France)	—
5	½	**Lila Des Planches (FR)** 7-10-7 .... (P Chemin, France)	—
6	4	**Julio Du Tao (FR)**[1254] 9-10-12 .... (Mme A Muilwijk, France)	—
P		**Liroquois (FR)** 7-10-12 .... (J Robic, France)	—
P		**Guichi (FR)**[1816] 8-10-12 .... (G Lecomte, France)	—
P		**Kalin Du Beury (FR)**[1401] 8-10-7 .... (P Chemin, France)	—
F		**Kaline Du Mou (FR)** 8-9-13 .... (4) (J Chapdelaine, Belgium)	—
P		**Lertxundi (FR)**[299] 7-10-6 .... (4) (Mme A Chayrigues, France)	—
U		**Manor Down (IRE)**[29] 8-10-7 .... JoffretHuet (Dolly Maude) *in touch when blundered and unseated rider at 7th (a bank)*	—

5m 50.9s **12** Ran
PARI-MUTUEL (including one euro stakes): WIN 9.40; PL 3.50, 3.20, 5.70; DF 31.80.
Owner Mme N Devilder **Bred** Mlle S Van Egroo **Trained** France

NOTEBOOK
Manor Down(IRE) had won a point-to-point on her previous start in Britain.

4527 KELSO (L-H)
Monday, April 3

OFFICIAL GOING: Soft (heavy in places)
Wind: Breezy, half-behind

4719 PAUL BURTON DRINKS WHOLESALE BEGINNERS' CHASE (19 fncs) 3m 1f
2:20 (2:22) (Class 4) 5-Y-0+ **£4,554** (£1,337; £668; £333)

Form				RPR
4PP2	1		**Profowens (IRE)**[26] 4300 8-11-2 95..........(b) RussGarritty (P Beaumont) *mde all: rdn bef 2 out: styd on strly fr last* **9/2**[2]	109+
3P2	2	7	**Trisons Star (IRE)**[15] 4516 8-10-11 106.......... DesFlavin(5) (Mrs L B Normile) *chsd wnr: mstke 14th: effrt and ev ch 2 out: one pce last* **2/1**[1]	103+
4P0F	3	9	**Kimbambo (FR)**[15] 4528 8-10-13 113..........(p) GaryBerridge(3) (J P L Ewart) *prom: outpcd 14th: rallied and cl up after 3 out: no ex bef last* **8/1**	95+
3453	4	dist	**Wild About Harry**[11] 4587 9-11-2 66.......... KeithMercer (A R Dicken) *towards rr: struggling 12th: no ch after: lft remote 4th last* **20/1**	—
P-	5	3 ½	**Crackadee**[43] 7-11-2 .... RichardMcGrath (Miss R Brewis) *bhd: struggling 1/2-way: t.o* **15/2**	—
2-P2	6	dist	**Icare D'Oudairies (FR)**[9] 4610 10-11-2 .... OllieMcPhail (A L Forbes) *mstkes: sn bhd: wknd fr 1/2-way* **16/1**	—
0	R		**Glen Harley (IRE)**[35] 4141 6-10-9 ....(t) TomSiddall (R T J Wilson, Ire) *ref to r* **40/1**	—
3U3	P		**More Flair**[15] 4518 9-10-9 75.......... LarryMcGrath (J B Walton) *a bhd: t.o whn p.u after 12th* **16/1**	—
-F5P	P		**Field Roller (IRE)**[50] 3877 6-11-2 110.......... GLee (P Monteith) *chsd ldrs: wknd after 13th: t.o whn p.u bef 3 out* **12/1**	—
2552	U		**Tandava (IRE)**[11] 4583 8-11-2 .... MarkBradburne (Mrs S C Bradburne) *prom: outpcd 13th: rallied and cl up bef 2 out: 6l down disputing 3rd and outpcd whn blnd and uns rdr last* **11/2**[3]	—

6m 38.8s (9.20) **Going Correction** +0.45s/f (Soft) **10** Ran SP% **116.4**
Speed ratings: **103,100,97,—,—** —,—,—,—,— CSF £14.52 TOTE £6.50: £2.10, £1.30, £2.90; EX 26.70.
Owner Trevor Hemmings **Bred** Charles McCann **Trained** Stearsby, N Yorks

FOCUS
A weak contest that took little winning.

NOTEBOOK
Profowens(IRE) has been transformed by the blinkers and, having finished second at Catterick last month, he was able to go one better, leading throughout and staying on strongly on the long run-in. As long as the headgear continues to have the same effect, there is no reason why he cannot follow up assuming the Handicapper treats him fairly. *(op 7-1 tchd 15-2)*
Trisons Star(IRE) has been pretty consistent since going chasing, but he has yet to win and proved no match for the winner here. He stays this trip well, but remains vulnerable. *(op 9-4)*
Kimbambo(FR) ran his best race for a while and should take some confidence from this, having fallen at the course last month. *(op 12-1)*
Wild About Harry faced little realistic chance and trailed in a well-beaten fourth. A return to low-grade handicaps is likely to see him in a better light.
Tandava(IRE), a pleasing runner-up on his fencing debut at Ayr last month, had a bit to prove on this rise in distance, but he was keeping on well enough when unseating at the last. He can find a race over fences, but it may be worth preserving his novice status until next term, given this season is nearly over. *(op 4-1)*
Field Roller(IRE), making his debut for the Monteith yard having been with Pipe, made a poor start for new connections and offered little hope with the future in mind. *(op 4-1)*

4720 KELSO MEMBERS "NATIONAL HUNT" NOVICES' HURDLE (8 hdls) 2m 110y
2:50 (2:52) (Class 4) 4-Y-0+ **£3,253** (£955; £477; £238)

Form				RPR
5023	1		**Boulders Beach (IRE)**[54] 3793 6-11-0 .... DominicElsworth (Mrs S J Smith) *chsd ldrs: drvn 3 out: styd on to ld nr fin* **8/13**[1]	99
4-0F	2	shd	**Harry Flashman**[24] 4342 5-11-0 .... WilsonRenwick (D W Whillans) *trckd ldrs: led after 3 out: kpt on wl: hdd nr fin* **16/1**	99
401	3	4	**Stagecoach Opal**[56] 3785 5-11-0 .... PadgeWhelan (Mrs S J Smith) *in tch: effrt 3 out: sn outpcd: kpt on fr last: nt rch first two* **8/1**[3]	95
05-6	4	4	**Fastaffaran (IRE)**[25] 4315 5-11-0 .... BrianHarding (I McMath) *keen: cl up: effrt bef 2 out: one pce last* **25/1**	92+
0	5	15	**Glen Oscar (IRE)**[15] 4527 7-11-0 .... NeilMulholland (Miss S E Forster) *midfield: hdwy and prom 4 out: outpcd fr next* **200/1**	76
50	6	shd	**Nonotreally**[106] 2906 5-11-0 .... GLee (B Mactaggart) *bhd tl sme hdwy 2 out: nvr on terms* **50/1**	76
	7	5	**Solway Bee** 6-10-0 .... GarethThomas(7) (Miss L Harrison) *a bhd* **200/1**	64
4-43	8	1 ¾	**Lady Speaker**[16] 4493 5-10-7 .... DavidO'Meara (T D Easterby) *trckd ldrs tl wknd fr 3 out* **6/1**[2]	62
055	9	14	**Floral Rhapsody**[22] 4387 5-10-7 .... TomSiddall (P Beaumont) *a bhd: no ch fr 1/2-way* **100/1**	48
6	10	1 ¾	**Ben Nelly (IRE)**[16] 4493 5-11-0 .... AlanDempsey (M Todhunter) *a in rr* **33/1**	53
00	11	1	**Young Blade**[35] 4147 5-11-0 .... RichardMcGrath (C Grant) *nt fluent: in tch to 1/2-way: sn lost pl* **100/1**	52
64	12	4	**Young Smokey (IRE)**[25] 4319 5-11-0 .... RussGarritty (P Beaumont) *sn towards rr: rdn 4 out: n.d* **20/1**	48
5046	13	7	**Overnight**[24] 4342 6-11-0 .... KeithMercer (Mrs A C Hamilton) *led to after 3 out: wknd bef next* **40/1**	41
06	14	8	**Windygate (IRE)**[15] 4519 6-10-9 .... TJDreaper(5) (A Parker) *a bhd: no ch fr 1/2-way* **200/1**	33
0	15	dist	**Teviot Brig**[68] 3563 5-10-11 .... GaryBerridge(3) (L Lungo) *nt fluent: nvr on terms* **40/1**	—
	F		**Speedro (IRE)**[834] 2885 8-11-0 .... PeterBuchanan (Miss Lucinda V Russell) *in tch: effrt 3 out: 6l down in sixth and outpcd whn fell next* **100/1**	—

4m 11.1s (7.40) **Going Correction** +0.45s/f (Soft) **16** Ran SP% **116.0**
Speed ratings: **100,99,98,96,89 89,86,85,79,78 78,76,72,69,—** — CSF £10.15 TOTE £1.70: £1.10, £3.40, £2.00; EX 15.40.
Owner R A Keogh **Bred** Thomas A O'Donnell **Trained** High Eldwick, W Yorks

FOCUS
Weak novice form.

NOTEBOOK
Boulders Beach(IRE) was forced to work harder than would have been expected, but he stayed on dourly and just got the better of Harry Flashman, getting on top late. Clearly in need of further, he looks the sort with more to offer and may yet be capable of better. *(op 8-11 tchd 4-5 in places)*
Harry Flashman, in the process of running a good race on his hurdling debut when falling at Ayr, showed no ill-effects of that experience and looked the winner for much of the way. He can find a similarly modest contest. *(op 14-1)*
Stagecoach Opal, a stablemate of the winner, got off the mark in his third bumper outing at Sedgefield back in February, but this trip proved to be inadequate on this hurdles debut and he could only muster the one pace. The step up to two and a half miles can be expected to see him in a better light.
Fastaffaran(IRE), expected to be suited by the drop in trip, raced a tad too keenly for his own good and ultimately found himself outpaced by the front trio. Two and a half mile handicap hurdles are likely to present him with his best chance of winning.
Lady Speaker dropped away tamely and she may find life easier against her own sex. *(op 11-2)*

4721 PAT DE CLERMONT H'CAP CHASE (FOR THE SCOTT BRIGGS CHALLENGE TROPHY) (12 fncs) 2m 1f
3:20 (3:22) (Class 4) (0-110,108) 5-Y-0+ **£6,506** (£1,910; £955; £477)

Form				RPR
4465	1		**Little Flora**[47] 3928 10-9-9 82 oh4.......... MichaelMcAlister(5) (S J Marshall) *midfield: hdwy 3 out: led run in: styd on wl* **14/1**	93+
0151	2	3 ½	**Silver Sedge (IRE)**[16] 4488 7-11-11 107.......... PeterBuchanan (Mrs A Hamilton) *prom: led 2 out: hdd run in: kpt on same pce* **11/2**[2]	114
3535	3	9	**Ideal Du Bois Beury (FR)**[11] 4587 10-10-0 82 oh8.......... NeilMulholland (P Monteith) *bhd: hit 2nd: effrt u.p bef 3 out: no imp fr next* **14/1**	80
3P62	4	2 ½	**Posh Stick**[15] 4520 9-11-9 105.......... BrianHarding (J B Walton) *in tch: outpcd whn hmpd 4 out: kpt on fr last: no imp* **10/1**	102+
013P	5	2 ½	**Isellido (IRE)**[16] 4495 7-11-1 107.......... JohnFlavin(10) (R C Guest) *chsd ldrs: lft in ld 4 out: hdd appr 2 out: outpcd bef last* **16/1**	101+
6143	6	½	**Sound Of Cheers**[15] 4531 9-11-12 108..........(t) KennyJohnson (F Kirby) *chsd ldrs: outpcd whn hit 2 out: sn btn* **7/1**[3]	104+
0022	7	17	**The Miner**[25] 4318 8-10-2 91..........(p) TomMessenger(7) (Miss S E Forster) *chsd ldrs: hmpd 4 out: sn lost pl* **15/2**	70+
4312	8	8	**Mr Prickle (IRE)**[16] 4502 6-11-8 104.......... RussGarritty (P Beaumont) *hld up: effrt bef 3 out: btn after next* **5/1**[1]	82+
3152	9	18	**Miss Pross**[16] 4489 6-11-5 101.......... RobertWalford (T D Walford) *bhd and sn detached: no ch fr 1/2-way* **8/1**	51
030	P		**College City (IRE)**[56] 3784 7-11-11 107..........(p) LarryMcGrath (R C Guest) *hld up: p.u bef 5th* **50/1**	—

F334 **F** **Loulou Nivernais (FR)**[79] 3380 7-11-0 **96** .... AlanDempsey —
(M Todhunter) *led tl fell heavily 4 out* **7/1**[3]

P/1- **P** **Barcham Again (IRE)**[697] 190 9-11-0 **96** ....(p) MarkBradburne —
(Mrs C J Kerr) *a bhd: t.o whn p.u bef 3 out* **66/1**

4m 28.1s (4.90) **Going Correction** +0.45s/f (Soft) **12** Ran SP% **111.7**
Speed ratings: **106,104,100,98,97 97,89,85,77,—** —,— CSF £85.96 CT £1089.51 TOTE £15.90: £4.80, £3.10, £3.80; EX 118.50.

Owner S J Marshall **Bred** Mrs S Gilchrist **Trained** Alnwick, Northumberland

FOCUS
They went a decent gallop and in the end Little Flora ground out a game win.

NOTEBOOK
Little Flora, taking a sharp drop in distance, took her time to get on top, but she ended up winning well. A proper test at the distance suits her and she should continue to run well under similar conditions. *(op 11-1)*

Silver Sedge(IRE), a winner over hurdles at Hexham last month, seems just as effective over fences and he appeared to run his race in second, plugging on for pressure without being able to hold the winner. This was a fair effort under his big weight. *(op 5-1)*

Ideal Du Bois Beury(FR) never really got involved and was struggling after an early error. He has not won for over four years when with Martin Pipe and he remains one to avoid. *(op 11-1)*

Posh Stick, still 4lb higher than when last winning, may have challenged for third had she not had her rhythm interrupted when hampered at the fourth last. *(op 14-1)*

Isellido(IRE) appeared to face a simpler task than when disappointing at Uttoxeter last time, but she was readily brushed aside from the second-last and ultimately well held. *(tchd 20-1)*

Mr Prickle(IRE), whose sole win came at two and a half miles, ran well enough when second back at this trip last time, but he was unable to get involved here having been held up and clearly failed to run to form. *Official explanation: jockey said gelding ran flat (op 11-2)*

4722 BANK OF SCOTLAND AGRI BUSINESS - BUCCLEUCH CUP (MAIDEN HUNTERS' CHASE) (19 fncs) 3m 1f
3:50 (3:50) (Class 5) 5-Y-O+ **£2,498** (£774; £387; £193)

Form RPR

P- **1** **Birkwood**[16] 7-11-7 .... MrRSBrown(7) 93+
(Ian D Stark) *led 2nd: mde rest: rdn and r.o strly fr 2 out* **6/1**[3]

P/6 **2** *8* **Natain**[16] 7-12-0 .... MissPRobson 88+
(Alistair M Brown) *cl up: blnd 11th: blnd and lost 2nd 4 out: chsd wnr bef last: kpt on same pce* **4/1**[1]

46P0 **3** *15* **High Expectations (IRE)**[26] 4305 11-11-9 62 .... MrTDavidson(5) 67
(J S Haldane) *chsd ldrs: lft 2nd 4 out: outpcd and hung rt bef last* **100/1**

PP4P **4** *3 ½* **Highland Brig**[35] 4144 10-11-7 76 ....(t) MrMEllwood(7) 64
(T Butt) *bhd: outpcd 1/2-way: kpt on fr 2 out: nvr rchd ldrs* **20/1**

0-2P **5** *29* **Carriage Ride (IRE)**[16] 8-11-7 94 .... MrCJCallow(7) 35
(N G Richards) *prom: lost pl 7th: sn rdn: no ch fr 1/2-way* **11/2**[2]

/6-5 **6** *18* **Old Rolla (IRE)**[43] 8-12-0 .... MrCStorey 17
(C Storey) *hld up: hdwy and prom 1/2-way: outpcd whn blnd 2 out: sn btn* **12/1**

3P-P **7** *dist* **Shining Tyne**[48] 3913 12-12-0 59 .... MrPJohnson —
(R Johnson) *bhd and detatched: nvr on terms* **100/1**

5-2 **F** **Solway Sunset**[41] 4044 7-11-4 .... MrDJewett(3) —
(David Alan Harrison) *hld up: fell 8th* **4/1**[1]

P/ **U** **I'm Willie's Girl**[15] 10-11-0 .... MrJARichardson(7) —
(Miss J Luton) *hld up: blnd and uns rdr 8th* **100/1**

P **Thunder Hawk (IRE)**[15] 6-11-7 .... MissJHollands(7) —
(J Burke) *in tch: outpcd whn blnd 12th: sn btn: t.o whn p.u bef 4 out* **20/1**

U **A Boy Named Sioux (IRE)**[15] 8-11-11 .... MissRDavidson(3) —
(Mrs E J Reed) *hld up: stdy hdwy: 4th and in tch whn blnd and uns rdr 15th* **13/2**

/U3- **P** **Just Barney Boy**[16] 9-11-7 .... MrAWaugh(7) —
(S G Waugh) *towards rr: hdwy 7th: hit and lost pl 10th: sn btn: p.u and dismntd run in: collapsed after line* **8/1**

6m 47.3s (17.70) **Going Correction** +0.75s/f (Soft) **12** Ran SP% **114.3**
Speed ratings: **101,98,93,92,83 77,—,—,—,— —,—** CSF £28.81 TOTE £7.60: £2.70, £1.40, £12.30; EX 36.20.

Owner R S Brown **Bred** Mrs M Armstrong **Trained** Ashkirk, Scottish Borders

■ The first training success under Rules for Ian Stark, the former three-day eventer.

■ Stewards' Enquiry : Mr T Davidson four-day ban: used whip with excessive frequency (Apr 15-18)

FOCUS
Not the worse hunter chase ever run and the front pair may well go on to better things.

NOTEBOOK
Birkwood ◆, a multiple winning pointer, pulled up on his only previous hunter chase outing, but that came on a fast surface and this softer ground clearly saw him in a better light. He always held the lead having taken it up at the second fence and stuck on dourly to win with plenty in hand. Still only seven, he looks to have more to offer and this proficient jumper can go on to better things. *(op 7-1)*

Natain has a formidable record in points and he too stepped up on his previous hunter chase effort with a keeping-on second. He can pick up a race if improving his jumping. *(op 7-2)*

High Expectations(IRE) finished well adrift of the front two and has yet to win a hunter chase. *(op 66-1)*

Highland Brig failed to show any real improvement for the first-time tongue-tie, but he was at least going on at the end of his race. *(op 25-1)*

Carriage Ride(IRE), twice a beaten-favourite in points, failed to make any impact on this hunter chase debut and he was well held back in fifth. *(op 9-2)*

4723 BETFAIR.COM H'CAP HURDLE (8 hdls) 2m 110y
4:20 (4:24) (Class 4) (0-105,105) 4-Y-O+ **£3,903** (£1,146; £573; £286)

Form RPR

5000 **1** **Acceleration (IRE)**[11] 4585 6-10-3 **82** ....(t) GLee 88
(R Allan) *midfield on ins: smooth hdwy 3 out: ev ch last: styd on to ld nr fin* **14/1**

044P **2** *½* **Fearless Foursome**[35] 4142 7-10-10 **89** ....(t) PeterBuchanan 95
(N W Alexander) *prom: led 3 out: rdn next: kpt on wl: hdd towards fin* **20/1**

FF3 **3** *1 ¾* **Robert The Bruce**[54] 3797 11-11-6 **102** .... GaryBerridge(3) 106
(L Lungo) *prom: effrt bef 2 out: ev ch run in: hld towards fin* **11/1**

12FF **4** *4* **Shares (IRE)**[15] 4531 6-11-2 **105** .... DavidDaSilva(10) 105
(P Monteith) *hld up: hdwy and prom 2 out: rdn and one pce last* **11/2**[2]

5123 **5** *1 ¼* **Bob's Buster**[16] 4489 10-10-11 **90** .... KennyJohnson 89
(R Johnson) *hld up: hdwy on outside and prom 3 out: rdn next: sn no ex* **10/1**

6232 **6** *4* **Lethem Air**[16] 4493 8-11-7 **103** ....(p) DougieCostello(3) 99+
(T Butt) *cl up: led 3rd to 3 out: rallied: ev ch last: wknd run in* **6/1**[3]

6-02 **7** *4* **Diamond Mick**[24] 4354 6-11-4 **104** .... MissRDavidson(7) 95
(Mrs R L Elliot) *in tch: outpcd 3 out: n.d after* **9/2**[1]

0542 **8** *½* **Lord Baskerville**[48] 3916 5-10-11 **90** .... NeilMulholland 80
(W Storey) *keen: in tch: effrt bef 2 out: btn last* **14/1**

00F- **9** *4* **Crosby Dancer**[400] 4084 7-9-8 **80** oh6 ow1 .... PhilKinsella(7) 66
(W S Coltherd) *hld up: hdwy bef 3 out: sn rdn: btn next* **100/1**

5000 **10** *nk* **Mr Twins (ARG)**[132] 2416 5-9-10 **80** ....(t) MichaelMcAlister(5) 66
(M A Barnes) *chsd ldrs tl wknd after 3 out* **10/1**

2P6P **11** *5* **Gospel Song**[25] 4317 14-10-1 **87** ow2 .... EwanWhillans(7) 68
(A C Whillans) *led to 3rd: cl up tl wknd 3 out* **25/1**

0-00 **12** *½* **Browneyes Blue (IRE)**[35] 4145 8-9-9 **79** oh8 .... DeclanMcGann(5) 59
(D R MacLeod) *midfield: rdn and wknd bef 3 out* **66/1**

000P **13** *¾* **Another Taipan (IRE)**[102] 2945 6-10-0 **79** oh5 .... BarryKeniry 58
(A C Whillans) *bhd: rdn 4 out: nvr on terms* **25/1**

P/6P **14** *2* **Maradan (IRE)**[48] 3918 10-10-7 **86** .... KeithMercer 63
(Mrs J C McGregor) *a bhd: no ch fr 1/2-way* **33/1**

14BF **15** *dist* **North Landing (IRE)**[48] 3918 6-11-6 **99** .... LarryMcGrath —
(R C Guest) *sn bhd: no ch fr 1/2-way* **9/1**

4m 8.70s (5.00) **Going Correction** +0.45s/f (Soft) **15** Ran SP% **115.6**
Speed ratings: **106,105,104,103,102 100,98,98,96,96 94,93,93,92,—** CSF £264.38 CT £3161.14 TOTE £16.30: £4.30, £6.80, £3.90; EX 303.90.

Owner Kim Marshall, Sue Rigby, Susan Warren **Bred** Cliveden Stud Ltd **Trained** Cornhill-on-Tweed, Northumberland

■ Stewards' Enquiry : Peter Buchanan two-day ban: used whip with excessive frequency (Apr 15-16)

FOCUS
Ordinary stuff though the pace was decent.

NOTEBOOK
Acceleration(IRE) had failed to shine in all previous starts over hurdles this season, but he received a fine ride from Lee and came through late to win with something in hand. He may be capable of finding a little improvement and it is also worth bearing in mind he is not badly handicapped on the Flat.

Fearless Foursome was always to the fore and appeared to run his race, but the winner proved too strong in the latter stages. This was a better effort and it is hoped he continues to go the right way.

Robert The Bruce kept on well enough in third, but he was not making it easy for his jockey and was always being held. He is slowly finding his form again. *(op 16-1)*

Shares(IRE) came through to hold every chance, but he was unable to go on with the front trio and was left a one-paced fourth. *(op 5-1)*

Bob's Buster looked set to play a major role as they took the fourth last, but he was beaten before two out and failed to see his race out as strongly as had once looked likely. *(op 7-1)*

Diamond Mick was unable to dominate and did not run up to form as a result. *(tchd 5-1)*

4724 PRINCESS ROYAL TRUST FOR CARERS OREGON H'CAP HURDLE (11 hdls) 2m 6f 110y
4:50 (4:52) (Class 4) (0-110,110) 4-Y-O+ **£3,903** (£1,146; £573; £286)

Form RPR

6221 **1** **Imtihan (IRE)**[15] 4517 7-10-7 **101** .... MichaelO'Connell(10) 109+
(Mrs S J Smith) *cl up: chal 6th: led next: mde rest: styd on strly fnl 2* **7/2**[1]

02P4 **2** *6* **Chief Dan George (IRE)**[80] 3376 6-10-9 **98** .... DeclanMcGann(5) 98+
(D R MacLeod) *keen early: chsd ldrs: effrt and chsd wnr 3 out: kpt on same pce run in* **10/1**

0P22 **3** *1* **Roobihoo (IRE)**[15] 4517 7-11-12 **110** ....(t) RichardMcGrath 109+
(C Grant) *prom: outpcd 3 out: rallied after next: kpt on run in* **7/1**[3]

1360 **4** *13* **Tobesure (IRE)**[24] 4344 12-10-13 **100** .... MichalKohl(3) 85
(J I A Charlton) *midfield: effrt bef 3 out: no imp fr next* **14/1**

4523 **5** *1 ½* **Sotovik (IRE)**[23] 4362 5-10-12 **103** .... EwanWhillans(7) 87
(A C Whillans) *hld up: hdwy after 4 out: rdn and no ex fr 2 out* **14/1**

5060 **6** *½* **Uptown Lad (IRE)**[25] 4314 7-11-0 **98** .... KennyJohnson 81
(R Johnson) *hld up: hit 4th: effrt 3 out: btn next* **16/1**

0204 **7** *3* **Le Millenaire (FR)**[11] 4582 7-10-11 **102** .... MissKBryson(7) 82
(S H Shirley-Beavan) *cl up: led 6th to next: rdn and wknd bef 2 out* **33/1**

-420 **8** *4* **Letitia's Loss (IRE)**[41] 4043 8-11-7 **105** .... TonyDobbin 81
(N G Richards) *hld up: hdwy after 4 out: rdn next: sn btn* **6/1**[2]

4220 **9** *18* **Miss Kilkeel (IRE)**[33] 4186 8-11-4 **102** .... TomSiddall 60
(R T J Wilson, Ire) *bhd: rdn bef 4 out: nvr on terms* **33/1**

0P35 **10** *13* **Crackleando**[16] 4488 5-10-5 **96** .... TomMessenger(7) 41
(A R Dicken) *led to 6th: wknd fr next* **14/1**

0P5- **11** *½* **Rosalyons (IRE)**[379] 4475 12-10-12 **103** .... MissRDavidson(7) 48
(Mrs H O Graham) *midfield: rdn 4 out: wknd bef next* **25/1**

5055 **12** *2 ½* **Try Catch Paddy (IRE)**[11] 4583 8-11-1 **109** .... DavidDaSilva(10) 51
(P Monteith) *hld up: hdwy bef 7th: rdn and wknd 3 out* **40/1**

2500 **13** *8* **Bodfari Signet**[47] 3929 10-11-3 **101** .... MarkBradburne 35
(Mrs S C Bradburne) *a bhd* **25/1**

-45P **P** **Wise Man (IRE)**[24] 4345 11-11-2 **100** .... GLee —
(N W Alexander) *bhd: t.o whn p.u bef 4 out* **14/1**

/00P **P** **Corbie Lynn**[16] 4491 9-10-9 **100** .... PhilKinsella(7) —
(W S Coltherd) *hld up: struggling bef 7th: t.o whn p.u bef 3 out* **50/1**

PFP3 **P** **Aberdare**[16] 4491 7-10-13 **100** ....(p) GaryBerridge(3) —
(J R Bewley) *midfield: rdn after 6th: wknd next: t.o whn p.u bef 3 out* **16/1**

F4P6 **P** **Kharak (FR)**[24] 4344 7-11-8 **106** .... WilsonRenwick —
(Mrs S C Bradburne) *chsd ldrs: drvn after 6th: wknd next: p.u bef 3 out* **20/1**

5m 50.1s (12.40) **Going Correction** +0.625s/f (Soft) **17** Ran SP% **119.3**
Speed ratings: **103,100,100,96,95 95,94,92,86,82 81,81,78,—,— —,—** CSF £33.87 CT £237.41 TOTE £5.60: £2.00, £2.40, £2.00, £3.90; EX 55.30.

Owner Keith Nicholson **Bred** Shadwell Estate Company Limited **Trained** High Eldwick, W Yorks

FOCUS
A smooth display from the improving Imtihan.

NOTEBOOK
Imtihan(IRE) ◆, 6lb higher than when winning at Carlisle last month, is clearly on the up and he surged clear in the final quarter-mile, winning with plenty in hand. The extra two furlongs caused no problems and, with there likely to be further improvement, he is one to keep on the right side of. *(tchd 4-1)*

Chief Dan George(IRE) showed improved form for this step up in distance, keeping on despite having failed to settle, and there should be a small race in him off this sort of mark. *(op 9-1)*

Roobihoo(IRE), behind the winner last time at Carlisle, had every chance but was well held on this occasion, looking anchored by his big weight.

Tobesure(IRE) was a bit adrift of the front trio and the veteran is unlikely to be winning off this mark.

Sotovik(IRE) has been running well and this was another reasonable effort. He is young enough to improve still.

Wise Man(IRE) *Official explanation: jockey said gelding never travelled*

4725 GG.COM HUNTERS' CHASE (19 fncs) 3m 1f
5:20 (5:20) (Class 5) 5-Y-O+ **£2,637** (£811; £405)

Form RPR

15-3 **1** **Jacksonville (FR)**[9] 9-11-9 85 ....(p) MissVickySimpson(7) 101
(Miss Vicky Simpson) *cl up: effrt after 3 out: kpt on run in to ld nr fin* **11/2**

1515 **2** 2 ½ **The Butterwick Kid**[15] 13-11-12 96................................(b) MrRTATate(7) 103+
(T P Tate) *sn led: pushed along 2 out: hdd and no ex towards fin* **15/8**[1]
21-P **3** *dist* **Mr Mahdlo**[9] 12-12-0 97.. MrBWoodhouse(5) —
(B R Woodhouse) *bhd and sn detached: kpt on fr 2 out: nvr on terms* **9/4**[2]
-66F **4** 7 **Nisbet**[16] 12-11-5 67.. MrAJFindlay(7) —
(Miss M Bremner) *chsd ldrs tl wknd fr 14th* **33/1**
U **Benny Boy (IRE)**[16] 6-11-5 .... MrAWaugh(7) —
(S G Waugh) *nt jump wl: sn bhd: blnd and uns rdr 12th* **9/2**[3]
6-53 **P** **Supreme Silence (IRE)**[9] 9-11-9 80................................. MrNickKent(7) —
(Nick Kent) *blnd 2nd: sn bhd: p.u bef 4th* **14/1**
PP0- **P** **Fisher Street**[9] 11-11-5 .... MissJHollands(7) —
(Mrs C J Kerr) *blnd 2nd: sn wl bhd: p.u bef 10th* **50/1**
PPP- **F** **Em's Guy**[363] 4737 8-11-5 64.. MissKBryson(7) —
(W Amos) *chsd ldrs tl wknd 11th: fell heavily 13th* **100/1**

6m 47.8s (18.20) **Going Correction** +0.75s/f (Soft) 8 Ran SP% **111.7**
Speed ratings: **100,99**,—,—,— —,—,— CSF £16.20 TOTE £7.60: £1.30, £1.40, £1.40; EX 16.40 Place 6 £272.44, Place 5 £180.75.
Owner Miss Vicky Simpson **Bred** F Cottin **Trained** North Berwick, East Lothian

FOCUS
An uncompetitive heat in which the front two finished clear.

NOTEBOOK
Jacksonville(FR) ◆, recently successful in a point at Mordon, has clearly taken confidence from that and he stuck on gamely on the long run-in to win going away from The Butterwick Kid. He seems to be going in the right direction and may yet be able to win again. *(op 9-2)*
The Butterwick Kid has a been a fair hunter for a few seasons now, but he is not getting any better at the of 13 and he had no answer to the winner close home. He was clear of the third in fairness and may yet be capable of poaching another race. *(tchd 2-1)*
Mr Mahdlo was struggling from an early stage and never got into it. This was disappointing. *(tchd 5-2, 11-4 in a place)*
Benny Boy(IRE) was never jumping with any fluency and it was no surprise to see him get rid of his rider at the 12th. *(op 5-1)*
T/Plt: £671.10 to a £1 stake. Pool: £58,058.65. 63.15 winning tickets. T/Qpdt: £403.90 to a £1 stake. Pool: £4,530.80. 8.30 winning tickets. RY

4556 EXETER (R-H)

Wednesday, April 5

OFFICIAL GOING: Good to soft (soft in places)
Last hurdle and first past winning post omitted all races. Two fences in back straight also omitted for all chases.
Wind: Light, against Weather: Sunny

4726 EXETER CITY COUNCIL NOVICES' H'CAP HURDLE (5 hdls 3 omitted) 2m 1f
2:30 (2:31) (Class 4) (0-110,110) 4-Y-0+ **£3,903** (£1,146; £573; £286)

Form RPR
P012 **1** **Dorneys Well (IRE)**[27] 4322 6-10-10 94.............................(t) PaulMoloney 102+
(Evan Williams) *hld up and bhd: hdwy on ins whn nt fluent 3rd: led last: drvn out* **4/1**[1]
-610 **2** 2 ½ **Kings Rock**[40] 4099 5-11-3 108.................................. MissFayeBramley(7) 110
(P A Blockley) *w ldr: led 1st tl after 3rd: led appr 2 out to last: no ex towards fin* **14/1**
635P **3** 3 ½ **Miss Midnight**[46] 3997 5-9-13 90....................................(b) JamesWhite(7) 90+
(R J Hodges) *hld up in tch: ev ch 2 out: sn rdn: hit last: one pce* **14/1**
4005 **4** 8 **Thenameescapesme**[24] 4396 6-11-0 98 .... NoelFehily 88
(T R George) *hld up in mid-div: kpt on same pce fr 2 out* **16/1**
33F0 **5** 5 **Corals Laurel (IRE)**[12] 4606 7-11-5 103.........................(t) WarrenMarston 89+
(R T Phillips) *hld up and bhd: hdwy 2nd: rdn and wknd appr 2 out* **17/2**
546 **6** 3 **Fuss**[23] 4425 5-10-2 86.. RichardJohnson 68
(P J Hobbs) *hld up in mid-div: hdwy appr 3rd: wknd appr 2 out* **8/1**
1310 **7** *hd* **Honan (IRE)**[48] 3944 7-10-13 104........................(v) AndrewGlassonbury(7) 86
(M C Pipe) *prom: led after 3rd tl appr 2 out: sn wknd* **12/1**
1463 **8** 1 ¼ **Coach Lane**[39] 4104 5-11-11 109... SamThomas 90
(Miss Venetia Williams) *led to 1st: rdn appr 2 out: wknd appr last* **9/2**[2]
0500 **9** 2 **Harcourt (USA)**[46] 3996 6-10-11 95.................................... JimmyMcCarthy 74
(M Madgwick) *prom: lost pl 1st: n.d after* **10/1**
060 **10** *nk* **Palamedes**[25] 4367 7-10-1 85.. OllieMcPhail 63
(B J Llewellyn) *hld up in tch: rdn and wknd appr 2 out* **20/1**
-041 **11** 2 ½ **Longstone Lady (IRE)**[15] 4556 9-10-3 90............................ ChrisHonour(3) 66
(J D Frost) *prom: hit 2nd: sn rdn and lost pl* **10/1**
-000 **12** *shd* **Jo's Sale (IRE)**[219] 1359 7-10-1 85................................. ChristianWilliams 61
(Evan Williams) *a bhd* **20/1**
6306 **13** 1 ½ **Red Moor (IRE)**[65] 3650 6-11-7 110.....................................(p) LiamHeard(5) 84
(Mrs D A Hamer) *hld up and bhd: hdwy appr 3rd: wknd appr 2 out* **15/2**[3]

4m 14.5s (5.30) **Going Correction** +0.40s/f (Soft) 13 Ran SP% **126.2**
Speed ratings: **103,101,100,96,94 92,92,91,91,90 89,89,88** CSF £62.86 CT £731.00 TOTE £5.50: £2.80, £8.10, £7.30; EX 83.90.
Owner Donal Keating **Bred** A McCarren **Trained** Cowbridge, Vale Of Glamorgan
■ What was usually the last flight on both circuits, plus the flight after winning post were omitted.

FOCUS
A low-grade affair won by an improver who was value for further and can win another. The third sets the standard for the form.

NOTEBOOK
Dorneys Well(IRE) won really nicely and has definitely improved since the application of a tongue tie - his Towcester defeat in between wins can be forgiven due to the heavy ground. He is probably still slightly in front of the Handicapper and can gain another success before the season is out. *(op 9-2)*
Kings Rock, 8lb higher in the weights than his course victory back in December, made the winner pull out all the stops on the run to the line but ideally needs further. *(op 20-1)*
Miss Midnight, who could not get into the race last time after being badly hampered, ran up to her best and had every chance. She is still a maiden but will enjoy the ground getting quicker in the coming months. *(op 16-1)*
Thenameescapesme gave the impression he needs stepping back up in trip. *(tchd 20-1)*
Corals Laurel(IRE) kept going for really strong pressure, after being off the pace, but did not give the impression he was enjoying himself on the ground. *(op 9-1)*
Honan(IRE) led into the straight, going well, but found nothing when challenged and threw the towel in fairly quickly. *(op 10-1)*

4727 KENMART LTD H'CAP HURDLE (8 hdls 3 omitted) 2m 6f 110y
3:00 (3:03) (Class 3) (0-125,120) 4-Y-0+ **£5,204** (£1,528; £764; £381)

Form RPR
4151 **1** **In Accord**[29] 4284 7-11-7 115... RichardJohnson 124+
(H D Daly) *hld up and bhd: hdwy 5th: rdn appr 2 out: styd on to ld flat: drvn out* **6/1**[1]
0410 **2** 4 **Bak To Bill**[18] 4497 11-10-7 108....................................... MissLGardner(7) 112
(Mrs S Gardner) *a.p: led after 6th: clr 2 out: sn rdn: hdd and no ex flat* **20/1**
U640 **3** 2 **Moscow Whisper (IRE)**[25] 4372 9-10-11 110................. MrTJO'Brien(5) 112
(P J Hobbs) *a.p: rdn after 6th: one pce fr 2 out* **25/1**
1/F0 **4** *shd* **Rosarian (IRE)**[88] 3289 9-11-7 120....................................(p) LiamHeard(5) 122
(V R A Dartnall) *hld up towards rr: hdwy 3rd: lost pl after 6th: styd on fr 2 out* **10/1**
-PF0 **5** 1 **Grey Brother**[15] 4561 8-11-5 113..................................... AndrewThornton 114
(Nick Williams) *hld up towards rr: hdwy appr 5th: btn whn edgd lft flat* **25/1**
/121 **6** 4 **Before Dark (IRE)**[29] 4285 8-10-13 110........................ DougieCostello(3) 108+
(Mrs H Dalton) *hld up and bhd: hdwy 4th: rdn appr 2 out: wknd flat* **9/1**
4P00 **7** 10 **Star Angler (IRE)**[25] 4372 8-11-0 108...........................(b[1]) MarkBradburne 100+
(H D Daly) *hld up towards rr: hdwy appr 4th: led after 5th tl after 6th: wknd appr last* **20/1**
2023 **8** 6 **Keepers Mead (IRE)**[15] 4559 8-11-8 116......................... RobertWalford 97
(R H Alner) *hld up in tch: wknd 6th* **16/1**
/630 **9** 6 **Euradream (IRE)**[69] 3581 8-10-9 103........................(b[1]) JimmyMcCarthy 78
(Jean-Rene Auvray) *hld up in tch: rdn 5th: sn bhd* **25/1**
6P01 **10** ¾ **Haloo Baloo**[15] 4557 6-10-9 103... NoelFehily 77
(Jonjo O'Neill) *hld up in mid-div: hdwy 4th: rdn after 6th: wknd 2 out* **9/1**
/301 **11** 16 **Carew Lad**[25] 4372 10-11-4 112..................................... ChristianWilliams 70
(Mrs D A Hamer) *led tl appr 2nd: led 4th tl after 5th: wknd appr 2 out* **11/1**
3P43 **12** *dist* **Kingsbay**[14] 4579 7-10-10 104...(p) JimCrowley —
(H Morrison) *prom: rdn after 3rd: wknd 4th: virtually p.u flat* **10/1**
000F **P** **Naja De Billeron (FR)**[12] 4606 5-10-10 107..................(t) TomMalone(3) —
(M C Pipe) *bhd fr 3rd: t.o whn p.u bef 4th* **50/1**
4P32 **P** **El Hombre Del Rio (IRE)**[29] 4284 9-10-10 104.................... JoeTizzard —
(V G Greenway) *a bhd: t.o whn p.u after 3rd* **8/1**[3]
2054 **P** **Westmeath Flyer**[39] 4119 11-11-0 115................(p) MissFayeBramley(7) —
(P A Blockley) *a bhd: t.o whn p.u bef 2 out* **33/1**
6401 **P** **Ask The Umpire (IRE)**[27] 4320 11-10-5 104............(b) LiamTreadwell(5) —
(N E Berry) *a bhd: rdn after 3rd: t.o whn p.u bef 2 out* **20/1**
4FPU **P** **Predestine (FR)**[36] 4165 6-10-11 105................................... AlanO'Keeffe —
(K C Bailey) *hld up in mid-div: mstke 4th: sn bhd: t.o whn p.u bef 2 out* **33/1**
P422 **P** **Heron's Ghyll (IRE)**[16] 4549 9-10-10 104............................ SamThomas —
(Miss Venetia Williams) *led appr 2nd to 4th: wknd after 6th: t.o whn p.u bef last* **7/1**[2]

5m 45.4s (6.10) **Going Correction** +0.40s/f (Soft) 18 Ran SP% **124.0**
Speed ratings: **105,103,102,102,102 101,97,95,93,93 87**,—,—,—,— —,—,— CSF £125.78 CT £2821.14 TOTE £6.90: £1.40, £8.50, £9.00, £2.30; EX 152.80 TRIFECTA Not won..
Owner T F F Nixon **Bred** T F F Nixon **Trained** Stanton Lacy, Shropshire

FOCUS
A competitive handicap and the form looks sound for the grade with the placed horses having run to their marks.

NOTEBOOK
In Accord, who came into the race having won two of his previous three races on heavy ground, took a really long time to get to the front but won nicely by the time he had passed the post. He looks a thorough stayer and should make a nice chaser next season. *(op 5-1)*
Bak To Bill, 8lb higher in the handicap than his win over the course in March on heavy ground, looked the most likely winner all the way up the straight until his stamina appeared to give out. He has won at up to three miles - over fences - but is probably better over two and a half miles over hurdles. *(op 25-1)*
Moscow Whisper(IRE) came to have every chance jumping the last but did not see the trip out as well as the first two. He could do with coming down the handicap a little bit more to have an obvious winning chance.
Rosarian(IRE) did not run too badly on his first run since early January, but at no stage did he ever look like winning. *(op 12-1)*
Grey Brother just kept galloping up the home straight and would probably appreciate a bit further. He is nicely handicapped on his winning form. *(tchd 28-1)*
Before Dark(IRE), usually ridden by the winning jockey and making his handicap debut, is better served by a longer trip and shaped accordingly. *(op 8-1)*
Haloo Baloo, up 10lb for his win last time out, was under pressure a long way from home and could not get competitive in this grade. *(op 17-2)*

4728 SIS H'CAP CHASE (13 fncs 4 omitted) 2m 7f 110y
3:30 (3:32) (Class 3) (0-125,122) 5-Y-0+ **£6,506** (£1,910; £955; £477)

Form RPR
36P3 **1** **Hever Road (IRE)**[15] 4558 7-10-2 105.............(b) AndrewGlassonbury(7) 115
(M C Pipe) *hld up in mid-div: hdwy appr 8th: led last: hung lft nr fin: all out* **16/1**
P5P6 **2** 1 **Holy Joe (FR)**[11] 4617 9-11-12 122.. SamThomas 131
(Miss Venetia Williams) *led tl after 5th: prom: rdn to ld after 2 out: hdd last: r.o* **17/2**
U522 **3** 6 **Bay Island (IRE)**[26] 4348 10-10-4 100...............................(tp) PaulMoloney 105+
(M Pitman) *prom: led after 5th: rdn and hdd after 2 out: hung lft and wknd flat* **7/2**[2]
-131 **4** 6 **On Y Va (FR)**[17] 4516 8-11-4 114....................................(t) WarrenMarston 111
(R T Phillips) *hld up and bhd: rdn and sme hdwy appr 4 out: nvr trbld ldrs* **14/1**
343- **5** *nk* **Dealer's Choice (IRE)**[420] 3761 12-10-13 109.......................... NoelFehily 106
(Miss Victoria Roberts) *prom: outpcd 9th: n.d after* **33/1**
0011 **6** 1 ¾ **Cousin Nicky**[15] 4559 5-11-2 121...................................... RichardJohnson 108+
(P J Hobbs) *prom tl wknd 4 out* **5/2**[1]
13U0 **7** *dist* **Gumley Gale**[193] 1550 11-11-10 120...(t) RJGreene —
(K Bishop) *a bhd: lost tch appr 8th: t.o* **33/1**
21UP **P** **Osiris (IRE)**[90] 3250 11-11-6 116..............................(t) ChristianWilliams —
(Evan Williams) *sn bhd: t.o whn p.u after 9th* **16/1**
PF22 **U** **Supreme Catch (IRE)**[25] 4374 9-10-12 113..................... MrTJO'Brien(5) —
(Miss H C Knight) *hld up in tch: cl 5th whn blnd and uns rdr 7th* **5/1**[3]
30F5 **U** **Trust Fund (IRE)**[18] 4496 8-11-7 117.................................. RobertWalford —
(R H Alner) *w ldr to 3rd: lost pl after 4th: blnd bdly and uns rdr 7th* **7/1**
6P3P **P** **Biliverdin (IRE)**[27] 4332 12-11-5 115.................................. MarkBradburne —
(J A Geake) *hld up: sltly hmpd 7th: bhd fr 9th: t.o whn p.u bef 2 out* **14/1**

5m 53.3s (-5.30) **Going Correction** 0.0s/f (Good)
WFA 5 from 7yo+ 4lb 11 Ran SP% **121.5**
Speed ratings: **108,107,105,103,103 102**,—,—,—,— — CSF £149.26 CT £593.65 TOTE £28.10: £6.20, £3.50, £1.60; EX 235.00.

Owner Professor D B A Silk & Mrs Heather Silk **Bred** Dr D B A Silk And H Jarvis **Trained** Nicholashayne, Devon

FOCUS
A low-grade handicap run at a fair pace and the form looks solid enough, rated through those in the frame behind the winner.

NOTEBOOK
Hever Road(IRE), from a stable struggling for form, travelled really until coming off the bridle. Once under pressure he tended to wander, but still found enough to win with a little bit in hand. He is almost certainly quite a bit better than his official mark but his attitude is questionable, and is not one to rely on. *(tchd 25-1)*

Holy Joe(FR) has not won since 2002, when trained in France, but came really close to finally adding to that tally. The drop in grade helped him and he only just failed to give lumps of weight away to the winner. He should go very close next time in similar company. *(op 8-1)*

Bay Island(IRE) is a model of consistency but just finds one or two good for him every time. He is considerably higher in the handicap still than his win earlier in the season. *(op 5-1)*

On Y Va(FR) never figured against his more experienced rivals and was firmly put in his place. He needs a return to novice company to gain more experience, and would probably benefit from a slight step up in trip. *(op 10-1)*

Dealer's Choice(IRE) shaped quite nicely after a huge absence, but never looked like winning at any stage. *(op 25-1)*

Cousin Nicky looked to be outdone by the rise in the weights for his last two wins, and the step up in trip. *(op 11-4 tchd 10-3, 7-2 in a place)*

Osiris(IRE) *Official explanation: jockey said gelding bled from the nose (op 14-1)*

4729 PERCY BROWNE MEMORIAL NOVICES' CHASE (13 fncs 2 omitted) 2m 3f 110y

4:00 (4:00) (Class 3) 5-Y-O+ **£7,156** (£2,101; £1,050; £524)

Form RPR

25F0 **1** **Chilling Place (IRE)**[20] 4456 7-11-6 139 .... RichardJohnson 118+
(P J Hobbs) *hld up in tch: led appr 4 out: pushed clr flat: comf* **11/10**[1]

40U4 **2** *7* **Le Rochelais (FR)**[29] 4289 7-11-0 103 .... AndrewThornton 106+
(R H Alner) *hld up: hdwy 6th: chsd wnr 9th tl j.rt 4 out: wnt 2nd again 2 out: no imp* **12/1**

112F **3** *6* **Preacher Boy**[20] 4456 7-11-10 131 .... ChristianWilliams 107
(R J Hodges) *led to 4th: led appr 8th: rdn and hdd appr 4 out: wknd 2 out* **11/2**[3]

0001 **4** *2* **Waltzing Beau**[27] 4323 5-11-1 129 .... JohnnyLevins(5) 102+
(B G Powell) *prom: outpcd 9th: no real prog fr 4 out* **6/1**

P5P6 **5** *1* **Jonanaud**[38] 4131 7-10-7 102 .... MrRMcCarthy(7) 94
(H J Manners) *nvr nrr* **25/1**

6140 **6** *dist* **Idole First (IRE)**[20] 4456 7-11-10 131 .... AlanO'Keeffe —
(Miss Venetia Williams) *hld up in mid-div: hit 6th: sn struggling: t.o* **10/3**[2]

U3P0 **7** *dist* **Glenkill (IRE)**[13] 4590 8-10-7 .... MarkGrant —
(S M Jacobs) *t.k.h: hdwy to ld 4th: hdd appr 8th: sn wknd: t.o whn j.rt 3 out* **200/1**

P0 **P** **Lincoln Leader (IRE)**[13] 4590 8-10-7 .... PaulMoloney —
(Evan Williams) *a bhd: nt fluent 2nd: lost tch appr 8th: t.o whn p.u bef 4 out* **100/1**

4m 50.1s (-3.80) **Going Correction** 0.0s/f (Good)
WFA 5 from 7yo+ 3lb **8** Ran SP% **113.4**
Speed ratings: **107,104,101,101,100** —,—,— CSF £14.93 TOTE £2.70: £1.10, £2.50, £1.60; EX 16.20.

Owner M J Tuckey **Bred** Wickfield Farm Partnership **Trained** Withycombe, Somerset

FOCUS
A reasonable novice chase run at a good tempo. The winner was rated well below his best with the runner-up to his hurdles form.

NOTEBOOK
Chilling Place(IRE), well beaten in the Jewson Novices' Handicap Chase at the Festival last time, collected his third course success with the minimum of fuss. His form entitled him to the greatest respect in this company, namely his first two efforts over fences, and he made no mistake. He handles quick ground and could add to this success if a suitable opportunity arose during the spring. *(op 6-4)*

Le Rochelais(FR), who is still a maiden, ran his best race for some time and could well have improved for the slightly quicker. He should be capable of getting his head in front if found a realistic opportunity on good ground. *(op 14-1 tchd 11-1)*

Preacher Boy, dropping back in trip and giving weight to a useful winner, was niggled along from an early stage and requires a stiffer test of stamina to be at his best. *(op 4-1)*

Waltzing Beau did not run too badly but found conditions vastly different to those he won in on his previous run. *(op 11-2 tchd 13-2)*

Jonanaud kept on well up the home straight but never figured with a chance. *(tchd 28-1)*

Idole First(IRE), who finished in front of the winner at Cheltenham, once again gave the impression that chasing is not his thing. He was niggled along from an early stage, after making a mistake, and does not look like a horse who enjoys jumping fences. *(op 7-2 tchd 4-1)*

4730 COUNTRYSIDE ALLIANCE OPEN HUNTERS' CHASE (13 fncs 2 omitted) 2m 3f 110y

4:30 (4:30) (Class 5) 5-Y-O+ **£2,637** (£811; £405)

Form RPR

230P **1** **Enitsag (FR)**[13] 4594 7-11-9 94 .... MrDMansell(3) 101
(S Flook) *a.p: led appr 4 out: rdn after 2 out: j.rt last: r.o* **20/1**

22-P **2** *3* **Bengal Bullet**[17] 9-11-7 107 .... MissTCave(5) 98
(C Blank) *a.p: chsd wnr appr 4 out: r.o one pce flat* **3/1**[1]

06-F **3** *6* **Whatashock**[11] 11-11-5 .... MissETory(7) 92
(Mrs H M Tory) *prom: lost pl 4th: rallied 4 out: wknd flat* **16/1**

340/ **4** *1* **Tuba (IRE)**[38] 11-11-7 .... MrRWoollacott(5) 91
(S A Hughes) *led tl appr 4 out: wknd 3 out* **33/1**

0002 **5** *12* **Dun An Doras (IRE)**[16] 4555 10-11-5 96 .... MrDMcKenna(7) 79
(Mrs N Frost) *hld up in mid-div: hdwy appr 8th: wknd appr 4 out* **9/2**[2]

5F/6 **6** *10* **Elgar**[16] 4555 9-11-12 ....(t) MrJMPritchard 69
(M Hammond) *hld up in tch: outpcd 9th: rallied appr 4 out: wkng whn hit 3 out* **12/1**

1P **7** *3 1/2* **Virgos Bambino (IRE)**[15] 4560 9-11-2 .... MrJBarnes(7) 63
(Miss V J Nicholls) *prom tl wknd 9th* **9/1**

5P40 **R** **Hot Plunge**[16] 4555 10-12-2 .... MrJSnowden —
(Mrs J P Lomax) *ref to r: tk no part* **25/1**

31-R **U** **Sir D'Orton (FR)**[10] 10-11-13 113 .... MissCTizzard(3) —
(A J Tizzard) *bhd tl blnd and uns rdr 8th* **7/1**[3]

000/ **P** **Langcourt Jester**[375] 8-10-12 .... MrPHockley(7) —
(N K Allin) *a bhd: t.o whn hit 8th: sn p.u* **150/1**

P-PB **P** **Polka**[18] 11-11-9 ....(t) MrDEdwards(3) —
(V G Greenway) *prom tl wknd 8th: t.o whn p.u bef 4 out* **50/1**

PP-U **P** **Curragh Gold (IRE)**[18] 6-10-12 71 ....(p) MrRMcCarthy(7) —
(Mrs P N Dutfield) *a bhd: t.o whn p.u bef 4 out* **100/1**

0-02 **P** **Polish Cloud (FR)**[8] 4660 9-11-5 109 .... MrsHKemp(7) —
(Mrs H M Kemp) *a bhd: t.o whn p.u and dismntd after 9th* **11/1**

33 **P** **Nailed On**[30] 4283 7-11-7 .... MrAndrewMartin(5) —
(Andrew J Martin) *mid-div: j.lft 5th (water): sn bhd: t.o whn p.u bef 4 out* **12/1**

51U- **P** **Mr Woodland**[39] 12-11-11 105 .... MissLGardner(5) —
(Miss L Gardner) *chsd ldrs: lost pl 8th: rallied appr 4 out: 5th whn p.u and dismntd bef 3 out* **10/1**

4m 54.4s (0.50) **Going Correction** 0.0s/f (Good) **15** Ran SP% **119.5**
Speed ratings: **99,97,95,95,90 86,84**,—,—,— —,—,—,—,— CSF £78.64 TOTE £22.30: £7.20, £2.80, £4.40; EX 142.40.

Owner Glyn Byard **Bred** Agence F I P S **Trained** Leominster, Herefordshire

FOCUS
A competitive, if low grade, event. The time was just over four seconds slower than the previous race.

NOTEBOOK
Enitsag(FR), who beat Oneway on his first run over hurdles for Martin Pipe in the distant past, won with plenty in hand but is not one to entirely trust to reproduce the same effort next time given his career profile. *(op 16-1)*

Bengal Bullet kept on well but never got to the runaway leader. He is a versatile sort with regards to trip but might be better suited by slightly further. *(op 9-2)*

Whatashock finished strongly from off the pace after losing his place early. He stays three miles and acts on quick ground, so there might be a race for him before the end of the season if the ground gets firmer.

Tuba(IRE) made most of the running before being readily outpaced by Enitsag just before the home straight. *(op 25-1)*

Dun An Doras(IRE) looked to be going well at the top of the home straight before finding less than *looked likely off the bridle. He may have found the course a bit too stiff for him given his best* form. *(op 5-1 tchd 11-2)*

Mr Woodland was staying on quite well when pulled up before three out, presumably with an injury. *Official explanation: jockey said gelding lost its action (op 12-1)*

4731 HAPPY BIRTHDAY ROBERT THOMAS CONDITIONAL JOCKEYS' H'CAP HURDLE (5 hdls 3 omitted) 2m 1f

5:00 (5:01) (Class 5) (0-100,100) 4-Y-O+ **£3,083** (£898; £449)

Form RPR

1536 **1** **Lorient Express (FR)**[33] 4213 7-10-7 **84** .... LiamTreadwell(3) 100+
(Miss Venetia Williams) *t.k.h in mid-div: hdwy 2nd: led on bit after 3rd: rdn out flat* **7/4**[1]

6P00 **2** *1 1/4* **Moon Catcher**[179] 1677 5-11-4 **97** .... JayPemberton(5) 103
(D Brace) *hld up and bhd: rdn and hdwy appr 2 out: styd on towards fin: nt rch wnr* **66/1**

2232 **3** *2* **Mistified (IRE)**[46] 3997 5-10-8 **90** .... WayneKavanagh(8) 94
(J W Mullins) *hld up: hdwy 3rd: rdn appr 2 out: one pce flat* **8/1**

0 **4** *1* **Longueville Manor (FR)**[231] 1242 5-11-5 **93** .... ShaneWalsh 96
(Jonjo O'Neill) *hld up in tch: ev ch 2 out: sn rdn: no ex flat* **6/1**[2]

PP/5 **5** *1 3/4* **Without Pretense (USA)**[39] 4101 8-10-0 **74** oh10 .... SamCurling 75
(N G Ayliffe) *hld up towards rr: hdwy appr 2 out: one pce flat* **100/1**

3P0- **6** *shd* **Dance With Wolves (FR)**[418] 3790 6-11-2 **90** .... PaddyMerrigan 91
(Jim Best) *hld up towards rr: hdwy appr 2 out: one pce flat* **12/1**

0620 **7** *3* **El Corredor (IRE)**[41] 4080 7-10-8 **88** .... AndrewGlassonbury(6) 86
(M C Pipe) *hld up in mid-div: rdn and hdwy on ins appr 2 out: wknd flat* **6/1**[2]

064F **8** *11* **Joli Classical (IRE)**[29] 4290 4-9-11 **83** .... JamesWhite(6) 64
(R J Hodges) *nvr nr ldrs* **25/1**

25F0 **9** *2* **Brown Fox (FR)**[138] 2314 5-10-3 **77** .... OwynNelmes 62
(C J Down) *hld up and bhd: hdwy 2nd: wknd 2 out* **40/1**

0055 **10** *4* **Harrival**[29] 4290 6-10-8 **82** .... DarylJacob 63
(Miss M Bragg) *mde most tl hdd after 3rd: sn rdn: wknd 2 out* **25/1**

-PP2 **11** *1/2* **Montesino**[14] 4570 7-11-7 **100** ....(p) RichardGordon(5) 81
(M Madgwick) *prom tl wknd appr 2 out* **50/1**

5200 **12** *1* **Backstreet Lad**[71] 3548 4-10-12 **92** ....(t) JohnnyLevins 66
(Evan Williams) *prom tl wknd appr 2 out* **7/1**[3]

FP45 **13** *15* **Georges Boy (IRE)**[15] 4556 8-11-3 **91** ....(v) TomGreenway 56
(P J Jones) *prom early: dropped rr 1st: n.d after* **50/1**

040P **14** *1 1/4* **Duke's View (IRE)**[86] 3321 5-9-9 **74** oh2 ....(p) DavidBoland(5) 37
(D C Turner) *bhd fr 2nd* **100/1**

/53- **U** **Border Star (IRE)**[547] 1601 9-9-11 **79** .... RichardKilloran(8) —
(B G Powell) *bhd tl blnd and uns rdr 2nd* **25/1**

4m 15.5s (6.30) **Going Correction** +0.40s/f (Soft)
WFA 4 from 5yo+ 5lb **15** Ran SP% **117.6**
Speed ratings: **101,100,99,99,98 98,96,91,90,88 88,88,80,80**,— CSF £142.59 CT £768.74 TOTE £2.40: £1.50, £13.70, £1.90; EX 72.20 Place 6 £160.06, Place 5 £46.06.

Owner Let's Live Racing **Bred** D Laupretre **Trained** Kings Caple, H'fords

FOCUS
A very poor race won by a horse 40lb well in on his chase form.

NOTEBOOK
Lorient Express(FR), running off a massive 40lb lower rating than his mark over fences, won as he should have after taking a really keen hold early. He will probably get a hefty rise in the weights for this success - given the official ratings of the next three home - but he should be more than capable of winning again in similar company. *(op 11-8 tchd 5-4)*

Moon Catcherhad every chance after taking an age to get going. She is now better handicapped over hurdles on her winning form, and is one to bear in mind next time, especially if raised in trip slightly. *(op 40-1)*

Mistified(IRE) is a consistent sort but never looked like winning at any stage. He is probably more effective over further and is still a maiden after 31 attempts. *(op 12-1)*

Longueville Manor(FR), making his debut for the stable, had every chance two from home but did not get home as well as the first three. It was not a bad effort after such a long absence, but his next run will tell us more about his current ability. *(op 12-1)*

Without Pretense(USA), running from 10lb out of the handicap, did not disgrace himself and probably has enough ability to win a seller.

El Corredor(IRE), making his debut for the stable, showed nothing to suggest he is about to win. *(tchd 7-1)*

T/Jkpt: Not won. T/Plt: £258.70 to a £1 stake. Pool: £65,325.50. 184.30 winning tickets. T/Qpdt: £27.90 to a £1 stake. Pool: £5,019.40. 132.80 winning tickets. KH

4549 HEREFORD (R-H)

Wednesday, April 5

OFFICIAL GOING: Good (good to firm in places) changing to good to firm after race 2 (2.40pm)

Wind: Light, across Weather: Fine and sunny

4732 EXPRESS CAFES MAIDEN HURDLE (9 hdls 1 omitted) 2m 3f 110y

2:10 (2:11) (Class 4) 4-Y-0+ **£3,578** (£1,050; £525; £262)

Form				RPR
1654	**1**		**Briscoe Place (IRE)**[15] 4564 6-11-2 .... MickFitzgerald (Jonjo O'Neill) *led to 2nd: led 4th: drvn out* **14/1**	109
4-4	**2**	*nk*	**Pass It On (IRE)**[26] 4359 7-11-2 .... APMcCoy (Jonjo O'Neill) *a.p: rdn to chse wnr last: sn ev ch: unable qck nr fin* **4/9**[1]	109
45	**3**	*10*	**The Rocking Dock (IRE)**[79] 3421 5-10-13 .... StephenCraine(3) (D McCain) *chsd ldrs: ev ch whn mstke 2 out: sn rdn: wknd last* **33/1**	101+
402/	**4**	*8*	**Irish Flight (IRE)**[807] 3414 9-10-13 .... WilliamKennedy(3) (Noel T Chance) *hld up: hdwy 7th: nt trble ldrs* **8/1**[2]	91
000	**5**	*14*	**Coorbawn Vic (IRE)**[13] 4595 5-11-2 .... LeightonAspell (S A Brookshaw) *hld up: hmpd after 2nd: n.d* **66/1**	77+
0	**6**	*¾*	**Saddlers' Son (IRE)**[21] 4455 5-10-13 .... TJPhelan(3) (Mrs H Dalton) *hld up: hdwy 5th: wknd appr 2 out: mstke last* **50/1**	76
5020	**7**	*1 ¼*	**The Boobi (IRE)**[150] 2070 5-10-4 .... MarkNicolls(5) (Miss M E Rowland) *hld up: hdwy 5th: wknd appr 2 out* **33/1**	68
000-	**8**	*dist*	**Nettleton Flyer**[440] 3439 5-11-2 ....(t) SeanCurran (Miss J S Davis) *chsd ldrs: rdn and hung lft after 6th: wknd next* **150/1**	—
0-3	**9**	*16*	**Eurydice (IRE)**[326] 349 6-10-9 .... KeithMercer (Ferdy Murphy) *bhd fr 4th* **25/1**	—
	P		**Dartanian**[577] 4-10-9 .... TomScudamore (M Scudamore) *hld up: a in rr: t.o whn p.u bef last* **66/1**	—
0	**P**		**Ciarans Lass**[283] 844 7-10-3 ow1 .... MrRHodges(7) (C Roberts) *nt jump wl: a bhd: t.o whn p.u bef 2 out* **125/1**	—
	P		**Flying Dick** 7-11-2 .... JamesDavies (A G Newcombe) *led 2nd to 4th: wknd after 7th: t.o whn p.u bef last* **100/1**	—
00	**P**		**Hold That Thought (IRE)**[100] 3001 6-11-2 .... TimmyMurphy (Miss H C Knight) *hld up: a in rr: t.o whn p.u bef last* **40/1**	—
662	**P**		**Wenlocks Wonder**[56] 3800 5-11-2 .... JohnMcNamara (K C Bailey) *hld up: hdwy 6th: wknd appr 2 out: t.o whn p.u bef last* **11/1**[3]	—

4m 47.5s (-0.40) **Going Correction** +0.025s/f (Yiel)

WFA 4 from 5yo+ 5lb **14** Ran SP% **114.9**

Speed ratings: **101,100,96,93,88 87,87,—,—,— —,—,—,—** CSF £19.89 TOTE £12.30: £2.00, £1.10, £5.90; EX 23.80.

Owner Mrs J Doyle & Mrs P Shanahan **Bred** Michael Croke **Trained** Cheltenham, Gloucs

FOCUS

A modest maiden, lacking strength in depth, and the first two came clear. The winner and the fourth are the best guides to the level. Third-last flight bypassed.

NOTEBOOK

Briscoe Place(IRE), who had shown just moderate form in both his previous hurdle outings to date, dug deep to repel his better-fancied stablemate close home and get off the mark at the third attempt in this sphere. Having won his bumper on fast ground, this surface was clearly much to his liking, and he did enough to suggest he may have a little more to offer when upped to a longer trip in due course. *(op 16-1)*

Pass It On(IRE), who on the form of his previous two outings looked to give him an obvious chance in this, had every chance yet did not appear that reluctant to go through with his effort when it mattered. This must rate a missed opportunity, but he now qualifies for a handicap mark, *and is not one to write off when encountering a stiffer test on easier ground in that sphere. (tchd 40-85 in places)*

The Rocking Dock(IRE), making his debut over timber, lost vital momentum when fluffing the penultimate flight, and is slightly better than the bare form, yet it made little difference to the overall result. He was in turn clear of the remainder and is entitled to improve for the experience. *(op 40-1)*

Irish Flight(IRE), last seen finishing second on his hurdling bow in 2004, was never a serious factor on this return to action. However, it will be a surprise were he not to better this form with the run under his belt. *(op 7-1)*

4733 CLASSIC HITS NOVICES' (S) HURDLE (8 hdls) 2m 1f

2:40 (2:41) (Class 5) 4-Y-0+ **£2,081** (£611; £305; £152)

Form				RPR
0206	**1**		**Glimmer Of Light (IRE)**[29] 4289 6-11-0 105 .... RobertThornton (A King) *trckd ldr: led appr 2 out: styd on wl: comf* **11/4**[1]	104+
F03P	**2**	*6*	**Madam Caversfield**[100] 2995 4-10-1 94 .... PJBrennan (P D Evans) *chsd ldrs: wnt 2nd 2 out: kpt on: no imp* **3/1**[2]	79
1060	**3**	*3 ½*	**Jack Durrance (IRE)**[9] 1742 6-10-9 81 .... EamonDehdashti(5) (G A Ham) *hdwy 4th: chsng ldrs 3 out: kpt on one pce* **12/1**	88
3451	**4**	*29*	**Mickey Pearce (IRE)**[16] 4550 4-10-9 84 ....(v) StevenCrawford(5) (J G M O'Shea) *hdwy 3rd: reminders next: nvr nr ldrs: lft remote 4th last* **9/1**	59
0	**5**	*2 ½*	**Venetian Romance (IRE)**[54] 3322 5-10-7 ....(tp) SeanCurran (M R Bosley) *mstke 2nd: sme hdwy 4th: nvr on terms* **16/1**	50
0	**6**	*2*	**Must Be So**[23] 4423 5-10-4 .... RichardYoung(3) (Mrs L J Young) *bhd: sme hdwy 5th: sn wknd* **66/1**	48
3/0P	**7**	*6*	**Adventino**[46] 3985 11-10-7 .... AdrianScholes(7) (P R Johnson) *bhd fr 5th* **66/1**	49
0	**8**	*6*	**Mount Butler (IRE)**[16] 4550 4-10-1 .... TomMessenger(7) (J W Tudor) *hdwy 3rd: hit 5th: sn lost pl* **50/1**	37
U	**9**	*10*	**Lieuday**[15] 4556 7-11-0 ....(p) TomScudamore (C L Tizzard) *hdwy 3rd: lost pl 5th: sn bhd* **33/1**	33
	P		**Hugo The Boss (IRE)**[112] 4-10-5 .... ColinBolger(3) (S T Lewis) *lost pl 2nd: sn bhd: t.o whn p.u bef 4th* **66/1**	—
	P		**Danger Bird (IRE)**[9] 6-9-11 .... AdamHawkins(10) (R Hollinshead) *hdwy 2nd: wknd 5th: bhd whn p.u bef 2 out* **33/1**	—
0/PP	**P**		**Steel Warrior**[48] 3948 9-11-0 .... WayneHutchinson (J S Smith) *mstkes: sn bhd: t.o whn p.u bef 2 out* **40/1**	—
0P00	**P**		**Judy The Drinker**[14] 4577 7-10-7 ....(b[1]) DaveCrosse (J G M O'Shea) *bhd and drvn along: t.o whn p.u bef 5th* **40/1**	—
2PP	**P**		**Herons Cove (IRE)**[60] 3731 7-11-0 .... AndrewTinkler (W M Brisbourne) *prom: lost pl 3rd: t.o 5th: p.u bef 2 out* **25/1**	—
1130	**P**		**Sunley Future (IRE)**[11] 4620 7-11-7 98 .... CharliePoste(5) (M F Harris) *led tl appr 2 out: 4th and wkng whn broke leg and p.u bef last: dead* **7/2**[3]	94

4m 3.20s (0.10) **Going Correction** +0.025s/f (Yiel)

WFA 4 from 5yo+ 5lb **15** Ran SP% **118.5**

Speed ratings: **100,97,95,81,80 79,76,74,69,—** ... CSF £10.16 TOTE £3.00: £1.30, £1.90; EX 8.30

The winner was bought in for 2,500gns. Madam Caversfield was claimed by [illegible] Flint for £5,000.\n\x\x

Owner The Norf 'N' Sarf Partnership **Bred** The Earl Of Harrington **Trained** Barbury Castle, Wilts

FOCUS

A dire event, run at a modest pace, and the winner is value for double the official margin with the placed horses to their marks.

NOTEBOOK

Glimmer Of Light(IRE), having his first outing in this lowly grade, came to win score pretty much as he pleased under a confident ride. He is value for further, but was entitled to win as he did according to official figures, and he has clearly found his sort of level now. *(op 5-2 tchd 2-1)*

Madam Caversfield, last seen pulling up at Fakenham in first-time cheekpieces on Boxing Day, showed her true colours on this first outing in selling company yet still ran well below her official mark in defeat. *(op 7-2 tchd 4-1)*

Jack Durrance(IRE), sixth on the All-Weather nine days previously, turned in his arguably his best effort to date over timber without seriously threatening at any stage. The drying ground was much in his favour. *(op 11-1)*

Mickey Pearce(IRE), off the mark in this grade over further at the track 16 days previously, posted a tame effort under his penalty. *(tchd 8-1 and 10-1)*

4734 RACING ADVERTISER CONDITIONAL JOCKEYS' NOVICES' H'CAP HURDLE (13 hdls) 3m 2f

3:10 (3:10) (Class 5) (0-95,95) 4-Y-0+ **£2,927** (£859; £429; £214)

Form				RPR
UR42	**1**		**Hill Forts Henry**[17] 4526 8-10-0 **74** ....(p) SimonElliott(5) (J W Mullins) *hld up: hdwy 9th: led flat: rdn out* **13/2**[3]	79+
132F	**2**	*3 ½*	**Bar Gayne (IRE)**[23] 4428 7-11-6 **95** .... WillieMcCarthy(6) (T R George) *led: rdn and hdd flat: styd on same pce* **9/2**[2]	98+
-033	**3**	*1 ¼*	**Scarface**[21] 4449 9-10-5 **77** .... JamesDiment(3) (J L Spearing) *chsd ldrs: rdn and ev ch after 2 out: no ex flat* **13/2**[3]	77
-0P4	**4**	*16*	**Star Time (IRE)**[30] 4277 7-10-0 **77** ....(v) JohnKington(8) (M Scudamore) *hld up: nvr nrr* **22/1**	61
2405	**5**	*1*	**Buz Kiri (USA)**[24] 4393 8-10-12 **86** .... ThomasBurrows(5) (P L Clinton) *chsd ldrs: rdn after 9th: wknd next* **16/1**	69
P00P	**6**	*8*	**Kayleigh (IRE)**[16] 4553 8-10-4 **81** ....(b[1]) KeiranBurke(8) (P R Rodford) *chsd ldrs: lost pl and mstke 4th: sn rdn: wknd after 9th* **25/1**	56
0230	**7**	*1*	**Carl's Boy**[36] 4164 10-10-8 **77** ....(t) WilliamKennedy (D A Rees) *hld up: hdwy 4th: wknd appr 2 out* **15/2**	51
303P	**8**	*¾*	**Carroll's O'Tully (IRE)**[38] 4133 6-10-1 **73** .... JustinMorgan(3) (L A Dace) *mid-div: hdwy 4th: wknd after 3 out* **14/1**	46
5006	**9**	*dist*	**Phar The Best (IRE)**[10] 4640 9-11-2 **85** ....(p) CharliePoste (Mrs A L M King) *hld up: rdn appr 8th: wknd after next* **16/1**	—
01	**P**		**The Small Farmer (IRE)**[30] 4277 9-10-6 **78** .... TomMessenger(3) (Mrs A E Brooks) *chsd ldrs: cl 3rd whn p.u and dismntd bef 10th* **4/1**[1]	—
03	**P**		**Shanteen Lass (IRE)**[26] 4341 6-10-12 **84** .... KeithMercer(3) (Ferdy Murphy) *bhd and rdn 6th: sme hdwy after 8th: sn wknd: t.o whn p.u bef 2 out* **10/1**	—

6m 32.0s (4.00) **Going Correction** +0.025s/f (Yiel) **11** Ran SP% **112.3**

Speed ratings: **94,92,92,87,87 84,84,84,—,— —** CSF £34.74 CT £196.03 TOTE £9.20: £2.80, £2.00, £2.50; EX 59.30.

Owner Mrs J C Scorgie **Bred** R L And Mrs Scorgie **Trained** Wilsford-Cum-Lake, Wilts

FOCUS

A modest winning time for the class and the form is ordinary but looks reasonable, with the first three within a couple of pounds of their pre-race marks.

NOTEBOOK

Hill Forts Henry found the race run to suit and finally broke his duck at the 25th time of asking. He has been improved since encountering a quick surface the last twice, and should be high on confidence now, but the fact he won as he did suggests this was a weak event. *(op 6-1 tchd 7-1)*

Bar Gayne(IRE) had every chance from the front, yet could not cope with the winner late on, and ultimately the burden of top weight proved too much. He is a fair yardstick for this form. *(tchd 5-1)*

Scarface again held every chance, yet again failed to find all that much when it mattered, and was readily held at the finish. This has to rate a slightly improved effort, however, and he has developed into a consistent performer of late. *(op 6-1 tchd 7-1)*

Star Time(IRE) would have been much better served by a more positive ride. *(op 25-1)*

The Small Farmer(IRE), 4lb higher than when beating Bar Gayne over course and distance last time, was quickly pulled up approaching the tenth flight with something presumably amiss. *(op 7-2)*

4735 EXPRESS CAFES NOVICES' H'CAP CHASE (14 fncs) 2m 3f

3:40 (3:40) (Class 4) (0-110,110) 5-Y-0+ **£4,554** (£1,337; £668; £333)

Form				RPR
1642	**1**		**Lubinas (IRE)**[11] 4620 7-11-3 **101** .... TomDoyle (F Jordan) *j.lft: w ldrs: led after 4th: hdd after next: led 2 out: clr last: eased towards fin* **7/2**[1]	112+
406P	**2**	*6*	**Dere Lyn**[45] 4012 8-10-4 **95** .... MrRhysHughes(7) (D Burchell) *in rr: hdwy 9th: disputing 2nd whn blnd last: kpt on* **10/1**	100+
/00P	**3**	*1 ¼*	**Plantaganet (FR)**[49] 3919 8-10-0 **84** .... GLee (Ian Williams) *trckd ldrs: led after 11th: hdd 2 out: kpt on same pce* **13/2**[3]	86
30/F	**4**	*11*	**Eljay's Boy**[14] 4572 8-10-1 **85** .... TomScudamore (C L Tizzard) *hdwy to chse ldrs 9th: wknd appr 2 out* **9/1**	77+
4603	**5**	*10*	**Mandica (IRE)**[24] 4396 8-10-11 **95** ....(v[1]) JasonMaguire (T R George) *j.lft: w ldrs: led after 5th: hdd after 11th: wknd appr 2 out* **8/1**	76
50FF	**6**	*2 ½*	**Fantastic Arts (FR)**[21] 4454 6-10-13 **104** .... MrWBiddick(7) (Miss Venetia Williams) *stdd s: hld up in rr: mstke 7th: nvr on terms* **14/1**	82
P40P	**7**	*28*	**Cadtauri (FR)**[27] 4331 5-10-0 **88** oh14 .... BenjaminHitchcott (Miss H C Knight) *hld up in rr: bhd fr 8th: t.o 11th* **18/1**	34
6PPP	**8**	*2 ½*	**Drive On Driver (IRE)**[16] 4552 9-9-8 **85** oh6 ow1 ....(p) MissLBrooke(7) (Lady Susan Brooke) *mid-div: outpcd 9th: sn bhd: t.o 11th* **50/1**	33
-P5P	**9**	*15*	**Top Gale (IRE)**[14] 4580 7-10-0 **84** oh3 .... HenryOliver (R Dickin) *led: blnd bdly and rdr lost irons temporarily 2nd: hdd after 4th: lost pl 8th: t.o 11th* **40/1**	17
PP6P	**10**	*2*	**The Rainbow Man**[47] 3955 6-9-7 **84** oh19 ....(p) MattyRoe(7) (J Ryan) *in rr: blnd 5th: t.o 10th* **66/1**	15
2PP3	**P**		**Supreme Tadgh (IRE)**[12] 4605 9-11-0 **105** .... SimonElliott(7) (J A Geake) *bhd fr 6th: t.o 11th: p.u bef 2 out* **11/2**[2]	—
5P0P	**U**		**Kirby's Vic (IRE)**[49] 3923 6-9-7 **84** oh9 .... MrDEngland(7) (N A Twiston-Davies) *in rr whn tried run out: blnd and uns rdr 4th* **25/1**	—
3F40	**P**		**Kimono Royal (FR)**[55] 3815 8-10-10 **97** .... GinoCarenza(3) (A King) *prom: lost pl after 7th: sn bhd: t.o whn p.u bef 3 out* **8/1**	—
0-PP	**P**		**Downpour (USA)**[57] 3788 8-11-12 **110** .... WayneHutchinson (Ian Williams) *wnt prom 6th: lost pl 8th: sn bhd: t.o whn p.u bef 2 out* **20/1**	—

4m 46.7s (0.10) **Going Correction** +0.125s/f (Yiel)

WFA 5 from 6yo+ 3lb **14** Ran SP% **118.7**

Speed ratings: **104,101,100,96,92 91,79,78,71,71 —,—,—,—** CSF £36.01 CT £221.95 TOTE £3.60: £1.80, £4.40, £1.90; EX 53.30.

Owner Paul Ratcliffe **Bred** Gestut Fahrhof Stiftung **Trained** Adstone, Northants

FOCUS

A poor bunch whose jumping left a lot to be desired in the main and they finished well strung out. Not that many got into it and the runner-up is the best guide to the level.

NOTEBOOK

Lubinas(IRE), in and out of the lead the whole way, appreciated this better ground and pulled right away from his two nearest rivals from the second last. He is a consistent sort and looks capable of winning off a higher mark given the right conditions. *(op 4-1 tchd 9-2)*

Dere Lyn, making his chasing debut with the visor dispensed with, did much the best of those that tried to come from off the pace but was already held when making a mess of the last. He has won on fast ground here over hurdles so could win a race like this in the coming months. *(op 11-1)*

Plantaganet(FR), pulled up on his chasing debut on soft ground, performed much better on this quicker surface and, after taking it up travelling well, he did not seem to quite get home. He is no world-beater, but given good ground a small chase may come his way. *(op 8-1)*

Eljay's Boy, a faller on his chasing debut last month following a lengthy absence, was entitled to 'bounce' and, after threatening to get into the contest on the final circuit, he eventually faded out of it. This effort may have been a bit better than it looks. *(tchd 10-1)*

Mandica(IRE), with a visor replacing the blinkers, helped force the pace before fading out of it over the last half-mile. This ground was probably faster than ideal. *(op 15-2)*

Fantastic Arts(FR), never got into the race, but at least he put in a clear round this time and that was probably the most important thing. *(op 11-1)*

4736 RACING POST H'CAP HURDLE (8 hdls) 2m 1f

4:10 (4:10) (Class 4) (0-115,114) 4-Y-0+ £4,228 (£1,241; £620; £310)

Form				RPR
5123	1		**Capitana (GER)**[96] 3128 5-11-2 **104** MickFitzgerald (N J Henderson) *hld up: hdwy 6th: led on bit appr last: readily* **13/8**[1]	128+
45P5	2	*8*	**Sabreur**[32] 4243 5-10-11 **99** WayneHutchinson (Ian Williams) *hld up: hdwy to join ldrs 5th: led after 3 out: rdn and hdd appr last: sn outpcd* **6/1**[3]	103
430	3	*2 ½*	**It's The Limit (USA)**[19] 4469 7-11-1 **103** (v[1]) CarlLlewellyn (W K Goldsworthy) *chsd ldrs: ev ch 3 out: sn rdn: wknd appr last* **12/1**	105
3404	4	*1 ¾*	**Desert Spa (USA)**[13] 4591 11-9-13 **94** MissIsabelTompsett[(7)] (G E Jones) *chsd ldrs: ev ch 3 out: wknd appr last* **40/1**	94
411F	5	*4*	**Mister Moussac**[192] 1559 7-10-6 **99** BrianHughes[(5)] (Miss Kariana Key) *chsd ldrs: led 4th: rdn and hdd after 3 out: wknd next* **28/1**	95
4334	6	*¾*	**Cruise Director**[18] 4503 6-10-12 **100** APMcCoy (Ian Williams) *hld up: hdwy 6th: rdn and wknd after 2 out* **9/2**[2]	95
2230	7	*6*	**A Bit Of Fun**[8] 4420 5-11-8 **110** JamieMoore (J T Stimpson) *prom: rdn after 3 out: wknd next* **25/1**	99
04-0	8	*1 ½*	**Silk Trader**[148] 2103 11-11-0 **109** MrGTumelty[(7)] (J Mackie) *hld up: rdn 5th: n.d* **50/1**	97
40F0	9	*9*	**Tom Bell (IRE)**[39] 4104 6-11-1 **103** DaveCrosse (J G M O'Shea) *hld up: rdn and wknd 5th* **14/1**	82
0012	10	*7*	**Nick's Choice**[15] 4566 10-11-1 **110** RyanCummings[(7)] (D Burchell) *mid-div: bhd fr 5th* **16/1**	82
0226	11	*11*	**Lupin (FR)**[269] 947 7-11-10 **112** TimmyMurphy (A W Carroll) *hld up: a in rr* **33/1**	73
2140	P		**Walsingham (IRE)**[14] 4569 8-10-11 **99** RobertThornton (R Lee) *led to 4th: wknd 3 out: bhd whn p.u bef next* **14/1**	—
2200	P		**Pirandello (IRE)**[118] 2716 8-11-6 **108** JohnMcNamara (K C Bailey) *chsd ldrs: rdn after 4th: wknd bef next: t.o whn p.u bef 2 out* **14/1**	—

3m 58.2s (-4.90) **Going Correction** +0.025s/f (Yiel) **13** Ran SP% **118.8**
Speed ratings: **112,108,107,106,104 104,101,100,96,92 87,—,—** CSF £11.21 CT £90.68 TOTE £2.90: £1.40, £2.10, £3.70; EX 16.80.
Owner P J D Pottinger **Bred** Gestut Hof Ittlingen **Trained** Upper Lambourn, Berks

FOCUS

The size of the field made this look a competitive handicap hurdle, but the winner made it anything but and is value for 20 lengths. The winning time was decent for a race of its class and the form looks solid rated through the placed horses.

NOTEBOOK

Capitana(GER), returning from a three-month break off a 3lb higher mark, was always travelling supremely well off the pace and eventually won without being asked any sort of a question. She would have expended more energy going down to the start, but the Handicapper is bound to hit her hard for this. *(op 2-1)*

Sabreur was unfortunate run into a horse like the winner in a race like this and, though he tried to hang on to her over the last couple of flights, it proved an unequal struggle. He is yet to win a race, but it should only be a matter of time given similarly good ground. *(op 13-2 tchd 7-1)*

It's The Limit(USA), last seen floundering behind Black Jack Ketchum in the Brit Insurance Novices' Hurdle at the Festival, was back at a more realistic level over a more suitable trip. Wearing a visor for the first time instead of blinkers and a tongue tie, he ran well for a long way on ground he likes but did not get home and may benefit from being ridden a little more patiently. *(op 14-1)*

Desert Spa(USA) likes this ground, but he is a plating-class veteran these days and probably achieved more than might have been expected. *(op 33-1)*

Mister Moussac, 8lb higher than when gaining the second of his two victories last September, ended up well beaten but should come on for this first run in seven months. *(op 25-1)*

Cruise Director, still relatively unexposed over hurdles, could never land a blow and may have found this ground too quick. *(tchd 4-1)*

4737 BET365 08000 322365 H'CAP CHASE (19 fncs) 3m 1f 110y

4:40 (4:40) (Class 4) (0-110,109) 5-Y-0+ £4,879 (£1,432; £716; £357)

Form				RPR
233F	1		**Dante Citizen (IRE)**[47] 3965 8-11-7 **104** JasonMaguire (T R George) *chsd ldrs: led appr 3 out: hrd rdn and edgd lft run-in: all out* **5/1**[2]	116+
05/U	2	*shd*	**Noble Buck (IRE)**[23] 4428 10-9-11 **83** oh2 RichardYoung[(3)] (Mrs L J Young) *bhd: hdwy 14th: chsng ldrs 3 out: wnt 2nd 2 out: upsides run-in: jst failed* **20/1**	94
2-04	3	*5*	**Metal Detector (IRE)**[16] 4549 9-11-3 **105** (p) MarkNicolls[(5)] (K C Bailey) *wnt prom 7th: rdn and one pce whn mstke 2 out* **9/1**	113+
15F3	4	*16*	**Ede'Iff**[13] 4592 9-11-6 **108** RobertLucey-Butler[(5)] (W G M Turner) *hdwy to chse ldrs 10th: wknd 3 out* **9/1**	101+
1-00	5	*6*	**Mounsey Castle**[146] 2143 9-11-11 **108** PJBrennan (P J Hobbs) *chsd ldrs: mstke 2nd: chal 4 out: wknd next: eased towards fin* **9/2**[1]	93+
4243	6	*2 ½*	**Treasulier (IRE)**[27] 4328 9-10-8 **98** KeiranBurke[(7)] (P R Rodford) *chsd ldrs: drvn along 7th: lost pl 12th* **13/2**	80
4330	7	*2 ½*	**Channahrlie (IRE)**[36] 4163 12-10-4 **87** (p) HenryOliver (R Dickin) *chsd ldr: led 5th tl appr 3 out: sn lost pl* **8/1**	66
4-0P	P		**Jackem (IRE)**[49] 3923 12-10-0 **83** oh2 WayneHutchinson (Ian Williams) *in rr: bhd fr 9th: t.o whn p.u bef 3 out* **10/1**	—
PPP	P		**Gallik Dawn**[23] 4419 8-11-5 **109** TomMessenger[(7)] (A Hollingsworth) *mid-div: drvn along 8th: sn lost pl: bhd whn p.u bef 3 out* **14/1**	—
524P	P		**Algarve**[93] 3204 9-10-9 **92** KeithMercer (Ferdy Murphy) *led: sn pushed along: hdd 5th: losing pl whn blnd bdly 10th: bhd whn mstke 12th: p.u after next* **11/2**[3]	—

6m 33.2s (-1.00) **Going Correction** +0.125s/f (Yiel) **10** Ran SP% **115.2**
Speed ratings: **106,105,104,99,97 96,96,—,—,—** CSF £89.85 CT £874.02 TOTE £7.30: £2.50, £5.30, £2.00; EX 173.40.
Owner Ryder Racing Ltd **Bred** E J O'Sullivan **Trained** Slad, Gloucs

FOCUS

A moderate handicap, run at a sound pace, and the first two came clear in a thrilling finish. The first three all ran close to their recent best.

NOTEBOOK

Dante Citizen(IRE) dug deep when it mattered on the run-in and just did enough to score in a bobbing finish. This success was thoroughly deserved, he enjoyed the decent ground, and his jumping was much more assured this time. *(tchd 11-2)*

Noble Buck(IRE) came from out of the clouds to challenge in the home straight and ultimately only lost out by the smallest of margins. This was a much-improved effort for his current connections and the return to a stiffer track in the coming weeks could see him go one better. *(tchd 22-1)*

Metal Detector(IRE) was held prior to making an error at the penultimate fence, yet still showed much-improved form for this return to chasing.

Mounsey Castle failed to sustain his effort in the home straight and ran close to his recent level. *(tchd 11-2)*

4738 LETHEBY & CHRISTOPHER H'CAP HURDLE (10 hdls) 2m 3f 110y

5:10 (5:10) (Class 4) (0-100,100) 4-Y-0+ £3,578 (£1,050; £525; £262)

Form				RPR
4613	1		**True Mariner (FR)**[79] 3416 6-11-7 **100** (t) MarkNicolls[(5)] (B I Case) *hld up: hdwy appr 4th: led bef 2 out: clr last* **14/1**	113+
P-54	2	*10*	**Boing Boing (IRE)**[55] 3818 6-11-0 **95** RichardSpate[(7)] (Miss S J Wilton) *chsd ldr tl led 3rd: hdd appr 2 out: sn wknd* **10/1**	96
604P	3	*3 ½*	**Absolutelythebest (IRE)**[43] 4036 5-11-1 **94** StevenCrawford[(5)] (J G M O'Shea) *hld up: hdwy appr 7th: wknd after 2 out* **9/2**[2]	92
	4	*7*	**Long Road (USA)**[193] 1557 5-11-5 **93** APMcCoy (Jonjo O'Neill) *hld up: hdwy after 6th: chsd wnr 2 out: rdn and wknd bef last* **5/2**[1]	89+
0623	5	*15*	**Twist The Facts (IRE)**[21] 4450 6-11-2 **97** MarcGoldstein[(7)] (N P Littmoden) *chsd ldrs tl rdn and wknd appr 2 out* **9/1**	73
	6	*16*	**Allaboveboard (IRE)**[94] 3191 7-11-12 **100** JamieMoore (P Bowen) *s.s: hdwy 6th: wknd 8th* **8/1**	60
0502	7	*10*	**Manolo (FR)**[23] 4427 6-11-6 **94** JodieMogford (Mrs H Dalton) *chsd ldrs tl rdn and wknd appr 2 out* **7/1**[3]	44
-030	8	*13*	**Snipe**[250] 1098 8-11-12 **100** WayneHutchinson (Ian Williams) *hld up: wknd 7th* **28/1**	37
F55P	9	*dist*	**Miss Skippy**[29] 4289 7-11-8 **96** JamesDavies (A G Newcombe) *mid-div: bhd fr 6th* **11/1**	—
500P	P		**Simonovski (USA)**[84] 3345 5-11-12 **100** GLee (Mrs A M Thorpe) *hld up: bhd fr 6th: t.o whn p.u bef 2 out* **12/1**	—
03UP	P		**Cresswell Willow (IRE)**[11] 4619 6-11-7 **95** (b) CarlLlewellyn (W K Goldsworthy) *led to 3rd: rdn and wknd 6th: t.o whn p.u bef 2 out* **25/1**	—

4m 44.3s (-3.60) **Going Correction** +0.025s/f (Yiel) **11** Ran SP% **119.4**
Speed ratings: **108,104,102,99,93 87,83,78,—,— —** CSF £147.46 CT £741.45 TOTE £17.80: £3.80, £2.90, £1.80; EX 147.80 Place 6 £35.42, Place 5 £27.83.
Owner D Allen **Bred** J P Philippe And Classic Breeding Sarl **Trained** Edgcote, Northants

FOCUS

A poor handicap, run at a strong gallop, and the field came home strung out behind the easy winner, who is rated to the level of his best chase run.

NOTEBOOK

True Mariner(FR) jumped fuently throughout and made a facile winning return from a 79-day break under a well-judged ride. A decent surface is key to him and he should still look feasibly treated after a rise in the weights in relation to his chase rating. *(op 16-1)*

Boing Boing(IRE) was made to look pedestrian when the winner swept past nearing the *penultimate flight and ran close to his official mark in defeat. He helps to set the level of this form.* *(op 12-1)*

Absolutelythebest(IRE) put a disappointing effort at Exeter last time behind him, mainly on account of this faster ground, yet still ran below his best. *(op 5-1)*

Long Road(USA), making his British debut for a new yard, failed to get home over the longer trip and was well beaten. *(tchd 3-1)*

T/Plt: £79.50 to a £1 stake. Pool: £48,511.75. 445.30 winning tickets. T/Qpdt: £33.50 to a £1 stake. Pool: £3,236.50. 71.30 winning tickets. CR

4739 - 4744a (Foreign Racing) - See Raceform Interactive

2367 AINTREE (L-H)

Thursday, April 6

OFFICIAL GOING: Grand national course - good (good to soft in places); mildmay & hurdle courses - good

The ground was at first described as 'on the easy side of good' but the rain was getting in late in the day.

Wind: Fresh 1/2 against Weather: Overcast and cool with persistent rain race 4 onwards.

4745 JOHN SMITH'S AND FLIXTON CONSERVATIVE CLUB LIVERPOOL HURDLE (THE LONG DISTANCE HURDLE) GRADE 2 (13 hdls) 3m 110y

2:00 (2:00) (Class 1) 4-Y-0+

£39,914 (£14,973; £7,497; £3,738; £1,876; £938)

Form				RPR
1223	1		**Mighty Man (FR)**[21] 4458 6-11-6 158 RichardJohnson (H D Daly) *lw: a.p: led 2 out: sn rdn: styd on wl* **11/4**[2]	169+
2111	2	*7*	**My Way De Solzen (FR)**[21] 4458 6-11-10 163 RobertThornton (A King) *lw: trckd ldrs: led 3 out: rdn and hdd next: no ex last* **6/4**[1]	166+
-150	3	*13*	**No Refuge (IRE)**[21] 4458 6-11-10 151 (v[1]) GLee (J Howard Johnson) *lw: hld up: hit 4th: hdwy next: rdn and outpcd when mstke 3 out: kpt on to take 3rd after last* **16/1**	153+
P430	4	*2 ½*	**Westender (FR)**[21] 4458 10-11-6 151 (p) TomScudamore (M C Pipe) *mid-div: rdn after 7th: well outpcd 3 out and no ch after: styd on again appr last* **50/1**	147+
1113	5	*¾*	**Dom D'Orgeval (FR)**[22] 4446 6-11-6 148 BJGeraghty (Nick Williams) *swtg: mid-div: hdwy 4th: rdn 10th: wknd bef next* **14/1**	146+
6020	6	*8*	**Carlys Quest**[21] 4461 12-11-10 140 (b) KeithMercer (Ferdy Murphy) *lw: bhd: styd on flat: n.d* **100/1**	141
40U0	7	*14*	**Redemption**[21] 4459 11-11-2 144 AntonyEvans (N A Twiston-Davies) *hld up: reminders 2nd: hdwy 9th: ev ch 3 out: sn rdn and wknd* **50/1**	119
-13F	8	*2 ½*	**Big Moment**[40] 4116 8-11-2 148 JimCrowley (Mrs A J Perrett) *swtg: mid-div: rdn and wknd appr 3 out* **66/1**	116

114/ **9** *2* **Classified (IRE)**^{1120} 4131 10-11-2 .... TimmyMurphy 139+
(M C Pipe) *hld up: hit 9th: hdwy appr 3 out: wknd next: disputing 3rd whn blnd last* **40/1**

/300 **10** *2* **Starzaan (IRE)**^{21} 4458 7-11-2 145... PCarberry 116+
(H Morrison) *lw: led to 7th: rdn to ld appr 3 out: sn hdd & wknd* **12/1**

-4FF **11** *3* **Fundamentalist (IRE)**^{22} 4445 8-11-2 ....(t) CarlLlewellyn 119+
(N A Twiston-Davies) *lw: hld up: hdwy appr 3 out: sn rdn and wknd* **20/1**

2214 **P** **Fire Dragon (IRE)**^{21} 4458 5-11-10 155...............................(b) APMcCoy —
(Jonjo O'Neill) *chsd ldr tl led 7th: mstke 9th: hdd & wknd appr 3 out: bhd whn p.u bef last* **7/1**^{3}

6m 5.50s (-10.90) **Going Correction** -0.075s/f (Good) **12** Ran SP% **113.0**
Speed ratings: **114,111,107,106,106 104,99,98,98,97 96,**— CSF £6.72 TOTE £3.90: £1.50, £1.30, £4.00; EX 6.30 Trifecta £104.50 Pool: £2,428.62 - 16.50 winning units.
Owner E R Hanbury **Bred** Evan Hanbury **Trained** Stanton Lacy, Shropshire

■ A second consecutive win for Mighty Man at this meeting, following last year's success in the two-mile novice event.

FOCUS
An interesting renewal with the World Hurdle winner and third re-opposing, but those two apart the race lacked any real strength in depth, especially with Cheltenham fourth Fire Dragon failing to run his race. With the pace pretty ordinary for much of the way, the field were still well bunched on the turn into the long straight, but the 'big two' had little trouble in pulling clear and Mighty Man was able to reverse form with My Way De Solzen. The latter would have appreciated more of a stamina test, but he and the third ran pretty much to their marks and Mighty Man can now be regarded as the best staying hurdler in training.

NOTEBOOK
Mighty Man(FR), just over four lengths behind My Way De Solzen when third in the World Hurdle at Cheltenham on his previous start, was ridden as positively as he has ever been this time, with the pace just ordinary, and reversed form in no uncertain terms. He would not have minded the way the race was run given he had the speed to win the two-mile novice event here at last year's National meeting, but the runner-up would have been better suited by more of an emphasis on stamina. Still, that one ran to a very smart level of form in defeat and this must rate as a very high-class performance. He will have every chance of improving on last year's third in the World Hurdle if continuing his progression next season. *(op 3-1 tchd 100-30 in a place)*

My Way De Solzen(FR) has progressed into a high-class staying hurdler this season and came here off the back of a fine win in the World Hurdle but, with the pace nowhere near as strong as it was at Cheltenham, he failed to confirm form with Mighty Man, who was just over four lengths away in third last time. He is an out-and-out-stayer, and the ordinary gallop on such an easy track might not have brought out the very best in him, although the first two were a long way clear and RPRs suggest he ran to a very similar level to Cheltenham. Connections will have the option of going chasing next year, and he will be schooled in the summer. If he goes over fences he could *go right to the top, but it will be tempting to allow him the chance to retain his stayers' crown. (tchd 11-8 and 7-4 in a place)*

No Refuge(IRE), last year's SunAlliance winner, has not progressed as one might have hoped this season and was disappointing when down the field in the World Hurdle on his most recent outing but, fitted with a visor for the first time (he wore blinkers on his final two runs on the Flat), this was a step in the right direction. His stable have not had a great season by their standards, and he can be given another chance to confirm the promise he initially showed over hurdles next term. They *will also have the option of going chasing, and he will be schooled in the summer. (tchd 20-1 and 12-1 in places)*

Westender(FR), nine and a half lengths in front of No Refuge in the World Hurdle on his previous start, has his own ideas about the game (he refused in this race last year) and made hard work of this, but he ultimately responded quite well to pressure to pass tired horses in the straight for a creditable fourth. *(op 40-1)*

Dom D'Orgeval(FR), who rattled up a hat-trick of wins in handicap company this winter at around two and a half miles on testing ground (the first off a mark of 123, the last off 136), deserved his chance in this following a fine third in the Coral Cup off a mark of 144. Given he has been winning over shorter and had never previously tried this trip, he should not have minded the steady pace, but he finished up well held and may just have been found out by the step up in class.

Carlys Quest has been largely disappointing since causing a surprise in the Grade One staying event at last year's Punchestown Festival, but he finished better than all bar the two principals, so there was some hope in this effort. He may be worth his chance back at Punchestown this term, but he will want soft ground to have a chance there.

Classified(IRE), not seen since running fourth to Baracouda in the 2003 Stayers' Hurdle 1120 days previously, travelled with some enthusiasm and was disputing third when making a tired mistake at the last. On this evidence, he retains plenty of ability and one hopes he will stand up to training.

Starzaan(IRE) was well beaten and failed to build on his seventh in the World Hurdle. It would be no surprise to see him drop in trip.

Fundamentalist(IRE), back over hurdles, having fallen on his last two starts over fences, and given another chance over a staying trip, was under pressure a long way out. He has had serious injury problems and it remains to be seen whether he retains all of his ability.

Fire Dragon(IRE), the World Hurdle fourth, travelled quite nicely for much of the way and could have been expected to play a hand in the finish, but he stopped quite quickly and presumably something was amiss. *Official explanation: jockey said gelding ran too freely (tchd 8-1)*

4746 BETFAIR BOWL CHASE GRADE 2 (19 fncs) 3m 1f (Mildmay)
2:35 (2:36) (Class 1) 5-Y-0+

£85,530 (£32,085; £16,065; £8,010; £4,020; £2,010)

Form RPR

30-U **1** **Celestial Gold (IRE)**^{20} 4470 8-11-8 160........................ TimmyMurphy 171+
(M C Pipe) *t.k.h under patient ride: wnt handy 3rd after 4 out: chalng whn lft in ld last: pushed clr* **8/1**

62U5 **2** *7* **Take The Stand (IRE)**^{20} 4470 10-11-2 157........................ TonyDobbin 165+
(P Bowen) *chsd ldrs: chal 4 out: led after next: jnd whn blnd last: nt rcvr* **6/1**^{3}

2424 **3** *2 1/2* **L'Ami (FR)**^{20} 4470 7-11-8 .... APMcCoy 161
(F Doumen, France) *lw: trckd ldrs: led 15th: hdd after 3 out: wknd appr last* **5/2**^{1}

2426 **4** *14* **Monkerhostin (FR)**^{20} 4470 9-11-8 169........................ RichardJohnson 155+
(P J Hobbs) *lw: prom: hmpd 1st: drvn along 13th: lost pl after 4 out* **9/2**^{2}

0640 **5** *8* **Ollie Magern**^{20} 4470 8-11-12 149....................................... CarlLlewellyn 145+
(N A Twiston-Davies) *w ldr: lost pl appr 4 out* **20/1**

0140 **6** *10* **See You Sometime**^{21} 4457 11-11-12 135.................... AndrewThornton 133
(J W Mullins) *led: drvn along 12th: hdd 15th: lost pl after 4 out* **50/1**

3234 **F** **My Will (FR)**^{21} 4457 6-11-7 149...(t) RWalsh —
(P F Nicholls) *fell 1st* **10/1**

2110 **U** **Beef Or Salmon (IRE)**^{20} 4470 10-11-12 ....(p) PCarberry —
(Michael Hourigan, Ire) *lw: hld up: last but wl in tch whn blnd and uns rdr 5th* **9/2**^{2}

P210 **F** **Royal Emperor (IRE)**^{20} 4470 10-11-2 143................. DominicElsworth 135
(Mrs S J Smith) *chsd ldrs: outpcd 13th: lost pl 15th: blnd next: poor 6th whn fell 2 out* **12/1**

6m 27.8s (-2.60) **Going Correction** +0.05s/f (Yiel) **9** Ran SP% **113.8**
Speed ratings: **106,103,102,98,95 92,**—,—,— CSF £54.80 TOTE £10.50: £2.70, £1.90, £1.40; EX 67.60 Trifecta £218.20 Pool: £2,797.42 - 9.10 winning units.
Owner D A Johnson **Bred** P Downes **Trained** Nicholashayne, Devon

FOCUS
The pace was not strong and the first three in the Cheltenham Gold Cup sat on the sidelines. The result was still in the balance until Take The Stand's final-fence blunder. The pair have been rated as having dead-heated, but with Celestial Gold conceding 6lb this is championship-class form.

NOTEBOOK
Celestial Gold(IRE) ◆, an early casualty in the Gold Cup, was keen to get on with it. Jumping with elan, he looked to be travelling just the better when handed it on a plate at the last, giving connections a welcome big-race winner. He is still relatively unexposed, and this was a championship-class performance, so he may yet be a major contender for the 2007 Gold Cup.

Take The Stand(IRE), inclined to get warm beforehand, set sail for home but looked to have a battle royal on his hands when he made a complete nonsense of the final fence. His habit of making at least one serious mistake has cost this talented horse dear. He may now go to Punchestown for the Guinness Gold Cup and a possible re-match with War Of Attrition. *(op 11-2)*

L'Ami(FR), sold to JP McManus since the Gold Cup and with McCoy aboard for the first time, didn't look at his very best beforehand. He travelled strongly and went on five out but he could *never stamp his authority and the needle was on empty going to the final fence. (op 7-2 tchd 4-1 in a place)*

Monkerhostin(FR), again not looking at his best, was knocked out of his stride by the faller at the first. He ran very flat and dropped right away up the final straight. His busy season has almost certainly caught up on him. *(tchd 4-1 and 5-1)*

Ollie Magern, taken out of the National to run in this, couldn't dominate and his season has been all downhill since his Wetherby success. *(tchd 22-1)*

See You Sometime set his own pace. Trying to wind it up with a circuit to go, he could never dominate and called it a day before the final turn. *(op 40-1)*

Beef Or Salmon(IRE), with cheekpieces tried, only got as far as the fifth fence before Carberry was on the ground. His confidence must be at a low ebb but after a possible outing over hurdles there is still time for him to bounce back on home ground at Punchestown. *(op 7-2)*

4747 THE SPORTSMAN ANNIVERSARY 4-Y-O NOVICES' HURDLE GRADE 1 (9 hdls) 2m 110y
3:10 (3:11) (Class 1) 4-Y-O

£68,424 (£25,668; £12,852; £6,408; £3,216; £1,608)

Form RPR

0111 **1** **Detroit City (USA)**^{20} 4468 4-11-0 146.......................(v) RichardJohnson 150+
(P J Hobbs) *lw: chsd ldrs: hdwy 6th: rdn to ld appr 3 out: drvn clr appr last: eased towards fin* **3/1**^{1}

215 **2** *8* **Premier Dane (IRE)**^{50} 3925 4-11-0 127.............................. TonyDobbin 140+
(N G Richards) *lw: hld up: smooth hdwy 6th: wnt 2nd appr 2 out: styd on same pce between last 2* **20/1**

2115 **3** *3* **Afsoun (FR)**^{20} 4468 4-11-0 144.. MickFitzgerald 137+
(N J Henderson) *lw: ears plugged in preliminaries: hld up in tch: effrt to chse ldrs whn hit 3 out: one pce fr next* **7/2**^{2}

111 **4** *7* **Opera De Coeur (FR)**^{24} 4416 4-11-0 .... MarkBradburne 129
(H D Daly) *lw: chsd ldrs: one pce fr 3 out* **16/1**

2216 **5** *1 3/4* **Turko (FR)**^{20} 4468 4-11-0 141..(t) RWalsh 127
(P F Nicholls) *lw: in rr: reminders after 3rd: sn lost pl: bhd tl kpt on fr 3 out* **7/1**

331 **6** *1 1/2* **Pseudonym (IRE)**^{12} 4616 4-11-0 110................................ DaveCrosse 126
(M F Harris) *hld up in rr: sme hdwy appr 3 out: nvr nr ldrs* **100/1**

3214 **7** *5* **Pace Shot (IRE)**^{20} 4468 4-11-0 136............................... JamieMoore 126+
(G L Moore) *prom: drvn along whn blnd 5th: n.d after* **16/1**

1342 **8** *2* **Fair Along (GER)**^{20} 4468 4-11-0 141.................................... PJBrennan 120+
(P J Hobbs) *mde most tl appr 3 out: wl btn whn hit 2 out* **9/2**^{3}

1013 **9** *4* **Aviation**^{137} 2367 4-11-0 115... BarryKeniry 115
(G M Moore) *in rr: drvn along and outpcd 4th: hit next: sn bhd* **200/1**

4P11 **10** *3* **Shamayoun (FR)**^{23} 4435 4-11-0 135...................................(b) APMcCoy 112
(C R Egerton) *lw: w ldr: lost pl appr 3 out: bhd whn eased run-in* **8/1**

6F **11** *dist* **Cogans Lake (IRE)**^{40} 4122 4-11-0 .... JMAllen —
(Kieran Purcell, Ire) *mid-div: effrt 6th: sn wknd: t.o: btn total 83 l* **28/1**

6153 **P** **Twist Magic (FR)**^{40} 4117 4-11-0 129......................... ChristianWilliams —
(P F Nicholls) *in rr: t.o 3 out: p.u bef next* **50/1**

4041 **P** **Lerida**^{50} 3925 4-11-0 107.. PeterBuchanan —
(Miss Lucinda V Russell) *prom: drvn and lost pl after 3rd: sn t.o: p.u after 6th* **200/1**

4m 1.40s (-3.20) **Going Correction** -0.075s/f (Good) **13** Ran SP% **112.9**
Speed ratings: **104,100,98,95,94 94,91,90,88,87** —,—,— CSF £62.92 TOTE £3.40: £1.60, £4.70, £1.90; EX 100.00 Trifecta £480.20 Pool: £3,179.44 - 4.70 winning tickets.
Owner Terry Warner **Bred** E J Kelly **Trained** Withycombe, Somerset

■ Detroit City was the first juvenile to complete the Cheltenham-Aintree double since Pollardstown in 1979.

FOCUS
A Grade 1 for the second year running, so no penalty for Detroit City, who confirmed his Cheltenham form almost to the pound with Afsoun and put up a performance that ranks behind only Bilboa and Hors La Loi III among recent winners of this race. Improved form from the second, fourth and sixth, but there were grounds for expecting it from the first two.

NOTEBOOK
Detroit City(USA), who didn't look quite as well as he had done at Cheltenham, was sent to the front on the final turn. In charge thereafter, he was value for another three or four lengths. He deserves great credit for translating his Cheltenham form to this very different track, but he is essentially a stayer, and Brave Inca and company will surely be too quick for him in the 2007 Champion Hurdle. In due course, however, he has the makings of a major contender for staying honours. *(op 11-4 tchd 10-3)*

Premier Dane(IRE) put his Musselburgh failure behind him. He travelled exceptionally well but after being sent in pursuit of the winner it was soon clear he was very much second best. This was much-improved form, but he was among the very best of these on the Flat, so there is no reason to doubt the form. He would have appreciated even quicker ground and can surely find a nice prize this spring.

Afsoun(FR), his ears plugged with cotton wool beforehand, was still inclined to get warm. Called on for an effort when clouting the third last, on the day he had no excuse. He has the ability but with him it is all in the mind. *(op 10-3 tchd 3-1)*

Opera De Coeur(FR), taking a big step up in class, lost his unbeaten record but was far from disgraced, especially as he would have appreciated even more give underfoot.

Turko(FR) seemed to sulk turning away from the stands and only consented to put his best foot forward late in the day. He looks to have more stamina than speed, but fences could be the making of him next term. *(op 8-1)*

Pseudonym(IRE) was biting off more than he could chew but even so this was still a big step up.

Pace Shot(IRE) was struggling to keep up when blundering away what little chance he still had. This was not his form. *(tchd 18-1, 20-1 in a place)*

Fair Along(GER) was expected to benefit from the return to this easier track, but he was hassled for the lead and had been hung out to dry when he put in a tired jump two out. His lack of size will always count against him.

4748 JOHN SMITH'S FOX HUNTERS' CHASE (18 fncs) 2m 5f 110y (Gd National)
3:45 (3:45) (Class 2) 6-Y-0+

£21,007 (£6,562; £3,279; £1,641; £819; £413)

Form RPR

U/1- **1** **Katarino (FR)**[364] [4750] 11-12-0 .... MrSWaley-Cohen 139+
(R Waley-Cohen) *lw: trckd ldrs: lft in ld 14th: styd on strly appr last* **11/2**[2]

4-12 **2** 7 **Christy Beamish (IRE)**[24] [4421] 9-12-0 .... MrWHill 130+
(P Jones) *lw: hld up: hdwy 14th: wnt 2nd appr last: no imp* **8/1**[3]

/0U- **3** 15 **Beachcomber Bay (IRE)**[11] 11-12-0 .... MrJTKeeling 114
(I J Keeling, Ire) *hld up in rr: hdwy 15th: one pce fr 2 out* **100/1**

4 **4** 2 ½ **Bothar Na (IRE)**[20] [4471] 7-12-0 .... MrKEPower 119+
(W P Mullins, Ire) *hld up in rr: hdwy whn bdly hmpd 14th: effrt 3 out: one pce* **9/2**[1]

-040 **5** ¾ **Junior Fontaine (FR)**[47] 9-12-0 .... MissJCoward 111
(David M Easterby) *lw: chsd ldrs: one pce fr 3 out* **66/1**

2111 **6** 7 **Bill Haze**[17] [4555] 10-12-0 .... MrPSheldrake 108+
(P Dando) *chsd ldrs: led 4th (water): hdd 6th: blnd 11th (Foinavon): wknd 2 out* **20/1**

-61F **7** 5 **Sikander A Azam**[12] 13-12-0 .... MrOGreenall 103+
(David M Easterby) *hld up: hdwy to trck ldrs 11th: lft 2nd 14th: hit next: wknd appr last* **12/1**

46-B **8** shd **Munster (IRE)**[25] 9-12-0 ....(t) MrJDMoore 99
(A L T Moore, Ire) *lw: mstkes: bhd: r.o fr 3 out: nvr on terms* **14/1**

3543 **9** 4 **Moving Earth (IRE)**[48] [3960] 13-12-0 114 .... MrCWard 95
(C E Ward) *hld up: stdy hdwy 14th: wknd 2 out* **100/1**

F/F- **10** 13 **Arctic Times (IRE)**[19] [4512] 10-12-0 ....(p) MrROHarding 82
(Eugene M O'Sullivan, Ire) *in rr whn mstke 10th (Becher's): nvr on terms* **14/1**

-240 **11** 1 **Cornish Gale (IRE)**[17] [4555] 12-12-0 .... MrRBurton 84+
(D McCain Jnr) *chsd ldrs: wkng whn hmpd 14th* **50/1**

0/0- **12** 1 ½ **Champagne Native (IRE)**[19] [4512] 12-12-0 .... MrAGCash 79
(D Broad, Ire) *led to 4th (water): lost pl 8th* **80/1**

F5P3 **13** 2 **Thieves'Glen**[17] [4555] 8-12-0 98 .... MrGTumelty 77
(H Morrison) *lw: nvr bttr than mid-div* **66/1**

2PU3 **14** ¾ **Ikdam Melody (IRE)**[12] 10-12-0 85 ....(p) MissJFoster 76
(Miss J E Foster) *a in rr* **150/1**

15 hd **Clear The Line (IRE)**[18] 8-12-0 .... MrBHassett 76
(J L Hassett, Ire) *w'like: mstkes: a in rr* **66/1**

10PU **16** ½ **Let's Fly (FR)**[17] [4555] 11-12-0 .... MissPGundry 76
(Ross Oliver) *a towards rr* **100/1**

6/03 **17** 8 **Danaeve (IRE)**[18] 11-12-0 .... MrLHicks 68
(R Harvey) *prom: lost pl 10th (Becher's): hmpd 14th* **100/1**

60-P **18** 18 **Arctic Copper (IRE)**[19] 12-12-0 ....(p) MrATDuff 50
(D M Christie, Ire) *prom to 4th: bhd fr 15th* **33/1**

P55P **19** 1 ¼ **Guignol Du Cochet (FR)**[13] [4607] 12-12-0 87 .... MrAWintle 48
(S Flook) *a towards rr* **200/1**

5P20 **20** 9 **Caught At Dawn (IRE)**[20] [4471] 12-12-0 120 .... MrTWeston 39
(M H Weston) *prom to 5th: bhd fr 11th (Foinavon)* **25/1**

-4U1 **21** 6 **Barryscourt Lad (IRE)**[27] [4347] 12-12-0 103 .... MrBWoodhouse 33
(R D E Woodhouse) *a bhd* **25/1**

4-35 **B** **Adolphus (IRE)**[12] 9-12-0 .... MrCStorey —
(C Storey) *in rr whn b.d 1st* **100/1**

4-24 **F** **Gielgud**[13] [4607] 9-12-0 105 .... MrJMaxse —
(B G Powell) *bhd whn fell 8th* **50/1**

2U-1 **F** **Satchmo (IRE)**[19] 14-12-0 109 .... MrPGHall —
(Mrs D M Grissell) *prom: fell 7th* **40/1**

3015 **F** **Galway Breeze (IRE)**[27] [4351] 11-12-0 104 .... MrMMackley —
(Mrs Julie Read) *prom whn fell 1st* **100/1**

3F10 **P** **Gatsby (IRE)**[20] [4471] 10-12-0 .... MrJMPritchard —
(J Groucott) *in rr: wl bhd whn p.u bef 2 out* **12/1**

5/P- **F** **Abbeytown (IRE)**[25] 9-12-0 .... MrJJCodd —
(Mrs Jeanette Riordan, Ire) *w ldrs: lft in ld 7th: fell 14th* **12/1**

00-P **F** **Venn Ottery**[5] 11-12-0 140 .... MrRQuinn —
(O J Carter) *hmpd 1st: t.k.h: hdwy to ld 6th: fell next* **66/1**

/110 **F** **Drombeag (IRE)**[20] [4471] 8-12-0 114 ....(b) MrJTMcNamara —
(Jonjo O'Neill) *chsd ldrs: tried run out bnd after 4th (water): fell 14th* **8/1**[3]

650- **U** **Hersov (IRE)**[12] 10-12-0 ....(p) MrDerekO'Connor —
(D M Christie, Ire) *hdwy to chse ldrs 4th (water): wknd 10th (Becher's): hmpd 14th: blnd and uns rdr next* **33/1**

5m 36.2s (-2.30) **Going Correction** +0.10s/f (Yiel) **30** Ran SP% **131.2**
Speed ratin**108,105,100,99,98 96,94,94,92,88 87,87,86,86,86 86,83,76,76,72** 70,—,—,—,— —,E CSF £44.27 TOTE £6.00: £3.10, £3.90, £22.60; EX 102.30 Trifecta £1649.80 Pool: £3,253.30 - 1.40 winning tickets.

Owner Robert Waley-Cohen **Bred** Haras Des Coudraies **Trained** Ratley, Warweick

FOCUS

No Irish whitewash this time, and Katarino became the first horse to win successive runnings since Spartan Missile in 1979. While it was not a vintage renewal, he looked different class. The form, which is solid enough, has been rated through the third.

NOTEBOOK

Katarino(FR), absent since winning this last year, has a well documented history of problems, but he retains a lot of class and he jumps these big fences for fun. After being left in charge, he raced with real enthusiasm and ran hard all the way to the line. The hat-trick must be a real possibility. *(op 6-1 tchd 7-1)*

Christy Beamish(IRE), given a patient ride, tended to brush through his fences rather than giving them air. He went in pursuit of the winner, and while he was never going to trouble that rival, he finished miles clear of the rest, showing much-improved form. It will come as little surprise to see him return and make a bold bid to go one better next year, but the Weatherbys Chase John Corbet Cup for novice hunters at Stratford looks the ideal short-term target, the sharp track the one doubt. *(op 9-1)*

Beachcomber Bay(IRE), who didn't get past the first fence a year ago, took a chance or two this time before finishing a remote third.

Bothar Na(IRE), almost brought down five out, flattened out from the final turn and the ground had probably turned against him.

Junior Fontaine(FR), placed in two points this year, gave his young rider a fine spin round.

Bill Haze made a wholesale error at the Foinavon fence, the smallest on the course bar the water, and his rider deserves full marks for keeping the partnership intact.

Sikander A Azam gave his teenage rider a great thrill, but after threatening the winner his legs turned to jelly going to the last. *(op 10-1)*

Munster(IRE), happy to sit way off the pace, fumbled his way round before keeping on in his own time late on. This looked something of a sighter. *(op 16-1)*

Drombeag(IRE), who tried to duck out on to the Mildmay course on the run down to what is the first fence in the Grand National itself, was still bang there when crashing out five from home. *(tchd 15-2)*

Abbeytown(IRE), a winner of four points, was still full of running when crashing out five from home. *(tchd 15-2)*

4749 JOHN SMITH'S RED RUM H'CAP CHASE GRADE 3 (12 fncs) 2m (Mildmay)
4:20 (4:21) (Class 1) 5-Y-0+

£39,914 (£14,973; £7,497; £3,738; £1,876; £938)

Form RPR

2121 **1** **Jacks Craic (IRE)**[12] [4618] 7-10-2 134 .... AntonyEvans 149+
(J L Spearing) *lw: hld up: hdwy 4 out: led appr last: drvn out* **10/1**

P524 **2** 2 ½ **Nyrche (FR)**[20] [4472] 6-10-7 139 .... RobertThornton 150+
(A King) *lw: chsd ldrs: led 6th: rdn and hdd appr last: styd on same pce flat* **7/1**[3]

261F **3** 4 **Andreas (FR)**[20] [4472] 6-10-12 144 ....(t) RWalsh 151+
(P F Nicholls) *hld up in tch: rdn and ev ch appr last: no ex flat* **7/2**[1]

0436 **4** 7 **Ground Ball (IRE)**[20] [4472] 9-10-11 143 .... APMcCoy 142
(C F Swan, Ire) *lw: hld up in tch: ev ch 3 out: rdn and wknd appr last* **11/1**

110F **5** 1 ½ **Town Crier (IRE)**[47] [3974] 11-10-13 145 .... DominicElsworth 143
(Mrs S J Smith) *prom: chsd ldr 4 out: ev ch next: rdn and wknd appr last* **20/1**

512P **6** shd **Armaturk (FR)**[21] [4457] 9-11-12 158 .... ChristianWilliams 155
(P F Nicholls) *chsd ldrs: lost pl after 4th: n.d after* **50/1**

-455 **7** 3 **Hand Inn Hand**[21] [4457] 10-10-13 145 .... RichardJohnson 140+
(H D Daly) *led and sn clr: blnd 3rd: hdd 6th: wknd 2 out* **14/1**

0/F **8** 2 ½ **Monjoyau (FR)**[46] [4018] 6-9-11 132 oh2 ....(v[1]) PWFlood[(3)] 125+
(E J O'Grady, Ire) *lw: neat: prom tl rdn and wknd after 3 out* **14/1**

3F61 **9** 27 **Mansony (FR)**[25] [4404] 7-10-7 139 .... DJCasey 104
(A L T Moore, Ire) *rangy: swtg: s.s: j.rt 5th: a bhd* **6/1**[2]

1040 **B** **Bambi De L'Orme (FR)**[20] [4472] 7-10-5 137 .... GLee —
(Ian Williams) *hld up: b.d 6th* **14/1**

0414 **P** **Palua**[68] [3619] 9-10-5 137 .... BarryFenton —
(Miss E C Lavelle) *hld up: hmpd 6th: a in rr: bhd whn p.u bef last* **66/1**

131P **P** **Tysou (FR)**[20] [4472] 9-11-1 147 .... MarcusFoley —
(N J Henderson) *lw: hld up: hmpd 6th: a in rr: t.o whn p.u bef 3 out* **40/1**

3-51 **P** **Greenhope (IRE)**[20] [4472] 8-10-9 141 .... MickFitzgerald —
(N J Henderson) *hld up: hdwy 7th: wknd next: bhd whn p.u bef last* **8/1**

222F **U** **Bleu Superbe (FR)**[20] [4472] 11-10-0 132 .... AlanO'Keeffe —
(Miss Venetia Williams) *chsd ldrs tl slipped and uns rdr after 6th* **20/1**

231F **P** **Demi Beau**[21] [4456] 8-10-3 135 .... PaulMoloney —
(Evan Williams) *lw: chsd ldrs: blnd 3rd: lost pl after next: t.o whn p.u bef 4 out* **20/1**

6014 **U** **Almaydan**[47] [3974] 8-10-3 135 ....(b) TimmyMurphy —
(R Lee) *lw: rdn after 4th: lost pl next: bhd fr 8th: t.o whn j. slowly and uns rdr last* **33/1**

3m 57.8s (-3.20) **Going Correction** +0.05s/f (Yiel) **16** Ran SP% **120.7**
Speed ratings: **110,108,106,103,102 102,100,99,86,—** —,—,—,—,— — CSF £72.71 CT £300.30 TOTE £11.90: £2.00, £2.20, £1.70, £2.20; EX 73.00 Trifecta £312.30 Pool: £3,299.20 - 7.50 winning tickets.

Owner Bbb Computer Services **Bred** Michael Murphy **Trained** Kinnersley, Worcs

■ Jacks Craic's success made it eight wins by novices in the last 12 runnings of this race.

FOCUS

A competitive renewal of this valuable handicap chase, and Hand Inn Hand ensured there was no hanging about. The good record of novices in this race was maintained by both the winner and second. Very solid form.

NOTEBOOK

Jacks Craic(IRE) ◆, still a novice, has progressed with pretty much every run this season, and though 9lb higher than when successful at Newbury on his previous start, he continued his improvement with another ready success. His effort is all the more creditable given all three of his previous wins came on ground with soft in the description, and he was held up well off the pace in a race many of the principals were never that far away from the action. He will go up again for this, but there is no sign of his improvement levelling out for the time being and he must be kept on the right side of. *(tchd 11-1)*

Nyrche(FR), fourth in the Grand Annual at Cheltenham on his previous start, confirmed form with all those who finished behind off a 2lb higher mark and found only the improving winner too good. Like the winner, he is still a novice and this was a very creditable effort. *(tchd 15-2)*

Andreas(FR), a beaten favourite when falling in the Grand Annual at Cheltenham on his latest start, got round this time but had his chance and did not appear to have any real excuses. *(op 4-1 tchd 9-2 in a place)*

Ground Ball(IRE), just over a length behind Nyrche in the Grand Annual at Cheltenham on his previous start, was 2lb better off but beaten further this time. He gave the impression that decent ground on a speed track did not quite suit, and he can be given another chance. *(op 12-1)*

Town Crier(IRE), who took a very nasty fall when a beaten favourite at Haydock on his most recent start, showed that has not left too much of a mark with a creditable enough effort. This could well have provided a welcome confidence boost.

Armaturk(FR) would have found this a more suitable race than the Ryanair Chase (pulled up), and though he struggled with the pace he ultimately did not fare badly.

Hand Inn Hand went off very quick in front this time, and yet again his jumping let him down. *(tchd 16-1)*

Mansony(FR), in good form in novice company on testing ground in Ireland lately, looked reluctant to jump off and was always trailing. He clearly has a lot of ability, but he appeared to sulk this time. *(op 5-1 tchd 13-2 and 11-2 in places)*

Demi Beau *Official explanation: jockey said gelding was never travelling having made mistake (tchd 9-1 in a place)*

Greenhope(IRE), the Johnny Henderson Grand Annual winner, ran no sort of race off a 9lb higher mark and Cheltenham was very much his day. *(tchd 9-1 in a place)*

4750 CITROEN C4 MERSEY NOVICES' HURDLE GRADE 2 (11 hdls) 2m 4f
4:55 (4:55) (Class 1) 4-Y-0+

£31,361 (£11,764; £5,890; £2,937; £1,474; £737)

Form RPR

1436 **1** **Natal (FR)**[23] [4430] 5-11-3 142 ....(t) RWalsh 156+
(P F Nicholls) *lw: hld up: hdwy 7th: rdn to ld appr last: styd on u.p: idled nr fin* **7/2**[1]

1123 **2** 1 ½ **Blazing Bailey**[20] [4468] 4-10-7 140 .... RobertThornton 143
(A King) *lw: trckd ldrs: led 3 out: rdn and hdd appr last: styd on u.p* **7/2**[1]

2111 **3** 28 **Harmony Brig (IRE)**[18] [4529] 7-11-3 132 .... TonyDobbin 125
(N G Richards) *led: hdd 3 out: rdn and wknd after next* **9/1**

1133 **4** shd **Boychuk (IRE)**[53] [3878] 5-11-8 134 .... RichardJohnson 130
(P J Hobbs) *hld up: pushed along 4th: n.d* **7/1**[3]

3631 **5** 8 **Chiaro (FR)**[15] [4569] 4-11-1 139 ....(b) PJBrennan 115
(P J Hobbs) *chsd ldr: rdn appr 3 out: sn wknd* **15/2**

1233 **6** 10 **Buena Vista (IRE)**[23] [4430] 5-11-5 140 ....(p) APMcCoy 109
(M C Pipe) *lw: chsd ldrs: hit 6th: rdn and wknd after 8th* **4/1**[2]

1133 **7** 3 **Regal Heights (IRE)**[27] [4359] 5-11-0 132 .... StephenCraine 101
(D McCain) *hld up: rdn and wknd 7th* **66/1**

5101 **8** 2 **Some Touch (IRE)**[28] [4313] 6-11-0 122 .... GLee 99
(J Howard Johnson) *hld up in tch: plld hrd: rdn and wknd appr 3 out* **16/1**

1303 **9** *dist* **Patman Du Charmil (FR)**[23] 4435 4-10-7 128................(t) CarlLlewellyn —
(N A Twiston-Davies) *chsd ldrs: lost pl after 5th: bhd fr 7th* **33/1**

2443 **P** **Marshalls Run (IRE)**[19] 4494 6-11-0 .... TimmyMurphy —
(A King) *lw: hld up: bhd and rdn 6th: t.o whn p.u bef 2 out* **66/1**

1120 **P** **Craven (IRE)**[53] 3881 6-11-0 120...................................... MickFitzgerald —
(N J Henderson) *hld up: hdwy 5th: wknd 7th: t.o whn p.u bef 3 out* **33/1**

4m 52.4s (-11.30) **Going Correction** -0.075s/f (Good)
WFA 4 from 5yo+ 6lb **11** Ran SP% **113.5**
Speed ratings: **119,118,107,107,103 99,98,97,—,— —** CSF £15.07 TOTE £5.00: £1.80, £1.50, £2.40; EX 19.00 Trifecta £240.70 Pool: £2,407.48 - 7.10 winning tickets.
Owner Mrs Monica Hackett **Bred** Yves D'Armaille **Trained** Ditcheat, Somerset

FOCUS
With the likes of Boychuk and Buena Vista running below form, and some of the less exposed runners failing to cope with the step up in class, this was not that competitive for a Grade Two. However, Natal and Blazing Bailey finished a mile clear of the rest after a good battle, and both showed a very smart level of form.

NOTEBOOK
Natal(FR) ◆, sixth to his stablemate Noland in the Supreme Novices' at Cheltenham on his previous start, showed much-improved form for the step up to two and a half miles and won convincingly. Having travelled strongly throughout, he saw this trip out really well when asked to go and get Blazing Bailey, who had moved with similar ease from the start, and he had the race won when wandering around a touch in front. While the pace was just ordinary, his stamina for this sort of trip is now well and truly assured and connections ought to have plenty of options next season when they send him chasing. He will be a most exciting recruit to the larger obstacles. *(tchd 4-1 in a place)*
Blazing Bailey, third in the Triumph Hurdle on his previous start, looked to get this longer trip well and found only the older Natal too good - he finished upwards of 28 lengths clear of the remainder. He is likely to find things harder in his second season over hurdles, but should have options with regards to trip and ground. *(op 3-1)*
Harmony Brig(IRE), who has progressed to win his last three starts in minor company, finished up well beaten and fortunate to hang on for third. This was both the furthest trip he has raced over, and the liveliest ground he has encountered to date, so perhaps conditions were not ideal. *(op 10-1)*
Boychuk(IRE) has not progressed as one might have hoped this season but, given another chance over two and a half miles, he ran a funny sort of race. Richard Johnson never looked happy on him and was niggling from some way out, but the response was minimal and turning into the straight his rider appeared to accept he would finish up well beaten. However, he began to get after him again when some the beaten horses started to come back and he eventually picked up to very nearly grab third. He may be a tricky customer who only decided to run on in his own time but, looking at it in black and white, he probably should have finished a clear third. Off the back of this unsatisfactory display, it would be no surprise to see headgear fitted next time. *(op 8-1)*
Chiaro(FR), an ex-French performer who won easily on his debut in Britain in minor company at Chepstow, could not produce his best and will be suited by a return to softer ground. *(tchd 7-1)*
Buena Vista(IRE) had today's winner behind when a fine third in the Supreme Novices' Hurdle at Cheltenham on his previous start but, upped to two and a half miles for the first time, he was in trouble some way out and beaten before stamina became an issue. Even though he wore cheekpieces when third at Cheltenham last time, he did not look comfortable with them fitted this time but, whatever the case, he has had a hard season and is probably due a break. *(op 9-2)*

4751 JOHN SMITH'S HBLB TBA MARES' ONLY STANDARD OPEN NATIONAL HUNT FLAT RACE (LISTED RACE) 2m 1f

5:30 (5:30) (Class 1) 4-6-Y-O

£17,106 (£6,417; £3,213; £1,602; £804; £402)

Form RPR

61 **1** **Rhacophorus**[77] 3468 5-11-4 .... RWalsh 108
(C J Down) *lw: hld up: hdwy over 3f out: rdn and hung lft fr over 1f out: styd on to ld nr fin* **7/1**

212 **2** *nk* **Wyldello**[26] 4376 5-11-4 .... RobertThornton 109+
(A King) *chsd ldrs: led over 3f out: rdn and hung lft over 1f out: hdd nr fin* **7/2**[1]

41 **3** *2* **Ring Back (IRE)**[25] 4398 5-10-13 .... MarkNicolls(5) 106
(B I Case) *hld up: hdwy over 3f out: rdn and hung lft over 2f out: styd on same pce ins fnl f* **50/1**

2 **4** *¾* **Strawberry (IRE)**[33] 4237 5-10-7 .... WayneKavanagh(7) 101
(J W Mullins) *hld up: hdwy over 5f out: rdn over 2f out: styd on same pce appr fnl f* **20/1**

5 *2½* **Callherwhatulike (IRE)**[19] 4514 5-10-13 .... MrCJSweeney(5) 103
(Robert Tyner, Ire) *neat: chsd ldrs: rdn and hmpd over 1f out: wknd towards fin* **12/1**

6 *2½* **Chomba Womba (IRE)**[70] 3590 5-10-13 .... MrPCashman(5) 100
(Ms Margaret Mullins, Ire) *wl grwn: chsd ldrs: led over 4f out: rdn and hdd over 3f out: wknd over 1f out* **6/1**[3]

7 *½* **River Tigris (IRE)**[18] 4-10-8 .... RichardJohnson 90
(O Sherwood) *w'like: scope: prom: outpcd over 3f out: n.d after* **33/1**

8 *2* **Mill House Girl (IRE)**[186] 1625 5-11-0 .... MrATDuff(7) 101
(S Donohoe, Ire) *w'like: hld up: hdwy over 5f out: wknd 2f out* **11/1**

46 **9** *6* **Classic Fantasy**[52] 3904 5-11-0 .... ChristianWilliams 88
(P F Nicholls) *hld up: hdwy 7f out: rdn over 3f out: wknd over 2f out* **66/1**

1 **10** *3* **Paix Eternelle (FR)**[46] 4011 5-11-4 .... MarcusFoley 89
(N J Henderson) *hld up: hdwy 6f out: wknd over 2f out* **20/1**

113 **11** *3* **Apollo Lady**[26] 4376 5-11-0 .... MrGTumelty(7) 89
(A King) *mid-div: hdwy 6f out: rdn and wknd over 1f out* **12/1**

12 *1½* **Seventh Sense** 5-10-11 .... MichalKohl(3) 80
(J I A Charlton) *lw: hld up: hdwy over 4f out: wknd wl over 1f out* **100/1**

15 **13** *10* **Scarvagh Diamond (IRE)**[26] 4376 5-10-11 .... MissRDavidson(7) 74
(Mrs R L Elliot) *lw: led: rdn and hdd over 4f out: wknd 3f out* **50/1**

1 **14** *2* **Amaretto Rose**[46] 4017 5-11-4 .... MickFitzgerald 72
(N J Henderson) *hld up: hmpd and stmbld after 2f: hdwy 10f out: wknd over 2f out* **11/2**[2]

060 **15** *1½* **Follow My Leader (IRE)**[17] 4554 6-10-11 ....(p) MissNCarberry(3) 67
(R Ford) *hld up: hdwy over 3f out: wknd over 2f out* **80/1**

4 **16** *10* **Miss Mitch (IRE)**[28] 4333 5-11-0 .... AndrewThornton 57
(R H Alner) *hld up: hdwy over 5f out: wknd over 2f out* **16/1**

556 **17** *3½* **Mrs O'Malley**[75] 3497 6-10-11 .... StephenCraine(3) 53
(D McCain) *mid-div: hdwy u.p 10f out: wknd over 6f out* **100/1**

002 **18** *5* **Lily Tara**[18] 4533 4-10-3 .... DeclanMcGann(5) 42
(A M Crow) *prom 10f* **100/1**

401 **19** *1½* **She's Humble (IRE)**[11] 4644 4-10-12 .... AntonyEvans 45
(P D Evans) *chsd ldrs over 11f* **28/1**

2 **20** *20* **Wensleydale Web**[29] 4304 4-10-8 .... GLee 21
(M E Sowersby) *hld up: bhd fr 1/2-way* **66/1**

21 *dist* **Anglerzar (IRE)** 6-11-0 .... DominicElsworth —
(J M Saville) *angular: prom: racd keenly: lost pl 1/2-way: sn bhd* **100/1**

126 **P** **Saratogane (FR)**[26] 4376 4-10-12 .... TomScudamore —
(M C Pipe) *mid-div: lost pl over 7f out: bhd whn p.u over 5f out* **16/1**

4m 11.0s (-6.60) **Going Correction** -0.075s/f (Good)
WFA 4 from 5yo+ 5lb **22** Ran SP% **127.9**
Speed ratings: 112,111,110,110,109 108,107,107,104,102 101,100,95,95,94 89,87,85,84,75 —,— CSF £29.35 TOTE £9.70: £3.00, £2.00, £13.80; EX 49.60 Trifecta £995.40 Place 6 £26.99, Place 5 £20.55.
Owner W A Bromley **Bred** Wood Farm Stud **Trained** Mutterton, Devon

FOCUS
As is to be expected in mares-only company, the bare form is just ordinary and it is unlikely we saw anything as good as last year's winner Senorita Rumbalita. Still, there was little between Rhacophorus and Wydello and they are both likeable types. The pace was steady for much of the way.

NOTEBOOK
Rhacophorus, who shaped well in a good Wincanton bumper on her debut before winning at Taunton, had the beating of Wyldello strictly on the form of her last run, given the three and a half-length runner-up that day, Korello Bay, went on to beat the King horse a neck at Sandown. She duly got that one's measure, but it took a perfectly-timed ride from Ruby Walsh and the runner-up's jockey also lost his whip. She should continue her progression in mares-only company over hurdles next season. *(op 9-1)*
Wyldello ran a game race in defeat and got closer to Rhacophorus than her latest running at Sandown entitled her to, given she was neck behind Korello Bay and that one had been beaten three and a half lengths by today's winner on her previous start. Her effort is all the more creditable given her rider lost his whip, and she could even be considered unlucky. A really tough, likeable type, she ought to do well in mares-only company over hurdles next season. *Official explanation: jockey said mare hung left (op 9-2)*
Ring Back(IRE) looked a nice prospect when winning a modest race at Warwick on her previous start and acquitted herself very creditably in defeat.
Strawberry(IRE), second on her debut in a Polytrack bumper at Lingfield, ran well in this tougher company. She really should pick up races in mares' company. *(op 25-1)*
Callherwhatulike(IRE), an Irish point winner who won a bumper at Gowran on her debut under Rules, was hampered when trying to throw down a challenge and is better than the bare form. However, she was given a pretty hard ride and it remains to be seen which way she will go from this. *(tchd 14-1)*
Chomba Womba(IRE), successful in a Punchestown bumper two starts previously, acquitted herself creditably on this step up in class. *(op 7-1)*
River Tigris(IRE), successful in a two and a half-mile point just 18 days previously, would have appreciated the decent ground and fared best of the four-year-olds by some way. A pleasing debut under Rules from a filly who was the first horse of her age ever to win a point-to-point in this country. *(op 28-1)*
Mill House Girl(IRE), twice a winner on fast ground in Ireland, travelled well for much of the way but disappointingly failed to pick up. *(op 12-1)*
Apollo Lady was just a length and a quarter behind Wyldello at Sandown on her previous start, so this was disappointing. *(op 11-1)*
Amaretto Rose, a promising winner on her debut at Towcester, travelled quite well for much of the way but did not pick up and was disappointing. Perhaps a return to softer ground will suit. *(op 4-1)*
T/Jkpt: Part won. £41,120.70 to a £1 stake. Pool: £57,916.50. 0.50 winning tickets. T/Plt: £30.20 to a £1 stake. Pool: £260,689.75. 6,299.60 winning tickets. T/Qpdt: £15.00 to a £1 stake. Pool: £11,106.40. 546.50 winning tickets. CR

4661 TAUNTON (R-H)

Thursday, April 6

OFFICIAL GOING: Good
Wind: Breezy across

4752 COMPARE PRICES AT GG-ODDS.COM CONDITIONAL JOCKEYS' (S) H'CAP HURDLE (12 hdls) 3m 110y

2:20 (2:21) (Class 5) (0-95,91) 4-Y-O+ **£2,192** (£639; £319)

Form RPR

-001 **1** **Le Forezien (FR)**[11] 4640 7-11-5 89 7ex......................(t) BernieWharfe(5) 93+
(C J Gray) *hld up towards rr: stdy hdwy fr 8th to trck ldrs after 3 out: led next: kpt on wl* **7/1**[1]

/44U **2** *3½* **Bonny Boy (IRE)**[8] 4666 11-10-13 78.........................(vt) WilliamKennedy 78
(D A Rees) *chsd ldr: led after 2nd: rdn and narrowly hdd 2 out: kpt on but no ex flat* **10/1**

0PUP **3** *1½* **Cosi Celeste (FR)**[17] 4549 9-11-11 90................................ CharliePoste 88
(John Allen) *mid div: tk clsr order 8th: rdn after next: styd on fr 2 out: wnt 3rd run-in* **66/1**

-04P **4** *1¼* **Emphatic (IRE)**[56] 3814 11-11-11 90.................................(b) DarylJacob 87
(J G Portman) *led tl after 2nd: chsd ldr: rdn and effrt after 3 out: one pce fr next* **8/1**[3]

40-P **5** *1¾* **Field Master (IRE)**[28] 4331 9-11-2 81...................... RobertLucey-Butler 76
(C J Gray) *hld up towards rr: hdwy after 6th: rdn to chse ldrs after 3 out: sn one pce* **16/1**

-P00 **6** *¾* **Big Max**[28] 4331 11-11-6 85...(p) PaddyMerrigan 81+
(Miss K M George) *chsd ldrs: rdn to ld briefly after 3 out: ev ch next: no ex* **20/1**

P-60 **7** *4* **La Professoressa (IRE)**[24] 4427 5-11-0 87............(t) AngharadFrieze(8) 79+
(Mrs P N Dutfield) *hld up towards rr: sme late hdwy: nvr a danger* **66/1**

P00U **8** *3½* **They Grabbed Me (IRE)**[31] 4277 5-10-10 78...............(t) TomMalone(3) 65
(M C Pipe) *chsd ldrs: rdn after 8th: wknd appr 2 out* **14/1**

0560 **9** *nk* **Killer Cat (FR)**[60] 3757 5-11-9 91......................... AndrewGlassonbury(3) 78
(G F Edwards) *hld up towards rr: hdwy after 8th into mid div: rdn after 3 out: wknd next* **16/1**

B360 **10** *1¾* **Penny's Crown**[17] 4549 7-11-4 86.............................. EamonDehdashti(3) 71
(G A Ham) *in tch: drvn along after 7th: outpcd after next: nt a threat after* **15/2**[2]

056P **11** *2* **Lunch Was My Idea (IRE)**[47] 3997 6-11-6 88...............(t) LiamHeard(3) 71
(P F Nicholls) *mid div tl wknd appr 3 out* **15/2**[2]

2200 **12** *22* **Knight Of Silver**[17] 4549 9-11-5 87.........................(b) TomMessenger(3) 48
(S C Burrough) *a bhd: t.o* **8/1**[3]

00P3 **13** *3½* **Silverpro**[17] 4550 5-9-9 68.. RyanCummings(8) 25
(D J Wintle) *mid div tl dropped rr after 6th: t.o* **9/1**

0-0P **14** *nk* **Homer (IRE)**[28] 4320 9-10-12 80............................... WillieMcCarthy(3) 37
(N M Babbage) *slowly away: a bhd: t.o* **14/1**

POPP **15** *1* **Oui Exit (FR)**[57] 3800 5-10-9 80.................................(t) MarcGoldstein(6) 36
(N A Twiston-Davies) *t.k.h in tch: wknd after 3 out: t.o* **25/1**

5m 57.6s (-11.00) **Going Correction** -0.45s/f (Good) **15** Ran SP% **114.0**
Speed ratings: **99,97,97,97,96 96,94,93,93,93 92,85,84,84,83** CSF £68.37 CT £4156.87 TOTE £3.40: £2.80, £2.50, £10.40; EX 79.00.The winner was bought in for 5,800gns.
Owner S C Botham **Bred** P Coyne-Bodin And Paul Coyne **Trained** Moorland, Somerset

FOCUS
A race that took little winning.

NOTEBOOK

Le Forezien(FR) ◆, a recent winner at Worcester, had little trouble defying the 7lb penalty, clearing away after the last to win comfortably. Held up wide throughout, he travelled strongly and readily made ground to race prominently leaving the back straight, the extra half a mile proving to be no problem. Open to further improvement at the age of seven, the tongue tie seems to have been the making of him and he is one to keep on-side at this sort of level. *(op 13-2 tchd 6-1)*

Bonny Boy(IRE), reverting to hurdles, kept on well in second having led for most of the way. He has never won under Rules, and is hardly getting any better at the age of 11. *(op 12-1)*

Cosi Celeste(FR)'s previous efforts left a lot to be desired, but the drop in grade brought about a better effort and he was keeping on in third. *(op 50-1)*

Emphatic(IRE) disputed it with Bonny Boy early before allowing that one to go on, and he was keeping on again at the end of his race, leaving behind a poor effort at Huntingdon back in February. *(op 10-1)*

Field Master(IRE) made a little headway down the back straight, but he was unable to get involved and could only keep on at the one pace.

Big Max showed up well for a long way before fading out of it in the straight.

La Professoressa(IRE) may have got closer with a little more assistance from the saddle. *(op 50-1)*

4753 NORMAN READING BEGINNERS' CHASE (17 fncs) 2m 7f 110y

2:55 (2:55) (Class 4) 5-Y-O+ **£5,855** (£1,719; £859; £429)

Form RPR

P161 **1** **Vingis Park (IRE)**[111] 2859 8-11-0 115..........(b) LiamHeard(5) 98+
(V R A Dartnall) *disp: mstke 6th: j.lft thereafter: wnt 2 l clr and hit 3 out: hit next: sn rdn: edgd lft but kpt on whn chal flat* **11/4**[2]

3/00 **2** ¾ **Isotop (FR)**[17] 4553 10-11-5 81.......... LeightonAspell 94
(John Allen) *disp tl appr 3 out: sn rdn to chse wnr: swtchd lft approching last: rallied flat: no ex cl home* **25/1**

20 **3** *10* **Dante's Promise (IRE)**[57] 3806 10-11-0..........(p) MrTJO'Brien(5) 86+
(C J Down) *disp tl 4th: chsd ldng pair: cl 3rd and rdn whn pckd 3 out: kpt on same pce* **28/1**

6020 **4** ¾ **Blue Business**[21] 4460 8-11-5 132..........(b) JoeTizzard 83
(P F Nicholls) *nvr travelled fluently bhd ldrs: reminders after 4th and 10th: rdn after 12th: no ch fr after 4 out* **8/13**[1]

P0-6 **5** ¾ **Russian Lord (IRE)**[156] 1969 7-11-5 77 ow5..........(p) MrNHarris(5) 88
(V R A Dartnall) *chsd ldrs tl outpcd after 12th: nt a danger after* **50/1**

P **U** **Barrshan (IRE)**[86] 3331 7-11-5..........(t) AndrewTinkler —
(N J Henderson) *trcking ldrs whn blnd bdly and uns rdr 3rd* **10/1**[3]

6m 2.40s (-2.70) **Going Correction** -0.45s/f (Good) **6** Ran SP% **106.9**

Speed ratings: **86,85,82,82,81** — CSF £39.64 TOTE £2.80: £1.50, £4.00; EX 59.50.

Owner Nick Viney **Bred** Victor Robinson **Trained** Brayford, Devon

FOCUS

With hot favourite Blue Business running a stinker, it is likely the form is worth little.

NOTEBOOK

Vingis Park(IRE), who has finally got his act together over hurdles, had to be respected on this return to fences and, although his jumping was a little suspect at times, it was hard to fault his resolution after the last, sticking his neck out to hold the runner-up. The form is not worth a great deal, but he has definitely improved since being fitted with blinkers and he is now likely to head to the three-day Perth festival. *(op 5-2)*

Isotop(FR), unable to get competitive in a couple of handicaps since returning from injury, found the less-competitive nature of this contest to his liking and it momentarily looked as though he would go by the winner after the last, but Vingis Park proved too strong. His current lowly rating should enable him to find a handicap if going on from this. *(op 33-1)*

Dante's Promise(IRE), an experienced pointer, ran well to finished second in a hunter chase at Exeter back in May of last year and a recent spin over hurdles would have put him straight for this. He ran well to a point, but finished a little tired and did well to hold third. *(op 20-1)*

Blue Business, not for the first time this season, looked thoroughly uninterested in the game and he was being ridden along with a circuit to go. The half-brother to Best Mate has not taken to fences as well as anticipated and he remains one to avoid. *Official explanation: trainer's representative had no explanation for poor form shown (op 4-6 tchd 8-11)*

Russian Lord(IRE), a sizeable gelding, failed to show anything in bumpers and hurdles, but the combination of cheekpieces and a switch to fences coaxed the gelding into showing a bit more. He is not an easy ride, but jumped well in the main and there will be other days for him. *(op 33-1)*

4754 TINCKNELL MITSUBISHI MAIDEN HURDLE (9 hdls) 2m 1f

3:30 (3:30) (Class 4) 4-Y-0+ **£5,204** (£1,528; £764; £381)

Form RPR

25 **1** **Traprain (IRE)**[53] 3883 4-10-5.......... MrTJO'Brien(5) 102+
(P J Hobbs) *plld hrd: hld up in mid div: sltly hmpd 1st: hdwy 3 out: narrow advantage and gng wl 2 out: kpt on: rdn out* **5/4**[1]

2 **2** 1¾ **The Composer**[12] 3355 4-10-10.......... JimmyMcCarthy 94
(M Blanshard) *trckd ldrs: led briefly appr 2 out: rdn and ev ch whn hit last: no ex* **8/1**

0 **3** *shd* **Wiggy Smith**[51] 3908 7-11-2.......... LeightonAspell 102+
(O Sherwood) *hld up towards rr: smooth prog fr 6th: ev ch whn mstke and pckd 2 out: kpt on flat* **13/2**[3]

-335 **4** *4* **Nocturnally**[113] 2821 6-10-11.......... LiamHeard(5) 96
(V R A Dartnall) *mid div: tk clsr order 5th: ev ch 2 out: sn rdn: kpt on same pce* **9/2**[2]

445 **5** *12* **Great Memories**[28] 4327 7-11-2.......... NoelFehily 86+
(Jonjo O'Neill) *trackd ldrs: led 6th: hung rt and hdd appr 2 out: sn wknd* **7/1**

0-34 **6** *4* **Xcentra**[302] 685 5-11-2.......... JohnMcNamara 80
(B G Powell) *hld up towards rr: hdwy after 6th: rdn after 3 out: wknd next* **20/1**

7 *11* **Zacatecas (GER)**[207] 6-10-9.......... JohnKington(7) 69
(M Scudamore) *hmpd 1st: towards rr: reminders and hdwy after 4th: wknd 6th* **33/1**

0P **8** ½ **Lord West**[156] 1968 5-11-2.......... JoeTizzard 69
(C L Tizzard) *led tl 6th: sn wknd* **40/1**

000/ **9** *shd* **Court Emperor**[182] 4213 6-11-2.......... WayneHutchinson 68
(Evan Williams) *j.rt 1st: in tch: stmbld 2nd: rdn and wknd after 6th* **40/1**

650 **10** *dist* **Handel With Care (IRE)**[28] 4333 4-10-10.......... TomDoyle —
(R A Farrant) *j. bdly rt 1st: t.o fr 5th* **100/1**

00 **11** *hd* **Bronze King**[28] 4333 6-11-2.......... JasonMaguire —
(J A B Old) *chsd ldrs tl wknd 6th: t.o* **80/1**

12 *6* **Cool Bathwick (IRE)**[62] 7-11-2.......... JodieMogford —
(G H Yardley) *a in rr: t.o fr 5th* **100/1**

3m 59.4s (-9.40) **Going Correction** -0.45s/f (Good) **12** Ran SP% **115.4**

WFA 4 from 5yo+ 5lb

Speed ratings: **104,103,103,101,95 93,88,88,88,—** —,— CSF £11.17 TOTE £1.70: £1.10, £1.60, £3.20; EX 9.60.

Owner R A Green **Bred** C J Foy **Trained** Withycombe, Somerset

FOCUS

An uncompetitive maiden hurdle and Traprain appreciated the better ground.

NOTEBOOK

Traprain(IRE) ◆, a fair sort on the Flat, was expected to prove good enough with the ground coming in his favour, and he did what was required despite the steady gallop that would not have helped. Keen throughout, he tanked into the straight, along with Wiggy Smith, but a mistake from that one at the second-last handed him the advantage and he found what was required to win comfortably. He is likely to be kept on the go through the summer and can probably win again, with the quickening ground in his favour. *(op 11-8)*

The Composer has taken well to hurdles and he confirmed the promise of his Ludlow second, keeping on well having raced prominently throughout. There is a small race in him if kept on the go during the summer. *(op 11-2)*

Wiggy Smith ◆ was perhaps the most interesting runner in the line-up and, despite racing keenly, he was able to build on his initial Folkestone effort. It could be said he made up his ground too quickly, and a mistake at the second-last did not help, but he is definitely one to keep on the right side of in future. *(op 7-1 tchd 15-2)*

Nocturnally came there to have every chance in the straight, but he lacked the pace of the front trio and it is unlikely he will be winning until contesting handicaps. *(op 6-1)*

Great Memories ran well to a point, but like so many from his stable this season, he stopped quickly under pressure. *(op 9-1 tchd 10-1)*

4755 KINGSTON VETERINARY GROUP H'CAP CHASE (14 fncs) 2m 3f

4:05 (4:05) (Class 3) (0-125,123) 5-Y-0+ **£7,807** (£2,292; £1,146; £572)

Form RPR

20U6 **1** **Terre De Java (FR)**[50] 3922 8-11-1 112.......... JodieMogford 130+
(Mrs H Dalton) *hld up and a travelling wl: hdwy to trck ldrs 5th: led 9th: in command after: eased flat* **12/1**

1015 **2** *4* **Magico (NZ)**[33] 4239 8-11-7 118..........(b) SamThomas 124
(Miss Venetia Williams) *led tl 2nd: styd prom: led briefly after 7th: cl up: rdn to chse wnr in vain fr 4 out* **9/2**[2]

U22P **3** *9* **Priscilla**[12] 4620 8-9-13 101.......... LiamHeard(5) 101+
(K Bishop) *hld up: tk clsr order 8th: rdn to go 3rd after 4 out: kpt on same pce* **4/1**[1]

-00P **4** *28* **Waterspray (AUS)**[68] 3619 8-11-3 114.......... HenryOliver 94+
(Ian Williams) *chsd ldrs: led after 7th: hdd 9th: wknd appr 4 out* **16/1**

6012 **P** **Runner Bean**[28] 4332 12-11-1 112.......... JohnMcNamara —
(R Lee) *bhd fr 7th: p.u bef 9th* **6/1**

2142 **P** **Smart Cavalier**[5] 4694 7-10-13 110..........(t) JoeTizzard —
(P F Nicholls) *led 2nd tl after 7th: wknd after 8th: p.u bef 10th* **4/1**[1]

4520 **U** **Ballyrobert (IRE)**[85] 3344 9-10-12 109.......... AndrewTinkler —
(A M Hales) *chsd ldrs: mstke 4th: cl 5th whn blnd and uns rdr 8th* **10/1**

4614 **P** **No Visibility (IRE)**[12] 4611 11-11-9 120.......... RobertWalford —
(R H Alner) *sn struggling: towards rr: sme hdwy appr 8th: wknd 9th: p.u bef 10th* **5/1**[3]

4m 42.3s (-10.50) **Going Correction** -0.45s/f (Good) **8** Ran SP% **111.8**

Speed ratings: **104,102,98,86,—** —,—,— CSF £63.01 CT £254.27 TOTE £17.50: £3.60, £1.60, £1.50; EX 112.10.

Owner Miss L Hales **Bred** C Guezet **Trained** Norton, Shropshire

FOCUS

They went a decent gallop and Terre De Java ran out an authoritative winner.

NOTEBOOK

Terre De Java(FR) had not shown a great deal since winning a poor race at Doncaster last season, but this step up in distance suited the gelding and he jumped soundly throughout under a fine ride from Mogford. He is lightly raced and it is hoped he goes on from this. *(tchd 11-1)*

Magico(NZ) raced prominently throughout and kept galloping away for a clear second. He has had a decent first season for new connections, going up 25lb in the weights, and this effort suggested he has not done winning yet. *(op 5-1 tchd 11-2)*

Priscilla left behind a poor effort at Newbury last month, but with only four completing it is debatable what she achieved.

Waterspray(AUS) was the last to finish, but he came home well held and remains below a winning level. *(op 14-1)*

No Visibility(IRE) *Official explanation: jockey said gelding was unsuited by good ground (tchd 11-2)*

Ballyrobert(IRE) was still in with every chance when unseating his rider in spectacular fashion down the back straight. *(tchd 11-2)*

Smart Cavalier, turned out quickly after a decent effort at Fontwell last week, pulled up sharply *suggesting something may have been amiss. Official explanation: jockey said gelding lost its action (tchd 11-2)*

4756 SOUTHWESTRACING.COM H'CAP HURDLE (9 hdls 1 omitted) 2m 3f 110y

4:40 (4:40) (Class 4) (0-110,110) 4-Y-0+ **£4,228** (£1,241; £620; £310)

Form RPR

1130 **1** **Businessmoney Jake**[47] 3993 5-11-5 108.......... LiamHeard(5) 111+
(V R A Dartnall) *prom: led after 5th: rdn after 2 out: blnd last: all out* **13/2**[2]

0060 **2** ½ **Mister Chatterbox (IRE)**[24] 4429 5-10-1 90.......... MrTJO'Brien(5) 91
(P J Hobbs) *chsd ldrs: hrd rdn after 2 out: chal and ev ch after last: no ex cl home* **10/1**

4F25 **3** 1½ **Buffalo Bill (IRE)**[89] 3282 10-11-2 103.......... WilliamKennedy(3) 102
(A M Hales) *hld up in tch: hdwy after 6th: rdn to go 3rd appr last: kpt on same pce* **25/1**

4345 **4** 1¼ **Hail The King (USA)**[75] 3510 6-11-0 103.......... RobertLucey-Butler(5) 101
(R M Carson) *hld up: hdwy after 7th: rdn and effrt appr last: kpt on same pce* **10/1**

0022 **5** 1¼ **Shalati Princess**[24] 4423 5-9-9 86 oh6 ow2.......... MrRhysHughes(7) 85+
(D Burchell) *chsd ldrs: jnd wnr 7th: rdn and ev ch after 2 out: 4th and hld whn blnd last* **20/1**

-055 **6** *5* **La Marette**[25] 4392 8-10-10 94.......... LeightonAspell 87+
(John Allen) *hld up: smooth hdwy after 6th: rdn after 2 out: sn one pce* **8/1**[3]

02-5 **7** *3* **Complete Outsider**[16] 4561 8-11-4 102.......... JoeTizzard 91
(Nick Williams) *hld up in tch: tk clsr order 7th: rdn and effrt after 2 out: sn btn* **8/1**[3]

2PP2 **8** *dist* **Manawanui**[24] 4429 8-10-11 95.......... RobertWalford —
(R H Alner) *prom tl after 5th: grad fdd: t.o fr 2 out* **7/4**[1]

0000 **9** *8* **Rift Valley (IRE)**[16] 4561 11-11-9 110..........(v) TomMalone(3) —
(P J Hobbs) *led tl after 5th: wknd after next* **20/1**

3645 **P** **Hilarious (IRE)**[28] 4331 6-10-0 84.......... JamieGoldstein —
(Dr J R J Naylor) *prom tl 3rd: sn wknd: p.u after 5th: b.b.v* **8/1**[3]

4m 33.3s (-12.70) **Going Correction** -0.45s/f (Good) **10** Ran SP% **114.6**

Speed ratings: **107,106,106,105,105 103,102,—,—,—** CSF £64.85 CT £1514.27 TOTE £9.20: £2.80, £3.90, £6.00; EX 119.40.

Owner Business Money Limited **Bred** Mrs I Lefroy **Trained** Brayford, Devon

FOCUS

The second-last was missed out here after being broken earlier on.

NOTEBOOK

Businessmoney Jake, a dual winner before the new year, made it a double on the day for the Dartnall/Heard team, bouncing back to his best on the back of a break. Winning here off a mark of 108, he remains open to a little improvement at the age of five, and could follow-up if kept on the go. *(op 15-2)*

Mister Chatterbox(IRE) ◆, who failed to shine on his handicap debut when tailed off at Exeter last month, ran a much better race here and pushed the winner right the way to the line. Running off a mark of 90, he will probably go up a couple of pounds, but should still be well enough weighted to pick up a small contest. *(op 11-1 tchd 12-1)*
Buffalo Bill(IRE), still 8lb higher than when winning at Warwick last season, ran a shocker when last seen at Fontwell back in January, but this was better and a little leniency from the Handicapper may see him winning again. *(op 16-1)*
Hail The King(USA) travelled with his usual gusto, but he does not often find a great deal for pressure and he failed to last out over this trip. *(tchd 11-1)*
Shalati Princess has been running well in lesser events and this was a respectable effort back up in grade. *(op 16-1)*
Manawanui was never travelling and failed to build on his recent Exeter second, possibly finding the ground too lively. *Official explanation: jockey said gelding was unsuited by good ground (op 9-4 after 10-3 in a place, 3-1 and 11-4 in places, tchd 5-2 and 13-8)*
Hilarious(IRE) was reported to have broken blood-vessels. *Official explanation: jockey said mare bled from nose (op 11-2)*

4757 CAPTAIN RONNIE WALLACE HUNTERS' CHASE (17 fncs) 2m 7f 110y
5:15 (5:16) (Class 6) 5-Y-O+ £1,977 (£608; £304)

Form RPR
1 **Highway Oak**[19] 10-12-0 .... MrMGMiller(3) 112+
(Ben White) *chsd ldrs: led 4th: 7 l clr 3 out: rdn appr last: idled and wnt lft 50yds out: drvn out* **7/1[3]**
11/0 2 ½ **Kestick**[20] [4471] 11-12-3 .... MissTCave(5) 112
(Mrs R Kennen) *mid div: stdy hdwy fr 11th: rdn appr 3 out: wnt 2nd at the last the last: styd on* **7/2[2]**
1 3 ¾ **Deep Pockets (IRE)**[16] [4560] 7-12-8 .... MrJSnowden 111
(Mrs Caroline Keevil) *mid div: hdwy after 10th: cl up whn hit 12th: sn pushed along : 4th and rdn appr 3 out: styd on flat* **11/8[1]**
4 ½ **La Griffe (IRE)**[26] 10-11-10 ....(t) MrTVaughan(7) 107+
(Mrs Abbi Vaughan) *led tl 4th: chsd wnr: rdn after 4 out: 2nd and looked hld whn nt fluent 2 out: no ex: lost 2nd at the last* **33/1**
43P0 5 9 **Fear Siuil (IRE)**[14] [4594] 13-11-10 88 ....(t) MrRBliss(7) 97
(Michael Blake) *hld up towards rr: mstke 7th: sme hdwy whn mstke 13th: styd on fr 3 out but nvr trbld ldrs* **50/1**
354- 6 ½ **Bush Park (IRE)**[18] 11-11-10 .... MrRTory(7) 96
(Mrs Monica Tory) *chsd ldrs tl outpcd 13th: nt a danger after* **16/1**
/12- 7 12 **Springford (IRE)**[11] 14-12-7 .... MrDAlers-Hankey(3) 91
(Mrs Caroline Keevil) *mid div: hit 7th and 10th: sn bhd* **10/1**
U **Rogue River**[410] 6-11-10 .... MrGLoader(7) —
(W G M Turner) *wl bhd whn blnd and uns rdr 5th* **33/1**
506/ P **Rosemead Tye**[12] 10-11-3 .... MrJMahot(7) —
(T Jewitt) *mstke 7th: a bhd: t.o and p.u bef 12th* **100/1**
-0P4 P **Jabiru (IRE)**[25] [4397] 13-12-5 96 ....(b) MrDEdwards(3) —
(Mrs K M Sanderson) *chsd ldrs tl after 10th: sn t.o: p.u bef 2 out* **16/1**
/26- P **West Paces (IRE)**[12] 12-11-10 .... MissETory(7) —
(S Dixon) *nvr fluent: blnd 1st: hit 6th: a bhd: tailed and p.u bef 12th* **16/1**
4P-4 P **Nickit (IRE)**[54] 10-12-0 ....(v[1]) MissAGoschen(3) —
(Mrs Susan Smith) *in tch: hit 3rd: mstke 7th: sn bhd: t.o and p.u bef 12th* **40/1**
P522 P **Mister Club Royal**[16] [4560] 10-12-1 82 .... MrMMunrowd(7) —
(Miss Emma Oliver) *chsd ldrs: mstke 13th: sn wknd: bhd and p.u bef 3 out* **20/1**

5m 57.8s (-7.30) **Going Correction** -0.45s/f (Good) **13** Ran SP% **119.6**
Speed ratings: **94,93,93,93,90 90,86,—,—,— —,—,—** CSF £31.09 TOTE £8.80: £2.10, £1.40, £1.20; EX 47.70.
Owner M White **Bred** M White **Trained** Hardington Moor, Somerset

FOCUS
A good hunter chase and, although the front four finished bunched, the form looks strong.

NOTEBOOK
Highway Oak ◆, successful in his last two points, was hanging on for dear life as they crossed the line as, having taken it up going towards the last, he idled on the run-in and nearly threw it away. He is clearly a very promising sort and, with the useful-looking Deep Pockets only managing third, it is likely it was a decent effort. He is one to keep on the right side of. *(tchd 6-1)*
Kestick, who ran a little better than his finishing position suggests in the Cheltenham Foxhunter's, found this easier and kept on well to hassle the winner after the last, but he was unable to get past. *(op 11-2)*
Deep Pockets(IRE), who did it impressively at Exeter last month, was not beaten far in third, but it was slightly disappointing he was unable to follow up and maybe the faster ground did not suit. *(op 6-4 and 13-8 in places)*
La Griffe(IRE) ran better than his price entitled him to and it was only in the final furlong that he began to tire, having been up there throughout. *(op 25-1)*
Fear Siuil(IRE) made a little late headway and ran better than could have been expected, but he is unlikely to be winning at this stage of his career. *(op 33-1)*

4758 PAS SOUND & COMMUNICATION INTERMEDIATE OPEN NATIONAL HUNT FLAT RACE 2m 1f
5:50 (5:50) (Class 6) 4-6-Y-O £2,055 (£599; £299)

Form RPR
4 1 **Kelv**[8] [4667] 5-11-4 .... JasonMaguire 94+
(J A B Old) *mde all: rdn clr over 2f out: drifted lft ins fnl f: drvn out* **1/2[1]**
0 2 1½ **Gandy Dancer (IRE)**[47] [3983] 6-10-6 .... SamCurling(5) 83
(Miss E C Lavelle) *hld up in 4th: wnt 2nd 1/2-way: jnd wnr 4f out: rdn over 3f out: reponded wl to press over 1f out: sn edgd rt: kpt on* **9/4[2]**
3 dist **Bricos Boy (IRE)** 5-11-4 .... JoeTizzard —
(Miss C J Williams) *chsd ldrs tl lost tch w ldng pair 7f out: btn 88 l* **7/1[3]**
P P **Wotabirthday**[125] [2611] 4-10-12 .... RJGreene —
(S C Burrough) *chsd wnr tl wknd rapidly 1/2-way: sn t.o and p.u* **25/1**

4m 1.30s (-7.30) **Going Correction** -0.45s/f (Good)
WFA 4 from 5yo 5lb 5 from 6yo 3lb **4** Ran SP% **113.8**
Speed ratings: **99,98,—,—** CSF £2.11 TOTE £1.60; EX 2.30 Place 6 £210.33, Place 5 £50.86.
Owner Peter Guntrip **Bred** J R Heatley **Trained** Barbury Castle, Wilts

FOCUS
A massively depleted field, with ten withdrawals mainly due to the drying ground, leaving Kelv with a fairly straightforward task.

NOTEBOOK
Kelv, who shaped well when fourth here on debut, had little left to beat with all the defections and he galloped on resolutely to win in workmanlike fashion. He will obviously need to raise his game if he is to defy a penalty, but that is not an impossibility. *(tchd 4-6)*
Gandy Dancer(IRE) appeared to step up on her initial effort on the Lingfield Polytrack, but she was receiving plenty of weight from the winner and it is hard to evaluate just what she achieved. *(tchd 11-4)*
Bricos Boy(IRE) was a mile adrift of the front two and is evidently going to struggle. *(op 9-1 tchd 11-2)*
Wotabirthday, who broke blood-vessels when pulling up on his debut, again stopped quickly and clearly has problems. *Official explanation: jockey said gelding bled from nose (op 16-1 tchd 12-1)*

T/Plt: £399.90 to a £1 stake. Pool: £44,567.30. 81.35 winning tickets. T/Qpdt: £21.20 to a £1 stake. Pool: £3,985.40. 138.80 winning tickets. TM

4745 AINTREE (L-H)
Friday, April 7

OFFICIAL GOING: Hurdle course - good to soft (good in places); mildmay & grand national courses - good (good to soft in places)
The rain the previous afternoon resulted in ground described as 'on the soft side of good, softer than that in places on the National course'.
Wind: Fresh, half-against Weather: Overcast and breezy.

4759 JOHN SMITH'S MILDMAY NOV CHASE GRADE 2 (19 fncs) 3m 1f (Mildmay)
2:00 (2:11) (Class 1) 5-Y-O+
£45,616 (£17,112; £8,568; £4,272; £2,144; £1,072)

Form RPR
2311 1 **Star De Mohaison (FR)**[23] [4444] 5-11-0 153 ....(t) BJGeraghty 152+
(P F Nicholls) *lw: a.p: trckd ldr 6th: led 11th: rdn appr last: styd on* **11/4[1]**
1325 2 2 **Turpin Green (IRE)**[22] [4456] 7-11-5 142 .... TonyDobbin 153+
(N G Richards) *hld up in tch: reminders 10th: chsd wnr 3 out: mstke next: hung lft flat: kpt on* **8/1[3]**
1212 3 2 **Copsale Lad**[22] [4456] 9-11-5 143 .... MarcusFoley 149+
(N J Henderson) *lw: hld up: hit 15th: hdwy and hung lft fr 3 out: rdn and nt fluent last: no ex* **8/1[3]**
1225 4 13 **Zabenz (NZ)**[23] [4444] 9-11-2 141 ....(b) RichardJohnson 132
(P J Hobbs) *w ldr tl led 3rd: hdd next: remained handy tl wknd after 4 out* **14/1**
311 5 4 **Montgermont (FR)**[48] [3976] 6-11-9 143 .... MarkBradburne 140+
(Mrs L C Taylor) *lw: hld up: hdwy 8th: hit 10th and 13th: chsd wnr 4 out: rdn and wknd after 2 out* **9/1**
41F 6 20 **Olney Lad**[41] [4112] 7-11-2 131 .... RussGarritty 116+
(Mrs P Robeson) *hld up: hit 13th: a bhd* **40/1**
13B4 P **Roman Ark**[22] [4459] 8-11-2 132 .... AndrewThornton —
(J M Jefferson) *prom to 13th: p.u bef 4 out* **40/1**
2110 P **Napolitain (FR)**[22] [4459] 5-11-0 138 .... RWalsh —
(P F Nicholls) *chsd ldrs: hit 8th: wknd 12th: bhd whn p.u bef 14th* **20/1**
F22U U **Tighten Your Belt (IRE)**[45] [4035] 9-11-2 138 .... AlanO'Keeffe —
(Miss Venetia Williams) *hld up: blnd and uns rdr 5th* **33/1**
14P P **Crozan (FR)**[48] [3976] 6-11-7 .... MickFitzgerald —
(N J Henderson) *prom: rdn and lost pl after 11th: t.o whn p.u bef 4 out* **16/1**
5/01 P **Lordofourown (IRE)**[33] [4271] 8-11-9 .... MrRWidger —
(S Donohoe, Ire) *tall: lw: hld up: a bhd: rdn 7th: t.o whn p.u bef 14th* **100/1**
1U U **Bold Bishop (IRE)**[23] [4444] 9-11-7 146 .... APMcCoy —
(Jonjo O'Neill) *replated bef s: mid-div: rdn 11th: sn lost pl: in rr whn hmpd and uns rdr 12th* **8/1[3]**
5-1P P **Commercial Flyer (IRE)**[23] [4444] 7-11-2 ....(t) TimmyMurphy —
(M C Pipe) *hld up: hdwy appr 4 out: sn rdn and wknd: j. bdly rt and hit 2 out: sn p.u* **13/2[2]**
2546 F **Kerryhead Windfarm (IRE)**[33] [4271] 8-11-5 .... AndrewJMcNamara —
(Michael Hourigan, Ire) *rangy: lw: hld up: hit 8th: rdn 11th: in rr whn fell next* **50/1**
1236 P **Bewleys Berry (IRE)**[23] [4444] 8-11-2 141 .... GLee —
(J Howard Johnson) *led: mstke 2nd: hdd next: led 4th to 6th: wknd after 4 out: bmpd next: bhd whn p.u bef last* **14/1**

6m 32.2s (1.80) **Going Correction** +0.325s/f (Yiel)
WFA 5 from 6yo+ 8lb **15** Ran SP% **118.1**
Speed ratings: **110,109,108,104,103 96,—,—,—,— —,—,—,—,—** CSF £22.37 TOTE £3.70: £1.70, £2.60, £2.80; EX 22.20 Trifecta £108.60 Pool: £3,029.57 - 19.80 winning tickets..
Owner Sir Robert Ogden **Bred** J Veau **Trained** Ditcheat, Somerset
■ Star de Mohaison became the first horse to complete the SunAlliance/Mildmay double since Monsieur le Cure in 1994.

FOCUS
A good novice chase, run at a sound pace after the start was delayed by 11 minutes. The highly progressive Star de Mohaison improved again on his splendid SunAlliance win, but there were several disappointing efforts behind and this still leaves him some 20lb off Gold Cup level.

NOTEBOOK
Star De Mohaison(FR) ◆, such an impressive winner of the Royal & SunAlliance Chase at Cheltenham, had to work harder to follow up under his Grade One penalty but improved once again. He was taken on for the lead but he again jumped fluently and saw off his rivals before idling going to the final fence. Once the placed horses got within striking distance he picked up again, and he never looked likely to be caught. Still only five, he has the potential to make up into a Gold Cup contender next season if making the expected improvement, although connections are adamant he doesn't want it too soft. *(op 10-3 tchd 7-2)*
Turpin Green(IRE), who disappointed when jumping moderately at the Festival, was more at home on this track, where he had won on his previous two visits over hurdles, and gave the winner a race. He looked a big danger turning in but spoilt his chance when hitting the penultimate fence before running on again. This was his first attempt at the trip and he got it well enough. Effective on most ground, he should make up into a decent handicapper next season.
Copsale Lad ◆, who finished ahead of today's runner-up in the Jewson at Cheltenham, was 7lb worse off. Held up to get the trip, the impression was his jockey overdid the waiting tactics as he still had at least ten lengths to make up turning in before an effort was made after the third last. He then reduced the margin to about three lengths at the final fence but landed flat-footed and had nothing left to give. He may not have quite got home, but it would have been interesting to see how he had fared under more positive tactics. *(tchd 15-2)*
Zabenz(NZ), fifth behind today's winner in the Royal & SunAlliance, ran a similar race and finished eight lengths closer on 8lb better terms, giving substance to the form. He does not look that well treated handicap-wise at present, but is the sort to win a decent staying handicap next season once re-assessed. *(tchd 16-1)*
Montgermont(FR) ◆, whose recent good efforts have been with more cut in the ground, ran really well despite making jumping errors. He was on the heels of the winner turning in, but then weakened out of contention. Like the winner he has age on his side, and with his ability to stay three miles and handle much more testing ground proven, could develop into the natural successor to the yard's Hennessy winner Gingembre next season. *(op 11-1)*
Bold Bishop(IRE), who had to be re-plated twice before the start, may well have been placed in the Royal & SunAlliance had he not been hampered. However, he was never really travelling this time and was behind when suffering the same fate as at the Festival. *(op 17-2 tchd 9-1)*
Crozan(FR) has gone backwards since making an impressive debut in this country at Cheltenham in the autumn. He has a fair bit to prove now, but he may need more time to acclimatise. *(op 17-2 tchd 9-1)*
Commercial Flyer(IRE), who disappointed in the Royal & SunAlliance, having won impressively on his chasing debut, produced another disappointing effort and has something to prove now. *(op 17-2 tchd 9-1)*

Bewleys Berry(IRE) ◆, despite pulling up, ran much better than the bare facts suggest for a yard that has been out of sorts for much of the season. A bold jumper, it would be no surprise to see him improve considerably with another summer behind him. *(op 17-2 tchd 9-1)*
Napolitain(FR), the only five-year-old in the race other than the winner, showed up early, but he *was struggling soon after giving the cross fence a mighty smack on the first circuit. (op 17-2 tchd 9-1)*

4760 CITROEN C6 SEFTON NOVICES' HURDLE GRADE 1 (13 hdls) 3m 110y
2:35 (2:43) (Class 1) 4-Y-0+
£51,318 (£19,251; £9,639; £4,806; £2,412; £1,206)

Form RPR
1111 **1** **Black Jack Ketchum (IRE)**[21] 4469 7-11-4 150................. APMcCoy 165+
(Jonjo O'Neill) *lw: hld up: hdwy to trck ldrs 9th: chal on bit 3 out: led between last 2: shkn up and qcknd clr run-in: eased nr fin: impressive* **8/13**[1]
111 **2** *5* **Money Trix (IRE)**[19] 4530 6-11-4 .... TonyDobbin 148
(N G Richards) *chsd ldrs: effrt appr 3 out: styd on to take 2nd nr fin* **12/1**
1211 **3** *½* **Neptune Collonges (FR)**[48] 3969 5-11-4 148........... ChristianWilliams 148+
(P F Nicholls) *set mod pce: qcknd 8th: hdd between last 2: kpt on same pce* **8/1**[2]
2142 **4** *12* **Powerstation (IRE)**[21] 4469 6-11-4 .... DNRussell 137+
(C Byrnes, Ire) *hld up: hdwy to chse ldrs after 10th: wknd appr last* **14/1**
2416 **5** *13* **Ungaro (FR)**[23] 4446 7-11-4 135.................................. PCarberry 122
(K G Reveley) *lw: hld up in last: hit 6th: hdwy 10th: nvr nr ldrs* **25/1**
3110 **6** *9* **Glasker Mill (IRE)**[23] 4443 6-11-4 130.......................... TimmyMurphy 113
(Miss H C Knight) *chsd ldrs: drvn along after 7th: lost pl after 9th* **40/1**
1212 **7** *25* **Gungadu**[48] 3993 6-11-4 140...................................... RWalsh 88
(P F Nicholls) *trckd ldrs: outpcd 9th: sn lost pl* **10/1**[3]
0213 **8** *12* **Rathowen (IRE)**[48] 3969 7-11-4 120.............................. MichalKohl 76
(J I A Charlton) *prom: pushed along 7th: lost pl and hmpd next: sn bhd* **200/1**
2123 **F** **Travino (IRE)**[21] 4469 7-11-4 .... JLCullen —
(Ms Margaret Mullins, Ire) *hld up towards rr: fell 8th* **12/1**
11 **P** **Hard Act To Follow (IRE)**[83] 3381 7-11-4 .... GLee —
(J Howard Johnson) *lw: trckd ldrs: lost pl appr 3 out: sn bhd and p.u* **33/1**
0422 **P** **Sharajan (IRE)**[27] 4373 6-11-4 124........................ RobertThornton —
(A King) *lw; chsd ldrs: outpcd 9th: sn lost pl: t.o whn p.u bef last* **100/1**
6m 19.1s (2.70) **Going Correction** +0.25s/f (Yiel) **11** Ran SP% **114.9**
Speed ratings: **105,103,103,99,95 92,84,80,—,— —** CSF £8.51 TOTE £1.60: £1.10, £2.40, £2.20; EX 8.80 Trifecta £84.00 Pool: £3,773.59 - 31.88 winning tickets..
Owner Mrs Gay Smith **Bred** E Morrissey **Trained** Cheltenham, Gloucs

FOCUS
Just a steady gallop and a tactical event, but the winner could hardly have been more impressive. Rated value for 17l, he is an outstanding novice and he could go to the very top, despite his lack of size.

NOTEBOOK
Black Jack Ketchum(IRE) ◆ may not be very big but he has a real engine. Never out of third gear, he came there running away and could hardly have won more easily, looking value for at least three times the winning margin. Next year's World Hurdle looks the logical long-term target, but it would be foolish to rule him out of the Champion Hurdle. *(tchd 4-6)*
Money Trix(IRE) ◆, taking a big step up in class, never gave up the fight and showed much-improved form to snatch second spot near the line. He will not run again this time but is a grand type should make a fine chaser next season. *(op 14-1 tchd 16-1)*
Neptune Collonges(FR) ◆, racing on much less testing ground, had his own way in front. He wound up the gallop, but it was clear the winner was simply toying with him and he lost out on second spot near the line. He will not run over hurdles again and looks another exciting prospect when put back over fences. *(op 15-2)*
Powerstation(IRE), who chased home the winner at Cheltenham, moved into contention on the *final turn but tired badly going to the final flight. His busy season seems to have caught up on* him. *(op 16-1)*
Ungaro(FR), likely to be suited by the step up to three miles, had plenty to find and was simply not up to the task. *(op 20-1)*
Glasker Mill(IRE) didn't match his Cheltenham effort but he too looks a chasing prospect for next term.

4761 JOHN SMITH'S MELLING CHASE GRADE 1 (16 fncs) 2m 4f (Mildmay)
3:10 (3:16) (Class 1) 5-Y-0+ **£85,932** (£32,487; £16,467; £8,412; £4,422)

Form RPR
1463 **1** **Hi Cloy (IRE)**[13] 4625 9-11-10 .... AndrewJMcNamara 165+
(Michael Hourigan, Ire) *lw: trckd ldr: led 4 out: kpt on gamely run-in: hld on towards fin* **14/1**
U212 **2** *¾* **Fota Island (IRE)**[23] 4445 10-11-10 .... APMcCoy 162
(M F Morris, Ire) *lw: hld up: wnt prom 8th: chsd wnr fr 3 out: kpt on towards fin* **4/1**[2]
0354 **3** *13* **Mariah Rollins (IRE)**[48] 3999 8-11-3 .... RWalsh 142
(P A Fahy, Ire) *lw: in rr: hdwy 12th: wnt 3rd 3 out: wknd between last 2* **40/1**
2115 **4** *6* **Don't Be Shy (FR)**[24] 4431 5-11-6 158.......................... TimmyMurphy 143+
(M C Pipe) *nt fluent in rr: reminders and hdwy 12th: wknd fr 3 out* **7/1**
13F3 **5** *2* **Strong Project (IRE)**[29] 4334 10-11-10 .... DNRussell 145+
(Sean O O'Brien, Ire) *mstkes: chsd ldrs: wkng whn blnd 11th: t.o 4 out* **66/1**
6-2U **P** **River City (IRE)**[23] 4445 9-11-10 147.......................... TomDoyle —
(Noel T Chance) *in rr: bhd whn hit 9th: p.u bef next* **16/1**
3414 **R** **Central House**[23] 4445 9-11-10 ....(v[1]) PCarberry —
(D T Hughes, Ire) *led: hdd and hit 4 out: wkng whn blnd next: t.o whn ref last* **7/1**
1133 **P** **Impek (FR)**[22] 4457 10-11-10 164.......................... PaulMoloney —
(Miss H C Knight) *trckd ldrs: wnt 2nd 7th: rdn 12th: sn wknd: bhd whn p.u bef last* **10/3**[1]
2333 **P** **Mister McGoldrick**[23] 4445 9-11-10 160.................. DominicElsworth —
(Mrs S J Smith) *chsd ldrs: hit 7th: lost pl next: bhd whn p.u bef 9th* **11/1**
0222 **P** **Jim (FR)**[48] 3999 9-11-10 .... RMPower —
(J T R Dreaper, Ire) *lw: chsd ldrs: blnd 5th: hmpd 7th: lost pl after next: bhd whn p.u bef 3 out* **12/1**
B131 **P** **Fondmort (FR)**[22] 4457 10-11-10 157...................... MickFitzgerald —
(N J Henderson) *lw: hld up in rr: drvn 8th: bhd whn blnd next: sn t.o: p.u bef 4 out* **6/1**[3]
5m 7.30s (-1.60) **Going Correction** +0.325s/f (Yiel)
WFA 5 from 8yo+ 4lb **11** Ran SP% **114.9**
Speed ratings: **116,115,110,108,107 —,—,—,—,— —** CSF £69.74 TOTE £18.70: £4.40, £1.80, £7.10; EX 89.80 Trifecta £2533.50 Part won. Pool: £3,568.41 - 0.50 winning tickets..
Owner Mrs S McCloy **Bred** Mrs Paul Finegan **Trained** Patrickswell, Co Limerick

FOCUS
A strongly-run Grade 1 but no Moscow Flyer this year and two-mile champion Newmill was another absentee. The runner-up looks the best guide in a below-par renewal.

NOTEBOOK
Hi Cloy(IRE), suited by the strong pace - he has won over three miles - went on at the cross fence, but he tended to idle in front and in the end had to be kept right up to his work. This was a new *personal best, and he could now head for the Guinness Gold Cup at Punchestown. (tchd 16-1 in a place)*
Fota Island(IRE), who took a handicap at this meeting a year ago, has never stopped improving *since and here he proved beyond doubt that he full stays this extended trip. He went down* fighting. *(op 5-1 tchd 11-2)*
Mariah Rollins(IRE), struggling to make an impact in her second season over fences, worked hard to get on to the heels of the first two but in the end she found them much too tough. This is probably as good as she is. *(op 33-1)*
Don't Be Shy(FR), a raw novice, clattered his way round in the rear. He tried hard to enter the picture but in the end was found sadly lacking. He will bounce back in the right grade. *(op 6-1)*
Strong Project(IRE) was unable to dominate, and as a result his jumping went to pieces. In the end he could only complete in his own time. *(op 50-1)*
Fondmort(FR), away from his beloved Cheltenham, was taken off his legs, and after a bad blunder his rider sensibly called it a day. Two miles five round Prestbury is made to measure for him and *he will be back there next term. Official explanation: trainer had no explanation for the poor form shown (tchd 13-2)*
Mister McGoldrick struggled after a mistake at the seventh. *(tchd 13-2)*
Impek(FR), who did not look anywhere near his best beforehand, was taken to post last. He took on the leader in a strongly-run race but he was unhappy leaving the back straight and was wisely pulled up. He will be back in the autumn. *(tchd 13-2)*
Central House set a fast and furious pace but when headed at the cross fence, which he hit, he stopped to nothing. Exhausted, he refused to take off at the last. *(tchd 13-2)*

4762 JOHN SMITH'S AND SPAR TOPHAM CHASE (H'CAP) (18 fncs) 2m 5f 110y
3:45 (3:51) (Class 2) (0-150,145) 5-Y-0+
£62,630 (£18,500; £9,250; £4,630; £2,310; £1,160)

Form RPR
0U50 **1** **Liberthine (FR)**[23] 4447 7-10-4 **130**.............. MrSWaley-Cohen[(7)] 147+
(N J Henderson) *chsd ldrs: chal 2 out: j.rt and led last: styd on gamely* **16/1**
1122 **2** *1 ½* **Hakim (NZ)**[70] 3596 12-10-6 **125**............................ PJBrennan 138
(J L Spearing) *hdwy to ld after 1st: mde most: hdd and bmpd last: no ex last 150yds* **13/2**[1]
3034 **3** *5* **Pak Jack (FR)**[27] 4378 6-10-0 **119** oh1........................ TimmyMurphy 127
(P J Hobbs) *hld up in mid-div: smooth hdwy to join ldrs 11th: nt qckn appr last* **25/1**
215P **4** *2 ½* **Dunbrody Millar (IRE)**[24] 4433 8-10-8 **127**.................... JamieMoore 133+
(P Bowen) *lw: led tl after 1st: w ldrs: kpt on same pce appr last* **16/1**
1F3F **5** *1 ½* **Euro Leader (IRE)**[22] 4459 8-11-9 **142**.......................... DJCasey 146
(W P Mullins, Ire) *bhd: styd on fr 3 out: nt rch ldrs* **20/1**
-004 **6** *5* **Cregg House (IRE)**[66] 3640 11-10-7 **126**........................ DNRussell 125
(S Donohoe, Ire) *lw: mid-div: hdwy 13th: kpt on fr 3 out: nvr trbld ldrs* **14/1**
-P0U **7** *5* **Polar Red**[20] 4496 9-10-4 **126**.......................................(t) TomMalone[(3)] 123+
(M C Pipe) *sn bhd: t.o 6th: styd on wl fr 3 out: nt rch ldrs* **33/1**
2340 **8** *1 ¼* **Lou Du Moulin Mas (FR)**[23] 4447 7-10-7 **126**.................(t) SamThomas 118
(P F Nicholls) *mid-div: hdwy to chse ldrs 7th: one pce fr 3 out* **25/1**
4640 **9** *hd* **Va Vavoom (IRE)**[24] 4433 8-10-0 **119**..........................(t) CarlLlewellyn 111
(N A Twiston-Davies) *mstke 3rd (Chair): bhd: hdwy 15th: styng on one pce whn blnd last* **33/1**
00P0 **10** *2 ½* **Mixsterthetrixster (USA)**[24] 4433 10-10-4 **123** ow3.... AndrewThornton 116+
(Mrs Tracey Barfoot-Saunt) *chsd ldrs: wknd after 2 out* **14/1**
10PP **11** *8* **Scots Grey**[23] 4447 11-11-2 **135**................................ MickFitzgerald 123+
(N J Henderson) *mid-div: hdwy to chse ldrs 8th: outpcd 15th: wknd 2 out* **66/1**
4260 **12** *17* **Le Passing (FR)**[22] 4459 7-11-12 **145**..............................(b) JoeTizzard 110
(P F Nicholls) *prom to 5th: sn lost pl* **33/1**
0223 **13** *10* **Better Days (IRE)**[48] 3988 10-10-8 **127**.................... DominicElsworth 82
(Mrs S J Smith) *chsd ldrs: j.lft and mstke 6th: wknd 9th* **10/1**[2]
5154 **14** *2* **Wain Mountain**[43] 4070 10-10-8 **127**............................(b) JasonMaguire 80
(J A B Old) *lw: mid-field: lost pl 7th: sn bhd* **28/1**
PP05 **15** *5* **The Bandit (IRE)**[13] 4617 9-10-1 **120**.......................... BarryFenton 68
(Miss E C Lavelle) *a in rr* **25/1**
1055 **16** *dist* **Sir Storm (IRE)**[48] 3974 10-10-0 **119** oh3..........................(p) BarryKeniry —
(G M Moore) *in tch to 8th: bhd fr 13th (Valentine's): t.o* **100/1**
P-P **17** *dist* **Lotomore Lad (IRE)**[26] 4400 8-10-0 **119** oh5..........................(t) JRBarry —
(Donal Hassett, Ire) *neat: w ldrs: lost pl after 4th (water): bhd fr 10th: hopelessly t.o* **33/1**
4323 **F** **Flight Command**[27] 4363 8-10-0 **119** oh1..........................(p) TomSiddall —
(P Beaumont) *mid-div: fell 1st* **66/1**
5130 **F** **Tamango (FR)**[22] 4459 9-10-13 **132**............................ RichardJohnson —
(P J Hobbs) *bhd whn fell 3rd (Chair)* **25/1**
0150 **F** **Star Clipper**[33] 4270 9-10-11 **130**.......................................(t) PCarberry —
(Noel Meade, Ire) *str: bhd whn fell 8th* **11/1**[3]
6522 **F** **Terivic**[29] 4323 6-10-0 **119** oh1................................. LeightonAspell —
(K C Bailey) *lw: w ldrs: fell 10th (Becher's): dead* **66/1**
U **Kings Glen (IRE)**[61] 3775 10-10-0 **119** oh3.......................... PACarberry —
(Thomas Carberry, Ire) *lw: in tch: blnd and uns rdr 8th* **16/1**
05-4 **B** **Burwood Breeze (IRE)**[28] 4356 10-10-0 **119** oh4..... WayneHutchinson —
(T R George) *chsd ldrs: b.d 10th (Becher's)* **80/1**
351P **F** **Almost Broke**[48] 3988 9-11-3 **136**.................................... RWalsh —
(P F Nicholls) *bhd: hmpd 3rd (Chair): fell 10th (Becher's)* **11/1**[3]
1P4P **U** **Dangerousdanmagru (IRE)**[66] 3661 10-10-6 **125**........... MarcusFoley —
(A E Jones) *bhd: hmpd and uns rdr 10th (Becher's)* **100/1**
00-0 **F** **The Last Cast**[62] 3739 7-10-11 **130**..........................(p) PaulMoloney —
(Evan Williams) *chsd ldrs: outpcd whn fell 10th (Becher's)* **66/1**
5211 **F** **Nycteos (FR)**[27] 4371 5-10-9 **132**............................ ChristianWilliams —
(P F Nicholls) *lw: mid-div: hdwy and prom whn fell 10th (Becher's)* **10/1**[2]
5FU0 **F** **I Hear Thunder (IRE)**[13] 4617 8-10-3 **122**................... BenjaminHitchcott —
(R H Buckler) *mid-div: whn prom 4th (water): fell 10th (Becher's)* **66/1**
B124 **F** **Be My Better Half (IRE)**[48] 3988 11-10-8 **127**................... APMcCoy —
(Jonjo O'Neill) *lw: mid-div: hdwy to chse ldrs 13th (Valentine's): fell 15th* **16/1**
5m 36.0s (-4.00) **Going Correction** +0.20s/f (Yiel)
WFA 5 from 6yo+ 4lb **29** Ran SP% **131.1**
Speed ratings: **112,111,109,108,108 106,104,104,104,103 100,94,90,89,87 —,—,—,—,— —,—,EM** CSF £101.03 CT £2659.20 TOTE £21.00: £4.90, £2.10, £7.30, £6.70; EX 186.20 TRIFECTA Not won..
Owner Robert Waley-Cohen **Bred** Benoit Gabeur **Trained** Upper Lambourn, Berks
■ A notable Aintree double for Sam Waley-Cohen, ruled out of the National because he has yet to ride the statutory 15 winners.

FOCUS
Liberthine was among the better handicapped runners but is a bit better than the bare result. It was a career best from the runner-up, and the third ran his best race for a while. The overall form is nothing special however. Becher's Brook reduced the field by seven.

NOTEBOOK

Liberthine(FR), warm beforehand as usual, was bang on the inside after Valentine's. Racing with real enthusiasm under a most capable ride, she collided with the runner-up at the final fence but would simply not be denied. She may now be retired to stud - a pity because she retains all her enthusiasm.

Hakim(NZ), who missed a beat at the anticipated start, is only small but he made jumping these big fences look simple. After collecting a bump from the winner at the last he never gave up fighting. A horse who needs a break between races, he will no doubt be back here in November for the Grand Sefton, which he took this term. *(op 7-1 tchd 15-2)*

Pak Jack(FR), appreciating the better ground, went round in cruise control. He looked a serious threat between the last two fences but in the end the first two saw it out the better.

Dunbrody Millar(IRE), first away from a tardy start, bounced back over a trip very much short of his best.

Euro Leader(IRE), a faller on two of his last three starts, seemed to find this trip too sharp even over these big fences. He was doing all his best work at the finish.

Cregg House(IRE), who took this in 2005 from a 2lb lower mark, has been in indifferent form so far this time but this was more encouraging. *(op 16-1)*

Polar Red, who took his chance in the National last year, seemed to sulk out of touch until deciding to put his best foot forward over the final three fences. *(op 40-1tchd 50-1 in a place)*

4763 JOHN SMITH'S IMAGINE APPEAL TOP NOVICES' HURDLE GRADE 2 (9 hdls) 2m 110y

4:20 (4:25) (Class 1) 4-Y-0+

£31,361 (£11,764; £5,890; £2,937; £1,474; £737)

Form				RPR
112	**1**		**Straw Bear (USA)**[24] 4430 5-11-3 142 .... APMcCoy (N J Gifford) *lw: hld up: hdwy 5th: led 3 out: clr last: comf* **2/1**[1]	159+
0-	**2**	*13*	**Conna Castle (IRE)**[26] 4401 7-11-3 .... BJGeraghty (James Joseph Mangan, Ire) *lw: chsd ldrs: ev ch 3 out: wknd last* **9/2**[3]	139+
3611	**3**	*5*	**The Duke's Speech (IRE)**[30] 4301 5-11-0 124 .... JasonMaguire (T P Tate) *lw: chsd ldrs: rdn and outpcd 3 out: styd on from next and went 3rd last* **100/1**	129
1311	**4**	*3*	**Senorita Rumbalita**[41] 4115 5-11-1 132 .... RobertThornton (A King) *hld up: hdwy 5th: mstke 3 out: sn rdn: wknd next* **10/1**	128+
2615	**5**	*nk*	**Circassian (IRE)**[83] 3388 5-11-0 122 .... GLee (J Howard Johnson) *prom: rdn whn hit 3 out: wknd next* **33/1**	126
135	**6**	*nk*	**Wanango (GER)**[40] 4137 5-11-8 .... WJLee (T Stack, Ire) *lw; hld up and bhd: sme hdwy appr 3 out: hmpd next: n.d* **66/1**	135+
1250	**7**	*3*	**Whispered Promises (USA)**[24] 4430 5-11-0 137 .... JohnMcNamara (R S Brookhouse) *chsd ldrs: ev ch appr 3 out: rdn and wknd next* **20/1**	123+
4	**8**	*6*	**Moon Over Miami (GER)**[13] 4621 5-11-0 .... NoelFehily (C J Mann) *lw: hld up: effrt appr 3 out: sn wknd* **66/1**	118+
P231	**9**	*12*	**Auenmoon (GER)**[19] 4527 5-11-0 120 .... MarkBradburne (P Monteith) *disp ld tl led 4th: hdd & wknd 3 out* **150/1**	104
1311	**10**	*2 1/2*	**Desert Quest (IRE)**[21] 4473 6-11-8 144 .... (b) RWalsh (P F Nicholls) *hld up: hdwy after 6th: mstke next: sn rdn and wknd* **11/4**[2]	112+
P41	**11**	*5*	**Yenaled**[26] 4388 9-11-0 .... PJBrennan (P S McEntee) *hld up: racd keenly: hdwy after 6th: wknd next* **300/1**	97
5431	**12**	*19*	**Temple Place (IRE)**[13] 4613 5-11-0 117 .... (t) StephenCraine (D McCain) *hld up: hdwy 6th: wknd bef next* **66/1**	78
2502	**13**	*7*	**Classic Role**[13] 4621 7-11-0 116 .... (b[1]) LeightonAspell (L Wells) *hld up: mstke 1st: a in rr* **100/1**	71
0F	**P**		**Arctic Cove**[32] 3912 5-11-0 .... WilsonRenwick (M D Hammond) *hld up: bhd fr 5th: t.o whn p.u bef 2 out* **400/1**	—
F211	**P**		**Bureaucrat**[18] 4551 4-10-8 135 .... RichardJohnson (P J Hobbs) *swtg: led to 4th: mstke and lost pl 5th: sn bhd: t.o whn p.u bef 3 out* **10/1**	—
1	**F**		**Welcome Stranger**[17] 4564 6-11-0 .... JamieMoore (G L Moore) *hld up: hit 4th and next: hdwy 6th: disputing 3rd and wkng whn fell 2 out* **14/1**	123

4m 2.40s (-2.20) **Going Correction** +0.25s/f (Yiel)

WFA 4 from 5yo+ 5lb **16** Ran SP% **118.4**

Speed ratings: **115,108,106,105,104 104,103,100,94,93 91,82,79,—,— —** CSF £10.69 TOTE £3.00: £1.50, £1.60, £12.90; EX 13.60 Trifecta £487.20 Pool: £4,117.27 - 6.00 winning tickets..

Owner John P McManus **Bred** Cyril Humphris **Trained** Findon, W Sussex

FOCUS

A high-class novice hurdle was turned into procession by the winner from the third-last flight. Straw Bear improved around a stone on his Cheltenham form and, although it might not be saying much, he can already be regarded the best British 2m hurdler. The third was also stepping up considerably, but the fourth, fifth and sixth all give the form a solid look.

NOTEBOOK

Straw Bear(USA) ◆, who looked unlucky to be caught close home in the Supreme Novices' at the Festival, gained compensation in impressive fashion. Tucked away off the pace, once he came through to lead the result was never in doubt and he drew right away from the second last. He could well attempt to supplement this success at Punchestown, where he is likely to get suitable ground, before a campaign next season that will be geared towards the Champion Hurdle. *(op 5-2 tchd 11-4 in a place)*

Conna Castle(IRE) ◆ has progressed nicely on testing ground over hurdles since the turn of the year, but seemed to handle this better surface well enough. He looked to be travelling as well as the winner when moving into contention, only to find that rival changing up a gear and leaving him for dead from two out. That said, he beat the rest well enough and, although it would be no surprise to see him taking his chance at Punchestown, he looks the type to develop into a good novice chaser next year. *(op 11-2)*

The Duke's Speech(IRE) ◆, who had won a couple of small novice hurdles in the north, stepped up considerably on those efforts. He won his bumpers on good and easy ground and that may well be the key to him. He would be very interesting if going for one of the novice events at Ayr later in the month, but ultimately should make up into a nice novice chaser for connections, who had the good chaser Aghawhadda Gold a few years ago. *(op 80-1)*

Senorita Rumbalita, who won a bumper at this meeting last year and was already a winner at this level, had to shoulder a 5lb penalty. She moved into contention looking likely to figure at the end of the back straight, but could not respond when the principals quickened. She looks capable of winning more good races and, if switching to fences next season, should be able to make hay against her own sex. *(op 9-1)*

Circassian(IRE) ◆, a stayer on that Flat who had disappointed on two attempts over longer trips over hurdles, ran with a fair amount of credit. His best Flat form was on a sound surface, so he could be the sort for a race such as the Betfred Swinton Hurdle at Haydock early next month. *(op 28-1 tchd 40-1)*

Wanango(GER), who has been lighlty raced since the autumn, ran well, having been out the back and then got impeded when staying on from the second last. He can be rated a little better than the form and, considering he was giving weight to all of those that finished in front of him, may have more to give on level terms. *(op 50-1)*

Whispered Promises(USA), eighth in the Supreme Novices', finished much further behind Straw Bear on this occasion and there appeared no excuses.

Desert Quest(IRE), winner of the County Hurdle at the Festival and on a roll prior to this, was held up as usual but, just when he was moving into contention, made a mistake at the first in the straight and stopped to nothing. It may be that he hurt himself or he has gone over the top, but he is much better than this performance indicates. *(op 3-1 tchd 5-2)*

Welcome Stranger, making only his second appearance over hurdles, had moved into contention but was beginning to feel the pinch when knuckling over and the second-last flight. He should be capable of winning good racs over hurdles. *(op 8-1 tchd 9-1 in places)*

Bureaucrat, the only four-year-old in the contest, found the ground against him and was unable to get an uncontested lead. He dropped away soon after halfway as if something was amiss. *(op 8-1 tchd 9-1 in places)*

4764 BETFAIR.COM H'CAP CHASE (19 fncs) 3m 1f (Mlldmay)

4:55 (4:58) (Class 2) 5-Y-0+

£31,315 (£9,250; £4,625; £2,315; £1,155; £580)

Form				RPR
1115	**1**		**State Of Play**[102] 2973 6-10-2 128 .... PaulMoloney (Evan Williams) *lw: led 3rd to 6th: led 13th: clr last: eased towards fin* **22/1**	156+
3402	**2**	*16*	**Lacdoudal (FR)**[22] 4457 7-11-12 152 .... RichardJohnson (P J Hobbs) *hld up: hdwy 11th: chsd wnr appr 3 out: rdn and wknd bef last* **13/2**[2]	160+
536U	**3**	*7*	**Aristoxene (FR)**[23] 4447 6-10-6 132 .... MarcusFoley (N J Henderson) *lw: hld up: mstkes 10th and 13th: hmpd 15th: styd on fr 3 out: nt trble ldrs* **40/1**	129+
1P24	**4**	*nk*	**Model Son (IRE)**[24] 4433 8-10-8 134 .... APMcCoy (P C Haslam) *hld up: hdwy and hit 13th: hit 15th: wknd 3 out* **5/1**[1]	132+
P000	**5**	*hd*	**Seebald (GER)**[24] 4433 11-10-11 137 .... (t) TomScudamore (M C Pipe) *lw: prom: rdn 13th: wkng whn mstke 3 out* **50/1**	133+
3050	**6**	*15*	**Supreme Prince (IRE)**[34] 4241 9-11-0 140 .... PJBrennan (P J Hobbs) *chsd ldrs: mstke 6th: rdn and wknd appr 2 out* **66/1**	120
P-60	**7**	*nk*	**Chauvinist (IRE)**[22] 4459 11-10-9 135 .... MickFitzgerald (N J Henderson) *swtg: chsd ldrs: led 6th to 13th: wknd appr 3 out* **20/1**	114
-200	**8**	*14*	**Tikram**[21] 4470 9-11-6 146 .... (b) JamieMoore (G L Moore) *mid-div: rdn after 11th: wknd 13th* **16/1**	111
44F6	**9**	*10*	**East Tycoon (IRE)**[22] 4459 7-10-2 128 .... (p) BrianHarding (Jonjo O'Neill) *hld up: rdn 12th: a in rr* **25/1**	83
21UF	**10**	*1 3/4*	**Ardaghey (IRE)**[22] 4460 7-10-8 134 .... (t) AntonyEvans (N A Twiston-Davies) *hld up: effrt and hit 4 out: sn wknd* **25/1**	87
4-P0	**11**	*dist*	**Whitenzo (FR)**[13] 4617 10-9-13 130 .... (t) MrJSnowden[(5)] (P F Nicholls) *lw: chsd ldrs: mstke 4th: hit 15th: wknd appr 3 out: j. slowly and rt next: virtually p.u run-in* **22/1**	—
1UP3	**U**		**Mckelvey (IRE)**[83] 3396 7-10-5 131 .... ChristianWilliams (P Bowen) *blnd and uns rdr 2nd* **16/1**	—
-1BF	**P**		**Joaaci (IRE)**[48] 3971 6-11-10 150 .... TimmyMurphy (M C Pipe) *lw: hld up: a bhd: t.o whn p.u after 11th* **8/1**[3]	—
-54P	**F**		**Limerick Boy (GER)**[21] 4470 8-11-3 143 .... SamThomas (Miss Venetia Williams) *prom to 14th: fell next* **18/1**	—
-P1P	**P**		**Dark'n Sharp (GER)**[132] 2492 11-10-11 137 .... WarrenMarston (R T Phillips) *mstkes: a in rr: t.o whn p.u bef 4 out* **66/1**	—
31/1	**P**		**Fair Prospect**[167] 1825 10-10-2 128 .... RWalsh (P F Nicholls) *lw: nt jump wl: hld up: hit 5th and 8th: t.o whn p.u bef 15th* **5/1**[1]	—
3410	**U**		**Billyvoddan (IRE)**[22] 4459 7-11-0 140 .... RobertThornton (H D Daly) *led 2nd to next: chsd ldrs: rdn 12th: wknd 15th: hmpd and uns rdr 2 out* **14/1**	—
F3P2	**P**		**Mount Clerigo (IRE)**[20] 4498 8-10-4 130 .... AlanO'Keeffe (V R A Dartnall) *led to 2nd: remained handy tl rdn and wknd 12th: blnd nxt: t.o whn p.u bef 3 out* **11/1**	—

6m 29.2s (-1.20) **Going Correction** +0.325s/f (Yiel) **18** Ran SP% **118.3**

Speed ratings: **114,108,106,106,106 101,101,97,93,93** —,—,—,—,— —,—,— CSF £143.22 CT £5621.84 TOTE £30.30: £4.30, £2.20, £12.40, £1.10; EX 148.10 Trifecta £1781.30 Part won. Pool: £2,508.96 - 0.10 winning tickets..

Owner William Rucker **Bred** Roland Lerner **Trained** Cowbridge, Vale Of Glamorgan

FOCUS

A decent handicap, but one that featured a number of out-of-form contenders and doubtful stayers. However it was run at a good pace and the inexperienced winner made a huge impression, scoring with plenty in hand after travelling strongly near the head of affairs throughout. Rated value for 20 lengths, this vastly improved form puts him upsides Darkness and The Listener among the top British staying novices and there is more still to come.

NOTEBOOK

State Of Play ◆, a decent winner of his first two chases in the autumn before being well beaten on quicker ground in the Grade One Feltham Novices' Chase at Christmas, had clearly benefited from the break and, always to the fore on the inside rail, jumping economically, galloped right away from his rivals in the straight to win as he pleased. He will go up a fair amount for this, but he is still unexposed and is already clearly a really smart staying novice. He is unlikely to run again this term but next season looks just the sort for the Welsh National, as there is more improvement in him when he steps up again in distance. *(tchd 25-1)*

Lacdoudal(FR), runner-up in the Ryanair Chase at the Festival, had to give weight away all round. He ran his usual honest race, but after chasing the winner into the straight, was left behind got as he very tired from the second last. He will not find it easy to win handicaps from his current mark. *(op 11-2 tchd 7-1)*

Aristoxene(FR), some of whose best efforts have been around Haydock's flat, left-handed circuit, ran better than of late on this similar track. However, he merely ran on past beaten horses to reach his final position, so it can hardly be said to have been a return to form.

Model Son(IRE), who has run so well in competitive handicaps of late, had the services of the champion jockey this time. However, he again did not help his chances with jumping errors and could not pick up in the latter stages. He has a future though and could well make up into a Welsh or Midlands National horse next season, when the more testing ground will not put so much pressure on his jumping. *(op 9-2)*

Seebald(GER), 7lb better off with Model Son for a near ten-length beating at Cheltenham, reduced the gap considerably. He is now 19lb lower than he was rated early last year, but although he is now being given a chance he still has a bit more to find to win again at this level.

Supreme Prince(IRE) has been below-par since running third to Impek here in the autumn and, although this was a bit better than of late, he was still beaten a fair way. Perhaps he will be better after a summer off, when connections can attempt an autumn campaign, possibly with the aid of some headgear.

Chauvinist(IRE), who has been relatively lightly raced of late, was made plenty of use of but dropped away from the turn in and is struggling for form at present.

Fair Prospect *Official explanation: trainer's rep said gelding had a breathing problem (op 15-2)*

Joaaci(IRE), who has not had the best of experiences in recent runs, was always out the back and pulled up early on the final circuit. He looked very useful at Cheltenham in January and is still young enough to bounce back when his stable finds some form. *Official explanation: trainer said gelding never travelled (op 15-2)*

4765 THE SPORTSMAN H'CAP HURDLE (LISTED RACE) (11 hdls) 2m 4f

5:30 (5:34) (Class 1) 4-Y-0+

£28,510 (£10,695; £5,355; £2,670; £1,340; £670)

Form	Pos	Dist	Horse	Jockey	RPR
1322	1		**Strangely Brown (IRE)**[23] 4446 5-11-0 **145**	BCByrnes(5)	152+
			(E McNamara, Ire) *lw: prom: hmpd and lost pl bnd after 5th: hdwy appr 3 out: rdn to ld bef last: r.o*	**10/1**	
0211	2	2	**Saltango (GER)**[8] 4678 7-9-11 **124** 4ex	WilliamKennedy(3)	130+
			(A M Hales) *chsd ldrs: rdn and ev ch 2 out: pckd last: styd on same pce*	**16/1**	
004B	3	1 3/4	**Penny Pictures (IRE)**[23] 4446 7-10-7 **133**	TimmyMurphy	134
			(M C Pipe) *hld up: hdwy 6th: ev ch 3 out: styd on same pce last*	**40/1**	
3110	4	2	**Zipalong Lad (IRE)**[21] 4469 6-10-2 **128**	PJBrennan	127
			(P Bowen) *led 2nd to next: chsd ldrs: rdn appr last: styd on same pce*	**16/1**	
0-P4	5	nk	**Back To Ben Alder (IRE)**[102] 2974 9-10-0 **126** oh6	MarcusFoley	125
			(N J Henderson) *chsd ldrs: lost pl 5th: r.o flat*	**66/1**	
P066	6	2 1/2	**Arrayou (FR)**[14] 4608 5-10-0 **126** oh6	(v) LeightonAspell	124+
			(O Sherwood) *hld up: hdwy 5th: outpcd 8th: styd on fr 2 out*	**100/1**	
6600	7	1/2	**Hasty Prince**[22] 4461 8-11-0 **140**	APMcCoy	137+
			(Jonjo O'Neill) *hld up: hdwy 8th: rdn appr 3 out: wknd flat*	**16/1**	
6210	8	1/2	**Alpha Royale (IRE)**[26] 4401 6-10-0 **126**	(b) DJCasey	122
			(C Byrnes, Ire) *neat: str: hld up: hdwy appr 3 out: wknd after next*	**8/1**[3]	
45/0	9	1 1/4	**Leaders Way (IRE)**[13] 4627 11-10-0 **129**	(p) RGeraghty(3)	123
			(T K Geraghty, Ire) *w'like: hld up: nvr nrr*	**100/1**	
3464	10	3/4	**Phar Bleu (FR)**[23] 4446 5-11-2 **142**	(t) RWalsh	136
			(P F Nicholls) *trckd ldrs: led after 3 out: hdd & wknd appr last*	**8/1**[3]	
3610	11	1/2	**Texas Holdem (IRE)**[41] 4110 7-9-9 **126** oh1	MichaelMcAlister(5)	119
			(M Smith) *led 3rd: mstke 7th: hdd after 3 out: wkng whn mstke last* **100/1**		
2240	12	5	**Lunar Crystal (IRE)**[21] 4473 8-10-4 **130**	TomScudamore	118
			(M C Pipe) *chsd ldrs: rdn appr 3 out: sn wknd*	**66/1**	
U550	13	1	**Akilak (IRE)**[23] 4446 5-10-9 **135**	GLee	122
			(J Howard Johnson) *trckd ldrs: racd keenly: ev ch 3 out: wkng whn hit next*	**33/1**	
11F1	14	1	**Motorway (IRE)**[14] 4608 5-10-0 **126**	RichardJohnson	112
			(P J Hobbs) *hld up: hdwy 7th: ev ch 3 out: wknd and eased next*	**7/1**[2]	
6224	15	1 1/4	**Pirate Flagship (FR)**[21] 4473 7-10-2 **128**	ChristianWilliams	113
			(P F Nicholls) *hld up: rdn after 8th: n.d*	**14/1**	
3110	16	2 1/2	**Bougoure (IRE)**[27] 4373 7-10-1 **127** oh4 ow1	DominicElsworth	109
			(Mrs S J Smith) *hld up: effrt appr 3 out: sn wknd: in rr whn blnd last* **50/1**		
4610	17	6	**Overstrand (IRE)**[41] 4110 7-9-9 **126** oh5	(b) TomGreenway(5)	104+
			(Robert Gray) *hld up: hdwy and edgd lft bnd after 5th: rdn and wknd appr 3 out*	**100/1**	
-250	18	1/2	**Blue Canyon (FR)**[22] 4458 8-11-12 **152**	BJGeraghty	128
			(F Doumen, France) *hld up: a in rr*	**66/1**	
	19	14	**Chelsea Harbour (IRE)**[43] 4083 6-10-0 **126** oh5	MissNCarberry	95+
			(Thomas Mullins, Ire) *str: mid-div: blnd 8th: sn wknd*	**40/1**	
2140	20	22	**Desert Air (JPN)**[23] 4446 7-11-0 **140**	(t) RJGreene	80
			(M C Pipe) *led to 2nd: rdn and wknd appr 6th*	**66/1**	
111	21	7	**Temoin**[35] 4215 6-11-0 **140**	MickFitzgerald	73
			(N J Henderson) *lw: hld up: hmpd bnd after 5th: n.d*	**9/4**[1]	
4130	U		**Mahogany Blaze (FR)**[21] 4468 4-10-0 **133** oh4	CarlLlewellyn	—
			(N A Twiston-Davies) *lw: mstke and uns rdr 2nd*	**20/1**	
1421	P		**Hernando's Boy**[7] 2716 5-10-0 **126** oh3	RichardMcGrath	—
			(K G Reveley) *prom tl rdn and wknd appr 3 out: bhd whn pu bef last* **40/1**		
2300	P		**Perle De Puce (FR)**[21] 4473 7-10-0 **133**	(p) MrSWaley-Cohen(7)	—
			(N J Henderson) *chsd ldrs: hit 5th: sn lost pl: t.o whn p.u bef 3 out* **100/1**		

4m 57.8s (-5.90) **Going Correction** +0.25s/f (Yiel)

WFA 4 from 5yo+ 6lb **24** Ran SP% **126.8**

Speed ratings: 121,120,119,118,118 117,117,117,116,116 116,114,113,113,112 111,109,109,103,94 92,—,—,**E** CSF £147.34 CT £6035.83 TOTE £11.30: £1.90, £4.00, £6.40, £3.40; EX 163.80 TRIFECTA Not won. Place 6 £80.36, Place 5 £44.47..

Owner We Didn't Name Him Syndicate **Bred** Barry Noonan **Trained** Rathkeale, Co. Limerick

FOCUS

Another competitive contest. It was run at a good gallop, but it was something of a rough race. Saltango's recent win had been upgraded amd Strangely Brown needed a personal best to beat him.

NOTEBOOK

Strangely Brown(IRE) is a tough, consistent sort who acts on any ground, and gained compensation for having finished runner-up in the Coral Cup at the Festival. Settled in the pack behind the leaders, he got involved in scrimmaging with the much bigger Temoin going out on the second circuit, but soon made his way back into contention. On the heels of the leaders turning in, he picked up best of all and never looked like being reeled in once getting to the front. He won a valuable Grade One at Auteuil last June, and it would be no surprise to see him turn up there after a trip to Punchestown. *(op 12-1)*

Saltango(GER) ◆ has been progressing steadily this winter, and this was another step up. Racing from 2lb out of the handicap despite a 4lb penalty, he raced handily throughout and was delivered to win his race, but found the classy winner too strong. There was no disgrace in this and, although the Handicapper is likely to put him up again, he could pick up a decent handicap while in this sort of form.

Penny Pictures(IRE), who was brought down behind today's winner at the Festival, had run his best race of the season over course and distance in the autumn. This was a return to something like that form and he kept on quite well without ever looking like winning. It is quite a while since he won over hurdles, but a drop of a few more pounds would make him interesting if this return to form can be sustained. *(op 50-1)*

Zipalong Lad(IRE) ◆, whose wins have been on softer ground, found this more to his liking than the Grade Two he contested at Cheltenham. He was up with the pace throughout and, after looking likely to drop away early in the straight, ran on again despite drifting right. He deserves plenty of credit for this performance, and looks one to bear in mind for novice chases on soft ground next season. *(op 14-1)*

Back To Ben Alder(IRE), having only his third race since this meeting last year and his first since December, ran a strange race but similar to how he had performed over Christmas. After showing up early he lost his place and looked set to finish tailed off on the home turn, but then ran on to such effect he nearly snatched fourth place. He was racing from 6lb out of the handicap and clearly retains ability, so it will be interesting to see if connections opt for some headgear next time to help him concentrate. *(op 50-1)*

Arrayou(FR) ran a similar race to Back To Ben Alder. He was in the pack when squeezed out and losing his pitch going onto the second circuit then looked to have little chance on the home turn before running on well in the straight to reach his final position. Good ground suits and he could well prove up to winning in lesser company. *(op 66-1)*

Hasty Prince has taken a big drop in the weights since the autumn, and put up a decent effort before tiring in the closing stages. This was something of a return to form, but he will not prove easy to place, even off his current mark.

Alpha Royale(IRE) *(tchd 15-2 and 9-1)*

Phar Bleu(FR), fourth behind the winner in the Coral Cup, travelled well for a long way but faded pretty quickly in the closing stages. He had reportedly had a wind operation before Cheltenham but on this evidence it may not have been altogether successful. *(op 11-1)*

Texas Holdem(IRE) showed up well for a long way, but got very tired in the closing stages and may be better ridden less positively.

Motorway(IRE), who has been tough and consistent this season, ran well to a point but seemed to find this longer trip beyond him and was wisely allowed to come home in his own time when beaten. If kept on the go a race like the Swinton Hurdle may be on the agenda. *(op 6-1)*

Pirate Flagship(FR) represented the County Hurdle form in this contest, but after losing his place early on the second circuit he finished up well beaten. He was beaten too early for the trip to have been a factor and may just have had enough for the time being.

Temoin, unbeaten in three runs over hurdles, was all the rage in the betting market. However, he was never travelling that well and, after getting into a barging match with the winner and Alpha Royale turning away from the stands seemed to lose enthusiasm for the job. He had looked potentially better than this previously and can be given a chance to atone. *(op 5-2)*

T/Jkpt: Not won. T/Plt: £51.20 to a £1 stake. Pool: £295,346.41. 4,205.25 winning tickets. T/Qpdt: £38.70 to a £1 stake. Pool: £11,849.60. 226.10 winning tickets. CR

4766 - 4772a (Foreign Racing) - See Raceform Interactive

4759 AINTREE (L-H)

Saturday, April 8

OFFICIAL GOING: Good to soft

The rain had got into the ground. The rails on the bends on the Mildmay track had been moved in, on the hurdles course out with the hurdles on the outside.

Wind: Strong, half-against Weather: Rain first race, then changeable and blustery

4773 JOHN SMITH'S EXTRA SMOOTH H'CAP HURDLE (LISTED RACE) (9 hdls) 2m 110y

1:45 (1:45) (Class 1) 4-Y-0+

£28,510 (£10,695; £5,355; £2,670; £1,340; £670)

Form	Pos	Dist	Horse	Jockey	RPR
3311	1		**Wellbeing**[18] 4561 9-10-2 **121**	PJBrennan	144+
			(P J Hobbs) *lw: hld up: hdwy appr 3 out: led 2 out: r.o wl*	**7/1**	
0012	2	9	**Noble Request (FR)**[22] 4473 5-11-5 **138**	RichardJohnson	146+
			(P J Hobbs) *hld up: hdwy appr 3 out: ev ch next: no ex last*	**9/1**	
2252	3	6	**Double Vodka (IRE)**[20] 4527 5-9-7 **119** oh10	PhilKinsella(7)	120
			(C Grant) *hld up: effrt appr 3 out: styd on same pce fr next*	**66/1**	
6-46	4	5	**Monte Cinto (FR)**[28] 4375 6-10-6 **125**	RWalsh	121
			(P F Nicholls) *hld up: hdwy appr 3 out: rdn and wknd bef last*	**6/1**[2]	
0-	5	hd	**Beautiful Vision (IRE)**[86] 3363 6-10-8 **127**	BJGeraghty	123
			(T J Taaffe, Ire) *chsd ldrs: hit 6th: wknd appr last*	**10/1**	
0020	6	nk	**Dusky Warbler**[22] 4473 7-11-7 **140**	(p) JamieMoore	138+
			(G L Moore) *hld up in tch: rdn appr 3 out: wknd appr last*	**12/1**	
UF-2	7	2	**Bound**[15] 4608 8-10-8 **127**	(t) LeightonAspell	122+
			(Mrs L Wadham) *hld up: hdwy appr 3 out: wkng whn mstke last*	**16/1**	
2222	8	1	**Saif Sareea**[22] 4478 6-10-0 **119**	PadgeWhelan	113+
			(R A Fahey) *chsd ldrs: mstke 6th: wknd appr last*	**20/1**	
1-30	9	1/2	**Lord Henry (IRE)**[22] 4473 7-10-1 **125**	MrTJO'Brien(5)	117
			(P J Hobbs) *led: rdn and hdd 2 out: sn wknd*	**20/1**	
50P	10	2 1/2	**Salut Saint Cloud**[36] 3993 5-10-1 **120**	(p) PhilipHide	112+
			(G L Moore) *hld up: hdwy 6th: rdn and wknd appr last*	**28/1**	
5-00	11	3 1/2	**Bongo Fury (FR)**[10] 4663 7-10-9 **128**	(v) TomScudamore	114
			(M C Pipe) *lw: chsd ldr: rdn appr 3 out: wknd next*	**40/1**	
12	12	5	**Neveesou (FR)**[43] 4097 5-10-9 **128**	TimmyMurphy	109
			(M C Pipe) *hld up in tch: rdn and wknd appr 3 out*	**13/2**[3]	
P-PP	13	3/4	**Astronomic**[70] 3618 6-11-4 **137**	GLee	117
			(J Howard Johnson) *plld hrd and prom: rdn and wknd appr 3 out*	**100/1**	
3333	14	3/4	**Pepe Galvez (SWE)**[15] 4608 9-10-2 **121**	(v[1]) MarcusFoley	101
			(Mrs L C Taylor) *hld up: mstke 4th: a in rr*	**33/1**	
3115	15	7	**Tarlac (GER)**[28] 4375 5-10-6 **125**	APMcCoy	98
			(N J Henderson) *lw: chsd ldrs: rdn and mstke 2 out: sn wknd: eased run-in*	**9/2**[1]	
0000	16	2	**Admiral (IRE)**[22] 4473 5-11-12 **145**	PCarberry	116
			(T J Pitt) *lw: hld up: rdn 5th: a bhd*	**50/1**	
1110	P		**Nippy Des Mottes (FR)**[62] 3761 5-10-6 **130**	(t) LiamHeard(5)	—
			(P F Nicholls) *swtg: hld up: a in rr: t.o whn p.u bef last*	**16/1**	

4m 18.3s (13.70) **Going Correction** +0.725s/f (Soft) **17** Ran SP% **119.6**

Speed ratings: **96,91,88,86,86 86,85,84,84,83 81,79,79,78,75 74,—** CSF £61.64 CT £3826.02 TOTE £5.80: £1.80, £2.70, £4.10, £2.30; EX 29.10 Trifecta £1594.90 Part won. Pool: £2,246.38 - 0.40 winning tickets..

Owner Gillian, Lady Howard De Walden **Bred** Lord Howard De Walden **Trained** Withycombe, Somerset

FOCUS

It was noticeable that there was a lack of early pace, and even allowing for alterations to the course and overnight rain, a time almost 16 seconds slower than that recorded by Straw Bear 24 hours earlier in the novice race was striking, to say the least. At least 12 of the field were covered by three lengths jumping the second last, but nothing was going to beat the very easy winner Wellbeing, who has been rated value for 15 lengths and has been raised another 17lb on RPRs.

NOTEBOOK

Wellbeing ◆, raised 11lb for his last success, moved into the race with ominous ease at the top of the straight before running right away from his rivals after the second last. By far his most impressive performance over timber to date, he has rediscovered some of his classy Flat form of yesteryear and has options of a race at Punchestown as well as the Swinton Hurdle before the end of the season. He also received a quote of 50/1 for next year's Champion Hurdle, but he would need to find another 20lb to be a serious contender and hardly has youth on his side.The trainer suggested that he might go chasing in any case, but whatever his future, he is one to follow until beaten. *(op 6-1)*

Noble Request(FR), who would have been a clear-cut victor without the winner, tried in vain to chase down Wellbeing in the final stages, but could never reel him back in. He had absolutely no chance giving weight to a well-treated winner, but still ran a good race, confirming the impression that he is now improving with every run. The Swinton Hurdle looks the most obvious race for him before the end of the season, where he should get his preferred ground. *(op 8-1)*

Double Vodka(IRE), who was a useful sort on the Flat, ran well above his best form over timber, keeping on really strongly throughout the final stages after being pushed along coming around the final turn. He has yet to win a race over hurdles but has been unlucky on at least one occasion.

Monte Cinto(FR) came with a promising effort up the straight but did not go through with his effort as looked likely, though a mistake at the second-last did not aid his cause. He has struggled over hurdles since being raised to a mark in the 120s, but he would have appreciated a stronger pace and still looks the sort who will do well over fences next season. *(op 13-2 tchd 7-1)*

Beautiful Vision(IRE) always looked to go a stride faster than his jockey wanted him to for most of the race, but still held every chance entering the home straight. However, once his jockey got serious with him, he found less than expected off the bridle, probably due to the way he travelled during the race. Only lightly raced in his native Ireland, he has scope for improvement and will be winning more races. *(tchd 11-1)*

Dusky Warbler has become a really hard ride for his jockey, and probably has more talent than he cares to show. A mistake at the third-last did not help him, but he kept on fairly well for strong pressure to finish just behind the placed horses. It would be interesting to see if a switch to chasing next season would see him recapture some of his best hurdling form. *(op 10-1)*

Bound confirmed the promise of his last run, which came after a huge absence, and may well have finished a place closer had he not made a bad error at the last. *(op 14-1)*

Saif Sareea raced with plenty of zest during the early stages and did well to finish as close as he did. He has enjoyed a good season for his small stable and can still be competitive off this mark in slightly less-exacting company. *(op 16-1)*

Lord Henry(IRE), who has run in some hot races despite having very little experience, was again was far too keen for his own good in the early stages. He has plenty of scope still and would probably be an even better prospect if learning to settle.

Neveesou(FR) moved nicely on the outside of the field in the early stages, but was readily left behind when the race took shape. It was yet another disappointment for a stable that has been struggling for winners recently. *(op 7-1 tchd 15-2)*

Tarlac(GER), made favourite for every run he has had in England, was quite keen in the early stages and dropped out of contention disappointingly after making a mistake at the second-last hurdle. The rise in the weights, the lack of early pace and the slightly quicker ground than he has been used to during the winter all probably contributed to his effort. *(tchd 4-1 and 5-1 in places)*

4774 JOHN SMITH'S MAGHULL NOV CHASE GRADE 1 (12 fncs) 2m (Mildmay)

2:15 (2:15) (Class 1) 5-Y-0+

£62,722 (£23,529; £11,781; £5,874; £2,948; £1,474)

Form					RPR
2-13	**1**		**Foreman (GER)**[25] [4431] 8-11-4	APMcCoy	164+
			(T Doumen, France) *trckd ldrs: hit 9th: wnt 2nd after 3 out: led sn after last: styd on*	**4/1**[2]	
1111	**2**	*1*	**Voy Por Ustedes (FR)**[25] [4431] 5-11-1 162	RobertThornton	160+
			(A King) *trckd ldrs: led 3 out: hdd after last: kpt on wl*	**10/11**[1]	
21F6	**3**	*13*	**Le Volfoni (FR)**[10] [4663] 5-11-1 141	JoeTizzard	146
			(P F Nicholls) *lw: led to 2nd: outpcd and lost pl 10th: rallied 2 out: tk modest 3rd nr fin*	**40/1**	
1521	**4**	*1 ¾*	**Hoo La Baloo (FR)**[28] [4377] 5-11-1 147	RWalsh	146+
			(P F Nicholls) *hld up in last: hdwy 9th: tk modest 3rd last: one pce*	**15/2**	
2110	**5**	*5*	**Green Tango**[22] [4472] 7-11-4 143	RichardJohnson	143+
			(H D Daly) *t.k.h: led 2nd tl 3 out: wknd between last*	**11/1**	
213F	**6**	*22*	**Accordion Etoile (IRE)**[25] [4431] 7-11-4	JLCullen	132+
			(Paul Nolan, Ire) *lw: t.k.h: wl in tch whn blnd bdly and lost pl 9th: nt rcvr: eased run-in*	**7/1**[3]	
1310	**P**		**Cerium (FR)**[25] [4431] 5-11-1 144	(t) PJBrennan	—
			(P F Nicholls) *nt fluent: w ldrs: lost pl 3 out: p.u bef next*	**50/1**	

4m 12.3s (11.30) **Going Correction** +0.80s/f (Soft)
WFA 5 from 7yo+ 3lb **7** Ran SP% **109.4**
Speed ratings: **103,102,96,95,92 81,—** CSF £7.74 TOTE £5.40: £2.20, £1.40; EX 10.30.
Owner John P McManus **Bred** Mrs B Neumann **Trained** France

FOCUS

A much smaller field than the one that lined up for the Arkle at Cheltenham, but the winner and third of that race turned up, giving the race a classy feel. Cheltenham form was reversed, with Foreman staying much closer to the pace than he had done in the Arkle, and showing all his battling qualities to hold on in a tight finish. Voy Por Ustedes jumped with his usual zest and lost very little in defeat. They were both well clear of the third, and Foreman has been rated behind only Ashley Brook among recent winners of this race.

NOTEBOOK

Foreman(GER) was possibly given a bit too much to do last time in the Arkle and reversed form with Voy Por Ustedes under a determined Tony McCoy ride. Showing admirable battling qualities up the home straight, he found plenty for pressure and always just had too many guns for the runner-up after the last. The jockey believed that the slight ease in the ground helped, while his smooth jumping of fences has always been an asset in the short time he has raced over them. He has the potential to a serious Champion Chase contender next season, but will need to be ridden *much closer to the pace than he was in the Arkle to make use of his stamina. (op 7-2 tchd 9-2 in a place)*

Voy Por Ustedes(FR) always moved sweetly during the race, as he usually does, and looked to be going really well at the top of the home straight. However, he faced a stern challenge by Foreman over the final three fences and never quite got back on terms after being headed. He met the winner on slightly worse terms than he had done at Cheltenham, but he lost little in defeat after a brilliant season and should take high rank amongst the two-mile chasers next season. *(op Evens)*

Le Volfoni(FR), sharpened up by a run over hurdles last time, kept on well after becoming outpaced turning for home. He was easily beaten by Foreman at Lingfield earlier in the season and is clearly not going to make it at the top level over a two-mile trip, but the way he stayed on suggests a step back up in trip by four furlongs, probably for new connections as the current owners have a policy of selling their horses, will pose him few problems and give him plenty of options. *(op 33-1)*

Hoo La Baloo(FR), held up in the rear for a second time after showing plenty of decent form when making the running, moved into contention before the third-last, looking to be going really well. However, when the pressure was applied, he emptied out really quickly and never landed a blow. *He is likely to take up an engagement at Sandown at the end of the season before having a break. (op 8-1 tchd 7-1)*

Green Tango , who was slightly disappointing in the Grand Annual Chase at the Cheltenham Festival last time, soon took up the running and jumped well in front for much of the race. He held his place for a long time but was readily left behind when the classier types made their moves three from home. Things will be tough for him next season off his current mark and he might not be easy to place unless he can handle a step back up in trip, which would at least give his trainer more options. *(op 12-1)*

Accordion Etoile(IRE) never got the opportunity to get involved in the Arkle after falling at a relatively early stage. He again ruined any chance he had with a really bad error at the fourth-last whilst still travelling on the bridle. He will need to eradicate the jumping errors if he is to make it at the top level over fences. *(op 6-1 tchd 5-1 in places)*

Cerium(FR) was going backwards when pulled up before the second-last. He was wearing a tongue tie for the first time, as the trainer was said to be worried about his wind, and may have been suffering from a problem. He is one to remember if having a wind operation during the summer given his trainer's success with those types in the past.

4775 SCOTTISH AND NEWCASTLE AINTREE HURDLE GRADE 1 (11 hdls) 2m 4f

2:50 (2:50) (Class 1) 4-Y-0+

£85,530 (£32,085; £16,065; £8,010; £4,020; £2,010)

Form					RPR
12F	**1**		**Asian Maze (IRE)**[25] [4432] 7-11-0	RWalsh	165+
			(Thomas Mullins, Ire) *lw: mde all: qcknd 7th: styd on wl to forge clr appr last: rdn out*	**4/1**	
-103	**2**	*17*	**Hardy Eustace (IRE)**[25] [4432] 9-11-7	(v) CO'Dwyer	160+
			(D T Hughes, Ire) *lw: trckd ldrs: wnt 2nd 3rd: rdn 3 out: no imp*	**5/2**[1]	
5021	**3**	*7*	**Sky's The Limit (FR)**[24] [4446] 5-11-7	(v) BJGeraghty	151+
			(E J O'Grady, Ire) *hld up: wnt prom 5th: effrt 3 out: one pce whn blnd next*	**11/4**[2]	
0U10	**4**	*2*	**Kawagino (IRE)**[25] [4432] 6-11-7 147	JamieMoore	146
			(J W Mullins) *wnt prom 5th: drvn and outpcd 8th: kpt on: no threat*	**125/1**	
-4F0	**5**	*18*	**Patriarch Express**[23] [4458] 9-11-7 158	DominicElsworth	128
			(Mrs S J Smith) *chsd ldrs: drvn along and outpcd 6th: lost pl next*	**16/1**	
1-14	**6**	*5*	**Al Eile (IRE)**[25] [4432] 6-11-7	TimmyMurphy	125+
			(John Queally, Ire) *in rr: mstke 4th: drvn and lost pl after next: bhd fr 8th*	**10/3**[3]	
4120	**7**	*25*	**Royal Shakespeare (FR)**[25] [4432] 7-11-7 150	TomScudamore	115+
			(S Gollings) *hld up: outpcd 7th: sn lost pl: bhd fr next: eased*	**40/1**	
P200	**P**		**Intersky Falcon**[25] [4432] 9-11-7 157	(bt) APMcCoy	—
			(Jonjo O'Neill) *prom: lost pl 6th: sn bhd: bhd fr 8th: p.u bef next*	**33/1**	
	P		**Timolino (GER)**[48] 8-11-7	PAJohnson	—
			(M Keller, Germany) *w'like: racd in last: mstke 4th: detached after next: t.o whn p.u bef 8th*	**200/1**	

5m 7.90s (4.20) **Going Correction** +0.725s/f (Soft) **9** Ran SP% **110.9**
Speed ratings: **120,113,110,109,102 100,90,—,—** CSF £13.85 TOTE £5.00: £1.50, £1.40, £1.50; EX 16.90 Trifecta £28.30 Pool: £3,598.60 - 90.00 winning tickets..
Owner Mrs C A Moore **Bred** Mrs C A Moore **Trained** Goresbridge, Co Kilkenny

FOCUS

A decent renewal of the Grade One feature. High-class form from Asian Maze, who made it a stiff test of stamina and was the only one who got home. She now heads to the ACC Bank Champion Hurdle at Punchestown at the end of the month to test her effectiveness at the minimum trip. Hardy Eustace, who will meet the winner again in Ireland, ran a bit below his best in defeat but Sky's The Limit was probably heading for a personal best when hitting the second-last hard.

NOTEBOOK

Asian Maze(IRE), receiving 7lb from her rivals, put up an outstanding performance under a strong front-running ride. The disappointment of her exit during the Champion Hurdle was banished as she steadily cleared away from her toiling opponents in the rain-affected ground, extending her advantage in a slow-motion finish the further she went. Connections still believe she is a live contender for honours at two miles and plan to drop her back to the minimum at Punchestown, where she would meet the runner-up again and probably Brave Inca. However, the Form Book strongly suggests otherwise, and she surely owed the wide margin of her success here to having outstayed her rivals in what developed into a real test of stamina.

Hardy Eustace(IRE) had no answer to the classy younger mare in the prevailing ground and ran around 8lb below his best. Although it should not be forgotten that he won a SunAlliance Hurdle over two miles five, his very best efforts have all been at two miles in the Champion Hurdle or the AIG Champion and he was outstayed here. He is an admirable sort and still more than capable of top-class form in the highest grade at that trip. *(op 11-4 tchd 9-4 and 3-1 in a place)*

Sky's The Limit(FR) ◆ was facing his stiffest task to date after a succesful season. His demolition of solid handicappers off top-weight in the Coral Cup showed him to be a very talented hurdler, and he ran a good race behind two top-class rivals. A clumsy mistake at the second-last ended the slim chance he had of claiming second, and he looked tired thereafter. He is due to go chasing next season and looks a fine prospect. *(op 5-2 tchd 3-1)*

Kawagino(IRE), who was a decent two-year-old on the Flat, is finding some amazing improvement from somewhere over timber, as he ran another fine race in the highest company. Although never having any chance of winning, he powered up the home straight for pressure, almost catching the weary Sky's The Limit in the process. It is safe to say that his last winning handicap mark of 108 is a distant memory, as he was raised to 147 after his run in the Champion Hurdle. Things will be incredibly tough for him but no doubt his connections will have enjoyed the fun he has given them in recent weeks. If he can sort his jumping out, a return to fences could see him have a more even chance of success.

Patriarch Express, like plenty in the race, was beaten by the time he was exiting the back straight. He has run some fair races without hitting the heights of the previous season, and he will surely be tried over fences next term. *(op 14-1)*

Al Eile(IRE) was a big disappointment, never getting into the race at any stage. Something must have been wrong with him as he was a fine fourth in the Champion Hurdle on his last run, and was defending a two-from-two record at the track, one of which was last season's renewal of this race *in which he beat the then reigning Ladbrokes World Hurdle winner Inglis Drever.Official explanation: jockey said gelding made a mistake and never travelled thereafter (op 3-1 tchd 7-2)*

Royal Shakespeare(FR) lost any chance he had when the rain fell overnight. He was not given a hard time. *(op 66-1)*

4776 JOHN SMITH'S EXTRA COLD H'CAP HURDLE (LISTED RACE) (13 hdls) 3m 110y

3:25 (3:25) (Class 1) 4-Y-0+

£28,510 (£10,695; £5,355; £2,670; £1,340; £670)

Form					RPR
1113	**1**		**Refinement (IRE)**[24] [4443] 7-10-12 **131**	(b) APMcCoy	147+
			(Jonjo O'Neill) *hld up: stdy hdwy 9th: led 2 out: rdn and styd on wl*	**11/4**[1]	
2-31	**2**	*3*	**Material World**[49] [3993] 8-10-6 **128**	ColinBolger[(3)]	137+
			(Miss Suzy Smith) *trckd ldrs: led 8th: j.rt and hdd 2 out: kpt on same pce*	**14/1**	
2340	**3**	*6*	**Mughas (IRE)**[24] [4446] 7-11-8 **141**	RobertThornton	144+
			(A King) *mid-div: drvn along 8th: hdwy 3 out: styd on same pce*	**16/1**	
P035	**4**	*7*	**Freetown (IRE)**[23] [4461] 10-10-9 **128**	(b) TonyDobbin	123
			(L Lungo) *chsd ldrs: one pce fr 2 out*	**16/1**	
111P	**5**	*1*	**Be Be King (IRE)**[63] [3727] 7-11-1 **134**	RWalsh	128
			(P F Nicholls) *hld up in rr: hit 8th: stdy hdwy next: effrt 3 out: wknd between last 2*	**13/2**[2]	
6426	**6**	*3*	**Rimsky (IRE)**[24] [4443] 5-10-11 **130**	(b) CarlLlewellyn	123+
			(N A Twiston-Davies) *hdwy 4th: sn chsng ldrs: wknd 2 out*	**14/1**	
5-01	**7**	*2*	**Albany (IRE)**[63] [3741] 6-10-7 **126**	GLee	115
			(J Howard Johnson) *chsd ldrs: drvn along after 10th: wknd 2 out*	**10/1**	
15/0	**8**	*6*	**Don Fernando**[23] [4461] 7-10-1 **127**	AndrewGlassonbury[(7)]	112+
			(M C Pipe) *hld up in rr: gd hdwy 9th: sn chsng ldrs: wknd 2 out*	**50/1**	
-000	**9**	*5*	**Mistanoora**[23] [4458] 7-11-7 **145**	(b) StevenCrawford[(5)]	126+
			(N A Twiston-Davies) *lw: chsd ldrs: rdn 3 out: wknd next: hit last*	**100/1**	
6-04	**10**	*dist*	**Liberman (IRE)**[23] [4461] 8-10-9 **128**	TimmyMurphy	—
			(M C Pipe) *in rr: t.o fr 8th: virtually p.u 10th: hopelessly t.o*	**14/1**	
3600	**F**		**Alikat (IRE)**[23] [4461] 5-10-12 **131**	(p) TomScudamore	—
			(M C Pipe) *in rr: fell 5th*	**50/1**	
5455	**P**		**Mythical King (IRE)**[4] [4497] 9-10-6 **125**	RichardJohnson	—
			(R Lee) *bhd and drvn 7th: p.u bef last*	**66/1**	
F000	**P**		**Campaign Trail (IRE)**[23] [4461] 8-10-11 **130**	(p) NoelFehily	—
			(Jonjo O'Neill) *bhd: t.o whn p.u after 8th*	**33/1**	
-F50	**P**		**Pole Star**[24] [4446] 8-11-7 **140**	PJBrennan	—
			(J R Fanshawe) *lw: prom: lost pl 8th: t.o whn p.u bef 3 out*	**28/1**	
0150	**P**		**Valley Ride (IRE)**[24] [4446] 6-11-4 **137**	TomDoyle	—
			(C Tinkler) *lw: prom to 8th: sn lost pl: t.o whn p.u bef 3 out*	**25/1**	

P **Dead Sound (IRE)**[42] 4125 6-10-13 **132**..............................(t) BJGeraghty —
(T J Taaffe, Ire) *chsd ldrs: wknd qckly appr 3 out: bhd whn p.u bef 2 out* **20/1**

-50P P **Loup Charter (FR)**[14] 4612 7-10-7 **126** ow1....................(t) SamThomas —
(Miss H C Knight) *mid-div: mstke 4th: bhd fr 7th: t.o whn p.u bef 3 out* **66/1**

P-F6 P **Paperprophet**[96] 3208 8-10-4 **130**.................................. EwanWhillans[(7)] —
(N G Richards) *mid-div: drvn along 7th: sn lost pl: t.o whn p.u bef 3 out* **33/1**

-012 P **Hordago (IRE)**[23] 4461 6-10-7 **131**....................................(p) BCByrnes[(5)] —
(E McNamara, Ire) *nvr gng wl: reminders and lost pl after 2nd: t.o whn p.u after 7th* **7/1**[3]

0121 P **Habitual Dancer**[21] 4491 5-10-11 **130**................................ BrianHarding —
(Jedd O'Keeffe) *led tl after 1st: lost pl appr 8th: t.o whn p.u bef 3 out* **25/1**

-130 P **Fair Question (IRE)**[24] 4446 8-10-11 **130**.......................... AlanO'Keeffe —
(Miss Venetia Williams) *lw: led after 1st: hdd 8th: sn lost pl: t.o whn p.u bef 3 out* **20/1**

6m 27.5s (11.10) **Going Correction** +0.725s/f (Soft) **21** Ran SP% **127.8**
Speed ratings: 111,110,108,105,105 104,103,102,100,— —,—,—,—,—,—,—,—,—,—,—
EM CSF £36.92 CT £557.96 TOTE £3.00: £1.30, £3.70, £5.60, £5.40; EX 52.70 Trifecta £2171.90 Part won. Pool: £3,059.10 - 0.90 winning tickets..
Owner Michael Tabor **Bred** M Tabor **Trained** Cheltenham, Gloucs

FOCUS
Something of a re-run of Cheltenham's Pertemps Final, but the most decisive winner emerged from another race at the Festival, the SunAlliance Novices' Hurdle. The form has a solid look, and has been rated through the third and fourth.

NOTEBOOK
Refinement(IRE), with the blinkers back on, jumped a shade left-handed at first but got better in that department as the race developed. She came there cruising but after an untidy jump at the last she had to be kept right up to her work against the strong headwind. The step up in distance suited her and this was improved form. She is already a prolific winner and there may be even better to come. *(op 3-1 tchd 100-30 in places)*
Material World went on with a circuit to go and soon had them strung out. She proved extra game and showed improved form, but the winner was simply too good for her. Though she has only one eye she should make a good-class novice chaser. *(op 12-1)*
Mughas(IRE), weighted to the hilt, ran right up to his best. He is not the biggest and it remains to be seen if he tries fences. *(tchd 18-1)*
Freetown(IRE), third in this in 2002, again gave a good account of himself in blinkers but this is as good as he is now.
Be Be King(IRE) ◆, absent for two months, was much happier on this ground. He travelled as well as the winner and made his move at the same time but he had no more to give between the last two. He should make a smart novice chaser next term. *(op 15-2)*
Rimsky(IRE), a novice, jumped better on this occasion but was still not nearly good enough. *(op 12-1)*
Albany(IRE) found a 7lb higher mark in a better-class race too much. *(op 11-1)*
Don Fernando, having his second race back after injury, went well for a long way and may be on the way back.
Hordago(IRE) never went a yard and something was clearly amiss. *Official explanation: jockey said gelding never travelled (op 9-1)*

4777 JOHN SMITH'S GRAND NATIONAL CHASE (H'CAP) GRADE 3 (30 fncs) 4m 4f (Gd National)

4:15 (4:20) (Class 1) 6-Y-0+

£399,140 (£149,730; £74,970; £37,380; £18,760; £9,380)

Form RPR

1-5B **1** **Numbersixvalverde (IRE)**[27] 4403 10-10-8 **138**.................. NPMadden 154+
(Martin Brassil, Ire) *lw: hld up: smooth hdwy 17th: sn trcking ldrs gng wl: led last: shaken up and styd on strly to forge clear* **11/1**

-422 **2** *6* **Hedgehunter (IRE)**[22] 4470 10-11-12 **156**................................ RWalsh 166+
(W P Mullins, Ire) *w ldrs: lft in ld 25th (2nd Valentine's): hdd last: no ex* **5/1**[1]

-531 **3** *1 ¼* **Clan Royal (FR)**[27] 4390 11-10-10 **140**.................................. APMcCoy 151+
(Jonjo O'Neill) *hld up: hdwy to chse ldrs 17th: blnd 19th: chal 3 out: rallied to take 3rd on line* **5/1**[1]

0P42 **4** *shd* **Nil Desperandum (IRE)**[22] 4483 9-10-7 **137**........................ TPTreacy 145
(Ms F M Crowley, Ire) *mid-div: hdwy to chse ldrs 20th: styd on same pce fnl 200yds* **33/1**

2S05 **5** *dist* **Risk Accessor (IRE)**[24] 4447 11-10-6 **136**........................ NoelFehily 114
(Jonjo O'Neill) *hld up: hdwy 13th: mstke 16th (water): sn chsng ldrs: wknd appr last* **66/1**

/60- **6** *16* **Puntal (FR)**[484] 2749 10-10-12 **142**..................................(t) BJGeraghty 97
(M C Pipe) *chsd ldrs: wknd 23rd (2nd Foinavon): kpt on fr 2 out* **66/1**

0440 **7** *2 ½* **Joes Edge (IRE)**[22] 4470 9-10-10 **140**................................ DNRussell 95
(Ferdy Murphy) *mid-div: hdwy 17th: mstke 19th: lost pl appr 2 out* **20/1**

1511 **8** *22* **Inca Trail (IRE)**[29] 4356 10-10-9 **139**..........................(b) BrianHarding 72
(D McCain) *hdwy after 16th (water): sn chsng ldrs gng wl: wknd 2 out: fin tired* **40/1**

-UPP **9** *3 ½* **Forest Gunner**[103] 2992 12-10-10 **140**........................ MissNCarberry 69
(R Ford) *mid-div: hdwy to chse ldrs 10th: wknd 27th* **33/1**

-FP2 F **Juveigneur (FR)**[25] 4433 9-10-9 **139**........................... MickFitzgerald —
(N J Henderson) *lw: fell 1st* **25/1**

0-11 F **Innox (FR)**[42] 4118 10-10-13 **143**.................................(b) RobertThornton —
(F Doumen, France) *fell 1st* **10/1**[3]

1520 F **Royal Auclair (FR)**[22] 4470 9-11-12 **156**...............(t) ChristianWilliams —
(P F Nicholls) *fell 1st* **33/1**

1F10 F **Ebony Light (IRE)**[49] 3971 10-10-10 **140**......................(p) StephenCraine —
(D McCain) *chsd ldrs: fell 5th* **50/1**

5000 P **Le Roi Miguel (FR)**[23] 4461 8-11-7 **151**................................(t) LiamHeard —
(P F Nicholls) *bhd tl p.u bef 19th* **150/1**

1F31 F **Ross Comm**[14] 4611 10-10-5 **135**................................ DominicElsworth —
(Mrs S J Smith) *in tch whn fell 4th* **16/1**

2140 U **Whispered Secret (GER)**[23] 4456 7-10-12 **142**...................... RJGreene —
(M C Pipe) *lw: blnd and uns rdr 1st* **100/1**

5000 P **Amberleigh House (IRE)**[19] 4549 14-10-9 **139**............................ GLee —
(D McCain) *chsd ldrs: bhd fr 7th: p.u bef 21st* **50/1**

-P4P U **Baron Windrush**[21] 4496 8-10-7 **137**.................................. CarlLlewellyn —
(N A Twiston-Davies) *blnd and uns rdr 3rd* **66/1**

3615 F **Haut De Gamme (FR)**[49] 3988 11-10-7 **137**........................ KeithMercer —
(Ferdy Murphy) *rr-div: sme hdwy 17th: fell 20th* **25/1**

5351 U **Jack High (IRE)**[22] 4483 11-10-7 **137**.................................. DJCasey —
(T M Walsh, Ire) *in rr tl blnd and uns rdr 15th (Chair)* **9/1**[2]

P360 F **Just In Debt (IRE)**[25] 4434 10-10-4 **134**........................ AlanDempsey —
(M Todhunter) *in rr whn fell 6th (1st Becher's)* **50/1**

P/64 F **Tyneandthyneagain**[49] 3971 11-10-7 **137**........................ PeterBuchanan —
(J Howard Johnson) *fell 1st: rn loose: dead* **100/1**

-4PP F **Silver Birch (IRE)**[42] 4105 9-10-12 **142**..............................(t) SamThomas —
(P F Nicholls) *in tch tl hmpd and fell 15th (Chair)* **40/1**

P-55 P **Colnel Rayburn (IRE)**[41] 4138 10-10-6 **136**............................. JLCullen —
(Paul Nolan, Ire) *bhd: mstke 16th (water): p.u bef 27th* **50/1**

-404 P **It Takes Time (IRE)**[49] 3977 12-11-8 **152**........................ TimmyMurphy —
(M C Pipe) *lw: hld up: mstke 8th: bhd whn p.u after 3 out* **50/1**

-624 U **Heros Collonges (FR)**[32] 4285 11-10-7 **137**................... JohnMcNamara —
(P F Nicholls) *lw: mid-div: hmpd and uns rdr 15th (Chair)* **66/1**

0-00 P **Iznogoud (FR)**[22] 4470 10-10-8 **138**................................ TomScudamore —
(M C Pipe) *mid-div: sme hdwy 13th: lost pl 16th: bhd whn p.u bef 27th* **200/1**

-02U U **Le Duc (FR)**[97] 3176 7-10-10 **140**.. JamieMoore —
(P F Nicholls) *mid-div: blnd, rdr lost iron and uns rdr 8th (1st Canal Turn)* **33/1**

-330 P **Cornish Rebel (IRE)**[22] 4470 9-11-9 **153**............................ JoeTizzard —
(P F Nicholls) *hld up: bhd whn hmpd 1st: j. slowly after: p.u bef 19th* **22/1**

0PP- P **Shotgun Willy (IRE)**[385] 4461 12-10-5 **135**..................(p) AndrewTinkler —
(R C Guest) *led to 9th (1st Valentine's): wknd 17th: p.u bef next* **33/1**

-001 P **Therealbandit (IRE)**[103] 2992 9-11-9 **153**................(p) RichardJohnson —
(M C Pipe) *chsd ldrs: mstke 16th (water): lost pl 26th: p.u bef next* **50/1**

65-4 R **Rince Ri (IRE)**[42] 4123 13-10-12 **142**........................ AndrewJMcNamara —
(T M Walsh, Ire) *lw: chsd ldrs to 22nd (2nd Becher's): bhd whn ref 27th* **100/1**

P020 P **Lord Of Illusion (IRE)**[22] 4470 9-10-11 **141**..................... JasonMaguire —
(T R George) *chsd ldrs: lost pl after 16th (water): p.u bef next: b.b.v* **33/1**

611F F **Sir Oj (IRE)**[23] 4457 9-10-10 **140**..(b) PCarberry —
(Noel Meade, Ire) *lw: mid-div: hmpd 15th (Chair): wl bhd whn fell 22nd (2nd Becher's)* **33/1**

60F5 P **Iris Royal (FR)**[49] 3995 10-10-6 **136**.................................... MarcusFoley —
(N J Henderson) *mid-div: j. slowly and lost pl 16th (water): bhd whn p.u bef next* **100/1**

5PUP U **First Gold (FR)**[49] 3971 13-10-10 **140**.........................(b) RichardMcGrath —
(F Doumen, France) *prom to 20th: bhd whn blnd and uns rdr 23rd (2nd Foinavon)* **100/1**

0350 F **Ballycassidy (IRE)**[22] 4470 10-10-9 **139**........................ LeightonAspell —
(P Bowen) *prom: led 9th (1st Valentine's): 6l clr whn fell 25th (2nd Valentine's)* **80/1**

4-F1 P **Direct Access (IRE)**[133] 2499 11-10-6 **136**........................ TonyDobbin —
(N G Richards) *in tch: mstke 7th (1st Foinavon): drvn along 12th: wknd 18th: p.u bef 19th* **25/1**

0253 R **Native Upmanship (IRE)**[55] 3895 13-11-0 **144**.................(b) CO'Dwyer —
(A L T Moore, Ire) *s.s: bhd: bdly hmpd 19th: hdwy 21st: j. bdly rt 26th: bhd whn ref next* **100/1**

6512 P **Garvivonnian (IRE)**[42] 4123 11-10-8 **138**.................................. GCotter —
(Edward P Mitchell, Ire) *lw: prom: lost pl 12th: mstke 15th (Chair): bhd whn p.u after 16th (water)* **11/1**

9m 41.0s (-379.5) **Going Correction** +1.00s/f (Soft) **40** Ran SP% **147.2**
Speed ratings: **117,115,115,115,— —,—,—,—,— —,—,—,—,— —,—,—,—,—** CSF £56.30 CT £337.70 TOTE £15.30: £3.80, £2.80, £2.40, £11.30; EX 98.90 Trifecta £401.30 Pool: £74,608.48 - 132.00 winning tickets..
Owner O B P Carroll **Bred** Major F B & J G B Boyd **Trained** Dunmurray, Co Kildare
■ Neither Martin Brassil or Niall 'Slippers' Madden had had a winner in Britain before.

FOCUS
A high-class renewal, with all forty runners running from the proper handicap. Numbersixvalverde, unexposed over extreme distances and campaigned largely over hurdles this season, showed much improved form to return the fifth Irish-trained winner in the last eight years. Hedgehunter reproduced last year's running but was slightly below his Gold Cup form. The first four finished miles clear. There was a false start after Ross Comm got his head over the tape, and a delay as the tape was repaired. Only Earth Summit and Red Marauder on heavy ground have recorded a slower time in the last ten years.

NOTEBOOK
Numbersixvalverde(IRE), last year's Irish National winner, was having just his eleventh start in chases. He really attacked these big fences, looking an Aintree natural, and he moved up simply running away. Sent to the front at the last, he finished as fresh as paint and was hardly blowing aftewards, giving trainer and jockey National glory at their first attempt. Red Rum was the last horse to win the National more than once, but if he returns in 12 months' time he will have better credentials than many of those who have failed in the interim.
Hedgehunter(IRE) was 12lb higher in the weights this year and had 11lb more on his back. Although dull in the paddock and from a stable without a winner for over a month, he hardly touched a fence. He was left in front at Valentine's second time, but in the end the winner was simply too strong for him on the run-in. The ground by now was not in his favour and he too will be back for another crack next year. *(op 11-2)*
Clan Royal(FR), seeking to make it third time lucky, somehow found a leg to save himself at the big ditch, the third fence on the second circuit. He found himself outpaced setting out up the long run-in but stuck to his task in willing fashion to snatch third spot on the line. He came back with a cut on his belly and was not asked to return to the unsaddling enclosure. A year older than the first two, his chance may have gone. *(op 11-2)*
Nil Desperandum(IRE), sixth last year, ran out of his skin on ground plenty soft enough for him and was only just caught for third. In his favour is that he is younger than the three ahead of him.
Risk Accessor(IRE), an early casualty on his two previous tries, gave a good account of himself but, after looking a real threat, he was dog tired when jumping badly right at the final fence and he finished some 37 lengths adrift of Nil Desperandum.
Puntal(FR), absent for 16 months, stopped to nothing at the Foinavon fence on the second circuit but got a second wind and stayed on to pass the three behind him at the line from two out.
Joes Edge(IRE), last year's Scottish National winner, was far from disgraced on ground too soft for him. He came back with cuts on his hind legs but hopefully will tackle the French Gold Cup at Auteuil in May. *(tchd 25-1 in a place)*
Inca Trail(IRE), having his first run for new connections, travelled strongly, but he emptied quickly after jumping two out and in the end struggled to reach the finishing line. This trip stretched him, but he took well to the fences and could be the type for the Becher Chase.
Forest Gunner, fifth last year, was running from a 4lb higher mark. He gave Nina Carberry a memorable ride but this trip is beyond him, especially on this ground. *(op 50-1)*
Amberleigh House(IRE), the 2004 winner, could never enter the argument this time and was wisely pulled up. He goes into honourable retirement, his eight other wins including two Graded races in Ireland and a Becher Chase. *(op 12-1 tchd 14-1 in places)*
Native Upmanship(IRE) was worst away at the second attempt after the false start, bringing back memories of Esha Ness and the void race in 1993. *(op 12-1 tchd 14-1 in places)*
First Gold(FR) is on the decline and all chance had long gone when he departed. The end of the road must be very close now. *(op 12-1 tchd 14-1 in places)*
Shotgun Willy(IRE), favourite when pulled up after breaking a blood-vessel in 2003, went well for a circuit and is due to reappear in the Scottish National. *(op 12-1 tchd 14-1 in places)*
Garvivonnian(IRE), who became upset beforehand, never looked like adding to his Becher Chase success. *(op 12-1 tchd 14-1 in places)*
Innox(FR), seventh last year, was one of a handful out of the contest at the very first fence this time. *(op 12-1 tchd 14-1 in places)*
Tyneandthyneagain fell at the first. He continued riderless but, ending up in the open ditch at the fourth last, was fatally injured. *(op 12-1 tchd 14-1 in places)*

Royal Auclair(FR) last year's runner-up and joint top-weight here, was on the deck at the first. *(op 12-1 tchd 14-1 in places)*

Ballycassidy(IRE) ◆, who is not very big, really enjoyed himself and held a useful advantage when tipping up at Valentine's second time round. Whether he would have held on is doubtful, but he will be of obvious interest if he turns up in the Betfred Gold Cup. *(op 12-1 tchd 14-1 in places)*

Jack High(IRE), runner-up in last year's Irish National, is not that big and was still biding his time when departing at The Chair. *(op 12-1 tchd 14-1 in places)*

Le Duc(FR) was unlucky to go out of the race at the Canal Turn first time round. *(op 12-1 tchd 14-1 in places)*

Ross Comm took a heavy fall at only the fourth fence. Happily he was reported none the worse. *(op 12-1 tchd 14-1 in places)*

Silver Birch(IRE) was a somewhat unlucky faller at The Chair. *(op 12-1 tchd 14-1 in places)*

4778 JOHN SMITH'S NOVICES' H'CAP CHASE (FOR AMATEUR RIDERS) (16 fncs) 2m 4f (Mildmay)

5:00 (5:03) (Class 2) 5-Y-0+ **£18,076** (£5,695; £2,881; £1,477; £772)

Form RPR

2112 **1** **Mon Mome (FR)**[24] 4447 6-11-5 **130** MrWBiddick(7) 143+
(Miss Venetia Williams) *chsd ldrs: led 10th: rdn appr last: styd on u.p* **15/2**[3]

2212 **2** *1 ½* **New Alco (FR)**[77] 3494 5-11-3 **125** MrROHarding 131
(Ferdy Murphy) *lw: chsd ldrs: ev ch 2 out: styd on u.p* **7/2**[1]

2F04 **3** *nk* **Direct Flight (IRE)**[23] 4456 8-11-7 **125** (t) MrTJO'Brien 135+
(Noel T Chance) *chsd ldrs: ev ch 2 out: sn rdn: no ex towards fin* **12/1**

6P1P **4** *10* **Lord Rodney (IRE)**[21] 4498 7-10-6 **117** MrSWByrne(7) 119+
(P Beaumont) *hit 1st: in rr: styd on flat: nt trble ldrs* **25/1**

52F6 **5** *dist* **Itsuptoharry (IRE)**[49] 3973 7-10-3 **114** MrRMcCarthy(7) —
(D McCain) *hld up: j.big and rdr lost iron 7th: effrt appr 4 out: sn wknd* **50/1**

1113 **F** **Roznic (FR)**[10] 4664 8-11-0 **121** MrGTumelty(3) —
(P Winkworth) *hld up in tch: fell 5th* **25/1**

2513 **P** **Alphabetical (IRE)**[29] 4355 7-10-9 **113** MrDHDunsdon —
(C J Mann) *hld up: a in rr: t.o whn p.u bef 4 out* **33/1**

3115 **F** **Bob The Builder**[25] 4433 7-11-3 **126** MrDEngland(5) —
(N A Twiston-Davies) *led to 5th: 2nd whn fell 7th* **15/2**[3]

F **Well Tutored (IRE)**[27] 4402 7-10-9 **113** MissNCarberry —
(A L T Moore, Ire) *hld up: hdwy 6th: mid-div whn fell 10th* **4/1**[2]

-1U6 **P** **Wicked Nice Fella (IRE)**[103] 2959 8-11-2 **120** MrTGreenall —
(C C Bealby) *hld up: bhd fr 10th: t.o whn p.u bef 3 out* **28/1**

62F1 **P** **Von Origny (FR)**[36] 4214 5-10-11 **124** MrPCallaghan(5) —
(H D Daly) *hld up: effrt appr 4 out: sn wknd: t.o whn p.u bef last* **10/1**

P **Nirvana Swing (FR)**[125] 5-10-12 **120** MrJSnowden —
(P F Nicholls) *str: hld up: hdwy 6th: wknd 11th: t.o whn p.u bef 3 out* **16/1**

35-0 **P** **New Field (IRE)**[34] 4270 8-11-11 **129** MrKEPower —
(Thomas Mullins, Ire) *hld up: hmpd 5th: hdwy 5 out: wknd 3 out: t.o whn p.u bef last* **9/1**

P **Symphonique (FR)**[305] 5-11-6 **133** MrSWaley-Cohen(5) —
(P J Hobbs) *w'like: lengthy: chsd ldr: sddle slipped and hit 3rd: led 5th: hdd 10th: wknd 5 out: t.o whn p.u bef 3 out* **16/1**

5m 19.0s (10.10) **Going Correction** +0.80s/f (Soft)
WFA 5 from 6yo+ 4lb **14** Ran SP% **120.3**
Speed ratings: **111,110,110,106,**— —,—,—,—,— —,—,—,— CSF £33.15 CT £321.53 TOTE £9.20: £2.80, £2.00, £3.90; EX 31.80 Trifecta £1558.50 Part won. Pool: £2,195.10 - 0.50 winning tickets..

Owner Mrs Vida Bingham **Bred** A Deschere **Trained** Kings Caple, H'fords

FOCUS

A solid-looking handicap in which the first three came well clear. It was run at a good pace and, despite the lack of finishers, the form ought to be solid.

NOTEBOOK

Mon Mome(FR) ◆, under a fine ride from his young amateur jockey, was in no mood to be passed all the way up the straight, and kept finding enough to repel the persistent challenges of the second and third. He has had a fine season and stays much further than two miles four, so his entry in the Scottish National looks very interesting. He is definitely one to consider if getting into the race. *(op 8-1 tchd 7-1)*

New Alco(FR) ◆, representing last season's winning connections, has not had much racing and performed with plenty of credit. He shaped as though he will appreciate a bit further and looks a progressive sort with time on his side. *(tchd 10-3)*

Direct Flight(IRE), who was a fine fourth in the Jewson Novices' Handicap at the Cheltenham Festival, gave his all up the straight but could never get past the tenacious leader. It was still a decent performance and he should win more races as long as his jumping problems do not resurface. *(op 11-1)*

Lord Rodney(IRE) kept on strongly up the straight but never had any chance of winning after losing his place very early in the race. *(op 20-1)*

Roznic(FR) took a heavy-looking fall early in the race. *(op 9-2 tchd 5-1 in places)*

Bob The Builder was still going well within himself when exiting in front of the stands on their first circuit. *(op 9-2 tchd 5-1 in places)*

New Field(IRE) was given an awful lot to do after being positioned towards the rear of the field. He moved smoothly into contention four from home, but the ground he had to make up to get into a challenging position clearly took its toll. He can be given another chance *(op 9-2 tchd 5-1 in places)*

Symphonique(FR) was pulled up quickly after making some of the running. Her saddle was found to have slipped. *(op 9-2 tchd 5-1 in places)*

Well Tutored(IRE) was still going well when getting the tenth fence all wrong, but it was too far out to know how he would have fared. *(op 9-2 tchd 5-1 in places)*

Nirvana Swing(FR), a huge horse, recently purchased from France, did not show a great deal on his first run for new connections and may possibly benefit from more time. It should also be noted that his best French form came when he was allowed to lead, something that never happened on this occasion. *(op 9-2 tchd 5-1 in places)*

Von Origny(FR) might not be the best ride for an amateur as he can take plenty of driving. He was struggling in the back straight on the final circuit and, although momentarily looking like getting back into things, soon weakened. *(op 9-2 tchd 5-1 in places)*

4779 JOHN SMITH'S CHAMPION STANDARD OPEN NATIONAL HUNT FLAT RACE GRADE 2 2m 1f

5:30 (5:33) (Class 1) 4-6-Y-0
£19,957 (£7,486; £3,748; £1,869; £938; £469)

Form RPR

2110 **1** **Pangbourne (FR)**[24] 4448 5-11-4 (be) RobertThornton 126
(A King) *chsd ldr: led 9f out: rdn and hdd over 2f out: sn outpcd: hung lft over 1f out: rallied u.p to ld nr fin* **28/1**

2 **2** *nk* **Tidal Bay (IRE)**[21] 4507 5-11-1 MichalKohl(3) 126
(J I A Charlton) *lw: hld up: hdwy over 2f out: rdn and hung lft ins fnl f: sn ev ch: styd on* **66/1**

113 **3** *1* **Kicks For Free (IRE)**[24] 4448 5-10-13 LiamHeard(5) 128+
(P F Nicholls) *hld up: hdwy over 3f out: rdn to ld over 1f out: hung rt and hdd towards fin* **4/1**[2]

111 **4** *nk* **Alfie Flits**[59] 3799 4-10-9 DougieCostello(3) 119+
(G A Swinbank) *w'like: medium-sized: lw: hld up: hdwy 6f out: led over 2f out: rdn and hdd over 1f out: styd on* **9/4**[1]

1102 **5** *5* **Sword Of Damascus (IRE)**[65] 3691 4-10-12 DominicElsworth 113
(D McCain) *prom: chsd wnr 1/2-way: rdn over 2f out: styd on same pce appr fnl f* **100/1**

11 **6** *1 ¼* **Ringaroses**[49] 3983 5-11-4 TimmyMurphy 118
(Miss H C Knight) *hld up: bhd and rdn 7f out: styd on fnl 2f: nvr nrr* **50/1**

21 **7** *2 ½* **Astarador (FR)**[86] 3353 4-10-12 GLee 110
(J Howard Johnson) *trckd ldrs: rdn over 2f out: wknd over 1f out* **40/1**

110 **8** *3* **Wichita Lineman (IRE)**[24] 4448 5-11-1 MrJPMagnier(3) 114+
(Jonjo O'Neill) *hld up: hdwy 10f out: wknd over 2f out* **12/1**

120 **9** *7* **Hennessy (IRE)**[63] 3742 5-11-4 CarlLlewellyn 106
(M Pitman) *hld up: bhd and rdn 10f out: nvr nrr* **50/1**

1 **10** *2* **Chaim (IRE)**[21] 4500 4-10-12 LeightonAspell 98
(Mrs L Wadham) *hld up: effrt over 4f out: sn wknd* **20/1**

1124 **11** *1 ½* **Heraldry (IRE)**[20] 4519 6-10-8 GaryBartley(10) 102
(P C Haslam) *chsd ldrs: rdn over 4f out: wknd over 2f out* **150/1**

12 *1 ¼* **Streetshavenoname (IRE)**[20] 4539 5-11-4 BJGeraghty 101
(T J Taaffe, Ire) *w'like: hld up: effrt over 3f out: sn wknd* **11/1**

1 **13** *2 ½* **Young Albert (IRE)**[107] 2948 5-11-4 TonyDobbin 98
(N G Richards) *lw: hld up: hdwy 10f out: rdn and wknd over 2f out* **25/1**

1-3 **14** *dist* **Round The Horn (IRE)**[84] 3392 6-11-4 JasonMaguire —
(J A B Old) *hld up: rdn and wknd over 4f out* **80/1**

13 **15** *½* **Pepporoni Pete (IRE)**[35] 4244 5-11-4 RWalsh —
(P F Nicholls) *lw: hld up: wknd 4f out: eased* **9/2**[3]

2 **16** *14* **Marine Life**[24] 4455 4-10-12 TomDoyle —
(P R Webber) *prom over 12f* **40/1**

1 **17** *5* **Sherwoods Folly**[46] 4038 4-10-12 RichardJohnson —
(H D Daly) *mid-div: rdn and lost pl after 4f: sn bhd* **50/1**

11 **18** *6* **Sir Jimmy Shand (IRE)**[24] 4455 5-11-4 MarcusFoley —
(N J Henderson) *prom over 11f* **22/1**

19 *7* **Pure Theatre (IRE)**[547] 1650 6-11-4 DNRussell —
(Eoin Griffin, Ire) *hld up: bhd fr 1/2-way* **20/1**

1 **20** *2 ½* **Mam Ratagan**[72] 3583 5-11-4 MickFitzgerald —
(N J Henderson) *hld up: sme hdwy 6f out: rdn and wknd over 4f out* **16/1**

1 **21** *18* **Risk Challenge (USA)**[16] 4595 4-10-12 PJBrennan —
(C J Price) *w'like: led 7f: sn rdn and wknd* **40/1**

01 **22** *dist* **Dancewiththedevil (IRE)**[19] 4554 5-11-4 (b[1]) NoelFehily —
(Jonjo O'Neill) *hld up: bhd fr 1/2-way* **50/1**

4m 17.2s (-0.40) **Going Correction** +0.725s/f (Soft)
WFA 4 from 5yo+ 5lb **22** Ran SP% **131.6**
Speed ratings: **113,112,112,112,109 109,108,106,103,102 101,101,100,—,— —,—,—,—,— —,E** CSF £1267.26 TOTE £45.30: £11.30, £31.10, £2.20; EX 1723.40 TRIFECTA Not won. Place 6 £22.57, Place 5 £5.60.

Owner Trevor Hemmings **Bred** Haras De Reuilly And Gerard Ben Lassin **Trained** Barbury Castle, Wilts

■ Hennessy, who finished unplaced, was Mark Pitman's last runner as a trainer.

FOCUS

A really strong running of the Champion Bumper, with plenty of winners taking part. Pangbourne is quirky but very talented. The runner-up improved for his debut effort, while the third and fourth give the form a solid look.

NOTEBOOK

Pangbourne(FR) put up another remarkable performance in only his first season of racing. Looking to be going nowhere but backwards with over a furlong to go, after leading into the home straight, he picked up as the eventual runner-up moved alongside him and found renewed enthusiasm to win all out. A horse that definitely has his quirks, he should get further when he goes over timber but will never be the safest of betting mediums. That said, the talent is there and he could easily make up into a decent sort if taking to hurdles. *(tchd 25-1)*

Tidal Bay(IRE), a chasing type, still had plenty to do at the top of the home straight, but came within an inch of a huge shock. The chances are that under stronger handling he would have gone one place better, but he still ran a big race for a once-raced horse and looks a really decent prospect for his small but capable yard. *(op 50-1)*

Kicks For Free(IRE) looked the clear winner passing the furlong pole, but hung right under pressure and gave away his advantage. He had not shown that tendency in the past so it was presumably tiredness that caused him to wander, even though he won on soft ground on his debut. Better ground will suit him much better and he looks sure to make up into a decent hurdler next season given his optimum conditions. *(tchd 9-2 in places)*

Alfie Flits had created a big impression in bumpers and looked to have a big chance as the race developed. However, he could not get away from his rivals when his jockey went for home and was passed before the furlong pole. A Flat campaign beckons for him and his astute trainer will no doubt place him to advantage in that sphere. *(op 5-2 tchd 11-4)*

Sword Of Damascus(IRE) has had a fine season for the McCain stable and produced a career-best effort. Bred to make a decent Flat horse, he should provide connections with plenty of fun next season over hurdles. *(op 150-1)*

Ringaroses ran with plenty of credit, making up masses of ground up the home straight. He will be better suited by further than two miles and will no doubt make up into a fair novice hurdler next season. *(op 40-1)*

Astarador(FR) had every chance coming into the straight but failed to get home as well as some. He looks a fair prospect and should win his share of hurdle races next season.

Wichita Lineman(IRE) has proved a disappointment in the Championship Bumpers at both Cheltenham and Aintree after looking a fair sort prior to that. He may well need much further than two miles when sent over hurdles. *(op 14-1)*

Hennessy(IRE), Mark Pitman's final runner as a trainer, was always towards the rear and never got into the race at any stage. *(op 66-1)*

Heraldry(IRE) looks a chasing type. *(tchd 100-1)*

Young Albert(IRE) is a real chasing type. *(op 28-1)*

Pepporoni Pete(IRE) has a big reputation but ran poorly. This was disappointing, but he may need better ground. *(op 6-1)*

Mam Ratagan, who won well on his debut, was firmly put in his place by some very decent bumper performers. He is, however, almost certainly a much better animal than this form suggests. *(op 12-1)*

T/Jkpt: Part won. £67,176.10 to a £1 stake. Pool: £94,614.25. 0.50 winning tickets. T/Plt: £22.40 to a £1 stake. Pool: £293,891.56. 9,552.85 winning tickets. T/Qpdt: £9.70 to a £1 stake. Pool: £16,873.30. 1,283.35 winning tickets. CR

[4569]CHEPSTOW (L-H)

Saturday, April 8

OFFICIAL GOING: Good to soft (soft in places)

Wind: Fresh, across

4780 JOHN SMITH'S EXTRA SMOOTH BEGINNERS' CHASE (16 fncs) 2m 3f 110y

2:00 (2:02) (Class 4) 5-Y-O+

£4,384 (£1,295; £647; £324; £161; £81)

Form RPR

U224 **1** **Give Me Love (FR)**[10] [4664] 6-10-9 119..............(bt) PaddyMerrigan(5) 109+
(P F Nicholls) *mstkes first 3: hld up: hdwy 8th: drew clr after next: j.rt 4 out: tired but a in command fr there* **10/11**[1]

45/P **2** *11* **Opal Ridge**[28] [4369] 9-11-0 .... OllieMcPhail 91+
(C Roberts) *trckd ldr: led 5th to 10th: no imp on wnr after next* **16/1**

1340 **3** *1 ½* **Ballyjohnboy Lord (IRE)**[28] [4375] 7-10-7 .... JohnKington(7) 91+
(M Scudamore) *in tch: outpcd appr 5 out: styng on whn hit 2 out* **3/1**[2]

36P4 **4** *19* **Rash Moment (FR)**[19] [4552] 7-10-7 97.................. RichardSpate(7) 70
(Mrs K Waldron) *bhd but in tch tl wknd 11th* **7/1**[3]

5F6F **5** *10* **Look To The Future (IRE)**[55] [3888] 12-10-9 72........... JamesDiment(5) 60
(M J M Evans) *in tch tl rdn 6th: sn wl bhd* **25/1**

0000 **6** *16* **Hayley's Pearl**[18] [4566] 7-10-0 .... WayneKavanagh(7) 37
(Mrs P Ford) *in tch tl wknd appr 5 out* **80/1**

U **7** *14* **The Well Lad (IRE)**[26] [4417] 7-11-0 .... MarkBradburne 30
(A M Balding) *led to 5th: wknd qckly fr 10th* **12/1**

0P60 **U** **Miss Jessica (IRE)**[31] [4302] 6-10-7 .... JodieMogford —
(Miss M E Rowland) *a bhd: blnd and uns rdr 5 out* **33/1**

5m 13.6s (2.30) **Going Correction** -0.45s/f (Good) **8 Ran SP% 111.5**

Speed ratings: **77,72,72,64,60 54,48,—** CSF £15.22 TOTE £1.70: £1.10, £2.90, £1.80; EX 19.50.

Owner C J Harriman **Bred** Janus Bloodstock Inc **Trained** Ditcheat, Somerset

FOCUS

A poor race in which the eased-down winner was value for 18l but was still 15lb below his mark.

NOTEBOOK

Give Me Love(FR) has been called some names in the past but he was much too good for this modest opposition and scored without needing to come under pressure. He jumped particularly well once he had he warmed to his task and this will not have harmed his confidence. *(op Evens)*

Opal Ridge was pulled up here last month on his first run for two years. Although no match for the winner, who was value for more than the actual margin, this was fairly encouraging and he he has now qualified for handicaps. *(op 12-1)*

Ballyjohnboy Lord(IRE), a fair hurdler, was a little disappointing on this chase bow, having been rather keen in the early stages, but he should have learned from the experience. *(op 2-1)*

Rash Moment(FR), back up in trip, was beaten before they reached the long home turn. *(op 15-2)*

The Well Lad(IRE) won a fast-ground point last May but has not shown much in two tries over regulation fences since. *(op 14-1)*

4781 JOHN SMITH'S CHEPSTOW RACE CLUB H'CAP HURDLE (11 hdls) 2m 4f

2:35 (2:36) (Class 3) (0-125,125) 4-Y-O+

£6,263 (£1,850; £925; £463; £231; £116)

Form RPR

4230 **1** **Jockser (IRE)**[10] [4663] 5-10-0 106.......................... WayneKavanagh(7) 113
(J W Mullins) *in tch: hdwy to ld 3 out: hung lft fr last: kpt on wl* **8/1**[2]

0303 **2** *1 ½* **Bonny Grey**[13] [4641] 8-10-5 104.............................. OllieMcPhail 110
(D Burchell) *keen: a cl up: disp ld fr 4 out: kpt on fr last* **14/1**

0-20 **3** *1 ½* **Almah (SAF)**[140] [2347] 8-10-11 115......................... LiamTreadwell(5) 119
(Miss Venetia Williams) *chsd ldrs: outpcd after 7th: rallied next: kpt on fr last: nt rch first two* **11/1**

0120 **4** *10* **Nick's Choice**[3] [4736] 10-10-4 110...................... MissIsabelTompsett(7) 104
(D Burchell) *in tch: effrt fr 4 out: one pce after next* **20/1**

2210 **5** *4* **Sunday City (JPN)**[70] [3622] 5-11-2 120..................... TomGreenway(5) 112+
(P Bowen) *in tch: smooth hdwy bef 4 out: ev ch whn blnd bdly next: nt rcvr* **8/1**[2]

1125 **6** *4* **What A Vintage (IRE)**[21] [4494] 6-10-10 109.................. WarrenMarston 95
(R T Phillips) *hld up: hdwy and in tch bef 4 out: outpcd fr next* **7/1**[1]

FPP3 **7** *7* **Cockatoo Ridge**[18] [4561] 9-9-11 99 oh1..................... OwynNelmes(3) 79+
(N R Mitchell) *cl up: led bef 5th to 3 out: sn wknd* **10/1**

6160 **8** *11* **Marrel**[10] [4663] 8-10-6 110...................................(v) PaddyMerrigan(5) 78
(D Burchell) *midfield tl rdn and wknd after 4 out* **20/1**

102 **9** *9* **Fleurette**[81] [3437] 6-9-9 99.................................... SamCurling(5) 64+
(D R Gandolfo) *hld up: hmpd 4th: effrt u.p after 7th: wknd next* **7/1**[1]

5003 **10** *6* **Spike Jones (NZ)**[16] [4593] 8-10-2 106 ow3.................. DerekLaverty(5) 61+
(Mrs S M Johnson) *hld up: hdwy 7th: hit and wknd next* **16/1**

-3PP **11** *1 ¾* **Greenfield (IRE)**[28] [4364] 8-11-3 116.....................(bt) JimmyMcCarthy 67
(R T Phillips) *bhd: reminders 6th: nvr on terms* **33/1**

2010 **12** *½* **Sunnyarjun**[86] [3360] 8-10-0 99 oh1............................ JodieMogford 50
(J C Tuck) *hld up: sme hdwy 7th: wknd fr next* **25/1**

00P4 **P** **Reservoir (IRE)**[98] [3152] 5-10-1 105.....................(p) ShaneWalsh(5) —
(J Joseph) *a bhd: t.o whn p.u bef 3 out* **50/1**

1/P **U** **Imazulutoo (IRE)**[291] [808] 6-11-12 125........................ PaulMoloney —
(Evan Williams) *stmbld and uns rdr 1st* **20/1**

0 **P** **Sha Bihan (FR)**[18] [4561] 5-10-9 108........................ WayneHutchinson —
(A King) *prom: effrt 4 out: wkng whn p.u bef next* **9/1**[3]

P324 **U** **Bright Green**[12] [4652] 7-9-10 102 ow2........................ BernieWharfe(7) —
(C J Gray) *midfield whn hmpd by loose horse and uns rdr 4th* **9/1**[3]

1250 **P** **Killing Me Softly**[49] [3986] 5-11-5 118.....................(v) JimCrowley —
(J Gallagher) *led to bef 5th: wknd after next: t.o whn p.u bef 3 out* **33/1**

4m 54.4s (-8.30) **Going Correction** -0.225s/f (Good) **17 Ran SP% 123.2**

Speed ratings: **107,106,105,101,100 98,95,91,87,85 84,84,—,—,— —,—** CSF £104.07 CT £1253.46 TOTE £10.60: £2.60, £3.80, £4.50, £5.20; EX 101.40.

Owner The D M L Partnership **Bred** Miss Barbara Phelan **Trained** Wilsford-Cum-Lake, Wilts

FOCUS

Quite a competitive handicap, and solid enough form.

NOTEBOOK

Jockser(IRE), who has been running creditably of late, showed in front with three to jump and kept on willingly. This was a return to his best and, a versatile sort as regards the ground, he can win again in his turn.

Bonny Grey ran her best race of the season and kept the winner up to his work. She seems to like this track and this longer trip held no terrors for her.

Almah(SAF) ◆, returning from a break since November, was keeping on strongly at the end. She is capable of winning off her current mark. *(op 12-1)*

Nick's Choice, back up in trip, was outpaced by the principals over the final three flights.

Sunday City(JPN) was in the firing line when blundering at the third last. Greenway made a good recovery, but the damage was done. *(op 9-1 tchd 10-1)*

What A Vintage(IRE), making her handicap debut, could not go with the leaders from the third last.

Marrel was not knocked about from the fourth last and might be one to keep an eye on. *(op 18-1)*

Fleurette, back in handicap company on this return from a break, was hampered early on and was never able to get into contention. *Official explanation: jockey said mare never travelled*

Reservoir(IRE) *Official explanation: jockey said gelding had a breathing problem (op 40-1)*

4782 JOHN SMITH'S EXTRA COLD H'CAP CHASE (12 fncs) 2m 110y

3:05 (3:05) (Class 4) (0-115,112) 5-Y-O **£4,400** (£1,311; £663; £340; £177)

Form RPR

F403 **1** **Fantasmic**[14] [4614] 10-10-5 91.................................. OllieMcPhail 107+
(M J M Evans) *j.w: trckd ldr: led 5th: drew clr fr 4 out: pushed out run-in* **5/1**[3]

30PP **2** *7* **Easibrook Jane**[28] [4372] 8-10-5 94......................... RichardYoung(3) 103+
(C L Tizzard) *hmpd 1st: in tch fr 4th: rdn and styd on to chse wnr fr 3 out but nvr nr to chal* **9/1**

2434 **3** *9* **Amadeus (AUS)**[14] [4614] 9-9-12 91......................... JohnKington(7) 89+
(M Scudamore) *hld up: styng on whn mstke 2 out but nvr on terms* **4/1**[2]

3322 **4** *1 ¼* **Jupon Vert (FR)**[26] [4426] 9-10-9 95.............................. JimCrowley 92+
(R J Hodges) *led to 5th: chsd wnr tl rdn 3 out: wknd qckly* **9/4**[1]

P64B **5** *1 ¾* **All Sonsilver (FR)**[63] [3733] 9-10-3 89.......................... HenryOliver 86+
(P Kelsall) *a in rr* **16/1**

46P1 **P** **Bel Ombre (FR)**[14] [4614] 6-10-7 96........................ OwynNelmes(3) —
(O Sherwood) *a bhd: t.o whn p.u bef 2 out* **4/1**[2]

4U6/ **P** **Oa Baldixe (FR)**[412] 12-11-12 112............................... SeanCurran —
(K J Burke) *blnd 1st: j. slowly next: sn bhd: t.o 6rh: p.u bef 5 out* **16/1**

4m 13.0s (-9.90) **Going Correction** -0.45s/f (Good) **7 Ran SP% 109.2**

Speed ratings: **105,101,97,96,96 —,—** CSF £41.54 TOTE £6.80: £2.40, £3.20; EX 53.40.

Owner M J M Evans **Bred** G G A Gregson **Trained** Kidderminster, Worcs

FOCUS

A modrate handicap won comfortably by Fantasmic, who was back to the level of his best form of 2004.

NOTEBOOK

Fantasmic, dropped 5lb despite signs of a revival at Bangor, jumped nicely and, in front before halfway, was never seriously challenged. *(op 4-1)*

Easibrook Jane, still a maiden over fences, shaped a little more encouragingly but was no match for the winner. A trip of around two and a half miles might prove best. *(op 12-1)*

Amadeus(AUS) stayed on to take third place on the run-in but is not firing at present. *(tchd 9-2)*

Jupon Vert(FR) is finding it hard to get his head in front and he was not at his best after a busy spell. *(op 2-1)*

Bel Ombre(FR) was 9lb higher than when scoring at Bangor, where he had today's winner back in third. *He did not seem to be enjoying himslef and was never in the hunt.Official explanation: jockey said gelding never travelled (op 9-2)*

4783 JOHN SMITH'S "NO NONSENSE" (S) H'CAP HURDLE (11 hdls) 2m 4f

3:35 (3:37) (Class 5) (0-90,90) 4-Y-O+ **£2,277** (£668; £334; £166)

Form RPR

54F- **1** **Sou'Wester**[403] [4113] 6-10-12 76.............................. AndrewThornton 97+
(C Roberts) *trckd ldrs: led gng wl 4 out: clr fr next: hit last: easily* **9/1**[3]

5P/3 **2** *10* **Yaiyna Tango (FR)**[13] [4640] 11-11-5 83......................... PaulMoloney 84+
(Miss L Day) *in tch: hdwy bef 4 out: chsd wnr next: no imp* **14/1**

00P3 **3** *9* **Breezer**[12] [4651] 6-10-9 73.................................(p) MarkBradburne 64
(J A Geake) *hld up: hdwy bef 4 out: kpt on fr next: no imp* **11/2**[1]

6P13 **4** *5* **Cullian**[14] [4609] 9-11-5 90..(p) JohnKington(7) 76
(J G M O'Shea) *midfield: outpcd bef 4 out: kpt on fr 2 out but no imp fr 2 out* **8/1**[2]

2152 **5** *2* **The Wife's Sister**[19] [4550] 5-11-3 88.....................(b) RichardSpate(7) 72
(Mrs K Waldron) *midfield: outpcd after 6th: kpt on fr 2 out: n.d* **11/2**[1]

5410 **6** *8* **Lazy Lena (IRE)**[21] [4487] 7-11-2 80............................... TomSiddall 56
(Miss L C Siddall) *hld up: hdwy and prom bef 4 out: edgd lft and outpcd fr next* **8/1**[2]

0PU **7** *hd* **Little Rort (IRE)**[17] [4570] 7-11-6 87............................ ChrisHonour(3) 65+
(S T Lewis) *cl up: ev ch 4 out: wkng whn nt fluent 2 out* **40/1**

-4PP **8** *1* **I'm For Waiting**[85] [3372] 10-11-0 83.......................... MarkNicolls(5) 58
(John Allen) *in tch: outpcd after 6th: n.d after* **33/1**

U060 **9** *27* **Sir Walter (IRE)**[28] [4368] 13-11-7 85............................ OllieMcPhail 33
(D Burchell) *nt fluent: bhd: hdwy and prom bef 4 out: sn rdn and wknd* **14/1**

0UUO **10** *¾* **Heatherlea Squire (NZ)**[12] [4651] 8-10-9 73.................. WarrenMarston 20
(D J Wintle) *cl up: led 7th to next: wknd* **50/1**

4514 **11** *2 ½* **Mickey Pearce (IRE)**[3] [4733] 4-10-6 84..................(b) ChrisDavies(7) 22
(J G M O'Shea) *midfield: rdn and wknd bef 4 out* **12/1**

PPRP **12** *9* **Kadlass (FR)**[99] [3125] 11-9-13 70........................... RyanCummings(7) 6
(Mrs D Thomas) *bhd: rdn 6th: nvr on terms* **100/1**

0000 **13** *5* **Secret Divin (FR)**[103] [2995] 6-11-11 89...................... BenjaminHitchcott 20
(Mrs D A Hamer) *cl up: led after 4th to 7th: wknd next* **20/1**

-P64 **14** *dist* **Thespian Lady**[17] [4570] 5-10-6 70................................ JamesDavies —
(P R Chamings) *bhd: rdn 6th: nvr on terms* **14/1**

0-30 **P** **Final Command**[318] [502] 9-11-7 85.............................. JimCrowley —
(J C Tuck) *a bhd: t.o whn p.u bef 4 out* **25/1**

-P45 **P** **Adalie**[17] [4577] 12-10-10 79...................................... ShaneWalsh(5) —
(J Joseph) *led to after 4th: wknd next: t.o whn p.u bef 2 out* **28/1**

0100 **P** **Irish Blessing (USA)**[27] [4392] 9-11-1 89............(tp) ThomasBurrows(10) —
(F Jordan) *prom tl wknd after 5th: t.o whn p.u bef 2 out* **12/1**

530/ **P** **Peggy Lou**[861] [1958] 6-10-4 75...............................(p) WillieMcCarthy(7) —
(B J Llewellyn) *hld up outside: hdwy and prom after 4th: wkng whn nt fluent 6th: t.o whn p.u bef 4 out* **25/1**

5m 1.00s (-1.70) **Going Correction** -0.025s/f (Good)

WFA 4 from 5yo+ 6lb **18 Ran SP% 122.6**

Speed ratings: **102,98,94,92,91 88,88,87,77,76 75,72,70,—,— —,—,—** CSF £116.15 CT £771.05 TOTE £11.10: £2.70, £4.10, £2.10, £2.40; EX 128.60.The winner was sold to Colin Tizzard for 11,500gns.

Owner E R Griffiths **Bred** Newgate Stud Co **Trained** Newport, Newport

FOCUS

Not a strong race, rated through the second, but a very easy winner, value for double the winning margin.

NOTEBOOK

Sou'Wester was having his first run for this yard and appearing for the first time since taking a fall over fences in March last year. He shrugged off the long absence to win very easily indeed, value for double the winning margin, and should be capable of winning again for new connections, having changed hands at the auction. *(op 10-1)*

Yaiyna Tango(FR) has now run two fair races since reverting to hurdling but on this occasion the winner was in a different league.

Breezer has been falling steadily down the handicap this term. He stayed on through beaten horses at the end but never promised to get to the first two. *(tchd 6-1 and 13-2 in a place)*

Cullian, back up in trip, merely stayed on past struggling rivals when it was all over.

The Wife's Sister kept on gain after getting her second wind. *(op 7-1)*

4784 THE CROWN AT WHITEBROOK NOVICES' HURDLE (8 hdls) 2m 110y

4:05 (4:09) (Class 4) 4-Y-0+ £2,927 (£859; £429; £214)

Form RPR

5-41 1 **Manners (IRE)**[43] 4088 8-11-2 .... MrAJBerry(7) 110+
(Jonjo O'Neill) *trckd ldrs: smooth hdwy to ld sn after 4 out: rdn appr last: kpt up to work run-in* 8/13[1]

360 2 *nk* **Sky Mack (IRE)**[14] 4621 5-11-2 .... PaulMoloney 100
(Evan Williams) *hld up in rr: hdwy 4th: rdn to go 2nd last: kpt on wl run-in* 50/1

00 3 *3 ½* **Charmatic (IRE)**[55] 3878 5-10-9 .... HenryOliver 90
(Andrew Turnell) *in tch: rdn 2 out: styd on one pce run-in* 66/1

P660 4 *¾* **Templer (IRE)**[46] 4033 5-11-2 .... AndrewThornton 97+
(P J Hobbs) *a.p: rdn 2 out: one pce run-in* 50/1

4125 5 *1 ½* **Kayceecee (IRE)**[30] 4329 5-11-9 111 .... MarkBradburne 102
(H D Daly) *a.p: ev ch 2 out: hung lft and wknd run-in* 4/1[2]

210 6 *11* **Sonnengold (GER)**[21] 4494 5-11-2 111 ....(b[1]) JimmyMcCarthy 85+
(Mrs L Wadham) *trckd ldrs: led appr 1st: hdd sn after 4 out: wknd appr 2 out* 7/1[3]

P0 7 *10* **Lorrelini (IRE)**[98] 3133 5-11-2 .... RobertWalford 75+
(R H Alner) *in rr: styd on fr 4 out but nvr on terms* 100/1

0250 8 *2* **Jobsworth (IRE)**[13] 4644 6-11-2 .... WayneHutchinson 72
(Evan Williams) *in tch tl wknd after 3 out* 33/1

9 *3* **Hello It's Me**[237] 5-11-2 .... RichardHobson 69
(K A Morgan) *trckd ldr tl wknd appr 4 out* 16/1

60 10 *1 ¼* **Arc Of Stone (IRE)**[17] 4569 6-11-2 .... WarrenMarston 67
(D J Wintle) *led to after 1st: behind fr 4th* 80/1

00 11 *2* **Honorary Citizen**[42] 4106 4-10-10 .... JamesDavies 59
(Evan Williams) *mid-div tl lost pl appr 4 out* 100/1

0 12 *¾* **Onslow Road (IRE)**[14] 4621 6-10-11 .... LiamTreadwell(5) 65
(Miss Venetia Williams) *a bhd* 66/1

00 13 *16* **Cool Society**[54] 3898 4-10-5 .... DarylJacob(5) 43
(R H Alner) *a bhd* 100/1

P/ 14 *19* **Sun Hill**[32] 3329 6-11-2 .... OllieMcPhail 30
(D Burchell) *a bhd* 25/1

15 *12* **Mystery Maid (IRE)**[565] 4-10-3 .... JodieMogford 5
(H S Howe) *plld hrd: led after 1st but rn wd on bnd and hdd bef next: sn bhd* 100/1

0P 16 *¾* **Ciarans Lass**[3] 4732 7-10-3 ow1 .... MrRHodges(7) 11
(C Roberts) *iin rr: rdn appr 3rd and sn wl bhd* 100/1

4m 10.0s (-0.40) **Going Correction** -0.025s/f (Good)
WFA 4 from 5yo+ 5lb **16** Ran SP% **120.2**
Speed ratings: **99,98,97,96,96 90,86,85,83,83 82,82,74,65,59 59** CSF £54.70 TOTE £1.70: £1.10, £13.20, £11.90; EX 52.10.
Owner Michael Tabor **Bred** M Tabor **Trained** Cheltenham, Gloucs

FOCUS
A fair novices' race but not an easy one to assess. The winner was 5lb below his best hurdles form.

NOTEBOOK
Manners(IRE) follwed up his Sandown win to make it four wins from six racecourse appearances. In front at the third last, he landed awkwardly over the final flight but was always holding the runner-up's challenge. *(op 8-15 tchd 4-6)*
Sky Mack(IRE) showed ability in bumpers but was beaten out of sight on his hurdles debut. This was much better and, after moving into second place at the last, he harried the winner all the way to the line.
Charmatic(IRE) ◆, four times a winner on the Flat at up to 11 furlongs, ran her best race to date over hurdles on this drop in grade. The way she was finishing suggests she will get further, and there are races to be won with her. *(op 50-1)*
Templer(IRE), who played up down at the start, had his chance but was held when landing flat-footed over the last. He has now qualified for handicaps.
Kayceecee(IRE) looked to be going well when challenging at the second last but was soon unable to quicken. He looks the type to make a chaser next season. *(op 9-2)*
Sonnengold(GER), tried in blinkers after a poor effort at Uttoxeter, ran a better race but her measure had been taken with two to jump. *(op 8-1)*

4785 JOHN SMITH'S PREMIER CLUB H'CAP CHASE (18 fncs) 3m

4:45 (4:51) (Class 5) (0-90,90) 5-Y-0+ £2,927 (£859; £429; £214)

Form RPR

366U 1 **Sissinghurst Storm (IRE)**[19] 4553 8-10-11 **75** .... HenryOliver 95+
(R Dickin) *hld up: hdwy to ld 5 out: sn clr: eased run in* 9/1

3033 2 *6* **Southerndown (IRE)**[28] 4370 13-10-13 **80** .... WilliamKennedy(3) 87+
(R Lee) *hld up: hdwy 1/2-way: wnt 2nd bef 3 out: kpt on: no imp* 10/1

F2P4 3 *6* **Zimbabwe (FR)**[19] 4553 6-11-1 **79** ....(p) AndrewThornton 79
(N J Hawke) *mde most to 11th: outpcd after next: kpt on fr 2 out: no ch w first two* 12/1

3424 4 *5* **Five Alley (IRE)**[15] 4603 9-11-10 **88** .... MarkBradburne 85+
(R H Buckler) *hld up: outpcd 10th: kpt on fr 2 out: n.d* 13/2[2]

P343 5 *5* **Supreme Sir (IRE)**[27] 4394 8-11-1 **79** .... MatthewBatchelor 69
(P G Murphy) *w ldrs: mstke 4th: led 11th to bef next: cl up tl outpcd fr 3 out* 15/2[3]

5P 6 *17* **Orbys Girl (IRE)**[40] 4151 6-11-7 **85** .... PaulMoloney 58
(M Pitman) *in tch: hdwy to ld bef 12th: hdd 5 out: wknd after next* 20/1

43PP P **Monsieur Georges (FR)**[74] 3547 6-10-11 **78** .... OwynNelmes(3) —
(F Jordan) *a bhd: t.o whn p.u bef 10th* 33/1

-663 P **Glashedy Rock (IRE)**[211] 1446 9-11-4 **87** .... CharliePoste(5) —
(M F Harris) *a bhd: t.o whn p.u bef 4 out* 16/1

-562 U **Sweet Minuet**[17] 4575 9-10-13 **82** .... RobertLucey-Butler(5) —
(M Madgwick) *prom whn blnd and uns rdr 9th* 20/1

4P/4 P **Dalcassian Buck (IRE)**[43] 4100 12-10-7 **74** .... RichardYoung(3) —
(Mrs L J Young) *a bhd: t.o whn p.u bef 4 out* 22/1

P-P5 P **Twotensforafive**[64] 3716 13-10-10 **81** .... KeiranBurke(7) —
(P R Rodford) *in tch tl wknd 7th: p.u bef next* 40/1

P312 P **Jacarado (IRE)**[29] 4353 8-10-6 **77** ....(v) JohnPritchard(7) —
(R Dickin) *w ldrs tl wknd fr 12th: t.o whn p.u bef 3 out* 5/1[1]

P4PP P **Tradingup (IRE)**[30] 4328 7-11-4 **85** .... GinoCarenza(3) —
(Andrew Turnell) *in tch to 7th: sn wknd: t.o whn p.u bef 11th* 20/1

63P3 P **Paddy The Optimist (IRE)**[19] 4553 10-10-7 **76** .... PaddyMerrigan(5) —
(D Burchell) *hld up: struggling and p.u bef 11th* 5/1[1]

P/2P P **Royal Scandal**[18] 4560 10-11-5 **90** .... TomMessenger(7) —
(C J Down) *in tch tl wknd fr 12th: t.o whn p.u bef 4 out* 20/1

6m 22.8s (7.90) **Going Correction** -0.25s/f (Good) **15** Ran SP% **119.9**
Speed ratings: **76,74,72,70,68 63,—,—,—,— —,—,—,—,—** CSF £84.37 CT £1096.34 TOTE £10.20: £4.40, £2.00, £2.90; EX 128.90.
Owner Brian Clifford **Bred** John Noonan **Trained** Atherstone on Stour, Warwicks

FOCUS
A low-grade handicap in which the winner has been rated value for 13l. The pace was sound.

NOTEBOOK
Sissinghurst Storm(IRE), largely consistent since recording her last victory a year ago, showed in front at the first fence in the home straight and was not unduly troubled thereafter, being value for around double the winning margin. *(op 8-1)*
Southerndown(IRE), whose last win came off this mark, plugged on in his usual fashion to secure second but was flattered by his proximity to the winner at the line. A pretty safe conveyance, he has only fallen once in 73 races over jumps. *(op 12-1)*
Zimbabwe(FR), back in cheekpieces, did best of those who had helped force the pace.
Five Alley(IRE) did not show much sparkle on this return to fences but did stay on late for fourth. *(op 15-2)*
Supreme Sir(IRE) ran his race again but was held from the third last. *(op 8-1)*
Orbys Girl(IRE), without the headgear, ran respectably on this return to fences but was found out by the trip. *(op 16-1)*
Paddy The Optimist(IRE) is well handicapped at present and is at his best in the spring, but he ran a lacklustre race. *(op 6-1)*
Jacarado(IRE), off the same mark as when runner-up at Leicester, did not really settle properly and eventually paid the price. *(op 6-1)*

4786 JOHN SMITH'S GRAND NATIONAL DAY "NATIONAL HUNT" NOVICES' HURDLE (11 hdls) 2m 4f

5:15 (5:24) (Class 4) 4-Y-0+ £3,083 (£898; £449)

Form RPR

02B 1 **Mars Rock (FR)**[17] 4581 6-10-9 .... LiamTreadwell(5) 97+
(Miss Venetia Williams) *lft in ld in bnd after 4th: mde rest: wandered in front fr 2 out but styd in command* 6/4[1]

53 2 *2 ½* **Black And Tan (IRE)**[94] 3240 6-11-0 .... AndrewThornton 90
(P J Hobbs) *a front rnk: wnt 2nd 4 out: rdn 2 out: kpt on but no imp run-in* 7/4[2]

0 3 *dist* **Southern Classic**[24] 4455 6-10-9 .... ShaneWalsh(5) —
(R M Stronge) *prom: trckd wnr appr 2nd tl 4 out: sn wknd and wl btn whn hit 2 out: t.o* 20/1

61- 4 *5* **Elbdoubleu**[594] 1249 6-10-4 .... ChrisHonour(3) —
(C J Down) *hld up: passed btn horses appr 4 out: nvr on terms: t.o* 12/1[3]

0650 5 *28* **Schindler's List**[7] 4691 6-11-0 .... OllieMcPhail —
(C Roberts) *led tl rn wd on bnd after 4th: sn bhd: t.o* 16/1

PP 6 *1 ½* **Conemara Breeze**[11] 4657 8-11-0 .... TomSiddall —
(Miss L C Siddall) *a bhd: t.o appr 4 out* 100/1

7 *5* **Morgan's Money** 7-11-0 .... WayneHutchinson —
(R T Phillips) *mid-div: wknd appr 4 out: t.o* 14/1

0 8 *dist* **Raki Rose**[30] 4326 4-10-0 .... JohnKington(7) —
(M Scudamore) *a bhd: t.o* 100/1

650 9 *7* **Flemens River (IRE)**[72] 3583 5-10-11 .... TomMalone(3) —
(C J Down) *hld up in tch: wknd after 7th: t.o* 25/1

0-0 F **Go Harvey Go (IRE)**[21] 4494 7-11-0 .... WarrenMarston —
(R T Phillips) *in tch whn fell 7th* 20/1

U F **Mister Sher (IRE)**[65] 3693 7-10-11 .... RichardYoung(3) —
(Mrs L J Young) *trckd ldrs tl fell 7th* 40/1

0 F **Scania Classic**[17] 4569 5-10-11 .... WilliamKennedy(3) —
(R Lee) *hit 2nd: bhd whn blnd & uns rdr 7th* 100/1

P **Curraheen Chief (IRE)**[1562] 3068 11-11-0 .... HenryOliver —
(J L Spearing) *hld up: a in rr: t.o whn p.u bef 3 out* 14/1

UP U **Story Arms**[48] 4015 4-10-0 .... AngharadFrieze(7) —
(D Burchell) *bhd and poor 5th whn tried to run out and uns rdr 4 out* 100/1

5m 1.80s (-0.90) **Going Correction** +0.05s/f (Yiel)
WFA 4 from 5yo+ 6lb **14** Ran SP% **123.0**
Speed ratings: **103,102,—,—,— —,—,—,—,— —,—,—,—** CSF £4.14 TOTE £2.90: £1.30, £1.50, £3.80; EX 4.50 Place 6 £532.07, Place 5 £434.67 .
Owner John Nicholls (Trading) Ltd **Bred** S C E A Haras De Mirande **Trained** Kings Caple, H'fords

FOCUS
The first two finished clear in this weak race, both running pretty close to their bumper marks. The pace was not strong.

NOTEBOOK
Mars Rock(FR), upped in trip, possessed too much pace for the runner-up from the second last. This was a poor race. *(op 13-8 tchd 7-4 in places)*
Black And Tan(IRE) looked a danger up the straight but ran a little green when the pressure was on and could not match his market rival for pace. He should stay three miles. *(op 9-4)*
Southern Classic, on his hurdling debut, turned into the long home straight in a close second but was already beginning to struggle. *(op 14-1)*
Elbdoubleu, off the track since landing a bumper in August 2004, was well beaten on this hurdles debut.
Schindler's List was in front when running very wide on the bend near the stable exit with a circuit or so to run. He continued tailed off but did pass some beaten rivals towards the end.
T/Plt: £454.80 to a £1 stake. Pool: £58,575.75. 94.00 winning tickets. T/Qpdt: £105.20 to a £1 stake. Pool: £3,543.00. 24.90 winning tickets. JS

4719 KELSO (L-H)

Sunday, April 9

OFFICIAL GOING: Good to soft (good in places)
Wind: Fresh across

4787 BLAEBERRYHILL INN "NATIONAL HUNT" NOVICES' HURDLE (DIV I) (11 hdls) 2m 6f 110y

2:30 (2:31) (Class 4) 4-Y-0+ £3,383 (£993; £496; £248)

Form RPR

2 1 **One Sniff (IRE)**[58] 3846 7-11-2 .... TonyDobbin 113+
(N G Richards) *a.p: led 3 out: drvn and styd on wl fr last* 8/11[1]

0215 2 *2 ½* **Supreme's Legacy (IRE)**[64] 3738 7-11-9 121 .... AndrewThornton 117+
(K G Reveley) *hld up: hdwy 4 out: chsd wnr run in: kpt on* 11/4[2]

30-2 3 *2* **Arctic Echo**[21] 4532 7-10-13 .... DougieCostello(3) 108+
(G A Swinbank) *in tch: drvn and outpcd after 3 out: rallied next: kpt on same pce run in* 10/1

-322 4 *10* **Blue Buster**[41] 4143 6-10-13 104 .... MrTGreenall(3) 97
(M W Easterby) *hld up: stdy hdwy bef 3 out: chsng ldrs and effrt after last: wknd run in* 8/1[3]

3610 5 *¾* **More Likely**[21] 4529 5-11-2 101 .... GLee 96
(Mrs A F Tullie) *led to 3 out: rdn and wknd after last* 33/1

U0 6 *18* **Mighty Fella**[53] 3925 4-10-0 ow2 .... StevenGagan(10) 72
(Mrs E Slack) *keen in rr: bhd tl stdy hdwy bef 2 out: kpt on run in: nvr nr ldrs* 200/1

00/ 7 *6* **Naughtynelly's Pet**[64] 7-10-9 .... BenOrde-Powlett(7) 72
(A M Crow) *hld up: hdwy and prom 4 out: rdn and wknd after next* 200/1

4 8 *9* **Dinnie Flanagan (IRE)**[31] 4315 6-11-2 .... BarryKeniry 63
(P C Haslam) *prom tl rdn and wknd bef 3 out* 33/1

0 **9** *9* **Floral Future**[21] 4519 6-10-2 .... EwanWhillans(7) 47
(A C Whillans) *a bhd: no ch fr 1/2-way* **200/1**

05 **10** *shd* **Glen Oscar (IRE)**[6] 4720 7-11-2 .... NeilMulholland 54
(Miss S E Forster) *hld up: wknd bef 4 out* **200/1**

0 **11** *dist* **Striking Silver**[41] 4147 5-11-2 .... BrianHarding —
(I McMath) *in tch tl wknd bef 4 out* **150/1**

50 **12** *27* **Hiddenfortune (IRE)**[30] 4342 6-11-2 .... PeterBuchanan —
(Miss Lucinda V Russell) *sn towards rr: no ch fr 1/2-way* **100/1**

5U **F** **Hold The Bid (IRE)**[28] 4386 6-10-9 .... MrTCollier(7) —
(Mrs S J Smith) *chsng ldrs whn fell 7th* **66/1**

0PP **P** **Givitago**[31] 4315 7-10-4 .... MichaelMcAlister(5) —
(B Storey) *pressed ldr tl wknd bef 7th: t.o whn p.u bef 3 out* **200/1**

000 **P** **Northern Quest (IRE)**[94] 3253 5-11-2 .... DavidO'Meara —
(H P Hogarth) *nt fluent towards rr: struggling 7th: t.o whn p.u bef 3 out* **200/1**

5m 39.9s (2.20) **Going Correction** +0.175s/f (Yiel)
WFA 4 from 5yo+ 6lb **15** Ran SP% **116.8**
Speed ratings: **103,102,101,97,97 91,89,86,83,83** —,—,—,—,— CSF £2.71 TOTE £1.70: £1.10, £1.40, £3.20; EX 3.40.
Owner J Hales **Bred** Eamonn Kelleher **Trained** Greystoke, Cumbria
■ Stewards' Enquiry : Steven Gagan ten-day ban: failed to take all reasonable and permissible measures to obtain the best possible placing (April 20-29)

FOCUS
A fair novices' event, run at just a moderate early gallop, and the form looks sound.

NOTEBOOK
One Sniff(IRE) ◆, runner-up on his hurdling debut behind the high-class novice Denman in February, duly went one better with a workmanlike display over this shorter trip. The lack of pace would have been against him over this shorter trip, he looked to idle when in front from the third last, and is value for slightly further than his winning margin. This former winning pointer will no doubt come into his own when going novice chasing next season, where the return to three miles should suit him well, yet he could defy a penalty in this sphere should connections opt to find him another race in the meantime. *(op 4-5)*
Supreme's Legacy(IRE), found out in Graded company last time, ran his race on this drop back in class yet was found out by his penalty. He may be slightly flattered by his official mark, and ideally wants softer ground, yet still sets the standard for this form. *(tchd 10-3)*
Arctic Echo, up in trip, posted another fair effort and got home well enough over the longer distance. He will be eligible for handicaps after his next assignment and, considering he won two bumpers on fast ground in 2004, could be interesting if kept in training during the summer. *(op 12-1)*
Blue Buster ran his race, yet did not get home as well as the principals over this longer trip. This was just the second occasion he had finished out of the frame in his career to date and he ought to fare better in handicaps from his current mark. *(op 17-2)*
Glen Oscar(IRE) *Official explanation: jockey said gelding bled from the nose*

4788 KELSO GOLF CLUB NOVICES' CHASE (19 fncs) 3m 1f
3:00 (3:11) (Class 4) 5-Y-O+ **£5,204** (£1,528; £764; £381)

Form RPR

3331 **1** **Bellaney Jewel (IRE)**[21] 4518 7-10-9 105 .... TonyDobbin 107
(J J Quinn) *chsd ldrs: led 12th: hdd after last: rallied and swtchd run in: styd on wl to regain ld nr fin* **10/3**[2]

1511 **2** *nk* **Jimmy Bond**[21] 4520 7-11-2 106 .... BrianHarding 114
(Mrs K Walton) *prom: wnt 2nd 14th: effrt and led after last: edgd lft run in: kpt on: hdd cl home* **7/1**

P435 **3** *11* **No Picnic (IRE)**[21] 4528 8-10-13 99 .... PaddyAspell(3) 103
(Mrs S C Bradburne) *in tch: outpcd 4 out: rallied after 2 out: kpt on run in: no ch w first two* **33/1**

5141 **4** *¾* **Snowy (IRE)**[112] 2905 8-11-2 110 .... GLee 105+
(J I A Charlton) *prom: blnd 5th: rallied and prom 13th: rdn 4 out: one pce after 2 out* **11/4**[1]

0550 **5** *2½* **Try Catch Paddy (IRE)**[6] 4724 8-10-6 98 .... DavidDaSilva(10) 103+
(P Monteith) *hld up: hdwy and in tch bef 3 out: mstke and rdn next: no ex last* **33/1**

30PF **6** *23* **Brundeanlaws**[32] 4302 5-9-11 82 .... DougieCostello(3) 61
(Mrs H O Graham) *bhd: hmpd 5th: nvr on terms* **100/1**

4P50 **7** *½* **Bramble Princess (IRE)**[41] 4145 7-10-9 80 .... PeterBuchanan 69
(Miss Lucinda V Russell) *led to 12th: cl up tl wknd bef 3 out* **66/1**

12P/ **8** *5* **Paphian Bay**[835] 2907 8-11-2 96 .... KeithMercer 71
(Ferdy Murphy) *a bhd: no ch fnl circ* **33/1**

2FU1 **9** *1¼* **Red Man (IRE)**[12] 4655 9-10-6 106 ....(p) StevenGagan(10) 70
(Mrs E Slack) *in tch: rdn 15th: outpcd whn mstkes 2 out and last* **8/1**

P-44 **F** **Fromragstoriches (IRE)**[94] 3253 10-11-2 105 .... DavidO'Meara —
(Mrs S J Smith) *hld up: fell 2nd* **8/1**

5P11 **P** **Skenfrith**[30] 4345 7-11-2 109 .... NeilMulholland —
(Miss S E Forster) *cl up: mstke 9th: p.u after next* **4/1**[3]

6m 27.1s (-2.50) **Going Correction** +0.10s/f (Yiel)
WFA 5 from 7yo+ 8lb **11** Ran SP% **115.8**
Speed ratings: **108,107,104,104,103 95,95,94,93,**— — CSF £25.51 TOTE £5.00: £1.80, £2.00, £3.50; EX 19.10.
Owner J W Rosbotham **Bred** J W Rosbotham **Trained** Settrington, N Yorks
■ Stewards' Enquiry : Brian Harding caution: careless riding

FOCUS
A modest novice, run at a decent pace, and the first two came clear. It has been rated through the third.

NOTEBOOK
Bellaney Jewel(IRE), off the mark as a novice chaser on her handicap bow last time, dug deep to follow up in game fashion and recorded a personal-best in the process. She handled this softer ground well, is clearly progressing, and the return to softer ground next time should see her make a bold bid for the hat-trick. *(op 7-2 tchd 4-1 in places)*
Jimmy Bond, bidding for his fourth success from his last five outings, was only just denied on this return to novice company and finished well clear of the rest. He got this longer trip well enough, despite ultimately getting outstayed by the winner, and is clearly in the form of his life at present. *(op 6-1)*
No Picnic(IRE), with the cheekpieces left off, needed plenty of driving yet responded to pressure and ran his best race for some time. He is not really a betting proposition, but could better this if encountering softer ground again in the coming weeks. *(op 50-1 tchd 25-1)*
Snowy(IRE), well backed for this return from a 112-day break, spoilt his chance with a bad error at the fifth fence and found just the same pace when it really mattered. He probably wants faster ground, and is entitled to have needed this outing, so should be given another chance if kept on the go through the summer. *(op 7-2)*
Skenfrith, who had won his last two outings in handicap company, was quickly pulled up after *making an error at the ninth fence with something presumably amiss. Official explanation: jockey said gelding was never travelling (tchd 9-2)*

4789 BOB BLAGG'S GLORIOUS 12TH JUVENILE NOVICES' HURDLE (8 hdls) 2m 110y
3:30 (3:43) (Class 4) 4-Y-O **£3,903** (£1,146; £573; £286)

Form RPR

0P0 **1** **Singhalongtasveer**[53] 3925 4-10-12 ....(tp) AlanDempsey 96
(W Storey) *keen: prom: led run in: styd on wl* **66/1**

1210 **2** *nk* **Patxaran (IRE)**[15] 4616 4-10-9 112 ....(t) GaryBartley(10) 103
(P C Haslam) *led to 4 out: cl up: effrt and ev ch run in: kpt on: hld cl home* **8/11**[1]

5225 **3** *3½* **Madge**[125] 2676 4-10-5 ....(v) NeilMulholland 85
(W Storey) *cl up: led 4 out: edgd rt and hdd run in: kpt on same pce* **14/1**

35 **4** *1½* **Dance The Mambo**[15] 4615 4-10-5 .... WilsonRenwick 84
(M W Easterby) *midfield: outpcd after 3 out: edgd lft and kpt on fr last* **28/1**

0100 **5** *5* **Insurgent (IRE)**[60] 3799 4-10-12 .... LarryMcGrath 86
(R C Guest) *hld up: effrt 3 out: one pce between last two* **33/1**

000 **6** *½* **Turtle Bay**[53] 3925 4-10-5 83 .... BrianHarding 78
(B Storey) *sn chsng ldrs: rdn and one pce bef 2 out* **66/1**

654P **7** *shd* **In Dream's (IRE)**[14] 4631 4-10-12 98 ....(t) PeterBuchanan 85
(M A Barnes) *hld up: drvn bef 3 out: kpt on run in: n.d* **16/1**

8 *shd* **High Dyke**[15] 4-10-12 .... GLee 85
(K A Ryan) *plld hrd in rr: hdwy and prom after 3 out: rdn and no ex after next* **8/1**[3]

9 *4* **Shamrock Bay**[224] 4-10-2 .... GaryBerridge(3) 74
(L Lungo) *nt fluent: hld up: hdwy 3 out: outpcd fr next* **9/2**[2]

00 **10** *3* **Thatlldoforme**[21] 4533 4-10-12 .... BarryKeniry 78
(A C Whillans) *in tch tl wknd fr 3 out* **200/1**

P61P **11** *nk* **Commanche Sioux**[17] 4582 4-10-9 103 .... MrTGreenall(3) 78
(M W Easterby) *chsd ldrs: hit 3 out: sn wknd: btn whn hit next* **20/1**

12 *¾* **Vision Victory (GER)**[408] 4-10-5 .... PatrickMcDonald(7) 77
(P Spottiswood) *a bhd* **200/1**

0 **13** *20* **Miss Iverley**[21] 4532 4-9-13 ow1 .... DavidDaSilva(7) 51
(J M Dun) *sn bhd: nvr on terms* **200/1**

4 **P** **Devils Delight (IRE)**[189] 1601 4-10-5 .... KeithMercer —
(James Moffatt) *sddle slipped and p.u bef 1st* **25/1**

4m 7.60s (3.90) **Going Correction** +0.175s/f (Yiel) **14** Ran SP% **119.2**
Speed ratings: **97,96,95,94,92 91,91,91,89,88 88,88,78,**— CSF £116.53 TOTE £109.00: £19.00, £1.10, £3.40; EX 243.80.
Owner W Storey **Bred** J O'Mulloy **Trained** Muggleswick, Co Durham

FOCUS
A weak juvenile event, run at a fair pace, and the first two came clear. The form looks suspect, though.

NOTEBOOK
Singhalongtasveer, despite running freely through the early parts, stepped up vastly on his previous form and got off the mark as a hurdler at the fourth time of asking. Indeed this was his first success of any kind at the 20th attempt and, while he has been improved by the recent application of cheekpieces, he will likely struggle to defy a penalty in this sphere.
Patxaran(IRE), back in trip, held every chance yet could not get past the winner on the run-in. This has to rate as a missed opportunity. *(op 4-5 tchd 5-6 in places)*
Madge, returning from a 125-day break, had her chance and did more than enough to suggest she ought to improve for the outing. *(op 16-1)*
Dance The Mambo, who showed ability in her two bumpers, was not given too hard a time of things on this hurdling bow. She will be of much more interest when eligible for handicaps in due course. *(tchd 25-1)*
Shamrock Bay, rated 69 on the Flat and making her hurdling bow after a 224-day layoff, did not look a natural over her hurdles and never really threatened to take a part in the finish. As a half-sister to Dancing Bay, she can be expected to do better in this sphere with further experience, but will need to brush up her jumping in order to do so. *(tchd 5-1)*
Devils Delight(IRE) *Official explanation: jockey said saddle slipped (op 33-1)*

4790 ALCAZAR LTD DEVELOPING OUTSTANDING BRANDS H'CAP CHASE (21 fncs) 3m 4f
4:00 (4:14) (Class 3) (0-125,119) 5-Y-O+ **£7,807** (£2,292; £1,146; £572)

Form RPR

1-3P **1** **Rosie Redman (IRE)**[57] 3851 9-11-9 **116** .... TonyDobbin 132+
(J R Turner) *hld up: stdy hdwy and in tch 1/2-way: outpcd after 4 out: rallied next: led bef last: styd on wl run in* **7/1**[3]

P3U3 **2** *2½* **Devil's Run (IRE)**[29] 4361 10-10-11 **107** .... PaddyAspell(3) 119
(J Wade) *a cl up: pushed along 15th: disp ld between last two to run in: kpt on same pce towards fin* **11/1**

P006 **3** *8* **Robbo**[5] 4496 12-11-2 **119** .... JamesReveley(10) 123
(K G Reveley) *bhd and sn outpcd: hdwy 3 out: kpt on wl run in: no ch w first two* **12/1**

0/1P **4** *9* **Move Over (IRE)**[21] 4518 11-10-12 **105** .... BarryKeniry 103+
(R C Guest) *trckd ldrs gng wl: led bef 3 out: mstke and rdn next: sn hdd: wknd last* **40/1**

0663 **5** *3½* **Strong Resolve (IRE)**[30] 4345 10-11-8 **115** .... PeterBuchanan 106
(Miss Lucinda V Russell) *in tch: outpcd 16th: n.d after* **9/1**

PP41 **6** *17* **Almire Du Lia (FR)**[29] 4361 8-10-12 **105** ....(v) WilsonRenwick 79
(Mrs S C Bradburne) *cl up: led 11th to bef 3 out: wknd next* **20/1**

P02P **7** *dist* **Harlov (FR)**[29] 4361 11-11-0 **107** ....(v) AlanDempsey —
(A Parker) *in tch: reminders and outpcd 12th: sn btn* **20/1**

R16P **P** **Huka Lodge (IRE)**[30] 4345 9-11-4 **111** .... BrianHarding —
(Mrs K Walton) *towards rr: p.u after 6th* **33/1**

0032 **P** **Wildfield Rufo (IRE)**[22] 4505 11-10-10 **110** ....(p) ColmSharkey(7) —
(Mrs K Walton) *sn bhd: t.o whn p.u bef 2 out* **14/1**

0312 **P** **Lazy But Lively (IRE)**[14] 4636 10-10-1 **94** .... KeithMercer —
(R F Fisher) *nt fluent: a bhd: t.o whn p.u bef last* **6/1**[2]

0615 **P** **Red Perk (IRE)**[47] 4042 9-10-4 **97** ....(p) LarryMcGrath —
(R C Guest) *sn bhd and outpcd: nvr on terms: p.u bef 3 out* **14/1**

502P **P** **Capybara (IRE)**[21] 4518 8-11-5 **115** .... DougieCostello(3) —
(H P Hogarth) *towards rr: reminders 4th: outpcd 14th: t.o whn p.u bef last* **33/1**

12 **F** **Weapons Inspector (IRE)**[89] 3336 7-10-12 **105** .... GLee —
(J Howard Johnson) *nt fluent: hld up: hdwy gng wl and in tch whn fell heavily 14th* **7/2**[1]

6401 **P** **Bang And Blame (IRE)**[14] 4636 10-10-8 **106** .... MichaelMcAlister(5) —
(M W Easterby) *cl up: led 7th to 11th: wknd 4 out: t.o whn p.u bef last* **9/1**

1245 **P** **Sharp Belline (IRE)**[22] 4505 9-11-2 **109** .... DavidO'Meara —
(Mrs S J Smith) *led to 7th: prom: mstke and outpcd 15th: sn btn: t.o whn p.u bef 2 out* **10/1**

7m 14.5s **15** Ran SP% **125.3**
CSF £78.83 CT £932.48 TOTE £7.50: £2.30, £3.20, £3.20; EX 135.70 Trifecta £560.20 Part won. Pool £789.02 - 0.10 winning units..

Owner Miss S J Turner **Bred** G W Turner **Trained** Norton-le-Clay, N Yorks

FOCUS

A fair staying handicap, run at an average pace, and the field came home strung out.

NOTEBOOK

Rosie Redman(IRE), whose latest success was in this event last year from a 5lb lower mark, duly bounced back to her best and followed up in typically game fashion. She is clearly back in top form now, and is capable of holding her form well enough, so may be able to add to this in the coming weeks. *(tchd 8-1)*

Devil's Run(IRE) had every chance but ultimately found the winner too determined and was well held by that rival at the finish. He is a dour stayer, but while this was an improved effort, he is likely to be raised in the weights now and may struggle. *(op 10-1)*

Robbo, unplaced in a gruelling test at Pontefract five days previously, gave himself too much to do through the first half of the contest and was staying on all too late in the day. He is weighted to win at present, but has his own ideas about racing nowadays. *(op 14-1)*

Move Over(IRE), pulled up at Carlisle last time, was starting to tire prior to making an error at the penultimate fence which effectively ended any chance he may have had. This was a much more encouraging effort, however, and he can find another race when reverting to a slightly shorter trip. *(op 33-1)*

Strong Resolve(IRE) turned in a fairly lifeless effort and really has regressed since running in the Grand National last year. *(tchd 10-1)*

Lazy But Lively(IRE) *Official explanation: jockey said gelding was unsuited by the good to soft (good in places) going (op 7-1)*

Weapons Inspector(IRE) had yet to be asked for a serious effort prior to his crashing fall, but he had been less than impressive with his jumping up to that stage, and it was not a total surprise to see him come to grief. *(op 7-1)*

4791 K.O.S.B. NOVICES' HUNTERS' CHASE (19 fncs) 3m 1f

4:30 (4:40) (Class 6) 5-Y-0+ **£1,249** (£387; £193; £96)

Form					RPR
2	1		**Coomakista**[21] 9-10-12	MrRMorgan(5)	90+
			(Mrs E J Reed) *cl up: led 3 out: sn clr: styd on wl*	**4/7**[1]	
6P03	2	6	**High Expectations (IRE)**[6] [4722] 11-11-5 62	MrTDavidson(5)	85
			(J S Haldane) *led to 3rd: chsd ldrs: outpcd 15th: rallied 3 out: chsd wnr run in: no imp*	**12/1**	
	3	12	**Anshan Spirit (IRE)**[7] 8-10-10	MrRWGreen(7)	68+
			(R W Green) *led 3rd: sn clr: hit 11th: hdd 3 out: no ex fr next*	**12/1**	
P4P4	4	½	**Highland Brig**[6] [4722] 10-11-3 76	(t) MrMEllwood(7)	73
			(T Butt) *mstkes in rr: wl bhd tl sme late hdwy: nvr on terms*	**16/1**	
42P	5	dist	**Boardsmill Rambler (IRE)**[32] [4305] 7-11-10	MrMThompson	—
			(V Thompson) *in tch to 11th: sn wknd*	**14/1**	
3543	6	dist	**Starbuck**[15] 12-11-5 72	MrWLMorgan(5)	—
			(Miss J Fisher) *prom tl wknd fr 14th: t.o*	**10/1**[3]	
P6P/	P		**Winnie Wild**[28] 9-10-12	MissTJackson(5)	—
			(Miss T Jackson) *in tch tl lost pl 6th: t.o whn p.u bef 14th*	**9/1**[2]	
00P/	U		**Kiora Bay**[50] 9-11-3	MrDThomas(7)	—
			(T S Sharpe) *mstkes in rr: hdwy and in tch bef 10th: hit and wknd 12th: t.o whn blnd and uns rdr 2 out*	**33/1**	

6m 33.3s (3.70) **Going Correction** +0.10s/f (Yiel) **8** Ran SP% **113.6**

Speed ratings: **98,96,92,92,—** —,—,— CSF £8.69 TOTE £1.70: £1.10, £2.90, £2.80; EX 8.40.

Owner I B Speke **Bred** I B Speke **Trained** Hexham, Northumberland

FOCUS

A weak event of its type which saw the field trail home behind the ready winner. It has been rated around the second, who has been taken as having run to the same mark as in this race last year.

NOTEBOOK

Coomakista ran out a comfortable winner and got off the mark under Rules at the second time of asking. She stays very well, loves good ground, and should be capable of adding to this in the coming weeks. *(tchd 8-13 and 4-6 in places)*

High Expectations(IRE) was made to look pedestrian when the winner went past, yet plugged on under pressure and finished a clear second-best. He remains a maiden under Rules.

Anshan Spirit(IRE), runner-up between the flags a week previously, failed to sustain her effort and finished legless.

Highland Brig made too many early mistakes and was again keeping on all too late as a result. *(op 20-1)*

4792 GG.COM H'CAP HURDLE (10 hdls) 2m 2f

5:00 (5:06) (Class 3) (0-130,124) 4-Y-0+ **£7,807** (£2,292; £1,146; £572)

Form					RPR
-310	1		**River Alder**[104] [2990] 8-11-5 117	PeterBuchanan	119
			(J M Dun) *a cl up: led bef 2 out: hld on wl run in*	**20/1**	
22P2	2	½	**Pay Attention**[22] [4490] 5-11-5 124	PatrickMcDonald(7)	125
			(T D Easterby) *prom: drvn along 3 out: chsd wnr run in: kpt on: hld nr fin*	**13/2**	
U315	3	6	**Turbo (IRE)**[29] [4364] 7-10-12 113	(t) MrTGreenall(3)	109+
			(M W Easterby) *hld up: hdwy after 3 out: hung rt and kpt on fr last: nt rch first two*	**11/2**[3]	
-106	4	1 ½	**October Mist (IRE)**[5] [4215] 12-10-5 113	JamesReveley(10)	107
			(K G Reveley) *bhd tl kpt on fr 2 out: n.d*	**20/1**	
1543	5	nk	**Culcabock (IRE)**[22] [4490] 6-11-0 112	GLee	105
			(Miss Lucinda V Russell) *keen: chsd ldrs: led briefly after 3 out: no ex run in*	**8/1**	
1213	6	2	**Stagecoach Diamond**[43] [4108] 7-11-8 120	DavidO'Meara	111
			(Mrs S J Smith) *midfield: outpcd 3 out: kpt on fr last: no imp*	**9/2**[2]	
4340	7	5	**Rising Generation (FR)**[22] [4490] 9-11-1 123	FearghalDavis(10)	110+
			(N G Richards) *hld up midfield: drvn 3 out: no imp fr next*	**16/1**	
P034	8	hd	**Andre Chenier (IRE)**[22] [4490] 5-11-2 114	NeilMulholland	100
			(P Monteith) *hld up: smooth hdwy and ev ch 3 out: sn rdn: outpcd fr next*	**4/1**[1]	
20-0	9	7	**Regal Setting (IRE)**[183] [1677] 5-11-1 118	(t) BrianHughes(5)	97
			(J Howard Johnson) *bhd: rdn after 4 out: n.d*	**20/1**	
20U-	10	½	**Indy Mood**[400] [4184] 7-11-5 120	DougieCostello(3)	99
			(Mrs H O Graham) *bhd on outside: rdn 4 out: nvr on terms*	**25/1**	
63P0	11	4	**Thoutmosis (USA)**[57] [3854] 7-10-12 113	GaryBerridge(3)	88
			(L Lungo) *chsd ldrs to 3 out: qckly lost pl*	**11/1**	
300P	12	8	**St Pirran (IRE)**[57] [3852] 11-11-6 118	LarryMcGrath	85
			(R C Guest) *in tch tl wknd bef 3 out*	**33/1**	
041P	13	15	**Front Rank (IRE)**[29] [4364] 6-10-10 115	StevenGagan(7)	67
			(Mrs Dianne Sayer) *mde most to after 3 out: sn wknd*	**100/1**	
21P0	P		**Dan's Heir**[26] [4435] 4-10-12 121	PaddyMerrigan(5)	—
			(P C Haslam) *w ldrs tl wknd: eased and p.u bef 2 out*	**14/1**	
3256	U		**Carapuce (FR)**[29] [4364] 7-11-6 118	(p) TonyDobbin	—
			(L Lungo) *prom tl wknd 4 out: bhd whn blnd and uns rdr next*	**14/1**	

4m 31.3s (-8.60) **Going Correction** +0.175s/f (Yiel)

WFA 4 from 5yo+ 5lb **15** Ran SP% **127.6**

Speed ratings: **109,108,106,105,105 104,102,102,99,98 97,93,86,—,—** CSF £143.97 CT £842.46 TOTE £26.60: £7.80, £2.10, £2.40; EX 220.60.

Owner J M Dun **Bred** Mrs A G Martin And R F And S D Knipe **Trained** Heriot, Borders

FOCUS

A competitive event for the class, run at a sound pace, and the first two came clear.

NOTEBOOK

River Alder, whose trainer won this race in 1996 with Coqui Lane, showed her true colours on this return from a 104-day break with a game peformance. The drop back to this trip proved no problem, her form figures at this course now read 131, and she is versatile as regards underfoot conditions. Considering she was racing from a career-high mark, this must rate as a personal-best, and she ought to have a little more to offer over hurdles yet. *(op 22-1)*

Pay Attention turned in her usual game effort, but could not get past the winner try as she might. She finished nicely clear of the remainder and really does deserve to go one better this season. *(op 7-1)*

Turbo(IRE) again advertised his quirks and was never a serious threat to the first two. He still helps to set the level of this form, however. *(op 13-2)*

October Mist(IRE), who beat just one home at Pontefract five day previously, was only really put into the race from three out on this return to hurdling and is better than the bare form suggests.

Culcabock(IRE) ultimately paid for refusing to settle through the early stages. This was still another sound enough effort, however, and he can find less competitive assignments from his current mark. *(tchd 17-2)*

Stagecoach Diamond failed to really improve as expected for this less taxing ground and drop back in trip. He ideally wants a stiffer test. *(tchd 5-1)*

Andre Chenier(IRE), well backed, failed to find what had looked likely when off the bridle and looked very one-paced. He is one to have reservations about. *(op 11-2 tchd 6-1)*

4793 BLAEBERRYHILL INN "NATIONAL HUNT" NOVICES' HURDLE (DIV II) (11 hdls) 2m 6f 110y

5:30 (5:37) (Class 4) 4-Y-0+ **£3,383** (£993; £496; £248)

Form					RPR
54-2	1		**Ally Shrimp**[21] [4530] 5-11-2	BrianHarding	110
			(T P Tate) *a cl up: drvn bef 2 out: led run in: drifted lft: styd on wl*	**7/2**[2]	
2315	2	½	**Laertes**[31] [4315] 5-11-6 114	MrTGreenall(3)	117
			(C Grant) *led to 3rd: led 6th to run in: rdn and hung lft: kpt on: hld towards fin*	**9/1**[3]	
1123	3	3	**King Of Confusion (IRE)**[90] [3316] 7-11-9 121	KeithMercer	114
			(Ferdy Murphy) *keen: chsd ldrs: shkn up bef 2 out: one pce run in*	**5/6**[1]	
	4	7	**Robbers Glen (IRE)**[126] 6-11-2	GLee	103+
			(J Howard Johnson) *keen in midfield: smooth hdwy and ev ch 3 out: hung bdly lft and wknd run in*	**12/1**	
-635	5	22	**Major Oak (IRE)**[67] [3677] 5-11-2	BarryKeniry	78
			(G M Moore) *hld up towards rr: effrt 4 out: outpcd after next*	**12/1**	
0-00	6	dist	**Nasstar**[87] [3347] 5-11-2	WilsonRenwick	—
			(M W Easterby) *bhd and sn struggling: nvr on terms*	**100/1**	
F5P/	7	11	**Very Very Noble (IRE)**[755] [4371] 12-11-2	(t) NeilMulholland	—
			(W Storey) *keen in rr: hdwy to ld 3rd: hdd 6th: wknd appr 3 out*	**50/1**	
060	8	10	**Justwhateverulike (IRE)**[21] [4532] 5-10-13	MrCStorey(3)	—
			(Miss S E Forster) *prom tl wknd bef 3 out*	**100/1**	
0/P	9	dist	**Sharp Exit (IRE)**[12] [4657] 7-10-13	PaddyAspell(3)	—
			(J Wade) *prom: rdn and lost pl 1/2-way: n.d after*	**200/1**	
0	10	dist	**The Ringer**[148] [2192] 6-10-13	MichalKohl(3)	—
			(J I A Charlton) *a bhd: struggling fr 7th*	**80/1**	
10	P		**Red Poker**[60] [3793] 6-11-2	AlanDempsey	—
			(G A Harker) *a bhd: t.o whn p.u bef 3 out*	**16/1**	
P-P0	P		**Just Jed**[87] [3352] 7-10-13	DougieCostello(3)	—
			(R Shiels) *midfield: wknd 4 out: t.o whn p.u bef 2 out*	**100/1**	

5m 36.9s (-0.80) **Going Correction** +0.175s/f (Yiel) **12** Ran SP% **114.7**

Speed ratings: **108,107,106,104,96** —,—,—,— —,— CSF £33.03 TOTE £4.00: £1.50, £2.20, £1.10; EX 27.80 Place 6 £78.29, Place 5 £69.52.

Owner The Ivy Syndicate **Bred** G G A Gregson **Trained** Tadcaster, N Yorks

FOCUS

A fair novice event, slightly stronger than the first division, and the form looks sound enough.

NOTEBOOK

Ally Shrimp, runner-up to Money Trix over the course and distance last time, produced a dogged display to lose his maiden tag at the fourth time of asking. He does stay very well, has scope, and may be able to defy a penalty in this division while his yard remains in decent form. *(op 4-1 tchd 9-2 in a place)*

Laertes turned in an improved effort and did little wrong in defeat, yet was ultimately found out by his penalty. He probably needs softer ground and a stiffer trip now, however. *(op 8-1 tchd 12-1 in a place)*

King Of Confusion(IRE), absent for 90 days previously, found just the same pace when push came to shove and paid for running too freely through the early parts. He is another who ideally wants easier ground, and while this rather confirms his limitations, there are races to be won with him as a novice chaser next term. *(op 4-5 tchd 10-11 and Evens in a place)*

Robbers Glen(IRE), last seen winning an Irish point on heavy ground at the second attempt 126 days previously, posted a fairly promising debut effort on ground he looked to find against him. He will need to learn to settle better, but he is entitled to improve a deal for this experience, and is one to keep an eye on.

T/Plt: £87.40 to a £1 stake. Pool: £52,496.00. 438.45 winning tickets. T/Qpdt: £35.70 to a £1 stake. Pool: £3,171.90. 65.70 winning tickets. RY

4631 MARKET RASEN (R-H)

Sunday, April 9

OFFICIAL GOING: Soft

6mm rain soon turned the ground 'very soft' with a total of twenty two non-runners because of the changed underfoot conditions.

Wind: Light, half against Weather: Persistent rain

4794 BUY YOUR TICKETS ONLINE @ MARKETRASENRACES.CO.UK (S) H'CAP HURDLE (8 hdls) 2m 1f 110y

2:20 (2:22) (Class 5) (0-95,93) 4-Y-0+ **£2,192** (£639; £319)

Form					RPR
-400	1		**Losing Grip (IRE)**[15] [4609] 7-10-9 76	DominicElsworth	92+
			(Mrs S J Smith) *mde all: wnt clr appr 2 out: styd on strly*	**16/1**	
3106	2	10	**Moyne Pleasure (IRE)**[22] [4487] 8-11-3 84	KennyJohnson	88
			(R Johnson) *trckd ldrs: wnt 2nd appr 2 out: no ch w wnr*	**11/2**[2]	
5040	3	4	**Only Words (USA)**[32] [4302] 9-10-5 79	PhilKinsella(7)	79
			(A J Lockwood) *chsd ldrs: kpt on same pce appr 2 out*	**10/1**	
F0/	4	6	**Belene Boy (IRE)**[116] [2831] 13-10-6 76	TJPhelan(3)	70
			(M Flannery, Ire) *in rr: hdwy 5th: one pce fr next*	**33/1**	
PPU0	5	13	**Loup Bleu (USA)**[19] [4566] 8-11-7 93	LiamTreadwell(5)	74
			(Mrs A V Roberts) *wnt prom 4th: hit 6th: rdn and wknd appr 2 out*	**20/1**	
040	6	4	**Gran Dana (IRE)**[12] [3328] 6-10-12 79	TomScudamore	56
			(G Prodromou) *hld up in rr: effrt 5th: sn btn*	**14/1**	

-051 **7** *1 1/4* **Ethan Snowflake**[23] [4475] 7-11-8 92..........(b) ChrisHonour(3) 68
(N B King) *hld up in rr: hdwy to chse ldrs 6th: lost pl appr next* **10/1**

0034 **8** *5* **Protocol (IRE)**[14] [4632] 12-10-10 82..........(tp) TJDreaper(5) 53
(Mrs S Lamyman) *chsd ldrs: rdn and lost pl 3 out* **11/1**

53PP **9** *2 1/2* **Desertmore Chief (IRE)**[14] [4640] 7-10-13 80..........(b) MarkBradburne 48
(G J Smith) *chsd wnr: lost pl after 6th* **25/1**

0-00 **10** *1 3/4* **Explode**[86] [3371] 9-10-9 76.......... TomSiddall 43
(Miss L C Siddall) *a detached in rr: t.o 5th* **25/1**

2204 **11** *1 1/2* **Seraph**[14] [4640] 6-10-13 83.......... LeeVickers(3) 48
(O Brennan) *mid-div: effrt 6th: sn rdn and btn* **5/1**[1]

454F **12** *1/2* **Jour De Mee (FR)**[40] [4165] 9-10-12 79.......... JodieMogford 44
(G J Smith) *chsd ldrs: j. slowly and lost pl 4th: sn bhd* **13/2**[3]

R-06 **R** **Golden Fields (IRE)**[32] [4299] 6-10-13 80..........(p) PaulMoloney —
(G A Harker) *ref to r: lft at s* **22/1**

U1PR **P** **Prairie Law (GER)**[31] [4320] 6-11-5 93.......... TomMessenger(7) —
(B N Pollock) *rel to r: hopelessly t.o: p.u bef 5th* **7/1**

00P0 **P** **Dormy Two (IRE)**[14] [4632] 6-11-2 83..........(p) AnthonyRoss —
(J S Wainwright) *bdly hmpd s: hopelessly t.o tl p.u bef 2nd* **33/1**

4m 28.7s (12.30) **Going Correction** +0.725s/f (Soft) **15** Ran SP% **119.6**
Speed ratings: **101,96,94,92,86 84,84,81,80,79 79,79,—,—,—** CSF £92.66 CT £940.04 TOTE £21.90: £5.60, £2.20, £3.00; EX 138.00.The winner was bought in for 3,600gns
Owner The Victory Salute Group **Bred** Mrs Mary Tyner **Trained** High Eldwick, W Yorks

FOCUS
The winner made it a true test in the deteriorating conditions. The race has been rated through the runner-up's Sedgefield win.

NOTEBOOK
Losing Grip(IRE), promoted to first in an Irish point, was warm beforehand and keen to post. She ran her rivals ragged and may be able to hold her own in slightly better company.
Moyne Pleasure(IRE), 5lb higher than when winning at Sedgefield, travelled strongly and looked a real threat three out but in the end he could not get in a blow. *(op 9-2 tchd 6-1)*
Only Words(USA), without a win for over two years, ran better than on his five previous starts this time without showing any real sparkle.
Belene Boy(IRE), an elderly Irish raider, had the blinkers left off and his career record now reads one win from 33 starts.
Seraph was making hard work of it some way out and the rain had turned the ground against him. *Official explanation: trainer said gelding was unsuited by the soft ground*

4795 SPORTING SUNDAY JUVENILE NOVICES' HURDLE (8 hdls) 2m 1f 110y
2:50 (2:53) (Class 4) 4-Y-O **£4,554** (£1,337; £668; £333)

Form RPR

14 **1** **Caribou (FR)**[98] [3182] 4-11-4 113.......... PJBrennan 111+
(O Sherwood) *trckd ldrs: led 5th: styd on u.p run-in* **6/4**[2]

5 **2** *6* **Osako D'Airy (FR)**[43] [4117] 4-10-12..........(t) TomScudamore 98
(S Gollings) *chsd ldrs: wnt 2nd appr 2 out: kpt on same pce run-in* **11/8**[1]

4 **3** *24* **Beautiful Night (FR)**[25] [4450] 4-10-5.......... RobertThornton 69+
(M D Hammond) *chsd ldrs: lft modest 3rd 2 out: hit last* **7/1**[3]

00 **4** *1 3/4* **Finnegans Rainbow**[45] [4077] 4-10-9.......... LeeVickers(3) 72
(M C Chapman) *j.lft: led to 5th: wknd appr 2 out* **66/1**

0P5P **5** *10* **Trappeto (IRE)**[46] [4057] 4-10-9 91.......... TJPhelan(3) 62
(C Smith) *stdd s: hld up in rr: sme hdwy 3 out: wl btn whn hmpd next* **16/1**

P4F **6** *nk* **Power Glory**[59] [3817] 4-10-9.......... ChrisHonour(3) 62
(M J Gingell) *t.k.h: wnt promient 4th: lost pl appr 2 out* **40/1**

0600 **7** *6* **Water Pistol**[14] [4631] 4-10-12 78.......... KennyJohnson 56
(M C Chapman) *chsd ldrs: lost pl after 6th* **80/1**

8 *dist* **House Martin**[36] 4-10-5.......... AndrewTinkler —
(C R Dore) *stdd s: hld up in rr: sme hdwy 6th: sn wknd: t.o* **25/1**

B **Maynooth Princess (IRE)**[324] 4-10-0.......... DeclanMcGann(5) —
(R Johnson) *in rr: bhd fr 6th: b.d last* **100/1**

P **The Last Sabo**[447] 4-10-5.......... MrSRees(7) —
(M Wigham) *stdd s: detached in last: nt fluent: t.o 4th: p.u after 6th* **100/1**

P **Eidsfoss (IRE)**[98] 4-10-9.......... ColinBolger(3) —
(T T Clement) *t.k.h in rr: sme hdwy whn mstke 5th: lost pl after next: t.o whn p.u bef 2 out* **100/1**

60 **F** **Smokey The Bear**[109] [2935] 4-10-12.......... JamieGoldstein 72
(Miss Sheena West) *sn trcking ldrs: modest 3rd whn fell 2 out: fell heavily loose last* **50/1**

4m 37.7s (21.30) **Going Correction** +1.10s/f (Heav) **12** Ran SP% **114.4**
Speed ratings: **96,93,82,81,77 77,74,—,—,— —,—** CSF £3.72 TOTE £2.50: £1.10, £1.10, £1.90; EX 5.10.
Owner It Wasn't Us **Bred** Haras De Nonant Le Pin **Trained** Upper Lambourn, Berks

FOCUS
No strength in depth and in the end just a two-horse race with the winner always holding the upper hand.

NOTEBOOK
Caribou(FR), absent for 98 days, went on and kept up the gallop all the way to the line. He looks every inch a potential chaser. *(tchd 15-8)*
Osako D'Airy(FR), a winner of a bumper and a chase in France, wore a tongue-tie on his second start here. He went in pursuit of the winner but never looked like getting the better of him. He can surely go one better in similar company. *(op 6-4)*
Beautiful Night(FR) looks to have but a fraction of her full-brother Sleeping Night's ability but a success, however small, will boost her paddock value. *(op 6-1)*
Finnegans Rainbow, reluctant to leave the paddock, took them along but continually gave away ground jumping to his left. *(op 100-1)*
Smokey The Bear, claimed at Ludlow, was third and tired when he fell two out. Running loose, he took a horrible-looking fall at the last. *(tchd 40-1)*

4796 RACING UK ON CHANNEL 432 NOVICES' CHASE (14 fncs) 2m 4f
3:20 (3:25) (Class 3) 5-Y-O+ **£6,506** (£1,910; £955; £477)

Form RPR

2134 **1** **Rebel Rhythm**[64] [3740] 7-11-8 135.......... DominicElsworth 137+
(Mrs S J Smith) *j.rt: led after 1st: wnt clr 3 out: eased towards fin* **2/5**[1]

-415 **2** *28* **Iron Man (FR)**[60] [3796] 5-11-8 129.......... RobertThornton 112+
(J Howard Johnson) *j.rt: led tl after 1st: chsd wnr: effrt and chal appr 3 out: sn btn: 18 l down last: eased* **5/2**[2]

P43 **3** *11* **Sandy Gold (IRE)**[74] [3558] 8-10-9.......... PhilKinsella(7) 87
(Miss J E Foster) *sn modest 3rd: mstke 4th: plodded rnd in own time* **18/1**[3]

36P4 **4** *dist* **Dalriath**[225] [1335] 7-10-9 85.......... KennyJohnson —
(M C Chapman) *t.k.h in modest 4th: wknd 8th: sn bhd: t.o 3 out* **33/1**

36 **P** **Delaware Trail**[60] [3796] 7-10-11.......... DeclanMcGann(5) —
(R Johnson) *j. bdly: t.k.h in last: t.o last whn p.u bef 3 out* **50/1**

5m 31.7s (29.00) **Going Correction** +1.425s/f (Heav) **5** Ran SP% **110.2**
Speed ratings: **99,87,83,—,—** CSF £1.89 TOTE £1.50: £1.10, £1.20; EX 1.90.
Owner The Fees R Us Syndicate **Bred** Five Horses Ltd **Trained** High Eldwick, W Yorks

FOCUS
The winner is gaining valuable experience and will be even better going left-handed. The race has been rated through the winner, who ran to his mark in beating a dubious stayer over this trip.

NOTEBOOK
Rebel Rhythm, whose five previous career victories have been on left-handed tracks, continually went off to his right at the fences. Keeping up the gallop in relentless fashion, he had it in the bag three from home. *(op 4-7)*
Iron Man(FR), friendless in the betting markets, need a right-handed track. Jumping that way, he emptied in a matter of strides going to three out and in the end was left to finish in his own time. He has yet to prove his stamina. *(op 2-1)*
Sandy Gold(IRE) couldn't live with the first two from an early stage and novices' handicaps are surely a better option. *(op 16-1)*
Dalriath, absent since August, took a grip for a circuit before falling in a heap. *(op 28-1)*
Delaware Trail *Official explanation: jockey said gelding was unsuited by the soft ground (op 33-1)*

4797 WEST LINDSEY DISTRICT COUNCIL EASTER CUP H'CAP HURDLE (10 hdls) 2m 6f
3:50 (3:54) (Class 4) (0-115,115) 4-Y-O+ **£5,204** (£1,528; £764; £381)

Form RPR

312- **1** **Malay**[355] [4920] 9-11-5 115.......... WillieMcCarthy(7) 120+
(Mrs Norma Pook) *hld up: smooth hdwy 7th: wnt 2nd after next: shkn up and chal 2 out: hung rt and led last: styd on towards fin* **14/1**

2211 **2** *1 1/4* **Imtihan (IRE)**[6] [4724] 7-10-9 108 7ex.......... MichaelO'Connell(10) 112
(Mrs S J Smith) *chsd ldrs: reminders and led 6th: hdd last: no ex last 75yds* **10/11**[1]

F446 **3** *25* **Titian Flame (IRE)**[22] [4488] 6-10-1 97..........(p) MrRhysHughes(7) 76
(D Burchell) *led: hdd 6th: outpcd after 3 out: tk modest 3rd 2 out* **14/1**

0321 **4** *4* **Emmasflora**[12] [4657] 8-11-6 114.......... AdamPogson(5) 89
(C T Pogson) *chsd ldrs: wnt 3rd after 3 out: sn hrd drvn and outpcd by 1st 2* **7/2**[2]

200P **5** *dist* **Sovereign State (IRE)**[23] [4478] 9-11-0 110.......... PhilKinsella(7) —
(D W Thompson) *mid-divsion: hdwy 5th: lost pl after 7th: sn bhd: t.o* **40/1**

P3F5 **P** **Common Girl (IRE)**[74] [3559] 8-11-2 105.......... JamieMoore —
(O Brennan) *chsd ldrs: lost pl 5th: bhd whn p.u bef 3 out* **14/1**

00UP **P** **Cha Cha Cha Dancer**[46] [4053] 6-10-9 98.......... DominicElsworth —
(G A Swinbank) *bhd fr 5th: 8th and t.o whn p.u bef 2 out* **20/1**

605 **P** **Fantastic Champion (IRE)**[72] [3593] 7-11-9 112..........(b) RichardHobson —
(J R Cornwall) *sn bhd and rdn along: t.o 6th: p.u bef 3 out* **50/1**

P-PP **P** **Kaparolo (USA)**[28] [4390] 7-10-8 97.......... AndrewTinkler —
(John A Harris) *chsd ldrs: outpcd 6th: wknd next: 6th and t.o whn p.u bef 2 out* **50/1**

2111 **P** **Charlie's Double**[266] [1026] 7-10-12 101.......... DaveCrosse —
(J R Best) *prom: lost pl 5th: bhd fr 7th: 9th and t.o last whn p.u bef 2 out* **9/1**[3]

42P2 **P** **Pride Of Finewood (IRE)**[22] [4491] 8-10-5 99.......... TJDreaper(5) —
(E W Tuer) *prom: drvn along 4th: lost pl next: bhd fr 7th: 7th and t.o whn p.u bef 2 out* **14/1**

5m 53.1s (24.80) **Going Correction** +1.10s/f (Heav) **11** Ran SP% **122.4**
Speed ratings: **98,97,88,87,— —,—,—,—,— —** CSF £28.74 CT £206.70 TOTE £15.90: £3.30, £1.10, £2.70; EX 37.70.
Owner Mrs Norma Pook **Bred** Temple Farming **Trained** Penn Bottom, Bucks
■ A first training success for Norma Pook.

FOCUS
A strongly-run race in the deteriorating conditions and the race could be rated 6lb higher.

NOTEBOOK
Malay, absent for a year and flying the flag for her rookie trainer, came there on the bridle. She hung fire when asked to go and win her race but was firmly in command at the line. With the runner-up penalised for his Kelso success both face a stiff rise in the ratings after this. *(op 12-1)*
Imtihan(IRE), pulled out under a 7lb penalty, stepped up the gallop early on the final circuit. He gave his all but in the end the winner had his measure. *(op 11-10)*
Titian Flame(IRE), who planted herself at the start, took them along at a sound gallop and kept on sufficiently well to regain a modest third spot. The ground had come in her favour. *(tchd 12-1)*
Emmasflora, who gets no respite, was left behind by the first two going to two out. *(op 6-1)*
Sovereign State(IRE), out of sorts, doesn't want conditions as testing as this and this trip looks beyond him. *(op 33-1)*
Charlie's Double *Official explanation: jockey said gelding was unsuited by the soft ground (op 40-1)*
Kaparolo(USA) *Official explanation: jockey said gelding was unsuited by the soft ground (op 40-1)*
Common Girl(IRE) *Official explanation: jockey said mare never travelled (op 40-1)*
Pride Of Finewood(IRE) *Official explanation: jockey said gelding hung left throughout (op 40-1)*

4798 LEGSBY ROAD H'CAP CHASE (14 fncs) 2m 4f
4:20 (4:22) (Class 4) (0-115,115) 5-Y-O+ **£3,665** (£1,137; £612)

Form RPR

4P01 **1** **Kirov King (IRE)**[13] [4653] 6-10-1 97.......... MrGTumelty(7) 108+
(R H York) *stdd s: keen and chsd ldr 2nd: led 5th: j.lft 7th: styd on wl run-in: rdn out* **7/4**[1]

031 **2** *7* **Kercabellec (FR)**[14] [4633] 8-10-8 97.......... RichardHobson 102+
(J R Cornwall) *wl away: led and clr to 2nd: hdd 5th: hit 7th: jnd wnr 9th: hit 3 out: upsides last: sn outpcd* **4/1**

F535 **3** *dist* **Sands Rising**[17] [4586] 9-10-12 101..........(t) KennyJohnson —
(R Johnson) *w.w: effrt 11th: chsng other 2 next: wknd 2 out: sn lost tch: t.o: fin tired* **3/1**[3]

3333 **U** **Before The Mast (IRE)**[10] [4675] 9-10-0 89.......... PJBrennan —
(M F Harris) *trckd ldrs fr 4th: unsighted: hmpd and uns rdr 7th* **11/4**[2]

5m 41.6s (38.90) **Going Correction** +1.425s/f (Heav) **4** Ran SP% **108.0**
Speed ratings: **79,76,—,—** CSF £8.39 TOTE £2.70; EX 6.50.
Owner K Tork **Bred** Mrs T V Ryan **Trained** Martyr's Green, Surrey

FOCUS
This was not much of a race but the first two ran pretty much to their marks.

NOTEBOOK
Kirov King(IRE), a headstrong individual, gave away ground at the start. He looked to have a battle royal on his hands jumping the last but in the end won going away. He went straight to the start, for which his rider was fined £130. *(op 2-1)*
Kercabellec(FR), hoisted a ridiculous 18lb after his runaway win in a bad race here last time, stole a march on his rivals at the start. Making a couple of jumping errors, after landing upsides at the last he was soon left trailing. *(op 3-1)*
Sands Rising, suited by heavy ground, has been off the boil. Hunted round, he stuck to the inner on the final turn but after getting within reach of the first two he stopped like a pricked balloon two out. *(op 4-1)*
Before The Mast(IRE) unluckily lost his rider at the last with a circuit to go having been left short of room by the first two. *(op 9-4 tchd 3-1)*

The Form Book, Raceform Ltd, Compton, RG20 6NL

4799 BEAUMONTCOTE HUNTERS' CHASE (17 fncs) 3m 1f
4:50 (4:50) (Class 6) 6-Y-O+ **£1,420** (£507)

Form RPR

5-P2 **1** **Sea Ferry (IRE)**[30] 4351 10-11-7 81 MrMBriggs(7) 101+
(Mrs Antonia Bealby) *chsd ldrs: hit 10th: c wd: led and blnd 3 out: styd on to forge clr last 150yds* **7/2**[3]

0/21 **2** *4* **Ramirez (IRE)**[16] 4607 8-12-0 MrNickKent(7) 102
(Nick Kent) *w ldrs: led briefly appr 3 out: upides last: no ex* **5/2**[2]

-435 **P** **Lucky Master (IRE)**[14] 14-11-7 MissGSwan(7) —
(Miss G Swan) *mstke 1st: in rr: t.o 6th: p.u bef 9th* **50/1**

P/ **P** **Tap The Father (IRE)**[14] 13-11-8 ow1 MrCWard(7) —
(Fred Farrow) *outpcd 5th: reminders 7th: t.o 9th: p.u bef 13th* **66/1**

010P **P** **Corkan (IRE)**[16] 4607 12-11-7 66 (p) MrABarlow(7) —
(Mrs F Kehoe) *led to 5th: outpcd 9th: bhd fr 11th: t.o 4th whn hit 14th: sn p.u* **40/1**

30/P **P** **Whitley Grange Boy**[21] 13-12-0 MrSWalker —
(C C Pimlott) *chsd ldrs: 4th and pushed along 11th: sn lost pl and bhd: t.o whn p.u bef next* **22/1**

2P **P** **Mage D'Estruval (FR)**[24] 4460 6-12-2 MrPCallaghan(5) —
(H D Daly) *chsd ldr: led 5th: mstke 14th: hdd and fnd nthing appr next: 3rd and wkng rapidly whn p.u bef 3 out* **11/10**[1]

7m 12.2s (34.80) **Going Correction** +1.425s/f (Heav) **7** Ran SP% **108.7**
Speed ratings: **101,99,—,—,—** —,— CSF £11.48 TOTE £4.70: £2.10, £2.30; EX 8.70.
Owner Mrs J A C Lundgren **Bred** T A Keating **Trained** Barrowby, Lincs
■ The first winner under Rules for Matt Briggs.

FOCUS
Only two finishers, but they ran to the level of their respective Leicester runs.

NOTEBOOK
Sea Ferry(IRE), a winner of two points this year, chanced his arm but, brought wide off the final turn, gained the upper hand in the closing stages. *(op 5-1)*
Ramirez(IRE) went down fighting but his rider wouldn't get many marks for style. *(op 6-4)*
Mage D'Estruval(FR) went on travelling easily, but a mistake four out finished him completely and *he looked out on his feet when pulled up before the next. He probably has a serious problem. Official explanation: trainer's represenative had no explanation for the poor form shown (op 6-5)*

4800 RASEN THE ROOF MARES' ONLY STANDARD OPEN NATIONAL HUNT FLAT RACE 2m 1f 110y
5:20 (5:20) (Class 6) 4-6-Y-O **£1,713** (£499; £249)

Form RPR

24-0 **1** **Autograph**[330] 349 5-11-0 DominicElsworth 96+
(Mrs S J Smith) *mde all: clr over 3f out: styd on wl: unchal* **9/2**[3]

2 *10* **Clifton** 4-10-1 MissJCoward(7) 78
(M W Easterby) *chsd ldrs: rn green and lost pl 7f out: poor 5th 3f out: styd on to go 2nd over 1f out* **12/1**

3 *8* **Jim Bobs Girl (IRE)**[56] 5-11-0 MarkBradburne 76
(W Jenks) *hdwy to chse ldrs 10f out: wnt 2nd 3f out: one pce* **15/2**

4 *9* **Single Handed** 4-10-8 RobertThornton 61
(H D Daly) *chsd ldrs: outpcd 7f out: rallied over 3f out: one pce* **4/1**[2]

5 *28* **Jessie May (IRE)** 5-11-0 TomDoyle 47+
(P R Webber) *trckd ldrs: wnt 2nd 8f out: rdn and wknd 3f out* **3/1**[1]

3 **6** *1 1/4* **Morning Roses**[32] 4304 4-10-1 PhilKinsella(7) 32
(K G Reveley) *hdwy to chse ldrs 10f out: lost pl over 4f out: sn bhd* **11/2**

7 *dist* **Panama Three Knots** 6-10-4 AndrewAdams(10) —
(J M Saville) *lost pl 10f out: sn bhd: t.o* **28/1**

8 *1 3/4* **Niza D'Alm (FR)** 5-10-11 ColinBolger(3) —
(Miss Suzy Smith) *chsd ldr: wknd 5f out: sn bhd: t.o* **14/1**

P **Bellaney House (IRE)** 5-11-0 DNolan —
(J J Quinn) *in rr: pushed along 10f out: bhd 7f out: sn t.o: p.u 4f out* **12/1**

P **Briyatha** 4-10-1 (t) MrCKester(7) —
(C N Kellett) *w.w off pce and racd wd: lost pl 6f out: sn t.o: p.u over 3f out* **50/1**

4m 34.8s (18.30) **Going Correction** +1.10s/f (Heav)
WFA 4 from 5yo+ 5lb **10** Ran SP% **117.8**
Speed ratings: **103,98,95,91,78 78,—,—,—,—** CSF £57.94 TOTE £5.80: £2.50, £3.50, £3.20; EX 71.30 Place 6 £30.56, Place 5 £6.32.
Owner Mrs B Ramsden **Bred** Longdon Stud Ltd **Trained** High Eldwick, W Yorks

FOCUS
A weak mares-only bumper turned into a true test by the winner.

NOTEBOOK
Autograph, runner-up on her debut, was having her fourth outing after nearly a year off. She ran them ragged and had this won turning in. *(op 7-2 tchd 5-1)*
Clifton, quite a rangy filly, looked green. After dropping right away she showed plenty of stamina to stay on and capture a remote second spot. The experience will not be lost on her. *(op 10-1)*
Jim Bobs Girl(IRE), who has shown form in Irish points, is up in the air and narrow. She looks to lack several gears. *(op 10-1)*
Single Handed, an active type, is from the dam line of the stable's useful chaser Hand Inn Hand. *(op 9-2)*
Jessie May(IRE), quite a tall filly, went well for a long way but tired badly on the testing ground turning for home. She is better than this. *(op 7-2)*
Morning Roses was on the retreat starting the home turn and seemed not to relish the testing conditions. *(op 6-1 tchd 5-1)*
T/Jkpt: £64,352.70 to a £1 stake. Pool: £90,637.62. 1.00 winning ticket. T/Plt: £31.90 to a £1 stake. Pool: £42,750.50. 978.05 winning tickets. T/Qpdt: £6.20 to a £1 stake. Pool: £2,550.30. 302.50 winning tickets. WG

4638 WORCESTER (L-H)
Sunday, April 9

OFFICIAL GOING: Good (good to soft in home straight)
This meeting was vastly over-subscribed and there were 182 eliminations.
Wind: Moderate behind Weather: Wintry showers

4801 RAINBOW CLEANING SERVICES MARES' ONLY MAIDEN HURDLE (10 hdls) 2m 4f
2:10 (2:10) (Class 5) 4-Y-O+ **£2,740** (£798; £399)

Form RPR

0-32 **1** **Ceoperk (IRE)**[31] 4324 7-11-0 WarrenMarston 97+
(D J Wintle) *a.p: led after 6th: rdn and 3 l ahd whn lft clr last: eased cl home* **6/4**[1]

3-2 **2** *3* **Blueland (IRE)**[347] 58 7-10-11 WilliamKennedy(3) 91+
(Noel T Chance) *hld up in mid-div: hdwy after 6th: rdn after 7th: mstke 3 out: lft 2nd last: no ch w wnr* **11/2**[3]

0 **3** *6* **Solway Bee**[6] 4720 6-10-7 GarethThomas(7) 82
(Miss L Harrison) *hld up and bhd: struggling 6th: hdwy appr 3 out: styd on fr 2 out: n.d* **150/1**

10 **4** *8* **Larkbarrow**[29] 4376 5-11-0 (t) AntonyEvans 74
(N A Twiston-Davies) *prom tl rdn and wknd after 7th* **12/1**

0-04 **5** *16* **Hiho Silver Lining**[29] 4376 5-11-0 JimCrowley 58
(H Morrison) *hld up: hdwy 5th: rdn after 6th: wknd 7th* **15/8**[2]

46 **6** *3* **Parthian Shot**[28] 4398 6-11-0 RichardJohnson 55
(R T Phillips) *led appr 2nd tl after 6th: wkng whn blnd 7th* **14/1**

6/6- **7** *24* **Heavenly Pleasure (IRE)**[683] 512 7-11-0 WayneHutchinson 31
(J Hetherton) *t.k.h in tch: wknd appr 7th: t.o* **66/1**

00 **8** *26* **Shoestodiefor**[49] 4017 6-11-0 LeightonAspell 5
(S A Brookshaw) *a bhd: t.o whn j.lft 2 out* **100/1**

0-P0 **P** **Fashion Shoot**[66] 3691 5-11-0 HenryOliver —
(P Kelsall) *a bhd: lost tch after 4th: t.o whn p.u bef 3 out* **200/1**

PF-0 **P** **Cillamon**[150] 2151 9-10-9 LiamHeard(5) —
(K Bishop) *led tl appr 2nd: chsd ldr: 2nd whn p.u and dismntd bef 5th* **80/1**

4004 **U** **Ausone**[20] 4551 4-10-4 OwynNelmes(3) 85
(Miss J R Gibney) *hld up: hdwy appr 6th: ev ch 3 out: sn rdn: 3 l 2nd and hld whn stmbld and uns rdr last* **20/1**

4m 54.5s (6.50) **Going Correction** +0.20s/f (Yiel)
WFA 4 from 5yo+ 6lb **11** Ran SP% **114.2**
Speed ratings: **95,93,91,88,81 80,71,60,—,—** — CSF £10.01 TOTE £2.20: £1.40, £1.30, £13.50; EX 8.80.
Owner Willijoman Partnership **Bred** Miss Annette McMahon **Trained** Naunton, Gloucs

FOCUS
A typically modest mares' maiden. The winner is rated value for 6l.

NOTEBOOK
Ceoperk(IRE) settled better this time and looked to have the upper hand when Ausone exited at the last. *(op 7-4 tchd 11-8)*
Blueland(IRE), off course for almost a year, was flattered by her proximity to the winner and may have been lucky to finish second. *(op 13-2)*
Solway Bee stepped up considerably on her recent Kelso debut and shaped as though she wants even further. *(op 125-1)*
Larkbarrow, highly tried last time after her successful bumper debut, was fitted with a tongue tie on this graduation to hurdles. *(op 10-1)*
Hiho Silver Lining had finished a long way ahead of Larkbarrow in a valuable Sandown bumper last time. It could be that she needs soft ground. *(tchd 2-1 and 9-4 in places)*
Cillamon *Official explanation: jockey said mare pulled up lame (op 100-1)*
Ausone appeared to be getting the worse of the argument when unshipping her rider at the last. This was a significant improvement on her previous efforts. *(op 100-1)*

4802 ARENA LEISURE BEGINNERS' CHASE (18 fncs) 2m 7f 110y
2:40 (2:40) (Class 4) 5-Y-O+ **£3,903** (£1,146; £573; £286)

Form RPR

-235 **1** **Ryders Storm (USA)**[16] 4605 7-11-2 105 JasonMaguire 113+
(T R George) *hld up: hdwy 12th: led 14th: sn edgd lft and hdd: led after 3 out: clr appr last: easily* **3/1**[2]

P04- **2** *16* **Blue Americo (IRE)**[353] 4948 8-11-2 ChristianWilliams 93+
(P F Nicholls) *nt jump wl: plld hrd in rr: hdwy 12th: rdn appr 3 out: wnt 2nd appr last: no ch w wnr* **5/1**[3]

12P0 **3** *3 1/2* **Herecomestanley**[28] 4396 7-10-11 CharliePoste(5) 89+
(M F Harris) *hld up: hdwy 9th: led after 14th: hit 3 out: sn hdd: blnd 2 out: sn wknd* **12/1**

00- **4** *3 1/2* **Captain Machell (IRE)**[520] 2012 8-11-2 WayneHutchinson 83
(Andrew Turnell) *hld up: hdwy after 14th: no imp whn mstke 2 out* **15/2**

6PF4 **5** *18* **Ashleybank House (IRE)**[30] 4350 9-10-9 80 (tp) AndrewGlassonbury(7) 65
(David Pearson) *hld up: hmpd 3rd: hdwy 9th: sn rdn: wknd 13th* **40/1**

P60 **6** *dist* **The Hardy Boy**[13] 4649 6-11-2 MatthewBatchelor —
(Miss A M Newton-Smith) *led: j.rt 3rd: hdd 4th: led after 9th: hit 13th: hdd 14th: sn wknd* **66/1**

P **Narval D'Avelot (FR)**[33] 5-10-7 JamesDavies —
(D G Bridgwater) *hld up in tch: hmpd after 14th: sn wknd: bhd whn p.u bef 2 out* **16/1**

/233 **U** **Supreme Toss (IRE)**[29] 4369 10-11-2 125 (b1) RichardJohnson —
(R T Phillips) *prom: bmpd 3rd: lost pl 4th: bhd whn blnd and uns rdr 11th* **6/4**[1]

/0P0 **P** **Adventino**[4] 4733 11-10-9 AdrianScholes(7) —
(P R Johnson) *sn prom: j.rt and led 4th: j.rt 5th: clr 6th: hdd after 9th: blnd 12th: sn wknd: p.u bef 4 out* **100/1**

6m 1.20s (6.30) **Going Correction** +0.20s/f (Yiel)
WFA 5 from 6yo+ 4lb **9** Ran SP% **111.9**
Speed ratings: **97,91,90,89,83** —,—,—,— CSF £17.91 TOTE £4.00: £1.10, £2.10, £2.30; EX 22.50.
Owner Ryder Racing Ltd **Bred** Stud Tnt **Trained** Slad, Gloucs
■ Stewards' Enquiry : Jason Maguire one-day ban: careless riding (Apr 20)

FOCUS
A moderate contest run in a slow time, and dubious form.

NOTEBOOK
Ryders Storm(USA) ◆ appeared to be suited by this slightly longer trip and the further he went the better he looked. Often let down by his jumping in the past, it seems as if he has got his act together and he is capable of defying a penalty on this sort of ground. *(op 7-2)*
Blue Americo(IRE) was reverting to fences on this first start for nearly a year. He found the combination of refusing to settle and some indifferent jumping eventually taking its toll. *(op 11-4)*
Herecomestanley, on his chasing debut, found that his jumping failed to come up to scratch when the chips were down. *(op 10-1)*
Captain Machell(IRE), an Irish point winner, never really looked like justifying being a springer in the market after a 520-day absence on first run for a new trainer. *(op 20-1)*
Supreme Toss(IRE), blinkered for the first time, was again an expensive failure. He may have *become unsettled after being bumped at the third and eventually departed at the third ditch. (op 13-8 tchd 7-4)*

4803 MISS WORCESTERSHIRE NIGHT 6TH MAY NOVICES' HURDLE (12 hdls) 3m
3:10 (3:10) (Class 4) 4-Y-O+ **£3,083** (£898; £449)

Form RPR

23P1 **1** **Blackergreen**[21] 4515 7-11-7 103 PadgeWhelan 124+
(Mrs S J Smith) *a.p: led 6th: clr appr 3 out: rdn and r.o wl flat* **8/1**[3]

1 **2** *6* **Teeton Babysham**[79] 3478 6-11-7 128 (t) ChristianWilliams 118
(P F Nicholls) *hld up in tch: sltly outpcd 8th: rallied and chsd wnr 3 out: no imp flat* **8/11**[1]

1-31 **3** *20* **Pontiff (IRE)**[22] 4501 6-11-1 MickFitzgerald 97+
(Carl Llewellyn) *led to 1st: a.p: chsd wnr 9th to 3 out: wknd appr last* **3/1**[2]

23 **4** *13* **Just For Men (IRE)**[33] 4284 6-10-10 LiamHeard(5) 79
(P F Nicholls) *a bhd: struggling fr 7th* **16/1**

6 5 26 **Jacksons Pier (IRE)**[22] [4500] 6-10-8 .... JohnKington(7) 53
(M Scudamore) *led 1st to 6th: rdn and wknd appr 3 out* **50/1**
6 dist **Carry Duff**[338] 5-11-1 .... TimmyMurphy —
(Ferdy Murphy) *hld up: hdwy 7th: rdn and wknd after 9th: t.o* **14/1**
014B P **Sistema**[17] [4593] 5-11-4 98.. OwynNelmes(3) —
(A E Price) *a bhd: rdn 7th: t.o whn p.u bef 9th* **100/1**
F P **Teddy's Song**[298] [763] 8-10-10 .... JamesDiment(5) —
(P A Pritchard) *hld up and plld hrd: bhd fr 7th: t.o whn mstke 3 out: p.u bef 2 out* **150/1**

5m 53.4s (4.20) **Going Correction** +0.20s/f (Yiel) **8** Ran SP% **110.2**
Speed ratings: **101,99,92,88,79** —,—,— CSF £13.83 TOTE £12.80: £2.50, £1.10, £1.50; EX 20.60.
Owner P England **Bred** Miss Leona Robertson **Trained** High Eldwick, W Yorks

FOCUS
The first three had all won in soft ground on their previous outings. The winner was quite impressive, although the time did not compare well with the later handicap.

NOTEBOOK
Blackergreen followed up his win at Carlisle in convincing fashion and showed that he does not require give in the ground to be seen at his best. *(op 9-1 tchd 11-1)*
Teeton Babysham, fitted with a tongue tie, was beaten fair and square having won his point on a similar surface to this. *(op 4-6 tchd 4-5 in places)*
Pontiff(IRE) may have been affected more than the first two by the fact that this was a quicker surface. *(op 9-2 tchd 5-1)*

4804 SEVERN SUITE RESTAURANT FOR SUNDAY LUNCH CONDITIONAL JOCKEYS' H'CAP CHASE (15 fncs) 2m 4f 110y
3:40 (3:40) (Class 5) (0-90,90) 5-Y-0+ **£3,253** (£955; £477; £238)

Form RPR
60P5 1 **Bayadere (GER)**[72] [3592] 6-11-10 88 .... ShaneWalsh 107+
(K F Clutterbuck) *hld up in tch: wnt 2nd 5th: lft in ld 11th: pckd 4 out: drvn out* **25/1**
P436 2 3 ½ **Ri Na Realta (IRE)**[13] [4653] 11-11-1 87..................... WayneKavanagh(8) 102
(J W Mullins) *hld up: hdwy 8th: ev ch 4 out: sn rdn: one pce fr 2 out* **16/1**
6P04 3 13 **Per Amore (IRE)**[40] [4165] 8-11-4 85.................(b) AndrewGlassonbury(3) 87
(David Pearson) *hld up in tch: outpcd 7th: styd on to take 3rd nr fin* **33/1**
0453 4 ½ **Scratch The Dove**[18] [4580] 9-11-6 84.............................. OwynNelmes 85
(A E Price) *hld up and bhd: sme hdwy 11th: no real prog fr 2 out* **9/1**
5222 5 4 **Lucky Sinna (IRE)**[27] [4428] 10-11-7 88......................... JohnnyLevins(3) 87+
(B G Powell) *j.rt: chsd ldr to 5th: reminders 6th: ev ch 4 out: wknd after 3 out* **7/1**[3]
4U01 6 23 **Sailor A'Hoy**[11] [4666] 10-11-8 86..(p) LiamHeard 60
(M Mullineaux) *rdn after 6th: a bhd* **7/1**[3]
PP31 7 dist **Pardini (USA)**[14] [4643] 7-11-9 90...............................(v) CharliePoste(3) —
(M F Harris) *chsd ldrs: rdn and lost pl 8th: t.o* **8/1**
4662 P **Pardon What**[22] [4497] 10-11-5 86...............................(b) RichardSpate(3) —
(S Lycett) *nt jump wl: bhd tl p.u bef 4th* **5/2**[1]
554P P **Patriarch (IRE)**[32] [4300] 10-11-11 89.............................. WilliamKennedy —
(P Bowen) *a bhd: pushed along after 6th: t.o whn p.u bef 10th* **5/1**[2]
2F0P F **Assumetheposition (FR)**[54] [3918] 6-11-2 88...............(b[1]) JohnFlavin(8) —
(R C Guest) *plld hrd: led: j.rt and hit 9th: pressed whn fell 10th* **20/1**
4P4 P **Scarlet Fantasy**[18] [4580] 6-11-10 88 .... JamesDiment —
(P A Pritchard) *j.rt: mid-div: mstke 3rd: bhd fr 8th: p.u bef 11th* **22/1**

5m 10.4s (2.90) **Going Correction** +0.20s/f (Yiel) **11** Ran SP% **113.1**
Speed ratings: **102,100,95,95,94 85**,—,—,—,— — CSF £327.42 CT £12439.60 TOTE £27.20: £8.80, £4.40, £13.40; EX 390.30.
Owner K F Clutterbuck **Bred** A Pereira **Trained** Exning, Suffolk

FOCUS
A low-grade affair but the time was decent and the the race has been rated positively.

NOTEBOOK
Bayadere(GER) had been the last winner for her trainer when causing a 100/1 shock in a Fontwell claiming hurdle nearly a year ago. Apart from pecking at the final ditch, she never put a foot wrong on this switch to fences although the form does not amount to much. *(op 18-1)*
Ri Na Realta(IRE) failed to cope with the winner despite having been dropped 3lb. *(op 12-1)*
Per Amore(IRE) appreciated the better ground but is only moderate these days. *(op 25-1)*
Scratch The Dove wants softer ground to be effective over this sort of trip on a course as easy as this. *(op 11-1)*
Lucky Sinna(IRE), without headgear of any description this time, did not help his cause by jumping right-handed. *(op 8-1)*
Pardon What was reported by his rider to have jumped poorly. *Official explanation: jockey said gelding jumped very poorly (tchd 11-4)*

4805 LETHEBY & CHRISTOPHER H'CAP HURDLE (12 hdls) 3m
4:10 (4:10) (Class 4) (0-100,100) 4-Y-0+ **£3,083** (£898; £449)

Form RPR
4122 1 **Rosses Point (IRE)**[64] [3732] 7-11-7 95.....................(p) ChristianWilliams 103
(Evan Williams) *hld up and bhd: hdwy appr 8th: swtchd rt after 2 out: styd on u.p to ld last strides* **3/1**[2]
3211 2 hd **Harry's Dream**[178] [1728] 9-11-12 100.............................. RichardJohnson 108
(P J Hobbs) *hld up and bhd: hdwy 7th: led appr 2 out: hrd rdn and hdd last strides* **4/5**[1]
0-PP 3 1 ¼ **Sir Rowland Hill (IRE)**[97] [3204] 7-11-0 95............................ MrSWByrne(7) 102
(Ferdy Murphy) *hld up and bhd: hdwy 8th: rdn and styd on same pce flat* **50/1**
65P0 4 7 **The Flyer (IRE)**[20] [4549] 9-11-3 98..................................(tp) RichardSpate(7) 98
(Miss S J Wilton) *hld up in mid-div: hdwy 8th: sn rdn: no imp fr 3 out* **16/1**
U11P 5 27 **Lonesome Man (IRE)**[243] [1189] 10-11-9 97.......................... SamThomas 70
(Tim Vaughan) *led: rdn appr 3 out: hdd appr 2 out: sn wknd* **16/1**
1P-P 6 14 **Mike Simmons**[73] [3581] 10-11-2 95..................................... DerekLaverty(5) 54
(L P Grassick) *prom: rdn after 9th: wkng whn hit 3 out* **66/1**
433- 7 21 **Solway Minstrel**[647] [857] 9-11-4 99..................................... MrDJewett(7) 37
(Miss L Harrison) *prom tl rdn and wknd appr 9th: t.o* **11/1**[3]
-4P0 8 8 **Jesper (FR)**[34] [4282] 9-11-3 98..(t) SeanQuinlan(7) 28
(R T Phillips) *a bhd: rdn 9th: t.o* **33/1**
306- 9 22 **Why The Big Paws**[371] [4710] 8-11-2 100............................. JohnFlavin(10) —
(R C Guest) *prom tl wknd 7th: t.o fr 9th* **22/1**
045 P **Cabrillo (IRE)**[28] [4388] 5-11-5 100...................................... MrRQuinn(7) —
(John A Quinn, Ire) *a bhd: t.o whn p.u bef 9th* **22/1**

5m 50.9s (1.70) **Going Correction** +0.20s/f (Yiel) **10** Ran SP% **115.7**
Speed ratings: **105,104,104,102,93 88,81,78,71**,— CSF £5.60 CT £87.51 TOTE £3.90: £1.90, £1.10, £7.70; EX 10.40.
Owner W Ralph Thomas **Bred** Simon Kearney Jnr **Trained** Cowbridge, Vale Of Glamorgan
■ Stewards' Enquiry : Christian Williams three-day ban: used whip with excessive frequency (April 20-22)

FOCUS
They went 11/1 bar the first two home in this fairly uncompetitive handicap. The form looks believable.

NOTEBOOK
Rosses Point(IRE) has had his jumping problems since winning over fences at Fontwell in January. The switch to these French-style hurdles paid off and he wore down the favourite at the death. *(op 7-2 tchd 4-1 in places)*
Harry's Dream, reverting to hurdles after a six-month absence, could not quite hold his chief market rival. *He lost little in defeat and the wintry showers would not have helped his cause. (op 10-11 tchd 8-11 and Evena in places)*
Sir Rowland Hill(IRE), pulled up over fences on his two previous outings, appreciated this much better ground and showed he still retains ability. *(op 33-1)*
The Flyer(IRE) has been unable to take advantage of a slipping handicap mark. *(op 14-1)*

4806 LETHEBY & CHRISTOPHER H'CAP CHASE (18 fncs) 2m 7f 110y
4:40 (4:40) (Class 4) (0-110,110) 5-Y-0+ **£3,903** (£1,146; £573; £286)

Form RPR
P43P 1 **Bubble Boy (IRE)**[8] [4690] 7-11-1 106.............................. CharlieStudd(7) 118+
(B G Powell) *hld up: rdn 11th: hdwy 14th: led 4 out: styd on wl* **8/1**
-550 2 9 **The Villager (IRE)**[15] [4617] 10-11-6 104.........................(t) JasonMaguire 109+
(T R George) *hld up and bhd: hdwy 10th: chsd wnr fr 2 out: no imp* **4/1**[1]
-3P3 3 9 **Mandingo Chief (IRE)**[78] [3499] 7-10-13 97.................. JimmyMcCarthy 92+
(R T Phillips) *hld up in tch: led 14th to 4 out: hit 2 out: sn wknd* **7/1**
3430 4 28 **Shannon's Pride (IRE)**[72] [3596] 10-10-13 107.............(p) JohnFlavin(10) 73
(R C Guest) *hld up in tch: rdn and wknd appr 4 out* **10/1**
-FPP 5 dist **Gingerbread House (IRE)**[50] [3992] 8-11-12 110....(bt[1]) RichardJohnson —
(R T Phillips) *led: mstke 9th: hdd 11th: wknd 13th: mstke 14th: sn t.o* **16/1**
1345 6 dist **Miss Shakira (IRE)**[19] [4568] 8-11-5 110.................... MarcGoldstein(7) —
(N A Twiston-Davies) *bhd: short-lived effrt 14th: t.o* **16/1**
P565 U **Cill Churnain (IRE)**[22] [4504] 13-11-6 104............................ PadgeWhelan —
(Mrs S J Smith) *mid-div tl blnd and uns rdr 6th* **10/1**
-P5F P **Cinnamon Line**[45] [4078] 10-11-0 98.................................. JohnMcNamara —
(R Lee) *nt jump wl after mstke 1st: t.o 4th: p.u after 9th* **6/1**[2]
335 P **Navarone**[270] [975] 12-11-7 105.................................... WayneHutchinson —
(Ian Williams) *chsd ldr: led 11th to 14th: sn wknd: t.o whn p.u bef last* **22/1**
P653 P **Martin Ossie**[18] [4572] 9-10-13 97..................................(p) WarrenMarston —
(J M Bradley) *chsd ldrs: mstke 6th: rdn and wknd qckly appr 10th: t.o whn p.u bef 13th* **8/1**
P2-1 P **Hold On Harry**[336] [244] 10-10-8 97....................................... LiamHeard(5) —
(Miss C J Williams) *hld up: mstke 1st: hdwy appr 10th: rdn appr 11th: sn wknd: t.o whn p.u bef 3 out* **13/2**[3]

5m 57.8s (2.90) **Going Correction** +0.20s/f (Yiel) **11** Ran SP% **116.6**
Speed ratings: **103,100,97,87**,— —,—,—,—,— — CSF £40.90 CT £238.62 TOTE £10.50: £2.70, £2.40, £2.40; EX 43.20.
Owner Exors of the late J G Plackett **Bred** J L Rothwell **Trained** Morestead, Hants

FOCUS
Not a strong handicap, this did not turn out to be as competitive as the betting suggested.

NOTEBOOK
Bubble Boy(IRE) showed his form at Fontwell last time, when reported to have been unsuited by the soft ground, to be all wrong on this sounder surface. *(tchd 9-1)*
The Villager(IRE), dropped in grade, simply met one much too good off an 8lb lower mark. *(op 11-2)*
Mandingo Chief(IRE), raised 5lb, was already just beginning to feel the pinch when missing out at the penultimate fence. *(tchd 13-2)*
Hold On Harry *Official explanation: jockey said gelding was unsuited by the good (good to soft, places) ground (op 9-1 tchd 6-1)*

4807 FIRST EVENING MEETING, WEDNESDAY 26TH APRIL MAIDEN OPEN NATIONAL HUNT FLAT RACE 2m
5:10 (5:11) (Class 6) 4-6-Y-0 **£1,713** (£499; £249)

Form RPR
24 1 **Mount Sandel (IRE)**[36] [4244] 5-11-2 .... LeightonAspell 102+
(O Sherwood) *hld up: hdwy 4f out: led 2f out: rdn out* **7/4**[1]
66 2 3 **Sexy Rexy (IRE)**[36] [4244] 5-10-11 .... StevenCrawford(5) 97
(N A Twiston-Davies) *hld up in mid-div: hdwy after 6f: rdn over 5f out: outpcd 4f out: rallied 2f out: styd on ins fnl f: nt trble wnr* **7/1**
0 3 3 **Ringo Cody (IRE)**[25] [4455] 5-10-11 ....(b[1]) SamCurling(5) 94
(D R Gandolfo) *hld up in tch: led 4f out: sn rdn: hung rt over 1f out: one pce* **100/1**
65 4 shd **Hot Zone (IRE)**[27] [4422] 4-10-10 .... APMcCoy 88
(Jonjo O'Neill) *hld up: hdwy 9f out: rdn and ev ch over 2f out: bmpd over 1f out: one pce* **5/1**[3]
02 5 4 **Just Smudge**[80] [3462] 4-10-7 .... OwynNelmes(3) 84
(A E Price) *hld up and bhd: hdwy 8f out: rdn and ev ch over 3f out: wknd fnl f* **16/1**
P3 6 ¾ **Accumulus**[162] [1922] 6-10-13 .... WilliamKennedy(3) 89
(Noel T Chance) *hld up and bhd: hdwy over 5f out: wknd fnl f* **14/1**
30 7 10 **Rapallo (IRE)**[66] [3691] 5-11-2 .... CarlLlewellyn 79
(Carl Llewellyn) *hld up: sn in tch: dropped rr over 6f out: n.d after* **25/1**
60 8 1 **Hue And Cry**[104] [2988] 5-11-2 .... MickFitzgerald 78
(N J Henderson) *a bhd* **14/1**
00 9 7 **Irish Guard**[31] [4326] 5-11-2 .... SeanCurran 71
(J G O'Neill) *hld up in mid-div: hdwy after 6f: ev ch 4f out: wknd 3f out* **100/1**
33 10 18 **Ellerslie George (IRE)**[25] [4455] 6-11-2 .... JasonMaguire 53
(T P Tate) *chsd ldr: led 8f out to 4f out: wknd 3f out* **3/1**[2]
0-0 11 3 ½ **Bonny Jago**[50] [3983] 5-11-2 .... AntonyEvans 50
(R Brotherton) *t.k.h: led 8f: wknd over 5f out* **50/1**

3m 45.9s (-1.90) **Going Correction** +0.20s/f (Yiel)
WFA 4 from 5yo+ 5lb **11** Ran SP% **117.5**
Speed ratings: **101,99,98,97,95 95,90,90,86,77 75** CSF £14.61 TOTE £3.10: £1.10, £3.00, £9.60; EX 18.70 Place 6 £257.93, Place 5 £157.00.
Owner Trevor Hemmings **Bred** Eamonn Walsh **Trained** Upper Lambourn, Berks

FOCUS
A fair bumper for the course with the first two having run well at Newbury last time. They both ran to their marks here and the form looks sound enough.

NOTEBOOK
Mount Sandel(IRE) probably had less to do this time and ran out a clear-cut winner. *(op 2-1)*
Sexy Rexy(IRE) had more use made of him and hung left when headed when also three lengths behind Mount Sandel at Newbury last month. *(op 12-1)*
Ringo Cody(IRE) showed much-improved form in the blinkers but was inclined to lean on the fourth.
Hot Zone(IRE) was done no favours by Ringo Cody but lack of the required turn of foot was the real problem. *(op 4-1 tchd 7-2)*
Just Smudge faded in the closing stages but at least showed that his second at Ludlow was no fluke. *(op 14-1)*
Accumulus, having his first run for five months, has presumably been waiting for the ground to dry up. *(op 16-1)*

T/Plt: £446.60 to a £1 stake. Pool: £43,353.90. 70.85 winning tickets. T/Qpdt: £143.70 to a £1 stake. Pool: £3,049.50. 15.70 winning tickets. KH

4808 - 4818a (Foreign Racing) - See Raceform Interactive

4689 FONTWELL (L-H)

Tuesday, April 11

OFFICIAL GOING: Good changing to good to soft after race 2 (2.30) changing to soft after race 5 (4.00)

Wind: Strong, half-behind Weather: Heavy rain

4819 SAFECOAT EUROPE LIMITED MAIDEN HURDLE (9 hdls) 2m 2f 110y

2:00 (2:00) (Class 5) 4-Y-O+ **£2,927** (£859; £429; £214)

Form RPR

5253 **1** **Tech Eagle (IRE)**[38] [4243] 6-11-0 105 TomDoyle 106+
(R Curtis) *hld up in midfield: hdwy 3 out: led last: pushed clr run-in: comf* **2/1**[1]

0 **2** *3 ½* **Ladino (FR)**[54] [3947] 6-11-0 RichardJohnson 98+
(P J Hobbs) *chsd ldrs: led appr 2 out: hdd and nt fluent last: one pce* **12/1**

P0 **3** *2 ½* **Song Of Vala**[17] [4621] 5-11-0 DaveCrosse 96+
(C J Mann) *hld up in midfield: gd hdwy after 3 out: no ex run-in* **50/1**

F023 **4** *3 ½* **Lysander (GER)**[29] [4420] 7-10-9 106 CharliePoste(5) 92+
(M F Harris) *prom: led 3 out tl appr next: 4th and btn whn blnd last* **11/4**[2]

23P **5** *nk* **Looking Great (USA)**[162] [1948] 4-10-7 AndrewTinkler 84
(R F Johnson Houghton) *chsd ldrs: hrd rdn and btn appr 2 out* **20/1**

0 **6** *1 ¾* **Otago (IRE)**[25] [4479] 5-11-0 NoelFehily 89
(C J Mann) *led: mstke 4th: hdd 3 out: wknd appr next* **14/1**

3-50 **7** *hd* **Ten Pressed Men (FR)**[60] [3842] 6-11-0 APMcCoy 89
(Jonjo O'Neill) *chsd ldr tl 5th: wknd appr 2 out* **10/1**

000 **8** *1 ¼* **Reflector (IRE)**[20] [4581] 5-11-0 TimmyMurphy 90+
(Miss H C Knight) *wd: hld up and bhd: sme hdwy whn blnd 2 out: nvr in chalng position* **33/1**

6P **9** *1 ½* **Saltrio**[18] [4604] 8-11-0 (t) RobertThornton 86
(A King) *chsd ldrs: effrt 6th: wknd appr 2 out* **13/2**[3]

60 **10** *7* **Marghub (IRE)**[24] [4493] 7-10-7 MissCDyson(7) 79
(Miss C Dyson) *prom to 6th: btn whn blnd 3 out: n.d whn rn wd home turn* **66/1**

562P **11** *1 ¾* **Hatteras (FR)**[23] [4523] 7-10-9 102 RobertLucey-Butler(5) 78
(Miss M P Bryant) *mid-div: outpcd and hrd rdn 3 out: n.d after* **25/1**

00 **12** *1* **Pagan Sky (IRE)**[36] [4280] 7-11-0 SamThomas 77
(Miss Venetia Williams) *bhd: pushed along 5th: nvr nr ldrs* **16/1**

0P **13** *1 ¾* **Public Eye**[56] [3906] 5-10-7 JustinMorgan(7) 75
(L A Dace) *hld up and bhd: mod effrt appr 2 out: sn wknd* **66/1**

40 **14** *8* **Hollandia (IRE)**[63] [3789] 5-11-0 PaulMoloney 67
(Miss H C Knight) *hld up and bhd: pushed along appr 2 out: nvr trbld ldrs* **66/1**

066 **15** *11* **Supreme Copper (IRE)**[75] [3583] 6-11-0 BarryFenton 56
(Miss E C Lavelle) *stdd s: several mstkes: hld up and a wl bhd* **33/1**

460 **P** **Viennchee Run**[52] [3983] 5-10-9 ShaneWalsh(5) —
(K F Clutterbuck) *a towards rr: blnd 2nd: t.o 3 out: p.u bef next* **50/1**

4m 25.6s (-10.40) **Going Correction** -0.725s/f (Firm)
WFA 4 from 5yo+ 5lb **16** Ran SP% **125.6**
Speed ratings: **92,90,89,88,87 87,87,86,85,82 82,81,81,77,73** — CSF £26.31 TOTE £2.70: £1.20, £3.80, £27.90; EX 51.60.
Owner The Tech Eagle Partnership **Bred** Gestut Wittekindshof **Trained** Lambourn, Berks

FOCUS
A typical end-of-season maiden hurdle and not a very good one. The pace was reasonable.

NOTEBOOK
Tech Eagle(IRE) is well exposed with a lowly rating of 105 and ran enough times on the Flat in Germany. However, he got bogged down in soft conditions, and showed on fast ground at Newbury that he is quite useful - that winner Wellbeing has gone on to better things. Travelling well before going on at the last, he cleared away for a cosy victory and should have a successful summer on his favoured sound surface. *(tchd 9-4)*
Ladino(FR), three times a winner on the Flat in Germany, appears to prefer a sound surface as he left behind his soft-ground hurdles debut form. He was forced to race on the outside of the pack chasing the pace and, while outpaced by the winner at the business end, beat the rest well enough.
Song Of Vala made rapid headway around the home bend after being well back and held a chance between the last two, before those exertions told. He looks to be getting the idea and is one to bear in mind for a summer handicap.
Lysander(GER) had no excuses, but could not match the pace of the front three from the home turn without being disgraced. His jumping still has room for improvement. *(op 3-1 tchd 10-3 in a place)*
Looking Great(USA), the only juvenile in the line-up, ran well after being unsuited to softer ground following some promise in his first two races. He looks another likely to do better summer jumping. *(op 25-1)*
Otago(IRE) cut out the running but faded once being headed three from home.
Saltrio, tried in a tongue strap for this third run, weakened out of contention on the home turn. *(op 7-1 tchd 6-1)*

4820 PETERS PLC NOVICES' CHASE (13 fncs) 2m 2f

2:30 (2:30) (Class 3) 5-Y-O+ **£7,828** (£2,312; £1,156; £578; £288; £145)

Form RPR

4315 **1** **The Local**[24] [4502] 6-11-5 120 APMcCoy 123+
(C R Egerton) *mde all: sn 6 l clr: rdn along fr 8th: hrd drvn and hld on gamely fr 2 out: all out* **4/1**[2]

0221 **2** *nk* **Lord On The Run (IRE)**[17] [4620] 7-10-12 117 WillieMcCarthy(7) 124+
(J W Mullins) *chsd ldrs: wnt 2nd at 5th: clsd on wnr and mstke 2 out: kpt on wl run-in: jst hld* **6/4**[1]

3221 **3** *1* **Lewis Island (IRE)**[10] [4692] 7-11-9 117 JamieMoore 126+
(G L Moore) *reluctant to line up: hld up: stmbld 1st: stdy hdwy fr 1/2-way: rdn to chal run-in: nt qckn nr fin* **13/2**

U3PP **4** *5* **Balladeer (IRE)**[39] [4214] 8-11-5 113 AndrewThornton 116
(Mrs T J Hill) *hld up in rr: rdn and hdwy fr 3 out: nt pce to chal* **14/1**

2U21 **5** *½* **Matthew Muroto (IRE)**[20] [4572] 7-11-0 109 DarylJacob(5) 116+
(R H Alner) *fair 4th most of way: hld whn nt fluent 3 out* **9/2**[3]

6033 **6** *20* **Lord Gunnerslake (IRE)**[55] [3922] 6-10-13 90 AnthonyCoyle 93+
(Miss C J E Caroe) *chsd wnr to 5th: wknd 8th* **50/1**

4216 **7** *26* **Kilindini**[198] [1559] 5-10-10 BarryFenton 60
(Miss E C Lavelle) *j. slowly in rr: sn wl bhd* **7/1**

4m 27.2s (-7.90) **Going Correction** -0.20s/f (Good)
WFA 5 from 6yo+ 3lb **7** Ran SP% **112.6**
Speed ratings: **109,108,108,106,105 97,85** CSF £10.64 TOTE £3.50: £2.50, £1.40; EX 10.30.
Owner Barry Marsden **Bred** Chippenham Lodge Stud And Rathbarry Stud **Trained** Chaddleworth, Berks

FOCUS
A fair novices' chase.

NOTEBOOK
The Local made all under a fine aggressive ride from McCoy. Quick enough to sulk if taken on for the lead, he got his way here under a most positive ride. He was often ten lengths clear but was also careful over some of his fences and he looked like being swamped into the straight being under strong pressure as his two rivals stalked him at a couple of lengths remove, but neither of those two opponents is particularly hearty in a finish and the line came in time. *(op 9-2)*
Lord On The Run(IRE) had broken his duck under a positive ride at Newbury after some near misses, but he gave best up front and could not quite get past his rival. While on official ratings he ran a shade above himself, he leaves the impression that he is best when dictating, and a return to those tactics can bring further reward. *(op 5-4 tchd 13-8)*
Lewis Island(IRE) needed revving up at the start, showing his usual tendencies of thinking about it. He slipped on landing over the first which was not his fault and thereafter he took a good grip and looked ready to strike, along with the runner-up, in the straight. He went left towards his rivals on the run-in but ran to within a few pounds of his rating. *(tchd 7-1)*
Balladeer(IRE) could never land a blow but was staying on best, as befits a horse with winning form over further. The ground is coming his way. *(op 16-1)*
Matthew Muroto(IRE) could never get into the shake-up but plodded on *(op 11-2)*

4821 GERRARD FINANCIAL PLANNING H'CAP HURDLE (10 hdls) 2m 4f

3:00 (3:00) (Class 3) (0-130,127) 4-Y-O+ **£8,768** (£2,590; £1,295; £648; £323; £162)

Form RPR

4031 **1** **Herakles (GER)**[54] [3943] 5-11-0 **115** MickFitzgerald 122+
(N J Henderson) *hld up towards rr: mstke 4th: hdwy 3 out: styd on to ld jst after last: drvn clr* **7/2**[2]

51P5 **2** *1 ½* **New Entic (FR)**[13] [4663] 5-11-9 **124** (p) JamieMoore 129+
(G L Moore) *mid-div: hdwy 7th: edged lft and bmpd between last 2: slt ld last: sn hdd and nt qckn* **14/1**

6630 **3** *4* **Cool Roxy**[26] [4461] 9-11-7 **125** ChrisHonour(3) 126+
(A G Blackmore) *prom: led 3rd: bmpd between last 2: hdd last: no ex* **12/1**

6030 **4** *2* **Hawadeth**[25] [4473] 11-11-12 **127** (p) JimCrowley 125
(V R A Dartnall) *in tch: mstke 7th: drvn to chse ldrs appr 2 out: no ex last* **10/1**

12P1 **5** *10* **Tora Bora (GER)**[10] [4691] 4-11-1 **123** (b) TimmyMurphy 104
(B G Powell) *prom tl wknd appr last* **11/2**[3]

0035 **6** *2* **Guru**[46] [4091] 8-10-12 **113** PhilipHide 99
(G L Moore) *t.k.h: in tch: wnt 3rd 1/2-way: mstke 7th: wknd 3 out* **25/1**

P041 **7** *¾* **Kandjar D'Allier (FR)**[20] [4573] 8-11-5 **120** RobertThornton 105
(A King) *hld up in midfield: rdn 7th: wknd 3 out* **5/2**[1]

0100 **8** *shd* **Screenplay**[25] [4469] 5-11-3 **118** JamieGoldstein 103
(Miss Sheena West) *chsd ldrs tl wknd 3 out* **9/1**

2040 **9** *10* **Enhancer**[25] [4473] 8-11-5 **120** LeightonAspell 95
(M J McGrath) *hld up towards rr: pushed along and n.d fr 3 out* **33/1**

0350 **10** *11* **Anatar (IRE)**[39] [4215] 8-10-9 **110** (v) TomScudamore 74
(M C Pipe) *bhd: rdn along fr 5th: nvr nr ldrs* **16/1**

55F0 **11** *10* **Wembury Point (IRE)**[17] [4616] 4-10-1 **114** ow1 JohnnyLevins(5) 61
(B G Powell) *prom to 3rd: bhd fr 6th* **66/1**

14P0 **12** *3* **Come Bye (IRE)**[21] [4561] 10-10-13 **114** (bt) MatthewBatchelor 65
(Miss A M Newton-Smith) *led to 3rd: wknd 7th: bhd whn j.rt 3 out* **33/1**

111/ **P** **Captain Zinzan (NZ)**[1018] [760] 11-11-7 **122** RichardJohnson —
(L A Dace) *hld up: a wl bhd: p.u bef 2 out* **25/1**

4m 46.6s (-17.20) **Going Correction** -0.725s/f (Firm)
WFA 4 from 5yo+ 6lb **13** Ran SP% **120.6**
Speed ratings: **105,104,102,102,98 97,96,96,92,88 84,83,—** CSF £48.32 CT £543.05 TOTE £5.60: £2.00, £3.70, £3.10; EX 68.70.
Owner Mrs Maureen Buckley & Mrs A M Halls **Bred** E Jahns **Trained** Upper Lambourn, Berks

FOCUS
The sustained rain which started for the first race looked to be getting into this well-raced ground now - officially changed to good to soft after this race. This looked a strong contest befitting its decent prize and the first four finished well clear.

NOTEBOOK
Herakles(GER) defied the handicapper in some style despite being slightly outpaced around the home bend, looking held before staying on well between the last two flights. He can go on to better things judged on this display and ran as if further would not be a problem. *(op 4-1 tchd 9-2 in places)*
New Entic(FR) was wanting to hang badly left up the straight - he had been reported unsteerable in a previous race - when challenging widest out towards the stands' side. He did not help his cause, or that of Cool Roxy, by barging him between the last two flights when they were ahead, and he is obviously not straightforward but has the ability.
Cool Roxy, soon in front, was only worn down at the final flight after taking a bump from the eventual runner-up. He can win again on genuinely good ground.
Hawadeth is now in the twilight of his career, but this was a decent effort and he could yet add to his tally granted good ground. *(op 16-1)*
Tora Bora(GER) could not cope with his more experienced rivals and looks lazy already, having to be shoved along in the back straight twitching his ears. He still matched it in the front rank before looking to find this longer trip just too far as he weakened from the second last. *(op 6-1)*
Kandjar D'Allier(FR) was found out by the 12lb higher mark. *(op 9-4)*
Screenplay *Official explanation: trainer said gelding struck into himself*
Captain Zinzan(NZ) completed a facile hat-trick in the summer of 2003 but has not been seen since. With the ground going against him, he was given an easy time out the back before being pulled up. He should not be written off.

4822 GERRARD INVESTMENT MANAGEMENT H'CAP CHASE (16 fncs) 2m 6f

3:30 (3:30) (Class 3) (0-125,122) 5-Y-O+ **£12,526** (£3,700; £1,850; £926; £462; £232)

Form RPR

3-61 **1** **Mr Boo (IRE)**[23] [4522] 7-10-9 **105** PhilipHide 132+
(G L Moore) *hld up in tch: led 3 out: sn clr: easily* **8/1**

5411 **2** *13* **Walcot Lad (IRE)**[10] [4694] 10-11-1 **114** (p) WilliamKennedy(3) 121+
(A Ennis) *led to 7th: rdn and lost pl 4 out: styd on to take 2nd run-in* **5/1**[3]

4F00 **3** *2* **Kosmos Bleu (FR)**[51] [4014] 8-10-11 **107** AndrewThornton 111
(R H Alner) *cl up: outpcd by wnr 3 out: sn btn* **16/1**

-062 **4** *shd* **Wakeup Smiling (IRE)**[20] [4571] 8-10-1 **97** BarryFenton 102+
(Miss E C Lavelle) *prom: led 7th to 3 out: nt pce of wnr: wknd and lost 2nd run-in* **7/2**[2]

3/1- **5** *10* **Sento (IRE)**[699] [303] 8-11-8 **118** RobertThornton 112
(A King) *hld up towards rr: hdwy 11th: rn wl tl fdd 3 out* **8/1**

5P62 **6** *9* **Holy Joe (FR)**[6] [4728] 9-11-12 **122** (p) SamThomas 107
(Miss Venetia Williams) *sn pressing ldr: rdn and lost pl 11th: mod rally whn mstke 3 out: n.d after* **11/4**[1]

0F30 **P** **One Cornetto (IRE)**[17] [4618] 7-11-9 **119** .... LeightonAspell —
(L Wells) *a bhd: p.u after 10th* **12/1**

0113 **P** **Touch Closer**[231] [1301] 9-11-9 **119** .... (p) APMcCoy —
(P Bowen) *sn bhd: rdn along fr 4th: p.u after 10th* **5/1**[3]

5m 37.8s (-6.00) **Going Correction** -0.125s/f (Good) **8** Ran SP% **118.0**
Speed ratings: **105,100,99,99,95 92,—,—** CSF £49.41 CT £634.15 TOTE £7.40: £2.20, £1.50, £4.50; EX 36.60.

Owner The Hon Mrs C Cameron **Bred** Mrs Eleanor Hadden **Trained** Woodingdean, E Sussex

FOCUS

This looked a competitive handicap beforehand but Mr Boo made it look easy.

NOTEBOOK

Mr Boo(IRE) turned what looked a competitive handicap into a procession up the straight, having always been travelling and jumping well in being taken slightly wide of his rivals throughout. This novice has taken exceptionally well to fences after a year off and as such remains a dark horse. He will no doubt pay with the handicapper although the strength of the opposition was hardly in keeping with the big prize.

Walcot Lad(IRE) was another 9lb higher on this hat-trick attempt. He still remains a force, as he beat the rest well enough, despite dropping away as if beaten into the final half-mile, before rallying strongly without seeing which way the winner went. *(op 11-2)*

Kosmos Bleu(FR) snatched third without threatening to land a telling blow, and is another who looks plenty high enough in the ratings.

Wakeup Smiling(IRE) paid late for being over-exuberant early in jumping ahead of Walcot Lad within a mile. The ground was also probably going against him and he looks ready to strike in summer jumping.

Sento(IRE) ran well enough on this comeback after nearly two years off as he has shown his best on good ground. He only tired from the home bend, having looked to enjoy himself. *(op 7-1)*

Holy Joe(FR) looked to lose interest running downhill across the course on the last circuit, but after some sharp reminders stayed on again into the home straight before being left behind again. He has not won for a long time. *(op 3-1 tchd 10-3)*

Touch Closer downed tools from an early stage and even the champion jockey had to admit defeat with a circuit to run. *(op 11-2)*

4823 GERRARD INVESTMENT MANAGEMENT NOVICES' HURDLE (10 hdls) 2m 4f

4:00 (4:04) (Class 4) 4-Y-0+ **£4,944** (£1,451; £725; £362)

Form				RPR
46/	**1**		**High Hope (FR)**[18] [3527] 8-11-0 .... PhilipHide (G L Moore) *hld up in tch: sltly hmpd 5th: led on bit 2 out: sn clr: easily* **8/1**	110+
0-40	**2**	6	**Best Actor (IRE)**[85] [3425] 7-11-0 .... MickFitzgerald (Carl Llewellyn) *led tl after 2nd: blnd 5th: led 6th tl 2 out: nt pce of wnr* **10/1**	100+
4	**3**	*hd*	**Onward To Glory (USA)**[56] [3908] 6-11-0 .... RichardJohnson (P J Hobbs) *t.k.h in midfield: hdwy 7th: styd on same pce fr 2 out: jst hld for 2nd* **2/1**[1]	99
64	**4**	4	**Angello (FR)**[20] [4569] 5-10-7 .... KeiranBurke(7) (N J Hawke) *chsd ldrs: one pce fr 2 out* **16/1**	95
3	**5**	5	**Silber Mond**[21] [4562] 4-10-7 .... JamieGoldstein (Miss Sheena West) *prom tl wknd 2 out* **20/1**	83
0-P6	**6**	1 1/4	**Poggenip**[27] [4450] 7-9-11 .... RichardKilloran(10) (B G Powell) *hld up in rr: hdwy into midfield 5th: no further prog fr 7th* **33/1**	82
2613	**7**	10	**Sweet Oona (FR)**[44] [4129] 7-11-0 103 .... SamThomas (Miss Venetia Williams) *hld up towards rr: promising hdwy 3 out: 6th and btn whn blnd next* **4/1**[3]	83+
PPP0	**8**	29	**It's Official (IRE)**[23] [4526] 7-10-7 71 .... (v) RyanCummings(7) (Miss A M Newton-Smith) *led after 2nd: mstke and hdd 6th: sn wknd: bhd whn hmpd 3 out* **50/1**	50
0PP5	**9**	*dist*	**Secret Jewel (FR)**[23] [4526] 6-10-7 71 .... AnthonyCoyle (Miss C J E Caroe) *a towards rr: wl bhd fr 6th* **66/1**	—
/22-	**10**		**Sintos**[528] [1912] 8-10-11 .... ColinBolger(3) (Miss A M Newton-Smith) *a bhd: no ch whn blnd 7th* **20/1**	—
P0P	**11**		**Redneck Girl (IRE)**[31] [4367] 7-10-2 .... CharliePoste(5) (A E Jones) *a bhd: no ch fr 6th* **66/1**	—
1-52	**F**		**Young Dude (IRE)**[16] [4638] 7-11-0 .... APMcCoy (Jonjo O'Neill) *prom: hit 3rd and 7th: cl 3rd whn fell 3 out* **3/1**[2]	—

4m 59.4s (-4.40) **Going Correction** +0.025s/f (Yiel)
WFA 4 from 5yo+ 6lb **12** Ran SP% **121.8**
Speed ratings: **109,106,106,104,102 102,98,86,—,— —,—** CSF £78.78 TOTE £9.00: £3.60, £3.30, £1.20; EX 64.00.

Owner Rdm Racing **Bred** Mme Danielle Merian-Fricker And Mr Julian Ince **Trained** Woodingdean, E Sussex

FOCUS

The change in going added to the dead wood in this race, which was weakened by four non-runners.

NOTEBOOK

High Hope(FR) was another easy winner for the Moore-Hide team. He had shown promise in decent novice races three years ago before cracking his pelvis and getting knee chips, but he has been just a modest handicapper (rated 70 for his last run) on the Flat this winter. He jumped well and should be able to win again. *(op 9-1 tchd 10-1)*

Best Actor(IRE) made much of the running but was put in his place by the winner from the second last. He could have done without the rain, but he again showed he should be winning soon when getting a sounder surface.

Onward To Glory(USA) found disappointingly little under pressure, having looked to be travelling as well as anything down the back straight, although he hugged the inside rail while the principals took the traditional soft-ground wider route. *(op 13-8)*

Angello(FR) looks to want even further as he showed improved form for this half-mile longer trip, *but was tapped for toe out of the back straight under strong pressure. He kept plugging away. (op 20-1)*

Silber Mond was not disgraced as an inexperienced juvenile against his elders. *(op 16-1)*

Poggenip, who was taken round the outer half of the course, again hinted at some ability. *(op 25-1)*

Young Dude(IRE) had not been asked a question, although he had made mistakes, when he stepped into the third-last and took a heavy fall when still in a close third. *(op 4-1)*

4824 GERRARD FINANCIAL PLANNING H'CAP HURDLE (11 hdls) 2m 6f 110y

4:30 (4:31) (Class 4) (0-105,105) 4-Y-0+ **£5,204** (£1,528; £764; £381)

Form				RPR
245	**1**		**Here We Go (IRE)**[66] [3729] 7-11-5 **98** .... JamieMoore (G L Moore) *wd: hld up in midfield: smooth hdwy 8th: styd on to ld on bit last: sn clr: easily* **4/1**[1]	115+
22-6	**2**	4	**San Hernando**[18] [4604] 6-11-11 **104** .... (v) BarryFenton (Miss E C Lavelle) *mde most to 5th: led 2 out to last: nt pce of wnr* **12/1**	106
65P	**3**	7	**Alderbrook Girl (IRE)**[30] [4391] 6-9-7 **79** oh4 .... CharlieStudd(7) (R Curtis) *chsd ldrs: led 5th tl 2 out: no ex* **66/1**	76+
01	**4**	10	**Brendar (IRE)**[15] [4652] 9-11-9 **105** .... WilliamKennedy(3) (Jim Best) *hld up and bhd: hdwy 8th: wnt fair 4th 3 out: no imp* **15/2**[3]	93+
6436	**5**	12	**Coleraine (IRE)**[47] [4071] 6-10-11 **90** .... LeightonAspell (O Sherwood) *hld up in midfield: rdn 8th: no imp* **8/1**	63
P613	**6**	*dist*	**Geography (IRE)**[15] [4652] 6-10-2 **86** .... (p) RobertLucey-Butler(5) (P Butler) *towards rr: mod hdwy after 7th: sn wknd* **14/1**	—
350P	**7**	11	**It's Rumoured**[95] [3276] 6-11-0 **93** .... (p) JamesDavies (Jean-Rene Auvray) *w ldrs to 3rd: wknd 7th* **33/1**	—
F16F	**P**		**Lahinch Lad (IRE)**[236] [1247] 6-10-6 **92** .... MrSPJones(7) (B G Powell) *a bhd: no ch 8th: p.u bef last* **33/1**	—
6003	**P**		**Trebello**[21] [4080] 5-10-10 **89** .... NoelFehily (J R Boyle) *a towards rr: no ch 8th: p.u bef 2 out* **10/1**	—
PP02	**P**		**Midnight Gold**[21] [4557] 6-11-7 **100** .... RobertThornton (A King) *in tch to 7th: wl bhd whn p.u bef 2 out* **5/1**[2]	—
0030	**P**		**Willy The Slip**[17] [4616] 4-10-8 **100** .... (v) DarylJacob(5) (R H Alner) *in tch to 4th: wl bhd fr 7th: p.u bef 2 out* **50/1**	—
-2P4	**P**		**Here Comes Harry**[23] [4526] 10-9-11 **79** oh1 .... OwynNelmes(3) (C J Down) *in tch tl wknd appr 3 out: bhd whn p.u bef next* **20/1**	—
3510	**P**		**Nobel Bleu De Kerpaul (FR)**[57] [3901] 5-11-5 **98** .... PhilipHide (P Winkworth) *hld up towards rr: j.lft 3rd: p.u bef next* **14/1**	—
0003	**F**		**Cambo (FR)**[21] [4564] 5-10-9 **95** .... MarcGoldstein(7) (Miss Sheena West) *wd: prom: hung rt most of way: j.rt 2nd: 4th and in tch whn fell 8th* **10/1**	—
3643	**P**		**Geordie Peacock (IRE)**[24] [4501] 7-11-12 **105** .... SamThomas (Miss Venetia Williams) *in tch: rdn along fr 3rd: wknd 7th: wl bhd whn p.u bef 2 out* **10/1**	—

5m 42.5s (-2.30) **Going Correction** +0.025s/f (Yiel)
WFA 4 from 5yo+ 6lb **15** Ran SP% **121.9**
Speed ratings: **105,103,101,97,93 —,—,—,—,— —,—,—,—,—** CSF £49.61 CT £2777.65 TOTE £5.80: £2.50, £2.90, £7.70; EX 50.30.

Owner D N Green **Bred** Seamus Murphy **Trained** Woodingdean, E Sussex

FOCUS

A strong pace in ground now officially soft, as the rain continued, strung out this field.

NOTEBOOK

Here We Go(IRE) appeared to be going best leaving the back straight with his rider looking round for dangers while still stalking the front pair, who were allowed to lead him on sufferance up the straight until a little nudge of the reins settled it on the run-in. He was value for considerably more than the bare margin and his future will depend on the handicapper. *(op 7-2)*

San Hernando, always prominent, battled on well for pressure on this drop back in trip and looks a dour stayer. He is lightly-raced.

Alderbrook Girl(IRE) was clear, together with the eventual third, with a circuit to run. Headed two from home, she has had plenty of chances, but she looks like another from her stable who will enjoy good ground through the summer so is worth bearing in mind next time. *(op 50-1)*

Brendar(IRE) was the only one able to make any headway from the pack. He sat well out of his ground and did well to raise hopes as he stayed on off the home bend but the exertions told up the run-in. *(op 8-1)*

Midnight Gold *Official explanation: jockey said gelding was unsuited by soft ground (tchd 9-1)*

Cambo(FR) took a heavy fall four out when still chasing the leaders. *(tchd 9-1)*

Nobel Bleu De Kerpaul(FR) *Official explanation: jockey said gelding was never travelling (tchd 9-1)*

4825 MOBILITY BUREAU STANDARD OPEN NATIONAL HUNT FLAT RACE 2m 2f 110y

5:00 (5:01) (Class 6) 4-6-Y-0 **£1,626** (£477; £238; £119)

Form				RPR
	1		**Benetwood (IRE)** 5-11-0 .... APMcCoy (V R A Dartnall) *t.k.h towards rr: hdwy 1/2-way: led and hung bdly lft ins fnl f: drvn out* **7/4**[1]	101+
	2	1 3/4	**Psychomodo** 4-10-7 .... TimmyMurphy (B G Powell) *in tch: led over 2f out tl ins fnl f: kpt on* **4/1**[2]	93
1	**3**	1 1/2	**Solid As A Rock**[33] [4326] 6-11-2 .... MrTJO'Brien(5) (J G Cann) *hld up in midfield: effrt 4f out: styd on fnl 3f: nt rch ldng pair* **4/1**[2]	105
30	**4**	1/2	**Trigger The Light**[33] [4333] 5-11-0 .... WayneHutchinson (A King) *hld up in tch: effrt 4f out: kpt on fnl 3f* **9/1**	98
0	**5**	15	**Nacho Des Uncheres (FR)**[24] [4500] 5-11-0 .... JodieMogford (D G Bridgwater) *chsd ldr: led after 6f tl over 2f out: sn wknd* **66/1**	86+
	6	10	**Bentinck (IRE)** 4-10-7 .... TomScudamore (M Scudamore) *towards rr: sme hdwy 6f out: no imp* **14/1**	66
0	**7**	2 1/2	**Bob Mountain (IRE)**[106] [2988] 5-11-0 .... TomDoyle (C Tinkler) *mid-div: rdn 5f out: sn outpcd* **14/1**	70
0	**8**	11	**Kevinsky Blue**[24] [4500] 4-10-2 .... MarkNicolls(5) (M J McGrath) *led 6f: prom tl wknd 4f out* **66/1**	52
5	**9**	8	**Chez Bleu**[17] [4623] 5-11-0 .... RichardJohnson (P J Hobbs) *sn chsng ldrs: wknd over 4f out* **6/1**[3]	51
	10	9	**Noscar (FR)** 5-10-7 .... CharlieStudd(7) (B G Powell) *prom tl wknd 4f out* **33/1**	42
	11	9	**Stansted (IRE)** 5-11-0 .... LeightonAspell (M J McGrath) *a bhd: no ch fnl 7f* **20/1**	33
	12	2	**Sir Ben** 5-10-11 .... ColinBolger(3) (A Ennis) *a bhd: t.o fnl 7f* **25/1**	31
	13	1	**Topajo (IRE)** 5-10-9 .... TomGreenway(5) (D G Bridgwater) *in tch: wknd 6f out: t.o* **50/1**	30

4m 38.0s (-1.30) **Going Correction** +0.025s/f (Yiel)
WFA 4 from 5yo 5lb 5 from 6yo 3lb **13** Ran SP% **130.5**
Speed ratings: **103,102,101,101,95 90,89,85,81,78 74,73,73** CSF £9.03 TOTE £2.90: £1.70, £2.10, £1.40; EX 14.40 Place 6 £205.24, Place 5 £95.45.

Owner John P McManus **Bred** Donal Casey **Trained** Brayford, Devon

FOCUS

A reasonable pace given the conditions for one of these contests, but there was little strength in depth with a strung-out finish. The first four finished well clear, and the first two on opposite sides of the track.

NOTEBOOK

Benetwood(IRE) came with a reputation from a stable which knows the time of day with bumper horses. He is physically impressive as well and looks sure to go on over hurdles and fences in time. He took the inside route up the straight and was green under pressure, hanging over to the inside rail, but still stayed on stronger than the runner-up. *(op 5-2)*

Psychomodo, a 26,000euros buy, is out of a mare who was second in the Cesarewitch. He gave up the outside to nobody throughout, but still turned into the straight with a two-length lead. He is not as physically impressive as the winner but he did nothing wrong and should soon make amends. *(op 6-1)*

Solid As A Rock did well under his penalty against two nice prospects. He travelled well but sat off the leaders before staying on steadily all the way up the straight to be nearest at the finish. *(op 7-2)*

Trigger The Light put his previous experience to good use, but was just found wanting. *(op 7-1)*

Nacho Des Uncheres(FR), the long-time leader, showed more than enough as a big chasing type to suggest he will be winning races. *(op 50-1)*

T/Jkpt: Not won. T/Plt: £50.50 to a £1 stake. Pool: £55,983.65. 808.75 winning tickets. T/Qpdt: £22.70 to a £1 stake. Pool: £4,443.50. 144.50 winning tickets. LM

4589 LUDLOW (R-H)

Thursday, April 13

OFFICIAL GOING: Good to firm (good in places)

Wind: Fresh, against Weather: Odd shower

4826 ROBERT HOLDEN NOVICES' HURDLE (12 hdls) 3m

2:30 (2:32) (Class 3) 4-Y-0+ **£5,204** (£1,528; £764; £381)

Form					RPR
121F	**1**		**Piran (IRE)**[21] 4593 4-11-5 125	PaulMoloney	108+
			(Evan Williams) *hld up towards rr: hdwy appr 7th: led last: rdn and styd on wl*	**11/8**[1]	
0142	**2**	*5*	**Waterloo Son (IRE)**[38] 4280 6-11-7 115	RichardJohnson	104+
			(H D Daly) *hld up in mid-div: hdwy 7th: led appr 3 out to last: one pce*	**9/4**[2]	
-UP0	**3**	*8*	**Allborn Lad (IRE)**[69] 3717 6-11-1	NoelFehily	92+
			(C J Mann) *hld up and bhd: hdwy appr 9th: btn whn blnd 2 out*	**50/1**	
0602	**4**	*1*	**Darn Good**[21] 4589 5-11-1 107	WayneHutchinson	90+
			(A King) *prom tl rdn and wknd 3 out*	**4/1**[3]	
FPF	**5**	*shd*	**Cloneybrien Boy (IRE)**[104] 3126 6-10-10 64	DerekLaverty(5)	89
			(Mrs A M Thorpe) *j.rt: prom: led after 1st tl appr 3 out: wknd appr last*	**150/1**	
0-00	**6**	*7*	**Alderman Rose**[20] 4604 6-11-1	SamThomas	83+
			(R T Phillips) *hld up in tch: rdn and wknd appr 3 out*	**16/1**	
50P6	**7**	*6*	**Oakfield Legend**[18] 4642 5-10-12	TomMalone(3)	78+
			(P S Payne) *hld up in mid-div: hdwy 8th: wknd 3 out*	**150/1**	
564P	**8**	*20*	**Little Word**[46] 4133 7-10-3 69	JamesDiment(5)	49
			(P D Williams) *hld up in mid-div: short-lived effrt 6th: bhd fr 7th*	**50/1**	
	9	*2*	**Hollywood Henry (IRE)**[79] 6-11-1	RJGreene	54
			(Mrs A M Thorpe) *prom: j. slowly 3rd: hit 2nd: rdn and wknd 9th*	**50/1**	
6P00	**10**	*15*	**Mr Smithers Jones**[22] 4569 6-11-1 85	JamesDavies	39
			(Mrs S M Johnson) *a towards rr*	**66/1**	
200P	**11**	*dist*	**Back With A Bang (IRE)**[56] 3941 7-11-1	JodieMogford	—
			(Mrs N S Evans) *prom: carried rt 4th: reminders 5th: wknd qckly 8th: t.o*	**80/1**	
60P	**P**		**Toothill Gunner**[19] 4613 5-11-1	AntonyEvans	—
			(J K Cresswell) *bhd tl p.u bef 7th*	**150/1**	
0/0-	**P**		**Fieldings Society (IRE)**[516] 2196 7-11-1	AlanO'Keeffe	—
			(Jennie Candlish) *a bhd: blnd 9th: t.o whn p.u bef 3 out*	**66/1**	
0P	**P**		**Tight Corner (IRE)**[50] 4052 7-11-1	DaveCrosse	—
			(Ian Williams) *t.k.h: hdwy after 3rd: wknd 8th: t.o whn p.u bef 3 out*	**28/1**	
-600	**P**		**Northern Link (IRE)**[53] 4005 7-11-1 82	MarcusFoley	—
			(Miss Tor Sturgis) *led tl after 3rd: wkng whn nt fluent 7th: t.o whn p.u bef 2 out*	**66/1**	

5m 40.0s (-14.60) **Going Correction** -0.65s/f (Firm)
WFA 4 from 5yo+ 7lb **15** Ran SP% **115.8**
Speed ratings: **98,96,93,93,93 90,88,82,81,76** —,—,—,—,— CSF £4.19 TOTE £2.40: £1.10, £1.40, £7.50; EX 4.80.
Owner The Welsh Valleys Syndicate **Bred** Michael Hurley **Trained** Cowbridge, Vale Of Glamorgan

FOCUS
Only three could be seriously fancied in this staying event and the race is rated around the first two about half a stone below their previous best.

NOTEBOOK
Piran(IRE), a progressive young staying hurdler, was none the worse for his fall here last time. He *did not mind the return to three miles and readily asserted his superiority on the run-in. (op 13-8 tchd 7-4)*
Waterloo Son(IRE), attempting this trip for the first time, found the winner too hot to handle from the final flight. *(op 11-4)*
Allborn Lad(IRE), stepping up in distance, ran by far his best race to date but was held when making a hash of the penultimate hurdle.
Darn Good was a shade disappointing and was the first of the three major players to crack. *(op 7-2)*
Cloneybrien Boy(IRE) was back over hurdles after failing to take to fences at the end of last year. This was his best performance so far. *(op 100-1)*
Alderman Rose failed to prove that he stays three miles. *(tchd 20-1)*
Toothill Gunner *Official explanation: jockey said gelding lost its action (op 100-1)*

4827 MILLICHOPE TRUST NOVICES' CHASE (19 fncs) 3m

3:00 (3:00) (Class 3) 5-Y-0+
£6,263 (£1,850; £925; £463; £231; £116)

Form					RPR
4533	**1**		**The Dark Lord (IRE)**[19] 4617 9-11-2 120	LeightonAspell	131+
			(Mrs L Wadham) *hld up in tch: nt fluent 11th (water): hit 2 out: led last: drvn out*	**4/1**[2]	
6023	**2**	*1 1/4*	**Mioche D'Estruval (FR)**[31] 4419 6-11-2 119	(v) APMcCoy	128+
			(M C Pipe) *j.lft: w ldr: led 10th: nt fluent 11th (water): hdd 12th: led and hit 13th: rdn appr 4 out: hdd last: nt qckn*	**9/2**[3]	
2321	**3**	*3 1/2*	**Martha's Kinsman (IRE)**[64] 3801 7-11-2 120	RichardJohnson	124+
			(H D Daly) *a.p: mstkes 13th and 14th: lft 3rd 3 out: one pce*	**10/3**[1]	
FP30	**4**	*10*	**Portavo (IRE)**[31] 4419 6-11-2 106	PaulMoloney	114+
			(Miss H C Knight) *hld up and bhd: hdwy 7th: hit 12th: no imp whn hit 2 out: j.lft last*	**16/1**	
00P5	**5**	*22*	**Barcelona**[21] 4591 9-10-9 80	(t) MissLBrooke(7)	95+
			(Lady Susan Brooke) *bhd fr 12th*	**100/1**	
5P65	**6**	*6*	**Jonanaud**[8] 4729 7-10-9 102	MrRMcCarthy(7)	85
			(H J Manners) *a bhd: mstke 7th: lost tch 9th*	**50/1**	
1305	**P**		**Go For Bust**[19] 4612 7-11-2 120	MarcusFoley	—
			(N J Henderson) *a bhd: blnd 14th: t.o whn p.u bef 3 out*	**6/1**	
5006	**P**		**Let's Rock**[21] 4590 8-10-9 67	MrRHodges(7)	—
			(Mrs A Price) *a bhd: mstke 5th: sn rdn: t.o whn p.u bef 4 out*	**100/1**	
-45P	**P**		**Mesmeric (IRE)**[22] 4579 8-11-2 112	JohnMcNamara	—
			(B G Powell) *hld up in tch: j. slowly 6th: hit 9th: wknd 12th: t.o whn p.u bef 4 out*	**16/1**	
412F	**U**		**Nayodabayo (IRE)**[82] 3506 6-11-2 120	(v) ChristianWilliams	—
			(Evan Williams) *mde most to 10th: led and hit 12th: hdd 13th: ev ch whn stmbld and uns rdr 3 out*	**9/2**[3]	

5m 54.3s (-17.80) **Going Correction** -0.65s/f (Firm) **10** Ran SP% **109.4**
Speed ratings: **103,102,101,98,90 88**,—,—,—,— CSF £20.95 TOTE £5.20: £1.80, £1.50, £1.50; EX 25.90.
Owner A E Pakenham **Bred** Thomas Barry **Trained** Newmarket, Suffolk

FOCUS
This did not look a great contest for the grade and is best rated around the placed horses.

NOTEBOOK
The Dark Lord(IRE) is proven on this sort of surface and took advantage of a return to novice company. *(op 3-1)*
Mioche D'Estruval(FR) confirmed that he stays three miles under a vintage ride by McCoy but did not help his cause by jumping left.
Martha's Kinsman(IRE) did well to finish so close after consecutive mistakes in the back straight on the second circuit. *(op 4-1 tchd 3-1)*
Portavo(IRE) had finished only a length and a quarter behind Martha's Kinsman when third over course and distance in February.
Nayodabayo(IRE) likes to force the pace and was still well in contention when unluckily getting rid of his rider at the third last. *(op 5-1)*

4828 TIGER DEVELOPMENTS & R STRACHAN PROPERTY CONSULTANTS (S) HURDLE (9 hdls) 2m

3:30 (3:30) (Class 4) 4-7-Y-0 **£3,253** (£955; £477; £238)

Form					RPR
00PP	**1**		**Simonovski (USA)**[8] 4738 5-11-0 100	(p) RichardJohnson	93+
			(Mrs A M Thorpe) *mde all: rdn whn j.rt 2 out and last: r.o wl*	**5/1**[2]	
3540	**2**	*7*	**Waziri (IRE)**[84] 3456 5-11-0 78	PaulMoloney	85
			(M Sheppard) *a.p: chsd wnr fr 3rd: rdn appr 2 out: no imp*	**8/1**	
05	**3**	*shd*	**City Of Manchester (IRE)**[18] 4631 4-10-3	PaddyMerrigan(5)	79
			(P C Haslam) *chsd ldrs: rdn 3 out: one pce fr 2 out*	**11/2**[3]	
0225	**4**	*7*	**Shalati Princess**[7] 4756 5-10-0 78	MrRhysHughes(7)	71
			(D Burchell) *chsd ldrs: rdn appr 3 out: sn wknd*	**9/2**[1]	
	5	*10*	**Lyrical Girl (USA)**[6] 5-10-0	WillieMcCarthy(7)	61
			(H J Manners) *chsd ldrs: no hdwy fr 6th*	**33/1**	
600	**6**	*7*	**Rabbit**[91] 3355 5-10-7 69	JamesDavies	54
			(Mrs A L M King) *no hdwy fr 6th*	**25/1**	
00P0	**7**	*2*	**Another Flint (IRE)**[104] 3131 6-10-7	(t) MrPSheldrake(7)	59
			(R Flint) *bhd: n.m.r 2nd: nvr nr ldrs*	**50/1**	
P04	**8**	*2*	**Oktis Morilious (IRE)**[24] 4550 5-10-7 74	AdrianScholes(7)	57
			(J A Danahar) *bhd: hmpd 3rd: n.d*	**25/1**	
P	**9**	*1/2*	**Danger Bird (IRE)**[8] 4733 6-9-11	AdamHawkins(10)	50
			(R Hollinshead) *j.rt 1st: nvr bttr than mid-div*	**66/1**	
0-PP	**10**	*19*	**Silk Appeal**[22] 4570 6-10-7	HenryOliver	31
			(D J Wintle) *hmpd 3rd: a bhd*	**50/1**	
00	**11**	*11*	**Showtime Faye**[17] 3730 4-9-8	(p) TomMessenger(7)	14
			(A Bailey) *j.rt 4th: a towards rr*	**50/1**	
	12	*1 1/4*	**Upirlande (IRE)**[145] 2362 6-11-0	LeightonAspell	25
			(D A Rees) *hmpd 1st: a towards rr*	**33/1**	
P00P	**B**		**Life Estates**[37] 4290 6-10-11 69	ChrisHonour(3)	—
			(J D Frost) *bhd tl b.d 4th*	**80/1**	
0F00	**U**		**Weet An Haul**[25] 5-11-0 70	RJGreene	—
			(T Wall) *bhd tl hmpd and uns rdr 4th*	**100/1**	
00-0	**U**		**Davnic**[187] 1674 6-10-0	MarcGoldstein(7)	—
			(T Wall) *j.big 1st: j. awkwardly and uns rdr 3rd*	**100/1**	
02P3	**P**		**Made In France (FR)**[21] 4591 6-11-10 100	(v) APMcCoy	—
			(M C Pipe) *hld up: hmpd 1st: hdwy 6th: lost pl and p.u bef 3 out*	**6/1**	
0502	**P**		**Weet Watchers**[21] 4591 6-11-0 85	JohnMcNamara	68
			(T Wall) *hld up in mid-div: hdwy after 6th: no imp whn hit 3 out: sn eased: p.u after 2 out*	**11/2**[3]	

3m 40.7s (-11.60) **Going Correction** -0.65s/f (Firm)
WFA 4 from 5yo+ 5lb No bid. Made In France clmd R. J. Price for £6,000 **17** Ran SP% **115.2**
Speed: **103,99,99,95,90 87,86,85,85,75,70,69,** CSF £38.45 TOTE £6.40: £2.10, £2.60, £2.80; EX 70.80
Owner Mrs A M Thorpe **Bred** Joanne Nor **Trained** Bronwydd Arms, Carmarthens

FOCUS
This was run at a good pace and only a few of this big field of platers got into it.

NOTEBOOK
Simonovski(USA), tried in cheekpieces for this drop into a seller, ensured there would be no hanging about. Apparently given a breather on the home turn, he proceeded to run his rivals ragged *despite rather running down the last two flights. Official explanation: trainer said, regarding the improved form shown, race was run to suit gelding and it was able to dominate (op 9-2)*
Waziri(IRE) could not react when the winner kicked again once in line for home and just managed to hold on for second. *(tchd 15-2)*
City Of Manchester(IRE), dropped in grade, kept plugging away in what turned into a separate race for the runner-up spot. *(op 6-1 tchd 13-2)*
Shalati Princess could not take advantage of a return to selling company. *(op 5-1)*
Lyrical Girl(USA), who had a pipe-opener on the Fibresand six days earlier, won a mile seller at Southwell and a ten-furlong claimer at Lingfield in the winter of 2003/4. *(op 25-1)*
Made In France(FR) stopped as if something was amiss. *(op 7-1)*

4829 BROMFIELD SAND & GRAVEL H'CAP CHASE (FOR THE OAKLY PARK CHALLENGE CUP) (17 fncs) 2m 4f

4:00 (4:00) (Class 3) (0-125,122) 5-Y-0+
£9,394 (£2,775; £1,387; £694; £346; £174)

Form					RPR
1150	**1**		**Saffron Sun**[119] 2847 11-11-1 **111**	ChristianWilliams	119+
			(J D Frost) *prom: lost pl 12th: n.m.r on ins after 13th: rallied appr 4 out: rdn to ld last: r.o wl*	**33/1**	
4221	**2**	*2*	**Cossack Dancer (IRE)**[21] 4590 8-11-4 **114**	(p) MatthewBatchelor	119
			(M Bradstock) *led 2nd: rdn and hdd last: nt qckn*	**6/1**[2]	
1110	**3**	*2 1/2*	**She's Our Native (IRE)**[29] 4443 8-10-0 **96** oh3	PaulMoloney	101+
			(Evan Williams) *hld up and bhd: hdwy whn sltly hmpd 4 out: r.o flat*	**9/4**[1]	
3431	**4**	*1 3/4*	**Lord Dundaniel (IRE)**[23] 4563 9-11-1 **111**	(p) APMcCoy	112
			(B De Haan) *hld up: hdwy 5th: rdn and ev ch 3 out: wknd flat*	**7/1**[3]	
0301	**5**	*3*	**Toulouse (IRE)**[21] 4592 9-11-8 **118**	(t) RobertWalford	117+
			(R H Alner) *hld up in mid-div: hit 4th: struggling appr 4 out: styd on fr 2 out*	**8/1**	
5153	**6**	*4*	**Rooster's Reunion (IRE)**[137] 2516 7-11-8 **118**	JohnMcNamara	114+
			(D R Gandolfo) *hld up and bhd: hdwy 12th: wknd 3 out*	**12/1**	
-322	**7**	*3/4*	**Jaffa**[27] 4476 14-10-12 **115**	MrRArmson(7)	112+
			(Miss J Wormall) *hld up in rr: hdwy 13th: 3l 5th whn blnd bdly 4 out: nt rcvr: mstke 2 out*	**8/1**	
PF4	**8**	*10*	**Gazump (FR)**[41] 4213 8-11-7 **117**	(t) AntonyEvans	106+
			(N A Twiston-Davies) *hld up and bhd: hdwy 12th: n.m.r after 13th: sn rdn: wknd 3 out*	**11/1**	
6565	**P**		**Kind Sir**[21] 4592 10-10-6 **102**	WayneHutchinson	—
			(A W Carroll) *prom tl wknd 10th: t.o whn p.u bef 4 out*	**20/1**	
042P	**P**		**Spring Lover (FR)**[19] 4611 7-11-12 **122**	(p) SamThomas	—
			(Miss Venetia Williams) *led to 2nd: prom: mstke 12th: wknd appr 4 out: p.u bef last*	**8/1**	

4m 53.9s (-16.80) **Going Correction** -0.65s/f (Firm) course record **10** Ran SP% **114.6**
Speed ratings: **107,106,105,104,103 101,101,97**,—,— CSF £218.82 CT £639.01 TOTE £37.40: £6.60, £2.20, £1.50; EX 256.00.
Owner Mrs J F Bury **Bred** G Blight **Trained** Scorriton, Devon
■ Stewards' Enquiry : Sam Thomas two-day ban: careless riding (Apr 24-25)

FOCUS
A fair, competitive handicap for some decent prizemoney run at sound gallop. The form looks solid enough rated around the principals.
NOTEBOOK
Saffron Sun, who usually runs over further, had lost his position prior to running out of room at the end of the back straight. Soon recovering, he ran out a decisive first winner for his trainer at the course.
Cossack Dancer(IRE) was soon in his favourite front-running position on this graduation to handicaps. He got the longer trip well enough and it was simply a case of meeting one too good. *(op 13-2)*
She's Our Native(IRE) ◆, 3lb out of a handicap for this return to fences, is now rated 29lb higher over hurdles after a successful time this winter. She can soon exploit her chase rating and a longer trip may help. *(op 5-2)*
Lord Dundaniel(IRE), again wearing cheekpieces, had more to do this time and could not overcome an 8lb hike in the ratings for his win at Warwick.
Toulouse(IRE), again in a tongue tie, had been raised 5lb for winning last time and was another taking on better company.
Rooster's Reunion(IRE) appeared to get found out by the longer trip. *(op 11-1)*
Jaffa did a demolition job on the fourth last and it was out of commission for the rest of the meeting *(op 10-1)*

4830 WELSH GUARDS ASSOCIATION NOVICES' H'CAP HURDLE (11 hdls) 2m 5f
4:30 (4:31) (Class 3) (0-115,113) 4-Y-0+ **£5,204** (£1,528; £764; £381)

Form RPR
6P16 **1** **Pure Magic (FR)**[23] 4557 5-10-3 **89** .... SeanCurran 92+
(Miss J S Davis) *mde all: rdn appr 3 out: edgd lft appr 2 out and flat: drvn out* **12/1**
216F **2** *3 ½* **Dearson (IRE)**[55] 3957 5-11-12 **112** .... NoelFehily 113+
(C J Mann) *hld up and bhd: hdwy on ins 6th: ev ch 2 out: sn rdn: j.lft last: one pce* **9/1**
316 **3** *1* **Pseudonym (IRE)**[7] 4747 4-11-3 **110** .... DaveCrosse 102
(M F Harris) *hld up in rr: hdwy after 8th: sn rdn: one pce fr 2 out* **6/4**[1]
6-P1 **4** *14* **Maljimar (IRE)**[25] 4521 6-11-5 **105** .... PaulMoloney 90
(Miss H C Knight) *hld up and bhd: hdwy appr 8th: wknd appr 3 out* **5/1**[3]
04P4 **5** *14* **Beau Supreme (IRE)**[21] 4589 9-11-12 **112** .... RichardJohnson 83
(C J Down) *prom tl wknd after 8th* **4/1**[2]
5F00 **6** *6* **Wembury Point (IRE)**[2] 4821 4-10-13 **113** .... CharlieStudd[(7)] 71
(B G Powell) *prom: reminders after 6th: wknd after 8th* **16/1**
6F03 **7** *11* **Presenter (IRE)**[38] 4282 6-9-10 **89** .... MrLRPayter[(7)] 43
(M Sheppard) *hld up: hdwy 3rd: nt fluent 6th: wknd after 8th* **10/1**
003F **8** *11* **Castle Frome (IRE)**[44] 4164 7-9-12 **87** .... OwynNelmes[(3)] 30
(A E Price) *prom: lost pl 4th: t.o fr 7th* **20/1**

5m 2.60s (-15.70) **Going Correction** -0.65s/f (Firm)
WFA 4 from 5yo+ 6lb **8** Ran SP% **114.1**
Speed ratings: **103,101,101,95,90 88,84,79** CSF £109.56 CT £255.90 TOTE £15.90: £3.20, £3.10, £1.10; EX 55.80.
Owner West Country Racing - Winter Warmer **Bred** Recent A/S **Trained** Codrington, S Gloucs
■ Stewards' Enquiry : Dave Crosse caution: used whip with excessive frequency
FOCUS
A modest novices' handicap in which Pseudonym looked a good thing after his run at Aintree last week but disappointed. The winner is the best guide to the level.
NOTEBOOK
Pure Magic(FR), 8lb higher than when scoring at Wincanton in February, found more than enough *despite being inclined to go left-handed.Official explanation: trainer said, regarding the improved form shown, gelding was allowed an uncontested lead*
Dearson(IRE) had shown he acts on good ground last autumn and may need to come down a few pounds. *(op 7-1)*
Pseudonym(IRE), 10lb higher than when successful at Newbury, would have had another 15lb to carry had his new mark been enforced after his effort at Aintree last week. It could be that this longest trip he has tackled so far was against him. *(tchd 13-8)*
Maljimar(IRE) dropeed away tamely over this longer distance and the Handicapper had appeared to take no chances with him. *(op 9-2 tchd 11-2)*

4831 ABBERLEY HALL OLD BOYS ASSOCIATION HUNTERS' CHASE (15 fncs 2 omitted) 2m 4f
5:00 (5:03) (Class 5) 5-Y-0+ **£2,400** (£750; £374; £187; £93; £47)

Form RPR
30P1 **1** **Enitsag (FR)**[8] 4730 7-11-11 94 .... MrDMansell[(3)] 105+
(S Flook) *hld up: hdwy 6th: led 10th: hit last: r.o* **14/1**
2453 **2** *½* **Wings Of Hope (IRE)**[18] 10-11-6 89 ....(b) MrDSJones[(3)] 97
(James Richardson) *prom: led 4th to 5th: led 7th to 10th: outpcd appr 3 out: rallied appr last: r.o flat* **50/1**
UP-4 **3** *¾* **Kerstino Two**[25] 9-11-6 .... MrDAlers-Hankey[(3)] 98+
(Mrs Caroline Keevil) *hld up in mid-div: hmpd 2nd: mstke 4th: hdwy 9th: kpt on flat* **10/1**
P-0R **4** *5* **Eskimo Jack (IRE)**[41] 4216 10-11-4 .... MrWLMorgan[(5)] 93+
(T R George) *hld up in mid-div: hdwy 7th: rdn appr 3 out: no ex flat* **9/1**[3]
/2-1 **5** *6* **Longstone Boy (IRE)**[19] 14-11-7 96 .... MrPSheldrake[(7)] 92+
(E R Clough) *hld up in tch: mstke 6th: sn hmpd and lost pl: hdwy 11th: no imp fr 3 out* **33/1**
00-6 **6** *3 ½* **Summer Stock (USA)**[25] 8-11-2 ....(t) MrCDawson[(7)] 82
(R A Mills) *hld up and bhd: hdwy 9th: wknd after 12th* **100/1**
-PP0 **7** *dist* **Barton Bandit**[24] 4555 10-11-2 ....(p) MrJSole[(7)] —
(Miss Sarah Kent) *prom tl wknd 10th: t.o* **200/1**
2 **F** **Lord Nellerie (FR)**[21] 4594 7-11-7 112 .... MrGOpperman[(7)] —
(B G Powell) *fell 2nd* **10/3**[2]
4PP/ **F** **Solvang (IRE)**[737] 4696 14-11-2 .... MrMWall[(7)] —
(Mrs J Marles) *prom tl fell 9th* **150/1**
23-P **P** **Iambe De La See (FR)**[12] 10-10-9 104 .... MrTWeston[(7)] —
(Mrs P Grainger) *bhd tl p.u bef 12th* **50/1**
P **P** **Pollerton Run (IRE)**[44] 4167 8-11-2 .... MrGDavies[(7)] —
(T G Williams) *t.o whn p.u bef 6th: b.b.v* **200/1**
111 **U** **Red Brook Lad**[21] 4594 11-11-11 107 .... MissCTizzard[(3)] —
(C St V Fox) *bhd tl blnd and uns rdr 5th* **5/4**[1]
P400 **P** **River Mere**[310] 673 12-11-2 69 .... MrWKinsey[(7)] —
(Mrs P A Rigby) *a bhd: j.rt 2nd: t.o whn p.u bef 3 out* **100/1**
53FU **P** **Knight's Emperor (IRE)**[21] 4594 9-11-9 95 .... MrRMorgan[(5)] —
(Miss Alexandra Lindner) *a bhd: t.o whn p.u bef 3 out* **66/1**
3 **U** **Alexander Fourball (IRE)**[21] 4594 12-11-2 .... MrRJagger[(7)] —
(R Teague) *hld up in tch: hmpd by loose horse and uns rdr 6th* **66/1**
/B-1 **U** **Albatros (FR)**[11] 9-11-7 .... MrRTrotter[(7)] —
(A R Trotter) *hld up in mid-div: hmpd 2nd: blnd 5th: hmpd and uns rdr after 6th* **11/1**
5650 **P** **Papua**[218] 1435 12-11-7 106 ....(b) MissSDuckett[(7)] —
(Geoffrey Deacon) *mid-div: hit rails after 7th: sn bhd: t.o whn p.u bef last* **40/1**
2U25 **P** **Deep King (IRE)**[169] 1881 11-11-2 109 .... MrJJarrett[(7)] —
(Col R I Webb-Bowen) *led to 4th: led 5th to 7th: blnd and sddle slipped 12th: sn lost pl: p.u bef 3 out* **18/1**

4m 58.0s (-12.70) **Going Correction** -0.65s/f (Firm) **18** Ran SP% **122.8**
Speed ratings: **99,98,98,96,94 92,—,—,—,— —,—,—,—,— —,—,—** CSF £532.43 TOTE £15.30: £3.80, £5.50, £3.40; EX 593.50.
Owner Glyn Byard **Bred** Agence F I P S **Trained** Leominster, Herefordshire
FOCUS
Much of the interest in this hunter chase was lost with the early exit of the consistent Red Brook Lad. The placed horses are the best guide to the form. First fence in the home straight omitted - damaged.
NOTEBOOK
Enitsag(FR) does not mind a sound surface and held on well under a typically flamboyant finish by his rider.
Wings Of Hope(IRE) likes fast ground and fought back well over a trip on the short side for him.
Kerstino Two, a winner over three miles at Larkhill last time, was another to find this distance short of his best. *(op 13-2)*
Eskimo Jack(IRE), who blotted his copy-book at the start at Newbury, also probably needs further *on a course as easy and ground as fast as this. Official explanation: vet said gelding finished distressed (op 17-2)*
Longstone Boy(IRE) had finished no less than 21 lengths in front of the winner when successful over course and distance in May last year. *(op 22-1)*
Red Brook Lad is normally a model of consistency and had the bookmakers breathing a sigh of relief for once with his early exit. *(op 14-1 tchd 20-1)*
Deep King(IRE) *Official explanation: jockey said saddle slipped (op 14-1 tchd 20-1)*
Pollerton Run(IRE) *Official explanation: trainer said gelding had bled from the nose (op 14-1 tchd 20-1)*

4832 J O HAMBRO INVESTMENT MANAGEMENT & LUDLOW R.P. H'CAP HURDLE (9 hdls) 2m
5:30 (5:30) (Class 3) (0-120,120) 4-Y-0+ **£6,263** (£1,850; £925; £463; £231; £116)

Form RPR
16 **1** **Political Intrigue**[47] 4117 4-10-10 **110** .... JimCrowley 117+
(T G Dascombe) *a.p: led appr 3 out: clr last: comf* **9/2**[3]
55UF **2** *8* **Dusty Dane (IRE)**[75] 3616 4-9-4 **100** oh1 .... RichardGordon[(10)] 97+
(W G M Turner) *hld up in mid-div: hdwy whn hmpd 3 out: r.o flat: no ch w wnr* **25/1**
222 **3** *½* **Vaughan**[23] 4564 5-11-2 **110** .... MarkBradburne 113+
(H D Daly) *hld up: hdwy appr 5th: one pce fr 2 out* **9/4**[1]
0631 **4** *nk* **Theatre Tinka (IRE)**[18] 4632 7-9-5 **95** .... AdamHawkins[(10)] 97+
(R Hollinshead) *hld up and bhd: hdwy whn hmpd 3 out: kpt on flat* **12/1**
0-20 **5** *5* **Zalda**[18] 4641 5-11-12 **120** .... RichardJohnson 116
(P J Hobbs) *nvr trbld ldrs* **8/1**
4204 **6** *shd* **Canadian Storm**[84] 3456 5-9-7 **94** oh4 ....(p) RichardSpate[(7)] 90
(A G Juckes) *t.k.h: hmpd 3 out: nvr nr ldrs* **50/1**
5-56 **7** *10* **Fortune Point (IRE)**[28] 1957 8-10-3 **97** ....(v) WayneHutchinson 85+
(A W Carroll) *prom: rdn appr 6th: wknd appr 3 out* **33/1**
4205 **8** *5* **Carte Sauvage (USA)**[67] 2147 5-9-12 **97** ....(v) CharliePoste[(5)] 86+
(M F Harris) *hld up in tch: rdn appr 6th: wkng whn hmpd 3 out* **16/1**
5064 **9** *dist* **Milligan (FR)**[22] 4573 11-11-3 **111** .... JodieMogford —
(Dr P Pritchard) *prom: lost pl appr 4th: t.o fr 6th* **40/1**
1624 **F** **Predator (GER)**[41] 4215 5-10-12 **106** ....(p) APMcCoy —
(Jonjo O'Neill) *led: rdn and hdd appr 3 out: 2l 2nd and hld whn fell 3 out* **5/2**[2]

3m 39.5s (-12.80) **Going Correction** -0.65s/f (Firm)
WFA 4 from 5yo+ 5lb **10** Ran SP% **113.4**
Speed ratings: **106,102,101,101,99 99,94,91,—,—** CSF £101.08 CT £314.13 TOTE £7.80: £2.30, £5.20, £1.10; EX 148.90 Place 6 £123.16, Place 5 £92.28.
Owner ONEWAY National Hunt Partnership **Bred** Juddmonte Farms **Trained** Lambourn, Berks
FOCUS
Quite an interesting little handicap and run at a solid pace. The form looks sound enough through the runner-up and fourth.
NOTEBOOK
Political Intrigue ◆ was highly tried on unsuitable soft ground at Sandown last time after winning here on a similar surface to this in January. He is clearly useful when conditions are in his favour. *(op 11-2)*
Dusty Dane(IRE) did well to prevail in the seperate battle for second but should not be considered unlucky. This should help his confidence. *(op 20-1)*
Vaughan appeared to be reasonably handicapped but proved no match for the useful winner. *(op 2-1 tchd 5-2)*
Theatre Tinka(IRE) had a shorter distance and totally different ground to contend with this time.
Zalda, dropped 2lb, again ran below par. *(tchd 9-1)*
Canadian Storm had a bit to do from 4lb 'wrong'. *(op 40-1)*
Predator(GER) had just started to play second fiddle to the useful winner when coming to grief at the third last. *(op 3-1 tchd 9-4 and 7-2 in places)*
T/Plt: £125.40 to a £1 stake. Pool: £52,311.55. 304.35 winning tickets. T/Qpdt: £65.20 to a £1 stake. Pool: £3,242.60. 36.80 winning tickets. KH

4674 WINCANTON (R-H)
Thursday, April 13
OFFICIAL GOING: Good (good to firm in places)
Wind: Strong, across

4833 ROLLIN CLONES ON 12 MAY NOVICES' CHASE (13 fncs) 2m
2:20 (2:20) (Class 3) 5-Y-0+ **£6,665** (£2,069; £1,114)

Form RPR
0-P **1** **Made In Montot (FR)**[133] 2593 6-11-0 ....(t) RWalsh 110+
(P F Nicholls) *racd keenly: hld up bhd ldng pair: rdn to chal and hung lft fr 2 out: v slt advantage last: drvn out* **4/1**[2]
3425 **2** *hd* **Without A Doubt**[28] 4460 7-11-6 134 .... MickFitzgerald 116+
(Carl Llewellyn) *led tl 2nd: styd prom: led 8th: nt fluent 4 out: rdn and hrd pressed fr 3 out:narrowly hdd last: rallied flat: no ex fnl st* **8/13**[1]
3212 **P** **Pardishar (IRE)**[23] 4559 8-11-6 120 ....(p) JamieMoore —
(G L Moore) *hld up bhd ldng pair: hit 2nd: p.u qckly bef 6th (dismntd)* **4/1**[2]

3m 57.2s (-4.70) **Going Correction** -0.50s/f (Good)
WFA 5 from 6yo+ 3lb **4** Ran SP% **104.9**
Speed ratings: **91,90,87,—** CSF £6.94 TOTE £4.50; EX 12.00.

Owner The Hon Mrs Townshend **Bred** J L Berger And Jean-Francois Lamborot **Trained** Ditcheat, Somerset

■ Stewards' Enquiry : Mick Fitzgerald caution: careless riding

FOCUS

A decent little novices' chase, run at a sound pace, and the first two came clear. THe third sets the standard for the form.

NOTEBOOK

Made In Montot(FR), disappointing when pulled up on his chasing debut at this track back in December, was equipped with a tongue strap on this return to action. Despite refusing to settle through the first half of the contest, he emerged full of running turning for home, and ultimately just did enough to get off the mark with a narrow success. He is clearly tricky, and it must be noted he was in receipt of 6lb from the runner-up, but he also has definite talent and it is hoped a breathing operation during the summer will help him fulfill his potential next season. *(op 7-2)*

Without A Doubt, fifth in the four miler at Cheltenham 28 days previously, was not aided by being taken on for the lead on this marked drop back in trip. He did little wrong in defeat in giving 6lb to the winner, and really does deserve to get his head back in front, but is surely in need of a stiffer test now. *(op 4-6 tchd 4-7)*

Imperial Rocket(USA), well beaten in handicap company the last twice, showed greatly-improved form and only cried enough from the penultimate fence. A fast surface is clearly key to him, he seemed to enjoy this sharper track, and really ought to win a race or two during the summer from his current mark. *(op 25-1)*

Pardishar(IRE) was quickly dismounted after being pulled up and clearly had a problem. *(op 7-2)*

4834 EASTER NOVICES' H'CAP HURDLE (8 hdls) 2m

2:50 (2:50) (Class 4) (0-105,101) 4-Y-O+ **£3,426** (£998; £499)

Form RPR

5361 **1** **Lorient Express (FR)**[8] 4731 7-10-4 **84** LiamTreadwell[(5)] 96+
(Miss Venetia Williams) *t.k.h in tch: hdwy after 3 out: led next: clr whn nt fluent last: readily* **10/11**[1]

66P **2** *2 ½* **Royal Stardust**[20] 4606 5-11-11 **100** (p) JamieMoore 103
(G L Moore) *hld up in tch: rdn and effrt appr 2 out: wnt 2nd appr appr last: hung rt and a hld by wnr run-in* **40/1**

0004 **3** *hd* **Post It**[64] 3800 5-11-3 **92** RobertThornton 95
(R J Hodges) *chsd ldrs: lost position 4th: rdn after 3 out: styd on to go 3rd run-in* **100/1**

4 *½* **Boulevin (IRE)**[23] 2303 6-11-1 **95** MarkNicolls[(5)] 97
(R J Price) *hld up towards rr: stdy prog after 3 out: styd on fr next: nrst fin* **100/1**

00F0 **5** *1 ¼* **Avesomeofthat (IRE)**[41] 4210 5-10-10 **92** WayneKavanagh[(7)] 94+
(J W Mullins) *hld up towards rr: pckd 4th: hdwy after 3 out: sn rdn: styd on* **20/1**

0100 **6** *1* **Muntami (IRE)**[30] 4430 5-11-11 **100** AndrewTinkler 100
(John A Harris) *mid div: making hdwy whn hit 3 out: ev ch 2 out: sn rdn: kpt on same pce* **20/1**

-1P4 **7** *3 ½* **Lawaaheb (IRE)**[27] 4478 5-11-3 **92** (p) RWalsh 89
(M J Gingell) *led 2nd tl 4th: chsd ldrs: rdn after 3 out: one pced fr next* **20/1**

000 **8** *3* **Brave Hiawatha (FR)**[86] 3429 4-10-6 **87** JasonMaguire 77+
(J A B Old) *hld up towards rr: stdy hdwy appr 3 out: ev ch whn nt fluent 2 out: wknd appr last* **50/1**

9 *5* **Rivertree (IRE)**[172] 1864 5-11-3 **97** DarylJacob[(5)] 86
(D P Keane) *towards rr: sme late hdwy: nvr a factor* **66/1**

060P **10** *nk* **Sharp Rally (IRE)**[79] 3548 5-10-10 **85** (t) WarrenMarston 73
(A J Wilson) *nt fluent 3rd: in rr: drvn along fr next: sme late hdwy: nvr trbld ldrs* **100/1**

632 **11** *shd* **Stocking Island**[76] 3597 5-11-5 **94** PJBrennan 82
(C R Egerton) *in tch: hit 2nd: rdn and effrt after 3 out: wknd next* **14/1**[3]

-0F0 **12** *½* **Salt Cellar (IRE)**[90] 3371 7-11-9 **98** TomSiddall 86
(R S Brookhouse) *mid div tl wknd appr 3 out* **100/1**

000 **13** *4* **Mylord Collonges (FR)**[20] 4604 6-11-6 **95** TomScudamore 79
(Mrs Susan Nock) *led tl 2nd: led 4th tl 3 out: sn rdn: wknd appr next* **40/1**

0040 **14** *shd* **Ericas Charm**[73] 3648 6-10-13 **93** MrTJO'Brien[(5)] 89+
(P Bowen) *in tch: led 3 out: rdn and hdd 2 out: 3rd whn blnd bdly and nrly uns rdr last: nt rcvr* **25/1**

4111 **15** *1 ¼* **Picot De Say**[14] 4674 4-11-6 **101** OllieMcPhail 77
(C Roberts) *hld up and a towards rr* **4/1**[2]

3 **16** *11* **All Square (IRE)**[31] 4423 6-10-8 **83** JoeTizzard 54
(R A Farrant) *prom tl 5th: sn bhd* **50/1**

1540 **17** *28* **Twist Bookie (IRE)**[89] 3386 6-11-7 **101** ShaneWalsh[(5)] 44
(J S Moore) *prom tl 5th: sn bhd: t.o* **40/1**

50B0 **18** *1 ¼* **Patronage**[41] 4211 4-10-12 **93** MickFitzgerald 29
(Jonjo O'Neill) *a bhd: t.o* **14/1**[3]

3m 39.9s (-9.20) **Going Correction** -0.50s/f (Good)
WFA 4 from 5yo+ 5lb **18** Ran SP% **120.5**
Speed ratings: **103,101,101,101,100 100,98,97,94,94 94,94,92,92,91 85,71,71** CSF £51.91 CT £2322.66 TOTE £2.30: £1.20, £12.20, £4.60, £17.00; EX 54.90.

Owner Let's Live Racing **Bred** D Laupretre **Trained** Kings Caple, H'fords

FOCUS

A moderate handicap, run at a sound gallop, and although the winner is value for further, the form is worth treating with a degree of caution.

NOTEBOOK

Lorient Express(FR) ◆, unpenalised for his recent success at Exeter in a conditional jockeys' event under today's rider on his return to hurdling, had the race in the bag nearing two out and followed-up in ready fashion. Considering he is due to race from a 13lb higher mark in the future and is rated 123 as a chaser, this must rate another shrewd piece of placing by his astute trainer and a bold bid for the hat-trick can be expected if he is kept over hurdles. *(op Evens tchd 11-10)*

Royal Stardust showed his best form for a long time and clearly appreciated the application of first-time cheekpieces. He is one to have reservations about, but he will not always bump into such a well-handicapped rival as the winner in this grade. *(op 33-1)*

Post It, making her handicap debut, again advertised her liking for quick ground and ran another improved race. She looks up to winning a race from her current mark now the ground is getting livelier, but probably needs a stiffer track.

Boulevin(IRE), fit from a recent spin on the Flat, was doing his best work at the finish and turned in an eye-catching display. He had not shown a great deal over hurdles in Ireland, but this faster ground was evidently more to his liking, and he is capable of better from this mark when getting a more positive ride. *(op 66-1)*

Picot De Say, chasing a four-timer from a 9lb higher mark, failed to raise his game on this much quicker ground and his fate was sealed from halfway. He can be given another chance to prove his worth when reverting to easier ground.

4835 AXMINSTER CARPETS H'CAP CHASE 3m 4f

3:20 (3:23) (Class 4) (0-115,115) 5-Y-O+ **£5,204** (£1,528; £764; £381)

Form RPR

3F00 **1** **Tom Sayers (IRE)**[84] 3469 8-11-3 **111** MrTJO'Brien[(5)] 125+
(P J Hobbs) *a.p: led 17th: clr 2 out: styd on wl: rdn out* **9/1**

1P-0 **2** *5* **Elenas River (IRE)**[33] 4374 10-11-8 **111** PJBrennan 120+
(P J Hobbs) *mid-div: hdwy to trck ldrs after 9th: hit 16th: drew clr w wnr appr 3 out: sn rdn: kpt on same pce* **11/2**[2]

-465 **3** *¾* **Walter's Destiny**[70] 3698 14-10-1 **97** KeiranBurke[(7)] 103
(C W Mitchell) *prom: led 9th tl after 14th: w wnr tl sltly otpced 4 out: lft 4th 3 out: styd on again fr next: tk 3rd fnl stride* **18/1**

2114 **4** *shd* **Lord Anner (IRE)**[108] 3000 7-11-9 **112** (bt) RWalsh 121+
(P F Nicholls) *nt fluent 1st: hld up bhd: stdy hdwy fr 15th: mstke 18th: rdn to chse ldrs appr 3 out: 3rd and hld whn hit last* **15/8**[1]

061F **5** *14* **Even More (IRE)**[37] 4287 11-11-11 **114** AndrewThornton 106
(R H Alner) *in tch: outpcd 15th: nvr a danger after* **14/1**

0142 **6** *4* **Lord Broadway (IRE)**[22] 4576 10-10-7 **99** TJPhelan[(3)] 87
(N M Babbage) *hld up towards rr: rdn and sme hdwy after 18th: no further imp fr 3 out* **8/1**[3]

2F02 **7** *24* **Special Conquest**[23] 4565 8-11-2 **108** RichardYoung[(3)] 72
(J W Mullins) *mid div: blnd 4th: bhd fr 15th* **33/1**

31PP **8** *22* **Fin Bec (FR)**[22] 4576 13-10-13 **102** (b) PhilipHide 44
(R Curtis) *led tl 9th: led after 14th tl 17th: sn wknd* **25/1**

F244 **P** **Jiver (IRE)**[22] 4579 7-11-6 **109** (v) TomScudamore —
(M Scudamore) *nvr gng in rr: lost tch 15th: p.u after 4 out* **14/1**

U11P **P** **Hehasalife (IRE)**[154] 2151 9-10-4 **96** (b) DougieCostello[(3)] —
(Mrs H Dalton) *towards rr: blnd 16th: sn wknd: p.u bef 4 out* **16/1**

2416 **F** **Charango Star**[12] 4690 8-11-12 **115** (b) JamieMoore 103
(W K Goldsworthy) *chsd ldrs: rdn appr 18th: wknd after 4 out: fell next* **33/1**

-431 **F** **Its Wallace Jnr**[23] 4565 7-11-11 **114** (t) JamieGoldstein 116
(Miss Sheena West) *mid-div: hdwy fr 15th: rdn in 3rd and styng on whn fell 3 out* **12/1**

-00F **P** **Tribal King (IRE)**[101] 3212 11-11-6 **109** RobertThornton —
(A King) *mid div: reminders fr 12th: hdwy 15th: rdn appr 18th: sn wknd: p.u bef 3 out* **14/1**

6m 56.8s (-23.20) **13** Ran SP% **119.8**
CSF £58.32 CT £880.77 TOTE £9.90: £3.10, £1.90, £3.40; EX 56.50.

Owner Capt E J Edwards-Heathcote **Bred** Noel James **Trained** Withycombe, Somerset

FOCUS

A fair staying handicap, run at just an average gallop, and the form looks sound enough.

NOTEBOOK

Tom Sayers(IRE), returning from an 84-day break, resumed winning ways in ready fashion under a fine ride. This was the longest trip he has won over to date, plus the highest official mark he has won from, and the key to him is clearly a decent surface. He ought to be high on confidence now and could build on this if kept going through the summer months. *(op 14-1)*

Elenas River(IRE), well backed, showed the benefit of his recent comeback at Sandown, and the return to a faster surface, but could not live with his winning stablemate from two out. His jumping was still less than convincing, but he certainly has a race within his compass on this sort of ground from his current mark. *(op 8-1)*

Walter's Destiny was ridden more prominently than has often been the case in the past and, having been outpaced when the first two went for home, he stayed on gamely to bag third. He really needs an even stiffer test nowadays, but he retains his ability, and really deserves to find another race. *(op 20-1)*

Lord Anner(IRE), returning from a 108-day break, was none too fluent over his fences and was never quite going the pace. He has an engine, and still has time on his side, but is clearly not that straightforward. *(op 9-4)*

Its Wallace Jnr, off the mark over fences last time in a match race, was in the process of running a big race prior to departing and would have most likely been third at worst. Providing his confidence is not dented by this experience, he ought to have more to offer in this sphere, and is worth another chance over this sort of trip. *(op 10-1)*

4836 COUNTRYSIDE DAY NEXT MARES' ONLY NOVICES' HURDLE (11 hdls) 2m 6f

3:50 (3:53) (Class 4) 4-Y-O+ **£3,426** (£998; £499)

Form RPR

05-P **1** **Colorado Pearl (IRE)**[324] 487 5-11-0 (t) RWalsh 99+
(P F Nicholls) *mid div: smooth prog after 3 out: led sn after 2 out: nt fluent last: kpt on wl* **7/1**[3]

430/ **2** *8* **Annie Fleetwood**[753] 8-11-0 AndrewThornton 91
(R H Alner) *mid-div: hdwy after 3 out: nt fluent 2 out: styd on to go 2nd run-in* **16/1**

53-1 **3** *2* **Hollywood**[70] 3692 5-11-2 LiamHeard[(5)] 96
(V R A Dartnall) *slowly away: bhd: steadily rcvrd into mid div 4th: hdwy to ld 3 out: rdn appr next: hdd sn after 2 out: lost 2nd flat* **5/4**[1]

0540 **4** *2 ½* **Flirty Jill**[41] 4210 5-10-9 89 (t) MarkNicolls[(5)] 88+
(P R Webber) *mid div: hdwy 3 out: rdn appr next: kpt on same pce* **7/2**[2]

004P **5** *3* **Milanshan (IRE)**[35] 4324 6-10-7 WayneKavanagh[(7)] 84
(J W Mullins) *led tl 3 out: sn rdn: kpt on same pce* **25/1**

P05 **6** *12* **Four In Hand**[31] 4425 8-10-9 88 MrTJO'Brien[(5)] 72
(Mrs K M Sanderson) *chsd ldrs: ev ch 3 out: sn rdn: wknd after next: tired whn wnt rt last* **25/1**

0F30 **7** *2* **The Laying Hen (IRE)**[54] 3997 6-10-9 87 DarylJacob[(5)] 70
(D P Keane) *mid-div: hdwy appr 3 out: rdn and effrt appr 2 out: sn wknd* **12/1**

004P **8** *2 ½* **Loose Morals (IRE)**[60] 3884 5-11-0 BarryFenton 67
(Miss E C Lavelle) *hld up towards rr: sme hdwy 3 out: wknd bef next* **18/1**

06PP **9** *7* **Lady Wurzel**[15] 4662 7-10-11 MissPGundry[(3)] 60
(J G Cann) *chsd ldrs: rdn appr 3 out: sn one pce* **33/1**

P-4P **10** *4* **Tenko**[126] 2718 7-11-0 BenjaminHitchcott 56
(M D McMillan) *prom tl lost pl after 6th: hdwy 8th: wknd after 3 out* **80/1**

600P **11** *4* **Hazzard A Guess**[14] 4680 5-10-7 SimonElliott[(7)] 52
(J W Mullins) *in tch tl wknd 3 out* **33/1**

500P **12** *2 ½* **Lansdowne Princess**[35] 4327 4-10-7 PhilipHide 43
(G A Ham) *a towards rr* **66/1**

00 **13** *8* **My Little Molly (IRE)**[35] 4333 4-10-4 RichardYoung[(3)] 35
(J W Mullins) *a towards rr* **66/1**

63-0 **14** *6* **Lurid Affair (IRE)**[94] 3322 5-10-7 MissLGardner[(7)] 36
(Mrs S Gardner) *chsd ldrs tl wknd after 8th* **40/1**

0 **P** **Miss Flossy (IRE)**[37] 4286 5-11-0 PJBrennan —
(Mrs S D Williams) *a bhd: t.o and p.u bef 2 out* **25/1**

0 **P** **Final Over**[21] 4595 6-11-0 JoeTizzard —
(W K Goldsworthy) *prom tl 6th: sn fdd: p.u bef 3 out* **50/1**

0000 **P** **She's No Muppet**[37] 4286 6-11-0 64 JimmyMcCarthy —
(N R Mitchell) *hld up towards rr: mstke 7th: sn lost tch: p.u bef 2 out* **66/1**

5m 19.0s (-6.10) **Going Correction** -0.50s/f (Good)
WFA 4 from 5yo+ 6lb 17 Ran SP% 125.5
Speed ratings: **91,88,87,86,85 81,80,79,76,75 73,73,70,67,— —,—** CSF £101.78 TOTE £8.50: £3.10, £5.50, £1.10; EX 102.40.
Owner Dr M Nicholls **Bred** Mrs B D Byrne **Trained** Ditcheat, Somerset

FOCUS
An uncompetitive event on paper, but not the result many may have expected. The third is the best guide to the level of the form.

NOTEBOOK
Colorado Pearl(IRE), down the field in three starts for a different trainer last season, had the tongue tie on once more and, although she had plenty to do with the favourite, she stepped up markedly and was able to run out a pretty authoritative winner. Evidently a stayer in the making, she may well be able to follow up given the uncompetitive nature of these races and her ability to handle good, fast ground will obviously be to her advantage. *(op 11-2 tchd 5-1)*
Annie Fleetwood has not been seen under Rules for virtually three years, but her efforts in points in the interim suggest she has enough ability to win at a modest level and she kept on nicely into second after the last. Three miles is going to suit to her, as will a return to handicaps. *(tchd 18-1)*
Hollywood, a modest bumper performer who did it well on her hurdling debut at the course back in February, got left at the start and was forced to race to race in rear. This clearly did not suit the five-year-old and, having made stealthy headway to come through and lead three out, she failed to last home. This was probably a better effort than it looks and she remains capable of winning again this season. *(op 11-8 tchd 13-8)*
Flirty Jill is not really progressing, but her handicap debut at Newbury last time came over an inadequate trip and she may be capable of landing a small race off this sort of mark. *(op 4-1)*
Milanshan(IRE) is a bit in and out, but she again demonstrated she has the ability to find a race if placed well. *(op 33-1)*

4837 PAT RUTHVEN & GUY NIXON MEMORIAL VASE AMATEUR RIDERS' H'CAP CHASE (17 fncs) 2m 5f
4:20 (4:22) (Class 4) (0-100,100) 5-Y-O+ **£3,747** (£1,162; £580; £290)

Form				RPR
2225	**1**		**Lucky Sinna (IRE)**[4] 4804 10-10-7 **88** MrSPJones(7) (B G Powell) *mde virtually all: rdn appr 3 out: briefly hdd last: kpt on wl to assert cl home: rdn out* **8/1**	96
3025	**2**	*nk*	**Joe Deane (IRE)**[31] 4426 10-11-4 **95** (p) MrsMRoberts(3) (M J Coombe) *chsd wnr: rdn to chal appr 3 out: gd jump to ld briefly last: no ex* **9/1**	103
44U4	**3**	*10*	**Terrible Tenant**[14] 4675 7-10-12 **86** MrJSnowden (J W Mullins) *slowly away: in tch: tk clsr order 10th: rdn and effrt after 4 out: one pce fr next* **5/1**[1]	84
0020	**4**	*hd*	**Kadam (IRE)**[107] 3018 6-11-5 **100** (b) MrWBiddick(7) (P F Nicholls) *chsd ldrs: rdn and effrt after 4 out: sn one pce* **6/1**[2]	98
3P00	**5**	*8*	**The Muratti**[64] 3801 8-9-9 **74** oh3 MissLHorner(5) (G Brown) *hld up towards rr and nvr trbld ldrs* **33/1**	64
545	**6**	*shd*	**Barton Hill**[63] 3815 9-11-4 **99** (b) MrRQuinn(7) (D P Keane) *hld up bhd: stdy prog fr 10th: rdn to chse ldng pair after 4 out: wknd next* **15/2**	91+
1500	**7**	*25*	**Scotch Corner (IRE)**[38] 4281 8-11-3 **96** (b[1]) MrDEngland(5) (N A Twiston-Davies) *nvr fluent: chsd ldrs tl 8th: grad fdd* **10/1**	61
P-6P	**8**	*6*	**Native Performance (IRE)**[49] 4078 11-11-5 **100** (tp) MrMGorman(7) (N J Gifford) *chsd ldrs tl 9th: sn bhd* **33/1**	59
00PU	**9**	*9*	**Star Galaxy (IRE)**[46] 4132 6-9-9 **76** oh5 ow2 MissIsabelTompsett(7) (Andrew Turnell) *mid div tl 9th: sn bhd* **33/1**	26
04P4	**U**		**Cloudy Blues (IRE)**[19] 4620 8-9-9 **74** MissLGardner(5) (R H Buckler) *in tch whn blnd and uns rdr 2nd* **33/1**	—
F4/0	**U**		**Kaluga (IRE)**[37] 4290 8-9-10 **77** ow1 (p) MrPHockley(7) (S C Burrough) *a towards rr: blnd and uns rdr 11th* **33/1**	—
3U43	**P**		**Calcot Flyer**[65] 3791 8-11-4 **95** MrGTumelty(3) (A King) *nvr travelling in rr: t.o and p.u after 11th* **5/1**[1]	—
05F2	**P**		**Master Billyboy (IRE)**[22] 4572 8-11-12 **100** MrNWilliams (Mrs S D Williams) *a towards rr: nt fluent 5th: t.o and p.u bef 3 out* **13/2**[3]	—

5m 14.4s (-8.70) **Going Correction** -0.50s/f (Good) 13 Ran SP% 117.6
Speed ratings: **96,95,92,92,88 88,79,77,73,— —,—,—** CSF £72.45 CT £394.16 TOTE £9.10: £2.50, £3.10, £2.10; EX 98.50.
Owner Exors of the late J G Plackett **Bred** Miss D And P Keating **Trained** Morestead, Hants

FOCUS
A poor handicap in which Lucky Sinna set a good gallop throughout and he found more than expected to record his first win at the 26th attempt. Unfortunately he injured a tendon in the process and it remains to be seen if this was a farewell victory. The first two set the level for the form.

NOTEBOOK
Lucky Sinna(IRE) has failed to live up to expectations and had acquired a reputation, but it was 26th time lucky for the ten-year-old as he found what was required under pressure to hold the persistent challenge of Joe Deane and record an all-the-way success. Having been second on nine previous occasions, the writing looked on the wall when he was challenged at the last, but he proved a few people wrong. Unfortunately for both horse and connections he badly injured a tendon in the process and it remains to be seen whether this was a farewell win. *(op 7-1)*
Joe Deane(IRE) himself is hardly a frequent winner, but he winged the last and looked set to outbattle Lucky Sinna. He was unable to go by however and connections are likely to rue this near miss. *(op 11-1)*
Terrible Tenant had the assistance of the very effective Snowden, but his mount was unable to gallop on with the front two although it was yet another reasonable effort in defeat for the seven-year-old. *(op 9-2)*
Kadam(IRE) tends to mix hurdles and fences, but he was unable to take advantage of his mark that has slipped back down to a winning one. *(op 7-1)*
The Muratti made a little late headway and is gradually improving over fences, but he was still comfortably held and it is likely he needs to drop in grade.
Barton Hill, who is on a fair mark, briefly threatened, but his effort came to nothing and he remains a little out of sorts. *(op 8-1)*
Master Billyboy(IRE) is proving to be rather inconsistent and he remains winless. *(op 8-1)*
Calcot Flyer appeared to hold solid claims, but he was never going and there was clearly *something amiss. Official explanation: trainer said gelding was unsuited by trip; vet said gelding lost a near-fore shoe (op 8-1)*

4838 SPONSOR AT WINCANTON H'CAP HURDLE (8 hdls) 2m
4:50 (4:57) (Class 4) (0-115,115) 4-Y-O+ **£5,204** (£1,528; £764; £381)

Form				RPR
-456	**1**		**L'Oudon (FR)**[70] 3696 5-11-12 **115** (t) RWalsh (P F Nicholls) *mid-div: pushed along and hdwy after 3 out: rdn to chal appr last: led fnl 75yds: all out* **4/1**[1]	124+
1U2	**2**	*hd*	**Anemix (FR)**[22] 4569 5-11-7 **115** HowieEphgrave(5) (L Corcoran) *chsd ldrs: led appr 3 out: rdn and narrow advantage last: rallied whn hdd fnl 75yds: no ex fnl strides* **4/1**[1]	124+
303	**3**	*7*	**It's The Limit (USA)**[8] 4736 7-11-0 **103** (b) CarlLlewellyn (W K Goldsworthy) *prom: led after 3 out: rdn and hdd appr next: 3rd and hld whn hit last* **12/1**	104
2134	**4**	*5*	**Take A Mile (IRE)**[23] 4561 4-11-1 **115** JohnnyLevins(5) (B G Powell) *led tl after 3 out: sn rdn: kpt on same pce: hit last* **7/1**[3]	105
512P	**5**	*7*	**North Lodge (GER)**[90] 3371 6-10-11 **100** RobertThornton (A King) *chsd ldrs: rdn and effrt appr 2 out: kpt on same pce* **4/1**[1]	89
150	**6**	*6*	**Reaching Out (IRE)**[103] 3132 4-11-0 **109** MickFitzgerald (N J Henderson) *mid-div: tk clsr order 3 out: rdn and effrt appr 2 out: wknd appr last* **9/2**[2]	86
054	**7**	*nk*	**Estate**[56] 3939 4-10-5 **100** TomSiddall (R S Brookhouse) *towards rr: short lived effrt after 3 out* **16/1**	77
1F06	**8**	*9*	**Space Cowboy (IRE)**[159] 2047 6-11-7 **110** PhilipHide (G L Moore) *hld up: rdn and wknd after 3 out* **14/1**	84
65P5	**9**	*1 ¼*	**Tianyi (IRE)**[59] 3899 10-9-7 **89** oh9 (v) JohnKington(7) (M Scudamore) *prom: hmpd 2nd: rdn after 3 out: sn btn* **66/1**	61
01P6	**10**	*9*	**Barton Park**[56] 3944 6-10-4 **98** (t) DarylJacob(5) (D P Keane) *bolted bef s: hld up: short lived effrt after 3 out* **20/1**	61
04P/	**11**	*8*	**Afadan (IRE)**[11] 2156 8-10-4 **93** TomScudamore (J R Jenkins) *a towards rr* **66/1**	48

3m 39.0s (-10.10) **Going Correction** -0.50s/f (Good)
WFA 4 from 5yo+ 5lb 11 Ran SP% 118.7
Speed ratings: **105,104,101,98,95 92,92,87,87,82 78** CSF £20.73 CT £177.41 TOTE £5.40: £1.70, £2.00, £3.70; EX 22.50 Place 6 £207.18, Place 5 £30.79.
Owner Gerry Mizel & Terry Warner **Bred** M Prod'Homme **Trained** Ditcheat, Somerset

FOCUS
A fair handicap hurdle in which two of the three co-favourites fought out a cracking finish, Ruby Walsh making all the difference. The placed horses set the level for the form.

NOTEBOOK
L'Oudon(FR) ◆, a useful juvenile who had not been getting home in his races this season, had been off since February in wait for this sort of ground and he was sporting the first-time tongue tie. A strong traveller throughout, he owes his success to a brilliant ride by Walsh as, having nursed him into contention, he was seen at his strongest in the finish, driving him ahead to narrowly prevail. Open to a deal of improvement at the age of five, his ability to see out races remains a *worry, but this ground is important to him and he may have a decent time of it in the summer. (tchd 5-1)*
Anemix(FR), a progressive five-year-old, always held a good position and he went on two from home, but the winner was soon on his tail and the jockeys made the difference after the last. He remains capable of winning more races. *(tchd 7-2)*
It's The Limit(USA) has been in fair form and he ran another sound race, holding every chance in the straight, but being unable to go on with front two. *(op 11-1)*
Take A Mile(IRE), who shaped most pleasing when a keeping-on fourth on returning from a break *at Exeter last month, failed to go on from that and was already held when blundering at the last. (op 10-1 tchd 13-2)*
North Lodge(GER), 12lb higher than when winning at Hereford in November, was last seen pulling up at Huntingdon in January, but he has clearly benefited from a break and this was a reasonable effort. *(op 11-2)*
Reaching Out(IRE) seems to be regressing and he again failed to live up to expectation on this return from a break. *(op 4-1)*
T/Jkpt: Not won. T/Plt: £554.90 to a £1 stake. Pool: £56,449.05. 74.25 winning tickets. T/Qpdt: £49.30 to a £1 stake. Pool: £5,607.10. 84.00 winning tickets. TM

4515 CARLISLE (R-H)
Saturday, April 15

OFFICIAL GOING: Soft
Wind: Almost nil

4840 THE SPORTSMAN BEGINNERS' CHASE (12 fncs) 2m
2:00 (2:02) (Class 4) 5-Y-O+ **£3,578** (£1,050; £525; £262)

Form				RPR
66-F	**1**		**Lucky Duck**[93] 3352 9-10-13 105 PaddyAspell(3) (Mrs A Hamilton) *cl up: led 4th: hrd pressed 3 out to next: kpt on wl* **11/2**[2]	106+
4422	**2**	*3 ½*	**Show Me The River**[23] 4586 7-11-2 112 KeithMercer (Ferdy Murphy) *prom: drvn 4 out: lft 2nd 2 out: kpt on run in* **8/11**[1]	102
0561	**3**	*3 ½*	**Political Cruise**[18] 4656 8-10-9 67 GarethThomas(7) (R Nixon) *hld up: hdwy bef 3 out: kpt on fr next: no imp run in* **25/1**	98
0606	**4**	*½*	**Uptown Lad (IRE)**[12] 4724 7-11-2 (t) KennyJohnson (R Johnson) *hld up midfield: rdn 3 out: kpt on run in: nt rch ldrs* **10/1**	98
0066	**5**	*17*	**Hialeah**[18] 4655 5-10-6 93 MrOGreenall(7) (M W Easterby) *keen: nt fluent in rr: kpt on fr 2 out: n.d* **33/1**	78
6/0-	**6**	*hd*	**Hollows Mist**[546] 1726 8-10-13 85 DougieCostello(3) (F P Murtagh) *in tch tl rdn and outpcd fr 3 out* **33/1**	80
500P	**7**	*13*	**Firion King (IRE)**[18] 4655 6-11-2 DavidO'Meara (W S Coltherd) *keen: nt fluent: led to 4th: wknd after 8th* **100/1**	67
-000	**8**	*1 ¾*	**Magic Bengie**[38] 4299 7-10-11 68 (t) DeclanMcGann(5) (F Kirby) *nt fluent: a bhd* **100/1**	66
0P6F	**9**	*5*	**Viking Song**[38] 4303 6-10-9 60 (p) DavidCullinane(7) (F Kirby) *a bhd: no ch fr 1/2-way* **200/1**	61
0P40	**10**	*½*	**Native Coll**[47] 4141 6-10-11 DesFlavin(5) (N W Alexander) *prom tl wknd fr 4 out* **100/1**	60
43-F	**F**		**Lunar Dram**[18] 4655 8-11-2 WilsonRenwick (M Dods) *hld up: hdwy 8th: chal 3 out: upsides whn fell next* **20/1**	98
P	**P**		**Komoto**[83] 3529 5-10-13 NeilMulholland (Liam Lennon, Ire) *midfield: outpcd after 5th: t.o whn p.u bef 8th* **40/1**	—
5134	**P**		**Air Of Affection**[27] 4529 5-10-6 GLee (J R Turner) *hld up: smooth hdwy 8th: in tch whn blnd next: sn btn: t.o whn p.u bef last* **6/1**[3]	—

4m 14.3s (-2.80) **Going Correction** -0.075s/f (Good)
WFA 5 from 6yo+ 3lb 13 Ran SP% 117.1
Speed ratings: **104,102,100,100,91 91,85,84,81,81 —,—,—** CSF £9.69 TOTE £6.50: £1.90, £1.10, £4.80; EX 15.50.
Owner Ian Hamilton **Bred** J Howard Johnson **Trained** Great Bavington, Northumbland

FOCUS
A race lacking strength and one in which the proximity of the third holds down the form. The pace was sound.

NOTEBOOK
Lucky Duck, a faller on his chase debut and first run for well over a year in January, showed himself none the worse for that experience and registered his second win at the track. He goes well on a sound surface and may be capable of better over fences.
Show Me The River looked to have a sound chance on the pick of his form over fences but proved a bit of a disappointment. He is well worth another try over two and a half miles but this run shows he is not one to lump on at shortish odds. *(op 4-5 tchd 5-6 and 10-11 in places)*
Political Cruise, an inconsistent performer who returned to winning ways last time, turned in his best effort over fences. His proximity casts a doubt over this form but he is likely to do better returned to further in ordinary handicaps. *(op 22-1)*

Uptown Lad(IRE), an inconsistent hurdler who has not won for over two years, fared much better than on his chase debut last month. However, he may well be flattered in this truly-run race and remains one to have reservations about. *(tchd 11-1)*
Hialeah, having his second start over fences, did not look the most straightforward and only hinted at ability in this modest race. He is flattered by his rating and is likely to remain vulnerable in this type of event.
Hollows Mist, off the course for over 500 days, shaped as though the run was needed on this chasing debut. He should be better for the outing and experience and may do better in due course. *(op 40-1)*
Lunar Dram, a lightly-raced sort who showed ability over hurdles, was in the process of running a career-best race when sadly falling fatally at the penultimate fence. *(op 13-2 tchd 15-2 in places)*
Air Of Affection shaped a bit better than the bare form of this chase debut suggests as she was still travelling strongly when clouting the fourth last and was not knocked about thereafter. She is worth another chance. *(op 13-2 tchd 15-2 in places)*

4841 NEWS & STAR NOVICES' CHASE (18 fncs) 3m 110y
2:30 (2:31) (Class 3) 5-Y-O+ **£6,506** (£1,910; £955; £477)

Form				RPR
U21P	**1**		**Pass Me By**[36] [4345] 7-11-2 120 .... (e) JohnFlavin[(10)] (R C Guest) *chsd ldrs: effrt and led 3 out: kpt on strly* **3/1**[2]	127+
21P4	**2**	*5*	**Russian Sky**[27] [4528] 7-10-11 .... TomGreenway[(5)] (Mrs H O Graham) *led: j.lft 1st: rdn and hdd 3 out: kpt on same pce next* **8/1**	109
0/4P	**3**	*dist*	**Chopneyev (FR)**[31] [4444] 8-11-2 122 .... TonyDobbin (R T Phillips) *prom: outpcd 12th: n.d after* **5/1**	73
4	**4**	*1 ¾*	**Drumintine (IRE)**[36] [4343] 5-10-0 .... NeilMulholland (Liam Lennon, Ire) *cl up: blnd 13th: hit and wknd 4 out* **33/1**	71
/PP0	**5**	*dist*	**Rainha**[47] [4141] 9-10-9 .... BrianHarding (A C Whillans) *sn bhd: no ch fr 1/2-way* **40/1**	—
36P	**P**		**Delaware Trail**[6] [4796] 7-11-2 .... KennyJohnson (R Johnson) *a wl bhd: t.o whn p.u bef 14th* **100/1**	—
	P		**Banbrook Hill (IRE)**[29] [4482] 7-10-13 .... (p) JMAllen[(3)] (C A McBratney, Ire) *sn towards rr: t.o 1/2-way: p.u bef last* **25/1**	—
213P	**P**		**Lord Olympia (IRE)**[28] [4498] 7-11-12 126 .... AlanO'Keeffe (Miss Venetia Williams) *prom: lost pl whn p.u after 4th* **4/1**[3]	—
-12F	**P**		**Julius Caesar**[70] [3740] 6-11-8 130 .... GLee (J Howard Johnson) *j.lft: hld up: hdwy 9th: rdn and wknd fr 14th: t.o whn p.u bef 2 out* **5/2**[1]	—

6m 36.4s
WFA 5 from 6yo+ 8lb **9** Ran SP% **111.6**
CSF £24.50 TOTE £3.60: £1.50, £2.30, £1.50; EX 48.70.
Owner Paul Beck **Bred** Miss Coreen McGregor **Trained** Brancepeth, Co Durham

FOCUS
A decent gallop but, with three of the market leaders running poorly, this did not take as much winning as seemed likely beforehand and is best rated through the winner.

NOTEBOOK
Pass Me By, who had a valid excuse (choked) when disappointing last time, did not have to be at his very best in a race where his market rivals disappointed for one reason or another. However, he stays well and showed the right attitude to land his third chase win at this course and he is the sort to win again over the larger obstacles. *(op 4-1)*
Russian Sky bettered the form of his chase debut with this greater emphasis on stamina. His jumping was sound in the main and, although this was not the most competitive of races, appeals as the type to win a small race over fences. *(tchd 9-1)*
Chopneyev(FR), having his third run over fences after a very lengthy break, was again soundly beaten and is not going to be easy to place from his current 122 mark. He remains one to tread carefully with at present. *(op 11-2 tchd 6-1)*
Drumintine(IRE), a maiden point winner, shaped with a little more promise than the distance beaten would imply as she was bang there when making her final error at the fourth last fence. Modest handicaps will be her forte when she gets her jumping together. *(op 25-1 tchd 40-1)*
Rainha offered no immediate promise on this chase debut. *(op 33-1 tchd 50-1)*
Julius Caesar again showed why he was one to be wary of at short odds over fences as his jumping was anything but fluent. A left-hand course may suit better but he is going to struggle from a mark of 130 unless his fencing improves markedly. *Official explanation: jockey said gelding had a breathing problem (op 3-1)*
Lord Olympia(IRE), a dual hurdle and chase winner, sadly lost his life after reportedly severing an artery. *(op 3-1)*

4842 FREDA ELLIOTT 90TH BIRTHDAY CELEBRATION H'CAP CHASE (12 fncs) 2m
3:00 (3:04) (Class 4) (0-105,105) 5-Y-O+ **£3,578** (£1,050; £525; £262)

Form				RPR
31U3	**1**		**Nifty Roy**[23] [4586] 6-10-9 **91** .... DougieCostello[(3)] (I McMath) *hld up: smooth hdwy bef 4 out: led between last two: sn clr* **8/1**	111+
0PF0	**2**	*13*	**Master Papa (IRE)**[23] [4594] 7-10-11 **90** .... DavidO'Meara (H P Hogarth) *hld up: hdwy 8th: effrt whn lft 3rd 3 out: chsd wnr run in: no imp* **16/1**	96+
4651	**3**	*hd*	**Little Flora**[12] [4721] 10-10-5 **89** .... MichaelMcAlister[(5)] (S J Marshall) *midfield: outpcd after 7th: kpt on fr 2 out: no imp run in* **13/2**	94
P	**4**	*7*	**Il Penseroso (IRE)**[60] [3909] 8-10-4 **83** .... (p) MarkGrant (P A Blockley) *led at decent gallop to between last two: sn no ex* **12/1**	85+
5U65	**5**	*2 ½*	**Get Smart (IRE)**[95] [3338] 9-10-0 **79** oh7 .... KeithMercer (Ferdy Murphy) *hld up: sme hdwy 2 out: nvr rchd ldrs* **7/1**	74
P514	**6**	*10*	**Hollows Mill**[28] [4489] 10-11-12 **105** .... TonyDobbin (F P Murtagh) *hld up in tch: outpcd after 7th: no ch after* **9/2**[1]	90
/51	**7**	*14*	**Lovely Native (IRE)**[23] [4587] 10-11-1 **101** .... MrNMcParlan[(7)] (L Lungo) *chsd ldrs: lost pl 7th: sn n.d* **15/2**	72
0336	**F**		**Tagar (FR)**[66] [3798] 9-10-6 **92** ow2 .... MrOGreenall[(7)] (C Grant) *cl up: 5l down and outpcd whn fell 3 out* **6/1**[3]	—
P624	**P**		**Posh Stick**[12] [4721] 9-11-11 **104** .... BrianHarding (J B Walton) *sn towards rr: t.o whn p.u bef 8th* **11/2**[2]	—
	P		**Hanko (GER)**[553] [1669] 10-11-12 **105** .... GLee (Jonjo O'Neill) *hld up: hdwy and prom 8th: wknd next: t.o whn p.u bef 2 out* **14/1**	—

4m 14.5s (-2.60) **Going Correction** -0.075s/f (Good) **10** Ran SP% **116.8**
Speed ratings: **103,96,96,92,91 86,79,—,—,—** CSF £119.64 CT £883.88 TOTE £10.80: £3.10, £5.30, £2.00; EX 324.30.
Owner Mrs A J McMath **Bred** Mrs Norma Peebles **Trained** Cumwhinton, Cumbria

FOCUS
An ordinary event and the decent gallop played to the strengths of those coming from off the pace. The race could be rated higher but does not compare well with the opening contest.

NOTEBOOK
Nifty Roy, who had been running creditably of late, had the race run to suit and turned in his best effort over fences. Things were in his favour here but he will find life much tougher after reassessment after this wide-margin win. *(tchd 9-1)*
Master Papa(IRE), who has not won for over two years and has yet to win over regulation fences, ran his best race for his capable trainer. He is on a fair mark at present and is one to keep an eye on granted a stiffer test of stamina. *(tchd 14-1)*
Little Flora, 7lb higher than her Kelso victory last time, turned in a laboured performance and may be flattered by the way the race unfolded. Consistency is not her strong suit and she remains one to tread carefully with. *(op 5-1)*
Il Penseroso(IRE) ◆, in the first-time cheekpieces, shaped better than the bare form in this strongly-run race on only this second start for the yard. He will be hard to peg back in similar company with similar tactics employed granted less of a test of stamina and is one to keep an eye on. *(tchd 14-1)*
Get Smart(IRE), an inconsistent chaser, fared better than at Sedgefield last time returned to this shorter trip. However, he may be flattered by his proximity given the way this race unfolded and remains one to tread carefully with. *(op 10-1)*
Hollows Mill, a triple course winner over fences, had been running creditably but, after getting the race run to suit, proved a disappointment back at his favourite course. Consistency has not always been his strongest suit. *Official explanation: jockey said gelding never travelled (op 4-1 tchd 5-1)*
Hanko(GER), easy to back, shaped as though this first run for over 500 days and first for this yard was very much needed. He travelled strongly for a long way and could be a different proposition next time. *(op 10-1)*
Tagar(FR) looked held but was nevertheless in the process of running creditably after chasing the strong pace when coming to grief. He is worth another chance away from progressive or well handicapped sorts. *(op 10-1)*
Posh Stick *Official explanation: jockey said mare never travelled (op 10-1)*

4843 THE SPORTSMAN'S H'CAP CHASE (18 fncs) 3m 110y
3:30 (3:31) (Class 3) (0-130,130) 5-Y-O+ **£13,012** (£3,820; £1,910; £954)

Form				RPR
1233	**1**		**Undeniable**[31] [4447] 8-11-4 **122** .... DavidO'Meara (Mrs S J Smith) *chsd ldrs: led 4 out: styd on strly* **7/2**[1]	134+
432	**2**	*6*	**Clemax (IRE)**[35] [4367] 5-10-0 **113** oh4 .... KeithMercer (Ferdy Murphy) *bhd tl hdwy fr 3 out: chsd wnr run in: no imp* **5/1**[2]	108
14UP	**3**	*nk*	**Supreme Breeze (IRE)**[49] [4111] 11-10-8 **115** .... PaddyAspell[(3)] (Mrs S J Smith) *led to 4 out: sn rdn: kpt on u.p fr last* **10/1**	120+
62	**4**	*1*	**Dungarvans Choice (IRE)**[59] [3921] 11-11-10 **128** .... MarcusFoley (N J Henderson) *hld up: smooth hdwy 12th: prom 14th: effrt 3 out: no ex run in* **7/2**[1]	131
4200	**5**	*9*	**Miss Mattie Ross**[28] [4505] 10-9-12 **107** .... MichaelMcAlister[(5)] (S J Marshall) *midfield: outpcd after 13th: no imp fr 4 out* **16/1**	102+
1143	**6**	*14*	**Silver Knight**[20] [4635] 8-11-8 **126** .... RussGarritty (T D Easterby) *prom: outpcd 14th: sn btn* **7/1**[3]	109+
PUP4	**7**	*9*	**Grattan Lodge (IRE)**[57] [3966] 9-11-12 **130** .... GLee (J Howard Johnson) *cl up tl wknd fr 13th* **12/1**	101
/1P4	**8**	*14*	**Move Over (IRE)**[6] [4790] 11-9-6 **106** ow1 .... JohnFlavin[(10)] (R C Guest) *hld up: hdwy and prom 14th: sn wknd* **10/1**	63
45PP	**P**		**Wise Man (IRE)**[12] [4724] 11-10-10 **114** .... TonyDobbin (N W Alexander) *in tch tl lost pl 7th: t.o whn p.u bef 10th* **20/1**	—
1-PF	**P**		**Imperial Dream (IRE)**[143] [2445] 8-10-10 **117** .... (b) DougieCostello[(3)] (H P Hogarth) *in tch: lost pl 9th: t.o whn p.u bef 13th* **33/1**	—
323P	**P**		**Pietro Vannucci (IRE)**[33] [4419] 10-10-4 **108** .... (p) BrianHarding (Jonjo O'Neill) *dropped rr 2nd: struggling 6th: p.u bef 10th* **33/1**	—

6m 32.3s
WFA 5 from 8yo+ 8lb **11** Ran SP% **116.0**
CSF £21.18 CT £156.48 TOTE £3.50: £1.20, £2.40, £3.30; EX 28.90.
Owner Keith Nicholson **Bred** Ahmed Al Shafar **Trained** High Eldwick, W Yorks

FOCUS
A fair handicap in which the pace seemed sound and this form should prove reliable rated around the third and fourth.

NOTEBOOK
Undeniable ◆, a tremendously tough and consistent sort, was another to provide a boost for the Kim Muir form. He is worth another chance over three and a quarter miles and, although things will be tougher in more competitive company after reassessment, he should continue to give a good account. *(op 5-2)*
Clemax(IRE) ran creditably from 4lb out of the handicap and left the impression that an even stiffer test of stamina would have suited. He looks sure to win a race or two for his current stable granted a suitable test. *(op 7-1)*
Supreme Breeze(IRE) got round for the first time since December and showed that he retains plenty of ability. A good test of stamina suits him ideally and he may be capable of winning again in ordinary company away from progressive sorts. *(tchd 11-1)*
Dungarvans Choice(IRE) was not disgraced in terms of form but, given the way he travelled for much of the way, ran as though he would not be inconvenienced by the return to distances around two and a half miles. *(tchd 11-4)*
Miss Mattie Ross fared better than on her two previous starts but had her limitations exposed in this company. She may do better when returned to Kelso and when able to dominate inferior rivals. *(op 12-1 tchd 20-1)*
Silver Knight was in good heart over this trip at the end of last year but was below that level for the third outing in succession. He had things in his favour here and remains one to watch rather than bet on for now. *(op 8-1)*

4844 CFM NOVICES' H'CAP CHASE (16 fncs) 2m 4f
4:05 (4:06) (Class 4) (0-100,99) 5-Y-O+ **£3,578** (£1,050; £525; £262)

Form				RPR
1P50	**1**		**Mikasa (IRE)**[28] [4487] 6-10-7 **80** .... KeithMercer (R F Fisher) *prom: outpcd 12th: rallied 3 out: led run in: hld on wl* **12/1**	83
5P3-	**2**	*nk*	**Coy Lad (IRE)**[28] 9-10-8 **81** .... (p) TonyDobbin (Miss P Robson) *nt fluent midfield: mstke 8th: outpcd 10th: rallied bef 2 out: chal run in: kpt on u.p: jst hld* **11/4**[1]	85+
F0PF	**3**	*3 ½*	**Assumetheposition (FR)**[6] [4804] 6-11-1 **88** .... LarryMcGrath (R C Guest) *j.lft: cl up: led 5th: hdd run in: no ex* **9/1**	89+
3003	**4**	*2*	**Ambition Royal (FR)**[37] [4318] 6-11-3 **93** .... PaddyAspell[(3)] (Miss Lucinda V Russell) *in tch: outpcd 10th: rallied 2 out: kpt on fr last* **16/1**	90
P505	**5**	*12*	**Trovaio (IRE)**[35] [4361] 9-9-9 **73** oh17 .... (p) DeclanMcGann[(5)] (Miss Lucinda V Russell) *nt fluent in rr: bhd tl sme late hdwy: n.d* **33/1**	58
5-0P	**6**	*3*	**Cash Bonanza (IRE)**[60] [3914] 6-11-12 **99** .... BrianHarding (N G Richards) *hld up: pushed along bef 12th: n.d* **20/1**	81
603	**7**	*1*	**Stand On Me**[82] [3532] 7-10-12 **85** .... GLee (P Monteith) *keen early: prom: effrt 4 out: wknd appr last* **6/1**[2]	66
400P	**8**	*22*	**Najca De Thaix (FR)**[56] [3990] 5-11-8 **99** .... RussGarritty (C N Allen) *chsd ldrs tl wknd bef 3 out* **8/1**	54
6P22	**9**	*21*	**The Masareti Kid (IRE)**[36] [4341] 9-10-4 **80** .... DougieCostello[(3)] (I McMath) *hld up: rdn 10th: n.d* **8/1**	18
22P4	**10**	*2*	**Not A Trace (IRE)**[59] [3928] 7-11-4 **91** .... (v) WilsonRenwick (Mrs S C Bradburne) *midfield: outpcd 9th: n.d after* **8/1**	27

4444 **11** *1 ½* **Barrons Pike**[38] 4300 7-10-11 **89**..........................(p) MichaelMcAlister(5) 24
(B Storey) *led to 5th: sn lost pl and bhd: no ch fr 1/2-way* **7/1**[3]

5m 29.1s (9.20) **Going Correction** -0.075s/f (Good)
WFA 5 from 6yo+ 4lb **11** Ran SP% **118.1**
Speed ratings: **78,77,76,75,70 69,69,60,52,51 50** CSF £46.98 CT £322.72 TOTE £18.20: £4.00, £1.90, £2.60; EX 58.30.

Owner Sporting Occasions 7 **Bred** Michael Fleming **Trained** Ulverston, Cumbria

■ Stewards' Enquiry : Tony Dobbin caution: used whip with excessive frequency

FOCUS
A very ordinary handicap rated around the winner and backed up by the placed horses.

NOTEBOOK
Mikasa(IRE), returned to fences, showed his first form since winning at Newcastle in February but had the race teed up for him to a certain extent and, given his record, would not be one to get stuck into at shortish odds next time.

Coy Lad(IRE) ◆, a winning pointer on his previous start, turned in his best effort over regulation fences tried in cheekpieces and appeals as the type to win races in this sphere for his capable handler when he brushes up his jumping. *(op 4-1)*

Assumetheposition(FR) had failed to complete in three of his four starts over obstacles this year and was well beaten on the other, but returned to form and fared the best of those up with the strong pace. A left-handed course may suit better and, although his win record is poor, he looks capable of winning a similar race over fences if this can be reproduced. *(op 8-1)*

Ambition Royal(FR) has only a debut bumper win in 2003 to his name but showed ability upped in trip on only this second start over fences. He is not the most consistent but should be suited by the step up to three miles in this sphere. *(op 14-1)*

Trovaio(IRE) seemed to show much improved form from 17lb out of the handicap but he is almost certainly flattered given the way things unfolded in this strongly-run race and will have to show more before he is worth a bet.

Cash Bonanza(IRE), who has become disappointing for his current yard over hurdles, was again well beaten on this chasing debut and, although in good hands, will have to show more before he is worth a bet. *(op 16-1)*

Stand On Me, a winning pointer, shaped as though a bit better than the bare form of this chase debut as he was up with the decent gallop for much of the way. He is in good hands and is one to keep an eye on. *(op 8-1 tchd 11-2)*

Not A Trace(IRE) *Official explanation: jockey said gelding hung right-handed throughout*

Barrons Pike *Official explanation: jockey said gelding hung left-handed throughout (op 8-1)*

4845 ROBERT ELLIOTT MEMORIAL H'CAP CHASE (20 fncs) 3m 2f

4:40 (4:40) (Class 5) (0-95,94) 5-Y-O+ **£3,578** (£1,050; £525; £262)

Form RPR

4P31 **1** **Recent Edition (IRE)**[37] 4316 8-10-13 **84**....................(b) PaddyAspell(3) 107+
(J Wade) *mde all: rdn 3 out: hld on gamely run in* **5/1**[2]

3PPP **2** *½* **Behavingbadly (IRE)**[47] 4144 11-10-4 **79**........................ MrSWByrne(7) 99
(A Parker) *hld up midfield: smooth hdwy and prom 13th: ev ch 3 out: hung rt after next: kpt on fr last: jst hld* **25/1**

F1 **3** *24* **Shrove Tuesday (IRE)**[37] 4321 7-10-11 **79**........................ TonyDobbin 87+
(A J Martin, Ire) *hld up: hdwy and prom 13th: rdn and wknd fr 3 out* **5/2**[1]

2612 **4** *16* **Matmata De Tendron (FR)**[37] 4316 6-11-2 **87**.......... DougieCostello(3) 67
(A Crook) *midfield: drvn and outpcd after 12th: plodded on fnl 4* **7/1**[3]

4534 **5** *2* **Wild About Harry**[12] 4719 9-10-1 **69** oh2 ow1.................. LarryMcGrath 47
(A R Dicken) *chsd ldrs tl wknd fr 4 out* **20/1**

3420 **6** *dist* **Celtic Flow**[59] 3930 8-10-0 **73**... BrianHughes(5) —
(C R Wilson) *in tch to 1/2-way: sn wknd: t.o* **20/1**

P023 **7** *28* **Red Alert Man (IRE)**[36] 4353 10-10-0 **73** oh7 ow5.....(b) DerekLaverty(5) —
(Mrs L Williamson) *in tch to 11th: sn lost pl and struggling* **16/1**

60FP **P** **Jack Lynch**[38] 4300 10-10-12 **80**.. KeithMercer —
(Ferdy Murphy) *a bhd: p.u 5 out* **33/1**

312P **P** **Lazy But Lively (IRE)**[6] 4790 10-11-12 **94**.................................... GLee —
(R F Fisher) *hld up: struggling 12th: p.u 14th* **9/1**

54-2 **P** **Best China (IRE)**[35] 4361 6-11-5 **87**............................... DavidO'Meara —
(Liam Lennon, Ire) *a bhd: t.o whn p.u bef 14th* **11/1**

PU04 **P** **Ta Ta For Now**[35] 4361 9-10-12 **80**.................................. AlanO'Keeffe —
(Mrs S C Bradburne) *a bhd: t.o whn p.u bef 14th* **25/1**

55PP **P** **Hugo De Grez (FR)**[47] 4144 11-11-7 **89**........................ WilsonRenwick —
(A Parker) *midfield: struggling 12th: p.u bef 4 out* **25/1**

F3PP **P** **Gimme Shelter (IRE)**[37] 4316 12-10-4 **77**.............. MichaelMcAlister(5) —
(S J Marshall) *midfield: outpcd whn blnd 12th: sn p.u* **25/1**

3U05 **P** **Harry Hooly**[27] 4517 11-11-0 **87**.............................. TomGreenway(5) —
(Mrs H O Graham) *a bhd: no ch fr 1/2-way: t.o whn p.u bef 2 out* **33/1**

P1-P **P** **Peterhouse**[18] 4659 7-10-0 **68**... BrianHarding —
(Mrs E Slack) *bhd: hdwy 14th: wknd after next: t.o whn p.u bef 2 out* **25/1**

P **Me Tows (IRE)**[27] 4543 10-10-11 **79**................................ NeilMulholland —
(Thomas Carberry, Ire) *chsd ldrs to 12th: sn wknd: t.o whn p.u bef 4 out* **16/1**

7m 4.20s (-4.00) **Going Correction** -0.075s/f (Good) **16** Ran SP% **122.5**
Speed ratings: **103,102,95,90,89** —,—,—,—,— —,—,—,—,— — CSF £126.54 CT £388.70 TOTE £6.90: £1.40, £6.50, £1.50, £2.20; EX 246.10.

Owner John Wade **Bred** J J O'Neill **Trained** Mordon, Co Durham

■ Stewards' Enquiry : Paddy Aspell two-day ban: used whip with excessive frequency (Apr 26-27)

FOCUS
No progressive sorts on show but a good gallop and a gutsy display from Recent Edition. The winner looks capable of scoring again and the runner-up sets the standard.

NOTEBOOK
Recent Edition(IRE) notched his second successive course and distance win and in doing so, showed the right attitude to beat a rival who did not look to have the same level of determination. A good test suits ideally and he should continue to go well. *(op 7-1)*

Behavingbadly(IRE) had been badly out of sorts but jumped better and showed much more this time. He is undoubtedly on a fair mark but, although not beaten far, looked anything but straightforward under pressure and his record suggests he would be no certainty to reproduce this next time. *(op 33-1)*

Shrove Tuesday(IRE), who turned in an improved effort when successful at Towcester last time, was below that level from this 8lb higher mark in these less testing conditions. Consistency has not proved her strongest suit so far. *(tchd 11-4)*

Matmata De Tendron(FR) had been in decent heart but was much further behind the winner this time than over the same course and distance on his previous start. He is suited by a thorough test of stamina. *(op 8-1)*

Wild About Harry, an inconsistent maiden (after 23 starts) ran well for a long way from just out of the handicap and with overweight but his record means he will remain one to tread carefully with.

Celtic Flow is an inconsistent sort who was again soundly beaten and she is rarely one to place much faith in.

Jack Lynch *Official explanation: jockey said gelding had a breathing problem (op 25-1)*

4846 ARCHIE RICHARDS 65TH BIRTHDAY CELEBRATION OPEN HUNTERS' CHASE (18 fncs) 3m 110y

5:15 (5:15) (Class 6) 6-Y-O+ **£1,977** (£608; £304)

Form RPR

P56- **1** **Mr Woodentop (IRE)**[435] 3679 10-11-12 .... MissPRobson 124+
(Dave Parker) *keen: prom: led 13th: drew clr fr 3 out* **9/4**[1]

5-31 **2** *28* **Jacksonville (FR)**[12] 4725 9-11-12 85..............(p) MissVickySimpson(7) 101+
(Miss Vicky Simpson) *chsd ldrs: outpcd 14th: rallied to chse wnr 2 out: kpt on: no imp* **11/4**[2]

U5U5 **3** *22* **Raiseapearl**[14] 11-11-9 .... MrDAFitzsimmons(7) 73
(Patrick Thompson) *led to 13th: wknd bef 2 out* **14/1**

-3P4 **4** *6* **Kilcaskin Gold (IRE)**[27] 11-11-5 .... MrGRSmith(7) 63
(R A Ross) *in tch: lost pl 8th: n.d after* **14/1**

20-P **5** *27* **The Lyme Volunteer (IRE)**[36] 4351 9-11-2 108..........(b) MrOGreenall(7) 33
(David M Easterby) *hld up: effrt 13th: wknd next* **11/2**[3]

P **Daffi (IRE)**[28] 6-10-12 .... MrMGarnett(7) —
(F Jestin) *sn bhd: t.o whn p.u after 9th* **25/1**

1-55 **P** **Natural (IRE)**[7] 9-11-9 77...(t) MrSWByrne(7) —
(Mrs J Williamson) *in tch tl wknd 1/2-way: t.o whn p.u bef 13th* **15/2**

-P62 **P** **Camp Hill**[36] 4347 12-11-5 77.. MrMEllwood(7) —
(J S Haldane) *in tch: struggling 10th: t.o whn p.u bef 2 out* **8/1**

/PP- **P** **Minster Blue**[21] 8-10-12 ....(p) MrCJCallow(7) —
(Mrs Susan Murtagh) *prom tl wknd after 13th: t.o whn p.u bef 2 out* **100/1**

6m 41.5s **9** Ran SP% **113.9**
CSF £8.89 TOTE £4.20: £1.40, £1.60, £3.10; EX 9.70 Place 6 £80.34, Place 5 £61.46.

Owner Hale Racing Limited **Bred** Mrs M Doran **Trained** Capheaton, Northumb

FOCUS
An uncompetitive event but a wide-margin winner in Mr Woodentop, who looks a useful recruit to this sphere. The runner-up sets the standard.

NOTEBOOK
Mr Woodentop(IRE) ◆, highly tried over fences after his course and distance win in 2003, did not settle but ran out an easy winner on his first start for over a year, his first for new connections and his first in this sphere. Although this was not much of a race, he appeals as the type to win more races at this level. *(op 11-4 tchd 3-1)*

Jacksonville(FR) had his limitations exposed but is a consistent sort who has been in good form and looks a good guide to the value of this form. Although vulnerable against the better sorts in this grade, he should continue to give a good account. *(op 5-2 tchd 3-1)*

Raiseapearl, a modest and inconsistent performer, ran creditably for a long way but is likely to remain vulnerable in this type of event. *(op 12-1)*

Kilcaskin Gold(IRE) seems devoid of pace and was again soundly beaten.

The Lyme Volunteer(IRE) was soundly beaten with the blinkers on for the first time over fences and remains one to tread carefully with on this evidence. *(tchd 6-1)*

Minster Blue *(op 66-1)*

T/Plt: £36.60 to a £1 stake. Pool: £47,842.45. 951.85 winning tickets. T/Qpdt: £7.80 to a £1 stake. Pool: £2,862.30. 271.10 winning tickets. RY

4067 HAYDOCK (L-H)

Saturday, April 15

OFFICIAL GOING: Good to soft (soft in places)
Wind: Virtually nil

4847 TABLEY NOVICES' CHASE (17 fncs) 2m 6f

1:50 (1:53) (Class 3) 5-Y-O+ **£6,506** (£1,910; £955; £477)

Form RPR

2150 **1** **Darina's Boy**[139] 2529 10-11-0 107................................ DominicElsworth 126+
(Mrs S J Smith) *a.p: hdwy to ld appr 2 out: rdn clr last: styd on wl flat* **11/1**

3414 **2** *5* **Bannister Lane**[36] 4355 6-11-0 106....................................... JasonMaguire 118+
(D McCain) *chsd ldrs: rdn along and outpcd 3 out: rallied after next: chsd wnr whn j.lft and hit last: drvn and kpt on flat* **14/1**

5551 **3** *1 ½* **Another Native (IRE)**[28] 4502 8-11-0 115.............................. NoelFehily 116
(C J Mann) *hld up and bhd: stdy hdwy 6 out: rdn along and in tch 3 out: kpt on u.p fr next* **5/1**[3]

31F1 **4** *3* **Nice Try (IRE)**[36] 4355 7-11-0 119.................................... SamThomas 115+
(Miss Venetia Williams) *hld up in tch: mstke 9th: hdwy to trck ldrs 4 out: rdn along after next: drvn and wknd appr last* **11/4**[2]

5212 **5** *4* **Launde (IRE)**[35] 4371 7-11-0 120............................... AndrewThornton 110+
(B N Pollock) *led: pushed along and mstke 4 out: rdn next: hdd appr 2 out and sn btn* **9/4**[1]

6521 **6** *4* **Squires Lane (IRE)**[52] 4054 7-10-11 119...................... GinoCarenza(3) 105
(Andrew Turnell) *chsd ldrs: rdn along 4 out: one pce fr next* **8/1**

135/ **7** *2 ½* **Americanconnection (IRE)**[383] 10-10-7 101................ MrGTumelty(7) 106+
(D McCain) *mstkes: blnd 4th and 10th: a rr* **66/1**

P512 **8** *14* **Beauchamp Prince (IRE)**[22] 4605 5-10-10 119...................... RJGreene 90+
(M Scudamore) *blnd 1st and nt jump wl after: chsd ldrs: mstke 6th and next rdn along whn blnd 10th: sn lost pl and bhd* **9/1**

36PU **9** *1 ¾* **Abzuson**[27] 4518 9-10-11 92..(p) LeeVickers(3) 86
(J R Norton) *a rr* **66/1**

5m 32.5s (-16.30) **Going Correction** -0.55s/f (Firm)
WFA 5 from 6yo+ 4lb **9** Ran SP% **113.2**
Speed ratings: **107,105,104,103,102 100,99,94,94** CSF £139.72 TOTE £10.90: £2.80, £2.90, £1.60; EX 144.90.

Owner Mrs C Steel **Bred** D O Walsh **Trained** High Eldwick, W Yorks

FOCUS
A modest novice event with the winner value for further and the race could rate higher.

NOTEBOOK
Darina's Boy, a winner over this distance at Market Rasen back in October, had not been seen since running moderately in November, but he was clearly straight for this reappearance and, having gone on before the second last, he gradually edged away. Although ten he is not totally exposed, but it remains to be seen whether he goes on from this. *(op 14-1)*

Bannister Lane comes from a stable who have had a cracking season and the six-year-old, who was slightly disappointing at Sandown last month, bounced back with a gallant effort. He is a tough sort and remains open to further progress.

Another Native(IRE), bidding for a fourth win of the campaign, travelled well, but he was unable to go with the winner and had to settle for a place. There is no reason why he cannot progress further next term and he could be the right type for the 2007 Topham Chase at the Grand National meeting. *(op 9-2)*

Nice Try(IRE), who had won both completed outings over fences prior to this, failed to see out his race having been held up by Thomas, the extra distance proving beyond him. This is his first season racing and the seven-year-old can do better back at shorter next season. *(tchd 3-1)*

Launde(IRE) has been in decent form but, having attempted to make all, he was another whom the distance seemed to find out. *(tchd 5-2)*

The Form Book, Raceform Ltd, Compton, RG20 6NL

4848 CHEADLE HULME H'CAP HURDLE (8 hdls) 2m

2:25 (2:26) (Class 3) (0-135,135) 4-Y-0+ **£9,759** (£2,865; £1,432; £715)

Form RPR

2061 **1** **Glimmer Of Light (IRE)**[10] 4733 6-9-7 **109** oh4 PhilKinsella(7) 118+
(S A Brookshaw) *hld up: hdwy 2 out: led and mstke last: rdn out* **12/1**

-110 **2** 2 **Swift Swallow**[139] 2519 8-10-11 **127** MrGTumelty(7) 131
(O Brennan) *hld up: hdwy 5th: led and mstke 2 out: hdd last: styd on same pce* **33/1**

-400 **3** nk **Papini (IRE)**[43] 4215 5-10-12 **121** MickFitzgerald 125
(N J Henderson) *a.p: led after 3 out: hdd next: sn rdn: styd on same pce last* **7/1**[2]

5121 **4** 1 ½ **Rojabaa**[33] 4420 7-9-10 **110** RobertLucey-Butler(5) 112
(B D Leavy) *hld up: hdwy 5th: rdn 2 out: no ex last* **8/1**[3]

2065 **5** 1 ¼ **Silver Prophet (IRE)**[22] 4608 7-10-2 **111** SeanCurran 112
(M R Bosley) *chsd ldrs: rdn 5th: ev ch appr 2 out: no ex last* **16/1**

2FF4 **6** ¾ **Shares (IRE)**[12] 4723 6-10-0 **109** oh4 TimmyMurphy 109
(P Monteith) *hld up: hdwy 2 out: rdn and hung rt appr last: no imp* **8/1**[3]

05F4 **7** 5 **Brave Vision**[63] 3853 10-10-1 **110** oh1 ow1 PadgeWhelan 106+
(A C Whillans) *hld up: hdwy 2 out: sn rdn: wkng whn mstke last* **33/1**

0300 **8** ¾ **Fait Le Jojo (FR)**[31] 4446 9-11-7 **135** HowieEphgrave(5) 130+
(L Corcoran) *led: hdd after 2nd: chsd ldrs: rdn after 3 out: wknd appr last* **12/1**

/00- **9** 4 **Travelling Band (IRE)**[5] 4204 8-9-8 **110** PatrickMcDonald(7) 101+
(J Mackie) *hld up: hdwy after 3 out: wkng whn mstke last* **16/1**

6455 **10** ¾ **Argento**[67] 3788 9-10-1 **110** BarryKeniry 101+
(G M Moore) *plld hrd: w ldrs: led 3rd: mstke 3 out: sn hdd & wknd* **33/1**

5435 **11** 1 **Culcabock (IRE)**[6] 4792 6-10-3 **112** JimCrowley 101
(Miss Lucinda V Russell) *mid-div: rdn and wknd 3 out* **18/1**

110 **12** 7 **Bogus Dreams (IRE)**[80] 3561 9-10-1 **113** ow1 GaryBerridge(3) 95
(L Lungo) *hld up: rdn and wknd appr 3 out* **13/2**[1]

3P15 **13** 2 **Torkinking (IRE)**[28] 4490 7-10-12 **128** (t) BenOrde-Powlett(7) 108
(M A Barnes) *w ldr: led after 2nd: hdd next: rdn and wknd appr 3 out* **7/1**[2]

6-P3 **14** 1 **Debbie**[19] 633 7-11-0 **123** LeightonAspell 102
(B D Leavy) *hld up: bhd fr 3rd* **12/1**

1204 **15** nk **Nick's Choice**[7] 4781 10-9-9 **109** MrTJO'Brien(5) 87
(D Burchell) *prom to 5th* **16/1**

63F0 **16** 4 **Through The Rye**[28] 4490 10-11-5 **128** JohnMcNamara 102
(E W Tuer) *hld up: bhd fr 3rd* **25/1**

24P5 **17** 4 **Fiori**[91] 3398 10-10-1 **120** GaryBartley(10) 90
(P C Haslam) *mid-div: rdn 4th: sn lost pl* **33/1**

PPPP **18** dist **Konker**[52] 4053 11-10-5 **114** RichardHobson —
(J R Cornwall) *bhd fr 3rd* **100/1**

3m 46.8s (-12.30) **Going Correction** -0.55s/f (Firm) **18** Ran SP% **123.1**

Speed ratings: **108,107,106,106,105 105,102,102,100,99 99,95,94,94,94 92,90,**— CSF £374.68 CT £2983.67 TOTE £17.80: £3.30, £6.30, £2.00, £2.40; EX 614.90 TRIFECTA Not won..

Owner T G K Construction Ltd **Bred** The Earl Of Harrington **Trained** Wollerton, Shropshire

FOCUS

A competitive-looking handicap won in good style by last week's selling hurdle winner Glimmer Of Light. The form looks solid rated through those in the frame behind the winner.

NOTEBOOK

Glimmer Of Light(IRE), who appreciated the better ground and drop in grade when winning cosily at Hereford last week, had a bit to prove on this softer surface on his first start for new connections, but he travelled strongly throughout and made light of the better class of opposition to win a shade comfortably. Likely to be kept on the go through the summer, he remains open to further improvement and previous connections may be regretting running him in the Hereford seller. *(op 11-1)*

Swift Swallow, having only his second start in 11 months, stepped up markedly on his Doncaster effort in November and battled on well for second. This time of year seems to suit the gelding and, although hardly well handicapped, he showed here he is up to winning off this sort of mark.

Papini(IRE) appeared to hold his best chance of the season so far on this return to two miles, but he was unable to quicken sufficiently under pressure and proved no match for the winner. Still only five, it may well be he is best over further, and he is in the right hands to make a chaser in time.

Rojabaa made some late headway and momentarily looked in with a chance, but the effort took its toll and he was not good enough off his 6lb higher mark. *(op 17-2)*

Silver Prophet(IRE) ran well for a long way, but is without a win over hurdles in two years and he probably needs his sights lowering.

Shares(IRE), a winner over fences earlier in the season, did not make life easy for Murphy, hanging away to his right as they came into the last, but he has had a couple of confidence boosters over hurdles now and may be ready for a return to fences. *(op 7-1)*

Bogus Dreams(IRE), on a roll this time last year, never got involved on his reappearance in January, but much better was expected here of the nine-year-old. However, having been held up, he made a little progress before weakening and may still have needed the run. *(op 8-1)*

4849 RED SQUARE VODKA "FIXED BRUSH" NOVICES' HURDLE FINAL BONUS RACE (H'CAP) (10 hdls) 2m 4f

2:55 (2:55) (Class 2) 4-8-Y-0 **£13,012** (£3,820; £1,910; £954)

Form RPR

2112 **1** **Cloudy Lane**[21] 4612 6-11-6 **124** JasonMaguire 133+
(D McCain) *trckd ldrs: hit 4th: hdwy to ld after 3 out: rdn along 2 out: styd on wl* **8/1**

1220 **2** 6 **Oscar Park (IRE)**[29] 4469 7-11-12 **130** TomDoyle 131
(C Tinkler) *trckd ldrs: hdwy and cl up 4 out: ev ch next: rdn 2 out: kpt on same pce appr last* **10/1**

2131 **3** ¾ **Brankley Boy**[28] 4494 8-11-6 **124** MickFitzgerald 124
(N J Henderson) *trckd ldrs: hdwy gng wl 4 out: cl up next: sn rdn: drvn after 2 out and kpt on same pce* **3/1**[1]

0234 **4** 3 **Lysander (GER)**[4] 4819 7-9-11 **106** CharliePoste(5) 103
(M F Harris) *hld up towards rr: stdy hdwy 1/2-way: in tch 4 out: rdn along and outpcd bef next: drvn and kpt on fr 2 out* **25/1**

2323 **5** 1 **Miko De Beauchene (FR)**[16] 4678 6-11-3 **121** AndrewThornton 117
(R H Alner) *hld up towards rr: stdy hdwy on inner 1/2-way: in tch: 4 out: rdn along bef next and kpt on same pce* **16/1**

2B1 **6** 16 **Mars Rock (FR)**[7] 4786 6-10-6 **110** SamThomas 90
(Miss Venetia Williams) *led to 2nd: cl up tl rdn along appr 3 out and grad wknd* **12/1**

1221 **7** hd **Livingonaknifedge (IRE)**[55] 4015 7-11-0 **121** PaulO'Neill(3) 101
(Ian Williams) *hld up towards rr: stdy hdwy on inner 1/2-way: in tch 4 out: chsd ldrs bef next: sn rdn and btn 2 out* **10/1**

3231 **8** 3 **Tous Chez (IRE)**[28] 4493 7-10-13 **117** DominicElsworth 96+
(Mrs S J Smith) *in tch on outer: hdwy to chse ldrs 4 out: rdn along next and wknd appr 2 out* **6/1**[2]

1P0P **9** 5 **Dan's Heir**[6] 4792 4-10-5 **121** PaddyMerrigan(5) 86
(P C Haslam) *hit 3rd: a towards rr* **50/1**

0231 **10** 1 ½ **Boulders Beach (IRE)**[12] 4720 6-10-10 **114** PadgeWhelan 85
(Mrs S J Smith) *prom: hdwy to ld 6th: rdn along and hdd after 4 out: wknd bef next* **20/1**

0233 **11** 3 **Brave Rebellion**[38] 4303 7-11-1 **119** RichardMcGrath 87
(K G Reveley) *hld up: a rr* **50/1**

3425 **12** ½ **Woodview (IRE)**[24] 4576 7-10-0 **104** oh1 (b[1]) TimmyMurphy 71
(K C Bailey) *midfield: rdn along 4 out: sn wknd* **20/1**

3P0 **13** 18 **Offemont (FR)**[22] 4603 5-10-1 **105** MarkBradburne 54
(Mrs L C Taylor) *a rr* **20/1**

1000 **14** 2 ½ **Smart Boy Prince (IRE)**[5] 3729 5-10-7 **114** TJPhelan(3) 61
(C Smith) *cl up: led 2nd: rdn along and hdd 6th: wknd fr 4 out* **50/1**

4P **15** 14 **Ouste (FR)**[32] 4435 4-10-11 **122** APMcCoy 58+
(F Doumen, France) *hld up: hdwy whn blnd bdly 6th: no ch after* **7/1**[3]

6102 **P** **Kings Rock**[10] 4726 5-10-2 **113** MissFayeBramley(7) —
(P A Blockley) *chsd ldrs to 1/2-way: bhd whn p.u bef 2 out* **33/1**

4m 52.0s (-17.20) **Going Correction** -0.55s/f (Firm)

WFA 4 from 5yo+ 6lb **16** Ran SP% **121.6**

Speed ratings: **112,109,109,108,107 101,101,100,98,97 96,96,88,87,82** — CSF £76.43 CT £296.73 TOTE £8.10: £1.90, £2.80, £1.10, £4.90; EX 78.20 Trifecta £699.20 Pool £27,771.04. - 28.20 winning units..

Owner Trevor Hemmings **Bred** Gleadhill House Stud Ltd **Trained** Cholmondeley, Cheshire

FOCUS

A competitive renewal of the final of the 'fixed brush' hurdles series, as one would have expected, and the highly-progressive Cloudy Lane ran out a worthy winner. The form looks decent rated around the placed horses.

NOTEBOOK

Cloudy Lane has not looked back since taking a heavy fall on his hurdling debut at Hexham in November, and although beaten in a three-mile handicap at Bangor on his most recent outing, his two previous victories over course and distance pointed to a good run here and he battled on in typically game fashion to win going away. Only a six-year-old, his stable has had a magnificent season and he has the potential to make up into a useful chaser in time.

Oscar Park(IRE), runner-up in a Grade Two event at Warwick before finishing down the field behind Black Jack Ketchum in the Brit Insurance at the Festival, this represented a less-arduous task, but he still had to shoulder top weight and he did so admirably, holding every chance in the straight but proving unable to concede 6lb the hardy winner. He has had a good season on the whole and should make a fine chaser.

Brankley Boy, an easy winner in heavy ground at Uttoxeter last month, travelled strongly into contention on this handicap debut, but he was unable to race on with the winner and, although keeping on well enough, did not find quite as much as had once looked likely. *(tchd 10-3 in places)*

Lysander(GER), without a win in seven previous attempts over hurdles, ran an absolute blinder, making good headway to chase the leaders early in the straight before keeping on well for pressure. He should have little trouble finding a race on this evidence, once having his sights lowered.

Miko De Beauchene(FR) has run many good races in defeat this season, but this future chaser was given too much to do and he never threatened to play a hand in the finish. He has plenty of size and scope and is one to look forward to seeing over the larger obstacles next term.

Mars Rock(FR), a winner at Chepstow latest, ran well to a point, but he was not up to the task in the end and needs his sights lowering. *(op 14-1)*

Livingonaknifedge(IRE) made some good headway before dropping away and this distance may have again proved beyond him. *(tchd 11-1)*

Tous Chez(IRE) was a touch disappointing considering his trainer's horses are going so well, but his future very much lies over fences. *(op 13-2)*

Ouste(FR), a disappointment in the Fred Winter at the Festival, again failed to live up to expectations, losing all chance with a bad mistake at halfway. He may yet be capable of better. *(op 13-2)*

4850 CASINO 36 STOCKPORT PAUL SUMMERS CLASSIC H'CAP CHASE (12 fncs) 2m

3:25 (3:26) (Class 3) (0-130,127) 5-Y-0+ **£7,156** (£2,101; £1,050; £524)

Form RPR

1111 **1** **Polar Gunner**[28] 4503 9-10-9 **115** TJDreaper(5) 133+
(J M Jefferson) *chsd ldrs: led 3 out: clr last: easily* **7/2**[1]

-016 **2** 8 **Executive Decision (IRE)**[35] 4378 12-11-2 **117** (v) LeightonAspell 120
(Mrs L Wadham) *hld up: rdn 8th: hdwy appr 3 out: chsd wnr next: wknd last* **12/1**

F21P **3** 1 ¾ **Brave Thought (IRE)**[35] 4363 11-11-1 **116** TimmyMurphy 117
(P Monteith) *prom: rdn after 2 out: wknd last* **10/1**

-1UP **4** 8 **Moor Spirit**[33] 4419 9-11-0 **115** AnthonyRoss 109+
(P Beaumont) *hld up: hdwy and hit 3 out: wknd appr last* **10/1**

P4PU **5** 6 **Dangerousdanmagru (IRE)**[8] 4762 10-11-10 **125** AndrewThornton 112
(A E Jones) *hld up: bhd 6th: hit 9th: nvr nrr* **14/1**

323F **6** 1 **Flight Command**[8] 4762 8-11-3 **118** (p) TomSiddall 104
(P Beaumont) *hld up: hdwy 6th: rdn and wknd 2 out* **12/1**

3P33 **7** 4 **Turgeonev (FR)**[21] 4618 11-11-8 **123** RichardMcGrath 105
(T D Easterby) *chsd ldrs to 3 out* **7/1**[3]

3P41 **8** 6 **Jericho III (FR)**[35] 4378 9-11-5 **123** (b) PaulO'Neill(3) 111+
(Miss Venetia Williams) *led: hdd 3 out: sn wknd and eased* **9/2**[2]

10PP **9** 18 **Vigoureux (FR)**[29] 4478 7-10-0 **101** oh2 (p) BarryKeniry 59
(S Gollings) *chsd ldrs: rdn after 9th: wknd bef next* **40/1**

3130 **P** **Tanikos (FR)**[29] 4472 7-11-12 **127** MickFitzgerald —
(N J Henderson) *hld up: hdwy 6th: rdn and hit 9th: sn wknd: t.o whn p.u bef 2 out* **9/2**[2]

3m 59.7s (-7.30) **Going Correction** -0.30s/f (Good) **10** Ran SP% **113.8**

Speed ratings: **106,102,101,97,94 93,91,88,79,**— CSF £42.94 CT £381.09 TOTE £3.70: £1.80, £3.40, £3.30; EX 68.50.

Owner Mrs M E Dixon **Bred** Mrs P Nicholson **Trained** Norton, N Yorks

FOCUS

A one-horse show with Polar Gunner destroying his rivals to record a five-timer. The runner-up sets the standard and the form makes sense.

NOTEBOOK

Polar Gunner, on a five-timer following three wins since the turn of the year over hurdles, started his run over fences at Wetherby in November and, off just a 3lb higher mark, he destroyed the opposition with another powerful display of galloping. At his best over two miles, he is now likely to head to Perth next week and will take some stopping there under a penalty, providing the ground does not firm up too much. *(op 3-1 tchd 4-1 in places)*

Executive Decision(IRE) ran best he could in second, but was never in with a chance of getting to the winner.

Brave Thought(IRE) bounced back from a poor effort at Ayr last time where he failed to jump fluently, but he was readily left trailing.

Moor Spirit could be the one to take from the race away from the winner as he began make headway before a mistake three-out and seemed to benefit from the drop back in trip. *(op 14-1)*

Dangerousdanmagru(IRE) never got into it and is probably in need of some assistance from the Handicapper.

Jericho III(FR) has never been consistent and he bombed badly off an 11lb higher mark than when winning at Sandown last month. *Official explanation: trainer said gelding had a breathing problem (op 6-1)*

Tanikos(FR), down the field in the Grand Annual latest, was unable to repeat his course effort from February and ran too badly to be true off top weight. *(op 4-1 tchd 5-1)*

4851 BET365 H'CAP CHASE (22 fncs) 3m 4f 110y

3:55 (3:55) (Class 4) (0-105,107) 5-Y-0+ **£4,879** (£1,432; £716; £357)

Form / RPR

1413 **1** **Another Club Royal**[38] 4300 7-11-4 **97**........................(bt) JasonMaguire 113+
(D McCain) *a.p: effrt 4 out: rdn 2 out: styd on to ld last: drvn clr flat* **10/1**

000P **2** *6* **Valleymore (IRE)**[72] 3688 10-10-8 **87**....................(p) LeightonAspell 98+
(S A Brookshaw) *hld up: hdwy to trck ldrs 10th: led 16th: rdn along 3 out:drvn and hdd last: kpt on same pce flat* **20/1**

1604 **3** *4* **Midnight Gunner**[24] 4576 12-11-6 **99**........................ APMcCoy 106+
(A E Price) *hld up: hdwy to trck ldrs 6th: rdn to chse ldng pair 3 out: swtchd lft and chal 2 out: sn drvn and one pce last* **6/1**[2]

0504 **4** *16* **Dante's Back (IRE)**[35] 4370 8-10-12 **91**.......................(t) AntonyEvans 81
(N A Twiston-Davies) *hld up in rr: hdwy 13th: rdn along to chse ldrs 4 out: drvn and no imp fr next* **9/1**

24P2 **5** *1* **Sir Cumference**[62] 3886 10-11-4 **97**..........................(b) SamThomas 86
(Miss Venetia Williams) *cl up: led 11th: pushed along and hdd 16th: sn rdn and grad wknd: j. bdly lft 3 out* **6/1**[2]

PP21 **6** *28* **Profowens (IRE)**[12] 4719 8-11-9 **107**..........................(b) TJDreaper[(5)] 78+
(P Beaumont) *in tch: pushed along 8th: sn lost pl and bhd fr 1/2-way* **11/2**[1]

612P **F** **Dickie Lewis**[37] 4316 8-9-7 **79** oh1........................ MrGTumelty[(7)] —
(D McCain) *in tch: cl up fr 5th tl pushed along and fell 17th* **10/1**

6032 **F** **Elegant Eskimo**[25] 4558 7-11-4 **97**.............................. JoeTizzard —
(S E H Sherwood) *led: hit 6th: hdd 11th: rdn along and wkng whn fell 15th* **9/1**

1PPP **P** **Briar's Mist (IRE)**[20] 4636 9-11-1 **94**.......................(p) RichardMcGrath —
(C Grant) *towards rr: mstke 6th: nt fluent next: sn bhd and p.u bef 18th* **25/1**

P564 **P** **Onyourheadbeit (IRE)**[24] 4578 8-11-4 **97**..................... JohnMcNamara —
(K C Bailey) *racd wd: chsd ldrs tl pushed along and lost pl 10th: bhd whn p.u bef 3 out* **20/1**

4643 **U** **Runaway Bishop (USA)**[20] 4636 11-10-9 **88**.............. RichardHobson —
(J R Cornwall) *towards rr: n.m.r and hit 5th: sn lost pl and bhd whn blnd and uns rdr 17th* **14/1**

3P24 **P** **Ironside (IRE)**[34] 4394 7-10-13 **92**.......................... AndrewThornton —
(H D Daly) *hld up in midfield: hdwy 12th: pushed along 15th: sn lost pl and bhd whn p.u bef 3 out* **7/1**[3]

7m 25.8s (-6.90) **Going Correction** -0.30s/f (Good) **12** Ran SP% **114.7**
Speed ratings: **97,95,94,89,89 81,—,—,—,— —,—** CSF £182.41 CT £1301.59 TOTE £9.90: £2.40, £7.30, £2.10; EX 402.50.
Owner Halewood International Ltd **Bred** Halewood International Ltd **Trained** Cholmondeley, Cheshire

FOCUS
A proper test of stamina and the progressive Another Club Royal showed he has bags of stamina with a dour display. The form could be rated a little higher.

NOTEBOOK
Another Club Royal, like so many from his yard this season, has progressed with racing and this once plating-class chaser was recording his third win of the campaign. Racing off a 22lb higher mark than when scoring at Musselburgh in January, he relished every yard of the trip and won going away. The seven-year-old is one to keep on side in this form and is likely to do even better next season with another summer over his back *(tchd 9-1 and 11-1)*
Valleymore(IRE) has returned from an unsuccessful spell in Ireland with several fair efforts in defeat and the first-time cheekpieces brought about another good effort, looking the likely winner at one stage before Another Club Royal began to fly. It will be disappointing if he cannot find a race off this sort of mark sooner rather than later.
Midnight Gunner is a gallant old stayer back on a reasonable mark and McCoy got a good run out of him. He will appreciate the quick ground through the summer. *(op 7-1)*
Dante's Back(IRE) has not improved as anticipated since going chasing this season and he was well held back in fourth, the tongue tie making little difference. *(op 8-1)*
Sir Cumference looked a tired horse when jumping left three out and he gradually faded. *(op 13-2 tchd 7-1)*
Profowens(IRE), 12lb higher than when winning at Kelso earlier in the month, was the only other to complete, but it is fair to say he was disappointing. *(tchd 6-1)*
Dickie Lewis came down at the 17th and, although he would not have won, it is hard to say he would not have disputed the placings. *(op 11-2)*
Ironside(IRE) *Official explanation: jockey said gelding was unsuited by the good to soft (soft in places) ground (op 11-2)*

4852 LES BUCKLEY "FIXED BRUSH" H'CAP HURDLE (10 hdls) 2m 4f

4:30 (4:30) (Class 4) (0-110,110) 4-Y-0+ **£4,879** (£1,432; £716; £357)

Form / RPR

3330 **1** **No Guarantees**[77] 3613 6-11-9 **107**........................ AntonyEvans 110+
(N A Twiston-Davies) *led: hdd after 1st: chsd ldr: led after 7th: rdn and nt fluent 2 out: drvn out* **14/1**

2300 **2** *1 3/4* **A Bit Of Fun**[10] 4736 5-11-11 **109**........................ JohnMcNamara 108
(J T Stimpson) *hld up: hdwy 5th: ev ch fr 3 out: sn rdn: no ex nr fin* **25/1**

11P0 **3** *3* **Catch The Perk (IRE)**[127] 2745 9-11-7 **110**...............(p) TJDreaper[(5)] 106
(Miss Lucinda V Russell) *prom: outpcd appr 3 out: styd on u.p fr last* **14/1**

0P24 **4** *2 1/2* **Heavy Weather (IRE)**[33] 4429 8-11-4 **102**..................... JasonMaguire 96
(Miss Joanne Priest) *plld hrd and prom: mstke 5th: outpcd appr 3 out: rallied and hung lft appr next: no ex last* **20/1**

-1F2 **5** *7* **Il'Athou (FR)**[39] 4289 10-11-11 **109**.............................. JoeTizzard 97+
(S E H Sherwood) *led after 1st: hdd 3rd: led next: rdn and hdd after 7th: styd on same pce fr 3 out* **3/1**[2]

1 **6** *4* **Fox Point (USA)**[28] 4487 6-11-5 **103**............................ APMcCoy 86
(P C Haslam) *hld up: hdwy 6th: rdn and wknd appr last* **5/2**[1]

503F **7** *2* **Jaloux D'Estruval (FR)**[19] 4652 9-11-7 **105**................ MarkBradburne 88+
(Mrs L C Taylor) *chsd ldrs: rdn and wknd after 7th* **20/1**

4-00 **8** *5* **Silk Trader**[10] 4736 11-11-2 **107**...................... PatrickMcDonald[(7)] 83
(J Mackie) *hld up: sme hdwy after 3 out: n.d* **33/1**

-5PP **9** *16* **Neidpath Castle**[121] 2840 7-10-10 **101**...................... EwanWhillans[(7)] 61
(A C Whillans) *hld up: hdwy 7th: rdn and wknd bef next* **50/1**

662P **10** *9* **Pardon What**[6] 4804 10-11-9 **107**...............................(b) MickFitzgerald 58
(S Lycett) *mid-div: lost pl after 3rd: sn bhd* **20/1**

2156 **11** *4* **Seymar Lad (IRE)**[27] 4529 6-11-4 **102**...................... DominicElsworth 49
(P Beaumont) *hld up in tch: rdn 5th: wknd next* **13/2**[3]

006P **P** **Powder Creek (IRE)**[59] 3922 9-11-5 **110**...................... PhilKinsella[(7)] —
(K G Reveley) *hld up: a in rr: t.o whn p.u bef 3 out* **33/1**

41-0 **P** **Hutch**[321] 571 8-11-2 **105**.. DesFlavin[(5)] —
(Mrs L B Normile) *hld up: bhd and rdn 5th: t.o whn p.u bef 3 out* **100/1**

4/0- **P** **Fighter Pilot**[511] 2353 7-11-4 **107**........................ RobertLucey-Butler[(5)] —
(Jim Best) *hld up: hdwy 6th: wknd next: t.o whn p.u bef 2 out* **20/1**

003P **P** **Treasured Memories**[28] 4491 6-11-3 **101**..................... AndrewThornton —
(Miss S E Forster) *hld up: hdwy 6th: wknd next: t.o whn p.u bef 3 out* **16/1**

P01P **P** **Old Feathers (IRE)**[23] 4593 9-11-10 **108**...................(b) NoelFehily —
(Jonjo O'Neill) *prom: led 3rd: j.rt and hdd next: wknd after 5th: t.o whn p.u bef 3 out* **20/1**

5m 0.90s (-8.30) **Going Correction** -0.30s/f (Good) **16** Ran SP% **122.6**
Speed ratings: **104,103,102,101,98 96,95,93,87,83 82,—,—,—,— —** CSF £313.12 CT £4926.26 TOTE £16.00: £2.20, £5.70, £2.70, £3.00; EX 328.80.
Owner Mrs M Slade and G MacEchern **Bred** Mrs S J Brasher **Trained** Naunton, Gloucs
■ Stewards' Enquiry : Antony Evans one-day ban: used whip with excessive frequency (Apr 26)

FOCUS
An ordinary handicap won in gritty fashion by the novice No Guarantees. The first four were all close to their marks, and although the form appears sound it may not be that strong.

NOTEBOOK
No Guarantees, whose stable has gone through quite a tough spell in recent weeks, put up a thoroughly genuine performance for a novice seeking his first win, and the little break he has had clearly helped. Always prominent under new stable jockey Evans, he and the runner-up were locked in battle for some way, but the attractive gelding pulled out plenty and connections must be looking forward to sending this winning pointer chasing next term. *(op 16-1)*
A Bit Of Fun looked to be getting the better of the winner at one stage, but he was conceding size to the winner and was simply outstayed. He has not won since 2004, but is only five and may yet be capable of better.
Catch The Perk(IRE) is a grand stayer who kept plugging away to come through again for a place. This was a decent effort over a trip half a mile short of his best.
Heavy Weather(IRE), a multiple winning pointer, ran a cracker considering he pulled so hard and seems to be heading the right way.
Il'Athou(FR), who is better known as a chaser, was readily brushed aside as they began the turn for home, but he kept plugging away and Tizzard, as was the case at Exeter last time, should have commited the gelding sooner. *(tchd 11-4)*
Fox Point(USA), a winner on his British debut at Newcastle last month, was up 8lb here and did *not look up to the task, McCoy unable to extract anything from the gelding in the final quarter mile. (op 3-1)*
Silk Trader *Official explanation: jockey said gelding bled from the nose*
Seymar Lad(IRE) has not progressed as expected and may not win again until switched to fences. *(op 11-2)*

4853 ABRAM STANDARD OPEN NATIONAL HUNT FLAT RACE (DIV I) 2m

5:05 (5:06) (Class 6) 4-6-Y-O **£1,713** (£499; £249)

Form / RPR

1 **Little Bit Of Hush (IRE)** 6-11-2 .... APMcCoy 98
(Noel T Chance) *hld up in midfield: hdwy on inner over 5f out: rdn to chse ldrs 2f out: styd on to ld ent last: sn drvn and kpt on wl* **4/1**[2]

2 *1 1/4* **The Hudnalls (IRE)** 5-11-2 .... JasonMaguire 97
(J A B Old) *hld up in rr: hdwy on outer 4f out: str run fr wl over 1f out: rdn and kpt on wl towards fin* **50/1**

2 **3** *1/2* **Ship's Hill (IRE)**[21] 4622 5-11-2 .... MickFitzgerald 96
(N J Henderson) *hld up in midfield: hdwy on outer over 4f out: rdn to chse ldrs 2f out: drvn to chal ent last: no ex towards fin* **7/2**[1]

4 *1 1/4* **Reel Charmer** 6-10-6 .... MichalKohl[(3)] 88
(J I A Charlton) *hld up in rr: hdwy 1/2-way: in tch 2f out: swtchd rt to wd outside 1f out: fin wl* **50/1**

5 *1 1/4* **Master Somerville** 4-10-10 .... MarkBradburne 88
(H D Daly) *trckd ldrs: effort over 4f out: rdn along wl over 2f out: kpt on same pce* **25/1**

012 **6** *1/2* **Stolen Moments (FR)**[35] 4366 5-11-6 .... MrTGreenall[(3)] 100
(P D Niven) *cl up: rdn along and outpcd over 3f out: styd on u.p fnl f* **16/1**

01 **7** *2* **Joyryder**[21] 4622 5-11-9 .... CarlLlewellyn 99+
(Carl Llewellyn) *sn led: rdn along over 3f out: hdd 2f out and grad wknd* **6/1**[3]

8 *shd* **Oxley (FR)** 4-10-3 .... MrPCallaghan[(7)] 85
(H D Daly) *chsd ldrs: rdn along over 6f out: sn lost pl and bhd tl styd on wl appr last* **50/1**

9 *1/2* **Tomillielou** 5-11-2 .... JimCrowley 90
(G A Swinbank) *in tch: stmbld after 5f: rdn along over 3f out: drvn and no imp fnl 2f* **9/1**

10 *1 1/2* **Pass The Class (IRE)** 6-11-2 .... DominicElsworth 90+
(Mrs S J Smith) *in tch: hdwy on outer 6f out: cl up 4f out: led 2f out: sn rdn and hdd ent last: sn wknd* **28/1**

11 *11* **Heavenly Leader** 5-11-2 .... TimmyMurphy 78
(D McCain) *hld up: gd hdwy on outer over 4f out: rdn along over 2f out and sn wknd* **8/1**

2 **12** *1* **Mr Shambles**[75] 3657 5-11-2 .... LeightonAspell 77
(S Gollings) *chsd ldrs: rdn along 4f out: wknd 3f out* **12/1**

13 *nk* **Vicars Court (IRE)** 6-11-2 .... TomDoyle 77
(O Brennan) *nvr bttr than midfield* **80/1**

14 *1/2* **Chimichurri (FR)** 4-10-3 .... PatrickCStringer[(7)] 83+
(M Bradstock) *keen: midfield: gd hdwy on outer to joing ldrs 6f out: rdn along 3f out: sn wknd* **14/1**

333 **15** *3* **Classic Harry**[35] 4366 5-11-2 .... AnthonyRoss 73
(P Beaumont) *nvr bttr than midfield* **20/1**

16 *1* **The Wicketkeeper (IRE)** 4-10-3 .... JohnKington[(7)] 66
(M Scudamore) *a rr* **50/1**

17 *1* **Makin A Fuss** 4-10-10 .... PadgeWhelan 65
(R M Whitaker) *midfield: hdwy and in tch 1/2-way: rdn along over 5f out and sn wknd* **100/1**

18 *nk* **Flora The Explora** 5-10-4 .... DesFlavin[(5)] 64
(Mrs L B Normile) *midfield on inner: rdn along over 6f out: sn wknd* **66/1**

19 *5* **Goliathe** 5-11-2 .... BarryKeniry 66
(G M Moore) *prom 5f: sn lost pl and bhd fr 1/2-way* **66/1**

20 *21* **Amberbury** 4-10-10 .... AlanDempsey 39
(J Parkes) *a rr* **100/1**

3m 56.0s (-0.40) **Going Correction** -0.175s/f (Good)
WFA 4 from 5yo+ 5lb **20** Ran SP% **124.0**
Speed ratings: **94,93,93,92,91 91,90,90,90,89 84,83,83,83,81 81,80,80,78,67** CSF £212.73 TOTE £5.30: £2.70, £13.20, £1.60; EX 503.30.
Owner John P McManus **Bred** Stuart Crowley **Trained** Upper Lambourn, Berks
■ A first winner at the first attempt for the Chance/McManus combination.

FOCUS
A good bumper likely to produce numerous winners, although the time was significantly slower than the second division. The fifth sets the standard but the form looks worth treating with caution.

NOTEBOOK
Little Bit Of Hush(IRE), a first runner for the Chance/McManus combination, was solid in the market beforehand and he settled nicely in the race, holding a nice position off the sound gallop. He did not pick up immediately however, and needed plenty of driving from McCoy to win, but he gave the impression he was just doing enough and it is safe to assume the scopey six-year-old will do even better once tackling obstacles. *(tchd 9-2)*

The Form Book, Raceform Ltd, Compton, RG20 6NL

The Hudnalls(IRE), whose stable have had another good year with their bumpers, was a non-runner on account of quick ground at Taunton the other day, but he was allowed to take his chance here on this more suitable surface and he ran a race full of promise, coming from some way back down the outside to get up for second close home. His price suggested little was expected, but he clearly has ability and it is to be hoped he goes on from this.
Ship's Hill(IRE), highly regarded by connections, ran well when a good second on his debut at Newbury behind Joyryder and he was able to reverse the form with the pull in the weights. He did not prove good enough to collect overall however, as he flattened out under pressure and had little left in the last 50 yards. He is likely to improve a good deal once tackling obstacles. *(op 10-3)*
Reel Charmer ◆, one of only two mares in the field, followed the runner-up through in the final furlong or so and was another to shape particularly well. This was a pleasing debut and she should have little trouble finding a race against her own sex. *(op 40-1)*
Master Somerville was up there from an early stage and he kept going to finish a creditable fifth. His stable's bumpers often improve with experience and the gelding will stay further over hurdles.
Stolen Moments(FR) ran another sound race under his penalty, but he remains vulnerable and needs a switch to hurdles. *(tchd 14-1)*
Joyryder, who won authoritatively at Newbury, was unable to repeat the effort and seemed to be found out by the 7lb penalty. He is only five and can make a fair hurdler next term. *(op 15-2)*
Oxley(FR) ◆, another debutant from the Daly yard, kept on under considerate handling and could be interesting in a similar event before going hurdling.
Chimichurri(FR) *Official explanation: jockey said gelding ran too free early and found nothing home straight*

4854 ABRAM STANDARD OPEN NATIONAL HUNT FLAT RACE (DIV II) 2m
5:35 (5:36) (Class 6) 4-6-Y-O £1,713 (£499; £249)

Form | | | | RPR
2 **1** **Bleak House (IRE)**[117] [2927] 4-10-10 .... JasonMaguire 101+
(T P Tate) *hld up: hdwy 6f out: led over 1f out: r.o wl* **9/2**[1]
2 *3 ½* **Shouldhavehadthat (IRE)** 4-10-10 .... MickFitzgerald 94
(N J Henderson) *hld up: hdwy 6f out: outpcd over 3f out: rallied over 1f out: r.o* **13/2**
3 *½* **Shelomoh (IRE)** 5-11-2 .... RichardMcGrath 100
(D M Forster) *a.p: led 9f out: hdd over 4f out: led 3f out: rdn and hdd over 1f out: styd on same pce* **33/1**
4 *2 ½* **Noble Raider (IRE)** 4-10-3 .... DavidCullinane(7) 92+
(T J Fitzgerald) *hld up in tch: rdn over 3f out: ev ch over 1f out: wknd ins fnl f* **66/1**
221 **5** *1 ¼* **Kealshore Lad**[70] [3742] 5-11-9 .... BarryKeniry 103
(G M Moore) *chsd ldrs: led over 4f out: hdd 3f out: rdn and wknd over 1f out* **12/1**
6 *2 ½* **Mr Strachan (IRE)** 5-10-6 .... MichaelO'Connell(10) 94
(Mrs S J Smith) *hdwy 12f out: rdn over 2f out: wknd over 1f out* **25/1**
7 *nk* **Little Paddy (IRE)** 5-11-2 .... DominicElsworth 93+
(Mrs K Walton) *hld up: hdwy and swtchd lft over 1f out: nrst fin* **40/1**
8 *5* **Gunnasayso** 5-10-9 .... LeightonAspell 81+
(J A B Old) *hld up: styd on appr fnl f: nvr nrr* **25/1**
9 *¾* **Kellbury** 4-10-3 .... MrPCallaghan(7) 81
(H D Daly) *hld up: racd keenly: styd on ins fnl f: nrst fin* **66/1**
10 *5* **Solid Silver** 5-11-2 .... JimCrowley 82
(K G Reveley) *hld up in tch: rdn over 3f out: wknd wl over 1f out* **25/1**
3 **11** *3 ½* **Top Cloud (IRE)**[23] [4588] 5-11-2 .... TimmyMurphy 79
(Ferdy Murphy) *chsd ldrs: lost pl over 6f out: sn bhd* **6/1**[3]
2 **12** *9* **Ordre De Bataille (FR)**[37] [4326] 4-10-10 .... MarkBradburne 64
(H D Daly) *hld up: hdwy 6f out: wknd 4f out* **10/1**
302 **13** *¾* **Master Eddy**[28] [4500] 6-11-2 .... AntonyEvans 69
(S Lycett) *led 7f: wknd 2f out* **25/1**
3 **14** *6* **High Moor**[37] [4319] 4-10-10 .... SamThomas 57
(J D Bethell) *hld up: a in rr* **50/1**
4 **15** *¾* **Amhairghin (IRE)**[23] [4588] 6-11-2 .... AlanDempsey 62
(G A Harker) *plld hrd and prom: wknd over 4f out* **16/1**
16 *shd* **Ravenstone Lad (IRE)** 4-10-10 .... JimmyMcCarthy 56
(Mrs P Robeson) *mid-div: rdn 1/2-way: sn lost pl* **40/1**
1 **17** *3* **Cockspur (IRE)**[61] [3904] 5-11-9 .... APMcCoy 66
(Jonjo O'Neill) *hld up: hdwy 1/2-way: wknd 3f out* **11/2**[2]
18 *30* **The Gay Gordons** 5-11-2 .... TomDoyle 29
(P R Webber) *prom 10f* **10/1**
19 *18* **China Bond (IRE)** 4-10-10 .... PadgeWhelan 5
(G R Oldroyd) *hld up: hdwy 11f out: rdn 1/2-way: wknd 6f out* **100/1**
20 *18* **My Friend Paul** 6-11-2 .... JohnMcNamara —
(O Brennan) *hld up: hdwy over 6f out: wknd over 4f out* **50/1**

3m 51.5s (-4.90) **Going Correction** -0.175s/f (Good)
WFA 4 from 5yo+ 5lb **20** Ran SP% **124.0**
Speed ratings: **105,103,103,101,101 99,99,97,96,94 92,88,87,84,84 84,82,67,58,49** CSF £28.50 TOTE £6.60: £2.70, £2.10, £9.70; EX 42.80 Place 6 £1,701.47, Place 5 £396.44.
Owner T P Tate **Bred** Eamonn Delaney **Trained** Tadcaster, N Yorks

FOCUS
The winning time was 4.5 seconds faster than the first division, despite it looking the the lesser contest of the two on paper. The winner and fifth set the standard and the race should produce future winners.

NOTEBOOK
Bleak House(IRE), runner-up in a junior bumper at Doncaster back in December, has clearly strengthened in the time since and he stayed on strongly to win with plenty in hand. This time of this was significantly quicker than the first division and he will stay further over hurdles. *(op 11-2)*
Shouldhavehadthat(IRE) ◆, who is reportedly a bit on the weak side, saw his race out in good fashion, getting up for second close home, and he has a bright future ahead of him with another summer on his back likely to bring about significant improvement. *(tchd 6-1)*
Shelomoh(IRE) will no doubt have delighted connections with this debut effort, taking it up some way out and plugging away gallanty. He was claimed for second close home, but wasn't stopping and he is another for whom two and a half miles over hurdles looks certain to suit.
Noble Raider(IRE) made a little headway from the rear and ran above market expectation. He is another four-year-old likely to imrpove over the summer.
Kealshore Lad, a winner at Wetherby last time at the third attempt, knew his job and was always prominent, but he failed to get home as well as the pricipals and was found out by his penalty.
Mr Strachan(IRE) shaped well under a far from hard ride and is going to come on for the experience.
Kellbury, as with Oxley in the previous race, he made some good late headway under a considerate ride and he would make some appeal in a similar race if competing again this season.
Top Cloud(IRE) failed to build on his Ayr third and it may be the best of him is not seen until he tackles hurdles. *(op 9-2)*
Ordre De Bataille(FR) appeared to hold obvious claims if building on his Towcester second, but he never landed a blow and was beaten some way from the finish. *(op 11-1)*
Cockspur(IRE), a winner at Plumpton on his debut, had a hard race that day and he was unable to build on it, stopping disappointingly quickly. *(op 5-1)*
T/Jkpt: Not won. T/Plt: £1,232.00 to a £1 stake. Pool: £83,798.90. 49.65 winning tickets. T/Qpdt: £75.20 to a £1 stake. Pool: £5,131.50. 50.45 winning tickets. JR

1380 NEWTON ABBOT (L-H)
Saturday, April 15
OFFICIAL GOING: Good to firm (good in places)
Wind: Virtually nil.

4855 ROLAND PEDRICK MEMORIAL MARES' ONLY MAIDEN HURDLE (8 hdls) 2m 1f
2:20 (2:20) (Class 5) 4-Y-0+ £2,927 (£859; £429; £214)

Form | | | | RPR
60 **1** **Cirrious**[21] [4621] 5-10-12 .... RichardJohnson 101+
(P J Hobbs) *hld up towards rr: hdwy after 5th: rdn in 3rd appr 2 out: styd on to ld last: rdn out* **20/1**
523 **2** *1* **Wee Dinns (IRE)**[51] [4074] 5-10-12 97 .... TomScudamore 101+
(M C Pipe) *trckd ldrs: rdn to ld after 3 out: wandered and nt fluent next: hdd and wnt lft last: no ex* **5/1**[3]
20 **3** *2* **Screen Test**[11] [3902] 4-10-6 .... RobertThornton 92+
(B G Powell) *led 2nd: rdn and hdd after 3 out: 3rd and hld whn hit last* **3/1**[2]
2232 **4** *2* **Barton Flower**[20] [4641] 5-10-7 104 .... DarylJacob(5) 95
(D P Keane) *prom: rdn and effrt after 3 out: kpt on same pce* **11/8**[1]
3256 **5** *3* **Adlestrop**[34] [4389] 6-10-12 .... WarrenMarston 92
(R T Phillips) *hld up mid-div: hdwy 5th: rdn and effrt after 3 out: sn one pce* **16/1**
506 **6** *hd* **Sturbury**[17] [4665] 4-10-3 .... RichardYoung(3) 86
(J W Mullins) *mid-div: lost pl 4th: styd on again fr 3 out* **66/1**
00P6 **7** *13* **Fair View (GER)**[25] [4566] 5-10-9 70 .... ColinBolger(3) 79
(Dr P Pritchard) *led tl 2nd: chsd ldrs: rdn and wknd after 3 out* **66/1**
03P2 **8** *3* **Madam Caversfield**[10] [4733] 4-10-6 92 .... ChristianWilliams 70
(J L Flint) *chsd ldrs: rdn after 3 out: sn wknd* **16/1**
P **9** *14* **Regal Fantasy (IRE)**[20] [4642] 6-10-12 .... WayneHutchinson 62
(P A Blockley) *in tch tl after 5th* **100/1**
10 *6* **Mademoiselle**[76] 4-10-6 .... DaveCrosse 50
(R Curtis) *a towards rr* **50/1**
11 *4* **Diafa (USA)**[11] 4-10-1 .... StevenCrawford(5) 46
(J G M O'Shea) *mstke 5th: a towards rr* **66/1**
35P3 **12** *3* **Miss Midnight**[10] [4726] 5-10-12 92 .... (b) BarryFenton 49
(R J Hodges) *in tch tl wknd appr 3 out* **12/1**
F-F0 **13** *10* **Aber Gale**[52] [4048] 7-10-12 .... JamesDavies 39
(Mrs S M Johnson) *towards rr: hdwy after 4th: wknd after next* **100/1**
00-0 **P** **Itsukate**[328] [463] 6-10-12 .... OllieMcPhail —
(J Rudge) *mid-div tl 3rd: sn t.o: p.u after 4th* **100/1**

3m 58.0s (-7.10) **Going Correction** -0.325s/f (Good)
WFA 4 from 5yo+ 5lb **14** Ran SP% **117.4**
Speed ratings: **103,102,101,100,99 99,93,91,85,82 80,78,74,—** CSF £114.64 TOTE £18.70: £4.40, £1.70, £1.70; EX 119.10.
Owner Peter Morgan **Bred** P K C Racing **Trained** Withycombe, Somerset

FOCUS
A modest mares' maiden, run at a sound enough gallop, and the form appears fair rated around the placed horses and the fifth.

NOTEBOOK
Cirrious got off the mark as a hurdler at the third time of asking under a well-judged ride. Having shown little in two outings in this sphere previously, the switch to this faster ground was clearly much to her liking, and she did more than enough to suggest she can build on this if kept going through the summer. *(op 16-1)*
Wee Dinns(IRE), easy to back, held every chance to open her account in this sphere, yet spoilt her chance by hanging both ways when in front nearing the penultimate flight. She is frustrating, but this better ground proved in her favour, and she clearly has a race of this nature within her compass during the summer. *(op 9-2 tchd 4-1)*
Screen Test, reverting to hurdling and making her debut for a new yard, shaped as though she needs a stiffer test and should be of more interest now she is eligible for a handicap mark. *(op 7-2 tchd 4-1)*
Barton Flower, runner-up in handicap company last time, turned in a below-par effort and was beaten with three to jump. She is the benchmark for this form, but this was the first occasion she had not managed to fill a place in this sphere, and it leaves her with a deal to prove in the future. *(op 13-8 tchd 7-4 in places)*
Adlestrop ran with more encouragement on this faster ground and now qualifies for a handicap mark. *(op 12-1)*
Itsukate *Official explanation: jockey said mare bled from the nose*

4856 HOT CROSS BUN (S) HURDLE (9 hdls) 2m 3f
2:50 (2:53) (Class 5) 4-Y-0+ £2,192 (£639; £319)

Form | | | | RPR
4604 **1** **Brochrua (IRE)**[33] [4423] 6-10-4 86 .... ChrisHonour(3) 89+
(J D Frost) *mid div: tk clsr order after 4th: led 6th: rdn appr 2 out: hit last: kpt on* **5/2**[1]
F04P **2** *nk* **Random Quest**[19] [4652] 8-11-6 98 .... (b[1]) RichardJohnson 101
(B J Llewellyn) *mid div: gd hdwy appr 6th: jnd wnr 3 out: rdn sn after: 1l down 2 out: renewed effrt flat: kpt on* **4/1**[2]
4305 **3** *3 ½* **Smilingvalentine (IRE)**[21] [4609] 9-9-11 90 .... RyanCummings(10) 84
(D J Wintle) *hld up towards rr: hdwy 6th: rdn after 3 out: wnt 3rd next: kpt on same pce* **7/1**
0603 **4** *3* **Jack Durrance (IRE)**[10] [4733] 6-10-9 86 .... EamonDehdashti(5) 88
(G A Ham) *mid div: hdwy 6th: rdn after 3 out: kpt on same pce* **7/1**
0F64 **5** *3* **Griffin's Legacy**[25] [4556] 7-10-7 85 .... JamesWhite(7) 85
(N G Ayliffe) *w ldr: led after 3rd tl 6th: sn rdn: one pce after* **16/1**
4350 **6** *14* **Ashgan (IRE)**[27] [4526] 13-11-1 77 .... DrPPritchard(5) 77
(Dr P Pritchard) *bhd: lost tch 6th: styd on again fr 3 out* **33/1**
40P0 **7** *shd* **Duke's View (IRE)**[10] [4731] 5-10-7 70 .... (p) MrRQuinn(7) 71
(D C Turner) *in tch: tk clsr order 6th: rdn appr 3 out: wknd bef 2 out* **33/1**
0000 **8** *10* **Galant Eye (IRE)**[106] [3128] 7-11-0 80 .... (b[1]) VinceSlattery 61
(R J Baker) *in tch tl 5th: sn bhd* **25/1**
40-P **9** *9* **Bayford Boy**[62] [3882] 6-10-11 .... ColinBolger(3) 52
(K Bishop) *towards rr: rdn and wknd after 3 out: (lame)* **25/1**
PP50 **10** *½* **Impero**[12] [4392] 8-10-7 64 .... (b) AndrewGlassonbury(7) 51
(G F Bridgwater) *uns rdr bef s: led tl 3rd: prom tl wknd bef 3 out* **100/1**
450/ **11** *11* **Allegiance**[787] [3880] 11-10-11 72 .... TomMalone(3) 40
(P Wegmann) *a towards rr* **50/1**
12 *28* **Rodd To Riches** 8-11-0 .... MatthewBatchelor 12
(Jamie Poulton) *nvr fluent and sn t.o* **25/1**
03F- **P** **Assignation**[513] [2300] 6-11-0 67 .... (p) WayneHutchinson —
(Miss M Bragg) *prom tl wknd bef 3 out: p.u bef 2 out* **40/1**

25F2 **P** **Darko Karim**[35] 4368 4-10-7 90..............................(b) TomScudamore —
(R J Hodges) *chsd ldrs: nt fluent 1st: rdn appr 3 out: sn one pce: btn 5th whn p.u run-in: (lame)* **5/1**[3]

4m 29.4s (-3.60) **Going Correction** -0.325s/f (Good)
WFA 4 from 5yo+ 5lb **14** Ran SP% **118.9**
Speed ratings: **94,93,92,91,89 83,83,79,75,75 71,59,—,—** CSF £11.03 TOTE £3.70: £1.70, £2.00, £1.60; EX 17.80.There was no bid for the winner.
Owner Ms H Vernon-Jones **Bred** Nicholas Teehan **Trained** Scorriton, Devon

FOCUS
A very weak event which saw the first two come clear. The form is easy to rate with the runner-up and the majority of the first seven close to their marks, so should prove sound enough.

NOTEBOOK
Brochrua(IRE) relished the return to a quick surface and deservedly got back to winning ways in gritty fashion. This is very much her level and she is capable of going in again granted decent ground. *(op 4-1)*
Random Quest, having his first outing at this level and sporting first-time blinkers, was only just denied yet appeared reluctant to fully go through with his effort under maximum pressure. He is regressive, but remains capable of winning a race in this class if putting it all in. *(op 9-2 tchd 5-1)*
Smilingvalentine(IRE), back down in grade with the blinkers left off, was not that surprisingly found lacking for speed over this trip yet still posted an improved effort. The return to a stiffer test in this class can see her get closer. *(op 6-1)*
Jack Durrance(IRE) failed to improve all that much on his most recent effort, yet still ran his race and helps set the level of this form. *(op 8-1)*

4857 SOUTH WEST RACING CLUB H'CAP CHASE (20 fncs) 3m 2f 110y
3:20 (3:22) (Class 3) (0-120,115) 5-Y-O+ £7,605 (£2,246; £1,123; £561; £280)

Form RPR

6P31 **1** **Hever Road (IRE)**[10] 4728 7-11-3 **113**.............(b) AndrewGlassonbury[(7)] 130+
(M C Pipe) *towards rr: blnd 7th: hdwy 11th: wnt 2nd 14th: led 2 out: sn rdn: drifted rt and rdr dropped whip run-in: rdn out* **13/2**[3]

4055 **2** 1 ¾ **Koquelicot (FR)**[32] 4434 8-11-11 **114**.............(b) RichardJohnson 126+
(P J Hobbs) *led: reminder after 10th: rdn after 3 out: hdd and mstke next: kpt on* **3/1**[1]

F020 **3** 20 **Special Conquest**[2] 4835 8-11-2 **108**.............(p) RichardYoung[(3)] 102+
(J W Mullins) *trckd ldrs: jnd ldr after 6th tl 10th: sn drvn along: 3rd whn mstke 16th: wknd after 4 out* **8/1**

3500 **4** 12 **Baloo**[25] 4561 10-10-9 **101**.. ChrisHonour[(3)] 80
(J D Frost) *hld up in tch: lost tch after 13th: styd on fr 3 out to take mod 4th flat* **4/1**[2]

25P2 **5** ½ **Spring Grove (IRE)**[47] 4152 11-11-12 **115**...................... RobertWalford 94
(R H Alner) *trckd ldrs: hit 1st: wnt 2nd 11th tl 14th: rdn after 16th: wknd after next: lost 4th flat* **7/1**

1453 **6** 3 ½ **Tommy Carson**[19] 4650 11-10-3 **95**.............................. ColinBolger[(3)] 70
(Jamie Poulton) *w ldr tl 5th: sn pushed along: lost pl on bnd after 7th: mstke 12th: bhd fr next* **7/1**

FU00 **7** 17 **Farlington**[66] 3803 9-11-10 **113**...................................... JamieMoore 71
(P Bowen) *chsd ldrs: jnd ldr 5th tl 8th: chsd ldrs: mstke next: rdn after 14th: sn btn: t.o* **10/1**

132- **8** dist **Mr Dow Jones (IRE)**[678] 662 14-11-1 **104**................ ChristianWilliams —
(W K Goldsworthy) *in tch: sltly hmpd 1st: grad lost tch fr 12th: t.o* **14/1**

6m 22.1s (-21.30) **Going Correction** -0.55s/f (Firm) **8** Ran SP% **110.2**
Speed ratings: **109,108,102,99,98 97,92,—** CSF £25.25 CT £147.38 TOTE £5.90: £1.70, £1.80, £2.90; EX 15.40.
Owner Professor D B A Silk & Mrs Heather Silk **Bred** Dr D B A Silk And H Jarvis **Trained** Nicholashayne, Devon

FOCUS
A fair handicap run at a good pace, which provided a thorough test of stamina, and the first pair came well clear. The form is rated around the placed horses.

NOTEBOOK
Hever Road(IRE), raised 8lb for winning at Exeter last time, followed-up in fairly ready fashion to record a career-best display. He looked happy on this fast ground and, while not appearing the most straightforward, he finally looks to be coming good for connections. The Handicapper should not put him up too much in the weights for this and he probably has more to offer on this sort of ground. *(op 8-1 tchd 10-1)*
Koquelicot(FR), fifth in the Cross Country Handicap at Cheltenham last time, posted a solid effort on ground he would have found plenty soft enough. He was well clear of the remainder, and is on a fair mark at present, so could well be placed to end his losing run if able to maintain this current mood. *(op 5-2)*
Special Conquest, unplaced at Wincanton two days previously and popular in the betting ring, was put firmly in his place nearing four out and finished tired. He is hard to catch right. *(op 12-1)*
Baloo, reverting to fences, failed to raise his game on this better ground and continues to look out of sorts. *(op 5-1)*
Spring Grove(IRE), agonisingly denied at Plumpton last time, would have found this ground too fast for his liking and failed to seriously figure. *(op 9-2)*

4858 INTER-LINE PEARL ANNIVERSARY H'CAP HURDLE (8 hdls 1 omitted) 2m 3f
3:50 (3:50) (Class 4) (0-115,115) 4-Y-O+ **£4,554** (£1,337; £668; £333)

Form RPR

-63F **1** **Gaelic Flight (IRE)**[140] 2488 8-10-10 **102**.............(t) WilliamKennedy[(3)] 109+
(Noel T Chance) *hld up mid-div: hdwy after 6th: cl 5th and nt clr run bef 2 out: sn rdn: styd on wl to ld sn after last: rdn out* **9/2**[1]

163 **2** 1 **Shiny Thing (USA)**[16] 4674 4-10-7 **103**...................... RobertThornton 103+
(A King) *trckd ldrs: hmpd 3rd: led appr 2 out: sn rdn and idled: hit last and sn hdd: no ex* **9/2**[1]

6 **3** 1 ¼ **Allaboveboard (IRE)**[10] 4738 7-10-11 **100**...................... JamieMoore 104
(P Bowen) *led tl after 1st: prom: rdn and ev ch 2 out: kpt on* **12/1**

1350 **4** 1 ¾ **College Ace (IRE)**[33] 4420 5-11-12 **115**...................... RichardJohnson 117
(P J Hobbs) *bhd: drvn along after 5th: styd on wl fr 2 out: wnt 4th at the last: nvr trbld ldrs* **9/1**[3]

0010 **5** 4 **Fard Du Moulin Mas (FR)**[117] 2925 13-11-1 **104**.............. BarryFenton 104+
(M E D Francis) *mid-div: hmpd 3rd: rdn after 6th: styd on* **16/1**

0314 **6** shd **Abraham Smith**[22] 4606 6-11-0 **110**...................... TomMessenger[(7)] 109+
(B J Eckley) *led tl after 1st: rdn and hdd appr 2 out: wkng whn hit last* **7/1**[2]

P360 **7** ½ **Aldiruos (IRE)**[17] 4663 6-10-11 **100**...................... WayneHutchinson 97
(A W Carroll) *bhd: rdn after 6th: styd on fr 2 out: nvr a danger* **25/1**

4050 **8** 4 **Devito (FR)**[17] 4663 5-11-0 **110**...................... MrDEdwards[(7)] 104+
(G F Edwards) *mid-div: rdn after 6th: sn one pce* **11/1**

1043 **9** 12 **Amanpuri (GER)**[14] 4693 8-11-6 **109**...................... ChristianWilliams 90
(Mrs A M Thorpe) *chsd ldrs: wnt 2nd after 6th: sn rdn: wknd wl bef 2 out* **9/1**[3]

0030 **10** 25 **Spike Jones (NZ)**[7] 4781 8-11-0 **103**...................... PhilipHide 59
(Mrs S M Johnson) *in tch: nt fluent 6th: sn wknd: t.o* **20/1**

40 **11** 4 **Lik Wood Power (NZ)**[21] 4621 9-10-13 **102**...................... HenryOliver 54
(D J Wintle) *prom tl 6th: sn wknd: t.o* **20/1**

2304 **12** 7 **Tell The Trees**[280] 768 5-11-5 **108**...................... TomScudamore 53
(M C Pipe) *nt a fluent: mstke 2nd: bhd thereafter: t.o fr 5th* **16/1**

001- **13** dist **Maldoun (IRE)**[421] 3684 7-11-8 **111**...................... BenjaminHitchcott —
(Mrs Barbara Waring) *a towards rr: t.o fr 5th* **66/1**

3-1F **F** **Friendly Request**[218] 1443 7-9-9 **91**...................... KeiranBurke[(7)] —
(N J Hawke) *trcking ldrs whn fell 3rd* **20/1**

4m 25.0s (-8.00) **Going Correction** -0.325s/f (Good)
WFA 4 from 5yo+ 5lb **14** Ran SP% **116.3**
Speed ratings: **103,102,102,101,99 99,99,97,92,82 80,77,—,—** CSF £21.86 CT £227.82 TOTE £6.30: £2.70, £1.90, £3.90; EX 24.30.
Owner Top Flight Racing 3 **Bred** Mrs M Skehan-O'Brien **Trained** Upper Lambourn, Berks

FOCUS
A modest handicap, run at a fair pace. The form is sound for the class and should work out. Third-last flight bypassed.

NOTEBOOK
Gaelic Flight(IRE), a faller over fences when last seen back in November, advertised his clear liking for fast ground and made a winning return in game fashion. He looked as though he may be ready to tackle further now, so more improvement should not be ruled out, and his confidence should be fully restored now should connections opt to put him back over fences during the summer. *(tchd 4-1)*
Shiny Thing(USA), up in trip, hit the front two out yet spoilt her chance with an error at the final flight and was reeled in by the winner on the run-in. She got the longer trip well, was helped by the faster ground, and is clearly up to winning a race from this mark. *(op 11-4)*
Allaboveboard(IRE) improved a deal on this form of his recent British debut for connections and left the definite impression that he ought to be placed to resume winning ways when faced with a stiffer test or the return to easier ground. *(op 16-1)*
College Ace(IRE) ran in snatches and, while this must rate an improved effort, he is a happier horse on softer ground. He has not progressed as expected this term, but this was no real disgrace under top weight. *(op 14-1)*

4859 GRAHAM DYMOND BIRTHDAY PRESENT H'CAP CHASE (13 fncs) 2m 110y
4:20 (4:21) (Class 4) (0-110,109) 5-Y-O+ **£5,204** (£1,528; £764; £381)

Form RPR

3513 **1** **Wild Power (GER)**[14] 4694 8-10-7 **93**...................... OwynNelmes[(3)] 100
(Mrs H R J Nelmes) *in tch: hdwy 7th: rdn after 3 out: styd on strly fr next: led run-in: rdn out* **9/2**[2]

3224 **2** ½ **Jupon Vert (FR)**[7] 4782 9-10-10 **93**...................... TomScudamore 100
(R J Hodges) *in tch: hdwy 7th: led after 4 out: rdn after 2 out: no ex whn hdd run-in* **9/1**

5656 **3** 1 ¾ **O'Toole (IRE)**[21] 4618 7-11-12 **109**...................... RichardJohnson 116+
(P J Hobbs) *trckd ldrs: wnt rt 7th: jnd ldr next: rdn after 3 out: ev ch whn wnt rt and hit 2 out: kpt on same pce* **13/8**[1]

F035 **4** 5 **Whaleef**[26] 4552 8-11-6 **103**...................... (t) ChristianWilliams 103
(B J Llewellyn) *towards rr: styd on fr 4 out: wnt 4th appr 2 out: nvr trbld ldrs* **14/1**

4F52 **5** 12 **Nagano (FR)**[21] 4614 8-11-5 **102**...................... RobertThornton 93+
(Ian Williams) *w ldr: mstke 6th: led next: rdn and hdd after 4 out: wknd next: lft 5th at the last* **11/2**[3]

U3F **P** **La Source A Gold (IRE)**[33] 4424 7-9-10 **86** ow3.....(t) WillieMcCarthy[(7)] —
(Nick Williams) *towards rr: lost tch 8th: t.o and p.u bef 2 out* **8/1**

3311 **F** **Better Moment (IRE)**[24] 4575 9-10-11 **101**......(v) AndrewGlassonbury[(7)] 101+
(M C Pipe) *led tl 7th: sn drvn along: one pce fr 4 out: 5th and btn whn fell last* **6/1**

3m 58.7s (-6.80) **Going Correction** -0.55s/f (Firm) **7** Ran SP% **113.7**
Speed ratings: **94,93,92,90,84 —,—** CSF £40.68 CT £91.22 TOTE £7.20: £2.20, £3.00; EX 30.60.
Owner K A Nelmes **Bred** M Ommer **Trained** Warmwell, Dorset

FOCUS
A modest winning time and the form is ordinary witrh the third the best guide to the level.

NOTEBOOK
Wild Power(GER) got back to winning ways under a well-judged ride. He enjoyed the faster ground and, while he is not one to overly rely upon, he should still be feasibly treated despite an inevitable rise in the weights. *(op 6-1)*
Jupon Vert(FR) turned in his usual game effort, and had every chance, but he still remains 2lb higher than his last winning mark. *(op 5-1)*
O'Toole(IRE), well-backed for this drop in class, failed to really improve for this return to quicker ground and did not appear too willing to fully go through with his effort under pressure. *(op 9-4)*
Whaleef failed to make any impression from off the pace and would have been closer granted a more positive ride. *(op 8-1)*

4860 ANNE MILLERS 50TH BIRTHDAY CELEBRATION NOVICES' H'CAP HURDLE (10 hdls) 2m 6f
4:55 (4:55) (Class 4) (0-105,105) 4-Y-O+ **£4,554** (£1,337; £668; £333)

Form RPR

2-50 **1** **Complete Outsider**[9] 4756 8-11-7 **100**...................... WayneHutchinson 105+
(Nick Williams) *in tch: trckd ldrs 7th: shkn up to ld appr 2 out: r.o wl: readily* **16/1**

06F4 **2** 4 **Sparklinspirit**[43] 4212 7-11-2 **95**...................... PhilipHide 96+
(J L Spearing) *mid-div: hdwy 7th: rdn and effrt appr 2 out: 2nd and hld whn hit last* **15/2**[3]

0602 **3** 1 ½ **Mister Chatterbox (IRE)**[9] 4756 5-11-0 **93**...................... RichardJohnson 91
(P J Hobbs) *trckd ldrs: rdn along after 7th: kpt on same pce fr 2 out* **11/4**[1]

40P0 **4** nk **Minster Park**[37] 4331 7-10-3 **85**...................... (t) ChrisHonour[(3)] 83
(S C Burrough) *mid-div: hdwy appr 3 out: sn rdn: hit next: styd on* **100/1**

0011 **5** 2 ½ **Le Forezien (FR)**[9] 4752 7-10-10 **96**...................... (t) BernieWharfe[(7)] 91
(C J Gray) *hld up bhd: styd on fr after 3 out: swtchd lft after 2 out: nt rch ldrs* **9/1**

5466 **6** ½ **Fuss**[10] 4726 5-10-6 **85**...................... PJBrennan 80
(P J Hobbs) *hld up towards rr: hdwy after 7th: rdn after 3 out: kpt on same pce* **12/1**

0015 **7** ¾ **Lord Ryeford (IRE)**[25] 4557 6-10-11 **97**...................... (t) WillieMcCarthy[(7)] 92+
(T R George) *led: mstke 5th: hit next: narrowly hdd 7th: led again 3 out: sn rdn: hdd appr 2 out: no ex* **10/1**

0-64 **8** nk **Lord Oscar (IRE)**[122] 2818 7-10-11 **97**...................... AndrewGlassonbury[(7)] 91
(M C Pipe) *restrained in rr: stdy prog fr 7th: rdn after 3 out: sn one pce* **14/1**

4000 **9** 1 **Able Charlie (GER)**[21] 4616 4-10-2 **95**...................... TomMessenger[(7)] 81
(Mrs Tracey Barfoot-Saunt) *towards rr: hdwy 7th: rdn after 3 out: kpt on same pce* **33/1**

10 6 **Paddleurowncanoe (IRE)**[45] 4182 7-11-1 **94**...................... SeanFox 81
(J C Fox) *mid-div tl lost pl 6th* **50/1**

0633 **11** ¾ **How Is The Lord (IRE)**[25] 4557 10-10-0 **82**...............(p) OwynNelmes[(3)] 68
(C J Down) *chsd ldrs: rdn after 7th: wkng whn hmpd 3 out* **10/1**

5600 **12** 11 **Killer Cat (FR)**[9] 4752 5-11-0 **100** ow10...................... (v) MrDEdwards[(7)] 75
(G F Edwards) *in tch: jnd ldrs 4th: hit 5th: j.rt and hit 7th: ev ch 3 out: wknd qckly* **50/1**

The Form Book, Raceform Ltd, Compton, RG20 6NL

3424 **13** *nk* **Lavenoak Lad**[17] 4661 6-10-9 **95**....................(p) JamesWhite(7) 70
(P R Rodford) *t.k.h: trckd ldrs: led 7th tl 3 out: sn wknd* **20/1**

/P64 **P** **Polyanthus Jones**[52] 4052 7-10-12 **91**.................... RobertThornton —
(H D Daly) *mid-div tl 6th: sn bhd: p.u bef 3 out* **14/1**

-021 **P** **Rude Health**[34] 4391 6-10-0 **86**.................... KeiranBurke(7) —
(N J Hawke) *hld up towards rr: making gd hdwy whn stmbld bdly and nrly uns rdr 3 out: nt rcvr and p.u bef next* **5/1**[2]

5m 16.8s (-3.50) **Going Correction** -0.325s/f (Good)
WFA 4 from 5yo+ 6lb **15** Ran SP% **122.8**
Speed ratings: **93,91,91,90,89 89,89,89,89,86 86,82,82,—,—** CSF £129.59 CT £441.02 TOTE £22.20: £5.50, £3.40, £1.40; EX 209.40 Place 6 £77.86, Place 5 £25.60.
Owner Mike Ford **Bred** M W Ford **Trained** George Nympton, Devon

FOCUS
A modest winning time for the grade, but the form still looks fair enough rated around the placed horses.

NOTEBOOK
Complete Outsider bounced back to form over this longer trip, appearing to relish the faster ground, and ran out a most ready winner. He comprehensively reversed his recent Taunton form with the third horse and, despite now facing an inevitable hike back up in the weights, he can be placed to go in again on this sort of ground.
Sparklinspirit, making his handicap debut, duly showed his best form to date and gave the *impression he ought to go one better during the summer. He may also prefer a stiffer test. (op 8-1 tchd 7-1)*
Mister Chatterbox(IRE), who had the winner well behind when narrowly denied at Taunton last time, was very well backed to go one better over this longer trip, yet failed to get home as well as the front pair. He is frustrating. *(op 9-2)*
Minster Park was never a serious threat, yet posted a much-improved effort in defeat, presumably on account of the quicker surface. He can build on this during the summer months. *(op 66-1)*
T/Plt: £191.00 to a £1 stake. Pool: £55,367.15. 211.60 winning tickets. T/Qpdt: £47.70 to a £1 stake. Pool: £4,216.60. 65.40 winning tickets. TM

4861 - 4867a (Foreign Racing) - See Raceform Interactive

4648 PLUMPTON (L-H)
Sunday, April 16

OFFICIAL GOING: Good to soft (soft in places)
Wind: Light against Weather: Fine but cloudy

4868 TOTEPLACEPOT NOVICES' HURDLE (12 hdls) 2m 5f
2:30 (2:30) (Class 4) 4-Y-0+ **£3,903** (£1,146; £573; £286)

Form RPR

32 **1** **Buster Collins (IRE)**[44] 4212 6-11-0 .... BarryFenton 110+
(Miss E C Lavelle) *mstkes: racd freely: mde all and mostly clr: briefly threatened bef 2 out: sn clr again: rdn out* **11/4**[2]

1200 **2** *7* **Mikado**[31] 4461 5-11-7 123.................... NoelFehily 107
(Jonjo O'Neill) *off the pce in midfield: mstke 3rd: reminders 5th: chsd clr ldng pair 7th: rdn after next: chsd wnr bef 2 out: no imp* **4/1**[3]

0 **3** *21* **Zacatecas (GER)**[10] 4754 6-10-7 .... JohnKington(7) 79
(M Scudamore) *hld up in last pair: prog 7th: chsd ldng trio bef 9th: outpcd after 3 out: kpt on to take 3rd flat* **25/1**

4601 **4** *2 1/2* **Witness Run (IRE)**[25] 4581 6-11-7 108.................... LeightonAspell 86+
(N J Gifford) *prom: chsd wnr 5th: clsd 7th: drvn and hld whn mstke 3 out: wknd bef next* **9/4**[1]

0-P **5** *8* **In No Hurry (IRE)**[76] 3646 5-11-0 .... AndrewThornton 69
(M G Quinlan) *hld up in rr: mstke 6th: sme prog after 8th but nvr on terms: shuffled along fr 3 out: kpt on steadily* **33/1**

4 **6** *dist* **Mister Completely (IRE)**[20] 4649 5-11-0 .... JamieGoldstein —
(Miss Sheena West) *a towards rr: wl bhd whn blnd 9th: t.o: btn 78l* **9/1**

P2 **7** *19* **Captain's Legacy**[20] 4649 5-11-0 .... JamesDavies —
(D B Feek) *chsd ldrs: drvn 8th: sn wknd: t.o: btn 96l* **6/1**

0 **8** *3/4* **Doctor Supremo (IRE)**[32] 4455 5-10-9 .... RobertLucey-Butler(5) —
(D B Feek) *stmbld bdly on landing 1st: mstkes and nvr gng wl after: t.o 8th: btn 97l* **50/1**

0-P **P** **Drongo**[143] 2461 5-11-0 .... MarkBradburne —
(Mrs P Robeson) *chsd ldrs: rdn and wknd v rapidly 8th: p.u bef next* **50/1**

05/ **P** **Henry Henbit**[70] 11-10-9 .... JamesDiment(5) —
(Mrs A E Brooks) *mstkes: chsd wnr to 5th: wknd rapidly 8th: t.o whn p.u bef next* **66/1**

5m 25.9s (1.10) **Going Correction** +0.35s/f (Yiel) **10** Ran SP% **113.9**
Speed ratings: **111,108,100,99,96 —,—,—,—,—** CSF £13.51 TOTE £3.60: £1.30, £1.60, £6.10; EX 12.30.
Owner Cockerell Cowing Scotland **Bred** Mrs W H Walter **Trained** Wildhern, Hants

FOCUS
A fair winning time for the grade and the field finished strung out behind the ready winner.

NOTEBOOK
Buster Collins(IRE), runner-up at Newbury last time, ran out a comfortable winner and lost his maiden tag at the fifth time of asking. He stays well, and despite not being the most natural of hurdlers, he should certainly have more to offer when going novice chasing next season. *(tchd 5-2)*
Mikado, easy to back despite dropping markedly in class, stayed on well enough yet never posed a threat to the winner. He has become a disappointing performer in this sphere and looks to be struggling for an optimum trip. *(op 11-4 tchd 9-2)*
Zacatecas(GER) improved a touch on his recent British debut and was doing his best work at the finish. He will no doubt fare better when eligible for a handicap mark after his next assignment.
Witness Run(IRE) failed to get home over this longer trip and has to rate disappointing under his penalty. *(op 11-4)*
Mister Completely(IRE) *Official explanation: jockey said gelding was unsuited by the good to soft (soft in places) ground (op 16-1)*
Captain's Legacy ran well below the form of his latest improved effort over course and distance, but may fare better now he is eligible for a handicap rating. *(op 7-1)*

4869 BRIGHT 106.4 CONDITIONAL JOCKEYS' (S) H'CAP HURDLE (12 hdls) 2m 5f
3:00 (3:00) (Class 5) (0-90,90) 4-Y-0+ **£2,398** (£698; £349)

Form RPR

44U2 **1** **Bonny Boy (IRE)**[10] 4752 11-11-2 **80**....................(vt) WilliamKennedy 81+
(D A Rees) *led 3rd: mde rest: drew clr bef 2 out: pushed out flat* **4/1**[1]

0-P6 **2** *8* **Pintail**[56] 4015 6-10-8 **72**.................... OwynNelmes 63
(Mrs P Robeson) *prom: mostly chsd wnr fr 5th: drvn and no imp bef 2 out* **10/1**

0P44 **3** *13* **Star Time (IRE)**[11] 4734 7-10-2 **74**....................(v) JohnKington(8) 52
(M Scudamore) *mstke 3rd and dropped to rr: reluctant after and sn detached: no ch fr 9th: styd on again fr 3 out to take 3rd flat* **6/1**[3]

0245 **4** *3* **Zeloso**[20] 4652 8-11-5 **86**....................(v) CharliePoste(3) 62+
(M F Harris) *chsd ldrs: rdn 8th: no imp and struggling bef next: mstke 3 out: one pce* **5/1**[2]

P0PP **5** *4* **Swazi Prince**[18] 4662 7-11-4 **90**....................(t) BernieWharfe(8) 61
(N A Twiston-Davies) *in tch: trckd ldng pair 7th: blnd next: effrt to chse wnr 3 out whn mstke: sn drvn and wknd rapidly* **9/1**

0PP6 **6** *13* **Fireside Legend (IRE)**[28] 4526 7-10-12 **76**.................... RobertLucey-Butler 34
(Miss M P Bryant) *hld up in detached last pair: brief effrt 8th: sn outpcd and bhd again* **14/1**

6530 **P** **Sungio**[25] 3125 8-11-3 **81**.................... LiamHeard —
(B P J Baugh) *in tch tl wknd 8th: t.o whn p.u bef 3 out* **8/1**

0602 **P** **Dirty Sanchez**[20] 4651 8-10-12 **76**....................(b[1]) ColinBolger —
(Miss A M Newton-Smith) *led to 3rd: chsd wnr tl stmbld bdly on landing 5th: wknd u.p: p.u bef 8th* **9/1**

5200 **P** **Joe Malone (IRE)**[37] 4341 7-11-2 **80**.................... JamesDiment —
(Mrs A E Brooks) *reluctant to post: s.s: rn in snatches: mstke 5th: drvn 8th : wkng whn slow next: t.o whn p.u bef 2 out* **7/1**

5m 30.1s (5.30) **Going Correction** +0.35s/f (Yiel) **9** Ran SP% **110.3**
Speed ratings: **103,99,95,93,92 87,—,—,—** CSF £39.79 CT £221.64 TOTE £3.90: £1.80, £3.80, £2.20; EX 55.90.There was no bid for the winner.
Owner D Rees **Bred** Airlie Stud **Trained** Clarbeston, Pembrokes

■ Stewards' Enquiry : Bernie Wharfe one-day ban: used whip when out of contention and also when mount showing no response (Apr 27)

FOCUS
A dire event that saw the field finish strung out.

NOTEBOOK
Bonny Boy(IRE) came home to win with authority under an enterprising ride over this shorter trip. He has found a new lease of life since switching back to hurdling and, while this was a very weak event, he may well go in again at this level in the coming weeks. *(tchd 9-2)*
Pintail, having his first outing in this grade, posted his most encouraging effort to date despite not *really looking to get home all that well over the longer trip. He has clearly now found his level. (op 12-1)*
Star Time(IRE) ran in snatches and continues to look out of sorts. *(tchd 13-2)*
Zeloso failed to raise his game on this drop back in grade and is one to avoid. *(op 4-1)*

4870 TOTESPORT.COM NOVICES' CHASE (12 fncs) 2m 1f
3:30 (3:33) (Class 4) 5-Y-0+ **£5,079** (£1,549; £809; £439)

Form RPR

-611 **1** **Mr Boo (IRE)**[5] 4822 7-11-7 105.................... PhilipHide 128+
(G L Moore) *trckd ldng pair: nt fluent 6th: wnt 2nd next: led on inner bef 2 out: mstke 2 out: cruised clr bef last* **1/2**[1]

30-1 **2** *19* **Appach (FR)**[291] 862 7-11-0 103.................... AndrewThornton 109+
(J W Mullins) *hld up in tch: mstke 3rd: trckd ldng pair 8th: effrt bef 2 out: no ch w wnr after* **7/2**[2]

00FP **3** *10* **Spiritual Society (IRE)**[22] 4618 6-10-7 103.................... JohnKington(7) 99+
(M Scudamore) *s.s: hld up in rr: effrt after 8th gng wl: mstke 3 out and outpcd: trying to cl whn hmpd 2 out: no ch after* **10/1**[3]

6602 **4** *dist* **Stopwatch (IRE)**[28] 4525 11-11-0 57....................(p) BenjaminHitchcott —
(Mrs L C Jewell) *chsd ldr to 7th: sn rdn: wknd 3 out: t.o: btn 60l* **33/1**

005U **R** **Tails I Win**[28] 4525 7-11-0 61.................... MarkBradburne —
(Miss C J E Caroe) *in tch tl wknd rapidly 7th: t.o whn blnd next: over a fence bhd whn ref 2 out* **40/1**

-F35 **F** **Prato (GER)**[48] 4150 6-11-0 98....................(b) JamieMoore 103+
(C Von Der Recke, Germany) *led at str pce: blnd 3rd: j.big next: hdd and btn whn crashing fall 2 out: winded* **14/1**

4m 26.5s (2.40) **Going Correction** +0.35s/f (Yiel) **6** Ran SP% **110.0**
Speed ratings: **108,99,94,—,—** — CSF £2.67 TOTE £1.50: £1.10, £1.60; EX 2.10.
Owner The Hon Mrs C Cameron **Bred** Mrs Eleanor Hadden **Trained** Woodingdean, E Sussex

FOCUS
A moderate novice chase and another event which again saw the field come home strung out.

NOTEBOOK
Mr Boo(IRE), reverting to novice company in this quest for the hat-trick, ultimately came home to score as he pleased and showed no signs of his exertions from having scored at Fontwell four days previously. He is clearly in the form of his life at present and it is unlikely we have seen the best of him just yet. *(op 4-7 tchd 4-6)*
Appach(FR), last seen breaking his duck at Worcester in June 2005, was eventually firmly put in his place by the winner and shaped as though the race was needed. He ought to be sharper next time. *(op 11-4 tchd 5-2)*
Spiritual Society(IRE) lost ground at the start and was never a serious player thereafter. He is a headstrong character, and has been disappointing since joining current connections, but he had some fair form over timber in Ireland and may fare better in handicaps from his current rating, so is not one to write off yet. *(op 14-1)*
Prato(GER) took a very heavy fall and does not look a natural over fences by any means. *(op 16-1)*

4871 TOTECOURSE TO COURSE CLASSIFIED HURDLE (9 hdls) 2m
4:00 (4:01) (Class 5) 4-Y-0+ **£2,740** (£798; £399)

Form RPR

P0-6 **1** **Dance With Wolves (FR)**[11] 4731 6-10-9 88....(p) RobertLucey-Butler(5) 94
(Jim Best) *trckd ldrs: pushed along 6th: drvn to chse ldng pair 2 out: hung lft flat: r.o to ld nr fin* **5/1**[3]

0P00 **2** *3/4* **Amnesty**[5] 4427 7-11-0 90....................(b) JamieMoore 94+
(G L Moore) *hld up: prog to trck ldrs 3 out: cruised into ld bef 2 out: idled in front and drvn: hdd nr fin* **7/2**[1]

30U0 **3** *2 1/2* **Cois Na Tine Eile**[32] 4450 4-10-6 90.................... AntonyEvans 83
(N A Twiston-Davies) *hld up in rr: pushed along bef 3 out: sn prog on inner: jnd ldr 2 out: nt qckn u.p fr last* **14/1**

1054 **4** *18* **Silistra**[48] 4153 7-11-0 87....................(p) BenjaminHitchcott 73
(Mrs L C Jewell) *chsd ldrs: rdn 6th: sn outpcd and struggling: plugged on again fr 2 out* **14/1**

3120 **5** *4* **Percipient**[250] 1188 8-10-9 89....................(v) SamCurling(5) 69
(D R Gandolfo) *disp ld to 5th: led again 6th to 3 out: wknd rapidly 2 out* **12/1**

2332 **6** *4* **Native Commander (IRE)**[26] 4556 11-10-9 90..... ChristopherMurray(5) 65
(Miss Sheena West) *trckd ldrs: led 3 out: hdd & wknd rapidly bef next* **6/1**

0000 **7** *5* **Allez Melina**[18] 4661 5-10-6 87.................... JohnnyLevins(5) 57
(Mrs A J Hamilton-Fairley) *lost tch 3rd and sn wl bhd: no ch after: plugged on u.p fr 3 out* **14/1**

603 **8** *7* **Positano (IRE)**[35] 4388 6-10-7 89....................(v[1]) JohnKington(7) 53
(M Scudamore) *t.k.h: trckd ldng pair: led and hit 5th: hdd next: wknd rapidly after 3 out* **20/1**

3413 **9** *2* **Isam Top (FR)**[75] 3661 10-11-0 89.................... LeightonAspell 51
(M J Hogan) *in tch to 6th: sn struggling and bhd* **9/2**[2]

605 **P** **Love Beauty (USA)**[49] 4128 4-10-4 88....................(v[1]) CharliePoste(5) —
(M F Harris) *disp ld to 5th: wknd rapidly and mstke next: t.o whn mstke 3 out and p.u* **16/1**

000 P **Nemetan (FR)**[26] 4564 5-11-0 88 AndrewThornton —
(R H Alner) *hld up: reminders 5th: prog on outer to press ldrs next: j. bdly rt 3 out: 7th and btn whn blnd 2 out and p.u* **25/1**

4m 9.00s (7.80) **Going Correction** +0.35s/f (Yiel)
WFA 4 from 5yo+ 5lb **11** Ran SP% **113.5**
Speed ratings: **94,93,92,83,81 79,76,73,72,—** — CSF £22.46 TOTE £5.50: £2.40, £1.90, £4.30; EX 24.10.
Owner Leon Best **Bred** E Libaud **Trained** Lewes, E Sussex
■ Stewards' Enquiry : Jamie Moore one-day ban: used whip with excessive frequency (Apr 27)

FOCUS
A modest winning time for a race of its class and the first three came well clear.

NOTEBOOK
Dance With Wolves(FR), with the cheekpieces back on, dug deep under pressure from the last flight and eventually reeled in the idling runner-up on the run-in to score. This was his first success since joining connections from France in 2004, and just his second overall, and he is unlikely to follow-up from a higher mark. *(op 9-2)*
Amnesty held every chance under top weight, but not for the first-time, he found very little when in front and really has become a fiendishly tricky ride. *(tchd 10-3)*
Cois Na Tine Eile had her chance, and posted an improved effort, but was still firmly put in her place after the last flight. *(op 10-1)*
Silistra ideally wants further, but she still ran close to her recent moderate level, and helps to set the level of this form.
Native Commander(IRE) was given a more positive ride than has often been the case in the past yet, after hitting the front seemingly full of running, he found nothing and faded very disappointingly thereafter. *(op 7-1)*

4872 RAY HUNT MEMORIAL NOVICES' H'CAP CHASE (18 fncs) 3m 2f
4:30 (4:31) (Class 5) (0-95,93) 5-Y-0+ £3,143 (£936; £474; £243; £127)

Form				RPR
PP43	1		**Roddy The Vet (IRE)**[18] 4662 8-10-8 75 (b) JimCrowley **5/1**[3] (A Ennis) *trckd ldr: shkn up after 13th: led sn after 3 out: forged clr*	90
4146	2	14	**Rosetown (IRE)**[36] 4370 8-11-2 83 (b) PJBrennan **10/3**[1] (T R George) *led: mstke 11th: narrow ld whn blnd 3 out: sn hdd and btn*	86+
2134	3	18	**Twenty Degrees**[20] 4653 8-11-12 93 (b) PhilipHide **6/1** (G L Moore) *trckd ldrs: nt fluent 13th and sn outpcd: n.d fr next: plugged on into modest 3rd 2 out*	76
3P3	4	13	**Waynesworld (IRE)**[118] 2922 8-11-3 91 JohnKington[(7)] **13/2** (M Scudamore) *hld up: mstke 5th: hmpd 11th: outpcd fr 13th: wnt modest 3rd 4 out to 2 out: wknd*	61
6035	5	4	**Mandica (IRE)**[11] 4735 8-11-5 93 (v) WillieMcCarthy[(7)] **4/1**[2] (T R George) *hld up: mstke 6th: j.lft 11th: chsd ldng pair 13th: sn outpcd: wknd 4 out*	59
FP3-	P		**Couldn't Be Phar (IRE)**[360] 4939 9-10-12 84 (b) SamCurling[(5)] **10/1** (D R Gandolfo) *trckd ldrs tl wknd 10th: t.o whn p.u after 13th*	—
0F02	P		**Unusual Suspect**[30] 4474 7-11-12 93 (b) JamieMoore **13/2** (G L Moore) *chsd ldrs: nt fluent 7th: u.p fr 9th: wknd 12th: p.u after next*	—

7m 5.50s (11.50) **Going Correction** +0.35s/f (Yiel)
WFA 5 from 6yo+ 8lb **7** Ran SP% **109.8**
Speed ratings: **96,91,86,82,80** —,— CSF £20.71 CT £92.74 TOTE £6.40: £3.20, £2.10; EX 16.70.
Owner A T A Wates **Bred** John O'Brien **Trained** Beare Green, Surrey

FOCUS
A weak novices' handicap which produced a modest winning time. The form should be treated with caution.

NOTEBOOK
Roddy The Vet(IRE) took full advantage of Rosetown's blunder three from home and ultimately ran out a clear-cut winner. He has been improved by the recent application of blinkers, but no doubt his connections will be praying the Handicapper does not take this form too literally. *(op 11-2)*
Rosetown(IRE), not for the first time, lost his chance with a blunder at a crucial stage and was eventually well beaten by the winner. He has the ability to win from this mark, but his jumping remains a real cause for concern. *(op 7-2)*
Twenty Degrees ran a fairly tame race and looked non-stayer over this longer trip. *(op 11-2 tchd 5-1)*
Waynesworld(IRE) put in what appeared a moody effort and still looks too high in the weights at present. *(op 6-1 tchd 7-1)*
Mandica(IRE) appeared to lose his confidence after a mistake at the sixth fence and is capable of better than this on a going day. *(op 9-2 tchd 5-1)*

4873 TOTEEXACTA H'CAP CHASE (14 fncs) 2m 4f
5:00 (5:00) (Class 4) (0-100,96) 5-Y-0+
£4,384 (£1,295; £647; £324; £161; £81)

Form				RPR
0460	1		**The Newsman (IRE)**[99] 3284 14-11-9 93 MickFitzgerald **16/1** (G Wareham) *chsd ldrs: outpcd after 9th and sn wl adrift: styd on again fr 4 out: chsd ldr 2 out: led last: drvn and kpt on gamely*	109
4362	2	¾	**Ri Na Realta (IRE)**[7] 4804 11-11-3 87 AndrewThornton **9/2**[2] (J W Mullins) *settled wl in rr: rapid prog 9th: hit 4 out: led sn after 3 out and drvn 5l clr: hdd last: nt qckn flat*	102+
562U	3	8	**Sweet Minuet**[8] 4785 9-10-7 82 RobertLucey-Butler[(5)] **14/1** (M Madgwick) *trckd ldrs: outpcd fr 3 out: kpt on same pce fr next*	89
0143	4	7	**Jack Fuller (IRE)**[21] 4639 9-11-12 96 (b) LeightonAspell **5/1**[3] (P Winkworth) *hld up: trckd ldrs fr 5th: mstke 6th: effrt to chse ldr 4 out to next: fdd next*	96
4UP2	5	12	**Myson (IRE)**[20] 4652 7-11-10 94 (b) JamesDavies **4/1**[1] (D B Feek) *hld up in rr: drvn and struggling in last after 8th: sn adrift: n.d fr 10th*	82
P2	6	10	**Ehab (IRE)**[18] 4662 7-10-7 80 (t) ColinBolger[(3)] **9/1** (Miss A M Newton-Smith) *chsd ldr to 4 out: wknd fr next*	58
U253	7	9	**Sett Aside**[20] 4653 8-10-6 76 (p) BenjaminHitchcott **8/1** (Mrs L C Jewell) *chsd ldr to 4 out: wkng whn blnd 3 out*	45
FP53	8	½	**Galapiat Du Mesnil (FR)**[80] 3582 12-10-12 82 PhilipHide **16/1** (R Gurney) *in tch to 9th: sn wknd and bhd*	51
0P22	P		**Major Belle (FR)**[19] 4659 7-10-13 83 HenryOliver **6/1** (John R Upson) *racd wd: mstke 4th: nvr gng wl after: t.o whn p.u bef 9th*	—
1420	P		**Julies Boy (IRE)**[34] 4426 9-11-5 96 (t) WillieMcCarthy[(7)] **12/1** (T R George) *led at gd pce: hdd sn after 3 out: wknd next: 5th and no ch last: p.u and dismntd nr fin*	—

5m 19.6s (1.15) **Going Correction** +0.35s/f (Yiel) **10** Ran SP% **116.4**
Speed ratings: **111,110,107,104,99 95,92,92,—,—** CSF £88.43 CT £1051.48 TOTE £24.20: £4.90, £1.50, £4.60; EX 100.40.
Owner G Wareham **Bred** Miss Maeve Chadwick **Trained** Findon, Sussex

FOCUS
This was a fair winning time for the class, and it produced a cracking finish between the first two, who finished clear.

NOTEBOOK
The Newsman(IRE) came from a long way off the pace to grind down his rivals in the home straight and eventually won this going away under a fine ride by Fitzgerald. He looks to have benefited from a recent break and, considering he is happiest on faster ground, may well be able to find another race during the summer despite a higher mark.
Ri Na Realta(IRE) looked all over the winner when sweeping to the front turning for home, but despite doing nothing wrong thereafter, he could not cope with the winner's late challenge. Ideally he needs to be produced as late as possible in his races and, considering he finished well clear of the rest, he ought to go one better before too long. *(op 3-1)*
Sweet Minuet ran her race and, when faced with a stiffer test, may be able to find a race during the summer from this mark. *(op 12-1)*
Jack Fuller(IRE) found just the same pace when it mattered and looks in need of some respite from the Handicapper on this evidence. *(op 13-2)*
Myson(IRE), raised 9lb for finishing second in first-time blinkers at this track previously, ran no sort of race and the headgear clearly failed to have the same effect

4874 TOTESPORT 0800 221 221 H'CAP HURDLE (14 hdls) 3m 1f 110y
5:30 (5:30) (Class 5) (0-95,96) 4-Y-0+ £3,083 (£898; £449)

Form				RPR
2235	1		**Kyno (IRE)**[56] 4012 5-11-12 95 (t) MickFitzgerald **7/2**[1] (M G Quinlan) *hld up in rr: stdy prog 11th: effrt after 3 out: led next: rdn clr fr last*	98+
0P-1	2	3½	**Festival Flyer**[38] 4331 11-11-2 90 DarylJacob[(5)] **4/1**[2] (Miss M Bragg) *prom: trckd ldr 7th: led after 10th: drvn and hdd 2 out: no ex fr last*	89
5/65	3	11	**Carthago (IRE)**[27] 4549 9-11-5 95 AndrewGlassonbury[(7)] **12/1** (Miss T McCurrich) *cl up: jnd ldr after 10th: stil upsides after 3 out: wknd next*	83
6136	4	6	**Geography (IRE)**[5] 4824 6-10-12 86 (p) RobertLucey-Butler[(5)] **10/1** (P Butler) *hld up wl in rr: stdy prog fr 11th to trck ldrs 3 out: wknd next*	68
40P0	5	8	**Dan's Man**[44] 4210 5-11-10 93 AntonyEvans **15/2** (N A Twiston-Davies) *in tch: prog to chse ldrs 8th: rdn 10th: wknd 3 out*	67
04P4	6	17	**Emphatic (IRE)**[10] 4752 11-11-7 90 (b) PJBrennan **6/1** (J G Portman) *unable to ld and sn dropped to rr: lost tch after 9th: t.o*	47
5P04	7	9	**Full On**[32] 4453 9-11-12 95 (b[1]) ChristianWilliams **5/1**[3] (A M Hales) *t.k.h: led: hdd after 10th: wknd rapidly bef 3 out*	43
0052	P		**Elle Roseador**[21] 4640 7-11-5 88 (p) JamieGoldstein **11/1** (M Madgwick) *racd wd: struggling fr 6th: wknd 8th: p.u after 10th*	—
00-0	P		**Boring Goring (IRE)**[343] 233 12-11-6 96 ow6 MrGordon[(7)] **33/1** (E J Farrant) *t.k.h: trckd ldr tl 7th: wkng in last whn p.u bef 8th*	—

6m 48.4s (12.50) **Going Correction** +0.35s/f (Yiel) **9** Ran SP% **113.0**
Speed ratings: **94,92,89,87,85 80,77,—,—** CSF £17.88 CT £147.11 TOTE £3.50: £1.80, £1.70, £4.40; EX 10.90 Place 6 £54.76, Place 5 £18.83.
Owner Liam Mulryan **Bred** Pat Tobin **Trained** Newmarket, Suffolk

FOCUS
A modest winning time and the first two came clear.

NOTEBOOK
Kyno(IRE), up in trip, belatedly lost his maiden tag at the tenth attempt in ready fashion under a strong ride by Fitzgerald - who is clearly riding at the top of his game at present. He ought to be high on confidence now and should have more to offer over this sort of distance. *(op 3-1)*
Festival Flyer, raised 8lb for winning at Wincanton last time, turned in a sound effort yet failed to get home all that well over the longer trip. He was nicely clear of the rest at the finish and remains capable of winning again from this mark. *(op 7-2)*
Carthago(IRE) ◆ did not appear to really get home, but still turned in his best effort since switching from France. He has clearly had his problems, yet considering he once beat Stormez over hurdles in 2001, he could interesting from this sort of mark should connections get him to rekindle old enthusiasm. *(tchd 14-1)*
Geography(IRE) looks to have gone off the boil at present and did little to convince he stays this far. *(tchd 11-1)*
Dan's Man *(op 11-1)*
Full On was lit-up by the first-time blinkers through the early parts and ultimately failed to get home. *(tchd 6-1)*
Boring Goring(IRE) *Official explanation: jockey said gelding had a breathing problem*
T/Plt: £37.10 to a £1 stake. Pool: £55,743.85. 1,095.55 winning tickets. T/Qpdt: £25.80 to a £1 stake. Pool: £3,786.50. 108.30 winning tickets. JN

4576 TOWCESTER (R-H)
Sunday, April 16

OFFICIAL GOING: Good to soft (good in places)
Wind: Fresh, across Weather: Sunny spells giving way to cloud

4875 GALA CASINO SOL CENTRAL, NORTHAMPTON MAIDEN HURDLE (10 hdls) 2m 3f 110y
2:10 (2:11) (Class 4) 4-Y-0+ £3,802 (£1,123; £561; £280; £140)

Form				RPR
4-53	1		**Giovanna**[41] 4280 5-10-9 WarrenMarston **9/2**[1] (R T Phillips) *hld up: hdwy 5th: led after 3 out: clr last: styd on*	96+
0602	2	5	**A Few Kind Words (IRE)**[18] 4665 5-10-9 RichardSpate[(7)] **12/1** (Mrs K Waldron) *hld up in tch: rdn appr 2 out: styd on same pce last*	95
4434	3	1	**Maryscross (IRE)**[21] 4644 6-10-9 TomSiddall **11/1** (O Brennan) *hld up: hdwy after 3 out: rdn appr last: styd on same pce*	87
4P14	4	10	**Top Ram (IRE)**[38] 4326 6-11-2 JasonMaguire **9/2**[1] (J A B Old) *chsd ldr tl led 3rd: hdd after 3 out: j.lft next: sn wknd*	86+
40	5	7	**Dinnie Flanagan (IRE)**[7] 4787 6-11-2 RichardJohnson **8/1**[2] (P C Haslam) *hld up in tch: j.lft 5th: wknd appr 2 out*	77
0P62	6	1¼	**Lookafterme (IRE)**[26] 4562 6-11-2 WayneHutchinson **16/1** (A W Carroll) *prom tl wknd after 3 out*	76
440	7	7	**Solent Sunbeam**[36] 4376 6-10-10 ow1 JohnMcNamara **14/1** (K C Bailey) *bhd fr 4th: nvr nrr*	63
4P	8	4	**Stoney Drove (FR)**[123] 2829 6-11-2 PaulMoloney **33/1** (Miss H C Knight) *hld up: hdwy 6th: wknd appr 3 out*	65
5	9	25	**Airgusta (IRE)**[41] 4280 5-11-2 JimmyMcCarthy **10/1** (C P Morlock) *hld up: hdwy 6th: wknd after 3 out*	40
	10	dist	**Just Buddy** 5-10-9 JohnPritchard[(7)] **66/1** (R Dickin) *a in rr: bhd fr 4th: t.o whn blnd last*	—
45	P		**Karrie**[58] 3961 5-10-2 TomMessenger[(7)] **66/1** (C C Bailey) *chsd ldrs to 7th: t.o whn p.u bef last*	—
4/	P		**Gingerslookingreat (IRE)**[1064] 334 7-11-2 TomDoyle **40/1** (O Brennan) *hld up: a in rr: t.o whn p.u bef 7th*	—

The Form Book, Raceform Ltd, Compton, RG20 6NL

	P	**Tout Les Sous**[655] 5-10-9 .... MrMWall(7)	—
		(B W Duke) *chsd ldrs: mstke 2nd: wknd and hit 6th: t.o whn p.u bef last* **80/1**	
/04-	P	**Midnight Spirit**[364] [4878] 6-11-2 .... SeanCurran	—
		(F E Sutherland) *led to 3rd: wknd 5th: t.o whn p.u bef 2 out* **100/1**	
	P	**Brave Benefactor (IRE)** 6-11-2 .... RobertThornton	—
		(B G Powell) *chsd ldrs: lost pl 3rd: bhd fr 5th: t.o whn p.u bef 7th* **10/1**	
	P	**Never So Blue (FR)**[308] 5-11-2 .... SamThomas	—
		(Miss Venetia Williams) *hld up: hdwy 6th: wknd appr 3 out: t.o whn p.u bef next* **9/1**[3]	

5m 1.50s (-14.30) **Going Correction** -0.725s/f (Firm) **16** Ran SP% **114.8**
Speed ratings: **99,97,96,92,89 89,86,84,74,**— —,—,—,—,— — CSF £54.55 TOTE £4.90: £1.70, £3.60, £4.90; EX 48.80.
Owner Dozen Dreamers Partnership **Bred** Crandon Park Stud **Trained** Adlestrop, Gloucs

FOCUS
A fair maiden hurdle and Giovanna did it extrremely well.

NOTEBOOK
Giovanna ◆, fourth in last season's Listed mares bumper at Antree, has taken her time to get going over hurdles, but she looked at her best here and came through to win comfortably under Marston, wandering around under pressure but always having things under control. She has the potential to be useful and may be one to keep on-side in the coming weeks. *(tchd 4-1)*
A Few Kind Words(IRE) has taken well to hurdles and he confirmed his recent 100/1 second at Taunton to be no fluke with a staying-on second. Three miles is likely to help the gelding in time and he can find a race of this nature. *(op 16-1)*
Maryscross(IRE), a winning pointer who ran many good races in defeat in bumpers, made a pleasing switch to hurdles and was going on at the end as if to suggest she will stay further in time.
Top Ram(IRE), successful in a bumper here back in February, for whatever reason seems a bit in-and-out and he failed to live up to expectations on this hurdling debut, dropping away tamely in the straight. *(op 7-2)*
Dinnie Flanagan(IRE) has yet to build on a promising debut effort, but he is now qualified for handicaps and may well do better in that sphere. *(op 15-2 tchd 9-1)*

4876 GALA CASINO - JOIN TODAY, PLAY TODAY H'CAP CHASE (18 fncs) 3m 110y
2:40 (2:41) (Class 4) (0-100,99) 5-Y-0+**£3,802** (£1,123; £561; £280; £140)

Form				RPR
5-51	**1**		**Would You Believe**[25] [4576] 10-11-12 99 .... RichardJohnson	121
			(P J Hobbs) *prom: led 9th tl 10th: nt fluent 12th: led again 14th: drew wl clr fr 2 out: drvn out: unchal* **10/3**[1]	
352U	**2**	*18*	**Dun Locha Castle (IRE)**[20] [4650] 11-10-7 80 .... TomScudamore	84
			(N R Mitchell) *rdn 7th: hdwy 11th: urged along to chse ldrs fr 14th: wnt 2nd bef last: no ch w wnr but plugged on* **9/1**	
445P	**3**	*6*	**Caper**[47] [4164] 6-10-9 82 .... TomDoyle	83+
			(R Hollinshead) *hld up and bhd: stdy prog 11th: 4l 5th and effrt whn mstke 3 out: one pce and no ch fr next* **16/1**	
5223	**4**	*1*	**Bay Island (IRE)**[11] [4728] 10-11-12 99 ....(tp) PaulMoloney	96
			(Carl Llewellyn) *led tl 8th and again 9th tl 14th: chsd wnr tl outpcd and j.rt 2 out: wkng whn j.rt last* **4/1**[2]	
U402	**5**	*24*	**Happy Hussar (IRE)**[37] [4356] 13-11-5 97 .... DrPPritchard(5)	70
			(Dr P Pritchard) *blnd 2nd: bhd: lost tch 6th: plugged rnd in hopeless pursuit: t.o* **12/1**	
31PP	**6**	*dist*	**Heartache**[49] [4130] 9-10-5 78 ....(b) RJGreene	—
			(R Mathew) *prom: rdn 14th: fdd bdly bef 2 out: crashed over last: btn 94l* **14/1**	
1115	**P**		**Tallow Bay (IRE)**[20] [4650] 11-10-10 90 .... MrGTumelty(7)	—
			(Mrs S Wall) *nvr gng wl: lost tch 6th: p.u 8th* **11/1**	
P0P	**P**		**Jesnic (IRE)**[87] [3460] 6-9-7 73 oh2 .... JohnPritchard(7)	—
			(R Dickin) *hdwy 9th: cl up 11th: sn drvn: wknd 13th: t.o and p.u 2 out* **22/1**	
6400	**P**		**Strong Magic (IRE)**[25] [4576] 14-11-3 90 .... RichardHobson	—
			(J R Cornwall) *chsd ldr tl 5th: wknd 8th: sn bhd: t.o and p.u 15th* **50/1**	
5502	**P**		**Moscow Leader (IRE)**[61] [3915] 8-11-10 97 .... WarrenMarston	—
			(R T Phillips) *midfield: hit 7th: lost pl next: struggling whn p.u 10th* **8/1**[3]	
3300	**P**		**Channahrlie (IRE)**[11] [4737] 12-10-0 83 ....(p) JosephStevenson(10)	—
			(R Dickin) *wnt 2nd 5th tl 8th: rdn bef 12th: sn wknd: t.o and p.u 2 out* **16/1**	
-0PP	**P**		**Jackem (IRE)**[11] [4737] 12-10-5 78 .... WayneHutchinson	—
			(Ian Williams) *towards rr: stuggling whn pckd 14th: mstke next: t.o and p.u 3 out* **20/1**	
44F4	**P**		**Mobasher (IRE)**[21] [4633] 7-11-10 97 .... SamThomas	—
			(Miss Venetia Williams) *j. modly: rdn 8th: nt gng wl after: lost tch 12th: mstke next: t.o and p.u 3 out* **10/1**	

6m 22.1s (-24.50) **Going Correction** -0.725s/f (Firm) **13** Ran SP% **118.8**
Speed ratings: **110,104,102,102,94** —,—,—,—,— —,—,— CSF £32.95 CT £427.59 TOTE £3.30: £1.60, £2.50, £8.00; EX 33.20.
Owner D Allen **Bred** Shade Oak Stud **Trained** Withycombe, Somerset

FOCUS
A poor handicap but a fair winning time for a race of its class.

NOTEBOOK
Would You Believe, finally off the mark at the course last month, was up 8lb, but he seems to have improved and had little trouble defying the rise, scooting clear in the straight to win with any amount in hand. The lightly-raced ten-year-old may yet be capable of better and a hat-trick is a distinct possibility in this sort of form. *(op 11-4)*
Dun Locha Castle(IRE) is a gallant old boy, but he finds winning tough and it was a shame to see his effort again go unrewarded. He is consistent at this sort of level, and it is hoped he gains a deserved win sooner rather than later. *(op 10-1)*
Caper ◆, whose lack of chasing experience, having completed only once from two starts, looked a major drawback here, loomed into a dangerous position only to make a blunder at the third-last which effectively ended his winning chance. It will be disappointing if he cannot find a race off this sort of mark. *(op 20-1 tchd 22-1)*
Bay Island(IRE), a tough gelding who often runs his race, took them along in his customary fashion, but he did not find a great deal once coming under maximum pressure and a string of hard races may have taken their toll. He has also gone up 13lb in the weights without winning and looks best left alone for the moment. *(op 11-2)*
Happy Hussar(IRE) kept going in his own time but was never in with a chance. *(op 10-1)*
Heartache ran well to a point, but he stopped abruptly under pressure and only just managed to get over the last. *(op 11-1)*
Tallow Bay(IRE) *Official explanation: jockey said gelding never travelled (op 12-1)*

4877 GALA CASINO REGENT STREET, NORTHAMPTON JUVENILE NOVICES' HURDLE (8 hdls) 2m
3:10 (3:10) (Class 4) 4-Y-0 **£4,436** (£1,310; £655; £327; £163)

Form				RPR
121	**1**		**Heathcote**[62] [3898] 4-11-3 116 .... EamonDehdashti(5)	116+
			(G L Moore) *a.p: chsd ldr 4th: led appr 2 out: styd on wl* **9/4**[2]	
5	**2**	*6*	**Paddys Tern**[34] [4416] 4-10-7 .... TJPhelan(3)	94+
			(N M Babbage) *led: clr 4th: hit 3 out: hdd bef next: no ex last* **33/1**	
6P	**3**	*7*	**Ngauruhoe (IRE)**[21] [4631] 4-10-3 ow7 .... MrMatthewSmith(7)	87+
			(John Berry) *hld up: hdwy and mstke 5th: wknd after 2 out* **20/1**	
4632	**4**	*½*	**Whistle Blowing (IRE)**[27] [4551] 4-10-10 105 .... GLee	86
			(D McCain) *chsd ldrs: rdn after 3 out: wknd bef next* **7/4**[1]	
2	**5**	*5*	**Almavara (USA)**[20] [4648] 4-10-10 .... JimmyMcCarthy	82+
			(C P Morlock) *chsd ldrs: rdn after 4th: wknd appr 2 out* **9/2**[3]	
	6	*12*	**Joey**[132] 4-9-7 .... AdamHawkins(10)	62
			(R Hollinshead) *hld up: mstke 4th: hdwy after next: wknd appr 2 out* **28/1**	
0	**7**	*11*	**Neardown Bishop**[21] [4631] 4-10-3 .... MrSRees(7)	58
			(M Wigham) *dwlt: sn mid-div: lost pl after next: sn wl bhd* **100/1**	
0	**8**	*21*	**Son Of Sophie**[21] [4631] 4-10-10 .... RJGreene	37
			(C N Kellett) *hld up: mstke 3rd: rdn next: wknd after 5th* **80/1**	
0	**9**	*15*	**Suivez Moi (IRE)**[44] [4211] 4-10-10 .... DaveCrosse	22
			(M F Harris) *hld up: effrt appr 3 out: sn wknd: bhd whn blnd last* **10/1**	
0	**10**	*3½*	**Callitquits (IRE)**[22] [4613] 4-10-10 .... AlanO'Keeffe	18
			(Jennie Candlish) *hld up: rdn 4th: sn lost tch* **100/1**	
P	**11**	*29*	**Zagreus (GER)**[186] [1718] 4-10-10 .... SeanCurran	—
			(F E Sutherland) *hld up: bhd fr 4th* **80/1**	
PP6	**P**		**Don Pasquale**[9] [1441] 4-10-10 .... JohnMcNamara	—
			(J T Stimpson) *chsd ldrs: mstke 3rd: wknd appr 3 out: t.o whn p.u bef next* **80/1**	

4m 3.80s (-7.60) **Going Correction** -0.725s/f (Firm) **12** Ran SP% **111.2**
Speed ratings: **90,87,83,83,80 74,69,58,51,49 35,**— CSF £69.51 TOTE £3.20: £1.30, £4.10, £6.60; EX 57.20.
Owner B Siddle & B D Haynes **Bred** Miss K Rausing **Trained** Woodingdean, E Sussex

FOCUS
A modest juvenile contest with a moderate winning time.

NOTEBOOK
Heathcote, who faced a simple task when winning his second race over hurdles at Plumpton in February, had a bit more to do here, but he did it just as cosily and failed to meet a challenge from his main rivals. *He will stay further than two miles in time, and could be of interest in handicaps (op 15-8)*
Paddys Tern stepped up markedly on his initial outing over hurdles and he kept on well enough to claim a clear second. Providing he can build on this, it is not hard to see him picking up a small race.
Ngauruhoe(IRE) had looked nothing better than poor in two previous starts, but this was better and she is now qualified for handicaps, a sphere she is likely to do better in. *(op 16-1)*
Whistle Blowing(IRE) appeared to hold obvious claims for his in-form stable and he was rightly made favourite in receipt of 7lb from Heathcote. He failed to run to form however and it is possible the stiff track did not suit the gelding. *(op 5-2)*
Almavara(USA) was unable to step up on his debut second and it may be he does not win until tackling handicaps, for which he will be qualified after another run. *(op 7-2)*

4878 GALA CASINO NORTHAMPTON - PLAY & PARTY NOVICES' H'CAP CHASE (13 fncs 1 omitted) 2m 3f 110y
3:40 (3:41) (Class 3) (0-120,116) 5-Y-0 **£6,338** (£1,872; £936; £468; £234)

Form				RPR
000U	**1**		**Mokum (FR)**[37] [4355] 5-10-0 94 oh4 .... WayneHutchinson	103+
			(A W Carroll) *bhd: reminders after 6th: nt fluent 8th: stl 6th and rdn 2 out: chal outer ent st: led bef last: drvn and r.o wl* **10/1**	
4240	**2**	*6*	**Rookery Lad**[21] [4639] 8-9-13 94 .... MrTJO'Brien(5)	100
			(C N Kellett) *led 2nd tl 4th: led again 6th: rdn and racd awkwardly and hdd bef last: wknd flat* **11/2**	
2110	**3**	*19*	**The Outlier (IRE)**[44] [4214] 8-11-12 116 .... SamThomas	105+
			(Miss Venetia Williams) *pressed ldrs: rdn and ev ch bef 3 out: fdd on v long run to last: fin tired* **4/1**[1]	
1U00	**4**	*6*	**Bishop's Bridge (IRE)**[43] [4239] 8-11-9 116 .... GinoCarenza(3)	97
			(Andrew Turnell) *prom: volley of reminders 4th: ev ch 3 out: 2nd briefly home turn: fdd on long run to last: fin v tired* **12/1**	
3421	**5**	*3½*	**Merry Storm (IRE)**[18] [4662] 7-10-4 101 ....(t) RichardSpate(7)	79
			(Mrs K Waldron) *hld up trcking ldrs: effrt and ev ch 3 out: sn wknd* **5/1**[3]	
3360	**6**	*20*	**Flying Fuselier**[129] [2733] 7-10-12 102 .... RichardJohnson	60
			(P J Hobbs) *midfield and cl up: rdn and lost tch bef 3 out: t.o* **8/1**	
P011	**F**		**Kirov King (IRE)**[7] [4798] 6-10-7 104 7ex .... MrGGallagher(7)	—
			(R H York) *taken down early: plld hrd: crashing fall 3rd: dead* **9/2**[2]	
060-	**P**		**Celtic Vision (IRE)**[507] [2447] 10-10-0 90 ....(t) BarryKeniry	—
			(P C Haslam) *a last: j. slowly 6th and lost tch: t.o and clambering over fences after tl p.u 3 out* **11/1**	
044P	**P**		**Prince Of Persia**[57] [3993] 6-11-9 113 ....(p) JohnMcNamara	—
			(R S Brookhouse) *led tl 2nd and 4th tl 6th: pressed ldr tl 3 out: wknd qckly: t.o and p.u bef omitted 2 out* **12/1**	

5m 6.20s (-13.80) **Going Correction** -0.725s/f (Firm) course record
WFA 5 from 6yo+ 3lb **9** Ran SP% **114.2**
Speed ratings: **98,95,88,85,84 76,**—,—,— CSF £63.90 CT £258.25 TOTE £11.80: £2.90, £2.30, £1.80; EX 83.20.
Owner Xunely Limited **Bred** Haras D'Ecouves And Ronald Reeves **Trained** Cropthorne, Worcs

FOCUS
A moderate novices' handicap, won in good style by five-year-old Mokum. Second-last fence bypassed final circuit.

NOTEBOOK
Mokum(FR) ◆, without a win in 25 starts on the Flat and over hurdles, was in the process of running well when unseating on his chasing debut at Sandown last month and it was not hard to see why he could be backed. He raced in typically lazy fashion, but the stiff finish suited him down to the ground and he powered home to win stylishly. Still only five, he could be open to plenty of improvement and is most definitely one to keep on-side. *(op 8-1)*
Rookery Lad, reported to have breathing troubles when disappointing latest, ran a fine race under a positive ride and kept plugging away for a clear second. He was no match for the winner, but is capable of winning a similar contest. *(op 7-1)*
The Outlier(IRE) has had a decent season and had definitely progressed, but he ran moderately at Newbury latest and top weight seemed to get him down here. He finished very tired and may have had enough for the season. *(op 9-2)*
Bishop's Bridge(IRE) ran a little better, but he ultimately finished very tired and stopped quickly in the straight. *(op 10-1)*
Merry Storm(IRE), an easy winner in the first-time tongue tie at Taunton, was up 10lb and he failed to reproduce the effort. He is better than this and deserves another chance. *(tchd 11-2)*
Flying Fuselier is not progressing and this second start over fences failed to bring about any improvement.

4879 GALA CASINO - ANYONE CAN BE A PLAYER H'CAP HURDLE (8 hdls) 2m
4:10 (4:25) (Class 4) (0-105,105) 4-Y-0 **£4,436** (£1,310; £655; £327; £163)

Form				RPR
31	**1**		**Elegant Clutter (IRE)**[35] [4392] 8-10-12 98 .... MrGTumelty(7)	101+
			(R N Bevis) *hld up: hdwy after 5th: led flat: rdn out* **15/2**[3]	

21F5 **2** *2 ½* **Make My Hay**[20] 3990 7-11-4 **97**..........(b) TomDoyle 98+
(J Gallagher) *reminders sn after s: jnd ldr 2nd: led appr last: hdd and unable qckn flat* **10/1**

3U13 **3** *1 ¼* **Merryvale Man**[29] 4503 9-11-2 **100**.......... BrianHughes(5) 98
(Miss Kariana Key) *mde most tl rdn and hdd appr last: no ex flat* **14/1**

P610 **4** *3 ½* **Etoile Russe (IRE)**[61] 3918 4-10-11 **105**..........(t) GaryBartley(10) 94
(P C Haslam) *a.p: ev ch fr 3 out: rdn and hung rt appr last: nt run on* **14/1**

0000 **5** *5* **Damarisco (FR)**[40] 4290 6-10-10 **89**.......... RichardJohnson 78
(P J Hobbs) *chsd ldrs: rdn 3 out: wknd after 2 out* **10/1**

0-51 **6** *1 ½* **Knockrigg (IRE)**[36] 4368 12-10-9 **93**.......... DrPPritchard(5) 81
(Dr P Pritchard) *hld up: styd on fr 2 out: nt rch ldrs* **14/1**

56F6 **7** *3 ½* **Porak (IRE)**[26] 4561 9-11-2 **100**.......... DerekLaverty(5) 84
(W Davies) *hld up: hdwy 5th: wknd next* **25/1**

60/P **8** *1* **Peerless Motion (IRE)**[57] 3997 11-10-11 **90**.......... KeithMercer 73
(S Lycett) *hld up: rdn 4th: hdwy appr 3 out: wknd bef next* **66/1**

-000 **9** *5* **Dark Society**[32] 4452 8-11-2 **95**.......... WayneHutchinson 73
(A W Carroll) *hld up: nvr nrr* **25/1**

F040 **10** *3 ½* **Murphy's Nails (IRE)**[44] 4210 9-10-12 **91**..........(p) JohnMcNamara 66
(K C Bailey) *chsd ldrs: ev ch 3 out: rdn and wknd next* **11/1**

05P1 **11** *½* **Andy Gin (FR)**[38] 4322 7-11-7 **105**.......... MrTJO'Brien(5) 79
(Miss E M England) *chsd ldrs: lost pl appr 4th: sn bhd* **7/1**[2]

4012 **12** *6* **Park City**[28] 4523 7-10-12 **96**.......... ShaneWalsh(5) 64
(J Joseph) *chsd ldrs: lost pl appr 3rd: rallied 3 out: sn wknd* **11/1**

400P **13** *3 ½* **Forzacurity**[18] 4663 7-10-13 **99**.......... TomMessenger(7) 64
(D Burchell) *hld up: rdn 5th: wknd appr 3 out* **33/1**

05PP **14** *shd* **Mnason (FR)**[38] 4322 6-11-9 **102**..........(v¹) MarcusFoley 67
(S J Gilmore) *hld up: a in rr* **33/1**

643 **P** **Inishturk (IRE)**[38] 4327 7-11-7 **100**.......... RobertThornton —
(A King) *sn drvn along in rr: t.o whn p.u bef 2 out* **9/2**[1]

0423 **P** **Shaman**[28] 4523 9-11-0 **93**.......... GLee —
(G L Moore) *mid-div: hdwy 5th: wknd after 3 out: bhd whn p.u bef next* **7/1**[2]

4m 1.10s (-10.30) **Going Correction** -0.725s/f (Firm)
WFA 4 from 5yo+ 5lb **16** Ran SP% **124.9**
Speed ratings: **96,94,94,92,89 89,87,86,84,82 82,79,77,77,— —** CSF £78.59 CT £1052.75 TOTE £8.70: £2.20, £3.00, £2.80, £4.50; EX 64.90.
Owner Kelvin Briggs **Bred** Limestone Stud **Trained** Threapwood, Cheshire

FOCUS
They went a fair gallop throughout in what was a moderate handicap.

NOTEBOOK
Elegant Clutter(IRE), up 14lb for his Warwick romp, handled the better ground well and put up a fair effort in coming from the rear of the field to win a shade comfortably. Tumelty was able to offset half of the 14lb rise and he came home strongly up the hill as the leaders tired. He may yet be open to further improvement, but needs to progress if he is to defy another rise. *(op 11-2)*
Make My Hay was woken up soon after the start to race prominently and he took it up coming into the last, but the winner had too much in reserve and he could only plod on for a place. *(tchd 11-1)*
Merryvale Man was always up there with Make My Hay, but he had nothing left to give after the last and may need to drop a few pounds before winning again. *(tchd 12-1)*
Etoile Russe(IRE) was never far off the gallop, but he was able to run better than when down the field at Newcastle. *(op 12-1)*
Damarisco(FR) offered hope of better to come following several poor efforts and he is gradually creeping back down to a fair mark. *(op 12-1)*
Dark Society *Official explanation: jockey said gelding was struck into (tchd 20-1)*
Andy Gin(FR), finally back to winning ways when bolting up here last month, had much more to do off a 12lb higher mark and he was unable to reproduce anything like the form he showed that day. *(tchd 6-1 and 15-2)*
Inishturk(IRE), a fascinating contender on this handicap debut, was never going from a very early *stage and there was presumably something amiss. He remains capable of better.Official explanation: jockey said gelding never travelled (op 6-1)*

4880 GALA CASINO - 0845 604 64 64 OPEN HUNTERS' CHASE (18 fncs) 3m 110y
4:40 (4:47) (Class 5) 5-Y-0+ **£2,186** (£677; £338; £169)

Form RPR

13UP **1** **Denvale (IRE)**[26] 4560 8-12-3.......... MrRCope(3) 117
(Mrs Caroline Bailey) *mde virtually all: j.lft 11th and again 2 out: sn drvn: styd on wl* **5/2**[2]

03P/ **2** *3 ½* **Moscow Court (IRE)**[22] 8-11-5.......... MrIanHowe(7) 107+
(Mrs David Plunkett) *chsd wnr fr 7th: sme awkward jumps: bmpd along 2 out: hung lft and nt qckn flat* **7/2**[3]

51 **3** *4* **Brer Bear**[34] 4421 7-12-6.......... MrJMPritchard 110
(Mrs E Insley) *trckd ldrs: 3rd fr 8th: rdn after 3 out: nvr able to cl* **11/8**[1]

63/0 **4** *21* **Toscanini (GER)**[15] 10-11-5.......... MrSGray(7) 83+
(Mark Doyle) *bhd: stdy prog 13th: 11l 4th 3 out: fdd bef next* **11/1**

-P60 **P** **Shellin Hill (IRE)**[15] 12-11-5 59..........(p) MrRHodges(7) —
(F L Matthews) *6th whn p.u and dismntd 6th* **66/1**

0UP- **P** **Parsons Fancy**[28] 8-11-2.......... MissAGoschen(3) —
(Mark Gillard) *midfield: lost tch 11th: t.o 14th: p.u last* **14/1**

P-FR **P** **Chaparro Amargoso (IRE)**[35] 4397 13-11-5.......... MrLEdwards(7) —
(F L Matthews) *bhd: lost tch 10th: t.o 13th: p.u 2 out* **50/1**

P/PP **P** **Come On Boy**[41] 4283 12-11-5.......... MrGDavies(7) —
(T G Williams) *led briefly bef 2nd: pressed wnr tl 7th: sn hopelessly t.o: eventually p.u 15th* **66/1**

6m 28.9s (-17.70) **Going Correction** -0.725s/f (Firm) **8** Ran SP% **112.8**
Speed ratings: **99,97,96,89,— —,—,—** CSF £11.73 TOTE £3.80: £1.40, £1.20, £1.10; EX 8.90.

Owner A & Mrs P Hurn **Bred** R R Clarke **Trained** Holdenby, Northants

FOCUS
An uncompetitive race in which only three could be given a serious chance in the absence of Cobreces.

NOTEBOOK
Denvale(IRE), who failed to run to form when pulled up at Exeter last month, appreciated the change in tactics and ground his rivals into submission, jumping boldly throughout. He is a decent *sort on his day and connections will presumably stick to forcing tactics. Official explanation: trainer said, regarding the improved form shown, gelding was able to dominate and was better suited by today's track (tchd 11-4 in places)*
Moscow Court(IRE), who had won two of his last three outings in points, never won over fences in Ireland, falling/unseating on several occasions, and his jumping once again hampered his winning chance. A useful performer over hurdles, he has the ability to win races in this sphere, but needs his jumping to be slicker. *(op 11-4)*
Brer Bear, winner of a hunter chase at Stratford last month, held strong claims with Cobreces being a non-runner, but he was most disappointing and seemed to be held down by his big weight. *(op 7-4)*
Toscanini(GER) was the only other to complete, but he never really threatened and was well held. *(op 10-1)*
Shellin Hill(IRE) *Official explanation: jockey said gelding pulled up lame (op 50-1)*

4881 GALA CASINO SOL CENTRAL, NORTHAMPTON STANDARD OPEN NATIONAL HUNT FLAT RACE 2m
5:10 (5:11) (Class 5) 4-6-Y-0 **£2,602** (£764; £382; £190)

Form RPR

1 **Bermuda Pointe (IRE)** 4-10-6.......... StevenCrawford(5) 100+
(N A Twiston-Davies) *chsd ldrs: wnt 2nd 1/2-way: led over 3f out: rn green and hung lft fr over 1f out: drvn and styd on wl* **7/1**

223 **2** *nk* **Bradley Boy (IRE)**[105] 3188 5-11-2.......... CarlLlewellyn 104
(Carl Llewellyn) *2nd tl led after 6f: hdd over 3f out: drvn and hung lft 1f out: kpt on* **2/1**[1]

4 **3** *13* **Nictos De Bersy (FR)**[25] 4574 5-11-2.......... JimmyMcCarthy 91
(C P Morlock) *chsd ldrs: rdn over 3f out: wnt mod 3rd over 1f out: unable to chal* **6/1**[2]

62 **4** *7* **Aubigny (FR)**[90] 3421 4-10-11.......... RobertThornton 79
(A King) *hld up towards rr: effrt to 4th and rdn 7f out: mod 3rd over 2f out: sn wl btn* **13/2**[3]

5 *½* **Red Rattle (IRE)** 4-10-11.......... PaulMoloney 79
(Miss H C Knight) *bhd: sme prog 3f out: no ch w ldrs fnl 2f* **12/1**

6 *13* **Mountain Of Dreams** 4-10-4.......... MrNKinnon(7) 66
(R H York) *chsd ldrs 11f* **40/1**

7 *1 ¼* **More Trouble (IRE)** 5-11-2.......... TomDoyle 69
(P R Webber) *midfield: racd awkwardly u.p 4f out: sn lost tch* **13/2**[3]

8 *12* **Run Dani Run (IRE)** 5-9-13.......... JamieBunsell(10) 50
(B W Duke) *immediately lost tch: passed sme stragglers in fnl 3f* **20/1**

9 *4* **Red Quest** 6-10-9.......... WayneKavanagh(7) 53
(Dr J R J Naylor) *bhd: drvn 1/2-way: sn btn: t.o* **50/1**

10 *4* **Sizeable Return** 5-11-2.......... JasonMaguire 49
(J A B Old) *bhd: prog to 3rd 6f out: n.m.r over 3f out: sn btn: heavily eased over 2f out* **9/1**

11 *6* **Sundawn Star** 5-10-9.......... RJGreene 36
(C P Morlock) *rdn 1/2-way: sn labouring: t.o* **33/1**

12 *19* **Rapid Lad** 5-11-2.......... MatthewBatchelor 24
(B R Johnson) *hdwy to 3rd 7f out: wknd 5f out: t.o* **50/1**

13 *9* **Danahill Lad (USA)** 5-10-9.......... MrDEngland(7) 15
(J A Danahar) *led 6f: struggling in rr 5f out: t.o fnl 3f* **33/1**

3m 57.9s (-14.00) **Going Correction** -0.725s/f (Firm)
WFA 4 from 5yo 5lb 5 from 6yo 3lb **13** Ran SP% **121.5**
Speed ratings: **106,105,99,95,95 89,88,82,80,78 75,65,61** CSF £20.48 TOTE £10.10: £2.40, £1.60, £2.30; EX 50.80 Place 6 £150.12, Place 5 £49.05.
Owner D J & S A Goodman **Bred** Edward Sexton **Trained** Naunton, Gloucs

FOCUS
A good bumper for the track run in a fair time, significantly faster than both hurdle contests over the same trip.

NOTEBOOK
Bermuda Pointe(IRE), whose stable had their first winner for a while the previous day at Haydock, put up a dour performance for a four-year-old, forging into the lead before the turn in and staying on well, despite running green, when pressed by the vastly more experienced runner-up. This was a taking performance and the gelding, who looks certain to improve with time, appears to have a bright future, with two and a half miles plus over hurdles likely to suit next season before a switch to fences. *(op 8-1)*
Bradley Boy(IRE) is most consistent, but it was just another good effort in defeat for the gelding. He stuck on willingly when the winner began to run around, but he was never quite getting there. He too will require a greater distance over hurdles and he should have little trouble finding a race. *(op 9-4 tchd 5-2 in a place)*
Nictos De Bersy(FR) appeared to step up on his initial effort at Chepstow, and kept on well enough in third. Two and a half miles will see him in a better light once hurdling. *(op 7-1)*
Aubigny(FR) has demonstrated enough ability to win a bumper, but he failed to get involved and it *now looks likely he will not be winning until tackling hurdles. Official explanation: jockey said gelding was hampered on bend into back straight (op 7-1)*
Red Rattle(IRE) comes from a stable who have had a very disappointing season and, as a result, the four-year-old shaped reasonably well. *(tchd 14-1)*
Sizeable Return, whose trainer has had another good season with his bumpers, was solid enough in the market, but he soon dropped away having been a bit squeezed for room when holding a prominent position. There was promise in the performance and he ran a bit better than his finishing *position suggests. Official explanation: jockey said gelding lost its action going up hill and failed to travel thereafter (op 17-2)*
T/Plt: £53.40 to a £1 stake. Pool: £51,748.80. 707.40 winning tickets. T/Qpdt: £17.90 to a £1 stake. Pool: £3,697.40. 152.70 winning tickets. IM

4882 - 4886a (Foreign Racing) - See Raceform Interactive

4121 FAIRYHOUSE (R-H)
Sunday, April 16

OFFICIAL GOING: Good to yielding

4887a IRISH STALLION FARMS EUROPEAN BREEDERS FUND (MARES) NOVICE HURDLE CHAMPIONSHIP FINAL (GRADE 3) (11 hdls) 2m 4f
2:45 (2:46) 4-Y-0+ **£23,346** (£6,849; £3,263; £1,111)

RPR

1 **Cailin Alainn (IRE)**[7] 4809 7-10-11.......... BMCash 119
(C Byrnes, Ire) *hld up: hmpd 5th: mstke 6th: hdwy after 4 out: led after 2 out: kpt on u.p fr last: all out* **12/1**

2 *2* **Celestial Wave (IRE)**[28] 4540 6-11-3.......... MissNCarberry 123
(Adrian Maguire, Ire) *led: rdn and hdd after 2 out: rallied after last: no imp cl home* **7/4**[1]

3 *4 ½* **La Marianne**[50] 4125 6-10-11 104.......... TGMRyan 113
(J R H Fowler, Ire) *mid-div: 6th 1/2-way: 5th and rdn bef 2 out: kpt on fr last* **10/1**

4 *1* **Clear Riposte (IRE)**[33] 4435 4-10-9.......... RWalsh 110
(W P Mullins, Ire) *mid-div: 8th 4 out: hdwy into cl 2nd bef 2 out: sn rdn and no imp: no ex after last* **8/1**[3]

5 *6* **Coolgreaney (IRE)**[9] 4767 5-10-10.......... MDarcy 105
(S J Treacy, Ire) *prom: 2nd 4 out: 4th and rdn bef 2 out: no ex fr last* **10/1**

6 *4* **Kylebeg Dancer (IRE)**[6] 4540 5-10-10 108.......... AndrewJMcNamara 101
(T Hogan, Ire) *hld up: mstke 7th: kpt on same pce fr bef 2 out* **20/1**

7 *4* **Gazza's Girl (IRE)**[50] 4125 6-11-3 119.......... TPTreacy 104
(Mrs John Harrington, Ire) *prom: 2nd to 5 out: wknd bef 2 out* **4/1**[2]

8 *¾* **Gemini Lucy (IRE)**[9] 4768 6-10-11 91.......... BJGeraghty 97
(Mrs John Harrington, Ire) *trckd ldrs: 5th 5 out: 4th after 4 out: no ex bef 2 out* **20/1**

9 *hd* **Tiarella (IRE)**[28] 4540 6-11-0 113.......... DNRussell 100
(Denis Ahern, Ire) *hld up: hmpd 5th: prog into 7th 4 out: no ex bef 2 out* **25/1**

10 2 **Maura's Legacy (IRE)**[30] 4480 6-10-11 .... AnthonyRoss 95
(I A Duncan, Ire) *a bhd* **50/1**
11 20 **Native House (IRE)**[45] 4205 8-10-11 106........................ JLCullen 75
(Edward Cawley, Ire) *hld up: sme prog after 4 out: no ex whn eased bef last* **20/1**
12 15 **Freemantle Doctor (IRE)**[42] 4266 6-10-11 .... RGeraghty 60
(J R H Fowler, Ire) *chsd ldrs: reminders briefly bef 1/2-way: 6th 4 out: sn wknd: eased fr 2 out: t.o* **20/1**
13 20 **Limestream (IRE)**[73] 3701 6-10-11 102........................ PACarberry 40
(John G Carr, Ire) *prom early: 7th 5 out: sn wknd: completely t.o* **25/1**
14 6 **Handfull Of Euros (IRE)**[84] 3524 6-10-11 .... RMPower 34
(W J Austin, Ire) *a bhd: trailing fr 1/2-way: completely t.o* **20/1**
F **Ceart Go Leor (IRE)**[36] 4384 9-10-11 89........................ DJCasey —
(Richard Francis O'Gorman, Ire) *fell 1st* **66/1**
F **Creme D'Arblay (IRE)**[36] 4380 4-10-1 .... DFO'Regan —
(Thomas Cooper, Ire) *trckd ldrs on inner: fell 5th* **10/1**
P **Thunder Road (IRE)**[17] 1534 6-11-0 108........................ APLane —
(P A Fahy, Ire) *hld up towards rr: impr to trck ldrs bef 1/2-way: wknd 4 out: p.u bef last* **40/1**

4m 52.2s **Going Correction** -0.40s/f (Good)
WFA 4 from 5yo+ 6lb **17** Ran SP% **139.8**
Speed ratings: **102,101,99,99,96 95,93,93,93,92 84,78,70,67,— —,—** CSF £34.60 TOTE £20.70: £3.60, £1.20, £2.10, £2.00; DF 97.30.
Owner Dewdrop Racing Syndicate **Bred** Michael P Keane **Trained** Ballingarry, Co Limerick

NOTEBOOK
Cailin Alainn(IRE), a winner at Tramore last time, overcame being hampered at the fifth flight to stay on well for victory. She likes good ground and this lightly-raced improving type looks capable of further progress. She will make a chaser next season. *(op 10/1)*
Celestial Wave(IRE), who was unbeaten in three previous starts over hurdles, made a brave attempt to make all. She would probably have preferred easier ground so this was a decent performance in the circumstances. *(op 7/4 tchd 2/1)*
La Marianne, more exposed than the first two, ran a solid race in defeat and, although still seeking her first win over hurdles, she keeps improving steadily. She looks a chasing prospect. *(op 8/1)*
Clear Riposte(IRE), a Grade Two winner in December, has been rated as having run to her best form. *(op 7/1)*
Coolgreaney(IRE), stepping up in grade, could not go with the principals from the second last.

4888a RATHBARRY & GLENVIEW STUDS FESTIVAL NOVICE HURDLE (GRADE 2) (11 hdls) 2m 4f
3:15 (3:15) 4-Y-0+ **£21,550** (£6,322; £3,012; £1,026)

RPR
1 **Vic Venturi (IRE)**[98] 3309 6-11-8 ....(t) APMcCoy 138
(Philip Fenton, Ire) *hld up in tch: 5th 3 out: hdwy on outer ent st: led after 2 out: strly pressed fr last: kpt on wl u.p* **5/1**[3]
2 ½ **Mounthenry (IRE)**[38] 4336 6-11-10 .... AndrewJMcNamara 139
(C Byrnes, Ire) *hld up in tch: 6th appr 3 out: 3rd after 2 out: 2nd and chal last: ev ch: no ex nr fin* **9/4**[1]
3 6 **Thyne Again (IRE)**[11] 4740 5-11-7 .... DNRussell 130
(W J Burke, Ire) *trckd ldrs: 3rd after 1/2-way: led on inner after 3 out: strly pressed next: hdd bef last: 3rd and no ex run-in* **11/2**
4 9 **Letterman (IRE)**[32] 4443 6-11-5 128........................ BJGeraghty 119
(E J O'Grady, Ire) *led: rdn and hdd after 3 out: 4th and no ex bef last* **14/1**
5 hd **Sir Overbury**[38] 4336 5-11-4 .... RMPower 118
(Daniel O'Connell, Ire) *trckd ldrs: 3rd early: 5th and drvn along 5 out: kpt on same pce fr 3 out* **10/1**
6 ½ **Drunken Disorderly (IRE)**[53] 4061 6-11-5 123........................ JLCullen 118
(David Wachman, Ire) *trckd ldrs on outer: 4th 4 out: rdn to chal appr 3 out: sn wknd* **12/1**
7 1½ **Back To Bid (IRE)**[30] 4469 6-11-5 .... DFO'Regan 117
(Noel Meade, Ire) *cl 2nd: chal 3 out: no ex after next: 5th and btn whn mstke last* **4/1**[2]
8 dist **Sizing America (IRE)**[64] 3871 5-11-4 .... RWalsh —
(Henry De Bromhead, Ire) *chsd ldrs early: dropped to rr bef 1/2-way: t.o fr 4 out* **20/1**
F **Mossbank (IRE)**[63] 3892 6-11-5 .... CO'Dwyer —
(Michael Hourigan, Ire) *hld up in rr: fell 4th* **8/1**

4m 52.6s **Going Correction** -0.40s/f (Good) **9** Ran SP% **122.1**
Speed ratings: **101,100,98,94,94 94,93,—,—** CSF £18.25 TOTE £6.20: £2.10, £2.10, £1.80; DF 12.20.
Owner J P Dunne **Bred** Mrs P & C Brabazon **Trained** Carrick-On-Suir, Co Waterford

FOCUS
A cracking contest, but the slow pace means the result has to be treated with a hint of caution. Vic Venturi, Mounthenry and Letterman are the ones to take from the race, with all three likely to develop into leading staying novices over fences. Thyne Again may well improve for the drop back to two miles.

NOTEBOOK
Vic Venturi(IRE) has quickly developed into a high-class novice this season, progressing from winning an ordinary event at Galway in October to landing this highly competitive end-of-season contest. Successful in a Grade Three at Limerick over Christmas, this represented a personal best and, considering he was held up off the modest tempo, he deserves even more credit. He could develop into a leading staying novice next season. *(op 11/2)*
Mounthenry(IRE), a dual Grade Two winner seeking his sixth win of the campaign, had to concede upwards of 2lb to all his rivals, but nonetheless he deserved his place at the head of the market. He came through to hold every chance, but the winner proved too strong and he had to make do with an honourable second. He too has the potential to make a top novice chaser next term. *(op 2/1)*
Thyne Again(IRE), who did not look good enough on his sole previous attempt at graded level, travelled strongly for a long way on this step back up in distance, but he again failed to get home. *His wins have come at shorter and the way he travels suggests a stiff two miles suits him best. (op 5/1)*
Letterman(IRE), down the field in the Royal & SunAlliance Hurdle, was at an advantage in making the running at a modest gallop, but he took some passing and ran above market expectations. He will stay three miles over fences and is another good chasing prospect.
Back To Bid(IRE), a creditable fourth to Black Jack Ketchum in the Brit Insurance, raced on the outer of leader Letterman, but he dropped away disappointingly under pressure and did not appear to be at his best. *(op 5/1)*
Mossbank(IRE) has not quite lived up to expectations this season and he got no further than the fourth.

4889a POWERS GOLD CUP CHASE (NOVICES') (GRADE 1) (15 fncs) 2m 4f
3:50 (3:50) 5-Y-0+ **£45,517** (£13,103; £6,206; £2,068)

RPR
1 **Justified (IRE)**[77] 3639 7-11-9 .... APMcCoy 154+
(E Sheehy, Ire) *mde all: j. bdly lft thrght: clr after 6 out: rdn bef 4 out: strly pressed 2 out: styd on wl* **5/1**[3]
2 3 **In Compliance (IRE)**[42] 4271 6-11-9 140........................ BJGeraghty 151+
(M J P O'Brien, Ire) *hld up: 5th 7 out: impr into 3rd next: 2nd and rdn after 4 out: chal 2 out: no imp fr bef last: kpt on u.p* **7/4**[1]
3 20 **The Railway Man (IRE)**[32] 4444 7-11-9 .... DNRussell 131+
(A L T Moore, Ire) *trckd ldrs in 4th: lost tch 4 out: kpt on same pce to go mod 3rd fr last* **10/1**
4 ½ **Davenport Democrat (IRE)**[30] 4472 8-11-9 143........................ TPTreacy 131
(W P Mullins, Ire) *trckd ldrs: 3rd 1/2-way: 2nd 6 out: 3rd and no ex 4 out: kpt on same pce* **16/1**
5 25 **Public Reaction**[7] 4334 8-11-9 .... JLCullen 106
(Edward U Hales, Ire) *chsd ldr in 2nd: u.p whn mstke 6 out: sn wknd: t.o* **66/1**
6 1½ **Arteea (IRE)**[33] 4431 7-11-9 .... AndrewJMcNamara 104
(Michael Hourigan, Ire) *hld up in tch: last and drvn along fr 9th: trailing fr 6 out: t.o* **10/1**
F **Missed That**[33] 4431 7-11-9 .... RWalsh —
(W P Mullins, Ire) *hld up in tch: fell 7th* **4/1**[2]
F **Wild Passion (GER)**[33] 4431 6-11-9 150........................ DFO'Regan —
(Noel Meade, Ire) *chsd ldrs: 5th whn fell at 5th* **13/2**

4m 59.2s **Going Correction** -0.40s/f (Good) **8** Ran SP% **111.9**
Speed ratings: **121,119,111,111,101 101,—,—** CSF £14.23 TOTE £5.40: £1.40, £1.40, £1.80; DF 10.90.
Owner Braybrook Syndicate **Bred** Miss Maura McGuinness **Trained** Graiguenamanagh, Kilkenny

FOCUS
A top event fought out between two high-class novices. Justified received an aggressive ride from McCoy and stayed on too strongly for the runner-up, despite jumping badly left under pressure. In Compliance is the horse to take from the race, and the way he travels suggests two miles could be more his trip. Of the two fallers, Missed That will require three miles next season, while Wild Passion may be difficult to place.

NOTEBOOK
Justified(IRE), who created an excellent impression when beating Wild Passion in a Grade Two event at Punchestown in November, has had mixed fortunes since and bypassed the Festival. In good shape for this, he was given a typically bold McCoy ride and had burned all bar the favourite off as they rounded into the straight. Despite jumping badly left over the last few, he stayed on too strongly for the runner-up, who was making no impression. He now has the Swordlestown Cup at Punchestown as his final target of the season. *(op 9/2)*
In Compliance(IRE), who created a huge impression in winning his two previous outings over fences, was bidding to compensate for the unfortunate defeat of connections' subsequent Gold Cup third Forget The Past in this 12 months ago, but having come through to hold every chance turning in, he was unable to stay on as strongly as Justified. Despite the winner jumping badly out to his left in the straight, he never looked like reeling him in. It could be argued Geraghty gave the winner too much rope, but the way he jumps and travels suggests two miles could be his trip and, although a long way off, it is not impossible to see him developing into a Champion Chase contender of the future. *(op 7/4 tchd 15/8)*
The Railway Man(IRE) failed to last home having raced keenly in the SunAlliance Chase at Cheltenham and, although running well here, he proved no match for the classy front pair. He is likely to develop into a top handicap chaser next term.
Davenport Democrat(IRE), a hugely creditable fifth in the Grand Annual, ran only a reasonable race back in fourth. He is in at Punchestown next week, and will appreciate the return to handicap company.
Wild Passion(GER) ran well for a long way in the Arkle, but he was not ridden as aggressively on this occasion and came down at the fifth. He may be hard to place next season. *(op 5/1)*
Missed That, who found the ground too lively and trip too short when disappointing in the Arkle, was not out of it, although there were others going stronger, when he fell at the seventh. He is likely to develop into a three miler next season. *(op 5/1)*

4890 - 4895a (Foreign Racing) - See Raceform Interactive

4474 FAKENHAM (L-H)
Monday, April 17

OFFICIAL GOING: Good (good to firm in places)
With a drying wind the going was described as 'mainly good to firm'.
Wind: Fresh, across Weather: Mainly fine but heavy shower race four

4896 JOAN AND JOHN SKELTON GOLDEN WEDDING ANNIVERSARY (S) H'CAP HURDLE (9 hdls) 2m
2:00 (2:00) (Class 5) (0-85,85) 4-Y-0+ **£2,398** (£698; £349)

Form RPR
UPO- 1 **Real Chief (IRE)**[28] 3261 8-10-9 **68**........................ JodieMogford 77+
(Miss M E Rowland) *hld up: hdwy to trck ldrs after 5th: led 2 out: rdn clr between last 2* **20/1**
-106 2 6 **Clydeoneeyed**[80] 3591 7-11-0 **78**........................ ShaneWalsh(5) 78
(K F Clutterbuck) *chsd ldrs: led after 5th: hdd 2 out: kpt on same pce* **5/1**[2]
4465 3 ¾ **Chariot (IRE)**[31] 4475 5-11-3 **76**........................(t) SeanCurran 75
(M R Bosley) *t.k.h: trckd ldrs: chal 2 out: kpt on same pce* **6/1**[3]
UR- 4 ¾ **Socarineau (FR)**[358] 8-11-0 **80**........................ MrMatthewSmith(7) 79
(N J Pomfret) *chsd ldrs: reminders and outpcd 6th: styd on fr 2 out* **33/1**
0002 5 1¼ **Theatre Belle**[35] 4418 5-11-7 **80**........................ AntonyEvans 77
(Ms Deborah J Evans) *hld up in rr: effrt 6th: kpt on fr 2 out: nvr nr ldrs* **9/2**[1]
000 6 3½ **Tiger Island (USA)**[80] 3603 6-10-9 **75**........................(p) KeiranBurke(7) 69
(A E Jones) *chsd ldrs: outpcd 5th: kpt on fr 2 out: nvr a real threat* **8/1**
-PP6 7 3½ **Maunby Roller (IRE)**[194] 1643 7-10-11 **75**........................(p) JohnnyLevins(5) 65
(K A Morgan) *led: reminders and hdd after 5th: sn outpcd* **20/1**
003P 8 10 **Polish Pilot (IRE)**[26] 4580 11-11-6 **79**........................ RichardHobson 59
(J R Cornwall) *in rr: rdn 6th: sn btn* **20/1**
0026 9 3 **Purr**[37] 4368 5-10-1 **67**........................(p) MrSRees(7) 44
(M Wigham) *racd wd: jnd ldrs 3rd: lost pl after 5th* **7/1**
10 21 **Level Par (IRE)**[19] 914 6-11-9 **82**........................(t) AlanO'Keeffe 38
(J A Supple) *t.k.h: trckd ldeers: lost pl 3rd: bhd fr 6th* **11/1**
2002 P **Aleemdar (IRE)**[31] 4475 9-11-7 **85**........................(p) DerekLaverty(5) —
(A E Jones) *w.r.s: detached in last: t.o whn p.u bef 3 out* **5/1**[2]
0U0 F **Tricky Venture**[16] 4149 6-11-0 **83**........................ CraigMessenger(10) —
(Mrs L C Jewell) *trckd ldrs: 4th and styng on same pce whn fell last* **12/1**

4m 0.70s (-8.20) **Going Correction** -0.60s/f (Firm) **12** Ran SP% **122.7**
Speed ratings: **96,93,92,92,91 89,88,83,81,71 —,—** CSF £117.56 CT £697.54 TOTE £38.10: £9.40, £2.40, £2.70; EX 247.80.The winner was bought in for 4,600gns.
Owner Miss M E Rowland **Bred** Janus Bloodstock **Trained** Lower Blidworth, Notts
■ Stewards' Enquiry : Derek Laverty 28-day ban: in breach of Rule 157 (Apr 28-May 2, May 4-6, May 8-27) A E Jones fined £5,000 under Rule 155 (ii), horse banned 40 days.

FOCUS
A sound pace and a much improved effort from the winner with the third the best guide to the level.

NOTEBOOK
Real Chief(IRE), fit from the Flat, settled better and came there on the bit. Shaken up coming off the final bend, he had this won in a matter of strides after having finished unplaced in eight previous starts under jumping rules. *(op 16-1)*

Clydeoneeyed, 13lb higher than when successful here in May, was having his first outing since January. After being sent on, he was joined by the winner who was simply running away and he was never going to finish anything better than second best.
Chariot(IRE) took a fierce grip and his stamina looks very limited even on a sharp track such as this. *(op 11-2 tchd 13-2)*
Socarineau(FR), last seen in a point at this track a year ago, was struggling to keep up with a full circuit to go and he needs a stiffer test of stamina. *(op 25-1)*
Theatre Belle, dropping back in trip, failed to land a blow.
Tiger Island(USA), back in selling company, sported first-time cheekpieces and was nibbled at in the market. Unplaced in a dozen previous tries, he was struggling to keep up with a circuit to go. *(op 20-1)*
Level Par(IRE) *Official explanation: jockey said gelding had a breathing problem (op 10-1)*
Aleemdar(IRE), kept in last at the start, whipped round losing many lengths. With his cause a hopeless one, he was eventually pulled up. His performance set the red lights flashing in the *Stewards' room and they came down with a heavy hand. It seemed a harsh decision. Official explanation: 40-day ban (Apr 20-May 30) (op 11-1)*
Tricky Venture, a winner twice on the All-Weather, was making his handicap debut on just his fourth start. He was on the heels of the placed horses when crashing out at the last. *(op 11-1)*

4897 HOOD, VORES AND ALLWOOD NOVICES' HUNTERS' CHASE (14 fncs 2 omitted) 2m 5f 110y
2:35 (2:35) (Class 6) 5-Y-O+ **£2,091** (£798)

Form — RPR
0F/1 **1** **Rhythm King**[16] 11-12-1 .... MrGMaundrell(3) 109+
(G C Maundrell) *trckd ldrs: led 11th: 2l up and in command whn blnd last* **1/1**[1]
0-P **2** 2½ **Ruggtah**[29] 5-10-8 .... (b[1]) MrMBriggs(7) 83
(Mrs Antonia Bealby) *prom: wnt 2nd 2 out: hld whn hit last* **12/1**
F **L'Or De Thou (FR)**[22] 7-11-9 .... (b[1]) MrNBloom(3) —
(W J Tolhurst) *prom: 5th whn fell 4th* **33/1**
/P0- **F** **Crystal Dance (FR)**[16] 6-11-7 .... MrDKemp(5) —
(D J Kemp) *chsd ldrs: 4th whn fell 8th* **6/1**[3]
F **Wainhill Lad**[16] 10-11-5 .... MissJKelly(7) —
(S G Allen) *set str pce: clr whn j.rt and fell heavily 3rd* **66/1**
0PP/ **P** **Pirate King (IRE)**[9] 9-11-5 .... MrABraithwaite(7) —
(H Hill) *mstke 3rd: bhd fr 11th: t.o whn p.u bef 2 out* **25/1**
3P/3 **U** **Gollinger**[20] 4660 10-11-5 .... MrRTierney(7) 74
(R H R Tierney) *chsd ldr: lft in ld 3rd: hdd 8th: wknd 3 out: 4th whn blnd and uns rdr last* **16/1**
F5/1 **U** **Abbey Days (IRE)**[9] 9-11-11 .... MrRhysHughes(7) 78
(S Flook) *in tch: hmpd 8th: outpcd whn blnd bdly 9th: modest 5th whn bdly hmpd and uns rdr last* **8/1**
/FR2 **R** **Cloudy Bay Boy**[38] 4349 8-11-5 .... (b) MrRJBarrett(7) 79
(Mrs Caroline Bailey) *j.rt: chsd ldrs: led 8th to 11th: wknd 2 out: 15l 3rd whn wnt rt and ref last* **11/2**[2]

5m 33.8s (-10.70) **Going Correction** -0.60s/f (Firm)
WFA 5 from 6yo+ 4lb **9** Ran SP% **112.6**
Speed ratings: **95,94**,—,—,— —,—,—,— CSF £13.48 TOTE £2.00: £1.60, £4.90; EX 20.10.
Owner G C Maundrell **Bred** Shade Oak Stud **Trained** Marlbrough, Wilts.

FOCUS
The winner idled in front and is value for further as he was lucky to keep his legs at the last. The gallop was sound and the time compared well with the later handicap chase. Second-last fence bypassed last two circuits.

NOTEBOOK
Rhythm King, possibly in front soon enough, seemed to idle and gave his supporters a fright at the last. This was his sixth successive success but he will have more on his plate at Stratford next time. *(op 4-5 tchd 11-10 in places)*
Ruggtah, winner of two of her last three starts in points, was blinkered for the first time uner Rules. She tried hard but looked held when the winner made a much worse mistake than her at the final fence. *(op 10-1)*
Gollinger found this much tougher and was booked for a distant third spot when giving his rider little chance at the last. *(op 7-1)*
Abbey Days(IRE), under his penalty, was a couple of lengths behind the third horse when given no chance of jumping the last. *(op 7-1)*
Cloudy Bay Boy continually gave away ground jumping to his right and had but a distant view of the first two when declining to jump the last. *(op 7-1)*

4898 SIS NOVICES' H'CAP HURDLE (11 hdls) 2m 4f
3:10 (3:10) (Class 4) (0-105,103) 4-Y-0+ **£3,253** (£955; £477; £238)

Form — RPR
431P **1** **Colophony (USA)**[38] 4344 6-11-4 **94** .... JohnnyLevins(5) 103+
(K A Morgan) *trckd ldrs: wnt 2nd appr 2 out: shkn up and led between last 2: eased towards fin* **7/1**[3]
050 **2** 6 **Bucks**[36] 4389 9-10-11 **82** .... WayneHutchinson 81+
(Ian Williams) *trckd ldrs: led appr 2 out: hdd between last 2: no ex* **5/1**[2]
PU05 **3** 10 **Loup Bleu (USA)**[8] 4794 8-11-8 **93** .... JodieMogford 81+
(Mrs A V Roberts) *hld up in rr: hdwy 7th: led after 8th: hdd appr 2 out: sn wl outpcd* **20/1**
-0P4 **4** 1¼ **Chilly Milly**[76] 3664 5-11-5 **90** .... JimCrowley 76
(V Smith) *sn detached in rr: hdwy 3 out: styd on run-in: nvr nr ldrs* **7/1**[3]
-3P0 **5** 1¼ **Greek Star**[67] 3814 5-11-6 **91** .... AntonyEvans 76
(K A Morgan) *w ldrs: lost pl 3 out* **7/1**[3]
F43 **6** 7 **Rainbow Tree**[22] 4634 6-10-11 **92** .... (b) JamesPeters(10) 70
(C C Bealby) *chsd ldrs: lost pl 3 out* **5/1**[2]
POP5 **7** 2½ **Deo Gratias (POL)**[22] 4640 6-10-12 **83** .... (p) CarlLlewellyn 58
(Carl Llewellyn) *nt fluent: led: rdn after 7th: hdd after next: lost pl 3 out* **4/1**[1]
6000 **8** ½ **Water Pistol**[8] 4795 4-9-12 **78** .... LeeVickers(3) 47
(M C Chapman) *chsd ldrs: outpcd 7th: wl btn whn hit 2 out* **14/1**
P4F6 **9** 4 **Power Glory**[8] 4795 4-10-12 **92** .... ChrisHonour(3) 57
(M J Gingell) *prom: hdwy 7th: lost pl after next* **14/1**
5-00 **F** **Homelife (IRE)**[81] 3577 8-11-0 **85** .... OllieMcPhail —
(Mrs J A Saunders) *t.k.h in mid-field: hdwy to chse ldrs whn fell 6th* **25/1**
05P **P** **Woolstone Boy (USA)**[128] 2460 5-10-12 **83** .... AlanO'Keeffe —
(K C Bailey) *stdd s: hld up in rr: lost pl 7th: bhd whn p.u bef next* **16/1**
2P04 **P** **Lord Of Adventure (IRE)**[23] 4616 4-11-7 **103** .... ShaneWalsh(5) —
(Mrs L C Jewell) *trckd ldrs: drvn along 5th: lost pl next: sn bhd: t.o whn p.u after 8th* **9/1**

4m 59.9s (-12.30) **Going Correction** -0.60s/f (Firm)
WFA 4 from 5yo+ 6lb **12** Ran SP% **128.7**
Speed ratings: **100,97,93,93,92 89,88,88,87**,— —,— CSF £46.39 CT £701.41 TOTE £9.10: £2.50, £4.90, £10.10; EX 62.70.
Owner H A Blenkhorn & Miss C J Blenkhorn **Bred** Juddmonte Farms Inc **Trained** Waltham on the Wolds, Leics

FOCUS
The winner made it look simple and is value for ten lengths, the runner-up, potentially well treated on his Flat form, ran easily his best race over hurdles so far.

NOTEBOOK
Colophony(USA), 8lb higher than Huntingdon, cruised round and made this look very simple, value double the official margin. This totally different ground to Ayr did not put such a strain on his wind. *(op 8-1)*
Bucks, stepping up in trip on his handicap debut on just his fourth start over hurdles, finished clear second best and deserves to go one better. *(tchd 11-2)*
Loup Bleu(USA), who ran in a selling hurdle a week earlier, burst through on the outer to take charge but the first two left him for dead on the run round to the last. *(op 25-1)*
Chilly Milly, on her handicap debut, was not fluent at the back. She stayed on late in the day and a stiffer test will suit her better.
Greek Star, who ran over much further last time, is still a maiden after nine attempts now and he dropped right out of contention at the third-last flight. *(op 15-2 tchd 8-1)*
Rainbow Tree, suited by fast ground, seems off the boil at present but should bounce back when returned to fences in time. *(op 6-1)*
Deo Gratias(POL), suited by fast ground, wore cheekpieces rather than a tongue tie. He was let down by his jumping and, after making the running, he stopped in a matter of strides. *(tchd 9-2 in a place)*

4899 CECIL AND SHEILA BUTTIFANT MEMORIAL H'CAP HURDLE (13 hdls) 2m 7f 110y
3:45 (3:45) (Class 4) (0-110,102) 4-Y-0+ **£4,554** (£1,337; £668; £333)

Form — RPR
4552 **1** **Siegfrieds Night (IRE)**[5] 3416 5-11-0 **93** .... (t) LeeVickers(3) 105+
(M C Chapman) *w ldrs: led 10th: drvn clr between last 2: eased fnl 50yds* **7/2**[1]
2242 **2** 12 **Di's Dilemma**[27] 4568 8-11-4 **94** .... WayneHutchinson 93
(C C Bealby) *trckd ldrs: wnt 2nd after 3 out: kpt on: no ch w wnr* **7/2**[1]
4245 **3** 7 **Honey's Gift**[33] 4453 7-11-12 **102** .... JimCrowley 94
(G G Margarson) *led tl after 6th: drvn along 9th: one pce fr 3 out* **9/2**[2]
-000 **4** 2½ **Valerun (IRE)**[87] 3487 10-10-4 **90** .... (p) JohnFlavin(10) 80
(R C Guest) *nt fluent: prom: drvn 10th: one pce* **15/2**
6P60 **5** ¾ **Red Granite**[62] 3906 6-10-9 **85** .... AlanO'Keeffe 74
(K C Bailey) *hld up in rr: hdwy and in tch 9th: one pce fr 3 out* **9/1**
41-6 **6** 29 **Flaming Cheek**[31] 4478 8-11-5 **98** .... ChrisHonour(3) 58
(A G Blackmore) *hld up: hdwy and in tch 9th: jnd ldrs next: wknd qckly appr 2 out* **8/1**
0003 **P** **Flemingstone (IRE)**[20] 4656 6-10-0 **81** ow5 .... DerekLaverty(5) —
(M J Gingell) *nt fluent:: blnd 3rd: sn drvn along: bhd fr 8th: t.o 10th: p.u after next* **9/1**
012- **P** **Khaysar (IRE)**[595] 1329 8-11-9 **99** .... CarlLlewellyn —
(N B King) *j.rt: t.k.h: trckd ldrs: led and qcknd after 6th: hdd 10th: sn lost pl: t.o whn p.u bef 2 out* **6/1**[3]

5m 54.9s (-11.50) **Going Correction** -0.60s/f (Firm) **8** Ran SP% **119.8**
Speed ratings: **95,91,88,87,87 77**,—,— CSF £17.47 CT £57.05 TOTE £4.00: £1.30, £1.30, £2.40; EX 9.10.
Owner K D Blanch **Bred** Barronstown Stud And Orpendale **Trained** Market Rasen, Lincs

FOCUS
The eased winner bounced back to his very best, the race has been rated through the runner-up.

NOTEBOOK
Siegfrieds Night(IRE), in action on the flat just five days earlier, raced with real enthusiasm and skipping clear was value for at least 20 lengths. He will shoot up in the ratings as a result though. *(op 3-1)*
Di's Dilemma, a maiden after 19 previous starts, does nothing wrong and here was achieving her tenth placing. The extra distance if anything suited her.
Honey's Gift made this a true test but on this ground she could not match the first two in the final half mile.
Valerun(IRE), absent since January, was ring rusty but, a winner over three miles on fast ground in Ireland, he looks a likely sort for summer jumping. *(op 8-1)*
Red Granite, absent since February, was switched off at the back. He kept on in his own time and may need fences.

4900 DAVID KEITH MEMORIAL H'CAP CHASE (16 fncs) 2m 5f 110y
4:20 (4:20) (Class 4) (0-110,110) 5-Y-0+ **£5,204** (£1,528; £764; £381)

Form — RPR
5P42 **1** **Jodante (IRE)**[101] 3272 9-10-3 **97** .... (p) JohnFlavin(10) 113+
(R C Guest) *hld up in rr: smooth hdwy to trck ldrs 12th: wnt 2nd 2 out: led on bit appr last: j.lft: sn qcknd clr: comf* **11/2**
1111 **2** 6 **New Perk (IRE)**[31] 4476 8-10-12 **99** .... ChrisHonour(3) 105
(M J Gingell) *chsd ldrs: drvn along 10th: outpcd after 2 out: kpt on to take 2nd nr line* **5/2**[1]
/642 **3** ½ **Lightning Strikes (IRE)**[31] 4477 12-10-0 **91** ow2 .... MrMatthewSmith(7) 100+
(Mrs L Wadham) *trckd ldrs: led 13th tl appr last: 1 1/2 l down whn hit last: lost 2nd towards fin* **11/4**[2]
/6UF **4** 5 **Longstone Loch (IRE)**[59] 3958 9-10-1 **85** .... (b[1]) WayneHutchinson 87+
(C C Bealby) *in rr: drvn along 7th: hdwy and prom 10th: one pce fr 13th: hit last* **9/1**
5 dist **Chain**[201] 1574 9-9-11 **84** oh7 .... LeeVickers(3) —
(O Brennan) *hld up in rr: hdwy and prom 10th: lost pl 13th: sn bhd: t.o* **33/1**
0511 **6** 1¾ **Tipp Top (IRE)**[26] 4580 9-9-8 **85** .... (t) MrGTumelty(7) —
(O Brennan) *chsd ldrs: reminders after 4th: lost pl 12th: sn bhd: t.o* **4/1**[3]
1415 **7** 1 **Reverse Swing**[108] 3129 9-10-12 **96** .... JodieMogford —
(Mrs H Dalton) *chsd ldr: led 4th: hit 13th: hdd next: wknd qckly 2 out: sn bhd: t.o* **15/2**
P61P **P** **Log On Intersky (IRE)**[23] 4618 10-11-12 **110** .... RichardHobson —
(J R Cornwall) *led to 4th: reminders 11th: lost pl 12th: sn bhd: t.o whn p.u bef 2 out* **18/1**

5m 28.8s (-15.70) **Going Correction** -0.60s/f (Firm) **8** Ran SP% **120.6**
Speed ratings: **104,101,101,99**,— —,—,— CSF £21.67 CT £47.29 TOTE £8.30: £2.40, £1.80, £1.50; EX 33.70.
Owner R C Guest **Bred** Mrs Margaret Fitzgerald **Trained** Brancepeth, Co Durham

FOCUS
The winner turned in a personal best, the runner-up, on his favourite stamping ground, ran to his mark.

NOTEBOOK
Jodante(IRE), with the cheepieces back on, went round in cruise control with his very promising young rider exuding confidence. He took it up hard on the steel and was value for double the official margin. *(op 5-1 tchd 6-1)*
New Perk(IRE), winner on his last five visits here, was racing from a 6lb higher mark. Under pressure with a full circuit to go, he stuck to his task to grab a fortuitous second spot near the line.
Lightning Strikes(IRE), runner-up to Rhythm King in a hunter chase here a month ago, found the winner cruising past him going to the last. Sadly he broke down and lost second spot near the line. *(op 5-2 tchd 3-1 in a place)*
Longstone Loch(IRE), in first-time blinkers, was soon being driven to keep up and he was left behind from four out. *(op 7-1)*
Tipp Top(IRE), 6lb higher, could not dominate and was soon being put about his job. He dropped right out at the first fence on the final circuit. *(tchd 9-2)*

The Form Book, Raceform Ltd, Compton, RG20 6NL

4901 THE QUEEN'S CUP, AN EASTERN COUNTIES HUNTERS' CHASE (18 fncs) 3m 110y

4:55 (4:55) (Class 6) 5-Y-0+ **£1,977** (£608; £304)

Form				RPR
-P21	**1**		**Sea Ferry (IRE)**^{8} [4799] 10-11-5 81 ... MrMBriggs$^{(7)}$ (Mrs Antonia Bealby) *trckd ldrs: wnt 2nd 7th: chal last: styd on to ld last 100yds* **3/1**^{2}	102+
-F22	**2**	*1 1/4*	**Montys Tag (IRE)**^{24} [4607] 13-11-9 ... MrNBloom$^{(3)}$ (S R Andrews) *led: jnd last: hdd and no ex run-in* **3/1**^{2}	99
5/1-	**3**	*11*	**Deckie (IRE)**^{22} 11-11-7 ... MrDKemp$^{(5)}$ (D J Kemp) *rel to r: wnt prom 6th: outpcd 13th: no threat after* **6/4**^{1}	94+
P/P	**4**	*dist*	**Tap The Father (IRE)**^{8} [4799] 13-11-3 ... MrMatthewSmith$^{(5)}$ (Fred Farrow) *chsd ldrs: lost pl 13th: sn bhd: t.o* **50/1**	—
PP/F	**5**	*5*	**Dunmanus Bay (IRE)**^{22} 9-11-5 ... MrRJBarrett$^{(7)}$ (Mrs Julie Read) *chsd ldrs: hit 2nd: drvn along 5th: wknd 12th: t.o* **9/1**^{3}	—
/3-4	**F**		**Bush Hill Bandit (IRE)**^{16} 11-11-5 ... MissALStennett$^{(7)}$ (Mrs Anne-Marie Hays) *trckd ldrs: pckd 2nd: fell heavily 3rd* **16/1**	—
00/	**P**		**Present Moment (IRE)**^{338} 8-11-1 ... MrABraithwaite$^{(7)}$ (Mrs Ruth Hayter) *bhd whn hmpd 3rd: drvn along and hit 7th: sn bhd: t.o whn p.u bef 13th* **18/1**	—

6m 25.0s (-12.60) **Going Correction** -0.60s/f (Firm) 7 Ran SP% **113.1**
Speed ratings: **96,95,92,—,—** —,— CSF £12.60 TOTE £4.70: £2.10, £2.00; EX 18.30.
Owner Mrs J A C Lundgren **Bred** T A Keating **Trained** Barrowby, Lincs
■ Stewards' Enquiry : Mr Matthew Smith two-day ban: careless riding (Apr 28,30)

FOCUS
Last year's winner Deckie fluffed his lines at the start, the first two ran to their pre-race marks.

NOTEBOOK
Sea Ferry(IRE) is not the most natural jumper but he still has a good attitude and finally won the argument on the run-in. *(op 5-2 tchd 10-3)*
Montys Tag(IRE), in his twilight years, tried hard to run them ragged but had to give best in the closing stages. He deserves bags of credit for this. *(op 7-2)*
Deckie(IRE), last year's winner, has been in fine form in points. He was reluctant to jump off and could not go with the first two from four out. *(op 11-8)*
Bush Hill Bandit(IRE), who this in 2003, fell heavily at the third fence and had to be put down.

4902 GG.COM MARES' ONLY MAIDEN OPEN NATIONAL HUNT FLAT RACE 2m

5:30 (5:30) (Class 6) 4-6-Y-0 **£1,713** (£499; £249)

Form				RPR
35	**1**		**The Music Queen**^{61} [3931] 5-11-0 ... JimCrowley (G A Swinbank) *chsd ldr: led over 1f out: hrd rdn and hld on towards fin* **11/4**^{1}	89
	2	*3/4*	**Maggie Mathias (IRE)** 5-10-4 ... RichardKilloran$^{(10)}$ (B G Powell) *chsd ldrs: outpcd 6f out: rallied 3f out: wnt 2nd ins last: no ex nr line* **7/1**	88+
	3	*2 1/2*	**Mardi Roberta (IRE)** 4-10-4 ... JohnnyLevins$^{(5)}$ (B G Powell) *led: qcknd 6f out: hdd over 1f out: kpt on same pce fnl f* **14/1**	82+
	4	*7*	**High Life** 4-10-9 ... WayneHutchinson (A King) *chsd ldrs: effrt over 3f out: wknd appr fnl f* **5/1**^{2}	74
	5	*9*	**Taipan Sue (IRE)** 5-11-0 ... AntonyEvans (Noel T Chance) *in tch: drvn along and outpcd 6f out: kpt on fnl 3f* **6/1**^{3}	70
	6	*2 1/2*	**Harissa (IRE)** 4-10-2 ... SimonElliott$^{(7)}$ (J W Mullins) *hld up in rr: hdwy 5f out: nvr nr ldrs* **33/1**	62
2	**7**	*4*	**True Dove**^{67} [3820] 4-10-9 ... AnthonyRoss (R A Fahey) *rn wd and lost pl bnd after 1f: in rr: sme hdwy 6f out: nvr a factor* **11/4**^{1}	58
6	**8**	*5*	**So Chic**^{54} [4059] 4-10-2 ... MrGTumelty$^{(7)}$ (A King) *chsd ldrs: drvn and outpcd 6f out: sn lost pl* **20/1**	53
-6	**9**	*3*	**Navelina**^{112} [2961] 6-11-0 ... AlanO'Keeffe (T J Fitzgerald) *hld up in rr: sme hdwy 6f out: nvr on terms* **16/1**	55
0	**10**	*17*	**Ellerslie Jackie**^{30} [4507] 6-11-0 ... JodieMogford (O Brennan) *racd wd thrght: in tch: drvn and lost pl 7f out: t.o 3f out* **50/1**	38
	11	*2*	**Lucky Pearl** 5-10-11 ... LeeVickers$^{(3)}$ (O Brennan) *a in rr: bhd fnl 7f: t.o 3f out* **20/1**	36
04/0	**P**		**Bonny Busona**^{59} [3961] 6-10-9 ... ShaneWalsh$^{(5)}$ (K F Clutterbuck) *w.r.s: a wl detached in last: t.o 6f out: eventually p.u over 1f out* **33/1**	—

3m 52.0s (-18.20) **Going Correction** -0.60s/f (Firm)
WFA 4 from 5yo+ 5lb 12 Ran SP% **126.7**
Speed ratings: **103,102,101,97,93 92,90,87,86,77 76,**— CSF £23.35 TOTE £3.40: £1.90, £2.90, £3.80; EX 49.80 Place 6 £60.89, Place 5 £20.12.
Owner Abbadis Racing Club **Bred** Wickfield Farm Partnership **Trained** Melsonby, N Yorks

FOCUS
The gallop was sound and the race has been rated through the winner.

NOTEBOOK
The Music Queen, who moved moderately to post, battled away and under severe pressure did just enough to take this modest mares-only bumper. *(op 9-4 tchd 3-1)*
Maggie Mathias(IRE), who moved poorly to post, came with a renewed effort and in the end was just held. *(op 8-1 tchd 13-2)*
Mardi Roberta(IRE), a sister to Big Rob, looks an embryo chaser. She quickened up the pace and soon had them strung out but she was leg weary near the line. *(op 16-1)*
High Life, a rangy filly, did not get home and will be seen to better advantage over hurdles in due course. *(op 9-2)*
Taipan Sue(IRE), who is not that big, was struggling soon after the halfway mark. *(op 7-1)*
Harissa(IRE), who is only small, stayed on when it was all over.
True Dove was on the backfoot after running wide on the first turn. She could never get back into the race and something was amiss here. *(op 7-2)*
Navelina *Official explanation: trainer said mare was found to be in season (op 12-1)*
T/Plt: £55.70 to a £1 stake. Pool: £24,666.15. 322.85 winning tickets. T/Qpdt: £11.80 to a £1 stake. Pool: £1,353.80. 84.55 winning tickets. WG

4449 HUNTINGDON (R-H)

Monday, April 17

OFFICIAL GOING: Good to firm (good in places)
Wind: Moderate, half behind Weather: Showers

4903 BETFRED MILLION (S) H'CAP HURDLE (8 hdls) 2m 110y

2:05 (2:08) (Class 5) (0-90,90) 4-Y-0+ **£2,740** (£798; £399)

Form				RPR
4600	**1**		**Quotable**^{53} [4074] 5-11-2 80 ... LeightonAspell (O Sherwood) *a.p: led sn after 3 out: clr last: rdn out* **6/1**^{3}	94+
004F	**2**	*3*	**After Lent (IRE)**^{27} [4556] 5-11-2 87 ... AndrewGlassonbury$^{(7)}$ (M C Pipe) *t.k.h in mid-div: hdwy 5th: chsd wnr appr 2 out: rdn appr last: no imp* **9/2**^{2}	98
0454	**3**	*14*	**Southern Bazaar (USA)**^{82} [3557] 5-9-12 69 ... PatrickMcDonald$^{(7)}$ (M E Sowersby) *hld up in mid-div: hdwy appr 4th: rdn and sltly outpcd 5th: one pce fr 3 out* **7/2**^{1}	66
F00U	**4**	*8*	**Weet An Haul**^{4} [4828] 5-10-6 70 ... RJGreene (T Wall) *hld up towards rr: rdn and hdwy after 5th: wknd after 3 out: hit last* **66/1**	59
4330	**5**	*1 1/4*	**Grand Prairie (SWE)**^{27} [4566] 10-11-0 83 ... (b) EamonDehdashti$^{(5)}$ (G L Moore) *hld up in mid-div: hdwy appr 4th: wknd appr 2 out* **6/1**^{3}	73+
0050	**6**	*shd*	**Trackattack**^{34} [3956] 4-11-7 90 ... JoeTizzard (P Howling) *w ldr tl appr 4th: wknd appr 3 out* **16/1**	73
0U6	**7**	*1 1/4*	**Carpet Ride**^{35} [4416] 4-10-6 82 ... CharlieStudd$^{(7)}$ (B G Powell) *hdwy after 2nd: led 4th: hit 3 out: sn hdd: wknd 2 out* **13/2**	63
PRPO	**8**	*2 1/2*	**Kadlass (FR)**^{9} [4783] 11-9-10 67 ... RyanCummings$^{(7)}$ (Mrs D Thomas) *bhd: rdn after 5th: sme hdwy whn mstke 3 out: n.d* **66/1**	51
3/PU	**9**	*25*	**General Hopkins (IRE)**^{29} [4526] 11-10-2 73 ... MrGPewter$^{(7)}$ (G R Pewter) *led to 4th: wknd after 5th* **50/1**	32
P/65	**10**	*7*	**Brunston Castle**^{64} [3885] 6-11-12 90 ... (t) NoelFehily (A W Carroll) *a bhd* **12/1**	42
0-PP	**11**	*dist*	**Mr Micky (IRE)**^{123} [2845] 8-11-4 82 ... PhilipHide (M B Shears) *a bhd: t.o* **20/1**	—
6PP/	**12**	*shd*	**Got Alot On (USA)**^{785} 8-10-0 64 oh1 ... HenryOliver (F E Sutherland) *t.k.h: prom: j.big 1st: wknd after 4th: t.o* **28/1**	—
55-P	**P**		**Arkholme**^{31} [4475] 5-11-4 89 ... (p) RichardSpate$^{(7)}$ (N A Dunger) *a bhd: t.o whn p.u bef 3 out* **25/1**	—
POP/	**P**		**Crusoe (IRE)**^{10} [2866] 9-10-1 65 ... AndrewTinkler (A Sadik) *bhd fr 5th: t.o whn p.u bef 2 out* **12/1**	—

3m 54.9s (-0.80) **Going Correction** 0.0s/f (Good)
WFA 4 from 5yo+ 5lb 14 Ran SP% **120.6**
Speed ratings: **101,99,93,89,88 88,88,86,75,71** —,—,—,— CSF £31.74 CT £110.86 TOTE £7.10: £2.40, £2.30, £2.10; EX 44.90.There was no bid for the winner
Owner P A Deal **Bred** Peter Deal **Trained** Upper Lambourn, Berks

FOCUS
A weak race in which the runners could muster just three previous hurdling wins between them. The third and fourth set the level for the form.

NOTEBOOK
Quotable is out of a half-sister to 1997 Champion Hurdle winner Make A Stand who raced in the same colours. Dropped into selling company for the first time, she moved to the front after the third last and stayed on well for a decisive victory. Now she has got off the mark there could be a bit more to come.
After Lent(IRE), keen once again, went into second place two from home but was soon making no impression on the mare, although he did finish clear of the rest. He needs to settle better. *(op 6-1)*
Southern Bazaar(USA), who will benefit from this first run since January, was keeping on at the end having been outpaced. On this showing he needs further. *(op 5-1)*
Weet An Haul, who is fully exposed, had never previously reached the frame over hurdles and was pulled up in a point-to-point last month, albeit with a slipping saddle.
Carpet Ride, headed by the winner after the third last, soon weakened but was still disputing third at the final flight. Stamina looks to be a problem. *(op 5-1)*
Crusoe(IRE) *Official explanation: jockey said gelding lost its action (op 9-1)*

4904 BETFRED MILLION NOVICES' CHASE (19 fncs) 3m

2:40 (2:40) (Class 4) 5-Y-0+ **£3,903** (£1,146; £573; £286)

Form				RPR
0143	**1**		**Party Games (IRE)**^{50} [4130] 9-11-4 110 ... (p) PhilipHide (G L Moore) *w ldr: led 12th: nt fluent 3 out: rdn clr last: eased considerably flat* **5/6**^{1}	112+
200P	**2**	*4*	**Pirandello (IRE)**^{12} [4736] 8-11-4 105 ... JohnMcNamara (K C Bailey) *hld up: hdwy 10th: hit 11th: lft 2nd 15th: rdn after 2 out: no ch w wnr* **8/1**	98
51-P	**3**	*2*	**Espresso Forte (IRE)**^{19} [4662] 7-11-4 95 ... PaulMoloney (Miss H C Knight) *hld up: hdwy and wnt 2nd 13th tl blnd bdly 15th: mstke 3 out: sn rdn: one pce* **11/2**^{3}	102+
224P	**4**	*dist*	**Superrollercoaster**^{59} [3965] 6-11-4 92 ... (v) LeightonAspell (O Sherwood) *led: mstke 9th: nt fluent and hdd 12th: wkng whn nt fluent 14th: t.o* **4/1**^{2}	—
PP-P	**F**		**Red Socialite (IRE)**^{22} [4639] 9-11-1 95 ... WilliamKennedy$^{(3)}$ (D R Gandolfo) *nt j.w: hld up: disputing 3rd whn fell 8th* **14/1**	—

6m 4.70s (-7.60) **Going Correction** -0.525s/f (Firm) 5 Ran SP% **107.7**
Speed ratings: **91,89,89,**—,— CSF £7.34 TOTE £1.60: £1.10, £2.90; EX 8.80.
Owner Goldfingers **Bred** G N Cannon **Trained** Woodingdean, E Sussex

FOCUS
A moderate winning time, 7.3 seconds slower than the later handicap chase over the same trip. Comfortable in the end for Party Games, whose four opponents had all been pulled up on their latest start, and he was value for 14 lengths.

NOTEBOOK
Party Games(IRE), back at the venue of his one previous chase success, had 5lb and more in hand on BHB figures. In front with a lap to go, he was momentarily headed after a slow jump at the third last but was soon back in command and ended up coasting home. He was value for considerably more than the final margin. *(op 10-11 tchd Evens)*
Pirandello(IRE) jumped soundly on this chase debut but, after looking a threat at the third last, he was soon put in his place. He has now finished runner-up on four of his last seven starts. *(op 7-1 tchd 13-2)*
Espresso Forte(IRE) was a close second when blundering badly five from home, Moloney doing well to stay aboard, and another error two fences later ended his hopes. *(op 7-1 tchd 5-1)*
Superrollercoaster had started to jump sketchily prior to losing his lead with a circuit to run. Soon dropping to the rear, he completed in his own time. *(op 7-2 tchd 9-2)*
Red Socialite(IRE) jumped poorly before departing. *(op 12-1 tchd 11-1)*

4905 BETFRED MILLION MAIDEN HURDLE (10 hdls) 2m 5f 110y

3:15 (3:15) (Class 4) 4-Y-0+ **£3,253** (£955; £477; £238)

Form				RPR
352	**1**		**Surface To Air**^{18} [4676] 5-10-4 ... AngharadFrieze$^{(10)}$ (Mrs P N Dutfield) *hld up in rr: hdwy appr 3 out: j.rt 2 out: sn rdn: j.rt last: hung rt and led flat: cleverly* **10/3**^{2}	102+
3453	**2**	*1*	**Cave Of The Giant (IRE)**^{23} [4616] 4-10-8 110 ... JoeTizzard (T D McCarthy) *a.p: led 3 out: hrd rdn and hdd flat: nt qckn* **7/4**^{1}	91
50	**3**	*5*	**Sea Wall**^{24} [4604] 4-10-8 ... NoelFehily (Jonjo O'Neill) *hld up in mid-div: hdwy appr 6th: rdn appr 2 out: one pce flat* **8/1**	87+
-0F4	**4**	*6*	**Double Law**^{24} [4604] 6-11-0 ... BarryFenton (Miss E C Lavelle) *sn led: hit 4th: hdd and hit 3 out: wknd 2 out* **9/2**^{3}	87+
F3PP	**5**	*14*	**Lescer's Lad**^{137} [2592] 9-11-0 69 ... JimmyMcCarthy (Mrs A M Woodrow) *hld up in mid-div: hdwy appr 6th: wknd 3 out* **100/1**	72

0P00 **6** 2 **Bob's Temptation**[83] 3545 7-11-0 75.........................(t) JohnMcNamara 70
(A J Wilson) *hld up towards rr: hdwy appr 6th: hit 3 out: sn wknd* **66/1**

5006 **7** 2 ½ **Cleymor House (IRE)**[60] 3938 8-10-7 72................ ThomasBurrows(7) 67
(John R Upson) *led early: chsd ldr tl rdn appr 6th: wknd appr 3 out* **66/1**

5/P **8** 1 ¼ **Mid Sussex Spirit**[38] 4359 7-11-0 .... PhilipHide 66
(G L Moore) *hld up towards rr: hdwy appr 6th: wknd appr 3 out* **20/1**

0 **9** 11 **Discomania**[7] 1397 4-10-8 ....(v) TomSiddall 49
(V Smith) *hld up and bhd: hdwy after 7th: wknd after 3 out* **66/1**

360 **10** 26 **Star Fever (IRE)**[139] 2559 5-11-0 .... PaulMoloney 29
(Miss H C Knight) *mid-div: mstke 6th: bhd fr 7th* **25/1**

0-04 **11** 23 **Quest On Air**[21] 4388 7-10-11 87.......................................(b) PaulO'Neill(3) 6
(J R Jenkins) *hld up in tch: rdn and hit 7th: sn wknd: t.o* **40/1**

-P00 **12** dist **Fort Royal (IRE)**[29] 4521 7-10-7 ....(p) MrGPewter(7) —
(G R Pewter) *hld up in tch: lost pl 3rd: t.o fr 6th* **100/1**

50 **P** **Seal Harbour (FR)**[23] 4623 6-11-0 ....(t) RobertThornton —
(A King) *a bhd: t.o 7th: p.u bef 3 out* **16/1**

0 **P** **Murrieta**[62] 3908 4-10-1 .... RJGreene —
(Miss J R Gibney) *bhd fr 3rd: hit 4th: p.u bef 5th* **50/1**

6 **P** **Executive Friend (IRE)**[123] 2844 7-11-0 .... HenryOliver —
(O Brennan) *a bhd: t.o whn p.u bef 2 out* **33/1**

PP **P** **Curate (USA)**[30] 4501 7-10-11 .... MrTGreenall(3) —
(M E Sowersby) *prom tl wknd 5th: bhd whn p.u bef 6th* **100/1**

0F- **P** **Yukon Jack**[453] 3414 8-10-7 .... AndrewGlassonbury(7) —
(N J Pomfret) *hld up in tch: blnd 2nd: wknd 5th: bhd whn p.u after 6th* **100/1**

0-6 **P** **Hermano Cordobes (IRE)**[112] 2968 6-11-0 .... JasonMaguire —
(Mrs J R Buckley) *hld up towards rr: hdwy appr 6th: wknd appr 3 out: p.u bef 2 out* **20/1**

5m 9.40s (-1.40) **Going Correction** 0.0s/f (Good)
WFA 4 from 5yo+ 6lb **18** Ran SP% **123.8**
Speed ratings: **102,101,99,97,92 91,90,90,86,77 68,—,—,—,— —,—,—** CSF £8.90 TOTE £4.90: £1.60, £1.80, £2.30; EX 9.20.
Owner Tim Urry **Bred** Kenneth Broom, Timothy Urry And Beverley Parker **Trained** Axmouth, Devon
■ Stewards' Enquiry : Mr G Pewter 10-day ban: improper riding - failed to dismount when appeared to be lame on pulling up (Apr 28,30, May 2-6, 9-11)

FOCUS

This was run at a decent pace and could be rated higher, but has been treated cautiously, using the fifth, sixth and seventh as the guides.

NOTEBOOK

Surface To Air was held up some 20 lengths off the pace before improving steadily leaving the back straight. He was stilll only third and under pressure over the final flight but, unlike at Wincanton, Frieze had timed things right and she was able to put down her stick and allow the gelding to coast home once he had struck the front. He had no problem with the sound surface and is progressing well. *(op 11-4 tchd 7-2)*

Cave Of The Giant(IRE), upped in trip and tackling a sound surface, looked sure to win on the home turn but, although he did nothing wrong, he was cut down by the winner after the last. His turn will come in ordinary company. *(op 2-1)*

Sea Wall, a useful middle-distance handicapper on the Flat for Roger Charlton, ran his best race so far over hurdles on this third start but was held in second when making a slight mistake at the final flight.

Double Law was responsible for setting a decent gallop but he could not pull out any extra when headed. *(op 6-1)*

Lescer's Lad is thoroughly exposed as a plating-class maiden.

Bob's Temptation showed a glimmer of promise but did not get home.

Fort Royal(IRE) *Official explanation: vet said gelding finished lame*

Curate(USA) *Official explanation: jockey said gelding bled from the nose (op 20-1)*

Seal Harbour(FR) *Official explanation: jockey said gelding had a breathing problem (op 20-1)*

4906 N B TOFTS PLUMBING AND HEATING CONTRACTORS LTD H'CAP CHASE (17 fncs 2 omitted) 3m

3:50 (3:51) (Class 3) (0-120,117) 5-Y-0+ **£6,506** (£1,910; £955; £477)

Form RPR

24PO **1** **Tribal Dancer (IRE)**[27] 4567 12-9-11 93..................... LiamTreadwell(5) 104+
(Miss Venetia Williams) *t.k.h: wnt prom 3rd: led 2 out: rdn and hung rt flat: r.o wl* **12/1**

43P1 **2** 5 **Bubble Boy (IRE)**[8] 4806 7-11-1 113 7ex........................ CharlieStudd(7) 118
(B G Powell) *a.p: led 10th to 2 out: one pce* **4/1**[2]

P514 **3** 10 **Magic Of Sydney (IRE)**[96] 3343 10-10-12 103.................. BarryFenton 100+
(R Rowe) *prom: led appr 4th to 10th: hit 11th: wknd appr 2 out* **9/1**

-650 **4** 7 **Zaffamore (IRE)**[112] 3000 10-11-8 113................................ PaulMoloney 101
(Miss H C Knight) *hld up: reminders after 9th: nvr nr ldrs* **15/2**

FF53 **5** 3 **Moonlit Harbour**[25] 4583 7-11-0 112................................ MrSWByrne(7) 97
(Ferdy Murphy) *hld up and bhd: hdwy after 3 out: sn rdn and no imp: 4th and no ch whn mstke last* **12/1**

5415 **6** 2 **Caribbean Cove (IRE)**[31] 4476 8-10-12 106..................... PaulO'Neill(3) 89
(Miss Venetia Williams) *hld up: hdwy 12th: hit 14th: wknd appr 2 out* **8/1**

/002 **7** 2 ½ **Pro Dancer (USA)**[25] 4593 8-11-7 117.....................(p) MrTJO'Brien(5) 98
(P Bowen) *hld up in tch: blnd 13th (water): blnd 3 out: sn wknd* **16/1**

1205 **8** 12 **Ultimate Limit**[130] 2717 6-10-5 96.................................. ChristianWilliams 65
(A Ennis) *a bhd* **7/2**[1]

523P **P** **Jackson (FR)**[33] 4447 9-11-11 116.................................. RobertThornton —
(A King) *hld up in tch: rdn 8th: blnd 9th: sn bhd: p.u bef 14th* **6/1**[3]

PPP6 **P** **Ankles Back (IRE)**[141] 2524 9-10-12 103............................... RJGreene —
(T Wall) *led tl appr 4th: rdn 14th: wknd after 3 out: p.u bef 2 out* **12/1**

5m 57.4s (-14.90) **Going Correction** -0.525s/f (Firm) **10** Ran SP% **118.3**
Speed ratings: **103,101,98,95,94 94,93,89,—,—** CSF £62.14 CT £464.66 TOTE £13.10: £2.70, £2.10, £2.70; EX 74.20.
Owner You Can Be Sure **Bred** J Ward **Trained** Kings Caple, H'fords

FOCUS

A modest handicap with the runner-up setting the standard. The fence at end of back straight omitted.

NOTEBOOK

Tribal Dancer(IRE), who won this event two years ago, was ending a long losing run. There was no repeat of the recalcitrance he showed last time at Warwick and, in front two out, he quickly cleared away on the flat.

Bubble Boy(IRE), under a 7lb penalty for his Worcester win, was in front with a circuit to run but the winner had his measure from the second last. He jumped particularly well and there is another race in him on his favoured sound surface. *(op 9-2)*

Magic Of Sydney(IRE), dropped 3lb but still 8lb above his last winning mark, ran a fair race on this seasonal debut and should benefit from the run.

Zaffamore(IRE), absent since Boxing Day, is now 10lb lower than at the start of the season but is still not firing. *(op 8-1 tchd 9-1)*

Moonlit Harbour made ground to tack on to the leading bunch but failed to stay this longer trip and was tired in fourth when making a mistake at the last. *(op 11-1)*

Caribbean Cove(IRE), a stablemate of the winner, has yet to convince that he wants this far.

Ultimate Limit had run lacklustre races on his last two starts and a four-month break did nothing to revitalise him. He never looked happy and was in the rear division throughout. *(op 4-1 tchd 9-2)*

Jackson(FR) *Official explanation: jockey said gelding never travelled (op 7-1)*

4907 BETFREDPOKER.COM H'CAP HURDLE (10 hdls) 2m 5f 110y

4:25 (4:27) (Class 4) (0-110,109) 4-Y-0+ **£3,426** (£998; £499)

Form RPR

3225 **1** **Vivante (IRE)**[225] 1410 8-9-7 83 oh2...............................(tp) MrDEngland(7) 84
(A J Wilson) *sn led: hdd after 5th: led appr 3 out: drvn out* **14/1**

U51 **2** 1 ¼ **Orange Street**[45] 4212 6-11-12 109............................ BenjaminHitchcott 110+
(Mrs L J Mongan) *hld up in mid-div: mstke 7th: hdwy appr 3 out: chsd wnr after 2 out: mstke last: kpt on* **4/1**[1]

0016 **3** 12 **Coralbrook**[33] 4453 6-10-12 95..................................(b) JimmyMcCarthy 84+
(Mrs P Robeson) *led early: prom: reminders after 5th: led 6th tl appr 3 out: wknd last* **11/2**[2]

P6F- **4** 1 ½ **Envious**[642] 953 7-10-3 89... OwynNelmes(3) 76
(Miss J Feilden) *hld up and bhd: hdwy 7th: rdn appr 3 out: wknd 2 out* **14/1**

-P46 **5** 2 ½ **Oyster Pearl (IRE)**[35] 4429 7-11-0 97.............................. ChristianWilliams 81
(P Bowen) *hld up in mid-div: hdwy after 5th: rdn appr 2 out: wknd appr last* **20/1**

3503 **6** 5 **Assoon**[26] 4570 7-11-3 100..(b) PhilipHide 81+
(G L Moore) *prom: hit 7th: wknd 3 out* **6/1**[3]

063P **7** 14 **Orki Des Aigles (FR)**[112] 2994 4-9-13 95................ PatrickMcDonald(7) 54
(Ferdy Murphy) *mid-div: pushed along after 1st: sn bhd* **20/1**

0656 **8** 3 **Simply Mystic**[98] 3318 6-11-6 103...................................... PadgeWhelan 65
(P D Niven) *prom tl wknd 6th* **9/1**

4350 **9** 3 ½ **Delightful Cliche**[93] 3393 5-11-6 103.............................. WarrenMarston 62
(Mrs P Sly) *hld up and bhd: hdwy appr 6th: mstke 7th: sn wknd* **10/1**

0P-3 **P** **Autumn Rain (USA)**[27] 4566 9-10-0 90.............................. MissLHorner(7) —
(G Brown) *prom to 5th: bhd whn p.u and dismntd bef 3 out* **15/2**

4P/0 **P** **Afadan (IRE)**[4] 4838 8-10-7 93.......................................(v[1]) PaulO'Neill(3) —
(J R Jenkins) *bhd: short-lived effrt 6th: t.o whn p.u bef 3 out* **66/1**

0004 **P** **Etendard Indien (FR)**[25] 4593 5-11-8 105........................ AndrewTinkler —
(N J Henderson) *prom: led after 5th to 6th: wknd 3 out: p.u bef 2 out* **11/2**[2]

5m 11.0s (0.20) **Going Correction** 0.0s/f (Good)
WFA 4 from 5yo+ 6lb **12** Ran SP% **120.3**
Speed ratings: **99,98,94,93,92 90,85,84,83,— —,—** CSF £70.18 CT £357.87 TOTE £19.00: £3.80, £1.40, £2.50; EX 55.90.
Owner The Up And Running Partnership **Bred** Patrick Kinsella **Trained** Ham, Gloucs
■ Jim Wilson's first winner for over four years.

FOCUS

A moderate contest rated around the second.

NOTEBOOK

Vivante(IRE), off the track since September, had the cheekpieces back on and a tongue-strap was fitted. She stays further and, having kicked for home, was always going to hold on although the runner-up was closing. *(op 16-1)*

Orange Street, making his handicap debut, took time to pick up. In second when making a mistake at the last, he stayed on to cut the deficit on the flat but appeared to be hanging. He will stay a bit further than this. *(op 7-2 tchd 9-2)*

Coralbrook, back down in trip, was on the end of reminders from the fifth but plugged on and was only seen off going to the last. *(op 6-1 tchd 13-2)*

Envious, previously with Dick Allan, was last seen in July 2004 when a last-flight fall denied him victory at Worcester. Without his customary cheekpieces, this was a pleasing return to the track after such a lengthy absence. *(op 16-1)*

Oyster Pearl(IRE) faced up to the last two flights in third place but could not find a change of gear. This ground might have been fast enough for him. *(op 25-1)*

Afadan(IRE) *Official explanation: jockey said gelding had a breathing problem (op 7-1)*

Etendard Indien(FR) weakened pretty quickly from the cross flight and looks one to be wary of. *(op 7-1)*

4908 BETFREDPOKER.COM NOVICES' H'CAP CHASE (10 fncs 2 omitted) 2m 110y

5:00 (5:01) (Class 4) (0-105,100) 5-Y-0+ **£3,903** (£1,146; £573; £286)

Form RPR

U432 **1** **Spinaround**[25] 4590 8-11-5 93.....................................(v) TomDoyle 112+
(P R Webber) *a.p: blnd 2nd: mstke 5th: rdn to ld appr 2 out: clr last: r.o wl* **4/1**[1]

-5PP **2** 12 **Cupla Cairde**[22] 4633 6-10-1 75.................................(b) HenryOliver 82
(O Brennan) *mstke 1st: hdwy 4th: led after 3 out tl appr 2 out: one pce* **25/1**

53U5 **3** 4 **Ground Breaker**[91] 3418 6-11-9 100.................................. MrTGreenall(3) 103
(M W Easterby) *hld up and bhd: hdwy appr 3 out: one pce fr 2 out* **10/1**

-406 **4** 1 ½ **Quarrymount**[44] 4243 5-11-4 95... JasonMaguire 93
(J A B Old) *hld up in mid-div: hdwy 6th: one pce fr 3 out* **8/1**

0445 **5** 1 **Darialann (IRE)**[57] 4013 11-10-10 84.................................... TomSiddall 84
(O Brennan) *sn wl bhd: late hdwy: nrst fin* **28/1**

00P3 **6** 4 **Plantaganet (FR)**[12] 4735 8-10-10 84............................. RobertThornton 81+
(Ian Williams) *prom tl rdn and wknd 2 out* **9/2**[2]

R062 **7** 12 **Kinkeel (IRE)**[18] 4675 7-9-10 77 oh1 ow3................(b) WillieMcCarthy(7) 66+
(A W Carroll) *prom: led 7th tl after 3 out: wknd 2 out: blnd last* **10/1**

-400 **8** 8 **Prince Of Aragon**[313] 686 10-10-5 79....................(t) BenjaminHitchcott 55
(Miss Suzy Smith) *sn wl bhd: hmpd 4th* **16/1**

4211 **U** **Moscow Gold (IRE)**[117] 2936 9-10-4 81............................... OwynNelmes(3) —
(A E Price) *mid-div: mstke and uns rdr 4th* **5/1**[3]

PFPP **P** **Terminology**[22] 4643 8-10-3 82...............................(tp) MarkNicolls(5) —
(K C Bailey) *mstke 1st: sn wl bhd: t.o whn p.u bef 2 out* **50/1**

4F0 **P** **French Direction (IRE)**[76] 3663 7-11-3 91............................ PaulMoloney —
(R Rowe) *led to 3rd: led appr 5th to 7th: wknd after 3 out: p.u bef 2 out* **15/2**

2562 **P** **Karakum**[179] 1805 7-11-3 91... SeanCurran —
(A J Chamberlain) *w ldr: led 3rd: mstke 4th: hdd appr 5th: nt fluent and wknd 6th: t.o whn p.u bef 2 out* **12/1**

4m 2.70s (-6.60) **Going Correction** -0.525s/f (Firm)
WFA 5 from 6yo+ 3lb **12** Ran SP% **118.7**
Speed ratings: **94,88,86,85,85 83,77,74,—,— —,—** CSF £95.41 CT £946.45 TOTE £4.70: £1.90, £8.90, £2.90; EX 113.50.
Owner D R Stoddart **Bred** D R Stoddart **Trained** Mollington, Oxon

FOCUS

The fence at the end of the back straight was omitted. A truly-run race which took place in driving rain and the form looks solid enough.

NOTEBOOK

Spinaround ◆ raced in touch but did not get too involved in the early stages as the leaders went off rather fast. Picking off the leader at the second last, he came away in ready style. He is on the upgrade.

Cupla Cairde, a winner in Grade 3 company as a juvenile hurdler for Dessie Hughes in Ireland, had been pulled up in two previous runs from this yard. It looked as if he might spring a shock when he took it up but the winner asserted at the second last.

Ground Breaker, without the tongue tie, stayed on from off the pace but was never in it. *(op 9-1)*

Quarrymount will have learned from this chase debut and a step up in trip might suit. *(op 10-1)*
Darialann(IRE), a stablemate of the second, was having his first run over fencdes since his days in Ireland. He was taken of his feet before staying on when it was all over. *(op 25-1)*
Plantaganet(FR) was somewhat disappointing with the drop in trip not really suiting. *(tchd 5-1)*
Kinkeel(IRE) did not get home after being partly responsible for the strong pace. *(op 11-1)*
Moscow Gold(IRE), returning from a four-month break and 10lb higher for this hat-trick attempt, did not get far.

4909 BETFRED MILLION INTERMEDIATE OPEN NATIONAL HUNT FLAT RACE — 2m 110y
5:35 (5:35) (Class 6) 4-6-Y-0 — **£2,055** (£599; £299)

Form				RPR
	1		**Grecian Groom (IRE)** 4-10-11 ..... NoelFehily (P D Niven) *a gng wl: led on bit over 3f out: shkn up and qckly clr fnl f: easily* **7/2**[1]	115+
10	**2**	*12*	**Mumbles Head (IRE)**[33] [4448] 5-11-4 ..... MrTJO'Brien[(5)] (P Bowen) *hld up in tch: ev ch 3f out: rdn and one pce fnl 2f* **4/1**[2]	112
	3	*6*	**Red Square Express** 4-10-8 ..... MrTGreenall[(3)] (M W Easterby) *hld up in mid-div: hdwy 9f out: rdn and one pce fnl 2f* **16/1**	94
23	**4**	*4*	**Medic (IRE)**[77] [3657] 5-10-9 ..... DavidCullinane[(7)] (T J Fitzgerald) *hld up in tch: rdn 5f out: one pce fnl 2f* **15/2**	95
	5	*2*	**Viper** 4-10-11 ..... PaulMoloney (R Hollinshead) *hld up and bhd: hdwy over 6f out: wknd over 1f out* **25/1**	88
	6	*½*	**Lord Morley (IRE)** 6-11-2 ..... AndrewTinkler (Karen McLintock) *hld up in tch: rdn 5f out: wknd over 2f out* **25/1**	93
335	**7**	*1 ½*	**Graphex**[57] [4011] 4-10-11 ..... (v[1]) RobertThornton (A King) *hld up in mid-div: rdn and hdwy 4f out: wknd over 2f out* **15/2**	86
6	**8**	*nk*	**Best Deal**[44] [4237] 5-10-11 ..... MarkNicolls[(5)] (B I Case) *hld up towards rr: styd on fnl 2f: nvr nrr* **33/1**	91
P36	**9**	*¾*	**Accumulus**[8] [4807] 6-10-13 ..... WilliamKennedy[(3)] (Noel T Chance) *hld up: hdwy over 6f out: wknd over 2f out* **10/1**	90
6	**10**	*11*	**Marlion (FR)**[23] [4623] 4-10-4 ..... AndrewGlassonbury[(7)] (B R Johnson) *hld up towards rr: sme hdwy over 5f out: n.d* **40/1**	74
0	**11**	*1 ½*	**Duke Of Kentford**[25] [4595] 4-10-11 ..... TomDoyle (P R Webber) *prom: led 5f out tl over 3f out: rdn and wknd over 2f out* **16/1**	73
0	**12**	*1 ½*	**Bowdlane Barb**[94] [3373] 5-10-4 ..... LiamTreadwell[(5)] (John A Harris) *t.k.h: prom tl wknd over 3f out* **100/1**	69
	13	*nk*	**Silver Feather (IRE)** 4-10-4 ..... PatrickMcDonald[(7)] (Ferdy Murphy) *hld up in mid-div: hdwy 9f out: wknd over 2f out* **25/1**	71
1	**14**	*3*	**Rocca's Boy (IRE)**[87] [3490] 4-10-11 ..... WillieMcCarthy[(7)] (M Wigham) *chsd ldr: led over 9f out to 5f out: wknd over 2f out* **11/2**[3]	75
0	**15**	*1 ¾*	**Gemini Storm**[22] [4637] 6-11-2 ..... HenryOliver (O Brennan) *hld up in mid-div: rdn over 5f out: sn bhd* **50/1**	71
0	**16**	*2 ½*	**Zaffarsson (IRE)**[23] [4622] 5-11-2 ..... BarryFenton (J S Moore) *a bhd* **33/1**	68
0	**17**	*3 ½*	**Zarbeau**[70] [3785] 4-10-8 ..... PaulO'Neill[(3)] (J M Jefferson) *t.k.h in mid-div: bhd fnl 5f* **40/1**	60
	18	*22*	**Galaxia (IRE)** 4-10-11 ..... JohnMcNamara (K C Bailey) *hld up in mid-div: hdwy 8f out: wknd over 3f out: t.o* **20/1**	38
0	**19**	*1 ¾*	**Headley (IRE)**[23] [4623] 5-11-2 ..... JimmyMcCarthy (J S Moore) *a bhd: t.o* **66/1**	41
0	**20**	*dist*	**Dottie West**[23] [4615] 6-10-9 ..... PadgeWhelan (Ms N M Hugo) *led: hdd over 9f out: wknd qckly: t.o* **100/1**	—

3m 49.4s (-7.10) **Going Correction** 0.0s/f (Good)
WFA 4 from 5yo+ 5lb — **20** Ran SP% **134.5**
Speed ratings: **102,96,93,91,90 90,89,89,89,84 83,82,82,81,80 79,77,67,66,—** CSF £16.29 TOTE £3.90: £1.90, £2.70, £5.30; EX 53.20 Place 6 £44.26, Place 5 £27.10.
Owner P D Niven **Bred** Ballymacoll Stud Farm Ltd **Trained** Barton-le-Street, N Yorks

FOCUS
A solid enough bumper with the runner-up and several outside the placings close to their pre-race marks.

NOTEBOOK
Grecian Groom(IRE) was bred for the Flat, being out of an unraced half-sister to high-class middle-distance performers Gamut and Multicoloured. He ran out an easy winner of this ordinary bumper, showing a nice turn of foot when asked to win his race, and should go on to better things. *(op 7-1)*
Mumbles Head(IRE), down the field at 200/1 behind Hairy Molly in the Champion Bumper at Cheltenham, ran a decent race under his penalty but probably came up against an above-average performer. *(tchd 9-2)*
Red Square Express is out of a winning hurdler who is a half-sister to smart hurdlers Anzum, Sh Boom and Jazilah. He stayed on in a manner which suggests that he has a future when stepped up in trip over hurdles.
Medic(IRE) made the frame for the third time in his many starts although he never looked a likely scorer here. *(op 13-2 tchd 8-1)*
Viper, a half-brother to winning hurdler Itcanbedone Again, travelled quite well before coming under pressure before the straight and is capable of improvement.
T/Plt: £30.80 to a £1 stake. Pool: £27,304.15. 646.70 winning tickets. T/Qpdt: £10.10 to a £1 stake. Pool: £1,607.50. 117.75 winning tickets. KH

4868 PLUMPTON (L-H)
Monday, April 17

OFFICIAL GOING: Good to soft
Race 7: charity Flat race not under Rules.
Wind: Light, half against Weather: Fine

4910 EASTER TREAT FOR LINDA'S BOY JUVENILE NOVICES' HURDLE (9 hdls) — 2m
2:30 (2:30) (Class 4) 4-Y-0 — **£3,903** (£1,146; £573; £286)

Form				RPR
P110	**1**		**Shamayoun (FR)**[11] [4747] 4-11-12 134 ..... (b) PJBrennan (C R Egerton) *led: hdd and hit 2nd: led again 5th and sn 5l clr: rdn and hanging lft fr 2 out: styd on wl: eased nr fin* **8/15**[1]	122+
5FF	**2**	*5*	**Mac Federal (IRE)**[45] [4211] 4-10-12 ..... AndrewThornton (M G Quinlan) *prom: chsd wnr after 5th: rdn and no real imp after 3 out: carried hd high fr 2 out* **9/1**[3]	100
205	**3**	*1 ¼*	**Ardglass (IRE)**[21] [4648] 4-10-12 ..... (p) MatthewBatchelor (Mrs P Townsley) *hld up: prog 5th: sn rdn: kpt on u.p after 3 out: no ch w wnr* **12/1**	99
2100	**4**	*17*	**Equilibria (USA)**[12] [3422] 4-11-5 105 ..... JamieMoore (G L Moore) *plld hrd early: hld up: prog after 5th: chsd ldng pair bef 3 out: wknd bef next* **11/2**[2]	89
5P	**5**	*2*	**Bilkie (IRE)**[22] [4631] 4-10-12 ..... SamThomas (John Berry) *chsd ldrs: stl in tch 3 out: wknd u.p bef next* **66/1**	80
060	**6**	*4*	**Hereditary**[56] [3714] 4-10-12 92 ..... TomScudamore (Mrs L C Jewell) *nt jump wl: hld up: outpcd after 5th and bhd: sme prog 3 out: no imp fr next* **25/1**	76
	P		**J'Adore (GER)**[120] 4-10-12 ..... DaveCrosse (R Curtis) *chsd ldrs: rdn 5th: wknd next and sn t.o: remote 8th whn p.u bef 2 out* **14/1**	—
4506	**P**		**Ghaill Force**[21] [4648] 4-10-7 93 ..... (t) RobertLucey-Butler[(5)] (P Butler) *a wl in rr: t.o after 6th: poor 7th whn p.u bef 2 out* **66/1**	—
P	**P**		**Maddox (POL)**[49] [4149] 4-10-9 ..... ColinBolger[(3)] (Mrs P Townsley) *plld hrd early: hld up: mstke 2nd: wknd 5th: t.o after next: p.u bef 2 out* **100/1**	—
300	**P**		**Laconicos (IRE)**[53] [4075] 4-10-5 93 ..... JustinMorgan[(7)] (W B Stone) *plld v hrd: led 2nd to 5th: wknd rapidly and t.o after next: p.u bef 2 out* **40/1**	—

4m 0.40s (-0.80) **Going Correction** +0.025s/f (Yiel) — **10** Ran SP% **115.2**
Speed ratings: **103,100,99,91,90 88,—,—,—,—** CSF £5.94 TOTE £1.60: £1.10, £2.10, £1.70; EX 5.40.
Owner Ronald Brimacombe **Bred** S A Aga Khan **Trained** Chaddleworth, Berks

FOCUS
An uncompetitive affair won as expected by Shamayoun with the placed horses running to their marks.

NOTEBOOK
Shamayoun(FR), a gutsy winner of the Fred Winter at the Festival, got involved in a suicidal speed duel at Aintree and this was a comparitively simple task. He had plenty of weight to shoulder, but went about his business in usual fashion. Despite hanging under pressure, he proved too strong for the opposition and was value for double the winning distance. He may not be that easy to place next season, but undoubtedly has an engine and could make an interesting chaser one day. *(op 4-9 tchd 4-7 in places)*
Mac Federal(IRE) was in the process of running a fair race when falling at the last at Newbury latest, second successive fall, and this would have done his confidence no harm at all. He looked a little reluctant under pressure, but deserves the benefit of the doubt for the time being. *(op 8-1)*
Ardglass(IRE) is a horse of modest ability and the first-time cheekpieces failed to make any real difference, but he will find easier opportunities than this. *(op 14-1)*
Equilibria(USA) has not yet built on his course win back in November and he pulled far too hard here to get home. *(op 10-1)*
Maddox(POL) *Official explanation: jockey said gelding was lame (op 66-1)*

4911 HARRY SANDLER MEMORIAL (S) H'CAP CHASE (12 fncs) — 2m 1f
3:05 (3:07) (Class 5) (0-90,89) 5-Y-0+
£3,131 (£925; £462; £231; £115; £58)

Form				RPR
5252	**1**		**Denarius Secundus**[21] [4653] 9-10-3 66 ow1 ..... (b) DaveCrosse (N R Mitchell) *mde most: drew clr fr 8th: hrd rdn after 2 out: unchal* **3/1**[1]	85+
3464	**2**	*12*	**Just Muckin Around (IRE)**[141] [2522] 10-11-4 86 ..... LiamHeard[(5)] (R H Buckler) *trckd ldrs: effrt 8th: chsd clr wnr 3 out: styd on but no imp fr next* **3/1**[1]	94
/000	**3**	*25*	**My Big Sister**[33] [4450] 7-10-12 82 ..... WayneKavanagh[(7)] (J W Mullins) *mstkes: prom: j.rt fnl circ: chsd wnr 8th tl blnd 3 out: v tired and j. wildly rt last* **20/1**	70+
-300	**4**	*12*	**Sarobar (IRE)**[53] [4080] 6-11-12 89 ..... (p) TomScudamore (M Scudamore) *prom: rdn and struggling 7th: hit next: sn wl adrift: hrd rdn to hold 4th nr fin* **9/2**[2]	60
54F0	**5**	*½*	**Jour De Mee (FR)**[8] [4794] 9-10-13 83 ..... MrSPJones[(7)] (G J Smith) *lost pl and rdn in rr after 4th: wl bhd 8th: t.o whn hmpd 3 out: modest rally fr next* **12/1**	54
P6P0	**6**	*5*	**The Rainbow Man**[12] [4735] 6-9-9 65 ..... (b[1]) MattyRoe[(7)] (J Ryan) *nvr on terms w ldrs: effrt to chse clr ldng trio 8th to 3 out: wknd* **40/1**	31
333U	**7**	*3*	**Before The Mast (IRE)**[8] [4798] 9-11-12 89 ..... PJBrennan (M F Harris) *hld up: rdn and effrt 7th but nvr on terms: disputing poor 4th whn blnd 3 out: wknd rapidly bef last* **11/2**[3]	52
U55P	**F**		**Mcsnappy**[37] [4370] 9-11-4 84 ..... RichardYoung[(3)] (J W Mullins) *a in rr: struggling fr 7th: poor 6th whn fell 3 out and knocked over as he got up* **10/1**	—
56F6	**P**		**Barnards Green (IRE)**[29] [4525] 8-10-6 69 ..... (p) JamieGoldstein (M Madgwick) *led briefly bef 2nd where mstke: w wnr to 7th: wknd rapidly next: crawled over 4 out and p.u* **14/1**	—

4m 24.7s (0.60) **Going Correction** -0.05s/f (Good) — **9** Ran SP% **114.2**
Speed ratings: **96,90,78,72,72 70,68,—,—** CSF £12.83 CT £147.50 TOTE £4.30: £1.50, £1.10, £3.70; EX 8.10.There was no bid for the winner
Owner Mrs Stephanie Atkinson **Bred** Stanley J Sharp **Trained** Piddletrenthide, Dorset

FOCUS
A poor event that took little winning and Denarius Secundus was finally able to get off the mark. The runner-up is the best guide.

NOTEBOOK
Denarius Secundus, winless in 30 previous attempts on the flat and over jumps, finally gained a deserved success after many solid efforts in defeat. Up there throughout, he galloped his rivals into submission, but he is hardly one to make a habit of backing and is worth opposing next time. *(op 11-4 tchd 10-3 and 7-2 in a place)*
Just Muckin Around(IRE) filled the same position as he had done in the corresponding race three years ago, and he was never in with a chance once the winner began to forge clear. This was his first start since November and he should come on for the outing. *(op 7-2)*
My Big Sister was well adrift of the front pair and simply made too many blunders. *(op 16-1)*
Sarobar(IRE) has been mixing hurdles and fences of late, but he was in trouble a long way out here. *(op 6-1)*
Jour De Mee(FR) would have certainly been fourth had he not collided with McSnappy after that one fell three from home, but he was well held anyhow and already in the process of disappointing. *(op 10-1)*

4912 PORTMAN BUILDING SOCIETY H'CAP HURDLE (12 hdls) — 2m 5f
3:40 (3:40) (Class 4) (0-105,105) 4-Y-0+ — **£5,204** (£1,528; £764; £381)

Form				RPR
PP20	**1**		**Manawanui**[11] [4756] 8-11-2 95 ..... RobertWalford (R H Alner) *racd wd: trckd ldrs: mstke 1st: effrt bef 3 out: drvn to ld narrowly bef 2 out: styd on* **7/1**[3]	100+
2323	**2**	*3 ½*	**Mistified (IRE)**[12] [4731] 5-10-9 91 ..... RichardYoung[(3)] (J W Mullins) *sn trckd ldrs: effrt bef 3 out: w wnr bef next: one pce u.p last* **5/1**[1]	92+
3/6	**3**	*nk*	**Stars Delight (IRE)**[251] [1188] 9-11-2 100 ..... RobertLucey-Butler[(5)] (Jim Best) *racd wd: hld up in midfield: prog to press ldrs 9th: led after 3 out to bef next: kpt on u.p* **11/2**[2]	100
0426	**4**	*5*	**Carly Bay**[21] [4652] 8-11-5 98 ..... TomScudamore (G P Enright) *hld up in rr: prog 9th: cl up 3 out: nt qckn and btn sn after* **14/1**	93

6030 **5** *12* **Esplendidos (IRE)**[103] 3242 7-10-2 **86**.......................(b[1]) DarylJacob[(5)] 69
(D P Keane) *w ldr: led 5th tl sn after 3 out: wknd* **14/1**

62P0 **6** *hd* **Lady Alderbrook (IRE)**[29] 4523 6-10-4 **83**..................... MarcusFoley 66
(C J Down) *lost pl 5th and sn in last pair: shuffled along at bk of main gp after 9th: nvr nr ldrs after* **20/1**

166U **7** *13* **Ressource (FR)**[29] 4523 7-10-2 **88**............................(b) MrWRussell[(7)] 58
(G L Moore) *hld up: prog to trck ldrs 7th: wknd 3 out: sddle slipped* **14/1**

620P **8** *20* **Maclean**[35] 4429 5-11-9 **102**...(b) JamieMoore 52
(G L Moore) *racd wd: hld up in rr: drvn and effrt 9th: mstke 3 out and wknd* **8/1**

P434 **9** *2 ½* **Soeur Fontenail (FR)**[18] 4677 9-11-10 **103**................. AndrewThornton 50
(N J Hawke) *racd wd: led to 5th: styd prom tl wknd and hit 3 out: sn eased* **5/1**[1]

6556 **10** *11* **Private Benjamin**[29] 4523 6-10-13 **92**.................... MatthewBatchelor 28
(M R Hoad) *racd wd: in tch in rr: mstke 8th: sn rdn and wknd: t.o* **16/1**

4506 **F** **Ridjit (FR)**[49] 4149 6-11-2 **95**.. PJBrennan —
(N J Gifford) *hld up: fell 2nd* **8/1**

2360 **P** **Corker**[60] 3943 4-11-4 **103**.. JamesDavies —
(D B Feek) *racd wd: rdn in rr bef 6th: t.o after 8th: p.u bef 3 out* **16/1**

4205 **P** **Sound Skin (IRE)**[182] 1773 8-10-11 **93**.......................(v) ColinBolger[(3)] —
(A Ennis) *prom: drvn and losing pl whn mstke 8th: t.o whn p.u bef 3 out* **16/1**

5m 24.7s (-0.10) **Going Correction** +0.025s/f (Yiel)
WFA 4 from 5yo+ 6lb **13** Ran SP% **125.8**
Speed ratings: **101,99,99,97,93 93,88,80,79,75** —,—,— CSF £44.95 CT £215.69 TOTE £9.40: £2.90, £1.70, £2.70; EX 32.90.
Owner J M Dare, T Hamlin, J W Snook **Bred** Mrs H A St Lo Stoddart **Trained** Droop, Dorset

FOCUS
An open handicap won in good fashion by Manawanui with the placed horses close to their marks.

NOTEBOOK
Manawanui showed no ill-effects of a poor run at Taunton earlier in the month, staying on dourly under pressure to grind out the result. Consistency is clearly not his strong point, but he is capable of his day and, although his record over fences is indifferent, he has twice won over them and he could be worth putting back over the larger obstacles. *(op 15-2 tchd 9-1)*
Mistified(IRE) has now finished either second or third on each of his last seven starts and he again did little wrong in defeat. He will find a race eventually and may be open to a little further improvement at the age of five. *(tchd 11-2)*
Stars Delight(IRE) was having only his second start since May 2003, has clearly had training difficulties, but he is evidently capable on his day and this was a fine effort. He has a race in him off this mark. *(op 15-2)*
Carly Bay is without a win in over three years, but she has run some fair races in defeat of late and this was another case in point. She is on a decent mark and can end the losing run before long.
Ressource(FR) *Official explanation: jockey said saddle slipped (op 16-1)*
Soeur Fontenail(FR), who is best known as a chaser, was racing over hurdles for the first time in over four years and she was already held when blundering at the third last. *(op 11-2)*

4913 FRIDAY-AD MAIDEN CHASE (14 fncs) 2m 4f
4:15 (4:16) (Class 5) 5-Y-O+ **£3,457** (£1,030; £521; £267; £139)

Form RPR

40PF **1** **Saddlers Cloth (IRE)**[31] 4474 6-10-7 .... MarcusFoley 97+
(J A Geake) *w ldr: led 4th to 8th and fr 10th: clr 3 out: v easily* **15/8**[1]

305P **2** *20* **Missyl (FR)**[41] 4288 6-11-0 105...................................... AndrewThornton 79
(R H Alner) *nt fluent and nvr gng wl in last trio: effrt after 10th: plugged on fr 2 out to snatch 2nd last strides* **10/3**[3]

505P **3** *nk* **Bally Rainey (IRE)**[76] 3660 7-11-0 77.................................. JamesDavies 79
(Mrs L C Jewell) *chsd ldrs: outpcd after 10th: rdn to chse wnr 3 out: no imp: lost 2nd last strides* **33/1**

P606 **4** *11* **The Hardy Boy**[8] 4802 6-11-0 66................................ MatthewBatchelor 68
(Miss A M Newton-Smith) *led to 4th: led 8th to 10th: sn hrd rdn: wknd 3 out* **16/1**

0FF6 **5** *16* **Fantastic Arts (FR)**[12] 4735 6-11-0 102.............................. SamThomas 52
(Miss Venetia Williams) *nt fluent in last trio: mstkes 6th and 7th: prog to join ldng pair 10th: wknd tamely 4 out* **5/2**[2]

3PP0 **U** **Desertmore Chief (IRE)**[8] 4794 7-10-7 ....(b) MrSPJones[(7)] —
(G J Smith) *j. ponderously: prom: u.p 8th: 7th and wkng whn uns rdr 10th* **25/1**

02P/ **F** **Koyaanisqatsi**[736] 4750 6-10-11 .... ColinBolger[(3)] —
(Jamie Poulton) *a in last pair: rdn and wknd 9th: wl t.o in last whn fell 3 out* **20/1**

/P-P **F** **Hidden Weapon**[16] 4689 9-10-7 .... JustinMorgan[(7)] —
(L Wells) *j. bdly: chsd ldrs: wkng whn blnd 4 out: hopelessly t.o whn fell last: winded* **16/1**

5m 13.0s (-5.45) **Going Correction** -0.05s/f (Good) **8** Ran SP% **109.7**
Speed ratings: **108,100,99,95,89** —,—,— CSF £7.93 TOTE £2.70: £1.20, £1.50, £5.00; EX 7.70.
Owner Lady G Wates **Bred** Edward Crow **Trained** Kimpton, Hants

FOCUS
A poor maiden chase won in emphatic style by the mare Saddlers Cloth who was value for more than the official margin.

NOTEBOOK
Saddlers Cloth(IRE), who appeared to have the race in the bag when taking a tired fall at the last at Fakenham last month, was dropping back half a mile in distance today and she seemed much more at home. Never far off the lead, she drew clear with the minimum of fuss to dispose of what was admittedly a moderate field. The former winning pointer remains unexposed and she can probably follow up, given the nature of this success. *(op 7-4 tchd 2-1)*
Missyl(FR), who did not appear to handle the heavy ground when disappointing on his recent chase debut at Exeter, was being niggled from a very early stage and failed to jump with the fluency of an Alner chaser. It is hoped he improves with experience, but the fact he struggled to get past 77-rated Bally Rainey does not augur well. *(op 7-2)*
Bally Rainey(IRE), winner of an Irish point, had not shown a great deal since arriving in Britain, but this was better and he was only just caught for second. His lowly rating would give him a chance in very low-grade handicaps. *(op 25-1)*
The Hardy Boy has not shown a great deal since coming from Ireland, but although his win there was on soft, he seems suited by better ground. *(op 20-1)*
Fantastic Arts(FR), who has twice fallen over fences, blundered his chance away and stopped worryingly quickly under pressure. *(op 2-1)*

4914 SPINAL RESEARCH H'CAP CHASE (18 fncs) 3m 2f
4:50 (4:51) (Class 5) (0-90,88) 5-Y-O+ **£3,492** (£1,065; £556; £302)

Form RPR

P-PP **1** **Test Of Friendship**[126] 2801 9-10-11 **76**.............................. TJPhelan[(3)] 83
(Mrs H Dalton) *wl plcd: trckd ldr 13th: rdn after 3 out: kpt on u.p to ld last: drvn out* **10/1**

5F00 **2** *1 ¾* **Peveril Pride**[38] 4353 8-9-11 **62** oh3.......................(t) RichardYoung[(3)] 67
(J A Geake) *t.k.h: prom: led 10th: hit 11th: gng bttr than rivals 3 out: rdn and hdd last: nt qckn* **33/1**

536 **3** *28* **Kappelhoff (IRE)**[26] 4576 9-10-4 **66**.........................(b) MatthewBatchelor 51+
(Mrs L Richards) *set off in last pair: reminders 7th: prog to chse ldrs and hit 9th: cl 3rd after 14th tl wknd and mstke 2 out: fin tired* **11/2**[3]

5224 **4** *dist* **Up The Pub (IRE)**[21] 4650 8-11-6 **82**............................(t) RobertWalford —
(R H Alner) *nvr gng wl in midfield: drvn after 10th: losing tch w ldrs whn hmpd 14th: plodded on: btn 61l* **10/3**[1]

-000 **F** **Great Benefit (IRE)**[140] 2555 7-11-4 **80**............................... SamThomas —
(Miss H C Knight) *hld up: 8th whn fell 2nd* **10/1**

P2P0 **F** **Buckland Gold (IRE)**[21] 4653 6-11-12 **88**.......................... JamesDavies —
(D B Feek) *settled in rr: prog to join ldrs 10th: wkng in 7th whn fell 14th* **20/1**

3332 **P** **Spider Boy**[21] 4650 9-10-3 **70**.........................(p) RobertLucey-Butler[(5)] —
(Miss Z C Davison) *several blunders and a in last trio: t.o 13th: p.u next* **9/2**[2]

PPPU **P** **Germany Park (IRE)**[26] 4578 8-9-12 **65**...................... TomGreenway[(5)] —
(W B Stone) *pressed ldr 2nd tl blnd 9th: lost pl: wknd and p.u on ins of fence 13th* **50/1**

435 **R** **Reach The Clouds (IRE)**[26] 4571 14-11-10 **86**............ JamieGoldstein —
(John R Upson) *a in rr: lost tch 12th: no ch whn nowhere to go and forced to refuse 13th* **14/1**

3435 **F** **Supreme Sir (IRE)**[9] 4785 8-11-0 **79**.............................. ColinBolger[(3)] —
(P G Murphy) *in tch in midfield: rdn at rr of main gp after 10th: prog u.p into cl 3rd whn fell 14th* **13/2**

/PP5 **P** **Designer Label (IRE)**[28] 4553 10-11-7 **83**.........................(p) PJBrennan —
(Carl Llewellyn) *led: mstke 9th: hdd next: drvn 12th: wkng whn hmpd 14th: t.o whn scrambled over 3 out and p.u* **10/1**

5U6P **P** **Multi Talented (IRE)**[39] 4321 10-10-12 **81**.................. JustinMorgan[(7)] —
(L Wells) *chsd ldrs to 7th: sn lost pl: struggling in last 9th: tailing off whn nrly c to a halt 13th: scrambled over and p.u* **16/1**

7m 2.30s (8.30) **Going Correction** -0.05s/f (Good) **12** Ran SP% **119.5**
Speed ratings: **85,84,75**,—,— —,—,—,— —,— CSF £281.53 CT £2001.19 TOTE £15.30: £3.90, £11.90, £1.80; EX 341.00.
Owner Severn River Racing **Bred** Mrs C J C Bailey **Trained** Norton, Shropshire

FOCUS
A slow time and those who did complete finished tired, so the race has been rated cautiously.

NOTEBOOK
Test Of Friendship, pulled up in both previous starts this season, had dropped 14lb as a result and he was able to rediscover his form on this return from a break. He found plenty for pressure and stayed on too strongly for the lightly-weighted runner-up, but the form is worth little with so few horses managing to complete. *(op 12-1)*
Peveril Pride, a poor performer on all previous evidence, looked the likeliest winner taking the third-last, but his early exertions took their toll and he failed to see his race out as strongly as the winner. He can find a race off this mark if it proves to be no fluke.
Kappelhoff(IRE) was soon in rear and, although he kept going for third, he was well beaten and never in the hunt. *(op 9-2)*
Up The Pub(IRE) was struggling a long way from the finish and was last to complete. *(op 4-1)*
Spider Boy *Official explanation: jockey said gelding was never travelling (op 11-2)*
Germany Park(IRE) *Official explanation: jockey said gelding was distressed (op 11-2)*
Supreme Sir(IRE), of those who failed to get around, was the only one still in with a winning chance and it is hoped this does not affect his confidence. *(op 11-2)*

4915 HOB BRITE MAIDEN HURDLE (9 hdls) 2m
5:25 (5:26) (Class 4) 4-Y-O+ **£2,927** (£859; £429; £214)

Form RPR

0/25 **1** **Ken's Dream**[31] 4479 7-11-3 115.................................. LeightonAspell 120+
(Mrs L Wadham) *trckd clr ldr after 2nd: clsd 5th: led after 3 out: sn drew clr: in n.d whn blnd last* **11/10**[1]

5020 **2** *18* **Classic Role**[10] 4763 7-11-3 114... JamieMoore 105+
(L Wells) *led and sn clr: wandered bef 2nd: stalked by rival fr 5th: hdd after 3 out: sn btn: hit last* **7/4**[2]

3 *20* **Escobar (POL)**[14] 5-11-3 ....(p) MatthewBatchelor 80
(Mrs P Townsley) *mstkes: chsd ldrs: rdn after 5th and outpcd: tk poor 3rd bef 3 out: no imp* **25/1**

62P0 **4** *4* **Hatteras (FR)**[6] 4819 7-10-12 102.......................(p) RobertLucey-Butler[(5)] 76
(Miss M P Bryant) *chsd ldr tl after 2nd: outpcd after 5th: no ch fr next* **16/1**

0-50 **5** *½* **Sister Grace**[26] 4581 6-10-7 .... RichardYoung[(3)] 69
(N J Gifford) *nvr on terms w ldrs: wl adrift after 5th: plugged on* **14/1**

6 *5* **Narlen (CZE)**[166] 4-10-9 .... TJPhelan[(3)] 66
(Mrs P Townsley) *restrained s: hld up and sn t.o: kpt on fr 3 out: nvr in the r* **33/1**

10PP **7** *½* **Slick (FR)**[54] 4048 5-11-3 .... MarcusFoley 70
(N J Henderson) *sn off the pce in midfield: wl adrift after 5th: plugged on* **9/1**[3]

PP **8** *29* **Buckland Bobby**[57] 4005 8-10-10 .... MarcGoldstein[(7)] 41
(M Madgwick) *mstke 2nd: chsd clr ldrs to 4th: sn struggling: t.o* **40/1**

P **P** **Hello Tiger**[7] 4479 5-10-12 .... TomGreenway[(5)] —
(J A Supple) *a wl in rr: t.o whn p.u bef 6th* **50/1**

4m 0.10s (-1.10) **Going Correction** +0.025s/f (Yiel)
WFA 4 from 5yo+ 5lb **9** Ran SP% **117.7**
Speed ratings: **103,94,84,82,81 79,79,64**,— CSF £3.27 TOTE £2.20: £1.10, £1.20, £3.00; EX 3.50 Place 6 £22.21, Place 5 £18.05.
Owner Michael Underwood **Bred** Colin Bothway **Trained** Newmarket, Suffolk

FOCUS
An uncompetitive maiden hurdle in which only two could be given a chance and it was Ken's Dream who ran out the impressive winner and sets the standard, although the form is not that solid.

NOTEBOOK
Ken's Dream, who failed to build on a promising reappearance when turned over at odds on at Fakenham last month, was back on song today and came clear in bloodless fashion. He is unexposed and remains capable of better once handicapping. *(new market op 9-4)*
Classic Role was given a positive ride, but he was readily brushed aside by the winner and is becoming disappointing. *(new market op 3-1)*
Escobar(POL), a poor Flat performer, ran well for a long way on this hurdling debut and should find some success at selling level. *(new market op 50-1)*
Hatteras(FR) failed to improve for the cheekpieces and will be better off back in handicaps. *(new market op 33-1)*
Sister Grace will not be winning until contesting low-grade handicaps. *(new market op 20-1 tchd 12-1)*
T/Plt: £35.70 to a £1 stake. Pool: £31,011.75. 633.10 winning tickets. T/Qpdt: £19.00 to a £1 stake. Pool: £1,947.30. 75.60 winning tickets. JN

4655 SEDGEFIELD (L-H)

Monday, April 17

OFFICIAL GOING: Good to firm

The race times and the jockeys description of the ground suggested strongly that the surface was riding much slower than the official.

Wind: Fairly strong, half-behind

4916 TOTEPLACEPOT NOVICES' HURDLE (DIV I) 2m 4f

2:20 (2:20) (Class 4) 4-Y-0+ **£3,253** (£955; £477; £238)

Form				RPR
2224	1		**Character Building (IRE)**49 [4141] 6-11-0 .... RussGarritty (J J Quinn) *keen: cl up: led bef 3 out: r.o fr next: idled nr fin* **11/10**1	95+
22-0	2	1	**General Hardi**49 [4147] 5-10-11 .... PaddyAspell(3) (J Wade) *cl up: effrt and ev ch 3 out: kpt on u.p fr last* **20/1**	90
15P	3	2	**Lindbergh Law (USA)**18 [4676] 6-10-11 .... DougieCostello(3) (Mrs H Dalton) *midfield: hdwy bef 3 out: effrt bef next: one pce last* **10/1**	88
00P	4	4	**Ad Murum (IRE)**62 [3914] 7-11-0 .... BarryKeniry (G M Moore) *hld up: hdwy 3 out: kpt on fr next: no imp* **50/1**	84
-000	5	¾	**Boxclever**40 [4301] 5-11-0 .... DavidO'Meara (J M Jefferson) *bhd tl hdwy bef 2 out: no imp fr last* **33/1**	83
1005	6	20	**Insurgent (IRE)**8 [4789] 4-10-8 .... LarryMcGrath (R C Guest) *midfield: hdwy to chse ldrs bef 3 out: wknd and eased after next* **15/2**3	65+
-12P	7	8	**Court One**62 [3918] 8-11-0 98 .... PhilKinsella(7) (R E Barr) *hld up: sme hdwy bef 3 out: wknd bef next* **12/1**	62
0P5P	8	8	**Yankee Holiday (IRE)**121 [2878] 6-11-0 74 .... MarkBradburne (Mrs S C Bradburne) *chsd ldrs tl wknd fr 4 out* **66/1**	47
0P4P	P		**Lethem Present (IRE)**65 [3855] 6-10-4 75 .... GaryBerridge(3) (T Butt) *sn bhd: t.o whn p.u bef 6th* **80/1**	—
	P		**Bestofthebrownies (IRE)**93 [3407] 5-11-0 .... GLee (J Howard Johnson) *plld hrd: sn led: hdd whn blnd 3 out: sn p.u* **10/3**2	—
0-00	P		**Only Millie**83 [3556] 5-10-7 .... (t) DominicElsworth (James Moffatt) *bhd: wnt lft and nrly uns rdr 3rd: sn p.u* **66/1**	—
000P	P		**Stormy Madam (IRE)**84 [3540] 6-10-0 74 .... ColmSharkey(7) (J R Turner) *towards rr: struggling 4 out: t.o whn p.u bef next* **100/1**	—
P0P0	P		**First Grey**30 [4487] 7-10-7 67 .... AlanDempsey (E W Tuer) *in tch: reminders 4th: outpcd whn hit 4 out: sn btn: t.o whn p.u bef 2 out* **80/1**	—

5m 1.30s (8.70) **Going Correction** +0.50s/f (Soft) **13** Ran SP% **115.4**

WFA 4 from 5yo+ 6lb

Speed ratings: **102,101,100,99,98 90,87,84,—,— —,—,—** CSF £26.92 TOTE £2.60: £1.10, £3.30, £3.30; EX 29.70.

Owner Mrs E Wright **Bred** P R Joyce **Trained** Settrington, N Yorks

FOCUS

An uncompetitive event in which the winner did not have to improve to win with more in hand than the official margin suggests. The pace seemed sound and the runner-up sets the level.

NOTEBOOK

Character Building(IRE), who again failed to settle early on, did not have to improve to win an ordinary event with more in hand than the winning margin suggests. He will now reportedly have a break before going over fences and can win races in that sphere. *(op 11-8 tchd 6-4 in places and 13-8 in a place)*

General Hardi, well beaten after a lengthy break on his fourth and final start in bumpers in February, shaped promisingly on this hurdle debut and, on this evidence, should have no problem winning an ordinary event in this sphere. *(tchd 18-1)*

Lindbergh Law(USA), back in trip, turned in his best effort to date over hurdles. While he may continue to look vulnerable in this type of event, he should stay a bit further and may do better in ordinary handicap company. *(op 8-1)*

Ad Murum(IRE) showed his first worthwhile form over hurdles and, on this evidence, will be suited by the step into modest handicap company and he should have no problems with three miles.

Boxclever hinted at ability without being knocked about on only this second start over hurdles. He is another that will benefit from the step into modest handicap company in due course. *(op 25-1)*

Insurgent(IRE) looked sure to be suited by the step up to this trip but proved a disappointment on ground that was softer than the official good to firm. However he has time on his side and is not one to write off yet. *(op 7-1)*

Only Millie *Official explanation: jockey said saddle slipped (op 3-1)*

Bestofthebrownies(IRE), who showed ability in Irish bumpers, looked anything but straightforward on this first run over hurdles and first run for new connections. He is not one to write off yet but will have to settle better if he is to progress. *(op 3-1)*

Stormy Madam(IRE) *Official explanation: jockey said mare bled from the nose (op 3-1)*

4917 TOTEPLACEPOT NOVICES' HURDLE (DIV II) 2m 4f

2:55 (2:55) (Class 4) 4-Y-0+ **£3,253** (£955; £477; £238)

Form				RPR
3214	1		**Emmasflora**8 [4797] 8-11-2 114 .... AdamPogson(5) (C T Pogson) *cl up: led after 6th: mde rest: edgd lft u.p last: kpt on* **2/1**1	103
-0PP	2	1½	**My Good Lord (IRE)**122 [2859] 7-11-0 .... BarryKeniry (G M Moore) *midfield: effrt whn lft 2nd 3 out: kpt on between last two: nt rch wnr* **50/1**	94
P0P0	3	10	**Macchiato**112 [2962] 5-10-0 77 .... PhilKinsella(7) (R E Barr) *prom: outpcd after 6th: rallied 3 out: rdn and no imp fr next* **40/1**	77
	4	3½	**Cedrus Libani (IRE)** 5-10-9 .... BrianHughes(5) (J Howard Johnson) *hld up: hdwy bef 2 out: nvr nr ldrs* **14/1**	81
F30-	5	11	**American President (IRE)**446 [3545] 10-11-0 105 .... RussGarritty (J J Quinn) *prom: lft 3rd 3 out: sn rdn and wknd* **10/3**2	70
3425	6	dist	**Fortune's Fool**192 [1663] 7-10-9 75 .... PaddyMerrigan(5) (I A Brown) *prom tl rdn and wknd fr 3 out* **8/1**	—
4-5P	7	12	**Destino**40 [4302] 7-11-0 83 .... DominicElsworth (Mrs S J Smith) *led to after 6th: wknd bef 3 out* **9/2**3	—
000	8	2½	**Silver Seline**33 [4450] 5-10-0 .... TomMessenger(7) (B N Pollock) *cl up tl wknd after 4 out* **66/1**	—
6-40	P		**Rhuna Red**326 [523] 7-10-7 .... (t) WilsonRenwick (J R Bewley) *sn bhd: t.o whn p.u bef 5th* **20/1**	—
	P		**Red Mountain**278 5-11-0 .... RichardMcGrath (Mrs K Walton) *a bhd: t.o whn p.u after 2 out* **33/1**	—
00	P		**Countrywide Dancer (IRE)**36 [4389] 6-10-4 .... PaddyAspell(3) (K W Hogg) *a bhd: t.o whn p.u bef 6th* **100/1**	—
6P	P		**Solway Cloud**177 [1839] 6-10-0 .... GarethThomas(7) (Miss L Harrison) *a bhd: t.o whn p.u after 2 out* **100/1**	—
66-0	P		**Belter**62 [3912] 6-11-0 .... AnthonyCoyle (S P Griffiths) *chsd ldrs to 4 out: sn wknd: t.o whn p.u bef 2 out* **66/1**	—
	F		**Guerilla (AUS)**649 6-11-0 .... LarryMcGrath (R C Guest) *racd wd: hld up: smooth hdwy to chse ldrs 4 out: ev ch and gng wl whn fell heavily next* **14/1**	—

5m 4.00s (11.40) **Going Correction** +0.50s/f (Soft)

WFA 4 from 5yo+ 6lb **77** Ran SP% **116.1**

Speed ratings: **97,96,92,91,86 —,—,—,—,— —,—,—,—** CSF £122.34 TOTE £3.00: £1.10, £7.50, £10.30; EX 321.10.

Owner C T Pogson **Bred** Mrs J D Goodfellow **Trained** Farnsfield, Notts

FOCUS

Another uncompetitive event in which the winner did not have to improve to notch her third win over hurdles and the placed horses are the best guides to the form.

NOTEBOOK

Emmasflora did not have to improve to win her third race over hurdles on ground that was softer than the official good to firm. She is a game and genuine sort but may be vulnerable from her current mark back in handicap company. *(op 15-8 tchd 9-4 in places)*

My Good Lord(IRE) turned in his best effort to date over hurdles after a four-month break. Stamina looks his strong suit and, although he is likely to remain vulnerable to the better types in this grade, looks the sort to win an ordinary handicap. *(op 33-1)*

Macchiato's proximity confirms the bare form of this race is modest at best. On this evidence she is worth a try over a bit further but, given her record, would not be one to lump on at shortish odds next time. *(op 33-1)*

Cedrus Libani(IRE), a half-brother to a winning pointer, showed ability on this racecourse debut, albeit at a modest level. He should stay three miles and is the type to improve again. *(op 12-1)*

American President(IRE), from a stable among the winners, shaped as though this first start since January of last year and first start for new connections was needed. Although he has not always looked straightforward, he is not one to write off yet. *(op 3-1 tchd 11-4)*

Fortune's Fool, mainly a consistent sort last year, had plenty to find on these terms on this first start since early October but was nevertheless disappointing. He should fare better back in modest handicaps. *(op 12-1)*

Guerilla(AUS), a consistent sort on the Flat in Australia, had caught the eye with the way he went through the race on this hurdle debut and first start for new connections and was bang there when taking a heavy tumble. Although too far out to say with certainty where he would have finished, he appeals as the type to win races if none the worse for this experience.

4918 TOTECOURSE TO COURSE BEGINNERS' CHASE (16 fncs) 2m 5f

3:30 (3:31) (Class 4) 5-Y-0+ **£4,086** (£1,217; £616; £316; £165)

Form				RPR
4222	1		**Show Me The River**2 [4840] 7-11-2 112 .... GLee (Ferdy Murphy) *chsd ldrs: drvn 3 out: rallied to ld after last: styd on wl* **11/10**1	96
2P03	2	3½	**Herecomestanley**8 [4802] 7-10-11 95 .... CharliePoste(5) (M F Harris) *hld up: hdwy 1/2-way: effrt after 3 out: chsd wnr run in: kpt on* **9/1**3	92
4/P-	3	2½	**Oneforbertandhenry (IRE)**711 [195] 7-11-2 .... BarryKeniry (G M Moore) *led: rdn whn mstke last: sn hdd and no ex* **12/1**	91+
R542	4	14	**Jimmys Duky (IRE)**20 [4655] 8-11-2 67 .... (p) RichardMcGrath (D M Forster) *prom: outpcd 10th: n.d after* **12/1**	76
3PPU	5	17	**Simoun (IRE)**22 [4633] 8-10-9 111 .... TomMessenger(7) (B N Pollock) *chsd ldrs: outpcd after 8th: n.d after* **10/1**	59
-P0P	P		**Just Jed**8 [4793] 7-11-2 .... WilsonRenwick (R Shiels) *a bhd: t.o whn p.u bef 2 out* **100/1**	—
P60U	F		**Miss Jessica (IRE)**9 [4780] 6-10-4 .... DeclanMcGann(5) (Miss M E Rowland) *in tch whn fell 3rd* **33/1**	—
3634	R		**Kempski**30 [4488] 6-10-9 .... (p) GarethThomas(7) (R Nixon) *hit 2nd and bhd: hmpd next: ref 6th* **16/1**	—
55PP	P		**Nomadic Blaze**20 [4659] 9-11-2 69 .... LarryMcGrath (P G Atkinson) *midfield: blnd and outpcd 7th: p.u bef next* **28/1**	—
PFP3	P		**Missoudun (FR)**20 [4655] 6-10-11 65 .... (p) MichaelMcAlister(5) (J R Weymes) *bhd: outpcd whn blnd 8th: t.o whn p.u bef 2 out* **50/1**	—
0PP0	P		**Charlie Castallan**31 [4475] 6-10-9 69 .... (v1) PhilKinsella(7) (D W Thompson) *bhd: hit 7th: sn btn: t.o whn p.u bef 10th* **100/1**	—
03FU	P		**Kingfisher Sunset**54 [4053] 10-11-2 90 .... DominicElsworth (Mrs S J Smith) *cl up: blnd and outpcd 10th: t.o whn p.u bef 2 out* **6/1**2	—

5m 30.5s (7.10) **Going Correction** +0.40s/f (Soft) **2** Ran SP% **112.6**

Speed ratings: **102,100,99,94,87 —,—,—,— —,—** CSF £10.54 TOTE £1.70: £1.10, £2.00, £3.60; EX 6.00.

Owner Mrs A N Durkan **Bred** B McHugh **Trained** West Witton, N Yorks

FOCUS

A race lacking any strength in depth but the pace seemed sound. The form is not strong with the fourth the best guide. Third-last fence omitted.

NOTEBOOK

Show Me The River, turned out quickly, proved well suited by the return to this longer trip and did not have to improve to get off the mark over obstacles. He should appreciate an even stiffer test over this trip and may do better back in handicaps. *(tchd Evens)*

Herecomestanley jumped better than on his chase debut at Warwick earlier in the month and turned in an improved effort. He looks capable of winning a minor event over fences on this evidence. *(op 10-1)*

Oneforbertandhenry(IRE), off the course for nearly two years, showed his first worthwhile form on this chasing debut and he is entitled to improve for the experience. He looks capable of winning a small event. *(op 10-1)*

Jimmys Duky(IRE) was not disgraced in the face of a very stiff task but is likely to remain vulnerable in this type of event. *(op 16-1)*

Simoun(IRE) has shown ability over fences but disappointed badly for the third successive outing and remains one to tread very carefully with at present. *(tchd 9-1)*

Kingfisher Sunset had a bit to find strictly at the weights but quickly capitulated after a blunder in the back straight and his jumping leaves a bit to be desired at present. *(op 11-2)*

4919 TOTEPOOL - A BETTER WAY TO BET NOVICES' H'CAP HURDLE (8 hdls) 2m 1f

4:05 (4:05) (Class 5) (0-90,90) 4-Y-0+ **£2,740** (£798; £399)

Form				RPR
1P00	1		**Suprendre Espere**55 [4033] 6-11-8 85 .... JosephByrne (Jennie Candlish) *prom chsng gp: led 2 out: drvn out* **18/1**	91
4000	2	1¼	**Filey Flyer**29 [4527] 6-11-1 85 .... ColmSharkey(7) (J R Turner) *hld up: hdwy 4 out: chsng ldrs next: kpt on fr 2 out* **16/1**	90
PP06	3	6	**Emerald Destiny (IRE)**71 [3757] 4-11-8 90 .... BrianHarding (Jedd O'Keeffe) *chsd clr ldr: led bef 3 out to next: outpcd run in* **11/1**	84
0U10	4	8	**Nuzzle**77 [3655] 6-11-6 83 .... TonyDobbin (N G Richards) *in tch chsng gp: rdn and outpcd 3 out: no imp fr next* **9/2**2	74
0365	5	¾	**Heversham (IRE)**22 [4632] 5-11-9 86 .... (p) RussGarritty (J Hetherton) *racd wd: hld up: outpcd 4 out: rallied 2 out: n.d* **20/1**	76
-004	6	shd	**Fiddlers Creek (IRE)**62 [3674] 7-11-5 85 .... (t) PaddyAspell(3) (R Allan) *in tch chsng gp: rdn 3 out: no imp bef next: btn whn hit last* **13/2**3	76+
0055	7	5	**Zaffie Parson (IRE)**39 [4313] 5-11-11 88 .... AlanDempsey (G A Harker) *hld up: outpcd 4 out: no ch after* **16/1**	73

Form	Pos	Dist	Horse	RPR
600	8	19	**Oh Mister Pinceau (FR)**^{116} [2954] 4-11-4 **86** RichardJohnson (H D Daly) *hld up: rdn 4 out: sme hdwy bef 2 out: n.d* **4/1**^{1}	47
053P	9	10	**Kalawoun (FR)**^{122} [2858] 4-11-6 **88** (p) RichardMcGrath (Ferdy Murphy) *midfield: outpcd 4 out: no ch after* **8/1**	39
2	10	½	**Pearl Fisher (IRE)**^{36} [4388] 5-11-5 **87** PaddyMerrigan(5) (D Carroll) *led and clr tl hdd bef 3 out: wknd* **11/1**	42
2FFP	11	dist	**Shakwaa**^{141} [2526] 7-11-12 **89** DominicElsworth (E A Elliott) *prom to 1/2-way: sn lost pl: virtually p.u fnl 3* **40/1**	—
-06R	L		**Golden Fields (IRE)**^{8} [4794] 6-11-3 **80** (p) BarryKeniry (G A Harker) *ref to r* **40/1**	—
0200	P		**The Boobi (IRE)**^{12} [4732] 5-11-7 **89** DesFlavin(5) (Miss M E Rowland) *a bhd: t.o whn p.u bef 2 out* **33/1**	—
05-P	P		**African Sunset (IRE)**^{22} [4632] 6-11-6 **83** GLee (A Parker) *in tch: hit 2nd: wknd bef 3 out: p.u bef next* **25/1**	—
0600	P		**Another Misk**^{54} [4056] 4-11-0 **85** DougieCostello(3) (M E Sowersby) *bhd: drvn 4 out: nvr on terms: t.o whn p.u bef 2 out* **33/1**	—

4m 13.5s (7.00) **Going Correction** +0.50s/f (Soft)
WFA 4 from 5yo+ 5lb **15** Ran SP% **115.7**
Speed ratings: **103,102,99,95,95 95,93,84,79,79** —,—,—,—,— CSF £241.03 CT £3280.88 TOTE £38.30: £6.50, £6.00, £3.90; EX 632.00.
Owner Ricochet Management Limited **Bred** T A F Neal **Trained** Basford Green, Staffs

FOCUS
A sound pace and the form should work out but, with the topweight only rated 89, this was a seller in all but name.

NOTEBOOK
Suprendre Espere, a heavy-ground bumper winner, showed his first worthwhile form over hurdles on this handicap debut on ground softer than the official. He should stay two and a half and, *although this was not much of a race, may be capable of better.Official explanation: trainer had no explanation for the improved form shown (tchd 16-1)*
Filey Flyer's form over hurdles had been patchy but she turned in her best effort yet back in handicap company and left the impression that a stiffer test would have suited. It remains to be see whether this will be reproduced next time, though. *(tchd 14-1)*
Emerald Destiny(IRE) is not the most consistent and has not always looked the easiest of rides, but did nothing wrong this time and ran creditably on this first start after a short break. The return to further should be in his favour. *(op 12-1)*
Nuzzle, who had won a poor event at Kelso, once again had her limitations firmly exposed in *handicap company and she remains one to field against at single-figure odds in this type of event. (tchd 4-1 and 5-1 in places)*
Heversham(IRE), an inconsistent sort on the Flat and over hurdles, shaped as though a stiffer test of stamina would be in his favour. However his record strongly suggests he is not one to be placing much faith in. *(op 25-1)*
Fiddlers Creek(IRE) again proved a disappointment with the cheekpieces left off and, given he has yet to win a race over hurdles, remains one to tread carefully with. *(op 17-2 tchd 9-1 in places)*
Oh Mister Pinceau(FR), who has reportedly undergone a breathing operation since his last run, proved a disappointment on this handicap debut in this weak race. It is too soon to write him off and a step up in trip may suit but he is one to go carefully with. *(op 7-2 tchd 5-1)*

4920 TOTESPORT.COM H'CAP CHASE (14 fncs 2 omitted) 2m 5f
4:40 (4:41) (Class 4) (0-110,107) 5-Y-0+
£4,384 (£1,295; £647; £324; £161; £81)

Form	Pos	Dist	Horse	RPR
4052	1		**Dead Mans Dante (IRE)**^{30} [4492] 8-11-10 **105** TonyDobbin (Ferdy Murphy) *hld up ins: hdwy 9th: led gng wl bef 2 out: sn clr: kpt on run in* **7/2**^{1}	115+
-PFP	2	2	**Dumadic**^{69} [3791] 9-10-9 **97** PhilKinsella(7) (R E Barr) *in tch: effrt 3 out: chsd wnr next: kpt on run in* **12/1**	102
FU10	3	1¾	**Red Man (IRE)**^{8} [4788] 9-11-1 **106** (p) StevenGagan(10) (Mrs E Slack) *chsd ldrs: drvn 4 out: kpt on fr 2 out* **8/1**	109
F006	4	19	**Celtic Blaze (IRE)**^{55} [4041] 7-10-10 **96** (tp) MichaelMcAlister(5) (B S Rothwell) *hld up: outpcd 4 out: kpt on fr 2 out: no imp* **33/1**	80
3PP5	5	6	**Classic Lash (IRE)**^{123} [2842] 10-9-13 **87** ColmSharkey(7) (P Needham) *bhd: hit 7th: drvn 10th: outpcd after next* **22/1**	65
4P5P	6	13	**Pams Oak**^{299} [812] 8-11-5 **100** DominicElsworth (Mrs S J Smith) *led: hit 6th: hdd 8th: cl up tl wknd after 3 out* **4/1**^{2}	65
0FP5	7	3	**Tunes Of Glory (IRE)**^{68} [3804] 10-11-9 **107** (b^{1}) PaddyAspell(3) (D McCain) *prom tl wknd bef 4 out* **28/1**	69
5420	8	15	**Renvyle (IRE)**^{61} [3930] 8-10-13 **94** (e) LarryMcGrath (R C Guest) *chsd ldrs: blnd 8th: sn btn* **9/1**	41
P-UP	P		**Looking Forward**^{62} [3915] 10-10-11 **92** GLee (Mrs S A Watt) *hld up: outpcd whn hit 7th: sn btn: p.u bef 9th* **11/2**^{3}	—
565U	F		**Cill Churnain (IRE)**^{8} [4806] 13-10-13 **104** MichaelO'Connell(10) (Mrs S J Smith) *nt fluent: sn bhd: no ch whn fell heavily 2 out* **11/1**	—
6640	U		**Drumossie (AUS)**^{71} [3757] 6-10-0 **81** oh2 (b) KennyJohnson (R C Guest) *chsd ldrs: led 8th to bef 2 out: 7l down and disputing 3rd whn hit and uns rdr 2 out* **10/1**	—

5m 28.8s (5.40) **Going Correction** +0.40s/f (Soft) **11** Ran SP% **114.6**
Speed ratings: **105,104,103,96,94 89,87,82,**—,— — CSF £41.90 CT £313.21 TOTE £2.90: £2.00, £4.10, £1.90; EX 80.00.
Owner S Hubbard Rodwell **Bred** P O'Connell **Trained** West Witton, N Yorks

FOCUS
A modest handicap featuring mainly exposed and disappointing types but the winner won with more in hand than the official margin suggests and along with the third sets the standard. Third-last fence omitted.

NOTEBOOK
Dead Mans Dante(IRE) looked anything but an easy ride when touched off at Newcastle but, apart from idling late on, put his best foot forward to land his second course and distance success. He *was value for more than the winning margin but remains one to tread carefully with at short odds. (op 3-1)*
Dumadic ◆ returned to form and showed more than enough on ground that was softer than the official and softer than ideal to suggest he is capable of winning a similar event on a sounder surface when returned to three miles. *(op 9-1)*
Red Man(IRE) seems best suited by sharp right-hand courses and returned to something like his best dropped in distance. However, he is likely to remain vulnerable to progressive or well handicapped types from his current mark *(op 14-1)*
Celtic Blaze(IRE), who had the cheekpieces back on, never threatened to take a hand and she is a *disappointing and inconsistent performer who remains one to tread very carefully with. (op 25-1 tchd 40-1)*
Classic Lash(IRE) proved a disappointment back over a trip that should have been in his favour on this first start since December and consistency does not seem to be his strongest suit. *(op 20-1)*
Pams Oak, a point winner having his first run for Sue Smith, is the type to do better for current connections but he again showed that he will have to brush up on his jumping if he is to progress in this sphere. *(tchd 7-2 and 9-2 in places)*
Drumossie(AUS) looked held but was nevertheless in the process of running creditably with the blinkers refitted for this return to fences. He should not mind a drop in distance and may be capable of better over the larger obstacles. *(op 12-1)*

4921 TOTEEXACTA H'CAP CHASE (16 fncs 5 omitted) 3m 3f
5:15 (5:15) (Class 5) (0-90,87) 5-Y-0+ **£3,492** (£1,065; £556; £302)

Form	Pos	Dist	Horse	RPR
-P45	1		**Middleway**^{199} [1589] 10-9-12 **64** MichaelMcAlister(5) (Miss Kate Milligan) *prom: drvn 11th: rallied to chse ldr after 3 out: led after next: hung bdly rt run in: hld on towards fin* **17/2**	75+
4PP	2	hd	**Place Above (IRE)**^{97} [3336] 10-11-10 **85** GLee (E A Elliott) *mde most to after 2 out: rallied and ev ch towards fin: jst hld* **16/1**	94
461P	3	28	**Sconced (USA)**^{17} [3928] 11-11-12 **87** (b) LarryMcGrath (R C Guest) *hld up: struggling 1/2-way: rallied and lft remote 4th 2 out: kpt on fr next: no ch w first two* **11/1**	68
-005	4	13	**Bright Present (IRE)**^{88} [3460] 8-9-10 **64** (tp) TomMessenger(7) (B N Pollock) *w ldr: outpcd 12th: wknd bef 3 out: lft remote 3rd next* **7/1**^{3}	32
P36	B		**Casalani (IRE)**^{20} [4659] 7-11-12 **87** JosephByrne (Jennie Candlish) *b.d 1st* **8/1**	—
60PP	F		**Zaffiera (IRE)**^{38} [4341] 5-10-0 **69** oh4 (t) NeilMulholland (M D Hammond) *fell 1st* **40/1**	—
P605	P		**Benefit**^{71} [3762] 12-10-7 **68** TonyDobbin (Miss L C Siddall) *a bhd: t.o whn p.u bef 9th* **5/1**^{1}	—
0P6P	P		**Barneys Reflection**^{54} [4056] 6-10-2 **70** (v) AdrianScholes(7) (A Crook) *sn bhd: struggling whn p.u bef 11th* **33/1**	—
05PP	P		**Sea Maize**^{97} [3338] 8-9-11 **61** oh8 (p) PaddyAspell(3) (C R Wilson) *chsd ldrs tl lost pl bef 8th: t.o whn p.u bef 10th* **50/1**	—
P005	P		**Stoneriggs Merc (IRE)**^{40} [4302] 5-10-4 **73** BrianHarding (Mrs E Slack) *a cl up: drvn bef 3 out: 3rd and wkng whn p.u appr next* **8/1**	—
U5P-	P		**Schoolhouse Walk**^{385} [4623] 8-10-4 **68** DougieCostello(3) (M E Sowersby) *nt fluent in rr: effrt 8th: wknd 10th: p.u bef 12th* **33/1**	—
P-3P	P		**Bobby Brown (IRE)**^{87} [3486] 6-9-13 **65** (bt^{1}) PaddyMerrigan(5) (P C Haslam) *hld up: hdwy and prom 8th: wknd 11th: t.o whn p.u bef 2 out* **11/1**	—
2PPP	P		**Jballingall**^{29} [4520] 7-11-1 **76** WilsonRenwick (N Wilson) *hmpd 1st bhd and early reminders: outpcd whn mstke 9th: t.o whn p.u after next* **12/1**	—
3366	P		**Arctic Lagoon (IRE)**^{62} [3915] 7-10-13 **74** (t) MarkBradburne (Mrs S C Bradburne) *hmpd 1st: midfield: blnd and lost pl 6th: n.d after: t.o whn p.u bef 2 out* **11/2**^{2}	—

7m 10.9s (4.10) **Going Correction** +0.40s/f (Soft)
WFA 5 from 6yo+ 8lb **14** Ran SP% **117.8**
Speed ratings: **109,108,100,96,**— —,—,—,—,— —,—,—,— CSF £126.22 CT £1508.41 TOTE £11.50: £3.80, £4.70, £3.50; EX 198.00.
Owner Mrs J M L Milligan **Bred** Mrs J M L Milligan **Trained** Middleham, N Yorks

FOCUS
A modest handicap but a decent gallop throughout ensured the premium was firmly on stamina and the winner sets the level. Third-last fence omitted all circuits, and penultimate fence in back straight bypassed last two circuits.

NOTEBOOK
Middlewayis not the most reliable (has failed to complete on four of his last nine starts) and did not look an easy ride late on but ran up to his best on this first start since September. Whether this will be reproduced next time remains to be seen, though.
Place Above(IRE), mainly disappointing since winning at Musselburgh in January of last year, jumped soundly in the main and showed more than enough to suggest a similar event can be found when his fencing holds up.
Sconced(USA) seemed to stay this longer trip but turned in a laboured performance and never threatened to get competitive at any stage. He is not the most straightforward and remains one for the layers rather than the backers. *(op 17-2)*
Bright Present(IRE), with the tongue-tie and cheekpieces fitted for the second time, was not ridden as though stamina was an issue but did not get home over this longer trip. The return to three miles should suit and he is not one to write off yet.
Bobby Brown(IRE), having his first start for his new stable, has yet to show much worthwhile form but did not get home in the first-time blinkers. *(op 12-1)*
Stoneriggs Merc(IRE), up markedly in distance and switched to fences for the first time, ran well for a long way and showed more than enough to suggest a small race at up to three miles should be within his compass. *(op 12-1)*

4922 TOTESPORT 0800 221 221 H'CAP HURDLE (8 hdls) 2m 1f
5:50 (5:50) (Class 4) (0-110,110) 4-Y-0+ **£3,903** (£1,146; £573; £286)

Form	Pos	Dist	Horse	RPR
6004	1		**Majorca**^{60} [3944] 5-10-11 **95** GLee (J Howard Johnson) *hld up: hdwy bef 3 out: led last: rdn out* **9/2**^{1}	104+
155	2	4	**Sir Night (IRE)**^{143} [2478] 6-11-2 **100** BrianHarding (Jedd O'Keeffe) *cl up: led 3 out to last: swtchd lft run in: kpt on same pce* **7/1**^{3}	102
4BF0	3	3½	**North Landing (IRE)**^{14} [4723] 6-10-6 **97** MichaelO'Connell(7) (R C Guest) *hld up: hdwy 3 out: rdn and no imp fr next* **20/1**	96
0630	4	2	**Bolshoi Ballet**^{62} [1153] 8-11-2 **100** (v) TonyDobbin (R A Fahey) *midfield: hdwy and ev ch 3 out: outpcd next* **15/2**	97
P000	5	1	**Ramblees Holly**^{146} [2417] 8-10-4 **95** TomMessenger(7) (R S Wood) *hld up: hdwy to chse ldrs 3 out: outpcd fr next* **33/1**	91
005P	6	5	**Vrisaki (IRE)**^{59} [3967] 5-10-8 **92** RichardMcGrath (M E Sowersby) *keen: prom tl rdn and wknd bef 2 out* **33/1**	83
4550	7	hd	**Argento**^{2} [4848] 9-11-9 **110** DougieCostello(3) (G M Moore) *prom: effrt 3 out: wknd bef next* **10/1**	100
12U6	8	nk	**Comical Errors (USA)**^{68} [3797] 4-10-9 **103** PaddyMerrigan(5) (P C Haslam) *hld up: hit 3rd: effrt u.p bef 2 out: sn rdn and btn* **6/1**^{2}	88
-020	9	¾	**Diamond Mick**^{14} [4723] 6-10-11 **102** MissRDavidson(7) (Mrs R L Elliot) *led to 3rd: cl up tl wknd fr 3 out* **17/2**	91
141	10	18	**Ball Games**^{125} [2567] 8-10-6 **100** MichaelMcAvoy(10) (James Moffatt) *hld up: rdn after 4 out: n.d* **9/1**	71
0046	11	3½	**Planters Punch (IRE)**^{40} [4301] 5-11-5 **103** BarryKeniry (G M Moore) *a bhd* **12/1**	71
5-P	12	8	**Red Cedar (USA)**^{84} [3534] 6-10-5 **92** PaddyAspell(3) (J Wade) *keen: cl up: led 3rd to 3 out: wknd* **33/1**	52
0456	13	30	**He's Hot Right Now (NZ)**^{192} [1665] 7-11-1 **99** (p) KennyJohnson (R C Guest) *prom: lost pl 5th: n.d after* **10/1**	29
PP	14	5	**Balasari (IRE)**^{22} [4634] 6-11-2 **100** WilsonRenwick (M D Hammond) *a bhd: no ch fr 1/2-way* **25/1**	25

4m 11.1s (4.60) **Going Correction** +0.50s/f (Soft)
WFA 4 from 5yo+ 5lb **14** Ran SP% **120.6**
Speed ratings: **109,107,105,104,104 101,101,101,101,92 91,87,73,70** CSF £33.82 CT £568.21 TOTE £5.10: £2.00, £3.20, £8.40; EX 49.40 Place 6 £589.00, Place 5 £345.83.
Owner Chiltern **Bred** Shadwell Estate Company Limited **Trained** Billy Row, Co Durham

FOCUS
A modest handicap in which the pace was fair and the winner looks the sort to progress again. The placed horses set the level for the form.

The Form Book, Raceform Ltd, Compton, RG20 6NL

NOTEBOOK
Majorca ◆ turned in his best effort yet on this second handicap start. He travelled strongly, showed the right attitude when asked for his effort and appeals strongly as the type to win more races over obstacles. *(op 6-1)*
Sir Night(IRE) extended his run of creditable efforts over hurdles and looks a good guide to the level of this form. Although vulnerable to progressive sorts in this sphere, he should continue to give a good account. *(op 8-1 tchd 9-1)*
North Landing(IRE) is not the most reliable and was well beaten last time but returned to form and shaped as though the return to two and a half miles would be in his favour.
Bolshoi Ballet travelled strongly for a long way on this return to hurdles but his response off the bridle was a little disappointing on this first start after a short break and he remains one to tread carefully with. *(op 9-1)*
Ramblees Holly, who goes well at this course, is back on a fair mark and shaped as though retaining a fair bit of ability on this first start after a five-month break. He is one to keep an eye on returned to further in similar company away from progressive sorts.
Vrisaki(IRE) was not totally disgraced given he failed to settle in the first half of the contest but his record of one Flat win from 30 career starts does not inspire too much confidence. *(op 40-1)*
T/Plt: £878.80 to a £1 stake. Pool: £21,911.60. 18.20 winning tickets. T/Qpdt: £286.10 to a £1 stake. Pool: £1,237.50. 3.20 winning tickets. RY

4926 - 4928a (Foreign Racing) - See Raceform Interactive

4886 FAIRYHOUSE (R-H)
Monday, April 17

OFFICIAL GOING: Good (good to yielding in places)

4929a POWERS WHISKEY IRISH GRAND NATIONAL H'CAP CHASE (GRADE A) (23 fncs) 3m 5f
3:50 (3:50) 5-Y-0+
£97,586 (£33,448; £16,206; £5,862; £4,137; £2,413)

RPR

1 **Point Barrow (IRE)**[23] [4627] 8-10-8 125 PACarberry 153+
(P Hughes, Ire) *mid-div: 8th 1/2-way: prog into 4th 8 out: led appr 4 out: sn rdn clr: kpt on wl u.p fr 2 out* **20/1**
2 *1* **Oulart**[32] [4461] 7-9-12 118 RLoughran(3) 145+
(D T Hughes, Ire) *trckd ldrs: 5th after 1/2-way: 3rd 4 out: mod 2nd and rdn bef next: kpt on wl u.p* **10/1**
3 *8* **A New Story (IRE)**[23] [4627] 8-10-6 123 AndrewJMcNamara 144+
(Michael Hourigan, Ire) *mid-div: 8th bef 6 out: 5th 4 out: 3rd 2 out: no ex after last* **16/1**
4 *1 ½* **American Jennie (IRE)**[29] [4542] 8-10-7 124 DNRussell 142+
(Michael Cullen, Ire) *mid-div: 9th after 1/2-way: 8th 5 out: kpt on u.p fr next* **16/1**
5 *10* **Solar System (IRE)**[43] [4270] 9-10-11 128 JRBarry 136+
(T J Taaffe, Ire) *hld up: prog 5 out: 6th bef 2 out: kpt on* **50/1**
6 *hd* **Coolnahilla (IRE)**[6] [3775] 10-10-4 124 KTColeman(3) 131
(W J Burke, Ire) *mid-div: 8th bef 5 out: 7th and no imp 3 out: kpt on same pce* **20/1**
7 *¾* **Dun Doire (IRE)**[34] [4433] 7-11-6 137 MickFitzgerald 144+
(A J Martin, Ire) *hld up towards rr: prog 6 out: mod 8th u.p bef 2 out: kpt on same pce* **9/2**[1]
8 *½* **Well Presented (IRE)**[43] [4270] 8-10-13 130 RMPower 136
(Mrs John Harrington, Ire) *led and disp: hdd 16th: 2nd and rdn 5 out: wknd appr 4 out* **25/1**
9 *1* **Doodle Addle (IRE)**[31] [4481] 10-10-3 120 APCrowe 125
(J T R Dreaper, Ire) *trckd ldrs: hdwy on outer to ld 16th: hdd appr 4 out: 4th and no ex bef 3 out: wknd* **66/1**
10 *25* **Black Apalachi (IRE)**[33] [4447] 7-10-8 125 NPMadden 105
(P J Rothwell, Ire) *trckd ldrs: 6th 1/2-way: 5th and rdn 5 out: wknd next: t.o* **14/1**
11 *hd* **Supreme Developer (IRE)**[37] [4374] 9-10-5 122 KeithMercer 102
(Ferdy Murphy) *nvr a factor: t.o* **33/1**
12 *2* **Coljon (IRE)**[57] [4022] 8-10-8 128 (p) RMMoran(3) 106
(Paul Nolan, Ire) *2nd and disp ld: slt mstke 9th: 4th and rdn 16th: sn wknd: t.o* **25/1**
13 *10* **Montayral (FR)**[12] [4742] 9-10-5 127 MrROHarding(5) 95
(P Hughes, Ire) *mid-div: 12th 1/2-way: wknd fr 6 out: t.o* **66/1**
14 *dist* **Star Clipper**[10] [4762] 9-10-11 128 (t) MissNCarberry —
(Noel Meade, Ire) *nvr a factor: wknd 6 out: completely t.o* **33/1**
P **Kymandjen (IRE)**[51] [4123] 9-11-1 132 JLCullen —
(Paul Nolan, Ire) *a bhd: p.u bef 5 out* **25/1**
F **One More Minute (IRE)**[224] [1423] 6-10-0 117 MDarcy —
(C F Swan, Ire) *mid-div: fell 14th* **40/1**
P **Romaha (IRE)**[8] [4483] 10-10-13 130 (t) TGMRyan —
(S J Mahon, Ire) *nvr a factor: p.u bef 5 out* **33/1**
P **Our Ben**[33] [4444] 7-11-12 143 RWalsh —
(W P Mullins, Ire) *towards rr: slt mstke 6th: p.u bef 5 out* **10/1**
P **Monterey Bay (IRE)**[141] [2539] 10-10-0 117 TimmyMurphy —
(Ms F M Crowley, Ire) *nvr a factor: p.u bef 5 out* **9/1**[3]
P **G V A Ireland (IRE)**[30] [4496] 8-11-0 131 BJGeraghty —
(F Flood, Ire) *prom: 4th 1/2-way: sn lost pl: p.u bef 7 out* **10/1**
P **Harbour Pilot (IRE)**[31] [4471] 11-11-6 137 DFO'Regan —
(Noel Meade, Ire) *prom early: mid-div 1/2-way: p.u bef 5 out* **40/1**
P **What A Native (IRE)**[31] [4483] 10-10-8 125 DJCasey —
(C F Swan, Ire) *trckd ldrs to 1/2-way: sn no ex: p.u bef 8 out* **33/1**
P **Colonel Monroe (IRE)**[43] [4270] 9-10-8 125 PWFlood —
(E J O'Grady, Ire) *rr of mid-div: no ex fr 7 out: p.u bef 5 out* **66/1**
P **What Odds (IRE)**[34] [4434] 10-10-1 118 RGeraghty —
(T K Geraghty, Ire) *cl up: 3rd 1/2-way: wknd after 16th: p.u bef 3 out* **66/1**
F **Far From Trouble (IRE)**[32] [4460] 7-10-10 127 APMcCoy —
(C Roche, Ire) *rr of mid-div: prog after 1/2-way: 6th travelling wl whn fell 6 out* **7/1**[2]
P **Manjoe (IRE)**[71] [3771] 8-10-6 123 TPTreacy —
(David Wachman, Ire) *trckd ldrs: prog into 2nd bef 1/2-way: 4th 6 out: wknd next: p.u bef 3 out* **33/1**

7m 41.7s **30** Ran SP% **135.0**
CSF £191.86 CT £3319.83 TOTE £29.30: £6.20, £2.30, £3.90, £3.60; DF 547.30.
Owner Mrs P Clune Hughes **Bred** Henry M Dunne **Trained** Bagenalstown, Co Carlow
■ The biggest winner to date for Philip Carberry.

NOTEBOOK
Point Barrow(IRE) looked a reformed character after a recent wind operation. On top before the fourth last, he was always containing the runner-up. He goes up 10lb for this.
Oulart, still a maiden over fences after six attempts, confirmed the notion that a novice can run well in this race. He was brave in his pursuit of the winner and was nearest him at the line but it was a task just beyond him. He goes up 9lb to 127.
A New Story(IRE) plies his trade over both fences and hurdles but just lacks that essential bit of finishing power. This was a career-best effort and he is raised 2lb to 125. *(op 14/1)*
American Jennie(IRE) was another novice to run with credit, staying on well over the last three fences. *(op 20/1)*
Solar System(IRE) was never involved but stayed on better than most.
Dun Doire(IRE) was well in the rear until beginning to creep closer from six out. Under pressure *after three out, he never held out any hope of getting on terms on ground that was too fast for him. (op 5/1 tchd 4/1)*
Supreme Developer(IRE) never factored.

4930 - 4933a (Foreign Racing) - See Raceform Interactive

4780 CHEPSTOW (L-H)
Tuesday, April 18

OFFICIAL GOING: Good
Wind: Moderate, across Weather: Showers

4934 32RED.COM "NATIONAL HUNT" MAIDEN HURDLE (DIV I) (8 hdls) 2m 110y
2:20 (2:20) (Class 4) 4-Y-0+ **£2,602** (£764; £382; £190)

Form RPR

F-23 1 **Northaw Lad (IRE)**[22] [4649] 8-11-3 108 AndrewTinkler 100+
(C Tinkler) *hld up in mid-div: hdwy 4th: led and j.lft last: drvn out* **5/4**[1]
3 2 *1 ½* **So Brash (IRE)**[20] [4665] 6-11-3 AndrewThornton 96
(P C Ritchens) *t.k.h: w ldr: led 4th to last: nt qckn* **10/1**[3]
-0P6 3 *5* **Creinch**[30] [4521] 5-10-12 CharliePoste(5) 91
(M F Harris) *hld up and bhd: rdn and hdwy appr 4 out: one pce fr 2 out* **33/1**
3662 4 *3 ½* **Haunted House**[27] [4581] 6-11-3 102 MarkBradburne 89+
(H D Daly) *hld up in mid-div: hdwy appr 4 out: rdn and hung lft whn hit 2 out: sn wknd* **5/2**[2]
1-0 5 *5* **Hop Fair**[56] [4032] 7-10-10 AntonyEvans 79+
(J L Spearing) *hld up in mid-div: hdwy appr 4 out: rdn and wknd after 2 out: pckd last* **22/1**
0F0P 6 *2 ½* **Another Penny**[40] [4324] 6-10-3 JohnPritchard(7) 73
(R Dickin) *hld up in tch: lost pl 4th: n.d after* **100/1**
440- 7 *2* **Flashy Sir**[523] [2143] 7-11-3 LeightonAspell 78
(John Allen) *hld up and bhd: hdwy 4 out: wknd 2 out* **66/1**
03 8 *6* **Honest Abe (IRE)**[37] [4387] 5-10-10 TomMessenger(7) 72
(B N Pollock) *hld up in tch: wknd after 4th* **16/1**
000 9 *4* **Bronze King**[12] [4754] 6-11-3 JasonMaguire 68
(J A B Old) *a bhd* **100/1**
2500 10 *shd* **Jobsworth (IRE)**[10] [4784] 6-11-3 PaulMoloney 68
(Evan Williams) *chsd ldrs tl wknd 4 out* **18/1**
0 11 *dist* **Sukey Tawdray (IRE)**[24] [4623] 5-11-3 WarrenMarston —
(D J Wintle) *a bhd: t.o fr 4th* **50/1**
P **Opium Des Pictons (FR)** 4-10-12 TomScudamore —
(M C Pipe) *t.k.h: led to 4th: wknd qckly appr 4 out: t.o whn p.u bef 2 out* **12/1**
UPU P **Story Arms**[10] [4786] 4-10-5 AngharadFrieze(7) —
(D Burchell) *hld up in mid-div: hdwy appr 4th: wknd 3 out: p.u bef last* **100/1**

4m 0.10s (-10.30) **Going Correction** -0.95s/f (Hard)
WFA 4 from 5yo+ 5lb **13** Ran SP% **114.7**
Speed ratings: **86,85,82,81,78 77,76,74,72,72** —,—,— CSF £14.08 TOTE £2.40: £1.10, £2.60, £12.20; EX 12.60.
Owner J Fishpool **Bred** Miss Ann Twomey **Trained** Compton, Berks

FOCUS
The winning time was pedestrian for the grade, 3.1 seconds slower than the second division, and the form is not strong.

NOTEBOOK
Northaw Lad(IRE) was reverting to the minimum trip on better ground and found what was required on the short run-in after going left at the last. He will be sent novice chasing next term with a combination of two miles and soft ground considered his ideal. *(op 13-8)*
So Brash(IRE) could have settled better but proved a tough nut to crack on this sounder surface. He is capable of taking a similar event. *(op 7-1)*
Creinch may have benefited from a change of scenery and this was a much better effort for his new stable. *(op 25-1)*
Haunted House was not helping his rider when missing out at the penultimate hurdle. *(op 10-3)*
Hop Fair was presumably unsuited by the soft ground on her hurdling debut in February having won a bumper on good to firm on her only other start. *(op 20-1)*
Jobsworth(IRE) *Official explanation: jockey said gelding lost its action (op 14-1)*

4935 32RED.COM "NATIONAL HUNT" MAIDEN HURDLE (DIV II) (8 hdls) 2m 110y
2:55 (2:55) (Class 4) 4-Y-0+ **£2,602** (£764; £382; £190)

Form RPR

104 1 **Star Shot (IRE)**[96] [3353] 5-11-3 TomDoyle 107+
(P R Webber) *hld up up in mid-div: hdwy appr 4 out: rdn appr last: r.o to ld cl home* **4/1**[1]
4 2 *1* **Turnberry Bay (FR)**[31] [4500] 5-11-3 TomScudamore 104
(M C Pipe) *hld up in mid-div: hdwy 4th: led 2 out: rdn and edgd lft flat: hdd cl home* **11/2**[3]
-065 3 *14* **Golden Crew**[78] [3646] 6-10-12 DarylJacob(5) 91+
(Miss Suzy Smith) *plld hrd: prom: j. slowly 1st: wkng whn hit 2 out* **9/2**[2]
/025 4 *hd* **Regal Term (IRE)**[52] [4106] 8-10-7 109 JosephStevenson(10) 90
(R Dickin) *hld up in tch: mstke 4 out: sn wknd* **9/2**[2]
00 5 *4* **Corble (IRE)**[43] [4280] 6-11-3 PJBrennan 88+
(P J Hobbs) *prom: led 4th: rdn appr 3 out: hdd 2 out: wknd appr last* **8/1**
0- 6 *8* **Celtic Prince (IRE)**[476] [3052] 8-11-3 JodieMogford 80+
(Miss H Lewis) *led to 2nd: hit 4 out: wkng whn nt fluent 3 out* **80/1**
U0 7 *½* **Worth A Glance**[40] [4333] 5-11-3 MarkBradburne 78
(H D Daly) *bhd: hmpd 1st: hdwy appr 4 out: wknd appr 3 out* **40/1**
P06 8 *1 ½* **Lyster (IRE)**[25] [4603] 7-10-12 90 (v[1]) JamesDiment(5) 76
(D L Williams) *prom: j.rt and led 2nd: hdd 4th: wknd appr 3 out* **16/1**
-U06 9 *11* **Pipers Legend**[27] [4570] 7-11-3 OllieMcPhail 65
(D Burchell) *prom tl wknd appr 3 out* **66/1**
P 10 *14* **Billy Bray**[19] [4676] 6-11-3 SamThomas 51
(Miss Venetia Williams) *a towards rr* **28/1**
000 11 *shd* **Miss Millfield**[29] [4554] 5-10-10 JamesDavies 44
(V J Hughes) *mid-div: rdn after 4th: sn struggling* **100/1**
/00P 12 *1 ½* **Barfleur (IRE)**[59] [3979] 6-10-10 JamieMoore 42
(P Bowen) *hmpd 1st: rdn after 2nd: mstke 4th: a bhd* **20/1**
13 *2 ½* **Zubrowsko (FR)** 5-11-3 JimmyMcCarthy 47
(J A Geake) *a bhd* **20/1**

0 **14** *29* **Extra Bold**[27] 4574 4-10-12 RobertThornton 13
(R Lee) *keen early: a bhd: t.o* **20/1**
000 **P** **Dryliner**[78] 3646 6-10-10 MrPCallaghan(7) —
(A E Price) *sn t.o: p.u bef 4th* **100/1**
3m 57.0s (-13.40) **Going Correction** -0.95s/f (Hard)
WFA 4 from 5yo+ 5lb **15** Ran SP% **113.6**
Speed ratings: **93,92,85,85,83 80,79,79,74,67 67,66,65,51,**— CSF £21.77 TOTE £5.40: £2.10, £1.70, £1.40; EX 19.40.
Owner Robert Kirkland **Bred** Oliver McLoughney **Trained** Mollington, Oxon

FOCUS
The winning time was 3.1 seconds faster than the first division, but still moderate and the form is rated around those in the frame.

NOTEBOOK
Star Shot(IRE) ◆, described as a bit nervy, made a successful transition to hurdling. He scored more decisively than the margin suggests and looks the type to improve with experience. *(tchd 9-2)*
Turnberry Bay(FR) ◆, on totally different ground to when making his bumper debut last month, may have come up against an above-average sort for this type of event. He can soon go one better. *(op 13-2)*
Golden Crew, dropping back to the minimum trip, appeared to pay the penalty for being headstrong early on. *(op 5-1 tchd 11-2)*
Regal Term(IRE), reverting to two miles, had only previously encountered soft ground. *(op 3-1)*
Corble(IRE), did not get home after having plenty of use made of him over this shorter distance. *(op 15-2)*
Celtic Prince(IRE) *Official explanation: trainer said gelding was unsuited by the good ground (op 40-1)*
Extra Bold *Official explanation: jockey said gelding was too keen early and ran green (op 16-1 tchd 22-1)*

4936 32RED.COM (S) H'CAP CHASE (16 fncs) 2m 3f 110y
3:30 (3:31) (Class 5) (0-90,89) 5-Y-0+ **£2,277** (£668; £334; £166)

Form RPR
0/ **1** **Collinstown (IRE)**[51] 10-10-12 **75** NoelFehily 87+
(Robert Tyner, Ire) *hld up towards rr: hdwy 11th: led 2 out: rdn out* **4/1**[1]
1P43 **2** *2* **Mill Bank (IRE)**[23] 4643 11-11-12 **89** (p) PaulMoloney 100+
(Evan Williams) *a.p: led after 5th to 7th: led 9th: hit 4 out: rdn and hdd 2 out: nt qckn flat* **13/2**[3]
0005 **3** *3* **Blazing Batman**[27] 4575 13-9-10 **64** ow1 DrPPritchard(5) 70
(Dr P Pritchard) *prom: lost pl 9th: rdn and rallied 3 out: styd on flat* **11/1**
0445 **4** *½* **Taksina**[17] 4694 7-10-10 **73** SamThomas 78
(R H Buckler) *hld up in mid-div: hdwy appr 6th: rdn after 5 out: swtchd rt appr 2 out: one pce* **8/1**
P134 **5** *1 ¼* **Cullian**[10] 4783 9-11-11 **88** (p) JamieMoore 92
(J G M O'Shea) *hld up and bhd: rdn and hdwy appr 5 out: one pce fr 2 out* **16/1**
P523 **6** *1* **Royale Acadou (FR)**[19] 4679 8-11-12 **89** (p) LeightonAspell 92
(Mrs L J Mongan) *hld up and bhd: hdwy on ins whn hit 9th: one pce fr 3 out* **17/2**
2521 **7** *2 ½* **Denarius Secundus**[1] 4911 9-10-9 **72** 7ex (b) DaveCrosse 73
(N R Mitchell) *prom: led 7th to 9th: rdn appr 4 out: j.rt 2 out: wknd last* **6/1**[2]
F6F5 **8** *7* **Look To The Future (IRE)**[10] 4780 12-10-4 **72** JamesDiment(5) 66
(M J M Evans) *nvr nr ldrs* **16/1**
406P **9** *dist* **Vanormix (FR)**[36] 4426 7-11-12 **89** (v) RichardHobson —
(C J Gray) *a bhd: t.o* **25/1**
P/PR **P** **Renaloo (IRE)**[81] 3602 11-10-0 **63** oh2 (b) MarkGrant —
(R Rowe) *a bhd: lost tch 8th: t.o whn p.u bef 5 out* **66/1**
2000 **P** **Knight Of Silver**[12] 4752 9-9-12 **68** (b) TomMessenger(7) —
(S C Burrough) *a bhd: t.o whn p.u after 5th* **33/1**
0P0P **F** **Adventino**[9] 4802 11-10-4 **74** AdrianScholes(7) —
(P R Johnson) *hld up in tch: lost pl 10th: 7th and no imp whn fell 4 out* **100/1**
FPPP **P** **Castle Oliver (IRE)**[183] 1776 8-10-0 **63** oh3 VinceSlattery —
(A J Chamberlain) *chsd ldrs: lost pl after 5th: t.o whn p.u bef 4 out* **50/1**
5PP- **P** **Wot No Cash**[583] 1414 14-10-4 **72** MarkNicolls(5) —
(R C Harper) *prom: led 4th tl after 5th: wknd 6th: t.o whn p.u bef 4 out* **66/1**
4PP5 **P** **Minat Boy**[20] 4666 10-10-5 **68** (p) JoeTizzard —
(C L Tizzard) *led: hit 2nd and 3rd: hdd 4th: rdn 9th: wknd 11th: bhd whn p.u bef 4 out* **10/1**
643- **P** **The Hearty Joker (IRE)**[553] 1689 11-10-10 **73** OllieMcPhail —
(M J M Evans) *hld up in mid-div: hdwy appr 6th: wknd appr 5 out: bhd whn p.u bef 2 out* **14/1**
4m 59.4s (-11.90) **Going Correction** -0.40s/f (Good) **16** Ran SP% **117.8**
Speed ratings: **107,106,105,104,104 103,102,100,**—,— —,—,—,—,— — CSF £28.53 CT £267.66 TOTE £4.00: £1.60, £2.00, £1.60, £1.70; EX 30.20.There was no bid for the winner. Royale Acadou was claimed by B. Pollock for £6,000.
Owner David Cotter **Bred** Tim and Michael McCarthy **Trained** Kinsale, Co Cork

FOCUS
A rare and typically poor selling handicap chase rated around the runner-up to his mark.

NOTEBOOK
Collinstown(IRE), second in his last two points in Ireland in February, came across for this seller because he kept getting balloted out at home. *(op 7-2)*
Mill Bank(IRE), dropped in both class and distance, was always keen to help force the pace. He clouted the last ditch and could not concede a stone to the winner after being tackled at the penultimate fence. *(op 6-1)*
Blazing Batman eventually found a second wind but could not overhaul the runner-up let alone the winner over this trip. *(op 10-1 tchd 12-1)*
Taksina does not want the ground too soft and was back in the right sort of grade. *(op 11-1)*
Cullian had not appeared to take to fences when last seen over them towards the end of 2003. *(op 20-1 tchd 25-1)*
Royale Acadou(FR) remains without a win since coming over from France two years ago. *(op 11-1 tchd 12-1)*
Denarius Secundus had won a similar event over a shorter trip at Plumpton the previous day and *his exertions there may eventually have caught up with him. Official explanation: jockey said gelding jumped right throughout (op 5-1)*

4937 32RED.COM BEGINNERS' CHASE (18 fncs) 3m
4:05 (4:05) (Class 4) 5-Y-0+ **£4,228** (£1,241; £620; £310)

Form RPR
-P66 **1** **Arceye**[29] 4553 9-10-12 60 DerekLaverty(5) 104+
(W Davies) *hld up: hdwy 7th: led 12th: drvn out* **20/1**
4550 **2** *4* **Chanticlier**[37] 4390 9-11-3 105 (t) RobertThornton 100
(R T Phillips) *hld up: hdwy 10th: chsd wnr fr 5 out: rdn appr 3 out: one pce flat* **3/1**[1]
/002 **3** *dist* **Isotop (FR)**[12] 4753 10-11-3 86 LeightonAspell 70
(John Allen) *prom: hit 5th: led 11th to 12th: wknd appr 4 out* **3/1**[1]
3P03 **4** *10* **Wayward Melody**[34] 4451 6-10-10 91 (b) JamieMoore 60
(G L Moore) *led to 2nd: mstke 9th: rdn and wknd 10th* **3/1**[1]
5P4P **5** *dist* **Uncle Ada (IRE)**[27] 4580 11-11-3 59 HenryOliver —
(D J Minty) *hld up in mid-div: dropped rr 8th: sn lost tch: t.o* **100/1**
PP **P** **Echo Blu (IRE)**[23] 4642 8-11-3 PaulMoloney —
(Miss Joanne Priest) *a bhd: lost tch after 7th: t.o whn p.u bef 13th* **25/1**
5536 **P** **Bosworth Gypsy (IRE)**[43] 4277 8-10-10 (p) OllieMcPhail —
(Miss J S Davis) *w ldrs: lost pl 4th: t.o whn p.u after 7th* **8/1**[2]
F6PP **P** **Run To The King (IRE)**[22] 4653 8-11-3 74 (b[1]) TomDoyle —
(P C Ritchens) *led 2nd to 5th: wknd 11th: t.o whn p.u bef 5 out* **16/1**
P03P **P** **Idbury (IRE)**[28] 4561 8-11-3 JamesDavies —
(V J Hughes) *sn prom: j.lft 4th: led 5th to 11th: rdn appr 5 out: wknd appr 4 out: p.u bef 3 out* **12/1**[3]
6m 2.30s (-12.60) **Going Correction** -0.40s/f (Good) **9** Ran SP% **109.3**
Speed ratings: **105,103,**—,—,— —,—,—,— CSF £75.46 TOTE £26.50: £5.40, £1.40, £1.70; EX 157.80.
Owner Bill Davies **Bred** L J Stockdale **Trained** Leominster, H'fords
■ A first training success for Bill Davies.

FOCUS
A weak affair rated around the second to his hurdle form.

NOTEBOOK
Arceye, a winner between the flags, jumped better than at Hereford last time. This was the first *winner for his trainer and even he admitted his charge was the best horse in a bad race. (op 16-1 tchd 25-1)*
Chanticlier was reverting to fences having failed to complete in three outings for Kim Bailey. He did appear capable of picking up the winner early in the home straight but things did not turn out that way. *(op 7-2)*
Isotop(FR) ran way below the form of his second at Taunton in a similar contest. *(tchd 11-4)*
Wayward Melody had also run below par when also blinkered over hurdles here last December. *(op 9-4)*
Bosworth Gypsy(IRE) *Official explanation: trainer said mare was unsuited by the good ground (op 20-1)*
Echo Blu(IRE) *Official explanation: jockey said gelding had lost its action (op 20-1)*

4938 32RED ONLINE CASINO H'CAP HURDLE (8 hdls) 2m 110y
4:40 (4:40) (Class 3) (0-130,127) 4-Y-0 **£6,338** (£1,872; £936; £468; £234)

Form RPR
1600 **1** **Marrel**[10] 4781 8-10-1 **109** (v) TomMessenger(7) 115
(D Burchell) *a.p: rdn appr 3 out: wnt lft and led last: r.o wl* **20/1**
2410 **2** *4* **Billyandi (IRE)**[38] 4373 6-10-5 **106** AntonyEvans 108
(N A Twiston-Davies) *led: rdn and hdd last: no ex* **11/2**
P2P5 **3** *5* **Mister Mustard (IRE)**[17] 4693 9-11-2 **117** WayneHutchinson 114
(Ian Williams) *hld up: outpcd 4 out: hdwy appr last: kpt on flat* **10/1**
3032 **4** *1* **Bonny Grey**[10] 4781 8-10-7 **108** OllieMcPhail 104
(D Burchell) *a.p: rdn appr 3 out: one pce* **4/1**[2]
460- **5** *¾* **Time To Shine**[409] 4188 7-11-12 **127** LeightonAspell 123+
(Mrs L J Mongan) *hld up: hdwy appr 3 out: no imp fr 2 out* **66/1**
1153 **6** *3 ½* **The Hairy Lemon**[51] 4131 6-10-12 **113** RobertThornton 105
(A King) *hld up: rdn 4 out: no rspnse* **5/1**[3]
0666 **7** *1* **Borora**[32] 4473 7-11-7 **127** PaddyMerrigan(5) 118
(R Lee) *hld up: hdwy appr 4 out: sn rdn: wknd 2 out* **7/2**[1]
5P/4 **8** *13* **Dumaran (IRE)**[25] 4608 8-10-4 **105** JasonMaguire 86+
(W J Musson) *hld up in rr: short-lived effrt 2 out* **6/1**
460 **F** **Shirazi**[83] 3128 8-9-11 **103** SamCurling(5) 95
(D R Gandolfo) *hld up: hdwy appr 3 out: nt fluent 2 out: wkng whn fell last* **10/1**
3m 50.4s (-20.00) **Going Correction** -0.95s/f (Hard) **9** Ran SP% **113.0**
Speed ratings: **109,107,104,104,103 102,101,95,**— CSF £124.02 CT £1175.98 TOTE £25.10: £4.60, £2.50, £2.50; EX 115.80.
Owner Don Gould **Bred** Hilborough Stud Farm Ltd **Trained** Briery Hill, Blaenau Gwent

FOCUS
It paid to be near the pace in a race run at a decent gallop producing the fastest time of the day compared with standard, and the form looks solid.

NOTEBOOK
Marrel bounced back to form with his trainer putting it down to a return to faster ground. *Official explanation: trainer said, regarding the improved form shown, gelding was better suited by today's quicker ground (op 16-1)*
Billyandi(IRE) likes to force the pace and eventually managed to burn them all off with the exception of the winner. *(op 6-1)*
Mister Mustard(IRE) got caught flat-footed once in line for home and really wants a longer trip. *(op 7-1)*
Bonny Grey, raised 4lb, did not seem to be suited by a return to two miles on this faster ground. *(op 9-2)*
Time To Shine, who did not take to fences last season, she could well come on for this first outing since being highly tried on her return to hurdles at Newbury over a year ago. *(op 33-1)*
Borora was sent off favourite on the strength of performing well in the County Hurdle for the second year running. He failed to deliver in a race where nothing was able to come from off the pace. *(op 4-1)*

4939 32RED ONLINE POKER ROOM H'CAP CHASE (18 fncs) 3m
5:15 (5:15) (Class 4) (0-110,106) 5-Y-0+ **£4,228** (£1,241; £620; £310)

Form RPR
66U1 **1** **Sissinghurst Storm (IRE)**[10] 4785 8-10-3 **83** HenryOliver 95+
(R Dickin) *hld up: hdwy appr 8th: rdn appr 3 out: styd on to ld nr fin* **4/1**[1]
P3PP **2** *nk* **Lucky Leader (IRE)**[27] 4571 11-10-1 **84** (b) OwynNelmes(3) 95+
(N R Mitchell) *hld up in tch: led 5 out: hdd nr fin* **17/2**
0145 **3** *hd* **Ebony Jack (IRE)**[38] 4370 9-10-6 **86** (p) JoeTizzard 96
(C L Tizzard) *led to 5 out: hrd rdn and ev ch flat: r.o* **8/1**
P3FP **4** *4* **Kausse De Thaix (FR)**[17] 4690 8-11-12 **106** (t) LeightonAspell 115+
(O Sherwood) *hld up: blnd 9th: hdwy 11th: hit 3 out: swtchd rt appr 2 out: no ex flat* **7/1**[3]
F1UP **5** *11* **Happy Shopper (IRE)**[42] 4287 6-11-8 **102** TomScudamore 97
(M C Pipe) *prom: rdn 13th: wknd appr 5 out* **6/1**[2]
-455 **6** *6* **Lord Seamus**[78] 3649 11-10-8 **93** MarkNicolls(5) 82
(K C Bailey) *w ldr: lost pl 12th: bhd fr 5 out* **9/1**
P5FP **7** *3 ½* **Cinnamon Line**[9] 4806 10-11-4 **98** TomDoyle 87+
(R Lee) *hld up in mid-div: blnd and lost pl 9th: short-lived effrt appr 5 out* **8/1**
-24P **8** *23* **Rudolf Rassendyll (IRE)**[97] 3345 11-11-12 **106** SamThomas 69
(Miss Venetia Williams) *hld up in mid-div: hdwy after 7th: blnd 8th: wknd appr 13th* **16/1**
24-2 **P** **Another Conquest**[40] 4321 7-11-0 **97** RichardYoung(3) —
(J W Mullins) *a bhd: t.o whn p.u bef 5 out* **7/1**[3]
21-4 **P** **Waimea Bay**[19] 4679 7-10-12 **97** DarylJacob(5) —
(D P Keane) *nt fluent: a in rr: t.o whn p.u bef 5 out* **20/1**

The Form Book, Raceform Ltd, Compton, RG20 6NL

6m 2.10s (-12.80) **Going Correction** -0.40s/f (Good) **10** Ran SP% **112.7**
Speed ratings: **105,104,104,103,99 97,96,89,—,—** CSF £36.61 CT £256.13 TOTE £3.20: £1.20, £3.40, £2.60; EX 33.30.
Owner Brian Clifford **Bred** John Noonan **Trained** Atherstone on Stour, Warwicks
■ Stewards' Enquiry : Joe Tizzard one-day ban: used whip with excessive frequency (Apr 29)

FOCUS
This turned out to be a pretty competitive affair and although low grade the form looks solid enough.

NOTEBOOK
Sissinghurst Storm(IRE) followed up her easy win over course and distance with a game effort of an 8lb higher mark and was one for the old adage of following a mare in form. She is likely to be aimed at one of the minor Nationals next season. *(tchd 7-2)*
Lucky Leader(IRE) emerged from the doldrums with the help of one of his better rounds of jumping and did not deserve to be beaten. Whether he can reproduce this performance next time remains to be seen. *(op 8-1)*
Ebony Jack(IRE) likes to dominate and was in no mood to concede defeat one headed. His rider can consider himself a shade fortunate to only pick up a one-day whip ban.
Kausse De Thaix(FR), who made a mess of the second ditch, only gave best from the final fence after failing to complete in cheekpieces and blinkers respectively on his two previous starts. *(op 8-1 tchd 17-2)*
Happy Shopper(IRE), who had only previously been campaigned in soft ground, found that the trolley was full once in line for home.
Another Conquest *Official explanation: trainer said mare lost her action after mistake (op 11-2)*

4940 32REDPOKER.COM STANDARD OPEN NATIONAL HUNT FLAT RACE 2m 110y
5:50 (5:51) (Class 6) 4-6-Y-0 **£1,626** (£477; £238; £119)

Form				RPR
	1		**Star Award (IRE)** 5-10-8 ... MickFitzgerald (N J Henderson) *hld up in tch: rdn and hung lft over 3f out: carried lft over 1f out: led ent fnl f: hrd rdn and edgd rt: r.o* **5/2**[1]	93+
	2	1 ½	**Mole's Chamber (IRE)** 5-11-1 ... JimCrowley (V R A Dartnall) *a.p: led and hung lft fr over 3f out: hld whn n.m.r ins fnl f* **5/1**[2]	100+
13	**3**	3 ½	**Ballykelly (IRE)**[23] 4644 5-11-8 ... RichardJohnson (R T Phillips) *hld up and bhd: hdwy over 5f out: rdn and edgd lft over 2f out: one pce* **5/1**[2]	102
	4	nk	**Or Sing About (FR)** 4-10-7 ... RichardYoung(3) (J W Mullins) *hld up towards rr: hdwy on ins over 4f out: kpt on same pce fnl 2f* **40/1**	90
30	**5**	7	**Silver Serg**[314] 685 5-10-10 ... DarylJacob(5) (Miss Suzy Smith) *led: hdd over 3f out: wknd over 1f out* **20/1**	88
	6	2 ½	**Mister Christian (IRE)** 5-10-8 ... MissJodieHughes(7) (W K Goldsworthy) *hld up towards rr: rdn 3f out: hdwy fnl f: nvr nrr* **66/1**	86
3	**7**	½	**Victor George**[40] 4326 6-10-10 ... StevenCrawford(5) (N A Twiston-Davies) *prom: lost pl 6f out: n.d after* **8/1**	85
	8	½	**St George's Day** 6-11-1 ... WarrenMarston (D J Wintle) *mid-div: rdn over 4f out: sn struggling* **33/1**	85
	9	nk	**True Star (IRE)** 6-10-12 ... WilliamKennedy(3) (Noel T Chance) *nvr nr ldrs* **6/1**[3]	84
6P2	**10**	6	**Le Burf (FR)**[36] 4422 5-10-8 ... TomMessenger(7) (G R I Smyly) *hld up and bhd: hdwy 9f out: rdn over 3f out: sn wknd* **11/1**	78
	11	16	**Bonney Flame** 6-10-8 ... AntonyEvans (J L Spearing) *hld up in mid-div: wknd over 3f out* **50/1**	55
	12	28	**The Rollerskater (IRE)**[346] 6-11-1 ... WayneHutchinson (Mrs A M Thorpe) *prom tl wknd over 5f out: t.o* **16/1**	34
	13	dist	**Regal Future** 4-9-10 ... JohnPritchard(7) (R Dickin) *a bhd: t.o* **66/1**	—

3m 52.4s (-17.80) **Going Correction** -0.95s/f (Hard)
WFA 4 from 5yo 5lb 5 from 6yo 3lb **13** Ran SP% **116.6**
Speed ratings: **103,102,100,100,97 96,95,95,95,92 85,71,—** CSF £13.21 TOTE £3.80: £1.50, £2.40, £1.70; EX 23.50 Place 6 £76.88, Place 5 £44.57.
Owner Mrs E Roberts **Bred** Patrick Joyce **Trained** Upper Lambourn, Berks
■ Stewards' Enquiry : Mick Fitzgerald caution: careless riding

FOCUS
With several newcomers and only one previous winner, only time will tell the value of this form. The form is rated around the third, fourth and seventh.

NOTEBOOK
Star Award(IRE)is out of a half-sister to Hardy Eustace who was placed over a mile as a juvenile. She showed signs of inexperience and had to work hard to justify favouritism. *(op 11-4 tchd 3-1 and 10-3 in places)*
Mole's Chamber(IRE) proved a difficult ride after striking the front and was inclined to lean on the winner before his ground was taken. *(op 7-1 tchd 8-1)*
Ballykelly(IRE) settled much better this time but could not give the weight away. *(op 10-3 tchd 3-1)*
Or Sing About(FR) kept plugging away after making his move one in line for home. *(op 28-1)*
Silver Serg had not been seen since June last year and eventually found lack of a recent outing catching up with him. *(op 16-1)*
Mister Christian(IRE) is a half-brother to the Midlands National winner and Grand National third Laura's Beau. He did his best work in the closing stages to show a little promise for the future. *(op 40-1)*
T/Plt: £93.90 to a £1 stake. Pool: £47,822.00. 371.50 winning tickets. T/Qpdt: £40.80 to a £1 stake. Pool: £3,618.30. 65.50 winning tickets. KH

4726 EXETER (R-H)
Tuesday, April 18

OFFICIAL GOING: Firm (good to firm in places)
The course had really dried out over the previous week and horses wanting any cut would have been at a big disadvantage.
Wind: Moderate, across

4941 ANITA MCCOY NOVICES' H'CAP HURDLE (8 hdls) 2m 1f
2:10 (2:10) (Class 4) (0-105,103) 4-Y-0+ **£3,426** (£998; £499)

Form				RPR
0000	**1**		**Young Tot (IRE)**[65] 3887 8-10-12 **89** ... ChristianWilliams (M Sheppard) *mde all: rdn clr appr last* **16/1**	95+
2446	**2**	8	**The Castilian (FR)**[24] 4616 4-10-10 **99** ...(v) AndrewGlassonbury(7) (M C Pipe) *hld up: hdwy after 4th: chsd wnr fr 2 out* **9/2**[1]	92
000	**3**	2	**Mr Tambourine Man (IRE)**[65] 3878 5-10-1 **78** ... TimmyMurphy (B J Llewellyn) *t.k.h: trckd ldrs: one pce fr 2 out* **5/1**[2]	75+
5F00	**4**	1 ¼	**Brown Fox (FR)**[13] 4731 5-10-0 **77** oh2 ...(t) MarcusFoley (C J Down) *hld up: styd on fr 3 out: nvr nr to chal* **9/1**	72
-326	**5**	6	**Loita Hills (IRE)**[87] 3505 6-11-12 **103** ... RichardJohnson (P J Hobbs) *trckd ldr: rdn appr 3 out: wknd sn after* **9/2**[1]	92
0-50	**6**	¾	**Cornish Orchid (IRE)**[87] 3505 5-9-11 **77** oh1 ... OwynNelmes(3) (C J Down) *bhd: sme hdwy 3 out: sn btn* **20/1**	65
0204	**7**	14	**Sunset King (USA)**[22] 4651 6-9-7 **77** ... KeiranBurke(7) (R J Hodges) *t.k.h: a bhd* **9/1**	51
440F	**8**	10	**Barella (IRE)**[23] 4639 7-10-13 **95** ...(b) HowieEphgrave(5) (L Corcoran) *trckd ldrs: rdn 5th: wknd appr 3 out* **14/1**	59
/013	**9**	6	**Dancing Hill**[226] 1413 7-10-7 **84** ... RJGreene (K Bishop) *rdn 3rd: a bhd* **7/1**[3]	42
0000	**F**		**Windyx (FR)**[42] 4290 5-10-5 **85** ... TomMalone(3) (M C Pipe) *hld up in rr: hdwy and 5th whn fell 3 out* **14/1**	—
P010	**P**		**Ghabesh (USA)**[24] 4616 4-10-0 **89** ...(p) MrRhysHughes(7) (Evan Williams) *mstke 1st: in tch: wknd qckly bef p.u 3 out: dismntd* **10/1**	—

3m 59.6s (-9.60) **Going Correction** -0.475s/f (Good)
WFA 4 from 5yo+ 5lb **11** Ran SP% **118.6**
Speed ratings: **103,99,98,97,94 94,87,83,80,—** — CSF £88.77 CT £424.29 TOTE £18.70: £2.70, £1.60, £1.70; EX 75.20.
Owner Out Of Bounds Racing Club **Bred** James Patrick Kelly **Trained** Eastnor, H'fords

FOCUS
A poor contest rated around the runner-up, but the form appears solid enough for the level.

NOTEBOOK
Young Tot(IRE) boasted one win in a couple of dozen tries previously, but that was on similar conditions and he bounced back to form after being beaten on softer. He races off the mark of a plater and, given these conditions and his favoured front-running tactics, may be able to score again this summer *(op 14-1)*
The Castilian(FR) continues to frustrate, as he travels so well before not finding anything. There probably is a bad race out there somewhere for him, but he is not one to waste money supporting. *(op 8-1)*
Mr Tambourine Man(IRE) did himself no favours on his first try in handicap company by running too freely. He will have to learn to settle better before he gets his head in front, but he is potentially well treated on Flat form. *(tchd 9-2)*
Brown Fox(FR) is ordinary but the tongue tie and faster ground seemed to help. *(op 14-1)*
Loita Hills(IRE) was uneasy in the market and faded pretty quickly in the closing stages. *(op 7-2 tchd 5-1)*
Windyx(FR) was running on from the rear and may have been placed but for his fall, though he would not have threatened the winner. *(op 10-1 tchd 16-1)*
Ghabesh(USA) *Official explanation: jockey said colt was lame (op 10-1 tchd 16-1)*

4942 MAURA BLAKE 70TH BIRTHDAY "NATIONAL HUNT" NOVICES' HURDLE (11 hdls) 2m 6f 110y
2:45 (2:45) (Class 4) 4-Y-0+ **£3,332** (£1,034; £557)

Form				RPR
-PBP	**1**		**Grande Creole (FR)**[120] 2922 7-10-9 109 ... LiamHeard(5) (P F Nicholls) *t.k.h: hdwy appr 3 out: led on bit next: clr whn hit last: easily* **7/4**[1]	104+
P00	**2**	13	**Call Out (IRE)**[31] 4494 6-10-7 ... MissLGardner(7) (Mrs S Gardner) *mde most tl hdd 2 out: hung lft and sn no ch w wnr* **16/1**	84
0/4	**3**	29	**Emma's Dream**[42] 4286 7-10-7 ... ChristianWilliams (P F Nicholls) *trckd ldr: led briefly appr 3 out: rdn and wknd sn after* **2/1**[2]	62+
5056	**P**		**So Long**[27] 4569 6-10-7 ... RobertWalford (C L Popham) *in tch tl wknd 8th. wknd qckly: p.u bef 3 out* **9/4**[3]	—

5m 32.5s (-6.80) **Going Correction** -0.475s/f (Good) **4** Ran SP% **106.3**
Speed ratings: **92,87,77,—** CSF £17.43 TOTE £2.40; EX 26.80.
Owner Sir Robert Ogden **Bred** Patrick Champion **Trained** Ditcheat, Somerset

FOCUS
A moderate winning time for this poor novices' hurdle that was greatly devalued by the withdrawal of Double Dizzy.

NOTEBOOK
Grande Creole(FR) was having his first outing since December and appreciated the fast surface. He was never off the bridle and scored as he pleased. He has a date at the sales. *(op 6-4 tchd 5-2)*
Call Out(IRE), a point winner on much softer ground, set the pace but had no chance with the easy winner. *(op 12-1 tchd 10-1 and 20-1)*
Emma's Dream, another ex-pointer, briefly threatened early in the straight but faded quickly from that point. *(op 11-8 tchd 5-4)*
So Long, whose best previous efforts have been on easier ground, dropped away and was pulled up as if something was amiss. *(op 5-1 tchd 2-1)*

4943 ELITE RACING CLUB BEGINNERS' CHASE (15 fncs) 2m 3f 110y
3:20 (3:20) (Class 4) 5-Y-0+ **£3,903** (£1,146; £573; £286)

Form				RPR
543P	**1**		**Latin Queen (IRE)**[69] 3802 6-10-6 ... ChrisHonour(3) (J D Frost) *hld up in rr: hdwy appr 8th: tk narrow ld bef lft clr last* **6/1**[3]	106+
3446	**2**	8	**Keepthedreamalive**[62] 3921 8-11-2 116 ... BenjaminHitchcott (R H Buckler) *blnd 2nd: prom: outpcd appr 4 out: styng on whn lft 2nd last* **11/4**[1]	105
1304	**3**	15	**Houlihans Free (IRE)**[55] 4048 7-11-2 ...(t) ChristianWilliams (P F Nicholls) *in tch to 11th: sn rdn no ch fr 4 out* **9/1**	94+
-5PP	**4**	3	**In Contrast (IRE)**[25] 4605 10-11-2 110 ... RichardJohnson (P J Hobbs) *trckd ldr: led 8th: hdd appr 4 out: sn wknd* **6/1**[3]	89+
15-P	**5**	½	**Cristophe**[29] 4549 8-10-11 ... MrTJO'Brien(5) (P Bowen) *in tch to 11th: sn wknd* **12/1**	87
P-04	**6**	dist	**Champagne Sundae (IRE)**[28] 4559 8-11-2 83 ...(t) RJGreene (Mrs S D Williams) *mstke 4th: a bhd: t.o* **40/1**	—
0UP	**7**	25	**A Monk Swimming (IRE)**[99] 3325 5-10-12 ... SeanCurran (Miss J S Davis) *led to 8th: wknd qckly 10th: t.o* **80/1**	—
0332	**P**		**Brooklyn's Gold (USA)**[67] 3844 11-10-11 102 ... LiamHeard(5) (Ian Williams) *hld up: hit 9th: wknd appr 11th: t.o whn p.u bef 4 out* **8/1**	—
4025	**F**		**Manx Royal (FR)**[36] 4417 7-10-9 ...(p) AndrewGlassonbury(7) (M C Pipe) *hld up: hdwy appr 9th: led appr 4 out: rdn and jst hdd whn fell last* **3/1**[2]	112+

4m 37.1s (-16.80) **Going Correction** -0.60s/f (Firm)
WFA 5 from 6yo+ 3lb **9** Ran SP% **112.7**
Speed ratings: **109,105,99,98,98 —,—,—,—** CSF £23.12 TOTE £7.90: £1.70, £1.60, £3.70; EX 30.20.
Owner B S Williams **Bred** Cooliney Stud **Trained** Scorriton, Devon

FOCUS
A fairly open looking beginners' chase, run at a fair gallop. The winner has been rated as improving to the level of her best hurdles form. Manx Royal has been treated as if he had dead heated, but still a long way off his hurdles form.

NOTEBOOK
Latin Queen(IRE) was gifted the prize by the last fence fall of Manx Royal but would very probably have scored in any case. She appeared just to have taken the measure of that rival at the time and, with her stable in cracking form at present, she bounced back to form following a short break. She has gone well fresh in the past and that may be the key to her. *(op 7-1)*
Keepthedreamalive has yet to get his act together together over fences and is flattered by his finishing position as he would have been a well-held third if Manx Royal had stood up. *(op 10-3 tchd 7-2 and 5-2)*

Houlihans Free(IRE), making his debut over fences, ran quite well but could not pick up in the straight. He looks the type who will do better over the summer when the competition is not too strong. *(op 6-1)*
In Contrast(IRE) is a shadow of his former self and stopped pretty quickly once headed at the first in the straight. *(op 8-1)*
Cristophe, making his chasing debut, was outpaced from the turn for home. *(tchd 14-1)*
Manx Royal(FR) was dropping slightly in trip and was in the process of running one of his better races since switching to chasing. Although the winner looked to be in the process of taking his measure, he would have been second at worst had he remained on his feet. *(op 4-1 tchd 5-1)*

4944 AGATHA CHRISTIE CHALLENGE TROPHY MARATHON H'CAP CHASE (21 fncs) 3m 6f 110y

3:55 (3:55) (Class 3) (0-125,123) 5-Y-0+ **£6,506** (£1,910; £955; £477)

Form RPR
P050 **1** **The Bandit (IRE)**[11] 4762 9-11-7 **118**................................ BarryFenton 138+
(Miss E C Lavelle) *j.w: mde all: drew clr fr 17th: unchal* **8/1**[3]
F001 **2** *11* **Tom Sayers (IRE)**[5] 4835 8-11-1 **117** 6ex......................... MrTJO'Brien[(5)] 125+
(P J Hobbs) *mid-div: hdwy 14th: wnt 2nd appr 4 out: kpt on but no ch w wnr* **5/4**[1]
4005 **3** *1 1/2* **Twisted Logic (IRE)**[42] 4287 13-10-9 **106**................... RobertWalford 111+
(R H Alner) *hld up in rr: hdwy appr 14th: styd on one pce fr 4 out* **7/1**[2]
1140 **4** *1 1/4* **Mrs Be (IRE)**[35] 4434 10-11-1 **115**............................... MissPGundry[(3)] 118
(J G Cann) *towards rr: hdwy to chse ldrs 5th: rdn appr 4 out: one pce after* **7/1**[2]
61F5 **5** *shd* **Even More (IRE)**[5] 4835 11-11-3 **114**..................... AndrewThornton 118+
(R H Alner) *in tch tl dropped rr 13th: nvr on terms after* **14/1**
P32P **6** *dist* **El Hombre Del Rio (IRE)**[13] 4727 9-10-0 **104**............... JamesWhite[(7)] —
(V G Greenway) *prom tl wknd rapidly fr 17th: j.rt last 4: t.o* **16/1**
FP45 **7** *4* **Kittenkat**[17] 4690 12-10-2 **99**.. SeanCurran —
(N R Mitchell) *trckd wnr to 10th: sn pushed along lost pl 14th: t.o* **20/1**
4102 **F** **Bak To Bill**[13] 4727 11-10-4 **108**.................................. MissLGardner[(7)] —
(Mrs S Gardner) *bhd whn fell 1st* **12/1**
41PP **P** **Le Jaguar (FR)**[45] 4240 6-11-7 **123**..............................(bt) LiamHeard[(5)] —
(P F Nicholls) *bhd whn hit 9th: rdn 13th: hit 16th: sn lost tch: p.u after next* **11/1**

7m 23.4s **9** Ran SP% **113.9**
CSF £19.12 CT £74.87 TOTE £9.80: £2.80, £1.10, £2.10; EX 27.20.
Owner R J Lavelle **Bred** Mrs V J Curl **Trained** Wildhern, Hants

FOCUS
A fair staying handicap. The Bandit was thrown in on his best form and was a runaway winner on this step up in distance.

NOTEBOOK
The Bandit(IRE) produced an excellent exhibition of front running and jumping on his first attempt at this far. He had no problems with the trip, and it opens up more options, with races such as the Summer National at Uttoxeter in June a possible target. However the Handicapper is unlikely to take kindly to the ease of the success, so things may not be as easy in future. *(tchd 10-1)*
Tom Sayers(IRE), trying to follow up last week's Wincanton win under a penalty, ran his race, but never looked likely to get to the winner. This type of ground obviously suits him better than the soft he was encountering in the winter when not getting home. *(tchd 6-4)*
Twisted Logic(IRE) does not know how to run a bad race around here when conditions are in his favour and, though he is not as good as he was, he has dropped to a decent mark so the form seems solid enough in the context of the race. *(op 15-2 tchd 8-1)*
Mrs Be(IRE)showed up for a long way, but even over this trip she was short of pace in the closing stages. *(op 15-2 tchd 6-1)*
Even More(IRE) is high enough in the weights at present and had nothing more to give in the straight. *(tchd 16-1)*

4945 ELITE RACING CLUB H'CAP HURDLE (10 hdls) 2m 3f

4:30 (4:30) (Class 3) (0-125,125) 4-Y-0+ **£5,204** (£1,528; £764; £381)

Form RPR
03P0 **1** **No Way Back (IRE)**[24] 4621 6-10-6 **105**........................... BarryFenton 110+
(Miss E C Lavelle) *trckd ldrs: wnt 2nd bef lft clr last* **8/1**[3]
511 **2** *5* **Flotta**[17] 1722 7-11-10 **123**... JohnMcNamara 125+
(B G Powell) *led tl hdd 2 out: wkng whn lft 2nd last* **1/1**[1]
0000 **3** *14* **Fontanesi (IRE)**[32] 4473 6-11-12 **125**.........................(p) TimmyMurphy 113+
(M C Pipe) *bhd: rdn after 7th: sme hdwy: no imp fr 3 out: lft poor 3rd last* **3/1**[2]
3600 **4** *9* **Goldbrook**[20] 4663 8-11-0 **120**..................................... JamesWhite[(7)] 97
(R J Hodges) *hld up: hdwy 6th: rdn after next: sn btn* **10/1**
01-0 **5** *dist* **Island Stream (IRE)**[87] 3510 7-11-5 **118**.................(b) ChristianWilliams —
(P F Nicholls) *hld up: a bhd: t.o* **14/1**
450P **F** **Legally Fast (USA)**[19] 4674 4-9-13 **107** oh2 ow2............ ChrisHonour[(3)] 106
(S C Burrough) *trckd ldr: led 2 out: rdn and fell last* **9/1**

4m 26.4s (-14.50) **Going Correction** -0.475s/f (Good)
WFA 4 from 6yo+ 5lb **6** Ran SP% **111.9**
Speed ratings: **111,108,103,99,—** — CSF £17.13 TOTE £9.60: £3.10, £1.30; EX 31.30.
Owner G P MacIntosh **Bred** Gerard McMahon **Trained** Wildhern, Hants

FOCUS
A decent little handicap hurdle and a fair winning time for the grade.

NOTEBOOK
No Way Back(IRE) facing ground this fast for the first time, put up an improved effort, although he may have been a somewhat fortunate winner. He is likely to be kept on the go now and further, *along with fences, would not go amiss, as he has the make and shape for that game.Official explanation: trainer said, regarding the improved form shown, gelding was better suited by today's faster ground (op 11-2)*
Flotta, having his first outing since last October, ran his race and should soon be able to get his head back in front as he handles this ground. *(op 5-4 tchd 11-8)*
Fontanesi(IRE) has dropped to a winning mark but was lacking in pace. This former Cheltenham Festival winner may need a rest, having been kept fairly busy. *(op 4-1 tchd 9-2)*
Legally Fast(USA) ran well and was just about in front when his rider let him guess at the final flight and he came down. Assuming his confidence is not too badly affected, this represents a better showing and he is not on a bad mark. *(op 15-2)*

4946 TOTNES AND BRIDGETOWN RACES FUTURE STARS NOVICES' HUNTERS' CHASE (17 fncs) 2m 7f 110y

5:05 (5:06) (Class 5) 5-Y-0+ **£2,498** (£774; £387; £193)

Form RPR
P3P0 **1** **Beauchamp Oracle**[25] 4607 9-11-8 .... MrDMansell[(3)] 101+
(S Flook) *led to 11th: rallied gamely 3 out: hit next: led last: styd on* **4/1**[2]
1116 **2** *1 1/4* **Bill Haze**[12] 4748 10-11-10 **96**...................................... MrPSheldrake[(7)] 105+
(P Dando) *w wnr: led 11th: rdn and hdd last: no ex run-in* **5/4**[1]
P-50 **3** *9* **Presentingthecase (IRE)**[9] 8-11-4 **61**......................... MissSarahWest[(7)] 90
(Miss S Mitchell) *hld up: racd wd: hdwy 9th: styd on to go 3rd appr last* **8/1**
UF4/ **4** *2 1/2* **Shobrooke Mill**[3] 13-11-4 .... MrsCFarrant[(7)] 89+
(Mrs S Prouse) *hld up: hdwy to trck ldrs 8th: rdn and hit 13th: wkng whn hit 2 out* **50/1**
5 *1* **Bally Blue**[24] 8-11-4 .... MrWBiddick[(7)] 86
(Mrs Monique Pike) *in tch: rdn appr 4 out: one pce after* **5/1**[3]
P-4P **6** *14* **Nickit (IRE)**[9] 10-11-11 ....(b) MissPGundry 72
(Mrs Susan Smith) *chsd ldrs: hit 12th: wknd after next* **16/1**
4 **7** *dist* **O'Ech**[9] 12-10-11 .... MrCWallis[(7)] —
(Mrs C Lawrence) *mstke 2nd: a bhd: t.o* **50/1**
0- **U** **Zesta Fiesta**[30] 6-11-8 .... MrDEdwards[(3)] —
(A R Finch) *bhd whn blnd and uns rdr 1st* **10/1**
0/U **P** **Golden Rivet**[26] 4594 9-11-8 .... MrMGMiller[(3)] —
(Miss Lisa Bebbington) *prom tl wknd appr 4 out: p.u bef last* **25/1**
P **Zakley**[715] 10-11-4 .... MrRQuinn[(7)] —
(Mrs C Lawrence) *hld up in tch: rdn appr 4 out: sn wknd: t.o and tired whn p.u run-in* **50/1**

5m 45.7s (-12.90) **Going Correction** -0.60s/f (Firm) **10** Ran SP% **116.9**
Speed ratings: **97,96,93,92,92 87,—,—,—,—** CSF £9.73 TOTE £5.20: £1.80, £1.10, £1.60; EX 11.60.
Owner E C Everall **Bred** E Penser **Trained** Leominster, Herefordshire

FOCUS
The title of this hunters' chase may be misleading as there did not appear to be too many future stars in the line-up. However, the form looks solid enough, rated around the first two.

NOTEBOOK
Beauchamp Oracle, whose best previous effort was third at Huntingdon back in February, only had to reproduce that to see off this lot. However, it took all his rider's persistence to get the better of the runner-up, who appeared to have his measure most of the way up the straight. *(op 5-1 tchd 10-3)*
Bill Haze, not disgraced in the Aintree Fox Hunters', ran well enough and looked sure to score *before being worried out of it on the flat. Unfortunately he was later reported to be lameOfficial explanation: jockey said gelding was lame (op 6-5 tchd 6-4)*
Presentingthecase(IRE) had won his last three points, but they were pretty moderate affairs and he found this beyond him, although he was plugging on at the death. *(op 10-1 tchd 12-1)*
Shobrooke Mill, who prefers to make the running, was held up this time and faded in the straight. *(op 33-1)*
Zakley *Official explanation: jockey said gelding was lame (op 28-1)*

4947 GG.COM/ODDS INTERMEDIATE OPEN NATIONAL HUNT FLAT RACE 2m 1f

5:35 (5:36) (Class 6) 4-6-Y-0 **£2,055** (£599; £299)

Form RPR
1 **Painter Man (FR)** 4-10-4 .... AndrewGlassonbury[(7)] 86+
(M C Pipe) *mde all: hung lft fnl 4f but clr over 2f out* **13/8**[1]
2 *5* **Schemer Fagan (IRE)**[199] 6-11-2 .... AndrewThornton 83
(P Henderson) *hld up: hdwy 7f out: styd on to chse wnr fnl f* **6/1**
0 **3** *1 1/2* **Topamendip (IRE)**[80] 3617 6-11-2 .... ChristianWilliams 81
(P F Nicholls) *hld up: hdwy to trck ldrs 6f out: chsd wnr over 2f out to 1f out: one pce* **4/1**[2]
0 **4** *7* **Aymard Des Fieffes (FR)**[80] 3617 4-10-6 .... LiamTreadwell[(5)] 69
(R A Harris) *trckd ldrs: chsd wnr 1/2-way to over 2f out: edgd lft and wknd over 1f out* **16/1**
5 *6* **Cornish Flame** 6-10-9 .... TO'Connor[(7)] 68
(J D Frost) *mid-div: hdwy 7f out: wnt 3rd 5f out: one pce ins fnl 2f* **16/1**
6 *5* **Classic Rarity** 4-10-11 .... VinceSlattery 58
(R J Baker) *chsd ldrs to 4f out: sn outpcd* **33/1**
7 *8* **Skistorm** 4-10-4 .... AlanO'Keeffe 43
(D A Rees) *in tch tl wknd over 2f out* **33/1**
6 **8** *5* **Cash Back**[20] 4667 6-10-13 .... ChrisHonour[(3)] 50
(J D Frost) *bhd: effrt 6f out: nvr on terms* **11/2**[3]
0 **9** *14* **High Minster (IRE)**[24] 4623 4-10-11 .... RJGreene 31
(S C Burrough) *a bhd* **14/1**
3 **10** *dist* **Bricos Boy (IRE)**[12] 4758 5-10-11 .... LiamHeard[(5)] —
(Miss C J Williams) *a bhd: t.o* **50/1**
0 **11** *3* **Delcombe**[58] 4011 5-11-2 .... SeanCurran —
(N R Mitchell) *w.r.s: sn w wnr: wknd over 4f out: t.o* **100/1**
P **Rainbow Venture** 5-11-2 .... JohnMcNamara —
(J D Frost) *bhd fr 1/2-way: t.o whn p.u 1f out* **25/1**

4m 0.80s (-6.00) **Going Correction** -0.475s/f (Good)
WFA 4 from 5yo+ 5lb **12** Ran SP% **118.9**
Speed ratings: **95,92,91,88,85 83,79,77,70,— —,—** CSF £11.09 TOTE £2.00: £1.30, £3.00, £1.50; EX 23.40 Place 6 £13.61, Place 5 £6.26.
Owner M C Pipe **Bred** Gaetan Gilles **Trained** Nicholashayne, Devon

FOCUS
Even though a couple of the top yards were represented, this bumper did not appear to have much strength in depth

NOTEBOOK
Painter Man(FR) won nicely enough on his debut, but showed a tendency to hang left for much of the race and he will probably be better suited going the other way round. He could no more than *beat what was put in front of him, but it will not be easy to follow up under a penalty. (op 6-4 tchd 15-8)*
Schemer Fagan(IRE), not disgraced in a couple of Irish points, ran with a little promise on his British debut but he looks the type who wants fences already. *(op 8-1)*
Topamendip(IRE) well beaten on his debut at Chepstow, ran with just a hint of promise this time, but his proximity holds the bare form down. *(tchd 10-3)*
Aymard Des Fieffes(FR), also well beaten on his debut at Chepstow, ran with just a hint of promise this time, but like the third holds the bare form down. *(op 12-1)*
T/Plt: £17.90 to a £1 stake. Pool: £42,387.95. 1,725.40 winning tickets. T/Qpdt: £3.70 to a £1 stake. Pool: £3,687.90. 734.10 winning tickets. JS

4948 - 4949a (Foreign Racing) - See Raceform Interactive

[4926]FAIRYHOUSE (R-H)

Tuesday, April 18

OFFICIAL GOING: Good to yielding

4950a DUNBOYNE CASTLE HOTEL & SPA NOVICE HURDLE (GRADE 2) (9 hdls) 2m

3:15 (3:15) 4-Y-0+ **£26,937** (£7,903; £3,765; £1,282)

RPR
1 **Glenfinn Captain (IRE)**[37] 4401 7-11-4 .... APMcCoy 137
(T J Taaffe, Ire) *led: hdd after 6th: regained ld 3 out: rdn and styd on fr next* **9/4**[2]
2 *4* **O'Muircheartaigh (IRE)**[35] 4430 6-11-7 .... BJGeraghty 136
(E J O'Grady, Ire) *cl 2nd: led after 6th: hdd 3 out: sn rdn: no ex appr last* **9/4**[2]

3 6 **Jazz Messenger (FR)**[35] [4430] 6-11-4 .... NPMadden 127
(Noel Meade, Ire) *hld up in tch: j. poorly: reminders 5 out: 4th after mstke 3 out: sn rdn and no imp* **11/8**[1]

4 ½ **Ballyagran (IRE)**[37] [4401] 6-11-4 ....(b[1]) DFO'Regan 127
(Noel Meade, Ire) *hld up in tch: 3rd and rdn 3 out: no imp: one pce* **16/1**[3]

4m 0.70s **5** Ran SP% **109.5**
CSF £7.70 TOTE £3.10; DF 9.40.
Owner John P McManus **Bred** Patrick McGinty **Trained** Straffan, Co Kildare

NOTEBOOK
Glenfinn Captain(IRE) dominated through his rider. Headed briefly after four out, he had his breather and landed in front again over the next and asserted between the last two flights. Good ground suits him. *(op 9/4 tchd 2/1)*
O'Muircheartaigh(IRE) had every chance but the winner left him struggling after the second last. *(op 7/4)*
Jazz Messenger(FR), whose hurdling technique let him down badly, was a spent force three out. *(op 6/4 tchd 7/4)*

4951a MENOLLY HOMES H'CAP HURDLE (GRADE B) (8 hdls 1 omitted) 2m
3:50 (3:50) 4-Y-0+ **£58,275** (£17,034; £8,068; £2,689)

RPR

1 **Wishwillow Lord (IRE)**[11] [4769] 7-9-9 116........................... NJO'Shea(5) 128
(Leonard Whitmore, Ire) *mde virtually all: strly pressed fr 2 out: styd on wl u.p cl home* **33/1**

2 1 ½ **Callow Lake (IRE)**[9] [1093] 6-10-12 128..............................(b[1]) BJGeraghty 138
(Mrs John Harrington, Ire) *mid-div: 10th appr 3 out: impr into 4th next: sn chal and ev ch: no ex cl home* **11/1**

3 4 **Pom Flyer (FR)**[93] [3411] 6-10-6 125.................................... KTColeman(3) 131
(F Flood, Ire) *in tch: nt fluent early: 5th 3 out: 3rd travelling wl appr 2 out: rdn and kpt on* **9/1**[3]

4 1 **Adamant Approach (IRE)**[32] [4473] 12-11-4 134........................ RWalsh 139
(W P Mullins, Ire) *towards rr: rdn 3 out: 11th 2 out: styd on wl* **14/1**

5 shd **Joueur D'Estruval (FR)**[31] [4511] 9-9-10 119........................... RJKiely(7) 124
(W P Mullins, Ire) *rr of mid-div: prog into 8th bef 3 out: 6th and rdn 2 out: kpt on u.p* **25/1**

6 1 **Khetaam (IRE)**[11] [4769] 8-10-12 128.. NPMadden 132
(Noel Meade, Ire) *settled 4th: impr into 2nd and chal 2 out: sn sltly hmpd: no ex cl home* **8/1**[2]

7 ¾ **The Last Hurrah (IRE)**[44] [4269] 6-9-3 112..........................(b) ADLeigh(7) 115
(Mrs John Harrington, Ire) *hld up: prog 3 out: 8th appr 2 out: kpt on same pce* **25/1**

8 ½ **Well Mounted (IRE)**[72] [3773] 5-9-10 112.................................. DJCasey 115
(A L T Moore, Ire) *in tch: 7th 4 out: 6th next: sn rdn: no imp after 2 out* **7/1**[1]

9 9 **Victram (IRE)**[23] [4375] 6-10-3 119...................................... MissNCarberry 113
(Adrian McGuinness, Ire) *towards rr: hdwy 3 out: 6th 2 out: sn no ex* **10/1**

10 2 ½ **Sirius Storm (IRE)**[93] [3411] 6-10-6 122..................................... JLCullen 113
(Paul Nolan, Ire) *towards rr: prog into 11th 3 out: rdn and no imp fr next* **25/1**

11 1 ½ **City Of Sails (IRE)**[52] [4126] 7-9-8 115.................................. BCByrnes(5) 105
(A J McNamara, Ire) *mid-div: 7th appr 1/2-way: no imp after 3 out* **20/1**

12 6 **Davenport Milenium (IRE)**[33] [4458] 10-10-13 129. AndrewJMcNamara 113
(W P Mullins, Ire) *rr of mid-div: no imp fr 3 out* **33/1**

13 1 ½ **Helensburgh (IRE)**[9] [4509] 5-10-2 118...................................... PACarberry 100
(P Hughes, Ire) *cl up: 2nd 4 out: rdn and wknd appr 2 out: sn eased* **7/1**[1]

14 7 **Ursis (FR)**[38] [4375] 5-11-3 133.. APMcCoy 108
(Jonjo O'Neill) *trckd ldrs: 9th 3 out: sn rdn: wknd bef next* **12/1**

15 3 **Cellarmaster (IRE)**[210] [1505] 5-9-5 112................................... EMButterly(5) 84
(K J Condon, Ire) *nvr a factor* **25/1**

16 ¾ **Silk Screen (IRE)**[65] [3894] 6-10-8 124...................................... RMPower 95
(W P Mullins, Ire) *nvr a factor* **33/1**

17 ½ **Dalton (FR)**[9] [4269] 5-10-0 116.. PWFlood 87
(E J O'Grady, Ire) *mid-div early: prog into 4th 4 out: 3rd next: sn wknd* **25/1**

18 1 **Diego Garcia (IRE)**[44] [4269] 6-9-13 115.................................... DJCondon 85
(W P Mullins, Ire) *in tch: 7th bef 3 out: sn wknd* **16/1**

19 dist **French Accordion (IRE)**[44] [4260] 6-9-12 117.......................... RMMoran(3) —
(Paul Nolan, Ire) *trckd ldrs to 1/2-way: sn wknd: t.o* **20/1**

20 4 ½ **Loughanelteen (IRE)**[11] [4771] 8-9-13 115................................ APCrowe —
(P J Rothwell, Ire) *cl up: 2nd 1/2-way: wknd 4 out: t.o* **33/1**

21 1 ½ **Out The Gap (IRE)**[9] [4260] 10-9-11 113..................................... JMAllen —
(C Hennessy, Ire) *a bhd: rdn and wknd fr 5th: t.o* **25/1**

22 11 **Studmaster**[32] [4473] 6-11-10 140.. TPTreacy —
(Mrs John Harrington, Ire) *hld up: bad mstke 4th: sn no ex: trailing bef 4 out: t.o* **11/1**

23 14 **Mise En Place**[30] [4540] 5-9-11 113 ow1... JRBarry —
(J Morrison, Ire) *nvr a factor: wknd 1/2-way: t.o* **20/1**

F **Dashing Home (IRE)**[184] [1534] 7-10-5 121.............................. DFO'Regan —
(Noel Meade, Ire) *fell 2nd* **20/1**

3m 56.1s **24** Ran SP% **146.0**
CSF £351.79 CT £3588.18 TOTE £96.40: £12.20, £2.10, £2.00, £3.40; DF 5225.00.
Owner Malachy McDaniel-Stone **Bred** Gerard Mullins **Trained** Enniscorthy, Co. Wexford

NOTEBOOK
Ursis(FR) raced comfortably until having to be ridden after three out. There was no response and he held no chance from the next.
Mise En Place *Official explanation: jockey said mare was in season post race; trainer said mare finished lame*

4952 - 4955a (Foreign Racing) - See Raceform Interactive

4468
CHELTENHAM (New Course) (L-H)
Wednesday, April 19

OFFICIAL GOING: Good
Wind: Virtually nil Weather: Steady rain throughout

4956 BYRNE BROS NOVICES' HURDLE (10 hdls) 2m 5f 110y
2:20 (2:21) (Class 2) 4-Y-0+
£9,394 (£2,775; £1,387; £694; £346; £174)

Form RPR

1211 1 **Oscatello (USA)**[38] [4386] 6-11-4 127........................... WayneHutchinson 126
(Ian Williams) *in tch: hdwy 3 out: trckd ldr 2 out: led wl bef last: hrd rdn and hld on gamely run-in* **7/1**

2165 2 ½ **Turko (FR)**[13] [4747] 4-11-2 138...(t) RWalsh 124+
(P F Nicholls) *chsd ldrs: rdn to chse wnr appr last: chal u.p sn after: kpt on but a hld* **9/4**[1]

1334 3 7 **Boychuk (IRE)**[13] [4750] 5-11-8 133................................ RichardJohnson 122
(P J Hobbs) *led: blnd 4th: rdn appr 2 out: hdd wl bef last: sn btn* **4/1**[2]

4261 4 6 **Aztec Warrior (IRE)**[40] [4359] 5-11-4 126........................... TimmyMurphy 112
(Miss H C Knight) *in tch: hdwy 3 out: sn rdn: wknd after 2 out* **8/1**

23P 5 6 **Art Virginia (FR)**[76] [3694] 7-11-0 .... MickFitzgerald 105+
(N J Henderson) *hld up in rr: hit 5th: hdwy and hit 4 out: mstke 2 out: kpt on again run-in but nvr in contenton* **16/1**

-U30 6 1 ½ **Easter Present (IRE)**[39] [4373] 7-11-0 103........................... SamThomas 101
(Miss H C Knight) *chsd ldrs: rdn 3 out: wknd next* **33/1**

130U 7 3 ½ **Mahogany Blaze (FR)**[12] [4765] 4-10-12 129...................... CarlLlewellyn 97+
(N A Twiston-Davies) *prom: chsd ldr 5th tl after 3 out: sn wknd* **9/2**[3]

F13P 8 nk **Sea The Light**[65] [3901] 6-11-4 115.................................. RobertThornton 101
(A King) *chsd leeders: hit 5th: rdn 3 out and sn wknd* **10/1**

P 9 11 **Considine (USA)**[26] [4603] 5-11-0 .... NoelFehily 88+
(C J Mann) *j. slowly 2nd: a bhd: no ch whn wnt bdly lft last* **100/1**

0-0P P **Hazel Mere**[28] [4581] 6-10-7 .... DerekLaverty —
(R Curtis) *j. poorly in rr and a t.o: p.u after 4 out* **250/1**

P0P P **Roseville (IRE)**[27] [4589] 6-10-7 59.................................. MarkNicolls —
(S T Lewis) *chsd ldr to 5th: sn wknd: t.o whn p.u bef 2 out* **250/1**

P P **Imperioli**[65] [3898] 4-10-8 .... MissFayeBramley —
(P A Blockley) *in tch to 5th: sn wknd: t.o whn p.u bef 2 out* **250/1**

5m 18.6s (2.00) **Going Correction** +0.325s/f (Yiel)
WFA 4 from 5yo+ 6lb **12** Ran SP% **112.7**
Speed ratings: **109,108,106,104,101 101,100,99,95,— —,—** CSF £22.68 TOTE £7.30: £2.20, £1.30, £1.70; EX 24.70 Trifecta £41.60 Pool: £550.76 - 9.39 winning tickets..
Owner Rye Braune **Bred** Highland Farms Inc **Trained** Portway, Worcs

FOCUS
A decent novice hurdle that could be rated higher, but the fifth and sixth set the standard with the placed horses below their best.

NOTEBOOK
Oscatello(USA) struggled in heavy conditions at Market Rasen, but this ground was much more suitable and he completed the hat-trick in game style, battling on after the runner-up threatened to swamp him on the run-in. He has enjoyed a good season, but while he remains progressive he *might not be easy to place from his revised mark next term and he may have to switch to fences.* *(op 11-2)*
Turko(FR), just out of the frame in the big juvenile hurdles at Cheltenham and Aintree, was taking a sizeable step up in trip. Closing on the long run to the final flight, he looked set to go past but the winner proved too tough. He is likely to go chasing next term. *(op 11-4 tchd 3-1)*
Boychuk(IRE), who ran a strange race at Liverpool, adopted different tactics. Attempting to make all, he was collared early on the long run to the final flight and had no more to give nearing the flight. *(op 7-2)*
Aztec Warrior(IRE), upped in trip, ran respectably but might have preferred better ground. He should make a nice chaser next season. *(tchd 7-1)*
Art Virginia(FR) is a winner of a three-mile point-to-point and might need stepping up to that trip. *(op 18-1)*
Mahogany Blaze(FR) had hinted at the Festival that he would be suited by this sort of trip but he did not appear to get home. *(tchd 5-1)*

4957 Q. EQUINE H'CAP CHASE (FOR THE GOLDEN MILLER TROPHY) (21 fncs) 3m 1f 110y
2:55 (2:59) (Class 2) (0-140,140) 5-Y-0+
£12,526 (£3,700; £1,850; £926; £462; £232)

Form RPR

1222 1 **Sweet Diversion (IRE)**[175] [1879] 7-11-2 **130**...........................(t) RWalsh 151+
(P F Nicholls) *trckd ldrs: wnt 2nd gng wl 2 out: led last: drvn and styd on strly run-in* **9/2**[1]

0P20 2 6 **Parsons Legacy (IRE)**[35] [4447] 8-10-10 **124**........................... PJBrennan 136+
(P J Hobbs) *chsd ldrs: nt fluent 13th: rdn 3 out: led appr next: narrowly hdd last: kpt on but sn no ch w wnr* **16/1**

33P6 3 5 **Fork Lightning (IRE)**[36] [4433] 10-11-7 **135**..................... RobertThornton 143+
(A King) *chsd ldrs: j.rt 17th and 4 out: rallied next: kpt on same pce fr 2 out* **15/2**[2]

1406 4 2 ½ **See You Sometime**[13] [4746] 11-11-7 **135**...................... AndrewThornton 139
(J W Mullins) *chsd ldrs: chal 4 out: led sn after: hdd appr 2 out and sn btn* **20/1**

-25P 5 4 **Ken'tucky (FR)**[102] [3296] 8-10-8 **122**........................... WayneHutchinson 123+
(A King) *j.big 3rd: bhd: hit 5th: hdwy 12th: styd on fr 3 out but nvr gng pce to rch ldrs* **20/1**

P2R0 6 shd **Tribal Venture (FR)**[36] [4434] 8-11-2 **130**......................(b) RichardJohnson 130+
(P J Hobbs) *bhd: hit 9th: drvn along sn after and nvr really travelling: kpt on fr 16th and styd on fr 2 out: nvr in contention* **11/1**

0P00 7 1 ¾ **Quazar (IRE)**[46] [4241] 8-10-9 **123**..(bt) APMcCoy 121
(Jonjo O'Neill) *mid-div: hdwy 12th: hit 17th: one pce fr 3 out: no ch w ldrs whn hit next* **11/1**

0224 8 ½ **Bee An Bee (IRE)**[35] [4447] 9-10-9 **123**............................(v) JasonMaguire 123+
(T R George) *led tl after 1st: chsd ldrs: hit 15th: no ch w ldrs fr 4 out* **10/1**[3]

1000 9 7 **Cassia Heights**[25] [4617] 11-10-0 **114** oh3.........................(t) LeightonAspell 104
(S A Brookshaw) *bhd: sme hdwy fr 4 out but nvr in contention* **33/1**

P3P3 10 6 **Jakari (FR)**[46] [4240] 9-11-1 **129**.. MarkBradburne 115+
(H D Daly) *led after 1st: hdd after 4 out: wknd next* **12/1**

1P1P 11 4 **Cruising River (IRE)**[35] [4447] 7-10-12 **126**........................ PaulMoloney 106
(Miss H C Knight) *rr: hit 5th and next: hdwy into mid-div 13th: wknd 17th* **25/1**

421U 12 ½ **Moorlands Again**[25] [4617] 11-10-3 **117**.........................(t) TomScudamore 97
(M Sheppard) *chsd ldrs to 14th: sn wknd* **25/1**

2010 13 20 **Koumba (FR)**[102] [3290] 8-10-3 **117**................................. ChristianWilliams 77
(Evan Williams) *broke wl: sn mid-div: blnd 9th: rr whn mstke 12th and nvr in contention after* **14/1**

11PP 14 nk **Sonevafushi (FR)**[60] [3995] 8-11-12 **140**.............................. SamThomas 99
(Miss Venetia Williams) *hit 7th and 11th: a in rr* **33/1**

P0F0 15 nk **Iris Bleu (FR)**[35] [4447] 10-11-9 **137**.................................... TimmyMurphy 96
(M C Pipe) *hld up in rr: hit 7th: sme hdwy 17th: nvr in contention: wknd sn after* **10/1**[3]

P613 16 11 **Naunton Brook**[43] [4287] 7-10-11 **125**..................................(t) AntonyEvans 73
(N A Twiston-Davies) *a bhd:t.o fr 15th* **11/1**

P434 P **Victory Gunner (IRE)**[32] [4496] 8-10-6 **120**.......................... OllieMcPhail —
(C Roberts) *hit 3rd: chsd ldrs: hit 8th: wknd 16th: t.o whn p.u bef 2 out* **25/1**

6m 29.5s **Going Correction** -0.30s/f (Good) **17** Ran SP% **120.3**
Speed ratings: **113,111,109,108,107 107,107,106,104,102 101,101,95,95,95 91,—** CSF £64.31 CT £532.78 TOTE £4.90: £1.70, £4.40, £2.30, £4.60; EX 114.70 Trifecta £653.40 Part won. Pool: £920.42 - 0.20 winning tickets..
Owner Ian Marshall **Bred** Con O'Keeffe **Trained** Ditcheat, Somerset

FOCUS
A well-contested handicap with the winner value for half as much again and the form appears solid.

NOTEBOOK

Sweet Diversion(IRE) ◆, fresh for this first run since October, always travelled nicely and stayed on well enough after jumping to the front at the final fence. On the upgrade, he could go for the Galway Plate, where the strong pace over 2m 6f would suit him. *(op 5-1)*

Parsons Legacy(IRE), 4lb lower than when fifth in this a year ago, ran his best race of the campaign and was unfortunate to come up against a progressive opponent.

Fork Lightning(IRE) has run some creditable races here this season and this was another of them. He was staying on well at the end and marathon trips could suit him next term. *(op 11-2 tchd 8-1)*

See You Sometime, eased in grade, ran well for a long way but could not counter when collared on the home turn.

Ken'tucky(FR) ran a better race after a break since early in the year, without quite being able to mount a challenge. *(op 33-1)*

Tribal Venture(FR), who has left Ferdy Murphy since his last run, was receiving reminders with a circuit to cover but consented to stay on late in the day. *(op 12-1)*

Quazar(IRE), who landed the Grade 2 event over 2m 5f on this card a year ago, had just entered the argument when he made a mistake at the top of the hill. His stamina failed him from the third last but he has become well handicapped. *(op 10-1)*

Iris Bleu(FR) *Official explanation: jockey said gelding had no more to give (op 12-1)*

4958 FAUCETS FOR MIRA SHOWERS SILVER TROPHY CHASE (LIMITED H'CAP) GRADE 2 (17 fncs) 2m 5f

3:30 (3:33) (Class 1) 5-Y-0+ **£28,644** (£10,829; £5,489; £2,804; £1,474)

Form RPR

1P10 **1** **Our Vic (IRE)**[34] 4457 8-11-1 **158** TimmyMurphy 165+
(M C Pipe) *w ldr: led 4th: hdd 13th: led again appr 2 out: rdn run-in: kpt on wl* **5/2**[1]

125U **2** *8* **Too Forward (IRE)**[34] 4459 10-10-4 **147** oh9 TonyDobbin 147+
(Carl Llewellyn) *chsd ldrs: chal 7th to next: chal again 12th: led next: hdd appr 2 out: sn no ch w wnr and one pce* **15/2**

4264 **3** *15* **Monkerhostin (FR)**[13] 4746 9-11-10 **167** RichardJohnson 153+
(P J Hobbs) *chsd ldrs: chal 8th to 11th: rdn sn after: wknd fr 13th* **13/2**[3]

-300 **4** *8* **Kadarann (IRE)**[102] 3299 9-10-4 **147** oh8 PJBrennan 124+
(P F Nicholls) *led to 4th: styd chalng to 8th: wknd 12th* **33/1**

1U02 **5** *20* **Kelrev (FR)**[34] 4459 8-10-4 **147** oh8 SamThomas 117+
(Miss Venetia Williams) *chsd ldrs: hit 8th: wknd 13th* **6/1**[2]

000P **U** **Le Roi Miguel (FR)**[11] 4777 8-10-1 **149** (t) LiamHeard(5) —
(P F Nicholls) *nt fluent and uns rdr 1st* **10/1**

2210 **F** **Cornish Sett (IRE)**[34] 4456 7-10-4 **147** (b) RWalsh —
(P F Nicholls) *hld up in rr: nt fluent 7th: hday 11th: 3l 3rd and gng comf whn fell 4 out* **5/2**[1]

5m 12.5s (-14.20) **Going Correction** -0.30s/f (Good) **7** Ran SP% **108.6**

Speed ratings: **115,111,106,103,95** —,— CSF £18.80 TOTE £3.00: £2.00, £2.70; EX 26.00.

Owner D A Johnson **Bred** Col W B Mullins **Trained** Nicholashayne, Devon

FOCUS

A good limited handicap but only four of these raced off their correct mark. The form is straightforward rated around the first two.

NOTEBOOK

Our Vic(IRE) is frustratingly inconsistent, but he has bags of talent and this was a going day. Appearing to enjoy racing handily in this small field, he jumped soundly and, moving easily past the runner-up on the home turn, stayed on well. *(tchd 9-4)*

Too Forward(IRE) tried to kick clear after the fourth last but was put in his place by the winner from the home turn. This was a good effort from 9lb out of the weights over a trip short of his best. *(op 8-1 tchd 7-1)*

Monkerhostin(FR) ran another lacklustre race, coming under pressure with six to jump and merely plugging on over the final four fences. Back on top of the BHB's Order of Merit but under threat from Royal Shakespeare, he may be asked to turn out at Sandown on the last day of the season. *(op 5-1)*

Kadarann(IRE) ran as well as could be expected from 8lb out of the weights, but he is hard to place now and this trip is really too far for him. *(op 25-1)*

Kelrev(FR) had a stiff task from 8lb out of the handicap. *(op 13-2 tchd 7-1)*

Cornish Sett(IRE) was rather sluggish in rear through the first part of the race, but he warmed to his task and had the leading pair in his sights when coming down at the fourth last. *(tchd 11-4)*

4959 MITIE GROUP H'CAP HURDLE (10 hdls) 2m 5f 110y

4:05 (4:06) (Class 2) 4-Y-0+

£12,212 (£3,607; £1,803; £902; £450; £226)

Form RPR

1130 **1** **Darrias (GER)**[157] 2209 5-10-10 **135** (t) RWalsh 137+
(P F Nicholls) *blnd 5th: rr: stdy hdwy after 2 out to chse ldr last: hrd drvn and one pce run-in: styd on to ld cl home as ldr wknd* **10/3**[1]

0666 **2** *1/2* **Arrayou (FR)**[12] 4765 5-10-0 **125** (v) LeightonAspell 126+
(O Sherwood) *hld up in rr: stdy hdwy 3 out: chal 2 out: led sn after: rdn last:2l clr run-in: wknd u.p and hdd cl home* **8/1**

04B3 **3** *8* **Penny Pictures (IRE)**[12] 4765 7-10-11 **136** TimmyMurphy 130+
(M C Pipe) *chsd ldrs: blnd 5th: styd front rnk: rdn 2 out: outpcd appr last* **11/2**[2]

2550 **4** *3/4* **Howle Hill (IRE)**[33] 4473 6-10-10 **135** WayneHutchinson 126
(A King) *chsd ldrs: rdn 3 out: outpcd appr last* **6/1**[3]

4304 **5** *3/4* **Westender (FR)**[13] 4745 10-11-12 **151** (p) TomScudamore 141
(M C Pipe) *chsd ldrs: wnt 2nd 4 out tl appr 2 out: sn outpcd u.p* **12/1**

660P **6** *10* **Flying Enterprise (IRE)**[25] 4612 6-10-5 **130** (b) SamThomas 110
(Miss Venetia Williams) *led tl hdd sn after 2 out: wknd qckly sn after* **16/1**

0031 **7** *6* **Spectrometer**[60] 3992 9-10-7 **135** PaulO'Neill(3) 109
(Ian Williams) *mid-div: rdn and effrt 3 out: nvr gng pce to trble ldrs: wknd next* **8/1**

340F **8** *3* **Penzance**[36] 4432 5-11-9 **148** RobertThornton 119
(A King) *chsd ldrs: rdn 3 out: styd prom tl wknd after 2 out* **9/1**

6000 **9** *1 1/4* **Hasty Prince**[12] 4765 8-11-0 **139** (t) APMcCoy 109
(Jonjo O'Neill) *mid-div: hit 5th and 6th: chsd ldrs and rdn after 3 out: nt fluent next and sn wknd* **6/1**[3]

/2-P **10** *11* **Amid The Chaos (IRE)**[69] 3815 6-9-4 **125** oh15 KevinTobin(10) 84
(C J Mann) *rdn 4 out: a bhd* **50/1**

010 **11** *1* **Jug Of Punch (IRE)**[30] 4549 7-9-12 **128** oh36 ow3 MarkNicolls(5) 86
(S T Lewis) *chsd ldr to 4 out: wknd qckly* **150/1**

5m 18.5s (1.90) **Going Correction** +0.325s/f (Yiel) **11** Ran SP% **115.5**

Speed ratings: **109,108,105,105,105 101,99,98,98,94 93** CSF £29.96 CT £142.70 TOTE £4.50: £2.00, £3.00, £2.30; EX 52.50 Trifecta £328.30 Pool: £739.96 - 1.60 winning tickets..

Owner Peter Hart **Bred** Gestut Rottgen **Trained** Ditcheat, Somerset

FOCUS

A competitive handicap run at a reasonable pace and the form is rated around the first two. There were plenty were in with a shout between the last two flights.

NOTEBOOK

Darrias(GER), like Nicholls' earlier winner on the card, had not run since the autumn. Held up and still with eight in front of him over the penultimate flight, he moved into second going to the last but appeared held until Walsh forced him past the flagging leader close home. He looks a very nice novice chase prospect for next season. *(op 7-2 tchd 3-1 and 4-1 in a place)*

Arrayou(FR) took up the running off the home turn and looked set to secure his first win for a year when a couple of lengths to the good halfway up the run-in, but he began to weaken in the last 50 yards and was just caught. *(op 11-1 tchd 12-1)*

Penny Pictures(IRE), who survived a blunder in the back straight, could not go with the first two on the long run to the final flight but did stay on to grab third place on the run-in. Raised 3lb after his good run at Aintree, this was another solid effort. *(op 6-1)*

Howle Hill(IRE) ran a decent race on this return to a more suitable trip but he is finding it hard to get his head in front. *(tchd 13-2)*

Westender(FR), back in handicap company, was off the bridle at times but was only seen off between the last two flights. He will remain difficult to win with. *(tchd 14-1)*

Flying Enterprise(IRE), wearing blinkers for the first time since his days in France, made the running but could never shake off his pursuers. He is edging back down the weights.

Spectrometer was successful in a handicap chase from a 21lb lower mark on his latest run two months ago. *(op 11-1)*

Penzance, raised 3lb after the Champion Hurdle and running in only his second handicap, failed to stay. *(op 4-1)*

Hasty Prince, who has dropped 18lb since the start of the season, was fitted with a tongue tie for the first time. He was another to fade after the second last. *(op 13-2)*

4960 APRIL NOVICES' CHASE (21 fncs) 3m 1f 110y

4:40 (4:41) (Class 2) 5-Y-0+ **£12,699** (£3,873; £2,023; £1,099)

Form RPR

110P **1** **Napolitain (FR)**[12] 4759 5-11-1 138 RWalsh 134+
(P F Nicholls) *trckd ldrs: j. slowly 6th: mstke 8th: outpcd 15th: hdwy 4 out: slt ld 3 out: hrd drvn fr 2 out: hld on all out* **6/1**

323 **2** *shd* **Unleash (USA)**[145] 2484 7-11-6 135 RichardJohnson 140+
(P J Hobbs) *rr:in tch: hit 9th and 10th: hdwy 4 out: chal 3 out:gng wl next: nt fluent last and lost 1/2l: nt get bk at wnr run-in* **7/2**[2]

P141 **3** *14* **Yardbird (IRE)**[25] 4617 7-11-9 127 RobertThornton 127
(A King) *chsd ldr 4th to 15th: pressing ldrs whn lft in ld 4 out: narrowly hdd next: wknd u.p fr 2 out* **7/2**[2]

1123 **4** *2 1/2* **De Blanc (IRE)**[32] 4495 6-11-2 125 SamThomas 119+
(Miss Venetia Williams) *led to 2nd: chsd ldrs: chal 14th: led 16th: hdd next: pressing ldrs whn hit 3 out: wknd next* **17/2**

1F10 **B** **Alderburn**[36] 4433 7-11-9 129 MarkBradburne —
(H D Daly) *chsd ldrs: hit 7th: rdn 17th: cl 4th and stl styng on whn b.d 4 out* **9/2**[3]

F13P **F** **Lough Derg (FR)**[35] 4444 6-11-6 144 (v[1]) TomScudamore —
(M C Pipe) *led 2nd: hit 9th and 10th: hdd 16th: led next: rdn and 1l clr whn fell 4 out* **3/1**[1]

6m 38.2s **Going Correction** -0.30s/f (Good)

WFA 5 from 6yo+ 8lb **6** Ran SP% **112.4**

Speed ratings: **99,98,94,93**,— — CSF £27.27 TOTE £6.90: £2.40, £2.20; EX 17.30.

Owner The Stewart Family **Bred** Francois Cottin **Trained** Ditcheat, Somerset

FOCUS

A decent novice chase run at just a steady pace and rated around the principals.

NOTEBOOK

Napolitain(FR), who had been sticky at a couple of fences on the first circuit, found himself outpaced as the tempo lifted with seven to jump but was right back in it as two rivals departed three fences later. Ahead three from home, he showed a gutsy attitude to hold on to his slim advantage as the runner-up rallied. The return to this less exalted grade helped him and he saw out *the trip well, albeit in this moderately-run race.Official explanation: trainer's representative said, regarding the improved form shown, gelding was better suited by today's extended trip and stiffer track and had made a bad mistake at Aintree (op 11-2)*

Unleash(USA), the equal of the winner on adjusted BHB ratings, had been off the track since the Hennessy meeting in November. He should have won, as he was travelling better than Napolitain from the second last but his rider failed to kick on. An error at the final fence cost him momentum and, although he kept on for pressure all the way to the line, the damage had been done. *(tchd 4-1)*

Yardbird(IRE), back in novice company, would have been 11lb better off with both the first two had this been a handicap. He ran a sound race and was only seen off between the last two fences. *(op 4-1 tchd 9-2)*

De Blanc(IRE), tackling stronger opposition, had every chance at the top of the hill but was found wanting from the second last. Softer ground is ideal for her and there was no disgrace in this. *(op 7-1 tchd 9-1)*

Lough Derg(FR), who was visored for the first time, was the pick on official figures. Not entirely fluent as he cut out the running, he held a narrow lead when getting in too close to the fourth last and coming down. *(op 4-1)*

Alderburn, travelling within himself and disputing third place, had nowhere to go when the leader fell in his path four out. He had jumped soundly enough before his unfortunate departure. *(op 4-1)*

4961 ENDSLEIGH INSURANCE NOVICES' H'CAP HURDLE (12 hdls) 3m

5:15 (5:15) (Class 3) (0-120,120) 4-Y-0+

£8,455 (£2,497; £1,248; £625; £311; £156)

Form RPR

451 **1** **Here We Go (IRE)**[8] 4824 7-10-11 **105** 7ex JamieMoore 115+
(G L Moore) *hld up rr: nt fluent 7th and 8th: hdwy 3 out: qcknd to chal last whn sprawled and lost 2l: rallied gamely to ld fnl 100yds:* **11/4**[1]

2452 **2** *1* **Best Profile (IRE)**[20] 4678 6-11-4 **112** (t) AntonyEvans 117
(N A Twiston-Davies) *chsd ldrs: led 3 out: narrowly hdd next: sn led again: hrd rdn last: hdd and no ex fnl 100yds* **16/1**

4223 **3** *3 1/2* **Original Thought (IRE)**[26] 4603 6-11-0 **108** NoelFehily 109
(B De Haan) *chsd ldrs: rdn 2 out: kpt on run-in but nt pce to chal* **10/1**

2141 **4** *shd* **Hot 'N' Holy**[24] 4642 7-11-0 **108** RWalsh 110+
(P F Nicholls) *mid-div: hdwy 3 out: styd on to chse ldrs fr 2 out: one pce and edgd lft run-in* **5/1**[2]

1301 **5** *5* **Businessmoney Jake**[13] 4756 5-11-0 **113** LiamHeard(5) 109
(V R A Dartnall) *in tch: rdn to chse ldrs after 3 out: wknd appr last* **7/1**[3]

-501 **6** *nk* **Complete Outsider**[4] 4860 8-10-13 **107** 7ex WayneHutchinson 103
(Nick Williams) *chsd ldrs: chal 2 out: chsd ldr sn after: wknd last* **14/1**

1402 **7** *nk* **Jaunty Times**[47] 4215 6-11-12 **120** MarkBradburne 117+
(H D Daly) *mid-div: hdwy 3 out: chsd ldrs and hit 2 out: wknd last* **16/1**

6P-1 **8** *19* **Wild Chimes (IRE)**[71] 3792 7-10-13 **107** (b) RichardJohnson 84
(P J Hobbs) *bhd and racd on outside: hdwy to chse ldrs 3 out: rdn next: wknd sn after* **12/1**

0423 **9** *1/2* **Hambaphambili**[21] 4661 6-10-11 **105** LeightonAspell 83+
(O Sherwood) *chsd ldrs: led 4 out: hdd next: slt ld 2 out: sn hdd: wknd qckly* **33/1**

3222 **10** *7* **Seeador**[57] 4036 7-10-4 **105** WayneKavanagh(7) 74
(J W Mullins) *led to 8th: wknd 3 out* **20/1**

065 **11** *8* **Keswick (IRE)**[46] 4238 6-10-13 **107** MickFitzgerald 68
(N J Henderson) *nt fluent 2nd: bhd most of way* **28/1**

/6P2 **12** *22* **Pertemps Timmy**[38] 4393 8-10-10 **111** SeanQuinlan(7) 50
(R T Phillips) *nvr bttr than mid-div: bhd fr 7th* **100/1**

0150 **P** **Huckster (ZIM)**[26] 4606 7-11-1 **109** SamThomas —
(Miss Venetia Williams) *bhd: rdn 6th: t.o whn p.u bef last* **33/1**

031 **P** **Doc Row (IRE)**[78] 3664 6-11-4 **112**.................................... TimmyMurphy —
(M C Pipe) *w ldr tl led 8th: hit 4 out and hdd: wknd after 3 out: p.u bef 2 out* **16/1**

0460 **P** **Nice Horse (FR)**[39] 4373 5-11-1 **109**.. APMcCoy —
(M C Pipe) *bhd: nt fluent: sme hdwy 3 out: mstke and wknd 2 out: t.o whn p.u bef last* **7/1**[3]

6m 5.00s (6.10) **Going Correction** +0.325s/f (Yiel) **15** Ran SP% **124.5**
Speed ratings: **102,101,100,100,98 98,98,92,92,89 87,79,—,—,—** CSF £46.33 CT £406.33 TOTE £3.70: £2.10, £7.00, £3.00; EX 80.00 Trifecta £498.20 Part won. Pool: £701.74 - 0.50 winning tickets..
Owner D N Green **Bred** Seamus Murphy **Trained** Woodingdean, E Sussex

FOCUS
The rain had certainly got into the ground by this stage. A solid enough handicap with the winner value for further and the third, fifth and sixth close to their marks.

NOTEBOOK
Here We Go(IRE) followed up his Fontwell win under a 7lb penalty. Patiently ridden, he was about to take it up when he lost his footing after an awkward jump at the last, but he recovered well to get back up. He would have won comfortably had he landed running at the last and there is more to come from him. *(tchd 3-1)*
Best Profile(IRE), back in front again at the second last, looked to have been handed the race when the challenging favourite sprawled at the last but was cut down in the last 75 yards. The tongue tie has had a positive effect. *(tchd 20-1)*
Original Thought(IRE) ran a sound race on this handicap debut but, while he stays well, he does lack anything in the way of a change in pace. *(op 9-1)*
Hot 'N' Holy is proven over this trip and he ran well with no excuses on this handicap debut. Chasing is going to be his game. *(tchd 4-1 and 11-2 in places)*
Businessmoney Jake has gained his victories over shorter but probably stayed this trip. *(op 8-1 tchd 13-2)*
Complete Outsider, turned out quickly under a penalty following his Newton Abbot win, travelled well enough but faded on the approach to the final flight. *(op 11-1)*

4962 CHELTENHAM JUVENILE NOVICES' HURDLE (8 hdls) 2m 1f

5:45 (5:48) (Class 2) 4-Y-0 **£8,768** (£2,590; £1,295; £648; £323)

Form RPR

6315 **1** **Chiaro (FR)**[13] 4750 4-11-6 139.....................................(b) RichardJohnson 121+
(P J Hobbs) *mde virtually all: hrd rdn whn strly chal last: forged clr u.p run-in* **8/11**[1]

2140 **2** *5* **Pace Shot (IRE)**[13] 4747 4-11-6 136.................................... JamieMoore 116+
(G L Moore) *trckd ldrs: hdwy to chal between horses bnd appr last: sn str chal: wknd u.p run-in* **11/4**[2]

1005 **3** *3 1/2* **Desert Secrets (IRE)**[20] 4674 4-10-9 94........................ RobertThornton 100
(J G Portman) *pressed ldr thrght and stl ev ch u.p last: wknd run-in* **50/1**

3163 **4** *19* **Pseudonym (IRE)**[6] 4830 4-11-6 125..................................... PJBrennan 93+
(M F Harris) *rr whn blnd 2nd: hdwy 4 out: chsd ldrs 2 out: sn wknd* **16/1**

12 **5** *7* **Tritonville Lodge (IRE)**[131] 2753 4-11-2 115...................... BarryFenton 85+
(Miss E C Lavelle) *trckd ldrs: nt fluent 4th: stl wl there whn hit 2 out and sn lost pl* **6/1**[3]

4m 11.9s **Going Correction** +0.325s/f (Yiel) **5** Ran SP% **106.7**
Speed ratings: **113,110,109,100,96** CSF £2.85 TOTE £1.80: £1.20, £1.60; EX 2.70 Place 6 £74.89, Place 5 £51.02 .
Owner Andrew L Cohen **Bred** Hans Peter Sorg **Trained** Withycombe, Somerset

FOCUS
This was run at just a steady pace and although it could be rated higher, has been rated cautiously with the third limiting the form.

NOTEBOOK
Chiaro(FR) had to battle to see off a pair of rivals but stamina came to his aid in the end. Likely to go chasing in the new season, he promises to stay further than this. *(op Evens tchd 4-6)*
Pace Shot(IRE), fourth in the Triumph Hurdle here before a lesser effort at Aintree, had 3lb to find with Chiaro on BHB figures. Briefly relegated to last place before closing again on the downhill run to the second last, he only gave best to the favourite on the run-in. *(op 9-4 tchd 3-1)*
Desert Secrets(IRE) had more than two stone to find with the first two on official figures yet was still alongside them at the last and only conceded defeat on the run-in. This was a very creditable effort but her handicap mark will be adversely affected. *(op 33-1)*
Pseudonym(IRE) , down in trip, was the first beaten of this quintet and has now run poorly twice since his improved effort at Aintree. He will struggle in handicaps from his revised mark but remains eligible for novice events until the end of October. *(op 14-1)*
Tritonville Lodge(IRE) faded from the second last and it might be that he needed this first run since December. *(op 5-1)*
T/Jkpt: £26,841.60 to a £1 stake. Pool: £170,123.00. 4.50 winning tickets. T/Plt: £41.50 to a £1 stake. Pool: £96,985.95. 1,705.65 winning tickets. T/Qpdt: £19.50 to a £1 stake. Pool: £5,185.20. 196.75 winning tickets. ST

4963 - 4969a (Foreign Racing) - See Raceform Interactive

4956 CHELTENHAM (New Course) (L-H)

Thursday, April 20

OFFICIAL GOING: Good (good to soft in places)
The card ended with a charity Flat race, not run under Rules.
Wind: Moderate, half-across

4970 COTSWOLD LIFE GLOUCESTERSHIRE TRAINERS' CHAMPIONSHIP NOVICES' HURDLE (8 hdls) 2m 1f

2:20 (2:21) (Class 2) 4-Y-0+

£9,081 (£2,682; £1,341; £671; £334; £168)

Form RPR

2240 **1** **Pirate Flagship (FR)**[13] 4765 7-11-8 126.................................... RWalsh 124+
(P F Nicholls) *w ldr tl after 2nd: styd 2nd: pushed along to chal 2 out: sn led: hdd wl bef last:sn chalng:led after last: drvn out* **2/5**[1]

4310 **2** *4* **Linnet (GER)**[34] 4468 4-10-6 110...............................(v[1]) RichardJohnson 105+
(Ian Williams) *chsd ldrs: nt fluent and rdn 2 out: styd on u.p run-in: tk 2nd cl home but no imp on wnr* **6/1**[2]

P465 **3** *1/2* **Amour Multiple (IRE)**[38] 4420 7-11-8 124........................... KeithMercer 120+
(S Lycett) *chsd ldrs: chal 2 out: led wl bef last: sn rdn and mstke: hdd sn after: no ex and lost 2nd cl home* **8/1**[3]

0544 **4** *7* **Reach For The Top (IRE)**[76] 3717 5-11-0 108................ TimmyMurphy 106+
(Miss H C Knight) *slt ld tl def advantage after 2nd: rdn and hdd sn after 2 out: wknd last* **16/1**

055 **5** *8* **John Diamond (IRE)**[97] 3369 5-11-0 .... SamThomas 96
(Miss H C Knight) *chsd ldrs: rdn to chal 2 out: wknd sn after* **33/1**

0 **6** *17* **Fisby**[125] 2860 5-11-0 .... PaddyMerrigan 79
(K J Burke) *nt fluent: rr: dropped off pce 4 out: pushed along after 3 out: wknd 2 out* **66/1**

4m 15.9s (3.70) **Going Correction** +0.425s/f (Soft)
WFA 4 from 5yo+ 5lb **6** Ran SP% **107.1**
Speed ratings: **108,106,105,102,98 90** CSF £2.95 TOTE £1.30: £1.20, £1.70; EX 2.50 Trifecta £7.50 Pool: £303.86 - 28.39 winning tickets..
Owner Mr & Mrs Mark Woodhouse **Bred** Haras De Preaux **Trained** Ditcheat, Somerset

FOCUS
The absence of both Acambo and Welcome Stranger left Pirate Flagship with a simple task. The third and fourth are the best guides to the form.

NOTEBOOK
Pirate Flagship(FR) has taken plenty of racing during the season, acquitting himself well on almost every occasion, and he did not pass up this simple opportunity. He won over course and distance back in January, when getting the race in the Stewards' room, and went on to run well in the County Hurdle. His effort when stepped up in trip at Aintree last time was slightly lacklustre and he had to work really hard to sign-off for the season with a win. Novice chasing beckons for him next season. *(op 4-9 tchd 1-2)*
Linnet(GER), representing the ladies and the juvenile generation in a first-time visor, was firmly put in her place last time when visiting Prestbury Park behind Detroit City, and was another who was under pressure quite a way from home. However, to her credit, under a strong Johnson ride, she kept on well to secure second place. Races over slightly further should be within her compass. *(op 5-1)*
Amour Multiple(IRE), who had shown the odd bit of form in England and took a Listed hurdle in France, can make the running, but was held up just behind the pace on this occasion. He looked to be going ominously well between the last two but did not seem to quite get home, and a mistake at the last ended his interest. It was a good effort all the same and he considerably closed the gap on the winner compared with their meeting at Newbury earlier in the season. *(op 9-1 tchd 7-1)*
Reach For The Top(IRE), ridden by Murphy after his original mount was taken out, had shown the odd piece of form, and took the field along early. A bad error at the second-last stopped him in his tracks, before staying on again. A half-brother to Rosslea, he has plenty of time on his side and, like many from his stable, chasing will be his game. *(op 14-1)*
John Diamond(IRE) is another unlikely to be winning until sent chasing. *(op 18-1)*

4971 MESSIER-DOWTY LANDING GEAR NOVICES' LIMITED H'CAP CHASE (17 fncs) 2m 5f

2:55 (2:56) (Class 3) (0-135,135) 5-Y-0+

£9,707 (£2,867; £1,433; £717; £358; £179)

Form RPR

1U11 **1** **Taranis (FR)**[21] 4679 5-11-10 **135**..(t) RWalsh 147+
(P F Nicholls) *hld up in rr: hdwy 11th: trckd ldrs on bit 3 out: qcknd to chal 2 out: sn led: clr last: easily* **5/4**[1]

2341 **2** *8* **Amicelli (GER)**[45] 4279 7-11-6 **127**................................ RichardJohnson 133+
(P J Hobbs) *rr: nt flunet 2nd: hit 7th and 9th: mstke 11th: hit 13th:hdwy after 3 out: styd on wl fr 2 out to take 2nd run-in: no ch w* **11/2**[3]

1U24 **3** *3* **Shining Strand**[27] 4605 7-10-13 **120**................................ AndrewTinkler 121
(N J Henderson) *led: rdn appr 2 out: hdd sn after: wknd last* **4/1**[2]

0014 **4** *6* **Mighty Matters (IRE)**[89] 3507 7-10-4 **111** oh1........... WayneHutchinson 106
(T R George) *chsd ldrs: wnt 2nd 11th: rdn 3 out: wknd 2 out* **8/1**

F1U0 **5** *25* **Florida Dream (IRE)**[36] 4447 7-11-0 **121**.........................(b) AntonyEvans 91
(N A Twiston-Davies) *chsd ldr 6th to 10th: sn wknd* **10/1**

4P32 **6** *3* **Iris's Prince**[25] 4633 7-10-1 **111** oh12........................(p) DougieCostello(3) 78
(A Crook) *in tch: rdn 5th: wknd 12th* **66/1**

31P **P** **Thistlecraft (IRE)**[63] 3942 7-11-2 **123**..................................... NoelFehily —
(C C Bealby) *chsd ldr to 6th: j. slowly 12th: wknd qckly 3 out: t.o whn p.u bef last* **16/1**

5m 21.3s (-5.40) **Going Correction** -0.05s/f (Good) **7** Ran SP% **107.4**
Speed ratings: **108,104,103,101,92 90,—** CSF £7.70 TOTE £1.80: £1.30, £2.50; EX 5.00.
Owner Foster Yeoman Limited **Bred** P De Maleissye Melun **Trained** Ditcheat, Somerset

FOCUS
Only three of the runners looked to hold realistic claims, and it was hot favourite Taranis that emerged superior and is value for more than the official margin.

NOTEBOOK
Taranis(FR), a progressive five-year-old unbeaten in completed starts over fences, jumped and travelled beautifully all the way around under a confident ride from Walsh. Having come there going easily, he moved away from his rivals after the last, winning with any amount in hand. He looks a horse to be on the right side of next season, with further improvement anticipated. *(op 11-8 tchd 6-5)*
Amicelli(GER), making his handicap debut, stays three miles and would have preferred much quicker ground, and did not really get going until coming up the hill - he was still a running-on fourth with two to jump. Arguably well-treated on his best hurdling form given the exploits of those who finished in front of him on his last two efforts over timber, he can win a race in handicap company, especially over further. *(tchd 13-2)*
Shining Strand has talent and temperament in equal shares given the racecourse evidence - and at the start. One can never be quite sure which horse will turn up but, to be fair, he did little wrong when jumping off. He raced prominently, as is his usual trait, and was bang there until two out, before not getting home. He should win more races but will always be a risky betting proposition. *(op 11-4)*
Mighty Matters(IRE), an ex-pointer, is lightly raced under Rules but managed to pick up a novice event over two miles six at Towcester back in December. He did not shape too badly in handicap company last time, and travelled well for a lot of the race. He was left behind after the third-last but still shaped with some promise for the future. *(op 10-1)*
Florida Dream(IRE), whose stable have found some form again, dropped out disappointingly after being prominent early. *(op 12-1 tchd 14-1)*
Thistlecraft(IRE) did not run too badly on this return from a break and will find easier opportunities. *(op 10-1)*

4972 YORKSHIRE BANK MARES' ONLY H'CAP HURDLE (LISTED RACE) (10 hdls) 2m 5f 110y

3:30 (3:30) (Class 1) 4-Y-0+

£13,969 (£5,240; £2,623; £1,308; £656; £328)

Form RPR

0-16 **1** **Golden Bay**[29] 4579 7-9-13 **113**.. DarylJacob(5) 114
(Miss Suzy Smith) *chsd ldrs: chal 2 out: led sn after: hrd rdn whn strly chal run-in: hld on gamely* **20/1**

1F32 **2** *hd* **Jontys'Lass**[26] 4619 5-9-11 **109** oh2............................... DougieCostello(3) 110
(A Crook) *hdwy to chse ldrs 4th: rdn appr 2 out: chal sn after: stl upsides last: kpt on but a jst hld by wnr run-in* **16/1**

3421 **3** *4* **Zaffaran Express (IRE)**[80] 3648 7-10-7 **116**........................ TonyDobbin 114+
(N G Richards) *in tch: hit 6th: hdwy 3 out: styng on one pce whn blnd last* **15/2**

4213 **4** *3* **Blaeberry**[22] 4663 5-9-9 **109** oh2... SamCurling(5) 103
(Miss E C Lavelle) *hld up rr: hit 6th: hdwy 4 out: chsd ldrs 3 out: one pce u.p fr next* **7/1**[3]

4313 **5** *1* **Reem Two**[71] 3802 5-9-7 **109** oh9...................................... MrGTumelty(7) 102
(D McCain) *in tch: outpcd 6th: rdn and styd on to chse ldrs 3 out: one pce fr next* **40/1**

-230 **6** *shd* **Silver Charmer**[27] 4608 7-10-9 **118**.................................. MickFitzgerald 111
(H S Howe) *hld up in rr: stdy hday fr 4 out: trckd ldrs gng wl 2 out: rdn appr last: no imp and sn one pce* **9/1**

-0F0 **7** *10* **Inch Pride (IRE)**[36] 4446 7-11-6 **129**................................. TimmyMurphy 114+
(M C Pipe) *led 3rd: hdd after 2 out: wknd bef last* **5/1**[2]

1541 **8** *1 1/4* **Novacella (FR)**[30] 4568 5-10-0 **109** oh5 RobertWalford 90
(R H Alner) *rr: rdn along fr 4th: kpt on fr 2 out but nvr in contention* **14/1**

2-P3 **9** *12* **Floreana (GER)**[157] 2240 5-10-6 **115** NoelFehily 84
(C J Mann) *bhd: hdwy 6th: rdn to chse ldrs after 3 out: nvr a danger: wknd fr next* **40/1**

-203 **10** *3 1/2* **Almah (SAF)**[12] 4781 8-10-9 **118** (b) SamThomas 84
(Miss Venetia Williams) *chsd ldrs: hit 7th: n.d after* **12/1**

1033 **11** *1 1/2* **Festive Chimes (IRE)**[80] 3648 5-9-13 **111** OwynNelmes[(3)] 75
(N B King) *in tch: hdwy 6th: rdn 3 out: sn wknd: no ch whn mstke next* **50/1**

P-P1 **12** *3* **Almnadia (IRE)**[340] 372 7-11-2 **125** (p) RobertThornton 86
(S Gollings) *chsd ldrs to 4 out: wknd next* **40/1**

2231 **13** *10* **Rowlands Dream (IRE)**[38] 4425 6-10-0 **109** oh6 PJBrennan 60
(R H Alner) *in tch whn hmpd and lost plcd bnd after 4th: sme hdwy and rdn 4 out: wknd next* **20/1**

1042 **14** *9* **Penneyrose Bay**[38] 4417 7-11-10 **133** RichardJohnson 75
(J A Geake) *chsd ldrs: rdn fr 5th: wknd after next* **10/1**

1P1U **P** **Topanberry (IRE)**[57] 4058 7-10-0 **109** BrianHarding —
(N G Richards) *bhd most of way: t.o whn p.u bef last* **33/1**

1121 **P** **Ile Maurice (FR)**[26] 4612 6-11-0 **123** APMcCoy —
(Ferdy Murphy) *chsd ldrs tl wknd qckly after 3 out: t.o whn p.u bef last* **9/2**[1]

5m 21.0s (4.40) **Going Correction** +0.425s/f (Soft) **16** Ran SP% **120.2**
Speed ratings: **109,108,107,106,106 105,102,101,97,96 95,94,90,87,—** — CSF £285.87 CT £2622.12 TOTE £29.50: £4.40, £3.30, £2.10, £1.90; EX 615.20 TRIFECTA Not won..
Owner Goldie's Friends **Bred** Mrs S D Watts **Trained** Lewes, E Sussex

FOCUS
An ultra-competitive mares' event that produced a cracking finish. The winner and the third are the best guides to the level of the form.

NOTEBOOK
Golden Bay, who appeared to struggle off this mark at Towcester last month, looked beaten turning for home but, under a strong ride from her capable claiming jockey, she battled on doggedly to deny Jontys' Lass. The rain during the day certainly did not harm her chances, and it is likely to seven-year-old can go on to better things, with a switch to fences next season a distinct possibility. *Official explanation: trainer said, regarding the improved form shown, mare was unsuited by the track at Towcester*
Jontys'Lass received a fine ride from Costello and the pair only just lost out. She was under serious pressure after the second last, but responded gamely and was not stopping as they reached the line. This tough mare is only five and may yet have more to offer. *(op 25-1)*
Zaffaran Express(IRE) is a consistent sort who created a good impression when winning at Ludlow last time. She looked to have a chance of sorts approaching the last, but a bad mistake there ended her challenge. In all likelihood she would not have got to the front two, but still ran well and should make a chaser next term. *(op 10-1 tchd 11-1)*
Blaeberry, who could have done without the rain, comes from an in-form stable and she ran a reasonable race back in fourth. She is the type to enjoy further success on fast ground during the summer months.
Reem Two ran above market expectation, as has been the case with many of her in-form stable's runners this season, but she will need to improve further to win off this mark.
Silver Charmer looked to have been aimed at this all season after running well in the race in previous years, but she was another that failed to get home when push came to shove. She is quite high in the weights and probably ran as well as she was entitled to do. *(op 7-1 tchd 10-1)*
Inch Pride(IRE) set off in front and ran well for a long way, but she got tired after the second last and came home in her own time. She too could make a smart chasing mare next year. *(tchd 11-2)*
Ile Maurice(FR) went well for a long way before a mistake three from home stopped her in her tracks. *Official explanation: trainer's representative said mare was in season (op 4-1)*

4973 NICHOLSON HOLMAN CUP H'CAP CHASE (14 fncs) 2m 110y

4:05 (4:18) (Class 3) (0-135,135) 5-Y-O+ **£6,057** (£2,997; £1,517; £777; £406)

Form RPR

22FU **1** **Bleu Superbe (FR)**[14] 4749 11-11-9 **132** SamThomas 140
(Miss Venetia Williams) *w ldr: nt fluent 6th: led next: hrd rdn fr 2 out: hld on all out* **6/1**[3]

2266 **2** *1 1/2* **Escompteur (FR)**[99] 3344 6-10-4 **113** TimmyMurphy 120
(M C Pipe) *pushed along after 4th in rr: hdwy to chse wnr fr 4 out: rdn next:styd on one pce u.p fr 2 out: a hld run-in* **3/1**[1]

414P **3** *16* **Palua**[14] 4749 9-11-12 **135** BarryFenton 127+
(Miss E C Lavelle) *bhd: hit 9th: nt fluent 4 out: 3rd and one pce after 3 out* **16/1**

214F **4** *8* **Saintsaire (FR)**[35] 4459 7-11-7 **130** (b) MickFitzgerald 117+
(N J Henderson) *led: hit 5th: hdd 7th: j. slowly and lost 2nd 4 out: sn no ch* **3/1**[1]

P005 **5** *dist* **Auditor**[29] 4580 7-9-12 **112** oh44 ow3 (b) MarkNicolls[(5)] —
(S T Lewis) *a in rr: lost tch 8th: t.o* **200/1**

5PP2 **F** **Bonus Bridge (IRE)**[48] 4213 11-11-6 **129** RobertThornton —
(H D Daly) *cl up whn fell 2nd* **7/2**[2]

4m 14.1s (6.60) **Going Correction** -0.05s/f (Good) **6** Ran SP% **92.9**
Speed ratings: **103,102,94,91,—** — CSF £16.66 CT £128.03 TOTE £5.90: £2.40, £2.30; EX 24.70 Trifecta £95.30 Pool: £349.06 - 2.60 winning tickets..
Owner P A Deal, A Hirschfeld & J Tyndall **Bred** Mr Michel Agelou **Trained** Kings Caple, H'fords
■ Lindsay (5/1) was withdrawn (unseated rider and bolted before start). R4 applies, deduct 15p in the £.

FOCUS
A deserved win for Bleu Superbe who along with the runner-up sets the standard. Quite a weak race for the money.

NOTEBOOK
Bleu Superbe(FR) took over at halfway and hung on under grim determination to record his first win since November 2003. Nobody could begrudge him this success, as he has run many cracking races in defeat since that last victory, but he will be doing well to defy a rise. *(tchd 5-1)*
Escompteur(FR) looked a huge danger at the top of the hill but failed to pick up as looked likely. He did keep on for pressure but never looked like troubling the winner.
Palua, who was pulled up last time when out of his depth at Aintree, was anchored at the back of the runners and never looked like getting involved. *(op 9-1)*
Saintsaire(FR), in the process of running a massive race when crashing out at the second-last in the Racing Post Plate, may still have had that incident on his mind and failed to reproduce the effort. *(tchd 11-4)*
Bonus Bridge(IRE), back to form at Newbury latest, got no further than the second. *(op 4-1)*

4974 RENAULT MASTERS H'CAP HURDLE (12 hdls) 3m

4:40 (4:48) (Class 2) (0-145,144) 4-Y-O+

£10,333 (£3,052; £1,526; £763; £381; £191)

Form RPR

11P0 **1** **Standin Obligation (IRE)**[35] 4461 7-11-12 **144** TimmyMurphy 155+
(M C Pipe) *hld up in rr: stdy hdwy 3 out: styd on to ld appr last: kpt on wl* **14/1**

4266 **2** *7* **Rimsky (IRE)**[12] 4776 5-10-12 **130** (b) AntonyEvans 133+
(N A Twiston-Davies) *bhd: hdwy 4 out: chsd ldrs and hit 2 out: kpt on to chse wnr run-in but no imp* **13/2**[2]

10P1 **3** *1* **Lyes Green**[28] 4589 5-10-0 **118** oh1 LeightonAspell 121+
(O Sherwood) *bhd: gd hdwy 3 out: led briefly bef last: narrowly hdd whn blnd bdly: nt rcvr* **8/1**[3]

-5PP **4** *1* **Lord Sam (IRE)**[75] 3727 10-11-3 **140** (p) LiamHeard[(5)] 140
(V R A Dartnall) *hld up mid-div: hdwy to trck ldrs appr 3 out: led after 2 out: hdd bef last: styd on same pce* **14/1**

2102 **5** *6* **Drumbeater (IRE)**[29] 4579 6-10-5 **123** RichardJohnson 118+
(P J Hobbs) *mid-div: hdwy 4 out: chsd ldrs 3 out: rdn next: wknd last* **9/2**[1]

0P00 **6** *1 1/4* **Quick**[35] 4461 6-10-13 **138** (v) AndrewGlassonbury[(7)] 131
(M C Pipe) *led: sn clr: hdd after 2 out: wknd last* **40/1**

01/2 **7** *hd* **Pipssalio (SPA)**[19] 4693 9-10-0 **118** oh3 MatthewBatchelor 111
(Jamie Poulton) *chsd ldrs: rdn appr 2 out: wknd sn after* **25/1**

3233 **8** *9* **Just Beth**[26] 4612 10-9-13 **122** DerekLaverty[(5)] 106
(G Fierro) *chsd ldrs to 3 out: wknd next* **10/1**

4606 **9** *1/2* **Heltornic (IRE)**[26] 4619 6-10-0 **118** oh1 TomScudamore 102
(M Scudamore) *chsd ldrs to 3 out: wknd sn after* **20/1**

121P **10** *11* **Harrycone Lewis**[47] 4240 8-10-2 **120** (b) WarrenMarston 93
(Mrs P Sly) *chsd clr ldr to 3 out: wknd next* **16/1**

2206 **11** *1/2* **Openide**[57] 4060 5-10-0 **118** oh1 (b) PJBrennan 90
(B W Duke) *chsd ldrs: hit 4 out: sn rdn and wknd* **16/1**

3205 **12** *4* **Bengo (IRE)**[48] 4215 6-10-0 **118** oh1 (b) DaveCrosse 86
(B De Haan) *mid-div: sme hdwy 4 out: j. slowly 3 out and sn wknd* **12/1**

2-40 **13** *18* **Glacial Sunset (IRE)**[35] 4461 11-11-1 **133** TomDoyle 83
(C Tinkler) *hld up rr: rdn and effrt into mid-div 3 out: sn wknd* **16/1**

0-0P **14** *7* **Ballyvaddy (IRE)**[26] 4617 10-10-6 **124** (v) MarcusFoley 67
(J A Geake) *chsd ldrs to 3 out* **33/1**

0000 **15** *6* **Tango Royal (FR)**[35] 4459 10-11-2 **134** (t) APMcCoy 71
(M C Pipe) *bhd: sme hdwy 4 out: sn rdn and wknd* **20/1**

P-00 **16** *12* **Chicuelo (FR)**[159] 2175 10-10-8 **126** (b) MickFitzgerald 51
(N J Henderson) *in tch early: mstke and wknd 7th* **40/1**

42P0 **17** *nk* **Rowley Hill**[26] 4612 8-10-12 **130** RobertThornton 55
(A King) *nvr bttr than mid-div: bhd fr 6th* **50/1**

0204 **P** **Blue Business**[14] 4753 8-11-5 **137** (b) RWalsh —
(P F Nicholls) *a bhd: rdn 7th: t.o whn p.u bef 2 out* **12/1**

6m 1.10s (2.20) **Going Correction** +0.425s/f (Soft) **18** Ran SP% **121.2**
Speed ratings: **113,110,110,110,108 107,107,104,104,100 100,99,93,90,88 84,84,—** CSF £93.93 CT £796.11 TOTE £14.40: £3.00, £2.60, £2.30, £4.00; EX 80.60 Trifecta £590.20 Part won. Pool: £831.28 - 0.50 winning tickets..
Owner D A Johnson **Bred** Mrs S Flood **Trained** Nicholashayne, Devon

FOCUS
A mixed bunch turned up for this competitive-looking handicap. It had an end-of-season feel to it, as it featured quite a few who have been doing their racing over fences recently, some badly handicapped sorts and plainly out-of-form horses. Some of the interest was lost before the race when the mare Material World was taken out and the form is slightly mixed.

NOTEBOOK
Standin Obligation(IRE) has not shown much in his last two runs after an impressive run of success. The stable has not been churning out winners as regularly as it often does, and his halt in form coincided with that spell, but, under a fine waiting ride, he moved slowly into contention and joined issue on the home turn. Under his big weight, he kept on really well and won in the manner of a nice horse. He could make a smart chaser next season.
Rimsky(IRE) is not an easy horse to predict, despite his talent. He did not run too badly behind Nicanor at the Festival in March and again showed his better side, staying on really well up the hill. He does look a hard ride and would probably get even further over timber if tried. *(op 7-1 tchd 15-2)*
Lyes Green, running from 1lb out of the handicap, has progressed fairly well after giving Denman a minor scare at Wincanton earlier in the season. Racing off a 1llb higher mark than when well beaten the last time he dipped his toe into handicap company, he had every chance coming to the last before a blunder cost him dearly. On this showing he is capable of winning a handicap, but only if the assessor does not take the form too literally.
Lord Sam(IRE), wearing cheekpieces for the first time, ran a big race after so many disappointments. He looked the winner coming around the home turn, but failed to get home under his big weight. It was a welcome return to form for such a talented animal and one hopes he can build on this effort. *(op 12-1)*
Drumbeater(IRE), taking a rise in grade, has never looked the easiest of rides despite his success. He stays really well but probably needs a drop into a slightly less-taxing event. *(op 4-1)*
Quick kept on surprisingly well after being under strong pressure at the top of the hill, and might be coming back to some form despite his battle with the Handicapper.
Blue Business was a huge disappointment, looking to lose interest at an early stage. He does not look entirely in love with the game at the moment and might feel better after a summer off. *(op 10-1)*

4975 COOLUS AIR CONDITIONING HUNTERS' CHASE (22 fncs) 3m 2f 110y

5:15 (5:20) (Class 4) 6-Y-O+ **£3,435** (£1,065; £532; £266)

Form RPR

4215 **1** **Knife Edge (USA)**[30] 4560 11-11-11 120 (p) MrAJBerry[(3)] 122
(Jonjo O'Neill) *chsd ldrs: hit 9th: 13th and 15th: rdn fr 17th: styd on u.p fr 3 out to ld last: drvn clr* **14/1**

-263 **2** *7* **Yeoman Sailor (IRE)**[27] 4607 12-12-0 MrNHarris 116+
(Miss Grace Muir) *chsd ldrs: led 7th: narrowly hdd 12th: led again 13th: lft clr 16th: rdn 3 out: hdd appr 2 out: styd on same pce last* **9/1**

14-3 **3** *3 1/2* **Joe Blake (IRE)**[34] 4471 11-11-9 MrMJO'Hare[(5)] 112+
(I R Ferguson, Ire) *in tch: lft chsng ldr 16th: styd on to ld appr 2 out: rdn and hdd last: wknd run-in* **5/4**[1]

0025 **4** *12* **Dun An Doras (IRE)**[15] 4730 10-11-7 94 MrDMcKenna[(7)] 101+
(Mrs N Frost) *bhd: hdwy fr 4 out: clsd on ldrs next: rdn and fnd little appr 2 out* **50/1**

1-1P **5** *3 1/2* **Mister Friday (IRE)**[75] 3736 9-12-4 112 (v) MrCMulhall[(3)] 105+
(C A Mulhall) *a in rr* **11/2**[3]

F110 **F** **Raregem**[34] 4471 8-11-10 MrWBiddick[(7)] —
(M Biddick) *rr: lost tch: 9th: fell 12th* **5/1**[2]

3P-5 **P** **Dunowen (IRE)**[234] 1362 11-12-0 MrNWilliams —
(Mark Doyle) *rdn 4th: a bhd: t.o whn p.u bef 15th* **66/1**

30/3 **P** **Handyman (IRE)**[30] 4560 12-11-11 MrDEdwards[(3)] —
(Michael M Watson) *in rr: no ch whn blnd 4 out: t.o whn p.u bef last* **40/1**

P5P/ **P** **Jolly Joe (IRE)**[18] 9-11-11 MrDMansell[(3)] —
(S T Lewis) *led to to 5th: bit c through and sn no ch: t.o whn p.u after 12th* **50/1**

/220 **U** **Bosham Mill**[34] 4471 8-12-0 112 MrTJO'Brien —
(P J Hobbs) *chsd ldrs: led 5th to 7th: led briefly 12th to next: upsides whn blnd and uns rdr 16th* **8/1**

7m 6.20s (9.10) **Going Correction** -0.05s/f (Good) **10** Ran SP% **112.1**
Speed ratings: **105,102,101,98,97** —,—,—,—,— CSF £121.09 TOTE £9.90: £2.10, £2.60, £1.20; EX 84.50 Trifecta £89.50 Pool: £365.80 - 2.90 winning tickets..

The Form Book, Raceform Ltd, Compton, RG20 6NL

Owner John P McManus **Bred** John R Gaines Thoroughbreds Llc & John G Sikura **Trained** Cheltenham, Gloucs

FOCUS

A good hunter chase likely to produce its share of winners although none of the first three ran to their best.

NOTEBOOK

Knife Edge(USA), who did not run at the Festival, stayed on too strongly for all his rivals and won with quite a bit to spare. He did not look to be going anywhere at the top of the hill, but his jockey persevered with him and grabbed the spoils after jumping the last. *(op 16-1)*

Yeoman Sailor(IRE) was another to keep on really well when the pressure was fully applied after being left in the lead down the back straight. He looked booked for third at one point but stayed on well to take second-place money. *(op 10-1)*

Joe Blake(IRE) looked a big danger to all in the Foxhunters' at Cheltenham before a mistake three out stopped his progress. Again, he looked like winning between the last two before fading badly after the last. The Form Book strongly suggests he does not stay this trip, and he would be worth a try at slightly shorter if a race can be found for him. *(tchd 6-5)*

Dun An Doras(IRE) ran well above expectations and if this run could be believed, he should win a normal hunter chase in the near future. *(op 40-1)*

Mister Friday(IRE) , the winner last year, was never really in with a chance from an early stage. He was held up at the rear and appeared to jump a bit deliberately, and although he stayed on well up *the hill, he never had a chance of placing, let alone winning.Official explanation: jockey said gelding was unsuited by the good (good to soft places) ground (op 13-2 tchd 7-1)*

Bosham Mill, who ran well for a long way in the Festival Foxhunters', was still enjoying himself in front when unseating halfway down the back straight on the final lap. It is hoped this does not affect confidence. *(op 11-2 tchd 9-2)*

Jolly Joe(IRE) *Official explanation: jockey said bit pulled through gelding's mouth (op 11-2 tchd 9-2)*

Raregem was towards the rear when falling in front of the stands' before their last circuit. Is is hoped this does not affect confidence. *(op 11-2 tchd 9-2)*

4976 RENAULT TRAFIC MARES' ONLY STANDARD OPEN NATIONAL HUNT FLAT RACE 2m 1f

5:45 (5:55) (Class 4) 4-6-Y-O **£3,578** (£1,050; £525; £262)

Form				RPR
1	**1**		**Classic Fiddle**[24] [4654] 4-11-2 .... MickFitzgerald (N J Henderson) *trckd ldrs: wnt 2nd over 3f out: drvn to ld ins fnl 2f: styd on strly* **4/1**[2]	112+
24	**2**	*9*	**Strawberry (IRE)**[14] [4751] 5-10-7 .... WayneKavanagh(7) (J W Mullins) *bhd: hdwy 1/2-way: styd on u.p fnl 2f to take 2nd wl ins last but no imp on wnr* **11/4**[1]	101
213	**3**	*shd*	**Tihui Two (IRE)**[70] [3820] 6-11-7 .... TomDoyle (G R I Smyly) *led in at s: sn clr: rdn 3f out: hdd ins fnl 2f: kpt on same pce and ct for 2nd wl ins last* **25/1**	108
	4	*3/4*	**Missis Potts** 5-11-0 .... RichardJohnson (P J Hobbs) *bhd: hdwy 6f out: r.o under presure fr over 2f out: kpt on ins last* **14/1**	100
10	**5**	*5*	**Sovietica (FR)**[40] [4376] 5-11-7 .... RobertThornton (S Pike) *chsd ldrs: wnt 2nd over 4f out tl over 3f out: wknd fnl f* **33/1**	102
	6	*1 1/2*	**Mountain Approach** 4-10-9 .... DaveCrosse (Jean-Rene Auvray) *bhd: hdwy 6f out: rdn to chse ldrs 4f out: one pce fr over 2f out* **100/1**	89
1	**7**	*15*	**Westgrove Berry (IRE)**[43] [4304] 6-11-7 .... TonyDobbin (N G Richards) *bhd: hdwy 4f out: kpt on fnl 2f but nvr in contention* **7/1**	86
341	**8**	*7*	**Inherent (IRE)**[127] [2830] 4-11-2 .... MarkBradburne (C G Cox) *bhd: sme hdwy 5f out: nt rch ldrs: wknd 3f out* **8/1**	74
61	**9**	*3/4*	**Delena**[22] [4667] 5-11-7 .... RWalsh (P F Nicholls) *mid-div: pushed along 6f out: nvr in contention* **6/1**[3]	78
	10	*5*	**Foxy Tales** 5-11-0 .... APMcCoy (T R George) *bhd: rdn and sme hdwy 7f out: nvr rch ldrs: bhd fnl 4f* **8/1**	66
0	**11**	*10*	**Silent City**[60] [4017] 6-10-7 .... AndrewGlassonbury(7) (P D Williams) *nvr bttr than mid-div* **100/1**	56
	12	*9*	**Fad Amach (IRE)**[172] [1947] 5-10-9 .... StevenCrawford(5) (G R I Smyly) *nvr bttr than mid-div* **80/1**	47
	13	*2 1/2*	**Jaunty Flight** 4-10-4 .... MarkNicolls(5) (B J Eckley) *chsd ldrs 12f* **50/1**	39
3	**14**	*9*	**Zuzu Summit (IRE)**[149] [2425] 4-10-9 .... TomScudamore (M Scudamore) *bhd fr 1/2-way* **33/1**	30
	15	*8*	**Cider's Niece** 5-11-0 .... WayneHutchinson (C J Price) *t.k.h: sn chsng ldr: wknd 5f out* **100/1**	27
	16	*1 1/4*	**Heebie Jeebie** 4-10-9 .... PJBrennan (P J Hobbs) *rdn 1/2-way: a bhd* **40/1**	21
0	**17**	*3/4*	**Mary Casey**[86] [3556] 5-10-11 .... DougieCostello(3) (C A Mulhall) *bhd fr 1/2-way* **100/1**	25

4m 10.2s

WFA 4 from 5yo 5lb 5 from 6yo 3lb **17** Ran SP% **121.7**

CSF £14.42 TOTE £4.40: £1.80, £1.50, £5.30; EX 13.40 Trifecta £180.60 Part won. Pool: £254.40 - 0.90 winning tickets. Place 6 £49.93, Place 5 £45.76 .

Owner Mrs E Roberts **Bred** Mrs E C Roberts **Trained** Upper Lambourn, Berks

FOCUS

A competitive mares' bumper on paper, but Classic Fiddle ran out an authoritative winner and looks to have a bright future. The form looks solid enough with the runner-up running to her mark.

NOTEBOOK

Classic Fiddle ◆ is certainly bred for the job, being out of that very useful racemare Fiddling The Facts. She sloshed through the mud to win at Plumpton and created an equally favourable impression here, going away from her rivals up the hill. She could be smart and certainly should get further, so her future looks particularly bright. *(op 3-1)*

Strawberry(IRE) really well in a Listed bumper at Aintree last time and gives the form a solid look. She stayed on strongly in the final stage and will get further as well. However, she lacks a little size and could do with growing a bit. *(op 9-2)*

Tihui Two(IRE) got a flyer at the start and took the field along at a good pace, but she was unable to prove any match for the winner and just got nabbed for second. *(op 16-1)*

Missis Potts will no doubt have pleased connections with this debut effort, keeping on nicely into fourth. She should have little trouble finding a race in this sphere. *(tchd 12-1)*

Sovietica(FR), a winner on her debut in October, has faced two vastly stiffer tasks since, but she has performed reasonably on both occasions and she should make a hurdler.

Mountain Approach made a little late headway, performing way above market expectations, and she should stay further over hurdles next term.

Westgrove Berry(IRE), representing the same trainer/jockey combination who landed the race last season, never got into it and failed to build on last month's Catterick win. *(op 8-1)*

Inherent(IRE), stepping up to this distance for the first time having previously contested junior bumpers, failed to last out the trip, but she is only four and may yet strengthen. *(op 15-2 tchd 7-1)*

Delena failed to build on her Taunton win and does not look one of her powerful stable's brighter prospects. *(op 9-2 tchd 13-2)*

Foxy Tales could have done without the rain, but the fact she was sent off at only 8/1 suggests she is well thought-of and she may be capable of better next season. *(op 11-1)*

T/Jkpt: Not won. T/Plt: £139.50 to a £1 stake. Pool: £82,504.65. 431.65 winning tickets. T/Qpdt: £45.60 to a £1 stake. Pool: £4,807.90. 78.00 winning tickets. ST

4977 - 4979a (Foreign Racing) - See Raceform Interactive

[4582] AYR (L-H)

Friday, April 21

OFFICIAL GOING: Good to soft (good in places)

Wind: Breezy; half behind

4980 ROYAL BANK OF SCOTLAND "NATIONAL HUNT" NOVICES' H'CAP HURDLE (12 hdls) 3m 110y

2:20 (2:20) (Class 2) 4-Y-0+ **£11,710** (£3,438; £1,719; £858)

Form				RPR
111	**1**		**According To John (IRE)**[43] [4315] 6-11-6 **123** .... TonyDobbin (N G Richards) *chsd ldrs: clsd 7th: led bef 3 out: edgd lft run in: pushed out* **6/4**[1]	135+
1104	**2**	*3 1/2*	**Zipalong Lad (IRE)**[14] [4765] 6-11-12 **129** .... APMcCoy (P Bowen) *cl up: led 4 out to bef next: sn outpcd: rallied 2 out: kpt on fr last: nt rch wnr* **13/8**[2]	132
3311	**3**	*15*	**Aces Four (IRE)**[29] [4582] 7-11-8 **125** .... KeithMercer (Ferdy Murphy) *set stdy pce to 4 out: wknd fr next* **9/2**[3]	116+
1232	**4**	*dist*	**Menchikov (FR)**[42] [4359] 6-11-10 **127** .... MickFitzgerald (N J Henderson) *prom: hit 6th: outpcd next: hit 8th: sn lost tch* **8/1**	—

6m 4.30s (-27.50) **Going Correction** -0.70s/f (Firm) **4** Ran SP% **107.4**

Speed ratings: **110,108,104,—** CSF £4.38 TOTE £2.40; EX 3.40.

Owner Sir Robert Ogden **Bred** John P Kiely **Trained** Greystoke, Cumbria

FOCUS

Not a competitive race and the gallop was only fair, but another step up the ladder for According To John, who was value for further and remains one to keep on the right side.

NOTEBOOK

According To John(IRE) ◆ maintained his unbeaten record over hurdles with a workmanlike success on this handicap debut. He really took the eye in the preliminaries and will be very much one to keep on the right side when sent over fences next term. *(tchd 11-8 and 13-8)*

Zipalong Lad(IRE) back up in trip, ran creditably and looks a fair guide to this form. A stronger gallop over this trip would have been in his favour but, in this sphere, he is likely to remain vulnerable to the more progressive sorts from his current mark. *(op 9-4)*

Aces Four(IRE), back up in trip and on this handicap debut, had the run of the race but dropped out disappointingly when the pressure was on. He is going to find life tough over hurdles from this mark. *(op 4-1)*

Menchikov(FR), up in trip for this handicap debut, proved most disappointing and was beaten before stamina became an issue. His hurdling was less than fluent but, given he is in good hands *and is only lightly raced, he may not be one to write off yet. Official explanation: jockey said gelding hung right-handed throughout (op 7-1)*

4981 BUSINESS SOLUTIONS SCOTLAND RUN FASTER WITH XEROX NOVICES' H'CAP CHASE (17 fncs) 2m 4f

2:55 (2:55) (Class 3) (0-115,115) 5-Y-0+ **£6,506** (£1,910; £955; £477)

Form				RPR
4123	**1**		**King Barry (FR)**[69] [3851] 7-11-5 **108** .... RichardMcGrath (Miss P Robson) *hld up: hdwy to chse ldrs 9th: led after 3 out: clr bef last: kpt on wl* **3/1**[1]	124+
6314	**2**	*10*	**Persian Point**[29] [4587] 10-10-0 **92** ow1 .... MrCStorey(3) (Miss S E Forster) *chsd ldrs: led 11th: blnd 3 out: sn hdd: no ch w wnr* **10/1**	96+
13P2	**3**	*1 3/4*	**Silver Jack (IRE)**[69] [3849] 8-10-12 **106** .... (p) TJDreaper(5) (M Todhunter) *chsd ldrs: hmpd 12th: rdn and outpcd 4 out: kpt on fr 2 out: no imp run in* **6/1**[3]	106+
4440	**4**	*3*	**Barrons Pike**[6] [4844] 7-9-11 **89** .... DougieCostello(3) (B Storey) *in tch: drvn fr 1/2-way: outpcd 12th: kpt on fr 2 out: no imp* **33/1**	85
-046	**5**	*1 1/2*	**Banchory Two (IRE)**[133] [2751] 6-11-2 **105** .... RWalsh (P F Nicholls) *prom: hmpd 12th: effrt bef 4 out: wknd bef 2 out* **7/1**	102+
F5PP	**6**	*nk*	**Field Roller (IRE)**[18] [4719] 6-11-2 **105** .... TimmyMurphy (P Monteith) *nt fluent: hld up: effrt after 5 out: hit and wknd next* **25/1**	99
040	**7**	*4*	**Beau De Turgeon (FR)**[28] [4604] 5-11-3 **110** .... WayneHutchinson (Ian Williams) *chsd ldrs: hmpd 12th: outpcd after next: n.d after* **20/1**	96
4/	**8**	*dist*	**Rob The Five (IRE)**[326] [597] 9-10-12 **101** .... APMcCoy (P C Haslam) *nt fluent: hld up: effrt u.p 13th: btn after next* **11/2**[2]	—
P0F3	**U**		**Kimbambo (FR)**[18] [4719] 8-10-7 **99** .... (b[1]) GaryBerridge(3) (J P L Ewart) *blkd 1st: rr: mstke next: blnd bdly and uns rdr 7th* **12/1**	—
1/F1	**P**		**Armaguedon (FR)**[102] [3317] 8-11-12 **115** .... TonyDobbin (L Lungo) *led tl hdd 11th: j.rt next: sn wknd: t.o whn p.u bef 4 out* **7/1**	—
3165	**P**		**Master Sebastian**[41] [4363] 7-11-10 **113** .... PeterBuchanan (Miss Lucinda V Russell) *mstkes: sn bhd: lost tch 9th: t.o whn p.u bef 2 out* **20/1**	—

5m 12.4s (-10.50) **Going Correction** -0.70s/f (Firm)

WFA 5 from 6yo+ 4lb **11** Ran SP% **112.8**

Speed ratings: **97,93,92,91,90 90,88,—,—,— —** CSF £29.20 CT £167.16 TOTE £4.00: £1.30, £3.60, £2.60; EX 46.90.

Owner Mr & Mrs Raymond Anderson Green **Bred** Mme Gilbert Gallot **Trained** Kirkharle, Northumberland

FOCUS

Not the most competitive of races but the pace was sound and the winner may be capable of better still. The winning time was almost eight seconds slower than the later handicap over the same trip.

NOTEBOOK

King Barry(FR) ◆ proved well suited by the return to this trip in these less testing conditions and turned in a career best effort. Although a stiff rise is imminent, he is the sort to progress again and he is sure to win another race over fences. *(op 9-2)*

Persian Point has been running creditably and turned in another decent effort against a progressive sort. He would have finished closer had he not ploughed through the third last and should continue to give a good account. *(op 8-1)*

Silver Jack(IRE), with the cheekpieces again fitted, was not disgraced after meeting trouble but left the impression that a stiffer test of stamina would have been in his favour. *(op 9-2)*

Barrons Pike did well to finish as close as he did given he was off the bridle a long way out. The return to further will be in his favour but he is inconsistent over fences and not one to put too much faith in at present. *(op 25-1)*

Banchory Two(IRE), with the headgear left off on this first run since December, shaped as though this run was just needed but may be one to watch till getting his head in front where it matters.

Field Roller(IRE) completed for the first time over fences but was anything but foot perfect and did not really show enough to suggest he is one to be interested in for the near future.

Armaguedon(FR) dropped out before stamina over this longer trip became an issue, but it *transpired that he lost a shoe and he may be worth another chance.Official explanation: jockey said gelding lost a back shoe and sustained a cut to its off fore (op 13-2)*

4982 WALKER LAIRD SOLICITORS AT PAISLEY & RENFREW H'CAP HURDLE (12 hdls) 3m 110y

3:25 (3:25) (Class 3) (0-125,122) 4-Y-0+ £6,506 (£1,910; £955; £477)

Form RPR
5235 1 Sotovik (IRE)[18] 4724 5-9-13 102 ow1 EwanWhillans(7) 116+
(A C Whillans) *chsd ldrs: lft 2nd 4th: led 4 out: drew clr fr 2 out* 16/1
F021 2 23 Prince Adjal (IRE)[42] 4341 6-9-11 96 oh2 DougieCostello(3) 89+
(Miss S E Forster) *mstkes: led and sn clr: hdd 4 out: outpcd bef next: rallied to chse clr wnr between last two: no imp* 5/1[2]
321P 3 hd Cash And New (IRE)[27] 4619 7-11-0 110 RichardJohnson 104+
(R T Phillips) *hld up midfield: hdwy and chsng ldrs bef 7th: effrt bef 3 out: chsng wnr but no imp whn blnd next* 14/1
11 4 6 Geeveem (IRE)[41] 4367 6-11-12 122 RWalsh 110+
(P F Nicholls) *chsd ldrs: pushed along bef 4 out: effrt u.p bef next: outpcd after 3 out* 4/6[1]
256U 5 10 Carapuce (FR)[12] 4792 7-11-8 118 TimmyMurphy 93
(L Lungo) *hld up: outpcd bef 7th: nvr on terms* 25/1
104F 6 5 Caesar's Palace (GER)[34] 4491 9-10-3 99 (p) PeterBuchanan 69
(Miss Lucinda V Russell) *towards rr: struggling fr 6th: t.o* 25/1
FP3P R Aberdare[18] 4724 7-10-0 96 oh1 WilsonRenwick —
(J R Bewley) *chsng clr ldr whn rn out 4th* 33/1
141P P Relix (FR)[150] 2417 6-10-4 105 (t) DeclanMcGann(5) —
(A M Crow) *prom tl wknd 7th: t.o whn p.u bef 3 out* 66/1
11F/ P Westmorland (IRE)[771] 4274 10-10-0 106 oh1 ow10 MichaelTurnbull(10) —
(D R MacLeod) *a bhd: t.o whn p.u bef 8th* 50/1
2230 P Better Days (IRE)[14] 4762 10-11-0 120 MichaelO'Connell(10) —
(Mrs S J Smith) *j. slowly and lost pl 1st: j. slowly 2nd: p.u bef next* 10/1[3]
12PP P Lazy But Lively (IRE)[6] 4845 10-11-7 117 TonyDobbin —
(R F Fisher) *hld up: shortlived effrt whn nt fluent 7th: sn btn: t.o whn p.u bef 3 out* 25/1

6m 2.80s (-29.00) **Going Correction** -0.70s/f (Firm) 11 Ran SP% **116.2**
Speed ratings: **112,104,104,102,99 97,—,—,—,—** — CSF £86.73 CT £1164.86 TOTE £18.10: £3.40, £1.80, £2.50; EX 162.40.
Owner C Bird **Bred** Timothy Fennessy **Trained** Newmill-On-Slitrig, Borders

FOCUS
The gallop was ordinary, and with the favourite disappointing this did not take as much winning as seemed likely. Much improved form nevertheless from the winner.

NOTEBOOK
Sotovik(IRE) proved well suited by this better ground and turned in a much improved effort. However the handicapper is not going to look too favourably on this demolition job and life is going to get much tougher. *(op 20-1)*
Prince Adjal(IRE), up 14lb for his recent course win, adopted the same tactics and, although put in his place, did well to hang on for second spot given his lack of fluency. He may be capable of winning again if brushing up his jumping.
Cash And New(IRE), down to a more realistic level, was not disgraced but left the impression that a stiffer overall test of stamina would have been in her favour. *(tchd 16-1)*
Geeveem(IRE), a progressive sort in testing ground this year, lost his unbeaten record on this handicap debut. Much softer ground may have suited better and, given his age and connections, he is not one to write off yet. *(op 8-11)*
Carapuce(FR) continues to slip in the weights but did not show enough returned to this longer trip to suggest he is one to be interested in at present.
Caesar's Palace(GER) is not the easiest of rides and is not very consistent. He ran poorly and remains one to tread carefully with.

4983 GALA CASINOS DAILY RECORD MARES' ONLY H'CAP HURDLE (9 hdls) 2m

3:55 (3:55) (Class 2) 4-Y-0+ £12,526 (£3,700; £1,850; £926; £462)

Form RPR
-153 1 Into The Shadows[9] 2765 6-10-5 112 RichardMcGrath 122+
(K G Reveley) *prom: effrt after 3 out: led run in: edgd lft: r.o wl* 1/1[1]
2411 2 3 ½ Tessanoora[26] 4641 5-10-11 118 MickFitzgerald 121
(N J Henderson) *cl up: led 3 out to run in: kpt on same pce* 11/4[2]
P-12 3 nk Diamond Sal[115] 3040 8-10-11 118 TonyDobbin 121
(J Howard Johnson) *hld up in tch: effrt 3 out: kpt on same pce last* 13/2[3]
136- 4 16 Golden Odyssey (IRE)[343] 4837 6-10-3 110 RobertThornton 97
(K G Reveley) *cl up tl hung lft and wknd fr 3 out* 7/1
P 5 2 Symphonique (FR)[13] 4778 5-11-5 133 MrSWaley-Cohen(7) 118
(P J Hobbs) *set stdy pce to 3 out: rdn and wknd next* 20/1

3m 52.1s (-5.20) **Going Correction** -0.70s/f (Firm) 5 Ran SP% **107.3**
Speed ratings: **79,77,77,69,68** CSF £4.03 TOTE £1.90: £1.10, £1.60; EX 5.40.
Owner R C Mayall **Bred** Mrs Linda Corbett And Mrs Mary Mayall **Trained** Lingdale, Redcar & Cleveland

FOCUS
An ordinary handicap in which the pace was on the steady side. The second and third ran close to their marks, and Into The Shadows is better than the bare result suggests.

NOTEBOOK
Into The Shadows ◆, returned to hurdles, won an ordinary handicap with more in hand than the official margin suggests. A stronger gallop and softer ground would have suited her even better, and she is the type to win again over obstacles. *(tchd 11-10 and 10-11 in places)*
Tessanoora in good form after wins at Huntingdon and Worcester this year, ran creditably from this 11lb higher mark, but she had the run of the race. She is lightly raced and may well be capable of better over obstacles in due course. *(tchd 3-1)*
Diamond Sal ran creditably on this first start since December but left the strong impression that a much stiffer test of stamina over this trip would have been in her favour. She is worth another try over two and a half miles. *(op 6-1)*
Golden Odyssey(IRE), having her first run over obstacles for a year, was well below her best form and did not impress with the way she hung to her left once coming off the bridle. She will have to show more before being worth a bet. *(op 12-1)*
Symphonique(FR), returned to hurdles, had the run of the race but folded very tamely once pressure was applied and is not going to be easy to place from her current mark. *(op 12-1)*

4984 HILLHOUSE QUARRY H'CAP CHASE (17 fncs) 2m 4f

4:30 (4:30) (Class 2) 5-Y-0+ £18,858 (£5,619; £2,844; £1,458; £762)

Form RPR
0506 1 Supreme Prince (IRE)[14] 4764 9-10-6 138 RichardJohnson 155+
(P J Hobbs) *cl up: led 5 out: drew clr fr 3 out* 7/2[1]
54P3 2 16 Edmo Yewkay (IRE)[27] 4611 6-10-0 132 oh5 (b) DavidO'Meara 134+
(T D Easterby) *in tch: hdwy to chse wnr bef 4 out: kpt on same pce next* 16/1
12P6 3 12 Armaturk (FR)[15] 4749 9-11-12 158 RWalsh 146
(P F Nicholls) *cl up: led bef 9th to 5 out: outpcd fr 4 out* 6/1[3]
P5FP 4 3 ½ Kadount (FR)[62] 3988 8-10-6 138 (b[1]) RobertThornton 127+
(A King) *mstkes in rr: hdwy and prom 9th: wknd 4 out* 10/1
0046 5 4 Cregg House (IRE)[14] 4762 11-9-9 132 oh8 MrTJO'Brien(5) 113
(S Donohoe, Ire) *hld up: rdn 10th: wknd next* 9/1
F-1P F Provocative (FR)[132] 2757 8-10-2 134 TimmyMurphy —
(M Todhunter) *hld up: 5l down in 5th pl whn fell 12th* 5/1[2]
PP31 P Horus (IRE)[48] 4241 11-10-6 138 (v) JamieMoore —
(M C Pipe) *led to bef 9th: dropped rr next: t.o whn p.u bef 4 out* 5/1[2]
10P2 P Noisetine (FR)[27] 4611 8-10-3 135 AlanO'Keeffe —
(Miss Venetia Williams) *bhd and sn pushed along: t.o whn p.u bef 13th* 10/1
-314 P Fool On The Hill[209] 1549 9-10-2 134 AndrewTinkler —
(P J Hobbs) *mstkes towards rr: hdwy 8th: wknd 10th: t.o whn p.u bef 4 out* 12/1

5m 4.70s (-18.20) **Going Correction** -0.70s/f (Firm) 9 Ran SP% **111.6**
Speed ratings: **112,105,100,99,97 —,—,—,—** CSF £51.22 CT £317.07 TOTE £4.10: £1.50, £4.70, £2.50; EX 95.00 Trifecta £476.20 Part won. Pool: £670.76 - 0.50 winning units..
Owner Mrs Karola Vann **Bred** R Kidd **Trained** Withycombe, Somerset

FOCUS
A fair gallop but, with a couple of the principals failing to get round, this race did not take as much winning as seemed likely. Not form one can be confident about, even though the winning time was nearly eight seconds faster than the earlier contest over the same trip.

NOTEBOOK
Supreme Prince(IRE), who looked a bit better than the bare form of his three runs this year implied and was back in trip, returned to something like his best to win a fair handicap with plenty in hand. He is another wide-margin winner on this card that can expect little respite from the handicapper, but will be interesting if turned out under a penalty at Sandown. *(op 4-1)*
Edmo Yewkay(IRE) ran creditably from 5lb out of the handicap, without being any threat to the wide-margin winner, but he is likely to continue to look vulnerable to progressive or well handicapped types.
Armaturk(FR) was not disgraced over a trip that stretches his stamina to the full. A return to two miles will be in his favour, but he has very little margin for error from his current mark of 158. *(op 11-2)*
Kadount(FR), who had failed to get round on three of his previous four starts, was well beaten on this first run in blinkers and will have to jump much better than he did here if he is to return to winning ways over fences. *(op 9-1 tchd 11-1)*
Cregg House(IRE), an inconsistent sort who ran creditably at Aintree on his previous start, was a long way below that level and does not seem one to place too much faith in. *(tchd 10-1 in places)*
Horus(IRE), who was allowed to dominate when running up to his best at Newbury on his previous start, showed the other side of his character this time and dropped himself out quickly once taken on for the lead. He remains one to tread carefully with. *(op 4-1)*
Provocative(FR) had yet to be asked for his effort when coming to grief but, given he has fallen three times in his last seven starts, does not really appeal as one to be taking a short price about. *(op 4-1)*

4985 THE GLENLIVET H'CAP CHASE (21 fncs) 3m 3f 110y

5:00 (5:01) (Class 3) (0-120,119) 5-Y-0+ £6,506 (£1,910; £955; £477)

Form RPR
331F 1 Calvic (IRE)[20] 4690 8-11-10 117 WayneHutchinson 135+
(T R George) *prom: led 5 out: drew clr after next* 14/1
4322 2 10 Clemax (IRE)[6] 4843 5-10-8 109 TonyDobbin 108+
(Ferdy Murphy) *midfield: hdwy 1/2-way: led 16th to next: one pce fr 3 out* 4/1[2]
3366 3 6 Theatre Knight (IRE)[36] 4460 8-11-0 107 PeterBuchanan 106
(J Howard Johnson) *chsd ldrs: outpcd 17th: n.d after* 16/1
P416 4 1 ¾ Almire Du Lia (FR)[12] 4790 8-10-12 105 (v) RichardMcGrath 102
(Mrs S C Bradburne) *cl up: led 4th to 16th: wknd bef 4 out* 66/1
14P4 5 14 D J Flippance (IRE)[26] 4636 11-10-8 101 (p) TimmyMurphy 84
(A Parker) *sn wl bhd: no ch fnl circ* 25/1
2231 6 23 Dark Ben (FR)[33] 4528 6-11-0 110 DougieCostello(3) 70
(Miss Kate Milligan) *chsd ldrs tl wknd fr 16th* 8/1
1314 F On Y Va (FR)[16] 4728 8-11-2 109 (t) RichardJohnson —
(R T Phillips) *bhd whn fell 6th* 9/1
3315 P Nykel (FR)[39] 4419 5-10-11 112 RobertThornton —
(A King) *bhd: shortlived effrt u.p bef 13th: p.u after next* 20/1
0232 P Mioche D'Estruval (FR)[8] 4827 6-11-12 119 (v) APMcCoy —
(M C Pipe) *led to 4th: sn lost pl: t.o whn p.u after 12th* 11/2[3]
-PFP P Imperial Dream (IRE)[6] 4843 8-11-10 117 (b) DavidO'Meara —
(H P Hogarth) *midfield: wknd 14th: t.o whn p.u bef 4 out* 33/1
0111 P Parkinson (IRE)[30] 4571 5-9-9 101 ShaneWalsh(5) —
(Jonjo O'Neill) *sn bhd: reminders 4th: nvr on terms: p.u bef 13th* 10/3[1]
FU0P P Celioso (IRE)[26] 4636 9-9-13 102 MichaelO'Connell(10) —
(Mrs S J Smith) *j.rt: chsd ldrs: wkng whn blnd 13th: sn p.u* 14/1

7m 7.80s
WFA 5 from 6yo+ 8lb 12 Ran SP% **111.8**
CSF £64.88 CT £905.67 TOTE £12.20: £4.20, £1.90, £4.50; EX 74.00.
Owner The Alchabas Partnership **Bred** Kevin Neville **Trained** Slad, Gloucs

FOCUS
An ordinary event, but a decent test of stamina and a much improved performance from the winner.

NOTEBOOK
Calvic(IRE) proved none the worse for his fall in first-time blinkers at Fontwell earlier in the month and turned in easily his best effort yet over the larger obstacles, confirming that stamina is his strong suit. He has a fair strike-rate and may be capable of still better next term.
Clemax(IRE), up in distance, ran creditably, ridden more prominently than at Carlisle. He looks sure to win an ordinary event from his current mark if he can avoid progressive or well handicapped types.
Theatre Knight(IRE), down in grade, again had his limitations exposed in handicap company. He has time on his side but will have to do better if he is to return to winning ways in the near future in this type of event. *(op 20-1)*
Almire Du Lia(FR), an inconsistent chaser, was again below his best and remains one to have reservations about.
D J Flippance(IRE) has been disappointing since winning at this course in December. He remains one to tread carefully with. *(op 20-1)*
Dark Ben(FR), who showed the right attitude to win at Kelso last time, was beaten before stamina became an issue over this longer trip on this handicap debut over fences. He is not one to write off yet, though. *(op 13-2)*
Parkinson(IRE), unbeaten in three starts over fences, had gone up 13lb in the weights but was never going at any stage and proved a big disappointment. Given his age and his progressive nature he has to be worth another chance. Official explanation: *jockey said gelding was never travelling (op 11-4)*

4986 WEST SOUND CONDITIONAL JOCKEYS' H'CAP HURDLE (11 hdls) 2m 4f

5:35 (5:36) (Class 3) (0-125,125) 4-Y-0+ £7,807 (£2,292; £1,146; £572)

Form RPR
040P 1 Reap The Reward (IRE)[41] 4362 6-10-0 102 oh2 ow3.. GaryBerridge(3) 110+
(L Lungo) *hld up: hdwy to chse ldrs 7th: led last: rdn and r.o strly* 14/1

-464 **2** *5* **Monte Cinto (FR)**[13] 4773 6-11-8 **124**................................ LiamHeard[(3)] 125
(P F Nicholls) *hld up in tch: hdwy bef 3 out: ev ch last: one pce run in* **2/1**[1]

P130 **3** *3/4* **Up Above (IRE)**[82] 3642 6-11-12 **125**.............................. PaddyMerrigan 127+
(S Donohoe, Ire) *led: hdd whn nt fluent last: no ex* **7/1**[3]

1521 **4** *16* **Aston Lad**[34] 4504 5-11-8 **121**.. DougieCostello 105
(M D Hammond) *in tch tl wknd fr 3 out* **3/1**[2]

6352 **5** *3 1/2* **Orang Outan (FR)**[34] 4506 4-9-9 **105** oh2....................(t) ScottMarshall[(5)] 80
(J P L Ewart) *prom tl rdn and wknd bef 3 out* **10/1**

-53P **6** *1* **Cordilla (IRE)**[63] 3965 8-10-5 **112**.............................. FearghalDavis[(8)] 92
(N G Richards) *keen early: prom: outpcd 7th: btn bef 3 out* **8/1**

431 **P** **Olival (FR)**[34] 4506 4-10-2 **107**... ShaneWalsh —
(Jonjo O'Neill) *chsd ldrs tl wknd 7th: t.o whn p.u after 4 out* **15/2**

1-2P **F** **Nolife (IRE)**[43] 4317 10-9-11 **99** oh3..................................... PhilKinsella[(3)] —
(Miss Lucinda V Russell) *cl up: rdn after 4 out: 4l down and disputing 4th whn fell heavily next* **25/1**

4m 55.7s (-17.00) **Going Correction** -0.70s/f (Firm) **8** Ran SP% **113.3**
WFA 4 from 5yo+ 6lb
Speed ratings: **100,98,97,91,89 89,—,—** CSF £42.87 CT £219.07 TOTE £19.40: £3.00, £1.40, £2.30; EX 69.80 Place 6 £123.48, Place 5 £49.84.
Owner Mr & Mrs Raymond Anderson Green **Bred** John Sweeney **Trained** Carrutherstown, D'fries & G'way

FOCUS
An ordinary event in which the pace was only fair. The winner was quite impressive, however.

NOTEBOOK
Reap The Reward(IRE) ◆, back in trip, turned in his best effort to win his first race over obstacles. He won with plenty in hand and appeals as the type to win more races around this trip on this sort of ground. *(op 16-1 tchd 20-1 in a place)*
Monte Cinto(FR) travelled like the best horse in the race for much of the way but did not find as much as seemed likely after the final flight. He has not won for a while and may remain vulnerable over hurdles from this mark. *(op 7-4)*
Up Above(IRE) ran creditably, returned to the scene of his previous hurdle win, but he had the run of the race and is another that is likely to remain vulnerable from this sort of mark. *(op 10-1)*
Aston Lad, 6lb higher than for his previous win, was below that level and may need testing conditions to show his best form. *(op 7-2 tchd 4 in places)*
Orang Outan(FR) had his limitations exposed on this handicap debut and will have to improve to win from this sort of mark. *(op 11-1 tchd 12 in a place)*
Cordilla(IRE) was well beaten returned to hurdles and will have to show a good deal more before he is a betting proposition in this sphere. *(op 7-1 thcd 9 in a place)*
Olival(FR), easy to back, was a big disappointment on this handicap debut but would not be one to *write off by any means just yet. Official explanation: trainer's representative had no explanation for poor form shown (op 7-1)*
T/Jkpt: Not won. T/Plt: £135.20 to a £1 stake. Pool: £62,767.45. 338.90 winning tickets. T/Qpdt: £48.60 to a £1 stake. Pool: £4,018.70. 61.10 winning tickets. RY

4916 SEDGEFIELD (L-H)
Friday, April 21

OFFICIAL GOING: Good to firm (good in final 3f)
The ground had dried out and with the late spring conditions were described as 'jump racing on dry mud'.
Wind: Light; half against Weather: Overcast

4987 OAKLEY FOR MITSUBISHI AT WEST AUCKLAND JUVENILE NOVICES' HURDLE (7 hdls 1 omitted) 2m 1f
5:15 (5:15) (Class 4) 4-Y-O
£5,010 (£1,480; £740; £370; £184; £92)

Form RPR

12P **1** **Parsley's Return**[58] 4057 4-11-2 112.. NoelFehily 107+
(M Wigham) *hdwy to chse ldrs 4th: chal appr last: bdly squeezed and hmpd run-in: led nr fin* **9/2**[2]

2160 **2** *3/4* **First Fought (IRE)**[70] 3848 4-11-2 108..............................(t) JasonMaguire 104+
(D McCain) *wnt prom 4th: led after omitted 2 out: edgd rt and crowded wnr run-in: hdd nr fin* **6/1**[3]

2200 **3** *12* **Eborarry (IRE)**[44] 4301 4-11-2 109...................................... RussGarritty 91
(T D Easterby) *trckd ldrs: led 5th: hdd after omitted next: wknd appr last* **15/2**

264 **4** *3* **Daldini**[26] 4631 4-10-10 .... DominicElsworth 82
(Mrs S J Smith) *trckd ldrs: chal 5th: wknd after omitted 2 out* **3/1**[1]

4P **5** *6* **Devils Delight (IRE)**[12] 4789 4-10-4 ow1........................... AlanDempsey 71+
(James Moffatt) *in rr: hdwy 5th: nvr nr to chal* **33/1**

54P0 **6** *2 1/2* **In Dream's (IRE)**[12] 4789 4-10-10 98..................................(t) JimCrowley 74
(M A Barnes) *j.lft: led to 2nd: cl up tl wknd after 5th* **16/1**

0 **7** *3* **Shamrock Bay**[12] 4789 4-10-3 .... BrianHarding 64
(L Lungo) *prom: lost pl 5th* **9/1**

P0 **8** *nk* **C'Est La Vie**[73] 3786 4-10-3 ....(t) PadgeWhelan 63
(Miss J E Foster) *in tch: effrt 5th: sn wknd* **66/1**

0 **9** *3* **Frith (IRE)**[20] 3925 4-10-5 .... DesFlavin[(5)] 67
(Mrs L B Normile) *in rr: sme hdwy 5th: sn wknd* **25/1**

0056 **10** *2* **Insurgent (IRE)**[4] 4916 4-10-10 .... LarryMcGrath 65
(R C Guest) *jnd ldrs 4th: wknd qckly 3 out* **14/1**

00 **11** *11* **Dantor**[33] 4532 4-10-3 ....(t) BenOrde-Powlett[(7)] 54
(M A Barnes) *a in rr* **100/1**

0501 **12** *2 1/2* **No Commission (IRE)**[99] 3349 4-11-2 98........................... PaddyAspell 58
(R F Fisher) *chsd ldrs: reluctant and lost pl 4th: sn t.o* **14/1**

B **13** *1 1/4* **Maynooth Princess (IRE)**[12] 4795 4-10-3 .... KennyJohnson 44
(R Johnson) *s.s: a bhd* **66/1**

P5P5 **F** **Trappeto (IRE)**[12] 4795 4-10-3 91...................................... MrSWByrne[(7)] —
(C Smith) *blnd 1st: fell 2nd* **22/1**

0 **F** **High Dyke**[12] 4789 4-10-10 .... BarryKeniry —
(K A Ryan) *t.k.h: sn w ldrs: led 2nd to 5th: bhd whn fell last* **25/1**

4m 1.50s (-5.00) **Going Correction** -0.30s/f (Good) **15** Ran SP% **117.4**
Speed ratings: **99,98,93,91,88 87,86,86,84,83 78,77,76,—,—** CSF £29.05 TOTE £4.30: £2.30, £2.40, £2.40; EX 39.70.
Owner D T L Limited **Bred** Baydon House Stud **Trained** Newmarket, Suffolk
■ Stewards' Enquiry : Kenny Johnson 10-day ban: failed to take all reasonable and permissible measures to obtain best possible placing (May 2, 4-6, 8-13)
Jason Maguire 10-day ban: improper riding - deliberate interference (May 2, 4-6, 8-13)

FOCUS
The first two came right away and after a barging match Jason Maguire was rightly handed a 10-day ban for improper riding. Not bad form for the track. Flight after winning post omitted.

NOTEBOOK
Parsley's Return, suited by the drying ground, improved a good deal on his selling-race success at *Ludlow despite Jason Maguire's unwelcome attentions. Official explanation: trainer said, regarding improved form shown, gelding was better suited by a return to faster ground (tchd 4-1)*
First Fought(IRE), who bled from the nose on his previous outing ten weeks earlier, went on starting down the hill. His rider seemed determined to cut off the winner, leaving him with no room at all on the run-in, and his ten-day ban was fully justified. *(tchd 7-1)*
Eborarry(IRE) ran better than of late but was still below his best. He should make a better chaser next term. *(op 8-1)*
Daldini, kept wide, seems to struggle to see out the trip over hurdles. *(op 4-1)*
Devils Delight(IRE) stayed on in her own time and seems to be learning to settle. *(op 40-1)*
In Dream's(IRE) continually jumped to his left. *(op 14-1)*
Maynooth Princess(IRE), brought down on her debut two weeks earlier, was dropped in at the start and was never on terms. The Stewards were not impressed and handed her rider a ten-day ban for making insufficient effort.

4988 SPEEDY HIRE SCOTLAND "NATIONAL HUNT" NOVICES' HURDLE (8 hdls 2 omitted) 2m 5f 110y
5:45 (5:46) (Class 4) 4-Y-O+ **£5,204** (£1,528; £764; £381)

Form RPR

0002 **1** **Willies Way**[40] 4387 6-11-0 96.. DominicElsworth 92+
(Mrs S J Smith) *mde all: j.lft: styd on wl between last 2: hrd rdn and hld on towards fin* **7/2**[2]

6355 **2** *1 3/4* **Major Oak (IRE)**[12] 4793 5-11-0 .... BarryKeniry 89
(G M Moore) *chsd ldrs: drvn along 4th: rallied to take 2nd sn after last: kpt on* **11/4**[1]

3-05 **3** *2* **Jeringa**[34] 4493 7-11-0 .... PaddyAspell 87
(J Wade) *chsd ldrs: wnt 2nd after 5th: nt qckn between last 2* **6/1**

5404 **4** *8* **Stroom Bank (IRE)**[63] 3957 6-11-0 .... NoelFehily 80+
(C C Bealby) *hld up in rr: hdwy 5th: one pce fr 2 out* **16/1**

000P **5** *5* **Nigwell Forbees (IRE)**[64] 3941 5-11-0 .... AlanDempsey 76+
(J Howard Johnson) *hdwy to chse ldrs 5th: lost pl appr 2 out* **33/1**

0205 **6** *3* **Primitive Poppy**[43] 4317 7-10-6 86........................... PatrickMcDonald[(7)] 70
(Mrs A Hamilton) *chsd ldrs: wknd appr 6th* **11/2**[3]

7 *14* **Himalayan Trail**[389] 7-11-0 .... BrianHarding 57
(Mrs S J Smith) *wnt prom 5th: lost pl after next* **40/1**

00/0 **8** *10* **Naughtynelly's Pet**[12] 4787 7-10-7 .... BenOrde-Powlett[(7)] 47
(A M Crow) *s.v.s: hdwy 4th: lost pl after next* **50/1**

0/P0 **9** *6* **Sharp Exit (IRE)**[12] 4793 7-10-10 ow3......................(b[1]) MrCDawson[(7)] 44
(J Wade) *wnt prom 5th: wknd after next* **66/1**

04 **10** *10* **Tartan Classic (IRE)**[24] 4657 5-10-9 .... BrianHughes[(5)] 31
(J Howard Johnson) *chsd ldrs: rdn 5th: sn lost pl and bhd* **20/1**

0-00 **F** **Saddlers Express**[128] 2821 5-10-2 .... CharliePoste[(5)] —
(M F Harris) *fell 1st* **12/1**

530- **P** **Ewe Beauty (FR)**[436] 3753 6-10-3 96 ow3........................ MrSWByrne[(7)] —
(Ferdy Murphy) *sn bhd: t.o whn p.u bef 2 out* **9/1**

-0PP **P** **Mountain Mix**[29] 4582 6-10-9 ....(b[1]) DesFlavin[(5)] —
(Mrs L B Normile) *t.k.h: hdwy to chse ldrs 3rd: lost pl after 5th: sn bhd: t.o whn p.u bef 2 out* **100/1**

5m 14.6s (-1.10) **Going Correction** -0.30s/f (Good) **13** Ran SP% **116.7**
Speed ratings: **90,89,88,85,83 82,77,74,71,68 —,—,—** CSF £12.84 TOTE £2.80: £1.50, £1.30, £2.40; EX 12.30.
Owner Keith Nicholson **Bred** Mrs Sharon Lee **Trained** High Eldwick, W Yorks

FOCUS
A weak novices' hurdle after the late withdrawal because of the drying ground of the winner's stablemate Stagecoach Opal, who would have started odds-on. Flight after winning post omitted.

NOTEBOOK
Willies Way jumped left in front. He looked well in command between the last two flights but at the line he had little to spare. *(op 11-4)*
Major Oak(IRE), struggling to keep up with a full circuit to go, stayed on up the final hill to snatch second spot near the line and he looks to just stay. *(op 7-2)*
Jeringa, a bumper winner here, went in pursuit of the winner, but on this drying ground he could never get in a telling blow, though keeping on all the way to the line. *(op 7-1)*
Stroom Bank(IRE), tailed off on his two previous starts over hurdles, at least shaped better this time.
Nigwell Forbees(IRE), unplaced on his four previous starts, had been absent since pulling up in February. *(op 16-1)*

4989 JOE RUTHERFORD MEMORIAL NOVICES' H'CAP CHASE (21 fncs) 3m 3f
6:15 (6:15) (Class 5) (0-90,87) 5-Y-O+ **£3,485** (£1,029; £514; £257; £128)

Form RPR

P241 **1** **Lambrini Bianco (IRE)**[31] 4567 8-10-8 **69**.................(b) TomScudamore 82+
(Mrs L Williamson) *led to 3rd: chsd ldrs: led after 4 out: styd on strly: readily* **3/1**[1]

PF45 **2** *10* **Ashleybank House (IRE)**[12] 4802 9-11-5 **80**............(tp) RichardHobson 81
(David Pearson) *sn bhd: hdwy 13th: styd on to take modest 3rd last: kpt on to take 2nd on line* **20/1**

0000 **3** *shd* **Tiger Talk**[44] 4302 10-9-11 **68**..(b) JohnFlavin[(10)] 70+
(R C Guest) *t.k.h: w ldr: led 3rd: j.lft: hdd after 4 out: wknd run-in* **9/1**

6050 **4** *2* **Celia's High (IRE)**[32] 4553 7-10-7 **68**..................................(t) PaddyAspell 69+
(D McCain) *chsd ldrs: blnd 5th: reminders 13th: sn outpcd: kpt on fr 4 out* **5/1**[2]

P-00 **5** *24* **Bourneagainkristen**[30] 4577 8-9-10 **64**.................... TomMessenger[(7)] 47+
(C C Bealby) *wnt prom 5th: wknd 4 out* **18/1**

663P **6** *dist* **Glashedy Rock (IRE)**[13] 4785 9-11-3 **83**........................ CharliePoste[(5)] —
(M F Harris) *hld up: hdwy and in tch 11th: lost pl 15th: sn bhd: t.o* **8/1**

61P3 **7** *2* **Sconced (USA)**[4] 4921 11-11-12 **87**...............................(b) LarryMcGrath —
(R C Guest) *sn bhd: t.o fr 11th* **8/1**

0/0P **P** **Troysgreen (IRE)**[75] 3762 8-9-10 **62** oh3 ow1.............(p) BrianHughes[(5)] —
(P D Niven) *chsd ldrs: wknd 16th: sn bhd: t.o whn p.u bef 2 out* **66/1**

P-00 **P** **Bullies Acre (IRE)**[196] 1663 6-10-0 **61** oh1........................... BrianHarding —
(F P Murtagh) *prom to 11th: sn lost pl: bhd whn p.u bef 14th* **25/1**

P36B **F** **Casalani (IRE)**[4] 4921 7-11-12 **87**....................................... JosephByrne —
(Jennie Candlish) *hdwy and prom 11th: 3rd and styng on whn fell 17th* **9/1**

504F **P** **Derainey (IRE)**[44] 4300 7-11-0 **75**.................................... KennyJohnson —
(R Johnson) *chsd ldrs: wknd 16th: bdly hmpd and lost pl next: p.u bef 4 out* **7/1**[3]

6m 54.8s (-12.00) **Going Correction** -0.30s/f (Good) **11** Ran SP% **111.8**
Speed ratings: **105,102,102,101,94 —,—,—,—,— —** CSF £57.08 CT £474.45 TOTE £2.70: £1.60, £5.70, £2.80; EX 55.20.
Owner Halewood International Ltd **Bred** John Brophy **Trained** Saighton, Cheshire

FOCUS
A true test, and in the end the winner saw it out much the best. Poor form, however.

NOTEBOOK
Lambrini Bianco(IRE), just 1lb higher, kept up the gallop in relentless fashion and in the end came right away. A late-developer, he is progressing nicely. *(op 5-2)*
Ashleybank House(IRE), off the boil for ages, struggled to keep up. He kept galloping in his own time and in the end just missed out on second spot.

Tiger Talk, bang out of form over both hurdles and fences, was keen to get on with it. He took them along at a strong pace but, dead tired up the final hill, held on to second spot by a whisker. *(op 12-1)*
Celia's High(IRE), absent for a month after bursting, blundered badly at the final fence first time round. He stuck on in his own time late in the day and looks to just stay. *(op 11-2 tchd 13-2)*
Bourneagainkristen, beaten in selling company over hurdles, was having his first outing over fences. *(op 16-1)*
Casalani(IRE), brought down at the first here on Easter Monday, was looking a likely candidate for second place when crashing out five from home. *(op 7-1)*

4990 WORLD BET EXCHANGE LAUNCHING SOON AT WBX.COM H'CAP HURDLE (8 hdls 2 omitted) 2m 5f 110y

6:45 (6:45) (Class 3) (0-130,124) 4-Y-O+

£13,778 (£4,070; £2,035; £1,018; £508; £255)

Form RPR

-F51 **1** **Presumptuous**[58] 4058 6-11-3 **115**.............................. DominicElsworth 120+
(Mrs S J Smith) *mid-div: hdwy 5th: effrt appr 2 out: led last: r.o strly* **7/4**[1]

2P22 **2** *2 ½* **Pay Attention**[12] 4792 5-11-5 **124**.............................. MrGTumelty(7) 125
(T D Easterby) *chsd ldrs: led 2 out: edgd lft appr last: sn hdd: nt qckn* **6/1**[2]

0102 **3** *3 ½* **Supreme Leisure (IRE)**[34] 4504 9-11-3 **120**.................. BrianHughes(5) 119+
(J Howard Johnson) *chsd ldrs: led after 3 out: hdd next: n.m.r appr last: styd on same pce* **12/1**

1442 **4** *shd* **Gidam Gidam (IRE)**[26] 4631 4-10-3 **114**...............(p) PatrickMcDonald(7) 105
(J Mackie) *in rr: wl outpcd 5th: hdwy next: styd on run-in* **13/2**[3]

1135 **5** *7* **Snow's Ride**[139] 2641 6-10-12 **110**.............................. NeilMulholland 100
(M D Hammond) *in rr: hdwy 6th: nvr nr ldrs* **16/1**

1U6P **6** *hd* **Wicked Nice Fella (IRE)**[13] 4778 8-10-11 **109**.................... NoelFehily 99
(C C Bealby) *chsd ldrs: wknd 2 out* **16/1**

P642 **7** *18* **Stormy Lord (IRE)**[34] 4488 10-10-10 **108**.......................... BrianHarding 80
(J Wade) *t.k.h: led and sn clr: hdd after 3 out: lost pl appr next* **16/1**

1125 **8** *10* **Rare Coincidence**[9] 2942 5-10-10 **108**............................(p) KeithMercer 70
(R F Fisher) *chsd ldrs: lost pl after 3 out: sn bhd* **12/1**

-112 **P** **Midnight Creek**[14] 1844 8-11-1 **120**.............................. AdrianScholes(7) —
(A Sadik) *in rr: t.o 5th: p.u bef 2 out* **25/1**

0006 **P** **Border Tale**[46] 3929 6-10-2 **100**.............................. JimCrowley —
(James Moffatt) *in rr: bhd fr 5th: t.o whn p.u bef 2 out* **25/1**

0556 **P** **Flame Phoenix (USA)**[70] 3848 7-10-11 **109**..................(t) JasonMaguire —
(D McCain) *in rr: sme hdwy 5th: lost pl and eased after next: t.o whn p.u bef 2 out* **7/1**

5m 4.30s (-11.40) **Going Correction** -0.30s/f (Good)
WFA 4 from 5yo+ 6lb 11 Ran SP% **117.2**
Speed ratings: **108,107,105,105,103 103,96,92,—,—** — CSF £13.07 CT £94.01 TOTE £2.70: £1.50, £2.00, £3.70; EX 8.50.
Owner Sam Berry,C Bradford-Nutter,J Berry **Bred** J And Mrs Berry **Trained** High Eldwick, W Yorks

FOCUS
A strongly-run race for what is a valuable handicap by Sedgefield standards, and Presumptuouswho looked very well in, was ultimately a decisive winner. The runner-up ran to his mark, and it was a slight personal best from the third. Flight after winning post omitted.

NOTEBOOK
Presumptuous, 10lb higher, made hard work of it but was firmly in command at the line. He will be even better suited by three miles. *(op 2-1)*
Pay Attention, who is finding it very hard to get her head in front, was taking a step up in trip but after going on, she ducked and dived and found the winner too strong on the run-in. *(tchd 13-2)*
Supreme Leisure(IRE), 4lb higher, was only keeping on at the same pace when the runner-up went across him going to the last. Considering the ground had turned against this mud-lark, this was a really good effort. *(op 11-1)*
Gidam Gidam(IRE), on his handicap debut, struggled badly early on the final circuit. He was staying on to some purpose at the death and is well worth a try over three miles. *(tchd 7-1)*
Snow's Ride, absent since December, appreciates fast ground and this extended trip seemed to suit him. *(op 14-1)*
Wicked Nice Fella(IRE), back over hurdles, seemed to find this trip in a strongly-run race beyond him. *(op 14-1)*
Stormy Lord(IRE), taken to post early, was keen to get on with it but after showing in a clear lead he was readily picked off. This is so far the way he runs his races. *(tchd 20-1)*

4991 OAKLEY FOR MITSUBISHI AT WEST AUCKLAND H'CAP CHASE (13 fncs) 2m 110y

7:15 (7:15) (Class 4) (0-100,104) 5-Y-O+

£6,263 (£1,850; £925; £463; £231; £116)

Form RPR

640U **1** **Drumossie (AUS)**[4] 4920 6-10-6 **79**..............................(v1) KennyJohnson 92+
(R C Guest) *chsd ldrs: styd on between last 2: r.o to ld last 75yds* **15/2**[3]

34F2 **2** *2 ½* **Ton-Chee**[41] 4365 7-11-12 **99**.............................. BrianHarding 108
(F P Murtagh) *hld up: wnt prom 7th: led 3 out: 5 l clr next: 3 l clr last: hdd and no ex run-in* **9/2**[2]

P043 **3** *7* **Per Amore (IRE)**[12] 4804 8-10-12 **85**..............................(b) RichardHobson 87
(David Pearson) *rdn and hdwy to chse ldrs 7th: kpt on same pce fr 3 out* **16/1**

5324 **4** *2 ½* **Pure Brief (IRE)**[123] 2926 9-11-2 **89**..............................(p) PaulMoloney 90+
(J Mackie) *chsd ldrs fr 7th: wknd 3 out* **8/1**

334F **5** *6* **Loulou Nivernais (FR)**[18] 4721 7-11-4 **96**.......................... TJDreaper(5) 91+
(M Todhunter) *hdwy and prom 7th: wknd 3 out* **15/2**[3]

566 **6** *18* **Apadi (USA)**[84] 3592 10-10-13 **86**.............................. LarryMcGrath 62
(R C Guest) *hld up: sn detached: t.o 8th: styd on run-in: snatched 6th nr line* **9/1**

P4 **7** *½* **Il Penseroso (IRE)**[6] 4842 8-10-10 **83**..............................(p) MarkGrant 58
(P A Blockley) *led 2nd to 3 out: sn wknd: eased and lost 6th nr fin* **9/1**

2-60 **8** *2* **Reseda (IRE)**[34] 4493 9-11-1 **93**..............................(t) MichaelMcAlister(5) 66
(M A Barnes) *sn detached in rr: t.o 7th* **40/1**

1504 **9** *20* **Mexican (USA)**[31] 4365 7-11-2 **89**..............................(b) NeilMulholland 42
(M D Hammond) *s.i.s: sn detached in rr: t.o 7th* **12/1**

0012 **F** **Winds Supreme (IRE)**[29] 4585 7-10-8 **81**..........................(t) KeithMercer —
(Ferdy Murphy) *hld up: fell 3rd* **4/1**[1]

0P5P **U** **Brave Effect (IRE)**[44] 4302 10-10-7 **80**.............................. BarryKeniry —
(Mrs Dianne Sayer) *led to 3rd: 2nd whn blnd bdly and uns rdr 6th* **14/1**

4m 9.40s (-4.80) **Going Correction** -0.30s/f (Good) 11 Ran SP% **115.5**
Speed ratings: **99,97,94,93,90 82,81,80,71,—** — CSF £41.57 CT £527.62 TOTE £8.30: £3.90, £3.00, £6.80; EX 63.30.
Owner Concertina Racing **Bred** Woodlands Stud Nsw **Trained** Brancepeth, Co Durham
■ Stewards' Enquiry : Mark Grant two-day ban: dropped hands and lost 6th place (May 2, 4)

FOCUS
The forecast favourite was a non-runner, and the eventual market leader was an early faller, but this still represents much improved form from Drumrossie.

NOTEBOOK
Drumossie(AUS), in a visor rather than blinkers, was really galvanised to cut down the runner-up up the final hill. This reppresents much improved form. *(op 9-1 tchd 10-1)*
Ton-Chee looked nailed on when taking it up three out. His stride shortened after the last and in the end the winner saw it out up the final hill much the better. He will soon go one better with a little more patient ride. *(op 7-1)*
Per Amore(IRE), potentially very well treated, appreciated the dry ground and may be on the way back to some sort of form. *(op 11-1)*
Pure Brief(IRE), absent since December, should be cherry ripe for summer jumping after this. *(op 6-1)*
Loulou Nivernais(FR) took a crashing fall two weeks earlier and this should have gone some way to restoring his confidence. *(op 13-2)*
Apadi(USA), soon out with the washing, flew up the final hill to snatch sixth place prize money. *(op 10-1 after early 16-1 in a place)*
Il Penseroso(IRE) took them along but very tired, was eased near the line forfeiting sixth place prize money and earning his rider a two-day ban. *(op 8-1)*
Winds Supreme(IRE) was soon on the deck. *(op 7-2)*

4992 WORLD BET EXCHANGE LAUNCHING SOON AT WBX.COM STANDARD OPEN NATIONAL HUNT FLAT RACE 2m 1f

7:45 (7:45) (Class 5) 4-6-Y-O **£2,277** (£668; £334; £166)

Form RPR

1 **Anchors Away** 4-10-10.............................. RussGarritty 89
(T D Easterby) *hld up: hdwy to trck ldrs 6f out: styd on to ld nr fin* **8/1**

20 **2** *½* **Riodan (IRE)**[61] 4017 4-9-10.............................. PatrickMcDonald(7) 81
(J J Quinn) *t.k.h: sn trcking ldrs: led over 1f out: hdd and no ex towards fin* **4/1**[1]

3 *2* **Camden George (IRE)** 5-11-1.............................. PadgeWhelan 91
(Mrs S J Smith) *chsd ldrs: led over 4f out: hdd over 1f out: kpt on same pce* **18/1**

4 *2* **Millbury** 5-10-8.............................. BrianHarding 82
(M Dods) *t.k.h in rr: stdy hdwy 6f out: chal over 1f out: fdd ins last* **15/2**[3]

5 *4* **Bow School (IRE)** 5-10-10.............................. BrianHughes(5) 86+
(J Howard Johnson) *trckd ldrs: chal 4f out: wknd appr fnl f* **16/1**

26- **6** *12* **The Longfella**[436] 3757 5-11-1.............................. BarryKeniry 73
(G M Moore) *led after 1f: hdd over 4f out: wknd fnl 3f* **16/1**

40 **7** *5* **Mr Ironman**[81] 3657 5-10-5.............................. JohnFlavin(10) 68
(R C Guest) *mid-div: outpcd 4f out: sn lost pl* **20/1**

35 **8** *8* **Sybarite Chief (IRE)**[74] 3785 4-10-10.............................. AnthonyRoss 55
(R A Fahey) *mid-div: effrt 6f out: sn lost pl* **7/1**[2]

9 *4* **King Of Slane** 5-11-1.............................. JimCrowley 56
(G A Swinbank) *led 1f: chsd ldrs: lost pl 4f out* **4/1**[1]

054 **10** *11* **Intersky Emerald (IRE)**[97] 3399 5-10-12.............................. MrTGreenall(3) 45
(G A Swinbank) *hld up in mid-div: hdwy to trck ldrs 6f out: lost pl over 3f out* **15/2**[3]

11 *11* **King Shaadi**[341] 6-11-1.............................. LarryMcGrath 34
(C A Mulhall) *sn bhd: detached fnl 6f* **40/1**

12 *7* **Big Bad Bill (IRE)** 6-10-8.............................. MrMBriggs(7) 27
(P T Midgley) *hld up in rr: sme hdwy 6f out: lost pl 4f out: sn bhd* **33/1**

13 *14* **Naughty Boy** 4-10-10.............................. TomScudamore 8
(J Pearce) *rn green and sn in rr: detached fnl 9f: t.o 6f out* **11/1**

4m 4.30s (-2.60) **Going Correction** -0.30s/f (Good)
WFA 4 from 5yo+ 5lb 13 Ran SP% **122.6**
Speed ratings: **94,93,92,91,90 84,82,78,76,71 66,62,56** CSF £40.29 TOTE £8.10: £2.70, £2.30, £6.70; EX 88.50 Place 6 £69.77, Place 5 £25.21.
Owner Habton Farms **Bred** M H Easterby **Trained** Great Habton, N Yorks

FOCUS
No gallop to halfway, and five in a line one and a half furlongs out. The form has been rated through the second.

NOTEBOOK
Anchors Away, from a dam line that has served this yard well, looked very inexperienced but travelled strongly. With the rail to help, he put his head in front where it really matters. He can only improve on this. *(op 9-1 tchd 10-1)*
Riodan(IRE), is a free-going sort. She went a length up at the start of the final hill but in the end just missed out. *(tchd 9-2)*
Camden George(IRE), who looks a long-term chasing prospect, went on and stepped up the gallop, but in the end the first two outspeeded him. *(op 14-1)*
Millbury, a half-sister to smart chaser Ashley Brook, is a lightly-made type. She took a keen grip, but after working her way upsides, she faded up the final hill. Hurdling will put less strain on her stamina. *(op 10-1 tchd 11-1)*
Bow School(IRE), a cheap buy, travelled strongly but was the first of the five contenders coming down the hill to crack. *(op 14-1)*
The Longfella, the reluctant leader, fell in a heap at the top of the hill turning for home.
King Of Slane, a brother to staying chaser Prince of Slane, found himself in front early, but he fell in a heap fully half a mile from home. The stable makes few mistakes and he must have been showing much better at home. *(op 13-2 tchd 7-1 in a place)*
T/Plt: £65.50 to a £1 stake. Pool: £40,293.80. 448.55 winning tickets. T/Qpdt: £20.30 to a £1 stake. Pool: £4,040.50. 147.00 winning tickets. WG

4997 - 4999a (Foreign Racing) - See Raceform Interactive

4893

AUTEUIL (L-H)

Friday, April 21

OFFICIAL GOING: Very soft

5000a PRIX JEAN GRANEL (HURDLE) 2m 4f 110y

2:05 (2:12) 5-Y-O+ **£23,172** (£11,586; £6,759; £4,586; £2,172)

RPR

1 **Rock And Palm (FR)**[152] 2403 6-11-1.............................. MDelmares —
(Mlle C Cardenne, France)

2 *2 ½* **Cheler (FR)**[14] 7-10-10.............................. SLeloup —
(B Secly, France)

3 *2* **Phonidal (FR)**[19] 4717 10-10-10..............................(b) GAdam —
(M Rolland, France)

4 *5* **Claymore (IRE)**[48] 4241 10-10-8.............................. LeightonAspell —
(O Sherwood) *held up, headway 8th (of 12), 4th 2 out, kept on same pace (17/1)* **17/1**[2]

5 *1 ½* **Luc Moriniere (FR)**[33] 4547 7-11-1.............................. —
(P Monfort, France)

6 *3* **Blue Canyon (FR)**[14] 4765 8-10-12.............................. —
(F Doumen, France)

7 *½* **Oundle Scoundrel (FR)**[14] 7-10-12.............................. —
(E Pilet, France)

The Form Book, Raceform Ltd, Compton, RG20 6NL

8 *dist* **Sarahs Quay (IRE)**[34] 4495 7-10-3 MrMatthewSmith —
(K J Burke) *tracked leader (winner), close 2nd when blundered 3rd, weakened from 8th, tailed off from before 2 out (16/1)* **16/1**[1]

5m 4.00s 8 Ran SP% **11.4**
PARI-MUTEL: WIN 8.50; PL 2.30, 1.30, 2.60; DF 10.50.
Owner Mme P Menard **Bred** Pierre Fontaine **Trained** France

NOTEBOOK
Claymore(IRE) was held up in rear until closing up starting down the back straight. The closest he got was third on the final turn, before two out, but he kept on gamely under pressure to the end. Connections took issue with the official description of the ground, calling it too fast for him.
Sarahs Quay(IRE), who raced in cheekpieces, was a bit keen early. She pressed the front-running winner and was almost upsides when blundering at the third. She dropped out from five out, but her trainer regards her as a mudlark and thinks she needs more testing ground.

4980 AYR (L-H)

Saturday, April 22

OFFICIAL GOING: Good (good to soft in places)
Wind: Fresh, across

5001 PURVIS MARQUEES JUVENILE NOVICES' HURDLE (9 hdls) 2m
1:50 (1:50) (Class 2) 4-Y-0 **£9,394** (£2,775; £1,387; £694)

Form RPR
4220 **1** **Royals Darling (GER)**[39] 4435 4-11-3 124 MickFitzgerald 129+
(N J Henderson) *mde all: rdn 2 out: hld on gamely run in* **7/2**[3]
1120 **2** *½* **Bold Fire**[39] 4435 4-10-13 132 RWalsh 125+
(P F Nicholls) *cl up: effrt and j. sltly rt fr 2 out: ev ch run in: kpt on: hld towards fin* **11/10**[1]
1101 **3** *3 ½* **Shamayoun (FR)**[5] 4910 4-11-6 134 (b) APMcCoy 126
(C R Egerton) *chsd ldrs: outpcd bef 3 out: no imp next* **7/4**[2]
041P **4** *dist* **Lerida**[16] 4747 4-11-3 107 PeterBuchanan —
(Miss Lucinda V Russell) *in tch tl wknd 4th: t.o* **66/1**

3m 49.3s (-8.00) **Going Correction** -0.60s/f (Firm) 4 Ran SP% **107.7**
Speed ratings: **106,105,104,—** CSF £7.97 TOTE £4.70; EX 9.20.
Owner Paul Green **Bred** Gestut Erlenhof **Trained** Upper Lambourn, Berks

FOCUS
Not a competitive race and only a fair pace with the first two close to their marks.

NOTEBOOK
Royals Darling(GER), a long way below his best when behind both the runner-up and the third at Cheltenham, returned to something like his best under a well-judged ride. He showed the right attitude when challenged and will be interesting when sent over fences next term. *(tchd 4-1 in places)*
Bold Fire, who had a big pull in the weights with Shamayoun on Cheltenham form from last month, again showed a slight tendency to jump to her right but lost little in defeat against a rival who was allowed to set his own pace. She is a lightly raced and useful performer from a top yard and is capable of winning again in this sphere. *(op 6-5 tchd 5-4 in places)*
Shamayoun(FR), who has not always looked the easiest of rides but is a much-improved performer, did not have to be at his best to win at Plumpton last time and, while running creditably, left the impression that a much stronger overall gallop would have been in his favour. He looks worth a try over a bit further. *(op 13-8 tchd 15-8 in places)*
Lerida faced a very stiff task on these terms and was predictably outclassed. *(op 50-1)*

5002 ASHLEYBANK INVESTMENTS FUTURE CHAMPION NOVICES' CHASE GRADE 2 (17 fncs) 2m 4f
2:20 (2:20) (Class 1) 5-Y-0+ **£23,076** (£8,824; £4,552; £2,404)

Form RPR
-112 **1** **Monet's Garden (IRE)**[39] 4431 8-11-7 TonyDobbin 160+
(N G Richards) *cl up: led 4th: hrd pressed bef 4 out: rdn and styd on wl fr 2 out* **2/7**[1]
1F63 **2** *4* **Le Volfoni (FR)**[14] 4774 5-11-3 148 RWalsh 150
(P F Nicholls) *chsd ldrs: ev ch bef 4 out: one pce between last two* **4/1**[2]
21U0 **3** *dist* **Kasthari (IRE)**[37] 4456 7-11-7 136 RichardJohnson 94
(J Howard Johnson) *led to 4th: cl up tl wknd fr 9th* **12/1**[3]
0P23 **4** *9* **Duke Orsino (IRE)**[30] 4582 6-11-3 PeterBuchanan 81
(Miss Lucinda V Russell) *in tch to 7th: sn struggling* **66/1**
44 **P** **Neuro (FR)**[25] 4655 5-10-13 BenOrde-Powlett —
(Jedd O'Keeffe) *plld hrd early: in tch to 7th: sn wknd: t.o whn p.u bef 4 out* **100/1**

5m 1.20s (-21.70) **Going Correction** -0.60s/f (Firm)
WFA 5 from 6yo+ 4lb 5 Ran SP% **107.9**
Speed ratings: **115,113,—,—,—** CSF £1.89 TOTE £1.40: £1.10, £1.50; EX 1.40.
Owner David Wesley Yates **Bred** William Delahunty **Trained** Greystoke, Cumbria

FOCUS
Only two serious runners but both posted very useful efforts and the winner looks the type to hold his own in the highest grade next term.

NOTEBOOK
Monet's Garden(IRE) ◆, whose only defeat over fences came in last month's Arkle at the Cheltenham Festival, returned to winning ways with a workmanlike display to give weight and a beating to a very useful rival. His jumping is sound, he has the right attitude, he is a versatile sort and, with further improvement likely, looks set to take rank with the best chasers around at up to three miles next term. The King George back at Kempton on Boxing Day could be right up his street. *(tchd 3-10 and 1-4 in places)*
Le Volfoni(FR), a very useful chaser who was stepping back up in trip, jumped soundly and lost nothing in defeat against a rival that has the potential to rank among the best chasers up to three miles next term. He has age on his side but, given he does fall short of top class, he may not be the easiest to place in handicaps from his current mark of 148. *(op 9-2)*
Kasthari(IRE) had conditions to suit but, although his previous form left him something to find with the first two, could have been expected to finish a bit closer than he did. He is another that may find things tough going from his current mark of 136 in handicaps next term. *(op 10-1)*
Duke Orsino(IRE) faced an impossible task on these terms and predictably struggled.

5003 SAMSUNG ELECTRONICS SCOTTISH CHAMPION HURDLE (A LIMITED H'CAP) GRADE 2 (9 hdls) 2m
2:50 (2:50) (Class 1) 4-Y-0+
£33,804 (£12,732; £6,372; £3,186; £1,596; £798)

Form RPR
0122 **1** **Noble Request (FR)**[14] 4773 5-10-9 143 RichardJohnson 146+
(P J Hobbs) *hld up: hdwy to ld 3 out: r.o strly fr next: readily* **7/2**[2]
2330 **2** *5* **Faasel (IRE)**[39] 4432 5-11-6 154 (v) TonyDobbin 149
(N G Richards) *hld up: hdwy after 3 out: chsd wnr run in: no imp* **11/2**[3]
4640 **3** *1 ½* **Phar Bleu (FR)**[15] 4765 5-10-8 142 (t) RWalsh 135
(P F Nicholls) *hld up in tch: lost pl 1/2-way: rallied after 2 out: kpt on run in: no imp* **7/1**
1400 **4** *3* **Desert Air (JPN)**[15] 4765 7-10-4 138 (t) RJGreene 132+
(M C Pipe) *cl up: ev ch and rdn 3 out: sn outpcd: hmpd last: kpt on run in* **25/1**
-10P **5** *hd* **United (GER)**[20] 4717 5-10-4 138 oh1 LeightonAspell 130+
(Mrs L Wadham) *prom: outpcd bef 2 out: no imp run in* **8/1**
1200 **6** *4* **Royal Shakespeare (FR)**[14] 4775 7-11-0 148 TomScudamore 144+
(S Gollings) *chsd ldrs: ev ch 3 out: 2l down and one pce whn blnd last: nt rcvr* **16/1**
333P **7** *1* **Mister McGoldrick**[15] 4761 9-10-12 146 DominicElsworth 133+
(Mrs S J Smith) *led to 3 out: wkng whn hit next* **10/1**
6100 **8** *2* **Overstrand (IRE)**[15] 4765 7-9-13 138 oh17 TomGreenway[(5)] 121
(Robert Gray) *prom tl rdn and wknd fr 3 out* **100/1**
-1P5 **9** *1* **Arcalis**[39] 4432 6-11-10 158 APMcCoy 141+
(J Howard Johnson) *in tch on ins: outpcd after 4 out: wknd next* **2/1**[1]

3m 47.1s (-10.20) **Going Correction** -0.60s/f (Firm) 9 Ran SP% **114.4**
Speed ratings: **111,108,107,106,106 104,103,102,102** CSF £23.17 CT £126.48 TOTE £4.50: £1.70, £1.90, £2.50; EX 25.00.
Owner Mrs Karola Vann **Bred** P Chedeville And Antoinette Tamagni **Trained** Withycombe, Somerset

FOCUS
A race that did not take as much winning as seemed likely beforehand with the market leader disappointing. The gallop was only fair but this race suited those coming from off the pace and the winner is value for further and to his Aintree mark.

NOTEBOOK
Noble Request(FR) ◆ is an improved performer over hurdles and turned in his best effort with a very smart performance in a race run at only an ordinary gallop. Life will be tougher after reassessment but he does look a bit better than the bare form and is the type to win a decent race over this trip next term. *(op 3-1)*
Faasel(IRE), with the visor back on to replace the blinkers he wore in the Champion Hurdle, found the drop in grade to his liking and confirmed himself a very smart performer over this trip. However, this run also showed he is vulnerable to the more progressive sorts from his current handicap mark.
Phar Bleu(FR) has not won since late 2004 but did not look entirely happy with the drop to this trip in a race run at a less than true gallop. A much stronger pace over this trip would have suited but he will be very interesting if sent over fences next term.
Desert Air(JPN) has not been at his best since winning a valuable handicap at Sandown in January but has failed to reproduce that level since and found the drop to this trip against him. A stiffer test of stamina would have suited better but he is another vulnerable to progressive sorts in this type of event.
United(GER), back in trip and on less testing ground than in France last time, has been a bit of a disappointment since an encouraging reappearance run. More of a test of stamina may have helped but she will do well to win a competitive handicap from her current mark. *(op 13-2)*
Royal Shakespeare(FR) ran a good deal better than the bare form suggested as, although held by the winner, he was heading the chasing pack and plugging on when ploughing through the final flight and losing all momentum. Some shoddy jumping has often proved his downfall but, while undoubtedly smart, has little margin for error from his 148 mark. *(tchd 18-1)*
Arcalis, fifth in the Champion Hurdle, looked to have sound claims for this handicap debut on ideal ground. However, he proved a big disappointment, coming off the bridle soon after leaving the back straight and dropping out tamely. His stable's form has been very patchy this year and it is far *too soon to write him off yet. Official explanation: trainer's representative was unable to offer any explanation for poor form shown (op 3-1 tchd 10-3 in a place)*

5004 GALA CASINOS DAILY RECORD SCOTTISH GRAND NATIONAL H'CAP CHASE (GRADE 3) (27 fncs) 4m 1f
3:30 (3:32) (Class 1) 5-Y-0+
£91,232 (£34,224; £17,136; £8,544; £4,288; £2,144)

Form RPR
0402 **1** **Run For Paddy**[57] 4098 10-10-2 135 CarlLlewellyn 147+
(Carl Llewellyn) *hld up bhd: gd hdwy and prom bef 4 out: effrt bef last: styd on wl to ld post* **33/1**
1F24 **2** *shd* **Ladalko (FR)**[56] 4118 7-10-4 137 RWalsh 148+
(P F Nicholls) *hld up: blnd 2nd: mstke 7th: hdwy 18th: shkn up to ld last: sn rdn: kpt on: hdd post* **7/1**[1]
210F **3** *½* **Royal Emperor (IRE)**[16] 4746 10-11-4 151 DominicElsworth 161+
(Mrs S J Smith) *hld up: hdwy after 18th: led 5 out: hdd last: rallied u.p: hld cl home* **50/1**
132 **4** *10* **Idle Talk (IRE)**[38] 4444 7-10-11 144 JasonMaguire 146+
(T R George) *in tch: mstke 15th: led 21st to 23rd: styd upsides: wknd after 2 out* **8/1**[2]
4111 **5** *18* **Halcon Genelardais (FR)**[60] 4035 6-11-2 149 RobertThornton 130
(A King) *mstkes: prom tl rdn and wknd fr 4 out* **14/1**
P21P **6** *1* **Philson Run (IRE)**[35] 4496 10-10-5 138 KeithMercer 118
(Nick Williams) *hld up: rdn 22nd: nvr rchd ldrs* **33/1**
4153 **7** *2* **L'Aventure (FR)**[35] 4496 7-10-1 139 (bt) PaddyMerrigan[(5)] 121+
(P F Nicholls) *led to 5th: led 20th to next: hit 5 out: wknd next* **25/1**
1613 **8** *½* **King Killone (IRE)**[35] 4505 6-10-0 133 oh6 DavidO'Meara 111
(H P Hogarth) *in tch tl wknd after 18th* **40/1**
2254 **9** *hd* **Zabenz (NZ)**[15] 4759 9-10-8 141 (b) RichardJohnson 118
(P J Hobbs) *towards rr: hdwy after 18th: wknd fr 21st* **66/1**
2161 **10** *1* **Kerry Lads (IRE)**[35] 4505 11-10-0 133 oh1 (p) PeterBuchanan 109
(Miss Lucinda V Russell) *a.p: effrt bef 4 out: wknd 2 out* **40/1**
P424 **11** *9* **Nil Desperandum (IRE)**[14] 4777 9-10-4 137 TPTreacy 104
(Ms F M Crowley, Ire) *sn towards rr: no imp fnl circ* **25/1**
F10F **12** *3* **Ebony Light (IRE)**[14] 4777 10-10-3 136 (p) BrianHarding 100
(D McCain) *cl up: led 5th to 15th: wknd qckly 19th* **100/1**
520F **13** *5* **Royal Auclair (FR)**[14] 4777 9-11-7 159 (t) LiamHeard[(5)] 118
(P F Nicholls) *hld up midfield: rdn and wknd after 22nd* **20/1**
P-P0 **14** *2 ½* **Calling Brave (IRE)**[37] 4457 10-10-8 141 MarcusFoley 98
(N J Henderson) *midfield on outside tl wknd fr 19th* **66/1**
P0U0 **15** *4* **Polar Red**[15] 4762 9-9-7 133 oh7 (vt) DarrenO'Dwyer[(7)] 86
(M C Pipe) *hld up: shortlived effrt 21st: sn btn* **150/1**
0063 **16** *20* **Robbo**[13] 4790 12-9-4 133 oh14 JamesReveley[(10)] 66
(K G Reveley) *a bhd* **200/1**
P244 **17** *11* **Model Son (IRE)**[15] 4764 8-10-1 134 BarryKeniry 56
(P C Haslam) *in tch to 18th: sn lost pl* **14/1**
F100 **18** *6* **Double Honour (FR)**[63] 3971 8-10-7 140 (b) PJBrennan 56
(P J Hobbs) *cl up: led 15th to 20th: sn struggling* **100/1**
3-4P **F** **Another Rum (IRE)**[38] 4447 8-10-0 133 (b[1]) AnthonyRoss —
(I A Duncan, Ire) *fell 1st* **22/1**
2U52 **U** **Take The Stand (IRE)**[16] 4746 10-11-10 157 JamieMoore —
(P Bowen) *hmpd and uns rdr 1st* **33/1**
3P36 **F** **Truckers Tavern (IRE)**[63] 3971 11-10-2 135 (t) LeightonAspell —
(Mrs S J Smith) *fell 1st* **100/1**
0F1P **P** **The Bajan Bandit (IRE)**[35] 4496 11-10-12 145 (b) TonyDobbin —
(L Lungo) *sn bhd: t.o whn p.u bef 15th* **25/1**

1113 **P** **Darkness**[38] 4444 7-11-5 **152**........ APMcCoy —
(C R Egerton) *midfield: outpcd after 18th: p.u bef 21st* **12/1**

P4PU **P** **Baron Windrush**[14] 4777 8-10-6 **139**........ AntonyEvans —
(N A Twiston-Davies) *a bhd: t.o whn p.u bef 20th* **66/1**

F-P4 **P** **Lord Atterbury (IRE)**[49] 4238 10-10-0 **133** oh3........(p) TomScudamore —
(M C Pipe) *towards rr: t.o whn p.u bef 21st* **100/1**

PP-P **P** **Shotgun Willy (IRE)**[14] 4777 12-10-2 **135**........(p) RichardMcGrath —
(R C Guest) *in tch tl wknd 18th: p.u bef 20th* **100/1**

1521 **P** **All In The Stars (IRE)**[63] 3995 8-10-3 **141**........ DarylJacob(5) —
(D P Keane) *mstkes in rr: nvr on terms: p.u bef 20th* **7/1**[1]

FP2F **P** **Juveigneur (FR)**[14] 4777 9-10-9 **142**........ MickFitzgerald —
(N J Henderson) *in tch tl wknd after 18th: p.u bef 21st* **14/1**

313P **P** **Korelo (FR)**[39] 4433 8-10-0 **133** oh1........(p) TimmyMurphy —
(M C Pipe) *hld up: struggling after 18th: t.o whn p.u bef 20th* **25/1**

1121 **U** **Mon Mome (FR)**[14] 4778 6-10-2 **135** 5ex........ AlanO'Keeffe —
(Miss Venetia Williams) *in tch: lost pl whn mstke and uns rdr 17th* **9/1**[3]

8m 35.1s **30** Ran SP% **124.5**
CSF £212.38 CT £11156.06 TOTE £37.20: £6.40, £3.00, £13.40, £3.30; EX 522.30 Trifecta £14406.00 Part won. Pool £20,290.17 - 0.30 winning units..
Owner B Perkins **Bred** D E S Smith **Trained** Upper Lambourn, Berks

■ A first success as a trainer for Carl Llewellyn, who has taken over the licence from Mark Pitman. He also rode the winner.

FOCUS
A competitive race run at a decent gallop and the first three pulled clear over the last three fences. This form should stand up at a similar level with the first three all close to recent efforts.

NOTEBOOK
Run For Paddy, a smart performer, survived an early scare and turned in a career-best effort on his first run over this trip to provide his rookie trainer with his first-ever win. He travelled strongly, showed the right attitude and, given he handles good and soft ground, appeals as the type to win another decent staying handicap next term.
Ladalko(FR) ◆, a progressive sort over fences, overcame a few early blunders but took the eye with the way he went through the race and responded well to pressure when asked for his effort approaching the final fence. He clearly stays well, has age on his side and appeals strongly as the type to win one of the top staying handicaps next term. *(op 15-2 tchd 8-1)*
Royal Emperor(IRE) proved himself none the worse for his Aintree fall and, on his first start over this trip, turned in a performance that ranks with his best over fences. His jumping was much more fluent than is often the case and he showed a determined attitude, but his patchy completion record over fences in the last two years means he is not really one to be going in head down for at shortish odds next time.
Idle Talk(IRE) ◆, runner-up in the Royal & SunAlliance Chase at Cheltenham last month, travelled really strongly for much of the way and ran a blinder for one of such limited chasing experience. Apart from one mistake his jumping was sound and he will be worth another try over this trip next season. He has age on his side and is another that appeals strongly as the type to win a decent handicap next term. *(tchd 10-1 in a place)*
Halcon Genelardais(FR), making his handicap debut, did well given his lack of chasing experience to last as long as he did especially as his fencing was anything but fluent. He has age on his side but he will have to brush up his jumping if he is to hold his own in the top staying handicaps from this sort of mark next term.
Philson Run(IRE), a quirky but very capable staying chaser, was beaten a similar distance as in this race last year and he seems much more effective in very testing conditions. *(tchd 40-1)*
L'Aventure(FR), back in less-testing ground, ran well for a long way but was again some way below the form of her Welsh National win. She reportedly collapsed after the finish suffering from heat stroke but soon recovered. *(op 20-1)*
Kerry Lads(IRE), for the fourth year in a row, ran well for a long way in this marathon event but once again failed to truly see out the trip. There are more races to be won with him returned to three miles next term away from progressive or well-handicapped types when his jumping holds up.
Nil Desperandum(IRE), fourth in the Aintree equivalent last time, failed to make an impact from off the pace and no doubt his previous exertions were a disadvantage. He is now due to remain in Britain in an attempt to find greater opportunities.
All In The Stars(IRE) had looked to be laid out for this race but was never going at any stage and was a big disappointment. Given he is usually a consistent sort this run is best overlooked and he *is worth another chance next term. Official explanation: jockey said gelding was never travelling; trainer was unable to offer any explanation for poor form shown (op 15-2 tchd 8-1)*

5005 4* WESTERN HOUSE HOTEL H'CAP HURDLE (12 hdls) 2m 6f

4:05 (4:08) (Class 2) (0-150,149) 4-Y-O+ **£13,012** (£3,820; £1,910; £954)

Form RPR

3403 **1** **Mughas (IRE)**[14] 4776 7-11-5 **142**........(v1) RobertThornton 148+
(A King) *hld up midfield: hdwy bef 3 out: led bef next: hung lft: r.o strly* **9/2**[2]

0U-0 **2** *10* **Indy Mood**[13] 4792 7-9-7 **123** oh3........ TomMessenger(7) 117
(Mrs H O Graham) *chsd ldrs: outpcd after 4 out: styd on strly fr between last two: no ch w wnr* **50/1**

5100 **3** *¾* **Afrad (FR)**[38] 4446 5-10-12 **135**........ MickFitzgerald 128
(N J Henderson) *cl up: led bef 3 out to bef 2 out: sn one pce* **6/1**[3]

0006 **4** *nk* **Inching Closer**[37] 4461 9-10-2 **125**........ RichardJohnson 119+
(J Howard Johnson) *in tch: drvn after 4 out: one pce after next* **12/1**

1064 **5** *½* **October Mist (IRE)**[13] 4792 12-9-4 **123** oh10........ JamesReveley(10) 116+
(K G Reveley) *prom: effrt bef 3 out: no ex whn mstke last* **66/1**

006P **6** *3 ½* **Monolith**[35] 4497 8-10-10 **133**........ TonyDobbin 122
(L Lungo) *hld up: effrt after 4 out: no imp fr next* **11/1**

2131 **7** *2* **The Luder (IRE)**[23] 4676 5-10-7 **130**........(b) RWalsh 118+
(P F Nicholls) *led to bef 3 out: wknd bef next* **9/4**[1]

3101 **8** *3 ½* **River Alder**[13] 4792 8-10-0 **123** oh2........ PeterBuchanan 106
(J M Dun) *chsd ldrs: outpcd 8th: n.d after* **11/1**

52P1 **9** *10* **Heir To Be**[35] 4497 7-10-2 **125**........ LeightonAspell 106+
(Mrs L Wadham) *hld up: outpcd 8th: nvr on terms* **8/1**

40-6 **10** *dist* **Mirjan (IRE)**[179] 1872 10-10-11 **134**........(b) TimmyMurphy —
(L Lungo) *hld up: rdn bef 4 out: btn bef next* **12/1**

3150 **F** **The French Furze (IRE)**[39] 4432 12-11-12 **149**........ BrianHarding —
(N G Richards) *hld up: fell 6th* **20/1**

5m 27.0s (-14.60) **Going Correction** -0.60s/f (Firm) **11** Ran SP% **114.6**
Speed ratings: **112,108,108,107,107 106,105,104,100,—** — CSF £195.53 CT £1354.30 TOTE £5.70: £1.70, £7.50, £2.60; EX 316.30.
Owner B Winfield, C Fenton & A Longman **Bred** Baronrath And Baroda Studs **Trained** Barbury Castle, Wilts

FOCUS
Few progressive sorts for the money but an improved performance from the winner, who was tried in a visor. The race could rate higher but is limited by the fifth.

NOTEBOOK
Mughas(IRE), tried in a visor, ran at least as well as he ever has done to break a losing run that stretched back to December 2003. He is a tough and consistent sort but, given the margin of this win, can expect little leniency from the handicapper. *(op 5-1 tchd 11-2 and 6-1 in a place)*
Indy Mood returned to something like his best from 3lb out of the handicap on only this second start since last March, and left the impression that the return to three miles would be in his favour. He will be interesting if sent over fences next term.
Afrad(FR) had the run of the race and put up his best performance since winning at Sandown in December. Given stamina was his strong suit on the Flat last year, he looks well worth a try over three miles in this sphere. *(tchd 13-2)*
Inching Closer ran creditably and may have preferred a stiffer test of stamina but, given he has not won over hurdles for over three years, may continue to look vulnerable from his current mark in this type of event. *(op 14-1)*
October Mist(IRE) had the run of the race and was not disgraced from 10lb out of the handicap, especially as his cause was not helped by a final flight blunder. He will be of more interest from his proper mark in lesser company.
Monolith, back under ideal conditions, would have been suited by a better overall gallop but again underlined his vulnerability in this type of event from his current mark. *(op 9-1)*
The Luder(IRE), an in-form sort who looked one of the few in this field open to further improvement, had the run of the race but found disappointingly little once taken on and, while worth another chance, does not look one for maximum faith. *(op 5-2 tchd 2-1 in places)*
River Alder *Official explanation: jockey said mare ran flat (op 10-1)*

5006 ALBERT BARTLETT AND SONS H'CAP CHASE (12 fncs) 2m

4:35 (4:36) (Class 2) 5-Y-O+

£18,789 (£5,550; £2,775; £1,389; £693; £348)

Form RPR

5242 **1** **Nyrche (FR)**[16] 4749 6-10-11 **143**........ RobertThornton 162+
(A King) *mde all: drew clr fr 4 out* **3/1**[2]

3B4P **2** *16* **Roman Ark**[15] 4759 8-10-0 **132**........ PJBrennan 133
(J M Jefferson) *cl up: rdn bef 4 out: kpt on fr next: no ch w wnr* **12/1**

1113 **3** *7* **Madison Du Berlais (FR)**[36] 4472 5-10-1 **136**........ TomScudamore 129+
(M C Pipe) *chsd ldrs: mstkes 5th and next: sn outpcd: sme late hdwy: no ch w first two* **7/2**[3]

10F5 **4** *¾* **Town Crier (IRE)**[16] 4749 11-10-11 **143**........ DominicElsworth 137+
(Mrs S J Smith) *trckd ldrs: mstke 6th: rdn and wknd fr 3 out* **9/1**

1050 **5** *6* **Caracciola (GER)**[36] 4472 9-10-10 **142**........ MickFitzgerald 129
(N J Henderson) *hld up in tch: outpcd 7th: no ch after* **11/2**

2310 **6** *dist* **Kalca Mome (FR)**[36] 4472 8-10-4 **136**........ RichardJohnson —
(P J Hobbs) *hld up: blnd and outpcd 6th: sn btn* **16/1**

1211 **F** **Jacks Craic (IRE)**[16] 4749 7-10-11 **143**........ AntonyEvans —
(J L Spearing) *hld up: rdn whn hit 5 out: wl btn whn fell 3 out* **11/4**[1]

3m 51.2s (-13.30) **Going Correction** -0.60s/f (Firm)
WFA 5 from 6yo+ 3lb **7** Ran SP% **112.8**
Speed ratings: **105,97,93,93,90** —,— CSF £33.73 CT £129.34 TOTE £4.40: £2.40, £5.00; EX 47.30.
Owner Tony Fisher & Mrs Jeni Fisher **Bred** M Dolic **Trained** Barbury Castle, Wilts

FOCUS
Not the most competitive race for the money and, with the favourite disappointing, this race did not take as much winning as seemed likely. The pace was just fair and the runner-up sets the standard.

NOTEBOOK
Nyrche(FR) confirmed the impression that he was better than the bare form at Aintree with his best effort to date. He had the run of the race to a large degree but, although he will find things tougher *in competitive handicap company after reassessment, he looks the type to do better in this sphere. (op 5-2 tchd 10-3 and 7-2 in places)*
Roman Ark was not disgraced in a race that placed too much of an emphasis on speed. Although high enough in the weights, his jumping was sound and he should appreciate the return to two and a half miles. *(op 14-1)*
Madison Du Berlais(FR), 7lb higher than at Cheltenham, could not confirm those placings with the winner (finished fourth that day) and his tendency to make errors cost him against a rival that was enjoying the run of the race. He is only lightly raced though, and looks well worth another try over two and a half miles. *(tchd 4-1)*
Town Crier(IRE) ran a typical race in that he travelled well to a certain point before fading and he is *likely to continue to look vulnerable from his current mark over fences in this type of event. (op 15-2 tchd 10-1)*
Caracciola(GER) had a pull in the weights with the winner and third but was below his best on this occasion. He may continue to look vulnerable from this mark over fences but looks more favourably treated over hurdles. *(tchd 5-1)*
Kalca Mome(FR), a long way behind a couple of these at the Cheltenham Festival, was most disappointing after a mid-race blunder and is best watched at present.
Jacks Craic(IRE) has risen dramatically through the ranks this year but did not jump as well as he can and did not get the strong pace he has for his last two wins. He was well beaten when coming to grief and may have had enough for the time being. *(op 4-1)*

5007 P B EVENTS NOVICES' H'CAP CHASE (19 fncs) 3m 1f

5:05 (5:05) (Class 2) 5-Y-O+ **£12,572** (£3,746; £1,896; £972; £508)

Form RPR

2-11 **1** **Kinburn (IRE)**[98] 3382 7-10-11 **125**........ RichardJohnson 145+
(J Howard Johnson) *nt a fluent: mde most to 4 out: regained ld next: styd on strly* **11/4**[2]

UP3U **2** *6* **Mckelvey (IRE)**[15] 4764 7-11-3 **131**........ PJBrennan 143+
(P Bowen) *cl up: disp ld 14th: led 4 out to next: sn rdn: kpt on fr last: no ch w wnr* **9/1**

P210 **3** *1 ½* **No Full (FR)**[37] 4456 5-10-7 **129**........ MickFitzgerald 134+
(P R Webber) *hld up: hdwy 5 out: ev ch 3 out: lost 2nd whn mstke last* **6/1**[3]

140U **4** *dist* **Whispered Secret (GER)**[14] 4777 7-11-12 **140**........ APMcCoy —
(M C Pipe) *chsd ldrs: mstke 12th: wknd 5 out* **7/1**

F623 **5** *12* **See You There (IRE)**[34] 4528 7-10-0 **114**........ PeterBuchanan —
(Miss Lucinda V Russell) *mstkes: sn bhd and pushed along: no ch fnl circ* **8/1**

2121 **F** **Stavordale Lad (IRE)**[29] 4605 8-10-9 **123**........ RWalsh —
(P F Nicholls) *trckd ldrs: disputing 3rd whn fell 12th* **5/2**[1]

0014 **P** **Waltzing Beau**[17] 4729 5-10-1 **128**........ JohnnyLevins(5) —
(B G Powell) *mstkes: hld up in tch: outpcd after 10th: t.o whn p.u bef 3 out* **20/1**

6m 18.3s (-27.40) **Going Correction** -0.60s/f (Firm)
WFA 5 from 7yo+ 8lb **7** Ran SP% **107.9**
Speed ratings: **115,113,112,—,—** —,— CSF £23.18 CT £116.61 TOTE £2.90: £1.90, £4.40; EX 24.90.
Owner W M G Black **Bred** Mrs A Kirkwood **Trained** Billy Row, Co Durham

FOCUS
A fair event and a fair gallop resulting in a decent time, but one weakened by the departure of Stavordale Lad before the race had really begun to take shape. The runner-up was rated close to his best and the contest has been rated positively.

NOTEBOOK
Kinburn(IRE) ◆, a progressive sort over fences, maintained his unbeaten record in this sphere with a workmanlike display. Stamina is clearly his forte and, given there is room for improvement *in his jumping and he is only lightly raced, is almost certainly the type to do better next term. (op 9-4)*
Mckelvey(IRE) jumped better than is sometimes the case and lost little in defeat against a progressive young staying chaser. He is a strapping individual and the type to do better, especially if his jumping holds up next term. *(op 6-1)*

No Full(FR) ran arguably his best race over fences. Given he had little to offer in the closing stages and the fact that he travelled strongly for much of the way, he may do better dropped back to around two and a half miles.
Whispered Secret(GER) has still to convince that a truly-run race over this trip is ideal, but he dropped out of contention plenty quick enough and he remains one to have reservations about, especially from his current mark of 140. *(op 8-1)*
See You There(IRE), who has yet to win a race over fences, was well beaten for the second time in succession and he will have to brush up his jumping if he is to win races over the larger obstacles. *(op 10-1)*
Stavordale Lad(IRE), a progressive stayer, has the tendency to make the odd mistake and it cost him this time. Although too far out to say with certainty where he would have finished, he would almost certainly have been involved and is well worth another chance, assuming he is none-the-worse for this mishap. *(op 11-4 tchd 3-1)*

5008 ASHLEYBANK INVESTMENTS STANDARD OPEN NATIONAL HUNT FLAT RACE 2m
5:35 (5:37) (Class 4) 4-6-Y-O £3,253 (£955; £477; £238)

Form					RPR
	1		**Phardessa** 5-10-6 ... DeclanMcGann(5) *(A M Crow) hld up: hdwy to chse ldrs 1/2-way: led gng wl 3f out: kpt on strly fnl f* **100/1**		104+
	2	2	**Skippers Brig (IRE)** 5-11-4 ... TonyDobbin *(L Lungo) midfield: hdwy over 4f out: effrt over 2f out: kpt on ins fnl f: nt rch wnr* **3/1**[3]		109
02	3	7	**Arctic Ghost**[87] [3563] 6-11-4 ... WilsonRenwick *(N Wilson) mde most to 3f out: rdn and nt qckn fr 2f out* **14/1**		102
	4	2 1/2	**Kokoschka (IRE)** 4-10-13 ... APMcCoy *(C R Egerton) prom: effrt over 2f out: no ex over 1f out* **2/1**[1]		95
	5	5	**Inverlochy Lad (IRE)** 5-11-4 ... AnthonyRoss *(I A Duncan, Ire) cl up: chal 1/2-way: no ex over 2f out* **33/1**		95
1	6	2 1/2	**Jean Le Poisson (FR)**[28] [4623] 4-11-6 ... MickFitzgerald *(N J Henderson) hld up: hdwy and in tch over 4f out: rdn and wknd over 2f out* **9/4**[2]		94
	7	18	**Gavz Boy (IRE)** 4-10-13 ... BarryKeniry *(A C Whillans) hld up: sme hdwy over 3f out: nvr on terms* **50/1**		69
020	8	10	**Cavers Glen**[30] [4588] 4-10-13 ... DominicElsworth *(A C Whillans) chsd ldrs to 1/2-way: sn lost pl* **66/1**		59
0	9	shd	**Billsgrey (IRE)**[73] [3799] 4-10-13 ... DavidO'Meara *(J S Haldane) cl up: dropped rr 1/2-way: no ch after* **100/1**		59
6	10	3	**Darazari Bay (IRE)**[44] [4319] 5-11-4 ... RichardMcGrath *(K G Reveley) hld up: pushed along 6f out: sn btn* **33/1**		61
0	11	5	**Contendo**[54] [4147] 5-10-13 ... DesFlavin(5) *(N W Alexander) in tch to 1/2-way: wknd 6f out* **100/1**		56
	12	1 1/4	**Palmerston Place (IRE)** 6-11-4 ... PeterBuchanan *(Miss Lucinda V Russell) in tch to 1/2-way: sn lost pl* **66/1**		55
0	13	5	**Sparky Boy (IRE)**[77] [3742] 5-11-1 ... MichalKohl(3) *(J I A Charlton) hld up: struggling over 6f out: sn btn* **16/1**		50

3m 45.1s (-14.10) **Going Correction** -0.60s/f (Firm)
WFA 4 from 5yo+ 5lb 13 Ran SP% 115.5
Speed ratings: **103,102,98,97,94 93,84,79,79,77 75,74,72** CSF £372.75 TOTE £185.00: £27.10, £1.50, £2.20; EX 1338.80 Place 6 £229.84, Place 5 £46.93.
Owner Mrs P C Stirling **Bred** R W Russell **Trained** Bonjedward, Borders
■ Stewards' Enquiry : Michal Kohl two-day ban: used whip whilst out of contention (May 4-5)

FOCUS
A decent gallop and, although a shock result, there looked no fluke about the winner's performance. The proximity of the third means this bare form is only ordinary, though.

NOTEBOOK
Phardessa ◆, a cheap purchase out of a middle-distance Flat winner, belied her starting price with a decent performance and the manner of it in what looked a fairly truly-run race suggested there was no fluke about it. She can only improve for this experience and is the type to win races over obstacles.
Skippers Brig(IRE) ◆, the first foal of an unraced half-sister to smart National Hunt performer Skippers Cleuch, shaped well on this racecourse debut. Stamina looks his strong suit and he is sure to win races over further when sent over obstacles. *(op 7-2)*
Arctic Ghost has improved with every outing and, although his proximity holds down this form, he did not do much wrong and he looks capable of winning a small event over obstacles. *(op 20-1)*
Kokoschka(IRE), related to Flat winners and to a winning chaser in France, attracted support and *showed enough on this racecourse debut to suggest an ordinary event can be found. (tchd 5-2 in a place)*
Inverlochy Lad(IRE), related to a winning Irish pointer and a winning Irish chaser, shaped with a bit of promise on this racecourse debut and is entitled to improve for the experience.
Jean Le Poisson(FR) could have been expected to fare better than he did after creating a favourable impression on his debut at Newbury but proved a bit of a disappointment. However, he is not one to be writing off yet. *(op 13-8 tchd 5-2 in places)*
T/Plt: £313.10 to a £1 stake. Pool: £92,602.15. 215.85 winning tickets. T/Qpdt: £45.80 to a £1 stake. Pool: £7,587.60. 122.50 winning tickets. RY

4609 BANGOR-ON-DEE (L-H)
Saturday, April 22

OFFICIAL GOING: Hurdle course - good to soft; chase course - soft (heavy in places)
Wind: Light, across Weather: Fine

5009 CHARITY DAY NOVICES' HURDLE (DIV I) (12 hdls) 3m
2:15 (2:15) (Class 4) 4-Y-0+ £3,187 (£935; £467; £233)

Form				RPR
2152	1		**Supreme's Legacy (IRE)**[13] [4787] 7-11-6 121 ... AndrewThornton *(K G Reveley) hld up in mid-div: hdwy appr 7th: lft in ld 8th: rdn after 3 out: hit 2 out and last: edgd lft flat: drvn out* **9/2**[2]	117+
331	2	1	**Triple Mint (IRE)**[63] [3984] 5-11-6 109 ... PaddyAspell *(D McCain) prom: rdn and outpcd appr 8th: rallied 3 out: wnt 2nd last: nt qckn flat* **8/1**[3]	112
6-6P	3	3	**Alformasi**[92] [3477] 7-11-0 ... JoeTizzard *(P F Nicholls) hld up and bhd: hdwy appr 7th: lft 2nd and sltly hmpd 8th: rdn after 9th: no ex flat* **14/1**	104+
6P46	4	23	**William Butler (IRE)**[30] [4589] 6-11-0 93 ... TomDoyle *(S A Brookshaw) hld up and bhd: stdy hdwy 3rd: wknd after 3 out: no ch whn hit last* **50/1**	80
P03P	5	6	**Marchensis (IRE)**[47] [4277] 8-10-11 90 ... OwynNelmes(3) *(O Sherwood) prom: reminders after 6th: wknd after 3 out: no ch whn hit last* **50/1**	74
6505	6	21	**Schindler's List**[14] [4786] 6-11-0 ... JimmyMcCarthy *(C Roberts) hld up towards rr: hdwy appr 8th: wknd 9th* **100/1**	53
-6FP	7	1 1/2	**Sylviesbuck (IRE)**[88] [3554] 9-11-0 85 ... AndrewTinkler *(G M Moore) hld up in tch: wknd after 7th* **66/1**	52
/1-0	8	29	**Chapel Times (IRE)**[35] [4494] 7-11-0 ... MarkBradburne *(H D Daly) nt jump wl: a bhd: reminders after 5th: t.o fr 9th* **25/1**	23
2F46	9	24	**Baron Romeo (IRE)**[57] [4099] 6-11-0 ... WarrenMarston *(R T Phillips) a bhd: t.o fr 8th* **25/1**	—
3116	F		**Dream Alliance**[36] [4469] 5-11-7 131 ... MrTJO'Brien(5) *(P J Hobbs) chsd ldr: led 3rd: 3l clr whn stmbld and fell 8th* **8/13**[1]	—
-PF5	P		**Comte De Chambord**[25] [4657] 10-10-9 74 ... (t) DerekLaverty(5) *(Mark Campion) nvr gng wl: sn bhd: t.o 7th: p.u bef 8th* **100/1**	—
6-	P		**Northern Spirit**[616] [1177] 5-11-0 ... (b) JosephByrne *(C W Moore) led to 3rd: w ldr to 7th: sn wknd: t.o whn p.u bef 9th* **66/1**	—
0	P		**Cool Bathwick (IRE)**[16] [4754] 7-11-0 ... JodieMogford *(G H Yardley) prom: lost pl and reminders after 5th: t.o 7th: p.u bef 8th* **125/1**	—

6m 5.10s (8.30) **Going Correction** +0.60s/f (Soft) 13 Ran SP% 115.3
Speed ratings: **110,109,108,101,99 92,91,81,73,— —,—,—** CSF £35.57 TOTE £5.10: £1.40, £1.90, £3.60; EX 25.00.
Owner The Supreme Alliance **Bred** J Mernagh **Trained** Lingdale, Redcar & Cleveland

FOCUS
The departure of the odds-on favourite Dream Alliance took quite a bit away from this event but the time was smart, more than two seconds faster than the following handicap and over 12 seconds quicker than the second division. The winner is value for further with the third to recent form.

NOTEBOOK
Supreme's Legacy(IRE) took advantage of the fall of Dream Alliance despite not being foot-perfect at the last two flights on this slightly softer ground. *(op 4-1)*
Triple Mint(IRE) looks the type who does not do anything in a hurry and was suited by a step up to three miles. However, he just lacked the required turn of foot to get past the winner on this better ground. *(op 9-1)*
Alformasi confirmed that his run when pulled up in testing ground at Chepstow was all wrong.
Dream Alliance was probably the one to catch when he unluckily came to grief four from home. *(tchd 4-6)*

5010 BROOKES BELL H'CAP HURDLE (12 hdls) 3m
2:45 (2:45) (Class 3) (0-120,120) 4-Y-0+ £6,180 (£1,814; £907; £453)

Form				RPR
0P00	1		**Always Waining (IRE)**[35] [4497] 5-11-2 110 ... BarryFenton *(R M Stronge) hld up and bhd: nt fluent 4th: hdwy on ins appr 8th: led after 2 out: clr whn j.rt and hit last: eased considerably flat* **16/1**	122+
112	2	4	**Desert Tommy**[42] [4372] 5-11-4 117 ... MrNWilliams(5) *(Evan Williams) w ldr: nt fluent 1st: j. slowly 2nd: rdn after 8th: led after 3 out tl after 2 out: one pce* **4/1**[1]	119+
220P	3	2 1/2	**Glacial Evening (IRE)**[146] [2529] 10-11-9 120 ... WilliamKennedy(3) *(R H Buckler) prom: outpcd 7th: rdn and rallied 3 out: one pce fr 2 out* **16/1**	117
4-F1	4	1 1/4	**Ranelagh Gray (IRE)**[31] [4579] 9-11-2 110 ... SamThomas *(Miss Venetia Williams) led tl appr 8th: rdn appr 3 out: one pce fr 2 out* **9/2**[2]	106
R662	5	2	**Business Traveller (IRE)**[11] [4453] 6-9-10 95 ow1 ... (vt) MarkNicolls(5) *(R J Price) bhd: styng on whn bdly hmpd appr 2 out: nt rcvr* **12/1**	92+
-PP0	6	1 1/4	**Columbus (IRE)**[28] [4612] 9-11-12 120 ... (b) JosephByrne *(Jennie Candlish) hld up in tch: cl 2nd whn swtchd rt appr 2 out: sn rdn: fnd nil* **25/1**	114+
P-1F	7	dist	**Bowleaze (IRE)**[186] [1781] 7-11-12 120 ... AndrewThornton *(R H Alner) hld up in mid-div: hdwy 7th: wknd 3 out: t.o* **11/2**[3]	—
3F05	8	3	**Corals Laurel (IRE)**[17] [4726] 7-10-8 102 ... (t) WarrenMarston *(R T Phillips) hld up towards rr: rdn appr 8th: t.o* **10/1**	—
4134	9	11	**Vicario**[44] [4323] 5-11-12 120 ... (b[1]) PaddyAspell *(D McCain) hld up in mid-div: rdn after 7th: sn struggling: t.o* **16/1**	—
5P13	F		**Three Lions**[116] [3018] 9-10-10 104 ... JohnMcNamara *(R S Brookhouse) hld up and bhd: hdwy on ins 7th: 5l 6th and stl gng wl whn fell 9th* **8/1**	—
4006	P		**Tiger Tips Lad (IRE)**[27] [4639] 7-11-2 110 ... (bt[1]) TomSiddall *(N A Twiston-Davies) prom: nt fluent 7th: sn rdn and lost pl: t.o whn p.u bef last* **20/1**	—
F300	F		**Mini Dare**[93] [3460] 9-10-7 104 ... OwynNelmes(3) *(O Sherwood) hld up in mid-div: hit 5th: hdwy on ins 7th: prom and rdn whn collapsed and died appr 2 out* **14/1**	—
12/P	P		**Lazerito (IRE)**[31] [4573] 8-11-1 112 ... PaulO'Neill(3) *(Miss Venetia Williams) hld up in mid-div: hdwy after 6th: led appr 8th tl after 3 out: rdn and wkng whn hit 2 out: p.u bef last* **20/1**	—

6m 7.30s (10.50) **Going Correction** +0.60s/f (Soft) 13 Ran SP% 119.1
Speed ratings: **106,104,103,103,102 102,—,—,—,— —,—,—** CSF £78.08 CT £1070.22 TOTE £20.00: £6.40, £1.90, £5.80; EX 147.60.
Owner Peter J Douglas Engineering **Bred** Barouche Stud Ireland Ltd **Trained** Beedon Common, Berks
■ Stewards' Enquiry : Mr N Williams two-day ban: used whip with excessive frequency (May 3-4)

FOCUS
Run at no great pace, the time was 2.2 seconds slower than the previous novice event. The winner is value for ten lengths and the placed horses were close to their marks, but the form is ordinary.

NOTEBOOK
Always Waining(IRE) has just come to himself according to his trainer after being badly out of sorts. He could have scored by a much wider margin and is now likely to go for a better grade *handicap at Uttoxeter. Official explanation: trainer said, regarding improved form shown, gelding was better suited by step up in trip*
Desert Tommy, raised another 2lb, again ran his race but was undoubtedly flattered by his proximity to the winner. *(tchd 7-2)*
Glacial Evening(IRE), who failed to complete in his three outings over fences, may have preferred a stronger gallop in this first start for five months.
Ranelagh Gray(IRE), raised 5lb after making all at Towcester, would probably have been better off setting a stronger pace on this much easier course.
Business Traveller(IRE) was just beginning to find his stamina coming into play when the ill-fated *Mini Dare keeled over right in front of him. Official explanation: jockey said gelding suffered interference approaching second-last hurdle*
Columbus(IRE) really wants a stiffer test of stamina but the fact remains he found precious little off the bridle.
Three Lions was waiting in the wings prior to making his entrance when coming to grief four out. *(op 15-2)*

5011 KEN & GILL'S 25TH ANNIVERSARY NOVICES' CHASE (12 fncs) 2m 1f 110y
3:20 (3:27) (Class 3) 5-Y-0+ £6,831 (£2,005; £1,002; £500)

Form				RPR
2314	1		**My World (FR)**[63] [3973] 6-10-7 116 ... AndrewThornton *(R H Alner) hld up: wnt 2nd after 6th: led after 2 out: drvn out* **6/5**[1]	122

1224 **2** *4* **In The Frame (IRE)**[183] [1817] 7-11-0 117 .... PaulMoloney 125
(Evan Williams) *hld up: rdn and hdwy after 3 out: ev ch 2 out: edgd rt flat: no ex* **9/2**[3]

2241 **3** *3* **Give Me Love (FR)**[14] [4780] 6-11-0 119 ....(bt) JoeTizzard 122
(P F Nicholls) *led: rdn and hdd after 2 out: wknd last* **2/1**[2]

2F65 **4** *20* **Itsuptoharry (IRE)**[14] [4778] 7-11-0 114 .... PaddyAspell 102
(D McCain) *chsd ldr tl after 6th: wknd 4 out* **13/2**

4m 37.1s (10.70) **Going Correction** +0.60s/f (Soft) **4** Ran SP% **110.3**
Speed ratings: **100,98,96,88** CSF £6.71 TOTE £1.80; EX 5.00.
Owner Nicky Turner, Penny Tozer, Lotte Schicht **Bred** J E Dubois And Frederic Sauque **Trained** Droop, Dorset

FOCUS
This was quite competitive despite the small field and the first three were all close to their marks.

NOTEBOOK
My World(FR), back to a more suitable trip, needs soft ground and ran out a clear-cut winner after a couple of months off. *(op 11-10 tchd 5-4)*
In The Frame(IRE) had the ground against him on this return after a six-month absence. This was *a good effort in the circumstances and he should again pay his way when it dries up. (op 7-2 tchd 5-1)*
Give Me Love(FR) did not get things his own way this time in this better company. *(op 5-2)*

5012 BROOKE HOSPITAL FOR ANIMALS H'CAP CHASE (18 fncs) 3m 110y
3:55 (3:56) (Class 3) (0-130,130) 5-Y-0+ **£10,409** (£3,056; £1,528; £763)

Form RPR
4121 **1** **Simon**[35] [4498] 7-11-3 **121** .... AndrewThornton 139+
(J L Spearing) *racd wd: hld up in mid-div: hdwy 10th: led appr 13th to 14th: rdn after 3 out: led appr last: r.o wl* **5/1**[1]

6541 **2** *5* **Sharp Jack (IRE)**[31] [4578] 8-10-7 **111** .... WayneHutchinson 121
(R T Phillips) *hld up and bhd: blnd 7th: hdwy 11th: led 4 out: rdn and hdd appr last: no ex flat* **15/2**[3]

124F **3** *16* **Be My Better Half (IRE)**[15] [4762] 11-11-9 **127** .... NoelFehily 123+
(Jonjo O'Neill) *a.p: mstke 11th (water): no imp fr 4 out* **11/1**

P-PP **4** *1* **Whitford Don (IRE)**[140] [2637] 8-11-8 **126** ....(b) JoeTizzard 119
(P F Nicholls) *hld up towards rr: mstke 8th: hdwy 12th: wknd appr 2 out* **8/1**

36U3 **5** *3 ½* **Aristoxene (FR)**[15] [4764] 6-11-12 **130** .... AndrewTinkler 120
(N J Henderson) *hld up in mid-div: lost pl appr 12th: hdwy 14th: wknd after 3 out* **8/1**

4-40 **6** *3* **Rum Pointer (IRE)**[21] [4690] 10-10-2 **109** .... WilliamKennedy(3) 96
(R H Buckler) *hld up and bhd: hdwy 5th: led 9th to 10th: led 14th to 4 out: wknd appr 2 out* **11/1**

245P **7** *11* **Sharp Belline (IRE)**[13] [4790] 9-10-3 **107** .... PadgeWhelan 83
(Mrs S J Smith) *hld up in tch: wknd appr 12th* **16/1**

21FP **P** **Bob Ar Aghaidh (IRE)**[129] [2825] 10-11-5 **123** .... TomDoyle —
(C Tinkler) *prom: rdn and lost pl 6th: t.o whn p.u bef 12th* **14/1**

5-4B **P** **Burwood Breeze (IRE)**[15] [4762] 10-10-4 **115** .... WillieMcCarthy(7) —
(T R George) *hld up and bhd: hdwy 13th: wknd appr 4 out: p.u bef 2 out* **11/1**

P432 **P** **Tana River (IRE)**[21] [4690] 10-11-7 **125** .... BarryFenton —
(Miss E C Lavelle) *hld up in mid-div: hdwy 11th: wknd after 12th: bhd whn p.u bef 4 out* **11/2**[2]

4PP6 **P** **Indalo (IRE)**[42] [4374] 11-10-11 **118** .... PaulO'Neill(3) —
(Miss Venetia Williams) *prom: nt fluent 2nd (water): rdn and wknd 8th: t.o whn p.u after 11th* **15/2**[3]

12PP **P** **Major Benefit (IRE)**[71] [3845] 9-10-10 **114** .... JimmyMcCarthy —
(Mrs K Waldron) *hld up: sn mid-div: hdwy after 7th: wknd 12th: t.o whn p.u bef 3 out: b.b.v* **28/1**

/PP0 **P** **Shardam (IRE)**[39] [4433] 9-11-6 **124** ....(bt[1]) TomSiddall —
(N A Twiston-Davies) *led to 9th: led 10th: mstke 11th (water): hdd & wknd qckly appr 13th: p.u bef 3 out* **16/1**

6m 32.1s (8.90) **Going Correction** +0.60s/f (Soft) **13** Ran SP% **124.7**
Speed ratings: **109,107,102,101,100 99,96,—,—,— —,—,—** CSF £45.12 CT £408.56 TOTE £4.60: £1.80, £3.20, £3.50; EX 20.80.
Owner Mrs Mercy Rimell **Bred** Mrs Mercy Rimell **Trained** Kinnersley, Worcs

FOCUS
The finish to this quite valuable handicap was fought out by a couple of improving novices. The winner is value for further and the form should work out.

NOTEBOOK
Simon, raised 7lb, is beginning to live up to coming from the same family as Gaye Brief and Gaye Chance, having been bred by Mercy Rimell. It is thought this progressive sort will get further but, with the prospect of the ground drying up, he will be put away until next season. *(op 11-2)*
Sharp Jack(IRE) ◆ came up against a progressive sort on his handicap debut. He seems to be going the right way and can make his mark in handicap company.
Be My Better Half(IRE) was trying to concede weight to a couple of rivals on the upgrade and could only plod on for third. *(op 14-1)*
Whitford Don(IRE), pulled up when highly tried in a couple of handicaps towards the end of last year, had dropped a total of 8lb as a consequence.
Aristoxene(FR), dropped 2lb, still looks high enough in the handicap.
Rum Pointer(IRE) is being given a chance by the Handicapper.
Major Benefit(IRE) *Official explanation: trainer said gelding bled from nose*

5013 JANE MCALPINE MEMORIAL HUNTERS' CHASE (18 fncs) 3m 110y
4:25 (4:25) (Class 6) 6-Y-0+ **£2,175** (£669; £334)

Form RPR
3154 **1** **An Capall Dubh (IRE)**[13] 10-11-11 .... MrCPHuxley(7) 111+
(Mrs Edward Crow) *hld up: hdwy 11th: hit 4 out: led appr 2 out: sn clr: blnd last: r.o* **4/1**[2]

0-P5 **2** *16* **The Lyme Volunteer (IRE)**[7] [4846] 9-12-0 108 ....(b) MrTGreenall 89
(David M Easterby) *led tl after 1st: chsd ldr: led 8th: rdn and hdd appr 2 out: sn btn* **12/1**

-PUP **3** *2 ½* **Kingston-Banker**[29] [4607] 10-11-7 102 .... MrlChanin(7) 87
(Mrs S Alner) *hld up in tch: chsd ldr after 9th: ev ch appr 2 out: sn btn* **14/1**

-P10 **4** *10* **Cobreces**[36] [4471] 8-12-0 116 .... MrWBiddick(7) 86+
(Mrs L Borradaile) *hld up in tch: rdn after 12th: wknd 4 out: mstke 3 out* **5/4**[1]

5/06 **5** *3* **Hip Pocket (IRE)**[7] 10-11-7 76 .... MrNSSaville(7) 77+
(Robert Bowling) *hld up: hdwy appr 8th: mstkes 14th and 4 out: sn wknd* **20/1**

P/U2 **F** **Ikemba (IRE)**[13] 9-11-7 .... MrWKinsey(7) —
(J Groucott) *fell 1st* **6/1**[3]

P **P** **Sarah's Party**[13] 10-12-0 .... MrSMorris —
(G D Hanmer) *a bhd: reminders 6th: lost tch 12th: t.o whn p.u bef last* **9/1**

6 **P** **Another Client (IRE)**[30] [4594] 10-11-7 .... MissTessaClark(7) —
(Mrs A R Hewitt) *a bhd: lost tch 12th: t.o whn p.u bef 2 out* **33/1**

435P **U** **Lucky Master (IRE)**[13] [4799] 14-11-7 .... MissGSwan(7) —
(Miss G Swan) *mstke 2nd (water): j. slowly 3rd: sn t.o: blnd and uns rdr 6th* **100/1**

400P **P** **River Mere**[9] [4831] 12-11-7 69 .... MrDAFitzsimmons(7) —
(Mrs P A Rigby) *led after 1st to 8th: rdn and wknd after 9th: t.o whn p.u bef 12th* **80/1**

6m 48.9s (25.70) **Going Correction** +0.60s/f (Soft) **10** Ran SP% **113.0**
Speed ratings: **82,76,76,72,71 —,—,—,—,—** CSF £44.99 TOTE £5.40: £1.40, £3.30, £5.50; EX 27.80.
Owner D Pugh **Bred** Thoroughbred Investments **Trained** Shrewsbury, Shropshire

FOCUS
Only the winner and the below-par Cobreces had shown any worthwhile form this year. The winning time was very moderate even for a hunter chase, almost 17 seconds slower than the preceding handicap. The form is rated through the winner to his best, but the time was very slow.

NOTEBOOK
An Capall Dubh(IRE) appreciated being back up to three miles and had no problem handling ground much softer than he is normally seen on. *(op 7-2)*
The Lyme Volunteer(IRE) seemed to be helped by a return to the sort of tactics that saw him successful at Hereford in March last year.
Kingston-Banker had been let down by his jumping when failing to complete in his three previous starts under Rules this year. *(op 18-1)*
Cobreces was disappointing and favourite backers already knew their fate when he missed out at the third last. *(tchd 11-8)*

5014 MAELOR H'CAP HURDLE (11 hdls) 2m 4f
5:00 (5:00) (Class 4) (0-100,100) 4-Y-0+ **£3,426** (£998; £499)

Form RPR
3143 **1** **Chickapeakray**[32] [4568] 5-10-13 **87** .... PaddyAspell 93
(D McCain) *hld up in mid-div: hdwy on ins to ld 6th: rdn after 2 out: hld on gamely* **4/1**[1]

04 **2** *nk* **Longueville Manor (FR)**[17] [4731] 5-11-5 **93** .... NoelFehily 99
(Jonjo O'Neill) *hld up and bhd: stdy hdwy 6th: sltly hmpd 8th: rdn and ev ch flat: nt qckn* **9/2**[2]

6F60 **3** *12* **Porak (IRE)**[6] [4879] 9-11-7 **100** .... DerekLaverty(5) 96+
(W Davies) *hld up in tch: rdn and ev ch appr 2 out: wkng whn lft 3rd and hmpd last* **20/1**

0556 **4** *3* **La Marette**[16] [4756] 8-10-13 **92** .... MarkNicolls(5) 83
(John Allen) *hld up towards rr: rdn after 6th: hdwy after 3 out: no imp fr 2 out* **15/2**

P001 **5** *shd* **Suprendre Espere**[5] [4919] 6-11-4 **92** 7ex .... JosephByrne 85+
(Jennie Candlish) *prom: blnd 8th and 3 out: rdn and swtchd rt 2 out: sn wknd* **8/1**

5P04 **6** *5* **The Flyer (IRE)**[13] [4805] 9-11-3 **98** ....(tp) RichardSpate(7) 90+
(Miss S J Wilton) *led to 6th: rdn and wknd appr 2 out* **9/1**

0F00 **7** *8* **Salt Cellar (IRE)**[9] [4834] 7-11-6 **94** .... TomSiddall 72
(R S Brookhouse) *a bhd* **20/1**

500P **8** *nk* **Shady Anne**[47] [4282] 8-10-8 **92** ....(p) ThomasBurrows(10) 69
(F Jordan) *chsd ldr tl after 5th: sn rdn: wknd 8th: mstke 3 out* **12/1**

1/ **9** *dist* **Blackies All (USA)**[755] [4605] 8-11-9 **97** .... AndrewTinkler —
(W M Brisbourne) *hld up and bhd: sme hdwy after 5th: rdn appr 7th: sn struggling: t.o* **25/1**

P-P6 **P** **Mike Simmons**[13] [4805] 10-11-4 **92** .... BarryFenton —
(L P Grassick) *a bhd: rdn appr 6th: t.o whn p.u bef 3 out* **28/1**

32P0 **P** **Baikaline (FR)**[101] [3345] 7-11-10 **98** .... WayneHutchinson —
(Ian Williams) *hld up in tch: wknd 6th: t.o whn p.u bef 8th* **11/1**

020 **F** **Fleurette**[14] [4781] 6-11-11 **99** .... TomDoyle 103
(D R Gandolfo) *hld up and bhd: hdwy on ins 8th: hrd rdn and ev ch whn fell last* **13/2**[3]

0P5P **P** **Sommelier**[33] [4549] 6-11-0 **95** .... BernieWharfe(7) —
(N A Twiston-Davies) *prom: hit 4th: mstke 6th: wknd appr 8th: bhd whn p.u bef 3 out* **12/1**

5m 5.30s (7.70) **Going Correction** +0.60s/f (Soft) **13** Ran SP% **124.9**
Speed ratings: **108,107,103,101,101 99,96,96,—,— —,—,—** CSF £22.47 CT £336.34 TOTE £4.10: £1.60, £2.20, £7.80; EX 16.80.
Owner Ray Pattison **Bred** J Singleton **Trained** Cholmondeley, Cheshire

FOCUS
Not many came into this race in form and the winner is the best guide to the form.

NOTEBOOK
Chickapeakray did not mind being back on ground with some give in it and showed the right sort of attitude to justify being a well-backed favourite. *(op 13-2)*
Longueville Manor(FR), trying a longer trip, found that the winner simply refused to be beaten when he was eventually let down. *(tchd 5-1)*
Porak(IRE) has yet to prove he can be effective at this sort of trip.
La Marette was 2lb higher than when possibly a lucky winner of this event on even softer ground last year. *(op 13-2)*
Suprendre Espere, penalised for his Sedgefield win earlier in the week, was let down by his jumping. *(op 15-2)*
The Flyer(IRE) did not find a drop back in distance the answer. *(op 11-1)*
Fleurette was one of three in line but flat to the boards when crashing out at the final flight. *(tchd 7-1)*

5015 CHARITY DAY NOVICES' HURDLE (DIV II) (12 hdls) 3m
5:30 (5:30) (Class 4) 4-Y-0+ **£3,187** (£935; £467; £233)

Form RPR
21 **1** **Nobody Tells Me (FR)**[29] [4604] 5-10-13 .... AndrewGlassonbury(7) 116+
(M C Pipe) *chsd ldrs: rdn appr 8th: chalng whn mstke 3 out: sn outpcd: rallied to ld bef last: styd on wl to draw clr* **8/11**[1]

2 *3 ½* **Travel Agent (IRE)** 6-10-9 .... MrTJO'Brien(5) 105
(P J Hobbs) *chsd ldrs: led after 6th: hdd after 7th: remained prom: rdn and ev ch appr last: no ex run-in* **22/1**

4244 **3** *½* **Five Alley (IRE)**[14] [4785] 9-10-11 97 .... WilliamKennedy(3) 104
(R H Buckler) *disp ld: hdd after 6th: sn rdn: regained ld after 7th: outpcd after 4 out: styd on again run-in* **18/1**

3126 **4** *2 ½* **Gritti Palace (IRE)**[63] [3969] 6-11-6 120 .... HenryOliver 108
(John R Upson) *disp ld: hdd after 6th: rdn appr 4 out: sn outpcd: kpt on again run-in* **10/1**

6302 **5** *2 ½* **Campaign Charlie**[41] [4386] 6-11-0 100 .... MarkBradburne 103+
(H D Daly) *in tch: led 4 out: mstke next: rdn whn mstke 2 out: hdd appr last: sn btn* **10/1**

443P **6** *nk* **Marshalls Run (IRE)**[16] [4750] 6-11-0 .... WayneHutchinson 101+
(A King) *prom: rdn and outpcd appr 3 out: no imp after* **9/1**[3]

50-6 **7** *27* **Acacia Avenue (IRE)**[43] [4359] 6-11-0 .... DaveCrosse 72
(Ian Williams) *hld up in midfield: lost tch w ldrs after 3 out* **50/1**

/0-P **8** *3 ½* **Fieldings Society (IRE)**[9] [4826] 7-11-0 .... JosephByrne 68
(Jennie Candlish) *hld up bhd: rdn after 7th: nvr on terms* **100/1**

6/6 **9** *14* **Christon Cane**[50] 4212 8-11-0 .... AndrewThornton 54
(Dr J R J Naylor) *t.k.h: a bhd* **100/1**

01 **10** *½* **Twofan (USA)**[24] 4661 5-11-6 .... (p) DNRussell 60
(C Byrnes, Ire) *hld up: blnd 5th: stdy hdwy whn mstke 8th: sn btn* **9/2**[2]

06P- **11** *dist* **Newgate Suds**[600] 1319 9-10-2 .... DerekLaverty[(5)] —
(Mark Campion) *plld hrd: sn in midfield: wknd 8th: t.o* **100/1**

000 **P** **Dark Rosalina**[33] 4554 5-10-2 .... LiamTreadwell[(5)] —
(C W Moore) *a bhd: t.o whn p.u bef 3 out* **100/1**

UPP0 **P** **Casas (IRE)**[35] 4487 9-11-0 67 .... (vt) PaddyAspell —
(J R Norton) *midfield: lost pl 5th: sn struggling and bhd: t.o whn p.u bef 2 out* **100/1**

6m 17.4s (20.60) **Going Correction** +0.60s/f (Soft) **13** Ran SP% **120.8**
Speed ratings: **89,87,87,86,86 85,76,75,71,70** —,—,— CSF £22.66 TOTE £1.70: £1.10, £3.90, £4.30; EX 23.00 Place 6 £311.05, Place 5 £77.54.
Owner B A Kilpatrick **Bred** D Pigouchet & Catherine Doucet **Trained** Nicholashayne, Devon

FOCUS
A slow pace meant the winning time was over 12 seconds slower than the first division. The form looks sound enough with the majority of the first five close to their marks.

NOTEBOOK
Nobody Tells Me(FR), stepping up to three miles, scored in the style of an out-and-out stayer who would have preferred a stronger gallop. *(op 4-5 after Evens and 10-11 in places, tchd 5-6)*
Travel Agent(IRE) ◆, a half-brother to the decent staying chaser Frantic Tan, made a highly satisfactory debut. Normal improvement should see him pick up a similar contest. *(op 25-1)*
Five Alley(IRE) would have preferred a stronger-run race on this switch back to hurdles. *(op 22-1)*
Gritti Palace(IRE) had been highly tried when last seen at Haydock in February. *(op 11-1)*
Campaign Charlie was let down by his jumping over this longer trip once he struck the front. *(op 9-1)*
Marshalls Run(IRE) was another attempting three miles for the first time.
Twofan(USA) *Official explanation: trainer was unable to offer any explanation for poor form shown (op 4-1 tchd 7-2)*
T/Plt: £91.10 to a £1 stake. Pool: £39,651.10. 317.40 winning tickets. T/Qpdt: £21.70 to a £1 stake. Pool: £3,201.00. 108.70 winning tickets. KH

4416 STRATFORD (L-H)
Sunday, April 23

OFFICIAL GOING: Good (good to firm in places)
The tricky second-last fence has been removed and a portable fence has been installed after what was the last fence, leaving a very short run-in.
Wind: Light, across Weather: Overcast

5016 TOTEPLACEPOT NOVICES' HURDLE (12 hdls) 2m 6f 110y
2:30 (2:29) (Class 3) 4-Y-0+

£6,263 (£1,850; £925; £463; £231; £116)

Form RPR

2002 **1** **Mikado**[7] 4868 5-11-6 123 .... APMcCoy 115+
(Jonjo O'Neill) *a.p: rdn to ld after 3 out: sn clr: styd on* **10/11**[1]

202P **2** *8* **French Envoy (FR)**[43] 4373 7-11-0 111 .... PJBrennan 103+
(Ian Williams) *hld up: hdwy 6th: rdn and outpcd 3 out: wnt 2nd 2 out: no imp whn nt fluent last* **6/4**[2]

P25 **3** *5* **Izzyizzenty**[76] 3779 7-10-9 .... TJDreaper[(5)] 97+
(J M Jefferson) *w ldr: led after 2nd tl after 3rd: led 5th tl after 3 out: sn wknd* **16/1**[3]

-614 **4** *12* **Forest Dante (IRE)**[129] 2841 13-11-0 91 .... (p) KennyJohnson 84
(F Kirby) *led tl after 2nd: led after 3rd to 5th: wknd 8th* **16/1**[3]

P0PP **5** *6* **Roseville (IRE)**[4] 4956 6-10-4 59 .... ChrisHonour[(3)] 71
(S T Lewis) *hld up: blnd 2nd: struggling fr 8th* **200/1**

P/0 **6** *½* **Sun Hill**[15] 4784 6-10-7 .... AdrianScholes[(7)] 78
(D Burchell) *hld up: nt fluent 1st: struggling fr 6th* **28/1**

00-0 **F** **Nettleton Flyer**[18] 4732 5-11-0 .... MatthewBatchelor —
(Miss J S Davis) *hld up: last tl fell 6th* **100/1**

0-0P **P** **Kossies Mate**[114] 3131 7-10-2 .... JamesDiment[(5)] —
(P W Hiatt) *plld hrd in tch: jnd ldrs 5th: wknd after 7th: t.o whn p.u bef 2 out* **100/1**

5m 26.2s (-3.50) **Going Correction** -0.05s/f (Good) **8** Ran SP% **110.1**
Speed ratings: **104,101,99,95,93 93**,—,— CSF £2.34 TOTE £2.00: £1.10, £1.30, £1.40; EX 2.60.
Owner John P McManus **Bred** Gerald W Leigh **Trained** Cheltenham, Gloucs

FOCUS
A fair novice event, lacking strength in depth, and the form looks straightforward.

NOTEBOOK
Mikado belatedly got back to winning ways as a hurdler with a commanding success under his penalty. It would come as little surprise should this trip turn out to be his optimum in this sphere, but while his confidence can only be boosted by this experience, he is still flattered by his current official rating and this must rate his easiest task for some time. *(op Evens tchd 11-10)*
French Envoy(FR), last seen pulling up at Sandown in March, disappointingly proved no match for the winner on this return to non-handicap company and did not appear all that straightforward. He may prove happier back over a shorter trip in the future, but he has not progressed from his seasonal debut as expected, and is one to avoid at present. *(op 13-8)*
Izzyizzenty turned in an improved display, yet did little to convince he stays this longer distance. He should find life easier when switching to handicaps and will no doubt appreciate being dropped back in trip. *(op 12-1)*
Forest Dante(IRE), returning from a four-month break, was having his first outing over timber since 2003 and shaped very much as though the race was needed. He can be expected to be sharper next time and will no doubt revert to chasing before long. *(op 12-1)*

5017 TOTECOURSE TO COURSE BEGINNERS' CHASE (18 fncs) 2m 7f
3:00 (3:00) (Class 3) 5-Y-0+

£6,889 (£2,035; £1,017; £509; £254; £127)

Form RPR

222P **1** **Dickensbury Lad (FR)**[29] 4617 6-11-2 115 .... PJBrennan 115+
(J L Spearing) *led: mstkes 11th and 4 out: sn hdd: rdn to ld after 3 out: drvn clr on short run-in* **1/1**[1]

22PP **2** *5* **Wild Is The Wind (FR)**[36] 4504 5-10-8 .... APMcCoy 104+
(Jonjo O'Neill) *hld up in tch: hit 11th: rdn to ld after 4 out: hdd after 3 out: no ex on short run-in* **5/2**[2]

0P55 **3** *17* **Barcelona**[10] 4827 9-10-9 80 .... (t) MissLBrooke[(7)] 95+
(Lady Susan Brooke) *hld up: struggling 13th: styd on fr 3 out: n.d* **50/1**

3-PP **4** *24* **Alphabetic**[100] 3372 9-11-2 100 .... MickFitzgerald 69
(N J Henderson) *prom tl wknd 4 out* **12/1**

05U3 **5** *½* **The Holy Bee (IRE)**[86] 3593 7-11-2 94 .... MarcusFoley 68
(Mrs S J Humphrey) *a bhd: struggling fr 13th* **12/1**

6040 **6** *nk* **Sandywell George**[87] 3577 11-10-11 69 .... (vt) DerekLaverty[(5)] 68
(L P Grassick) *prom tl wknd 14th: no ch whn mstke 3 out* **80/1**

P032 **F** **Herecomestanley**[6] 4918 7-10-11 95 .... CharliePoste[(5)] —
(M F Harris) *nt j.w: hld up: rdn and hdwy after 13th: 5 l 4th whn fell 14th* **7/1**[3]

5m 40.6s
WFA 5 from 6yo+ 4lb **7** Ran SP% **109.7**
CSF £3.60 TOTE £1.80: £1.60, £1.70; EX 5.10.
Owner Thomas D Goodman **Bred** Emmanuel Brac De La Perriere **Trained** Kinnersley, Worcs

FOCUS
A modest beginners' chase which saw the market leaders dominate and come well clear at the finish. The winner was 6lb off his best.

NOTEBOOK
Dickensbury Lad(FR), despite being none too fluent, dug deep approaching the third-last fence and eventually gained a most deserved first success as a chaser. This put an uncharacteristically poor display at Newbury well behind him, he enjoyed the better ground, and this looks to be his best trip. His confidence will have been boosted now and he should have more to offer. *(tchd 5-4)*
Wild Is The Wind(FR), making his chase debut with the cheekpieces left off, had been pulled up on his last two outings over hurdles and this obviously rates a much-improved effort. He ideally prefers softer ground, and was well clear of the rest at the finish, so he ought to build on this and go one better before long. *(op 11-4 tchd 9-4)*
Barcelona tended to run in snatches and never seriously threatened the first two. He was not totally disgraced at the weights, however, and while he remains one to have reservations about, he will find life easier when reverting to handicaps from his current rating. *(op 40-1)*
Alphabetic, pulled up on his last two outings and returning from a 100-day break, faded tamely when it mattered and shaped as though the race was much needed. *(op 9-1)*

5018 TOTESPORT.COM H'CAP CHASE (15 fncs) 2m 4f
3:30 (3:30) (Class 3) (0-130,130) 5-Y-0+

£10,020 (£2,960; £1,480; £740; £369; £185)

Form RPR

2010 **1** **Calatagan (IRE)**[7] 3761 7-11-2 125 .... TJDreaper[(5)] 133+
(J M Jefferson) *mde all: nt fluent 7th: clr appr 2 out: drvn out* **15/2**

6232 **2** *1* **Joey Tribbiani (IRE)**[24] 4677 9-10-11 115 .... WayneHutchinson 122+
(T Keddy) *hld up and bhd: hdwy 11th: rdn to chse wnr appr 2 out: r.o flat* **7/2**[1]

6344 **3** *14* **Cameron Bridge (IRE)**[158] 2272 10-11-7 125 .... PJBrennan 117
(P J Hobbs) *hld up: hdwy to chse wnr 11th: rdn and wknd appr 2 out* **7/2**[1]

04/0 **4** *½* **Ticket To Ride (FR)**[162] 2190 8-11-4 122 .... (tp) WarrenMarston 114
(A J Wilson) *chsd wnr to 11th: sn wknd* **40/1**

3-51 **5** *5* **Smart Savannah**[41] 4417 10-11-3 121 .... TomScudamore 109+
(C Tinkler) *prom: rdn 12th: hit 3 out: sn wknd* **6/1**[3]

0442 **6** *2½* **Saafend Rocket (IRE)**[31] 4592 8-10-7 111 .... MarkBradburne 97+
(H D Daly) *hld up and bhd: short-lived effrt on ins 4 out* **6/1**[3]

3FPU **7** *9* **Le Seychellois (FR)**[101] 3357 6-11-7 130 .... (t) LiamHeard[(5)] 105
(P F Nicholls) *hld up and bhd: short-lived effrt on outside 11th* **11/2**[2]

1436 **8** *5* **Sound Of Cheers**[20] 4721 9-10-3 107 .... (t) KennyJohnson 77
(F Kirby) *prom to 10th* **9/1**

4m 55.9s (-4.10) **Going Correction** -0.05s/f (Good) **8** Ran SP% **112.6**
Speed ratings: **106,105,100,99,97 96,93,91** CSF £33.77 CT £107.58 TOTE £9.20: £2.70, £1.80, £1.60; EX 31.40.
Owner Mr & Mrs J M Davenport **Bred** Mrs S Camacho **Trained** Norton, N Yorks

FOCUS
A decent prize for the class and the form looks fair with the first two coming well clear. The winner improved to the level of his hurdling form but this was probably not form to get carried away with.

NOTEBOOK
Calatagan(IRE), fit from a recent spin on the Flat and having his first outing in this sphere since January, was allowed an easy lead through the first half of the contest, and that proved most decisive, as he hung on to repel the runner-up. He is well suited by this track, showed improved jumping, and has now won twice from as many starts as a chaser. However, he is not as effective when taken on for the early lead, so while open to further improvement he will always be vulnerable. *(op 8-1 tchd 17-2)*
Joey Tribbiani(IRE) gave his all, but could not get past the winner try as he might when it mattered. He may have been better served by a more positive ride over this slightly shorter trip, yet he was still a long way clear of the rest at the finish, and really does deserve a change of fortune. *(op 3-1)*
Cameron Bridge(IRE), returning from a 158-day break, was put in his place from the third fence and, considering he has a decent record when fresh, this has to rate as disappointing. It may be that he needs further now. *(op 9-2)*
Ticket To Ride(FR), who finished last over hurdles on his British debut back in November, produced an improved effort on this return to fences yet still failed to rate a threat. His previous best efforts in France came on soft ground, but he still looks too high in the weights at present nevertheless.
Smart Savannah, making his handicap bow over fences having scored over course and distance in novice company last month, was starting to tread water prior to an error three out and proved disappointing. *(op 11-2)*
Saafend Rocket(IRE) failed to sustain what looked a promising effort from off the pace and ran well below his best. All bar one of his previous wins over jumps have come at Ludlow. *(op 9-2)*
Le Seychellois(FR), returning from a 101-day layoff, was ridden to get this longer trip and ultimately appeared a non-stayer. He is going the wrong way.

5019 TOTEPOOL "A BETTER WAY TO BET" MARES' ONLY H'CAP HURDLE (10 hdls) 2m 3f
4:00 (4:01) (Class 3) (0-120,105) 4-Y-0+

£6,889 (£2,035; £1,017; £509; £254; £127)

Form RPR

5232 **1** **Wee Dinns (IRE)**[8] 4855 5-11-8 101 .... TomScudamore 110+
(M C Pipe) *hld up: hdwy on ins 4th: squeezed through on ins to ld 2 out: readily* **5/1**[2]

0115 **2** *4* **Treaty Flyer (IRE)**[29] 4619 5-11-7 100 .... APMcCoy 101+
(P G Murphy) *hld up: hdwy 6th: rdn and ev ch 2 out: hld whn pckd last* **3/1**[1]

4542 **3** *nk* **Little Venus (IRE)**[41] 4425 6-11-7 100 .... MarkBradburne 100
(H D Daly) *hld up: rdn and hdwy after 3 out: hung lft appr last: one pce* **14/1**

3114 **4** *¾* **Cream Cracker**[246] 1263 8-11-12 105 .... JasonMaguire 104
(R H Alner) *hld up and bhd: hdwy 3 out: one pce fr 2 out* **12/1**

0-16 **5** *5* **Lilac**[268] 1099 7-10-11 90 .... WayneHutchinson 85+
(Evan Williams) *prom: rdn appr 2 out: wknd appr last* **5/1**[2]

6-01 **6** *4* **Up At Midnight**[55] 4151 6-11-9 102 .... MickFitzgerald 94+
(R Rowe) *w ldr: led 3rd: hdd and mstke 2 out: sn wknd* **12/1**

5655 **7** *1¾* **White Dove (FR)**[28] 4641 8-10-9 91 .... JoffretHuet[(3)] 79
(Ian Williams) *prom: mstkes 4th and 3 out: sn wknd* **10/1**

63PP **8** *2½* **Carraig (IRE)**[89] 3550 4-10-3 95 .... MrRhysHughes[(7)] 75
(Evan Williams) *hld up: blnd 1st: bhd fr 3 out* **33/1**

0053 **9** *11* **Desert Secrets (IRE)**[4] 4962 4-10-9 94 .... (p) PJBrennan 63
(J G Portman) *led to 3rd: w ldr tl wknd after 3 out* **11/2**[3]

4463 **R** **Titian Flame (IRE)**[14] 4797 6-10-10 **96**....................(p) TomMessenger(7) —
(D Burchell) *unruly s: ref to r: tk no part* **16/1**

214- **P** **Precious Lucy (FR)**[629] 1104 7-10-11 **90**.................... RichardHobson —
(G F Bridgwater) *hld up and bhd: hdwy appr 7th: wknd after 3 out: bhd whn p.u bef 2 out* **20/1**

4m 30.8s (-4.50) **Going Correction** -0.05s/f (Good)
WFA 4 from 5yo+ 5lb **11** Ran SP% **118.4**
Speed ratings: **107,105,105,104,102 101,100,99,94,**— — CSF £21.02 CT £200.38 TOTE £5.70: £2.40, £1.90, £3.90; EX 27.90 Trifecta £109.60 Pool: £648.52 - 4.20 winning units.
Owner Lord Donoughmore&Countess Donoughmore I **Bred** Swordlestown Stud **Trained** Nicholashayne, Devon

FOCUS
A moderate mares-only handicap, run at a solid pace, and the form looks sound for the grade.

NOTEBOOK
Wee Dinns(IRE), making her handicap debut over timber, opened her account as a hurdler at the fifth attempt and saw out the longer trip well. She had hung both ways when in front last time, but the aid of the rail in the straight negated any chance of a repeat of those antics, and she can be rated value for slightly further. *(op 4-1)*
Treaty Flyer(IRE), back down in trip, ran her race but was firmly put in her place by the winner. She is a decent benchmark for this form. *(tchd 10-3)*
Little Venus(IRE), having her first outing in a handicap, ran near to her recent level in defeat and shaped as though she will be better suited by a longer trip now. *(op 16-1)*
Cream Cracker ◆, making her reappearance after an eight-month break, was not disgraced under the burden of top weight and left the impression she would improve a deal for the outing. She loves fast ground and, on this evidence, looks sure to add to her tally during the summer.
Desert Secrets(IRE), third at Cheltenham four days previously and sporting first-time cheekpieces, *dropped out tamely when push came to shove and clearly found this coming too soon. Official explanation: trainer was unable to offer any explanation for poor form shown (op 9-2)*

5020 TOTESPORT 0800 221 221 HUNTERS' CHASE (FOR THE JOHN AND NIGEL THORNE MEMORIAL CUP) (18 fncs) 2m 7f

4:30 (4:30) (Class 5) 6-Y-O+ **£3,123** (£968; £484; £242)

Form RPR
4-1P **1** **Spring Margot (FR)**[72] 3847 10-12-4 127.......................... MrTGreenall 109+
(David M Easterby) *a.p: lft in ld 9th: hdd 10th: led appr 2 out: r.o* **9/2**[2]

00-P **2** *1* **Maximize (IRE)**[22] 12-11-7 127.................................... MrDEdwards(3) 98
(D M Edwards) *hld up in mid-div: hdwy 7th: led 10th: rdn and hdd appr 2 out: rallied u.p flat* **11/1**

-145 **3** *1* **Millenium Way (IRE)**[8] 12-11-8 .... MrsCLTaylor(7) 102
(Mrs C L Taylor) *hld up: hdwy 12th: styd on fr 2 out* **8/1**

6/U- **4** *20* **Wink And Whisper**[21] 11-10-10 .... MissETory(7) 70
(Mrs H M Tory) *hld up and bhd: hdwy 12th: wknd after 3 out* **7/1**[3]

P3P- **5** *28* **Springwood White**[14] 12-11-3 68.................................. MrTPark(7) 49
(Mrs V Park) *hld up and bhd: hdwy 7th: wknd 4 out* **100/1**

10PP **6** *8* **Corkan (IRE)**[14] 4799 12-11-3 66.............................(v[1]) MrABarlow(7) 41
(Mrs F Kehoe) *prom to 5th: bhd fr 8th* **100/1**

P/P- **7** *2 1/2* **Jarod (FR)**[8] 8-11-3 .... MrSGray(7) 39
(Mark Doyle) *hmpd 1st: a wl bhd* **66/1**

F/11 **U** **Rhythm King**[6] 4897 11-12-1 .... MrGMaundrell(3) —
(G C Maundrell) *bdly hmpd and uns rdr 1st* **5/2**[1]

2F **F** **Lord Nellerie (FR)**[10] 4831 7-11-8 112......................... MrGOpperman(7) —
(B G Powell) *led: blnd 6th: 3 l clr whn fell 9th* **7/1**[3]

15U- **U** **Lord Youky (FR)**[21] 12-11-3 108......................... MissJodieHughes(7) —
(Miss J Hughes) *prom whn blnd and uns rdr 3rd* **12/1**

-PPP **P** **Mustang Molly**[8] 14-11-3 72............................. MrAndrewMartin(5) —
(Andrew J Martin) *prom to 4th: t.o whn p.u bef 11th* **40/1**

20/P **U** **Gudlage (USA)**[8] 10-11-3 ....(t) MissVShaw(7) —
(Mrs P J Shaw) *plld hrd: sn prom: 3 l 3rd whn blnd and uns rdr 7th* **40/1**

4-13 **P** **Royal Snoopy (IRE)**[332] 512 13-11-8 93.................(b) MrABrahams(7) —
(R Tate) *prom tl wknd 10th: mstke 13th: t.o whn p.u bef 2 out* **20/1**

0F-6 **U** **The Granby (IRE)**[30] 4607 12-11-3 88.........................(p) MrsHKemp(7) —
(Mrs H M Kemp) *hld up and bhd: j.lft 1st: mstke 5th: hdwy 8th: 4 l 4th whn blnd and uns rdr 11th* **20/1**

5m 44.4s **14** Ran SP% **116.8**
CSF £47.86 TOTE £5.30: £2.80, £3.60, £3.00; EX 68.30.
Owner Gavin Macechern & Lord Daresbury **Bred** Yves Bourdin And Jean-Pierre Rouillay **Trained** Sheriff Hutton, N Yorks

FOCUS
A fair event of its type and, despite the favourite unseating at the first fence, the form still looks solid with the first three coming well clear. It has been rated through the third.

NOTEBOOK
Spring Margot(FR), who had achieved very little in two outings since joining his current connections, showed the benefit of a recent break and got his head back in front under a strong ride. It is interesting that he has now won on his last two outings at this venue and he should build on this now that his confidence will have been boosted. *(op 6-1)*
Maximize(IRE), making his debut in this sphere under Rules, showed there is still life left in him and proved game in defeat. He really needs further, however. *(op 8-1)*
Millenium Way(IRE), back to winning ways in a point eight days previously, was doing his best work at the finish and posted another sound effort. He is another who is happiest over a longer trip, however. *(op 15-2)*
Wink And Whisper ran her race, but has never been the stoutest of stayers, and not that surprisingly failed to make a serious impact over this trip in such company. *(op 13-2 tchd 15-2)*
Rhythm King, chasing a seventh straight success, has to rate as very unlucky to have been hampered at the first fence and is clearly well worth another chance. *(op 6-1)*
Lord Nellerie(FR), who departed early on when very well backed at Ludlow last time, was none too fluent before again coming to grief and is clearly going to be very low on confidence after this unfortunate experience. *(op 6-1)*

5021 TOTEEXACTA NOVICES' H'CAP HURDLE (9 hdls) 2m 110y

5:00 (5:02) (Class 3) (0-120,117) 4-Y-O **£5,704** (£1,684; £842; £421; £210)

Form RPR
364 **1** **Tamreen (IRE)**[37] 4479 5-10-12 **103**...........................(b[1]) JamieMoore 119+
(G L Moore) *hld up in tch: wnt 2nd after 5th: led after 3 out: shkn up and sn clr: eased flat* **16/1**

0540 **2** *6* **Estate**[10] 4838 4-9-10 **97**.. RobertLucey-Butler(5) 96+
(R S Brookhouse) *hld up and bhd: nt fluent 1st: hdwy after 3 out: wnt 2nd and hit 2 out: no ch w wnr* **20/1**

1214 **3** *1 1/4* **Rojabaa**[8] 4848 7-11-0 **110**.. LiamHeard(5) 112
(B D Leavy) *hld up in mid-div: lost pl appr 3 out: rdn and hdwy appr 2 out: r.o flat* **15/2**

2201 **4** *1* **Dhehdaah**[11] 4478 5-11-10 **115**.. WarrenMarston 117+
(Mrs P Sly) *a.p: mstke 5th: rdn after 3 out: one pce fr 2 out* **13/2**[3]

1121 **5** *1 3/4* **According To Pete**[61] 4040 5-10-11 **107**.............................. TJDreaper(5) 106
(J M Jefferson) *hld up in mid-div: rdn appr 6th: nt fluent 3 out: no real prog* **11/4**[1]

1006 **6** *1 3/4* **Muntami (IRE)**[10] 4834 5-10-9 **100**.. AndrewTinkler 98
(John A Harris) *prom: rdn 6th: wknd appr 2 out* **14/1**

123P **7** *1/2* **Almizan (IRE)**[179] 1880 6-11-4 **109**.. PhilipHide 106
(G L Moore) *mid-div: hit 6th: sn lost pl: n.d after* **20/1**

41 **8** *1/2* **Kingham**[25] 4665 6-11-12 **117**.. CarlLlewellyn 116+
(Mrs Mary Hambro) *led: sn clr: hit 3rd and 4th: hdd after 3 out: wknd 2 out* **9/2**[2]

6644 **9** *1/2* **Xamborough (FR)**[58] 4093 5-11-1 **106**.............................. MickFitzgerald 102
(B G Powell) *chsd ldr to 5th: wknd 3 out* **9/1**

0540 **10** *1 1/2* **Pawn Broker**[70] 3889 9-10-7 **98**.......................................(b) MarcusFoley 93
(Miss J R Tooth) *hit 3rd: a towards rr* **20/1**

P040 **11** *4* **Oktis Morilious (IRE)**[10] 4828 5-9-7 **91** oh17.................. MrDEngland(7) 82
(J A Danahar) *mid-div: rdn after 6th: sn struggling* **150/1**

F-36 **12** *13* **La Dolfina**[199] 1651 6-10-9 **100**.. PJBrennan 78
(P J Hobbs) *hld up and bhd: nt fluent 1st and 4th: mstke 5th: sn struggling* **12/1**

P01 **13** *3 1/2* **Benefit Fund (IRE)**[60] 4056 6-9-6 **93**.......................... RyanCummings(10) 67
(D J Wintle) *mstkes 3rd and 6th: a bhd* **33/1**

3m 53.7s (-4.70) **Going Correction** -0.05s/f (Good)
WFA 4 from 5yo+ 5lb **13** Ran SP% **118.1**
Speed ratings: **109,106,105,105,104 103,103,103,102,102 100,94,92** CSF £294.74 CT £2590.89 TOTE £12.40: £4.90, £7.00, £3.10; EX 370.10 Place 6 £71.54, Place 5 £67.22.
Owner Alan Brazil Racing Club Ltd **Bred** Shadwell Estate Company Limited **Trained** Woodingdean, E Sussex

FOCUS
A modest handicap, run at a solid pace, and the form looks fair enough for the class. A big step up from the winner, value for double the winning margin.

NOTEBOOK
Tamreen(IRE), with the cheekpieces replaced by first-time blinkers for this return to handicap company, ultimately ran out an easy winner and is value for around double his winning margin. This better ground played to his strengths, but it is more likely the blinkers that brought about the vast improvement, and his future hopes rest on them having the same effect in the future. *(op 12-1)*
Estate was none too convincing over his hurdles, but still emerged to finish a clear second best, and this must rate a personal-best effort as a hurdler. He could be ready to tackle further now, and *is at the right end of the handicap to progress, but must improve in the jumping department. (tchd 25-1)*
Rojabaa continues in good form at present and helps set the level of this form. He ideally wants easier ground, but may just be in the Handicapper's grip now. *(op 13-2)*
Dhehdaah, raised 5lb for his latest success in this sphere and runner-up on the Flat on his most recent start 11 days previously, is another who ideally wants softer ground and was beaten from the penultimate flight. On this sort of ground, he may well be capable of getting closer when faced with a stiffer test. *(op 7-1 tchd 6-1)*
According To Pete, making his handicap debut, never really looked like following up his Sedgefield success and failed to improve as expected for this less taxing ground. He looked attractively *handicapped prior to this, so must rate disappointing, but is not one to write off on this display. (op 3-1)*
Kingham, a clear-cut winner of a weak maiden last time, was not particularly fluent on this handicap bow and was put in his place with three to jump. He looks badly handicapped on this evidence. *(op 6-1)*
T/Jkpt: Not won. T/Plt: £84.50 to a £1 stake. Pool: £63,188.60. 545.60 winning tickets. T/Qpdt: £57.40 to a £1 stake. Pool: £3,444.00. 44.40 winning tickets. KH

4833 WINCANTON (R-H)

Sunday, April 23

OFFICIAL GOING: Good
Wind: Virtually nil

5022 BATHWICK TYRES CONDITIONAL JOCKEYS' H'CAP HURDLE (8 hdls) 2m

1:50 (1:50) (Class 4) (0-105,102) 4-Y-O+ **£3,083** (£898; £449)

Form RPR
0F05 **1** **Avesomeofthat (IRE)**[10] 4834 5-11-0 **93**.................. WayneKavanagh(3) 98+
(J W Mullins) *chsd ldr: led after 5th: rdn after 2 out: kpt on gamely: drvn out* **3/1**[1]

3454 **2** *1 1/2* **Hail The King (USA)**[17] 4756 6-11-12 **102**.......................... JohnKington 103
(R M Carson) *hld up in tch: hdwy after 5th: pressed wnr appr 2 out: sn rdn: swtchd lft appr last: no ex* **7/2**[2]

F004 **3** *5* **Brown Fox (FR)**[5] 4941 5-9-11 **76** oh1........................(t) JayPemberton(3) 72
(C J Down) *chsd ldrs: nt fluent 2nd: ev ch appr 2 out: sn rdn : one pce fr next* **8/1**[3]

5440 **4** *3* **Hunting Lodge (IRE)**[33] 4566 5-11-2 **95**.......................... DavidBoland(3) 88
(H J Manners) *in tch: rdn after 3 out: sn one pce* **8/1**[3]

/05P **5** *9* **Alf Lauren**[30] 4604 8-11-6 **96**.. SeanQuinlan 80
(A King) *chsd ldrs: rdn after 4th: wknd after 3 out* **10/1**

5300 **6** *7* **Tytheknot**[66] 3944 5-10-12 **91**...................................... RyanCummings(3) 69+
(O Sherwood) *chsd ldrs early: grad fdd fr 4th* **8/1**[3]

0P-4 **7** *1 3/4* **Royal Prodigy (USA)**[346] 310 7-11-2 **92**..........................(b) KeiranBurke 67
(R J Hodges) *led: clr 3rd: hdd after 5th: sn wknd* **12/1**

0-00 **P** **Heriot**[344] 357 5-10-5 **81**.. SimonElliott —
(S C Burrough) *bhd fr 4th: t.o and p.u bef 2 out* **66/1**

0U60 **F** **Carpet Ride**[6] 4903 4-9-9 **82**...(t) RichardKilloran(6) 50
(B G Powell) *hld up: rdn after 5th: btn 6th whn fell 2 out* **10/1**

3m 45.3s (-3.80) **Going Correction** -0.075s/f (Good)
WFA 4 from 5yo+ 5lb **9** Ran SP% **107.9**
Speed ratings: **106,105,102,101,96 93,92,**—,— CSF £12.60 CT £62.63 TOTE £4.30: £1.60, £1.40, £2.40; EX 12.80.
Owner K J Pike **Bred** Michael Dalton **Trained** Wilsford-Cum-Lake, Wilts

FOCUS
A moderate contest, but it may produce the odd winner at a similarly poor level.

NOTEBOOK
Avesomeofthat(IRE), one of six coming into this still a maiden, held an obvious chance on the best of his previous efforts and the weight difference between he and the runner-up told after the last. He should continue to pay his way at a moderate level. *(tchd 11-4)*
Hail The King(USA), expected to be helped by the drop back in trip, often travels strongly without finding much and today was no different. He was giving 12lb to the winner and that may have been the difference. *(op 3-1)*
Brown Fox(FR) has definitely improved since being fitted with a tongue tie and she plugged on into third. She can find a lowly contest in the summer months.
Hunting Lodge(IRE) is not really progressing and he remains winless over jumps. *(op 10-1)*
Alf Lauren continues to disappoint and probably needs switching to fences sooner rather than later. *(op 9-1 tchd 11-1)*

5023 BATHWICK TYRES BRIDGWATER NOVICES' HURDLE (DIV I) (8 hdls) 2m

2:20 (2:21) (Class 4) 4-Y-0+ **£2,740** (£798; £399)

Form RPR
665 **1** **Cold Mountain (IRE)**[64] 3996 4-10-6 104 RichardYoung(3) 98
(J W Mullins) *hld up mid dvision: smooth hdwy after 5th: trckd ldr appr 2 out: chal last: sn rdn into narrow advantage: drvn out* **16/1**[2]
211P **2** *nk* **Bureaucrat**[16] 4763 4-11-9 135 RichardJohnson 112
(P J Hobbs) *slowly away: led 2nd: rdn and hung lft fr 2 out: narrowly hdd sn after last: no ex* **2/11**[1]
P6 **3** *28* **Lord Of Methley**[33] 4564 7-11-0 (t) AntonyEvans 78+
(S Lycett) *hld up towards rr: hdwy after 5th: wnt 3rd appr 2 out but no ch w ldng pair: wnt rt last* **150/1**
PP2 **4** *3/4* **Bold Trump**[13] 4278 5-11-0 JodieMogford 74
(Mrs N S Evans) *prom tl 4th: chsd ldr: rdn after 3 out: wknd bef next* **25/1**[3]
00/0 **5** *6* **Court Emperor**[17] 4754 6-11-0 PaulMoloney 68
(Evan Williams) *a towards rr* **50/1**
-60R **6** *5* **Indigo Sky (IRE)**[18] 1774 5-10-9 64 JohnnyLevins(5) 63
(B G Powell) *led tl 2nd: chsd ldrs: rdn after 5th: wknd appr 2 out* **66/1**
5 **7** *13* **Lyrical Girl (USA)**[10] 4828 5-10-0 WillieMcCarthy(7) 43
(H J Manners) *chsd ldrs: hit 2nd: wknd 3 out* **50/1**
0P **8** *dist* **Barjou (NZ)**[64] 3996 5-11-0 (v[1]) RobertThornton —
(A King) *mid div: rdn after 4th: sn wknd: t.o* **25/1**[3]
0 **9** *1 1/2* **Roche Ecossaise (FR)**[45] 4327 7-10-7 AndrewThornton —
(R H Alner) *mid div tl 5th: sn t.o* **100/1**
0PP **P** **Valleyofthekings (IRE)**[114] 3131 5-11-0 LeightonAspell —
(O Sherwood) *a bhd: t.o and p.u after 3 out* **50/1**

3m 43.6s (-5.50) **Going Correction** -0.075s/f (Good) **10** Ran SP% **107.2**
Speed ratings: **110,109,95,95,92 89,83,—,—,—** CSF £18.60 TOTE £7.80: £1.50, £1.02, £10.80; EX 17.60.
Owner Woodford Valley Racing **Bred** Skymarc Farm **Trained** Wilsford-Cum-Lake, Wilts

FOCUS
A decent winning time for the grade, five seconds faster than the second division, and the front two pulled right away with Cold Mountain causing quite an upset.

NOTEBOOK
Cold Mountain(IRE), a poor performer on the Flat in Ireland, had already suggested he was going to make a better hurdler and he got off the mark at the fourth attempt over obstacles, battling on strongly after the last to cause an upset. He is likely to take a hike up the weights for this and, as a result, may find life tough in handicaps unless improving again. *(op 12-1)*
Bureaucrat, who found the jump into graded company beyond him at Aintree, had plenty of weight to shoulder, but he was still expected to capitalise on the drop in grade and it looked for much of the journey as though he was going to do so. However, Johnson began to shove away on the four-year-old rounding for home and the difference in weight told close home. This was disappointing, but it is entirely possible he has had enough for the season and it will be interesting to see which route connections take next term. *(op 1-5)*
Lord Of Methley did best of the rest, but that is not saying much and it is highly unlikely he will be winning until contesting low-grade handicaps. *(op 100-1)*
Bold Trump ran pretty much as expected on this return to hurdles and is another for whom moderate handicaps beckon. *(op 33-1)*
Barjou(NZ)

5024 BATHWICK TYRES BRIDGWATER NOVICES' HURDLE (DIV II) (8 hdls) 2m

2:50 (2:54) (Class 4) 4-Y-0+ **£2,740** (£798; £399)

Form RPR
0F00 **1** **Dreams Jewel**[10] 2455 6-11-0 OllieMcPhail 87+
(C Roberts) *mid div: outpcd after 5h: styng on whn lft 2nd and stmbld 2 out: led sn after last: rdn out* **20/1**
2 *2 1/2* **Magic Merlin**[92] 5-11-0 JimmyMcCarthy 84+
(C P Morlock) *mid div: stdy prog after 3 out: rdn whn lft in ld 2 out: hdd sn after last: no ex* **25/1**
P0-6 **3** *4* **Night Warrior (IRE)**[53] 2721 6-11-0 PaulMoloney 79
(N P Littmoden) *lost tch 4th: stdy prog fr 3 out: lft 4th 2 out: wnt 3rd at the last: kpt on* **20/1**
PP0 **4** *dist* **Mr Mayfair (IRE)**[34] 4550 4-10-9 BenjaminHitchcott —
(Miss L Day) *t.k.h: taked ldrs tl 5th: sn wknd: lft remote 4th at the last* **125/1**
P **Superfling**[519] 5-10-7 MrRMcCarthy(7) —
(H J Manners) *a bhd: t.o and p.u bef 2 out* **50/1**
P **U** **The Last Sabo**[14] 4795 4-10-2 MrSRees(7) —
(M Wigham) *sn t.o: blnd and uns rdr last* **150/1**
P **Polonius**[50] 5 11 0 TomDoyle —
(P R Webber) *t.k.h: trckd ldrs tl wknd qckly 3 out: p.u bef next* **13/2**[2]
00- **P** **Durnovaria (IRE)**[409] 4290 6-10-9 (t) DarylJacob(5) —
(D P Keane) *a bhd: lost tch 4th: t.o and p.u bef 2 out* **33/1**
-346 **F** **Xcentra**[17] 4754 5-10-7 CharlieStudd(7) 72
(B G Powell) *j.rt 1st: chsd ldr: rdn appr 2 out: sn wknd: 4th whn fell last* **14/1**[3]
F154 **U** **Blu Teen (FR)**[36] 4494 6-11-7 125 (t) ChristianWilliams 104+
(P F Nicholls) *led: in command and 10 l clr whn stmbld bdly and uns rdr 2 out* **1/3**[1]

3m 48.6s (-0.50) **Going Correction** -0.075s/f (Good)
WFA 4 from 5yo+ 5lb **10** Ran SP% **114.7**
Speed ratings: **98,96,94,—,— —,—,—,—,—** CSF £331.69 TOTE £28.60: £3.20, £3.40, £3.50; EX 266.70.
Owner Allan Ashcroft **Bred** Allan Ashcroft **Trained** Newport, Newport

FOCUS
A modest winning time, five seconds slower than the first division.

NOTEBOOK
Dreams Jewel, although well-supported in the market beforehand, could not have been expected to win, but he took advantage of the favourites misfortune and stayed on too strongly for the runner-up after the last. He would have finished a respectable second had Blu Teen not unshipped Williams, and it is highly likely there is more to come, with further expected to suit in time. *(op 40-1 tchd 50-1)*
Magic Merlin, a modest sort on the Flat, travelled well on this switch to hurdling but was unable to stay on as strongly as the winner once left in the lead. He is entitled to come on for the run, but gives the impression he barely stays two miles and, as a result, all his best efforts are likely to come on sharp tracks. *(op 20-1)*
Night Warrior(IRE) has been a bit out of sorts on the level in recent weeks, but he shaped well enough on this return to hurdles and may have a small handicap in him.
Polonius, whose best efforts on the Flat were recorded at six and seven furlongs, stopped quickly on turning in and to the naked eye it appeared he blatantly failed to stay. *(op 25-1)*
Blu Teen(FR) was well suited to this drop back down in distance and had the race in the bag when unseating Williams at the second-last. This is the second time this season he has thrown victory away, but nonetheless he remains a good chasing prospect. *(op 25-1)*

Xcentra had run his race and looked weary when falling at the last. It remains to be seen how this affects his confidence. *(op 25-1)*
Durnovaria(IRE) *Official explanation: jockey said gelding had breathing problem (op 25-1)*

5025 BATHWICK TYRES SALISBURY NOVICES' H'CAP CHASE (21 fncs) 3m 1f 110y

3:20 (3:20) (Class 4) (0-110,109) 5-Y-0+ **£5,204** (£1,528; £764; £381)

Form RPR
P431 **1** **Roddy The Vet (IRE)**[7] 4872 8-10-0 82 7ex (b) JimCrowley 103+
(A Ennis) *led: mstke and hdd 15th: prom: led after 17th: lft wl clr next: unchal after: hit 3 out* **6/4**[1]
2PUP **2** *25* **Petolinski**[33] 4558 8-9-11 83 oh6 (p) RichardYoung(3) 67
(C L Popham) *hld up bhd ldrs: wnt 3rd at the 9th: mstke 13th (water): wknd after 16th and j.rt thereafter: lft distant 2nd 4 out* **7/1**[3]
5414 **3** *24* **Roman Court (IRE)**[39] 4451 8-10-12 95 AndrewThornton 55
(R H Alner) *chsd ldrs tl hmpd and lost pl 2nd: sn niggled along: lost tch fr fr 14th: lft remote 3rd 4 out* **11/4**[2]
P656 **4** *6* **Jonanaud**[10] 4827 7-10-13 103 MrRMcCarthy(7) 57
(H J Manners) *hld up: tk clsr order 12th: wknd after 14th: lft remote 4th 4 out* **11/1**
004 **5** *30* **River Indus**[32] 4572 6-10-4 87 BenjaminHitchcott 11
(R H Buckler) *chsd ldrs tl 9th: t.o fr 13th* **7/1**[3]
15-6 **U** **Lowe Go**[12] 4593 6-10-8 91 SeanCurran —
(Miss J S Davis) *j.lft thrght: trckd ldr: led 15th tl after 17th: cl 2nd whn pckd bdly and uns rdr 4 out* **14/1**

6m 39.3s (-0.60) **Going Correction** -0.075s/f (Good) **6** Ran SP% **106.7**
Speed ratings: **97,89,81,80,70** — CSF £10.84 TOTE £2.60: £1.60, £3.80; EX 13.60.
Owner A T A Wates **Bred** John O'Brien **Trained** Beare Green, Surrey

FOCUS
A moderate contest and the debate rages on as to whether Roddy The Vet or Lowe Go, who was still in with every chance when unseating at the fourth last, would have triumphed.

NOTEBOOK
Roddy The Vet(IRE), shouldering a penalty for last weeks Plumpton win, was left with a simple task once Lowe Go unseated, but whether he would have won anyway is open to debate. He may well complete the hat-trick, but the form of his two wins are hardly exhilerating, and connections are toying with the idea of running him back over hurdles in a novice event while he is in good form. *(op 11-8 tchd 13-8)*
Petolinski ran his best race for a while and, although unable to get anywhere near the winner, he did at least manage to complete. *(op 10-1)*
Roman Court(IRE) was never going after being hampered at the second and deserves another chance. *(op 9-4 tchd 3-1)*
Jonanaud has not taken to fences and continues to disappoint. *(op 10-1)*
Lowe Go, who enjoyed a pipe-opener on the Flat earlier in the month, continually jumped out to the left on this chasing debut, but he was still in with every chance when pecking and unseating Curran at the fourth-last. He was booked for at least second, but whether he would have won or not is open to debate. *(op 12-1 tchd 16-1)*

5026 BATHWICK TYRES YEOVIL NOVICES' HURDLE (11 hdls) 2m 6f

3:50 (3:51) (Class 4) 4-Y-0+ **£3,426** (£998; £499)

Form RPR
2535 **1** **Macmar (FR)**[24] 4676 6-11-0 AndrewThornton 107+
(R H Alner) *chsd ldrs: shkn up to ld appr 2 out: clr whn mstke last: readily* **9/4**[1]
55 **2** *13* **Sir Bathwick (IRE)**[30] 4603 7-11-0 NoelFehily 91
(B G Powell) *racd green: hld up: hdwy after 6th: rdn after 3 out: styd on flat : wnt 2nd nr fin* **5/2**[2]
00- **3** *3/4* **Kourosh (IRE)**[540] 1912 6-11-0 JimmyMcCarthy 90
(C P Morlock) *w.r.s: led: rdn and hdd appr 2 out: kpt on same pce* **25/1**
6645 **4** *1 3/4* **Come What Augustus**[86] 3603 4-10-3 97 ShaneWalsh(5) 86+
(R M Stronge) *in tch: jnd ldrs after 8th: led briefly after 3 out: sn rdn: wnt rt and hit last 2 flights: no ex run-in* **10/1**[3]
-200 **5** *23* **Earl Of Forestry (GER)**[128] 2865 5-11-0 (t) ChristianWilliams 74+
(P F Nicholls) *hld up: pushed along fr 5th: wknd after 3 out* **5/2**[2]
P **6** *27* **Flying Dick**[18] 4732 7-11-0 JamesDavies 39
(A G Newcombe) *drvn along fr 6th: a bhd* **50/1**
7 *6* **Smoke Trail (IRE)**[154] 7-11-0 BenjaminHitchcott 33
(R H Buckler) *in tch tl 6th: sn wl bhd* **16/1**
00 **P** **My Mon Amour**[29] 4623 5-10-4 RichardYoung(3) —
(J W Mullins) *too kee hold trcking ldr: wnt rt 4th: mstke 7th and rdr lost iron: sn wknd: t.o and p.u bef 3 out* **40/1**

5m 32.2s (7.10) **Going Correction** -0.075s/f (Good)
WFA 4 from 5yo+ 6lb **8** Ran SP% **111.1**
Speed ratings: **84,79,79,78,70 60,58,—** CSF £7.86 TOTE £3.30: £1.40, £1.30, £4.90; EX 6.70.
Owner E W Carnell **Bred** Vicomte Roger De Soultrait **Trained** Droop, Dorset

FOCUS
A weak novices' hurdle unlikely to produce anything than the occasional future winner. The winning time was very moderate, 13 seconds slower than the later handicap over the same trip.

NOTEBOOK
Macmar(FR) had thus far been disappointing since arriving from France, albeit he had run several good races in defeat, but this was a fine opportunity on his second start over hurdles and, barring a mistake at the last, he never had a moments worry. He seems happy over the smaller obstacles for the time being, and it will be interesting to see what sort of handicap mark he gets. *(op 7-4)*
Sir Bathwick(IRE), expected to be helped by the drop in distance, still showed signs of inexperience and he got going all too late. He can probably pick up a small race if kept on the go through the summer, but will ultimately end up in handicaps. *(op 7-2)*
Kourosh(IRE), a well-bred gelding, shaped pleasingly on this hurdles debut, quickly recovering from whipping around at the start to lead, and he kept on well enough down the straight. There should be more to come.
Come What Augustus appeared to find this trip beyond him, but in fairness he blundered at each of the last two hurdles and maybe that took its toll. *(op 8-1)*
Earl Of Forestry(GER) is evidently one of his stables lesser lights and makes little future appeal after a poor effort. *(tchd 9-4 and 11-4)*
My Mon Amour *Official explanation: jockey said saddle slipped (op 66-1 tchd 33-1)*

5027 BATHWICK TYRES TAUNTON H'CAP CHASE (13 fncs) 2m

4:20 (4:22) (Class 3) (0-120,118) 5-Y-0+ **£6,506** (£1,910; £955; £477)

Form RPR
6-5P **1** **Uncle Wallace**[135] 2748 10-11-0 106 TomDoyle 113+
(P R Webber) *hld up: tk clsr order 9th: led 2 out: r.o wl: pushed out* **13/2**
1P60 **2** *1 1/2* **Barton Park**[10] 4838 6-10-6 98 (t) NoelFehily 102+
(D P Keane) *hld up: tk clsr order 9th: cl up whn mstke 4 out: sn rdn: styd on fr 2 out: wnt 2nd cl home* **14/1**
1536 **3** *hd* **Rooster's Reunion (IRE)**[10] 4829 7-11-10 116 RichardJohnson 118
(D R Gandolfo) *hld up bhd ldrs: tk clsr order 9th: led 3 out: rdn and hdd next: kpt on* **5/1**[3]

333F **4** *6* **Neltina**[29] 4618 10-11-8 **114**.............................. LeightonAspell 111+
(Mrs J E Scrase) *led tl 2nd: led after 4th tl 6th: led 7th: rdn and hdd after 4: swtchd lft and hit 3 out: kpt on same pce* **8/1**

P432 **5** *1 ¼* **Jurado Express (IRE)**[29] 4618 10-11-12 **118**.................... SamThomas 114+
(Miss Venetia Williams) *led 2nd tl after 4th: led 6th tl next: rdn to ld briefly after 4 out: grad fdd fr next* **7/4**[1]

2131 **6** *21* **Wizard Of Edge**[24] 4675 6-10-13 **105**........................(b) ChristianWilliams 79
(R J Hodges) *chsd ldrs: slow jump and lost pl 6th: nvr a danger after* **11/4**[2]

3m 57.8s (-4.10) **Going Correction** -0.075s/f (Good) **6** Ran SP% **110.8**
Speed ratings: **107,106,106,103,102 92** CSF £69.91 TOTE £9.60: £3.50, £3.40; EX 119.30.

Owner Mrs John Webber **Bred** Mrs J Webber **Trained** Mollington, Oxon

FOCUS
Suspect form with the favourites disappointing, but Uncle Wallace was able to return to winning ways and land quite a gamble in the process.

NOTEBOOK
Uncle Wallace ◆ has not raced over this distance since February of last year, but he travelled extremely well off the gallop and moved sweetly into a challenging position towards the end of the back straight. He hit the front two-out with a bold leap, and was never going to be denied once clearing the last, keeping on well under pressure to land quite a gamble. Two and a half miles is within his stamina range, but he seemed more than happy at this distance and would be of interest if turned out under a penalty. *(op 11-1 tchd 12-1)*

Barton Park, a surprise winner at the course over hurdles back in November, had been unable to go on from that, but the combination of the tongue tie and switch to fences appeared to work and he kept on well to claim second after the last. He can find a race off this sort of mark. *(op 16-1)*

Rooster's Reunion(IRE) has taken reasonably well to fences, but he gave the impression here he requires a further drop in the weights before scoring again. *(op 9-2)*

Neltina took them along early, but was always going to be vulnerable to something with a bit of speed in the straight and she found herself readily outpaced. *(op 13-2 tchd 6-1)*

Jurado Express(IRE) has been running well, but winning does not come easy to the ten-year-old these days and this was a bitterly disappointing effort. *(op 6-4)*

Wizard Of Edge has been quietly progressive and was expected to go well at a course he likes, but he was always struggling after a laboured leap at the sixth and the way he dropped away suggests all was not well. *(op 3-1 tchd 7-2)*

5028 BATHWICK TYRES DORCHESTER H'CAP HURDLE (11 hdls) 2m 6f
4:50 (4:50) (Class 4) (0-110,105) 4-Y-0+ **£3,426** (£998; £499)

Form RPR

5005 **1** **Penny Park (IRE)**[51] 4210 7-10-11 **90**.......................... RichardJohnson 101+
(P J Hobbs) *trckd ldrs: wnt prom 7th: led after 3 out: drifted lft after 2 out: styd on wl: eased cl home* **9/2**[1]

324U **2** *9* **Bright Green**[15] 4781 7-11-0 **100**.................................... BernieWharfe[(7)] 99+
(C J Gray) *hld up towards rr: gd hdwy appr 3 out: rdn to chse wnr whn stmbld 2 out: hld whn mstke last* **14/1**

4F-1 **3** *14* **Sou'Wester**[15] 4783 6-10-11 **90**.. JoeTizzard 77+
(C L Tizzard) *plld hrd in mid div: trckd ldrs after 5th: led after 8th: rdn and hdd appr 2 out: wkng whn wnt rt at the last* **5/1**[2]

P02P **4** *5* **Midnight Gold**[12] 4824 6-11-4 **97**.............................. RobertThornton 76
(A King) *chsd ldrs: rdn and effrt after 3 out: kpt on same pce fr next* **6/1**[3]

P201 **5** *nk* **Manawanui**[6] 4912 8-11-9 **102** 7ex.................................. RobertWalford 81
(R H Alner) *drvn along after 6th and nvr bttr than mid div* **8/1**

P161 **6** *8* **Pure Magic (FR)**[10] 4830 5-11-2 **95**.................................. SeanCurran 66
(Miss J S Davis) *led tl after 4th: prom: wknd after 3 out* **7/1**

1545 **7** *2 ½* **Azzemour (FR)**[104] 3325 7-11-2 **100**..........................(t) PaddyMerrigan[(5)] 68
(P F Nicholls) *mid div: hdwy after 7th: rdn after 3 out: wknd bef next* **15/2**

0 **8** *12* **Rivertree (IRE)**[10] 4834 5-10-11 **95**............................ DarylJacob[(5)] 51
(D P Keane) *mid div: gd hdwy after 7th: rdn after 3 out: sn wknd* **11/1**

0P60 **P** **Oakfield Legend**[10] 4826 5-10-12 **91**................................. OllieMcPhail —
(P S Payne) *mid div tl 7th: bhd and p.u bef 2 out* **50/1**

50P0 **P** **It's Rumoured**[12] 4824 6-10-11 **90**...............................(p) JamesDavies —
(Jean-Rene Auvray) *a towards rr: t.o and p.u bef 2 out* **16/1**

0P30 **P** **Finsbury Fred (IRE)**[30] 4606 5-11-12 **105**........................ AntonyEvans —
(N A Twiston-Davies) *nvr travelling in rr: p.u beore 5th* **33/1**

2P00 **P** **Optimistic Alfie**[64] 3997 6-10-10 **96**.............................. CharlieStudd[(7)] —
(B G Powell) *sn struggling: taied offand p.u after 6th* **33/1**

0-PP **P** **Mixed Marriage (IRE)**[39] 4453 8-11-2 **95**.......................... NoelFehily —
(Miss Victoria Roberts) *a towards rr: t.o and p.u after 7th* **66/1**

PP30 **P** **Cockatoo Ridge**[15] 4781 9-11-4 **97**..................................... DaveCrosse —
(N R Mitchell) *prom: led after 4th tl after 8th: wknd after 3 out: p.u bef next* **20/1**

5m 19.2s (-5.90) **Going Correction** -0.075s/f (Good) **14** Ran SP% **119.5**
Speed ratings: **107,103,98,96,96 93,92,88,—,— —,—,—,—** CSF £61.84 CT £331.98 TOTE £6.80: £1.90, £4.80, £2.60; EX 81.00 Place 6 £573.41, Place 5 £374.59.

Owner Patrick Bancroft **Bred** David Twomey **Trained** Withycombe, Somerset

FOCUS
A modest handicap hurdle won in good style by the unexposed Penny Park, who appreciated the step back up in distance.

NOTEBOOK
Penny Park(IRE) ◆, stepping up three furlongs in distance for this second try in handicaps, was a point winner over three miles and it was no surprise to see Johnson ride the gelding positively. He showed a good change of gear to go clear before two out and stayed on strongly, despite still showing signs of greeness, to win with plenty in hand. A future chaser, he has more to offer and can win again before being put away for the year. *(op 13-2)*

Bright Green is largely consistent and the better ground posed no problems. He came through late to claim a clear second, but was never in with a chance of catching the winner.

Sou'Wester, purchased for 11,500gns after winning a selling hurdle at Chepstow earlier in the month, raced very keenly early on, but he still came through to have every chance, going on with the winner, travelling equally as well, before those early exertions took their toll. He can pick up a similar race if settling better in future. *(tchd 11-2)*

Midnight Gold is largely inconsistent and he was well held back in fourth. He remains winless and may need some assistance from the Handicapper. *(op 9-1)*

Manawanui, shouldering a 7lb penalty for winning at Plumpton earlier in the week, was never travelling with any real fluency and gave a rather laboured effort. He would probably have preferred the ground a little slower.

Mixed Marriage(IRE) *Official explanation: jockey said gelding was lame (op 100-1)*

It's Rumoured *Official explanation: jockey said gelding moved poorly (op 100-1)*

Optimistic Alfie *Official explanation: jockey said gelding was never travelling (op 100-1)*

T/Plt: £986.10 to a £1 stake. Pool: £35,459.85. 26.25 winning tickets. T/Qpdt: £547.00 to a £1 stake. Pool: £1,996.00. 2.70 winning tickets. TM

5030 - 5035a (Foreign Racing) - See Raceform Interactive

2262 HEXHAM (L-H)
Monday, April 24

OFFICIAL GOING: Good (good to firm in places)
Wind: Fresh against

5036 LIVING NORTH H'CAP CHASE (15 fncs) 2m 4f 110y
2:30 (2:31) (Class 5) (0-95,95) 5-Y-0+ **£3,083** (£898; £449)

Form RPR

6545 **1** **Rifleman (IRE)**[69] 3915 6-11-1 **89**...............................(t) TomGreenway[(5)] 100+
(Robert Gray) *in tch: hdwy bef 10th: led between last two: styd on strly* **25/1**

5FP **2** *5* **Contract Scotland (IRE)**[153] 2413 11-11-9 **95**...........(p) GaryBerridge[(3)] 101
(L Lungo) *trckd ldrs: effrt between last two: kpt on: nt rch wnr* **12/1**

0PF3 **3** *4* **Assumetheposition (FR)**[9] 4844 6-10-11 **90**..............(p) JohnFlavin[(10)] 92
(R C Guest) *led tl hdd between last two: kpt on same pce* **9/1**

6235 **4** *9* **Gangsters R Us (IRE)**[68] 3930 10-11-5 **95**....................... PhilKinsella[(7)] 88
(A Parker) *in tch: outpcd bef 3 out: n.d after* **9/1**

S0F4 **5** *7* **Panmure (IRE)**[198] 1684 10-11-11 **94**.................................. TonyDobbin 81+
(P D Niven) *hld up towards rr: reminders 6th: outpcd next: rallied u.p after 4 out: no imp fr next* **6/1**[2]

1321 **6** *2 ½* **Now Then Sid**[209] 1570 7-11-9 **92**...................................... KeithMercer 76
(Mrs S A Watt) *chsd ldrs: hung lft 11th: wknd next* **7/2**[1]

-421 **7** *shd* **Primitive Way**[184] 1837 14-11-3 **89**..............................(p) DougieCostello[(3)] 72
(Miss S E Forster) *chsd ldrs to 4 out: sn rdn and wknd* **9/1**

413P **8** *3 ½* **Cedar Rapids (IRE)**[40] 4454 6-11-10 **93**............................ DavidO'Meara 73
(H P Hogarth) *in tch: outpcd whn hit 11th: sn btn* **7/1**[3]

0220 **9** *1* **The Miner**[21] 4721 8-11-0 **90**.....................................(p) TomMessenger[(7)] 69
(Miss S E Forster) *nt fluent in rr: struggling fr 9th* **8/1**

/1-P **10** *dist* **Barcham Again (IRE)**[21] 4721 9-11-5 **93**..................(p) DeclanMcGann[(5)] —
(Mrs C J Kerr) *nt fluent: sn bhd: lost tch fr 1/2-way* **33/1**

-UPP **P** **Looking Forward**[7] 4920 10-11-9 **92**................................. BarryKeniry —
(Mrs S A Watt) *prom tl lost pl and p.u after 2nd* **12/1**

5m 0.90s (-10.50) **Going Correction** -0.50s/f (Good) **11** Ran SP% **112.3**
Speed ratings: **100,98,96,93,90 89,89,88,87,—,—** CSF £278.12 CT £2890.40 TOTE £17.60: £5.10, £5.60, £2.60; EX 226.80.

Owner Naughty Diesel Ltd **Bred** James Hanly, Trevor Stewart And Anthony Stroud **Trained** Malton, N Yorks

FOCUS
A moderate handicap, run at a fair pace, and the field came home fairly strung out. The race has been rated through the second and third.

NOTEBOOK
Rifleman(IRE), returning from a 69-day break, ran out a very ready winner and at last broke his duck over jumps at the 23rd time of asking. He had proved fiendishly tricky since starting his National Hunt career, often throwing away his chances, but this was a taking display and he is value for further than his winning margin. While it should be noted that this was the lowest mark he has competed off in this sphere, it is impossible to know whether he will now go on from this, and his next outing will reveal more. *(op 20-1)*

Contract Scotland(IRE), last seen pulling up at Sedgefield five months previously, stuck to his task well from two out and made an encouraging return to action. He should be sharper for this experience and will appreciate the return to a suitably longer trip in the future. *(op 9-1)*

Assumetheposition(FR) ran his race from the front and helps set the level of this form. His *tendency to race freely through the early stages of his races remains his downfall, however. (op 8-1 tchd 10-1)*

Gangsters R Us(IRE) ran below his best on this return from a break and failed to threaten. He may well prove happier when returning to three miles, but he remains winless since 2004, and remains one to avoid in the main. *(op 8-1 tchd 10-1)*

Now Then Sid turned in a fairly lifeless effort on this first outing since September and has it to prove now. *(op 9-2)*

5037 GG MEDIA NOVICES' H'CAP CHASE (19 fncs) 3m 1f
3:00 (3:01) (Class 4) (0-105,102) 5-Y-0+ **£3,578** (£1,050; £525; £262)

Form RPR

066 **1** **Bafana Boy**[36] 4530 6-10-6 **82**.. AlanDempsey 88+
(N G Richards) *hld up in tch: prom 5th: led 3 out: styd on strly fr last* **14/1**

-233 **2** *2 ½* **Aston (USA)**[199] 1664 6-11-4 **94**.................................... KennyJohnson 99+
(R C Guest) *hld up in tch: prom 5th: effrt whn hmpd between last 2: kpt on fr last: nt rch wnr* **7/1**[3]

4144 **3** *2 ½* **Chabrimal Minster**[36] 4518 9-11-12 **102**....................... RichardMcGrath 104+
(R Ford) *lft in ld 1st: hdd 3 out: kpt on same pce bef last* **5/1**[2]

P3-2 **4** *26* **Coy Lad (IRE)**[9] 4844 9-10-10 **86**.. TonyDobbin 76+
(Miss P Robson) *keen in tch: bdly hmpd 5th: sn rcvrd: wknd fr 3 out* **7/2**[1]

P500 **5** *14* **Bramble Princess (IRE)**[15] 4788 7-9-12 **77**...........(p) DougieCostello[(3)] 37
(Miss Lucinda V Russell) *in tch: hmpd 5th: sn rcvrd: rdn and wknd after 4 out* **25/1**

5505 **6** *1 ¼* **Try Catch Paddy (IRE)**[15] 4788 8-10-12 **98**................ DavidDaSilva[(10)] 56
(P Monteith) *bhd: j. slowly 5th: sme hdwy bef 13th: wknd bef 4 out* **16/1**

1P40 **U** **Move Over (IRE)**[9] 4843 11-11-1 **101**.............................. JohnFlavin[(10)] —
(R C Guest) *led tl blnd and uns rdr 1st* **17/2**

-P4P **U** **Mickey Croke**[44] 4361 9-10-7 **83**.................................. DominicElsworth —
(M Todhunter) *chsd ldrs whn bdly hmpd and uns rdr 5th* **9/1**

/6P0 **U** **Batto**[47] 4302 6-10-1 **77**.. BarryKeniry —
(G M Moore) *chsd ldrs whn crossed by loose horse and uns rdr 5th* **40/1**

P365 **U** **Kings Square**[84] 3656 6-10-2 **78**...................................... WilsonRenwick —
(M W Easterby) *keen: chsd ldrs: bdly hmpd, no room and uns rdr 5th* **15/2**

-P34 **P** **Sports Express**[36] 4516 8-11-1 **91**..............................(p) PeterBuchanan —
(Miss Lucinda V Russell) *prom whn bdly hmpd, no room and p.u 5th* **20/1**

24PP **P** **Algarve**[19] 4737 9-10-12 **88**.. KeithMercer —
(Ferdy Murphy) *hld up in tch: bdly hmpd 5th: lost tch fr 1/2-way: p.u bef 4 out* **12/1**

6m 16.8s (-15.10) **Going Correction** -0.50s/f (Good) **12** Ran SP% **115.0**
Speed ratings: **104,103,102,94,89 89,—,—,—,— —,—** CSF £104.24 CT £563.92 TOTE £14.60: £5.60, £2.00, £2.30; EX 183.60.

Owner The Rennington Racing Club **Bred** George F White **Trained** Greystoke, Cumbria

FOCUS
An eventful novices' handicap, which saw several horses hampered by a loose horse at the fifth fence, and the overall form must rate as suspect.

NOTEBOOK
Bafana Boy, making his handicap debut on this first outing under Rules over the bigger obstacles, got off the mark with a clear-cut success. He proved suited by the faster ground, the return to this longer trip was right up his street, and he jumped with accuracy throughout. He may be a touch flattered by this form, but further improvement looks most likely while he is at this end of the handicap. *(op 12-1)*

Aston(USA), returning from a 199-day break, turned in an encouraging comeback effort and would have given the winner more to think about but for being hampered between the final two fences. This is his ground and, while he has a habit of finding one too good, he is handicapped to win at present. *(tchd 8-1)*
Chabrimal Minster ran very close to his official mark in defeat and was not disgraced under top weight. He just looks held by the Handicapper at present. *(tchd 6-1)*
Coy Lad(IRE) was done no favours when hampered at the fifth fence, yet still recovered to have a chance, and ultimately found nothing when it mattered. This was disappointing, but it may be that he prefers easier ground, and it would come as no surprise to see the cheekpieces re-applied after this. *(op 9-2)*

5038 DOUG MOSCROP NOVICES' HURDLE (8 hdls 2 omitted) 2m 4f 110y
3:30 (3:30) (Class 4) 4-Y-O+ **£3,083** (£898; £449)

Form RPR
0303 **1** **Silent Bay**[58] 4114 7-11-0 .... PaddyAspell 100
(J Wade) *chsd ldr: outpcd 6th: rallied bef 2 out: jst led whn lft wl clr last (won by 43l)* **6/4**[2]
-40P **2** *dist* **Rhuna Red**[7] 4917 7-10-7 .... WilsonRenwick 48
(J R Bewley) *chsd clr ldrs: outpcd fr 3rd: n.d after: lft remote 2nd last* **16/1**[3]
50 **3** *1 3/4* **Little Vantage**[304] 828 7-10-9 .... DeclanMcGann[(5)] 53
(A M Crow) *chsd clr ldrs: outpcd fr 3rd: lft poor 3rd last* **100/1**
0- **P** **Joyful Echo**[400] 4477 7-10-7 .... KennyJohnson —
(J E Dixon) *sn t.o: p.u bef 3 out* **100/1**
0 **U** **Red Square Run**[36] 4519 4-10-5 .... MrTGreenall[(3)] —
(M W Easterby) *in tch: uns rdr 2nd* **16/1**[3]
P **Smart Man** 4-10-3 .... MichaelMcAlister[(5)] —
(Mrs E Slack) *sn wl bhd: t.o whn p.u bef last* **16/1**[3]
60 **R** **Is There More**[64] 4017 5-10-7 .... DavidO'Meara —
(J M Jefferson) *sn wl bhd: t.o whn p.u 3 out* **16/1**[3]
5 **F** **Bally Brakes (IRE)**[123] 2948 6-11-0 .... TonyDobbin 97
(N G Richards) *led: clr fr 5th to 2 out: hdd and 1l down whn fell last* **5/4**[1]
4m 57.3s (-12.30) **Going Correction** -0.40s/f (Good) **8** Ran SP% **110.0**
WFA 4 from 5yo+ 6lb
Speed ratings: **95,—,—,—,— —,—,—** CSF £22.66 TOTE £3.10: £1.10, £2.70, £17.60; EX 20.70.
Owner John Wade **Bred** Temple Farming **Trained** Mordon, Co Durham

FOCUS
A weak novice event which saw the winner come home as he pleased after his main market rival fell at the final flight. The first flight in the back straight was omitted on both circuits.

NOTEBOOK
Silent Bay was well on top of Bally Brakes prior to that rival coming to grief at the final flight and came home to score as he pleased. He handled this faster ground without much fuss, shaped as though he is a staying chaser in the making, and should be high on confidence now after this career-first success. *(op 2-1 tchd 9-4)*
Rhuna Red is flattered by her finishing position, but at least completed on this occasion and shaped as though she needs a return to further and the switch to low-grade handicaps. *(op 12-1)*
Little Vantage did not accomplish a great deal in third, but should fare better when qualified for handicaps and upped in trip. *(op 50-1)*
Bally Brakes(IRE), fifth on his debut for connections in an Ayr bumper just before Christmas, tried to make all but was held by the winner prior to crashing out at the final flight. He would have finished a clear second with a clear round and, providing he recovers suffiently from this experience, is one to look out for when entering the handicap arena. *(tchd 13-8)*

5039 THORNTON FIRKIN MARES' ONLY H'CAP HURDLE (6 hdls 2 omitted) 2m 110y
4:00 (4:00) (Class 4) (0-105,105) 4-Y-O+ **£3,083** (£898; £449)

Form RPR
113U **1** **Parisienne Gale (IRE)**[119] 2963 7-11-1 **99** ....(t) TomGreenway[(5)] 110+
(R Ford) *mde all: sn wl clr: unchal* **10/1**[3]
3522 **2** *9* **Nobodys Perfect (IRE)**[40] 4450 6-10-13 **99** .... PatrickMcDonald[(7)] 100
(Ferdy Murphy) *chsd (clr) wnr: rdn after 2 out: kpt on fr last: no imp* **8/1**[2]
2- **3** *3/4* **Dunguaire Lady (IRE)**[269] 1101 7-10-11 **90** .... RichardMcGrath 90
(Mrs K Walton) *in tch: effrt bef last: edgd lft and kpt on run in: no imp* **20/1**
305P **4** *3/4* **Calomeria**[62] 4041 5-11-4 **97** .... JasonMaguire 97
(D McCain) *hld up in tch: outpcd bef 2 out: rallied appr last: no imp* **8/1**[2]
3550 **5** *1* **Buffy**[36] 4529 6-10-11 **90** .... NeilMulholland 89
(B Mactaggart) *cl up tl rdn and outpcd bef last* **14/1**
245P **6** *1 3/4* **Feanor**[214] 1530 8-11-0 **100** ....(t) MrSWByrne[(7)] 97
(Mrs S A Watt) *hld up: rdn after 2 out: nvr rchd ldrs* **20/1**
110 **7** *nk* **United Spirit (IRE)**[163] 2173 5-11-5 **98** .... RussGarritty 95+
(Jedd O'Keeffe) *hld up: rdn after 2 out: nvr rchd ldrs* **11/4**[1]
006 **8** *4* **Royal Glen (IRE)**[8] 3171 8-11-1 **94** .... DavidO'Meara 86
(W S Coltherd) *hld up: hdwy bef 2 out: wknd bef last* **8/1**[2]
6-65 **9** *8* **Baby Gee**[62] 4045 12-10-7 **93** .... PhilKinsella[(7)] 77
(D W Whillans) *chsd ldrs to 2 out: sn rdn and btn* **14/1**
4005 **10** *3/4* **Political Pendant**[56] 4143 5-10-4 **90** .... GarethThomas[(7)] 74
(R Nixon) *sn towards rr: struggling fr 3rd* **12/1**
/1-3 **F** **Monte Rosa (IRE)**[361] 85 7-11-5 **105** .... EwanWhillans[(7)] —
(N G Richards) *fell 1st* **12/1**
134P **P** **Air Of Affection**[9] 4840 5-11-10 **103** .... TonyDobbin —
(J R Turner) *hld up: struggling 2 out: t.o whn p.u bef last* **11/1**
3m 58.7s (-16.50) **Going Correction** -0.40s/f (Good) **12** Ran SP% **115.7**
Speed ratings: **110,105,105,105,104 103,103,101,97,97 —,—** CSF £85.97 CT £1555.09 TOTE £8.10: £3.10, £2.80, £7.40; EX 37.40.
Owner S J Manning **Bred** Edmond And Richard Kent **Trained** Cotebrook, Cheshire

FOCUS
A decent winning time for the grade, the winner coming home unchallenged from the front, and the overall form looks sound enough. The first flight in the back straight was omitted on both circuits, and the last flight in the back straight omitted on the final circuit.

NOTEBOOK
Parisienne Gale(IRE), last seen unseating over fences at Market Rasen on Boxing Day, resumed winning ways with a decisive success from the front. While she was gifted an early lead, and may be slightly flattered by her winning margin, there was still plenty to like about this display and she is clearly still ahead of the Handicapper over timber. *(op 11-2)*
Nobodys Perfect(IRE) tried to keep tabs on the winner throughout, but she started to feel the pinch before the penultimate flight, and failed to make an impression. She could do with some respite from the Handicapper on this evidence, but is a consistent enough sort, and helps set the level of this form. *(op 7-1)*
Dunguaire Lady(IRE), making her British debut for new connections after a 269-day break and with her usual tongue-tie abandoned, saw her effort short-lived and left the impression the race was much needed. She remains winless after 21 outings, but is entitled to improve for this run, and can build on this during the summer months.
Calomeria, pulled up over fences when last seen two months ago, turned in a more encouraging effort on this better ground yet still looks out of sorts at present. She may well need further now on this evidence. *(op 9-1)*
United Spirit(IRE), well backed for this return from a 163-day break, was not ideally suited by the way the race was run and never threatened from off the pace. She is capable of plenty better than this and is worthy of another chance with this outing under her belt. *(op 9-2)*
Air Of Affection *Official explanation: jockey said mare bled from the nose (op 14-1)*

5040 RACING WELFARE MAIDEN HUNTERS' CHASE (19 fncs) 3m 1f
4:30 (4:30) (Class 6) 5-Y-O+ **£1,249** (£387; £193; £96)

Form RPR
4P44 **1** **Highland Brig**[15] 4791 10-11-11 76........ MrMEllwood[(7)] 87
(T Butt) *in tch: rdn 4 out: no imp tl rallied between last two: styd on to ld towards fin* **5/1**[3]
P/40 **2** *1/2* **Scenic Storm (IRE)**[16] 11-12-4 .... MrNTutty 87
(Miss Lucinda Broad) *mde most to 13th: led after 2 out: kpt on wl: hdd towards fin* **4/1**[2]
3 **3** *3* **Anshan Spirit (IRE)**[15] 4791 8-11-4 .... MrRWGreen[(7)] 78+
(R W Green) *in tch: disp ld 9th: led 13th: hit 4 out: hdd after 2 out: one pce run in* **4/1**[2]
35 **4** *17* **Queenies Girl**[9] 10-11-4 .... MrPFrank[(7)] 62+
(Paul Frank) *hld up: effrt after 4 out: no imp fr last* **11/1**
P032 **5** *24* **High Expectations (IRE)**[15] 4791 11-11-13 62........ MrTDavidson[(5)] 43
(J S Haldane) *in tch: outpcd 4 out: n.d after* **7/2**[1]
6 *10* **Ofcoursehekhan (IRE)**[7] 8-12-4 .... MrCStorey 33
(Mrs N C Neill) *hld up: outpcd whn hit 15th: sn btn* **18/1**
P **Just A Man**[16] 8-11-11 ....(p) MrRWakeham[(7)] —
(Richard Mason) *in tch to 1/2-way: sn wknd: t.o whn p.u bef last* **15/2**
P-P0 **P** **Shining Tyne**[21] 4722 12-12-4 59........ MrPJohnson —
(R Johnson) *sn towards rr: lost tch and p.u bef 15th* **40/1**
6m 18.5s (-13.40) **Going Correction** -0.50s/f (Good) **8** Ran SP% **106.7**
Speed ratings: **101,100,99,94,86 83,—,—** CSF £22.43 TOTE £6.50: £2.00, £1.10, £1.70; EX 38.00.
Owner William Hamilton **Bred** William Hamilton **Trained** Jedburgh, Borders

FOCUS
A weak event of its type, run at a sound pace, and the form looks fairly sound.

NOTEBOOK
Highland Brig responded to his rider's urgings nearing the penultimate fence and fairly flew home on the run-in to collar the runner-up and ultimately win going away. The better ground was clearly to his liking, this was his first success since winning a point in 2003, and he comprehensively reversed Kelso form with High Expectations. *(op 6-1)*
Scenic Storm(IRE), back to winning ways in a point 16 days previously, turned in a brave effort from the front and only gave way to the winner on the run-in. A similar display can see him open his account under Rules before too long. *(tchd 10-3)*
Anshan Spirit(IRE) was given a slightly more patient ride this time, which suited, but she still found just the same pace when it really mattered and failed to confirm Kelso form with the winner. *(tchd 9-2)*
High Expectations(IRE), in front of the winner and the third horse at Kelso last time, turned in a tame effort and failed to run his race. Consistency has never been his strong suit, but he is capable of better than this. *(op 11-4 tchd 4-1)*

5041 AT THE RACES MAIDEN OPEN NATIONAL HUNT FLAT RACE (DIV I) 2m 110y
5:00 (5:00) (Class 6) 4-6-Y-O **£1,027** (£299; £149)

Form RPR
3 **1** **Sir Boreas Hawk**[29] 4637 4-10-7 .... MrTGreenall[(3)] 88
(G A Swinbank) *trckd ldrs: led 1f out: pushed out* **5/6**[1]
5 **2** *2 1/2* **Elaeagnus**[61] 4059 4-10-3 .... RichardMcGrath 79
(C Grant) *keen: cl up: led 1/2-way to 1f out: kpt on same pce* **25/1**
4 **3** *1/2* **Reel Charmer**[9] 4853 6-10-5 .... MichalKohl[(3)] 83
(J I A Charlton) *hld up towards rr: stdy hdwy over 2f out: rdn and kpt on fnl f: no imp* **9/4**[2]
5 **4** *5* **Mr Viaillie (IRE)**[102] 3353 4-10-7 .... DougieCostello[(3)] 80
(Karen McLintock) *cl up tl rdn and nt qckn over 1f out* **16/1**[3]
0 **5** *8* **Gunadoir (IRE)**[32] 4588 4-9-10 .... MrCJCallow[(7)] 65
(N G Richards) *keen: hld up: hdwy and prom 1/2-way: outpcd 3f out: n.d after* **20/1**
0 **6** *1 1/2* **Franceschiella (ITY)**[47] 4304 5-10-1 .... PhilKinsella[(7)] 69
(Lady Susan Watson) *hld up in tch: effrt over 2f out: sn no imp* **100/1**
00 **7** *13* **Indian Wind**[36] 4533 4-10-3 ....(t) MissAngelaBarnes[(7)] 58
(M A Barnes) *led to 1/2-way: cl up tl wknd over 2f out* **100/1**
00 **8** *1 1/2* **Zarbeau**[7] 4909 4-10-10 .... DavidO'Meara 56
(J M Jefferson) *hld up: rdn over 3f out: sn btn* **28/1**
0 **9** *2* **Bodell (IRE)**[86] 3623 4-10-5 .... DerekLaverty[(5)] 54
(Mark Campion) *hld up in tch: rdn and wknd over 3f out* **100/1**
0 **10** *dist* **Billy Row**[46] 4319 5-10-5 .... MichaelMcAvoy[(10)] —
(James Moffatt) *bhd: rdn over 5f out: sn wknd: t.o* **66/1**
4m 4.80s (-7.90) **Going Correction** -0.40s/f (Good) **10** Ran SP% **107.7**
Speed ratings: **102,100,100,98,94 93,87,86,86,—** CSF £28.17 TOTE £1.80: £1.10, £2.20, £1.10; EX 21.20.
Owner William A Powrie **Bred** R And Mrs Blackham **Trained** Melsonby, N Yorks

FOCUS
This first division of the bumper was run at just a moderate early pace and the first three came clear. A very modest race, rated through the winner.

NOTEBOOK
Sir Boreas Hawk, third on his debut a month ago, got off the mark with a straightforward success and is value for slightly further than his winning margin. He enjoyed this faster ground, and rates a nice future prospect for connections, but unfortunately he was found to have struck into himself and finished lame, so could face a spell on the sidelines. *(op 6-5)*
Elaeagnus, fifth on her debut at Southwell two months ago, proved keen at the head of affairs, and ultimately paid for that when it mattered, yet posted an improved effort nevertheless. She ought to be better suited by further in due course. *(tchd 20-1)*
Reel Charmer, a promising fourth at Haydock on her debut nine days previously, never seriously threatened and would have been better served by a more positive ride. She ought to be seen in a better light when racing off a stronger gallop and will benefit from stronger handling in the future. *(op 6-4)*
Mr Viaillie(IRE), fifth on her debut 102 days previously, enjoyed the run of the race and found just the one pace when push came to shove. This represented an improved effort and he should come on a bit for the outing. *(tchd 20-1)*

5042 AT THE RACES MAIDEN OPEN NATIONAL HUNT FLAT RACE (DIV II) 2m 110y
5:30 (5:30) (Class 6) 4-6-Y-O **£1,027** (£299; £149)

Form RPR
6 **1** **King Daniel**[77] 3785 5-10-10 .... MichaelMcAlister[(5)] 87
(Mrs E Slack) *cl up: led 4f out: qcknd over 2f out: kpt on wl* **10/1**
0 **2** *3/4* **Mister Etek**[60] 4072 5-11-1 .... PeterBuchanan 86
(T D Walford) *prom: effrt over 2f out: kpt on fnl f* **7/1**

50 **3** 9 **Sea Cadet**[42] [4422] 4-10-10 .... RussGarritty 72
(T D Easterby) *hld up in tch: effrt 3f out: no imp fr 2f out* **3/1**[2]

30 **4** 2 **High Moor**[9] [4854] 4-10-10 .... TonyDobbin 70
(J D Bethell) *hld up: niggled over 4f out: effrt over 2f out: nvr rchd ldrs* **4/1**[3]

0 **5** 3 ½ **Emski**[47] [4304] 5-10-5 .... MrTGreenall(3) 65
(P Beaumont) *hld up in tch: rdn over 3f out: sn outpcd* **20/1**

0 **6** 6 **Hello Noddy**[142] [2642] 4-10-10 .... AlanDempsey 61
(B Mactaggart) *prom tl rdn and wknd over 2f out* **20/1**

00 **7** ½ **Roman Gypsy**[77] [3785] 5-10-1 .... ColmSharkey(7) 58
(Mrs K Walton) *hld up: rdn over 5f out: n.d* **33/1**

0 **8** 1 ½ **Seventh Sense**[18] [4751] 5-10-5 .... MichalKohl(3) 57
(J I A Charlton) *hld up: rdn and wknd over 3f out* **15/8**[1]

00- **9** dist **Gala Queen**[16] 6-10-8 .... WilsonRenwick —
(W G Young) *led to 4f out: sn wknd* **100/1**

4m 6.10s (-6.60) **Going Correction** -0.40s/f (Good)
WFA 4 from 5yo+ 5lb **9** Ran SP% **114.8**
Speed ratings: **99,98,94,93,91 89,88,88,**— CSF £73.04 TOTE £10.80: £3.60, £2.90, £1.40; EX 65.20 Place 6 £357.66, Place 5 £47.51.
Owner A Slack **Bred** A Slack **Trained** Hilton, Cumbria

FOCUS
This second division of the bumper was another slowly-run affair. It has been rated through the second and the fourth. The first two came clear.

NOTEBOOK
King Daniel, sixth on his debut at Sedgefield in February, stepped up greatly on that effort by getting off the mark with a tidy success and showing a turn of foot in the process. He appreciated this quicker surface and is clearly going the right way. *(op 14-1)*
Mister Etek, ninth in a more competitive event on his debut at Haydock two months ago, had his chance but could not match the winner's turn of foot and shaped as though he really wants a stiffer test. *(op 11-2)*
Sea Cadet, well backed, was not really suited by racing off the average gallop and never rated a serious threat to the first two. He can be rated slightly better than the bare form. *(op 4-1)*
High Moor was another who would have been better served by a more prominent ride, and never looked a threat, but still turned in a more encouraging display all the same. *(op 9-2)*
Seventh Sense, well backed, failed to improve on the form she showed on her recent debut in a *much better contest at Aintree against her own sex and proved most disappointing.Official explanation: trainer had no explanation for the poor form shown (tchd 9-4)*
T/Plt: £3,419.00 to a £1 stake. Pool: £43,791.40. 9.35 winning tickets. T/Qpdt: £20.50 to a £1 stake. Pool: £4,405.10. 158.90 winning tickets. RY

[4752] TAUNTON (R-H)
Monday, April 24

OFFICIAL GOING: Firm
Wind: Almost nil Weather: Fine

5043 TAUNTON RACECOURSE GROUNDSTAFF "NATIONAL HUNT" NOVICES' HURDLE (9 hdls) 2m 1f
5:15 (5:15) (Class 4) 4-Y-0+ **£5,204** (£1,528; £764; £381)

Form RPR
130 **1** **Paro (FR)**[42] [4420] 5-11-5 110 .... APMcCoy 105+
(M C Pipe) *mde all: rdn after 3 out: pressed whn lft wl clr 2 out* **8/13**[1]

000 **2** dist **Cool Society**[16] [4784] 4-10-7 .... AndrewThornton 55
(R H Alner) *sn wl bhd: r.o to take poor 2nd flat* **22/1**

2660 **3** 1 ¾ **Blues Story (FR)**[258] [1187] 8-10-7 83 ....(t) MarkNicolls(5) 58
(N G Ayliffe) *prom: hit 1st: wknd 5th: lft poor 2nd 2 out* **33/1**

000 **4** dist **My Little Molly (IRE)**[11] [4836] 4-9-7 .... WayneKavanagh(7) —
(J W Mullins) *hld up and bhd: rdn after 3rd: hit 4th: sn struggling: t.o* **50/1**

U0-F **F** **The Last Over**[351] [230] 5-10-0 .... EamonDehdashti(5) —
(Miss K M George) *sn wl bhd: t.o 5th: fell 2 out* **100/1**

P **Ballybough Eddie (IRE)**[100] [3407] 7-10-12 .... PaulMoloney —
(Evan Williams) *hld up in mid-div: p.u lame bef 4th* **9/1**[3]

234P **R** **Chunky Lad**[65] [3996] 6-10-2 .... RichardGordon(10) —
(W G M Turner) *plld hrd: chsd wnr: cl 2nd whn rn out 3rd* **12/1**

0P63 **U** **Creinch**[6] [4934] 5-10-7 100 .... CharliePoste(5) 95
(M F Harris) *prom: lft 2nd 3rd: hit 6th: rdn after 3 out: ev ch whn blnd bdly and uns rdr 2 out* **4/1**[2]

3m 49.6s (-19.20) **Going Correction** -1.125s/f (Hard)
WFA 4 from 5yo+ 5lb **8** Ran SP% **109.9**
Speed ratings: **100,—,—,—,— —,—,—** CSF £16.60 TOTE £1.70: £1.02, £4.30, £9.30; EX 11.80.
Owner Ms Y Spencer-Thompson **Bred** M Lalanne **Trained** Nicholashayne, Devon

FOCUS
An uncompetitive event and favourite Paro was left clear after Creinch unseated two out. Poor for the grade.

NOTEBOOK
Paro(FR) had failed to build on February's Ludlow win in two subsequent starts, but this represented a much simpler task and he appeared to just be getting the better of Creinch when that one unseated at the second last. He had set a strong pace and kept going well enough, but does not make a great deal of appeal with the future in mind. *(op 5-6)*
Cool Society, having only his third start over hurdles, was soon trailing and was not asked for his effort until the front pair had gone beyond recall. He is more of a handicap prospect, and should improve for two and a half miles. *(op 16-1)*
Blues Story(FR), who had raced exclusively at Newton Abbot on his last seven outings, was having a rare visit away from the place, but achieved very little in finishing a well-beaten third.
Creinch, back to form at Chepstow earlier in the month, was pushing the winner and still had every chance when unshipping Poste after a bad mistake two out. He can pick up a race if continuing to head the right way. *(op 3-1)*

5044 ROYAL DEVON YEOMANRY BEGINNERS' CHASE (12 fncs) 2m 110y
5:45 (5:45) (Class 4) 5-Y-0+ **£6,338** (£1,872; £936; £468; £234)

Form RPR
6004 **1** **Goldbrook**[6] [4945] 8-11-1 120 .... TomScudamore 105+
(R J Hodges) *chsd ldr: rdn appr 3 out: led last: drvn out* **9/4**[2]

4003 **2** 2 **Predicament**[32] [4590] 7-11-1 .... APMcCoy 103
(Jonjo O'Neill) *hld up in tch: hit 7th: rdn appr last: kpt on to take 2nd cl home* **15/8**[1]

3463 **3** 1 **Imperial Rocket (USA)**[11] [4833] 9-11-1 102 ....(t) RichardJohnson 104+
(W K Goldsworthy) *led: mstke 3 out: rdn whn mstke and hdd last: nt rcvr: lost 2nd cl home* **7/2**[3]

0005 **4** dist **Simiola**[32] [4590] 7-10-5 73 .... ChrisHonour(3) 63
(S T Lewis) *a bhd: lft poor 4th bef 3 out* **33/1**

P0P **5** 3 ½ **Lincoln Leader (IRE)**[19] [4729] 8-9-12 .... TimothyBailey(10) 60
(Evan Williams) *a bhd: t.o* **33/1**

3043 **P** **Houlihans Free (IRE)**[6] [4943] 7-11-1 ....(t) ChristianWilliams —
(P F Nicholls) *hld up: hdwy after 5th: blnd 7th: mstke 8th: nt rcvr: poor 4th whn p.u bef 3 out* **13/2**

3m 55.5s (-20.00) **Going Correction** -1.125s/f (Hard) **6** Ran SP% **107.0**
Speed ratings: **102,101,100,—,—** — CSF £6.49 TOTE £3.50: £1.80, £2.00; EX 8.00.
Owner John & Greer Norman **Bred** G Norman **Trained** Charlton Adam, Somerset

FOCUS
A welcome first win over fences for Goldbrook, who was rated 25lb off his best chase figure. The second and thord ran to their recent marks.

NOTEBOOK
Goldbrook, returning to fences for the first time this term, handled the ground and found plenty under pressure to run out a workmanlike winner. He had run a couple of fair races over hurdles earier this season and may yet be capable of better over the larger obstacles. *(tchd 2-1 and 5-2)*
Predicament has taken well to fences and he recorded another sound effort, keeping on without *being able to make any impression on the winner. He will find a race if kept on the go. (op 9-4 tchd 7-4)*
Imperial Rocket(USA) continues to find at least one too good over fences, but there is no denying he would have been closer had his jumping been more fluent in the straight. *(op 4-1)*
Houlihans Free(IRE) is one of his stable's lesser lights, but he should have fared a lot better here and it would not surprise to learn that something was amiss. *(op 5-1)*

5045 BREWIN DOLPHIN SECURITIES NOVICES' H'CAP HURDLE (10 hdls) 2m 3f 110y
6:15 (6:15) (Class 3) (0-125,123) 4-Y-0+ **£10,140** (£2,995; £1,497; £748; £374)

Form RPR
5112 **1** **Flotta**[6] [4945] 7-11-12 123 .... TimmyMurphy 131+
(B G Powell) *mde all: pushed clr appr 2 out: hit last: wnt lame and eased flat* **7/2**[2]

3060 **2** 3 ½ **Red Moor (IRE)**[19] [4726] 6-10-11 108 .... BenjaminHitchcott 108
(Mrs D A Hamer) *hld up: hdwy after 5th: rdn 3 out: wnt 2nd last: kpt on: nt trble wnr* **14/1**

00P0 **3** 3 ½ **Barathea Blue**[102] [3358] 5-10-0 97 ....(t) TomScudamore 93
(M C Pipe) *chsd wnr: rdn appr 2 out: lost 2nd last: no ex* **13/2**

6422 **4** 1 ¼ **Hill Forts Timmy**[81] [3694] 6-10-12 109 .... AndrewThornton 105+
(J W Mullins) *hld up in tch: no real prog fr 3 out* **5/1**[3]

3124 **5** 1 **Armariver (FR)**[81] [3696] 6-11-0 111 .... ChristianWilliams 106+
(P F Nicholls) *prom: hit 6th and 7th: rdn appr 2 out: wknd appr last* **7/2**[2]

04P2 **6** 2 ½ **Random Quest**[9] [4856] 8-10-1 98 ....(b) PJBrennan 90+
(B J Llewellyn) *rdn appr 7th: a bhd* **12/1**

3033 **7** dist **It's The Limit (USA)**[11] [4838] 7-10-6 103 ....(b) RichardJohnson —
(W K Goldsworthy) *hld up: hdwy appr 6th: sn rdn: wknd 3 out: sn t.o* **3/1**[1]

4m 24.0s (-22.00) **Going Correction** -1.125s/f (Hard) **7** Ran SP% **113.8**
Speed ratings: **99,97,96,95,95 94,**— CSF £44.98 TOTE £3.50: £2.10, £9.60; EX 49.50.
Owner G Hatchard,R Gunn,L Gilbert & R Williams **Bred** W G R Wightman **Trained** Morestead, Hants

FOCUS
A nice performance by the fast ground-loving Flotta, who was value for a fair bit further.

NOTEBOOK
Flotta was recording a third hurdling victory of the season, but it came at a price as he finished lame and had to be eased down on the run-in. He had received a good front-running ride from Murphy and it is hoped the fast-ground lover is able to race on through the summer. *(op 11-4)*
Red Moor(IRE), who failed to shine in the first-time cheekpieces latest, came through late to take second off Barathea Blazer, but was never in with a chance of getting to the winner. He may need a little further help from the Handicapper before winning again. *(op 16-1 tchd 12-1)*
Barathea Blue had not been progressing, but this was a better effort on his return from a break *and the fast ground may well have helped. He can surely be found a race off this sort of mark. (op 9-1 tchd 10-1)*
Hill Forts Timmy has been in fair form, but this was slightly disappointing and maybe the firm ground did not suit the gelding. *(op 13-2 tchd 7-1)*
Armariver(FR), expected to be helped by this step back up in distance, has not really progressed since 'winning' (disqualified) at Cheltenham in January and, although returning from a break here, it was disappointing at how little fight he put up. *(op 11-4)*
Random Quest would have found this ground too lively. *(op 15-2)*
It's The Limit(USA) ran too badly to be true and there was presumably something amiss. *(op 11-2)*

5046 SETSQUARE RECRUITMENT H'CAP CHASE (17 fncs) 2m 7f 110y
6:45 (6:45) (Class 3) (0-120,119) 5-Y-0+ **£9,633** (£2,845; £1,422; £711; £355)

Form RPR
P1PP **1** **Glacial Delight (IRE)**[40] [4447] 7-11-10 117 .... BarryFenton 128+
(Miss E C Lavelle) *hld up in rr: hdwy 11th: led 12th: j.rt 3 out: clr whn nt fluent last: pushed out* **7/2**[2]

-453 **2** 1 ¾ **Menphis Beury (FR)**[60] [4078] 6-10-6 99 .... MarkBradburne 107+
(H D Daly) *hld up: hdwy 12th: hmpd and mstke 3 out: sn rdn: wnt 2nd last: kpt on: nt trble wnr* **4/1**[3]

5F34 **3** 2 ½ **Ede'Iff**[19] [4737] 9-10-8 106 .... RobertLucey-Butler(5) 112+
(W G M Turner) *a.p: led 11th: hdd and mstke 12th: rdn appr 3 out: no ex flat* **12/1**

614F **4** 18 **Castlemore (IRE)**[165] [2151] 8-10-9 102 .... RichardJohnson 93+
(P J Hobbs) *prom: wknd 13th: blnd bdly 4 out* **3/1**[1]

320P **5** 8 **Benrajah (IRE)**[75] [3803] 9-11-0 112 .... TJDreaper(5) 90
(M Todhunter) *led to 11th: sn rdn: wknd 13th* **9/2**

4F3P **P** **Team Tassel (IRE)**[25] [4677] 8-11-12 119 ....(v) APMcCoy —
(M C Pipe) *chsd ldr to 11th: wknd 12th: bhd whn p.u bef 4 out* **9/1**

533P **F** **Keltic Lord**[173] [1989] 10-11-4 111 .... RobertThornton —
(P W Hiatt) *hld up and bhd: short-lived effrt appr 11th: no ch whn fell 3 out* **12/1**

5m 39.8s (-25.30) **Going Correction** -1.125s/f (Hard) **7** Ran SP% **110.8**
Speed ratings: **97,96,95,89,86** —,— CSF £17.04 CT £140.01 TOTE £3.90: £1.60, £2.80; EX 27.20.
Owner The Friday Night Racing Club **Bred** Patrick Tarrant **Trained** Wildhern, Hants

FOCUS
A tricky contest on paper, but it was the inconsistent Glacial Delight who emerged victorious. He is on the upgrade and is value for a bit further.

NOTEBOOK
Glacial Delight(IRE) is anything but consistent, as his form figures of 161P1PP1 suggest, but he is useful on his day when getting dry ground and, although bungling the last, he won with something in hand. It is tempting to say he can follow up for his in-form stable, but he cannot be *trusted. Official explanation: trainer said, regarding the improved form shown, gelding was better suited by the firm ground (op 3-1)*
Menphis Beury(FR) is slowly dropping back down to a winning mark, and the way he kept on in second suggests he would have pushed the winner harder had he not been hampered by the fall of Keltic Lord three out. *(op 5-1)*
Ede'Iff is still 5lb higher than when winning at Ludlow back in December and did not shape like a short-term future winner here. *(op 11-1 tchd 10-1)*
Castlemore(IRE) goes well on a fast surface and connections have kept their powder dry since November, but he was already beaten when making a bad error at the fourth-last fence. He will obviously need to step up on this in future. *(tchd 11-4)*

Team Tassel(IRE) is a thoroughly disappointing sort who shows no hunger for the game. *(op 7-1 tchd 10-1)*

5047 SOMERSET RED CROSS H'CAP CHASE (9 fncs 3 omitted) 2m 110y

7:15 (7:16) (Class 5) (0-90,90) 5-Y-O+ **£3,768** (£1,098; £549)

Form				RPR
056F	**1**		**Twentytwosilver (IRE)**[19] 1900 6-11-1 **84** RobertLucey-Butler(5) (D B Feek) *hld up and bhd: gd hdwy after 7th: r.o to ld nr fin* **9/1**	97
0055	**2**	*nk*	**Auditor**[4] 4973 7-9-13 **66** ow1 (b) ChrisHonour(3) (S T Lewis) *hld up in mid-div: hdwy appr 6th: led after 7th: rdn and hdd nr fin* **12/1**	79
4U43	**3**	*3*	**Terrible Tenant**[11] 4837 7-11-2 **83** RichardYoung(3) (J W Mullins) *hld up in tch: jnd ldrs 6th: rdn and one pce fr 2 out* **5/2**[1]	93
40	**4**	*9*	**Wondersobright (IRE)**[35] 4552 7-11-3 **86** PaddyMerrigan(5) (K J Burke) *led to 4th: led appr 5th: j.lft 6th: mstke 7th: sn hdd: wknd 2 out* **16/1**	89+
0620	**5**	*4*	**Kinkeel (IRE)**[7] 4908 7-10-2 **73** (b) WillieMcCarthy(7) (A W Carroll) *chsd ldrs tl wknd 7th* **11/1**	70
-P6P	**6**	*7*	**Colmcille (IRE)**[123] 2955 6-11-6 **84** ChristianWilliams (Evan Williams) *nvr nr ldrs* **9/2**[2]	74
0-PU	**7**	*½*	**Logger Rhythm (USA)**[34] 4164 6-10-0 **64** HenryOliver (R Dickin) *nvr nr ldrs* **10/1**	54
23P5	**8**	*10*	**Green Gamble**[80] 3718 6-11-12 **90** JamesDavies (D B Feek) *bhd fr 7th* **7/1**[3]	70
6PPP	**9**	*9*	**Run To The King (IRE)**[6] 4937 8-10-10 **74** (b) AndrewThornton (P C Ritchens) *hld up in mid-div: mstke 4th: bhd fr 7th* **20/1**	45
2060	**B**		**Johnny Grand**[214] 1524 9-10-11 **75** NoelFehily (D W Lewis) *bhd whn b.d 4th: dead* **14/1**	—
UP0	**F**		**A Monk Swimming (IRE)**[6] 4943 5-10-13 **80** (t) SeanCurran (Miss J S Davis) *towards rr whn fell 4th* **50/1**	—
150-	**U**		**Eyes To The Right (IRE)**[501] 2724 7-10-4 **71** WilliamKennedy(3) (D Burchell) *prom: mstke 1st: led 4th tl appr 5th: 5 l 4th and wkng whn blnd and uns rdr 6th* **14/1**	—

3m 52.8s (-22.70) **Going Correction** -1.125s/f (Hard)
WFA 5 from 6yo+ 3lb **12** Ran SP% **120.3**
Speed ratings: **108,107,106,102,100 97,96,92,87,— —,—** CSF £112.03 CT £355.36 TOTE £12.10: £3.30, £3.90, £1.70; EX 117.80.
Owner Chegwidden Systems Ltd **Bred** Dr Paschal Carmody **Trained** Brightling, E Sussex

FOCUS
A moderate handicap chase won by chasing debutant Twentytwosilver. It has been rated through the second to the level of his best form in the last year. The last fence in the back straight was omitted on both circuits and the final fence was bypassed because of a fallen rider.

NOTEBOOK
Twentytwosilver(IRE), a tough gelding who often mixes Flat and hurdles, did not look an obvious contender, but he jumped tidily in rear before making ground into a challenging position and stayed on well to collar Auditor close home. Winning here off a mark of 84, he looks open to a little further improvement as his versatility is sure to see him continue to pay his way. *(tchd 8-1 and 10-1)*
Auditor, who ran from a mile out of the handicap at Cheltenham last time, stood more of a realistic chance here and he looked the likely winner approaching the last, but he was unable to repel the challenge of Twentytwosilver and had to make do with second. There is a race in him off this mark, which is 23lb lower than when he was last successful, but he is hardly progressive. *(op 11-1 tchd 16-1)*
Terrible Tenant appreciates a sound surface and it was no surprise to see him run into a place. He has not progressed as expected however and still gives the impression he needs to drop a few more pounds before winning. *(op 10-3)*
Wondersobright(IRE) stepped up on last month's Hereford effort, but still failed to jump fluently enough to suggest he is up to winning. *(op 11-1)*
Kinkeel(IRE) remains winless after 19 attempts under Rules and makes little appeal as a future winner. *(tchd 10-1 and 12-1)*
Colmcille(IRE) has moved to a stable who do well with other people's horses, but he will need to step up significantly on this if he is to be winning anytime soon. *(op 6-1)*

5048 LAST OF THE SEASON H'CAP HURDLE (12 hdls) 3m 110y

7:45 (7:45) (Class 5) (0-90,89) 4-Y-O+ **£3,083** (£898; £449)

Form				RPR
0400	**1**		**Charm Offensive**[307] 801 8-10-7 **70** RichardHobson (C J Gray) *prom: rdn appr 8th: outpcd appr 2 out: rallied flat: str run to ld last strides* **20/1**	68
0-P5	**2**	*hd*	**Field Master (IRE)**[18] 4752 9-10-12 **80** RobertLucey-Butler(5) (C J Gray) *hld up and bhd: stdy hdwy 8th: rdn and ev ch whn hit last: r.o towards fin* **13/2**[3]	78
065-	**3**	*½*	**Spanchil Hill**[633] 1080 6-9-8 **64** CharlieStudd(7) (L A Dace) *chsd ldr: led 8th: rdn flat: hdd last strides* **8/1**	62
6366	**4**	*hd*	**Giant's Rock (IRE)**[34] 4556 4-10-3 **73** (t) PJBrennan (B J Llewellyn) *hld up in mid-div: hdwy 9th: nt fluent 3 out: sn rdn: ev ch last: nt qckn* **8/1**	64+
00U0	**5**	*1 ¼*	**They Grabbed Me (IRE)**[18] 4752 5-10-5 **75** (tp) AndrewGlassonbury(7) (M C Pipe) *a.p: r.o one pce fr 2 out* **8/1**	72+
00PP	**6**	*5*	**My Retreat (USA)**[64] 4013 9-9-13 **69** JamesWhite(7) (R Fielder) *hld up and bhd: hdwy after 3 out: no further prog fr 2 out* **40/1**	61+
R421	**7**	*7*	**Hill Forts Henry**[19] 4734 8-10-10 **80** (p) SimonElliott(7) (J W Mullins) *hdwy into mid-div after 2nd: nt fluent 5th: bhd fr 7th* **9/4**[1]	66+
2300	**8**	*25*	**Carl's Boy**[19] 4734 10-10-11 **74** (t) TomScudamore (D A Rees) *led to 8th: mstke 9th: sn wknd* **13/2**[3]	33
346	**P**		**Lets Try Again (IRE)**[13] 4290 9-11-4 **81** TomDoyle (R A Farrant) *hld up: blnd and rdr lost reins 3rd: p.u bef 4th* **6/1**[2]	—

5m 46.5s (-22.10) **Going Correction** -1.125s/f (Hard)
WFA 4 from 5yo+ 7lb **9** Ran SP% **112.3**
Speed ratings: **90,89,89,89,89 87,85,77,—** CSF £139.06 CT £1133.21 TOTE £16.50: £5.20, £2.70, £2.40; EX 94.30 Place 6 £128.11, Place 5 £82.66 .
Owner A P Helliar And A J W Hill **Bred** Colin Bothway **Trained** Moorland, Somerset
■ A one-two for trainer Carroll Gray.

FOCUS
A modest winning time to a moderate contest.

NOTEBOOK
Charm Offensive, making her seasonal reappearance without the visor she had been wearing, was never far off the pace and she rallied strongly under Hobson to collar her seemingly more fancied stable companion in the dying strides. This was an improved effort, but she will need to progress further if she is to follow up. *(op 16-1 tchd 33-1)*
Field Master(IRE) is on a very decent mark and, although just coming up shy on this occasion, a win is surely not far off. *(tchd 11-2)*
Spanchil Hill seems to be heading the right way and a little further improvement should see him capable of winning a moderate contest. *(op 6-1 tchd 9-1)*
Giant's Rock(IRE) had a bit to prove on this step up to three miles, having appeared not to get home over 2m5f at Huntingdon last month, but the firm ground made a big difference to the gelding and he put up an improved effort. It will be a bad race he wins, but he should find one on this evidence. *(tchd 15-2 and 17-2)*
They Grabbed Me(IRE) ran a little better and can surely be found a race eventually. *(op 9-1 tchd 10-1 and 15-2)*
Hill Forts Henry, a winner at Hereford latest, struggled off a 6lb higher mark, but should still have done better. *Official explanation: trainer said gelding would not let himself down on the firm ground (op 10-3 tchd 7-2)*
T/Plt: £435.60 to a £1 stake. Pool: £40,278.25. 67.50 winning tickets. T/Qpdt: £101.10 to a £1 stake. Pool: £3,910.80. 28.60 winning tickets. KH

4875 TOWCESTER (R-H)

Tuesday, April 25

OFFICIAL GOING: Good
Wind: Light, behind Weather: Cloudy with sunny spells

5049 DREAD LTD BEGINNERS' CHASE (16 fncs) 2m 6f

5:25 (5:25) (Class 4) 5-Y-O+ **£4,436** (£1,310; £655; £327; £163)

Form				RPR
6P55	**1**		**Jonny's Kick**[80] 3732 6-11-2 89 RussGarritty (T D Easterby) *a.p: led 11th: drvn out* **10/1**	103
3P33	**2**	*8*	**Mandingo Chief (IRE)**[16] 4806 7-11-2 96 RichardJohnson (R T Phillips) *hld up: hdwy 8th: ev ch 2 out: sn rdn: no ex last* **9/2**[2]	95
0434	**3**	*4*	**Instant Appeal**[30] 4643 9-11-2 83 PhilipHide (P Winkworth) *hld up: hdwy 10th: styd on same pce fr 3 out* **20/1**	91
5/P2	**4**	*1*	**Opal Ridge**[17] 4780 9-11-2 OllieMcPhail (C Roberts) *hld up: hit 2nd: hdwy 6th: mstke 12th: styd on same pce fr 3 out* **11/2**[3]	91+
4250	**5**	*16*	**Woodview (IRE)**[10] 4849 7-11-2 96 TomScudamore (K C Bailey) *hld up: hdwy 6th: wknd after 3 out* **15/2**	74
3-46	**6**	*17*	**Murphy's Quest**[133] 2805 10-11-2 119 LeightonAspell (Lady Herries) *hld up in tch: hit 3 out: sn rdn and wknd* **11/4**[1]	69+
P000	**7**	*13*	**Fortanis**[68] 3951 7-10-9 AndrewThornton (P C Ritchens) *hld up: hdwy 7th: wknd 11th* **100/1**	37
PU	**U**		**Barrshan (IRE)**[19] 4753 7-11-2 (t) MarcusFoley (N J Henderson) *hld up: mstke and uns rdr 11th* **20/1**	—
0P0	**P**		**Hi Blue**[60] 4088 7-10-6 JosephStevenson(10) (R Dickin) *chsd ldrs to 7th: t.o whn p.u bef last* **150/1**	—
P42P	**P**		**Dramatic Quest**[30] 4633 9-10-9 93 (p) RichardSpate(7) (A G Juckes) *prom: hit 7th: sn wknd: t.o whn p.u bef 12th* **25/1**	—
PPP	**P**		**Echo Blu (IRE)**[7] 4937 8-11-2 JasonMaguire (Miss Joanne Priest) *hld up: nt jump wl: a in rr: t.o whn p.u bef 13th* **100/1**	—
	P		**Lutin Collonges (FR)**[16] 7-11-2 BenjaminHitchcott (M J Roberts) *chsd ldr to 7th: wkng whn hit next: t.o whn p.u bef 12th* **100/1**	—
2260	**P**		**Lupin (FR)**[20] 4736 7-11-2 WayneHutchinson (A W Carroll) *hld up: mstke 1st: hdwy 9th: wknd after 3 out: bhd whn p.u bef next* **9/1**	—
P4P	**P**		**Scarlet Fantasy**[16] 4804 6-10-11 87 JamesDiment(5) (P A Pritchard) *hld up: hdwy 6th: wknd 3 out: blnd next: bhd whn p.u bef last* **50/1**	—
00-4	**P**		**Captain Machell (IRE)**[16] 4802 8-11-2 PJBrennan (Andrew Turnell) *chsd ldrs: rdn after 7th: wkng whn hit next: t.o whn p.u bef 13th* **25/1**	—
U0	**P**		**The Well Lad (IRE)**[17] 4780 7-11-2 MatthewBatchelor (A M Balding) *led: hit 1st: hdd 11th: ev ch 3 out: wkng whn blnd next: bhd whn p.u bef last* **66/1**	—

5m 40.3s (-25.70) **Going Correction** -0.60s/f (Firm) **16** Ran SP% **115.4**
Speed ratings: **105,102,100,100,94 88,83,—,—,— —,—,—,—,—,—** CSF £49.17 TOTE £12.20: £3.10, £2.30, £4.30; EX 82.00.
Owner Seven Up Partnership **Bred** N E And Mrs Poole **Trained** Great Habton, N Yorks

FOCUS
Less than half the field completed in what was a modest event. The form looks sound enough.

NOTEBOOK
Jonny's Kick has had many opportunities over fences in the past and did not look to hold obvious claims here, but he took advantage of several below-par performances and stayed on well to win with plenty in hand. The lack of headgear seemed to help and he should stay three miles. *(op 14-1 tchd 16-1 in places)*
Mandingo Chief(IRE) again ran well in defeat, but he does not find winning easy and he failed to get home as well as the winner. He has yet to win over fences, but can find a race in handicaps. *(op 3-1)*
Instant Appeal made a little late headway into third, but was never near the front pair and it is likely a return to handicaps will help.
Opal Ridge has done well since returning from a lengthy lay-off and she would have been closer here had his jumping been more fluent. *(op 9-2)*
Woodview(IRE) is a generally disappointing sort and he remains one to take on. *(op 9-1)*
Murphy's Quest, a useful hurdler, is not progressing as expected over fences and this was yet another disappointing effort on his return from a break. He is better than this, but can hardly be backed with confidence in future. *(op 10-3 tchd 7-2)*

5050 MK SCAFFOLDING (S) H'CAP HURDLE (8 hdls) 2m

5:55 (5:55) (Class 5) (0-95,95) 4-Y-O+ **£2,602** (£764; £382; £190)

Form				RPR
0P33	**1**		**Breezer**[17] 4783 6-10-2 71 MarkBradburne (J A Geake) *hld up: hdwy 5th: led appr last: drvn out* **11/2**[1]	73
0034	**2**	*3*	**Too Posh To Share**[45] 4368 8-9-4 69 oh5 (t) RyanCummings(10) (D J Wintle) *hld up: hdwy 5th: led appr 2 out: hdd bef last: styd on same pce* **10/1**	68
0053	**3**	*1 ¾*	**Will She Spin**[34] 4577 5-9-9 71 WayneKavanagh(7) (J W Mullins) *hld up: j.rt: hdwy 3 out: ev ch next: sn rdn: styd on same pce* **12/1**	68
UU00	**4**	*hd*	**Heatherlea Squire (NZ)**[17] 4783 8-10-1 70 TomSiddall (D J Wintle) *hld up in tch: rdn appr last: styd on same pce* **28/1**	67
P30P	**5**	*4*	**Macreater**[39] 4475 8-10-4 73 (p) PJBrennan (K A Morgan) *prom: hmpd 1st: hit 4th: rdn 2 out: wkng whn hmpd flat* **10/1**	68+
6-PP	**6**	*nk*	**Kynance Cove**[106] 3321 7-9-7 69 oh8 (t) RichardSpate(7) (C P Morlock) *hld up: rdn after 3 out: nvr nrr* **40/1**	62
PU0	**7**	*5*	**Little Rort (IRE)**[17] 4783 7-10-13 85 ChrisHonour(3) (S T Lewis) *prom: led 4th: rdn and hdd appr 2 out: wknd bef last* **17/2**	74+
-0P0	**8**	*3*	**Just Filly (IRE)**[149] 2523 5-10-2 71 oh1 ow2 AnthonyCoyle (Miss C J E Caroe) *hld up: hdwy appr 3 out: wknd next* **40/1**	56
0260	**9**	*2*	**Purr**[8] 4896 5-9-7 69 oh2 (p) MrSRees(7) (M Wigham) *hld up: effrt appr 3 out: sn wknd* **33/1**	52
50/0	**10**	*½*	**Allegiance**[10] 4856 11-10-0 69 SeanCurran (P Wegmann) *a bhd* **100/1**	51

30/P **11** 1 ¼ **Peggy Lou**[17] [4783] 6-10-6 75......(p) ChristianWilliams 56
(B J Llewellyn) *led to 4th: wknd after 3 out* **16/1**

P00U **12** 1 ½ **Crystal Ka (FR)**[29] [4651] 4-10-5 79...... TomScudamore 54
(M R Hoad) *hld up: effrt appr 3 out: sn wknd* **12/1**

/PP2 **13** 9 **Watermouse**[34] [4577] 6-10-12 81...... HenryOliver 52
(R Dickin) *hld up: hmpd 1st and 3rd: effrt appr 3 out: sn wknd* **7/1**[2]

-0P **14** ¾ **Knightsbridge King**[140] [2687] 10-11-12 95...... LeightonAspell 65
(John Allen) *hld up: bhd fr 5th* **16/1**

3650 **U** **Twist N Turn**[34] [4575] 6-9-7 69 oh2...... PhilKinsella[(7)] —
(D McCain) *mstke and uns rdr 1st* **12/1**

6-0P **P** **Bravura**[56] [456] 8-11-3 86......(b) JamieMoore —
(G L Moore) *hld up: hdwy 4th: hmpd and wknd 3 out: bhd whn p.u bef next* **8/1**[3]

601F **P** **Thornton Bridge**[239] [1363] 8-9-13 75...... CharlieStudd[(7)] —
(R J Hewitt) *chsd ldrs: rdn after 4th: cl up whn p.u bef 3 out* **25/1**

0406 **P** **Gran Dana (IRE)**[16] [4794] 6-10-4 80 ow4......(t) MrMatthewSmith[(7)] —
(G Prodromou) *chsd ldrs: rdn after 5th: wkng whn p.u and dismntd bef 2 out* **16/1**

4m 3.80s (-7.60) **Going Correction** -0.50s/f (Good)
WFA 4 from 5yo+ 5lb **18** Ran SP% **124.5**
Speed ratings: **99,97,96,96,94 94,91,90,89,89 88,87,83,82,— —,—,—** CSF £56.67 CT £652.58 TOTE £4.60: £1.10, £2.30, £3.00, £15.50; EX 71.90. The winner was bought in (no amount given).
Owner Kimpton Down Racing Club **Bred** Mrs P D Gulliver **Trained** Kimpton, Hants

FOCUS
A typically competitive selling hurdle in which Breezer forged clear on the run-in. Poor form but solid enough at a low level.

NOTEBOOK
Breezer, 13lb lower than when last winning just over a year ago, has returned to form in recent weeks and this drop back down to two miles appeared to help the gelding. This is about his level these days and he can probably pick up a similar event if kept on the go. *(op 9-2 tchd 6-1)*
Too Posh To Share ran an improved race in the first-time tongue tie, finding just the one too good. She was a fair way out of the weights and a return to further may assist. *(op 12-1)*
Will She Spin ran a solid race for her in-form stable, holding every chance but being unable to go with the winner on the climb to the line.
Heatherlea Squire(NZ) ran his best race for some time and can probably pick up a small race if building on this. *(op 25-1)*
Macreater raced prominently in the early stages, but she had been brushed aside and was held when hampered on the run-in. *(op 12-1)*
Kynance Cove was putting in some good late work and he seems to have benefited from the application of a tongue tie. *(op 50-1)*
Knightsbridge King *Official explanation: jockey said gelding hung left (op 20-1)*
Thornton Bridge *Official explanation: jockey said gelding blew up (op 14-1)*
Gran Dana(IRE) *Official explanation: jockey said gelding lost its action (op 14-1)*

5051 MARSHALL AMPLIFICATION H'CAP CHASE (12 fncs) 2m 110y
6:25 (6:25) (Class 4) (0-105,102) 5-Y-0 **£5,070** (£1,497; £748; £374; £187)

Form RPR

0135 **1** **Glen Thyne (IRE)**[46] [4353] 6-10-0 76 oh1......(b) TomScudamore 90+
(K C Bailey) *hld up in tch: rdn to ld 2 out: clr last: styd on wl* **11/2**[2]

00U1 **2** 8 **Mokum (FR)**[9] [4878] 5-11-4 97 7ex...... WayneHutchinson 102+
(A W Carroll) *hld up: bhd and rdn 7th: hdwy appr 2 out: styd on same pce last* **9/2**[1]

0260 **3** 5 **Upswing**[48] [4303] 9-10-9 85...... KennyJohnson 87+
(R C Guest) *bhd: hdwy after 9th: mstke next: ev ch 2 out: sn rdn: wknd last* **20/1**

4560 **4** 1 ½ **He's Hot Right Now (NZ)**[8] [4922] 7-9-7 81......(p) JohnFlavin[(10)] 81
(R C Guest) *chsd ldr 3rd: rdn and ev ch 2 out: wknd last* **13/2**[3]

-160 **5** 2 **Just A Touch**[63] [4037] 10-11-12 102...... PhilipHide 101+
(P Winkworth) *prom: rdn 9th: hmpd 2 out: wknd appr last* **16/1**

13P3 **6** ¾ **Eau Pure (FR)**[39] [4476] 9-11-4 94......(bt) JamieMoore 91
(G L Moore) *chsd ldrs: rdn 9th: wknd after 2 out* **11/2**[2]

5P30 **7** 7 **Thieves'Glen**[8] 8-11-2 92...... JimCrowley 83+
(H Morrison) *led 2nd: rdn: hdd and hit 2 out: wknd qckly* **9/2**[1]

0336 **8** 5 **Lord Gunnerslake (IRE)**[14] [4820] 6-11-0 90...... AnthonyCoyle 75
(Miss C J E Caroe) *hld up: rdn 9th: wknd next: bhd whn j.rt last* **10/1**

43-P **9** 1 ¾ **The Hearty Joker (IRE)**[7] [4936] 11-10-0 76 oh3...... OllieMcPhail 59
(M J M Evans) *prom: lost pl 3rd: bhd fr 7th* **40/1**

2-00 **10** 3 ½ **Arctic Spirit**[45] [4378] 11-11-11 101...... BenjaminHitchcott 86+
(R Dickin) *led to 2nd: chsd ldrs: rdn and ev ch 3 out: wknd next: bhd whn blnd last* **8/1**

4m 8.00s (-11.30) **Going Correction** -0.60s/f (Firm)
WFA 5 from 6yo+ 3lb **10** Ran SP% **113.8**
Speed ratings: **102,98,95,95,94 93,90,88,87,85** CSF £30.50 CT £456.85 TOTE £6.00: £1.80, £2.00, £5.80; EX 23.70.
Owner Dream Makers Partnership **Bred** J J Harding **Trained** Preston Capes, Northants

FOCUS
A tight contest in which two progressive horses filled the first two placings. The winner was up 7lb on his course and distance win while the runner-up ran to a similar level to his recent course win.

NOTEBOOK
Glen Thyne(IRE), a course and distance winner back in February, has since been racing over farther without success, but the drop back to two miles did the trick and, despite remaining 9lb higher for the course win, he proved far too strong for Mokum. He does stay further, but a stiff two miles seems ideal and he may yet be capable of further progression. *(op 7-1 tchd 8-1)*
Mokum(FR), shouldering a 7lb penalty for his recent course victory, found the combination of a shorter trip and faster ground against him and he was unable to get near the winner. He remains capable of better under more of a stamina examination. *(op 11-4 tchd 5-2)*
Upswing has run a couple of sound races since returning for another crack at fences and his astute trainer can surely place the gelding to find a race before long. *(op 16-1)*
He's Hot Right Now(NZ) has been mixing hurdles and fences and he found disappointingly little here for pressure. He remains winless over fences. *(op 9-1 tchd 10-1)*
Just A Touch has struggled since winning at Huntingdon in January and he is evidently in need of some assistance from the Handicapper. *(op 14-1)*
Thieves'Glen is not the heartiest of characters and a blunder at the second last was enough to worry him out of it. *(op 6-1)*

5052 RED DOT SQUARE SOLUTIONS MARES' ONLY NOVICES' HURDLE (8 hdls) 2m
6:55 (6:55) (Class 4) 4-Y-0+ **£4,436** (£1,310; £655; £327; £163)

Form RPR

003 **1** **Charmatic (IRE)**[17] [4784] 5-10-12...... PJBrennan 101+
(Andrew Turnell) *hld up in tch: led after 3 out: drvn out* **13/2**[3]

2121 **2** 2 ½ **Colline De Fleurs**[47] [4324] 6-11-5 120...... MarkBradburne 105+
(J A B Old) *hld up in tch: rdn to chse wnr appr 2 out: no imp last* **6/5**[1]

4660 **3** 11 **Miss Pebbles (IRE)**[30] [4641] 6-11-5 110...... HenryOliver 95+
(R Dickin) *chsd ldrs: hmpd 3 out: wknd next* **9/1**

0P **4** ¾ **Another Burden**[47] [4324] 5-10-12...... RichardJohnson 86
(H D Daly) *hld up: hdwy 3 out: wknd next* **28/1**

-000 **5** 2 **Miss Sirius**[41] [4450] 6-10-7...... MarkNicolls[(5)] 84
(John R Upson) *chsd ldrs: ev ch 3 out: sn rdn and wknd* **150/1**

2106 **6** 5 **Sonnengold (GER)**[17] [4784] 5-11-5 108...... LeightonAspell 88+
(Mrs L Wadham) *hld up: rdn after 5th: sme hdwy appr 2 out: wknd bef last: eased flat* **8/1**

6130 **7** 5 **Sweet Oona (FR)**[14] [4823] 7-11-2 103......(b) PaulO'Neill[(3)] 81
(Miss Venetia Williams) *trckd ldrs: led 5th: hdd & wknd after 3 out* **9/2**[2]

-045 **8** 1 ¾ **Hiho Silver Lining**[16] [4801] 5-10-12...... JimCrowley 73
(H Morrison) *prom: mstke 4th: sn rdn: wknd 3 out* **16/1**

0 **9** 2 ½ **Glitter Ice**[31] [4621] 5-10-12...... JamieMoore 70
(G Haine) *w ldr tl led after 4th: hdd next: j.lft and wknd 3 out* **100/1**

466 **10** 1 ½ **Parthian Shot**[16] [4801] 6-10-12...... WarrenMarston 69
(R T Phillips) *hld up and bhd: plld hrd: hdwy appr 3 out: wknd bef next* **50/1**

00 **11** 5 **Celtic Flame**[138] [2720] 7-10-12...... TomSiddall 65+
(O Brennan) *hld up: hdwy 4th: mstke and wknd next* **100/1**

0-PP **12** 2 ½ **Getaway Girl**[170] [2082] 8-10-9...... LeeVickers[(3)] 61
(O Brennan) *j.lft and bmpd 1st: hld up: bhd fr 4th* **125/1**

00 **13** 10 **Migigi**[70] [3911] 6-10-12...... BenjaminHitchcott 51
(M J Roberts) *j.rt and bmpd 1st: bhd fr 3rd* **150/1**

-000 **14** 7 **Bamby (IRE)**[41] [4450] 6-10-12...... JasonMaguire 44
(R Ford) *hld up: eased after 5th* **80/1**

-0PP **15** 9 **Hazel Mere**[6] [4956] 6-10-12...... SeanCurran 35
(R Curtis) *led: hdd after 4th: wknd next* **125/1**

R **Moaning Myrtle**[571] 5-10-9......(b[1]) TJPhelan[(3)] —
(G Haine) *ref to r* **100/1**

4m 2.10s (-9.30) **Going Correction** -0.50s/f (Good) **16** Ran SP% **116.5**
Speed ratings: **103,101,96,95,94 92,89,89,87,87 84,83,78,74,70** — CSF £14.28 TOTE £7.00: £1.70, £1.10, £2.50; EX 17.10.
Owner T L Morshead **Bred** Patsy Byrne **Trained** Broad Hinton, Wilts

FOCUS
A typically ordinary mares' novice, but the front two pulled clear and remain capable of better. There is a case for rating the race up to 8lb higher.

NOTEBOOK
Charmatic(IRE) showed when finishing third at Chepstow last time that there is a race in her and, having been restrained early by Brennan, she gradually edged clear once coming through to lead. She is relatively unexposed and may yet be capable of defying a penalty against her own sex before ultimately moving into handicaps. *(op 8-1)*
Colline De Fleurs has taken well to hurdles, winning at this course last month, but having held every chance she was unable to give 7lb away to the winner, finding the combination of the drop in trip and faster surface against her. She may be kept on the go through the summer and remains capable of better back up in trip. *(op 11-8 tchd 11-10 and 6-4 in places)*
Miss Pebbles(IRE) has had excuses for several recent defeats and this was a little better. She can find a small race back in handicaps once the Handicapper eases her a fraction. *(op 8-1)*
Another Burden did not seem inconvenienced by the drop back down in trip, but is unlikely to be seen at her best until tackling handicaps. *(op 33-1)*
Sweet Oona(FR) failed to shine with the blinkers on for the first time over hurdles and dropped away tamely once headed. *(op 5-1)*
Bamby(IRE) *Official explanation: jockey said mare hung left*

5053 MESLYN MAIDEN HUNTERS' CHASE (14 fncs) 2m 3f 110y
7:25 (7:26) (Class 6) 6-Y-0+ **£1,873** (£581; £290; £145)

Form RPR

4 **1** **My Best Buddy**[16] 10-11-11...... MrRCope[(3)] 95
(Mrs Caroline Bailey) *a.p: jnd ldr 5th: led 9th to next: led 2 out: drvn out* **9/4**[2]

-225 **2** 2 **Coole Glen (IRE)**[16] 10-12-0...... MrSMorris 93
(W J Warner) *hld up: hdwy 9th: led next to 2 out: styd on same pce last* **6/4**[1]

P/ **3** 5 **Nominate (GER)**[10] 6-11-11......(t) MrDMansell[(3)] 88
(S Flook) *hld up: mstke 10th: hdwy after 3 out: sn rdn: styd on same pce* **25/1**

4 5 **Lah Di Dah Lad**[17] 12-11-7...... MrLHicks[(7)] 83
(G J Tarry) *prom: jnd ldrs 8th: rdn after 3 out: wknd next* **14/1**

FU/F **5** 16 **Tender Tangle**[16] 11-11-7...... MrRJBarrett[(7)] 67
(Miss S A Loggin) *led to 9th: rdn and wknd appr 2 out* **11/1**

4 **6** 6 **Knighton Combe**[23] 6-12-0...... MrJSnowden 61
(J W Dufosee) *prom: rdn 3 out: wkng whn blnd next* **13/2**[3]

/4-0 **U** **Heavenly King**[24] 8-11-7......(p) MrTVaughan[(7)] —
(Mrs Abbi Vaughan) *blnd and uns rdr 2nd* **16/1**

P **Madame Bavarde**[17] 9-11-0......(p) MissEmily-JaneHarbour[(7)] —
(Mrs S S Harbour) *sn bhd: t.o whn p.u bef 11th* **66/1**

P **Catalan Girl**[758] 7-11-0...... MrMWall[(7)] —
(Miss E J Murray) *hld up in tch: mstke and wknd 3 out: t.o whn p.u bef next* **100/1**

0PP/ **P** **Hornbill**[10] 8-11-7......(b) MrSPJones[(7)] —
(Mrs K Lawther) *chsd ldr to 5th: mstke 8th: wknd 11th: hit 3 out: t.o whn p.u bef next* **40/1**

5m 17.6s (-2.40) **Going Correction** -0.60s/f (Firm) **10** Ran SP% **113.8**
Speed ratings: **80,79,77,75,68 66,—,—,—,—** CSF £6.01 TOTE £2.70: £1.30, £1.20, £4.00; EX 5.90.
Owner Mrs Cyndy Aldridge **Bred** Major R P Thorman **Trained** Holdenby, Northants

FOCUS
A very ordinary hunter chase in which the front two drew five lengths clear of the third.

NOTEBOOK
My Best Buddy, who has been in good form in points, winning four since the turn of the year, was able to improve on his only previous hunter chase experience and ran out a ready winner having come through to take it up a quarter of a mile out. He is a good prospect and it will be both disappointing and surprising if he cannot win again in the short term. *(op 7-4 tchd 5-2 in places)*
Coole Glen(IRE) is a pretty consistent sort in these events and he again ran his race, but the unexposed winner proved too strong. He should continue to pay his way and can pick up another race eventually. *(op 15-8)*
Nominate(GER), an ex-Flat racer, has been performing inconsistently in points but this was a pleasing hunter chase debut and the way he was keeping on suggests he is worth another try at further.
Lah Di Dah Lad ran well for a long way on this hunter chase debut, despite failing to find a rhythm, but he is already 12 and may struggle to make a go of it in this sphere. *(op 20-1)*
Tender Tangle has yet to convince outside of points and this was another slightly disappointing effort. *(op 9-1)*
Knighton Combe had the man of the moment on board, but was another who failed to get home having raced prominently. *(op 7-1)*

5054 SHEPHERD INTERIORS MAIDEN OPEN NATIONAL HUNT FLAT RACE 2m

7:55 (7:56) (Class 5) 4-6-Y-O £2,602 (£764; £382; £190)

Form				RPR
0	1		**The Entomologist (IRE)**[38] [4500] 5-11-4 .... PJBrennan (C R Egerton) *trckd ldrs: led 3f out: rdn over 1f out: edgd rt ins fnl f: all out* **4/1**[1]	95
0	2	*shd*	**Lincoln's Inn (IRE)**[31] [4622] 4-10-13 .... RichardJohnson (P J Hobbs) *hld up: hdwy 6f out: rdn to chse wnr over 2f out: ev ch ins fnl f: styd on* **6/1**[3]	90
0	3	*½*	**Obaki De Grissay (FR)**[38] [4500] 4-10-13 .... MarkBradburne (H D Daly) *mid-div: hdwy 7f out: outpcd over 2f out: r.o wl ins fnl f* **12/1**	90
63	4	*6*	**Glinton**[31] [4622] 4-10-13 .... WarrenMarston (Mrs P Sly) *led: clr 12f out: hdd 3f out: sn rdn: wknd over 1f out* **9/2**[2]	84
5	5	*½*	**Lord Gee (IRE)**[30] [4637] 5-11-4 .... LeightonAspell (O Sherwood) *hld up: hdwy 6f out: rdn over 2f out: wknd over 1f out* **9/2**[2]	88
0	6	*7*	**Perky Peaks (IRE)**[38] [4500] 5-10-13 .... StevenCrawford[(5)] (N A Twiston-Davies) *chsd ldrs: rdn over 3f out: wknd over 1f out* **22/1**	82+
5	7	*3*	**Nobile (FR)**[120] [2987] 5-11-4 .... MatthewBatchelor (M Bradstock) *chsd ldr 10f: wknd over 2f out* **9/1**	78
00	8	*nk*	**Fine Edge**[26] [4680] 5-10-6 .... LiamHeard[(5)] (H E Haynes) *hld up: hdwy 7f out: wknd over 4f out* **66/1**	71
6	9	*1 ¼*	**Scarecrow (IRE)**[30] [4637] 5-11-4 .... AntonyEvans (Mrs P Sly) *hld up in tch: rdn and wknd over 3f out* **20/1**	76
0	10	*3*	**Gentle John (FR)**[104] [3346] 4-10-13 .... BarryFenton (R M Stronge) *s.s: a in rr* **12/1**	68
00-	11	*hd*	**Villa Mara (IRE)**[411] [4290] 6-11-4 .... JamieMoore (S Kirk) *hld up: effrt 1/2-way: n.d* **50/1**	73
6	12	*nk*	**Opare (FR)**[47] [4326] 4-10-6 .... MrPCallaghan[(7)] (H D Daly) *hld up: rdn 1/2-way: a in rr* **25/1**	68
0-0	13	*15*	**Tony's Pride**[346] [355] 6-11-4 .... AndrewThornton (P T Dalton) *chsd ldrs over 9f* **50/1**	58
00	14	*nk*	**Kevinsky Blue**[14] [4825] 4-10-8 .... MarkNicolls[(5)] (M J McGrath) *hld up in tch: rdn 7f out: wknd over 5f out* **100/1**	53
00	15	*9*	**Fingersthumbsngums (IRE)**[38] [4500] 5-11-4 .... AlanO'Keeffe (Jennie Candlish) *hld up: rdn 1/2-way: a in rr* **66/1**	49
0	16	*hd*	**Silk Rope (IRE)**[44] [4398] 6-10-11 .... WayneHutchinson (R T Phillips) *hld up: plld hrd: sme hdwy 1/2-way: wknd over 5f out* **40/1**	41

3m 56.3s (-15.60) **Going Correction** -0.50s/f (Good)
WFA 4 from 5yo+ 5lb **16** Ran SP% **119.3**
Speed ratings: **104,103,103,100,100 96,95,95,94,93 93,92,85,85,80 80** CSF £24.67 TOTE £5.40: £1.90, £3.10, £3.80; EX 46.20 Place 6 £64.58, Place 5 £15.01.
Owner Ronald Brimacombe **Bred** David Connors **Trained** Chaddleworth, Berks

FOCUS
An ordinary bumper likely to produce winners. It has been rated though the fifth.

NOTEBOOK
The Entomologist(IRE), a point winner who flopped on his bumper debut, seemed to appreciate this faster surface and stayed on well up the hill to hold the persistent challenge of Lincoln's Inn. *He had a hard enough race, but will stay further over hurdles and looks one to keep on side. (op 11-2)*
Lincoln's Inn(IRE) stepped up on his initial Newbury effort and seemed to appreciate the restrained tactics. He came through to have every chance and and kept on well up the hill, but could not get by the winner. He can find a bumper on this evidence, with further improvement likely. *(op 11-2)*
Obaki De Grissay(FR) was another who left his debut effort behind on this better ground and, judging by the way he was keeping on towards the finish, two and half miles is going to suit him once hurdling. *(op 11-1)*
Glinton ran a fair race from the front, but was always going to be vulnerable to the classier types and he had nothing left to offer on the climb to the line. *(op 4-1)*
Lord Gee(IRE) was unable to improve on his initial effort and looks the sort who will benefit from another summer on his back. *(op 5-1 tchd 4-1)*
T/Plt: £37.10 to a £1 stake. Pool: £42,162.85. 827.45 winning tickets. T/Qpdt: £7.80 to a £1 stake. Pool: £4,227.50. 398.00 winning tickets. CR

5055 - (Foreign Racing) - See Raceform Interactive

[4060]PUNCHESTOWN (R-H)

Tuesday, April 25

OFFICIAL GOING: Good

5056a VC BET CHAMPION NOVICE HURDLE (GRADE 1) 2m

2:40 (2:40) 5-Y-0+ £42,758 (£13,103; £6,206; £2,068; £1,379)

			RPR
1		**Iktitaf (IRE)**[79] [3772] 5-11-11 136........ (t) RWalsh (Noel Meade, Ire) *hld up in tch: 6th 3 out: 4th and smooth hdwy 2 out: led bef last: sn rdn clr: eased cl home* **8/1**	148+
2	*7*	**Straw Bear (USA)**[18] [4763] 5-11-11 .... APMcCoy (N J Gifford) *cl up: disp ld 4th: led next: rdn and strly pressed after 2 out: hdd bef last: kpt on same pce* **8/11**[1]	136
3	*1 ½*	**Jazz Messenger (FR)**[7] [4950] 6-11-12 .... DFO'Regan (Noel Meade, Ire) *led: jnd 4th: hdd next: dropped to 5th 3 out: styd on again fr bef last* **20/1**	135
4	*3 ½*	**Sublimity (FR)**[42] [4430] 6-11-12 138........ (t) PACarberry (John G Carr, Ire) *cl up: plld hrd early: 2nd 3 out: 3rd next: sn rdn: wknd bef last* **5/1**[3]	132
5	*1 ½*	**Middlemarch (GER)**[79] [3764] 5-11-11 116........ DJCondon (Gerard Cully, Ire) *hld up in rr: no imp fr 3 out: kpt on one pce* **50/1**	129
6	*2 ½*	**Sweet Wake (GER)**[42] [4430] 5-11-11 .... PCarberry (Noel Meade, Ire) *in tch: plld hrd early: impr into cl 3rd 3 out: 2nd whn slt mstke 2 out: sn rdn and no imp: eased after last* **7/2**[2]	127
7	*dist*	**Classic Role**[8] [4915] 7-11-12 .... MickFitzgerald (L Wells) *in tch: plld hrd early: 4th 4 out: wknd after next: eased fr 2 out: t.o* **200/1**	—

3m 50.5s **Going Correction** -0.50s/f (Good) **7** Ran SP% **115.1**
Speed ratings: **116,112,111,110,109 108,—** CSF £15.24 TOTE £7.10: £1.90, £1.50; DF 14.70.
Owner Mrs P Sloan **Bred** Shadwell Estate Company Ltd **Trained** Castletown, Co Meath

FOCUS
A cracking contest that brought together some of the best two-mile novices around.

NOTEBOOK
Iktitaf(IRE) produced a performance of some quality to run out a stylish winner of a race that was initially run at quite a sedate pace. Victorious in the Royal Bond Novice Hurdle earlier this season, he was having his first run since picking up an injury when second to Mounthenry at this track in February. He was travelling ominously well in Straw Bear's slipstream off the final turn and quickened up in fine style to move clear before the last. He had already shown himself to be a classy novice, but this was a career-best effort. He will be a fascinating addition to the Champion Hurdle mix next season. *(op 7/1)*
Straw Bear(USA) came into this off a second in the Supreme Novices and a 13-length success in an Aintree Grade Two several weeks ago. Like several of his rivals he raced a little keenly early on before picking up the tempo somewhat when jumping to the front at the fourth. He had most of his rivals in trouble after the second last but was unable to match Iktitaf when that horse launched his bid for victory. This was still a commendable effort on only his fifth start over hurdles. He too is a very exciting prospect for the coming years. *(op 1/1)*
Jazz Messenger(FR) turned in a fine effort, to finish several lengths closer to Straw Bear than when seventh in the Supreme Novices and he jumped much better than when third at Fairyhouse last week. After looking booked for fourth or fifth off the final bend he stayed on well again in the closing stages, looking like a horse that might improve for a step up in trip.
Sublimity(FR) would also have preferred a stronger pace on his first appearance since his fine fourth in the Supreme Novices. He held second after three out, and was still in contention after the next, but had no more to give from early in the straight. A classy sort on the Flat, he has taken well to hurdles and could land a big prize over hurdles next season. This was only his fourth start over hurdles and there should be further improvement to come.
Middlemarch(GER) was taking a major rise in class having won a maiden hurdle at Limerick on his previous start. He was starting to struggle nearing the third last but kept on in the closing stages and was not at all disgraced. He may prefer a longer trip.
Sweet Wake(GER), who also raced keenly, was an easy winner of his first two starts over hurdles before meeting with defeat at Cheltenham. He was a close third three out and he held second at the next, but was soon under pressure and could find no more in the straight. This was certainly not his true form and he can be expected to leave this effort well behind him next term. *(op 3/1)*
Classic Role finished second to Straw Bear at Folkestone in January, but found this level of competition beyond him. He had no more to give from the third last - he was found to be badly cut *behind from an incident that occurred at that hurdle.Official explanation: jockey said gelding sustained a bad cut behind three out (op 150/1)*

5057a KERRYGOLD CHAMPION CHASE (GRADE 1) 2m

3:15 (3:15) 5-Y-0+ £85,972 (£26,206; £12,413; £4,137; £2,482)

			RPR
1		**Newmill (IRE)**[41] [4445] 8-11-12 171........ AndrewJMcNamara (John Joseph Murphy, Ire) *mde all: mstke 2nd: hit 5 out: nt fluent 3 out: sn drew clr: styd on wl: easily* **5/4**[1]	171+
2	*15*	**Fota Island (IRE)**[18] [4761] 10-11-12 162........ APMcCoy (M F Morris, Ire) *cl 3rd: slt mstke 4 out: 2nd and no imp u.p next: mod 2nd whn slt mstke 2 out* **9/4**[2]	154
3	*¾*	**Central House**[18] [4761] 9-11-12 160........ (t) RLoughran (D T Hughes, Ire) *cl 2nd: rdn and outpcd 4 out: 3rd and one pce fr next* **6/1**[3]	153
4	*14*	**Steel Band**[7] [4949] 8-11-12 129........ GTHutchinson (Paul A Roche, Ire) *hld up: trailing fr 1/2-way: mod 5th 3 out: kpt on same pce* **66/1**	139
5	*¾*	**Mariah Rollins (IRE)**[18] [4761] 8-11-7 143........ RWalsh (P A Fahy, Ire) *chsd ldrs in mod 4th: j.lft thrght: no imp fr bef 4 out* **9/1**	134
6	*nk*	**Sir Oj (IRE)**[17] [4777] 9-11-12 148........ (b) NPMadden (Noel Meade, Ire) *hld up: trailing fr 1/2-way: u.p bef 4 out: kpt on same pce* **16/1**	138

4m 6.30s **Going Correction** -0.50s/f (Good) **6** Ran SP% **106.9**
Speed ratings: **108,100,100,93,92 92** CSF £4.09 TOTE £2.30: £1.70, £1.80; DF 3.00.
Owner Mrs Mary T Hayes **Bred** Mrs Veronica O'Farrell **Trained** Upton, Co. Cork

FOCUS
As was the case with the Champion Chase at Cheltenham, this was definitely substandard judged in terms of strength in depth.

NOTEBOOK
Newmill(IRE), whose last two performances have marked him down as a speed chaser out of the very top drawer, led at a strong gallop from start to finish and effectively had the race in safe-keeping a long way from home. Despite making at least three serious mistakes on his way round - which he did not do at Cheltenham - his momentum never seemed to be sapped, and up the straight he appeared to be dossing to a degree with ears pricked all the way. He came here with upwards of 9lb in hand of his rivals and was entitled to romp home, which is exactly what he did. Having emulated Klairon Davies by completing the Cheltenham-Punchestown double, Newmill now truly merits his place among the upper echelons of two-mile chasers, and while there remains the possibility that the eight-year-old could race over three miles next season, it would surely be wiser to keep him at two miles, as his style of racing and tremendous cruising speed are potent weapons over the minimum distance. He has every right to go into the summer as favourite for next year's Champion Chase. *(op 5/4 tchd 6/4)*
Fota Island(IRE) was beaten even more easily than he had been at Cheltenham. Perhaps a little jaded after another hard race over two and a half miles at Aintree, he jumped a tad sluggishly and never travelled like a horse who was about to pick up Newmill. As a ten-year-old going on 11, he is not going to suddenly start improving, so the likelihood of him winning at the highest grade is not great, and, given that his rating precludes him from going for handicaps, he might not be that easy to place next season. *(op 2/1 tchd 7/4)*
Central House was disappointing at Aintree and he was disappointing again. The usually consistent gelding was being ridden some way from home, although to be fair to him he was the only horse apart from Fota Island to even remotely match strides with Newmill through the race. Having been on the go for an awful long time this season, he can be excused a below-par effort on his ninth run of the campaign and on ground that was very probably quicker than he would have liked. *(op 11/2)*
Steel Band, the lowest-rated horse in the field, won that battle for fourth but he is surely flattered by his placing.
Mariah Rollins(IRE) was probably unsuited by the drop back in trip. *(op 10/1 tchd 8/1)*
Sir Oj(IRE), a faller in his last two starts, including in the Grand National last time, found everything happening too quickly on this ground over this minimum distance.

5058a ELLIER DEVELOPMENTS NOVICE CHASE (GRADE 2) 2m 5f

3:50 (3:50) 5-Y-0+ £24,693 (£7,244; £3,451; £1,175)

			RPR
1		**Missed That**[9] [4889] 7-11-10 .... DJCasey (W P Mullins, Ire) *hld up in tch: cl 4th bef 3 out: 2nd travelling best appr 2 out: sn swtchd to chal: led bef last: styd on strly: impressive* **4/1**[3]	149+
2	*5*	**Slim Pickings (IRE)**[10] [4864] 7-11-6 .... APMcCoy (Robert Tyner, Ire) *cl up: 3rd 1/2-way: led 3 out: rdn and strly pressed next: hdd bef last: kpt on same pce* **7/2**[2]	140+
3	*1 ½*	**Our Ben**[8] [4929] 7-11-3 143........ RWalsh (W P Mullins, Ire) *cl 2nd: disp ld appr 1/2-way: 4th 5 out: 5th u.p bef 2 out: kpt on same pce* **5/1**	135+
4	*5 ½*	**Public Reaction**[9] [4889] 8-11-3 .... DNRussell (Edward U Hales, Ire) *led: jnd bef 1/2-way: drvn along and strly pressed 4 out: hdd 3 out: 3rd and kpt on fr next* **25/1**	130
5	*5*	**Back In Front (IRE)**[41] [4444] 9-11-3 .... PWFlood (E J O'Grady, Ire) *cl up: nt fluent 9th: 2nd 5 out: rdn after slt mstke next: 3rd u.p 3 out: no ex whn mstke 2 out: eased last* **13/8**[1]	125
6	*4 ½*	**Ursumman (IRE)**[188] [1790] 7-11-3 124........ NPMadden (Niall Madden, Ire) *hld up in tch: no imp fr 4 out: eased fr last* **16/1**	120

5m 23.1s **Going Correction** -0.50s/f (Good) **7** Ran SP% **106.7**
Speed ratings: **113,111,110,108,106 104** CSF £16.65 TOTE £5.70: £2.40, £1.90; DF 18.50.

Owner Mrs Violet O'Leary **Bred** Exors Of The Late T F M Corrie **Trained** Muine Beag, Co Carlow

NOTEBOOK
Missed That was the only previous Grade One winner over fences in this field and he came back to form with a resounding victory. Given a patient ride in a well-grouped field, he jumped soundly and began a forward move nearing the fourth-last fence. He was still going quite well coming to the second-last and ran on strongly when switched to the inside to lead at the final fence. He kept on well to move nicely clear of Slim Pickings at the finish. A pair of top-flight victories earlier this season showed him to be one of the best novices around and he was back to his best here. A possible French Champion Hurdle bid is on the cards and he can be expected to take high rank over fences next season, whatever direction he is pointed in. *(op 7/2)*
Slim Pickings(IRE), whose most recent success came in a Listed three-mile chase at Cork, turned in a fine effort over this shorter trip. He had most of his rivals in trouble when jumping to the front at the third-last and it was only coming to the last that he gave best to the winner. A talented sort, he handled this ground well and has a bright future as a staying hurdler. *(op 7/2 tchd 4/1)*
Our Ben raced prominently and, after dropping back to fifth entering the straight, stayed on again at the finish. He confirmed himself to be a good novice when a close third to The Railway Man in the Dr P J Moriarty Novice Chase at Leopardstown in February and is open to further progress. He should do well over three miles next term. *(op 9/2)*
Public Reaction looked to be facing a stiff task but acquitted himself quite well. He made much of the running and kept on under pressure in the straight. A useful sort, he will continue to pay his way.
Back In Front(IRE) was running for the first time since departing at the second last in the SunAlliance when in second place. He was in close contention, but was under pressure after the fourth last, and he had no more to give from early in the straight. *(op 6/4 tchd 7/4)*
Ursumman(IRE) was running for the first time since October and also looked to be facing a stern examination. This was a solid effort and last season's Galway Plate runner-up can be expected to improve on this. *(op 25/1)*

5059a EVENING HERALD H'CAP HURDLE (LISTED RACE) 2m 4f
4:25 (4:25) (0-140,135) 4-Y-0+ **£33,672** (£9,879; £4,706; £1,603)

RPR
1 **Joueur D'Estruval (FR)**[7] [4951] 9-9-10 119 .... RJKiely(7) 128
(W P Mullins, Ire) *rr of mid-div: impr into 6th 5 out: cl 5th 3 out: led after 2 out: clr last: kpt on wl* **20/1**
2 2 **Adamant Approach (IRE)**[7] [4951] 12-11-5 135 .... RWalsh 142
(W P Mullins, Ire) *towards rr: prog 3 out: 10th 2 out: rdn st: mod 2nd last: kpt on wl* **14/1**
3 shd **Knight Legend (IRE)**[8] [4928] 7-10-12 128 .... RMPower 135
(Mrs John Harrington, Ire) *towards rr: hdwy 3 out: 7th bef 2 out: mod 2nd appr last: kpt on u.p* **16/1**
4 2 **Moore's Law (USA)**[51] [4269] 8-10-1 117 .... DFO'Regan 122
(M J Grassick, Ire) *towards rr: tk clsr order after 4 out: 9th after 2 out: rdn and kpt on* **12/1**
5 2 **All Star (GER)**[41] [4446] 6-11-0 130 .... MickFitzgerald 133
(N J Henderson) *trckd ldrs on inner: 9th 5 out: 4th 3 out: kpt on same pce fr next* **9/1**[3]
6 3 **Supreme Being (IRE)**[8] [4930] 9-10-0 116 .... (b) TimmyMurphy 116
(Michael Cunningham, Ire) *mid-div on outer: 9th 2 out: sn outpcd: kpt on fr last* **13/2**[2]
7 1 1/2 **Naples**[163] [2206] 7-10-4 120 .... NPMadden 118
(Noel Meade, Ire) *trckd ldrs on inner: 5th 1/2-way: impr to ld 3 out: hdd after 2 out: sn no ex* **16/1**
8 shd **Letterman (IRE)**[9] [4888] 6-10-11 127 .... PWFlood 125
(E J O'Grady, Ire) *mid-div: prog 5 out: 4th next: 2nd 3 out: chal 2 out: wknd st* **16/1**
9 2 1/2 **Burntoakboy**[16] [4126] 8-9-13 115 .... JMAllen 111
(Michael Cunningham, Ire) *prom: 2nd 4 out: cl 3rd: next: lost pl whn slt mstke 2 out: sn no ex* **20/1**
10 nk **Carthalawn (IRE)**[10] [4861] 5-9-7 112 .... KTColeman(3) 108
(C Byrnes, Ire) *hld up: prog after 3 out: 11th and rdn after 2 out: kpt on same pce* **6/1**[1]
11 2 **Khetaam (IRE)**[7] [4951] 8-10-12 128 .... (b) MissNCarberry 122
(Noel Meade, Ire) *hld up: hdwy on inner 3 out: 5th and rdn 2 out: no ex bef last* **11/1**
12 3 **Vintage Port (IRE)**[13] [4627] 6-9-11 113 ow1 .... WSlattery 104
(T J O'Mara, Ire) *towards rr: no imp fr 3 out* **20/1**
13 3 1/2 **Arc En Ciel (GER)**[9] [4882] 6-10-6 122 .... DJCondon 109
(Gerard Cully, Ire) *trckd ldrs: impr into cl 3rd 5 out: rdn and wknd fr 3 out* **16/1**
14 5 1/2 **City Of Sails (IRE)**[7] [4951] 7-9-7 114 .... BCByrnes(5) 96
(A J McNamara, Ire) *nvr a factor* **16/1**
15 5 **Miss Toulon (IRE)**[20] [4742] 8-9-11 113 .... GTHutchinson 90
(Thomas Mullins, Ire) *a towards rr* **16/1**
16 10 **Whatareyouhaving**[8] [4930] 10-10-1 122 .... NJO'Shea(5) 89
(Henry De Bromhead, Ire) *prom: 5th bef 1/2-way: wknd fr 5 out* **33/1**
17 5 1/2 **Spring Breeze**[31] [4612] 5-9-13 115 .... (b) JRBarry 76
(Ferdy Murphy) *led: jnd 1/2-way: hdd & wknd bef 4 out: mstke 3 out* **16/1**
18 3 **Rooftop Protest (IRE)**[9] [4461] 9-11-2 132 .... (tp) APMcCoy 90
(T Hogan, Ire) *cl 2nd: disp ld 6 out: hdd & wknd after 4 out* **14/1**
19 4 **Haggle Twins (IRE)**[10] [4866] 6-9-10 112 .... TPTreacy 66
(Ms F M Crowley, Ire) *prom: 6th appr 1/2-way: rdn and wknd 4 out* **25/1**
20 2 **The Spoonplayer (IRE)**[8] [4930] 7-9-11 113 .... APCrowe 65
(Henry De Bromhead, Ire) *trckd ldrs: 8th 5 out: wknd after 4 out* **25/1**
21 25 **Davenport Milenium (IRE)**[7] [4951] 10-10-10 126 (t) AndrewJMcNamara 53
(W P Mullins, Ire) *mid-div: wknd 4 out: sn eased: t.o* **33/1**
22 20 **Gemini Guest (IRE)**[8] [4931] 10-10-0 116 .... PACarberry 23
(P Hughes, Ire) *a bhd: trailing fr 1/2-way: t.o* **16/1**
23 13 **Forager**[185] [1828] 7-11-0 130 .... CO'Dwyer 24
(J Ryan) *nvr a factor: trailing 4 out: t.o* **33/1**
F **Alpha Royale (IRE)**[18] [4765] 6-10-8 124 .... DNRussell —
(C Byrnes, Ire) *fell 3rd* **9/1**[3]
P **Colnel Rayburn (IRE)**[17] [4777] 10-10-2 118 .... DJCasey —
(Paul Nolan, Ire) *chsd ldrs to 1/2-way: sn wknd: trailing whn p.u bef 5 out* **20/1**

4m 56.0s **Going Correction** -0.50s/f (Good)
WFA 4 from 5yo+ 6lb **25** Ran SP% **159.6**
Speed ratings: 107,106,106,105,104 103,102,102,101,101 100,99,98,96,94 90,87,86,85,84 74,66,61,—,— CSF £305.25 CT £4650.95 TOTE £17.10: £4.10, £2.60, £8.00, £3.10; DF 166.20.

Owner Mrs Violet O'Leary **Bred** M Bernard Le Gentil **Trained** Muine Beag, Co Carlow

NOTEBOOK
Joueur D'Estruval(FR) came good in this competitive handicap to win his first race for nearly 14 months. The nine-year-old indicated that a race like this could be within his grasp when fifth at Fairyhouse last week, and prior to that he had filled the runner-up spot on his four previous outings. After making his way into contention after halfway, he went to the front at the second last and stayed on well in the straight to make sure of victory. Trainer Willie Mullins feels that the winner is at his best on this ground, but will see how he comes out of this before making any plans for the coming weeks.
Adamant Approach(IRE) ran another cracking race in defeat. He had plenty to do leaving the back straight but made good progress to go second on the run to the last. He was unable to reel in his stable companion but this was yet another commendable effort from the veteran. A confirmed good-ground performer, he can come here on the back of fine runs in the County Hurdle and when just *in front of Joueur d'Estruval at Fairyhouse last week. He could be aimed at the Galway Hurdle. (op 12/1)*
Knight Legend(IRE) ran well on his handicap hurdle debut. He began his move after the fourth last and stayed on quite well in the straight. A lightly-raced sort, he is open to further improvement and could appreciate a slightly longer trip. *(op 20/1)*
Moore's Law(USA) was also putting in some good work towards the finish. He has been in good form since returning from a lengthy break in February and looks quite capable of landing a decent handicap. *(op 10/1)*
All Star(GER) would have finished in the frame in the Coral Cup last time but for running out at the second last. A close fourth at the third last, he was not able to go with the leaders, but kept on under pressure to post a solid effort. *(op 8/1)*
Supreme Being(IRE) was never able to land a blow at the leaders and did not seem to match the form of his second at Fairyhouse last week. *(op 7/1)*
Naples ran well on his first start since last November. A useful novice hurdler, he only gave best at the second last but should improve nicely from this run. He is one to keep in mind.
Letterman(IRE) ran better than his finishing position suggests as he was challenging for the lead at the second last before weakening in the straight.
Carthalawn(IRE) was never able to get involved. *(op 6/1 tchd 11/2)*
Khetaam(IRE) had no more to give in the straight having been fifth at the second last. *(op 10/1 tchd 12/1)*
Spring Breeze did not get home having made much of the running.
Gemini Guest(IRE) *Official explanation: jockey said gelding was outpaced throughout and was unable to lie up*
Colnel Rayburn(IRE) *Official explanation: jockey said gelding did not act on the ground*

5060a GOFFS LAND ROVER BUMPER 2m
5:00 (5:00) 4-5-Y-0
£30,517 (£9,827; £5,000; £2,241; £862; £172)

RPR
1 **Glencove Marina (IRE)**[61] [4087] 4-10-13 .... MsKWalsh(5) 109+
(W P Mullins, Ire) *mde all: rdn clr early st: styd on wl: comf* **7/1**[2]
2 2 1/2 **Powerberry (IRE)**[185] [1842] 5-11-0 .... MrATDuff(7) 109
(T K Geraghty, Ire) *rr of mid-div: hdwy 5f out: 4th 4f out: 3rd appr st: 2nd and kpt on wl fr 2f out* **12/1**
3 11 **Sally's Dream (IRE)**[37] [4540] 4-10-4 .... MrJPO'Farrell(5) 86
(Michael Hourigan, Ire) *mid-div: 9th 1/2-way: prog on outer 3f out: 7th into st: kpt on* **12/1**
4 3/4 **Chairmanforlife**[66] [4004] 5-11-2 .... MrMJO'Connor(5) 97
(J Motherway, Ire) *towards rr: hdwy under 4f out: 8th appr st: kpt on* **16/1**
5 3 **Gold Thread (IRE)**[33] [4588] 5-11-11 .... MissNCarberry 98
(J Howard Johnson) *trckd ldrs: 5th 6f out: 2nd 4f out: sn rdn: no ex early st* **7/1**[2]
6 4 **Minnesota Leader (IRE)**[72] [3897] 5-11-4 .... MrKEPower(3) 90
(Mrs John Harrington, Ire) *towards rr: hdwy 5f out: 4th appr st: no ex u.p 2f out* **10/1**[3]
7 hd **Rebel Chief (IRE)**[93] [3531] 5-11-7 .... MrDerekO'Connor 90
(T M Walsh, Ire) *hld up: kpt on fr over 3f out* **10/1**[3]
8 nk **The Grey Friend**[44] 4-10-7 .... MrRPQuinlan(7) 82
(Andrew Slattery, Ire) *chsd ldrs: 8th 6f out: 5th over 4f out: no ex st* **16/1**
9 2 **Rose Of Clare** 5-10-11 .... MrGJPower(5) 82
(Joseph Crowley, Ire) *trckd ldrs: 6th 1/2-way: rdn and outpcd 5f out: kpt on same pce fr 3f out* **25/1**
10 1 1/2 **Cala Levante (IRE)**[10] [4867] 5-11-7 .... MrPFahey 86
(Mrs John Harrington, Ire) *towards rr: kpt on fr 4f out* **25/1**
11 3/4 **Crottys Point (IRE)**[20] [4740] 4-10-7 .... MrJEBurns(7) 78
(Henry De Bromhead, Ire) *towards rr: kpt on same pce fr over 3f out* **25/1**
12 nk **Square Root (IRE)** 5-11-4 .... MrPGMurphy(3) 85
(Anthony Mullins, Ire) *prom: 4th 5f out: sn rdn and wknd* **10/1**[3]
13 2 1/2 **Theatre Prince (IRE)**[79] [3778] 4-11-0 .... MrAFitzgerald 75
(S J Treacy, Ire) *settled 2nd: rdn 5f out: sn wknd* **25/1**
14 20 **Shanahan (IRE)**[75] [3835] 5-11-2 .... MrLPFlynn(5) 62
(C F Swan, Ire) *prom: 4th on inner 1/2-way: wknd fr over 4f out* **14/1**
15 3 **Lumps And Cracks (IRE)** 5-11-0 .... MrJAFahey(7) 59
(Seamus Fahey, Ire) *rr of mid-div: no ex fr 3 1/2f out* **25/1**
16 2 1/2 **Kingsmaster (IRE)** 5-11-0 .... MrJPMcKeown(7) 57
(Mrs John Harrington, Ire) *hld up: prog into 7th after 1/2-way: no ex fr over 4f out* **16/1**
17 2 1/2 **Lord Killucan (IRE)**[117] [3111] 5-11-7 .... MrJTMcNamara 54
(M Halford, Ire) *rr of mid-div: no ex fr 4f out* **14/1**
18 4 **Darnay Lad (IRE)** 5-11-0 .... MrJKing(7) 50
(E J O'Grady, Ire) *a bhd* **25/1**
19 2 1/2 **Fond Of A Drop** 5-11-0 .... MrRMHennessy(7) 48
(D T Hughes, Ire) *trckd ldrs: 6th 6f out: wknd over 4f out* **12/1**
20 1 **Willow King** 5-11-0 .... MissLAHourigan(7) 47
(Michael Hourigan, Ire) *a bhd* **25/1**
P **Sininlaw (IRE)** 4-11-0 .... MrJJCodd —
(John Queally, Ire) *nvr a factor: p.u lame appr st* **25/1**
P **My Condor (IRE)** 5-11-4 .... MrCJSweeney(3) —
(W J Burke, Ire) *trckd ldrs: 5th 1/2-way: eased over 5f out: sn p.u* **6/1**[1]

3m 41.4s **Going Correction** -0.50s/f (Good)
WFA 4 from 5yo 5lb **23** Ran SP% **151.4**
Speed ratings: 115,113,108,107,106 104,104,104,103,102 102,101,100,90,89 87,86,84,83,82 —,— CSF £96.25 TOTE £5.90: £1.80, £2.30, £2.10, £4.30; DF 76.70.
Owner John J Brennan **Bred** John Murphy **Trained** Muine Beag, Co Carlow
■ Stewards' Enquiry : Mr M J O'Connor three-day ban: excessive and improper use of the whip (May 4-6)

NOTEBOOK
Gold Thread(IRE) found the task of giving weight to all beyond him. His sole outing prior to this had produced a defeat of a couple of promising sorts, and the booking of Nina Carberry suggested big things were expected, but after leaving the back in an attacking position he ran out of gas inside the final quarter-mile. Even so, this was not a bad run, and he should be more than capable of mopping up a few novice hurdles in the north of England. *(op 6/1)*
My Condor(IRE) *Official explanation: jockey said gelding swallowed its tongue in running; vet said gelding was blowing hard (op 10/1)*

The Form Book, Raceform Ltd, Compton, RG20 6NL

5061a **MASTERCHEFS HOSPITALITY H'CAP CHASE** 2m
5:35 (5:35) (0-140,134) 4-Y-0+ **£15,713** (£4,610; £2,196; £748)

RPR

1 **Wills Wilde (IRE)**[7] [4952] 7-10-5 118 APLane(3) 126
(P A Fahy, Ire) *trckd ldrs: 5th 1/2-way: prog after 4 out: 2nd travelling wl after 3 out: led bef next: clr whn slt mstke last: kpt on* **7/1**

2 *2* **Guilt**[7] [4952] 6-9-10 106 (bt) PWFlood 112
(D T Hughes, Ire) *trckd ldrs in 3rd: impr into 2nd 5 out: 3rd after 3 out: 2nd and kpt on u.p fr bef last* **25/1**

3 *2 1/2* **Another Joker**[120] [2998] 11-10-2 112 PaulMoloney 116
(J L Needham) *chsd ldrs in 4th: 5th u.p 5 out: 6th 3 out: kpt on fr next* **25/1**

4 *2 1/2* **Livingstonebramble (IRE)**[7] [4949] 10-11-10 134 RWalsh 135
(W P Mullins, Ire) *hld up: 6th 4 out: 5th next: rdn and no imp fr 2 out: kpt on same pce* **13/2**[3]

5 *4* **Lakil Princess (IRE)**[8] [4931] 5-11-2 126 JLCullen 123
(Paul Nolan, Ire) *chsd ldr in 2nd: 3rd after slt mstke 5 out: 4th 3 out: sn no ex* **7/1**

6 *10* **Kahuna (IRE)**[94] [3501] 9-10-13 123 (b[1]) JRBarry 110
(E Sheehy, Ire) *led: rdn after 3 out: hdd bef next: sn wknd* **10/1**

7 *25* **City Hall (IRE)**[18] [4769] 12-10-13 123 (b) CO'Dwyer 85
(Paul Nolan, Ire) *hld up: wknd 5 out: trailing next: t.o* **25/1**

F **Ivan De Vonnas (FR)**[38] [4511] 10-10-6 116 DJCasey —
(A L T Moore, Ire) *hld up in 6th: fell 3rd* **9/1**

P **Commonchero (IRE)**[7] [4949] 9-11-6 130 TimmyMurphy —
(M J P O'Brien, Ire) *hld up: bdly hmpd 3rd: trailing whn p.u after 5th* **9/4**[1]

P **Laureldean (IRE)**[9] [4890] 8-10-3 113 RMPower —
(Michael Cunningham, Ire) *slow 2nd: sn drvn along and lost tch: t.o 1/2-way: p.u after 4 out* **6/1**[2]

4m 5.90s **Going Correction** -0.50s/f (Good)
WFA 5 from 6yo+ 3lb **10** Ran SP% **114.0**
Speed ratings: **109,108,106,105,103 98,86,—,—,—** CSF £150.53 CT £4027.38 TOTE £10.40: £2.50, £4.60, £12.40; DF 426.40.
Owner T Curran **Bred** R R Clarke **Trained** Leighlinbridge, Co Carlow

NOTEBOOK
Wills Wilde(IRE) put up a gritty performance and continued a recent revival in form for the Pat Fahy stable. He improved to track the leader after the third-last, led before two out, and got away with a mistake at the last as two outsiders gave chase. An improving seven-year-old, he stays a bit further than this and seems well suited by good ground, indicating that he could continue on the go a bit longer despite having had his last three runs within a short period. *(op 6/1)*
Another Joker stepped up on the poor form he had shown towards the end of last year. The ground was probably a help, since three of his four career wins have come on good to firm.
Commonchero(IRE) *Official explanation: jockey said gelding was badly hampered by the fall of a rival (op 9/4 tchd 11/4)*
Laureldean(IRE) *Official explanation: jockey said gelding did not jump well due to the ground conditions (op 9/4 tchd 11/4)*

[1526]PERTH (R-H)

Wednesday, April 26

OFFICIAL GOING: Good (good to firm in places)
Wind: Breezy; half against

5063 **MEIKLEOUR HOTEL PARTY CONTINUES MAIDEN HURDLE** (9 hdls 1 omitted) 2m 4f 110y
2:30 (2:30) (Class 4) 4-Y-0+ **£5,204** (£1,528; £764; £381)

Form RPR

344- 1 **All Things Equal (IRE)**[433] [3907] 7-11-0 TJPhelan(3) 106+
(Mrs H Dalton) *keen: chsd ldrs: led gng wl bef 2 out: sn clr* **7/2**[2]

4-66 2 *10* **Troll (FR)**[103] [3376] 5-11-3 TonyDobbin 91+
(L Lungo) *chsd ldrs: led 3 out to bef next: kpt on same pce* **4/1**[3]

5-64 3 *4* **Fastaffaran (IRE)**[23] [4720] 5-11-3 RichardMcGrath 86+
(I McMath) *hld up: effrt 3 out: no imp whn mstke next* **7/2**[2]

0550 4 *3* **Floral Rhapsody**[23] [4720] 5-10-10 DominicElsworth 75
(P Beaumont) *in tch: drvn along bef 3 out: no imp bef next* **33/1**

0 5 *6* **Bobbing Cove**[71] [3912] 7-11-3 JimmyMcCarthy 76
(Mrs L B Normile) *bhd: hdwy and in tch after 3 out: rdn and outpcd bef next* **100/1**

0600 6 *18* **Justwhateverulike (IRE)**[17] [4793] 5-11-0 DougieCostello(3) 58
(Miss S E Forster) *blnd 1st: towards rr: rdn bef 3 out: n.d* **100/1**

6 7 *nk* **Aztec Prince (IRE)**[18] 6-11-0 MrCStorey(3) 58
(Miss S E Forster) *bhd: rdn bef 3 out: nvr on terms* **20/1**

00P- 8 *1 1/4* **Solway Larkin (IRE)**[665] [843] 8-10-3 GarethThomas(7) 49
(Miss L Harrison) *mstkes: chsd ldrs tl wknd after 3 out* **100/1**

2-02 9 *3/4* **General Hardi**[9] [4916] 5-11-3 RussGarritty 56
(J Wade) *sn w ldr: led 6th to 3 out: sn wknd* **11/4**[1]

40 10 *dist* **The Saltire Tiger**[38] [4533] 5-10-12 DesFlavin(5) —
(Mrs L B Normile) *midfield: rdn bef 3 out: sn btn* **16/1**

0PPP 11 *4* **Mountain Mix**[5] [4988] 6-11-3 (b) MarkBradburne —
(Mrs L B Normile) *led to 6th: wknd bef next* **100/1**

12 *27* **Royal Mackintosh** 5-11-3 AlanDempsey —
(A H Mactaggart) *a bhd* **33/1**

13 *10* **Tipu Sultan**[185] 6-11-3 NeilMulholland —
(M D Hammond) *midfield tl wknd after 6th* **25/1**

14 *dist* **Solway Ed (IRE)** 7-11-1 ow5 MrDJewett(7) —
(Miss L Harrison) *sn wl bhd* **66/1**

60 P **Madam Killeshandra**[38] [4533] 6-10-3 PhilKinsella(7) —
(A Parker) *nt fluent in rr: t.o whn p.u bef 3 out* **25/1**

5m 2.80s (-5.40) **Going Correction** -0.325s/f (Good)
WFA 4 from 5yo+ 6lb **15** Ran SP% **120.8**
Speed ratings: **97,93,91,90,88 81,81,80,80,— —,—,—,—,—** CSF £16.88 TOTE £4.70: £1.90, £1.90, £1.50; EX 23.60.
Owner J Hales **Bred** Thomas Earney **Trained** Norton, Shropshire

FOCUS
A moderate maiden, run at an average pace, and the field came home strung out behind the facile winner, who is value for further with the runner-up to his mark.

NOTEBOOK
All Things Equal(IRE) ♦, making his debut for a new yard on the back of a 433-day layoff, came right away from the runner-up after the penultimate flight and ultimately got off the mark as a hurdler at the third attempt with a facile success. This looks to be his optimum trip in this sphere - although he ought to get further when sent over fences in due course - and, given that his dam registered her only two wins on firm ground, it was little surprise that he relished this decent surface. One will have to be wary of the bounce factor ahead of his next assignment, but it is hard *to not be impressed by this return to action, and he looks ready to fulfill his potential now. (tchd 10-3 and 4-1)*
Troll(FR), returning from a 103-day break, travelled kindly enough until being made to look pedestrian when the winner asserted after the penultimate flight. This was his best effort to date as a hurdler and, while he has not progressed as may have been expected this season, he ought to find life easier now he is eligible for a handicap rating. He may also be happier when dropping back in trip on this evidence. *(op 7-2 tchd 9-2)*
Fastaffaran(IRE) settled better under restraint this time and, while never a danger to the first pair, this must rate an improved effort. This trip looks to be as far as he wants to go - his dam was successful at the minimum trip - and he should find his feet now that he qualifies for a handicap mark. *(op 9-2)*
Floral Rhapsody, up in trip, showed improved form for this switch to a faster surface and managed to finish a great deal closer to Fastaffaran than had been the case at Kelso last time out. She is related to a winning pointer and may well need even further.
General Hardi, well backed, dropped out tamely when push came to shove and has to rate very disappointing. He may have found this coming a touch too soon after his latest improved effort at Sedgfield and will be qualified for handicaps after his next outing. *(op 3-1 tchd 7-2 and 4-1 in a place)*

5064 **TULLIBARDINE DISTILLERY NOVICES' H'CAP HURDLE** (12 hdls) 3m 110y
3:05 (3:08) (Class 4) (0-110,110) 4-Y-0+ **£5,204** (£1,528; £764; £381)

Form RPR

656 1 **Noir Et Vert (FR)**[114] [3205] 5-10-7 **91** KeithMercer 100
(Ferdy Murphy) *trckd ldrs: led 4 out: hrd pressed fr between last two: hld on gamely run in* **25/1**

2P42 2 *shd* **Chief Dan George (IRE)**[23] [4724] 6-10-10 **99** DeclanMcGann(5) 109+
(D R MacLeod) *loose bef s: keen: hld up: hdwy bef 3 out: disp ld between last two: kpt on: hld nr fin* **11/1**

02PP 3 *13* **Capybara (IRE)**[17] [4790] 8-11-12 **110** DavidO'Meara 106
(H P Hogarth) *prom: outpcd 3 out: kpt on fr next: nt rch first two* **50/1**

40P1 4 *5* **Reap The Reward (IRE)**[5] [4986] 6-10-10 **97** GaryBerridge(3) 89+
(L Lungo) *hld up: hdwy bef 3 out: rdn and no imp fr next: fin lame* **15/8**[1]

3621 5 *4* **Powerlove (FR)**[34] [4584] 5-11-5 **103** MarkBradburne 90
(Mrs S C Bradburne) *prom: drvn after 4 out: rallied bef 2 out: sn no imp* **8/1**[2]

5423 6 *19* **August Rose (IRE)**[39] [4487] 6-10-7 **91** PeterBuchanan 59
(Miss Lucinda V Russell) *midfield: outpcd bef 3 out: n.d after* **14/1**

050 7 *shd* **Doris's Gift**[121] [2979] 5-10-0 **84** oh2 GLee 52
(J Howard Johnson) *mstkes: racd wd in midfield: rdn and wknd 3 out: btn whn blnd next* **50/1**

4431 8 *1 1/4* **Kirkside Pleasure (IRE)**[46] [4362] 5-11-9 **107** WilsonRenwick 74
(Mrs S C Bradburne) *prom tl rdn and wknd fr 3 out* **16/1**

U046 9 *11* **Irish Raptor (IRE)**[45] [4396] 7-11-1 **99** TomScudamore 55
(N A Twiston-Davies) *led: hdd whn hit 4 out: wknd next* **16/1**

0056 10 *18* **Phantom Major (FR)**[48] [4313] 5-10-1 **92** MissRDavidson(7) 30
(Mrs R L Elliot) *towards rr: rdn after 4 out: n.d* **25/1**

1216 11 *4* **Camden Bella**[96] [3484] 6-11-9 **107** DominicElsworth 41
(N G Richards) *hld up: rdn 4 out: nvr on terms* **20/1**

-131 12 *14* **Custom Design**[45] [4387] 5-11-1 **99** AlanDempsey 19
(G A Harker) *hld up: rdn 4 out: sn btn* **14/1**

-413 13 *shd* **Mags Two**[196] [1723] 9-9-11 **84** oh2 DougieCostello(3) —
(I McMath) *keen towards rr: struggling 4 out: sn btn* **16/1**

32F2 14 *10* **Bar Gayne (IRE)**[21] [4734] 7-10-13 **97** JasonMaguire 7
(T R George) *chsd ldrs tl wknd qckly 8th* **10/1**[3]

22FP P **Sergio Coimbra (IRE)**[71] [3918] 7-11-1 **99** (b[1]) TonyDobbin —
(N G Richards) *chsd ldrs tl wknd 8th: p.u after next: lame* **11/1**

0600 P **Super Revo**[58] [4141] 5-10-6 **90** RichardMcGrath —
(Mrs K Walton) *bhd: reminders 6th: wknd 8th: p.u after next* **33/1**

5m 57.1s (-13.80) **Going Correction** -0.325s/f (Good) **16** Ran SP% **121.9**
Speed ratings: **109,108,104,103,101 95,95,95,91,86 84,80,80,77,— —** CSF £264.18 CT £12894.20 TOTE £20.80: £4.30, £2.80, £9.50, £1.50; EX 409.00.
Owner D F O'Rourke **Bred** Scea La Chaussee **Trained** West Witton, N Yorks
■ Stewards' Enquiry : Keith Mercer two-day ban: used whip with excessive frequency and without giving gelding time to respond (May 8-9)

FOCUS
A moderate handicap, run at a solid pace, and the first two came well clear. The third sets the standard.

NOTEBOOK
Noir Et Vert(FR), absent for 114 days previously and making his handicap bow, took the race by the scruff of the neck nearing four out and eventuallly just had enough left in the locker to repel the fast-finishing runner-up and score a career-first success. The step-up to this trip played to his strengths, as did the switch to this faster surface, and he has clearly begun handicap life on a decent mark.
Chief Dan George(IRE), who got loose before the start, deserves extra credit as he was notably free through the early parts and was only just denied at the finish. He is a headstrong character, but this was another improved effort for yet another step-up in trip, and he is clearly versatile as regards underfoot conditions. Nicely clear of the rest at the finish, he deserves to lose his maiden tag. *(op 10-1 tchd 12-1)*
Capybara(IRE), pulled-up over fences the last twice, was not disgraced under top weight considering he found things happening all to quickly when the winner kicked for home three out. He really needs a stiffer test, plus he has shown all of his previous best form on easier ground, so hopefully his confidence will have been restored again now and he is capable of going in when getting his optimum conditions.
Reap The Reward(IRE), who escaped a penalty for his success in a conditional riders' event five days previously, weakened when the race became serious approaching the third last flight and was later found to have finished lame. He is capable of better on his day, but he is due to race from an *11lb higher mark in the future. Official explanation: jockey said gelding finished lame on left fore (op 5-2 tchd 7-4)*
Kirkside Pleasure(IRE) *Official explanation: jockey said gelding lost its action*
Sergio Coimbra(IRE) *Official explanation: jockey said gelding pulled up lame (op 10-1 tchd 12-1)*

5065 **S.B.J. NELSON STEAVENSON NOVICES' CHASE** (18 fncs) 3m
3:40 (3:40) (Class 2) 5-Y-0+ **£12,572** (£3,746; £1,896; £972; £508)

Form RPR

2351 1 **Ryders Storm (USA)**[17] [4802] 7-11-7 113 JasonMaguire 124
(T R George) *chsd ldrs: led 2 out: drvn out* **4/1**[3]

4210 2 *4* **Briery Fox (IRE)**[42] [4447] 8-11-10 128 MarkBradburne 123+
(H D Daly) *chsd ldrs: effrt bef 3 out: sn outpcd: kpt on fr next: nt rch wnr* **2/1**[1]

1P3F **3** *1 1/4* **Kid'Z'Play (IRE)**[31] 4635 10-11-10 130 RichardMcGrath 122
(J S Goldie) *mde most to 2 out: outpcd last* **7/1**

2130 **4** *dist* **Classic Capers**[43] 4433 7-11-7 125 DominicElsworth —
(J M Jefferson) *chsd ldrs tl wknd 4 out: n.d after* **5/1**

646P **5** *25* **Goodbadindiferent (IRE)**[71] 3915 10-11-7 77 KeithMercer —
(Mrs J C McGregor) *sn wl bhd: no ch fnl circ* **100/1**

-P51 **U** **Galero**[96] 3489 7-11-7 117 GLee —
(J Howard Johnson) *w ldr whn blnd and uns rdr 10th* **7/2**[2]

5613 **F** **Political Cruise**[11] 4840 8-11-2 80 GarethThomas —
(R Nixon) *sn bhd: mstke and struggling 9th: t.o last whn fell last* **50/1**

6m 9.80s (-2.80) **Going Correction** -0.225s/f (Good) **7** Ran SP% **107.7**
Speed ratings: **95,93,93,—,— —,—** CSF £11.46 TOTE £5.80: £2.70, £1.90; EX 11.90.
Owner Ryder Racing Ltd **Bred** Stud Tnt **Trained** Slad, Gloucs

FOCUS
A fair novice chase which saw the first three come clear, though the winning time was modest for the grade.

NOTEBOOK
Ryders Storm(USA), up in trip, followed-up his recent Worcester success in ready fashion under his 5lb penalty. He loves this sort of ground, stayed the longer trip without fuss, and is finally coming good as a chaser. *(op 7-2)*
Briery Fox(IRE), who made crucial mistakes when beaten in the Kim Muir at Cheltenham last time, found just the same pace when it mattered in the home straight and was staying on again all too late at the finish. His jumping was more assured this time, but this was still disappointing considering he would have been giving the winner 12lb if it were a handicap, and on this evidence he is flattered by his current official mark. *(op 11-4)*
Kid'Z'Play(IRE), who has registered five of his six previous wins over jumps at this venue and was officially the highest-rated runner in the line-up, had every chance from the front yet did not appear to get home over this longer trip. He is an unpredictable performer, but he is worthy of another chance when reverting to a shorter trip. *(op 5-1)*
Classic Capers again did little to convince that he wants this trip and is in danger of going the wrong way over fences. He needs to drop in distance in order to get a confidence boost. *(op 9-2)*
Galero, up in trip and popular in the betting ring on this return from a 96-day break, was bang in contention prior to unseating. *(op 4-1)*

5066 JOHN SMITH'S H'CAP HURDLE (8 hdls) 2m 110y
4:15 (4:15) (Class 3) (0-120,120) 4-Y-0+ **£7,807** (£2,292; £1,146; £572)

Form RPR

2140 **1** **Lennon (IRE)**[70] 3929 6-11-2 115 BrianHughes(5) 119
(J Howard Johnson) *midfield: hdwy 3 out: rdn bef next: styd on wl fr last to ld cl home* **9/1**

4410 **2** *1/2* **Sun King**[33] 4608 9-10-1 105 (t) JamesReveley(10) 109
(K G Reveley) *in tch: smooth hdwy bef 2 out: led run in: kpt on: hdd cl home* **9/1**

4102 **3** *1/2* **Billyandi (IRE)**[8] 4938 6-10-5 106 MarcGoldstein(7) 110+
(N A Twiston-Davies) *mde most at decent gallop tl hdd run in: rallied: hld cl home* **15/2**[3]

41P0 **4** *1* **Front Rank (IRE)**[17] 4792 6-11-4 112 RichardMcGrath 114
(Mrs Dianne Sayer) *bhd tl styd on wl fr 2 out: nrst fin* **66/1**

14B0 **5** *hd* **Crathorne (IRE)**[138] 2746 6-11-3 116 TJDreaper(5) 118
(M Todhunter) *bhd: hdwy bef 2 out: edgd rt: kpt on fr last* **12/1**

4-F4 **6** *14* **Rehearsal**[81] 2478 5-11-7 115 TonyDobbin 105+
(L Lungo) *in tch: effrt 2 out: sn wknd* **4/1**[1]

0200 **7** *3/4* **Diamond Mick**[9] 4922 6-10-1 102 (p) MissRDavidson(7) 89
(Mrs R L Elliot) *reluctant to line up: towards rr: drvn 1/2-way: nvr rchd ldrs* **20/1**

6420 **8** *1 1/2* **Stormy Lord (IRE)**[5] 4990 10-11-0 108 RussGarritty 94
(J Wade) *bhd: rdn after 4 out: n.d* **16/1**

-331 **9** *shd* **Beseiged (USA)**[322] 689 9-11-12 120 PadgeWhelan 105
(J L Spearing) *keen: chsd ldrs tl wknd fr 2 out* **9/1**

-050 **10** *1 3/4* **Its Crucial (IRE)**[48] 4329 6-11-6 114 TomScudamore 98
(N A Twiston-Davies) *midfield: struggling after 4 out: n.d after* **25/1**

45-0 **11** *hd* **Show No Fear**[19] 2566 5-10-5 102 (t) DougieCostello(3) 86
(G M Moore) *w ldr tl wknd bef 2 out* **33/1**

3331 **12** *9* **Nerone (GER)**[58] 4143 5-10-11 105 NeilMulholland 80
(P Monteith) *keen in midfield: hdwy and prom bef 3 out: rdn and wknd bef next* **11/2**[2]

1465 **13** *11* **Farne Isle**[4] 3853 7-11-1 109 (tp) AlanDempsey 73
(G A Harker) *in tch tl rdn and wknd after 3 out* **16/1**

2326 **14** *hd* **Lethem Air**[23] 4723 8-10-8 102 WilsonRenwick 65
(T Butt) *towards rr: struggling 1/2-way: nvr on terms* **22/1**

420P **P** **Templet (USA)**[79] 3783 6-10-1 95 (b) JimmyMcCarthy —
(W G Harrison) *sn wl bhd: t.o whn p.u bef 4 out* **66/1**

3m 52.5s (-8.10) **Going Correction** -0.325s/f (Good) **15** Ran SP% **115.5**
Speed ratings: **106,105,105,105,104 98,98,97,97,96 96,92,86,86,—** CSF £77.10 CT £637.71 TOTE £10.10: £3.50, £2.70, £2.50; EX 87.80.
Owner Andrea & Graham Wylie **Bred** Henry Phipps **Trained** Billy Row, Co Durham

FOCUS
A fair handicap, run at a sound gallop, and the form looks sound enough with the first five coming clear.

NOTEBOOK
Lennon(IRE), disappointing on his handicap debut in this sphere when last seen 70 days previously, showed his true colours on this return to quicker ground and scored in gritty fashion. He has not yet reproduced his smart bumper form over timber, but he should still look feasily treated after a rise in the weights for this, and could well go in again providing he can maintain this current mood. *Official explanation: trainer had no explanation for the improved form shown (op 10-1)*
Sun King was produced to lead on the run-in, yet proved powerless to resist the winner's late burst. This sort of ground is clearly the key to him and he is on a fair mark at present. *(op 10-1 tchd 8-1)*
Billyandi(IRE) turned in a brave effort from the front and proved game after being headed after the final flight. He remains in decent form and deserves to find another race. *(op 13-2)*
Front Rank(IRE) showed much-improved form and would have been closer under a more positive ride. He can build on this and will not mind the return to easier ground in the future. *(op 80-1)*
Crathorne(IRE), returning from a 138-day break, ran in snatches yet stuck to his task under pressure and left the impression he ought to be sharper for the outing. *(op 8-1)*
Rehearsal, having his first outing over timber for 152 days, never really looked a threat at any stage and has to rate disappointing. *(tchd 7-2)*
Nerone(GER) was well backed, but he once again paid for refusing to settle early on. *(op 7-1)*

5067 ALLIED IRISH BANK (GB) H'CAP CHASE (FOR THE SCOTTISH MEMORIES CHALLENGE CUP) (15 fncs) 2m 4f 110y
4:45 (4:45) (Class 3) (0-125,122) 5-Y-0+ **£13,012** (£3,820; £1,910; £954)

Form RPR

023P **1** **Key Phil (FR)**[46] 4371 8-11-5 115 JasonMaguire 128+
(D J Wintle) *chsd ldrs: led after 3 out: clr next: easily* **6/1**[3]

1240 **2** *13* **South Bronx (IRE)**[38] 4531 7-11-6 116 (t) MarkBradburne 114
(Mrs S C Bradburne) *hld up in tch: outpcd 8th: rallied 4 out: chsd wnr last: no imp* **20/1**

5F03 **3** *2 1/2* **Gone Too Far**[26] 3929 8-11-11 121 (v) JimmyMcCarthy 117
(P Monteith) *in tch: stdy hdwy 9th: effrt 4 out: one pce next* **12/1**

3211 **4** *10* **Polyphon (FR)**[34] 4586 8-11-9 119 WilsonRenwick 105
(P Monteith) *cl up: led 6th: hdd after 3 out: sn no ex: lost 2nd last* **7/1**

0U61 **5** *dist* **Terre De Java (FR)**[20] 4755 8-11-12 122 JodieMogford —
(Mrs H Dalton) *nt fluent: hld up: hdwy 11th: rdn after next: btn 3 out: mstke last* **9/2**[2]

2332 **F** **Billie John (IRE)**[211] 1570 11-10-4 100 RichardMcGrath —
(Mrs K Walton) *hld up: fell 7th* **6/1**[3]

1UP4 **P** **Moor Spirit**[11] 4850 9-11-3 113 RussGarritty —
(P Beaumont) *in tch tl wknd 11th: t.o whn p.u bef 3 out* **7/1**

4304 **P** **Shannon's Pride (IRE)**[17] 4806 10-10-8 104 LarryMcGrath —
(R C Guest) *chsd ldrs tl lost pl bef 10th: t.o whn p.u bef 3 out* **12/1**

6400 **P** **Va Vavoom (IRE)**[19] 4762 8-11-8 118 (bt[1]) TomScudamore —
(N A Twiston-Davies) *mde most to 6th: cl up tl wknd 9th: t.o whn p.u bef 3 out* **4/1**[1]

5m 6.50s (-8.80) **Going Correction** -0.225s/f (Good) **9** Ran SP% **111.9**
Speed ratings: **107,102,101,97,— —,—,—,—** CSF £99.87 CT £1371.50 TOTE £8.20: £3.10, £5.70, £3.70; EX 101.60.
Owner The Key Partnership **Bred** Phillipe Legault **Trained** Naunton, Gloucs

FOCUS
A fair handicap, run at a decent clip, with the winner value for more than the official margin and setting the standard, but the form should be treated with a degree of caution.

NOTEBOOK
Key Phil(FR), pulled up on heavy ground at Chepstow last time, finally resumed winning ways over fences and came home to score pretty much as he pleased. He handled this quicker ground without fuss, it is interesting that three of his four wins to date have all been in April, and he would *have to be of real interest if turned out under a penalty.Official explanation: trainer had no explanation for the improved form shown (op 7-1)*
South Bronx(IRE) turned in a much more encouraging effort, but surprisingly appeared to find this an insufficient test of stamina. *(op 14-1)*
Gone Too Far, having his first outing over fences since October last year, did not get home over this trip and should be capable of better when reverting to a shorter trip. *(op 10-1 tchd 14-1)*
Polyphon(FR) showed up well until being headed after the third last and looked to throw in towel thereafter. That said, all of his previous best efforts have been at the minimum trip. *(op 6-1)*
Terre De Java(FR), up 10lb for winning at Taunton 20 days previously, spoilt any chance he may have had by making too many jumping errors. He has it all to prove after this. *(tchd 5-1 in places)*
Va Vavoom(IRE), whose yard has an excellent strike-rate at this venue, stopped quickly down the *back straight as though something was amiss. Official explanation: trainer had no explanation for the poor form shown (op 5-1)*

5068 ATTHERACES.COM AMATEUR RIDERS' H'CAP HURDLE (12 hdls) 3m 110y
5:15 (5:15) (Class 4) (0-100,100) 4-Y-0+ **£4,996** (£1,549; £774; £387)

Form RPR

3506 **1** **Burren Moonshine (IRE)**[95] 3508 7-10-11 92 MrPSheldrake(7) 101+
(P Bowen) *in tch: hdwy 7th: led bef 3 out: hrd pressed next: hld on gamely run in* **9/2**[1]

-PP3 **2** *hd* **Sir Rowland Hill (IRE)**[17] 4805 7-11-5 100 MrSWByrne(7) 108
(Ferdy Murphy) *hld up midfield: hdwy bef 3 out: effrt and disp ld next: hung rt u.p last: kpt on: jst hld* **7/1**[3]

3000 **3** *12* **Speed Kris (FR)**[64] 4043 7-11-1 92 (v) MissRDavidson(3) 89+
(Mrs S C Bradburne) *chsd ldrs tl rdn and outpcd appr 2 out* **16/1**

665 **4** *2* **Syncopated Rhythm (IRE)**[67] 3997 6-10-5 84 MrDEngland(5) 80+
(N A Twiston-Davies) *chsd ldrs: led 5th to bef 3 out: rallied u.p and ev ch appr next: sn btn* **13/2**[2]

6000 **5** *6* **Political Sox**[96] 3487 12-10-9 90 MrMEllwood(7) 78
(R Nixon) *bhd tl hdwy bef 2 out: kpt on: no imp* **25/1**

04F6 **6** *5* **Caesar's Palace (GER)**[5] 4982 9-11-4 99 (p) MrDOakden(7) 82
(Miss Lucinda V Russell) *in tch: lost pl after 4th: sme late hdwy: n.d* **25/1**

33-0 **7** *1* **Solway Minstrel**[17] 4805 9-11-8 99 MrDJewett(3) 81
(Miss L Harrison) *chsd ldrs tl wknd after 3 out* **25/1**

P220 **8** *2* **The Masareti Kid (IRE)**[11] 4844 9-10-2 83 MrLeelnnes(7) 63
(I McMath) *midfield: hit 2nd: effrt 3 out: sn wknd* **16/1**

0P2/ **9** *7* **Fortunate Dave (USA)**[395] 7-11-6 97 MrMSeston(3) 70
(M Smith) *in tch tl rdn and wknd fr 3 out* **20/1**

5000 **10** *3/4* **Bodfari Signet**[23] 4724 10-11-3 98 MrSFMagee(7) 70
(Mrs S C Bradburne) *midfield: outpcd bef 8th: n.d after* **16/1**

0305 **11** *9* **Welsh Dream**[29] 4656 9-10-12 93 MissJRiding(7) 56
(Miss S E Forster) *hld up: rdn after 4 out: wknd after next* **16/1**

003P **12** *21* **Opal's Helmsman (USA)**[10] 3918 7-10-2 83 (v) MrCJCallow(7) 25
(W S Coltherd) *a bhd* **25/1**

5353 **13** *1/2* **Ideal Du Bois Beury (FR)**[23] 4721 10-11-1 96 ow4 MrJWallace(7) 38
(P Monteith) *a bhd* **20/1**

0004 **F** **Valerun (IRE)**[9] 4899 10-11-0 91 ow1 (p) MrCMulhall(3) —
(R C Guest) *hld up: fell 8th* **25/1**

5631 **P** **Oulton Broad**[42] 4449 10-11-5 96 (p) MrGTumelty(3) —
(R Ford) *hld up: rdn 4 out: sn btn: t.o whn p.u bef 2 out* **7/1**[3]

5F0- **P** **Keep Smiling (IRE)**[639] 1047 10-10-9 83 MrCStorey —
(Mrs C J Kerr) *bhd: outpcd whn hmpd 8th: t.o whn p.u bef 3 out* **100/1**

2040 **P** **Le Millenaire (FR)**[23] 4724 7-11-5 100 MissKBryson(7) —
(S H Shirley-Beavan) *led to 3rd: cl up tl wknd 7th: t.o whn p.u bef last* **33/1**

22-U **P** **Alice's Old Rose**[114] 3209 9-10-2 83 ow2 MrDAFitzsimmons(7) —
(Mrs H O Graham) *led 3rd to 5th: wknd 4 out: t.o whn p.u bef last* **25/1**

5m 59.6s (-11.30) **Going Correction** -0.325s/f (Good) **18** Ran SP% **116.6**
Speed ratings: **105,104,101,100,98 96,96,95,93,93 90,83,83,—,— —,—,—** CSF £27.69 CT £464.31 TOTE £5.10: £1.40, £2.50, £3.00, £2.10; EX 30.00 Place 6 £157.45, Place 5 £92.72.
Owner G P O'Gara **Bred** Gabriel O'Gara **Trained** Little Newcastle, Pembrokes

FOCUS
A moderate handicap, run at a decent gallop, and the form looks sound for the class, rated around the first two.

NOTEBOOK
Burren Moonshine(IRE), well backed on this debut for her new yard, did just enough to hold off the persistent challenge of the runner-up and score on this return from a 95-day break. She is a tough sort, who loves decent ground, and is capable of holding her form well so may well follow-up from a higher mark. *(op 4-1)*
Sir Rowland Hill(IRE), up 5lb for his improved showing at Worcester last time, ran another improved race and was only just denied under top weight. He was nicely clear of the rest and, while another weight rise is now inevitable, he has clearly been improved for the recent return to faster ground. *(op 15-2 tchd 8-1)*
Speed Kris(FR) had his chance, but was left behind when the first two asserted in the home straight. This was his best effort for some time, and he has slipped to a more realistic mark now, but he remains winless after 28 outings since coming over from France in 2004. *(tchd 20-1)*

Syncopated Rhythm(IRE) failed to really improve that much for this switch to faster ground and a longer trip and may have benefited from a more patient ride. *(tchd 6-1)*
T/Plt: £223.70 to a £1 stake. Pool: £48,494.25. 158.25 winning tickets. T/Qpdt: £96.70 to a £1 stake. Pool: £3,974.60. 30.40 winning tickets. RY

4801 WORCESTER (L-H)
Wednesday, April 26

OFFICIAL GOING: Good to firm (firm in places on back straight of hurdle course)
The drying ground produced a plethora of non runners.
Wind: Almost nil Weather: Fine

5069 BETFRED MILLION CONDITIONAL JOCKEYS' NOVICES' H'CAP HURDLE (12 hdls) 3m
5:10 (5:13) (Class 5) (0-95,102) 4-Y-0+ **£2,740** (£798; £399)

Form RPR
615P **1** **Red Perk (IRE)**[17] 4790 9-11-2 **93**....(p) JohnFlavin[(8)] 96
(R C Guest) *set slow pce: rdn appr last: hld on u.p flat* **15/2**
2351 **2** *1 ¼* **Kyno (IRE)**[10] 4874 5-12-5 **102** 7ex....(t) WilliamKennedy 104
(M G Quinlan) *hld up: hdwy appr 8th: chsd wnr 2 out: sn rdn: nt qckn flat* **4/1**[1]
0440 **3** *1 ¾* **Salopian**[81] 3733 6-11-10 **93**.... PaddyMerrigan 93
(H D Daly) *hld up in mid-div: sltly hmpd 3rd: outpcd appr 3 out: rallied appr last: swtchd lft flat: no ex towards fin* **11/2**[2]
6324 **4** *1 ¾* **Fight The Feeling**[28] 4662 8-11-4 **87**.... DarylJacob 87+
(J W Unett) *hld up: hdwy on ins 8th: rdn appr 2 out: cl 3rd whn mstke last: nt rcvr* **13/2**[3]
PS **5** *8* **Follow The Bear**[38] 4526 8-11-12 **95**....(b) LiamHeard 85
(D R Gandolfo) *chsd wnr tl after 6th: rdn after 3 out: wknd appr last* **16/1**
4055 **6** *5* **Buz Kiri (USA)**[21] 4734 8-10-11 **85**.... ThomasBurrows[(5)] 70
(P L Clinton) *hld up and bhd: rdn after 8th: nvr nr ldrs* **20/1**
/P2- **7** *1 ½* **Compton Commander**[639] 1049 8-10-13 **88**....(p) TomMessenger[(6)] 72
(B N Pollock) *hld up and bhd: mstke last: n.d* **11/2**[2]
FPF5 **8** *8* **Cloneybrien Boy (IRE)**[13] 4826 6-11-12 **95**.... DerekLaverty 73+
(Mrs A M Thorpe) *j.rt: prom: ev ch appr 3 out: mstke 2 out: sn wknd* **16/1**
6P0P **9** *4* **Novack Du Beury (FR)**[51] 4277 5-10-10 **85**.... PatrickMcDonald[(6)] 57
(Ferdy Murphy) *a bhd* **33/1**
0P0 **10** *14* **Public Eye**[15] 4819 5-11-2 **88**.... JustinMorgan[(3)] 46
(L A Dace) *hld up in mid-div: short-lived effrt appr last* **33/1**
63P0 **11** *1 ¼* **Nowa Huta (FR)**[71] 3918 5-11-2 **88**.... BenOrde-Powlett[(3)] 45
(Jedd O'Keeffe) *prom tl wknd qckly after 9th* **33/1**
04P5 **F** **Milanshan (IRE)**[13] 4836 6-11-0 **91**.... WayneKavanagh[(8)] —
(J W Mullins) *prom whn fell 3rd* **10/1**

5m 50.4s (1.20) **Going Correction** -0.35s/f (Good) 12 Ran SP% **110.3**
Speed ratings: **84,83,83,82,79 78,77,74,73,68 68,**— CSF £33.94 CT £167.79 TOTE £9.60: £4.70, £1.60, £2.40; EX 32.30.
Owner B Chorzelewski,P Davies & P Hodgkinson **Bred** Alex Heskin **Trained** Brancepeth, Co Durham

FOCUS
A slow pace led to a modest winning time for this moderate handicap. The form is rated around the third and fourth and looks suspect.

NOTEBOOK
Red Perk(IRE) went no gallop on this return to hurdles with connections concerned about the fast ground. Taking advantage of a soft lead, he found what was required when the chips were down. *(op 17-2)*
Kyno(IRE), penalised for his win at Plumpton, had much faster ground to contend with. The weight concession proved too much and his new mark may well mean he will have to go up in class. *(op 10-3)*
Salopian ran his best race so far on this step up to three miles and gave the impression he would not have minded a stronger-run race. *(op 6-1)*
Fight The Feeling, reverting to hurdles, was still in with a shout when an error at the last effectively ended his hopes. *(op 9-1)*
Follow The Bear did not seem to get the trip despite the fact the race was slowly-run. *(op 11-1)*

5070 BETFRED MILLION NOVICES' HURDLE (8 hdls) 2m
5:40 (5:41) (Class 4) 4-Y-0+ **£3,253** (£955; £477; £238)

Form RPR
2531 **1** **Tech Eagle (IRE)**[15] 4819 6-11-7 117.... TomDoyle 118+
(R Curtis) *hld up in mid-div: hdwy appr 5th: swtchd rt appr 2 out: led last: rdn and r.o wl* **4/1**[3]
5110 **2** *4* **Sunley Shines**[32] 4619 6-11-2 114.... JohnnyLevins[(5)] 110+
(B G Powell) *led: rdn and hdd last: one pce* **14/1**
3 *1* **King Gabriel (IRE)**[296] 4-10-9.... PJBrennan 96
(Andrew Turnell) *keen early: bhd tl hdwy appr 3 out: one pce flat* **66/1**
221P **4** *1 ½* **Rosecliff**[43] 4435 4-11-2 120.... RobertThornton 102
(A M Balding) *a.p: chsd ldr 3 out: one pce flat* **9/4**[2]
1F **5** *3* **Welcome Stranger**[19] 4763 6-11-7.... JamieMoore 105+
(G L Moore) *keen early: hld up in mid-div: hit 3rd: hdwy after 5th: hit 3 out: btn whn hit last* **11/8**[1]
3 **6** *1 ¾* **Akash (IRE)**[40] 4479 6-10-7.... MrMatthewSmith[(7)] 95
(Miss J Feilden) *hld up and bhd: hdwy appr 3 out: rdn and wknd appr 2 out* **25/1**
1PF0 **7** *dist* **Baie Des Flamands (USA)**[75] 3848 4-11-2 107.... HenryOliver —
(Miss S J Wilton) *chsd ldrs: mstke 4th: sn wknd: t.o* **80/1**
0-00 **8** *28* **Marys Moment**[45] 4398 6-10-2.... TomGreenway[(5)] —
(P A Pritchard) *plld hrd in rr: hmpd 2nd: t.o fr 6th* **100/1**
9 *26* **Spy Gun (USA)**[2] 6-11-0.... RJGreene —
(T Wall) *plld hrd in rr: nt fluent 4th: j.rt 5th: sn t.o* **80/1**
00 **U** **Tanners Grove**[48] 4333 5-10-7.... MissCDyson[(7)] —
(Miss C Dyson) *blnd bdly and bmpd and uns rdr 2nd* **125/1**
1344 **F** **Slalom (IRE)**[26] 1538 6-11-4 99....(p) WilliamKennedy[(3)] 100
(D Burchell) *chsd ldr to 3 out: wknd 2 out: fell last* **25/1**

3m 38.7s (-9.70) **Going Correction** -0.35s/f (Good)
WFA 4 from 5yo+ 5lb 11 Ran SP% **113.0**
Speed ratings: **110,108,107,106,105 104,**—,—,—,— — CSF £48.57 TOTE £6.10: £1.20, £4.30, £31.80; EX 27.30.
Owner The Tech Eagle Partnership **Bred** Gestut Wittekindshof **Trained** Lambourn, Berks

FOCUS
A good pace resulted in a fair winning time for what was a pretty decent novice event for the time of year and the winner could be rated higher.

NOTEBOOK
Tech Eagle(IRE), described by his trainer as a real top of the ground horse, did not have too much difficulty in following up his win at Fontwell. He will be kept on the go through the summer with the valuable handicap in mid-July at Market Rasen as his target.
Sunley Shines, who won his bumper on this sort of ground, did not do a lot wrong against a fair performer in these sort of conditions. *(op 15-2)*
King Gabriel(IRE) ◆, a modest maiden at up to a mile and a half on the Flat, had not been seen since July last year. He seems likely to prove a better proposition over hurdles on this evidence and normal improvement will see him off the mark.
Rosecliff, highly tried last time, had a big chance with the winner based on the form of his Ludlow win on a line through Wellbeing. *Official explanation: jockey said gelding was unsuited by the ground: good to firm, firm in places back straight (op 5-2 tchd 11-4 in a place)*
Welcome Stranger had ground conditions in his favour but was again let down by his jumping. *Official explanation: vet said gelding finished lame on the off fore (op 13-8 tchd 7-4)*
Spy Gun(USA) *Official explanation: trainer said gelding bled from the nose (op 66-1)*

5071 BETFRED MILLION NOVICES' H'CAP CHASE (18 fncs) 2m 7f 110y
6:10 (6:10) (Class 4) (0-105,106) 5-Y-0+ **£3,903** (£1,146; £573; £286)

Form RPR
-336 **1** **Meehan (IRE)**[34] 4592 6-11-4 **93**.... SeanCurran 109+
(Miss J S Davis) *j.rt: t.k.h: hdwy 5th: led 10th: rdn clr whn mstke 2 out: eased towards fin* **33/1**
16FP **2** *5* **Lahinch Lad (IRE)**[15] 4824 6-10-11 **93**.... MrSPJones[(7)] 96
(B G Powell) *hld up in mid-div: hdwy 12th: outpcd after 14th: styd on to take 2nd towards fin: no ch w wnr* **13/2**[3]
24 **3** *2 ½* **Fieldsofclover (IRE)**[76] 3815 9-10-13 **88**.... BarryFenton 90+
(Miss E C Lavelle) *mstke 1st: sn bhd: hdwy appr 12th: ev ch 4 out: sn rdn: btn whn j.rt 2 out and last* **15/8**[1]
2002 **4** *2 ½* **Irishkawa Bellevue (FR)**[31] 4643 8-10-10 **85**....(b) DaveCrosse 84+
(Jean-Rene Auvray) *led: j. slowly and hdd 2nd: led 4th to 10th: one pce fr 14th* **11/2**[2]
5F2P **5** *9* **Master Billyboy (IRE)**[13] 4837 8-11-7 **96**.... ChristianWilliams 85
(Mrs S D Williams) *prom tl wknd after 14th* **20/1**
45P3 **6** *2* **Caper**[10] 4876 6-10-7 **82**.... PaulMoloney 69
(R Hollinshead) *nvr nr ldrs* **9/1**
2-1P **7** *15* **Hold On Harry**[17] 4806 10-11-3 **97**.... LiamHeard[(5)] 69
(Miss C J Williams) *led 2nd to 4th: wknd appr 13th* **11/1**
203 **8** *2 ½* **Dante's Promise (IRE)**[20] 4753 10-10-12 **92**....(p) MrTJO'Brien[(5)] 61
(C J Down) *a bhd* **16/1**
P034 **9** *15* **Wayward Melody**[8] 4937 6-11-2 **91**.... JamieMoore 45
(G L Moore) *in rr: nvr gng wl after j. slowly 3rd: lost tch 7th* **12/1**
P40U **10** *11* **Move Over (IRE)**[2] 5037 11-11-2 **101**.... JohnFlavin[(10)] 44
(R C Guest) *prom to 8th: bhd whn mstkes 11th and 12th* **17/2**

5m 48.3s (-6.60) **Going Correction** -0.35s/f (Good) 10 Ran SP% **113.6**
Speed ratings: **97,95,94,93,90 90,85,84,79,75** CSF £230.43 CT £610.70 TOTE £39.50: £12.20, £2.80, £1.60; EX 411.20.
Owner John L Marriott **Bred** A S O'Brien And Lars Pearson **Trained** Codrington, S Gloucs

FOCUS
A poor handicap with the winner value for 13 lengths and the placed horses close to their marks.

NOTEBOOK
Meehan(IRE), who had broken a blood-vessel on his previous start, raced freely and was inclined to jump right-handed over the first six fences. Things did improve and he had it in the bag when making his only serious error at the penultimate obstacle. *(op 25-1)*
Lahinch Lad(IRE) was much more at home back on fast ground. He eventually found a second wind after getting caught flat-footed at the end of the back straight. *(op 8-1 tchd 9-1)*
Fieldsofclover(IRE) was given time to recover from an error at the first. The winner had taken his measure when he jumped out to the right over the last two. *(op 2-1)*
Irishkawa Bellevue(FR) remains a maiden over fences and could make no impression from five out. *(op 5-1)*

5072 BETFRED MILLION H'CAP HURDLE (10 hdls) 2m 4f
6:40 (6:40) (Class 5) (0-85,85) 4-Y-0+ **£2,927** (£859; £429; £214)

Form RPR
30 **1** **All Square (IRE)**[13] 4834 6-11-10 **83**....(t) TomDoyle 86
(R A Farrant) *hld up: hdwy appr 7th: swtchd lft appr last: rdn to ld flat: drvn out* **8/1**
600P **2** *2 ½* **Northern Link (IRE)**[13] 4826 7-11-9 **82**.... MarcusFoley 83
(Miss Tor Sturgis) *led to 2nd: chsd ldr: led after 7th: rdn appr last: hdd and nt qckn flat* **20/1**
2B36 **3** *1 ½* **Think Quick (IRE)**[42] 4452 6-11-1 **84**.... AdamHawkins[(10)] 83
(R Hollinshead) *hld up: hdwy appr 3 out: rdn appr last: kpt on towards fin* **4/1**[2]
565- **4** *19* **The Teuchter**[454] 3546 7-11-7 **85**....(p) DerekLaverty[(5)] 65
(Mrs S D Williams) *prom: reminders after 4th: j. slowly and lost pl 5th: sn struggling* **9/1**
05P3 **5** *1 ¼* **Hapthor**[34] 4584 7-11-7 **83**.... MrTGreenall[(3)] 62
(F Jestin) *j.rt: led 2nd: clr 3rd: hdd after 7th: sn wknd* **6/1**[3]
0434 **6** *6* **Greencard Golf**[188] 1800 5-11-12 **85**.... AlanO'Keeffe 58
(Jennie Candlish) *hld up in rr: mstke 3rd: hdwy 5th: hrd rdn after 7th: wknd appr 2 out: mstke last* **15/2**
12PP **P** **Paddy Boy (IRE)**[48] 4331 5-11-9 **82**.... JamieMoore —
(J R Boyle) *plld hrd: prom: hit 6th: rdn and wknd after 7th: j. bdly rt 3 out: sn p.u* **7/4**[1]

4m 45.0s (-3.00) **Going Correction** -0.35s/f (Good) 7 Ran SP% **108.3**
Speed ratings: **92,91,90,82,82 79,**— CSF £112.33 CT £652.57 TOTE £9.40: £5.20, £6.80; EX 45.90.
Owner Tom Treacy **Bred** Rathbarry Stud **Trained** Bampton, Devon

FOCUS
A modest winning time for this tightly-knit handicap which was little better than a seller and is best rated through the winner.

NOTEBOOK
All Square(IRE) found the combination of the first-time tongue tie and a longer trip doing the trick, *but the form does not amount to much. Official explanation: trainer said, regarding the improved form shown, gelding made a bad mistake at the fifth hurdle when travelling well (op 4-1)*
Northern Link(IRE), dropping back in distance on this handicap debut, ran by far his best race to date. He may be capable of winning a similarly weak affair. *(op 14-1)*
Think Quick(IRE) might be worth another try over further. *(op 11-2 tchd 7-2)*
The Teuchter, off course since January 2005, was reverting to a shorter distance on the fastest ground he has encountered over hurdles. *(tchd 11-1)*
Paddy Boy(IRE) refused to settle on this much faster surface. *Official explanation: vet said gelding was lame on the off fore (op 2-1)*

5073 BETFRED MILLION MAIDEN HURDLE (10 hdls) 2m 4f
7:10 (7:12) (Class 5) 4-Y-0+ **£2,740** (£798; £399)

Form RPR
1 **Broken Reed (IRE)**[73] 7-11-2.... WayneHutchinson 105+
(T R George) *hld up: hdwy appr 6th: chalng whn lft in ld 2 out: clr last: r.o wl* **2/1**[1]
3/ **2** *8* **Bressbee (USA)**[749] 1702 8-11-2.... RobertThornton 97
(J W Unett) *hld up: hdwy 4th: ev ch 3 out: lft 2nd 2 out: one pce* **7/1**

35 **3** *13* **Silber Mond**[15] 4823 4-10-10 JamieGoldstein 78
(Miss Sheena West) *hld up in mid-div: outpcd 7th: no real prog* **5/2**[2]

P **4** *1* **Return Fire**[67] 3984 7-11-2 PaulMoloney 83
(Miss H C Knight) *j.rt: led: hdd 5th: wknd 3 out* **12/1**

5 *17* **The Beduth Navi**[51] 6-11-2 JamesDavies 66
(D G Bridgwater) *prom to 5th* **25/1**

6 *18* **Grand Ideas**[16] 7-11-2 DavidVerco 48
(G J Smith) *plld hrd: prom to 6th* **33/1**

0 **P** **Hey You M'Lady**[350] 300 6-10-2 RichardSpate(7) —
(J Rudge) *bhd: mstke 5th: t.o whn p.u after 7th* **33/1**

20 **U** **Mungo Jerry (GER)**[25] 4691 5-10-9 (t) TomMessenger(7) 100+
(B N Pollock) *w ldr: led 5th: slt ld whn blnd and uns rdr 2 out* **9/2**[3]

0000 **P** **Mr Parson (IRE)**[121] 2987 6-10-13 ChrisHonour(3) —
(S T Lewis) *mid-div: blnd 4th: sn struggling: t.o whn p.u bef 6th* **100/1**

4m 39.0s (-9.00) **Going Correction** -0.35s/f (Good)
WFA 4 from 5yo+ 6lb **9** Ran SP% **111.0**
Speed ratings: **104,100,95,95,88 81,—,—,—** CSF £15.33 TOTE £2.90: £1.20, £1.80, £1.60; EX 13.80.
Owner M J Hoskins **Bred** John McGuinness **Trained** Slad, Gloucs

FOCUS
A poor maiden hurdle rated around the second and third.

NOTEBOOK
Broken Reed(IRE), a brother to the winning hurdler and chaser Before The Mast, had been placed in two Irish maiden points prior to winning one in February. The further he went the better he looked and the fast ground turned out to be no problem. *(op 3-1)*
Bressbee(USA), pulled up when last seen on the Flat just over two years ago, had shown signs of ability on his only previous outing over hurdles. He would probably not have finished second had Mungo Jerry completed. *(op 13-2 tchd 5-1)*
Silber Mond was going up and down on the spot from the fourth last. *(tchd 3-1 in places and 100-30 in a place)*
Return Fire, third in a point in March last year, had been pulled up in the much softer ground on his hurdling debut. He did not help his cause by jumping right-handed. *(op 8-1)*
Mungo Jerry(GER), fitted with a tongue tie for the first time over hurdles, was racing on faster ground. The winner was breathing down his neck but he had not been asked a serious question when unshipping his rider two out. *(op 10-3 tchd 5-1)*

5074 BETFRED MILLION H'CAP CHASE (15 fncs) 2m 4f 110y
7:40 (7:40) (Class 4) (0-100,104) 5-Y-0+ **£3,903** (£1,146; £573; £286)

Form RPR

421 **1** **Jodante (IRE)**[9] 4900 9-11-8 **104** 7ex (p) JohnFlavin(10) 119+
(R C Guest) *hld up in rr: hdwy 8th: chal on bit fr 4 out: rdn to ld cl home* **7/2**[1]

62P2 **2** *nk* **Classic Rock**[42] 4451 7-10-9 **81** WarrenMarston 92+
(J W Unett) *hld up: hdwy 7th: led 9th: rdn appr last: hdd cl home* **11/2**[3]

0P3 **3** *20* **Manoram (GER)**[159] 2323 7-11-12 **98** (v) PaulMoloney 89
(Ian Williams) *hld up in tch: lost pl 7th: kpt on fr 4 out: n.d* **10/1**

3065 **4** *1 ½* **Deliceo (IRE)**[84] 3676 13-11-9 **95** (p) ChristianWilliams 85
(M Sheppard) *hld up in mid-div: hdwy 5th: wknd after 4 out* **33/1**

211U **5** *8* **Moscow Gold (IRE)**[9] 4908 9-10-6 **81** OwynNelmes(3) 63
(A E Price) *t.k.h: chsd ldrs: ev ch 4 out: wknd appr 2 out* **6/1**

0-PP **6** *7* **Montu**[69] 3950 9-10-6 **78** ow1 AndrewThornton 53
(Miss K M George) *a bhd* **33/1**

2203 **7** *1* **Opportunity Knocks**[28] 4666 6-10-0 **72** (p) PJBrennan 46
(N J Hawke) *chsd ldrs: mstke and reminders 6th: rdn 8th: sn wknd* **9/2**[2]

565P **8** *shd* **Kind Sir**[13] 4829 10-11-12 **98** WayneHutchinson 71
(A W Carroll) *led: blnd 8th: hdd 9th: wknd 11th* **9/1**

0P51 **F** **Bayadere (GER)**[17] 4804 6-11-5 **96** ShaneWalsh(5) —
(K F Clutterbuck) *hld up: hdwy whn mstke 9th: wknd 4 out: fell 3 out* **13/2**

4m 57.6s (-9.90) **Going Correction** -0.35s/f (Good) **9** Ran SP% **108.4**
Speed ratings: **104,103,96,95,92 89,89,89,—** CSF £21.05 CT £151.28 TOTE £4.70: £1.70, £2.20, £1.60; EX 27.60.
Owner R C Guest **Bred** Mrs Margaret Fitzgerald **Trained** Brancepeth, Co Durham

FOCUS
They went a decent clip in a race which developed into a match over the last four fences and the race could be rated higher.

NOTEBOOK
Jodante(IRE) would have had another 2lb to carry had his new mark been in force. He gets on well with his young rider who was in no hurry to press the button. *(op 2-1)*
Classic Rock lost no caste in defeat and only got worn down at the death. He did not mind a return to a shorter trip and fully deserves to go one better. *(op 9-1 tchd 5-1)*
Manoram(GER) just plugged on to finish a modest third. *(op 12-1)*
Deliceo(IRE) had been dropped 4lb for this first outing since the beginning of February. *(op 28-1)*
Moscow Gold(IRE) may have needed this after his early exit at Huntingdon but another explanation could be that he is now in the grip of the Handicapper. *(tchd 11-2)*
Bayadere(GER), raised 8lb for her shock course and distance win, is set to go up another 2lb which does not augur well for the future. *(op 9-2)*

5075 BETFRED MILLION INTERMEDIATE NATIONAL HUNT FLAT RACE (CONDITIONAL JOCKEYS' AND AMATEUR RIDERS' RACE) 2m
8:10 (8:10) (Class 6) 4-6-Y-0 **£1,713** (£499; £249)

Form RPR

5 **1** **Go On Ahead (IRE)**[67] 3983 6-10-11 MrsMRoberts(7) 106+
(M J Coombe) *mde all: edgd lft over 1f out: r.o wl to draw clr fnl f* **11/2**[3]

102 **2** *7* **Mumbles Head (IRE)**[9] 4909 5-11-6 MrTJO'Brien(5) 108+
(P Bowen) *chsd wnr: slipped on bnd 4f out: sn rdn: outpcd over 2f out: styd on to go 2nd ins fnl f: no ch w wnr* **8/13**[1]

24 **3** *4* **Zhivago's Princess (IRE)**[155] 2425 4-10-3 WilliamKennedy(3) 84+
(P T Dalton) *hld up and bhd: hdwy 6f out: chsd wnr over 3f out: rdn over 2f out: wknd ins fnl f* **5/1**[2]

0 **4** *10* **Primitive Academy**[27] 4680 4-10-8 ShaneWalsh(5) 80
(Mrs H Dalton) *prom: lost pl over 5f out: n.d after* **14/1**

0 **5** *25* **Paul Superstar (FR)**[145] 2611 4-10-6 KeiranBurke(7) 55
(N J Hawke) *t.k.h in tch: wknd over 4f out* **25/1**

P **6** *11* **Boomerang Boy (IRE)**[27] 4680 5-10-11 MrTWeston(7) 49
(M H Weston) *a bhd* **50/1**

0 **7** *2* **Danahill Lad (USA)**[10] 4881 5-10-11 RichardSpate(7) 47
(J A Danahar) *hld up: rdn 7f out: bhd fnl 5f* **50/1**

3m 40.6s (-7.20) **Going Correction** -0.35s/f (Good)
WFA 4 from 5yo+ 5lb **7** Ran SP% **108.4**
Speed ratings: **104,100,98,93,81 75,74** CSF £8.35 TOTE £7.00: £2.60, £1.10; EX 9.90 Place 6 £541.41, Place 5 £293.86.
Owner Richard G Cuddihy **Bred** Miss D J Merson **Trained** Fleet, Dorset

FOCUS
An uncompetitive bumper that could be rated higher but has been rated cautiously.

NOTEBOOK
Go On Ahead(IRE) lived up to his name having shown that he was likely to handle this sort of surface when making his debut on the Polytrack at Lingfield. This was the first winner for his trainer for over five years. *(tchd 5-1 and 6-1)*
Mumbles Head(IRE) could not go with the winner on this fast ground early in the home straight although his stamina did eventually show through. *(op 8-11 tchd 5-6)*
Zhivago's Princess(IRE), graduating from junior bumpers, could not take advantage of the weight she was receiving over this longer trip. *(op 9-2 tchd 4-1)*
Primitive Academy, out of a half-sister to staying hurdler Mylo, had made his debut on much softer ground at Wincanton last month. *(op 18-1)*
T/Plt: £611.90 to a £1 stake. Pool: £37,512.65. 44.75 winning tickets. T/Qpdt: £82.40 to a £1 stake. Pool: £4,900.60. 44.00 winning tickets. KH

5055 PUNCHESTOWN (R-H)
Wednesday, April 26

OFFICIAL GOING: Good

5076a AON GROUP/SEAN BARRETT BLOODSTOCK INSURANCES HURDLE 2m
2:05 (2:06) 4-Y-O **£13,468** (£3,951; £1,882; £641)

RPR

1 **Josephine Cullen (IRE)**[38] 4540 4-11-2 RWalsh 116+
(W P Mullins, Ire) *cl up in 2nd: led after 3 out: rdn clr last: easily* **11/2**[2]

2 *8* **Very Green (FR)**[32] 4624 4-10-11 90 (t) RLoughran(3) 106
(D T Hughes, Ire) *mid-div: 6th and hdwy 3 out: 4th next: mod 2nd early st: no imp whn slt mstke last* **33/1**

3 *2* **Jack The Giant (IRE)**[53] 4243 4-11-7 MickFitzgerald 111
(N J Henderson) *cl 3rd: rdn 2 out: no imp: 4th bef last: kpt on same pce* **11/10**[1]

4 *1 ½* **Baileysunice (IRE)**[6] 4977 4-11-7 MrPFahey 110
(Seamus Fahey, Ire) *mid-div: 9th appr 3 out: 7th next: mod 5th bef last: kpt on* **20/1**

5 *¾* **Valley Of Giants**[8] 4948 4-11-0 104 (b[1]) ADLeigh(7) 109
(Mrs John Harrington, Ire) *rr of mid-div: prog after 4 out: 9th after 2 out: kpt on* **16/1**

6 *shd* **Dream Of Tomorrow (IRE)**[46] 4379 4-10-2 EFPower(7) 97
(John Joseph Murphy, Ire) *led: hdd after 3 out: rdn and outpcd next: mod 3rd last: sn no ex* **25/1**

7 *6* **Noble Concorde**[116] 3157 4-11-0 DJCasey 96
(D K Weld, Ire) *rr of mid-div: kpt on wout threatening fr bef 2 out* **8/1**[3]

8 *2* **Wild Wood (IRE)**[16] 4816 4-10-2 (b) RTDunne(7) 89
(M J P O'Brien, Ire) *chsd ldrs: 5th and rdn 3 out: no ex after 2 out* **50/1**

9 *1* **Waking Dream (USA)**[16] 4816 4-10-9 AndrewJMcNamara 88
(Henry De Bromhead, Ire) *mid-div on inner: kpt on same pce fr 3 out* **33/1**

10 *nk* **Yameell**[21] 4740 4-11-7 (t) DNRussell 99
(David Marnane, Ire) *trckd ldrs: 5th 1/2-way: 4th 3 out: wknd bef next* **14/1**

11 *2* **Roman Villa (USA)**[19] 4767 4-11-0 TPTreacy 90
(Mrs John Harrington, Ire) *hld up: prog into 10th 3 out: no ex fr next* **16/1**

12 *2* **Qassas**[80] 3764 4-10-9 BCByrnes(5) 88
(Michael David Murphy, Ire) *hld up: kpt on same pce fr 3 out* **25/1**

13 *nk* **Querido (USA)**[14] 4-11-0 PWFlood 88
(E J O'Grady, Ire) *nvr bttr than mid-div* **40/1**

14 *3 ½* **Only Make Believe**[8] 4948 4-10-7 TMolloy(7) 85
(J S Bolger, Ire) *nvr a factor* **20/1**

15 *4 ½* **Raintown (IRE)**[238] 1326 4-11-0 KHClarke(7) 87
(Peter McCreery, Ire) *nvr a factor* **50/1**

16 *2* **Garryowen Star (IRE)**[34] 4602 4-10-7 DGHogan(7) 78
(C F Swan, Ire) *nvr a factor* **66/1**

17 *1 ½* **Widely Accepted (IRE)**[8] 4948 4-11-7 100 JMAllen 84
(Joseph Crowley, Ire) *chsd ldrs: 4th 1/2-way: dropped to 7th 3 out: sn wknd* **25/1**

18 *5* **Turn Card (IRE)**[120] 3049 4-10-11 MPWalsh(3) 72
(Declan Gillespie, Ire) *a towards rr* **66/1**

19 *1 ½* **Take A Mile (IRE)**[13] 4838 4-11-7 TimmyMurphy 77
(B G Powell) *mid-div: wknd bef 3 out* **16/1**

20 *¾* **Rock Angel (IRE)** 4-10-9 JLCullen 64
(Paul Nolan, Ire) *a bhd* **50/1**

21 *15* **Zaccheus (IRE)**[8] 4948 4-11-0 GCotter 54
(Comdt W S Hayes, Ire) *rr of mid-div: prog into 8th bef 3 out: sn no ex and wknd* **25/1**

22 *2* **Three Buck Chuck (IRE)**[186] 4-10-11 SGMcDermott(3) 52
(E Sheehy, Ire) *nvr a factor: wknd bef 3 out: trailing fr next* **66/1**

23 *¾* **Borouj (IRE)**[11] 4861 4-11-0 APCrowe 52
(Philip Fenton, Ire) *a bhd: trailing fr 2 out* **50/1**

24 *7* **Druids Stone**[13] 4001 4-10-7 MrJEBurns(7) 45
(Henry De Bromhead, Ire) *chsd ldrs: 6th 1/2-way: wknd bef 3 out: trailing fr next* **100/1**

25 *dist* **Pekan One**[186] 4-11-0 PACarberry —
(John G Carr, Ire) *a bhd: trailing 1/2-way: t.o* **50/1**

3m 44.8s **Going Correction** -0.40s/f (Good) **25** Ran SP% **146.9**
Speed ratings: **103,99,98,97,96 96,93,92,92,92 91,90,90,88,86 85,84,81,81,80 73,72,71,68,—** CSF £193.33 TOTE £3.60: £1.10, £5.20, £1.40, £4.70; DF 589.70.
Owner Mrs J M Mullins **Bred** Mrs J M Mullins **Trained** Muine Beag, Co Carlow

NOTEBOOK
Jack The Giant(IRE) was sent off favourite on the strength of his second to subsequent Aintree winner Wellbeing at Newbury. He was given every chance but simply lacked a change of gear. He stayed on though, and a step up to two and a half miles should help. *(op 5/4 tchd 11/8)*
Take A Mile(IRE), whose British form was nothing special, was beaten well before the turn for home. *(op 14/1)*

5077a BEWLEYS HOTELS IRISH STALLION FARMS EUROPEAN BREEDERS FUND MARES HURDLE (GRADE 3) 2m 2f
2:40 (2:41) 4-Y-0+ **£23,346** (£6,849; £3,263; £1,111)

RPR

1 **Brogella (IRE)**[118] 3110 6-11-0 123 (b) RWalsh 125
(Ms F M Crowley, Ire) *trckd ldrs in 3rd: tk clsr order 3 out: chal after 2 out: led early st: styd on wl u.p* **11/2**[2]

2 *2* **Chicago Vic (IRE)**[81] 3743 7-11-3 119 DJCasey 126
(E McNamara, Ire) *hld up: 10th 4 out: hdwy after next: 3rd after 2 out: 2nd and kpt on u.p fr last* **14/1**

3 ½ **Grangeclare Lark (IRE)**[17] 4814 5-10-9 .... RLoughran 118
(D T Hughes, Ire) *rr of mid-div: hdwy after 3 out: 6th next: rdn and kpt on to go 3rd fr last* **25/1**

4 4 **Outlaw Princess (IRE)**[55] 4205 6-10-10 .... JMAllen 115
(Sean O O'Brien, Ire) *sn prom: led fr 3rd: strly pressed 2 out: hdd early st: no ex appr last* **16/1**

5 2 **Trompette (USA)**[30] 4648 4-10-6 .... MickFitzgerald 109
(N J Henderson) *hld up: 9th and prog 3 out: 7th next: kpt on fr last* **6/1**[3]

6 ¾ **Red Square Lady (IRE)**[10] 4882 8-11-3 127.......... AndrewJMcNamara 119
(Michael John Phillips, Ire) *chsd ldrs: 4th 5 out: 6th next: kpt on same pce* **11/1**

7 2 **Seagull Eile (IRE)**[298] 886 7-11-0 99............................(b) MDarcy 114?
(K F O'Brien, Ire) *mid-div: 10th after 1/2-way: impr into 5th 3 out: 3rd 2 out: no ex early st* **33/1**

8 1 ½ **Tiarella (IRE)**[10] 4887 6-11-0 111............................ DNRussell 112
(Denis Ahern, Ire) *chsd ldrs: 7th 4 out: rdn after next: kpt on same pce* **20/1**

9 ¾ **Creme D'Arblay (IRE)**[10] 4887 4-10-2 .... DFO'Regan 100
(Thomas Cooper, Ire) *prom: 4th whn j.lft at 4th: 6th 3 out: kpt on same pce* **12/1**

10 4 ½ **Prairie Moonlight (GER)**[86] 3650 6-11-0 .... TimmyMurphy 107
(C J Mann) *towards rr: prog on outer bef 4 out: 7th 3 out: sn rdn: no imp fr next* **9/4**[1]

11 3 **Threequarter Moon (IRE)**[11] 4865 8-11-3 106..................... EFPower 107
(A Seymour, Ire) *towards rr: prog 1/2-way: 9th 5 out: no ex after 3 out* **33/1**

12 *shd* **Kylebeg Dancer (IRE)**[10] 4887 5-10-9 107......................(p) MFMooney 99
(T Hogan, Ire) *chsd ldrs: 8th bef 1/2-way: no ex fr bef 3 out* **16/1**

13 2 ½ **Lala Nova (IRE)**[11] 4865 7-11-0 95............................ RMPower 101
(John Joseph Murphy, Ire) *chsd ldrs: 6th 5 out: 5th next: wknd fr 3 out* **50/1**

14 3 ½ **Banna's (IRE)**[69] 3952 5-10-9 98............................ JLCullen 93
(Ms Margaret Mullins, Ire) *nvr a factor* **25/1**

15 1 **Sweetwater (GER)**[11] 4863 6-10-10 76............................ ECMcCarthy 93
(Seamus Lynch, Ire) *nvr a factor* **100/1**

16 1 ½ **Atagirl (IRE)**[5] 4996 7-10-10 78............................ KTColeman 91
(Andrew Lee, Ire) *led: hdd 3rd: remained prom: 2nd appr 3 out: sn wknd* **100/1**

17 14 **Behlaya (IRE)**[17] 3520 5-10-9 .... JRBarry 76
(Liam P Cusack, Ire) *a towards rr* **25/1**

18 ¾ **Thunder Road (IRE)**[10] 4887 6-11-0 108............................ APLane 81
(P A Fahy, Ire) *chsd ldrs: 7th 1/2-way: wknd fr 4 out* **20/1**

19 *nk* **Longwhitejemmy (IRE)**[70] 3937 4-10-2 .... NJO'Shea 68
(D T Hughes, Ire) *a towards rr* **100/1**

20 *hd* **Ohmissymoss (IRE)**[5] 4993 7-10-10 90............................(t) BMCash 76
(Michael C Griffin, Ire) *a towards rr* **66/1**

21 *hd* **Blueland (IRE)**[17] 4801 7-10-10 .... NPMadden 76
(Noel T Chance) *mid-div: mstke 5 out: sn wknd* **16/1**

22 1 **Native House (IRE)**[10] 4887 8-10-10 104............................ PACarberry 75
(Edward Cawley, Ire) *mid-div: wknd fr 4 out* **25/1**

23 2 ½ **Young Elodie (FR)**[199] 1699 5-10-13 108............................ PWFlood 75
(M J P O'Brien, Ire) *nvr a factor: bhd fr 3 out* **14/1**

U **Sauterelle (IRE)**[10] 4890 6-10-10 98............................(t) GTHutchinson —
(Thomas Mullins, Ire) *uns rdr 3rd* **25/1**

4m 16.1s **Going Correction** -0.40s/f (Good)
WFA 4 from 5yo+ 5lb **24** Ran SP% **148.5**
Speed ratings: **95,94,93,92,91 90,90,89,89,87 85,85,84,82,82 81,75,75,75,75 74,74,73,—**
CSF £82.34 TOTE £3.70: £1.10, £4.30, £4.40, £4.50; DF 214.30.
Owner M J Hanrahan **Bred** Michael Hanrahan **Trained** Curragh, Co Kildare

FOCUS
A competitive mares' contest that attracted a sizeable field although the form is nothing special.

NOTEBOOK
Brogella(IRE) emerged victorious to win her first race since March 2005 and was perfectly entitled to take this on her recent form. Taking over in front after two out she stayed on well and she could run in a valuable handicap at Killarney next month before retiring to stud. *(op 5/1 tchd 6/1)*
Chicago Vic(IRE) was reverting to hurdles following a spell over fences. She ran a fine race and stayed on well under pressure after the third-last. There are certainly more races to be won with her. *(op 12/1)*
Grangeclare Lark(IRE), who was placed in two bumpers, ran with promise on what was only her second start over hurdles. She was putting in some good work towards the finish and will not have to wait long for her success.
Outlaw Princess(IRE) acquitted herself well after making much of the running. It was only after the *second last that she had to give best. Official explanation: trainer said mare suffered an overreach and was found to have lost a shoe during the race*
Trompette(USA) fared best of the British raiders, having plenty to do coming to the second last but staying on in the straight. *(op 11/2 tchd 13/2)*
Creme D'Arblay(IRE) started to make good progress on the outer nearing the end of the back straight but she had no more to give from the third last. She is capable of better. *(op 14/1)*
Prairie Moonlight(GER) started to make good progress on the outer nearing the end of the back straight but she had no more to give from the third last. She is capable of better. *(op 9/4 tchd 5/2)*
Threequarter Moon(IRE) *Official explanation: trainer said mare was found to be in season*
Blueland(IRE), stepping up in grade, lost her chance with a mistake after halfway.

5078a BLUE SQUARE 1800 905050 H'CAP HURDLE 2m
3:15 (3:16) (0-140,134) 4-Y-0+ **£14,591** (£4,281; £2,039; £694)

RPR

1 **The Last Hurrah (IRE)**[8] 4951 6-9-6 109............................(b) ADLeigh(7) 119+
(Mrs John Harrington, Ire) *mid-div: prog into 7th after 3 out: 6th and rdn next: hdwy early st: led appr last: kpt on wl* **16/1**

2 2 ½ **Manorson (IRE)**[42] 4446 7-11-7 131............................ LeightonAspell 139+
(O Sherwood) *trckd ldrs: 5th 4 out: 3rd and chal 2 out: kpt on fr last* **16/1**

3 *nk* **Feel Good Factor**[9] 4927 6-9-6 109............................ MrJJDoyle(7) 116+
(P M J Doyle, Ire) *cl up: 2nd 1/2-way: led appr 4 out: hdd appr last: kpt on u.p* **25/1**

4 3 ½ **Reisk Superman (IRE)**[6] 1690 8-10-2 112............................ RWalsh 116
(A J Martin, Ire) *towards rr: hdwy into 12th bef 2 out: styd on wl fr last* **10/3**[1]

5 *shd* **Diego Garcia (IRE)**[8] 4951 6-9-11 114............................ RJKiely(7) 118
(W P Mullins, Ire) *mid-div: prog 4 out: 5th whn mstke next: rallied 2 out: 3rd early st: no ex fr last* **20/1**

6 4 **Heronstown (IRE)**[11] 4865 7-9-7 106............................ KTColeman(3) 106
(William Coleman O'Brien, Ire) *hld up: prog 3 out: 10th after 2 out: kpt on* **20/1**

7 2 **Charyan (IRE)**[207] 1514 5-9-10 106............................ APCrowe 104
(C Roche, Ire) *bhd: mstke 3 out: styd on fr next* **12/1**

8 ½ **Mountain Snow (IRE)**[9] 2388 6-9-10 106............................ DJCondon 103
(W P Mullins, Ire) *trckd ldrs early: dropped to mid-div 1/2-way: 9th after 2 out: kpt on same pce* **16/1**

9 ¾ **Dbest (IRE)**[189] 1789 6-10-4 114............................(p) JMAllen 110
(Ms Joanna Morgan, Ire) *prom: 3rd 1/2-way: dropped to 7th bef 2 out: kpt on same pce* **20/1**

10 9 **Serious Weapon (IRE)**[121] 3002 7-9-10 106............................ GCotter 93
(Liam P Cusack, Ire) *chsd ldrs: 5th appr 1/2-way: no ex bef 2 out* **25/1**

11 *nk* **Yarra Maguire (IRE)**[129] 2910 7-9-13 109............................ NPMadden 96
(Noel Meade, Ire) *chsd ldrs: 10th 1/2-way: rdn and no imp fr bef 2 out* **25/1**

12 *shd* **Run Katie Chimes (IRE)**[130] 2898 9-9-10 106............................ GTHutchinson 93
(Paul Nolan, Ire) *towards rr: kpt on fr 3 out* **25/1**

13 ¾ **Jimmy Spot On (IRE)**[10] 4890 9-9-3 106............................ ECMcCarthy(7) 92
(Seamus Lynch, Ire) *nvr a factor: sme late prog* **33/1**

14 1 ½ **Pablo Du Charmil (FR)**[43] 4430 5-11-10 134............................(b[1]) APMcCoy 119
(M C Pipe) *cl 3rd: 2nd 3 out: chal next: wknd ent st: sn eased* **12/1**

15 *nk* **Kilbeggan Lad (IRE)**[10] 4882 8-10-13 123............................ TimmyMurphy 107
(Michael Hourigan, Ire) *nvr a factor: no ex bef 4 out* **11/1**[3]

16 8 **Articulation**[199] 1699 5-10-7 117............................(p) DNRussell 93
(C Byrnes, Ire) *mid-div: 13th bef 4 out: no ex fr 3 out* **9/1**[2]

17 3 ½ **Classic Approach (IRE)**[182] 1876 6-9-13 109............................ JRBarry 82
(John Queally, Ire) *nvr a factor* **20/1**

18 15 **Athlumney Lad (IRE)**[199] 1534 7-10-11 121............................ DFO'Regan 79
(Noel Meade, Ire) *a towards rr* **20/1**

19 *shd* **Helensburgh (IRE)**[8] 4951 5-10-7 117............................ PACarberry 75
(P Hughes, Ire) *towards rr: no imp after mstke 4 out* **14/1**

20 7 **Rights Of Man (IRE)**[11] 4865 7-10-3 113............................ PWFlood 64
(D E Fitzgerald, Ire) *led: hdd appr 4 out: sn wknd* **20/1**

21 12 **Zeroberto (IRE)**[247] 1288 6-10-5 115............................ DJCasey 54
(D K Weld, Ire) *mid-div on outer: 8th 4 out: sn wknd* **16/1**

P **Grande Jete (SAF)**[40] 4473 9-11-3 127............................ MickFitzgerald —
(N J Henderson) *mid-div: 9th 5 out: wknd after next: p.u bef 2 out* **12/1**

P **High Day**[40] 4473 6-10-12 122............................ AndrewJMcNamara —
(Ferdy Murphy) *chsd ldrs: 9th appr 1/2-way: no ex 4 out: p.u bef last* **16/1**

F **Dashing Home (IRE)**[8] 4951 7-10-11 121............................ MissNCarberry —
(Noel Meade, Ire) *trckd ldrs: 5th 1/2-way: 4th 3 out: chal next: 4th and no ex whn fell last* **16/1**

3m 41.3s **Going Correction** -0.40s/f (Good) **25** Ran SP% **153.3**
Speed ratings: 112,110,110,108,108 106,105,105,105,100 100,100,100,99,99
95,93,85,85,82 76,—,—,— CSF £254.42 CT £6378.35 TOTE £36.60: £7.60, £7.50, £5.70, £1.80; DF 945.20.
Owner Mrs Adam Gurney **Bred** V G O'Donoghue **Trained** Moone, Co Kildare

FOCUS
A cracking handicap hurdle run at a hectic pace.

NOTEBOOK
Manorson(IRE) ran a fine race under his big weight on his first start since the Coral Cup. He was never out of the leading half dozen and kept on well after the winner from the last. On this evidence he could well land a good handicap. *(op 14/1)*
Pablo Du Charmil(FR) ran better than his finishing position suggests. He raced prominently and challenged for the lead at the second last flight but could soon find no more and was allowed to come home in his own time. *(op 12/1 tchd 14/1)*
Grande Jete(SAF), lightly-raced, has since failed to post an effort anywhere near his performance in the 2005 County Hurdle.

5079a PUNCHESTOWN GUINNESS GOLD CUP (GRADE 1 CHASE) 3m 1f
3:50 (3:51) 5-Y-0+
£99,310 (£31,448; £14,896; £4,965; £3,310; £1,655)

RPR

1 **War Of Attrition (IRE)**[40] 4470 7-11-12 171............................ CO'Dwyer 173+
(M F Morris, Ire) *mde all: strly pressed appr 2 out: rdn clr last: styd on wl: eased nr fin* **4/5**[1]

2 2 ½ **Beef Or Salmon (IRE)**[9] 4926 10-11-12 167................(p) TimmyMurphy 167
(Michael Hourigan, Ire) *cl 3rd: 2nd 6 out: pushed along bef 3 out: 3rd 2 out: kpt on fr last* **9/2**[2]

3 1 ½ **Hi Cloy (IRE)**[19] 4761 9-11-12 162............................ AndrewJMcNamara 165
(Michael Hourigan, Ire) *hld up: prog into 3rd 5 out: 2nd after 3 out: rdn to chal next: no ex appr last* **15/2**

4 5 ½ **Watson Lake (IRE)**[32] 4625 8-11-12 157............................ RWalsh 160
(Noel Meade, Ire) *hld up in rr: prog into 4th after 4 out: slt mstke and rdn next: no imp fr 2 out* **12/1**

5 25 **Forget The Past**[40] 4470 8-11-12 159............................ BJGeraghty 135
(M J P O'Brien, Ire) *settled 2nd: slt mstkes 10th and 11th: bad mstke 6 out: 4th and drvn along after 5 out: wknd 3 out: sn eased* **11/2**[3]

6 20 **Native Upmanship (IRE)**[18] 4777 13-11-12 144................(b) DJCasey 115
(A L T Moore, Ire) *chsd ldrs in 4th: wknd fr 5 out: t.o* **80/1**

6m 17.7s **Going Correction** -0.30s/f (Good) **7** Ran SP% **109.8**
Speed ratings: **112,111,110,108,100 94** CSF £4.80 TOTE £1.80: £1.50, £2.90; DF 5.70.
Owner Gigginstown House Stud **Bred** Miss B A Murphy **Trained** Fethard, Co Tipperary

FOCUS
An all-Irish renewal of Punchestown's premier race was well up to standard as it included the Gold Cup first and third plus Beef Or Salmon and recent Grade 1 winner Hi Cloy. THe winner confirmed the Cheltenham form in easy fashion.

NOTEBOOK
War Of Attrition(IRE) emulated the sidelined Kicking King by following up his Cheltenham success.With no-one else wanting to lead, O'Dwyer's dictated the pace that suited him, and aided by his mount's accurate jumping, was at no point seriously threatened. He seems particularly effective on this quicker ground, while also being effective in the mud. He has age on his side and is still improving, and the prospect of clashes with Kicking King next season. *(op 9/10)*
Beef Or Salmon(IRE) returned to something approaching his best following his Gold Cup flop. Reunited with both Murphy and with cheekpieces re-applied, he travelled better through the race than he has in the past and his jumping was also more fluent, although ground this quick does not usually bring out the best in him. Races such as the Lexus Chase and Hennessy Gold Cup at Leopardstown should still play to all his strengths next season. *(op 4/1)*
Hi Cloy(IRE) came here in good heart having taken the Melling Chase at Aintree, but the longer trip was a question mark against him and, although he ran well looked as if he was less effective over this far. Nevertheless, this run did increase the options available to him, although the feeling remains that despite being a four-time Grade 1 winner he has a little to find with the very top chasers. *(op 8/1)*
Watson Lake(IRE), another with stamina doubts was ridden like a non-stayer by Walsh, and it was unfortunate that he got the third last wrong just as he was was not beaten at all far by the front three.
Forget The Past, the Gold Cup third, appeared to be going well through the first half of the race, but a very bad mistake at the sixth-last following minor blunders at the preceding two obstacles seemed to knock the stuffing out of him. This run has to be forgiven, and he should be a threat in the top races next season. *(op 11/2 tchd 6/1)*

5080a S.M.MORRIS LTD. H'CAP CHASE (GRADE B) 2m 4f
4:25 (4:25) (0-150,144) 5-Y-0+ £24,693 (£7,244; £3,451; £1,175)

RPR

1 **Euro Leader (IRE)**[19] 4762 8-11-6 140 .... RWalsh 148+
(W P Mullins, Ire) *hld up in tch: prog into 6th 5 out: 3rd travelling wl 3 out: led bef next: styd on wl fr last: comf* **10/3**[1]

2 1 1/2 **Ross River**[9] 4930 10-10-9 129 .... DNRussell 134+
(A J Martin, Ire) *hld up in tch: 8th 5 out: 6th 3 out: 4th next: 2nd and kpt on fr last* **10/3**[1]

3 3 **Strong Project (IRE)**[19] 4761 10-11-10 144 .... JMAllen 146
(Sean O O'Brien, Ire) *cl up: led fr 6th: strly pressed 3 out: hdd whn mstke 2 out: 3rd and no ex fr last* **16/1**

4 1 1/2 **Natural Storm (IRE)**[17] 4813 8-9-7 116 .... KTColeman(3) 117
(F Flood, Ire) *trckd ldrs: 5th 1/2-way: 4th 3 out: 3rd next: no ex fr last* **12/1**

5 3 1/2 **Sum Leader (IRE)**[363] 92 10-9-10 116 ....(p) DJHoward 113
(Miss Jane Thomas, Ire) *2nd early: 4th appr 1/2-way: lost pl 6 out: towards rr next: kpt on fr 3 out* **25/1**

6 3 **Prince Of Pleasure (IRE)**[39] 4511 12-9-10 116 .... PACarberry 110
(D Broad, Ire) *led: hdd 6th: remained cl up: 2nd 3 out: sn no ex and wknd* **25/1**

7 1 1/2 **Strike Back (IRE)**[8] 4949 8-10-5 132 ....(b) ADLeigh(7) 125
(Mrs John Harrington, Ire) *hld up: mstke 7 out: rdn after next: slt mstke 4 out: kpt on same pce* **12/1**

8 13 **Charging (IRE)**[45] 4400 10-9-10 116 .... NPMadden 96
(John Joseph Murphy, Ire) *hld up towards rr: sme prog 5 out: 8th and rdn 3 out: no imp whn hmpd next: eased fr last* **25/1**

P **Rand (NZ)**[60] 4123 12-10-1 121 .... JRBarry —
(Noel Meade, Ire) *in tch early: dropped to rr 5th: p.u appr 7th* **16/1**

P **Cane Brake (IRE)**[45] 4400 7-10-6 126 .... TPTreacy —
(David Wachman, Ire) *a bhd: trailing 1/2-way: p.u bef 7 out* **33/1**

F **Macs Flamingo (IRE)**[17] 4811 6-10-3 123 .... DFO'Regan 120+
(P A Fahy, Ire) *mid-div: 7th 5 out: rdn next: 6th u.p whn fell 2 out* **10/1**[3]

F **Direct Flight (IRE)**[18] 4778 8-10-8 128 ....(t) DJCasey —
(Noel T Chance) *mid-div: prog 6 out: 4th next: 5th and rdn 3 out: 7th whn fell 2 out* **7/1**[2]

P **Green Ideal**[46] 4363 8-10-0 120 ....(b) TimmyMurphy —
(Ferdy Murphy) *prom: 3rd 1/2-way: cl up bef 4 out: wknd 3 out: trailing whn p.u after 2 out* **10/1**[3]

5m 3.20s **Going Correction** -0.30s/f (Good) 15 Ran SP% **118.5**
Speed ratings: **113,112,111,110,109 108,107,102,—,— —,—,—** CSF £14.54 CT £156.81 TOTE £3.40: £1.50, £1.70, £8.00; DF 8.00.
Owner John Cox **Bred** Mrs Maureen Mullins **Trained** Muine Beag, Co Carlow

NOTEBOOK
Green Ideal, whose best form has been on much softer ground, showed up for a long way but was well behind when his rider drew stumps. *(op 6/1)*
Direct Flight(IRE), third in a novices' handicap at Aintree, ran a fair race but was on the retreat when departing at the penultimate fence. *(op 6/1)*

5081a PADDY POWER CHAMPION INH FLAT RACE (GRADE 1) (MARES & GELDINGS) 2m
5:00 (5:01) 4-Y-0+ £44,896 (£13,172; £6,275; £2,137)

RPR

1 **Leading Run (IRE)**[74] 3875 7-12-0 .... MissNCarberry 131
(Noel Meade, Ire) *mid-div: hdwy into 5th 4f out: 3rd u.p ent st: sn chal: led 1f out: kpt on wl* **4/1**[1]

2 1/2 **Hairy Molly (IRE)**[42] 4448 6-12-0 .... MrDerekO'Connor 130
(Joseph Crowley, Ire) *a.p: 5th 6f out: 2nd and chal 3f out: led 1 1/2f out: hdd 1f out: kpt on u.p* **11/2**[2]

3 shd **Lord Over**[42] 4448 5-11-13 .... MrJPO'Farrell 129
(Patrick J Flynn, Ire) *rr of mid-div: prog 4f out: 6th into st: 3rd under 1f out: styd on wl: jst failed* **9/1**

4 4 1/2 **Mill House Girl (IRE)**[20] 4751 5-11-8 .... MrATDuff 120
(S Donohoe, Ire) *towards rr: hdwy 3f out: 10th into st: kpt on wl* **40/1**

5 1 **Dasher Reilly (USA)**[275] 1070 5-11-13 .... MrPFahey 124
(D K Weld, Ire) *trckd ldrs: 6th 1/2-way: rdn over 3f out: kpt on same pce st* **12/1**

6 1 1/2 **Clopf (IRE)**[38] 4546 5-11-13 .... MrKEPower 122
(E J O'Grady, Ire) *trckd ldrs: 4th 6f out: rdn over 3f out: 5th into st: kpt on same pce* **7/1**[3]

7 1 **Supreme Builder** 5-11-13 .... MrROHarding 121
(Ferdy Murphy) *towards rr: kpt on fr 3f out* **33/1**

8 nk **Footy Facts (IRE)**[31] 4645 6-12-0 .... MrJOMcGrath 122
(Robert Tyner, Ire) *in tch: hdwy into 3rd 4f out: 4th u.p ent st: sn wknd* **8/1**

9 shd **Ballytrim (IRE)**[42] 4448 5-11-13 .... MsKWalsh 121
(W P Mullins, Ire) *sn led: strly pressed ent st: hdd 1 1/2f out: no ex and wknd* **10/1**

10 3/4 **Dancing Hero (IRE)**[42] 4448 5-11-13 .... MissAFoley 120
(Thomas Foley, Ire) *trckd ldrs in 3rd: 2nd over 4f out: rdn and wknd over 3f out* **9/1**

11 1 1/2 **My Turn Now (IRE)**[10] 4892 4-11-6 .... MrAMO'Brien 111
(Edward U Hales, Ire) *rr of mid-div: rdn and no imp fr over 4f out* **20/1**

12 6 **West Route (IRE)**[73] 3897 6-12-0 .... MrLPFlynn 113
(I Madden, Ire) *nvr a factor* **200/1**

13 8 **Saddleeruppat (IRE)**[31] 4645 5-11-8 .... MrDPFahy 99
(Ms Joanna Morgan, Ire) *nvr a factor* **25/1**

14 10 **Crackin' Liss (IRE)**[10] 4892 5-11-8 .... MrPCashman 89
(John E Kiely, Ire) *a towards rr: eased st* **14/1**

15 1/2 **Abbeybraney (IRE)**[17] 4814 5-11-13 .... MrJJCodd 94
(J A Berry, Ire) *settled 2nd: wknd over 4f out* **33/1**

16 3 1/2 **Golden Hare (IRE)** 5-11-13 .... MrAAHoward 90
(Aidan Anthony Howard, Ire) *a towards rr: trailing st* **100/1**

17 20 **Kevkat (IRE)**[182] 1882 5-11-13 .... MrAFitzgerald 70
(Eoin Griffin, Ire) *mid-div: impr to chsd ldrs 6f out: wknd fr 4f out* **25/1**

18 5 **Crossing**[164] 2211 5-11-8 .... MrJAFahey 60
(William J Fitzpatrick, Ire) *mid-div: wknd fr 5f out: trailing bef st* **40/1**

3m 38.6s **Going Correction** -0.40s/f (Good)
WFA 4 from 5yo 5lb 5 from 6yo+ 3lb 21 Ran SP% **127.1**
Speed ratings: **109,108,108,106,105 105,104,104,104,104 103,100,96,91,91 89,79,76** CSF £23.12 TOTE £4.20: £2.00, £1.50, £2.10, £9.50; DF 12.40.
Owner Mrs Moira McGrath **Bred** Michael D McGrath **Trained** Castletown, Co Meath

FOCUS
A fantastic bumper that brought together the best form that this sphere has to offer and one in which 15 of the 18 contestants were previous winners.

NOTEBOOK
Leading Run(IRE) ◆ completed the truly remarkable feat of winning four consecutive bumpers and in doing so he beat the same two horses that filled the minor placings behind him on his most recent start at Naas in February - albeit on this occasion it was Hairy Molly that filled second and Lord Over in third. After making good progress heading into the final half mile, he moved into a close third under pressure off the final turn. He eventually fought his way to the front at the furlong pole and kept on tenaciously all the way to the line. He looks a most exciting prospect for next season. Trainer Noel Meade said afterwards that he sees him as a two-and-a-half-mile novice hurdler for next season and it is a measure of the regard he is held in that he worked the other day in the company of Nicanor, Sweet Wake and Iktitaf. *(op 7/2)*
Hairy Molly(IRE) ◆ came here on the back of a tremendous Cheltenham bumper success and was also bidding for a fourth victory in this sphere. Always close to the pace, he was challenging for the lead before the straight and led with well over a furlong to run. He stayed on very well all the way to the line. This was another commendable effort from a horse who has progressed with every run and he has the makings of a very high-class staying hurdler. *(op 5/1)*
Lord Over finished sixth at Cheltenham but got much closer to Hairy Molly here with a career-best effort. He looked momentarily outpaced before the turn-in but stayed on best of all in the straight. He, too, will have a bright future as a staying novice. *(op 8/1 tchd 10/1)*
Mill House Girl(IRE) looked a fine prospect when winning two bumpers on good to firm ground last summer. She didn't have the ground to suit on both runs since then but was back to her best here. She can be expected to do well over hurdles. *(op 33/1)*
Dasher Reilly(USA) posted a good effort on his first run since making a winning debut in a Galway bumper last July. He came under pressure heading into the final half mile but stuck to his task and can be expected to improve on this. *(op 10/1)*
Clopf(IRE) won a pair of Limerick bumpers on his first two starts. He looked as if he might get into *the reckoning at one point in the straight but he could find no more heading into the final furlong. (op 7/1 tchd 8/1)*
Supreme Builder ◆, making his debut, travelled as well as anything for much of the way and this must rate as a highly-promising effort. He could be very nice.
Footy Facts(IRE) was not disgraced in his bid for a hat-trick. This was the fastest ground he has yet to run on and he will do well over hurdles on soft ground next winter.
Ballytrim(IRE) ran much better than his ninth place suggests. He set a good pace and it was only heading towards the furlong pole that he gave best. *(op 8/1)*
Dancing Hero(IRE) was fifth at Cheltenham but could find no more from before the turn-in. *(op 8/1 tchd 10/1)*

5082a AVON RI CORPORATE & LEISURE RESORT NOVICE CHASE 2m 2f
5:35 (5:35) 5-Y-0+ £12,346 (£3,622; £1,725; £587)

RPR

1 **Tigerlion (IRE)**[11] 4864 8-11-12 125 .... MDarcy 126+
(J Bleahen, Ire) *hld up in tch: 5th 4 out: 4th whn mstke and bdly hmpd 2 out: lft mod 2nd: lft disputing ld last: sn led and drifted rt u.p: kpt on wl* **10/1**[3]

2 2 **Chetwind Music (IRE)**[11] 4866 8-11-12 114 .... JLCullen 122
(William Coleman O'Brien, Ire) *hld up towards rr: 7th and rdn 3 out: lft mod 4th 2 out: lft disputing ld last: sltly hmpd run-in: no ex cl home* **25/1**

3 7 **Dalian Dawn (IRE)**[272] 1091 8-11-12 120 .... AndrewJMcNamara 115
(David A Kiely, Ire) *led: stumbld bef 4 out: hdd 3 out: 4th and no ex whn lft mod 2nd 2 out: lft disputing ld last: sn hdd and hmpd: eased cl hom* **12/1**

4 3 **Mr McAuley (IRE)**[77] 3812 8-11-12 114 .... MrDerekO'Connor 112
(I R Ferguson, Ire) *a bhd: 8th and no imp 3 out: lft mod 5th next: lft 4th fr last* **12/1**

5 25 **Some Timbering (IRE)**[9] 4931 7-11-5 .... JRBarry 80
(E Sheehy, Ire) *prom: cl 3rd 5 out: hmpd and stmbld bef next: no ex 3 out: eased after 2 out* **8/1**[2]

F **Wing Of Fire (GER)**[34] 4601 6-11-5 .... PACarberry —
(P Hughes, Ire) *prom on outer: bmpd 6th: wknd 6 out: bhd whn fell 5 out* **33/1**

F **Brutto Facie (IRE)**[9] 4931 7-11-5 124 .... ADLeigh(7) 126+
(Mrs John Harrington, Ire) *sn 2nd: rdn 3 out: cl 3rd u.p whn fell 2 out* **14/1**

F **Rubberdubber**[53] 4239 6-11-12 .... APMcCoy 126+
(C R Egerton) *in tch: 6th 1/2-way: hdwy 4 out: 2nd and rdn to chal after next: ev ch whn fell 2 out* **2/1**[1]

F **Tiger Cry (IRE)**[9] 4927 8-11-12 139 .... DJCasey 131+
(A L T Moore, Ire) *trckd ldrs: cl 4th bef 4 out: led travelling wl 3 out: rdn and strly pressed whn lft clr 2 out: 15 l advantage whn fell las* **2/1**[1]

4m 46.7s **Going Correction** -0.30s/f (Good) 10 Ran SP% **115.7**
Speed ratings: **77,76,73,71,60 —,—,—,—** CSF £185.83 TOTE £18.20: £3.20, £9.60, £2.10; DF 277.60.
Owner J F O'Malley **Bred** Cooliney Stud **Trained** Ballinasloe, Co Galway
■ Stewards' Enquiry : M Darcy two-day ban: careless riding (May 5-6)

FOCUS
An incident-packed race and the form should be treated with extreme caution.

NOTEBOOK
Tigerlion(IRE) was a fortunate winner. Lying fourth when badly hampered at the second-last, he was left a poor second, and was then left to scrap it out from the last, just pulling out enough to assert, despite drifting to the right under pressure. More of a staying type, he has not covered much mileage and might go on to build on this over further, though he does not look particularly well treated off a current handicap mark of 125.
Chetwind Music(IRE) was out of contention at the third-last, but circumstances combined to get him back in the hunt and he very nearly pulled it out of the fire on the run-in. He was slightly hampered as the winner edged towards him, but the stewards ruled that it had not helped Tigerlion to improve his position. *(op 20/1)*
Dalian Dawn(IRE) *Official explanation: jockey said gelding finished lame (op 10/1)*
Some Timbering(IRE) lost momentum when hampered before four out. *(op 10/1)*
Tiger Cry(IRE), the Grand Annual runner-up, had the race sewn up when falling at the last, but just a fence earlier he had begun to look vulnerable as the other joint-favourite Rubberdubber began to launch his challenge *(op 2/1 tchd 9/4)*
Rubberdubber, successful at Newbury on his previous start, looked in with a serious shout before falling two out. *(op 2/1 tchd 9/4)*

5083a COX'S CASH & CARRY CHAMPION HUNTERS CHASE 3m 1f
6:10 (6:11) 5-Y-0+ £10,101 (£2,963; £1,412; £481)

RPR

1 **Whyso Mayo (IRE)**[40] 4471 9-11-9 .... MrDMurphy(5) 126
(Raymond Hurley, Ire) *in tch: 6th 7 out: prog 5 out: led bef 4 out: clr 2 out: kpt on u.p fr last* **5/1**[3]

2 2 **General Striker**[8] 4954 6-12-0 ....(p) MissNCarberry 124+
(E Bolger, Ire) *trckd ldrs: 4th 6 out: 5th whn bad mstke 4 out: rdn next: mod 2nd bef last: styd on wl* **9/2**[2]

3 1 **First Down Jets (IRE)**[8] 4954 9-11-11 .... MrCJSweeney(3) 123
(W J Burke, Ire) *towards rr: prog 5 out: 6th after 3 out: kpt on wl fr last* **9/1**

4 1 1/2 **Bothar Na (IRE)**[20] 4748 7-11-11 .... MrKEPower(3) 122
(W P Mullins, Ire) *mid-div: prog 6 out: 3rd next: cl 2nd bef 3 out: rdn bef next: no imp: no ex appr last* **3/1**[1]

5 3 1/2 **No Discount (IRE)**[8] 4954 12-11-7 98 .... MrThomasCoyle(7) 118
(Edward Cawley, Ire) *towards rr: styd on wl fr 4 out* **33/1**

6 ½ **Back On Top (IRE)**[8] 4954 12-11-11 .... MrPCashman(3) 118
(J L Hassett, Ire) *rr of mid-div: 8th 5 out: hdwy into 3rd 3 out: no imp next: wknd last* **10/1**
7 7 **Glenduff Bridge (IRE)**[8] 4954 10-12-0 104.............(b) MrDerekO'Connor 111
(W J Burke, Ire) *hld up in rr: kpt on wout threatening fr 3 out* **20/1**
8 nk **Newbay Prop (IRE)**[32] 7-11-7 102.......................... MrJWFarrelly(7) 110
(A J Martin, Ire) *rr of mid-div: kpt on same pce fr 4 out* **12/1**
9 9 **Industrious**[8] 4954 7-11-7 ....(p) MrCMMurphy(7) 101
(Mrs D A Love, Ire) *cl up and disp ld: hdd bef 4 out: 5th 3 out: sn no ex* **40/1**
10 nk **Drombeag (IRE)**[20] 4748 8-12-0 114..........................(b) MrJTMcNamara 101
(Jonjo O'Neill) *mid-div: slt mstke 10th: 7th 5 out: 6th bef 2 out: sn wknd* **8/1**
11 20 **Western View (IRE)**[17] 14-11-7 116..............................(p) MrDJFoster(7) 81
(Cecil Ross, Ire) *prom: 3rd 7 out: wknd fr 5 out* **33/1**
12 2 **Final Target (IRE)**[24] 10-11-7 .... MrFPCunningham(7) 79
(Liam O'Donoghue, Ire) *a bhd* **66/1**
13 ½ **Penny Out (IRE)**[56] 4187 8-11-7 90...................................... MrATDuff(7) 78
(D M Christie, Ire) *a towards rr* **33/1**
14 9 **Hersov (IRE)**[10] 10-11-7 ....(p) MissCJMacmahon(7) 69
(D M Christie, Ire) *cl and disp ld: 3rd after 1/2-way: wknd fr 6 out* **33/1**
15 2 **Andiamo (IRE)**[24] 11-11-7 83.. MrMDHickey(7) 67
(John Joseph Murphy, Ire) *chsd ldrs: 6th 1/2-way: wknd bef 5 out* **33/1**
16 11 **Abbeytown (IRE)**[20] 4748 9-12-0 .... MrJJCodd 56
(Mrs Jeanette Riordan, Ire) *trckd ldrs on inner: 4th appr 1/2-way: wknd bef 6 out* **14/1**
P **Savati (FR)**[40] 4471 6-11-7 .... MrWGRankin(7) —
(R T J Wilson, Ire) *nvr a factor: bhd whn p.u bef 2 out* **14/1**
P **Fogonthetyne (IRE)**[4] 7-11-11 .... MrJDMoore(3) —
(Damien Lavery, Ire) *chsd ldrs: 4th appr 1/2-way: sn wknd: p.u bef 4 out* **66/1**
P **De Chirico (IRE)**[10] 10-11-7 .... MrJTCarroll(7) —
(Martin M Treacy, Ire) *led and disp: hdd & wknd bef 4 out: p.u bef 2 out* **50/1**

6m 21.4s **Going Correction** -0.30s/f (Good) **20** Ran SP% **137.9**
Speed ratings: **106,105,105,104,103 103,101,100,98,97 91,90,90,87,87 83,—,—,—** CSF £29.57 TOTE £4.10: £1.50, £1.40, £2.90, £1.30; DF 11.00.
Owner Mrs Kathleen O'Driscoll **Bred** Edward O'Driscoll **Trained** Clonakilty, Co Cork

NOTEBOOK
Whyso Mayo(IRE) followed up his Christie's Foxhunters' Chase success with a thoroughly game performance. Held up, the winner began to improve his position on the outside of the field starting down the back straight and was sent to the front approaching four out. Almost joined by Bothar Na soon afterwards, he saw off that rival's challenge after the last and was never in much danger thereafter. *(op 9/2)*
General Striker made a bad mistake four out when he was racing in fifth place and that arguably cost him the race.
First Down Jets(IRE), runner-up to Whyso Mayo at Cheltenham before finishing well adrift of General Striker in the Joseph O'Reilly at Fairyhouse, took a long time to warm to his task here although he did stay on well from two out. *(op 8/1)*
Bothar Na(IRE), fourth at Cheltenham before being badly hampered in the Aintree Fox Hunters, had every chance and there appeared to be no obvious excuses this time as he had the sort of ground he likes. He pressed the winner from before four out but he came under pressure after the third-last and was struggling from there although holding on to second place until nearing the final fence. *(op 7/2)*
Drombeag(IRE) got round this time but was well held. *(op 8/1 tchd 9/1)*
De Chirico(IRE) *Official explanation: jockey said gelding received interference on the second-last bend and lost ground*
T/Jkpt: @1,125.90. Pool of @45,039.50 - 30 winning units. T/Plt: @1,345.50. Pool of @10,764.00 - 6 winning units. II

4819 FONTWELL (L-H)
Thursday, April 27

OFFICIAL GOING: Good to firm
Wind: Virtually nil

5084 GILLIAN CHIVERS MARES' ONLY MAIDEN HURDLE (9 hdls) 2m 2f 110y
2:10 (2:10) (Class 4) 4-Y-0+ **£3,057** (£897; £448; £224)

Form RPR
203 1 **Screen Test**[12] 4855 4-10-12 .... RobertThornton 91
(B G Powell) *slowly away: bhd: plld hrd and hdwy after 3rd: hit next: led 5th: rdn and hdd 2 out: looked hld whn lft clr last* **4/6**[1]
00 2 5 **The Chequered Lady**[70] 3939 4-10-12 .... JamesDavies 89+
(T D McCarthy) *chsd ldrs: rdn to chse ldng pair after 3 out: kpt on same pce : nt fluent and hmpd whn lft 2nd at the last* **25/1**
30/2 3 5 **Annie Fleetwood**[14] 4836 8-11-4 98......................... AndrewThornton 87
(R H Alner) *led tl 5th: chsd ldrs: rdn after 3 out: plugged on same pce to go 3rd after last* **10/3**[2]
4F0 4 1½ **Joli Classical (IRE)**[22] 4731 4-10-12 81....................... TomScudamore 80
(R J Hodges) *mid-div: rdn and hdwy after 6th: one pce after next: lft 3rd briefly at the last* **8/1**[3]
3-2P 5 15 **Maarees**[114] 1596 5-11-4 ....(p) AndrewTinkler 71
(G P Enright) *chsd ldrs: rdn after 6th: wknd after 3 out* **25/1**
00P0 6 10 **Hazzard A Guess**[14] 4836 5-10-11 .... WayneKavanagh(7) 61
(J W Mullins) *hld up towards rr: hdwy after 5th: wknd after 3 out* **33/1**
PFP 7 dist **Rathcannon Beauty**[146] 2612 4-10-5 .... MarcGoldstein(7) —
(Mrs L P Baker) *a bhd: t.o fr 3 out* **66/1**
00P- P **Lady Blaze**[455] 3546 7-11-4 .... DaveCrosse —
(B De Haan) *bhd: lost tch 6th: p.u bef last* **100/1**
P **Gregs Girl**[206] 4-10-7 .... RobertLucey-Butler(5) —
(M Madgwick) *mid-div tl 5th: sn wl bhd: p.u bef 3 out* **100/1**
U **Beauchamp Star**[51] 5-11-1 .... OwynNelmes(3) 98
(N B King) *hld up towards rr: gd hdwy after 5th: led appr 2 out: 1 1/2 clr and styng on whn blnd bdly and uns rdr last* **16/1**

4m 25.5s (-10.50) **Going Correction** -0.60s/f (Firm)
WFA 4 from 5yo+ 5lb **10** Ran SP% **114.2**
Speed ratings: **98,95,93,93,86 82,—,—,—,—** CSF £24.44 TOTE £1.80: £1.10, £4.50, £1.30; EX 21.50.
Owner Christopher Shankland **Bred** Cheveley Park Stud Ltd **Trained** Morestead, Hants

FOCUS
A moderate mares-only maiden rated around the third and fourth.
NOTEBOOK
Screen Test, a bit of a character, was probably a lucky winner, but she is now to be switched back to the Flat, where her trainer thinks she can find a decent handicap for her. *(op 10-11)*
The Chequered Lady has her limitations, but is gradually getting there at a modest level. That said, she would have finished third had the leader stood up at the last. *(op 33-1)*
Annie Fleetwood did not reproduce the promise of her run a fortnight ago, and may have "bounced". *(op 9-4)*
Joli Classical(IRE) has been running in handicaps, so this was nothing special dropped in grade. *(op 10-1)*
Maarees was well held in an uninspiring contest.
Hazzard A Guess *(op 25-1)*
Lady Blaze *Official explanation: jockey said mare had a breathing problem (op 20-1)*
Beauchamp Star needs to improve her jumping, but she would probably have won but for ejecting her rider at the last, and deserves to find a similar race. *(op 20-1)*

5085 ANDREW FLINTOFF BENEFIT SUPPORTING CHASE HOSPICE NOVICES' CHASE (16 fncs) 2m 6f
2:40 (2:40) (Class 4) 5-Y-0+ **£5,204** (£1,528; £764; £381)

Form RPR
-0PP 1 **General Grey (IRE)**[64] 4052 6-11-0 99................................ SamThomas 107+
(Miss H C Knight) *chsd ldrs: rdn after 4 out: led sn after 3 out: drifted lft after last: styd on wl: rdn out* **9/1**
0521 2 3½ **Dead Mans Dante (IRE)**[10] 4920 8-11-2 105..................... TJDreaper(5) 111+
(Ferdy Murphy) *hld up bhd: tk clsr order 9th: trckd ldr after 4 out: hmpd 3 out: chsd wnr next: hung lft and fnd little run-in* **1/1**[1]
032F 3 6 **Herecomestanley**[4] 5017 7-10-9 95................................ CharliePoste(5) 99+
(M F Harris) *in tch: hdwy and hit 8th: led after 12th: blnd and hdd 3 out: sn rdn: hit next: sn btn* **15/2**
1343 4 12 **Twenty Degrees**[11] 4872 8-11-0 93..(b) PhilipHide 84
(G L Moore) *sn chsng ldrs: rdn appr 11th: outpcd after 4 out* **5/1**[2]
P26 5 6 **Ehab (IRE)**[11] 4873 7-11-0 80...(t) MatthewBatchelor 78
(Miss A M Newton-Smith) *chsd ldrs tl 12th: wknd next* **18/1**
P4P/ 6 29 **The Dream Lives On (IRE)**[886] 2338 10-10-9 85 RobertLucey-Butler(5) 49
(Miss Z C Davison) *led: blnd 12th: sn hdd: wknd after next* **66/1**
-P22 U **El Viejo (IRE)**[26] 4692 9-10-7 100...............................(b) JustinMorgan(7) —
(L Wells) *stmbld and uns rdr sn after s* **11/2**[3]

5m 25.9s (-17.90) **Going Correction** -0.90s/f (Hard) **7** Ran SP% **110.6**
Speed ratings: **96,94,92,88,86 75,—** CSF £18.32 TOTE £13.10: £4.10, £1.30; EX 35.40.
Owner Martin Broughton & Friends **Bred** James Barry **Trained** West Lockinge, Oxon

FOCUS
A modest turnout for the money and the form, rated around the winner, is not strong.
NOTEBOOK
General Grey(IRE), with conditions to suit, bounced back to form, taking full advantage when the runner-up was hampered three out. He is very much at home on fast ground, though he suffered a crack to a bone in a hind leg earlier in the season. *(op 10-1)*
Dead Mans Dante(IRE) looked really good on the bridle, but he was never going as well after jumping into the back of a weakening rival three out, and then tired up the final hill. He deserves another chance. *(op 5-6)*
Herecomestanley's hopes ended with a bungle at the final ditch, three from home. *(op 10-1)*
Twenty Degrees may be more effective on easier ground. *(op 6-1)*
The Dream Lives On(IRE) *Official explanation: vet said gelding returned lame right fore (tchd 50-1)*

5086 GALES NOVICES' HURDLE (11 hdls) 2m 6f 110y
3:10 (3:10) (Class 4) 4-Y-0+ **£3,253** (£955; £477; £238)

Form RPR
2021 1 **Smart Mover**[54] 4238 7-11-7 110... SamThomas 100+
(Miss H C Knight) *hld up in tch: tk clsr order 7th: shkn up after 3 out: led next: clr last: rdn out* **5/4**[1]
520U 2 10 **Ballyrobert (IRE)**[21] 4755 9-10-11 .... WilliamKennedy(3) 83
(A M Hales) *trckd ldrs: lft 2nd at the 3rd: jnd ldr 6th: rdn after 3 out : sn one pce: wnt lft last: tk 2nd run-in* **8/1**[3]
-P 3 nk **Monzon (FR)**[51] 4284 6-10-9 .... JohnnyLevins(5) 83
(B G Powell) *led: hit 5th: rdn after 3 out: hdd next: 2nd and wkng whn hit last* **12/1**
0 4 21 **Rodd To Riches**[12] 4856 8-11-0 .... MatthewBatchelor 62
(Jamie Poulton) *keen in rr: hit 5th: rdn after 7th: sn lost tch: t.o* **66/1**
0-0P P **Fine Enough (IRE)**[34] 4603 7-11-0 ....(b[1]) PJBrennan —
(R Rowe) *hit 4th: sn struggling: t.o and p.u bef 7th* **66/1**
0021 U **Mikado**[4] 5016 5-11-7 123.. MrAJBerry(7) —
(Jonjo O'Neill) *trcking ldr whn blnd bdly and uns rdr 3rd* **13/8**[2]
0 P **Hollywood Henry (IRE)**[14] 4826 6-11-0 .... RJGreene —
(Mrs A M Thorpe) *in tch: trckd ldrs 4th: rdn after 7th: hit next: wknd 3 out: p.u bef next (dismntd)* **33/1**

5m 27.8s (-17.00) **Going Correction** -0.60s/f (Firm) **7** Ran SP% **107.3**
Speed ratings: **105,101,101,94,— —,—** CSF £10.20 TOTE £2.30: £1.30, £2.50; EX 9.90.
Owner Rendezvous Racing **Bred** Richard Chugg **Trained** West Lockinge, Oxon

FOCUS
An uncompetitive novice, made more so when the second favourite departed at the third. The form is virtually unrateable and could be a fair way out.
NOTEBOOK
Smart Mover, helped by the early departure of his only serious market rival, looked better the further he went, so should be suited by three miles. He will have a summer campaign over hurdles before switching to fences. *(op 11-8 tchd 6-5)*
Ballyrobert(IRE) ran his race, but was outclassed by the winner. *(op 11-1)*
Monzon(FR) got round this time, which - if nothing else - will have helped his confidence a bit. *(op 9-1)*
Rodd To Riches *(op 50-1 tchd 100-1)*
Hollywood Henry(IRE) *Official explanation: vet said gelding had been struck into (op 25-1)*
Mikado's early departure left the way open for the eventual winner. *(op 25-1)*

5087 BGC H'CAP HURDLE (12 hdls 1 omitted) 3m 3f
3:40 (3:40) (Class 4) (0-110,110) 4-Y-0+ **£3,253** (£955; £477; £238)

Form RPR
4P50 1 **Ballyhoo (IRE)**[33] 4619 6-10-3 **94**............................(v) WayneKavanagh(7) 95+
(J W Mullins) *chsd ldrs: wnt 10l 2nd after 4th: clsd on ldr 9th: led next: rdn and 1l clr last: all out* **15/8**[1]
0-PP 2 nk **Ockley Flyer**[101] 3424 7-9-9 **84** oh12..................(p) RobertLucey-Butler(5) 84
(Miss Z C Davison) *hld up: hdwy 9th: chsd wnr after 3 out: rdn after next: styd on strly fnl 75yds: jst hld* **10/1**
0-0P 3 20 **Boring Goring (IRE)**[11] 4874 12-9-13 **90**..................... JayPemberton(7) 70
(E J Farrant) *hld up: hdwy 9th: rdn and effrt after 3 out: one pce fr next* **25/1**
06P0 4 12 **Vanormix (FR)**[9] 4936 7-11-12 **110**................................... RichardHobson 78
(C J Gray) *hld up: hit 2nd: reminders after 6th: short lived effrt after 3 out: wknd next* **14/1**
4P46 5 nk **Emphatic (IRE)**[11] 4874 11-10-1 **90**...............................(b) DarylJacob(5) 57
(J G Portman) *chsd clr ldr tl 4th: chsd ldrs tl 9th: sn bhd* **4/1**[3]
/PF- 6 dist **Keltic Heritage (IRE)**[33] 12-9-13 **90**............................ JustinMorgan(7) —
(L A Dace) *led: sn clr: hit 5th: hdd 10th: wkng whn hit 3 out: t.o* **8/1**

-640 **U** **Lord Oscar (IRE)**[12] 4860 7-10-5 **96**..................(t) AndrewGlassonbury(7) —
(M C Pipe) *hld up bhd: blnd and uns rdr 3rd* **10/3**[2]

6m 26.0s (-8.30) **Going Correction** -0.60s/f (Firm) **7** Ran SP% **108.6**
Speed ratings: **103,102,96,93,93** —,— CSF £18.04 CT £303.11 TOTE £2.70: £1.60, £4.10; EX 36.00.
Owner Ian M McGready **Bred** Miss Annette McMahon **Trained** Wilsford-Cum-Lake, Wilts

FOCUS
Just an ordinary handicap, even for the time of year, but run at a strong pace and rated through the winner to her mark.

NOTEBOOK
Ballyhoo(IRE) has done well in the visor, and appreciates good or faster ground. *(op 7-4 tchd 9-4)*
Ockley Flyer nearly got there with a strong finish, and can step up on this promising first effort for three months. *(op 14-1)*
Boring Goring(IRE) has been lightly raced in the last two seasons. He put in a fair effort, but is some way from his best. *(op 20-1)*
Vanormix(FR) was in trouble with a circuit remaining. *(op 9-1 tchd 8-1)*
Keltic Heritage(IRE), reverting to hurdles, could hardly believe his luck. However, he went off too fast, and that was that.

5088 FK ROOFING SERVICES SUPPORTING CHASE HOSPICE H'CAP CHASE (19 fncs) 3m 2f 110y
4:10 (4:11) (Class 5) (0-90,83) 5-Y-0+ **£3,253** (£955; £477; £238)

Form				RPR
0-65	**1**		**Russian Lord (IRE)**[21] 4753 7-11-8 **79**..............................(p) PJBrennan (V R A Dartnall) *mde virtually all: j.rt 8th: lft clr 15th: j.rt after: hit 3 out: idled and sn rdn: styd on wl: drvn out* **6/1**[3]	99+
5002	**2**	*2 ½*	**Lucky Luk (FR)**[37] 4567 7-11-2 **73**.................................. JimmyMcCarthy (K C Bailey) *in tch: hdwy 9th: rdn whn lft 3rd and hmpd 15th: styd on to chse wnr after 3 out: no ex fr last* **7/2**[1]	87+
2411	**3**	*6*	**Lambrini Bianco (IRE)**[6] 4989 8-11-5 **76** 7ex............(b) TomScudamore (Mrs L Williamson) *rn in snatches: chsd ldrs: drvn along after 10th: wnt 3rd at the 13th: lft 2nd at the 15th: sn hrd rdn: kpt on same pce fr* **7/2**[1]	84+
34	**5**	*25*	**Pangeran (USA)**[189] 1803 14-10-13 **73**......................... OwynNelmes(3) (N B King) *mid div: rdn after 13th: wknd after 16th: poor 5th whn bdly hmpd 2 out* **11/1**	—
PPP5	**P**		**Rutland (IRE)**[26] 4692 7-10-0 **64**....................................... RichardSpate(7) (C J Drewe) *a bhd: t.o and p.u after 10th* **100/1**	—
RR-0	**R**		**Tino (IRE)**[356] 201 10-11-8 **79**.................................... WayneHutchinson (Andrew Turnell) *chsd ldrs tl wknd after 15th: bhd whn ref 2 out* **12/1**	—
PP5P	**P**		**Designer Label (IRE)**[10] 4914 10-11-12 **83**.................(b[1]) AndrewTinkler (Carl Llewellyn) *nvr travelling in rr: t.o and p.u after 10th* **8/1**	—
0054	**F**		**Bright Present (IRE)**[10] 4921 8-10-0 **64**................(tp) TomMessenger(7) (B N Pollock) *w wnr: led 11th tl 13th: w wnr: jst being pushed along whn fell 15th* **12/1**	—

6m 30.9s (-30.20) **Going Correction** -0.90s/f (Hard) **9** Ran SP% **111.2**
Speed ratings: **108,107,105**,—,— —,—,—,— CSF £26.67 CT £81.24 TOTE £8.10: £2.60, £1.50, £1.80; EX 29.00.
Owner Plain Peeps **Bred** James Canty And John Moloney **Trained** Brayford, Devon

FOCUS
A modest race, but run at a sound gallop and solid enough form at a low level, rated through the placed horses.

NOTEBOOK
Russian Lord(IRE) , winning at the second time of asking over fences, is suited by fast ground. He is a late developer, and will have one more run before being rested. *(op 9-2)*
Lucky Luk(FR) was only beaten by an improving sort, and will find other opportunties. *(op 10-3)*
Lambrini Bianco(IRE) was never really travelling, and may be better suited by a more conventional track. *(op 11-4)*
Alfred The Grey was not at his best, but may have been unsettled by his early blunder. *(op 7-1)*
Bright Present(IRE) helped to set the pace and dominated most of the race with the eventual winner. Though just starting to come off the bridle when departing five from home, he had done well until then. *(op 16-1)*

5089 NCS LIMITED SUPPORTING CHASE HOSPICE STANDARD OPEN NATIONAL HUNT FLAT RACE 2m 2f 110y
4:40 (4:40) (Class 6) 4-6-Y-0 **£1,626** (£477; £238; £119)

Form				RPR
	1		**Or Jaune (FR)** 4-10-12 .... PhilipHide (G L Moore) *hld up in tch: tk clsr order 7f out: led appr fnl f: kpt on wl: readily* **10/3**[2]	91+
	2	*3*	**River Heights (IRE)** 5-11-4 .... TomDoyle (C Tinkler) *trckd ldrs: rdn 2f out: swtchd lft 1f out: kpt on to go 2nd cl home: no ch w wnr* **11/4**[1]	89
05	**3**	*½*	**Ma Burls**[77] 3820 6-10-6 .... ShaneWalsh(5) (K F Clutterbuck) *led: rdn over 2f out: hdd appr fnl f: no ex: lost 2nd cl home* **6/1**	81
6	**4**	*13*	**Mister Christian (IRE)**[9] 4940 5-11-4 .... ChristianWilliams (W K Goldsworthy) *chsd ldrs: outpcd 5f out: styd on again past btn horses fr over 1f out* **7/2**[3]	75
	5	*1*	**Indian Open** 5-11-1 .... RichardYoung(3) (J W Mullins) *hld up: hmpd on bnd 1/2 way: effrt 4f out: wknd 3f out* **12/1**	74
	6	*3*	**Honey Nut** 4-10-0 .... RobertLucey-Butler(5) (Miss Z C Davison) *hld up: sme hdwy 5f out: wknd wl over 2f out* **16/1**	58
00	**7**	*3 ½*	**Kyliemoss**[84] 3699 5-10-4 .... KeiranBurke(7) (N R Mitchell) *in tch: hdwy 6f out: rdn 4f out: hung lft 3f out: sn wknd* **10/1**	61

4m 22.1s (-17.20) **Going Correction** -0.60s/f (Firm)
WFA 4 from 5yo 5lb 5 from 6yo 3lb **7** Ran SP% **108.9**
Speed ratings: **90,88,88,83,82 81,79** CSF £11.63 TOTE £3.90: £2.70, £1.50; EX 8.00.
Owner G L Moore **Bred** B Guilossou And Christian Le Galliard **Trained** Woodingdean, E Sussex

FOCUS
Run at a modest pace, and hard to assess with confidence, but the first two home can build on this with the third setting the level.

NOTEBOOK
Or Jaune(FR), a half-brother to the chaser Iznogoud, appealed as a likely improver. His trainer will get the best out of him, and he should make a hurdler before long. *(op 7-2 tchd 4-1 and 5-1 in a place)*
River Heights(IRE) probably ran into a tough rival at this level, and can win a similar race following this promising debut. *(op 3-1)*
Ma Burls again tried to make all, only to be picked off by two horses of reasonable potential. This was a good effort. *(op 5-1)*
Mister Christian(IRE) was a shade disappointing following an encouraging debut at Chepstow. A switch to hurdles looks likely before long. *(op 10-3)*
Kyliemoss *Official explanation: jockey said mare hung both ways (op 9-1)*

5090 VIRGIN CASINO H'CAP CHASE (11 fncs 2 omitted) 2m 2f
5:10 (5:10) (Class 4) (0-110,106) 5-Y-0+ **£5,204** (£1,528; £764; £381)

Form				RPR
500P	**1**		**Haafel (USA)**[26] 4694 9-11-8 **102**...(b) PhilipHide (G L Moore) *chsd ldrs tl 3rd: in tch: hdwy into 2nd bef 7th: rdn to ld 3 out: clr 2 out: kpt on wl: eased nr fin* **10/1**	119+
P016	**2**	*9*	**River Amora (IRE)**[29] 4666 11-9-9 **80** oh2.........(p) RobertLucey-Butler(5) (Jim Best) *chsd ldrs tl outpcd 7th: styng on whn hit 3 out:wnt 3rd after 2 out* **11/4**[2]	88+
5002	**3**	*hd*	**Romany Dream**[37] 4563 8-11-7 **101**....................................(b) HenryOliver (R Dickin) *chsd ldrs: outpcd after 7th: styd on again fr 3 out: wnt 2nd after 2 out: no ch w wnr* **3/1**[3]	108
F0P	**4**	*12*	**French Direction (IRE)**[10] 4908 7-10-11 **91**......................... PJBrennan (R Rowe) *led at gd pce: hit 6th: rdn and hdd and mstke 3 out: 2nd and hld whn hit out: wknd* **4/1**	88+
4156	**5**	*shd*	**Caribbean Cove (IRE)**[10] 4906 8-11-9 **106**.....................(b) PaulO'Neill(3) (Miss Venetia Williams) *bhd: reminders after 6th: short lived effrt after 4 out* **5/2**[1]	101

4m 16.5s (-18.60) **Going Correction** -0.90s/f (Hard) **5** Ran SP% **109.3**
Speed ratings: **105,101,100,95,95** CSF £36.52 TOTE £14.60: £3.50, £2.10; EX 41.70 Place 6 £7.48, Place 5 £6.36.
Owner D R Hunnisett **Bred** Shadwell Farm Inc **Trained** Woodingdean, E Sussex

FOCUS
An ordinary contest, with some of the contestants below their best, but run at a good pace with the placed horses pretty much to their marks.

NOTEBOOK
Haafel(USA) had only previously scored on soft ground, but handled the quick conditions in *apparent comfort. He looks the type to win again. Official explanation: trainer had no explanation for the improved form shown (tchd 11-1)*
River Amora(IRE) goes well around here, but was beaten by a fair sort from a stable in top form. He is always one to consider at Fontwell. *(op 5-2 tchd 3-1)*
Romany Dream, a market drifter, made heavy weather of it, and was not at her best. *(op 9-4)*
French Direction(IRE) probably went off a bit too fast, but at least he made it a good test for the others. *(op 9-2 tchd 7-2)*
Caribbean Cove(IRE) had the blinkers back on, but he was disappointing on ground which should have suited. *(op 7-2)*
T/Plt: £4.30 to a £1 stake. Pool: £38,312.15. 6,387.05 winning tickets. T/Qpdt: £2.60 to a £1 stake. Pool: £2,140.20. 587.15 winning tickets. TM

5063 PERTH (R-H)
Thursday, April 27

OFFICIAL GOING: Hurdle course - good to firm (good in places); chase course - good (good to firm in places)
Wind: Light, behind

5091 BETDAQ.CO.UK - THE BETTING EXCHANGE NOVICES' HURDLE (8 hdls) 2m 110y
2:30 (2:32) (Class 3) 4-Y-0+ **£6,506** (£1,910; £955; £477)

Form				RPR
1150	**1**		**Rasharrow (IRE)**[44] 4430 7-11-8 132................................ TonyDobbin (L Lungo) *cl up: chal and rdn bef 2 out: edgd rt and led last: drvn out* **4/6**[1]	132+
2310	**2**	*1 ½*	**Auenmoon (GER)**[20] 4763 5-11-4 120.............................. MarkBradburne (P Monteith) *led: rdn bef 2 out: led last: kpt on: hld towards fin* **9/2**[3]	123
2110	**3**	*11*	**Masafi (IRE)**[44] 4430 5-11-3 .... BrianHughes(5) (J Howard Johnson) *cl up tl rdn and outpcd bef 2 out* **4/1**[2]	117+
405P	**4**	*9*	**Witch Power**[72] 3914 5-10-0 ....(t) DeclanMcGann(5) (A M Crow) *prom tl rdn and outpcd fr 3 out* **150/1**	90
36F3	**5**	*7*	**Hush Tiger**[48] 4342 5-10-5 95.. GarethThomas(7) (R Nixon) *in tch: outpcd whn nt fluent 3 out: sn btn* **66/1**	91+
F	**6**	*4*	**Speedro (IRE)**[24] 4720 8-10-12 .... PeterBuchanan (Miss Lucinda V Russell) *s.s: sn wl bhd: kpt on fr 2 out: nvr on terms* **100/1**	86
00	**7**	*16*	**Lowsha Green**[39] 4533 5-10-12 .... KennyJohnson (R Johnson) *hld up: rdn after 4 out: nvr on terms* **200/1**	70
0	**8**	*2 ½*	**Rightful Ruler**[97] 3488 4-10-7 .... DominicElsworth (M Todhunter) *hld up: rdn after 4 out: btn next* **50/1**	63
500P	**9**	*15*	**Talisker Rock (IRE)**[71] 3927 6-10-12 .... AlanDempsey (A Parker) *midfield: rdn 4 out: sn btn* **200/1**	53
/5-0	**10**	*12*	**Flame Of Zara**[59] 4143 7-10-2 .... GaryBerridge(3) (L Lungo) *hld up: pushed along 4 out: nvr on terms* **66/1**	34
6PP	**11**	*16*	**Solway Cloud**[10] 4917 6-10-2 .... DougieCostello(3) (Miss L Harrison) *bhd: no ch fnl circ* **200/1**	18
0	**P**		**Kalishka (IRE)**[23] 4527 5-10-12 ....(t) KeithMercer (R Allan) *a bhd: t.o whn p.u bef 2 out* **200/1**	—
00	**P**		**Dispol Peto**[40] 4493 6-10-12 .... LarryMcGrath (R Johnson) *sn wl bhd: t.o whn p.u bef 4 out* **200/1**	—
0	**P**		**Le Chiffre (IRE)**[104] 3374 4-10-7 .... RichardMcGrath (N G Richards) *hmpd s: a wl bhd: t.o whn p.u bef 2 out* **33/1**	—

3m 51.0s (-9.60) **Going Correction** -0.60s/f (Firm)
WFA 4 from 5yo+ 5lb **14** Ran SP% **110.2**
Speed ratings: **98,97,92,87,84 82,75,74,66,61 53**,—,—,— CSF £3.55 TOTE £1.50: £1.10, £1.60, £1.50; EX 3.40.
Owner Ashleybank Investments Limited **Bred** Mrs Elizabeth English **Trained** Carrutherstown, D'fries & G'way

FOCUS
A couple of useful sorts and a decent pace but, with Masafi disappointing, this race did not take as much winning as seemed likely. However, the form looks solid enough with most of the first five close to their marks.

NOTEBOOK
Rasharrow(IRE) ◆, dropped to a more realistic grade, looked to have solid claims at this level and showed a determined attitude, despite edging off a true line in the closing stages. Life will be tougher in handicaps from a 132 mark next term, but he should stay further and he will be an interesting recruit if switching to the chasing ranks next season. *(op 8-11 tchd 4-5)*
Auenmoon(GER), one of the few in this race with a realistic chance, had the run of the race and performed right up to his best. He looks a decent guide to the worth of this form but will have to improve next term to win a competitive handicap from his current mark. *(op 11-2)*
Masafi(IRE), found out in Grade 1 company at the Cheltenham Festival last month, was fairly easy to back returned to this relatively uncompetitive grade and proved a disappointment. His stable has been in patchy form this year and he is not one to write off yet. *(tchd 7-2)*
Witch Power, tried in a tongue-tie, turned in a much-improved effort in the face of a very stiff task and connections will be hoping that the Handicapper does not take this effort too literally. Modest handicaps over further next year will be her forte. *(op 100-1)*

Hush Tiger was not totally disgraced in the face of a very stiff task but is likely to continue to look vulnerable in this type of event. *(op 50-1)*
Speedro(IRE) hinted at ability but looked anything but straightforward and is unlikely to be seen to best effect in this type of event.
Flame Of Zara *Official explanation: jockey said mare lost its action (op 100-1)*
Kalishka(IRE) *Official explanation: jockey said gelding was lame right fore (op 150-1)*
Le Chiffre(IRE) *Official explanation: jockey said gelding finished distressed (op 150-1)*

5092 BILL AND BUNNY CADOGAN MEMORIAL H'CAP CHASE (12 fncs) 2m

3:00 (3:02) (Class 4) (0-110,107) 5-Y-O+ **£6,506** (£1,910; £955; £477)

Form	Pos	Dist	Horse	Jockey	SP	RPR
PF02	**1**		**Master Papa (IRE)**[12] [4842] 7-10-9 **90** (H P Hogarth) *in tch: effrt 2 out: led run in: readily*	DavidO'Meara	**6/1**[3]	108+
1420	**2**	*1 1/2*	**Karo De Vindecy (FR)**[148] [2570] 8-10-8 **89** (M D Hammond) *chsd ldrs: led 3 out: j.lft last: hdd run in: no ch w wnr*	NeilMulholland	**8/1**	103+
40U1	**3**	*7*	**Drumossie (AUS)**[6] [4991] 6-10-5 **86** 7ex	(v) KennyJohnson		93+
			(R C Guest) *w ldr: led 8th to 3 out: one pce next*		**9/2**[1]	
64F1	**4**	*7*	**Seeyaaj**[39] [4531] 6-11-11 **106** (Miss Lucinda V Russell) *prom: outpcd after 4 out: no imp fr 2 out*	(t) PeterBuchanan	**14/1**	105
0446	**5**	*2 1/2*	**The Frosty Ferret (IRE)**[35] [4587] 8-10-6 **87** (J M Jefferson) *led to 8th: rallied: outpcd bef 3 out*	(p) DominicElsworth	**5/1**[2]	85+
/33-	**6**	*4*	**Henrianjames**[705] [467] 11-11-7 **102** (K G Reveley) *hld up: hmpd by loose horse bnd after 5th: n.d*	RichardMcGrath	**12/1**	97+
5005	**7**	*1 1/4*	**Jallastep (FR)**[35] [4585] 9-10-8 **89** (J S Goldie) *hld up: effrt bef 4 out: wknd bef next*	WilsonRenwick	**10/1**	80
U421	**8**	*8*	**Kalou (GER)**[153] [2479] 8-11-9 **107** (C Grant) *midield: outpcd 4 out: sn btn*	MrTGreenall(3)	**7/1**	90
2P-2	**U**		**Minouchka (FR)**[50] [4303] 6-11-3 **105** (S H Shirley-Beavan) *chsd ldrs: blnd and uns rdr 4th*	MissKBryson(7)	**14/1**	—
0/P6	**P**		**Native Heights (IRE)**[114] [3234] 8-11-2 **97** (M Todhunter) *bhd: struggling 6th: t.o whn p.u bef 3 out*	TonyDobbin	**12/1**	—
PPPP	**P**		**Lion Guest (IRE)**[97] [3486] 9-9-11 **81** oh15 (Mrs S C Bradburne) *in tch to 1/2-way: sn wknd: t.o whn p.u bef 3 out*	DougieCostello(3)	**33/1**	—

3m 55.0s (-7.80) **Going Correction** -0.475s/f (Good) **11** Ran SP% **113.5**
Speed ratings: **100,99,95,92,91 89,88,84,**—,— — CSF £51.76 CT £234.92 TOTE £7.90: £2.30, £4.00, £1.60; EX 51.70.
Owner Hogarth Racing **Bred** Highfort Stud **Trained** Stillington, N Yorks

FOCUS
An ordinary event but a decent gallop throughout and this bare form should prove reliable, with the winner value for further and the next three close to their marks.

NOTEBOOK
Master Papa(IRE) ◆ fully confirmed his return to form on his first run for this yard at Carlisle and won with more in hand than the official margin suggested. This was his first success over the larger obstacles, and on this evidence he is capable of winning more races for his current stable. *(op 11-2)*
Karo De Vindecy(FR) is not really noted for his consistency but returned to something like his best persevered with over this trip. A sound surface suits him ideally but his record suggests he would be no good thing to put it all in next time. *(tchd 17-2)*
Drumossie(AUS), who wore a first-time visor when successful last time, ran creditably with the same headgear on again and left the impression that the return to a bit further would not inconvenience him. *(tchd 4-1)*
Seeyaaj, 7lb higher than when outbattling an habitual loser at Kelso last month, had his limitations exposed from this higher mark. He may continue to look vulnerable to progressive or well handicapped types. *(op 12-1)*
The Frosty Ferret(IRE), who disappointed with the cheekpieces left off (back on here) upped in trip at Ayr last time, again had his limitations exposed returned to what had looked a more suitable distance and he will have to improve to win from this mark. *(op 11-2)*
Henrianjames had conditions to suit but could never get competitive after being hampered by a loose horse around halfway on this first start for nearly two years. He is entitled to come on for this experience.

5093 EBF FUTURE CHAMPIONS "NATIONAL HUNT" NOVICES' HURDLE (FOR THE PERTH HUNT BALNAKEILLY CHALLENGE CUP) (12 hdls) 3m 110y

3:30 (3:30) (Class 3) 5-Y-O+ **£7,807** (£2,292; £1,146; £572)

Form	Pos	Dist	Horse	Jockey	SP	RPR
3113	**1**		**Aces Four (IRE)**[6] [4980] 7-11-6 125 (Ferdy Murphy) *keen: hld up: hdwy to chse ldrs 1/2-way: led bef 3 out: drew clr between last two*	KeithMercer	**5/1**[3]	130+
3P11	**2**	*7*	**Blackergreen**[18] [4803] 7-11-6 120 (Mrs S J Smith) *cl up: outpcd 3 out: rallied to chse wnr run in: no imp*	DominicElsworth	**5/2**[2]	124+
4113	**3**	*5*	**Scotmail (IRE)**[39] [4529] 5-11-1 116 (J Howard Johnson) *chsd ldrs: effrt and chsd wnr bef 2 out: sn no ex*	BrianHughes(5)	**8/1**	120+
2PP3	**4**	*2 1/2*	**Capybara (IRE)**[1] [5064] 8-10-12 110 (H P Hogarth) *mde most to bef 3 out: sn one pce*	DavidO'Meara	**12/1**	106
2662	**5**	*shd*	**Rimsky (IRE)**[7] [4974] 5-11-6 130 (N A Twiston-Davies) *hld up: outpcd 4 out: n.d after*	(b) AntonyEvans	**11/8**[1]	114
0036	**6**	*dist*	**Norminster**[35] [4585] 5-10-5 80 (R Nixon) *bhd: lost tch fr 7th*	GarethThomas(7)	**100/1**	—
PF00	**7**	*12*	**Romanov Rambler (IRE)**[39] [4527] 6-10-12 73 (Mrs S C Bradburne) *in tch tl lost pl after 3rd: t.o fr 7th*	WilsonRenwick	**200/1**	—
P5P0	**8**	*11*	**Yankee Holiday (IRE)**[10] [4916] 6-10-12 74 (Mrs S C Bradburne) *prom tl wknd fr 8th: t.o*	MarkBradburne	**200/1**	—
P0P-	**P**		**Burning Question**[389] [4707] 8-10-12 66 (J S Haldane) *sn wl bhd: t.o whn p.u bef 6th*	NeilMulholland	**200/1**	—
0/P-	**P**		**Mitey Perk (IRE)**[60] 7-10-9 (Mrs A F Tullie) *in tch tl wknd after 6th: t.o whn p.u after 8th*	DougieCostello(3)	**100/1**	—

5m 51.9s (-19.00) **Going Correction** -0.60s/f (Firm) **10** Ran SP% **109.6**
Speed ratings: **106,103,102,101,101** —,—,—,—,— CSF £16.88 TOTE £6.40: £1.50, £1.20, £1.50; EX 15.90.
Owner The DPRP Aces Partnership **Bred** J R And Mrs S Cox **Trained** West Witton, N Yorks

FOCUS
A fair event, decent form and an improved performance from the winner, who is the type to win races over fences next term.

NOTEBOOK
Aces Four(IRE) ◆, below his best in a muddling event - despite having the run of the race - at Ayr the previous week, showed that to be all wrong in a race run at a much better gallop. He stays well and will be interesting over fences next term. *(op 9-2)*
Blackergreen, in decent heart over hurdles this spring, ran creditably and left the impression a stiffer test of stamina over this trip would have been in his favour. He will be interesting returned to fences from a much lower mark next term. *(op 11-4)*
Scotmail(IRE), a steadily progressive sort, ran creditably upped in distance, especially as it transpired that he finished lame. He has age and time on his side and appeals as the sort to win more races in this sphere or when sent chasing. *Official explanation: vet said gelding finished lame (tchd 15-2 and 17-2)*
Capybara(IRE), disappointing over fences on his last two starts, ran creditably given he had a bit to find at the weights returned to hurdles. He is suited by a good test of stamina and will be of more interest in ordinary handicap company. *(op 14-1)*
Rimsky(IRE) looked to have strong claims on these terms but proved a disappointment and he may have been feeling the effects of a couple of recent hard races. He may have had enough for the time being but will be worth another chance next term. *(tchd 13-8 in a place)*
Norminster faced an impossible task on these terms.

5094 BETDAQXPRESS.CO.UK PERTH FESTIVAL H'CAP CHASE (FOR THE KILMANY CUP) (18 fncs) 3m

4:00 (4:00) (Class 2) 5-Y-O+
£18,789 (£5,550; £2,775; £1,389; £693; £348)

Form	Pos	Dist	Horse	Jockey	SP	RPR
350F	**1**		**Ballycassidy (IRE)**[19] [4777] 10-11-12 **140** (P Bowen) *mde all: rdn clr bef 3 out: styd on strly*	JasonMaguire	**5/1**[3]	152+
3213	**2**	*6*	**Martha's Kinsman (IRE)**[14] [4827] 7-10-5 **119** (H D Daly) *hld up: hdwy 4 out: chsd wnr bef 2 out: kpt on: no imp*	RichardJohnson	**3/1**[1]	124
0PP0	**3**	*6*	**Scots Grey**[20] [4762] 11-11-3 **131** (N J Henderson) *prom: rdn 4 out: one pce fr next*	MarcusFoley	**14/1**	130
6351	**4**	*7*	**Little Big Horse (IRE)**[32] [4635] 10-11-3 **131** (Mrs S J Smith) *cl up tl rdn and wknd bef 3 out*	DominicElsworth	**8/1**	123
1P03	**5**	*3*	**Catch The Perk (IRE)**[12] [4852] 9-10-6 **120** (Miss Lucinda V Russell) *in tch: outpcd bef 4 out: btn next*	(p) PeterBuchanan	**9/1**	109
4400	**6**	*3 1/2*	**Joes Edge (IRE)**[19] [4777] 9-11-9 **137** (Ferdy Murphy) *in tch: hit 6th: rdn 5 out: rallied and effrt bef next: sn btn: no ch whn blnd last*	KeithMercer	**9/2**[2]	123
-3P1	**F**		**Rosie Redman (IRE)**[18] [4790] 9-10-10 **124** (J R Turner) *hld up: fell 10th*	TonyDobbin	**6/1**	—
-1PF	**P**		**Provocative (FR)**[6] [4984] 8-11-6 **134** (M Todhunter) *hld up: outpcd whn mstke 12th: sn btn: p.u after 14th*	RichardMcGrath	**14/1**	—

5m 59.3s (-13.30) **Going Correction** -0.475s/f (Good) **8** Ran SP% **108.6**
Speed ratings: **103,101,99,96,95 94,**—,— CSF £18.96 CT £171.02 TOTE £4.30: £2.10, £1.70, £2.70; EX 18.10.
Owner R Owen & P Fullagar **Bred** Michael Griffin **Trained** Little Newcastle, Pembrokes

FOCUS
Not the most competitive of races but a sound pace throughout and a fine front-running performance from Ballycassidy, who showed himself none-the-worse for his Aintree exertions. The runner-up sets the level for the form.

NOTEBOOK
Ballycassidy(IRE), clear when falling in the Grand National earlier in the month, had conditions to suit and turned in a decent performance to win a race that was not the most competitive for the money on offer. Given he had little margin for error from his mark before this, life will be tough back in more competitive company after reassessment next term. *(tchd 9-2 and 11-2 in places)*
Martha's Kinsman(IRE) ◆, a lightly raced and steadily progressive sort, ran as well as he ever has done over fences. A sound surface suits him ideally and, given he has age on his side, is the type to win a decent handicap next term, especially if tried at a more galloping course. *(op 7-2)*
Scots Grey had not shown much in some tough races since winning at Wincanton after a break in November but, although running better in this less-competitive event, is likely to remain vulnerable to well handicapped or progressive types on this evidence. *(op 16-1)*
Little Big Horse(IRE), up in the weights and in grade, is from a stable among the winners and had conditions to suit but was comfortably held and he does seem a better horse at Market Rasen than anywhere else. *(op 13-2)*
Catch The Perk(IRE), returned to fences, had his limitations exposed from this higher mark in this better race and it may be wise to try and exploit a favourable hurdle mark if kept on the go this summer. *(op 8-1 tchd 10-1)*
Joes Edge(IRE), who reportedly returned with cuts after completing the Grand National earlier this month, ran as though feeling the effects of that race. Although this can easily be forgiven, he has been essentially disappointing since winning the Scottish National a year ago. *(op 4-1)*

5095 WEATHERBYS CHASE CHAMPION STAYERS HUNTERS' CHASE (FOR THE FIFE HUNT CUP) (23 fncs) 3m 7f

4:30 (4:30) (Class 4) 5-Y-O+ **£3,747** (£1,162; £580; £290)

Form	Pos	Dist	Horse	Jockey	SP	RPR
21	**1**		**Coomakista**[18] [4791] 9-10-13 (Mrs E J Reed) *in tch: effrt 4 out: led bef 2 out: kpt on strly*	MrRMorgan(5)	**7/4**[1]	90+
	2	*7*	**Thatlldoya**[9] 8-11-8 (P Grindrod) *cl up: effrt after 4 out: kpt on fr 2 out: no ch w wnr*	MrTGreenall	**7/1**[2]	86
-55P	**3**	*1*	**Natural (IRE)**[12] [4846] 9-11-6 73 (Mrs J Williamson) *cl up: led 7th: clr 17th to 3 out: hdd and no ex bef next*	(p) MrTDavidson(5)	**25/1**	88
004-	**4**	*3/4*	**Web Master (FR)**[10] 8-11-8 88 (Mrs Sandra Smith) *rel to r and lost 25l s: rcvrd 4th: hld up: outpcd 4 out: kpt on fr last: no imp*	MissPRobson	**7/4**[1]	85+
P05P	**5**	*25*	**Iron Express**[9] 10-11-1 84 (Mrs C A Coward) *led to 7th: nt fluent and outpcd fr 17th*	MissJCoward(7)	**7/1**[2]	59
PU30	**6**	*18*	**Ikdam Melody (IRE)**[12] 10-11-5 85 (Miss J E Foster) *in tch: lost pl 14th: struggling fr 17th*	(p) MrCMulhall(3)	**11/1**[3]	41

8m 11.0s (-191.1) **Going Correction** -0.475s/f (Good) **6** Ran SP% **109.9**
Speed ratings: **95,93,92,92,86 81** CSF £13.58 TOTE £2.70: £1.60, £2.00; EX 12.60.
Owner I B Speke **Bred** I B Speke **Trained** Hexham, Northumberland

FOCUS
An uncompetitive event in which Web Master's stubbornness at the start made things much easier for Coomakista. The first and third set the standard but the form is weak.

NOTEBOOK
Coomakista, who returned to winning ways in an ordinary event at Kelso last time, faced a straightforward task over this longer trip when main market rival Web Master lost 25 lengths at the start. Stamina is her forte and she is sure to win more races in either this or the point sphere. *(op 2-1)*
Thatlldoya, the winner of an uncompetitive point last time, ran creditably without being any threat to the wide-margin winner. He clearly stays well and is capable of winning another point or a small race in this sphere. *(op 10-1)*
Natural(IRE), with the cheekpieces refitted, ran creditably in the face of a tough task. The return to three miles may suit but his inconsistency means he would not be one for maximum faith next time. *(op 33-1)*
Web Master(FR), unbeaten in points for today's rider this season, uncharacteristically proved most stubborn as the tape went back and was always up against it thereafter. He was beaten much less than the ground he forfeited at the start and is well worth another chance in this sort of event. *(op 11-8)*
Iron Express, an inconsistent performer who returned to winning ways in an ordinary point last time, had his limitations exposed in this company and, although the return to three miles may suit, is not one for maximum faith. *(op 9-1)*

Ikdam Melody(IRE), an inconsistent performer with a modest recent completion record, was soundly beaten. *(op 10-1 tchd 12-1)*

5096 BETDAQ.CO.UK 24 HOUR TELEBET H'CAP HURDLE (10 hdls) 2m 4f 110y

5:00 (5:01) (Class 3) (0-120,120) 4-Y-0+ **£6,506** (£1,910; £955; £477)

Form | | | | RPR
015 **1** **Brooklyn Brownie (IRE)**[92] 3561 7-10-9 **110**................ PhilKinsella(7) 116
(J M Jefferson) *midfield: smooth hdwy to ld bef 2 out: kpt on strly fr last* **15/2**
10BF **2** *1 ½* **Muckle Flugga (IRE)**[47] 4364 7-10-4 **98**.............. DominicElsworth 102
(N G Richards) *hld up: hdwy to chse ldrs bef 2 out: kpt on fr last* **6/1**[2]
6131 **3** *½* **True Mariner (FR)**[22] 4738 6-10-12 **111**......................(t) MarkNicolls(5) 115
(B I Case) *hld up midfield: effrt bef 2 out: kpt on same pce run in* **11/1**
11F5 **4** *15* **Mister Moussac**[22] 4736 7-9-13 **98**.............................. BrianHughes(5) 87
(Miss Kariana Key) *chsd ldrs: chal 4 out: wknd bef 2 out* **14/1**
-006 **5** *2 ½* **Full Irish (IRE)**[92] 3561 10-11-12 **120**................................ TonyDobbin 106
(L Lungo) *hld up: rdn 4 out: kpt on fr 2 out: nvr rchd ldrs* **7/1**[3]
2112 **6** *3 ½* **Imtihan (IRE)**[18] 4797 7-10-10 **114**........................ MichaelO'Connell(10) 97
(Mrs S J Smith) *cl up: led 3rd: hit 3 out: hdd & wknd bef next* **9/2**[1]
0130 **7** *½* **Aviation**[21] 4747 4-11-1 **115**.. BarryKeniry 91
(G M Moore) *in tch: outpcd bef 4 out: no ch after* **12/1**
6F51 **8** *4* **Sesame Rambler (IRE)**[26] 4693 7-11-2 **115**.......... EamonDehdashti(5) 93
(G L Moore) *chsd ldrs tl rdn and wknd after 3 out* **9/1**
41PP **9** *1* **Relix (FR)**[6] 4982 6-10-6 **105**...................................(t) DeclanMcGann(5) 82
(A M Crow) *hld up: rdn 4 out: nvr on terms* **33/1**
5343 **10** *7* **Time To Roam (IRE)**[35] 4585 6-10-3 **97**....................(p) PeterBuchanan 67
(Miss Lucinda V Russell) *prom tl rdn and wknd fr 3 out* **12/1**
20P0 **11** *5* **Top Style (IRE)**[15] 4045 8-10-9 **103**...............................(p) AlanDempsey 68
(G A Harker) *hld up: drvn 4 out: sn btn* **50/1**
1-0P **12** *8* **Hutch**[12] 4852 8-10-2 **101**..(b[1]) DesFlavin(5) 58
(Mrs L B Normile) *in tch tl wknd after 4 out* **50/1**
P223 **13** *6* **Roobihoo (IRE)**[24] 4724 7-11-2 **110**............................(t) RichardMcGrath 61
(C Grant) *led to 3rd: cl up tl wknd fr 4 out* **15/2**

4m 53.7s (-14.50) **Going Correction** -0.60s/f (Firm)
WFA 4 from 5yo+ 6lb **13** Ran SP% **115.7**
Speed ratings: **103,102,102,96,95 94,94,92,92,89 87,84,82** CSF £50.47 CT £492.64 TOTE £9.70: £2.90, £2.20, £5.00; EX 51.70 Place 6 £33.89, Place 5 £33.81.
Owner P Gaffney & J N Stevenson **Bred** John P A Kenny **Trained** Norton, N Yorks

FOCUS
An ordinary event in which the pace was sound throughout and this form should stand up at a similar level.

NOTEBOOK
Brooklyn Brownie(IRE) ◆, who had conditions to suit, proved well suited by the decent gallop and showed the right attitude to notch his second course and distance win on this first start for three months. He should not be going up too much for this win and, given his record is one of steady improvement, may be capable of better. *(op 17-2)*
Muckle Flugga(IRE), who is on a fair mark, had plenty in her favour regarding ground and a decent gallop and she showed more than enough to suggest that a similar race can be found in the coming months. *(op 7-1)*
True Mariner(FR), who won on fast ground at Hereford earlier this month, ran at least as well from this 11lb higher mark. Decent ground seems the key to him and he should continue to give a good account. *(op 9-1)*
Mister Moussac, having his second outing after a break, travelled strongly for a long way and should be spot on next time. Effective between two and two and a half miles, he looks capable of winning again this summer. *(tchd 16-1)*
Full Irish(IRE) was not totally disgraced but was again below his best and, although too early to be writing him off just yet, may have to drop further in the weights before returning to winning ways. *(op 8-1)*
Imtihan(IRE) had been in good form but seemed to be found out from this even higher mark over this shorter trip on this much quicker ground. However, he has progressed well this year and is not one to write off back on more suitable ground. *(tchd 4-1)*
T/Plt: £50.90 to a £1 stake. Pool: £49,708.50. 712.10 winning tickets. T/Qpdt: £21.80 to a £1 stake. Pool: £2,711.10. 91.80 winning tickets. RY

5097 - 5098a (Foreign Racing) - See Raceform Interactive

5076 PUNCHESTOWN (R-H)

Thursday, April 27

OFFICIAL GOING: Hurdle & chase courses - good; bank course - good to firm

5099a TOTE.IE CHAMPION FOUR YEAR OLD HURDLE (GRADE 1) 2m

3:15 (3:15) 4-Y-0 **£47,034** (£14,413; £6,827; £2,275; £1,517)

RPR
1 **Quatre Heures (FR)**[44] 4430 4-11-0 .... MickFitzgerald 135+
(W P Mullins, Ire) *hld up in tch: 4th after 3 out: 3rd after 2 out: led travelling wl bef last: rdn clr: comf* **9/2**[3]
2 *8* **Artist's Muse (IRE)**[9] 4948 4-10-9 .... DNRussell 122
(T M Walsh, Ire) *trckd ldrs: 4th 4 out: 3rd next: cl 2nd and chal after 2 out: no imp appr last: lft mod 2nd run-in: kpt on same pce* **13/2**
3 *1 ½* **Breathing Fire**[41] 4468 4-11-0 .... RMPower 126
(Mrs John Harrington, Ire) *cl 3rd: 2nd 3 out: led 2 out: sn rdn and strly pressed: hdd and sltly hmpd early st: bdly hmpd last: kpt on same pce* **11/4**[2]
4 *1 ½* **Clear Riposte (IRE)**[11] 4887 4-10-9 .... TimmyMurphy 119
(W P Mullins, Ire) *led: jnd 1/2-way: led again 4 out: hdd 2 out: sn no ex: lft mod 4th fr last* **14/1**
5 *1* **Jagoes Mills (IRE)**[46] 4406 4-11-0 .... AndrewJMcNamara 123
(Thomas Gerard O'Leary, Ire) *hld up: slt mstke 1st: no imp after 3 out: kpt on same pce* **33/1**
6 *11* **First Row (IRE)**[18] 4468 4-11-0 .... RLoughran 112
(D T Hughes, Ire) *cl 2nd: disp ld 1/2-way: 2nd and rdn after 4 out: wknd fr next* **9/1**
7 *25* **Look No Further (IRE)**[47] 4380 4-11-0 .... EFPower 87
(John Joseph Murphy, Ire) *a towards rr: nt fluent jumping: reminders 4th: wknd after 4 out: t.o* **150/1**
F **Mister Hight (FR)**[41] 4468 4-11-0 128.. RWalsh 130+
(W P Mullins, Ire) *settled 5th: 4th travelling wl 2 out: nt clr run briefly early st: 2nd and no imp whn fell last* **9/4**[1]

3m 52.0s **Going Correction** -0.65s/f (Firm) **8** Ran SP% **109.2**
Speed ratings: **106,102,101,100,100 94,82,—** CSF £30.51 TOTE £6.60: £1.70, £1.50, £1.50; DF 38.60.
Owner John Mc's Winchester Syndicate **Bred** M Henri Blois **Trained** Muine Beag, Co Carlow

FOCUS
A good juvenile event, but there was a lack of English interest. Quatre Heures won in impressive fashion and looks a high-class prospect. Mister Hight looked held when falling at the last.

NOTEBOOK
Quatre Heures(FR) ◆ was a very easy winner of races at Naas and Fairyhouse before heading to Cheltenham where he finished 11th to Noland in the Supreme Novices. However, he was not beaten all that far and trainer Willie Mullins felt that he had actually run quite well. Never far off the pace and he moved into contention coming to the third-last, clearly going best, and he took up the running on the run to the last and quickly moved clear to settle the issue. This was an impressive display and, although stablemate Mister Hight would have given him a bit more to do had he stood up, he rates as a high-class prospect for next season. He now looks set to head to France to contest the Prix Alain Du Breil. *(op 4/1)*
Artist's Muse(IRE) came here in good form having finished second in the Fred Winter at Cheltenham and then captured a winner's hurdle at Fairyhouse last week. She improved to press Breathing Fire for the lead after the second-last but was unable to make any further impression nearing the final flight. This was a sound effort and she can continue to do well over hurdles. *(op 7/1)*
Breathing Fire was in the process of running a good race in theTriumph when he came down at the last and he took over in front coming to two out. He had to give best to Quatre Heures when that rival moved to the front but was still in the thick of the battle for second when hampered by the fall of Mister Hight. A smart juvenile, he has posted some good efforts over hurdles without winning and will go into next season as a novice. There are good races to be won with him. *(op 3/1)*
Clear Riposte(IRE) helped to force the pace but had no more to offer after the second-last. A Grade 2 winner at Leopardstown in December she is a useful sort and can continue to pay her way. *(op 16/1)*
Jagoes Mills(IRE) was an interesting runner as he came here having landed a Naas bumper on his debut last month. He ran quite well andremained in contention until the second- last. This experience will bring him on considerably and he looks another that can do well next term.
First Row(IRE), who won a Grade 3 earlier in the season, raced prominently but had no more to give from the third-last. *(op 10/1)*
Mister Hight(FR), a disappointment in the Triumph Hurdle at the Festival, ran well on ground that was quicker than he would have liked, but he looked set to have to make do with second when falling at the last. He could join the winner in the Alain du Breil if the none the worse for this experience. *(op 7/4 tchd 5/2)*

5100a SWORDLESTOWN CUP NOVICE CHASE (GRADE 1) 2m

3:50 (3:50) 5-Y-0+ **£42,758** (£13,103; £6,206; £2,068; £1,379)

RPR
1 **Accordion Etoile (IRE)**[19] 4774 7-11-12 149........................... JLCullen 153
(Paul Nolan, Ire) *trckd ldrs in 3rd: 4th 5 out: smooth prog next: 2nd travelling best 3 out: rdn to dispute ld 2 out: lft in ld last: kpt on* **9/4**[2]
2 *2 ½* **Justified (IRE)**[11] 4889 7-11-12 .... APMcCoy 151+
(E Sheehy, Ire) *cl up: led fr 3rd: j.lft and slt mstke 6th: drvn along bef 4 out: jnd 2 out: stl ev ch whn blnd and hdd last: no ex run-in* **13/8**[1]
3 *3* **In Compliance (IRE)**[11] 4889 6-11-12 149........................... BJGeraghty 148+
(M J P O'Brien, Ire) *trckd ldrs: hit 4th: impr into 2nd 5 out: rdn after next: 3rd 3 out: kpt on same pce u.p* **3/1**[3]
4 *nk* **Davenport Democrat (IRE)**[11] 4889 8-11-12 143.................... RWalsh 147
(W P Mullins, Ire) *hld up: impr into 4th 4 out: rdn and no imp bef 2 out: kpt on same pce* **10/1**
5 *dist* **Zum See (IRE)**[9] 4949 7-11-12 125.. NPMadden —
(Noel Meade, Ire) *hld up in rr: pckd 4th: trailing 4 out: t.o* **25/1**
6 *4* **Laoch Dubh (IRE)**[77] 3832 7-11-12 111.................................. DFO'Regan —
(Henry De Bromhead, Ire) *led: hdd 3rd: slt mstke 5 out: sn wknd: t.o* **50/1**

4m 2.50s **Going Correction** -0.575s/f (Firm) **6** Ran SP% **108.8**
Speed ratings: **115,113,112,112,—** — CSF £6.20 TOTE £3.20: £1.80, £1.50; DF 5.50.
Owner Banjo Syndicate **Bred** John McKeever **Trained** Enniscorthy, Co. Wexford

FOCUS
A cracking heat despite the lack of runners, and fast ground-loving Accordion Etoile came back to his best. He could develop into a high-class older chaser next season. Justified is a tough gelding likely to do well next season, while In Compliance did not look good enough on the day.

NOTEBOOK
Accordion Etoile(IRE), despite a fall at Cheltenham and a bad error at Aintree, Accordion Etoile attracted good support and repaid the faith of his supporters with an accurate round of jumping and an assured performance overall on ground that brings out the best in him. He retains the tactical speed that made him a force as a hurdler, and picked up well in the straight to score in good style. If all goes well he has the makings of a Champion Chase contender for next season. *(op 3/1)*
Justified(IRE) again showed the tendency to jump left that had marred his winning performance at Fairyhouse, though it was less marked this time. In front from the third, he had to be kept up to his work from the fourth-last but maintained his effort until a mistake at the last simplified the task for the winner who was already beginning to get on top. Barring two races at Leopardstown, he has enjoyed a very successful campaign but the flaws in his jumping technique will have to be sorted out if he is to prosper at the highest level when he graduates to the senior ranks. *(op 6/4 tchd 7/4)*
In Compliance(IRE) disappointed Michael O'Brien with his failure to make more of a race of it with Justified in the Powers, and the market indicated no great confidence in his ability to do better over the shorter trip on quicker ground. He ran an honest enough race but never really gave the impression that he was the likely winner through the middle stages of the race, and from three out he was basically treading water. In the end, he only just held off Davenport Democrat for third and was probably not good enough.
Davenport Democrat(IRE) was back to something more like his best after struggling in the Powers. He is probably best at this trip, though his current handicap rating of 143 could make him difficult enough to place.

5101a WHITEWATER CHAMPION STAYERS' HURDLE (GRADE 1) 3m

4:25 (4:25) 4-Y-0+ **£85,517** (£26,206; £12,413; £4,137; £2,758)

RPR
1 **Asian Maze (IRE)**[19] 4775 7-11-7 158.................................... RWalsh 159+
(Thomas Mullins, Ire) *mde all: clr after 2 out: rdn and styd on wl: comf* **8/13**[1]
2 *4 ½* **Kerryhead Windfarm (IRE)**[12] 4864 8-11-12 .... AndrewJMcNamara 15720
(Michael Hourigan, Ire) *hld up in tch: nt fluent early: 8th and drvn along 5 out: 5th and hdwy appr 2 out: mod 3rd st: styd on wl to go 2nd nr fin* **100/1**
4 *8* **Kadoun (IRE)**[42] 4461 9-11-12 144.................................... APMcCoy 148
(M J P O'Brien, Ire) *hld up: drvn along fr 7th: 8th and prog 4 out: mod 4th after 2 out: no ex bef last* **16/1**
5 *2 ½* **Strangely Brown (IRE)**[20] 4765 5-11-10 149........................ RMPower 144
(E McNamara, Ire) *mid-div: 6th 5 out: prog next: 3rd 3 out: no ex appr 2 out: one pced* **10/1**[3]
6 *20* **Travino (IRE)**[20] 4760 7-11-12 .... JLCullen 126
(Ms Margaret Mullins, Ire) *trckd ldrs: 5th 5 out: 6th next: sn drvn along: mod 4th bef 2 out: no ex st* **16/1**
7 *9* **Emotional Moment (IRE)**[42] 4458 9-11-12 151................... DFO'Regan 117
(T J Taaffe, Ire) *prom: 4th 1/2-way: rdn bef 3 out: sn wknd* **16/1**
8 *2* **Carlys Quest**[21] 4745 12-11-12 ....(b) TimmyMurphy 115
(Ferdy Murphy) *bhd: trailing bef 1/2-way: drvn along and kpt on fr 5 out: nvr a factor* **25/1**

9 *11* **Yogi (IRE)**[18] 4811 10-11-12 130 .... GCotter 104
(Thomas Foley, Ire) *a towards rr: wknd fr 6 out* **100/1**

10 *6* **Sky's The Limit (FR)**[19] 4775 5-11-10 158 ....(b) BJGeraghty 96
(E J O'Grady, Ire) *prom: 3rd to 4 out: dropped to 5th u.p next: sn wknd* **7/1**[2]

11 *6* **Royal Paradise (FR)**[43] 4446 6-11-12 135 .... MickFitzgerald 92
(Thomas Foley, Ire) *hld up in tch: wknd fr 6 out* **33/1**

12 *20* **Ambobo (USA)**[42] 4458 6-11-12 .... CO'Dwyer 72
(Martin Brassil, Ire) *hld up in tch: mstke 6th: drvn along and wknd fr 5 out: t.o* **14/1**

5m 44.2s **Going Correction** -0.65s/f (Firm) **13** Ran SP% **124.3**
Speed ratings: **115,113,113,110,109 103,100,99,95,93 91,85** CSF £133.60 TOTE £1.70: £1.50, £6.90, £4.20; DF 73.80.
Owner Mrs C A Moore **Bred** Mrs C A Moore **Trained** Goresbridge, Co Kilkenny

FOCUS
Another excellent performance by top-class mare Asian Maze, who could develop into a Chamion Hurder next season. She did not beat a great deal, and was much fresher than most of her rivals, but is only seven and has more to offer.

NOTEBOOK
Asian Maze(IRE), as had been the case when she won here 12 months ago and also at Aintree earlier in the month, she set out to make all and succeeded in her aim. Having seemingly quickened the pace on passing the stands for the first time, Ruby Walsh increased the tempo once again running past the four-furlong pole, although just about everything had been beaten off some way before that point. Asian Maze's constitution has to be admired, as does her jumping, and the French Champion Hurdle - a race run over three miles and a furlong - was mentioned as a possible end-of-season target, and the race would appear to be perfectly suited for a horse who also has the option of dropping down to two miles for next season's Champion Hurdle. *(op 4/6 tchd 8/11)*
Kerryhead Windfarm(IRE) had been a five-length second to Asian Maze at Punchestown last year, and he once again chased her home. While his proximity to the winner does to a degree hold down the form, he is a horse who has always been held in high regard by Michael Hourigan while regularly frustrating the trainer. *(op 66/1)*
Fire Dragon(IRE) deserves to be rated the second best horse in the race, as he was the only one who really chased Asian Maze down the back, and he suffered for his valiant exploits. This run, backed up by his World Hurdle fourth and his earlier Sandown win, confirmed him a top stayer, and, although just a smidgeon shy of the very best, he should still win plenty more good races, especially as he is still only five. *(op 10/1)*
Kadoun(IRE) gradually got back into the action without ever getting remotely close to the winner, having got behind down the back. This was a perfectly respectable effort, but with his new rating he might well be difficult to place next season. *(op 14/1)*
Strangely Brown(IRE) is flattered by his top-flight win gained at Auteuil last year, and is much better judged by his previous handicap victory and Coral Cup second. Perhaps a little below par after those two efforts, he was not at his best here but in all likelihood was a little outclassed as well. *(op 8/1)*
Travino(IRE) travelled nicely through the first half of the race, and was far from disgraced for a novice. He has bags of ability and should come into his own over fences next season. *(op 14/1)*
Sky's The Limit(FR) , whose victory in the Coral Cup had to be seen to believed, had a very hard *race behind Asian Maze at Aintree, and it looked to have left its mark here.Official explanation: vet said gelding was blowing hard (op 5/1)*

5102a TATTERSALLS (IRELAND) LTD. PAT TAAFFE H'CAP CHASE (GRADE B HANDICAP) 3m 1f

5:00 (5:00) (0-145,138) 5-Y-O+ **£24,693** (£7,244; £3,451; £1,175)

RPR

1 **One Four Shannon (IRE)**[46] 4400 9-10-2 116 .... PACarberry 126
(D J Ryan, Ire) *mid-div: lost pl 6 out: 9th bef 4 out: 6th and hdwy 3 out: 4th after 2 out: chal and led last: styd on wl* **14/1**

2 *1 1/2* **Monterey Bay (IRE)**[10] 4929 10-10-3 117 .... RWalsh 125
(Ms F M Crowley, Ire) *hld up in tch: smooth hdwy into 4th 6 out: 3rd bef 4 out: 2nd and rdn next: led after 2 out: hdd last: kpt on* **9/2**[1]

3 *2* **A New Story (IRE)**[10] 4929 8-10-11 125 .... AndrewJMcNamara 134+
(Michael Hourigan, Ire) *hld up in tch: prog 5 out: 5th 3 out: 3rd next: chalng whn hmpd appr last: 4th run-in: kpt on* **6/1**[3]

4 *2* **Colonel Monroe (IRE)**[10] 4929 9-10-10 124 ....(p) JLCullen 128
(E J O'Grady, Ire) *chsd ldrs: reminders 7th: 6th 7 out: hdwy 5 out: led after 4 out: strly pressed after next: hdd after 2 out: edgd rt appr l* **33/1**

5 *9* **Wests Awake (IRE)**[12] 4866 10-9-10 110 .... NPMadden 105
(I Madden, Ire) *hld up: prog into 7th 4 out: kpt on same pce fr next* **33/1**

6 *1 1/2* **New Alco (FR)**[19] 4778 5-11-1 129 .... TimmyMurphy 123
(Ferdy Murphy) *mid-div: prog into 6th 4 out: 4th bef next: no ex appr 2 out: wknd bef last* **13/2**

7 *25* **Quazar (IRE)**[8] 4957 8-10-6 120 ....(bt) DNRussell 89
(Jonjo O'Neill) *hld up in rr: prog into 8th bef 4 out: sn no ex* **10/1**

8 *7* **I Hear Thunder (IRE)**[20] 4762 8-10-8 122 .... PWFlood 84
(R H Buckler) *chsd ldrs: 6th appr 1/2-way: 4th 7 out: no ex fr 5 out* **25/1**

9 *2 1/2* **Heads Onthe Ground (IRE)**[10] 4932 9-10-0 117 ....(b[1]) RLoughran[(3)] 76
(D T Hughes, Ire) *prom: led 8th: hdd whn hit 4 out: sn wknd: eased 2 out* **10/1**

10 *2 1/2* **Aimees Mark (IRE)**[9] 4953 10-9-7 110 .... KTColeman[(3)] 67
(F Flood, Ire) *a towards rr: drvn along and no imp fr bef 1/2-way* **33/1**

11 *1 1/2* **Garvivonnian (IRE)**[19] 4777 11-11-5 138 .... MJFerris[(5)] 93
(Edward P Mitchell, Ire) *prom: 2nd to 5th: reminders 7th: 4th 1/2-way: wknd 6 out: towards rr whn hmpd 5 out: no ex* **16/1**

12 *1/2* **Rodalko (FR)**[33] 4617 8-10-10 124 .... LeightonAspell 79
(O Sherwood) *prom: 3rd bef 1/2-way: cl 2nd fr 10th: led briefly bef 4 out: 3rd whn slt mstke 3 out: sn wknd and eased* **5/1**[2]

U **Harbour Pilot (IRE)**[10] 4929 11-11-2 130 ....(b) DFO'Regan —
(Noel Meade, Ire) *sn led: hdd 8th: 3rd whn bad mstke and uns rdr 5 out* **25/1**

P **Well Presented (IRE)**[10] 4929 8-11-1 129 .... RMPower —
(Mrs John Harrington, Ire) *prom: slt mstke and reminders 3rd: lost pl 5th: trailing whn p.u bef 6 out* **9/1**

6m 9.40s **Going Correction** -0.575s/f (Firm)
WFA 5 from 8yo+ 8lb **15** Ran SP% **119.7**
Speed ratings: **114,113,112,112,109 108,100,98,97,97 96,96,—,—** CSF £73.48 CT £424.32 TOTE £14.00: £3.20, £2.00, £2.20; DF 80.20.
Owner David Pierce **Bred** Robert McLean **Trained** Tuam, Co. Galway
■ Stewards' Enquiry : D N Russell seven-day ban: tried to weigh out with banned stirrup irons and incomplete body protector
J L Cullen four-day ban: improper riding (May 6-9)

NOTEBOOK
New Alco(FR) was in with every chance nearing the third-last but was unable to raise his effort in the straight. *(op 5/1)*
Quazar(IRE) remains below his best and never really got into contention. *(op 8/1)*
I Hear Thunder(IRE) has lost his form and was struggling a long way from the finish.
Rodalko(FR) was the main disappointment of the race, dropping away tamely under pressure. It is hoped he has not flared up one of his old injuries. *(op 4/1)*

5103a CHRONICLE BOOKMAKERS H'CAP HURDLE 3m

5:35 (5:35) (88-130,130) 4-Y-O+ **£11,224** (£3,293; £1,568; £534)

RPR

1 **Roadmaker (IRE)**[39] 4534 6-10-4 108 .... PACarberry 116
(John G Carr, Ire) *hld up: hdwy after 4 out: 4th bef st: rdn to ld appr last: kpt on wl u.p* **20/1**

2 *1 1/2* **Santa's Son (IRE)**[22] 4742 6-10-6 113 ....(t) SGMcDermott[(3)] 122+
(J F O'Shea, Ire) *a.p: led 3 out: hmpd by loose horse and hdd appr st: 5th u.p bef last: styd on wl* **20/1**

3 *2* **Mac Three (IRE)**[10] 4926 7-11-4 122 .... DFO'Regan 126
(Noel Meade, Ire) *trckd ldrs: 5th 5 out: prog into 4th after 3 out: rdn st: kpt on fr last* **7/1**[2]

4 *1* **Kings Advocate (IRE)**[102] 3413 6-11-2 120 .... BJGeraghty 123
(T J Taaffe, Ire) *trckd ldrs: 4th 5 out: impr into 2nd after 3 out: lft in ld appr st: hdd appr last: 5th early run-in: kpt on u.p* **7/1**[2]

5 *shd* **Sir Frederick (IRE)**[22] 4742 6-11-7 128 .... KTColeman[(3)] 131
(W J Burke, Ire) *mid-div: 10th and drvn along 5 out: 10th next: 3rd after 3 out: cl 2nd into st: no ex after last* **14/1**

6 *1* **Piran (IRE)**[14] 4826 4-10-8 112 .... PaulMoloney 114
(Evan Williams) *towards rr: hdwy into 8th 4 out: 5th early st: kpt on same pce u.p* **9/1**[3]

7 *2* **Wine Fountain (IRE)**[11] 4891 6-10-12 116 .... DNRussell 116
(A J Martin, Ire) *towards rr: hdwy appr 3 out: 7th into st: rdn and no imp bef last* **10/1**

8 *1/2* **Ile Maurice (FR)**[7] 4972 6-11-0 123 .... PatrickMcDonald[(5)] 122
(Ferdy Murphy) *trckd ldrs: 5th 1/2-way: 10th 4 out: kpt on same pce fr next* **20/1**

9 *4* **Zamnah (IRE)**[10] 4932 8-10-0 104 .... DJHoward 99
(F J Bowles, Ire) *towards rr: kpt on wout threatening fr 3 out* **50/1**

10 *3/4* **Spring Breeze**[2] 5059 5-10-11 115 ....(b) TimmyMurphy 110
(Ferdy Murphy) *mid-div: no imp after 3 out: kpt on same pce* **25/1**

11 *7* **Willie The Shoe**[22] 4742 9-9-10 107 .... ADLeigh[(7)] 95
(Mrs John Harrington, Ire) *towards rr: kpt on fr bef 3 out* **12/1**

12 *3/4* **I See Icy (IRE)**[6] 4994 6-9-13 103 .... NPMadden 90
(Daniel Miley, Ire) *towards rr: kpt on same pce fr bef 3 out* **25/1**

13 *8* **Truly Gold (IRE)**[544] 1924 7-10-0 109 .... RJMolloy[(5)] 88
(R P Burns, Ire) *mid-div: 9th appr 1/2-way: no imp whn mstke 3 out: wknd bef st* **33/1**

14 *3/4* **Dow Jones (GER)**[201] 1691 8-11-2 120 .... CO'Dwyer 98
(M Halford, Ire) *led: hdd 3 out: sn wknd* **16/1**

15 *12* **Double Dizzy**[34] 4606 5-10-0 107 .... RLoughran[(3)] 73
(R H Buckler) *chsd ldrs: 6th appr 1/2-way: 5th 5 out: wknd after next* **20/1**

16 *1/2* **Muttiah**[8] 4965 6-10-2 106 .... PWFlood 72
(E J O'Grady, Ire) *mid-div: 9th 5 out: wknd after next* **14/1**

17 *2 1/2* **Constantine**[7] 3135 6-9-12 109 .... SJGray[(7)] 72
(Daniel Mark Loughnane, Ire) *nvr a factor: slt mstke 5th* **50/1**

18 *7* **Kilty Storm (IRE)**[34] 4603 7-11-4 122 .... APMcCoy 78
(M C Pipe) *prom: 3rd 1/2-way: hmpd and lost pl after 4 out: sn no ex* **12/1**

19 *3* **Rory Sunset (IRE)**[10] 4930 8-9-13 110 .... DGHogan[(7)] 63
(C F Swan, Ire) *a towards rr* **25/1**

20 *1 1/2* **Roundstone Lady (IRE)**[200] 1701 6-10-3 107 .... RWalsh 59
(W P Mullins, Ire) *a towards rr* **6/1**[1]

21 *8* **Forager**[2] 5059 7-11-12 130 .... AndrewJMcNamara 74
(J Ryan) *chsd ldrs early: wknd fr 5 out* **50/1**

22 *25* **Healy's Pub (IRE)**[10] 4930 10-10-3 114 ....(b) MrMJBolger[(7)] 33
(Oliver McKiernan, Ire) *nvr a factor: wknd bef 4 out: t.o* **33/1**

23 *4* **Hidden Talents (IRE)**[56] 4206 6-10-5 109 .... MDarcy 24
(M F Morris, Ire) *rr of mid-div: lost pl 6th: trailing after next: t.o* **20/1**

U **Chelsea Harbour (IRE)**[20] 4765 6-10-12 116 .... RMPower —
(Thomas Mullins, Ire) *mstke and uns rdr 5th* **16/1**

P **Lovely Present (IRE)**[10] 4930 7-10-10 114 .... RGeraghty —
(T K Geraghty, Ire) *nvr a factor: p.u bef 5 out* **20/1**

5m 47.9s **Going Correction** -0.65s/f (Firm)
WFA 4 from 5yo+ 7lb **25** Ran SP% **150.7**
Speed ratings: 109,108,107,107,107 107,106,106,104,104 102,102,99,99,95 95,94,91,90,90 87,79,78,—,— CSF £380.41 CT £3129.79 TOTE £20.40: £4.00, £7.00, £2.60, £2.20; DF 386.80.

Owner L Behan **Bred** Dermot Conroy **Trained** Maynooth, Co. Kildare

FOCUS
Second last bypassed.

NOTEBOOK
Roadmaker(IRE)came from a long way back to win, but the runner-up was an unlucky loser.
Piran(IRE) has largely been progressive and he held every chance turning for home, but was unable go on with the principals. *(op 10/1)*
Ile Maurice(FR), in season when pulling up at Cheltenham, was under pressure some way from home but she is a tenacious horse and stuck to her task to finish closer than one less brave might have done.
Spring Breeze appeared to be running out of his grade and he was never involved. *(op 20/1)*
Double Dizzy was a little disappointing, as she was entitled to go well on the best of her form.
Kilty Storm(IRE) dropped away tamely having raced up there early, losing all momentum once hampered.
Forager, turned out quickly having been well down the field two days earlier, was again well-beaten and had a pretty fruitless trip.

5104a KILDARE TRADERS/CLAIREFONTAINE RACECOURSE (PRO/AM) INH FLAT RACE (MARES & GELDINGS) 2m

6:10 (6:12) 4-Y-O+ **£8,577** (£1,998; £881; £508)

RPR

1 **Nesserian (IRE)** 6-11-7 .... MrDerekO'Connor 106+
(John E Kiely, Ire) *towards rr: hdwy over 3f out: 8th into st: qcknd to ld ins fnl f: kpt on wl u.p: all out* **15/2**

2 *shd* **Zenaide (IRE)**[10] 4924 5-11-1 .... MrPRParkhill[(7)] 107+
(Mrs Louise Parkhill, Ire) *rr of mid-div: 9th travelling wl early st: swtchd to outer 2f out: hdwy to chal ins fnl f: kpt on wl u.p: jst failed* **16/1**

3 *4 1/2* **Whitehills (IRE)**[32] 4645 5-11-8 .... MrJPO'Farrell[(5)] 107
(F Flood, Ire) *trckd ldrs: 5th 6f out: cl up on inner 3f out: chal ent st: led over 1f out: hdd ins fnl f: kpt on u.p* **6/1**[2]

4 *nk* **Hotel Hilamar (IRE)** 5-11-6 .... MissNCarberry 100
(Noel Meade, Ire) *mid-div: hdwy 5f out: 4th over 3f out: rdn to chal ent st: kpt on u.p fnl f* **11/2**[1]

5 *nk* **Fruits De Mer (IRE)** 5-10-8 .... MrRHFowler[(7)] 94
(J R H Fowler, Ire) *hld up towards rr: hdwy appr st: 10th over 1f out: kpt on wl* **40/1**

6 *nk* **War General**[110] 3300 5-10-13 ... MrPDCollins(7) 99
(T J Taaffe, Ire) *led: strly pressed ent st: hdd over 1f out: kpt on same pce* **15/2**

7 *shd* **Omas Glen (IRE)**[20] 4772 5-11-1 ... MrATDuff(7) 101
(Cecil Ross, Ire) *hld up: prog 5f out: 7th 3f out: kpt on u.p st* **14/1**

8 *1/2* **Le Toscan (FR)**[11] 4892 6-11-7 ... RTDunne(7) 107
(M J P O'Brien, Ire) *trckd ldrs: 4th 1/2-way: 3rd 4f out: 2nd over 3f out: rdn and n.m.r early st: kpt on same pce fr over 1f out* **16/1**

9 *1/2* **Well Run (IRE)**[12] 4867 5-10-13 ... MrJPMcKeown(7) 98
(Noel Meade, Ire) *trckd ldrs in 3rd: 2nd 4f out: rdn and outpcd over 3f out: 5th into st: no ex fr 1 1/2f out* **12/1**

10 *nk* **Grapevine Sally (IRE)**[33] 4624 5-11-1 ... MrJKing(7) 100
(E J O'Grady, Ire) *towards rr: kpt on fr 3f out* **14/1**

11 *13* **Un Hinged (IRE)**[196] 1734 6-11-0 ... RJKiely(7) 86
(John J Coleman, Ire) *chsd ldrs: 6th and rdn 3f out: no ex st* **10/1**

12 *8* **Blackson Zulu (IRE)** 5-11-3 ... MrKEPower(3) 77
(J R H Fowler, Ire) *nvr a factor: kpt on one pced fr 3f out* **25/1**

13 *2 1/2* **Don Castille (USA)**[45] 4422 4-10-13 ... MrJJDoyle(7) 74
(P R Webber) *chsd ldrs: 8th 6f out: no ex fr 4f out* **25/1**

14 *7* **Kilcash Demon (IRE)**[46] 4406 5-11-0 ow1 ... MrJOMcGrath(7) 68
(Michael David Murphy, Ire) *settled 2nd: wknd over 4f out* **20/1**

15 *hd* **Derravarra Eagle (IRE)**[67] 4024 6-11-7 ... MrDPFahy(7) 75
(Mark Leslie Fagan, Ire) *rr of mid-div: rdn 5f out: sn no ex* **33/1**

16 *12* **Irish Invader (IRE)**[32] 4645 5-11-8 ... MsKWalsh(5) 62
(W P Mullins, Ire) *trckd ldrs: 8th 1/2-way: prog 4f out: wknd bef st* **13/2**[3]

17 *20* **Gunnison (IRE)**[255] 1230 5-11-6 ... MrJWFarrelly(7) 42
(Eoin Griffin, Ire) *mid-div on inner: 9th 6f out: effrt 4f out: wknd bef st* **14/1**

18 *1* **Leaveittwomebob (IRE)**[91] 3590 5-10-13 ... MrNTSlevin(7) 34
(Joseph Fox, Ire) *mid-div: lost pl 1/2-way: no ex fr 6f out* **50/1**

19 *3/4* **Evidence First**[164] 2252 5-10-13 ... MrAConlon(7) 33
(Michael Hourigan, Ire) *a towards rr* **50/1**

20 *25* **Coilog Jac's Folli (IRE)**[41] 4486 5-10-13 ... MrTGFreyne(7) 8
(Miss Sabrina Joan Harty, Ire) *chsd ldrs: 6th 1/2-way: wknd 6f out: t.o* **50/1**

21 *2* **Ask Hym (IRE)** 6-11-2 ... MrPFahey 2
(John G Carr, Ire) *nvr a factor: t.o* **33/1**

3m 48.3s **Going Correction** -0.65s/f (Firm)
WFA 4 from 5yo+ 5lb **25** Ran SP% **141.7**
Speed ratings: 106,105,103,103,103 103,103,102,102,102 96,92,90,87,87 81,71,70,70,57 56 CSF £126.60 TOTE £8.60: £2.50, £4.50, £1.60, £1.60; DF 226.50.
Owner Mrs Margaret Haughey **Bred** Miss Carmel O'Brien **Trained** Dungarvan, Co Waterford

NOTEBOOK

Don Castille(USA), a winner at Stratford last month, faced a much stiffer task here and never really threatened to play a hand in the finish.

Leaveittwomebob(IRE) *Official explanation: trainer said gelding scoped abnormally post race*

T/Jkpt: @371.50. Pool of @40,626.50 - 82 winning tickets. T/Plt: @73.50. Pool of @11,278.00 - 115 winning tickets. II

[4934]CHEPSTOW (L-H)

Friday, April 28

OFFICIAL GOING: Good (good to firm in places in back straight)
Wind: Almost nil Weather: Fine

5105 DUNRAVEN WINDOWS (S) H'CAP CHASE (18 fncs) 3m

5:40 (5:41) (Class 5) (0-95,92) 5-Y-O+ **£2,277** (£668; £334; £166)

Form RPR

0053 **1** **Blazing Batman**[10] 4936 13-9-9 **66** oh3 ... CharliePoste(5) 79+
(Dr P Pritchard) *hld up in mid-div: rdn and hdwy 5 out: led 2 out: styd on* **9/1**

20-P **2** *1 1/2* **Autumn Mist (IRE)**[34] 11-11-5 **92** ... (v) RichardSpate(7) 101
(M Scudamore) *a.p: led appr 8th: rdn appr 4 out: hdd 2 out: styd on flat* **20/1**

62U3 **3** *5* **Sweet Minuet**[12] 4873 9-10-11 **82** ... RobertLucey-Butler(5) 87+
(M Madgwick) *a.p: mstke 9th: lft 2nd briefly appr 4 out: wknd appr last* **14/1**

54P0 **4** *hd* **Dr Mann (IRE)**[65] 4047 8-10-11 **77** ... LeightonAspell 81
(Miss Tor Sturgis) *hld up in mid-div: styd on fr 3 out: nvr able to chal* **8/1**[3]

06/P **5** *4* **Dome**[106] 3359 8-10-0 **66** ... CarlLlewellyn 68+
(Carl Llewellyn) *prom: wkng whn mstke 2 out* **25/1**

1345 **6** *1 1/2* **Cullian**[10] 4936 9-11-5 **88** ... (p) WilliamKennedy(3) 86
(J G M O'Shea) *bhd tl hdwy appr 5 out: no further prog fr 4 out* **16/1**

P432 **7** *3* **Mill Bank (IRE)**[10] 4936 11-11-9 **89** ... (p) PaulMoloney 86+
(Evan Williams) *led 2nd: pckd 6th: hdd appr 8th: wknd 4 out* **9/2**[1]

4/0U **8** *dist* **Kaluga (IRE)**[15] 4837 8-10-5 **76** ... (p) DarylJacob(5) —
(S C Burrough) *mid-div: mstke 9th: no imp whn blnd 4 out: t.o* **66/1**

-5PP **9** *17* **Lets Go Dutch**[69] 3981 10-11-10 **90** ... RJGreene —
(K Bishop) *mstke 9th: a bhd: t.o* **14/1**

30PU **10** *dist* **Maybeseven**[71] 3938 12-9-7 **66** oh3 ... (v) JohnPritchard(7) —
(R Dickin) *a in rr: j. slowly 2nd: t.o fr 5th* **33/1**

0PU0 **P** **Star Galaxy (IRE)**[15] 4837 6-9-7 **69** ow3 ... (p) JFavell(10) —
(Andrew Turnell) *a bhd: t.o whn pu bef 2 out* **28/1**

P-3F **P** **Tacita**[143] 2686 11-10-0 **66** oh2 ... BenjaminHitchcott —
(M D McMillan) *a bhd: t.o whn p.u bef 4 out* **14/1**

-P26 **P** **Icare D'Oudairies (FR)**[25] 4719 10-11-5 **85** ... (p) OllieMcPhail —
(A L Forbes) *a bhd: t.o whn p.u bef 5 out* **25/1**

PP60 **P** **Lunardi (IRE)**[128] 2936 8-9-7 **66** oh3 ... MissLHorner(7) —
(D L Williams) *a bhd: t.o whn p.u and dismntd bef 4 out: lame* **66/1**

-P46 **P** **Gee Aker Malayo (IRE)**[49] 4353 10-10-8 **81** ... SeanQuinlan(7) —
(R T Phillips) *mid-div: bhd fr 12th: t.o whn p.u bef 2 out* **12/1**

5000 **P** **Scotch Corner (IRE)**[15] 4837 8-11-9 **89** ... (b) AntonyEvans —
(N A Twiston-Davies) *j.rt: prom to 8th: t.o whn p.u bef 5 out* **14/1**

P325 **P** **Connemara Mist (IRE)**[240] 1385 11-10-6 **72** ... (b) JodieMogford —
(Mrs N S Evans) *led: hdd and blnd 2nd: wknd 6th: t.o whn p.u bef 5 out* **25/1**

3PP2 **U** **Lucky Leader (IRE)**[10] 4939 11-11-1 **84** ... (b) OwynNelmes(3) 97+
(N R Mitchell) *hld up: hit 1st: hdwy 4th: ev ch whn rdrs rt foot slipped out of iron and uns rdr appr 4 out* **5/1**[2]

5m 58.7s (-16.20) **Going Correction** -0.60s/f (Firm) **18** Ran SP% **121.9**
Speed ratings: **103,102,100,100,99 98,97,—,—,— —,—,—,—,— —,—,—** CSF £177.57 CT £2502.78 TOTE £12.50: £1.50, £4.50, £2.70, £2.80; EX 173.30.There was no bid for the winner.
Owner Timber Pond Racing Club **Bred** Mrs R G Henderson **Trained** Purton, Gloucs

FOCUS

A lowly affair, but pretty competitive with most of the field dropped into this grade for the first time. The form appears solid enough with the first four close to their marks.

NOTEBOOK

Blazing Batman was on target for only the fourth time in a career which began back in 1997. Third in another seller at this course last time and racing from 3lb out of the handicap, he stayed on under pressure after showing ahead two from home to make the most of his good fortune, Lucky Leader having been going best when departing.

Autumn Mist(IRE), quite a consistent chaser at a low level, won a four-runner point-to-point at Brampton Bryan last month after a lengthy absence. In front by halfway, he could not counter immediately when the winner passed him with two to jump but was cutting into the deficit on the flat. *(op 12-1)*

Sweet Minuet was never far away despite a couple of mistakes. She faded between the last two fences and just held on for third. This trip probably just stretches her.

Dr Mann(IRE), who was doing his best work at the end, is lightly raced over fences and could have a little improvement in him. *(tchd 15-2)*

Dome ran respectably on this second outing over fences but was held in fourth when blundering at the second last.

Mill Bank(IRE) had tonight's winner and sixth behind when runner-up in a similar event here last time, but he failed to see out this longer trip having raced clear with the eventual runner-up for some way. *(op 6-1)*

Lucky Leader(IRE), who was touched off in a slightly better race over course and distance last time, was about to challenge for the lead when his rider lost an iron and was unshipped on the flat approaching the fourth last. He appeared to be going best and, as he will race from 4lb higher in future, this was an opportunity missed. *(op 9-2)*

Lunardi(IRE) *Official explanation: vet said gelding was lame (op 9-2)*

5106 SUN TRADE WINDOWS NOVICES' HURDLE (11 hdls) 2m 4f

6:10 (6:15) (Class 4) 4-Y-O+ **£2,927** (£859; £429; £214)

Form RPR

3504 **1** **College Ace (IRE)**[13] 4858 5-11-7 115 ... RichardJohnson 108+
(P J Hobbs) *a.p: led 7th: hit 4 out: rdn clr 4 out: nt fluent 2 out: drvn out* **5/4**[2]

6500 **2** *2 1/2* **Flemens River (IRE)**[20] 4786 5-11-0 ... (p) LeightonAspell 91
(C J Down) *hld up in mid-div: hdwy appr 7th: rdn whn hit 4 out: chsd wnr appr 2 out: nt qckn appr last* **50/1**

2-P **3** *11* **The Glen Road (IRE)**[36] 4590 9-11-0 ... PaulMoloney 80
(A W Carroll) *w ldr: led 4th to 7th: wknd after 2 out* **25/1**

P60P **4** *2* **Oakfield Legend**[5] 5028 5-10-9 91 ... JamesDiment(5) 78
(P S Payne) *t.k.h: prom tl wknd 4 out* **50/1**

0-6 **5** *22* **Celtic Prince (IRE)**[10] 4935 8-11-0 ... RobertWalford 56
(Miss H Lewis) *prom: mstkes 5th and 7th: sn wknd* **25/1**

00 **6** *4* **Montenda**[37] 4569 5-11-0 ... RJGreene 52
(S C Burrough) *hit 1st: a bhd* **50/1**

06- **7** *21* **Play Master (IRE)**[21] 3517 5-11-0 ... OllieMcPhail 31
(C Roberts) *hld up and plld hrd: j.rt 6th: hdwy 7th: sn rdn: wknd 4 out: t.o* **16/1**[3]

3-00 **P** **Lurid Affair (IRE)**[15] 4836 5-10-7 ... AntonyEvans —
(Mrs S Gardner) *bhd tl p.u after 6th* **50/1**

12 **P** **Darasim (IRE)**[185] 1870 8-11-7 121 ... (v) MickFitzgerald —
(Jonjo O'Neill) *led to 4th: rdn and wknd appr 6th: p.u bef 7th* **1/1**[1]

25F- **P** **Straight Talker (IRE)**[555] 1777 7-11-0 75 ... (p) JodieMogford —
(H S Howe) *bhd fr 3rd: rdn appr 5th: t.o whn p.u bef 6th* **33/1**

4m 47.4s (-15.30) **Going Correction** -0.90s/f (Hard)
WFA 4 from 5yo+ 6lb **10** Ran SP% **118.8**
Speed ratings: **94,93,88,87,79 77,69,—,—,—** CSF £64.40 TOTE £2.50: £1.20, £8.90, £3.70; EX 66.00.
Owner Mrs Peter Prowting **Bred** Ailish Cunningham **Trained** Withycombe, Somerset

FOCUS

A modest event run in a moderate time and pretty much a match on paper, but it did not work out that way with Darasim pulling up. The fourth sets the level and the form does not look strong.

NOTEBOOK

College Ace(IRE) seemed to be left with a simple task once his market rival pulled up, but did not win as easily as he had threatened to when he came clear before the third last and had to be driven out to score, perhaps finding the ground a bit dead. He has won twice over hurdles now and has the build to make a chaser next term. *(op 13-8 tchd 7-4)*

Flemens River(IRE), who was last on his recent hurdles bow over course and distance, ran a considerably better race in the cheekpieces and might stay a bit further.

The Glen Road(IRE), a well-beaten second to Cornish Rebel on his chasing debut in October 2004, was having only his second run since and making his hurdling debut. After showing prominently, he was left behind by the winner in the home straight. *(tchd 40-1)*

Oakfield Legend was not entirely disgraced and made the frame for the first time, but he looks very moderate.

Play Master(IRE), who came here fit from the Flat, did not stay but may do better in handicap company back at two miles. *(op 14-1)*

Darasim(IRE), a former leading stayer on the Flat, was having his first run since finishing second over three miles plus at Cheltenham in October. He came under pressure in the back straight and, soon losing touch with the leaders, was pulled up. He had a valid excuse this time, but he became *unreliable on the Flat and is one to tread warily with. Official explanation: jockey said gelding overreached (tchd 11-10)*

Lurid Affair(IRE) *Official explanation: jockey said mare was never travelling (tchd 11-10)*

5107 BRACEYS "THE FRIENDLY BUILDERS MERCHANT" H'CAP CHASE (16 fncs) 2m 3f 110y

6:40 (6:47) (Class 4) (0-110,110) 5-Y-O **£4,436** (£1,310; £655; £327; £163)

Form RPR

0/F4 **1** **Eljay's Boy**[23] 4735 8-10-0 **84** oh1 ... DaveCrosse 95+
(C L Tizzard) *hld up in mid-div: hdwy 8th: led 3 out: hit 2 out: all out* **15/2**[3]

4343 **2** *3/4* **Amadeus (AUS)**[20] 4782 9-9-12 **89** ... JohnKington(7) 98+
(M Scudamore) *chsd ldrs: led 8th: mstke 5 out: hdd 3 out: hrd rdn and kpt on flat* **15/2**[3]

0455 **3** *28* **Idealko (FR)**[222] 1484 10-10-7 **91** ... JodieMogford 71
(Dr P Pritchard) *prom: mstke 4th: lost pl after 5th: n.d after* **25/1**

5436 **4** *shd* **Westernmost**[47] 4392 8-10-6 **90** ... OllieMcPhail 70
(K Bishop) *nvr nr ldrs* **12/1**

33UF **5** *13* **Hiers De Brouage (FR)**[50] 4332 11-10-11 **100** ... (p) DarylJacob(5) 67
(J G Portman) *chsd ldrs: wknd appr 5 out: blnd 4 out* **9/1**

00P4 **6** *27* **Waterspray (AUS)**[22] 4755 8-11-12 **110** ... HenryOliver 50
(Ian Williams) *t.k.h in mid-div: bhd fr 6th: no ch whn blnd 4 out: t.o* **28/1**

03PP **7** *22* **Idbury (IRE)**[10] 4937 8-10-8 **92** ... JamesDavies 10
(V J Hughes) *prom tl wknd 8th: t.o* **25/1**

P634 **P** **Barren Lands**[33] 4639 11-10-5 **89** ... RJGreene —
(K Bishop) *a towards rr: t.o whn p.u bef 11th* **16/1**

P5U5 **P** **Flahive's First**[178] 1978 12-10-13 **97** ... AntonyEvans —
(D Burchell) *a bhd: t.o whn p.u bef 11th* **25/1**

20PP **P** **Caesarean Hunter (USA)**[52] 4288 7-10-8 **99** ... SeanQuinlan(7) —
(R T Phillips) *a bhd: t.o whn p.u bef 5 out* **28/1**

2101 **P** **Nazimabad (IRE)**[39] 4552 7-11-4 **107**............................(t) MrNWilliams(5) —
(Evan Williams) *led to 6th: led 7th to 8th: rdn 9th: sn wknd: t.o whn p.u bef 2 out* **5/2**[1]

P0P4 **F** **Lulumar (FR)**[46] 4419 7-11-11 **109**..................................(t) LeightonAspell —
(O Sherwood) *hld up and bhd: mstke 2nd: hdwy 7th: wknd 11th: 4th and no ch whn fell 4 out* **4/1**[2]

3P00 **F** **Glenkill (IRE)**[23] 4729 8-9-7 **84** oh9.................................. CharlieStudd(7) —
(S M Jacobs) *t.k.h: blnd 2nd: hdwy 4th: rn wd bnd after 5th: led and j.rt 6th: wknd 10th: mstke 5 out: no ch whn fell 4 out* **100/1**

4m 47.2s (-24.10) **Going Correction** -0.60s/f (Firm) **13** Ran SP% **115.1**
Speed ratings: **109,108,97,97,92 81,72,—,—,— —,—,—** CSF £55.42 CT £1333.88 TOTE £8.80: £1.90, £1.60, £4.40; EX 29.50.

Owner Mrs Kay Harvey **Bred** Mrs J M F Dibben **Trained** Milborne Port, Dorset

■ Stewards' Enquiry : Dave Crosse one-day ban: used whip with excessive frequency (May 9)

FOCUS
An ordinary handicap chase, run at a decent pace. The first two finished well clear and set the standard.

NOTEBOOK
Eljay's Boy gradually picked off the runner-up before showing ahead at the final ditch, but he could never shake off his rival and did not have much to spare at the end. Still travelling strongly when falling foul of the second last here on his return to chasing last month, he put in a lesser effort next time at Hereford, his trainer inclined to blame the right-handed track. He is likely to be kept busy through the summer. *(op 17-2 tchd 9-1)*

Amadeus(AUS) ran a sound race off a mark just 3lb higher than when successful at Fakenham in November. Trying to stretch his field in the back straight, he was collared after blundering at the fifth from home but he never stopped trying and made the winner work hard for his victory. *(op 12-1)*

Idealko(FR) was fortunate to pick up third prize but should improve with this first run for seven months behind him.

Westernmost was never a factor on his chasing debut. *(op 8-1)*

Hiers De Brouage(FR) who has a good previous record at Chepstow, went without the usual tongue tie. More effective on easier ground, he was a well-beaten third when blundering at the final ditch. *(op 13-2 tchd 6-1)*

Waterspray(AUS) is well in on last season's form but is not shaping as if about to take advantage. *(op 20-1)*

Flahive's First *Official explanation: jockey said gelding was never travelling (op 7-1)*

Barren Lands *Official explanation: jockey said gelding hung right (op 7-1)*

Nazimabad(IRE) was 8lb higher than when winning at Hereford, form that has been boosted by *runner-up Misty Dancer. He could never claim an uncontested lead and was eventually pulled up. Official explanation: jockey said gelding was never travelling (op 7-1)*

Lulumar(FR), dropped 3lb, threatened to get into the race leaving the back straight but was held when coming down. He probably needs further. *(op 7-1)*

5108 SUN TRADE WINDOWS H'CAP HURDLE (11 hdls) 2m 4f

7:10 (7:14) (Class 4) (0-105,105) 4-Y-0+ **£3,903** (£1,146; £573; £286)

Form RPR

0043 **1** **From Dawn To Dusk**[50] 4331 7-10-6 **85**........................ RichardJohnson 103+
(P J Hobbs) *a.p: led on bit 4 out: clr 3 out: easily* **9/4**[1]

6005 **2** *13* **Future Legend**[46] 4427 5-10-12 **91**..................................(t) JasonMaguire 97+
(J A B Old) *hld up towards rr: hdwy 6th: rdn after 4 out: wnt 2nd after 3 out: no ch w wnr* **10/1**

0105 **3** *7* **Fard Du Moulin Mas (FR)**[13] 4858 13-11-11 **104**.............. BarryFenton 96
(M E D Francis) *led to 4 out: wknd appr 2 out* **14/1**

14 **4** *hd* **Brendar (IRE)**[17] 4824 9-11-9 **105**................................ WilliamKennedy(3) 97
(Jim Best) *hld up and bhd: rdn 7th: hdwy appr 4 out: no imp fr 3 out* **9/1**

P002 **5** *1 ½* **Moon Catcher**[23] 4731 5-11-7 **100**................................ MickFitzgerald 90
(D Brace) *hld up and bhd: hdwy after 7th: no further prog fr 3 out* **8/1**[3]

31P1 **6** *2 ½* **Colophony (USA)**[11] 4898 6-11-3 **101** 7ex..................... JohnnyLevins(5) 89
(K A Morgan) *hld up in mid-div: hit 4th: no hdwy fr 7th* **11/2**[2]

-150 **7** *shd* **Prestbury Knight**[39] 4549 6-11-11 **104**...............................(t) AntonyEvans 94+
(N A Twiston-Davies) *a.p: hit 5th: ev ch 4 out: wkng whn j.lft 3 out: j.lft and mstke 2 out* **12/1**

60F **8** *4* **Shirazi**[10] 4938 8-11-5 **103**... LiamHeard(5) 87
(D R Gandolfo) *hld up and bhd: hdwy 7th: wknd appr 3 out* **12/1**

0P4P **9** *2* **Reservoir (IRE)**[20] 4781 5-11-2 **100**.................................. ShaneWalsh(5) 82
(J Joseph) *prom tl wknd 4 out* **66/1**

10P **10** *10* **Over Bridge**[50] 4331 8-10-8 **87**.. JamesDavies 59
(Mrs S M Johnson) *hld up in mid-div: rdn after 7th: sn struggling* **16/1**

1P06 **11** *2 ½* **Erins Lass (IRE)**[39] 4549 9-10-7 **86**.................................. HenryOliver 55
(R Dickin) *a towards rr: rdn 6th: sn struggling* **25/1**

644 **12** *25* **Angello (FR)**[17] 4823 5-11-3 **96**.. RJGreene 40
(N J Hawke) *rdn 6th: a bhd: t.o* **28/1**

UP60 **13** *27* **Uncle Max (IRE)**[44] 4451 6-10-9 **95**..........................(b) MarcGoldstein(7) 12
(N A Twiston-Davies) *hld up in tch: wknd 6th: t.o* **33/1**

00P0 **14** *4* **Forzacurity**[12] 4879 7-11-1 **99**... MrNWilliams(5) 12
(D Burchell) *t.k.h towards rr: hdwy 5th: wknd 6th: t.o* **50/1**

4m 43.4s (-19.30) **Going Correction** -0.90s/f (Hard) **14** Ran SP% **118.0**
Speed ratings: **102,96,94,93,93 92,92,90,89,85 84,74,64,62** CSF £23.55 CT £262.22 TOTE £3.10: £2.10, £3.10, £4.90; EX 42.70.

Owner C G M Lloyd-Baker **Bred** Tweenhills Farm And Stud Ltd **Trained** Withycombe, Somerset

FOCUS
What looked quite an open handicap was rendered anything but as From Dawn To Dusk ran away with it and the race could be rated higher.

NOTEBOOK
From Dawn To Dusk ◆ , adopting different tactics after failing to get home over an extra quarter mile at Wincanton, showed in front once in the home straight and soon came clear to win as he pleased, value for a greater margin of victory. Although the Handicapper will step in, he ran off only 85 here and could well win again on this better ground, especially if turned out under a penalty. *(op 11-4 tchd 3-1)*

Future Legend had shaped as if worth a try over a trip like this and he was unfortunate to come up against a progressive rival. The tongue tie contributed to this improved display. *(op 11-1 tchd 12-1)*

Fard Du Moulin Mas(FR) rallied well for third after making the running to the fourth last, and obviously retains his enthusiasm. *(op 11-1)*

Brendar(IRE) has been running well on soft ground and produced a fair effort on this sounder surface. *(op 8-1)*

Moon Catcher ran her race back up in trip without getting close enough to land a blow. *(op 11-2)*

Colophony(USA) was still 4lb ahead of the Handicapper under his penalty, but the win came in a *weaker race and he was found wanting. Official explanation: jockey said gelding had a breathing problem (op 5-1 tchd 6-1)*

Over Bridge *Official explanation: trainer's representative said gelding was lame (op 11-1)*

5109 DUNRAVEN BOWL NOVICES' HUNTERS' CHASE (FOR THE DUNRAVEN WINDOWS S & W WALES P-T-P CHAMPIONSHIP) (18 fncs) 3m

7:40 (7:45) (Class 5) 6-Y-0+ **£2,498** (£774; £387; £193)

Form RPR

62/ **1** **Cannon Bridge (IRE)**[27] 8-12-2.. MrDSJones(3) 114+
(Mrs C Williams) *t.k.h: a.p: mstke 9th: led 12th: nt fluent last: drvn out* **7/4**[1]

406/ **2** *3 ½* **Gilzine**[19] 10-12-0.. MrJLLlewellyn 102
(E Parry) *hld up and bhd: hdwy appr 8th: chsd wnr fr 3 out: no imp* **8/1**[3]

3 *4* **Mike Golden (IRE)**[27] 8-11-7.. MrWOakes(7) 98
(R W J Willcox) *led tl appr 3rd: prom: one pce fr 2 out* **20/1**

00-P **4** *12* **Classi Maureen**[11] 6-11-7 .... MrsLucyRowsell(5) 84
(S A Hughes) *led appr 3rd to 12th: wknd 2 out* **9/1**

F04- **5** *1 ¼* **Gipsy Girl**[20] 11-11-4 .... MrJETudor(3) 77
(D O Stephens) *hld up in mid-div: hdwy 11th: wknd 13th* **4/1**[2]

6 *1 ¼* **Clarice Starling**[13] 8-11-0 ....(t) MrRhysHughes(7) 76
(L J Bridge) *hld up towards rr: mstke 11th: hdwy after 13th: wknd 4 out* **14/1**

7 *17* **Grey Kid (IRE)**[13] 8-11-7 .... MrKYates(7) 66
(E W Morris) *a bhd* **33/1**

36-P **P** **Bowd Lane Joe**[34] 7-11-7 70......................................(p) MrPSheldrake(7) —
(E R Clough) *a bhd: t.o whn p.u bef 10th* **14/1**

0 **P** **She's Little Don**[11] 6-11-2 .... MrRWoollacott(5) —
(S A Hughes) *a towards rr: t.o whn p.u bef 5 out* **25/1**

U **Cape Teal (IRE)**[13] 7-12-0 .... MrNWilliams —
(D Brace) *prom: hit 1st and 2nd: w ldrs 3rd tl j.lft and bmpd whn uns rdr 9th* **12/1**

24P/ **P** **Ballet Red**[34] 9-11-0 .... MrTVaughan(7) —
(Miss B J Thomas) *hld up in mid-div: hdwy appr 8th: wknd 11th: t.o whn p.u bef 4 out* **22/1**

PP00 **P** **Barton Bandit**[15] 4831 10-11-7 ....(t) MrJSole(7) —
(Miss Sarah Kent) *hld up in mid-div: hdwy appr 8th: wknd 12th: t.o whn p.u bef 2 out* **66/1**

5m 59.9s (-15.00) **Going Correction** -0.60s/f (Firm) **12** Ran SP% **115.9**
Speed ratings: **101,99,98,94,94 93,88,—,—,— —,—** CSF £14.68 TOTE £2.50: £1.90, £2.20, £6.40; EX 15.70.

Owner K Pritchard **Bred** Tony McKiernan **Trained** Llancarfan

FOCUS
An event confined to Welsh-based point-to-pointers, and few of the runners had much hunter chase experience. The winner was value for further and the form makes sense time-wise.

NOTEBOOK
Cannon Bridge(IRE) had never run over regulation fences before but racked up 14 consecutive victories between the flags - starting favourite each time- before he was pulled up with a broken blood-vessel in the prestigious Lady Dudley Cup earlier this month, a race won by his stablemate Unmistakably. Usually a front runner, he took a hold in the early stages as he was restrained behind the leaders. He survived a mistake at the ninth and dived over the final fence, but he was in command by that stage. He could no doubt win plenty more races in this sphere but it would be interesting to see how he was to fare if given a chance in novice/handicap company. *(op 2-1 tchd 13-8)*

Gilzine, making his hunter chase debut, came here in good form with a couple of pointing victories this term, but at a lower level than the winner. He chased the favourite over the last three fences but was never able to get to him. *(op 9-1 tchd 15-2)*

Mike Golden(IRE), an ex-Irish gelding, winner of a restricted on his British debut, stayed on well and looks to be on the upgrade. *(op 14-1)*

Classi Maureen, coming here on the back of a hat-trick of pointing wins, ran well for a long way but eventually paid the price for helping force the pace. *(op 6-1)*

5110 BRACEYS "THE FRIENDLY BUILDERS MERCHANT" MAIDEN HURDLE (8 hdls) 2m 110y

8:10 (8:16) (Class 5) 4-Y-0+ **£1,472** (£1,472; £334; £166)

Form RPR

2344 **1** **Lysander (GER)**[13] 4849 7-10-11 106.............................. CharliePoste(5) 100
(M F Harris) *hld up: hdwy appr 4 out: rdn appr last: r.o to join ldr post* **6/4**[1]

5 **1** *dht* **Smokey Mountain (IRE)**[155] 2462 5-10-11 .... DarylJacob(5) 100
(D P Keane) *led tl after 1st: chsd clr ldr: led 4 out: rdn appr last: jnd post* **20/1**

3 *¾* **Recount (FR)**[590] 6-11-2 .... DaveCrosse 100+
(C J Mann) *hld up: hdwy appr 4 out: rdn after 2 out: ev ch whn edgd lft and nt fluent last: nt qckn* **14/1**

4 *7* **Argonaut**[17] 6-11-2 .... VinceSlattery 92
(P Bowen) *hld up in mid-div: hdwy appr 4 out: wknd appr 2 out* **12/1**

0505 **5** *2 ½* **Smoothly Does It**[105] 3371 5-11-2 94................................ AndrewTinkler 90
(Mrs A J Bowlby) *hld up in mid-div: hdwy on ins 4 out: wknd appr 2 out* **12/1**

5-53 **6** *9* **Storm Of Applause (IRE)**[97] 3511 5-11-2 .... RichardJohnson 81
(P J Hobbs) *hld up and bhd: hdwy appr 4 out: mstke 3 out: wkng whn mstke 2 out* **5/2**[2]

0660 **7** *1 ½* **Supreme Copper (IRE)**[17] 4819 6-11-2 .... BarryFenton 79
(Miss E C Lavelle) *hld up and bhd: hdwy appr 4 out: wknd after 3 out* **50/1**

P/06 **8** *2* **Sun Hill**[5] 5016 6-10-9 .... MrRhysHughes(7) 77
(D Burchell) *hld up and bhd: hdwy appr 3 out: wknd appr 2 out* **66/1**

P060 **9** *1* **Lyster (IRE)**[10] 4935 7-10-11 90....................................(v) JamesDiment(5) 76
(D L Williams) *hld up in mid-div: rdn after 2nd: wknd appr 3 out* **66/1**

10 *14* **Gala Evening**[343] 4-10-11 .... JasonMaguire 57
(J A B Old) *hld up: hdwy appr 4 out: wknd 3 out* **9/1**[3]

00 **11** *11* **Mount Butler (IRE)**[23] 4733 4-10-4 .... RichardSpate(7) 46
(J W Tudor) *hld up in tch: wknd 4th* **100/1**

PP **12** *¾* **Chaplin**[99] 3464 5-10-6 .... TimothyBailey(10) 51
(Evan Williams) *a bhd* **80/1**

P **13** *21* **Mardonicdeclare**[68] 4015 5-10-11 .... ShaneWalsh(5) 30
(S Lycett) *prom to 4th: t.o* **100/1**

5000 **14** *dist* **Jobsworth (IRE)**[10] 4934 6-11-2 .... PaulMoloney —
(Evan Williams) *hld up in tch: rdn and wknd after 3rd* **33/1**

06FP **P** **Financial Future**[33] 4640 6-11-2 80...................................... OllieMcPhail —
(C Roberts) *a bhd: t.o whn p.u bef 4 out* **50/1**

0 **P** **Diafa (USA)**[13] [4855] 4-9-13 .... StevenCrawford(5) —
(J G M O'Shea) *led after 1st: sn clr: wknd and hdd 4 out: t.o whn p.u bef 2 out* **100/1**

3m 53.1s (-17.30) **Going Correction** -0.90s/f (Hard)
WFA 4 from 5yo+ 5lb **16** Ran SP% **119.4**
Speed ratings: **104,104,103,100,99 94,94,93,92,86 81,80,70,—,— —**WIN: Lysander £1.30, Smokey Mountain £11.50. PL: L £1.60, SM £3.80, Recount £3.60. EX: L/SM £43.00, SM/L £20.70. CSF: L/SM £17.95, SM/L £24.90. Place 6 £161.54, Place 5 £45.06.
Owner The Piranha Partnership **Bred** R Peters **Trained** Edgcote, Northants
Owner Roy Swinburne **Bred** William Durkan **Trained** North End, Dorset

FOCUS
A weak maiden event, but a cracking finish which resulted in a dead-heat. The form, rated through the sixth and eighth, is nothing special.

NOTEBOOK
Lysander(GER) came into the race with some solid placed form to his name. Joining Smokey Mountain three from home, he looked set to score after getting away best from the final flight, but could not quite get his head past a determined rival. *(op 7-4 tchd 2-1)*
Smokey Mountain(IRE) has changed stables since his hurdles debut in November. Moving to the front four from home, he was joined by Lysander at the next and, in a good tussle, proved very game to hold on for a share of the spoils. *(op 7-4 tchd 2-1)*
Recount(FR), a fair middle-distance handicapper on the Flat, looked the likeliest winner when closing between the last two flights, but he jinked left going into the last and lost vital momentum. A small race should come his way. *(op 12-1)*
Argonaut, who rather lost his way on the Flat, ran a fair race on this hurdles bow without ever quite being able to get into the action. *(tchd 11-1 and 14-1)*
Smoothly Does It, who has been tackling better company, not for the first time did not quite get home.
Storm Of Applause(IRE) would have been a bit closer had he not made a couple of mistakes in the straight. *(op 3-1)*
T/Plt: £355.20 to a £1 stake. Pool: £50,663.80. 104.10 winning tickets. T/Qpdt: £57.70 to a £1 stake. Pool: £5,079.50. 65.05 winning tickets. KH

[4855] NEWTON ABBOT (L-H)
Friday, April 28

OFFICIAL GOING: Good to firm (good in places)
Wind: Virtually nil

5111 CHEESE AND WINE SHOP, DARLINGTON NOVICES' H'CAP HURDLE (8 hdls) 2m 1f
4:55 (4:56) (Class 4) (0-105,105) 4-Y-0+ **£2,927** (£859; £429; £214)

Form RPR
251 **1** **Traprain (IRE)**[22] [4754] 4-11-7 **105** .... MrTJO'Brien(5) 116+
(P J Hobbs) *hld up: smooth hdwy after 3 out to take narrow advantage 2 out: gng the bttr whn lft clr last* **4/6**[1]
0000 **2** *9* **Brave Hiawatha (FR)**[15] [4834] 4-10-6 **85** .... JasonMaguire 83+
(J A B Old) *hld up: stdy hdwy after 4th: hmpd and rdr lost iron 3 out: sn rdn: kpt on same pce: lft 2nd at the last* **15/2**[3]
321P **3** *7* **Zarakash (IRE)**[20] [1202] 6-11-8 **96** .... TomScudamore 95+
(Jonjo O'Neill) *chsd ldr: blnd 3 out: sn rdn: one pce fr next: lft 3rd whn mstke last* **8/1**
P66 **4** *3 1/2* **Mount Benger**[44] [2148] 6-10-11 **90** ....(p) PaddyMerrigan(5) 81
(Mrs A J Hamilton-Fairley) *hld up: sme hdwy appr 3 out: sn rdn: no imp after* **16/1**
23P5 **5** *14* **Looking Great (USA)**[17] [4819] 4-11-12 **105** .... AndrewThornton 77
(R F Johnson Houghton) *mid div tl wknd 3 out* **25/1**
0043 **6** *2 1/2* **Post It**[15] [4834] 5-11-7 **95** .... JamieMoore 70
(R J Hodges) *chsd ldrs: sltly hmpd 3 out: sn rdn and wknd* **14/1**
2410 **7** *16* **Urban Dream (IRE)**[134] [2845] 5-11-2 **90** .... JimCrowley 49
(R A Farrant) *hld up: rdn appr 3 out: sn btn* **25/1**
0PP1 **F** **Simonovski (USA)**[15] [4828] 5-11-7 **95** ....(p) WayneHutchinson 102
(Mrs A M Thorpe) *j.rt thrght: led: narrowly hdd 2 out: sn rdn: rallying whn fell last* **7/1**[2]

4m 1.80s (-3.30) **Going Correction** -0.15s/f (Good) **8** Ran SP% **115.6**
Speed ratings: **101,96,93,91,85 84,76,—** CSF £6.94 CT £21.27 TOTE £1.80: £1.10, £2.50, £2.10; EX 7.90.
Owner R A Green **Bred** C J Foy **Trained** Withycombe, Somerset

FOCUS
A modest handicap, run at an ordinary pace, with the progressive winner value for further. The third and fourth set the level, and several of the others are capable of paying their way during the summer months.

NOTEBOOK
Traprain(IRE) was helped by the final flight fall of Simonovski, but would almost certainly have won anyway because he was never off the bridle. The Handicapper appears to have underestimated him. *(op 11-10 after 5-4 in a place)*
Brave Hiawatha(FR) was unluckily forced into a blunder three out when a rival jumped across him, from which point he was always fighting a losing battle. He looks capable of winning a similar handicap. *(op 6-1)*
Zarakash(IRE) had a recent pipe-opener on the Flat, but he still fell some way short. Though briefly threatening to get into contention on the home turn, he was already under pressure by then. *(op 6-1)*
Mount Benger, with a recent run on the Flat to help him, made only a brief effort. The ground may have been a bit faster than ideal. *(op 12-1)*
Looking Great(USA) had plenty of weight on the basis of his four previous outings. *(op 16-1)*
Post It failed to reproduce her recent Wincanton effort. *Official explanation: jockey said mare jumped right-handed througout (op 10-1)*
Simonovski(USA) was in the process of running an excellent race when departing at the last. He would probably have been beaten by the cantering winner, but deserves credit nonetheless, with the cheekpieces appearing to have transformed him in his last two races. *(op 13-2)*

5112 DESIGN@ARKLEPRINT.CO.UK H'CAP CHASE (13 fncs) 2m 110y
5:25 (5:27) (Class 4) (0-115,113) 5-Y-0+ **£4,554** (£1,337; £668; £333)

Form RPR
6563 **1** **O'Toole (IRE)**[13] [4859] 7-11-8 109 .... PJBrennan 116+
(P J Hobbs) *hld up in tch: hdwy 7th: led after 4 out: rdn and pckd 2 out: hit last: all out* **3/1**[1]
2242 **2** *nk* **Jupon Vert (FR)**[13] [4859] 9-10-8 95 .... TomScudamore 101+
(R J Hodges) *hld up in tch: tk clsr order appr 3 out: rdn to chal after 2 out: kpt on but no ex cl home* **13/2**
26F **3** *7* **New Bird (GER)**[107] [3344] 11-11-7 108 .... WayneHutchinson 107+
(Ian Williams) *prom: led 7th tl 9th: stydprom: led briefly 4 out: rdn after 3 out: one pce whn hit 2 out* **10/3**[2]
0-12 **4** *2* **Appach (FR)**[12] [4870] 7-11-2 103 .... AndrewThornton 101+
(J W Mullins) *hld up: hdwy 7th: rdn and effrt appr 2 out: kpt on same pce* **4/1**[3]
53-P **5** *4* **Alakdar (CAN)**[156] [2431] 12-9-11 87 oh13 .... TomMalone(3) 79
(Jane Southcombe) *j.lft 1st: prom: led tl 5th: led 9th tl 4 out: sn rdn: wknd appr 2 out* **66/1**
4S04 **6** *1 1/2* **Gipsy Cricketer**[155] [2463] 10-9-7 87 oh12 .... AdrianScholes(7) 81+
(M Scudamore) *chsd ldrs: hit 5th: mstke 8th: nt a danger after* **33/1**
P-12 **7** *12* **Haile Selassie**[33] [4639] 6-10-10 97 .... WarrenMarston 78+
(W Jenks) *hld up: lost tch fr 9th* **7/1**
1110 **8** *2 1/2* **Blakeney Coast (IRE)**[251] [1265] 9-11-12 113 ....(t) JoeTizzard 89
(C L Tizzard) *led 5th tl 7th: styd prom tl wknd appr 4 out* **11/2**

(-5.50) **Going Correction** -0.15s/f (Good) **8** Ran SP% **113.7**
Speed ratings: **106,105,102,101,99 99,93,92** CSF £22.62 CT £67.23 TOTE £3.30: £2.20, £1.80, £1.60; EX 22.40.
Owner Mrs L R Lovell **Bred** John Moclair **Trained** Withycombe, Somerset

FOCUS
A fair handicap containing a number of typical summer jumping types. The first two to their marks set the standard.

NOTEBOOK
O'Toole(IRE) travelled well, but carried his head rather high in the finish, so it was fortunate for him that the runner-up is developing a reputation for finishing second. *(op 10-3 tchd 4-1)*
Jupon Vert(FR) has now finished second in six of his last nine starts. He lacks race-winning acceleration, but his consistency cannot be faulted. *(op 6-1 tchd 7-1)*
New Bird(GER) goes well round here, and success on fast ground at this shaper track would be no surprise following this promising first outing for three months. *(op 4-1 tchd 9-2)*
Appach(FR) ran well enough without managing to quicken up in the final half-mile. He should find *some decent opportunities during the summer campaign.Official explanation: trainer said gelding lost a shoe (op 10-3)*
Alakdar(CAN), 13lb out of the handicap, seemed to enjoy himself in front, and ran better than expected. *(op 50-1)*
Gipsy Cricketer, 12lb out of the handicap, had a tough task in this first run for five months. *(op 25-1)*
Haile Selassie's best form is on easier ground than this. *(tchd 8-1)*
Blakeney Coast(IRE), 14lb above his last winning mark, was having his first run for eight months, and needs to step up on it significantly to become competitive again. *(tchd 5-1 and 6-1)*

5113 R2 PARTNERSHIP H'CAP HURDLE (10 hdls) 2m 6f
5:55 (5:55) (Class 4) (0-115,112) 4-Y-0+ **£4,554** (£1,337; £668; £333)

Form RPR
0055 **1** **Red Echo (FR)**[30] [4661] 5-10-3 **96** .... AndrewGlassonbury(7) 104+
(M C Pipe) *mid-div: hdwy 6th: hrd rdn to chse ldrs ldrs after 3 out : led next: wnt lft last: drvn out* **8/1**
-3P4 **2** *2 1/2* **Navado (USA)**[198] [1715] 7-11-7 **107** .... TomScudamore 110
(Jonjo O'Neill) *t.k.h in mid-div: stdy hdwy fr 3 out: rdn to chse wnr whn pckd 2 out: no ex fr last* **14/1**
3400 **3** *7* **Woody Valentine (USA)**[30] [4663] 5-11-12 **112** .... SamThomas 108+
(Miss Venetia Williams) *chsd ldrs: lft in ld 7th: rdn and hdd appr 2 out: wknd appr last* **9/2**[3]
2F00 **4** *3/4* **Little Tobias (IRE)**[208] [1607] 7-9-7 **86** oh1 .... WayneKavanagh(7) 82+
(D D Scott) *hld up: hdwy after 7th: rdn after 3 out: styd on fr next* **33/1**
0130 **5** *shd* **Dancing Hill**[10] [4941] 7-10-0 **86** oh2 .... WayneHutchinson 81
(K Bishop) *hld up: rdn and hdwy after 3 out: styd on but nvr trbld ldrs* **14/1**
102F **6** *1 1/2* **Bak To Bill**[10] [4944] 11-11-3 **110** .... MissLGardner(7) 104
(Mrs S Gardner) *chsd ldrs: rdn after 3 out: sn one pce* **12/1**
63 **7** *1 1/2* **Allaboveboard (IRE)**[13] [4858] 7-11-2 **102** .... JamieMoore 94
(P Bowen) *in tch: rdn to chse ldrs appr 3 out: wknd 2 out* **3/1**[1]
4P3- **8** *30* **Beau Coup**[390] [4717] 9-11-2 **102** .... WarrenMarston 64
(John R Upson) *led tl 2nd: chsd ldr: mstke 5th: wknd appr 7th* **16/1**
3FP0 **9** *2* **Tignasse (FR)**[23] [3592] 5-10-2 **93** .... EamonDehdashti(5) 53
(Miss K M George) *mid-div tl wknd 7th* **33/1**
4240 **R** **Lavenoak Lad**[13] [4860] 6-10-2 **95** .... KeiranBurke(7) —
(P R Rodford) *led 2nd tl rn out 7th* **20/1**
021P **P** **Rude Health**[13] [4860] 6-10-0 **86** .... PJBrennan —
(N J Hawke) *hld up bhd: stmbld on bnd after 6th: hdwy next: sn rdn: wknd after 3 out: p.u bef next* **10/3**[2]

5m 14.4s (-5.90) **Going Correction** -0.15s/f (Good) **11** Ran SP% **114.9**
Speed ratings: **104,103,100,100,100 99,99,88,87,— —** CSF £105.48 CT £561.47 TOTE £7.90: £1.80, £4.30, £2.30; EX 66.20.
Owner Terry Neill **Bred** Georges Trinquet **Trained** Nicholashayne, Devon

FOCUS
An ordinary handicap, won by a horse making his handicap debut who had never previously finished in the first four. The fourth and fifth are the best guides to the form.

NOTEBOOK
Red Echo(FR), making his handicap debut, stepped up on all four previous efforts to score a hard-earned success, coming wide to the stands' rail in the home straight. It would be a surprise if he could not be improved a bit more. *(op 10-1 tchd 15-2)*
Navado(USA), running for the first time since last October, gave the winner a good race. A stronger pace would have stopped him being so headstrong.
Woody Valentine(USA) is dropping to a winning mark, but this trip was stretching him after he appeared the most likely winner on the home turn. *(op 5-1 tchd 4-1)*
Little Tobias(IRE) showed enough to keep his connections optimistic during the coming months.
Dancing Hill was trying a longer trip and appeared to stay it alright, though she made little impression over the final two flights. *(op 12-1)*
Bak To Bill had a nice confidence booster following a recent fall over fences, and will be more effective when returned to the bigger obstacles. *(op 8-1)*
Allaboveboard(IRE) may be more effective at two and a half miles and less. *(op 7-2)*
Rude Health *Official explanation: vet said mare had been struck into (op 16-1)*
Lavenoak Lad bowled along in front until unexpectedly ducking to the left and dumping his rider four from home. *(op 16-1)*

5114 ARKLE PRINT NOVICES' CHASE (16 fncs) 2m 5f 110y
6:25 (6:25) (Class 3) 5-Y-0+ **£7,675** (£2,316; £1,193; £631)

Form RPR
U215 **1** **Matthew Muroto (IRE)**[17] [4820] 7-11-6 112 .... TomScudamore 113+
(R H Alner) *trckd ldrs: led 11th tl next: led 3 out: sn rdn: kpt on wl: rdn out* **14/1**
3145 **2** *1 1/2* **Goblet Of Fire (USA)**[140] [2743] 7-11-10 ....(b) ChristianWilliams 115
(P F Nicholls) *trckd ldrs: cl up and rdn after 4 out: chalng for 2nd whn lft 2nd last: r.o cl home* **3/1**[2]
3232 **3** *7* **Unleash (USA)**[9] [4960] 7-11-6 135 .... PJBrennan 108+
(P J Hobbs) *hld up: tk clsr order 11th: 3rd and rdn after 4 out: one pce fr next: 5th and btn whn lft 3rd at the last* **8/15**[1]
-PP0 **4** *dist* **Mr Micky (IRE)**[11] [4903] 8-11-0 .... SeanCurran —
(M B Shears) *led tl 11th: sn wknd: lft remote 4th at the last* **100/1**

40F0 **F** **Barella (IRE)**[10] 4941 7-10-9 95 HowieEphgrave(5) —
(L Corcoran) *chsd ldrs tl fell 8th* **33/1**
-P1P **F** **Joizel (FR)**[38] 4558 9-11-6 91 JoeTizzard 112
(V G Greenway) *trckd ldrs: led 12th tl 3 out: sn rdn: 1l 2nd whn fell last* **33/1**
43P1 **F** **Latin Queen (IRE)**[10] 4943 6-10-10 ChrisHonour(3) 106
(J D Frost) *hld up: hdwy 12th: cl 3rd and n.m.r whn hit 2 out: rdn to chal for 2nd whn fell last* **8/1**[3]

5m 22.2s (-0.50) **Going Correction** -0.15s/f (Good) **7** Ran SP% **114.9**
Speed ratings: **94,93,90,—,—** —,— CSF £56.56 TOTE £15.10: £4.20, £1.70; EX 29.80.
Owner Alvin Trowbridge **Bred** Patrick Gahan **Trained** Droop, Dorset

FOCUS
A decent and valuable race, though the favourite was well below his best, the time was slow and the form looks suspect.

NOTEBOOK
Matthew Muroto(IRE) was left with little to beat, with three of his opponents hitting the deck and the favourite running poorly, but he has had a good season and deserved this. He was a length in front, and just in charge, when Joizel and Latin Queen came down at the last. *(op 12-1)*
Goblet Of Fire(USA), though just held in the home straight, stayed on well and was closing at the finish. He appears to be coming back to form. *(op 7-2)*
Unleash(USA) was a complete flop. He made no serious jumping errors, but he was fighting a losing battle from the third last. *(tchd 4-6 in a place)*
Mr Micky(IRE), who briefly threatened to head for the paddock with a circuit remaining, otherwise seemed happy in front until capitulating quickly five from home.
Joizel(FR) took a heavy fall at the last, but for which he would have been involved in the finish following a spirited effort. Happily, he was quickly on his feet and appeared none the worse. *(op 10-1)*
Latin Queen(IRE) travelled well and would have gone close, though probably held by the winner, but for falling at the last. That tumble apart, she has taken well to fences and can win again if her confidence has not been affected. *(op 10-1)*

5115 COMEHORSERACING.COM (S) HURDLE (9 hdls) 2m 3f
6:55 (6:55) (Class 5) 4-6-Y-0 **£2,192** (£639; £319)

Form RPR
6041 **1** **Brochrua (IRE)**[13] 4856 6-10-10 87 ChrisHonour(3) 94+
(J D Frost) *trckd ldrs: jnd ldr 4th: led 6th: qckn d clr after 3 out: readily* **10/11**[1]
4 **2** *9* **Cash On (IRE)**[30] 4665 4-10-7 (b[1]) ChristianWilliams 75
(P F Nicholls) *in tch: hit 3rd: wnt 3rd after 6th: rdn and effrt after 3 out: sn nt pce of wnr* **10/3**[2]
6000 **3** *nk* **Killer Cat (FR)**[13] 4860 5-10-11 90 ow5 (v) MrDEdwards(7) 86
(G F Edwards) *led 2nd tl 6th: pressed wnr: rdn after 3 out: sn one pce* **7/1**[3]
2040 **4** *19* **Sunset King (USA)**[10] 4941 6-10-13 77 TomScudamore 62
(R J Hodges) *led tl 2nd: chsd ldrs tl wknd after 6th* **7/1**[3]
0400 **5** *¾* **Garhoud**[17] 4423 4-10-7 73 (p) AndrewThornton 55
(Miss K M George) *in tch tl wknd after 6th* **16/1**
6 *30* **Silver Island**[339] 5-10-13 (t) SeanCurran 31
(K Bishop) *hld up: hdwy into 4th after 6th: wknd after 3 out* **20/1**
PP0P **7** *dist* **Time To Succeed**[41] 4506 4-10-2 56 (b[1]) DerekLaverty(5) —
(Mrs A M Thorpe) *chsd ldrs: reminders after 4th: lost tch fr 6th: t.o* **66/1**

4m 30.9s (-2.10) **Going Correction** -0.15s/f (Good)
WFA 4 from 5yo+ 5lb **7** Ran SP% **112.6**
Speed ratings: **98,94,94,86,85 73,—** CSF £4.12 TOTE £1.70: £1.50, £1.70; EX 5.50.The winner was bought in for 6,400gns. Cash On was claimed by Miss K. George for £6,000.
Owner Ms H Vernon-Jones **Bred** Nicholas Teehan **Trained** Scorriton, Devon

FOCUS
A weak seller, won easily by a plating specialist who was value for further, and with the runner-up sets the standard.

NOTEBOOK
Brochrua(IRE) scored in the style her odds had suggested she would. An admirable plater, she is ideally suited by fast ground and this sharp track, and she will doubtless be back. *(tchd Evens)*
Cash On(IRE) has plenty of ability, and the blinkers were on today in an attempt to persuade him to use it. He ran reasonably, but he gives the impression he is capable of so much better if he felt like it. *(tchd 7-2)*
Killer Cat(FR), the highest rated of these, merely set the race up for the winner. He saw his race out well enough, but needs to remain in selling company to be competitive. *(op 9-1)*
Sunset King(USA) did little to suggest he is about to win in any company. *(op 8-1)*
Garhoud is becoming very exposed, and is below his best at present. *(op 14-1)*
Silver Island sat off the pace, travelling comfortably, but a promising forward move a mile from home came to nothing. *(op 14-1)*

5116 P4MARKETING.CO.UK NOVICES' HUNTERS' CHASE (16 fncs) 2m 5f 110y
7:25 (7:25) (Class 6) 5-Y-0+ **£1,054** (£324; £162)

Form RPR
34P0 **1** **River Dante (IRE)**[11] 9-12-0 (t) MrACharles-Jones 101+
(Miss L A Blackford) *mde all: 6l clr 12th: hit 2 out: kpt on wl: pushed out* **33/1**
2 *5* **Derosa**[328] 9-11-7 MrWWhite(7) 95
(Mrs E B Scott) *bhd: hdwy appr 10th: rdn after 11th: lot to do 4 out: styd on fr 3 out: wnt 2nd run-in: nvr trbld wnr* **33/1**
1 **3** *2* **Highway Oak**[22] 4757 10-12-1 MrMGMiller(3) 97
(Ben White) *chsd ldrs: chsd wnr fr 8th: rdn after 3 out: plugged on same pce: lost 2nd run-in* **4/5**[1]
63-0 **4** *6* **Betterware Boy**[33] 6-12-0 (t) MissPGundry 87
(Mrs Susan Smith) *mid-div: chsd ldrs 7th: rdn in 3rd after 4 out: one pce fr next* **14/1**
P/ **5** *2½* **Magnemite (IRE)**[13] 10-12-0 MrJSnowden 85
(Miss Julie Pocock) *chsd ldrs: rdn after 4 out: sn one pce* **25/1**
/05- **6** *8* **Vin Du Pays**[13] 6-11-11 MissAGoschen(3) 77
(Mrs F M Vigar) *bhd: hdwy into midfield 6th: wknd after 11th* **16/1**
6-3 **7** *1½* **Horizon Hill (USA)**[13] 6-11-7 MrWBiddick(7) 75
(T W Boon) *mid-div tl wknd 12th* **20/1**
0/PU **8** *15* **Gudlage (USA)**[5] 5020 10-11-7 (t) MissVShaw(7) 60
(Mrs P J Shaw) *mstke 8th: a bhd* **20/1**
0-U **9** *5* **Zesta Fiesta**[10] 4946 6-11-11 MrDEdwards(3) 55
(A R Finch) *a bhd: t.o fr 10th* **25/1**
U5-3 **P** **Kyalami (FR)**[20] 8-11-7 MrPMason(7) —
(B Tulloch) *chsd wnr: blnd 6th: rdn after 12th: sn wknd: t.o and p.u bef 2 out* **13/2**[3]
P/P- **P** **Traditional (IRE)**[13] 10-11-11 (tp) MissCTizzard(3) —
(A J Tizzard) *mid-div: lost pl 8th: bhd thereafter: t.o and p.u bef 2 out* **5/1**[2]

5m 16.9s (-5.80) **Going Correction** -0.15s/f (Good) **11** Ran SP% **121.2**
Speed ratings: **104,102,101,99,98 95,94,89,87,—** — CSF £765.81 TOTE £44.10: £4.00, £8.60, £1.20; EX 355.90.
Owner 18 Red Lions Partnership **Bred** Bernard And Thomas Murphy **Trained** Tiverton, Devon

FOCUS
A decent hunter chase for the time of year, with the winner setting a good pace and the form has been rated positively.

NOTEBOOK
River Dante(IRE) setting a solid pace, soon had the field strung out, and just kept on galloping. It was a much-improved effort, but there is no obvious reason why similar tactics under the same sort of conditions should not see him reproduce it. *(op 40-1 tchd 50-1)*
Derosa, making his hunter chase debut, ran a race full of promise but had given himself too much to do. A winner of two point-to-points, he would be one to consider in similar company next time, especially over a longer trip.
Highway Oak sat behind the winner, with his rider apparently unconcerned at the six lengths deficit developing five from home, and when it came to the crunch there was little in the locker. He has done really well, but has been very busy of late. *(op 4-6)*
Betterware Boy, a recent winner over two and a half miles between the flags, travelled smoothly and ultimately ran well enough to suggest he can continue to feature in hunter chases following this encouraging first attempt. *(op 16-1)*
Magnemite(IRE) is very effective in point-to-points, and this was a much better attempt at hunter chasing than when pulled up on his only previous effort. *(tchd 33-1)*
Vin Du Pays's attempt to get into a position did not come to much, but he is still young, and past form on the Flat and in point-to-points suggests there might be some improvement. *(op 10-1)*
Traditional(IRE), given a patient ride, was below his best. Formerly inconsistent in hunter chases, he has been doing well in point-to-points of late and has the ability to do better under Rules if he can make the transformation. *(op 6-1 tchd 13-2)*
Kyalami(FR) ran well for a long way, and is capable of lasting longer when at his best. *(op 6-1 tchd 13-2)*

5117 COMEHORSERACING.COM STANDARD NATIONAL HUNT FLAT RACE (CONDITIONAL JOCKEYS' AND AMATEUR RIDERS' RACE) 2m 1f
7:55 (7:56) (Class 6) 4-6-Y-0 **£1,713** (£499; £249)

Form RPR
00 **1** **Swift Half (IRE)**[73] 3911 4-10-0 WayneKavanagh(7) 87
(J W Mullins) *in tch: rdn to ld over 2f out: kpt on gamely fnl f: all out* **9/1**
52 **2** *½* **Gaelic Gift (IRE)**[32] 4654 4-9-9 MrTJO'Brien(5) 79
(J G Cann) *mid-div: hdwy over 5f out: rdn to chal over 1f out: kpt on* **1/1**[1]
3 **3** *1¼* **Vintage Fabric (USA)**[30] 4667 4-10-0 MrDBurton(7) 85
(N J Hawke) *mid-div: gd hdwy over 4f out: rdn 2f out: kpt on* **11/2**[2]
566 **4** *6* **Devonia Plains (IRE)**[29] 4680 4-9-11 AngharadFrieze(10) 79
(Mrs P N Dutfield) *prom: ev ch 3f out: sn hung lft: kpt on same pce* **7/1**[3]
5 *½* **Can't Wack It**[33] 6-10-5 MrJBarnes(7) 84
(R H Alner) *t.k.h toward rr: outpcd 4f out: styd on strly fnl 2f: nvr trbld ldrs* **11/1**
00 **6** *½* **Knapp Bridge Boy**[116] 3216 6-10-7 LiamTreadwell(5) 83
(J R Payne) *led: rdn 4f out: hdd over 2f out: wknd 1f out* **80/1**
00 **7** *5* **King's Silver (IRE)**[116] 3216 5-10-7 DerekLaverty(5) 78
(N I M Rossiter) *in tch: rdn 5f out: hung lft 2f out: one pce after* **25/1**
00- **8** *20* **Tall Paul**[597] 1395 6-10-11 ow6 MrDEdwards(7) 64
(L Corcoran) *a towards rr* **16/1**
0 **9** *1* **Pats Last**[114] 3244 4-10-0 KeiranBurke(7) 52
(P R Rodford) *a towards rr* **33/1**
10 *18* **Dotsnew Dawn** 5-10-2 TomMalone(3) 32
(N E Berry) *a bhd: t.o fnl 3f* **16/1**

4m 4.90s (-0.40) **Going Correction** -0.15s/f (Good)
WFA 4 from 5yo 5lb 5 from 6yo 3lb **10** Ran SP% **116.0**
Speed ratings: **94,93,93,90,90 89,87,78,77,69** CSF £18.07 TOTE £11.50: £1.90, £1.10, £2.20; EX 22.10 Place 6 £39.60, Place 5 £32.21 .
Owner Ian F Sandell **Bred** Pat Beirne **Trained** Wilsford-Cum-Lake, Wilts

FOCUS
A modest bumper, with a pedestrian pace to halfway, and although the form looks sound enough it does not amount to much.

NOTEBOOK
Swift Half(IRE), scoring at the third time of asking, gamely held off a final furlong challenge from the hot favourite. *(op 10-1 tchd 11-1)*
Gaelic Gift(IRE), under a patient ride, was slightly caught out but a sudden lifting of the tempo at halfway, giving her eight lengths to make up in the final mile. She gradually got there, without quite getting up, and can win a similar contest. *(op 4-5)*
Vintage Fabric(USA) again showing plenty of ability at this level, stayed near the centre in the home straight, while the first two home came wide. He travelled stylishly for a long way, and can win in the coming months. *(tchd 6-1)*
Devonia Plains(IRE), tackling faster ground than before, again showed some ability without sparkling where it mattered. A switched to hurdles is surely imminent. *(op 9-1)*
Can't Wack It, apparently a promising point-to-pointer who had been let down by his jumping in two attempts, is one to keep an eye on for signs of improvement. *(op 9-1)*
Knapp Bridge Boy took them along but folded quickly in the closing stages. A switch to hurdling might help. *(op 50-1 tchd 100-1)*
T/Plt: £61.60 to a £1 stake. Pool: £35,109.00. 415.80 winning tickets. T/Qpdt: £20.10 to a £1 stake. Pool: £2,961.30. 108.80 winning tickets. TM

5091 PERTH (R-H)
Friday, April 28

OFFICIAL GOING: Good to firm (good in places on chase course)
Wind: Almost nil

5118 SCOT ADS "NATIONAL HUNT" MAIDEN HURDLE (8 hdls) 2m 110y
2:00 (2:04) (Class 4) 4-Y-0+ **£5,204** (£1,528; £764; £381)

Form RPR
3260 **1** **Lethem Air**[2] 5066 8-11-0 102 (b[1]) DougieCostello(3) 88+
(T Butt) *led: rdn bef 2 out: kpt on wl run in* **7/1**[2]
P0 **2** *2* **It's A Roofer (IRE)**[40] 4527 6-11-3 RichardMcGrath 86
(Mrs K Walton) *hld up: hdwy 3 out: shkn up to chse wnr run in: nvr nrr* **66/1**
0026 **3** *1¾* **Persian Native (IRE)**[69] 3983 6-10-10 TomMessenger(7) 84
(C C Bealby) *trckd ldrs: effrt bef 2 out: one pce run in* **16/1**
-26F **4** *nk* **Divex (IRE)**[40] 4532 5-11-3 RussGarritty 84
(M D Hammond) *hld up: hdwy u.p 3 out: one pce fr next* **14/1**
6400 **5** *7* **Rothbury**[40] 4532 6-10-12 TJDreaper(5) 77
(J I A Charlton) *hld up: effrt bef 3 out: no imp bef next* **9/1**[3]
06 **6** *½* **Saddlers' Son (IRE)**[23] 4732 5-11-0 TJPhelan(3) 76
(Mrs H Dalton) *midfield: effrt bef 2 out: sn outpcd* **25/1**
033F **7** *3½* **Scarlet Cloak (USA)**[49] 4342 5-11-3 KeithMercer 73
(Mrs L B Normile) *hld up: effrt 3 out: nvr rchd ldrs* **10/1**
0402 **8** *7* **Silver Dollars (FR)**[51] 4301 5-10-12 115 BrianHughes(5) 66
(J Howard Johnson) *keen: chsd ldrs: drvn and wknd bef 2 out* **11/10**[1]

001F **9** *1 ½* **Topwell**[105] [3374] 5-11-3 .... AlanDempsey 64
(R C Guest) *hld up: rdn along bef 3 out: sn btn* **9/1**[3]

43 **10** *dist* **Beautiful Night (FR)**[19] [4795] 4-10-5 96.......... NeilMulholland —
(M D Hammond) *chsd ldrs: hit 3rd: outpcd whn blnd bdly 2 out: eased* **9/1**[3]

11 *dist* **Smooth Attraction**[11] 5-11-3 .... KennyJohnson —
(S G Waugh) *uns rdr and loose bef s: prom tl wknd after 3rd: t.o* **100/1**

0-00 **U** **Barons Knight**[105] [3373] 5-10-10 .... BenOrde-Powlett(7) —
(M A Barnes) *uns rdr 1st* **100/1**

3m 58.1s (-2.50) **Going Correction** -0.30s/f (Good)
WFA 4 from 5yo+ 5lb **12** Ran SP% **119.1**
Speed ratings: **93,92,91,91,87 87,85,82,81,— —,—** CSF £371.12 TOTE £10.40: £2.60, £5.60, £3.50; EX 1228.70.
Owner Tim Butt **Bred** R S A Urquhart **Trained** Jedburgh, Borders

FOCUS
A race lacking strength and, with the favourite disappointing, this race took very little winning. It is rated through the sixth and is not an event to be confident about.

NOTEBOOK
Lethem Air, turned out quickly and tried in blinkers after a disappointing run in handicap company earlier in the week, won a very modest event in workmanlike fashion but he is an exposed performer who will find things tougher back in handicaps. *(op 15-2 tchd 8-1)*
It's A Roofer(IRE) turned in his best effort to date without being at all knocked about on this first run on fast ground and, although this form is modest, left the impression that he would do better in ordinary handicap company. *Official explanation: jockey said, regarding the running and riding, his orders were to drop gelding in and get it to settle as it had been very keen in previous races, adding that gelding was flat out from the second last and he switched right-handed approaching the last flight to keep it away from the crowd noise and give it more room; he then gave it a couple of flicks after the last to keep it going to the line (op 100-1)*
Persian Native(IRE), who showed ability in bumpers, ran creditably in this modest event on this hurdle debut and left the impression that the step up to two and a half miles and ordinary handicap company would suit in due course. *(op 33-1)*
Divex(IRE) seems best on a sound surface and turned in his best effort yet over hurdles. He is another that may appreciate the step up to two and a half miles and into handicap company. *(op 16-1)*
Rothbury was not totally disgraced and, although he is likely to continue to look vulnerable in this type of event, may do better in time and over further. *(op 10-1)*
Saddlers' Son(IRE), easy to back on all his three starts, has not shown enough in two outings over hurdles to suggest he is of interest in similar company in the short term future, but may not be one to write off yet. *(op 20-1)*
Scarlet Cloak(USA) *Official explanation: jockey said gelding spread its right fore plate (op 11-1)*
Silver Dollars(FR) looked the clear pick on official ratings and on his improved Catterick run last time but he proved a big disappointment on this much quicker ground. His stable has endured a very patchy time this year but he remains capable of winning a similar event on easier ground. *(op 5-4 tchd 11-8)*

5119 TULLIBARDINE DISTILLERY NOVICES' H'CAP CHASE (15 fncs) 2m 4f 110y
2:30 (2:31) (Class 3) (0-115,115) 5-Y-O+ **£7,807** (£2,292; £1,146; £572)

Form RPR

1301 **1** **Clouding Over**[44] [4454] 6-11-8 **106**.......... RichardMcGrath 116+
(K G Reveley) *hld up: hmpd by faller 7th: hdwy bef 4 out: led bef 2 out: rdn and r.o run in* **7/2**[2]

1231 **2** *1* **King Barry (FR)**[7] [4981] 7-11-12 **115** 7ex.......... TJDreaper(5) 122+
(Miss P Robson) *j.lft 1st: in tch: effrt and ev ch 4 out: hung lft bnd bef next: sn outpcd: kpt on fr last: nt rch wnr* **11/8**[1]

2P40 **3** *3 ½* **Not A Trace (IRE)**[13] [4844] 7-10-5 **89**..........(v) MarkBradburne 93+
(Mrs S C Bradburne) *chsd ldrs: effrt 4 out: blnd and outpcd next: kpt on fr last* **8/1**[3]

64 **4** *3* **Neptune Joly (FR)**[48] [4377] 5-11-9 **111**.......... KeithMercer 107
(Ferdy Murphy) *led 3rd tl hdd bef 2 out: sn no ex* **12/1**

5PP6 **5** *18* **Field Roller (IRE)**[7] [4981] 6-11-7 **105**.......... WilsonRenwick 87
(P Monteith) *hld up: rdn 4 out: wknd bef next* **25/1**

462P **6** *17* **Mounthooley**[145] [2654] 10-10-0 **84** oh10.......... PaddyAspell 49
(B Mactaggart) *nt fluent: led to 3rd: cl up tl wknd fr 10th* **25/1**

6064 **7** *10* **Uptown Lad (IRE)**[13] [4840] 7-10-13 **97**..........(t) KennyJohnson 52
(R Johnson) *keen: hld up: hdwy and prom 10th: wknd after next* **16/1**

4P53 **F** **Italiano**[77] [3844] 7-11-5 **103**.......... AnthonyRoss —
(P Beaumont) *chsd ldrs: fell 7th* **14/1**

3U3P **F** **Cyborg De Sou (FR)**[36] [4586] 8-11-12 **110**.......... AlanDempsey 113
(G A Harker) *hld up: hdwy 4 out: rdn next: disputing 4th and no imp whn fell last* **14/1**

0034 **P** **Ambition Royal (FR)**[13] [4844] 6-10-9 **93**..........(p) PeterBuchanan —
(Miss Lucinda V Russell) *prom tl lost pl 1/2-way: sn struggling: t.o whn p.u bef 3 out* **11/1**

5m 8.20s (-7.10) **Going Correction** -0.10s/f (Good)
WFA 5 from 6yo+ 4lb **10** Ran SP% **118.4**
Speed ratings: **109,108,107,106,99 92,89,—,—,—** CSF £9.28 CT £33.98 TOTE £3.40: £1.60, £1.40, £2.00; EX 7.90.
Owner W D Hockenhull **Bred** Shade Oak Stud **Trained** Lingdale, Redcar & Cleveland

FOCUS
A decent gallop and the in-form types filled the first two placings. The form looks reasonable rated through the runner-up.

NOTEBOOK
Clouding Over ◆, a progressive sort, notched her fourth win from her last six starts under her ideal conditions and left the impression that she was value for more than the winning margin. She continues to go in the right direction and is almost certainly capable of better.
King Barry(FR) ◆ lost nothing in defeat under a penalty for his Ayr win, especially as he left the impression that this right-handed course did not play to his strengths. Two and a half miles on decent ground are his requirements and he is very much the type to win more races. *(tchd 7-4 in places)*
Not A Trace(IRE) is not the most consistent and has yet to win under Rules, but ran creditably and left the impression that the return to three miles would be in his favour. *(op 9-1)*
Neptune Joly(FR), the winner of a non-thoroughbred race in the French provinces, ran creditably up to two and a half miles on his handicap debut and showed enough to suggest a small race can be found this summer. *(op 9-1)*
Field Roller(IRE) again completed but again did not show enough to suggest he is one to be interested in for the near future.

5120 STEADFAST SCOTLAND NOVICES' H'CAP HURDLE (10 hdls) 2m 4f 110y
3:05 (3:05) (Class 3) (0-115,112) 4-Y-O+ **£6,506** (£1,910; £955; £477)

Form RPR

555P **1** **Scotmail Too (IRE)**[71] [3943] 5-10-3 **94**.......... BrianHughes(5) 100+
(J Howard Johnson) *chsd clr ldr: effrt bef 2 out: hung rt and led last: styd on wl* **14/1**

11U1 **2** *¾* **Bohemian Spirit (IRE)**[36] [4585] 8-11-0 **107**.......... MissRDavidson(7) 113+
(N G Richards) *keen: led and clr: rdn bef 2 out: hdd last: kpt on: hld towards fin* **11/10**[1]

0001 **3** *15* **Acceleration (IRE)**[25] [4723] 6-10-3 **89**..........(t) PaddyAspell 79
(R Allan) *prom: effrt 3 out: sn one pce* **15/2**[3]

2243 **4** *3* **Cloudless Dawn**[40] [4530] 6-11-12 **112**.......... RussGarritty 99
(P Beaumont) *hld up: hdwy and prom 1/2-way: rdn and no ex after 3 out* **15/2**[3]

3P60 **5** *12* **Bonchester Bridge**[34] [4619] 5-10-8 **94**.......... MarcusFoley 69
(N J Henderson) *prom: outpcd 4 out: n.d after* **6/1**[2]

4P00 **6** *shd* **King's Envoy (USA)**[18] [4584] 7-9-7 **86** oh6.......... PatrickMcDonald(7) 61
(Mrs J C McGregor) *hld up: rdn bef 4 out: nvr on terms* **40/1**

05P0 **7** *9* **King's Protector**[93] [3561] 6-10-11 **97**.......... NeilMulholland 63
(M D Hammond) *hld up: rdn 4 out: nvr on terms* **33/1**

F004 **8** *9* **Scarrabus (IRE)**[2] [4302] 5-9-10 **87**.......... DeclanMcGann(5) 44
(A Crook) *in tch: rdn 4 out: wknd bef next* **25/1**

020P **9** *8* **Timbuktu**[49] [4344] 5-10-2 **88**..........(p) RichardMcGrath 37
(B Storey) *hld up: rdn bef 4 out: sn btn* **25/1**

600 **10** *6* **Mr Albanello (ARG)**[140] [2749] 7-10-0 **86** oh2.......... KeithMercer 29
(Ferdy Murphy) *midfield: struggling 4 out: sn btn* **16/1**

0005 **F** **Easby Mandarin**[40] [4532] 5-10-7 **100**.......... PhilKinsella(7) —
(C W Thornton) *hld up: fell 4th* **16/1**

PP0 **P** **Balasari (IRE)**[11] [4922] 6-11-0 **100**.......... WilsonRenwick —
(M D Hammond) *bhd: hmpd 4th: sn btn: t.o whn p.u bef 3 out* **66/1**

3P32 **P** **Bromley Abbey**[36] [4584] 8-9-11 **90**..........(p) TomMessenger(7) —
(Miss S E Forster) *hld up: struggling 1/2-way: t.o whn p.u bef 2 out* **14/1**

4m 56.9s (-11.30) **Going Correction** -0.30s/f (Good) **13** Ran SP% **125.1**
Speed ratings: **109,108,103,101,97 97,93,90,87,85 —,—,—** CSF £31.01 CT £143.42 TOTE £17.20: £3.90, £1.40, £2.10; EX 80.80.
Owner Gordon Brown/bert Watson **Bred** James A Slattery **Trained** Billy Row, Co Durham

FOCUS
An ordinary novices' handicap in which the pace seemed sound throughout. The winner and second pulled clear in the last half mile and the race could rate higher.

NOTEBOOK
Scotmail Too(IRE), having his first start after a short break, wandered off a true line under pressure but showed the right attitude to notch his first win over hurdles. He should stay three miles and may be capable of better. *(op 12-1)*
Bohemian Spirit(IRE), 10lb higher than his Ayr win, ran at least as well, especially as he failed to settle in front and kept trying once headed. He finished clear of the remainder and appeals as the type to win more races on a sound surface. *(op 6-4)*
Acceleration(IRE) is not the most reliable but ran creditably on this sounder surface upped 7lb in the weights for his recent Kelso victory. He remains one to tread carefully with, though. *(op 9-1)*
Cloudless Dawn, returning after a short break, was not at her best on this handicap debut and may have to come down in the weights if she is to add to her Doncaster good-ground win in November. *(op 8-1)*
Bonchester Bridge down in grade for this second run in handicaps, was well beaten on this first start on fast ground and, although too early to be writing her off yet, especially given her connections, remains one to be wary of at shortish odds in the near future. *(op 11-2)*
King's Envoy(USA), returned to hurdles, is an inconsistent hurdler who was again well beaten in this sphere and is of little short term interest. *(op 33-1 tchd 50-1)*
Bromley Abbey *Official explanation: jockey said mare was never travelling (tchd 16-1)*

5121 GALA CASINO DUNDEE NOVICES' CHASE (12 fncs) 2m
3:40 (3:40) (Class 3) 5-Y-O+ **£6,506** (£1,910; £955; £477)

Form RPR

1105 **1** **Green Tango**[20] [4774] 7-11-8 143.......... MarkBradburne 133+
(H D Daly) *in tch: hdwy bef 4 out: rdn and led 2 out: in command whn lft 6l clr last: kpt on* **8/13**[1]

1F10 **2** *2* **Coat Of Honour (USA)**[45] [4431] 6-11-4 .... PeterBuchanan 123
(J Howard Johnson) *chsd ldrs: rdn and outpcd bef 3 out: 6l down and no imp whn lft 2nd last: hung lft u.p: kpt on* **10/3**[2]

/20- **3** *15* **The Biker (IRE)**[502] [2788] 9-10-2 107.......... DavidDaSilva(10) 102
(P Monteith) *bhd: rdn 1/2-way: kpt on fr 3 out: lft remote 3rd last: no imp* **20/1**

3142 **4** *12* **Persian Point**[7] [4981] 10-11-1 91.......... MrCStorey(3) 98+
(Miss S E Forster) *in tch tl wknd after 7th* **25/1**

36-P **5** *19* **Magic Box**[131] [2902] 8-10-7 72..........(t) DeclanMcGann(5) 71
(A M Crow) *chsd ldrs tl wknd appr 2 out* **66/1**

00P **6** *1* **Mr Attitude**[49] [4342] 6-10-7 .... MichaelMcAlister(5) 70
(W S Coltherd) *in tch tl wknd fr 7th* **100/1**

36PP **7** *dist* **Delaware Trail**[13] [4841] 7-10-12 .... KennyJohnson —
(R Johnson) *plld hrd: hld up: mstke 2nd: struggling fr 1/2-way* **200/1**

00P0 **P** **Firion King (IRE)**[13] [4840] 6-10-12 .... DavidO'Meara —
(W S Coltherd) *bhd: struggling 1/2-way: t.o whn p.u bef 4 out* **200/1**

133P **F** **Portavadie**[42] [4472] 7-11-3 127.......... TJDreaper(5) 129
(J M Jefferson) *led: hdd and rdn whn blnd 2 out: 2l down and hld whn fell last* **6/1**[3]

3m 57.3s (-5.50) **Going Correction** -0.10s/f (Good) **9** Ran SP% **111.4**
Speed ratings: **109,108,100,94,85 84,—,—,—** CSF £2.79 TOTE £1.60: £1.10, £1.20, £3.40; EX 3.30.
Owner Mrs Strachan,Gabb,Lady Barlow & Harford **Bred** Southill Stud **Trained** Stanton Lacy, Shropshire

FOCUS
A mixed bag and the winner did not have to improve to notch his third win over fences. The runner-up, fourth and faller were close to their marks and the form makes sense.

NOTEBOOK
Green Tango, a capable sort with a decent strike-rate under Rules, did not have to improve to win his third race over fences. He may well be capable of better next season but will have to be to win a competitive race from his current mark of 143. *(tchd 8-15 in places)*
Coat Of Honour(USA), out of his depth in the Arkle last month, ran creditably returned to this much more realistic level. However, he did not look the easiest of rides and, although worth a try over further, will have to improve next term to win a competitive handicap from a mark somewhere in the mid 120s. *(tchd 7-2)*
The Biker(IRE) was not disgraced in the face of a stiff task on only this third run for his stable and his first over fences. While his record has been patchy, he is the type that his stable does well with and is one to keep an eye on at a more realistic level. *(op 33-1)*
Persian Point was well beaten in the face of a stiff task and he will be seen to better effect back in modest handicap company. *(tchd 20-1 and 33-1)*
Magic Box faced a very tough task on these terms and was predictably outclassed.
Portavadie remains capable of better over fences but, while in the process of running to his best when coming to grief, will have to brush up his fencing if he is to progress in this sphere. *(tchd 11-2 and 7-1)*

The Form Book, Raceform Ltd, Compton, RG20 6NL

5122 PRESS & JOURNAL HIGHLAND NATIONAL (A H'CAP CHASE) (22 fncs 1 omitted) 3m 7f
4:15 (4:16) (Class 4) (0-110,110) 5-Y-0+
£15,657 (£4,625; £2,312; £1,157; £577; £290)

Form RPR
5/U2 **1** **Noble Buck (IRE)**[23] 4737 10-10-4 88 .... MarkBradburne 99+
(Mrs L J Young) *chsd ldrs: hit 18th: led 4 out: r.o strly fr next* **5/1**[2]
4210 **2** *2 ½* **Primitive Way**[4] 5036 14-10-2 89 .... (v) DougieCostello(3) 95
(Miss S E Forster) *hld up midfield: effrt bef 4 out: chsd wnr 2 out: kpt on run in* **14/1**
0031 **3** *3* **Moustique De L'Isle (FR)**[31] 4658 6-10-13 104 .....(b) TomMessenger(7) 109+
(C C Bealby) *cl up: lft in ld 10th: hdd 4 out: kpt on same pce fr next* **8/1**
U04P **4** *shd* **Ta Ta For Now**[13] 4845 9-10-0 84 oh8 .... KeithMercer 87
(Mrs S C Bradburne) *rn in snatches: effrt u.p bef 4 out: no imp fr next* **9/1**
-043 **5** *11* **Metal Detector (IRE)**[23] 4737 9-11-2 105 .... (p) MarkNicolls(5) 98+
(K C Bailey) *chsd ldrs: ev ch 4 out: wknd fr next* **8/1**
1P30 **6** *dist* **Sconced (USA)**[7] 4989 11-9-7 87 .... (b) JohnFlavin(10) —
(R C Guest) *sn wl bhd: no ch fnl circ* **16/1**
1414 **P** **Snowy (IRE)**[19] 4788 8-11-7 110 .... TJDreaper(5) —
(J I A Charlton) *in tch tl outpcd 11th: t.o whn p.u bef 4 out* **3/1**[1]
1PPP **U** **Interdit (FR)**[33] 4636 10-11-12 110 .... (v[1]) WilsonRenwick —
(Mrs B K Thomson) *led 3rd: blnd and uns rdr 10th* **12/1**
/P-P **P** **Mystic Lord (IRE)**[173] 2066 9-11-4 102 .... (tp) PeterBuchanan —
(Miss Lucinda V Russell) *bhd: t.o whn p.u after 17th* **25/1**
UPPU **P** **Pessimistic Dick**[72] 3930 13-9-7 84 oh9 .... PhilKinsella(7) —
(Mrs J C McGregor) *in tch tl wknd 16th: t.o whn p.u bef 18th* **25/1**
P302 **P** **Jexel (FR)**[36] 4587 9-10-11 95 .... DavidO'Meara —
(B Storey) *hld up: blnd 2nd: hdwy and prom bef 13th: wknd 18th: p.u bef next* **6/1**[3]
366P **P** **Arctic Lagoon (IRE)**[11] 4921 7-10-0 84 oh10 .... (t) PaddyAspell —
(Mrs S C Bradburne) *j.lft thrght: prom tl wknd 16th: t.o whn p.u bef 2 out* **16/1**

7m 57.0s (-25.10) **Going Correction** -0.10s/f (Good) **12** Ran SP% **122.0**
Speed ratings: **113,112,111,111,108** —,—,—,—,— —,— CSF £73.66 CT £557.03 TOTE £6.70: £1.70, £4.20, £2.90; EX 107.00.
Owner Mrs Karen Cox **Bred** Mrs M M Kelly **Trained** Bridgwater, Somerset

FOCUS
A modest race but a decent gallop and this bare form should prove reliable with the placed horses close to their marks.

NOTEBOOK
Noble Buck(IRE), having only his third run for this yard, fully confirmed previous promise and showed the right attitude to win his first race since 2002. His jumping was sound in the main, he relished the conditions and is the type to win again next term when the emphasis is on stamina. *(op 11-2)*
Primitive Way fared much better than at Hexham earlier in the week upped to this trip for the first time and he is capable of winning another small race on this evidence in the next couple of months. *(op 12-1)*
Moustique De L'Isle(FR), a stout stayer, ran up to his best returned to fences after a short break but, while this ground posed no problems, all his wins have been in very testing ground and he will be of more interest when conditions change.
Ta Ta For Now was beaten a similar distance as in this race last year but again ran a typical race in that he was rarely travelling well but just kept plugging on. There is no guarantee that this will be reproduced next time. *(op 12-1)*
Metal Detector(IRE) finished further behind the winner than he had done at Hereford on his previous start and left the impression that he did not last home over this longer trip. The return to three miles will suit but the two-year losing run is the worry. *(op 7-1)*
Sconced(USA) has been below form since his Fakenham win in January and turned in another poor display. His stable is in good form but he is one to tread carefully with. *(op 14-1)*
Snowy(IRE) whose four career wins have been at Kelso, was beaten before stamina became an issue upped to this trip for the first time. This may have come too quickly after a recent Kelso run following a four-month break and he will be of more interest back at that track.*Official explanation: trainer had no explanation for the poor form shown (op 4-1)*

5123 ATTHERACES.COM CONDITIONAL JOCKEYS' H'CAP HURDLE (20 hdls) 3m 3f
4:45 (4:47) (Class 3) (0-125,110) 4-Y-0+ £7,807 (£2,292; £1,146; £572)

Form RPR
6561 **1** **Noir Et Vert (FR)**[2] 5064 5-10-11 98 7ex .... KeithMercer(3) 106+
(Ferdy Murphy) *trckd ldrs: led bef 4 out: clr next: kpt on wl run in* **11/4**[1]
-303 **2** *3 ½* **Forever Eyesofblue**[72] 3928 9-10-12 99 .... PhilKinsella(3) 101
(A Parker) *hld up: hdwy to chse wnr bef 3 out: rdn and hung lft bef next: rallied after last: sn one pce* **6/1**[2]
1216 **3** *dist* **Before Dark (IRE)**[23] 4727 8-11-12 110 .... DougieCostello 68
(Mrs H Dalton) *in tch: outpcd 4 out: sn no imp (btn 48l)* **11/4**[1]
P3P0 **4** *hd* **Aberdare**[7] 4982 7-10-11 95 .... MichaelMcAlister 53
(J R Bewley) *in tch: outpcd 1/2-way: n.d after* **25/1**
4353 **5** *12* **No Picnic (IRE)**[19] 4788 8-11-9 110 .... TomMessenger(3) 56
(Mrs S C Bradburne) *chsd ldrs: outpcd and struggling 6th: n.d after* **16/1**
0006 **6** *8* **Altitude Dancer (IRE)**[31] 4658 6-10-6 90 .... DeclanMcGann —
(A Crook) *sn wl bhd: no ch fnl circ* **8/1**[3]
004F **7** *1 ½* **Valerun (IRE)**[2] 5068 10-9-12 90 .... (p) JohnFlavin(8) —
(R C Guest) *led to 9th: sn wknd* **16/1**
3-00 **8** *13* **Solway Minstrel**[2] 5068 9-11-1 99 .... GaryBerridge —
(Miss L Harrison) *chsd ldrs tl wknd fr 4 out* **12/1**
2535 **P** **Shady Baron (IRE)**[80] 3792 7-10-12 99 .... PaddyAspell(3) —
(J Wade) *bhd: struggling 6th: t.o whn p.u bef last* **12/1**
63P0 **P** **Orki Des Aigles (FR)**[11] 4907 4-9-12 95 .... PatrickMcDonald(6) —
(Ferdy Murphy) *cl up: led briefly 9th: wknd bef 3 out: plld up bef last* **20/1**

6m 37.2s (-17.80) **Going Correction** -0.30s/f (Good)
WFA 4 from 5yo+ 7lb **10** Ran SP% **114.5**
Speed ratings: **109,107**,—,—,— —,—,—,—,— CSF £19.63 CT £48.49 TOTE £3.20: £1.70, £1.90, £1.90; EX 18.80.
Owner D F O'Rourke **Bred** Scea La Chaussee **Trained** West Witton, N Yorks

FOCUS
A fair gallop and an improved effort from the winner, who appeals as the type to score again over hurdles. The runner-up sets the standard and the race could rate higher.

NOTEBOOK
Noir Et Vert(FR) ◆ turned out after his course win two days earlier, was always travelling strongly and showed improved form to defy a 7lb penalty. Only lightly raced, he appeals strongly as the type to win more races on a sound surface over obstacles. *(op 2-1)*
Forever Eyesofblue, returned to hurdles after a short break, ran creditably on ground that looked plenty quick enough for his liking. He has not won for some time but looks capable of winning a similar event away from progressive sorts. *(tchd 11-2 in places)*
Before Dark(IRE), a dual winner in testing ground this term, was not at his best in these much quicker conditions but is only lightly raced and will be worth another chance next term back in more suitable ground conditions. *(op 3-1)*
Aberdare has been very disappointing since winning on soft ground at this meeting last year and did not do enough on ground plenty quick enough for him to suggest he will be returning to winning ways in the near future.
No Picnic(IRE), an inconsistent performer with a poor strike rate, offered no immediate promise on this return to hurdles. *(op 25-1)*
Altitude Dancer(IRE) was in good form at this time last year but has shown very little in seven starts for current connections and remains one to tread carefully with. *(tchd 9-1)*
Orki Des Aigles(FR) *Official explanation: jockey said gelding lost its action*

5124 EVENING EXPRESS STANDARD OPEN NATIONAL HUNT FLAT RACE 2m 110y
5:20 (5:20) (Class 6) 4-6-Y-0 £2,055 (£599; £299)

Form RPR
4 **1** **Wee Bertie (IRE)**[82] 3763 4-10-8 .... BrianHughes(5) 88+
(J Howard Johnson) *keen: chsd ldrs: led over 2f out: kpt on wl fnl f* **9/2**[2]
4 **2** *nk* **Campli (IRE)**[48] 4366 4-10-13 .... NeilMulholland 86
(M D Hammond) *pld hrd: hld up: hdwy to chal whn edgd lft over 1f out: kpt on: hld towards fin* **17/2**
3 *3 ½* **Rashartic (IRE)** 4-10-10 .... DougieCostello(3) 82
(Mrs H Dalton) *hld up midfield: effrt 3f out: kpt on same pce fr 2f out* **10/1**
40 **4** *2* **Amhairghin (IRE)**[13] 4854 6-11-4 .... AlanDempsey 85
(G A Harker) *hld up: hdwy 4f out: sn pushed along: kpt on fnl 2f: nrst fin* **8/1**
205 **5** *2* **Mister Jungle (FR)**[40] 4533 4-10-13 .... MarkBradburne 78
(Mrs S C Bradburne) *mde most to over 2f out: kpt on same pce* **8/1**
6 *1 ¾* **Rainbow Lord (IRE)**[404] 6-10-11 .... TomMessenger(7) 81
(C C Bealby) *hld up: drvn over 4f out: kpt on fnl 2f: nvr rchd ldrs* **20/1**
7 *2 ½* **Make A Mark (IRE)** 6-10-11 .... MissRDavidson(7) 79
(Mrs R L Elliot) *plld hrd: chsd ldrs tl rdn and outpcd fr 2f out* **7/1**[3]
8 *2* **Mrdeegeethegeegee (IRE)** 4-10-13 .... KeithMercer 72
(E W Tuer) *hld up: pushed along over 4f out: n.d* **7/2**[1]
0 **9** *2 ½* **Clovella**[98] 3490 5-10-4 .... PhilKinsella(7) 67
(R Allan) *hld up in tch: rdn over 3f out: wknd over 2f out* **100/1**
10 *1 ½* **Jendali Lad** 5-10-8 .... JohnFlavin(10) 73
(R C Guest) *hld up: rdn over 3f out: sn n.d* **20/1**
11 *17* **Cassius Dio (IRE)** 4-10-13 .... PaddyAspell 51
(J Wade) *trckd ldrs tl wknd over 2f out* **25/1**
12 *5* **Sister Lucy (IRE)** 5-10-11 .... PeterBuchanan 44
(B Storey) *prom tl wknd over 4f out* **22/1**
13 *4* **Political Dancer** 5-10-11 .... KennyJohnson 40
(J I A Charlton) *w ldr tl wknd fr 4f out* **14/1**
14 *30* **Jayenar** 5-10-11 .... DavidO'Meara 10
(W S Coltherd) *hld up: rdn 1/2-way: sn struggling* **25/1**
200 **U** **Ruby Joy**[51] 4304 4-10-1 .... TomGreenway(5) —
(Mrs H O Graham) *plld hrd and sddle slipped early: cl up tl wknd over 4f out: sn t.o: p.u 1f out* **25/1**

4m 0.50s (-0.30) **Going Correction** -0.30s/f (Good)
WFA 4 from 5yo+ 5lb **15** Ran SP% **127.8**
Speed ratings: **88,87,86,85,84 83,82,81,80,79 71,69,67,53**,— CSF £40.96 TOTE £4.50: £1.80, £2.30, £4.00; EX 30.70 Place 6 £53.69, Place 5 £5.40.
Owner Mrs Audrey Watson **Bred** Edward And Joseph McCormack **Trained** Billy Row, Co Durham

FOCUS
This looked an ordinary event and the steady pace renders this as a suspect form guide.

NOTEBOOK
Wee Bertie(IRE) was always well placed in a race run at a modest gallop and showed the right attitude to better the form of his bumper debut. He will be well suited by the step up to two and a half miles and is the type to win races over obstacles. *(op 6-1)*
Campli(IRE), having his first run on fast ground, more than confirmed debut promise (despite again edging to his left) and looks better than the bare form given he failed to settle and was held up in a steadily-run race. He looks sure to win a race or two. *(op 8-1 tchd 9-1)*
Rashartic(IRE), the first foal of an unraced dam, shaped with a bit of promise on this racecourse debut and left the impression that a much stiffer test of stamina would have been in his favour. He looks sure to win a race. *(op 8-1)*
Amhairghin(IRE) returned to form back on a sound surface and again left the impression that a decent test of stamina would suit when sent over hurdles. *(op 13-2)*
Mister Jungle(FR) had the run of a very messy race and was again not disgraced. He may be capable of winning a small event upped in trip when sent over obstacles next term. *(op 7-1)*
Rainbow Lord(IRE), placed in an Irish point when last seen over a year ago, was not disgraced on this bumper debut and first run for new connections. A considerably stiffer test of stamina will suit in due course. *(tchd 25-1)*
Mrdeegeethegeegee(IRE), a half-brother to several winners in the States, failed by a long chalk to justify market support on this racecourse debut. However, he is in good hands and must have been showing a fair bit at home so may well be worth another chance. *(op 7-1)*
Ruby Joy *Official explanation: jockey said saddle slipped*
T/Jkpt: Not won. T/Plt: £109.40 to a £1 stake. Pool: £51,477.45. 343.40 winning tickets. T/Qpdt: £4.70 to a £1 stake. Pool: £4,208.10. 662.25 winning tickets. RY

4373 SANDOWN (R-H)
Friday, April 28

OFFICIAL GOING: Good (good to firm in places)
Wind: Moderate, across Weather: Fine Other races under Rules of Flat Racing

5125 BETFRED MILLION HURDLE (8 hdls) 2m 110y
1:10 (1:10) (Class 2) 4-Y-0+
£31,315 (£9,250; £3,470; £3,470; £1,155; £580)

Form RPR
1221 **1** **Noble Request (FR)**[6] 5003 5-11-8 143 .... RichardJohnson 154+
(P J Hobbs) *hld up in last pair: pushed along and prog bef 2 out: led bef last: drvn and r.o wl* **2/1**[1]
3302 **2** *1 ½* **Faasel (IRE)**[6] 5003 5-11-4 154 .... (v) TonyDobbin 150+
(N G Richards) *hld up in tch: smooth prog bef 2 out to chal between last 2: w wnr last: rdn and fnd little flat: readily hld* **9/4**[2]
200P **3** *1* **Intersky Falcon**[20] 4775 9-11-4 155 .... (bt) MickFitzgerald 148
(Jonjo O'Neill) *led to 3rd: led again after 3 out: hrd pressed 2 out: hdd bef last: kpt on same pce flat* **11/1**
40F0 **3** *dht* **Penzance**[9] 4959 5-11-4 148 .... RobertThornton 149+
(A King) *cl up: rdn to chal and upsides sn after 2 out: nt qckn and n.m.r sn after: kpt on again flat* **15/2**[3]
1P50 **5** *8* **Arcalis**[6] 5003 6-11-10 158 .... BarryFenton 146
(J Howard Johnson) *racd wd: in tch: rdn and outpcd bef 2 out: struggling after: mstke last* **9/1**

-650 **6** ½ **Publican (IRE)**[11] 4927 6-11-8 .... TimmyMurphy 145+
(P A Fahy, Ire) *lw: cl up: mstkes 4th and 3 out and dropped to last pair: effrt again and cl up 2 out: sn wknd* **14/1**

3120 **7** 5 **Alph**[48] 4375 9-11-4 135 .... MatthewBatchelor 135+
(B R Johnson) *pressed ldr: led 3rd tl after 3 out: wknd u.p bef 2 out* **20/1**

1301 **8** 7 **Darrias (GER)**[9] 4959 5-11-7 135 ....(t) ChristianWilliams 130
(P F Nicholls) *lw: nt fluent: trckd ldrs: rdn and wknd bef 2 out* **14/1**

3m 46.8s (-22.10) **Going Correction** -0.925s/f (Hard) **8** Ran SP% **112.3**
Speed ratings: **115,114,113,113,110 109,107,104**WIN: £2.60. PL: £1.30, £1.50, Intersky Falcon £1.30, Penzance £1.00. CSF £6.63; EX 6.10.
Owner Mrs Karola Vann **Bred** P Chedeville And Antoinette Tamagni **Trained** Withycombe, Somerset

FOCUS
A decent enough event, despite the top two-milers having run at Punchestown earlier in the week, and it was run at a sound pace. The first four came clear, but the second, third and fourth have all been rated a bit below their best and Noble Request still needs to improve a stone or more to be regarded a realistic Champion Hurdle contender.

NOTEBOOK
Noble Request(FR) dug deep to get on top nearing the final flight, and confirmed his Ayr form with the runner-up, despite being on 15lb worse terms with that rival. He has gone from strength to strength since winning from a mark of 118 at Wincanton in February, and further progress looks most likely on this evidence, with time very much still on his side. A decent surface is key to him and he is due to be kept to hurdling next season in the hope he could develop into a Champion Hurdle contender. *(op 15-8 tchd 9-4)*

Faasel(IRE), 15lb better off with the winner for a five-length beating at Ayr six days previously, looked the most likely winner when making ground to challenge approaching the penultimate flight but, not for the first time in his career, he found little when asked to win his race and was ultimately well held at the finish. He is clearly talented, but really has developed into a tricky character this season, and it will be no surprise to see him sent over fences in the autumn. *(tchd 5-2)*

Intersky Falcon, best in at the weights according to official figures, only gave way to the front pair nearing the final flight and turned in his best effort for some time. He enjoyed this better ground and being allowed the chance to dominate, but he is going to continue to prove hard to place from his current rating. *(op 12-1)*

Penzance, dropping back in trip, posted a much more encouraging display and would have been a touch closer but for meeting trouble in between the last two flights. He has not lived up to expectations this season, but his engine is clearly still intact, and it is hoped that the switch to novice chasing next term will see him back in a better light. *(op 12-1)*

Arcalis turned in another lacklustre performance and really has been very disappointing since his impressive success in the Fighting Fifth at the start of the current campaign. *(op 8-1)*

Publican(IRE), back to winning ways at Fairyhouse 11 days previously, faced a stiff task at the weights yet never really gave himself much chance with a sloppy round of jumping. He retains his novice status as a chaser for next season and that is most likely where his greatest chance of further success lies. *(op 12-1)*

Darrias(GER), who practically bolted to the start, never looked happy at any stage and ran no sort *of race. He was later reported to have finished lame.Official explanation: jockey said gelding finished lame*

5126 BETFREDPOKER.COM H'CAP CHASE (17 fncs) 2m 4f 110y
2:20 (2:24) (Class 2) (0-145,138) 5-Y-0+
£12,526 (£3,700; £1,850; £926; £462; £232)

Form RPR

1P60 **1** **Full House (IRE)**[55] 4241 7-11-7 133 .... TomDoyle 152+
(P R Webber) *t.k.h: hld up in last: prog to trck ldr 8th: led bef 3 out: sn clr: easily* **11/4**[1]

2230 **2** 15 **Winsley**[35] 4605 8-10-4 116 .... LeightonAspell 117
(O Sherwood) *hld up: effrt to chse ldng pair 12th: in tch bef 3 out: sn wl outpcd: styd on flat to take 2nd nr fin* **10/3**[2]

3160 **3** 1¼ **Duke Of Buckingham (IRE)**[42] 4472 10-11-12 138........ MickFitzgerald 138
(P R Webber) *t.k.h: trckd ldr 4th: led 7th: hdd bef 3 out: no ch w wnr after* **9/2**

130F **4** ¾ **Tamango (FR)**[21] 4762 9-11-6 132 .... RichardJohnson 131
(P J Hobbs) *chsd ldr to 4th: in tch after: rdn 4 out: outpcd next: disp 2nd fr 2 out to flat: wknd* **7/2**[3]

U14 **5** 4 **East Lawyer (FR)**[69] 3992 7-10-2 119 .... LiamHeard(5) 114
(P F Nicholls) *lw: settled in tch: nt fluent 8th: struggling fr 12th: one pce and no imp after* **7/1**

42PP **6** *dist* **Spring Lover (FR)**[15] 4829 7-10-9 121 ....(b[1]) SamThomas —
(Miss Venetia Williams) *tended to jump lft: led to 7th: blnd next: struggling after: wknd after 14th: t.o: btn 53l* **14/1**

5m 2.50s (-18.30) **Going Correction** -0.475s/f (Good) **6** Ran SP% **109.3**
Speed ratings: **115,109,108,108,107** — CSF £11.88 TOTE £3.20: £1.70, £2.10; EX 12.50.
Owner The Chamberlain Addiscott Partnership **Bred** Schwindibode Ag **Trained** Mollington, Oxon

FOCUS
Not the strongest of fields for the money, but hard not to be impressed by Full House, who put up easily his best effort yet.

NOTEBOOK
Full House(IRE), despite refusing to settle under restraint through the early stages, ultimately slammed his rivals with a most convining success and is value for even further. Winner of the novice handicap on the same card last year, he showed a nice change of pace to establish a significant lead, and fluent leaps at each of the last two fences allowed him to draw even further clear. He clearly relished the return to genuine fast ground and this was a personal best by some way. There are attractive targets for him this summer at Market Rasen, Galway and Newton Abbot. *(op 9-4)*

Winsley, who has just a maiden chase win at Towcester to his name over fences, stayed on strongly after the last to take second, but his habit of finding at least one too good continues to be *a turn-off from a punting perspective. However, he was later reported to have finished lame.Official explanation: jockey said gelding was lame (op 4-1 tchd 9-2 in a place)*

Duke Of Buckingham(IRE) was dropping significantly in class, having contested the Grand Annual on his most recent start, and he was yet another for whom the fast ground allowed a return to form. He took it up at the seventh and held every chance, but was readily outpaced from the Pond fence and lost second on the run-in. *(tchd 4-1)*

Tamango(FR) was below his best, but it is quite possible he was still remembering his fall in the Topham at Aintree earlier in the month and it is reasonable to expect better next time. His stable continues to churn out the winners and he can probably add to his tally in the coming months. *(op 9-2)*

East Lawyer(FR) turned in an uninspiring run following a break. He was struggling badly as they began to turn out of the back straight and it is quite possible the ground was on the lively side for him. *(op 5-1)*

Spring Lover(FR) was weighted to confirm February's Ludlow form with Winsley and he was soon in a clear lead, the first-time blinkers certainly waking him up, but he had already been headed when blundering the eighth and was soon beaten. He may be capable of better back on a softer surface, but is clearly tricky.

5127 BETFRED MILLION NOVICES' H'CAP CHASE (17 fncs) 2m 4f 110y
3:30 (3:32) (Class 3) (0-130,123) 5-Y-0+**£12,699** (£3,873; £2,023; £1,099)

Form RPR

131P **1** **Harris Bay**[35] 4605 7-11-5 116 ....(t) TimmyMurphy 125+
(Miss H C Knight) *hld up: nt fluent 1st: prog to trck ldng pair 14th: cl 3rd and gng wl whn lft in ld 2 out: sn clr* **7/2**[3]

6421 **2** 12 **Lubinas (IRE)**[23] 4735 7-11-0 111 .... TomDoyle 110+
(F Jordan) *j.lft: led and sn clr: pressed 3 out: j. bdly lft 2 out and hdd: no ch w wnr after* **3/1**[2]

1PP **3** 1¼ **Thistlecraft (IRE)**[8] 4971 7-11-12 123 .... RobertThornton 119
(C C Bealby) *chsd ldrs: rdn 13th: outpcd bef 3 out: n.d after: lft 3rd 2 out* **20/1**

P240 **4** 6 **Kyper Disco (FR)**[71] 3940 8-10-5 102 .... AndrewTinkler 92
(N J Henderson) *in tch in rr: mstkes 3rd and 6th: struggling fr 12th: n.d bef 3 out* **12/1**

P1P4 **P** **Lord Rodney (IRE)**[20] 4778 7-11-6 117 .... TonyDobbin —
(P Beaumont) *nvr gng wl: lost tch 7th: t.o 10th: p.u bef 12th* **11/2**

6111 **F** **Mr Boo (IRE)**[12] 4870 7-11-12 123 5ex .... PhilipHide 132+
(G L Moore) *hld up: prog to trck ldr 10th: gng easily and poised to chal whn hmpd and fell 2 out* **11/4**[1]

0PF1 **P** **Saddlers Cloth (IRE)**[11] 4913 6-10-12 112 5ex .... PaulO'Neill(3) —
(J A Geake) *mstkes 1st and 2nd: chsd ldr tl mstke 10th: struggling fr 12th: t.o whn p.u bef 2 out* **9/1**

5m 7.50s (-13.30) **Going Correction** -0.475s/f (Good) **7** Ran SP% **111.7**
Speed ratings: **106,101,100,98,**— —,— CSF £14.20 TOTE £4.50: £2.20, £2.00; EX 13.50.
Owner Mrs G M Sturges & H Stephen Smith **Bred** R J Spencer **Trained** West Lockinge, Oxon

FOCUS
A modest handicap, and the form should be treated with a degree of caution, although it was run at a decent clip. Mr Boo has been rated as if dead-heating with the winner.

NOTEBOOK
Harris Bay ultimately ran out a decisive winner. A progressive chaser until pulling up at Newbury last time - he evidently has to go right handed - he put fears that he needs softer ground firmly to rest and his jumping was much more assured this time. The wind operation he underwent pre-season has allowed him to fulfill his potential and, despite being flattered by his winning margin, he probably has even more to offer now connections seem to have found the key to him. *(op 9-2)*

Lubinas(IRE) faced a much stiffer task here off a 10lb higher mark, but he was soon in a clear lead and put up a bold show until two out, where he caused Mr Boo to fall. He is tough and consistent, and versatile with regards to ground, but it would not surprise to see him returned to a left-handed track in future as his jumping got progressively more crooked as the race went on. *(op 7-2 tchd 4-1 in a place)*

Thistlecraft(IRE) has understandably struggled off marks of 125 and 123 since winning at weak race at Fakenham back in January, and he was expected to find this trip on the sharp side, which he did. He could do with some assistance from the Handicapper.

Kyper Disco(FR) has long been a frustrating horse and his jumping was simply not up to it. He has yet to win in 16 starts now and remains one to take on. *(op 14-1)*

Mr Boo(IRE), seeking a four-timer, was still travelling well when getting on the wrong side of Lubinas taking two out. He looked the more likely victor, and it remains to be seen how this affects his confidence. *(tchd 6-1)*

Lord Rodney(IRE) *Official explanation: jockey said gelding hung left (tchd 6-1)*

Saddlers Cloth(IRE) won a bad race very easily at Plumpton and didn't jump well enough in this much better race. *(tchd 6-1)*

5097 PUNCHESTOWN (R-H)
Friday, April 28

OFFICIAL GOING: Hurdle & chase courses - good; bank course - good to firm

5128a KILDARE HUNT CLUB CHASE 3m (Banks Course)
2:05 (2:05) 5-Y-0+ **£7,624** (£1,776; £783; £452)

RPR

1 **Wonderkid**[3] 5055 6-11-0 81 .... MrJWFarrelly(7) 108+
(A J Martin, Ire) *hld up in tch: 6th after 4 out: smooth hdwy into 3rd bef 2 out: 2nd and chal after 2 out: led bef last: kpt on wl u.p* **4/1**[1]

2 4 **Abram's Bridge (IRE)**[3] 5055 7-11-12 ....(p) MrJTMcNamara 109+
(E Bolger, Ire) *a.p: mstke 5 out: led after 3 out: strly pressed fr 2 out: hdd appr last: kpt on u.p: no ex cl home* **5/1**[2]

3 2 **Star Performance (IRE)**[47] 4401 11-11-12 100 ....(p) RMPower 107
(Oliver McKiernan, Ire) *trckd ldrs: 6th 1/2-way: impr into cl 3rd 4 out: 2nd and chal after next: 3rd and no imp bef last: kpt on* **12/1**

4 20 **Never Compromise (IRE)**[45] 4434 11-11-12 120 .... MsKWalsh(5) 92
(T M Walsh, Ire) *prom: 4th 1/2-way: 5th u.p bef 3 out: kpt on same pce* **4/1**[1]

5 9 **Andrewjames (IRE)**[82] 3776 12-11-10 88 .... MrJCash(7) 83
(Peter McCreery, Ire) *chsd ldrs: dropped to mid-div 1/2-way: hdwy 4 out: cl 4th and chal next: no ex bef 2 out* **25/1**

6 7 **Tenshookmen (IRE)**[5] 12-11-7 91 .... MrJJCodd 66
(W F Codd, Ire) *led: reminders 5 out: hdd u.p after 3 out: no ex whn mstke next* **20/1**

7 4 **Groomsport (IRE)**[3] 5055 8-11-0 80 ....(p) MrATDuff(7) 62
(Mrs Denise Foster, Ire) *prom: 3rd 1/2-way: 6th 4 out: no imp fr next* **25/1**

8 8 **Take The Lot (IRE)**[57] 4207 13-11-7 63 ....(t) JRBarry 54
(Anthony Moloney, Ire) *prom: 2nd early: 5th u.p 6 out: wknd fr 4 out* **66/1**

9 15 **Haut De Gamme (FR)**[20] 4777 11-12-3 .... DNRussell 49
(Ferdy Murphy) *hld up in tch: bad mstke 5 out: no ex bef 3 out: virtually p.u fr 2 out* **6/1**[3]

10 8 **Native Beat (IRE)**[9] 4967 11-11-10 106 .... MrPDuggan(7) 41
(J R H Fowler, Ire) *nvr a factor* **25/1**

11 4 **Castlerueanna (IRE)**[19] 14-11-0 .... MrBJToomey(7) 27
(G M O'Neill, Ire) *a bhd: trailing fr 5 out* **50/1**

F **Itsonlyapuppet (IRE)**[19] 7-11-7 .... RPMcNally —
(A J Martin, Ire) *fell 5th* **16/1**

P **Another Deployment (IRE)**[47] 7-11-7 .... NPMadden —
(M N O'Riordan, Ire) *bhd: p.u bef 5 out* **66/1**

F **Code Of Silence (IRE)**[54] 4264 6-11-7 104 .... AndrewJMcNamara —
(Thomas Gerard O'Leary, Ire) *hld up: fell 5th* **20/1**

P **Red Nell (IRE)**[47] 11-11-0 .... MrMCostello(7) —
(Mrs Helen Sheehy, Ire) *nvr a factor: lost irons 7th: p.u bef 5 out* **50/1**

6m 11.7s **Going Correction** -0.40s/f (Good) **19** Ran SP% **112.5**
Speed ratings: **106,104,104,97,94 92,90,88,83,80 79,—,—,—,—** CSF £19.27 TOTE £4.50: £1.80, £2.10, £2.40; DF 18.60.
Owner W A Moffett **Bred** Crandon Park Stud **Trained** Summerhill, Co. Meath
■ Stewards' Enquiry : R P McNally seven-day ban: wore defective body protector (May 7-9,11-15)

The Form Book, Raceform Ltd, Compton, RG20 6NL

NOTEBOOK

Haut De Gamme(FR), much the best horse in the race, coped with most of the obstacles pretty well but two costly mistakes at a crucial stage effectively robbed him of his chance. Nevertheless, there was hope for the future here and he is very probably worth bringing back. *(op 7/2)*

5129a ELLEN CONSTRUCTION CONYNGHAM (Q.R.) CUP (HANDICAP CHASE) 4m

2:40 (2:40) (0-140,126) 5-Y-O+ **£22,448** (£6,586; £3,137; £1,068)

RPR

1 **Howaya Pet (IRE)**[92] 3587 10-11-13 121..............................(t) MrJJCodd 131
(Gerard Keane, Ire) *hld up: prog into 6th bef 6 out: 2nd travelling best 4 out: cl up next: led bef 2 out: rdn and styd on wl fr last* **16/1**

2 *3* **Hot Weld**[43] 4460 7-11-13 126.. MrROHarding[(5)] 133+
(Ferdy Murphy) *mod 2nd: tk clsr order bef 6 out: led after 5 out: bad mstke 4 out: sn rdn and strly pressed: hdd appr 2 out: kpt on u.p* **7/1**[3]

3 *6* **Rare Ouzel (IRE)**[10] 4953 10-10-2 103............................ MrJWFarrelly[(7)] 104
(A J Martin, Ire) *hld up in tch: impr into 7th 5 out: 5th 3 out: mod 3rd 2 out: kpt on* **11/1**

4 *20* **Boom Economy (IRE)**[10] 4953 10-10-6 107...................... MrNHalley[(7)] 88
(Paul A Roche, Ire) *prom: 3rd 1/2-way: rdn 4 out: 4th after 2 out: kpt on same pce* **10/1**

5 *1 1/2* **Coolnahilla (IRE)**[11] 4929 10-11-12 123....................(b) MrCJSweeney[(3)] 103
(W J Burke, Ire) *trckd ldrs on inner: 6th 4 out: 4th next: 5th and no imp fr 2 out* **12/1**

6 *7* **Brigadier Brown (IRE)**[43] 4460 9-10-1 102.................. MrDESplaine[(7)] 75
(John Joseph Murphy, Ire) *towards rr: hdwy 4 out: mod 6th 2 out: kpt on same pce* **12/1**

7 *11* **Karlo (IRE)**[13] 4866 9-10-13 107.................................... MrDerekO'Connor 69
(David A Kiely, Ire) *hld up in rr: sme prog 5 out: no ex fr 3 out* **13/2**[2]

8 *shd* **Hang Seng (IRE)**[13] 4866 8-9-11 98............................ MrRPMcLernon[(7)] 59
(Eugene M O'Sullivan, Ire) *chsd ldrs: 4th 7 out: 5th 4 out: sn no ex* **33/1**

9 *4* **Just Cruising (IRE)**[10] 4953 9-9-11 98.................................. MrJKing[(7)] 55
(A L T Moore, Ire) *prom: 4th 1/2-way: dropped to mid-div bef 7 out: no imp fr next* **40/1**

10 *1* **Logical Approach (IRE)**[12] 4886 9-9-13 100.................... MrJJDoyle[(7)] 56
(Edward U Hales, Ire) *hld up: sme prog bef 6 out: no ex after 5 out* **25/1**

11 *1* **Legendsofthefall (IRE)**[12] 4886 7-10-3 102................(p) MrDMurphy[(5)] 57
(Michael Cunningham, Ire) *trckd ldrs: 6th 1/2-way: wknd fr 6 out* **14/1**

12 *dist* **Rocking Ship (IRE)**[10] 4953 8-10-10 111............................ MrDPFahy[(7)] —
(Ms Joanna Morgan, Ire) *led: sn wl clr: reduced advantage whn rdn 6 out: hdd after next: wknd fr next* **16/1**

13 *11* **Mutineer (IRE)**[10] 4953 7-10-10 107..........................(bt) MrPCashman[(3)] —
(D T Hughes, Ire) *chsd ldrs: pushed along 5th: u.p bef 1/2-way: wknd bef 6 out: t.o* **20/1**

P **Ashstorm (IRE)**[16] 10-11-1 109...................................... MrJTMcNamara —
(G Ducey, Ire) *towards rr: rdn 1/2-way: p.u bef 7 out* **25/1**

P **Laragh House (IRE)**[19] 4811 7-11-3 111.............................. MissNCarberry —
(E J O'Grady, Ire) *mid-div: mstke 15th: p.u bef next* **3/1**[1]

P **Shivermetimber (IRE)**[47] 4400 8-11-0 113................... MrJPO'Farrell[(5)] —
(F Flood, Ire) *nvr a factor: trailing whn p.u bef 2 out* **12/1**

F **Native Cooper (IRE)**[19] 4812 8-10-1 102......................(t) MrCJMoran[(7)] —
(Miss A M Lambert, Ire) *prom: 5th appr 1/2-way: 4th at 15th: sn lost pl: fell next* **33/1**

8m 27.8s **18** Ran SP% **130.5**

CSF £124.21 CT £1329.76 TOTE £12.60: £2.40, £2.00, £3.40, £2.50; DF 138.70.

Owner Beautiful Syndicate **Bred** M J Halligan **Trained** Trim, Co Meath

NOTEBOOK

Hot Weld was conceding plenty of weight bidding for a hat-trick after wins at Musselburgh and Cheltenham last month. He got to the front at the fifth-last but clobbered the next. Pushed along to regain his slender advantage, the eventual winner was travelling much the better in behind and once her rider asked a serious question the outcome was never in doubt. He still lost little in defeat. *(op 6/1)*

Laragh House(IRE) *Official explanation: vet said gelding coughed post race (op 9/2)*

5130a ACC BANK CHAMPION HURDLE (GRADE 1) 2m

3:15 (3:15) 5-Y-O+ **£89,655** (£26,206; £12,413; £4,137)

RPR

1 **Macs Joy (IRE)**[45] 4432 7-11-12 166.................................... BJGeraghty 170+
(Mrs John Harrington, Ire) *trckd ldrs in 3rd: smooth hdwy to ld 3 out: edgd clr travelling easily after 2 out: rdn and styd on wl fr last: impressive* **11/4**[2]

2 *4* **Brave Inca (IRE)**[45] 4432 8-11-12 167..................................... APMcCoy 166
(C A Murphy, Ire) *cl 2nd: disp ld 1/2-way: nt fluent 4 out: 2nd and rdn bef 3 out: chal 2 out: sn outpcd: kpt on u.p fr last* **4/5**[1]

3 *1* **Hardy Eustace (IRE)**[20] 4775 9-11-12 163..........................(b) CO'Dwyer 165
(D T Hughes, Ire) *led: jnd 1/2-way: hdd 3 out: 3rd and no imp bef 2 out: kpt on same pce u.p* **4/1**[3]

4 *shd* **Essex (IRE)**[19] 4000 6-11-12 155..(p) RWalsh 165?
(M J P O'Brien, Ire) *hld up in rr: rdn bef 2 out: kpt on u.p* **16/1**

3m 51.8s **Going Correction** -0.525s/f (Firm) **5** Ran SP% **108.1**

Speed ratings: **112,110,109,109** CSF £5.59 TOTE £3.80; DF 5.40.

Owner Mac's J Racing Syndicate **Bred** Northern Breeders Association **Trained** Moone, Co Kildare

FOCUS

The most eagerly awaited race of the Punchestown Festival brought together the first three horses from the Champion Hurdle. The three horses in question were rated within only 4lb of each other. It promised another cracker and that is how it turned out.

NOTEBOOK

Macs Joy(IRE) benefited from a change of tactics by his rider and his ploy worked to perfection. Rather than producing him at the final flight, Geraghty chose to put him into the race a full three flights from home and set his mount alight at the same time. By doing so he opened up a long lead before heads were turned for home and, as a result, he held a virtually unassailable advantage of around five lengths going to the final hurdle. By exploiting his turn of foot - which is probably superior to Brave Inca's - he ensured that his ally did not have to get into a tussle with Brave Inca so that the latter did not really have the chance to outbattle him. Geraghty's tactical display should be considered of the very highest order.

Brave Inca(IRE) was on the face of it disappointing, but one cannot say that without making clear that he failed to run his race and probably had valid excuses for not doing so. The track and ground were more favourable to Macs Joy, but arguably of more significance was the fact that Tony McCoy reported after the race that his seven-time Grade 1-winning mount did not give him the same feel he had at Cheltenham. At the end of what has been a long, hard season for a horse who always gives his all, the failure to fire is perfectly understandable and it would be churlish and wrong to judge Brave Inca on what he did here. He has been the season's star hurdler and will once again be the horse to beat next season. *(op 8/11 tchd 5/6)*

Hardy Eustace(IRE) put in another below-par run and appears to be slightly in decline. Like the winner, he has not had a trouble-free campaign and his fair and square Champion Hurdle defeat was followed by a thrashing by Asian Maze in the Aintree Hurdle in which he seemed to have a hard race. That was hardly an ideal preparation for this run - in which a visor was replaced by blinkers - and although he enjoyed the luxury of setting the pace he wanted on ground he appreciates, he lacked the gears when push came to shove. He remains a hurdler of the highest order, but he is now a few pounds off some of his younger rivals and while he will no doubt continue to be campaigned in the top races, he might struggle to win one of them.

Essex(IRE), who looked a potential champion when hosing up in the 2005 Totesport Trophy, has not quite gone on as once looked likely. Having had only three runs this season, he came here with less taxed legs than his three opponents and that should be taken into account. While he may well have posted a personal best on a track that suits his speedy style, there seems no reason to believe he ran way above himself. *(op 14/1)*

5131a BETFAIR.COM NOVICE H'CAP CHASE (GRADE A) 3m 1f

3:50 (3:50) 5-Y-O+ **£42,758** (£13,103; £6,206; £2,068; £1,379)

RPR

1 **Olney Lad**[21] 4759 7-10-11 131....................................(b) JimmyMcCarthy 143+
(Mrs P Robeson) *led: rdn and jnd 3 out: rallied u.p next: regained ld after last: styd on wl* **25/1**

2 *1 1/2* **Wolf Creek (IRE)**[43] 4460 6-10-3 123.. PWFlood 134+
(E J O'Grady, Ire) *a.p: 2nd 1/2-way: disp ld travelling best 3 out: rdn next: hdd after last: no ex cl home* **7/1**

3 *5 1/2* **Oulart**[11] 4929 7-10-0 123.. RLoughran[(3)] 128+
(D T Hughes, Ire) *trckd ldrs: slow 3rd: 5th and drvn along 6 out: 4th 4 out: mod 3rd after 3 out: kpt on u.p* **10/3**[1]

4 *4* **Underwriter (USA)**[44] 4447 6-9-12 123......................... MrROHarding[(5)] 124
(Ferdy Murphy) *trckd ldrs on outer: 3rd 6 out: rdn after slt mstke 3 out: 4th and no imp fr next* **14/1**

5 *3* **Gallant Approach (IRE)**[62] 4116 7-10-12 132........................ APMcCoy 130
(C R Egerton) *towards rr: slt mstke 3rd: 6th and sme prog 4 out: 5th and rdn 3 out: kpt on same pce* **5/1**[2]

6 *7* **One More Minute (IRE)**[11] 4929 6-10-3 123.............................. RWalsh 114
(C F Swan, Ire) *hld up in rr: 6th and rdn after 3 out: no imp* **5/1**[2]

P **Tumbling Dice (IRE)**[43] 4456 7-11-3 137.........................(p) BJGeraghty —
(T J Taaffe, Ire) *hld up: mstke 2nd: 7th 6 out: drvn along next: sn no ex: p.u after 3 out* **7/1**

P **Church Island (IRE)**[68] 4022 7-11-10 144............... AndrewJMcNamara —
(Michael Hourigan, Ire) *prom: 3rd 1/2-way: rdn and dropped to 5th 4 out: sn no ex: p.u bef 2 out* **6/1**[3]

P **Loss Of Faith (IRE)**[117] 3194 8-9-10 123............................. RTDunne[(7)] —
(M J P O'Brien, Ire) *chsd ldrs: slt mstke 9th: 6th whn reminders 7 out: rdn and wknd 5 out: p.u after 3 out* **20/1**

6m 15.2s **Going Correction** -0.40s/f (Good) **10** Ran SP% **111.0**

Speed ratings: **112,111,109,108,107 105**,—,—,— CSF £178.44 CT £719.78 TOTE £64.20: £9.60, £2.30, £1.80; DF 313.30.

Owner The Tyringham Partnership **Bred** T H Rossiter **Trained** Tyringham, Milton Keynes

NOTEBOOK

Olney Lad made virtually all the running to record the only success for the British at the four-day festival. His trainer had expressed concern over the drying ground beforehand, but to his credit he never gave in and despite being a little untidy at the last, he came away running and that was enough to see off his only serious challenger. He had won four times over hurdles with cut in the ground and his sole previous victory over fences was on heavy, but he saw out this longer trip well on this sounder surface. *(op 25/1 tchd 33/1)*

Underwriter(USA) was one of six horses wrong at the weights and was struggling after an untidy leap at the third last.

Gallant Approach(IRE), lightly raced over fences, was held up before creeping closer after the fifth last, but he was soon going nowhere.

One More Minute(IRE) *Official explanation: trainer said gelding finished very lame (op 6/1)*

5132a DUNBOYNE CASTLE HOTEL & SPA CHAMPION NOVICE HURDLE (GRADE 1) 2m 4f

4:25 (4:25) 4-Y-O+ **£42,758** (£13,103; £6,206; £2,068; £1,379)

RPR

1 **Nicanor (FR)**[44] 4443 5-11-11 .... RWalsh 139+
(Noel Meade, Ire) *led bef 2nd: hit 6 out: qcknd clr after 2 out: nt fluent last: kpt on u.p run-in: all out* **9/10**[1]

2 *1* **Mounthenry (IRE)**[12] 4888 6-11-12 .... DNRussell 139
(C Byrnes, Ire) *settled 2nd: rdn to chal bef 2 out: sn outpcd: styd on wl u.p fr bef last* **11/2**[3]

3 *2 1/2* **Vic Venturi (IRE)**[12] 4888 6-11-12 ....(t) AndrewJMcNamara 137+
(Philip Fenton, Ire) *settled 3rd: dropped to 5th and rdn 5 out: styd on after 2 out to go 3rd fr last* **10/1**

4 *4* **Justpourit (IRE)**[11] 4928 7-11-12 .... RLoughran 133
(D T Hughes, Ire) *trckd ldrs: 4th 5 out: 3rd 3 out: sn rdn and no imp: no ex fr last* **66/1**

5 *shd* **Mossbank (IRE)**[12] 4888 6-11-12 .... MDarcy 132
(Michael Hourigan, Ire) *trckd ldrs on outer: 3rd 5 out: rdn after next: 4th and no imp 2 out: no ex fr last* **20/1**

P **Powerstation (IRE)**[21] 4760 6-11-12 .... DFO'Regan —
(C Byrnes, Ire) *sn bhd and trailing: t.o whn p.u bef 3 out* **16/1**

P **Refinement (IRE)**[20] 4776 7-11-7 ....(b) APMcCoy —
(Jonjo O'Neill) *hld up in tch: 6th 5 out: wknd next: p.u bef 2 out* **9/2**[2]

P **Parliament Square (IRE)**[54] 4268 5-11-11 .... BJGeraghty —
(M J P O'Brien, Ire) *trckd ldrs tl p.u injured after 4th: dead* **12/1**

4m 54.2s **Going Correction** -0.525s/f (Firm) **10** Ran SP% **115.1**

Speed ratings: **109,108,107,106,105** —,—,— CSF £6.52 TOTE £2.00: £1.30, £1.70, £2.00; DF 8.70.

Owner D P Sharkey **Bred** M Pierre Hayeau **Trained** Castletown, Co Meath

FOCUS

A good renewal of this Grade 1 contest that attracted the Cheltenham winner and leading novice Nicanor, the talented and prolific Refinement and the recent Grade 2 winner Vic Venturi, as well as Powerstation, who had run a highly creditable second to Black Jack Ketchum in the Brit Insurances Novice Hurdle. When the tapes went up nothing was keen to go on and the runners hardly broke out of a walk, but the tempo picked up when Nicanor was sent on before the second.

NOTEBOOK

Nicanor(FR) travelled and jumped well from the outset and leaving the backstraight a number of his rivals had already cried enough. He was still going easily coming to the second-last and quickened clear after that flight to open up a useful lead over Mounthenry. In the straight he always looked like keeping that rival's challenge at bay, but he did begin to tire on the run to the last and was eventually all-out to hold on. His trainer had his worries as to how he would handle the ground, but that proved no problem. He is now likely to be sent chasing and appeals as the type to develop into a top-class novice as he has plenty of pace, and it would be no surprise to see him become a leading Arkle contender. *(op 4/5 tchd 1/1)*

Mounthenry(IRE) chased the winner throughout and stuck to his task very well when coming under pressure before the second last. He has enjoyed an excellent season and already has a pair of Grade 2 victories to his name. Versatile in terms of ground and trip, he is a classy novice and looks a fine prospect for next season. *(op 8/1)*

Vic Venturi(IRE) ran well on ground that was probably as quick as he would like. Successful in a Grade 2 over this trip at Fairyhouse recently, he looked to be in trouble with five to jump but ran on well over the final half-mile. Still a lightly raced sort, he is open to further progress and has the makings of a very good staying chaser. *(op 8/1)*

Justpourit(IRE) looked to face a very tough assignment, but he acquitted himself well. After racing close to the pace, he moved into third with three to jump but was unable to raise his effort from the next. He campaigned with credit on soft ground throughout the winter, but this quicker surface did not present him with any problems. *(op 50/1)*

Mossbank(IRE) was still in contention at the fourth last, but was starting to struggle coming to the next. His victory over Powerstation at Limerick in October marked him down as a horse of some potential and he is certainly open to further progress. His trainer has long held him in high regard and it could be that we will not see the best of him until he goes over fences. *(op 16/1)*

Refinement(IRE) was ridden patiently, but she began to lose touch after five out and was well held when pulling up. She was probably feeling the effects of a busy season and, as her previous form shows, she is much better than this. *Official explanation: jockey said mare was never travelling (op 20/1)*

Powerstation(IRE), who had run so well at Cheltenham and has been in good form for much of the season, was soon struggling and was well adrift of the field heading down the backstraight. *Official explanation: jockey said gelding was never travelling; trainer said gelding was found to have a lung infection post race (op 20/1)*

5134a BEWLEYS HOTELS & EUROPEAN BREEDERS FUND NATIONAL HUNT FILLIES PREMIER BUMPER — 2m

5:35 (5:35) 4-5-Y-0

£33,793 (£13,103; £8,275; £4,827; £1,379; £689)

RPR

1 — **Shuil Aris (IRE)** 5-11-9 ... MrAFitzgerald 120
(Paul Nolan, Ire) *trckd ldrs: 6th after 1/2-way: 7th 3f out: hdwy into 2nd 1 1/2f out: styd on wl ins fnl f: led nr fin* **14/1**

2 nk **Female (IRE)**[44] 4448 5-11-4 ... MrPRoche(5) 120
(C Roche, Ire) *trckd ldrs on inner: 5th and hdwy 3f out: swtchd to chal early st: led under 2f out: rdn clr: strly pressed wl ins fnl f: h* **11/8**[1]

3 10 **Chico Time (IRE)**[29] 4681 5-11-2 ... MrSCByrne(7) 110
(Denis P Murphy, Ire) *chsd ldrs: 8th 4f out: styd on u.p st to go mod 3rd cl home* **33/1**

4 nk **Winning Counsel (IRE)** 4-10-9 ... MrCJMurray(7) 103
(K F O'Brien, Ire) *hld up: kpt on wl fr 3 1/2f out* **33/1**

5 2 **Corrig Caul (IRE)**[23] 4744 5-11-4 ... MrDMurphy(5) 108
(Raymond Hurley, Ire) *hld up: hdwy on inner 5f out: 9th under 4f out: kpt on st* **50/1**

6 nk **Nolans Joy (IRE)**[64] 4081 5-11-4 ... MrROHarding(5) 107
(W J Burke, Ire) *trckd ldrs: 5th 6f out: 4th and rdn appr st: sltly hmpd over 2f out: kpt on same pce* **20/1**

7 3 **Bronx Girl (IRE)**[23] 4740 4-11-2 ... MrDerekO'Connor 97
(F Flood, Ire) *hld up: kpt on fr over 3f out* **16/1**

8 hd **Callherwhatulike (IRE)**[22] 4751 5-11-6 ... MrCJSweeney(3) 104
(Robert Tyner, Ire) *trckd ldrs: prog into 4th over 6f out: cl 2nd over 3f out: led appr st: hdd under 2f out: sn no ex* **7/1**[3]

9 2 **Rose Of Clare**[3] 5060 5-11-4 ... MrGJPower(5) 102
(Joseph Crowley, Ire) *prom: 2nd after 1/2-way: cl 3rd appr st: no ex fr 2f out* **25/1**

10 2 **Berkeley Storm (IRE)**[29] 4682 5-11-2 ... MrJPMcKeown(7) 100
(S J Treacy, Ire) *rr of mid-div: 12th 6f out: kpt on same pce fr 3f out* **33/1**

11 10 **Tambourine Davis (FR)**[48] 4376 4-11-2 ... MissNCarberry 83
(N J Henderson) *led: strly pressed 4f out: hdd appr st: sn wknd* **8/1**

12 4 **Swift Post (IRE)**[11] 4924 5-11-2 ... MissKAMartin(7) 86
(M J P O'Brien, Ire) *sn 2nd: 4th over 4f out: wknd qckly over 3f out* **50/1**

13 1 1/2 **Brownie Points (IRE)** 4-10-11 ... MrLPFlynn(5) 78
(C F Swan, Ire) *nvr a factor: kpt on one pce fr 4f out* **20/1**

14 2 1/2 **Lady Taipan (IRE)** 5-11-4 ... MrRO'Sullivan(5) 82
(Michael Flynn, Ire) *nvr a factor* **33/1**

15 shd **Madmoiselle Etoile (IRE)**[36] 4602 4-10-9 ... MrMDHickey(7) 75
(John Joseph Murphy, Ire) *mid-div: no imp fr over 4f out* **20/1**

16 1 1/2 **Outdoor Sally (IRE)**[21] 4772 5-11-9 ... MrPFahey 81
(Mrs John Harrington, Ire) *mid-div: 10th 6f out: no ex fr 4f out* **25/1**

17 3/4 **Pallas Lass (IRE)**[79] 3813 5-11-2 ... MrATDuff(7) 80
(B P Galvin, Ire) *a bhd* **100/1**

18 2 **Tred On Air (IRE)**[26] 5-11-6 ... MrPCashman(3) 78
(Miss A M Lambert, Ire) *mid-div: no ex fr over 4f out* **50/1**

19 25 **Henrietta Hall (IRE)** 5-11-9 ... MrJTMcNamara 53
(M Halford, Ire) *a bhd* **20/1**

20 20 **Macs Form (IRE)** 5-11-4 ... MissAFoley(5) 33
(Thomas Foley, Ire) *nvr a factor: t.o* **25/1**

21 1 1/2 **Kilbrickensfirth (IRE)** 5-11-2 ... MrSMcGonagle(7) 31
(T K Geraghty, Ire) *a bhd: t.o* **33/1**

22 25 **A Bit Pleased** 4-10-11 ... MsKWalsh(5) —
(W P Mullins, Ire) *chsd ldrs to 1/2-way: sn wknd: completely t.o* **10/1**

S **Conor's Secret (IRE)**[12] 4885 4-10-11 ... MrJPO'Farrell(5) —
(F Flood, Ire) *mid-div: smooth hdwy into 6th appr st: cl 5th whn sltly hmpd and slipped up over 2f out* **13/2**[2]

3m 49.7s **Going Correction** -0.525s/f (Firm)
WFA 4 from 5yo 5lb — **23** Ran SP% **152.9**
Speed ratings: 108,107,102,102,101 101,100,99,98,97 92,90,90,88,88 88,87,86,74,64 63,51,— CSF £34.35 TOTE £35.70: £6.30, £1.40, £6.20, £18.40; DF 199.00.
Owner Martin O'Sullivan **Bred** Mrs Juliet Brown **Trained** Enniscorthy, Co. Wexford
■ Stewards' Enquiry : Mr P Roche five-day ban: careless riding (May 7-9, 11-12)

FOCUS
A successful debut for Shuil Aris in a race which had its share of drama in the straight.

NOTEBOOK
Shuil Aris(IRE) got the end of a chain reaction set off when runner-up Female was switched from the inside off the final bend to deliver her challenge, but she moved into second place over a furlong out and stayed on well under pressure to snatch the verdict close home. *(op 10/1)*

Female(IRE) went to the front under two furlongs out and looked all set to score until she was grabbed close home. Her rider's manoeuvre early in the straight slightly hampered a few of her rivals. *(op 6/4 tchd 7/4)*

Chico Time(IRE), fourth on her debut at Thurles last month, was well adrift of the first two although she did stay on steadily from half a mile out to take third place near the finish.

Winning Counsel(IRE), making her debut, caught the eye. Held up, she began to close before the straight and stayed on quite well.

Tambourine Davis(FR) made the running until giving best and weakeninon the final bend.

Conor's Secret(IRE), who was pushed out and bumped the eventual winner, was knocked down when poised to start her challenge. *(op 7/1)*

5133a (Foreign Racing) - See Raceform Interactive

4794 MARKET RASEN (R-H)

Saturday, April 29

OFFICIAL GOING: Good (good to firm in places)
The rails had been moved out to their furthest point. 18mm was put on the back straight, 12mm on the home straight resulting in 'easy ground'.
Wind: Light, against Weather: Mainly fine, light shower race two

5135 MARKET RASEN RACECOURSE (S) HURDLE (8 hdls) — 2m 1f 110y

2:00 (2:02) (Class 5) 4-6-Y-0 — £2,192 (£639; £319)

Form — RPR

053 1 — **City Of Manchester (IRE)**[16] 4828 4-10-7 ... BarryKeniry 82+
(P C Haslam) *chsd ldrs: led 2 out: styd on wl last 100yds* **5/2**[1]

0000 2 4 **Mr Twins (ARG)**[26] 4723 5-10-7 77 ... (t) MichaelMcAlister(5) 82
(M A Barnes) *chsd ldrs: led after 3 out: hdd next: kpt on same pce run-in* **14/1**

2040 3 15 **Seraph**[20] 4794 6-10-9 83 ... LeeVickers(3) 67
(O Brennan) *chsd ldrs: rdn and bdly outpcd 3 out: styd on between last 2: tk mod 3rd nr fin* **7/1**

50 4 1 1/2 **Airgusta (IRE)**[13] 4875 5-10-12 ... JimmyMcCarthy 66
(C P Morlock) *in rr: hdwy 5th: one pce fr next* **13/2**[3]

00 5 3 **Discomania**[12] 4905 4-10-7 ... TomSiddall 58
(V Smith) *in rr: hdwy 5th: sn chsng ldrs: lost pl appr 2 out* **14/1**

0P0P 6 1 1/2 **New Wish (IRE)**[74] 3916 6-10-12 66 ... PaddyAspell 61
(S B Clark) *stdd s: stdy hdwy 5th: wnt 2nd appr 2 out: wknd run-in* **50/1**

200P 7 9 **The Boobi (IRE)**[12] 4919 5-10-0 87 ... MarkNicolls(5) 45
(Miss M E Rowland) *hdwy 4th: sn chsng ldrs: lost pl appr 2 out* **12/1**

3-05 8 19 **Soviet Joy (IRE)**[10] 4418 5-10-12 102 ... RussGarritty 33
(J J Quinn) *trckd ldrs: led 5th: hdd after next: wknd qckly bef 2 out: bhd whn eased run-in* **11/4**[2]

P00 9 dist **Chisel**[95] 3545 5-10-5 64 ... MrSRees(7) —
(M Wigham) *prom: drvn 4th: sn lost pl: hopelessly t.o fr 3 out* **66/1**

P0 U — **Danger Bird (IRE)**[16] 4828 6-9-9 ... AdamHawkins(10) —
(R Hollinshead) *hld up in rr: blnd and uns rdr 2nd* **50/1**

600P P — **Another Misk**[12] 4919 4-10-4 82 ... DougieCostello(3) —
(M E Sowersby) *in rr: t.o 3 out: p.u bef next* **25/1**

PP P — **Swell Lad**[40] 2954 4-10-4 ... WilliamKennedy(3) —
(S Gollings) *chsd ldrs: drvn and lost pl after 3rd: bhd whn p.u bef next* **40/1**

P P — **King Henrik (USA)**[117] 3203 4-10-0 ... AdrianScholes(7) —
(A Crook) *led: clr to 3rd: hdd 5th: wknd qckly: t.o whn p.u bef 2 out* **80/1**

4m 23.4s (7.00) **Going Correction** +0.475s/f (Soft)
WFA 4 from 5yo+ 5lb — **13** Ran SP% **115.0**
Speed ratings: **103,101,94,93,92 91,87,79,—,— —,—,—** CSF £34.48 TOTE £3.70: £1.70, £2.20, £1.80; EX 66.30.The winner was sold to B.Leavy for 6,200gns.
Owner Middleham Park Racing XXXVII **Bred** Brendan McSorley **Trained** Middleham, N Yorks

FOCUS
A poor seller with the first two well clear and the race is rated through them to their marks.

NOTEBOOK
City Of Manchester(IRE) has been gradually improving. He really knuckled down to pull clear in the closing stages and changed hands at the auction. *(op 11-4)*

Mr Twins(ARG), down in grade, made the winner dig deep but was definitely second best at the line.

Seraph had the ground to suit but badly tapped for toe and only eighth going to two out, he stuck on in his own time to take a remote third spot. *(op 15-2 tchd 13-2)*

Airgusta(IRE), a modest stayer on the Flat, lacked the pace to enter the picture and will be better suited by two and a half miles plus. *(op 7-1)*

Discomania, on his toes beforehand, had the headgear left off this time.

New Wish(IRE), absent since February, cruised on to the heels of the first two starting the home turn but, a shadow of his former self, his stamina also looks strictly limited.

Soviet Joy(IRE), a positive on the exchanges, had finished runner-up in an All-Weather seller ten days earlier. He stopped to nothing going to two out and completed in his own time. *(op 5-2)*

5136 INGHAM H'CAP CHASE (17 fncs) — 3m 1f

2:35 (2:35) (Class 4) (0-105,104) 5-Y-0+ — £4,111 (£1,198; £599)

Form — RPR

PPPP 1 — **Over The Storm (IRE)**[45] 4451 9-10-13 91 ... (b[1]) DavidO'Meara 102+
(H P Hogarth) *w ldrs: lft in ld after 10th: hrd rdn run-in: all out* **12/1**

643U 2 1 **Runaway Bishop (USA)**[14] 4851 11-10-9 87 ... RichardHobson 97+
(J R Cornwall) *in rr: hdwy to chse ldrs 11th: wnt 2nd appr 3 out: 3l down whn hit last: kpt on towards fin* **10/1**

211P 3 8 **Tee-Jay (IRE)**[158] 2413 10-11-1 93 ... BarryKeniry 94
(M D Hammond) *in rr: hdwy appr 3 out: styd on to take 3rd run-in* **8/1**

312P 4 5 **Jacarado (IRE)**[21] 4785 8-9-7 78 oh1 ... (v) JohnPritchard(7) 76+
(R Dickin) *wnt prom 8th: wnt 2nd 12th: one pce fr 3 out* **7/1**[3]

06-0 5 9 **Why The Big Paws**[20] 4805 8-10-12 100 ... JohnFlavin(10) 91+
(R C Guest) *mde most: blnd 9th: hmpd by loose horse and hdd after 10th: wkng whn mstke 3 out* **9/1**

1P22 6 hd **Cool Song**[88] 3662 10-9-11 80 ... DarylJacob(5) 67
(Miss Suzy Smith) *in rr: reminders 8th: sme hdwy 13th: nvr a factor* **11/4**[1]

3004 7 2 1/2 **Sarobar (IRE)**[12] 4911 6-10-0 85 ... (v[1]) RichardSpate(7) 69
(M Scudamore) *in rr: sme hdwy 13th: nvr on terms* **25/1**

5-P5 F — **Cristophe**[11] 4943 8-11-0 97 ... MrTJO'Brien(5) —
(P Bowen) *keen: fell 1st* **13/2**[2]

433 P — **Sandy Gold (IRE)**[20] 4796 8-11-1 100 ... PhilKinsella(7) —
(Miss J E Foster) *in tch: wknd 4 out: bhd whn p.u bef next* **25/1**

UF0P P — **Stanway**[164] 2273 7-11-12 104 ... TomSiddall —
(Mrs Mary Hambro) *chsd ldrs: wknd 4 out: bhd whn p.u bef 2 out* **40/1**

1PP0 P — **Fin Bec (FR)**[16] 4835 13-11-9 101 ... (b) AndrewThornton —
(R Curtis) *w ldrs: reminders and lost pl 9th: bhd whn p.u after next* **12/1**

5116 P — **Tipp Top (IRE)**[12] 4900 9-10-0 85 ... (t) MrGTumelty(7) —
(O Brennan) *chsd ldrs: sn pushed along: lost pl 4 out: bhd whn p.u bef next* **9/1**

P5 P — **Lost In Normandy (IRE)**[42] 4499 9-10-12 90 ... (b) DaveCrosse —
(Mrs L Williamson) *in tch: reminders and lost pl 9th: sn bhd: p.u bef 12th* **16/1**

6m 34.2s (-3.20) **Going Correction** +0.475s/f (Soft) — **13** Ran SP% **124.1**
Speed ratings: **105,104,102,100,97 97,96,—,—,— —,—,—** CSF £128.32 CT £1038.75 TOTE £15.40: £5.10, £2.90, £3.10; EX 228.20.
Owner Hogarth Racing **Bred** D Hickey **Trained** Stillington, N Yorks

FOCUS
The winner was rated almost three stone better at his peak. The race has been rated through the runner-up's previous efforts here.

NOTEBOOK

Over The Storm(IRE), without a win for over two years and pulled up on his five previous outings this time, has a long list of problems. In first-time blinkers, he was left in charge with a circuit to go *and had nothing at all to spare at the line.Official explanation: trainer said, regarding the improved form shown, gelding had had niggling veterinary problems and wearing blinkers for the first time today made all the difference (tchd 14-1)*

Runaway Bishop(USA), on the same mark as his last success at Towcester in October, went in pursuit of the winner turning for home. He looked cooked when hitting the last but was closing the gap at the line.

Tee-Jay(IRE), absent since November, likes fast ground. This will have put him spot on and four of his last five wins have been at Hexham. *(op 10-1)*

Jacarado(IRE), suited by going right-handed, went in pursuit of the winner but on this ground simply proved too slow. *(op 8-1)*

Why The Big Paws, back over fences, made minor errors and one serious mistake. Almost carried off the track by a loose horse passing the winning line with a circuit to go, she was out on her feet when clouting the third last.

Cool Song, 5lb higher, was soon struggling to keep up and was found to have bled from the nose. *Official explanation: jockey said gelding bled from the nose (op 7-2)*

Tipp Top(IRE) was soon being driven along to keep up and, stopping to nothing starting the final *turn, was reported to have a breathing problem.Official explanation: jockey said gelding had a breathing problem*

Lost In Normandy(IRE) *Official explanation: jockey said gelding was never travelling*

5137 UK HYGIENE H'CAP HURDLE (10 hdls) 2m 6f
3:10 (3:10) (Class 4) (0-100,104) 4-Y-0+ **£3,426** (£998; £499)

Form				RPR
P000	**1**		**Talarive (USA)**[83] [3757] 10-11-0 **93**.....(tp) BrianHughes(5) (P D Niven) *trckd ldrs: led after 3 out: rdn clr next: edgd lft and kpt on run-in* **20/1**	101+
3065	**2**	1¾	**Gaelic Roulette (IRE)**[24] [4391] 6-11-4 **92**..... JamesDavies (J Jay) *hld up in rr: hdwy and prom 5th: wnt 2nd sn after last: kpt on wl towards fin* **9/1**	97
6F42	**3**	3½	**Sparklinspirit**[14] [4860] 7-11-7 **98**..... WilliamKennedy(3) (J L Spearing) *hdwy to trck ldrs 5th: led 3 out: sn hdd: one pce between last 2* **5/1**[1]	99
1401	**4**	1¾	**Tickateal**[113] [3271] 6-11-3 **98**..... MrBWoodhouse(7) (R D E Woodhouse) *hld up: hdwy to trck ldrs 7th: rdn next: one pce fr 2 out* **5/1**[1]	97
0005	**5**	½	**Ramblees Holly**[12] [4922] 8-11-0 **95**..... TomMessenger(7) (R S Wood) *chsd ldrs: kpt on same pce appr 2 out* **7/1**[3]	94
3/63	**6**	1½	**Stars Delight (IRE)**[12] [4912] 9-11-11 **104**..... RobertLucey-Butler(5) (Jim Best) *hld up: hdwy 6th: one pce fr 3 out* **11/2**[2]	102+
0525	**7**	8	**Wally Wonder (IRE)**[37] [4593] 8-11-4 **99**.....(v) PhilKinsella(7) (K G Reveley) *w ldr: led 3rd: hdd 3 out: wknd appr next* **9/1**	90+
0064	**8**	6	**Celtic Blaze (IRE)**[12] [4920] 7-11-3 **96**.....(tp) MichaelMcAlister(5) (B S Rothwell) *wnt prom 4th: wknd appr 2 out* **14/1**	79
2/05	**9**	22	**Jamaican Flight (USA)**[25] [3966] 13-11-7 **95**..... TomSiddall (Mrs S Lamyman) *led tl blnd and hdd 3rd: wknd qckly 7th: sn bhd* **28/1**	56
5546	**10**	26	**Dock Tower (IRE)**[42] [4506] 4-11-6 **100**.....(t) PeterBuchanan (M E Sowersby) *in rr: sn pushed along: bhd fr 6th* **14/1**	29
/PPP	**11**	2	**Icy River (IRE)**[52] [4300] 9-11-4 **92**..... AndrewThornton (K G Reveley) *chsd ldrs: reminders 1st: lost pl 7th: sn bhd* **22/1**	25
-3PP	**P**		**Cruising Clyde**[118] [3184] 7-11-7 **95**..... BarryKeniry (P Winkworth) *sn in rr: t.o 5th: sn p.u* **10/1**	—
20-3	**P**		**Own Line**[345] [429] 7-11-10 **98**..... PaddyAspell (J Hetherton) *chsd ldrs: reminders and lost pl 5th: t.o 3 out: p.u bef next* **16/1**	—

5m 36.1s (7.80) **Going Correction** +0.475s/f (Soft)
WFA 4 from 6yo+ 6lb **13** Ran SP% **122.1**
Speed ratings: **104,103,102,101,101 100,97,95,87,78 77,—,—** CSF £190.22 CT £1059.33 TOTE £24.40: £6.60, £2.70, £2.30; EX 152.70.
Owner Ian G M Dalgleish **Bred** Juddmonte Farms **Trained** Barton-le-Street, N Yorks

FOCUS

The winner took advantage of a lenient mark. The form looks solid and is rated through the runner-up and the fourth.

NOTEBOOK

Talarive(USA), absent since February, looked in good nick and has slipped to a lenient mark. He was put about his job going to two out and never really looked like being caught. He seems to run best after a break.

Gaelic Roulette(IRE), last seen in action on the Flat, appreciated the much better ground and if anything, the extended trip seemed to suit her. *(op 8-1)*

Sparklinspirit, 3lb higher, showed his improved Newton Abbot effort was no fluke.

Tickateal, fourth in this a year ago, was 3lb higher than when winning on his previous start at Musselburgh in January. He seems to be better over the full three miles. *(op 11-2)*

Ramblees Holly, having his second outing after a break, looks in good form ahead of a summer campaign. *(op 13-2)*

Stars Delight(IRE), 4lb higher, is a fragile type and here was having his second outing in less than two weeks after a break. *(op 6-1 tchd 13-2)*

Jamaican Flight(USA) *Official explanation: jockey said horse banged a knee (tchd 25-1)*

5138 MELVYN MOFFATT NOVICES' HURDLE (10 hdls) 2m 3f 110y
3:45 (3:45) (Class 4) 4-Y-0+ **£3,253** (£955; £477; £238)

Form				RPR
1250	**1**		**Rare Coincidence**[8] [4990] 5-11-6 106.....(p) KeithMercer (R F Fisher) *w ldrs: led 2 out: 3l clr whn hit last: jst hld on* **12/1**[3]	106+
0653	**2**	nk	**Golden Crew**[11] [4935] 6-10-9..... DarylJacob(5) (Miss Suzy Smith) *chsd ldrs: styd on to go 2nd after last: jst hld* **12/1**[3]	99
P124	**3**	5	**Irish Wolf (FR)**[18] [2850] 6-11-1 115.....(p) TomGreenway(5) (P Bowen) *trckd ldrs: led after 3 out: hdd next: edgd lft and kpt on same pce run-in* **5/4**[1]	101+
0000	**4**	2½	**Smart Boy Prince (IRE)**[14] [4849] 5-11-11 112..... WayneKavanagh(7) (C Smith) *led tl after 3 out: outpcd appr next: kpt on run-in* **16/1**	109
600	**5**	hd	**Falcon's Cliche**[42] [4507] 5-10-7.....(t) PeterBuchanan (P Beaumont) *chsd ldrs: one pce appr 2 out* **125/1**	84
0005	**6**	dist	**Coorbawn Vic (IRE)**[24] [4732] 5-11-0..... MarcusFoley (S A Brookshaw) *sn in rr: sme hdwy 7th: lost pl next: t.o* **100/1**	—
34	**7**	½	**Nannys Gift (IRE)**[71] [3961] 7-10-7..... TomSiddall (O Brennan) *sn bhd and pushed along: t.o 7th* **100/1**	—
031P	**8**	1	**Boris The Spider**[42] [4488] 5-11-6 101..... BarryKeniry (M D Hammond) *in rr: bhd fr 7th: t.o whn blnd last 2* **16/1**	—
0	**P**		**Cottam Eclipse**[89] [3657] 5-10-11..... MrTGreenall(3) (M W Easterby) *in rr: t.o 7th: p.u after next* **125/1**	—
3F5P	**P**		**Common Girl (IRE)**[20] [4797] 8-10-12 103..... MrGTumelty(7) (O Brennan) *chsd ldrs: drvn 6th: sn lost pl: t.o whn p.u bef 2 out* **14/1**	—
P	**P**		**Turftanzer (GER)**[52] [4299] 7-10-7..... PhilKinsella(7) (Lady Susan Watson) *chsd ldrs: wknd qckly after 3 out: bhd whn p.u bef next* **200/1**	—
411P	**P**		**Turnstile**[45] [4443] 5-11-7 127..... BrianHughes(5) (J Howard Johnson) *chsd ldrs: rdn 7th: sn lost pl and eased: t.o whn p.u bef 2 out* **7/4**[2]	—

5m 1.60s (11.60) **Going Correction** +0.475s/f (Soft) **12** Ran SP% **118.7**
Speed ratings: **95,94,92,91,91 —,—,—,—,— —,—** CSF £142.47 TOTE £13.60: £2.20, £3.40, £1.10; EX 173.80.
Owner A Kerr **Bred** D R Tucker **Trained** Ulverston, Cumbria

FOCUS

Just fair novice form rated through the winner with the third and fourth below form.

NOTEBOOK

Rare Coincidence, back in trip, had it in the bag when clouting the last but in the end the line came just in time. He is nothing if not tough.

Golden Crew seemed to turn in an improved effort and his persistence almost paid off. *(op 14-1)*

Irish Wolf(FR), runner-up on the Flat two weeks earlier, went on looking to be travelling best but in the end couldn't match the first two. He prefers much quicker ground than the heavily-watered surface he encountered here. *(op 11-10)*

Smart Boy Prince(IRE), who had a stiff task with three penalties to shoulder, took them along and ran much better than of late. He would have a much more realistic chance in handicaps. *(tchd 18-1)*

Falcon's Cliche, who showed little in three bumpers, showed a lot more on her hurdling debut but she looks to have more stamina than speed. *(op 100-1)*

Turnstile, pulled up in Grade 1 company at the Cheltenham Festival, suddenly came under *pressure four out and dropped right away in a matter of strides.Official explanation: trainer had no explanation for the poor form shown (op 2-1 tchd 9-4 in a place)*

5139 F A WOULD GROUP NOVICES' H'CAP CHASE (14 fncs) 2m 4f
4:15 (4:15) (Class 3) (0-115,107) 5-Y-0+ **£6,506** (£1,910; £955; £477)

Form				RPR
0254	**1**		**Regal Term (IRE)**[11] [4935] 8-11-10 **105**..... HenryOliver (R Dickin) *jnd ldrs 8th: led next: j.lft and styd on fr 3 out* **16/1**	115+
4032	**2**	3	**Elvis Returns**[41] [4518] 8-11-6 **106**..... TJDreaper(5) (J M Jefferson) *jnd ldrs 8th: wnt 2nd appr 3 out: blnd 2 out: kpt on* **7/2**[2]	113+
00P2	**3**	6	**Valleymore (IRE)**[14] [4851] 10-10-6 **87**.....(p) MarcusFoley (S A Brookshaw) *sn in rr: styd on fr 3 out: snatched 3rd nr fin* **9/2**[3]	87+
30P	**4**	¾	**College City (IRE)**[26] [4721] 7-11-2 **107**.....(p) JohnFlavin(10) (R C Guest) *hld up: stdy hdwy and prom 8th: shkn up 3 out: wknd run-in and lost 3rd nr line* **14/1**	106
P551	**5**	2½	**Jonny's Kick**[4] [5049] 6-11-1 **96** 7ex..... RussGarritty (T D Easterby) *prom: drvn along 8th: outpcd 4 out: styd on last 2* **3/1**[1]	93
300	**6**	4	**Caveman**[109] [3328] 6-10-9 **90**..... TomSiddall (O Brennan) *trckd ldrs: wknd fr 3 out: 4th and wl btn whn blnd last* **20/1**	86+
P501	**7**	7	**Mikasa (IRE)**[14] [4844] 6-10-6 **87**..... KeithMercer (R F Fisher) *chsd ldrs: lost pl 10th: n.d after* **15/2**	75+
312	**8**	23	**Kercabellec (FR)**[20] [4798] 8-11-2 **97**..... RichardHobson (J R Cornwall) *mde most to 9th: outpcd 4 out: sn lost pl* **15/2**	70+
05UR	**9**	18	**Tails I Win**[13] [4870] 7-10-2 **83** oh20 ow2..... AnthonyCoyle (Miss C J E Caroe) *a in rr: sme hdwy 8th: sn lost pl and bhd* **66/1**	28
6053	**P**		**Salhood**[42] [4502] 7-11-6 **104**..... WilliamKennedy(3) (S Gollings) *w ldrs: lost pl 6th: bhd whn p.u after next* **8/1**	—

5m 13.4s (10.70) **Going Correction** +0.475s/f (Soft) **10** Ran SP% **118.8**
Speed ratings: **97,95,93,93,92 90,87,78,71,—** CSF £75.09 CT £305.01 TOTE £19.10: £4.00, £2.00, £1.90; EX 117.00.
Owner R G & R A Whitehead **Bred** Mrs R Deane **Trained** Atherstone on Stour, Warwicks

FOCUS

A strong gallop and they came home well strung out. Doubtful form rated through the second for the time being.

NOTEBOOK

Regal Term(IRE), making his debut over fences, was in front six out. Still inexperienced he tended to jump right-handed over the last three but kept up the gallop all the way to the line. There should be even better to come. *(op 12-1)*

Elvis Returns, dropping back in trip, ran his best race to far over fences keeping on in dour fashion after a blunder two out looked to have cooked his goose. *(op 6-1)*

Valleymore(IRE), dropping back a mile in trip, has not won for over three years and this trip is insufficient for him. *(tchd 4-1)*

College City(IRE) went round in cruise control but shaken up going to three out, his stamina gave out and he lost third spot and his each-way backers' cash near the line. *(op 12-1)*

Jonny's Kick, making a quick return under his penalty, found this track a different cup of tea. To his credit he never gave up the fight. *(op 5-2 tchd 10-3 in a place)*

Caveman, placed in a point, has changed stables and was back over fences. He was out on his feet when hitting the last hard. *(op 16-1)*

Salhood *Official explanation: trainer said gelding lost its action but returned sound*

5140 BRITISH HARDWOOD TREE NURSERY H'CAP CHASE (14 fncs) 2m 4f
4:45 (4:47) (Class 4) (0-105,105) 5-Y-0+ **£3,903** (£1,146; £573; £286)

Form				RPR
031P	**1**		**Phildari (IRE)**[264] [1178] 10-10-0 **86**.....(t) MrDEngland(7) (N A Twiston-Davies) *mde all: drew clr appr 3 out: drvn out* **7/2**[1]	100+
314P	**2**	15	**Good Outlook (IRE)**[89] [3649] 7-11-2 **105**..... JohnFlavin(10) (R C Guest) *chsd wnr fr 5th: 12l 2nd whn blnd 3 out: kpt on* **9/2**[2]	106+
5P-P	**3**	1¼	**Schoolhouse Walk**[12] [4921] 8-10-0 **79** oh16..... PeterBuchanan (M E Sowersby) *in rr: hdwy 8th: wnt 3rd 4 out: disp 2nd 2 out: one pce* **50/1**	75+
4U5P	**4**	1¾	**Tacolino (FR)**[149] [2588] 12-11-2 **102**..... MrGTumelty(7) (O Brennan) *chsd ldrs: one pce fr 4 out* **12/1**	95
5	**5**	5	**Chain**[12] [4900] 9-9-11 **79** oh6..... LeeVickers(3) (O Brennan) *sn bhd: blnd 8th: kpt on fr 3 out: nvr a threat* **11/1**	67
4000	**6**	5	**Prince Of Aragon**[12] [4908] 10-9-9 **79** oh3.....(bt) DarylJacob(5) (Miss Suzy Smith) *prom: outpcd 4 out: no threat after* **14/1**	62
5004	**P**		**Now Then Auntie (IRE)**[99] [3484] 5-10-0 **83** oh3..... KeithMercer (Mrs S A Watt) *sn bhd: t.o 6th: p.u bef 3 out* **12/1**	—
U016	**P**		**Sailor A'Hoy**[20] [4804] 10-10-7 **86**.....(b) AlanO'Keeffe (M Mullineaux) *sn bhd: t.o 8th: p.u bef next* **10/1**	—
050	**P**		**Day Du Roy (FR)**[57] [4213] 8-11-6 **99**..... TomSiddall (Miss L C Siddall) *chsd ldrs: lost pl 9th: bhd whn p.u bef 3 out* **15/2**[3]	—
0312	**P**		**Lanmire Tower (IRE)**[149] [2588] 12-10-9 **91**.....(p) WilliamKennedy(3) (S Gollings) *prom: rdn 7th: sn bhd: t.o whn p.u bef 4 out* **7/2**[1]	—
/0-6	**P**		**Hollows Mist**[14] [4840] 8-10-3 **85**..... DougieCostello(3) (F P Murtagh) *hld up: sme hdwy 8th: nvr on terms: bhd whn p.u bef 3 out* **16/1**	—

5m 18.8s (16.10) **Going Correction** +0.475s/f (Soft)
WFA 5 from 7yo+ 4lb **11** Ran SP% **121.7**
Speed ratings: **86,80,79,78,76 74,—,—,—,— —** CSF £21.16 CT £687.38 TOTE £5.50: £2.10, £2.80, £17.60; EX 27.60.

Owner J C England **Bred** F Murray **Trained** Naunton, Gloucs

FOCUS

A very moderate winning time when compared with the previous contest. The proximity of the third, 16lb out of the handicap, casts a doubt over the value of the form.

NOTEBOOK

Phildari(IRE), absent since August, was 11lb higher than when scoring here last July. He took this race by the scruff of the neck and had it won turning for home. *(op 4-1 tchd 9-2)*

Good Outlook(IRE), 6lb higher than his last success, had finished lame when pulled up on his previous start at Ludlow in January. He was soon in pursuit of the winner but had been shaken off before three out and in the end struggled to hang on to second spot.

Schoolhouse Walk, pulled up on his two most recent outings, was running from 16lb out of the handicap. He was happy to sit off the strong pace and this may flatter him.

Tacolino(FR), absent since December, has won here three times in the past and he seems suited by the better ground. What he actually achieved though is open to doubt. *(op 17-2)*

Chain was out of contention when he blundered at the first fence on the final circuit. *(op 16-1)*

Prince Of Aragon, out of the handicap and with the blinkers tried again, seems better over two miles. *(op 11-1)*

Lanmire Tower(IRE), on his favourite stamping ground, was having his first outing since December and was struggling to keep up with a full circuit to go. *(op 9-2)*

5141 RASEN & SULTANA HBLB STANDARD NATIONAL HUNT FLAT RACE (CONDITIONAL JOCKEYS' & AMATEUR RIDERS' RACE) 2m 1f 110y

5:20 (5:20) (Class 6) 4-6-Y-0 **£1,713** (£499; £249)

Form				RPR
1		**Casewick Mist** 6-10-4 ... MrOWilliams(7) (J M Jefferson) *hld up in rr: hdwy 8f out: styd on wl fnl 3f: led last 75yds* **25/1**	97+
2	1 ½	**Red Scally** 6-10-8 ... JohnFlavin(10) (R C Guest) *hld up: hdwy to trck ldrs 8f out: led 3f out: hdd last 150yds: no ex* **10/1**	101
3	hd	**Bleu Pois (IRE)** 4-10-8 ... BrianHughes(5) (J Howard Johnson) *trckd ldrs: led over 4f out tl 3f out: led 150yds out: hdd and no ex last 75yds* **11/1**	95
4	6	**Lucinda Lamb** 4-10-1 ... PaddyMerrigan(5) (Miss S E Hall) *hdwy to chse ldrs 8f out: outpcd 6f out: kpt on fnl 3f* **8/1**	82
16	5	nk	**Spitfire Sortie (IRE)**[42] 4507 5-11-8 ... MrTGreenall(3) (M W Easterby) *in tch: n.m.r on inner over 4f out: sn outpcd and no threat* **7/4**[1]	101
6	8	**Silver Snitch (IRE)** 6-11-1 ... DougieCostello(3) (G A Swinbank) *in rr: hdwy 8f out: outpcd over 3f out* **6/1**[3]	86
20	7	6	**Mr Shambles**[14] 4853 5-11-1 ... WilliamKennedy(3) (S Gollings) *in rr: outpcd whn bdly hmpd over 4f out* **12/1**	80
8	3 ½	**Tully Cross (IRE)**[41] 4539 5-10-11 ... MrBConnell(7) (T M Walsh, Ire) *chsd ldrs: drvn along 6f out: lost pl and sltly hmpd over 4f out* **7/2**[2]	79+
9	2	**Nico's Dream (IRE)** 4-10-6 ... MrLWheatley(7) (M W Easterby) *hld up in rr: hdwy to chse ldrs 6f out: outpcd whn hmpd over 4f out: no threat after* **33/1**	73+
10	6	**Didbrook** 4-10-1 ... RobertLucey-Butler(5) (Mrs Mary Hambro) *chsd ldr: lft in ld bnd 9f out: hdd over 4f out: sn lost pl* **22/1**	57
U		**Lambrini Legend (IRE)** 4-10-6 ... MrOGreenall(7) (M W Easterby) *in rr: outpcd whn bdly hmpd and uns rdr over 4f out* **18/1**	—
0	R		**Harloes Coffee (IRE)**[132] 2906 6-11-6 ... (t) DerekLaverty(5) (Ronald Thompson) *led: hung bdly lft and rn out on bnd 9f out* **25/1**	—

4m 24.1s (7.60) **Going Correction** +0.475s/f (Soft)

WFA 4 from 5yo+ 5lb **12 Ran SP% 129.3**

Speed ratings: **102,101,101,98,98 94,92,90,89,87** —,— CSF £267.99 TOTE £36.40: £6.20, £3.60, £4.60; EX 677.00 Place 6 £219.85, Place 5 £110.77.

Owner J Cleeve **Bred** J M Cleeve **Trained** Norton, N Yorks

FOCUS

A fair gallop but very hard to know the true value of the form.

NOTEBOOK

Casewick Mist, a leggy half-sister to Elvis Returns, benefited from a patient ride and finished strongly to cut down the placed horses near the line. *(op 20-1)*

Red Scally, coming to the track quite late in life, is a decent type who will make a chaser in time. He went on looking all over a winner but had no answer to the winner's late burst. *(op 11-1 tchd 9-1)*

Bleu Pois(IRE), on the leg and narrow, took it up starting the home turn. He regain the lead inside *the last but was cut down near the line. He looks the type who may appreciate even more time.* (op 9-1)

Lucinda Lamb, whose dam has served this yard well, is a decent type and this will have taught her plenty. *(tchd 17-2)*

Spitfire Sortie(IRE), tapped for toe when left short of room on the inner starting the final turn, has not built on his debut success. *(op 5-2)*

Silver Snitch(IRE), a sturdy, backward type, may need plenty more time yet. *(tchd 13-2)*

Mr Shambles *Official explanation: jockey said he suffered interference*

T/Plt: £215.60 to a £1 stake. Pool: £42,622.75. 144.30 winning tickets. T/Qpdt: £24.50 to a £1 stake. Pool: £2,837.00. 85.40 winning tickets. WG

5125 SANDOWN (R-H)

Saturday, April 29

OFFICIAL GOING: Jumps courses - good to firm; flat course - good (good to firm in places)

Wind: Moderate, across Weather: Fine Other races under Rules of Flat Racing

5142 BETFRED MILLION H'CAP HURDLE (9 hdls) 2m 4f 110y

2:10 (2:11) (Class 2) (0-140,138) 4-Y-0+

£12,526 (£3,700; £1,850; £926; £462; £232)

Form				RPR
0000	1		**Hasty Prince**[10] 4959 8-11-12 138 ... APMcCoy (Jonjo O'Neill) *lw: hld up wl in rr: nt fluent 5th: shkn up and gd prog bef 2 out: led last: rdn clr* **14/1**	147+
0P0	2	4	**Salut Saint Cloud**[21] 4773 5-10-3 115 ... (b) PhilipHide (G L Moore) *prom: trckd ldr 3 out: rdn to ld narrowly 2 out: hdd last : outpcd by wnr* **14/1**	121+
6226	3	2 ½	**My Immortal**[46] 4435 4-10-8 126 ... RJGreene (M C Pipe) *t.k.h: mde most: drvn and hdd 2 out: hld whn blnd last: faded flat* **9/1**	123+
0311	4	½	**Herakles (GER)**[18] 4821 5-10-9 121 ... MickFitzgerald (N J Henderson) *trckd ldrs: rdn bef 2 out: sn no imp: btn whn mstke last: kpt on* **11/2**[1]	123+
1F10	5	nk	**Motorway (IRE)**[22] 4765 5-10-13 125 ... RichardJohnson (P J Hobbs) *trckd ldrs: rdn and nt qckn bef 2 out: btn whn nt fluent last: kpt on* **7/1**[3]	129+
0304	6	3	**Hawadeth**[18] 4821 11-11-0 126 ... (p) JimCrowley (V R A Dartnall) *hld up wl in rr: nt fluent 3 out: effrt u.p bef 2 out: kpt on: n.d* **16/1**	124
0003	7	½	**Fontanesi (IRE)**[11] 4945 6-10-11 123 ... (p) TimmyMurphy (M C Pipe) *hld up wl in rr: shkn up bef 2 out: styd on steadily after: nt rch ldrs* **16/1**	121
42U2	8	½	**Nanga Parbat (FR)**[31] 4663 5-10-10 122 ... (t) RWalsh (P F Nicholls) *lw: hld up wl in rr: pushed along bef 2 out: styd on steadily after: nvr nr ldrs* **13/2**[2]	119
6662	9	hd	**Arrayou (FR)**[10] 4959 5-11-6 132 ... (v) LeightonAspell (O Sherwood) *hld up wl in rr: drvn bef 2 out: no real imp on ldrs* **16/1**	129
1P52	10	1 ½	**New Entic (FR)**[18] 4821 5-11-2 128 ... (p) JamieMoore (G L Moore) *prom: rdn bef 3 out: wknd after 2 out* **20/1**	123
-400	11	½	**Glacial Sunset (IRE)**[9] 4974 11-11-5 131 ... TomDoyle (C Tinkler) *lw: hld up in midfield: rdn and no prog bef 2 out* **33/1**	126
-660	12	7	**Paddy The Piper (IRE)**[45] 4446 9-11-7 133 ... (t) TonyDobbin (L Lungo) *mstkes: prom: blnd 5th: wknd 2 out* **25/1**	123+
-P13	13	6	**Kilgowan (IRE)**[63] 4119 7-10-5 117 ... WayneHutchinson (Ian Williams) *hld up in midfield: mstke 3rd: no prog bef 2 out: wknd* **20/1**	99
5602	14	5	**Rainbows Aglitter**[38] 4573 9-10-6 118 ... PJBrennan (D R Gandolfo) *swtg: hld up in last: sme prog into midfield 6th: wknd bef 2 out* **33/1**	95
413	15	15	**Mith Hill**[65] 4077 5-10-4 116 ... JasonMaguire (Ian Williams) *prom: blnd 4th and lost pl: tried to rally after 3 out: btn whn mstke 2 out: eased* **13/2**[2]	93+
60-5	16	nk	**Time To Shine**[11] 4938 7-11-0 126 ... BenjaminHitchcott (Mrs L J Mongan) *racd wd: in tch to 5th: sn wknd: t.o after 3 out* **50/1**	88
60P6	17	8	**Flying Enterprise (IRE)**[10] 4959 6-11-3 129 ... (b) SamThomas (Miss Venetia Williams) *w ldr to 5th: sn rdn: wknd next: t.o after 3 out* **50/1**	83

4m 47.4s (-26.00) **Going Correction** -0.95s/f (Hard) course record

WFA 4 from 5yo+ 6lb **17 Ran SP% 118.7**

Speed ratings: **111,109,108,108,108 107,106,106,106,106 105,103,100,99,93 93,90** CSF £174.60 CT £1862.87 TOTE £18.60: £3.80, £2.70, £2.60, £1.70; EX 277.20 Trifecta £1097.30 Part won. Pool: £1,545.54 - 0.10 winning units..

Owner John P McManus **Bred** Cheveley Park Stud Ltd **Trained** Cheltenham, Gloucs

FOCUS

A competitive handicap, and pretty solid form. The first two were both very well in on old form.

NOTEBOOK

Hasty Prince, who had not won over hurdles since scoring at this fixture two years ago, ran his best race for a long time to take advantage of what had become a lenient mark. Without the tongue strap in which he had been tried last time, he was given a very patient ride until making rapid *progress to lead at the last and soon clear away. Official explanation: trainers representative said, regarding the improved form shown, gelding was possibly better suited by today's faster ground* (op 16-1)

Salut Saint Cloud, who wore blinkers instead of cheekpieces, had been tumbling down the handicap but was a winner on the Polytrack last month. Well supported, he showed ahead at the second last but was no match for the back-to-form winner from the final flight. He has become very well handicapped. *(op 16-1)*

My Immortal travelled to Punchestown in the week but did not run. Tackling this trip and taking on his elders for the first time, he was unlucky to run into two really well treated rivals and ran his best race yet, though held in third when landing awkwardly over the final flight. *(tchd 10-1)*

Herakles(GER) was pitching for a hat-trick off a 6lb higher mark. Never far away, he could not go with the leaders at the second last but found a second wind up the hill. *(op 9-2)*

Motorway(IRE), similarly placed throughout, ran a sound race and saw out the trip well enough. He could rate higher if jumping a bit better.

Hawadeth has become well handicapped and ran a fair race, keeping on without being able to pick up the leaders.

Fontanesi(IRE), third in this last season, stayed on from the rear and could be on the way back. He is now 5lb lower than when gaining his most recent win over hurdles, in last season's County Hurdle.

Nanga Parbat(FR) never threatened to take a hand but was not knocked about when beaten. *(op 11-2)*

Arrayou(FR), raised 7lb after his narrow defeat at Cheltenham, was never a factor.

Mith Hill, running for only the fourth time over hurdles and making his handicap debut, blundered badly at the fourth flight and dropped back through the field. He closed again with three to jump but his exertions told and he faded going to the next. He is potentially well treated. *(op 7-1 tchd 15-2)*

5143 BETFRED CELEBRATION CHASE GRADE 2 (13 fncs) 2m

2:40 (2:41) (Class 1) 5-Y-0+ **£57,020** (£21,390; £10,710; £5,340)

Form				RPR
-2UP	1		**River City (IRE)**[22] 4761 9-11-6 147 ... TomDoyle (Noel T Chance) *settled in 3rd pl tl trckd ldr fr 6th: rdn to chal 2 out: upsides last: drvn ahd flat* **9/1**	159+
2421	2	1 ¾	**Nyrche (FR)**[7] 5006 6-11-6 143 ... RobertThornton (A King) *lw: led at gd pce: hrd pressed 2 out: jnd last: hdd and one pce flat* **11/8**[1]	156
03-5	3	1 ¼	**Contraband**[179] 1970 8-11-6 153 ... TimmyMurphy (M C Pipe) *lw: t.k.h: hld up: nt fuent 3rd and 5th: trckd ldng pair next: urged along and no rspnse 2 out: styd on nr fin* **5/2**[2]	156+
5214	4	9	**Hoo La Baloo (FR)**[21] 4774 5-11-3 147 ... RWalsh (P F Nicholls) *trckd ldr tl terrible blunder 6th: dropped to last and nvr able to rcvr* **3/1**[3]	148+

3m 52.2s (-10.30) **Going Correction** -0.40s/f (Good)

WFA 5 from 6yo+ 3lb **4 Ran SP% 105.7**

Speed ratings: **109,108,107,103** CSF £21.29 TOTE £9.90; EX 21.90.

Owner Mrs S Rowley-Williams **Bred** Greenville House Stud And M Morgan **Trained** Upper Lambourn, Berks

FOCUS

Not a strong renewal but still an interesting event. The winner has been rated 6lb on his previous best but was still a stone below the level of a typical Champion Chase winner, while the runner-up was 6lb below his Ayr mark.

NOTEBOOK

River City(IRE), back at the minimum trip after pulling up at Aintree, is well suited by fast ground. Generally jumping soundly, he drew alongside the leader at the last and asserted on the flat to gain his biggest win to date. He will be aimed at the Champion Chase next season - incidentally he is by the same sire as this year's winner Newmill - but will need to make significant improvement if he is to win at Cheltenham. *(op 7-1)*

Nyrche(FR), bidding to follow up last week's win at Ayr, set a good pace and jumped really well. He was joined by the winner at the final fence and could pull out no extra on the run-in. *(tchd 6-4)*

Contraband had been ruled out for the season after injuring himself at Exeter in the autumn and it was surprising to see him turn out here. Held up, and a little slow at a couple of early fences, he was close enough from the Pond Fence but, carrying his head a little high and not helping his rider, he could not get to the first two. He is without a win since last season's Arkle, when he had River City five lengths away in third. *(tchd 9-4 and 11-4 in a place)*
Hoo La Baloo(FR) dropped back to last place after a bad blunder at an open ditch and, his confidence seemingly affected, could never get back into the race. *(tchd 10-3 in place)*

5144 BETFRED GOLD CUP CHASE (H'CAP) GRADE 3 (24 fncs) 3m 5f 110y

3:20 (3:20) (Class 1) 5-Y-O+

£91,232 (£34,224; £17,136; £8,544; £4,288; £2,144)

Form				RPR

4022 **1** **Lacdoudal (FR)**[22] 4764 7-11-5 **152** .... RichardJohnson 164+
(P J Hobbs) *wl plcd: bdly hmpd 8th: prog to trck ldng pair 14th: lft 2nd 17th: led after 4 out: 3 l clr last: drvn and hld on gamely* **10/1**[3]

6-P1 **2** *1 ¼* **Eric's Charm (FR)**[49] 4374 8-10-7 **140** .... LeightonAspell 149+
(O Sherwood) *lw: w ldr: led 10th: hdd sn after 4 out: drvn next: styd on wl flat: a hld* **8/1**[2]

234F **3** *hd* **My Will (FR)**[23] 4746 6-11-2 **149** .... RWalsh 158+
(P F Nicholls) *lw: hld up wl in rr: stdy prog fr 15th: sltly hmpd next: chsd ldng pair 3 out: rdn and kpt on wl fr next* **8/1**[2]

U501 **4** *10* **Liberthine (FR)**[22] 4762 7-9-13 **139** oh3 ow6........... MrSWaley-Cohen[(7)] 139+
(N J Henderson) *nt a fluent: wl in tch: effrt to chse ldng pair 19th: no imp and lost 3rd 3 out: fdd* **10/1**[3]

001P **5** *2* **Therealbandit (IRE)**[21] 4777 9-11-6 **153** ....(p) TimmyMurphy 150+
(M C Pipe) *often j.lft: settled in rr: effrt fr 16th: nt on terms w ldrs fr 19th: wl btn whn j. bdly lft 2 out: kpt on* **16/1**

404P **6** *1 ½* **It Takes Time (IRE)**[21] 4777 12-10-11 **151** .... AndrewGlassonbury[(7)] 146
(M C Pipe) *hld up wl in rr: prog into midfield fr 13th: no imp on ldrs 4 out: one pce after* **33/1**

-P00 **7** *19* **Calling Brave (IRE)**[7] 5004 10-10-8 **141** ....(bt[1]) MickFitzgerald 117
(N J Henderson) *trckd ldrs: rdn in 5th pl after 4 out: no imp after: wknd bef 2 out* **25/1**

S055 **8** *5* **Risk Accessor (IRE)**[21] 4777 11-10-3 **136** .... RobertThornton 107
(Jonjo O'Neill) *hld up in midfield: hmpd 8th: prog whn mstke 14th: wknd fr 20th* **16/1**

351U **9** *½* **Jack High (IRE)**[21] 4777 11-10-7 **140** .... GCotter 110
(T M Walsh, Ire) *a wl in rr: lost tch w ldng gp fr 17th: u.p and tail swishing furiously bef 2 out* **10/1**[3]

60-6 **10** *6* **Puntal (FR)**[21] 4777 10-10-9 **142** ....(t) TomScudamore 106
(M C Pipe) *trckd ldng pair to 11th: sn rdn: losing pl whn mstke 14th: toiling in rr fr 17th* **12/1**

5110 **11** *6* **Inca Trail (IRE)**[21] 4777 10-10-0 **133** ....(b) DominicElsworth 91
(D McCain) *hld up towards rr: no prog 15th: wl bhd fr 19th* **12/1**

20F0 **12** *2 ½* **Royal Auclair (FR)**[7] 5004 9-11-7 **159** ....(t) LiamHeard[(5)] 115
(P F Nicholls) *lw: a wl in rr: struggling and j. slowly 14th: wl bhd after* **25/1**

UPP3 **F** **Mr Fluffy**[196] 1735 9-10-0 **133** oh8................................ WayneHutchinson —
(A W Carroll) *trckd ldrs tl fell 8th* **50/1**

21P1 **F** **You're Special (USA)**[45] 4447 9-10-1 **134** ....(t) TonyDobbin —
(Ferdy Murphy) *trckd ldrs: 5th and wl in tch whn crumpled on landing 16th* **7/1**[1]

-FUP **F** **One Knight (IRE)**[43] 4470 10-11-6 **153** .... PJBrennan —
(P J Hobbs) *led to 10th: pressed ldr after: mstke 13th: blnd 16th: cl 2nd whn fell next* **14/1**

111U **P** **Presenting Express (IRE)**[35] 4617 7-10-0 **133** oh8........... BarryFenton —
(Miss E C Lavelle) *mstkes: a wl in rr: reminders 13th: wl bhd 15th: t.o whn p.u bef 20th* **12/1**

-050 **P** **Montayral (FR)**[12] 4929 9-10-0 **133** oh2.................................. TomDoyle —
(P Hughes, Ire) *nvr gng wl and sn pushed along in rr: lost tch in last pair 11th: t.o whn p.u bef 17th* **33/1**

2320 **P** **High Cotton (IRE)**[44] 4460 11-10-0 **133** oh19....................... JimCrowley —
(K G Reveley) *prom to 2nd: mstke next and reluctant after: wl in rr and slow jump 8th: t.o last fr 11th: p.u bef 17th* **66/1**

7m 18.8s (-4.60) **Going Correction** -0.40s/f (Good) **18** Ran SP% **120.5**
Speed ratings: **117,116,116,113,113 113,107,106,106,104 103,102,—,—,— —,—,—** CSF £81.52 CT £683.63 TOTE £11.20: £2.80, £2.80, £2.50, £2.60; EX 83.60 Trifecta £989.30 Pool: £64,101.96 - 46.00 winning units..
Owner Mrs R J Skan **Bred** Scea Terres Noires **Trained** Withycombe, Somerset

FOCUS
A decent renewal of what has always been one of the most competitive handicap chases of the season, devalued only a little by the late defection of Innox on account of the drying ground. It was run at a strong pace. The winner is even better than the bare result, the second ran to a similar mark to his recent course win and the third ran right up to his mark.

NOTEBOOK
Lacdoudal(FR) was racing off a career-high mark and tackling half a mile further than he had ever gone before. Never far away, he survived being turned sideways by the falling Mr Fluffy at the eighth and, in front after the fourth last, he stayed on bravely. Suited by decent ground, he has the Hennessy as his likely first target next term and could go for the Grand National, although he is not very big and his owners will need persuading. *(tchd 11- 1 in a place)*
Eric's Charm(FR) was 12lb higher than when scoring over half a mile shorter here last month. Connections were worried about the drying ground, but he handled the surface well enough and ran a big race, always up with the pace and rallying up the hill after the winner had headed him leaving the back straight. *(op 7-1 tchd 17-2 and 9-1 in a place)*
My Will(FR), without the tongue tie on this step up in trip, was switched off in rear until creeping closer down the back straight. Keeping on well from the second last but just unable to quicken, this was a solid effort on ground that did not really suit, but he is hard to place and has ended the season without a win from nine starts.
Liberthine(FR) was effectively 9lb higher than when landing the Topham at Aintree, with her rider being able to claim only a pound of his allowance. Travelling well in touch before closing on the leading pair with six to jump, her stamina ran out from the Pond Fence. She is now set to retire to the paddocks. *(op 8-1 tchd 11-1)*
Therealbandit(IRE), who showed a marked tendency to jump to his left on this fast ground, could never get into the action although he was staying on at the end.
It Takes Time(IRE), who was never able to get into contention, has been dropped just a pound in the course of the last year and is difficult to place.
Calling Brave(IRE), who got round in the previous week's Scottish National, was blinkered for the first time. He ran well for a long way but faded at the last of the Railway fences. *(op 20-1)*
Risk Accessor(IRE) travelled well, as he often does, but he found little when the pressure was on. Despite the fact that he got round in the Grand National, these long distances stretch him.
Jack High(IRE), successful last year when 11lb lower, was always in the rear division and flashed his tail alarmingly in the latter stages when under pressure. *(tchd 9-1)*
Puntal(FR), having only his fourth run since winning this off the same mark two years ago, ran as if he had not recovered from his Grand National exertions. *(op 10-1)*
Inca Trail(IRE), Ginger McCain's last big-race runner, was always towards the back of the field.
Royal Auclair(FR), who is in the grip of the Handicapper, has had a tough season and was always at the back of the field.
You're Special(USA), 9lb higher than when landing the Fulke Walwyn Kim Muir, was shooting for a £250,000 bonus, having scored at the Cheltenham Festival. He was very much in the hunt when getting in too close to the sixteenth and coming down. *(tchd 16-1)*
One Knight(IRE), taken on for the lead by Eric's Charm, survived a couple of errors before hitting the deck when in second. He is highly talented but has completed the course just once in six starts since winning the Royal & SunAlliance Chase in 2003. *(tchd 16-1)*
Presenting Express(IRE) was no less than 22lb higher than when completing a four-timer two starts back, including being 8lb out of the handicap. He made a number of mistakes and was always trailing before pulling up. *(tchd 16-1)*

5000 AUTEUIL (L-H)

Saturday, April 29

OFFICIAL GOING: Very soft

5154a PX LEON RAMBAUD (HURDLE) (GRADE 2) 2m 4f 110y

3:25 (3:25) 5-Y-O+

£54,310 (£26,552; £15,690; £10,862; £6,034; £4,224)

RPR

1 **River Charm (FR)**[27] 4717 6-10-6 .... PMarsac —
(G Cherel, France)

2 *2* **Rock And Palm (FR)**[8] 5000 6-10-6 .... MDelmares —
(Mlle C Cardenne, France)

3 *3* **Lycaon De Vauzelle (FR)**[27] 4717 7-10-10 .... BChameraud —
(J Bertran De Balanda, France)

4 *2* **Dom D'Orgeval (FR)**[23] 4745 6-10-6 .... DGallagher —
(Nick Williams) *raced in midfield, mistake 4th, ridden & outpaced after 3f out, kept on again from approaching last*

5 *2 ½* **Royale Cazoumaille (FR)**[27] 4717 7-9-13 .... —
(B Barbier, France)

6 *3* **King's Daughter (FR)**[8] 5-9-11 ow2.. —
(Robert Collet, France)

7 *5* **Mayev (FR)**[27] 6-10-4 .... —
(B Barbier, France)

8 *15* **Grand Canal (FR)**[13] 10-10-4 .... —
(J-V Toux, France)

F **Sunspot**[27] 4717 6-10-6 .... —
(A Chaille-Chaille, France)

F **Gold Magic (FR)**[11] 2403 8-10-8 .... —
(J-P Gallorini, France)

4m 59.0s **10** Ran
PARI-MUTUEL: WIN 5.40; PL 2.10, 2.90, 2.30; DF 19.00.
Owner Mlle I Catsaras **Bred** Gestut Sybille **Trained** France

NOTEBOOK
Dom D'Orgeval(FR), fifth at Liverpool in a Grade Two contest over three miles, is perhaps at his best over slightly shorter, and with the ground to suit he appeared to have conditions in his favour here. This was a solid effort in defeat and this progressive six-year-old may yet make his mark at Graded level.

INDEX TO MEETINGS JUMPS 2005-2006

† Abandoned
(M) Mixed meeting

INDEX TO STEEPLECHASING & HURDLE RACING

Figure underneath the horse's name indicates its age. The figures following the pedigree refer to the numbers of the races (steeplechases are in bold) in which the horse has run; parentheses () indicate a win; superscript figures denote other placings. Foreign races are denoted by the suffix 'a'. Horses withdrawn (not under orders) are shown with the suffix 'w'. The figures within arrows indicate Raceform Private Handicap MASTER ratings. The ratings are based on a scale of 0-175. The following symbols are used: 'h' hurdle rating, 'c' chase rating, '+' on the upgrade, 'd' disappointing, '?' questionable form. 't' tentative rating based on time.

Aaron's Run *M R Bosley* 74b
6 b g Karinga Bay—Malaia (IRE) (Commanche Run)
1323[9] 1799[12] 2288[7]

Aba Gold (IRE) *J Clements* 41h
6 b m Darnay—Abadila (IRE) (Shernazar)
302[P] 500[3] 643[P] 854[P] 3235[P]

Abalvino (FR) *Miss J Wickens* 111c
12 ch g Sillery(USA)—Abalvina (FR) (Abdos)
(4055) 4351[6]

Abbeybraney (IRE) *J A Berry* 98b
5 b g Moonax(IRE)—Balliniska Beauty (IRE) (Roselier (FR))
5081a[15]

Abbey Days (IRE) *S Flook* 71h 98+c
9 ch g Be My Native(USA)—Abbey Emerald (Baptism)
(4283) 4897[U]

Abbey Hill *W S Kittow* 14h
9 b m Then Again—Galley Bay (Welsh Saint)
1158[F] 1266[6]

Abbeymore Lady (IRE) *Paul John Gilligan* 53h
5 bb m Capolago—Secret Pound (IRE) (Namaqualand (USA))
517[P]

Abbey Princess *J Howard Johnson* 63h
6 b m Prince Daniel(USA)—Riverain (Bustino)
152[P]

Abbeytown (IRE) *Mrs Jeanette Riordan* 124+c
9 ch g Over The River(FR)—Call Queen (Callernish)
4748[F] 5083a[16]

Abbotsford (IRE) *J Howard Johnson*
6 gr g Arzanni—Cloughan Girl (IRE) (Yashgan)
2638[P] 3173[P]

Aberdare *J R Bewley* 100h
7 b m Overbury(IRE)—Temple Heights (Shirley Heights)
2264[P] 3234[F] 4344[P] 4491[3] 4724[P]4982[0] 5123[4]

Aberdeen Park *Mrs H Sweeting* 67h
4 gr f Environment Friend—Michelee (Merdon Melody)
3579[6]

Aber Gale *Mrs S M Johnson* 67h
7 gr m Thethingaboutitis(USA)—Twablade (IRE) (Strong Gale)
3130[F] 4048[7] 4855[13]

A Bit Of Fun *J T Stimpson* 108 h
5 ch g Unfuwain(USA)—Horseshoe Reef (Mill Reef (USA))
220[6] 488[5] 571[8] 1413[F] 1668[U]1804[P] 3360[P] 3687[2] 3889[2] 4058[3]4420[11] 4736[7] 4852[2]

A Bit Pleased *W P Mullins*
4 b f Alflora(IRE)—Lady High Sheriff (IRE) (Lancastrian)
5134a[22]

Ablastfromthepast (IRE) *C F Swan* 82h
6 bb g Anshan—Kouron (Pauper)
3757[6]

Able Baker Charlie (IRE) *J R Fanshawe* 115+h
7 b g Sri Pekan(USA)—Lavezzola (IRE) (Salmon Leap (USA))
2487[F]

Able Charlie (GER) *Mrs Tracey Barfoot-Saunt* 86h
4 ch g Lomitas—Alula (GER) (Monsun (GER))
1737[5] 1955[F] 2178[9] 2587[4] 3242[11]4392[8] 4616[7] 4860[9]

A Boy Named Sioux (IRE) *Mrs E J Reed* 70+c
8 b g Little Bighorn—Gayable (Gay Fandango (USA))
4722[U]

Abragante (IRE) *M C Pipe* 106h
5 b g Saddlers' Hall(IRE)—Joli's Girl (Mansingh (USA))
515[2] 696[3] 764[8] 1968[10] 2173[3]2530[P] 3876[2] 4557[P]

Abraham (IRE) *Michael Cunningham* 78h
4 b g Orpen(USA)—We've Just Begun (USA) (Huguenot (USA))
3401a[7] (Dead)

Abraham Smith *B J Eckley* 112+h
6 b g Lord Americo—Alice Smith (Alias Smith (USA))
2285[2] 2592[12] 3846[3] (4282) 4606[4] 4858[6]

Abrakadalpha (IRE) *Ms Jane Evans* 32c
12 b g Alphabatim(USA)—Ebonylass (Slip Anchor)
282[P]

Abram's Bridge (IRE) *E Bolger* 109+c
7 b g Moscow Society(USA)—Arctic Scale (IRE) (Strong Gale)
5128a[2]

Absolutelythebest (IRE) *J G M O'Shea* 90 h
5 b g Anabaa(USA)—Recherchee (Rainbow Quest (USA))
1750[3] 2070[6] 3023[11] 3729[4] 4036[P]4738[3]

Absolut Power (GER) *J A Geake* 113h
5 ch g Acatenango(GER)—All Our Dreams (Caerleon (USA))
177[2] 312[2] (629) 864[3] 1026[2] 1220[2](1431) 1559[3]

Ab Und Zu (GER) *O W Seiler*
8 b m Colon(GER)—Allenstein (GER) (San Vicente (GER))
590a[4]

Abzuson *J R Norton* 97h 86c
9 b g Abzu—Mellouise (Handsome Sailor)
2010[P] **2441[U] 2675[3]3041[U]** 3289[8] 3548[3] 3675[6]4012[P] **4518[U] 4847[9]**

Acacia Avenue (IRE) *Ian Williams* 76+h
6 b g Shardari—Ennel Lady (IRE) (Erin's Hope)
4359[6] 5015[7]

Acambo (GER) *M C Pipe* 142+h
5 gr g Acambaro(GER)—Artic Lady (FR) (No Pass No Sale)
(2455) (2871) 3328[3] 3761[5] 4473[23]

Acca Larentia (IRE) *Mrs H O Graham* 70h
5 gr m Titus Livius(FR)—Daisy Grey (Nordance (USA))
2108[9] 2658[P] 3267[7]

Acceleration (IRE) *R Allan* 88h
6 b g Groom Dancer(USA)—Overdrive (Shirley Heights)
821[2] (406) 784[10] 2657[5] 2843[8] 3782[7]4585[7] (4723) 5120[3]

Accepting *J Mackie* 107 h
9 b g Mtoto—D'Azy (Persian Bold)
1436[10]

Accipiter *J A Geake* 149+h
7 b g Polar Falcon(USA)—Accuracy (Gunner B)
2326[P]

Accomplish *W J Haggas* 63h
4 b f Desert Story(IRE)—Last Ambition (IRE) (Cadeaux Genereux)
1737[7]

Accordello (IRE) *K G Reveley* 106h
5 b m Accordion—Marello (Supreme Leader)
3491[4] 3969[4]

According To Billy (IRE) *E J O'Grady* 130h
7 b g Accordion—Graphic Lady (IRE) (Phardante (FR))
4461[16]

According To John (IRE) *N G Richards* 133+h
6 br g Accordion—Cabin Glory (The Parson)
(2678) (3205) (4315) (4980)

According To Pete *J M Jefferson* 110+h
5 b g Accordion—Magic Bloom (Full Of Hope)
(1889) (2572) 2844[2] (4040) 5021[5]

According To Plan (IRE) *A E Jones* 79b
6 br g Accordion—Clonaheen Joy (IRE) (Lafontaine (USA))
844[8] 963[5]

Accordion Etoile (IRE) *Paul Nolan* 164h 153c
7 b g Accordion—Royal Thimble (IRE) (Prince Rupert (FR))
(954a) 1093a[6] **1702a[2] (2208) 3774a[3] 4431[F] 4774[6](5100a)**

Accumulus *Noel T Chance* 90b
6 b g Cloudings(IRE)—Norstock (Norwick (USA))
131[P] *1922[3]* 4807[6]4909[9]

Ace Coming *D B Feek* 76h
5 b g First Trump—Tarry (Salse (USA))
21[7] 1774[P]

Acertack (IRE) *R Rowe* 65h 94+c
9 b g Supreme Leader—Ask The Madam (Strong Gale)
2210[13] 2577[2] 2827[7]3187[P] 3718[4] 4120[4]4694[P]

Aces Four (IRE) *Ferdy Murphy* 130+h
7 ch g Fourstars Allstar(USA)—Special Trix (IRE) (Peacock (FR))
1445[2] 1672[4] 1834[3] 2036[3] (4052) (4582) 4980[3](5093)

Achancyman (IRE) *Richard Mathias*
11 br g Beau Sher—Little Chance (Master Owen)
98[U]

Achilles Wings (USA) *Miss K M George* 118h 71c
10 b g Irish River(FR)—Shirley Valentine (Shirley Heights)
387[3] (633) 864[2]

Acropolis (IRE) *J Howard Johnson* 92+h
5 b h Sadler's Wells(USA)—Dedicated Lady (IRE) (Pennine Walk)
3374[4]

Across The Water *G H Jones* 59h
12 b m Slip Anchor—Stara (Star Appeal)
1154[7] 1317[8]

Action Strasse (IRE) *J Howard Johnson* 95+b
4 b g Old Vic—Platin Run (IRE) (Strong Gale)
3799[4]

Activist *D Carroll* 100h
8 ch g Diesis—Shicklah (USA) (The Minstrel (CAN))
1796[10]

Actual *P D Niven* 32h
6 b g Factual(USA)—Tugra (FR) (Baby Turk)
1757[P] 2295[11]

Acushnet *J M Jefferson* 69h
7 b g Ezzoud(IRE)—Flitcham (Elegant Air)
(917) 1048[8] 1543[8] 1794[9]

Adair Mohr (IRE) *Michael Hourigan* 50h
6 gr g Luso—Cullenstown Lady (IRE) (Wood Chanter)
44a[22]

Adalar (IRE) *P W D'Arcy* 73h
6 br g Grand Lodge(USA)—Adalya (IRE) (Darshaan)
279[8] 1562[6]

Adalari (IRE) *W J Codd* 96h
4 bb g Priolo(USA)—Adalya (IRE) (Darshaan)
4360[5]

Adalie *J Joseph* 91 h 98+c
12 b m Absalom—Allied Newcastle (Crooner)
916[P] 1981[4] 4577[5]4783[P]

Adamant Approach (IRE) *W P Mullins* 142h 149c
12 b g Mandalus—Crash Approach (Crash Course)
2209[4] 3411a[11] 4473[3] 4951a[4] 5059a[2]

Adam's Belle (IRE) *N B King* 22b
6 b m Fourstars Allstar(USA)—Electric Belle (IRE) (Electric)
2242[13] 2558[14]

Adarma (IRE) *C Roche* 126h 129c
8 b m Topanoora—Overtime (IRE) (Executive Perk)
45a[18] 2539a[4] 3053a[4]4447[P]

Addiction (IRE) *Michael Hourigan* 92h
9 bb g Woods Of Windsor(USA)—Star Cream (Star Appeal)
71a[F] (Dead)

Adecco (IRE) *G L Moore* 88h 102 c
7 b g Eagle Eyed(USA)—Kharaliya (FR) (Doyoun)
2459[7] 2734[3] 2940[6] **(3663) 3888[3]4454[3]**

Adelphie Lass *D B Feek* 81h 58c
6 b m Theatrical Charmer—Miss Adventure (Adonijah)
2011[5]

Adelphi Theatre (USA) *R Rowe* 101+h 111+c
9 b g Sadler's Wells(USA)—Truly Bound (USA) (In Reality (USA))
566[2] **2241[5] 2583[3]3326[10]**

Adjami (IRE) *A King* 104+h
5 b g Entrepreneur—Adjriyna (Top Ville)
243[2] (343) 680[2] 1407[5]

Adjawar (IRE) *J J Quinn* 99 h 127+c
8 b g Ashkalani(IRE)—Adjriyna (Top Ville)
78[P] 396[2] **(479) (714)**

Adlestrop *R T Phillips* 93h
6 ch m Alderbrook—Lady Buck (Pollerton)
2961[3] 3448[2] 3979[5] 4389[6] 4855[5]

Admiral (IRE) *T J Pitt* 132 h
5 b g Alhaarth(IRE)—Coast Is Clear (IRE) (Rainbow Quest (USA))
(1677) (2338) 2500[8] 3298[14] 4432[12] 4473[27] 4773[16]

Admiral Peary (IRE) *C R Egerton* 112 h 121+c
10 bb g Lord Americo—Arctic Brief (Buckskin (FR))
(168) **2375[3] 3142[2] 3343[3]3845[7] 4016[P] 4287[2]**

Ad Murum (IRE) *G M Moore* 95h
7 ch g Hubbly Bubbly(USA)—Cailin Cainnteach (Le Bavard (FR))
2948[15] 3559[7] 3914[P] 4916[4] 8[2]

Adolphus (IRE) *C Storey* 72h 88+c
9 b g Tidaro(USA)—Coxtown Queen (IRE) (Corvaro (USA))
151[3] 4347[5] 4748[B]

Adopted Hero (IRE) *J Howard Johnson* 131 h
6 b g Sadler's Wells(USA)—Lady Liberty (NZ) (Noble Bijou (USA))
2190[2] 2636[P] 3256[7] 4473[24]

Advance East *M J M Evans* 82 c
14 b g Polish Precedent(USA)—Startino (Bustino)
2183[3] 2465[P] 3274[P](3482)

Adventino *P R Johnson* 45h
11 gr g Neltino—My Miss Adventure (New Member)
3673[9] 3985[P] 4733[7] **4802[P]4936[F]**

Adventurist *P Bowen* 114 h
6 ch g Entrepreneur—Alik (FR) (Targowice (USA))
2763[10] 2923[4] 3342[P] 3646[2] (3806) 3993[4]4589[3]

Aegean *Mrs S J Smith* 112c
12 b g Rock Hopper—Sayulita (Habitat)
1276[2]

Aelred *R Johnson* 85 h 125 c
13 b g Ovac(ITY)—Sponsorship (Sparkler)
108[8] 3049 553[3] **648[6]**

Afadan (IRE) *J R Jenkins* 97h
8 br g Royal Academy(USA)—Afasara (IRE) (Shardari)
4838[11] 4907[P]

Afeef (USA) *J A Danahar* 92+h
7 bb g Dayjur(USA)—Jah (USA) (Relaunch (USA))
1751[P] 1977[10] 2582[P] (Dead)

A Few Kind Words (IRE) *Mrs K Waldron* 95h
5 b g Darazari(IRE)—Aussieannie (IRE) (Arapahos (FR))
7[7] 2185[6] 4280[11] 4665[2] 4875[2]

Afrad (FR) *N J Henderson* 144 h
5 gr g Linamix(FR)—Afragha (IRE) (Darshaan)
65a[2] 450[4] 2493[5] (2974) 3298[8] 4446[2]4500[53]

African Star *J M Bradley*
5 b g Mtoto—Pass The Rose (IRE) (Thatching)
1916[P] 2148[P]

African Sunset (IRE) *A Parker* 81h
6 b g Danehill Dancer(IRE)—Nizamiya (Darshaan)
4632[P] 4919[P]

Afro Man *C J Mann* 108 h 110 c
8 b g Commanche Run—Lady Elle (IRE) (Persian Mews)
2429[2] 2960[U] 3676[F] (Dead)

Afsoun (FR) *N J Henderson* 140+h
4 b g Kahyasi—Afragha (IRE) (Darshaan)
2178[2] (2756) (3817) 4468[5] 4747[3]

After Eight (GER) *Miss Venetia Williams* 129+h
6 br g Sir Felix(FR)—Amrei (GER) (Ardross)
(2010)

After Lent (IRE) *M C Pipe* 98h
5 b g Desert Style(IRE)—Yashville (Top Ville)
3355[5] 3673[7] 3945[7] 4278[4] 4556[F]4903[2]

After Me Boys *Mrs S J Smith* 118 h 112 c
12 b g Arzanni—Realm Wood (Precipice Wood)
525[8] **(759)** 1234[6] **1442[3]**

Agent Lois (IRE) *S Donohoe* 89b
5 b m Flying Legend(USA)—Gosheen (IRE) (Supreme Leader)
(2480) 3931[9]

Agincourt (IRE) *John R Upson* 79h 95+c
10 b g Alphabatim(USA)—Miss Brantridge (Riboboy (USA))
81[7] 1713[F]

A Glass In Thyne (IRE) *B N Pollock* 103h 140 c
8 br g Glacial Storm(USA)—River Thyne (IRE) (Good Thyne (USA))
2176[7] (3620) 4433[F]

Agnese *M Dods* 80h
6 ch m Abou Zouz(USA)—Efizia (Efisio)
1921[11] 415[8] 603[3] 718[4] 1002[3]1067[3] 8[5]

Agua Ardente *Mrs Caroline Bailey*
9 ch g Afzal—Armagnac Messenger (Pony Express)
4421[U]

Ah Yeah (IRE) *N B King* 22c
9 b g Roselier(FR)—Serena Bay (Furry Glen)
1819[7] 2011[U] 2506[4]2951[5] 2957[U] 3419[5]3602[5]

Aide De Camp (FR) *M Todhunter* 72h
7 b g Saint Preuil(FR)—Baraka De Thaix II (FR) (Olmeto)
843[5]

Ailsa *C W Thornton* 36b
4 b f Bishop Of Cashel—Mindomica (Dominion)
3259[10]

Aimees Mark (IRE) *F Flood* 124h 122c
10 bb g Jolly Jake(NZ)—Wee Mite (Menelek)
115a[U] 5102a[10]

Ain Tecbalet (FR) *N M Bloom* 88h 108c
8 b g Riverquest(FR)—La Chance Au Roy (FR) (Rex Magna (FR))
184[5]

Ain't That A Shame (IRE) *P F Nicholls* 115+h
6 ch g Broken Hearted—Alvinru (Sandalay)
1847[F] 2269[B]

Aires Rock (IRE) *Miss J E Foster* 67b
6 b g Courtship—Newgate Music (IRE) (Accordion)
616[8] 828[7]

Air Guitar (IRE) *M G Quinlan* 106+h
6 b g Blues Traveller(IRE)—Money Talks (IRE) (Lord Chancellor (USA))
1206[8] 1364[4] 1454[2] 1565[2] (2144) 2261[3]

Airgusta (IRE) *C P Morlock* 93h
5 b g Danehill Dancer(IRE)—Ministerial Model (IRE) (Shalford (IRE))
4280[5] 4875[9] 5135[4]

Air Of Affection *J R Turner* 91+h
5 b m Air Express(IRE)—Auntie Gladys (Great Nephew)
27[5] (2412) 2704[3] 4529[4] **4840[P]**5039[P]

Air Of Supremacy (IRE) *Mrs K Walton* 41h
5 gr g Royal Applause—Lap Of Luxury (Sharrood (USA))
418[11] 596[10]

Aisjem (IRE) *Evan Williams* 83h 86c
7 ch m Anshan—Emma's Way (IRE) (Le Bavard (FR))
1832[P] 3359[P] 3482[4]3716[3] 3938[U] 4047[3]4553[2]

Aitchjayem *H J Manners* 66h
6 b g Rakaposhi King—G W Supermare (Rymer)
1635[5] 1854[7] 1959[5]

Ajay (IRE) *T D Walford* 88+b
5 ch g Posidonas—Gothic Shadow (IRE) (Mandalus)
4072[8] 4533[3]

Akarem *K R Burke* 121h
5 b h Kingmambo(USA)—Spirit Of Tara (IRE) (Sadler's Wells (USA))
2627[3] 3003a[2] 3534[3]

Akash (IRE) *Miss J Feilden* 100h
6 b g Dr Devious(IRE)—Akilara (IRE) (Kahyasi)
4479[3] 5070[6]

Akilak (IRE) *J Howard Johnson* 145 h
5 br g Charnwood Forest(IRE)—Akilara (IRE) (Kahyasi)
88a[3] 2761[U] 2971[5] 3383[5] 4446[25]4765[13]

Akram (IRE) *Jonjo O'Neill* 68h
4 b g Night Shift(USA)—Akdariya (IRE) (Shirley Heights)
3340[P] 3431[7] 3939[P] 4149[5] 4632[P]

Akshar (IRE) *D K Weld* 129 h
7 b g Danehill(USA)—Akilara (IRE) (Kahyasi)
117a[4] 1093a[10]

Alabaster *N J Hawke* 65 c
11 gr m Gran Alba(USA)—Last Ditch (Ben Novus)
1122[3] 1713[4] 1832[P]1951[U]

Alagon (IRE) *Ian Williams* 104h
6 b g Alzao(USA)—Forest Lair (Habitat)
2207[15] 3289[11] 3982[8] 4612[4]

Alaipour (IRE) *Barry Potts* 85h
7 b h Kahyasi—Alaiyda (USA) (Shahrastani (USA))
1100[P]

Alakdar (CAN) *Jane Southcombe* 77h 98c
12 ch g Green Dancer(USA)—Population (General Assembly (USA))
2431[P] 5112[5]

Al Alba (USA) *Mrs H Dalton* 69h
4 b f Distant View(USA)—Noblissima (IRE) (Sadler's Wells (USA))
3550[6] 3985[P]

Alam (USA) *P Monteith* 126 h 126c
7 b g Silver Hawk(USA)—Ghashtah (USA) (Nijinsky (CAN))
1846[6] 2003[8] 2498[P]3172[8]

Alasil (USA) *Mrs N Smith* 86+h
6 bb g Swain(IRE)—Asl (USA) (Caro)
2015[7] 2995[P] 3899[7]

Alaskan Fizz *R T Phillips* 80+h
5 ch m Efisio—Anchorage (IRE) (Slip Anchor)
(375) 3550[9]

Albany (IRE) *J Howard Johnson* 121 h
6 ch g Alhaarth(IRE)—Tochar Ban (USA) (Assert)
3256[10] (3741) 4776[7]

Albarino (IRE) *M Scudamore* 122 h 117+c
7 ch g Royal Abjar(USA)—Miss Lee Ann (Tumble Wind)
(2298) 2533[9] 2730[3] (2969) 3297[3] 3510[10]

Albatros (FR) *A R Trotter* 96c
9 b g Shining Steel—Abalvina (FR) (Abdos)
(3758) 4831[U]

Alberoni (IRE) *Peter McCreery* 67b 113c
10 b g Magical Strike(USA) —Douriya (Brave Invader (USA))
112a[18]

Albertas Run (IRE) *Jonjo O'Neill* 115b
5 b g Accordion—Holly Grove Lass (Le Moss)
(2340) (3292) 4448[15]

Albert House (IRE) *R H Alner* 105h 107+c
8 ch g Carroll House—Action Plan (Creative Plan (USA))
1854[4] 2341[3] 3018[4] 3441[2] 3603[P]4357[6] 4558[5]

Albertino Lad *Miss Lucinda V Russell* 84h 102+c
9 ch g Mystiko(USA) —Siokra (Kris)
1835[2] 2026[6] 2943[3]3255[2] 3447[U] 4142[2]4365[F] (Dead)

Albert Mooney (IRE) *David Wachman* 125+h
6 b g Dr Massini(IRE) —Prudent Rose (IRE) (Strong Gale)
3515a[6]

Albuhera (IRE) *P F Nicholls* 142h 149 c
8 b g Desert Style(IRE) —Morning Welcome (IRE) (Be My Guest (USA))
(1911) 2208[3] (2531) 2759[3] 3039[2] 3726[4]4241[4]

Alcapone (IRE) *M F Morris* 113h 103c
12 b g Roselier(FR) —Ann's Cap (IRE) (Cardinal Flower)
69a[17] 1700a[7] 2304a[3]2786a[4] 3472a[6] 4123a[7]

Alcatras (IRE) *B J M Ryall* 68h 97 c
9 bb g Corrouge(USA) —Kisco (IRE) (Henbit (USA))
518[2] (632) 805[5]865[2] 916[5] (2931) 3129[3] 3459[7]

Alchemystic (IRE) *M A Barnes* 104h 87 c
6 b g In The Wings—Kama Tashoof (Mtoto)
5[P] 419[P] 524[4]688[F] 782[5] (Dead)

Alchimiste (FR) *Mrs E Langley* 59h
5 ro m Linamix(FR) —Alcove (USA) (Valdez (USA))
2002[5] 2419[15] 2816[15] 3483[10] 3656[P]

Alcopop *Miss Venetia Williams* 90h 116 c
7 b g Alderbrook—Albaciyna (Hotfoot)
2259[2] 2431[5] 2926[2]3459[F] 3596[3] 4592[4]

Alcott (FR) *J Jay* 13h
4 ch g Medaaly—Louisa May (IRE) (Royal Abjar (USA))
2752[13]

Aldea (FR) *Mrs S J Smith* 95b
5 b g Pistolet Bleu(IRE) —Heleda (FR) (Zino)
2844[4] 3319[6] 4507[4]

Alderbrook Girl (IRE) *R Curtis* 76h
6 bb m Alderbrook—Trassey Bridge (Strong Gale)
1950[5] 2486[10] 2704[6] 2985[P] 3184[7]3424[6] 3951[5] 4391[P] 4824[3]

Alderburn *H D Daly* 121 h 141 c
7 b g Alderbrook—Threewaygirl (Orange Bay)
1917[4] (2701) 3331[F](3816) 4433[7] 4960[B]

Alderclad Lad (IRE) *J Howard Johnson*
6 ch g Anshan—Novelist (Quayside)
147[P] 2690[P]

Alderley Girl *Dr P Pritchard* 37h
7 b m Footloose Esquire—Nearly A Mermaid (Nearly A Hand)
1543[13] 1616[6]

Alderman Rose *R T Phillips* 83h
6 b g Alderbrook—Rose Ravine (Deep Run)
3978[7] 4604[11] 4826[6]

Aldiruos (IRE) *A W Carroll* 105h
6 ch g Bigstone(IRE) —Ball Cat (FR) (Cricket Ball (USA))
1872[16] 2347[P] 3542[3] 4091[6] 4663[14]4858[7] 5[6]

Aleemdar (IRE) *A E Jones* 89 h
9 b g Doyoun—Aleema (Red God)
(592) 1520[P] 1756[2] 2314[9] 3330[7] 4475[2]4896[P]

Al Eile (IRE) *John Queally* 162h
6 b g Alzao(USA) —Kilcsem Eile (IRE) (Commanche Run)
(3492) 4432[4] 4775[6]

Alekhine (IRE) *P J Hobbs* 77h
5 b g Soviet Star(USA) —Alriyaah (Shareef Dancer (USA))
485[4] 729[12] 804[4] 1653[5] 1774[7]

Aleron (IRE) *J J Quinn* 122h 120 c
8 b g Sadler's Wells(USA) —High Hawk (Shirley Heights)
420[3] 2764[4] 3317[4](3558) 4076[F]

Alessandro Severo *Mrs D A Hamer* 89 h
7 gr g Brief Truce(USA) —Altaia (FR) (Sicyos (USA))
(167) 451[14] 3687[12] 4102[F] (Dead)

Alethea Gee *K G Reveley* 77h
8 b m Sure Blade(USA) —Star Flower (Star Appeal)
14[P] 613[10] 686[11] 822[2] 987[11]1046[2] 1209[P] 1375[8] 1483[3] 1605[9]

Alexander Fourball (IRE) *R Teague* 89c
12 ch g Phardante(FR) —Novelist (Quayside)
4594[3] 4831[U]

Alexander Musical (IRE) *S T Lewis* 78c
8 bb g Accordion—Love For Lydia (IRE) (Law Society (USA))
74[2] 271[6] 1749[3]1877[P] 2141[P] 2284[5]3460[P]

Alexander Sapphire (IRE) *N B King* 82h
5 gr m Pennekamp(USA) —Beautiful France (IRE) (Sadler's Wells (USA))
2343[5] 2683[P] 3281[2] 3415[4] 3959[P]14[14]

Alexander Taipan (IRE) *W P Mullins* 125 h
6 b g Taipan(IRE) —Fayafi (Top Ville)
2667a[4] 3309a[7] 3892a[6]

Alexanderthegreat (IRE) *Ferdy Murphy* 112h 139+c
8 b g Supreme Leader—Sandy Jayne (IRE) (Royal Fountain)
2499[8] 2656[5] 3180[12]

Alfadora *M F Harris* 68h
6 ch g Alflora(IRE) —Dorazine (Kalaglow)
21[U] 1553[P]

Al Falcon *M W Easterby* 91b
4 ch g Alflora(IRE) —Northern Falcon (Polar Falcon (USA))
4519[3]

Alfasonic *A King* 114+h
6 b g Alflora(IRE) —Lady Solstice (Vital Season)
128[7] 2815[4] (3277) (3598) 4099[5]

Alfa Sunrise *R H Buckler* 109 h 65c
9 b g Alflora(IRE) —Gipsy Dawn (Lighter)
1858[5] 3600[3] 3909[8]4353[P] 4693[4]

Alfie Bright *Mrs L B Normile* 15h
8 ch g Alflora(IRE) —Candlebright (Lighter)
782[P]

Alfie Flits *G A Swinbank* 119+b
4 b g Machiavellian(USA) —Elhilmeya (IRE) (Unfuwain (USA))
(2642) (3623) (3799) 4779[4]

Alfie's Connection *K G Reveley* 46h
5 ch g Danzig Connection(USA) —Lady Warninglid (Ela-Mana-Mou)
323[9] 870[12] 1377[5]

Alfie's Sun *D E Cantillon* 111+h 120c
7 b g Alflora(IRE) —Sun Dante (IRE) (Phardante (FR))
2464[P] 2701[2]

Alf Lauren *A King* 86h
8 b g Alflora(IRE) —Gokatiego (Huntercombe)
2528[7] 3240[5] 4604[P] 5022[5]

Alformasi *P F Nicholls* 104+h
7 b g Alflora(IRE) —Anamasi (Idiots Delight)
3023[6] 3477[P] 5009[3]

Alfred The Great (IRE) *P C Haslam* 101+h
4 b g King's Best(USA) —Aigue (High Top)
(2045) (3374) 3912[3] 4435[16] (Dead)

Alfred The Grey *Miss Suzy Smith* 85h 83c
9 gr g Environment Friend—Ranyah (USA) (Our Native (USA))
101[2] 503[8] 673[11]1752[6] 2019[3] 2808[9]2957[2] 3359[6] 3662[8]4524[4] 5088[4]

Alf's Spinney *Ian Williams* 95h
6 ch g Anshan—Netherdrom (Netherkelly)
2821[16] 3248[6] 4094[3] 4606[P]

Alfy Rich *M Todhunter* 50h 112 c
10 b g Alflora(IRE) —Weareagrandmother (Prince Tenderfoot (USA))
(1684) 2022[3] 2841[P]2977[8] 3487[16] (3798) 4145[15] 4520[3]

Algarve *Ferdy Murphy* 100h 100c
9 b g Alflora(IRE) —Garvenish (Balinger)
2039[5] 2266[2] 2874[4]3204[P] 4737[P] 5037[P]

Alghaazy (IRE) *M D Hammond* 77h
5 b g Mark Of Esteem(IRE) —Kentmere (FR) (Galetto (FR))
1587[4]

Algymo *S C Burrough* 77h
6 b m Tamure(IRE) —Red Point (Reference Point)
167[6] 2073[F]

Alice's Old Rose *Mrs H O Graham* 78h
9 b m Broadsword(USA) —Rosie Marchioness (Neltino)
3209[U] 5068[P]

Alikat (IRE) *M C Pipe* 132 h
5 b m Alhaarth(IRE) —Be Crafty (USA) (Crafty Prospector (USA))
127[4] 408[2] 633[5] 814[5] 1039[2]1270[6] 1548[6] (1727) 1830[3] 2336[6] 3727[14]4461[7] 4776[F]

Ali Shuffle (IRE) *J J Lambe* 96h
7 b g Ali-Royal(IRE) —Ediyrna (IRE) (Doyoun)
647[5] 870[6]

Alisons Treasure (IRE) *R Johnson* 50b
7 b g Treasure Hunter—The Long Bill (IRE) (Phardante (FR))
1688[6] 2572[13] 3374[12]

Alittlebitopower *C Storey* 81+c
9 ch g Alflora(IRE) —What A Moppet (IRE) (Torus)
322[9] 555[7]

Aljoash (IRE) *C Roberts* 47h
10 b m Unblest—Party Guest (What A Guest)
1454[5]

Aljumbo *Robert Gray*
12 b g Jumbo Hirt(USA) —Natina-May (Mandrake Major)
2475[P]

Allaboveboard (IRE) *P Bowen* 104h
7 ch m Alphabatim(USA) —Always Proud (IRE) (Supreme Leader)
4738[6] 4858[3] 5113[7]

All Bart Native (IRE) *L Wells*
11 gr g Be My Native(USA) —Bissie's Jayla (Zambrano)
3438[P]

All Bleevable *Mrs S Lamyman* 83h
9 b g Presidium—Eve's Treasure (Bustino)
370[12] 824[6] 1001[F] 1816[6] 2964[7]3592[4] 4478[5]

Allborn Lad (IRE) *C J Mann* 92+h
6 b g Fourstars Allstar(USA) —Billeragh Girl (Normandy)
2865[U] 3240[P] 3717[11] 4826[3]

Allegedly So (IRE) *D W Whillans* 79h
5 b g Flemensfirth(USA) —Celtic Lace (Celtic Cone)
2268[6] 2947[7]

Allegiance *P Wegmann* 61h
11 b g Rock Hopper—So Precise (FR) (Balidar)
4856[11] 5050[10]

Allez Melina *Mrs A J Hamilton-Fairley* 89+h
5 b m Cloudings(IRE) —Theme Arena (Tragic Role (USA))
27[4] 266[4] 1600[8] *2131[11]*2457[9] 3902[8] 4074[7] 4661[9] 4871[7]

Allez Mousson *A Bailey* 69h
8 b g Hernando(FR) —Rynechra (Blakeney)
1671[6] 2064[6] 2822[8] 3731[P]

Allez Petit Luis (FR) *C A Murphy* 118+h 117c
8 br g Grand Tresor(FR) —Galissima (FR) (Sicyos (USA))
67a[11] 3411a[7]

Allez Scotia *R Nixon* 88h
7 ch m Minster Son—Allez (Move Off)
317[7] 552[F]

All For A Reason (IRE) *Miss J R Gibney* 68+h
7 gr g Zaffaran(USA) —Cyrano Imperial (IRE) (Cyrano De Bergerac)
4212[7]

All Fun And Games (IRE) *John R Upson* 12b
5 b g Duky—Congress Lass (IRE) (Boreen (FR))
2987[12] 3583[8]

All Heart *Thomas Mullins* 110h 92c
5 ch m Alhaarth(IRE) —Meznh (IRE) (Mujtahid (USA))
2032a[4]

All In The Stars (IRE) *D P Keane* 111h 141 c
8 ch g Fourstars Allstar(USA) —Luton Flyer (Condorcet (FR))
2054[U] (2215) 2491[5]2744[2] (3995) 5004[P]

All Is Bright (IRE) *S J Treacy* 7b
6 b g Fourstars Allstar(USA) —Wakt (Akarad (FR))
44a[23]

All Marque (IRE) *S Gollings* 46h
6 b m Saddlers' Hall(IRE) —Buzzing Beauty (Junius (USA))
369[8]

All On My Own (USA) *I W McInnes* 67h
11 ch g Unbridled(USA) —Someforall (USA) (One For All (USA))
2816[14]

All Sonsilver (FR) *P Kelsall* 87h 86+c
9 b g Son Of Silver—All Licette (FR) (Native Guile (USA))
1907[P] 2210[P] 2623[P]2816[6] 3140[4] 3733[B] 4782[5]

All Square (IRE) *R A Farrant* 86h
6 ch g Bahhare(USA) —Intricacy (Formidable (USA))
4423[3] 4834[16] (5072)

All Star (GER) *N J Henderson* 140 h
6 b g Lomitas—Alte Garde (FR) (Garde Royale)
67a[4] 420[2] (2347) 2636[5] 3298[17] 4446[0]5059a[5]

Allstar Leader (IRE) *Michael Joseph Fitzgerald* 98h
9 b g Fourstars Allstar(USA) —Rugged Leader (Supreme Leader)
2166[17]

All Things Equal (IRE) *Mrs H Dalton* 102+h
7 b g Supreme Leader—Angel's Dream (King's Ride)
(5063)

Allumee *P J Hobbs* 115 h 108c
7 ch g Alflora(IRE) —Coire Vannich (Celtic Cone)
(1654) 2246[2] 4050[5] 4242[8]

Ally Shrimp *T P Tate* 128+h
5 b g Tamure(IRE) —Minigale (Strong Gale)
4530[2] (4793)

Al Mabrook (IRE) *N G Richards* 75 h
11 b g Rainbows For Life(CAN) —Sky Lover (Ela-Mana-Mou)
9[16] 412[5] 480[5] 768[7] 988[P]

Almah (SAF) *Miss Venetia Williams* 126 h
8 b m Al Mufti(USA) —Jazz Champion (SAF) (Dancing Champ (USA))
2053[2] 2347[12] 4781[3] 4972[10]

Almavara (USA) *C P Morlock* 106h
4 bb g Fusaichi Pegasus(USA) —Name Of Love (IRE) (Petardia)
4648[2] 4877[5]

Almaydan *R Lee* 137h 142c
8 b g Marju(IRE) —Cunning (Bustino)
219[4] 1913[2] 2489[10]2768[6] 3357[7] (3619) 3974[4] 4749[U]

Almier (IRE) *Michael Hourigan* 110h 108c
8 gr g Phardante(FR) —Stepfaster (Step Together (USA))
2334[F] 3894a[15]

Almire Du Lia (FR) *Mrs S C Bradburne* 92h 108c
8 ch g Beyssac(FR) —Lita (FR) (Big John (FR))
1837[8] 2170[7] (2495) 2877[4] 3315[P] 3917[P]4144[4] (4361) 4790[6]4985[4]

Almizan (IRE) *G L Moore* 114+h
6 b g Darshaan—Bint Albaadiya (USA) (Woodman (USA))
(1245) 1596[2] 1775[3] 1880[P] 5021[7]

Almnadia (IRE) *S Gollings* 119h
7 b m Alhaarth(IRE) —Mnaafa (IRE) (Darshaan)
127[P] (372) 4972[12]

Almost Broke *P F Nicholls* 97 h 143c
9 ch g Nearly A Hand—Teletex (Pollerton)
2368[F] 2619[3] 3019[5](3509) 3988[P] 4762[F]

Almutasader *J A B Old* 98h
6 b h Sadler's Wells(USA) —Dreamawhile (Known Fact (USA))
172[6] 1975[7] 2206[9]

Alotdone (IRE) *Mrs N S Evans* 66b
7 b g Fourstars Allstar(USA) —Gale Tan (IRE) (Strong Gale)
463[8] 816[7]

Alph *B R Johnson* 135+h
9 b g Alflora(IRE) —Royal Birthday (St Paddy)
1745[4] (2261) 2632[3] (3185) 3725[2] 4375[10] 5125[7]

Alphabetic *N J Henderson* 98h 107c
9 ch g Alflora(IRE) —Incamelia (St Columbus)
2874[P] 3372[P] 5017[4]

Alphabetical (IRE) *C J Mann* 98h 115 c
7 bb g Alphabatim(USA) —Sheeghee (IRE) (Noalto)
1859[3] 2206[11] 2591[2] 2818[5](3284) 4355[3] 4778[P]

Alpha Gamble (IRE) *R Rowe* 93+h
6 ch g Alphabatim(USA) —Caher Cross (IRE) (Phardante (FR))
2238[P] 2556[P] 2868[10] 4357[B]

Alpha Image (IRE) *Mrs L Williamson* 85+c
7 b g Alphabatim(USA) —Happy Image (Le Moss)
95[5]

Alpha Juliet (IRE) *C J Teague* 85+h
5 b m Victory Note(USA) —Zara's Birthday (IRE) (Waajib)
1336[4] 1566[3] 1723[B] 1910[4] 2107[2]2416[11]

Alpha Romana (IRE) *Mrs S E Busby* 38h 106c
12 b g Alphabatim(USA) —Stella Romana (Roman Warrior)
1109[12] 1900[11]

Alpha Royale (IRE) *C Byrnes* 126+h
6 b g Alphabatim(USA) —Barnearrig Lass (IRE) (Pollerton)
93a[6] 2228a[2] (2784a) 3086a[7] 4765[8] 5059a[F]

Alphazar (IRE) *Anthony Mullins* 111h 117c
11 br g Alphabatim(USA) —Ravaleen (IRE) (Executive Perk)
45a[4]

Alphecca (USA) *K G Reveley* 62h
5 b g Kingmambo(USA) —Limbo (USA) (A.P. Indy (USA))
82[13] 194[8] 406[9] 520[8]

Alphun (IRE) *G L Moore*
4 b g Orpen(USA) —Fakhira (IRE) (Jareer (USA))
1268[B]

Alpine Fox *T R George*
9 b g Risk Me(FR) —Hill Vixen (Goldhill)
901[F]

Alpine Hideaway (IRE) *J S Wainwright* 90h
13 b g Tirol—Arbour (USA) (Graustark)
1111[P] 1610[6] 1756[6] 2289[8]

Alpine Racer (IRE) *L J Williams* 66h
7 b g Lake Coniston(IRE) —Cut No Ice (Great Nephew)
635[P]

Alpine Slave *N J Gifford* 112h 112+c
9 ch g Alflora(IRE) —Celtic Slave (Celtic Cone)
439[5] 567[4] 1219[F]1398[6]

Alrafid (IRE) *G L Moore* 116h 115c
7 ch g Halling(USA) —Ginger Tree (USA) (Dayjur (USA))
450[3] 2213[5]

Alright Now M'Lad (IRE) *Jonjo O'Neill* 132+h
6 b g Supreme Leader—Chattering (Le Bavard (FR))
2142[P] 2849[12] (3422) (3901) 4497[6]

Alska (FR) *P L Southcombe* 88c
13 bb m Leading Counsel(USA) —Kolkwitzia (FR) (The Wonder (FR))
49[P]

Altareek (USA) *K Tork* 97h
9 b g Alleged(USA) —Black Tulip (FR) (Fabulous Dancer (USA))
4009[R]

Altenburg (FR) *Mrs N Smith*
4 b g Sadler's Wells(USA) —Anna Of Saxony (Ela-Mana-Mou)
3132[P] 4015[P] 4648[P]

Alternative Route (IRE) *T Doyle* 98?h
7 b m Needle Gun(IRE) —Miss Ironside (General Ironside)
2173[12]

Althrey Dandy (IRE) *P T Dalton* 89b 100c
11 ch g Good Thyne(USA) —Hawthorn Dandy (Deep Run)
280[R] 672[3] 728[F]812[2] 902[RR] 948[4]1041[P]

Altitude Dancer (IRE) *A Crook* 104h
6 b g Sadler's Wells(USA) —Height Of Passion (Shirley Heights)
(287) (298) (441) 652[4] 814[3] 1026[3] 2840[14] 2990[11]3487[8] 3966[8] 4390[7] 4658[6] 5123[6]

Alto Bold *P S Payne*
8 ch m Bold Fox—Alto Bella (High Line)
1454[P]

Alva Glen (USA) *B J Llewellyn* 101h
9 b g Gulch(USA) —Domludge (USA) (Lyphard (USA))
78[4] (275) 460[6] 751[3] 1016[6] 3467[10]3876[P] 5[11]

Alvaro (IRE) *B J Llewellyn* 105h 88c
9 ch g Priolo(USA) —Gezalle (Shareef Dancer (USA))
385[3] 1715[5] 1800[7]

Alvino *Miss H C Knight* 109+h 130+c
9 b g Alflora(IRE) —Rose Ravine (Deep Run)
1759[3]

Always *Noel Meade* 116h 148c
7 b g Dynaformer(USA) —Love And Affection (USA) (Exclusive Era (USA))
45a[F] (1692a) 2230a[5]

Always Esteemed (IRE) *K A Ryan* 80h
6 b g Mark Of Esteem(IRE) —Always Far (USA) (Alydar (USA))
1340[3]

Always Flying (USA) *N Wilson* 90+h
5 ch g Fly So Free(USA) —Dubiously (USA) (Jolie Jo (USA))
369[11] 1432[3] 1567[7] 1588[4]

Always In Debt (IRE) *P J Hobbs* 96+h
7 b g Norwich—Forever In Debt (Pragmatic)
169[P]

Always Waining (IRE) *R M Stronge* 122+h
5 b g Unfuwain(USA) —Glenarff (USA) (Irish River (FR))
2184[7] 2519[4] 2746[10] 3143[P] 4058[7]4497[7] (5010)

Always Waiting (IRE) *Mrs Dianne Sayer*
5 b g Darazari(IRE) —American Conker (IRE) (Lord Americo)
4319[9]

Amadeus (AUS) *M Scudamore* 84+h 98+c
9 ch g Brief Truce(USA) —Amazaan (NZ) (Zamazaan (FR))
389[2] 615[3] 904[4]1126[3] (2257) 2664[5]2816[2] 3784[4] 4045[3] 4614[4]4782[3] 5107[2]

Amadores *J Ryan* 54b
4 b f Hernando(FR) —Lena (USA) (Woodman (USA))
2520[8] 3259[9] 3787[P]

Amalfi Storm *M W Easterby* 81h
5 b m Slip Anchor—Mayroni (Bustino)
1593[2] 1688[2] 2012[6] 2674[6] 2991[11]4080[4]

Amanpuri (GER) *Mrs A M Thorpe* 105h
8 b g Fairy King(USA) —Aratika (FR) (Zino)
1587[P] 1800[10] 2285[6] 2428[2] 2605[8]2802[6] 3358[2] (3441) (3719) 3901[2] (4131) 4357[7]4504[4] 4693[3] 4858[9]

Amaretto Rose *N J Henderson* 98+b
5 b m Alflora(IRE) —Teenero (Teenoso (USA))
(4017) 4751[14]

Amarula Ridge (IRE) *P J Hobbs* 112h 111+c
5 b g Indian Ridge—Mail Boat (Formidable (USA))
2249[5] (2751) 3255[4] 4049[3]

Amaya Silva *S Dow*
4 b f Silver Patriarch(IRE) —Queen Of Tides (IRE) (Soviet Star (USA))
1404[F] 1519[P]

Amazing Valour (IRE) *P Bowen* 89h
4 b g Sinndar(IRE) —Flabbergasted (IRE) (Sadler's Wells (USA))
2191[2] 2578[4] 2994[6] 3325[3] 3814[5]3982[6]

Amberbury *J Parkes* 39b
4 b g Overbury(IRE) —Dark Amber (Formidable (USA))
4853[20]

Amber Dawn *J Gallagher* 74h 97c
7 ch m Weld—Scrambird (Dubassoff (USA))
111[7] 394[B] 1280[12] 1413[4] 1487[7]1631[5]

Amber Go Go *James Moffatt* 70h 49c
9 ch m Rudimentary(USA) —Plaything (High Top)
592[F] 1100[P] 1333[6]

Amberleigh House (IRE) *D McCain* 111h 144c
14 br g Buckskin(FR) —Chancy Gal (Al Sirat)
1676[P] 1924[5] 2370[7]3988[7] 4549[13] 4777[P]

Ambersong *A W Carroll* 104h
8 ch g Hernando(FR) —Stygian (USA) (Irish River (FR))
2008[3] 2139[3] 2560[4] (3804) 4050[7] 4591[6]1[4]

Amber Starlight *R Rowe* 108h
8 b m Binary Star(USA) —Stupid Cupid (Idiots Delight)
2125[2] 2621[4] 2985[P]

Ambition Royal (FR) *Miss Lucinda V Russell* 99h 90c
6 ch g Cyborg(FR) —Before Royale (FR) (Dauphin Du Bourg (FR))
1722[4] 2064[3] 2497[9] 3205[9] 4318[3]4844[4] 5119[P]

Ambobo (USA) *Martin Brassil* 154+h
6 b g Kingmambo(USA) —Bold Bold (IRE) (Sadler's Wells (USA))
4458[9] 5101a[12]

Ameeq (USA) *G L Moore* 108+h
4 bb c Silver Hawk(USA) —Haniya (IRE) (Caerleon (USA))
2612[4]

Ameras (IRE) *Miss S E Forster* 78h 79c
8 bb m Hamas(IRE) —Amerindian (Commanche Run)
122[3] 419[5]

Americanconnection (IRE) *D McCain* 102h 106+c
10 b g Lord Americo—Ballyea Jacki (Straight Lad)
4847[7]

American Jennie (IRE) *Michael Cullen* 110h 142+c
8 br m Lord Americo—Cathy's Girl (Sheer Grit)
66a[7] 3012a[U] 4022a[2](4542a) 4929a[4]

American President (IRE) *J J Quinn* 103h
10 br g Lord Americo—Deceptive Response (Furry Glen)
4917[5]

Amhairghin (IRE) *G A Harker* 102b
6 ch g Accordion—North Gale (Oats)
4588[4] 4854[15] 5124[4]

Amicelli (GER) *P J Hobbs* 125+h 133+c
7 b g Goofalik(USA) —Arratonia (GER) (Arratos (FR))
(178) 667[2] (1089) (1608) 2483[2] 2762[3]
3213[4](4279) 4971[2]

Amid The Chaos (IRE) *C J Mann* 109h 100c
6 ch g Nashwan(USA) —Celebrity Style (USA) (Seeking The Gold (USA))
3815[P] 4959[10] 5[P]

Amir Zaman *J R Jenkins* 99 h
8 ch g Salse(USA) —Colorvista (Shirley Heights)
838[12] 2487[13]

Amjad *Miss Kate Milligan* 74h 61c
9 ch g Cadeaux Genereux—Babita (Habitat)
480[P] 520[U]

Ammunition (IRE) *M Pitman* 65h
6 b g Needle Gun(IRE) —Flapping Freda (IRE) (Carlingford Castle)
241[7] 2720[4] 3216[2] 3664[7]

Amnesty *G L Moore* 94 h
7 ch g Salse(USA) —Amaranthus (Shirley Heights)
312[P] 2379[7] 2632[9] 2802[2] 3185[9]3371[P] 4243[7]
4427[7] 4871[2]

Among Thieves (IRE) *M D I Usher*
6 b m Among Men(USA) —Abbessingh (Mansingh (USA))
230[LFT]

A Monk Swimming (IRE) *Miss J S Davis* 76h
5 br g Among Men(USA) —Sea Magic (IRE) (Distinctly North (USA))
742[P] 901[3] 1717[10] 2940[U] 3325[P]4943[7] 5047[F]

Amour Multiple (IRE) *S Lycett* 120+h
7 b g Poliglote—Onereuse (Sanglamore (USA))
3133[2] 3383[P] 3996[4] 4242[6] 4420[5]4970[3]

Amptina (IRE) *Mrs S J Smith* 72h 83+c
11 b g Shardari—Cotton Gale (Strong Gale)
135[2] 395[5] 674[9]997[8] 1178[4] 1277[U]1359[5]

Amyroseisuppose *C P Morlock* 44b
7 b m Classic Cliche(IRE) —Fishki (Niniski (USA))
866[7] 1231[P]

Anaclone (IRE) *M Scudamore*
8 b g Zaffaran(USA) —Monteith (IRE) (Montekin)
271[P]

Anaczar (IRE) *P J Rothwell* 52b 57c
6 ch g Anshan—Another Rosy (IRE) (Yashgan)
44a[18]

Anatar (IRE) *M C Pipe* 108h 100c
8 b g Caerleon(USA) —Anaza (Darshaan)
766[5] 864[5] 1020[8] 1270[14] 1675[8]1872[11] 2166[8]
2633[3] 2999[5] 4215[7]4821[10]

An Capall Dubh (IRE) *Mrs Edward Crow* 111c
10 bb g Air Display(USA) —Lady Of Wales (Welsh Pageant)
6[2] 221[3] (3805) 4051[5] 4594[4] (5013)

Anchors Away *T D Easterby* 89b
4 b g Slip Anchor—Qurrat Al Ain (Wolver Hollow)
(4992)

An Culainn Beag (IRE) *Denis P Murphy* 104h 85c
10 b m Supreme Leader—Sallybank (Buckskin (FR))
66a[13]

Andiamo (IRE) *John Joseph Murphy* 87h 98c
11 bb g Homo Sapien—Cathy's Girl (Sheer Grit)
112a[P] 5083a[15]

Andreas (FR) *P F Nicholls* 139+h 151c
6 b g Marchand De Sable(USA) —Muscova Dancer (FR) (Muscovite (USA))
(286) 1822[2] 2163[6](4050) 4472[F] 4749[3]

Andre Chenier (IRE) *P Monteith* 118h
5 b g Perugino(USA) —Almada (GER) (Lombard (GER))
82[2] 1912[U] 3171[2] 3383[P] 3761[12]4110[3] 4490[4] 4792[8]

Andrewjames (IRE) *Peter McCreery* 85c
12 gr g Van Der Linden(FR) —Tolaytala (Be My Guest (USA))
87a[6] 5128a[5]

An Dun Ri (IRE) *J J Lambe* 81h 53c
7 br g King's Ride—Take Me Home (Amoristic (USA))
1887[P]

Andy Gin (FR) *Miss E M England* 102+h
7 b g Ski Chief(USA) —Love Love Kate (FR) (Saint Andrews (FR))
2659[6] 2813[9] 3687[5] 3990[P] (4322) 4879[11]

Andy Higgins (IRE) *E J O'Grady* 100h 107c
9 b g Eve's Error—Go In Hope (IRE) (Mandalus)
1515a[F]

Andy's Lad (IRE) *D Burchell* 34h 105c
14 br g Versailles Road(USA) —Ah Ye Know (Wolverlife)
725[P]

Anemix (FR) *L Corcoran* 124+h
5 gr g Linamix(FR) —Sallivera (IRE) (Sillery (USA))
(3947) 4282[U] 4569[2] 4838[2]

A New Story (IRE) *Michael Hourigan* 108h 144+c
8 b g Fourstars Allstar(USA) —Diyala (FR) (Direct Flight)
2539a[2] 3053a[8] 3587a[3]3971[R] 4929a[3] 5102a[3]

Anflora *B J Llewellyn* 65h 77c
9 b m Alflora(IRE) —Ancella (Tycoon II)
1655[3] (1832) 1983[2] 2282[3]2863[5] 3427[6]

Angel Delight *J L Spearing* 97 h 101 c
10 gr m Seymour Hicks(FR) —Bird's Custard (Birdbrook)
174[3]

Angello (FR) *N J Hawke* 95h
5 gr g Kaldounevees(FR) —Mount Gable (Head For Heights)
4005[6] 4569[4] 4823[4] 5108[12]

Angie's Double *Mrs K Waldron* 89+h
6 ch m Double Trigger(IRE) —Arch Angel (IRE) (Archway (IRE))
(237) 506[8] 839[5] (891) 905[6] (1000) 1181[5]
1436[8]1715[P]

Anglerzar (IRE) *J M Saville*
6 ch m Shernazar—Anglers Girl (IRE) (Don't Forget Me)
4751[21]

Ankles Back (IRE) *T Wall* 116c
9 b g Seclude(USA) —Pedalo (Legal Tender)
240[P] 489[P] 746[P]2524[6] 4906[P]

Anko (POL) *P J Hobbs* 95h
7 b h Saphir(GER) —Arietta (GER) (King's Lake (USA))
838[4] 982[3] 1235[3]

Anna Gee *K G Reveley* 30b
6 b m Cyrano De Bergerac—Elusive Star (Ardross)
616[10] 1048[10]

Annals *R C Guest*
4 b f Lujain(USA) —Anna Of Brunswick (Rainbow Quest (USA))
2949[9] 3349[U] 3539[8] 3594[P] 3759[F]

Anna Panna *R H Alner* 94+h
5 b m Piccolo—Miss Laetitia (IRE) (Entitled)
2455[10] 2804[5] 3322[4] 3550[3] 4153[2]4450[7]

Anna's Blue (FR) *J-L Henry* 79c
11 ch g Mansonnien(FR) —Anna's Queen (FR) (Dom Pasquini (FR))
1073a[2]

Annie Fleetwood *R H Alner* 103+h
8 ch m Anshan—Gold Luck (USA) (Slew O'Gold (USA))
4836[2] 5084[3]

Annie's Answer (IRE) *Mrs V J Makin* 97+b
6 b m Flemensfirth(USA) —As An Sli (IRE) (Buckskin (FR))
616[4]

Annie's Dream (IRE) *T Hogan* 55h
4 b f Lahib(USA) —Agent Scully (IRE) (Simply Great (FR))
2645a[7]

Anno Jubilo (GER) *C F Swan* 117h 105+c
9 bb g Lando(GER) —Anna Maria (GER) (Night Shift (USA))
954a[7]

Annshoon (IRE) *M G Holden* 89h 119+c
11 b m Jurado(USA) —Solanum (Green Shoon)
45a[19]

Another Burden *H D Daly* 86h
5 b m Alflora(IRE) —Dalbeattie (Phardante (FR))
2727[10] 4324[P] 5052[4]

Another Chat (IRE) *R T Phillips* 65h
6 ch g Executive Perk—Lucky Fiver (Tumble Gold)
2988[9] 3328[15] 3466[9] 3963[10]

Another Client (IRE) *Mrs A R Hewitt* 87h 80+c
10 ch g Denel(FR) —Proverbs Girl (Proverb)
4594[6] 5013[P]

Another Club Royal *D McCain* 74 h 113+c
7 b g Overbury(IRE) —Miss Club Royal (Avocat)
98[2] 211[2] 546[4]1905[F] 2039[4] 3338[P](3486) 3762[4]
(3928) 4300[3] (4851)

Another Conquest *J W Mullins* 82h 109+c
7 b m El Conquistador—Kellys Special (Netherkelly)
4321[2] 4939[P]

Another Deckie (IRE) *L Lungo* 111h
8 b g Naheez(USA) —Merry Friends (King's Ride)
940[2] 1204[5]

Another Deployment (IRE) *M N O'Riordan*
7 ch g Accordion—Vinegar Hill (Pauper)
5128a[P]

Another Flint (IRE) *R Flint* 63h
6 ch g Accordion—Island Run (Deep Run)
2075[7] 2528[13] 2663[P] 3131[7] 4828[7]

Another Jameson (IRE) *J M Jefferson* 83h
6 b m Good Thyne(USA) —Another Grouse (Pragmatic)
138[10] 693[P] 2024[4] 2674[5] 3795[10]

Another Joker *J L Needham* 97h 125 c
11 b g Commanche Run—Just For A Laugh (Idiots Delight)
1542[3] 1918[U] 2048[6]2998[P] 5061a[3]

Another Lord (IRE) *Mrs B K Thomson* 94b
7 bb g Mister Lord(USA) —Queen Ofthe Island (IRE) (Carlingford Castle)
1667[2]

Another Misk *M E Sowersby* 74h
4 ch g Storm Boot(USA) —Pure Misk (Rainbow Quest (USA))
1718[F] 2442[P] 2587[9] 2752[2] 3169[8]3349[6] 3485[7]
4056[8] 4919[P] 5135[P]

Another Mistress *R M Flower*
4 b f Slip Anchor—Mellow Miss (Danehill (USA))
2373[U] 2797[P]

Another Native (IRE) *C J Mann* 100h 127c
8 b g Be My Native(USA) —Lancastrian's Wine (IRE) (Lancastrian)
2323[5] (2874) (3144) 3290[5] 3507[5] 3973[5](4502)
4847[3]

Another Penny *R Dickin* 73h 56c
6 b m Petoski—Penlea Lady (Leading Man)
3657[10] 3884[F] 4088[8] 4324[P] 4934[6]

Another Promise (IRE) *J A Supple* 98h
7 b g Presenting—Snape (IRE) (Strong Gale)
283[4]

Another Raleagh (IRE) *Graeme P McPherson* 123h 120+c
12 b g Be My Native(USA) —Caffra Mills (Pitpan)
55[5] (4351)

Another Rum (IRE) *I A Duncan* 118h 136 c
8 b g Zaffaran(USA) —Sharp Fashion VII (Damsire Unregistered)
3851[4] 4447[P] 5004[F]

Another Superman (IRE) *Lindsay Woods* 86h
7 b g Beneficial—Royal Broderick (IRE) (Lancastrian)
936[7] 4145[2]

Another Taipan (IRE) *A C Whillans* 85h
6 b g Taipan(IRE) —Sheeghee (IRE) (Noalto)
82[10] 1834[7] 2024[9] 2945[P]4723[13]

Another Ticket (IRE) *Eoin Griffin* 77h
6 ch g Erin's Isle—Deerfield Fame (USA) (Quest For Fame)
1870[P]

Another Windfall *C P Morlock* 40h
7 gr m Executive Perk—Rymolbreese (Rymer)
134[10] 697[14] 3125[P] 3456[13]

Ansar (IRE) *D K Weld* 135h 141c
10 b g Kahyasi—Anaza (Darshaan)
954a[4] (1083a) 1621a[2] 1692a[3]

Ansari (IRE) *Patrick O Brady* 111h
9 b g Selkirk(USA) —Anaza (Darshaan)
67a[10]

Ansa The Question *A H Mactaggart* 69b
5 b m Overbury(IRE) —Olive Branch (Le Moss)
3237[10] 4304[5]

Ansells Legacy (IRE) *A Berry* 64 h
4 b g Charnwood Forest(IRE) —Hanzala (FR) (Akarad (FR))
1338[6] 2569[P]

Anshabil (IRE) *A King* 97h 103c
7 br g Anshan—Billeragh Thyne (IRE) (Good Thyne (USA))
436[F] 673[P]

Anshan Spirit (IRE) *R W Green* 88c
8 ch m Anshan—Saffron Spirit (Town And Country)
4791[3] 5040[3]

Anticipating *G L Moore* 114+h
6 b g Polish Precedent(USA) —D'Azy (Persian Bold)
(1480) 1642[2] 1775[5] 1880[6] (2573) 4242[3]

Antigiotto (IRE) *P Bowen* 97+h
5 ch g Desert Story(IRE) —Rofool (IRE) (Fools Holme (USA))
243[4] 451[7] 762[P] 895[P] 1045[6]1319[6]

Antigone's Fire *P D Niven*
7 b m Lycius(USA) —Buzzbomb (Bustino)
14[P] 192[F]

Antinomy (IRE) *N J Henderson* 86b
6 ch m Anshan—Ardentinny (Ardross)
77[P]

Antony Ebeneezer *C R Dore* 94h
7 ch g Hurricane Sky(AUS) —Captivating (IRE) (Wolfhound (USA))
237[3]

Anty Wren *Mary Meek*
4 gr g Tragic Role(USA) —Granny Nix (Zambrano)
4654[7]

Anxious Moments (IRE) *C F Swan* 129h 132 c
11 b g Supreme Leader—Ms Brooks (IRE) (Lord Ha Ha)
45a[7]

A One (IRE) *H J Manners*
7 b g Alzao(USA) —Anita's Contessa (IRE) (Anita's Prince)
2421[P] 2618[P] 3275[12]

Aoninch *Mrs P N Dutfield* 81h
6 ch m Inchinor—Willowbank (Gay Fandango (USA))
1740[4] 2309[12]

Apadi (USA) *R C Guest* 90h 94+c
10 ch g Diesis—Ixtapa (USA) (Chief's Crown (USA))
(135) 246[4] 874[5]1529[3] 1604[5] 2172[P]3274[5] 3379[6]
3592[6]4991[6]

Apanal (GER) *H Hack*
6 b g Macanal(USA) —Audley (GER) (Nebos (GER))
1073a[3]

Apatura Dik *N R Mitchell* 80b
5 b g Deltic(USA) —Apatura Hati (Senang Hati)
4574[6]

A Piece Of Cake (IRE) *J S Goldie* 123 c
13 gr g Roselier(FR) —Boreen Bro (Boreen (FR))
130[2] 423[4] 547[5]

Apollo Lady *A King* 104b
5 b m Alflora(IRE) —Stac-Pollaidh (Tina's Pet)
(2961) (3820) 4376[3] 4751[11]

Apollo Theatre *R Rowe* 110+h
8 b g Sadler's Wells(USA) —Threatening (Warning)
2271[P] 2633[P]

A Pound Down (IRE) *N G Ayliffe* 80c
9 b g Treasure Hunter—Ann's Queen (IRE) (Rhoman Rule (USA))
1980[P] 3126[P] 3946[6]4428[3] 4666[7]

Appach (FR) *J W Mullins* 80h 118+c
7 gr g Riche Mare(FR) —Simply Red (FR) (Rb Chesne)
(862) 4870[2] 5112[4]

Apple Joe *A J Whiting* 41h 90c
10 b g Sula Bula—Hazelwain (Hard Fact)
1832[5] 1960[P] 2465[P]4571[6] 4650[P]

Approaching Land (IRE) *M W Easterby* 61h
11 ch g Dry Dock—Crash Approach (Crash Course)
11[4] 180[2] 363[F] 1374[F] 1486[6]2256[2] 2567[P] 2688[P]
2962[6] 3557[9]3956[P]

April Rose *K G Wingrove* 15h
6 ch m Alderbrook—Wise 'N' Shine (Sunley Builds)
463[11] 917[9] 1158[U] 1302[13] 1454[P]1654[P]

April Showers *J C Tuck* 52b
6 b m Alderbrook—Preachers Popsy (The Parson)
266[5] 3327[P] 3904[11]

April Vision (IRE) *Paul John Gilligan* 33h
7 b m Pierre—Sum Vision (IRE) (Vision (USA))
519[P]

Apsara *G M Moore* 81h
5 br m Groom Dancer(USA) —Ayodhya (IRE) (Astronef)
1569[4] 1683[5]

Aqua *P T Midgley* 71b
4 b f Mister Baileys—Water Well (Sadler's Wells (USA))
3259[5] 3623[9]

Aqua Breezer (IRE) *Ms Caroline Hutchinson* 106h
7 b m Namaqualand(USA) —Lomond's Breeze (Lomond (USA))
3005a[12]

A Qui Le Tour *M R Hoad*
4 b g Pyramus(USA) —Dolphin Beech (IRE) (Dolphin Street (FR))
2236[F] 3132[P]

Arafan (IRE) *Michael Hourigan* 96h
4 b c Barathea(IRE) —Asmara (USA) (Lear Fan (USA))
4122a[9]

Arcalis *J Howard Johnson* 163 h
6 gr g Lear Fan(USA) —Aristocratique (Cadeaux Genereux)
(2500) 3492[P] 4432[5] 5003[9] 5125[5]

Arc En Ciel (GER) *Gerard Cully* 128h
6 b h Daun(GER) —Amarna (GER) (Nebos (GER))
5059a[13]

Arceye *W Davies* 69b 104+c
9 b g Weld—Flower Of Tintern (Free State)
3277[P] 3457[6] 4553[6](4937)

Archduke Ferdinand (FR) *A King* 106h
8 ch g Dernier Empereur(USA) —Lady Norcliffe (USA) (Norcliffe (CAN))
1680[6] 1991[6] 2421[2] 2714[2]

Archerfield (IRE) *R Johnson*
5 ch m Docksider(USA) —Willow River (CAN) (Vice Regent (CAN))
3442[P]

Archie Babe (IRE) *J J Quinn* 114+h
10 ch g Archway(IRE) —Frensham Manor (Le Johnstan)
4420[10]

Arch Rebel (USA) *Noel Meade* 127 h
5 b g Arch(USA) —Sheba's Step (USA) (Alysheba (USA))
3411a[14] 3641a[6] 4473[15]

Arc Of Stone (IRE) *D J Wintle* 74h
6 ch g Arc Bright(IRE) —Stoney Broke (Pauper)
4393[6] 4569[9] 4784[10]

Arctic Cherry (IRE) *R Ford* 99h 75 c
8 b g Arctic Lord—Cherry Avenue (King's Ride)
2284[3] 2692[5] 3320[7]3844[4]

Arctic Copper (IRE) *D M Christie* 66h 117c
12 b g Montelimar(USA) —Miss Penguin (General Assembly (USA))
68a[P] 4748[18]

Arctic Cove *M D Hammond* 85h
5 b g Vettori(IRE) —Sundae Girl (USA) (Green Dancer (USA))
2658[8] 3912[F] 4763[P]

Arctic Echo *G A Swinbank* 108+h
7 b g Alderbrook—Arctic Oats (Oats)
4532[2] 4787[3]

Arctic Ghost *N Wilson* 102b
6 gr g Environment Friend—Saxon Gift (Saxon Farm)
3353[9] 3563[2] 5008[3]

Arctic Glow *Mrs H Pudd* 73+h
7 ch m Weld—Arctic Mission (The Parson)
575[6]

Arctic Lagoon (IRE) *Mrs S C Bradburne* 86h 86 c
7 ch g Bering—Lake Pleasant (IRE) (Elegant Air)
(212) (554) 783[4] 1838[10] 2039[3]2266[3] 3268[6]
3915[6]4921[P] 5122[P]

Arctic Minster *G A Harker* 88b
7 ch g Minster Son—Celtic Tern (Celtic Cone)
484[2]

Arctic Moss (IRE) *E W Tuer* 88+h
7 ch m Moscow Society(USA) —Arctic Match (Royal Match)
854[10] 3442[10] 3927[2] 4302[P]

Arctic Sky (IRE) *T M Stephenson* 110+h 122+c
9 b g Arctic Lord—Lake Garden Park (Comedy Star (USA))
4051[U]

Arctic Spirit *R Dickin* 81h 106 c
11 b g Arctic Lord—Dickies Girl (Saxon Farm)
4088[7] 4378[7] 5051[10]

Arctic Times (IRE) *Eugene M O'Sullivan* 120c
10 ch g Montelimar(USA) —Miss Penguin (General Assembly (USA))
4748[10]

Ardaghey (IRE) *N A Twiston-Davies* 126 h 138 c
7 bb g Lord Americo—Mrs Pepper (Lancastrian)
1845[3] 2052[6] 2848[P]3148[2] (4016) 4444[U]4460[F] 4764[10]

Ardashir (FR) *Mrs S J Humphrey* 128 h 92 c
7 b g Simon Du Desert(FR) —Antea (FR) (Esprit Du Nord (USA))
207[8] 1988[3] 2104[3]2717[6] 2957[P] 3966[9] (Dead)

Ardasnails (IRE) *K G Wingrove* 45h
4 b g Spectrum(IRE) —Fey Lady (IRE) (Fairy King (USA))
1440[8] 1563[14] 1729[P] 1802[9]

Ardent Number *D A Nolan*
6 b g Alderbrook—Pretty Average (Skyliner)
1532[15] 4519[P]

Ardent Scout *Mrs S J Smith* 119c
14 b g Ardross—Vidette (Billion (USA))
330[P]

Ardglass (IRE) *Mrs P Townsley* 97h
4 b g Danehill Dancer(IRE) —Leggagh Lady (IRE) (Doubletour (USA))
3898[2] 4327[9] 4648[5] 4910[3]

Ardlea Star (IRE) *Patrick O Brady* 70+h
8 br m Glacial Storm(USA) —Jolly Style (IRE) (Jolly Jake (NZ))
4483a[P]

Ard Na Re (IRE) *Paul John Gilligan* 71h
7 b g Michelozzo(USA) —Ottadini (IRE) (Cardinal Flower)
515[6]

Ardwelshin (FR) *C J Down* 64 h
8 b g Ajdayt(USA) —Reem Dubai (IRE) (Nashwan (USA))
668[P]

Ardynagh (IRE) *J Howard Johnson* 83h
7 b g Aahsaylad—Night Matron (IRE) (Hatim (USA))
1508[P]

Areba Rocky (IRE) *P J Rothwell* 34h
5 b g Rock Hopper—Boleybawn (IRE) (King's Ride)
65a[21]

Argento *G M Moore* 108h 108 c
9 b g Weldnaas(USA) —Four M'S (Majestic Maharaj)
2190[5] 2443[3] 2754[6]3172[4] 3378[5] 3788[5]4848[10] 4922[7]

Argent Ou Or (FR) *M C Pipe* 94h
5 b g Mansonnien(FR) —Gold Or Silver (FR) (Glint Of Gold)
274[2] 485[2] 838[9] 1982[4] 2166[9]2632[4] 3997[F]

Argonaut *P Bowen* 92h
6 b g Rainbow Quest(USA) —Chief Bee (Chief's Crown (USA))
5110[4]

Arimero (GER) *J G Portman* 110h
6 b g Monsun(GER) —Averna (Heraldiste (USA))
78[P]

Arinos (GER) *B J Curley*
6 ch g Platini(GER) —Arionette (Lombard (GER))
2663[P]

Aristocratic Yank (IRE) *S G Chadwick*
7 bb g Lord Americo—Dixons Dutchess (IRE) (Over The River (FR))
4516[P]

Aristoxene (FR) *N J Henderson* 98+h 141c
6 b g Start Fast(FR) —Petite Folie (Salmon Leap (USA))
2003[2] 2532[5] 3293[3]3620[6] 4447[U] 4764[3]5012[5]

Arjay *S B Clark* 78h
8 b g Shaamit(IRE) —Jenny's Call (Petong)
238[2] 412[2] 551[3] 683[2] 826[4]915[7] 987[4] 1063[10]

Arkadian (IRE) *Mrs A M O'Shea* 42h
7 b g Danehill Dancer(IRE) —Sky Lover (Ela-Mana-Mou)
3585a[6]

Arkholme *N A Dunger* 91h
5 b g Robellino(USA) —Free Spirit (IRE) (Caerleon (USA))
4475[P] 4903[P]

Armageddon *O Sherwood* 84h 88c
9 b g Deploy—Arusha (IRE) (Dance Of Life (USA))
132[3] 1907[8] 2282[2]2686[P]

Armagh South (IRE) *J C Tuck* 88 h
7 ch g Topanoora—Mogen (Adonijah)
3422[11] 3997[F] 4453[9]

Armaguedon (FR) *L Lungo* 124+h 116+c
8 b g Garde Royale—Miss Dundee (FR) (Esprit Du Nord (USA))
2943[F] (3317) 4981[P]

Arm And A Leg (IRE) *Mrs D A Hamer* 110h
11 ch g Petardia—Ikala (Lashkari)
571[11] 726[12] 864[6] 1020[5] 1179[3]1250[4] (1319) 1525[5] 1641[F] 2271[3] (2466) 2731[9]3143[P]

Armariver (FR) *P F Nicholls* 116h
6 ch g River Mist(USA) —Armalita (FR) (Goodland (FR))
1671[3] 2374[3] 3175[2] 3360[2] 3696[4]5045[5]

Armaturk (FR) *P F Nicholls* 151h 164c
9 ch g Baby Turk—Armalita (FR) (Goodland (FR))
(1918) 2163[5] (3136) 3980[2] 4457[P] 4749[6]4984[3]

Armentieres *Mrs E Slack* 92h
5 b m Robellino(USA) —Perfect Poppy (Shareef Dancer (USA))
2567[6] 2843[5] 3169[2] 3351[14] 3557[3]3916[11] 4299[5] 4517[3] 4656[8] 12[8]

Armoury House *T R George* 56b
5 ch g Gunner B—Coire Vannich (Celtic Cone)
4333[14]

Arnbi Dancer *Mrs N S Evans*
7 b g Presidium—Travel Myth (Bairn (USA))
1654[P]

Arnold Layne (IRE) *R T Phillips* 95+h
7 gr g Roselier(FR) —Cotton Gale (Strong Gale)
2859[3] 3316[4]

Arno River *D Brace* 68h
4 ch g Halling(USA) —Moonlight Saunter (USA) (Woodman (USA))
1478[F] 1679[P] 1948[5] 2454[7]

Ar Nos Na Gaoithe (IRE) *Mrs A M Thorpe* 85b
7 b m Toulon—Sidhe Gaoth (Le Moss)
361[3] 490[3] 655[2]

Aroldo (FR) *J Bertran De Balanda* 118h
5 b g Mansonnien(FR) —Cambaria (FR) (Nice Havrais (USA))
778a[3]

Around Before (IRE) *Jonjo O'Neill* 103+h 125c
9 ch g Be My Native(USA) —Glynn Cross (IRE) (Mister Lord (USA))
974[7] 1192[4] 1267[2] 1398[3]

Around Nassau Town *C J Gray*
6 b m Bahamian Bounty—Sarouel (IRE) (Kendor (FR))
3468[P]

Arrayou (FR) *O Sherwood* 130h 102+c
5 b g Valanjou(FR) —Cavatine (FR) (Spud (FR))
1677[10] 2079[5] 2746[3] 2871[P] 3298[9]3622[6] 4608[6] 4765[6] 4959[2] 5142[9]

Arriman *J A Geake* 73b
4 ch g Bien Bien(USA) —Spellbinder (IRE) (Magical Wonder (USA))
3904[7] 4422[12]

Arry Dash *M J Wallace* 110+h
6 b g Fraam—Miletrian Cares (IRE) (Hamas (IRE))
2584[5] (2950) 3944[2] 4243[P]

Artane Boys *Jonjo O'Neill* 107 h 104+c
9 b g Saddlers' Hall(IRE) —Belleminette (IRE) (Simply Great (FR))
803[7] 904[5] 980[4]1263[3] 1366[2] 1409[2] 1675[10] 1804[5]1987[6]

Art Aurel (GER) *U Stoltefuss*
7 ch g Temporal(GER) —Aurikola (GER) (Nebos (GER))
471a[6]

Arteea (IRE) *Michael Hourigan* 134h 154c
7 b g Oscar(IRE) —Merric (IRE) (Electric)
40a[4] 1702a[3] (1944a) 2395a[4]3006a[4] 3639a[2] 4431[8]4889a[6]

Arthur Pendragon *Mrs S M Johnson* 5h
6 b g Botanic(USA) —Blue Room (Gorytus (USA))
943[P] 1085[8] 1180[P]

Arthurs Dream (IRE) *J G M O'Shea* 53h
4 b g Desert Prince(IRE) —Blueprint (USA) (Shadeed (USA))
2069[9]

Artic Jack (FR) *Mrs S J Smith* 131 c
10 b g Cadoudal(FR) —Si Jamais (FR) (Arctic Tern (USA))
2189[4] 2875[2] 3390[6]

Articulation *C Byrnes* 116h
5 b h Machiavellian(USA) —Stiletta (Dancing Brave (USA))
65a[6] 5078a[16]

Artic Web (IRE) *F Flood* 101h
6 b g Arctic Lord—Ballela Maid (Boreen (FR))
44a[10]

Artist's Muse (IRE) *T M Walsh* 122h
4 b f Cape Cross(IRE) —Naked Poser (IRE) (Night Shift (USA))
3004a[2] 3401a[5] 4435[2] 5099a[2]

Art Virginia (FR) *N J Henderson* 109+h
7 b g Art Bleu—Sweet Jaune (FR) (Le Nain Jaune (FR))
2049[2] 2865[3] 3694[P] 4956[5]

Aruba Dam (IRE) *A E Jones* 72h
8 br m Be My Native(USA) —Arumah (Arapaho)
1018[6] 1236[R] 1383[6] 4556[8]

Arumun (IRE) *M Scudamore* 105 h
5 b g Posidonas—Adwoa (IRE) (Eurobus)
1681[7] 2262[2] 2683[2] 3210[12] 3417[2]3800[3] 4604[P]

Asaateel (IRE) *G L Moore* 65h
4 br g Unfuwain(USA) —Alabaq (USA) (Riverman (USA))
2824[10] 2954[7] 3132[U]

Asabache (IRE) *Sean Regan* 109c
11 b g Alphabatim(USA) —Inga Murphy (IRE) (Buckskin (FR))
404[7]

Ascari *A L Forbes* 75h
10 br g Presidium—Ping Pong (Petong)
237[6]

Ascot (POL) *Z Matysik*
9 ch g Chef Supreme(USA) —Addis Abbeba (POL) (Dakota)
1710a[7]

A Sea Commander (GER) *J W Mullins* 74b
4 b g Winged Love(IRE) —As Tu As (USA) (Irish River (FR))
3181[11] 3720[3] 4644[P]

Ashamdil (IRE) *P Hughes* 89h
7 ch m Mukaddamah(USA) —Terzia (Elegant Air)
93a[5]

Ashfield Orchestra (IRE) *M Brown* 87c
10 bb m Orchestra—Colour Clown (Random Shot)
977[6]

Ashgan (IRE) *Dr P Pritchard* 80 h 63c
13 br g Yashgan—Nicky's Dilemma (Kambalda)
105[12] 508[3] 565[6] 801[12]839[7] 916[4] (978) 1040[9] 1156[6]1483[10] 1981[5] 2459[4] 2845[4]3125[3] 3283[5] 4526[9] 4856[6] 5[7]

Ashgar (USA) *Mrs Nicola Sheppard* 95h 98c
10 ch g Bien Bien(USA) —Ardisia (USA) (Affirmed (USA))
49[P]

Ashgreen *Miss Venetia Williams* 68h 112c
9 b g Afzal—Space Kate (Space King)
(1646) 1713[5] (2282) 2485[5]

Ashleybank House (IRE) *David Pearson* 80 h 81c
9 b g Lord Americo—Deep Perk (IRE) (Deep Run)
2660[P] 2861[P] 2990[P]3332[6] 3548[12] 3733[6] 4012[P] 4166[F]4350[4] 4802[5] 4989[2]9[5]

Ashley Brook (IRE) *K Bishop* 123+h 167 c
8 ch g Magical Wonder(USA) —Seamill (IRE) (Lafontaine (USA))
1970[3] 2635[2]

Ashnaya (FR) *G M Moore* 98+h 115+c
8 b m Ashkalani(IRE) —Upend (Main Reef)
(193) 430[2] (524) 1664[4]

Ashstorm (IRE) *G Ducey* 116h 124c
10 ch g Glacial Storm(USA) —Sandy Ash (IRE) (Boreen (FR))
5129a[P]

Ashwell (IRE) *C C Bealby* 98h 104+c
7 gr g Anshan—Willshego (Welsh Captain)
1819[2] 2951[F]

Asian Maze (IRE) *Thomas Mullins* 165h
7 ch m Anshan—Mazuma (IRE) (Mazaad)
(116a) 4000a[2] 4432[F] (4775) (5101a)

Ask Again *D G Bridgwater* 53h 35c
7 ch g Rakaposhi King—Boreen's Glory (Boreen (FR))
2805[10] 3480[P]

Askham Lad (IRE) *M Todhunter* 77b
5 b g Courtship—Raymylettes Niece (IRE) (Dock Leaf)
4366[6] 4588[P]

Ask Hym (IRE) *John G Carr* 2b
6 b m Un Desperado(FR) —Chantel Rouge (Boreen (FR))
5104a[21]

Ask The Gatherer (IRE) *M Pitman* 126h
8 b g Be My Native(USA) —Shean Bracken (IRE) (Le Moss)
(1950) (2421) 3174[6] 3738[3] 4469[16]

Ask The Natives (IRE) *Miss C Roddick* 122+c
12 br g Be My Native(USA) —Ask The Lady (Over The River (FR))
453[F]

Ask The Umpire (IRE) *N E Berry* 98+h 86c
11 b g Boyne Valley—Ask Breda (Ya Zaman (USA))
(96) 385[4] 1977[7] 2129[2] 2594[3]2748[F] 2862[5] (3279) 3367[6] 3731[6]3923[4] 3997[12] (4320) 4727[P]

Aspharasyousee (IRE) *J G Cosgrave* 95h
8 b g Phardante(FR) —Brave Express (Brave Invader (USA))
2032a[6]

Aspiring Actor (IRE) *P F Nicholls* 101h
6 b g Old Vic—Stasias Dream (IRE) (Montelimar (USA))
2809[3]

Aspra (FR) *C J Down* 90h
6 b m Green Tune(USA) —Ambri Piotta (FR) (Caerwent)
569[3] 911[4] 1037[4] (1154) 3876[5]

Asrar *Miss Lucinda V Russell* 79b
4 b f King's Theatre(IRE) —Zandaka (FR) (Doyoun)
2068[4] 3259[4] 3799[3]

Assignation *Miss M Bragg* 77h
6 b g Compton Place—Hug Me (Shareef Dancer (USA))
4856[P]

Assoon *G L Moore* 103 h
7 b g Ezzoud(IRE) —Handy Dancer (Green God)
2017[2] 2347[15] (2576) 2868[3] 3286[5] 3950[7]4570[3] 4907[6]

Assumetheposition (FR) *R C Guest* 92 h 92 c
6 gr g Cyborg(FR) —Jeanne Grey (FR) (Fast Topaze (USA))
499[2] 612[B] 1942[5]2022[F] 2187[4] 2440[4]3037[2] 3368[F] 3732[8]3918[P] 4804[F] 4844[3]5036[3]

Assumptalina *R T Phillips* 68b
6 b m Primitive Rising(USA) —New Broom (IRE) (Brush Aside (USA))
3328[P] 3466[P]

Assured Physique *A E Jones* 58h
9 b g Salse(USA) —Metaphysique (FR) (Law Society (USA))
681[8]

Astalanda (FR) *Garvan Donnelly* 94h
4 ch f Sendawar(IRE) —Ashkara (IRE) (Chief Singer)
2645a[5] 4122a[7]

Astarador (FR) *J Howard Johnson* 110b
4 b g Astarabad(USA) —Touques (FR) (Tip Moss (FR))
2642[2] (3353) 4779[7]

Asteem *M E Sowersby* 55h
4 b g Mark Of Esteem(IRE) —Amidst (Midyan (USA))
1339[7] 2569[P] 2753[11] 3485[P]

Aston (USA) *R C Guest* 96h 99+c
6 b g Bahri(USA) —Halholah (USA) (Secreto (USA))
1539[2] 1589[3] 1664[3]5037[2]

Aston Lad *M D Hammond* 118+h
5 b g Bijou D'Inde—Fishki (Niniski (USA))
596[5] (2064) 2639[2] (2994) 3854[5] 4364[2] (4504)4986[4]

Astonville (FR) *P Cottin*
12 b g Top Ville—Astonishing (BRZ) (Vacilante (ARG))
4432[13]

Astral Affair (IRE) *P A Pritchard* 73h
7 br m Norwich—Jupiters Jill (Jupiter Pluvius)
2503[6] 2810[5] 2985[6]

Astral Dancer (IRE) *J Mackie* 74h
6 b g Fourstars Allstar(USA) —Walk N'Dance (IRE) (Pennine Walk)
1714[8] 1903[15] 2561[P]

Astronaut *R C Guest* 70h
9 b g Sri Pekan(USA) —Wild Abandon (USA) (Graustark)
839[3] 1310[3] 2290[U] 2977[10] 3367[5]

Astronomic *J Howard Johnson* 131 h
6 b g Zafonic(USA) —Sky Love (USA) (Nijinsky (CAN))
2943[P] 3618[P] 4773[13]

Astronomical (IRE) *Miss S J Wilton* 99h
4 b g Mister Baileys—Charm The Stars (Roi Danzig (USA))
(2587) 3972[5] 4551[5]

Astyanax (IRE) *N J Henderson* 109+h
6 b g Hector Protector(USA) —Craigmill (Slip Anchor)
5[7] (1806) 2166[5] 2530[4] 2723[2] 3358[5](4606)

Asudo (IRE) *N A Twiston-Davies* 114+b
5 ch g Flemensfirth(USA) —Nugget Moss (Le Moss)
1681[2] (1985) 2211[14]

Atacama Star *B G Powell* 70+h
4 ch g Desert King(IRE) —Aunty (FR) (Riverman (USA))
1478[6] 1649[P]

Atagirl (IRE) *Andrew Lee* 91h 41c
7 b m Supreme Leader—Corcaigh (Town And Country)
5077a[16]

Atahuelpa *Jennie Candlish* 125h
6 b g Hernando(FR) —Certain Story (Known Fact (USA))
2716[P] 3360[12] 3650[13] 4050[P]

Athlumney Lad (IRE) *Noel Meade* 128h
7 b g Mujadil(USA) —Simouna (Ela-Mana-Mou)
1093a[8] 5078a[18]

Athnowen (IRE) *J R Payne* 107+c
14 b g Lord Americo—Lady Bluebird (Arapaho)
170[6] (518) 666[RR]3212[P]

Atlantic City *Mrs L Richards* 98+h
5 ch g First Trump—Pleasuring (Good Times (ITY))
100[7] 1480[8]

Atlantic Crossing (IRE) *P Beaumont* 113+h 95+c
9 b g Roselier(FR) —Ocean Mist (IRE) (Crash Course)
717[P]

Atlantic Jane *Mrs S J Smith* 115+h
6 b m Tamure(IRE) —Atlantic View (Crash Course)
3149[9] (3461) (3962) 4634[4]

Atlantic Point (IRE) *D W Macauley* 92h
9 b m Arctic Lord—Door Rapper (IRE) (Mandalus)
2688[P]

Atlantic Rhapsody (FR) *T M Walsh* 132h 123c
9 b g Machiavellian(USA) —First Waltz (FR) (Green Dancer (USA))
3411a[15]

Atlantis (HOL) *G L Moore* 90+h
7 ch g No Ski—File Moon (HOL) (Man In The Moon (USA))
1523[3]

At Loggerheads *B G Powell* 52b
5 b m Turtle Island(IRE) —Salty Girl (IRE) (Scenic)
1985[11] 3327[12] 3904[8]

A Toi A Moi (FR) *Miss Venetia Williams* 112+h
6 ch g Cyborg(FR) —Peperonelle (FR) (Dom Pasquini (FR))
4693[6]

Atomic Breeze (IRE) *D M Forster* 78c
12 bb g Strong Gale—Atomic Lady (Over The River (FR))
373[P] 554[10]

At The Double *P Winkworth* 86 h
10 b g Sure Blade(USA) —Moheli (Ardross)
218[5] 3428[3] 3715[7] 3905[7] 4526[8]4577[10]

Attitude *A King* 55b
5 ch m Riverwise(USA) —Came Cottage (Nearly A Hand)
2558[8]

Attorney General (IRE) *J A B Old* 151 h
7 b g Sadler's Wells(USA) —Her Ladyship (Polish Precedent (USA))
1828[7] (2747) (3179) 3723[10] 4458[14]

Atum Re (IRE) *P F Nicholls* 117+h 131+c
9 br g Be My Native(USA) —Collopy's Cross (Pragmatic)
864[7] 2272[2] 2577[5]

At Your Request *Ian Williams* 121 h
5 gr g Bering—Requesting (Rainbow Quest (USA))
(100) (175) (Dead)

Aubigny (FR) *A King* 87b
4 b g Tel Quel(FR) —La Beaumont (FR) (Hellios (USA))
2425[6] 3421[2] 4881[4]

Auburn Grey *M D I Usher* 68b
4 gr g Environment Friend—Odyn Dancer (Minshaanshu Amad (USA))
3346[9] 3617[11]

Auburn Lodge (IRE) *J J Lambe* 51h
5 ch m Grand Lodge(USA) —Hadawah (USA) (Riverman (USA))
1683[7] 2903[10]

Auburn Spirit *M D I Usher* 82h 110+c
11 ch g Teamster—Spirit Of Youth (Kind Of Hush)
1861[7] 2215[6] 2608[P]3212[7] 3578[5] 3886[4]3989[5] 4370[2] 4524[6]

Au Courant (IRE) *N J Henderson* 101h
6 b g Zaffaran(USA) —Thatsthefashion (IRE) (Roselier (FR))
(1979) (3466)

Audiostreetdotcom *R A Harris* 98h 85c
9 ch g Risk Me(FR) —Ballagarrow Girl (North Stoke)
1395[P] 1486[3] 1564[U] 1655[U] 1800[P]

Auditor *S T Lewis* 59+h 79c
7 b g Polish Precedent(USA) —Annaba (IRE) (In The Wings)
176[P] 246[7] 395[6]534[P] 1646[P] 1855[5]2074[4] 2984[P] 3274[4]3482[P] 3686[9] 3887[8]4580[5] 4973[5] 5047[2]

Auenmoon (GER) *P Monteith* 123h
5 ch g Monsun(GER) —Auenlady (GER) (Big Shuffle (USA))
2652[6] 2942[P] 3534[2] 4067[3] (4527) 4763[9]5091[2]

Auetaler (GER) *E McNamara* 100+h
12 gr g Niniski(USA) —Astica (GER) (Surumu (GER))
(2139) 2685[9]

Augherskea (IRE) *Noel Meade* 141h 129c
7 b g Oscar(IRE) —Closing Thyne (IRE) (Good Thyne (USA))
117a[7] 3639a[5] 4022a[P]

August Rose (IRE) *Miss Lucinda V Russell* 91 h
6 bb m Accordion—Lockersleybay (IRE) (Orchestra)
302[7] 1683[3] 2024[5] 3235[5] 3442[4]3918[2] 4487[3] 5064[6]

Auntie Kathleen *J J Quinn* 84+h
7 gr m Terimon—Lady High Sheriff (IRE) (Lancastrian)
261[2] 2036[4]

Aunty Lil (USA) *N J Gifford* 91h
6 bb m Swain(IRE) —Singular Broad (USA) (Broad Brush (USA))
3979[P]

Ausone *Miss J R Gibney* 78h
4 b f Singspiel(IRE) —Aristocratique (Cadeaux Genereux)
1785[4] 2425[10] 4074[11] 4551[4] 4801[U]

Autcaesar Autnihil (IRE) *Mrs J Jeynes* 82h 70c
11 b g Supreme Leader—Monagey (Pimpernel's Tune)
6^{P}

Autograph *Mrs S J Smith* 87+h
5 b m Polar Prince(IRE) —Seraphim (FR) (Lashkari)
349^{7} (4800)

Autumn Dream *Miss J E Foster*
4 b f Primo Dominie—Red Cascade (IRE) (Danehill (USA))
2921^{P}

Autumn Fantasy (USA) *M R Hoad* 85 h 69+c
7 b g Lear Fan(USA) —Autumn Glory (USA) (Graustark)
1247^{4} 1406^{7} 1952^{P}

Autumn Mist (IRE) *M Scudamore* 81h 105c
11 br g Phardante(FR) —Sprinkling Star (Strong Gale)
535^{P} 5105^{2}

Autumn Rain (USA) *G Brown* 97+h
9 br g Dynaformer(USA) —Edda (USA) (Ogygian (USA))
4566^{3} 4907^{P} (Dead)

Autumn Red (IRE) *P R Webber* 100+h
6 ch g Zaffaran(USA) —Ballygullen River (IRE) (Over The River (FR))
1968^{3} 2421^{3} 3595^{4} 4238^{3}

Aux Le Bahnn (IRE) *Noel T Chance* 118+b
5 b g Beneficial—Helvick Lass (IRE) (Mandalus) (2665)

Avadi (IRE) *P T Dalton* 80 h 95 c
8 b g Un Desperado(FR) —Flamewood (Touching Wood (USA))
913^{P} **1487^{10} 1620^{7}1852^{4} 2011^{2} (2080) 2630^{5} 3274^{2} 3398^{3}3732^{P}**

Avalanche (FR) *J R Best* 111+h 136c
9 gr g Highest Honor(FR) —Fairy Gold (Golden Fleece (USA))
130^{P} 2530^{P}

Avalon *Jonjo O'Neill* 94 h
4 b g Kingmambo(USA) —Lady Carla (Caerleon (USA))
3355^{3} 3714^{3} 3898^{3}

Avanti *Dr J R J Naylor* 91h
10 gr g Reprimand—Dolly Bevan (Another Realm)
251^{2}

Avanti Tiger (IRE) *C C Bealby* 71h
7 bb g Supreme Leader—Reign Of Terror (IRE) (Orchestra)
2181^{0} 2290^{3} 3042^{7} 3433^{2} 3540^{4}4320^{P}

Avas Delight (IRE) *R H Alner* 100h 95+c
8 b g Ajraas(USA) —Whothatis (Creative Plan (USA))
(1749)

Avenches (GER) *M J McGrath* 68h
6 ch m Dashing Blade—Altja (GER) (Acatenango (GER))
134^{8}

Avesomeofthat (IRE) *J W Mullins* 98+h
5 b g Lahib(USA) —Lacinia (Groom Dancer (USA))
220^{7} 571^{7} 753^{F} 4210^{11} 4834^{5}(5022)

Aviation *G M Moore* 115h
4 b g Averti(IRE) —Roufontaine (Rousillon (USA))
(1338) (1512) 1718^{8} (1923) 2367^{3} 4747^{9} 5096^{7}

Aviemore *J R Cornwall*
4 b g Selkirk(USA) —Film Script (Unfuwain (USA))
2587^{10} 2661^{P} 3594^{8}

Avitta (IRE) *Miss Venetia Williams* 118 h 120+c
7 b m Pennekamp(USA) —Alinova (USA) (Alleged (USA))
593^{2} 688^{2} (972) (2005) 2241^{2} 2812^{5}3440^{4} 4068^{5}

Avoca Mist (IRE) *W P Mullins* 95h
6 bb m Luso—Apicat (Buckskin (FR))
70a^{10}

Award Me An Oscar (IRE) *M C Pipe* 17h
6 b g Oscar(IRE) —Anshan Lady (IRE) (Anshan)
1018^{11} 1246^{10} 1266^{7}

Awwal Marra (USA) *E W Tuer* 75h
6 ch m King Of Kings(IRE) —Secretariat Lass (USA) (Secretariat (USA))
1566^{P} 1756^{P}

Aymard Des Fieffes (FR) *R A Harris* 69b
4 ch g Lute Antique(FR) —Margot Des Fieffes (FR) (Magistros (FR))
3617^{7} 4947^{4}

Azahara *K G Reveley* 72 h
4 b f Vettori(IRE) —Branston Express (Bay Express)
1339^{4} 1397^{12} 1601^{7} 1883^{8}

Aztec Prince (IRE) *Miss S E Forster* 57h
6 ch g King Persian—China Doll (IRE) (West China)
495^{6} 5063^{7}

Aztec Warrior (IRE) *Miss H C Knight* 119h
5 b g Taipan(IRE) —Eurocurrency (IRE) (Brush Aside (USA))
1849^{3} 2534^{4} 2865^{2} 3210^{6} (4359) 4956^{4}

Azure Wings (IRE) *K C Bailey* 75b
6 ch m Karinga Bay—Minora (IRE) (Cataldi)
1730^{4} *2131^{10}*

Azzemour (FR) *P F Nicholls* 100+h
7 ch g Morespeed—Tarde (FR) (Kashtan (FR))
(216) 441^{5} 1026^{4} 3325^{5} 5028^{7}

Baawrah *M Todhunter* 81h
5 ch g Cadeaux Genereux—Kronengold (USA) (Golden Act (USA))
(1336) 1605^{2} 2064^{4} 2440^{6}

Babarullah *B R Foster* 23b
8 ch g Lucky Wednesday—Hantergantic (Van Der Linden (FR))
1206^{P}

Baby Gee *D W Whillans* 98h
12 ch m King Among Kings—Market Blues (Porto Bello)
3395^{6} 4045^{5} 5039^{9}

Baby Run (FR) *N A Twiston-Davies* 134 h 140 c
6 b g Baby Turk—Run For Laborie (FR) (Lesotho (USA))
(1822)

Baby Sister *D W Whillans* 78h
7 ch m King Among Kings—Market Blues (Porto Bello)
2977^{11} 4145^{16} 4585^{8}

Bach Beauty (IRE) *N J Henderson*
4 b f Classic Cliche(IRE) —Melody Maid (Strong Gale)
4237^{8}

Back Among Friends *J A B Old* 97 h
7 b g Bob Back(USA) —Betty's Girl (Menelek)
2826^{F} 3328^{5} 3611^{7}

Backbeat (IRE) *J Howard Johnson* 111 h 144 c
9 ch g Bob Back(USA) —Pinata (Deep Run)
1735^{2} 3385^{4}

Backbord (GER) *Mrs L Wadham* 103h
4 b g Platini(GER) —Bukowina (GER) (Windwurf (GER))
3431^{4} 3786^{3} 4211^{2}

Backcraft (IRE) *Mrs S J Smith* 113+h
8 b g Bob Back(USA) —Bawnanell (Viking (USA))
1361^{7} 1444^{7} 1665^{P}

Back De Bay (IRE) *J R Cornwall* 19h 51c
6 b g Bob Back(USA) —Baybush (Boreen (FR))
1757^{P} 2081^{10} **2260^{6} 2966^{P}3652^{F} 4164^{C} 4352^{3}**

Back For The Craic (IRE) *N J Henderson* 67h
7 ch g Bob Back(USA) —Alice Brennan (IRE) (Good Thyne (USA))
3975^{4}

Backgammon *K G Reveley* 101h
5 b g Sadler's Wells(USA) —Game Plan (Darshaan)
1794^{7} 1927^{5} 2475^{3} 2766^{2}

Back In Front (IRE) *E J O'Grady* 157 h 149c
9 br g Bob Back(USA) —Storm Front (IRE) (Strong Gale)
2227a^{2} 2669a^{4} **4444^{U} 5058a^{5}**

Back In Vogue *J G Portman* 79b
5 ch m Bob Back(USA) —Cooks Lawn (The Parson)
3657^{7} 4017^{13}

Back Nine (IRE) *R H Alner* 121h 129 c
9 b g Bob Back(USA) —Sylvia Fox (Deep Run)
1917^{2} 2743^{4} 3134^{F}3879^{3} 4090^{2} 4356^{3}

Back On Top (IRE) *J L Hassett* 118c
12 b g Bob Back(USA) —Top Girl (IRE) (High Top)
5083a^{6}

Backpacker (IRE) *B G Powell* 70h 102c
9 b g Petoski—Yellow Iris (Le Bavard (FR))
2805^{4} 3218^{3}

Backscratcher *John R Upson* 57 h 81c
12 b g Backchat(USA) —Tiernee Quintana (Artaius (USA))
181^{5} 575^{9} **1277^{F}**

Backsheesh (IRE) *G Tuer*
11 b g Bob Back(USA) —Kottna (USA) (Lyphard (USA))
63^{P}

Backstreet Lad *Evan Williams* 72h
4 b g Fraam—Forest Fantasy (Rambo Dancer (CAN))
1332^{5} 1440^{2} 1679^{7} 3548^{10} 4731^{12}

Back To Ben Alder (IRE) *N J Henderson* 125h
9 bb g Bob Back(USA) —Winter Fox (Martinmas)
207^{P} 2974^{4} 4765^{5}

Back To Bid (IRE) *Noel Meade* 138+h
6 b g Mujadil(USA) —Cut It Fine (USA) (Big Spruce (USA))
(2782a) 3408a^{3} 4137a^{2} 4469^{4} 4888a^{7}

Back With A Bang (IRE) *Mrs N S Evans* 96b
7 b g Oscar(IRE) —Trapper Jean (Orchestra)
656^{3} 1048^{2} 1323^{10} 2864^{14} 3941^{P}4826^{11}

Baden Vugie (IRE) *S T Lewis* 47h 77c
9 bl g Hamas(IRE) —Bag Lady (Be My Guest (USA))
948^{P} 1725^{11}

Badgers Glory *Miss Z Anthony* 71b 79c
10 u g Neltino—Shedid (St Columbus)
401^{3}

Bafana Boy *N G Richards* 32h 99+c
6 br g Presenting—Lorna's Choice (Oats)
3376^{11} 3914^{6} 4530^{6} **(5037)**

Baffling Secret (FR) *L Lungo* 71h
6 gr g Kizitca(FR) —Kadroulienne (FR) (Kadrou (FR))
2448^{LFT} 2942^{11} 3314^{6} 3534^{9}

Bagan (FR) *C J Mann* 133 h
7 bb h Rainbow Quest(USA) —Maid Of Erin (USA) (Irish River (FR))
116a^{5}

Bagwell Ben *M J Coombe*
9 ch g Karinga Bay—Nine Hans (Prince Hansel)
3433^{P}

Bahama Boom *C W Thornton*
4 ch f J B Quick—Ladys Regret (IRE) (Orchestra)
4304^{15}

Bahamian Breeze *G Haine*
5 b g Piccolo—Norgabie (Northfields (USA))
1364^{11} 1614^{P}

Baie Des Flamands (USA) *Miss S J Wilton* 96h
4 b g Kingmambo(USA) —Isle De France (USA) (Nureyev (USA))
(2286) 2921^{P} 3645^{F} 3848^{15} 5070^{7}

Baikaline (FR) *Ian Williams* 99h 90+c
7 b m Cadoudal(FR) —Advantage (FR) (Antheus (USA))
767^{3} 1826^{2} **2243^{P}**3345^{7} 5014^{P}

Bailaora (IRE) *B W Duke* 27h
5 bb g Shinko Forest(IRE) —Tart (FR) (Warning)
563^{6}

Baileys Prize (USA) *P R Rodford* 95h 19c
9 ch g Mister Baileys—Mar Mar (USA) (Forever Casting (USA))
3433^{P} **3888^{P}**

Baileysunice (IRE) *Seamus Fahey* 110h
4 b g Mister Baileys—Shamneez (IRE) (Pharly (FR))
5076a^{4}

Baily Breeze (IRE) *M F Morris* 117h 142 c
7 b g Zaffaran(USA) —Mixed Blends (The Parson)
(3012a) 3893a^{P}

Baily Mist (IRE) *M F Morris* 109 h 131c
9 b m Zaffaran(USA) —Mixed Blends (The Parson)
69a^{P}

Bainoona *Evan Williams* 51h
4 gr f Linamix(FR) —Anam (Persian Bold)
1563^{U} 1594^{11} 1729^{10}

Baker Of Oz *D Burchell* 67h
5 b g Pursuit Of Love—Moorish Idol (Aragon)
2381^{0} 681^{6} 2463^{P}

Bakhtyar *A J Martin* 69h
5 gr g Daylami(IRE) —Gentilesse (Generous (IRE))
65a^{18} 1806^{P}

Bak To Bill *Mrs S Gardner* 112+h 118 c
11 b g Nicholas Bill—Kirstins Pride (Silly Prices)
2271^{P} 2609^{8} 3214^{8} 3876^{4} (4289) 4497^{8}4727^{2}
4944^{F} 5113^{6} **4^{P}**

Balakar (IRE) *J J Lambe* 96 h 86+c
10 b g Doyoun—Balaniya (USA) (Diesis)
1883^{7} **2900^{2}**

Balamory Dan (IRE) *G A Harker* 116b
5 b g Fort Morgan(USA) —Musical Horn (Music Boy)
(1532) 1849^{5} 2534^{3}

Balapour (IRE) *Patrick O Brady* 137h 120c
8 b g Kahyasi—Balaniya (USA) (Diesis)
69a^{18} 4138a^{P}

Balasari (IRE) *M D Hammond* 101h
6 b g Sri Pekan(USA) —Balaniya (USA) (Diesis)
2186^{P} 4634^{P} 4922^{14} 5120^{P}

Balgarth (USA) *K J Burke*
4 b g Zamindar(USA) —Vaguely Regal (IRE) (Sadler's Wells (USA))
2569^{11} 2935^{P} (Dead)

Balinahinch Castle (IRE) *Mrs L B Normile* 120h 85c
9 b g Good Thyne(USA) —Emerald Flair (Flair Path)
465^{5}

Balla D'Aire (IRE) *K F Clutterbuck* 83h 83c
11 bb g Balla Cove—Silius (Junius (USA))
368^{2} 896^{8} 1109^{9}1299^{8} 1819^{P}

Balladeer (IRE) *Mrs T J Hill* 115+h 118+c
8 b g King's Theatre(IRE) —Carousel Music (On Your Mark)
1595^{U} 1761^{4} (2682) 3323^{U} 3440^{3} 3921^{P}4214^{P} 4820^{4}

Ballard Lad (IRE) *Miss S Cox* 125+h
7 b g Dolphin Street(FR) —Borough Counsel (Law Society (USA))
3005a^{11}

Ball Boy *G Haine* 17h
4 b g Xaar—Tanz (IRE) (Sadler's Wells (USA))
2949^{F} 3340^{14}

Ballet Red *Miss B J Thomas* 57h
9 b m Sea Raven(IRE) —Cailin Rua (IRE) (Montelimar (USA))
5109^{P}

Ballez (FR) *P F Nicholls* 101+c
5 b g Villez(USA) —Aconit (FR) (Shining Steel)
2213^{2} 3215^{U} 3506^{P}4693^{P}

Ball Games *James Moffatt* 99+h
8 b g Mind Games—Deb's Ball (Glenstal (USA))
120^{4} 214^{3} 592^{2} 1308^{4} 1357^{F}1588^{P} (1883) 2139^{4} (2567) 4922^{10}

Ballinabearna (IRE) *Eoin Doyle* 80b
6 b g Germany(USA) —Ceannabhalla (IRE) (Mandalus)
4680^{7}

Ballinclay King (IRE) *Ferdy Murphy* 125c
12 b g Asir—Clonroche Artic (Pauper)
150^{P}

Ballinger Venture *N M Babbage* 42h
4 b f Vettori(IRE) —Branston Ridge (Indian Ridge)
2013^{5} 2520^{5} 3181^{13}

Ballinruane (IRE) *B S Rothwell* 85+h
7 br g Norwich—Katie Dick (IRE) (Roselier (FR))
192^{0} 425^{6} 2171^{16}

Ballintra Boy (IRE) *Noel Meade* 124h
7 b g Oscar(IRE) —Super Leg (Super Slip)
70a^{14} 2228a^{4}

Ballistic Boy *R W Thomson* 69h 81+c
9 ch g First Trump—Be Discreet (Junius (USA))
858^{9} 1150^{5} 1602^{9}

Ballistigo (IRE) *A King* 103h
7 br g Executive Perk—Herballistic (Rolfe (USA))
2301^{9} 2755^{8} 3814^{4}

Ballito (IRE) *John G Carr* 99+h 27c
7 ch g Flying Legend(USA) —Whatt Ya Doin (IRE) (Duky)
(1800) 2139^{5}

Balloch *Mary Meek* 74h
5 ch m Wootton Rivers(USA) —Balayer (Balidar)
2301^{1} 3902^{10} 4129^{P} 4368^{11}

Ball O Malt (IRE) *R A Fahey* 116h 129 c
10 b g Star Quest—Vera Dodd (IRE) (Riot Helmet)
248^{2} 1083a^{7} 1295^{4}(1435) 1881^{6} 2292^{3}
2571^{3}3205^{3}

Ballyaahbutt (IRE) *B G Powell* 64h 58c
7 b g Good Thyne(USA) —Lady Henbit (IRE) (Henbit (USA))
358^{P} 486^{3} 673^{P}1041^{P}

Bally Abbie *P Beaumont* 55h
5 b m Weldnaas(USA) —Bally Small (Sunyboy)
1674^{13} 3167^{P} 3347^{11} 3963^{11} 4527^{10}12^{9}

Ballyagran (IRE) *Noel Meade* 127h
6 b g Pierre—Promalady (IRE) (Homo Sapien)
93a^{2} 2228a^{U} 2909a^{6} 4950a^{4}

Ballybawn House *J C Fox* 92 h
5 b m Tamure(IRE) —Squeaky Cottage (True Song)
2486^{6} 2983^{8} 3275^{2} 3437^{4} 3997^{4}4429^{U} 4619^{11}

Ballybean (IRE) *K C Bailey*
6 b g Simply Great(FR) —Youthful Capitana (Hard Boy)
1950^{P} **3251^{P} 3457^{9}**

Bally Blue *Mrs Monique Pike* 86c
8 gr g Roselier(FR) —Layston Pinzal (Afzal)
4946^{5}

Ballyboe Boy (IRE) *R C Guest* 90 h 80c
7 b g Flying Spur(AUS) —Born To Fly (IRE) (Last Tycoon)
9^{12} **122^{8} 604^{U}674^{12}** 856^{7} (987) 1046^{8} **1098^{5}**1336^{3}

Ballyboley (IRE) *R T Phillips* 105h
8 b g Roselier(FR) —Benbradagh Vard (IRE) (Le Bavard (FR))
4099^{2} 4315^{3}

Bally Bolshoi (IRE) *Mrs S D Williams* 106h
6 b m Bob Back(USA) —Moscow Money (IRE) (Moscow Society (USA))
2012^{4} 2605^{2} (3483) 3577^{9} (4034) 4286^{2} 4619^{10}

Ballybough Billy (IRE) *Carl Llewellyn* 86b
5 b g Taipan(IRE) —Bramblehill Fairy (IRE) (Toulon)
7^{4}

Ballybough Eddie (IRE) *Evan Williams* 91b
7 b g John French—Jib (Welsh Pageant)
5043^{P}

Ballybough Rasher (IRE) *J Howard Johnson* 121h
11 b g Broken Hearted—Chat Her Up (Proverb)
2499^{P} 2990^{P}

Bally Brakes (IRE) *N G Richards* 97h
6 ch g Moonax(IRE) —Deep Solare (Deep Run)
2948^{5} 5038^{F}

Ballybrophy (IRE) *G Brown* 87c
11 gr g Roselier(FR) —Bavardmore (Le Bavard (FR))
2009^{P} 2282^{4} 2575^{P}

Ballycassidy (IRE) *P Bowen* 131dh 152+c
10 br g Insan(USA) —Bitofabreeze (IRE) (Callernish)
(423) (814) **1013^{3} 2491^{10}2744^{5} 2972^{7} 3697^{3}4118^{5} 4470^{14} 4777^{F}(5094)**

Ballycross (IRE) *N A Twiston-Davies*
6 b g Zaffaran(USA) —Iveagh Lady (IRE) (Spin Of A Coin)
3583^{P}

Ballycroy Girl (IRE) *A Bailey* 58h
4 ch f Pennekamp(USA) —Hulm (IRE) (Mujtahid (USA))
1737^{11} 2477^{7}

Ballydoyle Counsel (IRE) *T Wall*
8 b m Leading Counsel(USA) —Bernelle (IRE) (Don't Forget Me)
487^{P}

Ballyfin (IRE) *J A Geake* 88h 89c
8 b g Lord Americo—Scar Stream (Paddy's Stream)
2957^{6} 3239^{5}

Ballyfinney (IRE) *D T Hughes* 107h
5 ch g Good Thyne(USA) —Sounds Confident (IRE) (Orchestra)
3003a^{9} 4060a^{4}

Ballyfitz *N A Twiston-Davies* 123+h
6 b g Overbury(IRE) —Running For Gold (Rymer)
(1854) (2169)

Ballyfourlass (IRE) *James Cousins* 74b 60c
6 br m Anshan—Liskilnewabbey (IRE) (Supreme Leader)
3528a^{11}

Ballygally Bay *S J Mahon* 116h
4 b g Erhaab(USA) —Indigo Dawn (Rainbow Quest (USA))
2645a^{2} 3004a^{11} 3401a^{6}

Ballyhale (IRE) *P D Niven* 88h
8 br g Mister Lord(USA) —Deep Inagh (Deep Run)
2571^{6} 2755^{4} 2994^{P}

Bally Hall (IRE) *M J Gingell* 62+h
6 b g Saddlers' Hall(IRE) —Sally Rose (Sallust)
1158^{12} 1222^{7} 1415^{5} 1483^{11} 1814^{10}1883^{P}

Ballyhoo (IRE) *J W Mullins* 95 h
6 b m Supreme Leader—Ballyhouraprincess (IRE) (Mulhollande (USA))
1600^{4} 2212^{5} (2486) 2932^{4} 3424^{P} 3802^{5}4619^{7} (5087)

Ballyhurry (USA) *J S Goldie* 102h
9 b g Rubiano(USA) —Balakhna (FR) (Tyrant (USA))
2062^{8} 2475^{6} 2901^{4} 3267^{3} 3929^{7}

Ballyjohnboy Lord (IRE) *M Scudamore* 118+h 91+c
7 b g Arctic Lord—Mount Sackville (Whistling Deer)
(3257) 3598^{3} 4036^{4} 4375^{18} **4780^{3}**

Ballykelly (IRE) *R T Phillips* 102b
5 b g Insan(USA) —Lady Oakwell (IRE) (King's Ride)
(4237) 4644^{3} 4940^{3}

Ballykettrail (IRE) *Mrs Julie Read* 120h
10 b g Catrail(USA) —Ballykett Lady (USA) (Sir Ivor (USA))
824^{7} **4477^{P}**

Ballykiln (IRE) *Miss H C Knight*
5 br g Petoski—Hunt The Thimble (FR) (Relkino)
1950^{P} 2866^{P}

Ballykilthy (IRE) *Ms A E Embiricos* 49h 73+c
9 b g Un Desperado(FR) —Theyllallwin (IRE) (Le Bavard (FR))
401^{5}

Ballymena *C Roberts* 71h
5 b m Saddlers' Hall(IRE) —Ace Gunner (Gunner B)
(138) 2457^{6} 3690^{7}

Ballynattin Buck (IRE) *M Sheppard* 100h 131 c
10 b g Buckskin(FR) —Dikler Gale (IRE) (Strong Gale)
115a^{10} 1231^{2} 1413^{DSQ}

Ballynure (IRE) *Mrs L B Normile* 91h 37c
8 bb g Roselier(FR) —Fresh Partner (IRE) (Yashgan)
1838^{8} 2171^{3} 2653^{11} 4530^{P}

Ballyowen (IRE) *Mrs P Sly*
7 br g Houmayoun(FR) —Polocracy (IRE) (Aristocracy)
1990^{4} 2421^{13} 2638^{P} 3941^{P}

Bally Rainey (IRE) *Mrs L C Jewell* 90b 79c
7 bb g Carroll House—Foxborough Lady (Crash Course)
2579^{5} 2866^{12} **3329^{5} 3660^{P}4913^{3}**

Ballyrobert (IRE) *A M Hales* 89 h 115 c
9 bb g Bob's Return(IRE) —Line Abreast (High Line)
1795^{4} 2239^{5} 2827^{2}3344^{10} 4755^{U} 5086^{2}

Bally's Bak *Mrs S J Smith* 102h 87c
8 ch m Bob Back(USA) —Whatagale (Strong Gale)
2457 329^{S} 763^{F} (Dead)

Bally's Bro (IRE) *N A Twiston-Davies* 101+h
7 ch g Zaffaran(USA) —Dalaray (Dalesa)
179^{2} 1619^{3}

Ballyshan (IRE) *N A Twiston-Davies* 118+h
8 b g Synefos(USA) —Bramble Leader (IRE) (Supreme Leader)
2527[2] 2866[3] 3253[2] (3477) 3962[2] 4603[8]

Ballytrim (IRE) *W P Mullins* 123+b
5 b g Luso—Helynsar (Fidel)
4448[13] 5081a[9]

Ballyvaddy (IRE) *J A Geake* 126h 128c
10 gr g Roselier(FR) —Bodalmore Kit (Bargello)
311[7] 4617[P] 4974[14]

Balmoral Queen *D McCain* 87+h
6 br m Wizard King—Balmoral Princess (Thethingaboutitis (USA))
2721[P] (2858) 3395[3] 3951[F] 4320[P] 12[7]

Balmoral Star *D McCain* 67b
5 b m Wizard King—Balmoral Princess (Thethingaboutitis (USA))
917[6]

Baloo *J D Frost* 102 h 110 c
10 b g Morpeth—Moorland Nell (Neltino)
751[4] 1125[3] (1271) 1877[3] 2072[5] 3876[8] 4561[7] 4857[4]

Balto Rambler (IRE) *D M Leigh* 92c
9 b g Naiyli—Star Of Leighlin (IRE) (Saher)
112a[P]

Baltracy Cross (IRE) *C J Mann*
5 b g Shaamit(IRE) —Marconda (IRE) (Colonel Godfrey (USA))
1799[20]

Balyan (IRE) *J Howard Johnson* 104 h
5 b g Bahhare(USA) —Balaniya (USA) (Diesis)
3347[2] 3779[P]

Bambi De L'Orme (FR) *Ian Williams* 143 c
7 gr g True Brave(USA) —Princesse Ira (FR) (Less Ice)
(219) 2163[7] 3724[4] 4472[10] 4749[8]

Bamby (IRE) *R Ford* 69h
6 b m Glacial Storm(USA) —Ardfallon (IRE) (Supreme Leader)
1961[7] 2211[16] 4450[12] 5052[14]

Banaluso (IRE) *B G Powell* 57h
6 b g Luso—Trembling Lass (IRE) (Tremblant)
2126[U] 3187[P] 3499[P] 4571[P]

Banasan (IRE) *M J P O'Brien* 121h 138c
8 b h Marju(IRE) —Banaja (IRE) (Sadler's Wells (USA))
1083a[6] 1700a[4]

Banbrook Hill (IRE) *C A McBratney* 82c
7 b g Sharp Charter—Crook Lady (Croghan Hill)
4841[P]

Banchory Two (IRE) *P F Nicholls* 106h 105 c
6 b g Un Desperado(FR) —Theyllallwin (IRE) (Le Bavard (FR))
2144[7] 2516[4] 2751[6] 4981[5]

Bang And Blame (IRE) *M W Easterby* 54h 115 c
10 b g Be My Native(USA) —Miss Lucille (Fine Blade (USA))
1177[P] 1276[6] 1446[7] 1886[4] (2413) 2589[F] (2978) (3336) 3560[6] 4042[4] 4356[11] (4636) 4790[P]

Banjo Hill *Miss E C Lavelle* 100h 98c
12 b g Arctic Lord—Just Hannah (Macmillion)
105[P]

Banker Count *Miss Venetia Williams* 141c
14 b g Lord Bud—Gilzie Bank (New Brig)
1924[3] 2177[14]

Bankit *M G Hazell*
13 ch g Gildoran—Game Trust (National Trust)
51[U]

Banna's (IRE) *Ms Margaret Mullins* 98+h
5 b m Saddlers' Hall(IRE) —Banna's Retreat (Vitiges (FR))
5077a[14]

Banningham Blaze *A W Carroll* 81+h
6 b m Averti(IRE) —Ma Pavlova (USA) (Irish River (FR))
1486[9] (1643) 1753[9] 2146[5]

Bannister Lane *D McCain* 94h 118+c
6 b g Overbury(IRE) —Miss Club Royal (Avocat)
(210) 1714[6] 1938 [P] 2503[5] 2817[5] 3290[7] 3541[3] 3794[4] (4068) 4355[4] 4847[2]

Bannow Beach (IRE) *J Mackie* 45b
5 b m Saddlers' Hall(IRE) —Mullaghcloga (IRE) (Glacial Storm (USA))
3353[P] 4059[7]

Bannow Strand (IRE) *M C Pipe* 95h 140+c
6 b g Luso—Bid For Fun (IRE) (Auction Ring (USA))
(2210) 2339[2] (3288) 3988[P] 4459[P]

Baracouda (FR) *F Doumen* 165 h
11 b g Alesso(USA) —Peche Aubar (FR) (Zino)
2490[2] 4458[5]

Baranook (IRE) *B J Llewellyn* 90+h
5 b g Barathea(IRE) —Gull Nook (Mill Reef (USA))
2618[P] 4106[7] 4678[6]

Barathea Blazer *K C Bailey*
7 b g Barathea(IRE) —Empty Purse (Pennine Walk)
2627[P]

Barathea Blue *M C Pipe* 94h
5 ch g Barathea(IRE) —Empty Purse (Pennine Walk)
2455[7] 2624 [7] 2849[10] 3211[P] 3358[9] 5045[3]

Barati (IRE) *M J P O'Brien* 124h
5 b g Sadler's Wells(USA) —Oriane (Nashwan (USA))
3411a[22]

Barbers Shop *N J Henderson* 106b
4 b g Saddlers' Hall(IRE) —Close Harmony (Bustino)
(4333)

Barbilyrifle (IRE) *H H G Owen*
5 b g Indian Rocket—Age Of Elegance (Troy)
3415[P] 4056[P]

Barcelona *Lady Susan Brooke* 71h 94+c
9 b g Barathea(IRE) —Pipitina (Bustino)
2659[12] 2940[15] 3125[8] 4013[P] 4591[5] 4827[5] 5017[3]

Barcham Again (IRE) *Mrs C J Kerr* 97h 100c
9 b g Aristocracy—Dante's Thatch (IRE) (Phardante (FR))
4721[P] 5036[10]

Barclay Boy *A J Lidderdale* 104h
7 b g Terimon—Nothings Forever (Oats)
3248[8] 3719[3] 4210[6] 4557[7]

Barella (IRE) *L Corcoran* 94 h
7 b g Barathea(IRE) —Daniella Drive (USA) (Shelter Half (USA))
2995[11] 3137[5] (3456) 3673[4] 3804[4] 4427[8] 4639[F] 4941[8] 5114[F]

Barfleur (IRE) *P Bowen* 96+h
6 b m Anshan—Lulu Buck (Buckskin (FR))
2075[8] 2457[8] 3979[P] 4935[12]

Bargain Hunt (IRE) *W Storey* 88+h
5 b g Foxhound(USA) —Atisayin (USA) (Al Nasr (FR))
544[2] 1336[6] 1604[4] 1665[2] 1836[9] 2693[6] 3169[0] 3557[6] 14[12]

Bar Gayne (IRE) *T R George* 98h 99c
7 ch g Good Thyne(USA) —Annie's Alkali (Strong Gale)
2555[3] 2800[P] (3250) 3613[3] 4277[2] 4428[F] 4734[2] 5064[14]

Barjou (NZ) *A King* 70h
5 b g Al Akbar(AUS) —Glowing Satin (NZ) (Noble Bijou (USA))
3324[9] 3996[P] 5023[8]

Barking Mad (USA) *C R Dore* 105 h
8 bb g Dayjur(USA) —Avian Assembly (USA) (General Assembly (USA))
1235[10] (1952) 2261[9] 3985[P]

Barnards Green (IRE) *M Madgwick* 79h 98c
8 ch g Florida Son—Pearly Castle (IRE) (Carlingford Castle)
354[4] 725[F] 958[5] 1299[6] 1646[F] 4525[6] 4911[P]

Barnbrook Empire (IRE) *B J Llewellyn* 85h
4 b f Second Empire(IRE) —Home Comforts (Most Welcome)
1679[5] (1873) 3021[11] 3439[P]

Barney (IRE) *Mrs E Slack* 70+h
5 b g Basanta(IRE) —Double Or Nothing (IRE) (Doubletour (USA))
1889[11] 2062[12] 3168[8] 3347[13] 3782[6] 4142[P] 4487[P]

Barney Blue (IRE) *Ian Williams*
6 ch g Presenting—Six Of Spades (IRE) (Exactly Sharp (USA))
2301[11] 2815[P]

Barney McAll (IRE) *R T Phillips* 101h
6 b g Grand Lodge(USA) —Persian Song (Persian Bold)
117a[P] 2347[13] 2562[P]

Barneys Joy *O Brennan* 56b
7 ch g Keen—Tullow Lady (IRE) (Mazaad)
1613[7] 1762[12]

Barneys Reflection *A Crook* 102 h 81 c
6 b g Petoski—Annaberg (IRE) (Tirol)
126[4] 1971[4] 4794[6] 925[7] 1176[7] 2080[P] 3562[6] 4056[P] 4921[P] 13[U]

Baron Blitzkrieg *D J Wintle* 73h 85 c
8 b g Sir Harry Lewis(USA) —Steel Typhoon (General Ironside)
1969[7] 2592[5] 3147[6] 3367[3] (3888) 4053[3] 4653[P]

Baron De Feypo (IRE) *Patrick O Brady* 83h 130c
8 b g Simply Great(FR) —Fete Champetre (Welsh Pageant)
67a[5] 2650a[13] 2777a[3] 3006a[5]

Baron Monty (IRE) *C Grant* 120+h
8 b g Supreme Leader—Lady Shoco (Montekin)
1939 [P]

Baron Romeo (IRE) *R T Phillips* 85+h
6 gr g Baron Blakeney—Langretta (IRE) (Lancastrian)
(2864) 3024[2] 3496[F] 3545[4] 4099[6] 5009[9]

Barons Knight *M A Barnes* 28h
5 ch g Lahib(USA) —Red Barons Lady (IRE) (Electric)
2534[20] 3373[8] 5118[U]

Baron Windrush *N A Twiston-Davies* 146 c
8 b g Alderbrook—Dame Scarlet (Blakeney)
2992[P] 4111[4] 4496[P] 4777[U] 5004[P]

Barrack Buster *Martin Brassil* 139+h 115+c
7 b m Bigstone(IRE) —Tarkhana (IRE) (Dancing Brave (USA))
66a[14] 1702a[5]

Barranco (IRE) *G L Moore* 85h
5 b g Sadler's Wells(USA) —Belize Tropical (IRE) (Baillamont (USA))
78[8] 2552[4] 2750[12] 2934[2] 3137[3] 3321[3] 3433[5] 3905[8] (4423)

Barrell Rose (IRE) *Paul Magnier* 52h
5 ch m Definite Article—Hardshan (IRE) (Warrshan (USA))
3003a[F]

Barren Lands *K Bishop* 110h 114 c
11 b g Green Desert(USA) —Current Raiser (Filiberto (USA))
170[2] 3507[P] 3949[6] 4332[3] 4639[4] 5107[P]

Barrons Pike *B Storey* 59b 92+c
7 ch g Jumbo Hirt(USA) —Bromley Rose (Rubor)
594[6] 2689[4] 3170[4] 3553[4] 4300[4] 4844[11] 4981[4]

Barrow (SWI) *Ferdy Murphy* 97 h
9 br g Caerleon(USA) —Bestow (Shirley Heights)
480[P]

Barrow Drive *Anthony Mullins* 140h 150c
10 b g Gunner B—Fille De Soleil (Sunyboy)
3587a[4]

Barrow Walk (IRE) *Thomas Mullins* 105h
7 b g Alphabatim(USA) —No Dunce (IRE) (Nordance (USA))
43a[17]

Barrshan (IRE) *N J Henderson*
7 b g Anshan—Bula Beag (IRE) (Brush Aside (USA))
3331[P] 4753[U] 5049[U]

Barrys Ark (IRE) *J A B Old* 99+h
8 bb g Commanche Run—Hand Me Down (Cheval)
2130[4]

Barryscourt Lad (IRE) *R D E Woodhouse* 106+c
12 b g Glacial Storm(USA) —Clonana (Le Bavard (FR))
12[4] 430[U] (4347) 4748[21]

Bartercard (USA) *C J Mann* 96+b
5 b g Sir Cat(USA) —Pure Misk (Rainbow Quest (USA))
2432[7] 2823[8] 3657[5]

Barton Bandit *Miss Sarah Kent* 47c
10 ch g Sula Bula—Yamrah (Milford)
3805[P] 4283[P] 4555[12] 4831[7] 5109[P]

Barton Belle *G A Swinbank* 104+b
4 b f Barathea(IRE) —Veronica (Persian Bold)
(3259) 4507[3]

Barton Flower *D P Keane* 104h 116+c
5 br m Danzero(AUS) —Iota (Niniski (USA))
1614[2] 1794[2] 2515[3] 4641[2] 4855[4]

Barton Gate *D P Keane* 94h 92c
8 b g Rock Hopper—Ruth's River (Young Man (FR))
2217[F] 2685[P] (3141) 3661[5] 3990[P]

Barton Hill *D P Keane* 106h 104c
9 b g Nicholas Bill—Home From The Hill (IRE) (Jareer (USA))
1342[P] 1620[3] 1855[F] 2420[5] 2594[4] 3815[5] 4837[6]

Barton Legend *D P Keane* 100h
6 b g Midnight Legend—Home From The Hill (IRE) (Jareer (USA))
1980[6] 3238[4] 3466[2]

Barton Nic *D P Keane* 124 h 124+c
13 b g Nicholas Bill—Dutch Majesty (Homing)
2636[P] (3187) 3293[2] (3495) 3974[7]

Barton Park *D P Keane* 102+h 105c
6 b g Most Welcome—William's Bird (USA) (Master Willie)
1714[P] 1908[12] (2269) 2716[P] 3944[6] 4838[10] 5027[2]

Barton Sun (IRE) *R N Bevis* 84h
7 b g Indian Ridge—Sun Screen (Caerleon (USA))
345[F] 545[2]

Barum Belle *R A Farrant* 66+h
6 b m Thowra(FR) —La Belle Shyanne (Shy Groom (USA))
1383[8] 1640[5] 1779[P]

Basic Fact (IRE) *Jonjo O'Neill* 92b
4 b g Rudimentary(USA) —Native Emma (IRE) (Be My Native (USA))
3651[4] 4038[4]

Basilea Star (IRE) *M C Pipe* 135 h 142 c
9 b g Fourstars Allstar(USA) —Swiss Castle (IRE) (Carlingford Castle)
43a[10] 90a[3] (3148) 4035[2] 4460[F] (Dead)

Basinet *J J Quinn* 98 h
8 b g Alzao(USA) —Valiancy (Grundy)
1823[P] 2590[6]

Bassett Tiger (IRE) *W P Mullins* 115h 125c
10 b g Shardari—Bassett Girl (Brigadier Gerard)
842[P]

Bathwick Annie *B G Powell* 97 h 138dc
10 ch m Sula Bula—Lily Mab (FR) (Prince Mab (FR))
3509[P] 3995[U] 4111[P] 4374[U]

Baton Charge (IRE) *T R George* 80b
8 b g Gildoran—Frizzball (IRE) (Orchestra)
1877[U] 2561[P]

Batswing *G L Moore* 103h 128 c
11 b g Batshoof—Magic Milly (Simply Great (FR))
2379[10] 2576[7] 2868[14] 2969[P] 4618[7]

Batties Den (IRE) *P D Niven* 48h
6 br g Corrouge(USA) —Miner's Society (Miner's Lamp)
2496 431[4] 1834[12]

Battledress (IRE) *K J Condon* 117+h 87c
4 b g In The Wings—Chaturanga (Night Shift (USA))
2178[12] 2645a[8]

Battling Buster (IRE) *R H Buckler*
9 b g Glacial Storm(USA) —Flutter (IRE) (Floriferous)
2165[P] 2301[12] 2619[10] 2848[P]

Batto *G M Moore* 77 h
6 b g Slip Anchor—Frog (Akarad (FR))
2639[6] 2994[P] 4302[12] 5037[U]

Baudolino *R J Price* 66h
9 br g Bin Ajwaad(IRE) —Stos (IRE) (Bluebird (USA))
2073[P] 2424[P] 3126[5]

Bauhaus (IRE) *R T Phillips* 104+h
5 b g Second Empire(IRE) —Hi Bettina (Henbit (USA))
2070[3] 2423[2]

Bayadere (GER) *K F Clutterbuck* 82 h 107+c
6 br m Lavirco(GER) —Brangane (IRE) (Anita's Prince)
(102) 367[6] 2261[10] 2552[P] 3592[5] (4804) 5074[F]

Bayard (USA) *J R Fanshawe* 98+h
4 gr g Lord Avie(USA) —Mersey (Crystal Palace (FR))
1955[2] (2258) (3594) 4435[F]

Bayazid (IRE) *N J Henderson* 92h
4 b g Grand Lodge(USA) —Bayrika (IRE) (Kahyasi)
3714[5] 4128[6] 4604[12]

Bayford Boy *K Bishop* 52h
6 b g Miner's Lamp—Emma's Vision (IRE) (Vision (USA))
3882[P] 4856[9]

Bay Hawk *B G Powell* 75h
4 b c Alhaarth(IRE) —Fleeting Vision (IRE) (Vision (USA))
2274[6] 2481[10] 2597[8]

Bay Island (IRE) *Carl Llewellyn* 111 c
10 bb g Treasure Hunter—Wild Deer (Royal Buck)
1713[U] (1780) 2009[2] 2703[U] 3547[5] 3919[2] 4348[2] 4728[3] 4876[4]

Bayoss (IRE) *Mrs Tracey Barfoot-Saunt*
10 b g Commanche Run—Baylough Lady (IRE) (Lancastrian)
2506[P] 2848[P] 3252[P]

Bdellium *B I Case* 84h 93c
8 b m Royal Vulcan—Kelly's Logic (Netherkelly)
1906[7]

Beachcomber *J Groucott* 77c
11 b g Kuwait Beach(USA) —Miss Rupert (Solar Topic)
594[U]

Beachcomber Bay (IRE) *I J Keeling* 117c
11 ch g Un Desperado(FR) —Beachcomber Lass (Day Is Done)
4748[3]

Beamish Prince *G M Moore* 120 h
7 ch g Bijou D'Inde—Unconditional Love (IRE) (Polish Patriot (USA))
1911[F] 2190[9] 2976[P]

Beam Me Up *G J Smith*
6 b g Gildoran—Beamo (Oats)
242[P] 2507[13]

Beantown (IRE) *Sean Aherne* 123+c
8 ch g Glacial Storm(USA) —Doorslammer (Avocat)
4460[2]

Bearaway (IRE) *Mrs H Dalton* 102 h 123+c
9 b g Fourstars Allstar(USA) —Cruiseaway (Torus)
747[8] 1049[P] 1659[3] 1754[4] 1956[4]

Beardie's Dream (IRE) *Miss P Robson* 13h
6 b m Luso—Florida Bay (IRE) (Florida Son)
2942[16] 3314[12]

Beare Necessities (IRE) *M J Hogan* 109+h
7 ch g Presenting—Lady Laburnum (Carlingford Castle)
4128[2] (4649)

Beat The Boys (IRE) *N A Twiston-Davies* 89b
5 gr g Portrait Gallery(IRE) —Portia's Delight (IRE) (The Parson)
2665[6]

Beat The Heat (IRE) *Jedd O'Keeffe* 111h 118+c
8 b g Salse(USA) —Summer Trysting (USA) (Alleged (USA))
(413) 550[3] 1435[2] 1489[6] 1761[3] 2294[3] 2841[7]

Beau Bridget (IRE) *Henry De Bromhead* 88h
5 b m Oscar(IRE) —Woodbine Lady (IRE) (Fools Holme (USA))
3003a[7]

Beauchamp Gigi (IRE) *J Howard Johnson* 88 h
8 b m Bob Back(USA) —Beauchamp Grace (Ardross)
2714[P] 3487[7]

Beauchamp Oracle *S Flook* 115+c
9 gr g Mystiko(USA) —Beauchamp Cactus (Niniski (USA))
50[2] 281[3] 440[P] 3819[3] 4305[P] 4607[7] (4946)

Beauchamp Prince (IRE) *M Scudamore* 108h 108c
5 gr g Beauchamp King—Katie Baggage (IRE) (Brush Aside (USA))
1456[P] 3480[P] 3955[5] (4369) 4605[2] 4847[8]

Beauchamp Star *N B King* 94h
5 ch m Pharly(FR) —Beauchamp Cactus (Niniski (USA))
5084[U]

Beauchamp Trump *G A Butler* 45h
4 b g Pharly(FR) —Beauchamp Kate (Petoski)
3294[13]

Beauchamp Twist *M R Hoad* 60h
4 b f Pharly(FR) —Beauchamp Cactus (Niniski (USA))
3132[8] 3429[5]

Beau Colina (IRE) *A J Martin* 94h 113c
9 b g Jolly Jake(NZ) —Decent Daisy (Decent Fellow)
91a[F]

Beau Coup *John R Upson* 100h
9 b g Toulon—Energance (IRE) (Salmon Leap (USA))
5113[8]

Beau De Turgeon (FR) *Ian Williams* 111h 95c
5 b g Turgeon(USA) —Beluda (FR) (Beyssac (FR))
2559[2] 2923[3] 3253[7] 3962[4] 4604[8] 4981[7]

Beaufort County (IRE) *Evan Williams* 108h 79 c
9 b g Torus—Afternoon Tea (IRE) (Decent Fellow)
2620[4] 3329[4] 3946[7]

Beaugency (NZ) *R C Guest* 114+h 112+c
8 br g Prized(USA) —Naiades (NZ) (Beaufort Sea (USA))
345[6] 414[3] 605[5] 690[4] 767[U] 948[F] (1015) (1066) (1111) 1151[5]

Beau Largesse *A J Chamberlain* 83b
4 b g Largesse—Just Visiting (Superlative)
2105[4]

Beaumont Girl (IRE) *Miss M E Rowland* 59h
4 ch f Trans Island—Persian Danser (IRE) (Persian Bold)
2286[U] 3594[P] 3786[7] 4551[9]

Beau Peak *D W Whillans* 76h
7 ch m Meadowbrook—Peak A Boo (Le Coq D'Or)
124[7] 643[6] 3337[10]

Beau Saddler *A R Dicken* 47b
5 b g Accondy(IRE) —Wand Of Youth (Mandamus)
876[11]

Beau Supreme (IRE) *C J Down* 106h 127 c
9 b g Supreme Leader—Miss Sabreur (Avocat)
1972[8] 2485[4] 2828[P] 4589[4] 4830[5]

Beautiful Night (FR) *M D Hammond* 83h
4 b f Sleeping Car(FR) —Doll Night (FR) (Karkour (FR))
4450[4] 4795[3] 5118[10]

Beautiful Vision (IRE) *T J Taaffe* 123h
6 ch g Moscow Society(USA) —Rumi (Nishapour (FR))
4773[5]

Beau Torero (FR) *B N Pollock* 96+h
8 gr g True Brave(USA) —Brave Lola (FR) (Dom Pasquini (FR))
(3592) (4299)

Beauty Ballistic *Miss J Feilden*
6 br m Bigstone(IRE) —Mobile Miss (IRE) (Classic Secret (USA))
1922[12]

Beaver (AUS) *R C Guest* 101+h
7 b g Bite The Bullet(USA) —Mahenge (AUS) (Twig Moss (FR))
418[P] 838[11] 1182[4] 1591[4] 1687[3] 1793[6]

Beaver Lodge (IRE) *B P J Baugh* 120 h 111c
9 gr g Grand Lodge(USA) —Thistlewood (Kalamoun)
488[P] 1277[5] (Dead)

Bebe Factual (GER) *J D Frost* 68h
5 b h So Factual(USA) —Bebe Kamira (GER) (Kamiros II)
343[9] 1021[8] 1636[10] 1902[8] 2146[6] 2728[5] 3321[7]

Be Be King (IRE) *P F Nicholls* 135 h
7 b g Bob Back(USA) —Trimar Gold (Goldhill)
(2343) (3023) (3388) 3727P 47765

Becky's Hill *Mrs Mary Hambro* 62b
4 b f Mtoto—Neptunalia (Slip Anchor)
242511

Bede (IRE) *S H Marriage* 92h 77c
10 b g Spanish Place(USA) —Midnight Oil (Menelek)
278P

Bedford Leader *A P Jones* 74h
8 b m Bedford(USA) —Neladar (Ardar)
1906P 25057 2966P 3278P

Bedlam Boy (IRE) *N G Richards* 79h
5 br g Broken Hearted—Evening Fashion (IRE) (Strong Gale)
23403 29484

Bedtime Boys *Miss H Campbell* 114c
9 gr g Gran Alba(USA) —Path's Sister (Warpath)
(3968) 447111

Bee An Bee (IRE) *T R George* 115h 132 c
9 b g Phardante(FR) —Portia's Delight (IRE) (The Parson)
1305 19202 21622 24859 33432 39922 44474 49578

Bee Cee Gee *S J Gilmore* 41h
8 ch g Jupiter Island—True Divine (True Song)
6719

Beechcourt *M J P O'Brien* 129h 130c
9 b g Son Pardo—Calametta (Oats)
67a13 (Dead)

Beechwood *P R Rodford* 97+h
8 b g Fraam—Standard Rose (Ile De Bourbon (USA))
(356) 4609 7536

Beef Or Salmon (IRE) *Michael Hourigan* 171 c
10 ch g Cajetano(USA) —Farinella (IRE) (Salmon Leap (USA))
23372 (3081a) (3895a) 447011 4746U 5079a2

Bee Hawk *P F Nicholls* 106+h
7 b g Gunner B—Cupids Bower (Owen Dudley)
201F (359) 679 2 814P

Been Here Before *G A Harker* 84c
6 ch g Fearless Action(USA) —Mistral Magic (Crofter (USA))
28394 2976P 31706 37962 40534 4300F 4587P

Beet De Bob (IRE) *Mrs S E Busby* 83+h
8 bb g Bob Back(USA) —Beet Statement (IRE) (Strong Statement (USA))
1785 35944 6307

Bee Vee Pea (IRE) *Mrs S J Smith* 41b
6 b m Primitive Rising(USA) —Kates Castle (Carlingford Castle)
405910 430411

Before Dark (IRE) *Mrs H Dalton* 110+h
8 b g Phardante(FR) —Menebeans (IRE) (Duky)
(3249) 35982 (4285) 42726 51233

Before The Mast (IRE) *M F Harris* 84 h 93 c
9 br g Broken Hearted—Kings Reserve (King's Ride)
168011 1921P 20438 (2463) 25677 28583 (2962) 32234 33954 34324 (3887) 39643 44273 46323 46753 4798U 49117

Before Time *Mrs A M Thorpe* 94 h
4 ch g Giant's Causeway(USA) —Original Spin (IRE) (Machiavellian (USA))
1821U 25976 282411 34633 37144 39445 113

Behan *A J Chamberlain* 66h
7 ch g Rainbows For Life(CAN) —With Finesse (Be My Guest (USA))
9438 1364P

Behavingbadly (IRE) *A Parker* 105c
11 b g Lord Americo—Audrey's Turn (Strong Gale)
1837F 21706 25893 2946P 3336P 4144P 48452

Behlaya (IRE) *Liam P Cusack* 94h
5 b m Kahyasi—Behera (Mill Reef (USA))
5077a17

Bekstar *J C Tuck* 90h
11 br m Nicholas Bill—Murex (Royalty)
17848 25762 32839

Belene Boy (IRE) *M Flannery* 68 h
13 b g Good Thyne(USA) —Strong Tide (Strong Gale)
47944

Belisco (USA) *C A Dwyer*
5 b g Royal Academy(USA) —A Mean Fit (USA) (Fit To Fight (USA))
180P

Belita *Miss Sheena West* 99+b
4 b f Hernando(FR) —Anchorage (IRE) (Slip Anchor)
(2425) 31812

Bella Bonkers *N A Twiston-Davies* 83b
6 b m Gildoran—Easy Horse (FR) (Carmarthen (FR))
16742 1974P

Bella Cosa (IRE) *Mrs L B Normile* 61b
4 b f Darnay—Adjamiya (USA) (Shahrastani (USA))
325914 376311 39318

Bella Liana (IRE) *J Clements* 83+h 74c
6 b m Sesaro(USA) —Bella Galiana (ITY) (Don Roberto (USA))
5004 8547 8704 9872 13102 13562 2031a14 2653P

Bellalou *Mrs S A Watt* 67h
4 b f Vettori(IRE) —Spinning Mouse (Bustino)
13326 1512S 171810 20017 3349F (Dead)

Bellaney Hall (IRE) *J J Quinn*
6 b m Luso—Sister Of Gold (The Parson)
376314

Bellaney House (IRE) *J J Quinn*
5 b m Carroll House—Sister Of Gold (The Parson)
4800P

Bellaney Jewel (IRE) *J J Quinn* 104h 110+c
7 gr m Roselier(FR) —Sister Of Gold (The Parson)
(124) 2291P 31703 37603 40413 (4518) (4788)

Belledesaro (IRE) *Mrs H Dalton* 64h
6 br m Un Desperado(FR) —Cedarbelle (IRE) (Regular Guy)
442510

Bellefleur *N J Pomfret* 76+h
9 b m Alflora(IRE) —Isabeau (Law Society (USA))
465P

Bellino Empresario (IRE) *B Llewellyn* 67h
8 b g Robellino(USA) —The Last Empress (IRE) (Last Tycoon)
1541P

Bell Lane Lad (IRE) *D J Wintle* 109+h 106c
9 b g Wakashan—Busti Lass (IRE) (Bustineto)
106P 21003 23137 27172 31424 38165

Bell Rock *Mrs T J Hill* 79h 95+c
8 ch g Charmer—Sule Skerry (Scottish Rifle)
(404) (1044) 1178P 13439

Bel Ombre (FR) *O Sherwood* 93h 99 c
6 b g Nikos—Danse Du Soleil (FR) (Morespeed)
27515 32204 34186 3844P (4614) 4782P

Belovodsk (SU) *Dr R Vitek* 129c
14 b g Eten(SU) —Bavariya (SU) (Avat (SU))
1710a5

Belshazzar (USA) *D C O'Brien*
5 b g King Of Kings(IRE) —Bayou Bidder (USA) (Premiership (USA))
3133P 4691P

Belter *S P Griffiths* 55h
6 b g Terimon—Bellinote (FR) (Noir Et Or)
391212 4917P 1010

Belton *Ronald Thompson* 31h
4 b g Lujain(USA) —Efficacious (IRE) (Efisio)
275313 292115

Be Lucky Lady (GER) *N J Dawe* 23h
4 b f Law Society(USA) —Ballata (GER) (Platini (GER))
19048 3947P

Beluga (IRE) *M Pitman* 86 h 78c
7 gr g John French—Mesena (Pals Passage)
282113 31396 332812 36636 4549P

Be My Better Half (IRE) *Jonjo O'Neill* 86h 133c
11 b g Be My Native(USA) —The Mrs (Mandalus)
20483 2368F 29938 (3385) 35032 39884 4762F 50123

Be My Destiny (IRE) *M Pitman* 115+h
9 b g Be My Native(USA) —Miss Cali (Young Man (FR))
2532P 2870P 3326P (4396)

Be My Dream (IRE) *Mrs C Wilesmith* 105 c
11 b g Be My Native(USA) —Dream Toi (Carlburg)
(204) 4535 42166

Be My Friend (IRE) *G D Hanmer* 115 h 90c
10 ch g Be My Native(USA) —Miss Lamb (Relkino)
348U 4373

Be My Royal (IRE) *R H Alner* 123+h 113c
12 b g Be My Native(USA) —Royal Rehearsal (Pamroy)
33898 3877P 4374P

Ben Belleshot *P W Hiatt* 23h
7 gr g Vague Shot—Ballygriffin Belle (Another Realm)
2663P 286611 332818

Benbeoch *Dave Parker* 82c
7 ch g Hatim(USA) —Phantom Singer (Relkino)
1232

Benbridge *Mrs S M Johnson* 39b
5 b g Overbury(IRE) —Celtic Bridge (Celtic Cone)
462211

Ben Britten *N G Richards* 104+h
7 ch g Sabrehill(USA) —Golden Panda (Music Boy)
(718) 8593 (941)

Benbyas *D Carroll* 128 h
9 b g Rambo Dancer(CAN) —Light The Way (Nicholas Bill)
33838 36225 3986P 41108

Benedict Bay *J A Geake* 80h
4 b g In The Wings—Persia (IRE) (Persian Bold)
329412 34365 39396 46165

Benefit *Miss L C Siddall* 87h 80 c
12 b g Primitive Rising(USA) —Sobriquet (Roan Rocket)
240P 4303 48146 6908 2413P 26926 35479 37625 4921P

Benefit Fund (IRE) *D J Wintle* 79 h
6 b g Beneficial—Pampered Sally (Paddy's Stream)
3275P 367710 (4056) 502113

Benefit Of Caution (IRE) *Paul John Gilligan* 18h 92c
7 bb g Beneficial—Rockport Rosa (IRE) (Roselier (FR))
71aP

Beneking *P Bowen*
6 bb g Wizard King—Gagajulu (Al Hareb (USA))
629P

Benetwood (IRE) *V R A Dartnall* 101+b
5 b g Beneficial—Donegal Thyne (IRE) (Good Thyne (USA))
(4825)

Bengal Boy *Mrs Jane Knight* 86h 93c
10 b g Gildoran—Bengal Lady (Celtic Cone)
221P

Bengal Bullet *C Blank* 109c
9 b g Infantry—Indian Cruise (Cruise Missile)
48P 47302

Bengo (IRE) *B De Haan* 115h 109c
6 b g Beneficial—Goforroad (IRE) (Mister Lord (USA))
1976P 27013 35062 397011 42155 497412

Ben Gorm (IRE) *P A Pritchard*
6 ch g Tagula(IRE) —Regal Entrance (Be My Guest (USA))
123715

Benjamin Buckram (IRE) *C R Egerton* 97b
7 b g Topanoora—Red Bit (IRE) (Henbit (USA))
282312 31384

Ben Lomand *B W Duke*
6 ch g Inchinor—Benjarong (Sharpo)
1222P

Ben Nelly (IRE) *M Todhunter* 70h
5 b g Taipan(IRE) —Cothu Na Slaine (IRE) (Roselier (FR))
44936 472010

Benny *R H York* 66+h
5 b g New Frontier(IRE) —Drumkilly Lilly (IRE) (Executive Perk)
2353 6547 8616

Benny Boy (IRE) *S G Waugh* 57c
6 b g Beneficial—Seefin Lass (IRE) (Mandalus)
4725U

Benny The Piler (IRE) *N G Richards* 61h
6 bb g Beneficial—An Charraig Mhor (IRE) (Tremblant)
32375 43427

Benrajah (IRE) *M Todhunter* 100h 122c
9 b g Lord Americo—Andy's Fancy (IRE) (Andretti)
8235 101312 20034 236814 29383 33502 35608 3803P 50465

Bens Lady (IRE) *T R George* 51b
7 b m Beneficial—Prime Lady (IRE) (Pollerton)
2937P

Ben's Turn (IRE) *A King* 110 h
5 b m Saddlers' Hall(IRE) —Christines Gale (IRE) (Strong Gale)
(242) (2021) (2558) (3149) 36922

Ben Tally Ho *Ian Williams* 70h
5 ch g Classic Cliche(IRE) —Poussetiere Deux (FR) (Garde Royale)
2127F 28786 3685P

Ben The Brave (IRE) *Mrs A M Thorpe*
7 b g Ridgewood Ben—Shoot The Dealer (IRE) (Common Grounds)
179919 1968P

Bentinck (IRE) *M Scudamore* 86b
4 b g In The Wings—Bareilly (USA) (Lyphard (USA))
48256

Bentyheath Lane *M Mullineaux* 78h 71c
9 b g Puissance—Eye Sight (Roscoe Blake)
956 4146 10964 1203U

Be Positive *C J Down* 89b
6 b g Petoski—Go Positive (Profilic)
3005 8173

Bercaldoun (FR) *P Chatelain*
7 b g Balleroy(USA) —Bercale (FR) (Emerson (BRZ))
846a4

Berengario (IRE) *S C Burrough* 114h 114c
6 b g Mark Of Esteem(IRE) —Ivrea (Sadler's Wells (USA))
16517 20557 22703 25932 27332

Bergerac (NZ) *R C Guest* 105+h 116c
8 b g Just A Dancer(NZ) —Guiding Star (NZ) (Star Wolf)
592 (495) 5935 22944 (2570) 26794

Berkeley Court *G L Moore* 59+h
5 b g Croco Rouge(IRE) —Penultimate (USA) (Roberto (USA))
1387 8176 31387 346310

Berkeley House (IRE) *C F Swan* 93h
6 b m Beneficial—Danny's Charm (IRE) (Arapahos (FR))
2796a3 3110a6

Berkeley Storm (IRE) *S J Treacy* 100b
5 b m Glacial Storm(USA) —Lonizera (IRE) (Houmayoun (FR))
5134a10

Berkhamsted (IRE) *M F Harris*
4 b c Desert Sun—Accounting (Sillery (USA))
4416P 4631P

Berkley (IRE) *Patrick Michael Verling* 103h 119c
9 b g Arctic Lord—Coach Road (Brave Invader (USA))
91a5 1083a10 1515a9 1700aU

Bermuda Pointe (IRE) *N A Twiston-Davies* 100+b
4 ch g Lahib(USA) —Milain (IRE) (Unfuwain (USA))
(4881)

Bernardon (GER) *Barry Potts* 97h 99c
10 b g Suave Dancer(USA) —Bejaria (GER) (Konigsstuhl (GER))
13 246P 3707 21115 3798P

Berry Racer (IRE) *Mrs S D Williams* 66h
5 ch m Titus Livius(FR) —Opening Day (Day Is Done)
515F 7583 91112

Bertie Arms *J M Jefferson* 35h
6 gr m Cloudings(IRE) —Pugilistic (Hard Fought)
922 134P 613P

Bertiebanoo (IRE) *M C Pipe* 115h 123 c
8 ch g Be My Native(USA) —Gemeleks Gem (IRE) (Carlingford Castle)
(688) 960P 25964 3698F (Dead)

Bertocelli *K F Clutterbuck* 60h
5 ch g Vettori(IRE) —Dame Jude (Dilum (USA))
1037P 1107P

Beseiged (USA) *J L Spearing* 123+h
9 ch g Cadeaux Genereux—Munnaya (USA) (Nijinsky (CAN))
1973 3703 (689) 50669

Best Accolade *J Howard Johnson* 80h
7 b g Oscar(IRE) —Made Of Talent (Supreme Leader)
32573

Best Actor (IRE) *Carl Llewellyn* 99+h
7 b g Oscar(IRE) —Supreme Princess (IRE) (Supreme Leader)
25074 34258 48232

Bestam *Mrs A V Roberts* 86h
7 b g Selkirk(USA) —Showery (Rainbow Quest (USA))
456U 145810 15629 25852 27506 3185P

Best China (IRE) *Liam Lennon* 92+c
6 b g West China—Knights Pleasure (IRE) (Gallant Knight)
43612 4845P

Best Deal *B I Case* 91b
5 gr g Presenting—Miss Drury (Baron Blakeney)
42376 49098

Best Flight *N Wilson* 97h
6 gr g Sheikh Albadou—Bustling Nelly (Bustino)
192F 691F (Dead)

Best Game *D W Thompson* 91 h
4 b g Mister Baileys—Bestemor (Selkirk (USA))
22585 24773 29492 320310 37595

Best Mate (IRE) *Miss H C Knight*
11 b g Un Desperado(FR) —Katday (FR) (Miller's Mate)
1970P (Dead)

Bestofthebrownies (IRE) *J Howard Johnson* 93h
5 b g Bob Back(USA) —Just A Brownie (IRE) (Orchestra)
4916P

Best Profile (IRE) *N A Twiston-Davies* 117h
6 b g Flemensfirth(USA) —Lincoln Green (IRE) (Ela-Mana-Mou)
(1937) 24612 28784 39825 46782 49612

Besuto (IRE) *D D Scott* 89b
9 br g Fourstars Allstar(USA) —Mabbots Own (Royal Trip)
384P

Be Telling (IRE) *B J Curley* 69h 91c
7 b g Oscar(IRE) —Manhattan King (IRE) (King's Ride)
18183 21277 2556P 2862P 33677 41644

Be The Tops (IRE) *Jonjo O'Neill* 92h 112+c
8 br g Topanoora—Be The One (IRE) (Supreme Leader)
9892 (1110) 12053 16097

Beths Choice *J M Bradley* 88b
5 b h Midnight Legend—Clare's Choice (Pragmatic)
37202 401110 4569P

Better Days (IRE) *Mrs S J Smith* 118h 140 c
10 b g Supreme Leader—Kilkilrun (Deep Run)
19293 23687 26292 28768 33852 37392 39883 476213 4982P (Dead)

Better Moment (IRE) *M C Pipe* 100h 104+c
9 b g Turtle Island(IRE) —Snoozeandyoulose (IRE) (Scenic)
1299 11217 115313 13815 19007 21508 25763 32223 (3899) (4575) 4859F

Better Think Again (IRE) *Miss Susan A Finn* 110h
12 b g Brush Aside(USA) —Ride The Rapids (Bulldozer)
216613

Better Thyne (IRE) *Mrs S D Williams* 108h 121c
10 ch g Good Thyne(USA) —Cailin Cainnteach (Le Bavard (FR))
284510 3581P

Betterware Boy *Mrs Susan Smith* 78+h 87c
6 ch g Barathea(IRE) —Crystal Drop (Cadeaux Genereux)
42977 51164

Be Upstanding *Ferdy Murphy* 94h
11 ch g Hubbly Bubbly(USA) —Two Travellers (Deep Run)
240P 2863P 2986P 3654P

Beveller *W M Brisbourne*
7 ch g Beveled(USA) —Klairover (Smackover)
1097P 1360F (Dead)

Bewhatyouwanttobe *J D Frost*
5 b m Morpeth—Supreme Daughter (Supreme Leader)
4556P

Bewleys Berry (IRE) *J Howard Johnson* 135+h 143+c
8 ch g Shernazar—Approach The Dawn (IRE) (Orchestra)
(2441) 27592 29733 44446 4759P

Bewleys Guest (IRE) *Miss Venetia Williams* 47h 72 c
7 b g Presenting—Pedigree Corner (Pollerton)
1949P 29332 3221P

Bewleys Newlands *Perry Harding-Jones* 79b
9 b g Royal Vulcan—No Grandad (Strong Gale)
4477P

Beyond Borders (USA) *G F Edwards* 87h
8 bb g Pleasant Colony(USA) —Welcome Proposal (Be My Guest (USA))
75P 3634 7498 20738 21814 24287

Beyondtherealm *J D Frost* 90h
8 b g Morpeth—Workamiracle (Teamwork)
(2428) 40365

Bhaydalko (FR) *M Todhunter* 81b
6 b g Kadalko(FR) —Bhaydana (Sassafras (FR))
201P 1915P

Bica (FR) *R Waley-Cohen* 100c
6 b g Cadoudal(FR) —Libertina (FR) (Balsamo (FR))
28283

Bidou (FR) *P Cottin*
11 b g Seurat—Centadj (FR) (Tadj (FR))
845a4

Biennale (IRE) *Patrick O Brady* 104h
10 b g Caerleon(USA) —Malvern Beauty (Shirley Heights)
3513a4

Biens Nanti (IRE) *M Cheno*
4 b g Montjeu(IRE) —Trexana (Kaldoun (FR))
4548a4

Big-And-Bold (IRE) *N G Richards* 100h 106 c
10 b g Legal Circles(USA) —Kodak Lady (IRE) (Entre Nous)
33184 38515 43634

Big Bad Bill (IRE) *P T Midgley* 27b
6 gr g Entrepreneur—Chamonis (USA) (Affirmed (USA))
499212

Big Bertha *M D Hammond* 78+h
8 ch m Dancing Spree(USA) —Bertrade (Homeboy)
25154 31685

Big Bone (FR) *B N Pollock* 119 h 107 c
6 b g Zayyani—Bone Crasher (FR) (Cadoudal (FR))
33232 3788P 45927

Big Max *Miss K M George* 86+h
11 b g Rakaposhi King—Edwina's Dawn (Space King)
3214P 345811 43318 47526

Big Moment *Mrs A J Perrett* 147h 130 c
8 ch g Be My Guest(USA) —Petralona (USA) (Alleged (USA))
(2377) 27983 4116F 47458

Big Palooka *J A Geake*
4 ch g Great Palm(USA) —Penniless (IRE) (Common Grounds)
462313

Big Quick (IRE) *L Wells* 85 h 86c
11 ch g Glacial Storm(USA) —Furryvale (Furry Glen)
502[9] 801[P] (1262) 1525[7] **3907[5]**4526[11]

Big Rob (IRE) *B G Powell* 97h 133c
7 b g Bob Back(USA) —Native Shore (IRE) (Be My Native (USA))
1881[F] 2102[U] 2296[2]**4037[2] 4635[2]**

Big Tom (IRE) *B G Powell*
5 ch h Cadeaux Genereux—Zilayah (USA) (Zilzal (USA))
804[P]

Big Wheel *N G Richards* 115h 94c
11 ch g Mujtahid(USA) —Numuthej (USA) (Nureyev (USA))
766[9] 903[4] 1510[3] 1604[3] 1836[2]2566[15]

Biliverdin (IRE) *J A Geake* 117+c
12 b g Bob Back(USA) —Straw Beret (USA) (Chief's Crown (USA))
2272[6] 3507[P] 4120[3]4332[P] 4728[P]

Bilkie (IRE) *John Berry* 80+h
4 ch g Polish Precedent(USA) —Lesgor (USA) (Irish River (FR))
3898[5] 4631[P] 4910[5]

Bill Brown *R Dickin* 91+h 91c
8 b g North Briton—Dickies Girl (Saxon Farm)
488[9] **692[U]**

Billesey (IRE) *S E H Sherwood* 108+h
8 b g King's Ride—Rose Runner (IRE) (Roselier (FR))
2861[F] 3023[4] 3478[F]

Bill Haze *P Dando* 108+c
10 ch g Romany Rye—Brilliant Haze VII (Damsire Unregistered)
3924[2] (4167) (4349) (4555) 4748[6] 4946[2]

Billie John (IRE) *Mrs K Walton* 93b 111 c
11 ch g Boyne Valley—Lovestream (Sandy Creek)
195[8] 409[5] 714[4]840[6] 1049[3] 1221[2]1295[3] 1399[3] 1570[2]5067[F] 14[U]

Bill Owen *D P Keane* 104+c
10 ch g Nicholas Bill—Pollys Owen (Master Owen)
288[4]

Bill's Echo *R C Guest* 103h 130+c
7 br g Double Eclipse(IRE) —Bit On Edge (Henbit (USA))
571[5] **714[U]** 784[2] **1012[3]1049[2]** 1202[7] 1312[2]
1542[U]1666[2] (1739)

Billsgrey (IRE) *J S Haldane* 59b
4 gr g Pistolet Bleu(IRE) —Grouse-N-Heather (Grey Desire)
3799[11] 5008[9]

Billyandi (IRE) *N A Twiston-Davies* 110+h
6 ch g Zaffaran(USA) —Top Dart (Whistling Top)
1632[P] 1782[5] 2142[2] 2617[6] 3333[2]3650[4] (4067) 4373[13] 4938[2] 5066[3]

Billy Ballbreaker (IRE) *C L Tizzard* 93h 99 c
10 br g Good Thyne(USA) —Droichead Dhamhile (IRE) (The Parson)
(169) 398[4] (546) 916[P]948[P] 1832[2] 1983[6]2610[U] 2800[P]

Billy Bray *Miss Venetia Williams* 51h
6 b g Alflora(IRE) —Chacewater (Electric)
4676[P] 4935[10]

Billy Bush (IRE) *Ferdy Murphy* 98h
7 b g Lord Americo—Castle Graigue (IRE) (Aylesfield)
3653[F] 3781[P]

Billy Coleman (IRE) *D Brace*
8 b g Hollow Hand—Little Treat (Miner's Lamp)
1750[10] **1951[P]**

Billy Row *James Moffatt*
5 b g Keen—Arasong (Aragon)
4319[10] 5041[10]

Billyvoddan (IRE) *H D Daly* 129+h 141+c
7 b g Accordion—Derryclare (Pollerton)
(2344) 2743[3] 3178[4](3549) 4459[9] 4764[U]

Bilton's Nap *R H Alner* 66h
7 b g Relief Pitcher—Sheer Water (Vital Season)
1779[4] 1980[5]

Bindaree (IRE) *N A Twiston-Davies* 112+h 153 c
12 ch g Roselier(FR) —Flowing Tide (Main Reef)
2370[8]

Bin Farmin *N R Mitchell*
6 b g Riverwise(USA) —Cut Above The Rest (Indiaro)
4574[13]

Bint Sesaro (IRE) *Mrs L B Normile* 72h
5 b m Sesaro(USA) —Crazed Rainbow (USA) (Graustark)
349[10] 2903[8] 3267[6] 4582[5]

Bint St James *J T Stimpson* 58 h
11 b m Shareef Dancer(USA) —St James's Antigua (IRE) (Law Society (USA))
96[P]

Birchall (IRE) *Ian Williams* 93+h 38c
7 b g Priolo(USA) —Ballycuirke (Taufan (USA))
1957[10] 4075[9]

Birdwatch *K G Reveley* 110 h
8 b g Minshaanshu Amad(USA) —Eider (Niniski (USA))
(2523) 2994[2] (3234) 3384[4] (3853) 4067[8] 4634[5]

Birkwood *Ian D Stark* 90+c
7 b g Presidium—Wire Lass (New Brig)
(4722)

Birtley Boy *W Amos* 49b
7 ch g Le Moss—City Lighter (Lighter)
3751[4] 3855[P]

Biscar Two (IRE) *A E Jones* 101h
5 b g Daggers Drawn(USA) —Thoughtful Kate (Rock Hopper)
1827[5] (2624) 3023[7] 3174[8] (3332) 3673[P] 4046[P]4372[P]

Biscay Wind (IRE) *T R George* 47h
6 ch m Anshan—La Bise (Callernish)
1974[11] 2937[7]

Bishop's Bridge (IRE) *Andrew Turnell* 112h 115 c
8 b g Norwich—River Swell (IRE) (Over The River (FR))
59[4] (369) (553) 2595[2] **(2963) 3323[U]3803[9] 4239[7] 4878[4]**

Bishop's Brig *N W Alexander* 68h
6 ch g Accondy(IRE) —Lillie's Brig (New Brig)
2268[9] 2947[P] 3534[11] 3793[11] 4341[P]

Bit Of A Gift *Thomas Mullins* 96h
8 b g Henbit(USA) —Saxon Gift (Saxon Farm)
70a[16]

Bitta Dash *A J Wilson* 78b
6 ch g Bandmaster(USA) —Letitica (Deep Run)
138[9] 2288[9]

Bizarre Native *W K Goldsworthy*
6 ch g Dreams End—Celtic Bizarre (Celtic Cone)
1274[8]

Bizet (IRE) *F Flood* 117+h 139c
10 b g Zaffaran(USA) —Annie Sue VI (Snuff Matter)
71a[2] 1515a[8] 1700a[6]

Bjorling *M J Gingell*
5 ch g Opening Verse(USA) —Pola Star (IRE) (Un Desperado (FR))
2702[P] 3591[P]

Black And Tan (IRE) *P J Hobbs* 90h
6 bb g Presenting—Bold Glen (Bold Owl)
2565[5] 3240[3] 4786[2]

Black Apalachi (IRE) *P J Rothwell* 138h 133+c
7 b g Old Vic—Hattons Dream (IRE) (Be My Native (USA))
(3053a) 4447[6] 4929a[10]

Blackbriery Thyne (IRE) *H D Daly* 84 h
7 br m Good Thyne(USA) —Briery Gale (Strong Gale)
2446[2] 2961[8] 3884[4]

Black Bullet (NZ) *Jennie Candlish* 118c
13 br g Silver Pistol(AUS) —Monte D'Oro (NZ) (Cache Of Gold (USA))
305[5] 747[13] 1180[P] **1529[P]**

Blackbury *J W Unett* 9h
4 b f Overbury(IRE) —Fenian Court (IRE) (John French)
2425[14] 3[14]

Black Collar *K C Bailey* 71h
7 br m Bob's Return(IRE) —Rosemoss (Le Moss)
2501[5] 3287[6] 3905[5] 4277[P]

Blackcomb Mountain (USA) *M F Harris* 70h
4 bb f Royal Anthem(USA) —Ski Racer (FR) (Ski Chief (USA))
3645[10] 3787[8] 4074[14]

Black De Bessy (FR) *D R C Elsworth* 118 h 133 c
8 b g Perrault—Emerald City (Top Ville)
(1400) **1744[2] (2051) 2492[3]3000[2] 3507[2] 3995[P]4433[11]**

Blackergreen *Mrs S J Smith* 124+h 102+c
7 b g Zaffaran(USA) —Ballinderry Moss (Le Moss)
2966[2] 3382[3] 4300[P](4515) (4803) 5093[2]

Black Frost (IRE) *Mrs S J Smith* 65c
10 ch g Glacial Storm(USA) —Black Tulip (Pals Passage)
130[6]

Black Hills *J A Geake* 115+h
7 b g Dilum(USA) —Dakota Girl (Northern State (USA))
(1968) 2606[3] 3210[8] 4608[8]

Blackies All (USA) *W M Brisbourne* 105+h
8 b g Hazaam(USA) —Allijess (USA) (Tom Rolfe)
5014[9]

Black Jack Ketchum (IRE) *Jonjo O'Neill* 165+h
7 b g Oscar(IRE) —Cailin Supreme (IRE) (Supreme Leader)
(1619) (2206) (2762) (4469) (4760)

Black Optimist (IRE) *Mrs S J Maiden* 112c
12 br g Roselier(FR) —Borys Glen (Furry Glen)
4421[P]

Blackout (IRE) *J Barclay* 39h 75 c
11 b g Black Monday—Fine Bess (Fine Blade (USA))
3236[7] 4145[14] **4343[P]**

Black Ouzel (IRE) *H Rogers* 105h
6 b m Taipan(IRE) —Black Pheasant (IRE) (Sexton Blake)
1691a[10]

Black Shan (IRE) *A Ennis* 77h
6 br g Anshan—Singing Forever (Chief Singer)
1875[7] 1990[P] 2238[10]

Blackson Zulu (IRE) *J R H Fowler* 77b
5 b g Supreme Leader—Janet Lindup (Sabrehill (USA))
5104a[12]

Blackthorn *M Appleby* 87h
7 ch g Deploy—Balliasta (USA) (Lyphard (USA))
936[5] 1293[3] 2285[10] (2702) 2930[P] 3673[2]3985[4] 4322[P]

Blaeberry *Miss E C Lavelle* 108h
5 b m Kirkwall—Top Berry (High Top)
2730[2] 3127[P] 3354[4] 3902[2] (4429) 4663[3]4972[4]

Blairgowrie (IRE) *J Howard Johnson* 113+h 121+c
7 b g Supreme Leader—Parsons Term (IRE) (The Parson)
2078[P] 4058[4] **(4583)**

Blaise Wood (USA) *A L Forbes* 36 h 92c
5 b g Woodman(USA) —Castellina (USA) (Danzig Connection (USA))
980[P] 2008[7] **2246[4] 2561[P]**2702[3]

Blake Hall Lad (IRE) *P S McEntee*
5 b g Cape Cross(IRE) —Queen Of Art (IRE) (Royal Academy (USA))
2099[14]

Blakeney Coast (IRE) *C L Tizzard* 74 h 129+c
9 b g Satco(FR) —Up To More Trix (IRE) (Torus)
(234) (684) (946) 1265[11]5112[8]

Blakeney Run *Miss M Bragg* 85b
6 gr g Commanche Run—Lady Blakeney (Baron Blakeney)
4667[8]

Blakes Road (IRE) *Ms Lisa Stock* 67b 39c
9 bb g Be My Native(USA) —Joyau (IRE) (Roselier (FR))
404[P]

Blame The Ref (IRE) *C C Bealby* 96h 109c
9 ch g Aahsaylad—Nags Head (IRE) (Aristocracy)
(1914) 2982[F]

Blandings Castle *Nick Williams* 47h
5 ro g Cloudings(IRE) —Country House (Town And Country)
517[5] 1021[10]

Blank Canvas (IRE) *K C Bailey* 93+h 84c
8 b g Presenting—Strong Cloth (IRE) (Strong Gale)
4352[2] 4643[P]

Blast The Past *T D Walford* 55b
4 b f Past Glories—Yours Or Mine (IRE) (Exhibitioner)
3490[7] 3763[10]

Blayney James (IRE) *Gerard Keane* 89b
6 b g Saddlers' Hall(IRE) —Lady Blayney (IRE) (Mazaad)
93a[7]

Blazeaway (USA) *R S Brookhouse* 78h
6 bb g Hansel(USA) —Alessia's Song (USA) (Air Forbes Won (USA))
456[P] 664[10] **862[P]** 903[P]

Blaze On *R H York* 89c
7 ch g Minster Son—Clova (Move Off)
401[2] 728[F] 3819[P]4477[5]

Blazing Bailey *A King* 143h
4 b g Mister Baileys—Wannaplantatree (Niniski (USA))
(3436) (3714) 4117[2] 4468[3] 4750[2]

Blazing Batman *Dr P Pritchard* 70h 81c
13 ch g Shaab—Cottage Blaze (Sunyboy)
246[3] 439[7] 567[3]746[7] 981[10] 1122[6]1542[8] 2527[6]
2664[7]3285[4] 3482[3] 3887[9]4007[7] 4356[8] 4575[5]4936[3] (5105)

Blazing Ember *J W Tudor* 48b
4 b f Faustus(USA) —Into The Fire (Dominion)
2014[7] 2797[P] 3249[P]

Blazing Fire *M Wellings*
9 b g Derrylin—Shean Deas (Le Moss)
137[5]

Blazing Hills *P T Dalton* 101 c
10 ch g Shaab—Cottage Blaze (Sunyboy)
330[P] 572[3] 694[P]

Blazing Liss (IRE) *John E Kiely* 125h
7 b m Supreme Leader—Liss De Paor (IRE) (Phardante (FR))
(66a)

Blazing The Trail (IRE) *C J Mann* 88h
6 ch g Indian Ridge—Divine Pursuit (Kris)
384[P] 1431[P]

Bleak Friday *J G M O'Shea* 50b
7 ch m Snurge—Nikatino (Bustino)
3145[8]

Bleak House (IRE) *T P Tate* 101b
4 b g Rudimentary(USA) —Dannkalia (IRE) (Shernazar)
2927[2] (4854)

Bleu Pois (IRE) *J Howard Johnson* 95b
4 ch c Pistolet Bleu(IRE) —Peas (IRE) (Little Wolf)
5141[3]

Bleu Superbe (FR) *Miss Venetia Williams* 140 c
11 b g Epervier Bleu—Brett's Dream (FR) (Pharly (FR))
1918[2] 2339[3] 2489[5]2757[3] 3136[2] 3619[2]3974[2] 4472[F] 4749[U](4973)

Blind Smart (IRE) *M F Harris* 27h
8 br g Phardante(FR) —Smart Chick (True Song)
2866[10] 3611[P]

Blinis (IRE) *P R Rodford*
4 ch g Danehill Dancer(IRE) —Richly Deserved (IRE) (King's Lake (USA))
945[P]

Blitzy Boy (IRE) *G T Lynch* 83h 100c
12 gr g Merrymount—Rosy Waters (Roselier (FR))
1420a[6] 1825[U] 1855[2]2748[P]

Blizzard Beach (IRE) *J Parkes* 15h
5 gr m Saddlers' Hall(IRE) —Stepfaster (Step Together (USA))
3490[13]

Blow Me Down *F Jordan* 48h
7 b m Overbury(IRE) —Chinook's Daughter (IRE) (Strong Gale)
23[P]

Blue Americo (IRE) *P F Nicholls* 125 h 88+c
8 br g Lord Americo—Princess Menelek (Menelek)
4802[2]

Blue Bajan (IRE) *Andrew Turnell* 85+h
4 b g Montjeu(IRE) —Gentle Thoughts (Darshaan)
2597[4]

Blue Bar *G A Harker* 88h
8 gr m Norton Challenger—Royal Scarlet (Royal Fountain)
302[4] 649[9] 854[P]

Blueberry Boy (IRE) *Paul Stafford* 131h
7 b g Old Vic—Glenair Lady (Golden Love)
3052a[2] 3892a[4] 4430[15]

Blueberry Ice (IRE) *B G Powell* 107+h 61c
8 bb m Glacial Storm(USA) —Call Me Honey (Le Bavard (FR))
(77) 504[3] 693[4] **1038[4] 1232[4]1365[6]**

Blue Business *P F Nicholls* 138 h 136 c
8 br g Roselier(FR) —Miss Redlands (Dubassoff (USA))
1781[2] 2165[F] 2564[6]3179[11] **3946[2] 4460[11]4753[4]** 4974[P]

Blue Buster *M W Easterby* 100h
6 b g Young Buster(IRE) —Lazybird Blue (IRE) (Bluebird (USA))
2658[3] 2968[2] 4143[2] 4787[4]

Bluebyyou (IRE) *T Hogan* 106b
5 b g Lake Coniston(IRE) —Stony View (IRE) (Tirol)
2782a[3]

Blue Canyon (FR) *F Doumen* 150 h
8 b g Bering—Nini Princesse (IRE) (Niniski (USA))
2326[2] 4069[5] 4458[16] 4765[18] 5000a[6]

Blue Chip (FR) *P Quinton*
10 gr m Cadoudal(FR) —Frou Frou Lou (FR) (Groom Dancer (USA))
1373a[F]

Bluecoat (USA) *M W Easterby* 100b
6 b g Majestic Twoeleven(USA) —Elusive Peace (USA) (Proud Truth (USA))
656[2] (719) 1554[2] 1667[3] 2024[P]

Blue Corrig (IRE) *Joseph Crowley* 120h 92c
6 gr g Darnay—Myristica (IRE) (Doyoun)
3411a[23]

Bluefield (IRE) *Mrs K Walton*
5 b g Second Empire(IRE) —Imco Reverie (IRE) (Grand Lodge (USA))
418[P]

Bluegrass Boy *J A Geake* 71+h
6 b g Bluegrass Prince(IRE) —Honey Mill (Milford)
1745[9]

Blue Hawk (IRE) *R Dickin* 99h
9 ch g Prince Of Birds(USA) —Classic Queen (IRE) (Classic Secret (USA))
220[4] (762) 1400[5] 1675[P]

Blue Hills *P W Hiatt* 94 h
5 br g Vettori(IRE) —Slow Jazz (USA) (Chief's Crown (USA))
2070[4] 2343[4] 2663[6]

Blue Jar *M Mullineaux* 36h
8 b g Royal Abjar(USA) —Artist's Glory (Rarity)
119[P] 417[P]

Blueland (IRE) *Noel T Chance* 91+h
7 b m Bigstone(IRE) —Legally Delicious (Law Society (USA))
58[2] 4801[2] 5077a[21]

Blue Leader (IRE) *M B Shears* 105+h 69c
7 b g Cadeaux Genereux—Blue Duster (USA) (Danzig (USA))
220[8] 347[2] 389[5] 568[6] 668[8](743) 915[11] **1022[P]** 1153[4] 1250[5]1409[5] 1724[7]

Bluemantle Maggie *R Ford*
5 ch m Then Again—Nordic Dream (Miramar Reef)
131[P]

Blue Mariner *J Jay* 99h
6 b g Marju(IRE) —Mazarine Blue (Bellypha)
2245[4] (2560) 2940[5] 3371[P] (Dead)

Blue Morning *Mrs J C McGregor* 47h
8 b m Balnibarbi—Bad Start (USA) (Bold Bidder)
2042[7] 2657[10] 3209[P]

Blue Nun *C L Popham* 61+h
5 b m Bishop Of Cashel—Matisse (Shareef Dancer (USA))
389[12] 651[6] 4661[P]

Blue Rising *Ferdy Murphy* 82h
5 gr g Primitive Rising(USA) —Pollytickle (Politico (USA))
1826[4] 2416[10]

Blue Shark (FR) *N J Henderson* 138+h
4 bb g Cadoudal(FR) —Sweet Beauty (FR) (Tip Moss (FR))
(3021)

Blue Sovereign *J L Spearing* 92+c
6 gr g Sovereign Water(FR) —Slack Alice (Derring Rose)
2581[P]

Blue Splash (FR) *Evan Williams* 102h
6 b g Epervier Bleu—Harpyes (FR) (Quart De Vin (FR))
490[7] 816[3] 3478[5] 4106[4] 4367[3]

Blues Story (FR) *N G Ayliffe* 92 h 58c
8 b g Pistolet Bleu(IRE) —Herbe Sucree (FR) (Tiffauges)
284[S] 385[6] 668[2] 806[6] 1121[6]1187[7] 5043[3]

Blue Venture (IRE) *B Mactaggart* 87+h
6 ch g Alhaarth(IRE) —September Tide (IRE) (Thatching)
61[12] 319[5] 716[F] (Dead)

Blue Wing *R Flint* 52+h
5 b g Bluebird(USA) —Warbler (Warning)
1340[7] 1454[10]

Blue Yonder *Evan Williams* 67h
6 b m Terimon—Areal (IRE) (Roselier (FR))
905[4] 1046[15] 1075[F] 1156[13]

Blunham *M C Chapman* 56 h
6 b g Danzig Connection(USA) —Relatively Sharp (Sharpen Up)
369[12] 670[14]

Blunham Hill (IRE) *John R Upson* 101h 108 c
8 ch g Over The River(FR) —Bronach (Beau Charmeur (FR))
12[3] 1853[4] (2502) (2877) 3343[P] (3989) 4395[4]

Blushing Bull *P F Nicholls* 130 h 97+c
7 b g Makbul—Blush (Gildoran)
3502[8] **3946[4]**

Blushing Russian (IRE) *P C Haslam*
4 b g Fasliyev(USA) —Ange Rouge (Priolo (USA))
1207[P]

Blu Teen (FR) *P F Nicholls* 117h
6 ch g Epervier Bleu—Teene Hawk (FR) (Matahawk)
2618[F] (3133) 4115[5] 4494[4] 5024[U]

Blyth Brook *W T Reed* 110c
14 b g Meadowbrook—The Bean-Goose (King Sitric)
63[5] 453[P]

Boardroom Dancer (IRE) *Miss Suzy Smith* 74b 116+c
9 b g Executive Perk—Dancing Course (IRE) (Crash Course)
276[6] 511[P] 3129[4](3359) 3547[4] (3938)

Boardroom Fiddle (IRE) *Miss E C Lavelle* 91+b
7 ch g Executive Perk—Opera Time (IRE) (Orchestra)
1954[3] 2663[P]

Boardsmill Rambler (IRE) *V Thompson* 82c
7 b g Persian Mews—Trimmer Wonder (IRE) (Celio Rufo)
3926[4] 4146[2] 4305[P]4791[5]

Bobalong (IRE) *C P Morlock* 99h
9 b g Bob's Return(IRE) —Northern Wind (Northfields (USA))
10[P] 2812[P] 3345[P]

Bob Ar Aghaidh (IRE) *C Tinkler* 115 h 128 c
10 b g Bob Back(USA) —Shuil Ar Aghaidh (The Parson)
(10) 1634[2] (1893) 2644[F] 2825[P] 5012[P]

Bobaway (IRE) *M G Rimell* 74b
9 br g Bob Back(USA) —Baybush (Boreen (FR))
696[F]

Bobbing Cove *Mrs L B Normile* 79h
7 b g Bob's Return(IRE) —Candlebright (Lighter)
3912[10] 5063[5]

Bobbi Rose Red *P T Dalton* 76h 72c
9 ch m Bob Back(USA) —Lady Rosanna (Kind Of Hush)
129^8

Bobble *R N Bevis* 59h
6 ch m Bob's Return(IRE) —Grayrose Double (Celtic Cone)
769^6 866^5 4425^8

Bobble Wonder *J G M O'Shea* 31b
5 b m Classic Cliche(IRE) —Wonderfall (FR) (The Wonder (FR))
3145^9

Bob Bob Bobbin *C L Tizzard* 139h 139+c
7 gr g Bob Back(USA) —Absalom's Lady (Absalom)
1917^5 2165^U 2848^33020^4 **(3480) (3612) 3976^2 4498^P**

Bobby Brown (IRE) *P C Haslam* 66h 17c
6 b g Insan(USA) —Miss Sally Knox (IRE) (Erdelistan (FR))
1905^3 3486^P 4921^P

Bobby Buttons *Mrs J Jones* 76+c
9 b g Primitive Rising(USA) —Lady Buttons (New Brig)
123^F 281^U 4305^6

Bobby Icata *K W Hogg*
5 b g I'm Supposin(IRE) —Its My Turn (Palm Track)
4315^P 4386^P

Bobe Brick *B R Foster*
5 b g Dervish—Tilstock Maid (Rolfe (USA))
1323^16

Boberelle (IRE) *C Tinkler* 94+h
6 gr m Bob Back(USA) —Zephyrelle (IRE) (Celio Rufo)
1683^F 1898^6 2866^2 3149^3 3461^5 4689^P

Bobering *B P J Baugh* 65h
6 b g Bob's Return(IRE) —Ring The Rafters (Batshoof)
457^9 696^11 838^10 1202^P

Bob Justice (IRE) *J Howard Johnson* 140+h 128c
10 b g Bob Back(USA) —Bramdean (Niniski (USA))
91a^9 (2641) 4473^8

Bob Mountain (IRE) *C Tinkler* 86b
5 bb h Bob Back(USA) —Honey Mountain (Royal Match)
2988^8 4825^7

Bobosh *R Dickin* 103 h 118c
10 b g Devil's Jump—Jane Craig (Rapid Pass)
2487 534^5 690^91016^5 **1236^P**

Bobsbest (IRE) *R J Price* 84h 96 c
10 b g Lashkari—Bobs (Warpath)
744^U (815) 916^P1152^11 **4281^P**

Bob's Buster *R Johnson* 89h 99 c
10 b g Bob's Return(IRE) —Saltina (Bustino)
644^5 1592^3 2172^4 2754^5 (3320) 3447^2 4489^3 4723^5

Bob Scotton (IRE) *K A Ryan* 101b
7 b g Bob Back(USA) —Zephyrelle (IRE) (Celio Rufo)
8^P

Bob's Finesse *J W Mullins* 52b
6 ch m Gran Alba(USA) —High Finesse (High Line)
27^13 285^4 487^8 4005^P **4578^F 4692^4**

Bob's Gone (IRE) *B P J Baugh* 106+h
8 ch g Eurobus—Bob's Girl (IRE) (Bob Back (USA))
(410) 762^8 949^8 (Dead)

Bob's Lad *D J Richards* 78h 76+c
9 b g Weldnaas(USA) —Porte Belloch (Belfort (FR))
299^5

Bobsleigh *H S Howe* 77 h
7 b g Robellino(USA) —Do Run Run (Commanche Run)
668^5 1675^11

Bobsourown (IRE) *D McCain* 68h 70c
7 b g Parthian Springs—Suir Queen (Deep Run)
2191^5 2639^P **2839^8 3652^8**

Bobs Pride (IRE) *D K Weld* 109h
4 b g Marju(IRE) —Vyatka (Lion Cavern (USA))
4122a^2

Bob's Temptation *A J Wilson* 70h 78+c
7 br g Bob's Return(IRE) —Temptation (IRE) (Clearly Bust)
300^10 2269^8 2755^P 2873^11 3545^11 4905^6

Bob's The Business (IRE) *Ian Williams* 90 c
12 b g Bob Back(USA) —Kiora (Camden Town)
2293^4 2608^P 2965^7 3845^U

Bob The Builder *N A Twiston-Davies* 101 h 134 c
7 b g Terimon—True Clown (True Song)
1631^4 1855^3 2011^P (2581) 2825^3 (3459) (3803) 4433^5 4778^F

Bob The Piler *N G Richards* 124 h 100c
10 b g Jendali(USA) —Laxay (Laxton)
1940^4

Bob What (IRE) *Thomas Mullins* 118h 108c
12 b g Bob Back(USA) —Whatyawant (Auction Ring (USA))
114a^4

Boddidley (IRE) *P F Nicholls* 98h 108c
8 b g Be My Native(USA) —Boardwalker (IRE) (Waajib)
2592^8 **3129^2 3698^P 4007^P 4662^P**

Bodell (IRE) *Mark Campion* 54b
4 b g Turtle Island(IRE) —Reddish Creek (USA) (Mt. Livermore (USA))
3623^13 5041^9

Bodfari Creek *J G Portman* 114h
9 ch g In The Wings—Cormorant Creek (Gorytus (USA))
137^F 296^P (Dead)

Bodfari Rose *A Bailey* 92h
7 ch m Indian Ridge—Royale Rose (FR) (Bering)
343^5 574^3 (Dead)

Bodfari Sauvage *J J Lambe* 3b
6 b g Loup Sauvage(USA) —Petite Sonnerie (Persian Bold)
1688^10 1889^P

Bodfari Signet *Mrs S C Bradburne* 105 h 76c
10 ch g King's Signet(USA) —Darakah (Doulab (USA))
(319) 422^U 873^2 1010^12 2038^10 2478^8 2904^7 3271^2 3487^5 3761^15 3929^11 4724^13 5068^10

Bodkin Boy (IRE) *Mrs S C Bradburne* 44h
6 b g Darnay—Kristar (Kris)
1661^8 2036^6

Bogus Dreams (IRE) *L Lungo* 116+h 116+c
9 ch g Lahib(USA) —Dreams Are Free (IRE) (Caerleon (USA))
(99) **(213)** 3561^10 4848^12

Bohemian Boy (IRE) *M Pitman* 118h 108 c
8 gr g Roselier(FR) —Right Hand (Oats)
353^3 **3419^3 3900^5**

Bohemian Brook (IRE) *J Howard Johnson* 70h
5 ch g Alderbrook—Bohemian Return (IRE) (Hawaiian Return (USA))
2108^4 2448^8 2690^6 3782^P

Bohemian Spirit (IRE) *N G Richards* 113+h 125+c
8 b g Eagle Eyed(USA) —Tuesday Morning (Sadler's Wells (USA))
151^2 555^2 2416^3 **(2900) (3272)** 3757^U (4585) 5120^2

Boher Storm (IRE) *P A Fahy* 100h
6 bb g Glacial Storm(USA) —Conna Bride Lady (IRE) (Phardante (FR))
117a^U 3408a^5

Boing Boing (IRE) *Miss S J Wilton* 93h
6 b g King's Theatre(IRE) —Limerick Princess (IRE) (Polish Patriot (USA))
275^5 3818^4 4738^2

Bold As Brass (IRE) *James Keegan* 85h
7 ch m Un Desperado(FR) —Noisy Kiss (IRE) (Executive Perk)
3005a^4

Bold Bishop (IRE) *Jonjo O'Neill* 149 h 153 c
9 b g Religiously(USA) —Ladybojangles (IRE) (Buckskin (FR))
1155^2 1871^2 (2163) (2492) 4444^U 4759^U

Bold Century *S C Burrough*
9 b g Casteddu—Bold Green (FR) (Green Dancer (USA))
3141^P (Dead)

Bold Fire *P F Nicholls* 125+h
4 b f Bold Edge—Kirkby Belle (Bay Express)
(3511) (3621) 3972^2 4435^7 5001^2

Bold Investor *C Grant* 92h 106 c
9 b g Anshan—Shirlstar Investor (Some Hand)
1759^5 1941^P 2588^3 2955^7 3849^P (Dead)

Bold Momento *B De Haan* 69h
7 b g Never So Bold—Native Of Huppel (IRE) (Be My Native (USA))
388^F

Bold 'N' Brave *C C Bealby*
7 ch g Fearless Action(USA) —Quenby Girl (IRE) (Remainder Man)
4016^P

Bold Pursuit (IRE) *S B Clark* 91 h
4 br g Bold Fact(USA) —Lyphard Belle (Noble Patriarch)
1563^7 1718^7 1904^5 2442^P 2752^6 3557^P

Bold Trump *Mrs N S Evans* 83h
5 b g First Trump—Blue Nile (IRE) (Bluebird (USA))
1077^P 1158^P 4278^2 5023^4

Bollin Annabel *T D Easterby* 101 h
5 b m King's Theatre(IRE) —Bollin Magdalene (Teenoso (USA))
2629^P 2964^9

Bollin Thomas *R Allan* 106h
8 b g Alhijaz—Bollin Magdalene (Teenoso (USA))
59^5 2173^6 2478^9 2680^F 3783^2 4108^4 4346^2 4529^2

Bollitree Bob *M Scudamore* 82h
5 b g Bob's Return(IRE) —Lady Prunella (IRE) (Supreme Leader)
1445^P 1672^7 1968^8 2142^4 2606^9 2995^6 3371^9

Bolshoi Ballet *R A Fahey* 110 h 86c
8 b g Dancing Spree(USA) —Broom Isle (Damister (USA))
2177 695^6 1001^3 1153^14 4922^4

Bombaybadboy (NZ) *Ian Williams* 59+h
7 ch g Rodrigo De Triano(USA) —Vuma (NZ) (Vice Regal (NZ))
3354^P 3947^11 4106^11 4564^7

Bon Accord *Miss E C Lavelle*
6 b g Accordion—Park Athlete (IRE) (Supreme Leader)
1775^U 1859^P

Bonbon Rose (FR) *A Chaille-Chaille* 125 h
5 ch h Mansonnien(FR) —Rose Angevine (FR) (Master Thatch)
778a^7

Bonchester Bridge *N J Henderson* 92+h
5 b m Shambo—Cabriole Legs (Handsome Sailor)
1323^2 (1674) 1820^2 2486^3 2718^P 4286^6 4619^8 5120^5

Bond Millennium *B Smart* 39h
8 ch g Piccolo—Farmer's Pet (Sharrood (USA))
2763^P

Boneyarrow (IRE) *Eoin Griffin* 144h 125c
10 ch g Over The River(FR) —Apicat (Buckskin (FR))
4471^F

Bongo Fury (FR) *M C Pipe* 134 h
7 b m Sillery(USA) —Nativelee (FR) (Giboulee (CAN))
4375^12 4663^8 4773^11

Bonheur Du Rheu (FR) *P Rago*
3 b g Dounba(FR) —Dona Du Rheu (FR) (Dom Pasquini (FR))
4298a^6

Bonjour Bond (IRE) *J G M O'Shea* 67h
5 ro g Portrait Gallery(IRE) —Musical Essence (Song)
1750^8 1898^11 2560^5 3985^7 4101^9

Bonnell (IRE) *K J Burke* 85h 53c
7 b g Oscar(IRE) —Suelemar (IRE) (Montelimar (USA))
3279^4 3395^9 **3418^7** 3603^4

Bonne Noel'S (IRE) *C Roche* 104h
6 b g Saddlers' Hall(IRE) —Mursuma (Rarity)
93a^3

Bonnet's Pieces *Mrs P Sly* 90 h 90 c
7 b m Alderbrook—Chichell's Hurst (Oats)
1850^3 **2344^6 2715^2 2951^F 3418^F** 3655^9

Bonney Flame *J L Spearing* 57h
6 ch m Bonny Scot(IRE) —Fountain Of Fire (IRE) (Lafontaine (USA))
4940^11

Bonnie Blue *Mrs Norma Pook* 37h
7 ch m Karinga Bay—Last Shower (Town And Country)
2507^6 2727^3 3280^10

Bonnie Rock (IRE) *J I A Charlton* 85b
6 b m Oscar(IRE) —A'Dhahirah (Beldale Flutter (USA))
719^2 1667^4 2028^6 2480^2

Bonny Blink (IRE) *S B Bell*
6 b m Needle Gun(IRE) —Pas De Mot (Tender King)
3448^10

Bonny Boy (IRE) *D A Rees* 81+h 81 c
11 b g Bustino—Dingle Bay (Petingo)
4167^4 4353^4 4666^U 4752^2 (4869)

Bonny Busona *K F Clutterbuck* 55b
6 b m Abou Zouz(USA) —La Busona (IRE) (Broken Hearted)
3961^7 4902^P

Bonny Grey *D Burchell* 110h
8 gr m Seymour Hicks(FR) —Sky Wave (Idiots Delight)
77^2 2002^3 2379^9 2850^6 3247^9 3510^3 4420^8 4641^3 4781^2 4938^4 (Dead)

Bonny Grove *H J Evans* 76b
6 b g Bonny Scot(IRE) —Binny Grove (Sunyboy)
2432^13 3248^P

Bonny Jago *R Brotherton* 76b
5 ch g Bonny Scot(IRE) —Bold Honey (IRE) (Nearly A Nose (USA))
3983^8 4807^11

Bonnyjo (FR) *P R Webber* 77h
7 br g Cyborg(FR) —Argument Facile (FR) (Argument (FR))
352^8

Bonnykino *S C Burrough* 11b
4 ch f Meadowbrook—Jukino (Relkino)
4667^12

Bon Temps Rouler (FR) *A L T Moore* 120h
7 b g Hero's Honor(USA) —Top Nue (FR) (Top Ville)
3411a^5

Bonus Bridge (IRE) *H D Daly* 108h 141+c
11 b g Executive Perk—Corivia (Over The River (FR))
219^5 1739^P 2489^P 4213^2 4973^F

Boobee (IRE) *Robert Gray* 83h 114+c
10 b g Mister Lord(USA) —Who's She (Tall Noble (USA))
611^2 745^8 **1232^3 (1396) 1939^P**

Books Delight *J Wade* 43h
6 b m Alflora(IRE) —In A Whirl (USA) (Island Whirl (USA))
1508^P 1661^7 3337^P

Book's Way *D W Thompson* 79+h 69c
10 br g Afzal—In A Whirl (USA) (Island Whirl (USA))
152^4 429^10 469^3 686^13 781^5 839^11 988^11 **1062^7 1178^5** 1310^8

Boom Economy (IRE) *Paul A Roche* 94 h 110c
10 bb g Black Monday—Miss Bula (Master Buck)
5129a^4

Boomerang Boy (IRE) *M H Weston* 49b
5 ch g Carroll House—Clowater Lassie (IRE) (Phardante (FR))
4680^P 5075^6

Boomshakalaka (IRE) *N J Henderson* 93+b
6 ch g Anshan—Fairy Gale (IRE) (Strong Gale) (655)

Booster Divin (FR) *M J Gingell* 39h
4 b g Signe Divin(USA) —Shenedova (FR) (Hellios (USA))
4637^11

Bora Shaamit (IRE) *M Scudamore*
4 b f Shaamit(IRE) —Bora Bora (Bairn (USA))
2642^11 3181^16

Border Artist *B G Powell* 78 h
7 ch g Selkirk(USA) —Aunt Tate (Tate Gallery (USA))
1724^8

Border Castle *Miss Venetia Williams* 116h
5 b g Grand Lodge(USA) —Tempting Prospect (Shirley Heights)
(2627) 2849^3 3908^2 4420^4 4613^4

Border Craic (IRE) *B Mactaggart*
6 ch g Glacial Storm(USA) —Clare Maid (IRE) (Fidel)
2036^P 3232^P 3532^P

Border Sovereign *J S Haldane*
6 b g Sovereign Water(FR) —Skelton (Derrylin)
2480^9

Border Star (IRE) *B G Powell* 53+h
9 b g Parthian Springs—Tengello (Bargello)
4731^U

Border Tale *James Moffatt* 101h
6 b g Selkirk(USA) —Likely Story (IRE) (Night Shift (USA))
2479 (332) 422^7 647^P 947^10 2324^5 2478^12 2925^12 3761^7 3929^6 4990^P

Borehill Joker *V R A Dartnall* 97h 99+c
10 ch g Pure Melody(USA) —Queen Matilda (Castle Keep)
57^2 275^2 370^6 (502) **565^2 805^6** 915^13 **1076^2** 1405^7 **2684^P** 3719^P

Boring Goring (IRE) *E J Farrant* 90h 90c
12 b g Aristocracy—Coolrusk (IRE) (Millfontaine)
233^8 4874^P 5087^3

Boris The Spider *M D Hammond* 98+h
5 b g Makbul—Try Vickers (USA) (Fuzzbuster (USA))
2062^5 2448^9 2991^9 4040^3 (4346) 4488^P 5138^8

Born Leader (IRE) *A King* 90+h
8 b g Supreme Leader—Real Lace (Kampala)
3477^P

Borora *R Lee* 129h
7 gr g Shareef Dancer(USA) —Bustling Nelly (Bustino)
332^3 824^2 1010^3 1878^4 2209^13 2746^6 3298^6 4473^6 4938^7

Borouj (IRE) *Philip Fenton* 74h
4 ch c Unfuwain(USA) —Amanah (USA) (Mr Prospector (USA))
5076a^23

Bosham Mill *P J Hobbs* 120+c
8 ch g Nashwan(USA) —Mill On The Floss (Mill Reef (USA))
3819^2 4051^2 4471^10 4975^U

Boston Strong Boy (IRE) *C Tinkler* 105b
6 ch g Pennekamp(USA) —Cossack Princess (IRE) (Lomond (USA))
3244^4 3911^3

Bosworth Boy *Mrs H Sweeting* 52h
8 b g Deploy—Krill (Kris)
533^P 749^13 977^P

Bosworth Gypsy (IRE) *Miss J S Davis* 76+h
8 b m Aahsaylad—Googly (Sunley Builds)
2865^6 3149^5 3545^5 3951^3 4277^6 **4937^P**

Bothar Na (IRE) *W P Mullins* 122c
7 ch g Mister Lord(USA) —Country Course (IRE) (Crash Course)
4471^4 4748^4 5083a^4

Bottom Drawer *Mrs D A Hamer* 82h
6 b g My Best Valentine—Little Egret (Carwhite)
172^5 456^F 753^10

Bougoure (IRE) *Mrs S J Smith* 123 h
7 b g Oscar(IRE) —Jasmine Melody (Jasmine Star)
1885^3 (2571) (3789) 4373^12 4765^16

Boulders Beach (IRE) *Mrs S J Smith* 99h
6 b g Beneficial—Billie's Beauty (IRE) (Lord Americo)
2192^5 2844^11 3314^2 3793^3 (4720) 4849^10

Boulevardofdreams (IRE) *M C Pipe* 102h
5 b g Beau Sher—Cap The Waves (IRE) (Roselier (FR))
(384) 514^2 742^2 1270^12

Boulevin (IRE) *R J Price* 101+h
6 bb g Perugino(USA) —Samika (IRE) (Bikala)
4834^4

Bounce Back (USA) *M C Pipe* 113h 126c
10 ch g Trempolino(USA) —Lattaquie (FR) (Fast Topaze (USA))
1861^P 2483^9 **4240^4**

Bound *Mrs L Wadham* 130+h 117 c
8 b g Kris—Tender Moment (IRE) (Caerleon (USA))
4608^2 4773^7

Boundary House *J A B Old* 77 h 94c
8 ch g Alflora(IRE) —Preacher's Gem (The Parson)
2431^P (3241) 3698^P 4328^P 4571^P

Bourneagainkristen *C C Bealby* 54h 47+c
8 ch m Afzal—Miss Lawn (FR) (Lashkari)
3730^8 4577^7 **4989^5**

Bowdens Lane *D O Stephens*
7 b g Sovereign Water(FR) —Belhelvie (Mart Lane)
490^12

Bowdlane Barb *John A Harris* 69b
5 b m Commanche Run—Foxs Shadow (Neltino)
3373^9 4909^12

Bowd Lane Joe *E R Clough* 67h 65c
7 gr g Mazaad—Race To The Rhythm (Deep Run)
74^P 5109^P

Bowes Cross *Ferdy Murphy* 50h
6 b g Environment Friend—Fenian Court (IRE) (John French)
2690^P 2923^15 3316^F

Bowleaze (IRE) *R H Alner* 122+h 122+c
7 br g Right Win(IRE) —Mrs Cullen (Over The River (FR))
(201) **1781^F** 5010^7

Bowling Along *M E Sowersby* 53h
5 b m The West(USA) —Bystrouska (Gorytus (USA))
569^8 691^9 892^10 1063^P

Bow School (IRE) *J Howard Johnson* 86+b
5 b g New Frontier(IRE) —Sallaghan (IRE) (Hays)
4992^5

Boxclever *J M Jefferson* 83h
5 b g Accordion—Pugilistic (Hard Fought)
1532^7 2480^14 4301^8 4916^5

Box On (IRE) *B J Llewellyn* 97h 63c
9 bb g Un Desperado(FR) —Party Dancer (Be My Guest (USA))
239^P 893^P 1638^4

Boyackasha (IRE) *E McNamara* 58h 107c
8 b g Executive Perk—Lady Pauper (IRE) (Le Moss)
2143^6 (Dead)

Boychuk (IRE) *P J Hobbs* 135+h
5 b g Insan(USA) —Golden Flower (GER) (Highland Chieftain)
(1640) (1782) (2161) 3174^3 3878^3 4750^4 4956^3

Boy's Hurrah (IRE) *J Howard Johnson* 98b 116c
10 b g Phardante(FR) —Gorryelm (Arctic Slave)
1759^6 2616^5

Boysterous (IRE) *Mrs H Dalton* 75b
6 b g Lord Americo—Hells Angel (IRE) (Kambalda)
266^U 300^6

Boytjie (IRE) *Miss H C Knight* 79h
6 b g Un Desperado(FR) —Miss Cali (Young Man (FR))
175^6 1876^5

Brackenorah *S C Burrough* 33b
4 b f Double Trigger(IRE) —Little Preston (IRE) (Pennine Walk)
2425^16 (Dead)

Brackney Boy (IRE) *I A Duncan* 89h 92c
12 b g Zaffaran(USA) —Donard Lily (Master Buck)
2151^2 (595)

Bradders *J R Jenkins* 41h
4 b g Silver Patriarch(IRE) —Lolita (FR) (Hellios (USA))
2013[6] 2105[7] 3421[6] 3579[10] 4638[7]

Bradley Boy (IRE) *Carl Llewellyn* 104+b
5 ch g Presenting—Mistric (Buckley)
2242[2] 2823[2] 3188[3] 4881[2]

Brads House (IRE) *J G M O'Shea* 107 h
4 b g Rossini(USA) —Gold Stamp (Golden Act (USA))
3498[3] 3722[6] 4106[2]

Brady Boys (USA) *J G M O'Shea* 87h 90c
9 b g Cozzene(USA) —Elvia (USA) (Roberto (USA))
276[5] 461[P]

Bramantino (IRE) *T A K Cuthbert* 75 h
6 b g Perugino(USA) —Headrest (Habitat)
2027[5] 2657[12]

Bramblehill Duke (IRE) *Miss Venetia Williams* 104c
14 b g Kambalda—Scat-Cat (Furry Glen)
176[2] 297[2] 461[2]567[R] 896[P] 1122[R]

Bramble Princess (IRE) *Miss Lucinda V Russell* 81h 69c
7 b m Lord Americo—Bramble Ridge (IRE) (Remainder Man)
2678[4] 2979[4] **3375[P] 3553[5]**4145[8] **4788[7] 5037[5]**

Brandeston Ron (IRE) *M Pitman* 74+h
7 b g Presenting—Boolavogue (IRE) (Torus)
79[P] 1642[5] 1975[P]

Brandon Mountain (IRE) *Gordon Elliott* 106h
4 ch c Woodborough(USA) —Fleetwood Fancy (Taufan (USA))
4435[P]

Brandy Wine (IRE) *L Lungo* 99h 110+c
8 b g Roselier(FR) —Sakonnet (IRE) (Mandalus)
83[2] 2004[3] (2440) **2819[2](3204) 3382[P] 4361[P]**

Brankley Boy *N J Henderson* 124h
8 ch g Afzal—Needwood Fortune (Tycoon II)
2815[2] (3428) 3729[3] (4494) 4849[3]

Branodunum *M W Easterby* 76b
5 b g Bal Harbour—Hiding Place (Saddlers' Hall (IRE))
1762[9] 2112[11] 2591[6]

Branston Lily *D Brace*
4 ch f Cadeaux Genereux—Indefinite Article (IRE) (Indian Ridge)
2286[P]

Brasilia Prince *G P Enright* 87h
7 ch g Karinga Bay—Cappuccino Girl (Broadsword (USA))
671[5] 1246[5]

Brave Benefactor (IRE) *B G Powell*
6 b g Beneficial—Brown Forest (Brave Invader (USA))
4875[P]

Brave Dane (IRE) *L A Dace* 100 h
8 b g Danehill(USA) —Nuriva (USA) (Woodman (USA))
726[RR] 747[F] 915[6] 1087[5]

Brave Effect (IRE) *Mrs Dianne Sayer*
10 br g Bravefoot—Crupney Lass (Ardoon)
689[9] 784[9] 940[5] **1062[3]1147[5]** 1296[4] 1312[4] **1570[5]1666[6]** 2691[P] **2980[8]3338[P]** 3757[DSQ] 4302[P] **4991[U]**

Brave Hiawatha (FR) *J A B Old* 83+h
4 b g Dansili—Alexandrie (USA) (Val De L'Orne (FR))
2824[14] 3340[8] 3429[10] 4834[8] 5111[2]

Brave Inca (IRE) *C A Murphy* 173+h
8 b g Good Thyne(USA) —Wigwam Mam (IRE) (Commanche Run)
(114a) (2397a) 2669a[3] (3109a) (3641a) (4432) 5130a[2]

Brave Jo (FR) *N J Hawke* 58h
5 ch g Villez(USA) —Eau De Nuit (King's Lake (USA))
1681[12] 1755[4] 2152[9] 3248[10] 3806[8]

Brave Rebellion *K G Reveley* 105h 79+c
7 b g Primitive Rising(USA) —Grand Queen (Grand Conde (FR))
(1635) 2169[3] 2444[7] 2571[2] 3173[3] **4303[3]**4849[11]

Brave Spirit (FR) *C L Tizzard* 107 h 131 c
8 b g Legend Of France(USA) —Guerre Ou Paix (FR) (Comrade In Arms)
(2015) **2215[4] 2637[2] 3186[P]3469[2]** 3613[2] **4111[P]4496[P]** (Dead)

Brave Thought (IRE) *P Monteith* 79h 125+c
11 b g Commanche Run—Bristol Fairy (Smartset)
2944[8] **3233[F] 3852[2](4109) 4363[P] 4850[3]**

Brave Vision *A C Whillans* 110 h
10 b g Clantime—Kinlet Vision (IRE) (Vision (USA))
61[6] 332[9] 3234[5] 3378[F] 3853[4]4848[7]

Bravo *J Mackie* 92+h
8 bb g Efisio—Apache Squaw (Be My Guest (USA))
352[P] 697[13] 988[6] 1045[P] 1564[P]

Bravura *G L Moore* 81 h
8 ch g Never So Bold—Sylvan Song (Song)
203[9] 456[P] 5050[P]

Brazen Hooker (IRE) *Ms Joanna Morgan*
4 b f Desert Story(IRE) —Ballyhookeen Lass (IRE) (Balla Cove)
1955[P]

Brazil Nut *Mrs K Waldron* 10h
5 b g Deploy—Garota De Ipanema (FR) (Al Nasr (FR))
911[16]

Breaking Ball (IRE) *N G Richards* 67h
6 ch g Erin's Isle—Noorajo (IRE) (Ahonoora)
592[10]

Breaking Breeze (IRE) *Andrew Turnell* 105h 113+c
11 b g Mandalus—Knockacool Breeze (Buckskin (FR))
206[6] **511[3] 684[5](1650)**

Break The Ice *L A Dace* 79b
5 b m North Col—Frozen Pipe (Majestic Maharaj)
1954[4] 2461[P] 2683[P]

Breathing Fire *Mrs John Harrington* 143h
4 b g Pivotal—Pearl Venture (Salse (USA))
3890a[2] 4468[F] 5099a[3]

Bredon Hill *R T Phillips* 54b
6 b m Rakaposhi King—Society News (Law Society (USA))
4398[8]

Breema Donna *R Dickin* 70h
8 b m Sir Harry Lewis(USA) —Donna Del Lago (King's Lake (USA))
399[U] 487[9] 654[4]

Breezer *J A Geake* 75h
6 b g Forzando—Lady Lacey (Kampala)
2043[3] 2314[4] 2582[5] 2958[11] 3279[10]3905[P] 4651[3] 4783[3] (5050)

Breezy Betsy (IRE) *R J Armson*
10 br m Phardante(FR) —Aughclogeen Run (Deep Run)
672[8]

Breezy Warrior (IRE) *J M Saville* 27h
7 b g Commanche Run—Another Crash (Crash Course)
4501[P]

Bregogue (IRE) *Sean Regan* 100h 122c
12 ch g Alphabatim(USA) —Sandra's Joy (Pollerton)
3960[P]

Brendan's Surprise *K J Burke* 80h
4 b g Faustus(USA) —Primrose Way (Young Generation)
2345[8] 2481[8] 3436[11]

Brendar (IRE) *Jim Best* 101h
9 b g Step Together(USA) —Willabelle (Will Somers)
762[14] (4652) 4824[4] 5108[4]

Brer Bear *Mrs E Insley* 113+c
7 b g Perpendicular—Nessfield (Tumble Wind)
3910[5] (4421) 4880[3]

Bressbee (USA) *J W Unett* 97h
8 ch g Twining(USA) —Bressay (USA) (Nureyev (USA))
5073[2]

Breuddwyd Lyn *Mrs D A Hamer* 64h
8 br g Awesome—Royal Resort (King Of Spain)
2343[P] 2619[P] 2930[P]

Brewster (IRE) *Ian Williams* 150h
9 b g Roselier(FR) —Aelia Paetina (Buckskin (FR))
1925[5] 3020[5] 3723[11]

Briannie (IRE) *P Butler* 65h
4 b f Xaar—Annieirwin (IRE) (Perugino (USA))
1737[10] 1948[4] 2681[8] 2797[P]

Briareus *A M Balding* 154 h
6 ch g Halling(USA) —Lower The Tone (IRE) (Phone Trick (USA))
2765[2] 3298[13] (3994) 4432[6]

Briar's Mist (IRE) *C Grant* 103h 103c
9 gr g Roselier(FR) —Claycastle (IRE) (Carlingford Castle)
1848[F] 2413[P] 2819[6](3315) 4144[P] 4316[P]4636[P] 4851[P]

Brickland (IRE) *Mayne Kidd* 25h
5 b m Insan(USA) —Time Of The Lord (IRE) (Lord Americo)
876[6]

Bricos Boy (IRE) *Miss C J Williams*
5 b g Executive Perk—Moy Farina (Derrylin)
4758[3] 4947[10]

Bridge Pal *P Monteith* 91h
6 ch m First Trump—White Domino (Sharpen Up)
306[5]

Brief Decline (IRE) *J D Frost* 93h
11 b g Alzao(USA) —Uncertain Affair (IRE) (Darshaan)
863[6] 1075[P] 1187[3] 1362[2]

Briery Fox (IRE) *H D Daly* 111h 132 c
8 ch g Phardante(FR) —Briery Gale (Strong Gale)
1891[4] 2441[2] (2953) 4447[13] 5065[2]

Brigadier Benson (IRE) *R H Alner* 98h
6 b g Fourstars Allstar(USA) —Decent Enough (Decent Fellow)
(111) 353[5] 1488[4] 1647[3] 1773[3]

Brigadier Brown (IRE) *John Joseph Murphy* 114h 113c
9 b g Satco(FR) —Tarasandy (IRE) (Arapahos (FR))
92a[12] **4460[7] 5129a[6]**

Brigadier Du Bois (FR) *Mrs L Wadham* 85 h 92 c
7 gr g Apeldoorn(FR) —Artic Night (FR) (Kaldoun (FR))
126[6] 1816[3] 2043[0] **2257[2]**3147[3] **3252[2] (3602)**

Bright Approach (IRE) *J G Cann* 121c
13 gr g Roselier(FR) —Dysart Lady (King's Ride)
150[5] 311[6] 439[2]

Bright Green *C J Gray* 99+h 76 c
7 b g Green Desert(USA) —Shining High (Shirley Heights)
3345[P] 3997[3] 4331[2] 4652[4] 4781[U]5028[2]

Bright Present (IRE) *B N Pollock* 32h 64+c
8 bb g Presenting—Bright Rose (Skyliner)
1990[8] 2950[12] **3460[5] 4921[4]5088[F]**

Bright Spirit *N J Henderson* 95b
5 b g Petoski—Lunabelle (Idiots Delight)
2075[6] 3421[7]

Bright Steel (IRE) *M Todhunter* 81+h 77c
9 gr g Roselier(FR) —Ikeathy (Be Friendly)
1914[2] 2039[P] 2413[P]

Brilliant Cut *N J Henderson* 88b
6 gr g Terimon—Always Shining (Tug Of War)
656[4]

Bringewood Fox *J L Needham* 70b
4 gr g Cloudings(IRE) —Leinthall Fox (Deep Run)
4455[11]

Bring Me Sunshine (IRE) *C L Tizzard* 109+h
5 ch g Alderbrook—Hilarys Pet (Bonne Noel)
2152[3] 2579[4] 3024[4] 3882[4] (4148) 4494[6]

Bringontheclowns (IRE) *M F Harris* 109h
7 b g Entrepreneur—Circus Maid (IRE) (High Top)
695[3] 873[B] 1087[U] 1408[3]

Brinkmanship (USA) *Mrs H Dalton* 92b
4 b g Red Ransom(USA) —Whist (Mr Prospector (USA))
1785[2] 4554[3]

Brisbane Road (IRE) *B J Llewellyn* 88+h
9 b g Blues Traveller(IRE) —Eva Fay (IRE) (Fayruz)
(229) **2610[P]** 2862[P]

Briscoe Place (IRE) *Jonjo O'Neill* 109h
6 b g Dr Massini(IRE) —Laridissa (IRE) (Shardari)
(1543) 2211[6] 3881[5] 4564[4] (4732)

Bristol Bridge *Ms M L Byrom*
9 b g Shannon Cottage(USA) —Plassey Bridge (Pitpan)
4283[5]

Britesand (IRE) *J S Moore* 82h
6 ch g Humbel(USA) —The Hollow Beach (IRE) (Beau Sher)
2142[5] 2528[9]

Briyatha *C N Kellett* 43b
4 ch f Montjoy(USA) —Just One Way Vii (Damsire Unregistered)
4800[P] 7[P]

Broadband *Miss S E Forster* 52b
7 ch g Minster Son—Sound Bite (Say Primula)
1532[10] 1688[7]

Broadspeed *M J Gingell*
10 b m Broadsword(USA) —Bosom Friend (Bustomi)
893[7] 998[U] 1047[6]

Broadstone Road (IRE) *Paul John Gilligan* 110c
9 ch g Magical Wonder(USA) —Administer (Damister (USA))
3921[P] 3942[C]

Brochrua (IRE) *J D Frost* 94+h
6 b m Hernando(FR) —Severine (USA) (Trempolino (USA))
(284) 536[3] 1121[3] 1218[6] 1747[7] 2150[4]3804[6] 4290[8] 4423[4] (4856) (5115)

Brogella (IRE) *Ms F M Crowley* 138+h
6 b m King's Theatre(IRE) —Metroella (IRE) (Entitled)
3110a[2] (5077a)

Broken Gale (IRE) *P Budds* 88+h
6 b m Broken Hearted—Ballyclough Gale (Strong Gale)
1906[3]

Broken Knights (IRE) *N G Richards* 135+h
9 ch g Broken Hearted—Knight's Row (Le Bavard (FR))
207[5]

Broken Reed (IRE) *T R George* 110+h
7 b g Broken Hearted—Kings Reserve (King's Ride)
(5073)

Broken River (IRE) *P J Rothwell* 86h
5 b g City Honours(USA) —Pelm (IRE) (John French)
65a[19]

Broke Road (IRE) *Mrs H Dalton* 112 h 107 c
10 b g Deploy—Shamaka (Kris)
99[P] 1087[P] 3360[5] 3650[7] 4242[10](4591)

Bromley Abbey *Miss S E Forster* 87h
8 ch m Minster Son—Little Bromley (Riberetto)
9[11] 301[9] 406[8] 1834[8] 2027[7]3269[9] 3484[3] **3762[P]** 4302[3]4584[2] 5120[P]

Bromley Moss *Miss S E Forster* 38b
7 ch g Le Moss—Little Bromley (Riberetto)
80[P]

Bronco Charlie (IRE) *Jonjo O'Neill* 95+h
8 b g Be My Native(USA) —Cockney Bug (Torus)
1158[5] 1222[4] 1302[9] 1645[12]

Bronhallow *Mrs Barbara Waring* 60h 56c
13 b g Belmez(USA) —Grey Twig (Godswalk (USA))
2958[P] 3367[11] **3938[5] 4451[8]4567[R]**

Bronx Girl (IRE) *F Flood* 48h
4 ch f Quws—Mill Lane Lady (IRE) (Un Desperado (FR))
5134a[7]

Bronze Dancer (IRE) *G A Swinbank*
4 b g Entrepreneur—Scrimshaw (Selkirk (USA))
2263[P]

Bronze King *J A B Old* 68h
6 b g Rakaposhi King—Bronze Sunset (Netherkelly)
4072[18] 4333[11] 4754[11] 4934[9]

Bronzesmith *B J M Ryall* 107b 138+c
10 b g Greensmith—Bronze Age (Celtic Cone)
386[4] (634) (761) 1013[10]1265[4] 1561[6] 1881[4]4459[12]

Brooking (IRE) *R T Phillips*
8 b g Roselier(FR) —Kilkil Pin (Bowling Pin)
3906[P] 4285[P]

Brooklands Lad *J W Mullins* 96h 93+c
9 b g North Col—Sancal (Whistlefield)
170[5]

Brooklyn Breeze (IRE) *L Lungo* 133+h 147 c
9 bb g Be My Native(USA) —Moss Gale (Strong Gale)
(1823) **2177[12] 2760[4]**

Brooklyn Brownie (IRE) *J M Jefferson* 116h
7 b g Presenting—In The Brownies (IRE) (Lafontaine (USA))
111[4] (345) 521[2] 892[2] (938) 1796[3] 2347[16](2952) 3561[5] (5096)

Brooklyn's Gold (USA) *Ian Williams* 116h 104c
11 b g Seeking The Gold(USA) —Brooklyn's Dance (FR) (Shirley Heights)
247[6] **570[6]** 1743[8] **2141[3]2929[3] 3844[2] 4943[P]**

Broomers Hill (IRE) *L A Dace* 76h
6 b g Sadler's Wells(USA) —Bella Vitessa (IRE) (Thatching)
630[P]

Brora Sutherland (IRE) *Miss Lucinda V Russell* 80h 63c
7 b g Synefos(USA) —Downtotheswallows (IRE) (Boreen (FR))
1834[10] 2447[P] **3850[6] 4520[P]**

Brosie *L Lungo* 28b
5 b m Opening Verse(USA) —Sveltissima (Dunphy)
323[13]

Brother Ted *J K Cresswell* 82h
9 b g Henbit(USA) —Will Be Wanton (Palm Track)
1[10] **465[P]** 1084[6] 1322[6]1756[8] 2463[P]

Broughton Boy *G J Smith* 37b
6 br g Alhaatmi—Metabolic Melody (Creetown)
465[P] 1279[P] **1618[P]**

Broughton Knows *Mrs C J Ikin* 44 h
9 b g Most Welcome—Broughtons Pet (IRE) (Cyrano De Bergerac)
1302[10] 1395[9] 1520[8] 1655[9] 3674[P] (Dead)

Browneyes Blue (IRE) *D R MacLeod* 59h
8 b g Satco(FR) —Bawnard Lady (Ragapan)
2657[11] 4145[11] 4723[12]

Brown Fox (FR) *C J Down* 84h
5 b m Polar Falcon(USA) —Garmeria (FR) (Kadrou (FR))
1021[9] 1222[P] 1640[2] 1750[5] 1974[F]2314[8] 4731[9] 4941[4] 5022[3]

Brownie Points (IRE) *C F Swan* 78b
4 ch f Bob Back(USA) —Curzon Street (Night Shift (USA))
5134a[13]

Brownie Returns (IRE) *M F Morris* 78h 124c
13 b g Dry Dock—What A Brownie (Strong Gale)
112a[12]

Brown Teddy *R Ford* 111+h 121+c
9 b g Afzal—Quadrapol (Pollerton)
305[U] 2342[3]

Bruern (IRE) *Mrs Mary Hambro* 58h
9 b g Aahsaylad—Bob's Girl (IRE) (Bob Back (USA))
1540[U]

Brumous (IRE) *O Sherwood* 117h
6 b g Glacial Storm(USA) —Ath Leathan (Royal Vulcan)
(2809) (3545) 4634[2]

Brunate *J A Danahar* 72h
7 b g Chaddleworth(IRE) —Dawn Call (Rymer)
4052[P] 4562[F]

Brundeanlaws *Mrs H O Graham* 72+h 88c
5 b m Endoli(USA) —The Respondant (Respect)
1532[8] 2028[7] 2678[3] 2947[12] 3914[P]4302[F] **4788[6]**

Brunston Castle *A W Carroll* 70h
6 b g Hector Protector(USA) —Villella (Sadler's Wells (USA))
3673[6] 3885[5] 4903[10]

Brush A King *C T Pogson* 107 h 67c
11 b g Derrylin—Colonial Princess (Roscoe Blake)
109[8] 468[2] 652[2] 768[6] 1026[5]1181[P]

Brutto Facie (IRE) *Mrs John Harrington* 100+h 126c
7 b g Old Vic—Elas Image (IRE) (Ela-Mana-Mou)
5082a[F]

Bryans Bach (IRE) *C Tinkler* 44b
5 ch g Good Thyne(USA) —Swinging Single (IRE) (Ashford (USA))
1048[11] 1386[7]

Buachaill Eile (IRE) *E McNamara* 110h
6 b g Lord Americo—Suilvaun (Lafontaine (USA))
2690[3]

Buailtes And Fadas (IRE) *E Bolger* 116c
11 bb g Be My Native(USA) —Ballyline Dancer (Giolla Mear)
4434[3]

Bubba Boy (IRE) *P Monteith* 33 h
6 bb g Anshan—Royal Patrol (IRE) (Phardante (FR))
1307[P] 3205[8] 3376[10] 3855[P]

Bubble Boy (IRE) *B G Powell* 97b 118+c
7 ch g Hubbly Bubbly(USA) —Cool Charm (Beau Charmeur (FR))
2828[4] 3481[P] 3698[4]4007[3] 4690[P] (4806) 4906[2] 11[3]

Bubbling Fun *T Wall*
5 b m Marju(IRE) —Blushing Barada (USA) (Blushing Groom (FR))
3355[P]

Buchanan Street (IRE) *R Ford* 13h
5 b g Barathea(IRE) —Please Believe Me (Try My Best (USA))
758[11]

Buckie Briar (IRE) *Mrs H Dalton* 24h
6 ch m Carroll House—Buckie Thistle (IRE) (Buckskin (FR))
4052[10]

Buckland Bobby *M Madgwick* 41h
8 b g Rakaposhi King—Lichen Moss (Le Moss)
3660[P] 4005[P] 4915[8]

Buckland Gold (IRE) *D B Feek* 92 h 49c
6 b g Lord Americo—Beann Ard (IRE) (Mandalus)
1921[11] 2556[F] 2802[P] 3905[2] 4331[P]**4653[7] 4914[F]**

Bucks *Ian Williams* 81+h
9 b g Slip Anchor—Alligram (USA) (Alysheba (USA))
2968[13] 3947[5] 4389[7] 4898[2]

Buck Whaley (IRE) *Jonjo O'Neill* 128 h
6 ch g Fleetwood(IRE) —Kayzarana (IRE) (Generous (IRE))
(3005a) (3383) 4473[F]

Buddhi (IRE) *M Pitman* 91 h
8 b g Be My Native(USA) —Paean Express (IRE) (Paean)
2462[3] 3133[7]

Buddy Girie *P Cornforth* 91c
13 b g Lord Bud—Hatsu-Girie (Ascertain (USA))
123[6] (594)

Bude *S A Brookshaw* 94h 91c
7 gr g Environment Friend—Gay Da Cheen (IRE) (Tenby)
5[10]

Buena Vista (IRE) *M C Pipe* 141h
5 b g In The Wings—Park Special (Relkino)
(457) (654) (804) (1010) 2161[2] 2742[3] 4430[3] 4750[6]

Buffalo Bill (IRE) *A M Hales* 109 h 109+c
10 ch g Be My Native(USA) —Sylvia Fox (Deep Run)
1458[3] 1668[4] 1862[10] **2241[4]2719[F] 2867[2] 3282[5]**4756[3]

Buffers Lane (IRE) *N A Twiston-Davies* 92+h
7 b g Fourstars Allstar(USA) —River Of Wine (River Knight (FR))
1799[9] 2421[5] 3478[P] 3941[P]

Buffy *B Mactaggart* 90h
6 b m Classic Cliche(IRE) —Annie Kelly (Oats)
2497[10] 3231[5] 3442[3] 3795[5] 4346[5]4529[8] 5039[5]

Bugle *Evan Williams* 69b
6 b g Cyrano De Bergerac—Homemaker (Homeboy)
844[10]

Bula's Quest *L G Cottrell* 93b
7 b g Sula Bula—Dinkies Quest (Sergeant Drummer (USA))
277[8]

Buldaan (FR) *W Amos* 53h
4 ch g Muhtathir—Fee Eria (FR) (Always Fair (USA))
3925[12] 4527[15]

Bullies Acre (IRE) *F P Murtagh* 54h
6 b g Arctic Cider(USA) —Clonminch Lady (Le Bavard (FR))
1374[7] 1663[10] **4989[P]**

Bumper (FR) *M C Pipe* 109h
5 b g Cadoudal(FR) —Dame Blonde (FR) (Pampabird)
3500[7] 3664[2] 3842[4] (4036)

Bunkum *R Lee* 109 h 119 c
8 b g Robellino(USA) —Spinning Mouse (Bustino)
353[P] **1978[3] 2325[U]**2813[4] 3018[6] 4105[5]

Bunmahon (IRE) *Mrs John Harrington* 100 h
6 bb g Broken Hearted—Glenpatrick Peach (IRE) (Lafontaine (USA))
1623a[12]

Bureaucrat *P J Hobbs* 132+h
4 b g Machiavellian(USA) —Lajna (Be My Guest (USA))
3355[F] 3787[2] (4211) (4551) 4763[P] 5023[2]

Burgau (IRE) *A D Brown* 70b
7 b g Treasure Kay—Brava (IRE) (Satco (FR))
375[8] 484[7]

Burn Brook *R J Armson* 25h
6 br m Alderbrook—One Of Those Days (Soviet Lad (USA))
655[12] 1048[7] 4615[9]

Burning Moon *K A Morgan*
5 b g Bering—Triple Green (Green Desert (USA))
2249[P]

Burning Question *J S Haldane* 59h
8 ch g Alderbrook—Give Me An Answer (True Song)
5093[P] (Dead)

Burning Truth (USA) *M Sheppard* 115h 115c
12 ch g Known Fact(USA) —Galega (Sure Blade (USA))
248[6] (458) **725[5]** (863) 980[3]1153[9] 1218[P]

Burnside Place *C C Bealby* 50h
6 b m Alderbrook—Knowing (Lochnager)
242[8] 1714[9] 2718[12] (Dead)

Burnt Oak (UAE) *C W Fairhurst* 115+b
4 b g Timber Country(USA) —Anaam (Caerleon (USA))
2068[3] (2521) (3181) 4448[11]

Burntoakboy *Michael Cunningham* 124h 92c
8 b g Sir Harry Lewis(USA) —Sainte Martine (Martinmas)
5059a[9]

Burnt Out (IRE) *B G Powell* 121h
7 ch m Anshan—Lantern Lover (Be My Native (USA))
2053[5] 2240[5] **2846[6] 3218[U]**

Burren Moonshine (IRE) *P Bowen* 102+h
7 ch m Moonax(IRE) —Burren Beauty (IRE) (Phardante (FR))
1992[3] 2271[5] 2990[14] 3508[6] (5068)

Burundi (IRE) *A W Carroll* 120 h 115+c
12 b g Danehill(USA) —Sofala (Home Guard (USA))
5[5] 315[4] 762[7] (1300) (1488)

Burwood Breeze (IRE) *T R George* 100h 128c
10 b g Fresh Breeze(USA) —Shuil Le Cheile (Quayside)
4356[4] 4762[B] 5012[P]

Bush Hill Bandit (IRE) *Mrs Anne-Marie Hays* 94c
11 bb g Executive Perk—Baby Isle (Menelek)
184[4] 4901[F]

Bushido (IRE) *Mrs S J Smith* 124 h 130c
7 br g Brief Truce(USA) —Pheopotstown (Henbit (USA))
465[F] 893[3] (1177) 1342[4] (1568) (1759) 2292[11] **2643[P]**

Bush Park (IRE) *Mrs Monica Tory* 105h 123c
11 b g Be My Native(USA) —By All Means (Pitpan)
4757[6]

Businessmoney Jake *V R A Dartnall* 111+h
5 b g Petoski—Cloverjay (Lir)
1717[U] 1856[6] (2578) (2687) 3286[3] 3993[8] (4756)4961[5]

Business Traveller (IRE) *R J Price* 101+h
6 ch g Titus Livius(FR) —Dancing Venus (Pursuit Of Love)
1977[15] 2466[6] 2731[7] **3356[R]**3458[6] 3997[6] 4453[2] 5010[5]

Buster (IRE) *J Ryan* 83h
7 ch g Presenting—Chez Georges (Welsh Saint)
1565[6] 1921[4] (2181) (Dead)

Buster Collins (IRE) *Miss E C Lavelle* 110+h
6 bb g Alderbrook—Carmen (IRE) (Meneval (USA))
3978[3] 4212[2] (4868)

Bustisu *D J Wintle* 89 h
9 b m Rakaposhi King—Tasmin Gayle (IRE) (Strong Gale)
96[4] 745[2] 913[F] (1192) 1630[3] 2505[6]2862[10] 3279[P]

Bustling Bay *S Gollings*
5 b m Shaddad(USA) —Bustling Around (Bustino)
349[17]

Busy Henry *Jonjo O'Neill* 86+h
6 ch g Busy Flight—Haliguen Royal (Halyudh (USA))
1543[3] 1979[2] 3511[2]

Busy Man (IRE) *J R Jenkins* 58h 25c
7 b g Darnay—Make Or Mar (Daring March)
1237[16] 1565[8] 1818[5] 1991[11] **2807[8]**

Buthaina (IRE) *Mrs L Williamson* 36h
6 b m Bahhare(USA) —Haddeyah (USA) (Dayjur (USA))
1952[5] 2148[P] 2335[8] 2627[F]

Butler's Cabin (FR) *Jonjo O'Neill* 95+h
6 b g Poliglote—Strictly Cool (USA) (Bering)
2823[4] 2983[3] 3425[3] 3545[7]

Butler Services (IRE) *Jonjo O'Neill* 55h
6 b g Muroto—Toevarro (Raga Navarro (ITY))
2075[4] 2288[5] 2455[12] 3591[8] 3800[P]4040[8]

Butsadtohavetogo (IRE) *A E Jones* 86b
6 b g Accordion—Glittering Pan (Pitpan)
1882[7] 2211[18] **2798[P] 3329[P]**

Buttress *M W Easterby* 97+h
7 b g Zamindar(USA) —Furnish (Green Desert (USA))
331[3] 513[3] 936[4]

Buy Onling (IRE) *C J Mann* 75h
5 b g Fourstars Allstar(USA) —Meadow Lane (IRE) (Over The River (FR))
3393[6] 4521[5]

Buz Kiri (USA) *P L Clinton* 80h
8 b g Gulch(USA) —Whitecorners (USA) (Caro)
826[P] 1490[6] 1753[6] 1890[4] 2256[4]2582[3] 3125[2] 3222[4] 3985[9] 4393[5]4734[5] 5069[6]

Buzybakson (IRE) *J R Cornwall* 102 h 91 c
9 bb g Bob Back(USA) —Middle Verde (USA) (Sham (USA))
1615[5] 1893[5] 2293[P]2506[U] 2662[7] 3923[F]4163[6] 4353[9]

By Degree (IRE) *R J Hodges* 125h 123 c
10 gr g Roselier(FR) —Decent Enough (Decent Fellow)
(1984) 2336[P]

Byland *Miss L Day* 53b
6 b g Danzig(USA) —Coxwold (USA) (Cox's Ridge (USA))
2432[14]

By My Side (IRE) *M J Lethbridge* 87h 66c
12 bb g Brush Aside(USA) —Stay As You Are (Buckskin (FR))
171[P]

Bynack Mhor (IRE) *Miss H C Knight* 65b
5 b g Taipan(IRE) —Pride Of Poznan (IRE) (Buzzard's Bay)
179[7]

Bythehokey (IRE) *B P J Baugh* 91h
5 b g Barathea(IRE) —Regal Portrait (IRE) (Royal Academy (USA))
1745[8]

Bywell Beau (IRE) *J I A Charlton* 102h
7 b g Lord Americo—Early Dalus (IRE) (Mandalus)
8[6] 1661[4] 2036[2] 2653[2] 2944[S]3914[5] 4530[P]

Caballe (USA) *M Scudamore* 84h 83+c
9 ch m Opening Verse(USA) —Attirance (FR) (Crowned Prince (USA))
2297[F] 2561[P] 2715[4]

Cabopino Lad (USA) *Miss Tracy Waggott* 27h
4 b g Comic Strip(USA) —Roxanne (USA) (Woodman (USA))
3349[11] 3912[P] 4056[P]

Cabrillo (IRE) *John A Quinn* 83h
5 b m Indian Rocket—Cerosia (Pitskelly)
2950[11] 4015[4] 4388[5] 4805[P]

Cadeaux Rouge (IRE) *D W Thompson* 74+h
5 ch m Croco Rouge(IRE) —Gift Of Glory (FR) (Niniski (USA))
1293[2] 1510[U] 1590[5] 1814[2] 2515[8]

Cadogen Square *Mrs Marjorie Fife* 24h
4 ch f Takhlid(USA) —Mount Park (IRE) (Colonel Collins (USA))
2263[P] 2477[10] 3349[9]

Cadtauri (FR) *Miss H C Knight* 65h 34c
5 bb g Alpha Tauri(FR) —Cadmina (FR) (Cadoudal (FR))
179[9] 1407[P] 3246[4] 3789[11] 4331[P]**4735[7]**

Caesarean Hunter (USA) *R T Phillips* 105h
7 ch g Jade Hunter(USA) —Grey Fay (USA) (Grey Dawn II)
2171[6] (2605) (2750) 2822[2] 3445[9] **4053[P]4288[P] 5107[P]**

Caesar's Palace (GER) *Miss Lucinda V Russell* 94h
9 ch g Lomitas—Caraveine (FR) (Nikos)
304[8] 595[4] 768[10] 1796[2] 2066[4]2417[6] (3209) 3854[12] 4344[4] 4491[F] 4982[6]5068[6]

Caged Tiger *C J Mann* 105h
7 b g Classic Cliche(IRE) —Run Tiger (IRE) (Commanche Run)
3466[3] 4005[5] 4604[3]

Cailin Alainn (IRE) *C Byrnes* 119h
7 br m Mister Lord(USA) —Royal Toombeola (IRE) (Royal Fountain)
(4887a)

Caipiroska *Ferdy Murphy* 66h
7 b g Petoski—Caipirinha (IRE) (Strong Gale)
426[4]

Cala Levante (IRE) *Mrs John Harrington* 100h
5 gr g Supreme Leader—Mondeo Rose (IRE) (Roselier (FR))
5060a[10]

Calamintha *M C Pipe* 117h
6 b m Mtoto—Calendula (Be My Guest (USA))
2053[6]

Calamitycharacter *I McMath* 69h
7 b m Tragic Role(USA) —Shaa Spin (Shaadi (USA))
212[P]

Calatagan (IRE) *J M Jefferson* 129 h 133+c
7 ch g Danzig Connection(USA) —Calachuchi (Martinmas)
1878[5] 2334[2] 2765[7] **(3329)** 3761[10]**(5018)**

Calcar (IRE) *Mrs S Lamyman* 79h
6 b g Flying Spur(AUS) —Poscimur (IRE) (Prince Rupert (FR))
110[7] (Dead)

Calcot Flyer *A King* 89h 99+c
8 br g Anshan—Lady Catcher (Free Boy)
240[3] 2557[U] 3151[4]3791[3] 4837[P]

Calculaite *M Todhunter* 91h
5 b g Komaite(USA) —Miss Calculate (Mummy's Game)
2627[10] 3912[9] 4143[4]

Calfraz *M D Hammond* 100h
4 bb g Tamure(IRE) —Pas De Chat (Relko)
1797[14] 2494[4] 2753[7] (3203) 3539[3] 4143[3]4360[2] 4657[3]

Caliban (IRE) *Ian Williams* 113 h 88c
8 ch g Rainbows For Life(CAN) —Amour Toujours (IRE) (Law Society (USA))
232[2] 284[2] (695) **1147[6]**

Calin Royal (FR) *J Howard Johnson* 88+h
5 ch g Garde Royale—Caline De Froment (FR) (Grand Tresor (FR))
2755[2] 3443[P]

Calladine (IRE) *C Roche* 123h 123c
10 b g Erin's Isle—Motus (Anfield)
3894a[F]

Called To The Bar *Evan Williams* 94+h
13 b g Legal Bwana—Miss Gaylord (Cavo Doro)
353[6] 697[10]

Callherwhatulike (IRE) *Robert Tyner* 104b
5 b m Old Vic—Fleece Alley (IRE) (Brush Aside (USA))
4751[5] 5134a[8]

Calling Brave (IRE) *N J Henderson* 130c
10 ch g Bob Back(USA) —Queenie Kelly (The Parson)
4118[P] 4457[7] 5004[14]5144[7]

Callingwood (IRE) *Ferdy Murphy* 45b
6 ch g Pierre—Clonroche Artic (Pauper)
241[10] 3559[F] 3914[P]

Callitquits (IRE) *Jennie Candlish* 64h
4 b g Desert Story(IRE) —Quits (IRE) (Brief Truce (USA))
4613[8] 4877[10]

Callitwhatyoulike *Miss Kate Milligan*
5 b g Cayman Kai(IRE) —Jamimo (IRE) (Jareer (USA))
484[13]

Call Me Anything (IRE) *D Brace* 101h
7 br g Oscar(IRE) —Beaudel (Fidel)
3478[3]

Call Me Bobbi *Mrs S M Johnson* 76b
7 b m Executive Perk—Call-Me-Dinky (Mart Lane)
349[6] 1961[8]

Call Me Edward (IRE) *N A Twiston-Davies* 88h
5 b g Safety Catch(USA) —Smith's Cross (IRE) (Crash Course)
1975[4] 2426[8] 2815[P] 3997[P]

Call Me Jack (IRE) *M J M Evans* 94h 87c
10 b g Lord Americo—Tawney Rose (Tarqogan)
437[F] 2284[2] 2705[P]3887[F] 4281[8]

Call Of The Seas (IRE) *J G M O'Shea*
7 b g Hymns On High—Mystical Isle (IRE) (Black Minstrel)
133[P] 635[P] 680[5] 861[P] 1107[P]

Call Oscar (IRE) *C Tinkler* 110h
7 b g Oscar(IRE) —Athy Princess (IRE) (Over The River (FR))
131[5] 1908[3] 3354[2] (3842)

Call Out (IRE) *Mrs S Gardner* 84h
6 br g Dr Massini(IRE) —Parsons Storm (IRE) (Glacial Storm (USA))
3881[P] 4285[7] 4494[10] 4942[2]

Callow Lake (IRE) *Mrs John Harrington* 149+h
6 b g Bahhare(USA) —Sharayif (IRE) (Green Desert (USA))
67a[3] 1093a[3] 4951a[2]

Calomeria *D McCain* 111h
5 b m Groom Dancer(USA) —Calendula (Be My Guest (USA))
1443[4] 1658[4] 1906[6] 2314[5] 2625[3]2981[7] 3655[5] **4041[P]** 5039[4]

Calon Lan (IRE) *B J Llewellyn* 98+c
15 b g Bustineto—Cherish (Nashwan (USA))
(725) 975[4] 1620[F]1746[8]

Calorando (IRE) *Anthony Mullins* 130h 119+c
7 b g Green Desert(USA) —Key Change (IRE) (Darshaan)
954a[3] 1093a[4] 1204[7] 1621a[3] **1944a[F]**

Calusa Charlie (IRE) *B G Powell* 120+h
7 b g Old Vic—Star Cream (Star Appeal)
2426[4] 2878[3] 3253[3] 3901[U] 4058[2](4603)

Calver's Conquest *J A B Old* 47b
4 b g El Conquistador—Spinayab (King Of Spain)
4667[11]

Calvic (IRE) *T R George* 104h 135+c
8 ch g Old Vic—Calishee (IRE) (Callernish)
2046[5] 2724[3] 3186[3](3845) 4690[F] (4985)

Camaraderie *A W Carroll* 76h
10 b g Most Welcome—Secret Valentine (Wollow)
681[5] **827[P]**

Cambo (FR) *Miss Sheena West* 96h
5 bb g Mansonnien(FR) —Royal Lie (FR) (Garde Royale)
2212[11] 2421[14] 3659[11] 4564[3] 4824[F]

Cambrian Dawn *Mrs L B Normile*
12 b g Danehill(USA) —Welsh Daylight (Welsh Pageant)
3234[P]

Camdenation (IRE) *J R Jenkins* 94h 90+c
10 b g Camden Town—Out The Nav (IRE) (Over The River (FR))
106[P] 481[5]

Camden Bella *N G Richards* 99 h
6 b m Sir Harry Lewis(USA) —Camden Grove (Uncle Pokey)
(349) 2412[2] (3235) 3484[6] 5064[11]

Camden Carrig (IRE) *Simon Bloss* 112+c
11 bb g Camden Town—Tinnecarrig Grove (Boreen (FR))
(4107) 4471[18]

Camden George (IRE) *Mrs S J Smith* 96+b
5 b g Pasternak—Triple Town Lass (IRE) (Camden Town)
4992[3]

Camden Tanner (IRE) *Robert Tyner* 134h 139c
10 b g Camden Town—Poor Elsie (Crash Course)
3053a[2] 4459[15]

Cameron Bridge (IRE) *P J Hobbs* 108h 140 c
10 b g Camden Town—Arctic Raheen (Over The River (FR))
1265[10] 1434[6] **1561[3]1735[4] 2272[4] 5018[3]**

Camerons Future (IRE) *J A Geake* 73+h
4 b c Indian Danehill(IRE) —Wicken Wonder (IRE) (Distant Relative)
1785[9] 3182[11]

Campaign Charlie *H D Daly* 106h
6 b g Rakaposhi King—Inesdela (Wolver Hollow)
7[6] 3246[3] 3677[8] 4386[2] 5015[5]

Campaign Trail (IRE) *Jonjo O'Neill* 120h 89 c
8 b g Sadler's Wells(USA) —Campestral (USA) (Alleged (USA))
2292[4] **2637[F] 3728[10]3921[7]** 4461[11] 4776[P]

Campbells Lad *A Berry*
5 b g Mind Games—T O O Mamma'S (IRE) (Classic Secret (USA))
991[P]

Camp Hill *J S Haldane* 85c
12 gr g Ra Nova—Baytino (Neltino)
3736[P] 4073[6] 4347[2]4846[P]

Campli (IRE) *M D Hammond* 86b
4 b g Zafonic(USA) —Sept A Neuf (Be My Guest (USA))
4366[4] 5124[2]

Canada Street (IRE) *J Howard Johnson* 100+h
5 b g Old Vic—Saucy Sprite (Balliol)
2106[2] 3789[4] 4582[2] (8)

Canadian Storm *A G Juckes* 94+h
5 gr g With Approval(CAN) —Sheer Gold (USA) (Cutlass (USA))
696[6] 1541[12] 1724[U] 2146[4] 2560[2]2721[7] 3456[4] 4832[6] (1)

Canavan (IRE) *Ferdy Murphy* 86h 110 c
7 gr g Bob Back(USA) —Silver Glen (IRE) (Roselier (FR))
1884[2] 2073[5] **2415[8] 2689[2](3553) 4042[2]** 4372[6] 4453[P] (Dead)

Can Can Flyer (IRE) *J C Tuck* 88+h
5 ch g In The Wings—Can Can Lady (Anshan)
100[10] 504[P] 3423[8] (4570)

Candarli (IRE) *D R Gandolfo* 115 h
10 ch g Polish Precedent(USA) —Calounia (IRE) (Pharly (FR))
1633[7] 2459[2] 2716[9] (3944)

Candlelight Valley (IRE) *P J Hobbs* 81 h
7 b g Supreme Leader—Curragh Breeze (Furry Glen)
2301[7] 2865[5] 3253[10] 3613[5]

Cane Brake (IRE) *David Wachman* 122+h 118c
7 b g Sadler's Wells(USA) —Be My Hope (IRE) (Be My Native (USA))
3053a[P] 3587a[P] 4123a[5]5080a[P]

Canis Lupus *J A T De Giles* 29b
5 ch g Wolfhound(USA) —Gopi (Marju (IRE))
1237[12]

Canni Thinkaar (IRE) *P Butler* 82+h
5 b g Alhaarth(IRE) —Cannikin (IRE) (Lahib (USA))
1760[5] 2017[4] 2556[P] 3899[9] 4010[P]

Cannon Bridge (IRE) *Mrs C Williams* 70h 114+c
8 ch g Definite Article—Hit For Six (Tap On Wood)
(5109)

Cannon Fire (FR) *Evan Williams* 109h
5 ch h Grand Lodge(USA) —Muirfield (FR) (Crystal Glitters (USA))
229[F] 334[5] (614) 949[3] 1040[2] (1099) 1181[4]1434[3] 1675[4] 5[2]

Canny Scot *R Curtis* 90+h
9 b g Slip Anchor—Pomade (Luthier)
283[P]

Canon Barney (IRE) *Jonjo O'Neill* 111h 107c
11 bb g Salluceva—Debbie's Candy (Candy Cane)
974[P] (Dead)

Cansalrun (IRE) *R H Alner* 96h 98+c
7 b m Anshan—Monamandy (IRE) (Mandalus)
568[2] 1491[3] 1596[3] **1716[4]2297[4] 2526[2]**

Cantarinho *D J Kemp* 120 c
8 b g Alderbrook—Hot Hostess (Silly Season)
3960[2]

Cantbeatheyouth (IRE) *Noel Meade* 89h
7 b m Old Vic—Elegant Kate (IRE) (Good Thyne (USA))
1116a[11]

Cantemerle (IRE) *W M Brisbourne* 86+h
6 b m Bluebird(USA) —Legally Delicious (Law Society (USA))
1[P]

Canterbury Bell *P D Niven* 20h
6 b m Bishop Of Cashel—Old Flower (Persian Bold)
14[8]

Cantgeton (IRE) *M C Pipe* 127h
6 b g Germany(USA) —Lahana (IRE) (Rising)
178[6] 912[3] (1123) (1445) 1481[6] 1675[3] (1878)2207[6] 2990[7] 3360[4]

Can't Wack It *R H Alner* 84b
6 b g Relief Pitcher—Lonicera (Sulaafah (USA))
5117[5]

Capacoostic *Miss H E Roberts* 51h
9 ch m Savahra Sound—Cocked Hat Girl (Ballacashtal (CAN))
75[11]

Cap Classique *Mrs H Dalton* 87+h
7 b g Classic Cliche(IRE) —Champenoise (Forzando)
490[11] 811[6] 977[U] 1410[3] 1539[P]

Cape Guard *F Jordan* 41h
4 b g Benny The Dip(USA) —Cape Siren (Warning)
2014[4] 2425[12] 3579[11] 4521[8]

Caper *R Hollinshead* 92h 83c
6 b g Salse(USA) —Spinning Mouse (Bustino)
352[4] 614[2] 724[6] 1028[5] 1153[8]1280[U] 1539[4] 1648[4] 1751[4] **3888[5]4164[P] 4876[3] 5071[6]**

Cape Stormer (IRE) *Mrs C M Gorman* 109 h 113c
11 b g Be My Native(USA) —My Sunny South (Strong Gale)
280[3]

Cape Teal (IRE) *D Brace* 94h 25c
7 b g Sharifabad(IRE) —Careful Minstrel (Black Minstrel)
5109[U]

Capitana (GER) *N J Henderson* 127+h
5 ch m Lando(GER) —Capitolina (FR) (Empery (USA))
78[5] (2726) 2940[2] 3128[3] (4736)

Cappacurry (IRE) *Evan Williams* 50h
7 b g Taos(IRE) —Lompoa (Lomond (USA))
1487[P] 1560[P] 1636[9]

Cappanrush (IRE) *A Ennis* 83+h
6 gr g Medaaly—Introvert (USA) (Exbourne (USA))
230[6] (1896) 2261[7] 2950[8] 3286[6]

Caprice Du Hasard (FR) *E Leray*
8 b g Pure Hasard(FR) —Etoile Du Ponsac (FR) (Shafaraz (FR))
(362a)

Capricorn *Miss L Day*
8 b g Minster Son—Loch Scavaig (IRE) (The Parson)
3876[10] **4394[P]** 4526[P] **4643[P]**

Captain Aubrey (IRE) *J A B Old* 93b
7 b g Supreme Leader—Hamers Girl (IRE) (Strong Gale)
2127[F]

Captain Cloudy *Miss Sheena West* 97+h
6 b g Whittingham(IRE) —Money Supply (Brigadier Gerard)
863[2] 973[2] 1046[5] (1246) (1408) 1456[4]

Captain Corelli *P J Hobbs* 105h 149 c
9 b g Weld—Deaconess (The Parson)
2176[8] (2628) 3345[3]

Captain Flinders (IRE) *Miss H C Knight* 101h
9 b g Satco(FR) —Auburn Queen (Kinglet)
128[6] 384[3]

Captain Mac (IRE) *E McNamara* 103h 110+c
7 b g Witness Box(USA) —Shesamystery (Side Track)
1741[3] (2692)

Captain Machell (IRE) *Andrew Turnell* 69h 78c
8 bb g King's Ride—Flying Silver (Master Buck)
4802[4] 5049[P]

Captain Marlon (IRE) *C L Tizzard* 103b
5 b g Supreme Leader—Marlonette (IRE) (Jareer (USA))
3001[5] 3617[2] 4011[3] 4574[9]

Captain Miller *N J Henderson* 109+h
10 b g Batshoof—Miller's Gait (Mill Reef (USA))
2103[8]

Captain Ron (IRE) *S Lycett* 58h 54c
10 b g Marju(IRE) —Callas Star (Chief Singer)
47[F] 221[P]

Captain Saif *N Wilson* 63h
6 b g Compton Place—Bahawir Pour (USA) (Green Dancer (USA))
870[10]

Captain's Leap (IRE) *L Lungo* 72h
10 ch g Grand Plaisir(IRE) —Ballingowan Star (Le Moss)
2171[P] 3853[9]

Captain's Legacy *D B Feek* 98h
5 b g Bob's Return(IRE) —Tuppence In Clover (Petoski)
3219[P] 4649[2] 4868[7]

Captain Smoothy *M J Gingell* 82h
6 b g Charmer—The Lady Captain (Neltino)
1991[P] 2584[7] 2967[7] 3592[P]

Captains Table *F Jordan* 116c
13 b g Welsh Captain—Wensum Girl (Ballymoss)
2248[7] 2583[5] 2926[P]

Captain Windsor (IRE) *P F Nicholls* 80+h
5 ch g Windsor Castle—Change The Pace (IRE) (Lancastrian)
4284[5]

Captain Zinzan (NZ) *L A Dace* 80h
11 b g Zabeel(NZ) —Lady Springfield (NZ) (Sharivari (USA))
4821[P] 5[8]

Capybara (IRE) *H P Hogarth* 106h 120 c
8 b g Commanche Run—The Pledger (Strong Gale)
(2023) 2265[3] 2965[5]3560[9] 4315[2] **4518[P]4790[P]**
5064[3] 5093[4]

Caracciola (GER) *N J Henderson* 139 h 150c
9 b g Lando(GER) —Capitolina (FR) (Empery (USA))
450[13] (1919) **2489[9]** 2765[5] **4472[8]5006[5]**

Caraman (IRE) *J J Quinn* 115h
8 ch h Grand Lodge(USA) —Caraiyma (IRE) (Shahrastani (USA))
2765[9] 2964[U] 3967[3] 4420[2]

Carapuce (FR) *L Lungo* 117 h 112 c
7 ch g Bigstone(IRE) —Treasure City (FR) (Moulin)
121[4] 2706[3] 3208[2] 3384[5] 4364[6]4792[U] 4982[5]

Carbonado *H R Tuck* 96c
12 b g Anshan—Virevoite (Shareef Dancer (USA))
51[5]

Carbury Cross (IRE) *Jonjo O'Neill* 88 c
12 b g Mandalus—Brickey Gazette (Fine Blade (USA))
3921[P]

Cardi Lyn *Mrs D A Hamer*
6 b g Awesome—Amany (IRE) (Waajib)
1042[14]

Cardinal Sinn (UAE) *M Pitman* 88+b
5 ch g Gulch(USA) —Ines Bloom (IRE) (Sadler's Wells (USA))
2075[2] 2565[8] 4637[7]

Card'Son (FR) *B Secly* 117h
4 ch c Mansonnien(FR) —Cardwell (FR) (Gift Card (FR))
2085a[2] (4548a)

Carew Lad *Mrs D A Hamer* 112+h
10 b g Arzanni—Miss Skindles (Taufan (USA))
3611[3] 3882[7] (4372) 4727[11]

Caribbean Cove (IRE) *Miss Venetia Williams* 109 h 103 c
8 gr g Norwich—Peaceful Rose (Roselier (FR))
150[6] 1670[5] 1819[4](3676) 4476[5] 4906[6]5090[5]

Caribou (FR) *O Sherwood* 111+h
4 b g Epervier Bleu—Cardoudalle (FR) (Cadoudal (FR))
(2580) 3182[4] (4795)

Carlesimo (IRE) *Noel Meade* 120h 118c
8 bb g Erin's Isle—Diamond Display (IRE) (Shardari)
1790a[5]

Carl's Boy *D A Rees* 75h 57c
10 ch g Itsu(USA) —Adelbaran (FR) (No Pass No Sale)
105[7] 298[2] 519[3] **4164[7]**4734[7] 5048[8]

Carlton Scroop (FR) *J Jay*
3 ch g Priolo(USA) —Elms Schooldays (Emarati (USA))
4298a[P]

Carluccios Quest *Mrs H Dalton* 73h
8 gr g Terimon—Jindabyne (Good Times (ITY))
94[F] 351[4]

Carly Bay *G P Enright* 109+h
8 b m Carlton(GER) —Polly Minor (Sunley Builds)
2218[P] 2576[P] 2802[3] 3185[10] 3901[4]4151[2] 4652[6]
4912[4]

Carlys Quest *Ferdy Murphy* 142h
12 ch g Primo Dominie—Tuppy (USA) (Sharpen Up)
(90a) 1925[P] 2175[15] 2490[5] 3020[6] 3389[10]3970[2]
4461[15] 4745[6] 5101a[8]

Carnacrack *Miss S E Forster* 95c
12 b g Le Coq D'Or—Carney (New Brig)
421[2] 554[2] (989)

Carndale (IRE) *Noel Meade* 106c
9 b g Black Monday—Inamuddle (IRE) (Lafontaine (USA))
112a[3]

Carneys Cross (IRE) *S J Treacy* 108h 130c
8 b g Kahyasi—Cityjet (IRE) (Orchestra)
69a[P] 3053a[15]

Carnival Town *Jonjo O'Neill* 90b
5 b g Classic Cliche(IRE) —One Of Those Days (Soviet Lad (USA))
2961[5] 3963[P] 4280[P]

Carnt Spell *J T Stimpson* 71h
5 b g Wizard King—Forever Shineing (Glint Of Gold)
1794[8] 2006[4] 2179[7] 2462[7] 2816[9]4080[P] 4640[7]

Caroline's Rose *A P Jones* 69+h
8 br m Fraam—Just Rosie (Sula Bula)
279[U] 3333[P]

Carpe Momentum (USA) *R C Guest* 49h
7 b g Marlin(USA) —Carsona (USA) (Carson City (USA))
2444[18] 2749[12] 2901[8] 3167[9]

Carpenters Boy *C Roberts* 76b
6 b g Nomination—Jolly Girl (Jolly Me)
73[P]

Carpet Ride *B G Powell* 72h
4 ch g Unfuwain(USA) —Fragrant Oasis (USA) (Rahy (USA))
4211[10] 4327[U] 4416[6] 4903[7] 5022[F]

Carraig (IRE) *Evan Williams* 78+h
4 b f Orpen(USA) —Rose Of Mooncoin (IRE) (Brief Truce (USA))
1594[6] 2501[3] 3291[P] 3550[P] 5019[8]

Carriacou *Dermot Day* 90h
5 b m Mark Of Esteem(IRE) —Cockatoo Island (High Top)
66a[17]

Carriage Ride (IRE) *N G Richards* 87h 100+c
8 b g Tidaro(USA) —Casakurali (Gleason (USA))
546[2] 989[P] 4722[5]

Carrickbrack (IRE) *D Broad*
6 b m Grand Plaisir(IRE) —Becky's Angel (IRE) (Le Bavard (FR))
93a[25]

Carrickerry (IRE) *Michael Hourigan* 81h
6 ch g Fourstars Allstar(USA) —Joli's Girl (Mansingh (USA))
1882[10]

Carricklee Boy (IRE) *Mrs L C Jewell* 93h 30c
9 bb g Jurado(USA) —Garland (Night Star)
4522[3]

Carroll's O'Tully (IRE) *L A Dace* 68+h
6 b m Carroll House—Miss O'Tully (IRE) (Fidel)
2720[11] 2928[P] 3281[3] 3437[8] 3656[3]4133[P] 4734[8]

Carry Duff *Ferdy Murphy* 79+h
5 b g Deploy—Pink Brief (IRE) (Ela-Mana-Mou)
4803[6]

Carte Sauvage (USA) *M F Harris* 107+h
5 rg g Kris S(USA) —See You (USA) (Gulch (USA))
1480[4] 1642[4] 1745[2] 1880[9] 2147[5]4832[8]

Carthago (IRE) *Miss T McCurrich* 83h
9 b g Roselier(FR) —Hi Cousin (Condorcet (FR))
2182[6] 4549[5] 4874[3]

Carthalawn (IRE) *C Byrnes* 112h
5 ch g Foxhound(USA) —Pohutakawa (FR) (Affirmed (USA))
1623a[2] 5059a[10]

Carthys Cross (IRE) *T R George* 109 h 121 c
7 ch g Moscow Society(USA) —Sweet Tarquin (Lucifer (USA))
2213[3] 2516[2] 2959[3]3506[P]

Cartier Opera *Miss Venetia Williams* 50h
6 ch g Zilzal(USA) —Slipper (Suave Dancer (USA))
3133[13] 4128[11]

Carvilla (IRE) *Mrs B Ansell* 74h 20c
11 b g Cardinal Flower—Villawood (Quayside)
404[8]

Casadei (IRE) *T G McCourt* 99h 98c
7 ch h Great Commotion(USA) —Inishmot (IRE) (Glenstal (USA))
1728[5]

Casalani (IRE) *Jennie Candlish* 81h
7 br m Fourstars Allstar(USA) —Brandy Hill Girl (Green Shoon)
1611[11] 2937[P] 3843[P] 4071[3] **4659[6]4921[B] 4989[F]**

Casalese *M D Hammond* 73h
4 ch g Wolfhound(USA) —Little Redwing (Be My Chief (USA))
1512[6] 1718[14] 2167[P]

Casas (IRE) *J R Norton* 65h
9 b g Tenby—Clodagh (Thatching)
11[13] 2188[U] 2582[P] 3147[P] 4487[11]5015[P]

Case Equal (IRE) *N J Hawke* 69+h
6 b g Accordion—Gaye Humour (IRE) (Montelimar (USA))
913[5] 978[F] 3211[P] 3325[9]

Casewick Mist *J M Jefferson* 97+b
6 ch m Primitive Rising(USA) —Buckmist Blue (IRE) (Buckskin (FR))
(5141)

Cash And Carry (IRE) *E J O'Grady* 119h 115c
8 b g Norwich—Little And Often (IRE) (Roselier (FR))
117a[12] **1626a[3] 1790a[RR]**

Cash And New (IRE) *R T Phillips* 104h
7 b m Supreme Leader—Shannon Lough (IRE) (Deep Run)
2503[3] 3149[2] (3443) 4619[P] 4982[3]

Cash Back *J D Frost* 85b
6 b g Bob's Return(IRE) —Connie's Pet (National Trust)
4667[6] 4947[8]

Cashbar *J R Fanshawe* 86h
5 b m Bishop Of Cashel—Barford Sovereign (Unfuwain (USA))
4074[6]

Cash Bonanza (IRE) *N G Richards* 98+h 81c
6 ch g Beneficial—Vulcash (IRE) (Callernish)
3205[10] 3914[P] **4844[6]**

Cash Converter (IRE) *R T Phillips* 87h
8 ch g Houmayoun(FR) —Golden Symphony (Le Moss)
384[P]

Cashel Dancer *S A Brookshaw* 105+h
7 b m Bishop Of Cashel—Dancing Debut (Polar Falcon (USA))
329[8] 460[3] 1804[P] 2940[14] 3247[8]

Cashema (IRE) *D R MacLeod* 58+h
5 b m Cape Cross(IRE) —Miss Shema (USA) (Gulch (USA))
302[9] 3267[9] 3488[9] 4141[P]

Cash King (IRE) *Mrs S J Smith* 106h
6 b g Beneficial—On The Bridle (IRE) (Mandalus)
2192[6] 2631[P] 2923[6] 3173[2] (3559)

Cash Man (IRE) *Mrs E Slack* 94b
5 b g Flemensfirth(USA) —Bollero (IRE) (Topanoora)
4519[5]

Cash 'n Carrots *R C Harper* 21h
7 b g Missed Flight—Rhiannon (Welsh Pageant)
743[9]

Cash On (IRE) *P F Nicholls* 75h
4 ch g Spectrum(IRE) —Lady Lucre (IRE) (Last Tycoon)
4665[4] 5115[2]

Cash On Friday *R C Guest* 78b
5 b g Bishop Of Cashel—Til Friday (Scottish Reel)
375[3]

Cash Return *Mrs S Lamyman* 73h
7 b m Bob's Return(IRE) —We'Re In The Money (Billion (USA))
185[7] 613[3] 905[8] 1112[2] 1213[4]1490[11] 1607[5] 1818[P]

Casisle *Mary Meek*
5 ch m Wootton Rivers(USA) —Isle Maree (Star Appeal)
569[11] 811[9] 982[P] 1085[10]

Caspers Case *P F Nicholls* 100h 100c
13 gr g Neltino—Casket (Pannier)
204[F] (763)

Caspian Dusk *W G M Turner* 93h
5 b g Up And At 'Em—Caspian Morn (Lugana Beach)
1804[8] 1977[4] 2150[15] 2419[11] 2734[4]2845[P]

Cassia Green *P H Morris* 98c
12 gr g Scallywag—Casa's Star (Top Star)
221[5] 348[P]

Cassia Heights *S A Brookshaw* 79h 115c
11 b g Montelimar(USA) —Cloncoose (IRE) (Remainder Man)
150[P] 330[3] 765[3]2003[7] 2368[5] (2583) 2938[8] 3728[9]
4617[9]4957[9]

Cassius Dio (IRE) *J Wade* 51b
4 ch g Anshan—Roisin Beag (IRE) (Cardinal Flower)
5124[11]

Casterflo *W S Coltherd* 75h
7 b m Primitive Rising(USA) —Celtic Sands (Celtic Cone)
210[8] 320[7] (601) 649[3] 718[2]

Castle Arrow (IRE) *Miss R Williams* 72h 83c
13 b g Mansooj—Soulful (So Blessed)
400[P] 4107[P]

Castleboy (IRE) *P J Hobbs* 59h
8 b g King's Ride—Bissie's Jayla (Zambrano)
206[P]

Castle Dargan (IRE) *Mrs A M Thorpe* 90b
7 b g Arctic Cider(USA) —Carramore Lady (IRE) (Celio Rufo)
1600[2]

Castleford (IRE) *Mrs T R Kinsey* 95+h 92c
8 b g Be My Native(USA) —Commanche Bay (IRE) (Commanche Run)
282[8]

Castle Frome (IRE) *A E Price* 54h 86c
7 b g Spectrum(IRE) —Vendimia (Dominion)
2249[13] 2803[10] **3920[3] 4164[F]**4830[8]

Castlemainevillage (IRE) *M R Bosley* 84b
6 b g Supreme Leader—Jennys Castle (Carlingford Castle)
(266) 1882[16]

Castlemore (IRE) *P J Hobbs* 102h 110+c
8 b g Be My Native(USA) —Parsonetta (The Parson)
244[6] (1638) 1858[4]2151[F] 5046[4]

Castle Oliver (IRE) *A J Chamberlain* 80c
8 u g Andretti—Red City Rose (IRE) (Roselier (FR))
1109[F] 1446[P] 1631[P]1776[P] 4936[P]

Castle Richard (IRE) *G M Moore* 102h 111c
9 gr g Sexton Blake—Miss McCormick (IRE) (Roselier (FR))
2452[3] 2944[9] 3445[7]

Castle River (USA) *O O'Neill* 102+h
7 b g Irish River(FR) —Castellina (USA) (Danzig Connection (USA))
571[6] 726[7] 1250[8] 1400[3] 1458[5]1651[4] 1743[P] (Dead)

Castlerueanna (IRE) *G M O'Neill* 59c
14 b g Farhaan—Royal Party (Royal Buck)
5128a[11]

Castleshane (IRE) *S Gollings* 136h
9 b g Kris—Ahbab (IRE) (Ajdal (USA))
99[4] 766[6] 824[4] 947[3] 1179[2]1823[9]

Castletown Lad *M C Pipe* 41h
6 b g Afzal—Once Bitten (Brave Invader (USA))
2269[11] 2606[10] 2803[12] 3130[F] 3246[10]

Catalan Girl *Miss E J Murray*
7 ch m Lancastrian—Miss Vagabond (Scallywag)
5053[P]

Catalpa Cargo (IRE) *E Sheehy* 122h 145c
12 b g Buckskin(FR) —Money For Honey (New Brig)
3587a[P]

Catchthebug (IRE) *Jonjo O'Neill* 114+h
7 b g Lord Americo—Just A Maid (Rarity)
(971) (1097) **1489[F]**

Catch The Bus (IRE) *Mrs K Smyly* 86 c
9 b g Eurobus—Careful Biddy (IRE) (Buckskin (FR))
281[4] 3805[7]

Catch The Perk (IRE) *Miss Lucinda V Russell* 108h 127c
9 b g Executive Perk—Kilbally Quilty (IRE) (Montelimar (USA))
321[3] 1526[2] (1587) **(1798) 2189[P]2745[8]** 4852[3]
5094[5]

Catfish Hunter *Mrs L P Baker*
6 b g Safawan—Secret Account (Blakeney)
3425[P] (Dead)

Cathedral Rock (IRE) *N J Gifford* 95+b
4 b g New Frontier(IRE) —Cathadubh (IRE) (Naheez (USA))
4622[4]

Cathkin Lad (IRE) *John G Carr* 78h
7 ch g Fourstars Allstar(USA) —Judys View (King's Ride)
859[P] (Dead)

Caucasian (IRE) *Ian Williams* 75h
8 gr g Leading Counsel(USA) —Kemal's Princess (Kemal (FR))
137[F] 288[P] 860[9]913[10]

Caught At Dawn (IRE) *M H Weston* 130c
12 b g Supreme Leader—Pharisee (IRE) (Phardante (FR))
(51) 280[5] 453[P]842[2] 4471[19] 4748[20]

Caulkleys Bank *M W Easterby* 90+h
6 b g Slip Anchor—Mayroni (Bustino)
2967[5] 3168[4] 3393[4] 4585[4]

Cava Bien *B J Llewellyn* 106+h
4 b g Bien Bien(USA) —Bebe De Cham (Tragic Role (USA))
2069[7] 2286[4] 2580[2] 3021[9] 3436[3]3719[8] 4616[2]

Caveman *O Brennan* 86h 86+c
6 b g Primitive Rising(USA) —Ferneyhill Lady (Menelek)
2427[3] 2956[7] 3328[16] **5139[6]**

Cave Of The Giant (IRE) *T D McCarthy* 113h
4 b g Giant's Causeway(USA) —Maroussie (FR) (Saumarez)
1948[3] 2612[3] 3436[4] 3722[5] 4616[3]4905[2]

Cavers Glen *A C Whillans* 80b
4 b g Overbury(IRE) —Thorterdykes Lass (IRE) (Zaffaran (USA))
3799[9] 4319[2] 4588[9] 5008[8]

Caymanas Bay *A Parker* 36h
6 ch g Karinga Bay—Carribean Sound (Good Times (ITY))
2942[P]

Cayman Calypso (IRE) *Mrs P Sly* 92+h
5 ro g Danehill Dancer(IRE) —Warthill Whispers (Grey Desire)
3545[8] 3962[5] 4389[5] 14[2]

Caymans Gift *A C Whillans* 50h
6 ch g Cayman Kai(IRE) —Gymcrak Cyrano (IRE) (Cyrano De Bergerac)
2169[9] 4145[F]

Ceannairceach (IRE) *J M Jefferson* 119c
13 b g Strong Gale—Balingale (Balinger)
(894) 1012[2] 1221[6]1666[5] 1795[P] 2570[5]

Ceart Go Leor (IRE) *Richard Francis O'Gorman* 100h 92c
9 b m Montelimar(USA) —Bold Empress (Decent Fellow)
4887a[F]

Cedar *R Dickin* 80h 81+c
9 gr g Absalom—Setai's Palace (Royal Palace)
23[P] **95[4]**

Cedar Chief *K Tork* 88 c
9 b g Saddlers' Hall(IRE) —Dame Ashfield (Grundy)
1038[3] 1086[F] 1219[3]1271[2] 4090[5] 4356[6]

Cedar Rangers (USA) *G F Edwards* 83 h
8 b g Anabaa(USA) —Chelsea (USA) (Miswaki (USA))
802[P] (Dead)

Cedar Rapids (IRE) *H P Hogarth* 85h 93 c
6 bb g Lord Americo—Amys Girl (IRE) (Pauper)
1915[7] 2295[9] 2497[0] 3232[4] **(3562) 3784[3] 4454[P]**
5036[8]

Cedrus Libani (IRE) *J Howard Johnson* 81h
5 b h Beneficial—Cedar Castle (IRE) (Castle Keep)
4917[4]

Ceeawayhome *John E Kiely* 119 h
7 b g Nomadic Way(USA) —Dame Scarlet (Blakeney)
2782a[5] 3772a[5]

Cee Moor Biscuits *Mrs A Price*
6 ch g Young Ern—Cee Beat (Bairn (USA))
685[14]

Cehix Des Mottes (FR) *L Viel*
9 b g Abonski(FR) —Bilix (FR) (Bellypha)
1372a[3]

Ceiriog Valley *P R Webber* 35h
4 b f In The Wings—Bodfari Quarry (Efisio)
3645[13]

Celebration Town (IRE) *Miss E C Lavelle* 105h
107+c
9 bb g Case Law—Battle Queen (Kind Of Hush)
104[5] (511) 815[8]

Celestial Gold (IRE) *M C Pipe* 171+c
8 br g Persian Mews—What A Queen (King's Ride)
4470[U] (4746)

Celestial Heights (IRE) *O Sherwood* 88h
7 b g Fourstars Allstar(USA) —Aon Dochas (IRE) (Strong Gale)
501[10]

Celestial Wave (IRE) *Adrian Maguire* 130+h
6 b m Taipan(IRE) —Blossom World (IRE) (The Parson)
(3110a) 4887a[2]

Celia's High (IRE) *D McCain* 44h 75c
7 br g Hymns On High—Celia's Fountain (IRE) (Royal Fountain)
2653[9] **2978[P] 3460[6]4047[8] 4300[5] 4553[8]4989[4]**

Celioso (IRE) *Mrs S J Smith* 94h 123c
9 b g Celio Rufo—Bettons Rose (Roselier (FR))
2841[F] 3560[U] 4374[10]4636[P] 4985[P]

Cellarmaster (IRE) *K J Condon* 112h
5 ch g Alhaarth(IRE) —Cheeky Weeky (Cadeaux Genereux)
4951a[15]

Celtic Blaze (IRE) *B S Rothwell* 100h 100+c
7 b m Charente River(IRE) —Firdaunt (Tanfirion)
397[3] 1341[8] **(1888) 2267[4]2526[4] 2982[F]**
3318[10]3561[9] **4041[6]** 4920[4]5137[8]

Celtic Boy (IRE) *P Bowen* 125h 142+c
8 b g Arctic Lord—Laugh Away (Furry Glen)
239[U] (486) 728[3](857) 1013[F] (1234) **(1531) 1735[F] 2052[P]**

Celtic Flame *O Brennan* 65+h
7 ch m Bold Fox—Annie Bee (Rusticaro (FR))
2446[14] 2720[15] 5052[11]

Celtic Flow *C R Wilson* 68h 75c
8 b m Primitive Rising(USA) —Celtic Lane (Welsh Captain)
1723[8] **(1886) 2413[3] 2978[4]3444[2] 3930[7] 4845[6]**

Celtic Jem (IRE) *P Bowen* 42h
6 b g Norwich—Running Board (IRE) (Deep Run)
138[2] 2487[12] 2860[11] 3248[P]

Celtic Legend (FR) *K G Reveley* 93+h 103+c
7 br g Celtic Swing—Another Legend (USA) (Lyphard's Wish (FR))
84[6] 279[5] 429[6] **511[4]690[6]** (2191) **2570[2] 2719[U]2842[6] 3272[3] 3370[4]**

Celtic Major (IRE) *P Bowen* 93h 64c
8 gr g Roselier(FR) —Dun Oengus (IRE) (Strong Gale)
2130[5] 3345[P] **3499[F] 3815[9]**

Celtic Pride (IRE) *Jennie Candlish* 72 c
11 gr g Roselier(FR) —Grannie No (Brave Invader (USA))
1907[9] 2143[8] 2863[6]

Celtic Prince (IRE) *Miss H Lewis* 80+h
8 gr g Old Vic—No Slow (King's Ride)
4935[6] 5106[5]

Celtic Realm (IRE) *K G Reveley* 49b
4 b g Celtic Swing—Recherchee (Rainbow Quest (USA))
1785[10] 2521[11]

Celtic Romance *Ms Sue Smith* 79h
7 b m Celtic Swing—Southern Sky (Comedy Star (USA))
238[9] 574[4] 747[4] 947[13]

Celtic Ross (IRE) *Robert Tyner* 92c
10 gr g Toulon—Auction Piece (IRE) (Auction Ring (USA))
112a[F]

Celtic Ruffian (IRE) *R Rowe* 75h
8 b g Celio Rufo—Candid Lady (Arctic Lord)
229[5] 665[3] (Dead)

Celtic Saloon (IRE) *K G Reveley* 45h
4 b g Celtic Swing—Lasting Chance (USA) (American Chance (USA))
2642[7] 3273[6] 3786[11]

Celtic Society (IRE) *P C Ritchens* 83b
5 ch g Moscow Society(USA) —Final Peace (IRE) (Satco (FR))
3691[4] 4554[10]

Celtic Son (FR) *M C Pipe* 142 h 152 c
7 b g Celtic Arms(FR) —For Kicks (FR) (Top Ville)
(2052) 2165[2] 2759[4]3341[4] 3995[2] 4456[14]

Celtic Star (IRE) *Mrs L Williamson* 109+h 100c
8 b g Celtic Swing—Recherchee (Rainbow Quest (USA))
4[10] 360[7] 505[P]841[12] **989[6] 1267[4]1406[2] 1524[5] 1620[6]**

Celtic Starlight *R Dickin*
7 gr m Arzanni—Celtic Berry (Celtic Cone)
4642[7]

Celtic Vision (IRE) *P C Haslam* 64h
10 b g Be My Native(USA) —Dream Run (Deep Run)
4878[P]

Cemgraft *A J Lidderdale* 97h
5 b m In The Wings—Soviet Maid (IRE) (Soviet Star (USA))
4129[2] 4425[4]

Central House *D T Hughes* 139h 163c
9 b g Alflora(IRE) —Fantasy World (Kemal (FR))
41a[5] (2230a) (2786a) 3051a[3] 3527a[4] (3774a) 4445[4] 4761[R] 5057a[3]

Ceoperk (IRE) *D J Wintle* 97h
7 ch m Executive Perk—Golden Mela (Golden Love)
3906[3] 4324[2] (4801)

Ceresfield (NZ) *R C Guest* 99h 112+c
10 br m Westminster(NZ) —Audrey Rose (NZ) (Blue Razor (USA))
615[4] 1746[7] 2257[9]

Cerium (FR) *P F Nicholls* 133 h 142 c
5 b g Vaguely Pleasant(FR) —Tantatura (FR) (Akarad (FR))
(1958) (2371) 2634[3](3695) 4431[10] 4774[P]

C'Est La Vie *Miss J E Foster* 63h
4 ch f Bering—Action De Grace (USA) (Riverman (USA))
3038[P] 3786[9] 4987[8]

Cetshwayo *J M P Eustace*
4 ch g Pursuit Of Love—Induna (Grand Lodge (USA))
4057[7] 4551[11]

Cetti's Warbler *Mrs P Robeson* 98 h 111+c
8 gr m Sir Harry Lewis(USA) —Sedge Warbler (Scallywag)
1907[7] 2210[9]

Chabrimal Minster *R Ford* 104 h 116 c
9 b g Minster Son—Bromley Rose (Rubor)
333[2] (1848) 2180[2]2675[2] 3336[5] 3845[4](4095) 4328[4] 4518[4]5037[3]

Cha Cha Cha Dancer *G A Swinbank* 85h
6 ch g Groom Dancer(USA) —Amber Fizz (USA) (Effervescing (USA))
3171[11] 3487[10] **3794[U] 4053[P]**4797[P]

Chaga *W Jenks* 40b
5 b m Hector Protector(USA) —Santarem (USA) (El Gran Senor (USA))
1323[12] 1674[7]

Chailand (CZE) *Martina Ruzickova*
9 br g Friedland(USA) —Chalinia (POL) (Skunks (POL))
1710a[U]

Chaim (IRE) *Mrs L Wadham* 109+b
4 bb g Lord Americo—Furry Gran (Furry Glen)
(4500) 4779[10]

Chain *O Brennan* 94h 79+c
9 b g Last Tycoon—Trampship (High Line)
4900[5] 5140[5]

Chairmanforlife *J Motherway* 97b
5 b g Bob Back(USA) —Aunt Sadie (Pursuit Of Love)
5060a[4]

Chakra *C J Gray* 107+h
12 gr g Mystiko(USA) —Maracuja (USA) (Riverman (USA))
389[P] 1188[5] 1223[10] 1381[11]

Chamacco (FR) *M F Harris* 93h
6 b g Cadoudal(FR) —Awentina (FR) (Caerwent)
2928[3] 3425[5] 3733[3] 3943[P]

Champagne Harry *N A Twiston-Davies* 134h 120 c
8 b g Sir Harry Lewis(USA) —Sparkling Cinders (Netherkelly)
207[7] 814[6] (871) 1039[6] 1234[2]

Champagneism (IRE) *R A Wernham* 35b
9 b g Euphemism—Champagne Annie (Silly Season)
51[F]

Champagne Native (IRE) *D Broad* 79h 97c
12 b g Be My Native(USA) —The Race Fly (Pollerton)
4748[12]

Champagne Rossini (IRE) *M C Chapman* 54h
4 b g Rossini(USA) —Alpencrocus (IRE) (Waajib)
945[F] 1338[P] 2258[10] 2753[14] 3817[P]3956[3]

Champagne Sundae (IRE) *Mrs S D Williams* 73h 103c
8 b g Supreme Leader—Partners In Crime (Crofthall)
389[11] **4559[4] 4943[6]**

Champion Gold (IRE) *Charles Coakley* 110h
7 ch g Germany(USA) —Bent Al Fala (IRE) (Green Desert (USA))
3894a[11]

Champion's Day (GER) *Jonjo O'Neill* 92+h
5 ch g Valanour(IRE) —Courtly Times (Machiavellian (USA))
3342[6] 3496[8] 3646[9] 3962[3] 4243[F]

Chancers Dante (IRE) *Ferdy Murphy* 92+h 80+c
10 b g Phardante(FR) —Own Acre (Linacre)
262[5] 398[3] 535[P]1886[3] 2039[2] 2237[U]2413[P] 3554[7] **(3930)**

Chanfron *R H Buckler* 27h
5 ch g Double Trigger(IRE) —Mhargaidh Nua (Thowra (FR))
1021[11]

Channahrlie (IRE) *R Dickin* 93h 107c
12 gr g Celio Rufo—Derravarragh Lady (IRE) (Radical)
176[5] 430[5] 694[P]1960[2] (2243) 2583[4]2931[3] 3649[3] 4163[7]4737[7] 4876[P]

Chanteuse *Mrs Marjorie Fife* 51h
6 b m Rudimentary(USA) —Enchanting Melody (Chief Singer)
2106[P] 2838[12] 2901[7] **3760[U]**

Chanticlier *R T Phillips* 99+h 100c
9 b g Roselier(FR) —Cherry Crest (Pollerton)
2609[P] 2868[4] 3253[5] 3581[5] 4390[8]**4937[2]**

Chantilly Passion (FR) *B Storey*
5 b g Double Trigger(IRE) —Chantilly Fashion (FR) (Northern Fashion (USA))
323[16] 484[10]

Chantoue Royale (FR) *Mrs L J Mongan* 112+c
7 bb m Cadoudal(FR) —Royal Blessing (Phaeton)
1978[P] 2577[P]

Chaos Theory *John Cranage* 90+c
11 b g Jupiter Island—Indian Orchid (Warpath)
132[4] 3968[5] 4351[P]

Chaparro Amargoso (IRE) *F L Matthews* 86h 110c
13 b g Ela-Mana-Mou—Champanera (Top Ville)
4051[F] 4397[R] 4880[P]

Chapel Bay *Mrs H Dalton* 27h
6 b m Alflora(IRE) —Jack It In (Derrylin)
1660[5] 1854[6]

Chapel Times (IRE) *H D Daly* 80+h
7 b g Supreme Leader—Dippers Daughter (Strong Gale)
4494[7] 5009[8]

Chaplin *Evan Williams* 51h
5 b g Groom Dancer(USA) —Princess Borghese (USA) (Nijinsky (CAN))
3355[P] 3464[P] 5110[12]

Chapners Cross *A W Congdon* 53c
10 b g Primitive Rising(USA) —Holly (Skyliner)
299[8]

Character Building (IRE) *J J Quinn* 112 h
6 gr g Accordion—Mrs Jones (IRE) (Roselier (FR))
2112[3] 2572[2] 3237[2] 3779[2] 4141[4](4916)

Charalambous (USA) *C L Tizzard* 92+h
9 b g Hermitage(USA) —Hula Lei (USA) (State Dinner (USA))
2732[P] 2995[P]

Charango Star *W K Goldsworthy* 104h 119 c
8 b g Petoski—Pejawi (Strong Gale)
(977) 1231[4] **(1455) 1678[C] 1778[5]1893[F] 2215[P] 2731[8]**3018[8] 3249[3] **3438[2]** 3598[4]**(3886) 4690[6] 4835[F]**

Charging (IRE) *John Joseph Murphy* 91h 123 c
10 ch g Alphabatim(USA) —Gleann Ard (Deep Run)
2210[12] 5080a[8]

Chariot (IRE) *M R Bosley* 82+h
5 ch g Titus Livius(FR) —Battle Queen (Kind Of Hush)
1208[3] 1520[5] 1814[4] 2283[4] 2806[4]3456[6] 4475[5] 4896[3]

Charleston *R Rowe* 68h
5 ch g Pursuit Of Love—Discomatic (USA) (Roberto (USA))
229[8]

Charley Brown (IRE) *Mrs L Wadham*
6 b g Muroto—Ballinure Girl (Buckskin (FR))
2961[16]

Charlie Bear *W K Goldsworthy*
5 ch h Bahamian Bounty—Abi (Chief's Crown (USA))
3[5] 243[8]

Charlie Castallan *D W Thompson* 72h
6 gr g Wace(USA) —Castle Cary (Castle Keep)
716[11] **782[P]** 3656[P] 4475[7]**4918[P]**

Charlie Chapel *N J Hawke* 91h
7 b g College Chapel—Lightino (Bustino)
175[5] 273[3] 943[2]

Charlie Chestnut *Mrs P Townsley*
6 ch g Rakaposhi King—Manaolana (Castle Keep)
1777[11]

Charlie George *P Monteith* 32h
5 ch g Idris(IRE) —Faithful Beauty (IRE) (Last Tycoon)
2040[5] 2903[12]

Charliemoore *G L Moore* 90h 99+c
10 ch g Karinga Bay—Your Care (FR) (Caerwent)
1631[P] 1776[3] (1897) 2217[P] 2323[4] 2719[P]

Charlie's Cross (IRE) *J G Portman* 36h 24c
8 gr g Roselier(FR) —Estuary View (Prince Rheingold)
1751[P]

Charlie's Double *J R Best* 99+h
7 b g Double Eclipse(IRE) —Pendil's Niece (Roscoe Blake)
105[3] (365) 575[2] (724) (745) (1026) 4797[P]

Charlies First (IRE) *Peter Casey* 118h
6 ch g Prince Of Birds(USA) —Royal Cindy (IRE) (Red Sunset)
3411a[4]

Charlies Future *S C Burrough* 107 h 116 c
8 b g Democratic(USA) —Faustelerie (Faustus (USA))
1853[F] 1972[3] 2325[7]3144[4] 3326[F] 3688[4]4014[5] 4287[P]

Charlie Tango (IRE) *D W Thompson* 96+h
5 b g Desert Prince(IRE) —Precedence (IRE) (Polish Precedent (USA))
(2108) 2950[7] 3783[4] 4045[P]

Charlotte Vale *M D Hammond* 105+h
5 ch m Pivotal—Drying Grass Moon (Be My Chief (USA))
(2414) 3254[2]

Charlton Kings (IRE) *R J Hodges* 113 h
8 b g King's Ride—Grove Gale (IRE) (Strong Gale)
2044[U] 2247[F] 2595[6] 2850[7]3135[F] 3286[8]

Charmatic (IRE) *Andrew Turnell* 107h
5 br m Charnwood Forest(IRE) —Instamatic (Night Shift (USA))
3281[8] 3878[8] 4784[3] (5052)

Charm Indeed *N B King* 44b
6 b g Charmer—House Deed (Presidium)
249[F] 2579[12] 2950[P] 3433[P]

Charming Fellow (IRE) *Miss H C Knight* 88+h
6 b g Taipan(IRE) —Latest Tangle (Ragapan)
1672[P] 2142[3]

Charm Offensive *C J Gray* 68h
8 b m Zieten(USA) —Shoag (USA) (Affirmed (USA))
358[7] 519[4] 665[13] 801[10](5048)

Charnwood Street (IRE) *D Shaw* 82+h
7 b g Charnwood Forest(IRE) —La Vigie (King Of Clubs)
483[6]

Charyan (IRE) *C Roche* 104h
5 b m Danehill Dancer(IRE) —Great Pleasure (GER) (Star Appeal)
5078a[7]

Chase The Dawn *C J Mann* 77b
4 gr g Silver Patriarch(IRE) —Marquesa Juana (Lepanto (GER))
4622[8]

Chase The Sunset (IRE) *Miss H C Knight* 98h 115+c
8 ch g Un Desperado(FR) —Cherry Chase (IRE) (Red Sunset)
459[6] (635) 892[5] (1036) 1220[5] **1365[3]1801[F] 2732[4]**

Chasing The Bride *Miss A Goschen* 112c
13 b g Gildoran—Bride (Remainder Man)
(6) 272[2] 453[P]4560[7]

Chasing The Dream (IRE) *P R Webber*
5 b m Desert Sun—Dream Of Jenny (Caerleon (USA))
1745[P]

Chasing The Stars (IRE) *D R Gandolfo*
6 b m Fourstars Allstar(USA) —Brogeen Lady (IRE) (Phardante (FR))
2928[P] 3280[P]

Chateau (IRE) *G A Swinbank* 59b
4 ch g Grand Lodge(USA) —Miniver (IRE) (Mujtahid (USA))
2105[9] 2520[11]

Chateau Rose (IRE) *Miss E C Lavelle* 107h 116c
10 b g Roselier(FR) —Claycastle (IRE) (Carlingford Castle)
1973[P] 2556[P] **3481[F]**

Chateau Rouge (IRE) *M D Hammond* 94h
5 b g Tiraaz(USA) —Carolina Rua (USA) (L'Emigrant (USA))
2192[3] 2572[4] 3231[3]

Chaucers Miller *R Bryan* 57h 61c
10 ch g Baron Blakeney—Reine De Rosehill (Shack (USA))
79[6]

Chauvinist (IRE) *N J Henderson* 145 h 146c
11 b g Roselier(FR) —Sacajawea (Tanfirion)
2492[6] 4459[8] 4764[7]

Cheeky Lad *R C Harper* 77+c
6 b g Bering—Cheeky Charm (USA) (Nureyev (USA))
401[6] 564[3] 682[6]

Cheer Us On *M W Easterby* 100+b
4 b g Bahhare(USA) —Markapen (IRE) (Classic Music (USA))
2521[2] 4588[5] (7)

Cheery Martyr *P Needham* 87h
8 b m Perpendicular—Kate O'Kirkham (Le Bavard (FR))
569[4] 715[4] (854) 941[7] 1937[6] 2693[8]3167[4] 3351[6]

Chef De Cour (FR) *L Lungo* 126 h
5 b g Pistolet Bleu(IRE) —Cour De Rome (FR) (Cadoudal (FR))
(418) (645) (2106) 2765[6] 3256[2] 3378[6] 4108[7]

Chef Tartare (FR) *Mrs K Waldron* 109+h 119+c
6 b g Nikos—Rive Tartare (FR) (Riverquest (FR))
4282[P] **4351[3] 4555[5]**

Cheler (FR) *B Secly*
7 b g Epervier Bleu—Chely (FR) (Mad Captain)
585a[5] 779a[5] 5000a[2]

Chelsea Bridge (IRE) *Miss H C Knight* 96 h
8 b g Over The River(FR) —Anguillita (IRE) (King Of Clubs)
3881[4]

Chelsea Harbour (IRE) *Thomas Mullins* 124h
6 b g Old Vic—Jennyellen (IRE) (Phardante (FR))
4765[19] 5103a[U]

Cherry Gold *Evan Williams* 110h 118 c
12 b g Rakaposhi King—Merry Cherry (Deep Run)
(468) **694[6] 4103[F]**

Cherry's Echo *H P Hogarth* 67h
6 gr m Keen—Distant Cherry (General Ironside)
2446[18]

Cherrywood (IRE) *M C Pipe* 71h
7 gr g Roselier(FR) —Marbleade (IRE) (Over The River (FR))
802[4] 1018[10]

Cherub (GER) *Jonjo O'Neill* 136h
6 b g Winged Love(IRE) —Chalkidiki (GER) (Nebos (GER))
208[7] 2207[5] 2493[7] 2636[2] 3298[5]3411a[18]

Chesnut Annie (IRE) *Miss H E Roberts* 90b
5 ch m Weld—Leaden Sky (IRE) (Roselier (FR))
1755[6] 7[3]

Chestall *R Hollinshead* 64+h
5 b g Polar Prince(IRE) —Maradata (IRE) (Shardari)
1725[6]

Chetwind Music (IRE) *William Coleman O'Brien* 106+h 122c
8 b g Aristocracy—Mariners Music (Black Minstrel)
4136a[2] 5082a[2]

Chez Bleu *P J Hobbs* 96+b
5 bb g Pistolet Bleu(IRE) —Tourbelaine (FR) (Cadoudal (FR))
4623[5] 4825[9]

Chiaro (FR) *P J Hobbs* 139+h
4 b g Hamas(IRE) —Link Diamond (FR) (Diamond Prospect (USA))
777a[3] 1428a[3] 1705a[6] 2085a[3] (4569) 4750[5](4962)

Chicago Bulls (IRE) *A King* 128+h 130+c
8 b g Darshaan—Celestial Melody (USA) (The Minstrel (CAN))
4119[5] 4497[P]

Chicago Vic (IRE) *E McNamara* 129h 71c
7 b m Old Vic—Clearwater Glen (Furry Glen)
5077a[2]

Chickapeakray *D McCain* 93h
5 b m Overbury(IRE) —Nevermind Hey (Teenoso (USA))
23[2] 310[6] (2256) 2653[3] (2977) 3416[4] 4568[3](5014)

Chico Time (IRE) *Denis P Murphy* 110b
5 b m Presenting—Hilldalus (IRE) (Mandalus)
5134a[3]

Chicuelo (FR) *N J Henderson* 108h
10 b g Mansonnien(FR) —Dovapas (FR) (Paseo (FR))
1872[14] 2175[10] 4974[16]

Chief Chippie *A C Simpson* 78h 63c
13 b g Mandalus—Little Katrina (Little Buskins)
405[6]

Chief Dan George (IRE) *D R MacLeod* 109+h
6 b g Lord Americo—Colleen Donn (Le Moss)
323[3] 424[3] 1532[4] 1834[4] 2024[6]2475[9] 2944[2] 3234[P] 3376[4] 4724[2]5064[2]

Chief Mouse *Steve Isaac* 66c
13 b g Be My Chief(USA) —Top Mouse (High Top)
47[10] 3805[6]

Chief Predator (USA) *B J Llewellyn* 80c
12 ch g Chief's Crown(USA) —Tsavorite (USA) (Halo (USA))
1022[F]

Chief Yeoman *Miss Venetia Williams* 144h
6 br g Machiavellian(USA) —Step Aloft (Shirley Heights)
2871[2] 3298[4] 3994[8] 4473[12]

Chigorin *Miss S J Wilton* 77h
5 b g Pivotal—Belle Vue (Petong)
2179[8] 2460[5] 2624[5] 3367[8]

Chilling Place (IRE) *P J Hobbs* 138 h 148c
7 ch g Moscow Society(USA) —Ethel's Dream (Relkino)
(1783) 1971[2] 2208[5]2924[F] 4456[12] (4729)

Chilly Milly *V Smith* 76h
5 b m Shambo—Phrase 'n Cold (IRE) (Strong Statement (USA))
2718[9] 3277[P] 3664[4] 4898[4]

Chimichurri (FR) *M Bradstock* 83+b
4 ch g Nikos—Wackie (USA) (Spectacular Bid (USA))
4853[14]

China Bond (IRE) *G R Oldroyd* 5b
4 ch g Shahrastani(USA) —At Amal (IRE) (Astronef)
4854[19]

China Chase (IRE) *J L Spearing* 63h
7 b g Anshan—Hannies Girl (IRE) (Invited (USA))
202[P] 371[F] 506[S]724[8]

China Fare (IRE) *Miss Lucinda V Russell* 77h
6 b m Taipan(IRE) —Sindys Gale (Strong Gale)
2821[14]

Chiqitita (IRE) *Miss M E Rowland* 43h
5 b m Saddlers' Hall(IRE) —Funny Cut (IRE) (Sure Blade (USA))
1565[11] 1756[P] (Dead)

Chisel *M Wigham* 20h
5 ch g Hector Protector(USA) —Not Before Time (IRE) (Polish Precedent (USA))
3173[P] 3328[19] 3545[10] 5135[9]

Chita's Flight *S C Burrough* 74h 74c
6 gr m Busy Flight—Chita's Cone (Celtic Cone)
271[U] 459[4] 632[7]

Chives (IRE) *Mrs S J Smith*
11 b g Good Thyne(USA) —Chatty Actress (Le Bavard (FR))
1926[P] 3389[7] **3971[P]4111[P]**

Chivitanova (FR) *T Trapenard*
3 ch g Alamo Bay(USA) —Casaque Blue (FR) (Epervier Bleu)
4298a[P]

Chivite (IRE) *P J Hobbs* 129 h 109+c
7 b g Alhaarth(IRE) —Laura Margaret (Persian Bold)
(459) (750)

Chivvy Charver (IRE) *A C Whillans* 82h
9 ch g Commanche Run—Claddagh Pride (Bargello)
11[16] 215[4] 2025[3]

Chockdee (FR) *P F Nicholls* 121+h 113+c
6 b g King's Theatre(IRE) —Chagrin D'Amour (IRE) (Last Tycoon)
1878[3] **2456[3]**

Chocolate Bombe (IRE) *S Lycett* 34h 52c
9 ch g Un Desperado(FR) —Lady Nerak (Pitpan)
1619[5] 1876[6] 2285[P] **2522[9]2986[7]** 3250[10] **3612[P]**

Chocolate Boy (IRE) *G L Moore* 86h
7 b g Dolphin Street(FR) —Kawther (Tap On Wood)
1875[4] 2212[10]

Chomba Womba (IRE) *Ms Margaret Mullins* 105+b
5 b m Fourstars Allstar(USA) —Miss Muppet (IRE) (Supreme Leader)
4751[6]

Chopneyev (FR) *R T Phillips* 145h 94c
8 b g Goldneyev(USA) —Pierre De Soleil (FR) (Jefferson)
4102[4] 4444[P] 4841[3]

Chorizo (IRE) *P F Nicholls* 106+b
5 b g Kahyasi—Bayariyka (IRE) (Slip Anchor)
4011[2] 4644[2]

Chris And Ryan (IRE) *Mrs L B Normile* 56h 78+c
8 b g Goldmark(USA) —Beautyofthepeace (IRE) (Exactly Sharp (USA))
1886[2] 2689[P]

Christmas Truce (IRE) *Ian Williams* 82h
7 b g Brief Truce(USA) —Superflash (Superlative)
96[3]

Christom *Mrs Tracey Barfoot-Saunt* 8h
4 b g Groom Dancer(USA) —Throw Away Line (USA) (Assert)
2661[P] 2935[11]

Christon Cane *Dr J R J Naylor* 54h
8 b g El Conquistador—Dancing Barefoot (Scallywag)
4212[6] 5015[9]

Christopher *P J Hobbs* 129 h 129c
9 gr g Arzanni—Forest Nymph (NZ) (Oak Ridge (FR))
2210[11] 2748[P] 3293[4]3507[3] 4332[F] 4677[3]

Christy Beamish (IRE) *P Jones* 130+c
9 bb g Jolly Jake(NZ) —Ballinatona Bridge (Black Minstrel)
(4216) 4421[2] 4748[2]

Christy Jnr (IRE) *C J Teague* 64h 68c
12 b g Andretti—Rare Currency (Rarity)
480[P]

Chromboy (GER) *N B King* 48h
6 ch g Kornado—Chroma (GER) (Torgos)
671[11] 1432[11]

Chunky Lad *W G M Turner* 80h
6 ch g Karinga Bay—Madam's Choice (New Member)
1635[2] 1730[3] 2148[4] 3996[P] 5043[0]

Church Island (IRE) *Michael Hourigan* 107+h 146 c
7 ch g Erin's Isle—Just Possible (Kalaglow)
(1622a) (2165) 2668a[U]3079a[U] 3514a[2] (4022a) 5131a[P]

Ciacole *Mrs B K Thomson* 60h
5 b m Primo Dominie—Dance On A Cloud (USA) (Capote (USA))
1835[F]

Ciarans Lass *C Roberts* 7h
7 b m Factual(USA) —Tradespark (Vital Season)
844[11] 4732[P] 4784[16]

Cicatrice *D R Gandolfo* 60h
5 ch g Wolfhound(USA) —Capricious Lady (IRE) (Capricorn Line)
230[10] 274[R] 1814[8]

Cider Man *Mrs J Hughes* 85c
11 b g Romany Rye—Champagne Peri (The Malster)
313[P]

Cider's Niece *C J Price* 27b
5 b m Chaddleworth(IRE) —Farriana (Dutch Treat)
4976[15]

Cillamon *K Bishop* 85b 53c
9 b m Terimon—Dubacilla (Dubassoff (USA))
2151[7] 4801[P]

Cill Churnain (IRE) *Mrs S J Smith* 127 h 118 c
13 b g Arctic Cider(USA) —The Dozer (IRE) (Bulldozer)
1670[U] 1825[3] 2003[U]2451[4] 2640[P] 3350[5]3966[6] 4504[5] **4806[U] 4920[F]**

Cill Uird (IRE) *J J Lambe* 82h 82+c
8 ch m Phardante(FR) —Sandy Run (IRE) (Deep Run)
481[P] 859[4] **989[P]**

Cinema (FR) *B R Hamilton* 98+h
6 b m Bering—Laquifan (USA) (Lear Fan (USA))
3235[3] 3534[5]

Cinnamon Line *R Lee* 99 h 103+c
10 ch g Derrylin—Cinnamon Run (Deep Run)
2485[P] 3481[5] 4078[F]4806[P] 4939[7]

Circassian (IRE) *J Howard Johnson* 126h
5 b g Groom Dancer(USA) —Daraliya (IRE) (Kahyasi)
1927[2] 2206[6] (2873) 3388[5] 4763[5]

Circle Of Wolves *H J Manners* 96+h
8 ch g Wolfhound(USA) —Misty Halo (High Top)
2[10]

Circumspect (IRE) *P C Haslam* 94h
4 b g Spectrum(IRE) —Newala (Royal Academy (USA))
1718[6] 1797[3] 2001[11] 4585[9]

Circus Rose *Mrs P Sly* 63b
4 ch f Most Welcome—Rosie Cone (Celtic Cone)
3820[7]

Cirrious *P J Hobbs* 104h
5 gr m Cloudings(IRE) —Westfield Mist (Scallywag)
3883[6] 4621[13] (4855)

Cirrus (FR) *K G Reveley* 90h 92c
7 gr g Saint Preuil(FR) —Cirta De Champfeu (FR) (Cap Martin (FR))
1454[3] 1915[4] **2109[3] 2413[P]2689[P] 2922[4] 3928[7]**

Cisco (GER) *M E Sowersby*
6 b g Laroche(GER) —Carmelita (GER) (Surumu (GER))
1613[P]

Cita Verda (FR) *P Monteith* 101h
8 b m Take Risks(FR) —Mossita (FR) (Tip Moss (FR))
3853[P] 4110[10] 4490[6]

Citius (IRE) *R Rowe* 89h
10 b g Supreme Leader—Fancy Me Not (IRE) (Bulldozer)
387[P]

City Affair *C J Down* 78h
5 b g Inchinor—Aldevonie (Green Desert (USA))
295[4] 813[6]

City Deep (IRE) *Paul A Roche* 109b
6 br g Taipan(IRE) —Waterloo Ball (IRE) (Where To Dance (USA))
2782a[9]

City General (IRE) *J S Moore*
5 ch g General Monash(USA) —Astra (IRE) (Glenstal (USA))
396[F]

City Hall (IRE) *Paul Nolan* 107?h 133c
12 gr g Generous(IRE) —City Fortress (Troy)
45a[12] 5061a[7]

City Music (IRE) *Mrs S J Smith* 77b
5 b g City Honours(USA) —Rahanine Melody (IRE) (Orchestra)
1554[7]

City Of Manchester (IRE) *P C Haslam* 79h
4 b g Desert Style(IRE) —Nomadic Dancer (IRE) (Nabeel Dancer (USA))
2521[10] 4631[5] 4828[3] (5135)

City Of Sails (IRE) *A J McNamara* 120h
7 br g Flemensfirth(USA) —Palmrock Donna (Quayside)
43a[3] 3894a[5] 4951a[11] 5059a[14]

City Palace *Evan Williams* 83h
5 ch g Grand Lodge(USA) —Ajuga (USA) (The Minstrel (CAN))
1337[7] 1645[7] 2563[2] 2858[10]

Civil Gent (IRE) *M E Sowersby* 31h 88c
7 ch g Flying Spur(AUS) —Calamity Kate (IRE) (Fairy King (USA))
688[6] 1015[P]

Claim To Fame *M Pitman* 57h
5 b g Selkirk(USA) —Loving Claim (USA) (Hansel (USA))
456[P] 683[9]

Clan Law (IRE) *Mrs L B Normile* 80h
8 b g Danehill(USA) —My-O-My (IRE) (Waajib)
2678[P]

Clan Royal (FR) *Jonjo O'Neill* 118+h 151 c
11 b g Chef De Clan II(FR) —Allee Du Roy (FR) (Rex Magna (FR))
2609[5] 3581[3] (4390) **4777[3]**

Clanrye (IRE) *P G Murphy*
5 bb g Insan(USA) —Lake Majestic (IRE) (Mister Majestic)
3342[12]

Clare Galway *B G Powell* 80h
5 b m Compton Place—Oublier L'Ennui (FR) (Bellman (FR))
3127[9] 3281[4] 3423[5] 3655[11]

Clarice Starling *L J Bridge* 79c
8 b m Saddlers' Hall(IRE) —Uncharted Waters (Celestial Storm (USA))
5109[6]

Classical Ben *R A Fahey* 104 h
8 ch g Most Welcome—Stoproveritate (Scorpio (FR))
(1410)

Classical Love *C J Down* 82h
6 b m Classic Cliche(IRE) —Hard Love (Rambo Dancer (CAN))
128[3] 394[2] 665[5] 2687[7]

Classic Approach (IRE) *John Queally* 121h
6 b g Luso—Vital Approach (IRE) (Mandalus)
1876[4] 5078a[17]

Classic Calvados (FR) *P D Niven* 93h 82c
7 bb g Thatching—Mountain Stage (IRE) (Pennine Walk)
9[5] **604[6] 692[6]862[P]**

Classic Capers *J M Jefferson* 111 h 129c
7 ch g Classic Cliche(IRE) —Jobiska (Dunbeath (USA))
1891[3] 2291[2] (2764) 2953[3] 4433[16] 5065[4]

Classic Clover *C L Tizzard* 69h
6 ch g Classic Cliche(IRE) —National Clover (National Trust)
201[10] 1982[8] 2147[3] 2592[6] 3211[9]

Classic Croco (GER) *Mrs Jeremy Young* 86+h
5 gr g Croco Rouge(IRE) —Classic Light (IRE) (Classic Secret (USA))
279[3] 806[7] 1158[10]

Classic Echo *J J Davies* 48c
6 b m Classic Cliche(IRE) —Sunday News'N'Echo (USA) (Trempolino (USA))
4044[5]

Classic Event (IRE) *T D Easterby* 106h
5 ch g Croco Rouge(IRE) —Delta Town (USA) (Sanglamore (USA))
61[10] 1720[P]

Classic Fantasy *P F Nicholls* 103b
5 b m Classic Cliche(IRE) —Fantasy World (Kemal (FR))
3327[4] 3904[6] 4751[9]

Classic Fiddle *N J Henderson* 112+b
4 ch f Classic Cliche(IRE) —Fiddling The Facts (IRE) (Orchestra)
(4654) (4976)

Classic Harry *P Beaumont* 94b
5 b g Classic Cliche(IRE) —Always Shining (Tug Of War)
3145[3] 3742[3] 4366[3] 4853[15]

Classic Lash (IRE) *P Needham* 92h 103c
10 b g Classic Cheer(IRE) —Khaiylasha (IRE) (Kahyasi)
152[3] 1887[P] **2692[P] 2842[5]4920[5] 13[6]**

Classic Lease *P C Haslam* 39h
5 b g Cyrano De Bergerac—Vado Via (Ardross)
1794[F] 2249[16] 2444[F] 4493[P]

Classic Native (IRE) *Jonjo O'Neill* 116 h 132 c
8 bb g Be My Native(USA) —Thats Irish (Furry Glen)
2215[2]

Classic Quart (IRE) *M Scudamore* 83h
5 b m Classic Cliche(IRE) —Ganpati (IRE) (Over The River (FR))
1711[5] 4581[3]

Classic Rarity *R J Baker* 58b
4 b g Classic Cliche(IRE) —Gently Ridden (IRE) (King's Ride)
4947[6]

Classic Revival *Mrs A Price* 28b 58c
8 ch g Elmaamul(USA) —Sweet Revival (Claude Monet (USA))
79[P]

Classic Rock *J W Unett* 83dh 98+c
7 b g Classic Cliche(IRE) —Ruby Vision (IRE) (Vision (USA))
2419[6] **3653[2] 4016[P]4451[2] 5074[2]**

Classic Role *L Wells* 118h
7 b g Tragic Role(USA) —Clare Island (Connaught)
3658[2] 3878[5] 4242[11] 4621[2] 4763[13]4915[2] 5056a[7]

Classic Ruby *M R Bosley* 63+h
6 b m Classic Cliche(IRE) —Burmese Ruby (Good Times (ITY))
1903[13] 2866[8]

Classic Sight *C C Bealby* 89h
6 ch m Classic Cliche(IRE) —Speckyfoureyes (Blue Cashmere)
3544[3] 4012[2] 4390[6]

Classified (IRE) *M C Pipe* 139+h
10 b g Roselier(FR) —Treidlia (Mandalus)
4745[9]

Classify *R Barber* 101+h
7 b g Classic Cliche(IRE) —Slmaat (Sharpo)
440[F]

Classi Maureen *S A Hughes* 43h 87c
6 ch m Among Men(USA) —Hi-Hannah (Red Sunset)
4283[P] 5109[4]

Classy Chav (IRE) *P Monteith* 75b
4 b g Classic Cliche(IRE) —Gavotte Du Cochet (FR) (Urbain Minotiere (FR))
2068[6] 3237[6]

Classy Chick (IRE) *H D Daly* 76b
5 b m Classic Cliche(IRE) —Nova Rose (Ra Nova)
349[5] 2457[7]

Claude Greengrass *Jonjo O'Neill* 105h 94c
10 ch g Shalford(IRE) —Rainbow Brite (BEL) (Captain's Treasure)
633[12] **997[7] 1109[2]1178[P] 1203[P]**

Claudia May *Miss Lucinda V Russell*
5 gr m Cloudings(IRE) —Princess Maxine (IRE) (Horage)
2028[9] 2652[P] 3232[8]

Clawick Connection (IRE) *J N R Billinge* 77c
11 b g Torus—Katie Lowe (IRE) (Pollerton)
87a[U] 554[U]

Claydon Cavalier *P A Trueman* 70b
7 b g Regal Embers(IRE) —Marsdale (Royal Palace)
817[11]

Claymills (IRE) *P Beaumont* 68b
6 b g Presenting—Merry Watt (Last Fandango)
59[P]

Claymore (IRE) *O Sherwood* 144h 146 c
10 b g Broadsword(USA) —Mazza (Mazilier (USA))
2492[8] 3136[4] 3385[3](3739) 4241[5] 5000a[4]

Clear Dawn (IRE) *J M Jefferson* 95h 93 c
11 b g Clearly Bust—Cobra Queen (Dawn Review)
690[3] 896[P] 941[P]

Clearly Now (IRE) *Bernard Jones* 93+h
8 b g Clearly Bust—Paico Lane (Paico)
(129)

Clearly Oscar (IRE) *Seamus O'Farrell* 98h
7 b g Oscar(IRE) —Clear Bid (IRE) (Executive Perk)
2335[7] 2784a[P]

Clear Riposte (IRE) *W P Mullins* 119h
4 b f King's Theatre(IRE) —Niamh Cinn Oir (IRE) (King Of Clubs)
(3004a) 3401a[4] 4435[13] 4887a[4] 5099a[4]

Clear The Line (IRE) *J L Hassett* 101c
8 br g Satco(FR) —Casheral (Le Soleil)
4748[15]

Clear Thinking *Miss Venetia Williams* 128h
6 b g Rainbow Quest(USA) —Coraline (Sadler's Wells (USA))
4329[P]

Clearwaterdreamer (IRE) *Martin Brassil* 21h
5 ch g City Honours(USA) —Rugged Heart (IRE) (Broken Hearted)
65a[22]

Clemax (IRE) *Ferdy Murphy* 102h 108c
5 gr g Linamix(FR) —Chauncy Lane (IRE) (Sadler's Wells (USA))
1938 [4] 3984[3] 4367[2] **4843[2]4985[2]**

Cleopatras Therapy (IRE) *T H Caldwell* 95h
9 b g Gone Fishin—Nec Precario (Krayyan)
2464[P]

Cleric *N A Dunger*
5 ch g Inchinor—St Clair (Distant Relative)
3504[5]

Cleverality (IRE) *Evan Williams* 42h
6 b g John French—Apple Betty (Runnett)
2145[6] 3545[12] 4284[P] 4621[14]

Clever Thyne (IRE) *H D Daly* 105 h 113c
9 b g Good Thyne(USA) —Clever Milly (Precipice Wood)
765[P]

Clew Bay Cove (IRE) *C A Murphy* 119h
6 ch g Anshan—Crashrun (Crash Course)
70a[7]

Cleymor House (IRE) *John R Upson* 67+h 71c
8 ch g Duky—Deise Lady (Le Bavard (FR))
2181[P] 2517[5] **3460[10]** 3656[7]**3938[6]** 4905[7]

Clichy *Mrs S J Smith* 85 h
6 b m Classic Cliche(IRE) —Kentucky Tears (USA) (Cougar (CHI))
414[7] 613[8]

Clifford T Ward *D McCain* 78h
6 b g Silver Wizard(USA) —Moonduster (Sparkler)
7[11] 2007[6] 3347[8] 3842[8] 3985[8]4550[10]

Clifton *M W Easterby* 78b
4 b f Bal Harbour—Contradictory (Reprimand)
4800[2]

Clintos *G R I Smyly* 53b
5 b g Syrtos—Galava (CAN) (Graustark)
266[6] 817[10]

Clodagh Valley (IRE) *R J Hewitt*
11 b g Doubletour(USA) —Raise A Princess (USA) (Raise A Native)
98[P]

Cloneybrien Boy (IRE) *Mrs A M Thorpe* 90h
6 ch g Mister Lord(USA) —Lough Eagle (Deep Run)
1779[5] 2214[P] **2660[F] 2801[P]3126[F]** 4826[5] 5069[8]

Cloonavery (IRE) *B Llewellyn* 68h
4 b g Xaar—Hero's Pride (FR) (Hero's Honor (USA))
1679[P] 1802[8] 1955[6] 4551[P]

Cloone River (IRE) *Paul Nolan* 125h 122+c
10 bb g Un Desperado(FR) —Grangemills (Strong Gale)
1093a[F]

Clopf (IRE) *E J O'Grady* 122b
5 b g Dr Massini(IRE) —Chroma (IRE) (Supreme Leader)
5081a[6]

Closed Orders (IRE) *Robert Gray* 96h 100c
9 b g Phardante(FR) —Monks Lass (IRE) (Monksfield)
2479[6] 2570[P] 2900[9]

Closed Shop (IRE) *P J Hobbs* 106+b
5 b g Saddlers' Hall(IRE) —Roses Niece (IRE) (Jeu De Paille (FR))
(4615)

Cloth Of Gold *Miss T Spearing* 122h 96+c
9 b g Barathea(IRE) —Bustinetta (Bustino)
333[4]

Cloud Catcher (IRE) *M Appleby* 51h
5 br m Charnwood Forest(IRE) —Notley Park (Wolfhound (USA))
3[12] 232[P] 438[6] 563[5] 680[4]891[F] 1245[8]

Cloudina *P T Dalton* 88b
5 b m Cloudings(IRE) —Lucia Forte (Neltino)
2987[2] 3497[2] 4376[16]

Clouding Over *K G Reveley* 100 h 116+c
6 gr m Cloudings(IRE) —Wellwotdouthink (Rymer)
2041[4] 2476[4] (2715) (2902) 3489[3] 3815[7](4454) (5119)

Cloudless Dawn *P Beaumont* 109 h
6 b m Cloudings(IRE) —Charlotte's Emma (Oats)
1915[6] (2515) 2923[2] 3287[2] 3795[4] 4530[3]5120[4]

Cloudmor (IRE) *L Lungo* 80+h
5 b g Cloudings(IRE) —Glen Morvern (Carlingford Castle)
323[U] 484[8] 2497[8] 2942[8] 3314[5]4113[5] 4341[P]

Clouds Of Gold (IRE) *J S Wainwright* 62h
5 b m Goldmark(USA) —Tongabezi (IRE) (Shernazar)
14[7] 651[7] 854[P] 1357[P]

Cloud Venture *S E H Sherwood* 68h
6 gr g Cloudings(IRE) —Fantasy World (Kemal (FR))
2821[17] 3846[6]

Cloudy Bay Boy *Mrs Caroline Bailey* 93c
8 gr g Petoski—Smoke (Rusticaro (FR))
278[F] 3924[R] 4349[2]4897[R]

Cloudy Blues (IRE) *R H Buckler* 69h 80c
8 ro g Glacial Storm(USA) —Chataka Blues (IRE) (Sexton Blake)
202[P] 2296[9] **2827[4]3252[P] 4620[4] 4837[U]**

Cloudy Club (IRE) *P R Webber*
7 b g Moscow Society(USA) —Glenpatrick Peach (IRE) (Lafontaine (USA))
1323[F]

Cloudy Grey (IRE) *Miss E C Lavelle* 136h
9 gr g Roselier(FR) —Dear Limousin (Pollerton)
2369[P] 2636[4] 2971[6] 3298[16] 4375[7]4608[9]

Cloudy Lane *D McCain* 133+h
6 b g Cloudings(IRE) —Celtic Cygnet (Celtic Cone)
131[2] (470) 2262[F] 2690[2] (3291) (3975) 4612[2](4849)

Clovella *R Allan* 67b
5 b m Missed Flight—Royella (Royal Fountain)
3490[10] 5124[9]

Clover Pearl (IRE) *Michael Cullen* 84h
6 b m Luso—Clover Run (IRE) (Deep Run)
2796a[4]

Cluain Rua (IRE) *Liam P Cusack* 81h 112c
11 ch g Be My Native(USA) —Test Drive (Crash Course)
45a[2]

Club Royal *N E Berry* 80 h 80c
9 b g Alflora(IRE) —Miss Club Royal (Avocat)
389[4] 749[5] 806[P] 1075[5] 1187[9]

Clueless *N G Richards* 90+h
4 b g Royal Applause—Pure (Slip Anchor)
3203[4]

Clydeoneeyed *K F Clutterbuck* 86h
7 b g Primitive Rising(USA) —Holly (Skyliner)
(363) 2256[11] 3591[6] 4896[2]

Clyffe Hanger (IRE) *R H Buckler* 98+h
6 b g Taipan(IRE) —French Thistle (Kemal (FR))
2049[3] (2527)

Coach Lane *Miss Venetia Williams* 106+h
5 b g Barathea(IRE) —Emplane (USA) (Irish River (FR))
2081[3] (2618) 3333[4] 3603[6] 4104[3] 4726[8]

Coachman (IRE) *A J Lockwood* 61h
8 b g King's Ride—Royal Shares (IRE) (Royal Fountain)
1107[4] 1148[8] 1374[5] 1566[F] 1883[P]

Coastguard (IRE) *David Pearson* 90h 89c
12 b g Satco(FR) —Godlike (Godswalk (USA))
132[P]

Coast To Coast (IRE) *E J O'Grady* 108h 120c
7 ch g Moscow Society(USA) —Madame Vitesse (Le Bavard (FR))
3079a[4] 4022a[7]

Coat Of Honour (USA) *J Howard Johnson* 143h 123c
6 gr g Mark Of Esteem(IRE) —Ballymac Girl (Niniski (USA))
(208) **1758[F] (2989) 4431[11]5121[2]**

Cobbet (CZE) *T R George* 127h 131 c
10 b g Favoured Nations(IRE) —Creace (CZE) (Sirano (CZE))
1739[3] 1918[5] 2368[F]2768[10] 3299[10]

Cobreces *Mrs L Borradaile* 123c
8 b g Environment Friend—Oleada (IRE) (Tirol)
48[P] (4073) 4471[12]5013[4] 6[3]

Coccinelle (IRE) *K A Morgan* 105h
8 b m Great Marquess—Nuit D'Ete (USA) (Super Concorde (USA))
1116a[9] 1436[5] 1482[2] 1552[2]

Cockatoo Ridge *N R Mitchell* 100+h
9 ch g Riverwise(USA) —Came Cottage (Nearly A Hand)
1968[P] 3214[2] 3508[F] 3901[P] 4036[P]4561[3] 4781[7] 5028[P]

Cockspur (IRE) *Jonjo O'Neill* 107+b
5 b g Darazari(IRE) —Melarka (Dara Monarch)
(3904) 4854[17]

Coconut Beach *C Roche* 104h
5 b g Sadler's Wells(USA) —Eversince (USA) (Foolish Pleasure (USA))
3005a[7]

Coctail Lady (IRE) *B W Duke* 76h
6 ch m Piccolo—Last Ambition (IRE) (Cadeaux Genereux)
1156[15]

Code (IRE) *Miss Z C Davison* 84b
5 b g Danehill(USA) —Hidden Meaning (USA) (Gulch (USA))
242[7] 1596[P]

Code Of Rules (IRE) *T J Taaffe* 106h
5 b g Bob Back(USA) —Thistle Witch (IRE) (Be My Native (USA))
4060a[7]

Code Of Silence (IRE) *Thomas Gerard O'Leary* 99h 104c
6 b g Oscar(IRE) —Mrs Hill (Strong Gale)
5128a[F]

Code Sign (USA) *P J Hobbs* 115+h 115+c
7 b g Gulch(USA) —Karasavina (IRE) (Sadler's Wells (USA))
682[3]

Cody *James Moffatt* 86 h
7 ch g Zilzal(USA) —Ibtihaj (USA) (Raja Baba (USA))
152[5] 417[2] 500[2] 545[7] 1002[P]1887[4] 2025[8] **2975[P]** (4113) 4658[4]

Coeur D'Alene *Dr J R J Naylor* 84h
5 gr g Hernando(FR) —Chambre Separee (USA) (Cozzene (USA))
844[3] 963[3] 2928[4] 3238[6] 3478[6]3997[8] 4210[15]

Cogans Lake (IRE) *Kieran Purcell* 124+h
4 b g Even Top(IRE) —Imperial Comet (IRE) (Imperial Frontier (USA))
3890a[6] 4122a[F] 4747[11]

Coilog Jac's Folli (IRE) *Miss Sabrina Joan Harty* 81b
5 ch g Jackson's Drift(USA) —Take Me On (Wolverlife)
5104a[20]

Cois Na Tine Eile *N A Twiston-Davies* 84+h
4 br f Cois Na Tine(IRE) —Water Pixie (IRE) (Dance Of Life (USA))
3690[3] 3979[7] 4425[U] 4450[8] 4871[3]

Colca Canyon (IRE) *David P Myerscough* 112h 135c
9 b g Un Desperado(FR) —Golden Flats (Sonnen Gold)
41a[7] 2346[8] 2489[11]

Cold Call *C W Thornton* 69b
4 b g Cois Na Tine(IRE) —Kiss In The Dark (Starry Night (USA))
2521[12] 2927[11] 4533[15]

Cold Mountain (IRE) *J W Mullins* 100h
4 b g Inchinor—Streak Of Silver (USA) (Dynaformer (USA))
3436[6] 3714[6] 3996[5] (5023) 3[5]

Cold Play *C J Mann*
4 ch g Inchinor—Ice House (Northfields (USA))
1011[5] 1095[P]

Cold Turkey *G L Moore* 109+h
6 b g Polar Falcon(USA) —South Rock (Rock City)
(2374) 3597[3]

Coleorton Dane *K A Ryan* 72h
4 gr g Danehill Dancer(IRE) —Cloudy Nine (Norton Challenger)
1718[9] 2167[P]

Coleraine (IRE) *O Sherwood* 84h
6 b g Supreme Leader—Ring Mam (IRE) (King's Ride)
2288[6] 3240[4] 3685[3] 4071[6] 4824[5]

Coljon (IRE) *Paul Nolan* 137 c
8 br g Roselier(FR) —Native Ocean (IRE) (Be My Native (USA))
3012a[2] 3587a[2] 4022a[6]4929a[12]

College Ace (IRE) *P J Hobbs* 117h
5 b g Taipan(IRE) —Frantesa (Red Sunset)
(1895) 3248[3] 3717[5] 4420[7] 4858[4] (5106)

College City (IRE) *R C Guest* 91 h 114c
7 b g College Chapel—Polish Crack (IRE) (Polish Patriot (USA))
122[2] 213[2] 357[F]**548[3] (904) (999) 1088[P]1320[7] (1612) 1682[2]1716[5]** 2657[7] **3543[3]3784[7] 4721[P] 5139[4]**

College Cracker *J F Coupland* 68h
8 b m Environment Friend—Primo Panache (Primo Dominie)
11[5]

Colline De Fleurs *J A B Old* 110+h
6 b m Alflora(IRE) —B Greenhill (Gunner B)
470[5] 2558[2] (3435) 3884[2] (4324) 5052[2]

Collinstown (IRE) *Robert Tyner* 97h 87+c
10 bb g Mister Lord(USA) —Paddock Minstrel (Black Minstrel)
(4936)

Colmcille (IRE) *Evan Williams* 98h 94c
6 ch g Desert Story(IRE) —Lasting Peace (IRE) (Pennine Walk)
1884[P] 2341[6] **2955[P] 5047[6]**

Colnel Rayburn (IRE) *Paul Nolan* 119h 143c
10 b g Un Desperado(FR) —Super Boreen (Boreen (FR))
3587a[5] 4138a[5] 4777[P]5059a[P]

Colnside Brook *B G Powell* 95h
7 br m Sovereign Water(FR) —Armagnac Messenger (Pony Express)
693[5] 861[F]

Colombe D'Or *M F Harris* 73+h 57c
9 gr g Petong—Deep Divide (Nashwan (USA))
278[P] 503[5]

Colonel Bilko (IRE) *Miss S J Wilton* 69h
4 b g General Monash(USA) —Mari-Ela (IRE) (River Falls)
1729[8] 2935[6]

Colonel Bradley (IRE) *Jonjo O'Neill* 102h 121c
12 b g Un Desperado(FR) —Dora Frost (Stradavinsky)
761[P] 949[P]

Colonel Hayes (IRE) *J I A Charlton* 1h
6 b g Flemensfirth(USA) —Laura Daisy (Buckskin (FR))
2948[9] 3742[5] 4533[6] 8[13]

Colonel James (IRE) *R Johnson* 60h
5 br g Invited(USA) —Carrignaveen Queen (IRE) (Torenaga)
2690[P] 3314[8] 4114[6]

Colonel Monroe (IRE) *E J O'Grady* 128 h 133c
9 bb g Lord Americo—Fairy Blaze (IRE) (Good Thyne (USA))
69a[U] 4929a[P] 5102a[4]

Colony Hill (IRE) *R H Buckler* 86h
8 ch g Broken Hearted—Arctic Raheen (Over The River (FR))
5047 802[2]

Colophony (USA) *K A Morgan* 103+h
6 ch g Distant View(USA) —Private Line (USA) (Private Account (USA))
238[P] 2750[4] 2958[3] (4080) 4344[P] (4898) 5108[6]

Colorado Pearl (IRE) *P F Nicholls* 91h
5 br m Anshan—Flying Silver (Master Buck)
487[P] (4836)

Colourful Life (IRE) *P F Nicholls* 125h 146 c
10 ch g Rainbows For Life(CAN) —Rasmara (Kalaglow)
1676[2] 1926[U] 2491[P]3620[P] 4434[P]

Coltscroft *J C Fox* 90+h
6 b g Teenoso(USA) —Marquesa Juana (Lepanto (GER))
2528[12] 3277[7] 3500[9]

Columbus (IRE) *Jennie Candlish* 128 h 115+c
9 b g Sadler's Wells(USA) —Northern Script (USA) (Arts And Letters (USA))
92a[P] 814[P] 4612[7] 5010[6]

Colway Ritz *W Storey* 76+h
12 b g Rudimentary(USA) —Million Heiress (Auction Ring (USA))
1940 [11] 2191[6] 2657[9] 3169[5] (3557) 14[3]

Colwyn Jake (IRE) *Ian Williams* 69h 61c
7 bb g Jolly Jake(NZ) —Maggie's Beauty (IRE) (Seclude (USA))
2639[P] **2936[12]**

Comanche War Paint (IRE) *P F Nicholls* 118h 133 c
9 b g Commanche Run—Galeshula (Strong Gale)
842[5] 960[5] (2458) (2596) 2745[10] 4434[8]

Combat Drinker (IRE) *D McCain* 92h 92c
8 b g Mandalus—Auburn Park (Sonnen Gold)
94[2] 334[3] (523) 687[3] 1100[9] 1587[3]**1662[3] 2072[P]**

Combe Florey *H D Daly* 81h
7 ch m Alflora(IRE) —Celtic Slave (Celtic Cone)
462[4] 1977[P]

Combined Venture (IRE) *P O'Connor* 43h 43c
10 b h Dolphin Street(FR) —Centinela (Caerleon (USA))
902[9] 979[5]

Come Bye (IRE) *Miss A M Newton-Smith* 112 h
10 b g Star Quest—Boreen Dubh (Boreen (FR))
1784[9] (2017) 2218[5] 2871[13] (3286) 3428[4] 3901[P]4561[9] 4821[12]

Come On Boy *T G Williams*
12 ch g Henbit(USA) —Miss Rewarde (Andy Rew)
3693[P] 4283[P] 4880[P]

Come On Jim (IRE) *A J Whiting*
5 b g Goldmark(USA) —Galapagos (Pitskelly)
2941[17]

Comeonourfella (IRE) *R T J Wilson* 26h 12c
7 b g Shernazar—Beauchamp Grace (Ardross)
408[3]

Comete Du Lac (FR) *Mrs N Macauley* 68 h 87c
9 ch m Comte Du Bourg(FR) —Line Du Nord (FR) (Esprit Du Nord (USA))
238[P] 3330[P] 3674[5]

Come To The Bar (IRE) *W W Dennis* 42h
7 b g Witness Box(USA) —Copper Hill (IRE) (Zaffaran (USA))
236[6] 1857[6]

Come What Augustus *R M Stronge* 86+h
4 b g Mujahid(USA) —Sky Red (Night Shift (USA))
2069[6] 2373[6] 2681[4] 3603[5] 5026[4]

Comfortable Call *H Alexander* 64 h
8 ch g Nashwan(USA) —High Standard (Kris)
352[P] 480[3] 781[P] 2290[P] 2586[P]3335[4]

Comical Errors (USA) *P C Haslam* 95h
4 b g Distorted Humor(USA) —Fallibility (USA) (Tom Rolfe)
1512[3] 1601[2] (2477) 2569[2] 3485[U] 3797[6]4922[8]

Coming Again (IRE) *D McCain* 93h
5 b g Rainbow Quest(USA) —Hagwah (USA) (Dancing Brave (USA))
1377[2] 1750[4] 2261[13] 3171[8]

Commanche Dawn *G P Enright*
4 b f Commanche Run—Charlycia (Good Times (ITY))
4237[11]

Commanche General (IRE) *J F Panvert* 79h
9 b g Commanche Run—Shannon Amber (IRE) (Phardante (FR))
3416[P]

Commanche Girl *Miss S E Forster* 45b
6 b m Commanche Run—Birtley Girl (Le Coq D'Or)
424[9]

Commanche Gun *A E Price* 52b
6 b g Commanche Run—Busy Girl (Bustiki)
179[11] 490[18] (Dead)

Commanche Jim (IRE) *R H Alner* 103h 120c
10 b g Commanche Run—On A Dream (Balinger)
2019[2] 2623[P] 2686[P]

Commanche Sioux *M W Easterby* 78+h
4 ch f Commanche Run—Double Chimes (Efisio)
2927[10] 3314[U] 3442[P] 3786[6] (4389) 4582[P]4789[11]

Commanche Tryer (IRE) *C F Swan* 73h
8 b m Commanche Run—Troilena (Troilus)
3757[P]

Commander Kev (IRE) *Noel T Chance* 108 h
5 b g Needle Gun(IRE) —Grange Park (IRE) (Warcraft (USA))
2056[2] 2534[5] 3246[U] 3595[2] 3882[3]

Commaover *R Ford*
7 b m Overbury(IRE) —Commanche Lyn (IRE) (Commanche Run)
1674[15]

Commemoration Day (IRE) *M E Sowersby* 70 h
5 b g Daylami(IRE) —Bequeath (USA) (Lyphard (USA))
2289[7] 2566[12] 2967[P] 3173[4] 3540[P]

Commercial Flyer (IRE) *M C Pipe* 144+h 130+c
7 ch g Carroll House—Shabra Princess (Buckskin (FR))
(3946) 4444[P] 4759[P]

Commonchero (IRE) *M J P O'Brien* 125h 140+c
9 b g Desert Of Wind(USA) —Douala (GER) (Pentathlon)
2650a[10] **4138a[6] 5061a[P]**

Common Girl (IRE) *O Brennan* 106 h
8 gr m Roselier(FR) —Rumups Debut (IRE) (Good Thyne (USA))
(182) (367) 521[4] 1722[3] 1870[P] 2714[3] 3287[F]3559[5] 4797[P] 5138[P]

Compadre *P Monteith* 84h 93c
8 gr g Environment Friend—Cardinal Press (Sharrood (USA))
213[3]

Complete Outsider *Nick Williams* 111+h
8 b g Opera Ghost—Alice Passthorn (Rapid Pass)
4561[5] 4756[7] (4860) 4961[6]

Comply Or Die (IRE) *M C Pipe* 150h 155 c
7 b g Old Vic—Madam Madcap (Furry Glen)
2491[4] 3022[P]

Compo (IRE) *E McNamara* 106+h 112c
8 gr g Roselier(FR) —Noelbonne Femme (Bonne Noel)
(2688) **3816[2]**

Compton Bolter (IRE) *G A Butler* 104+h
9 b g Red Sunset—Milk And Honey (So Blessed)
3297[5]

Compton Classic *J S Goldie*
4 b c Compton Place—Ayr Classic (Local Suitor (USA))
2167[P]

Compton Commander *B N Pollock* 90h
8 ch g Barathea(IRE) —Triode (USA) (Sharpen Up)
5069[7]

Compton Dragon (USA) *R Johnson* 80h
7 ch g Woodman(USA) —Vilikaia (USA) (Nureyev (USA))
1527[11] 2444[11] 2749[6] 3443[6]

Compton Drake *G A Butler* 114 h
7 b g Mark Of Esteem(IRE) —Reprocolor (Jimmy Reppin)
(1235)

Compton Eagle *J J Lambe* 103h
6 b g Zafonic(USA) —Gayane (Nureyev (USA))
1375[7] 1567[2] 1823[8]

Compton Earl *J J Lambe*
6 ch h Efisio—Bay Bay (Bay Express)
645[P]

Compton Princess *Miss S E Forster* 56h
6 b m Compton Place—Curlew Calling (IRE) (Pennine Walk)
1064[7]

Compton Quay *Miss K M George* 79+h
4 ch g Compton Place—Roonah Quay (IRE) (Soviet Lad (USA))
945[4] 1207[2] 1404[2] 2274[9] 2454[3]2811[9]

Compton Star *R J Hodges* 82h
6 ch g Compton Place—Darakah (Doulab (USA))
25[10] 456[3] 753[4]

Comte De Chambord *Mark Campion* 28h 59c
10 gr g Baron Blakeney—Show Rose (Coliseum I)
107[P] 4054[F] 4657[5]5009[P]

Concert Pianist *P Winkworth* 107h 113 c
11 b g Rakaposhi King—Divine Affair (IRE) (The Parson)
2805[U] (3218) 3438[U]3581[P] **3900[3] 4287[P]**

Conemara Breeze *Miss L C Siddall* 66h
8 b g Old Vic—Belle Perk (IRE) (Executive Perk)
3443[P] 4657[P] 4786[6] 10[8]

Confluence (IRE) *Jonjo O'Neill* 85+h
5 gr g Linamix(FR) —River Swan (Nashwan (USA))
2421[7] 3423[P] (Dead)

Confuzed *A P Jones*
6 b g Pivotal—Times Of Times (IRE) (Distinctly North (USA))
1085[P] 1180[P]

Conna Castle (IRE) *James Joseph Mangan* 139+h
7 b g Germany(USA) —Mrs Hegarty (Decent Fellow)
4763[2]

Connaught Lady (IRE) *Ferdy Murphy* 58h
7 b m Flemensfirth(USA) —Finnuala Supreme (IRE) (Supreme Leader)
2412[10] 2674[P] (Dead)

Connemara Mist (IRE) *Mrs N S Evans* 83b 83c
11 ch g Good Thyne(USA) —Rainys Run (Deep Run)
746[P] 1041[3] 1191[2]1385[5] 5105[P]

Connemara Rose (IRE) *Francis Ennis* 94h
5 ch m Desert King(IRE) —Brillantina (FR) (Crystal Glitters (USA))
65a[15]

Conor's Pride (IRE) *B Mactaggart* 101h
9 ch g Phardante(FR) —Surely Madam (Torenaga)
412[P] 716[8] 784[7] 873[P] 1063[6]1151[7]

Conor's Secret (IRE) *F Flood* 85b
4 b f Pistolet Bleu(IRE) —Lorna's Beauty (IRE) (King's Ride)
5134a[S]

Conroy *F Jordan* 111h 108c
7 b g Greensmith—Highland Spirit (Scottish Reel)
347[3] 450[11] **1726[2] 2[F]**

Conscript (IRE) *A L T Moore* 103 h
4 b c Mujadil(USA) —Battle Queen (Kind Of Hush)
3515a[2]

Considine (USA) *C J Mann* 88+h
5 b g Romanov(IRE) —Libeccio (NZ) (Danzatore (CAN))
4603[P] 4956[9]

Constable Burton *Mrs A Duffield* 101+h
5 b g Foxhound(USA) —Actress (Known Fact (USA))
415[5] 691[2] (942) (1527)

Constant Husband *R N Bevis* 82 c
13 gr g Le Solaret(FR) —Miss Mirror (Magic Mirror)
2140[9] **2522[5] 3359[8]**

Constantine *Daniel Mark Loughnane* 118+h
6 gr g Linamix(FR) —Speremm (IRE) (Sadler's Wells (USA))
13[8] 332[7] 450[7] 1878[10] 2324[4]2525[5] 3135[P] 5103a[17]

Constantius *K C Bailey* 86b
5 b g Halling(USA) —Premier Night (Old Vic)
1323[4] 1849[13]

Contact Dancer (IRE) *C F Swan* 119h
7 b g Sadler's Wells(USA) —Rain Queen (Rainbow Quest (USA))
2762[5]

Contas (GER) *M F Harris* 79h
6 b h Lomitas—Cocorna (Night Shift (USA))
177[7] 312[4]

Contemporary Art *N J Dawe* 66h
8 b g Blushing Flame(USA) —Marie La Rose (FR) (Night Shift (USA))
79[P] 1017[9] 1075[P]

Contendo *N W Alexander* 81b
5 ch g Classic Cliche(IRE) —Madam Ross (Ardross)
4147[7] 5008[11]

Contraband *M C Pipe* 145 h 159c
8 b g Red Ransom(USA) —Shortfall (Last Tycoon)
1970[5] 5143[3]

Contract Scotland (IRE) *L Lungo* 100h 103+c
11 br g Religiously(USA) —Stroked Again (On Your Mark)
80[5] **1837[F] 2413[P]5036[2]**

Control Man (IRE) *M C Pipe* 137 h 142 c
8 ch g Glacial Storm(USA) —Got To Fly (IRE) (Kemal (FR))
2176[3] 2747[13] **3022[U]3390[3] 4496[7]**

Convent Girl (IRE) *Mrs P N Duffield* 95+h
6 b m Bishop Of Cashel—Right To The Top (Nashwan (USA))
203[5] 574[5] 804[2] 959[2] 1740[P]

Coogans Bluff (IRE) *Gerard Keane* 70h 13c
6 b g Sri Pekan(USA) —Pleasant Outlook (USA) (El Gran Senor (USA))
3528a[P]

Coola Boola (IRE) *Adrian Maguire* 64c
7 b g Prince Rooney(IRE) —Bios Brrin (Pitpan)
93a[21]

Coola Tagula (IRE) *C W Thornton* 40h
4 b g Tagula(IRE) —Second Craft (IRE) (Second Set (IRE))
1601[12]

Coolawarra (IRE) *D M Forster* 51h
7 b g Accordion—Cool Virtue (IRE) (Zaffaran (USA))
2923[14]

Cool Bathwick (IRE) *G H Yardley*
7 b g Entrepreneur—Tarafa (Akarad (FR))
4754[12] 5009[P]

Coolbythepool *M J Gingell* 63h
6 b g Bijou D'Inde—Alchi (USA) (Alleged (USA))
2043[5] 2261[12]

Cool Carroll (IRE) *Mrs Tracey Barfoot-Saunt* 79c
8 b m Carroll House—Sohot Whyknot (IRE) (Macmillion)
122[P] 1318[U] 1570[P]2018[4] 2936[15] 3278[5]

Cool Chilli *N J Pomfret* 49h 95+c
8 gr g Gran Alba(USA)—Miss Flossa (FR) (Big John (FR))
135[P] 2257[8] 2960[5]

Cool Cossack (IRE) *Mrs S J Smith* 98h 116+c
9 ch g Moscow Society(USA)—Knockacool Breeze (Buckskin (FR))
(430)

Cool Dante (IRE) *T R George* 105 h 98+c
11 b g Phardante(FR)—Mum's Girl (Deep Run)
354[P] 674[13] 941[9]1233[3] 1395[3] 1655[4]

Cool Dessa Blues *W Amos* 77h 100c
7 br m Cool Jazz—Our Dessa (Derek H)
1839[7] 2066[P] **3375[2] 3930[2]4528[2]**

Cooldine Boy (IRE) *P J Hobbs* 91b
5 b g Oscar(IRE)—Roouan Girl (IRE) (Tremblant)
4072[14] 4422[7] 4680[4]

Cooldine Lad (IRE) *J Howard Johnson* 93+h
6 b g Flemensfirth(USA)—Lotto Lady (Le Moss)
2638[P] 3496[6] 3927[3]

Coole Abbey (IRE) *W Amos* 112c
14 b g Viteric(FR)—Eleanors Joy (Sheer Grit)
411[3]

Coolefind (IRE) *W J Warner* 110 c
8 b g Phardante(FR)—Greavesfind (The Parson)
48[F] (280) 3693[4]

Coole Glen (IRE) *W J Warner* 100+c
10 b g Executive Perk—Cailin Liath (Peacock (FR))
278[2] 437[2] 4349[5]5053[2]

Coolgreaney (IRE) *S J Treacy* 105h
5 b m Bob Back(USA)—Brambleshine (IRE) (Phardante (FR))
4887a[5]

Cool Linnett *P A Blockley*
5 br g Cool Jazz—Dowdency (Dowsing (USA))
4106[P]

Coolnahilla (IRE) *W J Burke* 95b 135c
10 gr g Roselier(FR)—Reoss (King's Ride)
91a[2] 3587a[6] 4929a[6]5129a[5]

Cool Present (IRE) *K R Burke* 87+c
7 ch m Presenting—Cooladeerra Queen (IRE) (Remainder Man)
1414[4] 1560[2]

Cool Roxy *A G Blackmore* 127h 109+c
9 b g Environment Friend—Roxy River (Ardross)
1743[3] 2483[6] 2871[6] 3135[3] 4461[9]4821[3]

Cool Society *R H Alner* 55h
4 b g Atraf—Cool Run (Deep Run)
3188[9] 3898[7] 4784[13] 5043[2]

Cool Song *Miss Suzy Smith* 80h 81 c
10 ch g Michelozzo(USA)—Vi's Delight (New Member)
1713[2] 1960[4] (2424) 2863[P] 3359[2] 3662[2]5136[6]

Cool Spice *P J Hobbs* 124+h
9 b m Karinga Bay—Cool Run (Deep Run)
(387) 633[9] 1020[7]

Cool Trader (IRE) *Mrs C J Ikin*
8 b g Mister Lord(USA)—Costly Alyse (Al Sirat)
631[P] 728[P]

Coomakista *Mrs E J Reed* 98+c
9 b m Primitive Rising(USA)—Miss Eros (Royal Fountain)
281[2] (4791) (5095)

Coorbawn Vic (IRE) *S A Brookshaw* 77+h
5 ch g Old Vic—Double Harmony (IRE) (Orchestra)
3462[8] 4072[12] 4595[7] 4732[5] 5138[6]

Copper Bay (IRE) *A King* 93h
4 b g Revoque(IRE)—Bahia Laura (FR) (Bellypha)
2580[3] 3038[3] 3786[4] 4613[5]

Coppermalt (USA) *R Curtis* 77h 77+c
8 b g Affirmed(USA)—Poppy Carew (IRE) (Danehill (USA))
565[7] 1152[4] (1395) 1564[4] **1803[6]**2214[5]

Copsale Lad *N J Henderson* 123h 149c
9 ch g Karinga Bay—Squeaky Cottage (True Song)
(1917) 2531[2] (3134) 4456[2] 4759[3]

Copyerselfon (IRE) *A M Hales*
7 bb g Right Win(IRE)—Cedarbelle (IRE) (Regular Guy)
1182[P]

Coralbrook *Mrs P Robeson* 100 h
6 b g Alderbrook—Coral Delight (Idiots Delight)
194[5] 1921[10] 2563[9] (3818) 4453[6] 4907[3]

Coral Island *Mrs Bernice Stronge* 90h 90c
12 b g Charmer—Misowni (Niniski (USA))
181[P] 4216[5] 4607[P]

Corals Laurel (IRE) *R T Phillips* 106h
7 b g Accordion—Bold Tipperary (IRE) (Orchestra)
2821[8] 3393[3] 3881[3] 4104[F] 4606[10]4726[5] 5010[8]

Corbie Abbey (IRE) *B Mactaggart* 79+c
11 b g Glacial Storm(USA)—Dromoland Lady (Pollerton)
213[11]

Corbie Lynn *W S Coltherd* 71 h
9 ch m Jumbo Hirt(USA)—Kilkenny Gorge (Deep Run)
2417[7] 2990[10] 4491[P] 4724[P]

Corble (IRE) *P J Hobbs* 110+h
6 b g Broken Hearted—Itaparica (FR) (Mistigri)
3963[13] 4280[8] 4935[5] (Dead)

Cordial (IRE) *J J Quinn* 104 h
6 gr g Charnwood Forest(IRE)—Moon Festival (Be My Guest (USA))
3328[4] 3591[F] (Dead)

Cordilla (IRE) *N G Richards* 110+h 119c
8 b g Accordion—Tumble Heather (Tumble Wind)
2629[5] **2946[3] 3965[P]**4986[6]

Corkan (IRE) *Mrs F Kehoe* 73c
12 b g Torus—Broad Tab (Cantab)
673[8] 981[7] (1122) 1960[8] 4607[P] 4799[P]5020[6]

Corker *D B Feek* 91h
4 ch g Grand Lodge(USA)—Immortelle (Arazi (USA))
1737[4] 2045[4] 2236[2] 2578[2] 2803[3]3664[6] 3943[7] 4912[P]

Corlande (IRE) *Mrs S J Smith* 121 h
6 br g Teamster—Vaguely Deesse (USA) (Vaguely Noble)
13[7] 127[13] 2110[5] 2347[11] (3384) (3987)

Cornish Flame *J D Frost* 68b
6 b g Thowra(FR)—Regal Flame (Royalty)
4947[5]

Cornish Gale (IRE) *D McCain Jnr* 106c
12 br g Strong Gale—Seanaphobal Lady (Kambalda)
348[2] 512[4] 4555[9]4748[11]

Cornish Jack *J D Frost* 54h
6 b g Thowra(FR)—Melody Mine (Torus)
1681[10] 1968[9] 2212[12] 2309[13]

Cornish Jester *C J Down* 101h
7 b g Slip Anchor—Fortune's Girl (Ardross)
1903[6] 2683[6] 2859[P]

Cornish Orchid (IRE) *C J Down* 72+h
5 ch g Be My Guest(USA)—Nilousha (Darshaan)
3246[5] 3505[8] 4941[6]

Cornish Rebel (IRE) *P F Nicholls* 152 h 162 c
9 br g Un Desperado(FR)—Katday (FR) (Miller's Mate)
2491[3] 3022[3] 4470[16]4777[P]

Cornish Sett (IRE) *P F Nicholls* 131 h 150c
7 b g Accordion—Hue 'N' Cry (IRE) (Denel (FR))
1783[2] (2482) 3150[4]3341[2] 3879[2] (4241) 4456[7] 4958[F]

Coronado's Gold (USA) *V Smith* 93h
5 ch g Coronado's Quest(USA)—Debit My Account (USA) (Classic Account (USA))
1360[4] 1654[4] 1772[6] 2261[8]

Corporal Pete *Lady Connell*
5 b g Petoski—Smart Chick (True Song)
1777[F]

Corporate Player (IRE) *Noel T Chance* 101+h 112+c
8 b g Zaffaran(USA)—Khazna (Stanford)
(1479)

Correct And Right (IRE) *J W Mullins* 97+h 103c
7 b m Great Commotion(USA)—Miss Hawkins (Modern Dancer)
233[4] 399[4]

Corrib Drift (USA) *Jamie Poulton* 85+h 91c
6 ch g Sandpit(BRZ)—Bygones (USA) (Lyphard (USA))
1235[7] 1407[3] 1596[5] 1921[6] 2809[P]**3432[3] 3903[4]**

Corrib Lad (IRE) *L Lungo* 94h 109+c
8 b g Supreme Leader—Nun So Game (The Parson)
9[3] **(2026) 2945[F] 3533[3]**

Corries Wood (IRE) *J J Lambe* 85h 69c
7 b g Corrouge(USA)—Ewood Park (Wishing Star)
991[P] 1151[6] 1374[3] 1526[4] **1686[5]1886[P]**

Corrig Caul (IRE) *Raymond Hurley* 108b
5 b m Oscar(IRE)—Cats Corner (IRE) (Buckskin (FR))
5134a[5]

Corroboree (IRE) *N A Twiston-Davies* 106 h 83 c
9 b g Corrouge(USA)—Laura's Toi (Quayside)
2629[10] **3037[5] 3368[12]3887[4]**

Corsican Native (USA) *P Bowen* 107+h
5 b g Lear Fan(USA)—Corsini (Machiavellian (USA))
2659[2] 2952[2]

Corston Jigthyme (IRE) *P Bowen* 89c
8 bb g Good Thyne(USA)—Corston Dancer (IRE) (Lafontaine (USA))
1041[P]

Corton (IRE) *Jonjo O'Neill* 90h
7 gr g Definite Article—Limpopo (Green Desert (USA))
178[8]

Corton Denham *G P Enright*
5 ch g Wolfhound(USA)—Wigit (Safawan)
1480[P]

Cosi Celeste (FR) *John Allen* 97h
9 b g Apeldoorn(FR)—Lemixikoa (FR) (Mendez (FR))
441[11] 2552[P] 3146[U] 4549[P] 4752[3]

Cosmic Sky *Robert Abrey*
9 ch g Charmer—Silver Cirrus (General Ironside)
404[P]

Cosmocrat *R Lee* 105 h 121c
8 b g Cosmonaut—Bella Coola (Northern State (USA))
(4) 1831[2] 2210[6]2577[4]

Cossack Dancer (IRE) *M Bradstock* 122 h 120 c
8 b g Moscow Society(USA)—Merry Lesa (Dalesa)
247[8] **2044[4] 2732[3]3329[2] (4590) 4829[2]**

Costa Del Sol (IRE) *Miss Victoria Roberts*
5 ch g General Monash(USA)—L'Harmonie (USA) (Bering)
838[P]

Cotswold Rose *N M Babbage* 75h
6 b m Sovereign Water(FR)—Rosehall (Ardross)
77[7] 261[4] 629[5] 801[8] 1564[3]

Cottage Hill *C R Wilson* 29b
7 b m Primitive Rising(USA)—Celtic Lane (Welsh Captain)
591[P]

Cottam Eclipse *M W Easterby*
5 b g Environment Friend—Che Gambe (USA) (Lyphard (USA))
3657[13] 5138[P]

Cottam Grange *M W Easterby* 109h
6 b g River Falls—Karminski (Pitskelly)
372[2] 1760[U] 2079[3] 2292[10]

Cottam Phantom *M W Easterby* 58b
5 b g River Falls—William's Bird (USA) (Master Willie)
1613[6] 1762[11] 2192[14] 2838[P]

Cottingham (IRE) *M C Chapman* 92h
5 b g Perugino(USA)—Stately Princess (Robellino (USA))
2950[6] 3597[4] **3920[F]**

Cougar (IRE) *R Rowe* 82h
6 b g Sadler's Wells(USA)—Pieds De Plume (FR) (Seattle Slew (USA))
2934[P] 3905[P]

Could Be Alright (IRE) *Noel T Chance* 107b
7 b g Witness Box(USA)—Some Gossip (Le Bavard (FR))
1681[4] 1820[3]

Could It Be Legal *Evan Williams* 44h
9 b g Roviris—Miss Gaylord (Cavo Doro)
2140[F]

Couldn't Be Phar (IRE) *D R Gandolfo* 89h
9 ch g Phardante(FR)—Queenford Belle (Celtic Cone)
4872[P]

Coulthard (IRE) *Mrs P Sly* 112h 102c
13 ch g Glenstal(USA)—Royal Aunt (Martinmas)
197[12]

Counsellor Tim *C J Down* 24b
6 ch g Hatim(USA)—Miss Counsel (Leading Counsel (USA))
1042[12]

Countback (FR) *C C Bealby* 79h
7 b g Anabaa(USA)—Count Me Out (FR) (Kaldoun (FR))
1552[P] 1712[2] 1814[6]

Count Boris *J A Geake* 101h
5 b g Groom Dancer(USA)—Bu Hagab (IRE) (Royal Academy (USA))
2624[3] 3275[4] 3906[6] 4606[8]

Count Campioni (IRE) *M Pitman* 135h 114 c
12 br g Brush Aside(USA)—Emerald Flair (Flair Path)
439[P] 694[5]

Countess Kiri *P Bowen* 94b
8 b m Opera Ghost—Ballagh Countess (King's Ride)
1231[F]

Countess Trifaldi (IRE) *Michael John Phillips* 14b 103c
6 b m Flemensfirth(USA)—Course Royal (Crash Course)
4542a[3]

Count Fosco *M Todhunter* 111+h
8 b g Alflora(IRE)—Carrikins (Buckskin (FR))
1334[7]

Count Kearney (IRE) *S J Mahon* 111h
4 b g Imperial Ballet(IRE)—Doumayna (Kouban (FR))
4122a[3] 4435[12]

Count Oski *M J Ryan* 92h 100c
10 b g Petoski—Sea Countess (Ercolano (USA))
283[8] **522[3] (673) 746[F]865[P]**

Country Rally *Mrs S Gardner* 43b
7 b g North Col—Country Art (Country Retreat)
249[8] 656[13] 3342[P]

Countrywide Dancer (IRE) *K W Hogg*
6 b m Danehill Dancer(IRE)—Meadow Grass (IRE) (Thatching)
4301[12] 4389[8] 4917[P]

Countrywide Sun *A C Whillans* 79h
4 b g Benny The Dip(USA)—Sundae Girl (USA) (Green Dancer (USA))
1512[7] 1601[6] 1797[10] 2064[5] 2263[3]2639[P] 4045[4] 4360[3]

Count Tony *Mrs D A Hamer* 122 h
12 ch g Keen—Turtle Dove (Gyr (USA))
315[5] 633[7]

County Classic *T D Easterby* 100+h
7 b m Noble Patriarch—Cumbrian Rhapsody (Sharrood (USA))
2264[P] 2590[9] 2766[P] 3040[7]

County Final (IRE) *Noel Meade* 120 h 101+c
7 b g Norwich—Soul Lucy (Lucifer (USA))
3052a[4] 4336a[5]

Count Your Change (FR) *Y Fouin*
3 b g Pennekamp(USA)—Count Me Out (FR) (Kaldoun (FR))
4298a[2]

Courageous Dove *A Bailey* 82h
5 gr g Overbury(IRE)—Mazzelmo (Thethingaboutitis (USA))
1654[8] 2460[6]

Courage Under Fire *C C Bealby* 90h 124c
6 b g Risk Me(FR)—Dreamtime Quest (Blakeney)
240[P]

Courant D'Air (IRE) *Lucinda Featherstone* 100h 71+c
5 b g Indian Rocket—Red River Rose (IRE) (Red Sunset)
275[4] 2296[F] 2714[8] 3018[7] 3600[7]3959[F] 4429[5] **4633[3]**

Coursing Run (IRE) *H D Daly* 122+c
10 ch g Glacial Storm(USA)—Let The Hare Run (IRE) (Tale Quale)
12[P] 2875[R] 3614[5]3989[4] (4395)

Court Alliance *R J Price* 69h
7 ch g Alhijaz—Fairfields Cone (Celtic Cone)
911[9] 1745[P]

Court Award (IRE) *B G Powell* 72h 47c
9 b g Montelimar(USA)—Derring Lass (Derring Rose)
201[11] **486[U] 673[10]**801[7] 863[12] 978[12]

Court Emperor *Evan Williams* 68h
6 b g Mtoto—Fairfields Cone (Celtic Cone)
4754[9] 5023[5]

Court Empress *P D Purdy* 80h
9 ch m Emperor Fountain—Tudor Sunset (Sunyboy)
613[9] 801[P] 1089[4] 1445[3] 3483[R]

Court Leader (IRE) *Thomas Mullins* 112 h 120c
8 b m Supreme Leader—Droichidin (Good Thyne (USA))
66a[6] **4018a[F]**

Court Of Justice (USA) *K A Morgan* 117h 88c
10 b g Alleged(USA)—Captive Island (Northfields (USA))
425[8] **646[3]**

Court One *R E Barr* 97h
8 b g Shareef Dancer(USA)—Fairfields Cone (Celtic Cone)
(813) 913[2] 3918[P] 4916[7]

Court Storm (IRE) *F Flood* 115h
7 b g Flemensfirth(USA)—Storm Court (IRE) (Glacial Storm (USA))
2784a[4]

Cousin Nicky *P J Hobbs* 94h 122+c
5 ch g Bob Back(USA)—Little Red Spider (Bustino)
2530[13] 3175[11] 3508[7] **(4288) (4559) 4728[6]**

Coustou (IRE) *R M Stronge* 91h
6 b g In Command(IRE)—Carranza (IRE) (Lead On Time (USA))
105[2] 1949[2] 2214[4] 2685[2]

Covent Garden *J Howard Johnson* 136+h
8 b g Sadler's Wells(USA)—Temple Row (Ardross)
(2369) 2747[P]

Cowboyboots (IRE) *L Wells* 109 h 130 c
8 b g Lord Americo—Little Welly (Little Buskins)
2813[8] **3186[4] 3469[3]4103[P] 4690[4]**

Coxwell Cossack *Mark Campion* 89h
13 ch g Gildoran—Stepout (Sagaro)
237[2] 686[3]

Coy Lad (IRE) *Miss P Robson* 82h 85+c
9 ch g Be My Native(USA)—Don't Tutch Me (The Parson)
4844[2] 5037[4]

Coyote Lakes *M J McGrath* 82h
7 ch g Be My Chief(USA)—Oakbrook Tern (USA) (Arctic Tern (USA))
359[5] 523[9]

Cracboumwiz (FR) *Mrs H Dalton* 98 h
6 b g Baby Turk—Ellapampa (FR) (Pampabird)
2763[3]

Crackadee *Miss R Brewis*
7 bb g Alflora(IRE)—Carnetto (Le Coq D'Or)
4719[5]

Cracking Dawn (IRE) *Mrs S Alner* 114 c
11 b g Be My Native(USA)—Rare Coin (Kemal (FR))
3910[2] 4092[2] 4471[P]

Crackington (FR) *H Alexander* 31b
6 gr g Linamix(FR)—Ta Awun (USA) (Housebuster (USA))
484[11] 2591[P]

Crackin' Liss (IRE) *John E Kiely* 109b
5 b m Bob Back(USA)—Liss De Paor (IRE) (Phardante (FR))
5081a[14]

Crackleando *A R Dicken* 99 h
5 ch g Forzando—Crackling (Electric)
99[6] 667[4] 2452[9] 3208[5] 3378[8]3854[P] 4364[3] 4488[5] 4724[10]

Crackpot (IRE) *C Rae* 53b
6 b g Mohaajir(USA)—Next Case (IRE) (Bluffer)
2480[10] 3353[10]

Cracow (IRE) *W K Goldsworthy* 72h
9 b g Polish Precedent(USA)—Height Of Secrecy (Shirley Heights)
385[5] 745[5] 802[6]

Crafty Glen (IRE) *G F Edwards* 38b
6 b g Warcraft(USA)—Glenmullen Rose (IRE) (Roselier (FR))
655[14] 866[10]

Crafty Lady (IRE) *Miss Suzy Smith* 90b
7 bb m Warcraft(USA)—Kilmana (IRE) (Castle Keep)
316[3] 1762[5] *1922[5]*

Cragg Prince (IRE) *Mrs S J Smith* 87 h
7 b g Roselier(FR)—Ivory Queen (Teenoso (USA))
2571[10] 3042[4] 3554[5] **3781[P]**

Crashtown Hall (IRE) *C Tinkler* 97+b
5 b h Saddlers' Hall(IRE)—Crashtown Lucy (Crash Course)
4622[6]

Crashtown Leader (IRE) *C Tinkler* 100h
7 b g Supreme Leader—Crashtown Lucy (Crash Course)
1892[8] 2638[P]

Crathorne (IRE) *M Todhunter* 121+h
6 b g Alzao(USA)—Shirley Blue (IRE) (Shirley Heights)
(991) (1591) (1720) 1823[4] 2369[8] 2746[9] 5066[5]

Craven (IRE) *N J Henderson* 127 h
6 b g Accordion—Glen Dieu (Furry Glen)
(2056) (2826) 3369[2] 3881[9] 4750[P]

Crazy Flirt (IRE) *A E Jones*
4 b f King's Best(USA)—Itab (USA) (Dayjur (USA))
1207[P] 1268[4]

Crazy Horse (IRE) *L Lungo* 120 h
13 b g Little Bighorn—Our Dorcet (Condorcet (FR))
3378[2] 3966[P]

Crazy Like A Fool (IRE) *M G Quinlan*
7 b g Charnwood Forest(IRE)—Shanghai Girl (Distant Relative)
2967[P] 3985[P]

Crazy Mazie *K A Morgan* 77h
9 b m Risk Me(FR)—Post Impressionist (IRE) (Ahonoora)
237[P]

Creagh Bay (IRE) *R T Phillips* 87b
7 b g Tidaro(USA)—Martha Anne (IRE) (Brush Aside (USA))
1042[4]

Cream Cracker *R H Alner* 105+h
8 b m Sir Harry Lewis(USA)—Cream By Post (Torus)
220[3] 520[5] 664[3] (982) (1037) 1263[4] 5019[4]

Create A Storm (IRE) *J G Portman* 82b
6 bb m Bob Back(USA)—Elag (Strong Gale)
1799[14] 2082[P] 2486[8]

Credit (IRE) *J Howard Johnson* 100 h
5 b g Intikhab(USA)—Tycooness (IRE) (Last Tycoon)
2519[6] 2716[7] 3378[13] 3761[13] 3929[10]

Cregg House (IRE) *S Donohoe* 115 h 134 c
11 ch g King Persian—Loyal River (Over The River (FR))
45a[13] 2370[11] 2768[4]4762[6] 4984[5]

Creinch *M F Harris* 97+h
5 b g Overbury(IRE)—Kingsfold Blaze (Mazilier (USA))
2983[11] 3354[P] 4521[6] 4934[3] 5043[U]

Creme D'Arblay (IRE) *Thomas Cooper* 105+h
4 b f Singspiel(IRE) —Daleria (Darshaan)
4887aF 5077a9
Creon *Jonjo O'Neill* 130 h 119c
11 b g Saddlers' Hall(IRE) —Creake (Derring-Do)
3389P
Cresswell Gold *D A Rees* 68+h
9 b m Homo Sapien—Running For Gold (Rymer)
10795 12623 15397
Cresswell Willow (IRE) *W K Goldsworthy* 91 h
6 b m Witness Box(USA) —Mandoora (IRE) (Mandalus)
13238 14014 3149P 32816 346110 36468 38843 4429U 4619P 4738P
Crested Penguin *Brian Perry* 62h 55c
8 b g Rock Hopper—Welsh Secret (Welsh Captain)
985
Crimond (IRE) *G A Harker* 60b
4 b f Zaffaran(USA) —Bayalika (FR) (Kashtan (FR))
43046
Crimson Bow (GER) *J G Given* 91+h
4 ch f Night Shift(USA) —Carma (IRE) (Konigsstuhl (GER))
1551P 20762 24427 275210 3442P
Crimson Pirate (IRE) *B De Haan* 104+h 119+c
9 b g Phardante(FR) —Stroked Again (On Your Mark)
(3243)
Cristoforo (IRE) *B J Curley* 107+h
9 b g Perugino(USA) —Red Barons Lady (IRE) (Electric)
3477 (428)
Cristophe *P Bowen* 110+h 87c
8 b g Kris—Our Shirley (Shirley Heights)
4549P **49435 5136F**
Critical Stage (IRE) *J D Frost* 110h
7 b g King's Theatre(IRE) —Zandaka (FR) (Doyoun)
57110 11882 12632 18044 (2216) 27468312813
Croc An Oir (IRE) *R Ford* 111+h 122+c
9 ch g Treasure Hunter—Cool Mary (Beau Charmeur (FR))
(630) (697) 9063 **11102 12052**1294P **(1603)**
Crofters Lad (IRE) *Miss Venetia Williams* 103b
4 gr g Almutawakel—Hariyana (IRE) (Kahyasi)
33462
Crofton Arch *J E Dixon* 77h
6 b g Jumbo Hirt(USA) —Joyful Imp (Import)
2108 6025 643P 337613
Croghan Loch (IRE) *P G Murphy* 69c
9 br g Mister Lord(USA) —Croghan Katie (Croghan Hill)
2126P 23774 255510
Croix De Guerre (IRE) *P J Hobbs* 130h 135 c
6 gr g Highest Honor(FR) —Esclava (USA) (Nureyev (USA))
3442 761P (825) (1024) 12643 13003 14002(1743) **1918P** 220716
Croker (IRE) *S T Lewis*
11 ch g Rainbows For Life(CAN) —Almagest (Dike (USA))
863P
Cromwell (IRE) *M C Chapman* 69h 93c
11 b g Last Tycoon—Catherine Parr (USA) (Riverman (USA))
1817 2406 37364649 547P 9895156414 **20805**
22906
Crosby Dancer *W S Coltherd* 70h
7 b g Glory Of Dancer—Mary Macblain (Damister (USA))
47239
Crosby Don *J R Weymes* 33h 75c
11 b g Alhijaz—Evening Star (Red Sunset)
371P
Crossbow Creek *M G Rimell* 137+h 148c
8 b g Lugana Beach—Roxy River (Ardross)
2083 **(2456) 26348 2970F40763 4431P**
Crossing *William J Fitzpatrick* 89b
5 b m Cape Cross(IRE) —Piney River (Pharly (FR))
221117 5081a18
Cross My Shadow (IRE) *M F Harris*
4 b g Cape Cross(IRE) —Shadowglow (Shaadi (USA))
159412
Crottys Point (IRE) *Henry De Bromhead* 80h
4 ch g Rudimentary(USA) —Shuil Ura (IRE) (Phardante (FR))
5060a11
Crown Agent (IRE) *M E Sowersby* 56h
6 b g Mukaddamah(USA) —Supreme Crown (USA) (Chief's Crown (USA))
11088 1553U 1608P 1723P
Crown Trix (IRE) *C W Moore* 61b
7 b g Riverhead(USA) —Ballagh Trix (IRE) (Buckskin (FR))
715
Crow Wood *J J Quinn* 135 h
7 b g Halling(USA) —Play With Me (IRE) (Alzao (USA))
(1614) 17943 21614 (3761) 443012
Crozan (FR) *N J Henderson* 147 c
6 b g Sassanian(USA) —La Guyonniere (FR) (Silver Rainbow)
(2174) 29734 3976P4759P
Cruise Director *Ian Williams* 104+h
6 b g Zilzal(USA) —Briggsmaid (Elegant Air)
28264 34223 39483 45034 47366
Cruise Leader (IRE) *C Grant* 130 c
11 b g Supreme Leader—Ormskirk Mover (Deep Run)
2993P
Cruise The Fairway (IRE) *B G Powell* 106c
10 b g Insan(USA) —Tickhill (General Assembly (USA))
3304 522P
Cruising Clyde *P Winkworth* 95h
7 ch g Karinga Bay—Bournel (Sunley Builds)
21273 2503P 3184P 5137P
Cruising River (IRE) *Miss H C Knight* 112 h 117c
7 b g Over The River(FR) —Jellaride (IRE) (King's Ride)
18916 23772 (2729) 3213P (3942) 4447P495711
Crumbs *B Mactaggart* 58b
6 b m Puissance—Norska (Northfields (USA))
8217 418P (Dead)
Crusoe (IRE) *A Sadik* 45h
9 b g Turtle Island(IRE) —Self Reliance (Never So Bold)
4903P
Cruzspiel *J R Fanshawe* 120+h
6 br g Singspiel(IRE) —Allespagne (USA) (Trempolino (USA))
(1632) (1818)
Cryfield *N Tinkler* 49h
9 b g Efisio—Ciboure (Norwick (USA))
209911 258417 2873P
Cry Of The Wolf *R M Stronge*
4 ch g Loup Sauvage(USA) —Hopesay (Warning)
38988
Crystal D'Ainay (FR) *A King* 162h 135c
7 b g Saint Preuil(FR) —Guendale (FR) (Cadoudal (FR))
19254 24903 **30224 33904**40693 445812
Crystal Dance (FR) *D J Kemp* 72h
6 gr g Loup Solitaire(USA) —Somptueuse (FR) (Crystal Palace (FR))
4897F
Crystal Gift *A C Whillans* 121h
14 b g Dominion—Grain Lady (USA) (Greinton)
646 (499)
Crystal Haven *M W Easterby* 27b
5 ch m Bal Harbour—Gypsy Race (IRE) (Good Thyne (USA))
155413
Crystal Hollow *N R Mitchell*
6 b g Riverwise(USA) —Pallanda (Pablond)
321611 3511P 4005P 45219 4691P
Crystal Ka (FR) *M R Hoad* 57h
4 b g Northern Crystal—Kahuna Magic (FR) (Dancing Spree (USA))
1948P 28038 318210 4651U 505012
Crystal Runner *E J Jamieson* 63h
6 b m Glacial Storm(USA) —Swift Run (Deep Run)
323110 183411
Culbann (IRE) *C Rae* 97b
7 b m Religiously(USA) —Persian Gem (IRE) (Persian Heights)
15088 1915P 24747 3335P
Culcabock (IRE) *Miss Lucinda V Russell* 112 h
6 b g Unfuwain(USA) —Evidently (IRE) (Slip Anchor)
1513P 18367 20388 245211 32084(3378) 35425 41104 44903 47925 484811
Cullian *J G M O'Shea* 97h 92c
9 b m Missed Flight—Diamond Gig (Pitskelly)
36556 4331P (4577) 46093 47834 **4936551056**
Cultured *Mrs A J Bowlby*
5 b m Danzero(AUS) —Seek The Pearl (Rainbow Quest (USA))
3322P 3690P 4074F
Cumbrian Knight (IRE) *J M Jefferson* 116+h 106+c
8 b g Presenting—Crashrun (Crash Course)
1483 (604) 9391110494 14127 31715
Cunning Pursuit *N J Henderson* 109h
5 b g Pursuit Of Love—Mistitled (USA) (Miswaki (USA))
1004 57115 23247
Cupla Cairde *O Brennan* 119h 93c
6 b h Double Eclipse(IRE) —Four-Legged Friend (Aragon)
1116a5 **3955P 4633P49082**
Curate (USA) *M E Sowersby*
7 ch g Unfuwain(USA) —Carniola (Rainbow Quest (USA))
3962P 4501P 4905P
Curfew Tolls (IRE) *Henry De Bromhead* 119c
10 b g Denel(FR) —Takeaway Curry (Mandalus)
1420a3
Curly Spencer (IRE) *R J Hewitt* 116 h 117c
12 br g Yashgan—Tim's Brief (Avocat)
40734 43514
Curragh Gold (IRE) *Mrs P N Dutfield* 75h
6 b m Flying Spur(AUS) —Go Indigo (IRE) (Cyrano De Bergerac)
169U 4730P
Curraheen Chief (IRE) *J L Spearing* 112b 106c
11 b g Little Bighorn—Sprightly's Last (Random Shot)
4786P
Curtins Hill (IRE) *Mrs K Waldron* 107 h 127c
12 b g Roi Guillaume(FR) —Kinallen Lady (IRE) (Abednego)
(55) 3112 64828428 1301P
Cusp *Mrs A M Thorpe* 73h 92c
6 b m Pivotal—Bambolona (Bustino)
1226 18525 2522F26793 28188 3274P
Custom Design *G A Harker* 92+h
5 ch g Minster Son—Scotto's Regret (Celtic Cone)
(2112) 28443 (4387) 506412
Cutthroat *P J Hobbs* 103h
6 ch g Kris—Could Have Been (Nomination)
1668S 17455 (Dead)
Cutting Edge *A J Chamberlain* 61b
7 b m Golden Heights—Another Sword (Broadsword (USA))
2774 490116 763P
Cyanara *Dr P Pritchard* 61h 78c
10 b m Jupiter Island—Shamana (Broadsword (USA))
4642 6732 11224141411
Cybele Eria (FR) *John Allen* 90h 84c
9 b m Johann Quatz(FR) —Money Can't Buy (Thatching)
16 12189 20718 265911 28066
Cyborg De Sou (FR) *G A Harker* 113+h 113c
8 b g Cyborg(FR) —Moomaw (Akarad (FR))
(1509) 17583 2626431723 **3317U 39403**4586P **5119F**
Cyborsun (FR) *M F Harris* 106 c
9 ch g Cyborg(FR) —Kaprika (FR) (Cadoudal (FR))
28775 (3338) 4120S (Dead)
Cyindien (FR) *Evan Williams* 107h 84c
9 bb g Cyborg(FR) —Indiana Rose (FR) (Cadoudal (FR))
2337 **4647 67337835 8654 1321413854**
Cyrlight (FR) *A Chaille-Chaille* 133+h
6 ch g Saint Cyrien(FR) —Yellow Light (FR) (Lightning (FR))
585a2
Dabiroun (IRE) *Paul Nolan* 138+h
5 b g Desert Prince(IRE) —Dabaya (IRE) (In The Wings)
65a3 1093a11
Dabus *M C Chapman* 99 h 107c
11 b g Kris—Licorne (Sadler's Wells (USA))
26 239P 37011**466RR** 15598 16109 **1758LFT**1816P **19114 19586 2208P 24439 25165**
Dad's Elect (GER) *Ian Williams* 126h 103+c
7 b g Lomitas—Diamond Lake (USA) (Cox's Ridge (USA))
4592 7822
Dafarabad (IRE) *Jonjo O'Neill* 101h
4 b c Cape Cross(IRE) —Daftara (IRE) (Caerleon (USA))
24422 30384 33288
Daffi (IRE) *F Jestin*
6 b m Zaffaran(USA) —Bdoore (IRE) (Petoski)
4846P
Daggy Boy (NZ) *R C Guest* 68h
6 ch g Daggers Drawn(USA) —La Berceuse (NZ) (Kings Island)
591P 16718 18248 258412
Daguyda (FR) *Ferdy Murphy* 94h 94c
7 b g Northern Crystal—La Domizia (FR) (Tip Moss (FR))
4133 5545
Daihannah (IRE) *Miss H E Roberts* 60h
6 b m Shahanndeh—Deep Fresh (Deep Run)
8175 1018P 15386 19749 (Dead)
Daily Run (IRE) *G M Moore* 79h
8 b g Supreme Leader—Rugged Run (Deep Run)
4145 6877 1000P
Daisy Dale *S C Burrough* 73h
8 gr m Terimon—Quetta's Girl (Orchestra)
101710 1077P 17507 178210
Daisy Fay *G R I Smyly*
11 b m Broadsword(USA) —Lily Of The West (True Song)
6936
Dajazar (IRE) *Mrs K Walton* 90h
10 b g Seattle Dancer(USA) —Dajarra (IRE) (Blushing Groom (FR))
768P 859P 98812 10638 1379P
Dalaram (IRE) *J Howard Johnson* 125h 97+c
6 b g Sadler's Wells(USA) —Dalara (IRE) (Doyoun)
15094 22097 329818 372544473P
Dalawan *Mrs J C McGregor* 87h
7 b g Nashwan(USA) —Magdala (IRE) (Sadler's Wells (USA))
8762 15322 20629 24757 2901545848
Dalcassian Buck (IRE) *Mrs L J Young* 88c
12 ch g Buckskin(FR) —Menebeans (IRE) (Duky)
41004 4785P
Daldini *Mrs S J Smith* 95h
4 b g Josr Algarhoud(IRE) —Arianna Aldini (Habitat)
29212 35396 463114 49874
Daliadot *Miss M Bragg* 70b
6 ch g Jendali(USA) —Miss Polkadot (Beveled (USA))
21528
Dalian Dawn (IRE) *David A Kiely* 111+h 118c
8 ch g Topanoora—Lovely Deise (IRE) (Tate Gallery (USA))
5082a3
Dalida *Miss M E Rowland* 94+h
5 ch m Pursuit Of Love—Debutante Days (Dominion)
13752 (1510) 15674 2285P
Dalkeys Lass *Mrs L B Normile*
5 gr m Wolfhound(USA) —Dalkey Sound (Crash Course)
87011
Dallas Alice *Ian Williams* 84b
6 ch m Sir Harry Lewis(USA) —Run On Stirling (Celtic Cone)
27274
Dalriath *M C Chapman* 94h 102c
7 b m Fraam—Alsiba (Northfields (USA))
46734 5446 1280P **1335447964 2U**
Dalton (FR) *E J O'Grady* 113h
5 ch h Bering—Divination (FR) (Groom Dancer (USA))
65a10 4951a17
Dalus Park (IRE) *C C Bealby* 90 c
11 b g Mandalus—Pollerton Park (Pollerton)
25025 28639 327684321P
Daly Said It (IRE) *A J Martin* 114h
6 b g Old Vic—Wonder Bird (GER) (Days At Sea (USA))
117a14
Damarisco (FR) *P J Hobbs* 98+h
6 b g Scribe(IRE) —Blanche Dame (FR) (Saint Cyrien (FR))
3899 24599 321410 429012 48795
Dame Beezil *K Bishop* 56b
7 b m Man Among Men(IRE) —Cuillin (Emarati (USA))
2283P
Damien's Choice (IRE) *Dr P Pritchard* 70h 68c
14 b g Erin's Hope—Reenoga (Tug Of War)
1297 **5658** 76011 (Dead)
Danaeve (IRE) *R Harvey* 115h 113c
11 b g Camden Town—Niagara Belle (Beau Charmeur (FR))
1515a12 39683 474817
Danahill Lad (USA) *J A Danahar* 47b
5 b g Danehill(USA) —Carmen Trial (USA) (Skip Trial (USA))
488113 50757
Danaw (FR) *F Doumen* 149 h
5 b g Lomitas—Damanka (IRE) (Slip Anchor)
37274
Danbury (FR) *O Sherwood* 77+h
6 b g Lost World(IRE) —Dany Ohio (FR) (Script Ohio (USA))
3164 17255 2462P
Dance Hall Diva *M D I Usher* 76h
4 b f Zaha(CAN) —Eastwell Star (Saddlers' Hall (IRE))
23735 27972 31826
Dance Party (IRE) *M W Easterby* 106 h 95+c
6 b m Charnwood Forest(IRE) —Society Ball (Law Society (USA))
1976 20024 26254 30404 **3334241425 45024**
Dancer Life (POL) *Evan Williams* 111h 129+c
7 b g Professional(IRE) —Dyktatorka (POL) (Kastet (POL))
(1781) 26154 2938436122 44609
Dance The Mambo *M W Easterby* 84h
4 b f Benny The Dip(USA) —Debutante Days (Dominion)
32593 46155 47894
Dancewiththedevil (IRE) *Jonjo O'Neill* 103+b
5 bb g Dr Massini(IRE) —Hibba (IRE) (Doubletour (USA))
40727 (4554) 477922
Dance With Wolves (FR) *Jim Best* 97h
6 ch g Tel Quel(FR) —La Florian (FR) (River Mist (USA))
47316 (4871)
Dance World *Miss J Feilden* 110+h
6 b g Spectrum(IRE) —Dansara (Dancing Brave (USA))
24876 28044 29502 (3597) 4478P
Dancing Bay *N J Henderson* 145+h
9 b g Suave Dancer(USA) —Kabayil (Dancing Brave (USA))
2747U 31773 35026 40082 444613
Dancing Bear *Lucinda Featherstone* 48h
5 b g Groom Dancer(USA) —Sickle Moon (Shirley Heights)
390610
Dancing Hero (IRE) *Thomas Foley* 128b
5 ch g Simply Great(FR) —Buck And Roll (Buckskin (FR))
44485 5081a10
Dancing Hill *K Bishop* 82h
7 b m Piccolo—Ryewater Dream (Touching Wood (USA))
9437 (1187) 14133 49419 51135
Dancinginthestreet *J L Flint* 96+h
6 b g Groom Dancer(USA) —Usk The Way (Caerleon (USA))
2872 384P 652P 949P 174781984P (2071) (2283)
Dancing Partner (USA) *M W Easterby* 69h
5 b g Distant View(USA) —Bold Ballerina (Sadler's Wells (USA))
16132 2262F 31677
Dancing Pearl *C J Price* 123 h
8 ch m Dancing Spree(USA) —Elegant Rose (Noalto)
1444P 32953 3621P 38022
Dancing Rock *P J Hobbs* 117+h
8 b g Dancing High—Liblet (Liberated)
19503
Dancing Shirley *Miss A M Newton-Smith* 73h
8 b m Dancing Spree(USA) —High Heather (Shirley Heights)
2552P 28095 3222P 41514 46893
Dancing Water *Patrick O Brady* 87h
7 gr g Halling(USA) —Gleaming Water (Kalaglow)
3052a6 4336aP
Dan De Lion *R C Guest* 77h 64c
7 b g Danzig Connection(USA) —Fiorini (Formidable (USA))
254 **1265 2138**71610 76015 106317 110713 **11769**
Dand Nee (USA) *G A Swinbank* 96+b
4 b f Kabool—Zobaida (IRE) (Green Desert (USA))
(2927) 31819
Dandygrey Russett (IRE) *B D Leavy* 96+h
5 gr m Singspiel(IRE) —Christian Church (IRE) (Linamix (FR))
2462P 2860P 37305 46132
Danebank (IRE) *J Mackie* 99 h
6 b g Danehill(USA) —Snow Bank (IRE) (Law Society (USA))
13649 19088 24193 275017 33718
Danehill Diamond (IRE) *Michael Joseph Fitzgerald* 109 h
7 b m Danehill Dancer(IRE) —Mitsubishi Diamond (Tender King)
21617
Danehill Prince (IRE) *P Bowen*
7 ch g Danehill Dancer(IRE) —Shragraddy Lass (IRE) (Jareer (USA))
3464P
Danger Bird (IRE) *R Hollinshead* 50h
6 ch m Eagle Eyed(USA) —Danger Ahead (Mill Reef (USA))
4733P 48289 5135U
Dangerousdanmagru (IRE) *A E Jones* 105h 128+c
10 b g Forest Wind(USA) —Blue Bell Girl (Blakeney)
(170) 18314 (1986) (2183) 2622P 349543661P **4762U 48505**
Daniel's Dream *J E Dixon* 80h
6 b g Prince Daniel(USA) —Amber Holly (Import)
4316 26529
Danish Decorum (IRE) *Evan Williams* 91h 129c
7 ch g Danehill Dancer(IRE) —Dignified Air (FR) (Wolver Hollow)
(354) (840) 1221713202 14354 1918P (Dead)
Danny Leahy (FR) *M D Hammond* 78h
6 b g Danehill(USA) —Paloma Bay (IRE) (Alzao (USA))
545P **782P**
Dannymolone (IRE) *M D Hammond*
7 b g Anshan—Moy Farina (Derrylin)
24157 2689P 3236P4633P

Dan Ryan (IRE) *T G McCourt* 90h
6 b g Oscar(IRE) —Becca's Approach (IRE) (King Luthier)
4417^{F}

Dans Blarney (IRE) *V J Hughes*
9 b g Teenoso(USA) —Easby Mandrina (Mandalus)
1801^{P}

Dans Dealer (IRE) *S Donohoe* 114h 111+c
11 ch h Be My Native(USA) —Hi' Upham (Deep Run)
4363^{2}

Dans Edge (IRE) *Ferdy Murphy* 42h
6 b g Fourstars Allstar(USA) —Collopy's Cross (Pragmatic)
1915^{11} 2144^{10} 2527^{5}

Danse Macabre (IRE) *A W Carroll* 111+h
7 b g Flemensfirth(USA) —My Romance (Green Shoon)
2043^{2} 2633^{5} 3286^{9} 3548^{9} (4093) (4354) 4504^{3}

Dan's Heir *P C Haslam* 110 h
4 b g Dansili—Million Heiress (Auction Ring (USA))
(1011) 3038^{2} (3415) 3539^{P} 4435^{14} 4792^{P} 4849^{9}

Dan's Man *N A Twiston-Davies* 91 h
5 ch g Zaffaran(USA) —Solo Girl (IRE) (Le Bavard (FR))
241^{2} 2503^{4} 3466^{8} 3806^{P} 4210^{14}4874^{5}

Dante Citizen (IRE) *T R George* 97h 114+c
8 ch g Phardante(FR) —Boreen Citizen (Boreen (FR))
150^{P} 2273^{4} 2596^{2}3000^{3} 3509^{3} 3965^{F}(4737)

Danteco *Miss Kate Milligan* 95 h 82c
11 gr g Phardante(FR) —Up Cooke (Deep Run)
1065^{4} 1378^{5} 1570^{3}

Dante's Back (IRE) *N A Twiston-Davies* 107h 98 c
8 b g Phardante(FR) —Jordans Pet (IRE) (Vision (USA))
1780^{7} 1988^{5} 3888^{7}4370^{4} 4851^{4}

Dante's Battle (IRE) *Mrs K Waldron* 100h 78c
14 bb g Phardante(FR) —No Battle (Khalkis)
903^{5} **997^{4} 1044^{4}**1180^{3} **1299^{2}** 1800^{6}

Dante's Brook (IRE) *B Mactaggart* 92c
12 ch g Phardante(FR) —Arborfield Brook (Over The River (FR))
714^{5}

Dante's Diamond (IRE) *G A Swinbank*
4 b g Orpen(USA) —Flower From Heaven (Baptism)
2001^{U}

Dante's Promise (IRE) *C J Down* 66h 86c
10 b g Phardante(FR) —Lets Compromise (No Argument)
299^{2} 3806^{7} **4753^{3}5071^{8}**

Dantes Reef (IRE) *A J Martin* 123h 133c
10 b g Phardante(FR) —Thousand Flowers (Take A Reef)
69a^{4} 2210^{4}

Dantes Venture (IRE) *Miss I E Craig* 107+h 104+c
9 b g Phardante(FR) —Fast Adventure (Deep Run)
949^{6} **1232^{P}**

Danticat (USA) *John J Coleman* 101h
5 ch g Tale Of The Cat(USA) —Colonial Debut (USA) (Pleasant Colony (USA))
2173^{10}

Dantor *M A Barnes* 57h
4 b g Dansili—Shallop (Salse (USA))
1601^{11} 4532^{10} 4987^{11} 8^{11}

Dantys Hampshire (IRE) *Sean Aherne* 104 h
9 b g Phardante(FR) —Castle Hamshire (Green Shoon)
1623a^{10}

Danzare *Mrs A J Hamilton-Fairley* 34h
4 b f Dansili—Shot Of Redemption (Shirley Heights)
3340^{13} 3464^{P}

Darab (POL) *Mrs S J Smith* 95h
6 ch g Alywar(USA) —Damara (POL) (Pyjama Hunt)
109^{P} 425^{P} 2840^{10} 2977^{7}

Daraheen Noora (IRE) *Dermot Day* 18h
6 b m Topanoora—Daraheen Pearl (Mr Fordette)
93a^{22}

Darak (IRE) *Mrs K J Tutty* 62h 72c
10 b g Doyoun—Dararita (IRE) (Halo (USA))
688^{P}

Daramoon (IRE) *D J S Ffrench Davis* 75b
5 b m Darazari(IRE) —Yellow Moon (IRE) (Executive Perk)
1274^{5} 1674^{9} *2131^{6}*

Darasim (IRE) *Jonjo O'Neill* 119+h
8 b g Kahyasi—Dararita (IRE) (Halo (USA))
(1661) 1870^{2} 5106^{P}

Daraybad (FR) *N J Henderson* 104h
4 b g Octagonal(NZ) —Daraydala (IRE) (Royal Academy (USA))
3594^{4} 4211^{4} 4569^{5}

Darazari Bay (IRE) *K G Reveley* 67b
5 b g Darazari(IRE) —Conna Dodger (IRE) (Kemal (FR))
4319^{6} 5008^{10}

Darby Wall (IRE) *E Bolger* 106h 126?c
8 ch g Beveled(USA) —Nikkis Pet (Le Moss)
(1874)

Darcy *D C O'Brien* 80h
12 ch g Miswaki(USA) —Princess Accord (USA) (D'Accord (USA))
3222^{6}

Darcy Wells *T D Easterby* 63b
5 b g Saddlers' Hall(IRE) —Qurrat Al Ain (Wolver Hollow)
2192^{12} 3563^{7}

Dare To Dance *R Donohoe* 99h
8 b h Mtoto—Thea (USA) (Marju (IRE))
2173^{5} 2261^{4} (Dead)

Dare Too Dream *K Bishop* 106h
7 b g Thowra(FR) —Dubacilla (Dubassoff (USA))
2311^{P} 2663^{4} (2849) 3210^{P} 3978^{P}

Dargaville (NZ) *R C Guest* 99h
7 bl g Sakti(NZ) —Oak Invasion (NZ) (Oak Ridge (FR))
78^{2} 544^{5} 2261^{6}

Dargin's Lass (IRE) *B N Pollock*
5 b m Mister Mat(FR) —Dargin's Hill (IRE) (Le Bavard (FR))
3149^{P} 3550^{10} 3690^{9} 3956^{P} 4449^{P}

Darialann (IRE) *O Brennan* 81h 84c
11 b g Kahyasi—Delsy (FR) (Abdos)
2256^{10} 2843^{12} 2962^{4} 3367^{4} 4013^{5}**4908^{5} (9)**

Darina's Boy *Mrs S J Smith* 113 h 131+c
10 b g Sula Bula—Glebelands Girl (Burslem)
1334^{3} 1618^{2} (1761) 1928^{5} 2529^{7} (4847) 11^{U}

Daring Games *B Ellison* 5h
5 b m Mind Games—Daira (Daring March)
415^{14} 496^{P}

Darjeeling (IRE) *P F Nicholls* 110 h
7 b m Presenting—Afternoon Tea (IRE) (Decent Fellow)
1844 ^{4} 2053^{4} **2297^{F}** 4034^{6}

Dark Artist (IRE) *John E Kiely* 114h
7 b g Perugino(USA) —Black Ivor (USA) (Sir Ivor (USA))
70a^{12}

Dark Ben (FR) *Miss Kate Milligan* 111h 119c
6 b g Solar One(FR) —Reine D'Auteuil (FR) (Cap Martin (FR))
61^{2} 525^{3} 2110^{P} **2975^{2}3352^{2} 3781^{3} (4528) 4985^{6}**

Dark Character *G A Swinbank* 95h
7 b g Reprimand—Poyle Jezebelle (Sharpo)
2444^{6} 2981^{P}

Dark Corner *N A Twiston-Davies* 103b
4 b g Supreme Leader—Made For A King (Roselier (FR))
3181^{4} (3617) 4448^{17}

Dark Diva *W T Reed* 71+h
8 b m Royal Fountain—Little Greyside (Nearly A Hand)
523^{4} **2441^{P}**

Darkest Peru (IRE) *A S T Holdsworth*
6 b g Taipan(IRE) —Eurolink Sea Baby (Deep Run)
4285^{P}

Dark Island *Mary Meek* 12h 17c
11 b g Silver Season—Isle Maree (Star Appeal)
979^{7} 1084^{P}

Darkness *C R Egerton* 125h 156 c
7 ch g Accordion—Winnowing (IRE) (Strong Gale)
(1618) 2065^{2} (2484) (2743) (2973) 4444^{3}5004^{P}

Dark'n Sharp (GER) *R T Phillips* 67h 146 c
11 b g Sharpo—Daytona Beach (GER) (Konigsstuhl (GER))
91a^{P} (2102) 2492^{P}4764^{P}

Darko Karim *R J Hodges* 80+h
4 b g Groom Dancer(USA) —Russian Rose (IRE) (Soviet Lad (USA))
1380^{4} 1802^{P} 2245^{6} 2454^{5} 2723^{6}3222^{2} 3577^{5} 3985^{F} 4368^{2} 4856^{P}

Dark Parade (ARG) *G L Moore* 104+h
5 b g Parade Marshal(USA) —Charming Dart (ARG) (D'Accord (USA))
3464^{2} 3659^{3} 3883^{U}

Dark Rebel (IRE) *J Wade* 22b
6 bb g Lord Americo—Solo Girl (IRE) (Le Bavard (FR))
1532^{12} 1889^{9}

Dark Room (IRE) *Jonjo O'Neill* 120c
9 b g Toulon—Maudlin Bridge (IRE) (Strong Gale)
727^{2} 815^{4} 1025^{2}1759^{P}

Dark Rosalina *C W Moore* 69b
5 b m Defacto(USA) —Zihuatanejo (Efisio)
1799^{10} 2075^{10} 4554^{13} 5015^{P}

Dark Rum *M Scudamore* 67h
10 b g Hubbly Bubbly(USA) —Rose Sauvage (Little Wolf)
1298^{4} 1454^{8} 1725^{8} **1951^{P}**

Dark Shadows *W Storey* 101h
11 b g Machiavellian(USA) —Instant Desire (USA) (Northern Dancer)
425^{5}

Darkshape *Miss Venetia Williams* 88 h
6 b g Zamindar(USA) —Shapely (USA) (Alleged (USA))
691^{11} 892^{7} 1077^{7} 2585^{4} (2816) 2994^{P}

Dark Slaney (IRE) *P D Niven* 79 h
11 b g Meneval(USA) —Black Valley (IRE) (Good Thyne (USA))
2586^{P} (Dead)

Dark Society *A W Carroll* 95 h
8 b g Imp Society(USA) —No Candles Tonight (Star Appeal)
3848^{9} 4131^{7} 4452^{8} 4879^{9}

Dark Thunder (IRE) *Ferdy Murphy* 90+h 90c
9 bb g Religiously(USA) —Culkeern (Master Buck)
2151^{1} 4173 **(481) 1713^{U}2413^{U} 2978^{P}** 4043^{5}4113^{6} 4658^{7}

Darnay Boy (IRE) *Mrs P Ford* 44b
6 b g Darnay—Mumtaz Queen (IRE) (Emmson)
7^{13}

Darnay Lad (IRE) *E J O'Grady* 50b
5 b g Darnay—Abadila (IRE) (Shernazar)
5060a^{18}

Darnayson (IRE) *N A Twiston-Davies* 89+h 98 c
6 b g Darnay—Nakuru (IRE) (Mandalus)
1877^{4} 2282^{0} 3732^{7}4571^{P}

Darn Good *A King* 101h
5 ch g Bien Bien(USA) —Thimbalina (Salmon Leap (USA))
3342^{7} 3646^{6} 3806^{9} 4589^{2} 4826^{4}

Darrens Lass (IRE) *Robert Murphy* 76b 102c
10 b m Montelimar(USA) —Serpentine Artiste (Buckskin (FR))
112a^{P}

Darrias (GER) *P F Nicholls* 137+h
5 b g Sternkoenig(IRE) —Dark Lady (GER) (Lagunas)
(274) (450) (729) 1204^{2} 1222^{3} 1677^{4} (1740) (1876) 2055^{3}2209^{16} (4959) 5125^{8} (Dead)

Darsharp *Miss Jane Mathias* 25h
4 b f Josr Algarhoud(IRE) —Dizzydaisy (Sharpo)
3^{12}

Dartanian *M Scudamore*
4 b g Jurado(USA) —Blackpool Mamma's (Merdon Melody)
4732^{P}

Darwaz (IRE) *D R Gandolfo* 98+h
4 ch g Grand Lodge(USA) —Dawala (IRE) (Lashkari)
2661^{11} 2753^{3} 2921^{9}

Daryal (IRE) *A King* 131+h
5 b g Night Shift(USA) —Darata (IRE) (Vayrann) (2247) 2636^{6}

Dasher Reilly (USA) *D K Weld* 124b
5 b g Ghazi(USA) —Kutira (USA) (Dixieland Band (USA))
5081a^{5}

Dash For Cover (IRE) *J G Portman* 89+h
6 b g Sesaro(USA) —Raindancing (IRE) (Tirol)
25^{2} (295) 1028^{P}

Dashing Home (IRE) *Noel Meade* 127h
7 b g Lahib(USA) —Dashing Rose (Mashhor Dancer (USA))
4951a^{F} 5078a^{F}

Datbandito (IRE) *L Lungo* 65h
7 gr g Un Desperado(FR) —Most Of All (Absalom)
2062^{F} 2447^{7} 2627^{12} 3231^{7} 3540^{5}4346^{P}

Dateldoo (IRE) *P D Williams* 82b
7 ch m Glacial Storm(USA) —Tanti's Last (Ardoon)
1755^{2} 2941^{6}

Datito (IRE) *R T Phillips* 99h 113 c
11 b g Over The River(FR) —Crash Call (Crash Course)
(2623) 3151^{2} 3481^{P}4111^{U}

Dat My Horse (IRE) *Tim Vaughan* 102 h 102c
12 b g All Haste(USA) —Toposki (FR) (Top Ville)
1675^{P} 1800^{5} 2731^{11}

Dauphin Des Carres (FR) *T Civel*
8 ch g Dauphin Du Bourg(FR) —Hypne (FR) (Carmarthen (FR))
362a^{P}

Davenport Democrat (IRE) *W P Mullins* 99h 150+c
8 ch g Fourstars Allstar(USA) —Storm Court (IRE) (Glacial Storm (USA))
117a^{8} **2208^{4} 4472^{5}4889a^{4} 5100a^{4}**

Davenport Milenium (IRE) *W P Mullins* 154h 121c
10 b g Insan(USA) —Society Belle (Callernish)
42a^{3} 2668a^{5} 4458^{15}4951a^{12} 5059a^{21}

Davids Lad (IRE) *A J Martin* 104 h 118c
12 b g Yashgan—Cool Nora (IRE) (Lafontaine (USA))
87a^{P}

David's Symphony (IRE) *A W Carroll* 83h
4 ch g Almutawakel—Habemus (FR) (Bluebird (USA))
2101^{4} 2286^{7} 3132^{F} 3479^{3} 4104^{5}4506^{5} 4616^{14}

Davnic *T Wall* 25h
6 ch m Weld—Lahtico VII (Damsire Unregistered)
1674^{14} 4828^{U} 1^{14}

Davoski *Dr P Pritchard* 103h 124 c
12 b g Niniski(USA) —Pamela Peach (Habitat)
247^{P} 387^{P} 668^{6} 841^{P} 1027^{11}

Davy's Luck *J M Bradley* 81+h
6 ch m Zahran(IRE) —Cursneh Decone (Celtic Cone)
1562^{10} 1680^{9} (1750) 1921^{P}

Dawadari (IRE) *S J Mahon* 106h
6 b h Indian Ridge—Dawala (IRE) (Lashkari)
70a^{11}

Dawn Devoy (IRE) *G A Swinbank* 106h
7 b g Supreme Leader—Dawn Hunt (IRE) (Architect (USA))
301^{2} 4527^{6} (Dead)

Dawn For The Stars (IRE) *O O'Neill* 22b
6 b m Fourstars Allstar(USA) —Spanish Slave (IRE) (Spanish Place (USA))
685^{12}

Dawn Frolics *M J Gingell* 57h 65c
5 gr m Silver Patriarch(IRE) —Mighty Frolic (Oats)
1064^{P} 1112^{5} 1213^{5} 1297^{6} 1523^{6}1949^{10} **2526^{5} 2807^{6}**

Dawn's Cognac (IRE) *D Brace* 86+c
13 b g Glacial Storm(USA) —Misty Venture (Foggy Bell)
333^{3}

Dawn Wager *D B Feek* 85h
5 b m Silver Patriarch(IRE) —Gemma's Wager (IRE) (Phardante (FR))
2579^{6} 3902^{P} 4450^{10} 4621^{8}

Dawton (POL) *T R George* 120h 115+c
8 br g Greinton—Da Wega (POL) (Who Knows)
682^{2} 855^{2} (1019) 1264^{4}

Day Du Roy (FR) *Miss L C Siddall* 110 h 105 c
8 b g Ajdayt(USA) —Rose Pomme (FR) (Rose Laurel)
61^{9} 197^{7} 347^{5} 428^{4} 689^{3}2004^{5} **2443^{6} 2768^{7}3344^{7} 3596^{5} 4213^{7}5140^{P}**

Day Of Claies (FR) *N A Twiston-Davies* 117 h
5 b g Passing Sale(FR) —Dayoula (Mouktar)
(1892) 2327^{3} 2990^{4} 3458^{P} (3966) 4215^{P} 4634^{P}

Dayoff (IRE) *P D Evans* 87h
5 gr m Daylami(IRE) —Dabtara (IRE) (Kahyasi)
3254^{3} 3611^{8}

Days Of Gold *C L Popham*
7 ch m Past Glories—Flira (Lir)
861^{P}

Dbest (IRE) *Ms Joanna Morgan* 115h
6 b g Woodborough(USA) —Leopard Lily (IRE) (Belmez (USA))
5078a^{9}

Dead-Eyed Dick (IRE) *Nick Williams* 131 c
10 b g Un Desperado(FR) —Glendale Charmer (Down The Hatch)
(461) 960^{4} (1489) (2608) 3390^{F} 3877^{6}

Dead Mans Dante (IRE) *Ferdy Murphy* 79h 115 c
8 ch g Montelimar(USA) —Great Dante (IRE) (Phardante (FR))
1062^{P} 1147^{2} 1365^{4}1490^{0} 1566^{5} **1716^{U} 1817^{3}(2109) 2814^{4} 3377^{8}3794^{5} 4492^{2} (4920) 5085^{2}**

Dead Sound (IRE) *T J Taaffe* 124+h
6 ch g Bob Back(USA) —Tonto's Girl (Strong Gale)
4776^{P}

Dealer's Choice (IRE) *Miss Victoria Roberts* 109 h 119c
12 gr g Roselier(FR) —Cam Flower VII (Damsire Unregistered)
4728^{5}

Dear Boy *F P Murtagh* 26h 76c
7 ch g Anshan—Kev's Lass (IRE) (Kemal (FR))
1719^{4}

Dear Deal *C L Tizzard* 118+c
13 b g Sharp Deal—The Deer Hound (Cash And Carry)
55^{4} 205^{4} 516^{3}865^{P}

Dear Oh Dear *David Pearson*
5 ch g Alflora(IRE) —Flagg Flyer VII (Damsire Unregistered)
2665^{16}

Dearson (IRE) *C J Mann* 113+h
5 b g Definite Article—Petite Maxine (Sharpo)
1857^{5} 2322^{2} (2683) 3175^{6} 3957^{F} 4830^{2}

Dear Villez (FR) *P F Nicholls* 120 h
4 b g Villez(USA) —Distant Meteor (Distant Relative)
(3429) 3759^{3}

Debatable *N J Hawke* 74h 66c
7 ch g Deploy—Questionable (Rainbow Quest (USA))
203^{8} 1046^{9} **1076^{5} 1236^{P}** (Dead)

Debbie *B D Leavy* 125 h
7 b m Deploy—Elita (Sharpo)
247^{P} 633^{3} 4848^{14}

De Blanc (IRE) *Miss Venetia Williams* 126h 126 c
6 b m Revoque(IRE) —Queen's Share (Main Reef)
2044^{8} 2297^{3} 2682^{2}(3278) 3621^{5} **(3689) (3900)** 4034^{2} **4495^{3} 4960^{4}**

Debris (IRE) *S B Bell* 39h
7 bb g Norwich—Tipperary Star (Arcticeelagh)
1755^{3} 2956^{10} 4532^{P}

Decent Fellow (GER) *J Vana Jr*
11 b g Esclavo(FR) —Domicella (In Fijar (USA))
590a^{2} 1710a^{2}

De Chirico (IRE) *Martin M Treacy* 60b 101c
10 b g Eurobus—Erin Primrose (IRE) (Torus)
5083a^{P}

Decisive *P Bowen* 136+h
7 b g Alhaarth(IRE) —Alys (Blakeney)
(911) (1266) (1526)

Deckie (IRE) *D J Kemp* 110h 111c
11 b g Be My Native(USA) —Shannon Spray (Le Bavard (FR))
4901^{3}

Dedrunknmunky (IRE) *Miss Tor Sturgis* 92h 111+c
7 b m Rashar(USA) —Rostoonstown Lass (IRE) (Decent Fellow)
(2018) 3601^{4}

Deep King (IRE) *Col R I Webb-Bowen* 117 c
11 bb g King's Ride—Splendid Run (Deep Run)
360^{3} 634^{3} 761^{2}904^{2} 1273^{2} 1399^{U}1542^{2} 1881^{5} 4831^{P}

Deep Moon (IRE) *Miss H C Knight* 53h
6 b g Moonax(IRE) —Mrs Hegarty (Decent Fellow)
2507^{2} 2864^{8} 3466^{11} 4094^{7}

Deep Pockets (IRE) *Mrs Caroline Keevil* 114c
7 b g Fourstars Allstar(USA) —Pocket Price (IRE) (Moscow Society (USA))
(4560) 4757^{3}

Deep Reflection *J A Supple*
6 b g Cloudings(IRE) —Tudor Thyne (IRE) (Good Thyne (USA))
(3138) 3504^{8}

Deep Rising *S P Griffiths*
8 ch m Primitive Rising(USA) —Lindisfarne Rose (Deep Run)
3544^{P} 3912^{P} 4657^{P}

Deepritive *B D Leavy* 73b
9 b m Primitive Rising(USA) —Last Of The Deep (IRE) (Deep Run)
611^{P}

Deep Water (USA) *M D Hammond* 122h 126c
12 b g Diesis—Water Course (USA) (Irish River (FR))
2294^{2} 2640^{3}

Deerpark (IRE) *John F Gleeson*
4 ch g Orpen(USA) —Early Fin (IRE) (Mukaddamah (USA))
2645a^{10}

Deeshan (IRE) *I Madden* 69b
5 b m Anshan—Deirdres Pet (IRE) (Be My Native (USA))
2796a^{10}

Defenceoftherealm (IRE) *Miss J E Foster* 45b
6 b g Saddlers' Hall(IRE) —Thai Nang (Tap On Wood)
1554^{12}

Deferlant (FR) *K Bell* 108 h 113c
9 ch g Bering—Sail Storm (USA) (Topsider (USA))
633^{11} **815^{7}**

Definate Spectacle (IRE) *Noel Meade* 138+h
6 b g Spectrum(IRE) —Silver Bubble (USA) (Silver Hawk (USA))
67a^{18} 208^{2} 1093a^{F}

Definite Approach (IRE) *R T Phillips* 91h
8 b g Presenting—Crash Approach (Crash Course)
2327^{6} **3949^{F} 4095^{P}**

Deja Vu (IRE) *J Howard Johnson* 111+h 108+c
7 b g Lord Americo—Khalkeys Shoon (Green Shoon)
121^{P} **1568^{3} 1888^{2}2630^{2}**

Dekatell Le Dun (FR) *A Sannier*
15 b g Mistigri—Katell II (FR) (Over)
845a^{3} 1074a^{P}

Delaware (FR) *H S Howe* 90h
10 ch g Garde Royale—L'Indienne (FR) (Le Nain Jaune (FR))
298^{4} 517^{2} 665^{10} 947^{8} 1121^{5}

Delaware Trail *R Johnson* 68h 59c
7 b g Catrail(USA) —Dilwara (IRE) (Lashkari)
3394^{3} 3796^{6} 4796^{P}4841^{P} 5121^{7}

Delcombe *N R Mitchell*
5 b g Deltic(USA) —Nellie's Joy VII (Damsire Unregistered)
4011^{11} 4947^{11}

Delena *P F Nicholls* 97+b
5 b m Classic Cliche(IRE) —Formal Affair (Rousillon (USA))
3468^{6} (4667) 4976^{9}

Delgany Gale (IRE) *M Hill* 70h
7 b g Alphabatim(USA) —Glamorous Gale (Strong Gale)
1384[P]

Deliceo (IRE) *M Sheppard* 62h 97c
13 br g Roselier(FR) —Grey's Delight (Decent Fellow)
1825[7] 2140[5] **2524[3]**3358[12] **3459[6] 3676[5]5074[4]**

Delightful Cliche *Mrs P Sly* 98h
5 b g Classic Cliche(IRE) —Ima Delight (Idiots Delight)
355[4] 1895[4] 2343[3] 2571[5] 3393[7]4907[9]

Delightful Touch (FR) *C P Morlock*
5 gr g Villez(USA) —Fagaras (FR) (Kenmare (FR))
1922[6]

Delphine *T R George* 77h
7 ch m Old Vic—Oh So Bright (Celtic Cone)
201[6] 4874[4] 813[3]

Deltic Arrow *D L Williams* 89 c
8 b g Deltic(USA) —Jolly Girl (Jolly Me)
2109[P] 2260[5] 2869[5]3598[5] **3909[7] 4150[4]**

Del Trotter (IRE) *M E Sowersby* 77h 64c
11 b g King Luthier—Arctic Alice (Brave Invader (USA))
573[8] 839[10] 891[2]

Demesne *P Hogan* 104h
6 b g Thowra(FR) —Alice's Mirror (Magic Mirror)
43a[22] 2650a[11]

Demi Beau *Evan Williams* 135h 143+c
8 b g Dr Devious(IRE) —Charming Life (NZ) (Sir Tristram)
1411[2] 1487[3] (2939) 4456[F] 4749[P]

Dempsey (IRE) *M Pitman* 136 h 159 c
8 b g Lord Americo—Kyle Cailin (Over The River (FR))
(3299) 3724[2] 4445[B]

Denada *Mrs Susan Nock* 113c
10 ch g Bob Back(USA) —Alavie (FR) (Quart De Vin (FR))
2814[F] 3372[2] 3965[3]4419[7]

Denarius Secundus *N R Mitchell* 50h 85c
9 ch g Barathea(IRE) —Penny Drops (Sharpo)
167[3] 287[4] 1833[P] 2605[4] 2845[7]2934[10] 3211[7] 3424[4] 4010[5] **4132[2]4525[5] 4653[2] (4911) 4936[7]**

Denman (IRE) *P F Nicholls* 157+h
6 ch g Presenting—Polly Puttens (Pollerton)
(1859) (2301) (3174) (3846) 4443[2]

Dennick *P C Haslam* 95+h
4 b g Nicolotte—Branston Dancer (Rudimentary (USA))
1332[3] 1441[P] 2167[6] 2494[2] (2752) (3479)

Dennis The Mennis (IRE) *R Johnson* 80h
7 b g Fourstars Allstar(USA) —Farm Approach (Tug Of War)
11[18]

Denvale (IRE) *Mrs Caroline Bailey* 117 c
8 b g Denel(FR) —Brackenvale (IRE) (Strong Gale)
440[P] (3736) 4073[3]4325[U] 4560[P] (4880)

Deo Gratias (POL) *Carl Llewellyn* 86h
6 b g Enjoy Plan(USA) —Dea (POL) (Canadian Winter (CAN))
1856[2] 2552[P] 2934[7] 3367[P] 4640[5]4898[7]

Depth Perception (IRE) *Paul John Gilligan* 94 c
6 b g Kadeed(IRE) —Scrahans Touch (Skyliner)
3528a[9] 3920[2] 4417[P]

Derainey (IRE) *R Johnson* 68+h 80 c
7 b g Farhaan—Hurricane Hazel (Lorenzaccio)
8[P] 212[5] 1834[15] **2677[5]3317[8] 3760[4] 4300[F]4989[P]**

Derawar (IRE) *A L T Moore* 116h 98c
7 b g Kahyasi—Denizliya (IRE) (Sadler's Wells (USA))
43a[15] 92a[8]

Dere Lyn *D Burchell* 92h 100+c
8 b g Awesome—Our Resolution (Caerleon (USA))
2347[14] 2609[4] 3018[9] 3876[6] 4012[P]**4735[2]**

Derivative (IRE) *Miss Venetia Williams* 113 h
8 bb g Erin's Isle—Our Hope (Dancing Brave (USA))
2633[4] 3289[P] 3508[8]

Derosa *Mrs E B Scott* 95c
9 br g Little Wolf—Easter Carnival (Pardigras)
5116[2]

Derravarra Eagle (IRE) *Mark Leslie Fagan* 105b
6 br g Flemensfirth(USA) —Rathcolman Queen (IRE) (Radical)
5104a[15]

Derrinraw (IRE) *Stephen McConville* 46c
7 ch g Woods Of Windsor(USA) —Tacheo (Tachypous)
872[P]

Derrintogher Yank (IRE) *Miss R S Reynolds* 113+c
12 b g Lord Americo—Glenmalur (Black Minstrel)
184[2] 455[F]

Derry Dice *C T Pogson* 82h
10 b g Derrylin—Paper Dice (Le Dauphin)
1002[P] 1047[P]

Derryrose *T Butt* 100c
13 br g Derrylin—Levantine Rose (Levanter)
411[P]

Derwent (USA) *R H Buckler* 89h
7 bb g Distant View(USA) —Nothing Sweeter (USA) (Darby Creek Road (USA))
504[U] (Dead)

Desailly *J A Geake* 140 c
12 ch g Teamster—G W Superstar (Rymer)
3921[3] 4433[8]

Desert Air (JPN) *M C Pipe* 145 h
7 ch g Desert King(IRE) —Greek Air (IRE) (Ela-Mana-Mou)
2746[2] (3298) 3994[4] 4446[11] 4765[20] 5003[4]

Desert Buzz (IRE) *J Hetherton* 87 h
4 b g Desert Story(IRE) —Sugar (Hernando (FR))
1601[3] 1797[12] 2286[P] (Dead)

Desert Image (IRE) *C Tinkler* 83h
5 b g Desert King(IRE) —Identical (IRE) (Machiavellian (USA))
369[10] 729[5] 1046[6] 1297[3] 1541[7]

Desert Jim (FR) *F Doumen* 110+h
4 ch g Desert King(IRE) —Jimshine (FR) (Shining Steel)
2756[4] 3436[2]

Desert Moonbeam (IRE) *R J Hodges* 66h
4 b f Desert Prince(IRE) —Pip's Dream (Glint Of Gold)
2274[8] 2681[P] 2797[4] 3340[12] 3479[5]3945[5]

Desertmore Chief (IRE) *G J Smith* 83h
7 b g Broken Hearted—Mangan Lane (Le Moss)
2020[6] 2552[5] 3332[3] 3613[P] 4640[P]4794[9] **4913[U]**

Desertmore King (IRE) *J A Danahar*
6 ch g Shahrastani(USA) —Forest Mist (Dalsaan)
2075[11] **3356[F]** 4046[P]

Desert Quest (IRE) *P F Nicholls* 146 h
6 b g Rainbow Quest(USA) —Jumilla (USA) (El Gran Senor (USA))
1680[2] 1875[2] (1898) 2595[U] (2734) (2765) 2871[3](4242) (4473) 4763[10]

Desert Secrets (IRE) *J G Portman* 100h
4 b f Almutawakel—Shaping Up (USA) (Storm Bird (CAN))
2345[4] 2612[P] 2824[2] (3281) 3722[8] 4210[10]4674[5] 4962[3] 5019[9]

Desert Spa (USA) *G E Jones* 102h
11 b g Sheikh Albadou—Healing Waters (USA) (Temperence Hill (USA))
1[4] (681) (760) 1027[9] 1153[3] 1218[4] 3889[10]4591[4] 4736[4] 1[3]

Desert Tommy *Evan Williams* 120+h
5 b g Desert King(IRE) —Flambera (FR) (Akarad (FR))
3140[3] 3733[P] (3876) (4012) 4372[2] 5010[2]

Designer Label (IRE) *Carl Llewellyn* 79h 58c
10 ch g Insan(USA) —Belle Babillard (IRE) (Le Bavard (FR))
3285[P] 3430[P] 4553[5]4914[P] 5088[P]

Desiree (IRE) *John Berry*
5 b m Desert Story(IRE) —Elba (IRE) (Ela-Mana-Mou)
2249[18]

De Soto *P R Webber* 114+h
5 b g Hernando(FR) —Vanessa Bell (IRE) (Lahib (USA))
2742[4]

Desperate Dex (IRE) *G J Smith* 68h
6 b g Un Desperado(FR) —Too Sharp (True Song)
470[8] 1799[13] 2340[13] 4638[6]

Desperately Frisky (IRE) *D Broad* 3h 71c
13 b g Un Desperado(FR) —Ruemalus (Mandalus)
87a[R]

Destino *Mrs S J Smith* 85+h
7 ch g Keen—Hanajir (IRE) (Cadeaux Genereux)
1066[5] 4302[P] 4917[7]

Detonateur (FR) *Ian Williams* 110h 120+c
8 b g Pistolet Bleu(IRE) —Soviet Princess (IRE) (Soviet Lad (USA))
(1595) 2725[4] 2963[2]

Detroit City (USA) *P J Hobbs* 150+h
4 gr c Kingmambo(USA) —Seattle Victory (USA) (Seattle Song (USA))
2661[8] (3340) (3722) (4468) (4747)

Deuteronomy (IRE) *E A Elliott* 24b
5 b g Beneficial—Good Heavens (IRE) (Heavenly Manna)
131[11]

Dev (IRE) *M G Quinlan* 94h 82c
6 b g Anshan—Local Dream (Deep Run)
3792[9] **4053[5]**

Devils And Dust (IRE) *D McCain* 85b
5 b g Needle Gun(IRE) —Tartan Trouble (Warpath)
3691[3] 4500[16]

Devils Delight (IRE) *James Moffatt* 78h
4 b f Desert King(IRE) —Devil's Crown (USA) (Chief's Crown (USA))
1601[4] 4789[P] 4987[5]

Devil's Disguise *Ferdy Murphy* 89b
4 b g Atraf—Dunloe (IRE) (Shaadi (USA))
4615[3]

Devils River (IRE) *N A Twiston-Davies* 96+h
4 b g Anabaa(USA) —Riviere Du Diable (USA) (Irish River (FR))
3645[4]

Devil's Run (IRE) *J Wade* 125+c
10 b g Commanche Run—She Devil (Le Moss)
2037[5] 3258[P] 3917[3]4111[U] 4361[3] 4790[2]

Devil's Teardrop *C J Mann* 95h
6 ch g Hernando(FR) —River Divine (USA) (Irish River (FR))
2743[3]

Devious Ayers (IRE) *J M Bradley* 92h
5 br g Dr Devious(IRE) —Yulara (IRE) (Night Shift (USA))
1750[6] 1916[5] 2249[P]

Devito (FR) *G F Edwards* 108 h
5 ch g Trempolino(USA) —Snowy (FR) (Wollow)
(1900) 2150[7] (2459) 2734[5] 3143[3] 3467[4] 3675[7]4153[5] 4663[9] 4858[8]

Devolution (IRE) *Miss C Dyson*
8 b g Distinctly North(USA) —Election Special (Chief Singer)
2873[P] 3328[F]

Devon Blue (IRE) *Mrs J G Retter* 84b
7 ch m Hubbly Bubbly(USA) —Tuney Blade (Fine Blade (USA))
1961[11]

Devondale (IRE) *Ferdy Murphy* 97h 102 c
10 b g Be My Native(USA) —Lancastrian Rose (IRE) (Lancastrian)
1334[8] 1570[7] (2022) (2170) 2495[U] 2692[3]

Devonia Plains (IRE) *Mrs P N Dutfield* 79b
4 ch g Danehill Dancer(IRE) —Marlfield Lake (Cadeaux Genereux)
1785[5] 2105[6] 4680[6] 5117[4]

Dewasentah (IRE) *J M Jefferson* 110h
7 b m Supreme Leader—Our Sioux (IRE) (Jolly Jake (NZ))
210[2] (574) 715[3] (838) (1112) 1222[2] **1411[P]**

Dextrous *P T Midgley* 76 h
9 gr g Machiavellian(USA) —Heavenly Cause (USA) (Grey Dawn II)
1377[P] 1567[5] 1927[14] 2567[P]

Dhaudeloup (FR) *A G Juckes* 101h 110 c
11 ch g Mister Sicy(FR) —Debolouve (FR) (Yours)
682[LFT] 1180[2] **1618[P]**

Dhehdaah *Mrs P Sly* 120+h
5 b g Alhaarth(IRE) —Carina Clare (Slip Anchor)
2249[2] 2627[2] 3256[11] (4478) 5021[4]

Diafa (USA) *J G M O'Shea* 42h
4 b f Swain(IRE) —I'm Unapproachable (USA) (Distinctive Pro (USA))
4855[11] 5110[P]

Diagon Alley (IRE) *K W Hogg* 71h
6 ro g Petong—Mubadara (IRE) (Lahib (USA))
120[10] 1202[P] 1333[P]

Diamond Alpha (IRE) *Ms Jane Evans* 50b
12 b g Alphabatim(USA) —Nevada Lady (Trimmingham)
278[S]

Diamond Cottage (IRE) *S B Bell* 86h 72c
11 b g Peacock(FR) —Sea Bright (IRE) (King's Ride)
(83) 211[4] 2495[P]3377[5] 3554[6] **3917[9]4042[P]**

Diamond Cutter (NZ) *R C Guest* 102h
7 br g Strike Diamonds(NZ) —Lough Allen (NZ) (Omnicorp (NZ))
(549) 691[3] 841[8] 3171[9] 3561[12]

Diamond Jack (IRE) *J J Lambe* 83h
8 gr g Sexton Blake—Dockmaid (IRE) (Dock Leaf)
(1357) 1527[5] 1687[4] 1883[6]

Diamond Jim (IRE) *Mrs R L Elliot* 50h
6 ch g Lord Of Appeal—Smash N Lass (Crash Course)
2036[P]

Diamond Joshua (IRE) *N B King* 90+h 90c
8 b g Mujadil(USA) —Elminya (IRE) (Sure Blade (USA))
352[P] 988[13] **1249[2] 1365[5]1568[P] 1595[3]** 1655[5]**1815[F]**
1884[4]

Diamond Merchant *Ian Williams* 69c
7 ch g Vettori(IRE) —Tosca (Be My Guest (USA))
275[6] **1801[P] 3215[6]3672[P]**

Diamond Mick *Mrs R L Elliot* 111 h
6 ch g Pivotal—Miss Poll Flinders (Swing Easy (USA))
3853[7] 4354[2] 4723[7] 4922[9] 5066[7]

Diamond Sal *J Howard Johnson* 121h
8 b m Bob Back(USA) —Fortune's Girl (Ardross)
(2452) 3040[2] 4983[3]

Diamond Vein *S P Griffiths* 84h
7 b g Green Dancer(USA) —Blushing Sunrise (USA) (Cox's Ridge (USA))
192[7] 428[7] 1066[P]

Dianica (FR) *R Le Gal*
7 b m Nikos—Diamona (FR) (Diamond Shoal)
846a[5]

Diatonic *D Carroll*
4 b g Deploy—Vic Melody (FR) (Old Vic)
1563[16] 2263[P]

Dickens (USA) *Miss Venetia Williams* 112+h 105c
6 ch g King Of Kings(IRE) —Dellagrazia (USA) (Trempolino (USA))
2143[3] 2955[6] 3214[7]

Dickensbury Lad (FR) *J L Spearing* 108 h 120 c
6 b g Luchiroverte(IRE) —Voltige De Cotte (FR) (Saumon (FR))
3356[2] 3801[2] 4419[2]4617[P] (5017)

Dickie Lewis *D McCain* 96+h 45c
8 b g Well Beloved—Moneyacre (Veloski)
2859[6] (3140) 3540[2] **4316[P] 4851[F]**

Dictator (IRE) *D R Gandolfo* 84+h 99 c
5 ch g Machiavellian(USA) —Obsessed (Storm Bird (CAN))
1614[P] 1824[7] 2099[8] 2460[4] **2751[2]2929[2] 3243[P]**
4606[12]

Dictum (GER) *Mrs Susan Nock* 136dh 111+c
8 ch g Secret 'n Classy(CAN) —Doretta (GER) (Aspros (GER))
3991[3]

Didbrook *Mrs Mary Hambro* 57b
4 b f Alzao(USA) —Nedaarah (Reference Point)
5141[10]

Didifon *N P McCormack* 116h 107c
11 b g Zafonic(USA) —Didicoy (USA) (Danzig (USA))
121[P]

Didn't You Know (FR) *M C Pipe* 82+h
5 ch m Trempolino(USA) —Lattaquie (FR) (Fast Topaze (USA))
355[5] 574[F] 911[8] 1021[5] 1188[13]1381[4]

Die Fledermaus (IRE) *D J Wintle* 54h 104c
12 b g Batshoof—Top Mouse (High Top)
573[9] (Dead)

Diego Cao (IRE) *G L Moore* 127h
5 b g Cape Cross(IRE) —Lady Moranbon (USA) (Trempolino (USA))
2207[P]

Diego Garcia (IRE) *W P Mullins* 128h
6 b g Sri Pekan(USA) —Chapel Lawn (Generous (IRE))
4951a[18] 5078a[5]

Different Class (IRE) *Jonjo O'Neill* 97h
7 b g Shardari—Hollygrove Cezanne (IRE) (King's Ride)
1979[3] 2212[P]

Differentgear *P C Haslam* 37h
5 b g Robellino(USA) —Garconniere (Gay Mecene (USA))
82[15]

Diklers Rose (IRE) *K G Reveley* 99+h
7 gr m Roselier(FR) —Diklers Run (Deep Run)
2414[4] 2515[2] 3235[2] (3544) 4619[13]

Diktatit *R C Guest* 59h
4 b f Diktat—Mystique Smile (Music Boy)
1146[10] 1201[2] 1332[F]

Dileer (IRE) *D J Wintle* 105h
7 b g Barathea(IRE) —Stay Sharpe (USA) (Sharpen Up)
247[P] 571[13] (Dead)

Diletia *R H Alner* 103 h 101+c
9 b m Dilum(USA) —Miss Laetitia (IRE) (Entitled)
297[5] 1630[5] 1992[5] (2731)

Dillay Brook (IRE) *T R George* 93h
6 b m Supreme Leader—Anns Run (Deep Run)
1961[2] 2446[3] 3287[7] 3437[3] 3984[4]

Dilsaa *K A Ryan* 98h
9 ch g Night Shift(USA) —Llia (Shirley Heights)
9[9] 238[7] 891[5]

Dinan (IRE) *Mrs Joanne Brown*
14 gr g Step Together(USA) —Nobodys Lady (Nobody Knows)
151[P] 555[9]

Dinarelli (FR) *M C Pipe* 68h
7 gr g Linamix(FR) —Dixiella (FR) (Fabulous Dancer (USA))
973[P]

Dinarobin (USA) *Noel Meade* 109h
5 b g Dynaformer(USA) —Debby (USA) (Woodman (USA))
3003a[6]

Ding Dong Belle *Mrs S J Smith* 83+h
7 ch m Minster Son—Corn Lily (Aragon)
(603)

Dinnie Flanagan (IRE) *P C Haslam* 98+h
6 b g Windsor Castle—Princess Diga (IRE) (Black Minstrel)
4315[4] 4787[8] 4875[5]

Dinofelis *C W Moore*
8 b g Rainbow Quest(USA) —Revonda (IRE) (Sadler's Wells (USA))
681[P] 1724[P]

Dino's Dandy *B N Pollock*
7 ch g Midnight Legend—Edina (IRE) (The Parson)
3843[8] 4071[8]

Diplomatic Daisy (IRE) *D R Gandolfo* 83 h
7 b m Alflora(IRE) —Landa's Counsel (Pragmatic)
3690[5]

Direct Access (IRE) *N G Richards* 142+c
11 ch g Roselier(FR) —Spanish Flame (IRE) (Spanish Place (USA))
2370[F] (2499) 4777[P]

Direct Flight (IRE) *Noel T Chance* 117h 136c
8 ch g Dry Dock—Midnight Mistress (Midsummer Night II)
2100[U] (2287) 2734[2] **3323[F]**3622[12] **4456[4] 4778[3]5080a[F]**

Dirty Sanchez *Miss A M Newton-Smith* 73h
8 b g Manhal—Lady Poly (Dunbeath (USA))
3423[7] 3715[6] 4392[10] 4651[2] 4869[P]

Discomania *V Smith* 78h
4 b g Pursuit Of Love—Discomatic (USA) (Roberto (USA))
1397[11] 4905[9] 5135[5]

Discord *T H Caldwell* 22h
5 b g Desert King(IRE) —Lead Note (USA) (Nijinsky (CAN))
1459[10]

Di's Dilemma *C C Bealby* 94+h
8 b m Teenoso(USA) —Reve En Rose (Revlow)
1717[4] 1987[2] 2590[2] 2968[4] 4568[2]4899[2]

Dish *Miss C J E Caroe*
7 b m Distant Relative—Shalati (FR) (High Line)
23[P]

Dishdasha (IRE) *C R Dore* 73h
4 b g Desert Prince(IRE) —Counterplot (IRE) (Last Tycoon)
1339[6] 1478[P] (1563) 1774[5] 3939[9]

Dispol Peto *R Johnson* 62h
6 gr g Petong—Plie (Superlative)
3912[14] 4493[8] 5091[P]

Distant Prospect (IRE) *A M Balding* 123 h
9 b g Namaqualand(USA) —Ukraine's Affair (USA) (The Minstrel (CAN))
3993[P] 4375[11] 4663[12]

Distant Romance *Miss Z C Davison* 72h 95c
9 br m Phardante(FR) —Rhine Aria (Workboy)
217[P] 314[5] 651[10] 1520[4](1597) 2457[P] 2932[P]

Distant Thunder (IRE) *R H Alner* 125 c
8 b g Phardante(FR) —Park Breeze (IRE) (Strong Gale)
2054[P] 2491[P] 3296[P]3942[2] 4118[F]

Divet Hill *Mrs A Hamilton* 106 h 131 c
12 b g Milieu—Bargello's Lady (Bargello)
64[5] **423[P]** 859[12]

Divex (IRE) *M D Hammond* 84h
5 b g Taipan(IRE) —Ebony Countess (IRE) (Phardante (FR))
1799[2] 2497[6] 4532[F] 5118[4]

Dix Villez (FR) *Paul Nolan* 111h 110c
7 b g Villez(USA) —Dix Huit Brumaire (FR) (General Assembly (USA))
2162[7]

Dizzy Future *B J Llewellyn* 67h
4 b g Fraam—Kara Sea (USA) (River Special (USA))
1904[9] 3[7]

Dizzy Lizzy *Nick Williams*
4 gr f Sendawar(IRE) —Black Velvet (FR) (Black Tie Affair)
1649[6]

Django (IRE) *Mrs John Harrington* 116+h 118c
7 ch g Glacial Storm(USA) —Rathtrim (Strong Gale)
116a[P] **1790a[3] 3012a[6]**

D J Flippance (IRE) *A Parker* 93h 105c
11 b g Orchestra—Jane Bond (Good Bond)
1837[4] 2453[2] **(2946)** 3554[4]**4111[P] 4636[4] 4985[5]**

Dmitri *J D Frost* 65h
6 b g Emperor Jones(USA) —Shining Cloud (Indian Ridge)
1742[8]

Doce Vida (IRE) *A King* 113h
8 b m Montelimar(USA) —Miss The Post (Bustino)
239[P] 633[P] (Dead)

Dock Copper's Girl *J N R Billinge* 74b
6 b m Thowra(FR) —Reeling (Relkino)
301[P]

Dock Tower (IRE) *M E Sowersby* 102h
4 b g Docksider(USA) —Thakhayr (Sadler's Wells (USA))
1551[6] 1718[5] 1923[2] 2442[P] 2921[5]3539[5] 4057[4] 4506[6] 5137[10]

Doc Row (IRE) *M C Pipe* 105+h
6 b g Dr Massini(IRE) —Roberto Moss (Le Moss)
3210[11] 3500[3] (3664) 4961[P]

Doctored *D C O'Brien* 57h
5 ch g Dr Devious(IRE) —Polygueza (FR) (Be My Guest (USA))
3133[11]
Doctor Linton (IRE) *M J P O'Brien* 122h 135c
7 b g Norwich—Alannah Rose (IRE) (Roselier (FR))
43a[16] **1790a[2] 2174[5]3006a[F] 3261a[2]**
Doctor Supremo (IRE) *D B Feek* 48b
5 b g Dr Massini(IRE) —Supreme View (Supreme Leader)
4455[13] 4868[8]
Doctor Wood *Miss V A Stephens* 100+h
11 b g Joligeneration—Ladywood (Doctor Wall)
2150[9]
Dodger McCartney *K Bishop* 46h
8 ch g Karinga Bay—Redgrave Girl (Deep Run)
3130[8] 4327[13] 4638[5]
Doe Nal Rua (IRE) *T D Easterby* 89h 110+c
9 b g Mister Lord(USA) —Phardante Girl (IRE) (Phardante (FR))
176[P]
Does It Matter *Evan Williams* 24h
9 b g Carlingford Castle—Flopsy Mopsy (Full Of Hope)
2140[F]
Do Keep Up *J R Weymes* 78h 83c
9 b g Missed Flight—Aimee Jane (USA) (Our Native (USA))
2168[4] 2945[U] 3170[7]3338[U]
Dolans Bay (IRE) *G M Moore* 49h
5 b g Old Vic—Kyle House VII (Damsire Unregistered)
2447[6] 2690[9] 3168[9]
Do L'Enfant D'Eau (FR) *B Storey* 134 h 125 c
7 ch g Minds Music(USA) —L'Eau Sauvage (Saumarez)
2067[F] 2498[4] 3233[4](3852) 4109[P]
Dolly Devious *D I Turner*
11 ch m Cruise Missile—Into Song (True Song)
4009[U]
Dolly Mop *Miss V A Stephens* 56h
10 b m Nearly A Hand—Roving Seal (Privy Seal)
58[P]
Dolly Of Dublin (IRE) *J R H Fowler* 84h
8 br m Be My Native(USA) —Ar Ais Aris (IRE) (Orchestra)
93a[17]
Dolmur (IRE) *Ferdy Murphy* 109+h 113+c
6 br g Charnwood Forest(IRE) —Kawanin (Generous (IRE))
2701[4] (2922) 4460[P]
Dolzago *G L Moore* 100+h
6 b g Pursuit Of Love—Doctor's Glory (USA) (Elmaamul (USA))
(2379)
Domart (POL) *M Pitman* 88h
6 gr g Baby Bid(USA) —Dominet (POL) (Dixieland (POL))
180[6]
Dom D'Orgeval (FR) *Nick Williams* 147h
6 b g Belmez(USA) —Marie D'Orgeval (FR) (Bourbon (FR))
2207[3] 2493[2] 2746[5] (3135) (3502) (3986) 4446[3]4745[5] 5154a[4]
Dome *Carl Llewellyn* 89h 68+c
8 bb g Be My Chief(USA) —Round Tower (High Top)
3359[P] 5105[5]
Domenico (IRE) *J R Jenkins* 97h
8 b g Sadler's Wells(USA) —Russian Ballet (USA) (Nijinsky (CAN))
2187 1481[U] 2103[9] 2379[8]
Domesday (UAE) *W G Harrison* 55b
5 b g Cape Cross(IRE) —Deceive (Machiavellian (USA))
2906[9] 3763[13]
Dominican Monk (IRE) *C Tinkler* 122h
7 b g Lord Americo—Ballybeg Katie (IRE) (Roselier (FR))
450[5] 726[8] 1010[7] (1087)
Domirome (FR) *G Macaire* 121h 130c
8 b g Roi De Rome(USA) —Bold Senorita (IRE) (Pennine Walk)
(1073a)
Don And Gerry (IRE) *P D Evans* 102h
5 ch m Vestris Abu—She's No Tourist (IRE) (Doubletour (USA))
(844) 982[2] 1037[3] 1235[2] 1383[2] 1490[2]1541[4] 1875[3] 2173[4] 2726[2] 2997[2]3254[5]
Don Argento *Mrs A J Bowlby*
5 gr g Sri Pekan(USA) —Grey Galava (Generous (IRE))
804[F] 901[P]
Donatus (IRE) *Miss K M George* 67 h 80 c
10 b g Royal Academy(USA) —La Dame Du Lac (USA) (Round Table)
760[14] 915[12] **958[6]**
Don Castille (USA) *P R Webber* 89b
4 ch g Royal Anthem(USA) —Suzie Sparkle (USA) (High Brite (USA))
3292[6] 3651[5] (4422) 5104a[13]
Don De Matha (FR) *D Grandin* 95c
6 b g Villez(USA) —Santa Marta (FR) (Cadmus II) (846a) **1073a[P]**
Don Fernando *M C Pipe* 117h
7 b g Zilzal(USA) —Teulada (USA) (Riverman (USA))
4461[10] 4776[8]
Donie Dooley (IRE) *P T Dalton* 93+h
8 ch g Be My Native(USA) —Bridgeofallen (IRE) (Torus)
1319[7] 1675[12] 1977[8] 2466[5] 2714[P]
Donna's Double *Karen McLintock* 96h
11 ch g Weldnaas(USA) —Shadha (Shirley Heights)
149[5]
Donnybrook (IRE) *R D E Woodhouse* 109c
13 ch g Riot Helmet—Evening Bun (Baragoi)
151[6] 3736[6] 4660[4]

Donovan (NZ) *R C Guest* 109+h 101 c
7 b g Stark South(USA) —Agent Jane (NZ) (Sound Reason (CAN))
(61) 332[4] 1010[6] 1087[6] 1548[13] **1673[3](1852) 2655[4] 2874[6]3348[4] 3844[F]**
Don Pasquale *J T Stimpson* 22h
4 br g Zafonic(USA) —Bedazzling (IRE) (Darshaan)
1201[P] 1397[P] 1441[6] 4877[P]
Don Preuil (FR) *P Boisgontier*
4 gr g Saint Preuil(FR) —Spleen (FR) (Sillery (USA))
4548a[7]
Don Royal *J R Scott* 95 c
12 b g Rakaposhi King—Donna Farina (Little Buskins)
204[3] 440[P]
Dont Askim (IRE) *Patrick G Kelly* 45c
6 b g Kahyasi—Segolene (FR) (Insan (USA))
3528a[S]
Dont Ask Me (IRE) *M C Pipe* 105+h
5 b g Spectrum(IRE) —Edyrna (IRE) (Doyoun)
664[11] 1541[3] 1717[2] (1784) 1806[4] 2150[5]4080[9]
Don't Be Bitin (IRE) *Eoin Griffin* 137h
5 b g Turtle Island(IRE) —Shonara's Way (Slip Anchor)
88a[5] 2650a[2] 3894a[4]
Dontbebrushedaside (IRE) *R M Moore* 109h 82c
7 b g Pierre—Brushaside Spa (IRE) (Brush Aside (USA))
70a[18]
Don't Be Shy (FR) *M C Pipe* 134h 155 c
5 b g Trempolino(USA) —Be Claimed (FR) (Al Nasr (FR))
2209[11] 2747[10] **3251[2] (3494) (3980) 4431[5] 4761[4]**
Dont Call Me Derek *J J Quinn* 133 h
5 b g Sri Pekan(USA) —Cultural Role (Night Shift (USA))
2765[11] 3929[F] 4110[2] 4375[P]
Dontelldonandgerry *P D Evans* 85b
6 ch m Rakaposhi King—Queenford Belle (Celtic Cone)
817[9] 1237[3] 1386[2] 1543[4]
Don't Matter *A E Price* 54c
6 bb m Petong—Cool Run (Deep Run)
3141[P] **3457[8] 3647[F]**
Dontnock'Er (IRE) *R H Buckler* 63h 61c
8 br m Naheez(USA) —Castlemagner (IRE) (Hatim (USA))
1597[3]
Don't Push It (IRE) *Jonjo O'Neill* 125+h
6 b g Old Vic—She's No Laugh Ben (USA) (Alleged (USA))
(1554) (2878)
Don Valentino (POL) *T R George* 110h 106+c
7 ch g Duke Valentino—Dona (POL) (Dakota)
4607 **672[2] 8584[1]1049[P]**
Doodle Addle (IRE) *J T R Dreaper* 113+h 132c
10 ch g Good Thyne(USA) —Call Trish (IRE) (Callernish)
3053a[14] 3587a[8] 4929a[9]
Doof (IRE) *M C Pipe* 116+h
6 b g Old Vic—Ashpark Rose (IRE) (Roselier (FR))
111[P] 1000[4] 1125[5] 1187[F]
Dopey Bob *N A Twiston-Davies* 46b
5 b g Bob's Return(IRE) —Dopey Muck (Gunner B)
1882[14] 2432[12] 3948[P]
Dorans Lane *W M Brisbourne* 75h
8 b m Gildoran—Snitton Lane (Cruise Missile)
77[8] 838[5] 971[P] 1100[U] 1206[F]
Doringo *J L Spearing*
5 b g Prince Sabo—Mistral's Dancer (Shareef Dancer (USA))
2763[P]
Doris's Gift *J Howard Johnson* 60h
5 gr g Environment Friend—Saxon Gift (Saxon Farm)
2169[8] 2497[5] 2979[7] 5064[7]
Doris Souter (IRE) *D J Wintle* 81h
6 bb m Desert Story(IRE) —Hope And Glory (USA) (Well Decorated (USA))
729[7] 1021[3] (1158) 1272[4] 1977[9]
Dormy Two (IRE) *J S Wainwright* 89h
6 b m Eagle Eyed(USA) —Tartan Lady (IRE) (Taufan (USA))
2515[13] 2749[11] 3042[P] 4632[8] 4794[P]12[4]
Dorneys Well (IRE) *Evan Williams* 102+h
6 bb g Supreme Leader—Princess Millicent (Proverb)
1753[P] 3818[8] (4104) 4322[2] (4726)
Dosco (IRE) *D T Hughes* 86h 106c
7 bb g Oscar(IRE) —Broken Rein (IRE) (Orchestra)
3528a[F]
Dotsnew Dawn *N E Berry* 43b
5 b m Lord Americo—Dawn O'Er Kells (IRE) (Pitskelly)
5117[10]
Dottie Digger (IRE) *Miss Lucinda V Russell* 68h 62c
7 b m Catrail(USA) —Hint-Of-Romance (IRE) (Treasure Kay)
874[6] 1311[P] 1509[5]1592[U] 1883[P] 2041[6]
Dottie West *Ms N M Hugo*
6 ch m The West(USA) —Bedelia (Mr Fluorocarbon)
4615[15] 4909[20]
Double Account (FR) *D L Williams* 122 h 112c
11 b g Sillery(USA) —Fabulous Account (USA) (Private Account (USA))
4090[6] 4356[9]
Double Ange (FR) *Mrs Katie Baimbridge* 89c
8 b g Double Bed(FR) —La Mesange (FR) (Olmeto)
455[2] 4471[P]
Double Aspect (IRE) *Jonjo O'Neill* 91h
5 b g Dr Fong(USA) —Spring (Sadler's Wells (USA))
133[4] 811[3]
Double Belle *S C Burrough*
6 b m Double Trigger(IRE) —Bellara (Thowra (FR))
866[12]

Double Car (FR) *B De Watrigant*
10 b g Sleeping Car(FR) —Double Roots (FR) (Deep Roots)
779a[3]
Double Date (FR) *C P Morlock*
5 bb g Double Bed(FR) —Gay Native (FR) (Gay Minstrel (FR))
4094[P] 4676[P]
Double Dizzy *R H Buckler* 110 h
5 b g Double Trigger(IRE) —Miss Diskin (IRE) (Sexton Blake)
65a[11] 1677[6] 1876[2] 2166[15] 2799[2]3174[7] 3993[3] 4606[5] 5103a[15]
Double Ells *J M Jefferson* 65h
4 b f Yaheeb(USA) —Knayton Lass (Presidium)
2076[10] 2442[P] 2753[5] 4360[6]
Double Emblem (IRE) *B R Foster* 52b
9 ch m Weld—Sultry (Sula Bula)
8[P] 838[P]
Double Gem (IRE) *J I A Charlton* 97h
7 ch g Grand Plaisir(IRE) —Thatildofornow (IRE) (Lord Americo)
82[3] 418[3] 1847[3]
Double Gin *W Amos* 89h
6 gr g Double Trigger(IRE) —Belmore Cloud (Baron Blakeney)
2838[3]
Double Grace (IRE) *Mrs S Gardner* 55b
6 ch m Double Trigger(IRE) —Flame O'Frensi (Tudor Flame)
1459[8] 1755[0] 1961[9]
Double Header (IRE) *Mrs S D Williams* 111h
7 b g Old Vic—Ballybeggan Lady (IRE) (Le Bavard (FR))
2311[U] 2607[P] 2820[13]
Double Honour (FR) *P J Hobbs* 136h 149 c
8 gr g Highest Honor(FR) —Silver Cobra (USA) (Silver Hawk (USA))
423[2] 842[6] 2054[2]4237[F] (2875) 3390[7]3971[7] 5004[18]
Double Kudos (FR) *Jamie Poulton* 78h
4 gr g Highest Honor(FR) —Black Tulip (FR) (Fabulous Dancer (USA))
1190[3] 1397[10]
Double Law *Miss E C Lavelle* 99h
6 ch g Double Trigger(IRE) —Sister-In-Law (Legal Tender)
2049[7] 2269[F] 4604[4] 4905[4]
Double Measure *T D Walford* 28h
6 b g Double Eclipse(IRE) —Double Resolve (Gildoran)
375[7] 828[6] 892[9]
Double Ransom *Mrs L Stubbs*
7 b g Bahamian Bounty—Secrets Of Honour (Belmez (USA))
3355[F]
Double Royal (IRE) *Mrs T J Hill* 89h
7 b g Ali-Royal(IRE) —Royal Wolff (Prince Tenderfoot (USA))
1432[4] 1645[9] 2256[7] 2582[2] 3656[8]
Double Spectre (IRE) *Jean-Rene Auvray* 94 h
4 b g Spectrum(IRE) —Phantom Ring (Magic Ring (IRE))
1679[2] 2069[2] 2481[P] 2612[P]
Double Spread *M Mullineaux* 71b
7 b g Alflora(IRE) —Flora Louisa (Rymer)
2425 2987[9] 4661[P]
Double The Trouble *R H Buckler* 76+b
5 b g Double Trigger(IRE) —Upton Lass (IRE) (Crash Course)
1882[15] 3911[10] 4654[6]
Double Turn *Mrs S J Smith* 87+h
6 ch g Double Trigger(IRE) —Its My Turn (Palm Track)
2838[6] 3559[2]
Double Vodka (IRE) *C Grant* 120h
5 bb g Russian Revival(USA) —Silius (Junius (USA))
2444[F] 2942[2] 3488[2] 4110[5] 4527[2]4773[3]
Doughty *D J Wintle*
4 b g Bold Edge—Marquante (IRE) (Brief Truce (USA))
4416[P] 4551[P]
Dover Creek *Miss M E Rowland* 24h
6 bb m Dover Patrol(IRE) —Up The Creek (IRE) (Supreme Leader)
891[F] 1374[6]
Dovers Venture *Miss M E Rowland* 52b
5 b m Dover Patrol(IRE) —Love Venture (Pursuit Of Love)
1237[10] 1401[P] 1688[8]
Dow Jones (GER) *M Halford* 120h
8 b g Temporal(GER) —Dahsa's Dream (IRE) (Soviet Lad (USA))
1116a[3] 1691a[2] 5103a[14]
Downing Street (IRE) *Jennie Candlish* 116+h
5 b g Sadler's Wells(USA) —Photographie (USA) (Trempolino (USA))
(301) 680[3] (974) (1039) 1234[5]
Downpour (USA) *Ian Williams* 98 c
8 b g Torrential(USA) —Juliac (USA) (Accipiter (USA))
3135[P] **3788[P] 4735[P]**
Down's Folly (IRE) *H D Daly* 119+h
6 b g Darnay—Pils Invader (IRE) (Carlingford Castle)
1921[2] 2285[8] (2925) (3214) 3508[4] 4606[2]
Downtherefordancin (IRE) *M C Pipe* 90 h
6 b g Groom Dancer(USA) —Merlin's Fancy (Caerleon (USA))
352[R]
Down The Stretch *A Ennis* 95c
6 b g Rakaposhi King—Si-Gaoith (Strong Gale)
1047[7] 1521[4]
Down To The Woods (USA) *D McCain* 59h
8 ch g Woodman(USA) —Riviera Wonder (USA) (Batonnier (USA))
1724[6]
Doyounoso *R J Armson*
6 b g Teenoso(USA) —Karina's Carbon (Mr Fluorocarbon)
3657[P]

Draconian *Mrs L Pomfret*
7 ch g Lancastrian—Strong Attraction (Strong Gale)
4421[P]
Dragon Blue *G F H Charles-Jones*
6 b m Puget(USA) —Dragon Fire (Dragonara Palace (USA))
654[13] 1018[P] 1121[P]
Dragon King *P Bowen* 111 c
14 b g Rakaposhi King—Dunsilly Bell (London Bells (CAN))
276[7]
Dragon's Dream *R Barber* 91+h
8 b g Afzal—Another Relation (Relkino)
50[F] (Dead)
Dragut Torghoud (IRE) *N M Babbage* 89 h
10 b g Persian Mews—Artist's Jewel (Le Moss)
334[P]
Dramatic Quest *A G Juckes* 108+h 94c
9 b g Zafonic(USA) —Ultra Finesse (USA) (Rahy (USA))
486[F] 2701[6] 3480[P]3888[4] 4454[2] 4633[P]5049[P]
Dramatic Review (IRE) *P C Haslam* 85+h
4 b g Indian Lodge(IRE) —Dramatic Shift (IRE) (Night Shift (USA))
945[3] 1512[4] 1729[3] 2263[P]
Drat *R Mathew* 76+h 90+c
7 b g Faustus(USA) —Heresy (IRE) (Black Minstrel)
2313[5] 2610[P] 4016[P]4367[5]
Dr Cerullo *C Tinkler* 107h
5 b g Dr Fong(USA) —Precocious Miss (USA) (Diesis)
(1562) 1916[3] 2099[3] 2734[6] 3360[8] 3848[7]
Dr Charlie *Miss C Dyson* 107 h
8 ch g Dr Devious(IRE) —Miss Toot (Ardross)
6651[2]
Dream Alliance *P J Hobbs* 134+h
5 ch g Bien Bien(USA) —Rewbell (Andy Rew)
1882[2] 2829[3] (3611) (4071) 4469[6] 5009[F]
Dream Along *Mrs A J Perrett* 90h
4 b g Sinndar(IRE) —Dream Quest (Rainbow Quest (USA))
1190[4] (1268)
Dream Castle (IRE) *Barry Potts* 116h
12 b g Poet's Dream(IRE) —Kerry's Castle (Deep Run)
306[3] (544) (716) 873[4] 1099[2] 1312[3] 1668[P]2110[6] 3005a[17]
Dream Falcon *R J Hodges* 123h
6 b g Polar Falcon(USA) —Pip's Dream (Glint Of Gold)
1804[U] 1984[P] 2731[4] 2999[3] 3389[4]3727[13] 3987[4]
Dream Merchant (IRE) *P J Hobbs* 101h
6 b h Deputy Minister(CAN) —User Friendly (Slip Anchor)
1772[4] 1991[12] 2423[11] 2868[13]
Dream Of Tomorrow (IRE) *John Joseph Murphy* 97h
4 b f Revoque(IRE) —Golden Jorden (IRE) (Cadeaux Genereux)
3401a[8] 5076a[6]
Dream On Maggie *P Bowen* 90h
6 ch m Dreams End—Alto Bella (High Line)
1849[12] 2070[P] 2559[12] 3280[5] 3996[P]
Dream Seeker (USA) *F Weisgerber*
9 b g Lear Fan(USA) —Danseuse Du Soir (IRE) (Thatching)
846a[0]
Dreams Jewel *C Roberts* 87+h
6 b g Dreams End—Jewel Of The Nile (Glenstal (USA))
235[P] 1849[9] 2070[F] 2309[7] 2455[11](5024)
Dreams Of Zena *D Burchell*
7 b m Dreams End—Billan Tara (Nicholas Bill)
77[P] 651[P]
Dream With Me (FR) *J A Geake* 117h 105c
9 b g Johann Quatz(FR) —Midnight Ride (FR) (Fast Topaze (USA))
511[7] 1236[6]
Dreux (FR) *Thomas Cooper* 122h
4 b c Anabaa(USA) —Divination (FR) (Groom Dancer (USA))
3004a[3] 3401a[2] 3890a[4] 4435[8]
Dr Flight *H Morrison* 91b
4 b g Dr Fong(USA) —Bustling Nelly (Bustino)
2927[7] 3181[8] *3504[7]*
Dr Hellier (IRE) *J R Turner* 70b
6 b g Dr Massini(IRE) —Rossmill Lady (IRE) (Be My Native (USA))
4507[8]
Drift Away (USA) *J J Lambe* 99 h
6 b m Dehere(USA) —Flying Blind (IRE) (Silver Kite (USA))
873[F]
Drink Light (IRE) *P R Webber* 50b
6 ch m Anshan—Mid Day Chaser (IRE) (Homo Sapien)
2021[7]
Drive On Driver (IRE) *Lady Susan Brooke* 80h 79c
9 bb m Niels—Gay And Sharp (Fine Blade (USA))
3247[11] **3480[U] 3888[6]4016[P] 4279[P] 4552[P]4735[8]**
Dr Mann (IRE) *Miss Tor Sturgis* 84h 81c
8 bb g Phardante(FR) —Shuil Le Laoi (IRE) (Lancastrian)
3146[5] **3427[4] 3909[P]4047[7] 5105[4]**
Drombeag (IRE) *Jonjo O'Neill* 119+c
8 b g Presenting—Bula Beag (IRE) (Brush Aside (USA))
(3819) (4044) 4471[9]4748[F] 5083a[10]
Drom Island *Graham Richards*
12 b m Jupiter Island—Netherdrom (Netherkelly)
50[P]
Dromlease Express (IRE) *C Byrnes* 132+h 112c
8 ch g Fourstars Allstar(USA) —Niat Supreme (IRE) (Supreme Leader)
1622a[6]
Drongo *Mrs P Robeson* 36b
5 br g Sure Blade(USA) —Ardeola (Ardross)
2461[P] 4868[P]
Droumleigh Lad (IRE) *Miss Z C Davison* 88h 65c
11 b g Jurado(USA) —Myra Gaye (Buckskin (FR))
1019[9] 1483[13]

Druids Stone *Henry De Bromhead* 45h
4 b g Wizard King—Lady Westgate (Welsh Chanter)
5076a^{24}

Drumbeater (IRE) *P J Hobbs* 122+h
6 b g Supreme Leader—Ballydrummund (IRE) (Henbit (USA))
(1294) (1513) (1796) 2731^{2} (3018) 3970^{9} 4579^{2} 4974^{5}

Drumbo (IRE) *I Buchanan* 99h 85c
10 ch g Lashkari—Mountstuart Lady (Orchestra)
421^{P}

Drumintine (IRE) *Liam Lennon* 71c
5 b m Mister Mat(FR) —Ballytrustan Maid (IRE) (Orchestra)
4343^{4} 4841^{4}

Drumossie (AUS) *R C Guest* 77 h 96+c
6 ch g Strategic(AUS) —Migvie (NZ) (Sir Tristram)
870^{14} 1014^{4} 1097^{5} 1663^{6} **3348^{6}3562^{4}** 3757^{8} **4920^{U}(4991) 5092^{3}**

Drunken Disorderly (IRE) *David Wachman* 130h
6 b g Luso—Slave Hero (IRE) (Sandalay)
4888a^{6}

Dryliner *A E Price* 65b
6 gr g Terimon—Take The Veil (Monksfield)
1985^{7} 2941^{13} 3646^{12} 4935^{P}

Dry Old Party (IRE) *P Winkworth* 73+h
7 ch g Un Desperado(FR) —The Vine Browne (IRE) (Torus)
21^{6} 263^{5}

Dual Star (IRE) *L Waring* 99h 95c
11 b g Warning—Sizes Vary (Be My Guest (USA))
668^{P} 864^{P}

Dubai Ace (USA) *Miss Sheena West* 109h
5 b g Lear Fan(USA) —Arsaan (USA) (Nureyev (USA))
504^{2} (671) 861^{4} 2347^{6} 2633^{10}

Dubai Dreams *S R Bowring* 81h
6 b g Marju(IRE) —Arndilly (Robellino (USA))
843^{8} 1302^{3} 1745^{12} 2191^{4} 2419^{13}3557^{16}

Dubai Sunday (JPN) *P S McEntee* 58h
5 b g Sunday Silence(USA) —Lotta Lace (USA) (Nureyev (USA))
(3504) 3983^{3} 4455^{16}

Dubious Deal *R J Hodges*
9 ch g Seven Hearts—Heather Lane (Heres)
1898^{10}

Dubonai (IRE) *G M Moore* 100h
6 ch g Peintre Celebre(USA) —Web Of Intrigue (Machiavellian (USA))
149^{11} (1360) 1527^{2} 1661^{10} 2191^{F} 2838^{U}3347^{5} 3561^{F} 4301^{7}

Duc De Regniere (FR) *G Cherel*
4 b g Rajpoute(FR) —Gladys De Richerie (FR) (Le Pontet (FR))
777a^{7}

Duchamp (USA) *A M Balding* 110h 131c
9 b g Pine Bluff(USA) —Higher Learning (USA) (Fappiano (USA))
248^{9} 1012^{7}

Dujareva *J P Broderick* 92h
5 b m Mark Of Esteem(IRE) —All Is Fair (Selkirk (USA))
65a^{7} 954a^{9}

Duke Of Buckingham (IRE) *P R Webber* 110h 146 c
10 b g Phardante(FR) —Deselby's Choice (Crash Course)
840^{2} 1010^{11} **1265^{3}(1561) 1918^{6} 4472^{12}5126^{3}**

Duke Of Kentford *P R Webber* 82b
4 b g Shambo—Kentford Duchess (Jupiter Island)
4595^{8} 4909^{11}

Duke Of Stradone (IRE) *S Donohoe* 52h
6 b g Beneficial—Thethingtodo (Kambalda)
2480^{4} 3763^{3} 3927^{10}

Duke Orsino (IRE) *Miss Lucinda V Russell* 107h 81c
6 b g Old Vic—Deselby's Choice (Crash Course)
210^{3} 1927^{7} 2262^{8} 3853^{P} 4141^{2}4582^{3} **5002^{4}**

Du Kerroch (FR) *G Brillet*
3 b g Kahyasi—Iu Mi Nao (IRE) (Turtle Island (IRE))
4298a^{P}

Duke's View (IRE) *D C Turner* 71h
5 b g Sadler's Wells(USA) —Igreja (ARG) (Southern Halo (USA))
748^{P} 804^{5} 1021^{7} 1123^{4} 1188^{7}3321^{P} 4731^{14} 4856^{7}

Dulcigris (FR) *J-P Carnel*
10 b g Mistigri—Dulcisport (FR) (Gosport)
845a^{2} 1074a^{4}

Dumadic *R E Barr* 56h 109c
9 b g Nomadic Way(USA) —Duright (Dubassoff (USA))
83^{P} 3350^{F} 3791^{P}4920^{2}

Dumaran (IRE) *W J Musson* 105h
8 b g Be My Chief(USA) —Pine Needle (Kris)
4608^{4} 4938^{8}

Dumfries *T H Caldwell* 79h
5 ch g Selkirk(USA) —Pat Or Else (Alzao (USA))
192^{9} 238^{P} 764^{10} 987^{9} 1046^{P}

Dun An Doras (IRE) *Mrs N Frost* 101 h 117c
10 br g Glacial Storm(USA) —Doorslammer (Avocat)
386^{9} 946^{7} 1189^{9}4555^{2} 4730^{5} 4975^{4}

Dunaskin (IRE) *Karen McLintock* 114+h
6 b g Bahhare(USA) —Mirwara (IRE) (Darshaan)
4479^{2}

Dunbell Boy (IRE) *C J Mann* 97+h
8 bb g Over The River(FR) —Whipper Snapper (Menelek)
(1833) 2130^{P} 2815^{6}

Dunbrody Millar (IRE) *P Bowen* 94h 135 c
8 bb g Lord Americo—Salt Mills (Proverb)
1832^{6} 2126^{2} 2424^{2}(2686) 2922^{F} (3186) 3509^{2} (3728) 4111^{5}4433^{P} 4762^{4}

Duncanbil (IRE) *J J Bridger*
5 b m Turtle Island(IRE) —Saintly Guest (What A Guest)
2322^{P} 2632^{P} 3715^{8}

Duncliffe *R H Alner* 106h 150+c
9 b g Executive Perk—Ida Melba (Idiots Delight)
42a^{4} 2054^{F} 3210^{4}**3299^{11}**

Dundock *A C Whillans* 90b
5 gr g Cloudings(IRE) —Rakajack (Rakaposhi King)
3490^{2} 4533^{10}

Dun Doire (IRE) *A J Martin* 96h 144+c
7 b g Leading Counsel(USA) —Yes Boss (IRE) (Carlingford Castle)
(2187) (2630) (3587a) (4433) 4929a^{7}

Dundonald *M Appleby* 50h
7 ch g Magic Ring(IRE) —Cal Norma's Lady (IRE) (Lyphard's Special (USA))
2^{P}

Dundridge Native *M Madgwick* 82+h
8 b m Be My Native(USA) —Fra Mau (Wolver Hollow)
1775^{10} 2378^{7} 2592^{4} 3146^{2}

Dungarvans Choice (IRE) *N J Henderson* 140 c
11 ch g Orchestra—Marys Gift (Monksfield)
2532^{6} 3921^{2} 4843^{4}

Dunguaire Lady (IRE) *Mrs K Walton* 90h
7 ch m Toulon—Why Me Linda (IRE) (Nashamaa)
5039^{3}

Dunkerron *J Joseph* 80h 90c
9 b g Pursuit Of Love—Top Berry (High Top)
25^{8} 218^{2} 469^{4} 760^{4} 978^{4}1395^{8} 1520^{P}

Dun Locha Castle (IRE) *N R Mitchell* 90c
11 b g Cataldi—Decent Preacher (Decent Fellow)
2009^{5} 2575^{6} 2800^{3}3212^{5} 3481^{3} 3909^{5}4152^{3} 4321^{5} 4524^{2}4650^{U} 4876^{2}

Dunlo Society (IRE) *S J Treacy* 90h
5 ch g Moscow Society(USA) —Dunlo Cherry (IRE) (Montelimar (USA))
44a^{19}

Dunmanus Bay (IRE) *Mrs Julie Read* 86h 103c
9 gr g Mandalus—Baby Fane (IRE) (Buckskin (FR))
282^{F} 4901^{5}

Dunnicks Betsie *F G Tucker*
6 b m Opera Ghost—Country Magic (National Trust)
4398^{P}

Dunnicks Field *F G Tucker* 55h
10 b g Greensmith—Field Chance (Whistlefield)
2729^{P} 3126^{P} 3252^{P}

Dunowen (IRE) *Mark Doyle* 92h 99c
11 b g Be My Native(USA) —Lulu Buck (Buckskin (FR))
1362^{5} **4975^{P}**

Dun Rose *Mrs P Claxton* 85+c
12 bb m Roscoe Blake—Dun Gay Lass (Rolfe (USA))
125^{5}

Dunsemore *Mrs A F Tullie* 87+h
6 b m Prince Daniel(USA) —Admire-A-More (Le Coq D'Or)
1834^{14}

Dunsfold Duke *P Winkworth* 116 h
6 b g Cloudings(IRE) —Rositary (FR) (Trenel)
(3425) 3882^{6} 3978^{4} 4373^{P} 4691^{3}

Dunshaughlin (IRE) *J A B Old* 98b
9 b g Supreme Leader—Russian Gale (IRE) (Strong Gale)
3950^{P}

Dunster Castle *P J Hobbs* 106h 128 c
11 ch g Carlingford Castle—Gay Edition (New Member)
297^{3} (Dead)

Dunston Bill *Mrs K Smyly* 73h 122c
12 b g Sizzling Melody—Fardella (ITY) (Molvedo)
49^{7}

Dunston Durgam (IRE) *Ms Sue Smith* 66+h
12 b g Durgam(USA) —Blazing Sunset (Blazing Saddles (AUS))
458^{13} 1206^{P} 1564^{13}

Durante (IRE) *J A B Old* 106+h
8 ch g Shernazar—Sweet Tune (Welsh Chanter)
2619^{8} 3548^{F} 4396^{2}

Durba (AUS) *R C Guest* 67h
6 ch g Desert Prince(IRE) —Placate (AUS) (Brief Truce (USA))
1014^{8} 1084^{7} 1113^{7} 1302^{12} 3269^{8}

Durlston Bay *S Dow* 112c
9 b g Welsh Captain—Nelliellamay (Super Splash (USA))
2048^{2} 2616^{3} 3296^{8}3698^{P}

Durnovaria (IRE) *D P Keane* 55b
6 b g Fourstars Allstar(USA) —Solar Jet (Mandalus)
5024^{P}

Dusky Dame *S B Bell* 20h
6 ch m Sir Harry Lewis(USA) —Red Dusk (Deep Run)
3314^{11} 3442^{F} 3551^{6}

Dusky Dawn (IRE) *J M Jefferson* 56h
5 b g Desert Style(IRE) —Kaaba (Darshaan)
2340^{14} 3793^{14} 4114^{7} (Dead)

Dusky Lord *N J Gifford* 120+h
7 b g Lord Americo—Red Dusk (Deep Run)
(1772) (3717) 3957^{2}

Dusky Warbler *G L Moore* 141h
7 br g Ezzoud(IRE) —Bronzewing (Beldale Flutter (USA))
2493^{10} 3502^{9} 4375^{2} 4473^{14} 4773^{6}

Dusty Dane (IRE) *W G M Turner* 99h
4 b g Indian Danehill(IRE) —Teer On Eer (IRE) (Persian Heights)
1679^{3} 1904^{3} 2236^{5} 2597^{5} 3429^{U}3616^{F} 4832^{2}

Dutch Star *G P Enright* 72b
7 b m Alflora(IRE) —Double Dutch (Nicholas Bill)
2988^{6} 3437^{P} 3690^{P} 3979^{P}

Dynamic Bemmy *N M Babbage*
4 ch f Fleetwood(IRE) —Wigit (Safawan)
7^{P}

Dyneburg (POL) *T R George* 102+h
6 ch h Alywar(USA) —Dora Baltea (POL) (Beauvallon (FR))
870^{9} 1014^{3} 1182^{5} (1364) 1480^{6}

Eagle's Landing *W K Goldsworthy* 68h
8 b m Eagle Eyed(USA) —Anchorage (IRE) (Slip Anchor)
245^{P}

Eamon An Chnoic (IRE) *B W Duke*
5 gr g Lil's Boy(USA) —Caranina (USA) (Caro)
2967^{P}

Earcomesannie (IRE) *P A Pritchard* 72h
6 ch m Anshan—Play It By Ear (IRE) (Be My Native (USA))
245^{6} 679 ^{3} 801^{9}

Earl Of Forestry (GER) *P F Nicholls* 74+h
5 b g Dream For Future(IRE) —Effelie (FR) (Son Of Silver)
361^{2} 2152^{7} 2865^{10} 5026^{5}

Earl Of Spectrum (GER) *J L Spearing* 88h
5 b g Spectrum(IRE) —Evry (GER) (Torgos)
513^{7} 1717^{F} 2283^{2} 2563^{8} 2822^{7}

Earlsfield Raider *G L Moore* 121+h
6 ch g Double Trigger(IRE) —Harlequin Walk (IRE) (Pennine Walk)
(397) (566) 814^{2}

Earl Sigurd (IRE) *J K Magee* 106h 86c
8 ch g High Kicker(USA) —My Kind (Mon Tresor)
122^{7} 416^{P} 990^{6}1308^{6}

Earl's Kitchen *C L Tizzard* 107 h 121+c
9 ch g Karinga Bay—Rempstone (Coronash)
2273^{8} 2623^{P} 3481^{2}3614^{3} 4103^{P} (4287) 4690^{P}

Earls Rock *J K Cresswell* 89h
8 b g Gunner B—Will Be Wanton (Palm Track)
111^{5} 469^{P} 1084^{2} 1319^{5} 1415^{4}

Early Start *J W Mullins* 119+h 119c
8 ch m Husyan(USA) —Gipsy Dawn (Lighter)
1853^{2} 2053^{P}

Earn A Buck *B I Case* 65b
5 b m Young Ern—Buck Comtess (USA) (Spend A Buck (USA))
3373^{5}

Earnest (IRE) *Ian Williams* 65b
6 b g Oscar(IRE) —Unassisted (IRE) (Digamist (USA))
4613^{P}

Earn Out *M C Pipe* 84+h
5 b g Sovereign Water(FR) —Tudor Spartan (Spartan General)
167^{7} 352^{6} 749^{6} (860) 913^{4} 1002^{5}1100^{4} 1262^{7}

Earth Man (IRE) *P F Nicholls* 123h
7 b g Hamas(IRE) —Rajaura (IRE) (Storm Bird (CAN))
203^{2} 1880^{P}

Earth Moving (IRE) *P F Nicholls* 78+h
6 ch g Anshan—Jacks Sister (IRE) (Entitled)
2056^{6} 2432^{2} 3130^{4}

Easby Mandarin *C W Thornton* 100+h
5 b g Emperor Fountain—Beijing (USA) (Northjet)
2507^{10} 2821^{7} 3793^{8} 4532^{5} 5120^{F}

Easibet Dot Net *I Semple* 95+h
6 gr g Atraf—Silvery (Petong)
3488^{4}

Easibrook Jane *C L Tizzard* 110h 103+c
8 b m Alderbrook—Relatively Easy (Relkino)
2018^{3} 2297^{8} 3982^{P}4372^{P} **4782^{2}**

Eastender *Miss Venetia Williams* 66b
5 b m Opening Verse(USA) —Trude (GER) (Windwurf (GER))
1674^{8}

Eastern Dagger *Miss L V Davis* 66h
6 b g Kris—Shehana (USA) (The Minstrel (CAN))
1717^{6}

Eastern Point *R H York* 79h 71 c
12 b m Buckskin(FR) —Deep Creek (Deep Run)
3909^{11} 4324^{3} 4649^{5}

Eastern Tribute (USA) *A C Whillans* 122 h 115 c
10 b g Affirmed(USA) —Mia Duchessa (USA) (Nijinsky (CAN))
120^{9}

Easter Present (IRE) *Miss H C Knight* 106h
7 br g Presenting—Spring Fiddler (IRE) (Fidel)
1669^{U} 3369^{3} 4373^{11} 4956^{6}

East Lawyer (FR) *P F Nicholls* 82h 124 c
7 b g Homme De Loi(IRE) —East Riding (FR) (Fabulous Dancer (USA))
1831^{F} 1986^{3} 2312^{5}3440^{U} (3507) 3992^{4}5126^{5}

East Tycoon (IRE) *Jonjo O'Neill* 128 h 141 c
7 ch g Bigstone(IRE) —Princesse Sharpo (USA) (Trempolino (USA))
(1221) 1265^{8} 1550^{7}1744^{4} 1918^{4} 2177^{F}4459^{6} 4764^{9}

Eastwell Violet *Mrs A M Thorpe* 75h
6 b m Danzig Connection(USA) —Kinchenjunga (Darshaan)
23^{5} 310^{7}

Eastwood Drifter (USA) *Miss L Day* 78h
9 ch g Woodman(USA) —Mandarina (USA) (El Gran Senor (USA))
2071^{7} 2214^{P}

Easy Laughter (IRE) *A King* 94 h
5 b g Danehill(USA) —All To Easy (Alzao (USA))
3591^{2} 3883^{7}

Eau Pure (FR) *G L Moore* 98+h 100+c
9 b m Epervier Bleu—Eau De Nuit (King's Lake (USA))
1051^{0} 329^{5} 501^{8} **684^{2}805^{4} 1524^{2} 1599^{4}(2248) 2522^{3} 2931^{P}4476^{3} 5051^{6}**

Ebac (IRE) *J Howard Johnson* 91 h
5 ch g Accordion—Higher Again (IRE) (Strong Gale)
2475^{11} 2903^{3} 3793^{13}

Ebinzayd (IRE) *L Lungo* 135h 136+c
10 b g Tenby—Sharakawa (IRE) (Darshaan)
1013^{P} 2641^{4}

Ebony Jack (IRE) *C L Tizzard* 96 c
9 bb g Phardante(FR) —Ebony Jane (Roselier (FR))
169^{P} 2237^{2} 2424^{5}(2575) 2686^{2} 3129^{P}3427^{2} 3909^{9} (4007) 4152^{4} 4370^{5} 4939^{3}

Ebony Light (IRE) *D McCain* 101h 148 c
10 br g Buckskin(FR) —Amelioras Daughter (General Ironside)
(1670) 1941^{4} 2368^{9}(2819) 3258^{F} (3493) 3971^{8} 4777^{F} 5004^{12}

Ebony Queen *Miss H C Knight* 78b
5 br m Classic Cliche(IRE) —Queen Of Spades (IRE) (Strong Gale)
3468^{11} 4422^{8}

Eborarry (IRE) *T D Easterby* 105h
4 b g Desert Sun—Aztec Princess (Indian King (USA))
1339^{5} 1718^{P} 2076^{4} (2693) 3171^{10} 3539^{2}3737^{2} 4067^{9} 4301^{9} 4987^{3}

E Bride (USA) *T T Clement*
4 rg f Runaway Groom(CAN) —Fast Selection (USA) (Talinum (USA))
2949^{11} 3294^{U}

Echo Blu (IRE) *Miss Joanne Priest*
8 b g Sharifabad(IRE) —Muchsorrylady (IRE) (Boreen (FR))
3653^{P} 4642^{P} **4937^{P}5049^{P}**

Echo Point (IRE) *N G Richards* 127+h
6 b g Luso—Lady Desart (IRE) (Buckskin (FR))
(1885) 2335^{2}

Ecos De L'Orme (FR) *Ron Caget*
3 ch c Sabrehill(USA) —Ecossette (FR) (Ecossais (FR))
4298a^{8}

Ede'Iff *W G M Turner* 98h 112 c
9 b m Tragic Role(USA) —Flying Amy (Norwick (USA))
1906^{8} **2051^{5} 2273^{3}2568^{2} (2938) 3326^{5}3649^{F} 4592^{3} 4737^{4}5046^{3}**

Edenderry (IRE) *A D Brown* 60b
7 ch g Dock Leaf—Orwell Annie (Risk Me (FR))
355^{7} 523^{P}

Eden Linty *W Storey* 90b
5 b m Zaffaran(USA) —Rio Dancer (IRE) (Where To Dance (USA))
3563^{U} (3931)

Edgar Gink (IRE) *L Corcoran* 92h 100c
12 ch g Step Together(USA) —Turbo Run (Deep Run)
333^{P} 3478^{P}

Edgar Wilde (IRE) *R Rowe* 101+h
8 b g Invited(USA) —Ou La La (IRE) (Be My Native (USA))
384^{F} 514^{3} 3184^{P}

Edgehill (IRE) *R Ford* 107+h
5 b g Ali-Royal(IRE) —Elfin Queen (IRE) (Fairy King (USA))
2652^{2} 2838^{2}

Edgemoor Princess *R J Armson* 49h
8 b m Broadsword(USA) —Stubbin Moor (Kinglet)
94^{4} 236^{P} 651^{P}

Edict *C J Down* 50h
4 br f Diktat—Pericardia (Petong)
3645^{8}

Edith Bankes *W G M Turner*
4 ch f Woodborough(USA) —Mayday Kitty (Interrex (CAN))
3431^{P}

Edmo Heights *T D Easterby* 124h 114c
10 ch g Keen—Bodham (Bustino)
108^{5} 305^{6} 689^{7}

Edmo Yewkay (IRE) *T D Easterby* 103 h 140 c
6 bb g Sri Pekan(USA) —Mannequin (IRE) (In The Wings)
(2640) 3019^{2} 3385^{5}3739^{4} 3988^{P} 4611^{3}4984^{2}

Eggmount (IRE) *T R George* 76+h 106c
8 b g Riberetto—Brigade Leader (IRE) (Supreme Leader)
170^{4} (2594) 2984^{P}

Ehab (IRE) *Miss A M Newton-Smith* 68 h 78c
7 b g Cadeaux Genereux—Dernier Cri (Slip Anchor)
3715^{5} 4320^{P} **4662^{2} 4873^{6}5085^{5}**

Eidsfoss (IRE) *T T Clement* 42h
4 b g Danehill Dancer(IRE) —Alca Egeria (ITY) (Shareef Dancer (USA))
4795^{P}

Eight Fifty Five (IRE) *R T Phillips* 93h
6 gr g Wood Chanter—Electric View (IRE) (Electric)
616^{5} 1975^{3} 2461^{6} (Dead)

Eight Fifty Six (IRE) *Michael Hourigan* 70h
5 gr g General Monash(USA) —Mignonnette (FR) (Mtoto)
3003a^{12}

Eileens Comet *M E Sowersby*
6 br m Cosmonaut—Starnina (IRE) (Caerleon (USA))
4501^{P}

Eko Deauville (DEN) *I Madden* 36h
11 b g Fijar Tango(FR) —Eltsinea (FR) (Groom Dancer (USA))
3528a^{B}

Elaala (USA) *P A Blockley* 76h
4 ch f Aljabr(USA) —Nufuth (USA) (Nureyev (USA))
2676^{6} 2921^{11} 2935^{2} 3349^{B} 3485^{3}3804^{2} 4046^{F}

Elaeagnus *C Grant* 79b
4 b f Environment Friend—Angel Falling (Scottish Reel)
4059^{5} 5041^{2}

Ela Figura *M Appleby* 29h 63c
6 ch m The West(USA) —Chili Bouchier (USA) (Stop The Music (USA))
510^{P} 682^{5} 914^{10}979^{U} 1249^{4} 1363^{P}

Ela La Senza (IRE) *N A Twiston-Davies* 98h 45c
9 br g Lord Americo—Diamond Glow (Kalaglow)
1907^{P}

El Andaluz (FR) *Robert Gray* 63h 92 c
6 b g Baby Turk—Elise L'Ermitage (FR) (Quart De Vin (FR))
2108^{5} **2291^{P} 2476^{3}2902^{2} (2966) 3268^{3}**

Ela Re *Mrs S J Smith* 112h 79c
7 ch g Sabrehill(USA) —Lucia Tarditi (FR) (Crystal Glitters (USA))
914^{5} 1024^{P} 1111^{P}(1278) 1668^{F}

El Bandindos (IRE) *M C Pipe* 88b
5 b g Darazari(IRE) —Supreme Weasel (IRE) (Supreme Leader)
1882^{5}

El Bandito (IRE) *M J Footer* 87h 82 c
12 ch g Un Desperado(FR) —Red Marble (Le Bavard (FR))
360^{P} 4092^{4}

Elbdoubleu *C J Down* 83b
6 ch m Classic Cliche(IRE) —Bowling Fort (Bowling Pin)
4786[4]

El Cascador (FR) *T Trapenard* 86h
4 bl g Limnos(JPN) —Lady Suki (FR) (Caerwent (IRE))
777a[6]

El Corredor (IRE) *M C Pipe* 89h
7 b g Sadler's Wells(USA) —Meteor Stage (USA) (Stage Door Johnny (USA))
2968[12] 3355[7] 3659[6] 3950[2] 4080[11]4731[7]

Eleazar (GER) *Mrs L Wadham* 101+h
5 b g Alkalde(GER) —Eicidora (GER) (Surumu (GER))
1908[4] 2423[4] 2804[2] 3415[3]

Election Seeker (IRE) *G L Moore* 90 h
4 b g Intikhab(USA) —Scottish Eyes (USA) (Green Dancer (USA))
(1190) 1397[7] (Dead)

Electric Times (IRE) *D McCain* 70b
5 br g Good Thyne(USA) —Merry Watt (Last Fandango)
4072[15] 4615[10]

Elegant Clutter (IRE) *R N Bevis* 101+h
8 b g Petorius—Mountain Hop (IRE) (Tirol)
3990[3] (4392) (4879)

Elegant Eskimo *S E H Sherwood* 95h 97c
7 b m Elegant Monarch—Eskimo Slave (New Member)
1851[3] 2559[3] 3249[6] 3648[3] **3919[3]4558[2] 4851[F]**

Elenas River (IRE) *P J Hobbs* 112h 130 c
10 br g Over The River(FR) —Elena's Beauty (Tarqogan)
4374[7] 4835[2]

Elfkirk (IRE) *R H Buckler* 100 h 118 c
7 b m Zaffaran(USA) —Winter Sunset (Celio Rufo)
2240[2] **2553[0] 2798[5](3426) 3689[U] 4495[P]**

Elgar *M Hammond* 94h 109+c
9 ch g Alflora(IRE) —School Run (Deep Run)
4555[6] 4730[6]

El Hamra (IRE) *T R George* 70h
8 gr g Royal Abjar(USA) —Cherlinoa (FR) (Crystal Palace (FR))
172[F] 389[P] 506[P]

Elheba (IRE) *C J Down* 98+h
7 bb g Elbio—Fireheba (ITY) (Fire Of Life (USA))
206[7] 458[P] (Dead)

El Hombre Del Rio (IRE) *V G Greenway* 111h 117 c
9 ch g Over The River(FR) —Hug In A Fog (IRE) (Strong Gale)
289[4] **2623[P]** 3876[3] 4284[2]4727[P] **4944[6]**

Eljay's Boy *C L Tizzard* 84h 99c
8 b g Sir Harry Lewis(USA) —Woodland Flower (Furry Glen)
4572[F] 4735[4] (5107)

Eljutan (IRE) *J Joseph* 94h
8 b g Namaqualand(USA) —Camarat (Ahonoora)
1977[2] 2556[6] 2685[6] 3428[2] 3733[5]4652[7]

Ellandshe (IRE) *P R Webber* 98h
6 bb g Topanoora—Fox Glen (Furry Glen)
1903[7] 2421[12] 3248[13]

Ellas Recovery (IRE) *D B Feek* 74 h 47c
6 b g Shernazar—Nancys Wood (IRE) (Doubletour (USA))
2127[P] 2378[P] **2684[P] 2807[7]2933[P]**

Elle Roseador *M Madgwick* 81h
7 b m El Conquistador—The Hon Rose (Baron Blakeney)
1916[9] 2214[6] 2592[9] 3147[8] 3437[5]4640[2] 4874[P]

Ellerslie George (IRE) *T P Tate* 104b
6 br g Presenting—Proud Polly (IRE) (Pollerton)
2720[3] 4455[3] 4807[10]

Ellerslie Jackie *O Brennan* 40b
6 b m Supreme Leader—Swift Conveyance (IRE) (Strong Gale)
4507[10] 4902[10]

Ellerslie Tom *P Bowen* 110 h
4 br g Octagonal(NZ) —Tetravella (IRE) (Groom Dancer (USA))
1551[F] 1718[4] 2797[F] 3340[F] 3645[2]3817[4] 4551[6] 3[2]

Ellie Lou *A E Jessop*
5 b m Lord Americo—Flemings Delight (Idiots Delight)
3961[8]

Ellie Moss *A W Carroll* 23h
8 b m Le Moss—Kayella (Fine Blade (USA))
1850[9] 2179[P] 2937[P] **3329[P]3920[P] 4279[5]**

El Lute (IRE) *Mrs E M Collinson* 94b 77c
10 b g Abednego—Much Obliged (Crash Course)
98[4] 3913[P]

Ellway Prospect *M G Rimell* 103h
6 ch m Pivotal—Littlemisstrouble (USA) (My Gallant (USA))
2726[3] 3185[5] (3687) 3902[6]

El Paradiso (FR) *M Rolland*
9 b g Red Paradise—Norade (FR) (Shafaraz (FR))
585a[P]

El Rey Royale *M D Hammond*
4 b g Royal Applause—Spanish Serenade (Nashwan (USA))
1718[P]

Eluvaparty *D P Keane* 83b
6 b g El Conquistador—Ruby Celebration (New Member)
1909[5]

El Vaquero (IRE) *J Howard Johnson* 117 h 154 c
8 ch g Un Desperado(FR) —Marble Fontaine (Lafontaine (USA))
2346[P] 2615[3] 3039[U]

Elverys (IRE) *R A Fahey* 97 h
7 b g Lord Americo—Paddy's Babs (Little Buskins)
3789[3] 4052[5] 4613[3]

El Viejo (IRE) *L Wells* 92c
8 b g Norwich—Shuil Na Gale (Strong Gale)
2800[P] 4522[2] 4692[2]5085[U]

Elvis Returns *J M Jefferson* 103h 130+c
8 b g Alhaarth—Buckmist Blue (IRE) (Buckskin (FR))
2295[4] 2638[2] 2985[4] **3352[8]4163[3] 4518[2] 5139[2]**

Emali *G Chambers* 42c
9 b g Emarati(USA) —Princess Poquito (Hard Fought)
171[P]

Emanate *John Allen* 62h
8 ch g Nicholas Bill—Sleepline Princess (Royal Palace)
73[6] 654[8] 1028[8]

Emanic (FR) *P F Nicholls* 113 h 113+c
6 br g Video Rock(FR) —Una Volta (FR) (Toujours Pret (USA))
217[2] 364[3]

Ember Dancer *Ian Williams* 88h
4 b g Emarati(USA) —Bella Coola (Northern State (USA))
2105[5] 2927[13] 3645[15] 3787[6] 3939[P]4096[6]

Emerald Destiny (IRE) *Jedd O'Keeffe* 84h
4 b g Key Of Luck(USA) —Green Belt (FR) (Tirol)
1551[5] 1601[DSQ] 1718[P] 2263[P] 3349[8]3757[5] 4919[3]

Emile Zola *Miss Venetia Williams* 85+h
4 b c Singspiel(IRE) —Ellie Ardensky (Slip Anchor)
2373[10] 2824[5]

Emkanat (IRE) *K A Morgan* 77b
5 ch m Unfuwain(USA) —Raaqiyya (USA) (Blushing Groom (FR))
367[F] (Dead)

Emma Lilley (USA) *J G M O'Shea*
4 ch f Theatrical—Changed Tune (USA) (Tunerup (USA))
2069[10]

Emma's Dream *P F Nicholls* 77h
7 ch m Karinga Bay—Some Dream (Vitiges (FR))
4286[4] 4942[3]

Emmasflora *C T Pogson* 114+h 72c
8 b m Alflora(IRE) —Charlotte's Emma (Oats)
1611[2] (1851) 2173[15] 2501[4] **2976[5]3287[3]** 3621[7] 3792[3] 4494[2] (4657) 4797[4](4917)

Emmpat (IRE) *Anthony Mullins* 122h
8 b g Bigstone(IRE) —Nordic Abu (IRE) (Nordico (USA))
1093a[8]

Emotional Article (IRE) *T J Taaffe* 117h
6 ch g Definite Article—Cairo Lady (IRE) (Persian Bold)
43a[F] 2334[U]

Emotional Moment (IRE) *T J Taaffe* 159 h 136 c
9 b g Religiously(USA) —Rosceen Bui (IRE) (Phardante (FR))
90a[7] 2227a[4] 2777a[2] 3080a[2] (3585a) 4458[6]5101a[7]

Emperor Ross (IRE) *N G Richards* 120c
11 bb g Roselier(FR) —Gilded Empress (Menelek)
63[2] (411) 694[4]857[3] 4055[F]

Emperors Guest *C J Mann* 110h 133c
8 b g Emperor Jones(USA) —Intimate Guest (Be My Guest (USA))
452[P]

Emperor's Monarch *J Wade* 101+h
7 ch g Emperor Fountain—Shalta (FR) (Targowice (USA))
1940 [5] 2981[6]

Emphatic (IRE) *J G Portman* 87h
11 ch g Ela-Mana-Mou—Sally Rose (Sallust)
2341[8] 3325[4] 3814[P] 4752[4] 4874[6]5087[5]

Em'sgem *W Amos*
12 b m Germont—Gaelic Empress (Regular Guy)
1687[P]

Em's Guy *W Amos* 68b
8 b g Royal Fountain—Gaelic Empress (Regular Guy)
4725[F]

Emski *P Beaumont* 35h
5 b m Gunner B—Moheli (Ardross)
4304[9] 5042[5]

Em's Royalty *A Parker* 101h
9 b g Royal Fountain—Gaelic Empress (Regular Guy)
2169[7] **2689[U] 2945[P]3794[P]** 4515[3]

Encore Cadoudal (FR) *H P Hogarth* 115h 125 c
8 b g Cadoudal(FR) —Maousse (FR) (Labus (FR))
193[2] (2067) 2443[8]2768[P] 3495[10] 3922[5]4109[4]

Encounter *A D Brown* 80h
10 br g Primo Dominie—Dancing Spirit (IRE) (Ahonoora)
369[4]

Endless Power (IRE) *J Barclay* 77h
6 b g Perugino(USA) —Charroux (IRE) (Darshaan)
1834[6] 2062[7] 4143[P] 4342[P]

End Of An Error *A W Carroll* 90 h
7 b m Charmer—Needwood Poppy (Rolfe (USA))
215[6] 304[4] 606[3] 686[2] 781[F]941[5] 988[2] 1152[U] 1367[2] 1793[9]1856[3] 1884[3] 2341[P]

End Of Saga *J B Walton* 39h
7 ch g Endoli(USA) —Super Saga (Sagaro)
876[10] 942[P] 1108[7] 1337[8]

English Jim (IRE) *Miss A M Newton-Smith* 80 h
5 b g Saddlers' Hall(IRE) —Royal Folly (IRE) (King's Ride)
1775[8] 1950[6] (2214) 2687[4] 3424[2] 3905[4]4557[8]

Englishtown (FR) *Jonjo O'Neill* 115h 81+c
6 b g Mark Of Esteem(IRE) —English Spring (USA) (Grey Dawn II)
(806) 915[3] (980) 1270[2]

Enhancer *M J McGrath* 126+h
8 b g Zafonic(USA) —Ypha (USA) (Lyphard (USA))
194[2] 525[2] 766[3] (892) 1266[2] 3622[7]4091[4] 4473[25] 4821[9]

Enitsag (FR) *S Flook* 104 h 105+c
7 ch g Pistolet Bleu(IRE) —Rosala (FR) (Lashkari)
52[2] 313[3] 437[7]4594[P] (4730) (4831)

Ennemi D'Etat (FR) *M Rolland* 109h
7 br g Passing Sale(FR) —Best Of The Best (FR) (Cadoudal (FR))
585a[7] 779a[6]

Ennistown Lady (IRE) *R P Burns* 116h
7 b m Mujadil(USA) —Lady Be Magic (Burslem)
2650a[15] 3411a[19]

Entre Amis *G M Moore* 65h
6 ch m Prince Daniel(USA) —Audrina (Young Generation)
1590[4] 2414[9] 2674[P]

Entrelechambre *A J Chamberlain* 82b
4 b g Entrepreneur—Cambronne (Darshaan)
3181[10]

Envious *Miss J Feilden* 84h
7 ch g Hernando(FR) —Prima Verde (Leading Counsel (USA))
4907[4]

Enzo De Baune (FR) *G A Harker* 127c
9 b g En Calcat(FR) —Pure Moon (FR) (Pure Flight (USA))
108[3] 409[4]

Epsilo De La Ronce (FR) *Paul Morris* 95c
14 bb g Le Riverain(FR) —India Rosa (FR) (Carnaval)
47[9] 221[7] 313[7] (Dead)

Equilibria (USA) *G L Moore* 90h
4 b g Gulch(USA) —Julie La Rousse (IRE) (Lomond (USA))
2101[2] (2373) 3021[10] 3422[8] 4910[4]

Equivocate *R Mathew*
4 br f Karinga Bay—Heresy (IRE) (Black Minstrel)
2611[11] *3504[12]*

Equus Maximus (IRE) *W P Mullins* 123+b
6 b g Flemensfirth(USA) —Sambara (IRE) (Shardari)
4448[12]

Ericas Charm *P Bowen* 89+h
6 b m Alderbrook—Springaleak (Lafontaine (USA))
(1048) 1274[7] 2070[10] 2186[7] 2704[4] 3648[10]4834[14]

Eric's Charm (FR) *O Sherwood* 147h 150+c
8 b g Nikos—Ladoun (FR) (Kaldoun (FR))
3942[P] (4374) 5144[2]

Erins Lass (IRE) *R Dickin* 98h 96 c
9 b m Erin's Isle—Amative (Beau Charmeur (FR))
245[8] 536[6] 689[5] **862[P]1212[U] (1343) 1852[P]3888[9]** 4549[6] 5108[11]

Eriskay (IRE) *L Lungo* 107h
10 b g Montelimar(USA) —Little Peach (Ragapan)
121[P]

Ermine Grey *A W Carroll* 37h
5 gr g Wolfhound(USA) —Impulsive Decision (IRE) (Nomination)
3328[17]

Erritt (IRE) *John C Shearman* 42b
6 b g Luso—Raisin Turf (IRE) (Phardante (FR))
44a[20]

Errol *J F Coupland* 97 h
7 ch g Dancing Spree(USA) —Primo Panache (Primo Dominie)
149[3] 238[5] 370[8]

Escape Wall *K Bishop* 79b
5 ch g Kirkwall—Island Escape (IRE) (Turtle Island (IRE))
249[7] 656[5]

Escobar (POL) *Mrs P Townsley* 80h
5 b g Royal Court(IRE) —Escola (POL) (Dixieland (POL))
4915[3]

Escompteur (FR) *M C Pipe* 128 h 123 c
6 b g Poliglote—Escopette (FR) (Tourangeau (FR))
419[2] 564[2] 682[4]840[4] 946[2] 2488[2]2757[6] 3344[6] 4973[2]

Escrea (IRE) *Paul Nolan* 127h
7 b m Oscar(IRE) —Parsons Alert (IRE) (The Parson)
43a[9] 2650a[4] 3411a[6] 4375[14]

Eskimo Jack (IRE) *T R George* 121c
10 ch g Glacial Storm(USA) —Covette (Master Owen)
1515a[14] 4216[RR] 4831[4]

Eskimo Pie (IRE) *C C Bealby* 117 h 124+c
7 ch g Glacial Storm(USA) —Arctic Verb (Proverb)
2168[2] 2464[3] 2812[3]3494[3] (3955) 4496[P]

Esperance (IRE) *J Akehurst* 27h
6 ch g Bluebird(USA) —Dioscorea (IRE) (Pharly (FR))
3908[13]

Esplendidos (IRE) *D P Keane* 83h
7 b m Beneficial—Index Lady (Decent Fellow)
2244[6] 2632[7] 2932[3] 3242[7] 4912[5]

Espoir Du Printemp (FR) *P Peltier*
10 ch g April Night(FR) —Counsella (FR) (Leading Counsel (USA))
362a[U]

Espresso Forte (IRE) *Miss H C Knight* 94 h 102+c
7 ch g Anshan—Symphony Express (IRE) (Orchestra)
4662[P] 4904[3]

Esprit Du Chene (FR) *Mme D Guibourne*
9 b g Esprit Du Nord(USA) —Etoile Du Chene (FR) (Riverval (FR))
362a[P]

Esquillon *S Parr* 74+h
4 b f High Estate—Our Aisling (Blakeney)
1797[9] 2076[5] 2587[7] 2921[8] 3337[6]

Essennbee *Mrs J R Buckley* 53b
6 ch g Carlingford Castle—Polly B (Distinct Native)
266[7] 470[8]

Essex (IRE) *M J P O'Brien* 165h
6 b g Sadler's Wells(USA) —Knight's Baroness (Rainbow Quest (USA))
2397a[2] 3109a[5] 4000a[4] 5130a[4]

Estate *R S Brookhouse* 102h
4 b g Montjeu(IRE) —Fig Tree Drive (USA) (Miswaki (USA))
2921[7] 3340[5] 3939[4] 4838[7] 5021[2]

Esteban *J J Quinn* 78h 40c
6 b g Groom Dancer(USA) —Ellie Ardensky (Slip Anchor)
2627[11]

Estepona *J Howard Johnson* 105 h
5 ch g Polar Falcon(USA) —Kingdom Ruby (IRE) (Bluebird (USA))
2658[5] (3267)

Esterelle (USA) *H J Manners* 93h
11 ch m Trempolino(USA) —Duck Flighting (USA) (Far North (CAN))
1341[9] 1408[7] 1564[11] 1630[P] 1906[5]

Esters Boy *P G Murphy* 102+h
8 b g Sure Blade(USA) —Moheli (Ardross)
(105) 359[2] 566[8] 1079[4] 1436[3] (1630) 1826[6]

Estuary (USA) *Ms A E Embiricos* 70h
11 ch g Riverman(USA) —Ocean Ballad (Grundy)
363[R] 451[16] 670[9]

Etched In Stone (IRE) *N G Richards* 99+h
7 gr g Roselier(FR) —Wilton Castle (IRE) (Monksfield)
(323) 1990[3] (3314)

Etching (USA) *W Storey* 64h
6 b m Groom Dancer(USA) —Eternity (Suave Dancer (USA))
3167[P] 3347[10]

Etendard Indien (FR) *N J Henderson* 101 h
5 b g Selkirk(USA) —Danseuse Indienne (IRE) (Danehill (USA))
1677[P] 2734[7] 3360[9] 4215[10] 4593[4]4907[P]

Ethan Snowflake *N B King* 89+h 52c
7 b g Weld—Snow Child (Mandrake Major)
3592[10] 3956[5] (4475) 4794[7]

Etoile Des Iles (FR) *M Nigge* 107h
4 ch f Starborough—L'Antillaise (FR) (Generous (IRE))
1705a[4] 2085a[5]

Etoilerouge *P F Nicholls* 81b
5 b m Singspiel(IRE) —Bayrouge (IRE) (Gorytus (USA))
3435[5]

Etoile Russe (IRE) *P C Haslam* 104+h
4 b g Soviet Star(USA) —To The Skies (USA) (Sky Classic (CAN))
(1440) 1821[P] 3479[6] (3783) 3918[9] 4879[4]

Eudyptes *N E Berry*
7 b g Rock Hopper—Katchum (Jimsun)
*1922[9] 2131[12]*2428[8] 3463[P]

Euradream (IRE) *Jean-Rene Auvray* 107+h
8 ch g Eurobus—Its All A Dream (Le Moss)
2296[8] 2862[3] 3581[10] 4727[9]

Euro American (GER) *E W Tuer* 135+h
6 br g Snurge—Egyptale (Crystal Glitters (USA))
1836[4] (2639) 2925[8] (3318) 3622[2] 3966[2] (4108)4375[P]

Euro Bleu (FR) *M Sheppard* 112h 91+c
8 b g Franc Bleu Argent(USA) —Princess Card (FR) (Gift Card (FR))
451[12] **1831[5] 1983[P]2287[2]**

Euro Craft (IRE) *Mrs C J Robinson*
9 bb g Warcraft(USA) —Balda Girl (IRE) (Mandalus)
4594[P]

Euro Leader (IRE) *W P Mullins* 119h 148+c
8 b g Supreme Leader—Noreaster (IRE) (Nordance (USA))
89a[4] (1515a) 1700a[F]2195a[3] 4459[F] 4762[5](5080a)

Europa *Ferdy Murphy* 79h 146c
10 b g Jupiter Island—Dublin Ferry (Celtic Cone)
1721[8] 1846[P] 2492[2]2760[5] 3620[2] 4241[P]4433[P]

Europrime Games *M E Sowersby* 42h
8 b g Mind Games—Flower Princess (Slip Anchor)
1757[6] 1927[12] 2082[5] 2440[9] 2816[12]2967[U] 3169[12] 3335[8]

Euro Route (IRE) *G J Smith* 94h
5 b g Desert Style(IRE) —Fresh Look (IRE) (Alzao (USA))
(1432) 1541[10] 1614[3]

Eurotrek (IRE) *P F Nicholls* 127h 154 c
10 ch g Eurobus—Orient Jewel (Pollerton)
2046[4] (2828) (3390) 3971[P]

Euro Two (IRE) *N R Mitchell*
9 ch g Eurobus—Share The Dream (Green Shoon)
2311[F]

Eurydice (IRE) *Ferdy Murphy* 82b
6 bb m Heron Island(IRE) —Little Thunder (Whistling Deer)
349[3] 4732[9]

Eva's Edge (IRE) *B N Pollock*
5 b m Good Thyne(USA) —Right Dark (Buckskin (FR))
3461[12]

Even Flo *Jean-Rene Auvray* 75b
5 b m River Falls—Re-Spin (Gildoran)
249[2] 2534[18] 2987[4] 4059[3]

Even More (IRE) *R H Alner* 119 c
11 b g Husyan(USA) —Milan Moss (Le Moss)
205[3] 1972[9] 2273[7]2458[3] 2808[8] 3212[2]3469[7] 3698[6] (3949) 4287[F] 4835[5] 4944[5]

Eveon (IRE) *Ian Williams* 36h 88+c
6 b m Synefos(USA) —Lovely Grand (Le Bavard (FR))
2309[15] 2718[11] 3149[12] **4553[F]**

Ever Present (IRE) *N G Richards* 122h 123+c
8 ch g Presenting—My Grand Rose (IRE) (Executive Perk)
(64) 2629[3] **3317[3] (4343)**

Ever So Slightly (IRE) *Mrs S J Smith* 98+h
5 b g Good Thyne(USA) —Loch Lomond (IRE) (Dry Dock)
4507[5]

Everytime *M W Easterby* 73h
6 b g Vettori(IRE) —Flamingo Times (Good Times (ITY))
1344[6] 1526[5]

Evidence First *Michael Hourigan* 63h
5 b g Overbury(IRE) —Flo-Jo (DEN) (Pelton Lad)
5104a[19]

Ewar Bold *K G Wingrove* 90h
13 b g Bold Arrangement—Monaneigue Lady (Julio Mariner)
458[10] 573[7] 652[10] 1026[8]

Ewar Finch (FR) *C L Popham* 40h
4 b f Kayf Tara—Ewar Empress (IRE) (Persian Bold)
4556[7]

Ewe Beauty (FR) *Ferdy Murphy* 90h
6 b m Phantom Breeze—Baie De Chalamont (FR) (Balsamo (FR))
4988[P]

Excellent Vibes (IRE) *N A Twiston-Davies* 85h 101c
8 b g Doyoun—Hawait Al Barr (Green Desert (USA))
(746) **805[P]** (916) **1041[U]**1079[P] 1262[6] **1511[7] 1728[F]** (Dead)

Exceptionnel (FR) *Lady Connell* 98h 108c
7 b g Subotica(FR) —The Exception (FR) (Melyno)
3277[3] 3611[5] **4016[4] 4394[5]**

Exclusive Air (USA) *H H G Owen* 64h
7 ch g Affirmed(USA) —Lac Dessert (USA) (Lac Ouimet (USA))
384[7] 3222[5] 3330[P] 3415[P] 4101[P]

Executive Decision (IRE) *Mrs L Wadham* 121h 127c
12 ch g Classic Music(USA) —Bengala (FR) (Hard To Beat)
3299[9] (3922) 4378[6]4850[2]

Executive Friend (IRE) *O Brennan* 80b
7 b g Executive Perk—Highland Chain (Furry Glen)
2844[6] 4905[P]

Exhibit (IRE) *N J Hawke* 57h
8 b g Royal Academy(USA) —Juno Madonna (IRE) (Sadler's Wells (USA))
1750[P] 1900[P]

Exit Swinger (FR) *P F Nicholls*
11 b g Exit To Nowhere(USA) —Morganella (FR) (D'Arras (FR))
2370[U] 2744[P] 3176[P]

Exit To Saumur (FR) *B Storey* 64h
5 b g Exit To Nowhere(USA) —Mercalle (FR) (Kaldoun (FR))
424[7] 2658[11]

Exodous (ARG) *Mrs A Blaker* 97h 87c
10 ch g Equalize(USA) —Empire Glory (ARG) (Good Manners (USA))
400[2]

Exotic Dancer (FR) *Jonjo O'Neill* 161h 142 c
6 b g Turgeon(USA) —Northine (FR) (Northern Treat (USA))
1822[3] 2174[3] (2759) 2970[F]

Expensive Folly (IRE) *A J Chamberlain* 60h
8 b g Satco(FR) —Tarasandy (IRE) (Arapahos (FR))
1089[P] 1298[8] 1410[6]

Explode *Miss L C Siddall* 40h
9 b g Zafonic(USA) —Didicoy (USA) (Danzig (USA))
2873[12] 3371[10] 4794[10]

Explosive Fox (IRE) *C P Morlock* 105+h
5 gr g Foxhound(USA) —Grise Mine (FR) (Crystal Palace (FR))
(1047) 1108[5] 1220[9] 1298[2] 1431[2] 1522[5]1854[P]

Extra Bold *R Lee* 13h
4 b g Overbury(IRE) —Tellicherry (Strong Gale)
4574[7] 4935[14]

Extra Cache (NZ) *O Brennan* 85h 80c
13 br g Cache Of Gold(USA) —Gizmo (NZ) (Jubilee Wine (USA))
2080[2] 2957[4] 3791[P]13[2]

Extra Cover (IRE) *Ronald Thompson*
5 b g Danehill Dancer(IRE) —Ballycurrane (IRE) (Elbio)
2763[13]

Extra Smooth *C C Bealby* 104+h
5 gr g Cloudings(IRE) —Miss Ondee (FR) (Dress Parade)
1885[2] 2295[6] 2690[4] 3792[P] (4634)

Extremist (USA) *K C Bailey* 100h
7 b g Dynaformer(USA) —Strumming (IRE) (Ballad Rock)
237[4] (Dead)

Eye Candy (IRE) *Mrs Sandra McCarthy* 116 h
5 b h Princely Heir(IRE) —Timissa (IRE) (Kahyasi)
88a[4] 2209[19] 3894a[14]

Eye On The Ball *M F Morris* 57h
7 b g Slip Anchor—Elaine Tully (IRE) (Persian Bold)
70a[5]

Eyes Dont Lie (IRE) *D A Nolan* 78h
8 b g Namaqualand(USA) —Avidal Park (Horage)
942[P]

Eyes To The Right (IRE) *D Burchell* 77h
7 ch g Eagle Eyed(USA) —Capable Kate (IRE) (Alzao (USA))
5047[U]

Eyze (IRE) *B Mactaggart* 95h 117c
10 b g Lord Americo—Another Raheen (IRE) (Sandalay)
1606[P] **2037[6] 2495[P]**

Faasel (IRE) *N G Richards* 160 h
5 b g Unfuwain(USA) —Waqood (USA) (Riverman (USA))
2338[2] 2761[3] 3492[3] 4432[8] 5003[2]5125[2]

Fable (USA) *Noel Meade* 115h 125+c
10 b h Hansel(USA) —Aragon (USA) (Raconteur (USA))
69a[16]

Fabrezan (FR) *B D Leavy* 97h
7 b g Nikos—Fabulous Secret (FR) (Fabulous Dancer (USA))
353[P] 768[11]

Fabro (IRE) *P A Fahy* 74h
5 b m Darazari(IRE) —Sweet Tune (Welsh Chanter)
44a[21]

Fabulous Jet (FR) *Miss Venetia Williams* 105+h
6 ch g Starborough—Jetty (FR) (Fabulous Dancer (USA))
2950[3] (3355) 4067[4] 4561[11]

Fact Cat *Ernst Oertel* 66b
8 ch g So Factual(USA) —Zealous Kitten (USA) (The Minstrel (CAN))
1538[P]

Factor Fifteen *J C Tuck* 107 h
7 gr g Hector Protector(USA) —Catch The Sun (Kalaglow)
3458[P]

Fad Amach (IRE) *G R I Smyly* 65b
5 gr m Flemensfirth(USA) —Fortina's Angle (Buckskin (FR))
4976[12]

Faddad (USA) *Mrs A M Thorpe* 54h 89+c
10 b g Irish River(FR) —Miss Mistletoes (IRE) (The Minstrel (CAN))
1075[P] (1156) **1299[5] 1411[5]1479[3] 1659[4]**
1747[9]**1897[P] 2074[7] 2282[6]**4290[9]

Fae Taylor (IRE) *Ferdy Murphy*
6 b m Desert Style(IRE) —Aliyna (FR) (Vayrann)
2028[10] 2515[P]

Fair Along (GER) *P J Hobbs* 144h
4 b g Alkalde(GER) —Fairy Tango (FR) (Acatenango (GER))
1023[U] (1095) (1201) (2178) (2367) 2756[3] 3021[4]
4468[2]4747[8]

Fairfield *B Storey*
5 b m Alflora(IRE) —April City (Lidhame)
3556[11] 4304[14]

Fairlight Express (IRE) *D P Keane* 82b
6 ch g Carroll House—Marble Fontaine (Lafontaine (USA))
1554[8] 1730[7] 3001[10]

Fairly Glorious *Mrs K J Tutty*
5 b g Tina's Pet—Steamy Windows (Dominion)
1374[P]

Fairly High (IRE) *N G Ayliffe* 87h
6 b m Sri Pekan(USA) —Ecco Mi (IRE) (Priolo (USA))
(133) 356[4]

Fairmorning (IRE) *C N Kellett* 84h
7 b g Ridgewood Ben—The Bratpack (IRE) (Mister Majestic)
237[5] 813[7] 1279[4]

Fair Options *A P Jones* 31h
5 gr g Marju(IRE) —Silver Singing (USA) (Topsider (USA))
1890[9]

Fair Prospect *P F Nicholls* 116h 130+c
10 b g Sir Harry Lewis(USA) —Fair Sara (Mcindoe)
(1825) 4764[P]

Fair Question (IRE) *Miss Venetia Williams* 139 h
8 b g Rainbow Quest(USA) —Fair Of The Furze (Ela-Mana-Mou)
(3854) 3970[3] 4446[17] 4776[P]

Fair Shake (IRE) *Karen McLintock* 90h
6 b g Sheikh Albadou—Shamrock Fair (IRE) (Shavian)
2658[6]

Fair Spin *M D Hammond* 107 h
6 ch g Pivotal—Frankie Fair (IRE) (Red Sunset)
2190[11] 3040[8] 3737[5] 4503[5]

Fairtoto *Mrs N S Evans* 94dh 81c
10 b g Mtoto—Fairy Feet (Sadler's Wells (USA))
313[8] 455[P] 978[P]

Fair Touch (IRE) *C P Morlock* 73h
7 b g Air Display(USA) —Anns Touch (IRE) (Ragapan)
357[9] 2140[8]

Fair View (GER) *Dr P Pritchard* 78h
5 b m Dashing Blade—Fairy Tango (FR) (Acatenango (GER))
3238[P] 3281[9] 3550[7] 4393[P] 4566[6]4855[7]

Fairwood Nickle (IRE) *Miss Lucinda V Russell* 46h 28c
7 b g Shernazar—Hop Picker (USA) (Plugged Nickle (USA))
81[P] 213[10]

Fairy Skin Maker (IRE) *G A Harker* 109b 90 c
8 ch g Nomadic Way(USA) —Malvern Madam (Reesh)
1835[3] 2110[10] 2680[8] 2840[8]**2975[6] 3781[5]**

Fait Le Jojo (FR) *L Corcoran* 139h
9 b g Pistolet Bleu(IRE) —Pretty Davis (USA) (Trempolino (USA))
(1598) 1919[3] 2209[8] 2519[3] 3298[7] 4446[12]4848[8]

Fakima (IRE) *John G Carr* 98h
8 b g Commanche Run—El Scarsdale (Furry Glen)
334[6] 595[F]

Falchion *J R Bewley* 85 c
11 b g Broadsword(USA) —Fastlass (Celtic Cone)
2265[6] 2451[P] 2877[6]3315[5] 4042[6] 4144[P]

Falcon Beneficial (IRE) *G L Moore* 74+h
4 br f Beneficial—Winnie Wumpkins (IRE) (Roselier (FR))
2830[8] 3188[5] 3281[5] 3902[7] 4129[P]

Falcon's Cliche *P Beaumont* 84h
5 b m Classic Cliche(IRE) —Guinda (IRE) (Corvaro (USA))
3448[6] 4059[11] 4507[14] 5138[5]

Falcon's Tribute (IRE) *P Beaumont* 56h
4 b f Beneficial—Early Storm (IRE) (Glacial Storm (USA))
3490[11] 3931[S] 4304[12]

Faline Du Rocher (FR) *D Lenfant*
9 ch m Red Paradise—Gambadove (FR) (Beyssac (FR))
1373a[F]

Fallout (IRE) *J W Mullins* 87h 87+c
5 b m Goldmark(USA) —Tearful Reunion (Pas De Seul)
(58) 462[P] 753[11] 2486[5] **2846[5]3215[5]** 3437[P]

Falmer For All (IRE) *J Ryan* 84b
8 b g Warcraft(USA) —Sunset Walk (Le Bavard (FR))
3899[P]

False Tail (IRE) *J J Lambe* 88c
14 b g Roselier(FR) —Its Good Ere (Import)
321[6]

Fame *P J Hobbs* 111h
6 ch g Northern Amethyst—First Sapphire (Simply Great (FR))
1862[F] 2103[4] 2595[8] 3128[12]

Family Venture (IRE) *Ferdy Murphy* 107h 124c
9 br g Montelimar(USA) —Well Honey (Al Sirat)
4611[P] (Dead)

Fandani (GER) *C J Mann* 132+h
6 b g Lomitas—Fainting Spell (FR) (Top Ville)
(203) 438[3] 1880[3] 2487[2] 4242[F]

Fanion De Neulliac (FR) *M Sheppard* 92c
13 b g Perrault—Malis Creiomin (FR) (Dirak Creiomin (FR))
547[9]

Fanling Lady *Martin Brassil* 98h
5 gr m Highest Honor(FR) —Pain Perdu (IRE) (Waajib)
3003a[16]

Fantasmic *M J M Evans* 96h 107+c
10 ch g Broadsword(USA) —Squeaky Cottage (True Song)
108[P] 2239[P] 2562[F]2960[4] 4392[11] **4614[3](4782)**

Fantastic Arts (FR) *Miss Venetia Williams* 106h 112 c
6 b g Royal Applause—Magic Arts (IRE) (Fairy King (USA))
3243[5] 3418[8] 3844[F]4454[F] 4735[6] 4913[5]

Fantastic Champion (IRE) *J R Cornwall* 118h 81c
7 b g Entrepreneur—Reine Mathilde (USA) (Vaguely Noble)
1412[8] 1549[P] 1760[6]**2717[8] 3593[5]** 4797[P]

Fantastico (IRE) *Mrs K Walton* 95h
6 b m Bahhare(USA) —Minatina (IRE) (Ela-Mana-Mou)
499[4] 697[9] 1211[5] (1310)

Faraway Echo *James Moffatt* 46h
5 gr m Second Empire(IRE) —Salalah (Lion Cavern (USA))
334[10] (496) 649[6] 987[P] 3147[P] 3557[11]3782[9] 4609[P]

Farceur (FR) *M C Pipe* 71h 50c
7 bb g Anabaa(USA) —Fabulous Account (USA) (Private Account (USA))
295[7] **466[7] 673[P]**749[11] **958[8]** 1121[8] 1152[P]1262[9]

Fard Du Moulin Mas (FR) *M E D Francis* 106+h 99c
13 bb g Morespeed—Soiree D'Ex (FR) (Kashtan (FR))
275[9] 488[7] (2766) 2925[7] 4858[5] 5108[3]

Far From Trouble (IRE) *C Roche* 119h 132c
7 b g Good Thyne(USA) —Derry Girl (Rarity)
4460[3] 4929a[F]

Farington Lodge (IRE) *J M Saville* 86h 104+c
8 b g Simply Great(FR) —Lodge Party (IRE) (Strong Gale)
594[5] 998[2] 1100[2]**1232[P] 2978[U] (3444) 4492[F]**

Farlington *P Bowen* 103c
9 b g Alflora(IRE) —Annapuma (Rakaposhi King)
823[F] 2577[U] 2703[7]3803[8] 4857[7]

Farmer Brent (IRE) *C J Down* 90b
6 bb g Lord Americo—Highland Party (Deep Run)
2507[5]

Farmer Brown (IRE) *P Hughes* 104b
5 b g Bob Back(USA) —Magic Moonbeam (IRE) (Decent Fellow)
3763[5]

Farmer Grant (IRE) *A J Martin* 95+c
7 b g Flemensfirth(USA) —Strong Opinion (Strong Gale)
2686[F]

Farnaheezview (IRE) *O Sherwood* 111h 123+c
8 b g Naheez(USA) —Sweet View (King's Ride)
489[6] 2809[P]

Farne Isle *G A Harker* 110 h
7 ch m Midnight Legend—Biloela (Nicholas Bill)
302[2] (647) 3171[4] 3542[6] 3853[5] 5066[13]

Fasgo (IRE) *P F Nicholls* 110h 112 c
11 b g Montelimar(USA) —Action Plan (Creative Plan (USA))
2162[5] 3614[P]

Fashion Shoot *P Kelsall*
5 b m Double Trigger(IRE) —Paris Fashion (FR) (Northern Fashion (USA))
1543[P] 3691[11] 4801[P]

Fastaffaran (IRE) *I McMath* 92+h
5 b g Zaffaran(USA) —Break Fast (Prince Tenderfoot (USA))
4315[6] 4720[4] 5063[3]

Fast And Fiery (IRE) *I A Duncan* 86h
6 ch m Zaffaran(USA) —Shawiba (IRE) (Rainbows For Life (CAN))
3235[7]

Fast Cindy (USA) *Paul Morris* 53h
7 b m Fastness(IRE) —Forever Cindy (ARG) (Forever Sparkle (USA))
1220[6]

Fast Forward (NZ) *Miss Venetia Williams* 101+h
6 gr g Grosvenor(NZ) —Abachi (NZ) (Three Legs)
2665[2] 2988[3] 3664[3] 4033[2]

Fast King (FR) *Dr P Pritchard* 101h
8 b g Housamix(FR) —Fast Girl (FR) (Gay Minstrel (FR))
5[6]

Fastnet Light (IRE) *D T Hughes* 89h
6 b m Definite Article—Undiscovered (Tap On Wood)
2796a[9]

Father Abraham (IRE) *J Akehurst* 103h 97c
8 b g Idris(IRE) —Mothers Blessing (Wolver Hollow)
240[P] 511[6]

Father Jim *J A T De Giles* 100c
11 b g Seymour Hicks(FR) —Deaconess (The Parson)
50[4] 282[7] 3910[7]4325[U]

Father Matt (IRE) *Noel Meade* 112h 144 c
8 br g King's Ride—Honeydew (IRE) (Persian Mews)
2668a[2] 3409a[2] 3893a[2]4136a[U]

Fatherofthebride (IRE) *Joseph Crowley* 106 h 124c
10 gr g Roselier(FR) —Trendy Princess (Prince Tenderfoot (USA))
1420a[10] 1515a[P] 2539a[10]3053a[9] 3587a[12]

Fayr Firenze (IRE) *M F Harris* 13h
5 b g Fayruz—Shillay (Lomond (USA))
4423[10]

Feanor *Mrs S A Watt* 106+h
8 b m Presidium—Nouvelle Cuisine (Yawa)
197[5] 551[2] 784[P] 1001[2] 1223[4]1366[5] 1530[P] 5039[6]

Fearless Foursome *N W Alexander* 95h
7 b g Perpendicular—Harrietfield (Nicholas Bill)
80[3] 2064[9] 2680[6] 2944[12] 3231[4]3797[4] **4142[P]** 4723[2]

Fearless Mel (IRE) *Mrs H Dalton* 114+c
12 b g Mandalus—Milan Pride (Northern Guest (USA))
176[P] 346[P] 1041[4](1321) (1446) 1511[5]

Fear Siuil (IRE) *Michael Blake* 123c
13 b g Strong Gale—Astral River (Over The River (FR))
386[8] 653[3] 805[3]1025[4] 1189[6] 1219[4]1406[3] 1650[P]
4594[11]4757[5] 6[5]

Feathard Lady (IRE) *C A Murphy* 160+h
6 b m Accordion—Lady Rolfe (IRE) (Alzao (USA))
(2032a) (2650a) (2971)

Feathered Storm (IRE) *Michael J O'Connor* 94b 109c
8 ch g Glacial Storm(USA) —Carrigeen Wood (IRE) (Buckskin (FR))
42[P]

Federstar (GER) *M F Harris* 120h
4 b g In A Tiff(IRE) —Federspeil (Konigsstuhl (GER))
(1023) 1821[2]

Feel Good Factor *P M J Doyle* 116+h
6 b g Singspiel(IRE) —Colorspin (FR) (High Top)
5078a[3]

Feeling Fizzical *Mrs J C McGregor* 29h
8 b g Feelings(FR) —Stepdaughter (Relkino)
1307[P] (Dead)

Feel The Pride (IRE) *Jonjo O'Neill* 131+h 131c
8 b m Persian Bold—Nordic Pride (Horage)
(108) (195) (217) 1822[F]2371[3] (2516)
2757[7]3387[5] 3618[2] 3695[4]

Felix Darby (IRE) *Miss G Browne* 73 h 97 c
11 b g Buckskin(FR) —Cool Anne (Orchardist)
101[3] 276[4]

Felix Rex (GER) *J Pearce* 99+h
6 ch g Tempeltanz(GER) —Figlia D'Oro (GER) (Luigi (GER))
4015[3] 4604[5]

Felix The Fox (NZ) *N A Twiston-Davies* 76+h
6 b g Felix The Cat(USA) —Aristippe (AUS) (Twenty Four Karat (USA))
242[P] 696[5] 758[6] 911[10] 1233[4]1366[10]

Female (IRE) *C Roche* 120b
5 b m Saddlers' Hall(IRE) —Mursuma (Rarity)
4448[7] 5134a[2]

Femme D'Avril (FR) *Miss Lucy Bridges* 55h
4 b f Homme De Loi(IRE) —Free Demo (FR) (Hero's Honor (USA))
2236[9] 2597[7] 2797[5] 3483[7]

Fencethegap (IRE) *A E Price* 78h
9 b g Archway(IRE) —Sally Gap (Sallust)
860[12]

Fencote (IRE) *P Beaumont* 91h 89c
9 b g Norwich—Primrose Forest (Menelek)
59[U] 343[4] 521[5] **2630[7]2839[F]**

Fencote Gold *P Beaumont* 64h
6 ch g Bob's Return(IRE) —Goldaw (Gala Performance)
1885[10] 2571[9]

Fenix (GER) *Mrs L Wadham* 134 h
7 b g Lavirco(GER) —Frille (FR) (Shareef Dancer (USA))
67a[P] 2190[3] 2636[8] 3298[3] 3502[2]3727[5] 3986[6]
4375[16]

Fenney Spring *W Jenks* 74+h
6 b m Polish Precedent(USA) —Sliprail (USA) (Our Native (USA))
111[P] 178[7] 569[5] (613) 905[3] 1202[4]1336[7] 1645[14]

Ferimon *H D Daly* 125 h 109+c
7 gr g Terimon—Rhyming Moppet (Rymer)
1976[5] 2660[3]

Ferrara Flame (IRE) *R Brotherton* 58h
4 b f Titus Livius(FR) —Isolette (Wassl)
1023[3]

Ferryport House (IRE) *R J Hewitt*
9 bb g Over The River(FR) —Tusker Lady (Callernish)
3847[P]

Fertility *B J Llewellyn* 24b
6 ch m Queen's Soldier(USA) —Ruths Pride (Amboise)
1401[6]

Festival Flyer *Miss M Bragg* 98h
11 b g Alhijaz—Odilese (Mummy's Pet)
(4331) 4874[2]

Festive Chimes (IRE) *N B King* 110+h
5 b m Efisio—Delightful Chime (IRE) (Alzao (USA))
185[F] 367[2] 671[2] 892[3] (976) 1047[2]1089[3] 1213[2]
1434[4] (1485) 1522[2] 1987[3](2218) 2347[18] 2952[3]
3648[3] 4972[11]

Fibre Optics (IRE) *Jonjo O'Neill* 87h
6 b g Presenting—Hooch (Warpath)
3505[5] 3846[4] 4033[11]

Fiddlers Creek (IRE) *R Allan* 89+h
7 b g Danehill(USA) —Mythical Creek (USA) (Pleasant Tap (USA))
2657[15] 3534[7] 3674[4] 4919[6]

Fiddles Music *D Burchell* 95h
5 b m Fraam—Fiddles Delight (Colmore Row)
399[7] 568[5] 839[2] 1027[4] 1075[2]1223[2] 1361[2] 1488[5]
1658[5] 1856[5]1977[P]

Fieldings Society (IRE) *Jennie Candlish* 81+h
7 ch g Moscow Society(USA) —Lone Trail (IRE) (Strong Gale)
4826[P] 5015[8]

Field Master (IRE) *C J Gray* 78h
9 ch g Foxhound(USA) —Bold Avril (IRE) (Persian Bold)
4331[P] 4752[5] 5048[2]

Field Roller (IRE) *P Monteith* 105h 99+c
6 ch g High Roller(IRE) —Cathedral Road (Hard Boy)
1110[F] 2430[5] **3877[P]4719[P] 4981[6] 5119[5]**

Fieldsofclover (IRE) *Miss E C Lavelle* 103h 90c
9 br g Montelimar(USA) —Power Point (Pollerton)
3460[2] 3815[4] 5071[3]

Fields Of Home (IRE) *Jennie Candlish* 119c
8 b m Synefos(USA) —Homefield Girl (IRE) (Rahotep (FR))
1317[P]

Field Spark *J G Given* 71h
6 b g Sillery(USA) —On The Top (High Top)
2444[16] 2923[11] 3168[10]

Fiepes Shuffle (GER) *C Von Der Recke* 132h
6 b g Big Shuffle(USA) —Fiepe (EG) (Zigeunersohn (EG))
3725[F] 4432[14]

Fier Normand (FR) *Jonjo O'Neill* 120+h
7 b g Cyborg(FR) —Moomaw (Akarad (FR))
1895[2] (2821) 3369[4] (4048) 4420[6]

Fiery Lord (IRE) *Paul Nolan* 106h
5 b h Lord Americo—Fairy Blaze (IRE) (Good Thyne (USA))
3515a[7]

Fiery Peace *C Grant* 97h 121c
9 ch g Tina's Pet—Burning Mirage (Pamroy)
48 534[2] 1012[5]1529[U] 1673[4] (2294) 2478[3] **3172[F]**
(Dead)

Fiery Ring (IRE) *J R H Fowler*
11 b g Torus—Kakemona (Kambalda)
45a[11]

Fifteen Reds *J C Haynes* 84 h 51c
11 b g Jumbo Hirt(USA) —Dominance (Dominion)
2025[P] **2168[6] 2449[P]2978[P]** 3209[8] 3552[P] 4113[7]

Fifth Column (USA) *M V Coglan*
5 b g Allied Forces(USA) —Miff (USA) (Beau Genius (CAN))
4055[U]

Figaro Du Rocher (FR) *M C Pipe* 112h 132 c
6 ch g Beyssac(FR) —Fabinou (FR) (Cavan)
409[2] 726[4] 915[2] (1001) **1080[2]**1263[5] **1542[6] 2102[6]**

Fighter Command *Evan Williams*
5 ch g Docksider(USA) —Rose Alto (Adonijah)
1374[8]

Fighter Pilot *Jim Best* 108h 96c
7 ch g Alflora(IRE) —Gunna Be Precious (Gunner B)
4852[P]

Fight The Feeling *J W Unett* 87h 88c
8 ch g Beveled(USA) —Alvecote Lady (Touching Wood (USA))
78[P] 345[4] 630[2] 913[6] **3672[3]4054[2] 4662[4]** 5069[4]

Filey Flyer *J R Turner* 90h
6 ch m Weldnaas(USA) —Chasers' Bar (Oats)
2028[5] 2446[11] 2658[9] 2903[4] 3253[9]3782[8] 4527[7] 4919[2]

Fillameena *P T Midgley* 65h
6 b m Robellino(USA) —Lotus Moon (Shareef Dancer (USA))
2515[12] 2838[7] 3167[8] 3557[12]

Fille Detente *C J Gray* 85h
6 ch m Double Trigger(IRE) —Matoaka (Be My Chief (USA))
23[4] 182[RR] 1018[5] (Dead)

Fille D'Honfleur *M C Pipe* 85+h
5 ch m Classic Cliche(IRE) —M I Babe (Celtic Cone)
1027[10]

Fill The Bunker (IRE) *N A Twiston-Davies* 83h
6 bl g Detroit Sam(FR) —Midland Queen (Midland Gayle)
2559[8] 2821[15] 3275[11] 3800[7]

Filscot *P W Hiatt* 80h 100c
14 b g Scottish Reel—Fililode (Mossberry)
461[4]

Final Act (IRE) *John Joseph Murphy* 109h 130c
10 b g Tidaro(USA) —Night Course (Crash Course)
92a[3]

Final Command *J C Tuck* 89+h
9 ch g Gildoran—Fine Fettle (Final Straw)
75[3] 502[7] 4783[P]

Final Lap *H H G Owen* 68h
10 b g Batshoof—Lap Of Honour (Final Straw)
3433[P] 3956[6] 4101[7]

Final Melody *P Bowen*
6 b m Luso—Final Abby (Push On)
742[P]

Final Over *W K Goldsworthy* 68b
6 br m Overbury(IRE) —Final Pride (Push On)
4595[11] 4836[P]

Final Overture (IRE) *J S Wainwright* 27h
4 b f Rossini(USA) —Two Magpies (Doulab (USA))
1339[11] 1441[P]

Final Target (IRE) *Liam O'Donoghue* 107c
10 b g Executive Perk—Riseaway (Raise You Ten)
5083a[12]

Financial Future *C Roberts* 77h
6 b g Barathea(IRE) —In Perpetuity (Great Nephew)
3023[P] 3328[14] 3463[6] 4367[F] 4640[P]5110[P]

Fin Bec (FR) *R Curtis* 44 c
13 b g Tip Moss(FR) —Tourbrune (FR) (Pamponi (FR))
1989[P] 2293[5] 2502[3]2965[2] 3241[U] 3547[3](3649) 4287[P] 4576[P]4835[8] 5136[P]

Find Me Another (IRE) *Mrs Caroline Bailey* 107c
10 b g Shardari—Naujwan Too (Kafu)
280[2] 512[6]

Fine Edge *H E Haynes* 73b
5 ch m Keen—Cap That (Derek H)
3468[12] 4680[8] 5054[8]

Fine Enough (IRE) *R Rowe* 62b
7 br g Florida Son—Lodge Party (IRE) (Strong Gale)
2020[7] 4603[P] 5086[P]

Finely Tuned (IRE) *M Pitman* 115 h
7 b g Lord Americo—Gusserane Princess (Paddy's Stream)
1991[3] 3417[3] 4052[P]

Fine Palette *B J Llewellyn* 76+h
6 ch g Peintre Celebre(USA) —Filly Mignonne (IRE) (Nashwan (USA))
1077[4] 1742[13]

Finest Of Men *J B Walton* 80b 90c
10 b g Tina's Pet—Merry Missus (Bargello)
604[5] 783[P]

Finger Onthe Pulse (IRE) *T J Taaffe* 127h
5 b g Accordion—Quinnsboro Ice (IRE) (Glacial Storm (USA))
(3003a) 3642a[3]

Fingersthumbsngums (IRE) *Jennie Candlish* 82b
5 br g Oscar(IRE) —Smart Fashion (Carlburg)
4072[11] 4500[13] 5054[15]

Finland (UAE) *Mrs A Duffield* 105h
4 b g Timber Country(USA) —Najm Al Bahar (FR) (Caerleon (USA))
1551[2] 1718[3] (1797) 1923[3] 2921[6]

Finnegans Rainbow *M C Chapman* 72h
4 ch g Spectrum(IRE) —Fairy Story (IRE) (Persian Bold)
3787[7] 4077[8] 4795[4]

Finns Cross (IRE) *K G Reveley* 95h
7 b g Topanoora—Riancoir Alainn (Strong Gale)
(1401)

Finsbury Fred (IRE) *N A Twiston-Davies* 94+h
5 b g Clerkenwell(USA) —Kalifornia Katie (IRE) (Sharp Charter)
1849[10] 2127[4] 2829[10] 3789[P] 4099[3]4606[11] 5028[P]

Finzi (IRE) *M Scudamore* 85h 103c
8 b g Zaffaran(USA) —Sporting Talent (IRE) (Seymour Hicks (FR))
2465[2] 2662[2] 3424[3](3578) 3845[3] 4103[2]4395[2]

Fiori *P C Haslam* 88h 118 c
10 b g Anshan—Fen Princess (IRE) (Trojan Fen)
84[4] 305[3] 1221[5]1825[U] 2003[6] 2368[2]2502[4] 3293[P] 3398[5]4848[17]

Fireaway *O Brennan* 89h 108 c
12 b g Infantry—Handymouse (Nearly A Hand)
2955[2] 3596[6]

Fireball Macnamara (IRE) *M Pitman* 113h 124c
10 b g Lord Americo—Glint Of Baron (Glint Of Gold)
387[P] 751[P]

Firebird Rising (USA) *R Brotherton* 64h
5 b m Stravinsky(USA) —Capable (USA) (Capote (USA))
729[10] 943[3] 1085[9] 3804[8] 4570[P]

Fire Dragon (IRE) *Jonjo O'Neill* 158h
5 b g Sadler's Wells(USA) —Cattermole (USA) (Roberto (USA))
(1559) 1677[P] 1872[2] 2747[2] 2999[2] (3723) 4458[4]4745[P] 5101a[3]

Fire Ranger *J D Frost* 100h
10 ch m Presidium—Regal Flame (Royalty)
385[2] (651) 1187[2] (1383) 1641[2]

Fireside Legend (IRE) *Miss M P Bryant* 71+h
7 b g College Chapel—Miss Sandman (Manacle)
502[8] 4153[P] 4449[P] 4526[6] 4869[6]

Firion King (IRE) *W S Coltherd* 82b 67c
6 b g Earl Of Barking(IRE) —Miss Tan A Dee (Tanfirion)
1048[5] 1237[11] 1323[13] **4655[P]4840[7] 5121[P]**

Firmount (IRE) *B S Rothwell*
4 bb g Lujain(USA) —Monkey Business (Warning)
2494[P]

First Author (IRE) *Gerard O'Leary* 103b
5 b g Orpen(USA) —Welsh Brook (Caerleon (USA))
4448[23]

First Boy (GER) *D J Wintle* 102+h
7 b g Bering—First Smile (Surumu (GER))
2324[10]

First Centurion *Ian Williams* 81h
5 b g Peintre Celebre(USA) —Valley Of Hope (USA) (Riverman (USA))
2423[9] 3238[P] 3963[9] 4392[4]

First Cry (IRE) *N G Richards* 81+h
6 b g Topanoora—Open Cry (IRE) (Montelimar (USA))
424[2] 3927[P]

First De La Brunie (FR) *A King* 78+h 103 c
5 ch g Mansonnien(FR) —Samisti (BEL) (Mistigri)
2248[2] 2555[6] (3239) 3368[P] 3816[P] (4350)

First Down Jets (IRE) *W J Burke* 97h 126+c
9 b g Arctic Lord—Kentish Town (Camden Town)
4471[2] 5083a[3]

Firstflor *F Jordan* 66h
7 b m Alflora(IRE) —First Crack (Scallywag)
261[P] 1100[P] 1297[7] 2140[U] 2585[5]2816[5] 4010[9]

First Fought (IRE) *D McCain* 104+h
4 b g Germany(USA) —Royal Flame (IRE) (Royal Academy (USA))
1095[6] 1201[4] 1338[P] 1797[2] (2069) 2367[6]3848[11] 4987[2]

First Gold (FR) *F Doumen* 151h
13 b g Shafoun(FR) —Nuit D'Or II (FR) (Pot D'Or (FR))
68a[5] 2176[P] 2492[U]3971[P] 4777[U]

First Grey *E W Tuer* 32h
7 gr m Environment Friend—Myrtilla (Beldale Flutter (USA))
2171[P] 2693[10] 3782[P] 4487[8] 4916[P]

First Look (FR) *P Monteith* 127+h
6 b g Acatenango(GER) —First Class (GER) (Bustino)
2062[2] 2335[3] (2658) 3912[2] (4364) 4529[5]

First Love *N J Henderson* 138h 125c
10 br g Bustino—First Romance (Royalty)
1279[7] **(4092) (4358) (4677)**

First Row (IRE) *D T Hughes* 124h
4 b c Daylami(IRE) —Ballet Society (FR) (Sadler's Wells (USA))
3004a[5] 3401a[3] 3890a[3] (4122a) 4468[9] 5099a[6]

First Tee (IRE) *Jonjo O'Neill*
7 ch g Un Desperado(FR) —Bright Future (IRE) (Satco (FR))
2421[P]

Fisby *K J Burke* 79h
5 ch g Efisio—Trilby (In The Wings)
2860[10] 4970[6]

Fisherman Jack *G J Smith* 81c
11 b g Carlingford Castle—Troublewithjack (Sulaafah (USA))
2165[4] 2689[5] 3221[4]4130[2] 4321[3] (4610)

Fisher Street *Mrs C J Kerr* 28c
11 gr g Tigani—Pricket Walk (Amboise)
4725[P]

Fishki's Lad *E W Tuer* 107+h
11 b g Casteddu—Fishki (Niniski (USA))
121[8] 372[7] 595[P]

Five Alley (IRE) *R H Buckler* 104h 97 c
9 gr g Roselier(FR) —Panel Pin (Menelek)
1776[2] 1858[P] (1951) 2126[3] 2575[4] 2986[2]3427[3] 3900[4] 4285[2]4603[4] **4785[4]** 5015[3]

Five Colours (IRE) *A King* 123 h
6 bb g Lord Americo—Thousand Springs (IRE) (King's Ride)
(3248) 3677[2] 3969[2] 4469[11]

Five Gold (IRE) *A C Whillans* 83 h
5 b g Desert Prince(IRE) —Ceide Dancer (IRE) (Alzao (USA))
149[6] 320[U] (Dead)

Fixateur *C C Bealby* 86h
4 b g Anabaa(USA) —Fabulous Account (USA) (Private Account (USA))
2753[6] 3038[7] 3431[P] 4632[2]

Fixed Interest (IRE) *H D Daly* 85+b
4 b g Taipan(IRE) —Fixed Assets (Rare One)
4680[3]

Fizzical Fizz *Mrs D M Grissell*
7 b m Sir Harry Lewis(USA) —No Fizz (Broadsword (USA))
3924[4]

Flahive's First *D Burchell* 65 h 109 c
12 ch g Interrex(CAN) —Striking Image (IRE) (Flash Of Steel)
246[8] 634[7] 725[3](975) 1080[4] 1221[8]1358[4] 1489[P] 1754[5]1855[U] 1978[5] 5107[P]

Flake *Mrs S J Smith* 101 h 112c
6 ch g Zilzal(USA) —Impatiente (USA) (Vaguely Noble)
1887[7] **2111[2] 2443[5]**2566[13] 2994[5] (3737) 3967[4]

Flamand (FR) *C P Morlock* 74h
5 b g Double Bed(FR) —Rays Honor (Ahonoora)
2804[6] 3127[4] 3422[9]

Flame Creek (IRE) *Noel T Chance*
10 b g Shardari—Sheila's Pet (IRE) (Welsh Term)
1913[F]

Flame Of Zara *L Lungo* 74h
7 ch m Blushing Flame(USA) —Sierra Madrona (USA) (Woodman (USA))
4143[10] 5091[10]

Flame Phoenix (USA) *D McCain* 110h 94 c
7 bb g Quest For Fame—Kingscote (King's Lake (USA))
56[3] 604[3] 914[7]990[7] 1204[3] 1444[4] 1668[3]1720[7] 1878[7] 2369[5] 2766[5] 3848[6]4990[P]

Flamethrower (IRE) *E A Elliott* 73b
6 b g Warcraft(USA) —Gallic Flame (Cyrano De Bergerac)
2480[8]

Flaming Cheek *A G Blackmore* 108+h
8 b g Blushing Flame(USA) —Rueful Lady (Streetfighter)
4478[6] 4899[6]

Flaming Heck *Mrs L B Normile* 94 h 100c
9 b g Dancing High—Heckley Spark (Electric)
2064[2] 2372[9] **3398[4] (3555) 4318[4] (4489) 4614[P]**

Flaming Weapon *G L Moore* 114h
4 b g Unfuwain(USA) —Flame Valley (USA) (Gulch (USA))
(1948) 2367[4] 3021[8] 3714[2] 3939[2] 4648[3]

Flash Cummins (IRE) *M C Pipe* 93 h
6 bb g Corrouge(USA) —Corshanna River (IRE) (Over The River (FR))
2206[14] 2809[7] 2928[2] 3248[11] 3423[3]**4007[P]**

Flashy Filly *J C Haynes* 51h
6 b m Puissance—Tempted (IRE) (Invited (USA))
59[P] 602[10] 715[7] 822[10] 1064[4]1148[7] 1308[7] 4609[P]

Flashy Sir *John Allen* 78h
7 ch g Weld—Manx Princess (Roscoe Blake)
4934[7]

Flaxen Town (IRE) *Timothy Doyle* 87h 94c
11 ch g Camden Town—Garrenroe (Le Moss)
112a[17]

Fleet Anchor *J M Bradley* 48h
5 b g Fleetwood(IRE) —Upping The Tempo (Dunbeath (USA))
2826[15]

Fleetfoot Mac *B Storey* 87h
5 b g Fleetwood(IRE) —Desert Flower (Green Desert (USA))
2943[5] 3352[F]

Fleet Street *N J Henderson* 145h 124 c
7 ch g Wolfhound(USA) —Farmer's Pet (Sharrood (USA))
2798[4]

Fleetwood Bay *V R A Dartnall* 89h
6 b g Fleetwood(IRE) —Caviar And Candy (Soviet Star (USA))
811[4]

Flemens River (IRE) *C J Down* 91h
5 b g Flemensfirth(USA) —Miss River (IRE) (Lord Americo)
2864[6] 3216[5] 3583[7] 4786[9] 5106[2]

Flemingstone (IRE) *M J Gingell* 76h
6 b m Flemensfirth(USA) —Philly Athletic (Sit In The Corner (USA))
1889[5] 2515[11] 2690[7] 3337[7] 4656[3]4899[P]

Flemington House *A M Crow* 68b
5 ch m Captain Maverick(USA) —Sabica (Prince Sabo)
2906[6] 3273[9]

Flemming (USA) *I A Brown* 72h
9 ch g Green Dancer(USA) —La Groupie (FR) (Groom Dancer (USA))
2290[4] 2586[3] 3169[11]

Fleur Des Pres (FR) *B G Powell* 52h
4 gr f Robin Des Pres(FR) —Divine Rodney (FR) (Kendor (FR))
3346[5] 3884[7] 4450[13]

Fleur D'Oudon (FR) *D Cadot*
9 b m Le Pommier D'Or—Sartine (FR) (Gay Minstrel (FR))
4718a[3]

Fleurette *D R Gandolfo* 106+h
6 b m Alflora(IRE) —Miss Wrensborough (Buckskin (FR))
1982[2] (2127) 3175[9] 3437[2] 4781[9] 5014[F]

Flexible Concience (IRE) *J A B Old* 32h
11 br g Glacial Storm(USA) —Philly Athletic (Sit In The Corner (USA))
2985[5] 4012[P]

Flight Command *P Beaumont* 102h 129c
8 ch g Gunner B—Wing On (Quayside)
2656[P] 2768[8] 2993[4]3495[3] 4109[2] 4363[3]4762[F] 4850[6]

Flight Leader (IRE) *C L Tizzard* 104b
6 b g Supreme Leader—Stormy Petrel (IRE) (Strong Gale)
3699[6] 3904[2] 4333[5]

Flinders *R Rowe* 81h 91c
11 b m Henbit(USA) —Stupid Cupid (Idiots Delight)
101[4] 461[P]

Flinders Chase *C J Mann* 126c
11 gr g Terimon—Proverbial Rose (Proverb)
2664[9]

Flintoff (USA) *R C Guest* 105+h
5 ch g Diesis—Sahibah (USA) (Deputy Minister (CAN))
(261) (500) (596) 2706[P]

Flirty Jill *P R Webber* 90 h
5 b m I'm Supposin(IRE) —Gaye Mercy (Petoski)
1961[5] 2486[11] 3550[5] 3806[4] 4210[7]4836[4]

Floragalore *O Sherwood* 104+h
5 b m Dr Fong(USA) —Valagalore (Generous (IRE))
3281[F] 4450[5] 4691[2]

Floral Future *A C Whillans* 47h
6 b m Alflora(IRE) —Political Prospect (Politico (USA))
4519[8] 4787[9]

Floral Rhapsody *P Beaumont* 73h
5 b m Alflora(IRE) —Music Interpreter (Kampala)
3273[7] 3563[5] 4387[5] 4720[9] 5063[4]

Floranz *Mrs M Evans* 79+h
10 br m Afzal—Tuesday Member (New Member)
487[P] 1017[P] 1436[13] **1540[3]1781[F]**

Flora The Explora *Mrs L B Normile* 64b
5 gr m Alflora(IRE) —The Whirlie Weevil (Scallywag)
4853[18]

Florazine (IRE) *F J Bowles* 72h
5 gr m Alflora(IRE) —Dorazine (Kalaglow)
3552[6]

Floreana (GER) *C J Mann* 107h 99+c
5 b m Acatenango(GER) —Frille (FR) (Shareef Dancer (USA))
2053[P] 2240[3] 4972[9]

Florida Belle (IRE) *P A Fahy* 91h 82c
7 b m Florida Son—Life Of A Lady (IRE) (Insan (USA))
1116a[6]

Florida Coast (IRE) *James Bowe* 148h
11 b g Florida Son—Deep Peace (Deep Run)
1691a[9] 3513a[2] 4019a[2]

Florida Dream (IRE) *N A Twiston-Davies* 118+h 128+c
7 b g Florida Son—Ice Pearl (Flatbush)
1676[6] 2325[6] (2717) 3258[F] (3698) 4240[U]4447[11] 4971[5]

Florida Fiesta *Mrs H R J Nelmes* 43b
5 ch m Florida Son—Tootsie (Hotfoot)
507[8]

Floritchel (FR) *W McKeown* 43b
9 b g Dark Stone(FR) —Aktia (FR) (Lyphard's Special (USA))
893[P]

Flotta *B G Powell* 131+h
7 ch g Elmaamul(USA) —Heavenly Goddess (Soviet Star (USA))
1245[5] (1596) (1722) 4945[2] (5045)

Flower Haven *M J Gingell* 84h
4 b f Dr Fong(USA) —Daisy May (In The Wings)
1737[8] 2045[7] 2258[3] 2569[3] 3217[2]3655[2] 4479[6]

Flower Of Pitcur *T R George* 105 h 100 c
9 b g Alflora(IRE) —Coire Vannich (Celtic Cone)
1716[7] 2141[2] 2733[P]2958[P] **3844[P]**

Flowerpotman *M W Easterby* 70b
4 b g Zaffaran(USA) —Calabria (Neltino)
2927[9]

Flowonlovelyriver (IRE) *Patrick J Flynn* 126b
5 ch g Beneficial—Over The Pond (IRE) (Over The River (FR))
4448[21]

Flurry *C J Down* 74+b
7 gr m Terimon—Queen's Favourite (Sunyboy)
138[12] 361[4] 680[F] 912[P] 1036[5]1235[11]

Flying Dick *A G Newcombe* 39h
7 b g Thowra(FR) —Birbrook Girl (Henricus (AUT))
4732[P] 5026[6]

Flying Druid (FR) *Evan Williams* 93+h
6 b g Celtic Swing—Sky Bibi (FR) (Sky Lawyer (FR))
763[3]

Flying Enterprise (IRE) *Miss Venetia Williams* 140 h
6 b g Darshaan—Flying Kiss (IRE) (Sadler's Wells (USA))
1872[9] (2334) 2493[6] 2876[6] 3993[13] 4612[P]4959[6] 5142[17]

Flying Falcon *Miss Venetia Williams* 107+h
7 b g Polar Falcon(USA) —Lemon Balm (High Top)
(4032)

Flying Fortune (IRE) *Miss Tor Sturgis* 88h 105+c
10 b g Jolly Jake(NZ) —Dynamite Flyer (USA) (Explodent (USA))
1796[7] 2004[6]

Flying Fuselier *P J Hobbs* 88h 60c
7 ch g Gunner B—Wing On (Quayside)
1714[3] 1969[3] 2421[6] **2733[7]4878[6]**

Flying Jody (IRE) *Sir John Barlow Bt* 97h
7 b g Frimaire—Flying Flo Jo (USA) (Aloma's Ruler (USA))
2372[8]

Flying Patriarch *G L Moore* 100 h 94c
5 gr g Silver Patriarch(IRE) —Flying Wind (Forzando)
1921[5] 2173[P] 2578[6] **2867[3]3222[2] 3368[10] 4132[P]4525[F]**

Flying Spirit (IRE) *G L Moore* 130 h 137c
7 b g Flying Spur(AUS) —All Laughter (Vision (USA))
104[2] 286[2] (564) 650[2] (1871) 2174[6]2970[F] 4472[F]

Flying Spud *A J Chamberlain*
5 ch g Fraam—Lorcanjo (Hallgate)
1892[P] 2283[P]

Flying Spur (IRE) *M C Pipe* 85h
5 b g Norwich—Moorstown Rose (IRE) (Roselier (FR))
(1386) 1543[7] 1875[10] 2099[10] 3248[5] 3675[P]

Flying Trix (IRE) *P J Hobbs*
10 b g Lord Americo—Bannow Drive (IRE) (Miner's Lamp)
3578[P] 3698[8]

Flyingwithoutwings *A King* 91b
7 b g Komaite(USA) —Light Slippers (IRE) (Ela-Mana-Mou)
355[6] *2131[2] 3138[5]*

Fly Tipper *W Storey* 78+h
6 ch g Environment Friend—Double Birthday (Cavo Doro)
2007[9] 2480[6] 2652[10] 2901[6] 3927[5]10[12]

Fogonthetyne (IRE) *Damien Lavery* 58h 14c
7 b g Good Thyne(USA) —Swuzzlebubble (Bargello)
5083a[P]

Follow My Leader (IRE) *R Ford* 72b
6 br m Supreme Leader—Frankly Native (IRE) (Be My Native (USA))
2446[15] 3961[6] 4554[9] 4751[15]

Follow The Bear *D R Gandolfo* 96h
8 ch g Weld—Run Lady Run (General Ironside)
4331[P] 4526[S] 5069[5]

Follow The Flow (IRE) *P A Pritchard* 113 c
10 ch g Over The River(FR) —October Lady (Lucifer (USA))
55[6] 1893[7] 2293[P]2662[5] 2800[4] 3688[2]3886[6] 4395[5]

Follow Up *S B Clark* 88h
8 b g Phardante(FR) —Dashing March (Daring March)
1002[4] 1066[P]

Follow Your Heart (IRE) *N J Gifford* 92h
6 bb g Broken Hearted—Souled Out (IRE) (Noalto)
2127[6] 2554[4] 2866[6] **3368[8]**

Folly Mount *M W Easterby* 50h
4 b g Anabaa(USA) —Height Of Folly (Shirley Heights)
1339[8] (Dead)

Foly Pleasant (FR) *Mrs K Waldron* 117 c
12 ch g Vaguely Pleasant(FR) —Jeffologie (FR) (Jefferson)
3847[3] (4100) 4471[15]

Fondmort (FR) *N J Henderson* 165c
10 b g Cyborg(FR) —Hansie (FR) (Sukawa (FR))
2177[4] 2760[B] (3180) 3977[3] (4457) 4761[P]

Fond Of A Drop *D T Hughes* 48b
5 br g Overbury(IRE) —Pearl's Choice (IRE) (Deep Run)
5060a[19]

Fontanesi (IRE) *M C Pipe* 121h 127 c
6 b g Sadler's Wells(USA) —Northern Script (USA) (Arts And Letters (USA))
208[F] **803[F] (962) (1078) 1265[14] 1744[5]**
2209[17]2636[P] 3298[19] 3622[13] 3986[8] 4473[20]4945[3] 5142[7]

Foodbroker Founder *D R C Elsworth* 116h
6 ch g Groom Dancer(USA) —Nemea (USA) (The Minstrel (CAN))
2324[6] 2969[4]

Fool On The Hill *P J Hobbs* 136h 142+c
9 b g Reprimand—Stock Hill Lass (Air Trooper)
1078[3] (1292) 1549[4]4984[P]

Fools Entire *Miss J Feilden* 16h
5 ch g Fraam—Poly Blue (IRE) (Thatching)
1916[11] 2523[9]

Football Crazy (IRE) *P Bowen* 140 h
7 b g Mujadil(USA) —Schonbein (IRE) (Persian Heights)
1270[10] 1548[7]

Footy Facts (IRE) *Robert Tyner* 129b
6 b g Oscar(IRE) —Princess Henry (IRE) (Callernish)
5081a[8]

Forager *J Ryan* 134 h
7 ch g Faustus(USA) —Jolimo (Fortissimo)
1548[S] 1828[9] 5059a[23] 5103a[21]

For All Mankind *M Pitman* 90b
5 b g Zaffaran(USA) —Gilston Lass (Majestic Streak)
3583[4] 3911[7]

Forbearing (IRE) *K G Wingrove* 110h
9 b g Bering—For Example (USA) (Northern Baby (CAN))
1208[5] 1405[6] 2139[11] 1[10]

Foreign Field (FR) *Mrs Tracey Barfoot-Saunt* 23h
7 b g Sleeping Car(FR) —Dame Laurel (FR) (Rose Laurel)
1266[P] 1298[7] 1410[9] **1540[P]1736[3]**

Foreman *C J Down* 46h
13 b g Timeless Times(USA) —Skiddaw Bird (Bold Owl)
385[P] 681[9]

Foreman (GER) *T Doumen* 160 h 164+c
8 ch g Monsun(GER) —Fleurie (GER) (Dashing Blade)
(3501) 4431[3] (4774)

Forensic Investor (IRE) *P R Webber* 87b
6 ch g Topanoora—Phar Bolder (IRE) (Phardante (FR))
1777[7]

Forest Chief (IRE) *Evan Williams* 103+h 95c
10 b g Forest Wind(USA) —Cryptic Gold (Glint Of Gold)
1098[6] 1249[6] 2940[17] (Dead)

Forest Dante (IRE) *F Kirby* 84h 103 c
13 ch g Phardante(FR) —Mossy Mistress (IRE) (Le Moss)
2243[6] (2568) 2841[4]5016[4]

Forest Emerald (IRE) *J W Mullins* 81b
4 b f Desert Sun—Moonbi Range (IRE) (Nordico (USA))
2830[5] 3346[4] 3820[6]

Forest Fauna *J W Mullins* 95+h
6 b m El Conquistador—Busy Mittens (Nearly A Hand)
2486[2] 2932[5]

Forest Gunner *R Ford* 123h 153 c
12 ch g Gunner B—Gouly Duff (Party Mink)
2370[U] 2656[P] 2992[P]4777[9]

Forest Miller *R T Phillips* 97+h
7 b g Classic Cliche(IRE) —Its My Turn (Palm Track)
2432[6] 3906[7] 4284[4] 4642[2]

Forest Rail (IRE) *L Corcoran* 57h
6 b m Catrail(USA) —Forest Heights (Slip Anchor)
1654[9] 2728[P]

Forest Viking (IRE) *J S Wainwright* 47h
4 b g Orpen(USA) —Berhala (IRE) (Doyoun)
1146[5]

Forever Dream *P J Hobbs* 119h 110 c
8 b g Afzal—Quadrapol (Pollerton)
1598[5] **1801[2] (1899) 2577[F]2996[P] 3344[P]** 5[9]

Forever Eyesofblue *A Parker* 105+h 97c
9 b g Leading Counsel(USA) —Forever Silver (IRE) (Roselier (FR))
2417[3] 2691[7] **3928[3]** 5123[2]

Forfeiter (USA) *M F Harris* 60h
4 ch g Petionville(USA) —Picabo (USA) (Wild Again (USA))
1190[6]

Forget The Past *M J P O'Brien* 111h 165 c
8 b g Past Glories—Worth Matravers (National Trust)
(42a) 2177[11] 2793a[3]3081a[3] (3999a) (4123a) 4470[3] 5079a[5]

Fork Lightning (IRE) *A King* 143+c
10 gr g Roselier(FR) —Park Breeze (IRE) (Strong Gale)
2744[3] 3176[3] 4118[P]4433[6] 4957[3]

Form And Beauty (IRE) *C Roberts* 57h
4 b c Orpen(USA) —Formezza (IRE) (Cyrano De Bergerac)
3021[13] 3340[F] 3436[P] 3579[9] 4046[5]

Fortanis *P C Ritchens* 65h 37c
7 gr m Alflora(IRE) —Sister's Choice (Lepanto (GER))
2179[P] 3133[14] 3505[7] 3951[7] **5049[7]**

Forthright *G L Moore* 102+h
5 b g Cadeaux Genereux—Forthwith (Midyan (USA))
331[2]

Fortmassini (IRE) *C Roche* 120+h
5 b g Dr Massini(IRE) —Fortlawn Bay (IRE) (Tidaro (USA))
3411a[13]

Fort Royal (IRE) *G R Pewter* 20h
7 b g Commanche Run—Grainne Geal (General Ironside)
3184[P] 3597[9] 4521[7] 4905[12]

Fortuna Favente (IRE) *J Howard Johnson* 72+h
6 b m Supreme Leader—La Grande Dame (Niniski (USA))
3337[5] 3484[P]

Fortunate Dave (USA) *M Smith* 107h
7 b g Lear Fan(USA) —Lady Ameriflora (USA) (Lord Avie (USA))
5068[9]

Fortune Island (IRE) *M C Pipe* 116 h
7 b g Turtle Island(IRE) —Blue Kestrel (IRE) (Bluebird (USA))
2347[9] 2636[13]

Fortune Point (IRE) *A W Carroll* 104h 109+c
8 ch g Cadeaux Genereux—Mountains Of Mist (IRE) (Shirley Heights)
1668[5] 1957[6] 4832[7] **2[3]**

Fortune's Fool *I A Brown* 80h
7 b g Zilzal(USA) —Peryllys (Warning)
415[7] 592[8] 686[8] 1063[3] 1148[3]1375[4] (1566) 1663[5] 4917[6]

Forty Licks (IRE) *E J O'Grady* 122 h
9 b g Supreme Leader—Bridevalley (Deep Run)
2909a[5]

Forty Shakes (IRE) *J Wade*
7 ch g Moonax(IRE) —Forty Quid (IRE) (Exhibitioner)
2112[8]

Forzacurity *D Burchell* 104+h
7 ch g Forzando—Nice Lady (Connaught)
136[13] 247[2] (347) 450[10] 726[10] 841[11]915[5] 1001[F] 1087[4] 1179[8] 1366[9]4663[P] 4879[13] 5108[14]

Fota Island (IRE) *M F Morris* 157h 162c
10 b g Supreme Leader—Mary Kate Finn (Saher)
89a[U] 3051a[2] (3527a) 4445[2] 4761[2] 5057a[2]

Fountain Brig *N W Alexander* 70h 89c
10 bb g Royal Fountain—Lillie's Brig (New Brig)
2063[3] (2945) 3204[P]3533[2] 3849[P] 4144[P]

Fountain Crumble *P F Nicholls* 100+h
5 b m Dr Massini(IRE) —My Lisa Too (K-Battery)
1042[2] (1237) 2997[4] 3322[5] 3461[7]

Fourboystoy (IRE) *Miss H C Knight* 98+h
7 ch g Roselier(FR) —Little Twig (IRE) (Good Thyne (USA))
2725[P] 3508[P]

Four Eagles (USA) *D R C Elsworth* 81h 89c
8 b g Lear Fan(USA) —Bloomingly (ARG) (Candy Stripes (USA))
1742[4]

Four For A Laugh (IRE) *A King* 104+h
7 b g Fourstars Allstar(USA) —She's No Laugh Ben (USA) (Alleged (USA))
2288[10] 4048[2] 4649[P]

Four In Hand *Mrs K M Sanderson* 72h
8 b m Supreme Leader—Relkissimo (Relkino)
2849[P] 3240[7] 4425[5] 4836[6]

Four Kisses (IRE) *Ms Sue Smith* 68b
6 b m Supreme Leader—Danjo's Lady (IRE) (Carlingford Castle)
1674[12] 7[7]

Fourpointone *E McNamara* 74h
5 b g Overbury(IRE) —Praise The Lord (Lord Gayle (USA))
65a[20]

Four Schools (IRE) *Jonjo O'Neill* 110 h
4 b g Raise A Grand(IRE) —Haanem (Mtoto)
4096[5]

Fourswainby (IRE) *B Ellison* 33h
5 b g Foxhound(USA) —Arena (Sallust)
2991[13] 3257[F] 4299[P]

Fourth Dimension (IRE) *N Wilson* 86h
7 b g Entrepreneur—Isle Of Spice (USA) (Diesis)
(785) 875[2] 1436[14]

Fourty Acers (IRE) *M C Pipe* 112h
6 ch g Bob Back(USA) —Guest Cailin (IRE) (Be My Guest (USA))
(1459) 1895[3] 2309[2] 2821[2]

Fox In The Box *R H Alner* 106 h 131+c
9 gr g Supreme Leader—Charlotte Gray (Rolfe (USA))
2299[P] 2847[P] 3614[4]3877[5] (4103) 4395[P]

Foxmeade Dancer *P C Ritchens* 92+h 77+c
8 b g Lyphento(USA) —Georgian Quickstep (Dubassoff (USA))
1856[16] 2182[5] 2419[4] 2816[3] 3250[4]3577[4] **(4132) 4164[5] 4525[3]**

Fox 'N' Goose (IRE) *P C Ritchens* 95h
6 ch g Ashmolean(USA) —Creative Flight (IRE) (Creative Plan (USA))
294[2]

Fox Point (USA) *P C Haslam* 105h
6 b g Foxhound(USA) —Linklee (USA) (Linkage (USA))
(4487) 4852[6]

Foxtrot Yankee (IRE) *Andrew Turnell* 89+h
7 b g Lord Americo—Derby Fox (IRE) (King's Ride)
2269[2] 2742[F] 3355[6] 4075[5]

Foxxtrot Oscar (IRE) *Nick Williams*
5 b g Oscar(IRE) —Cush Maid (Black Minstrel)
4011[8]

Foxy Tales *T R George* 66b
5 b m Classic Cliche(IRE) —Hill Vixen (Goldhill)
4976[10]

Frambo (IRE) *J G Portman* 79+h
5 b m Fraam—Wings Awarded (Shareef Dancer (USA))
134[14] 263[6] 310[5] (Dead)

Framlingham *R Curtis* 50h
11 gr g Out Of Hand—Sugar Hall (Weatherbird)
2181[P] 2582[P]

Franceschiella (ITY) *Lady Susan Watson* 69b
5 gr m Beat Of Drums—Filicaia (Sallust)
4304[13] 5041[6]

Francies Fancy (IRE) *J J Lambe* 113+h
9 b g Imperial Frontier(USA) —Cheeky Maid (IRE) (Bob Back (USA))
647[7] (784)

Francken (ITY) *Lady Susan Watson* 74 h
7 ro g Petit Loup(USA) —Filicaia (Sallust)
11[8]

Franco (IRE) *Mrs A E Brooks* 110 h 69c
8 b g Rashar(USA) —Market Thyne (IRE) (Good Thyne (USA))
281[7] 2527[0] 2749[3] (2985) 3792[2]

Francolino (FR) *Dr P Pritchard* 65h 76c
13 b g Useful(FR) —Quintefeuille II (FR) (Kashtan (FR))
386[P] 464[P] 630[11]**669[5] 865[5] 1122[5]**1280[11] 1381[9] **1446[6]** 1539[8]**1615[4] 1713[B]** 1977[5]2147[4] **2506[2]**

Frankie Dori (IRE) *S Donohoe* 92h 116+c
7 b g Key Of Luck(USA) —Kitty's Sister (Bustino)
10[2] 112a[14] 3928[2]4345[2]

Frankincense (IRE) *A J Lockwood* 72 h
10 gr g Paris House—Mistral Wood (USA) (Far North (CAN))
11[12] 480[4] 781[7] 4656[12]

Fransiscan *P C Haslam* 38h
4 ch g Fraam—Ordained (Mtoto)
1095[7] (Dead)

Frazers Fortune *H J Manners* 53h
6 ch g Environment Friend—Safidar (Roan Rocket)
457[10] 635[9]

Freddie Ed *R N Bevis* 100h
5 b g Makbul—Miss Mirror (Magic Mirror)
3248[12] 3843[2] 4613[P]

Freddie Foster (IRE) *Noel Meade* 115h
7 ch g Carroll House—Buff's Express (Bay Express)
3005a[14] 3894a[2]

Fredensborg (NZ) *Miss Venetia Williams* 99b
5 b g Danske(NZ) —Showplace (AUS) (Palace Music (USA))
3911[2] 4422[6] 4654[P]

Freds Benefit (IRE) *W P Mullins* 114b
5 ch g Beneficial—Welsh Ana (IRE) (Welsh Term)
4448[16]

Fred's In The Know *Miss Tracy Waggott* 100 h 123c
11 ch g Interrex(CAN) —Lady Vynz (Whitstead)
2964[F] 3318[2] 3675[5] 4058[6]

Freedom Fighter *Mrs Rosemary Gasson* 99c
15 b g Fearless Action(USA) —Zuleika Hill (Yellow River)
49[P]

Freedom Now (IRE) *R H Alner* 115+h
8 b g Sadler's Wells(USA) —Free At Last (Shirley Heights)
1784[6] 2055[8] 2150[6] 2459[3]

Free Gift *R H Alner* 45b 123c
8 b g Presenting—Gladtogetit (Green Shoon)
1489[P] 1728[F] 1989[3]2342[2] (2733)

Freeline Fantasy (IRE) *Tim Vaughan* 95h
9 ch g Shernazar—Lollia Paulina (IRE) (Phardante (FR))
1680[8]

Freeline Fury *P R Webber* 35h
6 b g Sir Harry Lewis(USA) —Queen's Favourite (Sunyboy)
2144[9] 3238[10]

Freemantle Doctor (IRE) *J R H Fowler* 100h
6 b m Luso—Lottobuck (Buckskin (FR))
4887a[12]

Freetown (IRE) *L Lungo* 130 h 136c
10 b g Shirley Heights—Pageantry (Welsh Pageant)
2292[12] **2451[P]** 2820[7] 3289[3]4461[5] 4776[4]

Free Will *R C Guest* 84 h
9 ch g Indian Ridge—Free Guest (Be My Guest (USA))
1357[4] 1588[5]

Freeze Frame (IRE) *G A Kingston* 94h
5 b m Perugino(USA) —Simulcast (Generous (IRE))
2031a[12]

Freindlypersuasion *Paul Morris* 30b
6 gr g Shambo—Sea Sky (Oats)
1048[13] 1459[7]

French Accordion (IRE) *Paul Nolan* 115h
6 b g Accordion—Royal Thimble (IRE) (Prince Rupert (FR))
(1623a) 2161[6] 2650a[7] 4951a[19]

French Cedar *P Monteith* 88h 82c
10 b g Jupiter Island—Another Rumour (The Parson)
717[8]

French Direction (IRE) *R Rowe* 89+h 104+c
7 ch g John French—Shelikesitstraight (IRE) (Rising)
(505) 862[4] 2960[F]3663[7] 4908[P] 5090[4]

French Envoy (FR) *Ian Williams* 109h
7 bl g Cadoudal(FR) —Miss Merry (FR) (Pedege (FR))
1782[2] 2212[7] 3789[2] 4373[P] 5016[2]

French Executive (IRE) *P F Nicholls* 109h 130 c
11 br g Beau Sher—Executive Move (IRE) (Executive Perk)
842[P] 960[6] 2518[3]2745[9] 3186[P]

French Fashion (IRE) *I A Duncan* 86?h
7 ch m Jamesmead—Sharp Fashion VII (Damsire Unregistered)
591[6]

Frenchgate *M E Sowersby* 77b
5 br g Paris House—Let's Hang On (IRE) (Petorius)
1113[P]

French Gold *N Wilson* 34h
4 b f Bien Bien(USA) —Shalad'Or (Golden Heights)
1146[7]

French Lieutenant (FR) *L Corcoran*
7 b g Saint Cyrien(FR) —Midweek Melody (Lucky Wednesday)
4593[F]

French Risk (IRE) *Evan Williams*
6 b g Entrepreneur—Troyes (Troy)
1384[P]

French Tune (FR) *Miss S E Hall* 95h
8 ch g Green Tune(USA) —Guerre De Troie (Risk Me (FR))
147[4] 483[5]

Freshford (IRE) *N Tinkler* 49b
4 ch g Titus Livius(FR) —Gustavia (IRE) (Red Sunset)
2927[17] 3399[10] 3563[9]

Freteval (FR) *S J Gilmore*
9 b g Valanjou(FR) —La Beaumont (FR) (Hellios (USA))
1832[F] 2129[U]

Freydis (IRE) *S Gollings* 93+h
8 b m Supreme Leader—Lulu Buck (Buckskin (FR))
3375[P]

Friedhelmo (GER) *S B Clark* 49h
10 ch g Dashing Blade—Fox For Gold (Glint Of Gold)
903[7] 1111[P] 1760[P] 2079[7] 2289[9]2567[P] 2843[P] 2962[15] 3335[9] 3916[9]

Friendly Request *N J Hawke* 96+h
7 bb m Environment Friend—Who Tells Jan (Royal Fountain)
(1211) 1443[F] 4858[F]

Frith (IRE) *Mrs L B Normile* 67h
4 b g Benny The Dip(USA) —Melodist (USA) (The Minstrel (CAN))
3925[10] 4987[9]

Froghole Flyer *G L Moore* 101+h
7 ch g Presenting—Peptic Lady (IRE) (Royal Fountain)
3906[P] 4088[6] 4359[7] (4651)

From Dawn To Dusk *P J Hobbs* 103+h
7 b g Afzal—Herald The Dawn (Dubassoff (USA))
2663[9] 2873[10] 3246[8] 3496[4] 4331[3](5108)

Fromragstoriches (IRE) *Mrs S J Smith* 100 h
10 b g Supreme Leader—Family Birthday (Sandalay)
2994[4] 3253[4] **4788[F]**

Frontenac (IRE) *Mrs Mandy Hand* 84+c
10 ch g Mister Lord(USA) —Daffydown Dolly (IRE) (The Parson)
299[U]

Frontier *B J Llewellyn* 119h
9 b g Indian Ridge—Adatiya (IRE) (Shardari)
1481[2] 2636[12] 2871[F] (Dead)

Front Rank (IRE) *Mrs Dianne Sayer* 114h
6 b g Sadler's Wells(USA) —Alignment (IRE) (Alzao (USA))
(456) 1826[P] 2218[8] 2716[5] 2940[12] 3332[4](3797) 4364[P] 4792[13] 5066[4]

Frosty Jak *J D Frost* 77h
8 b g Morpeth—Allied Newcastle (Crooner)
(1779) 1973[4] 2845[6] 3211[P]

Frosty Moon (IRE) *B L Lay*
6 gr m Moonax(IRE) —Artanagh Rosa (IRE) (Roselier (FR))
138[17]

Frosty Run (IRE) *Mrs H Dalton* 99h 97+c
8 b g Commanche Run—Here To-Day (King's Equity)
3326[3] 3654[P]

Frosty's Cousin (IRE) *P R Webber* 88 h 39c
7 b g Arctic Lord—Farojina (IRE) (Farhaan)
1719[8]

Frou Frou Bere (FR) *P Montfort*
13 br g Rivelago(FR) —Princesse Dufrene (FR) (Pitchy Poi (FR))
1372a[4]

Fruits De Mer (IRE) *J R H Fowler* 94b
5 b m Presenting—Fine De Claire (Teenoso (USA))
5104a[5]

Fuel Cell (IRE) *M E Sowersby* 110h
5 b g Desert Style(IRE) —Tappen Zee (Sandhurst Prince)
2763[2] 2923[5] 2968[5]

Fu Fighter *Evan Williams* 103+h
5 b g Unfuwain(USA) —Runelia (Runnett)
295[2] 414[2] (913) (1002) 1192[5] 1552[5]

Fullards *Mrs P Sly* 101h 112c
8 b g Alderbrook—Milly Kelly (Murrayfield)
1988[6] 2717[4] 3289[7]**(4474)**

Full House (IRE) *P R Webber* 127h 152+c
7 br g King's Theatre(IRE) —Nirvavita (FR) (Highest Honor (FR))
1550[F] (1721) 2177[P]3299[6] 4241[8] (5126)

Full Irish (IRE) *L Lungo* 122 h 144+c
10 ch g Rashar(USA) —Ross Gale (Strong Gale)
450[12] **2163[10]** 3561[6] 5096[5]

Full Kwai Ma (IRE) *John G Carr* 31c
6 b g Night Shift(USA) —So Kind (Kind Of Hush)
591[P]

Full Magic (FR) *M Rolland*
4 br g Kahyasi—Full Contact (FR) (Cadoudal (FR))
777a[4]

Full Minty *Mrs Sarah Stafford* 113c
11 br g Phardante(FR) —Jouvencelle (Rusticaro (FR))
4079[F] 4607[U]

Full On *A M Hales* 89 h 96 c
9 b g Le Moss—Flighty Dove (Cruise Missile)
1761[5] 2011[4] 2863[2]3285[5] 3905[P] 4080[8] 4453[4]4874[7]

Fullopep *J R Holt* 84h 88c
12 b g Dunbeath(USA) —Suggia (Alzao (USA))
110[5] 469[5] 670[4] 839[P] **999[P]**

Fu Manchu *Jonjo O'Neill* 91h
4 b g Desert Style(IRE) —Robsart (IRE) (Robellino (USA))
1397[3] 1679[9] 1904[C] 2076[P] 2597[11]

Fundamental *W K Goldsworthy* 132h
7 ch g Rudimentary(USA) —I'll Try (Try My Best (USA))
1598[P] 1743[10]

Fundamentalist (IRE) *N A Twiston-Davies* 119h 153+c
8 b g Supreme Leader—Run For Shelter (Strong Gale)
3039[4] 3977[F] 4445[F]4745[11]

Funny Fellow *R Rowe* 26b
4 b g Defacto(USA) —Royal Comedian (Jester)
1785[12]

Funny Times *N G Richards* 98 h
5 b m Silver Patriarch(IRE) —Elegant City (Scallywag)
2062[F] 3795[2]

Furioso (FR) *T Yon*
13 b g Brezzo(FR) —Quenice (FR) (Quart De Vin (FR))
1372a[7]

Fuss *P J Hobbs* 83+h
5 b m Unfuwain(USA) —First Sapphire (Simply Great (FR))
2573[5] 4129[4] 4425[6] 4726[6] 4860[6]

Futoo (IRE) *G M Moore* 92 h
5 b g Foxhound(USA) —Nicola Wynn (Nicholas Bill)
2627[7] 2763[5] 2947[10] 4040[5] 4299[3]

Future Legend *J A B Old* 97+h
5 ch g Lomitas—Proudy (IRE) (Night Shift (USA))
1982[6] 2249[12] 3659[7] 4427[5] 5108[2]

Future To Future (IRE) *Miss E C Lavelle*
6 gr g Linamix(FR) —Finir En Beaute (FR) (Groom Dancer (USA))
4562[5] 4689[P]

Gabla (NZ) *R C Guest* 106 h 107 c
10 b g Prince Of Praise(NZ) —Dynataine (NZ) (Centaine (AUS))
1179[5] 1223[9] **1311[6]** 1571[10]

Gabor *D W Thompson* 97h 91c
7 b g Danzig Connection(USA) —Kiomi (Niniski (USA))
743[3] 863[4] 903[3] 1248[2] 1384[2]1510[4] 1571[6] 1685[7] 2008[4] 2071[3]

Gaelic Flight (IRE) *Noel T Chance* 109+h 106+c
8 bb g Norwich—Ash-Dame (IRE) (Strong Gale)
1682[6] 2103[3] **2488[F]**(4858)

Gaelic Gift (IRE) *J G Cann* 84b
4 b f Presenting—Gaelic Leader (IRE) (Supreme Leader)
3904[5] 4654[2] 5117[2]

Gaelic Jig *J I A Charlton* 72b
7 ch g Dancing High—Gaelic Charm (IRE) (Deep Run)
212[P] 2169[P] 4299[P]

Gaelic Roulette (IRE) *J Jay* 97h
6 b m Turtle Island(IRE) —Money Spinner (USA) (Teenoso (USA))
(1213) 1322[3] 3818[9] 4075[6] 4391[5] 5137[2]

Gaiac (FR) *Ms N M Hugo* 115+c
12 b g Passing Sale(FR) —Ustitine (FR) (Moshi (GER))
47[5] 437[8] (512)

Gaining Ground (IRE) *John R Upson* 62h
6 ch g Presenting—Lorglane Lady (IRE) (Lancastrian)
1671[9] 1859[5] 2503[7] 2956[11]

Galadhrim (IRE) *J J Lambe* 35h
9 b g Glacial Storm(USA) —La Mode Lady (Mandalus)
1824[10]

Gala Evening *J A B Old* 57h
4 b g Daylami(IRE) —Balleta (USA) (Lyphard (USA))
5110[10]

Galahad (FR) *B Storey* 49h
5 b g Apple Tree(FR) —Reine Elodie (FR) (Cadoudal (FR))
418[12] 602[P] 2627[13] 3231[U] 3534[5]4039[7]

Galandora *Dr J R J Naylor* 24h
6 b m Bijou D'Inde—Jelabna (Jalmood (USA))
2501[13] 2928[F]

Galant Eye (IRE) *R J Baker* 93h
7 ch g Eagle Eyed(USA) —Galandria (Sharpo)
2314[7] 2609[7] 2868[12] 3128[10] 4856[8]

Galapiat Du Mesnil (FR) *R Gurney* 106h 86c
12 b g Sarpedon(FR) —Polka De Montrin (FR) (Danoso)
1815[2] 2215[F] 2931[P]3430[5] 3582[3] 4873[8]

Gala Queen *W G Young* 7b
6 gr m Accondy(IRE) —Miss Jedd (Scallywag)
5042[9]

Gala Sunday (USA) *M W Easterby* 72h
6 b g Lear Fan(USA) —Sunday Bazaar (USA) (Nureyev (USA))
2444[14] 3912[13]

Galaxia (IRE) *K C Bailey* 38b
4 bb g Fourstars Allstar(USA) —Cool N Calm (Arctic Lord)
4909[18]

Galaxy Dancer (IRE) *N B King* 51h
4 b g Starborough—Missy Dancer (Shareef Dancer (USA))
1563[9] 1737[14] 2454[P]

Galaxy Sam (USA) *N J Gifford* 99 h 86 c
7 ch g Royal Academy(USA) —Istiska (FR) (Irish River (FR))
2593[F] 2717[P] 2868[15]

Gale Dancer *D W Whillans* 57b
4 b f Saddlers' Hall(IRE) —Barton Gale (IRE) (Strong Gale)
4304[10]

Galen (IRE) *Miss J Froggatt* 44h 88c
15 br g Roselier(FR) —Gaye Le Moss (Le Moss)
498[4] 4325[P]

Galero *J Howard Johnson* 109+h 122+c
7 b g Overbury(IRE) —Rare Luck (Rare One)
2496[P] 3352[5] (3489) 5065[U]

Gale Star (IRE) *O Brennan* 107h 91+c
13 b g Strong Gale—Fairly Deep (Deep Run)
(368) 511[2] 1609[6]1819[8]

Gallant Approach (IRE) *C R Egerton* 110+h 140 c
7 ch g Roselier(FR) —Nicks Approach (IRE) (Dry Dock)
(2099) **(2825) 4116[2] 5131a[5]**

Gallant Hero *P J Hobbs* 110+h
7 b g Rainbow Quest(USA) —Gay Gallanta (USA) (Woodman (USA))
1364[5] 1565[9] 1902[7]

Gallantian (IRE) *Alan Fleming* 21h
4 gr g Turtle Island(IRE) —Galletina (IRE) (Persian Heights)
2645a[9]

Gallik Dawn *A Hollingsworth* 78h 119c
8 ch g Anshan—Sticky Money (Relkino)
(240) (439) 572[2] 3614[P]3942[F] 4419[P] 4737[P]

Gallion's Reach (IRE) *M F Harris* 87h 65c
11 b g Good Thyne(USA) —Raise Our Hopes (IRE) (Salluceva)
2905[U] 2957[7] 3762[6]

Galteemountain Boy (IRE) *Evan Williams* 110+h
6 b g Oscar(IRE) —Shantalla Bay (Pollerton)
1969[2] (2663) (Dead)

Galtee View (IRE) *Evan Williams* 111h 122+c
8 b g Namaqualand(USA) —Miss Dolly (IRE) (Alzao (USA))
(1631) 1639[2] 1728[2]2151[5]

Galway (IRE) *M Scudamore* 103c
13 b g Jurado(USA) —Solanum (Green Shoon)
(52) 272[3] 437[4]634[6]

Galway Breeze (IRE) *Mrs Julie Read* 117 h 117 c
11 b g Broussard(USA) —Furena (Furry Glen)
195[2] 427[2] 497[3]761[7] (3960) 4351[5]4748[F]

Game Ball Ali (IRE) *M Halford* 102+h
5 b h Ali-Royal(IRE) —Tahaddi (USA) (Northern Baby (CAN))
3005a[3]

Game Gunner *Miss B Lewis* 102c
14 b g Gunner B—The Waiting Game (Cruise Missile)
350[P]

Game On (IRE) *B N Pollock* 90h 99 c
10 b g Terimon—Nun So Game (The Parson)
1553[P] **1860[8] 2342[5]2719[4] 2984[2] 3791[8]**

Gameset'N'Match *Miss M P Bryant* 69h
5 b g Hector Protector(USA) —Tanasie (Cadeaux Genereux)
1085[5] 1480[13] 2804[P] 4651[P]

Gamma-Delta (IRE) *C T Pogson* 90+h 67c
11 b g Alphabatim(USA) —Hardy Polly (Pollerton)
2256[P] 3140[P] **3652[P] (Dead)**

Ganache (IRE) *P R Chamings* 85b
4 ch g Halling(USA) —Granted (FR) (Cadeaux Genereux)
4038[3] 4554[6]

Gandiloo Gully *Mrs L B Normile*
5 ch m Master Willie—Happydrome (Ahonoora)
715[P]

Gandy Dancer (IRE) *Miss E C Lavelle* 86b
6 b m Dr Massini(IRE) —Muckride Lady (Deep Run)
3983[9] 4758[2]

Gan Eagla (IRE) *Miss Venetia Williams* 112+h
7 b g Paris House—Mafiosa (Miami Springs)
1598[P] 1784[5] 2166[P] 2868[8] (4593)

Gangsters R Us (IRE) *A Parker* 102+h 105c
10 br g Treasure Hunter—Our Mare Mick (Choral Society)
1795[P] 2495[3] 2568[3]3272[6] 3486[2] 3762[3]3930[5] 5036[4]

Ganymede *J G M O'Shea* 41h
5 gr g Daylami(IRE) —Germane (Distant Relative)
1680[P] 4106[9]

Gaora Bridge (IRE) *C J Mann* 104h
8 b g Warcraft(USA) —Miss Good Night (Buckskin (FR))
2827[P]

Gardasee (GER) *T P Tate* 125 h
4 gr g Dashing Blade—Gladstone Street (IRE) (Waajib)
1904[2] (2263) (2676) 3021[7] (3539) 4015[2] 4435[4]

Garde Bien *T D Easterby* 111+c
9 br g Afzal—May Lady (Deep Run)
1795[P] 2111[8]

Garde Champetre (FR) *Jonjo O'Neill* 146h 137 c
7 b g Garde Royale—Clementine Fleurie (FR) (Lionel (FR))
1958[2] 2174[4] 2482[5]4456[13]

Garde D'Estruval (FR) *M C Pipe* 64h
12 ch g Garde Royale—Sainte Lys (FR) (Don Roberto (USA))
3179[14]

Garhoud *Miss K M George* 64h
4 b g Grand Lodge(USA) —Puce (Darshaan)
1955[7] 2274[10] 2811[8] 3211[10] 3321[4]3479[7] 4423[7] 5115[5]

Garibaldi (GER) *D R C Elsworth* 95+h
4 ch g Acatenango(GER) —Guanhumara (Caerleon (USA))
2481[5] 3294[11]

Garnett (IRE) *D E Cantillon* 101+h
5 b g Desert Story(IRE) —In Behind (IRE) (Entitled)
(283) 429[2]

Garolsa (FR) *C L Tizzard* 114c
12 b g Rivelago(FR) —Rols Du Chatelier (FR) (Diaghilev)
535[R] 669[P]

Garrigon *P A Blockley*
5 b g Hector Protector(USA) —Queen Of The Keys (Royal Academy (USA))
1187[P]

Garryowen Star (IRE) *C F Swan* 78h
4 br g Supreme Leader—Swing Into Action (IRE) (Be My Native (USA))
5076a[16]

Garryvoe (IRE) *T R George* 107h 125+c
8 b g Lord Americo—Cottage Theme (Brave Invader (USA))
(2293)

Garth Engineer *R J Hodges* 57b
4 b g Petoski—Colette's Choice (IRE) (Alzao (USA))
1785[8]

Garvivonnian (IRE) *Edward P Mitchell* 101h 143c
11 b g Spanish Place(USA) —Garvivonne (Belfalas)
91a[11] 1515a[6] 1700a[5](2370) 4123a[2] 4777[P]5102a[11]

Garw Valley *M Wigham* 82 h
7 b m Mtoto—Morgannwg (IRE) (Simply Great (FR))
784[F] 1027[12] 1218[P]

Gatejumper (IRE) *R H Alner* 95h 95+c
8 b g Zaffaran(USA) —Nelly Don (Shackleton)
2808[7]

Gathering Storm (IRE) *P R Hedger* 79h
8 gr g Roselier(FR) —Queen Of The Rock (IRE) (The Parson)
2957[P] 3427[P]

Gatorade (NZ) *R C Guest* 107h 121 c
14 ch g Dahar(USA) —Ribena (NZ) (Battle-Waggon)
(97) 2498[P] 2993[5]

Gatsby (IRE) *J Groucott* 99b 120+c
10 gr g Roselier(FR) —Burren Gale (IRE) (Strong Gale)
48[3] 3736[F] (4009) 4471[8] 4748[P]

Gaucho *Miss T Jackson* 30h 81 c
9 b g Rambo Dancer(CAN) —Sioux Be It (Warpath)
3320[3] 3555[P] 3915[8]4142[6] 4303[6] 13[4]

Gavz Boy (IRE) *A C Whillans* 69b
4 b g Executive Perk—Waltzins Comma (IRE) (Commanche Run)
5008[7]

Gayble *Nigel Smith* 70b 58c
8 b g Good Times(ITY) —High Kabour (Kabour)
4305[P]

Gaye Dream *T R George* 88h 80c
8 b g Gildoran—Gaye Fame (Ardross)
2863[F] 3276[4]

Gay Gladys *T H Caldwell* 43h
6 b m Ridgewood Ben—Ovideo (Domynsky)
93a[15] 3496[P] 4074[13]

Gay Kindersley (IRE) *K G Reveley* 77h 44c
8 ch g Roselier(FR) —Ramble Bramble (Random Shot)
2717[P] 3037[6] 3316[5]3443[4] 3656[P] **3923[P]**

Gayle Abated (IRE) *W P Mullins* 114h 112c
7 b g Moscow Society(USA) —Hurricane Girl (IRE) (Strong Gale)
92a[10]

Gay Millenium *L A Dace*
6 gr m Silver Owl—Gay Abandon (Risk Me (FR))
3511[U] 3885[P] 4649[P]

Gazump (FR) *N A Twiston-Davies* 106 h 128 c
8 b g Iris Noir(FR) —Viva Sacree (FR) (Maiymad)
1513[5] **2210[P] 2489[F]4213[4] 4829[8] 4[4]**

Gazza's Girl (IRE) *Mrs John Harrington* 123h
6 bb m Norwich—Miss Ranova (Giacometti)
4887a[7]

Gebora (FR) *B R Foster* 66h
7 ch g Villez(USA) —Sitapanoki (FR) (Houston (FR))
9[23] 839[9] 973[P]

Gee Aker Malayo (IRE) *R T Phillips* 68h 93 c
10 b g Phardante(FR) —Flying Silver (Master Buck)
3662[P] 3919[4] 4353[6]5105[P]

Geeveem (IRE) *P F Nicholls* 117+h
6 b g Supreme Leader—Glacial Field (IRE) (Glacial Storm (USA))
(3238) (4367) 4982[4]

Gelot (GER) *Elfi Schnakenberg*
7 br g Colon(GER) —Gela (GER) (San Vicente (GER))
(590a)

Gemini Dancer *C L Tizzard* 106+h
7 b g Glory Of Dancer—Lamloum (IRE) (Vacarme (USA))
230[9] 517[4] (753) 864[4] 959[3] 1123[2]1272[3] 1480[5] 1651[5]

Gemini Guest (IRE) *P Hughes* 115h 100c
10 ch g Waajib—Aldhabyih (General Assembly (USA))
5059a[22]

Gemini Lady *Mrs J C McGregor* 70h
6 b m Emperor Fountain—Raunchy Rita (Brigadier Gerard)
649[7] 854[F] 1528[5] 1605[7] 3235[8]

Gemini Lucy (IRE) *Mrs John Harrington* 97h
6 ch m Glacial Storm(USA) —Jodi (IRE) (Phardante (FR))
4887a[8]

Gemini Storm *O Brennan* 71b
6 br g Jendali(USA) —Fanny Adams (Nicholas Bill)
4637[9] 4909[15]

General Claremont (IRE) *P F Nicholls* 103+h 128c
13 gr g Strong Gale—Kasam (General Ironside)
49[P]

General Cloney (IRE) *S Donohoe* 47h 84+c
10 ch h Simply Great(FR) —Kitty's Sister (Bustino)
3784[8] 3929[12] **4365[3]**

General Duroc (IRE) *B Storey* 115h
10 ch g Un Desperado(FR) —Satula (Deep Run)
54[P] 501[7] 1838[4] 2066[3] (2453) (2691) 3384[8]3854[7] (4043) 4491[P]

General Gossip (IRE) *R T Phillips* 111 h 120+c
10 bb g Supreme Leader—Sno-Sleigh (Bargello)
168[3] 2862[8] **3293[P] 4163[8]**

General Grey (IRE) *Miss H C Knight* 99+h 116+c
6 gr g Fourstars Allstar(USA) —Tara The Grey (IRE) (Supreme Leader)
2574[7] 3372[P] 4052[P]**(5085)**

General Hardi *J Wade* 90h
5 b g In Command(IRE) —Hardiprincess (Keen)
4147[14] 4916[2] 5063[9]

General Hopkins (IRE) *G R Pewter* 78h 61c
11 b g Cataldi—Kewanee (Kafu)
4013[P] 4526[U] 4903[9]

General Jist *Evan Williams*
4 ch g Opening Verse(USA) —Pharling (Pharly (FR))
2811[10]

General O'Keeffe *Mrs Susie Old* 69b 91 c
9 b g Alflora(IRE) —Rosie O'Keeffe (IRE) (Royal Fountain)
169[P] 1832[P] 3693[P]

General Oliver (IRE) *K G Wingrove*
6 b g General Monash(USA) —Sea Idol (IRE) (Astronef)
71[6]

Generals Laststand (IRE) *Mrs L B Normile* 69h
8 b g Little Bighorn—Our Dorcet (Condorcet (FR))
2036[5] 2653[4] 3209[5]

General Smith *H J Evans* 97+h
7 b g Greensmith—Second Call (Kind Of Hush)
356[2] 513[6] (895) 1017[5] 1272[6] 1553[6]3650[8]

General Striker *E Bolger* 124c
6 ch g Classic Cliche(IRE) —Springfield Girl (Royal Vulcan)
5083a[2]

General Tantrum (IRE) *Mrs Sue Popham* 77c
9 b g Ilium—Barna Havna (Crash Course)
3693[P]

Genghis (IRE) *P Bowen* 150+h
7 br g Persian Bold—Cindy's Baby (Bairn (USA))
208[6] 1738[2] 2500[5]

Gentle Beau *P J Hobbs* 113+h 84+c
8 b g Homo Sapien—Tapua Taranata (IRE) (Mandalus)
177[8] **1098[8] 1212[3]1363[P]**

Gentle John (FR) *R M Stronge* 74b
4 b g Le Balafre(FR) —Perky (FR) (Kendor (FR))
3346[7] 5054[10]

Gentleman Jimmy *H Morrison* 111h
6 br g Alderbrook—Irish Orchid (Free State)
(2152) 2866[7] (4327) 4606[6]

Gentle Warning *M Appleby* 71h
6 b m Parthian Springs—Manx Princess (Roscoe Blake)
356[P] 613[6] 683[5] 1158[6]

Genuine Article (IRE) *M Pitman* 114h 119 c
10 ch g Insan(USA) —Rosemount Rose (Ashmore (FR))
450[2] 947[12] 2765[10] 2969[7]

Geography (IRE) *P Butler* 82h
6 ch g Definite Article—Classic Ring (IRE) (Auction Ring (USA))
1949[8] 2130[6] **2375[U] 2555[P]**2687[P] 3428[P] 3905[6] (4526) 4652[3] 4824[6]4874[4]

Geordie Peacock (IRE) *Miss Venetia Williams* 100 h
7 gr g Roselier(FR) —Cotton Call (IRE) (Callernish)
1777[5] 3477[3] 3677[6] 3941[4] 4501[3]4824[P]

Geordies Express *G T Bewley* 112+c
14 b g Tina's Pet—Maestroes Beauty (Music Maestro)
(63)

George Custer (IRE) *M A Gunn* 37b
8 b h Supreme Leader—Light The Lamp (Miner's Lamp)
93a[20]

Georgedoubleyou (IRE) *Miss T Jackson* 34b
5 b g Lord Americo—Ballybeg Rose (IRE) (Roselier (FR))
3353[11]

Georges Boy (IRE) *P J Jones* 87h
8 b g Toulon—Glebelands Girl (Burslem)
3426[F] 4012[P] 4290[4] 4556[5]4731[13]

George Stubbs (USA) *B Ellison* 100 h
8 bb g Affirmed(USA) —Mia Duchessa (USA) (Nijinsky (CAN))
1569[2] 2179[6] 2444[5] 2904[3] 3267[4]3783[3]

George The Grey *S Gollings* 60b
5 gr g Silver Patriarch(IRE) —Miss Firecracker (Relkino)
4637[8]

Georgian Harry (IRE) *R T Phillips* 103h
9 b g Warcraft(USA) —Solo Player (Blue Refrain)
218[6] 949[P]

Georgie Girl Dove *C J Price* 53b
6 b m Busy Flight—Emerald Dove (Green Adventure (USA))
7[S] 1381[4] 3149[P]

Georgie's Lass (IRE) *C Roberts* 43b
7 gr m Flemensfirth(USA) —Rongai (IRE) (Commanche Run)
463[12] 656[11] 943[P]

Geos (FR) *N J Henderson* 149h 149c
11 bb g Pistolet Bleu(IRE) —Kaprika (FR) (Cadoudal (FR))
585a[9]

Geraldine *Mrs S Lamyman* 63h
5 ch m Minster Son—Church Leap (Pollerton)
1762[3] 2844[8] 3789[10]

Gerfaut (FR) *T Civel* 101h
5 b g Northern Crystal—Gentle Woman (FR) (Solicitor (FR))
778a[P]

Geri Roulette *S C Burrough* 43 h
8 b m Perpendicular—Clashfern (Smackover)
3467[9] 3889[P]

Germany Park (IRE) *W B Stone* 60b
8 ch g Germany(USA) —Lohunda Park (Malinowski (USA))
3598[P] **3781[F] 4016[P]4578[U] 4914[P]**

Gerrard (IRE) *Mrs A Barclay* 61h 89 c
8 b g Jurado(USA) —Vienna Waltz (IRE) (Orchestra)
2555[4] 2984[F] 3368[9]

Gessecapade *P S McEntee*
4 b f Largesse—Muscade (USA) (Spend A Buck (USA))
3259[12] *4237[13]*

Getaway Girl *O Brennan* 61h
8 b m Perpendicular—Viowen (IRE) (Denel (FR))
1340[P] 2082[P] 5052[12]

Getinbybutonlyjust *Mrs Dianne Sayer* 94h 91c
7 b g King's Ride—Madame President (IRE) (Supreme Leader)
(429) **2266[4] 2978[2]**

Geton (IRE) *M C Pipe* 101+h
6 b g Glacial Storm(USA) —Monavale (IRE) (Strong Gale)
2243[F] 4150[P]

Getoutwhenyoucan (IRE) *M C Pipe* 115+h
144+c
6 gr g Old Vic—Galice Du Soleil (FR) (Royal Charter (FR))
748[2] 843[2] 977[2] (1079) **(1269) (2162) 2615[P]**

Get Smart (IRE) *Ferdy Murphy* 65b 98c
9 ch g Nucleon(USA) —Dark Colleen (Kambalda)
1716[6] 1907[5] 2248[U]2495[6] 3338[5] 4842[5]

Get The Point *Perry Harding-Jones* 105c
12 b g Sadler's Wells(USA) —Tolmi (Great Nephew)
170[8] 725[P] 894[3](1126) 1273[7] 1659[5]3960[P]

Ghabesh (USA) *Evan Williams* 79+h
4 rg c Dumaani(USA) —Dish Dash (Bustino)
1873[U] 2001[13] 2756[8] 3291[P] 3429[P]3817[7] (4290) 4616[11] 4941[P] (Dead)

Ghadames (FR) *Miss Venetia Williams* 107+h
136+c
12 b g Synefos(USA) —Ouargla (FR) (Armos)
(452) 2247[6] 2625[5] **4677[P]**

Ghaill Force *P Butler* 82h
4 b g Piccolo—Coir 'A' Ghaill (Jalmood (USA))
1478[7] 1649[4] 2069[5] 2373[4] 2949[5]3182[9] 4648[6] 4910[P]

Ghost Buster *Mrs L B Normile* 64h
7 ch g Opera Ghost—Venetian Storm (Glacial Storm (USA))
120[6]

Giant's Rock (IRE) *B J Llewellyn* 64+h
4 ch g Giant's Causeway(USA) —En Garde (USA) (Irish River (FR))
1011[8] 3885[6] 4046[3] 4449[6] 4556[6]5048[4]

Gidam Gidam (IRE) *J Mackie* 112h
4 b g King's Best(USA) —Flamands (IRE) (Sadler's Wells (USA))
2587[2] (2921) 3759[4] 4301[4] 4631[2] 4990[4]

Gielgud *B G Powell* 100 h 113c
9 b g Faustus(USA) —Shirl (Shirley Heights)
3847[2] 4607[4] 4748[F]

Gift Voucher (IRE) *P R Webber* 67h
5 ch g Cadeaux Genereux—Highland Gift (IRE) (Generous (IRE))
2334[9] 3351[P] 4608[11]

Gigs Bounty *C C Bealby* 111+h
8 ch g Weld—City's Sister (Maystreak)
465[P] 864[P]

Gilded Ally *M Wigham* 62b
6 b g Gildoran—Allyfair (Scallywag)
2702[4] 4449[P]

Gilzine *E Parry* 66h 105c
10 b g Gildoran—Sherzine (Gorytus (USA))
5109[2]

Gimmeabreak (IRE) *Miss E C Lavelle* 74h
6 b g Beneficial—Gentle Eyre (IRE) (Aristocracy)
2826[P] 4033[4] 4665[8]

Gimme Shelter (IRE) *S J Marshall*
12 ch m Glacial Storm(USA) —Glen Dieu (Furry Glen)
80[2] 2066[P] 2171[11] **2265[8]2589[2] 3315[F]** 3554[3]**4042[P] 4316[P] 4845[P]**

Gingembre (FR) *Mrs L C Taylor* 127c
12 ch g Le Nain Jaune(FR) —Teuphaine (FR) (Barbotan (FR))
2828[P]

Gingerbread House (IRE) *R T Phillips* 121 h 124 c
8 b g Old Vic—Furun (IRE) (Deep Run)
2644[F] 3176[P] 3992[P]4806[5] (Dead)

Ginger For Pluck *J G Given* 29b
4 b f Revoque(IRE) —Naughty Pistol (USA) (Big Pistol (USA))
2014[10]

Gingerslookingreat (IRE) *O Brennan* 76b
7 ch g Ashkalani(IRE) —Just An Illusion (IRE) (Shernazar)
4875[P]

Gingko *P R Webber* 94h
9 b g Pursuit Of Love—Arboretum (IRE) (Green Desert (USA))
78[P]

Ginko Biloba (FR) *F-M Cottin*
7 b g Villez(USA) —Brune Babe (FR) (Fabulous Dancer (USA))
1073a[0]

Gin 'N' Fonic (IRE) *J D Frost* 92h 92c
6 ch g Zafonic(USA) —Crepe Ginger (IRE) (Sadler's Wells (USA))
388[3] 532[F] 803[F]860[P]

Giolla De (IRE) *F Flood* 109h 66c
7 b g Glacial Storm(USA) —Deep Inagh (Deep Run)
43a[20]

Giorgio (IRE) *Miss Lucinda V Russell* 103+h
120+c
8 b g Presenting—Billys Pet (Le Moss)
234[2] (427) 823[2]1012[P] 1489[2]

Giovanna *R T Phillips* 96h
5 b m Orpen(USA) —Red Leggings (Shareef Dancer (USA))
3902[5] 4280[3] (4875)

Gipsy Cricketer *M Scudamore* 65h 87c
10 b g Anshan—Tinkers Fairy (Myjinski (USA))
79[P] 681[11] 760[6] **999[5]1126[2] 1299[3] 1612[P]1805[4] 2074[S]** 2139[13]2463[4] **5112[6]**

Gipsy Girl *D O Stephens* 74h 100+c
11 b m Motivate—Young Gipsy (The Brianstan)
5109[5]

Girlie Power *P W Hiatt*
9 b m King Among Kings—Santo Star (Monsanto (FR))
976[7] 1317[P]

Gironde *Jonjo O'Neill* 108+h
5 b g Sadler's Wells(USA) —Sarah Georgina (Persian Bold)
172[2] (294)

Gitche Manito (IRE) *A King* 63h
4 b g Namid—Chasing Rainbows (Rainbow Quest (USA))
1821[5] (Dead)

Giunchiglio *W M Brisbourne*
7 ch g Millkom—Daffodil Fields (Try My Best (USA))
1097[P]

Giust In Temp (IRE) *Mrs K M Sanderson* 91+h
7 b g Polish Precedent(USA) —Blue Stricks (Bluebird (USA))
173[6] 1021[4] 1158[4] 1222[5] 1235[5](1302) 1458[6] 1541[5]

Giveasummerdance (IRE) *Barry Potts* 58h
7 ch m Glacial Storm(USA) —Shuil Ceoil (IRE) (Orchestra)
2107[P]

Give Me Love (FR) *P F Nicholls* 128 h
124+c
6 ch g Bering—Cout Contact (USA) (Septieme Ciel (USA))
1828[5] 1919[4] **2620[3] 3017[U]4102[U] 4162[2] 4424[2]4664[4] (4780) 5011[3]**

Given A Chance *Mrs S Lamyman* 91h
5 bb g Defacto(USA) —Milly Molly Mango (Mango Express)
369[3] 826[6] 1014[2] 1364[10]

Givitago *B Storey* 35b
7 b m Primitive Rising(USA) —Olive Branch (Le Moss)
3931[11] 4141[P] 4315[P] 4787[P]

Glabejet (IRE) *John Brassil* 77b 105c
8 b m Old Vic—Le Bavellen (Le Bavard (FR))
112a[8]

Glacial Delight (IRE) *Miss E C Lavelle* 104 h
128+c
7 b g Glacial Storm(USA) —Annagh Delight (Saint Denys)
201[3] (1637) 1773[6] **(2151) 2529[P](3326) 3942[P] 4447[P](5046)**

Glacial Evening (IRE) *R H Buckler* 117+h
10 bb g Glacial Storm(USA) —Cold Evening (IRE) (Strong Gale)
1773[2] 2010[2] 2175[14] **2529[P]**5010[3]

Glacial Sunset (IRE) *C Tinkler* 126+h
11 ch g Glacial Storm(USA) —Twinkle Sunset (Deep Run)
2747[4] 4461[21] 4974[13] 5142[11]

Glashedy Rock (IRE) *M F Harris* 91h 92+c
9 b g Shernazar—Classical Lady (IRE) (Orchestra)
1181[6] 1337[6] **1446[3] 4785[P]4989[6]**

Glasker Mill (IRE) *Miss H C Knight* 139+h
6 b g Old Vic—Lucey Allen (Strong Gale)
2238[3] 2426[3] (2928) (3496) 4443[7] 4760[6]

Glencove Marina (IRE) *W P Mullins* 109+b
4 b g Spectrum(IRE) —Specifiedrisk (IRE) (Turtle Island (IRE))
(5060a)

Glencoyle (IRE) *Miss L Day* 106h
6 b g In The Wings—Lucky State (USA) (State Dinner (USA))
1026[P] 1085[2] 1233[P] (Dead)

Glendara (IRE) *Miss H C Knight* 66b
5 b g Darazari(IRE) —Annie's Glen (IRE) (Glenstal (USA))
179[6]

Glenduff Bridge (IRE) *W J Burke* 112c
10 bb g Good Thyne(USA) —Rich Penny (Pollerton)
5083a[7]

Glenelly Gale (IRE) *M W Easterby* 109h 138c
12 bb g Strong Gale—Smart Fashion (Carlburg)
1721[3]

Glenfarclas Boy (IRE) *Miss Lucinda V Russell* 70h 92c
10 b g Montelimar(USA) —Fairy Blaze (IRE) (Good Thyne (USA))
305[4] 1795[7] 2172[3]2495[7] 3320[2] 3915[7]4144[6] 4318[P] 4587[7]

Glenfield Heights *W G M Turner* 96+h
11 b g Golden Heights—Cleeveland Lady (Turn Back The Time (USA))
1017[2]

Glenfinn Captain (IRE) *T J Taaffe* 137h
7 br g Alderbrook—Glenfinn Princess (Ginger Boy)
3892a[U] (4950a)

Glenfolan (IRE) *A J Martin* 48h 92c
8 ch g Montelimar(USA) —Donegal Thyne (IRE) (Good Thyne (USA))
855[4]

Glengarra (IRE) *D R Gandolfo* 89h 122 c
9 ch g Phardante(FR) —Glengarra Princess (Cardinal Flower)
(1457) 1542[P] (3418) 3580[2] 4213[5]

Glen Harley (IRE) *R T J Wilson* 78h 87c
6 br m Presenting—Asidewager (IRE) (Brush Aside (USA))
4141[7] **4719[RR]**

Glenisla Mist *Mrs S C Bradburne*
5 ch m Missed Flight—Glengolden (IRE) (Glenstal (USA))
2062[11] 2414[P] 3231[8]

Glenkill (IRE) *S M Jacobs* 65h
8 b m Beneficial—Parsons Choice (IRE) (The Parson)
3251[U] 3689[3] 4102[P]4590[7] 4729[7] 5107[F]

Glenmoss Rosy (IRE) *N G Richards* 91h
7 gr m Zaffaran(USA) —Rosy Posy (IRE) (Roselier (FR))
(80)

Glenogue (IRE) *K C Bailey* 102h 91 c
8 b m Hushang(IRE) —Glenamal (Kemal (FR))
2217[P] 2553[2] 3375[3]3689[P]

Glen Omen (IRE) *Jennie Candlish* 91h
6 b g Flying Legend(USA) —Miners Own (IRE) (Miner's Lamp)
2823[6] 3373[3] 4604[7]

Glen Oscar (IRE) *Miss S E Forster* 76h
7 b g Oscar(IRE) —Lady Ara (IRE) (Jurado (USA))
4527[12] 4720[5] 4787[10]

Glen Thyne (IRE) *K C Bailey* 33h 90+c
6 b g Good Thyne(USA) —Glen Laura (Kambalda)
2462[8] 2631[6] 2859[P] **3359[10]3547[10] (3686) 3923[3]4353[5] (5051)**

Glenview Lass (IRE) *T G McCourt* 75+h
7 bb m Un Desperado(FR) —Love For Lydia (IRE) (Law Society (USA))
1724[3] 2025[10]

Glenviews Surlami (IRE) *R C Guest* 50h
5 gr m Daylami(IRE) —Surmise (USA) (Alleged (USA))
1208[4] 1356[U] (Dead)

Glen Warrior *J S Smith* 125h 125 c
10 b g Michelozzo(USA) —Mascara VII (Damsire Unregistered)
3258[F] 3390[5] 3989[2]

Glide *J A B Old* 77h
5 ch g In The Wings—Ash Glade (Nashwan (USA))
2436[6] 1680[12] 1782[6]

Glimmer Of Light (IRE) *S A Brookshaw* 118h
6 b g Marju(IRE) —Church Light (Caerleon (USA))
3133[9] 3423[2] 3908[8] 4289[6] (4733) (4848)

Glimpse Of Glory *C W Thornton* 52h
6 b g Makbul—Bright-One (Electric)
3793[17] 4475[8] 4656[9]

Glinger (IRE) *N G Richards* 91h 128+c
13 b g Remainder Man—Harilla (Sir Herbert)
856[9]

Glingerbank (IRE) *N G Richards* 106+h
6 b g Supreme Leader—Mauradante (IRE) (Phardante (FR))
4532[3]

Glinton *Mrs P Sly* 99+b
4 ch g Most Welcome—Chichell's Hurst (Oats)
3623[6] 4622[3] 5054[4]

Glitter Ice *G Haine* 70h
5 b m Intikhab(USA) —Golden Circle (USA) (Theatrical)
4621[12] 5052[9]

Global Challenge (IRE) *P G Murphy*
7 b g Sadler's Wells(USA) —Middle Prospect (USA) (Mr Prospector (USA))
168[2] 814[7] 1039[3] 2483[10] 3600[P]

Globalized (IRE) *Mrs P Sly* 72+h
4 b g Spectrum(IRE) —Smaointeach (IRE) (Green Desert (USA))
2811[5] 3340[9] 3579[7] (Dead)

Global Party (IRE) *Miss C J Williams* 31b
4 b g Portrait Gallery(IRE) —Fionas Party (IRE) (Torenaga)
4038[U] 4333[17] 4554[14]

Globe Pearl (IRE) *F P Murtagh* 60h
6 b m Oscar(IRE) —Wolver Top (Wolver Heights)
3021[0]

Glorious Castlebar *J C Fox* 38h
5 b g Carlingford Castle—Glorious Day (Lepanto (GER))
3392[7] 3691[7] 4621[16]

Glory Be *Miss Venetia Williams* 106+h
6 ch m Gunner B—Geoffreys Bird (Master Willie)
(2704) 3149[7]

Glory Of Love *J A Supple* 75h
11 b g Belmez(USA) —Princess Lieven (Royal Palace)
363[5]

Glory Trail (IRE) *Mrs D M Grissell* 53c
12 b g Supreme Leader—Death Or Glory (Hasdrubal)
403[5]

Gloster Gunner *T R George*
7 ch g Gunner B—Blue Empress (Blue Cashmere)
4164[F]

Glowette (IRE) *I W McInnes*
4 ch f General Monash(USA) —Why Not Glow (IRE) (Glow (USA))
1904[P]

Glowing Dawn (IRE) *Miss J S Davis* 48h
4 b f Definite Article—Alizee (IRE) (College Chapel)
2580[8]

Glowing Ember *J F Panvert* 86h
6 b m Blushing Flame(USA) —California Dreamin (Slip Anchor)
1340[U] 1364[7] 1562[3] 2298[7]

Glynn Dingle (IRE) *A J Martin* 95h 132c
13 b g Millfontaine—Banner Lady (Milan I)
1083a[15]

Gneeve Hill (IRE) *O Sherwood* 31h
8 b g Phardante(FR) —Diklers Run (Deep Run)
2866[9]

Goblet Of Fire (USA) *P F Nicholls* 136h 122 c
7 b g Green Desert(USA) —Laurentine (USA) (Private Account (USA))
(1270) 1548[11] 1872[3] **(2260) 2484[4]2743[5] 5114[2]**

Goblin *D E Cantillon* 103+h
99+c
5 b g Atraf—Forest Fantasy (Rambo Dancer (CAN))
1726[4] 1958[4] 2344[3]

Go Classic *A M Hales* 90h
6 b m Classic Cliche(IRE) —Edraianthus (Windjammer (USA))
651[3]

Go Commercial (IRE) *M C Pipe* 31h
5 b g Supreme Leader—Mullaun (Deep Run)
2211[13] 2826[19] 3240[12]

Gods Token *Miss Venetia Williams* 134 h
8 gr g Gods Solution—Pro-Token (Proverb)
(2850) 2969[6] (3880) (4097) 4375[9]

Gofagold *A C Whillans* 88h 91+c
11 ch g Tina's Pet—Golden Della (Glint Of Gold)
81[P] (Dead)

Go For Bust *N J Henderson* 124h 85c
7 b g Sabrehill(USA) —Butsova (Formidable (USA))
2344[F] 2924[4] (3360) 3622[3]3993[14] 4612[5] **4827[P]**

Go For One (IRE) *D J Wintle* 74+h
7 b g Muroto—Barntown (Belfalas)
4642[3]

Gogetter Girl *J Gallagher* 36h
4 b f Wolfhound(USA) —Square Mile Miss (IRE) (Last Tycoon)
1563[11] 1729[P]

Go Green *P D Evans* 64+h
5 ch m Environment Friend—Sandra Mac (Marju (IRE))
173[3] 651[5]

Go Gwenni Go *Mrs D A Hamer* 64b
7 bb m Bold Fox—Landsker Pryde (Nearly A Hand)
1317[P]

Go Harvey Go (IRE) *R T Phillips* 63h
7 b g Supreme Leader—Python Wolf (IRE) (Jolly Jake (NZ))
4494[8] 4786[F]

Gohh *M W Easterby* 91c
10 ch g Alflora(IRE) —Lavenham's Last (Rymer)
2026[P] 2570[6] 2980[2]3348[3]

Go Johnny (IRE) *V R A Dartnall* 86b
6 b g Taipan(IRE) —Glenmore Memories (IRE) (Strong Gale)
4500[8]

Golano *P R Webber* 117h
6 gr g Linamix(FR) —Dimakya (USA) (Dayjur (USA))
127[F] **2377[F]**

Gola Supreme (IRE) *R Lee* 117+h 101c
11 gr g Supreme Leader—Coal Burn (King Sitric)
169[3] 2009[3] 2506[P]2848[6]

Gold Beach (IRE) *M G Rimell* 94b
6 b g Jurado(USA) —Grange Park (IRE) (Warcraft (USA))
2145[2] 2941[7] 3244[7]

Goldbrook *R J Hodges* 130h 130 c
8 b g Alderbrook—Miss Marigold (Norwick (USA))
3467[2] 3615[3] 3994[6] 4242[7] 4663[13]4945[4] **(5044)**

Golden Amber (IRE) *John R Upson* 58h
7 ch g Glacial Storm(USA) —Rigton Angle (Sit In The Corner (USA))
8[10]

Golden Bay *Miss Suzy Smith* 114h
7 ch m Karinga Bay—Goldenswift (IRE) (Meneval (USA))
(3600) 4579[6] (4972)

Golden Chalice (IRE) *Miss E C Lavelle* 105+h
7 ch g Selkirk(USA) —Special Oasis (Green Desert (USA))
136[16] 726[5] 824[8] 1366[6] 1481[8]

Golden Crest *W Amos*
6 ch g Rakaposhi King—Golden Aureole (Gildoran)
3779[F] 4530[P]

Golden Crew *Miss Suzy Smith* 99h
6 b h Busy Flight—Goldenswift (IRE) (Meneval (USA))
2242[11] 2720[6] 3646[5] 4935[3] 5138[2]

Golden Cross (IRE) *M Halford* 166+h
7 b g Goldmark(USA) —Fordes Cross (Ya Zaman (USA))
2669a[2] 3641a[3] (4019a) 4458[2]

Golden Crusader *J W Mullins* 108h 117+c
9 b g Gildoran—Pusey Street (Native Bazaar)
452[F]

Golden Exchange (IRE) *David Wachman* 107h 118c
6 ch g Polar Falcon(USA) —Melting Gold (USA) (Cadeaux Genereux)
117a[15]

Golden Feather *Miss Venetia Williams* 89 h
4 ch g Dr Fong(USA) —Idolize (Polish Precedent (USA))
1095[5] 1207[5] 1338[8] 2569[5] (3367) (3485) 3616[3]4010[7] 4427[P]

Golden Fields (IRE) *G A Harker* 76h
6 b m Definite Article—Quickstep Queen (FR) (Pampabird)
4056[7] 4299[6] 4794[RR] 4919[LFT]

Golden Fitz (ARG) *R M Stronge*
7 ch g Fitzcarraldo(ARG) —Good Last (ARG) (Good Manners (USA))
356[P]

Golden Hare (IRE) *Aidan Anthony Howard* 90b
5 ch g Bahhare(USA) —Ela's Gold (IRE) (Ela-Mana-Mou)
5081a[16]

Golden Hawk (USA) *R M Clark*
11 ch g Silver Hawk(USA) —Crockadore (USA) (Nijinsky (CAN))
319[P] 606[P]

Golden Inca *J Gallagher* 57b
6 b m Sovereign Water(FR) —Rabdanna (Rabdan)
2941[14]

Golden Jack (FR) *Mrs A L Tory*
12 b g Matahawk—Union Jack III (FR) (Mister Jack (FR))
49[U]

Golden Key *J Gallagher*
5 b g Rainbow Quest(USA) —Keyboogie (USA) (Lyphard (USA))
2860[P]

Golden Measure *G A Swinbank* 73h
6 b g Rainbow Quest(USA) —Dawna (Polish Precedent (USA))
2942^{10}

Golden Odyssey (IRE) *K G Reveley* 108h
6 ch m Barathea(IRE) —Opus One (Slip Anchor)
4983^{4}

Golden Parachute (IRE) *C C Bealby* 110+b
5 b g Executive Perk—Ardfallon (IRE) (Supreme Leader)
(3421) 4637^{4}

Golden Rambler (IRE) *Jonjo O'Neill* 108 h 120 c
10 br g Roselier(FR) —Goldiyana (FR) (Glint Of Gold)
694^{P} 865^{P}

Golden Remedy *A R Dicken* 1h
5 b m Dr Fong(USA) —Golden Daring (IRE) (Night Shift (USA))
2062^{P} 2652^{13}

Golden Rivet *Miss Lisa Bebbington* 54b
9 b g Weld—Golden Valley (Hotfoot)
4594^{U} 4946^{P}

Golden Row (IRE) *Miss Mary Louise Hallahan* 104h 124+c
12 b g Ore—Guelder Rose (Trimmingham)
45a^{16} 4138a^{7}

Golden Silver (FR) *H Hosselet*
4 b c Mansonnien(FR) —Gold Or Silver (FR) (Glint Of Gold)
1705a^{5}

Golden Square *A W Carroll* 94 h
4 ch g Tomba—Cherish Me (Polar Falcon (USA))
2045^{5} 2580^{4} 3132^{5}

Golden Squaw *Miss C J E Caroe*
4 ch f Grand Lodge(USA) —Wig Wam (IRE) (Indian Ridge)
2258^{P} 2661^{P}

Golden Storm (IRE) *Joseph Crowley* 133h 134c
9 ch g Magical Wonder(USA) —Independent Woman (IRE) (Carmelite House (USA))
69a^{10} 91a^{P} 1420a^{2}

Golden Streak (IRE) *C R Egerton* 94b
4 b g Indian Lodge(IRE) —Final Contract (IRE) (Shaadi (USA))
2642^{6} 3181^{5}

Golden Tamesis *R Dickin* 63h
9 b g Golden Heights—Escribana (Main Reef)
3146^{P} 3920^{P} 4575^{F}

Golden Tina *Mrs S M Johnson* 41h
8 ch m Tina's Pet—Gold 'n Soft (Whistling Deer)
1896^{5}

Golders Green *P W Hiatt* 79h
9 b g Gildoran—Mayfair Minx (St Columbus)
1302^{5} 1399^{P} 1562^{8} 1900^{10}

Gold Flo (IRE) *E McNamara* 98h
9 b m Fourstars Allstar(USA) —Moonshee (IRE) (Le Moss)
2691^{4} 3818^{2}

Gold For Me (FR) *A C Wilson* 89h
7 b g Solar One(FR) —Volcania (FR) (Neustrien (FR))
1565^{10} 1643^{9} (Dead)

Gold Guest *P D Evans* 98+h
7 ch g Vettori(IRE) —Cassilis (IRE) (Persian Bold)
(1077) 1491^{F} 1653^{2} 1862^{4}

Gold Heart (FR) *G Macaire* 110h
4 gr g Turgeon(USA) —Shannondore (FR) (Nashamaa)
1705a^{F} 2085a^{6}

Golding Hop *P Winkworth* 53b
6 b g Alflora(IRE) —Rainbow Fountain (Royal Fountain)
3904^{9}

Gold Magic (FR) *J-P Gallorini* 133h
8 b g Goldneyev(USA) —Djouza (FR) (Djarvis (FR))
5154a^{F}

Gold Quest (IRE) *Ian Williams* 114h 82+c
9 ch g Rainbow Quest(USA) —My Potters (USA) (Irish River (FR))
52^{7} 151^{4} 278^{F}1486^{2} 1560^{4} 1776^{F}

Goldseam (GER) *S C Burrough* 60h
7 gr g Neshad(USA) —Goldkatze (GER) (Czaravich (USA))
2620^{6} 2729^{F} 3341^{5}3602^{6} 3887^{P}

Goldsmeadow *O Brennan* 81b
7 b g Thowra(FR) —Fanny Adams (Nicholas Bill)
1554^{6} 1660^{3} 1820^{5}

Goldstar Dancer (IRE) *J J Quinn* 105h
4 b c General Monash(USA) —Ravensdale Rose (IRE) (Henbit (USA))
1011^{2} (1207) (1332) 1551^{4} (2569)

Gold Tariff (IRE) *P Winkworth* 68h
6 b g Good Thyne(USA) —Ashville Lady (IRE) (Le Bavard (FR))
2020^{5}

Gold Thread (IRE) *J Howard Johnson* 110+b
5 b g Oscar(IRE) —Queen Boadicea (IRE) (Farhaan)
(4588) 5060a^{5}

Gold Vic (IRE) *P Bowen* 76b
6 b g Old Vic—Harrys Legacy (IRE) (Supreme Leader)
1681^{14} 1909^{6} 2809^{P}

Golfagent *Mrs K Waldron* 102h 88c
8 b g Kris—Alusha (Soviet Star (USA))
272^{4} 573^{3} 841^{6} 906^{F}1045^{2} 1153^{6}

Goliathe *G M Moore* 66b
5 b g Moonax(IRE) —Florella (Royal Fountain)
4853^{19}

Gollinger *R H R Tierney* 84+c
10 b g St Ninian—Edith Rose (Cheval)
4660^{3} 4897^{U}

Golly (IRE) *D L Williams* 97 h 92c
10 b g Toulon—Tor-Na-Grena (Torus)
1000^{3} 1073a^{8} 1372a^{2}1856^{10} 2077^{P} 2939^{5}4014^{P} 4354^{5} 4592^{P}

Gollyhott (IRE) *Mrs S J Smith* 75h
11 gr g Roselier(FR) —Liffey Lady (Camden Town)
1661^{F} (Dead)

Gondolin (IRE) *G Brown* 87+h
6 b g Marju(IRE) —Galletina (IRE) (Persian Heights)
206^{9} 724^{2} 813^{F} 1409^{4}

Gone Far (USA) *M C Pipe* 98h 98 c
9 b g Gone West(USA) —Vallee Dansante (USA) (Lyphard (USA))
174^{U}

Gone Too Far *P Monteith* 123h 128+c
8 b g Reprimand—Blue Nile (IRE) (Bluebird (USA))
318^{3} 409^{3} 714^{2}1010^{5} 1296^{3} (1529) 1604^{2} 1913^{P}2904^{5} 3378^{F} 3761^{14} 3929^{3} 5067^{3}

Go Nomadic *P G Atkinson* 105c
12 br g Nomadic Way(USA) —Dreamago (Sir Mago)
(81) 481^{2} 3917^{P}

Goodandplenty *Mrs J C McGregor* 92b
8 b g Sovereign Water(FR) —Our Wilma (Master Willie)
3205^{11} 3855^{P}

Goodbadindiferent (IRE) *Mrs J C McGregor* 81c
10 bb g Mandalus—Stay As You Are (Buckskin (FR))
83^{4} (858) 1531^{4}1602^{5} 2476^{6} 2902^{4}3489^{6} 3915^{P} 5065^{5}

Good Bone (FR) *S Flook* 104+c
9 b g Perrault—Bone Crasher (FR) (Cadoudal (FR))
6^{P} 184^{6} 512^{P}3693^{F} 4051^{4} 6^{2}

Goodbye Chemo *Evan Williams* 57h
8 b g Greensmith—Bajina (Dancing Brave (USA))
25^{P}

Good Call (IRE) *Jonjo O'Neill* 84h
7 gr g Roselier(FR) —Melarka (Dara Monarch)
2327^{5} 2631^{8} 2799^{12} 3426^{P}3814^{P}

Good Citizen (IRE) *T R George* 121h
6 b g Good Thyne(USA) —Citizen Levee (Monksfield)
2309^{3} 2742^{2} 3175^{4} 3500^{F}

Good Heart (IRE) *R Ford* 79h 100c
11 ch g Be My Native(USA) —Johnstown Love (IRE) (Golden Love)
322^{2} 860^{4} (997) 1152^{5}(1277) 1359^{4}

Good Investment *P C Haslam* 74 h
4 b g Silver Patriarch(IRE) —Bundled Up (USA) (Sharpen Up)
1011^{6} 1146^{2} 1338^{9} (1605) 2064^{8} 3797^{10}4632^{10}

Good Judgement (IRE) *Jonjo O'Neill*
8 b g Good Thyne(USA) —Loch Na Mona (IRE) (King's Ride)
1928^{P} 2077^{4} 2623^{P}3382^{5} 4012^{P}

Goodleigh Buster *W S Kittow* 79b
6 ch g Prince Of Peace—Blue-Bird Express (Pony Express)
1730^{5}

Good Lord *J G Cann* 60b
5 b g Alflora(IRE) —Friendly Lady (New Member)
655^{10}

Good Lord Louis (IRE) *P J Hobbs* 93h 133+c
8 br g Presenting—Ash Queen (IRE) (Altountash)
(386) 1013^{4} 1265^{P} (Dead)

Good Man Again (IRE) *A Sadik* 95+h 103c
8 b g Arctic Lord—Amari Queen (Nicholas Bill)
2983^{3} 759^{U} (812) 1086^{F}1358^{F} 1616^{2} 1727^{5} 1803^{P}1848^{F}

Good Outlook (IRE) *R C Guest* 80h 119 c
7 b g Lord Americo—I'll Say She Is (Ashmore (FR))
2583^{2} 2842^{3} (3172) 3533^{4} 3649^{P} 5140^{2}

Good Potential (IRE) *D J Wintle* 53c
10 b g Petardia—Steel Duchess (IRE) (Yashgan)
1456^{3} 1796^{5} 2130^{3} 2556^{3} 2863^{10}3250^{2} 3577^{8} 4012^{P}

Good Samaritan (IRE) *M Pitman* 112+h
7 ch g Insan(USA) —Ballymave (IRE) (Jareer (USA))
654^{2} (1671) 1903^{5}

Good Sort (IRE) *B G Powell*
6 b g Oscar(IRE) —Rowlandstown Lass (Rowlandson)
2805^{P} 2928^{8} 3425^{P}

Good Step (IRE) *E Bolger* 112h 137c
8 ch g Be My Native(USA) —Shuil Alainn (Levanter)
(87a) 2164^{P} 2745^{3}4434^{6}

Good Thyne Jack (IRE) *E McNamara* 132+h
8 b g Good Thyne(USA) —Reynella Lass (IRE) (Torus)
2166^{10} 4446^{P}

Good Thyne Johnny (IRE) *Jennie Candlish* 99h
12 b g Good Thyne(USA) —Wiasma (Ashmore (FR))
508^{4}

Good Time Bobby *Miss Kate Milligan* 61h
9 b g Primitive Rising(USA) —Goodreda (Good Times (ITY))
1566^{F}

Good Vintage (IRE) *S R Andrews* 82c
11 b g Lashkari—Furry Hope (Furry Glen)
403^{3}

Go On Ahead (IRE) *M J Coombe* 106b
6 b g Namaqualand(USA) —Charm The Stars (Roi Danzig (USA))
3983^{5} (5075)

Goose Chase *C J Mann*
4 b g Inchinor—Bronzewing (Beldale Flutter (USA))
1594^{P} 1948^{P} 2481^{9} 3429^{P}

Gordon Highlander *Mrs P Robeson* 93+h
7 ch m Master Willie—No Chili (Glint Of Gold)
1851^{5} 2271^{P} 3648^{7}

Gordy's Joy *G A Ham* 31h
6 b m Cloudings(IRE) —Beatle Song (Song)
134^{P} 459^{P} 1076^{P}1155^{P} 2310^{6} 2560^{9} 2728^{P}

Gorthnacurra (IRE) *Patrick Morris* 87h 108c
10 b g Erin's Isle—Junijo (Junius (USA))
1860^{3}

Gortinard (IRE) *C Byrnes* 112h 124+c
8 b g King's Ride—The Lady's Last (IRE) (Brush Aside (USA))
(92a) 1622a^{P}

Gortumblo *K Bishop* 76 h
4 b g Sri Pekan(USA) —Evergreen (IRE) (Lammtarra (USA))
1190^{P} (1380) 1563^{8}

Goscar Rock (IRE) *P J Hobbs* 102+b
5 b g Synefos(USA) —Almost Regal (IRE) (Jurado (USA))
3024^{3} 4574^{3}

Go Silver Bullet (FR) *C F Swan* 117b
5 gr g Simon Du Desert(FR) —Bouge De La (USA) (Trempolino (USA))
2211^{4}

Gospel Song *A C Whillans* 87 h
14 ch g King Among Kings—Market Blues (Porto Bello)
9^{4} 1940 ^{14} 2264^{U} 2452^{10} 2680^{5}2944^{11} 3395^{2} 3552^{P} 3916^{6} 4317^{P}4723^{11}

Goss *Jonjo O'Neill* 107h 107c
9 gr g Linamix(FR) —Guillem (USA) (Nijinsky (CAN))
1020^{3} (1188) 1610^{5} 1668^{8}

Gosse D'Alleuds (FR) *G Lecomte*
12 b g Murmure(FR) —Quelle Belle Gosse (FR) (Pamponi (FR))
362a^{7}

Goss Hawk (NZ) *Jonjo O'Neill* 73h
6 br g Senor Pete(USA) —Stapleton Row (NZ) (Long Row)
801^{11} 913^{F}

Got Alot On (USA) *F E Sutherland* 80h
8 bb g Charnwood Forest(IRE) —Fleety Belle (GER) (Assert)
4903^{12}

Gotontheluckyone (IRE) *P R Rodford* 80h
6 b g Eagle Eyed(USA) —Notluckytochange (IRE) (King Of Clubs)
3321^{2} 3715^{P} 3945^{4} 4368^{P} 4550^{5}

Gotta Get On *R H Alner* 78h
5 br m Emperor Fountain—Lonicera (Sulaafah (USA))
2015^{8} 2457^{4} 2730^{11} 2997^{5}

Government (IRE) *M C Chapman* 55h
5 b g Great Dane(IRE) —Hidden Agenda (FR) (Machiavellian (USA))
279^{U} 428^{9} 1911^{U} 2082^{P}2099^{15} 2517^{10} 2967^{P}

Governor Daniel *Ian Williams* 112 h 110c
15 b g Governor General—Princess Semele (Imperial Fling (USA))
1180^{4} 1362^{4} 1636^{8}

Go White Lightning (IRE) *M Bradstock* 91h 115c
11 gr g Zaffaran(USA) —Rosy Posy (IRE) (Roselier (FR))
183^{P}

Grace Dieu *M Scudamore* 66+h
5 gr m Commanche Run—Race To The Rhythm (Deep Run)
399^{6} 613^{11} 1202^{P} 1297^{RR}

Graceful Dancer *B G Powell* 106 h 106c
9 b m Old Vic—Its My Turn (Palm Track)
(2986) 3481^{U} 4012^{4} 4395^{3}4636^{P}

Graffiti Tongue (IRE) *Evan Williams* 108+h 73c
13 b g Be My Native(USA) —Lantern Line (The Parson)
(289) 1067^{2} (3433)

Grafton Truce (IRE) *Miss Lucinda V Russell* 21h
9 gr g Brief Truce(USA) —Grafton Street (GER) (Pentathlon)
1308^{P} 2027^{9} 2453^{P} 3335^{P}

Graham (IRE) *P Bowen* 81b
6 b g Flemensfirth(USA) —Prudence Sarn (IRE) (Strong Gale)
1543^{10}

Graig Hill Cracker (IRE) *R L Brown* 48b
7 b g Michelozzo(USA) —Tuftarney (Mandalus)
1681^{11} 4570^{P}

Gran Dana (IRE) *G Prodromou* 62h
6 b g Grand Lodge(USA) —Olean (Sadler's Wells (USA))
2968^{8} 3219^{4} 3328^{13} 4794^{6} 5050^{P}

Grand Bay (USA) *Jonjo O'Neill* 94 h
5 b g Coronado's Quest(USA) —Buckeye Gal (USA) (Good Counsel (USA))
1875^{5} 2950^{4} 3464^{7} 3818^{6}

Grand Canal (FR) *J-V Toux* 134h
10 ch g Phantom Breeze—Merry Land (FR) (Goodland (FR))
5154a^{8}

Grand Daum (FR) *T P Tate* 78h
5 bb g Double Bed(FR) —Maousse (FR) (Labus (FR))
2480^{5} 2763^{11} 3253^{P} 3780^{6} 12^{2}

Grande Cascade *Lucinda Featherstone*
5 b m Riverhead(USA) —Tallulah (Puissance)
976^{6} 1231^{6}

Grande Creole (FR) *P F Nicholls* 104+h
7 b g Byzantium(FR) —Sclos (FR) (Direct Flight)
1959^{P} 2729^{8} 2922^{P}(4942)

Grandee Line *R H Alner* 95h 87c
11 gr g Gran Alba(USA) —Judys Line (Capricorn Line)
106^{5} 3212^{P} 3465^{P}3899^{6} 4290^{2}

Grande Jete (SAF) *N J Henderson* 139 h
9 ch g Jallad(USA) —Corps De Ballet (SAF) (Truely Nureyev (USA))
4473^{9} 5078a^{P}

Grand Finale (IRE) *Miss Venetia Williams* 129 h
9 b h Sadler's Wells(USA) —Final Figure (USA) (Super Concorde (USA))
4573^{3}

Grand Ideas *G J Smith* 48h
7 br g Grand Lodge(USA) —Afrafa (IRE) (Lashkari)
5073^{6}

Grand In The Hand (IRE) *J R Turner* 58b
6 b g Grand Plaisir(IRE) —Lady Clara (IRE) (Jolly Jake (NZ))
2948^{17}

Grand Lili *John Charles McConnell* 100h
5 gr m Linamix(FR) —Jabali (FR) (Shirley Heights)
1623a^{4}

Grand Manner (IRE) *K G Reveley* 85h
6 b g Desert Style(IRE) —Reacted (IRE) (Entitled)
352^{P}

Grandma's Girl *Robert Gray* 65h
4 b f Desert Style(IRE) —Sakura Queen (IRE) (Woodman (USA))
2477^{5} 2752^{3}

Grand Prairie (SWE) *G L Moore* 92+h
10 b g Prairie—Platonica (ITY) (Primo Dominie)
75^{8} 502^{4} 3899^{4} 4101^{3} 4452^{3}4566^{11} 4903^{5}

Grand Slam (IRE) *A C Whillans* 82c
11 b g Second Set(IRE) —Lady In The Park (IRE) (Last Tycoon)
2655^{3} 3379^{3} 3555^{3}3849^{P}

Grand Slam Hero (IRE) *P Bowen* 91+h
5 ch g Anshan—Tidal Princess (IRE) (Good Thyne (USA))
1985^{5} 2864^{11} 3646^{10} 4052^{3} 4589^{8}

Grangeclare Lark (IRE) *D T Hughes* 118h
5 b m Old Vic—Grangeclare Rose (IRE) (Gianchi)
5077a^{3}

Granit D'Estruval (FR) *Ferdy Murphy* 108 c
12 b g Quart De Vin(FR) —Jalousie (FR) (Blockhaus)
1941^{P} 3022^{6} 3390^{P}3560^{F}

Granite Man (IRE) *Jonjo O'Neill* 81+h
6 b g Glacial Storm(USA) —Silkaway (IRE) (Buckskin (FR))
1401^{2} 1562^{11} 1672^{8} 1895^{6} 2141^{7}

Granny Shona (IRE) *P R Webber* 65h
5 ch m Nashwan(USA) —Manuetti (IRE) (Sadler's Wells (USA))
(27) 2515^{9} 3254^{8} 3484^{5} 3689^{F}

Grapevine Sally (IRE) *E J O'Grady* 101+h
5 b m Saddlers' Hall(IRE) —Mrs Battleaxe (IRE) (Supreme Leader)
5104a^{10}

Graphex *A King* 88b
4 bb g Inchinor—Allegra (Niniski (USA))
2520^{3} 3216^{3} 4011^{5} 4909^{7}

Graphic Approach (IRE) *C R Egerton* 123 h 145 c
8 b g King's Ride—Sharp Approach (Crash Course)
2532^{2} (3296) 4118^{6}4459^{3}

Grasia (IRE) *K C Bailey* 94b
7 b g Glacial Storm(USA) —Bar Flute (IRE) (Orchestra)
1976^{P} 2631^{F} (Dead)

Grasp *G L Moore* 113+h
4 b g Kayf Tara—Circe (Main Reef)
2481^{7} 3429^{2} (4128) 4435^{P} 4691^{4}

Gratomi (IRE) *Mrs A E Lee* 84c
16 b g Bustomi—Granny Grumble (Politico (USA))
405^{5}

Grattan Lodge (IRE) *J Howard Johnson* 108 h 144 c
9 gr g Roselier(FR) —Shallow Run (Deep Run)
2176^{P} 2451^{P} 2840^{U}3018^{P} 3966^{4} 4843^{7}

Grave Doubts *K Bishop* 115 h
10 ch g Karinga Bay—Redgrave Girl (Deep Run)
1270^{13} 1548^{2} 1743^{9} 2533^{6} 2765^{12}2999^{10}

Gray Knight (IRE) *Mrs T J Hill* 86dh 72+c
9 gr g Insan(USA) —Moohono (IRE) (Roselier (FR))
52^{P} 1109^{8} 1362^{7}1520^{2} 1597^{5} 1779^{2}

Gray's Eulogy *D R Gandolfo* 85h 103c
8 ch g Presenting—Gray's Ellergy (Oats)
2104^{P} 2616^{2} 3000^{5}3434^{4}

Great Approach (IRE) *N G Richards* 94+h
5 b g Simply Great(FR) —Gayles Approach (Strong Gale)
2947^{5} 3912^{6} 4527^{4}

Great As Gold (IRE) *B Ellison* 121h 122 c
7 b g Goldmark(USA) —Great Land (USA) (Friend's Choice (USA))
2629^{11} 2990^{9} 3380^{2} 3653^{3}4016^{2} (4314) 4505^{6}

Great Benefit (IRE) *Miss H C Knight* 73h 54c
7 ch g Beneficial—That's Lucy (IRE) (Henbit (USA))
1950^{7} 2313^{8} 2555^{9}4914^{F}

Great Compton *B J Llewellyn* 78h
6 b g Compton Place—Thundercloud (Electric)
167^{5} 287^{U} 506^{3} 801^{2} 1977^{12}2214^{8}

Great Escape (IRE) *L Corcoran* 63h
10 b g Montelimar(USA) —Sallucevanna (IRE) (Salluceva)
1657^{3}

Greatest By Phar *J Akehurst* 82+h
5 b g Pharly(FR) —Greatest Friend (IRE) (Mandalus)
1490^{8} 1655^{7} 2043^{7} 2802^{7}

Great Expense *G R Pewter*
7 b g Shambo—Zoes Pet (Cisto (FR))
1616^{P} 1990^{P}

Great Game *A S T Holdsworth* 38h
6 b g Indian Ridge—Russian Grace (IRE) (Soviet Star (USA))
1017^{P}

Great Memories *Jonjo O'Neill* 92h
7 b g Alflora(IRE) —Four Thyme (Idiots Delight)
2432^{4} 3505^{4} 4327^{5} 4754^{5} (Dead)

Grecian Groom (IRE) *P D Niven* 115+b
4 b g Groom Dancer(USA) —Danse Grecque (IRE) (Sadler's Wells (USA))
(4909)

Greek Star *K A Morgan* 92h
5 b g Soviet Star(USA) —Graecia Magna (USA) (Private Account (USA))
2639^{3} 2994^{P} 3814^{9} 4898^{5}

Greenacre Legend *D B Feek* 61h
4 br g Faustus(USA) —Alice Holt (Free State)
2611^{9} 3132^{U} 3898^{6} 4521^{P}

Greenacres Boy *M Mullineaux* 75h 68c
11 b g Roscoe Blake—Deep Goddess (Deep Run)
96^{F} 238^{P} 412^{9} 697^{4} 906^{P}1099^{P} 1180^{9} 1233^{P} 1321^{6}1442^{5} 1568^{5} 1615^{6}1713^{8} 1855^{F} (Dead)

Greenawn (IRE) *M Sheppard* 88+h
7 ch g Anshan—Arctic Bead (IRE) (Le Moss)
1957^{P} 2620^{5} 2861^{P}3251^{10}

Green Belt Flyer (IRE) *Mrs John Harrington* 125h 144 c
8 b g Leading Counsel(USA) —Current Liability (Caribo)
45a^{8} 1702a^{6} 2195a^{2}3261a^{P} 4138a^{3} 4459^{18}

Greencard Golf *Jennie Candlish* 87+h
5 b g Foxhound(USA) —Reticent Bride (IRE) (Shy Groom (USA))
3[8] (351) 891[3] 1000[9] 1153[P] 1486[10]1616[4] 1712[3] 1800[4] 5072[6]

Green Collar *M Salaman* 47b
7 ch g Factual(USA) —Highmoor Scallyann (Scallywag)
2987[8] 3478[U] 3800[P]

Greenfield (IRE) *R T Phillips* 121 h
8 ch g Pleasant Tap(USA) —No Review (USA) (Nodouble (USA))
2813[3] 2974[P] 4364[P] 4781[11]

Green Finger *J J Quinn* 92h 113c
8 b h Environment Friend—Hunt The Thimble (FR) (Relkino)
2037[7] 2841[P] 3398[P]

Greenfort Brave (IRE) *J J Lambe* 83h
8 b g Bravefoot—Greenfort Belle (IRE) (Lafontaine (USA))
317[5] 781[0] 991[5] 1066[4] 1337[5]1374[2] 1566[4] 1685[P] 1884[6]

Green Gamble *D B Feek* 90 h 101c
6 gr g Environment Friend—Gemma's Wager (IRE) (Phardante (FR))
246[5] 1860[2] 2239[3]2719[P] 3718[5] 5047[8]

Greenhall Rambler (IRE) *P A Fahy* 119h 113c
7 ch m Anshan—Gentle Pressure (Ovac (ITY))
66a[3] **4018a[U]**

Greenhope (IRE) *N J Henderson* 134 h 144+c
8 b g Definite Article—Unbidden Melody (USA) (Chieftain)
4242[5] **(4472) 4749[P]**

Green Iceni *N J Henderson* 114+h
7 br g Greensmith—Boadicea's Chariot (Commanche Run)
1745[3] 2173[2] (2632) 3175[3]

Green Ideal *Ferdy Murphy* 129h 120+c
8 b g Mark Of Esteem(IRE) —Emerald (USA) (El Gran Senor (USA))
2111[7] 2445[4] 2640[2]2993[F] (3533) 3917[8](4363) 5080a[P]

Green Master (POL) *A Sadik* 64h
6 bl g Who Knows—Green Fee (GER) (Windwurf (GER))
469[P] 575[P]

Greenmoor House (IRE) *V R A Dartnall* 89h
8 b g Denel(FR) —No Reason (Kemal (FR))
1892[P]

Green 'N' Gold *M D Hammond* 91h 36c
6 b m Cloudings(IRE) —Fishki (Niniski (USA))
499[8] (1333) 1571[8] 1685[3] 1838[6] **2267[7]**4145[5] 4656[4] 12[P]

Green Ocean *J W Unett* 26h
6 gr m Environment Friend—Northern Swinger (Northern State (USA))
77[9]

Green Prospect (FR) *M J McGrath* 101h
6 b g Green Tune(USA) —City Prospect (FR) (Diamond Prospect (USA))
689[4] (1208) 1400[6] 1559[7] 1630[6] **1853[0]**1992[P]

Green River (IRE) *J T R Dreaper* 114h 117 c
12 ch g Over The River(FR) —Collopy's Cross (Pragmatic)
112a[11]

Green Smoke *Miss M J Benson* 82h 90c
10 gr g Green Adventure(USA) —Smoke (Rusticaro (FR))
4167[P]

Green Tango *H D Daly* 131 h 148 c
7 br g Greensmith—Furry Dance (USA) (Nureyev (USA))
1971[4] 2482[2] (3251) (3618) 4472[7] 4774[5](5121)

Green Valley (IRE) *P F O'Donnell* 95h
6 b g Daar Alzamaan(IRE) —Kittys Luck (IRE) (Torus)
3894a[12]

Greenwich *Mrs Marilyn Scudamore* 103c
12 br g Handsome Sailor—Praise The Lord (Lord Gayle (USA))
6[4] 402[R]

Gregs Girl *M Madgwick*
4 b f Bluegrass Prince(IRE) —Ninotchka (Niniski (USA))
5084[P]

Grenfell (IRE) *R T Phillips* 81h
7 br m Presenting—Arumah (Arapaho)
2486[U] 2983[5]

Grenoli (FR) *P F Nicholls* 43h
5 b g Garde Royale—Pietrosella (FR) (Alias Smith (USA))
3342[10] 4005[9]

Grey Abbey (IRE) *J Howard Johnson* 121 h 175 c
12 gr g Nestor—Tacovaon (Avocat)
1926[P] 2992[P]

Grey Admiral (USA) *B R Johnson* 1h
5 gr g Cozzene(USA) —Remarkable Style (USA) (Danzig (USA))
1235[12] 1742[14]

Grey Brother *Nick Williams* 118+h
8 gr g Morpeth—Pigeon Loft (IRE) (Bellypha)
3215[P] 3323[F] 4561[10]4727[5]

Grey Clouds *T D Easterby* 72+h
6 gr m Cloudings(IRE) —Khalsheva (Shirley Heights)
331[4]

Grey Court *P D Purdy*
11 ro g Gran Alba(USA) —Tudor Sunset (Sunyboy)
1123[R] 3477[0]

Grey Kid (IRE) *E W Morris* 84+c
8 gr g Roselier(FR) —Gala's Pride (Gala Performance)
5109[7]

Grey Kite *A E Jessop*
4 gr g Silver Patriarch(IRE) —Flemings Delight (Idiots Delight)
4455[17]

Grey Mistral *P R Chamings* 74h
8 gr m Terimon—Winnowing (IRE) (Strong Gale)
3280[6]

Grey Prince *G Prodromou* 33h
5 gr g Samraan(USA) —Scallys Queen Jay (Scallywag)
367[U] 513[8]

Grey Report (IRE) *P J Hobbs* 151 h 125 c
9 gr g Roselier(FR) —Busters Lodge (Antwerp City)
130[4] 360[6] 650[F]2175[13]

Grey Tornado *C G Cox* 74b
5 gr g My Best Valentine—Grey Baroness (Baron Blakeney)
4244[10]

Grey Tune (IRE) *M Scudamore* 100h
7 gr g Farhaan—Many A Tune (Charlaw)
(742) 861[P] (Dead)

Greywell (IRE) *Miss Elizabeth Doyle* 108h 114c
9 bb g Camden Town—Bellalma (Belfalas)
3005a[19]

Griffens Brook *Mrs P Sly* 77h
6 b g Alderbrook—Ima Delight (Idiots Delight)
2295[10] 3843[4] 4320[P]

Griffin's Legacy *N G Ayliffe* 85h
7 b g Wace(USA) —Griffin's Girl (Bairn (USA))
216[7] 384[4] 665[14] 3321[F] 4278[6]4556[4] 4856[5]

Grimshaw (USA) *Mrs D A Hamer* 81h 66c
11 ch g St Jovite(USA) —Loa (USA) (Hawaii)
681[12] 749[15]

Gripit N Tipit (IRE) *C F Swan* 94b
5 b g Saddlers' Hall(IRE) —Savanagh (IRE) (Brush Aside (USA))
3763[2]

Gritti Palace (IRE) *John R Upson* 111h
6 b g Duky—Glittering Grit (IRE) (Sheer Grit)
1833[2] 2461[3] (2815) 3277[2] 3969[6] 5015[4]

Groomsport (IRE) *Mrs Denise Foster* 95c
8 b g Hubbly Bubbly(USA) —Mistress Bella (Giolla Mear)
5128a[7]

Ground Ball (IRE) *C F Swan* 139h 150+c
9 bb g Bob's Return(IRE) —Bettyhill (Ardross)
41a[4] 1970[10] 2757[4]4000a[3] **4472[6] 4749[4]**

Ground Breaker *M W Easterby* 101h 107c
6 b g Emperor Jones(USA) —Startino (Bustino)
895[5] 942[5] **2751[3] 2839[U]3418[5] 4908[3]**

Grouse Moor (USA) *P Winkworth* 108h 90c
7 b g Distant View(USA) —Caithness (USA) (Roberto (USA))
3903[U] 4424[F]

Grouville *C J Mann* 97+h
5 b g Groom Dancer(USA) —Dance Land (IRE) (Nordance (USA))
243[3]

Grove Lodge *L A Dace*
9 b g Donna's Red—Shanuke (IRE) (Contract Law (USA))
4133[P] 4523[8]

Grumpyintmorning *M J Gingell*
7 b g Magic Ring(IRE) —Grecian Belle (Ilium)
2523[P] 2702[P]

Grumpy Stumpy *N A Twiston-Davies* 81h 96 c
11 ch g Gunner B—Moaning Jenny (Privy Seal)
1832[4] 2164[F] 2623[U]

Grunzig *Mrs C A Dunnett* 33b
4 ch g Danzig Connection(USA) —Great Exception (Grundy)
2105[10]

Gudasmum *J P Elliot* 87c
8 b m Primitive Rising(USA) —Comarch (Ancient Monro)
3758[2] 3926[2]

Gudlage (USA) *Mrs P J Shaw* 109+h 111c
10 b g Gulch(USA) —Triple Kiss (Shareef Dancer (USA))
4330[P] 5020[U] 5116[8]

Gue Au Loup (FR) *J Groucott* 74c
12 gr g Royal Charter(FR) —Arche D'Alliance (FR) (Pamponi (FR))
79[5] 437[P] 4055[4]4594[P]

Guerilla (AUS) *R C Guest* 98+h
6 bb g Octagonal(NZ) —Partisan (AUS) (Canny Lad (AUS))
4917[F] (10)

Guess What *Mrs S J Smith* 77b
6 b g Warcraft(USA) —Double Talk (Dublin Taxi)
2864[13] 3353[8]

Guichi (FR) *G Lecomte*
8 ch g Beaudelaire(USA) —Queen Lance (FR) (Djarvis (FR))
4718a[P]

Guignol Du Cochet (FR) *S Flook* 93 c
12 ch g Secret Of Success—Pasquita (FR) (Bourbon (FR))
79[3] 280[6] 453[P]3805[5] 3960[5] 4607[P]4748[19]

Guilsborough Gorse *T D Walford* 105c
11 b g Past Glories—Buckby Folly (Netherkelly)
368[4] 605[7] 725[6]896[7] 997[3]

Guilt *D T Hughes* 111 h 112c
6 b g Mark Of Esteem(IRE) —Guillem (USA) (Nijinsky (CAN))
69a[14] 5061a[2]

Guinelia (FR) *C Bertrand*
7 bl m Aureliano(FR) —Guinee (FR) (Argument (FR))
846a[0]

Gulabill *N A Twiston-Davies* 85+h
7 b g Safawan—Gulsha (Glint Of Gold)
2529[P]

Gullivers Travels *N J Gifford* 72h
7 ch g Un Desperado(FR) —Drivers Bureau (Proverb)
2683[8] 2983[12] 4581[9]

Gulshique *N A Twiston-Davies* 61h
6 b m Classic Cliche(IRE) —Gulsha (Glint Of Gold)
3149[8] 3692[10] 3795[7]

Gumlayloy *S Flook*
7 ch g Indian Ridge—Candide (USA) (Miswaki (USA))
4477[P]

Gumley Gale *K Bishop* 121+h 127+c
11 b g Greensmith—Clodaigh Gale (Strong Gale)
55[3] 297[P] 489[2](516) 842[3] 1013[U]1550[11] 4728[7]

Gunadoir (IRE) *N G Richards* 76b
4 b f Needle Gun(IRE) —Rent Day (Town And Country)
4588[8] 5041[5]

Gungadu *P F Nicholls* 141+h
6 ch g Beneficial—Tsarella (Mummy's Pet)
1827[3] (2427) 2762[2] (3694) 3993[2] 4760[7]

Gunnasayso *J A B Old* 81+b
5 b m Gunner B—Sayshar (Sayfar)
4854[8]

Gunner Getya *R Dickin*
5 b m Gunner B—Kinlet Vision (IRE) (Vision (USA))
4695[6]

Gunner Jack *N G Richards* 99+b
5 b g Gunner B—Wayuphill (Furry Glen)
(4366)

Gunnison (IRE) *Eoin Griffin* 94b
5 b g Accordion—Anaglogs Last (Over The River (FR))
5104a[17]

Gunship (IRE) *P J Hobbs* 69h 64+c
5 b g Needle Gun(IRE) —Teejay's Future (IRE) (Buckskin (FR))
1849[7] 2269[7] 2487[10] 2618[5] 2873[13]3211[2] 4133[6] **4571[3]**

Gunsmoke *Ms Caroline Walker* 38b
8 gr g Thethingaboutitis(USA) —Fairy Princess (IRE) (Fairy King (USA))
4283[4]

Gunson Hight *Miss Sarah E Gledson* 85+h 54c
9 b g Be My Chief(USA) —Glas Y Dorlan (Sexton Blake)
322[P] 604[LFT] 4044[P]

Gunther McBride (IRE) *P J Hobbs* 140c
11 b g Glacial Storm(USA) —What Side (General Ironside)
1861[4] 3296[6] 3560[4](3877) 4617[4]

Gun Tote (USA) *P Hughes* 49h
5 ch g Benny The Dip(USA) —Popularity (USA) (Blushing Groom (FR))
65a[17]

Gurteenoona (IRE) *Ian Williams* 90b
4 b g Insan(USA) —Copper Hill (IRE) (Zaffaran (USA))
4667[2]

Guru *G L Moore* 118h 118 c
8 b g Slip Anchor—Ower (IRE) (Lomond (USA))
1919[2] 2636[10] 2871[8] **3599[3]**4091[5] 4821[6]

Gus Berry (IRE) *Mrs Alison Christmas* 84c
13 ch g Montelimar(USA) —Eurolink Sea Baby (Deep Run)
498[P]

Gustavo *Miss Venetia Williams* 97 h
5 b g Efisio—Washita (Valiyar)
1671[P] 2006[6] 2249[14] 2584[14] (2822) (2940) 3592[P]

Guymur (FR) *P J Hobbs* 68+h
6 ch g Murmure(FR) —Meggy (FR) (Master Thatch)
2624 [U] 2873[8]

G V A Ireland (IRE) *F Flood* 128h 140+c
8 b g Beneficial—Dippers Daughter (Strong Gale)
115a[9] 2539a[P] 3053a[5](4496) 4929a[P]

Gwens Girl *J Rudge* 22b
6 b m Wizard King—Russian Project (IRE) (Project Manager)
3478[P] 3731[P] 3885[9]

Gwyn's Choice *R A Harris* 64b
5 b g Faustus(USA) —Shalholme (Fools Holme (USA))
655[9] 917[12] 4005[P]

Haadef *J Howard Johnson* 79h
5 b h Sadler's Wells(USA) —Taqreem (IRE) (Nashwan (USA))
551[6] (Dead)

Haafel (USA) *G L Moore* 119+c
9 ch g Diesis—Dish Dash (Bustino)
1953[8] (2128) 2577[P]2870[5] 3344[12] 3815[8]4694[P] (5090)

Habanero *Miss S J Wilton*
5 b h Cadeaux Genereux—Queen Of Dance (IRE) (Sadler's Wells (USA))
3354[P] 4613[P]

Habitual (IRE) *John A Quinn* 109+h 67c
5 b g Kahyasi—Kick The Habit (Habitat)
(1648) (1685) 1751[2] **3528a[13]**

Habitual Dancer *Jedd O'Keeffe* 135+h
5 b g Groom Dancer(USA) —Pomorie (IRE) (Be My Guest (USA))
1929[4] 2207[14] 2629[9] (3208) 3741[2] (4491) 4776[P]

Hadeqa *M J Brown* 67c
10 ch g Hadeer—Heavenly Queen (Scottish Reel)
4347[P] 4594[8] 6[8]

Hades De Sienne (FR) *Miss Tracey Watkins* 76h 105c
11 b g Concorde Jr(USA) —Aube De Sienne (FR) (Cupids Dew)
4107[2] 4325[2]

Haditovski *J Mackie* 106h 109c
10 b g Hatim(USA) —Grand Occasion (Great Nephew)
1957[9] 2247[3] 2525[2] 3256[8] 3445[2]3733[7] 3990[P] 4503[2]

Haenertsburg (IRE) *A L Forbes*
4 b f Victory Note(USA) —Olivia's Pride (IRE) (Digamist (USA))
1011[7] 4450[P]

Haggle Twins (IRE) *Ms F M Crowley* 110h 116c
6 b g Thowra(FR) —Orwell Gaye (IRE) (Strong Gale)
92a[16] 5059a[19]

Haikal *R H Buckler* 56h
9 b g Owington—Magic Milly (Simply Great (FR))
1949[11] (Dead)

Haile Selassie *W Jenks* 85 h 103c
6 b g Awesome—Lady Of The Realm (Prince Daniel (USA))
(3844) 4639[2] 5112[7]

Hail The King (USA) *R M Carson* 105h
6 gr g Allied Forces(USA) —Hail Kris (USA) (Kris S (USA))
1793[8] 2379[4] 2685[3] 3185[4] 3510[5]4756[4] 5022[2]

Hairball *B Secly* 112h
4 b g Highest Honor(FR) —Sail Storm (USA) (Topsider (USA))
2085a[4]

Hairy Molly (IRE) *Joseph Crowley* 133b
6 b g Shernazar—Ballilaurenka (IRE) (Buckskin (FR))
(4448) 5081a[2]

Hakim (NZ) *J L Spearing* 98h 138c
12 ch g Half Iced(USA) —Topitup (NZ) (Little Brown Jug (NZ))
747[14] **(1088) (1320) (1894) (2368) 2768[2] 3596[2]4762[2]**

Hakumatata *Miss Z C Davison* 74b
4 b g Zafonic(USA) —Hasta (USA) (Theatrical)
3181[14] 3346[10] 4554[8]

Halcon Genelardais (FR) *A King* 136 h 147 c
6 ch g Halcon—Francetphile (FR) (Farabi)
2369[F] 2820[4] **(3391) (3740) (4035) 5004[5]**

Halcyon Express (IRE) *Mary Meek* 78h
4 b g Mujadil(USA) —Hakkaniyah (Machiavellian (USA))
1955[8] 2101[5] 3431[U] 3645[12]

Halexy (FR) *Jonjo O'Neill* 133c
11 b g Iron Duke(FR) —Tartifume II (FR) (Mistigri)
1881[2] 2003[3] 2368[F]3739[7] 4118[P] 4504[P]

Halfajobjones *C W Moore* 30h
7 b m Tina's Pet—Hop The Twig (Full Of Hope)
905[P]

Half An Hour *P Bowen* 109h 118 c
9 b g Alflora(IRE) —Country Mistress (Town And Country)
666[3] 840[P] 946[P]1205[6] 1489[9] 2562[P]

Half Inch *B I Case* 98+h 82+c
6 b m Inchinor—Anhaar (Ela-Mana-Mou)
247[4] 451[5] 689[6] 905[7] **1124[3]1249[3] 1442[4] 1631[8]**3146[9] 3655[8]

Hallahoise Hydro (IRE) *B S Rothwell*
5 ch g Lake Coniston(IRE) —Flo Bear (IRE) (Prince Rupert (FR))
2523[P]

Hallyards Gael (IRE) *L Lungo* 116+h 142+c
12 br g Strong Gale—Secret Ocean (Most Secret)
97[7]

Haloo Baloo *Jonjo O'Neill* 97+h
6 b g Morpeth—Sky Baloo (Skyliner)
866[2] 2573[8] 3422[10] 3658[6] **3940[P]**4289[0] (4557) 4727[10]

Hamadeenah *C J Down* 107+h
8 ch m Alhijaz—Mahbob Dancer (FR) (Groom Dancer (USA))
451[11] 959[6]

Hambaphambili *O Sherwood* 101h
6 b g Cloudings(IRE) —Sun Dante (IRE) (Phardante (FR))
2242[4] 2865[8] 3184[4] 4501[2] 4661[3]4961[9]

Hamburg Springer (IRE) *M J Polglase* 90h
4 b g Charnwood Forest(IRE) —Kyra Crown (IRE) (Astronef)
1551[12] 1797[P] 1904[4] 2076[6] 2935[10]

Hamcon Bleu (FR) *T Poche*
11 ch g Dadarissime(FR) —Arlette Bleue (FR) (Mister Jack (FR))
362a[F]

Ham Stone *B J M Ryall* 52h
8 b g Picea—Blushing Belle (Local Suitor (USA))
459[P]

Handa Island (USA) *M W Easterby* 91 h
7 br g Pleasant Colony(USA) —Remote (USA) (Seattle Slew (USA))
1508[5] 1607[3] 2146[2] 3269[F] (Dead)

Handel With Care (IRE) *R A Farrant* 83b
4 b g King Of Kings(IRE) —La Pepite (USA) (Mr Prospector (USA))
3346[6] 4038[5] 4333[15] 4754[10]

Handfull Of Euros (IRE) *W J Austin* 104h
6 ch m Flemensfirth(USA) —Two Spots (Deep Run)
4887a[14]

Hand Inn Hand *H D Daly* 136+h 161 c
10 b g Alflora(IRE) —Deep Line (Deep Run)
2346[4] 2635[5] 4457[5]4749[7]

Handsuposcar (IRE) *S Donohoe* 18b 112c
7 bb g Oscar(IRE) —Partners In Crime (Crofthall)
2764[5]

Handyman (IRE) *Michael M Watson* 128c
12 b g Hollow Hand—Shady Ahan (Mon Capitaine)
4560[3] 4975[P]

Handy Money *A King* 135h 128+c
9 b g Imperial Frontier(USA) —Cryptic Gold (Glint Of Gold)
127[8] 2209[6] 3298[P] **3903[P]4679[2]**

Hang Seng (IRE) *Eugene M O'Sullivan* 28h 104c
8 b g Phardante(FR) —Portia's Delight (IRE) (The Parson)
3528a[6] 5129a[8]

Hanko (GER) *Jonjo O'Neill* 106h 116c
10 b g Surumu(GER) —Hankaretta (USA) (Pirate's Bounty (USA))
4842[P]

Hannah's Tribe (IRE) *C W Moore*
4 b f Daggers Drawn(USA) —Cala-Holme (IRE) (Fools Holme (USA))
1904[P] 4551[P]

Hanseat (GER) *Frau E Mader* 71h
9 b g Goofalik(USA) —Hanseatin (GER) (Pentathlon)
(471a)

Hanybald (FR) *P Cormier-Martin*
11 b g Passing Sale(FR) —Renny (FR) (Diaghilev)
4718a[4]

Happiest Days (IRE) *Oliver McKiernan* 109h 93c
8 b g Supreme Leader—Cromogue Lady (Golden Love)
3005a[20]

Happy Boy (IRE) *M A Barnes* 71h
5 b g Victory Note(USA) —Pepper And Salt (IRE) (Double Schwartz)
8[3] 1947 2440[P]

Happy Hussar (IRE) *Dr P Pritchard* 95h 105c
13 b g Balinger—Merry Mirth (Menelek)
727[P] 1027[8] 1279[3] 1751[P] 1874[5] 2164[7] 2524[U] 2662[4] 2745[13] 4356[2] 4876[5]

Happy Shopper (IRE) *M C Pipe* 76h 107+c
6 b g Presenting—Reach Down (IRE) (Cheval)
2606[5] 2849[8] 3246[7] 3499[F] (3981) 4152[U] 4287[P] 4939[5]

Hapthor *F Jestin* 82h
7 ch m Zaffaran(USA)—My Goddess (Palm Track)
241[8] 470[7] 687[P] 785[P] 1839[4] 2171[14] 2653[5] 3209[P] 4584[3] 5072[5]

Harapour (FR) *P F Nicholls* 124+h 130+c
8 b g Valanour(IRE)—Haratiyna (Top Ville)
454[P]

Harbour Bound (IRE) *Evan Williams* 104h
7 b g Sadler's Wells(USA)—Argon Laser (Kris)
812[P] 914[P] 1153[P]

Harbour Breeze (IRE) *Jennie Candlish* 100 b
4 b g Slip Anchor—New Wind (GER) (Windwurf (GER))
(4519)

Harbour Buoy *J Wade* 35b
5 ch g Bal Harbour—Elissa (Tap On Wood)
3563[11]

Harbour House *J J Bridger*
7 b g Distant Relative—Double Flutter (Beldale Flutter (USA))
1916[12] 2216[P]

Harbour King (FR) *N I M Rossiter*
7 bb h Darshaan—Zinarelle (FR) (Zino)
2804[P]

Harbour Pilot (IRE) *Noel Meade* 128h 126 c
11 b g Be My Native(USA)—Las-Cancellas (Monksfield)
4471[P] 4929a[P] 5102a[U]

Harbour Point (IRE) *M Scudamore* 89 h 88 c
10 b g Glacial Storm(USA)—Forest Jem (Croghan Hill)
2684[3] 2933[F]

Harbour Rock (IRE) *D J Wintle* 67h
7 b g Midhish—Annie's Glen (IRE) (Glenstal (USA))
2988[12] 3342[9] 3496[P] (Dead)

Harbour View (IRE) *E McNamara* 109 h 124+c
7 br g Tidaro(USA)—Lily Parson (The Parson)
(1751)

Harchibald (FR) *Noel Meade* 171 h
5 b g Perugino(USA)—Dame D'Harvard (USA) (Quest For Fame)
114a[2] (1621a) 2397a[3] (2761) 3109a[2]

Harcourt (USA) *M Madgwick* 93+h
6 b g Cozzene(USA)—Ballinamallard (USA) (Tom Rolfe)
2826[16] 3422[5] 3658[9] 3996[9] 4726[9]

Hard Act To Follow (IRE) *J Howard Johnson* 120+h
7 ch g Shernazar—Lauren's Gem (Over The River (FR))
(2947) (3381) 4760[P]

Harder Steel (IRE) *K C Bailey*
5 b g Mister Lord(USA)—All The Answers (Boreen (FR))
2145[7]

Hardi De Chalamont (FR) *Jennie Candlish* 85h 72c
11 gr g Royal Charter(FR)—Naita II (FR) (Dom Luc (FR))
614[5] 839[8] 978[9]

Hardknott (IRE) *R F Fisher* 76b
4 ch g Intikhab(USA)—Danita (IRE) (Roi Danzig (USA))
2068[5] 2521[8]

Hard N Sharp *Evan Williams* 96+h
6 ch g Rakaposhi King—Hardwick Sun (Dieu Soleil)
720[7] 917[5] 1042[11] 1323[3] 1407[P] 1485[3] 1632[4] 1784[3] 1977[3] 2310[F] 4277[P]

Hard Shoulder (IRE) *Noel Meade* 113h
6 b g Sri Pekan(USA)—Sakanda (IRE) (Vayrann)
43a[6] (Dead)

Hardwick *Adrian Maguire* 110 h
7 br g Oscar(IRE)—Paper Tigress (IRE) (King's Ride)
1623a[6] 3052a[5]

Hard Winter (IRE) *D T Hughes* 119h 113c
9 b g Arctic Lord—Lucycello (Monksfield)
91a[6]

Hardybuck (IRE) *N A Twiston-Davies* 65h 76+c
5 b g Saddlers' Hall(IRE)—Miss Beaufleur (IRE) (Good Thyne (USA))
1870[5] 3246[F] 3920[4] 4352[U] 4590[4]

Hardy Eustace (IRE) *D T Hughes* 168 h
9 b g Archway(IRE)—Sterna Star (Corvaro (USA))
(3154a) 3641a[7] 4432[3] 4775[2] 5130a[3]

Hardy Russian (IRE) *P R Rodford* 82c
9 b g Moscow Society(USA)—Catchmekiss (IRE) (Executive Perk)
231[3] 461[P] 631[P] 759[3] 1022[P] 1122[P]

Harik *G L Moore* 117c
12 ch g Persian Bold—Yaqut (USA) (Northern Dancer)
103[8] 725[P] 904[6] 1189[10] 1406[6]

Harissa (IRE) *J W Mullins* 62b
4 ch f King Luthier—Hollowfield Bug (IRE) (Magical Wonder (USA))
4902[6]

Harithabad (FR) *Noel Meade* 109h 119c
11 b g Ela-Mana-Mou—Haratiyna (Top Ville)
1691a[8]

Harlequin Chorus *H E Haynes*
16 ch g Jester—Raise The Dawn (Rymer)
566[P] 681[P]

Harley *Mrs P Sly* 96+h
8 ch g Alderbrook—Chichell's Hurst (Oats)
(2043)

Harloes Coffee (IRE) *Ronald Thompson* 96b
6 b g Shernazar—Beauchamp Grace (Ardross)
2906[7] 5141[0]

Harlov (FR) *A Parker* 104h 120 c
11 ch g Garde Royale—Paulownia (FR) (Montevideo)
547[4] 1941[7] 2265[4] 2819[P] 2965[8] 3560[2] 4361[P] 4790[7]

Harmony Brig (IRE) *N G Richards* 129+h
7 ch g Accordion—Bridges Daughter (IRE) (Montelimar (USA))
2444[4] 2631[2] (3231) (3912) (4529) 4750[3]

Harps Hall (IRE) *N I M Rossiter* 37h
12 ch g Yashgan—Parsons Glen (IRE) (Glen Quaich)
3885[7] 4285[6] 4661[8]

Harpurs Girl *J Mackie* 80b
5 b m Overbury(IRE)—Kingy's Girl (Makbul)
2864[9] 3145[7] 3497[5]

Harrihawkan *Mrs T J Hill* 93c
8 b g Alflora(IRE)—Beatle Song (Song)
1781[4] 2574[P] 3660[4] 3801[P]

Harringay *Miss H C Knight* 116+h
6 b m Sir Harry Lewis(USA)—Tamergale (IRE) (Strong Gale)
2012[5] 2718[2] (2937) (3322) (4619)

Harris Bay *Miss H C Knight* 88+h 125+c
7 b g Karinga Bay—Harristown Lady (Muscatite)
(2011) (2613) 3284[3] (3921) 4605[P] (5127)

Harrival *Miss M Bragg* 74h
6 ch g Hazaaf(USA)—Departure (Gorytus (USA))
2148[10] 3238[7] 4033[5] 4290[5] 4731[10]

Harrovian *Miss P Robson* 102 h 126+c
9 b g Deploy—Homeoftheclassics (Tate Gallery (USA))
2038[5] 2445[6] 2644[3] 2946[4] 3377[3] 3917[2] 4144[2]

Harry B *R J Price* 95h
7 b g Midyan(USA)—Vilcabamba (USA) (Green Dancer (USA))
457[6] 630[6] 747[11] 860[P]

Harry Blade *N A Twiston-Davies* 109+h
7 b g Karinga Bay—Sparkling Cinders (Netherkelly)
(1508) 1959[2]

Harry Boy (IRE) *N G Richards*
6 b g Glacial Storm(USA)—Flo Again (IRE) (Mister Lord (USA))
2497[P] (Dead)

Harry Bridges *R Lee* 20h
7 ch g Weld—Northern Quay (Quayside)
2831[2]

Harrycat (IRE) *V Smith* 107h
5 b g Bahhare(USA)—Quiver Tree (Lion Cavern (USA))
1037[2] (1222) 2247[7] 2716[10]

Harry Collins *B I Case* 92h 115+c
8 ch g Sir Harry Lewis(USA)—Run Fast For Gold (Deep Run)
183[2] 1953[F] 2325[U] 2466[P]

Harrycone Lewis *Mrs P Sly* 121+h 126 c
8 b g Sir Harry Lewis(USA)—Rosie Cone (Celtic Cone)
109[2] 468[F] 1735[9] 2703[6] (2956) 3420[2] (3941) 4240[P] 4974[10]

Harry Flashman *D W Whillans* 104+h
5 ch g Minster Son—Youandi (Silver Season)
3763[8] 4342[F] 4720[2]

Harry Harestone *P J Jones*
11 b g Miner's Lamp—Slipalong (Slippered)
3732[P]

Harry Hooly *Mrs H O Graham* 107+h 105+c
11 b g Lithgie-Brig—Drummond Lass (Peacock (FR))
2265[10] 2946[P] 3336[3] 3554[U] 4043[9] 4517[5] 4845[P]

Harry In A Hurry *Andrew Lee* 78h 99c
9 gr g Baron Blakeney—Ballytina (Rugantino)
87a[4]

Harry May *C L Tizzard* 68h
4 b g Lujain(USA)—Mrs May (Carlingford Castle)
2797[P] 3324[8] 3645[11]

Harry Potter (GER) *Evan Williams* 108+h 115+c
7 b g Platini(GER)—Heavenly Storm (USA) (Storm Bird (CAN))
(1180) 1319[2] (1724) 1919[5] 3357[9] 4049[2]2[U]

Harry's Dream *P J Hobbs* 105+h 127+c
9 b g Alflora(IRE)—Cheryls Pet (IRE) (General Ironside)
1025[3] 1398[2] (1657) (1728) 4805[2]

Harrys House *J J Quinn* 32h
4 gr g Paris House—Rum Lass (Distant Relative)
2569[P] 2752[12]

Harry's Simmie (IRE) *R C Harper*
4 ch f Spectrum(IRE)—Minstrels Folly (USA) (The Minstrel (CAN))
1679[P] 1802[F] 1955[9]

Harry The Hoover (IRE) *M J Gingell*
6 b g Fayruz—Mitsubishi Style (Try My Best (USA))
863[P]

Harwood Dale *T D Walford* 55b
6 b g Past Glories—Scalby Clipper (Sir Mago)
1799[15] 1915[P]

Has Scored (IRE) *Ferdy Murphy* 118+c
8 b g Sadler's Wells(USA)—City Ex (Ardross)
2170[4]

Hastaven (FR) *C Olehla*
11 b g Dastaan(FR)—Venus Deesse (FR) (Djarvis (FR))
1710a[U]

Hasty Prince *Jonjo O'Neill* 147+h 142 c
8 ch g Halling(USA)—Sister Sophie (USA) (Effervescing (USA))
1621a[4] 1738[3] 2500[6] 3389[6] 3727[11] 4461[14] 4765[7] 4959[9] (5142)

Hatch A Plan (IRE) *Mrs A J Hamilton-Fairley* 99h
5 b g Vettori(IRE)—Fast Chick (Henbit (USA))
911[6] 1804[2] 1902[9] 2324[8] 2595[9]

Hathlen (IRE) *G L Moore* 102h
5 b g Singspiel(IRE)—Kameez (IRE) (Arazi (USA))
1407[2]

Hatsnall *Miss C J E Caroe* 87h 83+c
8 b g Mtoto—Anna Of Brunswick (Rainbow Quest (USA))
181[P] 532[U]

Hatteras (FR) *Miss M P Bryant* 104+h
7 b g Octagonal(NZ)—Hylandra (USA) (Bering)
230[4] 2020[4] 2374[4] 2632[5] 2809[6] 3603[2] 4523[P] 4819[11] 4915[4]

Hattington *M F Harris* 107+h 101+c
8 b g Polish Precedent(USA)—Ruffle (FR) (High Line)
54[F] 451[2] 533[2] 726[9] 766[4] 875[4] 1019[6] 1396[F] 1479[5]

Hatton House (IRE) *D McCain* 93h
6 b g Dr Massini(IRE)—Chancy Gal (Al Sirat)
2288[11] 2821[6]

Haunted House *H D Daly* 96h
6 ch g Opera Ghost—My Home (Homing)
131[8] 2179[2] 2860[3] 3500[6] 3990[6] 4581[2] 4934[4]

Haut Cercy (FR) *G C Evans*
11 b g Roi De Rome(USA)—Mamoussia (FR) (Laniste)
4358[R]

Haut De Gamme (FR) *Ferdy Murphy* 130 h 144 c
11 ch g Morespeed—Chantalouette (FR) (Royal Charter (FR))
1929[2] 2370[5] 2876[3] 2990[6] (3397) 3988[5] 4777[F] 5128a[9]

Havetoavit (USA) *Thomas Cooper* 106h
5 b g Theatrical—Summer Crush (USA) (Summer Squall (USA))
2173[7]

Having A Party *J Mackie* 98 h
8 b m Dancing High—Lady Manello (Mandrake Major)
236[3]

Havit *Lady Susan Brooke*
8 b g Lucky Wednesday—Gouly Duff (Party Mink)
3249[P] 3477[P] 3801[P] 3885[P] 4590[P]

Hawadeth *V R A Dartnall* 131h
11 ch g Machiavellian(USA)—Ghzaalh (USA) (Northern Dancer)
2055[6] 3289[10] 4097[3] 4473[22] 4821[4] 5142[6]

Hawaii (FR) *Mme L Bellet*
11 b g Luchiroverte(IRE)—Polynesie (FR) (Baroque)
1074a[3]

Hawksbury Heights *J J Lambe* 66h
4 ch c Nashwan(USA)—Gentle Dame (Kris)
1512[8]

Hawk's Landing (IRE) *Jonjo O'Neill* 114b 120c
9 gr g Peacock(FR)—Lady Cheyenne (Stanford)
1972[7] 2293[6] 2577[P] 2818[11] 3965[2] 4163[2] 4348[3] 4636[P]

Hawkwell (IRE) *N G Richards* 85h
5 b g Topanoora—Royal Daisy (Crash Course)
2942[6]

Hawridge King *W S Kittow* 99h
4 b g Erhaab(USA)—Sadaka (USA) (Kingmambo (USA))
2286[2] 2661[4]

Hawthorn Prince (IRE) *Mrs P Sly* 114 h
11 ch g Black Monday—Goose Loose (Dual)
109[P] (353) (652)

Haydens Field *Miss H Lewis* 84 h
12 b g Bedford(USA)—Releta (Relkino)
54[P] 451[6] 488[11] 2731[10] 3458[9]

Haydens First (IRE) *Thomas Cooper* 105h
6 b m Flemensfirth(USA)—Womenofninetyeight (IRE) (Mandalus)
2796a[2]

Hayley's Pearl *Mrs P Ford* 55h 79c
7 b m Nomadic Way(USA)—Pacific Girl (IRE) (Emmson)
487[10] 613[12] 4106[10] 4566[10] 4780[6]2[4]

Haystacks (IRE) *James Moffatt* 91h
10 b g Contract Law(USA)—Florissa (FR) (Persepolis (FR))
121[5] 304[7]

Hazel Bank Lass (IRE) *Andrew Turnell* 51h 94c
10 b m Insan(USA)—Bonecastle Queen (Fitzpatrick)
2244[8] 2610[2] 2986[5] 3285[P] 3791[P] 3919[P]

Hazelhall Princess (IRE) *John Paul Brennan* 116c
7 b m Hubbly Bubbly(USA)—Princess Douglas (Bishop Of Orange)
4460[P]

Hazeljack *A J Whiting* 96h 110+c
11 b g Sula Bula—Hazelwain (Hard Fact)
1874[8] 2215[3] 2623[4] 2938[7] 4007[2] (4650) (4690)

Hazel Mere *R Curtis* 35h
6 b m Gildoran—After Time (Supreme Leader)
3024[8] 4581[P] 4956[P] 5052[15]

Hazzard A Guess *J W Mullins* 57h
5 ch m Primitive Rising(USA)—Handy Venture (Nearly A Hand)
3435[6] 3699[7] 4326[7] 4680[P] 4836[11] 5084[6]

Head Boy *S Dow* 87h
5 ch g Forzando—Don't Jump (IRE) (Entitled)
1480[10] 1565[4] 1742[5]

Head For The Hills *Niall Saville* 92c
13 ch g Scottish Reel—Merry Cherry (Deep Run)
333[P]

Headley (IRE) *J S Moore* 41b
5 ch g Grand Plaisir(IRE)—Donwood (IRE) (King Persian)
4623[9] 4909[19]

Heads Onthe Ground (IRE) *D T Hughes* 125h 123c
9 br g Be My Native(USA)—Strong Wings (Strong Gale)
5102a[9]

Healy's Pub (IRE) *Oliver McKiernan* 125h 129c
10 b g Accordion—Valary (Roman Warrior)
5103a[22]

Heartache *R Mathew* 61h 84 c
9 b g Jurado(USA)—Heresy (IRE) (Black Minstrel)
(57) 346[F] 2594[P] 2986[3] (3276) 3923[P] 4130[P] 4876[6]

Heartbeat *I A Wood*
5 b m Pursuit Of Love—Lyrical Bid (USA) (Lyphard (USA))
3804[P]

Hear The Echo (IRE) *David Wachman* 110h
5 b g Luso—Echo Creek (IRE) (Strong Gale)
2536a[5]

Heart Midoltian (FR) *M C Pipe* 101b 92c
9 gr g Royal Charter(FR)—Pride Of Queen (FR) (Saint Henri)
311[9] 761[6]

Heathcote *G L Moore* 116 h
4 b g Unfuwain(USA)—Chere Amie (USA) (Mr Prospector (USA))
(3132) 3498[2] (3898) (4877)

Heather Lad *C Grant* 96c
13 ch g Highlands—Ragged Rose (Scallywag)
688[4] 782[3] 872[3] 998[F] 1062[2] 1147[4] 1275[4] 1334[2] 1359[U]

Heatherlea Squire (NZ) *D J Wintle* 67h
8 b g His Royal Highness(NZ)—Misty Gleam (NZ) (Gleam Machine (USA))
724[P] 1717[8] 4053[U] 4392[U] 4651[0] 4783[10] 5050[4]

Heathers Girl *R Dickin* 64h 46c
7 ch m Superlative—Kristis Girl (Ballacashtal (CAN))
2826[F] 3275[P] 3550[8] 3730[6]

Heathy Gore *J K Cresswell*
7 ch m Environment Friend—Hazel Hill (Abednego)
128[P]

Heavenly Chorus *K G Reveley* 69+b
4 b f Key Of Luck(USA)—Celestial Choir (Celestial Storm (USA))
2830[11] 3563[3] 3931[6] 4304[4]

Heavenly King *Mrs Abbi Vaughan* 80h
8 b g Homo Sapien—Chapel Hill (IRE) (The Parson)
105[9] 5053[U]

Heavenly Leader *D McCain* 78b
5 b g Supreme Leader—Ashniader (IRE) (Buckskin (FR))
4853[11]

Heavenly Pleasure (IRE) *J Hetherton* 31h
7 b m Presenting—Galynn (IRE) (Strong Gale)
4801[7]

Heavenly Stride *P Bowen* 105h 98c
10 b g Karinga Bay—Chapel Hill (IRE) (The Parson)
747[U] 891[0] 1045[P]

Heavy Weather (IRE) *Miss Joanne Priest* 96+h
8 ch g Glacial Storm(USA)—Tinkers Lady (Sheer Grit)
3238[8] 3478[P] 4005[2] 4429[4] 4852[4]

Hedchester *Mrs A Hamilton* 76b
5 b g Missed Flight—Lady Manello (Mandrake Major)
2844[9]

Hedgehunter (IRE) *W P Mullins* 126h 170 c
10 b g Montelimar(USA)—Aberedw (IRE) (Caerwent)
3081a[4] 3895a[2] 4470[2] 4777[2]

Heebie Jeebie *P J Hobbs* 21b
4 bb f Overbury(IRE)—Avec Le Vent (IRE) (Strong Gale)
4976[16]

Heemanela (IRE) *Miss P Robson* 114+h
11 b g Classic Secret(USA)—Ela Man Hee (Ela-Mana-Mou)
247[5]

Hegarty (IRE) *Jonjo O'Neill* 103h
7 gr g Topanoora—Banderole (IRE) (Roselier (FR))
3737[6] 4093[6] 4420[P]

Hehasalife (IRE) *Mrs H Dalton* 101+c
9 b g Safety Catch(USA)—America River (IRE) (Lord Americo)
896[4] 1205[P] 1276[U] (1752) (1901) 2151[P] 4835[P]

Heidi III (FR) *M D Hammond* 122+c
11 b g Bayolidaan(FR)—Irlandaise (FR) (Or De Chine)
62[P] 1664[5] 2293[2] 2965[9] 3917[5] 4144[P] 4356[5] 4636[P]

Heir To Be *Mrs L Wadham* 124+h
7 b g Elmaamul(USA)—Princess Genista (Ile De Bourbon (USA))
1992[4] 2292[5] 3675[2] 3993[P] (4497) 5005[9]

Heisamodel (IRE) *J J Boulter* 11b
8 b g Balla Cove—Liffeyside Lady (IRE) (Cataldi)
50[R] 278[R]

Heisse *Ian Williams* 85h
6 b g Darshaan—Hedera (USA) (Woodman (USA))
457[7] 515[4] 696[13] 1750[2] 2714[7]

Helensburgh (IRE) *P Hughes* 108+h
5 ch h Mark Of Esteem(IRE)—Port Helene (Troy)
4951a[13] 5078a[19]

Helixir Du Theil (FR) *R H Buckler* 107h 108+c
11 ch g Aelan Hapi(USA)—Manolette (FR) (Signani (FR))
2800[F] 3212[P]

Hello Baby *A C Whillans* 88h
6 b g Jumbo Hirt(USA)—Silver Flyer (Silver Season)
152[8] 215[P] 552[4] 1685[2] 2171[12] 2474[U]

Hell Of A Time (IRE) *Mrs N S Evans* 81b
9 b g Phardante(FR)—Ticking Over (IRE) (Decent Fellow)
2461[P]

Hello It's Me *K A Morgan* 65h
5 ch g Deploy—Evening Charm (IRE) (Bering)
4784[9]

Hello Mrs *Mrs S J Smith* 16b
8 b m Sir Harry Lewis(USA)—Five And Four (IRE) (Green Desert (USA))
521[P]

Hello Noddy *B Mactaggart* 61b
4 ch g Double Trigger(IRE)—Setter Country (Town And Country)
2642[10] 5042[6]

Hello Tiger *J A Supple*
5 gr g Terimon—Blue Peru (IRE) (Perugino (USA))
4479[P] 4915[P]

Helm (IRE) *R Rowe* 103+h
5 b g Alhaarth(IRE)—Pipers Pool (IRE) (Mtoto)
1775[2] 2166[7]

Helmac (GER) *C Von Der Recke* 82h
5 br h Macanal(USA)—Helsinki (GER) (Konigsstuhl (GER))
3355[4]

Heltornic (IRE) *M Scudamore* 115 h
6 ch m Zaffaran(USA) —Majestic Run (Deep Run)
1619[F] (2125) 2486[F] (3287) 3388[4] 3621[4] 3802[6]4443[11] 4619[6] 4974[9]

Helvetius *W T Reed* 99h 106c
10 b g In The Wings—Hejraan (USA) (Alydar (USA))
64[9] 2836[5] **(522) 605[4]896[P] 1795[P] 2495[9]2900[7]** (Dead)

Hennessy (IRE) *M Pitman* 118b
5 b g Presenting—Steel Grey Lady (IRE) (Roselier (FR))
(1909) 3327[2] 3742[7] 4779[9]

Henrianjames *K G Reveley* 90+h 113 c
11 b g Tina's Pet—Real Claire (Dreams To Reality (USA))
5092[6]

Henrietta Hall (IRE) *M Halford* 53b
5 b m Saddlers' Hall(IRE) —Nanavits (IRE) (Lord Americo)
5134a[19]

Henry Henbit *Mrs A E Brooks*
11 bb g Henbit(USA) —Turn Mill (Latest Model)
4868[P]

Henry's Happiness *C P Morlock* 74h
7 b m Bob's Return(IRE) —Irish Mint (Dusky Boy)
665[16] 1395[P]

Henry's Luck Penny (IRE) *Mrs H Dalton* 70h
6 br g Muroto—Lady Sallyanna (IRE) (Be My Native (USA))
96[6] 310[2]

Henry's Pride (IRE) *P C Haslam* 85h 123 c
6 ch g Old Vic—Hightown Girl (IRE) (Over The River (FR))
3781[2] 4054[U] 4314[2]4610[3]

Heraclitean Fire (IRE) *J J Lambe* 102h 111c
9 b g Norwich—Mazovia (FR) (Taufan (USA))
320[2] 482[6]

Herakles (GER) *N J Henderson* 123+h
5 b g Lagunas—Haraka (FR) (Kahyasi)
1824[4] 2487[4] 2826[13] 3650[3] (3943) (4821) 5142[4]

Heraldry (IRE) *P C Haslam* 114+h
6 b g Mark Of Esteem(IRE) —Sorb Apple (IRE) (Kris)
(2007) (2507) 4072[2] 4519[4] 4779[11]

Here Comes Harry *C J Down* 81+h 92+c
10 ch g Sunley Builds—Coole Dolly Day (Arctic Lord)
665[2] 3656[P] 4526[4] 4824[P]

Herecomestanley *M F Harris* 94 h 99+c
7 b g Missed Flight—Moonspell (Batshoof)
2374[7] 2528[16] 2816[7] 3147[2] 3386[6](3577) 3733[2] 3901[P] 4396[8] **4802[3]4918[2] 5017[F] 5085[3]**

Hereditary *Mrs L C Jewell* 89h
4 ch g Hernando(FR) —Eversince (USA) (Foolish Pleasure (USA))
3294[8] 3429[6] 3714[8] 4910[6]

Here's Johnny (IRE) *V R A Dartnall* 89+h
7 ch g Presenting—Treble Base (IRE) (Orchestra)
(2049) 3248[9] 4212[3]

Heres The Plan (IRE) *M G Quinlan*
4 b f Revoque(IRE) —Fanciful (IRE) (Mujtahid (USA))
1201[6]

Here We Go (IRE) *G L Moore* 115+h
7 b g Bob Back(USA) —Bold Lyndsey (Be My Native (USA))
1681[13] 3210[9] 3246[2] 3478[4] 3729[5](4824) (4961)

Heriot *S C Burrough* 79h
5 br g Hamas(IRE) —Sure Victory (IRE) (Stalker)
243[9] 357[10] 5022[P]

Heritage Castle *A E Jones* 81+h 9c
7 b g Past Glories—Castle Claire (Carlingford Castle)
57[P] 286[P]

Hermano (IRE) *A M Hales*
9 bb g Malmsey(USA) —Ballyhornan VII (Damsire Unregistered)
654[P] 758[P] 863[P]

Hermano Cordobes (IRE) *Mrs J R Buckley* 83+h
6 b g Un Desperado(FR) —Queens Tricks (Le Bavard (FR))
2968[6] 4905[P]

Hermitage Court (USA) *M J McGrath* 96h
5 ch g Out Of Place(USA) —Russian Act (USA) (Siberian Express (USA))
563[4] 901[P] 1245[4] 1408[5] 1856[P]

Hernando's Boy *K G Reveley* 124+h
5 b g Hernando(FR) —Leave At Dawn (Slip Anchor)
(85) 2334[4] 2519[2] (2716) 4765[P]

Herne Bay (IRE) *R S Brookhouse* 113+h
6 b g Hernando(FR) —Charita (IRE) (Lycius (USA))
665[11] (841) (949) 1111[7] 1270[9] 1300[2] 1743[7]

Heroic (IRE) *C F Swan* 113h 120c
10 b g War Hero—Happy Patter (Pitpan)
91a[P]

Heron Marsh (IRE) *Miss Venetia Williams* 104+b
5 b m Heron Island(IRE) —Make Or Mar (Daring March)
4376[15]

Herons Cove (IRE) *W M Brisbourne* 83b
7 b g Top Of The World—Rathsallagh (Mart Lane)
3145[2] 3496[P] 3731[P] 4733[P]

Heron's Ghyll (IRE) *Miss Venetia Williams* 115h
9 b g Simply Great(FR) —Leisure Centre (IRE) (Tanfirion)
2877[P] 3600[4] 4357[2] 4549[2]4727[P]

Heronstown (IRE) *William Coleman O'Brien* 114h
7 b g Standiford(USA) —Eleckydo (Electric)
5078a[6]

Heros Collonges (FR) *P F Nicholls* 139 c
11 b g Dom Alco(FR) —Carmen Collonges (FR) (Olmeto)
2370[6] 3022[2] 4285[4]**4777[U]**

Hersov (IRE) *D M Christie* 129h 118c
10 gr g Roselier(FR) —Higher Again (IRE) (Strong Gale)
4748[U] 5083a[14]

He's A Leader (IRE) *M C Pipe* 113+h
7 b g Supreme Leader—Raise The Bells (Belfalas)
(2271)

He's A Rascal (IRE) *A J Lidderdale* 91h 45c
8 b g Fumo Di Londra(IRE) —Lovely Ali (IRE) (Dunbeath (USA))
2523[3] 2810[2] 3147[4] 3577[3] 4080[5]

He's A Star *Miss Gay Kelleway* 81h
4 ch g Mark Of Esteem(IRE) —Sahara Belle (USA) (Sanglamore (USA))
2236[4] 2580[5]

He's Hot Right Now (NZ) *R C Guest* 101+h 86c
7 b g Pentire—Philadelphia Fox (NZ) (Dahar (USA))
(149) (412) 482[2] **534[6] 862[7]939[8] 1335[10] 1433[4]1592[5]** 1665[6] 4922[13] **5051[4]**

He's The Biz (FR) *Nick Williams* 93+h 102 c
7 b g Nikos—Irun (FR) (Son Of Silver)
(137) 439[F] 516[P]652[11] **1678[3] 1858[3]2215[5] 2596[3]**

He's The Gaffer (IRE) *R H Buckler* 88h 111 c
6 b g Oscar(IRE) —Miss Henrietta (IRE) (Step Together (USA))
201[9] 1596[6] 1753[4] 1900[2] **2456[7](3126) (3718) 4214[U]4592[P]**

He's The Guv'Nor (IRE) *R H Buckler* 113 h 130 c
7 b g Supreme Leader—Love The Lord (IRE) (Mister Lord (USA))
1830[7] **2005[U]** 2609[2] **2825[2](3142) 3612[3] 3988[2]4498[F]**

Hestherelad (IRE) *R Johnson* 81h
7 b g Definite Article—Unbidden Melody (USA) (Chieftain)
1307[2] 1528[P] 1760[P]

Hever Road (IRE) *M C Pipe* 97h 130+c
7 ch g Anshan—The Little Bag (True Song)
2931[2] 3578[3] 3649[6]3943[P] **4558[3] (4728) (4857)**

Heversham (IRE) *J Hetherton* 92h
5 b g Octagonal(NZ) —Saint Ann (USA) (Geiger Counter (USA))
2658[7] 2763[9] 4056[3] 4346[6] 4632[5]4919[5]

Hey Bob (IRE) *Joseph G Murphy* 59h
5 b g Bob Back(USA) —Blue Stocking (IRE) (Bluebird (USA))
44a[14]

Hey Boy (IRE) *Mrs S J Humphrey* 96h 90c
7 b g Courtship—Make Me An Island (Creative Plan (USA))
465[3] 631[2] 1815[3]2259[P]

Heynewboy *J W Mullins* 85b
6 ch g Keen—Clown Around (True Song)
1600[5]

Hey You M'Lady *J Rudge* 54b
6 b m Sovereign Water(FR) —Sea Countess (Ercolano (USA))
300[9] 5073[P]

Hezaam (USA) *C W Fairhurst*
5 b g Red Ransom(USA) —Ashraakat (USA) (Danzig (USA))
3534[P]

Hialeah *M W Easterby* 81h 78c
5 ch g Bal Harbour—Tommys Dream (Le Bavard (FR))
1532[5] 1611[10] 2923[9] 3314[7] 3943[6]**4655[6] 4840[5]**

Hiawatha (IRE) *A M Hales* 88h
7 b g Danehill(USA) —Hi Bettina (Henbit (USA))
1772[11]

Hibernian (IRE) *O Sherwood* 113+h
6 br g Supreme Leader—Tullahought (Jaazeiro (USA))
2212[2] 2631[3] 3842[3] 4373[6] 4678[5]

Hi Blue *R Dickin* 5h
7 b g Weld—Winnie Lorraine (St Columbus)
685[13] 3685[P] 4088[9] **5049[P]**

Hickleton Club *R M Clark* 40h
8 b g Aragon—Honest Opinion (Free State)
551[P] 942[P]

Hickory Hill (IRE) *J Motherway* 104h
8 b g Standiford(USA) —Laharn Gale (Strong Gale)
43a[P]

Hi Cloy (IRE) *Michael Hourigan* 135h 165+c
9 b g Be My Native(USA) —Thomastown Girl (Tekoah)
2230a[3] (2793a) (3051a) 3472a[4] 4457[6] 4625a[3](4761) 5079a[3]

Hidden Bounty (IRE) *K G Reveley* 130 h 119 c
10 b g Generous(IRE) —Sought Out (IRE) (Rainbow Quest (USA))
1929[6] 2483[3] 2990[2] 3970[5]

Hiddenfortune (IRE) *Miss Lucinda V Russell* 59h
6 bb g Denel(FR) —Hidden Play (IRE) (Seclude (USA))
4147[5] 4342[8] 4787[12]

Hidden Smile (USA) *F Jordan* 79h
9 b m Twilight Agenda(USA) —Smooth Edge (USA) (Meadowlake (USA))
134[11] 822[9] 1156[8] 1375[U] 1483[5]1597[7] 1814[5]

Hidden Storm (IRE) *Mrs S J Humphrey* 68h
7 br m Jamesmead—Hidden Play (IRE) (Seclude (USA))
1611[8] 1854[5] 2181[5] 2378[2] 4043[6]4133[4] 4501[5]

Hidden Talents (IRE) *M F Morris* 116+h
6 b g Arctic Lord—Cherry Avenue (King's Ride)
5103a[23]

Hidden Weapon *L Wells*
9 b g Charmer—Bustellina (Busted)
4689[P] **4913[F]**

Hiers De Brouage (FR) *J G Portman* 112 c
11 b g Neustrien(FR) —Thalandrezienne (FR) (Le Correzien (FR))
1780[8] 2248[6] (2431) 2827[3] 3239[3] 3815[U]4332[F] 5107[5]

Hi Fi *Ian Williams* 91 h 102 c
8 b g Homo Sapien—Baroness Orkzy (Baron Blakeney)
26[4] 413[4] 2149[6]2594[P] 3950[4] 4215[11]

High Altitude (IRE) *A King* 95 h
5 b g Alhaarth(IRE) —Delphini (IRE) (Seattle Dancer (USA))
1895[5] 3175[10] 3548[5] 3729[8]

High Bird Humphrey *Miss V Scott* 82h
7 ch g Nomadic Way(USA) —Miss Kewmill (Billion (USA))
3173

High Calibre (IRE) *Jonjo O'Neill* 98+b
5 b g Definite Article—Pidgeon Bay (IRE) (Perugino (USA))
4680[2]

High Charter *J R Fanshawe* 77h
5 b g Polish Precedent(USA) —By Charter (Shirley Heights)
2082[P] 2826[9]

High Class Pet *F P Murtagh* 86 h
6 b m Petong—What A Pet (Mummy's Pet)
302[6] 715[5] 785[P]

High Cotton (IRE) *K G Reveley* 120c
11 gr g Ala Hounak—Planalife (Beau Charmeur (FR))
2689[3] 3315[2] 3560[3]4111[2] 4460[10] 5144[P]

High Country (IRE) *M D Hammond* 93+h
6 b g Danehill(USA) —Dance Date (IRE) (Sadler's Wells (USA))
(1374) 1591[3] 2517[P]

High Day *Ferdy Murphy* 123h
6 b g Monsun(GER) —All Time Great (Night Shift (USA))
(2024) (2179) 2335[4] 2991[5] 3761[4] 4473[11] 5078a[P] (Dead)

High Delight *W Amos* 25b
6 b g Dancing High—Dunrowan (Dunbeath (USA))
424[14]

High Drama *P Bowen* 106 h 105+c
9 bb g In The Wings—Maestrale (Top Ville)
632[2] 871[2] **981[4]**1153[P] (Dead)

High Dyke *K A Ryan* 85h
4 b g Mujahid(USA) —Gold Linnet (Nashwan (USA))
4789[8] 4987[F]

High Expectations (IRE) *J S Haldane* 87c
11 ch g Over The River(FR) —Andy's Fancy (IRE) (Andretti)
63[4] 322[6] 4044[P]4305[7] 4722[3] 4791[2]5040[5]

High Five *S G Waugh* 39h 76+c
6 ch g Dancing High—Political Diamond (Politico (USA))
3319[8] 3914[4] **4583[6]**

High Gear (IRE) *Jonjo O'Neill* 103h 110+c
8 br g Accordion—Holly Grove Lass (Le Moss)
998[U] 1086[U] 1191[3](1276) (1367) **1484[F]** 1630[2]

High Hope (FR) *G L Moore* 109+h
8 ch g Lomitas—Highness Lady (GER) (Cagliostro (GER))
(4823)

Highland Brief *Mrs A Duffield* 74b
6 ch g Endoli(USA) —Highland Miss (Highlands)
2844[10] **3553[P]**

Highland Brig *T Butt* 87c
10 b g Homo Sapien—Birniebrig (New Brig)
123[P] 322[P] 3850[4]4144[P] 4722[4] 4791[4](5040)

Highland Chief (IRE) *Miss H C Knight* 90h
6 bb g Taipan(IRE) —Catatonia (IRE) (Cataldi)
7[4] 1847[5] 2301[5] 3246[6] **4163[U]**

Highland Games (IRE) *P R Webber* 45h
6 b g Singspiel(IRE) —Highland Gift (IRE) (Generous (IRE))
3354[9] 3646[P] 4604[14]

Highland Rose (IRE) *Ms A E Embiricos* 95dh 51c
10 b m Roselier(FR) —Carrick Grinder (Sheer Grit)
280[7]

High Life *A King* 74b
4 br f Kayf Tara—By Line (High Line)
4902[4]

Highlight Girl *A W Carroll* 57h
5 ch m Forzando—Norska (Northfields (USA))
1156[16]

High Minster (IRE) *S C Burrough* 31b
4 b g Moscow Society(USA) —Kilballyowen (IRE) (Supreme Leader)
4623[11] 4947[9]

High Moor *J D Bethell* 70b
4 b g Vitus—Pyewacket (Belfort (FR))
4319[3] 4854[14] 5042[4]

High Peak *J W Mullins* 89 h 86c
9 b g Alflora(IRE) —High Heels (IRE) (Supreme Leader)
106[P] 358[3] 631[3]759[4] 902[3] (1178) 1412[4] 1479[2]

High Point (IRE) *G P Enright* 51h
8 b g Ela-Mana-Mou—Top Lady (IRE) (Shirley Heights)
3906[9]

High Priestess (IRE) *M J P O'Brien* 117h
7 b m Priolo(USA) —Boss Lady (IRE) (Last Tycoon)
2031a[2] 2667a[5] 2916a[2]

High Rank *J Mackie* 108+h 101+c
7 b g Emperor Jones(USA) —Hotel Street (USA) (Alleged (USA))
10[6] 239[3]

High Reef (FR) *C F Swan* 111h
8 b m Shareef Dancer(USA) —Debate (High Line)
2916a[6] 3411a[25] 3894a[P]

Highway Oak *Ben White* 115+c
10 b g Sula Bula—Highway Light (Lighter)
(4757) 5116[3]

High Window (IRE) *S Gollings* 17h
6 b g King's Theatre(IRE) —Kayradja (IRE) (Last Tycoon)
192[P] 696[12]

Highworth Lady *H J Manners*
6 b m Petrizzo—Westerlands Queen (Afzal)
1755[7]

Hiho Silver Lining *H Morrison* 73h
5 gr m Silver Patriarch(IRE) —By Line (High Line)
2727[7] 4376[4] 4801[5] 5052[8]

Hi Humpfree *Mrs H Dalton* 95+h
6 b g Thowra(FR) —White Flash (Sure Blade (USA))
1968[7] 2295[8] 2755[7] 2934[P] 3345[F]3487[9]

Hilarious (IRE) *Dr J R J Naylor* 90h
6 b m Petorius—Heronwater (IRE) (Ela-Mana-Mou)
185[8] 1974[4] 2244[7] (2934) 3211[3] 3439[6]3951[4] 4331[5] 4756[P]

Hi Laurie (IRE) *M Scudamore* 101+h 100+c
11 gr m Roselier(FR) —Oh June (Le Bavard (FR))
1645[6] 1753[5] **(1905) 2019[F]**2181[2] 2466[2] 2932[2] (3217) 3439[2]

Hillary Harbour (IRE) *J G Cosgrave* 45h
7 ch m Roselier(FR) —Last Wager (IRE) (Strong Gale)
2441[F] 3795[11]

Hillcrest (NZ) *Ian Williams* 101 h
7 b g Danasinga(AUS) —Centafair (NZ) (Centaine (AUS))
133[6] 696[2] 838[3]

Hill Forts Henry *J W Mullins* 79+h 60 c
8 ch g Karinga Bay—Maggie Tee (Lepanto (GER))
202[6] 1414[P] 1564[9]1637[5] **1951[2] 2237[R]**2378[4] **2801[4] 2986[U]3427[R]** 4331[4] 4526[2] (4734) 5048[7]

Hill Forts Timmy *J W Mullins* 110 h
6 b g Thowra(FR) —Queen Of The Suir (IRE) (Carlingford Castle)
235[5] (463) (685) 2127[P] 2374[6] 3131[4] 3505[2]3694[2] 5045[4]

Hills Of View *J M Jefferson* 60h
8 b g Sea Raven(IRE) —Hardwick Sun (Dieu Soleil)
213[P]

Hilltime (IRE) *J J Quinn* 119h
6 b g Danetime(IRE) —Ceannanas (IRE) (Magical Wonder (USA))
(370) 726[3] 1010[2]

Himalayan Trail *Mrs S J Smith* 103h
7 b g Nomadic Way(USA) —Hindu Lady (Doon Lad)
4988[7]

Hip Pocket (IRE) *Robert Bowling* 77+c
10 b g Ela-Mana-Mou—Ebony And Ivory (IRE) (Bob Back (USA))
221[9] 498[6] 5013[5]

Hirapour (IRE) *Doug Fout* 135+h
10 b g Kahyasi—Himaya (IRE) (Mouktar)
(1394a)

Hi Rudolf *H J Manners* 76h 93c
11 b g Ballet Royal(USA) —Hi Darlin' (Prince De Galles)
103[P] 684[6] 744[5]

Hirvine (FR) *P Bowen* 139 h 126 c
8 ch g Snurge—Guadanella (FR) (Guadanini (FR))
2747[P] 3389[12]

Hisar (IRE) *P C Ritchens* 78c
13 br g Doyoun—Himaya (IRE) (Mouktar)
181[P] 503[10]

His Nibs (IRE) *Miss Venetia Williams* 137 h
9 b g Alflora(IRE) —Mrs Jennifer (River Knight (FR))
2999[9] 3389[2]

Historg (FR) *Ferdy Murphy* 82c
11 b g Cyborg(FR) —Kalliste (FR) (Calicot (FR))
2164[9] 2993[P] 3315[P] (Dead)

Historic Place (USA) *J A Geake* 107h
6 b g Dynaformer(USA) —Captive Island (Northfields (USA))
3238[5] 3664[8] 4604[2]

Hi Tech Man (IRE) *D E Cantillon* 97h
8 ch g Presenting—Cherry Mist (IRE) (Aristocracy)
281[P] 763[2] 861[3] **998[P]**

Hobbs Hill *C R Egerton* 100+h
7 b g Alflora(IRE) —Rim Of Pearl (Rymer)
3238[2]

Hobbycyr (FR) *J A T De Giles* 94c
11 b g Saint Cyrien(FR) —Sauteuse De Retz (FR) (Funny Hobby)
3434[3] 3909[6]

Hockenheim (FR) *J Howard Johnson* 110+h
5 b g Kadalko(FR) —L'Inka (FR) (Rb Chesne)
1915[2] 2169[6] 3291[P]

Hoh Nelson *Mrs A Price* 96h
5 b g Halling(USA) —Birsay (Bustino)
1751[P] 3889[7] 4282[4]

Ho Ho Hill (IRE) *Miss Lucinda V Russell* 88h 110+c
8 b g Beneficial—Bale Out (Shackleton)
202[2] (271) 690[10]

Hoh Viss *C J Mann* 132 h
6 b g Rudimentary(USA) —Now And Forever (IRE) (Kris)
(2082) 2527[F] 2878[2] (3139) (3622) 3986[5]

Holding The Fort (IRE) *I Anderson* 37h 61c
12 b g Moscow Society(USA) —Lady Of Desmond (Menelek)
313[6]

Hold On Harry *Miss C J Williams* 96+c
10 ch g Endoli(USA) —Hold On Tight (Battlement)
(244) 4806[P] 5071[7]

Hold That Thought (IRE) *Miss H C Knight* 77+h
6 ch g Zaffaran(USA) —Tarasandy (IRE) (Arapahos (FR))
2565[7] 3001[14] 4732[P]

Hold The Bid (IRE) *Mrs S J Smith* 103h
6 bb g Luso—Killesk Castle (IRE) (Little Bighorn)
3975[5] 4386[U] 4787[F]

Holey Moley (IRE) *R T J Wilson* 102c
9 b g Religiously(USA) —Hillmount (Abednego)
4144[3] 4460[8]

Hollandia (IRE) *Miss H C Knight* 67h
5 gr g Needle Gun(IRE) —Steel Mariner (Kambalda)
3462[4] 3789[12] 4819[14]

Holland Park (IRE) *Mrs S D Williams* 145+h
9 gr g Roselier(FR) —Bluebell Avenue (Boreen Beag)
207[9] 2175[P]

Hollow Flight (IRE) *Mrs L B Normile* 41h 67c
8 b g Hollow Hand—Gers Pet (IRE) (Baragoi)
1835[F] 2063[P] 3209[P]

Hollows Mill *F P Murtagh* 97 h 112+c
10 b g Rudimentary(USA) —Strawberry Song (Final Straw)
84[P] 1836[6] **2067[3]2443[7] 2946[P] 3798[5](4318) 4489[4] 4842[6]**

Hollows Mist *F P Murtagh* 94h 85c
8 b g Missed Flight—Joyfulness (FR) (Cure The Blues (USA))
4840[6] 5140[P]

Holly Park *C N Kellett*
8 b m Syrtos—Mapleline (Shy Groom (USA))
236[P]

Holly Walk *A G Juckes* 84h
5 ch m Dr Fong(USA) —Holly Blue (Bluebird (USA))
1158[8] 1235[8] 1742[6] 2283[7] 3125[4]

Hollywood *V R A Dartnall* 88h
5 b m Bin Ajwaad(IRE) —Raaha (Polar Falcon (USA))
(3692) 4836[3]

Hollywood Critic (USA) *P Monteith* 99h
5 b g Theatrical—Lyphard's Starlite (USA) (Lyphard (USA))
82[F] 1661[2] 2447[3] 3206[4] 3853[6]

Hollywood Henry (IRE) *Mrs A M Thorpe* 55h
6 b g Bahhare(USA) —Takeshi (IRE) (Cadeaux Genereux)
4826[9] 5086[P] (Dead)

Holme Lane (IRE) *A D Brown*
5 b g Taos(IRE) —Orwell Annie (Risk Me (FR))
131[13] 375[15]

Holmwood Jack (IRE) *Miss C J Williams*
5 b g Aboo Hom—Looe (IRE) (Sexton Blake)
748[P]

Holmwood Legend *Miss C J Williams* 45b
5 b g Midnight Legend—West-Hatch-Spirit (Forzando)
1274[9] 1386[6]

Holy Joe (FR) *Miss Venetia Williams* 131 c
9 b g Pharly(FR) —Niffy Nora (Mandalus)
2532[P] 3176[5] 3296[P]4617[6] 4728[2] 4822[6]

Holy Orders (IRE) *W P Mullins* 138h
9 b g Unblest—Shadowglow (Shaadi (USA))
2227a[7] 3080a[5] 3585a[4] 4019a[3] 4458[P] (Dead)

Hombre *M D Hammond* 95c
11 ch g Shernazar—Delray Jet (USA) (Northjet)
81[6] 213[9]

Homebred Buddy *P Bowen* 38h
7 ch g Environment Friend—Royal Brush (King Of Spain)
1297[12] 1541[P]

Home James (IRE) *A King* 120 h 131c
9 b g Commanche Run—Take Me Home (Amoristic (USA))
2532[P]

Homeleigh Mooncoin *B G Powell* 82+h
11 ch g Jamesmead—Super Sol (Rolfe (USA))
110[2] 397[7] 508[R] 841[P]

Homeleigh Sun *N J Gifford* 47b
7 b m Minster Son—Riverain (Bustino)
2021[8]

Homelife (IRE) *Mrs J A Saunders* 84h
8 b g Persian Bold—Share The Vision (Vision (USA))
2249[15] 3577[10] 4898[F]

Home Made *Miss H Brookshaw* 58b 92c
8 b g Homo Sapien—Inch Maid (Le Moss)
348[3]

Homer (IRE) *N M Babbage* 69h
9 b g Sadler's Wells(USA) —Gravieres (FR) (Saint Estephe (FR))
4080[7] 4320[P] 4752[14]

Home Rule *G P Enright* 29b
6 b m Wizard King—Pastures Green (Monksfield)
1237[14]

Homer Wells (IRE) *W P Mullins* 143h 124c
8 b g Arctic Cider(USA) —Run And Shine (Deep Run)
90a[4] 585a[10] **3079a[2] 3514a[3]4022a[3]**

Honan (IRE) *M C Pipe* 99+h 110 c
7 b g College Chapel—Medical Times (IRE) (Auction Ring (USA))
173[2] **(388) (666) 752[5]1012[8]** 1188[8] **1273[P]**1384[4] 1432[6] (1483) 1645[3] 1742[2] (1890) 2585[3](3661) 3944[8] 4726[7]

Honest Abe (IRE) *B N Pollock* 83h
5 b g Houmayoun(FR) —Blasgan (IRE) (Yashgan)
3789[8] 4387[3] 4934[8]

Honest Endeavour *J M Jefferson* 101h 99 c
7 b g Alflora(IRE) —Isabeau (Law Society (USA))
13[P] **1568[P]** 1793[3] 1987[10](2525) 3256[12] **3558[5] 3964[4]**

Honest Injun *A G Juckes* 69 h
5 b h Efisio—Sioux (Kris)
1302[6] 4278[F]

Honest Yer Honour (IRE) *Mrs C J Robinson* 124 h 105+c
10 b g Witness Box(USA) —Castle Duchess (Abednego)
79[P] (333)

Honey Nut *Miss Z C Davison* 58b
4 ch f Entrepreneur—Nocciola (Cadeaux Genereux)
5089[6]

Honey's Gift *G G Margarson* 107h
7 b m Terimon—Honeycroft (Crofter (USA))
1816[9] 1957[4] 2218[7] 2685[7] 2868[3]3146[4] 3439[4] 3655[4] 3959[2] 4396[4]4453[5] 4899[3]

Honneur Fontenail (FR) *N J Hawke* 57b 80c
7 ch g Tel Quel(FR) —Fontanalia (FR) (Rex Magna (FR))
206[8] **503[3] 567[P](1041) 1191[P] 1219[5]1414[P]** 1539[12] **1652[3]**

Honor And Glory *Nick Williams* 57c
6 br g Past Glories—Scalby Anna (Sir Mago)
1618[5] 1971[7] 2213[P]4571[4]

Honorary Citizen *Evan Williams* 55h
4 b g Montjoy(USA) —Heart So Blue (Dilum (USA))
3947[10] 4106[8] 4784[11]

Honourable Collins (IRE) *Mrs Tracey Barfoot-Saunt* 27h
6 br g Glacial Storm(USA) —Club Caribbean (Strong Gale)
1206[P] 1266[P] 1454[9]

Honours English (IRE) *J J Lambe* 16h
6 b h Sadler's Wells(USA) —Modiyna (Nishapour (FR))
645[9]

Hoober *J Gallagher* 28b
5 b g Mind Games—Chlo-Jo (Belmez (USA))
2987[11] 3583[9]

Hooky's Quest *Mrs H O Graham* 44b
4 br f Environment Friend—Hooky's Treat (Dutch Treat)
3556[7] 4530[P]

Hoo La Baloo (FR) *P F Nicholls* 148+c
5 b g Unfuwain(USA) —Via Saleria (IRE) (Arazi (USA))
(1758) 2634[2] (2970) 3724[5] 3991[2] (4377) 4774[4] 5143[4]

Hopbine *J L Spearing* 104+h
10 ch m Gildoran—Haraka Sasa (Town And Country)
3297 689[2] 1760[P] 3648[6]

Hope Hill *M Salaman*
5 b m Karinga Bay—Chapel Hill (IRE) (The Parson)
3024[9]

Hope Sound (IRE) *B Ellison* 100 h 100 c
6 b g Turtle Island(IRE) —Lucky Pick (Auction Ring (USA))
482[5]

Hop Fair *J L Spearing* 87+h
7 ch m Gildoran—Haraka Sasa (Town And Country)
4032[11] 4934[5]

Hopkins (IRE) *H D Daly* 95b
5 ch g Topanoora—Derryclare (Pollerton)
3583[3] 4500[5]

Horcott Bay *M G Rimell* 76h 104c
6 b m Thowra(FR) —Armagnac Messenger (Pony Express)
2574[F] 2846[2] 3689[P]4095[P] 4279[3]

Hordago (IRE) *E McNamara* 129h 95c
6 gr g Highest Honor(FR) —Mirmande (Kris)
43a[18] (2207) 4461[2] 4776[P]

Horizon Hill (USA) *T W Boon* 84h 78+c
6 b g Distant View(USA) —Accadia Rocket (CAN) (Bold Ruckus (USA))
299[3] 5116[7]

Hornbill *Mrs K Lawther* 62h
8 b g Sir Harry Lewis(USA) —Tangara (Town Crier)
5053[P]

Hors La Loi (FR) *Ian Williams* 119h 129+c
10 ch g Exit To Nowhere(USA) —Kernia (IRE) (Raise A Cup (USA))
634[8] 946[9]

Hors La Loi III (FR) *P F Nicholls* 118h 146c
11 b g Cyborg(FR) —Quintessence III (FR) (El Condor (FR))
(2732) 3341[3] 3695[2]4241[9] 4456[6]

Horus (IRE) *M C Pipe* 141c
11 b g Teenoso(USA) —Jennie's First (Idiots Delight)
2628[6] 3296[P] 3620[P]3995[3] (4241) 4984[P]

Hot Air (IRE) *J I A Charlton* 39h 78c
8 b g Air Display(USA) —Lyraisa (Tumble Wind)
210[12] 1834[13] **2839[6] 3352[6]3760[5]**

Hotel Hilamar (IRE) *Noel Meade* 100b
5 b g Flemensfirth(USA) —Gypsy Lass (King's Ride)
5104a[4]

Hot Girl *S P Griffiths* 3h
8 b m State Diplomacy(USA) —Hundred Islands (Hotfoot)
8[12]

Hot Lips Page (FR) *Ian Williams* 86+h 57c
5 b m Hamas(IRE) —Salt Peanuts (IRE) (Salt Dome (USA))
1850[6] **2284[6]**

Hot 'N' Holy *P F Nicholls* 110+h
7 b g Supreme Leader—Clonmello (Le Bavard (FR))
2565[2] (3024) 3466[4] (4642) 4961[4]

Hot Plunge *Mrs J P Lomax* 71h 107c
8 b g Bustino—Royal Seal (Privy Seal)
52[5] 278[4] 4375[4]4216[P] 4349[4] 4555[8]4730[RR]

Hot Produxion (USA) *J Mackie* 108h 99c
7 ch g Tabasco Cat(USA) —Princess Harriet (USA) (Mt. Livermore (USA))
106[3] 416[P]

Hot Rod (IRE) *Jonjo O'Neill* 112h
6 b g Overbury(IRE) —Belle Rose (IRE) (Roselier (FR))
4280[P] 4581[P]

Hot Shots (FR) *M Pitman* 112c
11 b g Passing Sale(FR) —Uguette IV (FR) (Chamberlin (FR))
1970[8] 2346[P] 3357[10]

Hot Toddy (IRE) *G L Landau* 86+c
11 b g Glacial Storm(USA) —Technical Merit (Gala Performance)
(402)

Hot Weld *Ferdy Murphy* 119 h 133+c
7 b g Weld—Deb's Ball (Glenstal (USA))
(317) **1817[5] 2441[3] 2812[6](3760) (4460) 5129a[2]**

Hot Zone (IRE) *Jonjo O'Neill* 88b
4 b g Bob Back(USA) —Trixskin (IRE) (Buckskin (FR))
3799[6] 4422[5] 4807[4]

Houlihans Free (IRE) *P F Nicholls* 81+h 94+c
7 b g Gothland(FR) —Yawa Prince (IRE) (Yawa)
(817) 866[3] 1037[8] 4048[4] **4943[3]5044[P]**

House Martin *C R Dore*
4 bb f Spectrum(IRE) —Guignol (IRE) (Anita's Prince)
4795[8]

House Warmer (IRE) *A Ennis*
7 ch g Carroll House—Under The Duvet (IRE) (Brush Aside (USA))
1656[3] 1960[P] 2424[9]3672[6]

Howaboys Quest (USA) *Ferdy Murphy* 91h 77c
9 b g Quest For Fame—Doctor Black (USA) (Family Doctor (USA))
110[3] 2831[0] 781[3] **896[P]**

Howards Dream (IRE) *D A Nolan* 84h
8 b g King's Theatre(IRE) —Keiko (Generous (IRE))
645[3] 780[7] 936[6] 2064[7] 3267[P]

How Art Thou (IRE) *S Donohoe* 105h
5 b g Russian Revival(USA) —Bounty (IRE) (Cataldi)
(2475)

Howaya Pet (IRE) *Gerard Keane* 120h 131c
10 br m Montelimar(USA) —Sarahs Music (IRE) (Orchestra)
1515a[4] 3587a[P] (5129a)

How Is The Lord (IRE) *C J Down* 78h
10 b g Lord Americo—Joaney How (Crash Course)
3388[P] 3881[8] 4033[6] 4290[3] 4557[3]4860[11]

Howle Hill (IRE) *A King* 143h 97+c
6 b g Ali-Royal(IRE) —Grandeur And Grace (USA) (Septieme Ciel (USA))
1828[2] 2209[5] 3177[5] 4473[16] 4959[4]

Howrwenow (IRE) *Miss H C Knight* 116h 119 c
8 b g Commanche Run—Maythefifth (Hard Boy)
1829[P] 2375[2] 2812[2]

Howsham Lad *G P Kelly* 70b
7 b g Perpendicular—Sherwood Hope (Eborneezer)
2295[P] 2690[P] 3253[P]

Huckster (ZIM) *Miss Venetia Williams* 112 h
7 b g Tilden—Cavallina (SAF) (Best By Test (USA))
2455[9] (2763) 4093[5] 4606[7] 4961[P]

Hue *B Ellison* 101 h
5 ch g Peintre Celebre(USA) —Quandary (USA) (Blushing Groom (FR))
3351[13] 3534[4] 4478[3]

Hue And Cry *N J Henderson* 91+b
5 br g Monsun(GER) —So Rarely (USA) (Arctic Tern (USA))
2565[6] 2988[11] 4807[8]

Hugo De Grez (FR) *A Parker* 96 h 121c
11 b g Useful(FR) —Piqua Des Gres (FR) (Waylay)
1941[P] 2451[5] 3207[5]3917[P] 4144[P] 4845[P]

Hugo De Perro (FR) *Miss Lucinda V Russell* 131h
11 b g Perrault—Fontaine Aux Faons (FR) (Nadjar (FR))
121[3] 425[3] 766[8] 1606[8] 1887[5]

Hugo The Boss (IRE) *S T Lewis*
4 ch g Trans Island—Heartland (Northfields (USA))
4733[P] 3[P]

Hugs Destiny (IRE) *M A Barnes* 85h
5 b g Victory Note(USA) —Embracing (Reference Point)
1340[6] 1415[3] 1538[3] 1940 [B] 2478[7]2693[U] 2750[14]

Huka Lodge (IRE) *Mrs K Walton* 125 h 121c
9 gr g Roselier(FR) —Derrella (Derrylin)
1929[U] 2265[R] (3289) 3741[6] **4345[P]4790[P]**

Hum (IRE) *Miss D A McHale* 29h
5 ch m Cadeaux Genereux—Ensorceleuse (FR) (Fabulous Dancer (USA))
3[11]

Humdinger (IRE) *John A Harris* 36h
6 b m Charnwood Forest(IRE) —High Finish (High Line)
1340[9]

Hume Castle (IRE) *Mrs John Harrington* 104h 132c
10 b g Religiously(USA) —Clyde Avenue (Peacock (FR))
91a[P] 1083a[P]

Hume Theatre (IRE) *Mrs John Harrington* 96h
7 b g Old Vic—Carrig Conn (IRE) (Torus)
1116a[12]

Humid Climate *M Sheppard* 100h 94c
6 ch g Desert King(IRE) —Pontoon (Zafonic (USA))
192[6] **344[3] 604[2]2722[3] 2839[5] 2980[7]3562[5] 4281[RR]** 4591[8]

Humming *Miss M E Rowland* 85+h
9 b g Bluebird(USA) —Risanda (Kris)
152[P] 469[P]

Huncheon Paddy (IRE) *I R Ferguson* 107c
9 b g Bob's Return(IRE) —Waterland Lady (Strong Gale)
4345[4]

Hunipot *M E Sowersby*
4 ch f Aragon—Acinom (Rambo Dancer (CAN))
1011[P] 2569[P]

Hunter Pudding *C L Popham* 66h
6 b m Shambo—Pudding (Infantry)
384[5] 758[F] 961[5] 2283[6] 2523[7]2845[P] 3125[10]

Hunters Ridge (IRE) *O Sherwood* 79b
5 b g Saddlers' Hall(IRE) —Dandy Poll (Pollerton)
2961[9]

Hunters Tweed *P Beaumont* 134h 141c
10 ch g Nashwan(USA) —Zorette (USA) (Zilzal (USA))
64[3]

Hunting Lodge (IRE) *H J Manners* 99h
5 ch g Grand Lodge(USA) —Vijaya (USA) (Lear Fan (USA))
1908[11] 2216[P] 2423[P] 2584[8] 2721[2]2850[5] 3185[6] 3464[5] 3889[5] 4050[4]4322[4] 4566[9] 5022[4]

Hunting Yuppie (IRE) *N A Twiston-Davies* 123+c
9 ch g Treasure Hunter—Super Yuppie (Belfalas)
4166[F]

Huron (FR) *H D Daly* 78b
5 b g Nononito(FR) —L'Indienne (FR) (Le Nain Jaune (FR))
2507[8] 3145[6] 3478[P]

Hurricane Alley (IRE) *G M Lyons* 108h
5 b g Ali-Royal(IRE) —Trumped (IRE) (Last Tycoon)
65a[5]

Hurricane Coast *K McAuliffe* 79h
7 b g Hurricane Sky(AUS) —Tread Carefully (Sharpo)
2627[15] 4569[12]

Hurricane Francis *T D Walford* 24h
6 ch g Minster Son—Joe's Fancy (Apollo Eight)
355[3] 616[7] 4301[11] 4530[P] 8[9]

Hurry Bob (IRE) *Thomas Mullins* 116h 104c
11 b g Bob Back(USA) —Dundovail (Dunphy)
1691a[6]

Hush Tiger *R Nixon* 91+h
5 br g Moshaajir(USA) —Just Hush (Kind Of Hush)
3319[3] 3374[6] 4114[F] 4342[3] 5091[5]

Husky (POL) *B G Powell* 88h 76+c
8 b g Special Power—Hallo Bambina (POL) (Neman (POL))
510[5] 692[F] 979[P] (Dead)

Hussard Collonges (FR) *P Beaumont* 122h 114c
11 b g Video Rock(FR) —Ariane Collonges (FR) (Quart De Vin (FR))
62[6] 3258[P] 3851[7]

Hutch *Mrs L B Normile* 103h
8 b g Rock Hopper—Polly's Teahouse (Shack (USA))
571[17] 4852[P] 5096[12]

Huw The News *S C Burrough* 81 h 4c
7 b g Primo Dominie—Martha Stevens (USA) (Super Concorde (USA))
2610[U] 3129[P] 3482[7]3602[P] 3945[8] 4013[P]

Huxley (IRE) *M G Quinlan* 88h
7 b g Danehill Dancer(IRE) —Biddy Mulligan (Ballad Rock)
1331[4] 601[9]

Hylia *Mrs P Robeson* 89+h
7 ch m Sir Harry Lewis(USA) —Lady Stock (Crofter (USA))
245[4] 566[4] 697[7] 1525[8] 1856[15]

Hypark (IRE) *C Roberts* 64b
7 br m Oscar(IRE) —La Ronde (Common Grounds)
1042[10] 1237[9] 1386[4]

Iambe De La See (FR) *Mrs P Grainger* 106h 101+c
10 b m Useful(FR) —Reine Mati (SWI) (Matahawk)
284[P] **4831[P]**

Iberus (GER) *S Gollings* 113 h
8 b g Monsun(GER) —Iberica (GER) (Green Dancer (USA))
1610[3] 1987[8] 3967[8] 4354[4] 4566[7]

Icare D'Oudairies (FR) *A L Forbes* 108h 102c
10 ch g Port Etienne(FR) —Vellea (FR) (Cap Martin (FR))
2466[P] **4610[2] 4719[6]5105[P]**

Icarro (FR) *J-P Gallorini* 114h
5 br g Mansonnien(FR) —Trop Tard (FR) (Fabulous Dancer (USA))
778a[6]

Ice And Fire *J T Stimpson* 95 h 73c
7 b g Cadeaux Genereux—Tanz (IRE) (Sadler's Wells (USA))
696[7] 811[5] **914[6] 979[P]**1415[P] 1490[12]

Iceberg (IRE) *Ian Williams* 101+h 111+c
10 b g Glacial Storm(USA) —Laura Daisy (Buckskin (FR))
(1741)

Ice Bucket (IRE) *Miss H C Knight* 91h
6 ch g Glacial Storm(USA) —Tranbu (IRE) (Buckskin (FR))
1311[2] 2142[6] 2528[4] 2799[5]

Ice Cream (FR) *M E D Francis* 85h
5 ch m Cyborg(FR) —Icone (FR) (Nikos)
277[2] 490[10] 2528[14]

Ice Crystal *W K Goldsworthy* 115h 110c
9 b g Slip Anchor—Crystal Fountain (Great Nephew)
441[8] 652[12]

Ice Melted (IRE) *Jonjo O'Neill* 94h
5 ch g Old Vic—Warren Thyne (IRE) (Good Thyne (USA))
3617[8] 4094[4] 4327[4]

Ice Rain (IRE) *Evan Williams* 68h
6 gr g Zaffaran(USA) —Turbet Lass (IRE) (Carlingford Castle)
860[7] 1063[13]

Ice Tea (IRE) *M G Rimell* 113+b
6 ch g Glacial Storm(USA) —Kakemona (Kambalda)
(2579) 3188[2]

Ichi Beau (IRE) *A J Martin* 113h 133c
12 b g Convinced—May As Well (Kemal (FR))
1320[P]

Ichi Cavalo (IRE) *Ian Cobb* 77h 87c
9 b g Leading Counsel(USA) —Black Avenue (IRE) (Strong Gale)
112a[16] 3910[8]

Icomb (IRE) *Mrs Susan Nock* 33h
6 ch g Zaffaran(USA) —Alavie (FR) (Quart De Vin (FR))
2829[15] 4212[P]

Icy Belle (IRE) *W J Burke* 80b 109c
9 bb m Glacial Storm(USA) —Chancy Belle (Le Bavard (FR))
1901[3]

Icy Prospect (IRE) *N A Twiston-Davies* 89h 119 c
8 ch g Glacial Storm(USA) —Prospect Lady (IRE) (Boreen (FR))
(1620) 2102[P] 2938[P]

Icy River (IRE) *K G Reveley* 95+h
9 ch g Over The River(FR) —Icy Lou (Blue Rullah)
3798[P] 3915[P] 4300[P]5137[11]

Idaho D'Ox (FR) *M C Pipe* 121h 130c
10 bb g Bad Conduct(USA) —Queseda (FR) (Quart De Vin (FR))
315[2] 3880[6] 3970[13]

Idbury (IRE) *V J Hughes* 89h 10c
8 b g Zaffaran(USA) —Delcarrow (Roi Guillaume (FR))
3478[P] 3881[7] 4033[3] 4561[P] **4937[P]5107[7]**

Ideal Du Bois Beury (FR) *P Monteith* 89h 82c
10 bb g Useful(FR) —Pampa Star (FR) (Pampabird)
939[7] 1098[7] 1203[5]1359[3] 1602[3] 1686[3]1837[5] 2026[2] 2476[5]2655[2] 2905[3] 3270[U]3320[4] 3486[3] 3916[5]**4142[3] 4587[5] 4721[3]**5068[13]

Ideal Jack (FR) *G A Ham*
10 b g Agent Bleu(FR) —Nuit Des Fanges (FR) (Trac)
202[3] 2296[11] **2996[P]3465[P] 3647[P]**

Idealko (FR) *Dr P Pritchard* 100h 109+c
10 b g Kadalko(FR) —Belfaster (FR) (Royal Charter (FR))
111[10] **(346) 518[4] 761[8]946[8] 1157[4] 1267[5]1484[5] 5107[3]**

Idian Mix (FR) *M C Pipe* 107h
5 b g Indian River(FR) —Nashamix (FR) (Linamix (FR))
2850[8] 3214[6] 3950[10] 4289[P] 4561[2]

Idiome (FR) *Mrs L C Taylor* 121h 115c
10 b g Djarvis(FR) —Asterie L'Ermitage (FR) (Hamster (FR))
2850[3] 3135[6] 3675[3] 4119[7] **4419[6]**

Idle Journey (IRE) *M Scudamore* 99 h
5 b g Mujadil(USA) —Camassina (IRE) (Taufan (USA))
911[7] 971[3] 1607[7] (1902) 1987[11]

Idle Talk (IRE) *T R George* 130 h 149c
7 br g Hubbly Bubbly(USA) —Belon Breeze (IRE) (Strong Gale)
(1976) (3213) 3976[3]4444[2] 5004[4]

Idlewild (IRE) *C T Pogson* 65 h 87 c
11 br g Phardante(FR) —Delia Murphy (Golden Love)
11[2] 129[5] 467[6] 697[5] (839) 1040[8]1180[5] 1280[9] 1607[P] **1819[R]**2862[P] 3141[7] (Dead)

Idolaire (FR) *P Rago*
3 b g Epistolaire(FR) —Sharon Doll (IRE) (Shahrastani (USA))
4298a[P]

Idole First (IRE) *Miss Venetia Williams* 145 h 134 c
7 b g Flemensfirth(USA) —Sharon Doll (IRE) (Shahrastani (USA))
3251[6] (3903) 4076[4]4456[11] 4729[6]

Idris (GER) *G L Moore* 121h
5 ch g Generous(IRE) —Idraak (Kris)
1916[2] 2238[6] 2455[3] (3369) 3505[3] 3717[2]4088[2] 4521[3]

I D Technology (IRE) *G L Moore* 109+h 90c
10 ch g Commanche Run—Lady Geeno (IRE) (Cheval)
2044[10] 2239[7] 2574[4]3282[4]

Iffy *R Lee* 100 h
5 b g Orpen(USA) —Hopesay (Warning)
729[9] 1927[3] 2455[6] 3880[5]

Igloo D'Estruval (FR) *Mrs L C Taylor* 121+h 123 c
10 br g Garde Royale—Jalousie (FR) (Blockhaus)
3508[P]

Ignotus *G A Swinbank* 65h
4 b g Vitus—Linns Heir (Leading Counsel (USA))
1146[3]

I Got Rhythm *K G Reveley* 99 h
8 gr m Lycius(USA) —Eurythmic (Pharly (FR))
319[3] 3271[5] 3757[2] 4391[2]

I Hear Thunder (IRE) *R H Buckler* 91h 128 c
8 b g Montelimar(USA) —Carrigeen Gala (Strong Gale)
(1676) (1861) 2176[10]2628[5] 3000[F] 4434[U]4617[7] 4762[F] 5102a[8]

Ihuru *J G Portman* 49h
4 b g Atraf—E Sharp (USA) (Diesis)
2425[8] 2824[8] 3340[P]

Ikdam Melody (IRE) *Miss J E Foster* 95 c
10 b g Ikdam—Music Slipper (Orchestra)
196[4] 455[U] 498[2]717[P] 989[U] 4100[3]4748[14] 5095[6]

Ikemba (IRE) *J Groucott* 95b 90c
9 b g Executive Perk—Ardglass Pride (Golden Love)
3924[U] 4305[2] 5013[F]

Iktitaf (IRE) *Noel Meade* 148+h
5 b g Alhaarth(IRE) —Istibshar (USA) (Mr Prospector (USA))
(2667a) 3772a[2] (5056a)

Ilabon (FR) *M C Pipe* 87h
10 ch g Secret Haunt(USA) —Ahuille (FR) (Haltea (FR))
2595[P] 3467[P] 3715[4] **3844[P]**

Il'Athou (FR) *S E H Sherwood* 111h 138c
10 b g Lute Antique(FR) —Va Thou Line (FR) (El Badr)
(2003) 2368[F] 4289[2] 4852[5]

Il Capriccio (IRE) *B J M Ryall* 87b
6 b g Windsor Castle—Brogeen View (Kambalda)
138[3] 3210[P] (Dead)

Il De Boitron (FR) *Thomas Gerard O'Leary* 80h 117c
8 b g Sheyrann—Ilkiya (FR) (General Holme (USA))
2164[5] 2745[15] 4434[4]

Il Duce (IRE) *A King* 144 h 130+c
6 br g Anshan—Glory-Glory (IRE) (Buckskin (FR))
2207[2] 2483[F] 3179[6] 4446[20]

Ile De Paris (FR) *P J Hobbs* 109+h 117 c
7 b g Cadoudal(FR) —Sweet Beauty (FR) (Tip Moss (FR))
55[2] 330[P]

Ile Facile (IRE) *B De Haan* 92+h
5 b g Turtle Island(IRE) —Easy Pop (IRE) (Shernazar)
3354[7] 3591[3]

Ile Maurice (FR) *Ferdy Murphy* 122h
6 b m Dernier Empereur(USA) —Indesha (FR) (Top Ville)
2106[F] 2414[3] (2674) (3337) 3544[2] (4612) 4972[P]5103a[8]

Il En Reve (FR) *S J Treacy* 111h 123c
8 b g Denham Red(FR) —Itaparica (FR) (Mistigri)
1083a[F] 1420a[9] 1515a[11]

I'll Call You Back (IRE) *Mrs John Harrington* 114h 104+c
7 b g Zaffaran(USA) —Ben Tack (Lucifer (USA))
67a[F]

Illineylad (IRE) *Mrs N S Evans* 83h 75+c
12 b g Whitehall Bridge—Illiney Girl (Lochnager)
981[9] 1539[P] 1655[6] **1901[4]**

Illuminati *L Corcoran* 104+h
4 b g Inchinor—Selection Board (Welsh Pageant)
3294[5] 3878[9] 4280[6]

Il Mulino (IRE) *Denis Ahern* 116+h
6 bb g Dr Massini(IRE) —Marshalls Bridge (Croghan Hill)
3086a[P]

Ilongue (FR) *R Dickin* 73h
5 b m Nononito(FR) —Marie De Geneve (FR) (Nishapour (FR))
216[8] 1974[6] 2285[5] 2810[8]

Iloveturtle (IRE) *M C Chapman* 81h 78 c
6 b g Turtle Island(IRE) —Gan Ainm (IRE) (Mujadil (USA))
1816[P] 1910[P] 2081[6] 2206[17] 2292[14]2440[8] 2517[P] **2750[9] 2951[7]2966[F] 3419[6] 3593[4]3791[7] 3958[2] 4164[2]4460[P]**

Il Penseroso (IRE) *P A Blockley* 88h 89c
8 br g Norwich—Railstown Phairy (IRE) (Phardante (FR))
3909[P] 4842[4] 4991[7]

Ilringuback (IRE) *A J Chamberlain* 67h
6 b g Altountash—Lorens Joy (IRE) (Mandalus)
2242[7] 2432[9] *3138[11]*

Ilton *M E Sowersby* 18 h
7 ch g Dr Devious(IRE) —Madame Crecy (USA) (Al Nasr (FR))
2290[P] 2843[U] 2962[13] 3335[P]

Imaginaire (USA) *Miss Venetia Williams* 116 c
11 b g Quest For Fame—Hail The Dancer (USA) (Green Dancer (USA))
1831[6] 2128[3] 2626[5]3398[P] 3788[P] 4078[8]

Imago II (FR) *B R Summers* 102h 98c
10 b g Chamberlin(FR) —Pensee D'Amour (FR) (Porto Rafti (FR))
221[P]

Im A Tanner *Miss C Dyson* 39b
5 b g I'm Supposin(IRE) —Galix (FR) (Sissoo)
2288[U] 2823[13] 3462[10]

Im A Witness (IRE) *David Martin Kelly* 97h
6 b g Witness Box(USA) —Welsh Sitara (IRE) (Welsh Term)
4019a[5]

Imazulutoo (IRE) *Evan Williams* 118+h 95c
6 b h Marju(IRE) —Zapata (IRE) (Thatching)
43a[P] 4781[U]

I'm For Waiting *John Allen* 84h 88+c
10 ch g Democratic(USA) —Faustelerie (Faustus (USA))
107[4] 2555[P] 3372[P]4783[8]

I'm Free *M C Pipe* 71b
4 b g I'm Supposin(IRE) —Gaye Mercy (Petoski)
4680[9]

Imlaak *James Moffatt* 4h
4 ch c Giant's Causeway(USA) —Karen S (USA) (Kris S (USA))
3534[12] 4613[P]

I'm Lovin It (IRE) *P F Nicholls* 96b
6 b g Supreme Leader—Sparky Mary (IRE) (Strong Gale)
490[2] 816[2] 1985[6]

I'm No Fairy *P Beaumont* 47h
7 b g Efisio—Fairywings (Kris)
2678[5] 2979[P]

I'm On The Line (IRE) *Mrs D A Love* 95h 101c
10 b g Deep Society—Matilda Cave (King's Leap)
87a[3]

Impartial *S J Mahon* 96h
5 b h Polish Precedent(USA) —Always Friendly (High Line)
65a[8]

Impatient Lady *J D Frost* 59h
9 b m Morpeth—Miss Firecracker (Relkino)
1383[7] 1640[8] 1800[8]

Impek (FR) *Miss H C Knight* 143h 166 c
10 b g Lute Antique(FR) —Attualita (FR) (Master Thatch)
1013[2] 1550[2] (1846) (2346) 2972[3] 4457[3]4761[P]

Imperative (USA) *M J Gingell* 47 h 70c
6 ch g Woodman(USA) —Wandesta (Nashwan (USA))
11[15] 363[B]

Imperial Dream (IRE) *H P Hogarth* 94h 128 c
8 b g Roselier(FR) —Royal Nora (IRE) (Dromod Hill)
2189[P] 2445[F] 4843[P]4985[P]

Imperialistic (IRE) *K R Burke* 63h
5 b m Imperial Ballet(IRE) —Shefoog (Kefaah (USA))
3730[7]

Imperial Miss (IRE) *B W Duke* 54h
4 b f Imperial Ballet(IRE) —Miss Flite (IRE) (Law Society (USA))
945[P] 1023[4] 1095[8] 1190[5] 1404[7]

Imperial Rocket (USA) *W K Goldsworthy* 104h 104 c
9 bb g Northern Flagship(USA) —Starsawhirl (USA) (Star De Naskra (USA))
3878[7] 664[2] 747[3] (947) 1020[6] 1087[2]1263[P] 3128[14] 3360[13] **3457[4]3647[3] 4049[4] 4552[6]4833[3] 5044[3]**

Imperial Royale (IRE) *P L Clinton* 92h
5 ch g Ali-Royal(IRE) —God Speed Her (Pas De Seul)
369[5] 1671[F] 2081[2] 2285[9] 2859[8]2968[7] (3674) 3990[7]

Imperioli *P A Blockley*
4 b g Fraam—Jussoli (Don)
3898[P] 4956[P]

Impero *G F Bridgwater* 65h
8 b g Emperor Jones(USA) —Fight Right (FR) (Crystal Glitters (USA))
356[8] 749[14] 978[15] 1000[5] 1100[P]3279[P] 4133[5] 4392[12] 4856[10]

Important Boy (ARG) *D D Scott* 75h
9 ch g Equalize(USA) —Important Girl (ARG) (Candy Stripes (USA))
566[7] 665[15] 1018[9] 1192[7]

I'm Posh *P Beaumont* 42b
6 b g Rakaposhi King—I'm Fine (Fitzwilliam (USA))
4455[14] 4615[13]

Imps Way *Mrs T Corrigan-Clark* 109+c
11 br m Nomadic Way(USA) —Dalton's Delight (Wonderful Surprise)
(123) 196[2] 440[3](555) 3913[P]

Impulsivo *Simon Earle*
6 ch g Millkom—Joytime (John De Coombe)
742[P]

I'm Supreme (IRE) *C J Down* 82b
4 b g Supreme Leader—Imtheone (IRE) (Meneval (USA))
4680[5]

Imtihan (IRE) *Mrs S J Smith* 112h
7 ch g Unfuwain(USA) —Azyaa (Kris)
1742[11] 1890[3] 2071[6] 3542[2] 3854[2](4517) (4724) 4797[2] 5096[6]

Imtouchingwood *L Wells*
5 b m Fleetwood(IRE) —Shanuke (IRE) (Contract Law (USA))
912[P]

I'm Willie's Girl *Miss J Luton*
10 br m Royal Fountain—Milton Lass (Scallywag)
4722[U]

I'm Your Man *Mrs Dianne Sayer* 90h
7 gr g Bigstone(IRE) —Snowgirl (IRE) (Mazaad)
406[12] 687[4] **2415[9] 2689[P]**2977[P] 3339[P]

In Accord *H D Daly* 124+h
7 ch g Accordion—Henry's True Love (Random Shot)
1903[4] (2619) 2956[5] (4284) (4727)

Inagh *R C Harper*
4 b f Tipsy Creek(USA) —Compton Amber (Puissance)
1802[11] 1955[P]

Inagh Road (IRE) *S C Burrough* 75h 75+c
11 b g Broken Hearted—Fiodoir (Weavers Hall)
630[9] **750[3]** (Dead)

In Ainm De (IRE) *N Wilson* 40h
10 ch m Seclude(USA) —Majestic Dancer (Gleason (USA))
1000[8] 1279[P] **2023[P]**

Inaki (FR) *P Winkworth* 100 c
9 b g Dounba(FR) —Incredule (FR) (Concertino (FR))
2870[P] 3187[5] 3430[4]3663[2] 4694[4]

Inaro (IRE) *Jonjo O'Neill* 119h
5 b g Bahhare(USA) —Doo Han (IRE) (Doulab (USA))
1909[2] 2238[5] (2606) 3500[2] 3880[4]

Incalotte *J A Supple* 33b
4 br f Nicolotte—Blue Peru (IRE) (Perugino (USA))
2425[15] 3399[8] (Dead)

Incandescence (IRE) *Mrs P Robeson* 68b
5 b g Insatiable(IRE) —Glowing Embers (Nebbiolo)
3373[6] 3677[9]

Incas (FR) *A L T Moore* 98h 118+c
10 br g Video Rock(FR) —Amarante II (FR) (Brezzo (FR))
45a[3]

Inca Trail (IRE) *D McCain* 138+h 148+c
10 br g Un Desperado(FR) —Katday (FR) (Miller's Mate)
1735[5] 2054[6] (2299) 2745[5] (4090) (4356) 4777[8] 5144[11]

Inch'Allah (FR) *Jennie Candlish* 100+h
10 b g Royal Charter(FR) —Cadoudaline (FR) (Cadoudal (FR))
1047[P]

Inchcape Rock *J G M O'Shea* 91h
4 ch g Inchinor—Washm (USA) (Diesis)
1679[4] 1737[6] 1873[2] 2178[11] 2454[4]3479[2]

Inch High *J S Goldie* 82h
8 ch g Inchinor—Harrken Heights (IRE) (Belmez (USA))
1291[P] 2942[9] 3673[10] 4143[7] 4632[11]

Inching Closer *J Howard Johnson* 129h
9 b g Inchinor—Maiyaasah (Kris)
2336[4] 3208[7] 3741[7] 3970[16] 4461[6]5005[4]

Inching West *C J Down* 59b
4 ch f Inchinor—Key West (FR) (Highest Honor (FR))
3327[11] 4038[10]

Inch Island (IRE) *W P Mullins* 116h
6 b g Turtle Island(IRE) —Persian Light (IRE) (Persian Heights)
1626a[RR] 3411a[9]

Inchloch *Miss Venetia Williams* 78+h
4 ch g Inchinor—Lake Pleasant (IRE) (Elegant Air)
3948[4] 4648[P]

Inch Over *S A Brookshaw* 76b
5 b g Overbury(IRE) —Inch Maid (Le Moss)
616[9] 685[9]

Inch Pride (IRE) *M C Pipe* 127+h 113+c
7 b m Beneficial—Stradbally Bay (Shackleton)
1828[12] 2369[F] 4446[7] 4972[7]

In Compliance (IRE) *M J P O'Brien* 137h 151+c
6 b g Old Vic—Lady Bellingham (IRE) (Montelimar (USA))
40a[3] **4889a[2] 5100a[3]**

In Contrast (IRE) *P J Hobbs* 154 h 103+c
10 bb g Be My Native(USA) —Ballinamona Lady (IRE) (Le Bavard (FR))
1871[5] 2270[P] 4605[P]4943[4]

Incorporation *M Appleby* 86h 98c
7 b g In The Wings—Danishkada (Thatch (USA))
843[4] 912[P] **3183[5] 3549[6]3732[P]**

Incroyable Mais Vrai (FR) *G F White*
10 b g Morespeed—Urtica V (FR) (Tourangeau (FR))
322[P]

Incursion *A King* 102+h
5 b g Inchinor—Morgannwg (IRE) (Simply Great (FR))
1206[2] (1793)

Indalo (IRE) *Miss Venetia Williams* 133 c
11 b g Lord Americo—Parsons Princess (The Parson)
2847[4] 3022[P] 3877[P]4374[6] 5012[P]

In Deep *Mrs P N Dutfield* 92h
5 b m Deploy—Bobbie Dee (Blakeney)
1782[4]

Indiana Jaune (FR) *P Cottin*
10 b m Le Nain Jaune(FR) —Vienoise De Cene (FR) (Djarvis (FR))
(4718a)

Indian Beat *C L Popham* 77+h
9 ch g Indian Ridge—Rappa Tap Tap (FR) (Tap On Wood)
749[2] 978[5]

Indian Chance *O Sherwood* 56c
12 b g Teenoso(USA) —Icy Miss (Random Shot)
3981[P] 4358[3] 4576[8]

Indian Gunner *Dr J R J Naylor* 107c
13 b g Gunner B—Icy Miss (Random Shot)
4120[2] 4332[4] 4617[P]

Indian Laburnum (IRE) *C C Bealby* 97+c
9 b g Alphabatim(USA) —St.Cristoph (The Parson)
1713[7] 2465[4] 3276[U]

Indian Open *J W Mullins* 74b
5 b g Commanche Run—Golf World (IRE) (Mandalus)
5089[5]

Indian Solitaire (IRE) *B P J Baugh* 95h
7 b g Bigstone(IRE) —Terrama Sioux (Relkino)
2285[3] 2750[13]

Indian Squaw (IRE) *B De Haan* 76h 85c
7 b m Supreme Leader—Kemchee (Kemal (FR))
231[2] 535[P] 1652[2]

Indian Star (GER) *J C Tuck* 106+h
8 br g Sternkoenig(IRE) —Indian Night (GER) (Windwurf (GER))
(2008) 2523[2] (2930)

Indian Wind *M A Barnes* 58b
4 ch g Chocolat De Meguro(USA) —Helm Wind (North Col)
4147[13] 4533[14] 5041[7]

Indien Royal (FR) *P F Nicholls* 116 h 129 c
7 b g Dauphin Du Bourg(FR) —Royale Nabeysse (FR) (Beyssac (FR))
1881[P]

Indigo Sky (IRE) *B G Powell* 63h
5 gr h Adieu Au Roi(IRE) —Urban Sky (FR) (Groom Dancer (USA))
1407[6] 1562[12] 1774[R] 5023[6]

In Dream's (IRE) *M A Barnes* 94+h
4 b g Dr Fong(USA) —No Sugar Baby (FR) (Crystal Glitters (USA))
3925[6] 4039[5] 4506[4] 4631[P] 4789[7]4987[6]

Inducement *R M Stronge* 73h
10 ch g Sabrehill(USA) —Verchinina (Star Appeal)
136[11] 357[11] 681[10]

Industrial Star (IRE) *M D Hammond* 114h
5 ch g Singspiel(IRE) —Faribole (IRE) (Esprit Du Nord (USA))
(3347) 4621[3]

Industrious *Mrs D A Love* 120c
7 b g Flemensfirth(USA) —Miss Redlands (Dubassoff (USA))
5083a[9]

Indyana Run *A Hollingsworth* 67b
5 b m Commanche Run—An Bothar Dubh (Strong Gale)
490[13] 655[11] 866[8]

Indy Mood *Mrs H O Graham* 120h
7 ch g Endoli(USA) —Amanta (IRE) (Electric)
4792[10] 5005[2]

Infidel (IRE) *C J Mann* 95h
6 b g Spectrum(IRE) —Implicit View (Persian Bold)
3576[7] **511[P] 962[P]**1181[7]

Infini (FR) *Mrs S J Smith* 81h 108c
10 gr g Le Nain Jaune(FR) —Contessina (FR) (Mistigri)
(1358) 1609[F] 2170[P]2862[9] 3339[7] 3797[5]

Influential (IRE) *J J Lambe* 93h 89+c
10 b g Spanish Place(USA) —More Drama (Pragmatic)
939[9]

Infrasonique (FR) *Mrs L C Taylor* 133c
10 b g Teresio—Quatalina III (FR) (Chateau Du Diable (FR))
1893[4] 2557[3] 2800[2]3241[6]

Ingenu (FR) *P Wegmann* 87 c
10 b g Royal Charter(FR) —Una Volta (FR) (Toujours Pret (USA))
1796[P] 2004[7] **2562[6] 2733[4]2933[5] 4666[2]**

Inglewood *Miss Kate Milligan* 79+h 96+c
6 ch g Fleetwood(IRE) —Preening (Persian Bold)
211[7] 413[6] (783) 1067[P] (Dead)

Inglis Drever *J Howard Johnson* 167 h
7 b g In The Wings—Cormorant Creek (Gorytus (USA))
(1925) (2490) 3020[F]

In Good Faith (USA) *N J Henderson* 84+h
5 bb m Dynaformer(USA) —Healing Hands (Zafonic (USA))
58[P] 1717[P] 4392[7]

In Good Faith *R E Barr* 85h 72c
14 b g Beveled(USA) —Dulcidene (Behistoun)
11[9] 152[7] 429[5] (480) 606[2] 716[5]784[8] 1486[8] 1571[7] 1685[P] 2440[F]

Ingres *B G Powell* 115h 58c
6 b g Sadler's Wells(USA) —Bloudan (USA) (Damascus (USA))
841[9] 915[9] 1525[3] 1743[4] **2072[3]2213[7]** 2347[3] 2466[3] 2731[3]2999[6] 3458[2] 4058[5] 4579[7]

Inherent (IRE) *C G Cox* 90+b
4 ch f In The Wings—Serpentara (Kris)
2014[3] 2521[4] (2830) 4976[8]

Inishturk (IRE) *A King* 95h
7 bb g Glacial Storm(USA) —Judy Henry (Orchestra)
3789[6] 4032[4] 4327[3] 4879[P]

Inissam Storm *D Brace*
5 b g Dr Massini(IRE) —Sister Kit (IRE) (Glacial Storm (USA))
1755[10]

Inland Run (IRE) *R T Phillips* 88+h 97c
10 b g Insan(USA) —Anns Run (Deep Run)
137[3] 673[P] 759[2]

Inmate (IRE) *Mrs E Slack* 52h
5 b g Needle Gun(IRE) —Highland Spirit (Scottish Reel)
936[8] 1569[P] 1938[P] 2979[8] 4145[12]

In Media Res (FR) *N J Henderson* 122h
5 b g Dushyantor(USA) —Colour Scheme (FR) (Perrault)
(515) (2804) 3143[P] 3696[3] 4215[3]

Inmom (IRE) *S R Bowring* 26h
5 b m Barathea(IRE) —Zakuska (Zafonic (USA))
4074[P]

Inn For The Dancer *Mrs H Dalton* 86+h
4 b g Groom Dancer(USA) —Lady Joyce (FR) (Galetto (FR))
2597[U] 2661[10] 2949[4] 3423[4] 4057[5]

Inn From The Cold (IRE) *L Lungo* 91+h
10 ch g Glacial Storm(USA) —Silver Apollo (General Ironside)
3445[3] 4145[13]

Innisfree (IRE) *John G Carr* 89h 99c
8 ch g Presenting—Sweet Peach (IRE) (Glenstal (USA))
(1378) 1589[4]

Innocent Rebel (USA) *A King* 97h
5 ch g Swain(IRE) —Cadeaux D'Amie (USA) (Lyphard (USA))
78[6] 295[3]

In No Hurry (IRE) *M G Quinlan* 69h
5 b g Supreme Leader—South Quay Lady (Quayside)
3646[P] 4868[5]

Innox (FR) *F Doumen* 156 c
10 b g Lute Antique(FR) —Savane III (FR) (Quart De Vin (FR))
(2176) (4118) 4777[F]

Innpursuit *J M P Eustace* 56h
4 b g Inchinor—Quest For The Best (Rainbow Quest (USA))
2580[11] 3340[11] 3479[8]

Inse Bay (IRE) *Thomas O'Neill* 74h
7 bb m Presenting—Kilclareen Belle (IRE) (Duky)
592[16]

Instant Appeal *P Winkworth* 99+h 91c
9 gr g Terimon—Free Travel (Royalty)
2632[P] 2934[4] 3211[8] 3661[8] **3909[4] 4132[3] 4643[4] 5049[3]**

Insubordinate *J S Goldie*
5 ch g Subordination(USA) —Manila Selection (USA) (Manila (USA))
4143[P]

Insurgent (IRE) *R C Guest* 86h
4 b g Fasliyev(USA) —Mountain Ash (Dominion)
2642[8] (3273) 3651[7] 3799[7] 4789[5] 4916[6] 4987[10]

Insurrection (IRE) *J D Frost* 76h
9 b g Un Desperado(FR) —Ballycahan Girl (Bargello)
288[P] 665[17]

Intavac Flight *C W Thornton* 75b
6 b g Tamure(IRE) —Mossfield (Le Moss)
2497[U] 2631[P]

Intensity *S B Bell* 98+h
10 b g Bigstone(IRE) —Brillante (FR) (Green Dancer (USA))
64[P] 410[7]

Interdit (FR) *Mrs B K Thomson* 107h 120 c
10 bb g Shafoun(FR) —Solaine (FR) (Pot D'Or (FR))
1603[3] 2037[2] 2265[P] (3377) 3851[P] 4345[P] 4636[P] 5122[U]

Internationalguest (IRE) *D G Bridgwater* 52h
7 b g Petardia—Banco Solo (Distant Relative)
671[7] 861[P]

Intersky Emerald (IRE) *G A Swinbank* 88+b
5 b g Luso—Green Formation (Green Desert (USA))
1532[11] 1667[5] 3399[4] 4992[10]

Intersky Falcon *Jonjo O'Neill* 159 h 132+c
9 ch g Polar Falcon(USA) —I'll Try (Try My Best (USA))
2055[2] 2500[P] 2761[2] 2971[7] 4432[11] 4775[P] 5125[3]

Interstice *M J Gingell* 35 h
9 b g Never So Bold—Mainmast (Bustino)
2257[4] 2719[F] 2807[P] 3418[10] 3592[9]

In The Forge *M Halford* 149?h 102c
9 ch g Zilzal(USA) —Harir (Kris)
954a[8]

In The Frame (IRE) *Evan Williams* 117 h 125c
7 b g Definite Article—Victorian Flower (Tate Gallery (USA))
2[4] (364) (692) 894[2] 1442[2] 1817[4] 5011[2]

In The Hat (IRE) *J R Jenkins* 82h
10 br g Roselier(FR) —Cotton Gale (Strong Gale)
1816[7] (2341) 3416[5] 3959[4]

In The Morning (IRE) *A J Martin* 67h 57c
7 ch g Anshan—Wee Norex (IRE) (Roselier (FR))
3528a[12] 4427[P] (Dead)

In The Park (IRE) *Jonjo O'Neill* 45h 62+c
9 gr g Roselier(FR) —Gay Seeker (Status Seeker)
169[F]

Into The Shadows *K G Reveley* 122+h
6 ch m Safawan—Shadows Of Silver (Carwhite)
(2103) 2533[5] 2765[3] (4983)

Intra Vires (IRE) *J L Spearing* 69b
4 b f Shinko Forest(IRE) —Sveltana (Soviet Star (USA))
4038[9] 4554[7]

Introduction *R J Price* 65h
5 b g Opening Verse(USA) —Cartuccia (IRE) (Doyoun)
3354[P]

Inverlochy Lad (IRE) *I A Duncan* 101b
5 b g Mister Lord(USA) —Brogue Melody (IRE) (King's Ride)
5008[5]

Investment Force (IRE) *M Sheppard* 87+h
8 b g Imperial Frontier(USA) —Superb Investment (IRE) (Hatim (USA))
1188[10] 1233[P] **1411[P]**

Investment Wings (IRE) *M C Pipe* 105h
4 b g In The Wings—Superb Investment (IRE) (Hatim (USA))
3464[6] 3579[F] 3786[12] 4096[4] 4443[16]

Involved (IRE) *Mrs Edward Crow* 37b 110+c
10 b g Macmillion—Symphony Express (IRE) (Orchestra)
49[4]

Iowa (IRE) *Jedd O'Keeffe* 60h
6 b g Sadler's Wells(USA) —Puzzled Look (USA) (Gulch (USA))
2171[P]

Ipledgeallegiance (USA) *Miss Tracy Waggott* 69c
10 b g Alleged(USA) —Yafill (USA) (Nureyev (USA))
370[4] 1280[4] **2677[U] 2980[5] 3317[5] 3555[7]**

Iraklion (POL) *J Votava*
11 b g Jape(USA) —Ibrala (POL) (Beauvallon (FR))
1710a[U]

Ireland's Eye (IRE) *J R Norton* 74h
11 b g Shareef Dancer(USA) —So Romantic (IRE) (Teenoso (USA))
13[6] 2010[3] 2264[6] 2688[7] 3279[P] 3918[6] 4320[P]

Irenie *N R Mitchell* 96b
11 ch m Nicholas Bill—Porto Irene (Porto Bello)
3322[12] 3464[10]

Irilut (FR) *R Waley-Cohen* 107 c
10 br g Lute Antique(FR) —Patchourie (FR) (Taj Dewan)
3819[U] 4100[2] 4471[17]

Iris Bleu (FR) *M C Pipe* 150 c
10 ch g Beyssac(FR) —Dear Blue (FR) (Cyborg (FR))
(2054) 2491[P] 3728[7] 4118[F] 4447[7] 4957[15]

Irish Blessing (USA) *F Jordan* 81 h
9 b g Ghazi(USA) —Win For Leah (USA) (His Majesty (USA))
(11) 237[P] 1756[3] 2256[8] 2822[10] (3330) 4101[8] 4392[9] 4783[P]

Irish Flight (IRE) *Noel T Chance* 98h
9 ch g Duky—Arewehavingfunyet (Green Shoon)
4732[4]

Irish Grouse (IRE) *Miss H C Knight* 64+h
7 b g Anshan—Another Grouse (Pragmatic)
1990[5] 2378[3] **2933[P] 3460[P]**

Irish Guard *J G O'Neill* 105+h
5 b g Infantry—Sharp Practice (Broadsword (USA))
4072[17] 4326[9] 4807[9]

Irish Hawk (GER) *M F Harris*
4 ch g Platini(GER) —Irishfritter (USA) (Irish River (FR))
1201[P] 1332[8]

Irish Hussar (IRE) *N J Henderson* 141h 161c
10 b g Supreme Leader—Shuil Ard (Quayside)
2972[P] 4118[P] 4433[3]

Irish Invader (IRE) *W P Mullins* 103b
5 b g Bob Back(USA) —Idealist (Busted)
5104a[16]

Irishkawa Bellevue (FR) *Jean-Rene Auvray* 120 h 100c
8 bb g Irish Prospector(FR) —Strakawa (FR) (Sukawa (FR))
762[11] (1125) **1479[P]** (1715) 2430[2] 3389[14] 3987[7] **4643[2] 5071[4]**

Irish Legend (IRE) *C Roberts* 114+h
6 b g Sadler's Wells(USA) —Wedding Bouquet (King's Lake (USA))
2184[5]

Irish Playwright (IRE) *D G Bridgwater* 68h
6 b g King's Theatre(IRE) —Marino Waltz (Thatching)
457[8] 696[8] 811[P] 1222[6] 4550[11]

Irish Prince (IRE) *Robert Gray* 76h
10 b g Fresh Breeze(USA) —Kilivarig (Crozier)
1112[8] 1375[10] 1567[6] 1756[4] 1883[5] 1943[5]

Irish Raptor (IRE) *N A Twiston-Davies* 94+h
7 bb g Zaffaran(USA) —Brownskin (Buckskin (FR))
1669[P] 1917[U] 3342[8] 4099[4] 4396[6] 5064[9]

Irish Totty *C J Down* 46h
7 b m Glacial Storm(USA) —Elver Season (Vital Season)
3882[8] 4286[P]

Irish Wolf (FR) *P Bowen* 117h
6 b h Loup Solitaire(USA) —Erins Run (USA) (Irish River (FR))
(1182) 1431[3] 1671[P] (1987) 2716[2] 2850[4] 5138[3]

Iris Royal (FR) *N J Henderson* 125 c
10 b g Garde Royale—Tchela (FR) (Le Nain Jaune (FR))
2346[6] 3180[7] 3728[F] 3995[5] 4777[P]

Iris's Dream *Jonjo O'Neill* 14h
6 ch g Gunner B—Miss Shaw (Cruise Missile)
912[13]

Iris's Gift *Jonjo O'Neill* 176h 155 c
9 gr g Gunner B—Shirley's Gift (Scallywag)
(1549) (1669) (1879) 2484[2] 3391[F] 4470[P]

Iris's Prince *A Crook* 107h 112 c
7 ch g Gunner B—Colonial Princess (Roscoe Blake)
85[2] 317[2] 499[9] **1568[6] 1761[2] 1939 [R] 2441[4] 2976[P] 4516[3] 4633[2] 4971[6] 9[2]**

Iris's Queen *D McCain* 17h
6 b m Bob's Return(IRE) —Colonial Princess (Roscoe Blake)
273[5]

Iron Express *Mrs C A Coward* 82h 104 c
10 b g Teenoso(USA) —Sylvia Beach (The Parson)
12[P] 989[7] 1276[5] 1378[P] 5095[5]

Iron Maid *O Sherwood* 73b
5 b m Shambo—Brass Castle (IRE) (Carlingford Castle)
4695[4]

Iron Man (FR) *J Howard Johnson* 116 h 123 c
5 ch g Video Rock(FR) —Key Figure (FR) (Fast Topaze (USA))
2634[4] (3380) 3796[5] 4796[2]

Ironside (IRE) *H D Daly* 97h 103+c
7 b g Mister Lord(USA) —The Helmet (IRE) (Riot Helmet)
8[P] 2505[8] 2862[7] **3290[3] 3499[P] 4095[2] 4394[4] 4851[P]**

Iron Warrior (IRE) *G M Moore* 89+h
6 b g Lear Fan(USA) —Robalana (USA) (Wild Again (USA))
14[2] 212[P] 2639[5] 3042[11]

Isam Top (FR) *M J Hogan* 89h 95c
10 b g Siam(USA) —Miss Sic Top (FR) (Mister Sic Top (FR))
105[P] 232[8] 502[P] 1597[2] 2379[3] 2685[4] (3223) 3661[3] 4871[9]

Isard III (FR) *Mrs K Waldron* 111b
10 gr g Royal Charter(FR) —Aurore D'Ex (FR) (Mont Basile (FR))
407[3] 648[3] 842[7] 1013[6] 1265[13] 1489[5] 3693[F]

I See Icy (IRE) *Daniel Miley* 113h
6 b g Arctic Lord—Jennie Dun (IRE) (Mandalus)
5103a[12]

Isellido (IRE) *R C Guest* 91h 109 c
7 bb m Good Thyne(USA) —Souled Out (IRE) (Noalto)
10[F] (119) 239[P] 1940[9] 2264[9] 2452[7] 2964[8] **(3375) 3849[3] 4495[F] 4721[5]**

Ishka Baha (IRE) *T R George* 100 h 93+c
7 ch m Shernazar—Briongloid (Callernish)
2244[3] 2750[5] (2995) **3243[4]** 3889[P]

Isitloveyourafter (IRE) *G L Moore* 62+h
4 b f Orpen(USA) —Pericolo (IRE) (Kris)
2236[6] 2501[12] 2752[5] 2935[5]

Island Faith (IRE) *J Howard Johnson* 106 h 140 c
9 b g Turtle Island(IRE) —Keep The Faith (Furry Glen)
(2339) 3019[F] 3852[P]

Island Light (USA) *P Wegmann* 26h
6 ch g Woodman(USA) —Isla Del Rey (USA) (Nureyev (USA))
2070[11] 2455[F] 3464[9]

Island Of Memories (IRE) *D P Keane* 74h
6 ch m Beneficial—Coronea Sea Queen (IRE) (Bassompierre)
4676[P]

Island Stream (IRE) *P F Nicholls* 82h 82c
7 b g Turtle Island(IRE) —Tilbrook (IRE) (Don't Forget Me)
3510[11] 4945[5]

Island Warrior (IRE) *B P J Baugh* 78h 45c
11 b g Warcraft(USA) —Only Flower (Warpath)
75[4] 237[P] 458[P] 686[6] 891[P] 1279[5] 1362[10] (1636) 1900[6] 2419[10]

Isle De Maurice *D B Feek* 76h
4 b g Sinndar(IRE) —Circe's Isle (Be My Guest (USA))
2681[6] 3182[8] 3294[U]

Isleofhopeantears (IRE) *A E Jones* 62+h
7 b g College Chapel—Fontaine Lodge (IRE) (Lafontaine (USA))
806[4] 2146[P]

Isotop (FR) *John Allen* 95h 104c
10 b g Port Etienne(FR) —Clorane (FR) (Rahotep (FR))
3331[7] 4553[7] 4753[2] 4937[3]

Isou (FR) *V R A Dartnall* 86c
10 ch g Dom Alco(FR) —Aghate De Saisy (FR) (Rhapsodien)
262[4]

Is There More *J M Jefferson* 57b
5 br m Classic Cliche(IRE) —Larksmore (Royal Fountain)
3556[6] 4017[10] 5038[0]

Itador (FR) *E Leray*
10 b g Badolato(USA) —Emeraude De Laigne (FR) (Bojador (FR))
362a[4]

Italian Counsel (IRE) *P J Hobbs* 84c
9 b g Leading Counsel(USA) —Mullaghroe (Tarboosh (USA))
4426[4]

Italiano *P Beaumont* 108+h 107c
7 b g Emperor Jones(USA) —Elka (USA) (Val De L'Orne (FR))
82[8] **2449[5] 2764[U] 3037[4] 3352[P] 3380[5] 3844[3] 5119[F]**

Itcanbedone Again (IRE) *Ian Williams* 54h
7 b g Sri Pekan(USA) —Maradata (IRE) (Shardari)
1742[10]

It Happened Out (IRE) *J W Mullins* 98b
5 gr g Accordion—Miss Hawkins (Modern Dancer)
3699[4] 4244[5] 4455[9]

It Plays Itself (IRE) *Jonjo O'Neill* 61h
7 bb g Naheez(USA) —Adabiya (IRE) (Akarad (FR))
3941[P] 4148[6]

Itsachopperbaby (IRE) *James J Kelly*
6 b g Revoque(IRE) —Coast Is Clear (IRE) (Rainbow Quest (USA))
93a[24]

Its A Classic *Mrs N S Evans* 75b
5 b g Classic Cliche(IRE) —Mcmahons River (Over The River (FR))
1042[9] 1386[5] 1660[6] 1857[7]

Its A Cracker (IRE) *M C Pipe* 56h
7 br g Roselier(FR) —Lilliput Queen (IRE) (Drumalis)
4164[P] 4331[P]

Its A Dream (IRE) *N J Henderson* 127 h
6 b g Oscar(IRE) —Gra-Bri (IRE) (Rashar (USA))
(44a) (2617) 3174[5] (3882) 4469[13]

It's A Hottie *P Winkworth* 40b
4 b g Bahamian Bounty—Laser Light Lady (Tragic Role (USA))
2014[9] 2797[P]

Itsallupintheair *Miss A Meakins* 66c
10 b g Lion Cavern(USA) —Flora Wood (IRE) (Bob Back (USA))
4283[F]

It's A Roofer (IRE) *Mrs K Walton* 89+h
6 b g Topanoora—Chelsea Belle (IRE) (Supreme Leader)
4342[P] 4527[9] 5118[2]

It's Bertie *Mrs S J Smith* 93 h
6 b g Unfuwain(USA) —Legend Of Aragon (Aragon)
1762[4] 2186[6] 2528[10] 2968[3] 3792[8]

It's Blue Chip *Miss H C Knight* 105+h
5 b g Polar Falcon(USA) —Bellateena (Nomination)
99[7]

Its Crucial (IRE) *N A Twiston-Davies* 124h 79c
6 b g Beneficial—Balda Girl (IRE) (Mandalus)
1668[9] **1891[5]** 4329[7] 5066[10]

It's Definite (IRE) *P Bowen* 117h 111+c
7 b g Definite Article—Taoveret (IRE) (Flash Of Steel)
315[F] 422[5] 814[P] **(1038) 1177[4] 1341[7] 1678[5] 1780[4] 1988[P] 2458[P]**

Itsdowntoben *D McCain* 48h
5 b g Karinga Bay—Martins Lottee (Martinmas)
241[3] 484[4] 3843[7] 4048[P]

It's Ej *Mrs S J Smith* 86h
8 b g Karinga Bay—Merry Marigold (Sonnen Gold)
345[8] 1206[7]

It's Got Buckleys *L A Dace* 58h
7 b g El Conquistador—Saucey Pup (The Parson)
506[P]

It's Gwendolene *Miss Sheena West* 52h
6 ch m Bedford(USA) —Built In Heaven (Sunley Builds)
912[7] 976[4]

It's Harry *Mrs S J Smith* 65 h 61c
8 b g Aragon—Andbracket (Import)
9[21] 545[6] 1000[P] 1486[13]

It's In The Stars *H D Daly* 112+h
6 b g Teenoso(USA) —Sail By The Stars (Celtic Cone)
2127[2]

It's Just Harry *C R Egerton* 140h
9 b g Tragic Role(USA) —Nipotina (Simply Great (FR))
2493[8] 4458[10]

It's Just Sally *B G Powell* 72+h
9 b m Kylian(USA) —Hush It Up (Tina's Pet)
399[9] 502[10]

Its Mick (IRE) *Mrs S J Smith* 60h
9 bb g Duky—Pendarron (Green Shoon)
1445[P] 1611[9]

Itsmyboy (IRE) *M C Pipe* 133+h
6 br g Frimaire—Hawkfield Lass (IRE) (The Parson)
(172) (331) 531[U] 1617[2] 1775[4] (1880)

It's My Party *W G M Turner* 90h 89c
5 b g Danzero(AUS) —Addicted To Love (Touching Wood (USA))
7[5] (235) 1596[7] 1772[8] 1898[3] 2301[8] 2576[6] 2728[2] 3332[0] 3673[DSQ] 3885[2] 3945[3] **4424[4] 4525[4]**

It's No Easy (IRE) *N G Richards* 80h
5 b g Beneficial—Ballough Bui (IRE) (Supreme Leader)
1799[16] 2942[7] 3534[P] 4342[P]

It's Official (IRE) *Miss A M Newton-Smith* 79h
7 ch g Moscow Society(USA) —Irish Pride (IRE) (Mister Lord (USA))
1775[9] 1959[7] **2555[P]** 2956[F] 3656[P] 4526[10] 4823[8]

Itsonlyapuppet (IRE) *A J Martin* 101h
7 ch g Houmayoun(FR) —Adala (IRE) (Shardari)
5128a[F]

It's Rumoured *Jean-Rene Auvray* 93+h 93c
6 ch g Fleetwood(IRE) —Etourdie (USA) (Arctic Tern (USA))
1781[3] 1983[5] 2325[9] 3276[P] 4824[7] 5028[P]

It's The Limit (USA) *W K Goldsworthy* 105h
7 b g Boundary(USA) —Beside (USA) (Sportin' Life (USA))
1654[5] 2559[7] 2730[4] 3286[4] 3441[F] 3646[7] 3719[4] 4050[3] 4469[15] 4736[3] 4838[3] 5045[7]

Itsukate *J Rudge* 61b
6 b m Makbul—Kilvarnet (Furry Glen)
4631[10] 4855[P]

Itsuptoharry (IRE) *D McCain* 97+h 125c
7 b g Old Vic—Celtic Gale (Strong Gale)
(126) 344[P] 2003[5] 2874[2] 3255[F] 3973[6] 4778[5] 5011[4]

Its Wallace Jnr *Miss Sheena West* 116h 116+c
7 b g Bedford(USA) —Built In Heaven (Sunley Builds)
2999[4] **3907[3] (4565) 4835[F]**

Itsy Bitsy *W J Musson* 72b
4 b f Danzig Connection(USA) —Cos I Do (IRE) (Double Schwartz)
2521[6] 3820[4] 4654[9]

It Takes Time (IRE) *M C Pipe* 163h 161 c
12 b g Montelimar(USA) —Dysart Lady (King's Ride)
2370[4] 2744[7] 3977[4] 4777[P] 5144[6]

It Was'Nt Me (IRE) *M Sheppard* 101 h 104 c
9 bb g Persian Mews—Creek's Sister (King's Ride)
2141[6] 2562[2] 2725[3] 2938[F] (Dead)

Itworked *E M Treneer* 63c
11 b g Landyap(USA) —Workamiracle (Teamwork)
171[5]

It Would Appear (IRE) *Jonjo O'Neill* 92 h
7 b g Un Desperado(FR) —Toi-Dante (IRE) (Phardante (FR))
2145[3] 2527[3] 3717[8] 3843[5]

Ivana Illyich (IRE) *J S Wainwright* 81h
4 ch f Tipsy Creek(USA) —Tolstoya (Northfields (USA))
1718[11] 1797[7] (2076) 14[16]

Ivan De Vonnas (FR) *A L T Moore* 123h 120c
10 b g Cadoudal(FR) —Diana De Vonnas (FR) (El Badr)
5061a[F]

Ivanoph (FR) *S Flook* 88c
10 b g Roi De Rome(USA) —Veronique IV (FR) (Mont Basile (FR))
79[4] 3847[4] 4079[5] 4555[10]

Iverain (FR) *Sir John Barlow Bt* 136h 110 c
10 b g Le Riverain(FR) —Ursala (FR) (Toujours Pret (USA))
(330) 765[6] 1025[P] 1664[2] 1798[3] 2368[11] (Dead)

Ivoire De Beaulieu (FR) *Ferdy Murphy* 105+h 138+c
10 b g Port Etienne(FR) —Kashmonde (FR) (Kashneb (FR))
(2745) (2979)

Izmir Du Cosquet (FR) *E Leenders*
10 gr g April Night(FR) —Simoniaque (FR) (Rolling Bowl (FR))
362a[F]

Iznogoud (FR) *M C Pipe* 70h 123c
10 bb g Shafoun(FR) —Vancia (FR) (Top Dancer (FR))
4241[11] 4470[15] 4777[P]

Izzy Gets Busy (IRE) *G F Bridgwater* 18b
6 b m Flemensfirth(USA) —Builder's Line (IRE) (Sheer Grit)
1850[P] 2125[P]

Izzyizzenty *J M Jefferson* 97+h
7 b g Myfontaine—More To Life (Northern Tempest (USA))
2755[P] 2859[2] 3779[5] 5016[3]

Izzykeen *Mrs S J Smith* 107+h 104+c
7 b g Keen—Washita (Valiyar)
552[2] 841[2] 1016[3] **1155[6]1275[2]** 3561[13]
Jabiru (IRE) *Mrs K M Sanderson* 119 c
13 bb g Lafontaine(USA) —Country Glen (Furry Glen)
805[9] 1022[P] 4397[4]4757[P]
Jabo (FR) *N A Twiston-Davies* 74h
4 b g Epervier Bleu—Reine Zazou (FR) (Castle Guard)
1785[7] 2101[8]
Jac An Ree (IRE) *Mrs D M Grissell* 89h 78c
10 b g Supreme Leader—Nic An Ree (IRE) (King's Ride)
4283[2]
Jacarado (IRE) *R Dickin* 67h 88 c
8 b g Jurado(USA) —Lady Mearba (IRE) (Le Bavard (FR))
73[4] **2072[4] 2424[8]3274[P] 3460[3] (3923) 4353[2] 4785[P] 5136[4]**
Jaccout (FR) *R Johnson* 92+h 76c
8 b g Sheyrann—Jacottiere (FR) (Dom Racine (FR))
647[6]
Jacdor (IRE) *R Dickin* 86c
12 b g Be My Native(USA) —Bellalma (Belfalas)
12[P] 489[7] 2010[P]**2248[4] 2524[2]**
Jackadandy (USA) *B Storey* 90h
4 b g Lear Fan(USA) —Chandra (CAN) (Morning Bob (USA))
1512[2] 1601[5] 2753[12]
Jack De Traou Land (FR) *J Vana Jr*
9 b g Nikos—Belzebuth (FR) (Ti King (FR))
1710a[U]
Jack Durrance (IRE) *G A Ham* 88h
6 b g Polish Precedent(USA) —Atlantic Desire (IRE) (Ela-Mana-Mou)
681[2] 749[10] 863[7] 973[4] 1156[5]1223[3] (1381) 1490[7] 1653[6] 1742[12] 4733[3]4856[4]
Jackem (IRE) *Ian Williams* 106 h 83c
12 bb g Lord Americo—Laurence Lady (Laurence O)
2863[8] 3923[P] 4737[P]4876[P]
Jack Flush (IRE) *M E Sowersby* 64h
12 b g Broken Hearted—Clubhouse Turn (IRE) (King Of Clubs)
11[P]
Jack Fuller (IRE) *P Winkworth* 87h 107+c
9 b g Be My Native(USA) —Jacks Sister (IRE) (Entitled)
2502[6] 2808[5] 3276[6]3547[7] (3919) 4348[4]4639[3] 4873[4]
Jack High (IRE) *T M Walsh* 136+h 142c
11 br g Erdelistan(FR) —Lyntim (Fidel)
2176[9] 2777a[4] **3081a[5]**3585a[3] **3895a[5] (4483a) 4777[U]5144[9]**
Jackie Boy (IRE) *N A Twiston-Davies* 82+h 65+c
7 b g Lord Americo—Riverpauper (IRE) (Over The River (FR))
1713[U] 1960[7] 2592[P]3905[P] 4080[6] 4320[P]
Jack Lynch *Ferdy Murphy* 94+h 76c
10 ch g Lancastrian—Troublewithjack (Sulaafah (USA))
2675[P] 2982[U] 3652[6]3915[9] 4053[F] 4300[P]4845[P]
Jack Martin (IRE) *S Gollings* 114h 118 c
9 ch g Erin's Isle—Rolling Penny (IRE) (Le Moss)
2292[13] 3384[6] **3596[4] 3942[F]**4390[2] **4636[F]**
Jack Of Kilcash (IRE) *Nigel Benstead* 51c
12 br g Glacial Storm(USA) —Candora (Cantab)
404[9]
Jack Of Spades (IRE) *R Dickin* 99+c
10 b g Mister Lord(USA) —Dooney's Daughter (The Parson)
137[2] 439[P]
Jack Rolfe *G L Moore* 107h
4 b g Polish Precedent(USA) —Haboobti (Habitat)
3340[4] 4621[5]
Jacks Craic (IRE) *J L Spearing* 117h 149+c
7 b g Lord Americo—Boleree (IRE) (Mandalus)
2312[2] 2622[P] 3183[4]3357[2] 3457[2] (4089) 4378[2] (4618) (4749) 5006[F]
Jacks Helen *G J Smith*
9 b m Lancastrian—Troublewithjack (Sulaafah (USA))
1619[P]
Jacks Jewel (IRE) *C J Down* 76+h
9 b g Welsh Term—September Daydream (IRE) (Phardante (FR))
759[F] 4666[U]
Jack's Lad (IRE) *Mrs S M Johnson* 109h
7 ch g High Roller(IRE) —Captain's Covey (Captain James)
175[4]
Jackson (FR) *A King* 121h 116+c
9 b g Passing Sale(FR) —Tynia (FR) (Djarvis (FR)) (73) (1959) 2175[5] **2564[5] 3419[2]3955[3] 4447[P] 4906[P]**
Jacksons Pier (IRE) *M Scudamore* 49h
6 b g Accordion—Uhuru (IRE) (Jurado (USA))
4500[6] 4803[5]
Jacksonville (FR) *Miss Vicky Simpson* 80h 101c
9 b g Petit Montmorency(USA) —Quinine Des Aulnes (FR) (Air Du Nord (USA))
4347[3] (4725) 4846[2]
Jack The Blaster *J Howard Johnson* 87b
6 b g Alflora(IRE) —Marsden Rock (Tina's Pet) (4319)
Jack The Giant (IRE) *N J Henderson* 120+h
4 b g Giant's Causeway(USA) —State Crystal (IRE) (High Estate)
(3786) 4243[2] 5076a[3]
Jack The Hough (IRE) *Philip Walsh* 109h 116c
9 ch g Grand Plaisir(IRE) —Burnpark Lady (Kambalda)
92a[6]
Jack Weighell *J M Jefferson* 84h 72+c
7 b g Accordion—Magic Bloom (Full Of Hope)
152[P] 265[U] 414[P] 523[6] 2341[7]
Jack White *Mrs S J Smith* 66h
9 b g Teenoso(USA) —Frabjous Day (Broadsword (USA))
111[P]

Jacobin (USA) *M Scudamore*
5 b g Tamayaz(CAN) —Simply Follow Me (USA) (Green Dancer (USA))
3139[P] 3355[P] 3806[P]
Jacquemart Colombe (FR) *P Bowen* 122c
9 gr g Royal Charter(FR) —Tanie (FR) (Kashmir Ring)
150[4] 489[5] 765[4]
Jades Double *M Madgwick* 83h
5 b m Double Trigger(IRE) —Jaydeebee (Buckley)
1772[10] 2212[3] 2486[4]
J'Adore (GER) *R Curtis* 71h
4 b g Chato(USA) —Josa (GER) (Northjet)
4910[P]
Jaffa *Miss J Wormall* 126 c
14 ch g Kind Of Hush—Sip Of Orange (Celtic Cone)
97[3] 3459[2] 4476[2]4829[7]
Jagoes Mills (IRE) *Thomas Gerard O'Leary* 123h
4 b g Dr Massini(IRE) —Thistle Chat (Le Bavard (FR))
5099a[5]
Jago's Girl *B N Pollock* 21h
5 b m Bob's Return(IRE) —Swazi Princess (IRE) (Brush Aside (USA))
3393[9]
Jailbird Rocks (IRE) *Hugh Paul Finegan*
7 b m Little Bighorn—Saved By Paper (IRE) (Hawaiian Return (USA))
649[10]
Jakari (FR) *H D Daly* 103 h 137c
9 b g Apeldoorn(FR) —Tartifume II (FR) (Mistigri)
1013[9] 2492[P] 3296[3]3620[P] 4240[3] 4957[10]
Jake Black (IRE) *J J Quinn* 129 h
6 b g Definite Article—Tirhala (IRE) (Chief Singer)
1010[P] (2190) 2746[7] 3256[5]
Jakers (IRE) *P A Fahy* 106h 108c
9 b g Jolly Jake(NZ) —Catchthegoose (Tug Of War)
3408a[6]
Jallastep (FR) *J S Goldie* 101 h 97 c
9 b g Boston Two Step(USA) —Balladine (FR) (Rivelago (FR))
1295[2] 1529[4] 1825[4]2067[P] 2498[5] 2900[8]4302[9] 4585[5] **5092[7]**
Jallopy (IRE) *G A Harker* 66b
5 b g Midhish—Ody Morody (IRE) (Kefaah (USA))
375[9]
Jaloux D'Estruval (FR) *Mrs L C Taylor* 114 h 134 c
9 b g Kadalko(FR) —Pommette III (FR) (Trac)
2130[2] 2621[6] **2847[P]** 3289[12]3428[5] 3982[7] 4357[3] 4652[F] 4852[7]
Jamaaron *W G M Turner* 84 h
4 ch g Bachir(IRE) —Kentmere (FR) (Galetto (FR))
1594[10] 1729[9] 2454[2] 2935[3] 2995[7]3349[3] 3456[7] 3804[3]
Jamadast Roma *N A Twiston-Davies* 57b
4 b f Doubletour(USA) —Outfield (Monksfield)
2830[9] 3651[9]
Jamaican Flight (USA) *Mrs S Lamyman* 90h
13 b h Sunshine Forever(USA) —Kalamona (USA) (Hawaii)
3687[8] 3966[5] 5137[9]
Jamerosier (FR) *Mrs L C Taylor* 109h 116 c
9 b g The Wonder(FR) —Teuphaine (FR) (Barbotan (FR))
4054[4]
James Bay (IRE) *N G Richards* 69h
5 b g Bob Back(USA) —Slave Gale (IRE) (Strong Gale)
3273[3]
Jameson Prince (IRE) *B P Galvin*
6 ch g Old Vic—Kigali (IRE) (Torus)
44a[S]
James Victor (IRE) *N R Mitchell* 61b 113+c
8 b g Be My Guest(USA) —Antakiya (IRE) (Ela-Mana-Mou)
534[4] 666[U] (752) 946[3] 1221[U] 1273[4]1457[2] 1650[4]
Jamica Plane (IRE) *J J Lambe* 93c
13 b g Aristocracy—Petite Fee (Cut Above)
644[2] 874[3] (939) 1065[P]
Jamorin Dancer *S G Chadwick* 68h 89c
11 b g Charmer—Geryea (USA) (Desert Wine (USA))
1229 520[6] 601[7] 716[12]1148[4]
Jandal *C L Popham* 67h 83c
12 ch g Arazi(USA) —Littlefield (Bay Express)
565[9] 750[5] 812[P]
Jane's Rug Rat *C L Popham*
7 gr g Rebelsway—Noble Roxy (Touch Of Grey)
1274[10] 1459[9] 1730[9]
Jansue Charlie *R Nixon* 98 h 72c
12 ch g Ardar—Kincherinchee (Dunbeath (USA))
81[3] 554[7]
Jaoka Du Gord (FR) *P R Webber* 94b 113c
9 b g Concorde Jr(USA) —Theorie Du Cochet (FR) (Franc Ryk)
12[2] 430[F] 1920[P]2325[4] 3151[3] 3343[U]
Jaolins *M Appleby* 30h
5 b m Groom Dancer(USA) —On The Top (High Top)
3[F]
Jaquouille (FR) *A L T Moore* 109 h 131c
9 b g Agent Bleu(FR) —Topeka (FR) (Italic (FR))
3053a[18] 3587a[9]
Jardin De Beaulieu (FR) *Ian Williams* 110c
9 ch g Rough Magic(FR) —Emblem (FR) (Siberian Express (USA))
1848[2] 2151[4]
Jarod (FR) *Mark Doyle* 80h 39c
8 b g Scribe(IRE) —Somnambula (IRE) (Petoski)
5020[7]
Jarro (FR) *Miss Venetia Williams* 125c
10 b g Pistolet Bleu(IRE) —Junta (FR) (Cariellor (FR))
2870[4] 4037[6]
Jarvo *Mark Campion*
5 b g Pursuit Of Love—Pinkie Rose (FR) (Kenmare (FR))
1614[P] 2040[8]

Jaskini *L Corcoran* 72h
10 b g Lion Cavern(USA) —Sharka (Shareef Dancer (USA))
1801[P] 2314[P] **2456[8]**
Jasmin D'Oudairies (FR) *W P Mullins* 118h 137c
9 b g Apeldoorn(FR) —Vellea (FR) (Cap Martin (FR))
(69a)
Jasper *Evan Williams*
7 gr g Environment Friend—Fisima (Efisio)
2152[P]
Jasper Rooney *C W Mitchell* 56b
7 b g Riverwise(USA) —Miss Secret (El Conquistador)
3215[F] 4676[P]
Jass *K G Reveley* 100b
4 b g Robellino(USA) —Iota (Niniski (USA))
(2105) 3623[3]
Jaunty Flight *B J Eckley* 39b
4 b f Busy Flight—Jaunty June (Primitive Rising (USA))
4976[13]
Jaunty Times *H D Daly* 122h
6 b g Luso—Jaunty June (Primitive Rising (USA))
(2503) (2813) 3289[4] 3675[8] 4215[2] 4961[7]
Javelin *N J Hawke* 115h 88c
10 ch g Generous(IRE) —Moss (Alzao (USA))
129[P]
Javelot D'Or (FR) *Mrs B K Thomson* 85+c
9 bb g Useful(FR) —Flika D'Or (FR) (Pot D'Or (FR))
84[P] 354[U] 466[6]939[5] 999[P] 1308[P]
Jaybejay (NZ) *T R George* 120h 90c
11 b g High Ice(USA) —Galaxy Light (NZ) (Balios)
1986[5] 2294[P] 2957[P]
Jayed (IRE) *M Bradstock* 88 h
8 bb g Marju(IRE) —Taqreem (IRE) (Nashwan (USA))
389[P] 806[8] 2218[2] 2685[8] 2940[7]3661[2] 3889[4]
Jayenar *W S Coltherd* 10b
5 gr m Kadeed(IRE) —Anzarna (Zambrano)
5124[14]
Jay Lo (IRE) *James G Sheehan* 120h 101c
8 ch m Glacial Storm(USA) —Celestial Rose (IRE) (Roselier (FR))
4542a[5]
Jazz City *J L Spearing* 82b
6 br g Rock City—Hullo Mary Doll (Lidhame)
655[6] 963[4]
Jazz D'Estruval (FR) *N G Richards* 142 h 148 c
9 gr g Bayolidaan(FR) —Caro D'Estruval (FR) (Caramo (FR))
(2876)
Jazz Du Forez (FR) *John Allen* 65h 80 c
9 b g Video Rock(FR) —Ophyr Du Forez (FR) (Fin Bon)
76[4] 653[7] 1219[F]1395[7] **2243[3] 2686[P]**
Jazz Junior *M J Weeden*
7 ch g Romany Rye—Rising's Lass (IRE) (Rising)
2056[12]
Jazz Messenger (FR) *Noel Meade* 140+h
6 b g Acatenango(GER) —In The Saltmine (FR) (Damister (USA))
4430[7] 4950a[3] 5056a[3]
Jazz Night *S Lycett* 75h 112+c
9 b g Alhijaz—Hen Night (Mummy's Game)
52[4] 437[8] (1299) (1363) 1542[7]
Jballingall *N Wilson* 58b 92 c
7 b g Overbury(IRE) —Sister Delaney (Deep Run)
1928[2] 2877[P] 3338[2]3398[P] 3798[P] 4520[P]4921[P]
Jealous Mead (IRE) *J Howard Johnson* 62b
5 ro g I'm Supposin(IRE) —Spindle'S (Gran Alba (USA))
124[P]
Jeanie's Last *G J Smith* 46b
7 b m Primitive Rising(USA) —Jean Jeanie (Roman Warrior)
2179[P] **2701[P]**
Jean Le Poisson (FR) *N J Henderson* 104+b
4 b g Villez(USA) —Baladinine (FR) (Bering) (4623) 5008[6]
Jeepers Creepers *Mrs A M Thorpe* 59b
6 b g Wizard King—Dark Amber (Formidable (USA))
1635[3] 1777[10] 4128[13] 4284[F]
Jefertiti (FR) *Miss Lucinda V Russell* 100h 105 c
9 ch g Le Nain Jaune(FR) —Nefertiti (FR) (Tourangeau (FR))
1295[6] 1529[2] 1666[4]2067[5] 2818[9]
Jeffslottery *D W Lewis*
4 b g Rock City—Thieves Welcome (Most Welcome)
3238[P]
Jendali Lad *R C Guest* 73b
5 bb g Jendali(USA) —Magic Lake (Primo Dominie)
5124[10]
Jenkins Lane (IRE) *J J Lambe* 75h
4 b g Revoque(IRE) —Suzy Street (IRE) (Dancing Dissident (USA))
1512[5] 1821[6]
Jenna Stannis *W Storey* 21h
4 ch f Wolfhound(USA) —Darling Splodge (Elegant Air)
2245[U] 3349[10]
Jeremy Cuddle Duck (IRE) *N A Twiston-Davies* 125 h
5 b g Supreme Leader—Shean Bracken (IRE) (Le Moss)
(1323) (1672) (1847) 2206[P] 3969[5] 4469[10]
Jericho III (FR) *Miss Venetia Williams* 97b 126+c
9 b g Lute Antique(FR) —La Salamandre (FR) (Pot D'Or (FR))
1913[P] 2067[4] 2183[2]2339[8] 2626[3] 3387[P]3922[4] (4378) 4850[8]
Jeringa *J Wade* 81h
7 b g Karinga Bay—Jervandha (Strong Gale)
3789[7] 4493[5] 4988[3]
Jerom De Vindecy (FR) *Miss Lucinda V Russell* 84c
9 ch g Roi De Rome(USA) —Preves Du Forez (FR) (Quart De Vin (FR))
2065[F] 2449[P] 2989[3]3317[6] 3543[2] 3849[4]4489[5]

Jesnic (IRE) *R Dickin* 57h 74c
6 b g Kahyasi—Fur Hat (Habitat)
532[P] 2073[P] **3359[7]3460[P] 4876[P]**
Jesper (FR) *R T Phillips* 100+h 67c
9 b g Video Rock(FR) —Belle Des Airs (FR) (Saumon (FR))
1834 416[P] 4282[10]4805[8]
Jessie May (IRE) *P R Webber* 47+b
5 b m Supreme Leader—Polly Platinum (IRE) (Phardante (FR))
4800[5]
Jethro Tull (IRE) *G A Harker* 98h 67c
7 b g Witness Box(USA) —Country Project (IRE) (Project Manager)
1915[8] 2169[10] (2417) 2691[3] **3336[6]**3987[6]
Jetowa Du Bois Hue (FR) *T R George* 108h 116+c
9 b g Kadrou(FR) —Vaika (FR) (Cosmopolitan (FR))
666[7] 1399[5]
Jeune Loup *P C Haslam*
4 b g Loup Sauvage(USA) —Secret Waters (Pharly (FR))
3539[P]
Jeune Premier (FR) *Evan Williams*
9 ch g Jeune Homme(USA) —Misaine (FR) (Saint Cyrien (FR))
1520[P] 1655[P]
Jexel (FR) *B Storey* 106 h 106+c
9 b g Video Rock(FR) —Siesta (FR) (Prove It Baby (USA))
2629[4] 2944[B] 3234[P] **3850[3]4142[7] 4587[2] 5122[P]**
Jigsaw Jumper (IRE) *Andrew Turnell*
6 b m Shahrastani(USA) —Cockney Bug (Torus)
3354[P] 3947[P]
Jillanory *C W Moore* 11b
4 b f Riverhead(USA) —Very Ominous (Dominion)
4072[20] 4554[15]
Jim (FR) *J T R Dreaper* 131h 158 c
9 b g Glaieul(USA) —Beautywal (FR) (Magwal (FR))
69a[15] 2793a[2] 3774a[2]3999a[2] 4761[P]
Jim Bobs Girl (IRE) *W Jenks* 76b
5 b m Flemensfirth(USA) —Sinfonietta (Foolish Pleasure (USA))
4800[3]
Jim Lad *J W Mullins* 72h 89c
6 b g Young Ern—Anne's Bank (IRE) (Burslem)
724[11] **914[4] 1019[5]1176[2] 1275[5] 1363[3]**
Jimmy Bedney (IRE) *M G Rimell* 85h
5 bb g Simply Great(FR) —Double Token (Furry Glen)
2494 2288[2] 2755[3] 3248[7] 3975[P]
Jimmy Blues *Ferdy Murphy* 86h 68c
11 b g Durgam(USA) —Tibbi Blues (Cure The Blues (USA))
151[P]
Jimmy Bond *Mrs K Walton* 81h 114c
7 b g Primitive Rising(USA) —Miss Moneypenny (Silly Prices)
2187[2] (3037) 3255[5](3849) (4520) 4788[2]
Jimmy Byrne (IRE) *R C Guest* 98h
6 ch g Red Sunset—Persian Sally (IRE) (Persian Bold)
120[7] 826[2] 860[5] 1322[7] 1553[4]1717[3] 1816[10]
Jimmy Cricket *Ms Caroline Walker* 93c
9 ch g Primitive Rising(USA) —Norton Gale (IRE) (Le Bavard (FR))
440[4]
Jimmys Duky (IRE) *D M Forster* 38h 76+c
8 b g Duky—Harvey's Cream (IRE) (Mandalus)
2109[R] 2495[5] 3915[4]4655[2] 4918[4]
Jimmy Spot On (IRE) *Seamus Lynch* 116h
9 b g Rainbows For Life(CAN) —Lady Be Lucky (IRE) (Taufan (USA))
5078a[13]
Jimmy Tennis (FR) *Miss Venetia Williams* 120+c
9 bb g Video Rock(FR) —Via Tennise (FR) (Brezzo (FR))
454[P] 2518[4]
Jivaty (FR) *Mrs A J Hamilton-Fairley* 111h 108+c
9 b g Quart De Vin(FR) —Tenacity (FR) (Prove It Baby (USA))
244[2] 436[5] 669[P]805[P] 1232[P] 1405[5]**1595[F]** 1800[9]
Jiver (IRE) *M Scudamore* 117h 120 c
7 b g Flemensfirth(USA) —Choice Brush (IRE) (Brush Aside (USA))
1678[F] 1741[2] 1893[2]2162[6] 2608[P] 3000[6]3469[F] 3581[2] 3970[4] 4579[4]**4835[P]**
Joaci (IRE) *M C Pipe* 159 c
6 b g Presenting—Miss Sarajevo (IRE) (Brush Aside (USA))
(3176) 3390[B] 3971[F]4764[P]
Jobsworth (IRE) *Evan Williams* 68h
6 ch g Good Thyne(USA) —Brown Willows (IRE) (Kemal (FR))
2432[10] 3292[2] 4326[5] 4644[7] 4784[8]4934[10] 5110[14]
Jockie Wells *Miss Lucinda V Russell* 66h
8 b g Primitive Rising(USA) —Princess Maxine (IRE) (Horage)
85[6] 523[P]
Jockser (IRE) *J W Mullins* 121+h
5 b g Desert Story(IRE) —Pupa Fiorini (ITY) (Indian Ridge)
387[2] 1675[7] 2207[12] 2706[4] 3143[2]3880[3] 4663[7] (4781) 5[4]
Jo D'Alco (FR) *P Briard*
9 b g Dom Alco(FR) —Datilca (FR) (Italic (FR))
1074a[F]
Jodante (IRE) *R C Guest* 108+h 119+c
9 ch g Phardante(FR) —Crashtown Lucy (Crash Course)
108[P] 195[5] 354[P]2754[4] 3272[2] (4900) (5074) 13[U]
Joe Blake (IRE) *I R Ferguson* 135 c
11 b g Jurado(USA) —I'Ve No Idea (Nishapour (FR))
4471[3] 4975[3]
Joe Brown *Mrs H Dalton* 104 h
6 br g Overbury(IRE) —Miss Roscoe (Roscoe Blake)
1892[5] 2186[3] 2631[7] 3042[2] (3339) 3548[7]

Joe Cooley (IRE) *K A Ryan* 82b
6 b g Accordion—My Missy Molly (IRE) (Entitled)
369P

Joe Cullen (IRE) *Ian Williams* 123 h 110c
11 ch g River Falls—Moycullen (Le Moss)
63313

Joe Deane (IRE) *M J Coombe* 92 h 103c
10 ch g Alphabatim(USA) —Craic Go Leor (Deep Run)
205112 25945 2733F3285³ 36987 40472442657 48372

Joe Malone (IRE) *Mrs A E Brooks* 81h
7 br g Rashar(USA) —Bucktina (Buckskin (FR))
3437 4955 1528LFT 16855 2586²34467 43417 4869P

Joemanchie (IRE) *Thomas O'Neill* 29h
8 ch g Commanche Run—Head Of Affairs (English Prince)
5917

Joe McHugh (IRE) *C J Mann* 67h 95+c
7 ch g Topanoora—Run For Shelter (Strong Gale)
190311 220616 23765 2986P36722 (4394) 4650P

Joes Edge (IRE) *Ferdy Murphy* 115 h 145 c
9 bb g Supreme Leader—Right Dark (Buckskin (FR))
115a2 1926U 2491112744⁴ 2992⁴ 447013⁴777⁷ 50946

Joey *R Hollinshead* 73h
4 b f Polar Prince(IRE) —Understudy (In The Wings)
48776 39

Joey Dunlop (IRE) *J Clements* 75c
12 br g Maelstrom Lake—Middle Verde (USA) (Sham (USA))
17415 18866

Joey Tribbiani (IRE) *T Keddy* 81h 122c
9 b g Foxhound(USA) —Mardi Gras Belle (USA) (Masked Dancer (USA))
(1399) 33576 3788²40893 46772 50182

Jofi (IRE) *Miss Lucinda V Russell* 55b
7 b g Shernazar—Giolla Donn (Giolla Mear)
1938 5 2450P 2945P 13P

John Diamond (IRE) *Miss H C Knight* 100h
5 b g Un Desperado(FR) —Lessons Lass (IRE) (Doyoun)
25349 27205 33695 49705

John Foley (IRE) *D P Keane* 99h 108+c
8 b g Petardia—Fast Bay (Bay Express)
1976P 25228 38877

John Forbes *B Ellison* 84+h
4 b g High Estate—Mavourneen (USA) (Dynaformer (USA))
9456 10114 3539U 40393

John James (IRE) *J H Scott* 97h 134c
10 b g Bravefoot—Glitter Grey (Nishapour (FR))
69a8 4138a8

John Jorrocks (FR) *J C Tuck* 57+h
7 br g Chamberlin(FR) —Caryatide (FR) (Maiymad)
167111 3898 17177 33303 345614⁴3683

Johnnybarry *Thomas Gerard O'Leary* 97b
6 ch g Colonel Collins(USA) —Run Tiger (IRE) (Commanche Run)
44a12

Johnny Grand *D W Lewis* 83c
9 b g Kasakov—Richesse (FR) (Far Away Son (USA))
1355 3957 9587999² 11097 141461524⁹ 50478 (Dead)

John Oliver (IRE) *John Queally* 112+h 116c
8 gr g Lure(USA) —Glitter Grey (Nishapour (FR))
71a9

John Rich *M E Sowersby* 65c
10 b g Mesleh—South Lodge (Current Magic)
6905 8273 896010153 1110P 2077P22665 25680 2966R3486P 8P

Johns Legacy *Miss Sarah Robinson* 104+c
11 gr g Almoojid—Flying Joker (Kalaglow)
(98)

Johnston's Swallow (IRE) *M J P O'Brien* 103h
8 b g Commanche Run—Mirror Of Flowers (Artaius (USA))
117aP

John's Treasure (IRE) *M A Barnes* 65h
6 b g Entrepreneur—Misallah (IRE) (Shirley Heights)
6455 3496P 39856

John The Greek (IRE) *A M Hales* 68+h 88c
10 bb g Aristocracy—Lucky Minstrel (IRE) (Black Minstrel)
4320P

Johnyyouronlyjoken (IRE) *N F Glynn* 96b 71c
10 gr g Roselier(FR) —Badsworth Madam (Over The River (FR))
3654P

Joie Du Manoir (FR) *Mme L Bellet*
9 b m Sicyos(USA) —Orallis (FR) (Pot D'Or (FR))
845a5

Joint Agreement (IRE) *T M Walsh* 110h 98c
9 ch g Good Thyne(USA) —Vul Gale (Strong Gale)
43a14 3053a16

Joint Authority (IRE) *D L Williams* 95h 110 c
11 b g Religiously(USA) —Highway's Last (Royal Highway)
2344 (567) 7254845aP 1074a6 1373a5

Joizel (FR) *V G Greenway* 74h 112c
9 b g Fill My Hopes(FR) —Anne De Boizel (FR) (Dhausli (FR))
4036P (4428) 4558P 5114F

Jojo I (FR) *S Hamon*
9 b g Kadalko(FR) —Amarante II (FR) (Brezzo (FR))
1074a5

Jolejoker *R Lee* 110+c
8 b g Alflora(IRE) —Jolejester (Relkino)
2712 18293 2660P3920P (4639)

Joli Christmas *G Chambers* 74c
9 b g Joligeneration—Christmas Bash (Shaab)
2997

Joli Classical (IRE) *R J Hodges* 80h
4 b f Classic Cliche(IRE) —Mesp (IRE) (Strong Gale)
22744 26817 31326 34834 4290F47318 50844

Jolie Mome Deux (FR) *F Bellenger*
6 ch m Marignan(USA) —Rivilla (Glint Of Gold)
846aF

Jolika (FR) *L Lungo* 103 h 108c
9 b m Grand Tresor(FR) —Unika Ii (FR) (Rolling Bowl (FR))
1192 20272 24534 29443

Jolly Boy (FR) *Miss Venetia Williams* 61h 100 c
7 b g Franc Bleu Argent(USA) —Lady Charrecey (FR) (Fin Bon)
16725 1905P 22573(2561) (2684) (2719) (2801) (2867) 3533P 4053P

Jolly Joe (IRE) *S T Lewis* 69b
9 b g Jolly Jake(NZ) —The Bread Robber (Mandalus)
4975P

Jollyolly *P Bowen* 140 h
7 gr g Environment Friend—Off The Air (IRE) (Taufan (USA))
422¹0 814P

Jollyshau (IRE) *Miss A M Newton-Smith* 86+h 100 c
8 b g Jolly Jake(NZ) —Escheat (Torus)
2957P 35986 4557P

Jollys Pride *K F Clutterbuck* 41h
5 b g Orpen(USA) —Greek Night Out (IRE) (Ela-Mana-Mou)
11126

Joly Bey (FR) *N J Gifford* 138 h 150 c
9 ch g Beyssac(FR) —Rivolie (FR) (Mistigri)
20545 2499P

Jomacomi *C Byrnes* 116h
5 b h Hector Protector(USA) —Stylish Rose (IRE) (Don't Forget Me)
3515a3

Jomelamin *R J Hodges* 60b
4 gr f Silver Patriarch(IRE) —Jomel Amou (IRE) (Ela-Mana-Mou)
26117 32449

Jonanaud *H J Manners* 103h 94c
7 b g Ballet Royal(USA) —Margaret Modes (Thatching)
167513 22136 2682U3331F 3480P 380154016P 41316 4729548276 50254

Jones's Road (IRE) *Jonjo O'Neill* 93h 118+c
8 ch g Be My Native(USA) —Hill Blends (IRE) (Glacial Storm (USA))
330P 19207 2294P

Jongleur Collonges (FR) *R H Alner* 104 h 109c
9 gr g Royal Charter(FR) —Soubrette Collonge (FR) (Saumon (FR))
1855P

Jonny's Kick *T D Easterby* 92 h 103c
6 b g Revoque(IRE) —Prudence (Grundy)
1928P 20783 2187324153 26306 2966P36525 37325 (5049) 51395

Jontys'Lass *A Crook* 110h
5 b m Tamure(IRE) —Gay Muse (Scorpio (FR))
2414 (431) 22624 25155 31676 35403(3795) 4108F 43913 46192 49722

Jordans Lad (IRE) *M Scudamore* 101h 120 c
10 b g Camden Town—Clockonocra (Shall We Dance)
31445

Jordan's Ridge (IRE) *P Monteith* 102h 118c
10 bb g Indian Ridge—Sadie Jordan (USA) (Hail The Pirates (USA))
4235 12955 14357

Jordans Spark *P Monteith* 69h
5 ch g Opening Verse(USA) —Ribot's Pearl (Indian Ridge)
9369 15278 20406

Joris De Vonnas (FR) *Rob Hodges* 82h 94+c
9 ch g Dear Doctor(FR) —Carine De Neuvy (FR) (Shelley (FR))
109P 3348 455513

Jorobaden (FR) *Mrs H Dalton* 139+h
6 gr g Poliglote—Mercalle (FR) (Kaldoun (FR)) (1760) (1844) 2336P

Jorodama King *N J Hawke*
12 b g Lighter—Princess Hecate (Autre Prince)
31256 404710 4428P4666P

Josear *C J Down* 100 h
4 b g Josr Algarhoud(IRE) —Real Popcorn (IRE) (Jareer (USA))
1380R 14788 15195 15944 1729520693 22983 25973 (2797) 3021P 3422238893 41533 45513

Jose Bove *R Dickin* 72b
4 ch c So Factual(USA) —Dark Sirona (Pitskelly)
29278 362310

Joseph Beuys (IRE) *D P Keane* 78 h 96+c
7 ch g Flemensfirth(USA) —Final Countdown (King's Ride)
19853 242610 27997 31395 34994(3662) 3989P 43282

Josephine Cullen (IRE) *W P Mullins* 116+h
4 ch f Daggers Drawn(USA) —Moycullen (Le Moss)
(5076a)

Joshua's Bay *J R Jenkins* 115 h
8 b g Karinga Bay—Bonita Blakeney (Baron Blakeney)
2333 4880 6752 8417 1039P

Jo's Sale (IRE) *Evan Williams* 76h 59c
7 b g Germany(USA) —Clonmeen Lodge (IRE) (Buckskin (FR))
20310 10447 1359747261²

Joueur D'Estruval (FR) *W P Mullins* 135 h 132c
9 gr g Perrault—Alrose (FR) (Kalyan (FR))
69a3 2650a16 4951a5 (5059a)

Joung Man (POL) *V Luka*
9 b g Juror(POL) —Joung Girl (POL) (Valiant Heart (FR))
471a4

Jour De Mee (FR) *G J Smith* 72 h 89 c
9 ch g Beyssac(FR) —Une De Mee (FR) (Sarpedon (FR))
2431U 26924 2986435824 36865 401344165F 479412 49115

Journal Princess (IRE) *M Scudamore* 80h
7 b m Zaffaran(USA) —Bramble Hatch (Pry)
329P (Dead)

Journals Rosy (IRE) *M Scudamore*
5 gr m Clerkenwell(USA) —Rosy Posy (IRE) (Roselier (FR))
20219

Joyful Echo *J E Dixon*
7 ch m Jumbo Hirt(USA) —Joyful Star (Rubor)
5038P

Joyryder *Carl Llewellyn* 116+b
5 gr g Cloudings(IRE) —Knight Ryde (Broadsword (USA))
20498 (4622) 48537

Jubilant Note (IRE) *Michael David Murphy* 107h
4 b c Sadler's Wells(USA) —Hint Of Humour (USA) (Woodman (USA))
4122a8

Jubilee Dream *Mrs L J Mongan* 78h
4 b g Bluebird(USA) —Last Dream (IRE) (Alzao (USA))
38984 42119

Jubilee Prince *A E Jones* 16h
6 b g Petong—Efficacious (IRE) (Efisio)
901F 94310

Judaic Ways *H D Daly* 72h 92c
12 b g Rudimentary(USA) —Judeah (Great Nephew)
6P 1764 572512055 14464 17284

Judge'N'Thomas *M R Bosley* 25b
6 b g Sadler's Way—Stapleford Lady (Bairn (USA))
5071² 2826P 33559 3591P

Judy's Lad *Mrs H R J Nelmes* 19h
7 ch g Master Willie—Flexwing (Electric)
31389 35118 3948P4285P 4689P

Judy The Drinker *J G M O'Shea* 49h
7 b m Snurge—Mardessa (Ardross)
4634 6856 8160 1681P 255913457784733P

Jug Of Punch (IRE) *S T Lewis* 86h
7 ch g In The Wings—Mysistra (FR) (Machiavellian (USA))
16437 17245 18758 (2140) 281610 368763899⁸ (4046) 45497 495911

Jules Lee *W G M Turner*
4 ch g Bluegrass Prince(IRE) —Jade's Girl (Emarati (USA))
3349F

Julies Boy (IRE) *T R George* 72+h 102 c
9 b g Toulon—Chickmo (IRE) (Seclude (USA))
(2217) (2323) 2684832743 (3546) 366343964² 44267 4873P

Julio Du Tao (FR) *Mme A Muilwijk*
9 bb g Beyssac(FR) —Angelina (FR) (Brezzo (FR))
4718a6

Julius Caesar *J Howard Johnson* 124 h 130 c
6 b g Sadler's Wells(USA) —Stiletta (Dancing Brave (USA))
(2291) 26432 3740F4841P

July Bleue (FR) *L Bellet*
9 b m Art Bleu—Ultradouce (FR) (Kashneb (FR))
1373aF

Jumbo's Dream *J E Dixon* 56h 83c
15 b g Jumbo Hirt(USA) —Joyful Star (Rubor)
2022P 2978P 333844659P

Jumpty Dumpty (FR) *J C Tuck* 90 h 77+c
9 bb g Chamberlin(FR) —Caryatide (FR) (Maiymad)
50111 6736 805717805 2009P

June's River (IRE) *Dr P Pritchard* 56h 25c
13 ch g Over The River(FR) —June Bug (Welsh Saint)
3175P 38868 401010

Jungle Fever (FR) *P Chemin*
9 b m Lights Out(FR) —Star Dancer (FR) (Mitsoupam (FR))
(1074a)

Jungle Gingoes (IRE) *John G Carr* 64h
6 b g Lord Of Appeal—Whatt Ya Doin (IRE) (Duky)
306P

Jungle Jinks (IRE) *G M Moore* 120h 127c
11 b g Proud Panther(FR) —Three Ladies (Menelek)
126 17984 2189²26442 29466 (3396) 40705 4505P

Junior Des Ormeaux (FR) *S H Shirley-Beavan* 117c
9 b g Baby Turk—Chic D'Estruval (FR) (Cyborg (FR))
2689P 32362 3850245316

Junior Fontaine (FR) *David M Easterby* 124h 122c
9 b g Silver Rainbow—Blanche Fontaine (FR) (Oakland (FR))
69a9 1083a4 1515a154748⁵

Jupiter Jo *J B Walton* 90b 94+c
10 b g Jupiter Island—Marejo (Creetown)
1224 717U 858393961 11096 1335213763 16026

Jupiter's Fancy *M V Coglan* 82b 94c
11 ch m Jupiter Island—Joe's Fancy (Apollo Eight)
123DSQ (322) 440P37583 (3926) 43474

Jupon Vert (FR) *R J Hodges* 101h 101 c
9 b g Lights Out(FR) —Danse Verte (FR) (Brezzo (FR))
1766 3865 505366644 7444 2074322394 24202 27335(2960) 32396 3370234822 37183 388734281² 44262 47824485⁹2 51122

Jupsala (FR) *S B Bell* 75h 73c
9 ch g Video Rock(FR) —Belle D'Avril (FR) (Quart De Vin (FR))
3228 555P 3338P34866 39303 4659P

Jurado Express (IRE) *Miss Venetia Williams* 101h 125+c
10 b g Jurado(USA) —Express Film (Ashmore (FR))
37247 3852P 408944378³ 46182 50275

Jurrassique (FR) *F Doumen* 78c
9 b g Trebrook(FR) —Veves (FR) (Brezzo (FR))
362aP

Just (IRE) *Michael Hourigan* 107+h 114c
7 ch g Great Marquess—Gerdando Lady (IRE) (Exhibitioner)
39733

Just A Diamond *Mrs D Walton* 62h 104c
13 ch m Primitive Rising(USA) —Just Diamonds (Laurence O)
4660U

Just A Man *Richard Mason*
8 b g Primitive Rising(USA) —Pretty Tactfull (State Diplomacy (USA))
5040P

Just Anvil (IRE) *L Wells* 85c
8 ch g Baron Blakeney—Amy Just (IRE) (Bustomi)
25753 2986P 3427P36627

Just Ask *N R Mitchell* 51h
6 ch m Busy Flight—Last Shower (Town And Country)
19545 27187 314910 343711

Just A Splash (IRE) *N J Gifford* 96+h 113+c
6 ch g Synefos(USA) —Guitane Lady (IRE) (Commanche Run)
19823 (2376) 32184 41484 45783

Just A Touch *P Winkworth* 96 h 104c
10 ch g Rakaposhi King—Minim (Rymer)
(3370) 37186 4037750515

Just Barney Boy *S G Waugh*
9 b g Past Glories—Pablena (Pablond)
4722P (Dead)

Just Beth *G Fierro* 121+h
10 ch m Carlingford Castle—One For The Road (Warpath)
3532 4417 19844 22928 2369426212 28202 31793 39872 4497346123 49748

Just Beware *Miss Z C Davison* 67h
4 b f Makbul—Bewails (IRE) (Caerleon (USA))
15634 15945 21017 34315 366111

Just Bryan *P A Pritchard* 36h
7 ch g Southern Music—Prospect Of Whitby (True Song)
2640 3966

Just Buddy *R Dickin*
5 b g Chaddleworth(IRE) —Roscoe's Gemma (Roscoe Blake)
487510

Just Cruising (IRE) *A L T Moore* 107h 99c
9 ch g Be My Native(USA) —Lady Burnett (IRE) (Le Bavard (FR))
5129a9

Just Different (IRE) *P G Murphy* 81h 101c
9 ch g Be My Native(USA) —Just For A Laugh (Idiots Delight)
14339 14796 18607

Just Filly (IRE) *Miss C J E Caroe* 58h
5 ch m Woodborough(USA) —Good Aim (IRE) (Priolo (USA))
18519 2082P 25238 50508

Just For Fun (IRE) *Ferdy Murphy* 90+h 85c
8 br g Kahyasi—Copper Breeze (IRE) (Strong Gale)
2115

Just For Men (IRE) *P F Nicholls* 85h
6 gr g Glacial Storm(USA) —Regents Ballerina (IRE) (Commanche Run)
32402 42843 48034

Just For Now (IRE) *T R George* 97h
7 b g Flemensfirth(USA) —Sara's Pinkie (IRE) (Roselier (FR))
19502 23274

Just Freya *R Dickin*
5 b m Chaddleworth(IRE) —Country Kizzie (Ballacashtal (CAN))
816P 132315

Just Gabby (IRE) *M B Shears* 28b
7 ch m Goldmark(USA) —Slievroe (IRE) (Red Sunset)
86611

Justice Jones *Mrs P Ford* 42h
5 b g Emperor Jones(USA) —Rally For Justice (Dominion)
3249F 3611U 40527

Justified (IRE) *E Sheehy* 139h 154+c
7 b g Leading Counsel(USA) —Monkeylane (Monksfield)
(1790a) (2395a) 3006aU(3341) 3639a3 (4889a) 5100a2

Just In Debt (IRE) *M Todhunter* 113h 140c
10 bb g Montelimar(USA) —No Debt (Oats)
17217 1941P 2370327456 443410 4777F

Justino *J A Geake* 83h
8 b g Bustino—Jupiter's Message (Jupiter Island)
22142 259210 2936F

Just In Time *J Clements* 127h 120c
11 b g Night Shift(USA) —Future Past (USA) (Super Concorde (USA))
(1296) 17432

Just Jaffa (IRE) *Miss Venetia Williams* 58b
7 ch g Zaffaran(USA) —East Link (IRE) (Over The River (FR))
29877

Just Jed *R Shiels* 48b
7 b g Presidium—Carrapateira (Gunner B)
3170P 35327 4793P4918P

Just Jolly (IRE) *J R Cornwall* 75h 105 c
11 b g Jolly Jake(NZ) —Bulgaden Gypsy (Ballinamona Boy)
14147

Just Lark *Mrs V K Rickcord* 55+c
12 b g Rubicund—Shelley's Lark (Sir Lark)
4007

Just Libbi *Ferdy Murphy* 16h
6 b m Cloudings(IRE) —Tibbi Blues (Cure The Blues (USA))
20077 244616 452713

Just Magical *Mrs C A Dunnett* 80b
9 b m Emperor Jones(USA) —Magnetic Point (USA) (Bering)
729P

Just Midas *N M Babbage* 90h 78c
8 b g Merdon Melody—Thabeh (Shareef Dancer (USA))
1085P 12997 141161897P (Dead)

Just Muckin Around (IRE) *R H Buckler* 70h 100+c
10 gr g Celio Rufo—Cousin Muck (IRE) (Henbit (USA))
234[6] 518[U] 684[P]1189[2] 1342[5] 1489[4]1831[3] 1894[4] 2217[6]2522[4] 4911[2]

Just Poppytee *R H Alner* 59b
4 br f Emperor Fountain—State Lady (IRE) (Strong Statement (USA))
3216[10] 3468[10] 3720[4] 4038[8]

Just Posin *Mrs S Lamyman* 67b
5 ch m I'm Supposin(IRE) —We'Re In The Money (Billion (USA))
3292[7] 3417[P]

Justpourit (IRE) *D T Hughes* 133h
7 b g Glacial Storm(USA) —Gale Choice (IRE) (Strong Gale)
2784a[3] 3642a[4] 4137a[6] 5132a[4]

Just Reuben (IRE) *C L Tizzard* 97c
11 gr g Roselier(FR) —Sharp Mama VII (Damsire Unregistered)
1273[P] 1414[12] 1524[3]1650[5] 1901[2] 2151[6]2684[7]

Just Ruby *F Jordan* 63b
5 ch m Gunner B—First Crack (Scallywag)
349[13] 817[7] 2727[9] 4613[P]

Just Sal *R Nixon* 70 h
10 b m Silly Prices—Hanim (IRE) (Hatim (USA))
120[5] 781[P] 2025[7] 2453[9] 2657[6]3335[6] 3552[3]

Just Scooby *M D Hammond* 44b
5 b h Makbul—Cute Wedding (Remainder Man)
431[8]

Just Smudge *A E Price* 88+b
4 b g Fraam—Flakey Dove (Oats)
2425[13] 3462[2] 4807[5]

Just Sooty *S B Clark* 92h 118+c
11 br g Be My Native(USA) —March Fly (Sousa)
497[P] 785[P] 895[10] **1025[P]1219[P]**

Just Superb *P A Pritchard* 109h
7 ch g Superlative—Just Greenwich (Chilibang)
1957[3] 2247[4]

Just Supposin *M C Pipe* 94b
4 b g I'm Supposin(IRE) —Devinette (IRE) (Be My Native (USA))
4615[2]

Just Touch Wood *B G Powell* 67b
5 ch g Fraam—Versaillesprincess (Legend Of France (USA))
2961[13] 3369[13]

Justwhateverulike (IRE) *Miss S E Forster* 56h
5 b g Courtship—Rose Of Summer (IRE) (Taufan (USA))
3785[7] 4147[6] 4532[12] 4793[8] 5063[6]

Just Wiz *J Jay* 87+h
10 b g Efisio—Jade Pet (Petong)
2816[11]

Juveigneur (FR) *N J Henderson* 149c
9 ch g Funny Baby(FR) —Azurea (FR) (On My Way (USA))
2370[F] 3988[P] 4433[2]4777[F] 5004[P]

Kadabelle (FR) *Mme L Audon*
5 b m Kadalko(FR) —Diana La Belle (FR) (Synefos (USA))
4717a[7]

Kadam (IRE) *P F Nicholls* 111+h 104+c
6 b g Night Shift(USA) —Kadassa (IRE) (Shardari)
275[3] 751[5] **812[5]** 2296[7]**2733[9]** 2868[2] 3018[14] **4837[4]**

Kadanza *P Bowen* 78b
5 b g Darazari(IRE) —The Dark Walk (Kemal (FR))
2565[11] 2941[11]

Kadarann (IRE) *P F Nicholls* 145c
9 b g Bigstone(IRE) —Kadassa (IRE) (Shardari)
219[3] 1970[9] 3299[12]4958[4]

Kaddasan *D E Cantillon* 85b
4 b g Indian Lodge(IRE) —Kadassa (IRE) (Shardari)
2927[14] 4595[6]

Kadito *R Dickin* 71 h 62c
10 b g Petoski—Kadastra (FR) (Stradavinsky)
2074[P] 2419[12] **2827[6]3252[U] 3578[7] 3919[P]**

Kadlass (FR) *Mrs D Thomas* 51h
11 b g Kadounor(FR) —Brave Lass (Ridan)
237[P] 385[P] 1900[RR] 3125[P] 4783[12]4903[8]

Kadoun (FR) *H D Daly*
7 gr g Sleeping Car(FR) —Dea De Chalamont (FR) (Royal Charter (FR))
1872[P]

Kadoun (IRE) *M J P O'Brien* 148+h 134c
9 b h Doyoun—Kumta (IRE) (Priolo (USA))
90a[2] 2650a[8] (4461) 5101a[4]

Kadount (FR) *A King* 147c
8 b g Our Account(USA) —Une De Lann (FR) (Spoleto)
1970[7] 2489[P] 3136[5]3503[F] 3988[P] 4984[4]

Kahuna (IRE) *E Sheehy* 132+h 135c
9 b g Mister Lord(USA) —My Baloo (On Your Mark)
1626a[2] 1944a[F] 2195a[6]3261a[4] 3501[4] 5061a[6]

Kahysera *Mrs H Dalton* 82h
5 b m Kahyasi—Recipe (Bustino)
2446[7] 2720[8]

Kaid (IRE) *R Lee* 43h 43 c
11 b g Alzao(USA) —Very Charming (USA) (Vaguely Noble)
1319[8] 1486[12] 2073[9] 3279[6] 4368[7]

Kaikovra (IRE) *M F Harris* 99h 75 c
10 ch g Toulon—Drefflane Supreme (Rusticaro (FR))
1396[P] 1487[9] 1595[4]1746[P] 1956[2] 2074[6]2420[7] 2570[9] 2933[4]3221[8]

Kalabell Prince *R A Farrant* 53h
7 br g Bluegrass Prince(IRE) —Shikabell (Kala Shikari)
3885[P] 3945[6]

Kalamazoo (IRE) *Nick Williams* 99b
5 b g Flemensfirth(USA) —Cheryls Pet (IRE) (General Ironside)
2534[7] *3138[3]* 4011[7]

Kalambari (IRE) *J D Frost* 118h
7 b g Kahyasi—Kalamba (IRE) (Green Dancer (USA))
136[5] 571[4] 726[RR] 841[RR] 1270[3]1675[6] 1828[LFT] 1919[RR]

Kalawoun (FR) *Ferdy Murphy* 71+h
4 b g Highest Honor(FR) —Kalajana (USA) (Green Dancer (USA))
1797[16] 2167[5] 2494[3] 2858[P] 4919[9]

Kalca Mome (FR) *P J Hobbs* 130 h 143+c
8 b g En Calcat(FR) —Belle Mome (FR) (Grand Tresor (FR))
2048[7] 2492[F] 2871[10]**3019[6] 3387[2] 3724[3](3974) 4472[14] 5006[6]**

Kalderon (GER) *T Hogan* 121+h
6 b g Big Shuffle(USA) —Kreuzdame (GER) (Acatenango (GER))
4430[16]

Kaldouas (FR) *P F Nicholls* 103+h
5 bb g Kaldou Star—Popie D'Ecorcei (FR) (Balsamo (FR))
2211[7] (2866) 4678[4]

Kalexandro (FR) *Miss J E Foster* 36h 66c
8 b g Michel Georges—Dalexandra (FR) (Quain (FR))
827[P] 998[P]

Kalic D'Alm (FR) *W S Coltherd* 79h
8 b g Passing Sale(FR) —Bekaa II (FR) (Djarvis (FR))
306[13] 553[4]

Kalin Du Beury (FR) *P Chemin*
8 ch g Chef De Clan(FR) —Pampa Star (FR) (Pampabird)
4718a[P]

Kaline Du Mou (FR) *J Chapdelaine*
8 b m Lights Out(FR) —Olazur Du Clos Ry (FR) (Signani (FR))
4718a[F]

Kalishka (IRE) *R Allan* 10h
5 b g Fasliyev(USA) —Andromaque (USA) (Woodman (USA))
4527[14] 5091[P]

Kalmini (USA) *Miss Sheena West* 115h
4 bb f Rahy(USA) —Kilma (USA) (Silver Hawk (USA))
(2345) (3324) 3722[F] 3817[2] 4435[10]

Kalou (GER) *C Grant* 95 h 114+c
8 br g Law Society(USA) —Kompetenz (IRE) (Be My Guest (USA))
305[2] 479[6] 692[4]855[U] 939[4] 1509[2](2479) 5092[8]

Kaluga (IRE) *S C Burrough* 82h 82c
8 ch m Tagula(IRE) —Another Baileys (Deploy)
4290[7] **4837[U] 5105[8]**

Kandjar D'Allier (FR) *A King* 119+h 146c
8 gr g Royal Charter(FR) —Miss Akarad (FR) (Akarad (FR))
2177[3] 2491[P] 3180[8]3493[4] (4573) 4821[7]

Kanpai (IRE) *J G M O'Shea* 97h
4 br g Trans Island—David's Star (Welsh Saint)
2045[2] 2345[2] 2612[2] 3021[12] 4128[3]

Kaola Du Houx (FR) *E Lecoiffier*
8 b g Moon Madness—Misse Cancal (FR) (Nando (FR))
1373a[6]

Kaparolo (USA) *John A Harris* 105h
7 ch g El Prado(IRE) —Parliament House (USA) (General Assembly (USA))
2964[P] 4390[P] 4797[P]

Kappelhoff (IRE) *Mrs L Richards* 70dh 74c
9 b g Mukaddamah(USA) —Miss Penguin (General Assembly (USA))
503[6] 1855[4] 2575[7]2686[3] 3276[5] 3909[3]4576[6] 4914[3]

Karakum *A J Chamberlain* 82h 106+c
7 b g Mtoto—Magongo (Be My Chief (USA))
979[P] 1155[5] 1363[2]1521[5] 1659[6] 1805[2]4908[P]

Karanja *V R A Dartnall* 133+h
7 b g Karinga Bay—Proverbial Rose (Proverb)
1847[2] 2301[2] (2461) 3249[P] 4469[7]

Karathaena (IRE) *M E Sowersby* 110 h
6 b m Barathea(IRE) —Dabtara (IRE) (Kahyasi)
571[P] 1552[4] (1610) 1668[6] 1912[3] 2079[4]2519[5] 2766[3] 2964[4] 3542[U]

Karawa *C L Tizzard* 86b
7 ch m Karinga Bay—Lady Buck (Pollerton)
300[7] 2021[3] 2421[11]

Karelian *K A Ryan* 117+h
5 gr g Linamix(FR) —Kalikala (Darshaan)
420[4]

Karello Bay *N J Henderson* 102b
5 b m Kahyasi—Caramello (Supreme Leader)
3468[2] (4059) (4376)

Karine Des Ongrais (FR) *P Chemin*
11 ch m Cyborg(FR) —Miss De La Croix (FR) (Tip Moss (FR))
(845a) 1073a[4]

Kario De Sormain (FR) *J-P Gallorini* 133h
8 ch m Gunboat Diplomacy(FR) —Bialystok (FR) (Saint Henri)
4445[U]

Karlo (IRE) *David A Kiely* 109c
9 bb g Toulon—Sammies Dozer (IRE) (Bulldozer)
5129a[7]

Karo De Vindecy (FR) *M D Hammond* 72h 103+c
8 b g Mollicone Junior(FR) —Preves Du Forez (FR) (Quart De Vin (FR))
416[6] 605[2] 717[7]1109[3] (1359) 1570[4]2172[2] 2570[7] 5092[2]

Karoo *K Bishop* 84h
8 b g Karinga Bay—Cupids Bower (Owen Dudley)
2845[P] 3950[5] 4331[P]

Karrie *C C Bealby* 65b
5 ch m Karinga Bay—Riva La Belle (Ron's Victory (USA))
3421[4] 3961[5] 4875[P]

Karrnak *Miss J Feilden* 62 h
4 b g Hernando(FR) —Maiden Aunt (IRE) (Distant Relative)
2236[10] 2949[8] 4056[4]

Karyon (IRE) *Miss Kate Milligan* 62h
6 b m Presidium—Stealthy (Kind Of Hush)
213[P] 2567[8] 3557[10]

Kasbah Bliss (FR) *F Doumen* 140h
4 b g Kahyasi—Marital Bliss (FR) (Double Bed (FR))
1705a[3] 2178[3] (4117) 4468[F]

Kasbimy (FR) *J-P Carnel*
7 b g Kadrou(FR) —Space Meto (FR) (Olmeto)
845a[F] 1073a[9]

Kasilia (FR) *Tim Brown* 89c
8 b g Silver Rainbow—Basilia (FR) (Mont Basile (FR))
50[3] 333[5]

Kasthari (IRE) *J Howard Johnson* 140 h 135 c
7 gr g Vettori(IRE) —Karliyka (IRE) (Last Tycoon)
2344[2] (2924) 3850[U]4456[8] 5002[3]

Katarino (FR) *R Waley-Cohen* 139+c
11 b g Pistolet Bleu(IRE) —Katevana (FR) (Cadoudal (FR))
(4748)

Katesellie *J L Spearing*
6 b m Terimon—Kate's Girl (Lighter)
912[P]

Kate's Gift *P R Webber* 90b
5 b g Supreme Leader—Ardentinny (Ardross)
(7)

Kates Little Pearl (IRE) *Thomas Gerard O'Leary* 51h 82c
6 bb m Beneficial—Brown Pearl (Tap On Wood)
2796a[13]

Kathleen Kennet *Mrs H Sweeting* 45b
6 b m Turtle Island(IRE) —Evaporate (Insan (USA))
3138[8] 3820[10]

Katie Kai *Miss S E Forster* 70h
5 b m Cayman Kai(IRE) —Yemaail (IRE) (Shaadi (USA))
302[8] 496[5] 649[5]

Katy Jones *Noel T Chance* 50b
6 b m Alderbrook—Just Jodi (IRE) (Good Thyne (USA))
2131[3] 2558[9] 3244[10]

Katy's Classic (IRE) *K C Bailey* 13h
6 b g Classic Cliche(IRE) —Mrs Jennifer (River Knight (FR))
2663[P] 3685[8] 3941[P]

Katz Pyjamas (IRE) *G F H Charles-Jones* 40h
5 b m Fasliyev(USA) —Allepolina (USA) (Trempolino (USA))
385[8]

Kausse De Thaix (FR) *O Sherwood* 96b 121+c
8 ch g Iris Noir(FR) —Etoile De Thaix (FR) (Lute Antique (FR))
(2019) (2325) 2485[6]3186[P] 4103[3] 4505[F]4690[P] 4939[4]

Kauto Star (FR) *P F Nicholls* 169+c
6 b g Village Star(FR) —Kauto Relka (FR) (Port Etienne (FR))
1970[2] (2635) 4445[F]

Kavi (IRE) *Simon Earle* 91h 100+c
6 ch g Perugino(USA) —Premier Leap (IRE) (Salmon Leap (USA))
106[F] 744[2]

Kawagino (IRE) *J W Mullins* 154?h 120c
6 b g Perugino(USA) —Sharakawa (IRE) (Darshaan)
2047[2] **2488[4] 2798[U]**3510[8] 4242[U] (4329) 4432[7] 4775[4]

Kayceecee (IRE) *H D Daly* 113 h
5 b g Mister Mat(FR) —Maid Of Glenduragh (IRE) (Ya Zaman (USA))
131[9] 2070[9] 2584[6] 2983[4] (3386) 3848[2]4329[5] 4784[5]

Kayleigh (IRE) *P R Rodford* 69h
8 b m Kylian(USA) —Easter Baby (Derrylin)
3477[P] 3692[8] 3951[9] **4553[P]**4734[6]

Kaysglory *F P Murtagh* 10h
7 b g Glory Of Dancer—Kayartis (Kaytu)
780[P] 1794[16] 2447[P]

Kealshore Lad *G M Moore* 105b
5 b g Supreme Leader—Our Aisling (Blakeney)
2192[2] 2864[2] (3742) 4854[5]

Kedgeree *H D Daly* 93b
4 b g Fleetwood(IRE) —Coh Sho No (Old Vic)
4455[5]

Kedon (CZE) *J Vana Jr* 89c
11 gr g Mill Pond(FR) —Kelda (FR) (Northern Baby (CAN))
1710a[4]

Keenan's Future (IRE) *Ian Williams* 119 h
5 ch g Safety Catch(USA) —The Singer (IRE) (Accordion)
2665[3] (3393) (3881) 4393[U]

Keen Leader (IRE) *Jonjo O'Neill* 154h 167 c
10 b g Supreme Leader—Keen Gale (IRE) (Strong Gale)
1830[5] **1926[F] 2337[4]**

Keen Royal *Miss Suzy Smith* 61b
5 ch m Keen—Ropsley High Style (Superlative)
179[5] 1237[13]

Keen Warrior *Mrs S Lamyman* 88h
6 gr g Keen—Briden (Minster Son)
241[6] 2591[3] 3291[P] 3417[5] 3963[3]4389[P]

Keepakicker (IRE) *E McNamara* 104h 96c
10 bb g Beau Sher—Castlewarren Girl (IRE) (Mister Lord (USA))
3814[10]

Keepasharplookout (IRE) *C W Moore* 64h
4 b g Rossini(USA) —Zoyce (Zilzal (USA))
1332[P] 1441[8] 1729[11] 1802[4] 2069[P]2563[10] 2810[4] 2858[5] 12[P]

Keep Asking (IRE) *Mrs D A Hamer* 81h
10 b g Castle Keep—Melodic Belle (IRE) (Black Minstrel)
1084[5] 1202[2]

Keepatem (IRE) *M F Morris* 130h 138c
10 ch g Be My Native(USA) —Ariannrun (Deep Run)
4019a[4]

Keepers Mead (IRE) *R H Alner* 116+h 104+c
8 ch g Aahsaylad—Runaway Pilot (Cheval)
168[5] 1715[6] 1973[P] 2430[3] (2609) 3018[2]3581[9] 4105[2] **4559[3]** 4727[8]

Keep On Movin' (IRE) *N A Callaghan* 96 h
5 b m Danehill Dancer(IRE) —Tormented (USA) (Alleged (USA))
487[3] (696) 838[2] 1097[2] 1366[11] 1816[5]

Keep Smiling (IRE) *Mrs C J Kerr* 71c
10 b g Broken Hearted—Laugh Away (Furry Glen)
5068[P]

Keepthedreamalive *R H Buckler* 125h 120c
8 gr g Roselier(FR) —Nicklup (Netherkelly)
43a[11] 116a[8] 1598[4] 1872[4] **2213[4]2607[3] 3251[4] 3549[4]3921[6] 4943[2]**

Keevers (IRE) *W J Burke* 126h 106c
12 ch g Commanche Run—Toransha (Torus)
71a[8] (Dead)

Kelantan *K C Bailey* 100h 114+c
9 b g Kris—Surf Bird (Shareef Dancer (USA))
1853[3] 2046[3]

Kellbury *H D Daly* 81b
4 b g Overbury(IRE) —Kellamba (Netherkelly)
4854[9]

Kells Castle *Ms F M Crowley* 111h
4 gr g Fraam—Bit O' May (Mummy's Pet)
3004a[6]

Kelly (SAF) *Miss Venetia Williams* 116h 126+c
9 b g Ethique(ARG) —Dancing Flower (SAF) (Dancing Champ (USA))
(183) (653)

Kelly Bidewell *D B Feek*
4 b f Wace(USA) —Lady Millennium (IRE) (Prince Rupert (FR))
3720[5]

Kelly Pride *Niall Saville* 86h 51c
9 b g Alflora(IRE) —Pearly-B (IRE) (Gunner B)
123[7]

Kellys Fable *J W Mullins* 78h
6 b g Thowra(FR) —Kellys Special (Netherkelly)
201[5] 469[10] **2149[8] 2593[3]2805[P]**

Kelrev (FR) *Miss Venetia Williams* 116 h 141c
8 ch g Video Rock(FR) —Bellile II (FR) (Brezzo (FR))
2492[5] (2768) 3019[U]3385[9] 4459[2] 4958[5]

Keltic Bard *C J Mann* 140 c
9 b g Emperor Jones(USA) —Broughton Singer (IRE) (Common Grounds)
3620[3]

Keltic Blue (IRE) *R Dickin* 16h
7 b g Blues Traveller(IRE) —White Cap'S (Shirley Heights)
74[P]

Keltic Heritage (IRE) *L A Dace* 97h 124c
12 gr g Roselier(FR) —Peek-A-Step (IRE) (Step Together (USA))
5087[6]

Keltic Lord *P W Hiatt* 86h 119+c
10 b g Arctic Lord—Scarlet Dymond (Rymer)
455[4] 746[2] (896) (948) (1025) 1189[4]1398[4] 1549[5] 1637[3]**1778[3] 1989[P] 5046[F]**

Kelv *J A B Old* 94b
5 gr g Karinga Bay—Pendle Princess (Broxted)
4667[4] (4758)

Kempski *R Nixon* 90h
6 b g Petoski—Little Katrina (Little Buskins)
1937[P] 3232[5] 3381[4] 3532[2] 3854[3]4141[6] 4317[3] 4488[4] **4918[R]**

Kenny *Mrs S J Smith* 75b
6 b g Wizard King—Deirdres Dream (The Parson)
2268[7]

Ken's Dream *Mrs L Wadham* 120+h
7 b g Bin Ajwaad(IRE) —Shoag (USA) (Affirmed (USA))
3963[2] 4479[5] (4915)

Kentford Lady *J W Mullins* 77h
5 b m Emperor Fountain—Kentford Duchess (Jupiter Island)
285[2] 2012[7] 2486[7] 2995[12] 3692[9]

Kentmere (IRE) *P R Webber* 104h
5 b g Efisio—Addaya (IRE) (Persian Bold)
(177) 485[3] 695[F] 947[2] 1245[7]

Ken'tucky (FR) *A King* 115 h 130 c
8 b g Video Rock(FR) —La Salamandre (FR) (Pot D'Or (FR))
2046[2] 2518[5] 3296[P]4957[5] (Dead)

Kentucky Blue (IRE) *T D Easterby* 121 h
6 b g Revoque(IRE) —Delta Town (USA) (Sanglamore (USA))
1720[4] 1823[6] 1912[2] 2190[P] 2641[2]3256[4] 3383[P] 3561[3] 4504[6]

Kentucky Charm (FR) *E J O'Grady* 119h
5 gr g Linamix(FR) —Kentucky Kaper (USA) (The Prime Minister (USA))
67a[12]

Kentucky King (USA) *Mrs D A Hamer* 99h
6 b g Tale Of The Cat(USA) —Anna's Honor (USA) (Alleged (USA))
1018[2] 1206[3] 1322[2] 1523[4] 1653[3]1804[3] 1898[F]

Keralam (FR) *B G Powell* 102+b
6 ch g Ashkalani(IRE) —Keraka (USA) (Storm Bird (CAN))
(316)

Kercabellec (FR) *J R Cornwall* 108h 102+c
8 bb g Useful(FR) —Marie De Geneve (FR) (Nishapour (FR))
135[P] 239[2] 364[2]466[3] 1363[5] 1612[6]1819[P] 2257[5] 2705[3]3418[3] 3546[4] 4076[7]4162[3] (4633) 4798[2]5139[8]

Keresforth *Mrs L C Jewell* 48h
4 b g Mind Games—Bullion (Sabrehill (USA))
2373[8] 2681[10] 2949[P] 3939[11]

Kerne Bridge *Mrs S M Johnson* 21b
6 b m Sovereign Water(FR) —Plassey Bridge (Pitpan)
4072[19] 4595[12]

Kerrs Whin *P G Atkinson* 106b
6 b g Past Glories—Dreamago (Sir Mago)
2844[5] 4507[12]

Kerryhead Sunshine (IRE) *Michael Hourigan* 95h 83c
6 bb m Topanoora—Kerryhead Girl (IRE) (Be My Native (USA))
3086a[9]

Kerryhead Windfarm (IRE) *Michael Hourigan* 157h 126c
8 br g Bob Back(USA) —Kerryhead Girl (IRE) (Be My Native (USA))
116a[2] **2364a[2] 3012a[5]3409a[4] 3893a[6] 4759[F]**5101a[2]

Kerry Lads (IRE) *Miss Lucinda V Russell* 82h 139+c
11 ch g Mister Lord(USA) —Minstrel Top (Black Minstrel)
2445^{5} 2946^{2} (3258) 4111^{6} (4505) 5004^{10}

Kerry's Blade (IRE) *P C Haslam* 94 h
4 ch g Daggers Drawn(USA) —Treasure (IRE) (Treasure Kay)
1207^{P} 1397^{8} (1601) 1873^{5} 2372^{5} 3779^{P}

Kerry Zulu Warrior *M Sheppard*
9 ch g Aspect(USA) —Kerry Blue Nun (Fine Blue)
635^{P} 742^{P}

Kerstino Two *Mrs Caroline Keevil* 105+c
9 b g Cruise Missile—Cresswell (Push On)
3819^{4} 4831^{3}

Kestick *Mrs R Kennen* 115c
11 b g Roscoe Blake—Hop The Twig (Full Of Hope)
4471^{14} 4757^{2}

Kestle Mill (IRE) *M J Coombe*
10 ch g Be My Guest(USA) —Tatisha (Habitat)
3938^{P}

Keswick (IRE) *N J Henderson* 96h
6 bb g Taipan(IRE) —Tigrinium Splenden (Buckley)
2829^{7} 4052^{6} 4238^{5} 4961^{11}

Kettysjames (IRE) *John G Carr* 93c
8 ch g Over The River(FR) —Friendly Sea (Callernish)
546^{F}

Kety Star (FR) *A W Carroll* 69 h 125 c
8 b g Bojador(FR) —Danystar (FR) (Alycos (FR))
3719^{7} 4606^{13}

Kevinsky Blue *M J McGrath* 53b
4 ch g Opening Verse(USA) —Zaffre Bleu (IRE) (Zaffaran (USA))
4500^{14} 4825^{8} 5054^{14}

Kevins View (IRE) *A W Carroll* 80h
10 ch g Brief Truce(USA) —Day Dress (Ashmore (FR))
1156^{11}

Kevkat (IRE) *Eoin Griffin* 97b
5 br g Dushyantor(USA) —Diamond Display (IRE) (Shardari)
1882^{4} 5081a^{17}

Kew Jumper (IRE) *Andrew Turnell* 99h 118 c
7 b g Mister Lord(USA) —Pharisee (IRE) (Phardante (FR))
2051^{8} 2926^{5} 3344^{3}

Kewlake Lane *R H Alner* 10b
8 b m Afzal—Sheer Impulse (IRE) (Montelimar (USA))
2311^{U} 2553^{P}

Keyalzao (IRE) *A Crook*
4 b f Alzao(USA) —Key Partner (Law Society (USA))
1718^{P}

Key In *I W McInnes* 71h
5 ch m Unfuwain(USA) —Fleet Key (Afleet (CAN))
2082^{4} 2414^{8} 2663^{7} 3042^{P} 3367^{10}

Keyneema *Miss K M George* 70b
4 b g Kayf Tara—Nothings Forever (Oats)
4667^{9}

Key Of Gold (IRE) *A G Juckes*
5 b g Key Of Luck(USA) —Damaslin (Camden Town)
173^{P}

Key Phil (FR) *D J Wintle* 133c
8 ch g Beyssac(FR) —Rivolie (FR) (Mistigri)
97^{F} 2102^{5} 2577^{7}3344^{2} 4037^{3} 4371^{P}(5067)

Key To The Kingdom (IRE) *Eoin Doyle* 110+h
6 br g Key Of Luck(USA) —Admiralella (Dominion)
(1687) 4661^{6}

Khadija *R Dickin* 82+h
5 ch m Kadastrof(FR) —Dark Sirona (Pitskelly)
2075^{5} 2423^{13}

Khaladjistan (IRE) *Mrs S E Handley* 82c
8 gr g Tirol—Khaladja (IRE) (Akarad (FR))
176^{P} 916^{P} 978^{13}3805^{3}

Kharak (FR) *Mrs S C Bradburne* 114 h 115c
7 gr g Danehill(USA) —Khariyda (FR) (Shakapour)
2065^{3} 2449^{7} 2675^{F}3204^{4} 3849^{P} 4344^{6}4724^{P}

Khaysar (IRE) *N B King* 106h
8 br g Pennekamp(USA) —Khaytada (IRE) (Doyoun)
4899^{P}

Khetaam (IRE) *Noel Meade* 132h
8 b g Machiavellian(USA) —Ghassak (IRE) (Persian Bold)
4473^{5} 4951a^{6} 5059a^{11}

Kicasso *D G Bridgwater* 70h 98c
7 b g Environment Friend—Merry Jane (Rymer)
674^{8} 815^{P}

Kickahead (USA) *Ian Williams* 87 h
4 b g Danzig(USA) —Krissante (USA) (Kris)
2811^{2} 3579^{8} 4057^{U} 4096^{7}

Kickham (IRE) *E J O'Grady* 127 h 132c
10 b g Supreme Leader—Knocknagow (Buckskin (FR))
1083a^{F}

Kicking Bear (IRE) *J K Hunter* 48h
8 b g Little Bighorn—Rongo (IRE) (Tumble Gold)
1937^{8} 2690^{10} 3169^{13} 3335^{5} 3552^{7}4656^{11}

Kicking King (IRE) *T J Taaffe* 145h 177+c
8 b g Old Vic—Fairy Blaze (IRE) (Good Thyne (USA))
(68a) 1810a^{2} 2337^{3}(2972)

Kicks For Free (IRE) *P F Nicholls* 131b
5 b g Flemensfirth(USA) —Keep The Change (IRE) (Castle Keep)
(3244) (3699) 4448^{3} 4779^{3}

Kidithou (FR) *W T Reed* 90h 109+c
8 b g Royal Charter(FR) —De Thou (FR) (Trebrook (FR))
119^{4} 215^{3} 1606^{P} 1939 ^{4}2265^{U} 2445^{F}
2691^{9}3271^{11} 3918^{4} 4113^{3} 4341^{U} 4488^{P}

Kids Inheritance (IRE) *J M Jefferson* 103 h 115 c
8 b g Presenting—Princess Tino (IRE) (Rontino)
108^{6} 409^{6} 1529^{6}2339^{5} (2679) 3172^{5}3495^{6} 3784^{P}
4531^{5}

Kid'Z'Play (IRE) *J S Goldie* 121h 122+c
10 b g Rudimentary(USA) —Saka Saka (Camden Town)
(646) (855) (937) 1083a^{P}1531^{3} 4635^{F} 5065^{3}

Kiev (IRE) *D G Bridgwater* 44h
6 b g Bahhare(USA) —Badrah (USA) (Private Account (USA))
1410^{P} 1712^{P}

Kiftsgate *Mrs P Robeson* 81h 95+c
9 ch g Kris—Blush Rambler (IRE) (Blushing Groom (FR))
4451^{F}

Kiko (FR) *A Chaille-Chaille* 130h
5 b g Poliglote—Kirkla (FR) (Bikala)
778a^{4}

Kilbeggan Lad (IRE) *Michael Hourigan* 126h 125c
8 b g Doyoun—Parnala (USA) (Assert)
43a^{7} 2650a^{12} 3411a^{16} 5078a^{15}

Kilbrickensfirth (IRE) *T K Geraghty* 31b
5 b m Flemensfirth(USA) —Kilbricken Star (Mandalus)
5134a^{21}

Kilbride Lad (IRE) *J J Lambe* 12h
12 b g Mac's Imp(USA) —Cordon (Morston (FR))
304^{10} 988^{14} 1062^{4} (Dead)

Kilcash Demon (IRE) *Michael David Murphy* 73b
5 br g Lord Americo—All Set (IRE) (Electric)
5104a^{14}

Kilcaskin Gold (IRE) *R A Ross* 86c
11 ch g Ore—Maypole Gayle (Strong Gale)
125^{3} 498^{P} 3913^{4}4846^{4}

Kildee Lass *J D Frost* 101h 59+c
7 gr m Morpeth—Pigeon Loft (IRE) (Bellypha)
387^{5} 1749^{5} 2595^{7} 2930^{2}3247^{3} 3483^{5}

Kildonnan *J A B Old* 119+h
7 b g Bob's Return(IRE) —Celtic Tore (IRE) (Torus)
1980^{4} 2426^{2} 3277^{6} 3477^{2} (4099) (4393)

Kilfinny Cross (IRE) *Michael Hourigan* 96h 96c
7 b m Broken Hearted—Polls Joy (Pollerton)
4542a^{4}

Kilgowan (IRE) *Ian Williams* 119 h
7 b g Accordion—Gaiety Lass (Le Moss)
2166^{P} (3675) 4119^{3} 5142^{13}

Kilifi Creek (IRE) *J J Lambe* 75c
9 gr g Arctic Lord—Cummeen Girl (Celio Rufo)
322^{10} 646^{4} 782^{P}

Kilindini *Miss E C Lavelle* 110+h 60c
5 gr g Silver Patriarch(IRE) —Newlands Corner (Forzando)
(230) 457^{3} 742^{3} 1020^{4} 1154^{2} (1298) 1559^{6}4820^{7}

Kilkilian (IRE) *B G Powell* 90b
6 b g Norwich—Vultang Lady (Le Bavard (FR))
2941^{12} 3369^{12}

Killaghy Castle (IRE) *N J Gifford* 132+h
6 b g Topanoora—One Eyed Lucy (IRE) (Miner's Lamp)
1892^{F} (2238) 3023^{3} (4373)

Killard Point (IRE) *Mrs Caroline Bailey* 100+c
7 b g Old Vic—Chic And Elite (Deep Run)
3819^{7} 4477^{4}

Killarney Prince (IRE) *Mrs J M Mann* 80+h
7 b g Lord Americo—Henry Woman (IRE) (Mandalus)
53^{4} 724^{10}

Kill Devil Hill (IRE) *Paul Nolan* 139h 137c
6 b g Carroll House—Home In The Glen (Furry Glen)
40a^{2} (2668a) 3006a^{3} 3893a^{4}4136a^{3}

Killeaney (IRE) *John G Carr* 115h 120+c
9 b g Classic Memory—Welsh Duchy (Welsh Saint)
92a^{9}

Killenaule (IRE) *B G Powell* 107+h
6 b g Bob Back(USA) —Party Woman (IRE) (Sexton Blake)
3342^{5}

Killer (FR) *Miss Lucinda V Russell*
8 ch g Cupidon(FR) —Kaoutchka (FR) (Bakst (USA))
212^{P} 783^{P}

Killer Cat (FR) *G F Edwards* 97 h
5 b g Lost World(IRE) —Heat Storm (USA) (Storm Cat (USA))
451^{8} 2419^{5} 2687^{6} 3757^{11} 4752^{9}4860^{12} 5115^{3}

Killing Joke *J J Lambe* 38h
6 b h Double Trigger(IRE) —Fleeting Vision (IRE) (Vision (USA))
645^{8}

Killing Me Softly *J Gallagher* 119+h
5 b g Kingsinger(IRE) —Slims Lady (Theatrical Charmer)
1957^{11} 2247^{5} (2585) 2802^{5} (3143) 3397^{2}
3615^{5}3986^{10} 4781^{P}

Killonemoonlight (IRE) *D R Stoddart* 107h 84+c
7 b m Moonax(IRE) —Killone Brae (King's Ride)
283^{3} 487^{2} (611) 1711^{3} 1870^{3} 2260^{4}

Killultagh Storm (IRE) *Noel T Chance* 121+c
12 b g Mandalus—Rostrevor Lady (Kemal (FR))
97^{4} 360^{5} 653^{6}

Killwillie (IRE) *J I A Charlton* 71h
7 b g Carroll House—Home In The Glen (Furry Glen)
124^{P} 301^{P} 3927^{7} 4530^{P}

Killy Beach *J D Frost* 73h
8 b g Kuwait Beach(USA) —Spiritual Lily (Brianston Zipper)
1897^{5} 2429^{P} 2728^{7}2933^{P} (Dead)

Killy Lass (IRE) *B J Llewellyn* 81+c
10 b m Buckskin(FR) —Nataf (Whistling Deer)
1321^{5} 1646^{2}

Kilmackilloge *M Todhunter* 103h
7 b g Lancastrian—Garjun (IRE) (Orchestra)
2295^{5} 2821^{11} 2942^{F} 3231^{2} 4114^{2}4493^{4}

Kilmeena Magic *J C Fox* 37b
4 b f Fumo Di Londra(IRE) —Kilmeena Lady (Inca Chief (USA))
3346^{14}

Kilminchy Lady (IRE) *B Llewellyn*
5 b m Cape Cross(IRE) —Lace Flower (Old Vic)
485^{6} 651^{P}

Kilmucklin Girl (IRE) *A S T Holdsworth* 35h
7 ch m Gone Fishin—Actuate (IRE) (Shardari)
961^{P}

Kilrossanty (IRE) *R Flint* 69h
7 bb g Accordion—Baby Clair (Gulf Pearl)
458^{4} 943^{6}

Kilty Storm (IRE) *M C Pipe* 126+h
7 b g Glacial Storm(USA) —Hogan's Cherry (General Ironside)
216^{3} 643^{2} 2099^{5} (3345) 3458^{5} (4105)
4603^{2}5103a^{18}

Kimbambo (FR) *J P L Ewart* 102h 95+c
8 gr g Genereux Genie—Contessina (FR) (Mistigri)
1835^{4} 2976^{P} 3378^{10}4528^{F} 4719^{3} 4981^{U} (Dead)

Kim Buck (FR) *K A Morgan*
8 b g Ambroise(FR) —Darling Jouve (FR) (Some Buck)
1644^{P} 4166^{F}

Kim Fontenail (FR) *N J Hawke* 108 h 108 c
6 b m Kaldounevees(FR) —Fontanalia (FR) (Rex Magna (FR))
3507^{9} 3949^{P} 4332^{F}

Kimi (IRE) *Noel T Chance* 105b
5 b g Presenting—Hatherley (Deep Run)
2720^{2} 3244^{3} 4244^{2} 4623^{2}

Kimoe Warrior *M Mullineaux* 88 h 90+c
8 ch g Royal Abjar(USA) —Thewaari (USA) (Eskimo (USA))
176^{7} 373^{3}

Kimono Royal (FR) *A King* 100 h 96 c
8 bb g Garde Royale—Alizane (FR) (Mourtazam)
206^{2} 521^{3} 977^{3} 3129^{F}3460^{4} 3815^{10} 4735^{P}

Kims Pearl (IRE) *S Lycett* 104+h
8 b m Jurado(USA) —Blushing Pearl (Monksfield)
(462) (747) 1179^{4} 1300^{4} 1668^{11} 1804^{7}

Kinallen *B J Llewellyn*
6 b g Environment Friend—Creeping Jane (Rustingo)
463^{13}

Kinburn (IRE) *J Howard Johnson* 106 h 145+c
7 gr g Roselier(FR) —Leadaro (IRE) (Supreme Leader)
(2976) (3382) (5007)

Kinda Crazy *H J Manners* 83+h
6 b g Petoski—Margaret Modes (Thatching)
102^{7} 271^{7}

Kind Sir *A W Carroll* 96h 112c
10 b g Generous(IRE) —Noble Conquest (USA) (Vaguely Noble)
4^{5} 360^{2} 725^{2}(823) 1028^{6} 3459^{5} 3803^{6}4592^{5}
4829^{P} 5074^{8}

Kinfayre Boy *K W Hogg* 72h
4 b g Grey Eagle—Amber Gambler (ITY) (Nijin (USA))
945^{7} 1338^{5} 1601^{8}

King After *J R Best* 39h
4 b g Bahamian Bounty—Child Star (FR) (Bellypha)
2236^{11} 2373^{9} 2580^{13}

King Amber *A Crook* 38b
5 b g Wizard King—Dark Amber (Formidable (USA))
720^{8} 1616^{P}

King Barry (FR) *Miss P Robson* 101h 123+c
7 b g Cadoudal(FR) —Leonie Des Champs (FR) (Crystal Palace (FR))
2415^{4} (2839) 3207^{2}3851^{3} (4981) 5119^{2}

King Bee (IRE) *H D Daly* 104+h 131+c
9 b g Supreme Leader—Honey Come Back (Master Owen)
2445^{3} (3151) 3481^{F}(4070) 4496^{P}

King Carew (IRE) *Michael Hourigan* 129+h 138c
8 b g Fairy King(USA) —Kareena (Riverman (USA))
67a^{20} 3894a^{13}

King Claudius (IRE) *M C Banks* 90h
10 b g King's Ride—Lepida (Royal Match)
826^{P}

King Coal (IRE) *R Rowe* 90h 113+c
7 bb g Anshan—Lucky Trout (Beau Charmeur (FR))
(2313) 2613^{3} 3284^{5}3940^{P} 4355^{P}

Kingcombe Lane *P W Hiatt* 67+h
6 b g Superpower—Starlight Wonder (Star Appeal)
133^{11} 394^{4} 611^{P} 760^{8} 839^{4}

King Cyrus (IRE) *Evan Williams* 98b
4 br g Anshan—Miss Eurolink (Touching Wood (USA))
4595^{3}

King Daniel *Mrs E Slack* 87b
5 br g Prince Daniel(USA) —Panic Button (IRE) (Simply Great (FR))
3785^{6} (5042)

King Darshaan *N I M Rossiter*
6 b g Darshaan—Urchin (IRE) (Fairy King (USA))
2148^{P}

King Eider *B Ellison* 128 h 117c
7 bb g Mtoto—Hen Harrier (Polar Falcon (USA))
1010^{10} (1147)

Kingfisher Sunset *Mrs S J Smith* 83h 92c
10 b g Alflora(IRE) —Jack It In (Derrylin)
2566^{14} 2975^{3} 3336^{F}4053^{U} 4918^{P}

King Foraday (FR) *F Doumen*
4 ch g Vettori(IRE) —Zakota (IRE) (Polish Precedent (USA))
1705a^{2}

King Gabriel (IRE) *Andrew Turnell* 101h
4 b g Desert King(IRE) —Broken Spirit (IRE) (Slip Anchor)
5070^{3}

King Georges (FR) *J C Tuck* 103h 98 c
8 b g Kadalko(FR) —Djoumi (FR) (Brezzo (FR))
2100^{5} 2703^{8} 3143^{5}3901^{3} 4573^{6}

Kingham *Mrs Mary Hambro* 120+h
6 ch g Desert Prince(IRE) —Marie De Flandre (FR) (Crystal Palace (FR))
3883^{4} (4665) 5021^{8}

King Harald (IRE) *M Bradstock* 124 h 145 c
8 b g King's Ride—Cuilin Bui (IRE) (Kemal (FR))
2176^{4} 2491^{U} 3620^{U}

King Henrik (USA) *A Crook*
4 b g King Of Kings(IRE) —Ma Biche (USA) (Key To The Kingdom (USA))
3203^{P} 5135^{P}

King Killone (IRE) *H P Hogarth* 116 h 138c
6 b g Moonax(IRE) —Killone Brae (King's Ride)
2291^{F} (2496) 3178^{6}(4112) 4505^{3} 5004^{8}

Kingkohler (IRE) *K A Morgan* 114+h
7 b g King's Theatre(IRE) —Legit (IRE) (Runnett)
428^{2} 647^{2} (1444) 1610^{2}

King Louis (FR) *R Rowe* 94h
5 b g Nikos—Rotina (FR) (Crystal Glitters (USA))
2534^{13} 2829^{16} 3133^{8} 3658^{5} 4088^{3}

King Marrakech (IRE) *M D I Usher*
4 b g King's Best(USA) —Tenue D'Amour (FR) (Pursuit Of Love)
2454^{P}

King Of Confusion (IRE) *Ferdy Murphy* 123+h
7 br g Topanoora—Rich Desire (Grey Desire)
(1839) (2036) 2956^{2} 3316^{3} 4793^{3}

King Of Gothland (IRE) *K C Bailey* 73h 108 c
7 gr g Gothland(FR) —Rose Deer (Whistling Deer)
(1988) 2529^{2} 2717^{P}3886^{5}

King Of Java *M Bradstock*
5 br g Priolo(USA) —Krakatoa (Shirley Heights)
3138^{6}

King Of Merlia (USA) *E Sheehy* 112h
4 ch c High Yield(USA) —Fardus (IRE) (Danehill (USA))
3004a^{8}

King Of Scots *R J Price* 26b
5 ch g Halling(USA) —Ink Pot (USA) (Green Dancer (USA))
4278^{F} 4638^{P}

King Of Slane *G A Swinbank* 56b
5 b g Prince Daniel(USA) —Singing Slane (Cree Song)
4992^{9}

King Of The Arctic (IRE) *J Wade* 101+h 116+c
8 b g Arctic Lord—Ye Little Daisy (Prince Tenderfoot (USA))
2111^{6}

King On The Run (IRE) *Miss Venetia Williams* 127 c
13 b g King's Ride—Fly Run (Deep Run)
3614^{F}

Kings Advocate (IRE) *T J Taaffe* 126h
6 bb g Saddlers' Hall(IRE) —Definitely Maybe (IRE) (Brush Aside (USA))
92a^{2} 5103a^{4}

Kings Avenue *A J Chamberlain* 62h 71c
9 b g Gran Alba(USA) —G W Supermare (Rymer)
4016^{F} 4417^{P} 4577^{6}

Kingsbay *H Morrison* 102h 69c
7 ch m Beveled(USA) —Storm Of Plenty (Billion (USA))
2297^{7} 2660^{P} 2845^{2}3146^{3} 3581^{P} 4372^{4} 4579^{3}
4727^{12}

King's Bounty *T D Easterby* 112h 117 c
10 b g Le Moss—Fit For A King (Royalty)
62^{2} 430^{4} 1825^{5}2037^{8} 2588^{4} (3791)

Kings Brook *Nick Williams* 107+h 117c
6 br g Alderbrook—Kins Token (Relkino)
1382^{2} 1487^{4} 1542^{5}1871^{P} 2456^{2} 2732^{3}

Kings Castle (IRE) *R J Hodges* 105h
11 b g King's Ride—Kilmana (IRE) (Castle Keep)
(110) (385) 633^{4} (3283) 3508^{3} 3600^{5} 3993^{5}4289^{5}

Kingscliff (IRE) *R H Alner* 170 c
9 b g Toulon—Pixies Glen (Furry Glen)
68a^{4} 1926^{2} (2337) 2972^{P} 3493^{2} 4470^{10}

Kingscourt Lad (IRE) *Jonjo O'Neill* 75h
8 b g Norwich—Mrs Minella (Deep Run)
133^{B} 575^{7} 724^{3}

King's Daughter (FR) *Robert Collet*
5 b m King's Theatre(IRE) —Bint Bladi (FR) (Garde Royale)
778a^{8} 5154a^{6}

King's Envoy (USA) *Mrs J C McGregor* 82h
7 b g Royal Academy(USA) —Island Of Silver (USA) (Forty Niner (USA))
82^{14} 320^{P} 1291^{4} 1527^{4} 2478^{P}3488^{11} 4584^{7} 5120^{6}

Kings Glen (IRE) *Thomas Carberry* 100h 132c
10 b g King's Ride—Lady Of Aherlow (Le Bavard (FR))
4762^{U}

King Shaadi *C A Mulhall* 34b
6 b g Wizard King—Prim Ajwaad (Bin Ajwaad (IRE))
4992^{11}

Kings Leader (IRE) *Evan Williams* 60h
9 b g Supreme Leader—Tokay Lady (Furry Glen)
4638^{8}

Kings Linen (IRE) *B I Case* 81 h 71c
10 b g Persian Mews—Kings Princess (King's Ride)
1269^{4}

Kingsmaster (IRE) *Mrs John Harrington* 90h
5 b g Beneficial—Phar From Men (IRE) (Phardante (FR))
5060a^{16}

King's Mill (IRE) *Mrs L Wadham* 111h
9 b g Doyoun—Adarika (King's Lake (USA))
3978^{5}

King's Mountain (USA) *R M Stronge* 61h
6 b g King Of Kings(IRE) —Statistic (USA) (Mr Prospector (USA))
182^{3}

King's Protector *M D Hammond* 105h
6 b g Hector Protector(USA) —Doliouchka (Saumarez)
59^{3} 418^{DSQ} 691^{7} 2169^{11} 2475^{5}2839^{P} 3561^{14}
5120^{7}

Kings Rock *P A Blockley* 110h
5 ch g Kris—Both Sides Now (USA) (Topsider (USA))
2619^{6} (2845) 4099^{7} 4726^{2} 4849^{P}

Kings Signal (USA) *M J Hogan* 109+h
8 b g Red Ransom(USA) —Star Of Albion (Ajdal (USA))
1772^{5} 1916^{F} 2374^{2}

King's Silver (IRE) *N I M Rossiter* 87b
5 b g King Of Kings(IRE) —Almi Ad (USA) (Silver Hawk (USA))
2534^{15} 3216^{12} 5117^{7}

Kings Square *M W Easterby* 84h
6 b g Bal Harbour—Prime Property (IRE) (Tirol)
152[10] 2764[P] 2975[P]3351[3] 3540[6] 3656[5] 5037[U]

King's Thought *S Gollings*
7 b h King's Theatre(IRE) —Lora's Guest (Be My Guest (USA))
4479[P]

Kingston-Banker *Mrs S Alner* 117c
10 b g Teamster—Happy Manda (Mandamus)
3910[P] 4560[U] 4607[P]5013[3]

King's Travel (FR) *Miss Sarah Robinson*
10 gr g Balleroy(USA) —Travel Free (Be My Guest (USA))
517[7] 1017[8] 3847[U] 4555[P]

Kingtobee (IRE) *J A B Old* 12h
8 b g King's Ride—Zephyrelle (IRE) (Celio Rufo)
2618[P] 4569[F]

King Triton (IRE) *L Wells* 88h 95 c
9 br g Mister Lord(USA) —Deepwater Woman (The Parson)
2682[3] 2982[P] 3438[4]

Kinkeel (IRE) *A W Carroll* 95h 74c
7 b g Hubbly Bubbly(USA) —Bubbly Beau (Beau Charmeur (FR))
1645[11] 1805[U] 1956[6]2561[P] 3243[6] 3543[4]4132[R] 4278[7] 4575[6]4675[2] 4908[7] 5047[5]

Kiora Bay *T S Sharpe* 65b 94+c
9 b g Karinga Bay—Equasion (IRE) (Cyrano De Bergerac)
4791[U]

Kippour (FR) *S B Clark* 90h 75+c
8 b g Luchiroverte(IRE) —Obole III (FR) (Signani (FR))
148[4] 1066[P] 1344[10] 1458[9]1486[P]

Kipsigis (IRE) *Lady Herries* 114+h
5 b g Octagonal(NZ) —Kisumu (Damister (USA))
(2212) (4357)

Kirby's Vic (IRE) *N A Twiston-Davies* 72h
6 b g Old Vic—Just Affable (IRE) (Phardante (FR))
1714[5] 1910[5] 2723[P] 3367[13] 3923[P]4735[U]

Kirin *D E Cantillon*
4 b c Selkirk(USA) —Amaryllis (IRE) (Sadler's Wells (USA))
3594[6] 3817[8]

Kirkham Abbey *J J Quinn* 116 h
6 b g Selkirk(USA) —Totham (Shernazar)
568[7] 838[8] 1028[2] (1206) 1526[3]

Kirkhammerton (IRE) *M J Polglase*
4 ch g Grand Lodge(USA) —Nawara (Welsh Pageant)
4631[U]

Kirkside Pleasure (IRE) *Mrs S C Bradburne* 105+h
5 ch g Grand Plaisir(IRE) —Caldeon Mist (IRE) (Le Moss)
1834[5] 2497[4] 3205[4] 3855[3] (4362) 5064[8]

Kirless (FR) *P Quinton*
8 gr m Magistros(FR) —Vallee D'Or V (FR) (Pot D'Or (FR))
845a[6] 4718a[2]

Kirov King (IRE) *R H York* 94h 108+c
6 b g Desert King(IRE) —Nymphs Echo (IRE) (Mujtahid (USA))
568[4] 841[P] 1017[7] (4653) (4798) 4878[F] (Dead)

Kissinthepeach (IRE) *Mrs K Walton* 43b
5 b m Witness Box(USA) —Balinloop (IRE) (Balinger)
2572[11]

Kiss The Girls (IRE) *Jennie Candlish* 63+h
7 ch g Roselier(FR) —Cheeney's Gift (Quayside)
1671[P] 2073[3] 2517[P] 3042[10] 3330[6]

Kitebrook *Mrs Mary Hambro* 80b
5 b m Saddlers' Hall(IRE) —Neptunalia (Slip Anchor)
1882[11] 2446[13]

Kitski (FR) *Ferdy Murphy* 108h 115c
8 b g Perrault—Macyrienne (FR) (Saint Cyrien (FR))
1939 [3] 2294[F] 2976[3]3794[2] 4279[P] 4578[2]

Kittenkat *N R Mitchell* 111h 118c
12 b m Riverwise(USA) —Cut Above The Rest (Indiaro)
2325[P] 2608[4] 2847[5]3390[P] 3614[2] 3688[F]4103[P] 4287[4] 4690[5]4944[7]

Kitty *Miss J S Davis*
4 b f Kayf Tara—Dancing Bluebell (IRE) (Bluebird (USA))
2824[15]

Kitty John (IRE) *J L Spearing* 85h 77c
9 gr m Safety Catch(USA) —La Baladina (Modern Dancer)
688[5] 902[8] 1098[4]1203[6]

Kituhwa (USA) *R Shiels*
6 br g Cherokee Run(USA) —Ruhnke (USA) (Cox's Ridge (USA))
3173[P] 3782[P] 3916[P]

Kivotos (USA) *M C Pipe* 117+h
8 gr g Trempolino(USA) —Authorized Staff (USA) (Relaunch (USA))
3970[15]

Kiwi Babe *D P Keane* 110 h
7 b m Karinga Bay—Sunshine Gal (Alto Volante)
2609[P] 3214[11] 3439[P]

Kiwijimbo (IRE) *A C Whillans* 106+h
6 b g Germany(USA) —Final Touch (IRE) (Orchestra)
2572[15] 3374[F] 4143[9] 4532[7]

Kiwi Riverman *D P Keane* 50+h
6 b g Alderbrook—Kiwi Velocity (NZ) (Veloso (NZ))
2503[8] 3125[5] 3321[8]

Kjetil (USA) *Mrs Caroline Bailey* 106h 111c
6 b g King Of Kings(IRE) —I Wich (FR) (Kris)
441[4] 3968[4]

Kjjimmy (IRE) *J W Mullins* 71+c
9 ch g Sunley Builds—Cavity (True Song)
104[U] 231[4] 564[5]

Klimt (GER) *H Blume*
8 br g Second Set(IRE) —Konigsblute (GER) (Cortez (GER))
471a[P]

Kline (IRE) *N J Henderson* 89b
5 b g King's Theatre(IRE) —Royal River (Another River)
2534[11]

Klondike Charger (USA) *Miss J S Davis* 111c
12 b g Crafty Prospector(USA) —Forever Waving (USA) (Hoist The Flag (USA))
103[4] 366[P]

Knapp Bridge Boy *J R Payne* 83b
6 b g Wimbleball—Toll Bridge (New Member)
300[11] 3216[13] 5117[6]

Kniaz (FR) *A J Martin* 117h 110c
8 gr g Saint Preuil(FR) —Alberade (FR) (Un Desperado (FR))
(1311)

Knife Edge (USA) *Jonjo O'Neill* 122+c
11 bb g Kris S(USA) —My Turbulent Miss (USA) (My Dad George (USA))
3736[4] 4216[2] (4397) 4560[5] (4975)

Knight General Mac *N Bycroft* 39h
7 b g Presidium—Agnes Jane (Sweet Monday)
892[P] 1278[P]

Knight Legend (IRE) *Mrs John Harrington* 135h
7 b g Flying Legend(USA) —Well Trucked (IRE) (Dry Dock)
70a[8] 3642a[5] 4336a[6] 5059a[3]

Knight Of Silver *S C Burrough* 86h 61c
9 gr g Presidium—Misty Rocket (Roan Rocket)
206[3] 1800[2] 1973[2] 2296[8] 4549[11]4752[12] 4936[P]

Knight Of The Road (IRE) *P G Murphy* 69h
7 bb g Lord Americo—Trolly Dolly (IRE) (The Parson)
1833[P]

Knighton Combe *J W Dufosee* 76c
6 b g Midnight Legend—Cindercombe (Ra Nova)
401[4] 5053[6]

Knighton Lad (IRE) *A King* 107 h
6 b g Supreme Leader—Tarqueen (IRE) (King's Ride)
1990[B] 2322[4] 2809[2] 3249[5] (3814)

Knightsbridge Hill (IRE) *A King* 94h
4 b c Raise A Grand(IRE) —Desert Gem (Green Desert (USA))
1397[2] 1551[10] 2921[3] 3386[P] 4551[8]

Knightsbridge King *John Allen* 103h
10 ch g Michelozzo(USA) —Shahdjat (IRE) (Vayrann)
451[13] 2687[P] 5050[14]

Knight's Emperor (IRE) *Miss Alexandra Lindner* 103h 103 c
9 b g Grand Lodge(USA) —So Kind (Kind Of Hush)
747[12] 904[U] 958[2]1088[F] 1223[P] (1273) 1457[F]1673[5] 1746[5] 1805[3]1897[F] 4594[U] 4831[P]

Knockara Luck (IRE) *N G Richards* 105b
5 ch m Simply Great(FR) —Bonne Atthenagh (IRE) (Rontino)
(2796a) 3931[2] 4376[7]

Knock Bridge (IRE) *P D Evans* 73+h
4 b f Rossini(USA) —Touraneena (Robellino (USA))
2258[2] 2949[3]

Knock Davron (IRE) *V Thompson*
7 ch g Beneficial—Chestnut Shoon (Green Shoon)
4044[P]

Knockdoo (IRE) *J S Goldie* 95h
13 ch g Be My Native(USA) —Ashken (Artaius (USA))
129[2] 429[3] 697[2] 871[3] 941[4]

Knocker Jock (FR) *R Rowe* 87h
6 b g Medaaly—Glorieuse Shadows (FR) (Le Glorieux)
1777[8] 1991[14]

Knock Knock (IRE) *David Wachman* 62h 131c
9 b g Executive Perk—Knockananig (Pitpan)
3053a[F]

Knockrigg (IRE) *Dr P Pritchard* 90+h 98c
12 ch g Commanche Run—Gaiety Lass (Le Moss)
3141[5] (4368) 4879[6]

Knocktemple Lass (IRE) *D P Keane* 66+h
7 b m Executive Perk—What's In A Name (IRE) (Le Moss)
128[4] 665[8]

Knotty Ash Girl (IRE) *D J Wintle* 80h
7 ch m Ashkalani(IRE) —Camisha (IRE) (Shernazar)
2423[12] 2704[8] 3885[3]

Knowhere (IRE) *N A Twiston-Davies* 140h
8 b g Lord Americo—Andarta (Ballymore)
3178[P]

Known Maneuver (USA) *M C Chapman* 64h 64c
8 b g Known Fact(USA) —Northernmaneuver (USA) (Al Nasr (FR))
987[10] 1014[7] 1107[12] 1176[6]1275[U] 1335[U] 1357[2]1756[P]

Kobai (IRE) *A King* 83h
7 b g Florida Son—Helens Birthday (Quisling)
131[3] 2242[3] 2988[2] 3685[6] 4280[10]

Kock De La Vesvre (FR) *Miss Venetia Williams* 141c
8 b g Sassanian(USA) —Csardas (FR) (Maiymad)
130[3] 423[3] 648[5]842[P]

Kofi *Miss K M George* 63h
4 br g Emperor Fountain—La Vie En Primrose (Henbit (USA))
3340[10] 3948[5] 4569[11]

Kohinor *O Sherwood* 86+h 92c
7 b m Supreme Leader—Always Shining (Tug Of War)
2808[4]

Kokopelli Mana (IRE) *J M Jefferson* 65h
6 b m Saddlers' Hall(IRE) —Kachina (IRE) (Mandalus)
1683[P] 1895[7] 2515[14]

Kokoschka (IRE) *C R Egerton* 95b
4 b g Oscar(IRE) —Sibley (Northfields (USA))
5008[4]

Koln Stars (IRE) *Jennie Candlish* 95h
8 b g Fourstars Allstar(USA) —Fraulein Koln (IRE) (Mandalus)
2466[P] 2625[P] 2822[11] 3325[8]

Kombinacja (POL) *T R George* 117h 108+c
8 ch m Jape(USA) —Komancza (POL) (Dakota)
318[4] 570[3] 937[3]1631[6] 1743[6] 2553[P] (Dead)

Komena *J W Payne* 47h
8 b m Komaite(USA) —Mena (Blakeney)
180[P]

Komoto *Liam Lennon* 68h
5 b g Mtoto—Imperial Scholar (IRE) (Royal Academy (USA))
2027[P] 4840[P]

Kong King *A E Jones* 47b
6 ch g Classic Cliche(IRE) —Another Shuil (IRE) (Duky)
816[8]

Konker *J R Cornwall* 125 h 92c
11 ch g Selkirk(USA) —Helens Dreamgirl (Caerleon (USA))
1911[6] 2323[7] 2861[P]3329[P] 3549[P] 4053[P]4848[18]

Koodoo *M Todhunter* 69h
5 gr g Fasliyev(USA) —Karsiyaka (IRE) (Kahyasi)
2838[8] 2947[11]

Kopeck (IRE) *Mrs L Wadham* 88b 100c
8 ch g Moscow Society(USA) —Cashla (IRE) (Duky)
1829[P] 2044[6] 2344[B]

Koquelicot (FR) *P J Hobbs* 105 h 126+c
8 ch g Video Rock(FR) —Ixia Des Saccarts (FR) (Laniste)
330[2] 1670[7] 2299[2]2662[3] 2745[4] 3000[8]3469[5] 4434[5] 4857[2]

Koral Bay (FR) *R Waley-Cohen* 98h
5 bb m Cadoudal(FR) —Bigouden (What A Guest)
2878[8] 3461[8] 3800[5] 3979[2] 4149[3]4396[P] 4641[9]

Korelo (FR) *M C Pipe* 154 h 144 c
8 b g Cadoudal(FR) —Lora Du Charmil (FR) (Panoramic)
2490[4] 2747[6] 3389[3] (3614) 4111[3]4433[P] 5004[P]

Kosmos Bleu (FR) *R H Alner* 105 h 128+c
8 ch g Franc Bleu Argent(USA) —Fee Du Lac (FR) (Cimon)
1978[4] 2703[F] 3344[8]4014[7] 4822[3]

Kossies Mate *P W Hiatt* 37h
7 b m Cosmonaut—Pola Star (IRE) (Un Desperado (FR))
2507[12] 3131[P] 5016[P]

Koumba (FR) *Evan Williams* 95+h 121+c
8 b g Luchiroverte(IRE) —Agenore (FR) (Le Riverain (FR))
906[4] 1045[3] 1436[11] (1540) 1678[2]1874[7] (2529) 3290[9]4957[13]

Kourosh (IRE) *C P Morlock* 90h
6 b g Anshan—Pit Runner (Deep Run)
5026[3]

Kova Hall (IRE) *P J Hobbs* 60h
4 ch g Halling(USA) —My Micheline (Lion Cavern (USA))
3786[14] 4551[10]

Koyaanisqatsi *Jamie Poulton* 49+h
6 ch g Selkirk(USA) —Bogus John (CAN) (Blushing John (USA))
4913[F]

Krakow Baba (FR) *Miss Venetia Williams* 109 h
6 b g Sleeping Car(FR) —Babacha (FR) (Latnahc (USA))
2766[8] 3286[7] 3458[3]

Krasivi's Boy (USA) *G L Moore* 73h
4 bb g Swain(IRE) —Krasivi (USA) (Nijinsky (CAN))
1948[7] 4211[8] 4621[6]

Krismas Cracker *N J Henderson* 102h
5 b g Kris—Magic Slipper (Habitat)
2742[5] 3133[17] 4088[5]

Kristikhab (IRE) *A Berry*
4 ch g Intikhab(USA) —Alajyal (IRE) (Kris)
1737[P]

Kristinor (FR) *G L Moore* 89 h
4 ch g Inchinor—Kristina (Kris)
(1729) 1802[6] 2632[P] 3592[8]

Kristoffersen *Ian Williams* 111h
6 ch g Kris—Towaahi (IRE) (Caerleon (USA))
(352) (766) 901[2] 1026[P] 1220[4] 1538[2] 1596[4]1952[P] 2216[5] (5)

Kroisos (IRE) *R Curtis* 76h 95 c
8 b g Kris—Lydia Maria (Dancing Brave (USA))
101[P]

Kryena *Mrs P Robeson* 81h
4 gr f Kris—Tereyna (Terimon)
3340[7] 3645[6] 3817[5] 4568[4]

Kuka *R Hollinshead* 46h
5 b g Polar Prince(IRE) —Crissem (IRE) (Thatching)
4046[F]

Kung Hei Fat Choi (IRE) *J S Goldie* 105c
11 b g Roselier(FR) —Gallant Blade (Fine Blade (USA))
2170[5] 2495[4]

Kurbani (FR) *H Billot*
8 b g Apeldoorn(FR) —Urbanie (FR) (Pot D'Or (FR))
846a[7]

Kyalami (FR) *B Tulloch* 104c
8 gr g Royal Charter(FR) —Reine Margot III (FR) (Trenel)
51[3] 5116[P]

Kyathos (GER) *M F Harris*
5 br g Dashing Blade—Kajaana (Esclavo (FR))
4301[F]

Kyber *R F Fisher* 84+h
5 ch g First Trump—Mahbob Dancer (FR) (Groom Dancer (USA))
1100[P] 1337[P] 2171[5] 3271[3] 3656[P]

Kylebeg Dancer (IRE) *T Hogan* 112h
5 ch m General Monash(USA) —Glamour Stock (USA) (Marfa (USA))
1740[3] 2031a[4] 2173[14] 4887a[6] 5077a[12]

Kyle Of Lochalsh *J S Goldie* 84 h
6 gr g Vettori(IRE) —Shaieef (IRE) (Shareef Dancer (USA))
11[P] 306[2] 686[4] 856[5] 940[4]1528[P] 2171[P]

Kyliemoss *N R Mitchell* 73b
5 b m Riverwise(USA) —Kalamoss (Kalaglow)
3001[15] 3699[11] 5089[7]

Kymandjen (IRE) *Paul Nolan* 114+h 138c
9 b g Un Desperado(FR) —Marble Miller (IRE) (Mister Lord (USA))
69a[2] 3587a[P] 4123a[6]4929a[P]

Kynance Cove *C P Morlock* 62h
7 b g Karinga Bay—Excelled (IRE) (Treasure Kay)
2517[P] 3321[P] 5050[6]

Kyno (IRE) *M G Quinlan* 104h 91c
5 b g Accordion—Kelly Gales (IRE) (Strong Gale)
65a[16] 1903[9] 2517[2] 2951[2]3372[3] 4012[5] (4874) 5069[2]

Kyper Disco (FR) *N J Henderson* 110h 110 c
8 b g Epervier Bleu—Disconea (FR) (Bayolidaan (FR))
104[4] 2825[P] 3282[2]3465[4] 3940[7] 5127[4]

Labelthou (FR) *Mrs L Wadham* 100h
7 b m Saint Preuil(FR) —Suzy De Thou (FR) (Toujours Pret (USA))
1974[3]

La Bonne Vie *C Roberts* 51b
4 ch g Magic Ring(IRE) —Perfect Answer (Keen)
2927[16] 3346[13]

Lacdoudal (FR) *P J Hobbs* 138 h 164+c
7 gr g Cadoudal(FR) —Belfaster (FR) (Royal Charter (FR))
(1828) 2177[6] (2615) 2760[3]3179[4] 4118[7] 4457[2]4764[2] (5144)

Lac Leman (FR) *X Puleo*
7 b g Ganges(USA) —Kadrature (FR) (Kadrou (FR))
1372a[8]

La Concha (IRE) *M J McGrath* 85h
5 b g Kahyasi—Trojan Crown (IRE) (Trojan Fen)
100[6] 365[2] 566[3] 768[8] 949[4]

Laconicos (IRE) *W B Stone* 81+h
4 ch g Foxhound(USA) —Thermopylae (Tenby)
2373[3] 2797[3] 2954[9] 4075[7] 4910[P]

La Cuenta (IRE) *Miss Venetia Williams* 76b
6 b g Accordion—Foyle Wanderer (IRE) (Supreme Leader)
3001[12] 4604[P] (Dead)

Ladalko (FR) *P F Nicholls* 138h 148+c
7 b g Kadalko(FR) —Debandade (FR) (Le Pontet (FR))
1550[3] 1744[3] (2485) 3296[F] 3728[2] 4118[4]5004[2]

La Dame Brune (FR) *N J Henderson* 78b
4 b f Mansonnien(FR) —Madame Extra (FR) (Sir Brink (FR))
2927[5] 4422[10] 4695[3]

Lade Braes (IRE) *J Howard Johnson*
5 b g Luso—Madamme Highlights (Andretti)
2169[P] 3173[P]

Ladies From Leeds *A Crook* 81h
7 b m Primitive Rising(USA) —Keldholme (Derek H)
83[P] 236[4] 523[3] 941[8]1619[P] 1723[F]

Ladino (FR) *P J Hobbs* 98+h
6 b g Acatenango(GER) —Lauderdale (GER) (Nebos (GER))
3947[9] 4819[2]

La Dolfina *P J Hobbs* 108+h
6 b m Pennekamp(USA) —Icecapped (Caerleon (USA))
1480[3] 1651[6] 5021[12]

Ladro Volante (IRE) *S E H Sherwood* 72b
4 bb g Benny The Dip(USA) —Genoa (Zafonic (USA))
3651[8]

Lady Accord (IRE) *W P Mullins* 90h
6 b m Accordion—Lady Of Tara (Deep Run)
93a[13]

Lady Alderbrook (IRE) *C J Down* 80 h
6 b m Alderbrook—Madame President (IRE) (Supreme Leader)
3211[P] 3437[6] 4010[2] 4151[P] 4523[7]4912[6]

Lady At Leisure (IRE) *M J Ryan* 40h
6 ch m Dolphin Street(FR) —In A Hurry (FR) (In Fijar (USA))
860[P] 1107[11]

Lady Baronette *Ian Howe* 64 c
9 b m Baron Blakeney—Rueful Lady (Streetfighter)
4167[7]

Lady Blaze *B De Haan* 61b
7 ch m Alflora(IRE) —Lady Elle (IRE) (Persian Mews)
5084[P]

Lady Bling Bling *P J Jones* 96b
5 b m Midnight Legend—Slipmatic (Pragmatic)
2534[8] (2727) 4376[18]

Lady Ellendune *Andrew Turnell*
5 b m Piccolo—Eileen's Lady (Mtoto)
1562[P]

Lady Godson *B Mactaggart* 39h
7 ch m Bold Arrangement—Dreamy Desire (Palm Track)
82[F] 780[9] 1336[8] 1605[P]

Lady Harriet *C J Mann* 76b 42c
7 b m Sir Harry Lewis(USA) —Forever Together (Hawaiian Return (USA))
3439[3] 3790[6]

Lady Jay Jay *Mrs Norma Pook*
6 b m Commanche Run—Scally Belle (Scallywag)
3983[13]

Lady Lambrini *Mrs L Williamson* 51h 64c
6 b m Overbury(IRE) —Miss Lambrini (Henbit (USA))
594[2] 759[P] 902[2]1044[F] 1178[P] 1203[9]3732[4] 4474[3]

Lady Lisa (IRE) *M C Pipe* 93+h
7 b m Supreme Leader—Jennyellen (IRE) (Phardante (FR))
105[8] 287[3]

Lady Lola (IRE) *Miss J E Foster* 77+b
8 b m Supreme Leader—Regents Prancer (Prince Regent (FR))
715[P] 785[U] 1000[P]

Lady Loveday *Nick Williams* 25h
5 bb m Panoramic—Cadal Queen (FR) (Cadoudal (FR))
462[P]

Lady Maranzi *Mrs D A Hamer* 94 h
7 b m Teenoso(USA) —Maranzi (Jimmy Reppin)
2463[3] 2934[F] 3147[10] 3483[8] (4013) (4101)

Lady Misprint *Mrs Rebecca Jordan*
10 ch m Classic—Miss Primrose (Primitive Rising (USA))
3819[U]

Lady Of Fortune (IRE) *N J Henderson* 115 h
7 b m Sovereign Water(FR) —Needwood Fortune (Tycoon II)
(2240) 2813[5]

Lady Past Times *D W Whillans* 77 h
6 b m Tragic Role(USA) —Just A Gem (Superlative)
2944[18] 3339[P] 4113[P] 4517[4]

Lady Percy *V R A Dartnall*
6 ch m Double Trigger(IRE) —Dundeelin (Dunbeath (USA))
1969[F] (Dead)

Lady Predominant *Robert Gray*
5 b m Primo Dominie—Enlisted (IRE) (Sadler's Wells (USA))
2752[14]

Lady Racquet (IRE) *Mrs A J Bowlby* 111h
7 b m Glacial Storm(USA) —Kindly Light (IRE) (Supreme Leader)
(488)

Lady Radmore *J G M O'Shea* 55h
7 b m Overbury(IRE) —Val's Jem (Golden Love)
2343[P]

Lady Roania (IRE) *S C Burrough* 82b
6 b m Saddlers' Hall(IRE) —Ahead Of My Time (IRE) (Royal Fountain)
844[5]

Lady Shanan (IRE) *D A Rees* 60h
6 b m Anshan—Cothill Lady (IRE) (Orchestra)
1002[P]

Lady Speaker *T D Easterby* 84h
5 b m Saddlers' Hall(IRE) —Stormy Gal (IRE) (Strong Gale)
349[4] 4493[3] 4720[8]

Lady Spur (IRE) *J S Wainwright* 75b
7 b m Flying Spur(AUS) —Hasaid Lady (IRE) (Shaadi (USA))
656[9] 1459[11] 1619[F] 1847[P]

Lady Stratagem *E W Tuer* 75h
7 gr m Mark Of Esteem(IRE) —Grey Angel (Kenmare (FR))
592[15] 1567[P]

Lady Sunrize *P D Evans*
7 ch m Whittingham(IRE) —Scenic Air (Hadeer)
3254[F]

Lady Taipan (IRE) *Michael Flynn* 82b
5 b m Taipan(IRE) —Replica (IRE) (Roselier (FR))
5134a[14]

Lady Toff *B R Johnson*
4 ch f Beauchamp King—Lucylenco (Pitpan)
2830[19]

Lady Victoria *Karen McLintock* 35b
5 gr m Lord Americo—Minature Miss (Move Off)
2572[14]

Lady Wilde (IRE) *Noel T Chance* 89b
6 b m Oscar(IRE) —Lady Swinford (Ardross)
2446[6] 3435[3] 3911[4] 4398[2]

Lady Wurzel *J G Cann* 52h 78c
7 b m Dilum(USA) —Fly The Wind (Windjammer (USA))
3127[12] 3240[9] **3801[6] 4553[P]4662[P]** 4836[9]

Lady Zephyr (IRE) *N A Twiston-Davies* 129 h 120+c
8 b m Toulon—Sorimak Gale (IRE) (Strong Gale)
1618[F]

Laertes *C Grant* 117h
5 gr g Theatrical Charmer—Handmaiden (Shardari)
1593[6] 1915[3] 2186[2] 2638[3] (3914) 4315[5]4793[2]

Laetitia (IRE) *C Byrnes* 122h
6 b m Priolo(USA) —Licimba (GER) (Konigsstuhl (GER))
(2031a)

Lafayette (IRE) *R J Osborne* 124h
8 b h General Monash(USA) —Bezee (Belmez (USA))
67a[23]

La Folichonne (FR) *C G Johnson* 53h
7 b m Useful(FR) —Allure Folle (FR) (Kenmare (FR))
549[5] 715[6] 822[P] 1725[9] 1890[7]**4421[P]**

Lagan Gunsmoke *Dr J R J Naylor* 68b
4 b g Double Trigger(IRE) —Bichette (Lidhame)
2014[8] 3216[7]

Lagan Legend *Dr J R J Naylor* 37h
5 gr m Midnight Legend—Piecemeal (Baron Blakeney)
3244[8] 3468[9] 4425[9] 4676[P]

La Gessa *John Berry* 71h
4 gr f Largesse—En Grisaille (Mystiko (USA))
4450[11] 4648[P]

La Gitana *A Sadik* 61h
6 b m Singspiel(IRE) —Iberian Dancer (CAN) (El Gran Senor (USA))
467[P] 569[7] 635[5] 760[P] 976[P]

Lago *James Moffatt* 90h
8 b g Maelstrom Lake—Jugendliebe (IRE) (Persian Bold)
4656[2]

Lago D'Oro *Dr P Pritchard* 91h 92c
6 b m Slip Anchor—Salala (Connaught)
375[2] 521[P] (1113) 1383[5] 1614[6] 1876[3]2161[8] **2526[3]**
2742[6] **3278[4]3494[4] 4006[2] 4116[3]4460[13]**

Lago Nam (FR) *M C Pipe*
7 gr g Cardoun(FR) —Rivalago (FR) (Grey Dawn II)
1040[11]

Lagosta (SAF) *G M Moore* 84h
6 ch g Fort Wood(USA) —Rose Wine (Chilibang)
152[13]

La Griffe (IRE) *Mrs Abbi Vaughan* 94h 110+c
10 b g Un Desperado(FR) —Brigette's Secret (Good Thyne (USA))
4757[4]

Lagudin (IRE) *Paul John Gilligan* 102h
8 b h Eagle Eyed(USA) —Liaison (USA) (Blushing Groom (FR))
67a[9] 3005a[16] 3797[2] 3944[3]

Laharna *Miss E C Lavelle* 93 h
6 b g Overbury(IRE) —Royal Celt (Celtic Cone)
1903[8] 2301[6] 2617[3] 2934[3] 4427[4]

Lah Di Dah Lad *G J Tarry* 83c
12 b g Crested Lark—Classey (Dubassoff (USA))
5053[4]

Lahib The Fifth (IRE) *N G Richards* 99+h
6 br g Lahib(USA) —Bob's Girl (IRE) (Bob Back (USA))
(720) (936) (1291)

Lahinch Lad (IRE) *B G Powell* 87h 102+c
6 ch g Bigstone(IRE) —Classic Coral (USA) (Seattle Dancer (USA))
566[9] **672[6] 805[10]916[F] (981)** 1152[6] **1247[F]**4824[P]
5071[2]

Lahob *P Howling* 64h
6 ch g First Trump—Mystical Song (Mystiko (USA))
3804[9]

Lake Imperial (IRE) *Mrs H Dalton* 74h
5 b g Imperial Ballet(IRE) —Lakes Of Killarney (IRE) (Ahonoora)
1794[11] 1991[7] 3371[11]

Lake Merced (IRE) *Jonjo O'Neill* 108h 110c
6 b g Charente River(IRE) —Mitsubishi Art (Cure The Blues (USA))
629[4] 838[6] 911[3] (1084) 1296[2] **(1412)** 1552[P] **1761[P]**

Lakil Princess (IRE) *Paul Nolan* 124h 123c
5 gr m Bering—Russian Rebel (Machiavellian (USA))
3894a[7] **5061a[5]**

Lalagune (FR) *Miss E C Lavelle* 111h 93+c
7 b m Kadalko(FR) —Donatella II (FR) (Brezzo (FR))
1727[3] 2130[P] 3018[P] 3581[P]

La Lambertine (FR) *M C Pipe* 105h
5 b m Glaieul(USA) —Mesoraca (IRE) (Assert)
460[4] 1248[7] 1362[11]

Lala Nova (IRE) *John Joseph Murphy* 101h
7 br m Zaffaran(USA) —Tarasandy (IRE) (Arapahos (FR))
3110a[8] 5077a[13]

La Maestra (FR) *Miss L Day* 88h
8 b m Zayyani—Ginestra (USA) (L'Emigrant (USA))
1107[10] 1156[14] 1278[4] 1384[5] 1520[P]

La Mago *Mrs A M Naughton* 30b
6 b m Wizard King—Dancing Dancer (Niniski (USA))
1360[P]

La Mandragola *R J Osborne* 125h
9 b g Machiavellian(USA) —Wajd (USA) (Northern Dancer)
3894a[9]

La Marette *John Allen* 90h
8 ch m Karinga Bay—Persistent Gunner (Gunner B)
2659[8] 3152[5] 4392[5] 4756[6] 5014[4]

La Marianne *J R H Fowler* 113h
6 b m Supreme Leader—Belle Magello (FR) (Exit To Nowhere (USA))
4887a[3]

Lambrini Bianco (IRE) *Mrs L Williamson* 48h 86c
8 br g Roselier(FR) —Darjoy (Darantus)
10[5] (464) 546[3]989[P] 3938[2] 4316[4](4567) (4989)
5088[3]

Lambrini Legend (IRE) *M W Easterby* 92+b
4 br g Bob's Return(IRE) —Spur Of The Moment (Montelimar (USA))
5141[U]

Lambrini Mist *Mrs L Williamson* 69b 77c
8 gr g Terimon—Miss Fern (Cruise Missile)
998[P] 1219[7] 1269[5]1560[F] 1719[7] 1914[3]1951[5]

L'Ami (FR) *F Doumen* 163c
7 ch g Lute Antique(FR) —Voltige De Nievre (FR) (Brezzo (FR))
2491[2] 2972[4] 4118[2]4470[4] 4746[3]

Lampion Du Bost (FR) *A Parker* 86+h
7 b g Mont Basile(FR) —Ballerine Du Bost (FR) (Fast (FR))
3797[9] 4344[2] 4584[4]

Lampos (USA) *Miss J A Camacho* 73h
6 bb g Southern Halo(USA) —Gone Private (USA) (Private Account (USA))
152[9] 352[7] 483[4] 630[P]

Lamp's Return *A King* 98+h 113 c
7 ch m Bob's Return(IRE) —Lampstone (Ragstone)
2664[2] 3344[P] 3922[2]

La Muette (IRE) *M Appleby* 72h
6 b m Charnwood Forest(IRE) —Elton Grove (IRE) (Astronef)
651[F] 1816[8] 2283[5] 2625[6] 2962[10]3330[5] 3483[P]

Lanaken (IRE) *S Donohoe* 96?h 102 c
6 b g Capolago—Farriersfriend (IRE) (Tidaro (USA))
(2476) 2945[P] 3489[5]

Lancastrian Island *John A Harris* 38h
8 b m Lancastrian—Kelly's Island (Jupiter Island)
128[P] 396[5]

Lance Toi (FR) *G D Hanmer* 88h 78c
7 br g Lampon(FR) —Devant Spring (FR) (Spring To Mind (USA))
437[10]

Lancier D'Estruval (FR) *J C Tuck* 79h
7 ch g Epervier Bleu—Pommette III (FR) (Trac)
105[5] 573[10]

Landescent (IRE) *Miss K M George* 87+h
6 b g Grand Lodge(USA) —Traumerei (GER) (Surumu (GER))
2148[3] 3127[3] 3467[3]

Land Of Nod (IRE) *G Brown* 58h
5 b m Barathea(IRE) —Rafif (USA) (Riverman (USA))
185[P]

Land Rover Lad *C P Morlock* 89h 53c
8 ch g Alflora(IRE) —Fililode (Mossberry)
202[P] 2043[4] 2310[4]

Land Sun's Legacy (IRE) *J S Wainwright* 66h
5 b g Red Sunset—Almost A Lady (IRE) (Entitled)
1454[7] 1614[11] 1757[5] 2082[P]

Lane Marshal *M E Sowersby* 85h
4 gr g Danzig Connection(USA) —Evening Falls (Beveled (USA))
2076[3] 2263[5] 2587[6] 2810[6] 3349[5]3557[7]

Laneret (CZE) *C Olehla*
10 b g Dunbeath(USA) —Latimeria (CZE) (Anno (GER))
1710a[3]

Langcourt Jester *N K Allin* 76b
8 ch m Royal Vulcan—Singing Clown (True Song)
4730[P]

Langdon Lane *P R Webber* 71+h
5 b m Overbury(IRE) —Snowdon Lily (Town And Country)
1213[3] 1317[5]

Lanhel (FR) *J Wade* 62h
7 ch g Boston Two Step(USA) —Umbrella (FR) (Down The River (FR))
1291[F] 1374[U] 1508[6] 1569[8]

Lankawi *Jedd O'Keeffe* 105h
4 ch g Unfuwain(USA) —Zarma (FR) (Machiavellian (USA))
1904[U] 2001[3] (2442) 3203[2] 3539[4] 3990[4]

Lanmire Tower (IRE) *S Gollings* 101h 95 c
12 b g Celio Rufo—Lanigans Tower (The Parson)
81[5] (373) 464[3](690) 1615[7] 2080[3](2129) 2588[2]
5140[P]

Lannigans Lock *R Rowe* 93+h
5 b g Overbury(IRE) —Lacounsel (FR) (Leading Counsel (USA))
2238[8] 2803[6] 3425[7] 4210[P]

Lanos (POL) *W Davies* 80h
8 ch g Special Power—Lubeka (POL) (Milione (FR))
1875[9] 2139[14] 2560[7] 2721[14]

Lansdowne Princess *G A Ham* 35h
4 b f Cloudings(IRE) —Premier Princess (Hard Fought)
2014[5] 3181[15] 3884[9] 4327[P] 4836[12]

L'Antartique (FR) *Ferdy Murphy* 122h
6 b g Cyborg(FR) —Moomaw (Akarad (FR))
(2006) 2444[2] (2755) 3738[4]

Lantaur Lad (IRE) *A King* 98+c
12 b g Brush Aside(USA) —Gleann Oge (Proverb)
(106)

Lantern Lad (IRE) *R Ford* 83h 93+c
10 b g Yashgan—Lantern Lass (Monksfield)
2465[P] 3338[P] 3938[8]4499[8]

Lantern Leader (IRE) *M J Gingell* 90h 98c
11 b g Supreme Leader—Lantern Line (The Parson)
1564[12] 1648[5] 1884[P]

Lanzlo (FR) *James Moffatt* 106+h
9 bb g Le Balafre(FR) —L'Eternite (FR) (Cariellor (FR))
(215) 499[3] 595[2] 1513[P] (Dead)

Laoch Dubh (IRE) *Henry De Bromhead* 102h 111c
7 b g Magical Wonder(USA) —Jaziyah (IRE) (Lead On Time (USA))
117a[20] **5100a[6]**

La Petite Lulu (FR) *J-P Carnel*
6 b m Princeton(FR) —Green And Blue (FR) (Gallant Vert (FR))
846a[P]

Lappeenranta (IRE) *V R A Dartnall* 104b
5 b g Presenting—Millies Luck (Al Sirat)
4574[2]

La Professoressa (IRE) *Mrs P N Dutfield* 82h
5 b m Cadeaux Genereux—Fellwah (IRE) (Sadler's Wells (USA))
2298[6] 4427[10] 4752[7]

Laragh House (IRE) *E J O'Grady* 92+h 121c
7 bb g Hubbly Bubbly(USA) —Black Valley (IRE) (Good Thyne (USA))
1116a[F] **5129a[P]**

Lara's Girl *K G Wingrove* 62h
4 b f Tipsy Creek(USA) —Joe's Dancer (Shareef Dancer (USA))
1441[P] 1563[12] 1729[7] 1802[5] 1[12]

Laras Grey (IRE) *Martin Ward* 81c
13 gr g Celio Rufo—Persian Winter (Persian Bold)
282[P]

Larkbarrow *N A Twiston-Davies* 74h
5 b m Kahyasi—Gardana (FR) (Garde Royale)
(3497) 4376[13] 4801[4]

La Rose *Paul Morris* 55h
6 b m Among Men(USA) —Marie La Rose (FR) (Night Shift (USA))
1028[P]

Larry The Tiger (IRE) *Mrs S J Smith* 61b
6 b g Lahib(USA) —Tigora (Ahonoora)
1979[5] 2572[10] 3785[12]

Lascar De Ferbet (FR) *R Ford* 79h 94+c
7 br g Sleeping Car(FR) —Belle De Ferbet (FR) (Brezzo (FR))
126[F] 1176[5] 1311[4]1433[3] 1592[4] 2476[7]3270[4]

La Source A Gold (IRE) *Nick Williams* 87c
7 br g Octagonal(NZ) —Coral Sound (IRE) (Glow (USA))
3879[U] 4006[3] 4424[F]4859[P]

Last Hope (IRE) *Miss Jane Thomas* 89b
7 b m Jurado(USA) —Kentstown Girl (Prince Tenderfoot (USA))
93a[12]

Last Minute Goal (IRE) *Noel Meade* 92h 75c
7 b g Oscar(IRE) —Mont Eilat (IRE) (Montelimar (USA))
3528a[8]

Latalomne (USA) *N Wilson* 124h 124c
12 ch g Zilzal(USA) —Sanctuary (Welsh Pageant)
1012[P]

Late Arrival *M D Hammond* 76h
9 b g Emperor Jones(USA) —Try Vickers (USA) (Fuzzbuster (USA))
428[U]

Late Claim (USA) *R T Phillips* 85 h
6 ch g King Of Kings(IRE) —Irish Flare (USA) (Irish River (FR))
2940[13] 3214[P] 3818[7]

Latimer's Place *J A Geake* 110 h 136 c
10 b g Teenoso(USA) —Pennethorne Place (Deep Run)
1853[U] 2051[3] 2272[3](2616) 3296[7] 4374[8]4635[4]

Latin Player (IRE) *B G Powell* 69b
7 b g Vestris Abu—Legal Minstrel (IRE) (Legal Circles (USA))
2242[10] 2961[12]

Latin Queen (IRE) *J D Frost* 105 h 106+c
6 bb m Desert Prince(IRE) —Atlantic Dream (USA) (Muscovite (USA))
(285) 569[2] 1021[2] 1984[6] 2595[5] **2846[4]3017[3]** 3802[P]
(4943) 5114[F]

Latitude (FR) *M C Pipe* 102h 132 c
7 b m Kadalko(FR) —Diyala III (FR) (Quart De Vin (FR))
387[7]

Laudamus *R H Alner* 96+h
8 ch g Anshan—Faint Praise (Lepanto (GER))
1984[5] 2296[P]

Launde (IRE) *B N Pollock* 125c
7 b g Norwich—Carbia's Last (Palm Track)
2044[7] 2701[5] 3017[2](3920) 4371[2] 4847[5]

Laureldean (IRE) *Michael Cunningham* 115 h 109c
8 b g Shernazar—Power Run (Deep Run)
5061a[P]

Laurier D'Estruval (FR) *S E H Sherwood* 85h 110 c
7 ch g Ragmar(FR) —Grive D'Estruval (FR) (Quart De Vin (FR))
3344[P] 3815[P]

Lavenoak Lad *P R Rodford* 88h
6 b g Cloudings(IRE) —Halona (Pollerton)
3433[3] 4046[4] 4449[2] 4661[4] 4860[13]5113[0]

L'Aventure (FR) *P F Nicholls* 133 h 153 c
7 b m Cyborg(FR) —Amphitrite (FR) (Lazer (FR))
1830[6] **2164[4] (3022) 3971[5]4496[3] 5004[7]**

Lawaaheb (IRE) *M J Gingell* 89 h
5 b g Alhaarth(IRE) —Ajayib (USA) (Riverman (USA))
(180) 456[P] 4478[4] 4834[7] 14[4]

Lawgiver (IRE) *T J Fitzgerald* 102+h 94c
5 b g Definite Article—Marylou Whitney (USA) (Fappiano (USA))
197[2] 406[3]

Lawyer Des Ormeaux (FR) *P Bowen* 112+h
7 ch g Sky Lawyer(FR) —Chaouia (FR) (Armos)
(748) 841[3] 1099[5] 1192[3] (1436)

Lazerito (IRE) *Miss Venetia Williams* 111+h
8 b g Shernazar—Nemova (IRE) (Cataldi)
4573[P] 5010[P]

Lazy But Lively (IRE) *R F Fisher* 103c
10 br g Supreme Leader—Oriel Dream (Oats)
1844 [7] 2038[7] 2336[P] **2819[3]2946[5] 3315[6]**
3845[P]4042[7] 4316[3] (4492) 4636[2] 4790[P]
4845[P]4982[P]

Lazy Lena (IRE) *Miss L C Siddall* 84+h
7 b m Oscar(IRE) —Magnum Gale (IRE) (King's Ride)
180[3] 345[7] 686[12] 781[2] 839[12]1722[5] 2025[4] (2290)
4487[9] 4783[6]

Leaburn (IRE) *Miss J Houldey* 129+c
13 b g Tremblant—Conderlea (Scorpio (FR))
313[P]

Leadaway *Miss P Robson* 89+h
7 b g Supreme Leader—Annicombe Run (Deep Run)
4302[2]

Leaders Way (IRE) *T K Geraghty* 123h
11 b g Supreme Leader—Mind Me Back (Kambalda)
43a[12] 4765[9]

Leading Authority (IRE) *C L Tizzard* 110+b
5 br g Supreme Leader—Bonnie Thynes (IRE) (Good Thyne (USA))
1985[2] 2432[3] (3216)

Leading Contender (IRE) *P J Hobbs* 125+b
5 b g Supreme Leader—Flair Dante (IRE) (Phardante (FR))
(1681) (2211) 4448[18]

Leading Man (IRE) *Ferdy Murphy* 111 h 132c
6 b g Old Vic—Cudder Or Shudder (IRE) (The Parson)
2449[3] (2643) 3178[5]3391[4] 3851[P]

Leading Run (IRE) *Noel Meade* 131b
7 b g Supreme Leader—Arctic Run (Deep Run)
(5081a)

Lead Role (IRE) *D R Gandolfo*
8 b g Supreme Leader—Surely Madam (Torenaga)
1711[P] (Dead)

Leapogues Lady (IRE) *C A McBratney* 98h
10 b m Chakiris(USA) —Canhaar (Sparkler)
499[7]

Leap Year Lass *C Grant* 84h
6 ch m Fleetwood(IRE) —Lady Phyl (Northiam (USA))
2414[7] 2680[F] 3254[4] 3442[6] 3655[10]3985[5] 4299[4]

Lease Back (FR) *L Wells* 113 h
7 b g Sleeping Car(FR) —Salsepareille (FR) (Perouges (FR))
201[U] (514) **3877[P]**

L'Eau Du Nil (FR) *P J Hobbs* 103+h
5 b g Kadounor(FR) —Lamakara (FR) (Akarad (FR))
3[3] 1508[2] 1775[7] 2314[3]

Leave It To You *M Sheppard*
8 b m Alflora(IRE) —Dalbeattie (Phardante (FR))
3249[P] 3461[P]

Leaveittwomebob (IRE) *Joseph Fox* 89b
5 ch g Alderbrook—You Know The Score (Strong Gale)
5104a[18]

Le Biassais (FR) *L Lungo* 111h
7 b g Passing Sale(FR) —Petite Fanfan (FR) (Black Beauty (FR))
2630[F] (Dead)

Le Briar Soul (IRE) *V R A Dartnall* 98h
6 b g Luso—El Moss (IRE) (Le Moss)
2340[5] 2864[3] 4094[5] 4676[4]

Le Burf (FR) *G R I Smyly* 90b
5 b g Lute Antique(FR) —Fripperie (FR) (Bojador (FR))
1882[6] 3699[P] 4422[2] 4940[10]

Le Cavalier (USA) *Mrs L Williamson* 73h
9 b g Mister Baileys—Secret Deed (USA) (Shadeed (USA))
1153[P] 1206[P] 1322[U]

Le Chiffre (IRE) *N G Richards*
4 br g Celtic Swing—Implicit View (Persian Bold)
3374[11] 5091[P]

Le Cluzeau (FR) *G Macaire*
11 br g Big John(FR) —Mazzina (FR) (Mad Captain)
1074a[2]

Le Comte Est Bon (USA) *F Doumen* 101h
5 bb h King Of Kings(IRE) —Navratilovna (USA) (Nureyev (USA))
4443[14]

Le Corvee (IRE) *A King* 106+h
4 b c Rossini(USA) —Elupa (IRE) (Mtoto)
1923[F] (1955) 2178[4] 4211[6] 4435[P]

Le Coudray (FR) *C Roche* 135h
12 b g Phantom Breeze—Mos Lie (FR) (Tip Moss (FR))
2793a[P]

Le Duc (FR) *P F Nicholls* 136h 147c
7 b g Villez(USA) —Beberova (FR) (Synefos (USA))
1828[11] **2370[2] 3176[U]4777[U]**

Le Forezien (FR) *C J Gray* 93+h
7 b g Gunboat Diplomacy(FR) —Diane Du Forez (FR) (Quart De Vin (FR))
2605[9] 2994[9] (4640) (4752) 4860[5]

Le Galactico (FR) *A King* 96b
5 br g Sleeping Car(FR) —Guendale (FR) (Cadoudal (FR))
2804[F]

Legal Glory (IRE) *B G Powell* 90b
6 b g Bob Back(USA) —Native Shore (IRE) (Be My Native (USA))
(2288) 3001[11] 3911[9]

Legally Fast (USA) *S C Burrough* 106h
4 b c Deputy Minister(CAN) —Earthly Angel (USA) (Crafty Prospector (USA))
1873[3] 3324[6] 3464[4] 3943[5] 4443[10]4674[P] 4945[F]

Legal Spy *F Jordan* 52h
7 b g Weld—Run Lady Run (General Ironside)
533[4] 912[11] 1154[P]

Legal Warning *Mrs S Gardner* 36b
5 b g Contract Law(USA) —Carrie's Risk (Risk Me (FR))
300[12]

Legendsofthefall (IRE) *Michael Cunningham* 93+h 103c
7 b m Arctic Lord—Glen Dieu (Furry Glen)
5129a[11]

Le Grand Jeu (FR) *P Journiac*
7 gr g Video Rock(FR) —Almeida (FR) (Royal Charter (FR))
362a[3]

Le Gris (GER) *P R Rodford* 89h
7 gr g Neshad(USA) —Lady Pedomade (GER) (Mondrian (GER))
947[14] 1077[2] 1158[7]

Leinster (IRE) *D T Hughes* 138h 118c
9 br g Supreme Leader—Jennycomequick (Furry Glen)
71a[5]

Leith Hill Star *R Rowe* 102+h 102c
10 ch m Comme L'Etoile—Sunnyday (Sunley Builds)
1780[P] 2240[6]

Le Jaguar (FR) *P F Nicholls* 129 c
6 b g Freeland(FR) —Fee La Maline (FR) (Maalem (FR))
1676[5] 1861[3] 2299[4](2724) 3186[P] 4240[P]4944[P]

Le Maraudeur (FR) *J-C Obellianne*
10 b g Cyborg(FR) —Santa Tanara (FR) (Amen (FR))
1373a[3]

Le Millenaire (FR) *S H Shirley-Beavan* 90h 60c
7 bb g Ragmar(FR) —Ezaia (FR) (Iron Duke (FR))
2976[7] 3232[2] 4141[8] 4582[4]4724[7] 5068[P]

Le Milliardaire (FR) *C J Down*
7 b g General Holme(USA) —Vanila Fudge (USA) (Bold Bidder)
1909[9] (Dead)

Le Mino (FR) *C W Thornton* 76+h
7 b g Noblequest(FR) —Minouche (FR) (Fill My Hopes (FR))
149[P] (Dead)

Lemon Tree *N M Babbage* 77b
6 ch m Weldnaas(USA) —Go Gipsy (Move Off)
1985[4]

Lennon (IRE) *J Howard Johnson* 119h
6 bb g Beneficial—Stradbally Bay (Shackleton)
2082[2] (2591) 3297[4] 3929[9] (5066)

Len Ross *R Lee* 81b
7 b g Bob's Return(IRE) —Instabene (Mossberry)
138[13]

Lens Boy *D Burchell* 68b
7 b g Teenoso(USA) —Red Again (Then Again)
361[8] 655[8]

Leod'Or (FR) *P Cottin*
7 b g Hellios(USA) —Rangue (FR) (Tourangeau (FR))
1373a[2]

Leonia's Rose (IRE) *Miss Lucinda V Russell* 72h
7 gr m Roselier(FR) —Sanafaa (Wolverlife)
1663[P] 2171[13] 2674[9] 3209[U] 4145[4]4341[5] 4584[9]

Leopard Spot (IRE) *Miss Lucinda V Russell* 97h 98c
8 b g Sadler's Wells(USA) —Savoureuse Lady (Caerleon (USA))
211[8] 416[P]

Leopold (SLO) *M F Harris* 101h
5 b g Solarstern(FR) —Lucera (GER) (Orofino (GER))
369[2] 482[4] 691[4] 748[4] 870[3]991[4] 1084[3] 1307[3] (1409) 1481[4] 1559[4]1878[9] 2566[9]

Leo's Luckyman (USA) *R S Brookhouse* 94 h
7 bb g Woodman(USA) —Leo's Lucky Lady (USA) (Seattle Slew (USA))
2763[F] 2873[3] 3491[5] 4432[P]

Leo's Lucky Star (USA) *R S Brookhouse* 97+h
4 b g Forestry(USA) —Leo's Lucky Lady (USA) (Seattle Slew (USA))
2345[F]

Le Pacha De Cercy (FR) *H Billot*
7 ch g Ragmar(FR) —Alconea (FR) (Brezzo (FR))
846a[9]

Le Passing (FR) *P F Nicholls* 136h 150 c
7 b g Passing Sale(FR) —Petite Serenade (FR) (Trac)
1924[4] 2492[4] 2760[2]3180[6] 4459[7] 4762[12]

Leprechaun's Maite *P A Blockley* 67h
4 b g Komaite(USA) —Leprechaun Lady (Royal Blend)
1679[P] 2286[8] 2580[10]

Lerida *Miss Lucinda V Russell* 91h
4 ch g Groom Dancer(USA) —Catalonia (IRE) (Catrail (USA))
1512[P] 2477[4] 3203[7] 3485[4] (3925) 4747[P]5001[4]

Le Rochelais (FR) *R H Alner* 106h 106+c
7 ch g Goldneyev(USA) —Olympiade De Brion (FR) (Night And Day)
2619[4] 2868[9] **3426[U]** 4289[4]**4729[2]**

Le Roi Miguel (FR) *P F Nicholls* 125h 162c
8 b g Point Of No Return(FR) —Loumir (USA) (Bob's Dusty (USA))
1846[5] 2346[7] 2999[7]4461[13] **4777[P] 4958[U]**

Le Royal (FR) *K G Reveley* 109h 110 c
7 b g Garde Royale—Caucasie (FR) (Djarvis (FR))
1796[P] 1929[9] **2100[4] 2719[2]2874[5] 2975[5]** 3622[4]3814[6] 4390[4]

Leroy's Sister (FR) *P F Nicholls* 101+h
6 b m Phantom Breeze—Loumir (USA) (Bob's Dusty (USA))
(961)

Lertxundi (FR) *Mme A Chayrigues*
7 ch g Lesotho(USA) —Musica Del Mar (FR) (Kenmare (FR))
4718a[P]

Lerubis (FR) *F Jordan* 92+h
7 b g Ragmar(FR) —Perle De Saisy (FR) (Italic (FR))
1957[2]

Les Baux Belle (IRE) *D J Wintle* 90b
6 b m Supreme Leader—Sister Stephanie (IRE) (Phardante (FR))
4017[2]

Lescer's Lad *Mrs A M Woodrow* 75h
9 b g Perpendicular—Grange Gracie (Oats)
201[P] 533[3] 753[12] 860[P] 1018[P]**1638[F] 1899[3] 2149[P]**2592[P] 4905[5]

Lesdream *J D Frost* 115h 111+c
9 b g Morpeth—Lesbet (Hotfoot)
2848[9] 3879[6] 4037[5]4288[2]

Le Seychellois (FR) *P F Nicholls* 144 c
6 ch g Mansonnien(FR) —Adjirah (FR) (Sicyos (USA))
2489[3] 2757[F] 3136[P]3357[U] 5018[7]

Lesoquera (FR) *G Cherel* 101c
4 b f Lesotho(USA) —Lora Du Charmil (FR) (Panoramic)
4548a[P]

L'Etang Bleu (FR) *P Butler* 86 h 86c
8 gr g Graveron(FR) —Strawberry Jam (FR) (Fill My Hopes (FR))
233[6] **1249[5]** 1409[7] 1756[12]

Lethem Air *T Butt* 103 h
8 ch g Aragon—Llanddona (Royal Palace)
301[8] 3205[P] 3314[4] 3534[6] 3853[2]4141[3] 4493[2] 4723[6] 5066[14] (5118)

Lethem Present (IRE) *T Butt* 40h 89c
6 ch m Presenting—Present Tense (Proverb)
323[7] 2838[11] 3235[P] 3532[4] 3855[P]4916[P]

Letitia's Loss (IRE) *N G Richards* 110+h
8 ch m Zaffaran(USA) —Satin Sheen (Abednego)
3234[4] 3554[2] 4043[8] 4724[8]

Le Toscan (FR) *M J P O'Brien* 107b
6 br g Double Bed(FR) —La Toscanella (FR) (Riverton (FR))
5104a[8]

Let's Be Subtle (IRE) *W Amos* 64h
7 b m Oscar(IRE) —Raven Night (IRE) (Mandalus)
1839[6] **2023[P]**

Lets Cast Again *P R Webber* 77+b
4 ch g Mark Of Esteem(IRE) —Alcalali (USA) (Septieme Ciel (USA))
2425[9]

Let's Celebrate *F Jordan* 96h
6 b g Groom Dancer(USA) —Shimmer (Bustino)
75[5] 363[3] 670[11] 1483[2] 1724[2]1902[2]

Let's Fly (FR) *Ross Oliver* 110h 111c
11 b g Rose Laurel—Harpyes (FR) (Quart De Vin (FR))
(47) 437[9] 4349[P]4555[U] 4748[16]

Lets Get Busy (IRE) *J W Mullins* 81+h
6 ch m Presenting—Mindyourown (IRE) (Town And Country)
487[5] 1851[6] 2125[3] 2605[3] 3149[6]

Lets Go Dutch *K Bishop* 112 h 108c
10 b m Nicholas Bill—Dutch Majesty (Homing)
1972[5] 3614[P] 3981[P]5105[9]

Letsplay (IRE) *K J Burke* 96h
6 ch g Accordion—Pennine Sue (IRE) (Pennine Walk)
507[4] 654[5] 1827[6] 2829[8] 2956[9]

Let's Rock *Mrs A Price* 91h 76c
8 b g Rock City—Sizzling Sista (Sizzling Melody)
2[7] 174[6] 459[P]1749[2] 2284[P] 2722[F]3251[7] 3457[5] 3647[5]3803[10] 4281[11] 4590[6]4827[P]

Lets Try Again (IRE) *R A Farrant* 82h
9 b g Barathea(IRE) —Intricacy (Formidable (USA))
3283[3] 3687[4] 4290[6] 5048[P]

Letterman (IRE) *E J O'Grady* 133h
6 br g Presenting—Papoose (IRE) (Little Bighorn)
116a[9] 3086a[4] 4443[8] 4888a[4] 5059a[8]

Levallois (IRE) *P Winkworth* 92h 87 c
10 b g Trempolino(USA) —Broken Wave (Bustino)
2662[6] 3186[5] 3434[6]3791[6] 4007[4] 4524[3]4666[4]

Level Par (IRE) *J A Supple* 85h
6 ch g Cadeaux Genereux—Howaida (IRE) (Night Shift (USA))
4896[10]

Leviathan De Brule (FR) *J P Delbe*
6 br g Dabistan(IRE) —Graine De Brule (FR) (Mistigri)
846a[2]

Levitator *M J P O'Brien* 117h
5 b h Sadler's Wells(USA) —Cantilever (Sanglamore (USA))
65a[12] 3411a[21]

Le Volfoni (FR) *P F Nicholls* 128h 150c
5 b g Sicyos(USA) —Brume (FR) (Courtroom (FR))
1871[3] 2422[2] (2620) (2872) (3183) 3501[2](4006) 4456[F] 4663[6] **4774[3]5002[2]**

Lewis Island (IRE) *G L Moore* 113+h 126+c
7 b g Turtle Island(IRE) —Phyllode (Pharly (FR))
452[F] 2377[3] 2754[3]3945[2] 4131[2] **(4692) 4820[3]**

Lewsher *M Mullineaux* 23h
6 b m Sir Harry Lewis(USA) —Sheraton Girl (Mon Tresor)
175[P] 351[6]

Ley Preacher (IRE) *G M Moore* 76h
5 b g High Roller(IRE) —Chapel Field (Sayaarr (USA))
2450[F] 3927[6]

Liam (GER) *J Albrecht*
8 b g Dear Doctor(FR) —Little Lady (GER) (Tarik (GER))
590a[P]

Liamos (IRE) *R H York* 87b
6 br g Desert Story(IRE) —Lorme (Glenstal (USA))
816[4]

Liathroidisneachta (IRE) *Jonjo O'Neill* 110 h
6 b g Accordion—Anozira Gold (IRE) (Camden Town)
2554[2] 3496[2] 4149[2] 4501[4]

Liberia (FR) *N J Henderson* 92h 96 c
7 b g Kadalko(FR) —Unica IV (FR) (Quart De Vin (FR))
2751[F] 3220[3] 4243[8]4691[6]

Liberman (IRE) *M C Pipe* 126 h
8 br g Standiford(USA) —Hail To You (USA) (Kirtling)
3970[18] 4461[4] 4776[10]

Liberthine (FR) *N J Henderson* 147+c
7 b m Chamberlin(FR) —Libertina (FR) (Balsamo (FR))
2177[7] 2744[U] 3296[5]4447[8] (4762) 5144[4]

Liberty Ben (IRE) *R H Alner* 92 h
6 b g Beneficial—Silver Fairy (IRE) (Lancastrian)
3694[6] 3943[4] 4557[4]

Liberty Boy (IRE) *Jonjo O'Neill* 59h
8 b g Be My Native(USA) —Deep Estee (IRE) (Supreme Leader)
767[P] 813[10] 863[10]

Liberty Run (IRE) *Mrs A J Hamilton-Fairley*
4 ch g Grand Lodge(USA) —Bathe In Light (USA) (Sunshine Forever (USA))
3354[P] 3714[12]

Liberty Seeker (FR) *G A Swinbank* 127 h 121 c
7 ch g Machiavellian(USA) —Samara (IRE) (Polish Patriot (USA))
3761[8] **4472[P]**

Libre *F Jordan* 78h
6 b g Bahamian Bounty—Premier Blues (FR) (Law Society (USA))
1645[10]

Lickadoon (IRE) *P F O'Donnell* 71h
5 b m Lahib(USA) —Legally Delicious (Law Society (USA))
66a[19]

Lieuday *C L Tizzard* 29h
7 b g Atraf—Figment (Posse (USA))
4556[U] 4733[9]

Life Begins (IRE) *Jonjo O'Neill* 92 h 82c
7 ch g Old Vic—Forty One (IRE) (Over The River (FR))
3676[P]

Life Estates *J D Frost* 70h
6 b g Mark Of Esteem(IRE) —Chepstow Vale (USA) (Key To The Mint (USA))
1640[6] 1969[P] 2309[14] 3456[10] 4290[P]4828[8]

Life Match (FR) *John G Carr* 106h
8 b g Polish Precedent(USA) —Life Watch (USA) (Highland Park (USA))
549[3] 591[P]

Lifes A Beach (IRE) *J J Bridger*
5 ch g Germany(USA) —Run Or Bust (IRE) (Commanche Run)
2534[21]

Light Des Mulottes (FR) *C R Egerton* 99+h 116 c
7 gr g Solidoun(FR) —Tango Girl (FR) (Tip Moss (FR))
365[7]

Lightening Fire (IRE) *B J Llewellyn* 50h
4 b g Woodborough(USA) —Glowlamp (IRE) (Glow (USA))
2454[R] 2935[9] 3645[14] 3804[10] 4550[6]

Lightin' Jack (IRE) *Miss E C Lavelle* 85h 109c
8 ch g Beneficial—Cillrossanta (IRE) (Mandalus)
271[4] 486[P] 1521[3]1631[2] 1746[6]

Lightning Star (USA) *G L Moore* 102+h
11 b g El Gran Senor(USA) —Cuz's Star (USA) (Galaxy Libra)
903[2] (1248) 1405[3]

Lightning Strikes (IRE) *Mrs L Wadham* 109+c
12 b g Zaffaran(USA) —Nimbi (Orchestra)
3819[6] 4216[4] 4477[2]4900[3]

Light On The Broom (IRE) *Gerard Stack* 113h 119c
10 b g Aristocracy—Montevelle (IRE) (Montelimar (USA))
1083a[3] 1420a[4] 1515a[7]1700a[P]

Light Tackle (IRE) *A Ennis*
5 ch g Kadastrof(FR) —La Siciliana (IRE) (Thatching)
2242[12]

Like A Bee (IRE) *C Roche* 116h 117c
8 b g Montelimar(USA) —Dasdilemma (IRE) (Furry Glen)
91a[8] 3053a[6]

Like A Lord (IRE) *Mrs S J Smith* 110 h
8 bb g Arctic Lord—Likashot (Celtic Cone)
762[6] (861) 2990[8]

Lik Wood Power (NZ) *D J Wintle* 106h 134 c
9 b g Bigstone(IRE) —Lady Paloma (USA) (Clever Trick (USA))
108[F] 360[4] 4621[17]4858[11]

Lilac *Evan Williams* 85+h
7 ch m Alhijaz—Fairfield's Breeze (Buckskin (FR))
(905) 1099[6] 5019[5]

Lila Des Planches (FR) *P Chemin*
7 b m Dress Parade—Amie Des Planches (FR) (What A Joy (FR))
4718a[5]

Lile Na Casca (IRE) *Mrs A M Thorpe*
7 b m Anshan—Pristina (IRE) (Mandalus)
2727[13]

Lilian Alexander *J R Holt* 79b
4 b f Nomadic Way(USA) —Dowdency (Dowsing (USA))
2425[7] 2927[6] 3259[11] 3691[9]

Lily Tara *A M Crow* 78b
4 b f Kayf Tara—Apprila (Bustino)
2068[7] 2642[9] 4533[2] 4751[18]

Limerick Boy (GER) *Miss Venetia Williams* 153 h 151 c
8 b g Alwuhush(USA) —Limoges (GER) (Konigsstuhl (GER))
3180[5] 3728[4] 4470[P]4764[F]

Limerick Leader (IRE) *P J Hobbs* 135h 110+c
8 b g Supreme Leader—View Of The Hills (Croghan Hill)
1759[4] 2046[6] 2175[12]**2608[P] 2819[F]**

Limerick Lord (IRE) *T J Taaffe* 113h 109c
9 ch g Mister Lord(USA) —Limerick Lady (The Parson)
1691a[5]

Limestream (IRE) *John G Carr* 108h
6 ch m Old Vic—Miss Lime (Aristocracy)
93a[8] 2211[12] 4887a[13]

Limogos (GER) *Mrs S Gardner*
6 b g Roi Danzig(USA) —Limoges (GER) (Konigsstuhl (GER))
1680[P] 1750[12]

Lincam (IRE) *P O'Keeffe* 103h 107c
10 b g Broken Hearted—Nanogan (Tarqogan)
115a[4] 1700a[8] 3053a[13]

Lincoln Leader (IRE) *Evan Williams* 60c
8 b m Supreme Leader—Tokay Lady (Furry Glen)
3801[P] 4590[8] 4729[P]5044[5]

Lincoln Place (IRE) *Mrs Marilyn Scudamore* 95 h 117+c
11 ch g Be My Native(USA) —Miss Lou (Levanter)
4[9] 4555[P]

Lincoln's Inn (IRE) *P J Hobbs* 90b
4 b g Old Vic—Eurodawn (IRE) (Orchestra)
4622[7] 5054[2]

Lindamarie (IRE) *C C Bealby* 85b
5 b m Luso—Rookery Lady (IRE) (Callernish)
2446[10] 2864[10]

Linda's Theatre *N G Richards* 96+b
6 b g King's Theatre(IRE) —Sorara (Aragon)
(1667)

Lindbergh Law (USA) *Mrs H Dalton* 88h
6 b g Red Ransom(USA) —Not So Shy (USA) (Crafty Prospector (USA))
(484) 769[2] (828) 3842[5] 4676[P] 4916[3]

Lin D'Estruval (FR) *C P Morlock* 99h 105+c
7 b g Cadoudal(FR) —Recolte D'Estruval (FR) (Kouban (FR))
1959[P] **2581[P] 2805[3]3372[P]**

Lindsay (FR) *H D Daly* 116 c
7 b g Chamberlin(FR) —Oliday (FR) (Djarvis (FR))
(2074) 2420[4] (2926) 3344[5] (4049) 4[F]

Line Ball (IRE) *C Roche* 117+h
5 b g Good Thyne(USA) —Navaro (IRE) (Be My Native (USA))
3003a[3]

Lingo (IRE) *Jonjo O'Neill* 152 h
7 b g Poliglote—Sea Ring (FR) (Bering)
(2209) (Dead)

Linnet (GER) *Ian Williams* 113 h
4 b f Dr Fong(USA) —Lauderdale (GER) (Nebos (GER))
2921[4] 3722[3] (3939) 4468[12] 4970[2]

Linn Of Dee (IRE) *N J Henderson* 70b
5 b m Zaffaran(USA) —Another Tycoon (IRE) (Phardante (FR))
4398[5]

L'Interprete (FR) *T Trapenard* 122h
7 b g Poliglote—Gnosca (FR) (Matahawk)
585a[6]

Linus *C J Down* 101h
8 b g Bin Ajwaad(IRE) —Land Line (High Line)
5[8] 352[2]

Lion Guest (IRE) *Mrs S C Bradburne* 87+h
9 ch g Lion Cavern(USA) —Decrescendo (IRE) (Polish Precedent (USA))
306[11] 551[8] 859[5] 941[10] 1151[8]1308[2] 1606[7] **1835[5] 2026[4]2476[P] 2655[P] 3320[P]3486[P] 5092[P]**

Lion's Domane *K W Hogg* 32h
9 b g Lion Cavern(USA) —Vilany (Never So Bold)
4301[P] 4388[7]

Liroquois (FR) *J Robic*
7 b g Legend Of France(USA) —Vienoise De Cene (FR) (Djarvis (FR))
4718a[P]

Lisaroon (IRE) *Miss E C Lavelle*
8 ch g Insan(USA) —Natasha's Run (IRE) (Le Bavard (FR))
216[P]

Liscooney (IRE) *David A Kiely* 120h 92c
8 ch g Old Vic—Golden Ambition (Torus)
2784a[5]

Lisdante (IRE) *W G Young* 101c
13 b g Phardante(FR) —Shuil Eile (Deep Run)
3758[U]

Liss Ard (IRE) *John Joseph Murphy* 100h
5 b h In The Wings—Beguine (USA) (Green Dancer (USA))
3642a[P]

Lissbonney Project (IRE) *Philip Fenton* 121h 121c
8 b g Lord Americo—Katie Lowe (IRE) (Pollerton)
2395a[5] 2916a[5] **3528a[2]**

Listen To Reason (IRE) *J G Given* 68h
5 b g Mukaddamah(USA) —Tenalist (IRE) (Tenby)
1565[7]

Litron (IRE) *J J Lambe* 104+h 83c
9 bb g Satco(FR) —Cornamucla (Lucky Guy)
319[2] **783[6]** 1379[3] 1571[2]

Little Alfie (IRE) *B S Rothwell* 76h
9 b g Shahanndeh—Debbies Scud (IRE) (Roselier (FR))
686[P]

Little Big Horse (IRE) *Mrs S J Smith* 105+h 140c
10 b g Little Bighorn—Little Gort (Roselier (FR))
248[3] (727) 1013[7](1550) 1735[6] 2499[3]2767[5] (4635) 5094[4]

Little Bit Of Hush (IRE) *Noel T Chance* 98b
6 b g Oscar(IRE)—Florenanti (Floriferous)
(4853)

Little Blackie *S J Marshall*
9 br m Royal Fountain—Mother Machree (Bing II)
1835[6] 1939 [P] 3926[P]

Little Brave *C Roberts* 92h
11 b g Kahyasi—Littlemisstrouble (USA) (My Gallant (USA))
(23) 298[5] 724[4] (2285) 2578[5]

Little Chartridge *P R Webber* 56h
8 b m Anshan—Auntie Dot (Hallodri (AUT))
135[F]

Little Farmer *Mrs D M Grissell* 112c
12 b g Little Wolf—Sea Farmer (Cantab)
402[2]

Little Flora *S J Marshall* 93+c
10 ch m Alflora(IRE)—Sister's Choice (Lepanto (GER))
(84) 305[7] 1942[P]2041[5] 2267[6] 2980[4]3379[4] 3555[6] 3928[5](4721) 4842[3]

Little Gannet *T D McCarthy*
5 ro m Bien Bien(USA)—Lady Kalliste (Another Realm)
2573[F] 3133[P] 3422[P] 3658[P]

Little Herman (IRE) *J A B Old* 90h 79c
10 b g Mandalus—Kilbricken Bay (Salluceva)
464[P]

Littlejimmybrown (IRE) *Patrick J Flynn* 95b
8 b g Over The River(FR)—Morning Susan (Status Seeker)
70a[P] (Dead)

Little John *W S Coltherd* 68 h
10 b g Warrshan(USA)—Silver Venture (USA) (Silver Hawk (USA))
1065[P]

Little Laurita *B De Haan* 32b
4 b f Overbury(IRE)—Laura Lye (IRE) (Carlingford Castle)
2830[12]

Little Ora (IRE) *J Rudge* 59h
9 ch g Black Monday—Country Melody (IRE) (Orchestra)
681[13]

Little Paddy (IRE) *Mrs K Walton* 93+b
5 b g Flemensfirth(USA)—Minor Tantrum (IRE) (Executive Perk)
4854[7]

Little Rocker (IRE) *M Pitman* 93b
5 b g Rock Hopper—One Back (IRE) (Meneval (USA))
4072[5] 4615[6]

Little Rort (IRE) *S T Lewis* 78 h
7 b g Ali-Royal(IRE)—Florinda (CAN) (Vice Regent (CAN))
(25) 177[6] 265[4] 397[4] 915[15] 2008[P]4570[U] 4783[7] 5050[7]

Little Saltee (IRE) *J A B Old* 66h
6 ch g Anshan—Shuil Na Mhuire (IRE) (Roselier (FR))
2829[14] 2983[14]

Little Saxtead (IRE) *J A Supple* 45h
6 ch g Anshan—Snape (IRE) (Strong Gale)
3137[4] 3367[9]

Little Sioux (IRE) *L Lungo* 54b
6 b m Little Bighorn—Our Dorcet (Condorcet (FR))
2028[P]

Little Sport (IRE) *Miss V Scott*
9 ch g Moscow Society(USA)—Ath Dara (Duky)
2925[F]

Little Task *J S Wainwright* 95h 77c
8 b g Environment Friend—Lucky Thing (Green Desert (USA))
520[3] **874[P]** 988[4] (1100) 1151[2]1211[3] 1333[2] 1436[7] (1456) 1606[5] 1715[2]1760[4] 1844 [6]

Little Tobias (IRE) *D D Scott* 85h
7 ch g Millkom—Barbara Frietchie (IRE) (Try My Best (USA))
573[4] 859[3] 871[6] 1107[2] 1208[F]1344[8] 1607[9] 5113[4]

Little Vantage *A M Crow* 87h
7 br g Mutamarrid—Shermago (Humdoleila)
720[5] 828[8] 5038[3]

Little Venus (IRE) *H D Daly* 100h
6 b m Moscow Society(USA)—Irene Good-Night (IRE) (Shernazar)
2446[4] 3287[5] 3690[4] 4425[2] 5019[3]

Little Villain (IRE) *T Wall* 58h
8 b g Old Vic—Party Woman (IRE) (Sexton Blake)
251[3] 973[9] 1100[6] 1395[4] 3985[B]4101[6] 4368[8]

Little Word *P D Williams* 62h
7 b m Rakaposhi King—Preacher's Gem (The Parson)
1681[8] 1833[5] 2427[6] 2937[4] 4133[P]4826[8]

Little Worsall (IRE) *Mrs F Marshall* 88+c
13 ch g Broadsword(USA)—In My View (King's Ride)
278[3] 400[4]

Litzinsky *J G M O'Shea* 93+h
8 b g Muhtarram(USA)—Boulevard Girl (Nicholas Bill)
1751[P] 4105[P]

Liverpool Echo (FR) *Mrs K Waldron* 136+c
6 b g Poliglote—Miss Echo (Chief Singer)
1013[8] 2744[6]

Livingonaknifedge (IRE) *Ian Williams* 120h
7 bb g Classic Memory—Duhallow Fiveo (Black Minstrel)
769[3] 1892[6] (2860) 3257[2] 3491[2] (4015) 4849[7]

Livingstonebramble (IRE) *W P Mullins* 125h 139c
10 b g Supreme Leader—Killiney Side (General Ironside)
(71a) 3587a[11] 5061a[4]

Livret Bleu (FR) *A E Jessop* 85h
7 b g Panoramic—Azur Bleue (FR) (Djarvis (FR))
2344[5]

Lizarazu (GER) *C R Egerton* 80h
7 b g Second Set(IRE)—Lilly (GER) (Motley (USA))
415[4]

Lizzie Bathwick (IRE) *J G Portman* 93 h 103c
7 b m Glacial Storm(USA)—Protrial (Proverb)
2149[3] 2555[2] 2996[4]3239[P] 3790[2] (3951) **4495[2]**

Llamadas *C Roberts* 87+h
4 b g Josr Algarhoud(IRE)—Primulette (Mummy's Pet)
3436[7] 3579[5]

Llys Y Fran *W K Goldsworthy*
4 b f Alphabatim(USA)—Lingua Franca (Formidable (USA))
4695[5]

Loada Baloney *Lucinda Featherstone* 62b
5 b g Jumbo Hirt(USA)—A Sharp (Sharpo)
138[6]

Loaded Gun *W Storey* 23h
6 ch g Highest Honor(FR)—Woodwardia (USA) (El Gran Senor (USA))
2658[F] 3167[U]

Lobengula (IRE) *I W McInnes* 67h
4 b g Spectrum(IRE)—Playwaki (USA) (Miswaki (USA))
2076[9] 2258[4] 2949[P]

Lochanee (IRE) *Mrs L C Jewell*
6 br g Anshan—Sassy Sally (IRE) (Callernish)
3664[11] **4006[P]**

Lochiedubs *Mrs L B Normile* 89h 95 c
11 br g Cragador—Linn Falls (Royal Fountain)
81[2] 2182[2] 2453[8] **2877[3]** (Dead)

Loch Red *C W Thornton* 42h
7 ch g Primitive Rising(USA)—Lochcross (Lochnager)
209[5] 553[P]

Loch Torridon *James Moffatt* 42h
7 b g Syrtos—Loch Scavaig (IRE) (The Parson)
209[6] 545[P] **990[P] 2415[P]**2631[P] **2839[P]**

Locksmith *M C Pipe* 132 h 147 c
6 bb g Linamix(FR)—Zenith (Shirley Heights)
2635[6] 3724[6] 3980[4]4459[16]

Lockstockandbarrel (IRE) *R Shiels* 104b
7 b g Needle Gun(IRE)—Quill Project (IRE) (Project Manager)
2906[2]

Lodestar (IRE) *Ian Williams* 114+h 120+c
9 br g Good Thyne(USA)—Lets Compromise (No Argument)
150[2] 321[5] 1025[P]

Lodgician (IRE) *J J Quinn* 92h
4 b c Grand Lodge(USA)—Dundel (IRE) (Machiavellian (USA))
1797[4] 2167[4]

Lofty Leader (IRE) *Mrs H O Graham* 101h
7 b g Norwich—Slaney Jazz (Orchestra)
82[9] 320[3] 647[4] 1291[P] 1377[3]1530[3] 1604[8] (1665) 2042[5]

Logger Rhythm (USA) *R Dickin* 39h 54c
6 b g Woodman(USA)—Formidable Dancer (USA) (Danzig (USA))
73[P] **4164[U] 5047[7]**

Logical Approach (IRE) *Edward U Hales* 101h 102c
9 b g Shernazar—Approach The Dawn (IRE) (Orchestra)
4018a[3] 4483a[P] 5129a[10]

Logies Lass *J S Smith* 71h
7 b m Nomadic Way(USA)—Random Select (Random Shot)
361[7] 656[7] 1674[10] 2125[4] 2815[P]3130[5]

Logistical *Ferdy Murphy* 73h
6 b g Grand Lodge(USA)—Magic Milly (Simply Great (FR))
2652[12] 3267[8] 3347[14]

Log On Intersky (IRE) *J R Cornwall* 118 c
10 ch g Insan(USA)—Arctic Mo (IRE) (Mandalus)
1320[4] 1435[6] 1666[3]1894[3] 2588[P] 2754[7]3619[P] 3788[6] (3964) 4618[P] 4900[P]

Loi De Martiale (IRE) *J M Jefferson* 87h
8 br g Presenting—Thresa-Anita (IRE) (Over The River (FR))
212[P] 603[5] 718[P] 913[P] 1040[10]

Loi Martiale (FR) *P Quinton*
8 b m Homme De Loi(IRE)—Isola D'Elba (USA) (Diesis)
846a[RR]

L'Oiseau (FR) *J G Portman* 95+h 123+c
7 br g Video Rock(FR)—Roseraie (FR) (Quart De Vin (FR))
84[3] 345[3] (1746) (1860) 2016[3] 2300[P] 4049[5]

Loita Hills (IRE) *P J Hobbs* 98h 26c
6 b g Norwich—Gleann Oisin (IRE) (Le Bavard (FR))
2528[3] 3131[2] 3505[6] 4941[5]

Loitokitok *P D Cundell*
4 b g Piccolo—Bonita Bee (King Of Spain)
1478[P]

Lojo *Miss Sheena West* 69h
4 ch f Pivotal—Myhat (Factual (USA))
2101[6] 2373[7] 2681[9] 3217[4]

Lolanita *Tim Vaughan* 31h
8 b m Anita's Prince—Jimlil (Nicholas Bill)
843[9] 1108[P]

Loner *W S Coltherd* 79h
8 b g Magic Ring(IRE)—Jolis Absent (Primo Dominie)
1591[6] 1937[5] 2191[9] 2567[2] 3267[5]

Lone Rider (IRE) *Jonjo O'Neill* 64h
5 b g Anshan—Reen-O-Foil (IRE) (Strong Gale)
2242[6] 2873[9] 3463[11] 3597[8] 3963[14]

Lone Soldier (FR) *S B Clark* 85 h
10 ch g Songlines(FR)—Caring Society (Caerleon (USA))
238[6] 370[2] 412[6] (520) 681[U] 784[3](822) 915[8] 1027[5] 1111[4] 1179[7] 1223[5]1344[5] 1458[8] 1607[6] 1756[5]

Lonesome Man (IRE) *Tim Vaughan* 106h 118+c
10 ch g Broken Hearted—Carn-Na-Ros (Royal Trip)
106[U] (436) (767) 1189[P]4805[5]

Longdale *M Todhunter* 92+h 108+c
8 b g Primitive Rising(USA)—Gunnerdale (Gunner B)
210[4] (602) 780[P] **2655[U] 2842[8](2980) 3233[8] 3334[3]3562[P] 4318[F]**

Longhope Boy *W J Musson* 57b
7 b g Rock Hopper—Always A Pleasure (Chauve Souris)
1892[9]

Long Night *P J Hobbs* 58h 104+c
7 b g Alflora(IRE)—Twice A Night (Oats)
384[6]

Long Road (USA) *Jonjo O'Neill* 103+h 94+c
5 b g Diesis—Tuviah (USA) (Eastern Echo (USA))
4738[4]

Long Road Home (IRE) *Jonjo O'Neill* 97+b
7 b g Supreme Leader—Chelsea Native (Be My Native (USA))
(1274) 2987[6]

Longshanks *K C Bailey* 104 h 136 c
9 b g Broadsword(USA)—Brass Castle (IRE) (Carlingford Castle)
3176[7]

Long Shot *Miss L C Siddall* 45h
9 b m Sir Harry Lewis(USA)—Kovalevskia (Ardross)
2027[P] 2714[9] 3351[15] 3959[P]

Longstone Boy (IRE) *E R Clough* 107+c
14 br g Mazaad—Inger-Lea (Record Run)
(313) 4831[5]

Longstone Lady (IRE) *J D Frost* 84h 84c
9 b m Mister Lord(USA)—Monamandy (IRE) (Mandalus)
1921[8] 4034[4] (4556) 4726[11]

Longstone Lass *Miss Tracy Waggott* 100 h 57c
6 b m Wizard King—Kamaress (Kampala)
352[P] 480[P] 1107[7] 1148[5] 1180[8]1756[10] (1884) (2066) 2417[9] 3318[9] **3352[4]**

Longstone Loch (IRE) *C C Bealby* 96+h 97 c
9 b g Executive Perk—Lyre-Na-Gcloc (Le Moss)
3368[6] 3791[U] 3958[F]4900[4]

Longueville Manor (FR) *Jonjo O'Neill* 99h 99c
5 gr g Tel Quel(FR)—Longueville (FR) (Turgeon (USA))
65a[23] 4731[4] 5014[2]

Longwhitejemmy (IRE) *D T Hughes* 68h
4 b f Rashar(USA)—Queen Polly (IRE) (Pollerton)
5077a[19]

Lookafterme (IRE) *A W Carroll* 84h 56c
6 ch g Old Vic—Mrs Cullen (Over The River (FR))
2192[7] **3331[P] 3558[6]**4562[2] 4875[6]

Look At The Stars (IRE) *R Hollinshead* 52h
4 b g Bachir(IRE)—Pizzazz (Unfuwain (USA))
1729[12] 1802[7] 2752[11]

Look Between Us (IRE) *L J Archdeacon* 99h 123c
9 b g Lucky Guest—Royal Myth (USA) (Sir Ivor (USA))
1083a[8]

Looking Forward *Mrs S A Watt*
10 br g Primitive Rising(USA)—Gilzie Bank (New Brig)
3676[U] 3915[P] 4920[P]5036[P]

Looking Great (USA) *R F Johnson Houghton* 84h
4 b g Gulch(USA)—Shoofha (IRE) (Bluebird (USA))
1594[2] 1737[3] 1948[P] 4819[5] 5111[5]

Look No Further (IRE) *John Joseph Murphy* 90h
4 b g Orpen(USA)—Glow (Alzao (USA))
5099a[7]

Look No More *W G M Turner* 46h
5 ch g First Trump—Jadebelle (Beldale Flutter (USA))
1[12] 4591[9]

Looks The Business (IRE) *W G M Turner* 103h
5 b g Marju(IRE)—Business Centre (IRE) (Digamist (USA))
78[9] 1458[2] 1565[3] (1651) 1862[5]

Look To The Future (IRE) *M J M Evans* 71c
12 b g Roselier(FR)—Toevarro (Raga Navarro (ITY))
95[P] 1715[P] 1981[2]2429[5] 2818[F] 3582[6]3888[F] 4780[5] 4936[8]

Loose Morals (IRE) *Miss E C Lavelle* 73 h
5 b m Luso—Lacken Star (IRE) (Be My Native (USA))
2056[9] 2865[9] 3511[4] 3884[P] 4836[8]

L'Orage Lady (IRE) *Mrs H Dalton* 92h
8 ch m Glacial Storm(USA)—Commanche Glen (IRE) (Commanche Run)
245[P] 1367[4]

Loramore *J C Tuck* 65b
9 ch m Alflora(IRE)—Apsimore (Touching Wood (USA))
167[P] 806[P]

Lord Alphieross (IRE) *W J Burke* 102c
8 ch g Alphabatim(USA)—Carrig Ross (Lord Ha Ha)
112a[P]

Lord Anner (IRE) *P F Nicholls* 121+c
7 br g Mister Lord(USA)—Anner Lodge (IRE) (Capitano)
440[P] 1780[2] (1858) (2273) 3000[4] 4835[4]

Lord Archie (IRE) *M Sheppard* 54b 100c
8 b g Arctic Lord—Jim's Monkey (Monksfield)
1622a[4] 3343[6] 3803[7]

Lord Atterbury (IRE) *M C Pipe* 96h 143 c
10 ch g Mister Lord(USA)—Tammyiris (Arapahos (FR))
3941[P] 4238[4] **5004[P]**

Lord Attica (IRE) *M F Harris* 61h 78 c
7 b g Mister Lord(USA)—Brief Pace (IRE) (Riot Helmet)
229[6] 310[3] 686[10] 749[9] 1100[8]

Lord Baskerville *W Storey* 92+h
5 br g Wolfhound(USA)—My Dear Watson (Chilibang)
1661[3] 1937[4] 2448[0] 2901[9] 2991[12]3171[7] 3351[5] 3445[4] 3916[2] 4723[8]12[5]

Lord Beau (IRE) *A J Bateman* 113c
10 b g Beau Sher—Bonny Joe (Derring Rose)
(440)

Lord Broadway (IRE) *N M Babbage* 111+c
10 b g Shardari—Country Course (IRE) (Crash Course)
3241[P] 3547[8] (3688) 4103[4] 4576[2] 4835[6]

Lord Brock *N A Twiston-Davies* 105 h 125 c
7 b g Alderbrook—Mariner's Air (Julio Mariner)
(3290) 3614[P] 4068[4]

Lord Capitaine (IRE) *J Howard Johnson* 115+c
12 bb g Mister Lord(USA)—Salvation Sue (Mon Capitaine)
150[P] (Dead)

Lord Castle (IRE) *P W Hiatt* 41h
10 ch g Mister Lord(USA)—Amandas Castle (IRE) (Carlingford Castle)
763[P]

Lord Collingwood (IRE) *M D Hammond* 90h
5 ch g Accordion—Cracker Dawn (IRE) (Executive Perk)
3399[3] 3742[4] 4342[2]

Lord Dundaniel (IRE) *B De Haan* 119h 118+c
9 bb g Arctic Lord—Killoskehan Queen (Bustineto)
174[F] 386[2] 570[5]2005[3] 2529[3] 2748[4]4214[3] (4563) 4829[4]4[3]

L'Or De Thou (FR) *W J Tolhurst*
7 b g Sleeping Car(FR)—Va Thou Line (FR) (El Badr)
4897[F]

Lord Euro (IRE) *Mrs D M Grissell* 89+c
9 br g Lord Americo—Orchards Beauty (IRE) (Miner's Lamp)
404[4]

Lord Gee (IRE) *O Sherwood* 88+b
5 gr g Topanoora—Forever Bubbles (IRE) (Roselier (FR))
4637[5] 5054[5]

Lord Gunnerslake (IRE) *Miss C J E Caroe* 100c
6 ch g Flying Spur(AUS)—Cry In The Dark (Godswalk (USA))
2664[8] 3331[6] 3549[7]3676[3] 3922[3] 4820[6]5051[8]

Lord Henry (IRE) *P J Hobbs* 133 h
7 b g Lord Americo—Auntie Honnie (IRE) (Radical)
4091[3] 4473[7] 4773[9]

Lord Hopeful (IRE) *C P Morlock* 77+h
5 b g Lord Americo—Hidden Agenda (Abednego)
249[5] 1982[7] 2374[9]

Lordington Lad *B G Powell* 52h
6 br g Terimon—Fit For Firing (FR) (In Fijar (USA))
2507[7] 2829[13] 3133[15] 3369[F] 3677[P]**4525[F]**

Lord Jack (IRE) *N G Richards* 123 h 133c
10 ch g Mister Lord(USA)—Gentle Gill (Pollerton)
1844 [5] **2164[2] 2745[14]**3854[10] **4434[11]**

Lord Jay Jay (IRE) *Miss H C Knight* 89h 77c
9 b g Lord Of Appeal—Mesena (Pals Passage)
345[2] 1711[P]

Lord Joshua (IRE) *N J Henderson* 113h
8 b g King's Theatre(IRE)—Lady Joshua (IRE) (Royal Academy (USA))
247[P]

Lord Kernow (IRE) *C J Down* 98b
6 b g Lord Americo—Bramble Ridge (IRE) (Remainder Man)
2864[3] 3244[5]

Lord Killeshanra (IRE) *C L Tizzard* 117h 143 c
7 br g Mister Lord(USA)—Killeshandra Lass (IRE) (King's Ride)
1976[2] (2311) 2869[2]3213[P] 4035[3] 4444[4]

Lord Killucan (IRE) *M Halford* 54b
5 b g Bob Back(USA)—Azinter (IRE) (Magical Strike (USA))
5060a[17]

Lord Kilpatrick (IRE) *Mrs H J Houghton* 91c
12 ch g Mister Lord(USA)—Running Frau (Deep Run)
4090[4]

Lord Lamb *K G Reveley* 91h
14 gr g Dunbeath(USA)—Caroline Lamb (Hotfoot)
283[5] 425[7]

Lord Leonardo (IRE) *L Wells* 23h
6 b g Norwich—Sue's A Lady (Le Moss)
507[10] 2579[8] 2928[11] 3664[10] 4005[7]

Lord Lington (FR) *D J Wintle* 116+h 116+c
7 b g Bulington(FR)—Tosca De Bussy (FR) (Le Riverain (FR))
136[3] 247[3] 726[U] 1610[8] (1957) **(2246)** 2525[6] **3580[RR]** 4420[9] **4664[P]**

Lord Maizey (IRE) *N A Twiston-Davies* 139+b 136c
9 b g Mister Lord(USA)—My Maizey (Buckskin (FR))
2499[7] 2744[P] (3019) 3385[10] 4240[P]

Lord Morley (IRE) *Karen McLintock* 93b
6 br g Lord Americo—Minature Miss (Move Off)
4909[6]

Lord Musgrave (IRE) *L Wells* 68h
7 b g Lord Americo—Raisin Turf (IRE) (Phardante (FR))
1954[7] 2928[F] 3466[12] 3717[10]

Lord Nellerie (FR) *B G Powell* 122+c
7 b g Panoramic—Epsom Nellerie (FR) (Carmont (FR))
4594[2] 4831[F] 5020[F]

Lord Nellsson *Andrew Turnell* 105h 98c
10 b g Arctic Lord—Miss Petronella (Petoski)
315[3] 509[3] 2150[2] (2296) **2996[5]**

Lord 'N' Master (IRE) *R Rowe* 96h 120c
10 b g Lord Americo—Miss Good Night (Buckskin (FR))
205[5] 516[2] (669) 1025[P]

Lord Noelie (IRE) *Mrs Jeremy Young* 51 c
13 b g Lord Americo—Leallen (Le Bavard (FR))
423[F] 842[P]

Lord Norman (IRE) *L Wells* 94b
5 b g Norwich—Sue's A Lady (Le Moss)
4011[4] 4326[8]

Lord O'All Seasons (IRE) *J P Elliot* 120c
13 bb g Mister Lord(USA) —Autumn News (Giolla Mear)
63[3] 3913[3] (4660)

Lord Of Adventure (IRE) *Mrs L C Jewell* 85h
4 b g Inzar(USA) —Highly Fashionable (IRE) (Polish Precedent (USA))
2236[7] 2681[3] 2954[3] 3137[2] 3431[P]3714[10] 4616[4] 4898[P]

Lord Of Gortmerron (IRE) *C J Cosgrave* 109+c
7 b g Mister Lord(USA) —Lek-Lady (IRE) (Royal Fountain)
872[2] 1531[2]

Lord Of Illusion (IRE) *T R George* 108h 156 c
9 b g Mister Lord(USA) —Jellaride (IRE) (King's Ride)
2166[P] 2491[12] 3176[2]4470[18] 4777[P]

Lord Of Methley *S Lycett* 78+h
7 gr g Zilzal(USA) —Paradise Waters (Celestial Storm (USA))
3883[P] 4564[6] 5023[3]

Lordofourown (IRE) *S Donohoe* 115h 125c
8 b g Mister Lord(USA) —Twinkling (Star Appeal)
3893a[8] (4136a) 4759[P]

Lord Of The Bog (IRE) *B Tulloch*
7 bb g Mister Lord(USA) —Shakie Lady (Tug Of War)
4167[P]

Lord Of The Flies (IRE) *Ms Lisa Stock* 65h 120c
13 bb g Lord Americo—Beau's Trout (Beau Charmeur (FR))
405[2]

Lord Of The Hill (IRE) *G Brown* 50h 110c
11 b g Dromod Hill—Telegram Mear (Giolla Mear)
246[2] 840[7] 3805[P]4452[7] 13[F]

Lord Of The Land *Mrs E Slack* 93h 85+c
13 b g Lord Bud—Saint Motunde (Tyrant (USA))
149[7] 214[P] 480[7] 690[2]896[9] 988[9] 1065[P]

Lord Olympia (IRE) *Miss Venetia Williams* 125h 130 c
7 b g Lord Americo—Mooreshill (IRE) (Le Moss)
2564[2] (2805) 3396[F]3509[F] 3973[2] (4130) 4323[3] 4498[P] 4841[P] (Dead)

Lord On The Run (IRE) *J W Mullins* 96h 124+c
7 b g Lord Americo—Polar Crash (Crash Course)
1852[2] 2141[P] 2528[8]3418[2] 4239[2] (4620) 4820[2]

Lord Oscar (IRE) *M C Pipe* 90h 96c
7 b g Oscar(IRE) —Americo Rose (IRE) (Lord Americo)
1875[6] 2818[4] 4860[8] 5087[U]

Lord Over *Patrick J Flynn* 129b
5 b g Kahyasi—Santana Lady (IRE) (Blakeney)
4448[6] 5081a[3]

Lord Pat (IRE) *Miss Kate Milligan* 79h 79c
15 ch g Mister Lord(USA) —Arianrhod (L'Homme Arme)
480[P]

Lord Payne (IRE) *P Monteith* 102h 102+c
8 b g Alphabatim(USA) —Clash Boreen (Arapaho)
2023[3] 2449[8] 2654[5]2839[2] 3236[P] 3377[7]

Lord Raffles *P R Webber* 66b
4 b g Zafonic(USA) —Dawna (Polish Precedent (USA))
3346[11]

Lord Rex (IRE) *S G Waugh*
6 b g Arctic Lord—Ohgolly Miss Molly (IRE) (Mandalus)
3314[P] (Dead)

Lord Rochester *K F Clutterbuck* 86h 62 c
10 b g Distant Relative—Kentfield (Busted)
670[15]

Lord Rodney (IRE) *P Beaumont* 104+h 132+c
7 b g Hatim(USA) —Howcleuch (Buckskin (FR))
85[5] 549[6] 2874[P] (4053) 4498[P] 4778[4] 5127[P]

Lord Rosskit (IRE) *G M Moore* 93+h
6 bb g Lord Americo—Redstone Lady (IRE) (Buckskin (FR))
59[9] 1663[3] 1826[3] 2191[10] 2416[9]

Lord Ryeford (IRE) *T R George* 102 h
6 br g Arctic Lord—Killoskehan Queen (Bustineto)
2288[4] 2720[7] 3342[11] 3463[8] (3843) 4557[5]4860[7]

Lord Sam (IRE) *V R A Dartnall* 140h 160 c
10 bb g Supreme Leader—Russian Gale (IRE) (Strong Gale)
2177[5] 2744[P] 3727[P]4974[4]

Lord Saxbury *P L Clinton*
7 b g Overbury(IRE) —Saxon Gift (Saxon Farm)
2864[15]

Lordsbridge (USA) *D P Keane* 76h
4 b g Lord Avie(USA) —Victorian Style (Nashwan (USA))
3511[6] 3996[8] 4569[7]

Lord Seamus *K C Bailey* 88h 108 c
11 b g Arctic Lord—Erica Superba (Langton Heath)
2703[4] 3343[5] 3649[5]4939[6]

Lord Strickland *P J Hobbs* 109h 122+c
13 b g Strong Gale—Lady Rag (Ragapan)
386[7] 653[P] 1189[7]

Lord Thomas (IRE) *A J Wilson* 29b
8 b g Grand Lodge(USA) —Noble Rocket (Reprimand)
729[P] 1415[8]

Lord Tiddlypush (IRE) *Sir John Barlow Bt*
8 b g Lord Americo—Ag Rith Abhaile (Carlingford Castle)
343[P] (Dead)

Lord Transcend (IRE) *J Howard Johnson* 130h 155+c
9 gr g Aristocracy—Capincur Lady (Over The River (FR))
2628[2] 3493[P]

Lord Valnic (IRE) *Ms A E Embiricos*
10 b g Mister Lord(USA) —Any Wonder (Hard Boy)
282[P]

Lord West *C L Tizzard* 69h
5 ch g The West(USA) —Flair Lady (Chilibang)
1777[9] 1968[P] 4754[8]

Lord Who (IRE) *P J Hobbs* 118h 131c
9 b g Mister Lord(USA) —Le Bavellen (Le Bavard (FR))
2162[P] 2828[U]

Lord Youky (FR) *Miss J Hughes* 117 c
12 b g Cadoudal(FR) —Lady Corteira (FR) (Carvin II)
5020[U]

Lorgnette *R H Alner* 111h 104c
12 br m Emperor Fountain—Speckyfoureyes (Blue Cashmere)
168[4]

Lorient Express (FR) *Miss Venetia Williams* 97+h 129 c
7 b g Sleeping Car(FR) —Envie De Chalamont (FR) (Pamponi (FR))
(2239) (2754) 2939[2](2998) 3299[5] 3357[3]4213[6] (4731) (4834)

Loriko D'Airy (FR) *Miss C Dyson* 101h 114c
7 b g Oblat(FR) —Ursali D'Airy (FR) (Marasali)
170[7] 667[3] 901[4] 1154[5]

Lorio Du Misselot (FR) *Ferdy Murphy* 83h
7 gr g Dom Alco(FR) —Byrsa (FR) (Quart De Vin (FR))
1569[9] 2474[2] 3271[7]

Lorna Dune *J G M O'Shea* 72h
4 b f Desert Story(IRE) —Autumn Affair (Lugana Beach)
1679[8] 1729[4] 1904[7] 2245[P]

Lorna's Star (IRE) *F Flood* 96h
7 b m Fourstars Allstar(USA) —Lorna's Beauty (IRE) (King's Ride)
2031a[11]

L'Orphelin *C L Tizzard* 78h 118+c
11 ch g Gildoran—Balula (Balinger)
1978[P] 3212[P] 3616[2]

Lorrelini (IRE) *R H Alner* 71+h
5 ch h Among Men(USA) —Well Able (IRE) (Lahib (USA))
2849[P] 3133[16] 4784[7]

Loscar (FR) *L Lungo* 70h
7 b g General Holme(USA) —Unika Ii (FR) (Rolling Bowl (FR))
545[4]

Losing Grip (IRE) *Mrs S J Smith* 89+h
7 bb m Presenting—Executive Wonder (IRE) (Executive Perk)
3551[4] 3795[12] 4609[7] (4794)

Loss Of Faith (IRE) *M J P O'Brien* 109h 120c
8 b g Ajraas(USA) —Sharp Mistress (IRE) (Sharp Victor (USA))
5131a[P]

Los Suenos (IRE) *Nick Williams*
5 br g Supreme Leader—Stormy Miss (IRE) (Glacial Storm (USA))
3882[P]

Lost And Found *C Grant*
6 ch g Master Willie—Top Cover (High Top)
1532[13]

Lost Boy (IRE) *R Bastiman*
7 ch g Roselier(FR) —Stranger Still (Cragador)
3253[8] 3792[P] (Dead)

Lost In Normandy (IRE) *Mrs L Williamson* 57h 90 c
9 b g Treasure Hunter—Auntie Honnie (IRE) (Radical)
1276[P] 1321[P] 1446[2]1615[2] 1960[3] 2424[7]2686[4] (2818) 2933[3]3398[2] 3845[P] 4499[5]5136[P]

Lost In The Snow (IRE) *M Sheppard* 64h 84c
8 bb g Arctic Lord—Where Am I (Kambalda)
912[6] 982[8] 1037[10] 1236[3]1412[2] 1659[8] 1801[P]

Lost Time (IRE) *C Roche* 125h 130 c
9 b g Glacial Storm(USA) —Overtime (IRE) (Executive Perk)
3053a[7] 4498[4]

Lost Treasure (IRE) *Mrs M Evans* 74c
9 br g Treasure Hunter—Jury Box (Jukebox)
972[4] 1038[P] 1089[5]1376[P] 1412[6] 1832[P]4283[P]

Lothian Falcon *P Maddison* 95h 120+c
7 b g Relief Pitcher—Lothian Rose (Roscoe Blake)
124[5] 367[4] 426[2] 1928[P]2259[4] (2518) 2841[2]

Lotomore Lad (IRE) *Donal Hassett* 108h 115c
8 ch g Good Thyne(USA) —Chaunticlear (IRE) (Over The River (FR))
92a[P] 4762[17]

L'Oudon (FR) *P F Nicholls* 124+h
5 ch g Alamo Bay(USA) —Stella Di Corte (FR) (Lightning (FR))
2595[4] 3135[5] 3696[6] (4838)

Lou Du Moulin Mas (FR) *P F Nicholls* 107 h 138c
7 b g Sassanian(USA) —Houf (FR) (Morespeed)
1759[2] 2176[2] 2767[3]3296[4] 4447[10] 4762[8]

Lou Flight (FR) *G Cherel*
3 b g Poliglote—Green Emerald (Warning)
4298a[5]

Loughanelteen (IRE) *P J Rothwell* 120h 109c
8 b g Satco(FR) —Ruths Rhapsody (IRE) (Creative Plan (USA))
3005a[15] 3411a[F] 4951a[20]

Lough Derg (FR) *M C Pipe* 150 h 140 c
6 b g Apple Tree(FR) —Asturias (FR) (Pistolet Bleu (IRE))
2174[2] 2484[F] (2848) 3213[3] 4444[P] 4960[F]

Lough Rynn (IRE) *Miss H C Knight* 82h 111+c
8 b g Beneficial—Liffey Lady (Camden Town)
436[F] 532[3] 3282[3]4047[P]

Louisville (IRE) *C A McBratney* 107h
7 b g Grand Lodge(USA) —Megastart (USA) (Private Account (USA))
2110[P]

Loulou Nivernais (FR) *M Todhunter* 95h 106+c
7 b g Lights Out(FR) —Clemence (FR) (Vorias (USA))
874[4] 1335[5] (1433) 1529[5] 1592[7] (2111) 2479[2] 2655[F] 2980[3]3255[3] 3380[4] 4721[F]4991[5]

Loup Bleu (USA) *Mrs A V Roberts* 86h
8 b g Nureyev(USA) —Louve Bleue (USA) (Irish River (FR))
1818[4] 2574[P] 3943[P] 4452[U]4566[8] 4794[5] 4898[3]

Loup Charter (FR) *Miss H C Knight* 125 h 98 c
7 gr g Royal Charter(FR) —Easy III (FR) (Perrault)
2311[5] 2848[7] 4612[P]4776[P]

Louve Heureuse (IRE) *J R Boyle* 76+h
5 ch m Peintre Celebre(USA) —Louve Sereine (FR) (Sadler's Wells (USA))
2704[7]

Love Affair (IRE) *R Hannon*
4 b f Tagula(IRE) —Changing Partners (Rainbow Quest (USA))
3340[F]

Love Angel (USA) *J J Bridger* 104+h
4 bb g Woodman(USA) —Omnia (USA) (Green Dancer (USA))
3294[7] 4117[7] 4468[13]

Love At Dawn *J A T De Giles* 78c
12 b g Dawn Johnny(USA) —Grafton Maisey (Jimsun)
53[P]

Love Beauty (USA) *M F Harris* 76h
4 bb g Seeking The Gold(USA) —Heavenly Rhythm (USA) (Septieme Ciel (USA))
3294[9] 3431[6] 3645[9] 4128[5] 4871[P]

Love Diamonds (IRE) *Miss C Dyson* 73h
10 b g Royal Academy(USA) —Baby Diamonds (Habitat)
279[11]

Lovely Lulu *J C Tuck* 62h
8 b m Petrizzo—The Green Girls (USA) (Distinctive Pro (USA))
134[13] 1774[6] 2463[5] 2806[5] 3456[15]

Lovely Native (IRE) *L Lungo* 71h 108+c
10 b m Be My Native(USA) —Lovely Tyrone (Peacock (FR))
4144[5] (4587) 4842[7]

Lovely Present (IRE) *T K Geraghty* 119h
7 ch m Presenting—Lovely Run (Deep Run)
92a[11] 5103a[P]

Love Of Classics *O Sherwood* 113 h
6 b g Classic Cliche(IRE) —Ardent Love (IRE) (Ardross)
1892[10] 1990[2] 2327[2] 2985[2] 3477[6]3941[3] (4689)

Lovers Lane (FR) *M C Pipe*
6 b g Freedom Cry—Leafy Lane (FR) (Garde Royale)
294[5]

Lovers Tale *G A Ham* 74h
8 b g Pursuit Of Love—Kintail (Kris)
486[P] 681[14] 812[F]1187[U] 1233[5] 1395[F]

Love Supreme (IRE) *C F Swan* 84h
6 b m Supreme Leader—Tri Folene (FR) (Nebos (GER))
1968[5]

Love That Benny (USA) *J Wade* 123h
6 ch g Benny The Dip(USA) —Marie Loves Emma (USA) (Affirmed (USA))
1722[2] 3779[3] (4141)

Love Triangle (IRE) *N B King*
5 ch g Titus Livius(FR) —Kirsova (Absalom)
670[10] 895[P] 973[8] (1085) 1208[P] 1432[9]

Low Cloud *J J Quinn* 113 h 98+c
6 b g Danehill(USA) —Raincloud (Rainbow Quest (USA))
332[5] 1318[3] 1644[3]2519[P]

Lowe Go *Miss J S Davis* 94h 57c
6 b g First Trump—Hotel California (IRE) (Last Tycoon)
4593[6] 5025[U]

Lowsha Green *R Johnson* 70h
5 b g Foxhound(USA) —Super Times (Sayf El Arab (USA))
3399[7] 4533[12] 5091[7]

Loy's Lad (IRE) *Miss V Scott* 64h 105c
10 b g Glacial Storm(USA) —Missing Note (Rarity)
873[8] (1592) 2692[P] 2842[7]

Lubinas (IRE) *F Jordan* 116 h 112+c
7 b g Grand Lodge(USA) —Liebesgirl (Konigsstuhl (GER))
10[3] 354[3] 1716[3]1877[7] 2818[6] (3368) 3815[6] 4214[4] 4620[2](4735) 5127[2]

Luccombe Bay *M G Rimell* 84b
6 b m Karinga Bay—Bay Lough (IRE) (Lancastrian)
4554[5]

Lucent (IRE) *Miss H C Knight* 78h
5 b g Luso—Allenswood Girl (IRE) (Bulldozer)
3327[9] 4048[5] 4665[7]

Luchi *M Scudamore*
5 ch m Mark Of Esteem(IRE) —Penmayne (Inchinor)
2515[P]

Lucifer Du Montceau (FR) *A L T Moore* 64b
7 b g Video Rock(FR) —Une De Montceau (FR) (Vorias (USA))
3528a[F]

Lucinda Lamb *Miss S E Hall* 82b
4 b f Kayf Tara—Caroline Lamb (Hotfoot)
5141[4]

Lucken Howe *Mrs J K M Oliver* 49h
7 b g Keen—Gilston Lass (Majestic Streak)
210[10] 2023[P] 2415[P]

Luckos (FR) *T Trapenard*
3 b g Ultimately Lucky(IRE) —Kostra (FR) (Nikos)
4298a[P]

Lucky Angler (IRE) *Mark Campion* 87b
7 b g Gone Fishin—Lady By Chance (IRE) (Never Got A Chance)
2948[6]

Lucky Arthur (IRE) *Mrs L Williamson* 78h
5 ch m Grand Lodge(USA) —Soltura (IRE) (Sadler's Wells (USA))
1158[3] 1235[6] 1356[4] 1520[6] 1742[9]2146[11]

Lucky Bay (IRE) *Mrs H M Kemp* 98c
10 b g Convinced—Current Liability (Caribo)
439[F] 4079[2]

Luckycharm (FR) *R Dickin* 53h 76 c
7 ch g Villez(USA) —Hitifly (FR) (Murmure (FR))
398[8] 612[2] 827[4]948[U] 3672[4] 4164[8]4394[P]

Lucky Do (IRE) *V J Hughes* 106+h
9 b g Camden Town—Lane Baloo (Lucky Brief)
284[3] (749) (1121) 2173[9] 4606[P] 1[7]

Lucky Duck *Mrs A Hamilton* 114h 121+c
9 ch g Minster Son—Petroc Concert (Tina's Pet)
3352[F] (4840)

Lucky Judge *G A Swinbank* 110h
9 b g Saddlers' Hall(IRE) —Lady Lydia (Ela-Mana-Mou)
1940 [10] 2440[3] 2840[7]

Lucky Largo (IRE) *D A Nolan* 87 h
6 bb g Key Of Luck(USA) —Lingering Melody (IRE) (Nordico (USA))
3267[F] 3534[P]

Lucky Leader (IRE) *N R Mitchell* 111+c
11 b g Supreme Leader—Lucky House (Pollerton)
1972[6] 2273[5] 2623[P]3212[3] 3481[P] 4571[P]4939[2] 5105[U]

Lucky Luk (FR) *K C Bailey* 77h 91c
7 b g Lights Out(FR) —Citronelle II (FR) (Kedellic (FR))
1855[P] 2555[5] 2936[11]4047[9] 4567[2] 5088[2]

Lucky Master (IRE) *Miss G Swan* 100h 83c
14 b g Roselier(FR) —Golden Chestnut (Green Shoon)
125[4] 4107[3] 4397[5]4799[P] 5013[U]

Lucky Pearl *O Brennan* 36b
5 b m Jendali(USA) —Fardella (ITY) (Molvedo)
4902[11]

Lucky Penny *K Bishop* 68h
10 ch m Karinga Bay—Redgrave Rose (Tug Of War)
2313[U]

Lucky Pete *P J Jones* 72+h 98+c
9 b g Lyphento(USA) —Clare's Choice (Pragmatic)
234[5]

Lucky Piscean *C W Fairhurst* 78 h
5 b g River Falls—Celestine (Skyliner)
545[P] 718[6]

Lucky Shame (FR) *A J Whitehead* 56h
4 ch g Lesotho(USA) —Shame (IRE) (Priolo (USA))
3948[6] 4057[P] 4416[9]

Lucky Sinna (IRE) *B G Powell* 119h 97 c
10 bb g Insan(USA) —Bit Of A Chance (Lord Ha Ha)
1631[3] 1953[P] 2273[6]2575[4] 2682[5] 2957[5]3221[2] 3888[2] 4428[2]4804[5] (4837)

Lucky Third Time *M Scudamore* 53b
4 b f Terimon—Zanditu (Presidium)
3497[7] 4398[7]

Lucky Turf (IRE) *W K Goldsworthy* 41h
9 b g Wood Chanter—Teacloth (Raga Navarro (ITY))
3354[10]

Luc Moriniere (FR) *P Monfort*
7 b g Saint Cyrien(FR) —Perle De Moriniere (FR) (Gairloch)
5000a[5]

Lujain Rose *N M Babbage* 37h
4 b f Lujain(USA) —Rose Chime (IRE) (Tirol)
4074[12]

Lulumar (FR) *O Sherwood* 94h 110c
7 ch g Beyssac(FR) —Friandise II (FR) (Mistigri)
2622[P] 2768[9] 3186[P]4419[4] 5107[F]

Luminoso *J D J Davies* 91h
14 gr g Machiavellian(USA) —Light The Sky (FR) (Persepolis (FR))
458[7] 973[7] 1636[6] 1756[P]

Lumps And Cracks (IRE) *Seamus Fahey* 63b
5 b g Oscar(IRE) —Orospring (Tesoro Mio)
5060a[15]

Lunar Crystal (IRE) *M C Pipe* 131h 107+c
8 b g Shirley Heights—Solar Crystal (IRE) (Alzao (USA))
3696[2] 4091[2] 4375[4] 4473[17] 4765[12]

Lunardi (IRE) *D L Williams* 75c
8 b g Indian Ridge—Gold Tear (USA) (Tejano (USA))
1856[P] 2260[P] 2733[6]2936[14] 5105[P]

Lunar Dram *M Dods* 98+h 98c
8 ch g Cosmonaut—Moonshine Malt (Superlative)
4655[F] 4840[F]

Lunar Eclipse *J I A Charlton* 85b
6 b m Dancing High—Pauper Moon (Pauper)
349[2] 720[2] (876)

Lunar Exit (IRE) *Lady Herries* 108h
5 gr g Exit To Nowhere(USA) —Moon Magic (Polish Precedent (USA))
133[2] 671[6]

Lunar Fox *J L Needham* 49h
7 b m Roselier(FR) —Leinthall Fox (Deep Run)
2501[8] 2815[P]

Lunar Sovereign (USA) *M C Pipe* 87h
7 bb g Cobra King(USA) —January Moon (USA) (Apalachee (USA))
2573[4] 4327[12] 4621[9]

Lunch Was My Idea (IRE) *P F Nicholls* 82 h
6 bb g Tawrrific(NZ) —Equity Law (IRE) (Gunner B)
2212[9] 2559[5] 3611[6] 3997[P] 4752[11]

Luneray (FR) *P F Nicholls* 86h 122 c
7 b m Poplar Bluff—Casandre (FR) (Montorselli)
(360) 634[2] 946[4]1398[5] 1670[3] 1874[3](2143) 2938[5]

Lupin (FR) *A W Carroll* 114 h
7 b g Luchiroverte(IRE) —Amarante II (FR) (Brezzo (FR))
136[7] 488[2] 633[2] 947[6] 4736[11]5049[P]

Lurid Affair (IRE) *Mrs S Gardner* 64h
5 b m Dr Massini(IRE) —Miss Good Night (Buckskin (FR))
3322[8] 4836[14] 5106[P]

Luristan (IRE) *S T Lewis* 66h
6 b g Pennekamp(USA) —Linnga (IRE) (Shardari)
133[15] 396[3] 635[6] 743[7] 760[13]978[10] 1156[P]

Lusaka De Pembo (FR) *N A Twiston-Davies* 71h 105+c
7 b g Funny Baby(FR) —Crackeline (FR) (Prince Melchior (FR))
3018[12] 3495[8] 3973[7]4239[4] 4605[8]

Luscat (IRE) *A Crook* 18b
6 b g Luso—Shuil Shell (IRE) (Cataldi)
2340[15]

Luscious (IRE) *K C Bailey* 49h
6 b m Luso—Gaye Chatelaine (IRE) (Castle Keep)
2515[15] 2704[10] 2860[P] 3646[13]

Lustral Du Seuil (FR) *N J Henderson* 123 h 137 c
7 b g Sassanian(USA) —Bella Tennise (FR) (Rhapsodien)
2044^2 2482^4 (3017)

Lutea (IRE) *M C Pipe* 93h 86c
6 ch g Beneficial—Francie's Treble (Quayside)
418^4 (668) 801^4 **1273^6**

Luthello (FR) *J Howard Johnson* 94h
7 b g Marchand De Sable(USA) —Haudello (FR) (Marignan (USA))
3927^P 4527^5 14^{10} (Dead)

Lutin Collonges (FR) *M J Roberts* 57c
7 b g Ragmar(FR) —Ariane Collonges (FR) (Quart De Vin (FR))
5049^P

Lutin Des Bordes (FR) *J Vana Jr*
7 ch g Epervier Bleu—Gamine Royale (FR) (Garde Royale)
471a^2

Lutin Du Moulin (FR) *L Lungo* 103 h 105 c
7 br g Saint Preuil(FR) —Emeraude Du Moulin (FR) (Djarvis (FR))
319^4 (414) (483) 1796^8 **2170^3 2589^{4}2877^P** 3339^6 **3444^{U}3915^P** 4344^3 4584^6

Luxi River (USA) *Michael McElhone* 97h
6 b g Diesis—Mariella (USA) (Roberto (USA))
320^{10}

Luzcadou (FR) *Ferdy Murphy* 134+c
13 b g Cadoudal(FR) —Luzenia (FR) (Armos)
87a^F 362a^6 1710a^{R}2164^6

Lycaon De Vauzelle (FR) *J Bertran De Balanda* 127h
7 ch g Video Rock(FR) —Athena De L'Isle (FR) (Quart De Vin (FR))
(779a) 4717a^4 5154a^3

Lyes Green *O Sherwood* 121+h
5 gr g Bien Bien(USA) —Dissolve (Sharrood (USA))
1596^8 1859^2 (2081) 2530^8 3277^P (4589) 4974^3

Lyical Assassin (IRE) *Paul A Roche* 70b
6 ch g Anshan—Tot Em Up (Strong Gale)
70a^{15}

Lyon *O Sherwood* 91+h
6 ch g Pivotal—French Gift (Cadeaux Genereux)
216^5 3848^{13} 4386^P

Lyrical Girl (USA) *H J Manners* 61h
5 b m Orpen(USA) —Lyric Theatre (USA) (Seeking The Gold (USA))
4828^5 5023^7 1^P

Lyrical Lily *B J Llewellyn* 54h
8 b m Alflora(IRE) —Music Interpreter (Kampala)
1246^7 3131^5 3424^5

Lyricist's Dream *R L Brown* 71+h
7 b m Dreams End—Lyricist (Averof)
134^2 314^2 729^6

Lysander (GER) *M F Harris* 103 h
7 br g Monsun(GER) —Leoparda (GER) (Lagunas)
2803^4 3374^2 3597^F 3848^{12} 4329^{2}4420^3 4819^4 4849^4 (5110)

Lyster (IRE) *D L Williams* 93h
7 b g Oscar(IRE) —Sea Skin (Buckskin (FR))
4015^P 4212^8 4603^6 4935^8 5110^9

Ly's West *C L Tizzard* 48h
6 ch g The West(USA) —Lysithea (Imperial Fling (USA))
172^P 294^P 515^5 668^{10}

Lytham (IRE) *J J Quinn* 70h
5 b g Spectrum(IRE) —Nousaiyra (IRE) (Be My Guest (USA))
596^7 1757^4

Maarees *G P Enright* 67h
5 b m Groom Dancer(USA) —Shemaleyah (Lomond (USA))
235^2 1596^P 5084^5

Mabella (IRE) *B Llewellyn* 32h
4 b f Brave Act—Wee Merkin (IRE) (Thatching)
945^P 1023^6 1095^P

Ma Burls *K F Clutterbuck* 81b
6 b m Perpendicular—Isabeau (Law Society (USA))
375^{13} 3820^5 5089^3

Macaroni Gold (IRE) *D J Daly* 29h
6 b g Rock Hopper—Strike It Rich (FR) (Rheingold)
3883^9

Macchiato *R E Barr* 93h
5 br m Inchinor—Tereyna (Terimon)
569^6 780^4 1607^P 2191^{11} 2639^{P}2962^{11} 4917^3 103^4

Mac Dargin (IRE) *N A Twiston-Davies* 89 h 85+c
7 b g Religiously(USA) —Dargin's Hill (IRE) (Le Bavard (FR))
1833^4 2144^2 2638^4 2994^{10} **3276^{3}3652^4 3938^4** 4453^{10}

Mac Federal (IRE) *M G Quinlan* 100h
4 b g In The Wings—Tocade (IRE) (Kenmare (FR))
3645^5 3898^F 4211^F 4910^2 3^4

Macgeorge (IRE) *R Lee* 135c
16 b g Mandalus—Colleen Donn (Le Moss)
76^2

Macgyver (NZ) *D L Williams* 81h 103 c
10 b g Jahafil—Corazon (NZ) (Pag-Asa (AUS))
395^8 674^4 846a^{10}**999^7** 1156^{12} **1219^U**1645^{13} **1795^6 2257^7**

Mac Hine (IRE) *Jonjo O'Neill* 106h 118 c
9 b g Eurobus—Zoe Baird (Aragon)
111^6 1125^2

Machrihanish *Miss S Brine* 86h 82c
6 b g Groom Dancer(USA) —Goodwood Lass (IRE) (Alzao (USA))
404^2

Mackenzie (IRE) *Mrs C J Kerr* 82h
10 b g Mandalus—Crinkle Lady (Buckskin (FR))
303^P 406^{13}

Maclean *G L Moore* 105 h
5 b g Machiavellian(USA) —Celtic Cross (Selkirk (USA))
(563) 726^2 1598^P 1823^7 2099^{12} 2533^{7}3467^6 3719^2 3944^7 4429^P 4912^8

Macmar (FR) *R H Alner* 114h 114 c
6 b g Ragmar(FR) —Ex Des Sacart (FR) (Balsamo (FR))
1986^2 2312^4 2870^{2}3440^5 4371^3 4676^5(5026)

Macnance (IRE) *R Lee* 110h 111+c
10 b m Mandalus—Colleen Donn (Le Moss)
97^F

Macreater *K A Morgan* 71+h
8 b m Mazaad—Gold Caste (USA) (Singh (USA))
134^4 (399) 649^8 1028^P 2256^3 2843^{13}4475^P 5050^5

Mac Robin's Lass (IRE) *Gerard Keane* 86h
6 ch m Lycius(USA) —Daddy's Duchess (IRE) (Tender King)
3005a^{13}

Mac's Elan *A B Coogan* 97h 86c
6 b g Darshaan—Elabella (Ela-Mana-Mou)
1991^{13} 2099^7 2191^7 2563^5 **2959^5**

Macs Flamingo (IRE) *P A Fahy* 121h 128c
6 br g Rashar(USA) —Parkality (IRE) (Good Thyne (USA))
116a^{10} **4022a^4 5080a^F**

Macs Form (IRE) *Thomas Foley* 33b
5 br m Anshan—Fine Performance (Gala Performance)
5134a^{20}

Macs Gildoran *W P Mullins* 117h 132c
12 b g Gildoran—Shamrock Bridge (Golden Love)
43a^5

Macs Joy (IRE) *Mrs John Harrington* 172 h
7 b g Religiously(USA) —Snob's Supreme (IRE) (Supreme Leader)
114a^3 2397a^5 3109a^4 3641a^2 (4000a) 4432^2(5130a)

Macs Mandalus *W P Mullins* 102b
6 b g Presenting—My Gonny (IRE) (Mandalus)
44a^5

Macs Valley (IRE) *Miss A M Winters* 134h
9 b g Hubbly Bubbly(USA) —Black Valley (IRE) (Good Thyne (USA))
2777a^5 3894a^{10}

Mac Three (IRE) *Noel Meade* 126h 129+c
7 b g Lord Americo—Le Nuit (Le Bavard (FR))
5103a^3

Macy (IRE) *Martin Jones*
13 ch g Sharp Charter—Lumax (Maximilian)
51^P 350^P

Madam Caversfield *J L Flint* 87h
4 b f Pursuit Of Love—Madam Alison (Puissance)
1802^2 1873^F 2178^{10} 2811^3 2995^{P}4733^2 4855^8

Madame Bavarde *Mrs S S Harbour*
9 b m Henbit(USA) —La Princesse (Le Bavard (FR))
5053^P

Madam Fleet (IRE) *M J Coombe* 74h
7 ch m Carroll House—Bucktan (Buckskin (FR))
2021^6 4286^5 4689^2

Madam Killeshandra *A Parker* 64b
6 b m Jurado(USA) —Killeshandra Lass (IRE) (King's Ride)
3563^6 4533^8 5063^P

Madam's Man *N A Twiston-Davies* 106h 112c
10 b g Sir Harry Lewis(USA) —Madam-M (Tina's Pet)
240^P 857^U

Maddox (POL) *Mrs P Townsley*
4 b g Upper Heights(GER) —Muddy's Girl (SWE) (Muddy Blues)
4149^P 4910^P

Maddy The Hatter *Miss T Jackson* 28b
7 ch m Alfie Dickins—Radar Blue (Ardar)
4841^2

Made In Bruere (FR) *Ferdy Murphy* 53b
6 b g Villez(USA) —Altesse Bruere (FR) (Kashneb (FR))
1882^{13} 2099^P **4655^P**

Made In France (FR) *M C Pipe* 87 h
6 b g Luchiroverte(IRE) —Birgonde (FR) (Quart De Vin (FR))
452^P 2626^P 3804^{12}4056^2 4418^P 4591^3 4828^P

Made In Japan (JPN) *P J Hobbs* 140 h 151c
6 b g Barathea(IRE) —Darrery (Darshaan)
2163^3 2489^2 2757^{5}3180^3 4241^{10} 4433^{13}

Made In Montot (FR) *P F Nicholls* 94h 110c
6 b g Video Rock(FR) —Deep Turple (FR) (Royal Charter (FR))
2593^P (4833)

Mademoiselle *R Curtis* 49h
4 b f Efisio—Shall We Dance (Rambo Dancer (CAN))
4855^{10}

Madge *W Storey* 89h
4 br f Marju(IRE) —Aymara (Darshaan)
1338^7 1601^{10} 1797^5 2001^2 2477^{2}2676^5 4789^3

Madhahir (IRE) *M J Gingell* 46h
6 b g Barathea(IRE) —Gharam (USA) (Green Dancer (USA))
111^1 182^5 352^P 745^P **981^U**1066^7 1333^7 **1560^P**

Madison Avenue (GER) *T M Jones* 92h
9 b g Mondrian(GER) —Madly Noble (GER) (Irish River (FR))
102^4 502^2 670^3

Madison De Vonnas (FR) *Miss E C Lavelle* 106+h 107+c
6 bb g Epervier Bleu—Carine De Neuvy (FR) (Shelley (FR))
(1774) 2103^5 **3370^3 4281^{6}4620^3**

Madison Du Berlais (FR) *M C Pipe* 141+c
5 b g Indian River(FR) —Anais Du Berlais (FR) (Dom Pasquini (FR))
2874^U 3387^3 (3788) (4037) (4213) 4472^{3}5006^3

Mad Louie *Miss Z C Davison*
6 b g Perpendicular—Miss Bordeaux (IRE) (Try My Best (USA))
235^9

Mad Max Too *N Wilson* 78h
7 gr g Environment Friend—Marnworth (Funny Man)
1888^P 2923^{10} 3253^6 3393^{8}4302^6 8^F

Madmoiselle Etoile (IRE) *John Joseph Murphy* 75b
4 br f Bob Back(USA) —Royal Thimble (IRE) (Prince Rupert (FR))
5134a^{15}

Mae Moss *W S Coltherd* 76+h
5 b m Cayman Kai(IRE) —Miss Brook (Meadowbrook)
720^3 876^4 2903^9 3167^{10} 3381^{P}3782^4 4145^3 4341^4 4487^P

Maenflora *B J Llewellyn*
4 b f Alflora(IRE) —Liddy's Choice (IRE) (Buckskin (FR))
2611^{12} 2935^{12} 3246^P

Magdelaine *A M Hales* 45h
4 b f Sinndar(IRE) —Crystal Drop (Cadeaux Genereux)
945^8

Mage D'Estruval (FR) *H D Daly* 119c
6 b g Sheyrann—Ivresse D'Estruval (FR) (Synefos (USA))
4073^2 4460^P 4799^P

Magenta Rising (IRE) *W M Brisbourne* 75h
6 ch m College Chapel—Fashion Queen (Chilibang)
743^6

Maggie Mathias (IRE) *B G Powell* 88+b
5 b m Portrait Gallery(IRE) —The Marching Lady (IRE) (Archway (IRE))
4902^2

Maggies Brother *R Shail* 98c
13 b g Brotherly(USA) —Sallisses (Pamroy)
49^P 282^3 (403) 4079^6

Magical Fun (IRE) *Mrs J A Hayes* 46c
13 b g Magical Strike(USA) —Roundstone Lass (Montekin)
47^P

Magical Harry *P F Nicholls* 98+b
6 b g Sir Harry Lewis(USA) —Magic (Sweet Revenge)
2941^2 3462^5

Magical Legend *L Corcoran* 109+h
5 gr m Midnight Legend—Alice's Mirror (Magic Mirror)
1459^2 (1600) (1745) 3247^2 4429^3 4641^4

Magical Liaison (IRE) *W Jenks* 90 h
8 b g Mujtahid(USA) —Instant Affair (USA) (Lyphard (USA))
109^6 488^3 768^P 2659^{10} 2940^{16}3250^F 3577^U

Magic Amigo *J R Jenkins* 103h
5 ch g Zilzal(USA) —Emaline (FR) (Empery (USA))
485^5 2804^7 3415^2 4389^4

Magic Bengie *F Kirby* 70 h 66c
7 b g Magic Ring(IRE) —Zinzi (Song)
3334^8 3916^{10} 4299^9 **4840^8**

Magic Box *A M Crow* 82+h 96+c
8 b g Magic Ring(IRE) —Princess Poquito (Hard Fought)
2902^P 5121^5

Magic Brook *R Allan* 54b
7 b g Meadowbrook—Kittybird (Current Magic)
876^8 992^P

Magicien (FR) *Steve Isaac* 78c
10 b g Muroto—French Look (FR) (Green River (FR))
3805^4 4051^7

Magic Merlin *C P Morlock* 84+h
5 b g Magic Ring(IRE) —St James's Antigua (IRE) (Law Society (USA))
5024^2

Magico (NZ) *Miss Venetia Williams* 105h 124 c
8 b g Casual Lies(USA) —Majica (NZ) (Star Way)
192^2 247^{11} 465^2 603^2 **1620^5**1836^3 **1928^3 2248^5(2705) (3282) 3507^8(3940) 4239^5 4755^2**

Magic Of Sydney (IRE) *R Rowe* 126c
10 b g Broken Hearted—Chat Her Up (Proverb)
132^P 1920^5 (2808) 3343^4 4906^3

Magic Red *J Ryan* 84h
6 ch g Magic Ring(IRE) —Jacquelina (USA) (Private Account (USA))
1564^8 **2555^{11}** 2958^9 3433^P

Magic Sky (FR) *P F Nicholls* 106h 136+c
6 b g Simon Du Desert(FR) —Kailasa (FR) (Rb Chesne)
840^U 1013^U 1204^4**1265^7 (1542) 1739^6**

Magic Verse *I W McInnes*
5 ch m Opening Verse(USA) —Festival Sister (Belmez (USA))
1213^P

Magic Warrior *J C Fox* 62h
6 b g Magic Ring(IRE) —Clarista (USA) (Riva Ridge (USA))
758^7 863^{11}

Magnate (IRE) *Mrs S M Johnson* 29b
4 b g Entrepreneur—Hilbys Brite Flite (USA) (Cormorant (USA))
1785^{11} 2286^P 2454^F

Magnemite (IRE) *Miss Julie Pocock* 85c
10 b g Dromod Hill—Rostoonstown Lass (IRE) (Decent Fellow)
5116^5

Magnesium (USA) *B G Powell* 103h 54c
6 ch g Kris S(USA) —Proflare (USA) (Mr Prospector (USA))
2584^2 2860^2 3386^3 3880^{10} **4239^P**

Magnetic Pole *B I Case* 82h
5 b g Machiavellian(USA) —Clear Attraction (USA) (Lear Fan (USA))
1753^8

Magnificent Seven (IRE) *J Howard Johnson* 83h 104+c
7 ch g Un Desperado(FR) —Seven Hills (FR) (Reform)
174^5 2266^P (2588) 2946^P (3268)

Magnifico (FR) *M C Pipe* 125h
5 b g Solid Illusion(USA) —Born For Run (FR) (Pharly (FR))
(2559) (3219) 3727^8 3970^{17} 4461^{23}

Magnus Veritas (IRE) *Miss Gina Weare* 93c
8 br g Jolly Jake(NZ) —Goldens Monkey (Monksfield)
4421^3

Magot De Grugy (FR) *R H Alner* 119+h
6 b g Tzar Rodney(FR) —Hirlish (FR) (Passing Sale (FR))
(1921) (2310) (2706) 2850^2 3135^7 3986^9

Mags Benefit (IRE) *T Hogan* 119h
6 b m Beneficial—Moynetto (Bustineto)
66a^2 1093a^{14}

Mags Two *I McMath* 82+h
9 b g Jumbo Hirt(USA) —Welsh Diamond (High Top)
1310^4 (1564) 1723^3 5064^{13}

Maharaat (USA) *P J Hobbs* 94+h
5 b g Bahri(USA) —Siyadah (USA) (Mr Prospector (USA))
100^5 747^{10} (1018)

Mahogany Blaze (FR) *N A Twiston-Davies* 133h
4 b g Kahyasi—Mahogany River (Irish River (FR))
1785^6 2014^2 2442^3 3132^4 (4033) 4211^{3}4468^7 4765^U 4956^7

Maidstone Monument (IRE) *Mrs A M Thorpe* 96 h 104+c
11 b g Jurado(USA) —Loreto Lady (Brave Invader (USA))
416^2 (503) (805) 960^{3}1065^3 1189^5

Maid The Cut *A D Smith*
5 ch m Silver Wizard(USA) —Third Dam (Slip Anchor)
396^P

Maille Blu (FR) *T M Walsh* 95h
6 b g Epervier Bleu—Bric Mamaille (FR) (Bricassar (USA))
2536a^6

Maitre Levy (GER) *D A Nolan* 89+h
8 b g Monsun(GER) —Meerdunung (EG) (Tauchsport (EG))
937^P

Majed (FR) *Mrs L B Normile* 118c
10 b g Fijar Tango(FR) —Full Of Passion (USA) (Blushing Groom (FR))
150^P 1844^P 2038^{13} **2640^P**

Majestic (IRE) *Ian Williams* 128h 121+c
11 b g Belmez(USA) —Noble Lily (USA) (Vaguely Noble)
1234^3 **1744^6**

Majestic Bay (IRE) *J A B Old* 101 h 101c
10 b g Unfuwain(USA) —That'll Be The Day (IRE) (Thatching)
397^P

Majestic Class (USA) *M W Easterby* 69h
6 b g Majestic Twoeleven(USA) —Miss Count Fleet (USA) (Mr Cockatoo (USA))
331^P

Majestic Moonbeam (IRE) *Jonjo O'Neill* 86h 107 c
8 b g Supreme Leader—Magic Moonbeam (IRE) (Decent Fellow)
2557^2 2800^P 3434^{P}3940^6 4577^9

Major Belle (FR) *John R Upson* 87+c
7 ch m Cyborg(FR) —Mistine Major (FR) (Major Petingo (FR))
134^{17} 180^{10} **2960^F 3370^{7}3663^8 4014^P 4499^{2}4659^2 4873^P**

Major Benefit (IRE) *Mrs K Waldron* 125c
9 b g Executive Perk—Merendas Sister (Pauper)
2077^5 2502^P (2863) 3144^2 3614^P 3845^{P}5012^P

Major Bit *S A Brookshaw* 79h 68c
10 b g Henbit(USA) —Cute Pam (Pamroy)
6^P 398^P 464^P

Major Blade (GER) *Mrs H Dalton* 82h
8 b g Dashing Blade—Misniniski (Niniski (USA))
3848^{16} 4243^P

Majorca *J Howard Johnson* 104+h
5 b g Green Desert(USA) —Majmu (USA) (Al Nasr (FR))
1527^6 2081^{11} 2923^8 3944^4 (4922)

Major Catch (IRE) *C T Pogson* 110+h
7 b g Safety Catch(USA) —Inch Tape (Prince Hansel)
2663^{10} 2859^4 2979^6 3277^4 3545^2(3780) 3984^2 4393^4

Major Euro (IRE) *S J Gilmore* 114+h 120c
9 b g Lord Americo—Gold Bank (Over The River (FR))
217^4 (1978) 2664^{3}2814^F

Major Hayward (IRE) *E J O'Grady* 100h
5 br g Anshan—Miss Eurolink (Touching Wood (USA))
44a^8

Major Jon (IRE) *W J Burke* 104h 83c
6 br g Shardari—Slyguff Lord (IRE) (Lord Americo)
1902^4

Major League (USA) *K Bishop*
4 b g Magic Cat(USA) —Quick Grey (USA) (El Prado (IRE))
4327^P

Major Miller *N J Henderson* 105+h
5 b g Opera Ghost—Millers Action (Fearless Action (USA))
(2242) 2983^2 3906^4

Major Oak (IRE) *G M Moore* 94h
5 b g Deploy—Mahaasin (Bellypha)
2340^6 2823^3 3677^5 4793^5 4988^2

Major Reno (IRE) *R C Harper* 81h 58c
9 b g Little Bighorn—Make Me An Island (Creative Plan (USA))
395^9 565^F 674^{11}972^5

Major Royal (FR) *A Parker* 70h
6 ch g Garde Royale—Majorica Queen (FR) (Kaldoun (FR))
2042^6 2843^9

Major Shark (FR) *Jennie Candlish* 104+h
8 b g Saint Preuil(FR) —Cindy Cad (FR) (Cadoudal (FR))
92a^P 675^4

Major Sharpe (IRE) *B J M Ryall* 102h 105+c
14 b g Phardante(FR) —Winsome Doe (Buckskin (FR))
1022^U 1247^6

Major Speculation (IRE) *J M Bradley* 30h
6 b g Spectrum(IRE) —Pacific Grove (Persian Bold)
3719^P 3804^{15}

Major Vernon (IRE) *W P Mullins* 128h 124 c
7 b g Flemensfirth(USA) —Rainys Run (Deep Run)
116a^6 **3409a^5 3893a^9**

Makandy *R J Armson* 77h
7 b g Makbul—Derring Floss (Derring Rose)
173^4 743^5 2523^5 2702^2 3330^{2}3731^5 4013^P

Makeabreak (IRE) *C J Mann* 99h
7 ch m Anshan—Nilousha (Darshaan)
1974[5] 3322[2] 3461[3] 3902[4] 4129[5]4652[8]

Make A Mark (IRE) *Mrs R L Elliot* 79b
6 b g Victory Note(USA) —Election Special (Chief Singer)
5124[7]

Make Haste Slowly *H D Daly* 101h 119 c
9 b g Terimon—Henry's True Love (Random Shot)
311[U]

Make It A Double (IRE) *Noel T Chance* 102+h
8 ch g Zaffaran(USA) —La Danse (Le Moss)
(94)

Make It Easy (IRE) *D L Williams* 61h 68 c
10 bb g Alphabatim(USA) —Mammy's Friend (Miner's Lamp)
(181) 398[7] 1015[6]1110[4] 1191[4] 1262[4]1646[4] 1832[3] 1951[4]

Make My Hay *J Gallagher* 98h
7 b g Bluegrass Prince(IRE) —Shashi (IRE) (Shaadi (USA))
3152[2] (3371) 3687[F] 3990[5] 4879[2]

Makin A Fuss *R M Whitaker* 65b
4 gr g J B Quick—Shadi Lady (IRE) (Shardari)
4853[17]

Makin Air *J Howard Johnson*
5 ch g J B Quick—Shadi Lady (IRE) (Shardari)
2444[19] 2749[P]

Malaga Boy (IRE) *C L Tizzard* 106 h 92+c
9 b g Nordic Brave—Ardglass Mist (Black Minstrel)
(53) 201[2] 549[2] 2849[11] 3215[U]3694[3] 3993[7] 4322[P] 4522[U]4692[3]

Malay *Mrs Norma Pook* 120+h
9 b m Karinga Bay—Malaia (IRE) (Commanche Run)
(4797)

Maldoun (IRE) *Mrs Barbara Waring* 104+h
7 b g Kaldoun(FR) —Marzipan (IRE) (Green Desert (USA))
4858[13]

Malek (IRE) *K G Reveley* 118 h 122c
10 b g Tremblant—Any Offers (Paddy's Stream)
2628[3] 2992[P] 3258[4]4111[U]

Maletton (FR) *Miss Venetia Williams* 110h
6 b g Bulington(FR) —Reine Dougla (FR) (Faunus (FR))
2629[7] 3135[9] 3384[3] 3901[6]

Malibu (IRE) *S Dow*
5 b g Second Empire(IRE) —Tootle (Main Reef)
2212[P] 3948[8]

Maljimar (IRE) *Miss H C Knight* 93+h
6 b g Un Desperado(FR) —Marble Miller (IRE) (Mister Lord (USA))
178[P] (4521) 4830[4]

Malko De Beaumont (FR) *K C Bailey* 83h 110 c
6 bb g Gold And Steel(FR) —Givry (FR) (Bayolidaan (FR))
1892[4] 2663[8] 3241[F] 3430[2](3732) 4499[4]

Malt De Vergy (FR) *L Lungo* 98+h
6 br g Sleeping Car(FR) —Intense (FR) (Roi De Rome (USA))
(424) 2211[9] 2942[4] 3374[8]

Malthouse Master (IRE) *Oliver Finnegan* 93h
6 b h Sadler's Wells(USA) —Miss Arizona (IRE) (Sure Blade (USA))
3005a[8]

Malton *M W Easterby* 92b
6 b g Bal Harbour—Elissa (Tap On Wood)
655[3]

Malt Sunflower (IRE) *C J Mann* 100b
5 ch g Germany(USA) —Sunset Malt (IRE) (Red Sunset)
1777[2]

Mambo (IRE) *N J Henderson* 52h
6 b g Ashkalani(IRE) —Bold Tango (FR) (In Fijar (USA))
2969[P] 3880[11] 4058[P]

Mambo Des Mottes (FR) *Miss Venetia Williams* 126+c
6 b g Useful(FR) —Julie Des Mottes (FR) (Puma Des Mottes (FR))
71a[F]

Mamideos (IRE) *T R George* 110+c
9 br g Good Thyne(USA) —Heavenly Artist (IRE) (Heavenly Manna)
2162[P] 4240[6]

Mamore Gap (IRE) *M E Sowersby* 89h
8 b g General Monash(USA) —Ravensdale Rose (IRE) (Henbit (USA))
9[7] 895[P]

Mamouna Gale (IRE) *E J O'Grady* 101h 122c
8 b m Fairydel(IRE) —Stealth (Strong Gale)
1622a[3] 2364a[3]

Mam Ratagan *N J Henderson* 95+b
5 b g Mtoto—Nika Nesgoda (Suave Dancer (USA))
(3583) 4779[20]

Man About Town (IRE) *T J Taaffe* 130h 116c
7 b g Bob Back(USA) —Pollys Glow (IRE) (Glow (USA))
40a[7] (Dead)

Manawanui *R H Alner* 100+h 112 c
8 b g Karinga Bay—Kiwi Velocity (NZ) (Veloso (NZ))
1953[2] 3239[P] 3508[P]4429[2] 4756[8] (4912) 5028[5]

Manbow (IRE) *M D Hammond* 25h 118c
8 b g Mandalus—Treble Base (IRE) (Orchestra)
1798[2] 2445[2] 2993[P]4617[P] 11[2]

Mandhoor (IRE) *J Wade* 75h
6 b g Flying Spur(AUS) —Moy Water (IRE) (Tirol)
1112[9]

Mandica (IRE) *T R George* 95h 110 c
8 br g Mandalus—Mawtvica (Monksfield)
(132) 1761[P] 1983[4]2613[4] 3212[6] 3997[7]4396[3] 4735[5] 4872[5]

Mandingo Chief (IRE) *R T Phillips* 104h 103+c
7 b g Flying Spur(AUS) —Elizabethan Air (Elegant Air)
2011[3] 2623[P] 3499[3]4806[3] 5049[2]

Mandm (IRE) *P C O'Connor* 118h 91c
8 br g Air Display(USA) —Hello October (Callernish)
3261a[5]

Maneki Neko (IRE) *E W Tuer* 92 h
4 b g Rudimentary(USA) —Ardbess (Balla Cove)
2921[12] 3374[3] 3786[2] 3925[2] 4631[3]

Man From Highworth *H J Manners* 120 h 94c
7 b g Ballet Royal(USA) —Cavisoir (Afzal)
3801[7] 4424[3] 2[7]

Mange Tout (IRE) *K J Burke* 75b
7 br g Presenting—Nish Bar (Callernish)
2864[5] 2961[11] 3417[4] 3962[6]

Mango Catcher (IRE) *Paul Nolan* 103h 81c
6 b g Personal Flag(USA) —Sun Shines East (USA) (Eastern Echo (USA))
2478[6]

Manjoe (IRE) *David Wachman* 123h 127c
8 b g Mandalus—Henris Blaze (IRE) (Be My Native (USA))
4929a[P]

Manners (IRE) *Jonjo O'Neill* 106+h
8 b g Topanoora—Maneree (Mandalus)
3878[4] (4088) (4784)

Man Of Mine *Mrs H Dalton* 58h
5 gr g Classic Cliche(IRE) —Dawn Spinner (Arctic Lord)
3216[4] 4072[10] 4642[4]

Man Of Repute *S J Mahon* 95h
5 b g Polish Precedent(USA) —Renowned (IRE) (Darshaan)
93a[9]

Manolo (FR) *Mrs H Dalton* 97h 72c
6 b g Ragmar(FR) —Coriola (FR) (Brezzo (FR))
513[4] 762[10] 1805[5] 1987[12]4427[2] 4738[7]

Manoram (GER) *Ian Williams* 89 h 111+c
7 ch g Zinaad—Mayada (USA) (The Minstrel (CAN))
(246) 573[6] 946[6] 1236[7]1542[P] 2323[3] 5074[3]

Manor Down (IRE) *Dolly Maude* 36b
8 b g Moscow Society(USA) —Scalp Hunter (IRE) (Commanche Run)
50[P] 4718a[U]

Manorson (IRE) *O Sherwood* 139+h
7 ch g Desert King(IRE) —Familiar (USA) (Diesis)
2047[5] (2493) 2871[4] 4446[10] 5078a[2]

Manor Star *B D Leavy* 66h
7 b m Weld—Call Coup (IRE) (Callernish)
10[P]

Manoubi *M Todhunter* 109 h 85+c
7 b g Doyoun—Manuetti (IRE) (Sadler's Wells (USA))
855[8] 990[4] 1099[3]1296[6] 1361[5] 1606[9]

Man Overboard *T P Tate* 87b
4 b g Overbury(IRE) —Dublin Ferry (Celtic Cone)
4615[4]

Manque Neuf *Mrs L Richards* 82+h
7 b g Cadeaux Genereux—Flying Squaw (Be My Chief (USA))
105[4] 501[5] 1949[3] (2378) 2578[3]

Manque Pas D'Air (FR) *T R George* 87h
6 br m Kadalko(FR) —Chantalouette (FR) (Royal Charter (FR))
2142[8] 2486[9] 3648[9] 3938[F]4288[P]

Man Ray (USA) *Jonjo O'Neill* 108+h
5 ch g Theatrical—Irtifa (Lahib (USA))
1680[13] 1772[7] 2314[2] 2632[2]

Mansion Special (FR) *A King* 78h
6 b g Mansonnien(FR) —Edition Speciale (FR) (Useful (FR))
203[P]

Mansony (FR) *A L T Moore* 140h 149+c
7 b g Mansonnien(FR) —Hairly (FR) (Air De Cour (USA))
(43a) 2668a[3] 3006a[F] 3639a[6](4018a) 4749[9]

Mantilla *Ian Williams* 119h 83+c
9 b m Son Pardo—Well Tried (IRE) (Thatching)
436[P] 948[3] 1044[P]1218[8] 1754[3]

Mantles Prince *A G Juckes* 89h
12 ch g Emarati(USA) —Miami Mouse (Miami Springs)
96[2] (508) 675[3] 2008[6]

Mantras (FR) *M C Pipe* 105h
7 b g Solido(FR) —Mantra (FR) (Ti King (FR))
451[3] 762[13] 980[7] 1121[P] 1153[2]1187[5] 1384[3]

Manx Royal (FR) *M C Pipe* 135h 112+c
7 b g Cyborg(FR) —Badj II (FR) (Tadj (FR))
2207[4] 3289[13] 3760[2] 4417[5]4943[F]

Maori Legend *D P Keane* 70b
5 b m Midnight Legend—Hinemoa (IRE) (Mandalus)
4574[8]

Mapilut Du Moulin (FR) *C R Dore* 64h
6 b g Lute Antique(FR) —Api (FR) (El Badr)
375[11] 691[P] 742[4] 843[10] 1000[F]1107[9] 1333[8] 1362[8]

Mapuche (IRE) *A M Balding* 91b
6 b g Selkirk(USA) —Spurned (USA) (Robellino (USA))
490[5]

Maradamo (FR) *R Le Gal*
6 b m Alamo Bay(USA) —Maradadi (USA) (Shadeed (USA))
846a[6]

Maradan (IRE) *Mrs J C McGregor* 68h
10 b g Shernazar—Marmana (USA) (Blushing Groom (FR))
3206[6] 3918[P] 4723[14]

Maralan (IRE) *Patrick O Brady* 110h
5 b g Priolo(USA) —Marilaya (IRE) (Shernazar)
3005a[5]

Marathea (FR) *Miss Venetia Williams* 82+h
5 b m Marathon(USA) —Shahmy (USA) (Lear Fan (USA))
185[2] 399[2] 649[2] (1075) (1152) 1443[3] 1753[P]

Marbeuf (USA) *Noel Meade* 116+h
5 b g Bahri(USA) —Salon Prive (USA) (Private Account (USA))
3086a[5]

Marcel (FR) *M C Pipe* 145 h 131 c
6 b g Bateau Rouge—Une Risette (FR) (Air Du Nord (USA))
2055[9] 3215[3] 3501[3]3647[2] 4241[6] 4472[13]

Marchand De Reve (FR) *P Briard*
10 b g Quai Voltaire(USA) —Flute D'Or (FR) (Noir Et Or)
1073a[7]

Marchensis (IRE) *O Sherwood* 80h
8 ch g Great Marquess—Trelissick (Electric)
3210[P] 3664[9] 4005[3] 4277[P] 5009[5]

Marco Bonheur (FR) *D Lenfant*
12 b g Nimrod(USA) —Menara (FR) (Huntercombe)
1373a[DSQ]

Marcus *Miss E C Lavelle* 64b
5 gr g Silver Patriarch(IRE) —Loving Around (IRE) (Furry Glen)
4574[10]

Marcus Du Berlais (FR) *A L T Moore* 131h 125c
9 gr g Saint Preuil(FR) —Rosacotte (FR) (Rose Laurel)
2539a[11] 3053a[20] 3587a[P]4123a[3] 4496[P]

Mardereil (IRE) *N J Hawke* 37h
9 ch m Moscow Society(USA) —Slap Of The Stick (Weavers Hall)
1018[8]

Mardi Roberta (IRE) *B G Powell* 82+b
4 b f Bob Back(USA) —Native Shore (IRE) (Be My Native (USA))
4902[3]

Mardonicdeclare *S Lycett* 30h
5 b g Perpendicular—Daisy Girl (Main Reef)
4015[P] 5110[13]

Margarets Wish *T Wall* 80+h
6 gr m Cloudings(IRE) —Gentle Gain (Final Straw)
1[1] 613[4] (973) 1223[6] 1413[8] 1793[4]2726[6] 2940[10] 3650[P]

Marghub (IRE) *Miss C Dyson* 87+h
7 b g Darshaan—Arctique Royale (Royal And Regal (USA))
4327[6] 4493[10] 4819[10]

Marguerita (FR) *A J McNamara* 98h
5 gr m Sillery(USA) —Manchaca (FR) (Highest Honor (FR))
2031a[8]

Marhaba Million (IRE) *E McNamara* 123h
4 gr g Linamix(FR) —Modelliste (Machiavellian (USA))
(3401a) 3890a[5] 4435[9]

Maria Bonita (IRE) *C N Kellett* 69h
5 b m Octagonal(NZ) —Nightitude (Night Shift (USA))
1113[6] 1222[P] 1364[P] 1491[4] 2081[5]2463[2] 2806[3]

Mariah Rollins (IRE) *P A Fahy* 139 h 142 c
8 bb m Over The River(FR) —Clonloo Lady (IRE) (Nearly A Nose (USA))
89a[F] 1700a[3] 2177[8]2786a[3] 3051a[5] 3999a[4]4761[3] 5057a[5]

Mariday *L Wells* 90+h
5 br g Trifolio—Classic Hand (Some Hand)
563[3] 911[5] 1037[9] 1408[6] 1525[4]1774[3] 2015[6]

Marie Noune (FR) *T Civel*
6 b m Useful(FR) —Ptite Noune (Baptism)
1372a[6]

Marigolds Way *R J Hodges* 73b
4 b f Nomadic Way(USA) —Miss Marigold (Norwick (USA))
3468[3]

Marine Des Ongrais (FR) *P Chemin*
9 b m Sarhoob(USA) —Star Des Ongrais (FR) (Cyborg (FR))
1373a[4]

Marine Life *P R Webber* 100b
4 b g Unfuwain(USA) —Aquamarine (Shardari)
4455[2] 4779[16]

Marjina *Miss E C Lavelle* 115+h
7 b m Classic Cliche(IRE) —Cavina (Ardross)
(1906) 2240[4]

Marked Man (IRE) *R Lee* 113 h 133c
10 b g Grand Plaisir(IRE) —Teazle (Quayside)
454[4] 823[P] 1013[5]2102[2] (2664) 2814[2]3019[F]

Mark Equal *M C Pipe* 105+h 126 c
10 b g Nicholas Bill—Dissolution (Henbit (USA))
386[3] 489[4] 2210[3]2532[3] 2748[2] 2998[4]3992[P] 4677[P]

Marki (FR) *Jonjo O'Neill* 64h
6 b g Video Rock(FR) —Payse (FR) (Trenel)
1152[12]

Marlborough Sound *N G Richards* 109 h
7 b g Overbury(IRE) —Dark City (Sweet Monday)
(591) 1513[2] 1992[6]

Marlion (FR) *B R Johnson* 74b
4 gr g Linamix(FR) —Marzipan (IRE) (Green Desert (USA))
4623[6] 4909[10]

Marlowe (IRE) *R J Hodges* 77b
4 b c Sadler's Wells(USA) —Minnie Habit (Habitat)
2611[10] 3216[9] 4038[7]

Marmot D'Estruval (FR) *Mrs Tracey Barfoot-Saunt* 42h 42c
6 b g Epervier Bleu—Alrose (FR) (Kalyan (FR))
1178[P] 1262[P] 1410[8]

Marque Deposee (FR) *B G Powell* 35h
6 br m Cadoudal(FR) —Unextase (FR) (Quart De Vin (FR))
4423[11] 4550[7]

Marrasit (IRE) *H E Thorpe* 104 c
10 b m Zaffaran(USA) —Alligator Crawl (IRE) (Pollerton)
282[2] 440[2] 3736[2]4009[U] 4607[P]

Marrel *D Burchell* 115h 109c
8 b g Shareef Dancer(USA) —Upper Caen (High Top)
2334[P] 2621[10] 2813[10] 3177[7] 3458[13]3889[6] (3950) 4119[6] 4663[11] 4781[8] (4938) 5[5]

Marron Prince (FR) *R Rowe* 57h
6 ch g Cyborg(FR) —Colombine (USA) (Empery (USA))
2578[P]

Marshalls Run (IRE) *A King* 106h
6 b g Accordion—Lady's Bridge (USA) (Sir Ivor (USA))
2340[2] 3392[4] 3904[4] 4494[3] 4750[P]5015[6]

Marsh Orchid *C C Bealby* 38h
5 b g Lahib(USA) —Majalis (Mujadil (USA))
1415[7] 1654[12]

Marsh Run *M W Easterby* 110h 107c
7 b m Presenting—Madam Margeaux (IRE) (Ardross)
2004[2] 2264[3] 2590[5] 2964[3] 3548[8]4583[4]

Mars Rock (FR) *Miss Venetia Williams* 97+h
6 b g Video Rock(FR) —Venus De Mirande (FR) (Carmont (FR))
(1954) 2211[19] 3947[2] 4581[B] (4786) 4849[6]

Martha Reilly (IRE) *Mrs Barbara Waring* 84h
10 ch m Rainbows For Life(CAN) —Debach Delight (Great Nephew)
11[17]

Martha's Kinsman (IRE) *H D Daly* 110h 124c
7 b g Petoski—Martha's Daughter (Majestic Maharaj)
128[2] 2291[3] 3558[2](3801) 4827[3] 5094[2]

Martin House (IRE) *D W Thompson* 88h
7 b g Mujadil(USA) —Dolcezza (FR) (Lichine (USA))
192[10] 306[9] 544[3] 822[6] 1063[11]

Martin Ossie *J M Bradley* 60h 102 c
9 b g Bonny Scot(IRE) —So We Know (Daring March)
(281) 3372[P] 3732[6]4095[5] 4572[3] 4806[P]

Marton Jubilee *A D Brown* 33b
4 gr f Paris House—Peep O Day (Domynsky)
3259[13] 3353[12] 3931[10]

Marton Mere *Miss J E Foster* 29h
10 ch g Cadeaux Genereux—Hyatti (Habitat)
437[P] 1149[8]

Martovic (IRE) *K C Bailey* 103h
7 b m Old Vic—Martomick (Montelimar (USA))
27[2] 349[3] 1246[3] 1671[2] 1851[2]2166[P] 3884[5]

Maryannthedancer (IRE) *Ms M Flynn* 103h
6 ch m Un Desperado(FR) —Scorpio Girl (Scorpio (FR))
66a[9] (Dead)

Mary Casey *C A Mulhall* 80h
5 br m Accordion—Kosheen (IRE) (Supreme Leader)
3556[10] 4976[17]

Mary Chan *C W Fairhurst*
7 b m Savahra Sound—Lucky Relikon (Lucky Wednesday)
602[P]

Marylou Day (IRE) *O Brennan* 67b
7 bb m Lord Americo—Dark Phoenix (IRE) (Camden Town)
180[P]

Mary Macs Lad (IRE) *John G Carr* 87h 98c
7 b g Cois Na Tine(IRE) —Embustera (Sparkler)
334[2] 545[5] 595[3]

Mary's Baby *Mrs A M Thorpe* 66h
6 b m Magic Ring(IRE) —Everdene (Bustino)
1302[7]

Maryscross (IRE) *O Brennan* 95+h
6 b m Presenting—Willowmere (IRE) (King's Ride)
2961[4] 3373[4] 4017[3] 4644[4] 4875[3]8[3]

Marys Moment *P A Pritchard* 28b
6 ch m Southern Music—Arley Gale (Scallywag)
3583[10] 4398[12] 5070[8]

Masafi (IRE) *J Howard Johnson* 118+h
5 b g Desert King(IRE) —Mrs Fisher (IRE) (Salmon Leap (USA))
1740[2] (2903) (3488) 4430[18] 5091[3]

Masamix (FR) *J Vana Jr*
8 b g Housamix(FR) —Maskwaya (FR) (Synefos (USA))
590a[6]

Maskul (USA) *F Holcak*
12 b g Lear Fan(USA) —Hooriah (USA) (Northern Dancer)
(1710a)

Masrahi (IRE) *Noel Meade* 109h
5 ch h In The Wings—Onereuse (Sanglamore (USA))
2650a[14] 3411a[24]

Massif Centrale *D R C Elsworth*
5 ch g Selkirk(USA) —Madame Dubois (Legend Of France (USA))
3464[U]

Massini Expres (IRE) *Philip Fenton* 80h
6 b g Dr Massini(IRE) —Lantern Line (The Parson)
4010[11]

Massini's Maguire (IRE) *P J Hobbs* 131 h
5 b g Dr Massini(IRE) —Molly Maguire (IRE) (Supreme Leader)
1827[2] 2206[3] 2614[2]

Master Albert (IRE) *David Wachman* 119h
8 b g Supreme Leader—Mullaun (Deep Run)
1787a[2]

Master Billyboy (IRE) *Mrs S D Williams* 106h 103+c
8 b g Old Vic—Clonodfoy (Strong Gale)
1973[P] 2607[P] 3326[11]3879[5] 4288[F] 4572[2]4837[P] 5071[5]

Master Brew *J R Best* 39h 52c
8 b g Homo Sapien—Edithmead (IRE) (Shardari)
1631[7] 1832[P] 2419[14]

Master Bury *Miss T Jackson* 61b
5 gr g Overbury(IRE) —Kerry To Clare (Step Together (USA))
4072[16]

Master D'Or (FR) *P J Hobbs* 124+h 114+c
6 b g Cyborg(FR) —Une Pomme D'Or (FR) (Pot D'Or (FR))
54[2] (1953) 2313[6] 2929[U]

Master Eddy *S Lycett* 101b
6 b g Alflora(IRE) —Mistress Star (Soldier Rose)
3617[3] 4244[7] 4500[2] 4854[13]

Master Ellis (IRE) *R L Brown* 70h
7 b g Turtle Island(IRE) —Take No Chances (IRE) (Thatching)
982[10]

Master Farrier *Miss Lucinda V Russell* 73h
6 br g Milieu—Nikwill (IRE) (Le Bavard (FR))
1687[P] 1839[5] 2036[P]

Master Fox *T R George* 74h
8 bb g Puissance—Hill Vixen (Goldhill)
314[3] 654[12] 862[P]

Master Henry (GER) *Ian Williams* 110c
12 b g Mille Balles(FR) —Maribelle (GER) (Windwurf (GER))
999[P] 1273[3] 1659[7]1897[4]

Master Jackson *T D Walford* 93h 85+c
7 b g Jendali(USA) —Fardella (ITY) (Molvedo)
373[4] 464[6] 554[6]

Master Mahogany *R J Hodges* 106h
5 b g Bandmaster(USA) —Impropriety (Law Society (USA))
3133[3] 3510[6] 3650[11] 4243[P]

Master Marmalade *D Morris* 89b
5 ch g Trempolino(USA) —Miss Picol (Exit To Nowhere (USA))
(241) 769[5]

Master Massini (IRE) *P Hughes* 95h 58c
6 b g Dr Massini(IRE) —Aunt Rose (IRE) (Caribo)
3757[10]

Master Moneyspider *C J Price*
7 b g Regal Embers(IRE) —Mis-E-Fishant (Sunyboy)
2560[P]

Master Nimbus *J J Quinn* 96h
6 b g Cloudings(IRE) —Miss Charlie (Pharly (FR))
415[10] 601[2] (683) 987[6] (1322) (1490) 1541[8]1605[3]

Master Ofthe Chase (IRE) *C F Swan* 119h 134+c
8 b g Norwich—Beglawella (Crash Course)
117a[9] **(1626a) 2208[6]**

Master Of The Ward (IRE) *D McCain* 54h 43c
6 ch g King Persian—Sara Jane (IRE) (Brush Aside (USA))
2631[5] 3496[7] 3846[5] 4515[5]

Master Papa (IRE) *H P Hogarth* 119+h 114c
7 bl g Key Of Luck(USA) —Beguine (USA) (Green Dancer (USA))
4[4] 1271[2] 4055[P]4349[F] 4594[9] 4842[2](5092)

Master Pip *R F Fisher* 50b
4 b g Wizard King—Tachelle (IRE) (Elbio)
2068[8] 2520[12]

Master Rex *B De Haan* 130h 136 c
11 ch g Interrex(CAN) —Whose Lady (USA) (Master Willie)
1919[6] **2489[8] 2998[2]3357[4] 4213[3] 4618[5]**

Master Sebastian *Miss Lucinda V Russell* 110h 110c
7 ch g Kasakov—Anchor Inn (Be My Guest (USA))
1942[4] 2677[3] (3207) 4068[6] 4363[5] 4981[P]

Masters Of War (IRE) *Jonjo O'Neill* 118+h 83c
9 b g Sri Pekan(USA) —Velinowski (Malinowski (USA))
766[10] 864[10] 1016[4] 1234[P]

Master Somerville *H D Daly* 88b
4 b g Alflora(IRE) —Lucy Glitters (Ardross)
4853[5]

Master Speaker *G A Harker* 42b
8 b g Presidium—Miss Ritz (Robellino (USA))
1839[P]

Master T (USA) *G L Moore* 109h 113+c
7 b g Trempolino(USA) —Our Little C (USA) (Marquetry (USA))
103[6] 234[3] 511[8](672) 1524[8] 2016[2]2239[6] 2733[F] 2827[5]

Master Tanner *Miss C Dyson*
6 ch g Master Willie—Flaxen Tina (Beau Tudor)
2961[15] 3373[13]

Master Tern (USA) *Jonjo O'Neill* 144h 104c
11 ch g Generous(IRE) —Young Hostess (FR) (Arctic Tern (USA))
1157[2] 1301[2] 1670[6]1989[4]

Master Theo (USA) *Lucinda Featherstone* 75h
5 b g Southern Halo(USA) —Lilian Bayliss (IRE) (Sadler's Wells (USA))
3597[5]

Master Trix (IRE) *P J Hobbs* 128 h 109 c
9 br g Lord Americo—Bannow Drive (IRE) (Miner's Lamp)
2529[6] 2825[4]

Master Wells (IRE) *P J Hobbs* 108 h
5 b g Sadler's Wells(USA) —Eljazzi (Artaius (USA))
3291[2] 3806[3]

Matelot (FR) *F Doumen* 100 c
6 ch g Epervier Bleu—Gloria IV (FR) (Video Rock (FR))
3438[3]

Material World *Miss Suzy Smith* 137+h
8 b m Karinga Bay—Material Girl (Busted)
3727[3] (3993) 4776[2]

Matmata De Tendron (FR) *A Crook* 96h 96c
6 gr g Badolato(USA) —Cora Des Tamarix (FR) (Iron Duke (FR))
8[P] **858[10] 1015[7]**1294[5] 3381[3] **3553[2] 3923[6](4042) 4316[2] 4845[4]**

Matrix (AUS) *K McAuliffe* 83h 64c
9 b g Centaine(AUS) —Iced Lass (NZ) (Half Iced (USA))
358[6] 631[P] 724[P]

Matthew Muroto (IRE) *R H Alner* 102h 117+c
7 b g Muroto—Glenmore Star (IRE) (Teofane)
3215[4] 3465[3] 3718[2]3949[U] 4102[2] (4572) 4820[5] (5114)

Matthew My Son (IRE) *F P Murtagh* 73h
6 ch g Lake Coniston(IRE) —Mary Hinge (Dowsing (USA))
2108[P] 2903[7] 3534[13]

Matt Wood (IRE) *Paul Nolan* 103h 106c
7 ch m Woodborough(USA) —Mattira (FR) (Rheffic (FR))
1116a[2] **1622a[5]** 1691a[7]

Mattys Joy (IRE) *Daniel Mark Loughnane* 96h 110c
7 b m Beneficial—Moorstown Rose (IRE) (Roselier (FR))
1433[2] 2208[U]

Maunby Reveller *P C Haslam* 77h
4 b g Benny The Dip(USA) —Aunt Tate (Tate Gallery (USA))
1201[3] 1797[11] 1873[8] 2416[F] 3349[7]

Maunby Rocker *P C Haslam* 89h
6 ch g Sheikh Albadou—Bullion (Sabrehill (USA))
551[9] 716[9] 988[8] 1375[5] 1883[2](2025) 2566[6] 3446[3]

Maunby Roller (IRE) *K A Morgan* 69h 8c
7 b g Flying Spur(AUS) —Brown Foam (Horage)
1044[P] 1343[P] 1643[6]4896[7]

Maunsell's Road (IRE) *L Lungo* 93+h
7 b g Desert Style(IRE) —Zara's Birthday (IRE) (Waajib)
614[3] 913[3] 1100[7]

Maura's Legacy (IRE) *I A Duncan* 95h
6 b m Zaffaran(USA) —Sharp Fashion VII (Damsire Unregistered)
3556[4] 4887a[10]

Mauritania (USA) *R Valentine* 91h
9 b g Trempolino(USA) —Chinguetti (FR) (Green Dancer (USA))
1394a[8]

Maxamillion (IRE) *S Kirk* 83h
4 b g Mujadil(USA) —Manazil (IRE) (Generous (IRE))
2661[P] 2954[4] 3579[P]

Maxie McDonald (IRE) *N A Twiston-Davies* 110+c
13 b g Homo Sapien—Lovely Sanara (Proverb)
(176)

Maximinus *M Madgwick* 95 h
6 b g The West(USA) —Candarela (Damister (USA))
1862[11] 2296[3] 2868[7] **3465[P]**3997[10] 4523[5]

Maximize (IRE) *D M Edwards* 88h 136 c
12 b g Mandalus—Lone Run (Kemal (FR))
679 [P] **5020[2]**

Max 'n Limbo (IRE) *M W Easterby*
6 ch g Un Desperado(FR) —Imperial Blue (IRE) (Callernish)
147[P] 2295[P] 2571[P]

Max Time *I Madden* 92h 62c
9 br g Mr Confusion(IRE) —First Born (Be My Native (USA))
3005a[9]

Maxxium (IRE) *M Halford* 128+h
5 b h Orpen(USA) —Florinda (CAN) (Vice Regent (CAN))
88a[7] 3894a[6]

Mayadeen (IRE) *J G M O'Shea* 78h
4 b g King's Best(USA) —Inaaq (Lammtarra (USA))
2824[12] 3817[6] 4096[9]

Ma Yahab *Miss Venetia Williams* 106+h
5 ch g Dr Fong(USA) —Bay Shade (USA) (Sharpen Up)
(3)

Maya's Prince *M D I Usher*
4 b g Easycall—Delciana (IRE) (Danehill (USA))
3340[8] 3898[F]

May Be Possible (IRE) *R Bryan*
7 ch g Presenting—Definitely Maybe (IRE) (Brush Aside (USA))
4421[U]

Maybeseven *R Dickin* 58c
12 gr g Baron Blakeney—Ninth Of May (Comedy Star (USA))
224 276[3] 503[P]1752[P] 2009[P] 2506[3]3276[7] 3688[P] 3938[U]5105[10]

Maybe She Will *D W Whillans* 36h
8 b m Tudor Diver—Blue Mischief (Precocious)
603[P]

Mayev (FR) *B Barbier*
6 br g Goldneyev(USA) —Couignamama (IRE) (Groom Dancer (USA))
5154a[7]

Maylee (IRE) *Mrs H O Graham* 65b
4 br f Good Thyne(USA) —Ganpati (IRE) (Over The River (FR))
3259[7] 4319[7]

Maynooth Princess (IRE) *R Johnson* 69h
4 ch f Trans Island—Burren Breeze (IRE) (Mazaad)
4795[8] 4987[13]

Mayoun (IRE) *Evan Williams* 100 h 49 c
9 b g Houmayoun(FR) —Botswana (African Sky)
3279[2] (3613) 3814[2] 4105[6]

Mays Delight (IRE) *S G Waugh* 54c
9 b m Glacial Storm(USA) —Lady Pauper (IRE) (Le Moss)
123[4]

Mayyas *C C Bealby* 91h
6 b g Robellino(USA) —Amidst (Midyan (USA))
2249[8] 2460[2]

Mazileo *Ian Williams* 91h 117c
13 b g Mazilier(USA) —Embroglio (USA) (Empery (USA))
746[3] 981[5] 1110[5]

Mazzareme (IRE) *Miss Venetia Williams* 101b
8 b g Supreme Leader—Mazza (Mazzier (USA))
61[P] 3143[P] 3675[F] 3733[U] 4282[11]

Mcbain (USA) *P J Hobbs* 134h
7 br g Lear Fan(USA) —River City Moon (USA) (Riverman (USA))
1275 3874 1270[5] 1548[U] (1617) 1872[7](4663)

Mccormack (IRE) *M D Hammond* 14h
4 b g Desert Story(IRE) —La Loba (IRE) (Treasure Kay)
2676[P] 3038[8] 3488[15]

Mccrinkle (IRE) *Mrs C J Kerr* 51h
9 br g Mandalus—Crinkle Lady (Buckskin (FR))
419[6]

Mckelvey (IRE) *P Bowen* 124 h 146 c
7 b g Anshan—Chatty Actress (Le Bavard (FR))
(148) 407[2] 1670[2](2189) 2643[U] 3022[P]3396[3] 4764[U] 5007[2]

Mcmahon's Brook *Mrs N S Evans* 49b
7 br g Alderbrook—Mcmahons River (Over The River (FR))
1089[6]

Mcqueen (IRE) *Mrs H Dalton* 96 h
6 ch g Barathea(IRE) —Bibliotheque (USA) (Woodman (USA))
1957[P] 4566[5]

Mcsnappy *J W Mullins* 74c
9 ch g Risk Me(FR) —Nannie Annie (Persian Bold)
2800[U] 3140[5] **4152[5]4370[P] 4911[F]**

Mead (IRE) *D J Wintle* 86+h
9 b g Mujadil(USA) —Sweetest Thing (IRE) (Prince Rupert (FR))
129[3] 458[2] 745[P]

Meadow Hawk (USA) *A W Carroll* 108+h
6 ch g Spinning World(USA) —Sophonisbe (Wollow)
136[9] 571[14] 758[9] 895[6] 949[P]1991[2] (2150) 2632[P] 3242[P]

Meandmrsjones *J G M O'Shea* 29h
7 ch m Alderbrook—Dunbrody Abbey (Proverb)
73[5]

Meda's Song *D W Whillans* 85b
7 ch m Master Willie—Cala Conta (Deep Run)
424[10]

Media Man (IRE) *E J O'Grady* 75h
6 br g Presenting—Derravarragh Lady (IRE) (Radical)
93a[14]

Medic (IRE) *T J Fitzgerald* 103+b
5 b g Dr Fong(USA) —Elupa (IRE) (Mtoto)
3353[2] 3657[3] 4909[4]

Medici (FR) *Mrs Jeremy Young* 110+h 110+c
8 bb g Cadoudal(FR) —Marie De Valois (FR) (Moulin)
4674 **510[2]**

Medison (FR) *M C Pipe* 134 h 135+c
6 bb g Video Rock(FR) —Colombia III (FR) (Altayan)
2636[P] **3150[3] 3599[2]3903[3] 4664[2]**

Medkhan (IRE) *F Jordan* 76h
9 ch g Lahib(USA) —Safayn (USA) (Lyphard (USA))
2816[16]

Meehan (IRE) *Miss J S Davis* 101+h 109+c
6 bb g Spectrum(IRE) —Seeds Of Doubt (IRE) (Night Shift (USA))
3329[3] 3546[3] 4592[6](5071)

Meentagh Loch *Miss H Brookshaw*
9 ch g Never So Bold—Miss Pisces (Salmon Leap (USA))
3847[P]

Mega D'Estruval (FR) *M C Pipe* 101+h
6 ch m Garde Royale—Vocation I (FR) (Toujours Pret (USA))
2730[10] 3217[3]

Megalala (IRE) *J J Bridger* 54b
5 b g Petardia—Avionne (Derrylin)
235[8] 5077

Megapac (IRE) *Noel T Chance* 93h 93c
8 b g Supreme Leader—Mistress Gale (IRE) (Strong Gale)
1217 4514 **3243[3] 3426[P]**3792[P] 4396[P]

Megaton *P Bowen* 97+h
5 ch g Nashwan(USA) —Pan Galactic (USA) (Lear Fan (USA))
3463[4] 3947[3] 4301[10]

Meggie's Beau (IRE) *Miss Venetia Williams* 110+c
10 ch g Good Thyne(USA) —Romantic Rose (IRE) (Strong Gale)
1907[2] 2210[7] 2502[P]3434[P] 3791[9] (4451) 4576[3]

Meiklecantly Charm *G F Bridgwater*
7 b m White Sorrel—Forgotten Empress (Dowsing (USA))
1381[8]

Meilleur (NZ) *A J Whitehead* 80b
8 ch g Mellifont(USA) —Petite Cheval (NZ) (Engagement (USA))
1772[P]

Melford (IRE) *C J Mann* 101h 120 c
8 br g Presenting—Echo Creek (IRE) (Strong Gale)
103[P] (1795) 2368[8](3420)

Melford Red (IRE) *R F Marvin*
6 b g Sri Pekan(USA) —Sunflower (IRE) (Fairy King (USA))
1614[P]

Mel In Blue (FR) *R Waley-Cohen* 114+h 126+c
8 b g Pistolet Bleu(IRE) —Calligraphie (FR) (Rb Chesne)
1675[5] **1976[3] (2654)**

Melmount Star (IRE) *J Howard Johnson* 79+h
8 bb g Rashar(USA) —Bucktina (Buckskin (FR))
(1337) 2416[P] (Dead)

Melograno (IRE) *Mark Campion* 47h
6 ch g Hector Protector(USA) —Just A Treat (IRE) (Glenstal (USA))
764[9] 911[14]

Melrose *J Hetherton* 89b
7 bb m Past Glories—Meltonby (Sayf El Arab (USA))
828[2]

Meltonian *K F Clutterbuck* 91 h 96+c
9 ch g Past Glories—Meltonby (Sayf El Arab (USA))
674[2] 1363[4] 1612[4]1805[P]

Memories Of Gold (IRE) *J A Danahar* 69h
6 b m Carroll House—Sweet Harmony (IRE) (Altountash)
1753[P] **1988[F] 2660[P]3126[P]** 3358[10]

Menai Straights *P S Payne* 74h
5 ch g Alhaarth(IRE) —Kind Of Light (Primo Dominie)
764[5] 1454[6] 1538[5]

Menchikov (FR) *N J Henderson* 122+h
6 br g Garde Royale—Caucasie (FR) (Djarvis (FR))
(2142) 2749[2] 3677[3] 4359[2] 4980[4]

Mendip Manor *S C Burrough* 28h 92c
8 b g Rakaposhi King—Broughton Manor (Dubassoff (USA))
388[5]

Meneur De Jeu (FR) *M C Pipe* 116+h 113 c
6 b g Sleeping Car(FR) —Tanie (FR) (Kashmir Ring)
(667) **842[11]** 1047[4] 1154[3]

Men Of Destiny (IRE) *B G Powell* 89h
5 b g Sadler's Wells(USA) —Caladira (IRE) (Darshaan)
361[5] 667[5] 843[P] 912[12] 2322[3]

Menphis Beury (FR) *H D Daly* 102h 110+c
6 b g Art Bleu—Pampa Star (FR) (Pampabird)
2458[4] 3420[5] 4078[3]5046[2]

Mer Bihan (FR) *L Lungo* 43h
6 b m Port Lyautey(FR) —Unika Ii (FR) (Rolling Bowl (FR))
11[P] 414[U] 545[P]

Mercari *Mrs J C McGregor* 27h
4 ch f Bahamian Bounty—Aonach Mor (Anabaa (USA))
2263[P] 2477[8] 2676[8] 3203[P] 3925[14]

Mercato (FR) *J R Best* 125 h 103c
10 b g Mansonnien(FR) —Royal Lie (FR) (Garde Royale)
489[P] 2808[3] 2931[P]4090[3] 4356[10]

Merchants Friend (IRE) *C J Mann* 108h 137 c
11 b g Lord Americo—Buck Maid (Buckskin (FR))
1861[2] 2176[6] 2875[F]

Merci Papi (FR) *T Trapenard* 105h 70c
4 b g Indian Kean(IRE) —Sante De Fer (FR) (Shining Steel)
777a[8]

Mercuric *Mrs John Harrington* 119h
5 gr g Silver Patriarch(IRE) —Seymourswift (Seymour Hicks (FR))
3003a[5] 4060a[3] 4336a[7]

Merdeka (IRE) *T J Taaffe* 130+h
6 b g Luso—Gentle Reef (IRE) (Orange Reef)
3309a[3] (4137a)

Mere Conquest *R M Beckett*
8 b g El Conquistador—Merely (Little Wolf)
2421[U]

Merits Pride *B Storey*
6 b m Merit(IRE) —Gunnerdale (Gunner B)
3551[P] 4342[P]

Merriott's Oscar (IRE) *N J Hawke* 89h 114+c
6 b g Oscar Schindler(IRE) —Killone Lady (IRE) (High Estate)
3881[6] **4417[3]**

Merry Minstrel (IRE) *Mrs Jackie Hunt* 106c
13 b g Black Minstrel—Merry Lesa (Dalesa)
471[2] 221[8] 405[4]

Merry Path (IRE) *Evan Williams* 123c
12 br g Alphabatim(USA) —Smokey Path (IRE) (Scallywag)
(572) 842[9] 4009[P]

Merry Storm (IRE) *Mrs K Waldron* 100+c
7 b g Glacial Storm(USA) —Cap Reform (IRE) (Phardante (FR))
236[P] **2581[4] 2984[0](3221) (3252) 3359[3]4163[4] 4350[2] (4662) 4878[5]**

Merryvale Man *Miss Kariana Key* 113+h
9 b g Rudimentary(USA) —Salu (Ardross)
61[5] 197[4] 428[5] 482[3] 784[12]2190[8] 2452[14] 2590[8] 2625[7] 2843[7]2952[6] 2981[F] (3206) 3378[12] 3737[4] 3853[F]3918[3] 4045[U] (4302) 4503[3] 4879[3]

Mersey Mirage *R C Guest* 64h
9 b g King's Signet(USA) —Kirriemuir (Lochnager)
75[9] 180[P] 1148[6] 1357[5]

Mesmeric (IRE) *B G Powell* 115 h
8 b g Sadler's Wells(USA) —Mesmerize (Mill Reef (USA))
1116a[4] 4357[5] 4579[P] **4827[P]**

Messager (FR) *J A Supple* 89h
6 ch g Brier Creek(USA) —Contessina (FR) (Mistigri)
1921[4] 3675

Message Recu (FR) *C L Tizzard* 112h 96c
10 b g Luth Dancer(USA) —High Steppe (Petoski)
2733[P] 2996[3] 3482[P]3949[5] 4426[8] 4639[5]

Metal Detector (IRE) *K C Bailey* 89h 111c
9 b g Treasure Hunter—Las-Cancellas (Monksfield)
3458[14] 4549[4] **4737[3] 5122[5]**

Methodical *B G Powell* 88+h
4 b f Lujain(USA) —Simple Logic (Aragon)
2501[6] 2597[F] 2935[4] (3321) 3483[2] 3902[3]4129[F]

Meticulous (USA) *K J Burke* 93h
8 b g Theatrical—Sha Tha (USA) (Mr Prospector (USA))
1773[P] 1856[14]

Me Tows (IRE) *Thomas Carberry* 53h 87 c
10 b m Orchestra—Loaker Lady (Furry Glen)
4845[P]

Mevagissey (BEL) *J D Frost* 81h
9 bb g Sula Bula—Fowey (Grand Conde (FR))
389[10] 514[P] 806[5]

Mexican (USA) *M D Hammond* 88h 99 c
7 b g Pine Bluff(USA) —Cuando Quiere (USA) (Affirmed (USA))
84[5] 2111[4] (2842) 3233[5] 3788[7] 4365[4]4991[9]

Mexican Pete *A W Carroll* 130 h
6 b g Atraf—Eskimo Nel (IRE) (Shy Groom (USA))
(1366) (1633) 1720[2] 2765[8]

Mezereon *D Carroll* 101+h
6 b m Alzao(USA) —Blown-Over (Ron's Victory (USA))
(4609)

Mialyssa *M R Bosley* 57h
6 b m Rakaposhi King—Theme Arena (Tragic Role (USA))
463[5] 1042[8] 2997[11] 3322[11]

Miami Explorer *P R Webber* 117+h
6 b m Pennekamp(USA) —Elaine Tully (IRE) (Persian Bold)
(569) (715) (780)

Michaels Dream (IRE) *N Wilson* 113h
7 b g Spectrum(IRE) —Stormswept (USA) (Storm Bird (CAN))
1151[4] (1361) (1443) 1488[2] 1844 [3] 2166[11]

Michigan D'Isop (FR) *B J M Ryall* 100+h
6 b g Cadoudal(FR) —Julie Du Berlais (FR) (Rose Laurel)
3130[2]

Mickataine (IRE) *M F Morris* 109h
5 b g Presenting—Inamuddle (IRE) (Lafontaine (USA))
3003a[F]

Mick Divine (IRE) *C J Mann* 95h 102c
8 gr g Roselier(FR) —Brown Forest (Brave Invader (USA))
1907[6] 2151[3] 2458[2]2955[4]

Mickey Croke *M Todhunter* 108 h
9 b g Alflora(IRE) —Praise The Lord (Lord Gayle (USA))
1939 [P] 3781[4] 4361[P]5037[U]

Mickey Pearce (IRE) *J G M O'Shea* 82+h
4 b g Rossini(USA) —Lucky Coin (Hadeer)
1955^5 2286^9 2756^9 3479^P 3985^3 4101^4 4368^5 (4550) 4733^4 4783^11

Mick Jerome (IRE) *Rune Haugen* 107h
5 b h Kahyasi—Acquilata (USA) (Irish River (FR))
2455^4 2663^3

Mick Murphy (IRE) *V J Hughes* 78+h 78+c
9 b g Jurado(USA) —Lee Ford Lady (Kemal (FR))
(573) 614^6 745^7 1028^4 1272^7

Micky Cole (IRE) *P F Nicholls* 76h
6 b g Luso—Simple Mind (Decent Fellow)
1833^3 2426^5 2559^6 3211^6 3876^7

Midas Way *P R Chamings* 118+h
6 ch g Halling(USA) —Arietta's Way (IRE) (Darshaan)
(4621)

Mid Dancer (FR) *A Chaille-Chaille* 128c
5 b g Midyan(USA) —Dancer Lady (FR) (Pink (FR))
4431^12

Middleham Park (IRE) *J W Mullins* 110+h
6 b g Revoque(IRE) —Snap Crackle Pop (IRE) (Statoblest)
182^2 (533) 751^P 864^9 2271^2 2459^8 3214^9 3345^6

Middlemarch (GER) *Gerard Cully* 129 h
5 br h Alkalde(GER) —Morgenpirsch (GER) (Surumu (GER))
5056a^5

Middlethorpe *M W Easterby* 133+h
9 b g Noble Patriarch—Prime Property (IRE) (Tirol)
4490^8

Middleton Kate *John R Upson*
6 b m Thethingaboutitis(USA) —Koritsaki (Strong Gale)
178^P 314^6 426^P

Middleway *Miss Kate Milligan* 81+h 78+c
10 b g Milieu—Galway Gal (Proverb)
373^P 554^4 1589^5 (4921)

Midlem Melody *W S Coltherd* 69h 101+c
10 b m Syrtos—Singing Hills (Crash Course)
84^P 122^P

Midnight Arrival *Ian Howe*
6 b m Danzig Connection(USA) —Carousel Zingira (Reesh)
3924^U

Midnight Creek *A Sadik* 116+h
8 br g Tragic Role(USA) —Greek Night Out (IRE) (Ela-Mana-Mou)
(1341) (1616) 1844 ^2 4990^P

Midnight Fury *J G M O'Shea* 46b
4 b g Tipsy Creek(USA) —Anne's Bank (IRE) (Burslem)
2013^8 3651^11

Midnight Gift (IRE) *T Hogan* 99h
6 ch m Presenting—Midnight Pond (IRE) (Long Pond)
2211^3

Midnight Gold *A King* 93h 107+c
6 ch g Midnight Legend—Yamrah (Milford)
1711^6 1833^P 3428^P 3792^7 4557^2 4824^P 5028^4

Midnight Gunner *A E Price* 94h 120 c
12 b g Gunner B—Light Tonight (Lighter)
176^P 1778^2 (1960) 3186^6 3560^7 4576^4 4851^3

Midnight In Moscow (IRE) *P C Haslam* 39h
4 b g Soviet Star(USA) —Solar Display (USA) (Diesis)
1146^8 1201^P

Midnight Marine *J F Panvert* 62b
5 b g Midnight Legend—The Bizzo (Malaspina)
507^6

Midnight Spirit *F E Sutherland* 71b
6 b g Midnight Legend—West-Hatch-Spirit (Forzando)
4875^P

Midnight Star *M Mullineaux* 83b
5 b g Cloudings(IRE) —Blueberry Parkes (Pursuit Of Love)
2340^16 2941^10

Mid Summer Lark (IRE) *I McMath* 82c
10 b g Tremblant—Tuney Blade (Fine Blade (USA))
1564^15 1686^P 1723^P 1886^P

Mid Sussex Spirit *G L Moore* 87+h
7 b g Environment Friend—Ranyah (USA) (Our Native (USA))
4359^P 4905^8

Mi Fa Sol Aulmes (FR) *W T Reed* 92b
6 ch m Garde Royale—Bull Finch Aulmes (FR) (Rose Laurel)
2446^5 3742^6 4533^4

Mighty Fella *Mrs E Slack* 72h
4 gr g Cloudings(IRE) —Zany Lady (Arzanni)
3203^U 3925^11 4787^6

Mighty Fine *Mrs E Slack* 105h 125+c
12 gr g Arzanni—Kate Kimberley (Sparkler)
13^4

Mighty Man (FR) *H D Daly* 169+h
6 b g Sir Harry Lewis(USA) —Vanina II (FR) (Italic (FR))
2209^9 (2758) 3177^2 3723^2 4458^3 (4745)

Mighty Matters (IRE) *T R George* 94+b 115 c
7 b g Muroto—Hasaway (IRE) (Executive Perk)
2044^9 2482^7 (2982) 3507^4 4971^4

Mighty Montefalco *Mrs Alison De Lisle Wells* 109c
10 b g Mtoto—Glendera (Glenstal (USA))
47^3 272^5

Mighty Moose (IRE) *Nick Williams*
6 b g Mister Lord(USA) —Brief Pace (IRE) (Riot Helmet)
2311^P 4035^5

Mightymuller (IRE) *D R Gandolfo* 80h
4 b g Montjeu(IRE) —Anazara (USA) (Trempolino (USA))
2927^12 3594^5 4327^11 4521^2

Mighty Pip (IRE) *M R Bosley* 81h
10 b g Pips Pride—Hard To Stop (Hard Fought)
1483^7

Migigi *M J Roberts* 51h
6 b m Alflora(IRE) —Barton Bay (IRE) (Kambalda)
3435^7 3911^12 5052^13

Migration *Mrs S Lamyman* 95h 93c
10 b g Rainbow Quest(USA) —Armeria (USA) (Northern Dancer)
372^6 1001^U 1487^8 1720^10 1912^P 2925^9 2964^6 3687^9 3967^9

Migwell (FR) *Mrs L Wadham* 102 h 123 c
6 b g Assessor(IRE) —Uguette IV (FR) (Chamberlin (FR))
2047^7 2493^9 2633^7 (2959) 3942^P 4374^9

Mikado *Jonjo O'Neill* 116+h
5 b g Sadler's Wells(USA) —Free At Last (Shirley Heights)
1614^5 (1908) 2099^2 3389^13 4461^22 4868^2 (5016) 5086^U

Mikado Melody (IRE) *A King* 110+h
7 b g Supreme Leader—Double Symphony (IRE) (Orchestra)
(1916) 3175^13 4678^P

Mikasa (IRE) *R F Fisher* 85h 83c
6 b g Victory Note(USA) —Resiusa (ITY) (Niniski (USA))
(548) 1098^3 1277^3 1335^6 1612^5 1905^P 2063^P 2688^5 2945^2 3320^8 (3447) 3915^P 4318^5 4487^10 (4844) 5139^7

Mike Golden (IRE) *R W J Willcox* 101c
8 ch g Shardari—Dessie's Girl (IRE) (Orchestra)
5109^3

Mike Simmons *L P Grassick* 101 h
10 b g Ballacashtal(CAN) —Lady Crusty (Golden Dipper)
3581^P 4805^6 5014^P

Miko De Beauchene (FR) *R H Alner* 121+h
6 b g Nashamaa—Chipie D'Angron (FR) (Grand Tresor (FR))
(2130) 2633^8 3023^2 3388^3 3975^2 4678^3 4849^5

Milan Deux Mille (FR) *M C Pipe* 104+h
4 b g Double Bed(FR) —Uberaba (FR) (Garde Royale)
2105^2 (2611) 4032^U 4416^3 4691^5

Milan King (IRE) *A J Lockwood* 35h
13 b g King's Ride—Milan Moss (Le Moss)
3169^14 4299^11

Milanshan (IRE) *J W Mullins* 76h
6 b m Anshan—Milan Moss (Le Moss)
1386^3 1674^3 2558^11 3240^11 3692^4 4324^P 4836^5 5069^F

Mildon (FR) *J-L Pelletan*
3 b g Milford Track(IRE) —Donnedi (FR) (Shining Steel)
(4298a)

Militaire (FR) *J M Turner* 65c
8 ch g Bering—Moon Review (USA) (Irish River (FR))
184^P

Milk And Sultana *G A Ham* 49h
6 b m Millkom—Premier Princess (Hard Fought)
1750^F 1952^4

Millagros (IRE) *I Semple* 113h
6 b m Pennekamp(USA) —Grey Galava (Generous (IRE))
(302) 873^3 2904^4 3761^16 3929^5

Millanymare (IRE) *A J Martin* 114+h 98+c
7 b m Old Vic—Lucey Allen (Strong Gale)
(1116a) 2207^7

Mill Bank (IRE) *Evan Williams* 61h 100+c
11 b g Millfontaine—Mossy Bank (IRE) (Le Moss)
(1713) 2073^P 3656^4 4643^3 4936^2 5105^7

Millbury *M Dods* 82b
5 b m Overbury(IRE) —Seamill (IRE) (Lafontaine (USA))
4992^4

Millenaire (FR) *Jonjo O'Neill* 122h 136 c
7 bb g Mister Mat(FR) —Mille Perles (FR) (Kashtan (FR))
1608^4 1976^P (2241) (2703) 2953^F (4166) 4460^F (Dead)

Millenium Royal (FR) *F Doumen* 143 h
6 b g Mansonnien(FR) —Pink Champagne (FR) (Blue Courtier)
3723^P 4069^2 4458^P

Millenium Way (IRE) *Mrs C L Taylor* 102c
12 ch g Ikdam—Fine Drapes (Le Bavard (FR))
(400) 3910^4 4607^5 5020^3

Millennium Hall *Miss Lucinda V Russell* 100 h
7 b g Saddlers' Hall(IRE) —Millazure (USA) (Dayjur (USA))
1291^F 1527^9 2627^4 2991^3 3206^5 3797^8

Miller's Monarch *Andrew Turnell* 87h
6 b g El Conquistador—Gables Girl (Sousa)
2056^5 2606^8 3354^8 3996^7

Millestore *M Mullineaux* 3b
6 b g Superlative—Gildoran's Mill (Gildoran)
1799^17

Mill House Girl (IRE) *S Donohoe* 120b
5 ch m Basanta(IRE) —Karalee (IRE) (Arokar (FR))
4751^8 5081a^4

Millicent Cross (IRE) *R Ford* 84h
8 b g Executive Perk—Flynn's Girl (IRE) (Mandalus)
764^4 1916^6 2179^10

Millicent Fairways (IRE) *R C Guest* 98b
8 b g King's Ride—Dollyliner (Skyliner)
591^P

Millie Boon *L J Williams*
7 b m Petoski—Bartondale (Oats)
685^15 917^11 1459^12

Millie's Fortune *M Mullineaux* 70b
5 b m Classic Cliche(IRE) —Millies Misfortune (IRE) (Hamas (IRE))
4046^P

Milliesome *J I A Charlton* 74h
8 b m Milieu—Some Shiela (Remainder Man)
4342^U

Milligan (FR) *Dr P Pritchard* 109 h 106c
11 b g Exit To Nowhere(USA) —Madigan Mill (Mill Reef (USA))
1270^15 1396^4 1481^10 1726^6 1871^F 3492^5 3725^7 4050^6 4573^4 4832^9 2^6

Milli Wizz *W M Brisbourne* 58b
6 b m Wizard King—State Of Love (Northern State (USA))
917^8 1048^9

Mill Lane *R Hollinshead*
9 b m Tromeros—Holdtight VII (Damsire Unregistered)
500^5 654^11

Millquista D'Or *G A Ham* 76h
4 b f Millkom—Gild The Lily (Ile De Bourbon (USA))
1095^2 1201^5 1404^3 1519^2

Mill Tower *R Nixon* 93h
9 b g Milieu—Tringa (GER) (Kaiseradler)
123^P 322^U 411^P 550^8 872^P 937^U

Milord Lescribaa (FR) *M C Pipe* 110 h 110c
6 b g Cadoudal(FR) —Mona Lisaa (FR) (Karkour (FR))
465^2 750^2 (914)

Minat Boy *C L Tizzard* 66c
10 b g Gildoran—Childhay Millie (Idiots Delight)
2313^P 2801^2 3187^4 3430^P 4428^P 4666^5 4936^P

Minella Silver (IRE) *G L Landau* 114c
13 gr g Roselier(FR) —Mrs Minella (Deep Run)
47^2 4216^3

Miniballist (IRE) *R T Phillips* 100+h
8 b m Tragic Role(USA) —Herballistic (Rolfe (USA))
245^P 397^5 1280^3 1379^2

Mini Dare *O Sherwood* 102 h 103 c
9 b g Derrylin—Minim (Rymer)
488^4 (1989) 2104^F 2610^3 2938^9 3460^11 5010^F

Miniperse (FR) *G R I Smyly* 81+h
6 ch g Lyphard's Wish(FR) —Lady Persane (FR) (Roi De Perse II)
2070^P 2249^10 2730^9 2860^7 3147^P 4164^P

Mini Sensation (IRE) *Jonjo O'Neill* 92 h 127+c
13 b g Be My Native(USA) —Minorettes Girl (Strong Gale)
1941^P 2265^2

Minivet *R Allan* 90h
11 b g Midyan(USA) —Bronzewing (Beldale Flutter (USA))
871^P 1510^F 1836^8 2038^12 2474^P 2840^F 3271^P

Minnesinger *M Todhunter* 75h
4 b f Fraam—Rose Alto (Adonijah)
3484^P 3925^4 4301^P

Minnesota Leader (IRE) *Mrs John Harrington* 90b
5 b g Supreme Leader—Windfields Native (IRE) (Be My Native (USA))
5060a^6

Minnie The Moocher *J W Mullins* 64h
6 b m Karinga Bay—Slippery Fin (Slip Anchor)
1595^U 2018^P

Minnigaff (IRE) *N G Richards* 67h
6 b g Supreme Leader—Across The Pond (IRE) (Over The River (FR))
59^10

Minouchka (FR) *S H Shirley-Beavan* 91b 113c
6 bb m Bulington(FR) —Elbury (FR) (Royal Charter (FR))
4303^2 5092^U 2^2

Minsgill Glen *Mrs J K M Oliver* 76h 82c
10 b m Minster Son—Gilmanscleuch (IRE) (Mandalus)
1686^P 1837^6 2495^8

Minster Abbi *W Storey* 74h
6 b m Minster Son—Elitist (Keren)
14^5 496^2 1838^5 1943^2 2171^8 2453^5 2653^6 3042^6

Minster Blue *Mrs Susan Murtagh* 68h
8 b m Minster Son—Elitist (Keren)
4846^P

Minster Brig *A Parker* 33h
7 b g Minster Son—Royal Brig (Royal Fountain)
1663^11 1884^5 2413^P 3930^P

Minster Fair *A C Whillans* 90 h
8 b m Minster Son—Fair Echo (Quality Fair)
80^P 3375^F 3854^11 4041^P

Minster Lane *J M Saville* 51b
6 ch g Minster Son—Coverdale Lane (Boreen (FR))
4615^12

Minster Meadow *S G Chadwick* 40h
7 ch g Minster Son—Eddies Well (Torus)
418^13 553^5

Minster Park *S C Burrough* 83h
7 b g Minster Son—Go Gipsy (Move Off)
2665^10 3139^4 3466^10 4015^P 4331^7 4860^4

Minster York *H H G Owen* 82h 117c
12 ch g Minster Son—Another Treat (Derring-Do)
1212^4

Minstrel's Double *F P Murtagh* 60h
5 ch g Jumbo Hirt(USA) —Hand On Heart (IRE) (Taufan (USA))
197^11 4632^P

Mio Caro (FR) *Noel T Chance* 109h
6 ch g Bering—Composition (USA) (Sillery (USA))
127^P 525^P

Mioche D'Estruval (FR) *M C Pipe* 122h 124+c
6 bl g Lute Antique(FR) —Charme D'Estruval (FR) (Mistigri)
(570) 728^2 2847^6 3727^15 3900^2 4419^3 4827^2 4985^P

Mirant *M C Pipe* 118 h
7 b g Danzig Connection(USA) —Ingerence (FR) (Akarad (FR))
2629^8 3333^3

Mirjan (IRE) *L Lungo* 135h
10 b g Tenby—Mirana (IRE) (Ela-Mana-Mou)
1872^6 5005^10

Mirpour (IRE) *Eoin Griffin* 125h 127c
7 b g Turtle Island(IRE) —Mirana (IRE) (Ela-Mana-Mou)
1083a^13

Misbehaviour *Jim Best* 112h
7 b g Tragic Role(USA) —Exotic Forest (Dominion)
3223^2 3990^2 (4075) (4153) 4329^6

Mise En Place *J Morrison* 119+h
5 b m Dr Fong(USA) —Oleana (IRE) (Alzao (USA))
4951a^23

Misleain (IRE) *J R Turner* 88b
6 b m Un Desperado(FR) —Naar Chamali (Salmon Leap (USA))
3931^3

Miss Academy (FR) *M C Pipe* 122h
5 ch m Video Rock(FR) —Mademoiselle Wo (FR) (Prince Wo (FR))
3298^11 3621^F 4473^19

Miss Caruso *P J Prendergast* 101+h
4 b f Efisio—Roma (Second Set (IRE))
3004a^4

Miss Chippy (IRE) *T R George* 62h
6 ch m Mister Lord(USA) —My Alanna (Dalsaan)
2558^3 2941^8 3461^11 3692^5 4074^10

Miss Colmesnil (FR) *A E Jessop* 88c
6 b m Dear Doctor(FR) —Princesse Dolly (FR) (The Wonder (FR))
3251^P 3457^3 3920^P

Miss Defying *R Curtis* 33h
4 b f Shambo—Dugy (Risk Me (FR))
2069^11 2454^U 2824^9 3321^9

Miss Dinamite *Mrs C J Ikin* 39h
4 b f Polar Prince(IRE) —Over The Moon (Beveled (USA))
945^P 1095^P 1146^F 1339^10 1440^7 1519^P

Miss Domino *S J Gilmore*
5 b m Alderbrook—Mrs Moneypenny (Relkino)
3373^11 3979^P

Miss Doublet *J W Mullins* 82+h 52c
5 ch m Double Trigger(IRE) —Bournel (Sunley Builds)
1776^5 (4286) 4619^P

Missed That *W P Mullins* 136b 156 c
7 b g Overbury(IRE) —Not Enough (Balinger)
70a^4 (3006a) (3639a) 4431^6 4889a^F (5058a)

Miss Ellie *Mrs C J Kerr* 80h 41c
10 b m Elmaamul(USA) —Jussoli (Don)
306^15

Miss Fahrenheit (IRE) *C Roberts* 98h
7 b m Oscar(IRE) —Gunner B Sharp (Gunner B)
1984^7 2430^7 2609^6 3018^15 3548^13 4012^3 4105^3 4372^P 4662^P

Miss Flinders *D P Keane* 60b
9 b m Sula Bula—Pollys Owen (Master Owen)
667^6 750^P

Miss Flossy (IRE) *Mrs S D Williams* 57h
5 ch m Bob Back(USA) —Moscow Money (IRE) (Moscow Society (USA))
4286^7 4836^P

Miss Grace *J D Frost* 83h
6 ch m Atticus(USA) —Jetbeeah (IRE) (Lomond (USA))
3878^7 4425^7 4665^5

Miss Holly *Mrs S J Smith* 99 h
7 b m Makbul—Seraphim (FR) (Lashkari)
3967^7 4391^4

Missis Potts *P J Hobbs* 100b
5 b m Overbury(IRE) —Potter's Gale (IRE) (Strong Gale)
4976^4

Miss Iverley *J M Dun* 51h
4 b f Shambo—Blanche The Almond (Northern Park (USA))
4532^13 4789^13

Miss Jessica (IRE) *Miss M E Rowland* 81h
6 bb m Woodborough(USA) —Sarah Blue (IRE) (Bob Back (USA))
(147) 414^9 724^P 1275^6 4302^11 4780^U 4918^F

Miss Kilkeel (IRE) *R T J Wilson* 105h 89c
8 b m Religiously(USA) —Shakiyka (IRE) (Shardari)
406^4 715^2 1064^2 3761^11 4724^9

Miss Lauren Dee (IRE) *M Flannery* 108h
10 ch m Montelimar(USA) —Miss Daisy Dee (Baptism)
67a^14

Miss Lehman *J D Frost* 99+h
8 ch m Beveled(USA) —Lehmans Lot (Oats)
(389) (517) 753^9 1272^8 (1742) 2150^P

Miss Lewis *C J Down* 89h
8 b m Sir Harry Lewis(USA) —Teelyna (Teenoso (USA))
1152^14

Miss Mailmit *J A B Old* 91h 110+c
9 b m Rakaposhi King—Flora Louisa (Rymer)
3481^U 3949^F 4105^7 4395^6

Miss Man *N E Berry*
12 ch m Man Among Men(IRE) —Rustys Special (Rustingo)
749^P 1040^P 1121^P

Miss Mattie Ross *S J Marshall* 61h 120c
10 b m Milieu—Mother Machree (Bing II)
1837^3 (2037) 2451^2 2656^4 3377^2 4111^8 4505^7 4843^5

Miss Merenda *J F Panvert* 91h
5 b m Sir Harry Lewis(USA) —Cool Merenda (IRE) (Glacial Storm (USA))
279^10 1108^3 (1522) 1775^6 1859^4 2125^5 4568^6

Miss Midnight *R J Hodges* 90 h
5 b m Midnight Legend—Miss Marigold (Norwick (USA))
27^3 300^2 2152^2 2457^2 2730^P 2997^6 3131^3 3386^5 3997^P 4726^3 4855^12

Miss Millfield *V J Hughes* 44h
5 b m Hatim(USA) —Miss Millbrook (Meadowbrook)
2665^15 3024^10 4554^12 4935^11

Miss Mitch (IRE) *R H Alner* 100b
5 bb m King's Theatre(IRE) —Party Woman (IRE) (Sexton Blake)
4333^4 4751^16

Miss Mobility *A J Wilson* 80b
6 ch m Primitive Rising(USA) —Poshka (Rakaposhi King)
490^9

Miss Morfire *Mrs S Gardner* 73b
6 b m Morpeth—Miss Firedor (Gildoran)
1961^6

Miss Muscat *Evan Williams* 59h 89+c
6 b m Environment Friend—Fisima (Efisio)
357^P 632^F 902^U 979^4 (1203) 1277^F

Miss Nosey *Mrs E Slack* 59h
4 b f Danzero(AUS) —Miss Nosey Oats (Oats)
4657^P 10^6

Miss Ocean Monarch *Miss Tracy Waggott* 42h
6 ch m Blue Ocean(USA) —Faraway Grey (Absalom)
780[11] 1757[P]

Missoudun (FR) *J R Weymes* 72b 72c
6 b g Esteem Ball(FR) —Lisiana (FR) (Iris Noir (FR))
212[P] **2109[F] 2978[P]3170[F] 4042[P] 4655[3]4918[P]**

Miss Pebbles (IRE) *R Dickin* 114+h
6 ch m Lake Coniston(IRE) —Sea Of Stone (USA) (Sanglamore (USA))
(2070) 2559[3] 3295[4] 3621[6] 3979[6] 4641[8]5052[3]

Miss Pross *T D Walford* 95h 105c
6 b m Bob's Return(IRE) —Lucy Manette (Final Straw)
9[6] 2191[8] 2525[3] 2750[10] 2994[3]3339[3] **(3784) 4041[5] 4489[2]4721[9]**

Miss Rideamight *G Brown* 70+h
7 b m Overbury(IRE) —Nicolynn (Primitive Rising (USA))
2140[10]

Miss Shakira (IRE) *N A Twiston-Davies* 103+h
117+c
8 b m Executive Perk—River Water (Over The River (FR))
(1528) 1727[4] **1942[2] (2284) (2526)** 3358[3] **3649[4]** 4568[5]**4806[6]**

Miss Shontaine *B G Powell*
4 b f Fumo Di Londra(IRE) —Stockline (Capricorn Line)
3690[P]

Miss Sirius *John R Upson* 84h
6 ch m Royal Vulcan—Star Shell (Queens Hussar)
27[9] 3322[10] 4450[14] 5052[5]

Miss Skippy *A G Newcombe* 100h
7 b m Saddlers' Hall(IRE) —Katie Scarlett (Lochnager)
1153[12] (1384) 1658[2] 2166[F] 3648[5] 3959[5]4289[P] 4738[9]

Miss Toulon (IRE) *Thomas Mullins* 119h
8 b m Toulon—Miss Top (IRE) (Tremblant)
5059a[15]

Miss Trooper *F Jordan* 64h
6 b m Infantry—Mountain Glen (Lochnager)
487[P]

Miss Una (IRE) *M Halford*
4 b f Spectrum(IRE) —Fer De Lance (IRE) (Diesis)
2645a[11]

Miss Wizadora *Simon Earle* 91 c
11 ch m Gildoran—Lizzie The Twig (Precipice Wood)
132[2] 181[6] 3602[4]

Miss Wizz *W Storey* 28h
6 b m Wizard King—Fyas (Sayf El Arab (USA))
1794[13] 2040[9]

Missyl (FR) *R H Alner* 100h 79c
6 gr g Great Palm(USA) —Elite Dacadour (FR) (Sarpedon (FR))
1857[2] 2050[3] 2309[11] 2683[5] **4288[P]4913[2]**

Missy Moscow (IRE) *H J Evans* 78h 49c
8 b m Moscow Society(USA) —Bright Shares (IRE) (Mandalus)
426[5] 2457[5] 2718[8] **3252[8]**3656[P]

Mistanoora *N A Twiston-Davies* 154 h 47c
7 b g Topanoora—Mistinguett (IRE) (Doyoun)
3020[7] 3723[9] 4458[17] 4776[9]

Mister Apple's (FR) *Ian Williams* 82c
6 ch g Video Rock(FR) —Doryane (FR) (Bayolidaan (FR))
2327[P]

Mister Arjay (USA) *B Ellison* 113h
6 b g Mister Baileys—Crystal Stepper (USA) (Fred Astaire (USA))
1434[2] 1633[3] (1929) 2292[7] 2925[10] 3256[9]3384[7]

Mister Aziz (IRE) *J R Jenkins* 42h
4 b g Mister Baileys—Aziz Presenting (IRE) (Charnwood Forest (IRE))
2258[7]

Mister Bean (FR) *R Waley-Cohen* 91+c
9 bb g Roi De Rome(USA) —Maria Theresa (FR) (Iron Duke (FR))
1741[4]

Mister Chatterbox (IRE) *P J Hobbs* 91h
5 b g Presenting—Lotta Talk (IRE) (Le Moss)
2941[5] 3466[7] 3996[10] 4032[6] 4429[7]4756[2] 4860[3]

Mister Christian (IRE) *W K Goldsworthy* 86b
5 ch g Shernazar—Laurabeg (Laurence O)
4940[6] 5089[4]

Mister Club Royal *Miss Emma Oliver* 63b 96+c
10 b g Alflora(IRE) —Miss Club Royal (Avocat)
47[P] 204[P] 3693[5]4397[2] 4560[2] 4757[P]

Mister Completely (IRE) *Miss Sheena West* 83h
5 b g Princely Heir(IRE) —Blue Goose (Belmez (USA))
4649[4] 4868[6]

Mister Dave'S (IRE) *Mrs S J Smith* 78 c
11 ch g Bluffer—Tacovaon (Avocat)
2818[10] 2965[P] 3917[6]

Mister Du Bois (FR) *L Bellet*
6 b g Grand Tresor(FR) —Altesse Du Bois (FR) (Mister Jack (FR))
1372a[5]

Mister Etek *T D Walford* 86b
5 b g Defacto(USA) —Boulevard Girl (Nicholas Bill)
4072[9] 5042[2]

Mister Flint *P J Hobbs* 127 h
135+c
8 b g Petoski—National Clover (National Trust)
459[U] 803[2] (1096) (1124) (1442)

Mister Friday (IRE) *C A Mulhall* 129 c
9 bb g Mister Lord(USA) —Rebecca's Storm (IRE) (Strong Gale)
(48) 3736[P] 4975[5]

Mister Frog (FR) *G A Swinbank* 91b
5 b g Dress Parade—Baronne De Meucon (FR) (Master Thatch)
1889[3]

Mister Gyor (FR) *B Barbier*
6 ch g Cyborg(FR) —Miss Tigresse (FR) (Mistigri (IRE))
779a[P]

Mister Hight (FR) *W P Mullins* 133+h
4 bl g Take Risks(FR) —Miss High (FR) (Concorde Jr (USA))
(3890a) 4468[8] 5099a[F]

Mister Julius *P Bowen*
9 b g Mister Lord(USA) —Princess Pool (Push On)
236[P]

Mister Jungle (FR) *Mrs S C Bradburne* 78b
4 b g Saint Cyrien(FR) —Fabuleuse Histoire (FR) (Fabulous Dancer (USA))
3273[2] 3763[7] 4533[5] 5124[5]

Mister Kingston *R Dickin* 78c
15 ch g Kinglet—Flaxen Tina (Beau Tudor)
1044[6] 1232[P]

Mister Knight (IRE) *P F Nicholls* 95b
7 ch g Mister Lord(USA) —Knights Bounty (IRE) (Henbit (USA))
2152[4]

Mister Magnum (IRE) *P Monteith* 91h 89c
8 gr g Be My Native(USA) —Miss Henrietta (IRE) (Step Together (USA))
122[11]

Mister McGoldrick *Mrs S J Smith* 151 h 165 c
9 b g Sabrehill(USA) —Anchor Inn (Be My Guest (USA))
1970[6] 2346[5] 2499[4](3039) 3492[2] 3725[3] **3980[3]4445[3] 4761[P]** 5003[7]

Mister Moonax (IRE) *M G Rimell* 45b
6 ch g Moonax(IRE) —Edna Cottage (The Parson)
4011[6] 4500[12]

Mister Moss (IRE) *B P J Baugh* 89c
13 b g Don Tristan(USA) —Lindas Statement (IRE) (Strong Statement (USA))
632[P]

Mister Moussac *Miss Kariana Key* 103h
7 b g Kasakov—Salu (Ardross)
13[3] 61[7] 121[6] 304[5] 784[6]1040[P] 1361[4] (1413) (1458) 1559[F] 4736[5] 5096[4]

Mister Mustard (IRE) *Ian Williams* 121 h 103 c
9 b g Norwich—Monalma (IRE) (Montekin)
194[F] 1642[F] 1880[P] 3880[2] 4215[P]4693[5] 4938[3]

Mister Nelson (IRE) *N G Richards* 95+b
5 b g Mister Mat(FR) —Dalus Pearl (IRE) (Mandalus)
2268[3]

Mister Notorious (IRE) *N A Twiston-Davies* 95b
7 ch g Bob Back(USA) —Island Run (Deep Run)
2665[12]

Mister Pearly *T D B Underwood* 55b 96c
9 ch g Alflora(IRE) —Pearly Dream (Rymer)
404[5]

Mister Pink *R Rowe* 65b
6 ch g Accordion—Place Stephanie (IRE) (Hatim (USA))
4623[7]

Mister Quasimodo *C L Tizzard* 130h
6 b g Busy Flight—Dubacilla (Dubassoff (USA))
1980[2] (2426) 2762[4] (3210) 3878[2] 4115[2] 4446[21]

Mister Sher (IRE) *Mrs L J Young* 99+h
7 b g Shernazar—Running River (IRE) (Riverhead (USA))
3693[U] 4786[F]

Misters Sister *C A Dwyer* 73h
4 b f Robellino(USA) —Baileys On Line (Shareef Dancer (USA))
2345[7] 2661[7] 2954[6] 4449[P]

Mister Tibus (FR) *J A Geake* 50b
5 b g Signe Divin(USA) —Ferlia (FR) (Noir Et Or)
1791[0] 5071[3]

Mister Top Notch (IRE) *D E Fitzgerald* 123+h
7 b g Mister Lord(USA) —Turn A Coin (Prince Hansel)
2784a[2] 3086a[2] 3309a[6] 4469[12]

Mister Zaffaran (IRE) *Mrs N S Evans* 75 h
7 ch g Zaffaran(USA) —Best Served Cherry (IRE) (Sheer Grit)
1459[3] 1543[5] 1657[2] 1859[7]

Mistified (IRE) *J W Mullins* 92+h
5 b g Ali-Royal(IRE) —Lough N Uisce (IRE) (Boyne Valley)
229[3] 451[9] 671[3] 860[8] 1018[3]1079[P] 1806[6] 2017[3] 2552[2] 3577[2]3943[3] 3997[2] 4731[3] 4912[2]

Mistify Me (IRE) *T K Geraghty* 80h
5 gr m Needle Gun(IRE) —Rosie Fort (IRE) (Roselier (FR))
2796a[5]

Mist Opportunity (IRE) *P C Haslam* 77h
4 b g Danetime(IRE) —Lady Of The Mist (IRE) (Digamist (USA))
2263[P] 2442[6] 3443[P] 3985[10] 4656[13]

Mistral De La Cour (FR) *R Ford* 93h 118c
6 bl g Panoramic—Gracieuse Delacour (FR) (Port Etienne (FR))
2183[5] 2626[2] 3207[P]3974[6] 4611[P]

Mistress Nell *A J Lidderdale* 54h
6 b m Thethingaboutitis(USA) —Neladar (Ardar)
2212[8]

Misty Dancer *Miss Venetia Williams* 112 h
121+c
7 gr g Vettori(IRE) —Light Fantastic (Deploy)
332[P] **2100[F] 2488[F]4552[2] (4664)**

Misty Future *Miss Venetia Williams* 94h 118 c
8 b g Sanglamore(USA) —Star Of The Future (USA) (El Gran Senor (USA))
2808[6] 3326[2] 3688[5]3949[U]

Misty Ramble (IRE) *Ms Jill Carenza* 95c
11 b g Roselier(FR) —Ramble Bramble (Random Shot)
281[6]

Mitey Perk (IRE) *Mrs A F Tullie*
7 b g Executive Perk—More Dash (IRE) (Strong Gale)
5093[P]

Mith Hill *Ian Williams* 115 h
5 b g Daylami(IRE) —Delirious Moment (IRE) (Kris)
3659[4] (3883) 4077[3] 5142[15]

Mixed Marriage (IRE) *Miss Victoria Roberts*
8 ch g Indian Ridge—Marie De Flandre (FR) (Crystal Palace (FR))
3719[P] 4453[P] 5028[P]

Mixmen (FR) *F Nicolle*
3 br g Pinmix(FR) —Mary Golade (FR) (Son Of Silver)
4298a[7]

Mixsterthetrixster (USA) *Mrs Tracey Barfoot-Saunt* 134dh
127+c
10 b g Alleged(USA) —Parliament House (USA) (General Assembly (USA))
97[2] 2492[9] 2760[7]3019[7] 3620[P] 4433[10]4762[10]

Mizinky *W G M Turner* 85h
6 b m El Conquistador—Miss Pimpernel (Blakeney)
3211[4] 3283[6] (3715) 3951[P]

M'Lord *J A Geake* 96+h
8 b g Mister Lord(USA) —Dishcloth (Fury Royal)
2310[5] 2868[11]

Mnason (FR) *S J Gilmore* 102 h 74c
6 gr g Simon Du Desert(FR) —Mincing (FR) (Polyfoto)
2010[P] 2525[10] **3251[8] 3465[5]**3733[P] 4322[P] 4879[14]

Moaning Myrtle *G Haine*
5 br m Desert King(IRE) —Grinning (IRE) (Bellypha)
5052[RR]

Mobasher (IRE) *Miss Venetia Williams* 137h 101+c
7 b g Spectrum(IRE) —Danse Royale (IRE) (Caerleon (USA))
2247[8] 2820[8] 2990[P] **3955[4]4279[4] 4474[F] 4633[4]4876[P]**

Mobo-Baco *R J Hodges* 51h
9 ch g Bandmaster(USA) —Darakah (Doulab (USA))
2721[13]

Mo Chailin *D A Rees* 87b
7 ch m Lyphento(USA) —Cordiglia (Newski (USA))
2075[9] 3024[5] 3461[P]

Mocharamor (IRE) *J J Lambe* 116+h
107+c
8 bb g Distinctly North(USA) —Oso Sure (IRE) (Sure Blade (USA))
43a[19] (1151) **(1334) 1511[2]1845[P]**

Mocho (IRE) *Ian Williams* 101b
5 b g Accordion—Supreme Kellycarra (IRE) (Supreme Leader)
4554[2]

Model Son (IRE) *P C Haslam* 117h 143 c
8 b g Leading Counsel(USA) —Miss Mutley (Pitpan)
422[4] **(1719) (1939) 2311[P]3971[2] 4433[4] 4764[4]5004[17]**

Modicum (USA) *N G Richards* 97b
4 b g Chester House(USA) —Wandesta (Nashwan (USA))
2068[2] 3181[3] 4588[2]

Modulor (FR) *L R James* 82h 106c
14 gr g Less Ice—Chaumontaise (FR) (Armos)
429[P]

Moffied (IRE) *J Barclay* 33b
6 b g Nashwan(USA) —Del Deya (IRE) (Caerleon (USA))
2062[P] 2947[P] 3231[P]

Mohawk Star (IRE) *Miss Venetia Williams* 100+h
5 ch g Indian Ridge—Searching Star (Rainbow Quest (USA))
82[4] 279[6] 596[4]

Mohayer (IRE) *D McCain* 67h
4 gr c Giant's Causeway(USA) —Karlafsha (Top Ville)
2013[4] 3353[3] 3842[6]

Mokujin (FR) *P F Nicholls* 79b
6 b g Kizitca(FR) —Susana (FR) (Iveday (FR))
3216[8]

Mokum (FR) *A W Carroll* 90h 103+c
5 b g Octagonal(NZ) —Back On Top (FR) (Double Bed (FR))
1827[7] 2173[16] 2878[7] 3040[6] 3358[7]3729[11] 4067[7] **4355[U] (4878) 5051[2]**

Moldavia (GER) *N B King* 80+h
5 b m Lagunas—Moricana (GER) (Konigsstuhl (GER))
279[2] 596[3] 691[6] 826[P] 4075[10]

Mole's Chamber (IRE) *V R A Dartnall* 100+b
5 b g Saddlers' Hall(IRE) —Magic Gale (IRE) (Strong Gale)
4940[2]

Mollyalice *T D Easterby* 59b
4 b f Slip Anchor—Cumbrian Rhapsody (Sharrood (USA))
4304[7]

Mollycarrsbrekfast *K Bishop* 63h 89c
11 b g Presidium—Imperial Flame (Imperial Lantern)
503[2] 665[7] **1414[5]**1637[7] **1897[3]**

Mollycarrs Gambul *Miss Sarah Robinson* 25h 93+c
7 b m General Gambul—Emma's Vision (IRE) (Vision (USA))
204[P] 594[7] 4421[4]

Molly Massini (IRE) *Gerard Quirk* 116h
6 b m Dr Massini(IRE) —Molly Maguire (IRE) (Supreme Leader)
3110a[4]

Molly McGredy *G Haine* 48b
5 b m Overbury(IRE) —Oatis Rose (Oats)
3820[9] 4059[9]

Molly's Spirit (IRE) *P R Webber* 57+h
5 br m Anshan—Native Success (IRE) (Be My Native (USA))
235[6] 3275[10] 3550[11] 3979[P]

Molostiep (FR) *Mrs Susan Nock* 82 h
6 b g Video Rock(FR) —Unetiepy (FR) (Marasali)
2211[5] (3685)

Moment Of Clarity *R C Guest*
4 b g Lujain(USA) —Kicka (Shirley Heights)
2954[P] 3539[9] 3594[9] 3925[13]

Moment Of Madness (IRE) *T J Fitzgerald* 89h 113 c
8 ch g Treasure Hunter—Sip Of Orange (Celtic Cone)
3233[2] 3379[5] 3788[3]

Moments Madness (IRE) *Miss S E Forster* 57h
7 b m Corrouge(USA) —Treble Clef (IRE) (Supreme Leader)
645[6] 785[5] 854[8]

Monanore Melody (IRE) *W Harney* 37h
8 br g Be My Native(USA) —Jasmine Melody (Jasmine Star)
117a[U]

Monash Lad (IRE) *M H Tompkins* 100h
4 ch g General Monash(USA) —Story Time (IRE) (Mansooj)
3498[4] 3594[3] 3787[4]

Monbonami (IRE) *Mrs K Waldron* 71h 101c
9 b g Beau Sher—Hard Riche (Hard Fought)
23[3] 237[P]

Mondial Jack (FR) *Mrs K Waldron* 108c
7 ch g Apple Tree(FR) —Cackle (USA) (Crow (FR))
422[3] 814[4] 1715[P] **3693[U]4051[3] 4348[5]**

Moneamon *R Johnson* 25h
7 b g Mon Tresor—De Valera (Faustus (USA))
3779[P] 4532[11]

Monet's Garden (IRE) *N G Richards* 157h 165c
8 gr g Roselier(FR) —Royal Remainder (IRE) (Remainder Man)
(2065) (3796) 4431[2](5002)

Money Line (IRE) *Jonjo O'Neill* 104 h
7 b g Roselier(FR) —Pharleng (IRE) (Phardante (FR))
1600[6] (1938) 2127[5] 2262[7] **3465[P]**3675[P]

Money Trix (IRE) *N G Richards* 148h
6 gr g Old Vic—Deer Trix (Buckskin (FR))
(3376) (3855) (4530) 4760[2]

Monger Lane *K Bishop* 112 h 106 c
10 b m Karinga Bay—Grace Moore (Deep Run)
(54) 168[6] 2184[8] **(3547) 4163[5]**

Mongino (GER) *M F Harris* 54h
5 b g In A Tiff(IRE) —Mondalita (GER) (Alkalde (GER))
1714[U] 1745[13] 1910[P] 2552[P]

Monica Rose *K G Reveley* 24b
5 b m Defacto(USA) —Keldholme (Derek H)
4507[13]

Monifieth *D W Whillans* 70h
6 b m Double Eclipse(IRE) —Parslin (The Parson)
2948[8] 3448[4] 3795[8] 4114[5] 4582[P]

Monita Des Bois (FR) *Miss Venetia Williams* 110+c
6 b m Snurge—Fauvette Grise (FR) (Epervier Bleu)
497[2] 765[5] 1599[P]

Monjoyau (FR) *E J O'Grady* 111 h 129 c
6 b g Pistolet Bleu(IRE) —Ballet Dancer (FR) (Groom Dancer (USA))
4018a[F] 4749[8]

Monkerhostin (FR) *P J Hobbs* 152h 171c
9 b g Shining Steel—Ladoun (FR) (Kaldoun (FR))
(1970) 2177[2] 2346[2]2635[4] 2972[2] 4470[6]4746[4] 4958[3]

Monks Error (IRE) *B J Llewellyn* 76h 106+c
13 b g Eve's Error—Miss Outlaw (IRE) (Lancastrian)
2073[P] **2215[P] 2575[2]**

Mon Mome (FR) *Miss Venetia Williams* 107h 143+c
6 b g Passing Sale(FR) —Etoile Du Lion (FR) (New Target)
1877[U] 1978[2] (2180) 2504[2] (2800) (3438) 4447[2] (4778) 5004[U]

Monolith *L Lungo* 132 h
8 b g Bigstone(IRE) —Ancara (Dancing Brave (USA))
1271[4] 2369[8] 3970[6] 4497[P] 5005[6]

Monroe Gold *Jennie Candlish* 70h
6 ch g Pivotal—Golden Daring (IRE) (Night Shift (USA))
2585[8] 3371[4]

Monsal Dale (IRE) *Mrs L C Jewell* 78+h 65c
7 ch g Desert King(IRE) —Zanella (IRE) (Nordico (USA))
1[5] 102[2] 2930[5] 3223[3] 3441[3]3661[7] 3899[3] 4010[8] 4526[3]

Monsieur Delage *S Gollings* 101+h
6 b g Overbury(IRE) —Sally Ho (Gildoran)
1611[3] 1885[P] 2950[P] 3595[P]

Monsieur Georges (FR) *F Jordan* 100 h 79 c
6 b g Kadalko(FR) —Djoumi (FR) (Brezzo (FR))
73[3] 1796[6] 2010[4] **2717[3]2957[P] 3547[P] 4785[P]**

Monsieur Le Chouan (FR) *T Trapenard* 101c
6 b g Turgeon(USA) —Omaha II (FR) (Saumon (FR))
1073a[P]

Monsieur Monet (IRE) *Michael Flynn* 106+h
7 b g Norwich—Sue's A Lady (Le Moss)
3408a[4]

Monsieur Rose (IRE) *N J Gifford* 88h 66c
10 gr g Roselier(FR) —Derring Slipper (Derring Rose)
231[P] 3221[7]

Monster Mick (FR) *N A Twiston-Davies* 88 h
8 b g Turgeon(USA) —The Dream I Dream (USA) (Theatrical)
137[4] 398[P] 2506[U]3359[P]

Montanah Jet *C N Kellett*
4 b g Montjoy(USA) —Nashwanah (Nashwan (USA))
3188[10] 3623[14] 3800[10] 3[P]

Montara (IRE) *Barry Potts* 62h
7 b h Perugino(USA) —Tatra (Niniski (USA))
2108[6]

Montayral (FR) *P Hughes* 127h 132c
9 b g Lesotho(USA) —Demi Lune De Mars (FR) (Fast (FR))
1700a[9] 2176[5] 4929a[13]5144[P]

Montcalm (IRE) *J G Given*
4 b f Montjeu(IRE) —Autumn Fall (USA) (Sanglamore (USA))
2949[10]

Montebank (IRE) *Mrs O Bush* 94c
10 b g Montelimar(USA) —Lady Glenbank (Tarboosh (USA))
3805[2] 4051[6]

Monte Cinto (FR) *P F Nicholls* 129 h
6 br g Bulington(FR) —Algue Rouge (FR) (Perouges (FR))
4097[4] 4375[6] 4773[4] 4986[2]

Montecorvino (GER) *N A Twiston-Davies* 92 h
5 ch g Acatenango(GER) —Manhattan Girl (USA) (Vice Regent (CAN))
(3275) 3687^{7} 4012^{P} 4557^{P}

Monte Cristo (FR) *Mrs L C Taylor* 109h 129+c
8 ch g Bigstone(IRE) —El Quahirah (FR) (Cadoudal (FR))
109^{7} 2734^{8}

Monteforte *J A B Old* 117+h 117+c
8 b g Alflora(IRE) —Double Dutch (Nicholas Bill)
3018^{P} **4279^{2} 4610^{F}**

Montemoss (IRE) *B N Pollock* 100h 100c
9 ch g Montelimar(USA) —Gaye Le Moss (Le Moss)
1854^{P} **1960^{P}**

Montenda *S C Burrough* 73h
5 ch g Classic Cliche(IRE) —Polly Leach (Pollerton)
4327^{10} 4569^{10} 5106^{6}

Monterey Bay (IRE) *Ms F M Crowley* 110h 125c
10 ch g Montelimar(USA) —Glowing Embers (Nebbiolo)
(112a) 1515a^{2} 2539a^{3} 4929a^{P} 5102a^{2}

Monte Rosa (IRE) *N G Richards* 96 h
7 b m Supreme Leader—Green Thorn (IRE) (Ovac (ITY))
85^{3} 5039^{F}

Montesino *M Madgwick* 106h
7 b g Bishop Of Cashel—Sutosky (Great Nephew)
2969^{P} 3345^{P} 4570^{2} 4731^{11}

Montevideo *Jonjo O'Neill* 109 h
6 b g Sadler's Wells(USA) —Montessori (Akarad (FR))
1399^{F} 2166^{14} 2595^{F} 2871^{12} 3792^{4}

Monte Vista (IRE) *Jonjo O'Neill* 140h 123+c
9 b g Montelimar(USA) —Tarqogan's Rose (Tarqogan)
1917^{6} 2701^{F} 3331^{2}

Montezuma *Ms Kim Holmes* 69c
13 br m Beveled(USA) —Miss Kuwait (The Brianstan)
4560^{U}

Montgermont (FR) *Mrs L C Taylor* 115h 145+c
6 b g Useful(FR) —Blowin'In The Wind (FR) (Saint Cyrien (FR))
1669^{2} 1891^{2} 2488^{3}(3215) (3976) 4759^{5}

Monticelli (GER) *P J Hobbs* 126+h 104+c
6 b g Pelder(IRE) —Marcelia (GER) (Priamos (GER))
247^{10} (726) 1010^{P} (1263) **1509^{3} 1726^{5}**

Montifault (FR) *Andy Carter* 132c
11 ch g Morespeed—Tarde (FR) (Kashtan (FR))
48^{P} 313^{2} 727^{4}4960^{P} 4594^{P}

Monti Flyer *S B Clark* 101h 97c
8 b g Terimon—Coole Pilate (Celtic Cone)
1488^{P} **1609^{P} 1761^{F}**

Montpelier (IRE) *Ms A E Embiricos* 112c
13 b g Montelimar(USA) —Liscarton (Le Bavard (FR))
108^{F}

Montreal (FR) *M C Pipe* 140h 111 c
9 bb g Chamberlin(FR) —Massada (FR) (Kashtan (FR))
423^{6} 653^{5} 727^{6}1189^{3} 1265^{9} 1550^{10}1728^{8}

Montrolin *S C Burrough* 62h
6 ch g Classic Cliche(IRE) —Charmed I'm Sure (Nicholas Bill)
2427^{9} 3611^{4} 4032^{8}

Mont Saint Michel (IRE) *Miss Clare Judith Macmahon* 98h
4 b c Montjeu(IRE) —Band Of Angels (IRE) (Alzao (USA))
3515a^{5}

Montu *Miss K M George* 95b 53c
9 ch g Gunner B—Promitto (Roaring Riva)
3326^{P} 3950^{P} **5074^{6}**

Monty Be Quick *J M Castle* 84h 66c
10 ch g Mon Tresor—Spartiquick (Spartan General)
357^{P} **(532) 672^{7} 865^{P}948^{7} 1044^{8} 4014^{6}4323^{5} 4460^{P} 4650^{P}**

Monty Mint (IRE) *Thomas Foley* 65h
8 b g Broken Hearted—Montetan (IRE) (Montelimar (USA))
2667a^{P}

Montys Island (IRE) *C J Mann* 87+h 103+c
9 b g Montelimar(USA) —Sea Island (Windjammer (USA))
271^{3}

Monty's Quest (IRE) *M Smith* 89h 123 c
11 b g Montelimar(USA) —A Bit Of Luck (IRE) (Good Thyne (USA))
2841^{5} 3377^{4} 3560^{P}

Monty's Salvo (USA) *N J Henderson* 69h
7 bb g Supreme Leader—Likashot (Celtic Cone)
629^{6}

Montys Tag (IRE) *S R Andrews* 102c
13 b g Montelimar(USA) —Herbal Lady (Good Thyne (USA))
184^{F} 350^{2} 4607^{2}4901^{2}

Monzon (FR) *B G Powell* 83h
6 b g Kadalko(FR) —Queenly (FR) (Pot D'Or (FR))
4284^{P} 5086^{3}

Moon Catcher *D Brace* 109h
5 b m Kahyasi—Moonlight Saunter (USA) (Woodman (USA))
329^{6} 1482^{P} 1658^{7} 1677^{8} 4731^{2}5108^{5}

Moondancer (GER) *B G Powell*
7 br g General Assembly(USA) —Miskinissa (GER) (Esclavo (FR))
2423^{15}

Moon Emperor *J R Jenkins* 108 h 103 c
9 b g Emperor Jones(USA) —Sir Hollow (USA) (Sir Ivor (USA))
1987^{13}

Moonfleet (IRE) *M F Harris* 90+h
4 b f Entrepreneur—Lunasa (IRE) (Don't Forget Me)
1338^{2} (1397) 1478^{2} 1873^{4}

Moonlit Harbour *Ferdy Murphy* 106+c
7 b g Bal Harbour—Nuit De Lune (FR) (Crystal Palace (FR))
2168^{3} 2677^{F} 3558^{F}3850^{5} 4583^{3} 4906^{5}

Moon Mist *N W Alexander* 62 c
8 gr m Accondy(IRE) —Lillie's Brig (New Brig)
2267^{5} 3209^{2} **3444^{F}4042^{P} 4361^{P}**

Moon Over Miami (GER) *C J Mann* 122+h
5 b g Dashing Blade—Miss Esther (GER) (Alkalde (GER))
4621^{4} 4763^{8}

Moonshine Gap *R Ford* 56b
6 b g Millkom—Blossomville (Petong)
1688^{5} *1922^{10}*

Moonshine Surprise (IRE) *M C Pipe* 77+h 71c
6 b g Moonax(IRE) —Balliniska Beauty (IRE) (Roselier (FR))
2147^{2} **2581^{3}**

Moonshine Vixen *P W Hiatt* 76b
5 ch m Deploy—Monongelia (Welsh Pageant)
1274^{4}

Moon Shot *A G Juckes*
10 gr g Pistolet Bleu(IRE) —La Luna (USA) (Lyphard (USA))
2^{9} 286^{3} 510^{6}692^{F}

Moonside *J A Geake*
4 gr f Dockside(USA) —Moon Magic (Polish Precedent (USA))
1380^{5}

Moonzie Laird (IRE) *Miss Lucinda V Russell* 74+h
8 bb g Good Thyne(USA) —Sweet Roselier (IRE) (Roselier (FR))
1938 ^{P} 2169^{P} **4112^{P} 4314^{F}**

Mooramana *P Beaumont* 91+h 103+c
7 ch g Alflora(IRE) —Petit Primitive (Primitive Rising (USA))
209^{2} 553^{2} 718^{3} **990^{2}**

Mooresini (IRE) *N J Gifford* 87h
6 b g Dr Massini(IRE) —Mooreshill (IRE) (Le Moss)
2212^{6} 2683^{P} 2928^{7} 3279^{3} 3424^{P}4080^{P}

Moore's Law (USA) *M J Grassick* 126h
8 b g Technology(USA) —Brass Needles (USA) (Twice Worthy (USA))
3894a^{3} 5059a^{4}

Moorland Monarch *J D Frost* 82h 87+c
8 b g Morpeth—Moorland Nell (Neltino)
74^{4} 1637^{2} **1983^{7}2313^{2} 3126^{4} 3482^{5}4053^{P}**

Moorlands Again *M Sheppard* 115+h 130+c
11 b g Then Again—Sandford Springs (USA) (Robellino (USA))
1711^{2} 1830^{P} **2210^{8} (2662) 2819^{4} 3396^{2} (4098) 4617^{U} 4957^{12}**

Moorlands Milly *D Burchell* 77h
5 b m Sooty Tern—Sandford Springs (USA) (Robellino (USA))
1445^{4} 1680^{7} 1851^{7} 2822^{9} 3321^{P}

Moorlands Return *Evan Williams* 96+h
7 b g Bob's Return(IRE) —Sandford Springs (USA) (Robellino (USA))
801^{6} 977^{8}

Moor Lane *A M Balding* 116c
14 b g Primitive Rising(USA) —Navos (Tyrnavos)
204^{P}

Moorlaw (IRE) *D McCain* 96h 97 c
5 b g Mtoto—Belle Etoile (FR) (Lead On Time (USA))
243^{7} 415^{13} **1726^{8} 2246^{F}2751^{3} 3844^{F} 3920^{F}**4613^{6} 1^{5}

Moor Spirit *P Beaumont* 118+c
9 b g Nomadic Way(USA) —Navos (Tyrnavos)
(3379) 3922^{U} 4419^{P}4850^{4} 5067^{P}

Moral Justice (IRE) *S J Gilmore* 72c
13 b g Lafontaine(USA) —Proven Right (IRE) (Kemal (FR))
815^{6} 997^{5}

Moratorium (USA) *Noel Meade* 126h
11 b g El Gran Senor(USA) —Substance (USA) (Diesis)
1093a^{12}

More Equity *Mrs A F Tullie* 57b
4 b f Classic Cliche(IRE) —Sillymore (Silly Prices)
3799^{10} 4533^{9}

More Flair *J B Walton* 44b 81+c
9 ch m Alflora(IRE) —Marejo (Creetown)
2496^{3} 2839^{U} 2975^{7}3796^{3} 4041^{U} 4518^{3}4719^{P}

More Likely *Mrs A F Tullie* 96h
5 b m Shambo—Admire-A-More (Le Coq D'Or)
2446^{12} 3319^{4} 3376^{3} 3795^{6} (4342) 4529^{7}4787^{5}

More Rainbows (IRE) *Noel Meade* 125h
6 b g Rainbows For Life(CAN) —Musical Myth (USA) (Crafty Prospector (USA))
954a^{6} (1093a)

More Trouble (IRE) *P R Webber* 88b
5 b g Zaffaran(USA) —Athas Liath (IRE) (Roselier (FR))
4881^{7}

Morgan Be *Mrs K Walton* 121+h
6 b g Alderbrook—Vicie (Old Vic)
1231^{P} 1915^{9} 2006^{3} 2631^{4} 3205^{2}(3532) (4344)

Morgan's Money *R T Phillips*
7 ch g Karinga Bay—Another Rumour (The Parson)
4786^{7}

Moritz (FR) *K G Reveley* 27b
6 b g Video Rock(FR) —Nivernaise (FR) (Laniste)
2720^{13} 3677^{P}

Morning Roses *K G Reveley* 72b
4 b f Overbury(IRE) —Society News (Law Society (USA))
4304^{3} 4800^{6}

Morph *E W Morris* 78h
12 gr g Baron Blakeney—Amber Marsh (Arctic Kanda)
79^{F}

Morson Boy (USA) *Mrs K Waldron* 98h
6 b g Lear Fan(USA) —Esprit D'Escalier (USA) (Diesis)
(273) 501^{2}

Mortar *R Rowe* 47b
7 b g Weld—Rockmount Rose (Proverb)
3664^{P} 4128^{10}

Mort De Rire (FR) *R H Alner* 130 c
6 gr g Luchiroverte(IRE) —Fia Rosa (FR) (Royal Charter (FR))
(3331) 3740^{3}

Moscow Ali (IRE) *Miss Lucinda V Russell*
6 ch g Moscow Society(USA) —Down The Bog (IRE) (Down The Hatch)
2062^{13} 2901^{P} 3532^{P}

Moscow Blue *Robert Gray* 105dh
5 ch g Soviet Star(USA) —Aquamarine (Shardari)
(1231) 1410^{7} 3559^{8} 3780^{P}

Moscow Court (IRE) *Mrs David Plunkett* 121h 116c
8 b g Moscow Society(USA) —Hogan Stand (Buckskin (FR))
4880^{2} 6^{4}

Moscow Dancer (IRE) *P Monteith* 109+h 122c
9 ch g Moscow Society(USA) —Cromhill Lady (Miner's Lamp)
60^{6} (318) (409) 767^{P}855^{3} 1012^{U} 1292^{2}

Moscow Executive *W M Brisbourne* 72h
8 b m Moscow Society(USA) —Stylish Executive (IRE) (Executive Perk)
843^{7} 976^{3} 1097^{4} 1202^{5} 1317^{3}

Moscow Flyer (IRE) *Mrs John Harrington* 170h 180 c
12 b g Moscow Society(USA) —Meelick Lady (IRE) (Duky)
41a^{2} 2230a^{2} 3051a^{4}4445^{5}

Moscow Gold (IRE) *A E Price* 59h 87+c
9 ch g Moscow Society(USA) —Vesper Time (The Parson)
1776^{4} 2561^{2} (2807) (2936) 4908^{U} 5074^{5}

Moscow Leader (IRE) *R T Phillips* 107h 102 c
8 ch g Moscow Society(USA) —Catrionas Castle (IRE) (Orchestra)
2259^{6} 2495^{2} 2748^{5}2955^{5} 3654^{7} 3915^{2}4876^{P}

Moscow Parade (IRE) *Michael Hourigan* 89h 55c
8 b g Moscow Society(USA) —Corrie Lough (IRE) (The Parson)
71a^{12} (Dead)

Moscow Summit (IRE) *E McNamara* 88h
8 b g Moscow Society(USA) —Rath Caola (Neltino)
2140^{2} 2687^{2}

Moscowtastic (IRE) *S J Robinson* 62c
8 ch g Moscow Society(USA) —Martialette (Welsh Saint)
4044^{4} 4660^{F}

Moscow Whisper (IRE) *P J Hobbs* 113 h 120+c
9 b g Moscow Society(USA) —Native Woodfire (IRE) (Mister Majestic)
(296) 1678^{F} 1972^{U}2633^{6} **3212^{4}** 4372^{8} 4727^{3}

Mose Harper (IRE) *Thomas O'Neill* 98h 46c
14 b g Supreme Leader—Miss Rockaway (Le Moss)
87a^{P}

Mossbank (IRE) *Michael Hourigan* 132h
6 b g Kadeed(IRE) —Miromaid (Simply Great (FR))
2909a^{3} 3892a^{5} 4888a^{F} 5132a^{5}

Moss Bawn (IRE) *B Storey* 114h 88c
10 b g Jurado(USA) —Boylan (Buckskin (FR))
1592^{6} 1686^{P} 2022^{4}2679^{6}

Moss Campian *Mrs A V Roberts* 33h
8 ch g Le Moss—Rose Rambler (Scallywag)
1634^{4} 1719^{P}

Moss Harvey *J G M O'Shea* 140 c
11 ch g Le Moss—Wings Ground (Murrayfield)
1759^{P}

Mossy Green (IRE) *W P Mullins* 146h 149c
12 b g Moscow Society(USA) —Green Ajo (Green Shoon)
41a^{6} 3472a^{2}

Mostakbel (USA) *M D I Usher* 35h
7 bb g Saint Ballado(CAN) —Shamlegh (USA) (Flying Paster (USA))
1908^{P} 2343^{8} 2584^{P} 3673^{P}

Motcombe (IRE) *R H Alner* 93+h 107+c
8 ch m Carroll House—Cooks Lawn (The Parson)
(2297) 2529^{8} 3241^{F}3676^{4} 3981^{2} (4328) 4495^{4}

Mother Says *B W Duke* 78b
10 b g Landyap(USA) —Miami Blues (Palm Track)
2212^{13}

Motive (FR) *J Howard Johnson* 124 h
5 ch g Machiavellian(USA) —Mistle Song (Nashwan (USA))
2904^{2} (3171) 3761^{6}

Motorway (IRE) *P J Hobbs* 129+h
5 b g Night Shift(USA) —Tadkiyra (IRE) (Darshaan)
1527^{3} (1875) (2533) (2746) 2969^{F} (4608) 4765^{14} 5142^{5}

Mouftari (USA) *C Byrnes* 108h
5 b h Miswaki(USA) —Nature's Magic (USA) (Nijinsky (CAN))
2166^{2}

Moulin Riche (FR) *F Doumen* 146+h 143+c
6 b g Video Rock(FR) —Gintonique (FR) (Royal Charter (FR))
2758^{F} **4070^{2} 4433^{P}**

Mounsey Castle *P J Hobbs* 110h 114c
9 ch g Carlingford Castle—Gay Ticket (New Member)
489^{8} 2143^{7} 4737^{5}

Mountain Approach *Jean-Rene Auvray* 89b
4 b f Kayf Tara—Fortunes Course (IRE) (Crash Course)
4976^{6}

Mountain Mayhem (IRE) *M G Rimell* 88h
8 br g Be My Native(USA) —Arctic Lucy (Lucifer (USA))
2322^{5}

Mountain Mix *Mrs L B Normile* 77b
6 ch g Bigstone(IRE) —Cormorant Bay (Don't Forget Me)
3237^{7} 3855^{P} 4582^{P} 4988^{P} 5063^{11}

Mountain Of Dreams *R H York* 83b
4 ch g Primitive Rising(USA) —Coraletta (Buckley)
4881^{6}

Mountain Snow (IRE) *W P Mullins* 109+h
6 ch g Barathea(IRE) —Mountains Of Mist (IRE) (Shirley Heights)
5078a^{8}

Mount Arafat *M Salaman*
4 bb g Erhaab(USA) —Cache (Bustino)
1380^{U} 1594^{P}

Mount Benger *Mrs A J Hamilton-Fairley* 81h
6 ch g Selkirk(USA) —Vice Vixen (CAN) (Vice Regent (CAN))
1680^{P} 1975^{6} 2148^{6} 5111^{4}

Mount Butler (IRE) *J W Tudor* 46h
4 b g Celtic Swing—Baylands Sunshine (IRE) (Classic Secret (USA))
4550^{9} 4733^{8} 5110^{11}

Mount Clerigo (IRE) *V R A Dartnall* 128 h 132c
8 b g Supreme Leader—Fair Ava (IRE) (Strong Gale)
1830^{4} **(2464) 2869^{F} 3331^{3}4374^{P} 4498^{2} 4764^{P}**

Mount Ephram (IRE) *R F Fisher*
4 b g Entrepreneur—Happy Dancer (USA) (Seattle Dancer (USA))
1904^{P}

Mounthenry (IRE) *C Byrnes* 139h
6 ch g Flemensfirth(USA) —Tudor Lady (Green Shoon)
2667a^{3} (3772a) (4336a) 4888a^{2} 5132a^{2}

Mounthooley *B Mactaggart* 84h 82c
10 ch g Karinga Bay—Gladys Emmanuel (Idiots Delight)
301^{6} **593^{4} 858^{6}2063^{2} 2654^{P} 5119^{6}**

Mount Karinga *P F Nicholls* 128h 136c
8 b g Karinga Bay—Candarela (Damister (USA))
1669^{P}

Mount Kimble (IRE) *P Winkworth* 108h 109c
10 b g Montelimar(USA) —Sweet Thunder (Le Bavard (FR))
103^{3} 505^{P} 815^{P}

Mount Pekan (IRE) *J S Goldie* 62h
6 b g Sri Pekan(USA) —The Highlands (FR) (High Line)
9^{20}

Mount Sandel (IRE) *O Sherwood* 105b
5 b g Supreme Leader—Droichidin (Good Thyne (USA))
3742^{2} 4244^{4} (4807)

Mounts Bay *R J Hodges* 83h
7 ch m Karinga Bay—Sweet On Willie (USA) (Master Willie)
2140^{7}

Mountsorrel (IRE) *T Wall* 30h
7 b g Charnwood Forest(IRE) —Play The Queen (IRE) (King Of Clubs)
1318^{P}

Mount Vernon (IRE) *P Wegmann* 68h
10 b g Darshaan—Chellita (Habitat)
2624 ^{P} 2816^{17}

Mount Vettore *K G Reveley* 88h
5 br g Vettori(IRE) —Honeyspike (IRE) (Chief's Crown (USA))
1481^{9} 1604^{RR}

Mouseski *P F Nicholls* 116 h 150c
12 b g Petoski—Worth Matravers (National Trust)
1265^{12} (1675) 1984^{2} 2166^{4} 2621^{3}2974^{5} 3987^{3} 4357^{U} 4497^{P}

Moustique De L'Isle (FR) *C C Bealby* 102+h 109+c
6 gr g Dom Alco(FR) —Gratiene de l'Isle (FR) (Altayan)
1609^{2} (2077) 2529^{5}(2862) **2965^{P}** 3581^{11} 3982^{9} 4453^{3}(4658) **5122^{3}**

Move Over (IRE) *R C Guest* 100 h 113+c
11 ch g Buckskin(FR) —Move Forward (Deep Run)
(4300) 4518^{P} 4790^{4}4843^{8} 5037^{U} 5071^{10}

Movie King (IRE) *S R Bowring* 94 h
7 ch g Catrail(USA) —Marilyn (IRE) (King's Lake (USA))
1553^{7} 1607^{4} 3943^{RR}

Moving Earth (IRE) *C E Ward* 100c
13 b g Brush Aside(USA) —Park Breeze (IRE) (Strong Gale)
(311) 727^{3} 1025^{5}1248^{4} **3960^{3} 4748^{9}**

Moving On Up *C N Kellett* 73h
12 b g Salse(USA) —Thundercloud (Electric)
1^{8} 458^{11} **3549^{P}** 3889^{12}4012^{P}

Moyliscar *Capt J A George* 89+c
7 b m Terimon—Annie Kelly (Oats)
2074^{P} 2297^{5}

Moyne Pleasure (IRE) *R Johnson* 88h
8 b g Exit To Nowhere(USA) —Ilanga (IRE) (Common Grounds)
1938 ^{P} 2447^{4} 2652^{7} 3169^{3} (3552) 4302^{8}4487^{6} 4794^{2}

Mr Albanello (ARG) *Ferdy Murphy* 73h
7 b g Southern Halo(USA) —Heiress (USA) (Greinton)
1794^{6} 1937^{7} 2749^{9} 5120^{10}

Mr Attitude *W S Coltherd* 39h 80+c
6 b g Respect—Leighten Lass (IRE) (Henbit (USA))
3374^{10} 3912^{11} 4342^{P} **5121^{6}**

Mr Auchterlonie (IRE) *L Lungo* 93h 109c
9 b g Mister Lord(USA) —Cahernane Girl (Bargello)
317^{6}

Mr Babbage (IRE) *W P Mullins* 124h 134c
8 b g Carroll House—Winsome Doe (Buckskin (FR))
92a^{7} **2668a^{4} 3079a^{F}4022a^{5} 4460^{U}** (Dead)

Mr Banker *N Bush* 82 c
11 b g Cashwyn—Flaming Fox (Healaugh Fox)
101^{P} 4079^{4} 4560^{P}

Mr Bashir (IRE) *N B King*
7 ch g John French—Cuckaloo (Master Buck)
2581^{P}

Mr Bently *J D Frost*
7 b g Morpeth—Celtic Mist (Celtic Cone)
1959^{P}

Mr Bigglesworth (NZ) *R C Guest* 109 h 109 c
8 ch g Honor Grades(USA) —Panza Anne (NZ) (Sound Reason (CAN))
(9) **(95)** (197) **479^{2}**

Mr Bill *D B Feek*
6 ch g Cosmonaut—Latch On (IRE) (Dance Of Life (USA))
23[P]

Mr Boo (IRE) *G L Moore* 104h 132+c
7 b g Needle Gun(IRE) —Dasi (Bonne Noel)
4076[6] (4522) (4822) (4870) 5127[F]

Mr Buddy (IRE) *J Howard Johnson*
5 b h Zaffaran(USA) —Witchy Native (IRE) (Be My Native (USA))
3963[P] 4657[P]

Mr Cavallo (IRE) *Miss Lucinda V Russell* 86h 93c
14 b g The Bart(USA) —Mrs Guru (Le Bavard (FR))
417[7] 1310[P]

Mr Cee *Mrs S J Smith* 78b
6 b g Gothenberg(IRE) —Hobbs Choice (Superpower)
1237[8] 1491[U]

Mr Christie *Miss L C Siddall* 88h
14 b g Doulab(USA) —Hi There (High Top)
80[7]

Mr Cool *M C Pipe* 144h 148c
12 b g Jupiter Island—Laurel Diver (Celtic Cone)
(207) 1548[8] 1828[4] 2326[4] 2490[6]

Mr Cooney (IRE) *J Clements* 65c
12 b g Van Der Linden(FR) —Green Orchid (Green Shoon)
322[7] 594[U] 872[4]

Mr Cospector *D L Williams* 124h 136+c
9 b g Cosmonaut—L'Ancressaan (Dalsaan)
2215[P] (Dead)

Mr Crawford *Nick Williams* 10h 37c
7 b g Opera Ghost—Alice Passthorn (Rapid Pass)
1983[P] 2217[R] 2313[9]3499[P]

Mrdeegeethegeegee (IRE) *E W Tuer* 76b
4 b g Sadler's Wells(USA) —Department (USA) (Secretariat (USA))
5124[8]

Mr Dinglawi (IRE) *D B Feek* 123+h
5 b g Danehill Dancer(IRE) —Princess Leona (IRE) (Naiyli (IRE))
1828[13]

Mr Dip *L A Dace* 76h
6 b g Reprimand—Scottish Lady (Dunbeath (USA))
294[3] 394[6] 742[P] 913[8] 1040[6]1949[7] 2214[7]

Mr Dow Jones (IRE) *W K Goldsworthy* 114h 120c
14 b g The Bart(USA) —Roseowen (Derring Rose)
4857[8]

Mr Ed (IRE) *P Bowen* 152+h 138c
8 ch g In The Wings—Center Moriches (IRE) (Magical Wonder (USA))
207[2] **(872) 944[F] 1096[2]1265[5]**

Mr Ex (ARG) *G L Moore* 84+h
5 b g Numerous(USA) —Express Toss (ARG) (Egg Toss (USA))
1274[3] 1600[3] (1777) 2020[3] 2374[8] 2865[7]

Mr Eye Popper (IRE) *J T Stimpson* 67h
7 b g Sadler's Wells(USA) —Tipperary Tartan (Rarity)
861[P]

Mr Fast (ARG) *J Gallagher*
9 ch g Numerous(USA) —Speediness (ARG) (Etienne Gerard)
4638[P] **2[P]**

Mr Fernet *M F Harris* 98+h
9 b g Mtoto—Francfurter (Legend Of France (USA))
102[P] (232) 871[5] (1027)

Mr Fisher (IRE) *D Burchell* 75h
9 ch g Toulon—Parthian Opera (Dalsaan)
1298[6] 1539[9] 1753[F]

Mr Flowers (IRE) *Miss S Barkley* 37b 110c
14 b g Cardinal Flower—Miss Monksfield (Monksfield)
45a[14]

Mr Fluffy *A W Carroll* 121+h 128c
9 br g Charmer—Hinton Bairn (Balinger)
(751) 814[U] 1016[P] 1270[P] **1735[3]5144[F]**

Mr Freeze (IRE) *J T Stimpson*
6 b g Silver Hawk(USA) —Iviza (IRE) (Sadler's Wells (USA))
4574[12]

Mr Hawkeye (USA) *Mrs A Hamilton* 16c
7 ch g Royal Academy(USA) —Port Plaisance (USA) (Woodman (USA))
4044[P]

Mr Ironman *R C Guest* 26h
5 ch g Jendali(USA) —Carly-J (Cruise Missile)
2268[4] 3657[8] 4992[7]

Mr Jake *H E Haynes* 71c
13 b g Safawan—Miss Tealeaf (USA) (Lear Fan (USA))
276[P] 565[4] 744[7]

Mr Jawbreaker (IRE) *J T Stimpson* 90+b
7 b g Sadler's Wells(USA) —Abury (IRE) (Law Society (USA))
685[2] 817[2] 917[3] 1042[3] 1158[U]1222[P]

Mr Kalandi (IRE) *P W D'Arcy* 67h
4 gr c Grand Lodge(USA) —Singhana (IRE) (Mouktar)
945[5]

Mr Laggan *Miss Kate Milligan* 75c
11 b g Tina's Pet—Galway Gal (Proverb)
416[5] 605[3] 717[3]896[5] 1684[2] 2900[5]3486[8]

Mr Lear (USA) *J J Quinn* 111+h
7 b g Lear Fan(USA) —Majestic Mae (USA) (Crow (FR))
552[5] 784[4] 1444[3] 1604[P]

Mr Lehman *J D Frost* 73h
9 ch g Presidium—Lehmans Lot (Oats)
1745[10]

Mr Lewin *D McCain* 93h
5 ch g Primo Dominie—Fighting Run (Runnett)
3[4] 1824[5] 2462[6] **2872[U]**

Mr Mahdlo *B R Woodhouse* 103c
12 b g Rakaposhi King—Fedelm (Celtic Cone)
453[P] 4725[3]

Mr Marucci (USA) *B Ellison* 72+h
4 b g Miner's Mark(USA) —Appealing Style (USA) (...al (USA))

Mr Maxim *R M Whitaker* 65h
4 ch g Lake Coniston(IRE) —White Hare (Indian Ridge)
1821[3]

Mr Mayfair (IRE) *Miss L Day* 63h
4 ch g Entrepreneur—French Gift (Cadeaux Genereux)
4015[P] 4416[P] 4550[8] 5024[4]

Mr McAuley (IRE) *I R Ferguson* 108h 112c
8 b g Denel(FR) —Dusty Lane (IRE) (Electric)
2764[6] 2943[2] 3352[P]5082a[4]

Mr McDellon (IRE) *J F Panvert* 31h 85c
9 ch g Duky—Erin Brownie (Seclude (USA))
2682[U]

Mr Meyer (IRE) *S Donohoe* 95h 112c
9 b g Alphabatim(USA) —Parsons Alert (IRE) (The Parson)
3929[P]

Mr Micky (IRE) *M B Shears* 56h
8 b g Rudimentary(USA) —Top Berry (High Top)
2377[P] 2845[P] 4903[11] **5114[4]**

Mr Midaz *D W Whillans* 107+h
7 ch g Danzig Connection(USA) —Marmy (Midyan (USA))
64[8] 3206[3] (3445)

Mr Mighty (IRE) *G R Pewter* 80c
10 br g Montelimar(USA) —Laurie Belle (Boreen (FR))
944[2] 1210[P]

Mr Mischief *P C Haslam* 120+h
6 b g Millkom—Snow Huntress (Shirley Heights)
(21) (192) 312[3] 1528[2] (1571) 1854[2] 3780[2]

Mr Nemo (IRE) *Evan Williams* 31b 112+c
10 b g Doubletour(USA) —Snowdrifter (Strong Gale)
1219[P] 1359[6]

Mr Nick (IRE) *N J Gifford* 94b
6 b g Naheez(USA) —Brave Express (Brave Invader (USA))
1882[3]

Mr Nosie (IRE) *Noel Meade* 142h
5 b g Alphabatim(USA) —Cromogue Lady (Golden Love)
(3052a) (3892a) 4443[4]

Mr Parson (IRE) *S T Lewis* 39b
6 b g Bob Back(USA) —Queenie Kelly (The Parson)
300[13] 655[13] 917[10] 2987[14] 5073[P]

Mr Pilchard *Mrs S Lamyman*
6 gr g Terimon—Reel Rascal (Scallywag)
691[10]

Mr Pointment (IRE) *C R Egerton* 141h
7 b g Old Vic—Bettyhill (Ardross)
(2295) 2829[4] (3957) 4443[5]

Mr Postman *M Scudamore* 87b
5 ch g Private Despatch(USA) —Palm Lady (Palm Track)
4595[9]

Mr President (GER) *Miss Venetia Williams* 114h
7 br g Surako(GER) —Mostly Sure (IRE) (Sure Blade (USA))
3383[7]

Mr Prickle (IRE) *P Beaumont* 91h 115c
6 ch g Carroll House—Auntie Prickle Pin (IRE) (Sexton Blake)
545[8] **2975[4] 3444[3](3915) 4502[2] 4721[8]**

Mr Rhubarb (IRE) *C J Drewe* 17h
8 ch g Shardari—Gale Griffin (IRE) (Strong Gale)
75[P] 279[R] 2298[P] 2578[P] 3687[11]4128[9]

Mrs Be (IRE) *J G Cann* 97b 118c
10 ch m Be My Native(USA) —Kilbrack (Perspex)
49[3] (231) (453) 4098[4]4434[9] 4944[4]

Mrs Fizziwig *R T Phillips* 87b
7 b m Petoski—Dans Le Vent (Pollerton)
3342[F] 4099[F] 4324[F] 4603[P]

Mrs Goldfarb *Miss Venetia Williams* 87b
7 b m Alderbrook—Chacewater (Electric)
2727[2]

Mr Shambles *S Gollings* 102b
5 ch g Karinga Bay—Urban Lily (Town And Country)
3657[2] 4853[12] 5141[7]

Mrs Higham (IRE) *M Scudamore* 69b
5 ch m Pasternak—Crowther Homes (Neltino)
3145[5] 3435[9] 4609[P]

Mr Smithers Jones *Mrs S M Johnson* 80h
6 br g Emperor Jones(USA) —Phylian (Glint Of Gold)
2624 [6] 2859[P] 4071[7] 4569[13] 4826[10]

Mrs O'Malley *D McCain* 78b
6 b m Overbury(IRE) —Chapel Hill (IRE) (The Parson)
2727[5] 3448[5] 3497[6] 4751[17]

Mrs Philip *P J Hobbs* 93h
7 b m Puissance—Lightning Legacy (USA) (Super Concorde (USA))
1125[P] 1482[3] **1656[6]** 1784[10]1900[9]

Mrs Pickles *M D I Usher* 87h
11 gr m Northern Park(USA) —Able Mabel (Absalom)
1949[5] 2341[4] 2609[P] 2845[8]

Mr Splodge *Mrs T J Hill* 41h 120+c
12 b g Gildoran—Ethels Course (Crash Course)
(50) (1484) 1874[P]

Mrs Ritchie *Mrs S Lamyman* 94h
9 b m Teenoso(USA) —Material Girl (Busted)
468[P]

Mrs Sherman *Miss C Pennycook* 59h 59c
11 b m Derrylin—Temporary Affair (Mandalus)
123[P]

Mr Strachan (IRE) *Mrs S J Smith* 94b
5 b g Zaffaran(USA) —Call Girl (IRE) (Dromod Hill)
4854[6]

Mr Strowger *J C Fox*
5 b h Dancing Spree(USA) —Matoaka (Be My Chief (USA))
3945[P]

Mrs Wallensky (IRE) *Paul Nolan* 114h 91c
8 gr m Roselier(FR) —Shannon Dee (IRE) (Supreme Leader)
66a[12] 3110a[3]

Mrs White (IRE) *M S Wilesmith* 61b
6 b m Alflora(IRE) —Annicombe Run (Deep Run)
490[15]

Mr Tambourine Man (IRE) *B J Llewellyn* 75h
5 b g Rainbow Quest(USA) —Girl From Ipanema (Salse (USA))
3127[13] 3463[9] 3878[10] 4941[3]

Mr Tee Pee (IRE) *M C Pipe* 69b
6 b g Norwich—Msadi Mhulu (IRE) (Kambalda)
1459[5]

Mr Tim (IRE) *L Lungo* 99h
8 br g Naheez(USA) —Ari's Fashion (Aristocracy)
301[7] 2448[3] 2693[3]

Mr Twins (ARG) *M A Barnes* 85+h
5 ch g Numerous(USA) —Twins Parade (ARG) (Parade Marshal (USA))
1360[7] 1591[5] 1793[5] 1940 [8] 2066[7]2416[7] 4723[10] 5135[2]

Mr Viaillie (IRE) *Karen McLintock* 80b
4 b g Kayf Tara—Formidable Task (Formidable (USA))
3353[5] 5041[4]

Mr Whizz *A P Jones*
9 ch g Manhal—Panienka (POL) (Dom Racine (FR))
747[6] 1248[5]

Mr Wonderful (IRE) *P O'Connor* 43h
8 ch g Shernazar—Time To Smile (IRE) (Good Thyne (USA))
860[11] 1002[P] 1100[P] **1618[P]**

Mr Woodentop (IRE) *Dave Parker* 133h 133c
10 b g Roselier(FR) —Una's Polly (Pollerton)
(4846)

Mr Woodland *Miss L Gardner* 116h 110c
12 br g Landyap(USA) —Wood Corner (Sit In The Corner (USA))
4730[P]

Ms Freebee *M Mullineaux* 44b
7 ch m Gunner B—Luckifosome (Smackover)
742[P] 1047[P] 1097[P]

Mt Desert *C J Mann* 104h
4 b g Rainbow Quest(USA) —Chief Bee (Chief's Crown (USA))
3[3]

Muckle Flugga (IRE) *N G Richards* 102+h
7 ch m Karinga Bay—Dancing Dove (IRE) (Denel (FR))
(334) 2566[7] 3234[B] 4364[F] 5096[2]

Muckshifter *P A Blockley* 56b
5 b g Topanoora—Melody Maid (Strong Gale)
4644[8]

Muffler *J G M O'Shea* 21h
8 b h Next Boom(USA) —Public Offering (Warrshan (USA))
133[P] 396[8]

Mughas (IRE) *A King* 148+h
7 b g Sadler's Wells(USA) —Quest Of Passion (FR) (Saumarez)
2876[2] 3397[3] 4008[4] 4446[8] 4776[3](5005)

Muhtenbar *Miss H C Knight* 107h 130+c
6 b g Muhtarram(USA) —Ardenbar (Ardross)
2291[F] 2861[3] 3251[3]3695[3] 4377[2]

Muir Cottage *L P Grassick* 53b
5 br g Chaddleworth(IRE) —Lady Crusty (Golden Dipper)
1882[12]

Mujazaf *Miss Sheena West*
4 b g Grand Lodge(USA) —Decision Maid (USA) (Diesis)
2045[8]

Mujimac (IRE) *G F Edwards* 51h
4 b g Mujadil(USA) —Cross Dall (IRE) (Blues Traveller (IRE))
3[10]

Mulahen *Katherine McKenna* 98h
11 b g Robellino(USA) —Moon Watch (Night Shift (USA))
1394a[6]

Mullacash (IRE) *Noel Meade* 118h 125c
8 b g Supreme Leader—The Parson's Line (The Parson)
115a[3] 3053a[12]

Mullensgrove *R Hollinshead* 118c
12 b g Derrylin—Wedding Song (True Song)
48[2] 204[U] 453[4]694[2] (765) 823[P]

Muller (IRE) *R W Thomson*
6 gr g Bigstone(IRE) —Missie Madam (IRE) (Kenmare (FR))
147[P] 856[U] 1066[P] 1663[12]

Mulligan's Pride (IRE) *G A Swinbank* 45h
5 b g Kahyasi—Babs Mulligan (IRE) (Le Bavard (FR))
424[4] 719[3] 2112[6] 2947[P] 8[7]

Mulligatawny (IRE) *N J Gifford* 113h 115c
12 b g Abednego—Mullangale (Strong Gale)
2808[10] 3186[P]

Multeen Gunner *Evan Williams* 84h 86c
9 b g Homo Sapien—Sister Delaney (Deep Run)
26[3] (416) 632[P]948[2] 1076[P] 1375[P]

Multeen River (IRE) *Jonjo O'Neill* 115+h 131c
10 b g Supreme Leader—Blackwater Mist (IRE) (King's Ride)
1542[4] 1739[5] 1913[3]

Multi Talented (IRE) *L Wells* 87c
10 b g Montelimar(USA) —Boro Glen (Furry Glen)
205[6] 567[6] 2164[11]2557[5] 3241[U] 4007[6]4321[P] 4914[P]

Mumaris (USA) *Miss Lucinda V Russell* 98h 120+c
12 bb g Capote(USA) —Barakat (Bustino)
195[P] 714[3] 894[F]1320[P]

Mumbles Head (IRE) *P Bowen* 112b
5 ch g Flemensfirth(USA) —Extra Mile (Torus)
(3563) 4448[19] 4909[2] 5075[2]

Mumbling (IRE) *B G Powell* 110+h
8 ch g Dr Devious(IRE) —Valley Lights (IRE) (Dance Of Life (USA))
397[P] 1270[4]

Munaawesh (USA) *Mrs Marjorie Fife* 77h
5 b g Bahri(USA) —Istikbal (USA) (Kingmambo (USA))
891[U] 1000[2] 1278[5] 1663[8] 2962[3]3335[2] 3782[5] 4302[P] 4632[7]

Munadil *A M Hales* 75+h 102+c
8 ch g Nashwan(USA) —Bintalshaati (Kris)
2585[10] 2995[3] **3546[2] 3686[7]4675[P]**

Mungo Jerry (GER) *B N Pollock* 100+h
5 b g Tannenkonig(IRE) —Mostly Sure (IRE) (Sure Blade (USA))
4389[2] 4691[7] 5073[U]

Munny Hill *M Appleby* 59h
6 b g Golden Heights—More Laughter (Oats)
1485[7] 1616[5] 1647[5]

Munster (IRE) *A L T Moore* 111h 128c
9 b g Zaffaran(USA) —Delway (Fidel)
91a[6] 4748[8]

Muntami (IRE) *John A Harris* 108h
5 gr g Daylami(IRE) —Bashashah (IRE) (Kris)
2249[7] (3591) 3967[10] 4430[17] 4834[6] 5021[6]

Muntasir *P G Murphy* 79h
6 b g Rainbow Quest(USA) —Licorne (Sadler's Wells (USA))
1977[13] (Dead)

Muraqeb *Mrs Barbara Waring* 81h
6 ch g Grand Lodge(USA) —Oh So Well (IRE) (Sadler's Wells (USA))
343[11] 2749[7]

Murat (FR) *M C Pipe* 82h
6 b g Useful(FR) —La Marianne (FR) (Don Roberto (USA))
436[U] 916[P] 3792[P]

Murotoevation (IRE) *D G Bridgwater* 63b
7 b g Muroto—Toevarro (Raga Navarro (ITY))
2665[11] 2865[P] 3275[P] 3731[P]

Murphy's Magic (IRE) *Mrs T J Hill* 85+c
8 br g Hubbly Bubbly(USA) —Wishing Trout (Three Wishes)
1879[3] 2581[P] 2805[7]2986[F] 3427[F] 3662[3]4166[3] 4321[6]

Murphy's Nails (IRE) *K C Bailey* 97h 87c
9 b g Bob's Return(IRE) —Southern Run (Deep Run)
5[U] 265[2] 501[9] 1443[2] 1645[2]1725[2] 2173[F] 2723[8] 2958[4] 4210[13]4879[10]

Murphy's Quest *Lady Herries* 117h 114c
10 ch g Sir Harry Lewis(USA) —Rondeau (Orchestra)
2344[4] 2805[6] 5049[6]

Murrayfield (USA) *C Byrnes* 105c
9 b g Ghazi(USA) —Hawaiian Comic (USA) (Doonesbury (USA))
1790a[6]

Murrieta *Miss J R Gibney* 25h
4 ch f Docksider(USA) —Lafleur (IRE) (Grand Lodge (USA))
3908[12] 4905[P]

Murt's Man (IRE) *Mrs A Holland* 52h 129c
12 b g Be My Native(USA) —Autumn Queen (Menelek)
4560[4]

Musally *W Jenks* 100h 82c
9 ch g Muhtarram(USA) —Flourishing (IRE) (Trojan Fen)
5[3] 573[2] 841[13] 980[9] 5[F]

Muscat Du Turf (FR) *E Leenders*
10 gr g Murmure(FR) —Souveraine Grise (FR) (Numbi (FR))
362a[5]

Mushraag (IRE) *J J Lambe* 40h
6 ch g Grand Lodge(USA) —Slayjay (IRE) (Mujtahid (USA))
495[8] 645[10] 856[8] 1063[12]

Musical Chord (IRE) *B Storey* 37h
7 ch g Accordion—Slieveglagh Queen (Proverb)
266[2] 671[10] 2678[P] 3376[P] 3559[P]

Musicalish *R Mathew*
5 ch g Up And At 'Em—La Scala (Scallywag)
2720[16] 4418[P]

Musical Shares *J A Geake*
5 ch g Piccolo—Ring Of Love (Magic Ring (IRE))
2584[P] 2860[P]

Musical Stage (USA) *P R Webber* 114+h 115+c
7 b g Theatrical—Changed Tune (USA) (Tunerup (USA))
1012[P] 1179[P] 1263[P]

Music To My Ears (IRE) *Jonjo O'Neill* 98+h 113+c
8 ch g Phardante(FR) —Evas Charm (Carlburg)
(1219) 1309[3]

Musimaro (FR) *R J Price* 107h
8 b g Solid Illusion(USA) —Musimara (FR) (Margouillat (FR))
1984[P] **2562[P]** 2734[9]

Muslin *Liam McAteer* 49h
5 ch m Bien Bien(USA) —Moidart (Electric)
3003a[15]

Mustang Jack *M Wigham*
6 b g Danzig Connection(USA) —Quivira (Rainbow Quest (USA))
1922[14]

Mustang Molly *Andrew J Martin* 90c
14 br m Soldier Rose—Little 'N' Game (Convolvulus)
51[P] 1041[P] 1398[P]5020[P]

Must Be Keen *Ernst Oertel* 90b
7 b g Emperor Jones(USA) —As Mustard (Keen)
1237[6] 1543[6] 2185[4] 2579[11]

Must Be Mistaken *A L Forbes*
5 b m Wizard King—Royal Celt (Celtic Cone)
844[12] 917[13]

Must Be So *Mrs L J Young* 44h
5 b m So Factual(USA) —Ovideo (Domynsky)
4423[8] 4733[6]

Mutakarrim *D K Weld* 130h 126c
9 ch g Mujtahid(USA) —Alyakkh (IRE) (Sadler's Wells (USA))
1083a[12]

Mutineer (IRE) *D T Hughes* 132h 116c
7 gr g Highest Honor(FR) —Miss Amy R (USA) (Deputy Minister (CAN))
5129a[13]

Muttiah *E J O'Grady* 109h
6 ch g Muhtarram(USA) —Loving Around (IRE) (Furry Glen)
5103a[16]

Muttley Maguire (IRE) *B G Powell* 112 c
7 b g Zaffaran(USA) —Alavie (FR) (Quart De Vin (FR))
106[2] (358) 524[3]1877[8] (2557)

Mvezo *Evan Williams* 7h
8 ch g Karinga Bay—Queen Of The Celts (Celtic Cone)
398[F] 948[P] 1122[P]

My Ace *Miss J E Foster* 78h 78c
8 b m Definite Article—Miss Springtime (Bluebird (USA))
670[16] **990[3] 1147[P]1335[7]**

My Arch *K A Ryan* 88b
4 b g Silver Patriarch(IRE) —My Desire (Grey Desire)
4588[6]

My Best Buddy *Mrs Caroline Bailey* 95c
10 b g Vital Season—Trade Only (Andrea Mantegna)
282[4] (5053)

My Best Secret *L Lungo* 81b
7 ch g Secret Appeal—Mohibbah (USA) (Conquistador Cielo (USA))
2480[13]

My Big Sister *J W Mullins* 77h 70+c
7 gr m Thethingaboutitis(USA) —My Concordia (Belfort (FR))
2928[10] 3979[9] 4450[9] **4911[3]**

My Bold Boyo *K Bishop* 103 h 73c
11 b g Never So Bold—My Rosie (Forzando)
57[3] 275[10]

My Condor (IRE) *W J Burke*
5 b g Beneficial—Margellen's Castle (IRE) (Castle Keep)
5060a[P]

My Countess *A C Whillans* 36b
5 ch m Danzig Connection(USA) —Settlement (USA) (Irish River (FR))
424[12]

Mydante (IRE) *S Flook* 78c
11 b m Phardante(FR) —Carminda (Proverb)
6[F] 204[4] 455[5]3758[P]

My Final Bid (IRE) *Mrs A C Hamilton* 104+h
7 b g Supreme Leader—Mini Minor (IRE) (Black Minstrel)
2268[2] 2948[2] 3376[2] 3914[2] 4527[3]

My Friend Paul *O Brennan*
6 b g Bold Fox—Annie Bee (Rusticaro (FR))
4854[20]

My Galliano (IRE) *B G Powell* 93h 96+c
10 b g Muharib(USA) —Hogan Stand (Buckskin (FR))
505[4] 1366[7] 1559[2] **1805[P]**

My Good Lord (IRE) *G M Moore* 94h
7 br g Mister Lord(USA) —Glenstal Forest (IRE) (Glenstal (USA))
1921[3] 2460[P] 2859[P] 4917[2]

My Immortal *M C Pipe* 123+h
4 b g Monsun(GER) —Dame Kiri (FR) (Old Vic)
2481[2] 3021[6] 3594[DSQ] 3759[2] 4435[6]5142[3]

My Lady Link (FR) *Miss Venetia Williams* 101+h 92c
7 bl m Sleeping Car(FR) —Cadoudaline (FR) (Cadoudal (FR))
167[2] (329) 545[3] (768)

My Last Bean (IRE) *M R Bosley* 116h
9 gr g Soviet Lad(USA) —Meanz Beanz (High Top)
99[3] 387[9] 1878[11]

My Little Molly (IRE) *J W Mullins* 27h
4 b f Perpendicular—Madame Firefly (Lyphento (USA))
3504[9] 4333[12] 4836[13]5043[4]

Mylo *Jonjo O'Neill* 124 h 104c
8 gr g Faustus(USA) —Bellifontaine (FR) (Bellypha)
353[P] **972[2] 1232[2]1365[P] 1396[2] 1540[2]1595[2]** 1773[4]

Mylord Collonges (FR) *Mrs Susan Nock* 81h
6 bl g Video Rock(FR) —Diane Collonges (FR) (El Badr)
3240[8] 4077[7] 4604[10] 4834[13]

My Lucky Rose (IRE) *S Donohoe* 85h 92c
8 br m Glacial Storm(USA) —Clogheen Lucy (Sheer Grit)
2657[3] 2944[5] **3533[5]**

My Maite (IRE) *R Ingram* 83h
7 b g Komaite(USA) —Mena (Blakeney)
230[F]

My Mon Amour *J W Mullins*
5 b m Terimon—Roll Over Darling (Double Bed (FR))
4011[12] 4623[14] 5026[P]

My Native Lad (IRE) *Noel Meade* 105h 98c
8 ch g Be My Native(USA) —Stevies Girl (IRE) (Satco (FR))
1623a[11]

My Only Bid (IRE) *A J Whiting*
8 b g Carroll House—Brush Master (IRE) (Brush Aside (USA))
4005[P] 4521[10]

Myoss (IRE) *Mrs V J Makin* 60h
7 b g Arctic Lord—Lake Garden Park (Comedy Star (USA))
1757[9] 1885[7]

My Pal Val (IRE) *Miss H C Knight* 107+h
6 br g Classic Cliche(IRE) —Lessons Lass (IRE) (Doyoun)
(394)

My Retreat (USA) *R Fielder* 70 h
9 b g Hermitage(USA) —My Jessica Ann (USA) (Native Rythm)
167[P] 506[11] 681[7] 760[9] 2563[7]2995[P] 4013[P] 5048[6]

My Rosie Ribbons (IRE) *B W Duke* 91 h
7 b m Roselier(FR) —Georgic (Tumble Gold)
1922[8] 2021[5] 2718[O]2866[5] 3287[4] 3548[2] 3648[4] 4619[9]

My Sharp Grey *J Gallagher* 101+h
7 gr m Tragic Role(USA) —Sharp Anne (Belfort (FR))
1400[7] 1645[15] 1738[4] 1902[6] 2139[2]2726[7] 2940[8]

My Skipper (IRE) *Miss H C Knight* 110+b
5 b g Old Vic—Nil Faic (IRE) (King's Ride)
1611[P]

Myson (IRE) *D B Feek* 85h 107c
7 ch g Accordion—Ah Suzie (IRE) (King's Ride)
1953[3] 2325[3] 2577[3]2931[4] 4120[U] 4419[P]4652[2] **4873[5]**

Mystery (GER) *T R George* 103+h
8 br g Java Gold(USA) —My Secret (GER) (Secreto (USA))
488[P]

Mystery Lot (IRE) *A King* 110+h
4 b f Revoque(IRE) —Mystery Bid (Auction Ring (USA))
3422[6] 3594[2] (3948) 4435[11]

Mystery Maid (IRE) *H S Howe* 1h
4 b f King's Theatre(IRE) —Duly Elected (Persian Bold)
4784[15]

Mystical Memories (IRE) *W P Mullins* 103h
7 ch m Bob Back(USA) —Mystical City (IRE) (The Noble Player (USA))
117a[18]

Mystical Star (FR) *M J Hogan* 70h 101 c
9 b g Nicolotte—Addaya (IRE) (Persian Bold)
(1776) 2217[2] 2684[2]3187[2] 4150[2] 4653[5]

Mystic Glen *P D Niven* 77h
7 b m Vettori(IRE) —Mystic Memory (Ela-Mana-Mou)
469[6] 601[6]

Mystic Lord (IRE) *Miss Lucinda V Russell* 45h 102c
9 gr g Roselier(FR) —Ash-Dame (IRE) (Strong Gale)
2066[P] **5122[P]**

Mystic Native (IRE) *David Pearson* 66c
13 ch g Be My Native(USA) —Mystic River (IRE) (Over The River (FR))
594[U]

My Sunshine (IRE) *M E Sowersby* 75h
5 b m Alzao(USA) —Sunlit Ride (Ahonoora)
9[17]

Mythical King (IRE) *R Lee* 128 h 107 c
9 b g Fairy King(USA) —Whatcombe (USA) (Alleged (USA))
127[10] 2076 2184[2] 2483[8] 2633[9]**3142[U] 3549[5] 3879[4]4102[5]** 4497[5] 4776[P]

My Turn Now (IRE) *Edward U Hales* 111b
4 ch g In The Wings—Wishful (IRE) (Irish River (FR))
5081a[11]

My Vic (IRE) *D R Gandolfo* 50h
6 b g Old Vic—Bitabiz (IRE) (Nearly A Nose (USA))
4393[7]

My Way De Solzen (FR) *A King* 166+h
6 b g Assessor(IRE) —Agathe De Solzen (FR) (Chamberlin (FR))
2336[2] (3020) (4008) (4458) 4745[2]

My Will (FR) *P F Nicholls* 130h 158 c
6 b g Saint Preuil(FR) —Gleep Will (FR) (Cadoudal (FR))
1846[2] 2177[9] 2615[2]2992[3] 3977[2] 4118[3]4457[4] 4746[F] 5144[3]

My World (FR) *R H Alner* 105+h 124 c
6 b m Lost World(IRE) —Fortuna Jet (FR) (Highest Honor (FR))
2798[2] 3183[3] (3599) 3973[4] (5011)

Nabir (FR) *P D Niven* 96h
6 gr g Linamix(FR) —Nabagha (FR) (Fabulous Dancer (USA))
1927[11] 2027[8] 2858[4]

Nacho Des Uncheres (FR) *D G Bridgwater* 86+b
5 b g Bulington(FR) —Radieuse Gamine (FR) (Chateau Du Diable (FR))
4500[15] 4825[5]

Nadover (FR) *C J Mann* 105h 120+c
5 br g Cyborg(FR) —Djerissa (FR) (Highlanders (FR))
2078[2] 2488[5] (2817) (3394)

Nae Bother At All (IRE) *N G Richards* 101h
5 b g Luso—I'll Say She Is (Ashmore (FR))
2658[2]

Naemi (GER) *S L Keightley* 54b
4 b f Tannenkonig(IRE) —Noanah (GER) (Konigsstuhl (GER))
2105[8]

Nagam (FR) *A Ennis* 102+h
5 b g Denham Red(FR) —Gamaytoise (FR) (Brezzo (FR))
2295[7] 2619[2] 3023[P] 3978[P] 4367[4]4689[P]

Nagano (FR) *Ian Williams* 101 h 109 c
8 b g Hero's Honor(USA) —Sadinskaya (FR) (Niniski (USA))
248[4] 2298[2] (2659) 2802[4] **3922[F]4281[5] 4614[2] 4859[5]**

Nailed On *Andrew J Martin* 80+c
7 ch g Factual(USA) —Highlights (Phountzi (USA))
3924[3] 4283[3] 4730[P]

Naja De Billeron (FR) *M C Pipe* 60h
5 b g Video Rock(FR) —Valse De Billeron (FR) (Cupids Dew)
2826[14] 3658[12] 3963[12] 4606[F] 4727[P]

Najca De Thaix (FR) *C N Allen* 96h 89c
5 bb g Marmato—Isca De Thaix (FR) (Cimon)
2249[11] 2584[4] 3422[7] 3687[10] 3990[P]**4844[8]**

Nakatani (IRE) *Mrs A V Roberts*
4 b g Raphane(USA) —Cnocma (IRE) (Tender King)
1718[P]

Naked Flame *A G Blackmore* 35h
7 b g Blushing Flame(USA) —Final Attraction (Jalmood (USA))
2008[P]

Naked Oat *Mrs L Wadham* 94h
11 b g Imp Society(USA) —Bajina (Dancing Brave (USA))
(536) 747[7] 947[9] 1027[2]

Named At Dinner *Miss Lucinda V Russell* 81h 76c
5 ch g Halling(USA) —Salanka (IRE) (Persian Heights)
320[9] 1839[9] 2040[3] 2567[10] **2943[U]3320[6]** 3446[2] 3916[7]

Name For Fame (USA) *R Donohoe* 102h 84c
7 b m Quest For Fame—Berceau (USA) (Alleged (USA))
1623a[3] 2031a[6]

Nanard (FR) *M C Pipe* 87b
5 br g Double Bed(FR) —Isabellita (GER) (Cyborg (FR))
1909[4]

Nanga Parbat (FR) *P F Nicholls* 124+h
5 b g True Brave(USA) —Celeste (FR) (Amen (FR))
1677[3] (1862) 2533[4] 2969[2] **3323[U]**4663[2] 5142[8]

Nannys Gift (IRE) *O Brennan* 83b
7 b m Presenting—Last Royal (Kambalda)
3497[3] 3961[4] 5138[7]

Naos De Mirande (FR) *T Doumen* 115+h
5 b g Smadoun(FR) —Venus De Mirande (FR) (Carmont (FR))
3389[9] 3993[P]

Napalm (IRE) *C C Bealby*
5 b g Warcraft(USA) —Cross My Palm (IRE) (King Luthier)
3983[11]

Napapijri (FR) *W G M Turner*
4 gr f Highest Honor(FR) —Les Marettes (FR) (Baillamont (USA))
4665[P]

Naples *Noel Meade* 120 h
7 b g Tragic Role(USA) —Glow Again (The Brianstan)
2206[7] 5059a[7]

Napoleon (IRE) *P J Hobbs* 112+h
5 b g Sadler's Wells(USA) —Love For Ever (IRE) (Darshaan)
1908[5] 2309[6] (2923) 3342[4] 3561[11] 4050[F] (Dead)

Napolitain (FR) *P F Nicholls* 124h 134c
5 b g Ajdayt(USA) —Domage II (FR) (Cyborg (FR))
(1736) 2052[2] 2344[F]3178[2] (3726) (4116) 4459[13] 4759[P] (4960)

Narlen (CZE) *Mrs P Townsley* 66h
4 ch g Rainbows For Life(CAN) —Neris (POL) (Dniepr (POL))
4915[6]

Narval D'Avelot (FR) *D G Bridgwater* 56c
5 b g Video Rock(FR) —Reine Des Planches (FR) (Diaghilev)
4802[P]

Nar Valley *A King* 31b
5 b g Alflora(IRE) —Barton Bay (IRE) (Kambalda)
2720[12] *4237[10]*

Nashaab (USA) *P D Evans*
9 b g Zafonic(USA) —Tajannub (USA) (Dixieland Band (USA))
1222[P]

Nas Na Riogh (IRE) *N J Henderson* 122 c
7 b m King's Theatre(IRE) —Abstraite (Groom Dancer (USA))
(3212) 3507[6] 4419[P]

Nassaro (IRE) *M Halford* 109h
6 gr g Linamix(FR) —Dawnsio (IRE) (Tate Gallery (USA))
1691a[4] 2166[12]

Nasstar *M W Easterby* 54b
5 b g Bal Harbour—Prime Property (IRE) (Tirol)
3145[11] 3347[12] 4793[6]

Natal (FR) *P F Nicholls* 156+h
5 b g Funny Baby(FR) —Donitille (FR) (Italic (FR))
(243) (438) 2161[5] (2487) (2730) 2971[4] 3994[3] 4430[6](4750)

Nathos (GER) *C J Mann* 143 h 119 c
9 b g Zaizoom(USA) —Nathania (GER) (Athenagoras (GER))
1598[3] 1760[2] (2079) (2292) 2876[5] 3135[2] 3298[2]3502[4] 4008[6] 4446[16]

Natiain *Alistair M Brown* 88+c
7 ch g Danzig Connection(USA) —Fen Princess (IRE) (Trojan Fen)
123[5] 4722[2]

Native Beat (IRE) *J R H Fowler* 113h 117c
11 b g Be My Native(USA) —Deeprunonthepound (IRE) (Deep Run)
4625a[4] 5128a[10]

Native Chancer (IRE) *Jonjo O'Neill* 101h
6 ch g Anshan—Native Aughrim (IRE) (Be My Native (USA))
696[14] 804[3] 901[5] (1028) 1075[7] 1181[2]1408[2] 1525[6] 1784[P]

Native Coll *N W Alexander* 73h 60c
6 ch g Primitive Rising(USA) —Harrietfield (Nicholas Bill)
2948[19] 3232[P] 3855[4] 4141[13] **4840[10]**

Native Commander (IRE) *Miss Sheena West* 89+h
11 b g Be My Native(USA) —The Better Half (IRE) (Deep Run)
3283[P] 3673[5] 3804[7] 3985[2] 4278[3]4392[3] 4556[2] 4871[6]

Native Cooper (IRE) *Miss A M Lambert* 85h 106c
8 br g Be My Native(USA) —Moyheez (IRE) (Naheez (USA))
3528a[4] 5129a[F]

Native Coral (IRE) *N G Richards* 97 h 132c
8 ch g Be My Native(USA) —Deep Coral (IRE) (Buckskin (FR))
(303) 937[2] (1295) 1550[6]

Native Cunning *R H Buckler* 78h 72c
8 b g Be My Native(USA) —Icy Miss (Random Shot)
519[2]

Native Daisy (IRE) *C J Down* 109+c
11 b m Be My Native(USA) —Castleblagh (General Ironside)
1157[5] 1236[P] (1406)

Native Eire (IRE) *N Wilson* 62h 94+c
12 b g Be My Native(USA) —Ballyline Dancer (Giolla Mear)
4499[7] 4659[5]

Native Emperor *Jonjo O'Neill* 126h 126 c
10 br g Be My Native(USA) —Fiona's Blue (Crash Course)
2175[6] **2847[3] 3022[P]**3179[5]

Native Forest (IRE) *Miss H C Knight* 75h
5 ch g Insan(USA) —Oak Lodge (IRE) (Roselier (FR))
2534[19] 3462[7] 4048[6]

Native Guide (IRE) *Noel C Kelly* 91h
11 b g Be My Native(USA) —Lana Tee (IRE) (Kemal (FR))
856[10]

Native Heights (IRE) *M Todhunter* 102h 111c
8 b g Be My Native(USA) —Shirley's Dream (IRE) (Mister Majestic)
3172[P] 3234[6] **5092[P]**

Native House (IRE) *Edward Cawley* 108h 98+c
8 b m Carroll House—Accountancy Native (IRE) (Be My Native (USA))
2650a[18] 4887a[11] 5077a[22]

Native Ivy (IRE) *C Tinkler* 125 h 134+c
8 b g Be My Native(USA) —Outdoor Ivy (Deep Run)
(2046) 2875[3] 4098[P]4617[P]

Native Jack (IRE) *P J Rothwell* 130h 134+c
12 br g Be My Native(USA) —Dorrha Daisy (Buckskin (FR))
(4434)

Native Performance (IRE) *N J Gifford* 114h 123c
11 b g Be My Native(USA) —Noon Performance (Strong Gale)
3284[6] 4078[P] 4837[8]

Native Ray (IRE) *Miss Noreen Hayes* 69c
12 b g Be My Native(USA) —Narcone (Kambalda)
2164[10]

Native Stag (IRE) *P A Fahy* 123h
8 b g Be My Native(USA) —Celestial Dance (Scottish Reel)
67a[2] 1093a[7]

Native Upmanship (IRE) *A L T Moore* 114h 155c
13 ch g Be My Native(USA) —Hi' Upham (Deep Run)
41a[3] 2230a[4] 2793a[7]3154a[2] **3472a[5] 3895a[3]4777[R] 5079a[6]**

Natoumba (FR) *H D Daly* 100+b
5 ch g Hawker's News(IRE) —Vanella (FR) (Quart De Vin (FR))
4500[3]

Natural (IRE) *Mrs J Williamson* 99dh 88c
9 b g Bigstone(IRE) —You Make Me Real (USA) (Give Me Strength (USA))
151[5] 498[5] 4846[P]5095[3]

Natural Storm (IRE) *F Flood* 108h 117c
8 b g Glacial Storm(USA) —Clara Grahame (IRE) (Seclude (USA))
5080a[4]

Nature's Magic *R J Price*
5 ch m Private Despatch(USA) —Sally's Dove (Celtic Cone)
1755[8] 1985[10]

Naughty Boy *J Pearce* 8b
4 ch g Compton Place—Ballerina Bay (Myjinski (USA))
4992[13]

Naughtynelly's Pet *A M Crow* 72h
7 b g Balnibarbi—Naughty Nessie (Celtic Cone)
4787[7] 4988[8] 8[14]

Naunton Brook *N A Twiston-Davies* 112+h 130+c
7 b g Alderbrook—Give Me An Answer (True Song)
(1853) 2054[P] 2628[7]2875[P] 3469[6] (3965) 4287[3] 4957[16]

Nautic (FR) *R Dickin* 92h
5 b g Apple Tree(FR) —Bella Dicta (FR) (Vayrann)
(531)

Nautical *A W Carroll* 88h
8 gr g Lion Cavern(USA) —Russian Royal (USA) (Nureyev (USA))
2261[P]

Nautical Lad *J H Docker* 73c
11 b g Crested Lark—Spanish Mermaid (Julio Mariner)
50[5] 282[6] 440[P]

Navado (USA) *Jonjo O'Neill* 110 h
7 b g Rainbow Quest(USA) —Miznah (IRE) (Sadler's Wells (USA))
1488[3] 1617[P] 1715[4] 5113[2]

Naval Force *Ian Williams* 55 h
4 b g Forzando—Barsham (Be My Guest (USA))
1441[3] 1594[9]

Navarone *Ian Williams* 122 c
12 b g Gunner B—Anamasi (Idiots Delight)
489[3] 815[3] 975[5]4806[P]

Navelina *T J Fitzgerald* 79b
6 b m Presidium—Orange Imp (Kind Of Hush)
2961[6] 4902[9]

Navy Lark *M C Pipe* 85b
4 ch g Nashwan(USA) —Holly Blue (Bluebird (USA))
4244[8]

Nawamees (IRE) *G L Moore* 136 h 105c
8 b g Darshaan—Truly Generous (IRE) (Generous (IRE))
803[3] (1249) 1720[9] **2102[7]**

Nawow *P D Cundell* 102h 94 c
6 b g Blushing Flame(USA) —Fair Test (Fair Season)
(465) 672[P] 4605[6]

Nayodabayo (IRE) *Evan Williams* 101h 135+c
6 b g Definite Article—Babushka (IRE) (Dance Of Life (USA))
2141[F] 2456[4] (2725) 2938[2] 3506[F] 4827[U](4)

Nazimabad (IRE) *Evan Williams* 70h 110 c
7 b g Unfuwain(USA) —Naziriya (FR) (Darshaan)
388[P] 692[3] (979) 999[3] 1124[4] 1176[3]1433[5] 1659[2] (1877) 2149[7] (4552) 5107[P]

Ndola *B J Curley* 82h
7 b g Emperor Jones(USA) —Lykoa (Shirley Heights)
764[11] 2103[6] 2585[11] 2816[8] 3371[P]

Neagh (FR) *N G Richards* 82h
5 b g Dress Parade—Carlie II (FR) (Highlanders (FR))
2024[P] 2652[11]
Neardown Bishop *M Wigham* 79h
4 b g Imperial Ballet(IRE) —Firedancer (Nashwan (USA))
4631[9] 4877[7] 3[6]
Nearly A Bay *R Fielder*
9 gr m Nearly A Hand—Splash Of Red (Scallywag)
4425[P]
Nearly A Breeze *C J Down* 64b
6 b m Thowra(FR) —Nearly At Sea (Nearly A Hand)
1042[15]
Nearly Never *Mrs S J Smith* 74h
11 b g Minster Son—Lady Barnett (Daring March)
1445[5] 2024[8] 2295[12] 3559[6]
Nebraska City *D W Thompson*
5 b g Piccolo—Scarlet Veil (Tyrnavos)
4278[P] 4479[P]
Nechouka (FR) *Seamus Neville* 33h
5 b g Useful(FR) —Soniville (FR) (Ghost Buster'S (FR))
3003a[17]
Neckar Valley (IRE) *R M Whitaker* 105 h
7 b g Desert King(IRE) —Solar Attraction (IRE) (Salt Dome (USA))
895[3] 991[P]
Nectar De Guye (FR) *Ferdy Murphy*
5 ch g
8[8]
Ned Kelly (IRE) *E J O'Grady* 163h 151 c
10 ch g Be My Native(USA) —Silent Run (Deep Run)
2195a[5] 2793a[4]
Needle Prick (IRE) *N A Twiston-Davies* 80b
5 b g Needle Gun(IRE) —Emersonsupreme (IRE) (Supreme Leader)
1042[6]
Needtoknow (IRE) *M J Gingell* 69h
7 b g Perugino(USA) —Capplenastore (IRE) (Sayyaf)
913[U] (Dead)
Needwood *G A Swinbank*
5 b g Danzig Connection(USA) —Enchanting Kate (Enchantment I)
4588[P]
Needwood Spirit *Mrs A M Naughton* 74h
11 b g Rolfe(USA) —Needwood Nymph (Bold Owl)
2453[10] 2567[11] 3330[4] 3446[4] 3674[U](3956) 4320[R]
Nefertari *P R Webber* 66b
4 b f Sir Harry Lewis(USA) —Kota Tinggi (Tragic Role (USA))
3468[4] 4017[7]
Negas (IRE) *J Howard Johnson* 77 h
4 b g Titus Livius(FR) —Alzeam (IRE) (Alzao (USA))
1332[2] 1679[P] 1923[8]
Negociant (FR) *R M Stronge*
5 b g Roi De Rome(USA) —Quartaxie (FR) (Saumon (FR))
2849[P]
Negus De Beaumont (FR) *F Jordan* 80h
5 b g Blushing Flame(USA) —Givry (FR) (Bayolidaan (FR))
131[4] 2423[14] 2860[6] 3139[3] 3386[P]
Neidpath Castle *A C Whillans* 91h
7 b g Alflora(IRE) —Pennant Cottage (IRE) (Denel (FR))
82[5] 2024[P] 2840[P] 4852[9]
Nellie The Nod *M J Gingell*
7 br m Lir—Benen Royal (King's Ride)
3417[U] 3550[P] 4015[7] 4129[P]
Nelson (POL) *P J Hobbs*
4 br g Fourth Of June(USA) —Neustria (POL) (Who Knows)
945[P] 1095[P] (Dead)
Nelson Du Ronceray (FR) *P Monteith* 91h
5 b g Lute Antique(FR) —Trieste (FR) (Quart De Vin (FR))
2528[11] 2804[8] 3130[6] 3464[8] 3659[10]4487[2]
Neltina *Mrs J E Scrase* 105h 124 c
10 gr m Neltino—Mimizan (IRE) (Pennine Walk)
1958[3] 2300[3] 2870[3]4618[F] 5027[4]
Nemetan (FR) *R H Alner* 70h
5 ch g Port Lyautey(FR) —Annabelle Treveene (FR) (Spoleto)
3328[9] 3545[9] 4564[8] 4871[P]
Neodyme (FR) *M C Pipe* 81b
5 b g Cupidon(FR) —Schotsalla (FR) (Dauphin Du Bourg (FR))
300[3]
Neophyte (IRE) *M J M Evans* 51h
7 gr g Broken Hearted—Dunmahon Lady (General Ironside)
1824[P] 2179[P] **3599[P] 3647[P]**4278[9]
Nepal (IRE) *M Mullineaux* 68h
4 ch f Monashee Mountain(USA) —Zetonic (Zafonic (USA))
2286[10] 2587[5] 2752[4] 3330[P] 3557[14]4046[P] 4423[6] 4591[P]
Nephite (NZ) *Miss Venetia Williams* 75h 108c
12 b g Star Way—Te Akau Charmer (NZ) (Sir Tristram)
108[7] 395[2] (534) (644) 840[P] 1744[P]2183[4] 2583[P] 3919[P]
Neptune *J C Fox* 80h
10 b g Dolphin Street(FR) —Seal Indigo (IRE) (Glenstal (USA))
357[P]
Neptune Collonges (FR) *P F Nicholls*150 h 139c
5 gr g Dom Alco(FR) —Castille Collonges (FR) (El Badr)
(1980) 2206[4] (2614) 3020[2] (3738) (3969) 4760[3]
Neptune D'Anzy (FR) *Jonjo O'Neill* 96 c
5 b g Lights Out(FR) —Dory (FR) (Italic (FR))
4076[5]
Neptune Joly (FR) *Ferdy Murphy* 72h 109c
5 b g Chef De Clan II(FR) —Fortune Jolie (FR) (Un Numide (FR))
4039[6] **4377[4] 5119[4]**
Nerone (GER) *P Monteith* 103h
5 gr g Sternkoenig(IRE) —Nordwahl (GER) (Waajib)
1940 [7] 2191[3] 2680[F] 3040[3] 3378[3]3737[3] (4143) 5066[12]
Nero West (FR) *Miss Lucy Bridges* 95h
5 ch g Pelder(IRE) —West River (USA) (Gone West (USA))
2309[9] 2624 [4] (3240) 3441[P] 4372[7]
Nesnaas (USA) *M G Rimell* 97h
5 ch g Gulch(USA) —Sedrah (USA) (Dixieland Band (USA))
177[3] 664[5] 1541[6] (1653) 1747[3] 1862[3]
Nesserian (IRE) *John E Kiely* 106+b
6 b g Sadlers' Hall(IRE) —Caslain Nua (Seymour Hicks (FR))
(5104a)
Nettleton Flyer *Miss J S Davis*
5 b g Ajraas(USA) —Mybella Ann (Anfield)
4732[8] 5016[F]
Network Oscar (IRE) *M W Easterby* 89h
5 b g Oscar(IRE) —Just Wonderful (IRE) (Prince Rupert (FR))
1554[3] 1824[9] 2444[13] 2591[5] 3042[3]4067[P] 4362[P]
Neuro (FR) *Jedd O'Keeffe* 65+c
5 b g Passing Sale(FR) —El Serenade (FR) (Djarvis (FR))
4303[4] 4655[4] 5002[P]
Neutrino *P C Haslam* 53h
4 b g Mtoto—Fair Seas (General Assembly (USA))
4313[7]
Neutron (FR) *L Lungo* 80+b
5 ch g Ragmar(FR) —Valentia (FR) (Brezzo (FR))
4366[5]
Nevada Red *D McCain* 99h
5 ch g Classic Cliche(IRE) —Sovereign Belle (Ardross)
2423 1672[6] 1937[2] 2450[3] 2979[3]3914[3] 4315[7]
Neveesou (FR) *M C Pipe* 133 h
5 gr g Kaldounevees(FR) —Tugend (GER) (Priamos (GER))
(3127) 4097[2] 4773[12]
Neven *Miss Lucinda V Russell* 91h
7 b g Casteddu—Rose Burton (Lucky Wednesday)
82[11] 3061[4] 601[F] 7161[6] 1293[6]
Never (FR) *Jonjo O'Neill* 123 h 112c
9 b g Vettori(IRE) —Neraida (USA) (Giboulee (CAN))
1318[2] 1411[3] 1487[5]
Never Awol (IRE) *B N Pollock* 96c
9 ch g John French—Lark Lass (Le Bavard (FR))
1277[P] 1646[0] (2009) (2506) 2986[U] 3276[2]3909[10] 4321[P]
Never Compromise (IRE) *T M Walsh* 94h 119c
11 br g Glacial Storm(USA) —Banderole (IRE) (Roselier (FR))
4434[7] 5128a[4]
Never Cried Wolf *R Dickin* 45h
5 b g Wolfhound(USA) —Bold Difference (Bold Owl)
3963[P] 4320[P]
Never Forget Bowie *R Allan* 62h
10 b g Superpower—Heldigvis (Hot Grove)
602[9] 7161[3] 936[10]
Never So Blue (FR) *Miss Venetia Williams*73+h
5 gr g April Night(FR) —Etiane Bleue (FR) (Reve Bleu (FR))
4875[P]
Nevertika (FR) *Mrs K Walton* 100b
5 b g Subotica(FR) —Griotte De Coddes (FR) (Silver Rainbow)
1799[5] 2340[4] 3319[2] 4147[2]
Nevsky Bridge *D McCain* 94 h
4 b f Soviet Star(USA) —Pontressina (USA) (St Jovite (USA))
(3550) 3730[3]
New Alco (FR) *Ferdy Murphy* 120h 133c
5 b g Dom Alco(FR) —Cabira Des Saccart (FR) (Quart De Vin (FR))
(1824) 2169[2] **2764[2] (2975) 3494[2] 4778[2] 5102a[6]**
Newbay Prop (IRE) *A J Martin* 110c
7 b g Good Thyne(USA) —Geray Lady (IRE) (Roselier (FR))
5083a[8]
New Bird (GER) *Ian Williams* 116 c
11 b g Bluebird(USA) —Nouvelle Amour (GER) (Esclavo (FR))
1673[2] 2339[6] 3344[F]5112[3]
New Currency (USA) *M C Pipe* 91h
6 bb g Touch Gold(USA) —Ceirseach (IRE) (Don't Forget Me)
1774 5711[2] 959[4] 2734[P] 3848[P]
New Dancer *K A Ryan* 94b
4 b g Zafonic(USA) —Paradise Soul (USA) (Dynaformer (USA))
(3763)
New Diamond *Mrs P Ford* 74h
7 ch g Bijou D'Inde—Nannie Annie (Persian Bold)
3250[P] 3616[6] 4277[7] 4564[5]
New Entic (FR) *G L Moore* 129 h
5 b g Ragmar(FR) —Entiqua Des Sacart (FR) (Lute Antique (FR))
2636[P] 2871[11] 2969[5] (4119) 4215[P] 4663[5]4821[2] 5142[10]
New Field (IRE) *Thomas Mullins* 123h 129c
8 b g Supreme Leader—Deep Steel (Deep Run)
117a[11] **4778[P]**
Newgate Suds *Mark Campion* 50h
9 b m Kasakov—Newgate Bubbles (Hubbly Bubbly (USA))
5015[11]
Newick Park *Mrs D M Grissell* 94c
11 gr g Chilibang—Quilpee Mai (Pee Mai)
395[3] 511[5] 4092[3]
New Leader (IRE) *Mrs L Richards* 88 h 75+c
9 b g Supreme Leader—Two Spots (Deep Run)
1776[F] 1951[P] (2237) 2555[7] 3221[6] 4580[2]
Newmill (IRE) *John Joseph Murphy* 155h 172+c
8 br g Norwich—Lady Kas (Pollerton)
89a[5] 2397a[4] 3109a[3] **(3472a) (4445) (5057a)**
New Mischief (IRE) *Noel T Chance* 102 h
8 b g Accordion—Alone Party (IRE) (Phardante (FR))
3184[3] 3441[4] 3729[7] (4210) 4606[3]
New Perk (IRE) *M J Gingell* 93h 103c
8 b g Executive Perk—New Cello (IRE) (Orchestra)
181[3] 365[6] **1905[2](2259) (2951)** (3416) (3959) **(4476) 4900[2]**
Newratking (IRE) *C Byrnes* 86h 100c
10 b g Shardari—Carmen Lady (Torus)
2210[P]
New's Full (FR) *Ferdy Murphy* 68h
5 b m Useful(FR) —Goldkara (FR) (Glint Of Gold)
2028[8] 2515[6] 2674[8]
Newsplayer (IRE) *R T Phillips* 47h
10 br g Alphabatim(USA) —Another Tycoon (IRE) (Phardante (FR))
1202[P] **1433[8]** 3899[10]
New Team (FR) *R H Alner* 105+h
5 ch g Green Tune(USA) —Fortuna Jet (FR) (Highest Honor (FR))
1908[2]
New Time (IRE) *Jonjo O'Neill* 91h
7 b g Topanoora—Fast Time (IRE) (Be My Native (USA))
(1647) 1900[3]
Newtown *M F Harris* 87h
7 b g Darshaan—Calypso Run (Lycius (USA))
3658[8] 4131[5] 4320[2] 4526[7]
Newtown Dancer (IRE) *T Hogan* 110+h 112c
7 b m Danehill Dancer(IRE) —Patience Of Angels (IRE) (Distinctly North (USA))
2166[3] 2347[8]
New Wave *R Lee* 69h
4 b g Woodman(USA) —Vanishing Point (USA) (Caller I.D. (USA))
3939[8] 4416[8]
New Wish (IRE) *S B Clark* 58h
6 b g Ali-Royal(IRE) —False Spring (IRE) (Petorius)
1661[0] 1757[10] 2082[6] 2463[7] 2567[12]3335[P] 3557[15] 3916[P] 5135[6]
Next Lord (FR) *C Von Der Recke* 66 h
4 b c Lord Of Men—Next Victory (FR) (Akarad (FR))
2580[7] 3436[9]
Ngauruhoe (IRE) *John Berry* 87+h
4 b f Desert Sun—Snowcap (IRE) (Snow Chief (USA))
2258[6] 4631[P] 4877[3]
Nicanor (FR) *Noel Meade* 155+h
5 b g Garde Royale—Uthane (FR) (Baly Rockette)
70a[3] 2536a[F] 2909a[2] (3642a) (4443) (5132a)
Nice Baby (FR) *M C Pipe* 80h
5 b m Baby Turk—First Union (FR) (Shafoun (FR))
352[9] 575[11] 749[3] 978[7] 1637[8]2244[5] 2728[F]
Nice Horse (FR) *M C Pipe* 108 h
5 ch g River Bay(USA) —Tchela (FR) (Le Nain Jaune (FR))
1968[U] 2423[7] 2829[11] 3175[14] 3500[4]3729[6] 4373[7] 4961[P]
Nice Try (IRE) *Miss Venetia Williams*102h 127+c
7 b g Lord Americo—Lyntim (Fidel)
2617[4] 2821[3] 3219[3] **(3582) 3992[F](4355) 4847[4]**
Niciara (IRE) *M C Chapman* 93h
9 b g Soviet Lad(USA) —Verusa (IRE) (Petorius)
238[P] 429[11] 686[P]
Nickit (IRE) *Mrs Susan Smith* 84h 88c
10 gr g Roselier(FR) —Run Trix (Deep Run)
171[4] 4757[P] 4946[6]
Nick Junior (IRE) *Evan Williams* 116 c
7 b g Norwich—Paico Ana (Paico)
(998) 1879[P] 2825[P]
Nickname (FR) *Martin Brassil* 148 c
7 b g Lost World(IRE) —Newness (IRE) (Simply Great (FR))
(3409a) 3639a[P] 4138a[2]4625a[2]
Nick's Choice *D Burchell* 111+h
10 b g Sula Bula—Clare's Choice (Pragmatic)
372[3] 525[7] 633[6] 2334[8] 2621[P]2820[10] 3018[13] 3289[P] 3458[P] 3889[8]4105[8] 4282[9] (4490) 4566[2] 4736[10] 4781[4]4848[15]
Nick The Jewel *Andrew Turnell* 71h 118c
11 b g Nicholas Bill—Bijou Georgie (Rhodomantade)
178[9] 946[U] 1049[8]1189[8] (1659) 1746[2]2300[4]
Nick The Silver *Robert Gray* 84 h
5 gr g Nicolotte—Brillante (FR) (Green Dancer (USA))
218[U] 1552[6] 1643[2] (1887) 2110[8] 2964[11]3271[9] 3987[P]
Nicolas Mon Ami (FR) *J Howard Johnson*112+h
5 b g Sleeping Car(FR) —Veronique IV (FR) (Mont Basile (FR))
(1757)
Nico's Dream (IRE) *M W Easterby* 73+b
4 b g Old Vic—Magical Mist (IRE) (Be My Native (USA))
5141[9]
Nicozetto (FR) *N Wilson* 54h
6 b g Nicolotte—Arcizette (FR) (Sarhoob (USA))
2749[10] 3488[13] **4303[U]**
Nictos De Bersy (FR) *C P Morlock* 98b
5 b g Useful(FR) —Tropulka God (FR) (Tropular)
4574[4] 4881[3]
Niembro *K A Morgan* 91 h
6 b g Victory Note(USA) —Diabaig (Precocious)
14[13]
Nietzsche (IRE) *R J Hodges* 76h
5 b h Sadler's Wells(USA) —Wannabe (Shirley Heights)
2849[7]
Nifty Roy *I McMath* 88h 105+c
6 b g Royal Applause—Nifty Fifty (IRE) (Runnett)
14[3] (152) 949[P] 1112[4] 1149[7] 1336[9]1379[5] 1490[9] **1605[11]** 1663[9] 2171[10]3445[6] **3798[3] (4142) 4531[U]4586[3] (4842)**
Night Bridge (IRE) *John Joseph Murphy* 112+h
4 b g Quws—Gold Shift (USA) (Night Shift (USA))
(3408a) 4468[14]
Night Cap (IRE) *T D McCarthy* 53h
7 ch g Night Shift(USA) —Classic Design (Busted)
3659[P]
Nightfly (IRE) *M Pitman* 115b
5 b g Fourstars Allstar(USA) —Except Alice (IRE) (Orchestra)
(3657) 4448[14]
Night Mail *Miss J E Foster* 78h
6 b g Shaamit(IRE) —Penlanfeigan (Abutammam)
992[P] 1209[4] 1336[P]
Nightmare Bud (IRE) *T J Fitzgerald* 3b
5 b g Midhish—Alpine Accentor (IRE) (Nashamaa)
3399[11] 3563[13]
Night Pearl (FR) *B Storey* 41h
5 bb m April Night(FR) —Tarpeia (FR) (Suvero (FR))
1356[5] 1588[P]
Night Safe (IRE) *N A Twiston-Davies* 113b
5 b g Safety Catch(USA) —Rock All Night (IRE) (Orchestra)
1882[8] (2720) (4072)
Night Sight (USA) *Mrs S Lamyman* 96h
9 b g Eagle Eyed(USA) —El Hamo (USA) (Search For Gold (USA))
1553[3] 1642[3] 2766[7]
Night Warrior (IRE) *N P Littmoden* 88h
6 b g Alhaarth(IRE) —Miniver (IRE) (Mujtahid (USA))
2721[6] 5024[3]
Nightwatchman (IRE) *S B Clark* 99h
7 b g Hector Protector(USA) —Nightlark (IRE) (Night Shift (USA))
1218[3] 1322[5] 1456[2] 1488[P] 1608[P]
Nigwell Forbees (IRE) *J Howard Johnson*70+h
5 ch g Shernazar—Gender Gap (USA) (Shecky Greene (USA))
2444[17] 2923[13] 3376[12] 3941[P] 4988[5]
Nikola (FR) *N A Twiston-Davies* 124h
5 b g Roi De Rome(USA) —Envie De Chalamont (FR) (Pamponi (FR))
3328[2] 3793[4] (4114) 4430[19]
Nikolaiev (FR) *N J Henderson* 86 h
5 b g Nikos—Faensa (FR) (Fabulous Dancer (USA))
3843[3] 4665[10]
Nilang (FR) *C F Swan* 85h
5 b m Legend Of France(USA) —Armonie III (FR) (Neustrien (FR))
93a[19]
Nil Desperandum (IRE) *Ms F M Crowley*145h 146c
9 b g Un Desperado(FR) —Still Hoping (Kambalda)
2370[9] 3176[P] 3895a[4]4483a[2] 4777[4] 5004[11]
Nile Moon (IRE) *J Howard Johnson* 87h
5 b g Simply Great(FR) —Reasonable Time (IRE) (Reasonable (FR))
1849[11] 3793[6]
Nimvara (IRE) *Evan Williams* 90h
10 br m Lord Americo—Liskennett Girl (Master Owen)
287[U] 399[P] 839[6] 978[3]
Ninah *J M Bradley* 62h
5 b m First Trump—Alwal (Pharly (FR))
1916[10] 2148[9]
Nine De Sivola (FR) *Ferdy Murphy* 127 h 104c
5 b g Video Rock(FR) —Quine De Chalamont (FR) (Do Do (FR))
1937[3] (2186) 2417[P] (2638) (3173) (3389) 3987[5] 4461[19]
Nippy Des Mottes (FR) *P F Nicholls* 131 h
5 b g Useful(FR) —Julie Des Mottes (FR) (Puma Des Mottes (FR))
367[8] 563[2] 1784[2] (1969) 2207[F] 2530[7](3128) (3467) (3510) 3761[9] 4773[P]
Nirvana Swing (FR) *P F Nicholls*
5 b g Chamberlin(FR) —Ukrainia II (FR) (Tadj (FR))
4778[P]
Nisbet *Miss M Bremner* 79 c
12 b g Lithgie-Brig—Drummond Lass (Peacock (FR))
63[6] 555[6] 3758[F]4725[4]
Nite Fox (IRE) *Mrs H Dalton* 103h
7 ch m Anshan—New Talent (The Parson)
(236) 509[P] (1826)
Nitelite *Edward U Hales* 79b
4 ch f Bahamian Bounty—By Candlelight (IRE) (Roi Danzig (USA))
2830[6]
Niver Bai (FR) *Miss H C Knight* 100b
5 ch g River Bay(USA) —True Beauty (IRE) (Sun Prince)
4333[6] 4667[7]
Niza D'Alm (FR) *Miss Suzy Smith* 60b
5 bb m Passing Sale(FR) —Bekaa II (FR) (Djarvis (FR))
4800[8] 7[10]
Noaff (IRE) *Evan Williams* 85c
12 b g Mandalus—Good Sailing (Scorpio (FR))
1178[P]
Nobel (FR) *N G Richards* 110h
5 gr g Dadarissime(FR) —Eire Dancer (FR) (Useful (FR))
82[6] 301[5] 2289[3] (3269) 4584[5]
Nobel Bleu De Kerpaul (FR) *P Winkworth* 93h
5 b g Pistolet Bleu(IRE) —Gecika De Kerpaul (FR) (Sarpedon (FR))
1916[F] 2573[3] 2803[5] (3603) 3901[7] 4824[P]
Nobelmann (GER) *A W Carroll* 86h
7 ch g Lomitas—Ninova (GER) (Esclavo (FR))
2099[6] 2423[6] 2584[9] 3242[P] 3386[9]
Nobile (FR) *M Bradstock* 80b
5 b g Kadalko(FR) —Elione (FR) (Video Rock (FR))
2987[5] 5054[7]
Noble Baron *C G Cox* 120 c
10 gr g Karinga Bay—Grey Baroness (Baron Blakeney)
1972[F] 2273[2] 2847[P]3212[8] 3698[P]
Noble Bily (FR) *M C Pipe* 94+h
5 b g Signe Divin(USA) —Vaillante Bily (FR) (The Quiet Man (FR))
2618[2] 3659[5]
Noble Buck (IRE) *Mrs L J Young* 98h 99+c
10 b g Buckskin(FR) —Point The Finger (IRE) (Neshad (USA))
4428[U] 4737[2] (5122)

Noble Calling (FR) *R J Hodges* 106 h
9 b g Caller I.D.(USA) —Specificity (USA) (Alleged (USA))
1641^{6} 1784^{7} 2008^{2} 2071^{4} 2459^{6}2609^{3} 2731^{P} 3325^{6} 3876^{9}
Noble Colours *Mrs C J Ikin* 69c
13 b g Distinctly North(USA) —Kentucky Tears (USA) (Cougar (CHI))
1343^{10} 1433^{7} 1644^{4}1751^{P} **1803^{5} 1981^{P}**
Noble Concorde *D K Weld* 96h
4 gr c Daylami(IRE) —Place De L'Opera (Sadler's Wells (USA))
5076a^{7}
Noblefir (IRE) *L Lungo* 92+h 117+c
8 b g Shernazar—Chrisali (IRE) (Strong Gale)
1971^{0} **318^{2}**
Noble House *Mrs A Duffield* 93h 74c
9 ch g Gildoran—Trust To Luck (Mandamus)
1472 **550^{6}** 913^{9} (1308)
Noble Hymn *C A Mulhall* 87c
13 br g Arctic Lord—Soraway (Choral Society)
4633^{P}
Noble Justice (IRE) *R J Hodges* 96b 115c
10 b g Jurado(USA) —Furry Hope (Furry Glen)
946^{5} 1080^{3} 1236^{5}(1301) 1650^{3}
Noble Mind *P G Murphy* 68h
5 b g Mind Games—Lady Annabel (Alhijaz)
1975^{P}
Noble Pasao (IRE) *N G Richards* 100 h
9 b g Alzao(USA) —Belle Passe (Be My Guest (USA))
220^{5} 428^{P} 1793^{7} (Dead)
Noble Pursuit *R E Barr* 80h
9 b g Pursuit Of Love—Noble Peregrine (Lomond (USA))
1569^{6} 1756^{9} 1927^{10} 2567^{9}
Noble Raider (IRE) *T J Fitzgerald* 92+b
4 gr g Deploy—Smooth Princess (IRE) (Roi Danzig (USA))
4854^{4}
Noble Request (FR) *P J Hobbs* 154+h
5 gr g Highest Honor(FR) —Restless Mixa (IRE) (Linamix (FR))
1677^{7} 3510^{7} (3696) 4473^{2} 4773^{2} (5003) (5125)
Noble Sham *M C Pipe* 102+h
5 b g Shambo—Shamana (Broadsword (USA))
655^{4} 917^{2} 1274^{2} (1538)
Noble Spy (IRE) *Mrs D A Hamer* 81h
12 bb g Lord Americo—Flashey Blond (Buckskin (FR))
575^{P} 839^{P}
Nobodysgonanotice (IRE) *J J Lambe* 87h
8 b g Play'Ntothegallery(IRE) —Clear Bid (IRE) (Executive Perk)
643^{7} 875^{7} **1062^{8}** 1337^{4}1379^{6} 1508^{4} 1685^{8} 1884^{7}
Nobodys Perfect (IRE) *Ferdy Murphy* 100h
6 br m Heron Island(IRE) —Likeness (Young Generation)
1906^{10} 2240^{7} 2688^{2} 2981^{3} 3339^{5}3442^{2} 4450^{2} 5039^{2}
Nobody Tells Me (FR) *M C Pipe* 116+h
5 bb g Lute Antique(FR) —Becebege (FR) (Iron Duke (FR))
4032^{2} (4604) (5015)
No Can Do (IRE) *K J Burke* 52c
8 b m Mister Lord(USA) —Lady Bellaghy (IRE) (Salt Dome (USA))
2^{8} 52^{P}
Nocatee (IRE) *P C Haslam* 94h 102c
5 b g Vettori(IRE) —Rosy Sunset (IRE) (Red Sunset)
552^{3} 784^{13} 1571^{5} **1888^{3}(2675) 3489^{9} 3794^{7}4095^{3} 4492^{3}**
Nocivo (FR) *H D Daly* 88+h
5 b g Funny Baby(FR) —Esperance IV (FR) (Persifleur (USA))
(490) 2462^{4}
Nocloix (FR) *S B Bell* 75h
5 b g Brier Creek(USA) —Belle Gambette (FR) (Quart De Vin (FR))
4319^{8}
No Commission (IRE) *R F Fisher* 83h
4 b g General Monash(USA) —Price Of Passion (Dolphin Street (FR))
1797^{8} 2494^{5} 2569^{8} (3349) 4987^{12}
No Complications (IRE) *Paul Nolan* 125h 52c
8 b g Supreme Leader—Bramble Bird (Pitpan)
2650a^{5}
Nocturnally *V R A Dartnall* 102+h
6 b g Octagonal(NZ) —Arletty (Rainbow Quest (USA))
1777^{3} 2269^{3} 2821^{5} 4754^{4}
Nodforms Victoria (IRE) *Karen McLintock* 78b
5 b g Arctic Lord—Webb Find (IRE) (Over The River (FR))
4072^{13}
Nodform William *Karen McLintock* 90b
4 b g Prince Sabo—Periwinkle (FR) (Perrault)
2521^{3}
No Discount (IRE) *Edward Cawley* 138h 118c
12 b g Be My Native(USA) —Flameing Run (Deep Run)
5083a^{5}
Nod's Star *Mrs L C Jewell* 77h
5 ch m Starborough—Barsham (Be My Guest (USA))
1853 506^{2} 905^{P} 2552^{6}
Nod Ya Head *R E Barr* 74h
10 ch m Minster Son—Little Mittens (Little Buskins)
8^{4} 523^{5} 591^{5} 718^{8} 8^{4}
Noel's Pride *C C Bealby* 128 h 99c
10 b g Good Thyne(USA) —Kavali (Blakeney)
1568^{P} 1960^{5}
Noend (IRE) *Ms F M Crowley* 103h
4 ch g Entrepreneur—Lucky Fountain (IRE) (Lafontaine (USA))
3890a^{7}
No Full (FR) *P R Webber* 91h 134 c
5 b g Useful(FR) —Rosy Junior (FR) (Labus (FR))
2422^{4} 2869^{P} 3391^{2}(3973) 4456^{9} 5007^{3}

No Further Comment (IRE) *Mrs Jeremy Young* 89h 97c
6 b g Lord Americo—Saltee Star (Arapaho)
107^{2} 523^{2} **998^{3}**1152^{P}
Noggler *M J Brown* 87+c
7 b g Primitive Rising(USA) —Sun Goddess (FR) (Deep Roots)
4009^{P} 4146^{U} 4477^{P}
No Girls Allowed *D Shaw*
6 ch g Cotation—Marcroft (Crofthall)
1791^{3}
No Guarantees *N A Twiston-Davies* 110+h
6 b g Master Willie—Princess Hotpot (IRE) (King's Ride)
1938 ^{2} 2295^{3} 2614^{3} 3291^{3} 3613^{7}(4852)
No Half Session (IRE) *Noel Meade*121+h 123c
9 ch g Be My Native(USA) —Weekly Sessions (Buckskin (FR))
(91a) 4433^{14}
No Hesitation *Mrs S C Bradburne* 12h
5 b g Terimon—Just A Minute (Derrylin)
59^{P} 2091^{0} 301^{P}
Noir Et Vert (FR) *Ferdy Murphy* 106+h
5 b g Silver Rainbow—Danse Verte (FR) (Brezzo (FR))
2450^{6} 2859^{5} 3205^{6} (5064) (5123)
Noisetine (FR) *Miss Venetia Williams*107h 140+c
8 ch m Mansonnien(FR) —Notabilite (FR) (No Pass No Sale)
(2622) 3180^{11} 3503^{P}4611^{2} 4984^{P}
No Kidding *J I A Charlton* 87 c
12 b g Teenoso(USA) —Vaigly Fine (Vaigly Great)
213^{P} 2479^{F} 3486^{5}(3762) 3930^{6}
Noland *P F Nicholls* 144+h
5 b g Exit To Nowhere(USA) —Molakai (USA) (Nureyev (USA))
1857^{3} (2742) (3297) (3878) (4430)
Nolans Joy (IRE) *W J Burke* 72h
5 b m Shernazar—Murphy's Venture (IRE) (Pollerton)
5134a^{6}
Nolans Pride (IRE) *W J Burke* 106h 122c
9 b m Good Thyne(USA) —Saucy Gale (IRE) (Strong Gale)
112a^{P}
Noleens Moon (IRE) *P J Rothwell* 95h
8 ch m Un Desperado(FR) —Last Moon (IRE) (Montelimar (USA))
1116a^{7}
Nolife (IRE) *Miss Lucinda V Russell* 97+h
10 b g Religiously(USA) —Garnerstown Lady (Pitpan)
1838^{2} 4317^{P} 4986^{F} (Dead)
Nomadic Blaze *P G Atkinson* 49h 72c
9 b g Nomadic Way(USA) —Dreamago (Sir Mago)
148^{5} 413^{5} 550^{3}593^{7} 2109^{5} 2415^{P}2692^{F} 3268^{5} 3555^{5}3915^{P} 4659^{P} 4918^{P}
Nominate (GER) *S Flook* 88c
6 b g Desert King(IRE) —Northern Goddess (Night Shift (USA))
5053^{3}
Nonantais (FR) *M Bradstock* 125h 120 c
9 b g Nikos—Sanhia (FR) (Sanhedrin (USA))
(127) 1617^{P} 2336^{7} 2633^{2} 2974^{6} 3727^{12}3986^{11}
None-So-Pretty *Miss E C Lavelle* 47+h
5 b m Tamure(IRE) —Sweet Memory (Lir)
(277) 1725^{7}
Nonita (FR) *T Civel*
6 b m Nononito(FR) —Contesty (FR) (Sicyos (USA))
(1372a)
Nonotreally *B Mactaggart* 76h
5 b g Rakaposhi King—Wellwotdouthink (Rymer)
431^{5} 2906^{8} 4720^{6}
Non So (FR) *N J Henderson* 146h 155 c
8 b g Definite Article—Irish Woman (FR) (Assert)
2489^{4} 3136^{3} 3739^{3}(4459)
Nooska Tivoli (FR) *P Tual*
5 b g Rajpoute(FR) —Passe Chesne (FR) (Rb Chesne)
778a^{P}
Nopekan (IRE) *Mrs K Waldron* 105+c
6 b g Sri Pekan(USA) —Giadamar (IRE) (Be My Guest (USA))
2^{3} 217^{3} 510^{4}8934
No Picnic (IRE) *Mrs S C Bradburne* 113h 103c
8 ch g Be My Native(USA) —Emmagreen (Green Shoon)
441^{10} 1844 ^{P} **2654^{4} 4343^{3}4528^{5} 4788^{3}** 5123^{5}
Noras Legacy (IRE) *Miss Lucinda V Russell* 72h
8 b m Old Vic—Balda Girl (IRE) (Mandalus)
120^{8} 214^{5} 496^{3} 718^{F} 781^{P}1066^{9}
No Refuge (IRE) *J Howard Johnson* 153+h
6 ch g Hernando(FR) —Shamarra (FR) (Zayyani)
(2326) 3723^{5} 4458^{13} 4745^{3}
No Retreat (NZ) *J Groucott* 117 c
13 b g Exattic(USA) —Lerwick (NZ) (Thoreau (FR))
(49) (348) 453^{3} 3693^{2}(4079) 4471^{13}
No Reward (IRE) *Mrs D M Grissell* 74c
10 b g Persian Mews—Tara's Dream (Polar Jinks)
404^{U}
Norma Hill *R Hollinshead* 120 h 111 c
5 b m Polar Prince(IRE) —Smartie Lee (Dominion)
450^{8} **2422^{3} (3647)**
Norman's Glories *R J Baker* 61h
8 ch g Past Glories—Norman's Delight (IRE) (Idiots Delight)
1123^{P} 1782^{9} 1898^{8}
Norminster *R Nixon* 77h
5 ch g Minster Son—Delightfool (Idiots Delight)
720^{10} 2652^{5} 2947^{9} 3376^{9} 3757^{9}4346^{3} 4585^{6} 5093^{6}
Nor'Nor'East (IRE) *Jonjo O'Neill* 120 h
8 b g Supreme Leader—Force Seven (Strong Gale)
1672^{3} (1915) 2295^{2} (2633) 3970^{P}
Northaw Lad (IRE) *C Tinkler* 106+h
8 ch g Executive Perk—Black Tulip (Pals Passage)
4104^{2} 4649^{3} (4934)

Northern Deal (IRE) *Evan Williams* 96+h 123 c
11 b g Top Of The World—Amberley (Deep Run)
3249^{4} **3803^{5}**
Northern Echo *K S Thomas* 76h 46c
9 b g Pursuit Of Love—Stop Press (USA) (Sharpen Up)
11^{7} 152^{2} 552^{7} 781^{8} 941^{6}988^{7} **1062^{P} 1376^{8}1589^{9} 1686^{6} 1822^{8}**
Northern Endeavour *Simon Earle* 84b
7 b g Alflora(IRE) —Northern Jinks (Piaffer (USA))
138^{4} 2288^{3} 2665^{14} 3806^{P}
Northern Flash *J C Haynes* 71h 80c
12 b g Rambo Dancer(CAN) —Spinster (Grundy)
122^{5} 213^{5} 601^{5}716^{7} **874^{P} 1311^{8}**
Northern Friend *R C Guest* 85h
6 b g Distinctly North(USA) —Pharaoh's Joy (Robellino (USA))
370^{5} 520^{2}
Northern Link (IRE) *Miss Tor Sturgis* 83h
7 b g Distinctly North(USA) —Miss Eurolink (Touching Wood (USA))
2376^{6} 3238^{9} 4005^{10} 4826^{P} 5072^{2}
Northern Matriarch *H P Hogarth*
5 b m Defacto(USA) —Distant Cherry (General Ironside)
2572^{16}
Northern Minster *F P Murtagh* 100+h 101c
7 b g Minster Son—Hand On Heart (IRE) (Taufan (USA))
1662^{5} 1835^{F} 1911^{5}2449^{6} 2568^{U} 2945^{P}
Northern News (IRE) *G A Swinbank* 80b
6 b g Saddlers' Hall(IRE) —Some News (IRE) (Be My Native (USA))
2106^{P}
Northern Quest (IRE) *H P Hogarth* 48b
5 ch g Un Desperado(FR) —Strong Heather (IRE) (Strong Gale)
2192^{11} 2572^{12} 3253^{11} 4787^{P}
Northern Rambler (IRE) *K G Reveley*81h 65+c
9 gr g Roselier(FR) —Ramble Bramble (Random Shot)
81^{P} 601^{11} **998^{P}**1379^{4} **1433^{6} 1602^{8}**2188^{2} 2440^{7} 2517^{9} 2586^{7} 3042^{5}
Northern Shadows *K G Reveley* 89h
7 gr m Rock Hopper—Shadows Of Silver (Carwhite)
2750^{15} 3367^{2} 3918^{P}
Northern Spirit *C W Moore* 40h
5 b g Kadeed(IRE) —Elegant Spirit (Elegant Air)
5009^{P}
Northern Stars (IRE) *H P Hogarth* 38b
5 b g Fourstars Allstar(USA) —Corun Girl (Apollo Eight)
4455^{15}
North Landing (IRE) *R C Guest* 102+h
6 b g Storm Bird(CAN) —Tirol Hope (IRE) (Tirol)
2107^{3} 2453^{3} 2680^{4} (2843) 2952^{4} 3783^{8}3918^{F} 4723^{15} 4922^{3}
North Lodge (GER) *A King* 106 h
6 b g Grand Lodge(USA) —Nona (GER) (Cortez (GER))
2015^{5} (2563) 2750^{2} 3371^{P} 4838^{5}
North Roc *M Scudamore* 75b
6 b g North Col—Madam Advocate (Avocat)
1543^{12}
Norton Sapphire *V R A Dartnall* 81+h
7 ch m Karinga Bay—Sea Of Pearls (IRE) (King's Ride)
(1297)
Norwegian *Ian Williams* 76h
5 b g Halling(USA) —Chicarica (USA) (The Minstrel (CAN))
78^{P}
Nosam *R C Guest* 86h 97+c
16 b g Idiots Delight—Socher (Anax)
181^{4} 416^{4} 997^{6}1321^{2}
No Sam No *Miss Lucinda V Russell* 81h 81c
8 b m Reprimand—Samjamalifran (Blakeney)
859^{11} 941^{P}
Noscar (FR) *B G Powell* 42b
5 ch g Ragmar(FR) —Perle De Saisy (FR) (Italic (FR))
4825^{10}
Noshinannikin *Mrs S J Smith* 127h 129 c
12 ch g Anshan—Preziosa (Homing)
108^{4} 427^{3} 547^{8}765^{2}
No Sound (FR) *Noel Meade* 110+h
5 br m Exit To Nowhere(USA) —Sound Hill (FR) (Green Tune (USA))
2031a^{3} 3894a^{17}
Nostalgia (POL) *R Holcak*
9 ch m Jape(USA) —Norcja (POL) (Chiavari)
1710a^{P}
Nostra (FR) *M C Pipe* 97h
5 br m Limnos(JPN) —La Giudecca (FR) (Rb Chesne)
3495^{P} 4034^{P}
Not Amused (UAE) *Ian Williams* 86+h
6 ch g Indian Ridge—Amusing Time (IRE) (Sadler's Wells (USA))
412^{3} 760^{2} 806^{3} 1223^{7}
Notanotherdonkey (IRE) *M Scudamore*88h 110 c
6 b g Zaffaran(USA) —Sporting Talent (IRE) (Seymour Hicks (FR))
121^{P} 1715^{3} **1877^{2} 2623^{3}**2994^{7} 3613^{6} **4281^{7} 4552^{3}**
Notaproblem (IRE) *G A Harker* 104h
7 b g Oscar(IRE) —Smashed Free (IRE) (Carlingford Castle)
(14) 194^{6} 2262^{P} 2440^{2} 3316^{2} 3443^{3}3854^{6} 4390^{3}
Not A Trace (IRE) *Mrs S C Bradburne* 81h 98c
7 b g Gothland(FR) —Copmenow (IRE) (Mandalus)
1663^{4} **2945^{P} 3268^{2}3489^{2} 3762^{P} 3928^{4}4844^{10} 5119^{3}**
Not For Diamonds (IRE) *Mrs H Dalton* 70h
6 b g Arctic Lord—Black-Crash (Crash Course)
(1762) 3392^{5} 3789^{9}
No Time At All (IRE) *Mayne Kidd* 74h
6 b m Saddlers' Hall(IRE) —Time Of The Lord (IRE) (Lord Americo)
304^{6}

Not Left Yet (IRE) *M C Pipe* 128 h
5 bb g Old Vic—Dalus Dawn (Mandalus)
(2173) 2292^{2} 3298^{12} 3615^{6} 3993^{6} 4661^{2}
Notre Cyborg (FR) *P F Nicholls* 103+b
5 ch g Cyborg(FR) —Cate Bleue (FR) (Katowice (FR))
(3720) 4574^{11}
Not To Be Missed *R Dickin* 88h
8 gr m Missed Flight—Petinata (Petong)
25^{9} 506^{6} 613^{2} 811^{2} 1235^{4}
Not Today Sir (IRE) *S Donohoe* 121h 104+c
8 b g Be My Native(USA) —Scenic Gold (IRE) (Supreme Leader)
(2474) (3487)
No Turning Back (IRE) *C L Popham* 78b
7 b g Shernazar—Offaly Rose (IRE) (The Parson)
1892^{P}
Notwhatshewanted (IRE) *J W Mullins* 84h 52c
9 b g Supreme Leader—Wise Nellie (IRE) (Brush Aside (USA))
295^{5} 506^{10} **632^{6} 916^{6}**
Nougat De L'Isle (FR) *C L Tizzard* 107b
5 b g Kadalko(FR) —Ceres De L'Isle (FR) (Bad Conduct (USA))
3583^{5} 3911^{5} 4333^{3}
Noun De La Thinte (FR) *Miss Venetia Williams* 99h
5 b m Oblat(FR) —Belis De La Thinte (FR) (Marasali)
2501^{10} 2859^{P} 3280^{2} 3461^{9}
Nous Voila (FR) *M C Pipe* 142 h
5 b g Video Rock(FR) —Ability (FR) (Olmeto)
(2249) (2584) 2746^{11} (3491) 3986^{3} 4375^{17}
Novacella (FR) *R H Alner* 105+h
5 b m Beyssac(FR) —Une Risette (FR) (Air Du Nord (USA))
(1974) 2530^{5} (2932) 3247^{5} 3733^{4} (4568) 4972^{8}
Novack Du Beury (FR) *Ferdy Murphy* 61h
5 b g Epaphos(GER) —Pampa Star (FR) (Pampabird)
1927^{13} 2343^{6} 2527^{P} 4052^{8} 4277^{P}5069^{9}
Noviciate (!RE) *Simon Earle* 61b
6 b g Bishop Of Cashel—Red Salute (Soviet Star (USA))
2050^{5} 3800^{9}
No Visibility (IRE) *R H Alner* 104h 131+c
11 b g Glacial Storm(USA) —Duhallow Lady (IRE) (Torus)
2622^{3} 3019^{4} 3387^{6}(4332) 4611^{4} 4755^{P}
Nowa Huta (FR) *Jedd O'Keeffe* 77h
5 b m Passing Sale(FR) —Saperlipopette II (FR) (Prove It Baby (USA))
2106^{U} 2412^{6} 2674^{3} 2977^{P} 3918^{8}5069^{11}
Now And Again *I W McInnes* 79+h
7 b g Shaamit(IRE) —Sweet Allegiance (Alleging (USA))
602^{4} 670^{13} 781^{11}
Nowator (POL) *Robert Gray* 107+h 130+c
9 ch g Jape(USA) —Naradka (POL) (Dakota)
(305) 615^{2} 940^{3} **1221^{9}**2139^{6} **2498^{P} (2626) 3293^{P}3495^{2} 3619^{P} 3974^{B}** (Dead)
No Way Back (IRE) *Miss E C Lavelle* 107+h
6 b g Eve's Error—Janeyway (Bulldozer)
1772^{14} 1916^{7} 2683^{3} 3242^{P} 4621^{7}(4945)
No Where To Hyde (IRE) *C Roche* 131h
6 ch g Topanoora—Tahaddi (USA) (Northern Baby (CAN))
2650a^{3} 3411a^{2} 4446^{F} (Dead)
Now Then Auntie (IRE) *Mrs S A Watt* 77h
5 gr m Anshan—Tara's Lady (General Ironside)
1593^{5} 1839^{8} 2414^{5} 2571^{8} 3271^{10}3484^{4} **5140^{P}**
Now Then Katie *C Grant* 67b
4 b f Kayf Tara—Nativus (IRE) (Be My Native (USA))
2520^{6} 3259^{6}
Now Then Sid *Mrs S A Watt* 100h 99 c
7 ch g Presidium—Callace (Royal Palace)
119^{5} 554^{8} 717^{6}(1065) 1150^{3} 1376^{2}(1570) 5036^{6}
Nudge And Nurdle (IRE) *N A Twiston-Davies* 70h
5 b g Shernazar—Firey Comet (IRE) (Buckskin (FR))
2618^{4}
Nuit Sombre (IRE) *J G M O'Shea* 112+h 70c
6 b g Night Shift(USA) —Belair Princess (USA) (Mr Prospector (USA))
175^{3} 460^{5} 1675^{P} **1958^{7}**3128^{9}
Numbersixvalverde (IRE) *Martin Brassil*124h 154c
10 b g Broken Hearted—Queens Tricks (Le Bavard (FR))
115a^{5} 3053a^{8} (4777)
Numero Un De Solzen (FR) *J P L Ewart* 113 h
5 b g Passing Sale(FR) —Tiffany'S (FR) (Chamberlin (FR))
(2450) 3381^{2} 4313^{3}
Numidas (POL) *P J Hobbs* 32h
4 bl c Duke Valentino—Numata (POL) (Freedom's Choice (USA))
2274^{11} 2597^{12} 2824^{13}
Nurzyk (POL) *T R George* 81+h 83+c
9 ch g Freedom's Choice(USA) —Numeria (POL) (Dakota)
169^{2}
Nutley Queen (IRE) *M Appleby* 68h
7 b m Eagle Eyed(USA) —Secret Hideaway (USA) (Key To The Mint (USA))
173^{F} 263^{4} 467^{7} 822^{7} 973^{10}1814^{3} 2146^{9} 2567^{3} 3557^{13}
Nuzzle *N G Richards* 81+h
6 b m Salse(USA) —Lena (USA) (Woodman (USA))
1527^{10} 1683^{U} (2040) 3655^{7} 4919^{4}
Nycos Des Ormeaux (FR) *Ferdy Murphy* 68h
5 bl g Sheyrann—Don't Be Low (FR) (Goldneyev (USA))
323^{4} 1903^{10} (Dead)
Nycteos (FR) *P F Nicholls* 123h 133+c
5 ch g Chamberlin(FR) —Cynthia (FR) (Mont Basile (FR))
1823^{5} **3903^{2} (4102) (4371) 4762^{F}**

Nykel (FR) *A King* 107 c
5 ch g Brier Creek(USA) —Une Du Chatelier (FR) (Quart De Vin (FR))
1845[P] 3241[3] 3698[3](4078) 4419[5] 4985[P]

Nyrche (FR) *A King* 136 h 162+c
6 b g Medaaly—Thoiry (USA) (Sagace (FR))
(56) 1971[5] (2270) 2371[P] 2634[5] 4076[2]4472[4] 4749[2] (5006) 5143[2]

Oa Baldixe (FR) *K J Burke*
12 gr g Linamix(FR) —Bal D'Oa (FR) (Noir Et Or)
4782[P] (Dead)

Oakapple Express *G A Harker* 109b
6 b g Alflora(IRE) —Royal Scarlet (Royal Fountain)
2007[2] 2948[3] 4072[3]

Oakfield Legend *P S Payne* 78+h 80+c
5 b g Midnight Legend—Kins Token (Relkino)
1755[5] *1922[13]* 2144[P]4642[6] 4826[7] 5028[P] 5106[4]

Oakley Absolute *R Hannon*
4 ch c Bluegrass Prince(IRE) —Susie Oakley VII (Damsire Unregistered)
3340[F]

Oasis Banus (IRE) *M C Pipe* 67h
5 b g Shaamit(IRE) —Summit Else (El Conquistador)
1637[P] 1900[4] 2378[5]

Oasis Blue (IRE) *M C Pipe* 57h
5 gr g Norwich—Mini Fashion (IRE) (Roselier (FR))
1640[7] 1725[10] 1779[F] 1896[3] 2605[6]

Obaki De Grissay (FR) *H D Daly* 90b
4 b g Robin Des Pres(FR) —Topeka (FR) (Italic (FR))
4500[7] 5054[3]

Obara D'Avril (FR) *Miss Kate Milligan* 55h
4 gr f April Night(FR) —Baraka De Thaix II (FR) (Olmeto)
2569[7]

Obay *M Todhunter* 102h
5 ch g Kingmambo(USA) —Parade Queen (USA) (A.P. Indy (USA))
1360[9] 1588[P]

Obe One *J Howard Johnson*
6 b g Puissance—Plum Bold (Be My Guest (USA))
1510[P]

Oblivious *K J Burke* 17h
4 b g Rainbow Quest(USA) —Never A Care (USA) (Roberto (USA))
1146[11]

Obstreperous Way *P R Chamings* 41h
4 ch g Dr Fong(USA) —Fleet Key (Afleet (CAN))
1268[F] 1594[13] 1737[13]

Ocean Of Storms (IRE) *N I M Rossiter* 77h
11 bb g Arazi(USA) —Moon Cactus (Kris)
3023[13] 3283[2] 3611[9] 3905[P]

Ocean Tide *R Ford* 101+h
9 b g Deploy—Dancing Tide (Pharly (FR))
2862[P] 3250[3] 4043[2] (4453) 4658[2]

O Cinza (IRE) *B G Powell* 81b
8 gr g Norwich—Queenlier (IRE) (Roselier (FR))
2866[P]

Ockley Flyer *Miss Z C Davison* 88h
7 b g Sir Harry Lewis(USA) —Bewails (IRE) (Caerleon (USA))
2934[P] 3424[P] 5087[2]

Ocotillo *James Moffatt* 61h
6 b g Mark Of Esteem(IRE) —Boojum (Mujtahid (USA))
331[5] 418[10] 495[7]

Ocras Mor (IRE) *Miss S Cox* 119h
8 bb m Old Vic—Special Trix (IRE) (Peacock (FR))
66a[10]

October Mist (IRE) *K G Reveley* 116+h 112c
12 gr g Roselier(FR) —Bonny Joe (Derring Rose)
(2519) 3318[8] 4215[6] 4792[4] 5005[5]

Odagh Odyssey (IRE) *Miss E C Lavelle* 117h 128c
12 ch g Ikdam—Riverside Willow (Callernish)
108[2] 452[3] 726[P]**840[8]** 1250[P]

Oddington (IRE) *Mrs Susan Nock* 47h
6 b g Supreme Leader—Woodford Princess (Menelek)
2427[7] 2815[P] 4676[P]

Oddsmaker (IRE) *M A Barnes* 98+h
5 b g Barathea(IRE) —Archipova (IRE) (Ela-Mana-Mou)
2006[2] 2062[3] 2447[F]

Odiham *H Morrison* 117h
5 b g Deploy—Hug Me (Shareef Dancer (USA))
2487[3] 2755[5] 3342[3]

Odyseusz (POL) *F Zobal*
8 ch g Jape(USA) —Ombrelia (POL) (Dixieland (POL))
1710a[U]

O'Ech *Mrs C Lawrence* 65+c
12 gr m Baron Blakeney—Hand Maid (Some Hand)
299[4] 4946[7]

Of Course (FR) *Miss Kate Milligan* 81b
4 ch c Adnaan(IRE) —Intelectuelle (FR) (Montorselli)
2520[4]

Of Course (IRE) *W P Mullins* 112+h
8 ch g Montelimar(USA) —Linda's Course (IRE) (Crash Course)
93a[16]

Ofcoursehekhan (IRE) *Mrs N C Neill* 30c
8 b g Phardante(FR) —King's Gift (IRE) (King's Ride)
5040[6]

Offalevel *R J Hodges* 77h 61c
8 ch g Beveled(USA) —Taffidale (Welsh Pageant)
893[6] 1859[6] 1898[5]

Offemont (FR) *Mrs L C Taylor* 71+h 93+c
5 br g Bulington(FR) —La Guyonniere (FR) (Silver Rainbow)
2044[3] 2482[P] 4603[7]4849[13]

Officer Cadet (IRE) *P J Hobbs*
7 b g Warcraft(USA) —Flinging (Good Times (ITY))
3882[P] (Dead)

Off Spin *P R Webber* 94h
6 b g Petoski—Re-Spin (Gildoran)
(131) 2161[9]

Off The Edge (AUS) *Ian Williams* 79h
7 br g Hatta's Mill—Himalaya Vain (AUS) (Semipalatinsk (USA))
91[3] 320[8] **862[P]**

Oh Be The Hokey (IRE) *C F Swan* 113h 131c
8 b g Be My Native(USA) —Lucky Perk (IRE) (Executive Perk)
69a[5]

Oh Calin (FR) *A Chaille-Chaille* 124h 108c
4 b c Alamo Bay(USA) —Soicaline (FR) (Olmeto)
1428a[2] 4468[10]

Oh Golly Gosh *N P Littmoden* 82h 40c
5 ch g Exit To Nowhere(USA) —Guerre De Troie (Risk Me (FR))
2422[P] 2861[6] 3220[6]

Ohmissymoss (IRE) *Michael C Griffin* 91h
7 ch m Moscow Society(USA) —Knockacool Breeze (Buckskin (FR))
5077a[20]

Oh Mister Pinceau (FR) *H D Daly* 71h
4 bl g Cupidon(FR) —Altesse D'O (FR) (Tadj (FR))
2286[6] 2811[7] 2954[11] 4919[8]

Oh My Lord (IRE) *A J Martin* 49h 123c
8 b g Mister Lord(USA) —Ross Rag (Ragapan)
765[P] 857[2] 1803[2]2164[3] 2745[F]

Oh So Brave *Evan Williams* 97+h 102c
9 gr g Arzanni—Goodbye Roscoe (Roscoe Blake)
1041[2] (1062)

Oh So Hardy *M A Allen* 73h
5 bb m Fleetwood(IRE) —Miss Hardy (Formidable (USA))
1522[3]

Oh So Lively (IRE) *E J O'Grady* 82h 117c
8 b g King's Ride—Borgina (Boreen (FR))
1515a[10]

Oh Sunny Boy (IRE) *B G Powell* 67h
5 b g Desert Sun—Naivement (IRE) (Doyoun)
1028[P] 1432[8] 1482[7] 1520[3] 1597[8]

Ojays Alibi (IRE) *J D Frost* 102+h 107+c
10 b g Witness Box(USA) —Tinkers Lady (Sheer Grit)
346[P]

Okayman (FR) *A Parker* 58h
5 b g Mansonnien(FR) —Aykoku Saky (FR) (Baby Turk)
1605[10] 2858[P] 2962[P]

Oktis Morilious (IRE) *J A Danahar* 82h
5 b g Octagonal(NZ) —Nottash (IRE) (Royal Academy (USA))
3885[P] 4278[10] 4550[4] 4828[8] 5021[11]

Olaso (GER) *Jonjo O'Neill* 140 h
7 b g Law Society(USA) —Olaya (GER) (Acatenango (GER))
2175[3] (3970) 4461[P]

Olazuro Du Mou (FR) *T Doumen* 48h
4 b g Sleeping Car(FR) —Viviane Du Mou (FR) (Tin Soldier (FR))
4616[10]

Olchons Debut (IRE) *Miss A E Broyd*
8 ch g Denel(FR) —Buckskins Babe (IRE) (Buckskin (FR))
3249[F]

Old Barns (IRE) *G A Swinbank* 75h
6 b g Nucleon(USA) —Surfer Katie (IRE) (Be My Native (USA))
2444[12] 3793[P]

Old Bean (IRE) *O R Dukes* 100+h
10 b g Eurobus—Princess Petara (IRE) (Petorius)
3968[P]

Old Benny *A King* 98b
5 b g Saddlers' Hall(IRE) —Jack's The Girl (IRE) (Supreme Leader)
2565[4] 3399[2] 4333[7]

Old Buddy (IRE) *B G Powell* 79h 97c
10 br g Roselier(FR) —Tipperary Star (Arcticeelagh)
1178[2]

Oldenway *R A Fahey* 83 h
7 b g Most Welcome—Sickle Moon (Shirley Heights)
1569[5]

Old Feathers (IRE) *Jonjo O'Neill* 108 h
9 b g Hernando(FR) —Undiscovered (Tap On Wood)
2505[3] 2820[9] 2990[P] 3458[7] (3733) 4593[P]4852[P]

Old Flame (IRE) *Paul Nolan* 118h 141c
7 b g Oscar(IRE) —Flameing Run (Deep Run)
45a[6] 3527a[2] 3724[8]

Old Golden Bay *M Wellings*
6 b g Meqdaam(USA) —Modina April (New Member)
138[P] 742[P]

Old Marsh (IRE) *A W Carroll* 126 h 136+c
10 b g Grand Lodge(USA) —Lolly Dolly (Alleged (USA))
452[2] 1087[3]

Old Nosey (IRE) *B Mactaggart* 93h 93c
10 b g Muhanb(USA) —Regent Star (Prince Regent (FR))
80[8] 215[10] **407[5] 546[6]**1606[6] 2066[6] 2474[3] 2840[11]

Old Opry *Noel Meade* 124h 124c
9 b g Old Vic—Tina Rosa (Bustino)
45a[5]

Old Pike Girl (IRE) *G M O'Neill* 103h 100c
9 gr m Jurado(USA) —Nancy's Sister (The Parson)
112a[15] (Dead)

Old Rolla (IRE) *C Storey* 97h 77c
8 b g Old Vic—Criswood (IRE) (Chromite (USA))
595[3] **4722[6]**

Old Splendour (IRE) *D J Ryan* 78h
8 b g Old Vic—Miss Splendour (IRE) (Kemal (FR))
3325[P]

Olimpo (FR) *P J Hobbs* 85h
5 ch g Starborough—Emily Allan (IRE) (Shirley Heights)
517[F] 664[6] 1046[3] 1188[4] 1272[2]1366[3] 1862[12] 1902[P]

Olival (FR) *Jonjo O'Neill* 93+h
4 b g Le Balafre(FR) —Carvine D'Or (FR) (Pot D'Or (FR))
3963[4] 4389[3] (4506) 4986[P]

Oliverjohn (IRE) *Miss Lucinda V Russell* 107 c
9 ch g Denel(FR) —Graeme's Gem (Pry)
593[3] 858[P] 1062[P]2945[3] (3233) (3543) 3852[3]

Ollie Magern *N A Twiston-Davies* 128h 165dc
8 b g Alderbrook—Outfield (Monksfield)
(1926) 2337[7] 2972[6]3697[4] 4470[17] 4746[5]

Ol' Man River (IRE) *H D Daly* 84h
6 b g Dr Massini(IRE) —Nearly Married (Nearly A Hand)
490[8] 2249[6] 2619[9] 3139[P] 3577[4]4282[8]

Olmetta (FR) *J P L Ewart* 64h
4 bb f Baby Turk—Tarpeia (FR) (Suvero (FR))
2642[5] 3442[9] 3927[11]

Olney Lad *Mrs P Robeson* 135 h 143+c
7 b g Democratic(USA) —Alipampa (IRE) (Glenstal (USA))
1669[4] 1976[4] (3541) 4112[F] 4759[6] (5131a)

Olympian Time *Miss J E Foster* 40h
6 b m Luso—Little Time (Arctic Lord)
349[14] 1014[6] 1377[F] 1485[8] 2283[P]

Olympic Storm (IRE) *N G Richards* 94+h
8 b g Glacial Storm(USA) —Philly Athletic (Sit In The Corner (USA))
320[6] 414[P] 856[2] 941[2]

Omas Glen (IRE) *Cecil Ross* 75h
5 br m Naheez(USA) —Carrick Glen (IRE) (Orchestra)
5104a[7]

Omas Leader (IRE) *J J Lambe* 75h
8 b m Supreme Leader—Derby Fox (IRE) (King's Ride)
1683[4]

O'Muircheartaigh (IRE) *E J O'Grady* 136h
6 b g Accordion—Brian's Delight (IRE) (Celio Rufo)
(2228a) 2667a[2] 4430[10] 4950a[2]

Once (FR) *M G Rimell* 75h
6 gr g Hector Protector(USA) —Moon Magic (Polish Precedent (USA))
2826[11] 3127[7] 4005[8]

Once A Brownie (IRE) *Edward U Hales* 116+b
5 b g Oscar(IRE) —Chocolate Brownie (IRE) (Orchestra)
2782a[2]

Once Seen *O Sherwood* 111 h
6 b g Celtic Swing—Brief Glimpse (IRE) (Taufan (USA))
428[3]

One Alone *Jean-Rene Auvray* 65h
5 b m Atraf—Songsheet (Dominion)
3550[P] 4074[15]

One And Only (GER) *D W Thompson*
5 ch m Kornado—On My Guest (IRE) (Be My Guest (USA))
3442[P]

One Cool Cookie (IRE) *C F Swan* 116h
5 ch g Old Vic—Lady Bellingham (IRE) (Montelimar (USA))
4336a[3]

One Cornetto (IRE) *L Wells* 111 h 125 c
7 b g Eurobus—Costenetta (IRE) (Runnett)
(803) 1024[2] 1871[4]2163[8] 2634[F] 3601[3]4618[8] 4822[P]

One Day (NZ) *R C Guest* 102+h 104 c
8 ch g Stark South(USA) —Dragon Pearl (USA) (Ahonoora)
1678[4] 1837[7] 2465[3]2703[P]

One Dream (FR) *R H Alner*
4 b f Balleroy(USA) —Galene III (FR) (Bayolidaan (FR))
1948[P]

One Five Eight *M W Easterby* 100h 93c
7 b g Alflora(IRE) —Dark Nightingale (Strong Gale)
1928[6] 2187[F] (2655) **2966[P] 3398[P] 3928[P]**

Oneforbertandhenry (IRE) *G M Moore* 87h 91+c
7 b g Rashar(USA) —Roi Vision (Roi Guillaume (FR))
4918[3]

One For Terry (IRE) *Mrs S D Williams* 77b
6 b m Saddlers' Hall(IRE) —Crosschild (IRE) (Buckskin (FR))
748[P]

Onefortheroadpaddy (IRE) *F Costello* 57h
6 ch m Oscar Schindler(IRE) —Minster's Madam (Minster Son)
2784a[P]

One Four Shannon (IRE) *D J Ryan* 110h 126c
9 b g Arctic Lord—Moss Air (Le Moss)
2539a[8] (5102a)

One Knight (IRE) *P J Hobbs* 134h 167c
10 ch g Roselier(FR) —Midnights Daughter (IRE) (Long Pond)
3022[F] 3697[U] 4470[P]5144[F]

One Love (IRE) *P J Rothwell* 89h
8 b m Bravefoot—Powers Of Magic (IRE) (Fairy King (USA))
4052[2]

One More Minute (IRE) *C F Swan* 109h 122c
6 ch g Zaffaran(USA) —Wollongong (IRE) (King Persian)
43a[13] **4929a[F] 5131a[6]**

One More Step *R A Farrant* 115b
5 b g Parthian Springs—Brush Belle (IRE) (Brush Aside (USA))
(1688) 4244[9] 4595[4] (Dead)

One More Stride *H J Manners* 77+h
10 g g Beveled(USA) —Gem Of Gold (Jellaby)
629[9]

One More Time (FR) *J Howard Johnson* 92+h
4 b f Le Balafre(FR) —Une De Villeneuve (FR) (Montevideo II)
1923[4] 2178[P] 2676[2] 3442[5]

One Of The Boys (IRE) *P R Webber* 66h
5 ch g Shernazar—Easter Morning (FR) (Nice Havrais (USA))
2142[7]

One Of Them *M A Barnes* 88h 86c
7 ch g Pharly(FR) —Hicklam Millie (Absalom)
551[5] 603[6] 716[6] 780[5] 856[3]938[2] **1062[6] 1147[7]**1294[2] 1310[6] 1410[2] 1839[10]

One Of The Natives (IRE) *Miss J H Jenner* 90dc
12 b g Be My Native(USA) —Take Me Home (Amoristic (USA))
52[8] 404[P]

One Sniff (IRE) *N G Richards* 116 h
7 b g Mister Lord(USA) —Deep Fern (Deep Run)
3846[2] (4787)

Oneway (IRE) *M G Rimell* 103 h 161 c
9 b g Bob's Return(IRE) —Rendezvous (Lorenzaccio)
2635[3] 3039[3] 4445[U]

One Wild Night *J L Spearing* 83 h
6 b m Rakaposhi King—Teenero (Teenoso (USA))
58[5] 178[3] 285[3] 2592[11] 2937[9]3371[P]

Only For Gold *Dr P Pritchard* 50h
11 b g Presidium—Calvanne Miss (Martinmas)
1654[11] **1749[6] 2208[8]2620[F] 3126[6]**

Only Make Believe *J S Bolger* 93h
4 ch c Selkirk(USA) —Land Of Dreams (Cadeaux Genereux)
5076a[14]

Only Millie *James Moffatt* 76+h
5 b m Prince Daniel(USA) —Deb's Ball (Glenstal (USA))
349[16] 3556[9] 4916[P]

Only Vintage (USA) *Miss H C Knight* 140+h
6 b g Diesis—Wild Vintage (USA) (Alysheba (USA))
2493[3] 2974[2] 3986[4] 4446[23]

Only Wallis (IRE) *C L Tizzard* 65h
9 b g Supreme Leader—Laurdella Lady (Golden Love)
3879[F] (Dead)

Only Words (USA) *A J Lockwood* 88h
9 ch g Shuailaan(USA) —Conversation Piece (USA) (Seeking The Gold (USA))
9[18] 2981[5] 3395[8] 3916[4] 4302[7]4794[3] (14)

Onnix (FR) *F Doumen* 118+h
4 ch g Funny Baby(FR) —Elza III (FR) (Lazer (FR))
(3498) 3972[3]

Onslow Road (IRE) *Miss Venetia Williams* 70+h
6 b g Un Desperado(FR) —Suelemar (IRE) (Montelimar (USA))
4621[11] 4784[12]

Ontario Sunset *G M Moore* 30h
5 ch g Weldnaas(USA) —High Penhowe (Ardross)
1591[9] 2571[P]

On The Fairway (IRE) *Miss M P Bryant*
7 b m Danehill Dancer(IRE) —Asta Madera (IRE) (Toca Madera)
3281[P] 4149[P] 4450[P]

On The Forty *Jonjo O'Neill* 80 h 73c
9 b g Rakaposhi King—Edwina's Dawn (Space King)
902[6] 979[F] 999[P]

On The Mend (IRE) *Miss S Balshaw* 121h 127c
13 ch g Broken Hearted—Mugs Away (Mugatpura)
4073[P]

On The Net (IRE) *Eoghan O'Grady* 119h 136+c
8 b g Torus—Petted Slave (Sandalay)
3012a[3] 3639a[4]

On The Outside (IRE) *S E H Sherwood* 100h 120+c
7 ch m Anshan—Kate Fisher (IRE) (Over The River (FR))
174[4] (631) 812[P](1398) (1634)

On Tilt *M W Easterby* 6b
5 b g Bal Harbour—Matam (Cyrano De Bergerac)
3563[12] 3657[11]

On Top (IRE) *Mrs S E Busby* 70h
6 b g Topanoora—Ballyanne Supreme (IRE) (Supreme Leader)
133[12] 3567 635[4]

Onward To Glory (USA) *P J Hobbs* 111+h
6 b g Zabeel(NZ) —Landaria (FR) (Sadler's Wells (USA))
3908[4] 4823[3]

Onyourheadbeit (IRE) *K C Bailey* 83h 113 c
8 b g Glacial Storm(USA) —Family Birthday (Sandalay)
2005[2] 2502[P] 3541[5]4394[6] 4578[4] 4851[P]

On Your Way *Miss Elizabeth Doyle* 118h
7 b g Rakaposhi King—Sayshar (Sayfar)
3411a[8]

On Y Va (FR) *R T Phillips* 114+h 114+c
8 b g Goldneyev(USA) —Shakna (FR) (Le Nain Jaune (FR))
(2430) **4054[3] (4516) 4728[4]4985[F]**

Oodachee *C F Swan* 137h 130+c
7 b g Marju(IRE) —Lady Marguerite (Blakeney)
43a[4] 2175[2] 2747[3] 4461[3]

Oohourboo (IRE) *G J Smith*
6 b m Old Vic—Tearaway Lady (IRE) (Tidaro (USA))
3355[0]

Opal Ridge *C Roberts* 95b 95+c
9 ch g Jupiter Island—The Beginning (Goldhill)
4369[P] 4780[2] 5049[4]

Opal's Helmsman (USA) *W S Coltherd* 84h
7 b g Helmsman(USA) —Opal's Notebook (USA) (Notebook (USA))
85[4] 212[6] 410[4] 3271[8] 3487[14]3757[3] 3918[P] 5068[12]

Opare (FR) *H D Daly* 68b
4 b g Agent Bleu(FR) —Fine Light (FR) (Sissoo)
4326[6] 5054[12]

Open De L'Isle (FR) *J P L Ewart* 80b
4 bb g Funny Baby(FR) —Gratiene de l'Isle (FR) (Altayan)
3237[4] 4147[9]

Openide *B W Duke* 124h
5 b g Key Of Luck(USA) —Eyelet (IRE) (Satco (FR))
88a[6] 814[P] 912[2] 1036[3] 1872[12]2338[DSQ] 2964[2] 3408a[2] 3727[16] 4060a[6]4974[11]

Open Range (IRE) *Jennie Candlish* 56h
6 b g Saddlers' Hall(IRE) —L'Enfant Unique (IRE) (Phardante (FR))
1116a[10] 2466[P] 3325[10] 3950[P] 4517[P]

Opera De Coeur (FR) *H D Daly* 129h
4 b g East Of Heaven(IRE) —Eden De Coeur (FR) (Lampon (FR))
(3579) (4096) (4416) 4747[4]

Opera Hall *H D Daly* 87+h
6 b m Saddlers' Hall(IRE) —Opera Hat (IRE) (Strong Gale)
536[4]

Opera Knight *G H Yardley*
6 ch g In The Wings—Sans Escale (USA) (Diesis)
971[P]

Opera Mundi (FR) *P F Nicholls* 105h
4 b g Discover D'Auteuil(FR) —Gymnastique II (FR) (Aelan Hapi (USA))
3324[2] (3906) 4435[U]

Opera Singer *R A Fahey* 78b
5 b g Ali-Royal(IRE) —Wheeler's Wonder (IRE) (Sure Blade (USA))
1401[3] 2844[13]

Opera Villevert (FR) *L Corcoran*
4 b g Goldneyev(USA) —Jubilation (FR) (Boston Two Step (USA))
3436[P] 4551[P] 4665[P]

Ophistrolie (IRE) *J R Weymes* 82h
4 b g Foxhound(USA) —Thoughtful Kate (Rock Hopper)
2263[4] 3925[3]

Opium Des Pictons (FR) *M C Pipe* 48h
4 b g Grand Tresor(FR) —Ballaway (FR) (Djarvis (FR))
4934[P]

Opportunity Knocks *N J Hawke* 74h 80 c
6 gr g Wace(USA) —Madame Ruby (FR) (Homing)
2313[4] 2555[8] 2801[5]3285[6] 3652[2] 3791[2]4451[7] 4666[3] 5074[7]

Optimism (FR) *R H Alner* 61+h 80+c
6 b g Roakarad—Miss Daisy (FR) (Shirley Heights)
351[5] 629[11] 811[7] **979[3]1176[4] 1412[5] 1631[P]**

Optimistic Alfie *B G Powell* 99h 99+c
6 b g Afzal—Threads (Bedford (USA))
2503[2] 3277[P] 3500[8] 3997[11] 5028[P]

Optimistic Harry *R Ford* 77+h 87+c
7 b g Sir Harry Lewis(USA) —Miss Optimist (Relkino)
764[7] **(902) 979[7]**

Optimo (GER) *G L Moore* 62h
5 b g Kahyasi—Onanga (GER) (Acatenango (GER))
2322[8] 2799[11] 3424[7]

Optimum (IRE) *J T Stimpson* 56h
4 br g King's Best(USA) —Colour Dance (Rainbow Quest (USA))
1207[3] 1339[12] 1729[P]

Oracle Des Mottes (FR) *R Barber* 125+h 122c
7 b g Signe Divin(USA) —Daisy Des Mottes (FR) (Abdonski (FR))
4358[2]

Oran Climate (IRE) *John Paul Brennan* 108h
6 b g Oscar(IRE) —Approach The Dawn (IRE) (Orchestra)
3642a[6]

Orange Street *Mrs L J Mongan* 110+h
6 b g Primitive Rising(USA) —Arctic Oats (Oats)
490[6] 2554[7] 2809[U] 3664[5] (4212) 4907[2]

Orang Outan (FR) *J P L Ewart* 91 h
4 b g Baby Turk—Ellapampa (FR) (Pampabird)
2263[2] 3038[6] 3488[3] 4141[5] 4506[2]4986[5]

Oration *Mrs P Robeson* 63h
5 b g Singspiel(IRE) —Blush Rambler (IRE) (Blushing Groom (FR))
3[9]

Orbys Girl (IRE) *M Pitman* 71h 77c
6 b m Broken Hearted—Cherry Sal (IRE) (Yashgan)
2553[5] 4151[P] **4785[6]**

Orcadian *J M P Eustace* 126+h
5 b g Kirkwall—Rosy Outlook (USA) (Trempolino (USA))
(3963) 4430[13]

Orchard Fields (IRE) *Mrs A V Roberts* 92 h
9 b g Lord Americo—Art Lover (IRE) (Over The River (FR))
2958[P]

Ordre De Bataille (FR) *H D Daly* 96b
4 gr g Ungaro(GER) —Hache De Guerre (FR) (Royal Charter (FR))
4326[2] 4854[12]

Orenay (USA) *W B Stone*
4 ch g Grand Slam(USA) —Moonfire (Sadler's Wells (USA))
4057[P] 4550[P]

Orest (FR) *F-M Cottin*
4 b g Subotica(FR) —Gintonique (FR) (Royal Charter (FR))
2085a[P]

Original Fly (FR) *P F Nicholls* 103 h
4 b g Chef De Clan II(FR) —Ultim De Plaisance (FR) (Top Dancer (FR))
2824[3] 3132[3] 3431[3] 4104[4] 4674[2]

Original Thought (IRE) *B De Haan* 111+h
6 b g Entrepreneur—Troyanos (Troy)
2528[5] 2866[4] 3941[2] 4238[2] 4603[3]4961[3]

Orinocovsky (IRE) *N P Littmoden* 97+h 110+c
7 ch g Grand Lodge(USA) —Brillantina (FR) (Crystal Glitters (USA))
840[P] 1632[2] 1921[P]

Orion Express *M Hill* 76h
5 b g Bahhare(USA) —Kaprisky (IRE) (Red Sunset)
1541[11] 1637[4]

Orions Eclipse *M J Gingell* 48h
5 b m Magic Ring(IRE) —Belle De Nuit (IRE) (Statoblest)
655[16] 1851[10] 2501[14] 2704[F] 3597[7]4075[11]

Or Jaune (FR) *G L Moore* 95b
4 ch g Grand Tresor(FR) —Vancia (FR) (Top Dancer (FR))
(5089)

Orki Des Aigles (FR) *Ferdy Murphy* 83h
4 b g Le Balafre(FR) —Rose Des Aigles (FR) (Le Nain Jaune (FR))
2001[9] 2263[6] 2676[3] 2994[P] 4907[7]5123[P]

Orlando Blue *B Storey*
6 gr g Wizard King—Murray Grey (Be My Chief (USA))
4299[F] 4493[P]

Orleans (IRE) *S J Robinson* 92h 88c
11 b g Scenic—Guest House (What A Guest)
151[U] 594[P]

Ornella Speed (FR) *J R Weymes* 94h 98+c
6 b m Vertical Speed(FR) —Macyrienne (FR) (Saint Cyrien (FR))
321[F] 481[3] 783[F](2267) 2476[U] 2692[2]3375[U] 3551[2] **4041[2]**

Ornoir (FR) *T Doumen* 6b
4 b g Subotica(FR) —Fleche Noir II (FR) (Quart De Vin (FR))
4622[12]

Oro Street (IRE) *G F Bridgwater* 88h
10 b g Dolphin Street(FR) —Love Unlimited (Dominion)
237[P] 451[15] 839[P]

Or Passion (FR) *L Bellet*
8 b m Amthaal(USA) —Miss Natha (FR) (Pure Flight (USA))
1372a[P]

Orpen Guama (IRE) *John F Gleeson* 111h
4 b g Orpen(USA) —Guama Lass (IRE) (Krayyan)
3004a[10]

Orpen Wide (IRE) *M C Chapman* 111+h
4 b g Orpen(USA) —Melba (IRE) (Namaqualand (USA))
4416[2] 4631[6] (3)

Orrezzo (GER) *G E Jones* 73h
6 br g Zinaad—Ordessa (GER) (Perrault)
2070[8] 2559[10]

Or Sing About (FR) *J W Mullins* 90b
4 b g Le Balafre(FR) —Grande Folie (FR) (Highlanders (FR))
4940[4]

Orswell Crest *P J Hobbs* 113 c
12 b g Crested Lark—Slave's Bangle (Prince Rheingold)
572[4] 746[F]

Ortega (FR) *P J Hobbs* 102h
4 b g Useful(FR) —Madame Dabrovine (FR) (Vacarme (USA))
3294[6] 3579[4] 3972[4] 4616[15]

Orthence (FR) *M Rolland*
4 ch f Epervier Bleu—Tchela (FR) (Le Nain Jaune (FR))
4548a[8]

Orthodox *G L Moore* 78h
7 gr g Baryshnikov(AUS) —Sancta (So Blessed)
230[P]

Ortolan Bleu (FR) *J Howard Johnson* 112 h
4 ch g Epervier Bleu—Graine Des Sacart (FR) (Quart De Vin (FR))
2367[2] (3038) 3759[P] (Dead)

Osako D'Airy (FR) *S Gollings* 98h
4 b g Cachet Noir(USA) —Esaka D'Airy (FR) (Marasali)
4117[5] 4795[2]

Oscar Buck (IRE) *V R A Dartnall* 98+h
5 b g Oscar(IRE) —Rosey Buck (IRE) (Buckskin (FR))
3699[10]

Oscardeal (IRE) *C T Pogson* 113b
7 b g Oscar(IRE) —Sleepy Bye Byes (IRE) (Supreme Leader)
1990[7]

Oscar D'Hyrome (FR) *C Grant* 97h
4 gr g Myrakalu(FR) —Fluying (FR) (Luynes (USA))
3203[5] 3967[5] 4313[RR] 4506[3]

Oscar Foxbow (IRE) *C Tinkler* 88h
7 bb g Oscar(IRE) —Miss Fox Bow (IRE) (King's Ride)
2144[3]

Oscar Jack (FR) *Miss Venetia Williams*
5 b g Video Rock(FR) —Miss Noir Et Or (FR) (Noir Et Or)
4689[F]

Oscar Park (IRE) *C Tinkler* 131h
7 b g Oscar(IRE) —Parkavoureen (Deep Run)
(1903) (2322) 2829[2] 3388[2] 4469[9] 4849[2]

Oscar Pepper (USA) *M J Brown* 32c
9 b g Brunswick(USA) —Princess Baja (USA) (Conquistador Cielo (USA))
151[7] 374[3]

Oscar Performance (IRE) *R H Buckler* 73+c
11 gr g Roselier(FR) —Miss Iverk (Torus)
2180[P] 2502[7] 2682[P]3241[5] 3654[U] 4428[4]4650[P]

Oscar Royal (IRE) *Mrs S E Busby* 31b
5 gr g Oscar(IRE) —Stonehill Princess (IRE) (King's Ride)
2288[13] 3948[P]

Oscar's Advance (IRE) *C Roche* 124+h 127+c
7 b g Oscar(IRE) —Banna's Retreat (Vitiges (FR))
3086a[8] 4336a[4]

Oscar's Delight *J L Spearing* 68b
5 b m Oscar(IRE) —Vi's Delight (New Member)
1793 656[P] (Dead)

Oscar's Lady (IRE) *G A Swinbank* 74h
5 b m Oscar(IRE) —Sandy Forest Lady (IRE) (Creative Plan (USA))
470[5] 720[4] 917[7] 1340[4] 1590[3]2262[6] 2688[P]

Oscars Law *J L Spearing* 39h
5 b m Oscar(IRE) —Eloquent Lawyer (Law Society (USA))
1896[4] 2501[11] (Dead)

Oscars Vision (IRE) *B W Duke* 82h 81c
6 ch m Oscar Schindler(IRE) —Eyelet (IRE) (Satco (FR))
813[9] 905[5] 1028[3] 1100[5] 1152[9]**1275[3] 1414[8] 1560[P]**

Oscar The Boxer (IRE) *J M Jefferson* 89+h
7 b g Oscar(IRE) —Here She Comes (Deep Run)
215[P] 2843[4] 3269[2] 3487[4] (4145)

Oscatello (USA) *Ian Williams* 126h
6 bb g Woodman(USA) —Galea Des Bois (FR) (Persian Bold)
1889[2] 2663[2] (2967) 3729[2] (4280) (4386) (4956)

Osiris (IRE) *Evan Williams* 90h 120 c
11 b g Orchestra—Merry Servant (Giolla Mear)
112a[2] (648) 2688[U] 3250[P]**4728[P]**

Oso Magic *Mrs S J Smith* 104+h 134+c
8 b g Teenoso(USA) —Scottish Clover (Scottish Reel)
346[3] 1915[5] **(2172) (2498) 2768[F]** (3040) **3495[7] 3619[7]**

Osorno *W M Brisbourne*
6 ch g Inchinor—Pacifica (Robellino (USA))
2860[P] 3673[P]

Oso Tilley *Miss J E Foster* 60h 68+c
7 b m Teenoso(USA) —Brockton Light (Be My Chief (USA))
594[4] 861[5]

Ossmoses (IRE) *D M Forster* 71h 153+c
9 gr g Roselier(FR) —Sugarstown (Sassafras (FR))
91a[7] 1941[6] (2656) 3258[3] (3971) 4496[2]

Ostfanni (IRE) *M Todhunter* 121h
6 b m Spectrum(IRE) —Ostwahl (IRE) (Waajib)
(1307) (1356) (1590) (1870) 2483[4] 4215[P]

Ostrogoth (FR) *N J Henderson* 103h
4 b g Ungaro(GER) —Holding (FR) (Useful (FR))
2661[3] 3294[2] 4096[3]

Otago (IRE) *C J Mann* 89h
5 b g Desert Sun—Martino (Marju (IRE))
4479[7] 4819[6]

Otahuna *J W Mullins* 86h 36c
10 b g Selkirk(USA) —Stara (Star Appeal)
1949[4]

Otantique (FR) *Miss E C Lavelle* 88+h
4 b g Lute Antique(FR) —Gracieuse Antique (FR) (Mont Basile (FR))
3346[3] 4359[5]

O'Toole (IRE) *P J Hobbs* 127+h 116+c
7 b g Toulon—Legs Burke (IRE) (Buckskin (FR))
(136) **2044[5] 2488[6] 3357[5]4618[6] 4859[3] (5112)**

Oui Exit (FR) *N A Twiston-Davies* 64h
5 b g Exit To Nowhere(USA) —Forest Hills (FR) (Sicyos (USA))
277[9] 457[P] 1714[7] 2142[P] 3800[P]4752[15]

Oulan Bator (FR) *R A Fahey* 68h
6 b g Astair(FR) —Scarieuse (FR) (Crackao (FR))
1794[10] 2991[P] 3488[7]

Oulart *D T Hughes* 128+h 145+c
7 ch g Sabrehill(USA) —Gaye Fame (Ardross)
92a[F] 1787a[4] **3079a[6]** 4461[8]**4929a[2] 5131a[3]**

Oulton Broad *R Ford* 89 h 105c
10 b g Midyan(USA) —Lady Quachita (USA) (Sovereign Dancer (USA))
(24) 264[2] 672[5]1153[10] 1218[7] 1405[4] **1855[P]**2008[5] 2216[3] 2576[5] 3141[6] 3959[3](4449) 5068[P]

Oundle Scoundrel (FR) *E Pilet*
7 b g Spinning World(USA) —Tidal Treasure (USA) (Crafty Prospector (USA))
5000a[7]

Our Armageddon (NZ) *R C Guest* 146+c
9 b g Sky Chase(NZ) —Monte D'Oro (NZ) (Cache Of Gold (USA))
2760[10] 3385[7] 3620[4](3988)

Our Ben *W P Mullins* 144h 144 c
7 ch g Presenting—Forest Pride (IRE) (Be My Native (USA))
90a[P] **(3528a) 3893a[3] 4444[U]4929a[P] 5058a[3]**

Our Bill *David Pearson*
8 br g Alflora(IRE) —Flagg Flyer VII (Damsire Unregistered)
4167[P]

Ourcarl *G Brown* 35b
6 b g Parthian Springs—Flower Of Tintern (Free State)
1985[8] 2288[12] 3246[P]

Our Girl Kaz (IRE) *L Corcoran* 84h
6 b m Arctic Lord—Blackwood Castle (IRE) (Castle Keep)
1274[6] 1543[11] 2849[5] 3437[F]

Our Glenard *J E Long* 84h
7 b g Royal Applause—Loucoum (FR) (Iron Duke (FR))
2573[9]

Our Jasper *K G Reveley* 87h
6 ch g Tina's Pet—Dawn's Della (Scottish Reel)
2171[7] 2475[4]

Our Jolly Swagman *J W Mullins* 72c
11 b g Thowra(FR) —Queens Dowry (Dominion)
(288) 464[P] 2506[5]2801[P] 3434[P] 3582[5]4525[7]

Our Joycey *Mrs K Walton* 85h
5 b m Shernazar—Charisse Dancer (Dancing Dissident (USA))
1762[2] 2028[3] 2718[10] 3337[3] 3551[3]3918[P] 4658[3]

Our Man Dennis *Mrs P Ford* 85c
12 b g Arzanni—Pendocks Polly (Grey Steel)
464[P]

Our Men *Miss Lucinda V Russell* 90h
7 b g Classic Cliche(IRE) —Praise The Lord (Lord Gayle (USA))
323[6] 418[5] 643[9] 764[3]

Our Mr Navigator (IRE) *N R Mitchell* 75c
8 ch g Erin's Isle—Latin Quarter (North Summit)
1455[U] 1638[2]

Our Sion *Mrs A M Thorpe*
6 b g Dreams End—Millfields Lady (Sayf El Arab (USA))
2070[P] 2283[9] 2428[9]

Oursweetsurprise *A Ennis*
5 ch g Lord Of Appeal—Sweet Allegiance (Alleging (USA))
4237[12]

Our Tees Component (IRE) *K G Reveley* 77b
5 b m Saddlers' Hall(IRE) —Shaiymara (IRE) (Darshaan)
431[2]

Our Vic (IRE) *M C Pipe* 147h 166 c
8 b g Old Vic—Shabra Princess (Buckskin (FR))
(2177) 2760[P] (3977) 4457[9] (4958)

Ouste (FR) *F Doumen* 123 h
4 ch g Ragmar(FR) —Elbe (FR) (Royal Charter (FR))
3722[4] 4435[P] 4849[15]

Outdoor Sally (IRE) *Mrs John Harrington* 89b
5 b m Accordion—Outdoor Holly (IRE) (Be My Native (USA))
5134a[16]

Outlaw Princess (IRE) *Sean O O'Brien* 115h
6 b m Beneficial—All French (IRE) (Lepanto (GER))
3110a[7] 5077a[4]

Outside Half (IRE) *L Corcoran* 71h
4 ch g Raise A Grand(IRE) —Lindas Delight (Batshoof)
1563[3] 3238[P] 3908[11] (Dead)

Outside Investor (IRE) *P R Rodford* 102h 61c
6 bb g Cadeaux Genereux—Desert Ease (IRE) (Green Desert (USA))
2325 458[6] 668[4] 760[12] **862[6]1019[8]** 1187[4] (1233) (1405) 1641[5] 1651[2]1862[8]

Out The Gap (IRE) *C Hennessy* 110h
10 b g Little Bighorn—Rongo (IRE) (Tumble Gold)
4951a[21]

Overamorous *J L Needham* 82b
5 b m Overbury(IRE) —Random Romance (Eric)
2007[4] 2565[9] 3617[10]

Over Bridge *Mrs S M Johnson* 87h 84c
8 b g Overbury(IRE) —Celtic Bridge (Celtic Cone)
283[U] (575) 697[8] 4331[P] 5108[10]

Overbryn *D McCain* 40b
6 b g Overbury(IRE) —Nero's Gem (Little Wolf)
7[12]

Overbury Lady *Daniel O'Connell* 90h
5 b m Overbury(IRE) —Albertina (Phardante (FR))
2796a[8]

Overdrawn (IRE) *Mrs S J Smith* 89+h
5 b g Daggers Drawn(USA) —In Denial (IRE) (Maelstrom Lake)
2627[14] 4388[P]

Overfields *S R Bowring* 46h
6 b g Overbury(IRE) —Honey Day (Lucky Wednesday)
2192[8] 2844[7] 3145[4] 3353[6]

Overjoyed *Miss Suzy Smith* 53h
5 b m Overbury(IRE) —Silk Touch (Lochnager)
1961[10] 2558[7] 3280[9] 3692[6]

Overlut (FR) *F-M Cottin* 135+h
4 bl g Discover D'Auteuil(FR) —Lutsine (FR) (Zino) (3972) 4468[15]

Overnight *Mrs A C Hamilton* 81+h
6 b g Overbury(IRE) —Misty Night (Grey Desire)
1688[3] 2112[5] 3237[13] 3927[4] 4342[6]4720[13]

Over'n Out *A R Dicken* 36b
5 b m Overbury(IRE) —The Distaff Spy (Seymour Hicks (FR))
4241[3] 720[9] 4147[15]

Overserved *A Parker* 113 h
7 bb g Supreme Leader—Divine Comedy (IRE) (Phardante (FR))
(2184) 3289[6]

Overstrand (IRE) *Robert Gray* 121h
7 b g In The Wings—Vaison La Romaine (Arctic Tern (USA))
1010[14] 1204[9] (1293) 1548[5] 1720[5] 2500[7]2904[6] 3383[4] 3492[6] (3967) 4110[9] 4765[17]5003[8]

Over The Beck (IRE) *Mrs H D Marks* 65h
13 b g Over The River(FR) —Echo Creek (IRE) (Strong Gale)
498[P]

Over The Blues (IRE) *Jonjo O'Neill* 81h
6 b g Bob Back(USA) —Fiona's Blue (Crash Course)
1611[7] 1714[4]

Over The First (IRE) *C F Swan* 130h 135c
11 bb g Orchestra—Ruby Lodge (Peacock (FR))
69a[P]

Over The Flow *R H Buckler* 96b
4 br f Overbury(IRE) —Flow (Over The River (FR))
2611[2] 2830[15]

Over The Odds *W Storey* 57b
4 b f Overbury(IRE) —Ashniader (IRE) (Buckskin (FR))
3799[13]

Over The Storm (IRE) *H P Hogarth* 102 c
9 b g Over The River(FR) —Naas (Ballymore)
1941[P] 2518[P] 2875[P]3336[P] 4451[P] (5136)

Over To Joe *C Grant* 55h
6 br g Overbury(IRE) —Flo-Jo (DEN) (Pelton Lad)
14[6]

Over Zealous (IRE) *John R Upson* 59h 107c
14 ch g Over The River(FR) —Chatty Di (Le Bavard (FR))
(22) 262[3] 1321[P]

Ovide (FR) *J Howard Johnson* 100+b
4 b g Video Rock(FR) —Una Volta (FR) (Toujours Pret (USA))
3623[2] (4637)

Owennacurra Bobby (IRE) *Thomas Cooper* 116h
6 b g Kahyasi—Tadjnama (USA) (Exceller (USA))
2207[P]

Owen's Pet (IRE) *Mrs S Wall* 94h 99c
12 b g Alphabatim(USA) —Ballinlovane (Le Moss)
3910[P] 4607[P]

Own Line *J Hetherton* 97h
7 b g Classic Cliche(IRE) —Cold Line (Exdirectory)
429[3] 5137[P]

Oxley (FR) *H D Daly* 85b
4 b g Assessor(IRE) —Tartifume II (FR) (Mistigri)
4853[8]

Oxybau (FR) *T J Taaffe* 108h
7 ch g Beaudelaire(USA) —Foxy (FR) (Moulin)
2166[16]

Oyez (IRE) *J J Lambe* 104h 74c
9 b g Jurado(USA) —Gleann Oisin (IRE) (Le Bavard (FR))
873[10] **1147[8] 1376[P]1509[P]**

Oysterhaven (IRE) *D P Keane* 104h
8 b g Mister Lord(USA) —Haven's Glory (IRE) (Supreme Leader)
1796[9] **2313[P]**

Oyster Pearl (IRE) *P Bowen* 81h
7 ch g Karinga Bay—Latin Mistress (Scallywag)
3246[P] 3780[4] 4429[6] 4907[5]

Pablo Du Charmil (FR) *M C Pipe* 128+h
5 ch g Lyphard's Wish(FR) —Pacifie Du Charmil (FR) (Dom Pasquini (FR))
2617^{2} 3996^{2} 4430^{U} 5078a^{14}

Pace Shot (IRE) *G L Moore* 141+h
4 b g Montjeu(IRE) —Pacific Grove (Persian Bold)
(1821) 2345^{3} 2597^{2} (3182) 4468^{4} 4747^{7} 4962^{2}

Pace Stalker (USA) *M R Hoad* 87h 108c
10 b g Lear Fan(USA) —In The Habit (USA) (Lyphard (USA))
105^{P}

Pacharan Queen *V Smith* 57b
5 b m Terimon—Persian Fountain (IRE) (Persian Heights)
1042^{13}

Pacific Highway (IRE) *Mrs L B Normile* 73h
7 b g Sadler's Wells(USA) —Obeah (Cure The Blues (USA))
306^{P} 469^{P}

Packie Tam (IRE) *Patrick O Brady* 95h
4 b g Tipsy Creek(USA) —Blonde Goddess (IRE) (Godswalk (USA))
2645a^{4} 3004a^{12} 4122a^{6}

Pacolet (IRE) *Patrick J Flynn* 114+h
7 b g Revoque(IRE) —Elupa (IRE) (Mtoto)
67a^{22}

Padamul *J W Mullins* 48c
10 ch g Polish Precedent(USA) —Oxslip (Owen Dudley)
135^{7} 264^{3} 565^{5}

Paddleurowncanoe (IRE) *J C Fox* 85h
7 ch g Germany(USA) —Brogeen View (Kambalda)
4860^{10}

Paddy Boy (IRE) *J R Boyle* 86 h
5 br g Overbury(IRE) —Arts Project (IRE) (Project Manager)
1952^{P} 2216^{6} (2552) 2958^{2} 3279^{P} 4331^{P}5072^{P}

Paddy For Paddy (IRE) *G L Landau* 115c
12 b g Mandalus—Lady Rerico (Pamroy)
(49) 3910^{3} (4325)

Paddy George (IRE) *A J Lockwood* 51b
5 ch g Houmayoun(FR) —Pennine Way (IRE) (Waajib)
484^{6}

Paddys Tern *N M Babbage* 94+h
4 b g Fraam—Great Tern (Simply Great (FR))
4416^{5} 4877^{2}

Paddy The Optimist (IRE) *D Burchell* 86h 91 c
10 b g Leading Counsel(USA) —Erne Duchess (IRE) (Duky)
461^{3} 653^{4} 746^{4}2282^{5} 2562^{3} 2818^{7}3326^{8} 3547^{6} 3886^{3}4370^{P} 4553^{3} 4785^{P}

Paddy The Piper (IRE) *L Lungo* 138+h 129+c
9 b g Witness Box(USA) —Divine Dibs (Raise You Ten)
422^{6} 2369^{6} 4446^{22} 5142^{12}

Padre (IRE) *M Pitman* 63b 95+c
7 b g Mister Lord(USA) —Lee Valley Lady (IRE) (Boyne Valley)
239^{U} 650^{3}

Padre Nostro (IRE) *J R Holt* 79h
7 ch g Grand Lodge(USA) —Meglio Che Posso (IRE) (Try My Best (USA))
1816^{11} 1991^{9}

Pagan Sky (IRE) *Miss Venetia Williams* 97+h
7 ch g Inchinor—Rosy Sunset (IRE) (Red Sunset)
3883^{8} 4280^{7} 4819^{12}

Page Point (AUS) *R C Guest* 107h 111+c
8 b g Supremo(USA) —She's Fun (NZ) (Racing Is Fun (USA))
148^{2} 570^{4} 1334^{6}

Painter Man (FR) *M C Pipe* 86+b
4 b g Double Bed(FR) —Diana La Belle (FR) (Synefos (USA))
(4947)

Pairtree *Jamie Poulton* 95+b
6 ch m Double Trigger(IRE) —Forest Pride (IRE) (Be My Native (USA))
27^{7} (507)

Paix Eternelle (FR) *N J Henderson* 100+b
5 ch m Esprit Du Nord(USA) —Pierre Magique (FR) (Down The River (FR))
(4011) 4751^{10}

Pak Jack (FR) *P J Hobbs* 109 h 133c
6 ch g Pitchounet(FR) —Miss Noir Et Or (FR) (Noir Et Or)
175^{2} 1857^{4} **1918^{3} 2489^{7}3942^{3} 4378^{4} 4762^{3}**

Palace (FR) *R H Buckler* 40h 44c
10 b g Rahotep(FR) —La Musardiere (FR) (Cadoudal (FR))
2807^{5} 3243^{F}

Palace Pett *J R Best* 60b
6 ch m Alflora(IRE) —Black H'Penny (Town And Country)
769^{7}

Palace Walk (FR) *B G Powell* 98h
4 b g Sinndar(IRE) —Page Bleue (Sadler's Wells (USA))
1519^{7} 1594^{3} (1649) (1802) 2178^{7} 2372^{6}

Palais (IRE) *John A Harris* 63h 13 c
11 b g Darshaan—Dance Festival (Nureyev (USA))
1109^{P} 2962^{12} 3279^{P}

Palamedes *B J Llewellyn* 63h
7 b g Sadler's Wells(USA) —Kristal Bridge (Kris)
3488^{14} 4106^{6} 4367^{7} 4726^{10}

Palaver *G R I Smyly*
4 ro f Kris—Galava (CAN) (Graustark)
3346^{16}

Pallas Lass (IRE) *B P Galvin* 80b
5 b m Taipan(IRE) —Castle Dove (IRE) (Castle Keep)
5134a^{17}

Palmac's Pride *P G Murphy*
6 ch g Atraf—Nashwanah (Nashwan (USA))
457^{P}

Palmers Peak (IRE) *M Keighley* 93c
7 b g Arctic Lord—Shahreza (Nishapour (FR))
4607^{P}

Palmerston Place (IRE) *Miss Lucinda V Russell* 55b
6 b g Fourstars Allstar(USA) —Real Lace (Kampala)
5008^{12}

Palm Island (FR) *Noel T Chance* 105h
5 b g Priolo(USA) —L'Orpheline (FR) (Seattle Song (USA))
3139^{2} 3545^{3} 3906^{2} 4148^{2} 4393^{3}4676^{7}

Palouse (IRE) *R H Buckler* 116h 117+c
10 gr g Toulon—Hop Picker (USA) (Plugged Nickle (USA))
634^{9} (Dead)

Palua *Miss E C Lavelle* 139 h 140 c
9 b g Sri Pekan(USA) —Reticent Bride (IRE) (Shy Groom (USA))
452^{5} 1739^{4} 1918^{7}3299^{4} (3357) 3619^{4}4749^{P} 4973^{3}

Pams Oak *Mrs S J Smith* 103+c
8 b g Afzal—Kins Token (Relkino)
296^{4} 459^{P} 650^{5}812^{P} 4920^{6}

Panama At Once *J M Saville* 76b
6 ch g Commanche Run—Cherry Sip (Nearly A Hand)
4507^{9}

Panama Royale (IRE) *J R Holt* 26b
8 ch m Aristocracy—Boreen Girl (IRE) (Boreen (FR))
3550^{P} 3690^{P}

Panama Three Knots *J M Saville* 52h
6 b m Primitive Rising(USA) —Emu (IRE) (Strong Gale)
4800^{7}

Panchovillas Gleam (IRE) *Dermot Day* 101+c
12 b g Un Desperado(FR) —Shining Spear (Commanche Run)
87a^{P}

Pangbourne (FR) *A King* 126+b
5 b g Double Bed(FR) —Valgrija (FR) (Big John (FR))
2665^{13} 3001^{2} (3373) (3911) 4448^{9} (4779)

Pangeran (USA) *N B King* 55h 82c
14 ch g Forty Niner(USA) —Smart Heiress (USA) (Vaguely Noble)
101^{P} 366^{4} 673^{4}(1247) 1378^{3} 1484^{3}1646^{3} 1803^{4} 5088^{5}

Panmure (IRE) *P D Niven* 88h 85 c
10 b g Alphabatim(USA) —Serjitak (Saher)
321^{4} (605) 717^{4}1110^{6} 1280^{7} **1342^{8}1489^{7} 1570^{F} 1684^{5}5036^{5}**

Pantalaimon *H D Daly* 104b
5 b g Classic Cliche(IRE) —Threewaygirl (Orange Bay)
4455^{4}

Pan The Man (IRE) *J W Mullins* 87h 100+c
5 b g Muroto—Kilbally Quilty (IRE) (Montelimar (USA))
(300) 2376^{2} 3425^{9} 3978^{P} 4604^{P}

Panthers Run *Jonjo O'Neill* 94+h
6 b g Jendali(USA) —Dorado Beach (Lugana Beach)
2268^{F}

Panzer (GER) *D McCain* 95 h
5 b g Vettori(IRE) —Prompt (Old Vic)
2763^{4} 3167^{2} 3685^{4} 4210^{9}

Paparaazi (IRE) *R A Fahey* 85+h
4 b g Victory Note(USA) —Raazi (My Generation)
1729^{2} 2676^{F} 2954^{10}

Papawaldo (IRE) *R C Guest* 58h
7 ch g Presenting—Another Bless (Random Shot)
2262^{10} 2653^{12}

Paperchaser *F P Murtagh* 64h
6 ch g Minster Son—Eye Bee Aitch (Move Off)
1938^{P} 3042^{9} 4145^{9}

Paper Classic *A C Whillans*
6 ch m Classic Cliche(IRE) —Kiniohio (FR) (Script Ohio (USA))
3319^{11}

Paperprophet *N G Richards* 128 h
8 b g Glory Of Dancer—Living Legend (ITY) (Archway (IRE))
2876^{F} 3208^{6} 4776^{P}

Paphian Bay *Ferdy Murphy* 96h 72c
8 b g Karinga Bay—Bichette (Lidhame)
4788^{8}

Papillon De Iena (FR) *M C Pipe* 125h 118+c
6 ch g Varese(FR)—Belle du Chesne (FR) (Rb Chesne)
459^{3} 750^{4} 803^{4}2247^{2} 2636^{7} **4214^{7} 4694^{P}**

Papini (IRE) *N J Henderson* 125 h
5 ch g Lomitas—Pariana (USA) (Bering)
3135^{4} 3622^{11} 4215^{9} 4848^{3}

Papswoodmoss *Mrs A L M King* 67b
4 ch f Fleetwood(IRE) —Pab's Choice (Telsmoss)
2830^{7} 3623^{8}

Papua *Geoffrey Deacon* 117 c
12 ch g Green Dancer(USA) —Fairy Tern (Mill Reef (USA))
354^{2} (615) 840^{5}1049^{6} 1273^{5} 1435^{8}4831^{P}

Paradise Bay (IRE) *C J Mann* 92+h
5 b g Topanoora—Lady Chloris (Kampala)
7^{2} 2050^{4} 2528^{6} 2821^{9} 3137^{6}

Paradise Garden (USA) *P L Clinton* 65h
9 b g Septieme Ciel(USA) —Water Course (USA) (Irish River (FR))
1485^{5} 3141^{P}

Paradise's Boss (USA) *J R S Fisher* 116h
6 b g Thats Our Buck(USA) —Paradise Land (URU) (Paradise Bay)
1394a^{5}

Pardini (USA) *M F Harris* 94h 100 c
7 b g Quest For Fame—Noblissima (IRE) (Sadler's Wells (USA))
1870^{6} **1920^{6} 2164^{12}2524^{5} 2877^{2} 3144^{F}3276^{P} 3578^{4} 3965^{P}4428^{P} 4499^{3} (4643) 4804^{7}**

Pardishar (IRE) *G L Moore* 122+h 124+c
8 b g Kahyasi—Parapa (IRE) (Akarad (FR))
2959^{2} 3323^{3} 3907^{2}(4424) 4559^{2} 4833^{P}

Pardon What *S Lycett* 106h 96c
10 b g Theatrical Charmer—Tree Poppy (Rolfe (USA))
397^{2} 1436^{6} 1630^{8} (1977) 2166^{6} (2556)
2868 ^{6}3018^{5} 3548^{4} 3581^{6} 4012^{6} 4497^{2}**4804^{P}**
4852^{10}

Parish House (IRE) *B W Duke*
6 b g Arzanni—Penny Gold (IRE) (Millfontaine)
3138^{2} 3699^{13}

Parish Oak *Ian Williams* 80h 108 c
11 b g Rakaposhi King—Poppy's Pride (Uncle Pokey)
2419^{8} **2814^{5} 3676^{2}3815^{P} 4476^{6}**

Parisian Rose (IRE) *Mrs H O Graham* 56h
7 b m Norwich—Magar's Mandy (Mandalus)
85^{8} 418^{9}

Parisian Storm (IRE) *Evan Williams* 113 h 130 c
10 b g Glacial Storm(USA) —Lost In Paris (Deep Run)
311^{3} 648^{4} 1039^{7}**(1205) 1267^{3} 1550^{4}1676^{P}**

Parisienne Gale (IRE) *R Ford* 117+h 125+c
7 b m Lapierre—Elegant Gale (IRE) (Strong Gale)
1473^{3} 352^{5} **548^{2}** (649) 9873**(1335) 1682^{F} (1942) (2041)** (2289) 2457^{3} **2963^{U}**(5039)

Parisi Princess *D L Williams* 41h
5 ch m Shaddad(USA) —Crambella (IRE) (Red Sunset)
180^{7} 232^{9} 396^{7}

Park City *J Joseph* 94h
7 b g Slip Anchor—Cryptal (Persian Bold)
1717^{5} 1987^{4} 2324^{11} (4010) 4523^{2} 4879^{12}

Parkinson (IRE) *Jonjo O'Neill* 62h 97+c
5 br g Presenting—Be My Citizen (IRE) (Be My Native (USA))
3291^{5} 3496^{5} 3685^{7} **(4164) (4353) (4571) 4985^{P}**

Parliament Square (IRE) *M J P O'Brien* 125+h
5 b g Sadler's Wells(USA) —Groom Order (Groom Dancer (USA))
3003a^{8} 5132a^{P} (Dead)

Paro (FR) *M C Pipe* 108+h
5 b g Panoramic—Rozinsara (IRE) (Mouktar)
(3800) 4048^{3} 4420^{12} (5043)

Parsifal *P Wegmann* 91+h
7 b g Sadler's Wells(USA) —Moss (USA) (Woodman (USA))
133^{3} 369^{9}

Parsley's Return *M Wigham* 107+h
4 b g Danzero(AUS) —The Frog Queen (Bin Ajwaad (IRE))
(2935) 3485^{2} 4057^{P} (4987)

Parson Ploughman *P F Nicholls* 84+h 101+c
11 br g Riverwise(USA) —Pretty Pantoes (Lepanto (GER))
514^{4}

Parsons Fancy *Mark Gillard* 66b 57c
8 ch m Alflora(IRE) —Preachers Popsy (The Parson)
4880^{P}

Parsons Leap (IRE) *I McMath*
7 b g Detroit Sam(FR) —Parson's Lodge (IRE) (The Parson)
8^{P}

Parsons Legacy (IRE) *P J Hobbs* 122 h 139+c
8 b g Leading Counsel(USA) —The Parson's Girl (IRE) (The Parson)
2532^{7} 3509^{P} 4240^{2}4447^{9} 4957^{2}

Parthian Shot *R T Phillips* 69h
6 b m Parthian Springs—Lavenham's Last (Rymer)
4059^{4} 4398^{6} 4801^{6} 5052^{10}

Partners Choice (IRE) *John G Carr* 77h 85+c
9 bb g Lord Americo—Finest Edition (IRE) (Satco (FR))
858^{P} 872^{P} 1376^{4}1592^{P} 1602^{2}

Party Airs (USA) *T Voss* 133h
7 b g Geri(USA) —Elegant Champagne (USA) (Alleged (USA))
1394a^{3}

Party Games (IRE) *G L Moore* 104h 120 c
9 b g King's Ride—Shady Miss (Mandamus)
(202) 436^{3} 1877^{F}2100^{2} 2485^{8} (3372) 3509^{4} 4130^{3} (4904)

Pasghetti Hoops (IRE) *A J Martin* 56c
9 b m Gothland(FR) —Amys Girl (IRE) (Pauper)
2684^{P}

Passenger Omar (IRE) *Noel T Chance* 111+h
8 b g Safety Catch(USA) —Princess Douglas (Bishop Of Orange)
(3146) (3581) 4105^{4} 4372^{3}

Pass Go *J J Lambe* 88h
5 b g Kris—Celt Song (IRE) (Unfuwain (USA))
645^{7} 780^{P}

Passionate Knight (IRE) *B S Rothwell*
7 ch g Semillon—Knight's Maid (Giolla Mear)
691^{P} 891^{P}

Pass It On (IRE) *Jonjo O'Neill* 114h
7 br g Accordion—Windswept Lady (IRE) (Strong Gale)
4359^{4} 4732^{2}

Pass Me A Dime *C L Tizzard* 106 h 126+c
7 b g Past Glories—Hand Out (Spare A Dime)
1984^{3} **2241^{3} (2574) (2814)**

Pass Me By *R C Guest* 126 h 127+c
7 b g Balnibarbi—Errol Emerald (Dom Racine (FR))
974^{9} **(1662) 1795^{2} 1941^{3}2265^{5} 2656^{U} 3382^{2}(3794) 4345^{P} (4841)**

Pass The Class (IRE) *Mrs S J Smith* 90+b
6 b g Classic Cliche(IRE) —Passchendaele (IRE) (Phardante (FR))
4853^{10}

Past Heritage *A E Jones* 72h
7 b g Past Glories—Norman's Delight (IRE) (Idiots Delight)
1123^{5} 1636^{P} 1814^{P} (2146) 3441^{P}

Patches (IRE) *P F Nicholls* 118h 136c
7 bb g Presenting—Ballykilleen (The Parson)
1861^{8}

Pathughkenjo (IRE) *S Donohoe*
6 ch g Eagle Eyed(USA) —Deirdre's Music (Advocator)
3757^{P} 4346^{P}

Pat Malone *Lucinda Featherstone* 42h
6 b g Jumbo Hirt(USA) —A Sharp (Sharpo)
277^{6} 635^{8} 838^{P} 8916 **1801^{P}**

Patman Du Charmil (FR) *N A Twiston-Davies* 124h
4 b g Robin Des Pres(FR) —Pacifie Du Charmil (FR) (Dom Pasquini (FR))
(1904) 2178^{6} (2811) 3021^{3} 3986^{7} 4435^{3} 4750^{9}

Patriarch (IRE) *P Bowen* 97c
10 b g Alphabatim(USA) —Strong Language (Formidable (USA))
2764^{8} 3148^{5} 3368^{5}4078^{4} 4300^{P} 4804^{P}

Patriarch Express *Mrs S J Smith* 153 h
9 b g Noble Patriarch—Jaydeeglen (Bay Express)
3723^{4} 4069^{F} 4458^{8} 4775^{5}

Patricksnineteenth (IRE) *P R Webber* 112b 142 c
9 b g Mister Lord(USA) —Many Miracles (Le Moss)
3019^{3} 3503^{3}

Patriotism *P A Fahy* 100h
6 b g Machiavellian(USA) —Dream Ticket (USA) (Danzig (USA))
67a^{7}

Patrixprial *M H Tompkins* 120 h
5 gr g Linamix(FR) —Magnificent Star (USA) (Silver Hawk (USA))
1827^{4} 4077^{5} 4430^{14}

Patrixtoo (FR) *T J Fitzgerald* 98h
5 gr h Linamix(FR) —Maradadi (USA) (Shadeed (USA))
2991^{8} 3328^{11}

Patronage *Jonjo O'Neill* 91h
4 b g Royal Applause—Passionate Pursuit (Pursuit Of Love)
2274^{5} 3714^{7} 3939^{B} 4211^{7} 4834^{18}

Pats Last *P R Rodford* 52b
4 b g Emarati(USA) —Bride's Answer (Anshan)
3244^{11} 5117^{9}

Patsy Bee (IRE) *E J O'Grady* 111+h 42c
5 b g Saddlers' Hall(IRE) —Strong Profit (IRE) (Strong Gale)
4060a^{5}

Patsy Hall (IRE) *Michael Cunningham* 130h
6 b g Saddlers' Hall(IRE) —Clahada Rose (IRE) (Roselier (FR))
4137a^{4}

Patxaran (IRE) *P C Haslam* 106+h
4 b f Revoque(IRE) —Stargard (Polish Precedent (USA))
1551^{3} (2167) 4039^{2} (4360) 4616^{9} 4789^{2}

Paula Lane *R Curtis* 82h
6 b m Factual(USA) —Colfax Classic (Jareer (USA))
105^{11} 265^{6} 506^{5} 686^{9}

Paulinski *F Jordan*
5 b m Suluk(USA) —Tsu Hsi (Teofane)
1298^{9}

Paulo Dancer (FR) *P F Nicholls* 94+h
5 b g Epaphos(GER) —Hora Dancer (FR) (Lashkari)
4032^{3}

Pauls Plain *P W Hiatt* 86h
5 b g Young Buster(IRE) —On The Wagon (Then Again)
1614^{12} 1750^{U} 1975^{5} 2750^{8}

Paul Superstar (FR) *N J Hawke* 58b
4 gr g Kaldounevees(FR) —Lady Lieutenant (IRE) (General Holme (USA))
2611^{8} 5075^{6}

Pauntley Gofa *R C Harper* 97c
10 b g Afzal—Gotageton (Oats)
1342^{P} 3964^{U} 4281^{4}4592^{8}

Pavey Ark (IRE) *James Moffatt* 71h 82 c
8 b g King's Ride—Splendid Run (Deep Run)
210^{5} 414^{P} **497^{4} 717^{P}989^{P} 1150^{4} 1317^{7}1359^{2} 1570^{P} 1684^{5}2022^{6} 2323^{2} 2570^{4}3555^{P}**

Pawn Broker *Miss J R Tooth* 100 h
9 ch g Selkirk(USA) —Dime Bag (High Line)
1957^{8} 2659^{5} 3386^{4} 3889^{5} 5021^{10}

Paxford Jack *M F Harris* 102h 118c
10 ch g Alflora(IRE) —Rakajack (Rakaposhi King)
22^{3} 288^{2} (366) 518^{3}

Pay Attention *T D Easterby* 125h
5 b m Revoque(IRE) —Catch Me (Rudimentary (USA))
1912^{4} 2452^{2} 3295^{2} 3621^{2} 3986^{P}4490^{2} 4792^{2} 4990^{2}

Pay It Forward *Mrs John Harrington* 139 h 128c
8 b g Anshan—Kellsboro Kate (Paddy's Stream)
(115a) 842^{10}

Pay To Production (IRE) *C Roche* 77h
6 b g Alphabatim(USA) —Keen Gale (IRE) (Strong Gale)
93a^{4}

Peach Of A Citizen (IRE) *Eugene M O'Sullivan* 16h 83c
7 b m Anshan—Sweet Peach (IRE) (Glenstal (USA))
1752^{2}

Peachy (IRE) *S R Andrews* 96+h 106+c
11 b g Un Desperado(FR) —Little Peach (Ragapan)
4477^{3}

Pearl Fisher (IRE) *D Carroll* 72+h
5 ch m Foxhound(USA) —Naivity (IRE) (Auction Ring (USA))
4388^{2} 4919^{10}

Pearl Island (USA) *D J Wintle*
5 b g Kingmambo(USA) —Mother Of Pearl (IRE) (Sadler's Wells (USA))
4278^{U}

Pearl King (IRE) *P J Hobbs* 105+h
4 gr g Daylami(IRE) —Regal Opinion (USA) (Gone West (USA))
3645^{3}

Pearly Bay *M G Rimell* 95h
8 b m Karinga Bay—Marina Bird (Julio Mariner)
(2457) 3130^{3} 3648^{P}

Pearly Jack *D E Fitzgerald* 118h 128c
8 ch g Weld—Pearly Lady (Tycoon II)
69a^{6} 115a^{7} 1515a^{3} 1700a^{2} 2539a^{6} 3053a^{11}

Pearly Star *A King* 88h
5 br g Bob's Return(IRE) —Pearly-B (IRE) (Gunner B)
2288^{8} 2559^{P} 2749^{4} 2983^{6} 3358^{6} 4080^{P} 4282^{7} 4556^{3}

Pearson Glen (IRE) *James Moffatt* 93+h
7 ch g Dolphin Street(FR) —Glendora (Glenstal (USA))
343^{3} 495^{3} 1591^{7} 2106^{4} 2478^{11} 2822^{6} 3152^{6}

Pebble Bay *Mrs S J Smith* 111h 102+c
11 br g Perpendicular—Milly L'Attaque (Military)
13^{2} **413^{2} (593)** 1940 3236^{9} **2654^{U} 2922^{F}**

Peccadillo (IRE) *R H Alner* 138c
12 br g Un Desperado(FR) —First Mistake (Posse (USA))
1561^{P}

Pecheur D'Islande (FR) *G Macaire*
3 ch g Nikos—Reine Elodie (FR) (Cadoudal (FR))
4298a^{4}

Peddars Way *A King* 99h
7 b g Nomadic Way(USA) —Deep Selection (IRE) (Deep Run)
109^{4}

Pedina (IRE) *C J Mann* 130h 112c
8 b g Toulon—Bilberry (Nicholas Bill)
1988^{2}

Pedler's Profiles *Miss K M George* 79+h
6 br g Topanoora—La Vie En Primrose (Henbit (USA))
2146^{3} 2728^{4} 4423^{9}

Pedros Brief (IRE) *R T Phillips* 111+h 98+c
8 bb g Leading Counsel(USA) —Pedros Pet (IRE) (Good Thyne (USA))
(2865) 3388^{P} **3907^{4}**

Peejay Hobbs *C J Gray* 95+h 93c
8 ch g Alhijaz—Hicklam Millie (Absalom)
169^{P}

Peerless Motion (IRE) *S Lycett* 74h
11 b g Caerleon(USA) —Final Figure (USA) (Super Concorde (USA))
3997^{P} 4879^{8}

Peeyoutwo *Mrs D A Hamer* 95h 125c
11 b g Golden Heights—Nyika (Town And Country)
570^{2} 914^{3} 1038^{5} 1396^{3} 1783^{3} 1899^{2} 2150^{10}

Peggy Lou *B J Llewellyn* 73h
6 b m Washington State(USA) —Rosemary Nalden (Great Commotion (USA))
4783^{P} 5050^{11}

Peggy Naylor *Miss J E Foster* 26h
5 ch m Presidium—Bitch (Risk Me (FR))
1360^{10} 2627^{P} 3267^{11}

Peggy's Prince *J D Frost* 76h
8 b g Morpeth—Prudent Peggy (Kambalda)
913^{P} 2071^{5} 2605^{7} 2934^{6} 3125^{7}

Pekan One *John G Carr*
4 ch c Grand Lodge(USA) —Ballet (Sharrood (USA))
5076a^{25}

Pen-Almozon *N J Hawke* 62h
10 ch h Almoojid—Cornish Mona Lisa (Damsire Unregistered)
2610^{P}

Penalty Clause (IRE) *Lucinda Featherstone* 79h 75 c
6 b g Namaqualand(USA) —Lady Be Lucky (IRE) (Taufan (USA))
1609^{3} 1832^{P} 2522^{P} 2717^{7} 3602^{3} 3923^{5} 4632^{9}

Penarwel *F Jordan* 52b
7 b g Aydimour—Funny Sarah (Cawston's Clown)
1660^{7}

Pencil House (IRE) *M G Rimell* 37b
6 ch g Carroll House—Pencil (Crash Course)
4507^{11}

Pendil's Princess *S E H Sherwood* 60h
7 b m Afzal—Pendil's Delight (Scorpio (FR))
359^{6} 630^{P}

Penel (IRE) *P T Midgley* 82h
5 b g Orpen(USA) —Jayess Elle (Sabrehill (USA))
2444^{8} 2752^{8} 2838^{10} 2962^{14}

Penerak *Mrs L J Young*
6 b g Primo Dominie—Ansellady (Absalom)
4556^{P}

Pennestamp (IRE) *J G M O'Shea*
4 b c Pennekamp(USA) —Sopran Marida (IRE) (Darshaan)
1679^{P}

Penney Lane *Miss Kate Milligan* 61h
5 ch m Minster Son—Cullane Lake (IRE) (Strong Statement (USA))
375^{12} 2412^{9} 3337^{9}

Penneyrose Bay *J A Geake* 144+h 107+c
7 ch m Karinga Bay—Pennethorne Place (Deep Run)
(1658) (2053) 2207^{9} 2758^{4} **4417^{2}** 4972^{14}

Pennyahei *Miss H Brookshaw* 92c
15 b m Malaspina—Pennyazena (Pamroy)
282^{P}

Pennybid (IRE) *C R Wilson* 51b
4 b g Benny The Dip(USA) —Stamatina (Warning)
3799^{12}

Penny Island (IRE) *A King*
4 b g Trans Island—Sparklingsovereign (Sparkler)
1190^{P}

Penny King *F Jordan* 78b
5 b g Desert King(IRE) —Pennycairn (Last Tycoon)
1762^{8}

Penny Out (IRE) *D M Christie* 92h 92c
8 b g Shernazar—Tuney Lady (Boreen (FR))
5083a^{13}

Penny Park (IRE) *P J Hobbs* 101+h
7 ch g Flemensfirth(USA) —Penny Bride (IRE) (The Parson)
2144^{5} 2421^{8} 3963^{7} 4210^{5} (5028)

Penny Pictures (IRE) *M C Pipe* 139h 113 c
7 b g Theatrical—Copper Creek (Habitat)
208^{8} 422^{2} 1270^{7} 1872^{8} 2369^{2} 2999^{8} 3179^{8} **3801^{4}** 4446^{8} 4765^{3} 4959^{3}

Penny Rich (IRE) *T Hogan* 115h
12 br g Little Bighorn—Musical Puss (Orchestra)
3005a^{21}

Penny's Crown *G A Ham* 90+h
7 b m Reprimand—Two And Sixpence (USA) (Chief's Crown (USA))
96^{8} 1456^{5} 1486^{4} 1636^{7} (1712) 2043^{6} 2150^{12} 2576^{4} 2687^{5} (3125) 3325^{7} 3951^{8} 4151^{3} 4331^{6} 4549^{9} 4752^{10}

Pennys From Heaven *Mrs Tracey Barfoot-Saunt* 78h 88+c
12 gr g Generous(IRE) —Heavenly Cause (USA) (Grey Dawn II)
2^{5} 388^{U} 459^{5}

Penny Stall *Miss E C Lavelle* 90 h
5 b m Silver Patriarch(IRE) —Madiyla (Darshaan)
2714^{10} **2960^{F}**

Penny Strong *A J Whiting*
6 b m Thowra(FR) —An Bothar Dubh (Strong Gale)
1755^{9} 2212^{P}

Penric *J K Price* 95+h
6 b g Marju(IRE) —Nafhaat (USA) (Roberto (USA))
238^{3} (1753) 2285^{7} 2559^{4}

Penteli *C Grant* 84h
6 ch m Double Trigger(IRE) —Raglan Lady (Carlingford Castle)
192^{12} 418^{6} 602^{8} 854^{4} 938^{3} 1066^{2} 1211^{4} 1337^{3} 1528^{4} (1606)

Penthouse Melody *R J Hodges* 70c
8 b m Seven Hearts—Pentameron (Heres)
962^{F}

Penthouse Minstrel *R J Hodges* 112+c
12 bb g Seven Hearts—Pentameron (Heres)
522^{2} 694^{3} 761^{9} 1874^{2} 2051^{6} 2273^{P}

Penzance *A King* 154h 112+c
5 ch g Pennekamp(USA) —Kalinka (IRE) (Soviet Star (USA))
2338^{3} 2761^{4} 3994^{7} 4432^{F} 4959^{8} 5125^{3}

Pepe Galvez (SWE) *Mrs L C Taylor* 126+h
9 br g Mango Express—Mango Sampaquita (SWE) (Colombian Friend (USA))
1823^{3} 2533^{3} 2974^{3} 4608^{3} 4773^{14}

Peppershot *R Gurney* 67h
6 b g Vettori(IRE) —No Chili (Glint Of Gold)
261^{P} 504^{4} 763^{P} 2043^{P} 2214^{U} 2802^{8} 2934^{9} 3283^{4} 3433^{4} 3729^{9}

Peppery Pamela *V R A Dartnall* 82b
5 ch m Master Willie—Kingky's Cottage (Kinglet)
4017^{5} 4324^{P}

Pepporoni Pete (IRE) *P F Nicholls* 122+b
5 b g Un Desperado(FR) —Sister Shot (Celtic Cone)
(3001) 4244^{3} 4779^{15}

Pequenita *R C Guest* 108 h 111+c
6 b m Rudimentary(USA) —Sierra Madrona (USA) (Woodman (USA))
170^{3} (264) 466^{P}(497) 595^{6} **840^{P}** 864^{P} 1045^{5} 1211^{2} 1319^{4} 1436^{12} 1552^{7}

Per Amore (IRE) *David Pearson* 121h 87c
8 ch g General Monash(USA) —Danny's Miracle (Superlative)
1400^{P} 1617^{6} **2993^{P} 3922^{7} 4165^{4} 4804^{3} 4991^{3} 13^{3}**

Perange (FR) *Mrs D M Grissell* 94c
10 ch g Perrault—La Mesange (FR) (Olmeto)
3960^{4} 4351^{P}

Perce Rock *T Stack* 122b
4 b c Dansili—Twilight Secret (Vaigly Great)
4448^{4}

Percipient *D R Gandolfo* 84+h 84c
8 b g Pennekamp(USA) —Annie Albright (USA) (Verbatim (USA))
95^{3} 565^{3} (758) **979^{2}** 1188^{9} 4871^{5}

Percussionist (IRE) *J Howard Johnson* 113 h
5 b g Sadler's Wells(USA) —Magnificient Style (USA) (Silver Hawk (USA))
(2447) 2614^{P} (2991) 3491^{3}

Percy Beck *P Needham* 87+h
10 ch g Minster Son—Kate O'Kirkham (Le Bavard (FR))
148^{U} 413^{P} 570^{P} 781^{P}

Percy Jay (NZ) *W Jenks*
7 ch g Rainbow Myth(NZ) —Zillah Grace (NZ) (Otehi Bay (AUS))
2941^{16} 3800^{8} 4048^{P} 1^{P}

Perfect Balance (IRE) *D W Thompson* 92 h
5 bb g Shinko Forest(IRE) —Tumble (Mtoto)
2081^{4} 2416^{2} 2688^{3} 2967^{3} (3656) 4043^{4} 4277^{P}

Perfect Liaison *R H Alner* 109h
9 b g Alflora(IRE) —Connie's Pet (National Trust)
2621^{P} 2999^{F} **3341^{P}**

Perfectly Posh *J K Cresswell* 55b
5 ch m Rakaposhi King—Gunner Be Good (Gunner B)
3145^{10} 3462^{9} 4422^{14}

Perfect Punch *K G Reveley* 87h 97 c
7 b g Reprimand—Aliuska (IRE) (Fijar Tango (FR))
2415^{P} 2751^{7} 2989^{5}

Perfect Venue (IRE) *A J Wilson* 89h
13 b g Danehill(USA) —Welsh Fantasy (Welsh Pageant)
1218^{P} 1367^{8} 1900^{P}

Periwinkle Lad (IRE) *Miss Victoria Roberts* 107h 94c
9 b g Perugino(USA) —Bold Kate (Bold Lad (IRE))
697^{12}

Perky Peaks (IRE) *N A Twiston-Davies* 82+b
5 bb g Executive Perk—Knockea Hill (Buckskin (FR))
4500^{10} 5054^{6}

Perle De Puce (FR) *N J Henderson* 134 h 121 c
7 b m Snurge—Ma Puce (FR) (Tip Moss (FR))
2715^{U} 2846^{F} 3278^{2} 3621^{3} 4375^{13} 4473^{18} 4765^{P}

Perouse *P F Nicholls* 152h 130+c
8 ch g Alderbrook—Track Angel (Ardoon)
208^{5} **(682) 1024^{P}** 2055^{5} **2270^{F}**

Persian Genie (IRE) *Miss J S Davis* 51h
5 br m Grand Lodge(USA) —Persia (IRE) (Persian Bold)
1266^{3} 2928^{9}

Persian Native (IRE) *C C Bealby* 84h
6 br g Anshan—Natina (IRE) (Be My Native (USA))
2572^{9} 2961^{7} *3504^{2} 3983^{6}* 5118^{3}

Persian Point *Miss S E Forster* 88h 98+c
10 ch g Persian Bold—Kind Thoughts (Kashmir II)
643^{8} **2026^{5} 2655^{3} 3334^{6} 3562^{3} (4303) 4587^{4} 4981^{2} 5121^{4}**

Persian Prince (IRE) *J Wade* 90b
6 br g Anshan—Real Decent (IRE) (Strong Gale)
1532^{3} 1849^{6} 3742^{12}

Personal Assurance *Jonjo O'Neill* 127h 132c
9 bb g Un Desperado(FR) —Steel Typhoon (General Ironside)
(489) 765^{P}

Personal Impact (IRE) *J J Lambe* 59c
8 gr g Arctic Lord—Coolcroo Lady (Roselier (FR))
643^{10} **872^{5}**

Pertemps Timmy *R T Phillips* 101h
8 b g Petoski—Brilliant Future (Welsh Saint)
3545^{6} 4106^{P} 4393^{2} 4961^{12}

Peruvian Breeze (IRE) *Evan Williams* 85h 40c
5 b g Foxhound(USA) —Quietly Impressive (IRE) (Taufan (USA))
903^{P} 1077^{3} 1246^{2} 1336^{5} 1523^{8} 1564^{10}

Pessimistic Dick *Mrs J C McGregor*
13 b g Derrylin—Tycoon Moon (Tycoon II)
857^{4} 1309^{2} 1511^{3} 1603^{4} 1837^{2} 2905^{U} 3377^{P} 3486^{P} 3930^{U} 5122^{P}

Peter Elkra (IRE) *T Hogan* 79h
8 b m Aahsaylad—Miss Maina (Thatching)
2341^{P}

Peterhouse *Mrs E Slack* 63b 79+c
7 b g Persian Bold—Run With Pride (Mandrake Major)
4659^{P} 4845^{P}

Peter Parkgate *N R Mitchell* 32b
7 gr g Kuwait Beach(USA) —Nellie's Joy VII (Damsire Unregistered)
564^{P}

Peter's Imp (IRE) *A Berry* 97 h
11 b g Imp Society(USA) —Catherine Clare (Sallust)
499^{6} 592^{4} (988) **1334^{F}** 3395^{11} 3797^{12} 4517^{6} 14^{17}

Peterson's Cay (IRE) *C L Tizzard* 96h 97+c
8 b g Grand Lodge(USA) —Columbian Sand (IRE) (Salmon Leap (USA))
4150^{P}

Petertheknot (IRE) *Patrick Sinnott* 142h 128c
8 ch g Beneficial—A Woman's Heart (IRE) (Supreme Leader)
116a^{4}

Pete The Painter (IRE) *J W Tudor* 93+c
9 b g Detroit Sam(FR) —Rambling Moss (Le Moss)
76^{P} 262^{F} 461^{5} 746^{6} 916^{3} 981^{3} 1109^{U} 1203^{7} 1406^{P}

Petite Salou *C N Kellett* 38h
9 ch m Path Of Condie—Rock Of Ages (Blakeney)
429^{9}

Petitjean *P J Hobbs* 98+h
6 ch g Garde Royale—Sainte Etoile (FR) (Saint Cyrien (FR))
3001^{4} 3906^{5} 4032^{7} 4604^{9}

Petit Owen (FR) *F Weisgerber*
6 b g Dolpour—Pierrot De Sou (FR) (Cyborg (FR))
846a^{8}

Petolinski *C L Popham* 100h 94c
8 b g Petoski—Olnistar (FR) (Balsamo (FR))
98^{3} (398) 535^{2} 669^{P} 3359^{U} 4558^{P} 5025^{2}

Petrolero (ARG) *James Moffatt* 93+h 75+c
7 gr g Perfect Parade(USA) —Louise (ARG) (Farnesio (ARG))
1491^{0} 495^{2} 544^{4} 991^{6} **1335^{9}**

Petrovka (IRE) *S Gollings* 81+h
6 b m King's Theatre(IRE) —Adjacent (IRE) (Doulab (USA))
1323^{7} 3591^{5}

Petwick (IRE) *A King* 110+h
7 bb g Flemensfirth(USA) —Scottish Minnie (IRE) (Farhaan)
(2419) 2706^{2} 3214^{5} 4058^{9}

Peveril Pride *J A Geake* 103h 67c
8 b g Past Glories—Peveril Princess (Town And Country)
2607^{P} 2848^{P} 3220^{5} 3359^{F} 3909^{12} 4353^{8} 4914^{2}

Pewter Light (IRE) *B J M Ryall* 58h 69 c
9 gr g Roselier(FR) —Luminous Light (Cardinal Flower)
2686^{F} 3252^{6} 3886^{F} 4553^{P}

Phairy Storm (IRE) *J D Frost* 62h
7 bb g Glacial Storm(USA) —Railstown Phairy (IRE) (Phardante (FR))
1671^{0} 664^{7}

Phantom Footsteps *C N Kellett*
9 gr g Komaite(USA) —Hyperion Palace (Dragonara Palace (USA))
2179^{P}

Phantom Major (FR) *Mrs R L Elliot* 76h
5 gr g Phantom Breeze—Leone Des Pres (FR) (Tip Moss (FR))
484^{3} 719^{4} 2948^{11} 3376^{8} 3912^{5} 4313^{6} 5064^{10}

Phantom Plumber (IRE) *V Bowens* 67h
6 b g Dabali(IRE) —Siobhan's Patch (IRE) (Red Sunset)
93a^{11}

Pharagon (IRE) *Mrs C J Kerr* 29b
8 b g Phardante(FR) —Hogan (IRE) (Black Minstrel)
81^{P} 419^{7}

Pharbeitfrome (IRE) *W B Stone*
12 b g Phardante(FR) —Asigh Glen (Furry Glen)
221^{P} 999^{P} 1044^{P} 1180^{P}

Phar Bleu (FR) *P F Nicholls* 141 h
5 b g Agent Bleu(FR) —Guilt Less (FR) (Useful (FR))
2209^{3} 2493^{4} 2761^{6} 4446^{4} 4765^{10} 5003^{3}

Phar City (IRE) *R H Buckler* 90h 108 c
9 b g Phardante(FR) —Aunty Dawn (IRE) (Strong Gale)
205^{2} 505^{P} 805^{8} 1022^{3}

Phardessa *A M Crow* 104+b
5 b m Pharly(FR) —Mardessa (Ardross)
(5008)

Phareight Dei (IRE) *Ian Williams* 71h 85c
8 b g Leading Counsel(USA) —Mullaghroe (Tarboosh (USA))
4320^{3}

Phar From Frosty (IRE) *C R Egerton* 121 h 115c
9 br g Phardante(FR) —Cold Evening (IRE) (Strong Gale)
413^{P} 1177^{3} 1455^{2} 1872^{10} 1992^{2} 2175^{11} 2483^{7} 2820^{6} 3179^{10}

Pharly Green *G P Enright*
4 ch f Pharly(FR) —Pastures Green (Monksfield)
4654^{8}

Pharly Star *H D Daly* 103c
12 ch g Pharly(FR) —Norapa (Ahonoora)
358^{4} 631^{P}

Pharmistice (IRE) *Mrs N C Neill* 102c
15 b g Phardante(FR) —Lucylet (Kinglet)
411^{2}

Pharnoon *E M Caine*
10 b g Pharly(FR) —Mountain Willow (Doyoun)
8^{P}

Pharoah's Gold (IRE) *D Burchell* 64h
8 b g Namaqualand(USA) —Queen Nefertiti (IRE) (Fairy King (USA))
2803^{9}

Phar Out Phavorite (IRE) *Miss E C Lavelle* 120 h 133 c
7 b g Beneficial—Phar From Men (IRE) (Phardante (FR))
(78) (312) 460^{2} (1804) **2482^{3} 3329^{F} 3647^{F}** (Dead)

Pharpost (IRE) *A G Juckes* 103 h 77c
11 b g Phardante(FR) —Branstown Lady (Deep Run)
572^{P} 1236^{P}

Pharshu (IRE) *C L Tizzard* 44h 90c
9 gr m Phardante(FR) —Bruna Rosa (Roselier (FR))
763^{5} **803^{5} 1521^{2}**

Phar The Best (IRE) *Mrs A L M King* 86h 70c
9 ch g Phardante(FR) —Auling (Tarqogan)
630^{5} 745^{10} 4449^{8} 4640^{6} 4734^{9}

Phase Eight Girl *J Hetherton* 57h
10 b m Warrshan(USA) —Bugsy's Sister (Aragon)
468^{P} 768^{P} 905^{P} 1040^{4} 1152^{P} 1280^{8} 1564^{6} 1685^{4} 2256^{5} 3169^{9}

Phase Three (IRE) *T R George* 72h 95c
9 ch g Torus—Winning Fare (Le Bavard (FR))
110^{4} 514^{5} 668^{3} **862^{2} 939^{2}**

Phazar *N J Hawke* 80h
6 b g Zamindar(USA) —Ypha (USA) (Lyphard (USA))
1969^{8} 2554^{8} 3133^{10}

Phildari (IRE) *N A Twiston-Davies* 108h 115c
10 b g Shardari—Philosophical (Welsh Chanter)
437^{6} 512^{2} 762^{12} **896^{3} (1109) 1178^{P}(5140)**

Philippa Yeates (IRE) *M C Pipe* 86+h 95+c
7 b m Hushang(IRE) —Miss Bobby Bennett (King's Lake (USA))
(1076) 1271^{F}

Philomena *V R A Dartnall* 100+h
7 b m Bedford(USA) —Mandalay Miss (Mandalus)
(4129) 4324^{R}

Philosophic *Mrs L C Jewell* 72h
12 b g Be My Chief(USA) —Metaphysique (FR) (Law Society (USA))
232^{7} 502^{6}

Philson Run (IRE) *Nick Williams* 143 c
10 b g Un Desperado(FR) —Isis (Deep Run)
1676^{8} 2370^{F} 3022^{P} 3877^{2} (4111) 4496^{P} 5004^{6}

Phoenix Phlyer *Mrs Marilyn Scudamore* 111+c
12 b g Ardross—Brown Coast (Oats)
79^{P}

Phone Back (IRE) *G L Moore* 96h
7 b g Bob Back(USA) —Will Phone (Buckskin (FR))
3134^{2}

Phone Tapping *Mrs L B Normile*
5 b g Robellino(USA) —Miss Party Line (USA) (Phone Trick (USA))
2942^{17}

Phonidal (FR) *M Rolland* 123h
10 br g Cadoudal(FR) —Grande Symphonie (FR) (Big John (FR))
585a^{0} 4717a^{6} 5000a^{3}

Photographer (USA) *S Lycett* 101h
8 bb g Mountain Cat(USA) —Clickety Click (USA) (Sovereign Dancer (USA))
2015^{3} 2487^{7} 2730^{7}

Phriapatius *Dr J R J Naylor* 93b
5 b g Parthian Springs—Metafan (Last Fandango)
1660^{4} *1922^{4}* 2507^{11} 3327^{8}

Physical Force *Mrs Marjorie Fife*
8 b g Casteddu—Kaiserlinde (GER) (Frontal)
50^{P}

Pick Of The Crop *J R Jenkins* 83h
5 ch g Fraam—Fresh Fruit Daily (Reprimand)
1480^{11} 1562^{4} 2261^{5} 3371^{P} 3597^{6} 4640^{P}

Picot De Say *C Roberts* 101+h
4 b g Largesse—Facsimile (Superlative)
2286^{11} 2580^{9} 2811^{6} 3577^{7} 4010^{4}(4427) (4452) (4674) 4834^{15}

Picts Hill *P F Nicholls* 104h
6 ch g Romany Rye—Nearly A Brook (Nearly A Hand)
3327^{5} 4676^{P}

Piercing Sun (IRE) *Anthony Mullins* 123h 120c
7 b g Eagle Eyed(USA) —Out In The Sun (USA) (It's Freezing (USA))
43a^{8} **1515a^{6}**

Pietro Vannucci (IRE) *Jonjo O'Neill* 136h 115c
10 b g Perugino(USA) —Lady's Bridge (USA) (Sir Ivor (USA))
2102^{4} 2498^{P} 2814^{3} 3440^{2} 4014^{3} 4419^{P} 4843^{P}

Pikestaff (USA) *M A Barnes* 99+h 63c
8 ch g Diesis—Navarene (USA) (Known Fact (USA))
2157 417^{F} (606) 697^{6} 859^{7} 941^{3}(1067) 1341^{6} **1603^{U} 1719^{6}**

Pilca (FR) *R M Stronge* 81h
6 ch g Pistolet Bleu(IRE) —Caricoe (Baillamont (USA))
1^{2} 571^{9} 695^{2} 841^{4} 974^{5} 1434^{7} 2625^{8} 3141^{3} 3456^{11} 3731^{7} **4350^{6}**

Pillaging Pict *J B Walton* 114c
11 ch g Primitive Rising(USA) —Carat Stick (Gold Rod)
3172^7 4531^U

Pillar Of Fire (IRE) *Ian Williams* 101h 103c
12 gr g Roselier(FR) —Cousin Flo (True Song)
632^3 896^2 1109^4 1219^6

Pilot's Harbour *Mark Hughes* 91h 56c
10 b g Distant Relative—Lillemor (Connaught)
125^8 411^P

Pine Marten *J A Geake*
7 b g Karinga Bay—Rakaposhi Queen (Rakaposhi King)
3240^P 3941^P

Pingus (FR) *C Scandella*
3 b c Sendawar(IRE) —Desert Victory (Green Desert (USA))
4298a^3

Pin High (IRE) *Miss H C Knight* 100h 81c
7 b g Needle Gun(IRE) —Eva's Fancy (Distinctly (USA))
2427^5 2723^7 **3940^4**

Pinkerton Mill *J T Stimpson* 78h
6 b m Rudimentary(USA) —Real Silver (Silly Season)
2179^P 2460^P 2873^5 3730^9

Pink Harbour *D McCain* 66h 93+c
8 b m Rakaposhi King—Let Me Finish (Chantro)
3144^4 **997^P 1203^8** 1357^6

Pinmoor Hill *Mrs Diane Wilson* 56c
10 b g Saddlers' Hall(IRE) —Pennine Pink (IRE) (Pennine Walk)
299^6

Pinnacle Ridge *Mrs K Walton* 90h
6 ch g Bob's Return(IRE) —Canal Street (Oats)
1723^2

Pintail *Mrs P Robeson* 63h
6 b g Petoski—Tangara (Town Crier)
3685^P 4015^6 4869^2

Piper Paddy *P R Chamings* 87b
4 ch f Fumo Di Londra(IRE) —Anouska (Interrex (CAN))
2830^3 3651^6 *3983^4*

Pipers Legend *D Burchell* 90+h
7 b g Midnight Legend—Pipers Reel (Palace Music (USA))
4106^U 4278^11 4570^6 4935^9

Pip Moss *J A B Old* 85h 69+c
11 ch g Le Moss—My Aisling (John De Coombe)
2126^P 3662^9 4277^P

Pippilongstocking *E G Bevan* 34h
4 b f Makbul—Princess Ermyn (Shernazar)
1397^13

Pips Assertive Way *A W Carroll* 95+h
5 ch m Nomadic Way(USA) —Return To Brighton (Then Again)
1454^P 1750^9 1851^4 2244^P 2501^9

Pipssalio (SPA) *Jamie Poulton* 113+h 121+c
9 b g Pips Pride—Tesalia (SPA) (Finissimo (SPA))
4693^2 4974^7

Piraeus (NZ) *R Johnson* 101+h
7 b g Beau Zam(NZ) —Gull Mundur (NZ) (Icelandic)
(2171) 2416^5 (2653)

Piran (IRE) *Evan Williams* 115+h
4 b g Orpen(USA) —Dancing At Lunasa (IRE) (Dancing Dissident (USA))
1478^4 1594^8 1729^6 (2810) 3286^2 (3458) 4593^F(4826) 5103a^6

Pirandello (IRE) *K C Bailey* 117h 98c
8 ch g Shalford(IRE) —Scenic Villa (Top Ville)
460^8 633^U 1633^2 1862^2 2103^2 2150^13 2716^8 4736^P **4904^2**

Pirate Flagship (FR) *P F Nicholls* 128h
7 b g River Mist(USA) —Sacadu (Tyrant (USA))
2050^2 (2528) 2829^6 (3175) 4242^2 4473^4 4765^15(4970)

Pirate King (IRE) *H Hill* 54h
9 ch g Eurobus—Shakie Lady (Tug Of War)
4897^P

Pirouettes (IRE) *Ernst Oertel* 90h
6 b m Royal Applause—Dance Serenade (IRE) (Marju (IRE))
971^2

Piton (FR) *F-M Cottin*
3 gr g April Night(FR) —Fourmille (FR) (Rose Laurel)
4298a^P

Pitsi Kahtoh *P W Hiatt* 32h
4 b f Petoski—Plectrum (Adonijah)
1440^5 1563^13

Pitton Prince *N R Mitchell* 79h
7 gr g Classic Cliche(IRE) —Curious Feeling (Nishapour (FR))
1459^6 1779^P 2269^6 2683^F 3425^6

Pixley *T J Fitzgerald* 87b
6 ch g Saxon Farm—Lady Renton (Rolfe (USA))
241^9

Pizarro (IRE) *E J O'Grady* 147h 159c
9 ch g Broken Hearted—Our Swan Lady (Swan's Rock)
68a^3 1810a^3

Place Above (IRE) *E A Elliott* 45h 109 c
10 b g Alphabatim(USA) —Lucky Pit (Pitpan)
1723^6 **2524^4 2978^F 3336^P 4921^2**

Plain Chant *C Roberts* 64h 78c
9 b g Doyoun—Sing Softly (Luthier)
862^10 916^P 1076^P 1178^U 1247^5

Planet Ireland (IRE) *Mrs J L Wight* 70c
14 b g Mandalus—Seapatrick (The Parson)
594^P

Plantaganet (FR) *Ian Williams* 91h 86c
8 br g Cadoudal(FR) —Ever Young (FR) (Royal Charter (FR))
2309^8 2816^13 **3919^P 4735^3 4908^6**

Plantagenet Prince *M Scudamore* 69h
7 b g Lancastrian—Yuan Princess (Tender King)
457^11 683^4

Planters Punch (IRE) *G M Moore* 109 h
5 b g Cape Cross(IRE) —Jamaican Punch (IRE) (Shareef Dancer (USA))
(2448) 2942^3 3257^7 3912^8 4114^4 4301^6 4922^11

Platinum Point (IRE) *E W Tuer* 63h
7 b g Norwich—Blackhill Lass (IRE) (King's Ride)
3314^P 3488^12 3780^5 3927^9 4302^10 4487^4

Platium Starlight (IRE) *Thomas O'Neill* 80h
6 gr g Red Sunset—Mone Club (IRE) (King Of Clubs)
592^11

Playing Dirty *M C Pipe* 67b
6 b g Topanoora—Lady Nell (Teenoso (USA))
817^8

Play It Again *Simon Earle* 70b
6 b g Double Trigger(IRE) —Play For Time (Comedy Star (USA))
138^5

Play Master (IRE) *C Roberts* 88+h
5 b g Second Empire(IRE) —Madam Waajib (IRE) (Waajib)
5106^7

Play The Melody (IRE) *C Tinkler* 95+h
5 bb g Revoque(IRE) —Dumayla (Shernazar)
(3137) 3441^5

Pleased To Receive (IRE) *A M Hales* 50b
6 ch g Beneficial—Cheeney's Gift (Quayside)
490^17 1892^P

Plenty Courage *B Storey* 95+h 83+c
12 ch g Gildoran—Fastlass (Celtic Cone)
(781) **858^5** 1063^4

Plutocrat *L Lungo* 126 h 96+c
10 b g Polar Falcon(USA) —Choire Mhor (Dominion)
372^P

Pocket Sevens (IRE) *Miss E C Lavelle* 32h
6 b g Supreme Leader—Flutter (IRE) (Floriferous)
1990^P 2144^P

Pocketwood *Jean-Rene Auvray* 87+h
4 b g Fleetwood(IRE) —Pocket Venus (IRE) (King's Theatre (IRE))
1948^2 2661^6

Poggenip *B G Powell* 81h
7 b m Petoski—Princess Tria (Space King)
4129^P 4450^6 4823^6

Point *W Jenks* 98h 101 c
9 b g Polish Precedent(USA) —Sixslip (USA) (Diesis)
137^P 2144^8 2723^3 **2936^4 3290^P 3732^3 4047^5**

Point Barrow (IRE) *P Hughes* 130h 153+c
8 b g Arctic Lord—Credit Transfer (IRE) (Kemal (FR))
2539a^9 3053a^10 3587a^10(4929a)

Poirot *J Howard Johnson*
4 b g Montjeu(IRE) —Opari (IRE) (Night Shift (USA))
1923^P

Poker Pal (IRE) *D T Hughes* 118h 99c
9 b g Hollow Hand—Lady Dee (Kambalda)
71a^7

Polar Gunner *J M Jefferson* 119+h 133+c
9 b g Gunner B—Polar Belle (Arctic Lord)
2027^4 **(2443)** (3395) (4045) (4503) **(4850)**

Polar Passion *R Hollinshead* 86h
4 b f Polar Prince(IRE) —Priorite (IRE) (Kenmare (FR))
(945) 1397^5 1551^11 3990^P

Polar Red *M C Pipe* 88h 123+c
9 ch g Polar Falcon(USA) —Sharp Top (Sharpo)
2636^P **3620^7 4496^U 4762^7 5004^15**

Polar Scout (IRE) *C J Mann* 111+h 120c
9 b g Arctic Lord—Baden (IRE) (Furry Glen)
233^2

Pole Star *J R Fanshawe* 144h 113+c
8 bb g Polar Falcon(USA) —Ellie Ardensky (Slip Anchor)
3329^F 3618^5 4446^14 4776^P

Polesworth *C N Kellett*
4 b f Wizard King—Nicholas Mistress (Beveled (USA))
3939^P

Polish Cloud (FR) *Mrs H M Kemp* 112+h 106 c
9 gr g Bering—Batchelor's Button (FR) (Kenmare (FR))
387^10 **4660^2 4730^P**

Polished *V R A Dartnall* 108+h 110c
7 ch g Danzig Connection(USA) —Glitter (FR) (Reliance II)
120^3 (214) (263) (664) 1458^4 **(1716) 1795^3** 3185^2 3333^7 4561^12

Polish Legend *I A Brown* 92+h
7 b g Polish Precedent(USA) —Chita Rivera (Chief Singer)
14^20

Polish Pilot (IRE) *J R Cornwall* 59h 51 c
11 b g Polish Patriot(USA) —Va Toujours (Alzao (USA))
2080^4 2719^5 3370^8 3686^10 4165^3 4580^P 4896^8

Polish Rhapsody (IRE) *J A Supple*
5 b m Charnwood Forest(IRE) —Polish Rhythm (IRE) (Polish Patriot (USA))
2099^13

Political Cruise *R Nixon* 79h 98c
8 b g Royal Fountain—Political Mill (Politico (USA))
1838^P 2944^17 **3317^7 3380^6 3555^F 3850^7** 3918^5 4314^6 (4656) **4840^3 5065^F**

Political Dancer *J I A Charlton* 40b
5 b m Dancing High—Political Diamond (Politico (USA))
5124^13

Political Intrigue *T G Dascombe* 114+h
4 b g Dansili—Quandary (USA) (Blushing Groom (FR))
(3645) 4117^6 (4832) (Dead)

Political Pendant *R Nixon* 85h
5 br m Moshaajir(USA) —Political Mill (Politico (USA))
2028^2 2446^8 2674^7 3235^4 3337^4 3534^8 3795^9 4143^5 5039^10

Political Sox *R Nixon* 95+h
12 br g Mirror Boy—Political Mill (Politico (USA))
647 304^2 410^6 499^5 859^8 2038^11 2474^6 2840^12 3271^12 3487^15 5068^5

Polka *V G Greenway* 82h
11 b g Slip Anchor—Peace Dance (Bikala)
519^P 749^8 **4730^P**

Pollensa Bay *S A Brookshaw* 88h 88 c
7 b g Overbury(IRE) —Cloncoose (IRE) (Remainder Man)
74^3 358^5 611^7 **767^2 1713^9 2074^5 2561^5 2936^13**

Pollensa Lady *A Crook* 46b
6 b m Abzu—Whitegates Lady (Le Coq D'Or)
719^7 876^9

Pollerton Run (IRE) *T G Williams*
8 b g Executive Perk—Whitebarn Run (Pollerton)
4167^P 4831^P

Pollys Angel *C N Kellett* 48h
7 b m Makbul—Wayzgoose (USA) (Diesis)
1415^6

Polly Whitefoot *R A Fahey* 78 h
7 b m Perpendicular—Cream O The Border (Meadowbrook)
1834^2 2186^11 2680^3 3152^7 3351^12

Polonius *P R Webber*
5 b g Great Dane(IRE) —Bridge Pool (First Trump)
5024^P

Poly Amanshaa (IRE) *M C Banks* 100h 118 c
14 bb g Nashamaa—Mombones (Lord Gayle (USA))
368^P

Polyanthus Jones *H D Daly* 82h
7 b m Sovereign Water(FR) —Cindie Girl (Orchestra)
2718^P 3461^6 4052^4 4860^P

Polyarnoe Bay *T D Walford* 47h
6 b m Mesleh—Vickenda (Giacometti)
1661^6

Polyphon (FR) *P Monteith* 80h 120+c
8 b g Murmure(FR) —Petite Folie (Salmon Leap (USA))
84^7 306^U 1665^9 **2067^2 2479^3 2842^2 (4365) (4586) 5067^4**

Pomfisch Lad (IRE) *S Donohoe* 99h
8 b g Roselier(FR) —Lancastrians Dream (IRE) (Lancastrian)
4341^P

Pom Flyer (FR) *F Flood* 131h
6 b g Broadway Flyer(USA) —Pomme D'Emeraude (FR) (Margouillat (FR))
117a^13 2650a^17 (2916a) 3411a^3 4951a^3

Ponchatrain (IRE) *D J Wintle* 101+h
6 ch g Fourstars Allstar(USA) —Phardante Lilly (IRE) (Phardante (FR))
685^5 843^3 976^5 1538^U 1611^5

Ponderon *Mrs P Robeson* 108h
6 ch g Hector Protector(USA) —Blush Rambler (IRE) (Blushing Groom (FR))
(194) 1632^3

Pontiff (IRE) *Carl Llewellyn* 101h
6 b g Alflora(IRE) —Northwood May (Teenoso (USA))
3496^3 (4501) 4803^3

Pontius *N A Twiston-Davies*
9 b g Terimon—Coole Pilate (Celtic Cone)
4643^P

Pont Neuf (IRE) *A Crook* 88+h
6 b m Revoque(IRE) —Petite Maxine (Sharpo)
2335^6 2704^2 2873^7 3337^P 3442^11 3967^6

Poor Tactic's (IRE) *J J Lambe* 89h
10 b g Commanche Run—Hilary's Image (IRE) (Phardante (FR))
(306) 785^P 938^5

Popgoestheweasel *B Tulloch* 84h
11 b m Phardante(FR) —Poetic Light (Ardross)
79^F

Pop Gun *Mrs K Waldron* 84h
7 ch g Pharly(FR) —Angel Fire (Nashwan (USA))
2146^8 2419^2 3945^P 4046^P

Popinpeat *W G Young*
4 b g Peter Quince—Oleron (Darshaan)
4147^16

Pop Play Again *G A Swinbank* 49h
5 ch g Vettori(IRE) —Bellair (Beveled (USA))
1794^12

Poppy Smith *B J Eckley* 58b
4 ch f Busy Flight—Alice Smith (Alias Smith (USA))
3468^8

Popsi's Cloggs *D W Lewis* 75h
14 ch g Joli Wasfi(USA) —Popsi's Poppet (Hill Clown (USA))
3573 630^P

Popsleebobross (IRE) *P Butler* 34h
5 b m Revoque(IRE) —Flame Of Sion (Be My Chief (USA))
3188^8 3435^12 3717^12

Porak (IRE) *W Davies* 118 h 111 c
9 ch g Perugino(USA) —Gayla Orchestra (Lord Gayle (USA))
4097^5 4282^6 4429^F 4561^6 4879^7 5014^3

Pornic (FR) *A Crook* 77h 74 c
12 b g Shining Steel—Marie De Geneve (FR) (Nishapour (FR))
81^4 373^5 481^P 2289^6 2474^5 2688^8 **2900^6 3320^5** 3446^6 **3762^7 3964^5** 4299^7 **4659^3**

Portant Fella *Ms Joanna Morgan* 121h 108c
7 b g Greensmith—Jubilata (USA) (The Minstrel (CAN))
1093a^5 1204^6

Portavadie *J M Jefferson* 124h 129c
7 b g Rakaposhi King—Woodland Flower (Furry Glen)
(209) 438^2 1880^4 **(2677) 2872^3 3380^3 4472^P 5121^F**

Portavo (IRE) *Miss H C Knight* 85+h 118c
6 b g Luso—Inchriver (IRE) (Over The River (FR))
2144^4 **2732^F** 2934^P **3801^3 4419^8 4827^4**

Port D'Argent (IRE) *Mrs H O Graham* 43h
4 b f Dockside(USA) —Petite-D-Argent (Noalto)
1797^15 2167^P

Porthilly Bay *H D Daly* 80+h
6 b g Primitive Rising(USA) —Threewaygirl (Orange Bay)
2341^5

Portland Bill (IRE) *R H Alner* 103h
6 ch g Zaffaran(USA) —Donegal Moss (Le Moss)
3001^7 3466^5 3717^3 4106^3 4373^9 4676^3

Port Natal (IRE) *J Wade* 66h
8 b g Selkirk(USA) —Play Around (IRE) (Niniski (USA))
1662^P 1883^P 2025^P 4487^P

Porto (IRE) *B J M Ryall* 62h
11 bb g Torus—Fare Twist (IRE) (Phardante (FR))
912^5 977^7 1486^P

Port Sodrick *R H Alner* 76h
5 bb g Young Ern—Keepsake (IRE) (Distinctly North (USA))
1077^6 1158^9 1246^4 1367^5 1800^P

Porty Fox *N R Mitchell* 5b
5 b g Riverwise(USA) —Mildred Sophia (Crooner)
4667^13

Posh Act *Miss H C Knight* 86h
6 b g Rakaposhi King—Balancing Act (Balinger)
3369^10 3717^7 4094^P 4581^4

Posh Crack *F Jordan* 58b
6 b m Rakaposhi King—First Crack (Scallywag)
271^2 261^P

Posh Stick *J B Walton* 100h 109c
9 b m Rakaposhi King—Carat Stick (Gold Rod)
2264^3 **2498^2 2993^3 3385^P** 4108^6 **4520^2 4721^4 4842^P**

Positano (IRE) *M Scudamore* 73h
6 b h Polish Precedent(USA) —Shamaya (IRE) (Doyoun)
3947^6 4327^7 4388^3 4871^8

Possextown (IRE) *N G Richards* 75+h 128+c
8 b g Lord Americo—Tasse Du The (Over The River (FR))
550^2 858^2 (1309) (1511) 1568^2

Possible Gale (IRE) *John G Carr* 90h
8 b g Posen(USA) —Native Gale (IRE) (Be My Native (USA))
592^7 871^4 (1375) (1588) 1806^5

Post It *R J Hodges* 95h
5 b m Thowra(FR) —Cream By Post (Torus)
2727^12 2997^9 3322^7 3463^7 3800^4 4834^3 5111^6

Potoffairies (IRE) *Mrs S A Bramall*
11 ch g Montelimar(USA) —Ladycastle (Pitpan)
2863^P 3923^P

Potts Of Magic *R Lee* 90h
7 b g Classic Cliche(IRE) —Potter's Gale (IRE) (Strong Gale)
21^4 261^3 611^5 745^4 1152^8 1410^4 (1539) 1910^2 2505^2 3140^P

Pottsy's Joy *Mrs S J Smith* 92+h 55c
9 b g Syrtos—Orange Spice (Orange Bay)
106^F 211^9 1888^P 2413^4 2840^9 **3170^U 3336^P**

Pougatcheva (FR) *Miss Venetia Williams* 103h 98+c
7 ch m Epervier Bleu—Notabilite (FR) (No Pass No Sale)
441^P

Powder Creek (IRE) *K G Reveley* 106h 105 c
9 b g Little Bighorn—Our Dorcet (Condorcet (FR))
427^P 1929^P **2102^P 2443^4 2498^7** 3622^10 **3784^6 3922^P** 4852^P

Power And Demand *C W Thornton* 67h
9 b g Formidable(USA) —Mazurkanova (Song)
214^6 592^6 3169^4 3557^5 4475^4

Powerberry (IRE) *T K Geraghty* 109b
5 b g Shernazar—Bilberry (Nicholas Bill)
5060a^2

Power Elite (IRE) *Noel Meade* 140h
6 b g Linamix(FR) —Hawas (Mujtahid (USA))
2209^15 4473^13

Powerful Pearl (IRE) *P J Rothwell* 36b
5 br m Taipan(IRE) —Mystical Isle (IRE) (Black Minstrel)
4060a^P

Power Glory *M J Gingell* 79h
4 b g Namaqualand(USA) —Belamcanda (Belmez (USA))
3203^P 3349^4 3817^F 4795^6 4898^9

Powerlove (FR) *Mrs S C Bradburne* 102+h
5 b m Solon(GER) —Bywaldor (FR) (Magwal (FR))
2062^6 2412^4 2901^3 3269^6 3484^2(4584) 5064^5

Powerstation (IRE) *C Byrnes* 141h
6 b g Anshan—Mariaetta (IRE) (Mandalus)
2206^2 (2536a) 2909a^4 4469^2 4760^4 5132a^P

Power Strike (USA) *Mrs L B Normile* 61h
5 b g Coronado's Quest(USA) —Galega (Sure Blade (USA))
870^13 1432^13 3488^10 12^6

Power Unit *Mrs D A Hamer* 115 h 115 c
11 ch g Risk Me(FR) —Hazel Bee (Starch Reduced)
452^4 615^P 1088^2 1218^5 **1399^4 (1673) 1746^4**

Powra *R J Hodges* 66b
6 b g Thowra(FR) —Lake Mariner (Julio Mariner)
3130^9 **3457^F 3879^U 4102^P 4424^R**

Pragmatica *R M H Cowell*
5 b m Inchinor—Isabella Gonzaga (Rock Hopper)
3690^P

Prairie Law (GER) *B N Pollock* 103 h
6 b g Law Society(USA) —Prairie Charm (IRE) (Thatching)
1908^7 2249^9 2584^13 2858^2 3395^7 **3546^U** (3731) 3943^P 4320^R 4794^P

Prairie Minstrel (USA) *R Dickin* 91c
12 b g Regal Intention(CAN) —Prairie Sky (CAN) (Gone West (USA))
1855^6 2522^7 2926^6 3887^6

Prairie Moonlight (GER) *C J Mann* 132 h
6 b m Monsun(GER) —Prairie Princess (GER) (Dashing Blade)
2533^2 2765^4 (3650) 5077a^10

Prairie Sun (GER) *Mrs A Duffield* 123+h
5 b m Law Society(USA) —Prairie Flame (IRE) (Marju (IRE))
1552^3 (1668) 1823^10

Praise The Prince (NZ) *Sanna Hendriks* 101h
11 br g Prince Of Praise(NZ) —Dynataine (NZ) (Centaine (AUS))
1394a^7

Prato (GER) *C Von Der Recke* 105+h 103+c
6 ch h Kornado—Prairie Lila (GER) (Homing)
2574^F 3352^3 4150^{5}4870^F

Prayerful *J G M O'Shea* 84 c
7 b m Syrtos—Pure Formality (Forzando)
1658^9 1751^3 1906^2 2341^2 2845^{9}3140^P **3888^F**

Preacher Boy *R J Hodges* 133 c
7 b g Classic Cliche(IRE) —Gospel (IRE) (Le Bavard (FR))
(2593) (2996) 3740^{2}4456^F 4729^3

Precious Bane (IRE) *M Sheppard* 114 c
8 b g Bigstone(IRE) —Heavenward (USA) (Conquistador Cielo (USA))
(2126) (2266) 2623^{2}2874^3 (3481) 3845^{2}4498^3 4690^7

Precious Lucy (FR) *G F Bridgwater* 96h
7 gr m Kadrou(FR) —Teardrops Fall (FR) (Law Society (USA))
5019^P

Precious Mystery (IRE) *A King* 106+h
6 ch m Titus Livius(FR) —Ascoli (Skyliner)
3247^4 3648^2 4034^3

Precious Pride *M J Gingell*
4 b f Master Willie—Awesome Lady (Forzando)
2105^{13} 2642^{12}

Precious Sammi *Lucinda Featherstone*
4 b g Mark Of Esteem(IRE) —Night Over Day (Most Welcome)
3939^P

Predator (GER) *Jonjo O'Neill* 122+h
5 b g Protektor(GER) —Polish Affair (IRE) (Polish Patriot (USA))
764^2 (2749) 2991^6 3650^2 4215^4 4832^F

Predestine (FR) *K C Bailey* 103 h 93c
6 ch g Signe Divin(USA) —Smyrna (FR) (Lightning (FR))
2630^4 3239^F 3434^{P}4165^U 4727^P

Predicament *Jonjo O'Neill* 108 h 110+c
7 br g Machiavellian(USA) —Quandary (USA) (Blushing Groom (FR))
1823^F 2525^4 3510^4 3741^4 3966^{7}4242^9 **4590^3 5044^{2}2^{LFT}**

Premier Cheval (USA) *P R Hedger* 37h
7 ch g Irish River(FR) —Restikarada (FR) (Akarad (FR))
2930^U 3283^8 3658^{14}

Premier Dane (IRE) *N G Richards* 140+h
4 b g Indian Danehill(IRE) —Crystal Blue (IRE) (Bluebird (USA))
3267^2 (3759) 3925^5 4747^2

Premier Drive (IRE) *G M Moore* 99h 95c
13 ch g Black Minstrel—Ballyanihan (Le Moss)
215^{13} 429^8

Premier Hope (IRE) *Miss E C Lavelle* 71b
5 b m Second Empire(IRE) —Our Hope (Dancing Brave (USA))
3820^8 4398^4

Premium First (IRE) *Mrs H Dalton* 94h 99c
7 ch g Naheez(USA) —Regular Rose (IRE) (Regular Guy)
1719^2

Pre Ordained (IRE) *Mark Anthony Stafford*
14 br g Iron Duke(FR) —Miyana (FR) (Sanctus II)
87a^P

Presence Of Mind (IRE) *Miss E C Lavelle* 97h 121+c
8 ch g Presenting—Blue Rose (IRE) (Good Thyne (USA))
(297) 439^3 746^{U}1022^2

Presentandcorrect (IRE) *P J Hobbs* 116b
5 ch g Presenting—Friston (IRE) (Roselier (FR))
2534^2 3327^3 4595^2

Present Bleu (FR) *M C Pipe* 138h 106c
11 b g Epervier Bleu—Lointaine (USA) (Lyphard's Wish (FR))
3022^P 3469^9

Present Company (IRE) *Edward U Hales* 82b 88c
8 ch m Presenting—Calmount (IRE) (Callernish)
1622a^P

Presenter (IRE) *M Sheppard* 88h
6 ch g Cadeaux Genereux—Moviegoer (Pharly (FR))
2460^U 2618^3 3152^9 3333^6 3616^{F}3848^8 4282^3 4830^7

Presentforyou (IRE) *R Ford* 83b
7 b g Presenting—Killonerry (Croghan Hill)
1543^9

Present Glory (IRE) *C Tinkler* 112 h
7 br g Presenting—Prudent Rose (IRE) (Strong Gale)
8^2 (2147) 3458^4 3814^U

Presenting Alf (IRE) *Mrs S J Smith* 83+h
6 b g Presenting—Hilary's Penny (Avocat)
1118 3347

Presenting Express (IRE) *Miss E C Lavelle* 107 h 130+c
7 b g Presenting—Glenbane Express (IRE) (Roselier (FR))
2015^2 **(2555) (3129) (3434) (4240) 4617^U 5144^P**

Presenting Gayle (IRE) *F Flood* 43h
5 bb m Presenting—Black Gayle (IRE) (Strong Gale)
2796a^7

Presentingthecase (IRE) *Miss S Mitchell* 48h 90c
8 b g Presenting—Let The Hare Run (IRE) (Tale Quale)
673^5 827^7 4946^3

Present Moment (IRE) *Mrs Ruth Hayter* 73b
8 b g Presenting—Springphar (IRE) (Phardante (FR))
4901^P

Pressgang *P R Webber* 125+b
4 b g Unfuwain(USA) —Petralona (USA) (Alleged (USA))
(3346) 4448^2

Prestbury Knight *N A Twiston-Davies* 103+h
6 ch g Sir Harry Lewis(USA) —Lambrini (IRE) (Buckskin (FR))
(3131) 4282^5 4549^{10} 5108^7

Preston Hall *M J McGrath* 71+h
5 b g Accordion—Little Preston (IRE) (Pennine Walk)
21^P 100^8

Presumptuous *Mrs S J Smith* 121+h
6 ch g Double Trigger(IRE) —T O O Mamma'S (IRE) (Classic Secret (USA))
2766^F 2925^5 (4058) (4990)

Pretty Lady Rose *T Wall* 67b
6 b m Perpendicular—Pandessa (Blue Cashmere)
844^7 1036^7

Pretty Star (GER) *A King* 128 h
6 b g Lando(GER) —Pretty Ballerina (Sadler's Wells (USA))
2207^{20} (2999) 3622^8 4461^{18}

Pride Of Finewood (IRE) *E W Tuer* 95h
8 ch g Old Vic—Macamore Rose (Torus)
2638^P 2923^{12} 3257^4 3443^2 3914^{P}4491^2 4797^P

Prideoftheyankees (IRE) *W J Burke* 120h
5 b g Good Thyne(USA) —Lady Lock (IRE) (Executive Perk)
1898^2 4060a^2

Pridewood Dove *R J Price* 40 h
7 b m Alderbrook—Flighty Dove (Cruise Missile)
574^P 651^8 758^{10} 2460^7 2721^{15}

Prime Contender *O Sherwood* 113 h
4 b g Efisio—Gecko Rouge (Rousillon (USA))
2286^U (2661) 3132^8 3294^4 3714^9

Prime Course (IRE) *Mrs A Farrant* 86c
17 b g Crash Course—Prime Mistress (Skymaster)
403^4

Prime Powered (IRE) *G L Moore* 84h
5 b g Barathea(IRE) —Caribbean Quest (Rainbow Quest (USA))
1772^9

Primeshade Promise *D Burchell* 39h
5 ch m Opening Verse(USA) —Bonnie Lassie (Efisio)
3324^{10} 3730^P

Primitive Academy *Mrs H Dalton* 86b
4 b c Primitive Rising(USA) —Royal Fontaine (IRE) (Royal Academy (USA))
4680^{10} 5075^4

Primitive Cove *G A Swinbank* 48b
5 b g Primitive Rising(USA) —Katie-A (IRE) (Cyrano De Bergerac)
3399^9

Primitive Jean *C R Wilson* 38h
7 b m Primitive Rising(USA) —Gemma Jean (Derek H)
14^P 124^P 1108^6 1310^9 **1568^P**

Primitive Poppy *Mrs A Hamilton* 89h
7 b m Primitive Rising(USA) —Lady Manello (Mandrake Major)
1246 2124 (545) 2440^5 2653^8 3339^{2}4043^7 4317^5 4988^6

Primitive Rebel *H P Hogarth* 84b
7 gr g Primitive Rising(USA) —Distant Cherry (General Ironside)
2169^P

Primitive Rites *M J Brown* 98c
9 b g Primitive Rising(USA) —Sun Goddess (FR) (Deep Roots)
4146^U 4397^P

Primitive Way *Miss S E Forster* 101c
14 b g Primitive Rising(USA) —Potterway (Velvet Prince)
411^4 1603^2 (1837) 5036^7 5122^2

Primrose Park *K Bishop* 60h 95+c
7 b m Thowra(FR) —Redgrave Rose (Tug Of War)
3692^7 4425^{11}

Prince Adjal (IRE) *Miss S E Forster* 100+h
6 b g Desert Prince(IRE) —Adjalisa (IRE) (Darshaan)
1494 306^6 716^3 822^3 **1176^F(1212)** 1297^{13} **1682^4 2042^{3}2677^4 3348^F** 3757^{12}4045^2 (4341) 4982^2

Prince Among Men *N G Richards* 120h
9 b g Robellino(USA) —Forelino (USA) (Trempolino (USA))
766^7 873^7 1010^{15} 1312^P

Prince Bere (FR) *J Bertran De Balanda*
3 b c Epistolaire(IRE) —Known Alibi (USA) (Known Fact (USA))
4298a^P

Prince Dolois (FR) *A Bonin*
8 gr g Highest Honor(FR) —Clear Hero (USA) (Hero's Honor (USA))
585a^8 779a^7

Prince Dundee (FR) *M Keighley*
11 ch g Ecossais(FR) —Princesse Normande (FR) (Belgio (FR))
51^P

Prince Highlight (IRE) *Mrs Jeremy Young* 111 c
11 b g Lord Americo—Madamme Highlights (Andretti)
76^3 366^2

Prince Ickarus (IRE) *Mrs S J Smith* 91b
6 ch g Double Trigger(IRE) —Stripe (Bustino)
2340^8 2823^{10}

Princelet (IRE) *N J Henderson* 101+h
4 b g Desert Prince(IRE) —Soeur Ti (FR) (Kaldoun (FR))
(3463) 3939^F

Prince Minata (IRE) *M Appleby* 85h
11 b g Machiavellian(USA) —Aminata (Glenstal (USA))
279^9 513^5 670^6 1046^{13} 1156^{10}1297^{11} 1362^9 1483^6 1653^7

Prince Of Aragon *Miss Suzy Smith* 82h 77c
10 b g Aragon—Queens Welcome (Northfields (USA))
1354 357^7 686^{14} **4908^{8}5140^6**

Prince Of Persia *R S Brookhouse* 114 h 107c
6 b g Turtle Island(IRE) —Sianiski (Niniski (USA))
3876 4888 2347^4 3675^4 3993^P**4878^P**

Prince Of Pleasure (IRE) *D Broad* 107h 126c
12 b g Spanish Place(USA) —Oronocco Gift (Camden Town)
69a^{12} 1083a^9 1435^{3}2210^{10} 5080a^6

Prince Of Slane *G A Swinbank* 85+h 128 c
7 b g Prince Daniel(USA) —Singing Slane (Cree Song)
(150) 421^3 2653^7 **2841^U(3350) (3560)**

Prince Of Tara (IRE) *S J Mahon* 147h 129 c
9 b g Prince Of Birds(USA) —Fete Champetre (Welsh Pageant)
2227a^3 **(2539a) 3053a^P 3895a^{6}4123a^P**

Prince On The Ter *B Scriven* 93h 61c
11 b g Terimon—Princess Constanza (Relkino)
1123^3 **1678^7 1858^{P}1981^P**

Prince Roscoe *D E Fitzgerald* 114h 108+c
10 b g Roscoe Blake—Standard Breakfast (Busted)
2248^U

Princess Aimee *P Bowen* 78+h
6 b m Wizard King—Off The Air (IRE) (Taufan (USA))
25^6 245^P

Princess Commanche (IRE) *S J Mahon* 106h
7 b m Commanche Run—Wernlas (Prince Tenderfoot (USA))
3110a^5

Princesse Grec (FR) *M Scudamore* 101 h 106c
8 ch m Grand Tresor(FR) —Perimele (FR) (Mon Fils)
1906^4 **2267^3 2686^{P}2996^P 3654^P** 3950^{9}4641^6

Princess Morgane (USA) *P Alexanian*
6 b m Judge T C(USA) —Justine Au Jardin (USA) (Black Tie Affair)
846a^3

Princess Pea *M C Pipe* 73h
6 b m Shareef Dancer(USA) —Super Sol (Rolfe (USA))
569^{10} 651^4 758^2 973^P (Dead)

Princess Stephanie *M J Gingell* 67h
8 b m Shaab—Waterloo Princess (IRE) (Le Moss)
1347 363^8 670^8

Princess Yum Yum *J L Spearing* 92b
6 b m Carlingford Castle—Miss Sick Note (Respect)
316^2 685^7 2727^{11} 3466^P 3800^P

Prince Valentine *D B Feek* 78h
5 b g My Best Valentine—Affaire De Coeur (Imperial Fling (USA))
102^6 180^5 863^8

Principe Azzurro (FR) *H D Daly* 111+h
5 b g Pistolet Bleu(IRE) —Massalia (GER) (Leone (GER))
2665^5 3248^2 3611^2 (4094) 4373^{10}

Prins Willem (IRE) *J R Fanshawe* 136h
7 b g Alzao(USA) —American Gardens (USA) (Alleged (USA))
2758^3 3177^6 4446^{19}

Prioritisation (IRE) *Mrs K Waldron* 86+c
7 b g Shernazar—No One Knows (IRE) (Kemal (FR))
322^3 570^7 893^{P}998^P

Priors Dale *Miss E C Lavelle* 130 h 130c
6 br g Lahib(USA) —Mathaayl (USA) (Shadeed (USA))
(2324) 2871^9 **3183^F 4377^{3}4664^5**

Priscilla *K Bishop* 98+h 103c
8 b m Teenoso(USA) —Dubacilla (Dubassoff (USA))
2297^6 2610^P 2846^{3}3465^U 3815^2 3940^{2}4620^P 4755^3

Pristeen Spy *R Ford* 72h 78+c
9 b g Teenoso(USA) —Sikera Spy (Harvest Spirit)
348^4 767^P 1044^{2}1178^P 1376^U 1414^{3}1656^5 1897^2 2936^{10}

Private Be *P J Hobbs* 123h
7 b g Gunner B—Foxgrove (Kinglet)
1672^2 1968^2 2826^2 (3130) 3615^2

Private Ben (IRE) *Mrs John Harrington* 106h 109c
8 b g Ridgewood Ben—Timeless (Royal Academy (USA))
45a^{15}

Private Benjamin *M R Hoad* 99 h
6 gr g Ridgewood Ben—Jilly Woo (Environment Friend)
1400^P 1481^7 1598^S 1804^6 2379^{5}2685^5 4523^6 4912^{10}

Private Jessica *R C Guest* 71+h
5 ch m Cadeaux Genereux—Rose Bay (Shareef Dancer (USA))
1349 3991^0 496^4 592^{13} 1209^{13}1308^8 1553^9

Prize Fighter (IRE) *Jonjo O'Neill* 113 h
4 b g Desert Sun—Papal (Selkirk (USA))
2481^4 (2954) 3340^8 3594^{DSQ} 3817^3 4416^4

Prizeman (USA) *J A Geake*
8 b g Prized(USA) —Shuttle (USA) (Conquistador Cielo (USA))
2826^P

Prize Ring *G M Moore* 107h 101+c
7 ch g Bering—Spot Prize (USA) (Seattle Dancer (USA))
61^{11} 197^9 **479^3 688^{3}782^4 1062^5 1176^F** (Dead)

Probus Lady *C J Down* 65h
9 ch m Good Times(ITY) —Decoyanne (Decoy Boy)
3483^P 4133^P 4557^P

Procrastinate (IRE) *R F Fisher* 47h
4 ch g Rossini(USA) —May Hinton (Main Reef)
1332^7 1441^4

Pro Dancer (USA) *P Bowen* 113 h 122c
8 bb h Pleasant Tap(USA) —Shihama (USA) (Shadeed (USA))
2939^8 3880^7 4593^2 **4906^7**

Profowens (IRE) *P Beaumont* 99 h 109+c
8 b g Welsh Term—Cutty Sark (Strong Gale)
2109^4 2630^P 3928^{P}4300^2 (4719) 4851^6

Programme Girl (IRE) *G A Swinbank* 96+b
4 ch f Definite Article—Targhyb (IRE) (Unfuwain (USA))
(2068)

Progressive (IRE) *Jonjo O'Neill* 110+h
8 ch g Be My Native(USA) —Move Forward (Deep Run)
1542^P 2264^7

Projectfiveonefive *Mrs S D Williams*
7 b g Tout Ensemble—Jillywag (Scallywag)
3948^9 4367^6

Prokofiev (USA) *Jonjo O'Neill* 125+h 128+c
10 br g Nureyev(USA) —Aviara (USA) (Cox's Ridge (USA))
1039^9 **1599^3 1778^P**

Prominent Profile (IRE) *N A Twiston-Davies* 128 c
13 ch g Mazaad—Nakuru (IRE) (Mandalus)
55^7

Promise To Be Good *N J Henderson* 99b
5 b g Unfuwain(USA) —Kshessinskaya (Hadeer)
1799^3 (Dead)

Promotion *N J Henderson*
6 b g Sadler's Wells(USA) —Tempting Prospect (Shirley Heights)
4327^P

Proper Article (IRE) *D K Weld* 114h
4 b g Definite Article—Feather 'n Lace (IRE) (Green Desert (USA))
4435^5

Proper Poser (IRE) *M C Chapman* 61h 53c
10 b g Posen(USA) —Dahar's Love (USA) (Dahar (USA))
2^P 183^P 508^{P}670^{12} 822^{12} **990^U 1015^{8}1176^8 1275^F**

Proper Squire (USA) *C J Mann* 115 h 130 c
9 b g Bien Bien(USA) —La Cumbre (Sadler's Wells (USA))
3458^{10}

Proprioception (IRE) *A King* 89 h
4 ch f Danehill Dancer(IRE) —Pepper And Salt (IRE) (Double Schwartz)
2101^3 2286^5 3275^6 (3655) 4282^2 4609^6

Protagonist *B N Pollock* 98h 97c
8 bb g In The Wings—Fatah Flare (USA) (Alydar (USA))
2296^5 2556^4 3146^7 **3652^{3}3919^5 4451^6**

Protecting Heights (IRE) *M E Sowersby* 24h
5 br g Hector Protector(USA) —Height Of Fantasy (IRE) (Shirley Heights)
992^4 1108^9

Protection Money *L P Grassick* 82h
6 ch g Hector Protector(USA) —Three Piece (Jaazeiro (USA))
359^P 630^P

Protective *J G Given* 99h
5 ch g Hector Protector(USA) —You Make Me Real (USA) (Give Me Strength (USA))
2627^5 2968^9 3496^P

Protocol (IRE) *Mrs S Lamyman* 89 h
12 b g Taufan(USA) —Ukraine's Affair (USA) (The Minstrel (CAN))
695^5 1208^2 1344^7 1756^{11} 1814^{7}2962^7 3330^8 4475^3 4632^4 4794^8

Proud To Be Irish (IRE) *Seamus O'Farrell* 116h
7 b g Brief Truce(USA) —Just Little (Mtoto)
117a^6 2334^7

Proverbial Gray *D R Gandolfo* 73 h
9 ro m Norton Challenger—Clove Bud (Beau Charmeur (FR))
167^P 389^P

Provocative (FR) *M Todhunter* 129+h 142+c
8 bb g Useful(FR) —All Blue (FR) (Noir Et Or)
(1913) 2757^P 4984^{F}5094^P

Prudencio (FR) *L Bellet*
8 b g Amthaal(USA) —Miss Anais (FR) (Hellios (USA))
(1373a)

Pseudonym (IRE) *M F Harris* 126?h
4 ch g Daylami(IRE) —Stage Struck (IRE) (Sadler's Wells (USA))
1339^3 1404^5 1551^8 3650^{10} 3967^{2}4075^3 4354^3 (4616) 4747^6 4830^3 4962^4

Psychomodo *B G Powell* 93b
4 b g Mark Of Esteem(IRE) —En Vacances (IRE) (Old Vic)
4825^2

Publican (IRE) *P A Fahy* 145+h 125 c
6 b g Overbury(IRE) —Night Therapy (IRE) (Mandalus)
40a^6 114a^5 4473^{26} 5125^6

Public Eye *L A Dace* 75h
5 b g Zafonic(USA) —Stardom (Known Fact (USA))
3659^{14} 3906^P 4819^{13} 5069^{10}

Public Reaction *Edward U Hales* 114h 130c
8 b g Husyan(USA) —Corrie's Girl (Whistling Deer)
3261a^3 4889a^5 5058a^4

Pucks Court *I A Brown* 70h
9 b g Nomadic Way(USA) —Miss Puck (Tepukei)
9^{14} 214^P 2567^5 2843^6 4299^P

Puff At Midnight *D P Keane* 75h
6 b m Midnight Legend—Sulapuff (Sula Bula)
2015^P (Dead)

Pumpkin Pickle *P R Rodford* 51h
5 b m Wace(USA) —Gypsy Crystal (USA) (Flying Saucer)
463^7 866^4 1042^5 1154^6 1266^F

Puntal (FR) *M C Pipe* 146 h 149 c
10 b g Bering—Saveur (Ardross)
4777^6 5144^{10}

Pure Brief (IRE) *J Mackie* 77h 95c
9 b g Brief Truce(USA) —Epure (Bellypha)
238^4 412^7 681^3 973^5 **(1098) (1176) 1852^3 2141^{5}2570^3 2754^2 2926^{4}4991^4**

Pure Magic (FR) *Miss J S Davis* 92 h
5 b g Lake Coniston(IRE) —La Le Lu (FR) (Exit To Nowhere (USA))
2618^P 2826^{12} 3240^6 3477^P (3997) 4557^6(4830) 5028^6

Pure Palatial *D T Hughes* 100h
5 ch g Bijou D'Inde—Filigree (FR) (Great Nephew)
44a^{13}

Pure Pleasure (NZ) *N M Babbage* 80h
7 gr g Casual Lies(USA) —Pure Glory (NZ) (First Norman (USA))
356^F 1298^5

Pure Steel (IRE) *Miss L Day* 73c
12 b g Miner's Lamp—Mary Deen (Avocat)
948^P 1109^P 1262^P

Pure Theatre (IRE) *Eoin Griffin* 99b
6 b g King's Theatre(IRE) —Direct Lady (IRE) (Fools Holme (USA))
4779^{19}

Purple Dancer (FR) *G A Swinbank*
4 b g Daylami(IRE) —Stage Manner (In The Wings)
2076^U

Purple Patch *C L Popham* 105h
8 b m Afzal—My Purple Prose (Rymer)
1850[5] 2012[2] (2501) 2937[2] 3210[7] 3439[P]4329[3] 4619[4]

Purple Shuffle (IRE) *P A Fahy* 110h
8 b g Accordion—Penny Shuffle (IRE) (Decent Fellow)
3086a[3]

Purr *M Wigham* 63h
5 b g Pursuit Of Love—Catawba (Mill Reef (USA))
2216[P] 2523[10] 2582[6] 3169[10] 3330[9]3956[2] 4368[6] 4896[9] 5050[9]

Purslow *T Wall* 32b
6 b m Petoski—Return To Romance (Trojan Fen)
7[13]

Push The Port (IRE) *N J Gifford* 81b
4 bb g Dushyantor(USA) —Port Queen (IRE) (Nashamaa)
4654[3]

Putup Or Shutup (IRE) *K C Bailey* 101 h
10 br g Religiously(USA) —Nights Crack (Callernish)
215[P] 2556[2] **2938[P]** 3458[12]4453[8]

Pyleigh Lady *S C Burrough* 89+h
5 b m Zaffaran(USA) —Lady Callernish (Callernish)
3468[7] 3884[8] 4286[10] 4425[3] 4676[6]

Qabas (USA) *P Bowen* 112h
6 b g Swain(IRE) —Classical Dance (CAN) (Regal Classic (CAN))
(571) 726[P] 824[9] 1016[2] **1540[4]**

Qassas *Michael David Murphy* 88h
4 b c Nashwan(USA) —Hasanat (Night Shift (USA))
5076a[12]

Quadco (IRE) *P A Fahy* 126h 126c
12 b g Be My Native(USA) —Anega (Run The Gantlet (USA))
1083a[U] 1420a[8] (Dead)

Quainton Hills *D R Stoddart* 83h 104+c
12 b g Gildoran—Spin Again (Royalty)
509[P] 1910[3] 2440[P]

Qualitair Pleasure *J Hetherton* 99h
6 b m Slip Anchor—Qualitair Ridge (Indian Ridge)
415[6] 601[3] (826) 905[2] 1280[6] 1443[P]1571[4] 1663[2] 1753[2] 2347[10] (2517)

Quality First (IRE) *A N Dalton* 111h 124c
13 b g Un Desperado(FR) —Vipsania (General Ironside)
348[P]

Quango *Miss J E Foster* 69c
14 b g Charmer—Quaranta (Hotfoot)
512[P]

Quarrelsome Queen (IRE) *S Donohoe* 72h
4 ch f Entrepreneur—Alcadia (IRE) (Thatching)
3485[6]

Quarry Boy (IRE) *E Sheehy* 105h 116c
10 ch g Beau Sher—Kundalu (Never Return (USA))
71a[4]

Quarry Island (IRE) *M Todhunter* 76h
5 b m Turtle Island(IRE) —Last Quarry (Handsome Sailor)
59[7] 602[6] 2843[11] 3269[7] 3442[8]3782[P]

Quarrymount *J A B Old* 94 h 93c
5 b g Polar Falcon(USA) —Quilt (Terimon)
1916[4] 2372[7] 4243[6] **4908[4]**

Quartier Latin (USA) *C Von Der Recke* 99h
5 bb h Woodman(USA) —Qui Bid (USA) (Spectacular Bid (USA))
2573[2] 3347[3] 4148[5]

Quasimodo (IRE) *A W Carroll* 111 h
4 b g Night Shift(USA) —Daziyra (IRE) (Doyoun)
2661[5] 3038[5] (3294) 3436[10] 3722[7] 4211[11]

Quatrain (IRE) *D R Gandolfo* 93h 80+c
6 ch g Anshan—Gray's Ellergy (Oats)
2934[5] **3126[3] 3652[F]3940[5]**

Quatre Heures (FR) *W P Mullins* 135+h
4 b g Vertical Speed(FR) —Macyrienne (FR) (Saint Cyrien (FR))
4430[11] (5099a)

Quay Walloper *J R Norton* 36h
5 b g In Command(IRE) —Myrrh (Salse (USA))
11[14] 414[8] 1887[P] 2025[P]

Quazar (IRE) *Jonjo O'Neill* 121c
8 b g Inzar(USA) —Evictress (IRE) (Sharp Victor (USA))
42a[2] 1924[6] 2760[11]3180[P] 3739[8] 4241[7]4957[7] 5102a[7]

Queen Astrid (IRE) *D K Weld* 131+h 96c
6 b m Revoque(IRE) —Talina's Law (IRE) (Law Society (USA))
66a[5]

Queen Excalibur *C Roberts* 85+h
7 ch m Sabrehill(USA) —Blue Room (Gorytus (USA))
77[F] 457[5] 683[6] 982[5] (1046) 1223[F]1297[5] 1490[5] 1541[13] **1829[P]**

Queenies Girl *Paul Frank* 75c
10 b m Primitive Rising(USA) —Riverboat Queen (Rapid River)
4044[3] 4305[5] 5040[4]

Queen Nefitari *M W Easterby* 49h
4 b f Celtic Swing—Opalette (Sharrood (USA))
2001[12] 2076[8] 2442[9] 2587[8] (Dead)

Queens Brigade *Miss V A Stephens* 87h
14 b g K-Battery—Queen Of Dara (Dara Monarch)
102[5] 298[P]

Queen's Dancer *N J Henderson* 92h
4 b f Groom Dancer(USA) —Special Beat (Bustino)
(3690) 3979[4] 4616[12]

Queen Soraya *Miss H C Knight* 114+h 97+c
8 b m Persian Bold—Fairlead (Slip Anchor)
127[11] 372[5] **1411[4]**

Queenstown (IRE) *B A Pearce*
5 b g Desert Style(IRE) —Fanciful (IRE) (Mujtahid (USA))
1772[P] 1952[P]

Quel Fontenailles (FR) *L A Dace* 87h
8 b g Tel Quel(FR) —Sissi Fontenailles (FR) (Pampabird)
295[6] 630[10] 913[P]

Querido (USA) *E J O'Grady* 88h
4 b c Spectrum(IRE) —Polent (Polish Precedent (USA))
5076a[13]

Quest On Air *J R Jenkins* 71h
7 b g Star Quest—Stormy Heights (Golden Heights)
3591[9] 4388[4] 4905[11]

Quibble *A Bailey* 86h 88c
9 ch g Lammtarra(USA) —Bloudan (USA) (Damascus (USA))
95[2]

Quick *M C Pipe* 142 h 100c
6 b g Kahyasi—Prompt (Old Vic)
207[10] **759[P]** 3970[14] 4461[20]4974[6]

Quickswood (IRE) *G C Maundrell* 105h
13 b g Yashgan—Up To Trix (Over The River (FR))
4560[P]

Quid Pro Quo (FR) *P F Nicholls* 112+h 116+c
7 b g Cadoudal(FR) —Luzenia (FR) (Armos)
1917[P] 2729[2] 4214[5]

Quiet Millfit (USA) *R Ingram* 97h 100c
10 b g Quiet American(USA) —Millfit (USA) (Blushing Groom (FR))
234[F] 1524[10]

Quinmaster (USA) *M Halford* 100+h
4 gr c Linamix(FR) —Sherkiya (IRE) (Goldneyev (USA))
3004a[7]

Quintus (USA) *A King* 113h 102c
11 ch g Sky Classic(CAN) —Superbe Dawn (USA) (Grey Dawn II)
1641[3] 1900[8] 2296[4] 2687[P]

Quiteb'Chance (IRE) *Miss J S Davis*
5 ch m Aahsaylad—De-Veers Currie (IRE) (Glenstal (USA))
2565[12] 4046[P]

Quizzical *John G Carr* 87h 76c
8 ch g Indian Ridge—Mount Row (Alzao (USA))
875[P] (1379) 1800[3]

Quizzling (IRE) *B J M Ryall* 77h 89+c
8 b g Jurado(USA) —Monksville (Monksfield)
684[4] 812[3] 1015[P]2594[P] 2818[3] 3239[P](3716) (4047) 4571[P]

Quotable *O Sherwood* 94+h
5 b m Master Willie—General Comment (IRE) (Torus)
2558[4] 3322[6] 3690[8] 4074[8] (4903)

Rabbit *Mrs A L M King* 75h
5 b m Muhtarram(USA) —Ninia (USA) (Affirmed (USA))
574[6] 2721[12] 3355[8] 4828[6] 1[6]

Rab Cee *W G Young* 50b
6 bb g Tragic Role(USA) —Hilltop Lady (Puissance)
2480[11] 2906[10] 3237[11] 4141[U]

Racing Demon (IRE) *Miss H C Knight* 147 h 162 c
6 b g Old Vic—All Set (IRE) (Electric)
(1971) (2634) (3879) 4431[7]

Rackard *P Hughes* 102h 94c
7 b g Distant Relative—City Times (IRE) (Last Tycoon)
92a[4]

Radcliffe (IRE) *Miss Venetia Williams* 96h 107c
9 b g Supreme Leader—Marys Course (Crash Course)
1670[4] 1778[4]

Radigan Lane *J R Payne* 72b
6 b m Wimbleball—Spirit Level (Sunley Builds)
27[8]

Radnor Lad *Mrs S M Johnson* 78h
6 ch g Double Trigger(IRE) —Gabibti (IRE) (Dara Monarch)
2073[8] 3250[5]

Raffaello (FR) *P F Nicholls* 121+h
5 b g Roi De Rome(USA) —Lady Noa (FR) (No Pass No Sale)
(3505) 4077[2]

Raffish *M Scudamore* 71h
4 ch g Atraf—Valadon (High Line)
2921[10] 4551[P]

Ragasah *Ernst Oertel* 71h
8 b m Glory Of Dancer—Slight Risk (Risk Me (FR))
971[F]

Raging Torrent *Mrs H J Cobb* 91c
11 b g Meadowbrook—Charons Daughter (Another River)
281[5]

Rag Week (IRE) *Evan Williams* 85h 98+c
9 b g Roselier(FR) —Lady Rag (Ragapan)
1378[4] 1639[6]

Raheel (IRE) *Evan Williams* 75+h
6 ch g Barathea(IRE) —Tajawuz (Kris)
232[6] 943[4] 2146[U] 2463[P]

Raider Of The East (IRE) *K A Morgan* 79b
4 b g Darshaan—Convenience (IRE) (Ela-Mana-Mou)
2642[3]

Raikkonen (IRE) *W P Mullins* 121h 83c
6 b g Lake Coniston(IRE) —Jour Ferie (IRE) (Taufan (USA))
43a[2] 585a[P]

Rainbow Lord (IRE) *C C Bealby* 81b
6 b g Lord Of Appeal—Rainbow Alliance (IRE) (Golden Love)
5124[6]

Rainbow River (IRE) *M C Chapman* 110 h
8 ch g Rainbows For Life(CAN) —Shrewd Girl (USA) (Sagace (FR))
1971[3] 370[P]

Rainbows Aglitter *D R Gandolfo* 119 h 120 c
9 ch g Rainbows For Life(CAN) —Chalet Waldegg (Monsanto (FR))
1617[5] **2931[6] 3459[9]**4573[2] 5142[14]

Rainbow Tree *C C Bealby* 97 h 45c
6 b g Rainbows For Life(CAN) —Little Twig (IRE) (Good Thyne (USA))
1490[4] 1607[2] **2259[F]** 4452[4]4634[3] 4898[6]

Rainbow Venture *J D Frost*
5 b g Tamure(IRE) —Studio Venture (Camden Town)
4947[P]

Rainha *A C Whillans* 55h 66c
9 b m Alflora(IRE) —Political Prospect (Politico (USA))
2447[P] 2674[P] 4141[11] **4841[5]**

Raintown (IRE) *Peter McCreery* 105h
4 ch c Raise A Grand(IRE) —Lorella (IRE) (Fayruz)
5076a[15]

Raise A McGregor *Mrs S J Smith* 74h 83c
10 br g Perpendicular—Gregory's Lady (Meldrum)
213[6] 416[3] 690[7]997[2] 1109[5] 1203[3]1343[6]

Raiseapearl *Patrick Thompson* 87 c
11 bb g Pocketed(USA) —Little Anthem (True Song)
(350) 3736[U] 3913[5]4051[U] 4100[5] 4846[3]6[6]

Rajam *G A Harker* 118+h
8 b g Sadler's Wells(USA) —Rafif (USA) (Riverman (USA))
(870) (1014) (1312) 1548[12]

Rajati (USA) *K R Pearce* 24h
11 b g Chief's Crown(USA) —Charming Life (NZ) (Sir Tristram)
519[7] 749[F]

Rajayla (IRE) *T G McCourt* 102h
5 b m Dockside(USA) —Rajaiyma (IRE) (Kahyasi)
2031a[10] 2901[2]

Rajayoga *M H Tompkins* 124+h
5 ch g Kris—Optimistic (Reprimand)
21[3] (485) (811) 980[2] (1179)

Rakalackey *H D Daly* 123h 99c
8 br g Rakaposhi King—Celtic Slave (Celtic Cone)
2682[4] 3017[5] 3419[4]

Raki Rose *M Scudamore*
4 b g Rakaposhi King—Fortria Rosie Dawn (Derring Rose)
4326[10] 4786[8]

Ramblees Holly *R S Wood* 99h
8 ch g Alfie Dickins—Lucky Holly (General David)
13[5] 370[9] (552) 768[9] 1016[7] **1062[P]**1552[8] 1571[9] 1760[P] 2110[9] 2264[10]2417[8] 4922[5] 5137[5]

Rambling Allie *B I Case* 33b
5 b m Gildoran—Merrie Mariner (Little Wolf)
3435[11]

Rambling Minster *K G Reveley* 135 h 110+c
8 b g Minster Son—Howcleuch (Buckskin (FR))
1925[6] 2175[4] 2336[5] 2747[5] **(3170)**

Rambo Blue *G J Smith* 34h
6 b g Elmaamul(USA) —Copper Trader (Faustus (USA))
4564[9]

Ramirez (IRE) *Nick Kent* 100h 102c
8 ch g Royal Abjar(USA) —Flooding (USA) (Irish River (FR))
4167[2] (4607) 4799[2]

Ramsgill (USA) *N P Littmoden* 90h
4 b g Prized(USA) —Crazee Mental (Magic Ring (IRE))
1797[6] 3939[5]

Rand (NZ) *Noel Meade*
12 gr g Omnicorp(NZ) —Foreign Coin (NZ) (Amyntor (FR))
4123a[P] 5080a[P]

Randolph O'Brien (IRE) *N A Twiston-Davies* 90+h 115+c
6 b g Zaffaran(USA) —Gala's Pride (Gala Performance)
1615[U] 1914[F] 2960[3]3465[2] 3815[3] (4165)

Random Native (IRE) *N G Richards* 78 h
8 br g Be My Native(USA) —Random Wind (Random Shot)
2448[4] 2944[13] 3445[8]

Random Precision (IRE) *B G Powell* 85+h
7 ch g Presenting—Rendezvous (Lorenzaccio)
111[2]

Random Quest *B J Llewellyn* 101h
8 b g Rainbow Quest(USA) —Anne Bonny (Ajdal (USA))
1711[4] (1982) 2173[F] 3333[8] 3616[4] 4652[P]4856[2] 5045[6]

Randwick Roar (IRE) *P M J Doyle* 125h 122c
7 b g Lord Americo—Le Bavellen (Le Bavard (FR))
1515a[5] 3587a[7]

Raneen Nashwan *R J Baker* 94h
10 b g Nashwan(USA) —Raneen Alwatar (Sadler's Wells (USA))
1121[P] 1297[9] 1541[9] 1640[3] 1806[P]

Ranelagh Gray (IRE) *Miss Venetia Williams* 109+h 109+c
9 gr g Roselier(FR) —Bea Marie (IRE) (King's Ride)
2929[F] (4579) 5010[4]

Ransboro (IRE) *C F Swan* 119h 127c
7 br g Needle Gun(IRE) —Moylena (Bustomi)
91a[4] 1700a[P] 2539a[7]

Rapallo (IRE) *Carl Llewellyn* 91b
5 b g Luso—Sheeba Queen (Crozier)
2987[3] 3691[8] 4807[7]

Rapide Plaisir (IRE) *R Lee* 119h 119+c
8 b g Grand Plaisir(IRE) —Royal Well (Royal Vulcan)
71a[11] (2)

Rapid Lad *B R Johnson* 24b
5 b g Busy Flight—Liverton Lass (Rapid Pass)
4881[12]

Rapscallion (GER) *Mrs H Dalton* 100+h
7 b g Robellino(USA) —Rosy Outlook (USA) (Trempolino (USA))
3133[12] 4327[2]

Rare Coincidence *R F Fisher* 106h
5 ch g Atraf—Green Seed (IRE) (Lead On Time (USA))
1336[2] (1607) (2462) 2566[2] 2942[5] 4990[8] (5138)

Rarefied (IRE) *T D Easterby* 74+h
5 b g Danehill(USA) —Tenuous (Generous (IRE))
1340[5]

Raregem *M Biddick* 120+c
8 b g Syrtos—Ruby's Vision (Balinger)
50[F] 171[2] 440[F](3924) (4330) 4471[7]4975[F]

Rare Gold (IRE) *R H Alner* 109 h
6 br g Beneficial—Tara's Pride (IRE) (Montelimar (USA))
3425[2] 3881[2] (4562)

Rare Ouzel (IRE) *A J Martin* 108h 121+c
10 b g Be My Native(USA) —Ring Ouzel (Deep Run)
112a[10] 5129a[3]

Rare Society (IRE) *Mrs S J Smith* 93+h 110 c
8 b g Deep Society—Rare Glen (Glen Quaich)
1736[2] 2023[2] 2415[3]3037[F] 3170[F]

Rasharrow (IRE) *L Lungo* 134+h
7 ch g Rashar(USA) —Fleeting Arrow (IRE) (Commanche Run)
(1834) (2062) 3725[5] 4430[9] (5091)

Rashartic (IRE) *Mrs H Dalton* 82b
4 ch g Rashar(USA) —Gothic Ash (IRE) (Yashgan)
5124[3]

Rash Decision (IRE) *I W McInnes* 84c
11 b g Rashar(USA) —Lady Nethertown (Windjammer (USA))
354[P] 674[5]

Rashida *M Appleby* 67h
4 b f King's Best(USA) —Nimble Lady (AUS) (Fairy King (USA))
2274[7] 2569[10] 2954[8] 3730[P]

Rash Leader (IRE) *L Lungo* 50b
7 ch g Rashar(USA) —Leader Lady (IRE) (Supreme Leader)
2948[18]

Rash Moment (FR) *Mrs K Waldron* 113+h 106+c
7 b g Rudimentary(USA) —Ashura (FR) (No Pass No Sale)
912[10] 1047[3] **1155[P] 1232[5]**1485[P] **2504[3] 2583[6]2982[P] 4552[4] 4780[4]**

Rathbawn Prince (IRE) *Miss H C Knight* 120h 129 c
14 ch g All Haste(USA) —Ellis Town (Camden Town)
97[6]

Rathcannon Beauty *Mrs L P Baker*
4 b f Muhtarram(USA) —Bint Alhabib (Nashwan (USA))
2236[P] 2373[F] 2612[P] 5084[7]

Rathcannon Man (IRE) *A King* 85b
6 b g Anshan—Miss Fern (Cruise Missile)
3699[9]

Rathgar Beau (IRE) *E Sheehy* 133h 168 c
10 bb g Beau Sher—Salerina (Orchestra)
(41a) 2304a[2] 2786a[2]

Rathlin Island *Miss V Scott* 93h
8 b g Carroll House—Mermaid Bay (Jupiter Island)
895[9] 1566[DSQ] 1587[2]

Rathmore (IRE) *Eugene M O'Sullivan* 50h 29c
7 b g Right Win(IRE) —Flighty Miss (IRE) (Tornabuoni)
71a[F]

Rathowen (IRE) *J I A Charlton* 117h
7 b g Good Thyne(USA) —Owenageera (IRE) (Riot Helmet)
323[8] 1938 [3] 2186[9] 2678[2] (3316) 3969[3]4760[8]

Rattina (GER) *M F Harris* 24h 85c
10 b m Motley(USA) —Rottara (GER) (Flotow (GER))
57[4] 135[6] 388[4]674[6] 874[7] 999[6]1121[10] **1343[3]** 1486[P] **1560[3]**

Ratty's Band *Mrs L B Normile* 67h 84 c
12 ch g Gunner B—Arctic Ander (Leander)
874[P] 939[10] 1311[5]1433[P] 1592[8] 2479[P]

Raven Hall Lady (IRE) *M G Rimell* 74b
5 b m Saddlers' Hall(IRE) —Dunraven Lady (Rakaposhi King)
3421[3]

Ravenscar *C T Pogson* 93h 106c
8 b g Thethingaboutitis(USA) —Outcrop (Oats)
106[4] 1711[P]

Ravens Flight (IRE) *S A Brookshaw* 64b
5 br g I'm Supposin(IRE) —Cloncoose (IRE) (Remainder Man)
463[6]

Raven's Last *R T Phillips* 104+h
7 b g Sea Raven(IRE) —Lavenham's Last (Rymer)
2867[P]

Ravenstone Lad (IRE) *Mrs P Robeson* 56b
4 br g Presenting—Brown Gillette (Callernish)
4854[16]

Ravenswood (IRE) *M C Pipe* 120 h
9 b g Warning—Green Lucia (Green Dancer (USA))
2747[12]

Rawaabet (IRE) *P W Hiatt* 94 h
4 b g Bahhare(USA) —Haddeyah (USA) (Dayjur (USA))
1955[3] 3939[3] 4096[8]

Raybers Magic *J R Weymes*
5 b m Magic Ring(IRE) —Kirkadian (Norwick (USA))
369[P]

Ray Boy (IRE) *P C O'Connor* 125+h
7 bb g Oscar(IRE) —Cappagale (IRE) (Strong Gale)
40a[8] 117a[3] 2227a[6]

Ray Mond *M J Gingell* 46h
5 b g Midnight Legend—Kinsale Florale (IRE) (Supreme Leader)
1954[8] 2374[P] 2523[F] 2803[11] 2968[14]3417[7] 3956[4] 4475[6]

Rayshan (IRE) *N G Richards* 135 h
6 b g Darshaan—Rayseka (IRE) (Dancing Brave (USA))
67a[19] (3383) 3727[6]

Rays Venture (IRE) *D M Leigh* 103h
6 bb m Hubbly Bubbly(USA) —Paradise Little (Kambalda)
2031a[7]

Razzamatazz *R Dickin* 85h 104c
8 b g Alhijaz—Salvezza (IRE) (Superpower)
3146[P] **3686[2] 4162[P]**

Reach For The Top (IRE) *Miss H C Knight* 106+h
5 br g Topanoora—Burren Gale (IRE) (Strong Gale)
2211[10] 2617[5] 3248[4] 3717[4] 4970[4]

Reaching Out (IRE) *N J Henderson* 99 h
4 b g Desert Prince(IRE) —Alwiyda (USA) (Trempolino (USA))
(2101) 2345[5] 3132[7] 4838[6]

Reach The Clouds (IRE) *John R Upson* 95h 102c
14 b g Lord Americo—Dusky Stream (Paddy's Stream)
25[5] 232[4] **466[4] 536[7] 1299[9] 2842[4] 3958[3] 4571[5] 4914[R]**

Ready To Rumble (NZ) *Miss Suzy Smith* 91h 91c
9 ch g Danasinga(AUS) —Regal Odyssey (NZ) (Vice Regal (NZ))
406[6] **1673[6] 1855[P] 1942[3] 2026[3] 2141[P] 4614[P]**

Real Chief (IRE) *Miss M E Rowland* 80h
8 b g Caerleon(USA) —Greek Air (IRE) (Ela-Mana-Mou)
(4896)

Real Cracker (IRE) *Miss Venetia Williams* 94h
7 b g Lahib(USA) —Loreo (IRE) (Lord Chancellor (USA))
389[7] 575[P]

Real Definition *M G Rimell* 58h 71+c
7 gr g Highest Honor(FR) —Segovia (Groom Dancer (USA))
3984[6] **4426[6]**

Reap The Reward (IRE) *L Lungo* 110+h
6 ch g Presenting—Reapers Harvest (Carlingford Castle)
2006[10] 2450[4] 2821[10] 4362[P] (4986) 5064[4]

Reasonable Reserve (IRE) *B G Powell* 113+h 90c
9 ch g Fourstars Allstar(USA) —Alice O'Malley (The Parson)
109[P] 468[4] 814[P] (Dead)

Reasonably Sure (IRE) *David M Easterby* 105h 98c
6 b g Presenting—No Reason (Kemal (FR))
178[2] **3913[2] 4167[3]**

Rebel Army (IRE) *Mrs C J Robinson* 84c
7 ch g Mister Lord(USA) —Mandasari (Mandalus)
4305[4]

Rebel Chief (IRE) *T M Walsh* 97b
5 b g Oscar(IRE) —Limavady (IRE) (Executive Perk)
5060a[7]

Rebelle *P Bowen* 98h
7 bb g Reprimand—Blushing Belle (Local Suitor (USA))
635[2] 802[U] (875) 992[3]

Rebel Raider (IRE) *B N Pollock* 103h
7 b g Mujadil(USA) —Emily's Pride (Shirley Heights)
2261[2] 2750[3]

Rebel Rhythm *Mrs S J Smith* 135+h 138c
7 b g Robellino(USA) —Celt Song (IRE) (Unfuwain (USA))
1911[2] 2344[F] 2449[2](3041) 3391[3] 3740[4](4796)

Rebel Son *B J Llewellyn* 119h 89c
12 b g Minster Son—Rebrona (Rebel Prince)
2576[P]

Recent Edition (IRE) *J Wade* 105+c
8 b g Roselier(FR) —Hi Millie (Decent Fellow)
2978[P] 3336[4] 3444[P] 4042[3] (4316) (4845)

Recount (FR) *C J Mann* 100+h
6 b g Sillery(USA) —Dear Countess (FR) (Fabulous Dancer (USA))
5110[3]

Rectangle Blue *M D Hammond* 35b
4 b g Atraf—Golden Decoy (Decoy Boy)
2520[10]

Rectory (IRE) *Mrs S J Smith* 90h
7 b g Presenting—Billys Pet (Le Moss)
1885[6] 2169[4]

Red Alert Man (IRE) *Mrs L Williamson* 17h 70c
10 ch g Sharp Charter—Tukurua (Noalto)
2465[P] 2957[P] 3427[4] 4165[2] 4353[3] 4845[7]

Red Alf *Miss J Wormall* 12b
7 ch g Alflora(IRE) —Red Dust (Saxon Farm)
4052[P]

Red Autumn *K G Reveley* 68h
9 ch g Nomadic Way(USA) —Naturally Autumn (Hello Gorgeous (USA))
4267[7] 1000[P]

Red Bells *D J Wintle* 86b
5 b g Magic Ring(IRE) —Redgrave Devil (Tug Of War)
4654[4]

Red Bluff (IRE) *H Alexander* 35h
6 b g Waky Nao—Reine Rouge (GER) (Nebos (GER))
2108[12] 2763[12] 2923[17] 3335[F]

Red Brook Lad *C St V Fox* 119 c
11 ch g Nomadic Way(USA) —Silently Yours (USA) (Silent Screen (USA))
47[4] (272) (3693) (4051) (4594) 4831[U]

Red Canyon (IRE) *C L Tizzard* 98h 83+c
9 b g Zieten(USA) —Bayazida (Bustino)
665[6] 762[3] 949[7] (1017) 1075[3] 1192[6] **1271[3]** 1413[7] 1482[8] 1641[4] 1784[11]

Red Cedar (USA) *J Wade* 89h
6 ch g Woodman(USA) —Jewell Ridge (USA) (Melyno)
3534[P] 4922[12]

Red Chief (IRE) *Mrs A M Thorpe* 91+h
6 b g Lahib(USA) —Karayb (IRE) (Last Tycoon)
(856) 949[2] 1066[3] 1181[3]

Red Dahlia *M Pitman* 91h 32c
9 b m Alflora(IRE) —Redgrave Devil (Tug Of War)
(185) 399[3] 1250[2] (1482) 2150[3] 2556[P] 2731[6] 3128[7]

Red Dancer (FR) *C Olehla* 108c
10 b g Red Paradise—Majestic Dancer (FR) (What A Guest)
1710a[6]

Red Dawn (IRE) *Miss H C Knight* 51h
7 ch g Presenting—West Tour (Deep Run)
4094[8] 4649[6]

Redde (IRE) *Mrs J G Retter* 29h
11 ch g Classic Memory—Stoney Broke (Pauper)
2483[11] 2609[9] 3140[P] **3343[P]**

Red Devil Robert (IRE) *P F Nicholls* 113h 153+c
8 ch g Carroll House—Well Over (Over The River (FR))
2054[2] 2491[6]

Redditzio *C W Thornton* 82b
5 b m J B Quick—Ladys Regret (IRE) (Orchestra)
1554[4] 1688[4] 2112[9] 2752[15] 3337[P]

Red Echo (FR) *M C Pipe* 105+h
5 b g Subotica(FR) —Volniste (FR) (Olmeto)
3611[10] 4033[8] 4285[5] 4661[5] (5113)

Redemption *N A Twiston-Davies* 149 h 143c
11 b g Sanglamore(USA) —Ypha (USA) (Lyphard (USA))
1925[2] **2177[F] 2491[8] 2760[6] 3180[4] 3723[8] 4241[U] 4459[17]** 4745[7]

Redeswire Ruby *Mrs H O Graham* 25b
5 ch m Silver Patriarch(IRE) —Burmese Ruby (Good Times (ITY))
1688[9] 2268[10] 2674[P]

Red Flyer (IRE) *Ronald Thompson* 98 h 100c
7 br g Catrail(USA) —Marostica (ITY) (Stone)
(1376) 1602[4] 2900[10]

Red Georgie (IRE) *N A Twiston-Davies* 125h 130 c
8 ch g Old Vic—Do We Know (Derrylin)
(1829) 2165[3] 2643[P] 4035[P]

Red Granite *K C Bailey* 81h
6 gr g Rock City—Cherry Side (General Ironside)
1799[6] 2799[P] 3806[6] 3906[11] 4899[5]

Red Guard *George Hosier* 106c
12 ch g Soviet Star(USA) —Zinzara (USA) (Stage Door Johnny (USA))
221[2]

Redhouse Chevalier *B G Powell* 47b 98c
7 b g Pursuit Of Love—Trampolo (USA) (Trempolino (USA))
2805[9] 3148[P] 3653[P] 3672[5] 3938[7] 4353[P]

Redi (ITY) *A M Balding* 111 h
5 b g Danehill Dancer(IRE) —Rossella (Shareef Dancer (USA))
2047[4] 3128[6] 3360[10]

Red Jester *A E Jones* 27h
5 b g Thowra(FR) —Red Ebrel (IRE) (Red Sunset)
2309[U] 3422[12] 3659[13]

Red Lion (FR) *D McCain* 88h 83c
9 ch g Lion Cavern(USA) —Mahogany River (Irish River (FR))
2563[6] 3358[8]

Redlynch Spirit (IRE) *C L Tizzard* 67h
6 b g Executive Perk—Gently Ridden (IRE) (King's Ride)
816[5] 866[6] 2427[4] 2619[P] 3127[8] 3616[U]

Red Man (IRE) *Mrs E Slack* 105 h 109c
9 ch g Toulon—Jamie's Lady (Ashmore (FR))
1887[3] (2042) 2190[4] 2453[6] 2566[5] 2977[5] 3171[3] **3351[2] 3562[2] 3784[2] 3928[F] 4520[U] (4655) 4788[9] 4920[3]**

Red Marsala *Miss S E Forster* 47h 26c
8 bb g Tragic Role(USA) —Southend Scallywag (Tina's Pet)
322[P] 718[F] 856[P]

Red Moor (IRE) *Mrs D A Hamer* 113 h
6 gr g Eagle Eyed(USA) —Faakirah (Dragonara Palace (USA))
635[7] (901) 1182[2] 3127[6] 3360[3] 3510[9] 3650[6] 4726[13] 5045[2]

Red Mountain *Mrs K Walton*
5 b g Unfuwain(USA) —Red Cascade (IRE) (Danehill (USA))
4917[P]

Redneck Girl (IRE) *A E Jones*
7 b m Oscar(IRE) —Flamewood (Touching Wood (USA))
3425[P] 3902[11] 4367[P] 4823[11]

Red Nell (IRE) *Mrs Helen Sheehy* 90c
11 b g Meneval(USA) —Friendly Sea (Callernish)
5128a[P]

Red Nose Lady *G J Smith* 97 h
9 b m Teenoso(USA) —Red Rambler (Rymer)
96[P] 180[4] 425[4] 697[11] 863[3](903) (1218) 1405[2]

Redouble *W B Stone* 81h
10 b g First Trump—Sunflower Seed (Mummy's Pet)
282[P] 1066[P]

Red Perk (IRE) *R C Guest* 96h 108+c
9 b g Executive Perk—Supreme View (Supreme Leader)
81[F] 215[2] **546[5]**(1910) **2170[2]** 2840[5] 2994[8] **3377[6](3917) 4042[5] 4790[P]**(5069) **(11)** (Dead)

Red Poker *G A Harker* 74h
6 ch g Alflora(IRE) —Scarlet Ember (Nearly A Hand)
(2268) 3793[10] 4793[P]

Red Quest *Dr J R J Naylor* 53b
6 b g El Conquistador—Red Maid (Red Man)
4881[9]

Red Rain (IRE) *J Clements*
4 ch f General Monash(USA) —Polish Saga (Polish Patriot (USA))
3237[12]

Red Rampage *P H Hogarth* 87h 108c
11 b g King's Ride—Mighty Fly (Comedy Star (USA))
(125) 240[5] 3913[6] 4351[7]

Red Raptor *J A Geake* 64h
5 ch g Polar Falcon(USA) —Star Precision (Shavian)
3001[13] 3355[P] 3948[7]

Red Rattle (IRE) *Miss H C Knight* 79b
4 ch g Old Vic—Only Her Way (IRE) (Jurado (USA))
4881[5]

Red Rocky *R Hollinshead* 62h
5 b m Danzero(AUS) —Post Mistress (IRE) (Cyrano De Bergerac)
2139[12] 3885[4] 3985[P] 4591[7]

Red Ruffles (IRE) *Noel T Chance* 124h 115c
7 b g Anshan—Rosie Ruffles (IRE) (Homo Sapien)
2924[3]

Red Scally *R C Guest* 101b
6 b g Alflora(IRE) —Southend Scallywag (Tina's Pet)
5141[2]

Red September *D L Williams* 83h
9 b g Presidium—Tangalooma (Hotfoot)
822[11] 1000[7] **1176[P]**

Redskin Raider (IRE) *Miss S Sharratt* 105h 105 c
10 b g Commanche Run—Sheltered (IRE) (Strong Gale)
4594[5]

Red Socialite (IRE) *D R Gandolfo* 108+h 91c
9 ch g Moscow Society(USA) —Dees Darling (IRE) (King Persian)
4639[P] 4904[F]

Redspin (IRE) *J S Moore* 99 h
6 ch g Spectrum(IRE) —Trendy Indian (IRE) (Indian Ridge)
394[F] 1220[3] 1482[4] (1725) 2175[P]

Red Square Express *M W Easterby* 94b
4 b g Kayf Tara—Formal Affair (Rousillon (USA))
4909[3]

Red Square Lad (IRE) *Mrs L Williamson* 28h 95+c
10 ch g Toulon—Tempestuous Girl (Tumble Wind)
4095[P]

Red Square Lady (IRE) *Michael John Phillips* 125h
8 b m Moscow Society(USA) —Arctic Scale (IRE) (Strong Gale)
66a[18] 954a[2] 1621a[5] (1691a) 5077a[6]

Red Square Run *M W Easterby* 48h
4 gr g Commanche Run—Absolutley Foxed (Absalom)
4519[7] 5038[U]

Red Striker *Miss T Jackson* 123+c
12 ch g Gunner B—Cover Your Money (Precipice Wood)
3736[3] (4146) 4505[4] (Dead)

Red Sun *J Mackie* 118 h
9 b g Foxhound(USA) —Superetta (Superlative)
4058[P]

Red Tyrant *R Flint* 88h
8 b g Minster Son—By The Lake (Tyrant (USA))
813[P]

Redvic *G J Smith* 7h
6 b g Alhaarmi—Sweet Fortune (Dubassoff (USA))
24[P]

Red Wharf *J Wade*
5 b g Bal Harbour—Contradictory (Reprimand)
2106[P] 3559[P]

Redwood Grove (USA) *Miss Tor Sturgis* 87 h
10 b g Woodman(USA) —Ikebana (IRE) (Sadler's Wells (USA))
3905[3] 4368[9]

Reedsman (IRE) *R C Guest* 65h
5 ch g Fayruz—The Way She Moves (North Stoke)
263[0] 363[2] 601[4] 670[7] 822[8] 1107[6] 1278[6]

Reel Charmer *J I A Charlton* 88b
6 b m Dancing High—Gaelic Charm (IRE) (Deep Run)
4853[4] 5041[3]

Reelinga *G A Ham* 78h
7 b m Karinga Bay—Reeling (Relkino)
2014[4]

Reel Missile *C T Pogson* 112+h 123+c
7 b g Weld—Landsker Missile (Cruise Missile)
2764[3] 2924[2] 3618[4] 4417[4]

Reem Two *D McCain* 102h
5 b m Mtoto—Jamrat Samya (IRE) (Sadler's Wells (USA))
331[U] 574[2] (1064) 1149[3] 1317[2] 1443[5] 1590[2] 1880[5] 2372[4] 3269[3] (3484) 3802[3] 4972[5]

Refinement (IRE) *Jonjo O'Neill* 147+h
7 b m Oscar(IRE) —Maneree (Mandalus)
(70a) (1714) (1850) (2050) (3295) (4077) 4443[3] (4776) 5132a[P]

Reflected Glory (IRE) *P F Nicholls* 120 h 139 c
7 b g Flemensfirth(USA) —Clashdermot Lass (Cardinal Flower)
1829[2] 2311[3] (2847) 3213[2] 4035[4] 4166[2]

Reflector (IRE) *Miss H C Knight* 90+h
5 b g Alderbrook—Four Moons (IRE) (Cardinal Flower)
2961[10] 3699[12] 4581[8] 4819[8]

Reflex Blue *R J Price* 78h 86 c
9 b g Ezzoud(IRE) —Briggsmaid (Elegant Air)
1413[5] 1645[8] 1793[10] 1856[7] **2429[3] 2561[8] 2936[6]** 3279[5] **3359[5]**

Refutation (FR) *J J Napoli*
4 b c Muhtathir—Such Is Life (FR) (Akarad (FR))
4548a[3]

Regal Act (IRE) *Jennie Candlish* 74h
10 ch g Montelimar(USA) —Portal Lady (Pals Passage)
1[P]

Regal Bandit (IRE) *Miss H C Knight* 95h 107+c
8 b g Un Desperado(FR) —Rainbow Alliance (IRE) (Golden Love)
2733[8] 2996[2] 3420[3]

Regal Fantasy (IRE) *P A Blockley* 67h
6 b m King's Theatre(IRE) —Threesome (USA) (Seattle Dancer (USA))
4642[P] 4855[9]

Regal Future *R Dickin*
4 b f Regal Embers(IRE) —In The Future (IRE) (Phardante (FR))
4940[13]

Regal Heights (IRE) *D McCain* 126h
5 b g Grand Plaisir(IRE) —Regal Hostess (King's Ride)
1847[4] 3205[5] (3534) (3793) 4115[3] 4359[3] 4750[7]

Regal Leader *M A Barnes* 28b
7 b g Mistertopogigo(IRE) —Princess Zena (Habitat)
3231[4] 719[9]

Regal Repose *Miss K M George* 42h
6 b m Classic Cliche(IRE) —Ideal Candidate (Celestial Storm (USA))
533[5]

Regal River (IRE) *John R Upson* 83h 77c
9 b g Over The River(FR) —My Friend Fashion (Laurence O)
2129[3] 3662[6] 4353[7]

Regal Setting (IRE) *J Howard Johnson* 116h
5 br g King's Theatre(IRE) —Cartier Bijoux (Ahonoora)
1677[9] 4792[9]

Regal Term (IRE) *R Dickin* 97h 110+c
8 b g Welsh Term—Regal Hostess (King's Ride)
3275[7] 3685[2] 4106[5] 4935[4] **(5139)**

Regal Vision (IRE) *Miss C Dyson* 101h 94c
9 b g Emperor Jones(USA) —Shining Eyes (USA) (Mr Prospector (USA))
283[11] 519[8] **673[9] 981[8]** 1539[3] **(1803) 2522[6] (2957) 3938[3]**

Regents Walk (IRE) *B De Haan* 110 h
8 b g Phardante(FR) —Raw Courage (IRE) (The Parson)
4215[12]

Registana (GER) *C Olehla* 115+c
10 b m Tauchsport(EG) —Reklame (GDR) (Immer (HUN))
1710a[F]

Regulated (IRE) *P A Blockley* 89h
5 b g Alzao(USA) —Royal Hostess (IRE) (Be My Guest (USA))
1085[4] 1153[F] 1480[9] 1522[6] 1643[5] 1779[P] 1806[P]

Rehearsal *L Lungo* 111+h
5 b g Singspiel(IRE) —Daralaka (IRE) (The Minstrel (CAN))
1836[F] 2478[4] 5066[6]

Reine Des Reines (IRE) *John E Kiely* 102h
8 b m Supreme Leader—La Grande Dame (Niniski (USA))
117a[U]

Reinedoff (IRE) *Noel Lawlor* 117h
5 b g Frimaire—Kilmood Lass (IRE) (Tout Ensemble)
4060a[F] (Dead)

Reisk Superman (IRE) *A J Martin* 116h
8 b g Naheez(USA) —Forward Gal (The Parson)
5078a[4]

Reivers Moon *W Amos* 108h 110+c
7 bb m Midnight Legend—Here Comes Tibby (Royal Fountain)
3379[2] 4531[4]

Reiziger (FR) *P J Hobbs* 116h
10 gr g Balleroy(USA) —Dany Ohio (FR) (Script Ohio (USA))
1878[2]

Relative Hero (IRE) *Miss S J Wilton* 76+h
6 ch g Entrepreneur—Aunty (FR) (Riverman (USA))
75[6] 273[2] 1362[6] 1643[4] 4046[2]

Reliance Leader *D L Williams* 30h 71+c
10 ch g Weld—Swift Messenger (Giolla Mear)
692[0] 914[8]

Relix (FR) *A M Crow* 94+h
6 gr g Linamix(FR) —Resleona (Caerleon (USA))
8[5] 301[4] (426) 643[4] (687) 2417[P] 4982[P] 5096[9]

Remington (IRE) *Mrs A M Thorpe* 100h
8 ch g Indian Ridge—Sea Harrier (Grundy)
4591[F]

Reminiscent (IRE) *B P J Baugh* 97h
7 b g Kahyasi—Eliza Orzeszkowa (IRE) (Polish Patriot (USA))
2755[9]

Remus Lupin *F P Murtagh* 39h
5 b g Wolfhound(USA) —Incharder (IRE) (Slip Anchor)
1508[P] 2106[7]

Renada *J Howard Johnson* 68+h
4 b f Sinndar(IRE) —Asterita (Rainbow Quest (USA))
(2494) 3203[P]

Renaloo (IRE) *R Rowe*
11 gr g Tremblant—Rare Flower (Decent Fellow)
2594[P] 3602[R] 4936[P]

Renvyle (IRE) *R C Guest* 120 h 105 c
8 bb g Satco(FR) —Kara's Dream (IRE) (Bulldozer)
248[8] 946[P] 1039[8] **1684[3] 1815[P]** 2766[9] 2925[13] **3272[5] 3486[4] 3762[2] 3930[8] 4920[8]**

Repeat (IRE) *Lucinda Featherstone*
6 ch g Night Shift(USA) —Identical (IRE) (Machiavellian (USA))
629[P]

Repent At Leisure *R C Guest* 50h
6 b g Bishop Of Cashel—Sutosky (Great Nephew)
1014[5]

Replacement Pet (IRE) *Mrs S D Williams* 62+h
9 b m Petardia—Richardstown Lass (IRE) (Muscatite)
668[7] 758[5] 863[9]

Reseda (GER) *Ian Williams* 113 h 109 c
7 b m Lavirco(GER) —Reklame (GER) (Immer (HUN))
(314) **2018[2] 2722[F]**

Reseda (IRE) *M A Barnes* 94h 67c
9 b g Rock Hopper—Sweet Mignonette (Tina's Pet)
4143[6] 4493[9] **4991[8] 9[4]**

Reservoir (IRE) *J Joseph* 109+h
5 b g Green Desert(USA) —Spout (Salse (USA))
21[5] 243[5] 460[10] 947[11] 1099[P] 3152[4] 4781[P] 5108[9]

Resonance *N A Twiston-Davies* 89h
5 b m Slip Anchor—Music In My Life (IRE) (Law Society (USA))
1364[3] 1527[7] 1658[8] 2726[8]

Resplendent Star (IRE) *Mrs L Wadham* 109+h 112c
9 b g Northern Baby(CAN) —Whitethroat (Artaius (USA))
(513) 691[5] 824[3] 1001[4] 1245[2] **1365[2]** 1987[5]

Ressource (FR) *G L Moore* 89h
7 b g Broadway Flyer(USA) —Rayonne (Sadler's Wells (USA))
9[9] 283[9] (451) 3661[6] 4010[6] 4523[U] 4912[7]

Restart (IRE) *Lucinda Featherstone* 107+h
5 b g Revoque(IRE) —Stargard (Polish Precedent (USA))
1608[2] 1870[4]

Restless D'Artaix (FR) *N J Henderson* 120+h
4 b g Restless Carl(IRE) —Akente (FR) (Antheus (USA))
2481[3] (2824)

Restoration (FR) *Noel Meade* 120h
4 gr g Zafonic(USA) —Restless Mixa (IRE) (Linamix (FR))
4468[11]

Retro's Girl (IRE) *M Scudamore* 86+h
5 ch m Zaffaran(USA) —Highland Chain (Furry Glen)
1850^{4} 2461^{5} 2718^{4} 2985^{7}

Returned Un Paid (IRE) *Mrs V Park* 82+h 81c
9 b g Actinium(FR) —Claregalway Lass (Ardross)
348^{5}

Return Fire *Miss H C Knight* 83h
7 b g Bob's Return(IRE) —Light Your Fire (Bay Express)
3984^{P} 5073^{4}

Return Home *J S Smith* 101h
7 b g Bob's Return(IRE) —Welgenco (Welsh Saint)
(3147) (3242) 3561^{2} 4282^{12}

Return Ticket *R T Phillips* 106 h
7 br g Bob's Return(IRE) —Mrs Jennifer (River Knight (FR))
3001^{8} 3328^{6} 4128^{4} (4638)

Reveal (IRE) *H E Haynes* 78b
4 b f King's Best(USA) —Never Explain (IRE) (Fairy King (USA))
2013^{3} 2611^{4} 2830^{17} *3983^{10}*

Reveillez *J R Fanshawe* 144 h
150+c
7 gr g First Trump—Amalancher (USA) (Alleged (USA))
3215^{2} 3549^{2} (3907) (4456)

Reverse Swing *Mrs H Dalton* 80dh 101+c
9 b m Charmer—Milly Kelly (Murrayfield)
(134) 760^{5} 973^{3} 1483^{4} **1612^{3}(1819) 2562^{4} (2955) 3129^{5} 4900^{7}**

Reviewer (IRE) *M Meade* 100h 100c
8 b g Sadler's Wells(USA) —Clandestina (USA) (Secretariat (USA))
436^{4}

Revolve *O Sherwood*
6 b g Pivotal—Alpine Time (IRE) (Tirol)
971^{P}

Rhacophorus *C J Down* 108b
5 b m Classic Cliche(IRE) —Tree Frog (IRE) (Lomond (USA))
3001^{6} (3468) (4751)

Rhapsody In Bloom *L Wells* 49b
5 b g Botanic(USA) —Jazzy Refrain (IRE) (Jareer (USA))
1600^{7}

Rhapsody Rose *P R Webber* 96h 88+c
5 b m Unfuwain(USA) —Haboobti (Habitat)
66a^{15} **1911^{3} 2246^{3}**

Rheindross (IRE) *C J Mann* 135+c
11 gr g Ala Hounak—Ardcarn Girl (Ardross)
69a^{13} 761^{3} (842) 2370^{P}

Rhetoric (IRE) *Miss Sarah-Jayne Davies* 66 h
7 b g Desert King(IRE) —Squaw Talk (USA) (Gulch (USA))
437^{U}

Rhetorical *P Butler* 77h
5 b g Unfuwain(USA) —Miswaki Belle (USA) (Miswaki (USA))
1523^{2} 1648^{3} 1921^{9} 2073^{P} 2378^{P}

Rhossili (IRE) *Mrs L Wadham* 86+h
6 b g Perugino(USA) —Velinowski (Malinowski (USA))
1454^{4} 1616^{3} 2687^{8}

Rhuna Red *J R Bewley* 85h
7 ch m Good Thyne(USA) —Oh Dear (Paico)
124^{4} 523^{8} 4917^{P} 5038^{2}

Rhythm King *G C Maundrell* 86h 112+c
11 b g Rakaposhi King—Minim (Rymer)
(4477) (4897) 5020^{U}

Riccarton *D C Turner* 83 h 88c
13 b g Nomination—Legendary Dancer (Shareef Dancer (USA))
388^{F} 664^{9} **752^{6}803^{6} 958^{4}**

Rich Song (IRE) *Mrs S J Smith* 86 h 86c
8 b g Treasure Hunter—Sonnet Lady (Down The Hatch)
631^{P} 972^{3} 1177^{P}1615^{F} 1976^{P}

Riders Revenge (IRE) *Miss Venetia Williams* 104h
8 b g Norwich—Paico Ana (Paico)
2011^{P}

Ridjit (FR) *N J Gifford* 93h
6 b g Exit To Nowhere(USA) —Ridja Princess (FR) (Crystal Glitters (USA))
3422^{4} 3685^{5} 3908^{10} 4149^{6} 4912^{F}

Rien A Perdre (FR) *S Donohoe* 47h
5 b g Nikos—Kamirish (FR) (Assert)
3490^{5}

Riffles *Mrs A J Bowlby* 66h
6 br m Alderbrook—Idiot's Lady (Idiots Delight)
2242^{5} 2558^{5} 3149^{4} 3478^{P} 4638^{4}

Rifleman (IRE) *Robert Gray* 116h 100c
6 ch g Starborough—En Garde (USA) (Irish River (FR))
236^{2} 488^{6} 976^{2} 1108^{4} 1319^{3}1384^{6} 1528^{3} 2071^{2} **2245^{5}** 2289^{4}2523^{6} **2976^{6} 3334^{5}3558^{4} 3915^{5} (5036)**

Rifle Ryde (IRE) *K C Bailey* 38h
6 br g Needle Gun(IRE) —Nellsway (Neltino)
1975^{9} 2238^{11}

Rift Valley (IRE) *P J Hobbs* 114 h 127c
11 b g Good Thyne(USA) —Necochea (Julio Mariner)
5^{2} (315) (1016) 1341^{4} 3880^{8} 4119^{8} 4289^{7}4561^{13} 4756^{9}

Rigadoon (IRE) *Mrs J L Haley* 84h 97c
10 b g Be My Chief(USA) —Loucoum (FR) (Iron Duke (FR))
374^{U}

Right Direction (IRE) *J J Lambe* 75h
8 b g Song Of The Woods—Rio Rhythm (Jaazeiro (USA))
875^{5} 941^{P}

Rightful Ruler *M Todhunter* 74h
4 b g Montjoy(USA) —Lady Of The Realm (Prince Daniel (USA))
3488^{8} 5091^{8}

Rights Of Man (IRE) *D E Fitzgerald* 122?h
7 bb g Right Win(IRE) —Stiritup (IRE) (Mandalus)
1623a^{7} 2207^{10} 5078a^{20}

Rigmarole *P F Nicholls* 157 h 101c
8 b g Fairy King(USA) —Cattermole (USA) (Roberto (USA))
244^{U} 358^{2} 564^{4}

Rileys Dream *C J Price* 65h
7 b m Rudimentary(USA) —Dorazine (Kalaglow)
1^{9}

Rimsky (IRE) *N A Twiston-Davies* 138+h
5 gr g Silver Patriarch(IRE) —Mistinguett (IRE) (Doyoun)
(1680) (1827) 2161^{10} 2762^{6} 2956^{4} 3738^{2} 4443^{6}4776^{6} 4974^{2} 5093^{5}

Ri Na Realta (IRE) *J W Mullins* 112h 102c
11 b g King's Ride—Realteen (Deep Run)
202^{P} 465^{4} 4150^{3}4653^{6} 4804^{2} 4873^{2}

Rince Ri (IRE) *T M Walsh* 130h 126c
13 ch g Orchestra—Mildred's Ball (Blue Refrain)
4123a^{4} 4777^{R}

Rincoola (IRE) *J S Wainwright* 72h
7 br m Warcraft(USA) —Very Tense (IRE) (Orchestra)
11^{P} 152^{6} 417^{P} 1943^{P}

Ringagold *N J Hawke* 57+h
7 ch m Karinga Bay—Miss Marigold (Norwick (USA))
2846^{P} 3130^{7} 3505^{P}

Ringaroses *Miss H C Knight* 118b
5 b g Karinga Bay—Rose Ravine (Deep Run)
(2941) *(3983)* 4779^{6}

Ring Back (IRE) *B I Case* 106b
5 ch m Bob Back(USA) —Ardrom (Ardross)
4017^{4} (4398) 4751^{3}

Ringo Cody (IRE) *D R Gandolfo* 94b
5 b g Dushyantor(USA) —Just A Second (Jimsun)
4455^{12} 4807^{3}

Ring Of Destiny *J Jay* 87h
7 b g Magic Ring(IRE) —Canna (Caerleon (USA))
1245^{6} 1991^{8}

Rings Of Power (IRE) *N R Mitchell* 96c
9 ch g Mister Lord(USA) —Rainbow Gurriers (IRE) (Buckskin (FR))
202^{P} 296^{3} 461^{F}669^{P} 1638^{3}

Ring Street Roller (IRE) *J J Lambe* 87+h
6 b m High Roller(IRE) —Eyre Street Lady (Carlingford Castle)
854^{2} 936^{3}

Ring The Boss (IRE) *K G Reveley* 84h
5 b g Kahyasi—Fortune's Girl (Ardross)
2340^{11} 2838^{4} 3167^{5} 3912^{4}

Ring You Later *J Howard Johnson* 36h
5 b g Golden Lahab(USA) —Woody's Surprise (Wonderful Surprise)
2024^{10}

Riodan (IRE) *J J Quinn* 86b
4 ch f Desert King(IRE) —Spirit Of The Nile (FR) (Generous (IRE))
3556^{2} 4017^{9} 4992^{2}

Rio De Janeiro (IRE) *P R Chamings* 119+h
5 b g Sadler's Wells(USA) —Alleged Devotion (USA) (Alleged (USA))
729^{8}

Rioja Rally (IRE) *R T Phillips*
6 b g Anshan—Glentrasna Venture (IRE) (Brush Aside (USA))
3500^{10} **4369^{P} 4610^{P}**

Riolo (IRE) *K F Clutterbuck* 26b
4 ch g Priolo(USA) —Ostrusa (AUT) (Rustan (HUN))
4038^{11}

Rip Kirby *Mrs J Warwick* 91b
11 b g Derrylin—Preacher's Gem (The Parson)
123^{P}

Rising Generation (FR) *N G Richards* 128 h
9 ch g Risen Star(USA) —Queen's Victory (FR) (Carmarthen (FR))
332^{6} 525^{9} 689^{8} 873^{9} 1312^{7}1530^{2} (1836) 2334^{3} 3378^{4} 3761^{3} 3929^{4}4490^{9} 4792^{7}

Rising Tempest *Mrs S J Smith* 72h
5 gr m Primitive Rising(USA) —Stormswift (Neltino)
1237^{5} (1593) 1674^{4} 2414^{6} 3168^{6}

Risington *Miss Venetia Williams* 81 c
8 b g Afzal—Barton Rise (Raise You Ten)
3920^{5} 4162^{4} 4575^{3}4666^{F}

Risk Accessor (IRE) *Jonjo O'Neill* 148h 145c
11 b g Commanche Run—Bellatollah (Bellman (FR))
1550^{P} 1676^{6} 2499^{2}2760^{S} 4118^{0} 4447^{5}4777^{5} 5144^{8}

Risk Challenge (USA) *C J Price* 110+b
4 ch g Mt. Livermore(USA) —Substance (USA) (Diesis)
(4595) 4779^{21}

Risk Factor *Ian Williams* 25h
7 b g Classic Cliche(IRE) —Easy Risk (Risk Me (FR))
1340^{P}

Risky Patricia *T J Fitzgerald* 65b
5 b m Silver Patriarch(IRE) —Take A Risk (Risk Me (FR))
4615^{8}

Risky Rhythm *R Johnson* 60h
7 b m Primitive Rising(USA) —Heatheridge (IRE) (Carlingford Castle)
10^{7}

Risky Way *W S Coltherd* 84 h 96c
10 b g Risk Me(FR) —Hot Sunday Sport (Star Appeal)
(122) 2137 644^{3}(874) 939^{3} 1311^{3}1529^{7} 1592^{2} 1684^{U}2022^{5} 2570^{8}

Rival (IRE) *S Flook*
7 b g Desert Style(IRE) —Arab Scimetar (IRE) (Sure Blade (USA))
278^{P}

Rival Bidder *Mrs S J Smith* 103h 91+c
9 ch g Arzanni—Beltalong (Belfort (FR))
614^{4}

River Alder *J M Dun* 119h
8 b m Alderbrook—River Pearl (Oats)
61^{3} (422) 2990^{12} (4792) 5005^{8}

River Amora (IRE) *Jim Best* 86h 88 c
11 b g Willie Joe(IRE) —That's Amora (Paddy's Stream)
(565) 674^{7} 978^{P} 1156^{9}**(4525) 4666^{6} 5090^{2}**

River Bailiff (IRE) *S Garrott* 86+c
10 ch g Over The River(FR) —Rath Caola (Neltino)
1717^{7} 404^{3}

River Charm (FR) *G Cherel*
6 ch g River Mist(USA) —Schwarzente (IRE) (Entitled)
4717a^{2} (5154a)

River City (IRE) *Noel T Chance* 131+h
159+c
9 b g Norwich—Shuil Na Lee (IRE) (Phardante (FR))
219^{2} 4445^{U} 4761^{P}(5143)

River Dante (IRE) *Miss L A Blackford* 101+c
9 ch g Phardante(FR) —Astral River (Over The River (FR))
962^{3} 1019^{4} 3924^{P}4594^{10} (5116)

River Groom (FR) *J-P Carnel*
7 b g River Mist(USA) —Couignamama (IRE) (Groom Dancer (USA))
1073a^{P}

River Heights (IRE) *C Tinkler* 89b
5 bb g Kotashaan(FR) —Mrs Cullen (Over The River (FR))
5089^{2}

River Indus *R H Buckler* 88h 11c
6 b g Rakaposhi King—Flow (Over The River (FR))
2606^{4} 3175^{8} 3548^{11} **4572^{4}5025^{5}**

River Iris *Lucinda Featherstone* 26b
5 ch m Riverhead(USA) —Barkston Singer (Runnett)
138^{15} 971^{P} 1206^{R}

River Line (USA) *C W Fairhurst* 40h
5 b g Keos(USA) —Portio (USA) (Riva Ridge (USA))
1661^{9}

River Marshal (IRE) *C C Bealby* 97+h
107+c
8 b g Synefos(USA) —Marshallstown (Callernish)
1608^{7} (Dead)

River Mere *Mrs P A Rigby* 90h 102c
12 b g River God(USA) —Rupert's Daughter (Rupert Bear)
132^{P} 346^{4} 503^{9}673^{7} 4831^{P} 5013^{P}

River Mist (IRE) *Karen McLintock* 112+h 83c
7 ch m Over The River(FR) —Minature Miss (Move Off)
(121) 334^{4} 483^{2} 2566^{8} (2840) **2976^{4}**

River Of Fire *C N Kellett* 73+h
8 ch g Dilum(USA) —Bracey Brook (Gay Fandango (USA))
237^{P} 687^{5} 978^{6} 1367^{7}

River Of Light (IRE) *D P Keane* 78h 102+c
6 b g Flemensfirth(USA) —Stillbyherself (IRE) (Le Bavard (FR))
2799^{6} 3184^{5} **3427^{5} (4370)**

River Of Wishes *C W Mitchell*
8 b m Riverwise(USA) —Wishful Dream (Crawter)
3280^{P} **3879^{P}**

River Paradise (IRE) *Jamie Broom* 93h
10 ch g John French—Barbara Brook (Over The River (FR))
4090^{7} 4356^{12}

River Pirate (IRE) *David W Drinkwater* 104 c
9 b g Un Desperado(FR) —Kigali (IRE) (Torus)
4^{6} 3847^{P} 4055^{3}4555^{11}

River Quoile *R H Alner* 73h 73c
10 b g Terimon—Carrikins (Buckskin (FR))
805^{F} 981^{2} 1191^{5}1247^{2} 1414^{9} 1560^{5}1639^{3} 1780^{6} 1901^{6}

River Ripples (IRE) *T R George* 98+h
7 ch g Over The River(FR) —Aelia Paetina (Buckskin (FR))
1954^{2} 2376^{3} 2983^{9} 3275^{9} 3659^{3}3982^{3} 4634^{P}

River Role *J W Tudor* 69b
4 b f Tragic Role(USA) —Arian Spirit (IRE) (High Estate)
2611^{6} 2797^{P} 3246^{P}

River Tigris (IRE) *O Sherwood* 90b
4 b f Dr Devious(IRE) —La Riveraine (USA) (Riverman (USA))
4751^{7}

River Trapper (IRE) *Miss H C Knight* 94 h 109+c
7 b g Over The River(FR) —Mousa (Callernish)
2149^{2} 2613^{P}

Rivertree (IRE) *D P Keane* 93h
5 ch g Entrepreneur—French River (Bering)
4834^{9} 5028^{8}

Riyadh *T P Tate* 73h
8 ch g Caerleon(USA) —Ausherra (USA) (Diesis)
148^{P}

Road King (IRE) *Miss J Feilden* 80h 64 c
12 b g Supreme Leader—Ladies Gazette (London Gazette)
1856^{8} 2586^{5} 2810^{3} 3279^{8} 3540^{U}4449^{5}

Roadmaker (IRE) *John G Carr* 116h
6 ch g Old Vic—Lucifer's Way (Lucifer (USA))
2145^{5} (5103a)

Roadworthy (IRE) *W G Young* 63h 64c
9 b m Lord Americo—Henry Woman (IRE) (Mandalus)
2144 496^{6} 718^{5} 854^{9} 2674^{P}3209^{4} 3381^{6} 3552^{2} 3795^{P} 3916^{3}4145^{6} 4341^{6} 4656^{10}

Roan Raider (USA) *R C Guest* 62h
6 rg g El Prado(IRE) —Flirtacious Wonder (USA) (Wolf Power (SAF))
2040^{7} 2245^{8}

Roaringwater (IRE) *R T Phillips* 106 h 98 c
7 b g Roselier(FR) —Supreme Cherry (Buckskin (FR))
2109^{2} 3815^{11}

Robber (IRE) *P Bowen* 87h 101+c
9 ch g Un Desperado(FR) —Christy's Girl (IRE) (Buckskin (FR))
(101) 669^{2} 746^{P}989^{4} 1191^{P}

Robber Red *Miss Suzy Smith* 104+c
10 b g Mon Tresor—Starisk (Risk Me (FR))
1726^{7} 1801^{4}

Robbers Glen (IRE) *J Howard Johnson* 103+h
6 b g Muroto—Dante's Thatch (IRE) (Phardante (FR))
4793^{4}

Robbie Can Can *A W Carroll* 75h
7 b g Robellino(USA) —Can Can Lady (Anshan)
3674^{3}

Robbie On Tour (IRE) *M C Pipe* 82+h
7 b g Oscar(IRE) —Mystery Woman (Tula Rocket)
129^{4} 352^{3} **464^{10}** 519^{5}**1041^{5}** 1152^{13} 1262^{10}

Robbie's Adventure *D L Williams* 7c
12 ch g Le Coq D'Or—Mendick Adventure (Mandrake Major)
101^{5} 403^{P}

Robbie Will *F Jordan* 81h
5 b g Robellino(USA) —Life's Too Short (IRE) (Astronef)
2006^{8} 2423^{10} 2683^{7} 2958^{12}

Robbo *K G Reveley* 103h 127c
12 b g Robellino(USA) —Basha (USA) (Chief's Crown (USA))
1941^{P} 2110^{3} **2499^{9}(2841) 3560^{P}** 3970^{7} **4111^{7}4496^{6} 4790^{3} 5004^{16}**

Robert (IRE) *D T Hughes* 120h
7 ch g Bob Back(USA) —Mother Imelda (IRE) (Phardante (FR))
2206^{10}

Robert The Bruce *L Lungo* 106h
11 ch g Distinct Native—Kawarau Queen (Taufan (USA))
544^{F} 1940 ^{F} 3797^{3} 4723^{3}

Robert The Rascal *Mrs C M James* 81c
13 ch g Scottish Reel—Midnight Mary (Celtic Cone)
6^{P}

Robeson *G Haine* 66h
4 br g Primo Dominie—Montserrat (Aragon)
3275^{5}

Rob Leach *G L Moore* 128h
9 b g Robellino(USA) —Arc Empress Jane (IRE) (Rainbow Quest (USA))
102^{P} (Dead)

Robmantra *B J Llewellyn* 31h
4 b g Prince Sabo—Eliza Jane (Mistertopogigo (IRE))
1023^{7}

Rob Mine (IRE) *C Sporborg* 93c
14 b g Roselier(FR) —Noddi Fliw (Jasmine Star)
4358^{4}

Rob The Five (IRE) *P C Haslam* 111+c
9 b g Supreme Leader—Derravarragh Lady (IRE) (Radical)
4981^{8}

Robyn Alexander (IRE) *P F Nicholls* 101 h 101 c
8 ch m Sharifabad(IRE) —Flagship Ahoy (IRE) (Accordion)
220^{2}

Rocca's Boy (IRE) *M Wigham* 82+b
4 b g Spectrum(IRE) —Quiet Counsel (IRE) (Law Society (USA))
(3490) 4909^{14}

Roche Ecossaise (FR) *R H Alner*
7 b m Chef De Clan II(FR) —Manon De Roches (FR) (Plouk Vergoignan (FR))
4327^{14} 5023^{9}

Rock And Palm (FR) *Mlle C Cardenne*
6 b g Great Palm(USA) —Marie De Rocroi (FR) (Crystal Palace (FR))
(585a) (5000a) 5154a^{2}

Rock Angel (IRE) *Paul Nolan* 64h
4 b f Desert King(IRE) —Ramich John (Kampala)
5076a^{20}

Rockanroll *C A McBratney* 101h
10 b g Tragic Role(USA) —Last Note (Welsh Pageant)
870^{P} (Dead)

Rock Back (IRE) *Miss Lucinda V Russell* 75h
5 b m Bob Back(USA) —Tikarna (FR) (Targowice (USA))
2031a^{13} 3783^{5}

Rockerfella Lad (IRE) *M Todhunter* 77h 62+c
6 b g Danetime(IRE) —Soucaro (Rusticaro (FR))
987^{5}

Rocket Bleu (FR) *D Burchell* 88+h
6 ch g Epervier Bleu—Egeria (FR) (Baly Rockette)
75^{10} 1957^{7} 2806^{2}

Rocket Force (USA) *S Gollings* 86h
6 ch g Spinning World(USA) —Pat Us (USA) (Caucasus (USA))
369^{7} 687^{P}

Rocket Ship (IRE) *Noel Meade* 129+h
6 b h Pennekamp(USA) —Rock The Boat (Slip Anchor)
1787a^{3} 2032a^{5} 2916a^{3} 3411a^{12}

Rocking Ship (IRE) *Ms Joanna Morgan* 86h 112c
8 b g Leading Counsel(USA) —One More Try (Kemal (FR))
(1420a) 2368^{F} 5129a^{12}

Rockpiler *J Howard Johnson* 57h
4 b g Halling(USA) —Emma Peel (Emarati (USA))
2076^{7}

Rocksham (IRE) *E Sheehy* 106h 97c
6 b m Bluebird(USA) —Kates Choice (IRE) (Taufan (USA))
2939^{U}

Rockvale (IRE) *Mrs J A Saunders*
7 ch g Presenting—Vanhalensdarling (Green Shoon)
1976^{P}

Rocky Agenda (IRE) *G A Harker* 78b
5 b g Fort Morgan(USA) —Floating Agenda (USA) (Twilight Agenda (USA))
769^{8}

Rockys Girl *R Flint* 75h
4 b f Piccolo—Lady Rockstar (Rock Hopper)
2069^{P} 2661^{9} 2811^{4} 3367^{12} 4013^{2}4101^{U} 4392^{2} 4651^{5}

Rodalko (FR) *O Sherwood* 134+c
8 b g Kadalko(FR) —Darling Rose (FR) (Rose Laurel)
4240^{5} 4617^{2} 5102a^{12}

Rodd To Riches *Jamie Poulton* 62h
8 br g Manhal—Lovely Lilly (Arrasas (USA))
4856[12] 5086[4]

Roddy The Vet (IRE) *A Ennis* 103+c
8 ch g Be My Native(USA) —Caronia (IRE) (Cardinal Flower)
2966[3] 3427[P] 3547[P]3791[4] 4662[3] (4872) (5025)

Ro Eridani *Miss S E Forster* 68h
6 b m Binary Star(USA) —Hat Hill (Roan Rocket)
1683[6] 1883[9] 2040[4] 3443[5] 3554[8]

Rogue River *W G M Turner*
6 b g Star Of Persia(IRE) —Roving Seal (Privy Seal)
4757[U]

Rogues Gallery (IRE) *J Howard Johnson* 103h
6 b g Luso—Sarah May (IRE) (Camden Town)
124[2]

Rohan *R F Johnson Houghton* 92h 86+c
10 gr g Norton Challenger—Acushla Macree (Mansingh (USA))
51[4] 3460[P] 3923[P]

Roi Du Val (FR) *H Hosselet*
4 b g Astarabad(USA) —Vallee Bleue (FR) (Tip Moss (FR))
777a[5]

Roi Six (FR) *Mrs S A Bramall* 127c
8 b g Royal Charter(FR) —Six A Thou (FR) (Citheron)
1083a[16]

Rojabaa *B D Leavy* 112h
7 b g Anabaa(USA) —Slava (USA) (Diesis)
1653[4] 1856[4] 1902[3] 2015[4] 2428[3](2582) 2721[5] 2958[6] 3332[5] (3673) 4067[2] (4420)4848[4] 5021[3]

Roky Star (FR) *T R George* 99h 33c
9 b g Start Fast(FR) —Rosydolie (FR) (Dhausli (FR))
518[5] 3241[P]

Rolfes Delight *A E Jones* 56h 100+c
14 b g Rolfe(USA) —Idiot's Run (Idiots Delight)
(1022) 1385[3]

Roll Along (IRE) *M Pitman* 124+b
6 b g Carroll House—Callmartel (IRE) (Montelimar (USA))
(1820) (3392)

Rolling River (IRE) *J Wade* 49h 91c
9 b g Over The River(FR) —Paddy's Dancer (Paddy's Stream)
1334[5] 1719[5] 1939 [P]2109[P]

Rollo (IRE) *M F Harris* 99+h 51+c
8 gr g Roselier(FR) —Comeragh Queen (The Parson)
1599[P] 1638[5] 1773[7]2126[P]

Romaha (IRE) *S J Mahon* 114h 142+c
10 b g Storm Bird(CAN) —Eurobird (Ela-Mana-Mou)
3079a[5] 3409a[3] 4483a[F]4929a[P]

Roman Ark *J M Jefferson* 139 h 133+c
8 gr g Terimon—Larksmore (Royal Fountain)
2371[U] 2861[2] (3236) 3618[3] 3974[B] 4459[4]4759[P] 5006[2]

Roman Candle (IRE) *Lucinda Featherstone* 84+h 70c
10 b g Sabrehill(USA) —Penny Banger (IRE) (Pennine Walk)
357[2] (506) 724[5] 1277[4] (1523) 1753[7]

Roman Consul (IRE) *Jonjo O'Neill* 85h
8 ch g Alphabatim(USA) —Stella Romana (Roman Warrior)
1002[P]

Roman Court (IRE) *R H Alner* 93+h 99+c
8 b g Witness Box(USA) —Small Iron (General Ironside)
1988[4] 2805[5] 3326[4](3652) 4451[4] 5025[3]

Romangod (IRE) *J A Supple*
6 ch g Bahhare(USA) —Mystique Air (IRE) (Mujadil (USA))
1922[7] 2131[8]

Roman Gypsy *Mrs K Walton* 58b
5 b m Primitive Rising(USA) —Roman Moor (Owen Anthony)
3448[7] 3785[13] 5042[7]

Romanov Rambler (IRE) *Mrs S C Bradburne* 60h
6 b g Moscow Society(USA) —Roses Lady (IRE) (Buckley)
323[11] 2475[P] 2947[F] 4141[12] 4527[11]5093[7]

Roman Rampage *Miss Z C Davison* 86h 99c
11 b g Perpendicular—Roman Moor (Owen Anthony)
(3222) 3345[4] 3982[4] 4116[4] 4571[P]4690[3]

Roman Rebel *Mrs K Walton* 96h
7 ch g Primitive Rising(USA) —Roman Moor (Owen Anthony)
1910[F] 2024[7] 2266[P] 2978[P]4528[P]

Romantic Hero (IRE) *C R Egerton* 78h 116c
10 b g Supreme Leader—Right Love (Golden Love)
240[2] 805[P] 1041[R]

Romantique (GER) *C Von Der Recke*
5 b m Big Shuffle(USA) —Romanze (GER) (Surumu (GER))
3374[P]

Roman Villa (USA) *Mrs John Harrington* 91h
4 b g Chester House(USA) —Danzante (USA) (Danzig (USA))
5076a[11]

Romany Dream *R Dickin* 77h 110c
8 b m Nomadic Way(USA) —Half Asleep (Quiet Fling (USA))
103[2] 505[F] 823[4]1012[6] 1344[3] 1399[6]1524[4] 1647[2] 1754[2](1956) 2217[4] (2420) 3147[5] 3387[7] 4213[8]4563[2] 5090[3]

Romany Prince *S Gollings* 122h
7 b g Robellino(USA) —Vicki Romara (Old Vic)
(82) 343[F] 467[2] (992) 1089[2] 1108[2] (1220) 1341[2]

Rome (IRE) *G P Enright* 93+h
7 br g Singspiel(IRE) —Ela Romara (Ela-Mana-Mou)
1364[6] 1522[P] 1632[5] 1772[13]

Romney Marsh *R Curtis* 70h
5 br m Glacial Storm(USA) —Mirador (Town And Country)
2558[15] 3188[4] 3657[6] 4011[9]

Roobihoo (IRE) *C Grant* 109+h 104c
7 b g Norwich—Griffinstown Lady (Over The River (FR))
64[2] 1929[8] 2990[13] 3318[7] 3854[P]4317[2] 4517[2] 4724[3] 5096[13]

Rood Report *Andrew Turnell*
6 ch g Gunner B—Quiet Dawn (Lighter)
4500[17]

Roofing Spirit (IRE) *D P Keane* 99h 122 c
8 b g Beneficial—Vulcash (IRE) (Callernish)
71a[6] 2051[11] (2300) 2998[5] 3507[7] 3788[4]4037[4] 4618[4]

Rooftop Protest (IRE) *T Hogan* 134 h 115c
9 b g Thatching—Seattle Siren (USA) (Seattle Slew (USA))
(1548) (1787a) 2175[7] 3970[10] 4461[12] 5059a[18]

Rookery Lad *C N Kellett* 98h 124c
8 b g Makbul—Wayzgoose (USA) (Diesis)
1552[P] 1644[2] 1877[5]2074[F] 2149[4] (2429) 2705[2] 3187[3] 3418[4]3593[2] 4476[4] 4639[7]4878[2] (13)

Room Enough *S E H Sherwood*
6 b g Muhtarram(USA) —Salsita (Salse (USA))
1616[7]

Room To Room Gold (IRE) *R H Alner* 114+h 66c
10 b g Phardante(FR) —Kiwi Circle (IRE) (Strong Gale)
726[P] 959[5] (1020) 1111[5] 1234[4]

Roosevelt (GER) *U Stoltefuss*
8 gr g Neshad(USA) —Reine Rouge (GER) (Nebos (GER))
590a[5]

Rooster Booster *P J Hobbs*
12 gr g Riverwise(USA) —Came Cottage (Nearly A Hand)
208[4] (1738) 2209[14] (Dead)

Rooster's Reunion (IRE) *D R Gandolfo* 108 h 118c
7 gr g Presenting—Court Town (Camden Town)
1444[5] (1726) 2016[5] 2516[3]4829[6] 5027[3]

Rory Sunset (IRE) *C F Swan* 112h
8 b g Lord Americo—Dunany Star (IRE) (Salluceva)
1691a[3] 2207[13] 5103a[19]

Rosadare (IRE) *Mrs K Waldron* 82h
8 b g Roselier(FR) —Mosephine (IRE) (The Parson)
2181[3]

Rosaker (USA) *Noel Meade* 152h
9 b g Pleasant Tap(USA) —Rose Crescent (USA) (Nijinsky (CAN))
90a[6] (3080a)

Rosalyons (IRE) *Mrs H O Graham* 102 h 38c
12 gr g Roselier(FR) —Coffee Shop (Bargello)
4724[11]

Rosamio (IRE) *R Donohoe* 81h
10 gr m Roselier(FR) —Toramio (Torenaga)
3426[F]

Rosarian (IRE) *V R A Dartnall* 128 h
9 b g Fourstars Allstar(USA) —Only A Rose (Glint Of Gold)
2747[F] 3289[9] 4727[4]

Roscam *G A Ham* 67h
9 b g Son Pardo—Muznah (Royal And Regal (USA))
813[P] 1523[5] 1800[P]

Roschal (IRE) *Miss Lucinda V Russell* 94+h 108 c
8 gr g Roselier(FR) —Sunday World (USA) (Solford (USA))
1609[4] 1825[F] 2051[10]2368[F] 3239[4] 3459[3]4362[2] 4515[4]

Rose Amber *J J Bridger* 60b
5 ch m Double Trigger(IRE) —Sun Follower (Relkino)
235[7] 507[11] 2376[P] 2528[15]

Rose Bien *P J McBride*
4 bb f Bien Bien(USA) —Madame Bovary (Ile De Bourbon (USA))
3498[5]

Rosecliff *A M Balding* 110+h
4 b g Montjeu(IRE) —Dance Clear (IRE) (Marju (IRE))
2274[2] 2681[2] (3354) 4435[P] 5070[4]

Rosedale Gardens *M W Easterby* 65h
6 b g Fleetwood(IRE) —Freddie's Recall (Warrshan (USA))
1593[7] 2108[8] 2262[9] 2678[P] 14[9]

Rose Du Bourg (FR) *P Demercastel*
4 b f River Bay(USA) —Duchesse Du Bourg (FR) (Pampabird)
4548a[6]

Rosehill Lady *M J Polglase*
6 b m Mister Lord(USA) —Rosehill Dream (Rubicund)
4017[P]

Rosemary's Fancy *C N Kellett* 30b
5 b m Oscar(IRE) —Fancy Nancy (IRE) (Buckskin (FR))
2727[14] 2987[10] 3691[10]

Rosemauve (FR) *M C Pipe* 127 h 91+c
6 b g Cyborg(FR) —Sweet Jaune (FR) (Le Nain Jaune (FR))
3600[2] 3877[P]

Rosemead Tye *T Jewitt* 52h 50c
10 b m Kasakov—Nouvelle Cuisine (Yawa)
4757[P]

Rosemont (IRE) *N R Mitchell* 34h
11 b g Montelimar(USA) —Ryehill Rose (Prince Hansel)
295[9]

Rosemount King (USA) *Mrs D A Hamer* 29h
7 bb g Desert King(IRE) —Verily (Known Fact (USA))
943[9] 1218[P]

Rosenblatt (GER) *J C Tuck* 101+h
4 b c Dashing Blade—Roseraie (GER) (Nebos (GER))
4648[4]

Rosenfirth (IRE) *R Rowe* 34b
4 gr f Flemensfirth(USA) —Red City Rose (IRE) (Roselier (FR))
2830[18] 3346[15] (Dead)

Rose Of Clare *Joseph Crowley* 102b
5 b m Bob Back(USA) —Trixskin (IRE) (Buckskin (FR))
5060a[9] 5134a[9]

Rose Of The Hill (IRE) *M C Pipe* 100+h
7 gr g Roselier(FR) —Golden Leaf (Croghan Hill)
298[F] 535[U] 745[9] 1045[P]

Rose Of York (IRE) *Mrs A M Thorpe* 73+h
6 b m Emarati(USA) —True Ring (High Top)
25[3] 185[5] 399[5] 905[P] 973[6]1063[9] 1153[P] 1344[4] 1395[2]

Rosetown (IRE) *T R George* 100 h 86 c
8 gr g Roselier(FR) —Railstown Cheeky (IRE) (Strong Gale)
1973[3] (2505) 2687[3] 3252[4] (3460) 3662[4] 4370[6] 4872[2]

Roseville (IRE) *S T Lewis* 71h
6 b m Beneficial—Knockhouse Rose (IRE) (Roselier (FR))
77[P] 531[4] 3275[P] 3884[8] 4589[P]4956[P] 5016[5]

Rosewater Bay *P F Nicholls* 76b
5 b m Alderbrook—Blush (Gildoran)
2056[8] 3468[5]

Rosiella *M Appleby* 59h
4 b f Tagula(IRE) —Queen Of Silk (IRE) (Brief Truce (USA))
3[8]

Rosie Redman (IRE) *J R Turner* 97 h 132+c
9 gr m Roselier(FR) —Carbia's Last (Palm Track)
2656[3] 3851[P] (4790) 5094[F]

Rosina Copper *P Beaumont* 49h
6 ch m Keen—Emilymoore (Primitive Rising (USA))
349[18] 549[7] 3168[11] 3393[P]

Rosita Bay *O Sherwood* 89+h
5 b m Hernando(FR) —Lemon's Mill (USA) (Roberto (USA))
(2075) 2534[10] 3961[3] 4376[10]

Rossall Point *R Allan*
5 b g Fleetwood(IRE) —Loch Clair (IRE) (Lomond (USA))
1113[P]

Rossclare (IRE) *J J Lambe* 86h
6 b g Warcraft(USA) —Ivory Queen (Teenoso (USA))
323[2] 495[4] 942[3] 1360[2]

Ross Comm *Mrs S J Smith* 99h 151+c
10 gr g Minster Son—Yemaail (IRE) (Shaadi (USA))
(865) 975[2] (1157) 1205[4] (1664) (1941) 2491[F] 4488[3] (4611) 4777[F]

Rosses Folly (IRE) *Joseph Crowley* 103h 82c
9 ch m Roselier(FR) —Daddy's Folly (Le Moss)
112a[13]

Rosses Point (IRE) *Evan Williams* 100h 104 c
7 b g Roselier(FR) —Ballon Bombshell (IRE) (Supreme Leader)
1829[P] 1917[P] 2564[8]2863[4] (3285) 3499[2]3732[2] (4805)

Rossin Gold (IRE) *P Monteith* 102+h
4 b g Rossini(USA) —Sacred Heart (IRE) (Catrail (USA))
2001[5] 2494[7] 3203[3] 3349[2]

Rosslare (FR) *R A Fahey* 91b
7 b g Lute Antique(FR) —Baie De Chalamont (FR) (Balsamo (FR))
1687[P] 1885[P]

Rossmore Castle (IRE) *Noel Meade* 95b
6 b g Witness Box(USA) —Latin Quarter (North Summit)
44a[11]

Ross River *A J Martin* 134+h 135+c
10 gr g Over The River(FR) —Solo Rose (Roselier (FR))
91a[P] 2650a[9] 3053a[3]4459[F] 5080a[2]

Rostropovich (IRE) *P F Nicholls* 140h 83c
9 gr g Sadler's Wells(USA) —Infamy (Shirley Heights)
631[P]

Rothbury *J I A Charlton* 88 h
6 b g Overbury(IRE) —The Distaff Spy (Seymour Hicks (FR))
1849[2] 2211[11] 2572[6] 3490[4] 3793[7]4532[8] 5118[5]

Rotheram (USA) *C J Mann* 97h
6 b g Dynaformer(USA) —Out Of Taxes (USA) (Out Of Place (USA))
2212[4] 2809[4] 2958[8]

Roundstone Lady (IRE) *W P Mullins* 104h
6 b m Anshan—Young Preacher (Decent Fellow)
5103a[20]

Round The Bend *Miss Louise Allan* 81c
14 b g Revolutionary(USA) —No Love (Bustiki)
50[F] 278[6]

Round The Horn (IRE) *J A B Old* 116+b
6 ch g Master Willie—Gaye Fame (Ardross)
3392[3] 4779[14]

Rourke Star *S R Bowring* 89b
4 b g Presidium—Mirror Four Sport (Risk Me (FR))
2105[3] 2425[5] 2520[7]

Roussea (IRE) *S G Griffiths* 80h
8 ch g Boyne Valley—River Regent (Over The River (FR))
2826[7] 3017[P] 3885[P] 4278[8]

Rowan Castle *Sir John Barlow Bt* 93h 63c
10 ch g Broadsword(USA) —Brass Castle (IRE) (Carlingford Castle)
548[F] 1826[5] 2820[11] 3316[P]

Rowlands Dream (IRE) *R H Alner* 99 h
6 b m Accordion—Bettyhill (Ardross)
3435[2] 3730[2] 3979[3] (4425) 4972[13]

Rowley Hill *A King* 120 h 112 c
8 b g Karinga Bay—Scarlet Dymond (Rymer)
2464[F] 2660[5] 3148[4]3394[2] 4498[P] 4612[9]4974[17]

Royal Artisan (IRE) *I A Duncan* 87h
8 ch g Insan(USA) —Brown's Cantata (Grange Melody)
212[2] 591[3]

Royal Atalza (FR) *G A Huffer* 112h 138 c
9 gr g Saint Preuil(FR) —Crystalza (FR) (Crystal Palace (FR))
1559[5]

Royal Attraction *W M Brisbourne* 73b
5 b g Mon Tresor—Star Gal (Starch Reduced)
1849[8] 2823[9]

Royal Auclair (FR) *P F Nicholls* 96h 165 c
9 ch g Garde Royale—Carmonera (FR) (Carmont (FR))
2337[5] (2744) 2972[5]3697[2] 4470[9] 4777[F]5004[13] 5144[12]

Royal Cliche *R T Phillips* 96h
7 b g Classic Cliche(IRE) —Princess Hotpot (IRE) (King's Ride)
128[5] 1892[7] 2426[6] 2985[U]

Royal Coburg (IRE) *N A Twiston-Davies* 107h
6 b g Old Vic—Honeyed (IRE) (Persian Mews)
1980[3] 2450[2] 3277[5] 3792[10] 4453[P]

Royal Corrouge (IRE) *N J Henderson* 66b 124c
8 b g Corrouge(USA) —Time In Life (Bishop Of Orange)
(2660)

Royal Czarina *J W Dufosee* 84h 69c
9 ch m Czaravich(USA) —Sabrata (IRE) (Zino)
405[3]

Royaldou (FR) *A L T Moore* 130+h
5 bb g Cadoudal(FR) —Royale Sea (FR) (Garde Royale)
3892a[2]

Royale Acadou (FR) *Mrs L J Mongan* 96 h 97c
8 bb m Cadoudal(FR) —Girl Vamp (FR) (Kaldoun (FR))
1953[U] 2216[7] 2557[4]3285[P] 3662[5] 4355[2]4679[3] 4936[6]

Royale Athenia (FR) *B Barbier* 114h
5 b m Garde Royale—Crystalza (FR) (Crystal Palace (FR))
778a[2] (4717a)

Royale Cazoumaille (FR) *B Barbier* 77h
7 b m Villez(USA) —Atreide (FR) (Son Of Silver)
4717a[5] 5154a[5]

Royaleety (FR) *Ian Williams* 127 h 122c
7 b g Garde Royale—La Grive (FR) (Pharly (FR))
2177[10]

Royal Emperor (IRE) *Mrs S J Smith* 150 h 161 c
10 gr g Roselier(FR) —Boreen Bro (Boreen (FR))
3620[P] 3851[2] (4069) 4470[8]4746[F] 5004[3]

Royal Exposure (IRE) *H Alexander* 73 h
9 b g Emperor Jones(USA) —Blue Garter (Targowice (USA))
180[8] 369[P]

Royal Factor *C Smith* 52b
6 ch g Factual(USA) —Royal Rigger (Reprimand)
4637[12]

Royal Friend *C R Wilson*
7 b g Environment Friend—La Princesse (Le Bavard (FR))
8[F] 426[P]

Royal Glen (IRE) *W S Coltherd* 104+h
8 b m Royal Abjar(USA) —Sea Glen (IRE) (Glenstal (USA))
(120) 320[4] 406[5] (551) 784[5] (940) 1087[P] 1312[6]1530[6] 1604[6] 2478[10] 2904[8] 3171[6]5039[8]

Royal Hector (GER) *Jonjo O'Neill* 138 h 130c
7 b g Hector Protector(USA) —Rudolfina (CAN) (Pleasant Colony (USA))
(2213) 2531[P] 3150[2](3323) 3619[5] 4459[P]

Royal Hilarity (IRE) *Ian Williams* 84+h
6 bb g Zaffaran(USA) —Brown's Cantata (Grange Melody)
1882[9] 2421[10] 3240[13] 4088[4]

Royal Katidoki (FR) *N J Henderson* 111h 85c
6 b g Rochesson(FR) —Miss Coco (FR) (Bay Comeau (FR))
2488[P] 4239[6]

Royal Lustre *M Todhunter*
5 b g Deputy Minister(CAN) —Snow Bride (USA) (Blushing Groom (FR))
1097[P] 1360[P]

Royal Mackintosh *A H Mactaggart*
5 b g Sovereign Water(FR) —Quick Quote (Oats)
5063[12]

Royal Maid (FR) *P R Johnson* 94+h
8 b g Bakharoff(USA) —Swimming Maid (FR) (Esprit Du Nord (USA))
654[9]

Royal Man (FR) *C F Swan* 100 h
5 ch g Garde Royale—Fayolia (FR) (Tip Moss (FR))
1623a[9]

Royal Master *P C Haslam* 93h
4 b g Royal Applause—High Sevens (Master Willie)
1023[2] (1339) 2367[5] 2676[7]

Royal Niece (IRE) *D J Wintle* 90+h
7 b m Rakaposhi King—Sister Stephanie (IRE) (Phardante (FR))
2419[7] 3483[3] 3951[2] 4277[3]

Royal Paradise (FR) *Thomas Foley* 142h
6 b g Cadoudal(FR) —Crystalza (FR) (Crystal Palace (FR))
1621a[6] 2032a[3] 2669a[5] 4446[18] 5101a[11]

Royal Prodigy (USA) *R J Hodges* 93h
7 ch g Royal Academy(USA) —Prospector's Queen (USA) (Mr Prospector (USA))
310[4] 5022[7]

Royal Racer (FR) *J R Best* 88dh
8 b g Danehill(USA) —Green Rosy (USA) (Green Dancer (USA))
1299[U]

Royal Sailor (IRE) *Lucinda Featherstone*
4 b g Bahhare(USA) —Old Tradition (IRE) (Royal Academy (USA))
3328[20]

Royal Scandal *C J Down* 100c
10 b g Royal Fountain—Langton Lass (Nearly A Hand)
4369[2] 4560[P] 4785[P]

Royals Darling (GER) *N J Henderson* 129h
4 ch g Kallisto(GER) —Royal Rivalry (USA) (Sir Ivor (USA))
1428a[4] 3340[2] 3722[2] 4435[15] (5001)

Royal Shakespeare (FR) *S Gollings* 147 h
7 b g King's Theatre(IRE) —Persian Walk (FR) (Persian Bold)
208[P] (2055) 2326[3] 2500[2] 2761[5] 2971[3]3492[4] (3725) 3994[2] 4432[10] 4775[7] 5003[6]

Royal Snoopy (IRE) *R Tate* 109h 114+c
13 bb g Royal Fountain—Lovely Snoopy (IRE) (Phardante (FR))
(374) 512[3] 5020[P]

Royal Spell *M Appleby* 3b
4 b f Wizard King—Manadel (Governor General)
2927[18]

Royal Stardust *G L Moore* 103h
5 b g Cloudings(IRE) —Ivy Edith (Blakeney)
2487[9] 2683[4] 3133[5] 3717[6] 4067[6]4606[F] 4834[2]

Royaltea *J T Stimpson* 79h
5 ch m Desert King(IRE) —Come To Tea (IRE) (Be My Guest (USA))
971[P] 1037[5] 1064[P] 1113[3] 1206[5]1317[6] 1432[5] 1654[7] 1724[F] 1756[13]

Royal Tir (FR) *P J Hobbs* 74h 68c
10 b g Royal Charter(FR) —Tirtaine (FR) (Mad Captain)
842[P] 1013[11] 1157[6]

Royal Upstart *M B Shears* 18h
5 b g Up And At 'Em—Tycoon Tina (Tina's Pet)
861[P] 982[11]

Royal Wedding *N J Gifford* 86h
4 b g King's Best(USA) —Liaison (USA) (Blushing Groom (FR))
1397[6] 1478[3] 1594[7] 1737[2]

Roy McAvoy (IRE) *M A Barnes* 84h
8 b g Danehill(USA) —Decadence (Vaigly Great)
495[F] 549[4] 716[15]

Roymillon (GER) *R J Baker* 87 h 62c
12 b g Milesius(USA) —Royal Slope (USA) (His Majesty (USA))
1901[P]

Roznic (FR) *P Winkworth* 95h 129+c
8 b g Nikos—Rozamie (FR) (Azimut (FR))
2867[F] (3432) (3580) (4120) 4664[3] 4778[F]

Rubberdubber *C R Egerton* 109h 135+c
6 b g Teenoso(USA) —True Clown (True Song)
(3344) 3921[4] (4239) 5082a[F]

Ruby Dante (IRE) *Mrs A M Thorpe* 82b
8 b m Ajraas(USA) —Phar Glen (IRE) (Phardante (FR))
358[P]

Ruby Gale (IRE) *P F Nicholls* 128h 133c
10 b g Lord Americo—Well Over (Over The River (FR))
2051[2]

Ruby Joy *Mrs H O Graham* 70h
4 b f Overbury(IRE) —Safari Park (Absalom)
3259[2] 3799[8] 4304[8] 5124[U]

Rude Health *N J Hawke* 90+h
6 b m Rudimentary(USA) —Birsay (Bustino)
1782[7] 2244[2] (4391) 4860[P] 5113[P]

Rudetski *M Sheppard* 92 h 112+c
9 b g Rudimentary(USA) —Butosky (Busted)
78[7] 275[7] **461[F] 684[3](744) 815[9]** (Dead)

Rudolf Rassendyll (IRE) *Miss Venetia Williams* 103 h 117c
11 b g Supreme Leader—Chantel Rouge (Boreen (FR))
2325[2] 2616[4] 3345[P]**4939[8]**

Rufius (IRE) *P Kelsall* 42c
13 b g Celio Rufo—In View Lass (Tepukei)
1446[8] 1539[11] **1646[6]1832[P] 1960[6]**

Ruggtah *Mrs Antonia Bealby* 83c
5 gr m Daylami(IRE) —Raneen Alwatar (Sadler's Wells (USA))
693[P] **4897[2]**

Rule Supreme (IRE) *W P Mullins* 162h 170c
10 b g Supreme Leader—Book Of Rules (IRE) (Phardante (FR))
68a[2] 585a[3] 779a[2]

Rumbling Bridge *Miss J S Davis* 88h
5 ch g Air Express(IRE) —Rushing River (USA) (Irish River (FR))
5[9] 743[2] 903[8] 1523[P] 1636[P]

Rum Pointer (IRE) *R H Buckler* 89h 96c
10 b g Turtle Island(IRE) —Osmunda (Mill Reef (USA))
4357[4] **4690[9] 5012[6]**

Run Atim *K C Bailey* 107b
8 ch g Hatim(USA) —Run Pet Run (Deep Run)
2878[P] 3249[P]

Runaway Bishop (USA) *J R Cornwall* 94h 104+c
11 bb g Lear Fan(USA) —Valid Linda (USA) (Valid Appeal (USA))
1609[5] 1713[3] (1855) 2009[4] 2243[4] 2502[2]2858[6] 2965[6] 3333[5] **3688[3]4014[4] 4078[6] 4321[4]4636[3] 4851[U] 5136[2]**

Run Dani Run (IRE) *B W Duke* 58h
5 b m Saddlers' Hall(IRE) —Georgic (Tumble Gold)
4881[8] 7[8]

Runfar (IRE) *John Monroe* 79h 103c
10 ch m Phardante(FR) —Cherry Run (Deep Run)
1626a[5]

Run For Paddy *Carl Llewellyn* 122h 147+c
10 b g Michelozzo(USA) —Deep Selection (IRE) (Deep Run)
(1735) 2491[7] 3176[4]3728[8] 4098[2] (5004)

Run Junior (FR) *J P L Ewart* 51h
5 bb g Concorde Jr(USA) —Run For Laborie (FR) (Lesotho (USA))
2497[7]

Run Katie Chimes (IRE) *Paul Nolan* 109h 86c
9 br m African Chimes—Good Run Katie (IRE) (Tony Nobles (USA))
5078a[12]

Run Monty (IRE) *D J Lay* 83c
11 ch g Montelimar(USA) —Bridevalley (Deep Run)
400[3]

Runner Bean *R Lee* 84h 119 c
12 b g Henbit(USA) —Bean Alainn (Candy Cane)
305[P] 534[3] 894[4]1012[4] 1320[5] 1860[4]2300[2] (2562) 2939[6]3459[8] (3815) 4332[4]4755[P]

Running Hotter *N J Hawke* 64b
5 b m Wace(USA) —Running Cool (Record Run)
4667[10]

Running Lord (IRE) *D A Rees* 96+h
8 b g Mister Lord(USA) —Craic Go Leor (Deep Run)
1959[4] 2517[4]

Running Machine (IRE) *L Corcoran* 96 h 108+c
9 b g Classic Memory—Foxborough Lady (Crash Course)
3910[9]

Running Moss *A H Mactaggart* 113c
14 ch g Le Moss—Run'n Fly (Deep Run)
4316[P]

Running Times (USA) *H J Manners* 81 h
9 b g Brocco(USA) —Concert Peace (USA) (Hold Your Peace (USA))
233[9] 536[8]

Runningwiththemoon *M S Burman* 58h 72+c
10 b g Homo Sapien—Ardeal (Ardross)
400[5]

Runshan (IRE) *D G Bridgwater* 82h 88c
6 ch g Anshan—Whitebarn Run (Pollerton)
1608[P] 1959[6] 2421[9] **2936[8]**

Run To Me *Miss Gay Kelleway* 7b
4 b f Commanche Run—Uninvited (Be My Guest (USA))
2830[16]

Run To The King (IRE) *P C Ritchens* 81c
8 b g Woods Of Windsor(USA) —Miss Firion (Tanfirion)
3249[P] **3601[5] 3660[F]4016[6] 4553[P] 4653[P]4937[P] 5047[9]**

Rush'N'Run *Mrs S J Smith* 65h
7 b g Kasakov—Runfawit Pet (Welsh Saint)
133[10] 209[4] 521[7] 895[F]

Russe D'Ouilly (FR) *Ron Caget*
3 b g Man O West(FR) —Roulette Russe (IRE) (Bluebird (USA))
4298a[P]

Russian Around (IRE) *N J Gifford* 104+h
5 ch g Moscow Society(USA) —Irish Pride (IRE) (Mister Lord (USA))
(1857)

Russian Court *S E H Sherwood* 106h 60c
10 b g Soviet Lad(USA) —Court Town (Camden Town)
1153[11] (Dead)

Russian Gigolo (IRE) *N A Twiston-Davies* 120+c
9 b g Toulon—Nanogan (Tarqogan)
1670[P] 2143[2]

Russian Lord (IRE) *V R A Dartnall* 58h 99+c
7 br g Topanoora—Russian Gale (IRE) (Strong Gale)
1969[6] **4753[5] (5088)**

Russian Sky *Mrs H O Graham* 118 h 118+c
7 gr g Endoli(USA) —Anzarna (Zambrano)
1513[3] 1606[3] 1887[2] 2038[2] 2417[2](2990) 3987[P] **4528[4] 4841[2]**

Rustarix (FR) *A King* 99h
5 b g Housamix(FR) —Star Of Russia (FR) (Soviet Star (USA))
2462[2]

Rust En Vrede *D Carroll* 80h
7 b g Royal Applause—Souveniers (Relko)
1490[10] 1553[5]

Rustler *N J Henderson*
4 b g Green Desert(USA) —Borgia (Machiavellian (USA))
4117[P]

Ruthie's Star (IRE) *V Bowens* 57h
6 ch m Eurobus—Curragh Queen (IRE) (Lord Americo)
93a[23]

Rutland (IRE) *C J Drewe* 73h 61 c
7 b g Supreme Leader—I Remember It Well (IRE) (Don't Forget Me)
54[4] **296[5] 518[P]**2214[P] 2605[P] **2867[5] 3274[P]3432[P] 4525[P] 4692[5]5088[P]**

Ryders Hill *M Weir*
7 b m Zaffaran(USA) —Deirfiur (IRE) (Buckley)
299[P]

Ryders Storm (USA) *T R George* 113 h 124c
7 bb g Dynaformer(USA) —Justicara (Rusticaro (FR))
2976[2] 4239[3] 4605[5](4802) (5065)

Rydon Lane (IRE) *Mrs S D Williams* 100+h
10 br g Toca Madera—Polocracy (IRE) (Aristocracy)
387[P]

Ryhall (IRE) *T D Easterby* 97h
6 b m Saddlers' Hall(IRE) —Loshian (IRE) (Montelimar (USA))
(8) 194[4] 426[3]

Ryminster *J Wade* 66h 89+c
7 ch g Minster Son—Shultan (IRE) (Rymer)
1309[F]

Saafend Rocket (IRE) *H D Daly* 112h 121+c
8 b g Distinctly North(USA) —Simple Annie (Simply Great (FR))
(2) 174[2] 510[3]761[U] 840[3] 2664[6]2939[4] 3357[8] 3459[4]3803[4] 4592[2] 5018[6]

Sabreflight *J Howard Johnson* 105+h
6 ch m Sabrehill(USA) —Little Redwing (Be My Chief (USA))
2112[2] 2414[2] (3254) (3551) 4619[P]

Sabreur *Ian Williams* 103+h
5 b g Thowra(FR) —Sleepline Princess (Royal Palace)
249[3] 1968[4] 2821[4] 3210[5] 3944[P]4243[5] 4736[2]

Saby (FR) *P J Hobbs* 86 h 119 c
8 bb g Sassanian(USA) —Valy Flett (FR) (Pietru (FR))
246[6] 752[4] 958[3]1236[4] 1381[7] **1524[7]**

Sachsenwalzer (GER) *C Grant* 107+h 107c
8 ch g Top Waltz(FR) —Stairway To Heaven (GER) (Nebos (GER))
99[5] 947[5] 1179[6] **(1318) 1487[P]**

Sacrifice *K Bishop* 101c
11 b g Arctic Lord—Kellyann (Jellaby)
(1236) 1398[8] 2051[U]2151[8]

Saddleback Prince *B Storey*
7 b g Northern Legend—Tully's Rosemarie (Slim Jim)
147[F] 212[P]

Saddleeruppat (IRE) *Ms Joanna Morgan* 124+b
5 bb m Saddlers' Hall(IRE) —Cailin Supreme (IRE) (Supreme Leader)
2782a[7] 5081a[13]

Saddlers Boy *R Johnson* 75b
8 b g Saddlers' Hall(IRE) —Miss Poll Flinders (Swing Easy (USA))
1491[P] 1661[P]

Saddlers Cloth (IRE) *J A Geake* 68h 97+c
6 b m Saddlers' Hall(IRE) —Strong Cloth (IRE) (Strong Gale)
2021[4] 2829[3] **3218[P] 4474[F](4913) 5127[P]**

Saddlers Express *M F Harris* 78h
5 b m Saddlers' Hall(IRE) —Swift Conveyance (IRE) (Strong Gale)
1974[8] 2821[12] 4988[F]

Saddlers' Harmony (IRE) *K G Reveley* 79b
5 b g Saddlers' Hall(IRE) —Sweet Mignonette (Tina's Pet)
876[5] 4422[13]

Saddlers Lady (IRE) *R Curtis* 70+b
6 b m Saddlers' Hall(IRE) —Mirador (Town And Country)
316[5]

Saddlers' Mark *D M Christie* 109h 107c
11 b g Saddlers' Hall(IRE) —Bambolona (Bustino)
45a[10] 416[P]

Saddler's Quest *B P J Baugh* 82h 87+c
9 b g Saddlers' Hall(IRE) —Seren Quest (Rainbow Quest (USA))
1[7] **486[4] 632[U]902[7] 1203[2] 1318[4]**

Saddlers' Son (IRE) *Mrs H Dalton* 76h
5 b g Saddlers' Hall(IRE) —Polleroo (IRE) (Pollerton)
4455[10] 4732[6] 5118[6]

Sadler's Pride (IRE) *A J Deakin* 103h
6 b g Sadler's Wells(USA) —Gentle Thoughts (Darshaan)
1715[P]

Sadlers Wings (IRE) *W P Mullins* 156h
8 b g In The Wings—Anna Comnena (IRE) (Shareef Dancer (USA))
3641a[4]

Safari Adventures (IRE) *P Winkworth* 99+b
4 b g King's Theatre(IRE) —Persian Walk (FR) (Persian Bold)
(3188) 3911[11]

Safeguard (IRE) *S J Gilmore*
5 ch g Zaffaran(USA) —Some Pidgeon (IRE) (Strong Gale)
4237[9]

Safe Route (USA) *W J Austin* 124h 124c
8 br m Farma Way(USA) —Taiki Victoria (IRE) (Caerleon (USA))
2364a[5]

Safe Shot *Mrs J C McGregor* 67h
7 b g Salse(USA) —Optaria (Song)
1307[P] 1508[P] 2040[P]

Safe To Blush *P A Pritchard* 84h
8 gr m Blushing Flame(USA) —Safe Arrival (USA) (Shadeed (USA))
359[3] 611[4] 763[6] 2181[P] 3147[7]3367[P] 4277[5]

Saffron Sun *J D Frost* 106h 121c
11 b g Landyap(USA) —Saffron Bun (Sit In The Corner (USA))
653[8] (1639) (1972) 2299[5] 2847[7] (4829)

Sagardian (FR) *L Lungo* 67h 71c
7 b g Mister Mat(FR) —Tipnik (FR) (Nikos)
81[F] 417[4]

Saif Sareea *R A Fahey* 124+h
6 b g Atraf—Slipperose (Persepolis (FR))
903[6] 973[U] (2478) (2904) 3761[2] 3929[2] 4050[2]4478[2] 4773[8]

Sailor A'Hoy *M Mullineaux* 96h 94 c
10 b g Handsome Sailor—Eye Sight (Roscoe Blake)
10[4] 371[2] 2284[4]2522[U] 2936[9] (4666) 4804[6] 5140[P]

Saint Par (FR) *Tim Vaughan* 118h 112c
8 gr g Saint Preuil(FR) —Paris Or (FR) (Noir Et Or)
633[P] 689[P] 2621[9]

Saintsaire (FR) *N J Henderson* 144h 143+c
7 b g Apeldoorn(FR) —Pro Wonder (FR) (The Wonder (FR))
2[2] (2870) 3503[4]4459[F] 4973[4]

Saint Shabby (FR) *P Chemin*
10 ch g Epervier Bleu—Shabby (FR) (Carmarthen (FR))
1372a[P]

Sakenos (POL) *P J Hobbs* 106h
6 b g In Camera(IRE) —Sakaria (POL) (Rutilio Rufo (USA))
3324[5] 3948[2] 4280[4]

Sales Flow *M W Easterby* 50h
4 ch f Double Trigger(IRE) —New Dawn (Rakaposhi King)
3785[9] 3931[7] 4388[U] 4506[8] 4609[P]

Salford *Miss Chloe Newman* 75+h 96c
11 ch g Salse(USA) —Bustellina (Busted)
47[8]

Salhood *S Gollings* 101 h 99c
7 b g Capote(USA) —Princess Haifa (USA) (Mr Prospector (USA))
2334[6] 2716[6] 2964[10] **4355[5]4502[3] 5139[P]**

Salim *Miss J S Davis* 74+h 82+c
9 b g Salse(USA) —Moviegoer (Pharly (FR))
1653[9] **2561[P]**

Salinas (GER) *M F Harris* 97h 96+c
7 b g Macanal(USA) —Santa Ana (GER) (Acatenango (GER))
177[10] **(990)**

Salinger (USA) *Andrew Turnell* 42h
4 b g Lear Fan(USA) —Sharp Flick (USA) (Sharpen Up)
2661[P] 2921[14]

Salix Bay *P Butler* 63h 56c
10 b g Karinga Bay—Willow Gale (Strong Gale)
229[4]

Salliemak *A J Wilson* 75h
8 b m Makbul—Glenbrook Fort (Fort Nayef)
3652[P] 4277[P]

Sally's Dream (IRE) *Michael Hourigan* 89h
4 b f Key Of Luck(USA) —Winning Sally (IRE) (Lancastrian)
5060a[3]

Salopian *H D Daly* 93h
6 b g Rakaposhi King—Dalbeattie (Phardante (FR))
2455[8] 2723[4] 3358[4] 3733[8] 5069[3]

Saltango (GER) *A M Hales* 130+h
7 b g Acatenango(GER) —Salde (GER) (Alkalde (GER))
1782[3] (1975) 2020[2] 2292[6] 2530[3] 3179[7]3508[2] (4005) (4678) 4765[2]

Salt Cellar (IRE) *R S Brookhouse* 100h
7 b g Salse(USA) —Athene (IRE) (Rousillon (USA))
136[17] **1917[F]** 3371[7] 4834[12]5014[7]

Saltrio *A King* 95h
8 b g Slip Anchor—Hills' Presidium (Presidium)
3908[6] 4604[P] 4819[9]

Salute (IRE) *P G Murphy* 118h
7 b g Muhtarram(USA) —Alasib (Siberian Express (USA))
136[2] 332[2] 1444[6] 1598[6] 4357[P]

Salut Saint Cloud *G L Moore* 127 h
5 b g Primo Dominie—Tiriana (Common Grounds)
1828[10] 2207[11] 2871[5] 3135[8] 3993[P]4773[10] 5142[2]

Salvage *Mrs J C McGregor* 100h 100c
11 b g Kahyasi—Storm Weaver (USA) (Storm Bird (CAN))
874[P]

Sam Adamson *J W Mullins* 63h 103c
11 br g Domitor(USA) —Sardine (Saritamer (USA))
2074[8] 2594[F]

Samandara (FR) *A King* 99h
6 b m Kris—Samneeza (USA) (Storm Bird (CAN))
77[3] 274[4] 487[F] 693[3] 1862[13]2726[4] 3461[2] 3950[8] 4593[P]

Samara Sound *A G Newcombe*
5 b h Savahra Sound—Hosting (Thatching)
668[P]

Samby *O Sherwood* 120+h
8 ch g Anshan—Mossy Fern (Le Moss)
2764[7]

Sammagefromtenesse (IRE) *A E Jones* 82h 77c
9 b g Petardia—Canoora (Ahonoora)
1897[P]

Samsaam (IRE) *M C Pipe* 133 h
9 b g Sadler's Wells(USA) —Azyaa (Kris)
1548[P]

Sams Lad (IRE) *S Donohoe* 55h
5 b g Saddlers' Hall(IRE) —Cellatica (USA) (Sir Ivor (USA))
3785[2]

Samson Des Galas (FR) *Robert Gray* 69h
8 bb g Agent Bleu(FR) —Sarema (FR) (Primo Dominie)
763[P] 1047[P] 1357[3] 1883[3] 2025[2]2290[2] 2586[6] 2962[P] 3335[P] 3916[8]

Sams Way *Mrs S M Barker* 87c
9 b g Nomadic Way(USA) —Samonia (Rolfe (USA))
196[3]

Samuel Wilderspin *R Lee* 95c
14 b g Henbit(USA) —Littoral (Crash Course)
49[5]

San Angelo (IRE) *Patrick Mooney* 89h 109+c
9 b g Supreme Leader—Shaping (Deep Run)
1702a[P]

Sandabar *Miss Tracy Waggott* 84+h
13 b g Green Desert(USA) —Children's Corner (FR) (Top Ville)
784[P] 1148[U] 1375[6]

Sandhills Boy *E Stanners*
11 b g Meadowbrook—Stagshaw Belle (Royal Fountain)
555[P]

Sandmartin (IRE) *P J Hobbs* 98+h
6 b g Alflora(IRE) —Quarry Machine (Laurence O)
1671[5] 2142[9] 2309[10] (3211) 3325[P] 4557[P]

Sands Point (FR) *M Scudamore*
4 b g Trempolino(USA) —Mayreau (Slip Anchor)
4416[F] (Dead)

Sands Rising *R Johnson* 98 h 109 c
9 b g Primitive Rising(USA) —Celtic Sands (Celtic Cone)
1887[6] **2111[3] 2679[2]3379[F] 3784[5] 4109[3]4586[5] 4798[3]**

Sandy Bay (IRE) *W G Harrison* 72 h
7 b g Spectrum(IRE) —Karinski (USA) (Palace Music (USA))
306[12] 1605[6] 2657[17] **2902[F]**

Sandy Gold (IRE) *Miss J E Foster* 94c
8 ch g Carroll House—Autumn Vixen (IRE) (Trigon)
1662[P] 1758[4] 3558[3]4796[3] 5136[P]

Sandy Owen (IRE) *P A Fahy* 106h 129c
10 b g Insan(USA) —Daisy Owen (Master Owen)
71a[3] (Dead)

Sandysnowing (FR) *J Howard Johnson* 65h
4 b g Sendawar(IRE) —Snow White (Polar Falcon (USA))
2521[5] 2753[8] 4057[P] (Dead)

Sandywell George *L P Grassick* 88h 69c
11 ch g Zambrano—Farmcote Air (True Song)
357[5] 614[7] 697[3] 1152[10] 1456[6]1539[13] **1656[4]** 3577[11] **5017[6]**

San Francisco *Miss Freya Hartley* 95c
12 b g Aragon—Sirene Bleu Marine (USA) (Secreto (USA))
196[5]

Sangiovese *H Morrison* 106h
7 b g Piccolo—Kaprisky (IRE) (Red Sunset)
2249[3] 2573[14]

San Hernando *Miss E C Lavelle* 102h
6 b g Hernando(FR) —Sandrella (IRE) (Darshaan)
4604[6] 4824[2]

San Peire (FR) *J Howard Johnson* 110+h 115+c
9 b g Cyborg(FR) —Shakapoura (FR) (Shakapour)
2110[2] 2691[2] 2977[9] (3554) 4043[3] 4658[5]

Santarco (FR) *P Demercastel*
4 b c Antarctique(IRE) —Swissara (FR) (Akarad (FR))
2085a[9]

Santa Sheva *K F Clutterbuck*
5 ch g Rainbow Quest(USA) —Kundalini (USA) (El Gran Senor (USA))
3138[10]

Santa's Son (IRE) *J F O'Shea* 122+h
6 ch g Basanta(IRE) —Rivers Town Rosie (IRE) (Roselier (FR))
92a[13] 5103a[2]

Saorsie *J C Fox* 100 h 86c
8 b g Emperor Jones(USA) —Exclusive Lottery (Presidium)
136[10] 265[U] 357[8] 536[5] 806[2] 915[10] 1121[4] 1223[8] 1381[2] 1717[9] 1856[9] **1956[5] 2217[5] 2420[6]**

Sapient *M Scudamore* 86h 64c
5 b g Karinga Bay—Twenty Winks (Gunner B)
3369[9] 3423[6] 3996[13] 4427[9]

Saposcat (IRE) *Dr P Pritchard* 45h
6 b g Groom Dancer(USA) —Dance Of Joy (Shareef Dancer (USA))
743[8] 802[5] 863[13] **944[3] 1275[P] 1411[7]**

Saraba (FR) *Mrs L J Mongan* 99h
5 gr m Soviet Star(USA) —Sarliya (IRE) (Doyoun)
2573[6] 2804[3] 3280[2] (4450)

Saragann (IRE) *N B King* 77+h 77c
11 b g Danehill(USA) —Sarliya (IRE) (Doyoun)
135[P] 346[P] 891[4] 1180[6] **1343[8]**

Sarah's Party *G D Hanmer*
10 b g Supreme Leader—Maries Party (The Parson)
98[P] 5013[P]

Sarahs Quay (IRE) *K J Burke* 91+h 114+c
7 b m Witness Box(USA) —Artistic Quay (IRE) (Quayside)
998[4] 1269[3] 1455[3] 2553[U] 2859[9] **3438[P] 3601[6] (4041) 4152[F]** 4386[3] **(4495)** 5000a[8]

Sara Monica (IRE) *L Lungo* 108 h
9 ch m Moscow Society(USA) —Swift Trip (IRE) (Duky)
2264[8] 2691[6] 2944[10]

Sarasota (IRE) *P Bowen* 91+h
11 b g Lord Americo—Ceoltoir Dubh (Black Minstrel)
206[P]

Saratogane (FR) *M C Pipe* 105+b
4 b f Saratoga Springs(CAN) —Asturias (FR) (Pistolet Bleu (IRE))
(2013) 2425[2] 4376[6] 4751[P]

Sardagna (FR) *M C Pipe* 117h 133+c
6 gr m Medaaly—Sarda (FR) (Funambule (USA))
217[6] 646[U] (1012) 1264[2] 1435[5] 1658[6] **1986[4] 2532[4]** 3295[5] 3648[F]

Sarena Special *J D Frost* 81+h
9 b g Lucky Guest—Lariston Gale (Pas De Seul)
75[2] (396)

Sargasso Sea *J A B Old* 116 h 114 c
9 gr g Greensmith—Sea Spice (Precipice Wood)
172[4] 2632[8] **3239[2] (4352) 4572[P]**

Sargon *Robert Gray* 109h 108c
7 b g Oscar(IRE) —Syrian Queen (Slip Anchor)
1894[5] 2519[7] **3272[4] 3489[7]**

Sarin *Miss Venetia Williams* 89h
8 b g Deploy—Secretilla (USA) (Secreto (USA))
192[5] 643[3] 3658[7] 3950[6]

Sarn *M Mullineaux* 80h
7 b g Atraf—Covent Garden Girl (Sizzling Melody)
1565[5] 1671[7] 1793[11] 1856[13] 2283[8]

Sarobar (IRE) *M Scudamore* 89h 77c
6 gr g Sesaro(USA) —Khairka (IRE) (Tirol)
3782[3] **3888[8]** 4080[10] **4911[4] 5136[7]**

Saros (IRE) *W Amos*
5 bb g Desert Sun—Fight Right (FR) (Crystal Glitters (USA))
3912[P]

Sasso *Jonjo O'Neill* 106+h
4 b g Efisio—Sioux (Kris)
(2236) 2587[3] 3467[8] 4573[P]

Sasso Lungo (FR) *Mme C De La Soudiere-Niault*
4 b c Limnos(JPN) —Executive (FR) (Don Roberto (USA))
1428a[6]

Sastar (FR) *B Barbier* 94h
4 gr g Mendocino(USA) —Swing Star (FR) (Balsamo (FR))
2085a[8]

Satchmo (IRE) *Mrs D M Grissell* 109c
14 b g Satco(FR) —Taradale (Torus)
(405) 4748[F]

Satco Express (IRE) *E Sheehy* 139h 134c
10 b g Satco(FR) —Rosel Chris (Roselier (FR))
1420a[F] (Dead)

Satin Rose *K J Burke* 74h
4 b f Lujain(USA) —Shamwari (USA) (Shahrastani (USA))
2345[6] 2569[4] 2797[F] 3217[P]

Satin Turk (FR) *G Chaignon*
10 b g Baby Turk—Satin Town (FR) (Satingo)
362a[2]

Sativa Bay *J W Mullins* 100+h
7 ch g Karinga Bay—Busy Mittens (Nearly A Hand)
2606[11] 2829[P]

Saucy King *M W Easterby* 91h
6 b g Amfortas(IRE) —So Saucy (Teenoso (USA))
(1663)

Saucy Night *Simon Earle* 83+h 111+c
10 ch g Anshan—Kiss In The Dark (Starry Night (USA))
1648[2] (1949) 2140[4] 2687[P]

Saucynorwich (IRE) *J G Portman* 97h 57c
8 b g Norwich—Kelly Gales (IRE) (Strong Gale)
244[4] 398[P] 673[12]

Saunders Road (IRE) *P J Hobbs*
5 b g King's Theatre(IRE) —Shaunies Lady (IRE) (Don't Forget Me)
2665[P]

Sauterelle (IRE) *Thomas Mullins* 102h
6 br m Key Of Luck(USA) —Haysong (IRE) (Ballad Rock)
1623a[5] 2031a[5] 2916a[4] 5077a[U]

Savannah Bay *P J Hobbs* 117h 118 c
7 ch g In The Wings—High Savannah (Rousillon (USA))
611[3] **(1365) 1634[3]**

Savannah River (IRE) *Miss Kate Milligan* 73h
5 b m Desert King(IRE) —Hayward (Indian Ridge)
2693[9] 3446[5] 4656[6]

Savati (FR) *R T J Wilson* 81b 120c
6 b g Subotica(FR) —Tipsa (FR) (Tip Moss (FR))
4471[5] 5083a[P]

Saw Doctor (IRE) *J K Magee* 53h
6 b g Dr Massini(IRE) —Rosy Waters (Roselier (FR))
3534[10] 3780[8]

Sawpit Sunset *J L Spearing* 92b
5 br m Classic Cliche(IRE) —Moonlight Air (Bold Owl)
4595[5]

Saxe-Coburg (IRE) *K G Wingrove* 70h
9 b g Warning—Saxon Maid (Sadler's Wells (USA))
1[9] 458[5] 573[8] 652[9] 724[7] 978[8]

Saxon Kingdom *M Bradstock*
7 b g Petoski—Saxon Magic (Faustus (USA))
531[5] 804[P]

Saxon Leader (IRE) *T P Tate* 83b
4 b g Supreme Leader—Bronica (IRE) (Waajib)
3292[3]

Saxon Mill *T J Fitzgerald* 57h 77c
11 ch g Saxon Farm—Djellaba (Decoy Boy)
2967[6] **3555[4] 3798[7]** 4080[P]

Saxon Mist *P Bowen* 82+h
7 b g Slip Anchor—Ruby Venture (Ballad Rock)
843[P] 1047[5] 1206[6]

Saxon Victory (USA) *John A Harris*
11 b g Nicholas(USA) —Saxon Shore (USA) (Halo (USA))
278[P] 508[P]

Sayoun (IRE) *Mrs L B Normile* 54h
7 gr g Primo Dominie—Sarafia (Dalsaan)
120[P]

Say What You See (IRE) *M C Pipe* 126h
6 b h Charnwood Forest(IRE) —Aster Aweke (IRE) (Alzao (USA))
1093a[9] 1394a[P]

Scalini'S (IRE) *Jonjo O'Neill* 77 h
6 ch g Peintre Celebre(USA) —Sistadari (Shardari)
1681[3] 2528[U] 2799[8] 3595[5] 3717[9]

Scalloway (IRE) *D J Wintle* 115+h 123+c
6 b g Marju(IRE) —Zany (Junius (USA))
726[11] **1019[3] 1147[3] (1264) 1382[3]** 1633[5]

Scamp *R Shiels* 72h
7 b m Selkirk(USA) —Cut And Run (Slip Anchor)
120[11] 214[2] 496[7] 592[9] 781[9] 875[3] 941[P] 4530[P] 4656[7]

Scania Classic *R Lee*
5 gr g Thethingaboutitis(USA) —Gifted Gale (Aird Point)
4569[14] 4786[F]

Scaramouche *B De Haan* 89 h
6 b h Busy Flight—Laura Lye (IRE) (Carlingford Castle)
2554[5] 2983[7] 3291[4]

Scarecrow (IRE) *Mrs P Sly* 80b
5 b g Presenting—Rossacrowe Gale (IRE) (Strong Gale)
4637[6] 5054[9]

Scarface *J L Spearing* 84h
9 ch g Hernando(FR) —Scarlatine (IRE) (Alzao (USA))
506[13] 4133[3] 4449[3] 4734[3]

Scarlet Cloak (USA) *Mrs L B Normile* 87h
5 b g Red Ransom(USA) —Secret Seeker (USA) (Mr Prospector (USA))
2340[12] 3237[3] 4147[3] 4342[F] 5118[7]

Scarlet Dawn (IRE) *D A Rees* 90h
8 b m Supreme Leader—Dawn Appeal (Deep Run)
1220[8] 1317[4] 1892[2]

Scarlet Fantasy *P A Pritchard* 109+h 87c
6 b g Rudimentary(USA) —Katie Scarlett (Lochnager)
54[P] 2505[5] 2706[5] **2982[4] 3732[P] 4580[4] 4804[P] 5049[P]**

Scarlet Memory *G A Harker* 34h
7 b m Dancing High—Scarlet Ember (Nearly A Hand)
209[7]

Scarlet Mix (FR) *B G Powell* 97+h 36c
5 gr g Linamix(FR) —Scarlet Raider (USA) (Red Ransom (USA))
1784[P] 2216[4] 2930[3] **3482[6]**

Scarlet Romance *M W Easterby* 24b
4 ch f Pursuit Of Love—Scarlet Livery (Saddlers' Hall (IRE))
2105[11] 4059[13]

Scarrabus (IRE) *A Crook* 85h 91 c
5 b g Charnwood Forest(IRE) —Errazuriz (IRE) (Classic Music (USA))
843[6] 1037[7] 1182[6] 1364[8] 1482[6] **(1521) 3172[F] 3489[8]** 3757[13] 4302[4] 5120[8]

Scarthy Lad (IRE) *Thomas Gerard O'Leary* 151h 139 c
8 ch g Magical Wonder(USA) —Grangeclare Rose (IRE) (Gianchi)
115a[8]

Scarvagh Diamond (IRE) *Mrs R L Elliot* 96b
5 b m Zaffaran(USA) —Bucks Slave (Buckskin (FR))
(3448) 4376[5] 4751[13]

Scary Night (IRE) *M J Gingell* 30h
6 b g Night Shift(USA) —Private Bucks (USA) (Spend A Buck (USA))
369[13] 467[8] 729[P]

Scenic Storm (IRE) *Miss Lucinda Broad* 91c
11 b g Scenic—Sit Elnaas (USA) (Sir Ivor (USA))
123[3] 4305[8] 5040[2]

Schapiro (USA) *Jonjo O'Neill* 122+h
5 b g Nureyev(USA) —Konvincha (USA) (Cormorant (USA))
247[7] (864)

Schemer Fagan (IRE) *P Henderson* 83b
6 ch g Nucleon(USA) —Less Hassle (IRE) (Strong Gale)
4947[2]

Schindlers Hunt (IRE) *D T Hughes* 122h
6 ch g Oscar Schindler(IRE) —Snipe Hunt (IRE) (Stalker)
44a[7] 3892a[3]

Schindler's List *C Roberts* 53h
6 b g Oscar Schindler(IRE) —Prepare (IRE) (Millfontaine)
463[9] 655[7] 3024[6] 3617[5] 4691[8] 4786[5] 5009[6]

Schinken Otto (IRE) *J M Jefferson* 82h
5 ch h Shinko Forest(IRE) —Athassel Rose (IRE) (Reasonable (FR))
596[6] 716[4] 2750[16] 2858[P]

School Class *M Scudamore* 46h
6 b m Classic Cliche(IRE) —School Run (Deep Run)
2937[8] 3461[P]

Schoolhouse Walk *M E Sowersby* 83+h 88+c
8 b g Mistertopogigo(IRE) —Restandbejoyful (Takachiho)
4921[P] 5140[3]

Schooner (GER) *Lady Herries* 90h
6 b g Slip Anchor—Sweet Enough (Caerleon (USA))
2584[3]

Schuh Shine (IRE) *Miss Venetia Williams* 98h 138 c
9 gr g Roselier(FR) —Naar Chamali (Salmon Leap (USA))
(2048) 2628[4] (3293) 3739[6] 4118[P]

Schumann *M Pitman* 90h
5 b g Rainbow Quest(USA) —Dance Sequence (USA) (Mr Prospector (USA))
1613[3] *(1922)* 2617[P] 2967[4] 3806[5] 4128[7]

Scippit *Miss Tracy Waggott* 90h
7 ch g Unfuwain(USA) —Scierpan (USA) (Sharpen Up)
1278[3] 1432[14] 1553[P] 1756[7]

Scolboa Arctic (IRE) *Mrs S J Smith* 16h
6 b m Dr Massini(IRE) —Arctic Vista (Deep Run)
769[9] 861[P]

Sconced (USA) *R C Guest* 83+h 85+c
11 ch g Affirmed(USA) —Quaff (USA) (Raise A Cup (USA))
96[5] 167[4] 365[4] 603[4] 2416[4] **2951[3] 2966[4]** 3271[6] **(3593) 3928[P] 4921[3] 4989[7] 5122[6]**

Scorpio Sally (IRE) *M D Hammond*
4 b f Mujadil(USA) —Clear Procedure (USA) (The Minstrel (CAN))
1332[9]

Scotch Corner (IRE) *N A Twiston-Davies* 106h 106 c
8 b g Jurado(USA) —Quennie Mo Ghra (IRE) (Mandalus)
516[P] 1874[6] 2170[8] 2488[P] (2722) 3372[5] 3919[7] 4281[10] 4837[7] 5105[P]

Scotmail (IRE) *J Howard Johnson* 120+h
5 b g Old Vic—Snipe Singer (Tyrnavos)
1885[4] (2262) (2690) 4529[3] 5093[3]

Scotmail Boy (IRE) *S Garrott*
13 b g Over The River(FR) —Princess Paula (Smoggy)
4092[U]

Scotmail Lad (IRE) *C A Mulhall* 65h 98c
12 b g Ilium—Nicholas Ferry (Floriferous)
47[7] 437[P] 2688[6] **3447[4] 4659[4]**

Scotmail Too (IRE) *J Howard Johnson* 101h
5 b g Saddlers' Hall(IRE) —Kam Slave (Kambalda)
2262[5] 2690[5] 2979[5] 3943[P] (5120)

Scots Brook Terror *Mrs N S Evans* 29b
4 b f Terimon—Angie Marinie (Sabrehill (USA))
1785[8] 2830[14]

Scots Grey *N J Henderson* 131h 148c
11 gr g Terimon—Misowni (Niniski (USA))
422[8] **(2272) 2760[9] 3620[P] 4447[P] 4762[11] 5094[3]**

Scotts Court *N Tinkler* 98b
6 b g Case Law—Pennine Star (IRE) (Pennine Walk)
(355) 470[2] 2571[P]

Scout Leader *C Grant* 54h
7 b g Supreme Leader—Celtic Cygnet (Celtic Cone)
2268[8] 2571[11]

Scratch The Dove *A E Price* 100h 89c
9 b m Henbit(USA) —Coney Dove (Celtic Cone)
2553[4] 3278[3] 3460[7] 4041[4] 4328[5] 4580[3] 4804[4]

Screenplay *Miss Sheena West* 121 h
5 ch g In The Wings—Erudite (Generous (IRE))
729[3] 911[2] 1364[2] (1407) (1481) 1598[2] 1743[5] 2207[8] (2530) 4215[8] 4469[14] 4821[8]

Screen Test *B G Powell* 95h
4 b f Danzero(AUS) —Audition (Machiavellian (USA))
3579[2] 3902[9] 4855[3] (5084)

Scribano Eile (IRE) *N A Twiston-Davies* 116+b
5 b g Scribano—Ean Eile (IRE) (Callernish)
(4507)

Sculptor *K R Pearce* 96h
7 b g Salse(USA) —Classic Colleen (IRE) (Sadler's Wells (USA))
515[F] 1152[P]

Sea Cadet *T D Easterby* 25h
4 gr g Slip Anchor—Stormy Gal (IRE) (Strong Gale)
3623[5] 4422[9] 5042[3]

Sea Drifting *Miss M E Rowland* 101h 74c
9 b g Slip Anchor—Theme (IRE) (Sadler's Wells (USA))
2616[6] 3350[6] 3547[12]

Sea Eagle (IRE) *H D Daly* 75b
4 b g Sea Raven(IRE) —Roseocean (IRE) (Roselier (FR))
4333[9]

Sea Ferry (IRE) *Mrs Antonia Bealby* 116h 102+c
10 b g Ilium—Nicholas Ferry (Floriferous)
83[P] 4351[2] (4799) (4901)

Seafire Lad (IRE) *R Johnson* 83h
5 b g Portrait Gallery(IRE) —Act The Fool (IRE) (Always Fair (USA))
210[11] (1107) 1293[5] 1588[2]

Seagull Eile (IRE) *K F O'Brien* 114?h
7 b m Oscar(IRE) —Precious Juno (IRE) (Good Thyne (USA))
5077a[7]

Sea Haven *P Beaumont*
7 b m Sea Raven(IRE) —Another Delight (Politico (USA))
81[5]

Sea Knight (IRE) *Ms J M Findlay* 78+h
9 b g Beau Sher—Meaney (Delamain (USA))
123[P] 4044[P]

Sea Laughter (IRE) *J N R Billinge* 83 h
8 gr m Presenting—Bruna Rosa (Roselier (FR))
606[4]

Sealed Orders *Mrs S Lamyman* 71h
9 ch m Bustino—Royal Seal (Privy Seal)
1611[6]

Seal Harbour (FR) *A King*
6 b g Vertical Speed(FR) —Maraxalou (FR) (Lou Piguet (FR))
4237[5] 4623[12] 4905[P]

Seal Of Office *A M Hales* 66h
7 ch g Mark Of Esteem(IRE) —Minskip (USA) (The Minstrel (CAN))
133[5] 456[P]

Sea Maize *C R Wilson* 71h
8 b m Sea Raven(IRE) —Dragons Daughter (Mandrake Major)
211[P] 417[6] 545[9] 2290[5] **2495[P] 3338[P] 4921[P]**

Sea Map *D E Cantillon* 96h
4 ch g Fraam—Shehana (USA) (The Minstrel (CAN))
2824[4] 2954[2]

Sean (IRE) *Mrs L C Jewell* 79h
7 b g Arctic Lord—Sextons Road (IRE) (Commanche Run)
230[8] 504[6] 895[P] 1040[P] 1246[9]

Seaniethesmuggler (IRE) *S Gollings* 98+h 109c
8 b g Balla Cove—Sharp Shauna (Sayyaf)
10[P] (371) 827[2] 1086[2] 1210[3] 1321[3] 1342[2] 1560[6] (1609)

Sean Nos (IRE) *W K Goldsworthy* 51h
5 b g Sri Pekan(USA) —Coolaba Princess (IRE) (Danehill (USA))
1158[11] 1432[P] 1724[F] 2146[10]

Sea Otter (IRE) *N W Alexander*
9 b g King's Ride—Knockarctic (Quayside)
2652[14]

Search And Destroy (USA) *T R George* 107h 129 c
8 bb g Sky Classic(CAN) —Hunt The Thimble (USA) (Turn And Count (USA))
386[6] 634[5] 815[5] 975[6] 1901[5]

Sea Senor *M W Easterby* 81b
4 b g Sea Freedom—Portonia (Ascertain (USA))
4147[4]

Sea Skate (USA) *R Donohoe* 111h
6 b m Gilded Time(USA) —Sea Of Serenity (USA) (Conquistador Cielo (USA))
67a[15]

Sea The Light *A King* 114h
6 b g Blue Ocean(USA) —Lamper's Light (Idiots Delight)
2050[F] (2309) 3210[3] 3901[P] 4956[8]

Sea To Sky (FR) *Michael Joseph Fitzgerald* 110h 97c
6 b h Take Risks(FR) —Urban Sky (FR) (Groom Dancer (USA))
3005a[6]

Seattle Prince (USA) *S Gollings* 83h
8 gr g Cozzene(USA) —Chicken Slew (USA) (Seattle Slew (USA))
365[8] 687[2] 1002[P]

Sea Wall *Jonjo O'Neill* 88+h
4 b g Giant's Causeway(USA) —Spout (Salse (USA))
4211[5] 4604[13] 4905[3]

Secluded *N G Ayliffe* 44h
6 b g Compton Place—Secret Dance (Sadler's Wells (USA))
911[13] 1036[4] 2858[9]

Secret Dell (IRE) *R Brotherton*
10 b g Doyoun—Summer Silence (USA) (Stop The Music (USA))
3141[P]

Secret Divin (FR) *Mrs D A Hamer* 90h
6 bb g Signe Divin(USA) —Lady Darling (Darshaan)
1916[8] 2301[10] 2730[8] 2995[8] 4783[13]

Secret Drinker (IRE) *N P McCormack*
10 b g Husyan(USA) —Try Le Reste (IRE) (Le Moss)
3336[P] 3917[P]

Secret Jewel (FR) *Miss C J E Caroe* 58h
6 b m Hernando(FR) —Opalette (Sharrood (USA))
1850[8] 2081[7] 2527[4] 2934[8] 3332[P] 4320[P] 4526[5] 4823[9]

Secret Moment *C G Cox* 61b
4 b g Polar Prince(IRE) —Inchtina (Inchinor)
3346[12]

Secret Pact (IRE) *I McMath* 95h
4 br g Lend A Hand—Schust Madame (IRE) (Second Set (IRE))
3793[5] 4313[2] 4532[4]

Secret's Out *F Lloyd* 90h
10 b g Polish Precedent(USA) —Secret Obsession (USA) (Secretariat (USA))
1490[3] 1668[2] 1747[4]

Secured (IRE) *Ian Williams* 105h
6 b g Safety Catch(USA) —Monalma (IRE) (Montekin)
1799[11] 2829[12] (3646) 4589[5]

Seeador *J W Mullins* 103h 49c
7 b g El Conquistador—Shepani (New Member)
53[2] **271[5]** 519[6] 748[3] 861[2] 2592[3] 3249[2] 3478[2] 4036[2] 4961[10]

Seebald (GER) *M C Pipe* 83h 140c
11 b g Mulberry(FR) —Spartina (USA) (Northern Baby (CAN))
1846[U] 2163[9] 2346[P] 2876[11] **4241[13] 4433[9] 4764[5]**

Seejay *B R Johnson*
6 b m Bahamian Bounty—Grand Splendour (Shirley Heights)
651[U]

Seeking Shelter (IRE) *N G Richards* 67+h
7 b m Glacial Storm(USA) —Seeking Gold (IRE) (Lancastrian)
2653[10] 3209[3] **4041[U] 4528[F]**

See Me *Andrew Turnell* 90b
7 ch g Nomadic Way(USA) —Ruby Rheims (Paveh Star)
41288

Seemma *N I M Rossiter* 85+h
6 b m Romany Rye—Shepani (New Member)
583 285F 487P

See More Jock *Dr J R J Naylor* 100h
8 b g Seymour Hicks(FR) —Metafan (Last Fandango)
3477P 36944 40054 46787

Seemore Sunshine *M J Gingell* 77h
9 br g Seymour Hicks(FR) —Temporary Affair (Mandalus)
10P 135R 18093630 4699 6865 7603 8224978 11 104610 10635 1208P

See My Soul (IRE) *R Hollinshead* 65b
4 b f Mister Mat(FR) —Kawarau Queen (Taufan (USA))
46157

Seeyaaj *Miss Lucinda V Russell* 105 h
107+c
6 b g Darshaan—Subya (Night Shift (USA))
4288 **8555 93744053F (4531) 50924**

See You Sometime *J W Mullins* 142h 146c
11 b g Sharp Deal—Shepani (New Member)
19704 26155 318010(3697) 39954 445784746 6 49574

See You There (IRE) *Miss Lucinda V Russell* 113 h 124 c
7 br g Religiously(USA) —Bye For Now (Abednego)
1939 2 32042 3382F37946 43432 4528350075

Seize *Ian Williams* 76b
4 gr g Silver Patriarch(IRE) —Sleepline Princess (Royal Palace)
46446

Selassie *M Scudamore* 49h
7 ch g Alflora(IRE) —Zanditu (Presidium)
4589 6116 7456

Selective *A W Carroll* 109 h
7 b g Selkirk(USA) —Portelet (Night Shift (USA))
17723 24238 312710

Self Defense *Miss E C Lavelle* 152h
9 b g Warning—Dansara (Dancing Brave (USA))
220912 25004 29712 329810 37256

Semi Precious (IRE) *D P Keane* 86h 99+c
8 ch g Semillon—Precious Petra (Bing II)
24314 2733F

Sendonthecheque (IRE) *R Ford* 65h 79+c
8 b g Torus—Miss Riversfield (IRE) (Sandalay)
67410 10152

Senora Snoopy (IRE) *Ferdy Murphy* 98b
5 b m Un Desperado(FR) —Lovely Snoopy (IRE) (Phardante (FR))
25346 (2988) 34483 437612

Senor Bond (USA) *P C Haslam* 48h
5 ch g Hennessy(USA) —Troppa Freska (USA) (Silver Hawk (USA))
13608 143212

Senor Eduardo *S Gollings* 98b
9 gr g Terimon—Jasmin Path (Warpath)
2567P

Senor Gigo *Evan Williams* 68h 61c
8 b g Mistertopogigo(IRE) —Lady Carol (Lord Gayle (USA))
17815 2074P 24296

Senorita Rumbalita *A King* 128+h
5 b m Alflora(IRE) —Lavenham's Last (Rymer)
2269U (2554) 29973 (3884) (4115) 47634

Senor Sedona *N J Gifford* 120h 99c
7 b g Royal Vulcan—Star Shell (Queens Hussar)
20525 2484U

Senor Set (GER) *P A Blockley* 78h
5 b g Second Set(IRE) —Shine Share (IRE) (El Gran Senor (USA))
3277P 36850

Sento (IRE) *A King* 108+h
120+c
8 ch g Persian Bold—Esclava (USA) (Nureyev (USA))
48225

Seomra Hocht (IRE) *William Coleman O'Brien* 80 h 90c
9 b g Standiford(USA) —Woodbury Princess (Never So Bold)
220613

Separated (USA) *P J Hobbs* 90+h
5 b m Unbridled(USA) —Lemhi Go (USA) (Lemhi Gold (USA))
774 4876 7537 (1317) 16583 (Dead)

September Moon *Mrs A M Thorpe* 101h
8 b m Bustino—Lunabelle (Idiots Delight)
(859) 9742 10457 13415 14084 1525216304 17272

Seraph *O Brennan* 83h
6 ch g Vettori(IRE) —Dahlawise (IRE) (Caerleon (USA))
1340P 15538 16086 **2291P**25864 29622 35572 44798 4640447941 1 51353

Serbelloni *M D Hammond* 107 h
104+c
6 b g Spectrum(IRE) —Rose Vibert (Caerleon (USA))
(2652) 37794 45305

Serge (FR) *W Gulcher*
9 b g Beyssac(FR) —Ptite Noune (Baptism)
590a3

Sergeant Small (IRE) *John Berry* 50h
4 b g Dr Devious(IRE) —Yavarro (Raga Navarro (ITY))
11466 14048

Sergio Coimbra (IRE) *N G Richards* 99h
7 b g Moscow Society(USA) —Across The Pond (IRE) (Over The River (FR))
1526P 16872 23722 2994F 3918P5064P

Serious Man (IRE) *Mrs P Townsley* 80h 102c
9 b g Norwich—One Woman (IRE) (Remainder Man)
177212 **19178**

Serious Position (IRE) *F Jordan* 91h
11 ch g Orchestra—Lady Temba (Callernish)
1296 978P

Serious Weapon (IRE) *Liam P Cusack* 108h
7 b g Simply Great(FR) —Woolly (Giolla Mear)
5078a10

Serpentine Rock *P J Hobbs* 110h 123 c
6 ch g Hernando(FR) —Serpentara (Kris)
20473 **(2312) 26224 29983 3695P**

Serusier (IRE) *T J Arnold*
5 ch g Sillery(USA) —Allzi (USA) (Zilzal (USA))
3003aP

Sesame Rambler (IRE) *G L Moore* 114+h
7 gr g Roselier(FR) —Sesame Cracker (Derrylin)
2685P 37196 4357F 45735 (4693) 50968

Sett Aside *Mrs L C Jewell* 82c
8 b g Set Adrift—Fields Of Fortune (Anfield)
2213F 2376P **268262805 8 31343 3430U3660 2 44515 465334873 7**

Settlement Craic (IRE) *T G Mills* 110+h
5 b g Ela-Mana-Mou—Medway (IRE) (Shernazar)
2302 (504) 7292

Seveneightsix (IRE) *D J Wintle* 80+h 75+c
6 ch m Old Vic—Necochea (Julio Mariner)
17234 21403 (2244) 25856 **29367**

Sevens Delight *Mrs S J Smith* 85+b
6 b m Karinga Bay—Dante's Delight (Idiots Delight)
10483 12374

Seven Shirt *E G Bevan*
5 b g Great Dane(IRE) —Bride's Answer (Anshan)
2070P 224919

Seventh Sense *J I A Charlton* 80b
5 b m Pasternak—Sister Seven (IRE) (Henbit (USA))
475112 50428

Severn Air *J L Spearing* 97h
8 b m Alderbrook—Mariner's Air (Julio Mariner)
1099P

Sexy Rexy (IRE) *N A Twiston-Davies* 97b
5 b g Mister Lord(USA) —Cab On Time (IRE) (Alphabatim (USA))
33926 42446 48072

Seymar Lad (IRE) *P Beaumont* 104 h
6 b g Oscar(IRE) —Far And Deep (IRE) (Phardante (FR))
21868 263110 29672 33932 (3918) 41085 45296 485211

Seymour Weld *C T Pogson* 86+b
6 ch g Weld—Seymour News (Seymour Hicks (FR))
8174 17627 18896

Sgt Pepper (IRE) *O Sherwood* 96 h
5 b g Fasliyev(USA) —Amandine (IRE) (Darshaan)
16546 19915 21485 27495 29404

Shaaban (IRE) *R J Price* 55h
5 b g Woodman(USA) —Ashbilya (USA) (Nureyev (USA))
91111 9829 1097P 165510 1753P

Shaadiva *A King* 111+h
125+c
8 b m Shaamit(IRE) —Kristal Diva (Kris)
6344 (1189)

Shaamit The Vaamit (IRE) *M Scudamore* 101h
6 b g Shaamit(IRE) —Shocker (IRE) (Sabrehill (USA))
19776 26594 28107 32422 33716

Shaanbar (IRE) *J Hetherton* 55h
4 b f Darshaan—Barbara Frietchie (IRE) (Try My Best (USA))
200110 21677

Sha Bihan (FR) *A King* 84h
5 b g Villez(USA) —Shadrou (FR) (Kadrou (FR))
45618 4781P

Shady Anne *F Jordan* 96h 81+c
8 ch m Derrylin—Juno Away (Strong Gale)
27265 294011 384810 4282P 50148

Shady Baron (IRE) *J Wade* 91h
7 b g Lord Americo—Glint Of Baron (Glint Of Gold)
7196 8926 11494 13372 3257535593 37925 5123P

Shady Grey *C J Mann* 100+h
8 gr m Minster Son—Yemaail (IRE) (Shaadi (USA))
2452 (487) 6932 9066 9613 1356P (Dead)

Shady Lad (IRE) *E Bolger* 74h 136c
9 b g Aahsaylad—Pimberley Shades (Pollerton)
87a2 27452

Shady Man *J K Hunter* 48 h
8 b g Shaamit(IRE) —Miss Hardy (Formidable (USA))
59212 1940 15 256714

Shady Willow (IRE) *W P Mullins* 107 b
4 b g Unfuwain(USA) —Shady Leaf (IRE) (Glint Of Gold)
444820

Shah (IRE) *P Kelsall*
13 b g King Persian—Gay And Sharp (Fine Blade (USA))
3686P

Shaheer (IRE) *J Gallagher* 42h
4 b g Shahrastani(USA) —Atmospheric Blues (IRE) (Double Schwartz)
311

Shahnameh (IRE) *P R Webber* 54b
4 ch g Anshan—Novelist (Quayside)
711

Shaka's Pearl *N J Gifford* 92h 101c
6 ch g Infantry—Zulu Pearl (Sula Bula)
25546 (2983) 32753 372914 41536 4396P

Shakerattleandroll (IRE) *J Nicol* 94b
5 b g Dr Fong(USA) —Speedybird (IRE) (Danehill (USA))
2424 (816)

Shakwaa *E A Elliott* 87h
7 ch m Lion Cavern(USA) —Shadha (USA) (Devil's Bag (USA))
92 149F **2041F 2526P**491911 1411

Shalako (USA) *P J Hobbs* 124h 126c
8 ch g Kingmambo(USA) —Sporades (USA) (Vaguely Noble)
16752 18725 **22102 2485232962 37285 4240F** (Dead)

Shalati Princess *D Burchell* 85+h
5 b m Bluegrass Prince(IRE) —Shalati (FR) (High Line)
10775 11567 34839 41012 4423247565 48284

Shaman *G L Moore* 103h
9 b g Fraam—Magic Maggie (Beveled (USA))
2320 5176 7266 22162 259510 31858 36614 40752 45233 4879P

Shamawan (IRE) *Jonjo O'Neill* 108+h
11 b g Kris—Shamawna (IRE) (Darshaan)
24304 26217 **3019P**

Shamayoun (FR) *C R Egerton* 129h
4 b c Kahyasi—Shamanara (IRE) (Danehill (USA))
34294 3883P (4057) (4435) 474710 (4910) 50013

Shambolina *J W Mullins* 60h
5 b m Shambo—Game Dilemma (Sulaafah (USA))
299710 343710

Shamore *C Grant* 40h
7 b m Shambo—Admire-A-More (Le Coq D'Or)
60211

Shamrock Bay *L Lungo* 74h
4 b f Celtic Swing—Kabayil (Dancing Brave (USA))
47899 49877

Shamsan (IRE) *J Joseph* 89+h
9 ch g Night Shift(USA) —Awayil (USA) (Woodman (USA))
13614 397P 5087 7629 980611535 12486 (1362)

Shamwari Fire (IRE) *I W McInnes* 42h
6 ch g Idris(IRE) —Bobby's Dream (Reference Point)
210810

Shanahan (IRE) *C F Swan* 82b
5 b g Little Bighorn—Thomastown Girl (Tekoah)
5060a14

Shanbally Lad (IRE) *D P Keane*
7 b g Germany(USA) —Coolbawn Rose (IRE) (Supreme Leader)
962P 1096P

Shandrani (GER) *D G Bridgwater* 75h
7 b g Komtur(USA) —Strockida (GER) (Rocket)
9826

Shannon Gale Boy (IRE) *K R Pearce* 57b
7 ch g Old Vic—Jemma's Gold (IRE) (Buckskin (FR))
68510

Shannon Quest (IRE) *C L Popham*
10 bb g Zaffaran(USA) —Carrick Shannon (Green Shoon)
1751P **1981P 262072933P 3129P 3686P3946P**

Shannon's Pride (IRE) *R C Guest* 120 h 118 c
10 gr g Roselier(FR) —Spanish Flame (IRE) (Spanish Place (USA))
1193 17985 194122368 3 26444 3350335967 48064 5067P

Shannon Springs (IRE) *Andrew Turnell* 103 h
4 b g Darshaan—Our Queen Of Kings (Arazi (USA))
27566 33244 37873 4243P

Shanteen Lass (IRE) *Ferdy Murphy* 80h
6 b m Shahanndeh—Margurites Pet (IRE) (Roselier (FR))
414510 43413 4734P

Sharaab (USA) *D E Cantillon* 85h
5 bb g Erhaab(USA) —Ghashtah (USA) (Nijinsky (CAN))
13402 (1415) 15627 17476 195712

Sharajan (IRE) *A King* 125+h
6 b g Desert King(IRE) —Balakera (FR) (Lashkari)
30239 34254 38822 43732 4760P

Shardakhan (IRE) *G L Moore* 73h
4 b g Dr Devious(IRE) —Sharamana (IRE) (Darshaan)
28246 329410 34368

Shardam (IRE) *N A Twiston-Davies* 103c
9 b g Shardari—Knockea Hill (Buckskin (FR))
3022P 3390P 4433155012P

Shareef (FR) *A King* 120+c
9 b g Port Lyautey(FR) —Saralik (Salse (USA))
5242 1205P

Shares (IRE) *P Monteith* 107h 123 c
6 b g Turtle Island(IRE) —Glendora (Glenstal (USA))
1940 6 20422 245212 **(2943) 331723852F 4531F** 4723448486

Sharp Belline (IRE) *Mrs S J Smith* 114h 117 c
9 b g Robellino(USA) —Moon Watch (Night Shift (USA))
1760P **(2039) (2445) 299323396 4 45055 4790P50127**

Sharp Exit (IRE) *J Wade* 38h
7 ch g Fourstars Allstar(USA) —Dipper's Gift (IRE) (Salluceva)
4657P 47939 49889

Sharp Jack (IRE) *R T Phillips* 114 h 121c
8 b g Be My Native(USA) —Polly Sharp (Pollerton)
2504U 26296 32895 **43144(4578) 50122**

Sharp N Frosty *W M Brisbourne* 58h
4 b g Somayda(IRE) —Wily Miss (Teenoso (USA))
10953 1201P 13328

Sharp Rally (IRE) *A J Wilson* 83h
5 ch g Night Shift(USA) —La Pointe (Sharpo)
17451 1 199110 258410 28736 324210 3548P 483410

Sharp Rigging (IRE) *A M Hales* 136h 140 c
6 b g Son Of Sharp Shot(IRE) —In The Rigging (USA) (Topsider (USA))
18286 **26074 2861431832 (4076) 4472F**

Sharp Storm *B G Powell*
6 gr m Terimon—Whirlwind Romance (IRE) (Strong Gale)
46958

Shays Lane (IRE) *Ferdy Murphy* 78h 92c
12 b g The Bart(USA) —Continuity Lass (Continuation)
3930P 4659P 135

Sh Boom *S A Brookshaw* 143h
8 b g Alderbrook—Muznah (Royal And Regal (USA))
1925P 23265 27477 28767 3502537272 40694 4458U (Dead)

Sheer Guts (IRE) *Robert Gray* 96+h
7 b g Hamas(IRE) —Balakera (FR) (Lashkari)
12506 13333 (1520) 15976 16433 (1756) 1940 13(2107) 3339P 3966P

Shekel (IRE) *Miss H C Knight*
4 b g Shernazar—Last Hand (IRE) (Hollow Hand)
461514

Sheknowsyouknow *H J Manners*
5 b m Petrizzo—Margaret Modes (Thatching)
175511

She'll Be Lucky (IRE) *Michael Hourigan* 108h 90c
8 ch m Arctic Cider(USA) —Johnnys Girl (Orchestra)
3005aF

Shellin Hill (IRE) *F L Matthews* 51h 51c
12 ch g Sharp Victor(USA) —Queenspay (Sandhurst Prince)
1122P 12336 153910 **4880P**

Shelomoh (IRE) *D M Forster* 100b
5 b g Zaffaran(USA) —Parson's Run (The Parson)
48543

Shem Dylan (NZ) *R C Guest* 30h
7 ch g Stark South(USA) —Khozaderry (NZ) (Khozaam (USA))
167110 179414 1938 P 216912

Sher Beau (IRE) *Philip Fenton* 140h 138 c
7 b g Beau Sher—Welsh Ana (IRE) (Welsh Term)
116a7 **3012a4 3893a7**

Shergael (IRE) *J L Spearing* 62h
5 b g Barathea(IRE) —Shergress (Siberian Express (USA))
16149 18906

Sheriff Roscoe *P Winkworth* 96 h
6 b g Roscoe Blake—Silva Linda (Precipice Wood)
31334 35005 39068

Sherkin Island (IRE) *Jonjo O'Neill* 98 h 123 c
8 b g Shernazar—Tullerolli (IRE) (Barbarolli (USA))
19295 27145

Sherman Bay *G F Bridgwater*
6 b g Alderbrook—Romantic Melody (Battle Hymn)
2988P

Shernatra (IRE) *J A B Old* 90h
7 b g Shernazar—Miss Nancy (Giolla Mear)
2624 P 46659

Sher One Moor (IRE) *Joseph Crowley* 93b
5 ch g Shernazar—Lady Moorfield (Sallust)
44a6

Sherwood Rose (IRE) *Mrs N Field* 70h 109+c
10 gr m Mandalus—Cronlier (Roselier (FR))
512

Sherwoods Folly *H D Daly* 95+b
4 b g Classic Cliche(IRE) —Action De Balle (FR) (Cricket Ball (USA))
(4038) 477917

She's A Terror *N B King* 25h
7 gr m Terimon—Shedid (St Columbus)
34915 6519

She's Humble (IRE) *P D Evans* 98+b
4 ch f Humbel(USA) —She's No Tourist (IRE) (Doubletour (USA))
28304 32598 (4644) 475119

She's Little Don *S A Hughes* 29b
6 b m Gran Alba(USA) —Doubting Donna (Tom Noddy)
349112 **5109P**

She's My Girl (IRE) *John G Carr* 93+h 98+c
11 ch m Arctic Cider(USA) —Sinead's Princess (Sun Prince)
3294 8596 **18013 214142905F 32684 348944417F**

She's No Muppet *N R Mitchell* 50h
6 b m Teenoso(USA) —Persian Dream (IRE) (Mazaad)
22699 32817 39798 42869 4836P

She's Our Daisy (IRE) *R H Buckler* 71h
6 b m Supreme Leader—Tell A Tale (Le Bavard (FR))
70a17 250115 29376 29978 428684619P

She's Our Native (IRE) *Evan Williams* 126 h
101+c
8 b m Be My Native(USA) —More Dash (IRE) (Strong Gale)
(2723) 28453 (3247) (3358) (3802) 444313 **48293**

She's The Lady *R S Brookhouse* 105+b
6 b m Unfuwain(USA) —City Of Angels (Woodman (USA))
21315 (2446) 27276 437617

Shifting Alliance (IRE) *Paul Nolan* 109h
6 b g Oscar(IRE) —Duchess Of Cork (IRE) (Satco (FR))
3005a2

Shikoku Lass (IRE) *Mrs S Wall*
6 br m Muroto—Miss Josephine (IRE) (Kemal (FR))
1954P

Shiminnie (IRE) *J R H Fowler* 105h
7 b m Bob Back(USA) —Shining Willow (Strong Gale)
66a8

Shingle Street (IRE) *Miss Venetia Williams* 89h
4 b g Bahhare(USA) —Sandystones (Selkirk (USA))
9452 1023F 12682 13974 (1441) 15631518739 44298 4557P

Shining Strand *N J Henderson* 123h 137+c
7 ch g Karinga Bay—First Romance (Royalty)
2034 (521) 25302 2925RR 33422 **(3653) 3942U 42142 460554971 3**

Shining Tyne *R Johnson* 91c
12 b g Primitive Rising(USA) —Shining Bann (Bargello)
3913P 47227 5040P

Shinjiru (USA) *P A Blockley* 70b
6 b g Broad Brush(USA) —Kalwada (USA) (Roberto (USA))
13110 3008 30247 4032P 4638P

Shinko Femme (IRE) *M E Sowersby* 58h
5 b m Shinko Forest(IRE) —Kilshanny (Groom Dancer (USA))
19278 20827 251510 27529 296283335P

Shiny Thing (USA) *A King* 103+h
4 br f Lear Fan(USA) —Juliet's Jewel (USA) (Houston (USA))
(2753) 33406 46743 48582

Ship's Hill (IRE) *N J Henderson* 109b
5 b g Oscar(IRE) —Ballykea (IRE) (Montelimar (USA))
46222 48533

Shirazi *D R Gandolfo* 104 h
8 b g Mtoto—Al Shadeedah (USA) (Nureyev (USA))
2218[6] 2714[4] 2925[6] 3128[8] 4938[F]5108[8]

Shirostran *Paul Williamson*
8 ch g Primitive Rising(USA) —Bebe Hattie (Gracious Melody)
3926[P]

Shivermetimber (IRE) *F Flood* 118h 121+c
8 b m Arctic Lord—Cherry Dancer (Monksfield)
5129a[P]

Shobrooke Mill *Mrs S Prouse* 89+c
13 ch g Shaab—Jubilee Leigh (Hubble Bubble)
4946[4]

Shoestodiefor *S A Brookshaw* 5h
6 b m Overbury(IRE) —Sister Delaney (Deep Run)
2727[8] 4017[12] 4801[8]

Shogoon (FR) *N E Berry* 65h 75c
7 b g Rangoon(FR) —Touranlad (FR) (Tourangeau (FR))
2146[12] 2723[P]

Shoof (USA) *M J Gingell*
7 bb m Dayjur(USA) —Shemaq (USA) (Blushing John (USA))
4074[16]

Shootforthemoon (IRE) *S Donohoe*
6 ch g Flemensfirth(USA) —Knock Hill Lady (IRE) (Electric)
4342[P]

Shotacross The Bow (IRE) *Mrs H E Rees* 81h
9 b g Warning—Nordica (Northfields (USA))
683[7]

Shotgun Willy (IRE) *R C Guest* 128c
12 ch g Be My Native(USA) —Minorettes Girl (Strong Gale)
4777[P] 5004[P]

Shouette (IRE) *John Joseph Murphy* 129h
6 b m Sadler's Wells(USA) —Sumava (IRE) (Sure Blade (USA))
4469[5]

Shouldhavehadthat (IRE) *N J Henderson* 94b
4 b g Definite Article—Keep The Pace (IRE) (Shardari)
4854[2]

Shoulton (IRE) *G H Yardley* 35h 81 c
9 br g Aristocracy—Jay Joy (Double-U-Jay)
2464[P] 2957[3] 3252[F]

Shoveontommy (IRE) *Miss Gina Weare* 54c
11 b g Odin(FR) —Knockboy Glory (I'm A Star)
4477[6]

Shower Of Hail (IRE) *M C Pipe* 101+h
6 b g Luso—Hail To Home (IRE) (Soughaan (USA))
53[3] 468[U] 566[P]

Show Me The River *Ferdy Murphy* 96h 116 c
7 b g Flemensfirth(USA) —Quare Dream'S (IRE) (Strong Gale)
1845[4] 2023[4] 2989[2]4586[2] 4840[2] (4918)

Show No Fear *G M Moore* 103h
5 b g Groom Dancer(USA) —La Piaf (FR) (Fabulous Dancer (USA))
2566[16] 5066[11]

Show Of Hands (IRE) *J G M O'Shea* 87b
6 b g Zaffaran(USA) —New Technique (FR) (Formidable (USA))
179[4] 685[3]

Showtime Annie *A Bailey* 81h
5 b m Wizard King—Rebel County (IRE) (Maelstrom Lake)
1824[3] 2062[4] 2412[5]

Showtime Faye *A Bailey* 51h
4 b f Overbury(IRE) —Rebel County (IRE) (Maelstrom Lake)
3645[7] 3730[10] 4828[11]

Shrove Tuesday (IRE) *A J Martin* 87+c
7 b m Accordion—Lough Neagh Lady (Furry Glen)
3276[F] (4321) 4845[3]

Shuffling Pals (IRE) *S E H Sherwood* 61h 46c
9 b g Roselier(FR) —Penny Shuffle (IRE) (Decent Fellow)
2610[5] 3359[9] 4321[P]

Shugula (IRE) *Ms J S Doyle* 48h
4 ch f Tagula(IRE) —Rose Of Shuaib (IRE) (Caerleon (USA))
1023[5]

Shuhood (USA) *P R Webber* 136h 130+c
6 b g Kingmambo(USA) —Nifty (USA) (Roberto (USA))
1971[3] 4102[3]

Shuil A Maidin (IRE) *Peter M Kiely* 71h
4 ch f Good Thyne(USA) —Shuil Tintreach (IRE) (Electric)
2830[10]

Shuil Aris (IRE) *Paul Nolan* 120b
5 br m Anshan—Shuil Sionnach (IRE) (Mandalus)
(5134a)

Shuil Bob (IRE) *C Tinkler* 90b
6 bb m Bob Back(USA) —Shuil Ar Aghaidh (The Parson)
1674[5]

Shuil Mavourneen (IRE) *D P Keane* 38h
7 b m Welsh Term—Shuil A Cuig (Quayside)
569[9]

Shuil Monty (IRE) *R H York* 94h 104c
10 b g Montelimar(USA) —Shuil Run (Deep Run)
862[8]

Shulmin *J Wade* 56h
6 ch m Minster Son—Shultan (IRE) (Rymer)
1307[4] 1757[8]

Si Anthony (FR) *Ferdy Murphy* 71h
6 b g Siam(USA) —Nekhtabet (FR) (Fast Topaze (USA))
351[7] 602[7] 780[6] 1066[U] **1177[5]**

Siberian Highness (FR) *A King* 122 h
5 b m Highest Honor(FR) —Emblem (FR) (Siberian Express (USA))
(2423) 2803[2] (3464) 3878[6]

Sidcup's Gold (IRE) *M Sheppard* 69h 54c
6 ch g Rhoman Rule(USA) —Sidcup Star (IRE) (Riberetto)
1908[10] 2206[15] 2619[7] **2863[P]3252[F] 3460[9] 3801[P]**

Siegfrieds Night (IRE) *M C Chapman* 106+h
5 ch g Night Shift(USA) —Shelbiana (USA) (Chieftain)
372[4] 450[F] 689[10] 824[5] 947[4]1016[8] 1111[8] 1361[6] 1559 [B] 1610[4]1816[4] 2079[6] 2289[5] 2566[4] 2952[5]2964[5] 3416[2] (4899) 5[3]

Siena Star (IRE) *Robert Gray* 85h
8 b g Brief Truce(USA) —Gooseberry Pie (Green Desert (USA))
149[8] 410[2] 566[5] 813[4] 1017[3]1297[10] 2560[3] 2721[3] 2981[4] 3916[P]

Signature Tune (IRE) *P Winkworth* 97 h
7 b g Gothland(FR) —Divine Affair (IRE) (The Parson)
265[3] 2659[3] 3185[3] 3548[6] 4322[3]

Signed And Dated (USA) *Mrs E Slack* 80h
7 b g Red Ransom(USA) —Libeccio (NZ) (Danzatore (CAN))
306[8] 595[7]

Sigwells Club Boy *J L Flint* 97+h
6 b g Fayruz—Run With Pride (Mandrake Major)
947[7] 1027[6] 1111[6] 1250[3] 1413[F]

Sikander A Azam *David M Easterby* 116c
13 b g Arctic Lord—Shanlaragh (Gaberdine)
47[6] (184) 453[F]4748[7]

Sikasso (USA) *Mrs K Walton* 102h
10 bb g Silver Hawk(USA) —Silken Doll (USA) (Chieftain)
64[4] 483[3]

Silber Mond *Miss Sheena West* 82h
4 gr g Monsun(GER) —Salinova (FR) (Linamix (FR))
4562[3] 4823[5] 5073[3]

Silence Reigns *Mrs K Waldron* 111 c
12 b g Saddlers' Hall(IRE) —Rensaler (USA) (Stop The Music (USA))
(221) (437) 761[5] (1153)1248[3] **1435[P] 3847[5]**

Silencio (IRE) *A King* 126h
5 b g Sillery(USA) —Flabbergasted (IRE) (Sadler's Wells (USA))
3510[2] 4375[15] 4663[4]

Silent Age (IRE) *S Gollings* 71b
5 b g Danehill(USA) —Set Fair (USA) (Alleged (USA))
375[6] 1554[10] 1613[5]

Silent Bay *J Wade* 100h
7 b g Karinga Bay—Lady Rosanna (Kind Of Hush)
1799[7] 2007[3] 3793[9] 4114[3] (5038)

Silent City *P D Williams* 36h
6 ch m Karinga Bay—Gordons Girl (IRE) (Deep Run)
4017[8] 4976[11]

Silent Dream *Simon Earle* 93h
8 b g Alflora(IRE) —Silent Surrender (Nearly A Hand)
3023[8] 3477[5]

Silent Oscar (IRE) *C P Donoghue* 118+h
7 b g Oscar(IRE) —Silent Shot (Random Shot)
(93a) 2667a[6]

Silent Snipe *Miss L C Siddall* 39c
13 ch g Jendali(USA) —Sasol (Bustino)
3547[U] 3958[5]

Silent Sound (IRE) *C L Tizzard* 87h 95+c
10 b g Be My Guest(USA) —Whist Awhile (Caerleon (USA))
1076[4] 1187[P]

Silent Voice (IRE) *Sir John Barlow Bt* 80h
9 ch g Unfuwain(USA) —Symeterie (USA) (Seattle Song (USA))
135[F] 334[P] **1602[P]1662[P]**

Silistra *Mrs L C Jewell* 87 h
7 gr g Sadler's Wells(USA) —Dundel (IRE) (Machiavellian (USA))
279[7] 506[9] 895[7] 2379[2] (2802) 3185[7]3719[5] 4153[4] 4871[4]

Silk Appeal *D J Wintle* 31h
6 b m Lord Of Appeal—Amazing Silks (Furry Glen)
4280[P] 4570[P] 4828[10]

Silken Pearls *L Lungo* 104h 104+c
10 b m Leading Counsel(USA) —River Pearl (Oats)
2042[4] 2944[P] (4317)

Silkie Pekin *N R Mitchell* 48b
7 gr m Riverwise(USA) —Came Cottage (Nearly A Hand)
961[P]

Silk Rope (IRE) *R T Phillips* 53b
6 br m Presenting—Osiery Girl (IRE) (Phardante (FR))
4398[10] 5054[16]

Silk Screen (IRE) *W P Mullins* 130h
6 b h Barathea(IRE) —Sun Screen (Caerleon (USA))
67a[6] 2650a[P] 3894a[16] 4951a[16]

Silk Trader *J Mackie* 113h 115c
11 b g Nomadic Way(USA) —Money Run (Deep Run)
2103[7] 4736[8] 4852[8]

Silkwood Top (IRE) *V R A Dartnall* 101+h
7 b g Norwich—Brave Mum (Brave Invader (USA))
1973[P] (2868) 3214[3]

Silloth Spirit *Mrs A M Naughton*
6 b g Atraf—Gaelic Air (Ballad Rock)
2447[P] 2658[P] 2838[P]

Silly Miss Off (IRE) *M Scudamore* 59b
5 b m Clerkenwell(USA) —Little Hulton (Teenoso (USA))
71[2] 1543[14]

Silver Birch (IRE) *P F Nicholls* 109 h 148 c
9 b g Clearly Bust—All Gone (Giolla Mear)
3581[4] **3995[P]** 4105[P] **4777[F]**

Silver Bow *J M Jefferson* 91+h
5 b m Silver Patriarch(IRE) —Isabeau (Law Society (USA))
616[3] 828[4] 1674[11] 2412[8] 2718[6]3235[6] 3757[4] 4080[12]

Silverburn (IRE) *P F Nicholls* 114b
5 b g Presenting—Polly Puttens (Pollerton)
4333[2] (4680)

Silver Castle *R J Rowsell* 114c
10 gr g Roscoe Blake—Pendle Princess (Broxted)
48[0] 440[P]

Silver Chancelor (IRE) *J Howard Johnson* 48h
5 gr g Taipan(IRE) —Abstemious (Absalom)
3205[P] 3914[P] 8[6]

Silver Charmer *H S Howe* 122h
7 b m Charmer—Sea Dart (Air Trooper)
766[2] 1548[3] 4608[10] 4972[6]

Silver City *P J Hobbs* 91h
6 ro g Unfuwain(USA) —Madiyla (Darshaan)
(2148) 2419[9] 2940[9] 3242[5] 4427[P]

Silver Dagger *J C Haynes* 47h 90+c
8 gr g Dr Devious(IRE) —La Belle Affair (USA) (Black Tie Affair)
632[8] 988[10] 1310[5] 1486[11]1838[9] 2188[3] 2657[18] 3169[6] 3557[P]**3796[4] 4614[P]**

Silver Dollars (FR) *J Howard Johnson* 107h
5 gr g Great Palm(USA) —Marie Olga (FR) (Dom Pasquini (FR))
1889[7] 2571[4] 2942[13] 4301[2] 5118[8]

Silver Dreamer (IRE) *H S Howe* 23h
4 b f Brave Act—Heads We Called (IRE) (Bluebird (USA))
2597[10]

Silver Emperor (IRE) *P A Blockley* 28h
5 gr g Lil's Boy(USA) —Just Possible (Kalaglow)
1123[7] 1187[10] 1266[5] 1587[P]

Silver Feather (IRE) *Ferdy Murphy* 71b
4 gr g Silver Patriarch(IRE) —Merilena (IRE) (Roselier (FR))
4909[13]

Silver Gift *G Fierro* 94h
9 b m Rakaposhi King—Kellsboro Kate (Paddy's Stream)
245[5] 575[10] 652[P] 768[12] 906[9]1564[5] 1630[7] 3146[8] 3656[2]

Silvergino (IRE) *Mrs Jeremy Young* 102h 110c
6 b g Perugino(USA) —Silvretta (IRE) (Tirol)
193[3] 946[F] 1126[4]

Silver Hill Lad *C W Fairhurst*
5 gr g Petoski—Miss Madelon (Absalom)
3399[12] 3789[P] 4315[P]

Silverick Lady *B G Powell* 46b
4 gr f Silver Patriarch(IRE) —Limerick (ITY) (Nijin (USA))
2830[13] 3435[10]

Silverio (GER) *G L Moore* 85h
5 b g Laroche(GER) —Silvassa (IRE) (Darshaan)
507[2] 769[4] 2127[P] 2376[7] 2554[10]2799[10] (4133) 4210[8]

Silver Island *K Bishop* 31h
5 ch g Silver Patriarch(IRE) —Island Maid (Forzando)
5115[6]

Silver Jack (IRE) *M Todhunter* 95+h 115 c
8 gr g Roselier(FR) —Consharon (IRE) (Strong Gale)
1682[3] (2063) 2451[3]2945[P] 3849[2] 4981[3]

Silver Jade *C J Teague* 10b
5 b m Silver Patriarch(IRE) —Kinraddie (Wuzo (USA))
470[9]

Silver Knight *T D Easterby* 119h 137 c
8 gr g Simply Great(FR) —Hysteria (Prince Bee)
1798[6] 2189[3] (2451) (2644) 2875[4] 4635[3]4843[6]

Silver Lake (IRE) *C J Lawson*
12 gr g Roselier(FR) —Over The Pond (IRE) (Over The River (FR))
403[P]

Silver Man *D C Turner* 46h 46c
12 gr g Silver Owl—What An Experiance (Chance Meeting I)
668[9] 1018[7] 1121[9] 1192[P]

Silverpro *D J Wintle* 58h
5 ch m Hector Protector(USA) —Silver Gyre (IRE) (Silver Hawk (USA))
1851[8] 3332[7] 3673[8] 4013[P] 4550[3]4752[13]

Silver Prophet (IRE) *M R Bosley* 114 h
7 gr g Idris(IRE) —Silver Heart (Yankee Gold)
1263[6] 2324[2] 2716[2] 2871[7] 3360[6]4608[5] 4848[5]

Silver Reign *J A Geake*
5 gr g Prince Sabo—Primo Donna Magna (Primo Dominie)
2573[P]

Silver Rosa *C C Bealby* 70b
5 gr m Silver Patriarch(IRE) —Manzanilla (Mango Express)
2988[7] 3435[8]

Silver Samuel (NZ) *S A Brookshaw* 99+h 93+c
9 gr g Hula Town(NZ) —Offrande (NZ) (Decies)
(76) 276[2] 461[P]746[5]

Silver Sedge (IRE) *Mrs A Hamilton* 110+h 114c
7 gr g Aristocracy—Pollyfaster (Polyfoto)
1530[5] 1665[5] **2026[F]** 2171[2]2453[11] 2944[7] **(3334) 3543[5]**(4488) **4721[2]**

Silver Seeker (USA) *A R Dicken* 90h
6 gr g Seeking The Gold(USA) —Zelanda (IRE) (Night Shift (USA))
2027[3] 2475[8] 2693[5] 2944[6] 3209[7](3446) (3757) 4317[4]

Silver Seline *B N Pollock* 33h
5 gr m Silver Patriarch(IRE) —Rive-Jumelle (IRE) (M Double M (USA))
27[10] 3437[9] 4450[16] 4917[8]

Silver Serg *Miss Suzy Smith* 88+b
5 b g Silver Patriarch(IRE) —Ranyah (USA) (Our Native (USA))
507[3] 685[8] 4940[5]

Silver Sister *J D Frost* 87b
5 gr m Morpeth—Pigeon Loft (IRE) (Bellypha)
963[2] 2152[6]

Silver Snitch (IRE) *G A Swinbank* 86b
6 gr g Supreme Leader—Banderole (IRE) (Roselier (FR))
5141[6]

Silver Sparrow (IRE) *P Bowen* 87+h
5 b g Revoque(IRE) —Silver Spark (USA) (Silver Hawk (USA))
828[3] 977[4]

Silver Streak (IRE) *Milson Robinson* 101+c
12 gr g Roselier(FR) —Vulcash (IRE) (Callernish)
125[2] 453[P]

Silver Styx *J R Holt*
7 gr g Terimon—Sconie's Poppet (Alias Smith (USA))
107[5]

Simiola *S T Lewis* 53 h 77+c
7 b m Shaamit(IRE) —Brave Vanessa (USA) (Private Account (USA))
294[4] 394[P] 629[10] 729[4] 811[8]860[10] 982[7] 1037[P] **1742[7]** 1890[5]2139[10] 2560[P] 3456[12] 3804[13] 3956[7]**4590[5] 5044[4] 2[5]**

Simlet *E W Tuer* 112h 108 c
11 b g Forzando—Besito (Wassl)
468[6] 2110[P] 2417[P] 2840[13] **4300[P]**

Simon *J L Spearing* 125h 139+c
7 b g Overbury(IRE) —Gaye Memory (Buckskin (FR))
2464[4] 2817[3] 2959[4](3506) 4068[2] (4498) (5012)

Simonovski (USA) *Mrs A M Thorpe* 102h
5 b g Miswaki(USA) —Earthra (USA) (Rahy (USA))
1740[5] 2173[13] 3242[9] 3345[P] 4738[P](4828) 5111[F]

Simon's Heights *Miss P Robson* 75h
5 b g Weldnaas(USA) —Star Thyme (Point North)
59[8] 406[10]

Simon's Seat (USA) *S C Burrough* 85h
7 ch g Woodman(USA) —Spire (USA) (Topsider (USA))
182[4] 670[5] 1085[3] 1107[8] 1381[8]1539[6] 1636[3] **1783[4] 1897[P]**

Simonstown *M D Hammond* 50b
6 ch g Pivotal—Watership (USA) (Foolish Pleasure (USA))
1048[12]

Simon The Poacher *L P Grassick* 54h
7 br g Chaddleworth(IRE) —Lady Crusty (Golden Dipper)
133[8]

Simoun (IRE) *B N Pollock* 91+h 114c
8 b g Monsun(GER) —Suivez (FR) (Fioravanti (USA))
56[2] 286[4] 3549[3]3922[P] 4014[P] 4633[U]4918[5]

Simple Glory (IRE) *R Dickin* 86 h 91c
7 br m Simply Great(FR) —Cabin Glory (The Parson)
94[3] 441[9] 3247[F] **3790[3]4214[P] 4643[5]**

Simply Da Best (IRE) *J J Lambe* 104h 97+c
8 b g Lake Coniston(IRE) —Sakala (NZ) (Gold And Ivory (USA))
318[5] 646[5] 855[5]990[5] 1148[P] **1335[8]**

Simply Gifted *Jonjo O'Neill* 142 c
11 b g Simply Great(FR) —Souveniers (Relko)
69a[7] 3495[9]

Simplyirresistible (IRE) *S T Lewis* 40b
6 b m Simply Great(FR) —Woolly (Giolla Mear)
277[7] 656[12] 4595[13]

Simply Mystic *P D Niven* 95h
6 ch m Simply Great(FR) —Mystic Memory (Ela-Mana-Mou)
2525[7] 2766[6] 2990[5] 3318[6] 4907[8]

Simply St Lucia *J R Weymes* 78h
4 b f Charnwood Forest(IRE) —Mubadara (IRE) (Lahib (USA))
4074[4]

Singhalongtasveer *W Storey* 96h
4 b g Namaqualand(USA) —Felinwen (White Mill)
1797[13] 2167[P] 3925[7] (4789)

Sing High *Mrs Rosemary Gasson* 79c
10 b m Golden Heights—Ranee's Song (True Song)
455[3]

Singing Wizard *P J Hobbs* 47b
4 gr g Silver Patriarch(IRE) —Singing Citystreet (Rock City)
4615[11]

Single Handed *H D Daly* 61b
4 b f Cloudings(IRE) —Hand Inn Glove (Alflora (IRE))
4800[4]

Single Player (IRE) *Noel T Chance* 91b
6 br g Accordion—Alone Party (IRE) (Phardante (FR))
3001[9] 4422[3]

Sininlaw (IRE) *John Queally*
4 b g Shernazar—Bloomfield (IRE) (Alzao (USA))
5060a[P]

Sinjaree *Mrs S Lamyman* 68h
8 b g Mark Of Esteem(IRE) —Forthwith (Midyan (USA))
696[9] 4388[6]

Sintos *Miss A M Newton-Smith* 95+b
8 bb g Syrtos—Sindur (Rolfe (USA))
4823[10]

Sir Bathwick (IRE) *B G Powell* 91h
7 b g Oscar(IRE) —Karenda (Kambalda)
4212[5] 4603[5] 5026[2]

Sir Ben *A Ennis* 31b
5 b g Sir Harry Lewis(USA) —Jolejester (Relkino)
4825[12]

Sir Boreas Hawk *G A Swinbank* 88+b
4 b g Overbury(IRE) —Fringe Benefit (IRE) (Executive Perk)
4637[3] (5041)

Sir Brastias *K C Bailey* 115 h 124+c
7 b g Shaamit(IRE) —Premier Night (Old Vic)
3360[7] 4093[3]

Sir Cumference *Miss Venetia Williams* 100c
10 b g Sir Harry Lewis(USA) —Puki Puki (Roselier (FR))
398[2] (535) 1615[3]1752[5] 2243[2] 2424[4]2863[P] 3886[2] 4851[5]

Sir D'Orton (FR) *A J Tizzard* 118c
10 ch g Beyssac(FR) —Prime Target (FR) (Ti King (FR))
453[R] 4730[U]

Sir Frederick (IRE) *W J Burke* 132+h 108 c
6 b g Insan(USA) —Promotor Fidei (Prominer)
3086a[P] 4137a[7] 5103a[5]

Sir Frosty *B J M Ryall* 113 c
13 b g Arctic Lord—Snowy Autumn (Deep Run)
(547) 2608[P] 2819[P]3845[5] 4287[P]

Sir Guillaume (FR) *T Trapenard*
3 b c Epervier Bleu—Bisette (FR) (Star Maite (FR))
4298a[P]

Sir Harry Hall (IRE) *P Bowen* 47b
5 b g Saddlers' Hall(IRE) —Cool Virtue (IRE) (Zaffaran (USA))
1323[11]

Sir Haydn *J R Jenkins* 86h
6 ch g Definite Article—Snowscape (Niniski (USA))
1740[6]

Sir Henrik (IRE) *Mrs D H McCarthy*
8 b g Tidaro(USA) —Let'Shaveaparty (IRE) (Bowling Pin)
401[P]

Sirius Storm (IRE) *Paul Nolan* 122h 122c
6 ch g Prince Of Birds(USA) —Tender Time (Tender King)
117a[5] 3411a[20] 4951a[10]

Sir Jimmy Shand (IRE) *N J Henderson* 112+b
5 bb g Accordion—Morganone (IRE) (Supreme Leader)
(3462) (4455) 4779[18]

Sir Lamb *Miss S E Hall* 66h
10 gr g Rambo Dancer(CAN) —Caroline Lamb (Hotfoot)
152[12] 2688[4] 3209[P]

Sir Monty (USA) *Mrs A J Perrett* 64+h
4 ch g Cat's Career(USA) —Lady Of Meadowlane (USA) (Pancho Jay (USA))
1948[6]

Sir Night (IRE) *Jedd O'Keeffe* 102h
6 b g Night Shift(USA) —Highly Respected (IRE) (High Estate)
1366[4] (1604) 1957[5] 2478[5] 4922[2]

Sir Oj (IRE) *Noel Meade* 126 h 147+c
9 br g Be My Native(USA) —Fox Glen (Furry Glen)
42a[6] (2760) (4138a) 4457[F] 4777[F] 5057a[6]

Sir Overbury *Daniel O'Connell* 123+h
5 b g Overbury(IRE) —Susie's Money (Seymour Hicks (FR))
44a[4] (4060a) 4336a[F] 4888a[5]

Sir Pandy (IRE) *R H Alner* 99 h
6 b g Taipan(IRE) —Miss Pitpan (Pitpan)
1714[2] 1975[P] 3238[3] 3792[6]

Sir Rembrandt (IRE) *R H Alner* 113h 161 c
10 b g Mandalus—Sue's A Lady (Le Moss)
2176[P] 2628[P] 3022[F]3390[2] 3971[3] 4470[7]

Sirroco Wind *Mrs L B Normile*
6 b g Oscar(IRE) —Gale (Strong Gale)
687[P] 2475[P]

Sir Rowland Hill (IRE) *Ferdy Murphy* 108h
7 b g Kahyasi—Zaila (IRE) (Darshaan)
2675[P] 3204[P] 4805[3]5068[2]

Sir Storm (IRE) *G M Moore* 114h 125 c
10 b g Ore—Yonder Bay (IRE) (Trimmingham)
195[6] 1913[4] 2339[4]2640[4] (2993) 3293[7]3495[5] 3974[5] 4762[16]

Sir Walter (IRE) *D Burchell* 71h 78 c
13 b g The Bart(USA) —Glenbalda (Kambalda)
1[F] 136[8] 357[4] 571[3] **632[5]**1027[3] 1121[2] 1218[2] **1335[3]**1862[6] 2166[18] 2659[7] 3128[11] 3456[U]3650[12] 4013[6] 4368[10] 4783[9]

Sissinghurst Storm (IRE) *R Dickin* 86h 95+c
8 bb m Good Thyne(USA) —Mrs Hill (Strong Gale)
262[2] 535[3] 1646[S]2151[2] 2424[3] 3250[6]**4047[6] 4553[U] (4785) (4939)**

Sistema *A E Price* 89+h
5 b g Danzero(AUS) —Shahdiza (USA) (Blushing Groom (FR))
1982[9] 2809[P] 3673[3] 4104[8] (4278) 4418[4]4593[B] 4803[P]

Sister Bury *W K Goldsworthy* 57b
7 b m Overbury(IRE) —Chapel Hill (IRE) (The Parson)
349[8]

Sister Cinnamon *S Gollings* 102+h
8 ch m Karinga Bay—Cinnamon Run (Deep Run)
372[8]

Sister Grace *N J Gifford* 87+h
6 b m Golden Heights—Black Spring (IRE) (Mister Lord (USA))
4074[5] 4581[7] 4915[5]

Sister Lucy (IRE) *B Storey* 44b
5 ch m Old Vic—Pharlucy (IRE) (Phardante (FR))
5124[12]

Sithgaoithe (IRE) *Leonard Whitmore* 86b
6 b m Anshan—The Real Gael (IRE) (Strong Gale)
2796a[11]

Sitting Duck *B G Powell* 74 h 97+c
7 b g Sir Harry Lewis(USA) —Fit For Firing (FR) (In Fijar (USA))
356[5] 523[7] 671[4] **2104[2]2555[P] 2801[3] 2936[2]3602[2] (4426)**

Six Of One *R Rowe* 104 h 108c
8 b g Kahyasi—Ten To Six (Night Shift (USA))
567[2] 865[P]

Six Pack (IRE) *Andrew Turnell* 86+h 109c
8 ch g Royal Abjar(USA) —Regal Entrance (Be My Guest (USA))
195[9] 354[P] 826[P]**894[B] 1049[7]**

Siyaran (IRE) *D R Gandolfo* 75h
5 ch g Grand Lodge(USA) —Sinndiya (IRE) (Pharly (FR))
1714[10] 3508[9]

Sizeable Return *J A B Old* 49b
5 b g Bob's Return(IRE) —Dutch Czarina (Prince Sabo)
4881[10]

Sizing America (IRE) *Henry De Bromhead* 104h
5 b g Lord Americo—Annfield Lady (IRE) (Furry Glen)
4888a[8]

Skeheenarinky (IRE) *Sean O O'Brien* 110h
6 b g Oscar(IRE) —Vital Touch (Le Bavard (FR))
70a[13]

Skenfrith *Miss S E Forster* 118+h 118+c
7 b g Atraf—Hobbs Choice (Superpower)
2449[P] 2654[F] 2943[4]3236[5] 3382[P] (4144) (4345) 4788[P]

Skew Whip *C Brader* 94+c
8 b g Primitive Rising(USA) —Magic Whip (Current Magic)
281[U] (4305)

Skibereen (IRE) *Mrs A M Thorpe* 88+h
6 b g Ashkalani(IRE) —Your Village (IRE) (Be My Guest (USA))
21[F] 515[3] 664[4] 747[5] 813[5]

Skiddaw Jones *M A Barnes* 89h
6 b g Emperor Jones(USA) —Woodrising (Nomination)
418[7] 691[8] 870[7] 942[2] 1291[2]1530[4] 1591[2]

Skip 'N' Tune (IRE) *R N Miller* 74c
9 b m Mandalus—Molten (Ore)
455[6]

Skippers Brig (IRE) *L Lungo* 109b
5 b g Zaffaran(USA) —Mathewsrose (IRE) (Roselier (FR))
5008[2]

Skistorm *D A Rees* 43b
4 b f Petoski—Dai-Namic-Storm (IRE) (Glacial Storm (USA))
4947[7]

Sky By Night *B J M Ryall* 67b
5 b m Riverwise(USA) —Purbeck Polly (Pollerton)
3244[12] 4244[11]

Skye Blue (IRE) *M J Weeden* 69h
9 b g Blues Traveller(IRE) —Hitopah (Bustino)
2296[10] 2845[P]

Skyhawk (IRE) *Henry De Bromhead* 112h
5 b g In The Wings—Babushka (IRE) (Dance Of Life (USA))
65a[4]

Sky Mack (IRE) *Evan Williams* 104h
5 ch h Anshan—Ramona Style (IRE) (Duky)
2565[3] 3617[6] 4621[15] 4784[2]

Sky's The Limit (FR) *E J O'Grady* 155+h
5 gr g Medaaly—Highness Lady (GER) (Cagliostro (GER))
954a[5] 1093a[13] 2032a[2] (4446) 4775[3] 5101a[10]

Sky To Sea (FR) *Mrs A M O'Shea* 112h
8 b g Adieu Au Roi(IRE) —Urban Sky (FR) (Groom Dancer (USA))
117a[17] 3515a[4]

Sky Warrior (FR) *Evan Williams* 111h 134+c
8 b g Warrshan(USA) —Sky Bibi (FR) (Sky Lawyer (FR))
4[2] (248) 454[3]727[5]

Slade Supreme (IRE) *D A Rees* 46b
4 b f Ridgewood Ben—Suprememememories (IRE) (Supreme Leader)
4398[9]

Slalom (IRE) *D Burchell* 100h
6 b g Royal Applause—Skisette (Malinowski (USA))
826[7] 1040[3] 1158[2] (1280) 1361[3] 1485[4]1538[4] 5070[F]

Slaney Native (IRE) *Miss M Mullineaux* 61h
13 b g Be My Native(USA) —Mean To Me (Homing)
125[P]

Slave's Adventure *R J Price* 49h
12 b m Green Adventure(USA) —Stockton Slave (Bivouac)
861[7]

Slew Charm (FR) *Noel T Chance* 110 h
4 b g Marathon(USA) —Slew Bay (FR) (Beaudelaire (USA))
3182[2] 3429[3] (3787) 4096[2]

Slick (FR) *N J Henderson* 70h
5 br g Highest Honor(FR) —Seven Secrets (Ajdal (USA))
(249) 2211[8] 2683[P] 4048[P] 4915[7]

Slight Hiccup *C W Moore* 37h
6 ch m Alderbrook—Very Ominous (Dominion)
7[8] 343[8] 843[P] 1317[F] 1619[4]

Slightly Shifty (IRE) *J T Gorman* 97h
5 b g Revoque(IRE) —Tarliya (IRE) (Doyoun)
65a[13]

Slim Pickings (IRE) *Robert Tyner* 122h 140+c
7 b g Scribano—Adapan (Pitpan)
(2364a) 3079a[F] 3514a[4]5058a[2]

Slinky Malinky *D G Bridgwater* 64b
8 b m Alderbrook—Winnie The Witch (Leading Man)
1220[P] 1410[P]

Slip The Ring *P Senter* 62h 68c
12 ch g Belmez(USA) —Sixslip (USA) (Diesis)
51[P]

Slooghy (FR) *N J Henderson* 108c
10 br g Missolonghi(USA) —Lady Charrecey (FR) (Fin Bon)
1096[3]

Slyboots (GER) *C J Mann* 91h 95+c
7 gr g Neshad(USA) —Shanice (USA) (Highland Park (USA))
516[P] 948[P] 1192[8]**1358[3]**

Slyguff Rory (IRE) *Michael McCullagh* 122h
8 ch g Fourstars Allstar(USA) —Slyguff Rosey (IRE) (Roselier (FR))
92a[B]

Smart (SLO) *M Pitman* 75h
7 b g Glenstal(USA) —Satyra (POL) (Montcontour (FR))
2573[13]

Smart Boy Prince (IRE) *C Smith* 116 h
5 b g Princely Heir(IRE) —Miss Mulaz (FR) (Luthier)
596[2] 895[4] 991[3] (1340) 1541[2] (1642) 1880[7]2347[5] (2590) 2952[9] 3622[14] 3729[12] 4849[14]5138[4]

Smart Cavalier *P F Nicholls* 113+c
7 b g Terimon—Smart Topsy (Oats)
171[3] 2574[2] (3220) 3580[4] 4694[2] 4755[P]

Smart Design (IRE) *K Bishop* 95h 94c
11 ch g Good Thyne(USA) —Polly's Cottage (Pollerton)
666[5] 744[6] 1076[P]

Smart Guy *Mrs L C Jewell* 87 c
14 ch g Gildoran—Talahache Bridge (New Brig)
3285[2] 3716[2]

Smart Man *Mrs E Slack*
4 gr g Silver Patriarch(IRE) —Run Tiger (IRE) (Commanche Run)
5038[P]

Smart Mover *Miss H C Knight* 111 h
7 b g Supreme Leader—Rachel C (IRE) (Phardante (FR))
1383[4] 1619[2] 1903[2] 2530[9] 3806[2](4238) (5086)

Smart Savannah *C Tinkler* 130+h 123+c
10 b g Primo Dominie—High Savannah (Rousillon (USA))
3946[5] (4417) 5018[5]

Smart Street *K G Reveley* 69b
4 b g Silver Patriarch(IRE) —Smart Spirit (IRE) (Persian Bold)
2520[9] 3742[8]

Smart Tiger (GER) *N P Littmoden*
4 b g Tiger Hill(IRE) —Smoke Signal (IRE) (College Chapel)
1519[P]

Smeathe's Ridge *J A B Old* 81h 93c
8 b g Rakaposhi King—Mrs Barty (IRE) (King's Ride)
1921[7] 2862[4] 3146[6] **(3430) 3582[2]**

Smell The Coffee (IRE) *E McNamara* 91h 78c
8 b g Phardante(FR) —Morabito (IRE) (Mandalus)
1752[3]

Smemi An Nada *P Bowen* 56h
4 b g Selkirk(USA) —One Way Street (Habitat)
1207[P]

Smileafact *Mrs Barbara Waring* 87h
6 b g So Factual(USA) —Smilingatstrangers (Macmillion)
345[5] 509[6] 860[6] 1220[7] 1485[2]1711[7] 3729[13] 4469[P] 8[P]

Smile Pleeze (IRE) *M Sheppard* 63h 124 c
14 b g Naheez(USA) —Harkin Park (Pollerton)
1157[8]

Smiling Applause *Mrs Barbara Waring* 81+h
7 b g Royal Applause—Smilingatstrangers (Macmillion)
860[3]

Smilingvalentine (IRE) *D J Wintle* 97 h
9 b m Supreme Leader—Cool Princess (Proverb)
2663[5] **2848[P]** 3149[11] 3461[4]3715[3] 4396[7] 4609[5] 4856[3]

Smith N Allan Oils *P A Blockley*
7 b g Bahamian Bounty—Grand Splendour (Shirley Heights)
1121[P]

Smiths Landing *Mrs S J Smith* 130 h 127c
9 b g Primitive Rising(USA) —Landing Power (Hills Forecast)
(407)

Smith's Tribe *B J Eckley* 101h
8 gr g Homo Sapien—Alice Smith (Alias Smith (USA))
860[P]

Smoke Trail (IRE) *R H Buckler* 33h
7 b g Zaffaran(USA) —Ardee Princess (Monksfield)
5026[7]

Smokey Mountain (IRE) *D P Keane* 104h
5 b g Saddlers' Hall(IRE) —Coco Opera (IRE) (Lafontaine (USA))
2462[5] (5110)

Smokey The Bear *Miss Sheena West* 84h
4 ch g Fumo Di Londra(IRE) —Noble Soul (Sayf El Arab (USA))
2454[6] 2935[8] 4795[F]

Smokincanon *W G M Turner* 70h
4 ch g Fumo Di Londra(IRE) —Secret Miss (Beveled (USA))
2797[6] 3324[7] 3479[P]

Smokin Grey *L Wells* 59h
6 gr m Terimon—Wollow Maid (Wollow)
1974[10]

Smooth Attraction *S G Waugh*
5 b g Lord Of Appeal—Amazing Silks (Furry Glen)
5118[11]

Smoothly Does It *Mrs A J Bowlby* 96h
5 b g Efisio—Exotic Forest (Dominion)
2148[7] 2730[5] 2826[8] 3371[5] 5110[5]

Smurfit (IRE) *C C Bealby* 95h 82 c
7 ch g Anshan—Williams Girl (IRE) (Be My Native (USA))
3274[6] 3732[P] 4164[6]

Snails Castle (IRE) *E W Tuer* 64h
7 b g Danehill(USA) —Bean Island (USA) (Afleet (CAN))
11[10] 469[7]

Snakebite (IRE) *M Pitman* 124h
6 gr g Taipan(IRE) —Bee In The Rose (IRE) (Roselier (FR))
2238[2] (3500) 3978[2] 4373[4]

Snargate *T D Walford* 87b
6 b g Double Eclipse(IRE) —Loch Irish (IRE) (Lancastrian)
470[3] 844[9]

Sninfia (IRE) *G A Ham* 101+h
6 b m Hector Protector(USA) —Christmas Kiss (Taufan (USA))
352[5] 458[R] 980[5] 1099[8]

Snipe *Ian Williams* 110+h 105+c
8 ch g Anshan—Flexwing (Electric)
725[7] 904[3] 1098[9]4738[8]

Snob Wells (IRE) *Noel Meade* 114h 117c
9 b h Sadler's Wells(USA) —Galitizine (USA) (Riverman (USA))
92a[15] **1700a[10]**

Snoopy Loopy (IRE) *P Bowen* 127h 109+c
8 ch g Old Vic—Lovely Snoopy (IRE) (Phardante (FR))
(117a) **1038[2]**

Snooty Eskimo (IRE) *W T Reed* 90c
14 ch g Aristocracy—Over The Arctic (Over The River (FR))
60[3] 278[5] 604[4]717[5] 855[7] 893[5]

Snow Patrol *C F Swan* 105h
5 gr g Linamix(FR) —Overcast (IRE) (Caerleon (USA))
3003a[10]

Snow's Ride *M D Hammond* 109 h
6 gr g Hernando(FR) —Crodelle (IRE) (Formidable (USA))
14[4] 192[4] (415) (1569) 1720[3] 2641[5] 4990[5]

Snow Tempest (USA) *T G Mills* 103+h
4 b g Theatrical—January's Storm (USA) (Hennessy (USA))
1146[4] (1519)

Snowy (IRE) *J I A Charlton* 103 h 117+c
8 gr g Pierre—Snowy Gunner (Gunner B)
303[2] 550[5] (1602) 2037[4] (2905) 4788[4]5122[P]

Snowy Ford (IRE) *N J Gifford* 117h 131c
9 b g Be My Native(USA) —Monalee Stream (Paddy's Stream)
(1599) 1920[3] 3000[10]3614[P] 4356[7] 4690[8]

Sobers (IRE) *R C Guest* 83+h
5 b g Epervier Bleu—Falcon Crest (FR) (Cadoudal (FR))
1849[4] 2185[2] 2572[5] 3691[6] 4342[4]

Sobraon (IRE) *N G Richards* 111 h
7 b g Topanoora—Anniepepp (IRE) (Montelimar (USA))
2944[B] (Dead)

So Brash (IRE) *P C Ritchens* 96h
6 ch g Rashar(USA) —Oak Tavern Lady (Dublin Taxi)
4665[3] 4934[2]

Socarineau (FR) *N J Pomfret* 79h
8 b g Assessor(IRE) —Samya King (FR) (King Of Macedon)
4896[4]

So Chic *A King* 53b
4 b f Luso—Tres Chic (IRE) (Bob Back (USA))
4059[6] 4902[8]

Society Buck (IRE) *John Allen* 102 h
9 b g Moscow Society(USA) —Bucks Grove (IRE) (Buckskin (FR))
450[9] 652[7] 1026[7] 2813[7] 3345[F]4549[12]

So Cloudy *D McCain* 75h
5 gr m Cloudings(IRE) —Sotattie (Teenoso (USA))
349[11] 917[4] 1213[P] 1569[10] 1896[2]2560[6] 3456[3] 4609[4]

So Determined (IRE) *J J Lambe* 96h
5 b g Soviet Star(USA) —Memory Green (USA) (Green Forest (USA))
870[8]

Soeur Fontenail (FR) *N J Hawke* 91h 117 c
9 b m Turgeon(USA) —Fontanalia (FR) (Rex Magna (FR))
234[7] 1825[2] 2368[F](2577) (2827) 3019[P]3344[4] 3992[3] 4677[4]4912[9]

Sofisio *Miss S J Wilton* 93h
9 ch g Efisio—Legal Embrace (CAN) (Legal Bid (USA))
760[10] 2463[8]

Solar At'Em (IRE) *M Sheppard* 79c
8 b g Up And At 'Em—Inshad (Indian King (USA))
2722[2] 2939[7] 3356[4]3647[4] 3888[U] 4281[6]

Solarias Quest *A King*
4 b g Pursuit Of Love—Persuasion (Batshoof)
3021[P] 3787[P]

Solar King *Mrs J M Mann* 43c
10 ch g Sir Harry Lewis(USA) —Chancer's Last (Foggy Bell)
4167[6] (Dead)

Solar System (IRE) *T J Taaffe* 111h 136+c
9 b g Accordion—Fauvette (USA) (Youth (USA))
69a[11] 3053a[F] 4929a[5]

Soldati (IRE) *I R Ferguson* 68c
8 b g Valville(FR) —Knocans Pride (IRE) (Torus)
322[5]

Sole Agent (IRE) *G L Moore* 115 h
4 b g Trans Island—Seattle Siren (USA) (Seattle Slew (USA))
2236[3] 3182[5] (3431) 3908[7] 4117[4] 4674[4]

Soleil D'Hiver *C J Drewe* 49 h
5 b m Bahamian Bounty—Catriona (Bustino)
134[P] 2726[9] 3279[F] 3483[P] 4320[P]

Soleil Fix (FR) *N J Gifford* 107h
5 b g Mansonnien(FR) —Ifaty (FR) (Rose Laurel)
100[3] (2020) 2530[10]

Solemn Vow *P Maddison* 36h
5 b m Zaffaran(USA) —Quick Quick Sloe (Scallywag)
209[8] 523[10] 687[6]

Solent Sunbeam *K C Bailey* 63h
6 b m Sovereign Water(FR) —Sail On Sunday (Sunyboy)
1961[4] 3497[4] 4376[11] 4875[7]

Solerina (IRE) *James Bowe* 161 h
9 b m Toulon—Deep Peace (Deep Run)
90a[5] 1621a[F] (2227a) (2669a) (2777a) 3080a[4] (3513a)

Solid As A Rock *J G Cann* 105b
6 b g Bijou D'Inde—Post Impressionist (IRE) (Ahonoora)
(4326) 4825[3]

Solid Silver *K G Reveley* 82b
5 ch g Pharly(FR) —Shadows Of Silver (Carwhite)
4854[10]

So Long *C L Popham* 82 h
6 ch m Nomadic Way(USA) —Cherry Picker (Nearly A Hand)
1909[3] 2152[5] 2507[9] 3882[5] 4569[6]4942[P]

Sol Roc (FR) *J Bertran De Balanda* 124h
5 gr g Turgeon(USA) —Shannon (FR) (Fijar Tango (FR))
778a[5]

Solvang (IRE) *Mrs J Marles* 88c
14 b g Carlingford Castle—Bramble Bird (Pitpan)
4831[F]

Solve It Sober (IRE) *S G Griffiths* 49h 86c
12 b g Carefree Dancer(USA) —Haunted Lady (Trimmingham)
436[2] 684[P] 1832[P]4594[P]

Solway Bee *Miss L Harrison* 82h
6 ch m Gunner B—Lady Mag (Silver Season)
4720[7] 4801[3]

Solway Bob *L Lungo*
7 b g Bob's Return(IRE) —Solway Moss (IRE) (Le Moss)
209^U

Solway Cloud *Miss L Harrison* 53h
6 b m Cloudings(IRE) —Oh Dear (Paico)
1590^6 1839^P 4917^P 5091^{11}

Solway Ed (IRE) *Miss L Harrison*
7 b g Mister Lord(USA) —Eds Luck (IRE) (Electric)
5063^{14}

Solway Gale (IRE) *L Lungo* 63 h 83 c
9 b m Husyan(USA) —Some Gale (Strong Gale)
11^6

Solway Larkin (IRE) *Miss L Harrison* 82h
8 b m Supreme Leader—In Any Case (IRE) (Torus)
5063^8

Solway Minstrel *Miss L Harrison* 103h
9 ch g Jumbo Hirt(USA) —Spicey Cut (Cut Above)
4805^7 5068^7 5123^8

Solway Raki *B Storey* 12b
5 ch g Rakaposhi King—In Any Case (IRE) (Torus)
1889^8 2450^P

Solway Sunset *David Alan Harrison* 90+c
7 br m Primitive Rising(USA) —Just Jessica (State Diplomacy (USA))
4044^2 4722^F

Solway Willy *N G Richards* 30h
5 ch g Bob's Return(IRE) —No Problem Jac (Safawan)
1323^5 1527^P

Some Bob Back (IRE) *C F Swan* 96+h
5 b m Bob Back(USA) —Sarahlee (Sayyaf)
2782a^8

Somedo Somedont *P F Nicholls* 94b
6 b g Sovereign Water(FR) —My Purple Prose (Rymer)
3583^2

Something Cristal (FR) *M Bradstock* 79b
5 b g Baby Turk—Something Fun (FR) (Rusticaro (FR))
2534^{17} 2988^5

Something Gold (FR) *M Bradstock* 105+h
6 gr g Baby Turk—Exiled (USA) (Iron Ruler (USA))
2983^{10} 4077^4 4443^{15}

Something Silver *J S Goldie* 77h
5 gr g Silver Patriarch(IRE) —Phantom Singer (Relkino)
4342^5 10^5

Something Wells (FR) *Miss Venetia Williams* 111+h
5 b g Dolpour—Linsky Ball (FR) (Cricket Ball (USA))
2799^3

Some Timbering (IRE) *E Sheehy* 104h 118c
7 b g Accordion—Hard Buns (IRE) (Mandalus)
3528a^3 5082a^5

Some Touch (IRE) *J Howard Johnson* 118+h
6 b g Scribano—Sarahs Touch (IRE) (Mandalus)
2487^5 (2901) 3376^7 (4313) 4750^8

Some Trainer (IRE) *J G Cromwell* 84h 82c
10 b g Leading Counsel(USA) —Miss Polymer (Doulab (USA))
1686^7 1723^P **2900^3**

Somewhere My Love *P Butler* 62h
5 br m Pursuit Of Love—Grand Coronet (Grand Lodge (USA))
1952^2 2216^P 3433^P

Somewin (IRE) *Mrs K Waldron* 73+h
6 b m Goldmark(USA) —Janet Oliphant (Red Sunset)
134^6 (310) 462^3 575^8 839^{13} 1156^4

Sommelier *N A Twiston-Davies* 89h
6 gr g Tamure(IRE) —Dissolve (Sharrood (USA))
2584^{11} 3249^P 3694^5 4549^P 5014^P

Sonderborg *Miss A M Newton-Smith* 63h
5 b m Great Dane(IRE) —Nordico Princess (Nordico (USA))
504^P

Sonevafushi (FR) *Miss Venetia Williams* 129h 152 c
8 b g Ganges(USA) —For Kicks (FR) (Top Ville)
2499^F 2748^3 (3343) (3469) 3620^P 3995^{P}4957^{14}

Song Of Vala *C J Mann* 108+h
5 ch g Peintre Celebre(USA) —Yanka (USA) (Blushing John (USA))
3963^P 4621^{10} 4819^3 10^2

Sonic Sound *Mrs K Waldron* 95+h
7 b g Cosmonaut—Sophiesue (Balidar)
230^3 502^3 1431^P 1712^4

Sonnenglanz (GER) *C Von Der Recke* 51h
7 br g Lomitas—Standing Ovation (ITY) (Law Society (USA))
2584^{16}

Sonnengold (GER) *Mrs L Wadham* 106+h
5 b m Java Gold(USA) —Standing Ovation (ITY) (Law Society (USA))
3550^2 (3979) 4494^9 4784^6 5052^6

Son Of Bathwick (IRE) *Mrs Norma Pook* 33h
4 b g Dr Fong(USA) —Bathwick Babe (IRE) (Sri Pekan (USA))
3340^8 3429^9 3939^{12}

Son Of Flighty *Evan Williams* 81h
8 b g Then Again—Record Flight (Record Token)
997^F 1333^5 1655^8

Son Of Greek Myth (USA) *G L Moore* 101h
5 b g Silver Hawk(USA) —Greek Myth (IRE) (Sadler's Wells (USA))
1826^P 2218^9 2347^7 2731^5 2952^{8}3814^7 4453^7

Son Of Man (IRE) *B D Leavy* 78h
7 b g Turtle Island(IRE) —Zagreb Flyer (Old Vic)
2071^{10} 2188^4 **3923^P**

Son Of Samson (IRE) *R J Price*
5 ch g Diesis—Delilah (IRE) (Bluebird (USA))
3504^{11}

Son Of Sophie *C N Kellett* 41h
4 b g Band On The Run—Fair Enchantress (Enchantment)
4631^8 4877^8

Sooky *J D Frost* 6h
6 ch m Double Trigger(IRE) —High Kabour (Kabour)
4667^5

Sooty From Mitcham *R H Alner* 46h
6 ch g Dancing Spree(USA) —Betty Barlow (Sagaro)
294^6 514^P 758^8

Soroka (IRE) *C N Kellett* 98h 64c
7 b g Sadler's Wells(USA) —Ivy (USA) (Sir Ivor (USA))
469^P 891^P **2807^9 2984^{P}3142^3 3547^{11} 3938^{U}4499^6**

Sort It Out (IRE) *Ferdy Murphy* 99h 85c
9 br g Phardante(FR) —Call Girl (IRE) (Dromod Hill)
279^4 415^3 **1568^4**

Sososimple (IRE) *D Broad* 75h
6 b m Simply Great(FR) —Reasonable Time (IRE) (Reasonable (FR))
1432^{10}

Sotovik (IRE) *A C Whillans* 116+h
5 gr g Aahsaylad—Moenzi (IRE) (Paris House)
2450^5 2652^3 2947^4 3376^5 3855^{2}4362^3 4724^5 (4982)

Soul King (IRE) *Michael Blake* 67c
11 b g King's Ride—Soul Lucy (Lucifer (USA))
3693^U 4325^P

Sound Accord (IRE) *C Tinkler* 108+b
5 br g Accordion—Shuil Na Lee (IRE) (Phardante (FR))
(4574)

Sound And Vision (IRE) *J K Price* 70h
4 b g Fayruz—Lyrical Vision (IRE) (Vision (USA))
1332^4 1441^2 1718^{13} 1^8

Sound Of Cheers *F Kirby* 109h 118 c
9 br g Zilzal(USA) —Martha Stevens (USA) (Super Concorde (USA))
2498^6 2926^3 3172^6(3398) 3917^4 4531^{3}4721^6 5018^8

Sound Skin (IRE) *A Ennis* 96h
8 gr g Sexton Blake—Ballinlassa (IRE) (Mandalus)
394^3 504^5 758^4 860^2 1607^{8}1773^5 4912^P

Sound Witness (IRE) *Robert Tyner* 99h 122c
8 b g Witness Box(USA) —Brogue Melody (IRE) (King's Ride)
4136a^4

Southbound (IRE) *I McMath* 58 h
7 ch g Zaffaran(USA) —Soxess (IRE) (Carlingford Castle)
417^P

South Bronx (IRE) *Mrs S C Bradburne* 105h 129c
7 br g Anshan—Tender Tan (Tanfirion)
1312^8 **1662^4 (1835) 2654^{2}3207^4 4531^7 5067^2**

Southern Bazaar (USA) *M E Sowersby* 69+h
5 ch g Southern Halo(USA) —Sunday Bazaar (USA) (Nureyev (USA))
892^8 1757^{11} 2081^{12} 2567^4 2962^{5}3557^4 4903^3 12^3

Southern Classic *R M Stronge* 97b
6 b g Classic Cliche(IRE) —Southern Sky (Comedy Star (USA))
4455^8 4786^3

Southerncrosspatch *Mrs Barbara Waring* 79h
15 ch g Ra Nova—Southern Bird (Shiny Tenth)
(1655) 2341^9 3656^6 4449^7

Southerndown (IRE) *R Lee* 88h 87 c
13 ch g Montelimar(USA) —Country Melody (IRE) (Orchestra)
464^4 1122^2 (1385) 1752^4 2424^6 2863^{3}3252^7 3654^3 4370^{3}4785^2

Southern Shore (IRE) *D Burchell* 71 h
4 ch g Erhaab(USA) —Intisab (Green Desert (USA))
1380^U 1440^9 1563^6 3804^P

Southern Vic (IRE) *T M Walsh* 133h 155 c
7 bb g Old Vic—Hug In A Fog (IRE) (Strong Gale)
(3079a) (3514a) 3893a^5

South Sands (IRE) *M Scudamore* 76h
5 b m Shaamit(IRE) —Mariners Mirror (Julio Mariner)
3^6

South Shore One *C Grant* 55b
5 b m J B Quick—Staggering (IRE) (Daring March)
277^5 720^6 1569^U 1683^P

Sou'Wester *C L Tizzard* 115h 76c
6 b g Fleetwood(IRE) —Mayfair (Green Desert (USA))
(4783) 5028^3

Sovereign Gale (IRE) *Miss T McCurrich* 73h
12 b m Strong Gale—Sovereign Sox (Don)
2244^P

Sovereign Girl *A W Carroll* 76h
5 b m Sovereign Water(FR) —The Quaker (Oats)
3^7

Sovereign's Gift *Mrs S D Williams* 95+h
10 ch m Elegant Monarch—Cadeau D'Aragon (Aragon)
245^P

Sovereign State (IRE) *D W Thompson* 112h
9 b g Soviet Lad(USA) —Portree (Slip Anchor)
525^6 1111^2 1296^5 2478^2 2952^{7}3761^{17} 4478^P 4797^5

Soviet Committee *T J Fitzgerald* 96b
6 b g Presidium—Lady Magician (Lord Bud)
1048^6 1237^7 1722^P

Sovietica (FR) *S Pike* 102b
5 b m Subotica(FR) —Vieille Russie (Kenmare (FR))
(1961) 4376^8 4976^5

Soviet Joy (IRE) *J J Quinn* 93+h
5 b g Russian Revival(USA) —Danny's Joy (IRE) (Maelstrom Lake)
136^{12} 4418^5 5135^8

Sovietta (IRE) *A G Newcombe* 63h
5 b m Soviet Star(USA) —La Riveraine (USA) (Riverman (USA))
3611^P 4074^9

So Wise So Young *R H Buckler* 53h
5 br g Young Ern—Tendresse (IRE) (Tender King)
2056^{11} 2579^9 3244^6 3996^{12} 4327^{8}4604^P

Space Cowboy (IRE) *G L Moore* 115+h
6 b g Anabaa(USA) —Lady Moranbon (USA) (Trempolino (USA))
(568) 753^5 (1250) (1272) 1598^F 1878^8 2047^{6}4838^8

Space Star *P R Webber* 112 h 118+c
6 b g Cosmonaut—Sophiesue (Balidar)
(104) 825^2 1024^3

Spanchil Hill *L A Dace* 69 h
6 b g Sabrehill(USA) —War Shanty (Warrshan (USA))
5048^3

Spanish Don *D R C Elsworth* 111h
8 b g Zafonic(USA) —Spanish Wells (IRE) (Sadler's Wells (USA))
2455^2

Spanish Main (IRE) *N A Twiston-Davies* 84 c
12 b g Spanish Place(USA) —Willow Grouse (Giolla Mear)
547^7 1893^6 2265^{7}3886^7 4567^3

Spanish Tan (NZ) *Jonjo O'Neill* 81h
6 ch g Senor Pete(USA) —Cammeray (NZ) (Prince Echo)
1614^{10} 2573^{10} 2860^U 2991^7 **3430^P**

Sparkes *H J Manners* 23h
8 b g Ballet Royal(USA) —Saxon Lass (Martinmas)
273^6

Sparkey Smith (IRE) *Major General C A Ramsay* 92h 76c
14 b g Mister Majestic—Jim Says (Jaazeiro (USA))
151^P

Sparkling Sabrina *P Bowen* 69h
6 b m Classic Cliche(IRE) —Sparkling Yasmin (Derring Rose)
2937^3 3881^{10} 4238^8

Sparkling Spring (IRE) *Evan Williams* 107 h 107c
15 b g Strong Gale—Cherry Jubilee (Le Bavard (FR))
1191^P

Sparkling Taff *Mrs S J Smith* 87+h
7 b g Alderbrook—Sparkling Time (USA) (Olden Times)
2340^{10} 2838^5 3975^6 4493^7 10^4

Sparklinspirit *J L Spearing* 99h
7 b g Sovereign Water(FR) —Emilys Trust (National Trust)
2720^9 3466^6 3806^F 4212^4 4860^{2}5137^3

Sparky Boy (IRE) *J I A Charlton* 74b
5 b g Executive Perk—Our Lot (IRE) (Phardante (FR))
3742^9 5008^{13}

Sparky Rocket *B Storey* 79b
5 b m Overbury(IRE) —Viking Rocket (Viking (USA))
2906^5 3273^8 4143^P

Sparron Hawk (FR) *N G Richards* 95+b
6 b m Hawker's News(IRE) —Inmemoriam (IRE) (Buckskin (FR))
(3556) 3931^4 4376^{14}

Spartacus Bay (IRE) *Miss Venetia Williams* 117b
5 b g Simply Great(FR) —Decent Slave (Decent Fellow)
(1849) 3392^2 4448^{22}

Spartan Encore *Miss Suzy Smith* 79b
4 ch g Spartan Monarch—Debs Review (Grundy)
4654^5

Spartan Place *J A Geake* 105 h
6 b g Overbury(IRE) —Pennethorne Place (Deep Run)
2301^4

Spa Wells (IRE) *Barry Potts* 47h
5 ch g Pasternak—La Tache (Namaqualand (USA))
719^5 876^7

Spear Thistle *Mrs N Smith* 108+h
4 ch g Selkirk(USA) —Ardisia (USA) (Affirmed (USA))
3340^P 3431^2 3908^5

Special Agenda (IRE) *M J M Evans* 76h 76c
12 b g Torus—Easter Blade (IRE) (Fine Blade (USA))
1673^P 1754^7

Special Ballot (IRE) *G A Swinbank* 78b
5 br m Perugino(USA) —Election Special (Chief Singer)
2948^7 3490^6

Special Conquest *J W Mullins* 117h 113c
8 b g El Conquistador—Kellys Special (Netherkelly)
(107) 296^2 1877^{P}2529^P 3290^4 3578^{2}3900^F 4078^7 4565^{2}4835^7 4857^3

Special Constable *B I Case* 56h 51c
8 bb g Derrylin—Lavenham's Last (Rymer)
110^P

Special Rate (IRE) *A King* 117h
9 br g Grand Plaisir(IRE) —Clerical Artist (IRE) (The Parson)
3017^P 3389^{11} 3727^7 4497^P

Spectacular Hope *J W Mullins* 80+h
6 b m Marju(IRE) —Distant Music (Darshaan)
134^{15} 263^2 458^3 749^7 905^{P}1017^6 1233^8 1597^4

Spectested (IRE) *A W Carroll* 96h
5 ch g Spectrum(IRE) —Nisibis (In The Wings)
2186^4 (3042) 3559^4

Spectrometer *Ian Williams* 120 h 125+c
9 ch g Rainbow Quest(USA) —Selection Board (Welsh Pageant)
1204^8 1444^2 1548^9 1872^{13} **2312^3(3992)** 4959^7

Spectrum Star *F P Murtagh* 55h 80c
6 b g Spectrum(IRE) —Persia (IRE) (Persian Bold)
60^5 213^4 395^{F}548^5 717^2

Specular (AUS) *Jonjo O'Neill* 147 h 118 c
10 b g Danehill(USA) —Spyglass (NZ) (Sir Sian (NZ))
1320^3 1457^F 1529^8

Speed Kris (FR) *Mrs S C Bradburne* 95h 93c
7 b g Belmez(USA) —Pandia (USA) (Affirmed (USA))
304^3 410^3 1296^7 1513^6 1606^{4}2066^5 2417^4 3234^3 3487^{13} 3854^{8}4043^{10} 5068^3

Speedro (IRE) *Miss Lucinda V Russell* 86h
8 b g Glacial Storm(USA) —Sindys Gale (Strong Gale)
4720^F 5091^6

Speed Venture *J Mackie* 101h
9 b g Owington—Jade Venture (Never So Bold)
91^5 2585^9 2822^3 3152^3 (3848) (3990) 4322^U

Speedy Tactics (IRE) *Lindsay Woods* 22h
7 b m Flemensfirth(USA) —Hilary's Image (IRE) (Phardante (FR))
4141^{14}

Spence Appeal (IRE) *C Roberts* 71 h
4 b g Nicolotte—It's All Academic (IRE) (Mazaad)
1380^F 1441^7 1563^5 1649^3

Spes Bona (USA) *G M Moore* 60+h
5 b g Rakeen(USA) —Novelette (Darshaan)
192^{16}

Sphinx Du Berlais (FR) *F-M Cottin* 128c
7 b g Nikos—La Taiga (FR) (Labus (FR))
585a^4 779a^4

Spidam (FR) *P F Nicholls* 118+h
4 bb g Moon Madness—Spinage (FR) (Village Star (FR))
2274^3 (2612) 3294^3

Spider Boy *Miss Z C Davison* 69h 76c
9 b g Jupiter Island—Great Dilemma (Vaigly Great)
229^7 501^4 1018^4 1246^6 1482^{5}1645^5 **2561^7 2951^{6}3221^3 3430^3 3686^{3}4650^2 4914^P**

Spiders Web *G L Moore* 97 h
6 gr g Linamix(FR) —Cattermole (USA) (Roberto (USA))
167^8 506^4 683^{RR} 1409^3 1483^{8}2930^4

Spike And Divel (IRE) *Jonjo O'Neill* 96h
8 b g Zaffaran(USA) —Lady Go Marching (USA) (Go Marching (USA))
841^{10} 906^7

Spike Jones (NZ) *Mrs S M Johnson* 104 h
8 br g Colonel Collins(USA) —Gloss (NZ) (Kaapstad (NZ))
1774^P 2071^9 2182^3 2285^4 2592^{7}2822^4 3128^2 3360^F (3616) 3650^5 3880^{9}4280^9 4593^3 4781^{10} 4858^{10}

Spilaw (FR) *John Allen* 73h 77c
10 b g Sky Lawyer(FR) —Spinage (FR) (Village Star (FR))
464^8

Spinaround *P R Webber* 92h 112+c
8 gr g Terimon—Re-Spin (Gildoran)
2705^U 3368^4 4164^{3}4590^2 (4908)

Spinofski *D R Stoddart* 127 c
11 b g Petoski—Spin Again (Royalty)
1798^P 1989^P 3151^P

Spirit Of New York (IRE) *Jonjo O'Neill* 74b 135+c
7 b g Topanoora—Fiona's Blue (Crash Course)
(1613) **(1891) 2607^5**

Spirit Of Tenby (IRE) *W K Goldsworthy* 87+h
9 b g Tenby—Asturiana (Julio Mariner)
(501) (665) 906^5 949^5 1152^7 2845^{12}

Spiritual Dancer (IRE) *L Wells* 102+h
11 b g King's Ride—Arctic Tartan (Deep Run)
502^5 630^8

Spiritual Society (IRE) *M Scudamore* 104h 99+c
6 b g Moscow Society(USA) —Sniggy (Belfort (FR))
3175^7 3386^7 **3903^F 4618^{P}4870^3**

Spitfire Bob (USA) *M E Sowersby* 86h
7 b g Mister Baileys—Gulf Cyclone (USA) (Sheikh Albadou)
1949^5 **570^P**

Spitfire Sortie (IRE) *M W Easterby* 110+b
5 b g Sadler's Wells(USA) —Madame Est Sortie (FR) (Longleat (USA))
(3319) 4507^6 5141^5

Splash Out Again *P Bowen* 107+h 107+c
8 gr g River Falls—Kajetana (FR) (Caro)
(1232) 2344^F 3326^P (Dead)

Splendour (IRE) *Miss S Cox* 120h 134c
11 b g Broken Hearted—Black Trix (Peacock (FR))
1083a^P 1810a^5 2227a^P

Sporazene (IRE) *P F Nicholls* 139h
7 gr g Cozzene(USA) —Sporades (USA) (Vaguely Noble)
2055^4 **2635^F** 2761^7 3177^{F}3723^6 4008^3 4473^{21}

Sporting Chance *Mrs Jo Sleep* 103c
14 ch g Ikdam—Tumbling Ego (Abednego)
47^{11} 221^6 4216^P

Sports Express *Miss Lucinda V Russell* 95+h 94c
8 ch m Then Again—Lady St Lawrence (USA) (Bering)
3316^P **4314^3 4516^{4}5037^P**

Sportsfield Coogee (IRE) *D P Keane* 48h
7 b g Fourstars Allstar(USA) —Maiden Fair (Monseigneur (USA))
201^P 343^6 384^P 696^{10} **805^P**

Sportula *C Grant* 80h
5 b m Silver Patriarch(IRE) —Portent (Most Welcome)
1839^P 2186^5 2674^2 3235^P 3914^P

Spot Thedifference (IRE) *E Bolger* 94h 150 c
13 b g Lafontaine(USA) —Spotted Choice (IRE) (Callernish)
(2164) 2745^{11} 4434^2

Spreejinsky *K G Wingrove*
8 ch g Dancing Spree(USA) —Smooth Flight (Sandhurst Prince)
79^P 911^{17}

Spree Vision *P Monteith* 99+h 94c
10 b g Suave Dancer(USA) —Regent's Folly (IRE) (Touching Wood (USA))
420^5 647^3 784^{14} 871^7 940^9

Springaway *Miss Kate Milligan* 79h
7 ch g Minster Son—Galway Gal (Proverb)
2106^3 4530^4

Spring Bee *T Wall* 68h
6 b m Parthian Springs—First Bee (Gunner B)
96^F 462^P 1028^P

Spring Breeze *Ferdy Murphy* 114 h
5 ch g Dr Fong(USA) —Trading Aces (Be My Chief (USA))
1569^3 (1794) 2903^2 3561^7 4612^6 5059a^{17}5103a^{10}

Spring Chick *A J Whiting*
6 b m Thowra(FR) —Broughton Manor (Dubassoff (USA))
1961^{12} 3188^{11}

Springer The Lad *Miss M P Bryant* 34h
9 ch g Carlton(GER) —Also Kirsty (Twilight Alley)
3715^P 3899^{11} 4133^P

Springford (IRE) *Mrs Caroline Keevil* 46h 111 c
14 b g King's Ride—Tickenor Wood (Le Bavard (FR))
4757^{7}

Spring Gamble (IRE) *G M Moore* 99h 110+c
7 b g Norwich—Aurora Run (IRE) (Cyrano De Bergerac)
1662^{6} (1928) 2630^{8}3037^{3}

Spring Grove (IRE) *R H Alner* 112h 123 c
11 b g Mandalus—Lucy Lorraine (IRE) (Buckskin (FR))
130^{P} 2048^{4} 2492^{7}2828^{2} 3509^{5} 3988^{P}4152^{2} 4857^{5}

Spring Ice *M Scudamore* 52b
4 b f Parthian Springs—Sea Ice (Roscoe Blake)
2521^{9} 3468^{13}

Spring Junior (FR) *P J Hobbs* 91h
5 b g Concorde Jr(USA) —Top Spring (FR) (Top Ville)
490^{4} 1969^{4} 2849^{4} 3210^{10} 3876^{P}**4558^{P}**

Spring Lover (FR) *Miss Venetia Williams* 95h 129c
7 b g Fijar Tango(FR) —Kailasa (FR) (Rb Chesne)
97^{5} 2272^{5} 2530^{11}**3420^{4} 3803^{2} 4611^{P}4829^{P} 5126^{6}**

Spring Margot (FR) *David M Easterby* 113c
10 b g Kadalko(FR) —La Brunante (FR) (Chaparral (FR))
(454) 3847^{P} (5020)

Spring Pursuit *E G Bevan* 125h
10 b g Rudimentary(USA) —Pursuit Of Truth (USA) (Irish River (FR))
1828^{3} 2336^{8} 2876^{9} 3289^{P} 3397^{F}3615^{F}

Springvic (IRE) *G M Moore* 94+h
6 b g Old Vic—Spring Beauty (IRE) (King's Ride)
2444^{9} 2991^{4} 3314^{9}

Springwood White *Mrs V Park* 85c
12 gr g Sharkskin Suit(USA) —Kale Brig (New Brig)
5020^{5} 6^{7}

Spud's Fancy *D A Rees*
7 ch m You My Chief—Adelbaran (FR) (No Pass No Sale)
1619^{P} 1711^{P} 1782^{11}

Spuradich (IRE) *Jonjo O'Neill* 109+h
6 b g Barathea(IRE) —Svanzega (USA) (Sharpen Up)
991^{2} 1182^{3} 1415^{2}

Spy Gun (USA) *T Wall*
6 ch g Mt. Livermore(USA) —Takeover Target (USA) (Nodouble (USA))
5070^{9}

Squantum (IRE) *Miss Joanne Priest* 89+h 95c
9 b g Roselier(FR) —Cool Eile (IRE) (King's Ride)
469^{2} 630^{P} (3325) **3654^{6}** 3959^{6}

Square Dealer *J R Norton* 71b
5 b g Vettori(IRE) —Pussy Foot (Red Sunset)
2690^{8}

Square Mile (IRE) *Jonjo O'Neill* 112+h
6 ch g Bob Back(USA) —Mother Imelda (IRE) (Phardante (FR))
(1611) 3646^{3} 4212^{F}

Square Root (IRE) *Anthony Mullins* 94b
5 b g Darazari(IRE) —Fontaine Lodge (IRE) (Lafontaine (USA))
5060a^{12}

Squeaker *H E Haynes* 64b
5 br m Sovereign Water(FR) —Armagnac Messenger (Pony Express)
2579^{10}

Squeeze (IRE) *B N Pollock* 83b 111c
8 b g Old Vic—Petaluma Pet (Callernish)
3644^{4} 3432^{5} (Dead)

Squires Lane (IRE) *Andrew Turnell* 107c
7 b g Mister Lord(USA) —Perks Glory (IRE) (Executive Perk)
2311^{6} 2848^{5} 3480^{2}(4054) 4847^{6}

Sraid Na Cathrach (IRE) *C Byrnes* 98h 123c
10 ch g Insan(USA) —Credo's Campaign (IRE) (Le Moss)
91a^{P}

Stack The Pack (IRE) *T R George* 86h 110+c
9 ch g Good Thyne(USA) —Game Trix (Buckskin (FR))
(321) (612) 1988^{P}4558^{4}

Staff Nurse (IRE) *N Wilson* 84h
6 b m Night Shift(USA) —Akebia (USA) (Trempolino (USA))
192^{8} 854^{5} 1278^{2} 1432^{2} 1490^{P}1588^{7}

Stagecoach Diamond *Mrs S J Smith* 130+h 37c
7 b g Classic Cliche(IRE) —Lyra (Blakeney)
133^{9} 591^{2} (843) 992^{2} (3779) 4108^{3} 4792^{6}

Stagecoach Opal *Mrs S J Smith* 97+h
5 b g Komaite(USA) —Rag Time Belle (Raga Navarro (ITY))
1889^{4} 2572^{8} (3785) 4720^{3}

Stage Friendly (IRE) *N A Twiston-Davies* 89h 102+c
7 ch g Old Vic—Just Affable (IRE) (Phardante (FR))
177^{5} 334^{U} **692^{0} 815^{2}**

Stag Party (FR) *F Doumen*
5 ch g Exit To Nowhere(USA) —Marital Bliss (FR) (Double Bed (FR))
3388^{P}

Stakeholder (IRE) *Mrs H E Rees* 65h
8 ch g Priolo(USA) —Island Goddess (Godswalk (USA))
2605^{5} 3211^{5} 4010^{3}

Staley's Queen *K G Wingrove* 16b
5 b m Classic Cliche(IRE) —Mesp (IRE) (Strong Gale)
7^{14}

Stallone *N Wilson* 86 h 75+c
9 ch g Brief Truce(USA) —Bering Honneur (USA) (Bering)
1376^{6}

Stamparland Hill *J M Jefferson* 111h 130 c
11 b g Gildoran—Woodland Flower (Furry Glen)
353^{P} 525^{5}

Stan (NZ) *R C Guest* 124+h 124c
7 b g Super Imposing(NZ) —Take Care (NZ) (Wham (AUS))
(13) 127^{6} **(550)** 1617^{4} **1669^{3}**

Stance *G L Moore* 136h 132c
7 b g Salse(USA) —De Stael (USA) (Nijinsky (CAN))
(510) 2052^{4} 2371^{2}2869^{3} 3299^{8} 3726^{3}4456^{P}

Stand Easy (IRE) *J R Cornwall* 77h 102c
13 b g Buckskin(FR) —Geeaway (Gala Performance)
240^{4}

Standing Bloom *Mrs P Sly* 88 h 88 c
10 ch m Presidium—Rosie Cone (Celtic Cone)
2184^{6} 2505^{4} **2955^{3} 3368^{11}3814^{8}**

Standin Obligation (IRE) *M C Pipe* 155+h 116+c
7 ch g Pierre—Clonroche Floods (Pauper)
(128) (1830) (2175) 2336^{P} 4461^{17} (4974)

Stand On Me *P Monteith* 70h 66c
7 ch g Bob's Return(IRE) —Weldcome (Weld)
3231^{6} 3374^{7} 3532^{3} **4844^{7}**

Stansted (IRE) *M J McGrath* 33b
5 b g Mister Mat(FR) —Blackwater Lady (IRE) (Torus)
4825^{11}

Stantons Church *Mrs P Ford* 71h 55c
9 b g Homo Sapien—Valkyrie Reef (Miramar Reef)
1212^{P}

Stanway *Mrs Mary Hambro* 94h 75 c
7 b g Presenting—Nicklup (Netherkelly)
193^{U} 1634^{F} 1877^{9}2273^{P} 5136^{P}

Star Angler (IRE) *H D Daly* 113 h 103 c
8 b g Supreme Leader—So Pink (IRE) (Deep Run)
2504^{4} 2825^{P} 3581^{7}4372^{9} 4727^{7}

Star Award (IRE) *N J Henderson* 93+b
5 bb m Oscar(IRE) —Forgotten Star (IRE) (Don't Forget Me)
(4940)

Starbright *W G Young* 67h
5 b g Polar Falcon(USA) —Treasure Hunt (Hadeer)
301^{P} 596^{9} 645^{4} 716^{14} 780^{8}942^{P} 1307^{5} 1508^{7} 1605^{5} 1824^{6}2040^{P} (Dead)

Starbuck *Miss J Fisher* 80c
12 b g Brush Aside(USA) —Clonmello (Le Bavard (FR))
783^{2} 827^{6} 1589^{2}1686^{4} 1719^{3} 1886^{5}3758^{4} 3926^{3} 4791^{6}

Star Clipper *Noel Meade* 127h 133c
9 b g Kris—Anne Bonny (Ajdal (USA))
91a^{10} (1700a) 2539a^{5}3053a^{19} 4762^{F} 4929a^{14}

Star De Lambre (FR) *J-P Cordonnier*
7 b g True Brave(USA) —Rosileina (FR) (Policeman (FR))
846a^{0}

Star De Mohaison (FR) *P F Nicholls* 119h 152+c
5 b g Beyssac(FR) —Belle De Mohaison (FR) (Suvero (FR))
(1845) 2607^{2} 3178^{3}(3601) (4444) (4759)

Star Double (ITY) *N A Twiston-Davies* 76+h
6 ch g Bob Back(USA) —Among The Stars (Pharly (FR))
1779^{3}

Star Fever (IRE) *Miss H C Knight* 88h
5 b g Saddlers' Hall(IRE) —Phenics Allstar (IRE) (Fourstars Allstar (USA))
7^{9} 531^{3} 2144^{6} 2559^{11} 4905^{10}

Star Galaxy (IRE) *Andrew Turnell* 67h 66c
6 b g Fourstars Allstar(USA) —Raven Night (IRE) (Mandalus)
2269^{10} 2624 ^{P} 2983^{13} 3603^{7} 3997^{P}**4132^{U} 4837^{9} 5105^{P}**

Star Jack (FR) *Miss P Robson* 115c
11 b g Epervier Bleu—Little Point (FR) (Le Nain Jaune (FR))
1954 437^{F}

Stark Raven *Miss E C Lavelle* 60h
6 b g Sea Raven(IRE) —Hilly Path (Brave Invader (USA))
1782^{8} 1990^{6} 3941^{P}

Starlight Express (FR) *Miss E C Lavelle* 99+h
6 b m Air Express(IRE) —Muramixa (FR) (Linamix (FR))
2018^{P}

Star Member (IRE) *Ian Williams* 122 h
7 b g Hernando(FR) —Constellation (IRE) (Kaldoun (FR))
(1454) 2173^{8} (2964) 3214^{4}

Starmix *G A Harker* 39h
5 br g Linamix(FR) —Danlu (USA) (Danzig (USA))
273^{4}

Staroski *Simon Earle* 83b
9 b m Petoski—Olnistar (FR) (Balsamo (FR))
2461^{P}

Star Performance (IRE) *Oliver McKiernan* 96h 107c
11 ch g Insan(USA) —Leallen (Le Bavard (FR))
87a^{7} 2745^{12} 3513a^{P}**5128a^{3}**

Star Prize (IRE) *N J Henderson* 100 h
9 b g Fourstars Allstar(USA) —Dipper's Gift (IRE) (Salluceva)
111^{9}

Starry Mary *R J Price* 80h
8 b m Deploy—Darling Splodge (Elegant Air)
1906^{9} 2466^{4} 2862^{11} 3125^{11}

Stars Delight (IRE) *Jim Best* 102+h
6 ch g Fourstars Allstar(USA) —Celtic Cygnet (Celtic Cone)
1188^{6} 4912^{3} 5137^{6}

Star Shot (IRE) *P R Webber* 115h
5 b g Cloudings(IRE) —B Final (Gunner B)
(616) 2211^{15} 3353^{4} (4935)

Stars'N'Stripes (IRE) *W W Dennis* 58b 64c
8 b g Lord Americo—Drumdeels Star (IRE) (Le Bavard (FR))
1891^{P} 2848^{8} 3017^{P}4279^{P}

Star Storm (IRE) *F Flood* 49c
12 b g Glacial Storm(USA) —Star Whistler (Menelek)
112a^{P}

Star Time (IRE) *M Scudamore* 79h
7 b g Fourstars Allstar(USA) —Punctual (Lead On Time (USA))
2073^{7} **3252^{P}** 4277^{4} 4734^{4}4869^{3}

Starting Point *Miss Lucinda V Russell* 94b
4 br g Monashee Mountain(USA) —Louise Moillon (Mansingh (USA))
3799^{2} 4519^{2}

Star Trooper (IRE) *Miss S E Forster* 78 h 85c
10 bb g Brief Truce(USA) —Star Cream (Star Appeal)
11^{3} 480^{2} 592^{3} 781^{4} 988^{5}2025^{9} 2453^{13} 2657^{14} **2843^{10} 3270^{5}**(3335) 3552^{4} 3797^{7} 4045^{7} 4145^{7} **4655^{5}**

Star Wonder *G R I Smyly* 53h
6 b m Syrtos—Galava (CAN) (Graustark)
2179^{11} 2721^{9} **3653^{F}**

Starzaan (IRE) *H Morrison* 150+h
7 b g Darshaan—Stellina (IRE) (Caerleon (USA))
3020^{3} 3723^{7} 4458^{7} 4745^{10}

Star Zero *J Howard Johnson* 86h
5 b g Danzero(AUS) —Startino (Bustino)
4040^{4} 4657^{P}

Stately Progress (IRE) *C Grant*
8 b g Nashwan(USA) —Khamsin (USA) (Mr Prospector (USA))
8^{P}

State Of Play *Evan Williams* 103+h 156+c
6 b g Hernando(FR) —Kaprice (GER) (Windwurf (GER))
136^{4} (680) **(1678) (2375) 2973^{5}(4764)**

Statley Raj (IND) *B G Powell* 99 h
7 b g Mtoto—Donna Star (Stately Don (USA))
1250^{7} **1363^{P}**

Stavordale Lad (IRE) *P F Nicholls* 122+c
8 b g Mister Lord(USA) —Ath Trasna (Amoristic (USA))
2375^{U} 2808^{2} 3218^{2}(3672) 3949^{2} (4605) 5007^{F}

St Barchan (IRE) *A G Juckes*
5 ch g Grand Lodge(USA) —Moon Tango (IRE) (Last Tycoon)
2245^{P}

Steel Band *Paul A Roche* 117h 139c
8 ch g Kris—Quaver (USA) (The Minstrel (CAN))
2650a^{6} 3411a^{17} **4138a^{4} 5057a^{4}**

Steel Duke (IRE) *D Broad* 46b
5 bb g Luso—Lobby Nes (IRE) (Lanfranco)
44a^{17}

Steel Warrior *J S Smith* 63b
9 ch g Michelozzo(USA) —Iskra Bay (IRE) (Un Desperado (FR))
2821^{P} 3948^{P} 4733^{P}

Steely Dan *J R Best*
7 b g Danzig Connection(USA) —No Comebacks (Last Tycoon)
3996^{P}

Stepastray *R E Barr* 49h
9 gr g Alhijaz—Wandering Stranger (Petong)
10^{11}

Step In Line (IRE) *D W Thompson* 63h 73+c
14 gr g Step Together(USA) —Ballycahan Girl (Bargello)
110^{P} 414^{F} 480^{9} 781^{10} 822^{5}1066^{6} 1308^{3} 1333^{4} 1526^{P} **1686^{P}1819^{3} 2080^{P} 2257^{6}**

Step Perfect (USA) *G M Moore* 90h
5 b g Royal Academy(USA) —Gossiping (USA) (Chati (USA))
1794^{4} 2108^{2} 2444^{U} 2750^{11} 3167^{3}3779^{P}

Steppes Of Gold (IRE) *Jonjo O'Neill* 136+h 132 c
9 b g Moscow Society(USA) —Trysting Place (He Loves Me)
1736^{F} 2620^{2} 2989^{3}3601^{2} 4460^{12}

Step Quick (IRE) *Mrs S E Busby* 97+c
12 ch g All Haste(USA) —Little Steps (Step Together (USA))
313^{U}

Sterling Guarantee (USA) *N Wilson* 98h
8 b g Silver Hawk(USA) —Sterling Pound (USA) (Seeking The Gold (USA))
192^{3} 415^{2} 602^{2} 780^{3} 856^{4}1085^{DSQ} (1223) 1377^{P}

Sterling Heights (NZ) *Mrs Tracey Barfoot-Saunt*
7 br g Rainbow Myth(NZ) —Amrita (NZ) (Amyntor (FR))
4562^{4}

Sterling Supporter *D W Thompson* 26h
4 b f Josr Algarhoud(IRE) —Riyoom (USA) (Vaguely Noble)
2477^{9} 2954^{P}

Stern (IRE) *Miss E C Lavelle* 108h
7 bb g Executive Perk—Christian Lady (IRE) (Mandalus)
(1775)

Stewarts Dream (IRE) *B D Leavy* 6h
5 b g Eurobus—Lolas Dream (Palm Track)
2007^{10} 3885^{8}

St George's Day *D J Wintle* 85b
6 gr g Sir Harry Lewis(USA) —Steel Typhoon (General Ironside)
4940^{8}

St Helier *D O Stephens*
11 b m Gildoran—Belhelvie (Mart Lane)
759^{P}

Sticky End *J B Walton* 78h
5 b g Endoli(USA) —Carat Stick (Gold Rod)
2268^{5} 3319^{9} 3793^{15}

Still Solvent *J R Turner* 95b
5 b g Keen—Bad Start (USA) (Bold Bidder)
2906^{3} 3785^{11}

Stingray (IRE) *N I M Rossiter*
4 b c Danehill(USA) —Music And Dance (USA) (Northern Dancer)
3346^{P} 3699^{P}

St Kilda *Miss Lucy Bridges* 65h 77 c
9 b m Past Glories—Oiseval (National Trust)
1832^{P} 1951^{3} 2424^{P}2575^{P}

St Matthew (USA) *Mrs S J Smith* 145+h 140+c
8 b g Lear Fan(USA) —Social Crown (USA) (Chief's Crown (USA))
1721^{5} (1924) (2336) **2491^{9}2992^{F}**

Stock Exchange (IRE) *P Bowen*
4 b g King's Best(USA) —Queen's Ransom (IRE) (Last Tycoon)
1190^{P}

Stocking Island *C R Egerton* 93h
5 ch m Desert King(IRE) —Rawya (USA) (Woodman (USA))
2826^{6} 3322^{3} 3597^{2} 4834^{11} (Dead)

Stocks 'n Shares *Miss E C Lavelle* 92h 112+c
10 b m Jupiter Island—Norstock (Norwick (USA))
762^{2} 1234^{P}

Stockton Flyer *Mrs D A Butler*
5 b g I'm Supposin(IRE) —Orange Alert (Gildoran)
3617^{12}

Stokesies Boy *C Roberts* 78h
6 gr g Key Of Luck(USA) —Lesley's Fashion (Dominion)
1541^{P} 1724^{8}

Stolen Moments (FR) *P D Niven* 100b
5 gr g Villez(USA) —Brave Lola (FR) (Dom Pasquini (FR))
2572^{7} (3237) 4366^{2} 4853^{6}

Stolen Song *M J Ryan* 86h 64c
6 b g Sheikh Albadou—Sparky's Song (Electric)
218^{8} 1559^{P}

Stone Cold *T D Easterby* 97h 107c
9 ch g Inchinor—Vaula (Henbit (USA))
132^{P} 346^{P}

Stoneferry *R Johnson* 84b
6 b g Hatim(USA) —Richards Kate (Fidel)
1593^{4} 1762^{6} 2112^{10}

Stoneravinmad *Mrs E Slack* 68+h
8 ch g Never So Bold—Premier Princess (Hard Fought)
(1723) 1943^{3}

Stoneriggs *Mrs E Slack* 64+h
5 gr g Silver Patriarch(IRE) —Maid To Match (Matching Pair)
14^{P} 147^{P} 209^{3} 426^{6}

Stoneriggs Merc (IRE) *Mrs E Slack* 68h 74c
5 gr g Alderbrook—Betseale (IRE) (Step Together (USA))
484^{5} 2036^{P} 3780^{7} 3927^{8} 4302^{5}**4921^{P}**

Stoneriggs Silver *Mrs E Slack* 24b
5 gr g Silver Patriarch(IRE) —Carole's Crusader (Faustus (USA))
431^{7}

Stoneville (IRE) *E McNamara* 130+h
6 b g Flemensfirth(USA) —Clodas Pet (IRE) (Andretti)
4137a^{3}

Stonewall George (NZ) *Jonjo O'Neill* 95+h
8 ch g Stark South(USA) —Mother's Word (Mummy's Pet)
915^{14}

Stoney Drove (FR) *Miss H C Knight* 65h
6 b g Exit To Nowhere(USA) —Miss Naelle (FR) (Al Nasr (FR))
2049^{4} 2829^{P} 4875^{8}

Stoneyford Ben (IRE) *S Gollings* 103b
7 b g Beneficial—Rosie Rock (Swan's Rock)
2131^{9}

Stoop To Conquer *A W Carroll* 113 h
6 b g Polar Falcon(USA) —Princess Genista (Ile De Bourbon (USA))
1969^{5} 3219^{2} 3984^{5}

Stopwatch (IRE) *Mrs L C Jewell* 70h 90c
11 b g Lead On Time(USA) —Rose Bonbon (FR) (High Top)
104^{6} 283^{7} **503^{7}1524^{6} 1595^{5} 1776^{6}2323^{6}** 2958^{10} **4525^{2}4870^{4}**

Storm Clear (IRE) *D J Wintle* 89h
7 b g Mujadil(USA) —Escape Path (Wolver Hollow)
(75) 396^{4} 438^{U} 683^{3} 943^{P}

Stormez (FR) *M C Pipe* 111 h 140c
9 b g Ezzoud(IRE) —Stormy Scene (USA) (Storm Bird (CAN))
2176^{P} 2747^{11} 3179^{2} 3727^{10}**4496^{P}**

Storm Of Applause (IRE) *P J Hobbs* 85h
5 b g Accordion—Dolce Notte (IRE) (Strong Gale)
3127^{5} 3511^{3} 5110^{6}

Stormont Dawn (IRE) *Mrs L B Normile* 62b
5 b m Glacial Storm(USA) —Andros Dawn (IRE) (Buckskin (FR))
3556^{5} 4319^{5}

Stormy Bay (IRE) *R C Guest* 90b
5 b g Glacial Storm(USA) —Duffys Choice (IRE) (Yashgan)
2340^{9} 2844^{12} 3532^{P}

Stormy Beech *R Johnson* 83 h 97+c
10 b g Glacial Storm(USA) —Cheeny's Brig (New Brig)
122^{10} 497^{5} 592^{14}**644^{4}**

Stormy Lord (IRE) *J Wade* 129h 128+c
10 br g Lord Americo—Decent Shower (Decent Fellow)
1913^{P} 3256^{6} 3542^{4} 4488^{2}4990^{7} 5066^{8}

Stormy Madam (IRE) *J R Turner* 54h
6 b m Glacial Storm(USA) —Menelave (IRE) (Meneval (USA))
27^{6} 2704^{9} 2942^{14} 3254^{7} 3540^{P}4916^{P}

Stormy Row (IRE) *M B Shears* 49h
12 b g Phardante(FR) —Thistle Chat (Le Bavard (FR))
137^{6}

Stormy Skye (IRE) *G L Moore* 106h 106c
10 b g Bluebird(USA) —Canna (Caerleon (USA))
12^{7} 288^{P} (1920) 2557^{F} 3284^{4} 3434^{2}3981^{3} 4524^{P}

Story Arms *D Burchell*
4 b g Kayf Tara—Young India (Indian King (USA))
3878^{U} 4015^{P} 4786^{U} 4934^{P}

St Pirran (IRE) *R C Guest* 85h
11 bb g Be My Native(USA) —Guess Twice (Deep Run)
1720^{8} 2334^{5} 2641^{3} 2876^{12} 3378^{14}**3852^{P}** 4792^{12}

Straight On (IRE) *A H B Hodge* 95c
15 bb g Tremblant—Maybird (Royalty)
184^{P}

Straight Talker (IRE) *H S Howe* 85+h
7 b g Warcraft(USA) —The Mighty Midge (Hardgreen (USA))
5106^{P}

Strange Days (IRE) *Mrs K Waldron* 85b
6 b g Topanoora—Boro Bow (IRE) (Buckskin (FR))
1730^{6} 2185^{5} 2461^{P}

Strangely Brown (IRE) *E McNamara* 152+h
5 b g Second Empire(IRE) —Damerela (IRE) (Alzao (USA))
88a^{2} (778a) 3080a^{3} 3585a^{2} 4446^{2} (4765) 5101a^{5}

Strathtay *M Appleby* 80+h
4 ch f Pivotal—Cressida (Polish Precedent (USA))
945[F] 1095[4] 1380[2] 1873[7] 2245[2](2454) 2632[6] 2935[P] 3479[P]
Stravonian *G A Swinbank* 70h
6 b g Luso—In The Evening (IRE) (Distinctly North (USA))
418[8] 2447[5] 2944[P]
Straw Bear (USA) *N J Gifford* 159+h
5 ch g Diesis—Highland Ceilidh (IRE) (Scottish Reel)
(3328) (3658) 4430[2] (4763) 5056a[2]
Strawberry (IRE) *J W Mullins* 101b
5 b m Beneficial—Ravaleen (IRE) (Executive Perk)
4237[2] 4751[4] 4976[2]
Street Life (IRE) *W J Musson* 94 h
8 ch g Dolphin Street(FR) —Wolf Cleugh (IRE) (Last Tycoon)
438[5] 2487[11] 3328[7] 3658[10]
Streetshavenoname (IRE) *T J Taaffe* 107b
5 b g Old Vic—Glore River (IRE) (Broken Hearted)
4779[12]
Strident (USA) *J J Lambe* 89h
5 ch g Deputy Commander(USA) —Regrets Only (USA) (Black Tie Affair)
1824[2]
Strides Of Fire (IRE) *John A Codd* 117h
5 b h General Monash(USA) —Lagrion (USA) (Diesis)
(65a)
Strike An Ark (IRE) *Ms Caroline Hutchinson* 101+b
5 bb m Shernazar—Me Little Mot (IRE) (Masterclass (USA))
2782a[10]
Strike Back (IRE) *Mrs John Harrington* 140h 140c
8 b g Bob Back(USA) —First Strike (IRE) (Magical Strike (USA))
89a[3] 3527a[3] 3774a[5]3894a[8] **4472[P] 5080a[7]**
Striking Silver *I McMath* 76b
5 gr g Silver Patriarch(IRE) —Snowgirl (IRE) (Mazaad)
4147[10] 4787[11]
Stripe Me Blue *P J Jones* 95b
4 b g Miner's Lamp—Slipmatic (Pragmatic)
3699[2]
Strolling Vagabond (IRE) *John R Upson* 77h
7 ch g Glacial Storm(USA) —Found Again (IRE) (Black Minstrel)
1854[3] 2073[6] 2517[6] (3424) 4012[P] 4557[9]
Strong Magic (IRE) *J R Cornwall* 57h 75c
14 br g Strong Gale—Baybush (Boreen (FR))
366[3] 1489[8] 1620[2](1815) 1989[5] 2325[8](2524) 2703[5] 3420[6]3965[4] 4419[9] 4576[9]4876[P]
Strong Project (IRE) *Sean O O'Brien* 130h 146c
10 ch g Project Manager—Hurricane Girl (IRE) (Strong Gale)
42a[5] 1692a[2] 1810a[4]2195a[4] 2304a[U] 2793a[6](3261a) 3472a[3] 3895a[F]3999a[3] 4761[5] 5080a[3]
Strong Resolve (IRE) *Miss Lucinda V Russell* 99 h 106c
10 gr g Roselier(FR) —Farmerette (Teofane)
1941[P] 2066[2] **2370[F]3022[7] 3851[6] 4070[6]4345[3] 4790[5]**
Strong Tea (IRE) *Miss S Waugh* 77c
15 b g Electric—Cutty Sark (Strong Gale)
49[P]
Strongtrooper (IRE) *Mrs C A Coward* 109c
11 b g Doubletour(USA) —Moss Gale (Strong Gale)
196[6]
Stroom Bank (IRE) *C C Bealby* 92h
6 b g Warcraft(USA) —All Alright (Alzao (USA))
1554[5] 1820[4] 2950[10] 3957[4] 4988[4]
Student Night (IRE) *John E F Skelton*
7 b g Jolly Jake(NZ) —Coteri Run (Deep Run)
4055[P] 4421[F]
Studmaster *Mrs John Harrington* 146 h
6 ch g Snurge—Danlu (USA) (Danzig (USA))
(3411a) (3894a) 4473[10] 4951a[22]
Stunning Spark *S Dow*
4 b f Fraam—Lady Jo (Phountzi (USA))
2373[P]
Sturbury *J W Mullins* 82h
4 b f Topanoora—Carry Me (IRE) (Lafontaine (USA))
2681[5] 3280[7] 4665[6] 4855[6]
Stutter *John G Carr* 112h
8 ch h Polish Precedent(USA) —Bright Spells (Salse (USA))
(67a)
Stylish Prince *R Lee* 59h
6 b g Polar Prince(IRE) —Simply Style (Bairn (USA))
2423[16] 2721[11] **3251[P] 3356[U]**
Stylistic (IRE) *J J Lambe*
5 b m Daggers Drawn(USA) —Treasure (IRE) (Treasure Kay)
302[P] 496[P]
Sublimity (FR) *John G Carr* 142+h
6 b h Selkirk(USA) —Fig Tree Drive (USA) (Miswaki (USA))
3772a[4] 4430[4] 5056a[4]
Suchwot (IRE) *M C Pipe* 75h
5 b g Intikhab(USA) —Fairy Water (Warning)
517[3] 915[4] 1075[P] 1297[8] 1483[12]1636[2] 1900[P] (Dead)
Sue Sue *Gerard Stack* 101h
6 b m Elmaamul(USA) —Bawader (USA) (Danzig (USA))
2031a[9]
Suetsu (IRE) *R A Ross* 63c
10 b m Toulon—Aryumad (Goldhill)
555[4]
Sugitani (USA) *N B King* 59h
4 b g Kingmambo(USA) —Lady Reiko (IRE) (Sadler's Wells (USA))
2236[8]
Suits Me Fine (IRE) *Jonjo O'Neill* 87h
6 b g Saddlers' Hall(IRE) —She's Tough (Deep Run)
1040[5] 1280[5] **1414[P]**
Suivez Moi (IRE) *M F Harris* 23h
4 ch c Daggers Drawn(USA) —Pamiers (Huntercombe)
4211[12] 4877[9] 31[3]
Sukey Tawdray (IRE) *D J Wintle* 64b
5 b g Presenting—My Gonny (IRE) (Mandalus)
4623[8] 4934[11]
Sula's Legend *D P Keane* 82b
5 ch g Midnight Legend—Sulapuff (Sula Bula)
3617[4]
Sullivan's Cascade (IRE) *E G Bevan* 47h
8 b g Spectrum(IRE) —Sombre Lady (Sharpen Up)
2723[9] 2858[8] 3147[9] 4013[P]
Sully Shuffles (IRE) *M Todhunter* 123 h
11 b g Broken Hearted—Green Legend (IRE) (Montekin)
422[9] 1434[P]
Sultan Fontenaille (FR) *N J Hawke* 89+h
4 b g Kaldounevees(FR) —Diane Fontenaille (FR) (Tel Quel (FR))
3786[8] 3947[8] 4551[7]
Sum Leader (IRE) *Miss Jane Thomas* 127h 135c
10 b g Leading Counsel(USA) —Greenodd (Green Shoon)
92a[14] **5080a[5]**
Summer Liric *J W Mullins* 90b
5 b g Lir—Summerhouse (Sunley Builds)
1777[6] 1954[6] 2809[8]
Summer Special *Mrs S C Bradburne* 96h
6 b g Mind Games—Summerhill Special (IRE) (Roi Danzig (USA))
418[2] 645[2] 870[5] 936[2] 2475[10]
Summer Stock (USA) *R A Mills* 92+h 82c
8 b g Theatrical—Lake Placid (IRE) (Royal Academy (USA))
4044[6] 4831[6]
Sunami Storm (IRE) *W P Mullins* 120h 113c
8 b m Glacial Storm(USA) —Live It Up (Le Coq D'Or)
66a[4] **4542a[2]**
Sundarbob (IRE) *P R Webber* 93b
4 bl g Bob Back(USA) —Villian (Kylian (USA))
2927[4] 3651[2] *3983[2]4237[3]*
Sundawn Lady *C P Morlock* 86h
8 b m Faustus(USA) —Game Domino (Derring Rose)
801[P] 1152[3] 1367[3] 1564[2] 1751[5]2073[2] 2378[6]
Sundawn Star *C P Morlock* 40b
5 b m Sure Blade(USA) —Game Domino (Derring Rose)
4881[11]
Sunday City (JPN) *P Bowen* 124 h
5 ch g Sunday Silence(USA) —Diamond City (USA) (Mr Prospector (USA))
1562[2] 1745[7] (1991) 2347[2] 2925[2] (3351) 3622[9]4781[5]
Sunday Habits (IRE) *Dr P Pritchard* 88c
12 ch g Montelimar(USA) —Robertina (USA) (Roberto (USA))
1219[P] 1276[P] 1414[10]1484[6] 1639[5] 1803[3](1981)
Sundeck (FR) *Ronald O'Leary* 117h
6 br g Dr Devious(IRE) —Mystery Tune (IRE) (Commanche Run)
1623a[8]
Sungates (IRE) *C Tinkler* 114 h 105 c
10 ch g Glacial Storm(USA) —Live It Up (Le Coq D'Or)
168[P] 441[P] **2660[4] 3142[U]3331[4] 3578[P] 3845[6]4394[7]**
Sungio *B P J Baugh* 104h
8 b g Halling(USA) —Time Or Never (FR) (Dowsing (USA))
237[P] 1409[6] 1486[5] 2728[3] 3125[9]4869[P]
Sun Hill *D Burchell* 83+h
6 b g Robellino(USA) —Manhattan Sunset (USA) (El Gran Senor (USA))
4784[14] 5016[6] 5110[8]
Sunisa (IRE) *J Mackie* 96 h
5 b m Daggers Drawn(USA) —Winged Victory (IRE) (Dancing Brave (USA))
1908[6] 2179[3] 2412[3] (2625) 3347[4] 3730[4]
Sun King *K G Reveley* 109h
9 ch g Zilzal(USA) —Opus One (Slip Anchor)
2716[4] 3561[4] (3929) 4608[7] 5066[2]
Sunley Future (IRE) *M F Harris* 100 h 84+c
7 b g Broken Hearted—The Wicked Chicken (IRE) (Saher)
1458[7] 1672[F] 2379[6] **2722[F]2867[0]** 3152[10] 3223[6] 3592[3](3885) (3945) **4350[3] 4620[0]**4733[P] (Dead)
Sunley Shines *B G Powell* 122 h
6 ch m Komaite(USA) —Sunley Story (Reprimand)
2554[3] 2829[5] (3280) (3439) 4619[12] 5070[2]
Sunnyarjun *J C Tuck* 97 h
8 ch g Afzal—Hush Tina (Tina's Pet)
(265) 536[2] 1862[9] (2314) 3360[11] 4781[12]
Sunny Daze *D McCain* 60h
6 ch g Unfuwain(USA) —Light Ship (Warning)
1672[P] 1890[8] 3843[6] 4056[5] 4570[5]
Sunnyland *P J Hobbs* 107+h
7 b m Sovereign Water(FR) —Quadrapol (Pollerton)
462[2] (915) 1075[4] (1541) (1717)
Sunnyside Royale (IRE) *R Bastiman* 90+h
7 b g Ali-Royal(IRE) —Kuwah (IRE) (Be My Guest (USA))
306[7] 573[5] 980[P]
Sunny South East (IRE) *S Gollings* 59h 72c
6 gr m Gothland(FR) —Rose Deer (Whistling Deer)
1042[7] 1213[6] 1317[7] **1618[4]2260[3] (2553) 2715[3]3593[P] 3790[4] 4495[P]**
Sunny Winner (FR) *G Cherel* 92h
4 ch g Villez(USA) —Torche Solaire (FR) (Caerleon (USA))
(777a) 1705a[F]
Sun Of The Glen (IRE) *B D Leavy* 18b
4 b f Key Of Luck(USA) —Gaelic Foray (IRE) (Unblest)
3651[12]
Sun Pageant *M G Rimell* 95+b
5 ch m Double Trigger(IRE) —Summer Pageant (Chief's Crown (USA))
(1660)
Sunridge Fairy (IRE) *L R James* 93 h
7 b m Definite Article—Foxy Fairy (IRE) (Fairy King (USA))
428[6] 1567[F]
Sunrise Spirit (FR) *F Doumen* 108+h
5 b g Double Bed(FR) —Belle Chaumiere (Gildoran)
2974[7]
Sunset King (USA) *R J Hodges* 78h
6 b g King Of Kings(IRE) —Sunset River (USA) (Northern Flagship (USA))
1381[3] 1523[7] 1653[8] 2298[5] 2605[P]2995[5] 3242[3] 3456[8] 3899[2] 4290[11]4651[4] 4941[7] 5115[4]
Sunset Light (IRE) *C Tinkler* 124+h
8 b g Supreme Leader—Game Sunset (Menelek)
1959[3] 3581[8] 3970[12] 4497[F]
Sunshan *R J Hodges* 74 c
10 b g Anshan—Kyrenia Sunset (CYP) (Lucky Look (CYP))
805[2] 896[5] 1076[3]1265[P] 1650[2] 3716[6]3949[P] 4575[7] 4666[P]
Sunshine Rays *C Tinkler* 81+h
8 b m Alflora(IRE) —Ruby Rheims (Paveh Star)
2704[5]
Sunshine Story (IRE) *C Von Der Recke*
6 b m Desert Story(IRE) —Sweet Tern (GER) (Arctic Tern (USA))
471a[5]
Sunspot *A Chaille-Chaille*
6 b g Peintre Celebre(USA) —Schezerade (USA) (Tom Rolfe)
4717a[3] 5154a[F]
Super Baby (FR) *J P L Ewart* 75h
4 b g Baby Turk—Norma Jane (FR) (Rahotep (FR))
3925[F]
Super Boston *Miss L C Siddall* 83h
6 b g Saddlers' Hall(IRE) —Nasowas (IRE) (Cardinal Flower)
237[7] 686[P] 1000[6] 1180[7] (1279) 1723[7]
Supercharmer *M A Humphreys* 95c
12 ch g Charmer—Surpassing (Superlative)
278[P] 374[P]
Superclean *Mrs A L M King*
6 ch m Environment Friend—Star Mover (Move Off)
943[P]
Super Dolphin *R Ford* 97+h 95+c
7 ch g Dolphin Street(FR) —Supergreen (Superlative)
692[2] 874[2] 939[P]1299[4] 2479[4] 2705[U]
Super Dominion *R Hollinshead*
9 ch g Superpower—Smartie Lee (Dominion)
1222[P]
Superfling *H J Manners*
5 ch g Superpower—Jobiska (Dunbeath (USA))
5024[P]
Superior Dream *J F Panvert*
4 b g Superpower—California Dreamin (Slip Anchor)
2105[12]
Superior Weapon (IRE) *A Robson* 89+c
12 b g Riverhead(USA) —Ballytrustan Maid (IRE) (Orchestra)
1673[P] 2172[5]
Super Lord (IRE) *J A B Old* 119 h 125 c
8 br g Mister Lord(USA) —Daisy's Dream (Paddy's Stream)
(2327) **3148[3] 3480[P]** 4469[P]
Super Nomad *M W Easterby* 112h 121+c
11 b g Nomadic Way(USA) —Super Sue (Lochnager)
1913[5] 2443[2] 2768[5]3619[6] 3852[4] 4378[5]4531[2]
Super Revo *Mrs K Walton* 79h
5 b g Revoque(IRE) —Kingdom Princess (Forzando)
844[2] 2007[5] 2948[13] 3779[6] 3912[7]4141[9] 5064[P]
Super Road Train *O Sherwood* 94h 97+c
7 b g Petoski—Foehn Gale (IRE) (Strong Gale)
509[2] 745[3] 913[7] **(1086) 1247[3]1398[9] 2800[5]**
Superrollercoaster *O Sherwood* 102h 108c
6 b g Classic Cliche(IRE) —Foehn Gale (IRE) (Strong Gale)
236[5] **2072[2] 2581[2]2982[2] 3382[4] 3965[P]4904[4]**
Supershot (IRE) *O Brennan* 81+h
8 b g Son Of Sharp Shot(IRE) —One To Two (IRE) (Astronef)
1654[10]
Supply And Fix (IRE) *J J Lambe* 98 h 88c
8 b g Supreme Leader—Hannies Girl (IRE) (Invited (USA))
301[3] 319[DSQ] 643[5] 780[2] 856[6]940[7] (1149) (1377) 1569[7] 1880[P]
Supreme Being (IRE) *Michael Cunningham* 124+h 124c
9 b g Supreme Leader—Parsonetta (The Parson)
5059a[6]
Supreme Breeze (IRE) *Mrs S J Smith* 120 c
11 b g Supreme Leader—Merry Breeze (Strong Gale)
1941[P] (2265) 2965[4]3560[U] 4111[P] 4843[3]
Supreme Builder *Ferdy Murphy* 121b
5 b g Supreme Leader—Osocool (Teenoso (USA))
5081a[7]
Supreme Cara *C J Down* 93+b
6 b m Morpeth—Supreme Daughter (Supreme Leader)
1979[4] 2432[8] 4398[3] (4695)
Supreme Catch (IRE) *Miss H C Knight* 121c
9 b g Supreme Leader—Lucky Trout (Beau Charmeur (FR))
2938[P] 3509[P] 3877[F]4078[2] 4374[2] 4728[U]
Supreme Copper (IRE) *Miss E C Lavelle* 90h
6 br g Supreme Leader—Black Wind (IRE) (Good Thyne (USA))
1922[17] 3216[6] 3583[6]4819[15] 5110[7]
Supreme Destiny (IRE) *G A Swinbank* 46h
8 b g Supreme Leader—Shuil Le Gaoth (IRE) (Strong Gale)
2006[9]
Supreme Developer (IRE) *Ferdy Murphy* 125h 143 c
9 b g Supreme Leader—Bettys The Boss (IRE) (Deep Run)
1846[4] 2499[6] 2828[P]4374[4] 4929a[11]
Supreme Hope (USA) *H D Daly* 81+h
7 b g Supreme Leader—Flaming Hope (IRE) (Callernish)
133[F] (Dead)
Supreme Leisure (IRE) *J Howard Johnson* 119+h
9 b g Supreme Leader—Maid Of Leisure (Le Moss)
2449[P] 2876[10] (3542) 4058[10] 4504[2]4990[3]
Supremely Gifted (IRE) *Mrs S J Smith* 87b
5 b g Supreme Leader—Some Gift (Avocat)
2823[7]
Supremely Smart (IRE) *N A Twiston-Davies* 80b
6 b g Supreme Leader—Fair Lisselan (IRE) (Kemal (FR))
1681[6] 1990[F] 4052[P]
Supreme Nova *John Allen* 74b
6 b m Supreme Leader—Qurrat Al Ain (Wolver Hollow)
656[6] 2558[13] 3373[10]
Supreme Peace (IRE) *F Flood* 117h 28c
8 b m Supreme Leader—Peace Time Girl (IRE) (Buckskin (FR))
92a[5]
Supreme Piper (IRE) *Miss C Dyson* 112+h 98 c
8 b g Supreme Leader—Whistling Doe (Whistling Deer)
2820[12] 3179[12] 3508[5] 3982[2] 4357[F]4491[4]
Supreme Prince (IRE) *P J Hobbs* 146 h 155+c
9 b g Supreme Leader—Strong Serenade (IRE) (Strong Gale)
1846[3] 2492[11] 3977[5]4241[12] 4764[6] (4984)
Supreme Prospect *R Johnson* 49b
5 b m Supreme Leader—Dubai Dolly (IRE) (Law Society (USA))
3448[9]
Supreme Return *A King* 89h
7 b g Bob's Return(IRE) —Supreme Wonder (IRE) (Supreme Leader)
206[4] 575[5]
Supreme Rullah (IRE) *Mrs L Wadham* 82h
9 b m Supreme Leader—Trapper Jean (Orchestra)
105[6]
Supreme Serenade (IRE) *P J Hobbs* 133 h 128 c
7 b m Supreme Leader—Strong Serenade (IRE) (Strong Gale)
1845[2] 2297[2] (2846) 3288[2] 3993[10] 4495[5]
Supreme Silence (IRE) *Nick Kent* 89+c
9 b g Bluebird(USA) —Why So Silent (Mill Reef (USA))
4107[5] 4325[3] 4725[P]
Supreme Sir (IRE) *P G Murphy* 86c
8 b g Supreme Leader—Sirrah Madam (Tug Of War)
1983[3] 2506[P] 2623[P]3252[3] 3654[4] 4394[3]4785[5] 4914[F]
Supreme's Legacy (IRE) *K G Reveley* 117+h
7 b g Supreme Leader—Lucylet (Kinglet)
(2192) 2340[7] 2947[2] (3253) 3738[5] 4787[2] (5009)
Supreme Tadgh (IRE) *J A Geake* 100h 112+c
9 b g Supreme Leader—Mariaetta (IRE) (Mandalus)
202[U] (2149) 2313[F]2613[2] 3241[P] 3372[P]4605[3] 4735[P]
Supreme Toss (IRE) *R T Phillips* 118c
10 b g Supreme Leader—Sleemana (Prince Hansel)
2464[2] 4016[3] 4369[3]4802[U]
Suprendre Espere *Jennie Candlish* 91h
6 b g Espere D'Or—Celtic Dream (Celtic Cone)
(3145) 3545[P] 3793[12] 4033[9] (4919) 5014[5]
Surefast *K Bishop* 80h 105 c
11 ch g Nearly A Hand—Meldon Lady (Ballymoss)
1780[3] 2502[P] 4152[R]
Sure Future *R M Stronge* 110 h 99c
10 b g Kylian(USA) —Lady Ever-So-Sure (Malicious)
169[P]
Surface To Air *Mrs P N Dutfield* 105+h
5 b g Samraan(USA) —Travelling Lady (Almoojid)
2301[3] 2815[5] 4676[2] (4905)
Surfboard (IRE) *P A Blockley* 98 h
5 ch g Kris—Surfing (Grundy)
138[11] 361[6] (1755) 2426[7] 2618[6] 3477[P]3876[P] 4243[9]
Suspicious Minds *J W Mullins* 76h
5 b m Anabaa(USA) —Paloma Bay (IRE) (Alzao (USA))
177[11]
Sussex Mist *J E Long* 42b
7 b m Phountzi(USA) —Dumerica (Yukon Eric (CAN))
513[10] 2576[P]
Susy Wells (IRE) *C W Moore* 28h
11 b m Masad(IRE) —My Best Susy (IRE) (Try My Best (USA))
96[P]
Sutton Lion *P D Purdy*
14 b g Lyphento(USA) —Crescent Cottage (Cornuto)
802[U]
Swahili Dancer (USA) *M D Hammond* 57h
5 b g Swain(IRE) —Bella Ballerina (Sadler's Wells (USA))
2444[10] 2652[8] 2991[10] 3918[P] 4449[P]
Swallow Falls (IRE) *D McCain* 67h
4 b f Lake Coniston(IRE) —Common Cause (Polish Patriot (USA))
1146[9] 1440[4] 2001[8] 2569[9] 2935[7]
Swallow Magic (IRE) *Ferdy Murphy* 95+h 98+c
8 b g Magic Ring(IRE) —Scylla (Rock City)
152[11] **1015[5] 1065[2](1150) 1343[7] 1376[5]1589[7] 1686[2] 1905[P](2522) 2900[4] 3928[P]**
Swansea Bay *P Bowen* 103 h 127 c
10 b g Jurado(USA) —Slave's Bangle (Prince Rheingold)
768[3] **842[4]** 1039[5] **1157[3](1267) 1342[3] 1735[7]**

Swaythe (USA) *P R Webber*
5 b m Swain(IRE) —Caithness (USA) (Roberto (USA))
(2131)

Swazi Prince *N A Twiston-Davies* 96+h
7 b g Rakaposhi King—Swazi Princess (IRE) (Brush Aside (USA))
2530[P] 3943[8] 4277[P] **4662[P]**4869[5]

Sweep Home *P Bowen* 86b
6 ch g Safawan—Royal Brush (King Of Spain)
1048[4] 1730[2]

Sweet Az *S C Burrough* 56h
7 b m Averti(IRE) —Yen Haven (USA) (Lear Fan (USA))
1123[6] 1266[4] 1456[P]

Sweet Bird (FR) *Miss J R Gibney* 96h 107+c
9 ch g Epervier Bleu—Sweet Virginia (FR) (Tapioca II)
1719[P] (2104) 2375[4]

Sweet Chariot *Mrs H Dalton* 68h
7 b g Hatim(USA) —Evening Dusk (IRE) (Phardante (FR))
895[P] 1375[9]

Sweet Diversion (IRE) *P F Nicholls* 124+h 151+c
7 b g Carroll House—Serocco Wind (Roi Guillaume (FR))
(728) (944) 1265[2]1549[2] 1879[2] (4957)

Sweet Medicine *P Howling* 79b
4 ch f Dr Devious(IRE) —Crimley Crumb (Rainbow Quest (USA))
3623[4]

Sweet Minuet *M Madgwick* 45h 89c
9 b m Minshaansu Amad(USA) —Sweet N' Twenty (High Top)
3663[5] 3907[6] 4575[2]4785[U] 4873[3] 5105[3]

Sweet Oona (FR) *Miss Venetia Williams* 103h
7 gr m Kendor(FR) —Poplife (FR) (Zino)
1850[2] 2244[4] 2995[2] 3242[6] (3730) 4129[3]4823[7] 5052[7]

Sweet Sabastion *C A McBratney* 46b
8 b g Torus—My Little Doxie (IRE) (Supreme Leader)
872[P]

Sweet Shooter *M Madgwick* 76h
6 ch m Double Trigger(IRE) —Sweet N' Twenty (High Top)
506[12] 724[9]

Sweet Wake (GER) *Noel Meade* 139+h
5 ch h Waky Nao—Sweet Royale (GER) (Garde Royale)
(3515a) 4430[5] 5056a[6]

Sweetwater (GER) *Seamus Lynch* 93h
6 b m Goofalik(USA) —Safrane (GER) (Mister Rock'S (GER))
5077a[15]

Swell Lad *S Gollings*
4 b g Sadler's Wells(USA) —Lydara (USA) (Alydar (USA))
2494[P] 2954[P] 5135[P]

Swete Deva *C Roberts* 67b
6 b g El Conquistador—Swete Fudge (Push On)
2565[10] 2941[15]

Swift Half (IRE) *J W Mullins* 87b
4 b g Bahhare(USA) —Brief Interval (IRE) (Brief Truce (USA))
3327[7] 3911[8] (5117)

Swift Post (IRE) *M J P O'Brien* 86b
5 b m Needle Gun(IRE) —Miss The Post (Bustino)
5134a[12]

Swifts Hill (IRE) *T R George* 107+h
8 ch g Executive Perk—Tudor Lady (Green Shoon)
111[P] (509) 1870[P]

Swift Swallow *O Brennan* 129h
8 ch g Missed Flight—Alhargah (Be My Guest (USA))
(247) (525) 2519[8] 4848[2]

Swift Water (IRE) *T R George* 48b
6 bb g Flemensfirth(USA) —Supreme Alliance (IRE) (Supreme Leader)
866[8] 4359[P]

Swiftway *Miss J Fisher* 113+c
12 ch g Anshan—Solemn Occasion (USA) (Secreto (USA))
(151) 322[4]

Swincombe (IRE) *Mrs S J Hickman* 101+c
11 b g Good Thyne(USA) —Gladtogetit (Green Shoon)
(3910) 4471[P]

Sword Lady *Mrs S D Williams* 120 h 69c
8 b m Broadsword(USA) —Speckyfoureyes (Blue Cashmere)
2297[U] 2553[6] 3295[6]3439[5] 4034[5] 4579[8]

Swordlestown (IRE) *T M Walsh* 110h 100c
8 br g Zaffaran(USA) —Carrick Shannon (Green Shoon)
3528a[7]

Sword Of Damascus (IRE) *D McCain* 113b
4 b g Darshaan—Damascene (IRE) (Scenic)
(1785) (2014) 3181[7] 3691[2] 4779[5]

Swordplay *M J P O'Brien* 130h 128c
8 ch g Kris—Throw Away Line (USA) (Assert)
45a[9] (Dead)

Sworovski (IRE) *C Aubert* 104h
6 br g Darshaan—Tropicaro (FR) (Caro)
1073a[6]

Sybarite Chief (IRE) *R A Fahey* 88b
4 b g Sinndar(IRE) —Fancy Wrap (Kris)
2927[3] 3785[5] 4992[8]

Sydney Greenstreet (GER) *C R Egerton* 103b
5 b g Acatenango(GER) —Spartina (USA) (Northern Baby (CAN))
2579[2] 2988[4] 3785[4]

Sylcan Express *O O'Neill* 76h
13 br g Sylvan Express—Dercanny (Derek H)
75[7] 458[8] (686) 891[7] 1395[6]

Sylphide *H J Manners* 84h 99c
11 b m Ballet Royal(USA) —Shafayif (Ela-Mana-Mou)
399[8] **567[5] 746[P]**

Sylvan Shack (IRE) *S J Gilmore* 95h
8 bb g Grand Plaisir(IRE) —Caddy Shack (Precipice Wood)
216[2]

Sylvie D'Orthe (FR) *Cooper Wilson* 72h
5 b m Saint Preuil(FR) —Paola Santa (FR) (Son Of Silver)
1064[5] 1308[5] 1564[7] 2107[4] 2453[7]

Sylviesbuck (IRE) *G M Moore* 91h 92 c
9 b g Kasmayo—Sylvies Missiles (IRE) (Buckskin (FR))
2413[6] 2589[F] 3554[P]5009[7]

Symphonique (FR) *P J Hobbs* 118h
5 ch m Epervier Bleu—Septieme Symphonie (FR) (Top Ville)
4778[P] 4983[5]

Syncopated Rhythm (IRE) *N A Twiston-Davies* 80+h 80c
6 b g Synefos(USA) —Northern Elation (IRE) (Lancastrian)
1877[6] 2126[6] 3997[5]5068[4]

Syroco (FR) *A L T Moore* 99h
7 b g Homme De Loi(IRE) —La Pommeraie I (Miller's Mate)
3005a[10]

Szeroki Bor (POL) *M Pitman* 109h
7 b g In Camera(IRE) —Szuana (POL) (Five Star Camp (USA))
2010[P] 2685[11]

Tacin (IRE) *B G Powell* 119 h 114+c
9 bb g Supreme Leader—Nicat (Wolver Hollow)
1872[15] **2529[4]**

Tacita *M D McMillan* 49 h 67c
11 ch m Gunner B—Taco (High Season)
2248[3] 2686[F] 5105[P]

Tacolino (FR) *O Brennan* 95c
12 ch g Royal Charter(FR) —Tamilda (FR) (Rose Laurel)
195[7] 360[P] 1721[4]1815[U] 2294[5] 2588[P]5140[4]

Taffy *H J Manners*
9 b g Ballet Royal(USA) —Darlin' Again (Jolly Me)
231[P]

Tagar (FR) *C Grant* 95h 99c
9 b g Fijar Tango(FR) —Fight For Arfact (Salmon Leap (USA))
2679[7] 3233[3] 3447[3]3798[6] 4842[F]

Tagula Blue (IRE) *Ian Williams* 113h
6 b g Tagula(IRE) —Palace Blue (IRE) (Dara Monarch)
3658[3]

Tahaddi Turtle (IRE) *T P Tate* 70b
4 b g Turtle Island(IRE) —Tahaddi (USA) (Northern Baby (CAN))
2642[4] 3237[9]

Tails I Win *Miss C J E Caroe* 89 h 49c
7 b g Petoski—Spinayab (King Of Spain)
183[P] 511[P] 862[9]902[5] 972[U] 1109[11]2701[P] 3274[7] 3418[9]3686[8] 4350[5] 4525[U]4870[R] 5139[9]

Taipan Sue (IRE) *Noel T Chance* 70b
5 b m Taipan(IRE) —Deeco Valley (IRE) (Satco (FR))
4902[5]

Taipo Prince (IRE) *Miss Kate Milligan* 98h 81c
6 b g Entrepreneur—Dedicated Lady (IRE) (Pennine Walk)
3348[5] 3562[P]

Taj India (USA) *N J Hawke*
4 bb g Gone West(USA) —Circle Of Gold (IRE) (Royal Academy (USA))
1904[F]

Takagi (IRE) *Miss Clare Judith Macmahon* 129h 151c
11 b g Husyan(USA) —Ballyclough Gale (Strong Gale)
87a[U] 1710a[U]

Takeachanceonhim *Mrs Barbara Waring* 78h
8 b g Dilum(USA) —Smilingatstrangers (Macmillion)
629[8] 1154[4]

Take A Drop (IRE) *Seamus O'Farrell* 100 h
11 b g Farhaan—Misquested (Lord Ha Ha)
2166[P] **2174[P]**

Take A Mile (IRE) *B G Powell* 108h
4 ch g Inchinor—Bu Hagab (IRE) (Royal Academy (USA))
2286[3] 2661[2] (2949) 3182[3] 4561[4] 4838[4]5076a[19]

Take The Lot (IRE) *Anthony Moloney* 78c
13 ch g Commanche Run—Quilty Rose (Buckskin (FR))
5128a[8]

Take The Oath (IRE) *D R Gandolfo* 103h 83+c
9 b g Big Sink Hope(USA) —Delgany Chimes (IRE) (Kafu)
388[P] (674) 752[2]862[P] **999[4] 1044[3]1191[P] 1746[3]**

Take The Stand (IRE) *P Bowen* 121 h 165 c
10 b g Witness Box(USA) —Denys Daughter (IRE) (Crash Course)
1434[5] **1926[3] 2337[6]2992[2] 3977[U] 4470[5]4746[2] 5004[U]**

Take Time *M G Rimell* 89h
7 b g Teenoso(USA) —Fernessa (Roman Warrior)
3369[7]

Taking My Cut *Jonjo O'Neill* 114h
6 b g Classic Cliche(IRE) —Gaye Memory (Buckskin (FR))
1975[2] 3677[4] (4106) 4579[P]

Taksina *R H Buckler* 43h 79+c
7 b m Wace(USA) —Quago (New Member)
632[4] 1343[4] 1646[5]1981[3] (2594) 2684[5]2984[3] 3239[7] 3716[4]4575[4] 4694[5] 4936[4]

Talarive (USA) *P D Niven* 101+h
10 ch g Riverman(USA) —Estala (Be My Guest (USA))
120[2] (425) 480[8] 1510[2] 1836[P] 2525[9]3351[9] 3757[7] (5137)

Talbot Lad *Mrs H Dalton*
10 b g Weld—Greenacres Girl (Tycoon II)
4[P] 311[8] 3803[P]

Taleban *J Wade* 26h 61c
11 b g Alleged(USA) —Triode (USA) (Sharpen Up)
1065[5] 1150[7] 1570[8]

Tales Of Bounty (IRE) *R Barber* 123h 121c
11 b g Ela-Mana-Mou—Tales Of Wisdom (Rousillon (USA))
(455)

Talikos (FR) *Miss H C Knight* 87+h
5 b g Nikos—Talaya (FR) (Matahawk)
1895[8] 2269[4] 2826[10]

Talioso (IRE) *R Hollinshead* 64c
9 b g Teenoso(USA) —Mulloch Brae (Sunyboy)
4167[5] 4421[F]

Talisker Rock (IRE) *A Parker* 53h
6 gr g Tagula(IRE) —Hallatte (USA) (Trempolino (USA))
323[5] 424[8] 3490[12] 3927[P] 5091[9]

Talking Cents (IRE) *S Donohoe* 91h 129c
9 b g Good Thyne(USA) —Necochea (Julio Mariner)
42a[P]

Talk The Talk *Jonjo O'Neill*
6 gr m Terimon—Free Travel (Royalty)
4238[P]

Tallahassee (IRE) *D R MacLeod* 43h
8 ch g Moscow Society(USA) —Kemperstrat (The Parson)
2947[P] 3559[9]

Tallison *N R Mitchell* 24h
8 ch g First Trump—Clare Celeste (Coquelin (USA))
911[15] **1155[P]**

Tallow Bay (IRE) *Mrs S Wall* 96c
11 b g Glacial Storm(USA) —Minimum Choice (IRE) (Miner's Lamp)
2129[4] 3221[5] (3427) (3909) (4152) 4650[5]4876[P]

Tall Paul *L Corcoran* 64b
6 b g Shaamit(IRE) —Brave Vanessa (USA) (Private Account (USA))
5117[8]

Talpour (IRE) *M C Chapman* 75b
6 ch g Ashkalani(IRE) —Talwara (USA) (Diesis)
375[5] 656[8]

Tamango (FR) *P J Hobbs* 117 h 141 c
9 gr g Klimt(FR) —Tipmosa (FR) (Tip Moss (FR))
(103) 454[2] 634[P]946[8] (1080) (1265) 1550[5] (1744) 1881[3]4459[10] 4762[F] 5126[4]

Tamarinbleu (FR) *M C Pipe* 149h 149 c
6 b g Epervier Bleu—Tamainia (FR) (Lashkari)
2208[2] 2861[5] (3457) 4431[9]

Tambourine Davis (FR) *N J Henderson* 88b
4 b f Cadoudal(FR) —Trumpet Davis (FR) (Rose Laurel)
2830[2] 3961[2] 4376[9] 5134a[11]

Tam O'Shanter *J G M O'Shea* 88h 97c
12 gr g Persian Bold—No More Rosies (Warpath)
684[P]

Tamreen (IRE) *G L Moore* 119+h
5 b h Bahhare(USA) —Na-Ayim (IRE) (Shirley Heights)
2487[8] 2730[12] 3133[6] 3603[3] 3978[6]4479[4] (5021)

Tanager *Mrs K Lawther* 105c
11 ch g Carlingford Castle—Tangara (Town Crier)
49[8] 282[5]

Tana River (IRE) *Miss E C Lavelle* 121h 125c
10 b g Over The River(FR) —Home In The Glen (Furry Glen)
2492[P] 2813[2] 2974[P] 3993[4]**4374[3] 4690[2] 5012[P]**

Tancredi (SWE) *N B King* 69+h
4 b g Rossini(USA) —Begine (IRE) (Germany (USA))
2949[6] 3431[P]

Tandava (IRE) *Mrs S C Bradburne* 104h 108+c
8 ch g Indian Ridge—Kashka (USA) (The Minstrel (CAN))
(59) (643) 938[4] 1839[2] 2638[5] 3318[5] **4583[2]4719[U]**

Tandawizi *Mrs L B Normile* 57 h
9 b m Relief Pitcher—Arctic Ander (Leander)
591[P] **4583[U]**

Tangoroch (FR) *J P L Ewart*
5 bb g Rochesson(FR) —Fitanga (FR) (Fijar Tango (FR))
3319[10]

Tango Royal (FR) *M C Pipe* 130h 149 c
10 gr g Royal Charter(FR) —Nazia (FR) (Zino)
(1013) 1265[6] 1550[9]1676[7] 2760[12] 4459[11]4974[15]

Tanikos (FR) *N J Henderson* 115+h 135 c
7 b g Nikos—Tamana (USA) (Northern Baby (CAN))
1739[F] 2128[2] 2489[6]2969[3] (3387) 3974[3] 4472[11]4850[P]

Tank (IRE) *Miss Sheena West* 41h
5 ch g Woodborough(USA) —Fiddes (IRE) (Alzao (USA))
513[9] 971[5] 1248[8]

Tank Buster *Mrs E Langley* 84h 77c
6 b g Executive Perk—Macfarly (IRE) (Phardante (FR))
2763[7] 2956[8] **3356[3] 4095[4]**

Tanmeya *R C Guest* 66h
5 gr m Linamix(FR) —Ta Awun (USA) (Housebuster (USA))
1850[F] 2106[5] 2186[10] 2674[P] 2704[11]

Tanners Grove *Miss C Dyson* 21h
5 b g Theatrical Charmer—Heldigvis (Hot Grove)
2941[18] 4333[16] 5070[U]

Tano (CZE) *Mrs A E Brooks*
5 ch g Sapano—Talci (CZE) (Gosport)
3249[P]

Tanterari (IRE) *M C Pipe* 117 h 121 c
8 b g Safety Catch(USA) —Cobblers Crest (IRE) (Step Together (USA))
2368[4] 2637[3]

Tanzanite (IRE) *D W P Arbuthnot* 87+h
4 b f Revoque(IRE) —Resume (IRE) (Lahib (USA))
2481[6]

Tanzanite Dawn *Andrew Turnell* 72h
5 b m Gunner B—Quiet Dawn (Lighter)
2432[11] 2997[7] 3690[10] 4238[7]

Tap The Father (IRE) *Fred Farrow*
13 b g Glacial Storm(USA) —Sally McIntyre (Proverb)
4799[P] 4901[4]

Taranai (IRE) *B W Duke* 86h
5 ch m Russian Revival(USA) —Miss Flite (IRE) (Law Society (USA))
357[12] 568[3] (801) 949[P] 1017[4] 1408[8]

Taranis (FR) *P F Nicholls* 100+h 147+c
5 ch g Mansonnien(FR) —Vikosa (FR) (Nikos)
(2488) 2924[U] (3356) (4679) (4971)

Taras Knight (IRE) *J J Quinn* 69b
4 b g Indian Danehill(IRE) —Queen Of Art (IRE) (Royal Academy (USA))
2521[7]

Tarbolton Moss *M Todhunter* 101h 116+c
11 b m Le Moss—Priceless Peril (Silly Prices)
62[5]

Tarbuck (IRE) *Mrs D A Hamer* 103h 71c
13 bb g Buckskin(FR) —Tar Slave (Tarqogan)
862[5] 948[6]

Tardenois (FR) *J T R Draper* 118+h
7 b g Turgeon(USA) —Allee Sarthoise (FR) (Pampabird)
2536a[4]

Tarkar (IRE) *J Howard Johnson* 64h
4 ch g Priolo(USA) —Tarakana (USA) (Shahrastani (USA))
2167[P] 2477[6] 2921[13] 3485[5]

Tarlac (GER) *N J Henderson* 127+h
5 ch g Dashing Blade—Tintina (USA) (General Assembly (USA))
3324[3] (3659) (4091) 4375[5] 4773[15]

Tartan Classic (IRE) *J Howard Johnson* 25h
5 b g Classic Cliche(IRE) —Laboc (Rymer)
3780[9] 4657[4] 4988[10]

Tarwin *J R Norton* 86b
6 b g Danzig Connection(USA) —Persian Blue (Persian Bold)
521[8]

Tarzan Du Mesnil (FR) *N J Hawke* 90b
5 br g Turgeon(USA) —Ladies View (FR) (Comrade In Arms)
1968[P]

Tashkandi (IRE) *P Bowen* 73+h
6 gr h Polish Precedent(USA) —Tashiriya (IRE) (Kenmare (FR))
1527[P] 1875[11] 2343[7] 2860[9] 2995[13]

Tass Heel (IRE) *B J Llewellyn* 84h
7 b g Danehill(USA) —Mamouna (USA) (Vaguely Noble)
501[3] 724[12] 976[F]

Ta Ta For Now *Mrs S C Bradburne* 101 h 95+c
9 b g Ezzoud(IRE) —Exit Laughing (Shaab)
(421) 1511[4] 1589[8]2413[5] 2495[P] 3315[U]3917[7] 4361[4] 4845[P]5122[4]

Tates Avenue (IRE) *N A Twiston-Davies* 91h 81c
8 b g Zaffaran(USA) —Tate Divinity (IRE) (Tate Gallery (USA))
193[4] 354[P]

Taurus Oats *P F Nicholls* 67+b
7 b m Makbul—Aintree Oats (Oats)
1892[U]

Tawrific Laois (IRE) *Seamus Fahey* 114h
6 b g Tawrrific(NZ) —Pointe Fine (FR) (Homme De Loi (IRE))
3154a[3]

Taylor Maid *G A Ham*
4 b f First Trump—Island Maid (Forzando)
4416[10]

Teal Saqqara (FR) *Miss Venetia Williams*
7 b g Shaamit(IRE) —Legal Drama (USA) (Turkoman (USA))
3342[P]

Team Captain *C J Down* 105+c
12 ch g Teamster—Silly Sausage (Silly Answer)
(276) 746[P] 981[P]

Team Leader (IRE) *N A Twiston-Davies* 99b
6 b g Supreme Leader—Lyshie Lashie (Mandalus)
2823[5] 3911[6]

Team Resdev (IRE) *F P Murtagh* 43h
6 b m Zaffaran(USA) —Crabtreejazz (IRE) (Royal Fountain)
2414[10] 3173[5] 3446[F] 4113[P]

Team Tassel (IRE) *M C Pipe* 123h 112c
8 b g Be My Native(USA) —Alcmena's Last (Pauper)
2564[4] 3356[F] 3946[3]4677[P] 5046[P]

Tea's Maid *Mrs A M Thorpe* 83h
6 b m Wizard King—Come To Tea (IRE) (Be My Guest (USA))
854[3] 961[2] 1046[11] 1100[3] 1262[2]

Tech Eagle (IRE) *R Curtis* 118h
6 b h Eagle Eyed(USA) —Technik (GER) (Nebos (GER))
2148[2] 2573[12] 2826[5] 3371[2] 3616[5]4243[3] (4819) (5070)

Teddy Boy *Miss E Thompson* 68h 88+c
10 b g Midyan(USA) —Likeable Lady (Piaffer (USA))
(299)

Teddy's Song *P A Pritchard*
8 ch g Royal Vulcan—Ranee's Song (True Song)
763[F] 4803[P]

Tee-Jay (IRE) *M D Hammond* 111h 97 c
10 ch g Un Desperado(FR) —N T Nad (Welsh Pageant)
109[P] **211[3] 554[3]783[3] 1015[4] 1378[2](1589) (1686) 2413[P]5136[3]**

Teen House *Miss Suzy Smith* 49h
7 b m Teenoso(USA) —Last House (Vital Season)
216[6]

Teen Lady *Ferdy Murphy* 85b
7 bb m Teenoso(USA) —State Lady (IRE) (Strong Statement (USA))
3563[10] 3795[P]

Teeno Rossi (IRE) *J K Magee* 47h
8 b m Teenoso(USA) —Mistress Ross (Impecunious)
601[10] 715[8]

Tees Components *K G Reveley* 152 h
11 b g Risk Me(FR) —Lady Warninglid (Ela-Mana-Mou)
1925[3] 2336[3] **3041[U]**

Tees Mill *D W Thompson*
7 b g Lugana Beach—Hopperetta (Rock Hopper)
470^{10} 3381^{P} 3443^{P}
Teeswater *Mrs P Sly* 58h
6 b g Alderbrook—Ewe Lamb (Free State)
192^{15}
Teeton Babysham *P F Nicholls* 114+h
6 b g Shambo—Teeton Bubbley (Neltino)
(3478) 4803^{2}
Teeton Priceless *Mrs Joan Tice* 98c
11 b m Broadsword(USA) —Teeton Frolic (Sunley Builds)
6^{3} 374^{2} 512^{5}4100^{6}
Teknash (FR) *Niall Madden* 107h 96c
11 ch g Nashwan(USA) —Te Kani (USA) (Northern Dancer)
92a^{19}
Telemoss (IRE) *N G Richards* 125c
12 b g Montelimar(USA) —Shan's Moss (Le Moss)
1925^{P} **(3847) 3968^{2} 4471^{6}**
Tellem Noting (IRE) *B G Powell* 100dh 70c
9 b g Treasure Hunter—Imperial Butterfly (IRE) (Euphemism)
404^{6} 1521^{6} 1644^{U}1897^{U}
Tell Henry (IRE) *Evan Williams* 18h
6 ch g Broken Hearted—Valleymay (IRE) (King's Ride)
(1730) 2826^{18}
Tell Tale (IRE) *J G Cann* 107c
14 b g Tale Quale—Loobagh Bridge (River Beauty)
297^{4} 403^{2} 669^{3}
Tell The Trees *M C Pipe* 103h
5 br m Tamure(IRE) —Bluebell Copse (Formidable (USA))
329^{2} 441^{3} 652^{8} 768^{4} 4858^{12}
Teme Valley *R C Guest* 113h 102c
12 br g Polish Precedent(USA) —Sudeley (Dancing Brave (USA))
552^{6} 940^{8} (1567) 1816^{2} 2110^{4} 2566^{3}2981^{2}
Temoin *N J Henderson* 144+h
6 b g Groom Dancer(USA) —Kowtow (USA) (Shadeed (USA))
(3423) (3729) (4215) 4765^{21}
Temper Lad (USA) *J D Frost* 85+h
11 b g Riverman(USA) —Dokki (USA) (Northern Dancer)
(519) 749^{4} 1079^{2} (2073) 3250^{8}
Temple Place (IRE) *D McCain* 123+h
5 b g Sadler's Wells(USA) —Puzzled Look (USA) (Gulch (USA))
3374^{5} 3947^{4} 4301^{3} (4613) 4763^{12}
Templer (IRE) *P J Hobbs* 102h
5 ch g Charmer—Ballinamona Lady (IRE) (Le Bavard (FR))
1799^{4} 3216^{P} 3327^{6} 3800^{6} 4033^{10}4784^{4}
Templet (USA) *W G Harrison* 93h
6 b g Souvenir Copy(USA) —Two Step Trudy (USA) (Capote (USA))
942^{6} 1291^{3} 1360^{3} 1508^{3} 1605^{4}2693^{2} 3378^{7} 3783^{P} 5066^{P}
Tempsford (USA) *Jonjo O'Neill* 85h
6 b g Bering—Nadra (IRE) (Sadler's Wells (USA))
3611^{11} 4071^{5}
Tender Tangle *Miss S A Loggin* 75c
11 ch g Crested Lark—Red Tango (Legal Tender)
3819^{F} 5053^{5}
Tengo Ambro *E J O'Grady* 123h
7 b g Jupiter Island—Loving Around (IRE) (Furry Glen)
4336a^{2} (Dead)
Teninarow (IRE) *M Weir* 60c
12 b g Camden Town—Noellespir (Bargello)
171^{6}
Tenko *M D McMillan* 60h
7 ch m Environment Friend—Taco (High Season)
2376^{4} 2718^{P} 4836^{10}
Ten Pressed Men (FR) *Jonjo O'Neill* 89h
6 b g Video Rock(FR) —Recolte D'Estruval (FR) (Kouban (FR))
3511^{5} 3842^{7} 4819^{7}
Tenshookmen (IRE) *W F Codd* 112c
12 ch g Cardinal Flower—April Rise (Prominer)
5128a^{6}
Tensile (IRE) *R J Hodges* 114+h
11 b g Tenby—Bonnie Isle (Pitcairn)
102^{3} 425^{2} 3993^{P}
Teorban (POL) *D J S Ffrench Davis* 98h
7 b g Don Corleone—Tabaka (POL) (Pyjama Hunt)
1806^{2} 2271^{4} 3358^{11}
Tequinha *C P Morlock*
6 b g Petoski—Caipirinha (IRE) (Strong Gale)
2421^{P}
Terimons Daughter *E W Tuer* 60b
7 b m Terimon—Fun While It Lasts (Idiots Delight)
3751^{0} 484^{9} 719^{8} 1590^{7} 1683^{8}1834^{16}
Terivic *K C Bailey* 107+h 121c
6 br g Terimon—Ludoviciana (Oats)
1903^{3} 2179^{5} **(2504) 2817^{6}3580^{5} 4014^{2} 4323^{2}4762^{F}**
Terminology *K C Bailey* 98+h
8 gr g Terimon—Rhyming Moppet (Rymer)
2099^{P} 3943^{P} **4164^{F} 4553^{P}4643^{P} 4908^{P}**
Terramarique (IRE) *L Lungo* 78h 92+c
7 b g Namaqualand(USA) —Secret Ocean (Most Secret)
215^{9} 2171^{9} **3338^{P} 3486^{U}3930^{4}**
Terre De Java (FR) *Mrs H Dalton* 106+h 130+c
8 b g Cadoudal(FR) —Terre D'Argent (FR) (Count Ivor (USA))
343^{2} 571^{16} **3619^{U} 3922^{6}(4755) 5067^{5}**
Terrible Tenant *J W Mullins* 9h 94+c
7 gr g Terimon—Rent Day (Town And Country)
(26) (74) 395^{4} 2011^{P}2561^{3} 2807^{4} 2984^{4}3126^{U} 4675^{4} 4837^{3}5047^{3}
Tessanoora *N J Henderson* 121h
5 b m Topanoora—Club Sandwich (Phardante (FR))
2070^{2} 3280^{4} (4074) (4641) 4983^{2}
Test Of Faith *J N R Billinge* 76h
7 b g Weld—Gold Pigeon (IRE) (Goldhill)
319^{7} 551^{7} 643^{P} 1066^{8} 1310^{7}

Test Of Friendship *Mrs H Dalton* 58b 101c
9 br g Roselier(FR) —Grease Pot (Gala Performance)
2465^{P} 2801^{P} (4914)
Teutonic (IRE) *R F Fisher* 83h
5 b m Revoque(IRE) —Classic Ring (IRE) (Auction Ring (USA))
496^{8} 1360^{6} 1908^{S} 3442^{RR} 4040^{6}4632^{6}
Teviot Brig *L Lungo* 5h
5 b g Weldnaas(USA) —Here Comes Tibby (Royal Fountain)
3563^{8} 4720^{15}
Texas Holdem (IRE) *M Smith* 124h 57c
7 b g Topanoora—Lough N Uisce (IRE) (Boyne Valley)
2038^{3} (2264) 2925^{3} 3383^{6} (3561) 4110^{7} 4765^{11}
Text *C J Down* 101+h
5 b g Atraf—Idle Chat (USA) (Assert)
3^{2} 457^{2} 696^{4}
Thai Town *A E Jones* 76h
7 br g Afzal—Koo-Ming (Mansingh (USA))
389^{6} 753^{3}
Thalys (GER) *P R Webber* 107+h 107c
8 bl g Gold And Ivory(USA) —Tachira (Faraway Times (USA))
(1524) 1894^{2} 2287^{5} (Dead)
Thaticouldntsayno (IRE) *A E Jones*
8 b g Up And At 'Em—Canoora (Ahonoora)
4651^{P}
Thatlldoforme *A C Whillans* 78h
4 b g Dancing High—Bantel Bargain (Silly Prices)
4147^{8} 4533^{13} 4789^{10}
Thatlldoya *P Grindrod* 87c
8 ch g Montelimar(USA) —Sevso (Jupiter Island)
5095^{2}
That Man Fox *Lucinda Featherstone* 78+h
5 b g Sovereign Water(FR) —Oh No Rosie (Vital Season)
3188^{6} 3591^{7} 4521^{4}
That's An Idea (IRE) *David Wachman* 120+h 107c
8 b g Arctic Lord—Annsgrove Polly (IRE) (Pollerton)
3514a^{F}
That's Final *J C Tuck*
5 b g Komaite(USA) —Fine Fettle (Final Straw)
3001^{16}
That's For Sure *Evan Williams* 90b
6 bb g Forzando—Sure Flyer (IRE) (Sure Blade (USA))
1231^{5} 1298^{P}
That's My Charlie (NZ) *Jonjo O'Neill* 102b
5 b g Magic Of Sydney(AUS) —La Magnifique (NZ) (Kampala)
2056^{10} 2534^{16}
That's Racing *J Hetherton* 81 h
6 ch g Classic Cliche(IRE) —All On (Dunbeath (USA))
414^{4} 826^{5} 941^{11} 1943^{P} 2657^{2}3042^{8} 3395^{10} 3782^{2} 14^{8}
That's Rhythm (FR) *M Todhunter* 100+h
6 b g Pistolet Bleu(IRE) —Madame Jean (FR) (Cricket Ball (USA))
3168^{2}
The Ample Hamper *Mrs L B Normile*
8 gr g Alflora(IRE) —The Whirlie Weevil (Scallywag)
3236^{P} 3553^{U}
The Associate (IRE) *Miss Lucinda V Russell* 69c
9 bb g Religiously(USA) —Stormy Trip (Strong Gale)
2168^{P} 3236^{6} 3380^{7}4502^{P}
Theatre Belle *Ms Deborah J Evans* 77h
5 b m King's Theatre(IRE) —Cumbrian Rhapsody (Sharrood (USA))
1974^{7} 2515^{7} 2749^{8} 4418^{2} 4896^{5}
Theatre Dance (IRE) *C Tinkler* 102b
5 b g King's Theatre(IRE) —Dance Alone (USA) (Monteverdi)
2961^{2} 3373^{2}
Theatre Knight (IRE) *J Howard Johnson* 89h 113c
8 b g Old Vic—Musical View (IRE) (Orchestra)
(2415) 3204^{3} 3794^{3}3928^{6} 4460^{6} 4985^{3}
Theatre Prince (IRE) *S J Treacy* 75b
4 b g King's Theatre(IRE) —Nawasib (IRE) (Warning)
5060a^{13}
Theatre Rights (IRE) *J S Haldane* 29b
6 ch g Old Vic—Deep Perk (IRE) (Deep Run)
3231^{2} 2036^{P}
Theatre Tinka (IRE) *R Hollinshead* 94h
7 b g King's Theatre(IRE) —Orange Grouse (IRE) (Taufan (USA))
1614^{7} 1745^{6} 2940^{3} (4632) 4832^{4}
The Bag Man *P F Nicholls* 63h
7 b g Alflora(IRE) —Lady Claudia (IRE) (Good Thyne (USA))
201^{7}
The Baillie (IRE) *C R Egerton* 96b
7 b g Castle Keep—Regular Dolan (IRE) (Regular Guy)
1681^{5} 1777^{4}
The Bajan Bandit (IRE) *L Lungo* 142 h 150+c
11 b g Commanche Run—Sunrise Highway VII (Damsire Unregistered)
2336^{P} 2747^{9} 3397^{F} **(3851) 4496^{P}5004^{P}**
The Bandit (IRE) *Miss E C Lavelle* 116 h 138+c
9 b g Un Desperado(FR) —Sweet Friendship (Alleging (USA))
454^{P} 1676^{P} 1735^{8}4617^{5} 4762^{15} (4944)
The Bar Maid *O Sherwood* 111h 77+c
8 b m Alderbrook—Corny Story (Oats)
24^{2}
The Bay Bogle *M A Barnes*
5 b g Primitive Rising(USA) —Karena Park (Hot Spark)
2480^{12} 3353^{14}
The Bay Bridge (IRE) *Miss E C Lavelle* 80+h
7 bb g Over The River(FR) —Alamo Bay (Torenaga)
654^{P} 1036^{2} 1522^{4}

The Beaming Bandit (IRE) *M G Rimell* 69b
6 b g Shernazar—Celtic Smiles (IRE) (Nucleon (USA))
2665^{8}
The Beduth Navi *D G Bridgwater* 66h
6 b g Forzando—Sweets (IRE) (Persian Heights)
5073^{5}
The Bees Knees *M Appleby*
6 b g Bijou D'Inde—Dismiss (Daring March)
3677^{P}
Thebellinnbroadway *S C Burrough* 77b
6 b m El Conquistador—Ten Deep (Deep Run)
3904^{10}
The Big Canadian (IRE) *A King* 101b
5 b g Presenting—Glory-Glory (IRE) (Buckskin (FR))
(1799) 2534^{14} 4574^{5}
Thebigfellow (IRE) *Richard Mathias* 48h 65c
9 bb g Gothland(FR) —Callady (IRE) (Callernish)
6^{U} 313^{P}
The Biker (IRE) *P Monteith* 111 h 113c
9 br g Arctic Lord—Glenravel (Lucifer (USA))
5121^{3}
The Boobi (IRE) *Miss M E Rowland* 76h
5 b m Beneficial—Orogale (IRE) (Strong Gale)
816^{6} 1401^{5} 1554^{11} 1757^{2} 2070^{7}4732^{7} 4919^{P} 5135^{7}
The Boro Man (IRE) *Mrs Jeremy Young* 37h
8 b g Good Thyne(USA) —Boro Penny (Normandy)
1246^{8}
The Bo'sun *A E Jessop* 90h
9 b g Charmer—Sailors Joy (Handsome Sailor)
2556^{5} 2956^{6} 3600^{P}
The Boys In Green (IRE) *C Roche* 125+h 127c
9 b g Shernazar—Mursuma (Rarity)
(45a)
The Bushkeeper (IRE) *N J Henderson*
12 b g Be My Native(USA) —Our Little Lamb (Prince Regent (FR))
130^{P}
The Butterwick Kid *T P Tate* 105c
13 ch g Interrex(CAN) —Ville Air (Town Crier)
(196) 3736^{5} (3913) 4073^{5} 4725^{2}
The Cad (IRE) *R H Alner* 86h
6 b g Broken Hearted—Redondo Beach (Mandalus)
3982^{P} **4288^{4} 4662^{P}**
The Castilian (FR) *M C Pipe* 90 h
4 b g Enrique—Triciana (USA) (Afleet (CAN))
1190^{2} 1268^{3} 1380^{3} 1649^{2} 1774^{2}1921^{3} 2632^{P} 3242^{8} 3456^{2} 3592^{2}4075^{4} 4210^{4} 4616^{6} 4941^{2}
The Chequered Lady *T D McCarthy* 88h
4 b f Benny The Dip(USA) —Hymne D'Amour (USA) (Dixieland Band (USA))
3714^{11} 3939^{7} 5084^{2}
The Cliffe (IRE) *J Rudge* 84b
7 b g Alflora(IRE) —Northwood Star (IRE) (Henbit (USA))
300^{4} 685^{11}
The Composer *M Blanshard* 94h
4 b g Royal Applause—Superspring (Superlative)
3355^{2} 4754^{2}
The Connor Fella *F P Murtagh* 90h
5 b g Kris—Flower Fairy (FR) (Fairy King (USA))
424^{5} 991^{7} 2024^{3} 2444^{F}
The Cool Guy (IRE) *N A Twiston-Davies* 135+h
6 b g Zaffaran(USA) —Frostbite (Prince Tenderfoot (USA))
70a^{2} (1711) (2631) 3174^{2}
The Corby Glenn (IRE) *Barry Potts* 40h
5 b g Broken Hearted—Always Proud (IRE) (Supreme Leader)
3793^{16}
The Count (FR) *F P Murtagh* 70h
7 b g Sillery(USA) —Dear Countess (FR) (Fabulous Dancer (USA))
406^{7}
The Croppy Boy *Mrs N S Evans* 44h 80c
14 b g Arctic Lord—Deep Cut (Deep Run)
812^{4} 1178^{P}
The Culdee (IRE) *F Flood* 125dh 123+c
10 ch g Phardante(FR) —Deep Inagh (Deep Run)
91a^{F} 1420a^{5}
The Cute Won (USA) *W K Goldsworthy* 84h
8 b g Defensive Play(USA) —Alzabella (USA) (Top Command (USA))
1021^{6} 1156^{17}
The Dark Lord (IRE) *Mrs L Wadham* 137h 132 c
9 b g Lord Americo—Khalkeys Shoon (Green Shoon)
(1817) 2484^{5} 2953^{4}3331^{5} 3816^{3} 4617^{3}(4827)
The Dasher (IRE) *Sean Aherne* 88h
7 ch g Erin's Isle—Gorm (Majority Blue)
70a^{9}
The Dream Lives On (IRE) *Miss Z C Davison* 73h 44c
10 ch g Phardante(FR) —Rare Dream (Pollerton)
5085^{6}
Thedreamstillalive (IRE) *J A B Old* 91+h 113c
6 ch g Houmayoun(FR) —State Of Dream (IRE) (Carmelite House (USA))
(2592) **3547^{2}**
Thedublinpublican (IRE) *C C Bealby* 103 h 103+c
6 b g Beneficial—Ideal Woman (IRE) (King's Ride)
(1491) 1611^{4} 1818^{P} 2925^{4} 3818^{3}
The Duckpond (IRE) *J A B Old* 117h 126+c
9 ch g Bob's Return(IRE) —Miss Gosling (Prince Bee)
(2812)
The Duke's Speech (IRE) *T P Tate* 129h
5 b g Saddlers' Hall(IRE) —Dannkalia (IRE) (Shernazar)
2444^{3} 2755^{6} (3232) (4301) 4763^{3}
The Eens *D McCain Jnr* 18h 85c
14 b g Rakaposhi King—Snippet (Ragstone)
350^{3}
The Entomologist (IRE) *C R Egerton* 95b
5 b g Saddlers' Hall(IRE) —Winter Ground (IRE) (Montelimar (USA))
4500^{9} (5054)

The Extra Man (IRE) *A King* 113c
12 b g Sayaarr(USA) —Chez Georges (Welsh Saint)
346^{P} 1989^{P} 2431^{2}2748^{6} 2877^{7}
The Fast Frog (FR) *Lady Connell*
5 b g Kadalko(FR) —Alba Terra (FR) (Kashtan (FR))
3685^{P} 4032^{10}
The Fingersmith (IRE) *A J McNamara* 111+h 128+c
7 ch g Safety Catch(USA) —Dalus Rose (IRE) (Mandalus)
3411a^{10}
The Flyer (IRE) *Miss S J Wilton* 98h
9 b g Blues Traveller(IRE) —National Ballet (Shareef Dancer (USA))
109^{3} 468^{3} 2184^{4} 2621^{5} 2862^{6}3345^{5} 3548^{P} 4549^{8} 4805^{4} 5014^{6}
Theflyingscottie *J D Frost* 74+h
4 gr g Paris House—Miss Flossa (FR) (Big John (FR))
1679^{6} 1955^{4} 2597^{9} 3479^{4} 4056^{6}
The Footballresult *P R Johnson* 59h
5 b m The West(USA) —Bunny Gee (Last Tycoon)
749^{12} 1987^{9}
The French Furze (IRE) *N G Richards* 151h 124c
12 ch g Be My Guest(USA) —Exciting (Mill Reef (USA))
2500^{3} (3177) 3641a^{5} 4432^{9} 5005^{F}
The Frisky Friar *G A Harker* 67h
8 ch g Symbolic—Ring Of Flowers (Nicholas Bill)
2571^{7} 2838^{P} (Dead)
The Frosty Ferret (IRE) *J M Jefferson* 86h 96+c
8 b g Zaffaran(USA) —Frostbite (Prince Tenderfoot (USA))
2591^{3} **2839^{3} 2982^{3}3486^{7} 3798^{4} 4142^{4}4587^{6} 5092^{5}**
The Galway Man (IRE) *Anthony Mullins* 125b 147c
9 b g Zaffaran(USA) —Nestley River (IRE) (Over The River (FR))
3472a^{P} (Dead)
The Gangerman (IRE) *N A Twiston-Davies* 106h
6 ch g Anshan—Ivy Lane (IRE) (Be My Native (USA))
178^{4} 365^{3} 1647^{4} 2310^{2} (2621) 2985^{3}3345^{2} 3814^{3} 4372^{5}
The Gay Gordons *P R Webber* 29b
5 b g Accordion—No Chili (Glint Of Gold)
4854^{18}
The Gene Genie *R J Hodges* 104h 97c
11 b g Syrtos—Sally Maxwell (Roscoe Blake)
1784^{4} 1862^{7} 2139^{7} 2609^{10} 2802^{P}3128^{4} 3223^{5}
The Gerry Man (IRE) *D J Wintle* 73b
7 b g Arctic Lord—Soldeu Creek (IRE) (Buckskin (FR))
2426^{11} 2849^{P}
Thegirlfromclapham (IRE) *D Carroll*
6 b m Dr Massini(IRE) —Port Alley (Torus)
1593^{9}
The Gleaner *M W Easterby* 88+b
4 b g Kayf Tara—Handmaiden (Shardari)
3785^{3} (4533)
The Glen *R Lee* 109+h 116+c
8 gr g Mtoto—Silver Singer (Pharly (FR))
465^{8} 893^{2} 1155^{4}1487^{2} 1726^{3}
The Glen Road (IRE) *A W Carroll* 80h 100+c
9 ch g Star Quest—Claret Mist (Furry Glen)
4590^{P} 5106^{3}
The Graduate *A J Walker* 81+c
12 ch g Indian Ridge—Queen's Eyot (Grundy)
196^{P}
The Granby (IRE) *Mrs H M Kemp* 105h 105c
12 b g Insan(USA) —Elteetee (Paddy's Stream)
4607^{6} 5020^{U}
The Grey Baron *A Coveney* 94c
9 gr g Baron Blakeney—Topsy Bee (Be Friendly)
440^{P}
The Grey Butler (IRE) *B De Haan* 105h
9 gr g Roselier(FR) —Georgic (Tumble Gold)
387^{P}
The Grey Friend *Andrew Slattery* 82b
4 gr g Environment Friend—Dark City (Sweet Monday)
5060a^{8}
The Grocers Curate (IRE) *N J Henderson* 104h 114+c
6 b g Anshan—Shining Willow (Strong Gale)
2574^{3} 2922^{2}
The Hairy Lemon *A King* 113 h
6 b g Eagle Eyed(USA) —Angie's Darling (Milford)
(1856) (3152) (3333) 3696^{5} 4131^{3} 4938^{6}
The Hardy Boy *Miss A M Newton-Smith* 68c
6 br g Overbury(IRE) —Miss Nero (Crozier)
1775^{P} **2574^{6}** 4649^{7} **4802^{6}4913^{4}**
The Hearty Joker (IRE) *M J M Evans* 78h 88c
11 b g Broken Hearted—Furryway (Furry Glen)
4936^{P} 5051^{9}
The Hero Sullivan (IRE) *C C Bealby* 53h
5 bb g Muroto—You'll Never Know (IRE) (Un Desperado (FR))
4637^{10}
The Hill (IRE) *D M Christie* 78h 84c
7 b g Desse Zenny(USA) —Another Munchkin (IRE) (Nordance (USA))
413^{U}
The Hollow Bottom *N A Twiston-Davies* 105+b
5 b g Kadeed(IRE) —Leighten Lass (IRE) (Henbit (USA))
(2145) 2941^{3} 3462^{3}
The Holy Bee (IRE) *Mrs S J Humphrey* 101h 103c
7 ch g Un Desperado(FR) —Ballycahan Girl (Bargello)
1618^{3} 1988^{7} 2574^{5}3419^{U} 3593^{3} 5017^{5}
The Honey Guide *Mrs L B Normile* 31b 66c
10 gr g Homo Sapien—The Whirlie Weevil (Scallywag)
550^{7} 874^{P} 979^{6}1147^{P} 1433^{P}
The Hudnalls (IRE) *J A B Old* 97b
5 ch g Shernazar—Toposki (FR) (Top Ville)
4853^{2}

The Iron Giant (IRE) *Miss H C Knight* 76 h
4 b g Giant's Causeway(USA) —Shalimar (IRE) (Indian Ridge)
2580[P] 3354[5] 3787[10]
Thejamman (IRE) *Noel Meade* 69h 64c
7 b g Glacial Storm(USA) —Terracotta (GER) (Nebos (GER))
3528a[10]
The Joker (IRE) *J K Magee* 103h
8 ch g Montelimar(USA) —How Doudo (Oats)
3378[11] 3783[F]
The Kew Tour (IRE) *Mrs S J Smith* 114h 127 c
10 ch g Un Desperado(FR) —Drivers Bureau (Proverb)
12[5] 1972[2] 2518[2]2767[4] 3258[2] 3728[6]
The King Of Rock *A G Newcombe* 77+h
5 b g Nicolotte—Lv Girl (IRE) (Mukaddamah (USA))
230[7]
The Kings Fling *Miss E Thompson* 95c
10 b g Rakaposhi King—Poetic Light (Ardross)
4330[2]
The Kirk (NZ) *M Madgwick* 100+h
8 b g Grosvenor(NZ) —Margaux (NZ) (War Hawk)
(206) 501[6] 1675[F]
The Knockinocker *W M Brisbourne*
5 ch g My Generation—Andy Coin (Andy Rew)
1849[15]
The Laird's Entry (IRE) *J Howard Johnson* 112+c
11 b g King's Ride—Balancing Act (Balinger)
2443[P]
The Langer (IRE) *S T Lewis* 60h
6 b g Saddlers' Hall(IRE) —Minigirls Niece (IRE) (Strong Gale)
138[16] 179[8] 266[3] 912[8] 3957[3]4589[7] 4642[5]
The Last Cast *Evan Williams* 128c
7 ch g Prince Of Birds(USA) —Atan's Gem (USA) (Sharpen Up)
3739[8] 4762[F]
The Last Hurrah (IRE) *Mrs John Harrington* 119+h
6 b g In The Wings—Last Exit (Dominion)
4951a[7] (5078a)
The Last Mohican *A G Juckes* 79h
7 b g Common Grounds—Arndilly (Robellino (USA))
3141[4] 3731[3] 3945[P]
The Last Over *Miss K M George* 12h
5 b m Overbury(IRE) —Little Serena (Primitive Rising (USA))
230[F] 5043[F]
The Last Sabo *M Wigham*
4 b g Prince Sabo—Classic Fan (USA) (Lear Fan (USA))
4795[P] 5024[U] 1[15]
The Last Stand *Anthony Mullins* 120+h
4 b g Vettori(IRE) —Cassilis (IRE) (Persian Bold)
(2645a) 3004a[9]
The Last Viking *A Parker* 86h
6 b g Supreme Leader—Viking Rocket (Viking (USA))
2948[10] 4143[8] 4527[8]
The Laying Hen (IRE) *D P Keane* 71h
6 ch m Anshan—Glacial Run (IRE) (Glacial Storm (USA))
131[7] 2558[12] 3240[10] 3437[F] 3692[3]3997[9] 4836[7]
The Listener (IRE) *R H Alner* 132 h 156 c
7 gr g Roselier(FR) —Park Breeze (IRE) (Strong Gale)
(2607) (2869) (3178) 3976[F]4444[F]
The Local *C R Egerton* 120+h 123+c
6 b g Selkirk(USA) —Finger Of Light (Green Desert (USA))
2324[3] (2595) **3387[4] 3580[3](4162) 4502[5] (4820)**
The Longfella *G M Moore* 91b
5 b g Petong—Miss Tri Colour (Shavian)
4992[6]
The Luder (IRE) *P F Nicholls* 127+h
5 b g Naheez(USA) —Secret Sensation (IRE) (Classic Secret (USA))
2309[4] 2624 [2] 3210[2] (3508) 4036[3] (4676) 5005[7]
The Lyme Volunteer (IRE) *David M Easterby* 89c
9 b m Zaffaran(USA) —Dooley O'Brien (The Parson)
4351[P] 4846[5] 5013[2]
The Main Man *M G Rimell*
5 b g Double Trigger(IRE) —Papirusa (IRE) (Pennine Walk)
3983[12]
Themanfromcarlisle *S H Shirley-Beavan* 112+c
10 br g Jupiter Island—Country Mistress (Town And Country)
176[P]
Themanfromfraam *Mrs S M Johnson* 82b
4 b g Fraam—Whey's Star (Bold Arrangement)
1785[3] 2611[5] 3181[12]
The Manse Brae (IRE) *J M Jefferson* 113h 114c
10 b g Roselier(FR) —Decent Preacher (Decent Fellow)
97[P]
The Market Man (NZ) *N J Henderson* 142+h
6 ch g Grosvenor(NZ) —Eastern Bazzaar (IRE) (King Persian)
(1872) (2483) 2758[2]
The Masareti Kid (IRE) *I McMath* 90+h 18c
9 b g Commanche Run—Little Crack (IRE) (Lancastrian)
110[6] 1361[P] 4113[2] 4341[2] **4844[9]**5068[8]
The Maystone (IRE) *B Mactaggart* 74h
6 bb g Thowra(FR) —Peg O The Wood (IRE) (Be My Native (USA))
59[6] 317[8]
The Merry Mason (IRE) *Mrs S J Smith* 80h 121c
10 gr g Roselier(FR) —Busters Lodge (Antwerp City)
80[6] 468[5] **2841[6] 3921[5]**
The Mick Weston *R T Phillips* 116h
7 b g North Col—Zalina (Tyrnavos)
(2460) 3175[5] 4443[12]

The Mighty Dunne (IRE) *Evan Williams*
6 bb g Moscow Society(USA) —Exceptional Value (Red Regent)
3142[P] (Dead)
The Mighty Oak *P S Payne* 17b
5 b g Current Edition(IRE) —Officially Pensham (Official)
656[14]
The Mighty Sparrow (IRE) *A E Jones* 90h 100c
13 b g Montelimar(USA) —Tamers Belle (Tamerlane)
126[3] 666[2] 902[4](958) 1860[5] 1956[P]
The Miner *Miss S E Forster* 82h 99 c
8 ch g Hatim(USA) —Glen Morvern (Carlingford Castle)
318[6] 407[4] 1605[8]1839[3] **2022[2] 2679[5]**2944[16] **3379[7] 3798[2]4318[2] 4721[7] 5036[9]**
The Money Pit *J R Turner*
5 b g Keen—Popping On (Sonnen Gold)
2507[15]
The Moyne Machine (IRE) *Timothy Doyle* 111c
10 b m Elbio—Victoria Hall (Hallgate)
45a[P]
The Muratti *G Brown* 78+h 64c
8 b g Alflora(IRE) —Grayrose Double (Celtic Cone)
351[3] 1671[P] **3251[9] 3801[8]4837[5]**
The Music Queen *G A Swinbank* 89+b
5 ch m Halling(USA) —Sadly Sober (IRE) (Roi Danzig (USA))
3556[3] 3931[5] (4902)
Thenameescapesme *T R George* 94+h
6 b g Alderbrook—Gaygo Lady (Gay Fandango (USA))
355[2] *2131[7]* 2860[4]3369[8] 3947[7] 4396[5] 4726[4]
The Names Bond *N G Richards* 113+h 108+c
8 b g Tragic Role(USA) —Artistic Licence (High Top)
60[4] 217[5] 413[P]466[2] (2027) (2680) 3206[7] **4586[4]**
The Needler (IRE) *B N Pollock* 81h
6 b g Needle Gun(IRE) —Monteanna (IRE) (Montelimar (USA))
1112[7]
The Newsman (IRE) *G Wareham* 112h 124c
14 b g Homo Sapien—Miller Fall'S (Stubbs Gazette)
103[7] 534[7] 2016[4]2577[6] 3284[7] (4873)
Thenford Boy (IRE) *B L Lay*
6 b g Oscar(IRE) —Sky Deely (Skyliner)
3883[P]
Thenford Flyer (IRE) *D J S Ffrench Davis* 97b
6 b g Oscar(IRE) —Broadway Baby (Some Hand)
4455[7]
Thenford Lad (IRE) *D J S Ffrench Davis* 72b
5 b g Saddlers' Hall(IRE) —Lady Leona (Leander)
846[6]
Thenford Lord (IRE) *D J S Ffrench Davis* 94b
5 b g Saddlers' Hall(IRE) —Laura's Native (IRE) (Be My Native (USA))
1459[4] 1681[9] 2056[4] 2534[12]
Thenford Star (IRE) *D J S Ffrench Davis* 72+h
5 b m Zaffaran(USA) —Limavady Lady (IRE) (Camden Town)
2937[5] 3437[7] 4094[6] 4427[6]
Thenford Trout (IRE) *E J O'Grady* 55b
5 b g Midhish—Monteanna (IRE) (Montelimar (USA))
44a[16]
The Nobleman (USA) *D Shaw* 86h 65c
10 b g Quiet American(USA) —Furajet (USA) (The Minstrel (CAN))
827[5] 902[P] 1177[P]
The Noble Roman *T Ellis*
8 ch g Sir Harry Lewis(USA) —Antica Roma (IRE) (Denel (FR))
4421[6]
The Nomad *M W Easterby* 110 h 122+c
10 b g Nomadic Way(USA) —Bubbling (Tremblant)
195[3] 1825[6]
Theocritus (GER) *Nick Williams* 109h
5 b g Trempolino(USA) —Thyatira (FR) (Bakharoff (USA))
(1021) 1383[3] 1680[5] 1880[2] (2002) 2533[8] 3175[12]
The Old Spinner *P R Chamings*
4 ch f Bluegrass Prince(IRE) —Raghill Hannah (Buckskin (FR))
4017[14]
The Otmoor Fox (IRE) *P J Hobbs* 68b
6 ch g Shahrastani(USA) —Misty's Wish (Furry Glen)
3292[5]
The Outlier (IRE) *Miss Venetia Williams* 98h 115 c
8 gr g Roselier(FR) —Shuil A Cuig (Quayside)
2839[U] 3426[2] (3660) (4014) 4214[8] 4878[3]
The Pecker Dunn (IRE) *Mrs N S Evans* 33h
12 b g Be My Native(USA) —Riversdale Shadow (Kemal (FR))
169[P] (2188) 2582[4] 2845[P] 3250[7]4012[7] 4449[P]
The Pen *P C Haslam* 103 h
4 ch f Lake Coniston(IRE) —Come To The Point (Pursuit Of Love)
(1718) 1923[7]
The Pennys Dropped (IRE) *Jonjo O'Neill* 107h 128+c
9 ch g Bob's Return(IRE) —Shuil Alainn (Levanter)
823[3] (960)
The Persuader (IRE) *P F Nicholls* 121+h
6 b g Sadler's Wells(USA) —Sister Dot (USA) (Secretariat (USA))
2071[1] 2369[7]
The Phair Crier (IRE) *S A Hughes* 114 h 74c
11 ch g Phardante(FR) —Maul-More (Deep Run)
4560[6]
The Piker (IRE) *T R George* 49h
5 b g Darazari(IRE) —Top Step (IRE) (Step Together (USA))
2961[14] 3511[7] 4088[10] 4603[P]
The Pious Prince (IRE) *L Lungo* 115+b
5 ch g Shahrastani(USA) —Ara Blend (IRE) (Persian Mews)
(4147)

The Player *A M Balding* 71h
7 b g Octagonal(NZ) —Patria (USA) (Mr Prospector (USA))
2584[15] 2802[9]
The Premier Cat (IRE) *T Cahill* 118h 150c
10 b g Glacial Storm(USA) —Carraigaloe (Little Buskins)
3587a[P]
Theprideofeireann (IRE) *Jonjo O'Neill* 60h
7 b g Toulon—Slaney Queen (Ballad Rock)
1977[12]
Thepubhorse *Mrs H O Graham* 81h
6 ch g Endoli(USA) —Lady Insight (Belfort (FR))
59[12] 212[7] 591[P] 785[2] 941[P]1151[3] 1294[3] 1379[P]
The Quarry Man *A W Congdon*
8 b g Opera Ghost—Beauty's Imp (Impecunious)
4560[U]
The Railway Man (IRE) *A L T Moore* 142h 146c
7 b g Shernazar—Sparky Sue (IRE) (Strong Gale)
40a[5] 117a[2] **3409a[P] (3893a) 4444[7] 4889a[3]**
The Rainbow Man *J Ryan* 38b 31c
6 gr g Terimon—Swallowfield (Wattlefield)
1757[P] 1916[P] 3417[6] **3955[P]4735[10] 4911[6]**
Therealbandit (IRE) *M C Pipe* 143+h 157 c
9 b g Torus—Sunrise Highway VII (Damsire Unregistered)
2177[13] 2760[8] (2992) 4777[P] 5144[5]
The Real Deal (IRE) *Nick Williams* 87h
5 b g Taipan(IRE) —Forest Mist (Dalsaan)
1614[4]
The Real Solara (IRE) *Michael Hourigan* 98+h 105c
9 bb g Aahsaylad—Arctic Brief (Buckskin (FR))
71a[10] (Dead)
There Goes Wally *A Ennis* 82b
8 b g Lyphento(USA) —Dutch Majesty (Homing)
3148[P] 3480[P] 3885[P]
There Is No Doubt (FR) *Miss Lucy Bridges* 89h
5 b g Mansonnien(FR) —Ma Chance (FR) (Dancehall (USA))
1968[6] 2238[7] 2606[6] 2958[7]
The Reverend (IRE) *J Howard Johnson* 119 h
6 bb g Taipan(IRE) —Sounds Classical (IRE) (Over The River (FR))
3970[8]
The Right People (IRE) *L Lungo* 86h
6 ch g Deploy—Marlousion (IRE) (Montelimar (USA))
3232[6] 3374[9] 4039[4]
The Ringer *J I A Charlton* 41b
6 b g Milieu—Sister Seven (IRE) (Henbit (USA))
2192[9] 4793[10]
The Rip *R M Stronge* 85h
5 ch g Definite Article—Polgwynne (Forzando)
3061[0] 1774[4] 2298[4] 2995[10] 3603[8]
The Risen Lark (IRE) *Miss Venetia Williams* 57h
6 b m Celtic Swing—May Hills Legacy (IRE) (Be My Guest (USA))
77[6]
The Rising Moon (IRE) *Jonjo O'Neill* 122h 98c
7 br g Anshan—I'm So Happy (IRE) (Miner's Lamp)
1758[2] 2291[P] 4633[P]
The River Joker (IRE) *John R Upson* 91h 88 c
10 ch g Over The River(FR) —Augustaeliza (IRE) (Callernish)
1884[P] **2986[6] 3276[3]4042[8] 4321[7] 4576[P]**
The Rocking Dock (IRE) *D McCain* 101+h
5 gr g Dr Massini(IRE) —Ackle Backle (Furry Glen)
2941[4] 3421[5] 4732[3]
The Rollerskater (IRE) *Mrs A M Thorpe* 34b
6 b g High Roller(IRE) —Lashkari Rose (IRE) (Lashkari)
4940[12]
The Rooken (IRE) *P Spottiswood* 57h
7 b g Fourstars Allstar(USA) —Be My Sweetheart (IRE) (Be My Native (USA))
82[16] 210[7] 643[P] 785[4] 3797[11]4299[10] 10[9]
The Saltire Tiger *Mrs L B Normile* 43h
5 b g Busy Flight—Candlebright (Lighter)
3563[4] 4533[11] 5063[10]
Thesaurus *Mrs S J Smith* 34h
7 gr g Most Welcome—Red Embers (Saddlers' Hall (IRE))
1340[10]
The Sawdust Kid *R H Buckler* 64h 102c
12 ch g River God(USA) —Susie's Money (Seymour Hicks (FR))
669[4] 1022[P] 1191[P]
The Sawyer (BEL) *R H Buckler* 105h
6 ch g Fleetwood(IRE) —Green Land (BEL) (Hero's Honor (USA))
2507[3] 2849[2] 3023[5] 3277[8]
The Sham *Michael Hourigan* 94b
6 b g Perpendicular—Our Aisling (Blakeney)
44a[9]
The Shirley Hunt *R T Phillips* 80b
6 b m Rakaposhi King—Zalina (Tyrnavos)
4017[6] 4398[RR] 4500[11]
The Sister *Jonjo O'Neill* 112 h 126 c
9 b m Alflora(IRE) —Donna Farina (Little Buskins)
1026[6] **(1342) 1670[8] 1893[P]2143[F]**
The Small Farmer (IRE) *Mrs A E Brooks* 82+h
9 b g West China—Wee Maggie (Avocat)
3279[7] (4277) 4734[P]
The Sneakster (IRE) *S A Brookshaw* 42h
8 b m Jurado(USA) —Royal Star (IRE) (Orchestra)
843[F] **3278[P] 3356[F]**3461[P] **3689[U]**
Thespian Lady *P R Chamings* 53h
5 bb m Kirkwall—Drama School (Young Generation)
243[P] 804[6] 4570[4] 4783[14]
The Spieler (IRE) *N J Henderson* 112 c
7 bb g Un Desperado(FR) —Mettle Kettle (Cut Above)
2848[4]
The Spoonplayer (IRE) *Henry De Bromhead* 123h
7 b g Accordion—Jennie Dun (IRE) (Mandalus)
93a[10] 2206[5] 3086a[6] 5059a[20]

The Squatter (IRE) *V Clifford* 104h
7 b g Right Win(IRE) —Dells Dream (IRE) (Classic Music (USA))
2206[8]
The Stafford (IRE) *L Wells*
5 b g Selkirk(USA) —Bint Zamayem (IRE) (Rainbow Quest (USA))
2683[P] 3463[P]
The Staggery Boy (IRE) *M R Hoad* 51h 100c
10 b g Shalford(IRE) —Murroe Star (Glenstal (USA))
103[5] (395)
The Tall Guy (IRE) *N A Twiston-Davies*
10 bb g Zaffaran(USA) —Mullangale (Strong Gale)
1848[3] 2485[P] 2957[F] (Dead)
The Teuchter *Mrs S D Williams* 82+h
7 b g First Trump—Barefoot Landing (USA) (Cozzene (USA))
5072[4]
The Tinker *Mrs S C Bradburne* 45h 111c
11 b g Nomadic Way(USA) —Miss Tino (Relkino)
1666[7] 2037[U] 2498[3]3377[F]
The Trojan Horse (IRE) *Miss H C Knight* 60b
6 b g Ilium—Miss Cynthia (Dawn Review)
3505[P] 3685[P]
The Unamed Man *J Groucott* 76c
10 ch g Weld—Orange Spice (Orange Bay)
313[5] 594[3]
The Villager (IRE) *T R George* 126+h 131c
10 br g Zaffaran(USA) —Kitty Wren (Warpath)
2210[5] 3293[5] 4617[10]4806[2]
The Vintage Dancer (IRE) *Mrs Nicola Pollock* 87c
10 b g Riberetto—Strong Swimmer (IRE) (Black Minstrel)
50[P] 3924[U] 4397[3]
The Washerwoman *B I Case* 75h
6 b m Classic Cliche(IRE) —Olnistar (FR) (Balsamo (FR))
2718[5]
The Weaver (FR) *L Lungo* 95h
7 ch g Villez(USA) —Miss Planette (FR) (Tip Moss (FR))
334[P] 2474[4] 2840[6] 3269[4] 3487[3]
The Welder *Miss S Jackson* 70h
12 b g Buckley—Crystal Run VII (Damsire Unregistered)
313[P]
The Well Lad (IRE) *A M Balding* 30c
7 ch g Moonax(IRE) —Caribbean Rose (IRE) (Regular Guy)
4417[U] 4780[7] 5049[P]
The Whispering Oak (IRE) *P S Payne* 36b
4 b f Silver Patriarch(IRE) —Celtic Remorse (Celtic Cone)
2013[7]
The Wicketkeeper (IRE) *M Scudamore* 66b
4 b g Double Bed(FR) —Inmemoriam (IRE) (Buckskin (FR))
4853[16]
The Wife's Sister *Mrs K Waldron* 82 h
5 b m Classic Cliche(IRE) —Hard Love (Rambo Dancer (CAN))
58[4] 351[2] 591[P] 2244[9] 2428[6]2752[7] 3141[2] 3335[7] 3731[2] (3985) 4278[5]4550[2] 4783[5]
The Wipper (IRE) *Sean Aherne* 125c
10 b g Alphabatim(USA) —Musical Millie (IRE) (Orchestra)
1700a[P]
The Wizard Mul *W Storey* 57h
6 br g Wizard King—Longden Pride (Superpower)
3168[7]
The Wooden Spoon (IRE) *L Wells* 99h
8 b g Old Vic—Amy's Gale (IRE) (Strong Gale)
2799[9] 3477[4] 4285[3] 4661[7]
The Wrens Nest (IRE) *J A Berry* 94h
7 ch m Shernazar—Approach The Dawn (IRE) (Orchestra)
66a[16]
The Yellow Earl (IRE) *J M Jefferson* 65h 3c
6 b g Topanoora—Sweet Innocence (IRE) (King's Ride)
147[P] 261[P] 415[11] 971[4] 1209[2]1310[P] 2639[P] 4584[10]
They Grabbed Me (IRE) *M C Pipe* 72+h
5 bb m Presenting—Royal Gale (Strong Gale)
2427[8] 2845[P] 3250[9] 3951[8] 4277[U]4752[8] 5048[5]
Thievery *H D Daly* 74h
5 gr g Terimon—Piracy (Jupiter Island)
1311[4] 2295[F] 2631[9] 2859[7] 4210[12]
Thieves'Glen *H Morrison* 110h 114 c
8 b g Teenoso(USA) —Hollow Creek (Tarqogan)
21[2] 203[3] 531[2] 742[P] 912[4]**1157[F] 1406[5] 4358[P]4555[3] 4748[13] 5051[7]**
Thinking Of You (IRE) *Moses McCabe* 40b
6 b g Accordion—Limaheights (IRE) (Head For Heights)
44a[24]
Think Quick (IRE) *R Hollinshead* 87h
6 b m Goldmark(USA) —Crimson Ring (Persian Bold)
25[7] 134[3] 613[5] 826[8] 987[7]1156[2] 1297[2] 2140[8] 3655[3] 4452[6]5072[3]
Third Empire *C Grant* 102 h
5 b g Second Empire(IRE) —Tahnee (Cadeaux Genereux)
2108[3] 2658[4] 3347[6] 4040[2] 4532[6]
Thiseldo Us *M B Shears* 77h
11 ch g Silver Owl—Sunny Breeze (Roi Soleil)
1331[6] 458[12] 861[F] 977[5]
This Is It (IRE) *T G McCourt* 47h
5 b m Saddlers' Hall(IRE) —Rub Of The Court (IRE) (Law Society (USA))
1724[F]
This Is Serious (IRE) *C F Swan*
12 ch g Broken Hearted—Lady Virtue (Oats)
91a[P]
Thisisyourlife (IRE) *H D Daly* 99 h
8 b g Lord Americo—Your Life (Le Bavard (FR))
216[4] (Dead)
Thisthatandtother (IRE) *P F Nicholls* 148 h 164c
10 b g Bob Back(USA) —Baden (IRE) (Furry Glen)
2346[3] 2760[F]

Thistlecraft (IRE) *C C Bealby* 58h 120 c
7 b g Warcraft(USA) —Thistletopper (Le Bavard (FR))
2530^{12} **2963^{3} (3419) 3942^{P}4971^{P} 5127^{3}**

Thomo (IRE) *N E Berry* 93h
8 b g Faustus(USA) —Dawn O'Er Kells (IRE) (Pitskelly)
384^{2} 635^{3} 802^{3} 4606^{9}

Thorn *P W Hiatt*
4 ch g Alhaarth(IRE) —Datura (Darshaan)
4667^{14}

Thorn Of The Rose (IRE) *James Moffatt* 74h
5 gr m Terimon—Loch Scavaig (IRE) (The Parson)
828^{5} 1532^{9} 1688^{U} 1885^{5} 2108^{7}2412^{7} 3254^{6} 4341^{P}

Thornton Bridge *R J Hewitt* 73h
8 b g Presidium—Wire Lass (New Brig)
982^{12} 1036^{6} 1108^{10} (1209) **1363^{F}**5050^{P}

Thornton Charlotte *B S Rothwell* 35h
5 b m Defacto(USA) —Lindrick Lady (IRE) (Broken Hearted)
1357^{7}

Thorny Issue *M J Gingell*
7 gr g Thethingaboutitis(USA) —Rose Of Macmillion (Macmillion)
1521^{P} 1619^{P} 1757^{12} 1854^{F} (Dead)

Thorpeness (IRE) *P D Cundell* 88h
7 b g Barathea(IRE) —Brisighella (IRE) (Al Hareb (USA))
2555^{P} 2701^{P}

Thorsgill *M Todhunter* 63c
8 ch g Denel(FR) —Italian Princess (IRE) (Strong Gale)
2169^{P} **2839^{7}**

Thosewerethedays *Miss P Robson* 107 h
13 b g Past Glories—Charlotte's Festival (Gala Performance)
2452^{6} 3208^{3} 3854^{4} **4345^{P}**

Thoutmosis (USA) *L Lungo* 88h
7 ch g Woodman(USA) —Toujours Elle (USA) (Lyphard (USA))
61^{4} (304) 2038^{6} 2590^{3} 3383^{P} 3854^{9}4792^{11}

Thrashing *A E Jones* 97 h
11 b g Kahyasi—White-Wash (Final Straw)
959^{P} 1187^{6}

Three Boars *S Gollings* 39h
4 ch g Most Welcome—Precious Poppy (Polish Precedent (USA))
1551^{9}

Three Buck Chuck (IRE) *E Sheehy* 52h
4 b c Orpen(USA) —May We Dance (IRE) (Dance Of Life (USA))
5076a^{22}

Three Carat (USA) *J E Sheppard* 113h
6 b g Storm Broker(USA) —Gemini's Gem (USA) (Gemini Dreamer (USA))
1394a^{2}

Three Days Reign (IRE) *P D Cundell* 91h 114 c
12 br g Camden Town—Little Treat (Miner's Lamp)
1744^{P} 2342^{4} 2557^{6}

Three Guesses (IRE) *M Pitman* 99b
5 b g Supreme Leader—Guess Twice (Deep Run)
4623^{4}

Three Lions *R S Brookhouse* 103h
9 ch g Jupiter Island—Super Sol (Rolfe (USA))
275^{8} 665^{4} 768^{5} **893^{P}**(906) 3018^{3} 5010^{F}

Three Mill (IRE) *Thomas Cleary* 31h 82c
9 ch g Hubbly Bubbly(USA) —Glen Fuel (IRE) (Meneval (USA))
87a^{5}

Threepenny Bit *Mrs S M Johnson* 26h
8 b m Safawan—Tuppence In Clover (Petoski)
134^{16} 273^{7}

Threequarter Moon (IRE) *A Seymour* 116h
8 b m Presenting—Shining Dante (IRE) (Phardante (FR))
5077a^{11}

Three Ships *Miss J Feilden* 105+h
5 ch g Dr Fong(USA) —River Lullaby (USA) (Riverman (USA))
(279) 513^{2} (691)

Three Times A Lady *D W Thompson* 71h
6 b m Syrtos—Pure Formality (Forzando)
185^{P} 302^{5} 592^{5} 670^{2} 760^{7}1293^{4}

Through The Rye *E W Tuer* 117 h 137+c
10 ch g Sabrehill(USA) —Baharlilys (Green Dancer (USA))
2641^{6} **3207^{3} 4109^{F}**4490^{7} 4848^{16}

Thunder Child *John Allen* 69b
6 gr g Cloudings(IRE) —Double Dutch (Nicholas Bill)
470^{6} 2665^{9}

Thunder Hawk (IRE) *J Burke*
6 b g Saddlers' Hall(IRE) —Final Peace (IRE) (Satco (FR))
4722^{P}

Thunder Road (IRE) *P A Fahy* 102h
6 b m Mtoto—Shefoog (Kefaah (USA))
4887a^{P} 5077a^{18}

Thuringe (FR) *N G Richards*
5 b m Turgeon(USA) —L'Arme Au Poing (FR) (Comrade In Arms)
1839^{P}

Thyne Again (IRE) *W J Burke* 130h
5 ch g Good Thyne(USA) —Fine Affair (IRE) (Fine Blade (USA))
3309a^{5} 4888a^{3}

Thyne For Intersky (IRE) *Jonjo O'Neill* 108h
7 ch g Good Thyne(USA) —One Last Chance (Le Bavard (FR))
109^{5} 1039^{4} 1300^{5} 1513^{P}

Thyne Man (IRE) *J Mackie* 82b 85 c
8 br g Good Thyne(USA) —Showphar (IRE) (Phardante (FR))
107^{3} 1907^{4} 2259^{P}2415^{5} 3144^{3} 3732^{P}

Thyne Spirit (IRE) *S T Lewis* 47h 66c
7 ch g Good Thyne(USA) —Friston (IRE) (Roselier (FR))
532^{2} 1870^{P} 2983^{15} 3277^{P}**3457^{7} 3958^{4} 4576^{7}**

Tia Marnie *S Lycett*
8 b m Perpendicular—Hinton Bairn (Balinger)
1538^{7} 2560^{P}

Tianyi (IRE) *M Scudamore* 85h 74+c
10 b g Mujadil(USA) —Skinity (Rarity)
1852^{U} 2140^{6} **2561^{6}2936^{5} 3460^{P}** 3899^{5}4838^{9}

Tiarella (IRE) *Denis Ahern* 113+h
6 b m Supreme Leader—Dawn Appeal (Deep Run)
4887a^{9} 5077a^{8}

Tiasfourth *A M Hales* 27b
5 b m Contract Law(USA) —Nordic Crown (IRE) (Nordico (USA))
655^{15} 758^{12}

Tickateal *R D E Woodhouse* 97+h
6 ch g Emperor Fountain—Mary Hand (IRE) (Hollow Hand)
(417) 509^{4} 2517^{8} (3271) 5137^{4}

Tickers Way *C Drew* 95+b
5 gr g Cloudings(IRE) —Zany Lady (Arzanni)
241^{5} (656)

Ticket To Ride (FR) *A J Wilson* 49h 114c
8 ch g Pistolet Bleu(IRE) —Have A Drink (FR) (Hasty Tudor (USA))
2190^{12} **5018^{4}**

Tickford Abbey *Mrs P Robeson* 93b
4 br g Emperor Fountain—Flash-By (Ilium)
3651^{2} *4237^{7}*

Tickhill Tom *C W Fairhurst* 73b
6 ch g First Trump—Tender Loving Care (Final Straw)
1554^{9} 2007^{8} 2968^{11}

Tickton Flyer *M W Easterby* 101+h 93+c
8 b g Sovereign Water(FR) —Contradictory (Reprimand)
1210^{4}

Tidal Bay (IRE) *J I A Charlton* 126b
5 b g Flemensfirth(USA) —June's Bride (IRE) (Le Moss)
4507^{2} 4779^{2}

Tidal Fury (IRE) *J Jay* 123 h
4 b g Night Shift(USA) —Tidal Reach (USA) (Kris S (USA))
777a^{2} 1011^{3} (1428a) (1705a) (2085a) 4548a^{5}

Tierkely (IRE) *J J Lambe* 31h 91c
11 br g Yashgan—Island Dream (Lucifer (USA))
989^{3} 1067^{5} **1150^{6}1358^{2} 1378^{P} 1511^{6}**

Tiffin Brown *P C Haslam* 60h
4 br g Erhaab(USA) —Cockatrice (Petong)
1095^{P} 1201^{P} 1551^{7}

Tiffin Deano (IRE) *H J Manners* 50h
4 b g Mujadil(USA) —Xania (Mujtahid (USA))
1339^{9} 1404^{6} 1519^{6} 1563^{10}

Tiger Cry (IRE) *A L T Moore* 127h 143c
8 b g Germany(USA) —Dream Academy (Town And Country)
1093a^{2} **2163^{2} 4472^{2}5082a^{F}**

Tiger Frog (USA) *J Mackie* 101h 96 c
7 b g French Deputy(USA) —Woodyoubelieveit (USA) (Woodman (USA))
(220) 347^{6} 695^{4} 1366^{8} 2925^{11} 3152^{8}3351^{8}

Tiger Island (USA) *A E Jones* 77h
6 b h Grand Slam(USA) —Paris Wild Cat (USA) (Storm Cat (USA))
1784^{12} 2802^{10} 3603^{9} 4896^{6}

Tiger King (GER) *P Monteith* 96 h
5 b g Tiger Hill(IRE) —Tennessee Girl (GER) (Big Shuffle (USA))
2006^{7} 2448^{6} 2638^{6} 3168^{3} 3853^{P}3929^{8} 4346^{4}

Tigerlion (IRE) *J Bleahen* 119 h 126+c
8 b g Supreme Leader—Avida Dancer (Ballymore)
3079a^{F} 3514a^{F} (5082a)

Tiger Rock *Ms N M Hugo* 75b
5 b g Petoski—Whitepoint (Nicholas Bill)
3462^{6}

Tigers Lair (IRE) *Jonjo O'Neill* 116h 132 c
7 b g Accordion—Eadie (IRE) (Strong Gale)
(174) (344) (650) 1676^{4}

Tiger Talk *R C Guest* 63h 74c
10 ch g Sabrehill(USA) —Tebre (USA) (Sir Ivor (USA))
181^{9} 262^{U} 398^{6}480^{6} 1814^{9} 2025^{6} 2171^{15} 2463^{6}2962^{9} 3169^{7} 3557^{8} 4302^{13} **4989^{3}**

Tiger Tips Lad (IRE) *N A Twiston-Davies* 115h 107+c
7 b g Zaffaran(USA) —Halens Match (IRE) (Matching Pair)
2504^{F} 2664^{4} 3326^{9}3949^{7} 4639^{6} 5010^{P}

Tigger Too *B Storey*
8 b g Hatim(USA) —Kemaline (Kemal (FR))
2678^{P} 4313^{P}

Tighe Caster *P R Webber* 120h 128+c
7 b g Makbul—Miss Fire (Gunner B)
(1411) 1758^{F} 2270^{2}3991^{4}

Tight Corner (IRE) *Ian Williams*
7 b g Shardari—General Rain (General Ironside)
3145^{12} 4052^{P} 4826^{P}

Tighten Your Belt (IRE) *Miss Venetia Williams* 142h 138 c
9 b g Phardante(FR) —Hi' Upham (Deep Run)
2464^{F} 2848^{2} 3541^{2}4035^{U} 4759^{U}

Tignasse (FR) *Miss K M George* 97h
5 b m Double Bed(FR) —Off Guard (FR) (Bakharoff (USA))
1651^{3} 1774^{F} 1987^{P} 3592^{7} 5113^{9}

Tigu (IRE) *A Ennis* 29h
5 b g Tiraaz(USA) —Christy's Girl (IRE) (Buckskin (FR))
2865^{P} 3425^{10} 3658^{13}

Tihui Two (IRE) *G R I Smyly* 52h
6 b m Accordion—Maid Of Glenduragh (IRE) (Ya Zaman (USA))
616^{2} (866) 3820^{3} 4976^{3}

Tikram *G L Moore* 139h 150c
9 ch g Lycius(USA) —Black Fighter (USA) (Secretariat (USA))
3299^{2} 3724^{10} 4470^{12}4764^{8}

Tilla *Mrs A J Hamilton-Fairley* 62h
6 b m Bin Ajwaad(IRE) —Tosca (Be My Guest (USA))
2932^{P} 3321^{P}

Timberley *Miss R Brewis* 78+c
12 ch g Dancing High—Kimberley Rose (Monksfield)
555^{5}

Timber Scorpion (UAE) *P Hughes* 105h
4 b g Timber Country(USA) —Aqraba (Polish Precedent (USA))
2645a^{6}

Timbuktu *B Storey* 90 h
5 b g Efisio—Sirene Bleu Marine (USA) (Secreto (USA))
1591^{8} 2040^{2} 2416^{8} 2693^{7} 3206^{2}3853^{8} 4344^{P} 5120^{9}

Time Bandit (IRE) *M C Pipe* 96+h
6 b g Luso—Over The Green (IRE) (Over The River (FR))
629^{3} (802)

Time For You *J M Bradley* 76h
4 b f Vettori(IRE) —La Fija (USA) (Dixieland Band (USA))
1207^{4} 1268^{B} 1397^{P} 1478^{5} 1563^{2}1802^{3} 2069^{4} 2245^{3}

Time Marches On *K G Reveley* 101 h
8 b g Timeless Times(USA) —Tees Gazette Girl (Kalaglow)
9^{8} (233) 451^{10} 3351^{11}

Times Up Barney *C W Moore* 97h
6 b g Alderbrook—Give Me An Answer (True Song)
1323^{14} 1485^{9} 1903^{P} 2860^{8} 3846^{P}3975^{3} 4515^{P}

Time To Reflect (IRE) *R C Guest* 103h 111+c
7 ch g Anshan—Castlemitchle (IRE) (Roselier (FR))
(62) 150^{3} 11^{4}

Time To Relax (IRE) *R Dickin* 71h
5 b m Orpen(USA) —Lassalia (Sallust)
3963^{6}

Timetoring *B J Eckley* 87+b
4 ch g Karinga Bay—Little Time (Arctic Lord)
7^{5}

Time To Roam (IRE) *Miss Lucinda V Russell* 98 h
6 br g Darshaan—Minstrels Folly (USA) (The Minstrel (CAN))
1296^{P} 1665^{4} 1793^{2} 1940 ^{12} 2625^{2}2944^{14} 3445^{5} 3853^{3} 4364^{4} 4585^{3}5096^{10}

Time To Shine *Mrs L J Mongan* 123 h 99c
7 b m Pivotal—Sweet Jaffa (Never So Bold)
4938^{5} 5142^{16}

Time To Succeed *Mrs A M Thorpe*
4 b g Pennekamp(USA) —Ivory League (Last Tycoon)
1338^{P} 1440^{P} 4128^{12} 4506^{P} 5115^{7}

Timidjar (IRE) *Mrs D Thomas* 77h
13 b g Doyoun—Timissara (USA) (Shahrastani (USA))
681^{4} 801^{5} 1395^{5} 1636^{5}

Timolino (GER) *M Keller*
8 b h Monsun(GER) —Tilbury (USA) (Trempolino (USA))
4775^{P}

Tim's Moll *J B Walton* 62b
6 b m Hatim(USA) —Queen Of Dara (Dara Monarch)
124^{P}

Timucua (IRE) *D T Hughes* 79c
7 bb g Commanche Run—Morry's Lady (The Parson)
87a^{F}

Tina's Scallywag *H P Hogarth* 57h 79+c
9 br m Baron Blakeney—Southend Scallywag (Tina's Pet)
(211) 464^{5} 554^{9}

Tingshaw Ring (IRE) *Eoin Doyle* 99+h
6 b m Son Of Sharp Shot(IRE) —Highest Baby (FR) (Highest Honor (FR))
1683^{2} 1991^{4}

Tin Healy's Pass *I McMath* 69h
6 b g Puissance—Shaa Spin (Shaadi (USA))
209^{0} 369^{6} 415^{9} 1360^{11} **2026^{P}**

Tinian *Miss Tracy Waggott* 80h
8 b g Mtoto—Housefull (Habitat)
2658^{10} 2903^{5} 3488^{6} 3673^{C} 3916^{12}14^{6}

Tino (IRE) *Andrew Turnell* 72h 90+c
10 ch g Torus—Delphic Thunder (Viking (USA))
2018 **5088^{R}**

Tinstre (IRE) *P W Hiatt* 103+h
8 ch g Dolphin Street(FR) —Satin Poppy (Satin Wood)
(238) (357) 568^{U} 762^{4} 813^{2} 980^{8} 1413^{2}1488^{7}

Tinvane Rose (IRE) *J G M O'Shea* 70h
7 ch m Roselier(FR) —Grey's Delight (Decent Fellow)
3483^{6} 3951^{6} 4133^{7}

Tioga Gold (IRE) *L R James* 88h
7 b g Goldmark(USA) —Coffee Bean (Doulab (USA))
1067^{4} 1566^{2} 2256^{6} 3552^{5} 14^{19}

Tipp Top (IRE) *O Brennan* 90c
9 b g Brief Truce(USA) —Very Sophisticated (USA) (Affirmed (USA))
183^{3} 368^{3} 2926^{P}3368^{7} 3654^{5} (3958) (4580) 4900^{6} 5136^{P}

Tipsy Mouse (IRE) *R C Guest* 102 h 108c
10 ch g Roselier(FR) —Darjoy (Darantus)
439^{4} 1276^{3} 2037^{U}2143^{4} 2368^{13}

Tipu Sultan *M D Hammond*
6 ch g Kris—Eye Witness (IRE) (Don't Forget Me)
5063^{13}

Tirikumba *S G Griffiths* 94h
10 ch m Le Moss—Ntombi (Trasi's Son)
245^{3} 441^{2} (679) 2053^{3} 2430^{6} 3247^{7}3458^{8}

Tirley Gale *Mrs N D Smith* 83c
14 b g Strong Gale—Mascara VII (Damsire Unregistered)
184^{U}

Tirley Storm *J S Smith* 66h 85+c
11 b g Tirley Gale—Random Select (Random Shot)
181^{2} 368^{P} 1620^{8}1819^{6} 2248^{8}

Tisfreetdream (IRE) *P A Pritchard* 90+b
5 b g Oscar(IRE) —Gayley Gale (IRE) (Strong Gale)
2665^{7} 2988^{10} 4422^{4}

Tis She *N B King* 44h
8 b m Sir Harry Lewis(USA) —Shedid (St Columbus)
671^{8} 763^{P}

Titian Flame (IRE) *D Burchell* 98h
6 ch m Titus Livius(FR) —Golden Choice (Midyan (USA))
747^{2} 841^{5} 949^{F} 2459^{P} 2659^{9}3247^{10} (3548) 3733^{F} 3802^{4} 4131^{4} 4488^{6}4797^{3} 5019^{RR} 5^{U}

Titus Salt (USA) *M D Hammond* 81h
5 ch g Gentlemen(ARG) —Farewell Partner (USA) (Northern Dancer)
1588^{3} 2763^{8} 3347^{9} 14^{18} (Dead)

Tizi Ouzou (IRE) *M C Pipe* 92+h
5 ch m Desert Prince(IRE) —Tresor (USA) (Pleasant Tap (USA))
389^{13} 1381^{10} 1636^{4} 1900^{5} 2146^{7}2428^{5} 2845^{5} 3321^{6}

Toad Hall *Mrs L B Normile* 82 c
12 b g Henbit(USA) —Candlebright (Lighter)
125^{7} 411^{6} (717) 1343^{5} 1570^{6} 1589^{6}

Tobesure (IRE) *J I A Charlton* 101h 109c
12 b g Asir—Princess Citrus (IRE) (Auction Ring (USA))
215^{5} 410^{5} (1838) 2840^{3} 3487^{6} 4344^{7}4724^{4}

Toemac *M Bradstock* 83+h
7 b g Slip Anchor—Bobanlyn (IRE) (Dance Of Life (USA))
2269^{5}

Tofta Tilly *L R James*
6 ch m Muhtarram(USA) —Budding Prospect (Rudimentary (USA))
4059^{12}

Tog Go Boge (IRE) *R T Phillips* 59h
8 bb g Erin's Isle—Vision Of Spring (Cadeaux Genereux)
356^{6} 1077^{P} 1158^{13}

Toi Express (IRE) *R J Hodges* 115h 128+c
10 ch g Phardante(FR) —Toi Figures (Deep Run)
1020^{2} **1221^{3} 1320^{6}1399^{2} 1489^{3} 1561^{4}**

Tokala *B G Powell* 119+h
5 br g Be My Guest(USA) —Lypharitissima (FR) (Lightning (FR))
(361) (1882) 2211^{2} (3246) (3595) 4242^{4} 4373^{P} (Dead)

Tolcea (IRE) *A C Whillans* 38h
7 ch g Barathea(IRE) —Mosaique Bleue (Shirley Heights)
2453^{P} **2839^{U}**

Tollbrae (IRE) *J Howard Johnson* 107h 127+c
9 gr g Supreme Leader—Miss Henrietta (IRE) (Step Together (USA))
3207^{P}

Tolpuddle (IRE) *T Stack* 119h
6 b g College Chapel—Tabdea (USA) (Topsider (USA))
3772a^{3} 3994^{9}

Tom Bell (IRE) *J G M O'Shea* 110h
6 b g King's Theatre(IRE) —Nordic Display (IRE) (Nordico (USA))
78^{3} (460) 742^{F} 1113^{2} 1680^{4} 1880^{8}1982^{F} 4104^{7} 4736^{9}

Tom Costalot (IRE) *Mrs Susan Nock* 84h 106c
11 gr g Black Minstrel—Hop Picker (USA) (Plugged Nickle (USA))
1989^{P} 2485^{3} 3326^{6}

Tomenoso *Mrs S J Smith* 115+h
8 b g Teenoso(USA) —Guarded Expression (Siberian Express (USA))
633^{10} 864^{8} 974^{3} 1099^{7} (1181) 1341^{3}1617^{3}

Tom Fruit *T D Easterby* 106h 115c
9 b g Supreme Leader—Forever Mine (IRE) (Phardante (FR))
2077^{3} 2445^{8} 3965^{U}4070^{P}

Tomillielou *G A Swinbank* 90b
5 gr g I'm Supposin(IRE) —Belle Rose (IRE) (Roselier (FR))
4853^{9}

Tomina *Miss E C Lavelle* 138 h
6 b g Deploy—Cavina (Ardross)
(109) (1992)

Tommy Carson *Jamie Poulton* 104 c
11 b g Last Tycoon—Ivory Palm (USA) (Sir Ivor (USA))
22^{2} 1110^{3} 1398^{7}1484^{2} (1778) 1920^{4}3434^{5} 4650^{3} 4857^{6}

Tommy Spar *P Bowen* 100h 106+c
6 b g Silver Owl—Lady Of Mine (Cruise Missile)
630^{4} (1040) **1236^{2} 1412^{3}1728^{6} 2287^{4} 2951^{4}**

Tom'n Ed *D R Gandolfo* 28b
5 b g Shaamit(IRE) —Manhunt (Posse (USA))
1882^{17}

Tom Sayers (IRE) *P J Hobbs* 106h 125+c
8 b g Toulon—Jillie James (The Parson)
205^{F} 1599^{2} 1861^{5}2299^{3} 2596^{F} 3000^{9}3469^{8} (4835) 4944^{2}

Tom's Prize *J L Spearing* 130 h 130c
11 ch g Gunner B—Pandora's Prize (Royal Vulcan)
(12) 311^{4} 2485^{7}

Tom's Toybox *J M Jefferson* 74b
4 b g Classic Cliche(IRE) —Jobiska (Dunbeath (USA))
3763^{6}

Tom Tobacco *A S T Holdsworth*
9 b g Afzal—Monsoon (Royal Palace)
2309^{P} 2928^{12} 3283^{P} 3477^{P}

Tom Tug (NZ) *W Jenks* 75b
6 b g Flying Pegasus(IRE) —Flight Judge (AUS) (The Judge (AUS))
7^{10}

Ton-Chee *F P Murtagh* 103 h 106c
7 b g Vettori(IRE) —Najariya (Northfields (USA))
9^{10} 149^{2} (482) 947^{P} 1111^{9} 1312^{5}1488^{6} 1604^{7} 1665^{7} **2902^{3}3334^{4} 3562^{F} 4365^{2}4991^{2}**

Tongariro Crossing (IRE) *W T Reed* 78b
6 b g Old Vic—Miss Kertina (IRE) (Orchestra)
4246 1799^{18}

Toni Alcala *R F Fisher* 101h
7 b g Ezzoud(IRE) —Etourdie (USA) (Arctic Tern (USA))
591^{4} 1491^{2} 1608^{3} 2169^{5} 2461^{7}2691^{8} 2979^{2}

Tonic Du Charmil (FR) *M C Pipe* 114h 130+c
6 b g Mansonnien(FR) —Thrusting (FR) (Akarad (FR))
91[4] (1049) 1124[2]1210[2] 1320[8] (1487) 1817[2] (2016) 2459[5]

Tony's Pride *P T Dalton* 58b
6 b g Alderbrook—Lucia Forte (Neltino)
355[8] 5054[13]

Tony Tie *J S Goldie* 64h
10 b g Ardkinglass—Queen Of The Quorn (Governor General)
2903[P] 2942[15]

Toofarback (IRE) *Noel Meade* 126+h
6 b g Mister Lord(USA) —Lady Pharina (IRE) (Phardante (FR))
(3309a) 4469[17]

Too Forward (IRE) *Carl Llewellyn* 97h 147+c
10 ch g Toulon—One Back (IRE) (Meneval (USA))
2054[7] (2532) 3180[2]3620[5] 4459[U] 4958[2]

Tooka *J Gallagher* 64b
5 b g Sure Blade(USA) —Parsons Lass (IRE) (The Parson)
242[6] 2864[12] 3373[7]

Toomebridge (IRE) *Andrew Turnell* 101h 108c
8 b g Warcraft(USA) —The Foalicule (Imperial Fling (USA))
2313[3]

Toon Trooper (IRE) *R Lee* 107+h 114+c
9 ch g Bob Back(USA) —Salmoncita (Salmon Leap (USA))
244[3] 2180[F] 2630[U]2818[2] 3290[2] 3652[F] (Dead)

Too Posh To Share *D J Wintle* 68h
8 b m Rakaposhi King—Two Shares (The Parson)
680[6] 2206[12] 2578[7] 3147[11] 4013[3]4368[4] 5050[2]

Toothill Gunner *J K Cresswell* 72b
5 ch g Gunner B—Hazel Hill (Abednego)
131[6] 3657[9] 4613[P] 4826[P]

Tooting (IRE) *J Nicol* 94+b
4 b g Dr Devious(IRE) —Phantom Row (Adonijah)
2520[2] 3181[6] (3651)

Top Achiever (IRE) *C W Moore* 102 h
5 ch g Intikhab(USA) —Nancy Maloney (IRE) (Persian Bold)
99[2] 1444[8] 1488[8] 3848[14]

Topajo (IRE) *D G Bridgwater* 30b
5 b g Topanoora—Jodi's Money (The Parson)
4825[13]

Topamendip (IRE) *P F Nicholls* 57h
6 b g Topanoora—Bucks Cregg (IRE) (Buckskin (FR))
3617[9] 4947[3]

Topanberry (IRE) *N G Richards* 107h
7 ch m Topanoora—Mulberry (IRE) (Denel (FR))
329[3] (693) 2066[P] (2944) 4058[U] 4972[P]

Toparudi *M H Tompkins* 106+h
5 b g Rudimentary(USA) —Topatori (IRE) (Topanoora)
3659[2] (4479)

Top Brass (IRE) *K G Reveley* 99+h
5 ch g Night Shift(USA) —Opus One (Slip Anchor)
2131[4] 2755[P] 2901[10](3927) 4210[3] 4373[P]

Top Cloud (IRE) *Ferdy Murphy* 103+b
5 b g Cloudings(IRE) —Top Dresser (IRE) (Good Thyne (USA))
4588[3] 4854[11]

Top Dawn (IRE) *L Lungo* 58h
6 b g Topanoora—Andros Dawn (IRE) (Buckskin (FR))
1885[8] 2108[11] 3209[6] 4487[5]

Top Dog (IRE) *L Wells* 42h
7 b g Topanoora—Dun Oengus (IRE) (Strong Gale)
2242[9] 2554[9] **3903[5]**

Top Dressing (IRE) *J Howard Johnson* 88b
5 br g Rashar(USA) —Ross Gale (Strong Gale)
3490[3] 3785[8]

Top Gale (IRE) *R Dickin* 75h 66c
7 b m Topanoora—Amy's Gale (IRE) (Strong Gale)
3149[P] **3790[5] 4580[P]4735[9]**

Topkat (IRE) *M C Pipe* 117+h
5 b g Simply Great(FR) —Kitty's Sister (Bustino)
2455[5] 3464[3] (3908) 4242[F] (Dead)

Topless (IRE) *D P Keane* 91b
5 gr m Presenting—Tara The Grey (IRE) (Supreme Leader)
4455[6]

Top Man Tee *D J Daly* 44h
4 gr g Vettori(IRE) —Etienne Lady (IRE) (Imperial Frontier (USA))
2811[11] 2949[7] 3431[P] 3939[10] 4331[P]

Top Of The Agenda *M Pitman* 106b
7 b g Michelozzo(USA) —Expensive Lark (Sir Lark)
2579[3] 3415[P]

Top Pack (IRE) *N G Richards* 77h
7 b g Top Of The World—Mels Pride (IRE) (Ajraas (USA))
209[9] 988[3] 1294[4] 1663[7] **1886[P]**

Topple *P W Hiatt* 5 b m Master Willie—Top Cover (High Top)
2560[10]

Top Pursuit *J L Spearing* 55h
4 b g Pursuit Of Love—Top Of The Parkes (Mistertopogigo (IRE))
1440[6] 1649[5] 1802[10]

Top Ram (IRE) *J A B Old* 86+h
6 ch g Topanoora—Aries Girl (Valiyar)
2665[4] 3024[P] (3691) 4326[4] 4875[4]

Top Son *D W Lewis*
7 b g Komaite(USA) —Top Yard (Teekay)
274[P]

Top Stoppa *A J Whiting* 50b
8 gr g Environment Friend—Orchid Valley (IRE) (Cyrano De Bergerac)
1750[11]

Top Strategy (IRE) *T M Walsh* 138h 118c
6 b g Hernando(FR) —Sudden Stir (USA) (Woodman (USA))
67a[8] **1626a[4] 1944a[2]2395a[3]**

Top Style (IRE) *G A Harker* 107+h
8 ch g Topanoora—Kept In Style (Castle Keep)
120[P] (1530) 1836[B] 2002[2] 2452[8] 2629[P]4045[8] 5096[11]

Top Tenor (IRE) *V Thompson* 78h
6 b g Sadler's Wells(USA) —Posta Vecchia (USA) (Rainbow Quest (USA))
2106[6] 2657[16] 4040[7] 4141[10]

Top The Bill (IRE) *Mrs S A Watt* 83h
6 b g Topanoora—Rio Star (IRE) (Riot Helmet)
2566[11] 3271[13] 3918[7]

Top Trees *W S Kittow* 87h
8 b g Charnwood Forest(IRE) —Low Line (High Line)
1902[5] 2150[11]

Top Weld *K R Owen*
11 ch g Weld—Moya's Girl (Prince Titian)
98[P]

Topwell *R C Guest* 76h
5 b g Most Welcome—Miss Topville (FR) (Top Ville)
1593[3] 1799[8] 2112[7] (2844) 3374[F] 5118[9]

Tora Bora (GER) *B G Powell* 115+h
4 bb g Winged Love(IRE) —Tower Bridge (GER) (Big Shuffle (USA))
2373[2] (2681) 4057[2] 4289[P] (4691) 4821[5]

Torche (IRE) *M Scudamore* 106+h 127c
8 b g Taos(IRE) —Orchette (IRE) (Orchestra)
1676[3]

Torgiano (IRE) *P Monteith* 83b
5 b g Cadeaux Genereux—Delimara (IRE) (In The Wings)
424[11]

Torinmoor (USA) *Mrs A J Perrett* 79+h
5 ch g Intikhab(USA) —Tochar Ban (USA) (Assert)
2148[8]

Torkinking (IRE) *M A Barnes* 130 h
7 b g Supreme Leader—Nicola's News (IRE) (Buckskin (FR))
2190[10] (2981) 3383[3] 3986[P] (4110) 4490[5] 4848[13]

Torkin Wind *M A Barnes*
5 ch g Chocolat De Meguro(USA) —Helm Wind (North Col)
214[U] 2106[P]

Tornado Alley (IRE) *J J Lambe* 95h 96c
7 b g Warcraft(USA) —Lucky Fiver (Tumble Gold)
1566[6] **1682[5] 1888[U]**

Torn Silk *P England* 83c
12 b g Top Ville—Cut Velvet (USA) (Northern Dancer)
280[4] 512[P]

Torrid Kentavr (USA) *B Ellison* 137h 104 c
9 b g Trempolino(USA) —Torrid Tango (USA) (Green Dancer (USA))
208[9]

Tory Boy *D T Turner* 100h
11 b g Deploy—Mukhayyalah (Dancing Brave (USA))
370[10] 2525[8]

Tory Island (IRE) *S Donohoe* 90b
5 b g Oscar(IRE) —Blenheim Run (IRE) (Remainder Man)
2480[3] 2948[14]

Tosawi (IRE) *R J Hodges* 103h 106c
10 b g Commanche Run—Deep Satisfaction (Deep Run)
26[2] 202[4] 388[2]486[2] 666[8] 752[P]948[5] 1019[7]

Toscanini (GER) *Mark Doyle* 100h 87c
10 b g Goofalik(USA) —Tosca Stella (GER) (Surumu (GER))
4555[7] 4880[4]

Toss The Caber (IRE) *K G Reveley* 113h
4 ch g Dr Devious(IRE) —Celtic Fling (Lion Cavern (USA))
(1478) 1718[2] 1923[5] 2167[2]

Totally Scottish *K G Reveley* 117h 101+c
10 b g Mtoto—Glenfinlass (Lomond (USA))
2038[4] 2417[5] 2633[P] 2840[2] 2990[3]3741[5] 4491[5]

Total Turtle (IRE) *T D Easterby* 98+h
7 b g Turtle Island(IRE) —Chagrin D'Amour (IRE) (Last Tycoon)
2627[9] 2763[14]

To The Future (IRE) *A Parker* 65h 83c
10 ch g Bob Back(USA) —Lady Graduate (IRE) (Le Bavard (FR))
1943[4] **2413[2] 2863[P]3315[4]**

Totheroadyouvgone *A E Jones* 88+h 127+c
12 b g Carlingford Castle—Wild Rosie (Warpath)
575[3] **(694) 960[2] 1083a[14]1515a[13] 1874[4]**

To The Top *Alan Hill* 89+c
8 b g Petoski—Mrs Pepperpot (Kinglet)
4216[7]

Totland Bay (IRE) *B D Leavy* 107h 65c
10 br g Phardante(FR) —Seanaphobal Lady (Kambalda)
51[6] 717[9]

Toto Caelo *C Roche* 100c
10 b g Mtoto—Octavia Girl (Octavo (USA))
112a[9]

Touch And Weld (IRE) *B W Duke* 58b
5 ch m Weld—Princess Touchee (IRE) (Shernazar)
27[11]

Touch Closer *P Bowen* 128h 127c
9 b g Inchinor—Ryewater Dream (Touching Wood (USA))
92a[17] **(893) (1210) 1301[3]4822[P]**

Touch Of Ebony (IRE) *C Roberts* 101h
7 b g Darshaan—Cormorant Wood (Home Guard (USA))
762[5]

Touch Of Fate *R Rowe* 100+h 91+c
7 b g Sovereign Water(FR) —Coral Delight (Idiots Delight)
261[5] (1773) 2592[2] **2867[4]**

Tough Queen (IRE) *N J Hawke*
5 b m Diesis—Here To Eternity (FR) (Fairy King (USA))
4425[P]

Tough Tales (IRE) *J Mackie* 99b
7 b g Charente River(IRE) —Petite Port (IRE) (Decent Fellow)
1794[P]

Toulouse (IRE) *R H Alner* 114h 131+c
9 b g Toulon—Neasham (Nishapour (FR))
4[3] (466) 2051[9]2939[3] 3344[9] (4592) 4829[5]

Toulouse Express (IRE) *R Johnson* 93h
7 b g Toulon—Miss Ivy (IRE) (Le Bavard (FR))
4299[2] 4487[7] 1415

Toulouse-Lautrec (IRE) *T R George* 106+h 132c
10 ch g Toulon—Bucks Slave (Buckskin (FR))
(1973) **2608[2] 3186[2]**

Tour Card (IRE) *Jonjo O'Neill* 54h
4 br g Presenting—Mrs Byrne (IRE) (Mandalus)
3623[7] 4048[8]

Tous Chez (IRE) *Mrs S J Smith* 109+h
7 b g Carroll House—Sixfoursix (Balinger)
2112[4] 2572[3] 2991[2] 3314[3] (4493) 4849[8]

Tout Les Sous *B W Duke*
5 ch g Tout Ensemble—Suzie Sue (IRE) (Ore)
4875[P]

Town Crier (IRE) *Mrs S J Smith* 140 h 154 c
11 br g Beau Sher—Ballymacarett (Menelek)
1720[6] 1823[2] **(2489) (3256) 3724[9]3974[F] 4749[5] 5006[4]**

Toy Boy (IRE) *P W Hiatt* 93h 54c
8 b g Un Desperado(FR) —Too Sharp (True Song)
2593[4] 3148[P] 3499[5]

Trabolgan (IRE) *N J Henderson* 133 h 168+c
8 b g King's Ride—Derrella (Derrylin)
(2491)

Trackattack *P Howling* 82h
4 ch g Atraf—Verbena (IRE) (Don't Forget Me)
2101[9] 2258[8] 2954[5] 3956[8] 4903[6]

Trade Off (IRE) *Mrs S Alner* 87b 110c
8 br g Roselier(FR) —Lady Owenette (IRE) (Salluceva)
(401) 3693[3] 4330[3]

Tradingup (IRE) *Andrew Turnell* 88 h 98 c
7 b g Arctic Lord—Autumn Queen (Menelek)
2431[3] 3239[P] 3481[4]3949[P] 4328[P] 4785[P]

Traditional (IRE) *A J Tizzard* 89h 77c
10 ch g Erin's Isle—Noorajo (IRE) (Ahonoora)
5116[P]

Trafalgar Man (IRE) *M D Hammond* 33h
5 bb g Scribano—Call Over (Callernish)
431[3] 2192[4] 3314[10]

Trafalgar Night *H Morrison*
5 b g Emperor Fountain—Hollow Creek (Tarqogan)
3504[3]

Tragic Lover *Donal Kinsella* 115h
10 b g Tragic Role(USA) —Wild Lover (USA) (Lyphard (USA))
3005a[18]

Tragic Ohio *P F Nicholls* 125+h
7 b g Tragic Role(USA) —Kiniohio (FR) (Script Ohio (USA))
1891[P]

Tramantano *N A Twiston-Davies* 140 h
7 b g Muhtarram(USA) —Hatta Breeze (Night Shift (USA))
2209[2] 2636[11] 3179[9]

Transatlantic (USA) *H D Daly* 81h
8 gr g Dumaani(USA) —Viendra (USA) (Raise A Native)
683[8] 1028[7]

Transit *B Ellison* 111h 130 c
7 b g Lion Cavern(USA) —Black Fighter (USA) (Secretariat (USA))
45a[17] 1878[6] 2190[7] 2452[4]2636[9] 4354[P]

Translucid (USA) *C Von Der Recke* 119+h 135+c
8 bb g Woodman(USA) —Gossamer (USA) (Seattle Slew (USA))
3440[6]

Trappeto (IRE) *C Smith* 77h
4 b c Barathea(IRE) —Campiglia (IRE) (Fairy King (USA))
2345[9] 3579[P] 3786[5] 4057[P] 4795[5]4987[F] (Dead)

Traprain (IRE) *P J Hobbs* 116+h
4 b g Mark Of Esteem(IRE) —Nassma (IRE) (Sadler's Wells (USA))
3463[2] 3883[5] (4754) (5111)

Travel (POL) *T R George* 125+h
6 gr g Freedom's Choice(USA) —Transylwania (POL) (Baby Bid (USA))
(320) 675[F] (873) 1010[P] 1179[F]

Travel Agent (IRE) *P J Hobbs* 105h
6 b g Shernazar—Brownskin (Buckskin (FR))
5015[2]

Travelling Band (IRE) *J Mackie* 105 h
8 b g Blues Traveller(IRE) —Kind Of Cute (Prince Sabo)
4848[9]

Travelling Warrior *M F Harris* 86+b
7 b g Emperor Fountain—Gipsy Princess (Prince Daniel (USA))
655[5]

Travino (IRE) *Ms Margaret Mullins* 139+h
7 bb g Roselier(FR) —Call Catherine (IRE) (Strong Gale)
2536a[2] (2909a) 3642a[2] 4469[3] 4760[F] 5101a[6]

Trawbreaga Bay *P Beaumont* 46h
6 ch g Bijou D'Inde—Give Me A Day (Lucky Wednesday)
2192[10]

Treacysdream (IRE) *Mrs K Waldron* 100b
6 b g Broken Hearted—Paddy's Owen (Paddy's Stream)
242[2] 4632[2] 1077[P] 1246[P]

Treasulier (IRE) *P R Rodford* 106c
9 gr g Roselier(FR) —Flashy Treasure (Crash Course)
2729[3] 3241[2] 3480[4]3698[2] 3949[4] 4328[3]4737[6]

Treasured Memories *Miss S E Forster* 91 h
6 b m Cloudings(IRE) —Glen Morvern (Carlingford Castle)
2674[4] 2947[8] 3442[7] 3795[3] 4491[P]4852[P]

Treasure Trail *Ian Williams* 92h
7 b g Millkom—Forever Shineing (Glint Of Gold)
1645[4] 1977[14]

Treasury Counsel (IRE) *N J Henderson* 92b
4 br g Leading Counsel(USA) —Dunacarney (Random Shot)
4623[3]

Treaty Flyer (IRE) *P G Murphy* 101+h
5 ch m Anshan—Highways Daughter (IRE) (Phardante (FR))
1961[3] 2501[7] (2997) (3437) 4619[5] 5019[2]

Treaty Stone *Jonjo O'Neill* 84h
7 b g Bigstone(IRE) —Quiet City (True Song)
1206[4] 1298[3] **1433[P]**

Trebello *J R Boyle* 82h
5 b g Robellino(USA) —Trempkate (USA) (Trempolino (USA))
2928[6] 3275[8] 3659[8] 4080[3] 4824[P]

Tred On Air (IRE) *Miss A M Lambert* 78b
5 bb m Luso—Shining Mogul (IRE) (Good Thyne (USA))
5134a[18]

Trefoilalight *J D Frost* 44h
7 b m Morpeth—Imalight (Idiots Delight)
961[4] 1262[P] 1384[P]

Tregastel (FR) *R Ford* 88+c
11 b g Tel Quel(FR) —Myrtlewood (FR) (Home Guard (USA))
547[6]

Tremallt (IRE) *T R George* 102h 120c
15 b g Henbit(USA) —Secret Romance (Gala Performance)
516[4]

Trenance *T R George* 83h 104+c
8 b g Alflora(IRE) —Carmel's Joy (IRE) (Carlingford Castle)
1905[F] (2610) 2986[F](3499) 3981[4] 4394[2]

Tres Bien *P R Webber* 92b
4 b g Bien Bien(USA) —Zielana Gora (Polish Precedent (USA))
7[2]

Tresor Clementais (FR) *S Foucher*
8 b g Grand Tresor(FR) —Miss Langonnet (FR) (Over)
362a[F]

Tresor Preziniere (FR) *P J Hobbs* 114h 115c
8 bb g Grand Tresor(FR) —Rose De Martine (FR) (The Quiet Man (FR))
1675[9] **1907[3] 2259[5]**

Trianger (IRE) *P J Rothwell* 84h
7 b h Midhish—Mugnano (Seymour Hicks (FR))
2139[8]

Tribal Dancer (IRE) *Miss Venetia Williams* 102h 106c
12 ch g Commanche Run—Cute Play (Salluceva)
112a[6] 311[5] 1728[7]1848[8] 2077[2] 2724[2]2938[6] 3241[7] 3649[2]4047[4] 4321[P] 4567[0](4906)

Tribal Dancing *D R Gandolfo*
6 b m Primitive Rising(USA) —Foxtrot Pie (Shernazar)
2021[P] (Dead)

Tribal Dispute *T D Easterby* 114 h 137c
9 b g Primitive Rising(USA) —Coral Princess (Imperial Fling (USA))
(60) (419) 646[2] 1913[B]2339[7] 2757[2] 3299[7]4472[P]

Tribal King (IRE) *A King* 122 c
11 bb g Be My Native(USA) —Island Bridge (Mandalus)
2051[7] 2368[10] 3212[F]4835[P]

Tribal Run (IRE) *Miss S A Loggin* 108c
11 ch g Be My Native(USA) —Queen's Run (IRE) (Deep Run)
49[6]

Tribal Suspect (IRE) *Mrs S A Watt*
7 br m Namaqualand(USA) —Twin Suspect (IRE) (Phardante (FR))
496[P]

Tribal Venture (FR) *P J Hobbs* 135h 143 c
8 gr g Dom Alco(FR) —Babacha (FR) (Latnahc (USA))
1925[8] **2176[P] 2491[P]2767[2] 3176[R] 4434[12]4957[6]**

Trickstep *D McCain* 84+h
5 b g Imperial Ballet(IRE) —Trick Of Ace (USA) (Clever Trick (USA))
(173) 412[8] 743[4] 943[P]

Tricky Trevor (IRE) *Mrs H J Cobb* 89c
13 bb g Arctic Lord—Chancer's Last (Foggy Bell)
400[6]

Tricky Venture *Mrs L C Jewell* 74h
6 gr g Linamix(FR) —Ukraine Venture (Slip Anchor)
3658[11] 3978[U] 4149[7] 4896[F] 1[11]

Trigger Guard *G L Moore* 85 h
4 ch g Double Trigger(IRE) —Harlequin Walk (IRE) (Pennine Walk)
1404[4] 1519[3] (1594) 1873[5] 2178[8] 2803[7]

Triggernometry *C L Tizzard* 86b
5 b g Double Trigger(IRE) —Dubacilla (Dubassoff (USA))
2242[8] 3699[8] 4333[10]

Trigger The Light *A King* 103b
5 ch g Double Trigger(IRE) —Lamper's Light (Idiots Delight)
3904[3] 4333[8] 4825[4]

Triple Crown (IRE) *P W Hiatt*
13 bb g Tidaro(USA) —Noreen Beag (Thatching)
825[4] 999[P]

Triple Deal *N G Richards* 85b
4 ch g Deploy—Three More (USA) (Sanglamore (USA))
3799[5] 4533[7] (Dead)

Triple Mint (IRE) *D McCain* 112h
5 b g Flemensfirth(USA) —Bucktina (Buckskin (FR))
2185[3] 3232[3] (3984) 5009[2]

Trip To The Stars (IRE) *D P Keane* 59h
6 b m Fourstars Allstar(USA) —Nora Dante (IRE) (Phardante (FR))
4450[15] 4603[P]

Trisons Star (IRE) *Mrs L B Normile* 125h 112c
8 b g Roselier(FR) —Delkusha (Castle Keep)
2449[4] 3041[2] 3236[3]4144[P] 4516[2] 4719[2]

Tristar (IRE) *Daniel Miley* 51b
6 b m Fourstars Allstar(USA) —Bawn Beag (IRE) (Brush Aside (USA))
2796a[12]

Tristernagh (IRE) *J A O'Connell* 95h 106c
10 b g Treasure Hunter—Had Enough (Hadeer)
112a[4]

Tritonville Lodge (IRE) *Miss E C Lavelle* 107+h
4 b g Grand Lodge(USA) —Olean (Sadler's Wells (USA))
(2274) 2753[2] 4962[5]

Trizzy *H J Manners* 55b
6 b m Petrizzo—Cavisoir (Afzal)
1635[6] 1909[7]

Troll (FR) *L Lungo* 87h
5 b g Cadoudal(FR) —Miss Dundee (FR) (Esprit Du Nord (USA))
1927[6] 3376[6] 5063[2]

Trompette (USA) *N J Henderson* 118+h
4 b f Bahri(USA) —Bold Bold (IRE) (Sadler's Wells (USA))
3579[3] (3902) 4104[6] (4648) 5077a[5]

Troodos Jet *K W Hogg* 64h
5 b g Atraf—Costa Verde (King Of Spain)
991[P] 1113[4] 1149[6] 1202[P] 1336[10]

Troodos Valley (IRE) *H D Daly* 90+h
7 b g Executive Perk—Valleymay (IRE) (King's Ride)
521[6] 763[P]

Trooper Kit *Mrs L Richards*
7 b g Petoski—Rolling Dice (Balinger)
3219[P]

Trooper Lee (IRE) *Mrs H Dalton* 71b
4 b g Wizard King—Rubylee (Persian Bold)
3346[8] 3651[10]

Trotsky (IRE) *D T Hughes* 100h 108c
8 b g Jurado(USA) —Make Me An Island (Creative Plan (USA))
1420a[7]

Troublesome Gerri *S C Burrough*
4 b f Thowra(FR) —Sid's Pretence (Southern Music)
2824[P]

Trovaio (IRE) *Miss Lucinda V Russell* 95+h 92+c
9 b g Un Desperado(FR) —Hazy Fiddler (IRE) (Orchestra)
2266[F] 3204[5] 3917[10]4361[5] 4844[5] 9[3]

Troysgreen (IRE) *P D Niven* 80b
8 b g Warcraft(USA) —Moylena (Bustomi)
3042[12] **3762[P] 4989[P]**

Truckers Tavern (IRE) *Mrs S J Smith* 121h 130c
11 ch g Phardante(FR) —Sweet Tulip (Beau Chapeau)
2820[3] **2992[P] 3493[3]3971[6] 5004[F]**

Truckle *C W Fairhurst* 96 h
4 b g Vettori(IRE) —Proud Titania (IRE) (Fairy King (USA))
1338[4] 2001[4] 2167[3] 2569[6] 3395[5]3918[P]

True Dove *R A Fahey* 77b
4 b f Kayf Tara—Pasja (IRE) (Posen (USA))
3820[2] 4902[7]

True Grit (FR) *L Corcoran* 37h
4 b g Goldneyev(USA) —Midweek Melody (Lucky Wednesday)
4595[10]

True Lover (GER) *J W Mullins* 126+h
9 b g Winged Love(IRE) —Truneba (GER) (Nebos (GER))
2336[9] 2747[8] **3218[P]**

True Mariner (FR) *B I Case* 115h 113 c
6 b g True Brave(USA) —Miss Above (FR) (Houston (FR))
1318[5] 1561[5] 1644[F]1749[4] 2218[4] 2714[6] (2958) 3416[3](4738) 5096[3]

True North (IRE) *D R MacLeod* 109 h 85 c
11 b g Black Monday—Slip A Loop (The Parson)
2945[F] 3289[P] **3533[P]**

True Star (IRE) *Noel T Chance* 84b
6 ch g Fourstars Allstar(USA) —Scouts Honour (IRE) (Electric)
4940[9]

True Tara *J L Spearing* 61b
4 b f Kayf Tara—True Ring (High Top)
4059[8] 4554[11]

True Temper (IRE) *A M Crow* 76h 76c
9 b m Roselier(FR) —Diamond Rock (Swan's Rock)
785[3] 1307[DSQ] 1374[4] 1608[5] 1723[5]1838[3] 2639[4] 2977[4] **3915[3]4041[F] 4300[6]**

True To Yourself (USA) *J G Given* 29h
5 b g Royal Academy(USA) —Romilly (Machiavellian (USA))
2081[9]

True Venture *R Curtis*
6 b m Un Desperado(FR) —Millers Venture (Sunyboy)
816[0]

Truly Gold (IRE) *R P Burns* 118h
7 ch g Goldmark(USA) —Truly Flattering (Hard Fought)
5103a[13]

Trust Fund (IRE) *R H Alner* 129 c
8 ch g Rashar(USA) —Tuney Blade (Fine Blade (USA))
(130) 2054[P] 2608[3]3343[7] 3989[F] 4496[5]4728[U]

Trust Rule *M W Easterby* 91h
6 b g Selkirk(USA) —Hagwah (USA) (Dancing Brave (USA))
2335[5] 2627[6] 2873[4]

Try *A M Crow* 77b
7 b g Rakaposhi King—Wonky (Hotfoot)
1613[4]

Try Catch Paddy (IRE) *P Monteith* 110h 103+c
8 ch g Safety Catch(USA) —Blackwater Rose VII (Damsire Unregistered)
1973[5] **2458[5] 3850[8]**4344[5] **4583[5]** 4724[12] **4788[5]5037[6]**

Tsar's Twist *Miss L Gardner* 71h 95+c
7 b g Presidium—Kabs Twist (Kabour)
(6)

Tshukudu *Mrs A L M King* 52h
5 ch m Fleetwood(IRE) —Pab's Choice (Telsmoss)
943[5]

Tuatara Bay (IRE) *R A Fahey* 90b
6 b g Luso—Timely Reminder (IRE) (Phardante (FR))
3319[7] 3490[8] 3657[4]

Tuba (IRE) *S A Hughes* 91c
11 b g Orchestra—Princess Paula (Smoggy)
4730[4]

Tubber Roads (IRE) *M G Hazell*
13 b g Un Desperado(FR) —Node (Deep Run)
184[P]

Tubber Streams (IRE) *B A Pearce* 87h 87+c
9 b g Great Marquess—Much Obliged (Crash Course)
24[4] 982[4] **1024[4]**1037[6] 1084[P] 1223[P]

Tuckerman *A J Martin* 76h
5 b g Gulch(USA) —Remuria (USA) (Theatrical)
65a[24] 1483[9]

Tuckers Bay *J R Holt* 88b
5 b m Karinga Bay—Mainvalley Queen (IRE) (Jolly Jake (NZ))
2185[7] 3353[7] 4059[2] 4637[2]

Tuck In *P Winkworth* 86+h
9 b g Good Thyne(USA) —Always Shining (Tug Of War)
2799[4] 3184[6] **3599[4]**

Tudor Buck (IRE) *R Dickin* 105+h
6 bb g Luso—Tudor Doe (IRE) (Buckskin (FR))
2860[5]

Tudor King (IRE) *Andrew Turnell* 86+h 100+c
12 br g Orchestra—Jane Bond (Good Bond)
176[3] 503[4] 916[2]981[6] (1414) (1652) 1728[3] 1960[S] 2104[P]

Tudor Oak (IRE) *Mark Campion* 56h
4 b g Woods Of Windsor(USA) —Tacheo (Tachypous)
1601[9] 2580[12] 3786[13]

Tudor Rose (IRE) *Mrs N S Evans*
5 ch m Midhish—Boreen Girl (IRE) (Boreen (FR))
2727[P] 4554[16]

Tudorvic (IRE) *John Joseph Murphy* 73h
5 b g Old Vic—Gayephar (Phardante (FR))
44a[3] 3003a[8]

Tuesday Club (IRE) *J A B Old* 66h
7 ch g Old Vic—Asfreeasthewind (IRE) (Moscow Society (USA))
2249[17] 2849[13] 4015[5]

Tuesday's Child *Miss H C Knight* 83h 108 c
7 b g Un Desperado(FR) —Amazing Silks (Furry Glen)
457[4] 654[6] **1877[F] (2141) 2562[P]**

Tuff Joint (IRE) *Mrs A Price* 82b
8 bb g Good Thyne(USA) —The Furnituremaker (Mandalus)
4283[P]

Tufty Hopper *Ferdy Murphy* 110 h 112c
9 b g Rock Hopper—Melancolia (Legend Of France (USA))
3170[2] 3541[4] 3955[2]

Tulipa (POL) *T R George* 123h
7 ch m Jape(USA) —Truly Best (POL) (Omen (POL))
1010[4] 1204[10] 1481[5] 1633[4]

Tullimoss (IRE) *J N R Billinge* 77+h
11 b m Husyan(USA) —Ballynattin Moss (Le Moss)
319[P] 406[11]

Tully Cross (IRE) *T M Walsh* 86b
5 b g Luso—Some News (IRE) (Be My Native (USA))
5141[8]

Tullyhappy Lad (IRE) *I A Duncan* 55h
5 b g Shaamit(IRE) —Infinity (IRE) (Second Set (IRE))
210[6] 596[8]

Tumbleweed Glen (IRE) *P Kelsall* 85h 85c
10 ch g Mukaddamah(USA) —Mistic Glen (IRE) (Mister Majestic)
1396[P] 1540[5] 1644[F]1852[P] 2140[P]

Tumbling Dice (IRE) *T J Taaffe* 142+h 142+c
7 b h King's Theatre(IRE) —Eva Fay (IRE) (Fayruz)
2174[7] 3079a[3] 4456[3]5131a[P]

Tunes Of Glory (IRE) *D McCain* 99+h 69c
10 b g Symboli Heights(FR) —Coxtown Queen (IRE) (Corvaro (USA))
784[P] 2625[9] 2843[F] **3459[P]**3804[5] **4920[7]**

Tupgill Turbo *W J Tolhurst* 41h 85c
8 ch g Rudimentary(USA) —Persian Alexandra (Persian Bold)
4477[P]

Turaath (IRE) *A J Deakin* 61 h
10 b g Sadler's Wells(USA) —Diamond Field (USA) (Mr Prospector (USA))
1796[4] 2347[17] 2731[P] 3143[P] 3458[15]3731[U] 3889[11] 5[10]

Turange (FR) *J-P Gallorini* 100h
4 b g Turgeon(USA) —La Mesange (FR) (Olmeto)
2085a[7]

Turbo (IRE) *M W Easterby* 115h
7 b g Piccolo—By Arrangement (IRE) (Bold Arrangement)
1480[2] 1654[2] 1772[2] 3737[U] 3848[3](4039) 4364[5] 4792[3]

Turbulent Flight *Mrs L B Normile* 37h
5 b m Busy Flight—Pejawi (Strong Gale)
2906[4] 3490[9]

Turftanzer (GER) *Lady Susan Watson* 90h
7 b g Lomitas—Tower Bridge (GER) (Big Shuffle (USA))
4299[P] 5138[P]

Turgeonev (FR) *T D Easterby* 121 h 131c
11 gr g Turgeon(USA) —County Kerry (FR) (Comrade In Arms)
1721[6] 1924[P] 2177[U]2590[7] **2768[3] 2993[P]3619[3] 4618[3] 4850[7]**

Turkama (FR) *L A Dace* 116h
9 gr g Turgeon(USA) —Whampoa (FR) (Wittgenstein (USA))
1111[3] 1270[11] 1548[14] 1984[P] 2271[6]2714[P]

Turko (FR) *P F Nicholls* 139 h
4 gr g Turgeon(USA) —Cambaria (FR) (Nice Havrais (USA))
(2481) 2756[2] 3021[2] (3996) 4468[6] 4747[5] 4956[2]

Turnberry Bay (FR) *M C Pipe* 104h
5 b g Phantom Breeze—Carmonera (FR) (Carmont (FR))
4500[4] 4935[2]

Turn Card (IRE) *Declan Gillespie* 83h
4 ch g Docksider(USA) —Poleaxe (Selkirk (USA))
5076a[18]

Turnium (FR) *P Cottin*
11 bb g Turgeon(USA) —Royal Mia (FR) (Kashmir II)
4432[P]

Turnnocard (IRE) *Ian Williams* 59b
7 b m Air Display(USA) —Night Blade (Fine Blade (USA))
2295[P] 2878[P] 3884[P]

Turn Of Phrase (IRE) *Robert Gray* 110h 97c
7 b g Cadeaux Genereux—Token Gesture (IRE) (Alzao (USA))
1361[5] **479[5] 672[4]858[7]** 1552[P]

Turn On The Style *M J Polglase*
4 ch g Pivotal—Elegant Rose (Noalto)
3594[7] 3787[11]

Turnstile *J Howard Johnson* 122+h
5 gr g Linamix(FR) —Kissing Gate (USA) (Easy Goer (USA))
2652[4] (2838) (3168) 4443[P] 5138[P]

Turn The Corner (IRE) *J Clements* 83h
7 b g Bob Back(USA) —Tabu Lady (IRE) (Commanche Run)
2657[8] 2843[15] 3232[7]

Turpin Green (IRE) *N G Richards* 146h 153+c
7 b g Presenting—Coolshamrock (IRE) (Buckskin (FR))
(2449) 2654[3] 3726[2]4456[5] 4759[2]

Turthen (FR) *P F Nicholls* 115h 126c
5 ch g Turgeon(USA) —Majathen (FR) (Carmathen (FR))
2869[4] 3288[3] 3494[5]

Turtle Bay *B Storey* 78h
4 ch f Dr Fong(USA) —My Valentina (Royal Academy (USA))
2753[9] 3203[9] 3925[8] 4789[6]

Turtle Patriarch (IRE) *Mrs A J Perrett* 48h
5 b g Turtle Island(IRE) —La Doyenne (IRE) (Masterclass (USA))
2374[10]

Turtle Soup (IRE) *T R George* 146 h
10 b g Turtle Island(IRE) —Lisa's Favourite (Gorytus (USA))
127[2] 207[F] 2876[4] 3502[3] 4008[5]4446[15]

Tuscany Boy (IRE) *C A McBratney* 87h
6 ch g Up And At 'Em—Belle Savenay (Coquelin (USA))
601[12] 875[6]

Tushna (IRE) *E McNamara* 94h 94c
9 b g Erin's Isle—Smaointeach (IRE) (Green Desert (USA))
(1747) 2693[4]

Tusk *H P Hogarth* 120h 120+c
6 ch g Fleetwood(IRE) —Farmer's Pet (Sharrood (USA))
2482[6] 2677[2] 2872[2]3236[4]

Tweed *D McCain* 88h
9 ch g Barathea(IRE) —In Perpetuity (Great Nephew)
2810[P] (Dead)

Twelve Paces *M C Pipe* 108+h
5 b g Double Trigger(IRE) —Raise The Dawn (Rymer)
(963) 1680[3] 1908[9] 2426[9] 3131[6]

Twenti Twenti (IRE) *K C Bailey* 68b
5 ch g Topanoora—Ar Ais Aris (IRE) (Orchestra)
7[9]

Twenty Degrees *G L Moore* 105h 102+c
8 ch g Beveled(USA) —Sweet N' Twenty (High Top)
3134[U] 3426[3] 3660[3]4053[2] (4150) 4563[3]4653[4] 4872[3] 5085[4]

Twentytwosilver (IRE) *D B Feek* 93h 97c
6 rg g Emarati(USA) —St Louis Lady (Absalom)
203[7] 460[11] 753[8] 1272[5] 1381[6]1900[F] **(5047)**

Twilight Dancer (IRE) *Miss H E Roberts* 68h 79c
8 b m Sri Pekan(USA) —Manhattan Sunset (USA) (El Gran Senor (USA))
272[6] 487[7] 630[3]

Twist Bookie (IRE) *J S Moore* 99 h
6 br g Perugino(USA) —Twist Scarlett (GER) (Lagunas)
2179[9] 2573[11] (2721) 2950[5] 3242[4] 3386[8]4834[17]

Twisted Logic (IRE) *R H Alner* 81+h 126 c
13 b g Tremblant—Logical View (Mandalus)
439[6] 1599[P] 1778[6]1972[4] 2215[7] 3212[10]4287[5] 4944[3]

Twist Magic (FR) *P F Nicholls* 115 h
4 b g Winged Love(IRE) —Twist Scarlett (GER) (Lagunas)
1923[6] (2597) 3021[5] 4117[3] 4747[P]

Twist 'n Shout *Jonjo O'Neill* 113h 120c
9 ch g Never So Bold—Ravaro (Raga Navarro (ITY))
1668[10] 2324[9]

Twist N Turn *D McCain* 74+h 74c
6 b m Sir Harry Lewis(USA) —Gaye Gordon (Scottish Reel)
1345 263[3] 651[P] 2146[P] 2283[3]**2655[U] 2980[6] 3270[3]3686[6] 4303[5] 4575[8]**5050[U] (12)

Twist The Facts (IRE) *N P Littmoden* 92+h
6 ch m Un Desperado(FR) —Three In A Twist (IRE) (Meneval (USA))
463[3] 2021[2] 2558[6] 3188[7] 3690[6]4074[2] 4450[3] 4738[5]

Twofan (USA) *C Byrnes* 102h
5 b h Lear Fan(USA) —Double Wedge (USA) (Northern Baby (CAN))
65a[14] (4661) 5015[10]

Two Good (IRE) *P D Niven* 70b
6 b m Good Thyne(USA) —Good Rose (IRE) (Roselier (FR))
1323[6] 1532[6] 3235[P]

Two Hoots *C J Mann* 109h
8 b m Dancing High—Farm Track (Saxon Farm)
2486[P] 2956[3]

Two Miles West (IRE) *Jonjo O'Neill* 137 h
5 b g Sadler's Wells(USA) —User Friendly (Slip Anchor)
(1927) 2161[3] 3793[2] 4446[U]

Two Of A Kind (IRE) *Miss L V Davis*
6 ch g Ashkalani(IRE) —Dulcinea (Selkirk (USA))
1908[P]

Two Shillings *R Curtis* 82b
6 bb m Teenoso(USA) —Miss Muire (Scallywag)
3435[4] 3911[13]

Two Steps To Go (USA) *M A Barnes* 83+h
7 b g Rhythm(USA) —Lyonushka (CAN) (Private Account (USA))
987[8] (1063) 1149[5] 1377[4] 1567[8] 1588[6]1883[4] 2025[5] 2627[P]

Twotensforafive *P R Rodford* 61 c
13 b g Arctic Lord—Sister Of Gold (The Parson)
3430[P] 3716[5] 4785[P]

Twotiming Gent (IRE) *P D Niven* 83 h 66 c
13 b g Broken Hearted—Dual Express (Giolla Mear)
(1943) **2039[F] 2978[3]** (3540)4012[P]

Two T'Three Weeks *M G Rimell* 32b
5 b m Silver Patriarch(IRE) —Misowni (Niniski (USA))
4398[11]

Tycoon Hall (IRE) *Mrs John Harrington* 112h
6 ch g Halling(USA) —Tycooness (IRE) (Last Tycoon)
117a[19]

Tyndarius (IRE) *A Crook* 118 c
15 b g Mandalus—Lady Rerico (Pamroy)
572[P] 2518[6] 2692[P]3350[P]

Tyneandthyneagain *J Howard Johnson* 127 c
11 b g Good Thyne(USA) —Radical Lady (Radical)
3385[6] 3971[4] 4777[F] (Dead)

Tynedale (IRE) *Mrs A Hamilton* 119h
7 b g Good Thyne(USA) —Book Of Rules (IRE) (Phardante (FR))
1513[4] (2038) 2264[5] 3318[3] 3741[8]

Tyson Returns *A J Chamberlain* 39h
4 b g Mujahid(USA) —Mabrookah (Deploy)
1397[14]

Tysou (FR) *N J Henderson* 146h 150 c
9 bb g Ajdayt(USA) —Pretty Point (Crystal Glitters (USA))
2163[4] (2757) 3299[3](3724) 4472[P] 4749[P]

Tytheknot *O Sherwood* 93h
5 b g Pursuit Of Love—Bundled Up (USA) (Sharpen Up)
1614[8] 1982[5] 2460[3] 2685[10] 3944[9]5022[6]

Tyup Pompey (IRE) *Miss J S Davis* 76h 81+c
5 ch g Docksider(USA) —Cindy's Baby (Bairn (USA))
2958 1084[4] 1344[9] 1407[4] 1637[6]1806[7] **2456[6] 2807[3]2929[U] 3126[F]**

Ultimate Limit *A Ennis* 59h 107+c
6 b g Bonny Scot(IRE) —Second Call (Kind Of Hush)
202[5] 532[F] 674[3](827) 862[3] (1560) 1858[2] 2243[7] 2717[5]4906[8]

Ultramoderne (FR) *C C Bealby*
9 bb g Garde Royale—Wonderful Live (FR) (The Wonder (FR))
1976[P]

Ulusaba *Ferdy Murphy* 94 c
10 b g Alflora(IRE) —Mighty Fly (Comedy Star (USA))
2037[P] 2368[U]

Umbrella Man (IRE) *Miss E C Lavelle* 109h 133+c
10 ch g Insan(USA) —Askasilla (IRE) (Lucky Mickmooch)
1989[2] 2243[5] 2931[5]3368[2] (3654) (4419)

Un Autre Espere *C C Bealby* 75h 85+c
7 b g Golden Heights—Drummer's Dream (IRE) (Drumalis)
901[6] 1107[5] 1297[4] 1553[2] **1612[2]**(1816) **2257[U] 2561[4]**

Uncle Ada (IRE) *D J Minty* 60c
11 ch g Phardante(FR) —Park Belle (IRE) (Strong Gale)
244[5] 2313[P] 4369[4]4580[P] 4937[5]

Uncle Al (IRE) *K Bishop* 89+h
7 br g Allegoric(USA) —Aunty Rosie (IRE) (Roselier (FR))
203[6] 629[7]

Uncle Arthur (IRE) *Mrs D Haine* 117h 99c
12 b g Satco(FR) —Lady-Easton (Oats)
366[P]

Uncle Batty *Mrs L Williamson* 68h
6 b g Bob Back(USA) —Aunt Sadie (Pursuit Of Love)
1158[P] 1202[8] 1333[9]

Uncle John *M E Sowersby* 91 h
5 b g Atraf—Bit O' May (Mummy's Pet)
764[6] 838[7] 1046[7] (1553) 1747[5] 1987[7]2517[7] 2750[7] (3169) 3351[4] 3818[F] (Dead)

Uncle Max (IRE) *N A Twiston-Davies* 100+h 100c
6 b g Victory Note(USA) —Sunset Park (IRE) (Red Sunset)
2429[4] 2936[3] 3274[U]3430[P] 3919[6] 4451[9]5108[13]

Uncle Mick (IRE) *C L Tizzard* 117h 100 c
11 b g Ikdam—Kandy Kate (Pry)
(262) 547[3] 1022[4](1191) 1385[2] 1484[4]1639[4] 1893[U] 4007[5]4325[4] 4524[5]

Uncle Neil (IRE) *P Monteith*
9 gr g Roselier(FR) —Bobs My Uncle (Deep Run)
440[P] 3914[P] **4112[P]**

Uncle Wallace *P R Webber* 114h 117 c
10 b g Neltino—Auntie Dot (Hallodri (AUT))
2048[5] 2748[P] (5027)

Undeniable *Mrs S J Smith* 123 h 135+c
8 b g Unfuwain(USA) —Shefoog (Kefaah (USA))
2037[3] (2342) 2656[2]4070[3] 4447[3] (4843)

Under Oath *Mrs John Harrington* 106h 79c
5 b g Selkirk(USA) —Wosaita (Generous (IRE))
65a[9]

Understood (USA) *R Valentine* 115h
10 ch g Pistolet Bleu(IRE) —Divi (Bustino)
1394a[4]

Underwriter (USA) *Ferdy Murphy* 97h 129 c
6 b g With Approval(CAN) —Night Risk (USA) (Wild Again (USA))
117a[10] **1888[U] (2072) 2180[F]2724[4] 3728[3] 4447[12]5131a[4]**

Uneven Line *Miss S E Forster* 82h 86c
10 b m Jurado(USA) —Altovise (Black Minstrel)
124[3] 317[4] 591[P] 649[4] 854[6]1884[8] **2041[2]**
2267[2]2657[4] 3375[4] 3553[3](4659)

Unexplored (IRE) *J Howard Johnson* 111h
6 b g Taipan(IRE) —White Lady Club (Callernish)
2024[2] 2450[F] 3173[F] 4039[P]

Unfair Dismissal (IRE) *M D Hammond* 87b
5 b g Broken Hearted—Annilogs Daughter (IRE) (Yashgan)
3319[5] 4147[11]

Ungaretti (GER) *Ian Williams* 105h 91+c
9 b g Law Society(USA) —Urena (GER) (Dschingis Khan)
76[P] 289[2] 397[6] 652[3]906[8] 974[4] 1152[P] 1279[2]

Ungaro (FR) *K G Reveley* 135 h
7 b g Epervier Bleu—Harpyes (FR) (Quart De Vin (FR))
194[3] (1990) (2110) 2497[2] 3174[4] (3727) 4446[6]4760[5]

Un Hinged (IRE) *John J Coleman* 103b
6 b g Danetime(IRE) —Classic Silk (IRE) (Classic Secret (USA))
5104a[11]

Un Intello (IRE) *E J O'Grady* 107h
8 gr g Funambule(USA) —Une Pensee (FR) (Kenmare (FR))
67a[21]

Union Deux (FR) *T D Easterby* 105+h
7 ch g Nikos—Sanhia (FR) (Sanhedrin (USA))
1796[P]

United (GER) *Mrs L Wadham* 136+h
5 b m Desert King(IRE) —Una Kasala (GER) (Law Society (USA))
(88a) 4375[8] 4717a[P] 5003[5]

United Nations *N Wilson* 93h
5 ch g Halling(USA) —Congress (IRE) (Dancing Brave (USA))
1149[2] 1360[5]

United Spirit (IRE) *Jedd O'Keeffe* 95+h
5 b m Fasliyev(USA) —Atlantic Desire (IRE) (Ela-Mana-Mou)
(1565) (1683) 2173[11] 5039[7]

Unjust Law (IRE) *N J Henderson* 120h
5 b g Dushyantor(USA) —Go Tally-Ho (Gorytus (USA))
(179) 2145[4] (2823) (3417) 3842[2] 4581[6]

Unleash (USA) *P J Hobbs* 146+h 140 c
7 ch g Benny The Dip(USA) —Lemhi Go (USA) (Lemhi Gold (USA))
631[P] 962[2] (1155) 2052[3] 2260[2] 2484[3]4960[2] 5114[3]

Un Nononito (FR) *G Macaire* 111c
4 b g Nononito(FR) —Basket Gironde (FR) (Iron Duke (FR))
1428a[5]

Unshakable (IRE) *Bob Jones* 89h
7 b g Eagle Eyed(USA) —Pepper And Salt (IRE) (Double Schwartz)
2763[6]

Unusual Suspect *G L Moore* 99+h 9c
7 b g Syrtos—Sally Maxwell (Roscoe Blake)
233[5] 441[6] **1917[7] 2325[F]2717[9] 4474[2] 4872[P]**

Up Above (IRE) *S Donohoe* 127+h
6 ch g Avarice—Amy Just (IRE) (Bustomi)
2228a[3] 2667a[P] (2942) 3513a[3] 3642a[7] 4986[3]

Up At Midnight *R Rowe* 101+h
6 b m Midnight Legend—Uplift (Bustino)
3661[10] (4151) 5019[6]

Upham Lord (IRE) *P Beaumont* 112 c
13 b g Lord Americo—Top O The Mall (Don)
184[3]

Up In The Sky (IRE) *Mrs R L Elliot* 61b
6 gr m Cloudings(IRE) —Littledrunkgirl (Carlingford Castle)
301[P]

Upirlande (IRE) *D A Rees* 74h
6 b g Up And At 'Em—Amiga Irlande (Whistling Deer)
4828[12]

Upright Ima *Mrs P Sly* 86+h
7 b m Perpendicular—Ima Delight (Idiots Delight)
185[4] 283[2] 429[U] 1856[12] 2182[4]2816[4] 2958[5] 3371[3] 3674[2] 4452[2](4566)

Upswing *R C Guest* 81h 96+c
9 b g Perpendicular—Moorfield Lady (Vicomte)
2027[6] 2289[2] 2585[7] **3270[2]3370[6] 4303[7] 5051[3]**

Up The Glen (IRE) *A W Carroll* 105 h 117+c
8 b g Tale Quale—Etrenne (Happy New Year)
248[P]

Up The Pub (IRE) *R H Alner* 67h 90 c
8 ch g Carroll House—Brave Ruby (Proverb)
(1983) 2126[4] 2610[4]3252[5] 3654[2] 3909[2]4650[4] 4914[4]

Uptown Lad (IRE) *R Johnson* 103 h 98c
7 b g Definite Article—Shoka (FR) (Kaldoun (FR))
1836[5] 2110[7] 2452[5] 2680[2] 3040[5]3378[9] 4110[6] **4314[7] 4724[6]4840[4] 5119[7]**

Urban (IRE) *Joseph Crowley* 113h
5 b g Second Empire(IRE) —Second Revolution (IRE) (On Your Mark)
43a[21] 2207[17]

Urban Dream (IRE) *R A Farrant* 86+h
5 ch g Foxhound(USA) —She's My Love (Most Welcome)
1302[8] 1432[7] 1724[F] 1742[3] 1890[2]2428[4] (2728) 2845[11] 5111[7]

Urowells (IRE) *S J Mahon* 94+h
6 b g Sadler's Wells(USA) —Highest Accolade (Shirley Heights)
(4418)

Ursis (FR) *Jonjo O'Neill* 136+h
5 b g Trempolino(USA) —Bold Virgin (USA) (Sadler's Wells (USA))
1677[5] (1912) (3615) 4375[P] 4951a[14]

Ursumman (IRE) *Niall Madden* 96h 122c
7 b g Leading Counsel(USA) —Canverb (Proverb)
1083a[2] 1790a[4] 5058a[6]

Usk Valley (IRE) *P R Chamings* 88+h 92 c
11 b g Tenby—Penultimate (USA) (Roberto (USA))
276[P]

Valance (IRE) *C R Egerton* 116h 111+c
6 br g Bahhare(USA) —Glowlamp (IRE) (Glow (USA))
(1801)

Valassini *J L Needham* 92b
6 b m Dr Massini(IRE) —Running Valley (Buckskin (FR))
1543[2]

Valderrama *L Waring* 3h
6 ch g Lahib(USA) —Silky Heights (IRE) (Head For Heights)
2075[12] 3001[P] 3881[P] 4423[P]

Vale De Lobo *P F Nicholls* 95 h
4 b f Loup Sauvage(USA) —Frog (Akarad (FR))
(1679) 1821[4] 3185[11]

Valerun (IRE) *R C Guest* 79h
10 b g Commanche Run—Glenreigh Moss (Le Moss)
1715[7] 2038[9] 3487[12] 4899[4] 5068[F]5123[7]

Valeureux *J Hetherton* 114h 91c
8 ch g Cadeaux Genereux—La Strada (Niniski (USA))
2590[10] **2975[8]**

Valhuec (FR) *Mrs J R Buckley* 85b
6 b g Nikos—Marie De Geneve (FR) (Nishapour (FR))
375[4] 470[4]

Valley Ger (IRE) *Rodger Sweeney* 94h
7 b g Naheez(USA) —Moving Valley VII (IRE) (Damsire Unregistered)
1902[10] (Dead)

Valley Hall (IRE) *C J Mann* 89+b
5 b m Saddlers' Hall(IRE) —Here She Comes (Deep Run)
4695[2]

Valley Henry (IRE) *R Gurney*
11 b g Step Together(USA) —Pineway VII (Damsire Unregistered)
1846[P] 1992[P]

Valleymore (IRE) *S A Brookshaw* 98+c
10 br g Jolly Jake(NZ) —Glamorous Brush (IRE) (Brush Aside (USA))
1928[4] 2180[3] 2630[3]2874[7] 3290[8] 3460[8]3688[P] 4851[2] 5139[3]

Valley Of Giants *Mrs John Harrington* 111h
4 ch c Giant's Causeway(USA) —Karri Valley (USA) (Storm Bird (CAN))
5076a[5]

Valleyofthekings (IRE) *O Sherwood*
5 b g Beauchamp King—Nell Valley (Neltino)
1730[8] 2826[P] 3131[P] 5023[P]

Valley Ride (IRE) *C Tinkler* 135h
6 bb g Glacial Storm(USA) —Royal Lucy (IRE) (King's Ride)
1743[U] 2207[18] (2820) 3389[5] 4446[9] 4776[P]

Valley Warrior *J S Smith* 86h 84c
9 b g Michelozzo(USA) —Mascara VII (Damsire Unregistered)
630[P] 679 [4] **1656[2] 2126[5]2966[P] 3359[4] (4553)**

Vallica *Mrs A M Thorpe* 85h
7 b m Bishop Of Cashel—Vallauris (Faustus (USA))
73[2] 229[2] 417[P]

Valman (IRE) *P J Millington* 72c
10 bb g Valville(FR) —Ornania (Runnett)
333[P]

Valprimo *G L Moore*
4 b g Primo Dominie—Valbra (Dancing Brave (USA))
3983[14] 4237[4] (Dead)

Valuable (IRE) *R Johnson* 95h 73c
9 b m Jurado(USA) —Can't Afford It (IRE) (Glow (USA))
370[13] 480[P] 784[11] 1063[2] 1148[2]1375[3] 1567[3] **2041[3]**

Valuso (IRE) *Noel T Chance* 53h
6 b g Luso—Regal Grove (IRE) (King's Ride)
3248[14] **3546[P]**

Van Cleef (IRE) *M Todhunter* 79b
5 b g Bob Back(USA) —Queenie Kelly (The Parson)
2948[12] 3532[P]

Vandante (IRE) *R Lee* 100b 91c
10 b g Phardante(FR) —Vanessa's Princess (Laurence O)
135[3] 288[3] 605[6]916[P] 1178[3] 1414[2]1615[P] 1960[P] 2562[P]

Vandas Choice (IRE) *Miss Lucinda V Russell* 121h 144c
8 b g Sadler's Wells(USA) —Morning Devotion (USA) (Affirmed (USA))
318[7] 1721[2] 1924[2]2499[5] 3385[8] 4459[14]

Van Ness (IRE) *Michael John Phillips* 101h 111c
7 ch g Hubbly Bubbly(USA) —Brown Trout (IRE) (Beau Charmeur (FR))
2364a[4]

Vanormix (FR) *C J Gray* 102 h 103 c
7 gr g Linamix(FR) —Vadsa Honor (FR) (Highest Honor (FR))
2609[P] **2989[4] 3426[4]3652[7] 4102[6] 4426[P]4936[9]** 5087[4]

Varuni (IRE) *P L Clinton* 69h
5 b m Ali-Royal(IRE) —Sauvignon (IRE) (Alzao (USA))
1850[7] 2245[7] 2463[P]

Vaughan *H D Daly* 114 h
5 b g Machiavellian(USA) —Labibeh (USA) (Lyphard (USA))
3127[2] 3883[2] 4564[2] 4832[3]

Va Vavoom (IRE) *N A Twiston-Davies* 94b 127 c
8 b g Supreme Leader—Shalom Joy (Kemal (FR))
870[2] **1716[2] (1831) 2208[7]2492[10] (2748) 2817[4]3176[6] 3816[4] 4433[12]4762[9] 5067[P]**

Venetian Romance (IRE) *M R Bosley* 46h
5 ch m Desert Story(IRE) —Cipriani (Habitat)
3322[9] 4733[5]

Vengeance *S Dow* 114+h
6 b g Fleetwood(IRE) —Lady Isabell (Rambo Dancer (CAN))
2322[7] 2573[7] 3996[6] 4243[4] (4523)

Venn Ottery *O J Carter* 87h 107c
11 b g Access Ski—Tom's Comedy (Comedy Star (USA))
4092[P] 4748[F]

Venture More *Mrs A F Tullie* 60h
10 b g Green Adventure(USA) —Admire-A-More (Le Coq D'Or)
85[7] 301[P]

Venture To Fly (IRE) *N W Alexander* 112h 112c
12 ch g Roselier(FR) —Fly Run (Deep Run)
498[U]

Verasi *G L Moore* 138h
5 b g Kahyasi—Fair Verona (USA) (Alleged (USA))
100[9] (2047) (2636) 3298[15] 4375[3] 4446[5]

Verchoyles Lad (IRE) *John G Carr* 112 h 116 c
9 b g Treasure Hunter—Lucifer's Way (Lucifer (USA))
857[5]

Verstone (IRE) *R F Fisher* 71+h
4 b f Brave Act—Golden Charm (IRE) (Common Grounds)
1338[3] 1440[3] 1904[6] 2494[P] 3337[2]3544[4] 3914[P]

Versus (GER) *C J Mann* 109h
6 gr g Highest Honor(FR) —Very Mighty (FR) (Niniski (USA))
54[3] 2483[8] 2820[5] 3018[10]

Vertical Bloom *Mrs P Sly* 117h
5 b m Perpendicular—Rosie Cone (Celtic Cone)
2012[3] 2501[2] (2718) 3595[3] 4619[3]

Very Green (FR) *D T Hughes* 109+h
4 b g Barathea(IRE) —Green Bend (USA) (Riverman (USA))
5076a[2]

Very Optimistic (IRE) *Jonjo O'Neill* 135+h 138 c
8 b g Un Desperado(FR) —Bright Future (IRE) (Satco (FR))
1271[5] 207[3] **2311[2] 3017[4]3653[P]**

Very Special One (IRE) *K C Bailey* 97h 99 c
6 b m Supreme Leader—Bright News (Buckskin (FR))
1974[2] 2552[3] **3887[2] 4639[F]**

Very Tasty (IRE) *M Todhunter* 87+h 59+c
9 ch g Be My Native(USA) —Jasmine Melody (Jasmine Star)
197[8] **548[6]** 988[P]

Very Very Noble (IRE) *W Storey* 101c
12 ch g Aristocracy—Hills Angel (IRE) (Salluceva)
4793[7]

Vesta Flame *Miss L V Davis* 46h
5 b m Vettori(IRE) —Ciel De Feu (USA) (Blushing John (USA))
601[8] 822[13] 1148[9] 1431[4]

Vesuve (FR) *G Macaire* 120h 107+c
7 b g Villez(USA) —Razzamatazz (FR) (Always Fair (USA))
2805[2]

Vettorious *Mrs P Sly* 44h
4 ch g Vettori(IRE) —Sleepless (Night Shift (USA))
1737[12] 2258[9]

Viable *Mrs P Sly* 66h
4 b g Vettori(IRE) —Danseuse Davis (FR) (Glow (USA))
1718[12]

Viana (FR) *E Lecoiffier* 105c
6 b m Signe Divin(USA) —Taviana (FR) (Don Roberto (USA))
1073a[5]

Vibe *R J Price* 33h
5 gr g Danzero(AUS) —Courting (Pursuit Of Love)
2826[17]

Vicario *D McCain* 120 h 114c
5 gr g Vettori(IRE) —Arantxa (Sharpo)
5[4] 1665[3] (2004) 2292[P] (2629) 2820[P] 3143[4]3397[4] **(3781) 4068[3] 4323[4]5010[9]**

Vicars Court (IRE) *O Brennan* 77b
6 b g Lord Of Appeal—Lady Temba (Callernish)
4853[13]

Vicars Destiny *Mrs S Lamyman* 120h
8 b m Sir Harry Lewis(USA) —Church Leap (Pollerton)
1929[7] 2292[9] 2590[4] 3289[2] 3741[3]3966[3] 4390[5] 4579[F]

Vicentio *T J Fitzgerald* 92h 75+c
7 br g Vettori(IRE) —Smah (Mtoto)
(218) 575[4] 859[2] 1045[4] 1436[4]

Viciana *Mrs L Wadham* 107h 103 c
7 b m Sir Harry Lewis(USA) —Ludoviciana (Oats)
(2012) 2238[4] 2718[3] **3689[2] (3790)**

Vicky Bee *M G Quinlan* 86h
7 b m Alflora(IRE) —Mighty Frolic (Oats)
1344[2] 1566[P]

Vic The Piler (IRE) *N G Richards* 116h 117+c
7 ch g Old Vic—Strong Gale Pigeon (IRE) (Strong Gale)
2264[2] 2813[6]

Victom's Chance (IRE) *Noel T Chance* 125+h
8 b g Old Vic—Lady Swinford (Ardross)
3502[7] 3986[2] 4497[4]

Victor Daly (IRE) *Mrs H Dalton* 98b
5 b g Old Vic—Murphys Lady (IRE) (Over The River (FR))
(2987) 3691[5]

Victor George *N A Twiston-Davies* 86+b
6 b g Entrepreneur—National Treasure (Shirley Heights)
4326[3] 4940[7]

Victoria's Boy (IRE) *Mrs W Wild* 92c
13 b g Denel(FR) —Cloghroe Lady (Hard Boy)
49[P] (498)

Victorias Groom (GER) *Mrs L Wadham* 116 h
4 bb g Lavirco(GER) —Valda (RUS) (Dotsero (USA))
2045[3] 3132[2] 3340[3] 4057[3] (4631)

Victoria's Pet *F P Murtagh*
10 b g Kasakov—Lonely Lass (Headin' Up)
1374[P]

Victor One (IRE) *J Wade* 36h
6 b g Victory Note(USA) —Another Baileys (Deploy)
1885[9]

Victory Gunner (IRE) *C Roberts* 127 h 125 c
8 ch g Old Vic—Gunner B Sharp (Gunner B)
1830[8] **2311[F] 2564[3]2825[5] (2965) 3290[6]3390[P] 3877[4] 4098[3]4496[4] 4957[P]**

Victory Lap (GER) *G T Lynch* 61h
5 ch m Grand Lodge(USA) —Vicenca (USA) (Sky Classic (CAN))
65a[25]

Victory Roll *Miss E C Lavelle* 104h 104c
10 b g In The Wings—Persian Victory (IRE) (Persian Bold)
2827[P] 3432[2] 3663[3]3888[P]

Victram (IRE) *Adrian McGuinness* 121+h
6 b g Victory Note(USA) —Lady Tristram (Miami Springs)
2636[3] 3411a[P] (4375) 4951a[9]

Victree (IRE) *L Wells* 68h
7 b g Old Vic—Boro Glen (Furry Glen)
235[4] 763[4]

Vic Venturi (IRE) *Philip Fenton* 138h
6 ch g Old Vic—Carmen Lady (Torus)
2536a[3] (3086a) 3309a[2] (4888a) 5132a[3]

Vic Ville (IRE) *Michael Hourigan* 118+h 122c
7 b g Old Vic—N T Nad (Welsh Pageant)
1702a[4]

Viennchee Run *K F Clutterbuck* 85h
5 b g Commanche Run—Lucky Vienna (Lucky Wednesday)
1635[4] 1820[6] *3983[7]*4819[P]

Vigna Maggio (FR) *R H Alner* 57h
4 b f Starborough—Viva Vodka (FR) (Crystal Glitters (USA))
2824[7]

Vigoureux (FR) *S Gollings* 100+h 105c
7 b g Villez(USA) —Rouge Folie (FR) (Agent Bleu (FR))
126[2] 466[5] 692[U]825[3] 2128[F] 2963[C](3255) 3334[7] 3580[P]4478[P] **4850[9]**

Viking Song *F Kirby* 27h 61c
6 b g Savahra Sound—Relikon (Relkino)
2571[P] **2839[9] 3338[P]3781[6] 4303[F] 4840[9]**

Viking Star (IRE) *A D Brown* 37h
5 b g Indian Rocket—Nordic Flavour (IRE) (Nordico (USA))
2444[15] 2658[P] 3804[14]

Villago (GER) *E W Tuer* 95 h
6 b g Laroche(GER) —Village (GER) (Acatenango (GER))
167[9] 509[5] 2171[4] (2416) 2691[5] 2977[3]3487[2] 4113[4]

Villair (IRE) *C J Mann* 84h 116c
11 b g Valville(FR) —Brackenair (Fairbairn)
2293[3] (2589) 2819[5]

Villa Mara (IRE) *S Kirk* 73b
6 b g Alflora(IRE) —Claudia Electric (IRE) (Electric)
5054[11]

Villon (IRE) *L Lungo* 123 h 132+c
7 b g Topanoora—Deep Adventure (Deep Run)
(2861)

Vinando *C R Egerton* 114+h
5 ch h Hernando(FR) —Sirena (GER) (Tejano (USA))
2826[3] 3996[3] 4115[4]

Vincere *L R James* 11b
7 b g Tigani—Katy Keys (Tepukei)
2192[13] 3145[P] (Dead)

Vin Du Pays *Mrs F M Vigar* 77h 77c
6 b g Alzao(USA) —Royale Rose (FR) (Bering)
5116[6]

Vingis Park (IRE) *V R A Dartnall* 116+h 101+c
8 b g Old Vic—Lady Glenbank (Tarboosh (USA))
172[3] **1595[U] 1891[P]**(2372) 2530[6] (2859) **(4753)**

Viniyoga *M H Tompkins*
4 b g Cadeaux Genereux—Optimistic (Reprimand)
3579[P]

Vinmix De Bessy (FR) *D B Feek* 116h
5 gr g River Bay(USA) —Hesse (FR) (Linamix (FR))
100[P]

Vinnie Boy (IRE) *Mrs O Bush* 116c
9 bb g Detroit Sam(FR) —Castle Ita (Midland Gayle)
48[4] (282) 440[F]4009[2] 4471[16]

Vino Venus *Miss Sheena West*
4 b f Tipsy Creek(USA) —Galaxy Glow (Kalaglow)
1478[F]

Vintage Fabric (USA) *N J Hawke* 89b
4 b g Royal Anthem(USA) —Sandalwood (USA) (El Gran Senor (USA))
4667[3] 5117[3]

Vintage Port (IRE) *T J O'Mara* 115h
6 ch g In The Wings—Gay Bentley (USA) (Riverman (USA))
5059a[12]

Viper *R Hollinshead* 88b
4 b g Polar Prince(IRE) —Maradata (IRE) (Shardari)
4909[5] 7[6]

Virginia Preuil (FR) *P Hughes* 110h
5 br g Saint Preuil(FR) —Sweet Jaune (FR) (Le Nain Jaune (FR))
44a[2]

Virgin Soldier (IRE) *G A Swinbank* 122 h 122c
10 ch g Waajib—Never Been Chaste (Posse (USA))
1550[8] 2841[3] 3350[4]3560[5]

Virgos Bambino (IRE) *Miss V J Nicholls* 90c
9 ch m Perugino(USA) —Deep In September (IRE) (Common Grounds)
(171) 4560[P] 4730[7]

Virtue *C F Swan* 74h
4 ch f Vettori(IRE) —Zenith (Shirley Heights)
3401a[9]

Virtus *Mrs B K Thomson* 85 h
6 ch g Machiavellian(USA) —Exclusive Virtue (USA) (Shadeed (USA))
456[2] 664[8] 813[8] 1156[3] (1202) 1297[15]1836[F] 2042[8] 2903[11]

Viscount Bankes *Mrs Rosemary Gasson* 33h 92+c
8 ch g Clantime—Bee Dee Dancer (Ballacashtal (CAN))
52[3] (278) 437[P]4055[2] 4330[P] 4555[4]

Visibility (FR) *M C Pipe* 116 h 98 c
7 gr g Linamix(FR) —Visor (USA) (Mr Prospector (USA))
2312F 26218 317913 346774093² 42893

Vision Victory (GER) *P Spottiswood* 77h
4 b g Dashing Blade—Val D'Isere (GER) (Surumu (GER))
478912

Vital Spark *J M Jefferson* 59+h
7 b g Primitive Rising(USA) —Enkindle (Relkino)
1915P **2415F**

Vitelucy *Miss S J Wilton* 91h
7 b m Vettori(IRE) —Classic Line (Last Tycoon)
110P 352P

Vitray (FR) *J Bertran De Balanda*
4 ch g Morespeed—Tarde (FR) (Kashtan (FR))
4548a2

Viva Forever (FR) *A M Hales* 85+h
7 br m Lando(GER) —Very Mighty (FR) (Niniski (USA))
23811 7479

Vivante (IRE) *A J Wilson* 84h
8 b m Toulon—Splendidly Gay (Lord Gayle (USA))
2065 8013 10022 11522 14105(4907)

Vivre Aimer Rire (FR) *M Scudamore* 64h
5 b m Cyborg(FR) —Badj II (FR) (Tadj (FR))
775 245P 575P 1002P 128010

Vocative (GER) *P C Haslam* 97+h
4 gr f Acatenango(GER) —Vadinaxa (FR) (Linamix (FR))
14415 (2001) 24424 40576 43624 46092

Voir Dire *Mrs P N Dutfield* 90+h
4 b g Vettori(IRE) —Bobbie Dee (Blakeney)
13979 (1737)

Volaire *A J Lidderdale* 20b
4 b f Zaha(CAN) —Appelania (Star Appeal)
462310

Vonadaisy *R A Harris* 16h
5 b m Averti(IRE) —Vavona (Ballad Rock)
10856

Von Origny (FR) *H D Daly* 101+h 128+c
5 gr g Blushing Flame(USA) —Forza Malta (FR) (Royal Charter (FR))
(2078) 26076 28172 3506F (4214) 4778P

Vox Populi (USA) *S J Mahon* 117 h
4 ch g Distant View(USA) —Popularity (USA) (Blushing Groom (FR))
2645a3 3890a8 4122a4 4435P

Voy Por Ustedes (FR) *A King* 126 h 162c
5 b g Villez(USA) —Nuit D'Ecajeul (FR) (Matahawk)
(2422) (2798) (3150) (3991) (4431) 47742

Vracca *M C Pipe*
4 ch f Vettori(IRE) —Crystal Cavern (USA) (Be My Guest (USA))
945RR

Vrisaki (IRE) *M E Sowersby* 92h
5 b g Docksider(USA) —Kingdom Queen (IRE) (Night Shift (USA))
20818 292316 296810 34885 3967P49226 147

Vrubel (IRE) *J R Holt* 46h
7 ch g Entrepreneur—Renzola (Dragonara Palace (USA))
1735 760P

Vulcan Lane (NZ) *R C Guest* 77h 90 c
9 ch g Star Way—Smudged (NZ) (Nassipour (USA))
848 2655 **39510**5207 33353 **35552 39644**40456 42998

Wages *Evan Williams* 91h 108 c
6 b g Lake Coniston(IRE) —Green Divot (Green Desert (USA))
1779 102710 10857 12787 **1805F20742 2561U 28072(3274) 33705**

Wahiba Sands *Miss Lucy Bridges* 71c
13 b g Pharly(FR) —Lovely Noor (USA) (Fappiano (USA))
313P 405P

Waimea Bay *D P Keane* 96+h
7 b m Karinga Bay—Smart In Sable (Roscoe Blake)
46794 4939P

Wainak (USA) *Miss Lucinda V Russell*
8 b g Silver Hawk(USA) —Cask (Be My Chief (USA))
385413 **4343P**

Wainhill Lad *S G Allen*
10 b g Suluk(USA) —The-Adstone-Lodge (Royal Vulcan)
4897F

Wain Mountain *J A B Old* 114h 134c
10 b g Unfuwain(USA) —Mountain Memory (High Top)
23686 28472 30225(3503) 37395 40704476214

Wait For The Will (USA) *G L Moore* 115 h
10 ch g Seeking The Gold(USA) —You'd Be Surprised (USA) (Blushing Groom (FR))
12637 14004 14813

Wakeup Smiling (IRE) *Miss E C Lavelle* 95 h 105+c
8 b g Norwich—Blackmiller Lady (Bonne Noel)
334411 42146 457114 48224

Waking Dream (USA) *Henry De Bromhead* 88h
4 b f Grindstone(USA) —Glorious Diamond (USA) (His Majesty (USA))
5076a9

Walcot Lad (IRE) *A Ennis* 83h 120+c
10 b g Jurado(USA) —Butty Miss (Menelek)
1039 505U 181952217P 22593 252226844 (2933) 32842(3440) 3596P 412054371 4 (4524) (4694) 48222

Waldo's Dream *P Bowen* 85+b
6 b g Dreams End—Landsker Pryde (Nearly A Hand)
16602

Walking Sunday (IRE) *K C Bailey* 85h 87+c
8 bb g Denel(FR) —Blue Mount (IRE) (Merrymount)
2116

Wally Wonder (IRE) *K G Reveley* 99 h 61c
8 ch g Magical Wonder(USA) —Sally Gap (Sallust)
237P 7816 9782 (1148) (1344) 15713 183811256610 27664 335110 38185 408024593 5 51377

Walsingham (IRE) *R Lee* 94h
8 b g Presenting—Lets Compromise (No Argument)
3655 (469) 9129 25277 **3274F**33862 (3889) 43294 45698 4736P

Walter (IRE) *P Winkworth* 85h
7 ch g Presenting—Siberian Princess (Northfields (USA))
19504 22389 29285

Walter's Destiny *C W Mitchell* 103c
14 ch g White Prince(USA) —Tearful Sarah (Rugantino)
32414 35096 3698548353

Waltons Mountain (IRE) *Anthony Mullins* 109+c
8 b g Norwich—Alzena (Persian Bold)
1622a2

Walton Way *P W Hiatt* 67h
6 b g Charmer—Needwood Poppy (Rolfe (USA))
6166 816P 21858 2663P 312711364611 4013P 4320P 44183 45774

Waltzing Along (IRE) *L Lungo* 71h 88+c
8 b g Presenting—Clyduffe Fairy (Belfalas)
24795 33482

Waltzing Beau *B G Powell* 113 h 120+c
5 ch g Dancing Spree(USA) —Blushing Belle (Local Suitor (USA))
220719 37279 399312 **(4323) 472945007P**

Wanango (GER) *T Stack* 135 h
5 ch g Acatenango(GER) —Wanateluthspilgrim (USA) (Pilgrim (USA))
(2335) 3052a3 4137a5 47636

Wandering Act (IRE) *A W Carroll* 60h
4 b g Brave Act—Cwm Deri (IRE) (Alzao (USA))
20456

Wantage Road (IRE) *N J Henderson* 49b
4 br g Pistolet Bleu(IRE) —Glowing Lines (IRE) (Glow (USA))
462210

Wardash (GER) *M C Chapman* 90 h 66 c
6 b g Dashing Blade—Warusha (GER) (Shareef Dancer (USA))
(670) 7532 8069 (943) 10289 12729 **13636**16404 17244 (1814) 226111 36746 40758 4632F

War General *T J Taaffe* 106h
5 gr g Classic Cliche(IRE) —Absalom's Lady (Absalom)
5104a6

Warlord *R H Buckler* 100b
5 b g Bob Back(USA) —Martomick (Montelimar (USA))
30013 *35044* 46225

Warningcamp (GER) *Lady Herries* 121h
5 b g Lando(GER) —Wilette (GER) (Top Ville)
23745 (2803) 4621F

War Of Attrition (IRE) *M F Morris* 152h 173+c
7 br g Presenting—Una Juna (IRE) (Good Thyne (USA))
(89a) (1810a) (2304a) 2793a53081a2 (4470) (5079a)

Warpath (IRE) *Anthony Mullins* 87h
5 b g Alderbrook—Blake's Fable (IRE) (Lafontaine (USA))
3003a14

Warrens Castle (IRE) *W P Mullins* 118 h 117c
9 b g Fourstars Allstar(USA) —Jerusalem Cruiser (IRE) (Electric)
1083a5

Washington Lad (IRE) *P A Fahy* 122h
6 ch g Beneficial—Kyle Lark (Miner's Lamp)
116a3

Washington Pink (IRE) *C Grant* 75h
7 b g Tagula(IRE) —Little Red Rose (Precocious)
1838P 2107P 265713 284314 3271434871 1 3656P

Watch The Wind *J B Walton* 61b
5 ch m High Kicker(USA) —Marejo (Creetown)
284414 35568

Waterberg (IRE) *H D Daly* 92h 109c
11 b g Sadler's Wells(USA) —Pretoria (Habitat)
2057 6532 115712764 18933 232552965 3 3886P

Watercress *Miss M E Rowland* 69b
6 b m Slip Anchor—Theme (IRE) (Sadler's Wells (USA))
176210 32734 365712

Water King (USA) *R M Stronge* 120h
7 b g Irish River(FR) —Brookshield Baby (IRE) (Sadler's Wells (USA))
(5) 3534 1675F (2166) 29990 33975 36006

Waterlaw (IRE) *Mrs D C Faulkner* 120+c
12 b g Kahyasi—Shuss (USA) (Princely Native (USA))
313F

Waterlily (IRE) *Mrs John Harrington* 111h 111+c
7 b m Revoque(IRE) —Cochineal (USA) (Vaguely Noble)
66a11

Waterline Blue (IRE) *P Bowen* 52h
5 b g Mujadil(USA) —Blues Queen (Lahib (USA))
237P 76016

Waterloo Leader (IRE) *Mrs S Kellard-Smith*
11 b g Supreme Leader—Victor's Valley (Deep Run)
50P

Waterloo Son (IRE) *H D Daly* 112+h
6 b g Luso—Waterloo Sunset (Deep Run)
343110 196811 (2968) 36464 42802 48262

Watermouse *R Dickin* 81h
6 b g Alhaarth(IRE) —Heavenly Waters (Celestial Storm (USA))
4013P 4392P 45772 505013

Water Pistol *M C Chapman* 73h
4 b g Double Trigger(IRE) —Water Flower (Environment Friend)
15194 34156 378610 40776 44167463117 47957 48988

Water Quirl (GER) *M F Harris* 96h 134 c
7 ch g Dr Devious(IRE) —Water Quest (IRE) (Rainbow Quest (USA))
3893 **471a3 590a7**

Watershed (IRE) *Seamus G O'Donnell* 111h 100c
11 gr g Beau Sher—Jirao (Walshford)
4321P (Dead)

Waterspray (AUS) *Ian Williams* 105c
8 ch g Lake Coniston(IRE) —Forain (NZ) (Nassipour (USA))
6338 281311 **3619P 475545107 6**

Water Taxi *Ferdy Murphy* 108+h
5 ch g Zafonic(USA) —Trellis Bay (Sadler's Wells (USA))
16615 19274 24752 28404 297763943 2 (4532) 46572

Watson Lake (IRE) *Noel Meade* 132 h 160c
8 b g Be My Native(USA) —Magneeto (IRE) (Brush Aside (USA))
89a2 (1702a) (2195a) 3774a4 44456 (4625a) 5079a4

Waverley Road *M Madgwick* 84h 90 c
9 ch g Pelder(IRE) —Lillicara (FR) (Caracolero (USA))
5067

Wave Rock *A W Carroll* 95 c
11 br g Tragic Role(USA) —Moonscape (Ribero)
47 761P 108831236P

Waydale Hill *T D Walford* 78h
7 ch m Minster Son—Buckby Folly (Netherkelly)
1113 2184 4698 1002P

Waynesworld (IRE) *M Scudamore* 90 h 107 c
8 b g Petoski—Mariners Mirror (Julio Mariner)
3349 **612F 1446514794 (1615) (1656) 17136** 22143 2517P **292234872 4**

Wayward Melody *G L Moore* 93+h 94c
6 b m Merdon Melody—Dubitable (Formidable (USA))
(245) 5666 **19179 223732553 3 2808P** 301811**44513 49374 50719**

Wayward Shot (IRE) *M W Easterby*
4 b g Desert Prince(IRE) —Style Parade (USA) (Diesis)
1718P

Waziri (IRE) *M Sheppard* 85h
5 b g Mtoto—Euphorie (GER) (Feenpark (GER))
25633 27235 29954 34569 4828212

Waziya *Mrs L Williamson* 82h
7 ch m Hurricane Sky(AUS) —Serration (Kris)
13313 3316 **990F** 104614 15207 17125 19523 2146P

Weapons Inspector (IRE) *J Howard Johnson* 107+c
7 bb g Sacrament—Delnac (Lucifer (USA))
(2689) 33362 4790F

Wearerich *D J Wintle* 54h
9 ch m Alflora(IRE) —Weareagrandmother (Prince Tenderfoot (USA))
13412

Webbow (IRE) *T D Easterby*
4 b g Dr Devious(IRE) —Ower (IRE) (Lomond (USA))
362312

Web Master (FR) *Mrs Sandra Smith* 99 h 85+c
8 b g Arctic Tern(USA) —Inesperada (Cariellor (FR))
50954

Wednesday Club *N M Babbage* 41h
5 ch g Shahanndeh—Fleur De Tal (Primitive Rising (USA))
3945

Wednesday Country (IRE) *J A T De Giles* 97b
5 ch g Carroll House—Mettle Kettle (Cut Above)
332710 36995 4212P

Wee Anthony (IRE) *Jonjo O'Neill* 108+h
7 gr g Roselier(FR) —Arctic Alice (Brave Invader (USA))
24325 26195 28496 332810 **3663P**(3982) 4357F

Wee Bertie (IRE) *J Howard Johnson* 88+b
4 b g Sea Raven(IRE) —Commanche Glen (IRE) (Commanche Run)
37634 (5124)

Wee Danny (IRE) *L A Dace* 89+h
9 b g Mandalus—Bonne Bouche (Bonne Noel)
105P 2986 6525

Wee Dinns (IRE) *M C Pipe* 114+h
5 b m Marju(IRE) —Tir-An-Oir (IRE) (Law Society (USA))
34635 36902 40743 48552 (5019)

Wee Robbie *N J Gifford* 121+h
6 b g Bob Back(USA) —Blast Freeze (IRE) (Lafontaine (USA))
18182 23432 (2829)

Wee Sean (IRE) *Miss Lucinda V Russell* 72h
6 b g Rashar(USA) —Mrs Blobby (IRE) (Rontino)
1307P 1528P 15660 2416P

Weet A Head (IRE) *R Hollinshead* 100 h
5 b g Foxhound(USA) —Morale (Bluebird (USA))
72911

Weet An Haul *T Wall* 62h
5 b g Danzero(AUS) —Island Ruler (Ile De Bourbon (USA))
310 457 12 729F 104612 1156184828U 49034

Weet N Measures *T Wall*
4 b g Weet-A-Minute(IRE) —Weet Ees Girl (IRE) (Common Grounds)
1190P 172913

Weet Watchers *T Wall* 85h
6 b g Polar Prince(IRE) —Weet Ees Girl (IRE) (Common Grounds)
21399 25234 25608 27214 285873456 5 380411 45912 4828P

Wee William *T D Walford* 100+c
6 b g Bollin William—Our Amber (Kabour)
16622 21685 3170537915 43007

Welcome Stranger *G L Moore* 123h
6 b g Most Welcome—Just Julia (Natroun (FR))
(4564) 4763F 50705

Welcome To Unos *K G Reveley* 116 h 116c
9 ch g Exit To Nowhere(USA) —Royal Loft (Homing)
21906 (2566) (2714) **31722 (3352)** 399311 **4419P**

Weldiva *B N Pollock* 19h
6 ch m Weld—Bivadell (Bivouac)
16574 190314 2503P 31418 3416P

Weldman *K G Reveley* 73h
7 b g Weld—Manettia (IRE) (Mandalus)
406P 6032 1002P (Dead)

Well Actually (IRE) *B G Powell* 85h
6 b g Luso—Lake Garden Park (Comedy Star (USA))
23226

Wellbeing *P J Hobbs* 144+h
9 b g Sadler's Wells(USA) —Charming Life (NZ) (Sir Tristram)
33543 39083 (4243) (4561) (4773)

Well Disguised (IRE) *D W Whillans* 77b
4 b f Beneficial—Executive Move (IRE) (Executive Perk)
45887

Wellfield *N A Twiston-Davies*
6 b m Primitive Rising(USA) —Ellerton Song (Cree Song)
16746

We'll Meet Again *M W Easterby* 88h
6 b g Bin Ajwaad(IRE) —Tantalizing Song (CAN) (The Minstrel (CAN))
3064 4062 5204 32695

Well Mounted (IRE) *A L T Moore* 115h
5 b g Saddlers' Hall(IRE) —Granny Clark (IRE) (Welsh Term)
3003a4 4951a8

Wellpict One (IRE) *N A Twiston-Davies* 97+h
6 b g Taipan(IRE) —Emily Bishop (IRE) (The Parson)
24272 2849P (Dead)

Well Presented (IRE) *Mrs John Harrington* 125h 136c
8 ch g Presenting—Casualty Madame (Buckskin (FR))
115a6 2304a4 2539a123053a17 4929a8 5102aP

Well Run (IRE) *Noel Meade* 98b
5 b g Saddlers' Hall(IRE) —Arctic Run (Deep Run)
5104a9

Wellstream Blue *Mrs H O Graham*
5 b g River Falls—Tugra (FR) (Baby Turk)
376312 4527P

Well Tutored (IRE) *A L T Moore* 120+c
7 b g Master Willie—Knockaverry (IRE) (Kemal (FR))
4778F

Welsh Dane *M Sheppard* 85h
6 b g Chaddleworth(IRE) —Dane Rose (Full Of Hope)
2183 17533 18063 25173 3325236134 45493

Welsh Doll (IRE) *D Brace* 65h
7 b m Flemensfirth(USA) —Give Me A Name (Pollerton)
12337 148012 1751P 19499

Welsh Dream *Miss S E Forster* 94h
9 b g Mtoto—Morgannwg (IRE) (Simply Great (FR))
3196 18387 245213 28433 335174656 5 506811

Welsh Gold *S T Lewis* 31h 77c
7 ch g Zafonic(USA) —Trying For Gold (USA) (Northern Baby (CAN))
243 276P 39851754 8

Welsh Main *Miss Tor Sturgis* 112h 114+c
9 br g Zafonic(USA) —Welsh Daylight (Welsh Pageant)
344U 6504 9149(1754) (1805) 242032725 5

Wembury Point (IRE) *B G Powell* 107+h
4 gr g Monashee Mountain(USA) —Lady Celina (FR) (Crystal Palace (FR))
(1146) (1404) 18736 21785 26125 27565 4593F461613 482111 48306

Wenceslas (IRE) *Miss H C Knight* 93+h 112 c
6 b g Un Desperado(FR) —Lady Of The West (IRE) (Mister Lord (USA))
2100P (2929) 3816645634

Wendys Dynamo *Mrs Jo Sleep* 85c
9 b g Opera Ghost—Good Appeal (Star Appeal)
44215

Wenger (FR) *P Winkworth* 100h
6 b g Unfuwain(USA) —Molly Dance (FR) (Groom Dancer (USA))
220F 5688 192112 22183 (2685) 3128536873 45234

Wenlocks Wonder *K C Bailey* 88h
5 b g I'm Supposin(IRE) —Idiots Money (Idiots Delight)
20496 33546 38002 4732P

Wenrus Lady *A W Carroll*
5 b m Overbury(IRE) —Persian Symphony (IRE) (Persian Heights)
432611

Wensleydale Web *M E Sowersby* 75b
4 b f Kayf Tara—Little Red Spider (Bustino)
43042 475120

Were In Touch (IRE) *P F Nicholls* 95+h 132+c
8 b g Old Vic—Winterland Gale (IRE) (Strong Gale)
(205)

Were Not Stoppin *R Bastiman* 87h 98c
11 b g Mystiko(USA) —Power Take Off (Aragon)
3732 572P

Weresmimum *Mrs S Lamyman*
6 b g Nile Delta(IRE) —Elite Bliss (IRE) (Tirol)
1182P

West Bay Mist *Mrs H R J Nelmes*
5 b m Relief Pitcher—West Bay Breeze (Town And Country)
255816 46957

West Bay Storm *Mrs H R J Nelmes* 75b
6 br m Relief Pitcher—West Bay Breeze (Town And Country)
5075

West Coaster (IRE) *M W Easterby* 88h 99+c
8 gr g Be My Native(USA) —Donegal Grey (IRE) (Roselier (FR))
1818

Westcraft (IRE) *A Ennis* 77h
6 b g Warcraft(USA) —Copperhurst (IRE) (Royal Vulcan)
15969 17253

Westender (FR) *M C Pipe* 152h 130 c
10 b g In The Wings—Trude (GER) (Windwurf (GER))
207^{4} 2209^{10} 2761^{P} 3177^{4} 3723^{3}4458^{11} 4745^{4} 4959^{5}

West End Pearl *C G Cox* 69h
5 ch m The West(USA) —Raghill Hannah (Buckskin (FR))
1725^{4} 1898^{9}

West End Wonder (IRE) *D Burchell* 111+h 106+c
7 b g Idris(IRE) —Miss Plum (Ardross)
133^{7} 356^{3} 629^{2} (912) 1680^{10} 1975^{8}3291^{P}

Western Bluebird (IRE) *Miss Kate Milligan* 51h
8 b g Bluebird(USA) —Arrastra (Bustino)
417^{5} 781^{P} **1062**^{U} 1588^{P}

Western Dasher (IRE) *Thomas Gerard O'Leary* 87h 72c
5 b g Saddlers' Hall(IRE) —Devil Worship (Yashgan)
44a^{15}

Westernmost *K Bishop* 93h 70c
8 b g Most Welcome—Dakota Girl (Northern State (USA))
2314^{6} 2595^{3} 3467^{5} 3731^{4} 3950^{3}4392^{6} **5107**^{4}

Western Roots *I W McInnes* 68h
5 ch g Dr Fong(USA) —Chrysalis (Soviet Star (USA))
1112^{3} 1340^{8}

Western View (IRE) *Cecil Ross* 86h 114c
14 br g Montelimar(USA) —Regency View (Royal Highway)
5083a^{11}

Westgate (IRE) *S Gollings* 48b
4 gr g Saddlers' Hall(IRE) —Jasmin Path (Warpath)
3392^{8} 3623^{11}

Westgrove Berry (IRE) *N G Richards* 88+b
6 br m Presenting—Mulberry (IRE) (Denel (FR))
(4304) 4976^{7}

West Hill (IRE) *D McCain* 78 h 85c
5 b g Gone West(USA) —Altamura (USA) (El Gran Senor (USA))
238^{8} 1202^{6} 1322^{4} 2006^{5} 2563^{4}2822^{5} (3782) 4566^{4}

Westmeath Flyer *P A Blockley* 112h 99+c
11 b g Deploy—Re-Release (Baptism)
2820^{P} 3332^{2} 3600^{8} 3901^{5} 4119^{4}4727^{P}

Westmorland (IRE) *D R MacLeod* 108+h
10 b g Phardante(FR) —Ticking Over (IRE) (Decent Fellow)
4982^{P}

Weston Rock *T D Walford* 112 h
7 b g Double Eclipse(IRE) —Mossberry Fair (Mossberry)
895^{8} 974^{6} (1045) (1108) 1231^{3}

West Paces (IRE) *S Dixon* 105+c
12 br g Lord Americo—Spanish Royale (Royal Buck)
4757^{P}

West Ridge *B G Powell* 102b
5 ch g Ridgewood Ben—Western Ploy (Deploy)
3699^{3}

West Route (IRE) *I Madden* 113b
6 b g Accordion—O Tuk Deep (Deep Run)
5081a^{12}

Wests Awake (IRE) *I Madden* 94h 120c
10 b g King's Ride—Letterfore (Strong Gale)
1083a^{11} 1116a^{8} **1420a**^{P}**5102a**^{5}

Wet Lips (AUS) *R C Guest* 121h 137+c
8 ch g Grand Lodge(USA) —Kissing (AUS) (Somalia (AUS))
121^{2} **371**^{3} **419**^{3}**(782)** 1548^{10} **(1666) 1739**^{2}3561^{8}

Whaleef *B J Llewellyn* 112 h 109+c
8 br g Darshaan—Wilayif (USA) (Danzig (USA))
(3348) 3562^{F} 4050^{8} **4281**^{3}**4552**^{5} **4859**^{4}

What A Blaze (IRE) *Robert Gray*
6 b m Oscar(IRE) —Imightn'Imightn'T (IRE) (Executive Perk)
1889^{10} 2446^{19}

What A Gift (IRE) *C Roche* 40b
6 bb m Erin's Isle—Motus (Anfield)
93a^{18}

What A Monday *M Pitman* 96h
8 b g Beveled(USA) —Raise Memories (Skyliner)
2730^{P}

What A Native (IRE) *C F Swan* 46h 128c
10 b g Be My Native(USA) —Yukon Lil (Yankee Gold)
3971^{P} **4483a**^{3} **4929a**^{P}

What A Night *Mrs A C Hamilton* 61h
7 gr g Environment Friend—Misty Night (Grey Desire)
59^{11}

Whatareyouhaving *Henry De Bromhead* 127h 88c
10 b g Derrylin—Simple Mind (Decent Fellow)
92a^{18} 5059a^{16}

Whatashock *Mrs H M Tory* 110 c
11 b g Never So Bold—Lady Electric (Electric)
4607^{F} **4730**^{3}

What A Vintage (IRE) *R T Phillips* 105h
6 ch m Un Desperado(FR) —The Vine Browne (IRE) (Torus)
(2185) (2799) 3184^{2} 4494^{5} 4781^{6}

Whatcanisay *J D Frost* 73h
7 b g Morpeth—Supreme Daughter (Supreme Leader)
2075^{3} 2606^{7} 2849^{9} 4032^{9}

Whatcanyasay *Mrs E Slack* 26h
5 br g Prince Daniel(USA) —Snowys Pet (Petong)
1885^{P} 2062^{10} 3205^{P} 3779^{7} 12^{10}

Whatdo You Want (IRE) *G M Moore* 39b
6 b m Spectrum(IRE) —Soviet Pretender (USA) (Alleged (USA))
147^{P}

What If (IRE) *I Buchanan* 101h 94+c
9 b g Lord Americo—Romany River (Over The River (FR))
419^{4} **2655**^{F}

What Odds (IRE) *T K Geraghty* 131 c
10 b g Torus—Merrywell (Mugatpura)
91a^{3} **2370**^{10} **3053a**^{2}**4434**^{U} **4929a**^{P}

What Perk (IRE) *A L T Moore* 100h 103c
7 b g Executive Perk—Milford Run (Deep Run)
92a^{P}

What's A Filly *R C Guest* 88+h 102+c
6 b m Bob's Return(IRE) —Pearly-B (IRE) (Gunner B)
185^{6} 613^{7} **862**^{P} **904**^{U}

What's Ahead *Mrs J C McGregor* 68h
6 ch m Emperor Fountain—Our Wilma (Master Willie)
323^{15} 2480^{7} 2903^{6}

Whatsinitforme (IRE) *W K Goldsworthy* 56b
4 ch g Tagula(IRE) —Sauvignon (IRE) (Alzao (USA))
2014^{6} 2927^{15} 3479^{P} 4423^{U} 4550^{P} (Dead)

What'sonyourmind (IRE) *Jonjo O'Neill* 88h
6 b g Glacial Storm(USA) —Granny Clark (IRE) (Welsh Term)
2179^{4} 3023^{12} 3393^{5} 3613^{P} 4067^{5}4282^{P} 4515^{2}

Whats Up Maid *Mrs Jo Sleep* 61c
9 b m Emperor Fountain—Roman Maid (Roman Warrior)
171^{P}

What You Know (IRE) *Mrs D A Hamer* 88+h
12 bb g Be My Guest(USA) —Flamme D'Amour (Gift Card (FR))
1040^{7}

Wheel Tapper (IRE) *P W Hiatt* 45b
5 bb g Humbel(USA) —Sananjella (IRE) (Rusticaro (FR))
1820^{7} 1909^{8}

When Your Readyles (IRE) *M Todhunter* 67h
6 b g Oscar(IRE) —Bellusis (Belfalas)
2838^{9} 3253^{P} 4052^{9}

Whereareyounow (IRE) *N A Twiston-Davies* 115h 110 c
9 ch g Mister Lord(USA) —Angies Delight (London Gazette)
1941^{5} **2368**^{12} **3180**^{9}**3988**^{6} **4434**^{13}

Wheresben (IRE) *Seamus Fahey* 123h
7 b g Flemensfirth(USA) —Chataka Blues (IRE) (Sexton Blake)
70a^{6}

Where's My Baby (IRE) *M Pitman* 85b
4 bb g Good Thyne(USA) —Furry Dream (Furry Glen)
4038^{2}

Where's Sally *J Mackie* 74b
6 b m Polar Prince(IRE) —Mustang Scally (Makbul)
2864^{7} 3373^{12}

Which Pocket (IRE) *A D Peachey* 97+c
8 br g Norwich—Toran Pocket (Proverb)
204^{2} **3819**^{U}

Whirling *M C Pipe* 106 h
4 ch f Groom Dancer(USA) —Supersonic (Shirley Heights)
1339^{2} (1551) 1679^{P}

Whisky In The Jar (IRE) *S J Marshall* 67c
5 b g Right Win(IRE) —Princess Cellina (IRE) (Jolly Jake (NZ))
785^{P} 991^{P}

Whispered Promises (USA) *R S Brookhouse* 138h
5 b g Real Quiet(USA) —Anna's Honor (USA) (Alleged (USA))
(764) 892^{4} (2444) 3297^{2} 3994^{5} 4430^{8} 4763^{7}

Whispered Secret (GER) *M C Pipe* 124h 145c
7 b g Selkirk(USA) —Wells Whisper (FR) (Sadler's Wells (USA))
353^{7} (675) 751^{2} **1019**^{2} **1155**^{3}**(1275) (1382) 1561**^{2}**(1881) 2531**^{4} **4456**^{10}**4777**^{U} **5007**^{4}

Whispering John (IRE) *W G M Turner*
10 b g Grand Plaisir(IRE) —London Anne (London Bells (CAN))
1615^{P} 1779^{P} 1859^{P}

Whistle Blowing (IRE) *D McCain* 100 h
4 b g Forzando—Philgwyn (Milford)
2753^{4} 3203^{6} 3883^{3} 4551^{2} 4877^{4}

Whistle Dixie *K Bishop* 85b
5 ch g Double Trigger(IRE) —Sendai (Le Moss)
4644^{5}

Whistling Fred *B De Haan* 93+h
7 b g Overbury(IRE) —Megabucks (Buckskin (FR))
230^{5} 1480^{7}

White Dove (FR) *Ian Williams* 93h 87c
8 b m Beaudelaire(USA) —Hermine And Pearls (FR) (Shirley Heights)
462^{5} 3247^{6} 3848^{5} 4641^{5} 5019^{7}

Whitehills (IRE) *F Flood* 92h
5 b g Oscar(IRE) —Carrigpreme (IRE) (Supreme Leader)
5104a^{3}

Whitenzo (FR) *P F Nicholls* 133h 145 c
10 b g Lesotho(USA) —Whitengy (FR) (Olantengy (FR))
2299^{P} **4617**^{8} **4764**^{11}

White On Black (GER) *G L Moore* 107+h
5 b h Lomitas—White On Red (GER) (Konigsstuhl (GER))
3658^{4} (4149) 4569^{3}

Whitewater Dash *J A B Old* 93b
6 b g Bob Back(USA) —Skiddaw Samba (Viking (USA))
4072^{6} 4422^{11}

Whitford Don (IRE) *P F Nicholls* 111h 137 c
8 b g Accordion—Whitford Breeze (Le Bavard (FR))
2176^{P} **2637**^{P} **5012**^{4}

Whitley Grange Boy *C C Pimlott* 55h 77c
13 b g Hubbly Bubbly(USA) —Choir (High Top)
151^{P} **4799**^{P}

Whitsun *Miss Kate Milligan* 56b
6 b g Gods Solution—Rasmoor Song (Cree Song)
1593^{8} 1889^{P} 3347^{F} 3559^{P} 4299^{P}

Who Cares Wins *J R Jenkins* 104h
10 ch g Kris—Anne Bonny (Ajdal (USA))
863^{4} 4452^{5}

Who Dares (IRE) *Jonjo O'Neill* 92h 101c
8 b g Toulon—Rare Weed (Frigid Aire)
1098^{2} **1176**^{B} **1212**^{2}**1277**^{2}

Who Dares Wins *Ms S Duell* 112h 90c
13 b g Kala Shikari—Sarah's Venture (Averof)
125^{6}

Who's Eddie (IRE) *H W Wheeler*
9 b g Jolly Jake(NZ) —Rare Choice (IRE) (Rare One)
4421^{P}

Whose Line Is It *N J Hawke* 82h
8 gr g Sharp Deal—Madame Ruby (FR) (Homing)
1153^{7} 1486^{7}

Whosethatfor (IRE) *J A B Old* 95h
6 b g Beneficial—Native Craft (IRE) (Be My Native (USA))
2049^{5} 2606^{2} 4613^{7}

Whyso Mayo (IRE) *Raymond Hurley* 126+c
9 b g Kasmayo—Why Cry (Pry)
(4471) (5083a)

Why The Big Paws *R C Guest* 89h 91 c
8 ch m Minster Son—Springdale Hall (USA) (Bates Motel (USA))
4805^{9} **5136**^{5}

Why The Long Face (NZ) *R C Guest* 116 h 108 c
9 ch g Grosvenor(NZ) —My Charm (NZ) (My Friend Paul (USA))
248^{5} 347^{4} 525^{4} 1610^{7}1668^{7} 1823^{P} 1940 ^{2} 3339^{4}

Wichita Lineman (IRE) *Jonjo O'Neill* 122+b
5 b g King's Theatre(IRE) —Monumental Gesture (Head For Heights)
(2534) (4244) 4448^{10} 4779^{8}

Wicked Nice Fella (IRE) *C C Bealby* 99h 126 c
8 b g Warcraft(USA) —Down Town To-Night (Kambalda)
(2100) 2768^{U} **2959**^{6}**4778**^{P} 4990^{6}

Widely Accepted (IRE) *Joseph Crowley* 111h
4 b g Mujadil(USA) —Costume Drama (USA) (Alleged (USA))
5076a^{17}

Widemouth Bay (IRE) *Miss H C Knight* 84h 104c
8 br g Be My Native(USA) —Lisaleen River (Over The River (FR))
3622^{F} 4215^{13}

Wiggy Smith *O Sherwood* 102+h
7 ch g Master Willie—Monsoon (Royal Palace)
3908^{9} 4754^{3}

Wild About Harry *A R Dicken* 72h 74c
9 ch g Romany Rye—Shylyn (Hay Chas)
83^{3} **2023**^{P} **2266**^{F}**3338**^{3} **3444**^{4} **4314**^{5}**4587**^{3} **4719**^{4} **4845**^{5}

Wild Cane Ridge (IRE) *L Lungo* 131 h 138+c
7 gr g Roselier(FR) —Shuil Na Lee (IRE) (Phardante (FR))
(2168) 2496^{2} **(3850) 4112**^{F} 4612^{8}

Wild Chimes (IRE) *P J Hobbs* 111 h
7 b g Oscar(IRE) —Jingle Bells (FR) (In The Mood (FR))
(3792) 4961^{8}

Wild Edgar (IRE) *A R Trotter* 76c
9 ch g Invited(USA) —Ou La La (IRE) (Be My Native (USA))
411^{5} **555**^{8}

Wildfield Rufo (IRE) *Mrs K Walton* 114h 117c
11 b g Celio Rufo—Jersey Girl (Hard Boy)
12^{P} **62**^{3} **547**^{2}**1603**^{5} **2164**^{8} **2745**^{7}**3315**^{3} **4505**^{2} **4790**^{P}

Wild Is The Wind (FR) *Jonjo O'Neill* 130 h 125+c
5 ch g Acatenango(GER) —Whirlwind (FR) (Leading Counsel (USA))
136^{6} (1940) 2079^{2} 3384^{2} 3970^{P} 4504^{P}**5017**^{2}

Wild Knight (IRE) *R J Hodges* 111h 120+c
9 b g Jurado(USA) —Knight's Maid (Giolla Mear)
1406^{4}

Wild Lass *J C Fox*
5 ch m Bluegrass Prince(IRE) —Pink Pumpkin (Tickled Pink)
3504^{10}

Wild Oats *B J M Ryall* 105+h 105+c
8 b g Primitive Rising(USA) —Miss Nosey Oats (Oats)
2149^{5} **2562**^{5} **2729**^{4}**3949**^{3} **(4558)**

Wild Ocean (IRE) *E Sheehy* 118h
5 b g Old Vic—Gaye Chatelaine (IRE) (Castle Keep)
3309a^{4} (Dead)

Wild Passion (GER) *Noel Meade* 139h 159c
6 b g Acatenango(GER) —White On Red (GER) (Konigsstuhl (GER))
(40a) **2395a**^{2} **3006a**^{2} **4431**^{4}**4889a**^{F}

Wild Power (GER) *Mrs H R J Nelmes* 90 h 99c
8 b g Turtle Island(IRE) —White On Red (GER) (Konigsstuhl (GER))
505^{2} **752**^{3} **1236**^{P}**1956**^{3} **2217**^{3} **2719**^{3}**3887**^{5} **(4281) 4694**^{3}**(4859)**

Wild Spice (IRE) *Miss Venetia Williams* 121h 114c
11 b g Mandalus—Curry Lunch (Pry)
421^{P} 906^{2} 974^{8}

Wild Tempo (FR) *M C Pipe* 99h
11 ch g Irish River(FR) —Fast Queen (FR) (Bon Sang (FR))
232^{3} 385^{7} 665^{9} 974^{10} 1079^{3}1192^{2} 1262^{5} 1436^{9} 1539^{5} 1655^{2}

Wild Wood (IRE) *M J P O'Brien* 89h
4 ch f Shinko Forest(IRE) —Kawanin (Generous (IRE))
5076a^{8}

Wilfie Wild *Mrs Lynne Ward* 89+c
10 b g Nomadic Way(USA) —Wild Child (Grey Ghost)
123^{U} **498**^{3} **4305**^{3}

Wilfred (IRE) *Jonjo O'Neill* 107h 89c
5 b g Desert King(IRE) —Kharaliya (FR) (Doyoun)
488^{10} 1211^{6} 1413^{6} **1958**^{5}**2422**^{P}

Wilful Lord (IRE) *J Wade* 70h 87+c
9 b g Lord Americo—Dotties Girl (IRE) (Remainder Man)
2022^{U}

Wiljen (IRE) *B S Rothwell* 36h
6 bb m Taipan(IRE) —Powleyvale (Roi Guillaume (FR))
3448^{8} 4017^{11} 10^{13}

Willhebemyguy *Mrs H R J Nelmes* 86+b
7 b g Master Willie—Right You Be (Sunyboy)
1237^{P} 2056^{7} 2720^{10}

William Bonney (IRE) *Anthony Mullins* 109b
6 b g Oscar(IRE) —Beaudel (Fidel)
3763^{9}

William Butler (IRE) *S A Brookshaw* 87h
6 b g Safety Catch(USA) —Rosie Josie (Trombone)
2941^{9} 3292^{4} *3504*^{6}3975^{P} 4071^{4} 4589^{6} 5009^{4}

William's Way *I A Wood* 80b
4 b g Fraam—Silk Daisy (Barathea (IRE))
4038^{6}

William Tell (IRE) *M D Hammond* 102h
4 b g Rossini(USA) —Livry (USA) (Lyphard (USA))
3203^{8} 3787^{5} 4506^{7}

Williamtown Lad (IRE) *Paul A Roche* 98h
5 b g Anshan—Hazy River (Over The River (FR))
3003a^{11}

Willie John Daly (IRE) *P J Hobbs* 129 h 137 c
9 b g Mister Lord(USA) —Murphys Lady (IRE) (Over The River (FR))
1861^{6} **2162**^{3} **(2637) 3176**^{P} **4098**^{5} **4374**^{5}**4496**^{P}

Willie Pep (IRE) *C R Egerton* 112b
5 b g Saddlers' Hall(IRE) —Favorable Exchange (USA) (Exceller (USA))
(3327)

Willies Way *Mrs S J Smith* 92+h
6 ch g Nomadic Way(USA) —Willies Witch (Bandmaster (USA))
138^{8} 2627^{8} 2923^{7} 4387^{2} (4988)

Willie The Shoe *Mrs John Harrington* 109h
9 b g Pyramus(USA) —Me Neither (Risk Me (FR))
5103a^{11}

Will Of The People (IRE) *M C Pipe* 130+h 71c
11 b g Supreme Leader—Another Partner (Le Bavard (FR))
127^{7} **2608**^{P} **3955**^{6}

Willou (FR) *E Lemartinel*
3 b g Cardoun(FR) —Hatica (FR) (Subotica (FR))
4298a^{P}

Willow King *Michael Hourigan* 47b
5 ch g Bijou D'Inde—Willowbank (Gay Fandango (USA))
5060a^{20}

Willows Gate *P R Webber* 73h
8 b g Petoski—Croix Val Mer (Deep Run)
438^{4}

Will She Spin *J W Mullins* 68h
5 b m Master Willie—Spinayab (King Of Spain)
2558^{10} 2997^{12} 3283^{7} 4423^{5} 4577^{3}5050^{3}

Wills Wilde (IRE) *P A Fahy* 81b 126c
7 b g Oscar(IRE) —Meadow Lane (IRE) (Over The River (FR))
3528a^{5} **(5061a)**

Will Tell *S R Bowring* 50+h
8 b g Rainbow Quest(USA) —Guillem (USA) (Nijinsky (CAN))
654^{10} 1297^{14} **1741**^{P}

Willy The Slip *R H Alner* 84+h
4 b g Benny The Dip(USA) —Miss Laetitia (IRE) (Entitled)
2611^{3} 3182^{7} 3429^{8} 4033^{7} 4148^{3}4616^{8} 4824^{P}

Willy Willy *Mrs Caroline Keevil* 90c
13 ch g Master Willie—Monsoon (Royal Palace)
(79) 313^{4} **437**^{F}

Wilson Blyth *R Ford*
8 b g Puissance—Pearls (Mon Tresor)
4278^{P}

Wimbledonian *R T Phillips* 93h
7 b m Sir Harry Lewis(USA) —Ardent Love (IRE) (Ardross)
289^{3} 652^{F} 1192^{P} 1262^{8} 1367^{6}

Win Alot *M C Chapman* 89h 75+c
8 b g Aragon—Having Fun (Hard Fought)
181^{P} 370^{14} **548**^{4}**593**^{6} **674**^{P}

Winapenny (IRE) *Ferdy Murphy* 109 h
7 b g Right Win(IRE) —Penny Pauper (Pauper)
2249^{4} 2448^{2} 2878^{5} 3855^{P}

Winchester *K A Ryan* 104 h 125c
11 ch g Gunner B—Tracy Jack (David Jack)
12^{P}

Winding River (IRE) *C R Egerton* 99+h 104+c
9 b g Montelimar(USA) —Bellora (IRE) (Over The River (FR))
1233^{2}

Wind Instrument (IRE) *T R George* 125b
5 ch g Accordion—Windy Bee (IRE) (Aristocracy)
(2565) (3399) 4448^{8}

Windmill View (IRE) *F Flood* 73h
6 b m Glacial Storm(USA) —Kemchee (Kemal (FR))
2796a^{6}

Windsor Boy (IRE) *M C Pipe* 121h 134 c
9 b g Mtoto—Fragrant Belle (USA) (Al Nasr (FR))
2054^{3} **2993**^{F} **(3596) 4241**^{3} **4459**^{5}

Winds Supreme (IRE) *Ferdy Murphy* 90h 54c
7 b g Supreme Leader—Richmond Breeze (Deep Run)
1606^{P} **1835**^{U} 2453^{12} 2944^{15}(3916) 4585^{2} **4991**^{F} 14^{5}

Windygate (IRE) *A Parker* 33h
6 bb g Supreme Leader—Moscow Maid (IRE) (Moscow Society (USA))
3237^{8} 4519^{6} 4720^{14}

Windy Hills *N G Richards* 101+h
6 bl g Overbury(IRE) —Chinook's Daughter (IRE) (Strong Gale)
2262^{3} 2947^{3} 4313^{4}

Windy Spirit (IRE) *Evan Williams* 93 h 108c
11 br g Religiously(USA) —Golden Gale (Strong Gale)
413^{P} **746**^{U} **865**^{3}**1078**^{2} **1177**^{2} **1269**^{2}**1334**^{4} **1829**^{4} **2005**^{4}**2458**^{P} **3017**^{6} 3715^{2}

Windyx (FR) *M C Pipe* 73h
5 gr g Linamix(FR) —Windy Gulch (USA) (Gulch (USA))
3463[12] 3685[9] 3963[8] 4290[10] 4941[F]

Wine Fountain (IRE) *A J Martin* 116h
6 bb g Supreme Leader—Millflower (Millfontaine)
5103a[7]

Wine River (IRE) *John R Upson*
7 b g Muroto—Croom River (IRE) (Over The River (FR))
2507[14] 3685[P]

Wing Of Fire (GER) *P Hughes* 105h
6 ch g Waky Nao—Windbraut (GER) (Big Shuffle (USA))
5082a[F]

Wings Of Hope (IRE) *James Richardson* 97 c
10 b g Treasure Hunter—She's Got Wings (Bulldozer)
79[2] 221[4] 3819[5]4079[3] 4831[2]

Wink And Whisper *Mrs H M Tory* 90h 114c
11 b m Gunner B—Lady Hannah (Daring March)
5020[4]

Winnie Wild *Miss T Jackson*
9 b m Primitive Rising(USA) —Wild Child (Grey Ghost)
4791[P]

Winning Counsel (IRE) *K F O'Brien* 103b
4 br f Leading Counsel(USA) —Dainty Daisy (IRE) (Buckskin (FR))
5134a[4]

Winning Dream (IRE) *Oliver McKiernan* 116c
12 b g Hollow Hand—Lottosprite (IRE) (Sandalay)
69a[P]

Winsley *O Sherwood* 124h 124c
8 gr g Sula Bula—Dissolve (Sharrood (USA))
104[3] (1644) 2239[2]2725[2] 3803[3] 4605[7]5126[2]

Winslow Boy (USA) *P Monteith* 84+h
5 bb g Expelled(USA) —Acusteal (USA) (Acaroid (USA))
942[4] 1097[3] 1202[3] 1293[7]

Wins Now *T Doumen* 87+h
5 ch h Croco Rouge(IRE) —Valdaia (Sadler's Wells (USA))
3388[6] 3996[11]

Winsome Wendy (IRE) *P A Pritchard*
6 b m Mister Lord(USA) —Gayley Gale (IRE) (Strong Gale)
2507[16] 2720[17] 4017[P]

Winter Brook *J A Geake* 50b
8 b m Alderbrook—Oats For Notes (Oats)
201[P]

Winter Coral (FR) *Mrs N S Evans* 80h
4 ch f Pennekamp(USA) —Winter Water (FR) (No Pass No Sale)
1095[9] 2069[8] 2580[6] 3280[8] 3550[4]4013[P]

Winter Garden *Miss Lucinda V Russell* 100h 107+c
12 ch g Old Vic—Winter Queen (Welsh Pageant)
303[3] 421[4] 717[P]873[5] 940[6] **1292[P]**

Winter Sport (IRE) *P J Hobbs* 78h
5 b g Oscar(IRE) —Amber Ballad (Ballad Rock)
2056[3] 2579[7] 3023[10]

Winter Star *J J Lambe* 100b
6 b g Overbury(IRE) —Pepper Star (IRE) (Salt Dome (USA))
(2906)

Win The Toss *P York* 47h 91c
14 b g Idiots Delight—Mayfield (USA) (Alleged (USA))
52[6]

Wiscalitus (GER) *Miss Venetia Williams* 118h
7 b g Lead On Time(USA) —Wiscaria (GER) (Ashmore (FR))
117a[16] 571[2] 1010[9] 3650[9]

Wise Counsel (IRE) *T J Taaffe* 92c
8 bb g Leading Counsel(USA) —Lilly's Way (Golden Love)
112a[7]

Wiseguy (IRE) *J Howard Johnson* 95h
7 b g Darshaan—Bibliotheque (USA) (Woodman (USA))
147[5] (Dead)

Wise Man (IRE) *N W Alexander*
11 ch g Mister Lord(USA) —Ballinlonig Star (Black Minstrel)
62[4] 3855[5] **4345[P]**4724[P] **4843[P]**

Wise Tale *P D Niven* 101 h
7 b g Nashwan(USA) —Wilayif (USA) (Danzig (USA))
1319[P] (1486) (1552) 1606[2] 1760[3]

Wishin And Hopin *A G Newcombe* 94b
5 b g Danzig Connection(USA) —Trina's Pet (Efisio)
1969[U]

Wishwillow Lord (IRE) *Leonard Whitmore* 128h
7 b g Lord Americo—The Mrs (Mandalus)
(4951a)

Witch Power *A M Crow* 90h
5 b m Accondy(IRE) —Apprila (Bustino)
2028[4] 2948[16] 3381[5] 3914[P] 5091[4]

Witch Wind *A M Crow* 101+h
6 b g Accondy(IRE) —Marie Zephyr (Treboro (USA))
2447[2] 2947[6] 3205[7] 4529[P]

With Due Respect *N A Twiston-Davies*
6 b g Classic Cliche(IRE) —Sparkling Cinders (Netherkelly)
2815[P] 3277[P]

With Honours *T J Fitzgerald* 49h
4 b f Bien Bien(USA) —Fair Test (Fair Season)
2167[P] 2494[6] 2753[10] 3787[9]

Without A Doubt *Carl Llewellyn* 122h 134c
7 b g Singspiel(IRE) —El Rabab (USA) (Roberto (USA))
(2044) 2531[3] 3288[4]4089[2] 4460[5] 4833[2]

Without Pretense (USA) *N G Ayliffe* 75h
8 b g St Jovite(USA) —Spark Of Success (USA) (Topsider (USA))
4101[5] 4731[5]

Witness Run (IRE) *N J Gifford* 103+h
6 b g Witness Box(USA) —Early Run (Deep Run)
2865[4] 3369[6] 3677[7] (4581) 4868[4]

Witness Time (IRE) *B J Eckley* 104+h 90c
10 b g Witness Box(USA) —Lisnacoilla (Beau Chapeau)
289[F] 652[6] 814[8] **2564[7]3148[P]** (4549)

Wizard Of Edge *R J Hodges* 116 h 103+c
6 b g Wizard King—Forever Shineing (Glint Of Gold)
1971[P] 2488[P] 2729[5]3126[2] 3243[2] (3465) 4288[3] (4675) 5027[6]

Wizard Roc *N E Berry* 33b
4 b g Wizard King—Rocky Revival (Roc Imp)
2425[17]

Wizards Princess *D W Thompson* 29h
6 b m Wizard King—Chalice (Governor General)
715[P] 780[10] 991[P]

Wiz The Dove *C J Price*
5 b m Wizard King—Deadly Dove (Little Wolf)
2704[B] 2937[P]

Wizzical Lad *B N Pollock* 43h
6 ch g Selkirk(USA) —Entente Cordiale (USA) (Affirmed (USA))
1445[P] 1565[12] 1857[8] 2298[8]

Wogan *N J Henderson* 123+h
6 b g Presenting—Fall About (Comedy Star (USA))
2528[2] (3342) 4094[2] 4373[5]

Wolds Way *T D Easterby* 79h
4 b g Mujahid(USA) —Off Camera (Efisio)
(2520) 4072[4] 4507[7]

Wold Top *M W Easterby*
5 ch m Defacto(USA) —Mrs Mills (Ballad Rock)
3353[13] (Dead)

Wolf Creek (IRE) *E J O'Grady* 107h 134+c
6 b g Anshan—Sleeven Lady (Crash Course)
4460[4] 5131a[2]

Wolf Hammer (USA) *J Howard Johnson*
4 ch g Diesis—Polly's Link (USA) (Phone Trick (USA))
2076[P]

Wonderkid *A J Martin* 108+c
6 b g Classic Cliche(IRE) —Mulloch Brae (Sunyboy)
(5128a)

Wondersobright (IRE) *K J Burke* 83+h 98c
7 br g Magical Wonder(USA) —Brightness (Elegant Air)
4387[4] **4552[7] 5047[4]**

Wont Leave An Oat (IRE) *William P Murphy* 86h 110c
7 b m Beneficial—Playwright (Furry Glen)
4542a[F]

Woodbine Willie (IRE) *Philip Fenton* 119b
5 b g Zaffaran(USA) —Good Foundation (IRE) (Buckskin (FR))
2782a[4]

Woodenbridge Dream (IRE) *R Lee* 59h 94 c
9 b g Good Thyne(USA) —Local Dream (Deep Run)
744[3] 896[P] 2287[3]2684[6] 2960[2] 3368[3]4426[3]

Woodford Consult *M W Easterby* 83h
4 b f Benny The Dip(USA) —Chicodove (In The Wings)
2001[P] 2442[5] 2676[4] (3442) 3674[0] 4360[4]

Woodlands Genpower (IRE) *P A Pritchard* 125 h 125+c
8 gr g Roselier(FR) —Cherished Princess (IRE) (Kemal (FR))
2184[3] **2660[2] 2812[4]3480[3] 4016[5] 4287[6]**4579[5]

Woodstock Express *P Bowen* 66h
6 b g Alflora(IRE) —Young Tess (Teenoso (USA))
1454[P]

Woodview (IRE) *K C Bailey* 97h 97c
7 ch g Flemensfirth(USA) —Marys Bard (Le Bavard (FR))
2461[4] 2815[3] **3372[4]** 4071[2]**4576[5]** 4849[12] **5049[5]**

Woody Glen (IRE) *A J Martin* 86h 44c
9 b g Wood Chanter—Gipsey Jo (Furry Glen)
859[10]

Woody Valentine (USA) *Miss Venetia Williams* 121h
5 ch g Woodman(USA) —Mudslinger (USA) (El Gran Senor (USA))
100[2] (467) 2746[4] 3256[3] 3615[4] 4058[8]4663[10] 5113[3]

Woolfall Princess *G G Margarson* 56b
7 b m Double Eclipse(IRE) —Emerald Dawn (Seymour Hicks (FR))
179[12] 507[9] 656[10]

Woolstone Boy (USA) *K C Bailey* 75h
5 ch g Will's Way(USA) —My Pleasure (USA) (Marfa (USA))
1302[11] 1562[5] 2460[P] 4898[P]

Word Gets Around (IRE) *L Lungo* 105+h 101+c
8 b g King's Ride—Kate Fisher (IRE) (Over The River (FR))
61[8] 320[5] 1838[P] **2476[2](3270) 3489[P]**

Workaway *M Keighley* 94h 105+c
10 b g Alflora(IRE) —Annicombe Run (Deep Run)
437[F]

Working Class Hero *J M Jefferson* 63c
7 b g Royal Applause—Dream Baby (Master Willie)
593[8]

Worlaby Dale *Mrs S Lamyman* 93h 103 c
10 b g Terimon—Restandbethankful (Random Shot)
1210[5] 1343[2] 1549[3]

World Vision (IRE) *Ferdy Murphy* 99+h 117c
9 ch g Denel(FR) —Dusty Lane (IRE) (Electric)
112a[5] 321[2] 1664[6]1989[P] 2143[5] 2905[2]3350[P]

World Wide Web (IRE) *Jonjo O'Neill* 122h 105c
10 b g Be My Native(USA) —Meldrum Lass (Buckskin (FR))
2175[9] 2483[5] **3022[P] 3877[3]4496[P]**

Worth A Glance *H D Daly* 78h
5 b g Thowra(FR) —Henry's True Love (Random Shot)
3583[U] 4333[13] 4935[7]

Worthy Man *Mrs E England* 64 h 52+c
9 b g Homo Sapien—Marnworth (Funny Man)
79[7] 278[P]

Wotabirthday *S C Burrough*
4 b g Makbul—Surfers Paradise (Safawan)
2611[P] 4758[P]

Wot About Me (IRE) *Mrs C J Ikin*
11 b g Jolly Jake(NZ) —Time Please (Welsh Saint)
632[P]

Wotabroad *K G Reveley*
8 b m Broadsword(USA) —Bosom Friend (Bustomi)
1722[P]

Wotan (IRE) *R Curtis* 57h
8 ch g Wolfhound(USA) —Triple Tricks (IRE) (Royal Academy (USA))
903[P] 978[14]

Wotashambles (IRE) *P R Webber* 61h
5 b g Shambo—Rent Day (Town And Country)
7[3] 3246[9] 3369[11]

Wotchalike (IRE) *R J Price* 84+h
4 ch c Spectrum(IRE) —Juno Madonna (IRE) (Sadler's Wells (USA))
2756[7]

Wot No Cash *R C Harper* 82c
14 gr g Ballacashtal(CAN) —Madame Non (My Swanee)
4936[P]

Wot Way Chief *J M Jefferson* 87h
5 b g Defacto(USA) —Wych Willow (Hard Fought)
2720[14] 2987[13] 3347[7] 3963[5] 4532[9]

Would You Believe *P J Hobbs* 121c
10 gr g Derrylin—Ramelton (Precipice Wood)
4078[5] (4576) (4876)

Wozani Dancer (IRE) *G A Huffer* 68h
4 b g Danehill Dancer(IRE) —Lauretta Blue (IRE) (Bluebird (USA))
1737[9]

Wozzeck *R H Buckler* 83h
6 b g Groom Dancer(USA) —Opera Lover (IRE) (Sadler's Wells (USA))
683[10] 1075[6] 1187[8]

Wrags To Riches (IRE) *J D Frost* 102h 132c
9 b g Tremblant—Clonea Lady (IRE) (Lord Ha Ha)
1881[P] 2310[3] **2622[2]3019[P]**

Wrangel (FR) *Mrs S M Johnson* 90+h 66c
12 ch g Tropular—Swedish Princess (Manado)
458[P] 573[F]

Wraparound You (IRE) *Norman Sanderson* 20h
9 b g Shernazar—Wraparound Sue (Touch Paper)
4146[3] 4347[P]

Wrapitup (IRE) *Mrs Joanne Brown* 71c
8 ch g Aristocracy—Lanesboro Lights (IRE) (Millfontaine)
3847[F] 4594[7]

Wrens Island (IRE) *R Dickin* 83c
12 br g Yashgan—Tipiton (Balboa)
865[P] 975[3] 1041[P]1178[P] 1321[P]

Wun Chai (IRE) *A E Jones* 95+h 88+c
7 b g King's Theatre(IRE) —Flower From Heaven (Baptism)
288[U] 389[P] **666[6]**

Wychbury (USA) *Mrs H Dalton* 77h
5 ch g Swain(IRE) —Garden Rose (IRE) (Caerleon (USA))
2070[5] 2950[9]

Wyldello *A King* 109+b
5 b m Supreme Leader—Clonmello (Le Bavard (FR))
3244[2] (3961) 4376[2] 4751[2]

Wyle Post (IRE) *Mrs K Waldron* 88h 74c
7 ch g Mister Lord(USA) —Daffydown Dolly (IRE) (The Parson)
4167[F] 4349[3] 4638[3]

Wyn Dixie (IRE) *W Amos* 95+h
7 b g Great Commotion(USA) —Duchess Affair (IRE) (Digamist (USA))
551[4] 716[2] 873[6] 1665[8]

Wynford Eagle *R H Alner*
7 b g Sula Bula—Tawny Silk (Little Buskins)
1781[6] 1976[P] 2607[7]

Wynyard Dancer *Miss T Jackson* 74c
12 b m Minster Son—The White Lion (Flying Tyke)
555[3]

Wyoming *John Allen* 84h
5 ch m Inchinor—Shoshone (Be My Chief (USA))
251[1] 651[2]

Xaipete (IRE) *R C Guest* 104h 118c
14 b g Jolly Jake(NZ) —Rolfete (USA) (Tom Rolfe)
84[2] 346[2] 761[4]1049[5] 1099[4] **1150[P]** (Dead)

Xamborough (FR) *B G Powell* 108h
5 b g Starborough—Sudden Spirit (FR) (Esprit Du Nord (USA))
2099[4] 2423[3] 2730[6] 3257[6] 3848[4]4093[4] 5021[9]

Xcentra *B G Powell* 80h
5 b g Docksider(USA) —Dicentra (Rambo Dancer (CAN))
277[3] 685[4] 4754[6] 5024[F]

Xellance (IRE) *P J Hobbs* 128h 118c
9 b g Be My Guest(USA) —Excellent Alibi (USA) (Exceller (USA))
450[6] (824) 1010[13] 1270[8] (1434) 1548[4]
1744[F]2051[4] 4[2]

Xila Fontenailles (FR) *N J Hawke* 97h
5 gr m Turgeon(USA) —Miss Fontenailles (FR) (Kautokeino (FR))
1491[5] 1898[7] 2309[5] 2850[9] 2995[9]3950[P]

Yaboya (IRE) *P J Hobbs* 128+h
7 b g King's Theatre(IRE) —Oh Jemima (Captain James)
2421[4] 2873[2] (3677) 4373[3]

Yaiyna Tango (FR) *Miss L Day* 84+h 77c
11 br g Fijar Tango(FR) —Yaiyna (FR) (Lashkari)
4640[3] 4783[2]

Yakareem (IRE) *D G Bridgwater* 101h 84c
10 b g Rainbows For Life(CAN) —Brandywell (Skyliner)
1219[2] 1414[P]

Yameell *David Marnane* 99h
4 b g King's Best(USA) —Maid Of Kashmir (IRE) (Dancing Brave (USA))
5076a[10]

Yammy Wilson (IRE) *S Donohoe* 92h
5 b g Lord Americo—Katie Lowe (IRE) (Pollerton)
4344[P]

Yankee Crossing (IRE) *Ferdy Murphy* 82+h
8 b g Lord Americo—Ath Leathan (Royal Vulcan)
147[P] (Dead)

Yankeedoodledandy (IRE) *B G Powell* 135 h
5 b g Orpen(USA) —Laura Margaret (Persian Bold)
1828[P]

Yankee Holiday (IRE) *Mrs S C Bradburne* 75+h
6 b g Oscar(IRE) —Parloop (IRE) (Buckley)
1532[14] 1834[9] 2024[P] 2448[5] 2878[P]4916[8] 5093[8]

Yann's (FR) *R T Phillips* 125h 116 c
10 b g Hellios(USA) —Listen Gyp (USA) (Advocator)
516[P] 2703[3] 3212[9]3326[7] 3578[6]

Yardbird (IRE) *A King* 114 h 134+c
7 b g Moonax(IRE) —Princess Lizzie (IRE) (Homo Sapien)
2174[P] (3000) 3469[4](4617) 4960[3]

Yarra Maguire (IRE) *Noel Meade* 116h
7 b g Shernazar—Balingale (Balinger)
5078a[11]

Yassar (IRE) *D J Wintle* 97c
11 b g Yashgan—Go Hunting (IRE) (Abednego)
1191[P] (1907) 2465[P](2984) 3686[4] 4348[6]

Yellow Soil Star (IRE) *J J Lambe* 91h
7 b m Perugino(USA) —Standing Ovation (Godswalk (USA))
1064[3] 1356[3]

Yenaled *P S McEntee* 99+h
9 gr g Rambo Dancer(CAN) —Fancy Flight (FR) (Arctic Tern (USA))
3978[P] 4149[4] (4388) 4763[11]

Yeoman (FR) *D J Ryan* 76h
5 b g Valanjou(FR) —Yamashina (IRE) (Kahyasi)
3003a[13]

Yeoman Sailor (IRE) *Miss Grace Muir* 119c
12 gr g Roselier(FR) —Liffey Lady (Camden Town)
453[2] 3910[6] 4607[3]4975[2]

Yer Father's Yacht (IRE) *Lady Connell* 96+h
6 b g Desert Story(IRE) —Alchiea (Alzao (USA))
451[P]

Yes My Lord (IRE) *M C Pipe* 102 h 116+c
7 b g Mister Lord(USA) —Lady Shalom (IRE) (Aylesfield)
2934[P] (3905) **(4163) 4690[P]**

Yes Ses Les *G Fierro* 81h
7 b g El Conquistador—Kellsboro Queen (Rakaposhi King)
1485[6] 2099[9]

Yes Sir (IRE) *P Bowen* 152 h 130 c
7 b g Needle Gun(IRE) —Miss Pushover (Push On)
127[3] (408) (420) (1204) 1828[8] **1971[6]**2209[18] 2758[5] **2953[2] 3251[5]3558[F]**

Yogi (IRE) *Thomas Foley* 152h 104c
10 ch g Glacial Storm(USA) —Good Performance VII (Damsire Unregistered)
90a[P] 1925[7] 2227a[5] 3585a[5] 5101a[9]

York Dancer *A D Smith* 67b
5 ch m Dancing Spree(USA) —York Street (USA) (Diamond Shoal)
490[14] 4680[11]

Yorker (USA) *Ms Deborah J Evans* 23h
8 b g Boundary(USA) —Shallows (USA) (Cox's Ridge (USA))
1794[15] 1890[P]

York Rite (AUS) *R C Guest* 77 h 89c
10 ch g Grand Lodge(USA) —Amazaan (NZ) (Zamazaan (FR))
858[8] 1044[5] 1065[U]1109[10] 1150[2] 1203[4]1277[6] 1376[7] 1602[7]1685[6]

You Do The Math (IRE) *L Lungo* 107h
6 b g Carroll House—Ballymave (IRE) (Jareer (USA))
82[7] 212[3] 1794[5] 2416[6] (2657) 2843[2]3234[2] 4108[2]

Youknowtheanswer *Miss L C Siddall* 39b
6 b m Brief Truce(USA) —Perfect Answer (Keen)
242[P]

Youlbesolucky (IRE) *Jonjo O'Neill* 116h
7 b g Accordion—Gaye Humour (IRE) (Montelimar (USA))
(1042) 1237[2] 1671[4] 1892[3] 2082[3] (2497) 3729[10]4119[2] 4373[8] 4589[P]

Young Albert (IRE) *N G Richards* 103b
5 br g Taipan(IRE) —Smooth Leader (IRE) (Supreme Leader)
(2948) 4779[13]

Young Blade *C Grant* 52h
5 b g Cloudings(IRE) —Lady Shoco (Montekin)
3742[11] 4147[12] 4720[11]

Young Bobby *P Beaumont* 78b
6 b g Gunner B—Trikkala Star (Tachypous)
3399[5] 3742[10]

Young Chevalier *J R Adam* 78h 107+c
9 b g Alflora(IRE) —Mrs Teasdale (Idiots Delight)
939[P] 1088[P] 1311[2]1457[P]

Young Collier *J A B Old* 110h 128+c
7 b g Vettori(IRE) —Cockatoo Island (High Top)
4037[P]

Young Dude (IRE) *Jonjo O'Neill* 99+h
7 b g Oscar(IRE) —Shuil Realt (IRE) (Jolly Jake (NZ))
4032[5] 4638[2] 4823[F]

Young Elodie (FR) *M J P O'Brien* 103h
5 ch m Freedom Cry—Irish Beauty (FR) (Irish River (FR))
5077a[23]

Young Guns (IRE) *J G M O'Shea* 92b
5 b g Turtle Island(IRE) —Glorious Bid (IRE) (Horage)
1985[9] 4554[4]

Young Lorcan *Mrs K Waldron* 91h 112c
10 ch g Bay Tern(USA) —Naughty Nessie (Celtic Cone)
(2182) **(2465)** 2862[2] 3140[2] **3578[RR]3989[3] (4348) (4499)**

Young Mr Grace (IRE) *T D Easterby*
6 b h Danetime(IRE) —Maid Of Mourne (Fairy King (USA))
1794[U]

Young Murf (IRE) *N A Twiston-Davies*
7 b g Alphabatim(USA) —Miss Iverk (Torus)
1976[P]

Young Owen *A G Juckes* 83h 102+c
8 b g Balnibarbi—Polly Potter (Pollerton)
1221[4] 1457[3] 1620[4]1754[6] 1956[LFT]

Young Patriarch *C J Mann* 108 h 81c
5 b g Silver Patriarch(IRE) —Mortify (Prince Sabo)
467[5]

Young Rocky (IRE) *C Grant* 71b
5 ch g Rock Hopper—Auntie Prickle Pin (IRE) (Sexton Blake)
1849[14] 2823[11] 3273[5]

Young Roscoe *M Mullineaux* 26h
7 b g Roscoe Blake—Royal Heiress (Amboise)
3842[9]

Young Scotton *J Howard Johnson* 72h
6 b g Cadeaux Genereux—Broken Wave (Bustino)
149[P]

Young Siouxsie *N A Twiston-Davies* 79h
6 b m Environment Friend—Rare Detail (IRE) (Commanche Run)
2446[17] 3884[6] 4286[3]

Young Smokey (IRE) *P Beaumont* 48h
5 gr g Cloudings(IRE) —Miss Aylesbury (IRE) (Le Moss)
3399[6] 4319[4] 4720[12]

Young Thomas (IRE) *James Moffatt*
4 ch g Inchinor—Splicing (Sharpo)
2442[8] 2569[P]

Young Tomo (IRE) *Miss C J Goodall* 64c
14 b g Lafontaine(USA) —Siege Queen (Tarqogan)
350[P] 512[7]

Young Tot (IRE) *M Sheppard* 93+h 85+c
8 b g Torus—Lady-K (IRE) (Rock Chanteur)
149[9] 412[4] 686[7] 1046[4] 1107[3](1645) 1856[11]
2150[14] 2721[8] **3887[10]**(4941)

Young Warrior (IRE) *M D Hammond*
5 b g Desert Style(IRE) —Arctic Splendour (USA) (Arctic Tern (USA))
691[F] 903[P]

You Owe Me (IRE) *N A Twiston-Davies* 94h 122 c
9 b g Jurado(USA) —Bodyline (Crash Course)
(239) 1879[U] 2162[4]2724[P] 3293[6] 3989[P]4476[P]

Youpeeveecee (IRE) *Miss L V Davis* 91 h
10 b g Little Bighorn—Godlike (Godswalk (USA))
1711[8] 1903[12] 2073[P]

Your Advantage (IRE) *Miss Lucinda V Russell* 112+h 109c
6 b g Septieme Ciel(USA) —Freedom Flame (Darshaan)
60[2] 1487[6] (1682)

Your A Gassman (IRE) *Ferdy Murphy* 109 h 117 c
8 b g King's Ride—Nish Bar (Callernish)
1941[P] 2265[9] 2747[14]**4111[P]**

You're Special (USA) *Ferdy Murphy* 122h 146+c
9 b g Northern Flagship(USA) —Pillow Mint (USA) (Stage Door Johnny (USA))
1881[P] 2102[3] 2451[6]2703[2] (2767) 3420[P](4447)
5144[F]

You'Re The Man (IRE) *Mrs E Slack* 86h
9 b g Lapierre—Another Advantage (IRE) (Roselier (FR))
80[4] 215[8] 2066[P] 3209[P] **3338[F]**

Yourman (IRE) *M C Pipe* 126h
6 b g Shernazar—Lantern Lover (Be My Native (USA))
1125[4] 1436[2] (1525) (1641) 1830[2]

Your My Angel (IRE) *J A Supple* 72h
10 b m Commanche Run—Marshtown Fair (IRE) (Camden Town)
1367[P]

Your The One (IRE) *Joseph Crowley* 108h 100c
7 b g Eurobus—Saphfinna (IRE) (Satco (FR))
2782a[6]

Yufo (IRE) *N J Gifford*
6 ch g Invited(USA) —Smart Lass (Martinmas)
1922[2]

Yukon Jack *N J Pomfret* 44h
8 b g Tharqaam(IRE) —Spanish Mermaid (Julio Mariner)
4905[P]

Yvanovitch (FR) *Mrs L C Taylor* 98 h 113+c
8 b g Kaldounevees(FR) —County Kerry (FR) (Comrade In Arms)
76[F] 386[P]

Zabadou *F Kirby* 56h
5 b g Abou Zouz(USA) —Strapped (Reprimand)
2245[9] 2567[13]

Zabenz (NZ) *P J Hobbs* 132 h 143+c
9 b g Zabeel(NZ) —In The Country (NZ) (In The Purple (FR))
1917[3] 2311[4] (2564) 2743[2] 2973[2] 4444[5]4759[4]
5004[9]

Zacatecas (GER) *M Scudamore* 79h
6 gr g Grand Lodge(USA) —Zephyrine (IRE) (Highest Honor (FR))
4754[7] 4868[3]

Zaccheus (IRE) *Comdt W S Hayes* 104h
4 b g Zafonic(USA) —Sudeley (Dancing Brave (USA))
4122a[5] 5076a[21]

Zadok The Priest (IRE) *B S Rothwell* 72h
6 bb g Zafonic(USA) —Valencay (IRE) (Sadler's Wells (USA))
1643[8]

Zaffamore (IRE) *Miss H C Knight* 90b 120 c
10 ch g Zaffaran(USA) —Furmore (Furry Glen)
2299[6] 2724[5] 3000[7]4906[4]

Zaffaran Express (IRE) *N G Richards* 114+h
7 b m Zaffaran(USA) —Majestic Run (Deep Run)
302[3] 2004[4] 2977[2] (3648) 4972[3]

Zaffarsson (IRE) *J S Moore* 68b
5 ch g Zaffaran(USA) —Sheelin Bavard (Le Bavard (FR))
4622[9] 4909[16]

Zaffie Parson (IRE) *G A Harker* 73h
5 b m Zaffaran(USA) —Katie Parson (The Parson)
(2028) 2446[9] 3337[8] 3551[5] 4313[5] 4919[7]

Zaffiera (IRE) *M D Hammond* 25h
5 b g Zaffaran(USA) —Kiera's Gale (IRE) (Strong Gale)
1915[10] 2186[12] **2415[6] 2764[9]3553[P]** 4341[P] **4921[F]**

Zaffisfaction *K C Bailey* 49h
6 b m Zaffaran(USA) —Anaconda (IRE) (Le Moss)
464[P]

Zaffre (IRE) *Miss Z C Davison* 97h
7 gr m Mtoto—Zeferina (IRE) (Sadler's Wells (USA))
367[3] 654[3] 1014[P] 1245[3]

Zaffre D'Or (IRE) *M J McGrath* 65h 67c
9 b g Zaffaran(USA) —Massinetta (Bold Lad (IRE))
3907[P] 4321[P]

Zagreus (GER) *F E Sutherland*
4 gr g Fasliyev(USA) —Zephyrine (IRE) (Highest Honor (FR))
1718[P] 4877[11]

Zahunda (IRE) *M J Gingell* 75h
7 b m Spectrum(IRE) —Gift Of Glory (FR) (Niniski (USA))
14[9] 1064[6] 1113[5] 1209[P] 1297[16]1883[P] 2256[9] 2806[P]

Zaiyad (IRE) *A Chaille-Chaille* 133h
5 b g Sadler's Wells(USA) —Zaila (IRE) (Darshaan)
4443[9]

Zakley *Mrs C Lawrence*
10 b g Sula Bula—Summer Bride (Harvest Sun)
4946[P]

Zalda *P J Hobbs* 122h
5 ch m Zilzal(USA) —Gold Luck (USA) (Slew O'Gold (USA))
1677[2] 4641[7] 4832[5]

Zamnah (IRE) *F J Bowles* 118 h 84c
8 ch m Naheez(USA) —Shazam (IRE) (Magical Strike (USA))
5103a[9]

Zandeed (IRE) *A C Whillans* 59h
8 b g Inchinor—Persian Song (Persian Bold)
2448[7] 2942[12]

Zando *E G Bevan* 82h
4 b g Forzando—Rockin' Rosie (Song)
2001[6] (2245) 2481[P]

Zanzibar Boy *H Morrison* 86+h
7 gr g Arzanni—Bampton Fair (Free Boy)
(2432) 3789[5] 4238[6] 4581[5]

Zarakash (IRE) *Jonjo O'Neill* 95+h
6 b g Darshaan—Zarannda (IRE) (Last Tycoon)
826[3] 895[2] (959) 1202[P] 5111[3]

Zarbeau *J M Jefferson* 60b
4 ch g Zaha(CAN) —Isabeau (Law Society (USA))
3785[10] 4909[17] 5041[8]

Zaydar (IRE) *Paul Nolan* 96h
6 br g Dr Devious(IRE) —Zayana (IRE) (Darshaan)
67a[16]

Zealand *R A Fahey* 60h
6 ch g Zamindar(USA) —Risanda (Kris)
1757[7] 1927[9]

Zeis (IRE) *Miss J R Gibney* 83 h
6 ch g Bahhare(USA) —Zoom Lens (IRE) (Caerleon (USA))
1233[U] 1302[4] 1362[3] 2721[10] 2958[P]

Zeitgeist (IRE) *J Howard Johnson* 108 h
5 b g Singspiel(IRE) —Diamond Quest (Rainbow Quest (USA))
(3167) 3780[3] 4301[5]

Zeloso *M F Harris* 90 h
8 b g Alzao(USA) —Silk Petal (Petorius)
1747[2] 1949[6] 2073[4] (2586) (2806) 2964[U]
3279[9]3661[9] 4133[2] 4449[4] 4652[5] 4869[4]

Zenaide (IRE) *Mrs Louise Parkhill* 107+b
5 bb m Zaffaran(USA) —Native Craft (IRE) (Be My Native (USA))
5104a[2]

Zen Garden *W M Brisbourne* 80b
5 b m Alzao(USA) —Maze Garden (USA) (Riverman (USA))
844[4]

Zeroberto (IRE) *D K Weld* 110h
6 ch g Definite Article—Blazing Soul (IRE) (Common Grounds)
5078a[21]

Zesta Fiesta *A R Finch* 35b 55c
6 b g El Conquistador—Little Lemon (Spartan Jester)
4946[U] 5116[9]

Zeta's River (IRE) *M C Pipe* 144 c
8 ch g Over The River(FR) —Laurebon (Laurence O)
1879[P] 3296[P] 4447[P]

Zeydnaa (IRE) *C R Wilson* 30h
6 b g Bahhare(USA) —Hadawah (USA) (Riverman (USA))
415[12] 1722[P]

Zhivago's Princess (IRE) *P T Dalton* 89b
4 b f Orpen(USA) —Collage (Ela-Mana-Mou)
2013[2] 2425[4] 5075[3]

Zibeline (IRE) *B Ellison* 113+h 102c
9 b g Cadeaux Genereux—Zia (USA) (Shareef Dancer (USA))
2175[8] **2456[5]** 2747[15]

Ziggy Zen *C J Mann* 111h
7 br g Muhtarram(USA) —Springs Welcome (Blakeney)
(1) 332[8] 1633[6]

Zilla (FR) *Miss Lucy Bridges* 60+h
5 ch m Gold Away(IRE) —Zarah (FR) (Zino)
2148[11] 2619[P] 2728[6] 3321[5]

Zimbabwe *G L Moore* 118 h
6 b g Kahyasi—Zeferina (IRE) (Sadler's Wells (USA))
2247[U]

Zimbabwe (FR) *N J Hawke* 93 h 93+c
6 b g Turgeon(USA) —Razzamatazz (FR) (Always Fair (USA))
1780[9] 2610[6] 2863[7]3252[F] 3923[2] 4328[P]4553[4]
4785[3]

Zipalong Lad (IRE) *P Bowen* 134+h
6 b g Zaffaran(USA) —Rosy Posy (IRE) (Roselier (FR))
1833[P] 2497[3] (3184) (3978) 4469[8] 4765[4] 4980[2]

Zola (IRE) *Mrs J Sidebottom* 55c
10 ch g Indian Ridge—Fluella (Welsh Pageant)
3805[8] 4107[4]

Zolash (IRE) *Mrs L C Jewell* 34h
4 b g General Monash(USA) —Zolba (IRE) (Classic Secret (USA))
3429[7] 3659[12]

Zoltano (GER) *M Todhunter* 92 h
8 b g In The Wings—Zarella (GER) (Anatas)
2372[3] 2944[4]

Zonergem *Lady Herries* 125+h
8 ch g Zafonic(USA) —Anasazi (IRE) (Sadler's Wells (USA))
450[14] 1010[8]

Zonic Boom (FR) *Mrs H Dalton* 98+h
6 bb g Zafonic(USA) —Rosi Zambotti (IRE) (Law Society (USA))
1364[P] 2423[5] 3591[4]

Zouave (IRE) *C J Mann* 92h
5 b g Spectrum(IRE) —Lady Windley (Baillamont (USA))
1757[3] 1898[4] 2147[P] 3415[5] 4210[2]

Zubrowsko (FR) *J A Geake* 47h
5 b g Nikos—Tinozakia (FR) (General Holme (USA))
4935[13]

Zuleta *B D Leavy* 70h
5 ch m Vettori(IRE) —Victoria (Old Vic)
3[F] 943[F]

Zumrah (IRE) *P Bowen* 101+h
5 b g Machiavellian(USA) —The Perfect Life (IRE) (Try My Best (USA))
(769) 876[3] 1235[9] 1302[2] 1654[3]

Zum See (IRE) *Noel Meade* 122 h 130c
7 ch g Perugino(USA) —Drew (IRE) (Double Schwartz)
67a[17] **1626a[6] 4018a[2]4472[9] 5100a[5]**

Zurs (IRE) *J J Lambe* 104h 93+c
13 b g Tirol—Needy (High Top)
644[F] 874[P] 989[P]1065[P]

Zuzu Summit (IRE) *M Scudamore* 89b
4 ch f Pasternak—Summit Else (El Conquistador)
2425[3] 4976[14]

Zygomatic *R F Fisher* 90h
8 ch g Risk Me(FR) —Give Me A Day (Lucky Wednesday)
768[2] 1280[2]

Owner Season Statistics - British Jumps 2005-2006

NAME	WINS-RUNS	2nd	3rd	4th	WIN PRIZE	TOTAL PRIZE	£1 STAKE
John P McManus	66-463 (14%)	61	47	43	597,729.60	1,060,965.27	-85.74
D A Johnson	57-392 (15%)	48	41	31	678,202.78	921,343.53	-117.48
Trevor Hemmings	36-254 (14%)	32	20	22	323,541.07	733,333.66	-27.64
Sir Robert Ogden	29-156 (19%)	26	18	14	411,481.35	526,689.88	-15.08
Andrea & Graham Wylie	36-180 (20%)	23	13	14	298,336.94	401,572.60	-19.53
O B P Carroll	1-1 (100%)	0	0	0	399,140.00	399,140.00	+11.00
The Stewart Family	14-69 (20%)	14	6	8	147,549.75	337,342.87	-32.41
Mrs Gay Smith	17-89 (19%)	13	5	11	240,128.24	294,212.46	+7.63
Gigginstown Ho'se Stud	1-2 (50%)	0	0	0	228,080.00	228,080.00	+6.50
J Hales	11-32 (34%)	3	5	6	171,465.71	221,502.46	+4.09
Winfield,Longman et al	3-5 (60%)	2	0	0	185,009.00	212,932.00	+18.91
Novices Syndicate	1-1 (100%)	0	0	0	202,683.30	202,683.30	+1.75
Mrs R J Skan	4-20 (20%)	4	1	3	135,749.74	194,066.50	+7.50
W J Brown	5-15 (33%)	1	2	3	150,677.48	172,759.77	+16.67
Terry Warner	9-49 (18%)	3	8	4	159,074.72	172,314.88	-10.67
Paul Barber/Mrs Findlay	7-20 (35%)	6	3	1	60,315.19	168,386.17	-3.68
M G St Quinton	2-20 (10%)	6	6	2	41,167.75	165,712.00	-5.50
Mrs Mary T Hayes	1-1 (100%)	0	0	0	165,358.00	165,358.00	+16.00
Jim Lewis	7-42 (17%)	2	4	7	89,618.61	155,201.60	+3.37
Paul Beck	20-154 (13%)	15	15	17	105,829.75	146,309.63	-45.03
Ashleybank Inv. Limited	18-95 (19%)	12	11	6	106,584.00	144,084.65	-33.95
J B Webb	7-49 (14%)	11	5	2	72,169.55	143,279.35	-20.90
Keith Nicholson	11-85 (13%)	12	13	7	102,912.64	141,911.64	-12.50
Mrs Karola Vann	5-31 (16%)	6	3	0	95,265.50	139,264.90	-10.27
Clive D Smith	2-24 (8%)	3	2	2	99,785.00	139,154.90	-13.00
Million In Mind Partners.	10-37 (27%)	6	4	2	80,022.77	137,838.47	-4.85
Conor Clarkson	1-2 (50%)	0	1	0	114,040.00	130,105.00	+0.38
Paul Green	10-37 (27%)	7	1	1	106,936.47	122,094.47	+1.97
A J Sendell	1-5 (20%)	2	0	0	85,530.00	120,825.00	+4.00
B Perkins	3-17 (18%)	4	1	2	109,452.80	118,038.94	+30.50
Jim Ennis	6-33 (18%)	7	4	2	38,941.75	117,615.16	-6.42
A Fisher/Mrs JFisher	3-23 (13%)	6	2	5	31,336.49	110,358.15	-15.31
B A Kilpatrick	7-36 (19%)	2	2	2	98,175.39	110,097.03	+18.61
Robert Waley-Cohen	3-31 (10%)	3	4	2	91,144.92	109,403.63	-1.50
D M Forster	2-13 (15%)	2	1	2	82,495.86	109,226.84	+8.50
E R Hanbury	5-13 (38%)	3	1	0	69,210.51	107,881.27	+9.85
Mrs Jane Williams	7-44 (16%)	1	9	5	78,799.41	106,708.14	+12.75
Peter Hart	6-18 (33%)	4	2	2	81,899.55	102,971.06	-1.59
Mr & Mrs Peter Orton	8-26 (31%)	2	3	2	82,735.91	101,777.56	+18.53
Mrs M Findlay	10-33 (30%)	4	4	3	89,309.14	101,594.47	+10.29
D Allen	15-59 (25%)	6	10	4	79,644.81	100,600.33	+47.75
D P Sharkey	2-4 (50%)	0	0	0	99,785.00	99,785.00	+7.41
Alan Peterson	5-29 (17%)	7	3	2	42,410.11	94,996.64	-12.47
Lady Lloyd-Webber	4-7 (57%)	1	1	0	72,144.49	89,498.81	+16.50
Mr & Mrs R A Green	10-125 (8%)	14	5	19	53,530.86	88,594.46	-68.58
Mrs S McCloy	1-2 (50%)	0	0	0	85,932.00	87,942.00	+13.00
Jack Joseph	11-76 (14%)	12	7	10	54,585.55	87,710.33	+7.61
George Ward	11-69 (16%)	11	6	2	58,790.28	86,870.03	-4.56
C J Harriman	2-16 (13%)	2	3	3	61,404.10	86,231.57	+0.91
Mrs C A Moore	1-2 (50%)	0	0	0	85,530.00	85,530.00	+3.00

Trainer Season Statistics - British Jumps 2005-2006

NAME	WINS-RUNS	2nd	3rd	4th	WIN PRIZE	TOTAL PRIZE	£1 STAKE
P F Nicholls	148-651 (23%)	103	71	68	1,565,591	2,404,288	-113.02
P J Hobbs	112-659 (17%)	82	79	66	1,058,393	1,631,939	-107.95
M C Pipe	112-880 (13%)	107	84	77	1,083,999	1,578,888	-287.58
Jonjo O'Neill	105-711 (15%)	88	65	60	759,693	1,194,883	-176.52
N J Henderson	85-390 (22%)	44	43	36	791,736	1,058,137	+43.42
A King	63-415 (15%)	61	43	41	616,152	967,442	-1.45
Mrs S J Smith	60-412 (15%)	45	42	35	484,000	713,556	-20.64
Miss V Williams	77-475 (16%)	67	42	41	432,630	662,814	-43.79
J H Johnson	58-331 (18%)	35	22	25	420,916	568,327	-46.71
N G Richards	59-277 (21%)	41	31	19	322,242	566,026	-16.86
G L Moore	63-452 (14%)	51	56	35	324,062	495,213	+17.04
R H Alner	38-352 (11%)	44	39	44	309,879	494,239	-94.13
N A Twiston-Davies	59-472 (13%)	36	36	46	327,147	486,192	-83.27
P Bowen	41-314 (13%)	38	33	27	286,603	485,662	-112.63
Ferdy Murphy	45-384 (12%)	48	34	31	300,373	461,267	-84.13
R C Guest	55-515 (11%)	49	48	60	311,995	451,180	-99.39
Martin Brassil	1-1 (100%)	0	0	0	399,140	399,140	+11.01
H D Daly	35-272 (13%)	36	23	40	242,077	390,951	-103.71
Evan Williams	56-340 (16%)	43	28	27	296,385	390,330	+97.90
Miss H C Knight	28-245 (11%)	18	23	26	243,018	359,087	-96.80
M F Morris	1-3 (33%)	2	0	0	228,080	322,598	+5.51
T R George	34-262 (13%)	31	33	33	166,938	321,740	-61.62
C R Egerton	21-85 (25%)	13	11	12	213,249	281,999	+72.45
K G Reveley	32-269 (12%)	28	26	32	169,577	272,987	-75.53
D McCain	35-300 (12%)	25	39	38	190,164	262,554	+92.04
C A Murphy	2-2 (100%)	0	0	0	259,703	259,703	+3.26
Miss E C Lavelle	30-197 (15%)	22	23	20	166,752	258,913	-15.42
W P Mullins	0-23	2	1	4	0	256,771	-23.00
C J Mann	23-181 (13%)	23	28	9	161,301	255,179	-16.91
F Doumen	4-39 (10%)	7	4	5	107,600	251,499	-14.75
Ian Williams	28-336 (8%)	40	36	33	144,657	246,320	-56.44
J L Spearing	14-113 (12%)	19	10	8	164,440	223,256	+5.51
O Sherwood	20-183 (11%)	22	21	20	117,097	218,161	-50.42
C L Tizzard	24-198 (12%)	26	26	22	113,425	211,509	-25.38
J W Mullins	22-300 (7%)	42	31	36	101,819	209,651	-84.47
B G Powell	32-330 (10%)	33	30	31	125,678	203,666	-103.27
Noel Meade	3-23 (13%)	1	0	3	162,507	203,036	+5.42
L Lungo	27-227 (12%)	18	20	19	129,896	188,239	-112.76
P C Haslam	28-157 (18%)	19	17	12	108,056	188,174	-10.76
S Gollings	13-124 (10%)	16	13	9	101,551	187,012	-28.90
Nick Williams	11-80 (14%)	5	12	6	137,918	182,473	+12.09
J M Jefferson	28-191 (15%)	17	16	18	126,739	180,933	-11.45
P R Webber	23-157 (15%)	12	21	13	109,300	168,361	+6.83
John Joseph Murphy	1-5 (20%)	0	0	0	165,358	167,368	+12.01
M Pitman	19-133 (14%)	19	16	8	97,808	162,788	+14.26
N J Gifford	14-89 (16%)	6	10	8	115,860	155,325	+26.48
Miss Lucinda V Russell	12-285 (4%)	27	29	29	72,095	150,240	-144.80
T J Taaffe	1-10 (10%)	0	2	0	114,040	143,095	-7.63
Noel T Chance	11-85 (13%)	16	17	9	93,169	134,777	-14.06
J J Quinn	19-94 (20%)	12	13	11	97,223	132,739	+7.36

Jockey Season Statistics - British Jumps 2005-2006

NAME	WINS-RUNS	2nd	3rd	4th	WIN PRIZE	TOTAL PRIZE	£1 STAKE
A P McCoy	178-828 (21%)	125	99	79	1,690,132.17	2,429,792.32	-138.48
Richard Johnson	167-911 (18%)	131	117	101	1,324,934.72	1,945,670.74	-30.48
G Lee	108-752 (14%)	88	74	71	629,123.31	907,434.56	-236.77
Tony Dobbin	91-510 (18%)	68	46	44	502,514.33	900,949.72	-122.16
Timmy Murphy	87-563 (15%)	63	56	51	925,755.69	1,252,108.08	-154.91
Christian Williams	77-548 (14%)	65	53	47	517,841.66	788,663.70	-38.12
Robert Thornton	73-605 (12%)	83	67	58	652,751.03	1,077,812.60	-84.79
R Walsh	69-236 (29%)	45	22	22	919,758.55	1,565,207.34	+20.22
Mick Fitzgerald	62-370 (17%)	37	40	39	641,846.17	921,406.30	-44.40
P J Brennan	60-557 (11%)	48	56	56	437,120.46	704,777.96	+38.13
Andrew Thornton	58-540 (11%)	64	46	61	331,092.94	508,230.94	-102.77
Tom Doyle	56-476 (12%)	61	53	38	300,233.16	472,203.58	-91.47
Leighton Aspell	55-545 (10%)	62	66	63	351,402.80	567,340.31	-124.60
Sam Thomas	55-400 (14%)	44	29	35	306,951.69	456,970.76	-86.99
Jamie Moore	52-443 (12%)	54	46	40	316,633.80	492,547.07	-55.21
Noel Fehily	52-441 (12%)	54	43	29	318,499.49	500,210.86	+35.00
Dominic Elsworth	46-319 (14%)	38	33	31	347,526.30	517,306.92	-35.02
Wayne Hutchinson	43-441 (10%)	50	36	37	226,436.65	355,057.41	+44.05
Jason Maguire	42-387 (11%)	44	42	41	254,623.20	436,497.21	-68.08
Carl Llewellyn	40-395 (10%)	29	34	38	335,762.16	465,155.15	-91.13
Richard McGrath	40-394 (10%)	42	33	42	252,257.41	386,129.64	-93.97
Joe Tizzard	39-351 (11%)	38	44	30	228,239.51	465,368.17	-105.81
Philip Hide	39-296 (13%)	21	37	26	177,412.79	258,787.96	+22.12
William Kennedy	37-298 (12%)	44	38	20	157,515.51	261,662.65	-32.11
Keith Mercer	36-390 (9%)	44	37	38	167,696.03	289,198.45	-101.12
Tom Scudamore	35-469 (7%)	60	47	45	224,267.11	497,355.56	-252.73
Mark Bradburne	35-417 (8%)	53	40	41	197,436.94	339,928.67	-191.79
Jim Crowley	33-314 (11%)	20	39	29	153,148.24	243,500.34	-104.34
Paul O'Neill	31-240 (13%)	20	26	28	155,689.77	214,045.99	-51.91
Marcus Foley	31-208 (15%)	21	21	21	177,808.80	267,606.13	+17.71
Paul Moloney	30-365 (8%)	30	45	48	153,157.32	259,421.77	-69.38
Paddy Merrigan	29-200 (15%)	19	18	22	110,533.38	179,375.93	-14.33
Liam Heard	28-206 (14%)	20	22	25	179,465.75	289,305.08	-85.18
Brian Harding	26-342 (8%)	21	23	31	158,184.18	236,645.00	-123.67
Andrew Tinkler	26-283 (9%)	19	31	24	142,529.37	209,773.91	-85.84
John McNamara	25-385 (6%)	57	27	43	101,231.29	229,337.05	-44.92
Stephen Craine	25-242 (10%)	18	27	28	143,894.62	199,747.56	+36.92
Russ Garritty	24-226 (11%)	23	29	33	113,189.20	190,130.85	-60.82
Dougie Costello	23-334 (7%)	34	34	33	107,236.40	190,664.97	-103.19
Barry Fenton	23-161 (14%)	14	17	10	124,610.99	180,670.28	+0.58
Mr T J O'Brien	22-157 (14%)	24	17	7	105,139.72	156,464.04	-7.21
T J Dreaper	21-217 (10%)	22	25	10	118,969.39	189,065.18	-89.95
Barry Keniry	20-262 (8%)	14	30	18	100,838.53	161,088.63	+10.45
Mr T Greenall	20-220 (9%)	31	29	23	96,272.87	169,221.38	-33.92
Peter Buchanan	19-388 (5%)	36	35	40	112,380.70	220,220.15	-189.30
Owyn Nelmes	19-344 (6%)	24	38	30	70,154.07	130,122.76	-185.75
Warren Marston	19-305 (6%)	23	42	31	76,784.83	158,650.48	-73.37
Daryl Jacob	19-147 (13%)	13	13	17	117,826.93	167,105.22	+53.33
Jodie Mogford	18-247 (7%)	16	13	20	66,186.07	99,559.85	-2.75
Henry Oliver	17-235 (7%)	15	18	23	78,814.98	120,058.70	-130.76

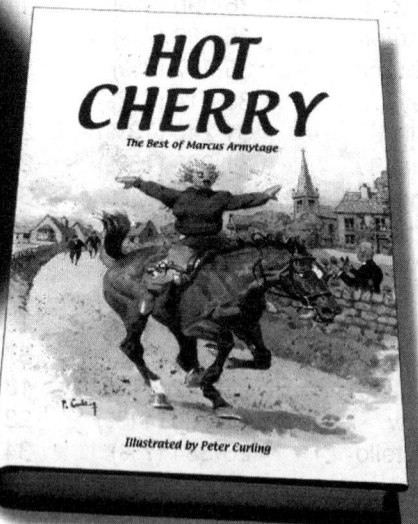

RACEFORM JUMP MEDIAN TIMES 2005-2006

Some distances have been omitted where insufficient data exists to establish a reliable median times

AINTREE

Chase (Mildmay)

2m 3m 58.7
2m4f 5m 7.3
3m1f 6m 29.2

Chase (National)

2m 6f 5m 40.1
3m3f 7m 15.7
4m4f 9m 8.6

Hurdles

2m110y 4m 7.2
2m4f 4m 59.2
3m110y 6m 11.7

ASCOT

Chase

2m 3m 59.2
2m3f110y 4m 58.2
3m110y 6m 23.5

Hurdles

2m110y 4m 2.9
2m4f 4m 59.9
3m 5m 58.1
3m1f 110y 6m 22.7

AYR

Chase

2m 4m 3.7
2m4f 5m 18.5
2m5f110y 5m 57.5
3m1f 6m 38
3m3f110y 7m 7.9
4m1f 8m 20.8

Hurdles

2m 3m 54.5
2m4f 5m 7.7
2m6f 5m 41.5
3m110y 6m 20.9
3m2f110y 6m 37.7

BANGOR

Chase

2m1f110y 4m 26.2
2m4f110y 5m 15.6
3m110y 6m 23.7
3m6f 8m 22.7
4m1f 9m 16.7

Hurdles

2m1f 4m 9
2m4f 4m 53.8
3m 5m 54.3

CARLISLE

Chase

2m 4m 13.1
2m4f 5m 15.2
3m 6m 23.9
3m2f 7m 8.2

Hurdles

2m1f 4m 22.6
2m4f110y 5m 16.5
3m110y 6m 18.6

CARTMEL

Chase

2m1f110y 4m 21.6
2m5f110y 5m 22.3
3m2f 6m 37.9

Hurdles

2m1f110y 4m 11
2m6f 5m 29.2
3m2f 6m 21.7

CATTERICK

Chase

2m 4m 2.6
2m3f 4m 55.5
3m1f110y 6m 45.8
3m4f110y 7m 46.8

Hurdles

2m 3m 55.4
2m3f 4m 48.2
3m1f110y 6m 33.8

CHELTENHAM (NEW)

Chase

2m110y 4m 10.6
2m5f 5m 28.9
3m1f110y 6m 47.8
3m2f110y 6m 50.8
4m1f 8m 57.2

Hurdles

2m1f 4m 14.6
2m5f110y 5m 28.6
3m 6m 1.2

CHELTENHAM (OLD)

Chase

2m 3m 59.3
2m4f110y 5m 12.4
3m110y 6m 26.1
3m3f110y 7m 17.3
4m 8m 23.6

Hurdles

2m110y 4m 1.7
2m5f 5m 14.3
3m1f110y 6m 36.5

Cross Country Chases

3m 6m 19
3m7f 8m 37.4

CHEPSTOW

Chase

2m110y 4m 19.5
2m3f110y 5m 12.9
3m 6m 16.3
3m2f110y 7m 21.7
3m5f110y 8m 11

Hurdles

2m110y 4m 11.6
2m4f 5m 4.6
3m 6m 17.7

DONCASTER

Chase

2m110y 4m 7.2
2m3f110y 4m 59.4
3m 6m 13.3
3m2f 6m 38.1

Hurdles

2m110y 4m 4.5
2m4f 4m 54
3m110y 6m 2.5

EXETER

Chase

2m1f110y 4m 20
2m3f110y 4m 52.3
2m7f110y 5m 59.3
3m1f110y 6m 26.4

Hurdles

2m1f 4m 6.7
2m3f 4m 33
2m6f110y 5m 33.5
3m110y 6m

FAKENHAM

Chase

2m110y 4m 14.4
2m5f110y 5m 34
3m110y 6m 28

Hurdles

2m 4m 3
2m4f 5m 0.7
2m7f110y 5m 47.8

FOLKESTONE

Chase

2m 4m 7.4
2m5f 5m 28.3
3m1f 6m 32.8
3m2f 6m 44.8
3m7f 7m 58.1

Hurdles

2m1f110y 4m 28.7
2m4f110y 5m 24.8
2m6f110y 6m 1.2

FONTWELL

Chase

2m2f 4m 38.6
2m4f 5m 2.3
2m6f 5m 37.4
3m2f110y 7m 4.5

Hurdles

2m2f110y 4m 33.3
2m4f 4m 59.8
2m6f110y 5m 38.8
3m3f 6m 37.5

HAYDOCK

Chase

2m 4m 13.9
2m4f 5m 27.5
2m6f 5m 45.7
3m 6m 33.4
3m4f110y 7m 39.9
4m110y 9m 11.2

Hurdles

2m 3m 59.2
2m4f 5m 6.1

2m6f 5m 48.1
2m7f110y 6m 9.4

HEREFORD

Chase

2m 4m 3.7
2m3f 4m 48.7
3m1f110y 6m 33.8

Hurdles

2m1f 4m 4
2m3f110y 4m 48.5
3m2f 6m 29.1

HEXHAM

Chase

2m110y 4m 10.1
2m4f110y 5m 13.2
3m1f 6m 32.8
4m 9m 12.4

Hurdles

2m110y 4m 14
2m4f110y 5m 6.9
3m 6m 11.2

HUNTINGDON

Chase

2m110y 4m 9.1
2m4f110y 5m 4.9
3m 6m 12
3m6f110y 8m 10.1

Hurdles

2m110y 3m 55.7
2m4f110y 4m 49.9
2m5f110y 5m 10
3m2f 6m 20.6

KELSO

Chase

2m1f 4m 20.5
2m6f110y 5m 55
3m1f 6m 28.4

3m4f 7m 24.1
4m 8m 39

Hurdles

2m110y 4m
2m2f 4m 31.5
2m6f110y 5m 37.8
3m3f 6m 34.7

KEMPTON

Chase

2m 3m 56.3
2m4f110y 5m 15.1
3m 6m 12.2

Hurdles

2m 3m 57.1
2m5f 5m 15.9
3m110y 6m 10.9

LEICESTER

Chase

2m 4m 16.5
2m4f110y 5m 24.3
2m7f110y 6m 7.3

Hurdles

2m 4m 6
2m4f110y 5m 21.8
3m 6m 17.1

LINGFIELD

Chase

2m 4m 20.5
2m4f110y 5m 34.8
3m 6m 36.8

Hurdles

2m110y 4m 14.6
2m3f110y 5m10.7
2m7f 6m 8.3

LUDLOW

Chase

2m 4m 4.2
2m4f 5m 5.8
3m 6m 9.1

Hurdles

2m 3m 47.6
2m5f 5m 13.5
3m 5m 54.6

MARKET RASEN

Chase

2m1f110y 4m 28.7
2m4f 5m 6.5
2m6f110y 5m 44.6
3m 6m 28
3m1f 6m 34
3m4f110y 7m 54.3
4m1f 9m 12.1

Hurdles

2m1f110y 4m 16.1
2m3f110y 4m 49
2m5f110y 5m 25.3
3m 6m 6.8

MUSSELBURGH

Chase

2m 3m 58.2
2m4f 5m 4.2
3m 6m 9.1

Hurdles

2m 3m 49.7
2m4f 4m 53.6
3m 5m 55.2

NEWBURY

Chase

2m1f 4m 15.5
2m2f110y 5m 41.4
2m4f 5m 11.8
2m6f110y 5m 47.3
3m 6m 9.9
3m2f110y 6m 51.9

Hurdles

2m110y 4m 3.7
2m3f 4m 47.5
2m5f 5m 15.2
3m110y 6m 9.4

NEWCASTLE

Chase

2m110y 4m 17.5
2m4f 5m 17
3m 6m 10.8
3m6f 8m 6.2
4m1f 8m 48.1

Hurdles

2m 4m 2.9
2m4f 5m 10.2
3m 6m 7.9

NEWTON ABBOT

Chase

2m110y 4m 7.2
2m5f110y 5m 25
3m2f110y 6m 49

Hurdles

2m1f 4m 7.1
2m6f 5m 21.7
3m3f 6m 46

PERTH

Chase

2m 3m 59.9
2m4f110y 5m 9.8
3m 6m 12.4

Hurdles

2m110y 3m 56.7
2m4f110y 5m 2.4
3m110y 6m 5.8

PLUMPTON

Chase

2m1f 4m 23.6
2m4f 5m 23.2
3m2f 7m 5.4

Hurdles

2m 3m 50.3
2m5f 5m 30.3
3m1f110y 6m 57.1

SANDOWN

Chase

2m 4m 3.2
2m4f110y 5m 21.3
3m110y 6m 31.2
3m5f110y 7m 41

Hurdles

2m110y 4m 7.2
2m4f110y 5m 23.3
2m6f 5m 33.5

SEDGEFIELD

Chase

2m110y 4m 11.6
2m5f 5m 19.3
3m3f 7m 2.4
3m4f 7m 11.3

Hurdles

2m1f 4m 2.7
2m5f110y 5m 10.7
3m3f110y 6m 56.5

SOUTHWELL

Chase

2m1f 4m 11.7
2m5f110y 5m 28.4
3m2f 6m 38.8

Hurdles

2m1f 4m 4.9
2m5f110y 5m 22.7
3m2f 6m 29.4

STRATFORD

Chase

2m1f110y 4m 14.7
2m4f 5m 1.2
2m5f110y 5m 22.6
3m 6m 4.2
3m4f 7m 11.7

Hurdles

2m110y 3m 59.9
2m3f 4m 34.9
2m6f110y 5m 33.7
3m3f 6m 33.8

TAUNTON

Chase

2m110y 4m 9.4
2m3f 4m 55
3m 6m 16.3
3m3f 7m 18.6
4m2f110y 9m 38.9

Hurdles

2m1f 4m 3.5
2m3f110y 4m 43.3
3m110y 6m 9.8

TOWCESTER

Chase

2m110y 4m 16.3
2m6f 5m 52.2
3m1f 6m 42.3

Hurdles

2m 4m 2.8
2m5f 5m 32.3
3m 6m 16.6

UTTOXETER

Chase

2m 4m 2.2
2m4f 5m 14.7
2m5f 5m 19.3
2m7f 5m 54.1
3m 6m 30.4
3m2f 6m 55
4m2f 8m 54.3

Hurdles

2m 3m 52.4
2m4f110y 5m 2.6
2m6f110y 5m 36.5
3m110y 5m 58.7

WARWICK

Chase

2m110y 4m 0.3
2m4f110y 5m 16.5
3m110y 6m 13.8
3m2f 6m 48.4
3m5f 7m 47.3

Hurdles

2m 3m 54.1
2m3f 4m 38.7
2m5f 5m 13.1
3m1f 6m 23

WETHERBY

Chase

2m 4m 3.5
2m4f110y 5m 19.4
2m7f110y 5m 55
3m1f 6m 36.1
3m5f 7m 23.1

Hurdles

2m 3m 57.2
2m4f110y 5m 7.5
2m7f 5m 59.6
3m1f 6m 14

WINCANTON

Chase

2m 4m 4.4
2m5f 5m 22.6
3m1f110y 6m 44.4

Hurdles

2m 3m 48
2m6f 5m 23.4

WORCESTER

Chase

2m 3m 58.6
2m4f110y 5m 15.5
2m7f110y 6m 1.1

Hurdles

2m 3m 50.2
2m4f 4m 53
3m 5m 51.9

RACEFORM JUMPS RECORD TIMES 2005-2006

AINTREE

Distance	Time	Age	Weight	Going	Horse	Date
2m C	3m 45.2	9	10-7	Firm	Nohalmdun	Apr 7 ,1990
2m 110y H	3m 44.6	6	10-7	Firm	Spinning	Apr 3 ,1993
2m 4f C	4m 47.5	8	11-6	Gd to firm	Wind Force	Apr 2 ,1993
2m 4f H	4m 37.1	5	10-11	Gd to firm	Gallateen	Apr 2 ,1993
2m 5f 110y C	5m 25.6	10	10-12	Good	Its Time For A Win	Apr 5 , 2002
3m 110y H	5m 50.6	6	10-2	Gd to firm	Andrew s First	Apr 1 ,1993
3m 1f C	6m 3.4	7	11-3	Gd to firm	Cab on Target	Apr 2 ,1993
3m 3f NC	6m 54.4	8	12-0	Gd to firm	Young Hustler	Nov18,1995
4m 4f NC	8m 47.8	11	10-6	Firm	Mr Frisk	Apr 7 , 1990

ASCOT

Distance	Time	Age	Weight	Going	Horse	Date
2m C	3m 45.8	6	10-3	Gd to firm	With Gods Help	May 1 ,1990
2m 110y H	3m 43.4	6	10-3	Gd to firm	Fred The Tread	Apr 13,1988
2m 3f 110y C	4m 38.2	9	10-0	Gd to firm	Wise King	Apr 7 , 1999
2m 4f H	4m 38.5	5	11-7	Firm	Babil	Mar 31, 1990
3m H	5m 25.2	5	10-6	Gd to firm	Shah's Choice	Apr 13 ,1988
3m 110y C	6m 2.1	7	11-7	Gd to firm	Lord Seamus	Apr 3 , 2002
3m 1f 110y H	6m 6.4	10	11-7	Gd to firm	Floyd	Dec 15, 1990

AYR

Distance	Time	Age	Weight	Going	Horse	Date
2m H	3m 27.4	6	10-7	Firm	Secret Ballot	Apr 19,1980
2m C	3m 38.7	6	11-0	Gd to firm	Clay County	Oct 12,1991
2m 4f C	4m 44.1	8	12-2	Firm	Chandigar	May 15,1972
2m 4f H	4m 35.0	8	9-10	Firm	Moss Royal	Apr 19,1974
2m 5f 110y C	5m 10.2	6	11-5	Gd to firm	Star To The North	May 9, 2001
2m 6f H	5m 6.8	11	10-0	Firm	Any Second	Apr 19,1980
3m 110y H	5m 42.0	13	10-11	Firm	Nautical Lad	Apr 6 ,1964
3m 1f C	5m 57.7	9	11-0	Gd to firm	Top N Tale	May 12,1982
3m 2f 110y H	6m 26.9	13	10-0	Good	Meditator	Apr 18,1997
3m 3f 110y C	6m 50.2	5	10-12	Good	Joaaci	Apr 15, 2005
4m 1f C	8m 0.4	7	10-2	Firm	Young Ash Leaf	Apr 17,1971

BANGOR-ON-DEE

Distance	Time	Age	Weight	Going	Horse	Date
2m 1f H	3m 44.5	9	10-2	Firm	Andy Rew	Apr 24,1982
2m 1f 110y C	4m 7.7	5	11-0	Gd to firm	Bunrannoch House	Aug16,1986
2m 4f H	4m 34.1	5	11-13	Good	Smithy s Choice	Apr 25,1987
2m 4f 110y C	4m 55.3	7	10-12	Gd to firm	Alqairawaan	Aug 17,1996
3m H	5m 34.0	5	11-2	Gd to firm	General Pershing	Apr 20,1991
3m 110y C	5m 57.7	8	11-0	Gd to firm	Tartan Trademark	Spt 15,1990
3m 6f C	7m 34.1	6	12-0	Good	Kaki Crazy (FR)	May 23,2001
4m 1f C	8m 50.7	6	10-11	Gd to soft	Nazzaro	Dec 13,1995

CARLISLE

Distance	Time	Age	Weight	Going	Horse	Date
2m C	3m 55.8	8	11-2	Firm	Cape Felix	Apr 20,1981
2m 1f H	4m 2.6	9	11-3	Firm	Supertop	Oct 25,1997
2m 4f 110y H	4m 45.4	4	10-12	Firm	Sujud (IRE)	Spt 21,1996
2m 4f 110y C	5m 1.9	6	11-11	Firm	Pentlands Flyer (IRE)	Oct 25,1997
3m C	5m 59.9	8	10-8	Firm	The Blue Boy (IRE)	Spt 21,1996
3m 110y H	5m 46.5	8	11-2	Firm	Kinda Groovy	Oct 25, 1997
3m 2f C	6m 40.4	8	11-3	Good	Lady of Gortmerron (IRE)	Oct 6, 2000

CARTMEL

Distance	Time	Age	Weight	Going	Horse	Date
2m 1f 110yH	3m 57.8	7	11-4	Good	Sayeh (IRE)	Aug 28,1999
2m 1f 110yC	4m 7.5	12	11-13	Hard	Clever Folly	May 27,1992
2m 5f 110y C	5m 6.1	10	10-10	Firm	Corrarder	May 30,1994
2m 6f H	5m 14.5	6	11-6	Gd to firm	Woodstock Wanderer (IRE)	May 23,1998
3m 2f C	6m 21.3	12	11-12	Good	Better Times Ahead	Aug 29,1998
3m 2f H	5m 57.9	10	11-3	Firm	Portonia	May 30,1994

CATTERICK

Distance	Time	Age	Weight	Going	Horse	Date
2m C	3m 44.6	6	10-0	Firm	Preston Deal	Dec 18,1971
2m H	3m 36.5	7	11-3	Firm	Lunar Wind	Apr 22,1982
2m 3f C	4m 41.9	8	10-8	Gd to firm	Fear Shuil (IRE)	Nov 24, 2001
2m 3f H	4m 33.0	7	11-6	Gd to firm	Sovereign State (IRE)	Dec 1, 2004
2m 3f H	4m 34.0	4	11-0	Gd to firm	Lady Netbetsports (IRE)	Nov 22, 2003
3m 1f 110y C	6m 14.0	10	10-1	Gd to firm	Clever General	Nov 7 , 1981
3m 1f 110y H	6m 3.8	6	10-9	Gd to firm	Seamus O Flynn	Nov 7 , 1981
3m 4f 110y C	7m 15.3	11	11-7	Gd to firm	The Wilk	Jan 19, 1990
3m 6f C	7m 48.4	9	10-8	Good	Harlov (FR)	Jan 24, 2004

CHELTENHAM

Distance	Time	Age	Weight	Going	Horse	Date
2m OldC	3m 44.6	8	12-0	Good	Edredon Bleu (FR)	Mar 15, 2000
2m110y OldH	3m 48.1	8	12-0	Good	Istabraq (IRE)	Mar 14, 2000
2m110y NwC	3m 52.4	7	10-11	Gd to firm	Samakaan (IRE)	Mar 16, 2000
2m 1f NwH	3m 51.2	5	11-2	Gd to firm	Moody Man	Mar 15, 1990
2m 4f NwH	4m 45.0	6	10-4	Gd to firm	Sir Dante (IRE)	Apr 15, 1997
2m4f110yOC	4m 49.6	9	10-3	Good	Dark Stranger (FR)	Mar 15, 2000
2m 5f OldH	4m 52.0	6	11-7	Good	Monsignor (IRE)	Mar 15, 2000
2m 5f NwC	5m 1.6	9	11-10	Gd to firm	Barnbrook Again	Apr 18, 1990
2m 5f 10yNH	4m 53.6	4	10-9	Good	Fashion House	Spt 19, 1968
3m 110yNwH	5m 36.6	6	11-10	Gd to firm	Bacchanal (IRE)	Mar16, 2000
3m 1f OldC	5m 59.7	8	10-3	Good	Marlborough (IRE)	Mar14, 2000
3m 1f110yNC	6m 13.4	9	10-11	Gd to firm	Bigsun	Mar15, 1990
3m 2f OldH	6m 3.4	9	11-2	Good	Rubhahunish (IRE)	Mar 14, 2000
3m 2f110yNC	6m 30.3	8	12-0	Good	Looks Like Trouble (IRE)	Mar 16, 2000
3m 3f110yOC	7m 1.0	6	10-2	Good	Shardam (IRE)	Nov15, 2003
4m OldC	8m 0.6	8	12-0	Good	Relaxation (IRE)	Mar 15, 2000
4m 1f NwC	8m 33.2	7	11-11	Good	Hot Weld	Mar 16, 2006

CHEPSTOW

Distance	Time	Age	Weight	Going	Horse	Date
2m 110y H	3m 43.2	4	10-1	Firm	Tingle Bell	Oct 4 ,1986
2m 110y C	3m 54.1	8	12-0	Firm	Panto Prince	May 9 ,1989
2m 3f 110y C	4m 45.0	11	9-12	Firm	Armala	May 14,1996
2m 4f 110y H	4m 36.2	9	11-3	Firm	Aileen s Cacador	Apr 23,1957
3m H	5m 33.5	10	10-0	Firm	Chucklestone	May 11,1993
3m C	5m 47.9	9	10-11	Firm	Broadheath	Oct 4 ,1986
3m 2f 110y C	6m 39.4	7	12-0	Firm	Jaunty Jane	May 26,1975
3m 5f 110y C	7m 24.0	9	10-5	Firm	Creeola	Apr 23,1957

DONCASTER

Distance	Time	Age	Weight	Going	Horse	Date
2m 110y H	3m 46.6	6	10-0	Gd to firm	Good for a Loan	Feb 24,1993
2m 110y C	3m 51.9	12	10-9	Gd to firm	Itsgottabealright	Jan 28,1989
2m 3f C	4m 48.7	6	11-8	Good	Kalca Mome (FR)	Dec 11, 2004
2m 3f 110y H	4m 42.0	10	12-0	Gd to soft	Moving Earth (IRE)	Feb 28,2003
3m C	5m 52.4	8	10-9	Good	Dalkey Sound	Jan 26,1991
3m 110yH	5m 45.3	6	10-12	Firm	Pandolfi	Nov 4 , 1972
3m 2f C	6m 18.4	7	10-0	Good	Saggarts Choice	Mar 25,1970

EXETER

Distance	Time	Age	Weight	Going	Horse	Date
2m 1f H	3m 52.2	4	10-10	Gd to firm	Made In France (FR)	Sep 28 , 2004
2m 1f 110y H	3m 53.8	5	10-0	Firm	Valtaki	Aug 24,1990
2m 1f 110y C	4m 6.8	8	11-5	Hard	Some Jinks	Aug 23,1984
2m 2f H	4m 3.1	4	11-4	Firm	Major Dundee (IRE)	Apr 15, 1997
2m 2f C	4m 13.9	7	11-0	Gd to firm	Travado	Nov 2 , 1993
2m 3f H	4m 16.5	5	11-11	Firm	Il Capitano	Oct 9 , 2002
2m 3f C	4m 31.4	8	10-8	Hard	James Pigg	Aug 25,1995
2m 6f H	4m 59.9	10	11-11	Firm	Owenius	Aug 21,1980
2m 6f 110y H	5m 20.0	7	10-10	Firm	Dandonell	May 16, 2001
	5m 20.0	4	10-9	Firm	Sammy Samba	Oct 9 , 2002
	5m 20.0	7	10-11	Gd to firm	Americanconnection (IRE)	Oct 21, 2003
2m 6f 110yC	5m 22.8	8	12-0	Hard	James Pigg	Spt 6 , 1995
2m 7f 110yC	5m 31.8	12	11-9	Firm	Noyan	Apr 23, 2002
3m 110y H	5m 42.3	5	11-7	Firm	Il Capitano	Oct 1, 2002
3m 1f C	6m 7.3	8	11-9	Gd to firm	Hand Woven	May 17, 2000
3m 1f 110yC	6m 8.3	10	11-5	Firm	Saffron Sun	Oct 5, 2005
3m 2f H	6m 26.9	9	12-1	Gd to soft	Rufus	Mar 22,1995
3m 2f C	6m 30.6	10	11-10	Gd to firm	The Leggett	Mar 24,1993

FAKENHAM

Distance	Time	Age	Weight	Going	Horse	Date
2m H	3m 45.7	5	10-9	Gd to firm	Cobbet (CZE)	May 9, 2001
2m 110y C	3m 44.9	11	12-4	Firm	Cheekio Ora	Apr 23,1984
2m 4f H	4m 41.1	4	10-8	Gd to firm	Ayem (IRE)	May 16,1999
2m 5f 110yC	5m 10.1	13	12-2	Gd to firm	Skipping Tim	May 25, 1992
2m 7f 110yH	5m 37.1	6	11-3	Good	Laughing Gas (IRE)	May 20,1995
3m 110y C	5m 57.0	7	11-1	Gd to firm	Specialize	May 16, 1999

FOLKESTONE

Distance	Time	Age	Weight	Going	Horse	Date
2m C	3m 48.7	7	12-0	Gd to firm	High Gale (IRE)	Apr 30,1999
2m 1f 110yH	3m 56.2	5	11-5	Firm	Super Tek	Nov14,1983
2m 4f 110yH	4m 57.0	6	11-0	Gd to firm	Circus Colours	Apr 2,1996
2m 5f C	5m 6.4	11	11-12	Firm	Silver Buck	Nov11,1983
2m 6f 110y H	5m 18.2	6	10-0	Firm	Royalty Miss	Apr 30,1985
3m 1f Ch	6m 11.4	7	11-0	Gd to firm	Highland	May 23, 2001
3m 2f C	6m 23.1	9	10-13	Firm	Bolt Hole	Apr 26,1988
3m 7f C	7m 55.4	9	12-0	Gd to firm	Apatura King	May 12,1999

FONTWELL

Distance	Time	Age	Weight	Going	Horse	Date
2m 2f C	4m 14.5	12	10-1	Gd to firm	A Thousand Dreams (IRE)	Jun 3 , 2002
2m 2f 110y H	4m 6.8	7	10-2	Gd to firm	Hyperion du Moulin II (FR)	Jun 3 , 2002
2m 3f C	4m 32.0	9	11-10	Firm	Connaught Cracker	May 3, 1999
2m 4f C	4m 38.1	6	11-0	Gd to firm	Chalcedony	Jun 3, 2002
2m 4f H	4m 30.5	8	10-7	Gd to firm	Hillswick	Aug 27, 1999
2m 6f C	5m 13.9	10	10-0	Gd to firm	Contes (IRE)	Jun 3, 2002
2m 6f 110y H	5m 6.7	7	10-1	Gd to firm	Mister Pickwick (IRE)	Jun 3, 2002
3m 2f 110y C	6m 24.3	5	10-2	Gd to firm	Il Capitano	May 6, 2002
3m 3f H	6m 21.6	5	11-2	Gd to firm	Lord Of The Track (IRE)	Aug 18, 2003
3m 4f C	7m 14.1	8	9-7	Good	General Tantrum (IRE)	Mar 20, 2005

HAYDOCK

Distance	Time	Age	Weight	Going	Horse	Date
2m H	3m 32.3	6	10-0	Good	She s Our Mare (IRE)	May 1 ,1999
2m C	3m 51.5	9	10-8	Good	Chergan (IRE)	Mar 30,2002
2m 4f C	4m 56.5	6	10-0	Firm	Hallo Dandy	May 5 ,1980
2m 4f H	4m 35.3	7	10-10	Gd to firm	Moving Out	May 6 ,1995
2m 6f C	5m 27.7	8	11-10	Good	Arlequin de Sou (FR)	Oct 24, 2002
2m 6f H	5m 12.7	5	10-10	Firm	Peter the Butcher	May 3 ,1982
2m 7f 110yH	5m 32.3	9	11-0	Gd to firm	Boscean Chieftain	May 3 ,1993
3m C	6m 1.6	11	11-5	Gd to firm	Eau De Cologne	Mar 29, 2003
3m 4f 110yC	7m 0.4	7	10-6	Good	Jurancon II (FR)	Feb 28,2004
4m 110y C	8m 37.4	8	10-4	Good	Jer (USA)	Nov 29,1979

HEREFORD

Distance	Time	Age	Weight	Going	Horse	Date
2m C	3m 46.0	6	10-9	Gd to firm	Smolensk (IRE)	Mar 21,1998
2m 1f H	3m 42.2	10	10-1	Hard	Tasty Son	Spt 11, 1973

2m 3f C	4m 30.0	9	10-11	Good	Kings Wild	Sep 28,1990
2m 3f 110y H	4m 22.2	7	11-3	Gd to firm	Polden Pride	May 6 , 1995
3m 1f 110y C	6m 10.7	8	10-10	Gd to firm	Gilston Lass	Apr 8 ,1995
3m 2f H	6m 2.8	6	10-1	Gd to firm	Wee Danny (IRE)	Spt 10, 2003

HEXHAM

Distance	Time	Age	Weight	Going	Horse	Date
2m 110y H	3m 58.4	4	9-11	Gd to firm	Covent Garden	Spt 15, 2002
2m 110y C	3m 53.6	9	11-9	Gd to firm	Adamatic	Jun17, 2000
2m 4f 110y H	4m 31.5	6	11-0	Gd to firm	Pappa Charlie (USA)	May27,1997
2m 4f 110y C	4m 55.4	8	9-11	Gd to firm	Mr Laggan	Spt 14,2003
3m H	5m 45.4	7	9-9	Firm	Fingers Crossed	Apr 29,1991
3m 1f C	6m 7.6	9	9-11	Gd to firm	Silent Snipe	Jun 1, 2002
4m C	8m 37.6	7	11-3	Good	Rubika	Mar 15,1990

HUNTINGDON

Distance	Time	Age	Weight	Going	Horse	Date
2m 110y H	3m 34.9	6	12-0	Gd to firm	Wakeel (USA)	Spt 18, 1998
2m 110y C	3m 54.2	12	10-9	Gd to firm	Who s To Say	Spt 18, 1998
2m 4f 110y C	4m 46.4	10	10-13	Gd to firm	Peccadillo	Sep 26, 2004
2m 4f 110y H	4m 32.9	6	10-12	Gd to firm	Richie's Delight (IRE)	Aug 30,1999
2m 5f 110y H	4m 45.8	6	11-5	Firm	Sound of Laughter	Apr 14, 1984
3m C	5m 44.3	7	11-9	Gd to firm	Ozzie Jones	Spt 18, 1998
3m 2f H	5m 54.6	6	10-13	Gd to firm	Weather Wise	Spt 18, 1998
3m 6f 110y C	8m 2.7	9	10-4	Gd to soft	Kinnahalla (IRE)	Nov 24, 2001

KELSO

Distance	Time	Age	Weight	Going	Horse	Date
2m 110y H	3m 39.6	5	10-0	Firm	The Premier Expres	May 2 , 1995
2m 1f C	4m 2.6	8	11-9	Firm	Mr Coggy	May 2 , 1984
2m 2f H	4m 11.5	7	11-0	Firm	All Welcome	Oct 15, 1994
2m 6f 110y H	5m 12.2	4	11-3	Firm	Hit The Canvas (USA)	Sep 30, 1995
2m 6f 110y C	5m 29.6	10	10-13	Good	Bas De Laine (FR)	Nov 13, 1996
3m 1f C	6m 1.2	13	12-0	Gd to firm	Mcgregor The Third	Sept 19, 1999
3m 3f H	6m 10.1	8	11-5	Firm	Ambergate	Oct 21, 1989
3m 4f C	7m 2.3	7	10-6	Good	Seven Towers (IRE)	Dec 2 , 1996
4m C	8m 7.4	8	10-0	Good	Seven Towers	Jan 17, 1997

KEMPTON

Distance	Time	Age	Weight	Going	Horse	Date
2m C	3m 42.9	6	11-0	Gd to firm	Young Pokey	Dec 27,1991
2m H	3m 37.0	5	11-8	Firm	Freight Forwarder	Oct 20, 1979
2m 4f 110y C	4m 55.8	8	10-6	Gd to firm	Mr Entertainer	Dec 27, 1991
2m 5f H	4m 51.6	7	11-8	Firm	Grand Canyon (NZ)	Oct 15, 1977
3m C	5m 45.3	8	11-10	Gd to firm	One Man (IRE)	Dec 26, 1996
3m 110yH	5m 45.6	7	10-6	Hard	Esmenella	Oct 17, 1964

LEICESTER

Distance	Time	Age	Weight	Going	Horse	Date
2m H	3m 39.6	6	10-11	Gd to firm	Ryde Again	Nov 20, 1989
2m C	3m 55.40	5	10-9	Good	Got One Too (FR)	Nov 30, 2002
2m 4f 110y C	5m 0.5	9	9-6	Firm	Prairie Minstrel (USA)	Dec 4 , 2003
2m 4f 110y H	4m 45.5	4	11-7	Gd to firm	Prince of Rheims	Dec 5 , 1989
2m 7f 110y C	5m 51.1	8	11-10	Good	Macgeorge (IRE)	Feb 17, 1998
3m H	5m 48.0	5	10-6	Gd to firm	King Tarquin	Apr 1 , 1967

LINGFIELD

Distance	Time	Age	Weight	Going	Horse	Date
2m C	3m 51.9	8	11-1	Firm	Cotapaxi	Mar 19, 1993
2m 110y H	3m 47.2	5	11-0	Firm	Va Utu	Mar 19, 1993
2m 3f 110y H	4m 37.4	6	10-3	Firm	Bellezza	Mar 20, 1993
2m 4f 110y C	5m 4.0	8	11-7	Good	Copsale Lad	Oct 29, 2005
2m 7f H	5m 38.8	6	11-12	Good	His Nibs	Nov 11, 2003
3m C	5m 58.4	6	11-3	Firm	Mighty Frolic	Mar 19, 1993

LUDLOW

Distance	Time	Age	Weight	Going	Horse	Date
2m H	3m 36.4	10	10-11	Gd to firm	Desert Fighter	Oct 11, 2001
2m C	3m 48.6	8	11-6	Gd to firm	Marked Man (IRE)	Mar 25, 2004
2m 4f C	4m 51.3	7	10-12	Good	Cosmocrat	May 24, 2005
2m 5f H	4m 54.7	8	11-0	Gd to firm	Willy Willy	Oct 11, 2001
3m H	5m 36.6	10	10-11	Gd to firm	Rift Valley (IRE)	May 12, 2005
3m C	5m 50.5	6	11-12	Good	Rodalko (FR)	Mar 4, 2004
3m 2f 110y H	6m 7.3	8	12-0	Gd to firm	Gysart (IRE)	Oct 9, 1997
3m 3f 110y C	6m 58.5	9	11-2	Good	Act In Time (IRE)	Dec 13, 2001

MARKET RASEN

Distance	Time	Age	Weight	Going	Horse	Date
2m 1f 110yH	3m 54.4	4	10-9	Firm	Border River	Jly 30, 1977
2m 1f 110yC	4m 11.9	9	12-7	Gd to firm	Cape Felix	Aug 14, 1982
2m 3f 110yH	4m 30.7	7	10-10	Gd to firm	Coble Lane	May 29, 1999
2m 4f C	4m 42.8	7	10-13	Gd to firm	Fleeting Mandate (IRE)	Jly 24, 1999
2m 5f 110yH	5m 3.8	4	10-0	Firm	Pandolfi	Aug 3 , 1970
2m 6f H	5m 13.8	9	10-11	Good	Hopbine	Apr 3, 2005
2m 6f 110yC	5m 24.2	8	11-9	Good	Annas Prince	Oct 19, 1979
3m H	5m 38.8	6	12-5	Firm	Trustful	May 21, 1977
3m 1f C	6m 1.0	7	11-8	Gd to firm	Allerlea	May 1 , 1985
3m 4f 110y C	7m 17.5	10	11-1	Good	Fin Bec (FR)	Nov 20, 2003
4m 1f C	8m 51.2	8	10-0	Good	Barkin	Nov 23, 1991

MUSSELBURGH

Distance	Time	Age	Weight	Going	Horse	Date
2m H	3m 35.9	3	10-7	Gd to firm	Joe Bumpas	Dec 11, 1989
2m C	3m 48.1	8	10-12	Gd to firm	Sonsie Mo	Dec 6, 1993
2m 1f H	4m 4.6	5	10-8	Gd to firm	Bodfari Signet	Apr 3, 2001
2m 4f C	4m 44.5	7	11-9	Gd to firm	Bohemian Spirit (IRE)	Dec 18, 2005
2m 4f H	4m 40.7	4	10-11	Gd to firm	Old Feathers (IRE)	Apr 3 , 2001
3m C	5m 47.7	7	11-10	Firm	Snowy (IRE)	Dec 18, 2005
3m H	5m 39.1	8	11-5	Firm	Supertop	Dec 17, 1996

NEWBURY

Distance	Time	Age	Weight	Going	Horse	Date
2m 110y H	3m 45.2	5	10-2	Gd to firm	Dhofar	Oct 25, 1985
2m 1f C	3m 58.2	8	12-0	Gd to firm	Barnbrook Again	Nov 25, 1989
2m 2f 110y C	4m 31.9	6	11-12	Gd to firm	Rubberdubber	Mar 4, 2006
2m 3f H	4m 30.5	4	11-11	Gd to soft	Schapiro (USA)	Apr 2, 2005
2m 4f C	4m 47.9	8	11-12	Gd to firm	Espy	Oct 25, 1991
2m 5f H	4m 51.2	6	10-4	Gd to soft	Penneyrose Bay	Apr 2, 2005
2m 6f 110y C	5m 35.5	5	11-0	Good	Von Origny (FR)	Mar 3, 2006
3m C	5m 43.5	7	11-3	Gd to soft	Red Devil Robert (IRE)	Apr 2, 2005
3m 110y H	5m 45.4	8	10-9	Good	Lansdowne	Oct 25, 1996
3m 2f 110y C	6m 27.1	10	12-0	Firm	Topsham Bay	Mar 26, 1993

NEWCASTLE

Distance	Time	Age	Weight	Going	Horse	Date
2m H	3m 40.7	7	10-10	Good	Padre Mio	Nov 25, 1995
2m 110y C	3m 56.7	7	11-12	Firm	Greenheart	May 7 , 1990
2m 4f C	4m 46.7	7	9-13	Firm	Snow Blessed	May 19, 1984
2m 4f H	4m 42.0	4	10-10	Hard	Mils Mij	May 13, 1989
3m C	5m 48.1	8	10-4	Firm	Even Swell	Oct 30, 1975
3m H	5m 40.1	6	10-5	Gd to firm	Withy Bank	Nov 29, 1986
3m 6f C	7m 30.0	8	12-0	Good	Charlie Potheen	Apr 28, 1973
4m 1f C	8m 30.4	7	10-0	Good	Domaine de Pron (FR)	Feb 21, 1998

NEWTON ABBOT

Distance	Time	Age	Weight	Going	Horse	Date
2m 110y C	3m 49.5	6	10-8	Gd to firm	Mrs Em	Jly 30, 1998
2m 1f H	3m 45.0	5	11-0	Firm	Windbound Lass	Aug 1 , 1988
2m 5f 110y C	5m 6.3	8	10-10	Gd to firm	Karadin (FR)	Aug 13, 2002
2m 6f H	4m 55.4	7	10-0	Firm	Virbian	Jun 30, 1983
3m 2f 110y C	6m 21.5	8	10-12	Gd to firm	Just In Business	May 14, 2001
3m 3f H	6m 17.6	7	12-0	Firm	Le Carotte	Jly 31, 1989

PERTH

Distance	Time	Age	Weight	Going	Horse	Date
2m C	3m 47.5	7	11-10	Gd to firm	Beldine	Aug 22, 1992
2m 110y H	3m 40.4	4	11-8	Hard	Molly Fay	Spt 23, 1971
2m 4f 110y H	4m 41.2	8	10-2	Firm	Valiant Dash	May 19, 1994
2m 4f 110y C	4m 56.3	9	11-12	Good	General Chandos	Aug 17, 1990
3m C	5m 52.0	7	11-5	Gd to firm	Montreal (FR)	Jun 6, 2004
3m 110y H	5m 43.1	5	12-0	Gd to firm	Mystic Memory	Aug 20, 1994

PLUMPTON

Distance	Time	Age	Weight	Going	Horse	Date
2m H	3m 31.0	3	11-1	Firm	Royal Derbi	Sep 19, 1988
2m 1f C	4m 5.9	6	10-13	Gd to firm	Janiture (FR)	Apr 19, 2003
2m 4f C	4m 48.2	8	9-11	Gd to firm	Blakeney Coast	May 8, 2005
2m 5f H	4m 50.1	4	10-11	Gd to firm	Majestic (IRE)	Oct 18, 1999
3m 1f 110y H	6m 0.1	5	10-9	Gd to firm	Bali Strong (IRE)	Oct 18, 1999
3m 2f C	6m 23.5	9	9-7	Gd to firm	Sunday Habits	Apr 19, 2003

SANDOWN

Distance	Time	Age	Weight	Going	Horse	Date
2m C	3m 44.3	8	12-0	Firm	News King	Apr 23, 1982
2m 110yH	3m 42.0	6	10-0	Firm	Olympian	Mar 13, 1993
2m 4f 110y C	4m 57.2	8	11-7	Gd to firm	Coulton	Apr 29, 1995
2m 4f 110y H	4m 43.8	6	11-9	Good	Yes Sir	Apr 23, 2005
2m 6f H	5m 5.6	8	11-3	Firm	Kintbury	Nov 5 ,1983
3m H	5m 39.1	6	11-5	Gd to firm	Rostropovich	Apr 27, 2002
3m 110y	5m 59.0	8	12-7	Good	Arkle	Nov 6 , 1965
3m 5f 110y	7m 9.1	9	10-0	Gd to firm	Cache Fleur (FR)	Apr 29, 1995

SEDGEFIELD

Distance	Time	Age	Weight	Going	Horse	Date
2m 1f C	4m 0.3	8	10-10	Firm	Stay Awake	May 18, 1994
2m 1f 110y H	3m 51.7	4	10-13	Gd to firm	Byzantine	Spt 4 , 1992
2m 5f C	4m 59.2	8	11-10	Gd to firm	Pennybridge	Spt 30, 1997
2m 5f 110y H	4m 46.3	7	10-0	Gd to firm	Palm House	Spt 4 , 1992
3m 3f C	6m 29.3	7	11-8	Gd to firm	The Gallopin' Major	Sept 14, 1996
3m 3f 110y H	6m 19.7	7	9-13	Firm	Pikestaff (USA)	Jly 25, 2005
3m 4f C	6m 46.5	10	11-1	Gd to firm	Mister Muddypaws	May 5, 2000

SOUTHWELL

Distance	Time	Age	Weight	Going	Horse	Date
2m C	3m 51.0	8	11-1	Gd to firm	Stay Awake	May 11, 1994
2m H	3m 36.2	5	11-8	Gd to firm	Merlins Wish (USA)	May 2 , 1994
2m 2f H	4m 19.5	6	11-2	Gd to firm	Heresthedeal (IRE)	May 8 , 1995
2m 4f 110y C	5m 2.8	9	10-0	Gd to firm	Bally Parson	May 8 , 1995
2m 4f 110y H	4m 47.8	8	11-13	Gd to firm	Man of the Grange	May 2 , 1994
3m 110y H	5m 46.5	5	10-0	Gd to firm	Soloman Springs (USA)	May 8 , 1995
3m 110y C	6m 9.0	7	11-8	Gd to firm	Strong Medicine	May 2 , 1994

STRATFORD-ON-AVON

Distance	Time	Age	Weight	Going	Horse	Date
2m 110y H	3m 40.4	6	11-12	Hard	Chusan	May 7 , 1956
2m 1f 110y C	4m 0.2	7	11-8	Good	Money In	Spt 5 , 1981
2m 4f C	4m 42.0	8	11-1	Gd to firm	Stately Home (IRE)	Jly 11, 1999
2m 5f 110y C	5m 3.0	10	10-13	Gd to firm	Father Rector (IRE)	Oct 16, 1999
2m 6f 110y H	5m 6.8	6	11-0	Firm	Broken Wing	May 31, 1986
3m C	5m 41.8	9	10-11	Gd to firm	Keltic Lord	Jul 17 , 2005
3m 2f H	6m 21.3	8	10-5	Firm	Space Kate	Jun 3 , 1989
3m 4f C	6m 44.8	8	10-0	Firm	Gold Castle	Jun 1 , 1985

TAUNTON

Distance	Time	Age	Weight	Going	Horse	Date
2m 110y C	3m 49.5	8	10-9	Firm	I Have Him	Apr 28, 1995
2m 1f H	3m 39.5	4	12-0	Hard	Indian Jockey	Oct 3, 1996
2m 3f C	4m 30.7	9	11-7	Firm	Harik	Mar 24, 2003

2m 3f 110y H	4m 21.7	7	11-0	Gd to firm	Nova Run	Nov 14, 1996
3m C	5m 38.4	9	11-8	Gd to firm	Art Prince (IRE)	Oct 4, 1999
3m 110y H	5m 30.4	7	10-4	Firm	On My Toes	Oct 15, 1998
3m 3f C	6m 44.2	9	11-9	Good	Even More (IRE)	Nov 25, 2004
4m 2f 110y C	9m 1.5	12	10-0	Gd to firm	Woodlands Genhire	Jan 16, 1997

TOWCESTER

Distance	Time	Age	Weight	Going	Horse	Date
2m H	3m 39.5	4	10-0	Firm	Nascracker (USA)	May 22, 1987
2m 110y C	3m 59.0	6	10-1	Hard	Silver Night	May 25, 1974
2m 5f H	5m 0.9	7	11-2	Gd to firm	Mailcom	May 3 , 1993
2m 6f C	5m 30.0	7	11-13	Firm	Whiskey Eyes	May 10, 1988
3m H	5m 44.0	9	9-10	Firm	Dropshot	May 25, 1984
3m 1f C	6m 12.3	9	10-8	Firm	Veleso	May 22, 1987

UTTOXETER

Distance	Time	Age	Weight	Going	Horse	Date
2m H	3m 37.2	4	10-9	Gd to firm	Flying Eagle	Jun 11, 1995
2m C	3m 41.5	6	11-0	Good	Tapageur	Aug 8 , 1991
2m 4f 110y H	4m 39.1	8	10-9	Gd to firm	Chicago s Best	Jun 11, 1995
2m 5f C	4m 54.2	8	11-8	Firm	McKenzie	Apr 27, 1974
2m 6f 110y H	5m 14.9	7	10-6	Good	Springfield Scally	Mar 18, 2000
2m 7f C	5m 26.8	7	10-13	Gd to firm	Certain Angle	Jun 9 , 1996
3m 110y H	5m 35.3	5	10-4	Gd to firm	Volcanic Dancer	Spt 19, 1991
3m 2f C	6m 23.5	10	11-13	Gd to firm	Mcgregor the Third	Oct 5 , 1996
3m 4f C	7m 33.9	8	10-6	Soft	Ottawa (IRE)	Feb 7 , 1998
4m 2f C	8m 33.7	8	11-4	Good	Seven Towers (IRE)	Mar 15, 1997

WARWICK

Distance	Time	Age	Weight	Going	Horse	Date
2m H	3m 34.6	5	11-4	Gd to firm	Arabian Bold	May 22, 1993
2m 110y C	3m 46.3	6	11-0	Gd to firm	Bambi De L'Orme (FR)	May 7, 2005
2m 3f H	4m 14.9	6	11-7	Gd to firm	Runaway Pete	Nov 2, 1996
2m 4f 110y C	4m 53.3	9	9-12	Gd to firm	Dudie	May 16, 1987
2m 5f H	4m 43.6	5	10-10	Firm	Three Eagles (USA)	May 11, 2002
3m 110y Ch	6m 3.9	10	11-2	Gd to firm	Shepherds Rest	Apr 2, 2002
3m 1f H	5m 53.5	7	11-0	Gd to firm	City Poser	Apr 2, 2002
3m 2f C	6m 16.1	12	10-12	Gd to firm	Castle Warden	May 6 , 1989
3m 5f C	7m 13.2	8	11-0	Firm	Purple Haze	Spt 18, 1982
4m 1f 110y C	8m 36.4	10	10-6	Firm	Jolly s Clump	Jan 24, 1976

WETHERBY

Distance	Time	Age	Weight	Going	Horse	Date
2m H	3m 38.0	9	10-1	Firm	Gimmick	Oct 15, 2003
2m C	3m 47.3	6	11-0	Gd to firm	Cumbrian Challenge (IRE)	Oct 22,1995
2m 4f 110y H	4m 45.3	9	11-12	Gd to firm	Master Sandy (USA)	May 8 , 1996
2m 4f 110y C	4m 52.0	7	10-6	Gd to firm	Toogood to Be True	Oct 11, 1995
2m 7f H	5m 40.2	5	11-2	Gd to firm	Frankie Anson	Apr 21, 2003
2m 7f 110y C	5m 43.7	12	10-13	Gd to firm	Joint Account	Apr 23, 2002
3m 1f C	6m 3.5	9	11-12	Good	See More Business (IRE)	Oct 30,1999
3m 1f H	5m 56.5	8	11-0	Good	Gralmano	Nov 1 , 2003

WINCANTON

Distance	Time	Age	Weight	Going	Horse	Date
2m H	3m 28.1	4	10-5	Gd to firm	Well Chief (GER)	Nov 8 , 2003
2m C	3m 43.7	8	12-7	Firm	Kescast	May 11, 1988
2m 5f C	4m 59.2	11	11-10	Firm	Edredon Bleu (FR)	Oct 26, 2003
2m 6f H	5m 1.9	6	11-0	Firm	St Mellion Green (IRE)	May 9 , 1995
3m 1f 110yC	6m 9.7	7	11-6	Gd to firm	Swansea Bay	Nov 8 , 2003

WINDSOR

Distance	Time	Age	Weight	Going	Horse	Date
2m H	3m 41.8	4	10-12	Firm	Skylander	Nov 21, 1983
2m C	3m 54.0	7	10-10	Gd to firm	Guiburn's Nephew	Nov 20, 1989
2m 4f H	4m 47.7	6	11-7	Good	Dream Leader (IRE)	Nov 16, 1996
3m C	5m 56.2	9	12-0	Gd to firm	Acarine	Nov 18, 1985

WORCESTER

Distance	Time	Age	Weight	Going	Horse	Date
2m H	3m 35.3	6	11-7	Hard	Santopadre	May 11, 1988
2m C	3m 45.2	6	12-0	Gd to firm	Lord Esker (IRE)	Jly 15, 1998
2m 2f H	4m 2.5	5	11-13	Gd to firm	Lady For Life (IRE)	Aug 5, 2000
2m 4f H	4m 34.5	5	11-5	Firm	Wottashambles	Sept 13, 1996
2m 4f 110y C	4m 54.3	8	10-8	Gd to firm	Ross Comm	Sep 5, 2004
2m 5f 110y H	4m 48.4	4	12-2	Firm	Elite Reg	May 19, 1993
2m 7f C	5m 37.6	12	10-7	Firm	Tanora	May 2 , 1981
2m 7f 110yC	5m 43.0	6	12-0	Firm	Arlas (FR)	Sep 15, 2001
3m H	5m 29.8	7	11-11	Gd to firm	Polar Champ	Aug 5 , 2000

SPLIT SECOND SPEED RATINGS

The following list shows the fastest performances of chasers and hurdlers which have recorded a speed figure of 100 or over during the 2005-2006 season. Additional information in parentheses following the speed figure shows the distance of the race in furlongs, course, state of going and the date on which the figure was achieved.

CHASING

A Glass In Thyne 115 (24½f,Sth,GS,Jan 28)
A New Story 112 (25f,Pun,G,Apr 27)
A Piece Of Cake 105 (24f,Utt,S,Apr 30)
Abram s Bridge 104 (24f,Pun,GF,Apr 28)
Accordion Etoile 115 (16f,Pun,G,Apr 27)
Acertack 105 (20f,Plu,G,Nov 30)
Adarma 109 (24f,Leo,YS,Dec 27)
Adecco 107 (16f,Fol,GS,Jan 31)
Adelphi Theatre 101 (20½f,Lei,G,Dec 1)
Adjawar 104 (16½f,Hex,GF,Jun 11)
Admiral Peary 105 (26f,Plu,GS,Nov 20)
Advance East 103 (16½f,Chp,S,Jan 20)
Afro Man 106 (16½f,Chp,GS,Nov 23)
Ah Yeah 100 (24½f,Tow,S,Nov 26)
Aimees Mark 104 (21f,Leo,YS,Mar 5)
Aisjem 104 (25½f,Her,G,Mar 20)
Albertini 100 (20f,Clo,Y,Mar 5)
Albuhera 112 (20f,Nby,G,Nov 27)
Alcatras 106 (20½f,Wor,GF,Jun 4)
Alcopop 108 (21½f,Fak,G,Nov 15)
Alderburn 112 (24½f,Chl,GS,Mar 14)
Aleron 103 (19f,Cat,G,Jan 25)
Alfie s Sun 110 (20½f,Lei,G,Dec 7)
Alfred The Grey 106 (28f,Fon,GF,Mar 19)
Alfy Rich 101 (16f,Crl,S,Feb 8)
Algarve 110 (25f,Hex,GS,Nov 16)
All In The Stars 109 (25½f,Chl,GS,Dec 9)
Allez Petit Luis 106 (16f,Naa,HY,Mar 12)
Almaydan 108 (16f,Wet,S,Oct 28)
Almire Du Lia 105 (25f,Ayr,S,Feb 27)
Almost Broke 112 (25½f,Wcn,GS,Jan 21)
Alphabetical 108 (20f,Fon,GS,Jan 7)
Alpine Slave 108 (24f,Str,G,Sep 3)
Alvino 100 (25f,Mar,G,Oct 16)
Always 110 (16f,Nav,S,Nov 13)
Amadeus 108 (19½f,Chp,G,Apr 28)
Amarula Ridge 107 (16½f,Don,G,Dec 9)
Amber Dawn 103 (16f,Utt,GF,Sep 18)
Amicelli 108 (25½f,Her,G,Mar 6)
Amptina 101 (16f,Wor,GF,Apr 30)
Andreas 111 (16f,Ain,GS,Oct 22)
Another Club Royal 104 (24f,Mus,GF,Feb 5)
Another Conquest 102 (24½f,Tow,HY,Mar 9)
Another Joker 106 (16f,Pun,G,Apr 25)
Another Native 110 (20f,Hay,S,Dec 17)
Another Raleagh 100 (23½f,Exe,HY,Apr 27)
Another Rum 108 (25f,Ayr,S,Feb 11)
Apadi 105 (16f,Wor,GF,Apr 30)
Appach 102 (16f,Wor,G,Jun 29)
Arceye 105 (24f,Chp,G,Apr 18)
Arctic Cherry 104 (17½f,Ban,GS,Feb 10)
Arctic Lagoon 107 (25f,Hex,GS,Nov 16)
Ardaghey 105 (24½f,Tow,S,Feb 19)
Argento 102 (16f,Wet,GS,Nov 23)
Aristoxene 108 (20f,Hay,S,Jan 7)
Armaguedon 103 (16½f,Ncs,S,Jan 9)
Armaturk 114 (16f,Lin,HY,Feb 18)
Around Before 109 (24f,Str,G,Sep 3)
Arteea 107 (17f,Leo,YS,Jan 29)
Artic Jack 106 (28½f,Hay,S,Dec 17)
Ashgreen 106 (25½f,Her,G,Nov 17)
Ashley Brook 117 (16f,San,S,Dec 3)
Ashleybank House 102 (27f,Sed,GF,Apr 21)
Ashnaya 108 (20½f,Wet,G,May 5)
Ashwell 107 (21½f,Fak,G,Oct 21)
Aston 103 (25f,Hex,G,Apr 24)
Athnowen 104 (21½f,Nab,G,May 26)
Atum Re 108 (21f,Wcn,G,Nov 16)
Auburn Spirit 104 (28f,Fon,GF,Mar 19)
Auditor 107 (16½f,Tau,F,Apr 24)
Autumn Mist 102 (24f,Chp,G,Apr 28)
Avadi 106 (20½f,Wet,HY,Jan 14)
Avitta 109 (21½f,Crt,G,May 30)

Baby Run 112 (16f,Ain,GS,Oct 22)
Back In Front 106 (21f,Pun,G,Apr 25)
Back Nine 105 (20½f,Lin,G,Oct 29)
Backbeat 111 (24f,Hun,G,Oct 15)
Backpacker 105 (25f,Fol,G,Dec 13)
Bafana Boy 104 (25f,Hex,G,Apr 24)
Ball O Malt 111 (20f,Utt,GF,Sep 7)
Balladeer 106 (18f,Fon,G,Apr 11)
Ballycassidy 116 (24½f,San,S,Feb 25)
Ballyfin 101 (21f,Wcn,S,Jan 4)
Baloo 103 (20½f,Chl,G,Oct 26)
Bambi De L Orme 108 (16f,San,GF,Feb 4)
Bang And Blame 107 (28½f,Mar,S,Mar 26)
Banker Count 105 (20½f,Wet,S,Oct 29)
Bannister Lane 107 (22f,Hay,HY,Feb 23)
Bannow Strand 113 (20½f,Chl,GS,Nov 13)
Bar Gayne 105 (21f,Fol,G,Nov 28)
Barren Lands 100 (20½f,Wor,G,Mar 26)
Barrow Drive 107 (24f,Gow,GY,Jan 26)
Barryscourt Lad 102 (25f,Wet,G,Apr 24)
Barton Nic 108 (20f,Hay,S,Jan 7)
Barton Park 106 (16f,Wcn,G,Apr 23)
Basilea Star 108 (25½f,Exe,S,Feb 21)
Battlefield 106 (20f,Clo,Y,Mar 5)
Bay Island 113 (23½f,Exe,GS,Oct 18)
Bayadere 102 (20½f,Wor,G,Apr 9)
Be My Better Half 109 (22½f,Utt,HY,Feb 18)
Be My Bonne 101 (18f,Pun,S,Apr 30)
Be The Tops 108 (25f,Mar,GF,Jly 31)
Bearaway 101 (16f,Wor,G,Oct 6)
Beat The Heat 110 (20f,Utt,GF,Sep 7)
Beau Supreme 101 (24f,Nby,G,Nov 25)
Beauchamp Prince 109 (22½f,Nby,G,Mar 24)
Beaugency 100 (20½f,Hex,F,May 31)
Bee An Bee 108 (24½f,Chl,G,Mar 15)
Beef Or Salmon 118 (24f,Hay,GS,Nov 19)
Before The Mast 107 (16f,Her,GS,Feb 12)
Behavingbadly 102 (26f,Crl,S,Apr 15)
Bell Lane Lad 110 (24f,Hun,G,Dec 8)
Bellaney Jewel 108 (25f,Kel,GS,Apr 9)
Benefit 105 (25f,Wet,GF,May 19)
Bengo 106 (20½f,Lei,G,Dec 7)
Bennie s Pride 102 (21f,Leo,YS,Mar 5)
Benrajah 110 (25½f,Cat,G,Jan 12)
Berengario 105 (19f,Tau,G,Dec 8)
Bergerac 105 (16f,Cat,G,Nov 30)
Berkley 100 (25f,Pun,S,Apr 28)
Bernardon 103 (16½f,Sed,S,Nov 8)
Bertiebanoo 110 (22½f,Mar,GF,Jun 8)
Better Days 111 (22½f,Utt,HY,Feb 18)
Better Moment 104 (16½f,Chp,G,Mar 22)
Bewleys Berry 110 (21f,Chl,GS,Dec 10)
Big Bone 104 (19f,Tau,G,Jan 9)
Big Moment 105 (17f,Plu,S,Dec 12)
Big Rob 107 (17½f,Exe,S,Feb 21)
Big-And-Bold 107 (25f,Ayr,S,Feb 11)
Bill s Echo 106 (16½f,Hun,G,Oct 15)
Billie John 106 (20½f,Per,GF,Aug 23)
Billy Ballbreaker 103 (26f,Crt,G,May 28)
Billyvoddan 113 (21f,Chl,GS,Jan 1)
Black Apalachi 111 (24f,Leo,YS,Dec 27)
Black Bullet 101 (16f,Per,G,May 11)
Black De Bessy 111 (24½f,Chl,GS,Mar 14)
Blackergreen 102 (25f,Mar,S,Dec 26)
Blakeney Coast 109 (20f,Str,GF,Jly 10)
Blazing Batman 105 (19½f,Chp,G,Apr 18)
Blazing Hills 101 (26f,Utt,GF,May 29)
Bleu Superbe 111 (16f,Lin,G,Oct 29)
Blue Business 106 (23½f,Tau,GS,Feb 16)
Blunham Hill 107 (29f,War,HY,Mar 12)
Boardroom Dancer 104 (24f,Hun,G,Feb 16)
Bob Ar Aghaidh 110 (24f,Hun,G,Oct 4)
Bob Bob Bobbin 109 (24f,Lin,HY,Feb 18)
Bob The Builder 114 (24½f,Chl,GS,Mar 14)
Bob s Buster 102 (16½f,Ncs,HY,Mar 18)
Bob s The Business 101 (28½f,Mar,S,Dec 26)
Bobsbest 107 (20½f,Wor,GF,Jun 22)
Boddidley 100 (23½f,Tau,G,Dec 30)
Bogus Dreams 107 (16½f,Hex,G,May 7)
Bohemian Boy 103 (24½f,Fak,G,Jan 16)
Bohemian Spirit 106 (20f,Mus,GF,Jan 6)
Bold Bishop 109 (16f,Chl,GS,Nov 11)
Bonnet s Pieces 100 (20½f,Hun,G,Dec 8)
Bonus Bridge 102 (17f,Nby,G,Mar 3)
Boobee 106 (21½f,Str,G,Sep 3)
Bordante 102 (24f,Naa,S,Jan 21)
Bounce Back 103 (24f,Nby,GF,Mar 4)
Boundary House 106 (25½f,Wcn,S,Jan 4)
Bramblehill Duke 105 (25½f,Exe,GF,May 11)
Brandy Wine 107 (25f,Ayr,S,Jan 2)
Brave Spirit 107 (27f,Tau,GS,Jan 19)
Brave Thought 107 (16½f,Ncs,HY,Feb 25)
Breaking Breeze 105 (21f,Wcn,F,Oct 6)
Briar s Mist 106 (30f,Ncs,S,Jan 9)
Briery Fox 104 (24½f,Fak,G,Dec 22)
Brigadier Du Bois 100 (20f,Fon,GS,Jan 27)
Bright Approach 106 (28f,Str,G,May 20)
Bronzesmith 108 (21½f,Nab,G,Aug 20)
Brooklyn Breeze 117 (21f,Chl,GS,Dec 10)
Brooklyn s Gold 107 (17½f,Ban,GS,Feb 10)
Brown Teddy 102 (20½f,Hun,G,Nov 19)
Brutto Facie 102 (20f,Pun,S,Nov 20)
Buailtes And Fadas 111 (31f,Chl,GS,Mar 14)
Bubble Boy 107 (26½f,Fon,HY,Feb 19)
Buffalo Bill 103 (16f,Wcn,GS,Dec 16)
Burning Truth 102 (20½f,Wor,GF,May 8)
Burwood Breeze 102 (24½f,San,S,Mar 10)
Bushido 107 (25f,Mar,G,Oct 16)

Calatagan 107 (16f,Lei,G,Jan 10)
Calcot Flyer 103 (26f,Utt,G,May 8)
Call Me Jack 100 (16f,Her,G,Nov 17)
Calling Brave 107 (29½f,San,GF,Apr 29)
Calon Lan 108 (20f,Str,G,Jun 12)
Calvic 112 (30f,Ban,GS,Feb 10)
Camden Tanner 110 (24f,Leo,YS,Dec 27)
Cameron Bridge 109 (24f,Hun,G,Oct 15)
Canavan 104 (27f,Sed,S,Jan 24)
Cane Brake 101 (25f,Fai,SH,Feb 25)
Cansalrun 100 (21f,Wcn,G,Nov 17)
Caper 102 (24½f,Tow,GS,Apr 16)
Captain Corelli 119 (24f,Hay,S,Dec 3)
Captain Mac 103 (21f,Sed,HY,Dec 6)
Capybara 101 (25f,Hex,S,Nov 4)
Caracciola 105 (16½f,Chl,G,Mar 17)
Caribbean Cove 105 (20½f,Lei,G,Feb 1)
Carnacrack 108 (26f,Crt,G,Jly 14)
Carndale 106 (25f,Pun,S,Apr 29)
Carneys Cross 108 (24f,Leo,YS,Dec 27)
Carriage Ride 102 (26f,Crt,G,May 28)
Carthys Cross 105 (16½f,Don,G,Nov 27)
Casadei 101 (24f,Lud,GF,Oct 13)
Cassia Heights 104 (25½f,Chl,G,Apr 19)
Catch The Perk 102 (31f,Chl,GS,Dec 9)
Ceannairceach 106 (17½f,Mar,G,Jly 16)
Celestial Gold 106 (25f,Ain,G,Apr 6)
Celestial Light 103 (18f,Pun,S,Apr 30)
Celia s High 101 (27f,Sed,GF,Apr 21)
Celtic Boy 100 (20½f,Per,GS,Sep 22)
Celtic Flow 100 (24f,Ncs,S,Jan 18)
Celtic Legend 104 (16f,Cat,G,Nov 30)
Celtic Son 106 (21f,Wcn,G,Nov 5)
Celtic Star 101 (22f,Fon,GF,Sep 4)
Central House 117 (16f,Nav,S,Nov 13)
Cerium 113 (16f,San,S,Dec 3)
Cetti s Warbler 101 (20½f,Chl,GS,Nov 13)
Chabrimal Minster 111 (30f,Ban,GS,Feb 10)
Chancers Dante 101 (24f,Mus,G,Feb 15)
Channahrlie 105 (26f,War,G,Oct 31)
Chanticlier 103 (24f,Chp,G,Apr 18)
Charango Star 110 (24f,Str,S,Sep 11)
Charging 103 (19f,Leo,YS,Jan 29)
Charlies Future 103 (24½f,Tow,GS,Feb 2)
Chase The Sunset 101 (20½f,Hun,GF,Aug 29)
Chauvinist 104 (21f,Chl,G,Mar 16)
Chilling Place 107 (19½f,Exe,GS,Apr 5)
Chivite 106 (21½f,Nab,GF,Jun 14)
Christopher 106 (20f,Hay,S,Jan 7)
Church Island 113 (24f,Naa,S,Jan 21)
Cill Churnain 103 (25½f,Cat,G,Jan 12)
Clan Royal 115 (36f,Ain,GS,Apr 8)
Classic Capers 108 (19f,Don,GS,Dec 10)
Classic Native 102 (28f,Fon,GS,Nov 13)
Classic Rock 107 (24f,Hun,G,Mar 15)
Claymore 108 (16f,Lin,S,Dec 31)
Clouding Over 109 (20½f,Per,GF,Apr 28)
Coat Of Honour 109 (16f,Wet,S,Dec 26)
Cobbet 102 (16f,Lin,G,Oct 29)
Colca Canyon 104 (16f,Pun,S,Apr 26)
Coljon 108 (24f,Gow,GY,Jan 26)
College City 105 (17½f,Mar,G,Oct 2)
Collinstown 107 (19½f,Chp,G,Apr 18)
Colnel Rayburn 106 (24f,Gow,GY,Jan 26)
Colonel Monroe 112 (25f,Pun,G,Apr 27)
Colourful Life 108 (24f,Chp,G,Oct 8)
Comanche War Paint 107 (27f,Tau,GF,Nov 24)
Commercial Flyer 108 (23½f,Tau,GS,Feb 16)
Compadre 102 (16½f,Hex,G,May 7)
Comply Or Die 109 (26½f,Nby,G,Nov 26)
Compo 109 (24f,Hun,G,Feb 9)
Concert Pianist 105 (25f,Fol,S,Jan 2)
Contraband 107 (16f,San,GF,Apr 29)
Control Man 106 (29f,War,S,Jan 14)
Cool Cossack 106 (25f,Wet,GF,May 19)
Cool Dessa Blues 103 (25f,Kel,GS,Mar 19)
Cool Song 105 (26f,War,G,Oct 31)
Coolnahilla 105 (24f,Gow,GY,Jan 26)
Copsale Lad 112 (21f,Chl,G,Mar 16)
Cordilla 106 (25f,Ayr,S,Dec 22)
Cornish Rebel 109 (26½f,Nby,G,Nov 26)
Cornish Sett 110 (20f,Nby,GF,Mar 4)
Corrib Drift 103 (16f,Fol,S,Jan 17)
Corrib Lad 104 (20f,Ayr,HY,Jan 23)
Cosmocrat 105 (20½f,Chl,GS,Nov 13)
Cossack Dancer 106 (16f,Lei,G,Jan 10)
Count Oski 106 (24f,Hun,GF,Jun 7)
Coursing Run 111 (29f,War,HY,Mar 12)
Cousin Joe 103 (24f,Pun,S,Apr 29)
Cousin Nicky 110 (19½f,Exe,GS,Mar 21)
Cowboyboots 108 (29f,Plu,S,Jan 1)
Cregg House 106 (21½f,Ain,G,Apr 7)
Crimson Pirate 107 (16f,Wcn,S,Jan 4)
Croc An Oir 107 (25f,Mar,GF,Jly 31)
Croix De Guerre 113 (17½f,Mar,G,Jun 24)
Crossbow Creek 103 (16½f,Tau,GF,Nov 24)
Crozan 110 (20½f,Chl,GS,Nov 12)
Cruising River 110 (24f,Hun,G,Feb 16)
Crystal D Ainay 104 (29f,War,S,Jan 14)
Cullian 104 (19½f,Chp,G,Apr 18)
Cupids Flyer 103 (20f,Clo,Y,Mar 5)
Curtins Hill 107 (23½f,Exe,HY,Apr 27)
Cyanara 104 (24f,Hun,GF,Jun 7)
Cyborg De Sou 106 (16f,Per,G,Sep 21)
Cyborsun 101 (21f,Sed,S,Jan 10)
Cyindien 104 (24f,Hun,GF,Jun 7)

D J Flippance 107 (25f,Ayr,S,Dec 22)
Dad s Elect 100 (20½f,Hex,GF,Jun 19)
Dance Party 103 (16½f,Sed,S,Jan 10)
Dancer Life 107 (24f,Lud,G,Dec 21)
Dangerousdanmagru 109 (16½f,Chp,HY,Nov 2)
Danish Decorum 106 (16f,Utt,G,May 14)
Dante Citizen 106 (25½f,Her,GF,Apr 5)
Dante s Back 103 (23½f,Exe,GS,Oct 18)
Dantes Reef 106 (20½f,Chl,GS,Nov 13)
Darby Wall 107 (24½f,Chl,G,Oct 25)
Darina s Boy 107 (22f,Hay,GS,Apr 15)
Dark Ben 104 (25f,Kel,GS,Mar 19)
Dark Room 110 (24f,Str,GF,Jly 17)
Dark Thunder 104 (27f,Sed,GS,May 24)
Dark n Sharp 112 (20½f,Hun,GS,Nov 8)
Darkness 117 (24f,Nby,G,Nov 25)
Datito 103 (24f,Chp,HY,Dec 3)
Davenport Democrat 112 (16f,Pun,G,Apr 27)
Davenport Milenium 110 (21f,Pun,S,Apr 26)
Davids Lad 109 (24f,Pun,YS,Apr 26)
Dawton 103 (16½f,Nab,GF,Jly 17)
Day Du Roy 104 (21½f,Fak,G,Jan 27)
De Blanc 107 (22f,Tow,GS,Feb 2)
Dead Mans Dante 105 (16½f,Sed,GF,Aug 5)
Dead-Eyed Dick 103 (25½f,Her,GS,May 22)
Dealer s Choice 103 (23½f,Exe,GS,Apr 5)
Dear Deal 102 (25½f,Wcn,G,May 6)
Dedrunknmunky 105 (20f,Fon,S,Nov 4)
Deep King 109 (16f,Wor,GF,Sep 23)
Deja Vu 100 (21f,Sed,GF,Sep 27)
Deltic Arrow 103 (20f,Plu,S,Feb 27)
Demi Beau 107 (16f,Utt,GF,Sep 18)
Dempsey 110 (16f,San,GF,Feb 4)
Denarius Secundus 102 (19½f,Chp,G,Apr 18)
Dere Lyn 101 (19f,Her,GF,Apr 5)
Desailly 112 (24½f,Chl,GS,Mar 14)
Detonateur 108 (20f,Lud,G,Dec 8)
Devil s Run 101 (24f,Ncs,S,Feb 14)
Devondale 104 (24f,Ncs,GS,Nov 11)
Diamond Joshua 103 (18f,Fon,GF,Aug 18)
Dickensbury Lad 106 (24f,Str,GS,Mar 13)
Dictator 106 (16½f,Don,G,Dec 9)
Direct Access 107 (24f,Ncs,S,Nov 26)
Direct Flight 110 (20f,Ain,GS,Apr 8)
Distant Thunder 109 (24f,Hun,G,Feb 16)
Dix Villez 107 (25f,Pun,G,Apr 29)
Django 103 (17f,Nav,S,Nov 13)
Do L Enfant D Eau 101 (16f,Ayr,S,Jan 3)
Doctor Linton 106 (16f,Pun,S,Dec 11)
Dolmur 102 (20½f,Lei,G,Dec 7)
Don t Be Shy 115 (16f,Lin,HY,Feb 18)
Donovan 102 (17½f,Ban,GS,Oct 8)
Doodle Addle 108 (24f,Leo,YS,Dec 27)
Dosco 100 (16f,Naa,HY,Mar 12)
Double Honour 111 (25½f,Wcn,G,Nov 5)
Dr Mann 100 (24f,Lud,G,Feb 22)
Duke Of Buckingham 108 (21½f,Nab,G,Aug 20)
Dumadic 104 (21f,Sed,GF,Apr 17)
Dun Doire 117 (24½f,Chl,GS,Mar 14)
Dun Locha Castle 109 (28f,Fon,GF,Mar 19)
Dunbrody Millar 113 (29f,Plu,S,Jan 1)
Duncliffe 110 (21f,Pun,S,Apr 26)
Dungarvans Choice 105 (23½f,Lei,S,Feb 15)
Dunster Castle 104 (25½f,Exe,GF,May 11)
Durlston Bay 102 (24½f,San,GS,Jan 7)

Earl s Kitchen 104 (24f,Chp,S,Jan 20)
Early Start 110 (22f,Tow,G,Oct 23)
Easibrook Jane 101 (16½f,Chp,GS,Apr 8)
East Lawyer 107 (20½f,San,G,Apr 28)
East Tycoon 107 (16f,Lin,G,Oct 29)
Eau Pure 102 (21½f,Nab,GF,Jun 21)
Ebony Jack 111 (26½f,Fon,HY,Feb 19)
Ebony Light 118 (24f,Hay,HY,Jan 21)
Ede Iff 111 (24f,Lud,G,Dec 21)
Edmo Yewkay 107 (20½f,Wet,HY,Dec 3)
El Andaluz 103 (25f,Mar,S,Dec 26)
El Vaquero 108 (24½f,San,S,Dec 2)
Elegant Eskimo 106 (23½f,Exe,GS,Mar 21)
Elenas River 101 (24½f,San,S,Mar 11)
Elfkirk 104 (20f,Plu,S,Jan 16)
Eljay s Boy 109 (19½f,Chp,G,Apr 28)
Encore Cadoudal 105 (16f,Ayr,S,Nov 6)
Endless Magic 106 (18f,Pun,S,Apr 30)
Eric s Charm 118 (24½f,San,S,Mar 11)
Escompteur 106 (20f,Fon,GF,May 29)

Eskimo Pie 105 (24½f,Fak,GS,Feb 17)
Euro Bleu 101 (19f,Her,G,Nov 17)
Euro Leader 113 (16f,Naa,HY,Nov 12)
Europa 115 (21f,Chl,GS,Dec 10)
Eurotrek 111 (29f,War,S,Jan 14)
Even More 106 (23½f,Tau,GS,Feb 16)
Ever Present 103 (25f,Ayr,S,Mar 10)
Excellent Vibes 109 (25½f,Her,GF,Jun 14)
Executive Decision 102 (16f,Lei,S,Feb 15)
Exotic Dancer 111 (21f,Chl,GS,Dec 10)
Extended Favour 102 (24f,Pun,Y,Feb 5)
Extra Cache 100 (24f,Hun,G,Dec 26)
Eyze 100 (22½f,Kel,GS,Nov 5)

Faddad 100 (16f,Wor,G,Oct 6)
Fair Prospect 103 (20f,Ain,GS,Oct 22)
Falchion 100 (30f,Ncs,S,Jan 9)
Fantasmic 105 (16½f,Chp,GS,Apr 8)
Farington Lodge 103 (24f,Ncs,S,Jan 18)
Father Matt 114 (20f,Fai,HY,Dec 4)
Fatherofthebride 108 (24f,Leo,YS,Dec 27)
Fear Siuil 110 (24f,Str,GF,Jly 17)
Fearless Mel 101 (24½f,Ban,G,Sep 9)
Feel The Pride 111 (16f,Wet,G,May 5)
Felix Darby 104 (26½f,Fon,G,Apr 29)
Figaro Du Rocher 106 (17f,Kel,GF,May 18)
Fin Bec 105 (28½f,Mar,S,Dec 26)
Finzi 111 (30f,Ban,GS,Feb 10)
Fiori 106 (21½f,Ain,GS,Nov 20)
First De La Brunie 107 (21f,Wcn,S,Jan 4)
First Love 109 (21f,Wcn,S,Mar 30)
Fisherman Jack 105 (24½f,Ban,S,Mar 25)
Five Alley 105 (24f,Lin,S,Nov 9)
Flahive s First 100 (21f,Utt,G,Jly 13)
Flake 109 (16½f,Sed,S,Nov 8)
Flaming Heck 105 (16½f,Sed,S,Jan 24)
Fleet Street 105 (17f,Plu,S,Dec 12)
Flight Command 106 (16½f,Ncs,HY,Feb 25)
Flinders 100 (26½f,Fon,G,Apr 29)
Florida Dream 111 (24f,Hun,G,Dec 8)
Flower Of Pitcur 105 (16f,Lud,G,Nov 10)
Flying Patriarch 101 (16f,Fol,S,Jan 2)
Flying Spirit 110 (20f,Fon,GF,May 29)
Follow The Flow 105 (24½f,Tow,GS,Feb 2)
Fondmort 117 (21f,Chl,G,Mar 16)
Fool On The Hill 101 (20½f,Per,GF,Aug 23)
Foreman 113 (16f,Chl,GS,Mar 14)
Forest Dante 105 (25½f,Cat,G,Dec 15)
Forest Leader 102 (20f,Pun,Y,Feb 5)
Forever Dream 100 (20f,Lud,GF,Oct 20)
Forever Eyesofblue 101 (24f,Mus,G,Feb 15)
Forget The Past 116 (26½f,Chl,G,Mar 17)
Fork Lightning 113 (24½f,Chl,GS,Mar 14)
Fota Island 118 (17f,Fai,S,Jan 22)
Fountain Brig 106 (20f,Ayr,HY,Jan 23)
Fox In The Box 108 (26½f,Chp,S,Feb 25)
Francolino 106 (24½f,Tow,S,Nov 26)
Frankie Dori 104 (25f,Ayr,S,Mar 10)
Free Gift 108 (20½f,Hun,G,Nov 19)
French Executive 105 (26f,Don,G,Nov 27)
Full House 115 (20½f,San,G,Apr 28)
Fullards 101 (24f,Hun,G,Dec 8)

G V A Ireland 112 (33½f,Utt,HY,Mar 18)
Galero 103 (20f,Mus,G,Jan 20)
Gallant Approach 107 (24f,Nby,GS,Dec 14)
Gallik Dawn 111 (26f,Utt,G,May 8)
Gallion s Reach 100 (24f,Mus,GF,Feb 5)
Galtee View 107 (25½f,Exe,F,Oct 5)
Galway 101 (20½f,Wor,GF,Jun 4)
Galway Breeze 109 (16f,Wet,G,May 5)
Gangsters R Us 105 (24f,Mus,GF,Feb 5)
Garde Champetre 104 (20½f,Chl,GS,Nov 12)
Garryvoe 100 (28½f,Mar,GS,Nov 17)
Garvivonnian 109 (25f,Fai,SH,Feb 25)
Gatorade 111 (20½f,Ban,GS,Apr 29)
Gerrard 105 (21f,Fol,G,Nov 28)
Getinbybutonlyjust 105 (25f,Hex,GS,Nov 16)
Getoutwhenyoucan 107 (26½f,Nab,GF,Aug 21)
Ghadames 107 (17½f,Str,S,May 21)
Giolla An Bhaird 103 (24f,Naa,HY,Mar 12)
Giorgio 106 (20½f,Wet,GF,May 19)
Give Me Love 108 (16½f,Tau,GS,Mar 29)
Glabejet 102 (25f,Pun,S,Apr 29)
Glacial Delight 100 (23½f,Tau,GF,Nov 10)
Glen Thyne 102 (16½f,Tow,G,Apr 25)
Glenelly Gale 102 (20½f,Wet,GF,Oct 12)
Glenfarclas Boy 101 (16f,Per,G,May 11)
Glenfolan 106 (25f,Pun,G,Apr 29)
Glengarra 109 (16½f,Fak,G,Jan 16)
Gleninagh 106 (25f,Pun,G,Apr 29)
Go Nomadic 107 (22½f,Kel,GS,Apr 28)
Goblet Of Fire 102 (24f,Nby,GS,Nov 25)
Gola Supreme 102 (22f,Tow,S,Nov 3)
Goldbrook 102 (16½f,Tau,F,Apr 24)
Gone Too Far 109 (16f,Per,GS,Sep 22)
Good Heart 100 (21½f,Crt,G,Aug 29)
Good Judgement 110 (25f,Mar,HY,Nov 6)
Good Lord Louis 110 (22½f,Mar,G,Jly 16)
Good Outlook 104 (19f,Cat,G,Jan 1)
Good Step 111 (34f,Pun,S,Apr 28)
Goodbadindiferent 103 (22½f,Kel,GF,Oct 2)
Gorthnacurra 100 (16f,Wcn,G,Oct 23)
Graceful Dancer 109 (29f,War,HY,Mar 12)
Grand Slam 100 (16½f,Sed,S,Jan 24)
Graphic Approach 111 (24½f,San,GS,Jan 7)
Gray s Eulogy 103 (25½f,Wcn,G,Dec 26)
Great As Gold 105 (20f,Crl,HY,Mar 9)
Green Belt Flyer 113 (16f,Naa,HY,Nov 12)
Green Gamble 101 (16f,Wcn,G,Oct 23)
Green Ideal 107 (20f,Ayr,HY,Jan 23)
Green Tango 111 (19f,Her,S,Jan 5)
Greenhope 109 (16½f,Chl,G,Mar 17)
Groomsport 100 (24f,Pun,Y,Feb 5)
Ground Ball 116 (16f,Pun,S,Apr 26)
Ground Breaker 105 (16½f,Don,G,Dec 9)
Guilt 108 (16f,Pun,G,Apr 25)
Gumley Gale 108 (23½f,Wor,G,May 24)
Gunther McBride 105 (24f,Nby,GS,Mar 25)

Haafel 107 (16f,Lin,S,Nov 9)
Haile Selassie 109 (17½f,Ban,GS,Feb 10)
Hakim 111 (21½f,Ain,G,Apr 7)
Halcon Genelardais 109 (25½f,Exe,S,Feb 21)
Halexy 103 (20½f,Chl,G,Oct 26)
Half Inch 102 (18f,Fon,GF,Aug 18)
Hand Inn Hand 114 (20½f,Hun,G,Nov 19)
Handsuposcar 106 (20f,Fai,SH,Feb 25)
Hang Seng 103 (17f,Fai,S,Jan 22)
Happy Hussar 106 (24½f,San,S,Mar 10)
Hard Winter 101 (25f,Fai,S,Jan 22)
Harlov 100 (28½f,Mar,S,Dec 26)
Harris Bay 106 (23½f,Lei,S,Feb 15)
Harrovian 106 (25f,Ayr,S,Feb 27)
Harry Collins 104 (24½f,Fak,G,May 4)
Harry In A Hurry 101 (34f,Pun,S,Apr 28)
Harry Potter 100 (16f,Lud,G,Feb 22)
Harry s Dream 110 (24f,Str,GF,Jly 17)
Harrycone Lewis 100 (24½f,Fak,G,Jan 16)
Haut De Gamme 105 (22½f,Utt,HY,Feb 18)
Have A Perk 106 (20f,Clo,Y,Mar 5)
Hawk s Landing 106 (25f,Mar,S,Feb 17)
Hazel Bank Lass 102 (23½f,Exe,S,Dec 2)
Hazelhall Princess 108 (24f,Naa,S,Jan 21)
Hazeljack 109 (26½f,Fon,HY,Feb 19)
He s The Biz 100 (25½f,Wcn,G,Oct 23)
He s The Gaffer 106 (18f,Fon,G,Feb 3)
He s The Guv Nor 113 (22½f,Utt,HY,Feb 18)
Heartache 104 (24½f,Tow,S,Jan 6)
Hedgehunter 118 (26½f,Chl,G,Mar 17)
Heez A Wonder 108 (21f,Leo,S,Dec 29)
Hehasalife 107 (23½f,Tau,F,Oct 27)
Helvetius 102 (23½f,Wet,G,May 26)
Henry s Pride 104 (20f,Crl,HY,Mar 9)
Herecomestanley 100 (21f,Sed,GF,Apr 17)
Hever Road 109 (26½f,Nab,GF,Apr 15)
Hi Cloy 118 (17f,Leo,YS,Dec 27)
Hi Laurie 108 (24f,Utt,S,Oct 28)
Hiers De Brouage 103 (23½f,Exe,GS,Oct 18)
High Cotton 105 (30f,Ncs,S,Jan 9)
High Drama 103 (20½f,Wor,GF,Jun 4)
High Peak 102 (20f,Utt,GS,Jly 5)
Hit The Net 106 (20f,Pun,Y,Feb 5)
Ho Ho Hill 105 (19f,Her,GF,May 10)
Holey Moley 106 (25f,Ayr,S,Feb 27)
Hollows Mill 103 (16f,Ayr,S,Nov 6)
Holy Joe 107 (23½f,Exe,GS,Apr 5)
Homer Wells 108 (24f,Leo,YS,Dec 28)
Honan 100 (16½f,Nab,G,Jun 6)
Hoo La Baloo 118 (16f,San,S,Dec 3)
Horcott Bay 104 (25½f,Her,G,Mar 6)
Hors La Loi III 111 (16f,Wcn,G,Feb 2)
Horus 110 (20f,Nby,GF,Mar 4)
Howrwenow 105 (26f,Plu,GS,Nov 20)

I Hear Thunder 109 (24f,Chp,G,Oct 8)
I m On The Line 107 (34f,Pun,S,Apr 28)
Icare D Oudairies 104 (24½f,Ban,S,Mar 25)
Iceberge 106 (24f,Str,G,Oct 15)
Icy Belle 106 (23½f,Tau,F,Oct 27)
Ideal Du Bois Beury 105 (22½f,Kel,GF,Oct 2)
Idealko 104 (20½f,Ban,G,May 14)
Idiome 101 (24f,Str,GS,Mar 13)
Idle Talk 113 (23½f,Wor,G,Nov 1)
Idole First 112 (17f,Plu,GS,Feb 13)
Il De Boitron 109 (31f,Chl,GS,Mar 14)
Il Athou 106 (20f,Hay,S,Nov 3)
Ile De Paris 105 (23½f,Exe,HY,Apr 27)
Illineylad 103 (23½f,Tau,F,Oct 27)
Illoveturtle 101 (24½f,Fak,S,Feb 17)
Imaginaire 104 (16f,Lin,S,Nov 9)
Impek 119 (20½f,Hun,G,Nov 19)
Imperial Rocket 102 (16f,Lud,GF,Jan 30)
In Compliance 119 (20f,Fai,GY,Apr 16)
In The Frame 102 (20½f,Ban,G,Sep 9)
Inaki 105 (16f,Fol,GS,Jan 31)
Inca Trail 109 (24f,Hun,G,Oct 15)
Incas 103 (17f,Fai,HY,Dec 4)
Indalo 107 (24½f,San,S,Mar 11)
Indian Squaw 101 (26f,Plu,GF,May 8)
Infrasonique 100 (25½f,Wcn,S,Jan 4)
Inglewood 106 (25f,Hex,GF,Jun 19)
Innisfree 105 (27f,Sed,GF,Aug 30)
Innox 118 (24½f,San,S,Feb 25)
Instant Appeal 100 (22f,Tow,G,Apr 25)
Interdit 108 (22½f,Kel,GS,Nov 5)
Iris Bleu 116 (25½f,Wcn,G,Nov 5)
Iris Royal 105 (20½f,Hun,G,Nov 19)
Iris s Gift 113 (24½f,Chl,G,Oct 26)
Iris s Prince 100 (20f,Crl,S,Mar 19)
Irish Hussar 115 (24½f,Chl,GS,Mar 14)
Iron Man 103 (16f,Crl,HY,Jan 14)
Isard III 107 (22½f,Mar,G,Jly 16)
Isellido 105 (22½f,Kel,GS,Jan 13)
Island Supreme 106 (16f,Naa,HY,Mar 12)
It Takes Time 113 (29½f,San,GF,Apr 29)
It Was Nt Me 108 (20f,Lud,G,Dec 8)
It s Definite 106 (23½f,Wor,GF,Jly 20)
Italiano 106 (17½f,Ban,GS,Feb 10)
Its Wallace Jnr 101 (21f,Fol,GS,Feb 14)
Itsuptoharry 108 (20f,Hay,S,Dec 17)
Iverain 101 (25f,Ain,G,May 13)
Ivoire De Beaulieu 109 (31f,Chl,GS,Dec 9)
Iznogoud 104 (26½f,Chl,G,Mar 17)

Jacarado 105 (23½f,Lei,S,Feb 15)
Jack Fuller 105 (20½f,Lei,S,Feb 15)
Jack High 106 (24f,Leo,Y,Feb 12)
Jack Martin 105 (21½f,Fak,G,Jan 27)
Jacks Craic 110 (16f,Ain,G,Apr 6)
Jackson 106 (24½f,Fak,G,Jan 16)
Jacquemart Colombe 102 (28f,Sed,G,May 2)
Jaffa 109 (20½f,Ban,GS,Apr 29)
Jakari 109 (24½f,San,GS,Jan 7)
Jallastep 106 (20½f,Per,GF,Aug 23)
James Victor 103 (20f,Str,GF,Jly 10)
Jamica Plane 102 (16f,Per,GF,Jly 10)
Jaoka Du Gord 106 (25f,Wet,G,Apr 24)
Jaquouille 108 (24f,Leo,YS,Dec 28)
Jaybejay 100 (16½f,Chp,HY,Nov 2)
Jazz Du Forez 102 (25½f,Her,GF,Apr 28)
Jazz Night 102 (16f,Wor,GF,Aug 23)
Jefertiti 105 (16f,Per,GS,Sep 22)
Jeff De Chalamont 100 (20f,Pun,S,Nov 20)
Jericho III 101 (16f,San,S,Mar 11)
Jetowa Du Bois Hue 102 (17½f,Str,G,Sep 3)
Jexel 104 (21½f,Ayr,G,Mar 23)
Jim 114 (20f,Pun,S,Dec 11)
Jimmy Bond 107 (20f,Crl,S,Mar 19)
Jiver 105 (24f,Str,G,Oct 15)
Joaaci 101 (26½f,Chl,GS,Jan 1)
Jodante 105 (20f,Mus,GF,Jan 6)
Joe Deane 103 (24f,Lud,G,Feb 22)
Joe McHugh 100 (23½f,Lei,G,Feb 1)
Joes Edge 109 (25f,Pun,S,Apr 29)
Joey Tribbiani 108 (17½f,Mar,G,Feb 7)
John Rich 103 (25f,Hex,GS,Nov 16)
Johnny Grand 102 (17f,Sth,G,Jly 15)
Joint Agreement 108 (24f,Leo,YS,Dec 27)
Jolejoker 110 (20½f,Wor,G,Mar 26)
Jolika 101 (25f,Hex,G,Apr 30)
Jolly Boy 106 (16f,Her,G,Nov 29)
Joly Bey 110 (25½f,Wcn,G,Nov 5)
Jonanaud 100 (19½f,Exe,GS,Apr 5)
Jonny s Kick 105 (22f,Tow,G,Apr 25)
Jordan s Ridge 105 (20½f,Per,GF,Aug 23)
Joseph Beuys 101 (25½f,Wcn,S,Mar 9)
Judaic Ways 104 (24f,Lud,GF,Oct 13)
Julies Boy 104 (16f,Fol,GS,Jan 31)
Julius Caesar 105 (22½f,Mar,GS,Nov 17)
Jumpty Dumpty 105 (23½f,Exe,GS,Oct 18)
Jungle Jinks 109 (25f,Wet,HY,Jan 14)
Junior Des Ormeaux 106 (20f,Ayr,S,Jan 3)
Jupiter Jo 102 (22½f,Kel,GF,Oct 2)
Jupon Vert 105 (16½f,Nab,GF,Apr 28)
Jurado Express 105 (16f,San,S,Feb 24)
Just 107 (20f,Pun,Y,Feb 5)
Just A Splash 103 (22f,Tow,G,Mar 22)
Just In Debt 103 (31f,Chl,GS,Dec 9)
Just Muckin Around 108 (21½f,Nab,GF,Aug 9)
Just Reuben 106 (23½f,Tau,F,Oct 27)
Justified 121 (20f,Fai,GY,Apr 16)
Juveigneur 116 (24½f,Chl,GS,Mar 14)

Kadarann 103 (21f,Chl,G,Apr 19)
Kadount 100 (16f,Lin,S,Dec 31)
Kahuna 104 (16f,Pun,S,Dec 11)
Kalca Mome 109 (16f,Hay,HY,Feb 18)
Kalou 107 (16f,Mus,GF,Nov 25)
Kandjar D Allier 113 (20½f,Chl,GS,Nov 12)
Kappelhoff 103 (24½f,Tow,G,Mar 22)
Karakum 100 (16½f,Hun,GF,Aug 29)
Karo De Vindecy 107 (21½f,Crt,G,Aug 29)
Kasthari 110 (20½f,Hun,G,Nov 19)
Kausse De Thaix 104 (24f,Wdr,G,Nov 18)
Kauto Star 118 (16f,San,S,Dec 3)
Keen Leader 112 (24f,Hay,GS,Nov 19)
Keepers Mead 103 (19½f,Exe,GS,Mar 21)
Keepthedreamalive 105 (19½f,Exe,F,Apr 18)
Kelantan 110 (22f,Tow,G,Oct 23)
Kelly 105 (24½f,Fak,G,May 4)
Kelrev 108 (21f,Chl,G,Mar 16)
Keltic Bard 111 (24½f,Sth,GS,Jan 28)
Keltic Lord 112 (24f,Str,GF,Jly 17)
Ken tucky 108 (24½f,San,GS,Nov 5)
Kercabellec 103 (16½f,Fak,G,Jan 16)
Kerry Lads 111 (25f,Wet,HY,Mar 18)
Kerryhead Windfarm 106 (21f,Leo,HY,Jan 15)
Kew Jumper 103 (18½f,Nby,GS,Jan 11)
Key Phil 107 (20½f,Per,G,Apr 26)
Kicking King 118 (25f,Pun,YS,Apr 27)
Kid Z Play 106 (16f,Per,HY,Jun 5)
Kids Inheritance 107 (17f,Kel,GS,Mar 19)
Kill Devil Hill 115 (20f,Fai,HY,Dec 4)
Killultagh Storm 108 (20½f,Ban,GS,Apr 29)
Kilty Lass 104 (24½f,Tow,GF,Oct 5)
Kimoe Warrior 100 (22½f,Mar,G,May 15)
Kinburn 115 (25f,Ayr,G,Apr 22)
Kind Sir 107 (20f,Str,G,Jun 12)
King Barry 109 (25f,Ayr,S,Feb 11)
King Bee 109 (24f,Hay,HY,Feb 23)
King Eider 107 (16½f,Sed,GF,Aug 5)
King Harald 104 (27½f,Chl,GS,Nov 12)
King Johns Castle 110 (16f,Naa,HY,Mar 12)
King Killone 110 (25f,Wet,HY,Mar 18)
King Of Gothland 104 (24f,Hun,G,Nov 2)
King Of Killeen 107 (18f,Pun,S,Apr 30)
King Of The Arctic 101 (16½f,Sed,S,Nov 8)
King s Bounty 105 (25f,Kel,S,Apr 27)
Kings Brook 107 (16f,Utt,GF,Sep 18)
Kingscliff 119 (24f,Hay,GS,Nov 19)
Kinkeel 100 (16½f,Tau,F,Apr 24)
Kirov King 106 (20f,Plu,S,Mar 27)
Kitski 104 (22f,Tow,G,Mar 22)
Kittenkat 109 (26½f,Chp,S,Jan 28)
Kniaz 102 (16f,Per,G,Aug 24)
Knight s Emperor 106 (16½f,Nab,GF,Aug 21)
Kock De La Vesvre 103 (24f,Utt,S,Apr 30)
Koquelicot 109 (31f,Chl,GS,Mar 14)
Korelo 110 (26½f,Chp,S,Jan 28)
Koumba 102 (24f,Chp,GS,Oct 8)
Kyper Disco 104 (18f,Fon,GS,Jan 7)

L Ami 117 (24½f,San,S,Feb 25)
L Aventure 117 (29½f,Chp,GS,Dec 27)
L Oiseau 103 (16f,Wcn,G,Oct 23)
Lacdoudal 117 (21f,Chl,GS,Dec 10)
Ladalko 116 (24½f,San,S,Feb 25)
Lady Lambrini 104 (20f,Utt,GS,Jly 5)
Lahinch Lad 101 (23½f,Wor,GF,Jly 13)
Lakil Princess 103 (16f,Pun,G,Apr 25)
Lambrini Bianco 105 (29f,War,GF,Mar 21)
Lamp s Return 101 (16½f,War,S,Dec 4)
Lanmire Tower 101 (22½f,Mar,G,May 15)
Latimer s Place 106 (21f,Wcn,G,Nov 16)
Latin Queen 109 (19½f,Exe,F,Apr 18)
Launde 105 (19½f,Chp,HY,Mar 11)
Lazy But Lively 106 (28½f,Mar,S,Mar 26)
Le Jaguar 100 (24f,Chp,G,Oct 8)
Le Passing 119 (21f,Chl,GS,Dec 10)
Le Rochelais 104 (19½f,Exe,GS,Apr 5)
Le Roi Miguel 104 (20f,Ain,S,Oct 23)
Le Seychellois 106 (17f,Nby,G,Nov 26)
Le Volfoni 113 (20f,Ayr,G,Apr 22)
Leading Man 109 (21f,Chl,GS,Jan 1)
Levallois 107 (28f,Fon,GF,Mar 19)
Lewis Island 108 (18f,Fon,G,Apr 11)
Liberthine 113 (29½f,San,GF,Apr 29)
Lightning Strikes 101 (21½f,Fak,G,Apr 17)
Lik Wood Power 102 (20½f,Wor,GF,May 14)
Like A Bee 108 (24f,Leo,YS,Dec 27)
Limerick Boy 108 (24½f,San,GF,Feb 4)
Limerick Leader 100 (25f,Mar,G,Oct 16)
Limerick Lord 105 (16f,Naa,HY,Nov 12)
Lin D Estruval 105 (25f,Fol,G,Dec 13)
Lincam 108 (24f,Leo,YS,Dec 27)
Lindsay 103 (16f,Her,GS,Nov 6)
Lisaan 104 (21f,Leo,S,Dec 29)
Lissbonney Project 111 (17f,Fai,S,Jan 22)
Little Big Horse 111 (22½f,Mar,G,Sep 24)
Little Flora 106 (17f,Kel,S,Apr 3)
Liverpool Echo 105 (22½f,Mar,G,Jly 16)
Livingstonebramble 105 (16f,Pun,G,Apr 25)
Lizzie Bathwick 106 (21f,Fol,G,Nov 28)
Lochiedubs 104 (22½f,Kel,GS,Apr 28)
Locksmith 104 (16f,San,GF,Feb 4)
Lodestar 108 (28f,Sed,G,May 2)
Log On Intersky 105 (17½f,Mar,S,Feb 17)
Lonesome Man 109 (20f,Ain,G,Jun 16)
Longdale 102 (16½f,Sed,S,Jan 10)
Look To The Future 100 (19½f,Chp,G,Apr 18)
Lord N Master 106 (26½f,Nab,G,Jun 6)
Lord Alphieross 101 (20f,Pun,Y,Feb 5)
Lord Anner 112 (23½f,Exe,GS,Oct 18)
Lord Broadway 109 (24½f,Tow,G,Mar 22)
Lord Brock 102 (24f,Hay,S,Jan 7)
Lord Dundaniel 105 (21½f,Nab,G,May 16)
Lord Gunnerslake 101 (20½f,Lei,G,Feb 1)
Lord Jack 108 (31f,Chl,G,Nov 11)
Lord Killeshanra 112 (23½f,Exe,GS,Nov 18)
Lord Maizey 103 (19½f,Chp,GS,Dec 27)
Lord Of Illusion 100 (26½f,Chl,GS,Jan 1)
Lord Of The Hill 102 (16f,Wor,GF,May 8)
Lord Olympia 110 (20f,Hay,HY,Feb 18)
Lord On The Run 108 (18f,Fon,G,Apr 11)
Lord Rodney 106 (20f,Ain,GS,Apr 8)
Lord Sam 110 (20½f,Chl,GS,Nov 12)
Lord Transcend 112 (24f,Hay,S,Dec 3)
Lorient Express 107 (16f,Wcn,G,Dec 26)
Loss Of Faith 108 (20f,Pun,S,Nov 20)
Lost In Normandy 108 (20½f,Wet,HY,Jan 14)

Lost In The Snow 102 (20½f,Wor,GF,Aug 17)
Lost Time 108 (24f,Leo,YS,Dec 27)
Lothian Falcon 107 (25½f,Cat,G,Dec 15)
Lotomore Lad 108 (24f,Naa,HY,Mar 12)
Lou Du Moulin Mas 106 (25f,Mar,G,Oct 16)
Lough Derg 107 (20½f,Chl,GS,Nov 12)
Loulou Nivernais 112 (16½f,Sed,S,Nov 8)
Lovely Native 105 (21½f,Ayr,G,Mar 23)
Loy s Lad 101 (16½f,Hex,GF,Sep 30)
Lubinas 106 (20½f,Hun,GS,Jan 13)
Lucky Duck 104 (16f,Crl,S,Apr 15)
Lucky Leader 104 (24f,Chp,G,Apr 18)
Lucky Luk 107 (26½f,Fon,GF,Apr 27)
Lulumar 105 (24f,Str,GS,Mar 13)
Luneray 108 (24f,Str,G,Sep 3)
Lustral Du Seuil 104 (16f,San,GS,Nov 5)
Luzcadou 104 (31f,Chl,G,Nov 11)

Macgeorge 106 (25½f,Her,GF,Apr 28)
Macmar 107 (16½f,Chp,HY,Nov 2)
Made In Japan 111 (21f,Chl,GS,Jan 1)
Madison Du Berlais 109 (17½f,Mar,G,Feb 7)
Magic Mark 103 (18f,Pun,S,Apr 30)
Magic Of Sydney 100 (25f,Fol,G,Dec 13)
Magic Sky 110 (16f,Wor,GF,Sep 23)
Magico 107 (18f,Fon,GS,Jan 7)
Magnificent Seven 106 (24f,Mus,GF,Jan 6)
Maidstone Monument 108 (21½f,Nab,GF,Jun 21)
Majella s Boy 105 (20f,Clo,Y,Mar 5)
Majestic Moonbeam 101 (25f,Fol,G,Nov 28)
Majlis 110 (16f,Naa,HY,Mar 12)
Major Belle 102 (21f,Sed,HY,Mar 28)
Major Benefit 109 (25f,Mar,HY,Nov 6)
Major Vernon 101 (21f,Leo,HY,Jan 15)
Make It Easy 101 (24½f,Tow,GF,Oct 5)
Malek 110 (24f,Hay,S,Dec 3)
Malko De Beaumont 105 (21f,Utt,GS,Feb 4)
Mamideos 101 (24f,Nby,GF,Mar 4)
Manawanui 102 (20f,Plu,GS,Oct 31)
Mandica 102 (20f,Utt,S,Apr 30)
Mandingo Chief 102 (22f,Tow,G,Apr 25)
Manoram 103 (16f,Wor,GF,May 8)
Mansony 112 (20f,Fai,HY,Dec 4)
Marcel 108 (16f,Lud,GF,Jan 30)
Marcus Du Berlais 108 (24f,Leo,YS,Dec 27)
Mariah Rollins 110 (20f,Ain,G,Apr 7)
Maristania 107 (24f,Naa,S,Jan 21)
Mark Equal 107 (20½f,Chl,GS,Nov 13)
Marked Man 110 (20½f,Hun,GS,Nov 8)
Martha s Kinsman 101 (24f,Lud,GF,Apr 13)
Master D Or 106 (20f,Plu,GS,Oct 31)
Master Henry 101 (16½f,Nab,GF,Aug 21)
Master Papa 100 (16f,Per,G,Apr 27)
Master Rex 103 (16f,Wcn,G,Dec 26)
Master Sebastian 103 (16½f,Ncs,HY,Dec 5)
Master Tern 102 (23½f,Wor,GF,Aug 5)
Matmata De Tendron 107 (26f,Crl,HY,Mar 9)
Matthew Muroto 105 (18f,Fon,G,Apr 11)
Maxie McDonald 104 (24f,Lud,G,May 3)
Maybeseven 101 (24½f,Tow,S,Nov 26)
Mazileo 103 (25½f,Her,GF,Jun 14)
Mckelvey 113 (25f,Ayr,G,Apr 22)
Me Tows 105 (24f,Naa,S,Jan 21)
Medison 110 (16½f,Tau,GS,Mar 29)
Megapac 101 (16f,Wcn,S,Jan 4)
Meggie s Beau 110 (24f,Hun,G,Mar 15)
Mel In Blue 109 (23½f,Wor,G,Nov 1)
Melford 104 (20f,Hay,G,Oct 20)
Merchants Friend 103 (27½f,Chl,GS,Nov 12)
Merriott s Oscar 105 (20f,Str,GS,Mar 13)
Merry Path 103 (26f,Utt,GF,May 29)
Metal Detector 108 (31f,Per,GF,Apr 28)
Mexican 105 (16½f,Sed,S,Nov 8)
Mexico Way 105 (24f,Naa,HY,Nov 12)
Mick Divine 103 (27f,Tau,GF,Nov 24)
Middleway 109 (27f,Sed,GF,Apr 17)
Midnight Gunner 110 (26f,War,G,Oct 31)
Mighty Matters 108 (22f,Tow,GS,Dec 26)
Migwell 100 (24½f,San,S,Mar 11)
Mikasa 103 (20f,Ncs,S,Jan 18)
Mill Bank 106 (19½f,Chp,G,Apr 18)
Millenaire 105 (23½f,Lei,G,Dec 7)
Milord Lescribaa 103 (21½f,Nab,GF,Jun 14)
Mini Dare 106 (24f,Hun,GS,Nov 2)
Mioche D Estruval 105 (24f,Str,GS,Mar 13)
Miss Mattie Ross 112 (22½f,Kel,GS,Nov 5)
Miss Pross 102 (16½f,Sed,S,Feb 6)
Miss Shakira 103 (16f,Her,G,Nov 17)
Missed That 113 (21f,Pun,G,Apr 25)
Missyl 100 (20f,Plu,GS,Apr 17)
Mister Flint 109 (20½f,Ban,GS,Jly 29)
Mister McGoldrick 118 (16f,Wet,S,Dec 27)
Misty Dancer 111 (16½f,Tau,GS,Mar 29)
Misty Future 101 (24½f,Tow,GS,Feb 2)
Mixsterthetrixster 113 (21f,Chl,GS,Dec 10)
Mobasher 100 (25½f,Her,G,Mar 6)
Model Son 115 (24½f,Chl,GS,Mar 14)
Moment Of Madness 107 (17½f,Mar,G,Feb 7)
Mon Mome 111 (24½f,Chl,G,Mar 15)
Monet s Garden 116 (16f,Chl,GS,Mar 14)
Monger Lane 103 (23½f,Lei,GS,Jan 24)
Monita Des Bois 107 (21½f,Crt,HY,May 25)
Monkerhostin 117 (20½f,Hun,G,Nov 19)
Monsieur Georges 104 (24f,Hun,G,Dec 8)
Montayral 103 (27½f,Chl,GS,Nov 12)
Monteforte 105 (25½f,Her,G,Mar 6)
Monterey Bay 113 (25f,Pun,G,Apr 27)
Montgermont 113 (24f,Lin,HY,Feb 18)
Monticelli 101 (16f,Per,G,Sep 21)
Montifault 100 (24f,Str,G,Jun 12)
Montreal 105 (21½f,Nab,GF,Aug 9)
Monty s Quest 103 (25½f,Cat,G,Dec 15)
Moorlands Again 108 (25f,Wet,HY,Jan 14)
Moorlaw 105 (16½f,Don,G,Dec 9)
Moscow Dancer 111 (17f,Kel,GF,May 18)
Moscow Flyer 118 (16f,Pun,S,Apr 26)
Moscow Gold 100 (16f,Her,G,Nov 29)
Moscow Whisper 100 (23½f,Exe,GF,May 11)
Mossy Green 109 (16f,Pun,S,Apr 26)
Motcombe 106 (21f,Wcn,G,Nov 17)
Moulin Riche 107 (24f,Hay,HY,Feb 23)
Mount Clerigo 108 (24f,Utt,HY,Mar 18)
Mountgarry 106 (20f,Clo,Y,Mar 5)
Mounthooley 103 (21½f,Crt,G,May 30)
Moustique De L Isle 112 (25f,Mar,HY,Nov 6)
Move Over 100 (25½f,Cat,GS,Mar 8)
Moving Earth 104 (24f,Str,G,Jun 12)
Moyliscar 100 (21f,Wcn,G,Nov 17)
Mr Babbage 112 (20f,Pun,S,Nov 20)
Mr Bigglesworth 101 (16½f,Sed,GS,May 24)
Mr Boo 108 (17f,Plu,GS,Apr 16)
Mr Ed 108 (20½f,Ban,GS,Jly 29)
Mr Fluffy 111 (24f,Hun,G,Oct 15)
Mr Laggan 102 (20½f,Hex,F,May 31)
Mr Prickle 101 (20f,Ncs,S,Feb 14)
Mrs Be 106 (31f,Chl,GS,Mar 14)
Muhtenbar 110 (16f,Wcn,G,Feb 2)
Mullacash 108 (25f,Pun,S,Apr 29)
Mullensgrove 107 (24f,Utt,GF,Jun 9)
Multeen River 106 (16f,Wet,S,Oct 28)
Multi Talented 100 (26½f,Fon,HY,Feb 19)
Music To My Ears 106 (24f,Str,GF,Aug 14)
Muttley Maguire 103 (23½f,Wor,GF,May 14)
My Lucky Rose 101 (20f,Ayr,HY,Jan 23)
My Will 117 (24½f,San,S,Feb 25)
My World 109 (17f,Plu,S,Dec 12)
Mylo 102 (20f,Utt,G,Jly 13)
Myson 105 (20f,Plu,G,Nov 30)
Mystical Star 106 (20f,Plu,S,Feb 27)

Nadover 107 (20½f,Ban,S,Dec 14)
Nagano 105 (20½f,Wor,GF,May 8)
Napolitain 114 (21f,Chl,GS,Jan 1)
Native Beat 107 (24f,Pun,YS,Apr 26)
Native Cooper 105 (17f,Fai,S,Jan 22)
Native Coral 108 (20½f,Per,GF,Aug 23)
Native Daisy 103 (22f,Fon,GF,Sep 4)
Native Ivy 109 (24½f,San,GS,Nov 5)
Native Jack 113 (31f,Chl,GS,Mar 14)
Native Upmanship 118 (16f,Pun,S,Apr 26)
Natural Storm 110 (20f,Pun,G,Apr 26)
Naunton Brook 112 (22f,Tow,G,Oct 23)
Navarone 105 (23½f,Wor,G,May 24)
Nawamees 104 (18f,Fon,GF,Aug 18)
Nayodabayo 110 (20f,Lud,G,Dec 8)
Nazimabad 108 (20½f,Chl,G,Oct 26)
Ned Kelly 112 (20f,Pun,S,Dec 11)
Neltina 103 (16f,Wcn,G,Apr 23)
Nephite 101 (16f,Per,HY,Jun 5)
Neptune Joly 106 (20½f,Per,GF,Apr 28)
Never 106 (16f,Utt,GF,Sep 18)
Never Awol 107 (24½f,Tow,S,Nov 26)
Never Compromise 108 (31f,Chl,GS,Mar 14)
New Alco 110 (20f,Ain,GS,Apr 8)
New Bird 102 (17½f,Ban,GS,Oct 8)
New Field 107 (21f,Leo,YS,Mar 5)
New Perk 109 (21½f,Fak,G,Nov 15)
Newmill 112 (16f,Chl,G,Mar 15)
Nice Try 107 (20½f,San,S,Mar 10)
Nick Junior 100 (26f,Sth,G,Jly 15)
Nick The Jewel 106 (16f,Wor,G,Oct 6)
Nickname 113 (21f,Leo,HY,Jan 15)
Nifty Roy 103 (16f,Crl,S,Apr 15)
Nil Desperandum 115 (36f,Ain,GS,Apr 8)
No Full 113 (20f,Hay,HY,Feb 18)
No Half Session 105 (24½f,Chl,GS,Mar 14)
No Kidding 106 (24f,Mus,GF,Feb 5)
No Picnic 104 (25f,Kel,GS,Apr 9)
No Visibility 111 (21f,Wcn,S,Mar 9)
Noble Baron 103 (25½f,Wcn,G,Nov 16)
Noble Buck 113 (31f,Per,GF,Apr 28)
Noble Justice 103 (21f,Wcn,F,Oct 6)
Noisetine 107 (19½f,Chp,HY,Dec 3)
Nomadic Blaze 100 (21½f,Crt,G,May 30)
Non So 112 (21f,Chl,G,Mar 16)
Nonchalant 105 (16f,Naa,HY,Nov 12)
Nopekan 102 (16f,Lud,G,Apr 24)
Norma Hill 109 (16f,Lud,GF,Jan 30)
Northern Deal 103 (20f,Lud,GF,Feb 8)
Northern Flash 101 (16½f,Hex,G,May 7)
Noshinannikin 102 (20½f,Wet,GF,May 19)
Not A Trace 107 (20½f,Per,GF,Apr 28)
Notanotherdonkey 103 (20½f,Chl,G,Oct 26)
Now Then Sid 107 (21f,Sed,F,Jly 25)
Nowator 106 (16f,Utt,GS,Jun 2)
Numbersixvalverde 117 (36f,Ain,GS,Apr 8)
Nycteos 110 (17f,Plu,GS,Feb 13)
Nykel 103 (25½f,Wcn,S,Jan 4)
Nyrche 109 (16f,Wcn,G,Nov 16)

O Toole 106 (16½f,Nab,GF,Apr 28)
Odagh Odyssey 100 (17f,Sth,G,Apr 29)
Oh My Lord 107 (31f,Chl,G,Nov 11)
Old Flame 116 (17f,Fai,S,Jan 22)
Old Marsh 103 (17½f,Str,S,May 21)
Oliverjohn 108 (21½f,Crt,G,May 30)
Ollie Magern 119 (25f,Wet,S,Oct 29)
Olney Lad 112 (25f,Pun,G,Apr 28)
On The Outside 112 (24f,Hun,G,Oct 4)
On Y Va 107 (20f,Crl,S,Mar 19)
One Cornetto 105 (22f,Fon,GS,Jan 27)
One Four Shannon 114 (25f,Pun,G,Apr 27)
One More Minute 105 (25f,Pun,G,Apr 28)
Oneway 113 (16f,San,S,Dec 3)
Opal Ridge 100 (22f,Tow,G,Apr 25)
Optimistic Harry 108 (20f,Utt,GS,Jly 5)
Ornella Speed 102 (21f,Sed,HY,Feb 21)
Oscar Performance 100 (25½f,Wcn,S,Jan 4)
Osiris 107 (25f,Pun,S,Apr 29)
Oso Magic 104 (20f,Ncs,GS,Nov 26)
Ossmoses 117 (28½f,Hay,HY,Feb 18)
Oulart 109 (25f,Pun,G,Apr 28)
Our Armageddon 115 (22½f,Utt,HY,Feb 18)
Our Ben 114 (21f,Leo,Y,Feb 12)
Our Jolly Swagman 103 (21½f,Nab,GF,May 10)
Our Vic 117 (20½f,Lin,HY,Feb 18)
Over Siberia 103 (20f,Fai,SH,Feb 25)
Over The Storm 105 (25f,Mar,G,Apr 29)

Paddy Fitz 101 (20f,Pun,Y,Feb 5)
Paddy The Optimist 102 (25½f,Her,G,Mar 20)
Page Point 104 (21f,Sed,G,May 2)
Pak Jack 110 (16f,Lin,G,Oct 29)
Palua 110 (16f,Lud,G,Jan 12)
Pangeran 103 (24½f,Tow,GF,Oct 5)
Panmure 104 (20½f,Hex,F,May 31)
Papua 111 (16f,Utt,GS,Jun 2)
Pardishar 107 (21f,Fol,GS,Feb 14)
Parish Oak 104 (20½f,Lei,G,Feb 1)
Parisian Storm 108 (24½f,Ban,G,Aug 13)
Parisienne Gale 102 (17½f,Crt,G,Aug 27)
Parkinson 101 (20½f,Lei,S,Feb 28)
Parsons Legacy 111 (25½f,Chl,G,Apr 19)
Partners Choice 105 (22½f,Kel,GF,Oct 2)
Party Games 104 (26½f,Fon,HY,Feb 26)
Pass Me A Dime 111 (20½f,War,S,Dec 13)
Pass Me By 103 (20f,Hay,G,Oct 20)
Patriarch 100 (20½f,Hun,GS,Jan 13)
Patricksnineteenth 101 (19½f,Chp,GS,Dec 27)
Pavey Ark 105 (21½f,Crt,G,Aug 29)
Paxford Jack 106 (24½f,Fak,GF,May 15)
Pay It Forward 110 (25f,Pun,S,Apr 29)
Peach Of A Citizen 103 (25½f,Her,GF,Oct 16)
Pearly Jack 108 (24f,Leo,YS,Dec 27)
Pebble Bay 110 (21½f,Crt,G,May 30)
Pedina 103 (24f,Hun,G,Nov 2)
Penneyrose Bay 106 (20f,Str,GS,Mar 13)
Penny Hall 100 (18f,Pun,S,Apr 30)
Penthouse Minstrel 106 (24½f,Chl,G,Oct 25)
Pequenita 108 (21½f,Crt,HY,May 25)
Perle De Puce 101 (19½f,Tow,S,Jan 6)
Perouse 107 (16f,Her,GF,Jun 8)
Persian Point 102 (16f,Cat,GS,Mar 8)
Personal Assurance 109 (23½f,Wor,G,May 24)
Pessimistic Dick 103 (25f,Kel,GS,Oct 22)
Pete The Painter 103 (23½f,Wor,G,Jly 6)
Petolinski 104 (24½f,Tow,G,May 17)
Phar City 105 (25½f,Wcn,G,May 6)
Phar From Frosty 109 (24f,Str,S,Sep 11)
Phar Out Phavorite 100 (17f,Nby,G,Nov 25)
Phase Three 101 (16f,Per,GF,Jly 10)
Phildari 101 (20f,Mar,GF,Jly 31)
Philson Run 100 (25½f,Exe,GS,Feb 12)
Pietro Vannucci 107 (20½f,Hun,GS,Nov 8)
Pizarro 112 (25f,Pun,YS,Apr 27)
Place Above 108 (27f,Sed,GF,Apr 17)
Plantaganet 100 (19f,Her,GF,Apr 5)
Point 102 (21f,Utt,GS,Feb 4)
Point Barrow 108 (24f,Leo,YS,Dec 27)
Polar Gunner 109 (16f,Wet,GS,Nov 23)
Polar Red 104 (21½f,Ain,G,Apr 7)
Polished 103 (16f,Utt,GS,Oct 12)
Political Cruise 100 (16f,Crl,S,Apr 15)
Pollensa Bay 100 (20f,Ain,G,Jun 16)
Polyphon 105 (16f,Ayr,S,Mar 11)
Pornic 101 (21f,Sed,HY,Mar 28)
Portavadie 111 (16½f,Ncs,HY,Dec 5)
Posh Stick 106 (20f,Crl,S,Mar 19)
Possextown 102 (24f,Per,G,Sep 21)
Power Unit 103 (17½f,Str,G,Sep 3)
Preacher Boy 107 (21f,Wcn,GS,Dec 1)
Precious Bane 111 (24f,Lin,S,Nov 9)
Predicament 101 (16½f,Tau,F,Apr 24)
Presence Of Mind 109 (25½f,Exe,GF,May 11)
Presenting Express 107 (21f,Fol,G,Nov 28)
Presentingthecase 101 (24f,Hun,GF,Jun 7)
Primitive Way 112 (31f,Per,GF,Apr 28)
Prince Adjal 104 (17½f,Mar,S,Aug 13)
Prince Highlight 102 (25½f,Her,GF,Apr 28)
Prince Of Pleasure 109 (20f,Utt,GF,Sep 7)
Prince Of Slane 111 (25½f,Cat,G,Jan 12)
Priors Dale 104 (16½f,Tau,GS,Mar 29)
Prize Ring 102 (22½f,Mar,GF,Jun 8)
Profowens 103 (25f,Kel,S,Apr 3)
Provocative 109 (16f,Wet,S,Oct 28)
Public Reaction 108 (21f,Pun,G,Apr 25)
Puntal 104 (29½f,San,GF,Apr 29)
Pure Brief 102 (16½f,Don,G,Dec 9)

Quazar 111 (21f,Pun,S,Apr 26)
Queen Astrid 101 (16f,Naa,HY,Mar 12)
Quid Pro Quo 104 (23½f,Tau,G,Dec 8)
Quizzling 104 (24f,Lud,G,Feb 22)

Racing Demon 120 (16f,San,S,Dec 3)
Radcliffe 101 (24½f,Ban,GS,Oct 8)
Rambling Minster 102 (25½f,Cat,G,Jan 1)
Randolph O Brien 107 (20½f,Lei,S,Feb 28)
Randwick Roar 105 (24f,Gow,GY,Jan 26)
Ransboro 105 (21f,Leo,YS,Mar 5)
Rare Ouzel 111 (25f,Fai,S,Jan 22)
Rare Society 106 (21f,Sed,GS,Nov 22)
Rathbawn Prince 100 (20½f,Ban,GS,Apr 29)
Rathcolman Storm 104 (24f,Pun,S,Apr 29)
Rathgar Beau 119 (16f,Pun,S,Apr 26)
Reach The Clouds 101 (24½f,Fak,S,Feb 17)
Rebel Rhythm 109 (25f,Wet,S,Dec 27)
Recent Edition 109 (26f,Crl,HY,Mar 9)
Red Devil Robert 114 (25½f,Wcn,G,Nov 5)
Red Flyer 104 (22½f,Kel,GF,Oct 2)
Red Georgie 105 (24f,Chp,S,Oct 22)
Red Man 105 (16½f,Sed,HY,Mar 28)
Red Perk 104 (24f,Ncs,S,Feb 14)
Red Ruffles 104 (19f,Don,G,Dec 19)
Red Striker 109 (25f,Wet,HY,Mar 18)
Redemption 113 (21f,Chl,GS,Dec 10)
Reel Missile 105 (19f,Don,G,Dec 19)
Reflected Glory 107 (23½f,Exe,GS,Nov 18)
Reflex Blue 105 (16½f,Chp,GS,Nov 23)
Regal Vision 104 (24f,Hun,G,Dec 26)
Reivers Moon 107 (17f,Kel,GS,Mar 19)
Renvyle 105 (24f,Mus,GF,Feb 5)
Reseda 104 (20f,Fon,S,Nov 4)
Resplendent Star 102 (20½f,Hun,GF,Aug 29)
Reveillez 113 (21f,Chl,G,Mar 16)
Reverse Swing 108 (21½f,Fak,G,Oct 21)
Rheindross 103 (20½f,Wor,G,Jun 15)
Ri Na Realta 110 (20f,Plu,GS,Apr 16)
Rifleman 100 (20½f,Hex,G,Apr 24)
Rince Ri 103 (25f,Fai,SH,Feb 25)
Ring Of Beara 104 (21f,Leo,S,Dec 29)
Risington 101 (16½f,Chp,G,Mar 22)
Risk Accessor 108 (24½f,Chl,G,Mar 15)
Risky Way 103 (16½f,Hex,G,Apr 30)
River Amora 101 (18f,Fon,GF,Apr 27)
River City 109 (16f,San,GF,Apr 29)
River Of Light 103 (26½f,Chp,HY,Mar 11)
River Quoile 103 (25½f,Exe,F,Oct 5)
River Trapper 103 (19f,Tau,GF,Nov 10)
Robber 105 (26½f,Fon,G,Apr 29)
Robbo 108 (25½f,Cat,G,Dec 15)
Rocking Annie 102 (18f,Pun,S,Apr 30)
Rockspring Hero 102 (20f,Pun,S,Dec 11)
Rodalko 110 (24f,Nby,GS,Mar 25)
Roddy The Vet 101 (25f,Mar,S,Dec 26)
Rolfes Delight 102 (26½f,Nab,GF,Jly 17)
Romaha 106 (21f,Leo,HY,Jan 15)
Roman Ark 108 (20f,Ayr,S,Jan 3)
Roman Court 104 (25f,Fol,G,Dec 13)
Roman Rampage 108 (28f,Fon,S,Apr 1)
Romantic Hero 105 (26f,Utt,G,May 8)
Romany Dream 102 (17½f,Str,G,Sep 3)
Roofing Spirit 103 (17½f,Exe,S,Feb 21)
Rookery Lad 107 (16½f,Chp,GS,Nov 23)
Rooster s Reunion 106 (16f,Wcn,G,Apr 23)
Roschal 102 (21f,Wcn,S,Jan 4)
Rosie Redman 104 (25f,Kel,S,Dec 4)
Ross Comm 112 (20½f,Ban,S,Mar 25)
Ross River 112 (20f,Pun,G,Apr 26)
Rosses Point 103 (21f,Utt,GS,Feb 4)
Royal Auclair 114 (26½f,Chl,G,Mar 17)
Royal Corrouge 108 (26f,War,S,Dec 4)
Royal Emperor 114 (26½f,Chl,G,Mar 17)
Royal Hector 107 (19f,Tau,G,Jan 9)
Royale Acadou 106 (20½f,San,S,Mar 10)
Royaleety 105 (20½f,Chl,GS,Nov 12)
Roznic 108 (16f,Fol,S,Jan 17)
Rubberdubber 106 (18½f,Nby,GF,Mar 4)
Ruby Gale 101 (21f,Wcn,G,Nov 5)
Rudolf Rassendyll 100 (24f,Wdr,G,Nov 18)
Rule Supreme 117 (25f,Pun,YS,Apr 27)
Run For Paddy 112 (24f,Hun,G,Oct 15)
Runaway Bishop 104 (22f,Tow,S,Nov 26)
Runner Bean 100 (16f,Wcn,G,Nov 17)
Russian Lord 108 (26½f,Fon,GF,Apr 27)
Ryders Storm 101 (21f,Sed,S,Dec 26)

Saafend Rocket 107 (16f,Lud,G,Apr 24)

Sacrifice 107 (24f,Str,G,Sep 3)
Saddlers Cloth 108 (20f,Plu,GS,Apr 17)
Saffron Sun 108 (25½f,Exe,F,Oct 5)
Saintsaire 104 (16f,Lud,G,Apr 24)
Sands Rising 106 (16½f,Sed,S,Nov 8)
Sarahs Quay 105 (21f,Sed,HY,Feb 21)
Sardagna 107 (17½f,Mar,G,Jly 16)
Sargasso Sea 103 (21f,Wcn,S,Jan 4)
Savannah Bay 109 (24f,Hun,G,Oct 4)
Scalloway 101 (16½f,Nab,G,Aug 20)
Scarthy Lad 105 (25f,Pun,S,Apr 29)
Schuh Shine 109 (20f,Hay,S,Jan 7)
Sconced 100 (27f,Sed,GF,Apr 17)
Scotch Corner 103 (24½f,Chl,G,Oct 25)
Scots Grey 114 (21f,Wcn,G,Nov 16)
Seaniethesmuggler 102 (25f,Mar,G,Aug 27)
Search And Destroy 101 (20½f,Wor,GF,Jun 4)
See You Sometime 108 (25½f,Chl,G,Apr 19)
See You There 104 (25f,Ayr,S,Jan 2)
Seebald 112 (24½f,Chl,GS,Mar 14)
Seeyaaj 110 (17f,Kel,GS,Mar 19)
Seisiun Eile 108 (20f,Clo,Y,Mar 5)
Serpentine Rock 100 (16f,Wcn,G,Dec 26)
Shaadiva 109 (21½f,Nab,GF,Aug 9)
Shady Lad 110 (34f,Pun,S,Apr 28)
Shalako 109 (20½f,Chl,GS,Nov 13)
Shannon s Pride 106 (25½f,Cat,G,Jan 12)
Shardam 104 (24½f,Chl,GS,Mar 14)
Shareef 100 (23½f,Wet,G,May 26)
Shares 102 (16½f,Ncs,S,Jan 9)
Sharp Belline 103 (25f,Wet,HY,Jan 14)
Sharp Jack 107 (24½f,Ban,S,Apr 22)
Sharp Rigging 107 (16½f,Hun,S,Feb 23)
She s My Girl 102 (16f,Lud,G,Nov 10)
She s Our Native 105 (20f,Lud,GF,Apr 13)
Sher Beau 110 (20f,Gow,GY,Jan 26)
Shining Strand 114 (24½f,Sth,G,Jan 30)
Shoulton 102 (24f,Hun,G,Dec 26)
Show Me The River 107 (16f,Wet,S,Dec 26)
Shrove Tuesday 103 (24½f,Tow,HY,Mar 9)
Silver Jack 102 (21½f,Ayr,S,Nov 6)
Silver Knight 108 (25f,Wet,HY,Dec 3)
Silver Samuel 107 (25½f,Her,GF,Apr 28)
Silver Sedge 105 (16½f,Sed,S,Jan 10)
Silvergino 100 (20½f,Wet,G,May 5)
Simon 109 (24f,Utt,HY,Mar 18)
Sir Cumference 106 (24½f,Tow,GF,May 27)
Sir Frosty 109 (30f,Ban,GS,Feb 10)
Sir Oj 120 (21f,Chl,GS,Dec 10)
Sir Rembrandt 115 (26½f,Chl,G,Mar 17)
Sir Storm 105 (16f,Wet,S,Oct 28)
Sissinghurst Storm 105 (24f,Chp,G,Apr 18)
Sitting Duck 100 (24f,Hun,GS,Nov 8)
Skenfrith 109 (25f,Ayr,S,Feb 27)
Sky Warrior 108 (20½f,Wor,GF,May 8)
Slim Pickings 111 (21f,Pun,G,Apr 25)
Slow To Part 107 (25f,Fai,S,Jan 22)
Smart Cavalier 104 (20f,Plu,G,Nov 30)
Smart Savannah 107 (20f,Str,GS,Mar 13)
Smeathe s Ridge 103 (21f,Fol,S,Jan 17)
Snoopy Loopy 105 (23½f,Wor,GF,Jly 20)
Snowy 106 (22½f,Kel,GF,Oct 2)
Snowy Ford 105 (26½f,Fon,G,Oct 1)
Soeur Fontenail 106 (20f,Plu,G,Nov 30)
Solar System 106 (19f,Leo,YS,Jan 29)
Solve It Sober 102 (21½f,Str,G,May 20)
Some Timbering 110 (17f,Fai,S,Jan 22)
Sonevafushi 109 (24f,Nby,GS,Jan 11)
Sound Of Cheers 109 (20½f,Wet,HY,Jan 14)
Sound Witness 109 (24f,Naa,HY,Mar 12)
South Bronx 104 (17f,Kel,GS,Oct 22)
Southern Vic 117 (24f,Naa,S,Jan 21)
Southerndown 102 (24½f,Sth,G,Jan 30)
Space Star 109 (17½f,Mar,G,Jun 24)
Special Conquest 102 (26f,War,S,Jan 26)
Spectrum Star 101 (16½f,Hex,G,May 7)
Specular 100 (17½f,Ban,G,Aug 25)
Spider Boy 100 (26f,Plu,S,Mar 27)
Spinaround 103 (20½f,Hun,GS,Jan 13)
Spirit Of New York 105 (20f,Str,S,Oct 27)
Splash Out Again 100 (23½f,Wor,GF,Aug 17)
Spot Thedifference 112 (31f,Chl,GS,Mar 14)
Spring Grove 102 (26f,Plu,S,Feb 27)
Spring Lover 107 (20f,Lud,GF,Feb 8)
Spring Margot 108 (21½f,Str,S,May 21)
Squires Lane 100 (26½f,Chp,S,Jan 20)
St Matthew 106 (20½f,Wet,S,Oct 29)
Stack The Pack 103 (24f,Per,GF,May 12)
Stage Friendly 106 (20½f,Wor,GF,Jun 22)
Stance 106 (16f,Ain,GS,Nov 20)
Stand Easy 103 (26f,Utt,G,May 8)
Star Clipper 108 (24f,Leo,YS,Dec 27)
Star De Mohaison 114 (21f,Chl,GS,Jan 1)
Star Jack 108 (16f,Wet,G,May 9)
Star Performance 104 (24f,Pun,GF,Apr 28)
Starbuck 103 (25f,Hex,GF,Jun 19)
State Of Play 114 (25f,Ain,G,Apr 7)
Stavordale Lad 110 (22½f,Nby,G,Mar 24)
Steel Band 104 (16f,Naa,SH,Feb 26)
Step In Line 102 (21½f,Fak,G,Oct 21)
Steppes Of Gold 109 (22f,Fon,GS,Jan 27)
Strike Back 115 (17f,Fai,S,Jan 22)
Strong Project 111 (20f,Pun,G,Apr 26)
Sum Leader 109 (20f,Pun,G,Apr 26)
Sungates 103 (30f,Ban,GS,Feb 10)
Sunshan 104 (21½f,Nab,GF,Jun 21)
Super Dolphin 101 (16f,Per,GS,Jun 30)
Super Nomad 109 (17f,Kel,GS,Mar 19)
Super Road Train 100 (24f,Str,G,Sep 3)
Superrollercoaster 106 (22f,Tow,GS,Dec 26)
Supreme Breeze 103 (28½f,Mar,S,Dec 26)
Supreme Catch 111 (24½f,San,S,Mar 11)
Supreme Developer 109 (24½f,San,S,Mar 11)
Supreme Prince 112 (20f,Ayr,GS,Apr 21)
Supreme Serenade 106 (20f,Hay,S,Jan 7)
Supreme Sir 102 (24½f,Sth,G,Jan 30)
Supreme Tadgh 106 (22½f,Nby,G,Mar 24)
Surefast 106 (23½f,Exe,GS,Oct 18)
Swallow Magic 104 (21f,Sed,F,Jly 25)
Swansea Bay 106 (26½f,Nab,G,Aug 20)
Sweet Bird 103 (24f,Hun,GS,Nov 8)
Sweet Diversion 113 (25½f,Chl,G,Apr 19)
Sweet Minuet 107 (20f,Plu,GS,Apr 16)
Swordlestown 101 (17f,Fai,S,Jan 22)

Ta Ta For Now 111 (31f,Per,GF,Apr 28)
Tacolino 103 (16f,Wet,G,May 5)
Tagar 101 (16f,Ayr,S,Jan 3)
Tails I Win 101 (20f,Utt,GS,Jly 5)
Take The Oath 100 (17f,Sth,G,Jly 15)
Take The Stand 118 (25f,Wet,S,Oct 29)
Taksina 104 (19½f,Chp,G,Apr 18)
Tallow Bay 104 (25f,Fol,GS,Feb 14)
Tamango 110 (21½f,Nab,G,Aug 20)
Tamarinbleu 109 (16f,Chl,GS,Nov 13)
Tana River 109 (24½f,San,S,Mar 11)
Tango Royal 115 (22½f,Mar,G,Jly 16)
Tanikos 106 (16f,Lin,S,Nov 9)
Tanterari 102 (21½f,Ain,GS,Nov 20)
Taranis 108 (21f,Chl,G,Apr 20)
Tee-Jay 102 (27f,Sed,GF,Aug 30)
Tell Tale 105 (26½f,Nab,G,Jun 6)
Terivic 105 (16½f,Tow,S,Nov 26)
Terre De Java 104 (19f,Tau,G,Apr 6)
Terrible Tenant 106 (16½f,Tau,F,Apr 24)
Thalys 104 (17½f,Str,S,Oct 27)
The Bajan Bandit 114 (25f,Ayr,S,Feb 11)
The Bandit 105 (24f,Nby,GS,Mar 25)
The Biker 100 (16f,Per,GF,Apr 28)
The Boys In Green 102 (17f,Leo,Y,Dec 26)
The Dark Lord 107 (24f,Nby,GS,Mar 25)
The Fox Regan 105 (25f,Pun,G,Apr 29)
The Glen 108 (16f,Utt,GF,Sep 18)
The Grocers Curate 101 (20f,Plu,G,Nov 30)
The Kew Tour 108 (25f,Wet,S,Jan 5)
The Listener 115 (21f,Chl,GS,Jan 1)
The Local 109 (18f,Fon,G,Apr 11)
The Merry Mason 103 (23½f,Lei,S,Feb 15)
The Mighty Sparrow 101 (20f,Utt,GS,Jly 5)
The Names Bond 101 (17f,Sth,G,May 22)
The Newsman 111 (20f,Plu,GS,Apr 16)
The Nomad 108 (16f,Wet,G,May 5)
The Outlier 102 (20f,Plu,S,Jan 16)
The Pennys Dropped 107 (26½f,Nab,GF,Jly 11)
The Railway Man 115 (21f,Leo,Y,Feb 12)
The River Joker 101 (24½f,Tow,S,Jan 6)
The Royal Dub 103 (21f,Leo,S,Dec 29)
The Sister 104 (25f,Mar,G,Aug 27)
The Villager 106 (20½f,Chl,GS,Nov 13)
The Wipper 106 (24f,Naa,HY,Nov 12)
Theatre Knight 107 (21f,Sed,GS,Nov 22)
Theatre Lane 104 (20f,Pun,S,Nov 20)
Theboyfrombulawayo 105 (20f,Fai,SH,Feb 25)
Thedreamstillalive 102 (23½f,Lei,GS,Jan 24)
Therealbandit 113 (21f,Chl,GS,Dec 10)
Thisthatandtother 115 (20½f,Hun,G,Nov 19)
Thistlecraft 107 (24½f,Fak,G,Jan 16)
Three Mill 100 (34f,Pun,S,Apr 28)
Tierkely 106 (26f,Crt,G,Jly 14)
Tiger Cry 108 (16½f,Chl,G,Mar 17)
Tiger Talk 102 (27f,Sed,GF,Apr 21)
Tigers Lair 107 (20f,Str,G,Jun 5)
Tighe Caster 107 (16f,Wor,GF,Sep 4)
Tighten Your Belt 105 (23½f,Exe,GS,Dec 15)
Tikram 108 (26½f,Chl,G,Mar 17)
Time To Reflect 106 (25f,Kel,S,Apr 27)
Tipp Top 102 (24½f,Fak,S,Feb 17)
Tipsy Mouse 103 (28f,Str,G,May 20)
To The Future 100 (30f,Ncs,S,Jan 9)
Toi Express 105 (17½f,Str,G,Sep 3)
Tom Costalot 102 (24f,Nby,G,Nov 25)
Tom Fruit 110 (25f,Mar,HY,Nov 6)
Tom Sayers 104 (26½f,Fon,G,Oct 1)
Tom s Prize 107 (25f,Wet,G,Apr 24)
Tommy Carson 107 (24f,Str,G,Sep 3)
Tommy Spar 104 (20½f,Wor,GF,Aug 17)
Tonic Du Charmil 109 (16f,Utt,GF,Sep 18)
Too Forward 112 (21f,Chl,GS,Jan 1)
Top Strategy 102 (16f,Pun,S,Nov 20)
Torche 106 (24f,Chp,G,Oct 8)
Tosawi 102 (16½f,Tow,GF,Apr 25)
Totheroadyouvgone 109 (24f,Utt,GF,Jun 9)
Toto Caelo 102 (25f,Pun,S,Apr 29)
Touch Closer 104 (20f,Mar,S,Aug 13)
Toulouse 106 (20f,Lud,G,Mar 23)
Toulouse-Lautrec 110 (29f,Plu,S,Jan 1)
Town Crier 108 (17f,Nby,G,Nov 26)
Trabolgan 111 (26½f,Nby,G,Nov 26)
Treasulier 104 (25½f,Wcn,S,Jan 4)
Trenance 103 (23½f,Exe,S,Dec 2)
Tribal Dancer 111 (25f,Mar,HY,Nov 6)
Tribal Dispute 105 (17f,Kel,GF,May 19)
Tribal Venture 107 (25½f,Chl,G,Apr 19)
Trisons Star 106 (20f,Crl,S,Mar 19)
Tristernagh 105 (25f,Pun,S,Apr 29)
Truckers Tavern 110 (24f,Hay,HY,Jan 21)
Trust Fund 111 (24f,Utt,S,Apr 30)
Try Catch Paddy 103 (25f,Kel,GS,Apr 9)
Tudor King 105 (24f,Lud,GF,Oct 13)
Tuesday s Child 107 (16f,Lud,G,Nov 10)
Tufty Hopper 101 (25½f,Cat,G,Jan 1)
Tumbling Dice 109 (21f,Chl,G,Mar 16)
Turgeonev 101 (20½f,Wet,GF,Oct 12)
Turpin Green 109 (25f,Ain,G,Apr 7)
Turthen 106 (20f,Hay,S,Jan 7)
Tusk 110 (16½f,Ncs,HY,Dec 5)
Twenty Degrees 107 (20f,Plu,S,Feb 27)
Twentytwosilver 108 (16½f,Tau,F,Apr 24)
Tyneandthyneagain 103 (28½f,Hay,HY,Feb 18)
Tysou 111 (16f,San,GF,Feb 4)

Ultimate Limit 104 (25½f,Wcn,G,Oct 23)
Umbrella Man 111 (24f,Str,GS,Mar 13)
Un Autre Espere 102 (17½f,Mar,G,Oct 2)
Uncle Max 101 (16½f,Chp,GS,Nov 23)
Uncle Mick 106 (28f,Fon,GF,Mar 19)
Uncle Wallace 107 (16f,Wcn,G,Apr 23)
Undeniable 111 (25f,Kel,S,Dec 4)
Underwriter 109 (24½f,San,GF,Feb 4)
Uneven Line 103 (21f,Sed,HY,Mar 28)
Unleash 112 (24f,Nby,G,Nov 25)
Up The Pub 103 (24½f,Sth,G,Jan 30)
Uptown Lad 100 (16f,Crl,S,Apr 15)
Ursumman 104 (21f,Pun,G,Apr 25)

Va Vavoom 111 (24½f,Chl,GS,Mar 14)
Valance 106 (20f,Lud,GF,Oct 20)
Valley Warrior 106 (25½f,Her,G,Mar 20)
Vandante 102 (21½f,Nab,GF,May 10)
Vandas Choice 105 (20½f,Wet,GF,Oct 12)
Vanormix 100 (16f,Wet,S,Dec 26)
Verchoyles Lad 100 (19f,Leo,YS,Jan 29)
Very Optimistic 111 (23½f,Exe,GS,Nov 18)
Very Special One 105 (16f,Her,GS,Feb 12)
Vesuve 106 (25f,Fol,G,Dec 13)
Vicario 104 (21f,Sed,S,Feb 6)
Vicars Way 107 (24f,Naa,HY,Nov 12)
Viciana 101 (22f,Tow,GS,Feb 2)
Victory Gunner 107 (28½f,Mar,S,Dec 26)
Victory Roll 106 (16f,Fol,S,Jan 17)
Villair 103 (28½f,Mar,S,Dec 1)
Villon 102 (16f,Utt,HY,Dec 16)
Virgin Soldier 106 (25½f,Cat,G,Dec 15)
Von Origny 107 (22½f,Nby,G,Mar 3)
Voy Por Ustedes 119 (16f,Wcn,S,Feb 18)
Vulcan Lane 102 (16½f,Sed,S,Jan 24)

Wages 102 (16½f,Tow,S,Jan 6)
Wain Mountain 111 (20½f,Lin,S,Jan 21)
Walcot Lad 111 (28f,Fon,GF,Mar 19)
Walter s Destiny 103 (25½f,Wcn,S,Jan 4)
Waltzing Beau 101 (19½f,Exe,GS,Apr 5)
War Of Attrition 119 (26½f,Chl,G,Mar 17)
Waterberg 104 (28½f,Mar,S,Dec 26)
Watson Lake 115 (16f,Naa,HY,Nov 12)
Waynesworld 101 (24f,Utt,G,Oct 2)
Wayward Melody 106 (24f,Hun,G,Mar 15)
Weapons Inspector 103 (27f,Sed,HY,Dec 6)
Welcome To Unos 103 (19f,Cat,G,Jan 1)
Well Presented 108 (24f,Leo,YS,Dec 27)
Well Tutored 109 (24f,Pun,S,Apr 29)
Wenceslas 104 (20f,Fon,G,Dec 20)
Were In Touch 106 (25½f,Wcn,G,May 6)
Were Not Stoppin 100 (22½f,Mar,G,May 15)
Wests Awake 109 (25f,Pun,G,Apr 27)
Wet Lips 107 (16f,Crl,GF,Oct 7)
What A Native 109 (24f,Leo,HY,Jan 15)
What Odds 108 (24f,Leo,YS,Dec 27)
Whereareyounow 101 (21f,Chl,GS,Jan 1)
Whispered Secret 110 (16½f,Nab,GF,Aug 31)
Whitenzo 103 (24f,Nby,GS,Mar 25)
Whitford Don 101 (24½f,Ban,S,Apr 22)
Why The Long Face 105 (20½f,Wor,GF,May 8)
Wild About Harry 102 (21½f,Ayr,G,Mar 23)
Wild Cane Ridge 107 (20f,Ayr,S,Feb 11)
Wild Oats 107 (23½f,Exe,GS,Mar 21)
Wild Passion 112 (16f,Chl,GS,Mar 14)
Wild Power 101 (18f,Fon,S,Apr 1)
Wildfield Rufo 110 (25f,Wet,HY,Mar 18)
Willie John Daly 107 (24½f,San,S,Mar 11)
Wills Wilde 109 (16f,Pun,G,Apr 25)
Win Alot 100 (21½f,Crt,G,May 30)
Windsor Boy 111 (25½f,Wcn,G,Nov 5)
Windy Spirit 106 (26½f,Nab,GF,Aug 21)
Winsley 109 (20½f,San,G,Apr 28)
Wise Counsel 102 (25f,Pun,S,Apr 29)
Wise Man 104 (25f,Kel,S,Apr 27)
Without A Doubt 108 (16f,San,S,Feb 24)
Wizard Of Edge 106 (16f,Wcn,S,Jan 4)
Wolf Creek 111 (25f,Pun,G,Apr 28)
Wonderkid 106 (24f,Pun,GF,Apr 28)
Wondersobright 102 (16½f,Tau,F,Apr 24)
Woodenbridge Dream 103 (20½f,Hun,GS,Jan 13)
Woodlands Genpower 107 (26f,War,S,Dec 4)
Woodview 104 (24½f,Tow,G,Mar 22)
World Vision 104 (25f,Pun,S,Apr 29)
Would You Believe 110(24½f,Tow,G,Mar 22)
Wrags To Riches 105 (19½f,Chp,HY,Dec 3)

Xaipete 103 (20½f,Wor,G,Jun 15)

Yakareem 102 (24f,Str,GF,Aug 14)
Yardbird 111 (24f,Nby,GS,Mar 25)
Yassar 101 (21f,Utt,S,Oct 28)
Yes My Lord 103 (23½f,Lei,S,Feb 28)
Yes Sir 103 (24½f,Fak,G,Dec 22)
York Rite 102 (22½f,Kel,GF,Oct 2)
You re Special 113 (24½f,Chl,G,Mar 15)
Young Chevalier 101 (16f,Per,G,Aug 24)
Young Lorcan 107 (20½f,Lei,HY,Mar 10)
Your Advantage 104 (16f,Utt,GF,Sep 18)

Zabenz 110 (25½f,Chl,GS,Dec 9)
Zaffamore 101 (25½f,Wcn,G,Dec 26)
Zaffran Lady 104 (24f,Naa,S,Jan 21)
Zamnah 100 (20f,Clo,Y,Mar 5)
Zimbabwe 104 (23½f,Lei,S,Feb 15)
Zum See 107 (17f,Fai,HY,Dec 4)

HURDLES

A Bit Of Fun 103 (20f,Hay,GS,Apr 15)
Aberdare 100 (24f,Ncs,HY,Mar 18)
Abragante 103 (16½f,Chl,GS,Nov 12)
Abraham Smith 106 (19½f,Her,G,Mar 6)
Absolut Power 107 (22½f,Str,GF,Jly 17)
Absolutelythebest 102 (19½f,Her,GF,Apr 5)
Abzuson 100 (20½f,Lei,HY,Jan 24)
Acambo 112 (17f,Tau,GF,Nov 24)
Acceleration 106 (16½f,Kel,GF,May 18)
Accordello 103 (23½f,Hay,HY,Feb 18)
According To John 110 (24½f,Ayr,GS,Apr 21)
According To Pete 104 (16½f,Str,G,Apr 23)
Aces Four 106 (24½f,Per,GF,Apr 27)
Achilles Wings 111 (19f,Nab,G,May 16)
Adamant Approach 112 (16½f,Chl,GS,Nov 13)
Adelphi Theatre 108 (22½f,Fon,GF,May 29)
Adjami 100 (16f,Wor,GF,May 8)
Admiral 109 (16½f,Chp,GS,Oct 8)
Adopted Hero 103 (16f,Wet,S,Nov 12)
Adventurist 106 (21f,Lud,GF,Feb 8)
Afrad 113 (16½f,San,S,Jan 7)
Afsoun 112 (17f,Chl,GS,Dec 10)
After Eight 111 (21f,Tow,S,Nov 3)
Afterburn 101 (19f,Naa,HY,Nov 12)
Air Guitar 102 (16f,Fak,G,Nov 15)
Akash 104 (16f,Wor,GF,Apr 26)
Akilak 116 (16f,Pun,S,Apr 28)
Akshar 114 (16f,Pun,S,Apr 29)
Al Eile 116 (16½f,Chl,GS,Mar 14)
Al Mabrook 103 (24½f,Ain,G,Jun 16)
Albany 110 (23f,Wet,S,Feb 4)
Albarino 110 (17f,Tau,G,Dec 8)
Albert House 106 (24f,Chp,GS,Dec 27)
Alderbrook Girl 101 (22½f,Fon,S,Apr 11)
Aldiruos 105 (16f,Wet,HY,Jan 23)
Aleemdar 104 (17½f,Mar,G,Oct 16)
Alekhine 101 (16f,Wcn,F,Oct 6)
Alessandro Severo 101 (19f,Exe,HY,May 3)
Alexander Taipan 106 (16f,Fai,SH,Dec 4)
Alfa Sunrise 101 (22½f,Fon,GS,Jan 27)
Alformasi 108 (24f,Ban,GS,Apr 22)
Alikat 113 (19½f,Mar,G,Sep 24)
All Heart 108 (20f,Pun,GF,Apr 29)
All Square 102 (17f,Tau,GS,Mar 13)
All Star 115 (20½f,Hun,G,Nov 19)
Allaboveboard 102 (19f,Nab,GF,Apr 15)
Allez Petit Luis 110 (16f,Leo,HY,Jan 15)
Allumee 107 (16f,Wor,GF,Oct 6)
Ally Shrimp 108 (22½f,Kel,GS,Apr 9)
Almah 105 (20f,Chp,GS,Apr 8)
Almavara 108 (16f,Plu,S,Mar 27)
Almizan 103 (16½f,Str,G,Apr 23)
Alph 109 (16f,Fak,G,Nov 15)
Alpha Royale 117 (20f,Ain,GS,Apr 7)
Alphabetical 102 (22f,Wcn,G,Oct 23)
Alpine Hideaway 100 (17½f,Mar,G,Oct 2)
Alrafid 104 (16½f,Str,S,May 21)
Alright Now M Lad 107 (21f,Plu,GS,Feb 13)
Altitude Dancer 107 (22½f,Str,GF,Jly 17)
Alva Glen 108 (19½f,Her,GF,May 10)
Always Esteemed 100 (17½f,Mar,G,Aug 27)
Always Waining 107 (19½f,Don,G,Nov 27)

Amalfi Storm 100 (20½f,Hun,S,Feb 23)
Amanpuri 105 (20f,Fon,S,Jan 17)
Amazing Valour 102 (24½f,Tau,G,Jan 9)
Amber Dawn 104 (20f,Wor,GF,Sep 4)
Amber Point 101 (16f,Leo,Y,Mar 5)
Amber Starlight 108 (23f,Lin,HY,Nov 9)
Ambersong 103 (16f,Lud,G,Nov 10)
Ambobo 111 (24f,Chl,G,Mar 16)
American Jennie 108 (24f,Pun,S,Apr 30)
Amicelli 108 (21f,Lud,G,May 3)
Amnesty 102 (16f,Plu,S,Dec 12)
Amour Multiple 105 (17f,Chl,G,Apr 20)
Anatar 102 (21f,Chl,G,Oct 25)
Andre Chenier 106 (16½f,Kel,GS,Apr 28)
Andreas 111 (16f,Lud,G,Feb 22)
Andy Gin 103 (16f,Tow,HY,Mar 9)
Anemix 106 (17f,Tau,GS,Feb 16)
Angello 104 (20f,Fon,GS,Apr 11)
Angie s Double 100 (22f,Mar,GF,Jly 3)
Anna Panna 100 (16f,Plu,S,Feb 27)
Another Deckie 101 (16½f,Per,GF,Jly 10)
Another Superman 104 (20f,Ayr,S,Feb 27)
Ansari 107 (16f,Pun,YS,Apr 27)
Anticipating 106 (16½f,Nby,GF,Mar 4)
Approaching Land 102 (16f,Fak,G,May 4)
Arc En Ciel 108 (24f,Leo,HY,Jan 15)
Arcalis 115 (16f,Ncs,S,Nov 26)
Arch Rebel 104 (17f,Chl,G,Mar 17)
Arctic Echo 101 (22½f,Kel,GS,Apr 9)
Arctic Lagoon 104 (24f,Hex,G,May 7)
Arctic Moss 100 (20f,Mus,G,Feb 15)
Ardashir 103 (23½f,Hay,GS,May 7)
Ardglass 103 (16f,Plu,GS,Feb 13)
Argent Ou Or 100 (17f,Her,GF,May 10)
Argento 105 (16½f,Kel,GS,Jan 13)
Argonaut 100 (16½f,Chp,G,Apr 28)
Arjay 102 (17f,Sed,GF,May 18)
Arm And A Leg 104 (19f,Nab,GF,Jly 17)
Armariver 109 (17f,Chl,GS,Jan 1)
Armentieres 101 (16f,Cat,G,Jan 25)
Arnold Layne 102 (20½f,Utt,HY,Dec 16)
Around Before 102 (27f,Nab,GF,Aug 9)
Arrayou 117 (20f,Ain,GS,Apr 7)
Arry Dash 108 (16f,Fak,G,Dec 22)
Art Virginia 107 (20f,Wdr,GS,Dec 16)
Artane Boys 103 (17f,Nab,G,Aug 20)
Arteea 108 (16f,Pun,S,Apr 26)
Articulation 106 (16f,Pun,YS,Apr 27)
Artist s Muse 103 (16f,Leo,Y,Dec 26)
Arumun 109 (20f,Fon,S,Dec 6)
Ashgan 100 (20f,Wor,GF,Jly 13)
Asian Maze 120 (20f,Ain,GS,Apr 8)
Ask The Umpire 101 (20f,Ban,GS,Apr 29)
Aspiring Actor 106 (22½f,Fol,S,Dec 13)
Assoon 103 (21f,Plu,G,Nov 30)
Assumetheposition 100 (23f,Wet,GS,Nov 23)
Aston Lad 107 (20½f,Wet,HY,Mar 18)
Astronaut 100 (24½f,Per,G,Aug 24)
Astronomical 104 (17½f,Mar,GS,Dec 1)
Astyanax 111 (21f,Nby,G,Nov 27)
At The Double 105 (21f,Plu,S,Jan 16)
At Your Request 109 (18½f,Fon,G,Apr 29)
Atlantic Jane 103 (24f,Mar,GS,Feb 17)
Atlantic Rhapsody 101 (16f,Leo,S,Dec 29)
Atlantis 100 (20f,Fon,GF,Sep 22)
Attorney General 105 (20f,Chp,S,Oct 22)
Audiostreetdotcom 103 (22½f,Utt,GF,Sep 18)
Auenmoon 106 (16f,Hay,HY,Feb 23)
Auetaler 107 (16f,Lud,G,Nov 10)
Augherskea 104 (16f,Pun,S,Apr 29)
Avalon 102 (18½f,Fon,G,Feb 3)
Avesomeofthat 106 (16f,Wcn,G,Apr 23)
Aviation 107 (16f,Wet,S,Oct 29)
Axinit 108 (20f,Pun,GF,Apr 29)
Aztec Warrior 109 (20f,Wdr,GS,Dec 16)
Azzemour 105 (22½f,Str,GF,Jly 17)

Baawrah 101 (17½f,Crt,G,Aug 27)
Back In Front 111 (20f,Nav,S,Nov 13)
Back To Ben Alder 118 (20f,Ain,GS,Apr 7)
Back To Bid 105 (20f,Leo,HY,Jan 15)
Backbord 103 (16½f,Nby,G,Mar 3)
Badgerlaw 103 (20f,Leo,S,Dec 29)
Bagan 114 (20f,Pun,S,Apr 29)
Bak To Bill 105 (19f,Exe,HY,Mar 7)
Ball Games 101 (16f,Lud,G,Nov 10)
Ball O Malt 106 (22f,Mar,GS,Nov 17)
Ballintra Boy 112 (24f,Leo,HY,Jan 15)
Ballito 101 (16f,Lud,G,Nov 10)
Bally Bolshoi 109 (19f,Exe,S,Feb 21)
Bally Scanlon 102 (16f,Leo,YS,Dec 28)
Bally s Bro 100 (22½f,Utt,G,Oct 2)
Ballyboe Boy 105 (17½f,Crt,G,Jly 14)
Ballycassidy 108 (24f,Wor,GF,Jun 22)
Ballyfitz 103 (24f,Tow,G,Oct 23)
Ballyhoo 108 (21f,Nby,GS,Mar 25)
Ballyrobert 101 (22½f,Fon,GF,Apr 27)
Ballyshan 102 (24f,Chp,S,Jan 20)
Balmoral Queen 103 (16f,Utt,HY,Dec 16)
Baloo 102 (22f,Nab,GF,Jun 14)
Bar Gayne 104 (24f,Chp,S,Jan 28)
Baracouda 117 (24f,Chl,G,Mar 16)
Barathea Blue 102 (17f,Tau,GF,Nov 24)
Barclay Boy 101 (18½f,Fon,G,Feb 3)
Barella 101 (16f,Lud,G,Jan 19)
Bargain Hunt 101 (17½f,Crt,G,May 28)
Barney McAll 100 (20½f,Hun,G,Nov 19)
Baron De Feypo 111 (16f,Pun,YS,Apr 27)
Barranco 104 (17f,Tau,GS,Mar 13)
Barton Flower 107 (16f,Utt,G,Oct 2)
Barton Park 103 (16f,Wcn,G,Nov 16)
Basilea Star 112 (20f,Pun,S,Apr 26)
Bayazid 102 (18½f,Fon,G,Feb 3)
Be Be King 105 (24½f,Ain,GS,Apr 8)
Be My Royal 102 (25f,War,S,Jan 14)
Beare Necessities 104 (21f,Plu,S,Mar 27)
Beau De Turgeon 103 (19½f,Her,G,Nov 29)
Beau Memories 109 (16f,Naa,SH,Feb 26)
Beau Torero 106 (16f,Fak,G,Jan 27)
Beaugency 110 (19½f,Mar,GF,Jly 31)
Beaver 105 (16½f,Hex,GF,Sep 30)
Beechwood 106 (16f,Wor,GF,May 14)
Before Dark 101 (22½f,Exe,GS,Apr 5)
Before The Mast 107 (17½f,Mar,GS,Dec 26)
Before Time 102 (17f,Tau,GS,Jan 19)
Bekstar 102 (21f,Plu,G,Nov 30)
Bella Liana 101 (17½f,Crt,GF,Jly 14)
Bella s Bailey s 108 (16f,Fai,GY,Apr 16)
Ben Britten 103 (24½f,Per,GF,Jun 29)
Ben s Turn 100 (21f,War,S,Dec 31)
Benbyas 101 (20½f,Sth,GS,Jan 28)
Bengo 103 (23½f,Hay,HY,Feb 18)
Berengario 104 (16f,Wcn,G,Nov 5)
Bergerac 108 (17½f,Crt,HY,May 25)
Beseiged 109 (19½f,Mar,GF,Jun 8)
Best Actor 106 (20f,Fon,GS,Apr 11)
Best Game 101 (16f,Fak,G,Dec 22)
Best Profile 104 (20f,Crl,HY,Oct 30)
Bestam 106 (16½f,Don,G,Dec 9)
Better Days 110 (20f,Hay,S,Dec 3)
Better Moment 106 (17f,Nab,GF,Aug 31)
Beyondtherealm 100 (16½f,Chp,GS,Nov 23)
Big Wheel 102 (16½f,Kel,GF,Oct 2)
Bill s Echo 103 (16f,Utt,GF,May 29)
Billyandi 107 (16f,Hay,HY,Feb 23)
Birdwatch 104 (20f,Ayr,S,Jan 3)
Biscar Two 103 (16½f,Chp,HY,Dec 3)
Bishop s Bridge 101 (20½f,Hex,GF,May 28)
Black And Tan 102 (20f,Chp,GS,Apr 28)
Black De Bessy 110 (16½f,Str,G,Sep 3)
Black Hills 103 (17f,Exe,GS,Nov 1)
Black Jack Ketchum 106 (21f,Chl,GS,Nov 13)
Blackergreen 103 (24½f,Per,GF,Apr 27)
Blackthorn 100 (16f,Lei,HY,Dec 7)
Blaeberry 110 (17f,Tau,G,Dec 8)
Blazing Bailey 118 (20f,Ain,G,Apr 7)
Blu Teen 104 (16½f,Lin,S,Dec 31)
Blue Buster 102 (16f,Ayr,S,Feb 27)
Blue Canyon 111 (20f,Wdr,G,Nov 18)
Blue Hawk 107 (20f,Wor,G,Jun 15)
Blue Leader 100 (20f,Wor,GF,Aug 5)
Blue Shark 112 (16½f,Chp,GS,Dec 27)
Blueberry Boy 116 (16f,Leo,YS,Dec 27)
Bob Bob Bobbin 109 (24f,Chp,GS,Dec 27)
Bob Justice 110 (16f,Wet,HY,Dec 3)
Bob s Buster 102 (16½f,Kel,S,Apr 3)
Bobs Pride 107 (16f,Leo,YS,Jan 29)
Bodakker 107 (19f,Naa,S,Jan 21)
Bodfari Signet 105 (16f,Mus,GF,Nov 25)
Bogus Dreams 105 (17f,Ban,GS,Apr 29)
Bohemian Boy 105 (24f,Utt,G,May 14)
Bohemian Spirit 108 (20½f,Per,GF,Apr 28)
Boing Boing 104 (19½f,Her,GF,Apr 5)
Bold Fire 108 (16f,Sth,GS,Jan 28)
Bollin Thomas 105 (16f,Mus,GF,Nov 25)
Bolshoi Ballet 104 (17f,Sed,GF,Apr 17)
Bon Temps Rouler 112 (16f,Leo,HY,Jan 15)
Bonchester Bridge 105 (21f,Nby,GS,Mar 25)
Bongo Fury 106 (16½f,San,S,Mar 11)
Bonny Boy 103 (21f,Plu,GS,Apr 16)
Bonny Grey 106 (20f,Chp,GS,Apr 8)
Border Castle 107 (19f,Exe,GS,Dec 15)
Border Tale 109 (16½f,Ain,G,May 13)
Borehill Joker 105 (19½f,Her,GF,May 10)
Boris The Spider 101 (16f,Ayr,S,Mar 10)
Borora 113 (16½f,San,S,Jan 7)
Bougoure 111 (20f,Ain,GS,Apr 7)
Boulders Beach 100 (16½f,Kel,S,Apr 3)
Boulevardofdreams 100 (19½f,Her,GF,Jun 14)
Boulevin 101 (16f,Wcn,G,Apr 13)
Bound 104 (16½f,Nby,G,Mar 24)
Boychuk 109 (16½f,Chl,GS,Nov 11)
Brads House 101 (20f,Chp,S,Feb 25)
Brandy Wine 107 (23f,Wet,GS,Nov 23)
Brankley Boy 109 (20f,Hay,GS,Apr 15)
Brave Effect 100 (20½f,Per,GF,Aug 23)
Brave Inca 123 (16f,Leo,S,Dec 29)
Brave Spirit 110 (24f,Chp,S,Jan 28)
Brave Villa 102 (16f,Pun,S,Nov 20)
Brave Vision 104 (18f,Kel,S,Apr 27)
Breathing Fire 109 (16f,Leo,Y,Feb 12)
Brendar 106 (21f,Plu,S,Mar 27)
Bressbee 100 (20f,Wor,GF,Apr 26)
Brewster 107 (24f,Chp,GS,Dec 27)
Briareus 117 (16f,Wcn,GS,Feb 18)
Bricks And Porter 105 (16f,Pun,S,Nov 20)
Brief Decline 103 (19f,Nab,GF,Aug 9)
Brigadier Benson 106 (21½f,Sth,G,Apr 29)
Brigadier Du Bois 104 (19f,War,S,Dec 31)
Bright Gas 111 (24f,Pun,S,Apr 30)
Bright Green 103 (21f,Plu,S,Mar 27)
Bringontheclowns 100 (16f,Utt,GF,Jun 9)
Brisbane Road 101 (25½f,Plu,GF,May 8)
Briscoe Place 101 (19½f,Her,G,Apr 5)
Brochrua 106 (17f,Nab,GF,May 10)
Brogella 104 (20f,Leo,S,Dec 29)
Broke Road 100 (16f,Lud,G,Jan 12)
Broken Gale 102 (24f,Utt,GS,Oct 28)
Broken Knights 108 (23½f,Hay,GS,May 7)
Broken Reed 104 (20f,Wor,GF,Apr 26)
Bromley Abbey 100 (16½f,Kel,GF,May 18)
Brooklyn Breeze 113 (16½f,Ain,GS,Oct 22)
Brooklyn Brownie 111 (20½f,Wet,G,May 26)
Brooklyn s Gold 105 (16f,Wor,GF,May 8)
Broom Maker 109 (24f,Pun,GF,Apr 29)
Brouling 101 (16f,Pun,S,Apr 30)
Brown Fox 102 (16f,Wcn,G,Apr 23)
Brumous 109 (22½f,Fol,S,Dec 13)
Brush A King 104 (24½f,Ain,G,Jun 16)
Buachaill Eile 100 (21½f,Sed,HY,Dec 6)
Buck Whaley 108 (17f,Crl,HY,Jan 14)
Buddhi 102 (16f,Utt,GS,Nov 24)
Buena Vista 110 (16½f,Chl,GS,Mar 14)
Buffalo Bill 106 (19½f,Tau,G,Apr 6)
Buffy 104 (16½f,Hex,G,Apr 24)
Bumper 102 (22½f,Exe,S,Feb 21)
Bunkum 105 (24f,Chp,GS,Dec 27)
Bureaucrat 110 (17f,Her,G,Mar 20)
Burning Truth 105 (16f,Wor,G,Jun 29)
Burntoakboy 107 (20f,Pun,S,Apr 30)
Burren Moonshine 105 (24½f,Per,G,Apr 26)
Burundi 111 (20f,Wor,GF,Aug 23)
Business Traveller 102 (24½f,Tau,G,Dec 8)
Businessmoney Jake 107 (19½f,Tau,G,Apr 6)
Buster 101 (24f,Utt,HY,Nov 12)
Buster Collins 111 (21f,Plu,GS,Apr 16)
Bustisu 105 (27f,Nab,GF,Aug 9)
By Degree 108 (20f,Chp,HY,Nov 2)
Bywell Beau 102 (22½f,Kel,S,Dec 4)

Cadeaux Rouge 100 (16f,Fak,G,Oct 21)
Caesar s Palace 106 (24½f,Ayr,S,Nov 6)
Caesarean Hunter 111 (16½f,Don,G,Dec 9)
Caged Tiger 104 (21f,Nby,G,Mar 24)
Cailin Alainn 102 (20f,Fai,GY,Apr 16)
Calatagan 107 (16f,Hay,GS,Nov 19)
Calfraz 104 (16f,Ayr,S,Jan 2)
Caliban 104 (16f,Utt,GF,Jun 9)
Call Oscar 105 (17f,Ban,G,Feb 10)
Callow Lake 112 (16f,Pun,YS,Apr 27)
Calomeria 105 (16½f,Hex,G,Apr 24)
Calusa Charlie 100 (24½f,Nby,G,Mar 24)
Camden Bella 102 (20f,Ayr,S,Jan 3)
Campaign Charlie 100 (19½f,Mar,HY,Mar 12)
Campaign Trail 106 (22f,Mar,GS,Nov 17)
Canada Street 101 (17f,Sed,S,Nov 8)
Candarli 109 (19½f,Tau,GF,Nov 24)
Cannon Fire 105 (20f,Ban,GS,Jly 29)
Cantgeton 106 (16½f,Chl,G,Oct 26)
Cap Classique 104 (24f,Wor,GF,Sep 4)
Caper 104 (19f,Str,GF,Jly 17)
Capitana 112 (17f,Her,GF,Apr 5)
Captain s Legacy 103 (21f,Plu,S,Mar 27)
Capybara 104 (24½f,Per,G,Apr 26)
Caracciola 109 (16½f,Lin,S,Oct 29)
Caraman 108 (16½f,Str,GS,Mar 13)
Carapuce 108 (20f,Ayr,S,Jan 2)
Carew Lad 109 (24f,Chp,HY,Mar 11)
Caribou 105 (16f,Lei,S,Dec 1)
Carly Bay 106 (21f,Plu,S,Feb 27)
Carlys Quest 114 (23½f,Hay,HY,Feb 18)
Carraig 103 (16f,Tow,S,Nov 26)
Carte Sauvage 101 (16½f,Str,GF,Oct 15)
Carthalawn 101 (20f,Pun,G,Apr 25)
Cash And Carry 100 (16f,Pun,S,Apr 29)
Cash And New 105 (24f,Ncs,S,Jan 18)
Caspers Case 103 (24f,Wor,G,Jun 15)
Castle River 103 (16f,Utt,GF,May 29)
Castleshane 108 (17f,Sth,GF,Aug 8)
Catch The Perk 103 (24f,Hex,GF,Sep 30)
Catchthebug 106 (16f,Utt,G,Jly 13)
Cava Bien 104 (16f,Lei,S,Dec 1)
Cave Of The Giant 104 (19f,Nby,GS,Mar 25)
Ceart Go Leor 106 (24f,Fai,HY,Feb 15)
Celestial Wave 108 (20f,Leo,S,Dec 29)
Celtic Boy 105 (24f,Wor,GF,Aug 17)
Celtic Romance 106 (17f,Her,GF,Jun 14)
Celtic Ruffian 103 (22f,Nab,G,Jun 6)
Central Arch 105 (19f,Naa,S,Jan 21)
Ceoperk 103 (20½f,Fol,S,Feb 14)
Champagne Harry 106 (23½f,Hay,GS,May 7)
Chanticlier 101 (25f,War,S,Jan 26)
Chapeaux Bas 111 (20f,Pun,GF,Apr 29)
Character Building 102 (20f,Ayr,S,Feb 27)
Charango Star 100 (24½f,Tau,G,Dec 8)
Chariot 100 (16f,Fak,G,Oct 21)
Charlie s Double 108 (22½f,Str,GF,Jly 17)
Charlies First 112 (16f,Leo,HY,Jan 15)
Charlotte Vale 102 (17f,Sed,GS,Nov 22)
Charmatic 103 (16f,Tow,G,Apr 25)
Charyan 105 (16f,Pun,G,Apr 26)
Cheery Martyr 101 (20½f,Per,GF,Jun 29)
Chef De Cour 109 (16f,Wet,S,Jan 5)
Chelsea Harbour 112 (24f,Pun,GF,Apr 29)
Cherub 114 (16½f,San,S,Jan 7)
Chiaro 113 (17f,Chl,G,Apr 19)
Chickapeakray 108 (20f,Ban,GS,Apr 22)
Chicuelo 104 (25½f,Chl,GS,Nov 12)
Chief Dan George 108 (24½f,Per,G,Apr 26)
Chief Yeoman 116 (16½f,San,S,Jan 7)
Chives 102 (25f,War,S,Jan 14)
Chivvy Charver 105 (24f,Hex,G,May 7)
Chockdee 102 (16½f,Chl,G,Oct 26)
Cill Churnain 102 (22f,Mar,GS,Feb 17)
Cill Uird 101 (24½f,Per,GF,Jun 29)
Circassian 110 (16f,Wet,S,Oct 29)
Circumspect 100 (16f,Wet,GF,Oct 12)
Cirrious 103 (17f,Nab,GF,Apr 15)
City Of Manchester 103 (17½f,Mar,G,Apr 29)
City Of Sails 117 (20f,Pun,S,Apr 26)
City Storm 101 (16f,Clo,S,Mar 5)
Clan Royal 107 (24f,Mar,HY,Mar 12)
Classic Croco 100 (16½f,Hun,GF,May 10)
Classic Role 104 (17½f,Fol,S,Jan 31)
Classic Sight 102 (24f,Tow,S,Feb 19)
Classical Ben 107 (24f,Wor,GF,Sep 4)
Classical Love 101 (22f,Nab,G,Jun 6)
Clear Riposte 105 (16f,Leo,Y,Dec 26)
Clemax 101 (20½f,Utt,HY,Feb 18)
Clever Bird 101 (24f,Pun,S,Apr 30)
Cloudless Dawn 105 (19½f,Don,G,Nov 27)
Cloudy Grey 112 (16½f,San,S,Mar 11)
Cloudy Lane 112 (20f,Hay,GS,Apr 15)
Clydeoneeyed 101 (16f,Fak,G,Jan 27)
Clyffe Hanger 103 (20½f,Lei,GS,Nov 27)
Coat Of Honour 106 (16f,Hay,GS,May 7)
Coccinelle 105 (21f,Plu,GF,Sep 18)
Cockatoo Ridge 105 (17f,Exe,GS,Mar 21)
Cockneys Revival 106 (16f,Fai,GY,Apr 16)
Code Of Rules 108 (24f,Pun,GF,Apr 29)
Cody 100 (27½f,Sed,HY,Mar 28)
Cold Mountain 110 (16f,Wcn,G,Apr 23)
Cold Turkey 103 (16f,Plu,GS,Nov 20)
College Ace 101 (19f,Nab,GF,Apr 15)
Colline De Fleurs 105 (21f,Tow,HY,Mar 9)
Colophony 108 (16½f,Don,G,Dec 9)
Columbus 102 (24f,Ban,GS,Apr 22)
Colway Ritz 102 (16f,Cat,G,Jan 25)
Combat Drinker 100 (24f,Hex,GF,Sep 30)
Come Bye 108 (20f,Fon,GS,Jan 7)
Comical Errors 101 (17f,Sed,GF,Apr 17)
Commanche Sioux 104 (17½f,Mar,HY,Mar 12)
Commander Kev 104 (19f,Exe,GS,Feb 12)
Common Girl 102 (20½f,Wet,G,May 26)
Commonchero 108 (16f,Pun,S,Nov 20)
Complete Outsider 102 (19½f,Tau,G,Apr 6)
Compo 107 (20f,Pun,GF,Apr 29)
Compton Drake 104 (16f,Wor,GF,Aug 17)
Compton Eagle 102 (16½f,Ain,GS,Oct 22)
Conna Castle 110 (16f,Naa,HY,Mar 12)
Connaught Hall 104 (20f,Pun,GF,Apr 29)
Constable Burton 101 (16½f,Per,GF,Jly 10)
Constantine 101 (16f,Lei,GS,Nov 27)
Contact Dancer 109 (24f,Leo,HY,Jan 15)
Contract Scotland 101 (27f,Kel,GS,Apr 28)
Convent Girl 107 (17f,Nab,GF,Jly 11)
Cool Blues 104 (16f,Leo,YS,Dec 28)
Cool Roxy 105 (19f,Str,GF,Oct 15)
Cool Running 102 (24f,Leo,HY,Jan 15)
Cool Spice 113 (19f,Nab,G,May 16)
Copper Bay 104 (16f,Lei,S,Dec 1)
Copper Moon 103 (20f,Pun,GF,Apr 29)
Coppermalt 100 (24f,Wor,GF,Aug 5)
Cordial 101 (16f,Lei,S,Jan 10)
Cordilla 100 (20f,Hay,S,Dec 3)
Corker 101 (21f,Plu,G,Nov 30)
Corlande 110 (24f,Utt,HY,Feb 18)
Coronado s Gold 100 (16f,Wor,GF,Oct 6)
Correct And Right 100 (21f,Plu,GF,May 8)
Corrib Boy 107 (20f,Pun,S,Apr 30)
Corsican Native 100 (16f,War,S,Dec 4)
Cosmic String 107 (16f,Gow,Y,Jan 26)
Cossack Dancer 102 (16f,Wor,GF,May 8)
Count Boris 102 (16½f,Chp,HY,Dec 3)
Count Tony 100 (20f,Wor,GF,Jun 4)
County Final 107 (16f,Leo,YS,Dec 27)
Courant D Air 104 (19½f,Her,GF,May 10)
Court Storm 107 (20f,Leo,S,Dec 29)
Coustou 102 (18½f,Fon,S,Dec 6)
Covent Garden 114 (20f,Ain,GS,Nov 20)
Crackleando 101 (20f,Ayr,S,Jan 2)
Crathorne 112 (16f,Wet,GF,Oct 12)
Craven 103 (16½f,Nby,GS,Dec 14)
Crazy Horse 106 (16½f,Kel,GS,Jan 13)
Cream Cracker 104 (19f,Str,G,Apr 23)
Credit 102 (19½f,Don,G,Nov 27)
Creme D Arblay 107 (16f,Nav,HY,Mar 11)
Crimson Bow 106 (17½f,Mar,HY,Nov 6)
Cristoforo 107 (16f,Wet,GF,May 19)
Critical Stage 105 (17f,Chl,GS,Dec 9)
Croc An Oir 100 (24f,Wor,GF,Jun 4)
Croix De Guerre 110 (20f,Wor,GF,Aug 23)
Crossbow Creek 103 (16f,Hay,GS,May 7)
Crow Wood 110 (16f,Utt,G,Oct 2)
Cruise Director 104 (17f,Her,GF,Apr 5)
Cruzspiel 105 (20½f,Hun,G,Oct 4)
Crystal D Ainay 108 (24f,Chl,G,Mar 16)

Crystal Gift 100 (22f,Crt,S,May 25)
Culcabock 111 (16½f,Kel,GS,Jan 13)
Cunning Pursuit 102 (18½f,Fon,G,Apr 29)

D J Flippance 101 (20f,Crl,S,Nov 24)
Dabiroun 111 (16f,Pun,YS,Apr 27)
Dalaram 110 (16½f,Chl,GS,Nov 13)
Dalida 102 (16½f,Per,G,Sep 21)
Dalton 103 (16f,Pun,YS,Apr 27)
Dan s Heir 105 (20f,Fak,G,Jan 16)
Danaw 115 (22f,San,G,Feb 4)
Dance Party 100 (16f,Wet,G,May 5)
Dance World 107 (16f,Fak,G,Dec 22)
Dancing Bay 113 (20f,Fon,HY,Feb 19)
Dancing Hill 107 (19f,Nab,GF,Aug 9)
Dancing Pearl 100 (21f,Lud,GF,Feb 8)
Dancing Water 102 (16f,Leo,YS,Dec 27)
Dancinginthestreet 101 (17f,Her,G,Nov 17)
Danse Macabre 105 (16½f,San,S,Mar 10)
Darasim 105 (25½f,Chl,G,Oct 25)
Dare To Dance 101 (16½f,Chl,GS,Nov 12)
Dare Too Dream 109 (19f,Exe,GS,Dec 15)
Dargaville 107 (17f,Her,GF,Apr 28)
Darialann 101 (17½f,Mar,GS,Dec 26)
Darjeeling 104 (24½f,Ain,S,Oct 23)
Dark Ben 106 (18f,Kel,S,Apr 27)
Darko Karim 101 (22½f,Fol,HY,Jan 2)
Darrias 115 (16f,Wcn,G,Nov 5)
Darwaz 103 (16½f,Don,G,Dec 9)
Daryal 111 (16f,Lei,GS,Nov 14)
Dash For Cover 103 (19f,Exe,GF,May 11)
Davenport Democrat 104 (16f,Pun,S,Apr 29)
Dawn Devoy 103 (20½f,Per,G,May 11)
Day Du Roy 100 (16f,Wet,G,May 5)
Day Of Claies 112 (22f,Mar,GS,Feb 17)
Dbest 105 (16f,Pun,G,Apr 26)
De Blanc 108 (19f,Exe,S,Feb 21)
De Soto 101 (17f,Chl,GS,Dec 9)
Dead Sound 109 (24f,Pun,Y,Feb 5)
Dear Villez 110 (17½f,Fol,HY,Jan 17)
Dearson 111 (20f,Fon,S,Dec 6)
Debbie 105 (20f,Wor,GF,Jun 4)
Decisive 106 (19f,Nab,G,Aug 20)
Definate Spectacle 103 (16f,Hay,GS,May 7)
Delaware 103 (17f,Nab,G,May 26)
Denman 116 (21f,Chl,G,Mar 15)
Dennick 102 (16½f,Don,G,Dec 9)
Derawar 105 (20f,Pun,S,Apr 26)
Derivative 101 (22f,San,HY,Dec 3)
Desert Air 121 (16½f,San,S,Jan 7)
Desert Image 103 (16f,Wor,GF,Sep 23)
Desert Jim 104 (18½f,Fon,S,Jan 17)
Desert Quest 112 (16½f,Nby,GF,Mar 4)
Desert Secrets 109 (17f,Chl,G,Apr 19)
Desert Spa 106 (17f,Her,GF,Apr 5)
Desert Tommy 107 (24f,Chp,HY,Mar 11)
Detroit City 116 (17f,Chl,G,Mar 17)
Devil s Teardrop 100 (17f,Her,GF,May 10)
Devito 111 (19½f,Tau,GF,Nov 24)
Dhehdaah 111 (16f,Fak,G,Mar 17)
Di s Dilemma 105 (16½f,Hun,G,Nov 2)
Diamond Merchant 101 (19½f,Her,GF,May 10)
Diamond Mick 102 (16½f,San,S,Mar 10)
Diamond Sal 104 (16f,Wet,S,Dec 27)
Dickie Lewis 108 (24f,Utt,HY,Dec 31)
Didn t You Know 106 (17f,Nab,GF,Aug 31)
Diego Garcia 108 (16f,Pun,G,Apr 26)
Diklers Rose 101 (19½f,Don,G,Nov 27)
Diletia 106 (24½f,Tau,G,Dec 8)
Direct Flight 103 (19½f,Tau,G,Dec 8)
Distant Prospect 107 (16½f,San,S,Mar 11)
Dock Tower 106 (16f,Wet,S,Oct 29)
Doctor Linton 103 (20f,Pun,S,Apr 26)
Dolzago 101 (16f,Plu,GS,Nov 20)
Dom D Orgeval 112 (21f,Chl,G,Mar 15)
Dominican Monk 107 (16½f,Str,GS,Jly 28)
Don And Gerry 105 (16f,Wor,GF,Sep 23)
Don Fernando 102 (24f,Chl,G,Mar 16)
Don t Be Bitin 116 (16f,Pun,S,Apr 28)
Don t Be Shy 107 (16½f,Chl,GS,Nov 13)
Don t Push It 101 (20f,Hay,S,Dec 17)
Donovan 108 (18f,Kel,S,Apr 27)
Dont Ask Me 109 (16f,Wor,GF,Sep 23)
Dont Call Me Derek 108 (16f,Ncs,HY,Feb 25)
Doris Souter 100 (17f,Nab,GF,Aug 21)
Dorneys Well 103 (17f,Exe,GS,Apr 5)
Double Dizzy 109 (22f,Wcn,GS,Feb 18)
Double Gem 105 (16½f,Kel,GS,Apr 28)
Double Law 102 (21f,Nby,G,Mar 24)
Double Vodka 102 (16f,Ncs,HY,Feb 25)
Down s Folly 104 (19½f,Don,GF,Dec 19)
Downing Street 104 (20½f,Per,G,May 11)
Dr Cerullo 104 (16½f,Hun,GF,Sep 25)
Dream Alliance 107 (19f,Nby,GS,Dec 14)
Dream Castle 103 (17½f,Crt,G,May 28)
Dream Falcon 105 (24½f,Tau,G,Dec 8)
Dream Of Tomorrow 102 (16f,Nav,HY,Mar 11)
Dreux 109 (16f,Leo,Y,Feb 12)
Druids Cross 108 (24f,Fai,YS,Jan 22)
Drumbeater 110 (24½f,Per,G,Sep 21)
Drummer First 105 (20f,Pun,GF,Apr 29)
Dubai Ace 108 (20½f,Hun,G,Nov 19)
Dujareva 105 (16f,Pun,YS,Apr 27)
Duke Orsino 105 (20f,Ayr,S,Feb 27)
Dulgodti Bob 107 (16f,Leo,YS,Dec 28)
Duncliffe 108 (19f,Exe,GS,Jan 2)
Dunguaire Lady 105 (16½f,Hex,G,Apr 24)
Dunsfold Duke 102 (21f,Plu,S,Jan 16)
Dusky Lord 105 (20f,Fak,S,Feb 17)
Dusky Warbler 115 (16½f,San,S,Mar 11)
Dusty Dane 102 (16f,Lud,GF,Apr 13)

Eagles High 103 (24f,Leo,HY,Jan 15)
Earl Of Spectrum 100 (17f,Her,G,Nov 17)
Earls Rock 100 (21½f,Sth,G,Apr 29)
Earlsfield Raider 110 (22½f,Fon,GF,May 29)
Earlyinthemorning 100 (16f,Naa,GF,Jly 20)
Earn Out 100 (20f,Wor,G,Jun 29)
Earth Magic 113 (16f,Pun,G,Apr 28)
Earth Man 110 (16f,Wcn,G,May 6)
Ease The Way 102 (16f,Leo,S,Dec 29)
Easter Present 101 (21½f,Chl,G,Apr 19)
Easy Laughter 108 (16f,Fak,G,Jan 27)
Eau Pure 105 (20f,Ain,G,May 13)
Eborarry 104 (17½f,Mar,HY,Nov 6)
Echo Point 103 (17f,Sed,GS,Oct 26)
Edgehill 111 (16½f,Kel,S,Dec 4)
Eight Fifty Five 100 (20f,Wor,G,Nov 1)
Ela Re 101 (17f,Sth,G,Aug 21)
Election Seeker 103 (17f,Nab,GF,Aug 9)
Elegant Clutter 107 (16f,War,HY,Mar 12)
Eljutan 105 (21f,Plu,S,Jan 16)
Ellerslie Tom 106 (16f,Lud,GF,Jan 30)
Ellway Prospect 106 (16f,Plu,GS,Feb 13)
Elvis Returns 102 (23f,Wet,HY,Dec 3)
Emeranna 106 (20f,Pun,GF,Apr 29)
Emmasflora 106 (22f,Mar,G,Feb 7)
Emotional Moment 117 (24f,Chl,G,Mar 16)
Emperor Titus 107 (16f,Fai,GY,Apr 16)
End Of An Error 106 (24f,Hex,F,May 31)
English Jim 104 (22½f,Fon,GS,Nov 13)
Englishtown 105 (17f,Nab,GF,Jun 21)
Enhancer 104 (19f,Nab,G,Aug 20)
Ennistown Lady 106 (16f,Leo,YS,Dec 28)
Errol 101 (17f,Sed,G,May 2)
Escrea 112 (20f,Pun,S,Apr 26)
Esquillon 102 (17½f,Mar,HY,Nov 6)
Essex 113 (16f,Leo,S,Dec 29)
Estate 106 (16½f,Str,G,Apr 23)
Etendard Indien 100 (21f,Lud,G,Mar 23)
Etoile Russe 105 (17f,Sed,S,Feb 6)
Euro American 110 (22f,Mar,GS,Feb 17)
Euro Flyer 106 (16f,Naa,GF,Jly 20)
Euro Route 101 (16f,Utt,GF,Sep 7)
Ever Present 108 (20f,Hay,S,Dec 3)
Exile 104 (16f,Naa,SH,Feb 26)
Extra Smooth 108 (22f,Mar,S,Mar 26)
Eye Candy 116 (16f,Pun,S,Apr 28)

Faasel 121 (17f,Chl,GS,Dec 10)
Fabulous Jet 104 (16f,Fak,G,Dec 22)
Faddad 102 (16f,Wor,GF,Aug 5)
Fair Along 113 (17f,Chl,G,Mar 17)
Fair Question 114 (23½f,Hay,HY,Feb 18)
Fait Le Jojo 113 (16½f,San,S,Jan 7)
Fakima 106 (24f,Fai,SH,Dec 4)
Fame 101 (16½f,Hun,GS,Nov 8)
Fandani 112 (16f,Wcn,G,May 6)
Fantastico 103 (24½f,Per,G,Aug 24)
Fard Du Moulin Mas 101 (19½f,Don,GF,Dec 19)
Farne Isle 101 (16½f,Per,HY,Jun 5)
Father Matt 109 (20f,Pun,S,Apr 30)
Feanor 105 (17f,Sth,G,Jly 15)
Fearless Foursome 106 (27f,Kel,GS,Apr 28)
Feathard Lady 119 (16½f,San,GS,Dec 26)
Federstar 107 (16½f,Ain,GS,Oct 22)
Feel Good Factor 110 (16f,Pun,G,Apr 26)
Felix Rex 102 (21f,Nby,G,Mar 24)
Fenix 117 (16½f,San,S,Jan 7)
Fenney Spring 103 (16f,Utt,GS,Jun 2)
Festive Chimes 103 (16½f,Hun,G,Nov 2)
Fiddles Music 100 (19f,Nab,GS,Jly 27)
Fier Normand 107 (17f,Ban,G,Dec 14)
Fiery Peace 110 (16f,Mus,GF,Nov 25)
Figaro Du Rocher 110 (17f,Sth,G,Jly 15)
Filey Flyer 102 (17f,Sed,GF,Apr 17)
Final Act 110 (24f,Pun,S,Apr 28)
Finely Tuned 101 (16f,Fak,G,Jan 16)
Finland 105 (16f,Wet,GF,Oct 12)
Fire Dragon 118 (24f,Chl,G,Mar 16)
Fire Ranger 106 (19f,Nab,GF,Aug 9)
First Centurion 100 (16f,War,HY,Mar 12)
First Fought 102 (17f,Her,GS,Nov 6)
First Look 104 (16f,Ayr,S,Nov 6)
First Row 110 (16f,Fai,SH,Feb 25)
Firth Of Forth 109 (20f,Leo,S,Dec 29)
Firthgreen Lady 100 (19f,Naa,HY,Nov 12)
Five Colours 105 (19½f,Her,S,Jan 5)
Flame Phoenix 109 (20f,Ain,GS,Nov 20)
Flaming Weapon 107 (16½f,Hun,G,Feb 16)
Flash Cummins 100 (22½f,Fon,G,Dec 20)
Fleurette 101 (17f,Chl,GS,Jan 1)
Flintoff 103 (21f,Tow,G,May 9)
Floragalore 100 (18½f,Fon,S,Apr 1)
Florida Coast 110 (19f,Naa,S,Jan 21)
Flotta 108 (19f,Exe,F,Apr 18)
Flower Haven 102 (16f,Sth,G,Jan 30)
Flying Enterprise 111 (16f,Hay,GS,Nov 19)
Flying Fuselier 101 (16f,Utt,GS,Oct 12)
Flying Johnny M 110 (24f,Pun,GF,Apr 29)
Flying Paragan 104 (16f,Naa,HY,Nov 12)
Fontanesi 106 (20½f,San,GF,Apr 29)
Foodbroker Founder 101 (16½f,San,GS,Dec 26)
Fools Rush In 102 (16f,Leo,Y,Mar 5)
Football Crazy 111 (19½f,Mar,G,Sep 24)
Forest Fauna 100 (21f,Nby,G,Nov 25)
Forever Eyesofblue 107 (27f,Per,GF,Apr 28)
Fortmassini 101 (16f,Leo,HY,Jan 15)
Fortune Island 107 (20½f,Hun,G,Nov 19)
Fortune Point 102 (16f,War,G,Oct 31)
Forty Licks 110 (19f,Naa,HY,Nov 12)
Forzacurity 108 (16f,Wor,GF,May 8)
Four For A Laugh 102 (16f,Lud,G,Feb 22)
Fourty Acers 106 (17f,Ban,G,Dec 14)
Fox Point 104 (20f,Pun,S,Dec 11)
Francies Fancy 104 (16½f,Hex,GF,Jun 19)
Franco 107 (22f,Mar,G,Feb 7)
Freddie Ed 105 (17f,Ban,G,Feb 10)
Freddie Foster 110 (16f,Leo,Y,Feb 12)
Freedom Now 103 (16f,Wcn,G,Nov 5)
Freetown 105 (24½f,Ain,GS,Apr 8)
French Envoy 101 (22½f,Str,G,Apr 23)
From Dawn To Dusk 102 (20f,Chp,G,Apr 28)
Front Rank 105 (16½f,Hun,G,Dec 8)
Frontier 108 (16f,Plu,GF,Sep 18)
Fu Fighter 101 (19f,Exe,GF,May 11)
Fuel Cell 103 (16½f,Don,GS,Dec 10)
Full Irish 100 (19f,Cat,G,Jan 25)
Funny Times 103 (20f,Crl,S,Feb 8)
Futoo 100 (16f,Cat,GS,Mar 8)

Gabor 103 (22f,Nab,GF,Aug 31)
Gaelic Flight 103 (19f,Nab,GF,Apr 15)
Gaelic Roulette 103 (17½f,Mar,S,Aug 13)
Gallant Approach 106 (16½f,Hun,GS,Nov 8)
Galteemountain Boy 103 (21f,War,S,Dec 4)
Game Ball Ali 103 (16f,Pun,GF,Apr 29)
Gan Eagla 107 (21f,Lud,G,Mar 23)
Gardasee 111 (16½f,Hex,GS,Nov 16)
Gaspar 106 (16f,Leo,HY,Jan 15)
Gayle Abated 100 (24f,Pun,S,Apr 28)
Gazza s Girl 110 (18f,Leo,Y,Feb 12)
Geeveem 102 (24½f,Ayr,GS,Apr 21)
Geill Sli 107 (20f,Leo,S,Dec 29)
Gemini Dancer 107 (17f,Nab,GF,Jly 11)
Gemini Lucy 112 (20f,Pun,GF,Apr 29)
General Alarm 105 (16f,Pun,S,Nov 20)
General Duroc 106 (24½f,Ayr,S,Nov 6)
General Hardi 101 (20f,Sed,GF,Apr 17)
Genghis 112 (16½f,Hun,GF,Oct 15)
Gentleman Jimmy 103 (16f,Wcn,S,Mar 9)
Genuine Article 105 (16½f,Str,S,May 21)
Geography 104 (21f,Plu,S,Mar 27)
George Stubbs 102 (16f,Mus,F,Dec 18)
Gidam Gidam 105 (21½f,Sed,GF,Apr 21)
Gimme Shelter 108 (27f,Kel,GS,Apr 28)
Giovanna 106 (16f,Plu,GS,Feb 13)
Gironde 104 (17f,Exe,HY,May 3)
Giust In Temp 104 (16f,Wor,GF,Sep 23)
Give Me Love 108 (20f,Chp,S,Oct 22)
Glacial Evening 107 (21f,Tow,S,Nov 3)
Glacial Sunset 105 (20½f,San,GF,Apr 29)
Glasker Mill 110 (21f,Chl,G,Mar 15)
Glenbane Lady 102 (19f,Naa,S,Jan 21)
Glenfield Heights 101 (19f,Nab,GF,Jly 17)
Glenfinn Captain 100 (16f,Naa,HY,Mar 12)
Gleninagh 109 (24f,Fai,SH,Dec 4)
Glenmoss Rosy 109 (27f,Kel,GS,Apr 28)
Glentorpe 109 (24f,Pun,GF,Apr 29)
Glimmer Of Light 108 (16f,Hay,GS,Apr 15)
Global Challenge 101 (24f,Wor,GF,Jly 20)
Glory Be 105 (16f,Lei,HY,Dec 7)
Go For Bust 102 (16f,Lud,G,Jan 12)
Go My Dream 108 (18f,Leo,Y,Feb 12)
Goblet Of Fire 107 (21f,Chl,G,Oct 25)
Gods Token 113 (16f,War,HY,Feb 24)
Gold Guest 107 (16f,Wcn,F,Oct 6)
Gold Quest 104 (22½f,Utt,GF,Sep 18)
Goldbrook 107 (17f,Tau,GS,Jan 19)
Golden Bay 109 (21½f,Chl,G,Apr 20)
Golden Chalice 102 (16½f,Str,G,Jun 12)
Golden Cross 120 (24f,Chl,G,Mar 16)
Golden Feather 106 (16f,Mus,G,Jan 20)
Golden Square 100 (16½f,Lin,S,Dec 31)
Goldstar Dancer 100 (16f,Cat,G,Nov 30)
Gone Too Far 106 (17½f,Mar,G,Jly 16)
Good Citizen 106 (17f,Chl,GS,Dec 9)
Good Heart 100 (24f,Wor,GF,Aug 5)
Good Investment 101 (18f,Kel,GF,Oct 2)
Good Potential 101 (22½f,Fol,GS,Nov 28)
Good Samaritan 104 (16½f,Str,GF,Jun 5)
Good Thyne Jack 104 (20f,Fai,SH,Feb 25)
Gortatlea 100 (19f,Naa,S,Jan 21)
Gortinard 113 (24f,Pun,S,Apr 28)
Gospel Song 102 (16f,Wet,HY,Jan 14)
Goss 105 (19f,Nab,GF,Jly 17)
Grand Bay 101 (16f,Fak,G,Dec 22)
Grande Jete 105 (17f,Chl,G,Mar 17)
Grangehill Dancer 101 (16f,Leo,YS,Dec 28)
Grasp 107 (17½f,Fol,HY,Jan 17)
Grattan Lodge 107 (22f,Mar,GS,Feb 17)
Grave Doubts 115 (19½f,Mar,G,Sep 24)
Great Compton 101 (20f,Fon,GF,May 25)
Green N Gold 108 (22f,Crt,G,Aug 27)
Green Black 102 (16f,Leo,YS,Dec 28)
Green Iceni 107 (17f,Chl,GS,Jan 1)
Green Prospect 100 (17½f,Mar,S,Aug 13)
Greenfield 104 (21f,War,S,Dec 13)
Greenhope 104 (16½f,Nby,GF,Mar 4)
Grey Brother 102 (22½f,Exe,GS,Apr 5)
Grey Tune 101 (19½f,Her,GF,Jun 14)
Gritti Palace 102 (25f,War,S,Dec 13)
Ground Ball 108 (16f,Leo,YS,Dec 28)
Gungadu 112 (22f,Wcn,GS,Feb 18)
Guru 108 (16½f,Lin,S,Oct 29)
Gustavo 103 (16f,Lud,G,Dec 21)
Gypsy Lord 105 (16f,Leo,YS,Jan 29)

Habitual 109 (24f,Hex,GF,Oct 8)
Habitual Dancer 109 (20f,Ayr,S,Jan 2)
Haditovski 107 (16f,Lei,GS,Nov 14)
Hail The King 105 (19½f,Tau,G,Apr 6)
Halcon Genelardais 101 (24f,Ban,G,Dec 14)
Half Inch 106 (16f,Wor,GF,May 8)
Haloo Baloo 100 (22½f,Exe,GS,Mar 21)
Hambaphambili 105 (24½f,Tau,GS,Mar 29)
Handa Island 101 (17½f,Mar,G,Oct 2)
Handy Money 110 (16½f,Chl,GS,Nov 13)
Harbour View 108 (24f,Fai,SH,Dec 4)
Harchibald 125 (17f,Chl,GS,Dec 10)
Hard Act To Follow 105 (20f,Ayr,S,Dec 22)
Hard N Sharp 105 (19f,Exe,GS,Oct 18)
Hard Shoulder 115 (20f,Pun,S,Apr 26)
Hardwick 102 (16f,Leo,YS,Dec 27)
Hardy Eustace 118 (16½f,Chl,GS,Mar 14)
Harley 103 (20½f,San,HY,Nov 5)
Harmony Brig 108 (18f,Kel,GS,Mar 19)
Harringay 113 (21f,Nby,GS,Mar 25)
Harry Blade 107 (25f,War,G,Oct 31)
Harry Potter 100 (17f,Sth,GF,Aug 8)
Harry s Dream 104 (24f,Wor,G,Apr 9)
Harrycat 101 (16f,Wor,GF,Jly 20)
Harrycone Lewis 106 (26f,Sth,G,Apr 29)
Hasanpour 100 (16f,Naa,HY,Nov 12)
Hasik 102 (16f,Naa,GF,Jly 20)
Hasty Prince 117 (20f,Ain,GS,Apr 7)
Hasty Second 103 (20f,Pun,S,Apr 30)
Hatch A Plan 106 (16f,Lud,GF,Oct 20)
Hathlen 106 (18½f,Fon,GF,Sep 4)
Hattington 102 (19½f,Tow,GF,May 27)
Haut De Gamme 109 (20f,Hay,S,Dec 17)
Hawadeth 107 (20½f,San,GF,Apr 29)
Hawridge King 102 (16f,War,S,Dec 4)
Hawthorn Prince 108 (24f,Utt,G,May 14)
He s A Rascal 103 (19f,War,S,Dec 13)
He s Hot Right Now 105 (17f,Sed,G,May 2)
He s The Gaffer 105 (19½f,Tau,F,Oct 27)
He s The Guv Nor 104 (22½f,Exe,S,Dec 2)
Heathcote 109 (16½f,Lin,S,Dec 31)
Heavy Weather 101 (22½f,Fon,HY,Feb 19)
Heemanela 105 (16f,Wor,GF,May 8)
Heir To Be 109 (22½f,Utt,HY,Mar 18)
Hello Baby 107 (24f,Hex,GF,Oct 8)
Helm 101 (21f,Plu,G,Oct 17)
Heltornic 109 (23f,Lin,HY,Nov 9)
Herakles 108 (20½f,San,GF,Apr 29)
Here Comes Harry 105 (22f,Nab,G,Jun 6)
Here We Go 105 (22½f,Fon,S,Apr 11)
Herecomestanley 108 (19f,War,S,Dec 31)
Hereditary 100 (18½f,Fon,G,Feb 3)
Hernando s Boy 111 (16½f,Hun,G,Dec 8)
Herne Bay 110 (20f,Wor,GF,Aug 23)
Heron s Ghyll 108 (22f,San,S,Mar 10)
Heronstown 106 (16f,Pun,G,Apr 26)
Hi Laurie 102 (22½f,Utt,S,Nov 24)
Hi Tech Man 101 (24f,Wor,G,Jun 15)
Hibernian 102 (20½f,San,S,Mar 11)
Hidden Bounty 109 (23½f,Hay,HY,Feb 18)
Hidden Storm 102 (25½f,Plu,GS,Nov 20)
High Altitude 100 (20½f,Lei,HY,Jan 24)
High Country 106 (16½f,Hex,GF,Sep 30)
High Day 105 (17f,Chl,G,Mar 17)
High Drama 103 (20½f,Per,GS,Jun 30)
High Hope 109 (20f,Fon,GS,Apr 11)
High Priestess 102 (16f,Fai,SH,Dec 4)
Hilarious 101 (20f,Fon,G,Dec 20)
Hill Forts Henry 101 (22½f,Fon,GF,Mar 19)
Hill Forts Timmy 105 (16f,Wcn,GS,Jan 21)
Hilltime 108 (17½f,Mar,G,Jly 16)
His Nibs 106 (25f,War,S,Jan 14)
Historic Place 105 (21f,Nby,G,Mar 24)
Hoh Viss 109 (19½f,Mar,HY,Nov 6)
Holland Park 101 (23½f,Hay,GS,May 7)
Hollywood Critic 100 (17f,Crl,S,Nov 24)
Holy Orders 105 (24f,Gow,Y,Jan 26)
Homer Wells 102 (24f,Pun,S,Apr 28)
Honan 100 (22f,Nab,GF,Aug 31)
Honest Endeavour 107 (16f,Lei,GS,Nov 27)
Honey s Gift 106 (23½f,Fak,S,Feb 17)
Hopbine 100 (19½f,Mar,GF,Jun 8)
Hordago 107 (21f,Chl,GS,Nov 13)
Hot N Holy 100 (24f,Chl,G,Apr 19)
How Art Thou 107 (16f,Fai,GY,Apr 16)
Howle Hill 114 (20f,Chp,S,Oct 22)
Huckster 104 (16½f,Don,GS,Dec 10)

Hue 100 (16f,Fak,G,Mar 17)
Hugo De Perro 102 (20½f,Hex,G,Apr 30)
Hugs Destiny 106 (16f,Mus,GF,Nov 25)
Huka Lodge 100 (23f,Wet,S,Feb 4)
Hunters Tweed 100 (22½f,Kel,S,Apr 27)
Hunting Lodge 102 (17f,Exe,GS,Dec 15)
Hurricane Alley 107 (16f,Pun,YS,Apr 27)
Hylia 106 (22½f,Fon,GF,May 29)

I Got Rhythm 101 (20f,Mus,GF,Feb 5)
I See Icy 104 (20f,Pun,S,Dec 11)
Iberus 101 (17½f,Mar,G,Oct 2)
Idian Mix 110 (17f,Exe,GS,Mar 21)
Idiome 103 (17f,Exe,GS,Dec 15)
Idle Journey 103 (17f,Tau,F,Oct 27)
Idris 108 (17f,Tau,GF,Nov 24)
Iffy 104 (16f,Wet,S,Oct 29)
Iktitaf 116 (16f,Pun,G,Apr 25)
Il Duce 106 (21f,Chl,GS,Nov 13)
Il Athou 104 (19f,Exe,HY,Mar 7)
Ilabon 100 (22½f,Fon,G,Feb 3)
Ile Facile 107 (16f,Fak,G,Jan 27)
Ile Maurice 106 (24f,Pun,G,Apr 27)
Iloveturtle 101 (16½f,Don,G,Dec 9)
Impartial 105 (16f,Pun,YS,Apr 27)
Imperial Rocket 106 (17f,Her,GF,Jun 14)
Imtihan 109 (20f,Crl,S,Mar 19)
In Accord 107 (20f,Chp,HY,Dec 3)
In Compliance 110 (16f,Pun,S,Apr 26)
In Good Faith 106 (21½f,Sed,GS,May 24)
In Media Res 106 (21f,Nby,G,Mar 3)
Inaro 104 (17½f,Fol,GS,Nov 14)
Inch Island 107 (16f,Leo,Y,Mar 5)
Inch Pride 110 (21f,Chl,G,Mar 15)
Inching Closer 107 (22f,Ayr,G,Apr 22)
Incidential 101 (16f,Fai,GY,Apr 16)
Incursion 100 (16f,Hay,G,Oct 20)
Indian Star 104 (16f,Tow,S,Nov 3)
Indy Mood 108 (22f,Ayr,G,Apr 22)
Inglis Drever 112 (25f,Wet,S,Oct 29)
Ingres 109 (20½f,Hun,G,Nov 19)
Innocent Rebel 101 (19f,Exe,GF,May 11)
Intersky Falcon 124 (17f,Chl,GS,Dec 10)
Into The Shadows 105 (16½f,Hun,GS,Nov 8)
Ipledgeallegiance 101 (21½f,Sth,G,Aug 21)
Ireland s Eye 101 (21f,Tow,S,Nov 3)
Irish Blessing 100 (17½f,Mar,G,Oct 16)
Irish Grouse 100 (25½f,Plu,GS,Nov 20)
Irish Legend 100 (24f,Utt,HY,Nov 12)
Irish Wolf 110 (16½f,Hun,G,Dec 8)
Irishkawa Bellevue 104 (24f,Utt,GS,Oct 12)
Isam Top 100 (18½f,Fon,S,Dec 6)
Ishka Baha 107 (16½f,Don,G,Dec 9)
Island Warrior 103 (19f,Exe,F,Oct 5)
It Would Appear 100 (20½f,Lei,GS,Nov 27)
It s Definite 108 (22½f,Kel,GF,May 19)
It s Just Harry 111 (24f,Chl,G,Mar 16)
It s My Party 101 (17f,Tau,GS,Feb 16)
It s The Limit 109 (17f,Tau,G,Dec 8)
Its A Dream 107 (19f,Exe,GS,Feb 12)
Itsmyboy 106 (17f,Exe,HY,May 3)
Ivana Illyich 107 (17½f,Mar,HY,Nov 8)
Ivoire De Beaulieu 100 (27½f,Sed,S,Dec 26)
Izzyizzenty 103 (20½f,Utt,HY,Dec 16)

Jack Durrance 109 (17f,Nab,GF,Aug 31)
Jack High 108 (24f,Gow,Y,Jan 26)
Jack Martin 106 (24f,Mar,HY,Mar 12)
Jack The Giant 109 (16½f,Nby,GF,Mar 4)
Jack The Hough 103 (24f,Pun,S,Apr 28)
Jackson 109 (25½f,Chl,GS,Nov 12)
Jagoes Mills 100 (16f,Pun,G,Apr 27)
Jake Black 108 (16f,Wet,S,Nov 12)
Jaloux D Estruval 102 (23f,Lin,HY,Nov 9)
Jamaican Flight 105 (22f,Mar,GS,Feb 17)
Jamie s Boy 110 (16f,Fai,GY,Apr 16)
Jaquouille 109 (24f,Fai,SH,Dec 4)
Jaunty Times 108 (21f,Nby,G,Mar 3)
Jayed 101 (18½f,Fon,GS,Nov 13)
Jazz D Estruval 112 (20f,Hay,S,Dec 17)
Jazz Messenger 111 (16f,Pun,G,Apr 25)
Jeremy Cuddle Duck 105 (20f,Ain,S,Oct 23)
Jethro Tull 105 (27½f,Sed,GS,Nov 22)
Jexel 100 (20f,Hay,S,Dec 3)
Jimmy Spot On 100 (16f,Pun,G,Apr 26)
Jiver 111 (23½f,Hay,HY,Feb 18)
Jockser 112 (19f,Nab,G,May 16)
Joe Brown 108 (21½f,Sed,S,Jan 10)
Joe Malone 102 (24f,Hex,GF,Oct 8)
Joint Agreement 110 (20f,Pun,S,Apr 26)
Jolika 106 (16½f,Hex,S,Nov 4)
Jontys Lass 112 (21f,Nby,GS,Mar 25)
Jorobaden 108 (24½f,Ain,S,Oct 23)
Josear 103 (16f,Wcn,G,Nov 17)
Josephine Cullen 103 (16f,Pun,G,Apr 26)
Joshua s Bay 100 (21f,Plu,GF,May 8)
Joueur D Estruval 107 (16f,Pun,S,Nov 20)
Just 109 (19f,Naa,S,Jan 21)
Just A Splash 110 (21f,Plu,GS,Nov 20)
Just Beth 110 (20f,Ain,GS,Nov 20)
Just In Time 106 (19f,Str,GF,Oct 15)
Just Sal 100 (20f,Sed,S,Jan 24)
Just Superb 104 (16f,War,G,Oct 31)
Justino 103 (22½f,Fon,GS,Nov 13)
Justpourit 107 (19f,Naa,HY,Nov 12)

Kadam 104 (19½f,Her,GF,May 10)
Kadoun 110 (24f,Pun,S,Apr 28)
Kalambari 105 (16f,Utt,GF,May 29)
Kalderon 107 (16f,Leo,Y,Mar 5)
Kaldouas 100 (20f,Wdr,GS,Dec 16)
Kalmini 107 (16½f,Hun,GF,Feb 9)
Kanpai 102 (18½f,Fon,HY,Feb 26)
Karanja 104 (20f,Ain,S,Oct 23)
Karathaena 108 (17½f,Mar,G,Oct 2)
Kasbah Bliss 113 (16½f,San,S,Feb 25)
Kawagino 111 (16½f,Chl,GS,Mar 14)
Kayceecee 105 (16f,War,S,Jan 14)
Keaveney 110 (24f,Pun,GF,Apr 29)
Keep On Movin 103 (17f,Ban,GS,Jly 29)
Keepers Mead 108 (24f,Chp,GS,Dec 27)
Keepthedreamalive 111 (20f,Pun,S,Apr 26)
Kells Castle 115 (20f,Pun,GF,Apr 29)
Kells Harps 101 (20f,Pun,S,Dec 11)
Kempski 101 (20f,Ayr,HY,Jan 23)
Ken s Dream 109 (17½f,Mar,GS,Feb 17)
Kentmere 107 (16f,Lud,G,May 3)
Kentucky Blue 109 (16f,Wet,HY,Dec 3)
Kentucky Charm 103 (16f,Pun,YS,Apr 27)
Kentucky King 106 (16f,Lud,GF,Oct 20)
Kerryhead Windfarm 117 (20f,Pun,S,Apr 29)
Key To The Kingdom 101 (24½f,Tau,GS,Mar 29)
Khetaam 108 (17f,Chl,G,Mar 17)
Kickahead 100 (16f,War,S,Dec 13)
Kidithou 108 (24f,Hex,G,May 7)
Kilbeggan Lad 114 (20f,Pun,S,Apr 26)
Kilbreena 102 (16f,Naa,HY,Nov 12)
Kildee Lass 106 (19f,Nab,G,May 16)
Kilfinny Cross 108 (18f,Leo,Y,Feb 12)
Kilgowan 100 (20½f,San,GF,Apr 29)
Kilindini 105 (19f,Nab,GF,Jly 17)
Kill Devil Hill 111 (16f,Pun,S,Apr 26)
Killaghy Castle 108 (17½f,Fol,GS,Nov 14)
Killeaney 101 (24f,Pun,S,Apr 28)
Killing Me Softly 106 (20½f,Wet,HY,Jan 14)
Killonemoonlight 106 (22½f,Utt,GS,Oct 12)
Kilty Storm 110 (24f,Chp,S,Feb 25)
Kimono Royal 109 (20½f,Wet,G,May 26)
Kims Pearl 110 (20f,Wor,GF,Aug 23)
Kind Sir 102 (19f,Str,GF,Jly 17)
King Gabriel 107 (16f,Wor,GF,Apr 26)
King Georges 103 (21f,Plu,GS,Feb 13)
King Of Confusion 107 (22½f,Kel,GS,Nov 5)
King s Protector 101 (16½f,Kel,GF,May 19)
Kinger Rocks 114 (16f,Pun,G,Apr 28)
Kingham 104 (17f,Tau,GS,Mar 29)
Kingkohler 109 (17f,Ban,GS,Sep 9)
Kings Advocate 112 (24f,Pun,S,Apr 28)
Kings Castle 107 (22f,Wcn,GS,Feb 18)
Kings Glen 100 (16f,Pun,S,Nov 20)
Kings Rock 101 (17f,Exe,GS,Apr 5)
Kings Signal 102 (16f,Plu,GS,Nov 20)
Kings Square 106 (19f,Cat,G,Jan 12)
Kingsbay 109 (24f,Tow,G,Mar 22)
Kipsigis 111 (22f,San,S,Mar 10)
Kirkham Abbey 107 (19f,Str,GF,Jly 17)
Kirkside Pleasure 105 (24½f,Ayr,S,Mar 11)
Kjetil 103 (27f,Str,G,May 20)
Knight Legend 107 (19f,Naa,S,Jan 21)
Knight Of Silver 101 (24½f,Exe,GS,Nov 1)
Knighton Lad 106 (22½f,Fol,S,Dec 13)
Knockersally Flyer 111 (20f,Pun,GF,Apr 29)
Kombinacja 102 (19f,Str,GF,Oct 15)
Koral Bay 102 (16f,Plu,S,Feb 27)
Korelo 105 (25f,War,S,Jan 14)
Krakow Baba 101 (24f,Lud,G,Jan 19)
Kristoffersen 108 (20½f,Utt,G,May 14)
Kyber 102 (24½f,Mus,GF,Jan 6)
Kyle Lord 100 (16f,Pun,GF,Apr 29)
Kyle Of Lochalsh 100 (16½f,Per,G,May 11)
Kylebeg Dancer 101 (16f,Leo,Y,Mar 5)
Kylegarra Lady 104 (24f,Fai,HY,Feb 15)
Kyno 100 (24½f,Don,G,Nov 27)

L Antartique 100 (16f,Wet,GS,Nov 23)
L Eau Du Nil 101 (20½f,Per,G,Sep 21)
L Oudon 105 (16f,Wcn,G,Apr 13)
La Concha 107 (22½f,Fon,GF,May 29)
La Marette 103 (19½f,Tau,G,Apr 6)
La Marianne 102 (24f,Fai,SH,Feb 25)
Labelthou 100 (16f,Wor,G,Nov 1)
Lacdoudal 115 (20f,Chp,S,Oct 22)
Lady Maranzi 100 (16f,Tow,S,Feb 19)
Lady Of Fortune 102 (21f,War,S,Dec 13)
Lady Racquet 109 (20f,Wor,G,May 24)
Laertes 108 (24f,Ncs,S,Feb 14)
Lagudin 107 (16f,Pun,YS,Apr 27)
Lahib The Fifth 107 (16½f,Per,GF,Aug 23)
Lahinch Lad 100 (24f,Wor,GF,Aug 5)
Lake Merced 103 (20½f,Per,GF,Aug 23)
Lakil Princess 102 (16f,Leo,Y,Feb 12)
Lala Nova 105 (16f,Naa,SH,Feb 26)
Landescent 102 (17f,Tau,GS,Jan 19)
Lane Marshal 105 (17½f,Mar,HY,Nov 6)
Lankawi 102 (16f,Ayr,S,Jan 2)
Lanzlo 109 (24f,Hex,G,May 7)
Latin Queen 100 (17f,Nab,GF,Jly 17)
Latitude 102 (19f,Nab,G,May 16)
Laureldean 112 (16f,Fai,GY,Apr 16)
Lavenoak Lad 104 (24½f,Tau,GS,Mar 29)
Lawaaheb 104 (16f,Fak,G,May 4)
Lawgiver 106 (16f,Wet,G,May 5)
Lawyer Des Ormeaux 102 (27f,Nab,GF,Aug 9)
Le Briar Soul 100 (22f,Wcn,S,Mar 30)
Le Corvee 100 (16½f,Chl,GS,Nov 12)
Le Coudray 102 (24f,Leo,YS,Dec 27)
Le Royal 104 (24f,Mar,HY,Mar 12)
Le Volfoni 102 (19½f,Tau,GS,Mar 29)
Leaders Way 116 (20f,Ain,GS,Apr 7)
Learn To Dance 102 (19f,Naa,S,Jan 21)
Legally Fast 102 (21f,Chl,G,Mar 15)
Lemagurut 108 (16f,Naa,SH,Feb 26)
Lennon 107 (19½f,Mar,HY,Nov 6)
Lenrey 104 (16f,Leo,YS,Dec 28)
Leonia s Rose 102 (20f,Ayr,S,Feb 27)
Leopold 104 (16½f,Per,GS,Jun 30)
Lerida 105 (16f,Mus,G,Feb 15)
Leroy s Sister 106 (22f,Nab,GF,Jly 11)
Lerubis 105 (16f,War,G,Oct 31)
Let s Celebrate 100 (17f,Tau,F,Oct 27)
Lethem Air 103 (20f,Ayr,S,Feb 27)
Letitia s Loss 103 (27½f,Sed,S,Jan 24)
Letterman 109 (21f,Chl,G,Mar 15)
Levitator 102 (16f,Leo,S,Dec 29)
Lewis Island 102 (17f,Tau,GS,Feb 16)
Liathroidisneachta 107 (20f,Hay,HY,Jan 21)
Liberman 104 (24f,Chl,G,Mar 16)
Liberty Seeker 102 (16f,Mus,GF,Feb 5)
Liffey 103 (16f,Fai,GY,Apr 16)
Lightning Star 101 (16f,Utt,GS,Jly 5)
Lilac 102 (19f,Str,G,Apr 23)
Limestream 100 (19f,Naa,S,Jan 21)
Lindbergh Law 100 (20f,Sed,GF,Apr 17)
Lingo 115 (16½f,Chl,GS,Nov 13)
Linnet 108 (16½f,Hun,G,Feb 16)
Linus 107 (20½f,Utt,G,May 14)
Little Brave 100 (19½f,Her,G,Nov 17)
Little Rort 101 (16f,Lud,G,May 3)
Little Task 105 (22f,Crt,G,Aug 27)
Little Tobias 100 (22f,Nab,GF,Apr 28)
Little Venus 105 (19f,Str,G,Apr 23)
Livingonaknifedge 103 (16f,Hay,HY,Jan 21)
Loita Hills 102 (19½f,Tau,G,Dec 30)
Lone Soldier 106 (16f,Wet,G,May 26)
Loner 103 (16½f,Hex,GF,Sep 30)
Long Journey 101 (16f,Leo,YS,Dec 28)
Longstone Lady 101 (17f,Exe,GS,Mar 21)
Longstone Lass 111 (24½f,Ayr,S,Nov 6)
Longueville Manor 107 (20f,Ban,GS,Apr 22)
Looks The Business 105 (16f,Wcn,F,Oct 6)
Lord Baskerville 103 (19f,Cat,G,Jan 12)
Lord Henry 107 (17f,Chl,G,Mar 17)
Lord Jack 101 (24½f,Ain,S,Oct 23)
Lord Lington 107 (16f,War,G,Oct 31)
Lord Nellsson 101 (22f,Wcn,G,Nov 17)
Lord Of Adventure 100 (19f,Nby,GS,Mar 25)
Lord Of The Band 100 (20f,Pun,S,Dec 11)
Lord Ryeford 106 (17f,Ban,G,Feb 10)
Lord Sam 110 (24f,Chl,G,Apr 20)
Lorient Express 103 (16f,Wcn,G,Apr 13)
Lorio Du Misselot 102 (24½f,Mus,GF,Nov 25)
Losing Grip 101 (17½f,Mar,S,Apr 9)
Lost Time 108 (24f,Pun,S,Apr 30)
Love Of Classics 103 (22½f,Fon,S,Apr 1)
Love That Benny 107 (20f,Ayr,S,Feb 27)
Lovely Present 113 (24f,Fai,SH,Dec 4)
Loyal Focus 108 (20f,Pun,S,Apr 30)
Lucky Do 103 (17f,Nab,GS,Aug 1)
Lucky Judge 102 (23f,Wet,GS,Nov 23)
Lucky Spirit 102 (16f,Leo,YS,Dec 28)
Lunar Crystal 115 (16½f,San,S,Mar 11)
Lunar Sea 100 (24f,Fai,SH,Feb 25)
Lupin 108 (20f,Wor,G,May 24)
Lutin Du Moulin 102 (21½f,Sed,GS,May 24)
Lyes Green 110 (24f,Chl,G,Apr 20)
Lysander 108 (20f,Hay,GS,Apr 15)

Mac Federal 100 (16f,Plu,GS,Apr 17)
Mac Three 107 (24f,Pun,G,Apr 27)
Maclean 103 (16½f,Str,G,Jun 12)
Macs Flamingo 103 (20f,Pun,S,Apr 29)
Macs Gildoran 115 (20f,Pun,S,Apr 26)
Macs Joy 120 (16½f,Chl,GS,Mar 14)
Macs Valley 102 (16f,Leo,S,Dec 29)
Madge 101 (16f,Hay,S,Nov 3)
Mae Moss 103 (20f,Ayr,S,Feb 27)
Magic Amigo 102 (20f,Fak,G,Jan 16)
Magic Sky 100 (17f,Ban,GS,Aug 13)
Magical Legend 103 (16½f,Str,GF,Oct 15)
Magical Liaison 107 (20f,Wor,G,May 24)
Magnesium 105 (16f,Lei,S,Dec 1)
Magnifico 111 (22f,San,G,Feb 4)
Mago Santhai 102 (16f,Nav,HY,Mar 11)
Magot De Grugy 103 (19½f,Lin,S,Oct 29)
Mahdi De Coeur 114 (20f,Pun,GF,Apr 29)
Mahogany Blaze 108 (17f,Chl,G,Mar 17)
Majestic 100 (24f,Wor,GF,Aug 17)
Major Catch 106 (20½f,Lei,HY,Jan 24)
Major Miller 102 (20½f,Fol,S,Feb 14)
Major Vernon 109 (20f,Pun,S,Apr 29)
Majorca 109 (17f,Sed,GF,Apr 17)
Make My Hay 105 (16f,War,S,Dec 31)
Makeabreak 107 (16f,Plu,GS,Feb 13)
Malaga Boy 106 (22f,Wcn,GS,Feb 18)
Maljimar 103 (18½f,Fon,GF,Mar 19)
Malko De Beaumont 101 (22½f,Str,GS,Oct 27)
Man About Town 105 (16f,Pun,S,Apr 26)
Man Ray 100 (16½f,San,HY,Dec 3)
Manawanui 101 (21f,Plu,GS,Apr 17)
Maneki Neko 103 (16f,Mus,G,Feb 15)
Mango Catcher 106 (16f,Mus,GF,Nov 25)
Manjoe 100 (24f,Pun,Y,Feb 5)
Manorson 112 (16½f,Nby,G,Nov 26)
Manoubi 100 (20f,Ban,GS,Jly 29)
Manque Neuf 103 (25½f,Plu,GS,Nov 20)
Mansony 118 (20f,Pun,S,Apr 26)
Mantras 105 (20f,Wor,GF,Aug 5)
Manx Royal 103 (21f,Chl,GS,Nov 13)
Marathea 106 (24f,Wor,GF,Aug 5)
Marcel 103 (16f,Wcn,G,Nov 5)
Marhaba Million 107 (16f,Leo,Y,Feb 12)
Marjina 104 (24f,Utt,GS,Oct 28)
Marlborough Sound 111 (22f,Crt,G,May 30)
Marrel 109 (16½f,Chp,G,Apr 18)
Mars Rock 103 (20f,Chp,GS,Apr 8)
Marsh Run 103 (20f,Hay,S,Nov 3)
Martha s Kinsman 102 (22½f,Utt,S,Apr 30)
Masafi 103 (16½f,Hun,GF,Oct 15)
Masrahi 100 (16f,Fai,GY,Apr 16)
Massini s Maguire 103 (21f,Chl,GS,Nov 13)
Master D Or 102 (22½f,Exe,HY,Apr 27)
Master Mahogany 102 (16f,Wcn,GS,Jan 21)
Master Nimbus 100 (16f,Wor,GF,Sep 23)
Master Ofthe Chase 103 (24f,Pun,S,Apr 29)
Master Wells 104 (20f,Hay,S,Jan 7)
Material World 115 (22f,San,G,Feb 4)
Mattock Ranger 104 (19f,Naa,S,Jan 21)
Maunby Rocker 103 (19f,Cat,G,Nov 30)
Maxxium 105 (16f,Leo,Y,Feb 12)
Mayoun 111 (24f,Chp,S,Jan 28)
Mcbain 111 (20½f,Utt,S,Apr 30)
Meadow Hawk 104 (16½f,Hun,G,Nov 2)
Medical Debenture 105 (16f,Pun,G,Apr 28)
Mel In Blue 102 (20f,Chp,G,Oct 8)
Menchikov 105 (16f,Lud,G,Nov 10)
Menelaus 100 (20f,Pun,GF,Apr 29)
Merdeka 106 (20f,Naa,SH,Feb 26)
Merryvale Man 105 (18f,Kel,S,Apr 27)
Methodical 107 (16f,Plu,GS,Feb 13)
Mexican Pete 111 (16f,Wet,GF,Oct 12)
Mezereon 105 (17f,Ban,GS,Mar 25)
Michaels Dream 105 (24½f,Ain,S,Oct 23)
Michigan D Isop 100 (19½f,Tau,G,Dec 30)
Mick Jerome 108 (17f,Tau,GF,Nov 24)
Mick Murphy 105 (19f,Str,GF,Jly 17)
Midas Way 100 (16½f,Nby,GS,Mar 25)
Middleham Park 104 (19½f,Tow,GF,May 27)
Middlemarch 109 (16f,Pun,G,Apr 25)
Midnight Creek 111 (24f,Mar,G,Aug 27)
Midnight Gold 101 (22f,Mar,G,Feb 7)
Mighty Man 119 (24f,Chl,G,Mar 16)
Mightymuller 101 (18½f,Fon,GF,Mar 19)
Mikado 108 (21f,Plu,GS,Apr 16)
Mikado Melody 106 (16½f,Lin,S,Oct 29)
Miko De Beauchene 109 (20f,Hay,HY,Feb 18)
Milan Deux Mille 104 (16½f,Str,GS,Mar 13)
Millagros 103 (16½f,Per,GS,Jun 30)
Millanymare 101 (21f,Chl,GS,Nov 13)
Millennium Hall 100 (16f,Wet,S,Dec 26)
Mini Dare 103 (20f,Wor,G,May 24)
Miniballist 102 (21½f,Sth,G,Aug 21)
Minnesinger 100 (16f,Mus,G,Feb 15)
Minnie Turbo 104 (20f,Pun,GF,Apr 29)
Mioche D Estruval 101 (22f,San,G,Feb 4)
Mirjan 105 (21f,Chl,G,Oct 25)
Misbehaviour 103 (16f,Plu,S,Feb 27)
Miss Academy 112 (16½f,San,S,Jan 7)
Miss Caruso 100 (16f,Pun,GF,Apr 29)
Miss Fahrenheit 101 (24f,Chp,S,Feb 25)
Miss Kilkeel 105 (16½f,Kel,GF,May 18)
Miss Lehman 108 (17f,Nab,G,May 26)
Miss Merenda 101 (22½f,Fon,GF,Sep 22)
Miss Midnight 101 (19½f,Tau,G,Dec 30)
Miss Pebbles 106 (17f,Her,GS,Nov 6)
Miss Pross 103 (16f,Lei,GS,Nov 27)
Miss Shakira 107 (20½f,Per,GS,Sep 22)
Miss Skippy 106 (22f,Nab,GF,Aug 31)
Miss Toulon 111 (20f,Pun,S,Apr 30)
Missyl 102 (20f,Fon,S,Dec 6)
Mistanoora 106 (24f,Chp,GS,Dec 27)
Mister Arjay 106 (16½f,Hun,G,Oct 4)
Mister Chatterbox 106 (19½f,Tau,G,Apr 6)
Mister Hight 112 (16f,Leo,Y,Feb 12)
Mister McGoldrick 103 (16f,Ayr,G,Apr 22)
Mister Month 101 (19f,Naa,S,Jan 21)
Mister Moussac 110 (20f,Wor,GF,Sep 4)
Mister Mustard 104 (16½f,Chp,G,Apr 18)
Mister Quasimodo 112 (19f,Exe,GS,Jan 2)
Mitchelstown 101 (16f,Nav,HY,Mar 11)
Mith Hill 107 (17f,Her,GS,Feb 12)
Mizinky 103 (22½f,Fon,G,Feb 3)
Model Son 108 (22½f,Kel,GF,May 19)
Mohawk Star 101 (16½f,Kel,GS,Apr 28)
Moldavia 100 (16½f,Hun,GF,May 10)
Molly Massini 107 (18f,Leo,Y,Feb 12)

Molostiep 107 (19½f,Tow,GS,Feb 2)
Mondial Jack 108 (22½f,Kel,GF,May 19)
Money Trix 103 (18f,Kel,GS,Jan 13)
Monger Lane 106 (22½f,Exe,HY,Apr 27)
Monolith 108 (23½f,Hay,HY,Feb 18)
Monsal Dale 100 (22½f,Fon,GF,Mar 19)
Monte Cinto 112 (16½f,San,S,Mar 11)
Montevideo 105 (22f,Mar,G,Feb 7)
Monticelli 105 (16½f,Str,G,Jun 12)
Monzon 101 (22½f,Fon,GF,Apr 27)
Moon Catcher 100 (17f,Exe,GS,Apr 5)
Moon Over Miami 100 (16½f,Ain,GS,Apr 7)
Mooramana 100 (20½f,Hex,GF,May 28)
Moore s Law 109 (16f,Leo,Y,Feb 12)
Moorlands Again 107 (22½f,Utt,GS,Oct 12)
More Likely 100 (18f,Kel,GS,Jan 13)
Morgan Be 105 (20f,Ayr,HY,Jan 23)
Moscow Whisper 102 (22½f,Exe,GS,Apr 5)
Mossbank 105 (20f,Pun,G,Apr 28)
Motive 104 (16f,Cat,G,Jan 1)
Motorway 114 (17f,Chl,GS,Dec 9)
Mouftari 107 (21f,Chl,GS,Nov 11)
Mount Clerigo 101 (24f,Chp,S,Oct 22)
Mountain Snow 105 (16f,Pun,G,Apr 26)
Mounthenry 110 (16f,Fai,SH,Dec 4)
Mouseski 107 (20f,Chp,HY,Nov 2)
Moustique De L Isle 103 (27½f,Sed,HY,Mar 28)
Movie King 100 (17½f,Mar,G,Oct 2)
Moyne Pleasure 103 (20f,Sed,S,Jan 24)
Mr Babbage 102 (24f,Pun,S,Apr 28)
Mr Bigglesworth 107 (16f,Wet,G,May 5)
Mr Cool 115 (23½f,Hay,GS,May 7)
Mr Ed 113 (23½f,Hay,GS,May 7)
Mr Fluffy 106 (22f,Nab,GF,Jun 14)
Mr Lear 108 (17f,Ban,GS,Sep 9)
Mr Midaz 105 (16f,Ncs,S,Jan 18)
Mr Mischief 106 (20½f,Per,GS,Sep 22)
Mr Nosie 119 (16f,Leo,YS,Dec 27)
Mr Pointment 112 (21f,Chl,G,Mar 15)
Mr Tim 101 (17f,Crl,S,Nov 24)
Mr Twins 103 (16½f,Hex,GF,Sep 30)
Mr Whizz 100 (17f,Her,GF,Jun 14)
Mrs Philip 104 (21f,Plu,GF,Sep 18)
Mrs Wallensky 100 (20f,Leo,S,Dec 29)
Muckle Flugga 102 (19f,Cat,G,Nov 30)
Mughas 112 (22f,Ayr,G,Apr 22)
Munaawesh 105 (17½f,Mar,GS,Dec 26)
Munadil 101 (16f,Wcn,G,Dec 26)
Mungo Jerry 101 (17½f,Mar,HY,Mar 12)
Muntami 109 (16f,Fak,G,Jan 27)
Murphy s Nails 103 (21f,Lud,GF,Oct 13)
My Final Bid 106 (24f,Ncs,S,Feb 14)
My Galliano 102 (20½f,Hun,GF,Sep 25)
My Immortal 111 (16½f,Nby,G,Nov 25)
My Lady Link 109 (20f,Ain,G,May 13)
My Last Bean 104 (17f,Ban,GS,Apr 29)
My Rosie Ribbons 105 (21f,Nby,GS,Mar 25)
My Sharp Grey 106 (16f,Lud,G,Nov 10)
My Way De Solzen 121 (24f,Chl,G,Mar 16)
Myson 105 (21f,Plu,S,Mar 27)
Mystery Lot 109 (17f,Tau,GS,Feb 16)
Mythical King 107 (23½f,Hay,GS,May 7)

Nagam 103 (20f,Chp,HY,Dec 3)
Nagano 105 (16f,Wcn,G,Nov 17)
Najca De Thaix 102 (16f,Lei,S,Dec 1)
Nanga Parbat 106 (20½f,San,GF,Apr 29)
Nanny Nunny Nac 109 (24f,Pun,GF,Apr 29)
Naos De Mirande 102 (25f,War,S,Jan 14)
Naples 102 (20f,Pun,G,Apr 25)
Napoleon 101 (17f,Exe,GS,Nov 18)
Nassaro 111 (20f,Pun,GF,Apr 29)
Natal 119 (20f,Ain,G,Apr 6)
Nathos 120 (16½f,San,S,Jan 7)
Native Chancer 110 (19f,Str,GF,Jly 17)
Native Commander 101 (16f,War,HY,Mar 12)
Native Emperor 107 (25½f,Chl,GS,Nov 12)
Native Stag 113 (16f,Pun,YS,Apr 27)
Navado 103 (22f,Nab,GF,Apr 28)
Neptune Collonges 117 (20½f,San,HY,Dec 2)
Nerone 105 (16½f,Kel,GS,Jan 13)
Nesnaas 109 (16f,Wcn,F,Oct 6)
Nevada Red 103 (20f,Crl,HY,Oct 30)
Neveesou 109 (16f,War,HY,Feb 24)
New Alco 102 (20f,Ncs,GS,Nov 11)
New Currency 102 (16f,Lud,G,May 3)
New Entic 106 (20½f,San,GF,Apr 29)
New Field 102 (16f,Pun,S,Apr 29)
New Mischief 101 (21f,Plu,S,Jan 1)
New Perk 107 (23½f,Fak,S,Feb 17)
New Team 100 (16f,Utt,GS,Oct 28)
New Time 100 (19½f,Tau,F,Oct 27)
Newmill 119 (16f,Leo,S,Dec 29)
Newtown Dancer 108 (20½f,Hun,G,Nov 19)
Nicanor 117 (21f,Chl,G,Mar 15)
Nice Try 102 (22½f,Fol,HY,Jan 2)
Nick s Choice 109 (16f,Ncs,HY,Mar 18)
Night Bridge 109 (20f,Leo,HY,Jan 15)
Night Sight 100 (16f,Tow,GF,Oct 5)
Nightwatchman 107 (19f,Str,GF,Aug 14)
Nikola 112 (16f,Lei,S,Jan 10)
Nine De Sivola 107 (25f,War,S,Jan 14)
Nippy Des Mottes 110 (17f,Tau,GS,Jan 19)
No Guarantees 104 (20f,Hay,GS,Apr 15)
No Half Session 108 (19f,Naa,S,Jan 21)
No Refuge 112 (20f,Wdr,G,Nov 18)
No Time At All 101 (24½f,Per,G,May 11)
No Way Back 111 (19f,Exe,F,Apr 18)
No Where To Hyde 115 (16f,Leo,HY,Jan 15)
Nobel 107 (20f,Mus,GF,Jan 6)
Noble Calling 104 (22½f,Exe,S,Dec 2)
Noble House 100 (20½f,Per,G,Aug 24)
Noble Request 115 (16½f,San,G,Apr 28)
Nobody Tells Me 107 (21f,Nby,G,Mar 24)
Nobodys Perfect 105 (16½f,Hex,G,Apr 24)
Nocturnally 101 (17f,Tau,G,Apr 6)
Nod Ya Head 106 (22f,Crt,G,May 30)
Nod s Star 101 (20f,Fon,GF,May 25)
Noend 101 (16f,Gow,Y,Jan 26)
Noir Et Vert 109 (24½f,Per,G,Apr 26)
Noland 111 (16½f,Chl,GS,Mar 14)
Nonantais 116 (20½f,Utt,S,Apr 30)
Nor Nor East 107 (22f,San,HY,Dec 3)
North Landing 105 (17f,Sed,GF,Apr 17)
North Lodge 110 (16½f,Don,G,Dec 9)
Northaw Lad 101 (21f,Plu,S,Mar 27)
Northern Friend 105 (16f,Wet,G,May 26)
Norton Sapphire 108 (16f,Wor,GF,Aug 23)
Not Amused 104 (17f,Nab,GF,Jun 21)
Not Left Yet 110 (16½f,San,S,Jan 7)
Not To Be Missed 102 (16f,Utt,GS,Jun 2)
Not Today Sir 103 (24½f,Mus,GF,Nov 25)
Notaproblem 106 (23f,Wet,GS,Nov 23)
Noun De La Thinte 103 (18½f,Fon,GS,Jan 7)
Nous Voila 109 (16f,Hay,HY,Jan 21)
Novacella 111 (21f,Nby,G,Nov 27)
Nowator 101 (16½f,Per,GF,Jly 10)
Numbersixvalverde 110 (24f,Fai,SH,Dec 4)
Numero Un De Solzen 103 (20f,Crl,S,Nov 24)
Nutley King 104 (16f,Leo,YS,Dec 28)
Nutley Queen 100 (16f,Fak,G,Oct 21)
Nycteos 111 (16½f,Ain,GS,Oct 22)

O Muircheartaigh 113 (16f,Nav,S,Nov 13)
O Toole 102 (16f,Wor,GF,Apr 30)
Oasis Banus 100 (19½f,Tau,F,Oct 27)
Ocean Tide 102 (27½f,Sed,HY,Feb 21)
Ockley Flyer 102 (27f,Fon,GF,Apr 27)
October Mist 110 (19½f,Don,G,Nov 27)
Of Course 104 (20f,Leo,S,Dec 29)
Oh Calin 103 (17f,Chl,G,Mar 17)
Oktis Morilious 100 (16½f,Str,G,Apr 23)
Olaso 115 (23½f,Hay,HY,Feb 18)
Old Nosey 102 (24½f,Mus,GF,Nov 25)
Olimpo 105 (17f,Nab,GF,Aug 21)
Olival 100 (17½f,Mar,HY,Mar 12)
Olympic Storm 101 (24½f,Per,GF,Jly 10)
On Y Va 100 (24f,Chp,GS,Nov 23)
On Your Way 105 (16f,Leo,HY,Jan 15)
Once Seen 100 (16f,Wet,GF,May 19)
One More Minute 110 (20f,Pun,S,Apr 26)
One Of Them 105 (24f,Wor,GF,Sep 4)
One Sniff 103 (24f,Ban,G,Feb 10)
One Wild Night 101 (21f,Lud,G,May 3)
Only Vintage 110 (16½f,Nby,G,Nov 26)
Onward To Glory 106 (20f,Fon,GS,Apr 11)
Oodachee 115 (20f,Pun,S,Apr 26)
Opal s Helmsman 100 (20f,Mus,GF,Feb 5)
Openide 114 (16f,Pun,S,Apr 28)
Opera De Coeur 109 (16½f,Str,GS,Mar 13)
Opera Mundi 105 (20½f,Fol,S,Feb 14)
Ophistrolie 100 (16f,Mus,G,Feb 15)
Orange Street 100 (21f,Nby,G,Mar 3)
Orcadian 110 (17½f,Mar,GS,Feb 17)
Orchestral Dream 112 (24f,Pun,S,Apr 30)
Original Fly 105 (16½f,Lin,S,Dec 31)
Original Thought 101 (26f,Hun,G,Feb 16)
Orinocovsky 103 (20½f,Hun,G,Oct 4)
Ornella Speed 101 (21½f,Sed,S,Jan 24)
Orpen Wide 108 (16½f,Str,GS,Mar 13)
Oscar Park 109 (20f,Hay,GS,Apr 15)
Oscar The Boxer 105 (20f,Mus,GF,Jan 6)
Oscars Vision 105 (19f,Str,GF,Jly 17)
Oscatello 109 (21½f,Chl,G,Apr 19)
Oso Magic 105 (16f,Wet,S,Dec 27)
Ostfanni 106 (25½f,Chl,G,Oct 25)
Ostrogoth 103 (16f,War,S,Dec 4)
Oulart 102 (24f,Chl,G,Mar 16)
Oulton Broad 101 (23½f,Fak,S,Feb 17)
Our Girl Kaz 102 (19f,Exe,GS,Dec 15)
Our Joycey 101 (27½f,Sed,HY,Mar 28)
Outside Investor 103 (16f,Wcn,F,Oct 6)
Over The First 106 (16f,Clo,S,Mar 5)
Overlut 103 (16f,Hay,HY,Feb 18)
Overserved 105 (24f,Utt,HY,Nov 12)
Overstrand 113 (19½f,Mar,G,Sep 24)

Pablo Du Charmil 106 (16f,Wcn,GS,Feb 18)
Pace Shot 111 (17f,Chl,G,Mar 17)
Pacolet 109 (16f,Naa,SH,Feb 26)
Paddy Mo 100 (16f,Nav,HY,Mar 11)
Paddy The Piper 108 (20f,Ain,GS,Nov 20)
Palm Island 105 (20½f,Lei,HY,Jan 24)
Pan The Man 107 (21f,Plu,GS,Nov 20)
Papillon De Iena 109 (16f,Lei,GS,Nov 14)
Papini 106 (16f,Hay,GS,Apr 15)
Pardon What 105 (24f,Chp,GS,Dec 27)
Parisienne Gale 110 (16½f,Hex,G,Apr 24)
Park City 103 (16½f,Hun,G,Nov 2)
Parliament Square 104 (16f,Leo,Y,Mar 5)
Paro 101 (16f,Lud,G,Feb 22)
Parsley s Return 105 (16f,Mus,G,Jan 20)
Pass It On 100 (19½f,Her,G,Apr 5)
Passenger Omar 107 (25f,War,S,Jan 26)
Patman Du Charmil 103 (16½f,Chp,GS,Dec 27)
Patriarch Express 113 (24f,Chl,G,Mar 16)
Patriotism 108 (16f,Pun,YS,Apr 27)
Patronage 102 (18½f,Fon,G,Feb 3)
Patsy Hall 113 (24f,Leo,HY,Jan 15)
Pauls Plain 104 (16½f,Don,G,Dec 9)
Pawn Broker 102 (16½f,Str,G,Apr 23)
Pay Attention 108 (18f,Kel,GS,Apr 9)
Pearl King 103 (16f,Lud,GF,Jan 30)
Pearly Bay 100 (19½f,Tau,G,Dec 30)
Pearson Glen 102 (17½f,Crt,HY,May 25)
Pebble Bay 111 (20f,Ain,GS,Nov 20)
Peddars Way 100 (26f,Sth,G,Apr 29)
Pedrobob 108 (16f,Pun,G,Apr 28)
Pedros Brief 111 (20f,Wdr,GS,Dec 16)
Penneyrose Bay 108 (20f,Wor,GF,Oct 6)
Penny Park 107 (22f,Wcn,G,Apr 23)
Penny Pictures 119 (20f,Ain,GS,Apr 7)
Penny Rich 103 (16f,Pun,S,Nov 20)
Penny s Crown 103 (22½f,Utt,GF,Sep 18)
Penric 102 (19½f,Her,GF,Oct 16)
Penteli 100 (21½f,Sed,F,Jly 25)
Penzance 116 (17f,Chl,GS,Dec 10)
Pepe Galvez 111 (16½f,Ain,GS,Oct 22)
Percussionist 104 (17f,Crl,S,Nov 24)
Perfect Balance 101 (21½f,Sed,GS,Nov 22)
Perle De Puce 105 (16f,Sth,GS,Jan 28)
Perouse 111 (16f,Wcn,G,Nov 5)
Peter s Imp 103 (22f,Crt,GF,Jly 14)
Petertheknot 114 (20f,Pun,S,Apr 29)
Petitjean 100 (20½f,Fol,S,Feb 14)
Petrolero 104 (17½f,Crt,HY,May 25)
Petrovka 102 (16f,Fak,G,Jan 27)
Petwick 101 (19f,War,G,Nov 22)
Phar Bleu 116 (20f,Ain,GS,Apr 7)
Phar From Frosty 102 (21f,Chl,G,Oct 25)
Phar Out Phavorite 108 (17f,Her,GF,Apr 28)
Phase Eight Girl 102 (24f,Hex,GF,Oct 8)
Photographer 104 (17f,Tau,G,Dec 8)
Picot De Say 103 (17f,Tau,GS,Mar 13)
Piercing Sun 114 (20f,Pun,S,Apr 30)
Pikestaff 107 (24f,Hex,F,May 31)
Pilca 101 (16f,Utt,GF,May 29)
Pipssalio 107 (24f,Chl,G,Apr 20)
Piraeus 103 (22½f,Kel,S,Dec 4)
Piran 107 (20f,Fon,GS,Jan 7)
Pirandello 106 (16½f,Hun,G,Oct 4)
Pirate Flagship 112 (20f,Ain,GS,Apr 7)
Pirouettes 104 (16f,Utt,G,Jly 13)
Planters Punch 109 (17f,Crl,S,Nov 24)
Pocketwood 102 (16f,Plu,GS,Oct 31)
Poggenip 102 (20f,Fon,GS,Apr 11)
Poker Pal 106 (24f,Pun,S,Apr 30)
Polar Gunner 109 (16f,Wet,HY,Jan 14)
Polar Scout 101 (21f,Plu,GF,May 8)
Pole Star 106 (21f,Chl,G,Mar 15)
Polished 103 (17f,Nab,G,Jun 6)
Political Intrigue 107 (16f,Lud,GF,Jan 30)
Political Sox 106 (24½f,Per,G,May 11)
Polly Whitefoot 101 (16½f,Kel,GS,Oct 22)
Polly s Dream 101 (20f,Pun,S,Apr 30)
Pom Flyer 114 (16f,Leo,HY,Jan 15)
Ponderon 103 (20½f,Hun,G,Oct 4)
Pont Neuf 100 (16f,Lei,HY,Dec 7)
Poor Tactic s 102 (16½f,Per,G,May 11)
Porak 103 (20f,Ban,GS,Apr 22)
Portavadie 100 (16½f,Chl,G,Oct 26)
Portland Bill 100 (22f,Wcn,S,Mar 30)
Posh Stick 103 (20½f,Hex,GS,Nov 16)
Post It 101 (16f,Wcn,G,Apr 13)
Potts Of Magic 108 (23f,Wet,S,Oct 28)
Power Elite 104 (17f,Chl,G,Mar 17)
Power Unit 101 (19f,Str,GF,Aug 14)
Powerlove 101 (20f,Mus,GF,Jan 6)
Powerstation 105 (21f,Chl,GS,Nov 13)
Prairie Law 104 (20½f,Utt,GS,Feb 4)
Prairie Moonlight 104 (16f,Lud,GF,Jan 30)
Prairie Sun 105 (17f,Ban,GS,Oct 8)
Prayerful 103 (24f,Utt,GS,Oct 28)
Precious Mystery 104 (19f,Exe,S,Feb 21)
Predator 103 (21f,Nby,G,Mar 3)
Predicament 106 (23f,Wet,S,Feb 4)
Preists Leap 108 (24f,Pun,S,Apr 30)
Premier Dane 100 (16½f,Ain,G,Apr 6)
Premier Rouge 111 (16f,Naa,SH,Feb 26)
Present Glory 109 (24½f,Tau,GF,Nov 10)
Prestbury Knight 104 (19½f,Tau,G,Dec 30)
Presumptuous 108 (21½f,Sed,GF,Apr 21)
Pretty Star 104 (22f,Wcn,G,Dec 26)
Pride Of Finewood 104 (24f,Ncs,S,Jan 18)
Prime Contender 108 (16f,War,S,Dec 4)
Primitive Poppy 107 (21½f,Sed,S,Jan 10)
Prince Adjal 104 (24½f,Ayr,GS,Apr 21)
Prince Of Persia 109 (20½f,Hun,G,Nov 19)
Prince Of Tara 108 (20f,Nav,S,Nov 13)
Princelet 106 (17f,Tau,GS,Jan 19)
Princess Commanche 100 (20f,Pun,S,Dec 11)
Principe Azzurro 103 (19f,War,HY,Feb 24)
Priors Dale 105 (16f,Wdr,G,Nov 18)
Private Be 103 (19½f,Tau,G,Dec 30)
Prize Fighter 104 (16½f,Hun,GF,Feb 9)
Pro Dancer 103 (21f,Lud,G,Mar 23)
Proper Article 100 (16½f,Chl,GS,Mar 14)
Proprioception 103 (16f,Sth,G,Jan 30)
Protagonist 100 (22½f,Fol,GS,Nov 28)
Proud To Be Irish 106 (16f,Pun,S,Apr 29)
Pseudonym 107 (19f,Nby,GS,Mar 25)
Publican 109 (16½f,San,G,Apr 28)
Pure Magic 103 (21f,Lud,GF,Apr 13)
Purple Patch 110 (21f,Nby,GS,Mar 25)
Purple Shuffle 106 (16f,Pun,G,Apr 28)
Putup Or Shutup 102 (22½f,Fol,GS,Nov 28)

Qabas 107 (16f,Utt,GF,May 29)
Qualitair Pleasure 107 (20½f,Hun,G,Nov 19)
Quarantine 107 (16f,Pun,G,Apr 28)
Quartier Latin 100 (16f,Plu,G,Nov 30)
Quasimodo 102 (16½f,San,S,Jan 7)
Quatre Heures 106 (16f,Pun,G,Apr 27)
Quick 107 (24f,Chl,G,Apr 20)
Quinmaster 103 (16f,Nav,HY,Mar 11)
Quotable 101 (16½f,Hun,GF,Apr 17)

Rackard 109 (24f,Pun,S,Apr 28)
Raffaello 107 (16f,Wcn,GS,Jan 21)
Raikkonen 117 (20f,Pun,S,Apr 26)
Rainbow Tree 102 (17½f,Mar,G,Oct 2)
Rajam 108 (16½f,Per,GS,Jun 30)
Rajayoga 112 (17f,Sth,GF,Aug 8)
Ramblees Holly 104 (17f,Sed,GF,Apr 17)
Rambling Minster 110 (25½f,Chl,GS,Nov 12)
Random Precision 105 (21½f,Sth,G,Apr 29)
Random Quest 103 (22½f,Utt,GS,Oct 12)
Raneen Nashwan 100 (16f,Wor,GF,Sep 23)
Ranelagh Gray 111 (24f,Tow,G,Mar 22)
Rapscallion 101 (16f,Wcn,S,Mar 9)
Rare Coincidence 108 (16f,Utt,GS,Nov 24)
Rare Ouzel 112 (24f,Fai,SH,Dec 4)
Rasharrow 106 (16½f,Chl,GS,Mar 14)
Rathlin Island 102 (24f,Hex,GF,Sep 30)
Rathowen 110 (24f,Ncs,S,Jan 9)
Rawaabet 100 (16½f,Hun,G,Feb 16)
Ray Boy 115 (16f,Pun,S,Apr 29)
Rayshan 114 (22f,San,G,Feb 4)
Reach For The Top 102 (17f,Chl,G,Apr 20)
Ready To Rumble 104 (16½f,Kel,GF,May 18)
Reap The Reward 103 (24½f,Per,G,Apr 26)
Reasonably Sure 101 (21f,Lud,G,May 3)
Rebel Raider 108 (16f,Fak,G,Nov 15)
Recount 103 (16½f,Chp,G,Apr 28)
Red Canyon 104 (20f,Wor,G,Jun 15)
Red Chief 104 (22½f,Str,GF,Jly 10)
Red Dahlia 106 (21f,Plu,GF,Sep 18)
Red Echo 104 (22f,Nab,GF,Apr 28)
Red Man 106 (19f,Cat,G,Jan 12)
Red Moor 100 (16f,Lud,G,Jan 12)
Red Nose Lady 108 (19f,Str,GF,Aug 14)
Red Perk 109 (23f,Wet,S,Oct 28)
Redemption 111 (25f,Wet,S,Oct 29)
Redi 101 (16½f,San,HY,Nov 5)
Redspin 104 (21f,Lud,GF,Oct 13)
Reem Two 106 (21½f,Chl,G,Apr 20)
Refinement 113 (21f,Chl,G,Mar 15)
Reflex Blue 103 (20f,Wor,GF,Sep 4)
Regal Force 102 (19f,Naa,HY,Nov 12)
Regal Heights 100 (16f,Ayr,HY,Jan 23)
Regal Term 106 (19½f,Tow,GS,Feb 2)
Rehearsal 108 (16f,Mus,GF,Nov 25)
Reinedoff 104 (19f,Naa,S,Jan 21)
Reisk Superman 108 (16f,Pun,G,Apr 26)
Reiziger 104 (16½f,Chl,G,Oct 26)
Relix 102 (20½f,Per,G,May 11)
Renvyle Society 109 (24f,Fai,SH,Dec 4)
Resplendent Star 103 (16½f,Hun,G,Nov 2)
Restart 102 (25½f,Chl,G,Oct 25)
Restless D Artaix 106 (16½f,Nby,G,Nov 25)
Restoration 102 (17f,Chl,G,Mar 17)
Return Home 109 (19f,War,S,Dec 31)
Return Ticket 101 (18½f,Fon,HY,Feb 26)
Reve De Rose 101 (16f,Leo,YS,Dec 28)
Rhetorical 101 (20f,Fon,GF,Sep 22)
Rifleman 101 (17½f,Mar,GS,Nov 17)
Rift Valley 104 (24f,Mar,G,Aug 27)
Rights Of Man 100 (21f,Chl,GS,Nov 13)
Rimsky 111 (21f,Chl,G,Mar 15)
Rince Donn 100 (16f,Nav,HY,Mar 11)
Ring Street Roller 100 (20½f,Per,GF,Jun 29)
Rising Generation 106 (16f,Hay,GS,Nov 19)
River Alder 110 (22½f,Kel,GF,May 19)
River Indus 102 (17f,Chl,GS,Jan 1)
River Mist 105 (20½f,Hex,G,Apr 30)
River Ripples 101 (21f,Plu,GS,Nov 20)
Roadmaker 109 (24f,Pun,G,Apr 27)
Roadworthy 101 (20f,Sed,S,Jan 24)
Robbers Glen 104 (22½f,Kel,GS,Apr 9)
Robbie On Tour 100 (20½f,Utt,G,May 14)
Robbo 107 (23½f,Hay,HY,Feb 18)
Robert The Bruce 104 (16½f,Kel,S,Apr 3)
Robyn Alexander 100 (16f,War,GF,May 7)
Rocket Bleu 102 (16f,War,G,Oct 31)
Rocket Ship 103 (16f,Leo,S,Dec 29)

Rockfield Dancer 101 (16f,Leo,HY,Jan 15)
Rockview Lad 103 (20f,Pun,GF,Apr 29)
Rockys Girl 104 (16f,War,HY,Mar 12)
Rojabaa 109 (16½f,Str,GS,Mar 13)
Romaha 102 (24f,Fai,SH,Dec 4)
Roman Candle 103 (20f,Fon,GF,May 25)
Roman Rampage 102 (22½f,Fol,HY,Jan 2)
Romany Prince 110 (24f,Mar,G,Aug 27)
Rome 101 (20½f,Hun,G,Oct 4)
Roobihoo 108 (20f,Crl,S,Mar 19)
Rooftop Protest 119 (19½f,Mar,G,Sep 24)
Room To Room Gold 108 (19f,Nab,GF,Jly 17)
Rooster Booster 115 (16½f,Hun,GF,Oct 15)
Rosaker 104 (24f,Leo,YS,Dec 28)
Rosarian 102 (22½f,Exe,GS,Apr 5)
Roschal 104 (24½f,Ayr,S,Mar 11)
Rosecliff 106 (16f,Wor,GF,Apr 26)
Rosemauve 103 (22½f,Fon,GS,Jan 27)
Rosenblatt 105 (16f,Plu,S,Mar 27)
Rosetown 101 (24½f,Exe,GS,Nov 1)
Rosses Point 105 (24f,Wor,G,Apr 9)
Rossin Gold 101 (16f,Ayr,S,Jan 2)
Royal Artisan 109 (22f,Crt,G,May 30)
Royal County Star 111 (16f,Fai,GY,Apr 16)
Royal Emperor 106 (23½f,Hay,HY,Feb 23)
Royal Glen 106 (16½f,Hex,G,Apr 30)
Royal Niece 103 (26f,Her,G,Mar 6)
Royal Paradise 102 (20f,Fai,SH,Dec 4)
Royal Shakespeare 116 (16f,Wcn,G,Nov 5)
Royal Stardust 104 (20f,Fon,S,Dec 6)
Royaldou 110 (18f,Leo,Y,Feb 12)
Royals Darling 106 (16½f,Nby,GS,Jan 11)
Rude Health 102 (20½f,Lei,GS,Nov 14)
Rudetski 100 (19½f,Her,GF,May 10)
Rum Pointer 100 (22f,San,S,Mar 10)
Run Katie Chimes 107 (16f,Pun,S,Nov 20)
Running Lord 102 (25f,War,G,Oct 31)
Russian Sky 107 (23f,Wet,S,Dec 26)
Rustarix 107 (16f,Utt,GS,Nov 24)
Ryhall 101 (23f,Wet,G,Apr 24)

Sabreflight 102 (21½f,Sed,S,Jan 24)
Sabreur 108 (17f,Her,GF,Apr 5)
Saby 105 (17f,Nab,GF,Aug 31)
Sachsenwalzer 102 (16½f,Str,GF,Jly 10)
Sadlers Wings 100 (16f,Leo,YS,Jan 29)
Saif Sareea 112 (16f,Mus,GF,Nov 25)
Saipan 102 (16f,Fai,HY,Feb 15)
Sakenos 101 (17f,Tau,GS,Feb 16)
Salhood 101 (16½f,Hun,G,Dec 8)
Salopian 102 (17f,Tau,GF,Nov 24)
Saltango 120 (20f,Ain,GS,Apr 7)
Salut Saint Cloud 109 (20½f,San,GF,Apr 29)
Salute 108 (16½f,Ain,G,May 13)
San Hernando 103 (22½f,Fon,S,Apr 11)
San Peire 105 (27½f,Sed,S,Jan 24)
Sangiovese 103 (16f,Lei,GS,Nov 14)
Sans Souci Boy 104 (20f,Pun,S,Apr 30)
Santa s Son 111 (24f,Fai,SH,Dec 4)
Saorsie 107 (17f,Nab,GF,Aug 31)
Saraba 103 (18½f,Fon,GS,Jan 7)
Sarena Special 102 (17f,Her,GF,Apr 28)
Sasso 103 (17½f,Mar,GS,Dec 1)
Saucy Night 102 (21f,Plu,GS,Oct 31)
Sauterelle 104 (16f,Fai,GY,Apr 16)
Scalloway 102 (16½f,Hun,G,Oct 4)
Scarlet Dawn 106 (22½f,Str,GS,Oct 27)
Scarrabus 101 (21f,Plu,GF,Sep 18)
Schapiro 106 (20f,Wor,G,Jun 29)
Schindlers Hunt 110 (16f,Leo,YS,Jan 29)
Schooner 103 (16f,Lei,S,Dec 1)
Sconced 100 (21½f,Sed,GS,Nov 22)
Scotmail 102 (21½f,Sed,HY,Dec 6)
Scotmail Too 109 (20½f,Per,GF,Apr 28)
Screen Test 101 (17f,Nab,GF,Apr 15)
Screenplay 112 (21f,Nby,G,Nov 27)
Sea Diva 107 (20f,Leo,S,Dec 29)
Sea Skate 104 (18f,Leo,Y,Feb 12)
Sea The Light 109 (19f,Exe,GS,Jan 2)
Sea To Sky 107 (16f,Naa,SH,Feb 26)
Secret Divin 102 (17f,Tau,G,Dec 8)
Secret Pact 104 (20f,Crl,HY,Mar 9)
Secretofshambhala 101 (24f,Fai,SH,Feb 25)
Secured 100 (21f,Lud,GF,Jan 30)
Seeador 101 (22½f,Exe,S,Feb 21)
Self Defense 113 (16½f,San,GS,Dec 26)
Senorita Rumbalita 106 (17½f,Fol,GS,Nov 28)
Seomra Hocht 102 (24f,Pun,S,Apr 30)
Separated 101 (20f,Wor,GF,Oct 6)
September Moon 105 (24½f,Per,GF,Jun 29)
Seraph 106 (17½f,Mar,GS,Dec 26)
Serbelloni 112 (16½f,Kel,S,Dec 4)
Sergio Coimbra 100 (20f,Ain,GS,Nov 20)
Serious Weapon 100 (16f,Pun,G,Apr 26)
Serpentine Rock 101 (16½f,San,HY,Nov 5)
Sesame Rambler 103 (22½f,Fon,S,Apr 1)
Settlement Craic 102 (16f,Plu,GF,May 8)
Seveneightsix 105 (20½f,Lei,GS,Nov 14)
Seymar Lad 101 (20f,Ncs,S,Feb 14)
Sh Boom 116 (22f,San,G,Feb 4)
Shaamit The Vaamit 106 (16f,Wcn,S,Jan 4)
Shady Baron 101 (22f,Mar,G,Feb 7)
Shady Grey 104 (20f,Wor,G,May 24)
Shalako 105 (21f,Chl,G,Oct 25)
Shalati Princess 105 (19½f,Tau,G,Apr 6)
Shaman 102 (18½f,Fon,GF,Mar 19)
Shamayoun 107 (16f,Sth,S,Feb 22)
Shannon Springs 107 (17½f,Mar,G,Feb 7)
Sharaab 100 (17½f,Mar,G,Aug 27)
Sharajan 106 (19f,Exe,GS,Feb 12)
Shares 105 (16f,Hay,GS,Apr 15)
Sharp Rigging 107 (20f,Chp,S,Oct 22)
She ll Be Lucky 104 (16f,Pun,S,Nov 20)
She s My Girl 106 (20f,Ain,G,May 13)
She s Our Native 105 (21f,Lud,GS,Dec 8)
Sheebadiva 103 (24f,Fai,YS,Jan 22)
Sheer Guts 105 (17½f,Mar,G,Oct 16)
Sher Beau 108 (20f,Pun,S,Apr 29)
Sher Why Not 109 (16f,Leo,YS,Jan 29)
Shifting Alliance 101 (18f,Leo,Y,Dec 26)
Shining Strand 113 (20½f,Wet,G,May 26)
Shiny Thing 105 (16½f,Don,G,Dec 9)
Shirazi 101 (19½f,Don,GF,Dec 19)
Siberian Highness 104 (17½f,Fol,S,Dec 13)
Siegfrieds Night 104 (19f,Cat,G,Nov 30)
Siena Star 101 (22½f,Fon,GF,May 29)
Signature Tune 101 (16f,Tow,G,May 9)
Silber Mond 102 (20f,Fon,GS,Apr 11)
Silence Reigns 106 (20f,Wor,GF,Aug 5)
Silencio 105 (16f,Wcn,GS,Jan 21)
Silistra 103 (16f,Plu,S,Dec 12)
Silk Screen 111 (16f,Pun,S,Nov 20)
Silk Trader 100 (17f,Her,GF,Apr 5)
Silken Pearls 103 (20f,Crl,HY,Mar 9)
Silkwood Top 100 (20f,Wdr,GS,Dec 16)
Silver Birch 102 (25f,War,S,Jan 26)
Silver Bow 100 (20f,Mus,GF,Feb 5)
Silver Charmer 114 (19½f,Mar,G,Sep 24)
Silver City 100 (16f,Wcn,S,Jan 4)
Silver Dollars 101 (16f,Cat,GS,Mar 8)
Silver Prophet 110 (16½f,Hun,G,Dec 8)
Silver Seeker 103 (16½f,Hex,S,Nov 4)
Silverio 104 (22½f,Fon,HY,Feb 26)
Simon s Seat 105 (17f,Nab,GF,Aug 31)
Simonovski 103 (16f,Lud,GF,Apr 13)
Simply Mystic 101 (23f,Wet,S,Dec 26)
Sir Frederick 107 (24f,Pun,G,Apr 27)
Sir Night 107 (16f,Mus,GF,Nov 25)
Sir Overbury 113 (24f,Pun,GF,Apr 29)
Sir Pandy 102 (16f,Utt,GS,Oct 12)
Sir Rowland Hill 104 (24f,Wor,G,Apr 9)
Sir Walter 107 (19f,Str,GF,Aug 14)
Sirius Storm 111 (16f,Pun,S,Apr 29)
Skeheenarinky 105 (20f,Leo,S,Dec 29)
Skibereen 104 (17f,Her,GF,Jun 14)
Skiddaw Jones 106 (16½f,Hex,GF,Sep 30)
Sky s The Limit 114 (21f,Chl,G,Mar 15)
Skyhawk 110 (16f,Pun,YS,Apr 27)
Slalom 106 (21½f,Sth,G,Aug 21)
Slaney Eagle 107 (16f,Leo,YS,Dec 28)
Slew Charm 109 (17½f,Mar,G,Feb 7)
Smart Boy Prince 109 (16f,Wor,GF,Sep 23)
Smart Mover 105 (22½f,Fon,GF,Apr 27)
Smilingvalentine 102 (22½f,Fon,G,Feb 3)
Smokey Mountain 104 (16½f,Chp,G,Apr 28)
Smoothly Does It 105 (17f,Tau,G,Dec 8)
Snakebite 105 (17½f,Fol,GS,Nov 14)
Snoopy Loopy 118 (16f,Pun,S,Apr 29)
Snow Tempest 104 (18½f,Fon,GF,Sep 22)
Snow s Ride 104 (16f,Wet,GF,Oct 12)
So Cloudy 100 (16f,Lud,G,Jan 19)
Soleil Fix 103 (18½f,Fon,G,Apr 29)
Solerina 116 (20f,Fai,SH,Dec 4)
Some Touch 106 (20f,Crl,HY,Mar 9)
Something Wells 102 (21f,Plu,S,Dec 12)
Son Of Greek Myth 108 (20½f,Hun,G,Nov 19)
Sonnengold 102 (16½f,Lin,HY,Feb 18)
Sonnyanjoe 102 (20f,Pun,S,Apr 30)
Sotovik 112 (24½f,Ayr,GS,Apr 21)
Sou Wester 102 (20f,Chp,GS,Apr 8)
Sound Witness 105 (24f,Pun,S,Apr 30)
Southern Bazaar 100 (16f,Cat,G,Jan 25)
Southern Command 111 (20f,Pun,GF,Apr 29)
Sovereign State 110 (16f,Mus,GF,Nov 25)
Space Cowboy 106 (17f,Nab,GF,Aug 21)
Spanish Don 110 (17f,Tau,GF,Nov 24)
Sparklinspirit 102 (22f,Mar,G,Apr 29)
Special Rate 111 (22f,San,G,Feb 4)
Spectrometer 109 (19½f,Mar,G,Sep 24)
Speed Kris 105 (24½f,Per,G,May 11)
Speed Venture 103 (16f,War,S,Dec 31)
Spidam 102 (16½f,San,HY,Dec 2)
Spider Boy 101 (21f,Plu,GF,Sep 18)
Spiders Web 101 (20f,Fon,GF,May 25)
Spike Jones 106 (17f,Tau,G,Dec 30)
Spirit Of Tenby 106 (22f,Nab,G,Jun 6)
Spiritual Society 102 (17f,Chl,GS,Jan 1)
Sporazene 113 (16f,Wcn,G,Nov 5)
Spring Breeze 108 (16f,Hay,G,Oct 20)
Spring Junior 102 (19f,Exe,GS,Dec 15)
Spring Pursuit 114 (20f,Chp,S,Oct 22)
Spuradich 100 (17½f,Crt,GF,Jly 14)
Squantum 103 (24½f,Tau,G,Jan 9)
Square Mile 103 (19½f,Mar,G,Oct 2)
St Pirran 105 (16f,Hay,GS,Nov 19)
Stacumny Bridge 105 (20f,Pun,GF,Apr 29)
Stage Friendly 102 (16f,Lud,G,May 3)
Stagecoach Diamond 110 (22f,Crt,G,May 30)
Stan 110 (20½f,Utt,S,Apr 30)
Standin Obligation 113 (25½f,Chl,GS,Nov 12)
Standing Bloom 100 (24f,Utt,HY,Nov 12)
Star Member 106 (19½f,Mar,GS,Dec 26)
Star Trooper 105 (21½f,Sed,GS,May 24)
Starry Mary 101 (22½f,Utt,S,Nov 24)
Stars Delight 100 (22f,Mar,G,Apr 29)
Starzaan 115 (24f,Chl,G,Mar 16)
Step In Line 102 (22f,Crt,G,Aug 27)
Stern 102 (21f,Plu,G,Oct 17)
Stocks n Shares 106 (20f,Wor,G,Jun 15)
Stoneville 103 (20f,Naa,SH,Feb 26)
Stoop To Conquer 106 (22½f,Fol,HY,Jan 2)
Storm Clear 104 (17f,Her,GF,Apr 28)
Stormez 106 (22f,San,G,Feb 4)
Strangely Brown 121 (20f,Ain,GS,Apr 7)
Straw Bear 116 (16f,Lei,S,Jan 10)
Strides Of Fire 116 (16f,Pun,YS,Apr 27)
Strike Back 101 (16f,Leo,Y,Feb 12)
Strong Resolve 109 (24½f,Ayr,S,Nov 6)
Studmaster 117 (16f,Leo,HY,Jan 15)
Stutter 116 (16f,Pun,YS,Apr 27)
Sublimity 110 (16f,Pun,G,Apr 25)
Suchwot 102 (19f,Exe,F,Oct 5)
Suits Me Fine 100 (21½f,Sth,G,Aug 21)
Sun King 110 (16f,Mus,G,Feb 15)
Sundawn Lady 102 (24f,Wor,GF,Aug 5)
Sunday City 110 (19f,Cat,G,Jan 12)
Sundeck 107 (19f,Naa,S,Jan 21)
Sungio 102 (22½f,Utt,GF,Sep 18)
Sunley Future 103 (17f,Tau,GS,Feb 16)
Sunley Shines 108 (16f,Wor,GF,Apr 26)
Sunnyarjun 103 (16f,Tow,G,May 9)
Sunnyland 110 (16f,Wor,GF,Sep 23)
Sunset King 106 (17f,Nab,GF,Aug 31)
Sunset Light 106 (25f,War,G,Oct 31)
Super Boston 104 (26f,Sth,G,Aug 21)
Super Road Train 102 (26f,Hun,GF,May 26)
Supply And Fix 102 (20½f,Per,G,May 11)
Supreme Being 103 (20f,Pun,G,Apr 25)
Supreme Justice 109 (16f,Leo,HY,Jan 15)
Supreme Leisure 108 (16f,Wet,HY,Jan 23)
Supreme Peace 103 (24f,Pun,S,Apr 28)
Supreme Piper 101 (23f,Lin,HY,Feb 18)
Supreme Serenade 102 (22f,Wcn,GS,Feb 18)
Supreme s Legacy 110 (24f,Ban,GS,Apr 22)
Suprendre Espere 103 (17f,Sed,GF,Apr 17)
Surface To Air 103 (22f,Wcn,S,Mar 30)
Swansea Bay 107 (24½f,Ain,G,Jun 16)
Sweet Oona 106 (16f,Wcn,G,Dec 26)
Sweet Wake 109 (16½f,Chl,GS,Mar 14)
Swift Swallow 109 (16f,Wor,GF,May 8)
Swifts Hill 104 (26f,Hun,GF,May 26)
Swiss Hall 102 (20f,Pun,GF,Apr 29)
Syncopated Rhythm 100 (24½f,Per,G,Apr 26)

Tagula Blue 103 (17½f,Fol,S,Jan 31)
Take A Mile 106 (16f,War,S,Dec 4)
Take Your Mark 105 (16f,Fai,HY,Feb 15)
Taking My Cut 104 (20½f,Lei,S,Feb 1)
Talarive 104 (16½f,Hex,G,Apr 30)
Tamreen 109 (16½f,Str,G,Apr 23)
Tana River 108 (22f,Wcn,GS,Feb 18)
Tandava 103 (20½f,Per,HY,Jun 5)
Tanikos 102 (16½f,San,GS,Dec 26)
Taranai 101 (22f,Nab,GF,Jun 21)
Tardenois 107 (24f,Fai,YS,Jan 22)
Tarlac 114 (16½f,San,S,Mar 11)
Tawrific Laois 104 (20f,Pun,GF,Apr 29)
Tazmana 109 (16f,Leo,YS,Dec 28)
Tech Eagle 110 (16f,Wor,GF,Apr 26)
Tees Components 108 (25f,Wet,S,Oct 29)
Teeton Babysham 100 (24f,Chp,S,Jan 20)
Tell The Trees 107 (20f,Ain,G,May 13)
Teme Valley 105 (19f,Cat,G,Nov 30)
Temoin 109 (21f,Nby,G,Mar 3)
Temple Place 101 (17f,Ban,GS,Mar 25)
Templelusk 100 (16f,Pun,GF,Apr 29)
Templet 102 (16½f,Kel,GS,Jan 13)
Teragram 101 (20f,Pun,S,Apr 30)
Terinka 104 (24f,Pun,S,Apr 30)
Terivic 100 (20½f,Utt,GS,Oct 28)
Tessanoora 109 (16f,Wor,G,Mar 26)
Texas Holdem 116 (20f,Ain,GS,Apr 7)
That Man Fox 100 (16f,Fak,G,Jan 27)
That s Rhythm 100 (19f,Cat,G,Jan 1)
The Black Tiger 102 (20f,Pun,S,Apr 30)
The Bulb 108 (24f,Pun,GF,Apr 29)
The Castilian 105 (16f,Fak,G,Jan 27)
The Composer 103 (17f,Tau,G,Apr 6)
The Cool Guy 110 (22½f,Utt,GS,Oct 12)
The Count 101 (16½f,Kel,GF,May 18)
The Deadly 104 (20f,Pun,S,Dec 11)
The Duke s Speech 106 (16½f,Ain,GS,Apr 7)
The Fingersmith 103 (16f,Leo,HY,Jan 15)
The Flyer 105 (26f,Sth,G,Apr 29)
The French Furze 112 (16f,Ncs,S,Nov 26)
The Gangerman 106 (24f,Chp,HY,Mar 11)
The Gene Genie 100 (17f,Tau,G,Dec 30)
The Hairy Lemon 106 (16f,War,S,Dec 31)
The Last Hurrah 112 (16f,Pun,G,Apr 26)
The Local 101 (16f,Wdr,G,Nov 18)
The Luder 111 (19f,Exe,GS,Jan 2)
The Market Man 109 (21f,Chl,G,Oct 25)
The Mick Weston 104 (17f,Chl,GS,Jan 1)
The Names Bond 108 (16½f,Hex,S,Nov 4)
The Pen 107 (16f,Wet,GF,Oct 12)
The Persuader 107 (20f,Ain,GS,Nov 20)
The Railway Man 116 (16f,Pun,S,Apr 29)
The Real Deal 101 (16f,Utt,G,Oct 2)
The Reverend 106 (23½f,Hay,HY,Feb 18)
The Roney Man 101 (20f,Pun,S,Dec 11)
The Sawyer 108 (19f,Exe,GS,Dec 15)
The Sister 101 (22½f,Str,GF,Jly 17)
The Small Farmer 104 (26f,Her,G,Mar 6)
The Weaver 102 (20f,Mus,GF,Jan 6)
The Wife s Sister 101 (16f,Utt,HY,Feb 18)
Theatre Diva 101 (18f,Leo,Y,Feb 12)
Theatre Tinka 101 (16f,Lud,GF,Apr 13)
Thedreamstillalive 104 (22f,Wcn,GS,Dec 1)
Thedublinpublican 102 (19½f,Don,GF,Dec 19)
Themanfromnenagh 100 (24f,Fai,YS,Jan 22)
Theocritus 105 (16½f,Chl,G,Oct 26)
Thepubhorse 100 (24½f,Per,GF,Aug 23)
Thieves Glen 105 (16f,Wcn,G,May 6)
Think Quick 101 (16f,Wor,GF,Aug 5)
Thosewerethedays 106 (20f,Ayr,S,Jan 2)
Thoutmosis 107 (24½f,Per,G,May 11)
Three Lions 108 (24f,Chp,GS,Dec 27)
Three Ships 101 (16½f,Hun,GF,May 10)
Threequarter Moon 102 (16f,Naa,HY,Nov 12)
Tickateal 103 (24½f,Mus,GF,Jan 6)
Tiger Frog 101 (16f,War,GF,May 7)
Tignasse 103 (16f,Wcn,F,Oct 6)
Time Marches On 103 (21f,Plu,GF,May 8)
Time To Shine 103 (16½f,Chp,G,Apr 18)
Times Up Barney 105 (20f,Hay,HY,Feb 18)
Tinstre 106 (20f,Wor,GF,Sep 4)
Tippeenan Lass 110 (24f,Pun,GF,Apr 29)
Tipper Road 113 (20f,Pun,GF,Apr 29)
Tirikumba 103 (27f,Str,G,May 20)
Titian Flame 107 (17f,Her,GF,Jun 14)
Tobesure 105 (24f,Hex,G,May 7)
Toi Express 105 (19f,Nab,GF,Jly 17)
Tokala 106 (19½f,Her,S,Jan 5)
Tom Bell 109 (17f,Her,GS,May 22)
Tomenoso 110 (24f,Mar,G,Aug 27)
Tomina 108 (26f,Sth,G,Apr 29)
Tommy Spar 101 (20f,Wor,GF,Jly 20)
Tomorrow s Dream 108 (16f,Leo,YS,Dec 28)
Ton-Chee 104 (17f,Sed,G,May 2)
Toni Alcala 109 (22f,Crt,G,May 30)
Tonic Du Charmil 100 (19½f,Tau,GF,Nov 24)
Toofarback 109 (20f,Pun,S,Dec 11)
Top Achiever 104 (17f,Ban,GS,Apr 29)
Top Brass 102 (20f,Mus,G,Feb 15)
Top Pack 100 (22f,Crt,GF,Jly 14)
Top Strategy 107 (16f,Pun,YS,Apr 27)
Topanberry 107 (20f,Ain,G,May 13)
Topkat 108 (17f,Tau,GF,Nov 24)
Tora Bora 103 (18½f,Fon,S,Apr 1)
Torkinking 109 (16f,Ncs,HY,Feb 25)
Toss The Caber 106 (16f,Wet,GF,Oct 12)
Totally Scottish 106 (23f,Wet,S,Dec 26)
Touch Of Ebony 103 (20f,Wor,G,Jun 15)
Touch Of Fate 101 (22f,Wcn,GS,Dec 1)
Toulouse Express 100 (16f,Cat,GS,Mar 8)
Toulouse-Lautrec 103 (24½f,Exe,GS,Nov 1)
Tous Chez 102 (16f,Wet,S,Dec 26)
Town Crier 115 (16f,Wet,S,Jan 5)
Tragic Lover 107 (24f,Fai,HY,Feb 15)
Tramantano 113 (16½f,Chl,GS,Nov 13)
Transit 101 (16½f,San,HY,Dec 3)
Traprain 105 (17f,Tau,GS,Jan 19)
Travel 108 (16½f,Per,GS,Jun 30)
Travelling Band 100 (16f,Hay,GS,Apr 15)
Travino 109 (19f,Naa,HY,Nov 12)
Treasured Memories 103 (20f,Crl,S,Feb 8)
Treaty Flyer 110 (21f,Nby,GS,Mar 25)
Trebello 101 (20½f,Hun,S,Feb 23)
Triple Mint 109 (24f,Ban,GS,Apr 22)
Tritonville Lodge 104 (16½f,Don,G,Dec 9)
Trompette 111 (16f,Plu,S,Mar 27)
Truckers Tavern 101 (24f,Ban,G,Dec 14)
True Mariner 108 (19½f,Her,GF,Apr 5)
Tulipa 106 (17½f,Mar,G,Jly 16)
Turbo 106 (16f,Wor,GF,Oct 6)
Turkama 102 (19½f,Mar,GF,Jly 31)
Turko 112 (16½f,Nby,G,Nov 25)
Turnstile 107 (16½f,Kel,S,Dec 4)
Turtle Soup 115 (20½f,Utt,S,Apr 30)
Tushna 111 (20f,Pun,GF,Apr 29)
Twentytwosilver 105 (17f,Nab,GF,Aug 31)
Twist Bookie 102 (16f,Lud,GS,Dec 8)
Twist Magic 102 (16f,Wcn,GS,Dec 1)
Two Hoots 102 (26f,Hun,G,Dec 26)
Two Miles West 111 (16f,Wet,S,Oct 29)
Two Steps To Go 102 (17f,Sed,F,Jly 25)
Twofan 107 (24½f,Tau,GS,Mar 29)
Twostrongmen 102 (16f,Leo,Y,Mar 5)
Twotiming Gent 104 (23f,Wet,HY,Jan 23)
Tynedale 104 (22½f,Kel,GS,Nov 5)

Un Autre Espere 104 (16f,Fak,G,Oct 21)
Uncle John 106 (16½f,Don,G,Dec 9)
Under Oath 104 (16f,Pun,YS,Apr 27)

Undergraduate 108 (16f,Nav,HY,Mar 11)
Underwriter 103 (16f,Pun,S,Apr 29)
Ungaretti 102 (26f,Sth,G,Aug 21)
Ungaro 117 (22f,San,G,Feb 4)
Unicorn Reward 103 (16f,Naa,SH,Feb 26)
United 123 (16f,Pun,S,Apr 28)
United In Spirit 106 (16f,Fai,GY,Apr 16)
United Spirit 103 (16½f,Hex,G,Apr 24)
Unjust Law 106 (16f,Fak,G,Jan 16)
Unusual Suspect 102 (27f,Str,G,May 20)
Up Above 109 (16f,Nav,S,Nov 13)
Up At Midnight 109 (21f,Plu,S,Feb 27)
Upright Ima 105 (16f,War,GF,Mar 21)
Upswing 107 (17½f,Mar,GS,Nov 17)
Uptown Lad 102 (16f,Ncs,HY,Dec 5)
Urban Rebel 110 (16f,Fai,HY,Feb 15)
Ursis 111 (16f,Wet,S,Oct 28)

Va Vavoom 105 (16½f,Per,GS,Jun 30)
Vale De Lobo 103 (16½f,Chp,GS,Oct 8)
Valley Ride 109 (21f,Chl,G,Mar 15)
Valuable 100 (17f,Sed,F,Jly 25)
Vaughan 106 (17f,Her,GS,Feb 12)
Vengeance 109 (18½f,Fon,GF,Mar 19)
Verasi 115 (16½f,San,S,Mar 11)
Versus 101 (24f,Ban,G,Dec 14)
Vertical Bloom 111 (21f,Nby,GS,Mar 25)
Very Optimistic 112 (23½f,Hay,GS,May 7)
Very Special One 103 (16f,Wor,G,Nov 1)
Vic The Piler 103 (20½f,Hex,GS,Nov 16)
Vic Venturi 107 (20f,Pun,G,Apr 28)
Vicario 111 (20f,Hay,S,Dec 3)
Vicars Destiny 108 (22f,Mar,GS,Feb 17)
Vicentio 104 (24½f,Per,GF,Jun 29)
Viciana 104 (17½f,Fol,GS,Nov 14)
Victom s Chance 109 (20½f,Utt,HY,Feb 18)
Victorias Groom 107 (16½f,Lin,S,Dec 31)
Victram 116 (16½f,San,S,Mar 11)
Villago 104 (21½f,Sed,GS,Nov 22)
Vinando 104 (16f,Wcn,GS,Feb 18)
Vingis Park 111 (21f,Nby,G,Nov 27)
Vintage Gold 111 (16f,Leo,YS,Jan 29)
Vintage Port 104 (20f,Pun,S,Apr 30)
Vintox 106 (16f,Gow,Y,Jan 26)
Vivante 105 (24f,Wor,GF,Aug 5)
Vocative 104 (16f,Hay,S,Nov 3)
Vrisaki 101 (17f,Sed,GF,Apr 17)

Wait For The Will 105 (16f,Plu,GF,Sep 18)
Waittillitellyou 106 (16f,Leo,YS,Dec 28)
Walkin Aisy 101 (19f,Naa,S,Jan 21)
Wally Wonder 105 (20½f,Hun,S,Feb 23)
Walsingham 103 (16f,War,S,Jan 14)
Waltzing Beau 111 (22f,San,G,Feb 4)
Wanango 109 (16f,Leo,YS,Dec 27)
Wardash 104 (16½f,Hun,GF,Jun 7)
Warningcamp 106 (17½f,Fol,S,Dec 13)
Washington Lad 115 (20f,Pun,S,Apr 29)
Washington Pink 101 (24½f,Mus,GF,Jan 6)
Water King 108 (21f,Chl,GS,Nov 11)
Water Taxi 102 (16f,Wet,S,Oct 29)
Waterspray 100 (20f,Wor,GF,Jun 4)
Waydale Hill 105 (21½f,Sth,G,Apr 29)
Waynesworld 101 (22½f,Fon,GS,Nov 13)
Wayward Melody 101 (24f,Wor,GF,May 8)
We ll Meet Again 105 (16½f,Kel,GF,May 18)
Wee Anthony 104 (23f,Lin,HY,Feb 18)
Wee Dinns 107 (19f,Str,G,Apr 23)
Wee Robbie 109 (19f,Nby,GS,Dec 14)
Welcome Stranger 105 (16f,Wor,GF,Apr 26)
Welcome To Unos 110 (19f,Cat,G,Nov 30)
Wellbeing 112 (17f,Exe,GS,Mar 21)
Welsh Dane 102 (24½f,Tau,G,Jan 9)
Wembury Point 100 (16½f,Chl,GS,Nov 12)
Wenger 103 (18½f,Fon,S,Dec 6)
West End Wonder 102 (20f,Wor,G,Jly 6)
Westender 111 (24f,Chl,G,Mar 16)
Weston Rock 104 (22f,Mar,GF,Jly 31)
Wet Lips 107 (19½f,Mar,G,Sep 24)
What A Benefit 100 (19f,Naa,HY,Nov 12)
What A Vintage 105 (21f,Plu,S,Dec 12)
What sonyourmind 100 (16f,Hay,HY,Feb 23)
Whatadifference 107 (16f,Naa,GF,Jly 20)
Where s Eddie 110 (20f,Pun,S,Apr 30)
Wheresben 102 (16f,Nav,HY,Mar 11)
Whirling 103 (17½f,Mar,G,Sep 24)
Whispered Promises 108 (16½f,Chl,GS,Mar 14)
Whispered Secret 104 (22f,Nab,GF,Jun 14)
Whistle Blowing 103 (17f,Her,GS,Feb 12)
White Dove 102 (17f,Ban,G,Feb 10)
White On Black 106 (16f,Plu,S,Feb 27)
Whosethatfor 100 (17f,Exe,S,Dec 2)
Wicked Nice Fella 103 (21½f,Sed,GF,Apr 21)
Wiggy Smith 103 (17f,Tau,G,Apr 6)
Wild Chimes 108 (22f,Mar,G,Feb 7)
Wild Is The Wind 105 (17f,Crl,HY,Oct 30)
Wild Passion 112 (16f,Pun,S,Apr 26)
Wild Tempo 104 (27f,Nab,GF,Aug 9)
Will Of The People 107 (20½f,Utt,S,Apr 30)
William Butler 101 (24f,Ban,GS,Apr 22)
Willie The Shoe 102 (24f,Pun,G,Apr 27)
Winapenny 108 (17f,Crl,S,Nov 24)
Windy Hills 100 (20f,Crl,HY,Mar 9)
Windy Spirit 102 (22½f,Fon,G,Feb 3)
Wine Fountain 107 (20f,Pun,S,Dec 11)
Winner Take All 106 (20f,Pun,S,Dec 11)
Winter Garden 100 (16½f,Per,GS,Jun 30)
Wiscalitus 106 (16f,Utt,GF,May 29)
Wise Tale 107 (22½f,Utt,GF,Sep 18)
Wishwillow Lord 101 (16f,Clo,S,Mar 5)
Witch Wind 101 (17f,Crl,S,Nov 24)
Witness Time 103 (26f,Her,G,Mar 20)
Wogan 103 (20½f,San,S,Mar 11)
Wolf Creek 103 (20f,Leo,S,Dec 29)
Woodford Consult 100 (16f,Ncs,S,Jan 18)
Woodhouse 105 (19f,Naa,HY,Nov 12)
Woodlands Genpower 103 (24f,Utt,HY,Nov 12)
Woodview 100 (20f,Hay,HY,Feb 23)
Woody Valentine 108 (17f,Chl,GS,Dec 9)
World Wide Web 104 (25½f,Chl,GS,Nov 12)
Wyoming 103 (16½f,Str,GF,Jun 5)

Xamborough 105 (17f,Tau,G,Dec 8)
Xellance 113 (19½f,Mar,G,Sep 24)
Xila Fontenailles 102 (17f,Exe,GS,Nov 18)

Yaboya 105 (20½f,Lei,S,Feb 1)
Yarra Maguire 100 (16f,Pun,G,Apr 26)
Yenaled 101 (16f,Plu,S,Feb 27)
Yes Sir 115 (20½f,Utt,S,Apr 30)
Yogi 105 (24f,Gow,Y,Jan 26)
You Do The Math 103 (20f,Ayr,S,Jan 3)
You Re The Man 103 (27f,Kel,GS,Apr 28)
Youlbesolucky 105 (20f,Ncs,GS,Nov 26)
Young Tot 103 (17f,Exe,F,Apr 18)
Yourman 108 (24f,Chp,S,Oct 22)

Zacatecas 100 (21f,Plu,GS,Apr 16)
Zaffaran Express 107 (21½f,Chl,G,Apr 20)
Zaffran Lady 101 (24f,Fai,HY,Feb 15)
Zaffre 101 (16½f,Str,GF,Jun 5)
Zaiyad 109 (21f,Chl,G,Mar 15)
Zalda 107 (16½f,Chp,GS,Oct 8)
Zamnah 104 (24f,Pun,G,Apr 27)
Zarakash 108 (17f,Nab,GF,Jly 11)
Zeloso 102 (22½f,Fon,HY,Feb 26)
Zibeline 105 (25½f,Chl,GS,Nov 12)
Ziggy Zen 101 (16½f,Hun,G,Oct 4)
Zipalong Lad 118 (20f,Ain,GS,Apr 7)
Zoltano 100 (20f,Ain,GS,Nov 20)
Zonergem 101 (17½f,Mar,G,Jly 16)
Zonic Boom 102 (16f,Fak,G,Jan 27)
Zouave 100 (19f,Nby,G,Mar 3)
Zumrah 102 (16f,Wor,GF,Oct 6)
Zygomatic 107 (24½f,Ain,G,Jun 16)

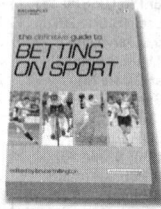

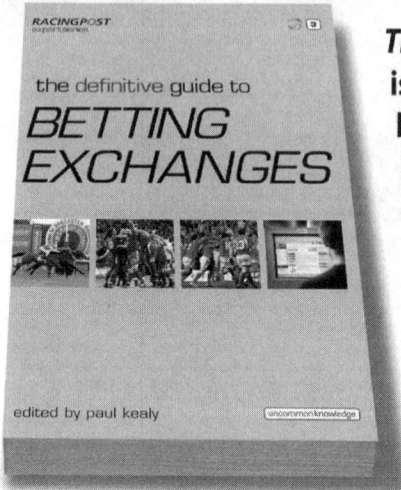

WINNERS OF PRINCIPAL RACES (LAST TEN YEARS)

PADDY POWER GOLD CUP (HANDICAP CHASE)

formerly Thomas Pink, Murphy's & Mackeson Gold Cup

Cheltenham 2m 4f 110y

1996	Challenger du Luc	6-10-02	12
1997	Senor El Betrutti	8-10-00	9
1998	Cyfor Malta	5-11-03	12
1999	The Outback Way	9-10-00	14
2000	Lady Cricket	6-10-13	15
2001	Shooting Light	8-11-03	14
2002	Cyfor Malta	9-11-09	15
2003	Fondmort	7-10-13	9
2004	Celestial Gold	6-10-02	14
2005	Our Vic	7-11-07	18

HENNESSY COGNAC GOLD CUP (HANDICAP CHASE)

Newbury 3m 2f 110y

1996	Coome Hill	7-10-00	11
1997	Suny Bay	8-11-08	14
1998	Teeton Mill	9-10-05	16
1999	Ever Blessed	7-10-00	13
2000	King's Road	7-10-07	17
2001	What's Up Boys	7-10-12	14
2002	Gingembre	8-10-13	25
2003	Strong Flow	6-11-00	21
2004	Celestial Gold	6-10-05	14
2005	Trabolgan	7-11-12	19

WILLIAM HILL - TINGLE CREEK TROPHY CHASE

Sandown 2m

1996	Sound Man	8-11-07	4
1997	Ask Tom	8-11-07	7
1998	Direct Route	7-11-07	10
1999	Flagship Uberalles	5-11-07	6
2000*	Flagship Uberalles	6-11-07	7
2001	Flagship Uberalles	7-11-07	6
2002	Cenkos	8-11-07	6
2003	Moscow Flyer	9-11-07	7
2004	Moscow Flyer	10-11-07	7
2005	Kauto Star	5-11-07	7

(* Run at Cheltenham)

ROBIN COOK MEMORIAL H'CAP CHASE (formerly Bonusprint.com and Tripleprint Gold Cup)

Cheltenham 2m 4f

1996	Addington Boy	8-11-10	10
1997	Senor El Betrutti	8-11-03	9
1998	Northern Starlight	7-10-01	13
1999	Legal Right	6-10-13	9
2000	Go Roger Go	8-11-00	12
2001	Abandoned due to frost		
2002	Fondmort	6-10-05	9
2003	Iris Royal	7-10-13	17
2004	Monkerhostin	7-10-02	13
2005	Sir OJ	8-10-00	16

STAN JAMES CHRISTMAS H'DLE

Kempton 2m

1996	Abandoned due to frost		
1997	Kerawi	4-11-07	5
1998	French Holly	7-11-07	5
1999	Dato Star	8-11-07	4
2000	Geos	5-11-07	7
2001	Landing Light	6-11-07	5
2002	Intersky Falcon	5-11-07	6
2003	Intersky Falcon	6-11-07	6
2004	Harchibald	5-11-07	7
2005*	Feathard Lady	5-11-00	7

(* Run at Sandown)

STAN JAMES KING GEORGE VI CHASE

Kempton 3m

1996	One Man	8-11-10	5
1997	See More Business	7-11-10	8
1998	Teeton Mill	9-11-10	9
1999	See More Business	9-11-10	9
2000	First Gold	7-11-10	9
2001	Florida Pearl	9-11-10	8
2002	Best Mate	7-11-10	10
2003	Edredon Bleu	11-11-10	12
2004	Kicking King	6-11-10	13
2005*	Kicking King	7-11-10	9

(*Run at Sandown)

CORAL WELSH NATIONAL (HANDICAP CHASE)

Chepstow 3m 5f 110y

1996	Abandoned due to frost		
1997	Earth Summit	9-10-13	14
1998	Kendal Cavalier	8-10-08	14
1999	Edmond	7-10-00	16
2000	Jocks Cross	9-10-04	19
2001	Supreme Glory	8-10-00	13
2002	Mini Sensation	9-10-04	16
2003	Bindaree	9-10-09	14
2004	Silver Birch	7-10-05	17
2005	L'Aventure	6-10-04	18

PIERSE HANDICAP HURDLE

(formerly Ladbroke Handicap Hurdle)

Leopardstown 2m

1997	Master Tribe	7-10-04	23
1998	Graphic Equaliser	6-10-00	20
1999	Archive Footage	7-11-08	25
2000	Mantles Prince	6-9-12	14
2001	Grinkov	6-10-07	24
2002	Adamant Approach	8-11-01	26
2003	Xenophon	7-10-11	28
2004	Dromlease Express	6-10-04	19
2005	Essex	5-10-08	21
2006	Studmaster	6-10-03	27

VICTOR CHANDLER HANDICAP CHASE

Ascot 2m

1997*	Ask Tom	8-10-10	8
1998	Jeffell	8-10-11	9
1999*	Call Equiname	9-11-03	7
2000	Nordance Prince	9-10-00	10
2001	Function Dream	9-10-11	10
2002	Turgeonev	7-10-04	8
2003**	Young Devereaux	10-10-04	9
2004	Isio	8-10-05	13
2005***	Well Chief	6-11-10	10
2006****	Tysou	9-11-02	10

(*Run at Kempton)
(**Run at Kempton as Tote Exacta Chase)
(***Run at Cheltenham)
(****Run at Sandown)

TOTESPORT TROPHY (HANDICAP HURDLE)

Newbury 2m 110y

1997	Make a Stand	6-11-07	18
1998	Sharpical	6-11-01	14
1999	Decoupage	7-11-10	18
2000	Geos	5-11-03	17
2001	Landing Light	6-10-02	20
2002	Copeland	7-11-07	16
2003	Spirit Leader	7-10-00	27
2004	Geos	9-10-9	25
2005	Essex	5-11-6	25
2006	Abandoned due to frost		

HENNESSY COGNAC GOLD CUP CHASE

Leopardstown 3m

1997	Danoli	9-12-00	8
1998	Dorans Pride	9-12-00	8
1999	Florida Pearl	7-12-00	7
2000	Florida Pearl	8-12-00	7
2001	Florida Pearl	9-12-00	7
2002	Alexander Banquet	9-12-00	5
2003	Beef Or Salmon	7-12-00	5
2004	Florida Pearl	12-11-12	7
2005	Rule Supreme	9-11-12	7
2006	Beef Or Salmon	10-11-12	7

RACING POST CHASE (HANDICAP)

Kempton 3m

1997	Mudahim	11-10-02	9
1998	Super Tactics	10-10-10	7
1999	Dr Leunt	8-11-05	8
2000	Gloria Victis	6-11-10	13
2001	Young Spartacus	8-11-03	15
2002	Gunther McBride	7-10-03	14
2003	La Landiere	8-11-07	14
2004	Marlborough	12-11-12	11
2005	Farmer Jack	9-11-12	16
2006*	Innox	10-11-00	15

(*Run at Sandown)

SUNDERLANDS IMPERIAL CUP (HANDICAP HURDLE)

Sandown 2m 110y

1997	Carlito Brigante	5-10-00	18
1998	Blowing Wind	5-11-10	15
1999	Regency Rake	7-10-07	9
2000	Magic Combination	7-10-00	18
2001	Ibal	5-9-09	23
2002	Polar Red	5-11-01	16
2003	Korelo	5-11-06	17
2004	Scorned	9-10-03	23
2005	Medison	5-10-01	19
2006	Victram	6-9-12	21

IRISH INDEPENDENT ARKLE CHALLENGE TROPHY CHASE (NOVICES)

(formerly Guinness Arkle Challenge Trophy)

Cheltenham 2m

1997	Or Royal	6-11-08	9
1998	Champleve	5-11-00	16
1999	Flagship Uberalles	5-11-00	14
2000	Tiutchev	7-11-08	12
2001	Abandoned- Foot & Mouth		
2002	Moscow Flyer	8-11-08	12
2003	Azertyuiop	6-11-08	9
2004	Well Chief	5-11-03	16
2005	Contraband	7-11-07	19
2006	Voy Por Ustedes	5-11-02	14

SMURFIT CHAMPION HURDLE CHALLENGE TROPHY

Cheltenham 2m 110y

1997	Make a Stand	6-12-00	17
1998	Istabraq	6-12-00	18
1999	Istabraq	7-12-00	14
2000	Istabraq	8-12-00	12
2001	Abandoned - Foot & Mouth		
2002	Hors La Loi III	7-12-00	15
2003	Rooster Booster	9-12-00	17
2004	Hardy Eustace	7-11-10	14

2005	Hardy Eustace	8-11-10	14
2006	Brave Inca	8-11-10	18

QUEEN MOTHER CHAMPION CHASE

Cheltenham 2m

1997	Martha's Son	10-12-00	6
1998	One Man	10-12-00	8
1999	Call Equiname	9-12-00	13
2000	Edredon Bleu	8-12-00	13
2001	Abandoned - Foot & Mouth		
2002	Flagship Uberalles	8-12-00	12
2003	Moscow Flyer	9-12-00	11
2004	Azertyuiop	7-11-10	8
2005	Moscow Flyer	11-11-10	8
2006	Newmill	8-11-10	12

ROYAL & SUNALLIANCE CHASE (NOVICES)

Cheltenham 3m

1997	Hanakham	8-11-04	14
1998	Florida Pearl	6-11-04	10
1999	Looks Like Touble	7-11-04	14
2000	Lord Noelie	7-11-04	9
2001	Abandoned - Foot & Mouth		
2002	Hussard Collonges	7-11-04	19
2003	One Knight	7-11-04	9
2004	Rule Supreme	8-11-04	10
2005	Trabolgan	7-11-04	9
2006	Star De Mohaison	5-10-08	15

LADBROKES WORLD HURDLE

(formerly Bonusprint Stayers' Hurdle)
Cheltenham 3m

1997	Karshi	7-11-10	17
1998	Princeful	6-11-10	9
1999	Anzum	8-11-10	12
2000	Bacchanal	6-11-10	10
2001	Abandoned - Foot & Mouth		
2002	Baracouda	7-11-10	16
2003	Baracouda	8-11-10	11
2004	Iris's Gift	7-11-10	10
2005	Inglis Drever	6-11-10	12
2006	My Way De Solzen	6-11-10	20

JCB TRIUMPH HURDLE

(formerly Daily Express & Elite Racing Club Triumph Hurdle)
Cheltenham 2m 1f (4-y-o)

1997	Commanche Court	11-00	28
1998	Upgrade	11-00	25
1999	Katarino	11-00	23
2000	Snow Drop	10-09	28
2001	Abandoned - Foot & Mouth		
2002	Scolardy	11-00	28
2003	Spectroscope	11-00	27
2004	Made In Japan	11-00	23
2005	Penzance	11-00	23
2006	Detroit City	11-00	17

TOTESPORT CHELTENHAM GOLD CUP (CHASE)

Cheltenham 3m 2f

1997	Mr Mulligan	9-12-00	14
1998	Cool Dawn	10-12-00	17
1999	See More Business	9-12-00	12
2000	Looks Like Trouble	8-12-00	12
2001	Abandoned - Foot & Mouth		
2002	Best Mate	7-12-00	18
2003	Best Mate	8-12-00	15
2004	Best Mate	9-11-10	10
2005	Kicking King	7-11-10	15
2006	War Of Attrition	7-11-10	22

BETFAIR BOWL CHASE

Aintree 3m 1f

1997	Barton Bank	11-11-05	5
1998	Escartefigue	6-11-13	8
1999	Macgeorge	9-11-05	5
2000	See More Business	10-12-00	4
2001	First Gold	8-12-00	7
2002	Florida Pearl	10-11-12	6
2003	First Gold	10-11-2	7
2004	Tiutchev	11-11-12	8
2005	Grey Abbey	11-11-12	8
2006	Celestial Gold	8-11-08	9

THE SPORTSMAN ANNIVERSARY HURDLE (4-y-o)

(formerly John Smith's, Unwins Wine Group and Glenlivet Anniversary Hurdle)
Aintree 2m 110y

1997	Quakers Field	11-00	12
1998	Deep Water	11-00	14
1999	Hors La Loi III	11-04	6
2000	Lord Brex	11-00	12
2001	Bilboa	10-13	14
2002	Quazar	11-04	17
2003	Le Duc	11-00	19
2004	Al Eile	11-00	18
2005	Faasel	11-00	12
2006	Detroit City	11.00	13

JOHN SMITH'S MELLING CHASE

(formerly Martell Cognac Melling Chase)
Aintree 2m 4f

1997	Martha's Son	10-11-10	4
1998	Opera Hat	10-11-05	5
1999	Direct Route	8-11-10	6
2000	Direct Route	9-11-10	5
2001	Fadalko	8-11-10	7
2002	Native Upmanship	9-11-10	8
2003	Native Upmanship	10-11-10	6
2004	Moscow Flyer	10-11-10	7
2005	Moscow Flyer	11-11-10	6
2006	Hi Cloy	9-11-10	11

JOHN SMITH'S RED RUM CHASE

(formerly Martell Cognac Chase)
Aintree 2m

1997	Down the Fell	8-10-07	10
1998	Jeffell	8-12-00	5
1999	Flying Instructor	9-11-05	7
2000	Jungli	7-10-07	7
2001	Aghawadda Gold	9-11-02	12
2002	Dark'n Sharp	7-10-08	15
2003	Golden Alpha	9-10-13	16
2004	Tidour	8-10-11	14
2005	Fotas Island	9-11-10	15
2006	Jacks Craic	7-10-02	16

SCOTTISH AND NEWCASTLE AINTREE HURDLE

(formerly Martell Aintree Hurdle)
Aintree 2m 4f

1997	Bimsey	7-11-07	7
1998	Pridwell	8-11-07	6
1999	Istabraq	7-11-7	7
2000	Mister Morose	10-11-07	10
2001	Barton	8-11-07	8
2002	Ilnamar	6-11-07	14
2003	Sacundai	6-11-07	5
2004	Rhinestone Cowboy	8-11-07	11
2005	Al Eile	5-11-07	9
2006	Asian Maze	7-11-00	9

JOHN SMITH'S GRAND NATIONAL (HANDICAP CHASE)

(formerly Martell Grand National)
4m 4f

1971	Specify	9-10-13	42
1972	Well To Do	9-10-01	42
1973	Red Rum	8-10-05	38
1974	Red Rum	9-12-00	42
1975	L'Escargot	12-11-03	31
1976	Rag Trade	10-10-12	32
1977	Red Rum	12-11-08	42
1978	Lucius	9-10-09	37
1979	Rubstic	10-10-00	34
1980	Ben Nevis	12-10-12	30
1981	Aldaniti	11-10-13	39
1982	Grittar	9-11-05	39
1983	Corbiere	8-11-04	41
1984	Hallo Dandy	10-10-02	40
1985	Last Suspect	11-10-05	40
1986	West Tip	9-10-11	40
1987	Maori Venture	11-10-13	40
1988	Rhyme 'N' Reason	9-11-00	40
1989	Little Polveir	12-10-03	40
1990	Mr Frisk	11-10-06	38
1991	Seagram	11-10-06	40
1992	Party Politics	8-10-07	40
1993	Void Race		
1994	Miinnehoma	11-10-08	36
1995	Royal Athlete	12-10-06	35
1996	Rough Quest	10-10-07	27
1997	Lord Gyllene	9-10-00	36
1998	Earth Summit	10-10-05	37
1999	Bobbyjo	9-10-00	32
2000	Papillon	9-10-12	40
2001	Red Marauder	11-10-11	40
2002	Bindaree	8-10-04	40
2003	Monty's Pass	10-10-07	40
2004	Amberleigh House	12-10-10	39
2005	Hedgehunter	9-11-01	40
2006	Numbersixvalverde	10-10-08	40

GALA CASINOS DAILY RECORD SCOTTISH GRAND NATIONAL (HANDICAP CHASE)

Ayr 4m 1f

1997	Belmont King	9-11-10	17
1998	Baronet	8-10-00	18
1999	Young Kenny	8-11-10	15
2000	Paris Pike	8-11-00	18
2001	Gingembre	7-11-02	30
2002	Take Control	8-10-06	18
2003	Ryalux	10-10-05	19
2004	Grey Abbey	10-11-12	28
2005	Joes Edge	8-9-11	20
2006	Run For Paddy	10-10-02	30

BETFRED GOLD CUP (HANDICAP CHASE)

(formerly Attheraces & Whitbread Gold Cup)
Sandown 3m 5f 110y

1996	Life of a Lord	10-11-10	17
1997	Harwell Lad	8-10-00	9
1998	Call It A Day	8-10-10	19
1999	Eulogy	9-10-00	19
2000	Beau	7-10-09	20
2001	Ad Hoc	7-10-04	25
2002	Bounce Back	6-10-09	20
2003	Ad Hoc	9-10-10	16
2004	Puntal	8-11-04	18
2005	Jack High	10-10-00	19
2006	Lacdoudal	7-11-05	18

RACEFORM TOP RATED CHASERS AND HURDLERS 2005-2006

CHASERS

Kicking King (IRE)	177
Beef Or Salmon (IRE)	174
War Of Attrition (IRE)	173
Newmill (IRE)	172
Monkerhostin (FR)	171
Celestial Gold (IRE)	171
Hedgehunter (IRE)	170
Rule Supreme (IRE)	170
Kingscliff (IRE)	170
Kauto Star (FR)	169
Trabolgan (IRE)	168
Impek (FR)	166
Ashley Brook (IRE)	166
Our Vic (IRE)	166
Fondmort (FR)	165
One Knight (IRE)	165
Mister McGoldrick	165
Royal Auclair (FR)	165
Take The Stand (IRE)	165
Hi Cloy (IRE)	165
Ollie Magern	165
Monet s Garden (IRE)	165
Forget The Past	165

HURDLERS

Brave Inca (IRE)	173
Macs Joy (IRE)	172
Harchibald (FR)	171
Mighty Man (FR)	169
Hardy Eustace (IRE)	168
Golden Cross (IRE)	166
My Way De Solzen (FR)	166
Essex (IRE)	165
Asian Maze (IRE)	165
Black Jack Ketchum (IRE)	165

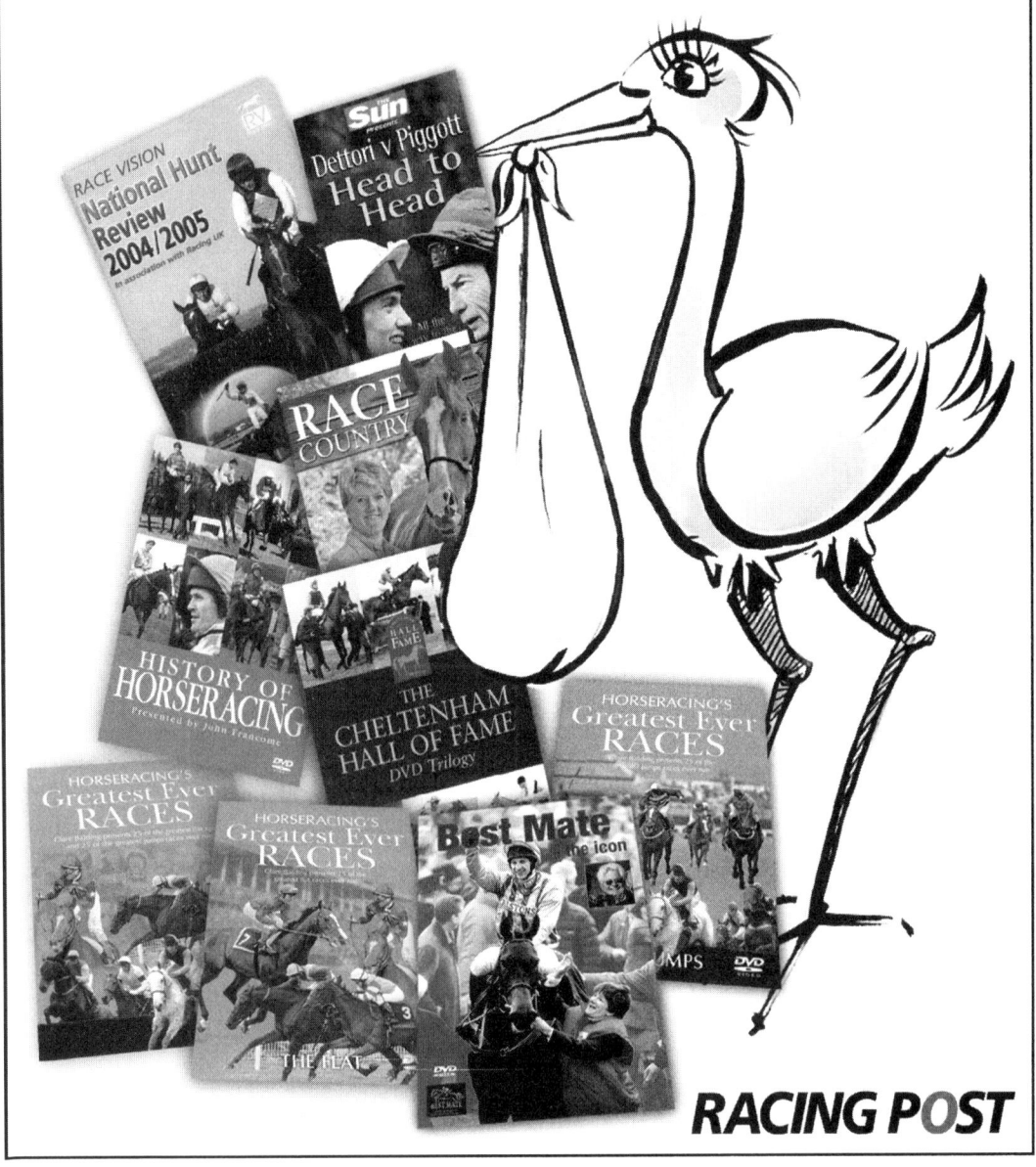